# ROTHMANS
# FOOTBALL
# YEARBOOK
# 1998-99

**EDITOR: GLENDA ROLLIN**
**EXECUTIVE EDITOR: JACK ROLLIN**

HEADLINE

First published in 1998
by HEADLINE BOOK PUBLISHING

10 9 8 7 6 5 4 3 2 1

**Front cover photographs:** (left) Gary Pallister (Manchester U) – *Action Images*; (centre and background) John Scales (Tottenham H) and Dennis Bergkamp (Arsenal) – *Colorsport*; (right) Chris Sutton (Blackburn R) – *Action Images*.

**Back cover photographs:** (top) Gareth Southgate (Aston Villa), Emile Heskey (Leicester C) and Andy Townsend (Aston Villa) – *Action Images*; (bottom) Faustino Asprilla (Newcastle U) and Des Walker (Sheffield W) – *Action Images*.

**British Library Cataloguing in Publication Data**
Rothmans Football Yearbook.—1998–99
1. Association Football—Serials
796.334'05

ISBN 0 7472 2125 1 (hardback)
ISBN 0 7472 7652 8 (softback)

Typeset by Wearset, Boldon, Tyne and Wear

Printed and bound in Great Britain by
Mackays of Chatham PLC,
Chatham, Kent

HEADLINE BOOK PUBLISHING
A division of Hodder Headline PLC
338 Euston Road
London NW1 3BH

# CONTENTS

# INTRODUCTION

The 29th edition of Rothmans Football Yearbook includes several new features, notably an article by our guest writer Terry Venables, and a more user-friendly guide to the book's sections indicated at the top of each page. There is full coverage of the World Cup, both for the qualifying matches and final tournament in France. For both English and Scottish League football, the position in which each club finished in 1996–97 is included along the same line as that for the 1997–98 season for comparative purposes.

Detailed and varied coverage involves the FA Premier League, Football League, Scottish, Welsh and Irish football, amateur, schools, university, reserve team, extensive non-league information, awards, records and international directory, the Football Trust, Football and the Law, coaching, referees and the work of chaplains.

Transfer fees are given where known. When two clubs have differed as to the amount of a record move, the lower figure has been quoted in both instances. Also the date when a player is signed often varies from the one given as his registration.

It is our intention for next year's edition to double the amount of historical and record information for the English clubs. Because of the pressures this will make on space, it is regretted that we will be unable to continue including the team pictures which are, in any case, not as up-to-date as we would have liked to present them. Doncaster Rovers did not have a team group picture taken at any time before or during the season!

The Editors would also like to thank Alan Elliott for the Scottish section, Norman Barrett for the Milestones Diary and Ian Vosper for the Obituaries. Thanks are also due to John English who provided his invaluable and conscientious reading of the proofs.

The Editors would like to pay tribute to the various organisations who have helped to make this edition complete, especially Sheila Andrew from the Football League, Mike Foster of the FA Premier League and the secretaries of all the FA Premier, Football League and Scottish League clubs for their kind co-operation. The ready availability of Football League secretary David Dent and his staff to answer queries was as usual most appreciated, as was Chris Hull's help from the press office. Thanks are also due in equal measure to the Scottish Football Association, Scottish Football League, as well as Adrian Cook and Mike Kelleher of the FA Premier League.

# ACKNOWLEDGEMENTS

The Editors would also like to express appreciation of the following individuals and organisations for their co-operation: Glynis Firth, Sandra Whiteside, Lorna Parnell, Debbie Birch, Jonathan Hargreaves (all from the Football League), David C. Thompson of the Scottish League, Alan Dick, Malcolm Brodie, Bob Hennessy, Peter Hughes (English Schools FA), Wally Goss (AFA), Ken Scott for Football Conference information, Rev. Nigel Sands, Edward Grayson, Ken Goldman, Grahame Lloyd, Marshall Gillespie, Sean Creedon, Manuel Màrquez, Adriano Stabile, Heather Elliott and Zöe Gilbert (Headline Books).

Special thanks are due to Lorraine Jerram, Headline's House Editor, for her expertise, constant support, unflagging patience, sincerity, understanding, perspicacity and appreciation, not to mention her unfailing humour and quick-wittedness.

Finally, sincere thanks to John Anderson, Simon Dunnington and Geoff Turner and the staff at Wearset for their efforts in the production of this book, which was much appreciated throughout the year.

---

### Lord Howell and John Camkin

During the lifetime of the 28th edition of Rothmans Football Yearbook, we were saddened to learn of the passing of two of the original members of the book's Editorial Board. Denis Howell was the chairman, a sitting Member of Parliament at the time and the first such to become a Football League referee. He was Minister for Sport and a champion of all good causes sporting. John Camkin had been a respected journalist, football commentator and sporting administrator as well as being an accomplished games player himself. He also contributed last year's article on the League Managers Association.

# VIEWPOINT

by Terry Venables

The start of a new season is always full of excitement for players, managers and fans alike. Hopes and dreams run rampant and all too often, for a few, they are dashed by the end of what is now a long campaign. For me, one of the tell-tale signs that all is about to start up again is the smell of freshly mowed grass on the training field. Its sweet, almost innocent aroma reminds me of my childhood and the games in the local park or at my school.

The other better known signal that battle is about to commence is the publication of *Rothmans Football Yearbook*. This is an institution and when I first moved from playing to coaching at Crystal Palace, it was always the first reference book I turned to when I needed accurate statistics on players' records, important matches and scores. Now the book is indispensable and contains so much more.

As a mark of its importance, you would not be able to walk into any professional manager's office or, for that matter, any self-respecting football journalist's office without seeing the book there in its distinctive cover.

Now, of course, I am back at Crystal Palace and, although I have had the odd job in between, the ever constant in this changing world has been the quality of *Rothmans Football Yearbook*. What is also true since I first started coaching some 23 years ago is that the game of football has changed enormously. When I was a player, it was still the number one game in the country. The pay was good but not great and as young men we could move between professionalism and playing for enjoyment very easily. Now it is the world's biggest sport as this summer in France has shown us again and the rewards are huge. Only the other month, David Beckham's earnings were purported to be £8.1 million.

These changes have also brought new demands of professionalism to bear. With the improvement of sports medicine, so far removed from the old magic sponge, and the greater understanding of the importance of diet and nutrition, a player can easily add some two or three years to his career. With the wages now being paid in the Premiership this, in some cases, could amount to an additional earning potential of £1 million, £2 million or even £3 million. Players know they have got to look after themselves.

The flip side of this is that the competition for first-team places is now not simply from the youth team or players from other clubs. Just as a lot of the medical and nutritional improvements have been imported from abroad, increasingly clubs here are recruiting players from overseas. Of the 704 players from all teams in the 1998 World Cup, 48 were registered in England – that represents 6 per cent of all who went to France. It just won't be so easy for players today to be sure of their positions.

One of the definite advantages of this influx of foreign players is that, in many cases, the quality of the football is getting higher. Our own players will learn from playing alongside a Bergkamp, a Laudrup or a Zola and this talent and skill factor should in time spill down to the lower leagues.

As to the effect on the national team, our best players can always learn from the best of the rest. However, as the world gets smaller England has no divine right to say we are the best in the world unless we actively learn from the best. It is fine to say we have the best league in the world in the Premiership but one of the key reasons foreigners come here is because the money is so high.

You may say, why pay the wages? The Italian clubs, for example, have suffered as they have paid too much for players and, although transfers have generated a lot of revenue, many clubs there have still paid out in wages more than they have earned. We have to be careful not to flatter ourselves too much about the attractions of our game as some foreigners have come to realise that they can just get better deals here than in their own countries. Some of the players from Italy who come here have probably been off-loaded by their clubs to reduce the wage bill and our league is one of the few places they can come to earn the same amount of money.

But herein lies a dangerous spiral for our clubs at the moment. In an ideal world, we probably do not want foreign players in our clubs as the problems of assimilation can be great and an unsettled player is no good to a manager. But with the financial pressures on the smaller clubs, who need every penny from the sale of their promising youngsters, it is now just as easy to gamble abroad on buying players of the same ability if not better for the same money or cheaper.

If you are not the manager of Manchester United or one of the top six clubs, you have got to look for deals. It is now too expensive to buy an English player rather than a foreign player and I can see this influx increasing until it evens out. I also predict that when the Bosman ruling finally bites, the transfer prices will naturally be reduced. Also, the prices for English players during their contract will start to come down as common sense will prevail. The clubs have got to come to their senses about prices and they have to sit down with the PFA and work out a solution. If English player A cost the same as foreign player B and they were the same ability you would always buy English to avoid the risks of assimilation.

In Germany, you do not find many of their players going abroad as they are well paid at home, and the same goes for Spain. In France, however, the small gates and lower revenue of the clubs inevitably lead to the better players being attracted overseas. Obviously, one of the key factors for enabling our clubs to purchase overseas is the television income from Sky.

The other key issue for us to decide is whether we are in Europe or not. By that I mean we either allow as many foreigners in per club as we like or cap it to, say, three or four per team. The work permit restrictions here are sometimes so onerous that it is difficult to secure the players to push the quality of the game up whereas the rest of Europe finds it easier to allow in all sorts of players from the rest of the world.

Personally, I would prefer a situation where we are more selective about the number of foreigners we allow per club. Not only would this ensure that only the best players from around the world were bought to add to the quality of the game but it would also perhaps encourage some caution on the prices paid. Also you do not want a structure like it is at Chelsea now where some of the young domestic players are finding it very hard to break through.

The immediate effect of our clubs getting more realistic on prices for players would be to slow down the rate of foreigners coming into our game. More importantly, this will also accelerate the inevitable that we have delayed for many, many years. The smaller clubs just will not have the financial resources to survive and most of them will become part-time. Although this sounds doom-laden, I feel it could be beneficial for many of the players who will perhaps never be the best. They will be able to play part-time and earn from that as well as having other jobs.

One of the fascinating things for me about the 1998 World Cup was that some of the traditional powerhouses of world football such as Germany, with Klinsmann and Matthaus, Brazil, with Dunga and Bebeto, and Italy, with Roberto Baggio, have ageing squads and few signs of youngsters coming through. We were all disappointed about the manner and stage of England's exit but I feel we have real cause for optimism that youngsters such as Owen, Campbell, Scholes and Beckham were blooded at an early point in their careers. The experience has served them and their country well and it bodes well for the forthcoming European Championships in Holland/Belgium and the World Cup in 2002.

As to the new season, I think the Premiership will be fascinating again. In my *News of the World* column at the start of last season, I said it would be between Manchester United and Arsenal and I just fancied Manchester as I was not sure how quickly Arsenal's skilful foreigners would take to settle in. The turning point for me was the Arsenal v Manchester United game where you saw a host of gifted players, a veritable array of talent lined up on both sides. What really stood out for me was that for all the expertise on display, not one player was looking for a free lunch that day on either side. You saw the ideal: quality players using their skill to the best of their advantage but allied to great hard work for the benefit of their teams.

Work-rate is all too often dismissed as a dirty word and treated as a poor substitute for flair. But if you are a talented writer but do not file any copy, what use are your talents?

Hopefully, this season will see our domestic and national game continuing to provide the excitement we all hope for and our players will have learnt from what they have seen at the World Cup. As to how the Premiership will finish, I cannot see beyond Liverpool, Chelsea, Manchester United and Arsenal competing for the top honour. I also feel that these last two clubs are perhaps better equipped now than at any other time in recent years to perform well in the Champions' League this coming season and it would not surprise me if one of them got to the final and won it.

# EDITORIAL

The penalty shoot-out must be ditched before the next World Cup. Originally introduced as a quick fix to avoid replays, its continued use is at variance with the spirit of the game and well past any credibility.

Play must carry on until a goal is scored. Experiments could be carried out in a serious competition well in advance of the next tournament.

While penalties may not possess much aesthetic appeal for the aficionado, they are the catalyst for immediate reaction. Victory ensures elation, defeat in strange contrast, the means of a lasting conviction of unfair robbery. In fact, the next best option to winning the World Cup is to lose a penalty shoot-out. Naturally England, Italy and Holland can all claim that they might have fared better but were forced into the lottery of penalties. For England, it seemed much worse having had to survive with ten men against Argentina.

The theory that we were playing for penalties once a player short is not entirely substantiated given our wretched record from spot kicks, the unfortunate Paul Ince and David Batty being added to the list, but the record books always refer to matches involving a penalty shoot-out as a draw. Yet surely one day we must be given the opportunity to prove just how good we believe we are in the context of the match itself without the seemingly inevitable lottery.

Legislation has come some way towards solving the problem with the introduction of sudden death, the more clinical way of explaining the so-called 'golden goal'. Concern for the needs of television, or more pointedly, the money derived from this source, is probably the main reason why games are not permitted to carry on indefinitely until the crucial goal.

However, there has been noticeable flexibility over allowing extended injury time, which once would have been totally taboo.

Once again some England supporters have brought the name into disrepute. This is becoming a tiresome repetition almost beyond words, whenever England plays abroad. As one commentator reflected, during the miners' dispute the police were able to restrict the movement of thousands of people involved in legitimate industrial action, yet in France 98, they were apparently powerless to prevent known football hooligans from crossing the channel. But presumably there is one law for the pits, another for the bore.

The conduct of many players themselves in the World Cup was questionable. How the world's idolising youth viewed the shirt-pulling, pushing, diving and theatrical behaviour is too frightening to envisage. You can blame referees, but the pace of the game is such that they cannot see everything that goes on. There are three possible alternatives. Firstly, make better use of the assistant referees, who have scarcely improved as a body since they changed their title from linesmen and make better use of the extra official than merely to lift a board indicating the amount of extra time to be played, without infringing the fourth protocol. Secondly, use all the modern technology available to pinpoint the culprits. This could be effected without interrupting the match, much the same way as an official will allow play to continue and then book an offender at a suitable moment. Thirdly, employ two referees.

Experiments towards this particular end were first made in the 1930s, when serious problems were almost non-existent. In *England's World Cup Triumph* in 1966, I recommended the use of two referees, because players were already taking every possible unfair advantage, though nothing as bad as today's deplorable situation.

After all it is the standard at the top which will be copied by the next generation. This needs to be addressed as a priority. The argument that all levels of the game cannot benefit from such changes is not valid; video replays are already provided as evidence even though few games outside first-class matches have this availability.

However, congratulations to England on sharing the Fair Play Award in France 98, along with the hosts and winners. We only had one player sent off, the French three. Such things are relative. C'est la vie.

# Coming soon . . .

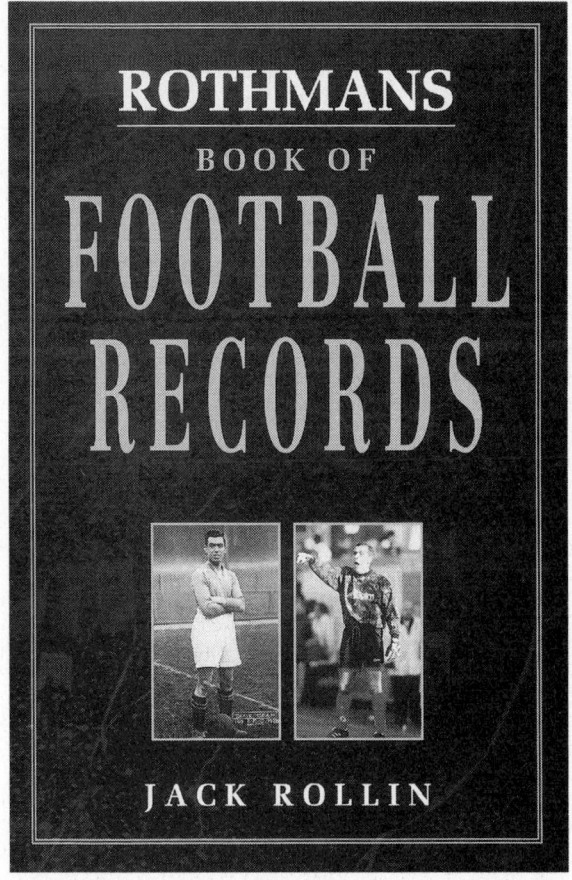

*A comprehensive glossary of the game's most important domestic and international records. The ideal historical companion to the sport's bestselling statistical bible,* Rothmans Football Yearbook.

Published by Headline on 8 October 1998, price £25.00
(ISBN 0 7472 1954 0)

# ROTHMANS FOOTBALL HONOURS

For the third consecutive year, members of the Football Writers' Association selected their team of the season for Rothmans Football Yearbook. Once again, players eligible had to have appeared in FA Carling Premiership matches during the season.

In contrast to last year when only 34 different players received votes, a record 61 were supported, 11 more than in the first season. While in 1996-97 there had been a switch to a 3-5-2 formation, this time there was a return to the original 4-4-2 favoured in the initial year of voting.

Understandably after Arsenal's double triumph, players from the Highbury club dominated the voting. In fact, 12 of them received nominations including Alex Manninger, the reserve goalkeeper. The final selection featured no fewer than nine Arsenal players: David Seaman, Martin Keown, Tony Adams, Nigel Winterburn, Ray Parlour, Patrick Vieira, Emmanuel Petit, Marc Overmars and Dennis Bergkamp. The other two collecting votes were Lee Dixon and Nicolas Anelka. Arsenal captain Adams received more votes than any other player, but was closely followed by Bergkamp. Even Parlour edged out David Beckham for the right side of midfield role in the most closely contested position in the team.

The remaining places were completed by Gary Neville at right-back as the only representative from Manchester United to make the final selection. Interestingly enough, he is the only player to have featured in each of the three seasons the award has been made. Liverpool's exciting prospect Michael Owen won the nomination as Bergkamp's striking partner.

Players in close contention for the final analysis included Peter Schmeichel and Ryan Giggs (both Manchester United), Chris Sutton (Blackburn Rovers), David Ginola (Tottenham Hotspur), Frank Leboeuf (Chelsea), Paul Ince (Liverpool) and Alan Shearer (Newcastle United), whose injury-hit season probably cost him a third consecutive appearance. Neil Redfearn, who made an impact in Barnsley's brief but memorable season in the Premier League, also gained recognition.

Such was the voting that the choice of substitutes gave the overall squad a strong attacking flavour with Beckham, Giggs and Sutton completing the selection for the season on the bench.

Not surprisingly, Arsenal's manager Arsène Wenger received overwhelming support as manager. Alex Ferguson (Manchester United) and Coventry City's Gordon Strachan were also featured.

### Rothmans Football Yearbook Team of the Season

David Seaman
*(Arsenal)*

| Gary Neville | Martin Keown | Tony Adams | Nigel Winterburn |
|:---:|:---:|:---:|:---:|
| *(Manchester U)* | *(Arsenal)* | *(Arsenal)* | *(Arsenal)* |
| Ray Parlour | Patrick Vieira | Emmanuel Petit | Marc Overmars |
| *(Arsenal)* | *(Arsenal)* | *(Arsenal)* | *(Arsenal)* |

Dennis Bergkamp      Michael Owen
*(Arsenal)*              *(Liverpool)*

**Manager:**
Arsène Wenger *(Arsenal)*

*Substitutes:*
David Beckham (Manchester U)
Ryan Giggs (Manchester U)
Chris Sutton (Blackburn R)

# MILESTONES DIARY 1997–98

**June 1997**
**No replays in Coca-Cola Cup ... Arsenal pay £7m for Overmars ... World record fee for Ronaldo ... Kendall back at Goodison after Gray stays at Sky ... Spurs lose Sheringham to Man U**

15  The Football League decide to do away with replays in the Coca-Cola Cup, although the 1st and 2nd rounds and the semi-finals will remain two-legged.

16  Larisa Nechayeva, business manager of Spartak Moscow, is gunned down in her car in a suspected Russian 'Mafia' contract killing. Graeme Souness signs a 2-year contract to coach Italian Serie B side Torino.

17  Arsenal pay £7m for Dutch international winger Marc Overmars from Ajax, taking their spending on foreign stars in the last fortnight to over £14m.

18  In official receivership since January and having survived eight winding-up orders, Bournemouth become Europe's first community-owned club after a takeover by a trust funded by public donations.

19  Don Howe quits his post as technical co-ordinator at the FA to rejoin Arsenal as head youth coach.

20  Stellican, a London-based company, buys troubled Italian Serie A club Vicenza for £8.2m at auction. Southampton announce Stockport boss David Jones, former Everton and Coventry player, as their new manager. Raith appoint Jimmy Nicholl manager. Inter-Milan sign 20-year-old striker Ronaldo, currently playing for Brazil in the Copa America, for a reported world record £17m, although his club Barcelona may contest the move.

22  Howard Wilkinson, the FA's first technical director, proposes a massive shake-up in coaching methods, including starting with children as young as 3-5 and transferring coaching from the FA to the League clubs.

23  The anticipated appointment of former star Andy Gray as the new Everton manager falls through as he does a complete U-turn and decides to stay with Sky TV, prompting a stinging personal attack from Goodison chairman Peter Johnson. David Jones is confirmed as Southampton manager, with Stockport receiving £200,000 compensation.

24  Howard Kendall fills the hot seat at Goodison, in charge for his third spell as Everton manager, while his club Sheff Utd will receive compensation for 2 years' contract remaining. Hull are taken over by British Davis Cup captain David Lloyd in a £2.4m deal. The transfer of Ronaldo, who claims he has bought-out his own contract from Barcelona, to Inter for a now reported £18m is blocked by the Spanish Football Federation.

25  Sheff Utd demand £1m compensation from Everton for Howard Kendall. Former Danish international Jan Sorensen takes over as manager of Walsall.

26  Matt Le Tissier signs a new 4-year contract that will keep him at Southampton till he is nearly 33.

27  Man Utd sign England striker Teddy Sheringham for £3.5m from Spurs, a hugely unpopular move with Tottenham fans. Adrian Heath resigns as Burnley manager to return to Everton to assist Howard Kendall, who officially takes charge at Goodison today.

30  Despite the appointment of Dutchman Louis van Gaal as Barcelona coach, Bobby Robson will stay with the Spanish Cup winners as director of recruitment rather than take over as Celtic boss. QPR sign striker Mike Sheron from Stoke for £2.5m. Lincoln's assistant manager John Still is to take over at Barnet from Terry Bullivant, who moves to Reading as manager.

**July**
**Middlesbrough sign Merson and sell Juninho ... Ginola and Ferdinand go to Spurs ... Ince joins Liverpool ... Shearer out till next year ... injuries and dismissals galore in friendlies**

1  Bolton sign Newcastle defender Robbie Elliott for £2.2m (rising to £2.5m). Gary Megson leaves Blackpool to take over at Stockport. Ronnie Whelan resigns as manager of Southend.

2  Atletico Madrid sign striker Christian Vieri from Juventus for £12m.

3  Celtic appoint former Dutch international Wim Jansen, 53, as manager. Forest sign midfielder Andy Johnson from Norwich for £2.2m.

4  Forest sign Tranmere full-back Alan Rogers for £2m.

5  Argentina beat Uruguay 2-1 in the final of the World Youth (U-20) Championships in Malaysia and Ireland beat Ghana 2-1 to take 3rd place.

6  Australia, coached by Terry Venables, beat New Zealand 2-0 (5-0 on aggregate) to win the Oceania zone of the World Cup qualifying competition, but still have to meet an Asian loser to make it to France 98.

7  Relegated Middlesbrough sign England international Paul Merson from Arsenal in a £5m deal.

8  Atletico Madrid sign Brazil midfield star Juninho from Middlesbrough for £12m, £1m more than Spurs bid. Former England winger Chris Waddle becomes player-manager of Burnley, and former N.Ireland left-back Nigel Worthington leaves Stoke to take over as Blackpool boss.

10  Arsenal striker Ian Wright escapes with a £15,000 fine, the FA punishment for remarks made to the referee and gestures to the crowd, respectively, in matches last April, but is warned that similar transgressions in the future are likely to attract a lengthy suspension. Former Wales, Swansea, Cardiff and Newcastle inside-forward Ivor Allchurch dies at 67.

11  The replica Jules Rimet Trophy, passed off for two years as the real thing after it was won by England in 1966, fetches £254,500 at Sotheby's. Blackburn complete the signing of Sweden striker Martin Dahlin from Roma for £2.5m.

14    Spurs finally clinch a transfer – ex-France international David Ginola, 30, from Newcastle for £2.5m. The FA change disciplinary procedure for cautions, replacing the totting-up process of 1-4pts for various misdemeanours with a suspension for 5 (then 8, then 11) bookings of any kind, but with the last booking erased for going 5 games without one. Hull sack manager Terry Dolan after 5 years. Diego Maradona makes his fifth comeback, at 36, for Boca Juniors.

15    Former West Ham stalwart Alvin Martin becomes manager of Southend. Rangers release striker Mark Hateley to take over as player-manager of Hull. Palace release Ray Houghton on a free transfer to Reading as player-coach. Liverpool complete the signing of England youth midfielder Danny Murphy from Crewe for £1.5m (rising to £3m).

16    Alex Ferguson makes Roy Keane captain of Man Utd on a trial basis.

17    Southampton's Matt Le Tissier breaks an arm in a friendly in Germany and is set to miss 2 months of the season. Fabrizio Ravanelli may return to Middlesbrough as his £7.5m move to Everton collapses when they refuse to meet his demand for £50,000 a week wages. But Everton do sign up a new shirt sponsor – One-2-One – for a 3-year deal worth £2m.

18    Liverpool complete the signing of England midfielder Paul Ince from Inter for £4.2m. England left-back Stuart Pearce, 35, signs a 2-year, £15,000 a week contract for Newcastle on a free transfer from Forest.

21    Leeds complete the signing of Scotland midfielder David Hopkin from Palace for £3.25m.

22    Unable to find another club to match his salary, Ravanelli decides to stay at Middlesbrough. FIFA inform Inter that the £18m they have paid for Ronaldo does not constitute a full fee, but the Italian club reject Barcelona's claims for an extra £11m.

23    Scotland's big guns easily account for minor opposition in away ties in the opening fixtures of European competition, Ally McCoist scoring twice in Rangers' 5-0 defeat of Faroes champions Gotu in the European Cup to take his European tally to 20, a Scottish record.

24    Celtic sign versatile Scotland international Craig Burley from Chelsea for £2.5m. Sheff Utd agree £0.4m compensation from Everton for the loss of manager Howard Kendall. After late payment of a £0.5m bond, the Football League reject a motion to expel homeless Brighton, who hope to share first with Gillingham and then Millwall.

25    Newcastle sign Inter defender Alessandro Pistone for £4.5m, while encouraging reluctant striker Les Ferdinand to discuss terms with Spurs.

26    Newcastle and England striker Alan Shearer suffers a serious ankle injury in the pre-season Umbro tournament at Goodison.

27    While Shearer undergoes a ligament operation that will keep him out of action for several months – a blow to club and country – Les Ferdinand rejects a Newcastle move to keep him and completes his £6m transfer to Spurs. Chelsea beat Everton 3-1 in the Umbro final. £18m Brazil striker Ronaldo makes his debut for Inter, a 17-min appearance at San Siro in a friendly against Man Utd which the Italian club win 4-1 on penalties.

28    Former Tory cabinet minister David Mellor is the government choice to head the new Football Task Force. Police authorities urge managers and players to tone down goal celebrations, particularly in front of rival supporters, to avoid inciting the fans.

29    Celtic cruise through to the 2nd qualifying round of the UEFA Cup with a 5-0 win (8-0 agg) over Inter Cable-Tel. Blackburn agree to Graeme Le Saux's transfer request and slap a £7.5m price-tag on the 28-year-old England left-back.

30    Scottish clubs rubber-stamp their progress in Europe, Rangers with a 6-0 defeat of Gotu (11-0 agg) in the European Cup and Dundee Utd with a 9-0 annihilation (17-0 agg) of Principat, Andorra, in the UEFA Cup. Barry have Dean Ryan dismissed against Dynamo Kiev after 35min and concede 4 second-half goals to go down 6-0 on aggregate in the European Cup. Arsenal striker Ian Wright is the controversial choice to front a new advertising campaign to promote the FA. Arsenal sign a 7-year deal with Nike worth potentially £40m, but their day is spoilt during the Heroes of Grass Nike Challenge, which they lose 1-0 to PSV in Holland, when they have 2 players sent off, Patrick Vieira and Matthew Upson. In another 'friendly', Chelsea's Frank Sinclair, Mark Hughes and Paul Hughes are asked to 'leave the field' in a bad-tempered 4-1 win at Portsmouth. Another friendly with a down side is Man United's 1-1 draw with Inter at Old Trafford, where striker Ole Gunnar Solskjaer damages ankle ligaments and will be out for about a month and Gary Neville and Ronny Johnsen both come off with injuries.

31    Speaking at the *Rothmans* launch, Chelsea chairman Ken Bates inveighs against all and sundry – UEFA, for pressing for a reduction in Premiership clubs, FIFA for planning an extended biannual World Club Championship, but particularly the Sports Council, on which there was no football representative and who, he warned, were incapable of building a national stadium for the 2006 World Cup. Another friendly causes grief, to Liverpool this time, as striker Robbie Fowler is carried off with a twisted knee against a Norway XI in Oslo. Man City complete the signing of Portsmouth forward Lee Bradbury for £3m. Southend and West Ham strike up a 'special relationship' in which the Hammers will have first option on any emerging talent from Roots Hall and will play their reserve matches there. There are signs of disarray at Newcastle as the board, because of the sudden lack of strikers, veto manager Kenny Dalglish's decision to sell Peter Beardsley to Bolton.

**August**
**Man Utd win Charity Shield ... Pride Park début ends in the dark ... Barcelona spurn £12m McManaman to sign £16m Rivaldo ... Newcastle in Champions' League, Rangers fail to qualify ... Maradona's hat-trick of positive drug tests**

1     Premiership clubs capture more foreign talent, as two Italian forwards arrive for under £2m apiece, Attilio Lombardo from Juventus to Palace and Francesco Baiano from Fiorentina to Derby. Man Utd

manager Alex Ferguson decides to rest young England star David Beckham for the first three weeks of the season.
2 With the big guns missing from the start of the Scottish season, Motherwell, the only winning side in 3 matches, find themselves 'top' of the Premier table.
3 Man Utd beat Chelsea 4-2 on penalties after a bad-tempered 1-1 draw at Wembley in the Charity Shield. The FA announce the setting up of a Medical Research Project to investigate the growing list of casualties in the game. Celtic go down 2-1 at Hibs in Wim Jansen's first League match in charge.
4 Champions Rangers begin their Premier League programme with a 3-1 win over Hearts. David Webb moves 'upstairs' at Brentford, from manager to chief executive. Wimbledon and Ireland striker Jon Goodman will be out for 6 months with damaged cruciate knee ligaments.
5 Arsenal chairman Peter Hill-Wood warns of future financial crisis if wages continue to spiral, citing the increase in Arsenal's wage bill from £8.7m to £13.3m in a year.
6 Unhappy Celtic allow Italian striker Paolo Di Canio to leave for Sheff Wed, who pay a club-record fee of £4.5m for him.
7 In the 'replayed' bribe case at Winchester Crown Court, footballers Bruce Grobbelaar, John Fashanu and Hans Segers and Malaysian businessman Heng Suan Lim are cleared of conspiring to throw matches, although one charge against Grobbelaar will be settled tomorrow.
8 Grobbelaar is acquitted of the remaining charge against him. As Blackburn drop their £7m asking price, England left-back Graeme Le Saux makes a surprise return to Chelsea for £5m.
9 The Premiership opens with a splendid hat-trick from Dion Dublin, equalising twice against Chelsea before hitting a late winner to put Coventry theoretically top of the League. Macclesfield make their League debut with a 2-1 win over Torquay in Div 3. There are no big shocks in the Scottish Coca-Cola Cup 2nd round; Celtic's 7-0 win at Berwick is the top score.
10 Teddy Sheringham is barracked throughout his quick return to White Hart Lane and misses a penalty, but he has the last laugh as Man Utd beat Spurs 2-0 and go straight back to the top of the Premiership.
11 Ian Wright scores both goals in Arsenal's 2-0 victory over Coventry at Highbury to take him within a goal of Cliff Bastin's club record and Arsenal temporarily to the top of the League. Man Utd sign Norway defender Henning Berg, 29, from Blackburn for £5m. Wolves break their transfer sale record, receiving £2m from Palace for defender Neil Emblen. Forest, surprisingly required to play in the 1st round of the Coca-Cola Cup, take their 1st-leg tie at Doncaster 8-0.
12 Celtic and Dundee Utd suffer 1-goal defeats in their UEFA Cup away ties. Barnsley enjoy their first victory in the top echelon, 1-0 at Palace. In the Coca-Cola Cup, a 21-man brawl late in the 2-2 draw between Peterborough and Portsmouth sees a player from each side sent off. Former Cardiff boss Eddie May takes the vacant job at Brentford.
13 In the 2nd qualifying round of the European Cup, Newcastle take a 2-1 lead away from Croatia Zagreb, with wing-back John Beresford scoring both their goals, while Rangers slump again, beaten 3-0 in Gothenburg. Blackburn scored a splendid 4-0 win at Villa with Chris Sutton contributing 3 to take them to the top of the Premiership. Leicester's shock 2-1 win at Anfield sees them level on a maximum 6pts, a position shared by Man Utd, who need to bring David Beckham off the sub's bench to score the only goal of the game against Southampton, and West Ham. The first match at Derby's new ground, Pride Park, is abandoned after 56min owing to floodlight failure with the home side 2-1 ahead of Wimbledon. Newcastle snap up Liverpool's John Barnes, 33, on a free transfer. Only 1,073 turn up to see Brighton's first home game at Gillingham's Priestfield Stadium, a 1-1 draw with Orient.
14 Barcelona sign Brazil midfielder Rivaldo from La Coruna for £16m, giving heart to Liverpool fans who feared losing Steve McManaman to the Spanish club in a £12m deal.
15 Sheff Utd appoint caretaker Nigel Spackman manager with a 3-year contract.
16 There are no Premiership matches in England, but in Scotland St Johnstone's 1-0 win at leaders Motherwell leapfrogs them into 1st place. England coach Glenn Hoddle is furious that the Premiership have vetoed his plans to retain players for an extra day after internationals. Unless Islington council allow Arsenal to redevelop, the club may have to move from 38,500-capacity Highbury. Former Leeds striker Phil Masinga blasts a goal in front of a capacity 90,000 crowd at Johannesburg that gives S.Africa a win over Congo and sees the Republic through to the World Cup finals for the first time. After Doncaster's second crushing home defeat in less than a week, 5-0 to Peterborough, manager Kerry Dixon offers to leave.
17 Hibs' 1-1 draw at Dundee Utd takes them top of the Scottish Premier on goal difference. Cameroon qualify for their 3rd World Cup running when they beat Zimbabwe 2-1 at Harare.
18 One of Newcastle's Old Brigade, Peter Beardsley, signs for Bolton, who also announce the capture of S.Africa centre-half Mark Fish from Lazio for £2m.
20 In World Cup qualifiers, N.Ireland are beaten by Germany for the first time in 6 games going back 20 years, losing 3-1 at Windsor Park to a Bierhoff hat-trick in 7 second-half minutes after taking a 59th-min lead. Meanwhile Ireland suffer a serious blow to their qualification hopes, held to a 0-0 draw at home by Lithuania, and Wales are involved in a see-saw 10-goal thriller in Istanbul before going down 6-4, Hakan Sukur scoring 4 for Turkey. Little more than 2,000 people see the big shock of the Scottish Coca-Cola Cup at Div 1 Stirling, where Premier side Kilmarnock go down 6-2 in the 3rd round.
21 Doncaster and player-manager Kerry Dixon part by mutual consent. Norwegian agent Rune Hauge, the man responsible for George Graham's disgrace, has been banned from Highbury even though his ban ended this month.
23 Blackburn stay top of the Premiership despite being held at home 1-1 by Liverpool. Only Newcastle, with a game in hand, retain their 100% record. Macclesfield go top of Div 3 with a 3-0 win over hapless Doncaster. A spectator runs onto the pitch and attacks referee Phil Richards in the match between Notts County and Lincoln. Marco Negri scores all Rangers' goals as they beat Dundee Utd 5-1 and retain their

100% record, but they remain a point behind Hibs, who stay top of the Scottish Premier with a 4-0 win over Kilmarnock. A collector's item from Div 3: Albion Rovers, leading 1-0 at Queen's Park, have keeper Stevie Ross sent off after 70min for protesting a booking under the 6sec rule, then have another 3 players dismissed; meanwhile, Queen's Park score 5 in the last 13min.

24  Chelsea, in their second match, break their Premiership duck in style, a 6-0 win at Barnsley with Gianluca Vialli scoring 4.

25  The one match tonight provides enough thrills and controversy for a full programme as Blackburn hammer Sheff Wed 7-2 and shoot to the top of the Premiership; Wednesday's Benito Carbone is sent off after 60min and Rovers' keeper John Filan suffers a broken arm after 63.

26  Celtic are through to the UEFA Cup proper, beating Tirol Innsbruck 6-3 (7-5 agg) with 2 goals in the last 3min, but Dundee Utd are out, held 1-1 at home by Trabzonspor (1-2 agg). England win a bonus 4th club in next year's UEFA Cup thanks to winning the Fair Play Trophy. In the Premiership, Liverpool break their duck with a 2-0 win at Leeds.

27  A goal by Temuri Ketsbaia in the last minute of extra time in Zagreb sees Newcastle through 4-3 on aggregate to the European Champions' League, but Rangers fail again, held 1-1 by Gothenburg at Ibrox and going out 4-1. Man Utd win 2-0 at Everton and go 2nd to Blackburn as the only two clubs with 10pts from 4 Premiership games, although Newcastle with 6 from 2 are the only 100% side. Arsenal, 2-0 up with 6min to go at Filbert Street, miss joining the leaders as Leicester grab a point in the 6th minute of stoppage time after Dennis Bergkamp completes a splendid hat-trick; Ian Wright, previously subbed, is involved with others in a fracas at the final whistle and could be in serious trouble, facing a 12-match ban. Gary Mabbutt returns for Spurs over a year after his left leg was shattered, coming on as sub at White Hart Lane and helping them come back from 1-2 to beat Villa 3-2.

29  Glenn Hoddle backs Ian Wright, picking him for the England squad despite the FA charge hanging over the errant Arsenal striker. Diego Maradona, 36, fails a drug test for the 3rd time in his career after making his comeback for Boca Juniors.

30  Wins for Blackburn and Man Utd takes them 3pts clear in the Premiership. Villa gain their first points after 5 matches with a 1-0 win over Leeds. In Div 3, Hull win their first points in 4 games and score their first goals with a 7-4 win over Swansea. The 1-1 draw at Ibrox between Rangers and Celtic reserve sides attracts 33,800 fans, only 164 fewer than the 3 Premier matches put together in which Hibs lose 1-0 at home to Hearts but still stay top.

31  Sunday fixtures, including Liverpool v Newcastle, are postponed because of the death of Diana, Princess of Wales.

## September

**SFA U-turns ... Rangers out of Coca-Cola Cup and Europe ... England lead their World Cup group ... Wright beats Bastin's record ... Asprilla hat-trick as Newcastle beat Barcelona ... 'bung-buster' report out ... racism at Leeds ... Arsenal overtake Man Utd ... Keegan new Fulham supremo ... Ravanelli goes to Marseille ... Roy Keane out for season ... Liverpool overcome Celtic**

1  Bolton open their new Reebok Stadium with a 0-0 draw against Everton, a 'goal' scored (according to TV replay) by Nathan Blake but not given, and the loss of newly acquired Robbie Elliott with a double leg fracture. Zoltan Czibor, left-winger of the great Hungarian side of the 50s, dies at 69. The Scottish FA controversially ignore calls to have their World Cup match against Belarus on Saturday postponed, all other major events being cancelled for Princess Diana's funeral.

2  West Ham defender Rio Ferdinand, 18, in line to become the youngest England cap since Duncan Edwards in 1955, is dropped from the squad by Glenn Hoddle for being banned from driving after failing a breath test.

3  Scotland, facing a revolt led by Rangers players, are off the hook as Belarus lift their objections to putting their match back to Sunday.

6  Ireland's 4-2 win in Iceland improves their chances of a World Cup play-off spot, while Holland's 3-1 victory over Belgium means they are virtually certain of qualifying for France 98. Norway qualify after winning 1-0 in Azerbaijan.

7  Scotland beat Belarus 4-1 and are looking good to qualify for France.

8  Glenn Hoddle names Arsenal keeper David Seaman captain for Wednesday's match. The top 10 Scottish clubs announce their intention to form a breakaway, autonomous Premier League next season under the auspices of the SFA. FIFA order Inter to pay Barcelona £1.17m in addition to the £17m they have already paid to release Ronaldo from his contract.

9  Liverpool striker Michael Owen is sent off in England U-18s 0-0 draw with Yugoslavia at Rotherham. N.Ireland coach Bryan Hamilton appoints West Ham midfielder Steve Lomas captain. Rangers make a shock exit from the Scottish Coca-Cola Cup, beaten 1-0 at home by Dundee Utd, while Hearts lose 1-0 at Dunfermline in the other quarter-final, both matches going to extra time.

10  Not only do a Gascoigne-inspired England beat Moldova 4-0 at Wembley but they have the added bonus of Georgia holding Italy 0-0, which means England now need only a draw in Rome to clinch their spot in France 98. Two free-kicks from Steve Staunton provide 2 goals for Tony Cascarino as Ireland win 2-1 in Lithuania and virtually book a place in the play-offs. Germany beat Armenia 4-0, with 2 goals by Jürgen Klinsmann in his 100th international. Albania do pick up their first win, 1-0 against hapless N.Ireland in Zurich. Bulgaria qualify with a 1-0 win over Russia, who must now contest the play-offs. In the Scottish Coca-Cola Cup quarter-finals, Celtic beat Motherwell 1-0 and Aberdeen win 2-0 at Stirling. Wolves chairman Jonathan Hayward moves down to let his father and owner of the club Sir Jack back as chairman.

11  The Premiership clubs promise to donate £3m over 3 years towards the £9m required for England's bid for the 2006 World Cup. A shake-up at faltering Carlisle sees manager Mervyn Day sacked and youth coach David Wilkes in temporary charge, with chairman Michael Knighton promising a more hands-on approach.

12  Despite Secretary Jim Farry's assertion yesterday that they were immovable on the issue, the SFA announce the transfer of their final World Cup tie from Easter Road to Celtic Park.

13  Hitting a hat-trick in a 4-1 win over Bolton at Highbury, Ian Wright takes his goal tally for Arsenal to 180, finally beating Cliff Bastin's 58-year-old record (178) for the club. With Blackburn playing tomorrow, Man Utd go top after a 2-1 win over West Ham, although John Hartson's goal for the visitors is the first conceded by the leaders this season, Peter Schmeichel having kept a clean sheet for 11hr 34min dating back to April. Newcastle lose their first points, a calamitous 3-1 home defeat by Wimbledon. Edinburgh rules the roost in Scotland, Hibs with 10pts thanks to their 5-2 defeat of Dunfermline and Hearts with 9 after winning 2-1 at St Johnstone. Rangers, held 3-3 at home by bottom club Aberdeen after going 2 up, are on 7pts but have 2 games in hand.

14  Blackburn suffer their first defeat, 4-3 at home to Leeds, with all goals coming in the first 34min, and stay 3pts behind Man Utd. Birmingham's Barry Horne, former captain of Wales, is the new PFA chairman.

15  Newcastle chairman Sir John Hall announces he will step down at the end of the season.

16  A stunning goal by Steve McManaman after a run from the half-way touchline a minute from time gives Liverpool a 2-2 draw at Celtic in their 1st round 1st leg UEFA Cup tie. Villa get a 0-0 draw at Bordeaux, but Arsenal, Leicester and Rangers all lose their away ties by a single goal. Arsenal have skipper Tony Adams back for the first time since May. In the 2nd round of the Coca-Cola Cup, 3 Premiership sides suffer 1-0 defeats away to lower-division clubs, Coventry, West Ham and Palace to Blackpool (Div 2), Huddersfield (bottom of Div 1) and Hull (Div 3), respectively.

17  England's clubs open their European Champions' League programme with splendid victories, Man Utd 3-0 over Kosice in Slovakia and Newcastle 3-2 at home to Barcelona thanks to a hat-trick by Faustino Asprilla and an inspired wing display by Keith Gillespie. In the Coca-Cola Cup, Blackburn slam Preston 6-0, but Sheff Wed go down 2-0 at Div 2 Grimsby.

18  Chelsea beat Slovan Bratislava 2-0 in their home leg of the Cup-Winners' Cup, but Kilmarnock lose 3-1 in Nice. Ian Wright will be available for England's Rome match as he, Arsenal team-mate Patrick Vieira and Leicester captain Steve Walsh are cleared of misconduct in the aftermath of their Premiership match at Filbert Street and just warned as to their future conduct, but Arsenal's assistant manager Pat Rice is fined £500. Goalkeepers Bruce Grobbelaar and Hans Segers, cleared last month of match-fixing, are charged by the FA with breaching rules on betting. West Ham sign Blackburn centre-half Ian Pearce for a fee that could reach £2.3m depending on appearances.

19  The Premier League report into corruption, a 500-page document compiled by the team of Rick Parry, Robert Reid QC and Steve Coppell over 4 years, has unearthed a cult of dishonesty within the game, including 'bungs', financial inducements, illegal payments to agents, false invoices and double dealing, and has caught several witnesses attempting to mislead the inquiry. FA charges are expected to follow.

20  Premiership leaders Man Utd are held 0-0 at Bolton, where Gary Pallister (Man U) and Nathan Blake (Bolton) are sent off. Blackburn, held 0-0 at Spurs, still trail by 3pts along with Leicester, 1-0 winners at Leeds, where racism again rears its ugly head in the crowd. Hearts beat Dundee Utd 2-1 to go top of the Scottish Premier by a point from Hibs, who are held 1-1 at Motherwell. Rangers, 2-0 winners at St Johnstone, are a further point behind but still with 2 games in hand.

21  In a bruising derby in which Chelsea's Frank Leboeuf is sent off, a rare goal from Nigel Winterburn a minute from time helps Arsenal to a 3-2 victory at Stamford Bridge and 2nd place in the Premiership, 2pts behind Man Utd.

22  Anderlecht's punishment from UEFA for bribing the referee in their match with Forest 13 years ago is a ban from the next European competition they qualify for, a decision that will encourage the Forest players suing for compensation.

24  Arsenal beat West Ham 4-0 and go top of the Premiership, on goal difference from Man Utd who can only draw 1-1 at Chelsea at Old Trafford, where a running feud between the players spills over into the tunnel at half-time. Newcastle, who beat Everton 1-0, are 6pts behind in 7th place, but have 3 games in hand. Derby beat Sheff Wed 5-2 at Hillsborough, where Wednesday's David Hirst and Benito Carbone are involved in an unseemly scuffle. Rangers win 3-0 at Kilmarnock to go top in Scotland, a point above Hearts. Spain's 2-1 victory in Slovakia puts them into the World Cup draw barring a disaster against the Faroes. The news surfaces that Kevin Keegan is about to take charge at Fulham, and their manager Micky Adams is absent as they are eliminated from the Coca-Cola Cup at Wolves tonight.

25  Kevin Keegan is officially presented to the media at Craven Cottage as the 'chief operating officer' of 2nd Div Fulham by owner Mohamed Al Fayed, along with Ray Wilkins as team manager. Fabrizio Ravanelli finally finds a new club, agreeing a £25,000 a week contract with Marseille, as Middlesbrough retrieve £5.5m of the £7m they paid for him 15 months ago. Following video evidence, the FA overturn the 3-match suspension Man United's Gary Pallister incurred for his harsh dismissal against Bolton.

27  Arsenal are held 2-2 at Everton after going 2 up, but move a point ahead of Man Utd who suffer their first defeat of the season, 1-0 at Leeds, and see their captain Roy Keane leave on crutches after a self-inflicted injury. Leicester, with a 2-0 win at Barnsley, move up to 3rd behind Man Utd on goal difference. The Keegan-Wilkins duo make an inauspicious start with Fulham, who lose 2-1 at Wigan after taking an early lead. Hearts emulate Rangers' 3-0 win at Kilmarnock in midweek and go back on top of the Scottish Premier as Rangers are held at home 2-2 by Motherwell.

28  High-scoring Blackburn, held 0-0 at home by Coventry despite their numerical superiority between the 42nd-min dismissal of Dion Dublin and the 68th-min sending-off of Jason Wilcox, miss their chance to go 2nd. Everton's Scottish striker Duncan Ferguson announces his retirement from international football.

29 Liverpool duo Steve McManaman and Robbie Fowler return to the England squad for the first time since they pulled out of the summer tour of France. John Hartson hits a hat-trick as West Ham beat Huddersfield 3-0, overturning their goal deficit in the Coca-Cola Cup.
30 In a physical game at Anfield, Liverpool hold on for a 0-0 draw and an away-goals victory over Celtic in the UEFA Cup. A Savo Milosevic goal in extra time gives Villa a 1-0 aggregate win over Bordeaux, but a late strike by PAOK at Highbury puts the Greek side through 2-1 after Dennis Bergkamp levelled the tie in the first half. Leicester controversially have Garry Parker sent off at Filbert Street – the first of his 2 yellow cards apparently for taking a free-kick too quickly – 10min after Atletico Madrid lose Juan Lopez, and succumb to 2 late goals for a 4-1 overall loss. Rangers go out of their second European competition this season, losing 2-1 at Ibrox to give Strasbourg a 4-2 aggregate. In the Coca-Cola Cup, Hull, 2nd bottom of Div 3, lose 2-1 to Palace at Selhurst Park but beat their Premiership opponents on away goals after extra time. Orient share an 8-goal thriller at Bolton but lose the tie 7-5. While Man Utd announce record profits of £27.6m and a link-up with BSkyB and Granada to create a club TV channel, their captain Roy Keane's injury turns out to be a snapped cruciate ligament which will keep him out for the rest of the season.

## October
**Man U beat Juventus ... Ferdinand and Fox locked in the lavatory ... England and Scotland qualify for World Cup ... police and England fans clash in Rome ... Ireland in play-offs ... Yugoslavia win 7-1 in Hungary ... Grimsby oust Coca-Cola holders Leicester ... Coca-Cola record for Rush**

1 A great night for English clubs in Europe as Man Utd chalk up a stirring 3-2 win over Juventus at Old Trafford despite losing a goal in the 1st minute, and Newcastle, thanks to 2-goal John Beresford, battle back for a draw in Kiev after trailing 2-0 with only 13min left. In the Coca-Cola Cup, Coventry come back from 2 down overall to score 3 goals in the last half-hour, including 2 Gary McAllister penalties, to beat Blackpool. But Sheff Wed fail to make up a 2-goal deficit and go out to Grimsby 4-3 on aggregate.
2 Chelsea make impressive progress in Europe, beating Slovan 2-0 again, this time in Bratislava, in the Cup-Winners' Cup. But Kilmarnock go out to Nice, who take the tie 4-2. Bolton pay a club record £3.5m for Wimbledon striker Dean Holdsworth, 28.
3 UEFA order Spartak Moscow to replay their UEFA Cup match against Swiss side Sion because their goals were 4.7in (12cm) too low. West Ham full-back Julian Dicks, sidelined since March, needs another op on his knee and will probably be out for the season.
4 Premiership leaders Arsenal enjoy a 5-0 win over Barnsley, who drop to bottom spot. But Man Utd, a point behind, keep up the pressure with a 2-0 victory over Palace. Newcastle beat Spurs 1-0 at St James' Park, where Spurs start the second half with 9 men, leaving strikers Les Ferdinand and Ruel Fox locked in the toilet. Steve Ogrizovic makes his record 488th League appearance for Coventry and keeps a clean sheet as they draw at home to Leeds. Hearts stay top in Scotland with a 4-1 away win over Motherwell, but Rangers, coming back from 3-1 down at Hibs to win 4-3, are still a point behind with a game in hand.
5 Patrik Berger scores 3 as Liverpool beat Chelsea 4-2 at Anfield. Middlesbrough's Paul Merson replaces the injured Rob Lee in England's squad.
6 Derby's 2-1 win at Leicester, their 5th in 6 outings, moves them up to 6th, 7pts behind leaders Arsenal but with 2 games in hand. Huddersfield, bottom of Div 1, sack manager Brian Horton and 3 coaches. Rangers announce a turnover of £32m, a profit of £6m and assets of £56m. Torino, in Italy's Serie B, sack coach Graeme Souness after just 6 games this season, but he comes away with £750k compensation.
7 Souness explains that he is not leaving Torino, but has agreed to play a wider role in the club's development. Halifax player Peter Jackson is confirmed as new Huddersfield manager. The German FA order a match to be replayed, ruling that the goal scored by Sean Dundee to give Karlsruhe a 2-2 draw against Munich 1860 crossed the line after the referee had blown for time.
8 FIFA secretary Sepp Blatter is reported as calling for the abolition of the tackle, but director of communications Keith Cooper explains that in German the word means something more sinister, although the sliding tackle is under review. Swansea, who have dropped to 20th in Div 3 after losing 6 of their last 8 matches, sack manager Jan Molby. Peterborough and Portsmouth are each fined £12,500 (£10,000 suspended) for the brawl during a Coca-Cola Cup match in August.
9 Micky Adams, sacrificed as Fulham player-manager to make way for the Keegan-Wilkins regime, makes a speedy return to management with Swansea.
10 Glenn Hoddle makes Paul Ince captain for tomorrow's vital match rather than Tony Adams. Ryan Giggs is to captain Wales tomorrow for the first time, taking over from the suspended Gary Speed.
11 After weeks of hype, England are through to the World Cup finals, gaining a momentous 0-0 draw in Rome with Italy, who now face the play-offs. The game is marred by scenes of violence on the terraces, with baton-wielding police wading into a section of England fans. Scotland beat Latvia 2-0 and are also through, as best runners-up, behind Austria. Ireland draw 1-1 at home to runaway group winners Romania, who lose their first points, and qualify for the play-offs having avoided the 12-goal defeat that might have kept them out. N.Ireland are beaten 1-0 by Portugal, who are themselves eliminated as both Germany and Ukraine win, the former with an extraordinarily difficult 4-3 home victory over Albania. Wales, making an academic trip to Belgium, salvage some pride in 3-2 defeat after being 3 down at half-time. Holland qualify from this group despite being held 0-0 at home by Turkey. Spain do no more than they have to against the Faeroes, winning 3-1, so Yugoslavia contest the play-offs.
12 Allegations and counter-allegations about yesterday's crowd trouble in Rome look set to rage for some time.
14 The FA announce that England manager Glenn Hoddle, a committed family man, has split with his wife Anne after 18 years of marriage. Man Utd, fielding a virtual 2nd XI, albeit with 7 internationals starting,

go down 2-0 at Ipswich in the Coca-Cola Cup, but manager Alex Ferguson does not seem bothered. Arsenal's mostly reserve side manage to beat Birmingham 4-1, although they need extra time in which débutant Jason Crowe is sent off 33sec after coming on for Lee Dixon, evening up the numbers following Darren Wassall's dismissal for Birmingham 7min earlier. Holders Leicester are beaten 3-1 at 2nd Div Grimsby after leading at half-time. Sheff Utd suffer their first defeat of the season, losing 2-1 at 2nd Div Walsall. Bolton win for the first time at their new Reebok Stadium, beating Wimbledon 2-0 after extra time.

15   In all-Premiership clashes in the Coca-Cola Cup, Chelsea beat Blackburn 4-1 on penalties despite having Gianluca Vialli dismissed in extra time, Coventry beat Everton 4-1, and West Ham beat Villa 3-0, while Spurs are the only home failures, going down 2-1 to Derby. Liverpool, Leeds and Newcastle come through safely against lower-division opposition. One of Newcastle's goals in their 2-0 win over Hull is scored by Ian Rush to equal Geoff Hurst's record of 49 in the League Cup. In the North-East derby, Middlesbrough beat Sunderland 2-0 and some of the home fans attack the Sunderland team coach after the game with bricks and concrete missiles. Dundee Utd beat Aberdeen 3-1 at Tynecastle to reach the final of the Scottish Coca-Cola Cup. Former England star Colin Bell will receive undisclosed compensation after Man City admit he was unfairly sacked from his youth development post.

17   Southampton gamble a club record £2m on injury-prone Sheff Wed striker David Hirst. Following a protest from Leicester, the referee of their UEFA Cup home defeat by Atletico Madrid, Frenchman Remi Harrel, has been dropped from the rest of this season's competition.

18   The big guns in the Premiership are held, Arsenal 0-0 at Palace, where Dennis Bergkamp's 5th caution means an automatic 3-match suspension, and Man Utd 2-2 at Derby after going 2-0 down. So Blackburn, who beat Southampton 1-0, split them by taking 2nd place. Everton emerge from the doldrums in the best possible way, a 2-0 victory over Liverpool in the Merseyside derby at Goodison. Newcastle crumble 4-1 at Leeds. In Scotland, Celtic beat leaders Hearts 2-1 away, handing top spot for the first time this season to deadly rivals Rangers who thrash Dunfermline 7-0, with 4 for the prolific Marco Negri.

19   Spurs beat Sheff Wed 3-2 to ease the pressure on manager Gerry Francis. After 17 months out with injury, Southampton midfielder and former England cap Barry Venison, 33, announces his retirement.

20   Barnsley, after 6 defeats on the trot, ease themselves off the bottom of the Premiership with a 2-0 victory over Coventry.

21   In the UEFA Cup Liverpool are shattered by a 3-0 reverse in Strasbourg but Villa come away from Athletic Bilbao with a creditable 0-0 draw and praise for their fans from a top police officer. With both matches shown live on TV, 18 Nationwide clubs suffer their worst gate of the season so far. Italy's Serie A leaders Inter have their 11-match unbeaten run ended by Olympique Lyon, 2-1 winners at the San Siro. Wolves chairman Sir Jack Hayward forks out more cash to keep his club afloat, a further £8m.

22   A brilliantly taken goal by Paul Scholes is the feature of Man United's unflattering 2-1 victory over Feyenoord in the Champions' League which maintains their 100% record, while Juventus keep up the pressure with a 1-0 win at Kosice. But Newcastle suffer their first defeat, 1-0 by PSV in Eindhoven, to drop 3pts behind Dinamo Kiev, 3-0 victors over Barcelona in front of 100,000. Manager Micky Adams walks out on Swansea 13 days after his appointment on finding that money promised for new signings is not there; his assistant Alan Cork is immediately promoted to manager.

23   Chelsea, struggling after conceding 2 early goals on a snow-covered pitch in Tromso, in the Arctic Circle, survive a hectic 2nd half played in a snowstorm to finish only 3-2 behind in their Cup-Winners' Cup tie after 3 goals in the last 6min, Gianluca Vialli driving through heroically for two solo goals either side of Tromso's third. N.Ireland sack manager Bryan Hamilton. Four Liverpool fans who attacked a passer-by in Strasbourg before Tuesday's UEFA Cup match are jailed by a French court as an example to other English hooligans.

24   In an official report, the FA blame the Italian police for the crowd trouble in Rome, a view immediately contradicted by the Italian embassy in London. A judge, sentencing the former Spurs general manager Eddie Ashby to 4 months for a flagrant breach of a bankruptcy ban, dismisses Terry Venables' evidence as intended dishonestly to mislead the jury.

25   Andy Cole hits 3 as Man Utd thrash Barnsley 7-0 and, with Arsenal playing tomorrow, go top of the Premiership. Blackburn draw 1-1 at Newcastle and stay 3rd. Liverpool come back after their midweek debacle in Europe to confound the knockers with a 4-0 beating of Derby. Celtic beat St Johnstone 2-0 to take over at the top in Scotland as Rangers suffer a shock 2-1 defeat at lowly Dundee Utd, their first in the League. Nevertheless, their scorer Marco Negri finds the net for the 9th consecutive League game – his 20th in the 9 matches – to beat the record set in 1977 by Hibs' Ally MacLeod.

26   Arsenal, held 0-0 at home by Villa, fail to regain top spot. The dismissal of Arsenal's Emmanuel Petit near the end for touching referee Paul Durkin adds to the club's poor disciplinary record.

27   News is out, prior to tomorrow's official announcement from Rangers, that manager Walter Smith is to stand down at the end of the season. Referee John Brandwood, who sent Forest keeper Dave Beasant off for the first time in his career during Forest's draw with Reading on Friday, reverses his decision after studying the match video and changes it to a caution.

28   Less than two years, 27 appearances and 4 goals after his £4.5m signing from Parma, Leeds decide to cut their losses on Sweden striker Tomas Brolin, granting him a free transfer and a reported pay-off of £140k. Man City's mercurial Georgia midfielder Georgi Kinkladze crashes his Ferrari but suffers only minor injuries. Referee Mike Reed threatens legal action against John Hartson for comments the West Ham striker made after Monday's defeat at Leicester.

29   In the World Cup play-offs, Ireland scrape a 1-1 draw with Belgium in Dublin thanks to Shay Given's heroics in goal, while Italy weather a snowstorm and a Russian onslaught in Moscow to come back with the same result. The scoreline that must have sent shudders round the rest of the world, however, was Hungary 1 Yugoslavia 7. In a damage limitation exercise, West Ham striker John Hartson faxes

apologies to referee Mike Reed and the FA for 'heat-of-the-moment' comments last Monday, which Reed accepts immediately. Winless Doncaster, bottom Nationwide club, are now managerless again, as Dave Cowling resigns after just 10 days in protest at interference from within the club, which, a few hours later, agrees a takeover by a consortium for £2m. Hearts beat Dunfermline 3-1 to go above Rangers in the Scottish Premier to 2nd, just behind Celtic on goal difference.

30  Sir John Smith, appointed by the FA to look into betting within football, reaches the conclusion that there is a widespread cult of betting in the game which is cause for serious concern, and that the anti-betting rules should be clarified. As Doncaster appoint Danny Bergara caretaker manager, the League are to investigate their takeover because of the presence on the consortium of Anton Johnson, banned for life 13 years ago from owning a League club. Coventry manager Gordon Strachan, recently linked with Benfica, scotches all such rumours by signing a new contract that will tie him to Highfield Road until 2003.

31  The FA decide to reopen their inquiry into gambling following revelations made by David Howells of Spurs on Radio 5.


**November**
**Arsenal beaten ... Negri scores in 10th game on trot ... David Pleat sacked ... Irwin clogged ... Arsenal halt march of United ... 'Big Ron' back at Wednesday ... Ireland out of World Cup, Jamaica and Japan in ... Francis out at Spurs, Gross in ... Man U reach knock-out stage of European Cup ... heartbreak for Venables Down Under ... Celtic win Coca-Cola Cup**

1   The last unbeaten record in the League is smashed as Arsenal go down 3-0 at Derby, while leaders Man Utd score their 13th goal in 2 matches, beating Sheff Wed 2-0 to go 4pts clear. Blackburn stay 3rd, held 1-1 at Barnsley, who move off the bottom, above Wednesday. Hearts go top in Scotland, beating Aberdeen 4-1 away to edge ahead on goal difference as Celtic win 2-0 at Dunfermline. Scoring in his 10th match running, the prolific Marco Negri hits another 3 for Rangers, who remain a point behind. Former Rangers boss Graeme Souness is named new coach of Benfica.

2   News leaks out of David Pleat's sacking by Sheff Wed, to be announced tomorrow.

3   The Premiership match between West Ham and Palace at Upton Park is abandoned after 65min because of floodlight failure with the score 2-2. Villa manager Brian Little gives captain Gareth Southgate a dressing-down for his public remarks yesterday that he and other leading players could be forced to leave because of the club's lack of ambition.

4   Putting their domestic troubles behind them, Villa beat Athletic Bilbao 2-1 to go through to the 3rd round of the UEFA Cup, but Liverpool's 2-0 win over Strasbourg is not quite enough. An industrial tribunal finds Chester manager Kevin Ratcliffe guilty of racial discrimination and awards former apprentice James Hussaney £2,500 for 'injury to feelings'.

5   Despite an unpleasant atmosphere in Rotterdam, where rival fans fought a 300-a-side pre-match battle, Man Utd come away with a perfect result, Andy Cole hitting a hat-trick in their 3-1 defeat of Feyenoord, to keep the only 100% record in the Champions' League. On the down side is a nasty injury to Denis Irwin, the result of a disgraceful challenge by Paul Bosvelt for which he is not even booked. Sadly, Newcastle have virtually blown their chances, losing 2-0 at home to PSV Eindhoven. Their group is still headed by unbeaten Dynamo Kiev, impressive 4-0 winners over Barcelona in Spain, Andriy Shevchenko scoring 3. Swindon, forced to play the fittest of their 3 crocked keepers, Fraser Digby, beat QPR 3-1 to go top of Div 1. Micky Adams takes over from Eddie May at Brentford, his 3rd club in 6 weeks. Preston, the first ever League Champions, win a £7.5m Lottery grant to build a national football museum at Deepdale.

6   Chelsea cruise through to the Cup-Winners' Cup semi-finals, beating Tromso 7-1 (9-4 agg), although it is not until the part-timers are down to 10 men that they score the last 4 and Gianluca Vialli completes his hat-trick.

7   Glenn Hoddle picks strikers Andy Cole and Chris Sutton and defender Rio Ferdinand in the England squad for the friendly with Cameroon.

8   With Man Utd at Highbury tomorrow, Blackburn slip in between the two leaders, scraping past Everton with 2 late goals for a 3-2 win. Leeds produce the comeback of the season, hitting 4 past Derby at Elland Road after going 3 behind in 34min. Sheff Wed climb off the bottom in style, slamming fellow-strugglers Bolton 5-0, all goals in the 1st half including an Andy Booth hat-trick. Spurs' 4-0 defeat at Anfield almost certainly spells the end for hapless manager Gerry Francis. Home sides win the big derbies in Scotland, Hearts beating Hibs 2-0 to stay in front as Rangers beat Celtic for the 9th time in succession, with Richard Gough scoring the only goal and Marco Negri failing to score in the League for the first time this season.

9   In a thriller at Highbury, Man Utd come back from two early reverses to draw level by the interval, but David Platt scores a late winner for Arsenal to take them within a point of the leaders and give heart to the rest of the challengers. Repercussions might follow incidents, however, in which Schmeichel and Winterburn were struck by missiles from the crowd. At Stamford Bridge, where two West Ham players, John Moncur and Eyal Berkovic, have to be pulled apart on the field, Chelsea win 2-1 and are now 3pts behind Man Utd with a game in hand. In Vancouver, the USA beat Canada 3-0 to clinch a place in the World Cup finals. Argentine-born former manager of Inter-Milan, Helenio Herrera dies at the age of 81.

10  Languishing in mid-table in Div 1, QPR sack manager Stewart Houston, while his assistant Bruce Rioch learns of his own dismissal on Ceefax. Former Scotland captain Roy Aitken is dismissed as manager of Aberdeen following yesterday's 5-0 defeat by Dundee Utd.

11  John Hollins takes over as caretaker at QPR.

12　In friendly internationals against World Cup favourites, Scotland lose 2-1 in France, Wales 3-0 in Brazil. Saudi Arabia qualify for the finals with a 1-0 win over Qatar.

13　Ron Atkinson is enticed back as manager of Sheff Wed, the details to be announced tomorrow. The Premier League agree a £100m 3-year contract with Mark McCormack's TWI and French TV company Canal Plus to televise their matches overseas. England U-21s lose the 1st leg of their play-off for a place in the UEFA finals by 2-0 in Greece, and have Man Utd teenage defender John Curtis sent off near the close on his U-21 début.

14　Rejecting a 3-year deal, Ron Atkinson signs to the end of the season as Sheff Wed boss with a brief to keep them in the Premiership. UEFA fine Feyenoord £11,000 for the conduct of their fans after crowd disturbances at the match against Man Utd, who in turn have been fined £1,700.

15　Ireland make a sad but courageous exit from the World Cup, beaten 2-1 in Belgium (3-2 agg) in the European play-offs. Other qualifiers are Italy, Croatia and Yugoslavia. Meanwhile England win their friendly with Cameroon at Wembley 2-0, Glenn Hoddle giving débuts to subs Rio Ferdinand and Chris Sutton. In the 1st round of the FA Cup, financially strapped Hereford take revenge on Brighton, beating the team that sent them into the Vauxhall Conference in the last match of last season by 2-1. The only other non-Leaguers to triumph over Nationwide opponents are last season's Cup heroes Hednesford, 2-0 winners at Hull, but Solihull draw 1-1 at Darlington, Gainsborough 1-1 at Lincoln City and Basingstoke 2-2 at Wycombe, and Hendon and Slough earn away replays. Blyth Spartans go down fighting at Blackpool, and after their last-minute 4-3 defeat player-manager John Burridge, 46-year-old veteran goalkeeper of 24 clubs including Blackpool, announces his retirement from the playing side. With the big Glasgow clubs slipping up against the Premier's bottom sides, Rangers held 1-1 at Aberdeen and Celtic losing 2-0 at home to Motherwell, Hearts take a 3pt lead after a last-minute penalty gives them a 2-1 victory over St Johnstone.

16　A 0-0 home draw with Mexico is enough to clinch Jamaica's place in France 98, the first West Indies team ever to reach the World Cup finals. Japan also reach the finals for the first time with a 3-2 'golden goal' defeat in Malaysia of Iran, who must now meet Australia for the last finals spot. Chile are the last S.American country to qualify, beating Bolivia 3-0 in Santiago. In the FA Cup, Fulham leave it late before winning 2-1 at Margate.

17　Barnsley reserve Dean Jones, 20, is charged by the FA with misconduct after failing a random drugs test, the first player with a Premier League club to do so.

18　Gerry Francis, who apparently had his resignation as Spurs manager rejected 2 weeks ago after their defeat at Liverpool, will resign officially at a press conference tomorrow and be replaced by disciplinarian Swiss coach Christian Gross of Grasshopper Zurich. Meanwhile, down the road at Highbury, Dennis Bergkamp, in the middle of a 3-match Premiership suspension, scores the winner in extra time as Arsenal, fielding half a reserve side, beat Coventry 1-0 in the Coca-Cola Cup. Reading, only 4pts from bottom of Div 1, cause an upset at Elland Road, beating Leeds 3-2, while Div 1 Middlesbrough beat Bolton 2-1 after extra time.

19　Teenage midfielder Jody Morris scores Chelsea's winner against Southampton 3min from the end of extra time to put them in the quarter-finals of the Coca-Cola Cup. West Ham are also through, Frank Lampard scoring 3 in their 4-1 win over Walsall. Paul Gascoigne is sent off for Rangers in the 57th minute at Celtic Park, but the 10 men take the lead through Marco Negri after 71min and it is only in the last minute that Alan Stubbs equalises for Celtic, enabling Hearts to stay top of the League. England climb to 6th in the FIFA world rankings, their highest position to date.

20　Paul Gascoigne incurs a 5-match ban for what was his first dismissal in Scottish domestic football, the 12pt penalty taking him past the 21pt mark. Andy Cole signs a new 5yr contract with Man Utd.

21　In an effort to pay off debts of over £10m and prevent closure, Oxford put their complete playing staff up for sale. West Ham's John Hartson escapes with a £1,000 fine for his verbal attack on referee Mike Reed last month.

22　Man Utd win 5-2 at Wimbledon, all goals coming in the 2nd half, while Blackburn stay within a point by beating Chelsea 1-0. But Arsenal crash 2-0 at Hillsborough, Sheff Wed playing their first match under Ron Atkinson this time round. The big upset is Barnsley's 1-0 win at Anfield to climb off the bottom. Hearts, without a game, stay top of the Scottish Premier as Rangers are held 1-1 at Motherwell. Celtic beat Dundee Utd 4-1 to stay in close contention in what has developed into a clear 3-horse race. Australia draw the 1st leg of their World Cup play-off with Iran 1-1 in Teheran, their goal scored by Leeds Utd teenager Harry Kewell.

23　Hearts, with a hat-trick from Stephane Adam, beat Kilmarnock 5-3 and extend their lead to 4pts.

24　New Spurs manager Christian Gross sees the extent of his task at White Hart Lane as the side, picked by assistant Chris Hughton, slip to a 1-0 defeat by Palace.

25　A Dwight Yorke 'away' goal gives Villa hope after they go 2 down to Steaua Bucharest in their UEFA Cup 3rd round tie. In the FA Cup 1st round replays, Orient are stunned 1-0 at home by Ryman League side Hendon and Wycombe lose on penalties at Basingstoke. Arsenal's French midfielder Emmanuel Petit receives a further 1-match ban and a fine of £1,000 for the pushing incident with referee Paul Durkin in last month's match with Villa.

26　In the Champions' Cup, Newcastle lose their last slim chance of qualifying for the knock-out stage as they go down 1-0 to Barcelona, bottom club in their group. Juventus's 2-0 defeat at Feyenoord leaves Man Utd virtually certain to win their group. In the Premiership, Chelsea go 3rd but need 2 penalties in the last 11min to beat bottom club Everton, who have Slaven Bilic expelled for the 2nd time this season. Solihull lose their home FA Cup replay to Darlington on penalties.

27　Man Utd clinch their Champions' League group with their 5th straight win, 3-0 over Kosice at Old Trafford.

29　Chelsea draw level behind Man Utd on goal difference with a 4-0 hammering of Derby, Gianfranco Zola notching 3. Leeds stage another comeback, winning 3-2 at Barnsley after going 2 down, and go 4th. Relishing his first match in charge of Spurs, Christian Gross presides over a 2-0 win at Goodison over bottom club Everton. Another new manager Ron Atkinson sees Sheff Wed chalk up their first away win of the campaign, 3-2 at Southampton. With Hearts not playing, Rangers move to within a point of the leaders after beating St Johnstone 3-2, Marco Negri netting another brace. Terry Venables is mortified to see his Australian side lose a 2-goal lead in Melbourne to Iran, who win their World Cup play-off on away goals.

30 Man Utd demonstrate their superiority with an overwhelming 4-0 victory over challengers Blackburn to go 3pts clear again, while Arsenal's challenge subsides with their first home defeat, 1-0 by Liverpool. In Scotland, Celtic gain a rare 3-0 triumph at Ibrox – not over rivals Rangers but in the final of the Coca-Cola Cup over Dundee Utd.

## December
**Honorary knighthood for Pelé ... Chelsea win 6-1 at Spurs ... Villa reach UEFA Cup last 8 ... Klinsmann and Pleat return to Tottenham ... third floodlight failure: Far East betting syndicates suspected ... England 4th in rankings ... Tom Finney knighted**

1 Ireland supporters win the 1997 FIFA Fair Play award for their exemplary behaviour during the World Cup qualifiers. Fulham sign Blackburn defender Chris Coleman for £2.1m. The PFA, celebrating their 90th birthday, announce a £30m TV deal over 4 years split 3 equal ways to help Premiership players and clubs, League players and clubs, and injured or retiring players. Coach Vanessa Hardwick wins her case against the FA in front of an industrial tribunal, who ruled that she had been deliberately failed and refused an advanced licence at a top FA coaching course because of her sex.

2 Following an investigation of the Italy-England World Cup tie in Rome, FIFA fine both countries, apportioning blame to both the English fans and the Italian police. The fines are thought to be relatively small, but any repeat by either party will lead to stiffer punishment. The 8 seeds for Thursday's World Cup draw do not include England despite their high FIFA ranking. It emerges that Portsmouth were unable to pay their players and staff their November wages. Borussia Dortmund beat Cruzeiro (Brazil) 2-0 in the final of the World Club Championship in Tokyo. Bottom League club Doncaster win their first match of the season and have a new manager, general manager Mark Weaver taking over from the newly appointed Danny Bergara, who decided not to attend any more games! Ten players are sent off in the Nationwide programme, half of them at Wigan, where visitors Bristol R play the last 20min with 7 players against 10 and lose 3-0. Also in Div 2 there is a mass brawl in injury time at the Luton–Gillingham game (2-2), and police have to intervene at the final whistle when fans try to attack a visiting player.

3 Pelé, now Brazilian sports minister, in London on a state visit with the Brazilian president, receives an honorary knighthood from the Queen at Buckingham Palace, becoming a Knight Commander of the British Empire (KBE). Hungarian Sandor Puhl, the referee who failed to punish Feyenoord's Paul Bosvelt for his crippling tackle on Man United's Denis Irwin, has been dropped as a UEFA referee for the rest of the season.

4 In the curtain-raiser to the World Cup draw in Marseille, with tackling off the menu, Europe are beaten 5-2 by the Rest of the World, Ronaldo scoring twice and putting on a dazzling first-half display – ominous for Scotland who are again drawn with Brazil. England find themselves in Romania's group. West Brom reject manager Ray Harford's resignation and take out an injunction to prevent his taking the vacant QPR job. Liverpool captain of the mid-60s, Ron Yeats, now the club's chief scout, unveils a statue of legendary manager Bill Shankly at Anfield in a ceremony that also honours his successor Bob Paisley, and the two widows open the new visitors' centre at the Kop end. Former England striker Paul Walsh, 35, now with Portsmouth, announces his retirement due to a long-standing knee injury.

5 Jamie Stuart, 21, becomes the 4th Charlton player to fail a drugs test, and is suspended by the club pending an FA inquiry. West Brom drop their legal action to prevent Ray Harford's appointment as QPR boss, the amount of compensation not being disclosed.

6 Man Utd outclass Liverpool 3-1 at Anfield to maintain their 3pt lead at the top of the Premiership over Chelsea, who humiliate Spurs at White Hart Lane to the tune of 6-1, with 3 from Tore Andre Flo, scoring 5 without reply in a 2nd half that wrecks Christian Gross's first home match in charge – their worst home defeat since Arsenal beat them 6-0 in 1935. Blackburn, a further point adrift, keep up their challenge with a 3-1 win over Bolton. Five non-League sides earn replays in the FA Cup, all after drawing away: Stevenage, Hereford, Emley, Basingstoke and Ilkeston at Cambridge, Colchester, Lincoln, Northampton and Scunthorpe. League newcomers Macclesfield, however, are thrashed 7-0 at home by Walsall of Div 2. In Scotland, Hearts beat Motherwell 2-0 to go 4pts clear of gameless Rangers, who have played the same number of matches now, while Celtic, held 0-0 at Kilmarnock, are 3pts further adrift.

7 Terry Venables resents press insinuations that a £300k payment from Portsmouth was a 'bung', openly paid as it was as a belated fee due on taking over as chairman more than a year ago. There is still confusion, however, as to whether he owns the 51% of the club's shares he claims are his. Rangers beat Hibs 1-0 to cut Hearts' Scottish Premier lead to 1pt. Former Leeds and Scottish dynamo Billy Bremner dies at 54.

8 While Portsmouth players finally get their November wages paid, thanks to a loan from the PFA, the speculation about chairman Terry Venables shifts to whether or not he will land the Nigeria job, coaching the African team in the World Cup. A brief meeting with Martin Gregory, the sale of whose Portsmouth shares to Venables is in dispute, proves inconclusive.

9 With their goals coming in the last 20min, Villa beat Steaua Bucharest 2-0 (3-2 agg) to reach the UEFA Cup quarter-finals. Inter, the favourites, overturn a 2-0 deficit to beat Strasbourg 3-2 overall. In the Nationwide Div 1, Portsmouth put their troubles behind them to beat Wolves 3-2 and climb off the bottom. Held 0-0 at Dundee Utd, their first draw of the campaign, Hearts go 2pts clear of Rangers in the

Scottish Premier, while Celtic's 2-0 win at Aberdeen leaves them a further 3pts away, all three leaders now having played 16 games.

10 Man Utd lose their 100% record in the Champions' League, going 1-0 down in Turin and thus, thanks also to Rosenborg's failure to win, allowing Juventus into the last 8 'by the back door', as a runner-up. Newcastle inflict the first defeat (2-0) on already-qualified Dynamo Kiev, and ensure Barcelona finish last in their group. Charlton cancel U-21 defender Jamie Stuart's contract as a result of his positive drugs test.

11 The Football League meet to examine proposals for 'reinvigorating' their competition; these include altering the structure of the competition and the points system, introducing double-header week-ends, and abolishing the transfer deadline.

12 After admitting breaching FA rules on betting, keepers Bruce Grobbelaar and Hans Segers are given bans (6mo) and fines (£10k) by the FA, suspended for 2 years because of the financial hardship they have already suffered and the 3-year blight on their careers as a result of the 'bribery' court cases.

13 Man Utd, playing on Monday, sit back and watch their nearest 4 challengers locked together in battle. Blackburn come out best, winning 3-1 at Arsenal to go 2nd, 1pt behind United, and above Chelsea who are held 0-0 at home despite Leeds being reduced to 9 men for the whole of the 2nd half. Ian Wright, who earned a senseless late booking, could be in trouble again after a confrontation from the dressing-room window with Arsenal fans outside. Coventry push hapless Spurs deeper into trouble with a 4-0 victory, leaving them 3pts adrift in 3rd-from-bottom place. Scottish leaders Hearts lose 1-0 at Celtic, but Rangers, held 0-0 at Dunfermline, fail to take advantage and remain 1pt behind, with Celtic 1pt behind them. Man City midfielder Georgi Kinkladze is banned for one international and fined SFr5,000 for assaulting an opponent in Georgia's World Cup qualifier against Poland.

15 Man Utd move away from the field again with a 1-0 win over Villa, despite Teddy Sheringham's penalty miss. In a 2nd round Cup replay, Cambridge take the lead at non-League Stevenage, but lose 2 men by 41min and the match 2-1.

16 In Cup replays, both non-League home sides are taken to penalties, Hereford beating Colchester, but Basingstoke losing to Northampton. Cheltenham win the all non-League replay 2-0 at Boreham Wood. Former England star Alan Hudson, 46, is critically ill in hospital after being struck by a car last night near his home in east London.

17 England U-21s beat Greece 4-2 at Norwich but lose on away goals and fail to qualify for the UEFA finals. In Cup replays, little Emley beat Lincoln on penalties after coming back from 2-0 down in normal time and drawing 3-3 aet. The other non-League club Ilkeston go down 2-1 at home to Scunthorpe. The Nigeria World Cup coaching job goes to Bora Milutinovic, not Terry Venables.

19 After 3 months' trying, Liverpool succeed where Newcastle, Sunderland and Southampton failed, obtaining a work permit for US keeper Brad Friedel, who costs them £1m from Columbus Crew. Inter's Brazilian striker Ronaldo is the 1997 Golden Ball European Footballer of the Year, awarded by *France Football*; the highest placed Premiership player is Arsenal's Dennis Bergkamp, 4th.

20 Blackburn beat West Ham 3-0 and Chelsea win 4-1 at Sheff Wed to close up within 1 and 2pts, respectively, of Man Utd. Two-goal David Ginola fires Spurs to a 3-0 win over bottom club Barnsley, but Spurs stay in the 3rd relegation position, above Everton who notch their first away win in more than a year, their first goal in a month and their first win in 9 games, 1-0 at Leicester. Rangers show who's boss in Scotland, overtaking leaders Hearts by 2pts with a crushing 5-2 victory at Tynecastle (Gordon Durie 3), even more remarkable having lost Italian teenager Rino Gattuso in the 69th minute for a second caution when they were leading only 3-1. Celtic's 5-0 defeat of Hibs also takes them past Hearts.

21 Andy Cole goes back to Newcastle and scores the winner for Man Utd to restore their 4pt lead in the Premiership. Brazil beat Australia 6-0 in the final of the much-maligned FIFA/Confederations' Cup in Riyadh, having drawn with them in the group matches, but this time are down to 10 men when 2-0 down and have no answers to hat-trick strikers Ronaldo and Romario.

22 Spurs hit the headlines with two signings, both old boys – inspirational German striker Jürgen Klinsmann, 33, relegated to the bench at Sampdoria, returns on a 6-month contract, leaving chairman Alan Sugar to eat humble pie, and former manager David Pleat is appointed director of football. The Wimbledon-Arsenal game at Selhurst Park is abandoned immediately after the start of the 2nd half at 0-0 because of floodlight failure, the 3rd such occurrence in the Premiership this season. Arsenal captain Tony Adams, who missed the match, is expected to be out for 6 weeks in order to clear up a back injury that threatens his fitness for the World Cup. It is reported that the FA's lawyers Freshfields have recommended that the FA take action against certain individuals named in the FA's 'bung' inquiry and that the FA are seeking further advice from a QC.

23 Police are to investigate claims that last night's floodlight failure at Selhurst Park was the work of Far East betting syndicates. England rise to 4th in the FIFA World Rankings. Coventry sign Romania striker Viorel Moldovan for a club record £3.25m from Swiss club Grasshopper. Oxford's Denis Smith agrees a 3-year contract to manage West Brom. Crisis-hit Portsmouth, bottom of Div 1 and with chairman Terry Venables and director Martin Gregory still battling for control, are banned by the League from buying players until they have paid back their PFA loan.

24 Villa striker Stan Collymore is bailed after being charged with an assault on a former girlfriend.

26 Man Utd widen their Premiership lead to 6pts with an effortless 2-0 victory over Everton, while Blackburn are held 0-0 at Sheff Wed and Chelsea 1-1 at home to Wimbledon. Stan Collymore answers his critics with 2 late strikes to kill Spurs off 4-1 at Villa Park and double his season's goal tally. Watching Portsmouth for the first time in 3 months, chairman Terry Venables sees his side beat QPR 3-1 and move off the bottom of Div 1 on goals from three other clubs.

27 Rangers beat Dundee Utd 4-1 to go 2pts ahead in the Scottish Premier, with Hearts, 3-1 winners at Dunfermline, now 2nd, 2pts in front of Celtic, 1-0 losers at St Johnstone. Graeme Souness signs Man United's underused Czech midfielder Karel Poborsky for Benfica in a £3m deal.

28    On a full Sunday programme in England, Man Utd slip up at Coventry, conceding 2 goals in the last 5min to lose 3-2, but they lead by 5pts as Blackburn, held 1-1 at home to Palace, fail to take advantage. Jürgen Klinsmann makes a low-key return for Spurs in a 1-1 draw with Arsenal at White Hart Lane, and his arrival is tempered by the news of injury blows to England stars Darren Anderton and Les Ferdinand, manager Christian Gross's refusal to deny he will quit if fitness trainer Fritz Schmidt is not granted a work permit, and wins for the 2 clubs below them – Everton, indeed, push Spurs into 2nd-bottom place with a 3-2 victory over Bolton, Duncan Ferguson scoring 3, all with his head. Spurs' problems are nothing, however, to those of Doncaster, falling apart at the bottom of Div 3 with 9pts from 24 games, having suffered another heavy defeat, 8-0 at Orient.

29    Chelsea's Premiership challenge receives a serious setback with their 1-0 defeat at Southampton, leaving them in 3rd place trailing 7pts behind Man Utd. With coach Christian Gross wanted by the Swiss national team, Spurs deny that the appointment of fitness trainer Fritz Schmidt was a condition of Gross's contract, and Gross himself feels it necessary to confirm his commitment to the club. Meanwhile Les Ferdinand blames the new training regime at Spurs for the aggravation of a leg injury that could sideline him for a month. Div 1 leaders Middlesbrough fine transfer-seeking Brazilian midfielder Emerson two weeks' wages for going AWOL in Rio and threaten to sack him if he does not return this week.

30    There's a long-overdue knighthood for Preston's Tom Finney, in the New Year's Honours List, along with an MBE for Wales and Chelsea striker Mark Hughes. Man United's Denis Irwin, back from his bad knee injury, comes through a full reserve game. West Ham's England defender Rio Ferdinand, 19, signs a lucrative extension to his contract that will keep him at the club until 2005.

## January 1998

**Giant-killers Stevenage rattle Magpies … Man U crush Cup-holders at Bridge … Gazza pipes up again … Ronaldo FIFA Player of the Year once more … Venables humbled in High Court … Emerson and Asprilla go … Shearer comeback … Arsenal eye Wembley as new home … Clough and Forest charged over 'bungs' … Bryan Robson hangs up his boots … Man U stutter in Premiership**

1    Hearts miss their chance to go top in Scotland held 2-2, leaving them a point behind Rangers. Man Utd fans accuse the club's security staff of brutality and call for a meeting to clear the air following incidents on Boxing Day when fans were ejected for standing up in seating areas.

2    Paul Gascoigne returns after a month out for the last 20min at Parkhead, but he cannot prevent Rangers losing their first Old Firm game (2-0) since May 1995 and allowing Celtic to get within a point of them in 2nd place; meanwhile Gazza might be in trouble again after another flute-playing mime.

3    Non-League Stevenage are the giant-killers of the 3rd round of the Cup, winning 2-1 at Swindon. But West Ham squeeze through 2-1 against Emley. Liverpool crash out 3-1 to Coventry at Anfield. Port Vale hold Arsenal 0-0 at Highbury thanks to a blinder from keeper Paul Musselwhite. Villa get a fright at Fratton Park as Portsmouth go 2-0 up but they recover to force a replay. Barnsley win the battle of the Premiership strugglers, beating Bolton 1-0, but police and stewards are needed to break up a brawl just before the end which involves players and coaching staff from both teams, and a steward is arrested for allegedly throwing a punch at Bolton's Jamie Pollock. The individual performance of the day belongs to Kevin Phillips, who hits 4 in Sunderland's 5-1 win at Rotherham. Five Cup ties are postponed and much of the rest of the programme in England and Scotland is disrupted by snow and storms.

4    An awesome Man Utd display in the Cup at Stamford Bridge leaves holders Chelsea gasping, goals from David Beckham (2), Andy Cole (2) and Teddy Sheringham putting United 5 up before Cup-holders Chelsea give the scoreline some respectability with 3 goals in the last 12min. Newcastle win 1-0 at Everton thanks to an Ian Rush goal, extending his FA Cup record to 43, and cup-fighters Wrexham hold Wimbledon 0-0 at Selhurst Park.

5    After a shaky spell Spurs emerge 3-1 victors over Fulham in the Cup, but add David Ginola and keeper Ian Walker to their lengthy injured list. Chelsea Village, owners of Chelsea, see their shares fall £13m as a result of yesterday's Cup defeat. Middlesbrough's Brazilian star Emerson, returning late from Rio, runs into a furious Bryan Robson, who fines him, bans him from training with the other players and leaves him out of his League and Cup squads.

6    Arsenal and Middlesbrough reach the semi-finals of the Coca-Cola Cup with away wins over West Ham and Reading, respectively. A row begins to simmer over the Stevenage-Newcastle 4th round Cup tie, with the Premier side inviting themselves down to inspect the non-Leaguer's ground after the FA approves it. Div 1 Bradford City sack manager Chris Kamara after a poor run of results.

7    Two FA Cup croppers win their Coca-Cola Cup quarter-finals: Chelsea lose a 2-0 lead at Ipswich but eventually win 4-1 on penalties as Ed De Goey makes 2 saves to set up a semi-final with Arsenal, while Liverpool need extra time to win 2-0 at Newcastle – so all quarter-finals go to the away team. After inspecting the Stevenage ground, Cup opponents Newcastle still consider it unsuitable for staging their tie and are to appeal to the FA, precipitating wide-ranging criticism and accusations of being frightened to play there.

8    Spurs sign former Italian International midfielder Nicola Berti on loan from Inter for the rest of the season.

9    Rangers discipline Paul Gascoigne for his flute-playing antics at the Old Firm game, but refuse to reveal details of his punishment.

10    Man Utd beat 2nd-from-bottom Spurs 2-0 at Old Trafford without breaking sweat and increase their Premiership lead to 7pts. Chelsea beat Coventry 3-1 and go 2nd. In Div 1, the fans at Stoke riot after a 7-0 thrashing by Birmingham, for whom Paul Furlong hits 3. Notts Cty, founded in 1862, become the first League club to play 4,000 matches. In Scotland, with Celtic held 1-1 at Motherwell, Rangers extend their

lead to 3pts with a 2-0 victory over lowly Aberdeen, after which Paul Gascoigne makes an abject apology for last-week's flute gaffe and reveals he was privately fined £20,000 by the club to go to charity.

11  Blackburn lose 3-1 at Derby and stay 3rd.

12  Chairman Terry Venables negotiates a pay-off from Portsmouth, relinquishing his claim for 51% of the club's shares for a reported half the £0.5m he had demanded. Hearts win 3-2 at St Johnstone to go 2nd in Scotland, a point behind Rangers. FIFA name their inaugural Hall of Champions. Inter's Brazilian striker Ronaldo (480pts) is voted FIFA World Player of the Year for the second time, with compatriot Roberto Carlos (65) of Real Madrid 2nd and Arsenal's Dennis Bergkamp (62) 3rd. Preston manager Gary Peters resigns and is replaced by assistant David Moyes.

13  Wimbledon, the only Premiership side involved in nine 3rd-round Cup ties and replays, survive a dangerous replay, winning 3-2 at Wrexham. Middlesbrough, 2-0 victors over QPR, finally unload unsettled Brazilian star Emerson to Tenerife for £4.2m. Portsmouth, in the process of parting company with chairman Terry Venables, sack manager Terry Fenwick by phone, replacing him temporarily by assistant Keith Waldon.

14  Facing 19 specific allegations of serious misconduct, Terry Venables reaches a settlement with the DTI, agreeing to a High Court order banning him from holding company directorships for 7 years and agreeing to pay their estimated costs of £0.5m. Held 1-1 at Port Vale after extra-time goals, Arsenal survive their Cup replay 4-3 on penalties, while 10-man Sheff Wed hold Watford 0-0 at Hillsborough before going through 5-3 in a shoot-out.

15  Manager Kenny Dalglish has to let the popular but unhappy Colombian star Faustino Asprilla go back to Parma for £6.1m, leaving Newcastle desperately short of strikers. Palace pay a club record £2.75m for French U-21 central defender Valerien Ismael from Strasbourg. Peter Coates, Stoke chairman for 12 years, steps down as unrest grows among fans.

16  With the two leaders not playing, a Kevin Gallacher hat-trick helps Blackburn humiliate Villa 5-0 and go 2nd, 5pts behind Man Utd. After the match, Villa striker Savo Milosevic is accused of spitting at his own disgruntled fans. Alan Shearer makes his much-heralded comeback for Newcastle as a 72nd-min sub after 6 months out. Jürgen Klinsmann scores his first goal for Spurs since his comeback, and it proves enough to beat West Ham 1-0 at White Hart Lane where there is an on-field confrontation between West Ham boss Harry Redknapp, beckoned on by referee David Elleray to escort dismissed Samassi Abou off the pitch, and Spurs midfielder Colin Calderwood. Highfield Road sees two players sent off, Patrick Vieira for visitors Arsenal and Paul Williams controversially for Coventry, in the 2-2 draw, the latter dismissal provoking furious Coventry boss Gordon Strachan to sound off to the press after the match about the refereeing. Much of the Scottish programme is lost because of blizzards, but Rangers, who scrape a 1-0 victory over Motherwell, take a 3pt lead over Hearts, who are held 2-2 at Kilmarnock. Nottingham Fraud Squad clear Forest of malpractice over transfers in the Brian Clough era, the Teddy Sheringham deal in particular having been under investigation, but in their report they criticise former chairman Fred Reacher and secretary Paul White.

18  The Euro 2000 draw takes place in Ghent and England are to meet Poland for the 5th time running in a major qualifying competition.

19  Kevin Davies gives the Premiership chasers hope as he scores an early goal for Southampton who again claim victory (1-0) at the Dell over Man Utd (playing in white). Arsenal consider another, controversial option in their quest to increase their capacity – a move to Wembley. Oxford manager Malcolm Crosby steps down after only 5 matches in charge.

20  Shearer plays the last half-hour for Newcastle at Anfield but is unable to prevent them going down 1-0 to an early Michael Owen goal. Reading beat Cheltenham 2-1 in their Cup replay. Villa manager Brian Little bows to fan pressure and transfer-lists striker Savo Milosevic following the spitting incident.

21  A chipped finger-bone suffered against Coventry on Saturday will keep England and Arsenal keeper David Seaman out for 3-4 weeks.

22  As a result of their 'bung' inquiry, set up in October 1993, and further advice from their lawyers and a QC, the FA finally decide to take action, charging retired Forest manager Brian Clough and his assistant Ronnie Fenton, and former Arsenal chief scout Steve Burtenshaw. Forest are also charged as a club with making payments outside the FA's rules and with misconduct for failing to properly supervise employees, all charges which the new board intend to fight vigorously. Another England keeper is sidelined, Spurs' Ian Walker, expected to be out for 3 months with a shoulder injury. Scientific research in Madrid on the speed of focusing of the human eye, with particular reference to offside in football, published in the *The Lancet*, suggests that linesmen will inevitably have a false picture of players' relative positions at the moment the ball is passed – which explains a lot. Two weeks after his dismissal as Bradford manager, Chris Kamara takes over at Stoke.

23  Cardiff sack manager Russell Osman, leaving director of football Kenny Hibbitt in temporary charge. Oxford appoint Barnsley reserve coach Malcolm Shotton, their former captain, as manager in place of Malcolm Crosby, who reverts to coaching.

24  No surprises in Saturday's FA Cup matches, although Palace, still without a home win in the Premiership, beat Leicester 3-0, with Bruce Dyer scoring all 3. In the Scottish Cup, Rangers made to struggle for their 2-1 win against Hamilton (playing their home tie at Motherwell's Fir Park). Andy Smith scores 5 in Dunfermline's 7-2 rout of non-League Edinburgh City. Former Portsmouth boss Alan Ball is announced as the new manager by the consortium taking over the club.

25  Stevenage Borough give Newcastle a big fright in their much-hyped Cup tie despite a 3min goal from Alan Shearer on his first start of the season, Giuliano Grazioli equalising in the 41st minute as the part-timers from the Vauxhall Conference match the Tyneside giants in every department.

26  West Ham's French striker Samassi Abou is charged with misconduct by the FA over his brush with referee David Elleray at Spurs when he was sent off. Middlesbrough player-manager Bryan Robson announces his retirement from the playing side.

27 In the 1st leg Coca-Cola Cup semi at Anfield, Middlesbrough hold out until the 82nd minute, when Robbie Fowler ends his barren streak to give Liverpool a 2-1 win. Celtic's 2-1 victory at Dundee Utd in the Scottish Premier takes them to within 3pts of leaders Rangers, above Hearts on goal difference. Newcastle complete the signing of AC Milan's Sweden striker Andreas Andersson for £3.6m. Bradford confirm caretaker-boss Paul Jewell as their new manager.

28 Outplayed by Arsenal in their Coca-Cola Cup 1st leg semi at Highbury, Chelsea score a late goal through sub Mark Hughes to come away just 2-1 down.

29 West Ham complete the transfer of forward Trevor Sinclair from QPR for £3m, with striker Iain Dowie and defender Keith Rowland moving to Rangers as part of the deal. Unsettled Everton skipper Gary Speed refuses to travel on the team bus for Saturday's game at Upton Park and is stripped of the club captaincy.

30 The League announce the success of their campaign to have the UEFA Cup berth for the Coca-Cola Cup winners restored, and it is now safe for 3 years. England back Andy Hinchcliffe moves from Everton, signing for Sheff Wed on a £3m transfer. West Ham skipper Steve Lomas, having already served a ban for his dismissal at Blackburn last month, receives a further match suspension for misconduct, for laying hands on referee Gerald Ashby.

31 At Fratton Park, where Portsmouth draw 1-1 with Sheff Utd in Div 1, a linesman is felled by what appears to be a Sheffield fan and is taken to hospital. Man Utd suffer their first defeat at Old Trafford, 1-0 to Leicester, and the chasing pack all move up on them, Liverpool and Blackburn albeit by only a point after reaching a 0-0 deadlock with each other at Anfield, where Jason McAteer breaks a leg. Chelsea, however, move above them both on goal difference, 4pts behind United, after their 2-0 victory over Barnsley, with Arsenal 4pts further back with a game in hand after beating Southampton 3-0. Coventry move away from the danger zone with a 5-1 win at Bolton. In Div 1, Tranmere, at home to Man City, create a dubious all-time League record of 5 consecutive 0-0 draws. Burnley move off the bottom of Div 2 in style, up 3 places by dint of their 7-2 thrashing of York. In Scotland, Rangers go down 2-0 at St Johnstone, enabling Hearts, 2-0 victors over Dundee Utd, to draw level on points, but the Gers have a superior goal difference. Motherwell leave Hibs deeper in the relegation mire, beating them 6-2 after going 2-0 down in 9min. Former England and Arsenal keeper George Marks dies at 82.

**February**
**Lawrie McMenemy is new N.Ireland supremo ... Michael Owen youngest England cap this century ... USA beat Brazil ... Vialli replaces sacked Gullit at Chelsea ... Middlesbrough shock Liverpool in Coca-Cola semi ... Steve Bull notches 300th goal for Wolves ... Robbie Fowler out for season ... Villa boss Brian Little resigns ... Barnsley knock Man U out of Cup**

2 Glenn Hoddle names 43 players for his senior and B squads to play Chile, the inclusion of in-form Coventry striker Dion Dublin in the seniors for the first time being the chief talking-point. Young Michael Owen is retained, preferred to his out-of-form Liverpool colleague Robbie Fowler up front. Paul Durkin of Portland, Dorset, is England's representative in the 34 FIFA referees for France 98, Hugh Dallas of Motherwell is Scotland's. Celtic beat Aberdeen 3-1 to go into a triple tie at the top of the Scottish Premier, 2nd behind Rangers. Hibs sack manager Jim Duffy following Saturday's humiliating defeat at Motherwell.

3 In a 4th-round Cup replay, Reading beat Cardiff on penalties after a match marred by rioting Cardiff fans before and during the game.

4 Spurs' season is in tatters – not only do they go down 3-1 at Barnsley in their Cup replay after Steve Clemence is controversially sent off for 'diving' (his 2nd bookable offence), but Jürgen Klinsmann is carried off and fellow striker Les Ferdinand is bound to be in trouble for his comments on the referee afterwards to the media. In the other tie, Stevenage refuse to lie down even after Shearer puts Newcastle 2-0 up and a 74th-min goal from Gary Crawshaw keeps the Premiership side on tenterhooks till the final whistle.

5 Blackburn striker Chris Sutton, piqued at being left out of England's senior squad, withdraws from the B side despite the efforts of club and country managers to persuade him otherwise.

6 Newcastle complete the £5.5m signing of Wales skipper Gary Speed from Everton.

7 After an emotional ceremony at Old Trafford in remembrance of those killed 40 years ago yesterday in the Munich air crash, Man Utd need a late Andy Cole goal to draw 1-1 with struggling Bolton. Yet they increase their lead in the Premiership as other sensational results see two of their closest challengers beaten at home, Blackburn 3-0 by crisis-ridden Spurs and Liverpool 3-2 by the improving Southampton. Mirroring the events south of the border, Scottish leaders Rangers are held 1-1 at home by lowly Dunfermline to go 1pt ahead of Celtic and Hearts, who play tomorrow.

8 Arsenal, with midfield stand-in Stephen Hughes scoring both goals in a bruising 2-0 defeat of Chelsea at Highbury, remain 5th, but only 6pts behind Man United with a game in hand. Celtic concede a late goal in their 1-1 draw at Tynecastle, so neither they nor Hearts overtake Rangers, who remain top on goal difference from the other two.

9 Lawrie McMenemy, who has been out of football since resigning as Southampton manager last summer, becomes the first non-Ulsterman to manage N.Ireland, with Joe Jordan and Pat Jennings his assistants. Leeds promise life bans for any of their supporters found guilty of making racist chants at Leicester on Saturday.

10 Glenn Hoddle omits Paul Gascoigne and selects Michael Owen for the Chile friendly tomorrow, when the Liverpool striker will become England's youngest (18y 59d) international this century. Leicester keeper Kasey Keller is the hero of the United States' sensational 1-0 victory over Brazil in Los Angeles to take them to the final of the CONCACAF Gold Cup.

11    Debut boy Michael Owen shines in a disjointed England performance at Wembley where Chile win 2-0 thanks to 2 goals from Marcelo Salas. Motherwell boss Alex McLeish takes over as manager of Hibs.

12    Chelsea shock the football world by replacing high-flying player-manager Ruud Gullit with their Italian striker Gianluca Vialli. The Scottish Football League vote to allow the 10 Premier League clubs to form their own organization next season, thus rubber-stamping the long-awaited breakaway.

13    Sheff Utd beat fellow Div 1 club Reading 1-0 to become the first side to reach the FA Cup quarter-finals. Chile captain Marcelo Salas completes his £12m transfer to Italian club Lazio, but will stay with Argentinian club River Plate until after the World Cup.

14    Three more clubs go through to the FA Cup last 8, Coventry with a 1-0 win over Villa, their first ever at Villa Park, Newcastle with a 1-0 victory over Tranmere thanks to a 1st-half Alan Shearer goal, and Leeds, who beat Birmingham 3-2. Liverpool are the only leading Premiership team in action, and they come back from 3-1 down at Sheff Wed as Michael Owen completes his hat-trick to force a draw and go 2nd, 4pts behind Man U. In the Scottish Cup, Ayr, joint bottom of Div 1, beat holders Kilmarnock 2-0, while Rangers salvage a 2-2 draw at Motherwell.

15    In the FA Cup, Premiership high-flyers Man U and Arsenal are both held at home by relegation strugglers, Barnsley and Palace, respectively. Mexico beat USA 1-0 in the final of the CONCACAF Gold Cup in Los Angeles in front of a 92,000 crowd.

16    Rangers confirm that PSV manager Dick Advocaat will succeed Walter Smith as manager at the end of the season. West Ham first-team coach Frank Burrows succeeds Russell Osman at Cardiff for his second spell as manager of the club. Chelsea announce a huge hike in season-ticket prices (up to 40% more next season).

17    Rangers drop Paul Gascoigne but beat Motherwell 3-0 in their Cup replay to reach the quarter-finals. Arsenal and England receive a blow with the news that striker Ian Wright, recovering from a hamstring injury, now needs a cartilage operation.

18    First-leg leads are overturned in both Coca-Cola Cup semi-finals, Arsenal having Patrick Vieira sent off soon after half-time and going down 3-1 (4-3 agg) to an inspired Chelsea at Stamford Bridge, while 2 goals in the first 4min are enough to see Middlesbrough through 3-2 on aggregate over Liverpool. The two losing semi-finalists receive a further blow with Man United's 2-0 Premiership victory at Villa. In Div 1 at Maine Road, 2nd-from-bottom Man City sack manager Frank Clark, and his replacement Joe Royle sees 2 goals from Ipswich in the last 8min snatch a 2-1 win to leave City in the doldrums. Steve Bull returns to action after 15 weeks as a sub and scores Wolves' winner in their 2-1 defeat of Bradford at Molineux – his 300th goal for the club. Llanelli player-manager Robbie James, 40, a former Wales international, collapses during a Welsh League match and is found to be dead on arrival at hospital.

19    Premiership prize money is increased again, more than 50% up on last season, with £3.25m going to the champions. Former manager Lou Macari loses his £0.4m damages claim against Celtic for breach of contract when they sacked him in 1994 after 8 months.

20    George Male, former England captain and right-back for the great Arsenal side of the 1930s, dies at 87.

21    Man U stretch their Premiership lead to 9pts, beating Derby 2-0, but they lose match-winner Ryan Giggs with a pulled hamstring and sub Jordi Cruyff with a hairline fracture. Arsenal, with 13 of their first-team squad out of action and playing Palace at Highbury again, just manage to beat them this time with defender Gilles Grimandi's first goal for the club and emerge in 2nd place as the strongest Championship challengers, 9pts adrift but with 2 away games in hand. There is no change in Scotland as the three runaway leaders all win and stand on 52pts, 19 ahead of the pack: Rangers stay top with a last-gasp 2-1 victory at bottom club Hibs, while Celtic hammer Kilmarnock 4-0, Norwegian striker Harald Brattbakk scoring all 4, and Hearts come back from 2 down at Motherwell to win 4-2.

23    Still without a derby League win since March 94, Liverpool are held 1-1 by Everton in a thriller at Anfield to join Arsenal in 2nd place in the Premiership with an identical goal record. Spurs complete the £2.3m signing of Algerian international midfielder Moussa Saib from Valencia. The FA suspend FIFA referee Dermot Gallagher for one match because his handling of the Arsenal–Chelsea Premiership game on 8 Feb was 'not up to the Premier League standard'. South Africa join the competition for the 2006 World Cup.

24    Liverpool and England striker Robbie Fowler will miss the rest of the season and the World Cup, having suffered a knee injury in yesterday's Premiership match. Villa announce the shock resignation of Brian Little, manager since 1994. With their rivals inactive, Rangers, who lose both Paul Gascoigne and Gordon Durie with injuries, can only scrape a 1-1 draw at Kilmarnock to lead the Scottish Premier by a point.

25    Barnsley produce the shock of the 4 FA Cup 5th-round replays with a 3-2 defeat of a suspiciously understrength Man U in a thriller at Oakwell. Div 1 Wolves beat Wimbledon 2-1 at Molineux after going behind, West Ham surprise Blackburn at Ewood Park with a penalties win, and a courageous 10-man Palace nevertheless go down 2-1 at home to Arsenal. Former Brian Little assistant John Gregory leaves Wycombe to succeed him as manager of Villa. Struggling Brighton sack manager Steve Gritt. Celtic storm to the top of the Scottish Premier with a 5-1 win over Dunfermline, on goal difference from Hearts, 3-1 victors over Aberdeen.

26    A nationwide poll of supporters finds much racial abuse exists in the game, its particular focus on black players keeping black fans away. Former Brighton captain Brian Horton is appointed their new manager.

27    Former Sheff Utd and England inside-forward Jimmy Hagen dies at 80.

28    Phil Neville's first goal in senior football is enough to give Man U a 1-0 win at Stamford Bridge, increasing their Premiership lead to 11pts and snuffing out Chelsea's faint hopes of the title. Blackburn go 2nd, beating Leicester 5-3 with the help of a Chris Sutton hat-trick. Liverpool, too, blow their diminishing Championship aspirations with a 2-1 defeat at Villa Park, where Stan Collymore takes great delight in scoring both goals to silence the jeers from the fans of his former club. There's bad news for England

coach Glenn Hoddle at Ibrox Park, where Paul Gascoigne limps off with a pulled hamstring, not the least of Rangers' worries, however, as Richard Gough is sent off twice – first for a second yellow and then for continuing to argue when summoned to the ref's dressing-room: Rangers just manage to save their unbeaten home record with a 2-2 draw against rivals Hearts, so Celtic, 1-0 winners at bottom club Hibs, take a 2pt lead over Hearts, with Rangers trailing by a further 2.

### March
**Manchester bookie pays up bets on Man U for the title ... Newcastle directors in scandal ... Man U and Villa go out of Europe, but Chelsea reach semis ... Gascoigne leaves Rangers for Middlesbrough ... hooliganism returns as fan is knifed to death ... Chelsea win Coca-Cola Cup ... Arsenal challenge Man U**

1　Spurs win their crucial relegation battle with Bolton 1-0 at White Hart Lane.
2　Arsenal can only draw 0-0 at West Ham, and although it's enough to take them past Blackburn on goal difference into 2nd place it now leaves them 11pts adrift of Man U with 2 away games in hand – a gap wide enough to persuade one Manchester-based bookie to pay up bets on Man U for the title. Nigel Spackman, upset at having to sell his best players, quits as manager of 1st Div Sheff Utd after 9 months in charge.
3　Keeper Mark Bosnich restricts Atletico's win over Villa in Madrid to 1-0 to keep hopes alive for the 2nd leg of their UEFA Cup quarter-final. Villa striker Stan Collymore confirms there was a bust-up with Liverpool's Steve Harkness after Saturday's match and accuses his former team-mate of racial abuse.
4　Man U manager Alex Ferguson gets the result he wants in their 1st-leg European Cup quarter-final in Monaco, but fumes after their goalless draw that the poor pitch leaves 8 of his players injured.
5　Striker Tore Andre Flo scores twice to give Chelsea a 2-1 advantage from their Cup-Winners' Cup 1st-leg tie with Real Betis in Seville. Sheff Utd chairman Mike McDonald resigns.
6　Lincoln sack manager John Beck after 29 months in the job. The simmering feud between Spurs manager Christian Gross and Jürgen Klinsmann takes a new turn as it emerges that chairman Alan Sugar had asked the German striker to take an interest in tactics.
7　A jaded Man U go down 2-0 at Sheff Wed and Liverpool, who beat Bolton 2-1 at Anfield, cut their lead to 9pts. Div 1 clubs cause upsets in the two Cup quarter-finals played, Wolves winning 1-0 at Leeds, thanks to a fine save by Hans Segers of a late penalty, and Sheff Utd, under stand-in boss Steve Thompson, drawing 1-1 at Coventry.
8　Newcastle reach the FA Cup semi-finals with a controversial 3-1 win over Barnsley at St James' Park, where the visitors' Adrian Moses is sent off, while Arsenal are held 1-1 at Highbury by West Ham. Celtic reach the Scottish semis with a 3-2 win at Dundee Utd thanks to a last-minute own goal.
9　Rangers are held 0-0 at home by Div 1 leaders Dundee in the Scottish Cup quarter-finals. Caretaker Steve Thompson is appointed manager of Sheff Utd for the rest of the season. Stan Collymore and Steve Harkness refuse to shake hands after 3 hours of attempted mediation at PFA headquarters in the racism row in which Harkness denies he called Collymore a 'coon'.
10　Newcastle complete the £2m signing of Greek international central defender Nikolaos Dabizas from Olympiakos.
11　Chris Wreh scores his first goal in his first Premiership start as Arsenal secure a 1-0 win at Wimbledon that takes them within 9pts of Man U, who come away from West Ham with a 1-1 draw, Arsenal's 3 games in hand all being away.
12　Unable to expand at Highbury, Arsenal make a £120m bid for Wembley Stadium.
14　Arsenal throw down the gauntlet at Old Trafford as Marc Overmars blows the title race wide open with a goal in the 79th minute to give Arsenal a 1-0 victory over Man U, taking them to within 6pts of the leaders with 3 games in hand. To add injury to insult, Man U keeper Peter Schmeichel damages a hamstring racing back after a last-ditch foray into the attack, and will miss the European Cup return with Monaco. In Scotland, Hearts are held at home 1-1 by Kilmarnock, leaving them 1pt behind leaders Celtic, who play tomorrow, while Rangers are shocked 2-1 at lowly Motherwell. Newcastle face a potential scandal with revelations about chairman Freddie Shepherd and director Doug Hall, allegedly filmed in a Spanish brothel boasting about ripping off the fans with shirt prices, selling a crocked Andy Cole to Man U, and making disparaging remarks about Alan Shearer, Kevin Keegan and Newcastle girls.
15　Celtic stumble in their quest for the Scottish title, held at home 1-1 by Dundee Utd and stretching their lead over Hearts to just 2pts.
16　Under pressure from disillusioned fans, Man City chairman and former star Francis Lee resigns after 4 years. England coach Glenn Hoddle omits Paul Gascoigne from the squad to play Switzerland with the message to sort himself out if he wants to go to the World Cup.
17　A dramatic 2nd-half revival by Villa after going 2-0 down on aggregate is not enough and they lose to Atletico Madrid on away goals in the UEFA Cup quarter-finals. Both FA Cup 6th-round replays go to penalties, Sheff Utd of Div 1 beating Coventry and Arsenal winning at West Ham despite having Dennis Bergkamp sent off in the 34th minute.
18　Man U are out of Europe again, an early goal from Monaco proving too much as, despite a second-half equalizer, their depleted side are beaten on away goals. Juventus reach the semis with a devastating 4-1 away victory (5-2 agg) over Dynamo Kiev featuring a hat-trick from Filippo Inzaghi. Newcastle succumb 2-1 to a Crystal Palace chalking up their 6th away win – only Man U and Leeds have won more (7) than the bottom club – and are now by no means safe from relegation. Rangers come back from a goal down at Dundee with 2 from Ally McCoist to reach the Scottish Cup semis where they will play Celtic, while Paul Gascoigne is severely censured by the Scottish FA for his flute-playing mime in the New Year Old Firm clash at Parkhead. Terry Bullivant resigns as manager of Reading, 2nd bottom of Div 1.
19　Despite an early shock, Chelsea come through 3-1 (5-2 agg) against Real Betis to reach the semis of the Cup-Winners' Cup.

21 There are no weekend Premiership games because of England's training, and in Scotland the three Premier League leaders all win by a single goal. Jimmy Scoular, former Portsmouth, Newcastle, and Scotland right-half and Cardiff manager, dies at 73.

23 Fan power, allied to a threat by the board to resign, forces disgraced Newcastle chairman Freddy Shepherd and vice-chairman Douglas Hall to quit, the latter's father Sir John Hall returning as chairman to plug the gap.

24 Paul Gascoigne leaves Rangers to sign for Div 1 Middlesbrough for a fee of £3.45m on a 3-yr contract worth £1.5m a year.

25 An experimental England side draw 1-1 with Switzerland in Berne thanks to a Paul Merson equalizer, but Scotland, under new captain Colin Hendry, are beaten 1-0 at Ibrox by Denmark, whose goal is scored by Brian Laudrup on his home ground. N.Ireland, with Lawrie McMenemy in charge for the first time, beat Slovakia 1-0, their first win for 13 months. Former Celtic manager Tommy Burns leaves the Newcastle coaching staff to take charge at Reading. Vinnie Jones leaves Wimbledon to join QPR as player-coach, Bolton allow Peter Beardsley to join Fulham on loan, and Michael Thomas, on loan to Middlesbrough, returns to Liverpool.

27 FIFA secretary Sepp Blatter throws his hat into the ring for the presidential election. Arsenal drop their plans to move to Wembley.

28 Hooliganism returns to English football with a vengeance as a Fulham fan is knifed to death outside Gillingham's Priestfield Stadium after their 2-0 defeat, and many other supporters are taken to hospital. At Oakwell, referee Gary Willard flees and suspends the game for several minutes when angry Barnsley fans invade the pitch: Liverpool finish 3-2 winners and Barnsley finish with 8 men after 3 are sent off. At Goodison, a home fan is intercepted as he goes for the referee in Everton's 4-1 defeat by Villa. At the top, Man U maintain their 6pt lead in the Premiership with a 2-0 win over Wimbledon, albeit both goals coming in the last 8min, in front of 55,306, Old Trafford's biggest gate of the season. Arsenal, with David Seaman back for the undefeated Alex Manninger in goal, keep up the pressure with a 1-0 win over Sheff Wed, also in front of a nervous crowd at Highbury, Dennis Bergkamp hitting the winner in his last match before suspension. Palace look goners as they crash to their 10th home defeat of the season, 3-1 to Spurs. Notts County become the first League club since the war to win promotion in March. As Celtic and Hearts fight out a goalless draw at Parkhead, Rangers come back into the Scottish picture with a 3-2 win at Dunfermline, Ally McCoist's pair taking his League tally to 250 goals.

29 Paul Gascoigne makes his debut for Middlesbrough as a 64th-min sub, but they are beaten by Chelsea 2-0 at Wembley for the second season running, this time after extra time in the final of the Coca-Cola Cup: 'Gazza' collects a yellow card and a losers medal, which he promptly gives to Craig Hignett who had played in most of the games leading up to the final.

30 Leeds' European ambitions take a knock as they crash 3-0 at West Ham, and they are then involved in a crash-landing at Stansted Airport as one engine of their plane explodes and catches fire on take-off: Leeds assistant manager David O'Leary is commended for his coolness in helping to evacuate the aircraft. After yesterday's serious eruptions of football mayhem, the government promises a strong clampdown on soccer hooliganism, and, welcoming the Task Force report, a swift amendment to the Football Offences Act to make racial abuse by individuals a criminal offence.

31 Arsenal win 1-0 at Bolton to move to within 3pts of Man U with still 2 games in hand, but have Martin Keown dismissed 15min after Chris Wreh's spectacular 25-yarder proves the 48th-min winner: Arsenal's 8th consecutive clean sheet equals the club record (1902–03) and sets a new Premiership record.

**April**
**Bergkamp PFA Player of the Year ... Chelsea reach Cup-Winners' Cup final ... Arsenal overtake Man U to top Premiership ... Shearer in kicking controversy**

1 An Alessandro Del Piero hat-trick is the feature of Juventus's 4-1 demolition of Man U's conquerors Monaco in the 1st leg of the European Cup semis. The other semi, in which Real Madrid beat Borussia Dortmund 2-0, is delayed for 75min for a replacement goal to be fitted after fans climbing the fencing supporting the goal contrive to break the posts. Rangers beat Hibs 3-0 to go 2nd in the Scottish Premier behind leaders Celtic on goal difference with a game more played.

2 A lacklustre Chelsea come back from Italy with a 1-0 deficit against Vicenza after their 1st-leg semi in the Cup-Winners' Cup. Wembley plc, the stadium's owners, agree to sell it to English National Stadium Trust for £103m. Scotland manager Craig Brown signs a new 4-year contract.

4 The Premiership relegation situation is largely unchanged as Everton draw 1-1 at Spurs but Bolton draw and Barnsley lose. Falkirk equalize an early Hearts goal in their Scottish Cup semi in the 85th min, but 2 goals from Hearts in the last 2min put them out.

5 Stand-in striker Chris Wreh's early goal – his third winner for Arsenal in a month – is enough to put them into the Cup final at the expense of 1st Div Wolves, while Newcastle beat the other 1st Div side Sheff Utd with an Alan Shearer goal after an hour. Suspended Arsenal striker Dennis Bergkamp is voted PFA Player of the Year. In the Scottish Cup, Rangers, having lost the toss for venue, beat Celtic 2-1 at Parkhead to reach the final.

6 Undeterred by Arsenal's great run, Man U refuse to lie down, coming back from a first-half in which they are outplayed and one down to win 3-1 at Blackburn and restore their 6pt lead.

7 Having collected bookings in his first two matches for Middlesbrough, Paul Gascoigne limps out of his third as Boro go down 1-0 to Sheff Utd. Spurs striker Les Ferdinand, fined £2,500 for calling ref Gerald Ashby 'an absolute disgrace' after their Cup defeat at Barnsley in February, defies the FA and calls for Ashby to be fined for his performance.

8    Celtic's 2-1 win at Kilmarnock puts them back 3pts ahead of Rangers, while Hearts' challenge fades as they are held 1-1 at home by Motherwell. Chris Kamara parts company with bottom Div 1 club Stoke after a disastrous 14-match reign and Alan Durban, manager 17 years ago, is put in charge for the remaining 5 games.

10   Playing on Friday, Man U miss the chance of going 9pts ahead of Arsenal as they are held 1-1 at home by Liverpool despite playing 50min against 10 men following the dismissal of Michael Owen who scored Liverpool's equalizer. With Grimsby failing to win, Div 2 leaders Bristol City are promoted without playing.

11   Arsenal brush Newcastle aside at Highbury in a Cup final rehearsal, Frenchmen scoring all 3 goals, 2 from Nicolas Anelka and a fabulous strike from Patrick Vieira, although a consolation goal scored by Newcastle's Warren Barton is the first conceded in 9 League matches. Now 4pts behind Man U with 3 games in hand, Arsenal have their odds for the title cut from 6-4 to 1-2, replacing United as favourites for the first time this season. At the other end of the table, Spurs' 2-0 defeat at Chelsea leaves them just 1pt ahead of Bolton and Barnsley, who both win 2-1 at home, with Palace now 8pts adrift after their 11th home defeat, 3-0 to Leicester. Doncaster's 2-1 defeat at Chester in Div 3 condemns them to Vauxhall Conference football next season.

12   Rangers beat Celtic 2-0 at Ibrox to overhaul them at the top on goal difference with 4 matches to play.

13   Arsenal continue their unrelenting charge for the Premiership title at Ewood Park, hitting 3 goals in the first 14min – the first from back-again Dennis Bergkamp in 70sec – 4 by half-time, before a snowstorm slows them down and Blackburn score a consolation goal: the Gunners are now just a point behind Man U with 2 games in hand. Watford clinch promotion from Div 2 with a 1-1 draw at leaders Bristol C.

14   England manager Glenn Hoddle's brings back Paul Gascoigne and the recuperating Ian Wright into his extended squad for the friendly against Portugal.

15   Juventus and Real Madrid reach the European Cup final.

16   Mark Hughes comes on as sub and scores a typical buccaneering goal to climax Chelsea's recovery from 2-0 down to beat Vicenza 3-1 (3-2 agg) and reach the final of the Cup-Winners' Cup.

18   As Man U slip up at home, held 1-1 by Newcastle with Ole Gunnar Solskjaer averting a last-minute defeat with a red-card tackle (and being cheered off by United fans for his effort), Arsenal (with left-back Nigel Winterburn playing his 500th game for the club) sweep past Wimbledon, who had not lost at Highbury since 1987, 5-0, to knock Man U off the top of the Premiership for the first time in 6 months: they lead by a point with 2 games still in hand. Spurs grab a vital 1-1 draw at Barnsley in the relegation battle despite having Ramon Vega sent off, while Bolton go down 3-2 at home to Leeds and Palace belatedly chalk up their first home victory of the season, 3-1 over Derby. In Scotland, Celtic's 4-1 defeat of Motherwell takes them 3pts clear of Rangers.

19   Rangers go down to a shock 1-0 defeat at Aberdeen and have centre-half Lorenzo Amoruso dismissed, so they trail Celtic by 3pts still. Halifax clinch promotion to the Football League with a 2-0 win at Kidderminster in the Vauxhall Conference.

20   England manager Glenn Hoddle reveals that faith healer Eileen Drewery has been working with the squad at their Burnham Beeches hotel.

21   Matt Le Tissier presses his claim for a World Cup place with a hat-trick in England's 4-1 'B' international defeat of Russia at Loftus Road.

22   England enjoy an encouraging 3-0 win over Portugal at Wembley, with their 'SAS' attack, Alan Shearer (2) and Teddy Sheringham, getting the goals.

25   Arsenal take another giant step towards the Premiership title, cruising through a potentially tricky fixture at Barnsley 2-0 to go 4pts clear of Man U (playing Monday) with a home match in hand: they just need to win their remaining 2 home games to clinch the title. Macclesfield beat Chester 3-2 in Div 3 to win promotion in their first season in the League, and are the only side in the League to finish with an undefeated home record. Celtic stumble within sight of the Scottish title, held 0-0 at Parkhead by bottom-club Hibs, who are now a whisker away from relegation. Rangers, keeping their hopes alive of a record 10th consecutive title, outclass Hearts 3-0 at Tynecastle despite having Craig Moore sent off and, with 2 matches to go, are a point behind the leaders.

26   Leicester win 4-0 at Derby, all scored with headers from right-wing crosses in the first 15min.

27   Refusing to make it easy for Arsenal, Man U win 3-0 at Selhurst Park, sending Crystal Palace into the 1st Division and moving to within a point of the leaders. France coach Aime Jacquet rules Spurs star David Ginola out of World Cup contention. Arsenal's Ian Wright makes his comeback for the reserves after 3 months on the injured list. Villa striker Stan Collymore is cleared in court of striking his former girlfriend.

28   Nottm Forest go straight back to the Premiership, promoted without playing as Ipswich beat Sunderland 2-0. West Brom terminate defender Shane Nicholson's contract following his admission of a drugs misconduct charge last week at an FA hearing.

29   Despite a fired-up Derby, stung into action by recent heavy defeats, Arsenal squeeze a 1-0 win thanks to a goal from midfielder Manu Petit to go 4pts clear of Man U and one victory away from the title – but a pulled hamstring makes Dennis Bergkamp (who also suffered his first penalty miss for Arsenal) doubtful for the Cup final. Attilio Lombardo steps down as coach at troubled Palace, leaving chairman Ron Noades and coach Ray Lewington to pick the team, while the long-running £30m takeover of the club has still not gone through. Newcastle grab a valuable point with a 0-0 draw at Leicester, but Alan Shearer brings down the wrath of the home fans – if not of ref Martin Bodenham – on him as he appears to kick N.Ireland midfielder Neil Lennon in the face.

30   An unhappy Mike Walker's second spell as Norwich manager is ended after nearly 2yr 'by mutual consent'. Spurs manager Christian Gross enters the Shearer debate, claiming the Newcastle striker and England captain broke Ramon Vega's nose on Saturday, while Shearer defends himself claiming that it

was not a kick and there was certainly no intent. UEFA president Lennart Johansson is re-elected unopposed for another 4yr term, while FA chairman Keith Wiseman fails to be elected to the full executive committee.

**May**
**Arsenal march to record 10th consecutive win to clinch Premiership and beat Newcastle at Wembley to complete League and Cup double ... Injured Bergkamp misses Arsenal triumphs but completes own 'double' as Footballer of the Year ... Celtic win Scottish Premier to foil a record 10th on trot for Rangers ... Wenger and Jansen first foreign managers to win English and Scottish titles, respectively ... Keegan sacks Wilkins at Fulham ... Sub Zola inspires Chelsea to Cup-Winners' Cup glory ... FA absolve Shearer ... Hearts win Scottish Cup to leave Rangers without a trophy ... Real Madrid Kings of Europe again ... Hoddle gives Gascoigne the chop**

1 Arsenal striker Dennis Bergkamp is voted FWA Footballer of the Year, with club captain Tony Adams 2nd and Michael Owen (Liverpool) 3rd.

2 With Saturday's Premiership matches concentrated towards the bottom end, the chief issue decided is the relegation of the popular Barnsley following their 1-0 defeat at Leicester. Spurs virtually guarantee their survival as Jürgen Klinsmann finds his golden touch with 4 goals in their 6-2 thrashing of Wimbledon at Selhurst Park. Watford win 2-1 at Fulham to take the Div 2 title. Burnley escape relegation with a 2-1 win over Plymouth, who go down with Brentford. In Div 3, Lincoln grab the 3rd automatic promotion place. In Scotland, the unbelievable happens at Ibrox, where Rangers crash to their first home defeat of the season, 1-0 to Kilmarnock who score an injury-time goal. Hibs 2-1 home defeat by Dundee Utd seals their relegation fate. Justin Fashanu, brother of John and former Norwich and Forest striker, is found dead, aged 37.

3 Arsenal clinch their 11th Championship with a flamboyant 4-0 win over Everton at Highbury, climaxed by an outrageous volleyed goal from captain Tony Adams from a pass by fellow central defender Steve Bould. It is Arsenal's 10th consecutive win, equalling the old Woolwich Arsenal record and setting a new Premiership mark, and Arsène Wenger is the first foreign manager to win the English title. It is sub Ian Wright's first game since January. The result is even welcomed by Spurs fans in as much at it secures their place (and Wimbledon's) in the Premiership, leaving Everton a point behind Bolton in the battle for survival. The last round of Div 1 matches is played, completing the Nationwide programme apart from play-offs. Middlesbrough beat Oxford 4-1 to deny Sunderland the 2nd automatic promotion place despite their 2-1 victory at Swindon. Man City are relegated to the third tier of English football for the first time in their history, going out in dramatic fashion with a thumping 5-2 win at Stoke, who accompany them to Div 2, as Port Vale and Portsmouth climb to safety with comprehensive away wins, 4-0 over Huddersfield and 3-1 over Bradford, respectively. Celtic fail to clinch the Scottish title: their 1-1 draw at Dunfermline means the race will go to the wire.

4 Man U hide their disappointment and beat Leeds 3-0 in front of the usual 55,000 crowd at Old Trafford which includes Jaap Stam, Dutch international due for a medical tomorrow before completing his transfer from PSV Eindhoven.

5 Man U sign Stam, 25, on a 7yr contract (worth £12m to the player) for £10.75m, a record for Man U and a world record for a defender. The Scottish FA formally approve the new Scottish Premiership, to kick off next season with 10 clubs.

6 Arsenal's 18-match unbeaten run in the Premiership comes to an end at Anfield, where several players are rested, Liverpool winning 4-0. England captain Alan Shearer is unhappy about having to face an FA misconduct charge for allegedly kicking Leicester's Neil Lennon, despite no mention of the incident in the ref's report.

7 Fulham chief operating officer Kevin Keegan sacks his friend Ray Wilkins, the manager, after just 7 months, and will take care of team affairs in the 1st Div play-offs. Two other Div 2 managers part company with their clubs, Billy Bonds with Millwall and Neil Warnock with Oldham. Spurs give their two longest-serving players, Gary Mabbutt and David Howells, free transfers, along with Dean Austin.

8 Man U give Brian McClair a free transfer in recognition of 11 years' service.

9 On the last day of the regular Scottish season, Celtic keep their nerve to beat St Johnstone 2-0 at Parkhead and take their first Premier title for 10 years, preventing Rangers, who win 2-1 at Dundee Utd, from attaining a record 10th: Celtic's Dutch coach Wim Jansen emulates Arsène Wenger in England by becoming the first foreign manager to win the Scottish League title.

10 Everton stay up on goal difference despite only drawing 1-1 at Goodison with Coventry as Bolton go down 2-0 at Chelsea and drop straight back to Div 1. Man U, with a sprinkling of youngsters, win 2-0 at Barnsley to finish just a point behind Arsenal, who, playing their best available side, lose 1-0 at Villa. Villa will qualify for the last UEFA Cup place if Chelsea win the Cup-Winners' Cup on Wednesday, Blackburn having qualified with their 1-0 defeat of Newcastle, whose David Batty is sent off for the 3rd time this season.

11 As expected, successful Celtic coach Wim Jansen resigns, differences in opinion with general manager Jock Brown as to the way the club should proceed being the apparent cause. Ajax confirm the signing of Georgian international Georgiou Kinkladze from Man City for a reported £5m.

12 The FA absolve Newcastle's Alan Shearer from deliberately injuring Leicester's Neil Lennon, who spoke out in the England captain's defence. Glenn Hoddle's 30-man squad for the last three friendlies before he selects the World Cup 22 omits such hopefuls as Andy Cole, Matt Le Tissier, Stuart Pearce, and Ray Parlour. Oldham name former striker Andy Ritchie as their new manager, while Keith Stevens, 33, takes over at Millwall. Player-manager Chris Waddle parts company with Burnley by mutual consent.

13    Chelsea bring back memories of 1971 as they win the Cup-Winners' Cup in Stockholm, beating Stuttgart 1-0 with a spectacular 71st-min strike from Gianfranco Zola just 22sec after he comes on as sub. Scotland manager Craig Brown omits stalwarts Ally McCoist and Stuart McCall from his provisional World Cup party. Former Villa boss Brian Little is confirmed as the new Stoke manager. Leicester chairman Tom Smeaton resigns because of outside commitments.

14    Former Villa forward Ray Graydon is the new Walsall manager.

15    Footballer of the Year Dennis Bergkamp fails his fitness test to play for Arsenal in tomorrow's Cup final.

16    Arsenal beat Newcastle 2-0 at Wembley to complete the League and Cup double and emulate Man U's achievement of two doubles. But in the Scottish Cup final, played at Celtic Park, Rangers fail to win a trophy for the first time in 11 season after a shock 2-1 defeat by Hearts, winning their first major trophy for 36 years.

17    Ron Atkinson, 59, having kept Sheff Wed in the Premiership, leaves the club for the second time as they announce their intention to appoint a long-term manager. After Paul Gascoigne is photographed on a 'boozy' night out in Soho following his promise to knuckle down for the World Cup, England coach Glenn Hoddle makes it clear his errant midfielder is not a certainty to be chosen.

18    Cup final ref Paul Durkin, England's representative in the World Cup, starts a week in which he will take part in England training sessions to help them prepare for the new interpretation of the laws FIFA have laid down for France, stipulating mandatory dismissal for dangerous tackles from behind.

19    The 1-yr European ban on Anderlecht for their admitted bribery of the ref in their 1984 UEFA Cup semi against Forest (who have demanded the Belgian club's place in 1998–99) has been overturned by the Court of Arbitration for Sport, who rule UEFA did not have the authority.

20    Real Madrid beat hot favourites Juventus 1-0 in the European Cup final to win the trophy for the 7th time – but the first since 1966.

21    The FA sign a new 5-year kit and sponsorship deal with Umbro worth £50m of which £20m will go to youth development.

22    Time runs out on Liverpool midfielder Jamie Redknapp, as he fails a fitness test on his knee and has to drop out of England's squad, while Darren Anderton and Andy Hinchcliffe are named in Glenn Hoddle's starting line-up for tomorrow's friendly against Saudi Arabia.

23    England are booed off at Wembley after being held to a 0-0 draw by Saudi Arabia in their last home try-out before the World Cup, while manager Glenn Hoddle reveals that his preparations will involve no smoking on the team coach and a ban on alcohol. Scotland do rather better, earning a 2-2 draw with one of England's 1st-round opponents, Colombia, in New York.

24    Grimsby beat Northampton 1-0 in the Div 2 play-off final at Wembley, where the crowd of 62,988 is only 745 fewer than for yesterday's international. Sports minister Tony Banks urges the Football Task Force to investigate the increasing cost of season tickets.

25    In arguably the finest and certainly the most exciting play-off final yet, Charlton beat Sunderland 7-6 on penalties as keeper Sasa Ilic stops Michael Gray's spot-kick, a save calculated to be worth at least £10m to the London club who win promotion to the Premiership, after a see-saw match which finishes 4-4 (3-3 after 90min): Clive Mendonca's hat-trick for the winners is the first in a play-off. England fly out to their La Manga training camp in Spain, where they will prepare for two flying visits to play in a tournament in Casablanca and Glenn Hoddle will whittle the party down to 22 for the World Cup. Derby sign Argentinian defender Horacio Carbonari for a club record £2.7m.

26    Maverick keeper Andy Goram quits the Scotland squad in their New Jersey training camp because of press reports about his private life and retires from international football.

27    Michael Owen returns to the pitch after an accidental kick on the head from the Moroccan keeper to become England's youngest ever scorer (beating Tommy Lawton's 60-yr-old record) and give them a 1-0 win in Casablanca, having come on in the first place for Ian Wright, whose hamstring injury looks like spelling the end of his World Cup hopes. Two more Newcastle directors resign, including plc chairman Sir Terence Harrison.

28    A devastated Ian Wright is forced out of World Cup contention after a scan on his hamstring injury. Chelsea complete the signing of Italy striker Pierluigi Casiraghi from Lazio for £5.4m. European Cup winners Real Madrid sack manager Jupp Heynckes and give him £1m compensation just 8 days after their triumph.

29    In their last try-out before the World Cup, England are beaten by Belgium on penalties after a 0-0 draw in Casablanca, where Paul Gascoigne is in the wars, first with a head injury and then a dead leg, and has to come off soon after the interval. The Premier League chairmen reject Sky TV's offer of pay-per-view next season: the offer was £16m for a 1-yr Pay-TV experiment which would have required shifting an extra three games to Sundays. The Scottish League Challenge Cup (formerly B & Q Cup), for teams from the lower three divisions, is scrapped for want of a sponsor after 7 seasons.

30    Scotland are held 0-0 by the USA in Washington DC in their last friendly before the World Cup.

31    Paul Gascoigne's omission from Glenn Hoddle's England 22 causes a minor sensation. Blackburn pay a club-record £7.5m for Southampton's 21-yr-old striker Kevin Davies.

**June**
**Ryan Green youngest Welsh cap ... Palace takeover completed with Venables as head coach ... Sheringham shame ... Sepp Blatter the new FIFA supremo ... Chelsea sign Brian Laudrup, Ferrer and Desailly ... Uneasy World Cup opens with riots and red cards ... Geoff Hurst knighted**

1    Newcastle lose their second chairman in 6 days as Sir John Hall, earlier than expected, steps down from the football club board.

2   QPR assistant player-manager Vinnie Jones is released on bail pending sentence after being found guilty of an attack on a neighbour last November. Injury rules striker Romario out of Brazil's World Cup squad.

3   Defender Ryan Green, 7 months a pro and yet to make his senior debut for Wolves, becomes the youngest player (at 17yr 226d) to represent Wales, who win 3-0 in Malta, eclipsing Ryan Giggs's record by 96 days. The Scottish Premier League sell their TV rights to Sky in a 4-yr deal worth £45m.

4   The long-drawn-out saga of the Crystal Palace takeover is completed and Mark Goldberg's successful bid for the club is £22.85m, with a 5-yr option to buy Selhurst Park for £10m, while Terry Venables is confirmed as the new head coach. England striker Teddy Sheringham, photographed drinking and smoking with the proverbial blonde in a Portuguese nightclub instead of relaxing quietly at home, plunges the squad into a potential World Cup scandal, whether or not the non-smoking player was set up.

5   Villa sign Bolton midfielder Alan Thompson, 24, for £4.5m. Liverpool complete the signing of South-African-born naturalized-German striker Sean Dundee from Karlsruhe for £2m. The FA switch their support in the FIFA presidential election from Lennart Johansson to Sepp Blatter – a stab in the back for the Swedish supremo of UEFA. Gottfried Dienst, the Swiss referee who officiated at the 1966 World Cup final, dies at 76.

6   Disgraced England star Teddy Sheringham reads out a public apology for his lapse of discipline.

7   Chelsea complete the signing of Danish international midfielder Brian Laudrup, whose contract with Rangers expired on 31 May. The Football League end fears of a breakaway as a settlement is agreed giving Div 1 the lion's share, in the event of a 'mega-deal', of any income over £100m – 90% to 6% for Div 2 and 4% Div 3.

8   Sepp Blatter is the new president of FIFA, beating Lennart Johansson, the only other candidate, by a surprising margin of 111 votes to 80, a victory approved by the FA who feel they stand more chance of establishing chairman Keith Wiseman as the British vice-president in place of Scot David Will and consequently improving England's chance of hosting World Cup 2006. Chelsea sign Spain right-back Albert Ferrer from Barcelona for £2.2m.

9   An evening pageant in Paris to celebrate the opening of the World Cup is marred by football fans fighting and rioting, with police forced to use tear gas. Villa striker Stan Collymore is involved in an incident in a Paris bar in which he assaults his girlfriend, TV presenter Ulrika Jonsson, and later makes a humiliating public apology. Chelsea secure yet another European star, France defender Marcel Desailly from AC Milan for £4.6m.

10  Scotland have the honour of kicking off the first game of the 1998 World Cup against Brazil and they put up a sterling performance to hold the champions to 2-1, the winner an unfortunate own goal when a blocked shot bounces off Tommy Boyd over the Scottish line. In the other match in Gp A, Norway escape with a 2-2 draw after Morocco, whose Mustapha Hadji is the star of the show, twice take the lead. Fabrizio Ravanelli is out of the World Cup with a chest infection, his place in Italy's squad taken by Parma's Enrico Chiesa.

11  Roberto Baggio, whose penalty miss in the 1994 World Cup final shoot-out decided the result in Brazil's favour, courageously steps up to convert a late spot-kick to give Italy a 2-2 draw with Chile in their opening match in Gp B, and in the evening game a stoppage-time goal gives Austria a 1-1 draw against Cameroon.

12  England World Cup hero of 1966 Geoff Hurst is knighted in the Queen's Birthday Honours. Day 3 of the World Cup sees the first of the expected deluge of red cards, Bulgarian Anatoli Nankov walking in the sterile 0-0 draw against Paraguay in Gp D. Hosts France open their account with a 3-0 win over South Africa, a result that leaves home fans relieved if not ecstatic about a scrappy victory. Norwich appoint Bruce Rioch as their new manager.

NORMAN BARRETT

# ENGLISH LEAGUE TABLES 1997–98

## FA CARLING PREMIERSHIP

| | | | Home | | Goals | | Away | | Goals | | | | |
|---|---|---|---|---|---|---|---|---|---|---|---|---|---|
| | | P | W | D | L | F | A | W | D | L | F | A | GLS | Pts |
| 1 | Arsenal | 38 | 15 | 2 | 2 | 43 | 10 | 8 | 7 | 4 | 25 | 23 | +35 | 78 |
| 2 | Manchester U | 38 | 13 | 4 | 2 | 42 | 9 | 10 | 4 | 5 | 31 | 17 | +47 | 77 |
| 3 | Liverpool | 38 | 13 | 2 | 4 | 42 | 16 | 5 | 9 | 5 | 26 | 26 | +26 | 65 |
| 4 | Chelsea | 38 | 13 | 2 | 4 | 37 | 14 | 7 | 1 | 11 | 34 | 29 | +28 | 63 |
| 5 | Leeds U | 38 | 9 | 5 | 5 | 31 | 21 | 8 | 3 | 8 | 26 | 25 | +11 | 59 |
| 6 | Blackburn R | 38 | 11 | 4 | 4 | 40 | 26 | 5 | 6 | 8 | 17 | 26 | +5 | 58 |
| 7 | Aston Villa | 38 | 9 | 3 | 7 | 26 | 24 | 8 | 3 | 8 | 23 | 24 | +1 | 57 |
| 8 | West Ham U | 38 | 13 | 4 | 2 | 40 | 18 | 3 | 4 | 12 | 16 | 39 | −1 | 56 |
| 9 | Derby Co | 38 | 12 | 3 | 4 | 33 | 18 | 4 | 4 | 11 | 19 | 31 | +3 | 55 |
| 10 | Leicester C | 38 | 6 | 10 | 3 | 21 | 15 | 7 | 4 | 8 | 30 | 26 | +10 | 53 |
| 11 | Coventry C | 38 | 8 | 9 | 2 | 26 | 17 | 4 | 7 | 8 | 20 | 27 | +2 | 52 |
| 12 | Southampton | 38 | 10 | 1 | 8 | 28 | 23 | 4 | 5 | 10 | 22 | 32 | −5 | 48 |
| 13 | Newcastle U | 38 | 8 | 5 | 6 | 22 | 20 | 3 | 6 | 10 | 13 | 24 | −9 | 44 |
| 14 | Tottenham H | 38 | 7 | 8 | 4 | 23 | 22 | 4 | 3 | 12 | 21 | 34 | −12 | 44 |
| 15 | Wimbledon | 38 | 5 | 6 | 8 | 18 | 25 | 5 | 8 | 6 | 16 | 21 | −12 | 44 |
| 16 | Sheffield W | 38 | 9 | 5 | 5 | 30 | 26 | 3 | 3 | 13 | 22 | 41 | −15 | 44 |
| 17 | Everton | 38 | 7 | 5 | 7 | 25 | 27 | 2 | 8 | 9 | 16 | 29 | −15 | 40 |
| 18 | Bolton W | 38 | 7 | 8 | 4 | 25 | 22 | 2 | 5 | 12 | 16 | 39 | −20 | 40 |
| 19 | Barnsley | 38 | 7 | 4 | 8 | 25 | 35 | 3 | 1 | 15 | 12 | 47 | −45 | 35 |
| 20 | Crystal Palace | 38 | 2 | 5 | 12 | 15 | 39 | 6 | 4 | 9 | 22 | 32 | −34 | 33 |

## NATIONWIDE FOOTBALL LEAGUE DIVISION 1

| | | | Home | | Goals | | Away | | Goals | | | | |
|---|---|---|---|---|---|---|---|---|---|---|---|---|---|
| | | P | W | D | L | F | A | W | D | L | F | A | GLS | Pts |
| 1 | Nottingham F | 46 | 18 | 2 | 3 | 52 | 22 | 10 | 8 | 5 | 30 | 22 | 82 | 94 |
| 2 | Middlesbrough | 46 | 17 | 4 | 2 | 51 | 12 | 10 | 6 | 7 | 26 | 29 | 77 | 91 |
| 3 | Sunderland | 46 | 14 | 7 | 2 | 49 | 22 | 12 | 5 | 6 | 37 | 28 | 86 | 90 |
| 4 | Charlton Ath | 46 | 17 | 5 | 1 | 48 | 17 | 9 | 5 | 9 | 32 | 32 | 80 | 88 |
| 5 | Ipswich T | 46 | 14 | 5 | 4 | 47 | 20 | 9 | 9 | 5 | 30 | 23 | 77 | 83 |
| 6 | Sheffield U | 46 | 16 | 5 | 2 | 44 | 20 | 3 | 12 | 8 | 25 | 34 | 69 | 74 |
| 7 | Birmingham C | 46 | 10 | 8 | 5 | 27 | 15 | 9 | 9 | 5 | 33 | 20 | 60 | 74 |
| 8 | Stockport Co | 46 | 14 | 6 | 3 | 46 | 21 | 5 | 2 | 16 | 25 | 48 | 71 | 65 |
| 9 | Wolverhampton W | 46 | 13 | 6 | 4 | 42 | 25 | 5 | 5 | 13 | 15 | 28 | 57 | 65 |
| 10 | WBA | 46 | 9 | 7 | 6 | 27 | 26 | 7 | 5 | 11 | 23 | 30 | 50 | 61 |
| 11 | Crewe Alex | 46 | 10 | 2 | 11 | 30 | 34 | 8 | 3 | 12 | 28 | 31 | 58 | 59 |
| 12 | Oxford U | 46 | 12 | 6 | 5 | 36 | 20 | 4 | 4 | 15 | 24 | 44 | 60 | 58 |
| 13 | Bradford C | 46 | 10 | 9 | 4 | 26 | 23 | 4 | 6 | 13 | 20 | 36 | 46 | 57 |
| 14 | Tranmere R | 46 | 9 | 8 | 6 | 34 | 26 | 5 | 6 | 12 | 20 | 31 | 54 | 56 |
| 15 | Norwich C | 46 | 9 | 8 | 6 | 32 | 27 | 5 | 5 | 13 | 20 | 42 | 52 | 55 |
| 16 | Huddersfield T | 46 | 9 | 5 | 9 | 28 | 28 | 5 | 6 | 12 | 22 | 44 | 50 | 53 |
| 17 | Bury | 46 | 7 | 10 | 6 | 22 | 22 | 4 | 9 | 10 | 20 | 36 | 42 | 52 |
| 18 | Swindon T | 46 | 9 | 6 | 8 | 28 | 25 | 5 | 4 | 14 | 14 | 48 | 42 | 52 |
| 19 | Port Vale | 46 | 7 | 6 | 10 | 25 | 24 | 6 | 4 | 13 | 31 | 42 | 56 | 49 |
| 20 | Portsmouth | 46 | 8 | 6 | 9 | 28 | 30 | 5 | 4 | 14 | 23 | 33 | 51 | 49 |
| 21 | QPR | 46 | 8 | 9 | 6 | 28 | 21 | 2 | 10 | 11 | 23 | 42 | 51 | 49 |
| 22 | Manchester C | 46 | 6 | 6 | 11 | 28 | 26 | 6 | 6 | 11 | 28 | 31 | 56 | 48 |
| 23 | Stoke C | 46 | 8 | 5 | 10 | 30 | 40 | 3 | 8 | 12 | 14 | 34 | 44 | 46 |
| 24 | Reading | 46 | 8 | 4 | 11 | 27 | 31 | 3 | 5 | 15 | 12 | 47 | 39 | 42 |

## NATIONWIDE FOOTBALL LEAGUE DIVISION 2

| | | | Home | | | Goals | | Away | | | Goals | | | |
|---|---|---|---|---|---|---|---|---|---|---|---|---|---|---|
| | | P | W | D | L | F | A | W | D | L | F | A | GLS | Pts |
| 1 | Watford | 46 | 13 | 7 | 3 | 36 | 22 | 11 | 9 | 3 | 31 | 19 | 67 | 88 |
| 2 | Bristol C | 46 | 16 | 5 | 2 | 41 | 17 | 9 | 5 | 9 | 28 | 22 | 69 | 85 |
| 3 | Grimsby T | 46 | 11 | 7 | 5 | 30 | 14 | 8 | 8 | 7 | 25 | 23 | 55 | 72 |
| 4 | Northampton T | 46 | 14 | 5 | 4 | 33 | 17 | 4 | 12 | 7 | 19 | 20 | 52 | 71 |
| 5 | Bristol R | 46 | 13 | 2 | 8 | 43 | 33 | 7 | 8 | 8 | 27 | 31 | 70 | 70 |
| 6 | Fulham | 46 | 12 | 7 | 4 | 31 | 14 | 8 | 3 | 12 | 29 | 29 | 60 | 70 |
| 7 | Wrexham | 46 | 10 | 10 | 3 | 31 | 23 | 8 | 6 | 9 | 24 | 28 | 55 | 70 |
| 8 | Gillingham | 46 | 13 | 7 | 3 | 30 | 18 | 6 | 6 | 11 | 22 | 29 | 52 | 70 |
| 9 | Bournemouth | 46 | 11 | 8 | 4 | 28 | 15 | 7 | 4 | 12 | 29 | 37 | 57 | 66 |
| 10 | Chesterfield | 46 | 13 | 7 | 3 | 31 | 19 | 3 | 10 | 10 | 15 | 25 | 46 | 65 |
| 11 | Wigan Ath | 46 | 12 | 5 | 6 | 41 | 31 | 5 | 6 | 12 | 23 | 35 | 64 | 62 |
| 12 | Blackpool | 46 | 13 | 6 | 4 | 35 | 24 | 4 | 5 | 14 | 24 | 43 | 59 | 62 |
| 13 | Oldham Ath | 46 | 13 | 7 | 3 | 43 | 23 | 2 | 9 | 12 | 19 | 31 | 62 | 61 |
| 14 | Wycombe W | 46 | 10 | 10 | 3 | 32 | 20 | 4 | 8 | 11 | 19 | 33 | 51 | 60 |
| 15 | Preston NE | 46 | 10 | 6 | 7 | 29 | 26 | 5 | 8 | 10 | 27 | 30 | 56 | 59 |
| 16 | York C | 46 | 9 | 7 | 7 | 26 | 21 | 5 | 10 | 8 | 26 | 37 | 52 | 59 |
| 17 | Luton T | 46 | 7 | 7 | 9 | 35 | 38 | 7 | 8 | 8 | 25 | 26 | 60 | 57 |
| 18 | Millwall | 46 | 7 | 8 | 8 | 23 | 23 | 7 | 5 | 11 | 20 | 31 | 43 | 55 |
| 19 | Walsall | 46 | 10 | 8 | 5 | 26 | 16 | 4 | 4 | 15 | 17 | 36 | 43 | 54 |
| 20 | Burnley | 46 | 10 | 9 | 4 | 34 | 23 | 3 | 4 | 16 | 21 | 42 | 55 | 52 |
| 21 | Brentford | 46 | 9 | 7 | 7 | 33 | 29 | 2 | 10 | 11 | 17 | 42 | 50 | 50 |
| 22 | Plymouth Arg | 46 | 10 | 5 | 8 | 36 | 30 | 2 | 8 | 13 | 19 | 40 | 55 | 49 |
| 23 | Carlisle U | 46 | 8 | 5 | 10 | 27 | 28 | 4 | 3 | 16 | 30 | 45 | 57 | 44 |
| 24 | Southend U | 46 | 8 | 7 | 8 | 29 | 30 | 3 | 3 | 17 | 18 | 49 | 47 | 43 |

## NATIONWIDE FOOTBALL LEAGUE DIVISION 3

| | | | Home | | | Goals | | Away | | | Goals | | | |
|---|---|---|---|---|---|---|---|---|---|---|---|---|---|---|
| | | P | W | D | L | F | A | W | D | L | F | A | GLS | Pts |
| 1 | Notts Co | 46 | 14 | 7 | 2 | 41 | 20 | 15 | 5 | 3 | 41 | 23 | 82 | 99 |
| 2 | Macclesfield T | 46 | 19 | 4 | 0 | 40 | 11 | 4 | 9 | 10 | 23 | 33 | 63 | 82 |
| 3 | Lincoln C | 46 | 11 | 7 | 5 | 32 | 24 | 9 | 8 | 6 | 28 | 27 | 60 | 72 |
| 4 | Colchester U | 46 | 14 | 5 | 4 | 41 | 24 | 7 | 6 | 10 | 31 | 36 | 72 | 74 |
| 5 | Torquay U | 46 | 14 | 4 | 5 | 39 | 22 | 7 | 7 | 9 | 29 | 37 | 68 | 74 |
| 6 | Scarborough | 46 | 14 | 6 | 3 | 44 | 23 | 5 | 9 | 9 | 23 | 35 | 67 | 72 |
| 7 | Barnet | 46 | 10 | 8 | 5 | 35 | 22 | 9 | 5 | 9 | 26 | 29 | 61 | 70 |
| 8 | Scunthorpe U | 46 | 11 | 7 | 5 | 30 | 24 | 8 | 5 | 10 | 26 | 28 | 56 | 69 |
| 9 | Rotherham U | 46 | 10 | 9 | 4 | 41 | 30 | 6 | 10 | 7 | 26 | 31 | 67 | 67 |
| 10 | Peterborough U | 46 | 13 | 6 | 4 | 37 | 16 | 5 | 7 | 11 | 26 | 35 | 63 | 67 |
| 11 | Leyton Orient | 46 | 14 | 5 | 4 | 40 | 20 | 5 | 7 | 11 | 22 | 27 | 62 | 66* |
| 12 | Mansfield T | 46 | 11 | 9 | 3 | 42 | 26 | 5 | 8 | 10 | 22 | 29 | 64 | 65 |
| 13 | Shrewsbury T | 46 | 12 | 3 | 8 | 35 | 28 | 4 | 10 | 9 | 26 | 34 | 61 | 61 |
| 14 | Chester C | 46 | 12 | 7 | 4 | 34 | 15 | 5 | 3 | 15 | 26 | 46 | 60 | 61 |
| 15 | Exeter C | 46 | 10 | 8 | 5 | 39 | 25 | 5 | 7 | 11 | 29 | 38 | 68 | 60 |
| 16 | Cambridge U | 46 | 11 | 8 | 4 | 39 | 27 | 3 | 10 | 10 | 24 | 30 | 63 | 60 |
| 17 | Hartlepool U | 46 | 10 | 12 | 1 | 40 | 22 | 2 | 11 | 10 | 21 | 31 | 61 | 59 |
| 18 | Rochdale | 46 | 15 | 3 | 3 | 43 | 15 | 2 | 4 | 17 | 13 | 40 | 56 | 58 |
| 19 | Darlington | 46 | 13 | 6 | 4 | 43 | 28 | 1 | 6 | 16 | 13 | 44 | 56 | 54 |
| 20 | Swansea C | 46 | 8 | 8 | 7 | 24 | 16 | 5 | 3 | 15 | 25 | 46 | 49 | 50 |
| 21 | Cardiff C | 46 | 5 | 13 | 5 | 27 | 22 | 4 | 10 | 9 | 21 | 30 | 48 | 50 |
| 22 | Hull C | 46 | 10 | 6 | 7 | 36 | 32 | 1 | 2 | 20 | 20 | 51 | 56 | 41 |
| 23 | Brighton & HA | 46 | 3 | 10 | 10 | 21 | 34 | 3 | 7 | 13 | 17 | 32 | 38 | 35 |
| 24 | Doncaster R | 46 | 3 | 3 | 17 | 14 | 48 | 1 | 5 | 17 | 16 | 65 | 30 | 20 |

*Leyton Orient deducted three points.*
*Goals scored determine Nationwide Football League position where clubs are level on points.*
*If teams still cannot be separated, the team that has conceded fewer goals is placed higher.*

# FOOTBALL LEAGUE PLAY-OFFS 1997–98

### DIV 2 SEMI-FINALS FIRST LEG

**9 MAY**

**Fulham (1) 1** *(Beardsley 45 (pen))*
**Grimsby T (0) 1** *(Smith 53)*      13,954
*Fulham:* Taylor; Lawrence, Brevett, Trollope, Coleman (Blake), Morgan, Beardsley (Smith), Bracewell, Moody, Peschisolido (Thorpe), Collins.
*Grimsby T:* Davison; McDermott, Gallimore, Handyside, Lever (Jobling), Burnett, Donovan, Smith, Nogan (Clare), Lester (Black), Groves.

### DIV 1 SEMI-FINALS FIRST LEG

**10 MAY**

**Ipswich T (0) 0**
**Charlton Ath (1) 1** *(Clapham 12 (og))*      21,681
*Ipswich T:* Wright; Stockwell, Taricco, Dyer, Venus, Cundy, Clapham (Uhlenbeek), Holland, Johnson, Mathie, Petta (Scowcroft).
*Charlton Ath:* Ilic; Mills, Bowen, Jones K (Brown), Rufus, Youds, Newton, Kinsella, Bright (Jones S), Mendonca, Heaney (Barness).

**Sheffield U (0) 2** *(Marcello 57, Borbokis 76)*
**Sunderland (1) 1** *(Ball 17)*      23,800
*Sheffield U:* Tracey; Borbokis, Quinn, Ford, Sandford, Holdsworth, Saunders, Marker, Devlin, Taylor (Marcello), Hamilton.
*Sunderland:* Perez; Holloway (Rae), Makin (Ord), Clark, Craddock, Williams, Summerbee, Ball, Dichio, Phillips, Johnston.

### DIV 2 SEMI-FINALS FIRST LEG

**10 MAY**

**Bristol R (2) 3** *(Beadle 30 (pen), Bennett 37, Hayles 46)*
**Northampton T (0) 1** *(Gayle 74)*      9173
*Bristol R:* Jones; Pritchard, Lockwood, Penrice, Foster, Tillson, Bennett (Hayfield), Ramasut (Power), Beadle, Zabek, Hayles.
*Northampton T:* Woodman; Clarkson, Frain, Sampson, Warburton, Hunt, Bishop (Peer), Dozzell (Gibb), Freestone, Gayle, Hill (Seal).

### DIV 3 SEMI-FINALS FIRST LEG

**10 MAY**

**Barnet (0) 1** *(Heald 48)*
**Colchester U (0) 0**      3858
*Barnet:* Harrison; Stockley, Harle, Heald, Howarth, Basham, Goodhind, Searle, Devine, McGleish (Charley), Simpson (Manuel).
*Colchester U:* Emberson; Dunne, Betts, Skelton, Greene, Branston, Forbes, Buckle, Sale, Gregory N (Lock), Gregory D.

**Scarborough (1) 1** *(Rockett 40)*
**Torquay U (1) 3** *(Jack 22, Gittens 50, McFarlane 72)* 5246
*Scarborough:* Elliott; Kay, Sutherland (Atkin), Snodin (Robinson), Bennett G, Rockett, Williams (Bennett T), McElhatton, Campbell, Brodie, Worrall.
*Torquay U:* Veysey; Gurney, Gibbs, Robinson, Gittens, Watson, Clayton, Leadbitter, Jack (Bedeau), McFarlane (Thomas), McCall.

### DIV 1 SEMI-FINALS SECOND LEG

**13 MAY**

**Charlton Ath (1) 1** *(Newton 36)*
**Ipswich T (0) 0**      15,585
*Charlton Ath:* Ilic; Bowen, Barness, Jones K, Rufus, Youds, Newton, Kinsella, Jones S (Mortimer), Bright, Heaney.
*Ipswich T:* Wright; Stockwell (Sonner), Taricco, Dyer, Venus, Cundy, Uhlenbeek, Holland, Johnson, Mathie (Scowcroft), Petta.
*Charlton Ath won 2-0 on aggregate.*

**Sunderland (2) 2** *(Marker 21 (og), Phillips 38)*
**Sheffield U (0) 0**      40,092
*Sunderland:* Perez; Holloway, Gray, Clark, Craddock, Williams, Summerbee, Ball, Quinn, Phillips (Dichio), Johnston.
*Sheffield U:* Tracey; Wilder, Quinn, Ford (Dellas), Sandford, Holdsworth, Saunders, Marker (Stuart), Devlin, Marcello (Morris), Hamilton.
*Sunderland won 3-2 on aggregate.*

Sasa Ilic the Charlton Athletic goalkeeper, saves the crucial Sunderland penalty attempt from Michael Gray at Wembley. (Action Images)

Stripe-shirted Grimsby players Wayne Burnett and John McDermott sandwich Northampton's Carl Heggs in the play-off at Wembley. (Action Images)

**DIV 2 SEMI-FINALS SECOND LEG**

**13 MAY**

**Grimsby T (0) 1** *(Donovan 81)*
**Fulham (0) 0**                                       8689

*Grimsby T:* Davison; McDermott, Gallimore (Livingstone), Handyside, Lever, Burnett, Donovan, Smith, Nogan (Black), Lester, Groves.
*Fulham:* Taylor; Lawrence, Brevett, Trollope, Coleman, Morgan, Hayward, Bracewell, Peschisolido, Thorpe, Collins (Brooker).
*Grimsby T won 2-1 on aggregate.*

**Northampton T (1) 3** *(Heggs 34, Clarkson 61, Warburton 77)*
**Bristol R (0) 0**                                    7501

*Northampton T:* Woodman; Clarkson, Frain, Sampson, Warburton, Hunt, Peer, Heggs, Freestone (Brightwell), Gayle, Hill.
*Bristol R:* Jones; Pritchard, Lockwood, Penrice, Foster, Tillson, Bennett (Hayfield), Ramasut (Power), Beadle, Zabek, Hayles.
*Northampton T won 4-3 on aggregate.*

**DIV 3 SEMI-FINALS SECOND LEG**

**13 MAY**

**Colchester U (1) 3** *(Gregory D 12 (pen), 95, Greene 65)*
**Barnet (1) 1** *(Goodhind 41)*                       5863

*Colchester U:* Emberson; Dunne, Betts, Forbes (Skelton), Greene, Gregory D, Wilkins, Buckle, Sale, Gregory N (Duguid), Abrahams (Lock).
*Barnet:* Harrison; Stockley, Harle, Heald, Howarth, Basham, Goodhind, Searle (Simpson), Charlery, McGleish (Samuels), Wilson (Manuel).
*Colchester U won 3-2 on aggregate.*

**Torquay U (3) 4** *(Jack 6, 7, McCall 38, Gibbs 55)*
**Scarborough (1) 1** *(Rockett 22)*                   5386

*Torquay U:* Veysey; Gurney, Gibbs, Robinson, Gittens, Watson, Clayton, Leadbitter, Jack (Bedeau), McFarlane (Thomas), McCall (Hill).
*Scarborough:* Elliott; Kay, Tate (Robinson), Bennett T (Mitchell), Atkin (Sutherland), Rockett, Williams, McElhatton, Campbell, Brodie, Worrall.
*Torquay U won 7-2 on aggregate.*

**DIV 3 FINAL (at Wembley)**

**22 MAY**

**Torquay U (0) 0**
**Colchester U (1) 1** *(Gregory D 22 (pen))*          19,486

*Torquay U:* Gregg; Gurney, Gibbs, Robinson, Gittens, Watson, Clayton, Leadbitter, Jack, McFarlane (Thomas), McCall (Bedeau).
*Colchester U:* Emberson; Dunne, Betts, Skelton (Duguid), Greene, Forbes, Wilkins, Buckle, Sale, Gregory N (Lock), Gregory D.

**DIV 2 FINAL (at Wembley)**

**23 MAY**

**Grimsby T (1) 1** *(Donovan 19)*
**Northampton T (0) 0**                                62,988

*Grimsby T:* Davison; McDermott, Gallimore, Handyside, Lever, Burnett, Donovan, Smith (Livingstone), Nogan (Black), Lester, Groves.
*Northampton T:* Woodman; Clarkson, Frain, Sampson, Warburton, Hunt, Peer, Heggs, Freestone, Gayle (Seal), Hill (Gibb).

**DIV 1 FINAL (at Wembley)**

**25 MAY**

**Charlton Ath (1) 4** *(Mendonca 23, 71, 103, Rufus 85)*
**Sunderland (0) 4** *(Quinn 50, 73, Phillips 58, Summerbee 99)*                                             77,739

*Charlton Ath:* Ilic; Mills (Robinson), Bowen, Jones K, Rufus, Youds, Newton, Kinsella, Bright (Brown), Mendonca, Heaney (Jones S).
*Sunderland:* Perez; Holloway (Makin), Gray, Clark (Rae), Craddock, Williams, Summerbee, Ball, Quinn, Phillips (Dichio), Johnston.
*Charlton Ath won 7-6 on penalties.*

# LEADING GOALSCORERS

## LEADING GOALSCORERS 1997–98

| | League | FA Cup | Coca-Cola Cup | Other Cups | Total |
|---|---|---|---|---|---|
| **FA CARLING PREMIERSHIP** | | | | | |
| Dion Dublin *(Coventry C)* | 18 | 4 | 1 | 0 | 23 |
| Michael Owen *(Liverpool)* | 18 | 0 | 4 | 1 | 23 |
| Chris Sutton *(Blackburn R)* | 18 | 2 | 1 | 0 | 21 |
| Dennis Bergkamp *(Arsenal)* | 16 | 3 | 2 | 1 | 22 |
| Jimmy Floyd Hasselbaink *(Leeds U)* | 16 | 4 | 2 | 0 | 22 |
| Andy Cole *(Manchester U)* | 16 | 5 | 0 | 5 | 26 |
| Kevin Gallacher *(Blackburn R)* | 16 | 3 | 1 | 0 | 20 |
| John Hartson *(West Ham U)* | 15 | 3 | 6 | 0 | 24 |
| Darren Huckerby *(Coventry C)* | 14 | 1 | 0 | 0 | 15 |
| Paulo Wanchope *(Derby Co)* | 13 | 0 | 4 | 0 | 17 |
| Francesco Baiano *(Derby Co)* | 12 | 1 | 0 | 0 | 13 |
| Dwight Yorke *(Aston Villa)* | 12 | 2 | 0 | 2 | 16 |
| Marc Overmars *(Arsenal)* | 12 | 1 | 2 | 0 | 15 |
| Nathan Blake *(Bolton W)* | 12 | 0 | 2 | 0 | 14 |
| Paolo Di Canio *(Sheffield W)* | 12 | 0 | 2 | 0 | 14 |
| **NATIONWIDE DIVISION 1** | | | | | |
| Kevin Phillips *(Sunderland)* | 29 | 4 | 0 | 2 | 35 |
| Pierre Van Hooijdonk *(Nottingham F)* | 29 | 1 | 4 | 0 | 34 |
| Clive Mendonca *(Charlton Ath)* | 23 | 1 | 1 | 3 | 28 |
| Kevin Campbell *(Nottingham F)* | 23 | 0 | 0 | 0 | 23 |
| David Johnson *(Ipswich T)* | 20 | 2 | 0 | 0 | 22 |
| *(Also 5 League, 3 Coca-Cola goals for Bury)* | | | | | |
| Brett Angell *(Stockport Co)* | 18 | 2 | 3 | 0 | 23 |
| Paul Furlong *(Birmingham C)* | 15 | 2 | 2 | 0 | 19 |
| Marcus Stewart *(Huddersfield T)* | 15 | 1 | 0 | 0 | 16 |
| Lee Mills *(Port Vale)* | 14 | 0 | 2 | 0 | 16 |
| Niall Quinn *(Sunderland)* | 14 | 1 | 0 | 0 | 15 |
| Mikkel Beck *(Middlesbrough)* | 14 | 0 | 1 | 0 | 15 |
| Chris Hay *(Swindon T)* | 14 | 0 | 0 | 0 | 14 |
| Lee Hughes *(West Bromwich Albion)* | 14 | 0 | 0 | 0 | 14 |
| Joey Beauchamp *(Oxford U)* | 13 | 0 | 6 | 0 | 19 |
| Alex Mathie *(Ipswich T)* | 13 | 0 | 2 | 0 | 15 |
| Andy Hunt *(West Bromwich Albion)* | 13 | 0 | 1 | 0 | 14 |
| Craig Bellamy *(Norwich C)* | 13 | 0 | 0 | 0 | 13 |
| Lee Clark *(Sunderland)* | 13 | 0 | 0 | 0 | 13 |
| Paul Dalton *(Huddersfield T)* | 13 | 0 | 0 | 0 | 13 |
| Colin Little *(Crewe Alexandra)* | 13 | 0 | 0 | 0 | 13 |
| **DIVISION 2** | | | | | |
| Barry Hayles *(Bristol R)* | 23 | 2 | 0 | 1 | 26 |
| Ade Akinbiyi *(Gillingham)* | 21 | 1 | 0 | 0 | 22 |
| Tony Thorpe *(Fulham)* | 17 | 0 | 3 | 2 | 22 |
| *(All except 3 League goals for Luton T)* | | | | | |
| Shaun Goater *(Bristol C)* | 17 | 0 | 1 | 0 | 18 |
| *(Also 3 League goals for Manchester C)* | | | | | |
| Ian Stevens *(Carlisle U)* | 17 | 0 | 0 | 2 | 19 |
| Mark Stallard *(Wycombe W)* | 17 | 0 | 0 | 1 | 18 |
| Kevin Donovan *(Grimsby T)* | 16 | 1 | 1 | 3 | 21 |
| Andy Cooke *(Burnley)* | 16 | 1 | 1 | 2 | 20 |
| David Lowe *(Wigan Ath)* | 16 | 1 | 0 | 1 | 18 |
| Carlo Corazzin *(Plymouth Arg)* | 16 | 0 | 0 | 0 | 16 |
| Peter Beadle *(Bristol R)* | 15 | 2 | 0 | 1 | 18 |
| Paul Moody *(Fulham)* | 15 | 0 | 0 | 1 | 16 |
| Lee Ashcroft *(Preston NE)* | 14 | 2 | 0 | 0 | 16 |
| Jeroen Boere *(Southend U)* | 14 | 0 | 0 | 0 | 14 |
| Robert Taylor *(Brentford)* | 13 | 2 | 3 | 0 | 18 |
| Phil Clarkson *(Blackpool)* | 13 | 2 | 0 | 1 | 16 |
| Jamie Cureton *(Bristol R)* | 13 | 0 | 0 | 1 | 14 |
| Paul Peschisolido *(Fulham)* | 13 | 0 | 0 | 0 | 13 |
| *(Also 3 League and 3 Coca-Cola goals for WBA)* | | | | | |
| **DIVISION 3** | | | | | |
| Gary Jones *(Notts Co)* | 28 | 0 | 0 | 0 | 28 |
| Steve Whitehall *(Mansfield T)* | 24 | 1 | 0 | 1 | 26 |
| Darren Rowbotham *(Exeter C)* | 20 | 1 | 0 | 0 | 21 |
| Jimmy Quinn *(Peterborough U)* | 20 | 3 | 1 | 1 | 25 |
| Carl Griffiths *(Leyton Orient)* | 18 | 0 | 3 | 0 | 21 |
| Lee Glover *(Rotherham U)* | 17 | 1 | 0 | 0 | 18 |
| Robbie Painter *(Rochdale)* | 17 | 0 | 1 | 0 | 18 |
| Sean Devine *(Barnet)* | 16 | 0 | 2 | 0 | 18 |
| Martin Carruthers *(Peterborough U)* | 15 | 2 | 1 | 0 | 18 |
| Sean Farrell *(Notts Co)* | 15 | 1 | 0 | 0 | 16 |
| Gareth Williams *(Scarborough)* | 15 | 0 | 0 | 0 | 15 |
| Tony Bird *(Swansea C)* | 14 | 0 | 0 | 0 | 14 |
| Steve Flack *(Exeter C)* | 14 | 0 | 0 | 0 | 14 |
| Lee Thorpe *(Lincoln C)* | 14 | 0 | 0 | 0 | 14 |

*Other matches consist of European games, Auto Windscreens Shield and Football League play-offs.*

# REVIEW OF THE SEASON

On 20 March 1971, Arsenal were six points behind the leaders Leeds U with two matches in hand. Twenty-seven years later to the day, ironically as Leeds were losing 3-0 at West Ham, Arsenal were six points behind Manchester United with three games to spare. All those years ago, Arsenal lost only one other match – and to Leeds of all teams – but still pulled off the title with a point to spare. In 1971 they went on to win the FA Cup and last season again completed the double.

The club's latest triumph in the Premier League did not seem even a remote possibility on 30 November after they were beaten 1-0 by Liverpool at Highbury. This followed a 2-0 defeat at Sheffield Wednesday. To underline the considerable improvement made, Arsenal lost just two more matches and those when the title was already in their grasp. Lying just fifth at the end of November, they managed to win 1-0 at Newcastle the following week, only to fail again on home territory when Blackburn beat them 3-1. Boxing Day saw a change in the club's fortunes, albeit with the aid of an own goal. It sparked a run of 18 matches without defeat.

Arsène Wenger's influx of French and Dutch players had not been an instant success. From mid October, six games produced just one win and this an incredible 3-2 victory over Manchester United, the only goals Arsenal managed during this bleak spell.

The absence through injury of captain Tony Adams and striker Ian Wright had to be taken into account. However, once the team achieved a level of consistency which the calibre of the players merited, they became stronger in all departments, notably defence, where only two goals were conceded in one sequence of 14 matches.

Confirmation of the seriousness with which Arsenal were to challenge Manchester United's previous supremacy in the Premier League came when the Gunners went to Old Trafford on 14 March and completed a double with a 1-0 win. On 18 April, Arsenal defeated Wimbledon 5-0 to take over from United at the top and it was academic after that because the challengers were a point ahead and had two games in hand of the defending champions. On 3 May, Arsenal's 4-0 win over Everton deservedly clinched the championship for them.

They went on to Wembley to win the Cup, beating Newcastle 2-0, dominating the match for long periods but uncharacteristically allowing their opponents the opportunity to fight back.

It may be argued that Manchester United lost their grip on yet another Premier League title in January when they were beaten 1-0 at Southampton and then by a single goal at home to Leicester. This was in a run of five games which produced just one win. It was not exactly an injury-free season at Old Trafford and goals never flowed freely in the second half of the season. While many of their rivals had invariably failed to take advantage of slips by United in the past, Arsenal showed a greater tenacity of purpose this time round.

Such are the pressures of the Premiership that third place for Liverpool represented something of a crisis at Anfield. The emergence of Michael Owen undoubtedly the find of the season, was offset by injury to Robbie Fowler and though they lost only three of the games after 13 December until the championship was decided, these defeats came at a crucial time and cost them any realistic hope of challenging for honours. Moreover, they conceded too many goals for championship material.

Teddy Sheringham (Manchester United) is surrounded by three Arsenal players, Patrick Vieira, David Platt and Nigel Winterburn. Arsenal achieved the double over United in the League. (Colorsport)

The pre-war complaint that Chelsea were consistently inconsistent, again could have been coupled to their performances in 1997-98. Their best League spell came in a six game run to Boxing Day and they were second on a number of occasions. But they seemed better equipped for the requirements of cup football and they deservedly achieved the double in this respect, beating Middlesbrough 2-0 in the Coca-Cola Cup Final, a repeat victory against the same opposition in the previous season's FA Cup and then going on to add the European Cup-Winners' Cup for their first European trophy for 27 years.

Leeds put a slow start behind them and lying fourth on 20 December with prospects of improvement looking good, they won only one of the next eight games to emphasize their failure to substantiate a promising position.

A useful beginning for Blackburn was sustained and having beaten Aston Villa 5-0 on 17 January and tucked neatly in second place, there seemed justification for further optimism. Alas, they won only four more matches. After losing their opening four games, Aston Villa made something of a recovery, but they were still as low as 15th on 21 February. The disappointments at Villa Park produced a change of manager with Brian Little giving way to John Gregory and thereafter they won nine of their last 11 games.

Good spells with successive wins were not enough for West Ham and the defence let them down towards the end of the season after sixth place had been reached in mid-April. For Derby County, a disappointing last quarter of the season erased much that had been worthwhile earlier on. A top six place had appeared the least of their ambitions, but then goals became difficult to obtain. Twenty-five of Leicester's matches produced either one or no goals. December was a particularly poor month and it was obvious where the problems needed to be addressed.

Having made something of a reputation of late escapes from relegation, Coventry had decided to tunnel their way out of trouble before the turn of the year. A 3-2 win over Manchester United was significant and they lost only two more games during the rest of the season.

Southampton, too, reached the heady heights of tenth place in March, a tribute to manager David Jones in his first season and a solitary win from their last seven games took much of the glory away from his leadership after just one win in the first nine games.

Goals were few and far between for Newcastle and from December, only four more matches were won. The absence of Alan Shearer with injury until the last third of the season, contributed to a lack of goals but in the cup final they were unlucky to the extent that having been outplayed for much of the game, they still managed to hit the woodwork twice. Uncomfortably near the relegation zone for much of the season, a modest run of five unbeaten matches at the end of the campaign saved injury-hit Tottenham.

The goals dried up for Wimbledon in the last ten games, only four being scored. They were never able to inflict even the odd defeat on any of the top teams and 11th was the highest all season for Sheffield Wednesday. They almost found themselves dragged into the relegation zone, had an uninspiring start and an undistinguished end of the season. Everton scraped a 1-1 draw at home to Coventry on the last day to escape the drop on goal difference. Three successive wins at the turn of the year was the sole bright spot at Goodison Park, though they did take four points from Liverpool.

Bolton had to win at Chelsea in the last game to stand any chance of survival. They lost 2-0 having won half of their last ten games. But the 12 matches without a win to 7 March had been their undoing. Barnsley had been everyone's favourites to go down but they produced some spirited performances. Three successive wins to mid-March gave some real hope, but it was not to be. The dice rolled against them in the next game when they had three players sent off against Liverpool, who only won 3-2 in the last minute. The third promoted team from the previous season, Crystal Palace made it a trio to go down. They only won their first home game on 18 April beating Derby 3-1. By then, they were dropping like a stone, courtesy of 15 games without a win to mid-March.

In the Football League, Nottingham Forest were headed only once from January and were never lower than fifth which they reached on 13 September, having taken just one point from a possible nine. Apart from the odd slip here and there, they were strong in most departments and worthy champions. Middlesbrough bounced back after relegation. Generally reliable in defence apart from two extraordinary results, losing 4-0 at Nottingham Forest and 5-0 at Queens Park Rangers in successive games.

Charlton, having finished two points behind Sunderland in the League, pipped them for promotion through the play-offs at Wembley when it was decided on penalties. For Sunderland, losing 2-0 at Ipswich in the penultimate League game cost them automatic promotion. It was their first defeat after 13 games. Meanwhile Charlton had been there or thereabouts from mid-December. They tightened up their defence and conceded no goals at all in the last seven League games.

Still as low as 20th on 29 November, Ipswich enjoyed a tremendous revival in the second half of the season with only one defeat in 23 games, only to fail in the play-offs as did Sheffield United, who won only one of their last seven matches. They were third as late as the end of December after a 4-1 win over Charlton, arguably their best performance of the season. For Birmingham, a promising start was spoiled by nine games without a victory and too many drawn matches. Stockport needed a consistent run to take them above 8th or 9th place.

Aspirations were dashed again for Wolverhampton who were never able to push higher than the last play-off place and even this failed them when they won only one of their last eight matches. Neighbours West Bromwich Albion were second on 23 November after beating their other local rivals Birmingham 1-0. But they fell away badly afterwards and a run of ten without a win ended after a single goal defeat at Birmingham.

A finishing position of 11th for Crewe represented their highest all season. Just one win in a sequence of 12 to early December had caused some problems. On 22 November, Oxford were 22nd but redeemed themselves when only two defeats came in 11 matches to mid-March.

Top briefly in September, Bradford were only able to hover in the top half of the table until late on in the season. Seven games with no goals plunged Tranmere into the bottom four in the New Year. An indifferent season for Norwich appeared to be developing into a crisis, when they experienced 14 matches without a win to mid-April but 16th position for Huddersfield did not seem possible since their first win did not arrive until 1 November.

A late improvement pulled Bury away from the brink of relegation following 14 games without a win in mid-season. Swindon looked enterprisingly resourceful in the first half of the season but vulnerable afterwards, slipping

Roberto Di Matteo scores the second Chelsea goal against Middlesbrough in the Coca-Cola Cup Final at Wembley.
(Colorsport)

to just above the relegation zone after failing to win any of their last eight games. Even though Port Vale won only one of their last five matches, this 4-0 success at Huddersfield saved them.

Alan Ball's arrival revived the Aussie-dominated playing staff at Portsmouth when the club was locked at the foot of the table. They faltered again but recovered to win the last two matches. But the end of the season probably arrived at the right time for Queens Park Rangers, having failed to win any of their last ten matches. All this, after being third at the end of September.

Even though Manchester City won 5-2 at Stoke on the last day, they were relegated. Only once did they win as many as two games in succession. Stoke had a new ground, but familiar problems. They never recovered from a sequence of 11 games without a win to mid-March. This came shortly after crashing 7-0 at home to Birmingham. They were joined in relegation by Reading, whose change of manager came too late to save them. From their last 13 games, they had 12 defeats.

Second Division champions Watford were never out of the top two, though a run of eight games with only one win from February caused a flutter. They were joined in automatic promotion by Bristol City, whose prospects had looked bleak in early October when they were 15th. Only one win in the last five cost them the title.

Distracted by reaching Wembley in the Auto Windscreens Final, Grimsby's hopes were put in some jeopardy with just one win in the last nine and only four goals scored. But they came alive in the play-offs. An unimpressive spell of five games from mid-March meant no automatic promotion after a steady season for Northampton. Then came the play-off disappointment. Five consecutive defeats from the end of February cost Bristol Rovers a chance of the play-offs and free-spending Fulham found their form deserting them when the they lost their last three games.

Third on 21 March following a 2-0 success over Wycombe, Wrexham managed only one other win and that in the last game. Gillingham needed a touch more consistency than the nine unbeaten games which came from the end of December and drawing four of the last six did not help.

Bournemouth drifted into mid-table, having been fourth in October, following a 2-1 win over Fulham and a promising start for Chesterfield was eroded halfway through the season when they failed to score in four successive matches. Wigan were too far down to benefit from just one defeat in the last nine, and seventh place on 7 September the best Blackpool contrived.

After beating Fulham 1-0 on 14 February, Oldham drifted down to below halfway. Wycombe drew too many games to mount a serious assault on the play-offs after a good start and though Preston were fifth at the beginning of October, a run of 11 without a win to February ended their hopes.

York were third in November but only one win in the next 12 came as a blow. Luton appeared outside candidates for relegation for much of the time before a turn round from March, and though Millwall were fourth halfway through December, a slump produced just four more wins. Walsall were unable to score at all in 19 games and never more than three goals in any one game, though incredibly they beat Macclesfield 7-0 away in the FA Cup.

Burnley managed their first goal after 552 minutes of play and struggled thereafter. A draw and a win in the last two matches edged them to safety. Not so for Brentford, Plymouth, Carlisle and Southend. A mini-revival for Brentford in March was not sustained, Plymouth flirted with relegation for most of the season following a poor start and Carlisle achieved only one win in their last ten matches. For Southend it was relegation in successive seasons.

Third Division champions Notts County were promoted as early as March. They failed to score in only four games and were never headed after early December. Newcomers Macclesfield remained unbeaten at home, the only team in the four divisions so to do. Once they succeeded in winning away – inevitably at Doncaster in January – it was rarely a problem for them.

For Lincoln losing 5-3 at home to Notts County on 24 January had a beneficial effect. The defence was noticeably tightened and no defeats in the last five games ensured automatic promotion. They were joined by Colchester who were still only half way well into the New Year and only 10th on 7 March. The 5-1 win over Macclesfield proved a turning point and the play-offs did the rest.

Eight successive wins in early March set Torquay into second place, but only one win came in the last eight. A fine second half of the campaign shot Scarborough into a play-off berth, while Barnet were rarely out of these positions until failing at the last hurdle. But for eight successive defeats to mid-January, Scunthorpe might have made the play-offs themselves and even three periods of seven unbeaten games failed to get Rotherham to the same destination.

On 31 January Peterborough were well placed, lying second. Then came the crash with just one win in the next nine games, and confidence drained away. For Leyton Orient, the loss of three points for fielding suspended players hit them badly late in the season. Eighth place on 7 March was their highest. Mansfield drew 17 games and even a late unbeaten sequence contained seven out of 11.

Twice as low as 20th, four successive wins in April for Shrewsbury improved their situation. Even by the end of January, the play-off position was not out of the question for Chester until they fell away badly, while Exeter faded themselves at the same time.

An unproductive 13 games without a win for Cambridge from 13 September set the pattern for them and Hartlepool's mid-term improvement was also handicapped by too many drawn games. Rochdale failed to score in 19 games, ninth was their highest position all season and they never had more than two wins in a row. A wretched start for Darlington produced only one win in the first 11 games while 19th place in February was the highest Swansea managed after September.

A useful start for Cardiff featuring six unbeaten matches was soon undone as the next victory did not arrive until November. Hull kicked off the season with just one win in the first ten, but this was a spectacular 7-4 affair against Swansea. Goals were never as easy after that. For Brighton playing home games at Gillingham, victories were few and far between. It was perhaps fortunate for them that Doncaster had such a disasterous time, otherwise they might have finished bottom themselves. Doncaster made the record books for all the wrong reasons. They conceded eight goals at Leyton Orient, seven at Cardiff and five on four occasions. Their first win came on 2 December.

Paul Ince of Liverpool makes progress in a Premier League clash with Chelsea for whom Gustavo Poyet (8) keeps a watchful eye on his opponent. (Action Images)

# INTRODUCTION TO THE CLUB SECTION

For this year's Rothmans Football Yearbook the players again appear under the club with whom they finished the season and in an A–Z form for easy reference (see pages 412–538). The names of Trainees and Associated Schoolboys are also included under each club's name.

The club section again comprises four pages, the first features the team photograph depicting those players and officials taken at the commencement of the 1997–98 season. On the second page which gives historical and record details for each club there are new entries in the 'Did you know?' series. Record Transfer fees are usually left to the discretion of the club concerned.

The third and fourth pages of this section present a complete record of the League season, including date, venue, opponents, results, half-time score, League position, goalscorers, attendances and complete line-ups including substitutes where used, for every League game in the 1997–98 season. Again goal times have been added, though not official they give an indication of when goals were scored. These appear as superior figures [10, 20, 30].

Squad numbers in the Premier League have been ignored; those used are the familiar ones, 1–11 while the introduction of a third outfield substitute has been recognised as follows:- the first substitute No. 12, the second No. 13 and the third No. 14. However, if there is a substitute goalkeeper he is represented by No. 15 but *only* if he replaces the first choice goalkeeper. Otherwise he adopts one of the other three substitute numbers, as there have been several instances where a goalkeeper has been used as an outfield player because of injuries during the game. Players replaced are respectively noted with superior figures [1], [2], [3] and [g] for goalkeeper. These third and fourth pages also include consolidated lists of goalscorers for the club in League, Coca-Cola Cup and FA Cup matches plus a summary of results in these two main domestic competitions.

The continued increase in the number of matches played on Sundays has resulted in the League positions shown after every League result being taken on that day. Full holiday programmes are also recorded, but the position after mid-week fixtures will not normally have been updated. Attendance figures quoted for the Nationwide Football League are those which appeared in the Press at the time. But those in the FA Carling Premiership are official. The attendance statistics published on pages 575–577 are those officially issued by the FA Premier League and the Football League at the end of the season.

In the totals at the top of each column on page 4, substitute appearances are listed separately by the '+', but have been amalgamated in the totals which feature in the players historical section in the directory mentioned above. Thus these appearances include those as substitute. In fact the directory again features those names appearing on the FA Premier League and Football League's Retained list, which is published at the end of May. Each player's height and weight where known, plus birth place, birth date and source together with total League goals and appearances for each club he has represented, can be found as in previous editions. The player's details remain under the club which retained him at the end of the season. An asterisk '*' by a player's name indicates that he was given a free transfer at the end of the 1997–98 season, a dagger '†' against a name means that he is a non-contract player, a double dagger '‡' indicates that the player's registration was cancelled during the season and a section mark '§' shows the player to be a trainee or associated schoolboy who has made League appearances. The symbol # indicates players aged 24 and over who are out of contract but who were offered re-engagement by their clubs. Appearances by players in the play-offs are not included in their career totals.

There is also a directory of all League club managers to be found on pages 555–564.

ARSENAL 1997–98    *Back row (left to right):* Ian Wright, Chris Kiwomya, Vince Bartram, Alex Manninger, John Lukic, David Seaman, Steve Bould, Gilles Grimandi.
*Middle row:* Gary Lewin (Physio), Colin Lewin (Assistant Physio), Pat Rice (Assistant Manager), Boro Primorac (Coach), Rémi Garde, Luis Boa Morte, Glenn Helder, Nicolas Anelka, Emmanuel Petit, Ray Parlour, Scott Marshall, Matthew Upson, Stephen Hughes, Bob Wilson (Goalkeeping Coach), George Armstrong (Reserve Coach), Mark James (Masseur), Vic Akers (Kit Manager).
*Front Row:* Alberto Mendez, Lee Dixon, Dennis Bergkamp, Jason Crowe, Marc Overmars, Martin Keown, Arsène Wenger (Manager), Tony Adams, Patrick Vieira, Nigel Winterburn, Ian Selley, Paul Shaw, David Platt.

# FA Premiership     **ARSENAL**

*Arsenal Stadium, Highbury, London N5 1BU.* Telephone: (0171) 704 4000. Fax: (0171) 704 4001. Box Office: (0171) 413 3366. Commercial and Marketing: (0171) 704 4100. Recorded information on (0171) 704 4242. Clubline: 0891 202021.

*Ground capacity:* 38,500 all seated.

*Record attendance:* 73,295 v Sunderland, Div 1, 9 March 1935.

*Record receipts:* £392,726.50 v Sampdoria, European Cup-Winners' Cup, semi-final first leg, 6 April 1995.

*Pitch measurements:* 110yd × 73yd.

*Life President:* Sir Robert Bellinger GBE, D.SC.

*Chairman:* P. D. Hill-Wood. *Vice-Chairman:* D. Dein.

*Directors:* R. G. Gibbs, C. E. B. L. Carr, R. C. L. Carr, D. D. Fiszman.

*Managing Director:* K. J. Friar.

*Manager:* Arsène Wenger. *Assistant Manager/Coach:* Pat Rice. *Head Youth Coach:* Don Howe. *Head of Youth Development:* Liam Brady.

*Physio:* Gary Lewin. *Reserve Coach:* George Armstrong. *Youth Coach:* Don Givens.

*Company Secretary:* David Miles. *Commercial Manager:* John Hazell.

*Stadium Manager:* John Beattie.

*Year Formed:* 1886. *Turned Professional:* 1891. *Ltd Co.:* 1893.

*Previous Names:* 1886, Dial Square; 1886–91, Royal Arsenal; 1891–1914, Woolwich Arsenal.

*Club Nickname:* 'Gunners'.

*Previous Grounds:* 1886–87, Plumstead Common; 1887–88, Sportsman Ground; 1888–90, Manor Ground; 1890–93, Invicta Ground; 1893–1913, Manor Ground; 1913, Highbury.

*Foundation:* Formed by workers at the Royal Arsenal, Woolwich in 1886 they began as Dial Square (name of one of the workshops) and included two former Nottingham Forest players Fred Beardsley and Morris Bates. Beardsley wrote to his old club seeking help and they provided the new club with a full set of red jerseys and a ball. The club became known as the "Woolwich Reds" although their official title soon after formation was Woolwich Arsenal.

*First Football League game:* 2 September 1893, Division 2, v Newcastle U (h) D 2-2 – Williams; Powell, Jeffrey; Devine, Buist, Howat; Gemmell, Henderson, Shaw (1), Elliott (1), Booth.

*Record League Victory:* 12–0 v Loughborough T, Division 2, 12 March 1900 – Orr; McNichol, Jackson; Moir, Dick (2), Anderson (1); Hunt, Cottrell (2), Main (2), Gaudie (3), Tennant (2).

*Record Cup Victory:* 11–1 v Darwen, FA Cup 3rd rd, 9 January 1932 – Moss; Parker, Hapgood; Jones, Roberts, John; Hulme (2), Jack (3), Lambert (2), James, Bastin (4).

*Record Defeat:* 0–8 v Loughborough T, Division 2, 12 December 1896.

*Most League Points (2 for a win):* 66, Division 1, 1930–31.

*Most League Points (3 for a win):* 83, Division 1, 1990–91.

*Most League Goals:* 127, Division 1, 1930–31.

*Highest League Scorer in Season:* Ted Drake, 42, 1934–35.

*Most League Goals in Total Aggregate:* Cliff Bastin, 150, 1930–47.

*Most Capped Player:* Kenny Sansom, 77 (86), England.

*Most League Appearances:* David O'Leary, 558, 1975–93.

*Record Transfer Fee Received:* £5,000,000 from West Ham U for John Hartson, February 1997.

*Record Transfer Fee Paid:* £7,500,000 to Internazionale for Dennis Bergkamp, June 1995.

*Football League Record:* 1893 Elected to Division 2; 1904–13 Division 1; 1913–19 Division 2; 1919–92 Division 1; 1992– FA Premier League.

*Honours:* FA Premier League Champions: 1997–98. *Football League:* Division 1 – Champions 1930–31, 1932–33, 1933–34, 1934–35, 1937–38, 1947–48, 1952–53, 1970–71, 1988–89, 1990–91; Runners-up 1925–26, 1931–32, 1972–73; Division 2 – Runners-up 1903–04. *FA Cup:* Winners 1930, 1936, 1950, 1971, 1979, 1993, 1998. Runners-up 1927, 1932, 1952, 1972, 1978, 1980. *Double performed:* 1970–71, 1997–98. *Football League Cup:* Winners 1987, 1993; Runners-up 1968, 1969, 1988. **European Competitions:** *Fairs Cup:* 1963–64, 1969–70 (winners), 1970–71; *European Cup:* 1971–72, 1991–92; *UEFA Cup:* 1978–79, 1981–82, 1982–83, 1996–97, 1997–98; *European Cup-Winners' Cup:* 1979–80 (runners-up), 1993–94 (winners), 1994–95 (runners-up).

*Colours:* Red shirts with white sleeves, white shorts, red and white hooped stockings. *Change colours:* Yellow with navy band, navy shorts, navy stockings with yellow band.

**Did you know?**
On 13 September 1997, Ian Wright scored three times against Bolton Wanderers taking his total of League and Cup goals to 179, a club record.

## ARSENAL 1997–98 LEAGUE RECORD

| Match No. | Date | Venue | Opponents | Result | H/T Score | Lg. Pos. | Goalscorers | Attendance |
|---|---|---|---|---|---|---|---|---|
| 1 | Aug 9 | A | Leeds U | D 1-1 | 1-1 | — | Wright [35] | 37,993 |
| 2 | 11 | H | Coventry C | W 2-0 | 1-0 | — | Wright 2 [29, 47] | 37,324 |
| 3 | 23 | A | Southampton | W 3-1 | 1-1 | 2 | Overmars [20], Bergkamp 2 [57, 79] | 15,246 |
| 4 | 27 | A | Leicester C | D 3-3 | 1-0 | — | Bergkamp 3 [9, 61, 90] | 21,089 |
| 5 | 30 | H | Tottenham H | D 0-0 | 0-0 | 5 | | 38,102 |
| 6 | Sept 13 | H | Bolton W | W 4-1 | 3-1 | 4 | Wright 3 [20, 25, 81], Parlour [44] | 38,138 |
| 7 | 21 | A | Chelsea | W 3-2 | 1-1 | 2 | Bergkamp 2 [45, 59], Winterburn [89] | 31,290 |
| 8 | 24 | H | West Ham U | W 4-0 | 4-0 | — | Bergkamp [12], Overmars 2 [39, 45], Wright (pen) [42] | 38,012 |
| 9 | 27 | A | Everton | D 2-2 | 2-0 | 1 | Wright [32], Overmars [41] | 35,457 |
| 10 | Oct 4 | H | Barnsley | W 5-0 | 3-0 | 1 | Bergkamp 2 [25, 32], Parlour [45], Platt [63], Wright [76] | 38,049 |
| 11 | 18 | A | Crystal Palace | D 0-0 | 0-0 | 1 | | 26,180 |
| 12 | 26 | H | Aston Villa | D 0-0 | 0-0 | 2 | | 38,061 |
| 13 | Nov 1 | A | Derby Co | L 0-3 | 0-0 | 2 | | 30,004 |
| 14 | 9 | H | Manchester U | W 3-2 | 2-2 | 2 | Anelka [7], Vieira [27], Platt [83] | 38,205 |
| 15 | 22 | A | Sheffield W | L 0-2 | 0-1 | 3 | | 34,373 |
| 16 | 30 | H | Liverpool | L 0-1 | 0-0 | 5 | | 38,094 |
| 17 | Dec 6 | A | Newcastle U | W 1-0 | 1-0 | 4 | Wright [36] | 36,751 |
| 18 | 13 | H | Blackburn R | L 1-3 | 1-0 | 5 | Overmars [18] | 38,147 |
| 19 | 26 | H | Leicester C | W 2-1 | 1-0 | 6 | Platt [36], Walsh (og) [56] | 38,023 |
| 20 | 28 | A | Tottenham H | D 1-1 | 0-1 | 6 | Parlour [62] | 29,601 |
| 21 | Jan 10 | A | Leeds U | W 2-1 | 0-0 | 5 | Overmars 2 [60, 72] | 38,018 |
| 22 | 17 | H | Coventry C | D 2-2 | 0-1 | 5 | Bergkamp [50], Anelka [58] | 22,777 |
| 23 | 31 | H | Southampton | W 3-0 | 0-0 | 5 | Bergkamp [62], Adams [67], Anelka [68] | 38,056 |
| 24 | Feb 8 | H | Chelsea | W 2-0 | 2-0 | 5 | Hughes 2 [4, 42] | 38,083 |
| 25 | 21 | H | Crystal Palace | W 1-0 | 0-0 | 2 | Grimandi [49] | 38,094 |
| 26 | Mar 2 | A | West Ham U | D 0-0 | 0-0 | — | | 25,717 |
| 27 | 11 | A | Wimbledon | W 1-0 | 1-0 | — | Wreh [21] | 22,291 |
| 28 | 14 | A | Manchester U | W 1-0 | 0-0 | 2 | Overmars [79] | 55,174 |
| 29 | 28 | A | Sheffield W | W 1-0 | 1-0 | 2 | Bergkamp [35] | 38,087 |
| 30 | 31 | H | Bolton W | W 1-0 | 0-0 | — | Wreh [47] | 25,000 |
| 31 | Apr 11 | H | Newcastle U | W 3-1 | 1-0 | 2 | Anelka 2 [41, 64], Vieira [72] | 38,102 |
| 32 | 13 | A | Blackburn R | W 4-1 | 4-0 | 2 | Bergkamp [2], Parlour 2 [7, 14], Anelka [42] | 28,212 |
| 33 | 18 | H | Wimbledon | W 5-0 | 3-0 | 1 | Adams [12], Overmars [17], Bergkamp [19], Petit [54], Wreh [88] | 38,024 |
| 34 | 25 | A | Barnsley | W 2-0 | 1-0 | 1 | Bergkamp [23], Overmars [76] | 18,691 |
| 35 | 29 | H | Derby Co | W 1-0 | 1-0 | — | Petit [34] | 38,121 |
| 36 | May 3 | H | Everton | W 4-0 | 2-0 | 1 | Bilic (og) [6], Overmars 2 [28, 57], Adams [89] | 38,269 |
| 37 | 6 | A | Liverpool | L 0-4 | 0-3 | — | | 44,417 |
| 38 | 10 | A | Aston Villa | L 0-1 | 0-1 | 1 | | 39,372 |

**Final League Position: 1**   1996–97 PREM 3

### GOALSCORERS

*League (68):* Bergkamp 16, Overmars 12, Wright 10 (1 pen), Anelka 6, Parlour 5, Adams 3, Platt 3, Wreh 3, Hughes 2, Petit 2, Vieira 2, Grimandi 1, Winterburn 1, own goals 2.
*Coca-Cola Cup (10):* Bergkamp 2 (1 pen), Boa Morte 2, Overmars 2, Hughes 1, Mendes 1, Platt 1 (pen), Wright 1.
*FA Cup (8):* Bergkamp 3 (1 pen), Anelka 2, Overmars 1, Parlour 1, Wreh 1.

| Seaman D 31 | Garde R 6 + 4 | Winterburn N 35 + 1 | Vieira P 31 + 2 | Bould S 21 + 3 | Grimandi G 16 + 6 | Parlour R 34 | Wright I 22 + 2 | Petit E 32 | Bergkamp D 28 | Overmars M 32 | Platt D 11 + 20 | Hughes S 7 + 10 | Marshall S 1 + 2 | Boa Morte L 4 + 11 | Dixon L 26 + 2 | Anelka N 16 + 10 | Adams T 26 | Mendez A 1 + 2 | Wreh C 7 + 9 | Keown M 18 | Rankin I — + 1 | Upson M 5 | Manninger A 7 | Vernazza P 1 | McGowan G — + 1 | Match No. |
|---|---|---|---|---|---|---|---|---|---|---|---|---|---|---|---|---|---|---|---|---|---|---|---|---|---|---|
| 1 | 2 | 3 | 4$^{1}$ | 5 | 6 | 7 | 8 | 9 | 10 | 11$^{12}$ | 12 | 13 |  |  |  |  |  |  |  |  |  |  |  |  |  | 1 |
| 1 | 2 | 3 | 4 |  | 6 | 7 | 8 | 9$^{1}$ | 10 | 11$^{2}$ | 12 | 13 | 5 |  |  |  |  |  |  |  |  |  |  |  |  | 2 |
| 1 | 2 | 3 | 4 | 5 | 6$^{2}$ | 7 | 8 | 9$^{1}$ | 10 | 11$^{13}$ | 12 |  | 13 | 14 |  |  |  |  |  |  |  |  |  |  |  | 3 |
| 1 |  | 3 | 4 | 5 | 6 | 7$^{1}$ | 8$^{9}$ | 9 | 10 | 11$^{12}$ | 12 | 13 |  |  | 2 | 14 |  |  |  |  |  |  |  |  |  | 4 |
| 1 |  | 3 | 4 | 5 | 6 | 7$^{2}$ | 8 | 9$^{1}$ | 10 | 11 | 12 |  |  |  | 2 | 13 |  |  |  |  |  |  |  |  |  | 5 |
| 1 |  | 3 | 4 | 5 | 6 | 7$^{1}$ | 8$^{2}$ | 9 | 10 | 11$^{3}$ | 12 |  |  | 14 | 2 | 13 |  |  |  |  |  |  |  |  |  | 6 |
| 1 |  | 3 | 4 | 5 | 12 | 7$^{2}$ | 8 | 9 | 10 | 11$^{1}$ |  |  |  |  | 13 | 2 | 6 |  |  |  |  |  |  |  |  | 7 |
| 1 |  | 3$^{2}$ | 4 | 5 | 12 | 7 | 8$^{9}$ | 9 | 10 | 11 |  | 13 |  |  | 2$^{1}$ | 14 | 6 |  |  |  |  |  |  |  |  | 8 |
| 1 | 12 | 3 | 4$^{1}$ | 5 | 2 | 7$^{2}$ | 8 | 9 | 10 | 11$^{13}$ |  | 13 |  |  | 14 |  | 6 |  |  |  |  |  |  |  |  | 9 |
| 1 |  | 3 | 4 | 5 |  | 7$^{1}$ | 8$^{3}$ | 9 | 10 | 11$^{2}$ | 12 |  |  | 14 | 2 | 13 | 6 |  |  |  |  |  |  |  |  | 10 |
| 1 |  | 3 | 4 | 5 | 2 | 7$^{2}$ | 8 | 9 | 10 |  | 12 |  |  | 11$^{1}$ |  |  | 6 | 13 |  |  |  |  |  |  |  | 11 |
| 1 |  | 3 | 4 | 5 |  | 7$^{1}$ | 8 | 9 | 10 |  | 12 |  |  | 11$^{2}$ | 2 | 13 | 6 |  |  |  |  |  |  |  |  | 12 |
| 1 |  | 3$^{1}$ | 4 | 5 |  | 7 | 8 | 9 |  |  |  |  |  | 11 | 12 | 2 | 10$^{2}$ | 6 |  |  |  |  |  |  | 13 | 13 |
| 1 |  | 3 | 4$^{1}$ | 12 | 5 | 7 | 8 |  |  | 11 | 9 |  |  |  | 2 | 10$^{2}$ | 6 |  |  |  |  |  |  | 13 | 14 |
| 1 |  | 3 |  | 5$^{2}$ |  | 7$^{1}$ | 8 |  |  | 11 | 9 | 12 | 13 |  | 2 |  | 6 | 10$^{3}$ | 14 | 4 |  |  |  |  |  | 15 |
| 1 |  | 3 |  | 12 |  |  | 8 | 9$^{1}$ | 10 | 11 | 4 | 7$^{2}$ |  |  | 2 |  | 6 | 13 | 5 |  |  |  |  |  |  | 16 |
| 1 |  | 3 |  |  |  | 7 | 8 | 9 | 10 | 11 | 4 |  |  |  | 2 |  | 6 |  | 5 |  |  |  |  |  |  | 17 |
| 1 | 12 | 3 |  |  |  | 7$^{1}$ | 8 | 9 | 10 | 11 | 4$^{2}$ |  |  | 13 | 2 |  | 6 |  | 5 |  |  |  |  |  |  | 18 |
| 1 |  | 3 | 4 | 5 |  | 7 | 8$^{2}$ |  | 10 | 11 | 9$^{1}$ | 12 |  |  | 2 | 13 |  | 6 |  |  |  |  |  |  |  | 19 |
| 1 |  | 3 | 4 | 5 | 12 | 7 |  | 9 | 10$^{2}$ | 11 |  | 13 |  |  | 2$^{1}$ | 8$^{2}$ |  | 6 | 14 |  |  |  |  |  |  | 20 |
| 1 |  | 3 | 4 | 5 |  | 7 | 8 | 9 | 10 | 11 |  |  |  |  | 2 |  |  | 6 |  |  |  |  |  |  |  | 21 |
| 1 |  | 3 | 4 | 5 | 12 | 7 |  | 9 | 10 |  |  |  |  |  | 13 | 2 |  | 6$^{1}$ | 11 |  |  |  |  |  |  | 22 |
|  |  | 3 |  | 5 | 2 | 7 |  | 9 | 10 | 11 | 12 |  | 4$^{1}$ |  |  | 8$^{2}$ | 6 | 13 |  |  |  |  | 1 |  |  | 23 |
|  |  | 3 |  | 5 | 2$^{3}$ | 7 | 12 | 9 | 10 | 11$^{2}$ | 13 |  | 4 |  | 14 | 8$^{1}$ | 6 |  |  |  |  |  | 1 |  |  | 24 |
|  |  |  | 4 |  | 6 |  |  |  |  |  | 7 | 9 | 11 | 2 | 8 |  | 5 | 3 | 1 | 10$^{1}$ | 12 |  |  |  |  | 25 |
|  | 12 | 4 |  |  |  |  | 9 |  | 11 | 7$^{2}$ | 10 | 13 |  | 2 | 8 | 6 |  | 5 | 3$^{1}$ | 1 |  |  |  |  |  | 26 |
|  | 12 | 3 | 4 |  |  | 7$^{1}$ |  | 9 | 10 | 11$^{2}$ |  | 13 |  | 2 | 8$^{3}$ | 5 |  | 6 |  | 1 |  |  |  |  |  | 27 |
|  | 12 | 3 | 4 |  |  | 7$^{1}$ |  | 9 | 10 | 11 |  |  |  | 2 | 13 | 6 |  | 8$^{2}$ | 5 | 1 |  |  |  |  |  | 28 |
| 1 | 12 | 3 | 4 |  | 13 | 7$^{2}$ |  | 9 | 11 |  |  |  |  | 2$^{1}$ | 14 | 6 |  | 8$^{3}$ | 5 |  |  |  |  |  |  | 29 |
| 1 |  | 3 | 4 | 12 | 2 | 7 |  | 9 | 11$^{2}$ | 14 | 13 |  |  |  |  | 8$^{3}$ | 6 | 10$^{1}$ | 5 |  |  |  |  |  |  | 30 |
| 1 | 2 | 3 | 4 | 5 |  | 7 |  | 9 | 11$^{2}$ | 12 | 13 |  |  | 14 |  | 8$^{3}$ | 6 | 10$^{1}$ |  |  |  |  |  |  |  | 31 |
| 1 | 2 | 3 | 4 | 5 |  | 7 |  | 9 | 10 | 11$^{2}$ | 12 | 13 |  |  |  | 8$^{1}$ | 6 |  |  |  |  |  |  |  |  | 32 |
| 1 | 2$^{2}$ | 3 | 4$^{1}$ |  |  | 7 |  | 9 | 10 | 11 | 12 |  |  | 13 | 8$^{3}$ | 6 |  | 14 |  | 5 |  |  |  |  |  | 33 |
| 1 |  | 3 | 4 |  |  |  |  | 9 | 10 | 11 | 7 |  |  | 2 | 8$^{1}$ | 6 |  | 12 | 5 |  |  |  |  |  |  | 34 |
| 1 |  | 3 | 4 |  |  | 7 |  | 9 | 10$^{2}$ | 11 | 12 |  |  | 2 | 8$^{1}$ | 6 |  | 13 | 5 |  |  |  |  |  |  | 35 |
| 1 |  | 3 | 4 | 12 |  | 7 | 13 | 9$^{3}$ |  | 11 | 14 |  |  | 2 | 8$^{2}$ | 6 |  | 10$^{1}$ | 5 |  |  |  |  |  |  | 36 |
|  | 12 | 5 | 6 |  | 7$^{1}$ | 8$^{2}$ |  |  | 4 | 9 |  | 11 | 2 | 13 |  | 14 | 10$^{3}$ |  |  | 3 | 1 |  |  |  |  | 37 |
| 1 |  | 3 | 4 |  | 2 | 7$^{1}$ | 8$^{2}$ | 9 |  | 11 | 12 |  |  |  | 10 | 6 |  | 13 | 5 |  |  |  |  |  |  | 38 |

**Coca-Cola Cup**

| | | | |
|---|---|---|---|
| Third Round | Birmingham C | (h) | 4-1 |
| Fourth Round | Coventry C | (h) | 1-0 |
| Fifth Round | West Ham U | (a) | 2-1 |
| Semi-Final | Chelsea | (h) | 2-1 |
| | | (a) | 1-3 |

**FA Cup**

| | | | |
|---|---|---|---|
| Third Round | Port Vale | (h) | 0-0 |
| | | (a) | 1-1 |
| Fourth Round | Middlesbrough | (a) | 2-1 |
| Fifth Round | Crystal Palace | (h) | 0-0 |
| | | (a) | 2-1 |
| Sixth Round | West Ham U | (h) | 1-1 |
| | | (a) | 1-1 |
| Semi-Final | Wolverhampton W (at Villa Park) | | 1-0 |
| Final | Newcastle U (at Wembley) | | 2-0 |

ASTON VILLA 1997–98    *Back row (left to right)*: Scott Murray, Neil Davis, Ben Petty, David Hughes, Simon Grayson, Riccardo Scimeca, Darren Byfield, Lee Hendrie.
*Middle row*: Paul Barron (Fitness Coach), Fernando Nelson, Gareth Southgate, Ugo Ehiogu, Michael Oakes, Ian Taylor, Gary Charles, Sasa Curcic, Jim Walker (Physio).
*Front row*: Julian Joachim, Steve Staunton, Stan Collymore, Mark Draper, Brian Little (Manager), Allan Evans (Assistant Manager), Savo Milosevic, Dwight Yorke, Andy Townsend, Alan Wright.
(Photograph: Mike Smith)

# FA Premiership

## ASTON VILLA

*Villa Park, Trinity Rd, Birmingham B6 6HE.* Telephone: (0121) 327 2299. Fax: (0121) 322 2107. Commercial Dept: (0121) 327 5399. Commercial Fax: (0121) 328 2099. Clubcall: 0891 121148. Ticketline: 0891 121848. Ticket information: (0121) 327 5353. Club shop: (0121) 327 2800.

*Ground capacity:* 39,372.

*Record attendance:* 76,588 v Derby Co, FA Cup 6th rd, 2 March 1946.

*Record receipts:* £1,196,712 Portugal v Czech Republic, Euro '96, 23 June 1996.

*Pitch measurements:* 115yd × 72yd.

*President:* J. A. Alderson. *Chairman:* H. D. Ellis.

*Directors:* S. M. Stride, M. J. Ansell, D. M. Owen, A. Hales.

*Manager:* John Gregory. *First Team Coach:* Steve Harrison. *Coach:* Kevin MacDonald.

*Physio:* Jim Walker. *Reserve Team Manager:* Malcolm Beard.

*Chief Scout:* Frank Upton. *Head of European Scouting:* Peter Withe. *Fitness Consultant:* Paul Barron.

*Youth Development Officer:* Alan Miller. *Director of Youth:* Bryan Jones.

*Secretary:* Steven Stride. *Commercial Manager:* Abdul Rashid. *Stadium Manager:* E. Small.

*Football Academy Director:* Bryan Jones. *Assistant Academy Director:* Steve Burns.

*Year Formed:* 1874. *Turned Professional:* 1885. *Ltd Co.:* 1896.

*Previous Grounds:* 1874–76, Aston Park; 1876–97, Perry Barr; 1897, Villa Park.

*Club Nickname:* 'The Villans'.

*Foundation:* Cricketing enthusiasts of Villa Cross Wesleyan Chapel, Aston, Birmingham decided to form a football club during the winter of 1873–74. Football clubs were few and far between in the Birmingham area and in their first game against Aston Brook St. Mary's Rugby team they played one half rugby and the other soccer. In 1876 they were joined by a Scottish soccer enthusiast George Ramsay who was immediately appointed captain and went on to lead Aston Villa from obscurity to one of the country's top clubs in a period of less than 10 years.

*First Football League game:* 8 September 1888, Football League, v Wolverhampton W, (a) D 1-1 – Warner; Cox, Coulton; Yates, H. Devey, Dawson; A. Brown, Green (1), Allen, Garvey, Hodgetts.

*Record League Victory:* 12–2 v Accrington S, Division 1, 12 March 1892 – Warner; Evans, Cox; Harry Devey, Jimmy Cowan, Baird; Athersmith (1), Dickson (2), John Devey (4), L. Campbell (4), Hodgetts (1).

*Record Cup Victory:* 13–0 v Wednesbury Old Ath, FA Cup 1st rd, 30 October 1886 – Warner; Coulton, Simmonds; Yates, Robertson, Burton (2); R. Davis (1), A. Brown (3), Hunter (3), Loach (2), Hodgetts (2).

*Record Defeat:* 1–8 v Blackburn R, FA Cup 3rd rd, 16 February 1889.

*Most League Points (2 for a win):* 70, Division 3, 1971–72.

*Most League Points (3 for a win):* 78, Division 2, 1987–88.

*Most League Goals:* 128, Division 1, 1930–31.

*Highest League Scorer in Season:* 'Pongo' Waring, 49, Division 1, 1930–31.

*Most League Goals in Total Aggregate:* Harry Hampton, 215, 1904–15.

*Most Capped Player:* Paul McGrath, 51 (83), Republic of Ireland.

*Most League Appearances:* Charlie Aitken, 561, 1961–76.

*Record Transfer Fee Received:* £5,500,000 from Bari for David Platt, July 1991.

*Record Transfer Fee Paid:* £7,000,000 to Liverpool for Stan Collymore, May 1997.

*Football League Record:* 1888 Founder Member of the League; 1936–38 Division 2; 1938–59 Division 1; 1959–60 Division 2; 1960–67 Division 1; 1967–70 Division 3; 1970–72 Division 2; 1972–75 Division 3; 1975–87 Division 1; 1987–88 Division 2; 1988–92 Division 1; 1992– FA Premier League.

*Honours: FA Premier League:* – Runners-up 1992–93. *Football League: Division 1* – Champions 1893–94, 1895–96, 1896–97, 1898–99, 1899–1900, 1909–10, 1980–81; Runners-up 1888–89, 1902–03, 1907–08, 1910–11, 1912–13, 1913–14, 1930–31, 1932–33, 1989–90; *Division 2* – Champions 1937–38, 1959–60; Runners-up 1974–75, 1987–88; *Division 3* – Champions 1971–72. *FA Cup:* Winners 1887, 1895, 1897, 1905, 1913, 1920, 1957; Runners-up 1892, 1924. *Double Performed:* 1896–97. *Football League Cup:* Winners 1961, 1975, 1977, 1994, 1996; Runners-up 1963, 1971. **European Competitions:** *European Cup:* 1981–82 (winners), 1982–83; *UEFA Cup:* 1975–76, 1977–78, 1983–84, 1990–91, 1993–94, 1994–95, 1996–97, 1997–98. *World Club Championship:* 1982; European Super Cup: 1982–83 (winners).

*Colours:* Claret shirts with sky blue sleeves, white shorts, sky blue stockings. *Change colours:* Turquoise shirts with black panel, black shorts with turquoise panel, turquoise stockings.

**Did you know?**
After signing from Leeds United, Con Martin played in 213 League and FA Cup games for Aston Villa between 1948 and 1956. These comprised 176 at centre-half, eight at right-back, two at left-back and 27 in goal.

## ASTON VILLA 1997–98 LEAGUE RECORD

| Match No. | Date | Venue | Opponents | Result | H/T Score | Lg. Pos. | Goalscorers | Atten-dance |
|---|---|---|---|---|---|---|---|---|
| 1 | Aug 9 | A | Leicester C | L 0-1 | 0-1 | — | | 20,304 |
| 2 | 13 | H | Blackburn R | L 0-4 | 0-3 | — | | 37,122 |
| 3 | 23 | A | Newcastle U | L 0-1 | 0-1 | 20 | | 36,783 |
| 4 | 27 | A | Tottenham H | L 2-3 | 1-1 | — | Yorke 27, Collymore 58 | 26,316 |
| 5 | 30 | H | Leeds U | W 1-0 | 0-0 | 19 | Yorke 67 | 39,027 |
| 6 | Sept13 | A | Barnsley | W 3-0 | 1-0 | 13 | Ehiogu 25, Draper 50, Taylor 72 | 18,649 |
| 7 | 20 | H | Derby Co | W 2-1 | 0-1 | 9 | Yorke 73, Joachim 75 | 35,444 |
| 8 | 22 | A | Liverpool | L 0-3 | 0-0 | — | | 34,843 |
| 9 | 27 | A | Sheffield W | D 2-2 | 1-2 | 14 | Staunton 32, Taylor 49 | 32,044 |
| 10 | Oct 4 | A | Bolton W | W 1-0 | 1-0 | 9 | Milosevic 12 | 24,196 |
| 11 | 18 | H | Wimbledon | L 1-2 | 1-1 | 12 | Taylor 45 | 32,087 |
| 12 | 26 | A | Arsenal | D 0-0 | 0-0 | 13 | | 38,061 |
| 13 | Nov 1 | H | Chelsea | L 0-2 | 0-1 | 14 | | 39,372 |
| 14 | 8 | A | Crystal Palace | D 1-1 | 0-1 | 15 | Joachim 86 | 21,097 |
| 15 | 22 | H | Everton | W 2-1 | 1-1 | 11 | Milosevic 36, Ehiogu 56 | 36,389 |
| 16 | 29 | A | West Ham U | L 1-2 | 0-1 | 13 | Yorke 47 | 24,976 |
| 17 | Dec 6 | H | Coventry C | W 3-0 | 1-0 | 12 | Collymore 21, Hendrie 71, Joachim 85 | 33,250 |
| 18 | 15 | A | Manchester U | L 0-1 | 0-0 | — | | 55,175 |
| 19 | 20 | H | Southampton | D 1-1 | 0-0 | 12 | Taylor 64 | 29,343 |
| 20 | 26 | H | Tottenham H | W 4-1 | 1-0 | 11 | Draper 2 38, 68, Collymore 2 81, 89 | 38,644 |
| 21 | 28 | A | Leeds U | D 1-1 | 0-0 | 10 | Milosevic 85 | 36,909 |
| 22 | Jan 10 | H | Leicester C | D 1-1 | 0-0 | 10 | Joachim 87 | 36,429 |
| 23 | 17 | A | Blackburn R | L 0-5 | 0-2 | 12 | | 24,834 |
| 24 | Feb 1 | H | Newcastle U | L 0-1 | 0-0 | 15 | | 38,266 |
| 25 | 7 | A | Derby Co | W 1-0 | 0-0 | 13 | Yorke 90 | 30,251 |
| 26 | 18 | H | Manchester U | L 0-2 | 0-0 | — | | 39,372 |
| 27 | 21 | A | Wimbledon | L 1-2 | 1-2 | 15 | Milosevic 41 | 13,131 |
| 28 | 28 | H | Liverpool | W 2-1 | 1-1 | 14 | Collymore 2 10, 65 | 39,372 |
| 29 | Mar 8 | A | Chelsea | W 1-0 | 0-0 | 13 | Joachim 51 | 33,018 |
| 30 | 11 | H | Barnsley | L 0-1 | 0-1 | — | | 29,519 |
| 31 | 14 | H | Crystal Palace | W 3-1 | 3-0 | 12 | Taylor 1, Milosevic 2 (1 pen) 15 (p), 36 | 33,781 |
| 32 | 28 | A | Everton | W 4-1 | 1-1 | 11 | Joachim 12, Charles 62, Yorke 2 (1 pen) 72 (p), 81 | 36,471 |
| 33 | Apr 4 | H | West Ham U | W 2-0 | 0-0 | 9 | Joachim 77, Milosevic 83 | 39,372 |
| 34 | 11 | A | Coventry C | W 2-1 | 1-0 | 8 | Yorke 2 5, 48 | 22,790 |
| 35 | 18 | A | Southampton | W 2-1 | 1-1 | 8 | Hendrie 6, Yorke 60 | 15,238 |
| 36 | 25 | H | Bolton W | L 1-3 | 0-2 | 8 | Taylor 57 | 38,392 |
| 37 | May 2 | A | Sheffield W | W 3-1 | 2-0 | 7 | Yorke 21, Hendrie 25, Joachim 50 | 34,177 |
| 38 | 10 | H | Arsenal | W 1-0 | 1-0 | 7 | Yorke (pen) 37 | 39,372 |

**Final League Position: 7**          1996–97 PREM 5

### GOALSCORERS

*League (49):* Yorke 12 (2 pens), Joachim 8, Milosevic 7 (1 pen), Collymore 6, Taylor 6, Draper 3, Hendrie 3, Ehiogu 2, Charles 1, Staunton 1.
*Coca-Cola Cup (0)*
*FA Cup (7):* Grayson 2, Yorke 2, Collymore 1, Milosevic 1, Staunton 1.

| Oakes M 8 | Nelson F 21 + 4 | Wright A 35 + 2 | Southgate G 32 | Ehiogu U 37 | Townsend A 3 | Taylor I 30 + 2 | Draper M 31 | Milosevic S 19 + 4 | Collymore S 23 + 2 | Yorke D 30 | Grayson S 28 + 5 | Joachim J 16 + 10 | Charles G 14 + 4 | Scimeca R 16 + 5 | Bosnich M 30 | Staunton S 27 | Curcic S 3 + 4 | Hendrie L 13 + 4 | Byfield D 1 + 6 | Walker R — + 1 | Barry G 1 + 1 | Match No. |
|---|---|---|---|---|---|---|---|---|---|---|---|---|---|---|---|---|---|---|---|---|---|---|
| 1 | 2 | 3 | 4 | 5 | 6 | 7 | 8 | 9 | 10 | 11 | | | | | | | | | | | | 1 |
| 1 | 2 | 3 | 4 | 5[1] | 7 | 12 | 8 | 9[2] | 10 | 11 | | 6 | 13 | | | | | | | | | 2 |
| 12 | 13 | | 4 | 5 | | 7 | 8 | | 10 | 11 | | 9[3] | 14 | 2 | 6[2] | 1 | 3[1] | | | | | 3 |
| | | | 4 | 5[1] | 9 | 7 | 8 | | 10 | 11 | | | | 2 | 6 | 1 | 3 | 12 | | | | 4 |
| 12 | | 3 | 4 | 5 | | 7 | 8 | | 10 | 11 | 9 | | | 2[1] | | 1 | 6 | | | | | 5 |
| | 2 | 3 | 4 | 5 | | 7[2] | 8 | | 10 | 11 | 9 | | | 12 | | 1 | 6[1] | 13 | | | | 6 |
| | 2 | 3 | 4 | 5 | | 7 | 8 | 12 | 10[1] | 11 | | 13 | | 14 | | 1 | 6[3] | 9[2] | | | | 7 |
| | 2 | 3 | 4 | 5 | | 7[1] | 8 | | 10 | 11 | 9 | 12 | | | | 1 | 6 | | | | | 8 |
| | 2[2] | 3 | 4 | 5 | | 7 | 8 | 12 | 10 | 11 | | 13 | | | | 1 | 6 | 9[1] | | | | 9 |
| | 2[3] | 3 | 4 | 5 | | 7 | | 9[1] | 10 | 11 | 8 | | 14 | 13 | | 1 | 6[2] | 12 | | | | 10 |
| | 12 | | 4 | 5 | | 7 | | 9 | | 11 | 10 | 13 | | 2 | 6[1] | 1 | 3 | 8[2] | | | | 11 |
| | 7 | 3 | 4 | 5 | | 8 | | | 9 | 10 | 11 | | 2 | | 6 | 1 | | | | | | 12 |
| 1 | 7[1] | 3 | 4 | 5 | | 12 | 8 | 13 | | 9 | 10 | 11[2] | | 2 | 6 | | | | | | | 13 |
| | 2 | 3 | 4 | | | 7 | | 9 | | 11 | | 8 | 12 | 5[1] | 10 | 1 | 6 | | | | | 14 |
| 1 | 7 | 3 | | 5 | | | 8 | 9 | 10 | 11 | | | | 2 | 4 | 6 | | | | | | 15 |
| 1 | 7 | 3 | | 5 | | | 8 | 9 | 10 | 11 | 12 | | | 2 | 4[1] | 6 | | | | | | 16 |
| | | 3 | 4 | 5 | | | 8 | 9[1] | 10[2] | 11[3] | 7 | 12 | | 2 | | 1 | 6 | 13 | 14 | | | 17 |
| 1 | | 3 | 4 | 5 | | 7 | 8 | 9[1] | 10 | | 11[2] | 12 | | 2 | | | 6 | 13 | | | | 18 |
| 1 | | 3 | 4 | 5 | | 7 | 8 | 9 | 10 | | 11[1] | | 2 | | | | 6 | 12 | | | | 19 |
| | 2 | 3 | | 5 | | 7 | 8 | 9 | 10 | | 11 | | | 4 | 1 | 6 | | | | | | 20 |
| | 2 | 3 | | 5 | | 7 | 8 | 9 | | | 11 | | | 4 | 1 | 6 | | 10[1] | 12 | | | 21 |
| | 2[1] | 3 | | 5 | | 7 | 8 | 9 | 10 | | 11 | 12 | | 4 | 1 | 6 | | | | | | 22 |
| | 2 | 3 | | 5 | | 7 | 8 | 9 | 10 | 11 | 4 | | | | 1 | 6 | | | | | | 23 |
| | | 3[1] | 4 | 5 | | 7 | 8 | | 10 | 9 | 2 | 12 | | 6 | 1 | | 11 | | | | | 24 |
| | 12 | 3 | 4 | 5 | | 8 | | 10 | 9[2] | 2 | 7 | | 6 | 1 | | 11[1] | 13 | | | | | 25 |
| | 2 | 3 | 4 | 5 | | 7 | | 9 | 10 | 8 | 11 | | 6 | 1 | | | | | | | | 26 |
| | 2[2] | 3 | 4 | 5 | | 7 | | 9[1] | 10 | 8 | 11 | | 6 | 1 | | 12 | 13 | | | | | 27 |
| | | 3 | 4 | 5 | | 7 | | 10[1] | 9 | 2 | 11 | | 6 | 1 | | 8 | 12 | | | | | 28 |
| | | 3 | 4 | 5 | | 7 | 8 | | 9 | 2 | 11 | | | 1 | 6 | 10 | | | | | | 29 |
| | 12 | 3[1] | 4 | 5 | | 7 | 8 | | 9 | 2[2] | 11 | | | 1 | 6 | 10 | 13 | | | | | 30 |
| | 2[2] | 3 | 4 | 5 | | 7 | 8[1] | 9 | | 12 | 11 | 13 | | 1 | 6 | 10 | | | | | | 31 |
| | | 3 | 4 | 5 | | 7 | 8 | | 9 | 12 | 11[2] | 2 | | 1 | 6 | 10[1] | 13 | | | | | 32 |
| | | 3 | 4 | 5 | | 7 | 8[2] | 12 | 9 | 13 | 11 | 2[1] | | 1 | 6 | 10 | | | | | | 33 |
| | | 3 | 4 | 5 | | 7 | | 9[1] | 11 | 2 | 8 | 12 | | 1 | 6 | 10 | | | | | | 34 |
| | | 3 | 4 | 5 | | 7 | 8 | | 9 | 2[1] | 11 | 12 | | 1 | 6 | 10 | | | | | | 35 |
| | | 3 | 4[1] | 5 | | 7 | 8 | 9[2] | 13 | 11 | 12 | 10 | 14 | 1 | 6[3] | 2 | | | | | | 36 |
| 1 | 2 | 3 | 4 | 5 | | 7[2] | 8 | | 9 | 6 | 11 | | | | | 10[1] | 12 | | 13 | | | 37 |
| | 2 | 3 | 4 | 5 | | | 8 | | 12 | 9 | 6 | 11[1] | | | 1 | | 10 | | 7 | | | 38 |

**Coca-Cola Cup**
Third Round    West Ham U    (a)    0-3

**FA Cup**
Third Round    Portsmouth    (a)    2-2
                                    (h)    1-0
Fourth Round    WBA    (h)    4-0
Fifth Round    Coventry C    (h)    0-1

BARNET 1997–98    *Back row (left to right):* Gary Anderson (Physio), Udo Onwere, Stevie Searle, Robert Sawyers, Michael Basham, John Doolan, Lee Howarth, Lee Harrison, Greg Heald, Matt Brady, Paul Wilson, Dean Samuels, Tarkan Mustafa.
*Front row:* Tom McMenemy, Sean Devine, Ken Charlery, Scott McGleish, Kieran Adams, Phil Simpson, Sam Stockley, Warren Goodhind, Billy Manuel, Michael Harle, John Ford.

# Division 3     **BARNET**

*Underhill Stadium, Barnet Lane, Barnet, Herts EN5 2BE.* Telephone: (0181) 441 6932. Fax: (0181) 447 0655.
Ticket Office: (0181) 449 6325. Club Call: 0891 121544

*Ground capacity:* 4057.

*Record attendance:* 11,026 v Wycombe Wanderers. FA Amateur Cup 4th Round 1951–52.

*Record Receipts:* £31,202 v Portsmouth, FA Cup 3rd Round, 5 January 1991.

*Pitch measurements:* 113yd × 72yd.

*Chairman:* A. Kleanthous. *Vice-Chairman:* D. J. Buchler FCA.

*Director:* J. Barnett.

*Manager:* John Still.

*Coach:* Mick Halsall. *Secretary:* David Stanley.

*Year Formed:* 1888. *Turned Professional:* 1965. *Ltd Co:*

*Club Nickname:* The Bees.

*Previous Names:* 1906–19 Barnet Alston FC.

*Previous Grounds:* 1888-1901, Queens Road; 1901-07, Totteridge Lane.

*Foundation:* Barnet Football Club was formed in 1888, disbanded in 1901. A club known as Alston Works FC
was then formed and in 1906 changed its name to Barnet Alston FC. In 1912 it combined with The Avenue to
become Barnet and Alston.

*First Football League game:* 17 August 1991, Division 4, v Crewe Alex (h) L 4-7 – Phillips; Blackford, Cooper
(Murphy), Horton, Bodley (Stein), Johnson, Showler, Carter (2), Bull (2), Lowe, Evans.

*Record League Victory:* 6–0 v Lincoln C (away), Division 4, 4 September 1991 – Pape; Poole, Naylor, Bodley,
Howell, Evans (1), Willis (1), Murphy (1), Bull (2), Lowe, Showler (1 og).

*Record Cup Victory:* 6–1 v Newport Co, FA Cup 1st rd, 21 November 1970 – McClelland; Lye, Jenkins, Ward,
Enbery, King, Powell (1), Ferry, Adams (1), Gray, George (3) (1 og).

*Record Defeat:* 0–6 v Port Vale, Division 2, 21 August 1993.

*Most League Points (3 for a win):* 79, Division 3, 1992–93.

*Most League Goals:* 81, Division 4, 1991–92.

*Highest League Scorer in Season:* Gary Bull, 20, Division 4, 1991–92.

*Most League Goals in Total Aggregate:* Sean Devine, 46, 1995–98.

*Most Capped Player:* None

*Most League Appearances:* Paul Wilson, 213, 1991–98.

*Record Transfer Fee Received:* £800,000 from Crystal Palace for Dougie Freedman, September 1995.

*Record Transfer Fee Paid:* £130,000 to Peterborough U for Greg Heald, August 1997.

*Football League Record:* Promoted to Division 4 from GMVC 1991; 1991–92 Division 4; 1992–93 Division 3;
1993–94 Division 2; 1994– Division 3.

*Honours: Football League:* best season 24th, Division 2, 1993–94. *FA Amateur Cup:* Winners 1946. *GM
Vauxhall Conference:* Winners 1990–91. *FA Cup:* best season; never past 3rd rd. *League Cup:* never past 2nd rd.

*Colours:* Amber and black striped shirts, black shorts, black stockings. *Change colours:* All azure blue.

**Did you know?**
On 13 December 1997, Barnet defeated Macclesfield Town 3-1, the losers becoming the 50th different club to
meet Barnet in the Football League.

## BARNET 1997–98 LEAGUE RECORD

| Match No. | Date | Venue | Opponents | Result | | H/T Score | Lg. Pos. | Goalscorers | Attendance |
|---|---|---|---|---|---|---|---|---|---|
| 1 | Aug 9 | A | Rotherham U | W | 3-2 | 1-1 | — | Harle [3], Goodwin (og) [83], Devine [85] | 4220 |
| 2 | 16 | H | Exeter C | L | 1-2 | 0-2 | 7 | Charlery [60] | 2137 |
| 3 | 22 | A | Colchester U | D | 1-1 | 0-0 | — | Howarth [59] | 3286 |
| 4 | 30 | H | Chester C | W | 2-1 | 0-0 | 6 | Wilson (pen) [75], Devine [76] | 1790 |
| 5 | Sept 2 | H | Swansea C | W | 2-0 | 2-0 | — | Charlery [8], Wilson (pen) [43] | 1946 |
| 6 | 7 | A | Peterborough U | L | 1-5 | 0-2 | 8 | Samuels [59] | 7243 |
| 7 | 13 | A | Cambridge U | W | 3-1 | 1-0 | 6 | Charlery [40], Devine [73], Heald [80] | 3395 |
| 8 | 20 | H | Scunthorpe U | L | 0-1 | 0-1 | 9 | | 1951 |
| 9 | 27 | H | Lincoln C | D | 0-0 | 0-0 | 8 | | 1734 |
| 10 | Oct 4 | A | Cardiff C | D | 1-1 | 0-1 | 8 | Charlery [49] | 3938 |
| 11 | 11 | A | Shrewsbury T | L | 0-2 | 0-1 | 14 | | 2112 |
| 12 | 18 | H | Hull C | W | 2-0 | 1-0 | 9 | Howarth [31], McGleish [62] | 2315 |
| 13 | 21 | H | Rochdale | W | 3-1 | 1-0 | — | Harle [39], Heald [48], Samuels [84] | 1310 |
| 14 | 25 | A | Mansfield T | W | 2-1 | 1-1 | 5 | McGleish [18], Wilson (pen) [60] | 2340 |
| 15 | Nov 1 | H | Notts Co | L | 1-2 | 0-0 | 6 | McGleish [60] | 2530 |
| 16 | 5 | A | Brighton & HA | W | 3-0 | 1-0 | — | Searle [44], Wilson [57], Howarth [76] | 1025 |
| 17 | 8 | H | Doncaster R | D | 1-1 | 1-0 | 5 | Charlery [38] | 2015 |
| 18 | 18 | H | Torquay U | D | 3-3 | 1-1 | — | McGleish [29], Devine 2 [59, 66] | 1246 |
| 19 | 22 | A | Hartlepool U | L | 0-2 | 0-1 | 7 | | 2225 |
| 20 | 29 | H | Darlington | W | 2-0 | 2-0 | 6 | McGleish [11], Devine [24] | 1726 |
| 21 | Dec 2 | A | Leyton Orient | L | 0-2 | 0-1 | — | | 2598 |
| 22 | 13 | H | Macclesfield T | W | 3-1 | 2-0 | 4 | Searle [56], Adams [70], Devine [84] | 1710 |
| 23 | 19 | A | Scarborough | L | 0-1 | 0-1 | — | | 1714 |
| 24 | 26 | H | Peterborough U | W | 2-0 | 0-0 | 6 | Simpson [57], Devine [80] | 3449 |
| 25 | 28 | A | Swansea C | W | 2-0 | 1-0 | 5 | McGleish [32], Simpson [90] | 3987 |
| 26 | Jan 10 | H | Rotherham U | D | 0-0 | 0-0 | 6 | | 2558 |
| 27 | 17 | A | Chester C | W | 1-0 | 0-0 | 4 | Devine [51] | 2479 |
| 28 | 20 | A | Exeter C | D | 0-0 | 0-0 | — | | 3697 |
| 29 | 24 | H | Colchester U | W | 3-2 | 1-1 | 3 | Devine 2 [44, 65], McGleish [60] | 2471 |
| 30 | 31 | H | Cambridge U | W | 2-0 | 1-0 | 3 | Heald [27], Simpson [63] | 2455 |
| 31 | Feb 7 | A | Scunthorpe U | D | 1-1 | 0-0 | 2 | McGleish [73] | 2313 |
| 32 | 14 | H | Cardiff C | D | 2-2 | 1-2 | 4 | Wilson (pen) [43], McGleish [68] | 2406 |
| 33 | 21 | A | Lincoln C | L | 0-2 | 0-0 | 5 | | 2945 |
| 34 | 24 | A | Hull C | W | 2-0 | 0-0 | 5 | McGleish [24], Samuels [85] | 3296 |
| 35 | 28 | H | Shrewsbury T | D | 1-1 | 1-1 | 4 | McGleish [16] | 2322 |
| 36 | Mar 3 | A | Doncaster R | W | 2-0 | 0-0 | — | Basham [51], McGleish [59] | 739 |
| 37 | 7 | A | Notts Co | L | 0-2 | 0-1 | 4 | | 6180 |
| 38 | 14 | H | Brighton & HA | W | 2-0 | 1-0 | 3 | Simpson [7], Howarth [71] | 2845 |
| 39 | 21 | A | Torquay U | D | 0-0 | 0-0 | 4 | | 4020 |
| 40 | 28 | H | Hartlepool U | D | 1-1 | 1-0 | 4 | Devine [5] | 2344 |
| 41 | Apr 4 | A | Darlington | W | 3-2 | 2-0 | 4 | Devine 3 [10, 30, 87] | 1880 |
| 42 | 11 | H | Leyton Orient | L | 1-2 | 0-0 | 4 | Goodhind [55] | 3437 |
| 43 | 13 | A | Macclesfield T | L | 0-2 | 0-2 | 6 | | 4171 |
| 44 | 18 | H | Scarborough | D | 1-1 | 1-1 | 6 | Devine [15] | 2353 |
| 45 | 25 | H | Mansfield T | L | 0-1 | 0-0 | 7 | | 2792 |
| 46 | May 2 | A | Rochdale | L | 1-2 | 0-2 | 7 | McGleish [90] | 2102 |

**Final League Position: 7**　　　　1996–97 DIV3 15

### GOALSCORERS

*League (61):* Devine 16, McGleish 13, Charlery 5, Wilson 5 (4 pens), Howarth 4, Simpson 4, Heald 3, Samuels 3, Harle 2, Searle 2, Adams 1, Basham 1, Goodhind 1, own goal 1.
*Coca-Cola Cup (4):* Devine 2, Heald 1, own goal 1.
*FA Cup (1):* Charlery.

| Harrison L 46 | Stockley S 40 + 1 | Harle M 42 + 1 | McDonald D 1 | Howarth L 45 | Ford J 19 | Manuel B 10 + 7 | Onwere U 11 + 6 | Charlery K 18 + 14 | Devine S 37 + 3 | Mills D 5 + 1 | Wilson P 34 + 5 | Goodhind W 22 + 13 | Heald G 43 | Mustafa T 2 + 9 | Simpson P 27 + 4 | Samuels D — + 22 | Searle S 26 + 4 | McGleish S 37 | Adams K 4 + 7 | Basham M 19 + 1 | Doolan J 17 | Devito C — + 1 | Sawyers R 1 | Match No. |
|---|---|---|---|---|---|---|---|---|---|---|---|---|---|---|---|---|---|---|---|---|---|---|---|---|
| 1 | 2 | 3 | 4 | 5 | 6 | $7^1$ | $8^2$ | 9 | 10 | 11 |  | 13 |  |  | 12 |  |  |  |  |  |  |  |  | 1 |
| 1 | $2^3$ | 3 |  | 5 | 6 | $7^2$ |  | 9 | 10 | $11^3$ | 8 |  | 4 | 12 | 13 | 14 |  |  |  |  |  |  |  | 2 |
| 1 | $2^3$ | $3^1$ |  | 5 | 6 | $7^3$ | 13 | 9 | 10 | 11 |  | 12 | 4 | 14 | 8 |  |  |  |  |  |  |  |  | 3 |
| 1 | 2 | 3 |  | 5 | $6^3$ | $7^2$ | 13 | 9 | 10 | 11 |  | 12 | $4^1$ | 14 | 8 |  |  |  |  |  |  |  |  | 4 |
| 1 | 2 | 3 |  | 5 | 6 |  |  | 9 | 10 | 11 |  | 12 | 4 |  | $7^1$ | 8 |  |  |  |  |  |  |  | 5 |
| 1 | 2 | 12 |  | 5 | 6 |  | 13 | 9 | 10 | 11 | 8 | $3^1$ | $4^3$ | 14 | $7^2$ |  |  |  |  |  |  |  |  | 6 |
| 1 | 2 | 3 |  | 5 | 6 |  |  | $9^1$ | 10 | 11 | 8 |  | 4 | 12 |  |  | 7 |  |  |  |  |  |  | 7 |
| 1 | 2 | $3^1$ |  | 5 | $6^3$ |  | 13 | 9 | 10 | 11 | 8 | 12 | 4 | 14 | $7^2$ |  |  |  |  |  |  |  |  | 8 |
| 1 | 2 |  |  | 5 | 6 | $7^3$ |  | 9 | 10 | 11 | $8^2$ | $3^1$ | 4 | 12 | 13 |  |  |  | 14 |  |  |  |  | 9 |
| 1 | 2 |  |  | 5 | 6 |  |  | 9 | $3^2$ | 11 | 8 | 12 | 4 | 14 | 13 |  | $7^1$ | $10^3$ |  |  |  |  |  | 10 |
| 1 | 2 | 3 |  | 5 | $6^2$ |  |  | 9 |  | $11^3$ | $8^1$ | 12 | 4 | 14 | 13 |  | 7 | 10 |  |  |  |  |  | 11 |
| 1 | 2 | 3 |  | 5 | 6 |  |  | 9 |  | $11^2$ | 8 | 12 | 4 |  | 13 |  | 7 | $10^1$ |  |  |  |  |  | 12 |
| 1 | 2 | $3^2$ |  | 5 | 6 |  |  | 9 |  | $11^3$ | 8 | 12 | 4 | 14 | 13 |  | $7^1$ | 10 |  |  |  |  |  | 13 |
| 1 | 2 | 3 |  | 5 | 6 |  |  | 9 |  |  | 8 | 12 | 4 |  | 13 | $11^2$ | 7 | $10^1$ |  |  |  |  |  | 14 |
| 1 | $2^2$ | 3 |  | 5 | 6 |  |  | 9 |  |  | $8^1$ | 12 | 4 |  | 13 | 11 | 7 | 10 |  |  |  |  |  | 15 |
| 1 | 2 | 3 |  | 5 | 6 |  |  | 9 |  |  | 8 |  | 4 |  |  | 11 | 7 | 10 |  |  |  |  |  | 16 |
| 1 | 2 | 3 |  | 5 | 6 |  |  | 9 |  |  | 8 |  | 4 |  |  | 11 | 7 | 10 |  |  |  |  |  | 17 |
| 1 | 2 | $3^2$ |  | 5 | 6 |  |  | 9 |  | $11^1$ | 8 | 12 | 4 |  | 13 |  | 7 | 10 |  |  |  |  |  | 18 |
| 1 | 2 | 3 |  | 5 | 6 |  |  | 9 |  | 11 | 8 | 12 | 4 |  |  |  | $7^1$ | 10 |  |  |  |  |  | 19 |
| 1 | 2 | 3 |  | 5 | 6 |  |  | 9 |  | 11 | $8^1$ | 12 | 4 | 14 | 13 |  | $7^2$ | $10^3$ |  |  |  |  |  | 20 |
| 1 | 2 | 3 |  | 5 | $6^1$ |  |  | 9 |  | $11^2$ | 8 | 12 | 4 |  | 13 |  | 7 | 10 |  |  |  |  |  | 21 |
| 1 | 2 | 3 |  | 5 |  |  |  | 9 |  | $11^3$ | 8 | 12 | $4^2$ |  | 13 |  | 7 | $10^1$ | 14 | 6 |  |  |  | 22 |
| 1 | 2 | $3^1$ |  | 5 |  |  |  | 9 |  |  | 8 | 12 | 4 |  | 13 | 11 | 7 | 10 |  | $6^2$ |  |  |  | 23 |
| 1 | $2^1$ | 3 |  | 5 |  |  |  | 9 |  |  | 8 | $12^2$ | 4 | 14 | 13 | 11 | 7 | $10^3$ |  | 6 |  |  |  | 24 |
| 1 |  | 3 |  | 5 |  |  |  | 9 |  |  | 8 | 2 | 4 | $12^2$ | 13 | 11 | $7^1$ | 10 |  | 6 |  |  |  | 25 |
| 1 |  | 3 |  | 5 |  |  |  | 9 |  |  | 8 | 2 | 4 |  |  | 11 | 7 | 10 |  | 6 |  |  |  | 26 |
| 1 | 12 | 3 |  | 5 |  |  |  | 9 |  |  | 8 | 2 | 4 |  | 13 | 11 |  | $10^2$ |  | $6^1$ | 7 |  |  | 27 |
| 1 | 6 | 3 |  | 5 |  |  |  | 9 |  |  | 8 | 2 | 4 | 12 | 13 | $11^2$ |  | $10^1$ |  |  | 7 |  |  | 28 |
| 1 | 6 | 3 |  | 5 |  |  |  | 9 |  |  | 8 | 2 | 4 |  |  | 11 |  | 10 |  |  | 7 |  |  | 29 |
| 1 | 6 | 3 |  | 5 |  |  |  | 9 |  |  | 8 | 2 | 4 | 12 |  | 11 |  | $10^1$ |  |  | 7 |  |  | 30 |
| 1 |  | 3 |  | 5 |  |  |  | 9 |  |  | 8 | 2 | 4 | 12 |  | 11 |  | 10 |  | $6^1$ | 7 |  |  | 31 |
| 1 | 6 | $3^1$ |  | 5 |  |  |  | 9 |  |  | $8^3$ | 2 | 4 | 12 | 13 | $11^2$ | 14 | 10 |  |  | 7 |  |  | 32 |
| 1 | 2 | $3^2$ |  | 5 |  |  |  | 9 |  |  | $8^1$ |  | 4 | 12 | 13 | 11 |  | 10 |  | 6 | 7 |  |  | 33 |
| 1 | 2 | 3 |  | 5 |  |  |  | $9^2$ |  |  | $8^2$ |  | 4 | 12 | 13 | $11^1$ |  | 10 | 14 | 6 | 7 |  |  | 34 |
| 1 | 2 | $3^2$ |  | 5 |  |  |  | 9 |  |  | $8^1$ |  | 4 | 12 | 13 | 11 |  | 10 |  | 6 | 7 |  |  | 35 |
| 1 |  | 3 |  | 5 |  |  |  | $9^1$ |  |  | 8 | 2 | 4 | 12 | 13 | $11^2$ |  | $10^3$ | 14 | 6 | 7 |  |  | 36 |
| 1 |  | 3 |  | 5 |  |  |  | $9^1$ |  |  | 8 | $2^2$ | 4 | 12 | 13 | $11^2$ |  | 10 | 14 | 6 | 7 |  |  | 37 |
| 1 | $2^1$ | 3 |  | 5 |  |  |  | $9^3$ |  |  | $8^2$ |  | 4 | 12 | 13 | 11 |  | 10 | 14 | 6 | 7 |  |  | 38 |
| 1 | 2 | 3 |  | 5 |  |  |  | 9 |  |  | $8^2$ |  | 4 | 12 | 13 | $11^1$ |  | 10 |  | 6 | 7 |  |  | 39 |
| 1 | 2 | 3 |  | 5 |  |  |  | 9 |  |  | $8^1$ |  | 4 | 12 | 13 | 11 | 7 | 10 |  | $6^2$ |  |  |  | 40 |
| 1 | 2 | 3 |  | 5 |  |  |  | 9 |  |  | $8^1$ |  | 4 | 12 | 13 | $11^3$ | 7 | $10^2$ | 14 | 6 |  |  |  | 41 |
| 1 | 2 | 3 |  | 5 |  |  |  | 9 |  |  | 8 |  | 4 | 12 | 13 | $11^1$ | 7 | $10^2$ |  | 6 |  |  |  | 42 |
| 1 | 2 | $3^2$ |  | 5 |  |  |  | 9 |  |  | 8 |  | 4 | 12 | 13 | 11 |  | $10^1$ | 14 | $6^3$ | 7 |  |  | 43 |
| 1 | 2 | $3^2$ |  | 5 |  |  |  | 9 |  |  | 8 |  | 4 | 12 | 13 | 11 |  | 10 |  | $6^1$ | 7 |  |  | 44 |
| 1 | $2^3$ | 3 |  |  | $6^1$ |  | 11 | 9 | 5 |  | $8^2$ |  | 4 | 12 | 13 |  |  | 10 | 14 |  | 7 |  |  | 45 |
| 1 | $2^1$ |  |  | 5 | 6 |  | 11 | 9 |  |  | $8^2$ |  | 4 | 12 | 13 |  |  | 10 |  |  | 7 |  | 3 | 46 |

**Coca-Cola Cup**  
First Round        Norwich C        (a)    1-2  
                                    (h)    3-1  
Second Round        Middlesbrough    (a)    0-1  
                                    (h)    0-2  

**FA Cup**  
First Round        Watford        (h)    1-2

BARNSLEY 1997–98   *Back row (left to right):* Paul Smith (Physio), Sean McClare, Shane Hulson, Chris Morgan, Paul Wilkinson, Tony Bullock, Lars Leese, David Watson, Steve Davis, Mark Hume, Paul Bagshaw, Darren Sheridan, Mick Tarmey (Physio).

*Middle row:* Eric Winstanley (First Team Coach), Dean Jones, Rory Prendergast, Luke Beckett, Jonathan Perry, Carl Rose, Andy Gregory, Danny Shenton, Arjan De Zeeuw, Eric Tinkler, Laurens Ten Heuvel, Adrian Moses, Neil Thompson, Norman Rimmington (Kit Manager), Malcolm Shotton (Reserve Team Coach).

*Front row:* Peter Shirtliff (Player/Coach), Clint Marcelle, Andrew Liddell, Nicky Eaden, Martin Bullock, Neil Redfearn, Danny Wilson (Manager), Matty Appleby, John Hendrie, Jovo Bosancic, Ales Krizan, Georgi Hristov, Colin Walker (Youth Team Coach).

# Division 1 **BARNSLEY**

*Oakwell Ground, Grove St, Barnsley, South Yorkshire S71 1ET.* Telephone: (01226) 211211. Fax: (01226) 211444. Clubcall: 0891 121152.

*Ground capacity:* 18,806.

*Record attendance:* 40,255 v Stoke C, FA Cup 5th rd, 15 February 1936.

*Record receipts:* Not disclosed.

*Pitch measurements:* 110yd × 75yd.

*President:* Arthur Raynor. *Chairman:* J. A. Dennis.

*Directors:* C. B. Taylor (Vice-Chairman), C. H. Harrison, M. R. Hayselden, J. N. Kelly, S. M. Hall, I. D. Potter.

*Player-Manager:* John Hendrie.

*First Team Coach:* Eric Winstanley. *Physios:* Michael Tarmey, Paul Smith.

*General Manager/Secretary:* Michael Spinks. *Lotteries Manager:* Gerry Whewall. *Sales and Marketing Manager:* Graham Barlow.

*Year Formed:* 1887. *Turned Professional:* 1888. *Ltd Co.:* 1899.

*Previous Name:* Barnsley St Peter's, 1887–97.

*Club Nickname:* 'The Tykes', 'Reds' or 'Colliers'.

*Foundation:* Many clubs owe their inception to the church and Barnsley are among them, for they were formed in 1887 by the Rev. T. T. Preedy, curate of Barnsley St. Peter's and went under that name until it was dropped in 1897 a year before being admitted to the Second Division of the Football League.

*First Football League game:* 1 September 1898, Division 2, v Lincoln C (a) L 0-1 – Fawcett; McArtney, Nixon; King, Burleigh, Porteous; Davis, Lees, Murray, McCullough, McGee.

*Record League Victory:* 9–0 v Loughborough T, Division 2, 28 January 1899 – Greaves; McArtney, Nixon; Porteous, Burleigh, Howard; Davis (4), Hepworth (1), Lees (1), McCullough (1), Jones (2). 9–0 v Accrington S, Division 3 (N), 3 February 1934 – Ellis; Cookson, Shotton; Harper, Henderson, Whitworth; Spence (2), Smith (1), Blight (4), Andrews (1), Ashton (1).

*Record Cup Victory:* 6–0 v Blackpool, FA Cup 1st rd replay, 20 January 1910 – Mearns; Downs, Ness; Glendinning, Boyle (1), Utley; Bartrop, Gadsby (1), Lillycrop (2), Tufnell (2), Forman. 6–0 v Peterborough U, League Cup 1st rd, 2nd leg, 15 September 1981 – Horn; Joyce, Chambers, Glavin (2), Banks, McCarthy, Evans, Parker (2), Aylott (1), McHale, Barrowclough (1).

*Record Defeat:* 0–9 v Notts Co, Division 2, 19 November 1927.

*Most League Points (2 for a win):* 67, Division 3 (N), 1938–39.

*Most League Points (3 for a win):* 80, Division 1, 1996–97.

*Most League Goals:* 118, Division 3 (N), 1933–34.

*Highest League Scorer in Season:* Cecil McCormack, 33, Division 2, 1950–51.

*Most League Goals in Total Aggregate:* Ernest Hine, 123, 1921–26 and 1934–38.

*Most Capped Player:* Gerry Taggart, 35 (45), Northern Ireland.

*Most League Appearances:* Barry Murphy, 514, 1962–78.

*Record Transfer Fee Received:* £1,500,000 from Nottingham F for Carl Tiler, May 1991.

*Record Transfer Fee Paid:* £1,500,000 to Partizan Belgrade for Georgi Hristov, June 1997.

*Football League Record:* 1898 Elected to Division 2; 1932–34 Division 3 (N); 1934–38 Division 2; 1938–39 Division 3 (N); 1946–53 Division 2; 1953–55 Division 3 (N); 1955–59 Division 2; 1959–65 Division 3; 1965–68 Division 4; 1968–72 Division 3; 1972–79 Division 4; 1979–81 Division 3; 1981–92 Division 2; 1992–97 Division 1; 1997–98 FA Premier League; 1998– Division 1.

*Honours: Football League:* Division 1 – Runners-up 1996–97; Division 3 (N) – Champions 1933–34, 1938–39, 1954–55; Runners-up 1953–54; Division 3 – Runners-up 1980–81; Division 4 – Runners-up 1967–68; Promoted 1978–79. *FA Cup:* Winners 1912; Runners-up 1910. *Football League Cup:* best season: 5th rd, 1982.

*Colours:* Red shirts, white shorts, red stockings. *Change colours:* Royal blue and black striped shirts, black shorts, black stockings.

**Did you know?**
Russell Wainscoat scored a hat-trick on his debut for Barnsley v Fulham on 6 March 1920 in a 4-1 win and he was brought down in the penalty area before Barnsley were awarded the penalty leading to the other goal.

## BARNSLEY 1997–98 LEAGUE RECORD

| Match No. | Date | Venue | Opponents | Result | | H/T Score | Lg. Pos. | Goalscorers | Atten-dance |
|---|---|---|---|---|---|---|---|---|---|
| 1 | Aug 9 | H | West Ham U | L | 1-2 | 1-0 | — | Redfearn [9] | 18,667 |
| 2 | 12 | A | Crystal Palace | W | 1-0 | 0-0 | — | Redfearn [56] | 21,547 |
| 3 | 24 | H | Chelsea | L | 0-6 | 0-3 | 14 | | 18,177 |
| 4 | 27 | H | Bolton W | W | 2-1 | 1-1 | — | Tinkler [12], Hristov [47] | 18,661 |
| 5 | 30 | A | Derby Co | L | 0-1 | 0-1 | 10 | | 27,232 |
| 6 | Sept 13 | H | Aston Villa | L | 0-3 | 0-1 | 15 | | 18,649 |
| 7 | 20 | A | Everton | L | 2-4 | 1-2 | 17 | Redfearn [32], Barnard [78] | 32,659 |
| 8 | 23 | A | Wimbledon | L | 1-4 | 1-0 | — | Tinkler [41] | 7688 |
| 9 | 27 | H | Leicester C | L | 0-2 | 0-0 | 19 | | 18,660 |
| 10 | Oct 4 | A | Arsenal | L | 0-5 | 0-3 | 20 | | 38,049 |
| 11 | 20 | H | Coventry C | W | 2-0 | 1-0 | — | Ward [11], Redfearn (pen) [66] | 17,476 |
| 12 | 25 | A | Manchester U | L | 0-7 | 0-4 | 20 | | 55,142 |
| 13 | Nov 1 | H | Blackburn R | D | 1-1 | 0-1 | 19 | Bosancic [79] | 18,687 |
| 14 | 8 | A | Southampton | L | 1-4 | 1-3 | 20 | Bosancic (pen) [37] | 15,018 |
| 15 | 22 | A | Liverpool | W | 1-0 | 1-0 | 19 | Ward [35] | 41,011 |
| 16 | 29 | H | Leeds U | L | 2-3 | 2-1 | 19 | Liddell [8], Ward [28] | 18,690 |
| 17 | Dec 8 | A | Sheffield W | L | 1-2 | 1-1 | — | Redfearn [29] | 29,086 |
| 18 | 13 | H | Newcastle U | D | 2-2 | 1-1 | 20 | Redfearn [9], Hendrie [75] | 18,694 |
| 19 | 20 | A | Tottenham H | L | 0-3 | 0-3 | 20 | | 28,232 |
| 20 | 26 | A | Bolton W | D | 1-1 | 1-1 | 20 | Hristov [20] | 25,000 |
| 21 | 28 | H | Derby Co | W | 1-0 | 0-0 | 20 | Ward [67] | 18,686 |
| 22 | Jan 10 | A | West Ham U | L | 0-6 | 0-2 | 20 | | 23,714 |
| 23 | 17 | H | Crystal Palace | W | 1-0 | 1-0 | 20 | Ward [26] | 17,831 |
| 24 | 31 | A | Chelsea | L | 0-2 | 0-1 | 20 | | 34,442 |
| 25 | Feb 7 | H | Everton | D | 2-2 | 1-1 | 20 | Fjortoft [24], Barnard [63] | 18,654 |
| 26 | 21 | A | Coventry C | L | 0-1 | 0-0 | 20 | | 20,262 |
| 27 | 28 | H | Wimbledon | W | 2-1 | 1-0 | 18 | Fjortoft 2 [25, 63] | 17,172 |
| 28 | Mar 11 | A | Aston Villa | W | 1-0 | 1-0 | — | Ward [17] | 29,519 |
| 29 | 14 | A | Southampton | W | 4-3 | 3-2 | 18 | Ward [17], Jones [32], Fjortoft [42], Redfearn (pen) [57] | 18,366 |
| 30 | 28 | H | Liverpool | L | 2-3 | 1-1 | 18 | Redfearn 2 (1 pen) [37, 85 (p)] | 18,687 |
| 31 | 31 | A | Blackburn R | L | 1-2 | 0-1 | — | Hristov [67] | 24,179 |
| 32 | Apr 4 | A | Leeds U | L | 1-2 | 1-1 | 19 | Hristov [44] | 37,749 |
| 33 | 11 | H | Sheffield W | W | 2-1 | 0-0 | 19 | Ward [65], Fjortoft [72] | 18,692 |
| 34 | 13 | A | Newcastle U | L | 1-2 | 0-1 | 19 | Fjortoft [50] | 36,534 |
| 35 | 18 | H | Tottenham H | D | 1-1 | 1-0 | 18 | Redfearn [19] | 18,692 |
| 36 | 25 | H | Arsenal | L | 0-2 | 0-1 | 19 | | 18,691 |
| 37 | May 2 | A | Leicester C | L | 0-1 | 0-0 | 19 | | 21,293 |
| 38 | 10 | H | Manchester U | L | 0-2 | 0-1 | 19 | | 18,694 |

**Final League Position: 19**          1996–97 DIV1 2

### GOALSCORERS

*League (37):* Redfearn 10 (3 pens), Ward 8, Fjortoft 6, Hristov 4, Barnard 2, Bosancic 2 (1 pen), Tinkler 2, Hendrie 1, Jones 1, Liddell 1.
*Coca-Cola Cup (7):* Liddell 2, Redfearn 2 (1 pen), Hristov 1, Sheridan 1, Ward 1.
*FA Cup (10):* Barnard 2, Hendrie 2, Jones 2, Redfearn 2 (1 pen), Liddell 1, Ward 1.

| Watson D 30 | Eaden N 32 + 3 | Barnard D 33 + 2 | Shirtliff P 4 | Moses A 32 + 3 | De Zeeuw A 26 | Hendrie J 7 + 13 | Redfearn N 37 | Wilkinson P 3 + 1 | Bullock M 23 + 10 | Tinkler E 21 + 4 | Marcelle C 9 + 11 | Hristov G 11 + 12 | Liddell A 13 + 13 | Appleby M 13 + 2 | Sheridan D 20 + 6 | Leese L 8 + 1 | Ward A 28 + 1 | Ten Heuvel L — + 2 | Krizan A 12 | Thompson N 3 | Bosancic J 13 + 4 | Markstedt P 6 + 1 | Morgan C 10 + 1 | Fjortoft J 12 + 3 | Jones S 12 | Match No. |
|---|---|---|---|---|---|---|---|---|---|---|---|---|---|---|---|---|---|---|---|---|---|---|---|---|---|---|
| 1 | 2 | 3 | 4¹ | 5 | 6 | 7 | 8 |  | 9² | 10³ | 11 | 12 | 13 | 14 |  |  |  |  |  |  |  |  |  |  |  | 1 |
| 1 | 2 | 3 |  | 5 | 6 | 7 | 8 |  | 9 | 10 |  |  |  | 4 | 11 |  |  |  |  |  |  |  |  |  |  | 2 |
| 1 | 2 | 3 |  | 5 | 6 | 7³ | 8 |  | 9² | 10 | 11 | 12 | 13 | 14 | 4 |  | 15 |  |  |  |  |  |  |  |  | 3 |
| 1⁶ | 2 | 3 |  | 5 | 6 | 7 | 8 |  | 12 | 11 | 10¹ | 9² | 13 |  | 4 |  | 15 |  |  |  |  |  |  |  |  | 4 |
|  | 2 | 3¹ |  | 5 | 6 | 13 | 8 | 14 | 11 | 7² | 9³ | 10 |  |  | 4 | 12 | 1 |  |  |  |  |  |  |  |  | 5 |
|  | 2 | 3 |  | 5 | 6 |  | 8 | 12 | 11² | 9³ | 7¹ | 4 | 13 | 1 | 10 | 14 |  |  |  |  |  |  |  |  |  | 6 |
| 1 |  | 3 | 4 | 5 | 6 |  | 8 | 12 | 11¹ | 13 | 14 | 10 | 2³ | 7 | 9² |  |  |  |  |  |  |  |  |  |  | 7 |
| 1 |  | 3 |  | 5 | 6 |  | 8 | 9 | 7¹ | 12 | 13 | 10² | 2 | 11 | 4 |  |  |  |  |  |  |  |  |  |  | 8 |
|  |  | 3 |  | 5 | 6 |  | 8 | 12 | 7¹ | 13 | 10² | 2 | 11 |  | 4 | 1 | 9 |  |  |  |  |  |  |  |  | 9 |
| 1 | 12 | 3 |  | 2⁵ | 6 |  | 8 | 13 | 7 | 14 | 10³ | 4² | 9 | 5 | 11 |  |  |  |  |  |  |  |  |  |  | 10 |
| 1 | 2 | 3 |  | 12 | 5 |  | 8 | 7¹ | 13 | 10² | 4 | 9 | 6 | 11 |  |  |  |  |  |  |  |  |  |  |  | 11 |
| 1 | 2 | 3 |  | 12 | 5 | 13 | 8 | 7 | 9² | 4 | 10 | 6¹ | 11³ | 14 |  |  |  |  |  |  |  |  |  |  |  | 12 |
| 1 | 12 | 13 | 4 | 2 | 5 | 7 | 8 | 10 | 9³ | 14 | 11¹ | 6² | 3 |  |  |  |  |  |  |  |  |  |  |  |  | 13 |
| 1 | 2 | 12 | 4² | 5 | 6 | 7³ | 9 | 11 | 10 | 13 | 14 | 8¹ | 3 |  |  |  |  |  |  |  |  |  |  |  |  | 14 |
|  | 2 | 3 |  | 5 | 6 | 12 | 8 | 11 | 7 | 10² | 13 | 9¹ | 4 |  |  |  |  |  |  |  |  |  |  |  |  | 15 |
|  | 2 | 3 |  | 12 | 5 | 8 | 9² | 7 | 14 | 10³ | 13 | 1 | 11 | 6¹ | 4 |  |  |  |  |  |  |  |  |  |  | 16 |
|  | 2 | 3 |  | 5 | 12 | 8 | 13 | 10¹ | 6² | 4 | 1 | 9 | 7 | 11 |  |  |  |  |  |  |  |  |  |  |  | 17 |
|  | 2 | 3 |  | 5 | 12 | 8 | 13 | 11 | 10¹ | 6² | 14 | 1 | 9 | 7 | 4³ |  |  |  |  |  |  |  |  |  |  | 18 |
|  | 2 | 3 |  | 5 | 6 | 8 | 12 | 11 | 13 | 10² | 7 | 1 | 9 | 4¹ |  |  |  |  |  |  |  |  |  |  |  | 19 |
| 1 | 2 | 3 |  | 5 | 6 | 12 | 8 | 11 | 7² | 9¹ | 13 | 4 | 10 |  |  |  |  |  |  |  |  |  |  |  |  | 20 |
| 1 | 2 | 3 |  | 5 | 6 | 8 | 12 | 11 | 7¹ | 9² | 13 | 4 | 10 |  |  |  |  |  |  |  |  |  |  |  |  | 21 |
| 1 | 2 | 3 |  | 12 | 8 | 11 | 13 | 9¹ | 5³ | 7 | 10 | 6² | 14 | 4 |  |  |  |  |  |  |  |  |  |  |  | 22 |
| 1 | 2 | 3 |  |  | 8 | 11 | 7 | 12 | 4 | 10 | 5 | 6 | 9¹ |  |  |  |  |  |  |  |  |  |  |  |  | 23 |
| 1 | 2 | 3 |  | 5 | 6 | 12 | 8 | 7 | 13 | 4³ | 10 | 11² | 14 | 9¹ |  |  |  |  |  |  |  |  |  |  |  | 24 |
| 1 | 2 | 3 |  | 5 | 6 | 12 | 8 | 7 | 13 |  | 10 | 11 | 4² | 9¹ |  |  |  |  |  |  |  |  |  |  |  | 25 |
| 1 | 2 |  |  | 5 | 12 | 8 | 7² | 13 | 14 | 4³ | 10 | 11 | 6 | 9¹ | 3 |  |  |  |  |  |  |  |  |  |  | 26 |
| 1 | 2 | 3 |  | 5 | 8 | 12 | 7 | 13 | 10 | 11² | 4¹ | 6 | 9 |  |  |  |  |  |  |  |  |  |  |  |  | 27 |
| 1 | 2 | 3¹ |  | 5 | 8 | 7 | 12 | 13 | 11 | 10 | 4 | 9² | 6 |  |  |  |  |  |  |  |  |  |  |  |  | 28 |
| 1 | 2 | 3 |  | 5 | 8 | 7 | 12 | 14 | 13³ | 11 | 10² | 4 | 9 | 6¹ |  |  |  |  |  |  |  |  |  |  |  | 29 |
| 1 | 2 | 3 |  | 8 | 7² | 10¹ | 12 | 14 | 5 | 11 | 13 | 4 | 9³ | 6 |  |  |  |  |  |  |  |  |  |  |  | 30 |
| 1 | 2 | 3 |  | 5 | 8 | 7¹ | 12² | 9 | 14 | 13 | 10 | 11 | 4 | 6³ |  |  |  |  |  |  |  |  |  |  |  | 31 |
| 1 | 2 | 3 |  | 5 | 8 | 7¹ | 12 | 9 | 10 | 11 | 4 | 13 | 6² |  |  |  |  |  |  |  |  |  |  |  |  | 32 |
| 1 | 2 |  |  | 5 | 6 | 7¹ | 8 | 9 | 10 | 3 | 11 | 12 | 4 |  |  |  |  |  |  |  |  |  |  |  |  | 33 |
| 1 | 2 |  |  | 5 | 6 | 12 | 8 | 7² | 14 | 13 | 10 | 3³ | 11 | 9¹ | 4 |  |  |  |  |  |  |  |  |  |  | 34 |
| 1 | 2 | 3 |  | 5 | 6 | 12 | 8 | 7 | 11² | 13 | 10 | 9 | 4¹ |  |  |  |  |  |  |  |  |  |  |  |  | 35 |
| 1 | 2 | 3 |  | 5 | 6 | 12 | 8 | 7 | 11² | 10³ | 14 | 13 | 9¹ | 4 |  |  |  |  |  |  |  |  |  |  |  | 36 |
| 1 | 2 | 3 |  | 5 | 6 | 8 | 12 | 11³ | 7 | 13 | 10 | 14 | 9² | 4¹ |  |  |  |  |  |  |  |  |  |  |  | 37 |
| 1 | 12 | 3 |  | 5 | 8 | 2 | 9² | 11¹ | 7 | 10 | 4 | 13 | 6 |  |  |  |  |  |  |  |  |  |  |  |  | 38 |

**Coca-Cola Cup**

| | | | |
|---|---|---|---|
| Second Round | Chesterfield | (a) | 2-1 |
| | | (h) | 4-1 |
| Third Round | Southampton | (h) | 1-2 |

**FA Cup**

| | | | |
|---|---|---|---|
| Third Round | Bolton W | (h) | 1-0 |
| Fourth Round | Tottenham H | (a) | 1-1 |
| | | (h) | 3-1 |
| Fifth Round | Manchester U | (a) | 1-1 |
| | | (h) | 3-2 |
| Sixth Round | Newcastle U | (a) | 1-3 |

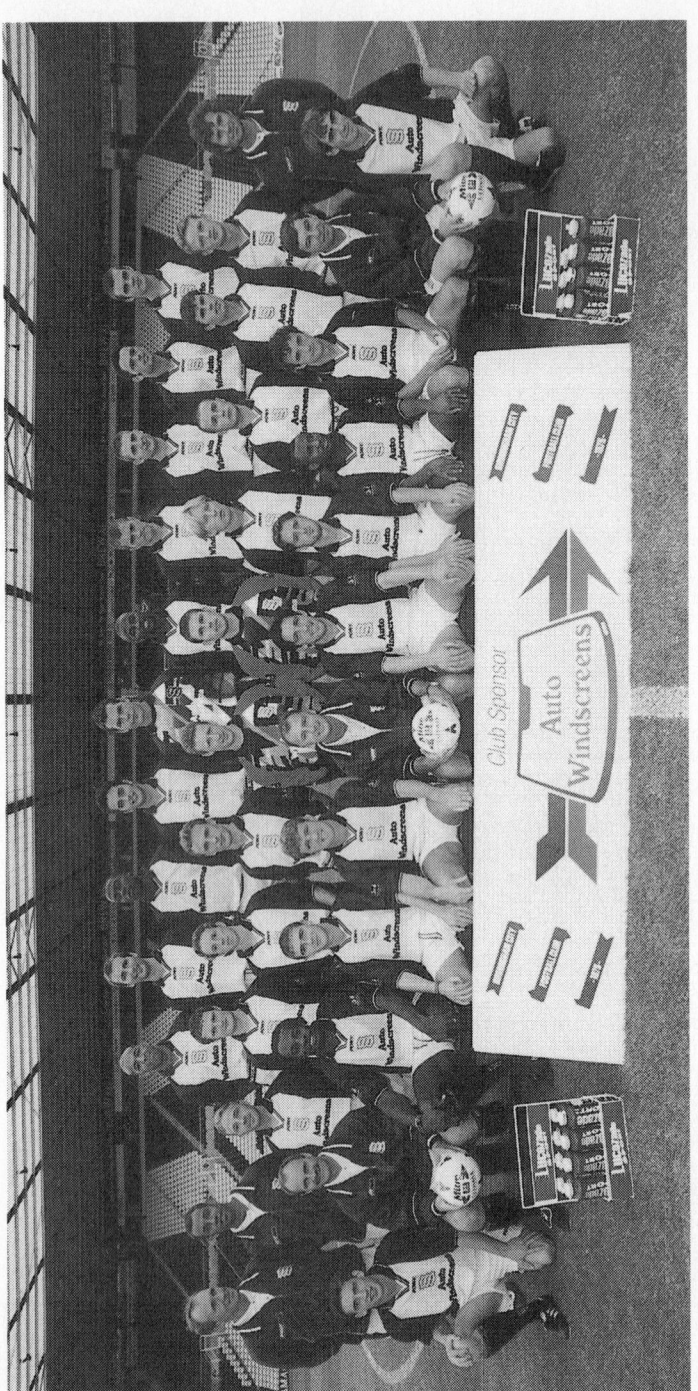

BIRMINGHAM CITY 1997–98    *Back row (left to right):* Martin O'Connor, Darren Wassall, Paul Furlong, Jon Bass, Richard Moore, Michael Johnson, Martin Grainger, Nicky Forster, Jerry Gill, Paul Hatton.

*Middle row:* Ian Bowyer (Reserve Coach), Arvel Lowe (Fitness Coach), Steve Barnes, Chris Holland, Steve Robinson, Tony Hey, Kevin Poole, Ian Bennett, Paul Tait, Paul Devlin, Howard Forinton, Simon Rea, Neil McDiarmid (Physio).

*Front row:* Craig Hinton, Mick Mills (Assistant Manager), Kevin Francis, Bryan Hughes, Steve Bruce, Trevor Francis (Manager), Gary Ablett, Jason Bowen, Peter Ndlovu, Barry Horne, Frank Barlow (Assistant Manager), James Dyson.

# Division 1     **BIRMINGHAM CITY**

*St Andrews, Birmingham B9 4NH.* Telephone: (0121) 772 0101. Fax: (0121) 766 7866. Lottery Office/Souvenir Shop: (0121) 772 1245. Clubcall: 0891 121188. Club Soccer Shop: (0121) 766 8274.

*Ground capacity:* 25,812.

*Record attendance:* 66,844 v Everton, FA Cup 5th rd, 11 February 1939.

*Record receipts:* £230,000 v Aston Villa, Coca-Cola Cup 2nd rd 1st leg, 21 September 1993.

*Pitch measurements:* 115yd × 75yd.

*Chairman:* D. Gold. *Vice-Chairman:* J. F. Wiseman

*Directors:* D. Sullivan, R. Gold, B. Gold, H. Brandman, A. G. Jones. *Managing Director:* K. R. Brady.

*Manager:* Trevor Francis. *Coach:* Mick Mills. *Physio:* N. McDiarmid.

*Commercial Manager:* Allan Robson. *Stadium Manager:* Brian Tew.

*Secretary:* A. G. Jones BA, MBA.

*Year Formed:* 1875. *Turned Professional:* 1885. *Ltd Co.:* 1888.

*Previous Names:* 1875–88, Small Heath Alliance; 1888, dropped 'Alliance'; became Birmingham 1905; became Birmingham City 1945.

*Club Nickname:* 'Blues'.

*Previous Grounds:* 1875, waste ground near Arthur St; 1877, Muntz St, Small Heath; 1906, St Andrews.

*Foundation:* In 1875 cricketing enthusiasts who were largely members of Trinity Church, Bordesley, determined to continue their sporting relationships throughout the year by forming a football club which they called Small Heath Alliance. For their earliest games played on waste land in Arthur Street, the team included three Edden brothers and two James brothers.

*First Football League game:* 3 September 1892, Division 2, v Burslem Port Vale (h) W 5-1 – Charsley; Bayley, Speller; Ollis, Jenkyns, Devey; Hallam (1), Edwards (1), Short (1), Wheldon (2), Hands.

*Record League Victory:* 12–0 v Walsall T Swifts, Division 2, 17 December 1892 – Charsley; Bayley, Jones; Ollis, Jenkyns, Devey; Hallam (2), Walton (3), Mobley (3), Wheldon (2), Hands (2). 12–0 v Doncaster R, Division 2, 11 April 1903 – Dorrington; Goldie, Wassell; Beer, Dougherty (1), Howard; Athersmith (1), Leonard (3), McRoberts (1), Wilcox (4), Field (1). Aston. (1 og).

*Record Cup Victory:* 9–2 v Burton W, FA Cup 1st rd, 31 October 1885 – Hedges; Jones, Evetts (1); F. James, Felton, A. James (1); Davenport (2), Stanley (4), Simms, Figures, Morris (1).

*Record Defeat:* 1–9 v Sheffield W, Division 1, 13 December 1930 and v Blackburn R, Division 1, 5 January 1895.

*Most League Points (2 for a win):* 59, Division 2, 1947–48.

*Most League Points (3 for a win):* 89, Division 2, 1994–95.

*Most League Goals:* 103, Division 2, 1893–94 (only 28 games).

*Highest League Scorer in Season:* Joe Bradford, 29, Division 1, 1927–28.

*Most League Goals in Total Aggregate:* Joe Bradford, 249, 1920–35.

*Most Capped Player:* Malcolm Page, 28, Wales.

*Most League Appearances:* Frank Womack, 491, 1908–28.

*Record Transfer Fee Received:* £2,500,000 from Coventry C for Gary Breen, January 1997.

*Record Transfer Fee Paid:* £1,500,000 to Chelsea for Paul Furlong, July 1996.

*Football League Record:* 1892 elected to Division 2; 1894–96 Division 1; 1896–1901 Division 2; 1901–02 Division 1; 1902–03 Division 2; 1903–08 Division 1; 1908–21 Division 2; 1921–39 Division 1; 1946–48 Division 2; 1948–50 Division 1; 1950–1955 Division 2; 1955–65 Division 1; 1965–72 Division 2; 1972–79 Division 1; 1979–80 Division 2; 1980–84 Division 1; 1984–85 Division 2; 1985–86 Division 1; 1986–89 Division 2; 1989–92 Division 3; 1992–94 Division 1; 1994–95 Division 2; 1995– Division 1.

*Honours: Football League:* Division 1 best season: 6th, 1955–56; Division 2 – Champions 1892–93, 1920–21, 1947–48, 1954–55, 1994–95; Runners-up 1893–94, 1900–01, 1902–03, 1971–72, 1984–85. Division 3 Runners-up 1991–92. *FA Cup:* Runners-up 1931, 1956. *Football League Cup:* Winners 1963. *Leyland Daf Cup:* Winners 1991. *Auto Windscreens Shield:* Winners 1995. **European Competitions:** *European Fairs Cup:* 1955–58, 1958–60 (runners-up), 1960–61 (runners-up), 1961–62.

*Colours:* Blue shirts, white shorts, blue and white hooped stockings. *Change colours:* White shirts with black stripes, black shorts.

**Did you know?**
Freddie Wheldon was the first Birmingham player to score as many as four goals in a League game. He achieved this feat on 2 December 1893 in an 8-0 win over Northwich Victoria.

## BIRMINGHAM CITY 1997–98 LEAGUE RECORD

| Match No. | Date | Venue | Opponents | Result | H/T Score | Lg. Pos. | Goalscorers | Attendance |
|---|---|---|---|---|---|---|---|---|
| 1 | Aug 9 | H | Stoke C | W 2-0 | 1-0 | — | Devlin [33], Ndlovu [87] | 20,608 |
| 2 | 23 | H | Reading | W 3-0 | 1-0 | 6 | Devlin [38], Bruce [81], Ndlovu [88] | 16,495 |
| 3 | 29 | A | Stockport Co | D 2-2 | 0-1 | — | Devlin [68], Francis [72] | 6260 |
| 4 | Sept 2 | A | Tranmere R | W 3-0 | 2-0 | — | Hughes [11], Furlong [44], Ndlovu [65] | 6620 |
| 5 | 9 | A | Huddersfield T | W 1-0 | 0-0 | — | Furlong [70] | 9477 |
| 6 | 14 | H | Sunderland | L 0-1 | 0-0 | 4 | | 17,478 |
| 7 | 20 | A | Middlesbrough | L 1-3 | 0-3 | 8 | Furlong [51] | 30,125 |
| 8 | 27 | A | Sheffield U | D 0-0 | 0-0 | 7 | | 20,553 |
| 9 | Oct 4 | H | Crewe Alex | L 0-1 | 0-0 | 10 | | 16,548 |
| 10 | 12 | H | Wolverhampton W | W 1-0 | 1-0 | 6 | Marsden [8] | 17,822 |
| 11 | 18 | A | Bury | L 1-2 | 0-2 | 9 | Grainger [90] | 5700 |
| 12 | 22 | A | Charlton Ath | D 1-1 | 0-0 | — | Devlin [83] | 10,072 |
| 13 | 25 | H | Oxford U | D 0-0 | 0-0 | 13 | | 16,352 |
| 14 | 28 | H | Ipswich T | D 1-1 | 0-1 | — | Bruce [81] | 16,778 |
| 15 | Nov 1 | A | QPR | D 1-1 | 1-1 | 11 | Furlong [42] | 12,715 |
| 16 | 4 | H | Bradford C | D 0-0 | 0-0 | — | | 14,552 |
| 17 | 8 | H | Norwich C | L 1-2 | 1-2 | 14 | Devlin (pen) [27] | 16,464 |
| 18 | 15 | A | Nottingham F | L 0-1 | 0-1 | 14 | | 19,610 |
| 19 | 23 | A | WBA | L 0-1 | 0-0 | 14 | | 18,444 |
| 20 | 29 | H | Portsmouth | W 2-1 | 1-1 | 14 | Furlong 2 [36, 73] | 17,738 |
| 21 | Dec 6 | A | Port Vale | W 1-0 | 1-0 | 11 | Cottee [18] | 7509 |
| 22 | 13 | H | Manchester C | W 2-1 | 0-0 | 11 | Forster [89], O'Connor [90] | 21,014 |
| 23 | 20 | A | Swindon T | D 1-1 | 1-1 | 11 | Forster [22] | 10,334 |
| 24 | 26 | A | Ipswich T | W 1-0 | 0-0 | 10 | McCarthy [83] | 17,459 |
| 25 | 28 | H | Tranmere R | D 0-0 | 0-0 | 10 | | 19,533 |
| 26 | Jan 10 | A | Stoke C | W 7-0 | 3-0 | 8 | Hughes 2 [4, 9], Forster [26], Furlong 3 [50, 69, 87], McCarthy [56] | 14,940 |
| 27 | 17 | H | Huddersfield T | D 0-0 | 0-0 | 8 | | 17,850 |
| 28 | 27 | H | Stockport Co | W 4-1 | 3-0 | — | Furlong 3 [7, 31, 90], McCarthy [16] | 17,118 |
| 29 | 31 | A | Reading | L 0-2 | 0-0 | 9 | | 10,315 |
| 30 | Feb 7 | H | Middlesbrough | D 1-1 | 1-1 | 9 | McCarthy [3] | 20,639 |
| 31 | 17 | A | Crewe Alex | W 2-0 | 2-0 | — | Adebola [42], Hughes [45] | 5559 |
| 32 | 22 | A | Sheffield U | W 2-0 | 1-0 | 8 | Grainger [31], Johnson [66] | 17,965 |
| 33 | 25 | H | Bury | L 1-3 | 0-1 | — | Johnson [90] | 20,021 |
| 34 | 28 | A | Wolverhampton W | W 3-1 | 1-1 | 6 | Ndlovu 2 (1 pen) [35, 77 (p)], Adebola [71] | 25,591 |
| 35 | Mar 4 | A | Norwich C | D 3-3 | 2-0 | — | Ndlovu 2 [13, 88], Adebola [44] | 9819 |
| 36 | 7 | H | QPR | W 1-0 | 1-0 | 7 | Adebola [16] | 18,298 |
| 37 | 10 | H | Sunderland | D 1-1 | 0-0 | — | Adebola [50] | 37,602 |
| 38 | 14 | A | Bradford C | D 0-0 | 0-0 | 7 | | 16,392 |
| 39 | 21 | H | Nottingham F | L 1-2 | 0-0 | 7 | Ndlovu (pen) [61] | 24,663 |
| 40 | 28 | H | WBA | W 1-0 | 0-0 | 7 | Johnson [90] | 23,260 |
| 41 | Apr 4 | A | Portsmouth | D 1-1 | 0-0 | 7 | Adebola [84] | 14,591 |
| 42 | 11 | H | Port Vale | D 1-1 | 0-0 | 7 | Ndlovu [87] | 17,193 |
| 43 | 13 | A | Manchester C | W 1-0 | 0-0 | 7 | Adebola [90] | 29,569 |
| 44 | 18 | A | Swindon T | W 3-0 | 2-0 | 7 | Furlong 2 (1 pen) [9, 34 (p)], Hughes [82] | 17,016 |
| 45 | 25 | A | Oxford U | W 2-0 | 0-0 | 7 | Ford (og) [73], Furlong [85] | 8818 |
| 46 | May 3 | H | Charlton Ath | D 0-0 | 0-0 | 7 | | 25,877 |

**Final League Position: 7**     1996–97 DIV1 10

## GOALSCORERS

League (60): Furlong 15 (1 pen), Ndlovu 9 (2 pens), Adebola 7, Devlin 5 (1 pen), Hughes 5, McCarthy 4, Forster 3, Johnson 3, Bruce 2, Grainger 2, Cottee 1, Francis 1, Marsden 1, O'Connor 1, own goal 1.
Coca-Cola Cup (10): Devlin 3 (1 pen), Furlong 2 (1 pen), Francis 1, Hey 1, Hughes 1, Ndlovu 1, Robinson 1.
FA Cup (6): Furlong 2 (1 pen), Hughes 2, Ablett 1, Ndlovu 1.

| Bennett I 45 | Wassall D 14 | Grainger M 27 + 6 | Bruce S 40 | Ablett G 34 + 2 | O'Connor M 32 + 1 | Devlin P 13 + 9 | Hey T 8 + 1 | Hughes B 34 + 6 | Robinson S 17 + 8 | Ndlovu P 29 + 10 | Holland C 2 + 8 | Francis K 2 + 18 | Johnson M 22 + 16 | Furlong P 24 + 1 | McCarthy J 41 | Bass J 30 | Marsden C 31 + 1 | Forster N 12 + 16 | Cottee T 4 + 1 | Charlton S 23 + 1 | Adebola D 16 + 1 | Purse D 2 + 6 | Forinton H — + 1 | Gill J 3 | Poole K 1 | Match No. |
|---|---|---|---|---|---|---|---|---|---|---|---|---|---|---|---|---|---|---|---|---|---|---|---|---|---|---|
| 1 | 2 | 3 | 4 | 5 | $6^1$ | $7^2$ | $8^3$ | 9 | 10 | 11 | 12 | 13 | 14 | | | | | | | | | | | | | 1 |
| 1 | 2 | 3 | 4 | 5 | 6 | $7^1$ | $8^2$ | 10 | 11 | 12 | 14 | 13 | | $9^3$ | | | | | | | | | | | | 2 |
| 1 | 2 | 3 | 4 | 5 | $6^1$ | 7 | $8^2$ | 9 | 10 | 11 | 12 | 13 | | | | | | | | | | | | | | 3 |
| 1 | 2 | 3 | 4 | 5 | 6 | $7^3$ | $8^2$ | 10 | 11 | 12 | 14 | 13 | | $9^1$ | | | | | | | | | | | | 4 |
| 1 | 2 | 3 | 4 | 5 | 6 | $7^2$ | $8^1$ | 10 | 11 | 12 | | 13 | | 9 | | | | | | | | | | | | 5 |
| 1 | 2 | 3 | $4^2$ | 5 | $6^1$ | 7 | 8 | 9 | 10 | $11^3$ | 12 | 13 | 14 | | | | | | | | | | | | | 6 |
| 1 | $2^2$ | $3^2$ | 4 | 5 | $6^1$ | 7 | 8 | 9 | 10 | 11 | 12 | 13 | 14 | | | | | | | | | | | | | 7 |
| 1 | 2 | 3 | 4 | 5 | 6 | $7^2$ | 8 | $9^2$ | 10 | $11^1$ | 12 | 13 | 14 | | | | | | | | | | | | | 8 |
| 1 | 2 | 3 | 4 | 5 | 6 | $7^1$ | 8 | 9 | 10 | 11 | 12 | | | | | | | | | | | | | | | 9 |
| 1 | | 3 | 4 | 5 | 6 | 7 | 8 | $9^2$ | $10^1$ | 11 | 12 | 13 | | | | 2 | 6 | | | | | | | | | 10 |
| 1 | 2 | 3 | 4 | $5^3$ | 6 | 7 | $8$ | $9^2$ | $10^1$ | 11 | 12 | 13 | 14 | | | | | | | | | | | | | 11 |
| 1 | 2 | 3 | 4 | 5 | 6 | $7$ | $8^2$ | $9^3$ | 10 | $11^1$ | 12 | 13 | 14 | | | | | | | | | | | | | 12 |
| 1 | 2 | 3 | 4 | 5 | 6 | 7 | 8 | $9^2$ | $10^1$ | 11 | 12 | 13 | | | | | | | | | | | | | | 13 |
| 1 | | 3 | 4 | 5 | 6 | 7 | 8 | 9 | 10 | $11^1$ | 12 | | | | | 2 | 6 | | | | | | | | | 14 |
| 1 | | 3 | 4 | 5 | 6 | 7 | 8 | 9 | $10^1$ | 11 | 12 | | | | | 2 | 6 | | | | | | | | | 15 |
| 1 | | 3 | 4 | 5 | 6 | $7^2$ | 8 | 9 | 10 | $11^1$ | 12 | 13 | | | | 2 | 6 | | | | | | | | | 16 |
| 1 | | 3 | 4 | 5 | 6 | 7 | 8 | 9 | $10^1$ | $11^2$ | 12 | 13 | | | | 2 | 6 | | | | | | | | | 17 |
| 1 | $2$ | $3^2$ | 4 | 5 | 6 | $7^3$ | 8 | 9 | 10 | $11^1$ | 12 | 13 | 14 | | | | | | | | | | | | | 18 |
| 1 | | 3 | 4 | 5 | 6 | 7 | 8 | 9 | $10^2$ | $11^1$ | 12 | 13 | | | | 2 | 6 | | | | | | | | | 19 |
| 1 | | 3 | 4 | 5 | 6 | 7 | 8 | 9 | $10^2$ | $11^1$ | 12 | 13 | | | | 2 | 6 | | | | | | | | | 20 |
| 1 | | 3 | 4 | 5 | 6 | 7 | 8 | 9 | $10^3$ | $11^1$ | $12^2$ | 13 | | | | 2 | 6 | | | | | 14 | | | | 21 |
| 1 | | 3 | 4 | 5 | 6 | $7$ | 8 | $9^3$ | 10 | $11^1$ | 12 | 13 | | | | $2^2$ | 6 | 14 | | | | | | | | 22 |
| 1 | | 3 | 4 | 5 | 6 | 7 | $8^1$ | 9 | 10 | $11^2$ | 12 | 13 | | | | 2 | | | | | | | | | | 23 |
| 1 | | 3 | 4 | 5 | 6 | 7 | 8 | 9 | $10^1$ | $11^2$ | 12 | 13 | | | | 2 | | | | | | | | | | 24 |
| 1 | | 3 | 4 | 5 | | 7 | 8 | $9^2$ | 10 | $11^1$ | 12 | 13 | 14 | | | 2 | $6^3$ | | | | | | | | | 25 |
| 1 | | 3 | $4^2$ | 5 | | 7 | 8 | 9 | 10 | $11^1$ | 12 | 13 | | | | 2 | 6 | | | | | | | | | 26 |
| 1 | | 3 | 4 | 5 | | 7 | $8^1$ | 9 | 10 | $11^3$ | 12 | 13 | 14 | | | $2^2$ | 6 | | | | | | | | | 27 |
| 1 | | 3 | $4^2$ | 5 | | 7 | 8 | 9 | 10 | $11^1$ | 12 | 13 | | | | 2 | 6 | | | | | | | | | 28 |
| 1 | | 3 | $4^1$ | 5 | | 7 | 8 | 9 | $10^3$ | $11^2$ | 12 | 13 | 14 | | | 2 | 6 | | | | | | | | | 29 |
| 1 | | 3 | 4 | 5 | | 7 | 8 | 9 | $10^1$ | $11^3$ | 12 | 13 | | | | 2 | 6 | | | $3^2$ | 14 | | | | | 30 |
| 1 | | 3 | $4^3$ | 5 | 6 | 7 | 8 | $9^2$ | $10^1$ | 11 | 12 | 13 | 14 | | | 2 | | | | 3 | | | | | | 31 |
| 1 | | | $4$ | 5 | 6 | 7 | 8 | 9 | $10^1$ | $11^2$ | 12 | 13 | 14 | | | 2 | | | | 3 | | | | | | 32 |
| 1 | | | 4 | 5 | $6^1$ | 7 | 8 | 9 | 10 | 11 | 12 | 13 | 14 | | | $2^2$ | | | | $3^3$ | | | | | | 33 |
| 1 | | | 4 | 5 | 6 | 7 | $8^1$ | 9 | $10^2$ | $11^3$ | 12 | 13 | 14 | | | 2 | 6 | | | 3 | | | | | | 34 |
| 1 | | | 4 | 5 | | $7^1$ | 8 | 9 | 10 | 11 | 12 | | | | | 2 | 6 | | | 3 | | | | | | 35 |
| 1 | | | 4 | 5 | 6 | 7 | 8 | 9 | $10^1$ | $11^2$ | 12 | 13 | | | | 2 | | | | 3 | | | | | | 36 |
| 1 | | | 4 | 5 | 6 | 7 | 8 | 9 | 10 | $11^1$ | 12 | | | | | 2 | | | | 3 | | | | | | 37 |
| 1 | | | 4 | 5 | 6 | 7 | 8 | 9 | $10^1$ | $11^2$ | 12 | 13 | | | | 2 | | | | 3 | | | | | | 38 |
| 1 | | | 4 | 5 | $6^3$ | $7^2$ | 8 | 9 | 10 | $11^1$ | 12 | 13 | | | | 2 | | | | 3 | | 14 | | | | 39 |
| 1 | | | 4 | 5 | 6 | $7^1$ | 8 | 9 | 10 | $11^2$ | 12 | | 14 | | | 2 | | | | 3 | | $13^3$ | | | | 40 |
| 1 | | | 4 | 5 | 6 | $7^3$ | 8 | 9 | $10^1$ | 11 | $12^2$ | 13 | 14 | | | 2 | | | | 3 | | | | | | 41 |
| 1 | | | 4 | 5 | 6 | $7^2$ | 8 | 9 | $10^1$ | 11 | 12 | 13 | | | | 2 | | | | 3 | | | | | | 42 |
| 1 | | | 4 | 5 | 6 | 7 | 8 | 9 | $10^1$ | $11^2$ | 12 | 13 | 14 | | | $2^3$ | | | | 3 | | | | | | 43 |
| 1 | | | $4^3$ | 5 | 6 | 7 | $8^1$ | 9 | 10 | $11^2$ | 12 | 13 | 14 | | | | | | | 3 | | | | 2 | | 44 |
| 1 | | | 4 | 5 | 6 | 7 | $8^2$ | 9 | $10^1$ | 11 | 12 | 13 | 14 | | | | | | | 3 | | | | $2^3$ | | 45 |
| 1 | | | 4 | 5 | 6 | $7^1$ | 8 | 9 | 10 | $11^2$ | 12 | 13 | 14 | | | | | | | 3 | | | | $2^5$ | 1 | 46 |

**Coca-Cola Cup**

| | | | |
|---|---|---|---|
| First Round | Gillingham | (a) | 1-0 |
| | | (h) | 3-0 |
| Second Round | Stockport Co | (h) | 4-1 |
| | | (a) | 1-2 |
| Third Round | Arsenal | (a) | 1-4 |

**FA Cup**

| | | | |
|---|---|---|---|
| Third Round | Crewe Alex | (a) | 2-1 |
| Fourth Round | Stockport Co | (h) | 2-1 |
| Fifth Round | Leeds U | (a) | 2-3 |

BLACKBURN ROVERS 1997–98    *Back row (left to right):* Jason Wilcox, Lars Bohinen, Tore Pedersen, Alan Fettis, Tim Flowers, John Filan, Anthony Williams, Stuart Ripley, Per Pedersen, Jeff Kenna.

*Middle row:* Arnoldo Longaretti, Roy Tunks, Martin Dahlin, Tim Sherwood, Chris Coleman, Stephane Henchoz, Chris Sutton, Colin Hendry, Patrik Valery, Mark Taylor, Alan Smith.
*Front row:* Kevin Gallacher, Anders Andersson, Marlon Broomes, Tony Parkes, Roy Hodgson (Manager), Derek Fazackerley, Gary Croft, Damien Duff, Billy McKinlay.
(Photograph: Action Images)

# FA Premiership    BLACKBURN ROVERS

*Ewood Park, Blackburn BB2 4JF.* Telephone: (01254) 698888. Fax: (01254) 671042. Ticket Hotline: 0321 101010. Clubcall: 0891 121179. Club Shop-Mail Order: (01254) 672333.

*Ground capacity:* 31,367.

*Record attendance:* 62,522 v Bolton W, FA Cup 6th rd, 2 March 1929.

*Record receipts:* £333,067 v Liverpool, Coca-Cola Cup 4th rd, 30 November 1994.

*Pitch measurements:* 115yd × 72yd.

*Chairman:* R. D. Coar BSC. *Vice-Chairman:* R. L. Matthewman. *Directors:* J. O. Williams BSC. (Chief Executive), K. C. Lee, I. R. Stanners, G. R. Root FCMA. T. M. Finn.

*Manager:* Roy Hodgson. *Physio:* Mark Taylor. *Assistant Manager:* Tony Parkes. *Coach:* Derek Fazackerley.

*Commercial Manager:* Ken Beamish.

*Secretary:* Tom Finn. *Stadium Manager:* M. Highmore.

*Year Formed:* 1875. *Turned Professional:* 1880. *Ltd Co.:* 1897.

*Club Nickname:* Rovers.

*Previous Grounds:* 1875-76, all matches played away; 1876, Oozehead Ground; 1877, Pleasington Cricket Ground; 1878, Alexandra Meadows; 1881, Leamington Road; 1890, Ewood Park.

*Foundation:* It was in 1875 that some Public School old boys called a meeting at which the Blackburn Rovers club was formed and the colours blue and white adopted. The leading light was John Lewis, later to become a founder of the Lancashire FA, a famous referee who was in charge of two FA Cup Finals, and a vice-president of both the FA and the Football League.

*First Football League game:* 15 September 1888, Football League, v Accrington (h) D 5-5 – Arthur; Beverley, James Southworth; Douglas, Almond, Forrest; Beresford (1), Walton, John Southworth (1), Fecitt (1), Townley (2).

*Record League Victory:* 9–0 v Middlesbrough, Division 2, 6 November 1954 – Elvy; Suart, Eckersley; Clayton, Kelly, Bell; Mooney (3), Crossan (2), Briggs, Quigley (3), Langton (1).

*Record Cup Victory:* 11–0 v Rossendale, FA Cup 1st rd, 13 October 1884 – Arthur; Hopwood, McIntyre; Forrest, Blenkhorn, Lofthouse; Sowerbutts (2), J. Brown (1), Fecitt (4), Barton (3), Birtwistle (1).

*Record Defeat:* 0–8 v Arsenal, Division 1, 25 February 1933.

*Most League Points (2 for a win):* 60, Division 3, 1974–75.

*Most League Points (3 for a win):* 89, FA Premier League, 1994–95.

*Most League Goals:* 114, Division 2, 1954–55.

*Highest League Scorer in Season:* Ted Harper, 43, Division 1, 1925–26.

*Most League Goals in Total Aggregate:* Simon Garner, 168, 1978–92.

*Most Capped Player:* Bob Crompton, 41, England.

*Most League Appearances:* Derek Fazackerley, 596, 1970–86.

*Record Transfer Fee Received:* £15,000,000 from Newcastle U for Alan Shearer, July 1996.

*Record Transfer Fee Paid:* £7,250,000 to Southampton for Kevin Davies, June 1998.

*Football League Record:* 1888 Founder Member of the League; 1936–39 Division 2; 1946–48 Division 1; 1948–58 Division 2; 1958–66 Division 1; 1966–71 Division 2; 1971–75 Division 3; 1975–79 Division 2; 1979–80 Division 3; 1980–92 Division 2; 1992– FA Premier League.

*Honours: FA Premier League:* – Champions 1994–95; Runners-up 1993–94. *Football League: Division 1* – Champions 1911–12, 1913–14; *Division 2* – Champions 1938–39; Runners-up 1957–58; *Division 3* – Champions 1974–75; Runners-up 1979–80. *FA Cup:* Winners 1884, 1885, 1886, 1890, 1891, 1928; Runners-up 1882, 1960. *Football League Cup:* Semi-final 1962, 1993. *Full Members' Cup:* Winners 1987. **European Competitions:** *European Cup:* 1995–96. *UEFA Cup:* 1994–95.

*Colours:* Blue and white halved shirts, white shorts with blue trim, white stockings with blue trim.
*Change colours:* Yellow and royal blue.

**Did you know?**
When Blackburn Rovers beat Everton 5-1 on 16 September 1922, Johnny McIntyre scored four second half goals in five minutes: 55, 56, 57, 59 minutes.

## BLACKBURN ROVERS 1997–98 LEAGUE RECORD

| Match No. | Date | Venue | Opponents | Result | H/T Score | Lg. Pos. | Goalscorers | Attendance |
|---|---|---|---|---|---|---|---|---|
| 1 | Aug 9 | H | Derby Co | W | 1-0 | 1-0 | — | Gallacher 20 | 23,557 |
| 2 | 13 | A | Aston Villa | W | 4-0 | 3-0 | — | Sutton 3 21, 25, 41, Gallacher 71 | 37,122 |
| 3 | 23 | H | Liverpool | D | 1-1 | 0-0 | 1 | Dahlin 84 | 30,187 |
| 4 | 25 | H | Sheffield W | W | 7-2 | 5-1 | — | Gallacher 2 3, 7, Hyde (og) 10, Wilcox 20, Sutton 2 24, 74, Bohinen 53 | 19,618 |
| 5 | 30 | A | Crystal Palace | W | 2-1 | 2-0 | 1 | Sutton 23, Gallacher 31 | 20,849 |
| 6 | Sept 14 | H | Leeds U | L | 3-4 | 3-4 | 2 | Gallacher 8, Sutton (pen) 16, Dahlin 33 | 21,956 |
| 7 | 20 | A | Tottenham H | D | 0-0 | 0-0 | 3 | | 26,573 |
| 8 | 24 | A | Leicester C | D | 1-1 | 1-1 | — | Sutton 36 | 19,921 |
| 9 | 28 | H | Coventry C | D | 0-0 | 0-0 | 5 | | 19,086 |
| 10 | Oct 4 | A | Wimbledon | W | 1-0 | 1-0 | 3 | Sutton 6 | 15,600 |
| 11 | 18 | H | Southampton | W | 1-0 | 1-0 | 2 | Sherwood 26 | 24,130 |
| 12 | 25 | A | Newcastle U | D | 1-1 | 0-1 | 3 | Sutton 57 | 36,716 |
| 13 | Nov 1 | A | Barnsley | D | 1-1 | 1-0 | 3 | Sherwood 30 | 18,687 |
| 14 | 8 | H | Everton | W | 3-2 | 1-1 | 3 | Gallacher 37, Duff 81, Sherwood 84 | 25,397 |
| 15 | 22 | H | Chelsea | W | 1-0 | 1-0 | 2 | Croft 11 | 27,683 |
| 16 | 30 | A | Manchester U | L | 0-4 | 0-1 | 3 | | 55,175 |
| 17 | Dec 6 | H | Bolton W | W | 3-1 | 2-0 | 3 | Gallacher 4, Sutton 21, Wilcox 90 | 25,503 |
| 18 | 13 | A | Arsenal | W | 3-1 | 0-1 | 2 | Wilcox 57, Gallacher 65, Sherwood 89 | 38,147 |
| 19 | 20 | H | West Ham U | W | 3-0 | 1-0 | 2 | Ripley 22, Duff 2 51, 72 | 21,653 |
| 20 | 26 | A | Sheffield W | D | 0-0 | 0-0 | 2 | | 33,502 |
| 21 | 28 | H | Crystal Palace | D | 2-2 | 1-1 | 2 | Gallacher 27, Sutton 78 | 23,872 |
| 22 | Jan 11 | A | Derby Co | L | 1-3 | 0-2 | 3 | Sutton 87 | 27,823 |
| 23 | 17 | H | Aston Villa | W | 5-0 | 2-0 | 2 | Sherwood 22, Gallacher 3 30, 54, 69, Ripley 81 | 24,834 |
| 24 | 31 | A | Liverpool | D | 0-0 | 0-0 | 3 | | 43,890 |
| 25 | Feb 7 | H | Tottenham H | L | 0-3 | 0-1 | 4 | | 30,388 |
| 26 | 21 | A | Southampton | L | 0-3 | 0-1 | 5 | | 15,162 |
| 27 | 28 | H | Leicester C | W | 5-3 | 3-0 | 2 | Dahlin 11, Sutton 3 25, 45, 47, Hendry 63 | 24,854 |
| 28 | Mar 11 | A | Leeds U | L | 0-4 | 0-0 | — | | 32,935 |
| 29 | 14 | A | Everton | L | 0-1 | 0-0 | 6 | | 33,423 |
| 30 | 31 | H | Barnsley | W | 2-1 | 1-0 | — | Dahlin 8, Gallacher 87 | 24,179 |
| 31 | Apr 6 | H | Manchester U | L | 1-3 | 1-0 | — | Sutton (pen) 32 | 30,547 |
| 32 | 11 | A | Bolton W | L | 1-2 | 0-1 | 6 | Duff 51 | 25,000 |
| 33 | 13 | H | Arsenal | L | 1-4 | 0-4 | 6 | Gallacher 51 | 28,212 |
| 34 | 18 | A | West Ham U | L | 1-2 | 1-2 | 7 | Wilcox 45 | 24,733 |
| 35 | 25 | H | Wimbledon | D | 0-0 | 0-0 | 6 | | 24,848 |
| 36 | 29 | A | Chelsea | W | 1-0 | 0-0 | — | Gallacher 48 | 33,311 |
| 37 | May 2 | A | Coventry C | L | 0-2 | 0-2 | 6 | | 18,792 |
| 38 | 10 | H | Newcastle U | W | 1-0 | 0-0 | 6 | Sutton 88 | 29,300 |

**Final League Position: 6**          1996–97 PREM 13

### GOALSCORERS
*League (57):* Sutton 18 (2 pens), Gallacher 16, Sherwood 5, Dahlin 4, Duff 4, Wilcox 4, Ripley 2, Bohinen 1, Croft 1, Hendry 1, own goal 1.
*Coca-Cola Cup (7):* Dahlin 2, Andersson 1, Bohinen 1, Gallacher 1, McKinlay 1, Sutton 1.
*FA Cup (10):* Gallacher 3, Sherwood 2, Sutton 2, Duff 1, Ripley 1, own goal 1.

| Filan J 7 | Valery P 14 + 1 | Kenna J 37 | Henchoz S 36 | Hendry C 34 | McKinlay B 26 + 4 | Ripley S 25 + 4 | Gallacher K 31 + 2 | Sutton C 35 | Flitcroft G 28 + 5 | Wilcox J 24 + 7 | Pearce I 11 + 4 | Andersson A 1 + 3 | Dahlin M 11 + 10 | Bohinen L 6 + 10 | Flowers T 24 + 1 | Duff D 17 + 9 | Sherwood T 29 + 2 | Croft G 19 + 4 | Pedersen T 3 + 2 | Beattie J — + 3 | Fettis A 7 + 1 | Broomes M 2 + 2 | Davidson C 1 | Match No. |
|---|---|---|---|---|---|---|---|---|---|---|---|---|---|---|---|---|---|---|---|---|---|---|---|---|
| 1 | 2 | 3 | 4 | $5^1$ | 6 | $7^2$ | 8 | $9^3$ | 10 | 11 | 12 | 13 | 14 | | | | | | | | | | | 1 |
| 1 | 2 | 3 | $4^1$ | 5 | 6 | $7^2$ | $8^3$ | 9 | 10 | 11 | 12 | | 14 | 13 | | | | | | | | | | 2 |
| 1 | 2 | 3 | $4^1$ | 5 | $6^3$ | 7 | 8 | 9 | 10 | $11^{12}$ | 12 | | 13 | 14 | | | | | | | | | | 3 |
| $1^6$ | 2 | 3 | | 5 | $6^2$ | 7 | 8 | 9 | 10 | $11^1$ | 4 | | 12 | 13 | 15 | | | | | | | | | 4 |
| | 2 | 3 | 4 | $5^1$ | | 7 | 8 | 9 | 10 | | | 12 | 13 | $11^2$ | 1 | | 6 | | | | | | | 5 |
| | $2^3$ | 3 | 4 | 5 | | | 8 | 9 | 10 | $11^1$ | | 14 | 7 | $6^2$ | 1 | 12 | 13 | | | | | | | 6 |
| | 2 | 3 | 6 | 5 | 12 | | | 9 | 10 | $11^1$ | | | $8^2$ | 7 | 1 | 4 | 13 | | | | | | | 7 |
| | $2^2$ | 3 | $4^1$ | 5 | 13 | 7 | | 9 | 10 | 11 | | | 8 | 12 | 1 | | 6 | | | | | | | 8 |
| | $2^2$ | 3 | 4 | 5 | | | 8 | 9 | 10 | 11 | | | $7^1$ | 12 | 1 | 13 | 6 | | | | | | | 9 |
| | 2 | | 4 | 5 | | 7 | 8 | 9 | 10 | 11 | | | | | 1 | | 6 | 3 | | | | | | 10 |
| | 2 | | 4 | 5 | 12 | 7 | 8 | 9 | 10 | | | | | | 1 | 11 | 6 | 3 | | | | | | 11 |
| | 2 | | 4 | 5 | 6 | $7^1$ | 8 | 9 | | | 12 | | | $11^2$ | 1 | 13 | 10 | 3 | | | | | | 12 |
| | 2 | | 4 | $5^2$ | 6 | 7 | 8 | 9 | | | 12 | | | | 1 | $11^1$ | 10 | 3 | 13 | | | | | 13 |
| | 2 | | 4 | | 11 | 7 | 8 | 9 | $10^2$ | | 12 | | | | 1 | 13 | 6 | $3^1$ | 5 | | | | | 14 |
| | 2 | | 4 | | 11 | $7^1$ | 8 | 9 | 10 | | 12 | | | | 1 | | 6 | 3 | 5 | | | | | 15 |
| | 2 | | 4 | | $6^1$ | 7 | 12 | 9 | 10 | $11^3$ | | | 13 | | 1 | 14 | 8 | 3 | 5 | | | | | 16 |
| | 2 | | 4 | 5 | 6 | $7^3$ | 8 | 9 | | | 12 | 13 | 14 | | 1 | $11^2$ | $10^1$ | 3 | | | | | | 17 |
| | 2 | | 4 | 5 | 6 | $7^1$ | 8 | 9 | | | 12 | | | 11 | 1 | | 10 | 3 | | | | | | 18 |
| | 2 | | 4 | 5 | 6 | $7^1$ | $8^3$ | | | | 12 | | 13 | 11 | 1 | $9^1$ | 10 | 3 | 14 | | | | | 19 |
| | 2 | | 4 | 5 | 6 | $7^1$ | 8 | 9 | | | 12 | 13 | | $11^2$ | | | 10 | 3 | | | 1 | | | 20 |
| | 2 | | 4 | $5^2$ | | 7 | 8 | 9 | 10 | | 12 | | | | 1 | 11 | 6 | $3^1$ | 13 | | | | | 21 |
| | 2 | | 4 | 5 | | 7 | 8 | 9 | 10 | | 12 | | | | 1 | 11 | 6 | $3^1$ | | | | | | 22 |
| | 2 | | 4 | 5 | 12 | 7 | $8^2$ | 9 | $10^1$ | | 3 | | | | 1 | 11 | 6 | 13 | | | | | | 23 |
| | 2 | | 4 | 5 | 6 | 7 | $8^1$ | 9 | | 11 | | | | | 1 | 12 | 10 | 3 | | | | | | 24 |
| | 2 | | 4 | 5 | $6^1$ | 7 | | 9 | | 11 | 12 | 13 | | | 1 | 10 | 8 | $3^2$ | | | | | | 25 |
| | 2 | | | 5 | | 7 | 8 | $9^2$ | $10^1$ | | 12 | | | | 1 | 11 | 6 | 3 | 4 | 13 | | | | 26 |
| | 2 | | $4^2$ | 5 | | | $8^1$ | 9 | 10 | 11 | 12 | | 7 | | | | 6 | 3 | 13 | | 1 | | | 27 |
| | 2 | | 4 | 5 | 12 | | 8 | 9 | 10 | 11 | | | 7 | | | | 6 | $3^1$ | | | 1 | | | 28 |
| | 2 | | 4 | 5 | 11 | $7^1$ | 8 | 9 | 10 | | | | | | 1 | 12 | 6 | 3 | | | | | | 29 |
| | 2 | | 4 | 5 | 6 | $7^2$ | | 9 | 10 | | 12 | | | | 16 | $11^1$ | 8 | 3 | 13 | | 15 | | | 30 |
| | 2 | | 4 | 5 | 6 | | 8 | 9 | 10 | | | | 7 | | 1 | 11 | | 3 | | | | | | 31 |
| | 2 | | 4 | 5 | 6 | | $8^2$ | 9 | 10 | | 12 | | $7^1$ | | 1 | 11 | | 3 | 13 | | | | | 32 |
| 12 | 2 | | 4 | 5 | 13 | $7^2$ | 8 | | 10 | 11 | | | | | $9^3$ | | 6 | $3^1$ | 14 | | 1 | | | 33 |
| | $2^1$ | 3 | 4 | 5 | 6 | $7^2$ | 8 | 9 | 10 | 11 | | | | | | 13 | | | 12 | | 1 | | | 34 |
| 1 | 2 | 3 | 4 | | | 7 | 8 | 9 | $10^1$ | | 12 | | | | | 11 | 6 | | | | | 5 | | 35 |
| 1 | 2 | 3 | 4 | 5 | 6 | | 8 | 9 | 10 | | | | | | | $11^2$ | $7^1$ | 12 | | | | 13 | | 36 |
| 1 | $2^2$ | 7 | 4 | 5 | $6^1$ | | 8 | 9 | 10 | 11 | | | | | | 13 | 12 | 3 | | | | | | 37 |
| | 2 | | 4 | 5 | 6 | $7^1$ | 8 | 9 | 10 | | | | 13 | | 1 | 11 | $12^2$ | 3 | | | | | | 38 |

**Coca-Cola Cup**

| | | | |
|---|---|---|---|
| Second Round | Preston NE | (h) | 6-0 |
| | | (a) | 0-1 |
| Third Round | Chelsea | (a) | 1-1 |

**FA Cup**

| | | | |
|---|---|---|---|
| Third Round | Wigan Ath | (h) | 4-2 |
| Fourth Round | Sheffield W | (a) | 3-0 |
| Fifth Round | West Ham U | (a) | 2-2 |
| | | (h) | 1-1 |

BLACKPOOL, 1997–98    *Back row (left to right):* Phil Robinson, Robbie Talbot, Gary Brabin, James Quinn, Chris Malkin, Tony Butler, Henry Heighton, Steve Banks, Phil Barnes, Clarke Carlisle, Phil Clarkson, Jamie Cross, Mike Davies (Reserve Manager), Tamas Byrne, Simon Seaton.

*Middle row:* Michael Bamber, Chris Ellis, Ian Dickinson, Mick Hennigan (Assistant Manager), Alan Crawford (Youth Manager), Paul Carden, Darren Bradshaw, Brett Ormerod, Anton Rogan, Keith Russell, Ben Dixon, John Reed, Jason Lydiate, Tony Ellis, Paul Kelly (Physio), Jason Jarrett, Lee Shockledge, Phil Thompson.

*Front row:* Jackie Burke (Kit Man), Fred O'Donoghue (Youth Liaison Officer), Paul Haddow, Marvin Bryan, Mark Bonner, Nigel Worthington (Player/Manager), David Linighan, Micky Mellon, Andy Preece, Lee Philpott, Jack Chapman (Chief Scout).

*Kneeling:* Chris Lazenby, Adam Nowland, Simon Bridges, Scott Sugden, Steve Longworth, Jamie Skeoch.

# Division 2 **BLACKPOOL**

***Bloomfield Rd Ground, Blackpool FY1 6JJ.*** Telephone: (01253) 404331 (Ticket/Credit Bookings), (01253) 405331 (Shop/General Enquiries). Fax: (01253) 405011. Clubcall: 0891 121648.

***Ground capacity:*** 11,295.

***Record attendance:*** 38,098 v Wolverhampton W, Division 1, 17 September 1955.

***Record receipts:*** £73,046 v Chelsea, Coca-Cola Cup 2nd rd 1st leg, 18 September 1996.

***Pitch measurements:*** 112yd × 74yd.

***Chairman:*** Mrs V. Oyston. ***Deputy Chairman:*** K. Chadwick.

***Managing Director:*** Mrs G. Bridge.

***Directors:*** C. Muir OBE, O. J. Oyston, G. Warburton, M. Joyce.

***Manager:*** Nigel Worthington.

***Secretary:*** Carol Banks.

***Commercial Director:*** Geoff Warburton.

***Commercial Manager:*** Frank Layton.

***Physio:*** Paul Kelly. ***Stadium Manager:*** John Turner.

***Year Formed:*** 1887. ***Turned Professional:*** 1887. ***Ltd Co.:*** 1896.

***Previous Name:*** 'South Shore' combined with Blackpool in 1899, twelve years after the latter had been formed on the breaking up of the old 'Blackpool St John's' club.

***Club Nickname:*** 'The Seasiders'.

***Previous Grounds:*** 1887, Raikes Hall Gardens; 1897, Athletic Grounds; 1899, Raikes Hall Gardens; 1899, Bloomfield Road.

***Foundation:*** Old boys of St. John's School who had formed themselves into a football club decided to establish a club bearing the name of their town and Blackpool FC came into being at a meeting at the Stanley Arms Hotel in the summer of 1887. In their first season playing at Raikes Hall Gardens, the club won both the Lancashire Junior Cup and the Fylde Cup.

***First Football League game:*** 5 September 1896, Division 2, v Lincoln C (a) L 1-3 – Douglas; Parr, Bowman; Stuart, Stirzaker, Norris; Clarkin, Donnelly, R. Parkinson, Mount (1), J. Parkinson.

***Record League Victory:*** 7–0 v Reading (home), Division 2, 10 November 1928 – Mercer; Gibson, Hamilton, Watson, Wilson, Grant, Ritchie, Oxberry (2), Hampson (5), Tufnell, Neal. 7–0 v Preston NE (away), Division 1, 1 May 1948 – Robinson; Shimwell, Crosland; Buchan, Hayward, Kelly; Hobson, Munro (1), McIntosh (5), McCall, Rickett (1). 7–0 v Sunderland (home), Division 1, 5 October 1957 – Farm; Armfield, Garrett, Kelly (J), Gratrix, Kelly (H), Matthews, Taylor (2), Charnley (2), Durie (2), Perry (1).

***Record Cup Victory:*** 7–1 v Charlton Ath, League Cup 2nd rd, 25 September 1963 – Harvey; Armfield, Martin; Crawford, Gratrix, Cranston; Lea, Ball (1), Charnley (4), Durie (1), Oates (1).

***Record Defeat:*** 1–10 v Small Heath, Division 2, 2 March 1901 and v Huddersfield T, Division 1, 13 December 1930.

***Most League Points (2 for a win):*** 58, Division 2, 1929–30 and Division 2, 1967–68.

***Most League Points (3 for a win):*** 86, Division 4, 1984–85.

***Most League Goals:*** 98, Division 2, 1929–30.

***Highest League Scorer in Season:*** Jimmy Hampson, 45, Division 2, 1929–30.

***Most League Goals in Total Aggregate:*** Jimmy Hampson, 246, 1927–38.

***Most Capped Player:*** Jimmy Armfield, 43, England.

***Most League Appearances:*** Jimmy Armfield, 568, 1952–71.

***Record Transfer Fee Received:*** £750,000 from QPR for Trevor Sinclair, August 1993.

***Record Transfer Fee Paid:*** £275,000 to Millwall for Chris Malkin, October 1996.

***Football League Record:*** 1896 Elected to Division 2; 1899 Failed re-election; 1900 Re-elected; 1900–30 Division 2; 1930–33 Division 1; 1933–37 Division 2; 1937–67 Division 1; 1967–70 Division 2; 1970–71 Division 1; 1971–78 Division 2; 1978–81 Division 3; 1981–85 Division 4; 1985–90 Division 3; 1990–92 Division 4; 1992–Division 2.

***Honours:*** *Football League:* Division 1 – Runners-up 1955–56; Division 2 – Champions 1929–30; Runners-up 1936–37, 1969–70; Division 4 – Runners-up 1984–85. *FA Cup:* Winners 1953; Runners-up 1948, 1951. *Football League Cup:* Semi-final 1962. *Anglo-Italian Cup:* Winners 1971; Runners-up 1972.

***Colours:*** All tangerine. ***Change colours:*** All royal blue.

**Did you know?**
Mike Conroy was Blackpool's Man of the Match on 28 March 1998 at York City. He made a goal after five minutes, had to go into goal after 55 minutes when the goalkeeper was sent off and was only beaten by the equaliser in injury time.

## BLACKPOOL 1997–98 LEAGUE RECORD

| Match No. | Date | Venue | Opponents | Result | H/T Score | Lg. Pos. | Goalscorers | Attendance |
|---|---|---|---|---|---|---|---|---|
| 1 | Aug 9 | H | Luton T | W 1-0 | 1-0 | — | Lydiate [11] | 6547 |
| 2 | 16 | A | Bristol C | L 0-2 | 0-0 | 12 | | 9043 |
| 3 | 23 | H | Wycombe W | L 2-4 | 1-2 | 20 | Quinn [23], Brabin [90] | 4733 |
| 4 | 30 | A | Bournemouth | L 0-2 | 0-1 | 22 | | 4196 |
| 5 | Sept 2 | A | Wrexham | W 4-3 | 0-2 | — | Ellis 3 [62, 69, 76], Bonner [82] | 3763 |
| 6 | 7 | H | Carlisle U | W 2-1 | 1-0 | 7 | Ellis [19], Carlisle [90] | 7259 |
| 7 | 13 | A | Wigan Ath | L 0-3 | 0-0 | 14 | | 5517 |
| 8 | 20 | H | Oldham Ath | D 2-2 | 1-1 | 14 | Quinn [42], Philpott [53] | 7174 |
| 9 | 27 | H | Southend U | W 3-0 | 1-0 | 7 | Bonner [12], Ellis [80], Clarkson [88] | 4542 |
| 10 | Oct 4 | A | Millwall | L 1-2 | 0-0 | 13 | Ellis [86] | 7042 |
| 11 | 11 | A | Fulham | L 0-1 | 0-1 | 17 | | 7760 |
| 12 | 18 | H | Grimsby T | D 2-2 | 1-1 | 17 | Quinn [44], Ellis [77] | 5234 |
| 13 | 21 | H | Chesterfield | W 2-1 | 1-0 | — | Clarkson [42], Quinn (pen) [47] | 3682 |
| 14 | 25 | A | Bristol R | W 3-0 | 1-0 | 9 | Bonner [30], Clarkson [48], Preece [53] | 6183 |
| 15 | Nov 1 | A | Watford | L 1-4 | 0-1 | 12 | Preece [74] | 9723 |
| 16 | 4 | H | Northampton T | D 1-1 | 1-0 | — | Clarkson [37] | 3685 |
| 17 | 8 | H | Burnley | W 2-1 | 1-1 | 10 | Clarkson [41], Preece [74] | 7429 |
| 18 | 18 | A | Gillingham | D 1-1 | 0-1 | — | Ellis [90] | 5045 |
| 19 | 22 | H | York C | W 1-0 | 0-0 | 8 | Strong [68] | 4508 |
| 20 | 29 | A | Walsall | L 1-2 | 1-0 | 9 | Clarkson [35] | 3933 |
| 21 | Dec 2 | H | Plymouth Arg | D 0-0 | 0-0 | — | | 3281 |
| 22 | 13 | A | Brentford | L 1-3 | 1-1 | 11 | Preece [4] | 3725 |
| 23 | 20 | H | Preston NE | W 2-1 | 2-0 | 9 | Preece [21], Philpott [37] | 8342 |
| 24 | 26 | A | Carlisle U | D 1-1 | 0-1 | 11 | Ormerod [53] | 8010 |
| 25 | 28 | H | Wrexham | L 1-2 | 1-0 | 12 | Ormerod [17] | 5424 |
| 26 | Jan 10 | A | Luton T | L 0-3 | 0-1 | 14 | | 5574 |
| 27 | 17 | H | Bournemouth | W 1-0 | 0-0 | 12 | Clarkson [19] | 4550 |
| 28 | 24 | A | Wycombe W | L 1-2 | 1-1 | 14 | Preece [20] | 5073 |
| 29 | 31 | H | Wigan Ath | L 0-2 | 0-2 | 15 | | 5288 |
| 30 | Feb 3 | H | Bristol C | D 2-2 | 0-0 | — | Preece [54], Bent [88] | 3724 |
| 31 | 7 | A | Oldham Ath | W 1-0 | 0-0 | 13 | Bent [56] | 6576 |
| 32 | 14 | H | Millwall | W 3-0 | 3-0 | 11 | Bryan [7], Malkin [18], Preece [39] | 4455 |
| 33 | 21 | A | Southend U | L 1-2 | 0-2 | 12 | Brabin [49] | 3340 |
| 34 | 24 | A | Grimsby T | L 0-1 | 0-0 | — | | 4924 |
| 35 | 28 | H | Fulham | W 2-1 | 0-1 | 12 | Preece [77], Clarkson [85] | 5183 |
| 36 | Mar 7 | H | Watford | D 1-1 | 0-0 | 12 | Clarkson [88] | 5237 |
| 37 | 14 | A | Northampton T | L 0-2 | 0-1 | 15 | | 6586 |
| 38 | 21 | H | Gillingham | W 2-1 | 0-0 | 13 | Malkin [73], Clarkson [83] | 4165 |
| 39 | 28 | H | York C | D 1-1 | 1-0 | 11 | Preece [5] | 3650 |
| 40 | Apr 4 | H | Walsall | W 1-0 | 0-0 | 11 | Preece [48] | 4451 |
| 41 | 7 | A | Burnley | W 2-1 | 1-1 | — | Clarkson [45], Bent [51] | 13,413 |
| 42 | 11 | A | Plymouth Arg | L 1-3 | 1-0 | 10 | Heathcote (og) [28] | 5655 |
| 43 | 13 | H | Brentford | L 1-2 | 0-2 | 10 | Taylor [81] | 3926 |
| 44 | 18 | A | Preston NE | D 3-3 | 2-1 | 11 | Clarkson 2 [3, 65], Hills [45] | 13,500 |
| 45 | 25 | H | Bristol R | W 1-0 | 0-0 | 12 | Brabin [68] | 7057 |
| 46 | May 2 | A | Chesterfield | D 1-1 | 0-0 | 12 | Carlisle [86] | 4462 |

**Final League Position: 12**          1996–97 DIV2 7

## GOALSCORERS

League (59): Clarkson 13, Preece 11, Ellis 8, Quinn 4 (1 pen), Bent 3, Bonner 3, Brabin 3, Carlisle 2, Malkin 2, Ormerod 2, Philpott 2, Bryan 1, Hills 1, Lydiate 1, Strong 1, Taylor 1, own goal 1.
Coca-Cola Cup (3): Linighan 2, Preece 1.
FA Cup (5): Clarkson 2, Ellis 1, Linighan 1, Preece 1.

| Banks S 45 | Bryan M 43 | Bradshaw D 6 | Butler T 37 | Lydiate J 22+1 | Brabin G 15+9 | Bonner M 32 | Clarkson P 42+3 | Quinn J 11+3 | Philpott L 27+8 | Preece A 42+2 | Malkin C 13+7 | Linighan D 26+3 | Mellon M 9+1 | Rogan A 1 | Bent J 25+11 | Ellis T 18 | Worthington N 4+5 | Carlisle C 8+3 | King P 6 | Dixon B 6+1 | Strong G 11 | Ormerod B 5+4 | Hughes I 20+1 | Foster M 1 | Reed J —+3 | Hills J 19 | Longworth S —+2 | Haddow P —+1 | Greenacre C 2+2 | Conroy M 5+1 | Taylor S 3+2 | Barnes P 1 | Thompson P 1 | Nowland A —+1 | Match No. |
|---|---|---|---|---|---|---|---|---|---|---|---|---|---|---|---|---|---|---|---|---|---|---|---|---|---|---|---|---|---|---|---|---|---|---|---|
| 1 | 2 | 3 | 4 | 5 | 6 | 7 | 8 | 9 | 10 | 11 | | | | | | | | | | | | | | | | | | | | | | | | | 1 |
| 1 | 2¹ | 3 | 4 | 5 | 6 | 7 | 8 | | 10 | 11 | 9 | 12 | | | | | | | | | | | | | | | | | | | | | | | 2 |
| 1 | 2 | 3¹ | 4 | 5 | 6 | 7³ | 8 | 9 | 10² | 11 | 13 | 12 | 14 | | | | | | | | | | | | | | | | | | | | | | 3 |
| 1 | 2 | | 4 | 5 | 6 | 7¹ | 8² | | | 11 | 12 | | 9 | | 3 | 13 | 10 | | | | | | | | | | | | | | | | | | 4 |
| 1 | 2 | | 4 | | | 7 | 6¹ | | 12 | 11 | | | 8 | | 9 | 10 | 3 | 5 | | | | | | | | | | | | | | | | | 5 |
| 1 | 2 | 4² | | 12 | | 7 | 6 | | 13 | 11 | | | 8 | | 9 | 10 | 3¹ | 5 | | | | | | | | | | | | | | | | | 6 |
| 1 | 2 | | 3 | 4² | | 7 | 6 | 12 | 13 | 11 | | | 8 | | 9¹ | 10 | | 5 | | | | | | | | | | | | | | | | | 7 |
| 1 | 2² | 3 | | 4 | | 7 | | 9 | 6 | 11¹ | | 5 | 8 | 12 | 10 | | 13 | | | | | | | | | | | | | | | | | | 8 |
| 1 | 2 | 3 | | 4 | | 7¹ | 12 | 9² | | 11 | 13 | 5⁴ | 8 | | 6 | 10 | 14 | | | | | | | | | | | | | | | | | | 9 |
| 1 | 2 | 3² | | 4 | | 7 | 6 | | 11 | 9¹ | 5 | | 8 | | 12 | 10 | 13 | | | | | | | | | | | | | | | | | | 10 |
| 1 | 2 | | | 4 | | 7 | 12 | 9 | 6¹ | 11 | | 5 | | | 10 | | 3 | | | | | | | | | | | | | | | | | | 11 |
| 1 | 2 | | | 4 | | 7 | 12 | 9 | 6¹ | 11 | | 5 | | | 13 | 10 | 3² | | | | | | | | | | | | | | | | | | 12 |
| 1 | 2 | | | 4 | | 7 | 8 | 9 | 6 | 11 | | 5 | | | 12 | 10 | 3¹ | | | | | | | | | | | | | | | | | | 13 |
| 1 | 2 | | | 4 | 12 | 7 | 8 | 9² | 6 | 11¹ | | 5 | | | 13 | 10 | 14 | 3³ | | | | | | | | | | | | | | | | | 14 |
| 1 | 2 | | | 4 | | 7 | 8 | 9¹ | 6 | 11 | | 5 | | | 12 | 10 | 3 | | | | | | | | | | | | | | | | | | 15 |
| 1 | 2 | | | 4 | | 7 | 8 | 9 | 6 | 11 | | 5 | | | | 10 | 3 | | | | | | | | | | | | | | | | | | 16 |
| 1 | 2 | | | 4 | 12 | 7 | 8 | 9 | 6 | 11 | | 5 | | | | 10 | 3¹ | | | | | | | | | | | | | | | | | | 17 |
| 1 | | | 4 | 2 | 6 | 7 | 8 | | 11 | 12 | | 5¹ | | | 9 | 10 | 3² | 13 | | | | | | | | | | | | | | | | | 18 |
| 1 | | | 4 | 2 | | 7 | 8 | | 11 | 6¹ | | | | | 9 | 10 | | | | | 3 | 5 | 12 | | | | | | | | | | | | 19 |
| 1 | | | 4 | 2 | | 7 | 8 | | 11¹ | 6² | 13 | | | | 9 | 10 | 12 | | | | 3 | 5 | | | | | | | | | | | | | 20 |
| 1 | 2 | | 4 | | 12 | 7 | 8 | | 11 | 9² | 6¹ | | | | | 10 | | | | | 3 | 5 | 13 | | | | | | | | | | | | 21 |
| 1 | 2 | | 4 | | | | 8 | | 11² | 10 | 9 | | | | 12 | | | | | | 3 | 5 | 6 | 7¹ | 13 | | | | | | | | | | 22 |
| 1 | 2 | | 4 | | | | 8 | | 11¹ | 10 | 9³ | 12 | | | 7² | | | | | | 3 | 5 | 13 | 6 | 14 | | | | | | | | | | 23 |
| 1 | 2 | | 4 | | | | 8 | | 11 | 10 | 9¹ | | | | 7 | | | | | | 3 | 5 | 12 | 6 | | | | | | | | | | | 24 |
| 1 | 2 | | 4 | | | 7 | 8 | | 11 | 10¹ | | 5 | | | 12 | | | | | | 9 | 3 | | 6 | | | | | | | | | | | 25 |
| 1 | 2 | | 4 | 5 | | 7 | 8 | | 11 | 10 | 6⁴ | | | | 12 | | 13 | | | | 9 | 3¹ | | | | | | | | | | | | | 26 |
| 1 | 2 | | 4 | | 6 | 7¹ | 8 | | 11 | 10 | | 5 | | | | | | | | | 9² | | | | | | 12 | | 3 | 13 | | | | | 27 |
| 1 | 2 | | | | 6 | 7² | 8 | | 11 | 12 | | | | | 10 | | | 4 | | | 9¹ | 5 | | | | 3 | | | 13 | | | | | | 28 |
| 1 | 2 | | | 12 | 6 | 7 | 8 | | 11 | 13 | | | | | 10 | | | 4¹ | | | 9² | 5 | | | | 3 | | | | | | | | | 29 |
| 1 | 2 | | 4 | | | 7 | 8 | | 12 | 11 | 9¹ | 6 | | | 10 | | | | | | | 5 | | | | 3 | | | | | | | | | 30 |
| 1 | 2 | | 4 | | | 7 | 8 | | 12 | 11 | 9² | 6 | | | 10 | | | | | | | 5¹ | | | | 3 | | | 13 | | | | | | 31 |
| 1 | 2 | | 4 | | 12 | 7 | 8 | | 13 | 11 | 9² | 6 | | | 10¹ | | | | | | | 5 | | | | 3 | | | | | | | | | 32 |
| 1 | 2 | | 4 | 6² | 12 | 7¹ | 8 | | 13 | 11 | 9 | | | | 10 | | | | | | | 5 | | | | 3 | | | | | | | | | 33 |
| 1 | 2 | | 4 | 5¹ | 10 | | 8 | | 12 | 11 | 9 | 6 | | | | | | | | | | 7 | | | | 3 | | | | | | | | | 34 |
| 1 | 2³ | | 4 | 5¹ | 10 | | 8 | | 12 | 11 | 9² | 6 | | | 13 | | | 14 | | | | 7 | | | | 3 | | | | | | | | | 35 |
| 1 | 2 | | 4 | 5¹ | 10 | | 8 | | 6 | 11 | 9 | | | | | | | | | | | 7 | | | | 3 | | | 12 | | | | | | 36 |
| 1 | 2 | | 4 | 5² | 10 | 7 | 8 | | 11 | 12 | | 6 | | | 13 | | | | | | | | | | | 3 | | | 9¹ | | | | | | 37 |
| 1 | 2 | | 4 | | | 7 | 8 | | 11 | 12 | | 6 | | | 10 | | | | | | | 5 | | | | 3 | | | 9¹ | | | | | | 38 |
| 1 | 2 | | 4 | | 7¹ | | 8 | | 11 | | | 6 | | | 10² | | | | | | | 5 | | | | 3 | | | 12 | 9 | 13 | | | | 39 |
| 1 | 2 | | 4 | | | | 8 | | 7 | 11 | | 6 | | | 10 | | | | | | | 5 | | | | 3 | | | | 9 | | | | | 40 |
| 1 | 2 | | 4 | | 7 | | 8 | | 11 | | | 6 | | | 10 | | | | | | | 5 | | | | 3 | | | | 9¹ | 12 | | | | 41 |
| | 2 | | 4 | | 12² | 7 | 8 | | 13 | 11 | | 6 | | | 10 | | | | | | | 5¹ | | | | 3 | | | | 9 | | 1 | | | 42 |
| 1 | 2¹ | | 4 | | 12 | | 8 | | 7 | 11 | | 6 | | | 10 | | | | | | | 5 | | | | 3 | | | | | 9 | | | | 43 |
| 1 | 2 | | 4 | | 12 | | 8 | | 7 | 11 | | 6 | | | 10¹ | | | | | | | 5 | | | | 3 | | | | 13 | 9² | | | | 44 |
| 1 | 2 | | | | 10 | | 8 | | 7 | 11 | | | | | | | 5 | | | | | 6 | | | | 3 | | | | | 9 | | 4 | | 45 |
| 1 | 2 | | 4 | | 10 | | 8 | | 11 | 9¹ | | 6 | | | | | | | | | | | 5 | | | 3 | 12 | | | | 7² | | | 13 | 46 |

**Coca-Cola Cup**

| | | | | |
|---|---|---|---|---|
| First Round | Manchester C | (h) | 1-0 | |
| | | (a) | 0-1 | |
| Second Round | Coventry C | (h) | 1-0 | |
| | | (a) | 1-3 | |

**FA Cup**

| | | | | |
|---|---|---|---|---|
| First Round | Blyth S | (h) | 4-3 | |
| Second Round | Oldham Ath | (a) | 1-2 | |

BOLTON WANDERERS 1997–98     *Back row (left to right):* Nicky Spooner, John Sheridan, Per Frandsen, Andy Todd, Neil Cox, Keith Branagan, Matthew Glennon, Gavin Ward, Nathan Blake, Scott Taylor, Simon Coleman, Alan Thompson.
*Middle row:* Ewan Simpson (Physio), Stephen McAnespie, John McGinlay, Chris Fairclough, Gerry Taggart, Hasney Aljofree, Mark Fish, Greg Strong, Stuart Whitehead, Martin Doherty, Lee Potter, Peter Beardsley, Scott Sellers, Colin Dyson (Kit Man).
*Front row:* Steve Carroll (Coach), Michael Johansen, Arnar Gunnlaugsson, Gudni Bergsson, Colin Todd (Manager), Jamie Pollock, Dean Holdsworth, Jimmy Phillips, Phil Brown (Coach).

# Division 1 BOLTON WANDERERS

**Reebok Stadium, Burnden Way, Lostock, Bolton BL6 6JW.** Telephone: (01204) 673673. Fax: (01204) 673773. Ticket Office: (01204) 673601.

**Ground capacity:** 25,000.

**Record attendance:** 69,912 v Manchester C, FA Cup 5th rd, 18 February 1933.

**Record receipts:** £202,031 v Tottenham H, Coca-Cola Cup 4th rd, 27 November 1996.

**Pitch measurements:** 114yd × 74yd.

**President:** Nat Lofthouse.

**Chairman:** G. Hargreaves.

**Directors:** P. A. Gartside, G. Ball, G. Seymour, G. Warburton, W. B. Warburton, B. Scowcroft.

**Team Manager:** Colin Todd. **Physio:** E. Simpson.

**Chief Executive & Secretary:** Des McBain. **Commercial Manager:** T. Holland.

**Year Formed:** 1874. **Turned Professional:** 1880. **Ltd Co.:** 1895.

**Previous Name:** 1874–77, Christ Church FC; 1877 became Bolton Wanderers.

**Club Nickname:** 'The Trotters'.

**Previous Grounds:** Park Recreation Ground and Cockle's Field before moving to Pike's Lane ground 1881; 1895–1997, Burnden Park.

**Foundation:** In 1874 boys of Christ Church Sunday School, Blackburn Street, led by their master Thomas Ogden, established a football club which went under the name of the school and whose president was Vicar of Christ Church. Membership was 6d (two and a half pence). When their president began to lay down too many rules about the use of church premises, the club broke away and formed Bolton Wanderers in 1877, holding their earliest meetings at the Gladstone Hotel.

**First Football League game:** 8 September 1888, Football League, v Derby Co (h), L 3-6 – Harrison; Robinson, Mitchell; Roberts, Weir, Bullough, Davenport (2), Milne, Coupar, Barbour, Brogan (1).

**Record League Victory:** 8–0 v Barnsley, Division 2, 6 October 1934 – Jones; Smith, Finney; Goslin, Atkinson, George Taylor; George T. Taylor (2), Eastham, Milsom (1), Westwood (4), Cook. (1 og).

**Record Cup Victory:** 13–0 v Sheffield U, FA Cup 2nd rd, 1 February 1890 – Parkinson; Robinson (1), Jones; Bullough, Davenport, Roberts; Rushton, Brogan (3), Cassidy (5), McNee, Weir (4).

**Record Defeat:** 1–9 v Preston NE, FA Cup 2nd rd, 10 December 1887.

**Most League Points (2 for a win):** 61, Division 3, 1972–73.

**Most League Points (3 for a win):** 98, Division 1, 1996–97.

**Most League Goals:** 100, Division 1, 1996–97.

**Highest League Scorer in Season:** Joe Smith, 38, Division 1, 1920–21.

**Most League Goals in Total Aggregate:** Nat Lofthouse, 255, 1946–61.

**Most Capped Player:** Nat Lofthouse, 33, England.

**Most League Appearances:** Eddie Hopkinson, 519, 1956–70.

**Record Transfer Fee Received:** £4,500,000 from Liverpool for Jason McAteer, September 1995.

**Record Transfer Fee Paid:** £3,500,000 for Dean Holdsworth from Wimbledon, October 1997.

**Football League Record:** 1888 Founder Member of the League; 1899–1900 Division 2; 1900–03 Division 1; 1903–05 Division 2; 1905–08 Division 1; 1908–09 Division 2; 1909–10 Division 1; 1910–11 Division 2; 1911–33 Division 1; 1933–35 Division 2; 1935–64 Division 1; 1964–71 Division 2; 1971–73 Division 3; 1973–78 Division 2; 1978–80 Division 1; 1980–83 Division 2; 1983–87 Division 3; 1987–88 Division 4; 1988–92 Division 3; 1992–93 Division 2; 1993–95 Division 1; 1995–96 FA Premier League; 1996–97 Division 1; 1997–98 FA Premier League; 1998– Division 1.

**Honours:** *Football League:* Division 1 – Champions 1996–97; Division 2 – Champions 1908–09, 1977–78; Runners-up 1899–1900, 1904–05, 1910–11, 1934–35, 1992–93; Division 3 – Champions 1972–73. *FA Cup:* Winners 1923, 1926, 1929, 1958; Runners-up 1894, 1904, 1953. *Football League Cup:* Runners-up 1995. *Freight Rover Trophy:* Runners-up 1986. *Sherpa Van Trophy:* Winners 1989.

**Colours:** White shirts, navy blue shorts, blue stockings. **Change colours:** Dark/sky blue shirts, navy blue shorts, blue stockings.

**Did you know?**
Ted Vizard a Bolton Wanderers left-winger, made over 500 League and Cup appearances, not including wartime matches, for the club between November 1910 and March 1931.

## BOLTON WANDERERS 1997–98 LEAGUE RECORD

| Match No. | Date | Venue | Opponents | Result | H/T Score | Lg. Pos. | Goalscorers | Attendance |
|---|---|---|---|---|---|---|---|---|
| 1 | Aug 9 | A | Southampton | W 1-0 | 1-0 | — | Blake [43] | 15,206 |
| 2 | 23 | A | Coventry C | D 2-2 | 0-2 | 8 | Blake 2 [69, 76] | 16,640 |
| 3 | 27 | A | Barnsley | L 1-2 | 1-1 | — | Beardsley [31] | 18,661 |
| 4 | Sept 1 | H | Everton | D 0-0 | 0-0 | — | | 23,131 |
| 5 | 13 | A | Arsenal | L 1-4 | 1-3 | 17 | Thompson [13] | 38,138 |
| 6 | 20 | H | Manchester U | D 0-0 | 0-0 | 16 | | 25,000 |
| 7 | 23 | H | Tottenham H | D 1-1 | 1-0 | — | Thompson (pen) [20] | 23,433 |
| 8 | 27 | A | Crystal Palace | D 2-2 | 1-2 | 17 | Beardsley [36], Johansen [66] | 17,134 |
| 9 | Oct 4 | H | Aston Villa | L 0-1 | 0-1 | 17 | | 24,196 |
| 10 | 18 | A | West Ham U | L 0-3 | 0-0 | 18 | | 24,864 |
| 11 | 26 | H | Chelsea | W 1-0 | 0-0 | 17 | Holdsworth [72] | 24,080 |
| 12 | Nov 1 | H | Liverpool | D 1-1 | 0-1 | 18 | Blake [84] | 25,000 |
| 13 | 8 | A | Sheffield W | L 0-5 | 0-5 | 18 | | 25,027 |
| 14 | 22 | A | Leicester C | D 0-0 | 0-0 | 18 | | 20,464 |
| 15 | 29 | H | Wimbledon | W 1-0 | 0-0 | 18 | Blake [89] | 22,703 |
| 16 | Dec 1 | H | Newcastle U | W 1-0 | 1-0 | — | Blake [22] | 24,494 |
| 17 | 6 | A | Blackburn R | L 1-3 | 0-2 | 14 | Frandsen [84] | 25,503 |
| 18 | 14 | H | Derby Co | D 3-3 | 0-0 | 16 | Thompson (pen) [50], Blake [73], Pollock [77] | 23,027 |
| 19 | 20 | A | Leeds U | L 0-2 | 0-0 | 17 | | 31,184 |
| 20 | 26 | H | Barnsley | D 1-1 | 1-1 | 16 | Bergsson [38] | 25,000 |
| 21 | 28 | A | Everton | L 2-3 | 2-2 | 17 | Bergsson [42], Sellars [43] | 37,149 |
| 22 | Jan 10 | H | Southampton | D 0-0 | 0-0 | 18 | | 23,333 |
| 23 | 17 | A | Newcastle U | L 1-2 | 0-1 | 19 | Blake [72] | 36,767 |
| 24 | 31 | H | Coventry C | L 1-5 | 1-1 | 19 | Sellars [21] | 25,000 |
| 25 | Feb 7 | A | Manchester U | D 1-1 | 0-0 | 19 | Taylor [60] | 55,156 |
| 26 | 21 | H | West Ham U | D 1-1 | 0-0 | 19 | Blake [86] | 25,000 |
| 27 | Mar 1 | A | Tottenham H | L 0-1 | 0-1 | 19 | | 29,032 |
| 28 | 7 | A | Liverpool | L 1-2 | 1-0 | 19 | Thompson [7] | 44,532 |
| 29 | 14 | H | Sheffield W | W 3-2 | 1-1 | 19 | Frandsen [31], Blake [53], Thompson (pen) [69] | 24,847 |
| 30 | 28 | H | Leicester C | W 2-0 | 0-0 | 19 | Thompson 2 [52, 89] | 25,000 |
| 31 | 31 | H | Arsenal | L 0-1 | 0-0 | — | | 25,000 |
| 32 | Apr 4 | A | Wimbledon | D 0-0 | 0-0 | 18 | | 11,356 |
| 33 | 11 | H | Blackburn R | W 2-1 | 1-0 | 18 | Holdsworth [20], Taylor [67] | 25,000 |
| 34 | 13 | A | Derby Co | L 0-4 | 0-4 | 18 | | 29,126 |
| 35 | 18 | H | Leeds U | L 2-3 | 0-2 | 19 | Thompson [56], Fish [89] | 25,000 |
| 36 | 25 | H | Aston Villa | W 3-1 | 2-0 | 18 | Cox [18], Taylor [41], Blake [84] | 38,392 |
| 37 | May 2 | H | Crystal Palace | W 5-2 | 3-2 | 17 | Blake [7], Fish [20], Phillips [30], Thompson [70], Holdsworth [79] | 24,449 |
| 38 | 10 | A | Chelsea | L 0-2 | 0-0 | 18 | | 34,845 |

**Final League Position: 18**    1996–97 DIV1 1

### GOALSCORERS

*League (41):* Blake 12, Thompson 9 (3 pens), Holdsworth 3, Taylor 3, Beardsley 2, Bergsson 2, Fish 2, Frandsen 2, Sellars 2, Cox 1, Johansen 1, Phillips 1, Pollock 1.
*Coca-Cola Cup (10):* Blake 2, McGinlay 2 (1 pen), Frandsen 1, Gunnlaugsson 1, Pollock 1, Thompson 1, Todd 1, own goal 1.
*FA Cup (0).*

| Branagan K 34 | Cox N 20 + 1 | Elliott R 4 | Frandsen P 38 | Taggart G 14 + 1 | Bergsson G 34 + 1 | Pollock J 25 + 1 | Sellars S 22 | Blake N 35 | McGinlay J 4 + 3 | Thompson A 33 | Phillips J 21 + 1 | Beardsley P 14 + 3 | Johansen M 4 + 12 | McAnespie S 1 + 1 | Todd A 23 + 2 | Gunnlaugsson A 2 + 13 | Fish M 22 | Whitlow M 13 | Holdsworth D 17 + 3 | Carr F — + 5 | Ward G 4 + 2 | Fairclough C 10 + 1 | Taylor B 10 + 2 | Sheridan J 12 | Salako J — + 7 | Aljofree H 2 | Giallanza G — + 3 | Match No. |
|---|---|---|---|---|---|---|---|---|---|---|---|---|---|---|---|---|---|---|---|---|---|---|---|---|---|---|---|---|
| 1 | 2 | 3 | 4 | 5 | 6 | 7 | 8 | 9 | 10 | 11 | | | | | | | | | | | | | | | | | | 1 |
| 1 | 2¹ | 3 | 4 | 5 | 6 | 7 | 8 | 9 | 10² | 11 | 12 | 13 | | | | | | | | | | | | | | | | 2 |
| 1 | | 3¹ | 4 | 5 | 6 | 7² | 10 | 9 | 12 | 11 | 2 | 8 | 13 | | | | | | | | | | | | | | | 3 |
| 1 | | 3³ | 4² | 5 | 6 | 7 | 10 | 9 | 12 | 11 | 2 | 8¹ | 13 | 14 | | | | | | | | | | | | | | 4 |
| 1 | | | 4 | 5 | 6 | 7 | 10 | 9 | | 11 | 3 | 8² | | | 2¹ | 12 | 13 | | | | | | | | | | | 5 |
| 1 | | | 4 | 5 | 2 | 7 | 8¹ | 9 | 10 | 11 | 12 | | | | 6 | | | 3 | | | | | | | | | | 6 |
| 1 | | | 4 | 5 | 2 | 7 | 10 | 9 | | 11 | | 8 | | | 6 | | | 3 | | | | | | | | | | 7 |
| 1 | | | 4 | 5 | 2 | 7¹ | 10 | 9 | | 11 | | 8 | 12 | | 6 | | | 3 | | | | | | | | | | 8 |
| 1 | | | 4 | 5 | 2 | 7 | 10¹ | | | 11 | | 8 | | | 6 | 12 | | 3 | 9 | | | | | | | | | 9 |
| 1 | | | 4 | 5 | 6 | 7 | 10 | | 12 | 11² | 2 | 8¹ | 13 | | | | | 3 | 9 | | | | | | | | | 10 |
| 1 | | | 4 | 5 | 2 | 12 | 7 | 9 | | 11 | 3 | 8¹ | | | 6 | | | | 10 | | | | | | | | | 11 |
| 1 | | | 4² | 5 | | 7 | | 9 | | 11 | 2 | 8¹ | | | 6 | 12 | | 3 | 10 | | | 13 | | | | | | 12 |
| 1 | | | 4² | 5 | | 7 | | 9 | | 11 | 2¹ | 8 | 12 | | 6 | | | 3 | 10 | | | 13 | | | | | | 13 |
| 1 | | | 4 | | 2 | 7 | | 9 | | 11 | | 8¹ | | | 6 | 12 | 5 | 3 | 10 | | | | | | | | | 14 |
| 1 | | | 4 | | 2 | 7 | 8 | 9 | | 11¹ | | | | | 6 | 12 | 5 | 3 | 10 | | | | | | | | | 15 |
| 1 | | | 4 | | 2 | 7 | 8 | 9 | | 11 | | | | | 6 | | 5 | 3 | 10 | | | | | | | | | 16 |
| 1⁶ | | | 4 | | 2 | 7 | 8 | 9 | | 11 | | | | | 6 | 12 | 5 | 3 | 10¹ | | 15 | | | | | | | 17 |
| | | | 4 | | 2 | 7 | 10² | 9 | | 11 | 3 | 8¹ | 13 | | 6 | | | | 12 | | 1 | 5 | | | | | | 18 |
| | | | 4 | | 2 | 7 | 10 | 9 | | 11¹ | 3 | 8 | | | 6 | | | | 12 | | 1 | 5 | | | | | | 19 |
| 13 | | | 4 | 12² | 2 | 7 | 10 | 9 | | 11³ | | 8 | | 14 | 6¹ | | 5 | 3 | | | 1 | | | | | | | 20 |
| 2 | 11 | | 6 | | | 7 | 10 | 9 | | | | 8² | 12 | | 13³ | | 4¹ | 3 | | | 14 | 1 | 5 | | | | | 21 |
| 1 | 2 | | 4 | 5 | | 7² | 8¹ | 9 | | 11 | 3 | | | | 6 | 12 | | | 10 | | | 13 | | | | | | 22 |
| 1 | 2 | | 4 | | | 7 | 10 | 9 | | | 3 | 8 | | | 6 | 12 | 5 | | | | | | 11¹ | | | | | 23 |
| 1 | 2 | | 4 | | | 7² | 8 | 9 | | | 3 | | 12 | | 6 | | | | | | | 13 | 5 | 11¹ | 10 | | | 24 |
| 1 | 2 | | 4 | | 3 | 7 | 8 | 9 | | 11 | | | | | 6 | 12 | | | | | | | 5 | 10¹ | | | | 25 |
| 1 | 2 | | 4 | | 3 | 7 | | 9 | | 11 | | 8 | | | 6 | 12 | | | | | | 10 | 5¹ | | | | | 26 |
| 1 | 2 | | 4 | | 8 | 7³ | | 9 | | 11 | 3 | | 13 | | 6 | 12 | | | | | | 10 | 5² | | | | | 27 |
| 1 | 2 | | 4 | | 3 | | | 9 | | 11 | | | | | 6 | | 8 | | | | | 10 | 5 | 7 | | | | 28 |
| 1 | 2 | 8 | | | 4 | | | 9 | | 11 | 3 | | | | 5 | | 6 | | | | | 10 | | 7 | | | | 29 |
| 1 | 2 | 8 | | | 4 | | | | | 11 | 3 | 13 | | | 5 | | 6 | | | | | 10¹ | 9 | 7 | 12² | | | 30 |
| 1 | 2 | 8 | | | 4 | | | 9 | | 11 | 3¹ | | 12 | | 5² | | 6 | | | | | 10 | 13 | 7 | | | | 31 |
| 1 | 2 | 8 | | | 4² | | | 9 | | 11 | 3 | | | | 5 | | 6 | | | | | 10¹ | 12 | 7 | 13 | | | 32 |
| 1 | 2 | 8 | | | | | | 9 | | 11 | | | | | 6 | | 4 | | | | | 10¹ | 5 | 12 | 7 | | 3 | 33 |
| 1⁶ | 2 | 8 | 12 | | | | | 9 | | 11 | | | | | 6 | | 4¹ | | | | 15 | 5² | 10 | 7 | 13 | | 3 | 34 |
| 1 | 2 | 8 | | | 4 | | | 9 | | 11 | 3¹ | | | | 5 | | 6 | | | | | 10 | 7² | 12 | | 13 | | 35 |
| 1 | 2 | 8¹ | | 5 | 6 | | | 9 | | 11 | 3 | | 12 | | 4² | | | | | | | 13 | 10³ | 7 | | 14 | | 36 |
| 1 | 2 | 8 | | 5 | 6 | | | 9³ | | 11 | 3 | | 12 | | 4 | | | | | | | 13 | 10² | 7¹ | | 14 | | 37 |
| 1 | 2 | 8 | | 5 | 6¹ | | | 9 | | 11 | 3 | | 12 | | 4 | | | | | | | | 10³ | 7² | 13 | 14 | | 38 |

**Coca-Cola Cup**
Second Round — Leyton Orient (a) 3-1 / (h) 4-4
Third Round — Wimbledon (h) 2-0
Fourth Round — Middlesbrough (a) 1-2

**FA Cup**
Third Round — Barnsley (a) 0-1

AFC BOURNEMOUTH 1997–98　*Back row (left to right)*: Eddie Howe, Antony Griffin, Owen Coll, David Wells, Jimmy Glass, Steve Fletcher, Robert Murray, Franck Rolling. *Middle row*: Sean O'Driscoll (Youth Manager), Justin Harrington, Russell Beardsmore, Leo Cotterell, John Williams (Assistant Manager), Jamie Vincent, John O'Neill, Neil Young, Steve Hardwick (Physio). *Front row*: James Hayter, Michael Dean, Jamie Jenkins, Steve Robinson, Mel Machin (Manager), Ian Cox, John Bailey, Mark Rawlinson, David Town.
(Photograph: Mick Cunningham)

# Division 2     **AFC BOURNEMOUTH**

*Dean Court Ground, Bournemouth, Dorset BH7 7AF.* Telephone: (01202) 395381. Fax: (01202) 309797.

*Ground capacity:* 10,770.

*Record attendance:* 28,799 v Manchester U, FA Cup 6th rd, 2 March 1957.

*Record receipts:* £80,267 v Walsall, Auto Windscreens Shield Southern Area Final, 17 March 1998.

*Pitch measurements:* 112yd × 74yd.

*Chairman:* T. S. Watkins.

*Directors:* A. H. Kaye (Vice-Chairman), K. R. Dando, P. W. Aldersey, I. D. F. Griffiths.

*Secretary:* K. R. J. MacAlister.

*Manager:* Mel Machin. *Assistant Manager:* John Williams. *Youth Team Coach:* Sean O'Driscoll. *Physio:* Steve Hardwick. *Corporate Manager:* Miss D. Edwards. *Stadium Manager:* S. Baker.

*Year Formed:* 1899. *Turned Professional:* 1912. *Ltd Co.:* 1914.

*Previous Names:* Boscombe St Johns, 1890–99; Boscombe FC, 1899–1923; Bournemouth & Boscombe Ath FC, 1923–71.

*Club Nickname:* 'Cherries'.

*Previous Grounds:* 1899–1910, Castlemain Road, Pokesdown; 1910, Dean Court.

*Foundation:* There was a Bournemouth FC as early as 1875, but the present club arose out of the remnants of the Boscombe St John's club (formed 1890). The meeting at which Boscombe FC came into being was held at a house in Gladstone Road in 1899. They began by playing in the Boscombe and District Junior League.

*First Football League game:* 25 August 1923, Division 3 (S), v Swindon T (a), L 1-3 – Heron; Wingham, Lamb; Butt, C. Smith, Voisey; Miller, Lister (1), Davey, Simpson, Robinson.

*Record League Victory:* 7–0 v Swindon T, Division 3 (S), 22 September 1956 – Godwin; Cunningham, Keetley; Clayton, Crosland, Rushworth; Siddall (1), Norris (2), Arnott (1), Newsham (2), Cutler (1). 10–0 win v Northampton T at start of 1939–40 expunged from the records on outbreak of war.

*Record Cup Victory:* 11–0 v Margate, FA Cup 1st rd, 20 November 1971 – Davies; Machin (1), Kitchener, Benson, Jones, Powell, Cave (1), Boyer, MacDougall (9 incl. 1p), Miller, Scott (De Garis).

*Record Defeat:* 0–9 v Lincoln C, Division 3, 18 December 1982.

*Most League Points (2 for a win):* 62, Division 3, 1971–72.

*Most League Points (3 for a win):* 97, Division 3, 1986–87.

*Most League Goals:* 88, Division 3 (S), 1956–57.

*Highest League Scorer in Season:* Ted MacDougall, 42, 1970–71.

*Most League Goals in Total Aggregate:* Ron Eyre, 202, 1924–33.

*Most Capped Player:* Gerry Peyton, 7 (33), Republic of Ireland.

*Most League Appearances:* Sean O'Driscoll, 423, 1984–95.

*Record Transfer Fee Received:* £800,000 from Everton for Joe Parkinson, March 1994.

*Record Transfer Fee Paid:* £210,000 to Gillingham for Gavin Peacock, August 1989.

*Football League Record:* 1923 Elected to Division 3 (S). Remained a Third Division club for record number of years until 1970; 1970–71 Division 4; 1971–75 Division 3; 1975–82 Division 4; 1982–87 Division 3; 1987–90 Division 2; 1990–92 Division 3; 1992– Division 2.

*Honours: Football League:* Division 3 – Champions 1986–87; Division 3 (S) – Runners-up 1947–48. Promotion from Division 4 1970–71 (2nd), 1981–82 (4th). *FA Cup:* best season: 6th rd, 1957. *Football League Cup:* best season: 4th rd, 1962, 1964. *Associate Members' Cup:* Winners 1984. *Auto Windscreens Shield:* 1998 (Runners-up)

*Colours:* Red shirts with black 3" stripe and white pinstripe, white shorts, white stockings.
*Change colours:* Blue/yellow halved shirts, blue shorts, yellow stockings.

**Did you know?**
Bournemouth's first professional footballer was Harry Baven Penton, who joined the club in January 1912 for a fee of £10 and thirty shillings a week (£1.50).

## AFC BOURNEMOUTH 1997–98 LEAGUE RECORD

| Match No. | Date | Venue | Opponents | Result | H/T Score | Lg. Pos. | Goalscorers | Attendance |
|---|---|---|---|---|---|---|---|---|
| 1 | Aug 9 | A | Northampton T | W 2-0 | 0-0 | — | Vincent [68], Fletcher S [75] | 6384 |
| 2 | 16 | H | Wigan Ath | W 1-0 | 0-0 | 1 | Rolling [89] | 3799 |
| 3 | 23 | A | Oldham Ath | L 1-2 | 0-1 | 5 | Robinson [63] | 4986 |
| 4 | 30 | H | Blackpool | W 2-0 | 1-0 | 1 | Tomlinson [30], Robinson [79] | 4196 |
| 5 | Sept 2 | H | Bristol R | D 1-1 | 1-1 | — | Robinson (pen) [20] | 5550 |
| 6 | 5 | A | Gillingham | L 1-2 | 1-0 | — | Fletcher S [44] | 5168 |
| 7 | 13 | H | Luton T | D 1-1 | 0-1 | 6 | O'Neill [83] | 4561 |
| 8 | 20 | A | Bristol C | D 1-1 | 0-1 | 7 | Robinson [63] | 8330 |
| 9 | 27 | H | Grimsby T | L 0-1 | 0-0 | 11 | | 3712 |
| 10 | Oct 4 | A | Chesterfield | D 1-1 | 1-0 | 14 | Rolling [14] | 4482 |
| 11 | 11 | A | Preston NE | W 1-0 | 0-0 | 10 | Warren [72] | 8531 |
| 12 | 18 | H | Fulham | W 2-1 | 1-0 | 4 | Cox 2 [17, 65] | 7606 |
| 13 | 21 | H | Millwall | D 0-0 | 0-0 | — | | 4752 |
| 14 | 25 | A | Burnley | D 2-2 | 0-1 | 8 | Howe [58], Vincent [68] | 9501 |
| 15 | Nov 1 | H | Brentford | D 0-0 | 0-0 | 7 | | 4772 |
| 16 | 4 | A | Wrexham | L 1-2 | 0-2 | — | Warren [89] | 2462 |
| 17 | 8 | A | Plymouth Arg | L 0-3 | 0-2 | 13 | | 5067 |
| 18 | 18 | H | Southend U | W 2-1 | 1-1 | — | Fletcher S [44], Warren [47] | 3019 |
| 19 | 22 | H | Carlisle U | W 3-2 | 2-1 | 9 | Fletcher S [5], Beardsmore [35], O'Neill [64] | 3709 |
| 20 | 29 | A | Wycombe W | D 1-1 | 0-0 | 8 | Robinson (pen) [77] | 4340 |
| 21 | Dec 2 | H | York C | D 0-0 | 0-0 | — | | 3365 |
| 22 | 13 | A | Walsall | L 1-2 | 0-0 | 10 | Robinson [72] | 3548 |
| 23 | 20 | H | Watford | L 0-1 | 0-0 | 14 | | 6081 |
| 24 | 26 | H | Gillingham | W 4-0 | 1-0 | 12 | Jones 2 [15, 88], Robinson [53], Young [78] | 5672 |
| 25 | 28 | A | Bristol R | L 3-5 | 1-4 | 13 | Jones [9], Cox [75], Robinson (pen) [84] | 7256 |
| 26 | Jan 10 | A | Northampton T | W 3-0 | 0-0 | 11 | Jones [63], Fletcher S [78], Young [83] | 4257 |
| 27 | 17 | A | Blackpool | L 0-1 | 0-1 | 13 | | 4550 |
| 28 | 24 | H | Oldham Ath | D 0-0 | 0-0 | 12 | | 4079 |
| 29 | 31 | A | Luton T | W 2-1 | 1-0 | 9 | Brissett [10], Fletcher S [59] | 5466 |
| 30 | Feb 7 | H | Bristol C | W 1-0 | 1-0 | 8 | Fletcher S [41] | 6623 |
| 31 | 14 | H | Chesterfield | W 2-0 | 2-0 | 8 | Warren 2 [13, 41] | 4271 |
| 32 | 21 | A | Grimsby T | L 1-2 | 1-0 | 9 | Warren [24] | 5456 |
| 33 | 24 | A | Fulham | W 1-0 | 1-0 | — | Robinson [38] | 7708 |
| 34 | 28 | H | Preston NE | L 0-2 | 0-2 | 10 | | 5009 |
| 35 | Mar 3 | H | Plymouth Arg | D 3-3 | 1-2 | — | Fletcher S 2 [17, 89], Vincent [80] | 3545 |
| 36 | 7 | A | Brentford | L 2-3 | 2-2 | 9 | Rolling 2 [36, 42] | 4973 |
| 37 | 14 | H | Wrexham | L 0-1 | 0-0 | 9 | | 5512 |
| 38 | 21 | A | Southend U | L 3-5 | 0-0 | 12 | Stein [58], Bailey [75], Fletcher S [90] | 4823 |
| 39 | 28 | A | Carlisle U | W 1-0 | 1-0 | 10 | Stein [23] | 4951 |
| 40 | Apr 4 | H | Wycombe W | D 0-0 | 0-0 | 10 | | 4271 |
| 41 | 7 | A | Wigan Ath | L 0-1 | 0-0 | — | | 2798 |
| 42 | 11 | A | York C | W 1-0 | 1-0 | 11 | O'Neill [33] | 2840 |
| 43 | 14 | H | Walsall | W 1-0 | 0-0 | — | Fletcher S [71] | 3404 |
| 44 | 25 | H | Burnley | W 2-1 | 0-0 | 10 | Robinson (pen) [56], Fletcher S [61] | 6527 |
| 45 | 28 | A | Watford | L 1-2 | 1-0 | — | Stein [14] | 12,834 |
| 46 | May 2 | A | Millwall | W 2-1 | 2-1 | 9 | Witter (og) [11], Stein [45] | 7872 |

**Final League Position: 9**      1996–97 DIV2 16

### GOALSCORERS
*League (57):* Fletcher S 12, Robinson 10 (4 pens), Warren 6, Jones 4, Rolling 4, Stein 4, Cox 3, O'Neill 3, Vincent 3, Young 2, Bailey 1, Beardsmore 1, Brissett 1, Howe 1, Tomlinson 1, own goal 1.
*Coca-Cola Cup (1):* Rolling 1.
*FA Cup (6):* Robinson 2, Beardsmore 1, Fletcher S 1, O'Neill 1, own goal 1.

| Glass J 46 | Young N 43 + 1 | Vincent J 43 + 1 | Rolling F 26 + 4 | Cox I 46 | Bailey D 30 + 2 | Beardsmore R 28 + 1 | Robinson S 45 | O'Neill J 34 + 9 | Fletcher S 42 | Rawlinson M 16 + 9 | Tomlinson G 6 + 1 | Howe E 31 + 9 | Brissett J 13 + 18 | Harrington J 4 + 4 | Murray R — + 4 | Warren C 29 + 1 | Dean M 3 + 5 | Town D — + 7 | Hayter J — + 5 | Teather P 5 + 5 | Jones S 5 | Fletcher C — + 1 | Stein M 11 | Match No. |
|---|---|---|---|---|---|---|---|---|---|---|---|---|---|---|---|---|---|---|---|---|---|---|---|---|
| 1 | 2 | 3 | 4 | 5 | 6 | 7 | 8 | $9^1$ | 10 | 11 | 12 | | | | | | | | | | | | | 1 |
| 1 | 2 | 3 | 4 | 5 | 6 | | 8 | $9^1$ | 10 | 11 | | 7 | $12^2$ | 13 | | | | | | | | | | 2 |
| 1 | 2 | 3 | 4 | 5 | 6 | | 8 | 9 | 10 | $11^1$ | | 7 | 12 | | | | | | | | | | | 3 |
| 1 | 2 | 3 | 4 | 5 | 6 | 7 | 8 | 9 | | 11 | $10^1$ | | 12 | | | | | | | | | | | 4 |
| 1 | 2 | 3 | 4 | 5 | $6^3$ | 7 | 8 | 9 | | $11^2$ | $10^1$ | 13 | 12 | | 14 | | | | | | | | | 5 |
| 1 | 2 | 3 | 4 | 5 | | 7 | 8 | 6 | 10 | 11 | $9^1$ | | 12 | | | | | | | | | | | 6 |
| 1 | 2 | 3 | $4^1$ | 5 | 6 | 7 | 8 | 11 | 10 | | $9^2$ | 12 | | | | 13 | | | | | | | | 7 |
| 1 | 2 | 3 | | 5 | 6 | 7 | 8 | $9^1$ | 10 | 12 | $11^2$ | 4 | 13 | | | | | | | | | | | 8 |
| 1 | 2 | 3 | $4^2$ | | 6 | 7 | 8 | 11 | 10 | | $9^1$ | 13 | 12 | | | | | | | | | | | 9 |
| 1 | 2 | 3 | 4 | 5 | 6 | $7^1$ | 8 | $9^2$ | 10 | 11 | | 12 | 13 | | | | | | | | | | | 10 |
| 1 | 2 | 3 | | 5 | 6 | 7 | 8 | | 10 | 11 | | 4 | | | | 9 | | | | | | | | 11 |
| 1 | 2 | 3 | | 5 | $6^1$ | 7 | 8 | 12 | 10 | 11 | | 4 | | | | 9 | | | | | | | | 12 |
| 1 | 2 | 3 | | 5 | | 7 | 8 | $6^1$ | 10 | 11 | | 4 | 12 | | | 9 | | | | | | | | 13 |
| 1 | 2 | 3 | 12 | 5 | | 7 | 8 | $6^1$ | 10 | $11^2$ | | 4 | 13 | | | 9 | | | | | | | | 14 |
| 1 | 2 | 3 | 4 | 5 | | 7 | $8^3$ | 12 | $10^2$ | 13 | | 6 | $11^1$ | | 14 | 9 | | | | | | | | 15 |
| 1 | 2 | 3 | $4^1$ | 5 | | 7 | 8 | 13 | 10 | 12 | | 6 | $11^2$ | | | 9 | | | | | | | | 16 |
| 1 | 2 | 3 | 12 | 5 | | 7 | $8^1$ | $6^2$ | 10 | $11^3$ | | 4 | 13 | | | 9 | 14 | | | | | | | 17 |
| 1 | 2 | 3 | | 5 | | 7 | 8 | 6 | 10 | 12 | | 4 | | $11^1$ | | 9 | | | | | | | | 18 |
| 1 | 2 | 3 | | 5 | | 7 | 8 | 6 | 10 | 12 | | 4 | | $11^1$ | | $9^2$ | 13 | | | | | | | 19 |
| 1 | 2 | 3 | | 5 | | 7 | 8 | 6 | 10 | | | 4 | | $11^1$ | | 9 | 12 | | | | | | | 20 |
| 1 | 2 | 3 | | 5 | 12 | 7 | 8 | 6 | 10 | | | 4 | | $11^1$ | | $9^2$ | 13 | | | | | | | 21 |
| 1 | 2 | 3 | | 5 | 6 | | 8 | 11 | 10 | | $7^1$ | 4 | | | | 9 | | | 12 | | | | | 22 |
| 1 | 2 | 3 | 12 | 5 | 6 | | 8 | $7^1$ | 10 | | | 4 | | | 13 | 9 | | | | $11^2$ | | | | 23 |
| 1 | 2 | 3 | | 5 | | | 8 | 7 | $10^2$ | 12 | | 4 | | | | 11 | | 13 | | $6^1$ | 9 | | | 24 |
| 1 | 2 | 3 | 12 | 5 | | | 8 | $6^2$ | $10^1$ | $7^3$ | | 4 | | | | 11 | 14 | 13 | | | 9 | | | 25 |
| 1 | 2 | 3 | | 5 | | | 8 | 7 | 10 | | | 4 | | | | 11 | | | | 6 | 9 | | | 26 |
| 1 | 2 | $3^2$ | | 5 | 12 | | 8 | 7 | 10 | | | 4 | 13 | 14 | | $11^1$ | | | | $6^2$ | 9 | | | 27 |
| 1 | 2 | 3 | | 5 | 6 | | 8 | 7 | 10 | | | 4 | | | | $11^1$ | | 12 | | | 9 | | | 28 |
| 1 | 2 | 3 | | 5 | 6 | | 8 | 7 | 10 | | | 4 | | | | $11^1$ | 9 | 12 | | | | | | 29 |
| 1 | 2 | 3 | 4 | 5 | 6 | | 8 | 7 | 10 | | | | | | | $11^1$ | 9 | 12 | | | | | | 30 |
| 1 | 2 | $3^1$ | 4 | 5 | 6 | | 8 | 7 | 10 | 14 | | | | | | $11^3$ | $12^2$ | 9 | | | 13 | | | 31 |
| 1 | 2 | | 4 | 5 | 6 | | 8 | $7^1$ | 10 | | | $3^2$ | | | | $11^1$ | 9 | 12 | 13 | | | 14 | | 32 |
| 1 | 2 | 3 | 4 | 5 | 6 | | 8 | 7 | 10 | | | | | | 13 | $11^1$ | 9 | $12^2$ | | | | | | 33 |
| 1 | 2 | 3 | 4 | 5 | 6 | | 8 | $7^1$ | 10 | | | | | | 12 | $11^2$ | 9 | 13 | | | | | | 34 |
| 1 | 2 | $3^2$ | 4 | 5 | 6 | | 8 | $7^1$ | 10 | | | | | | 14 | 11 | | 13 | 12 | | $9^1$ | | | 35 |
| 1 | 2 | 3 | 4 | 5 | 6 | | 8 | $7^1$ | 10 | | | | | | 14 | 12 | $11^2$ | | | $13^3$ | | | 9 | 36 |
| 1 | 2 | $3^3$ | 4 | 5 | $6^1$ | 11 | 8 | $7^2$ | 10 | 13 | | | | | 14 | 12 | | | | | | | 9 | 37 |
| 1 | 2 | $3^1$ | $4^2$ | $5^3$ | 6 | 11 | 8 | 14 | 10 | 12 | | | | | | 7 | | 13 | | | | | 9 | 38 |
| 1 | 2 | 3 | 4 | 5 | | 11 | 8 | | 10 | | | 7 | | | | | 6 | | | | | | 9 | 39 |
| 1 | 12 | | 4 | 5 | | $11^1$ | 8 | 13 | $10^3$ | $2^2$ | | 7 | 3 | | | 6 | 14 | | | | | | 9 | 40 |
| 1 | 2 | 3 | $4^1$ | 5 | 6 | $11^2$ | 8 | 13 | | | | 7 | 10 | | | | 12 | | | | | | 9 | 41 |
| 1 | 2 | 3 | | 5 | 6 | 12 | | | | | | 4 | 7 | 10 | | $11^1$ | 8 | | | | | | 9 | 42 |
| 1 | 2 | 3 | | 5 | $6^3$ | 7 | 8 | 12 | 10 | | | 4 | 13 | | | $11^1$ | 14 | | | | | | $9^2$ | 43 |
| 1 | $3^1$ | 2 | | 5 | 6 | 7 | 8 | 13 | 10 | | | 4 | 12 | | | 11 | | | | | | | $9^2$ | 44 |
| 1 | 12 | 3 | $2^1$ | 5 | 6 | $7^4$ | 8 | | 10 | | | 4 | 14 | | | 11 | $13^3$ | | | | | | 9 | 45 |
| 1 | 2 | $3^1$ | | 5 | $6^2$ | 7 | 8 | 13 | 10 | | | 4 | 12 | | | 11 | | | | | | | 9 | 46 |

**Coca-Cola Cup**
First Round　　　Torquay U　　　(h)　0-1
　　　　　　　　　　　　　　　　　 (a)　1-1

**FA Cup**
First Round　　　Heybridge S　　　(h)　3-0
Second Round　　Bristol C　　　　　(h)　3-1
Third Round　　　Huddersfield T　　(h)　0-1

BRADFORD CITY 1997-98    *Back row (left to right):* Nicky Mohan, John Dreyer, Robert Steiner, Eddie Youds, Dennis Sepp.
*Third row:* Richard Liburd, Jamie Lawrence, Andrew O'Brien, Lawrence Davies, George Kulcsar, Edinho, Wayne Jacobs, Robbie Blake, Shaun Murray.
*Second row:* David Donaldson, Ian McLean, Nigel Pepper, Craig Midgley, Mark Prudhoe, Darren Moore, Jonathan Gould, Gordon Watson, Andy Kiwomya, Chris Wilder, Craig Ramage.
*Front row:* Ole Bjorn Sundgot, Chris Hutchings (Youth Development Officer), Steve Redmond (Physio), Martin Hunter (First Team Coach), Chris Kamara (Manager), Paul Jewell (First Team
Coach), Mark Ellis (Kit Manager), Steve Smith (Youth Team Manager), Peter Beagrie.
(Photograph: *Bradford Telegraph & Argus*)

# Division 1      **BRADFORD CITY**

*Valley Parade, Bradford BD8 7DY.* Telephone: (01274) 773355 (Office). Fax: (01274) 773356. e-mail: bradfordcityfc@compuserve.com

*Ground capacity:* 18,018.

*Record attendance:* 39,146 v Burnley, FA Cup 4th rd, 11 March 1911.

*Record receipts:* £164,567 v Sheffield Wednesday, FA Cup 5th rd, 16 February 1997.

*Pitch measurements:* 110yd × 73yd.

*Chairman:* Geoffrey Richmond. *Vice-Chairman:* David Thompson FCA.

*Directors:* David Richmond, Elizabeth Richmond, Terry Goddard, Michael Richmond, Julian Rhodes.

*Managing Director:* Shaun Harvey.

*Manager:* Paul Jewell. *Assistant Manager:* Chris Hutchings.

*Youth Coach:* Steve Smith. *Physio:* Steve Redmond.

*Secretary:* Jon Pollard. *Stadium Manager:* Allan Gilliver.

*Year Formed:* 1903. *Turned Professional:* 1903. *Ltd Co.:* 1908.

*Club Nickname:* 'The Bantams'.

*Foundation:* Bradford was a rugby stronghold around the turn of the century but after Manningham RFC held an archery contest to help them out of financial difficulties in 1903, they were persuaded to give up the handling code and turn to soccer. So they formed Bradford City and continued at Valley Parade. Recognising this as an opportunity of spreading the dribbling code in this part of Yorkshire, the Football League immediately accepted the new club's first application for membership of the Second Division.

*First Football League game:* 1 September 1903, Division 2, v Grimsby T (a), L 0-2 – Seymour; Wilson, Halliday; Robinson, Millar, Farnall; Guy, Beckram, Forrest, McMillan, Graham.

*Record League Victory:* 11–1 v Rotherham U, Division 3 (N), 25 August 1928 – Sherlaw; Russell, Watson; Burkinshaw (1), Summers, Bauld; Harvey (2), Edmunds (3), White (3), Cairns, Scriven (2).

*Record Cup Victory:* 11–3 v Walker Celtic, FA Cup 1st rd (replay), 1 December 1937 – Parker; Rookes, McDermott; Murphy, Mackie, Moore; Bagley (1), Whittingham (1), Deakin (4 incl. 1p), Cooke (1), Bartholomew (4).

*Record Defeat:* 1–9 v Colchester U, Division 4, 30 December 1961.

*Most League Points (2 for a win):* 63, Division 3 (N), 1928–29.

*Most League Points (3 for a win):* 94, Division 3, 1984–85.

*Most League Goals:* 128, Division 3 (N), 1928–29.

*Highest League Scorer in Season:* David Layne, 34, Division 4, 1961–62.

*Most League Goals in Total Aggregate:* Bobby Campbell, 121, 1981–84, 1984–86.

*Most Capped Player:* Harry Hampton, 9, Northern Ireland.

*Most League Appearances:* Cec Podd, 502, 1970–84.

*Record Transfer Fee Received:* £2,000,000 from Newcastle U for Des Hamilton, March 1997.

*Record Transfer Fee Paid:* £625,000 to Bolton W for John McGinlay, November 1997.

*Football League Record:* 1903 Elected to Division 2; 1908–22 Division 1; 1922–27 Division 2; 1927–29 Division 3 (N); 1929–37 Division 2; 1937–61 Division 3; 1961–69 Division 4; 1969–72 Division 3; 1972–77 Division 4; 1977–78 Division 3; 1978–82 Division 4; 1982–85 Division 3; 1985–90 Division 2; 1990–92 Division 3; 1992–96 Division 2; 1996– Division 1.

*Honours: Football League:* Division 1 best season: 5th, 1910–11; Division 2 – Champions 1907–08; Promoted from Division 2 1995–96 (play-offs); Division 3 – Champions 1984–85; Division 3 (N) – Champions 1928–29; Division 4 – Runners-up 1981–82. *FA Cup:* Winners 1911. *Football League Cup:* best season: 5th rd, 1965, 1989.

*Colours:* Claret and amber shirts, black shorts, black stockings. *Change colours:* Light blue shirts and shorts, blue stockings.

**Did you know?**
Albert Whitehurst's 24 League goals for Bradford City stood for 30 years as a club record until John McCole finished with 28 in 1958-59 season.

## BRADFORD CITY 1997–98 LEAGUE RECORD

| Match No. | Date | | Venue | Opponents | Result | | H/T Score | Lg. Pos. | Goalscorers | Atten-dance |
|---|---|---|---|---|---|---|---|---|---|---|
| 1 | Aug | 9 | H | Stockport Co | W | 2-1 | 1-0 | — | Edinho 23, Steiner 74 | 14,312 |
| 2 | | 15 | H | Stoke C | D | 0-0 | 0-0 | — | | 13,823 |
| 3 | | 23 | H | Ipswich T | W | 2-1 | 1-0 | 5 | Steiner 10, Cundy (og) 52 | 13,913 |
| 4 | | 30 | A | Reading | W | 3-0 | 2-0 | 2 | Lawrence 10, Pepper 2 17, 66 | 7163 |
| 5 | Sept | 2 | A | Huddersfield T | W | 2-1 | 1-0 | — | Edinho 19, Blake 67 | 13,159 |
| 6 | | 5 | H | Sunderland | L | 0-4 | 0-4 | — | | 16,484 |
| 7 | | 13 | H | Middlesbrough | D | 2-2 | 1-1 | 1 | Steiner 16, Edinho 62 | 17,767 |
| 8 | | 21 | A | Charlton Ath | L | 1-4 | 1-3 | 4 | Edinho 12 | 11,583 |
| 9 | | 27 | A | Oxford U | D | 0-0 | 0-0 | 4 | | 6468 |
| 10 | Oct | 4 | A | Wolverhampton W | W | 2-0 | 2-0 | 2 | Steiner 34, Kulcsar 40 | 15,236 |
| 11 | | 18 | A | Port Vale | D | 0-0 | 0-0 | 5 | | 7148 |
| 12 | | 21 | A | Portsmouth | D | 1-1 | 1-1 | — | Edinho 40 | 6827 |
| 13 | | 25 | H | Crewe Alex | W | 1-0 | 0-0 | 4 | Edinho 74 | 15,333 |
| 14 | Nov | 1 | H | WBA | D | 0-0 | 0-0 | 7 | | 16,212 |
| 15 | | 4 | A | Birmingham C | D | 0-0 | 0-0 | — | | 14,552 |
| 16 | | 8 | A | Swindon T | L | 0-1 | 0-1 | 10 | | 10,029 |
| 17 | | 15 | H | Tranmere R | L | 0-1 | 0-0 | 12 | | 16,494 |
| 18 | | 18 | H | Sheffield U | D | 1-1 | 0-0 | — | McGinlay 70 | 16,127 |
| 19 | | 22 | A | Manchester C | L | 0-1 | 0-0 | 13 | | 29,746 |
| 20 | | 29 | H | Norwich C | W | 2-1 | 1-0 | 10 | Steiner 2 13, 48 | 16,637 |
| 21 | Dec | 6 | A | Nottingham F | D | 2-2 | 0-1 | 10 | Steiner 72, Pepper 90 | 17,943 |
| 22 | | 13 | H | Bury | W | 1-0 | 1-0 | 10 | McGinlay 25 | 15,812 |
| 23 | | 21 | A | QPR | L | 0-1 | 0-1 | 10 | | 8853 |
| 24 | | 26 | A | Sunderland | L | 0-2 | 0-1 | 11 | | 40,055 |
| 25 | | 28 | H | Huddersfield T | D | 1-1 | 1-1 | 11 | Blake 10 | 17,842 |
| 26 | Jan | 10 | A | Stockport Co | W | 2-1 | 2-0 | 11 | Jacobs 32, Blake 43 | 8460 |
| 27 | | 16 | A | Stoke C | L | 1-2 | 1-2 | — | McGinlay 21 | 10,459 |
| 28 | | 24 | H | Swindon T | D | 1-1 | 1-0 | 11 | Edinho 23 | 15,130 |
| 29 | | 27 | H | Reading | W | 4-1 | 2-1 | — | Lawrence 24, Edinho 2 32, 68, Blake 62 | 13,021 |
| 30 | | 31 | A | Ipswich T | L | 1-2 | 0-0 | 11 | Blake 56 | 11,864 |
| 31 | Feb | 7 | H | Charlton Ath | W | 1-0 | 1-0 | 10 | Blake 19 | 14,851 |
| 32 | | 14 | A | Middlesbrough | L | 0-1 | 0-1 | 10 | | 30,165 |
| 33 | | 18 | A | Wolverhampton W | L | 1-2 | 0-1 | — | Blake 58 | 21,510 |
| 34 | | 21 | H | Oxford U | D | 0-0 | 0-0 | 12 | | 14,190 |
| 35 | | 24 | H | Port Vale | W | 2-1 | 1-1 | — | Melville 34, Pepper 58 | 13,293 |
| 36 | | 28 | A | Sheffield U | L | 1-2 | 0-1 | 11 | Steiner 85 | 17,848 |
| 37 | Mar | 7 | A | WBA | D | 1-1 | 1-0 | 11 | Steiner 39 | 13,281 |
| 38 | | 14 | H | Birmingham C | D | 0-0 | 0-0 | 11 | | 16,392 |
| 39 | | 21 | A | Tranmere R | L | 1-3 | 1-0 | 13 | Youds 20 | 9463 |
| 40 | | 28 | H | Manchester C | W | 2-1 | 0-1 | 11 | Pepper 49, Edinho 66 | 17,099 |
| 41 | Apr | 4 | A | Norwich C | W | 3-2 | 1-0 | 9 | Jacobs 41, Lawrence 46, Blake (pen) 47 | 13,260 |
| 42 | | 11 | H | Nottingham F | L | 0-3 | 0-1 | 11 | | 17,248 |
| 43 | | 13 | A | Bury | L | 0-2 | 0-1 | 12 | | 6570 |
| 44 | | 19 | H | QPR | D | 1-1 | 1-0 | 11 | Steiner 18 | 14,871 |
| 45 | | 25 | A | Crewe Alex | L | 0-5 | 0-4 | 12 | | 5054 |
| 46 | May | 3 | H | Portsmouth | L | 1-3 | 0-1 | 13 | Ramage 87 | 15,890 |

**Final League Position: 13**  1996–97 DIV1 21

### GOALSCORERS
*League (46):* Edinho 10, Steiner 10, Blake 8 (1 pen), Pepper 5, Lawrence 3, McGinlay 3, Jacobs 2, Kulcsar 1, Melville 1, Ramage 1, Youds 1, own goal 1.
*Coca-Cola Cup (2):* Edinho 1, Steiner 1.
*FA Cup (0).*

| Prudhoe M 8 | Wilder C 31+4 | Jacobs W 36 | Kulcsar G 14+3 | Youds E 38 | Dreyer J 15+2 | Lawrence J 38+5 | Pepper N 31+1 | Blake R 23+11 | Edinho 34+7 | Murray S 29+9 | Steiner R 26+11 | Beagrie P 31+3 | Ramage C 24+8 | Sundgot O —+5 | Zabica R 3 | O'Brien A 23+3 | Walsh G 35 | Moore D 18 | O'Kane J 7 | McGinlay J 12+5 | Small B 5 | Bolland P 2+8 | Midgley C —+2 | Melville A 6 | Sepp D —+3 | Davies L 1+3 | McAnespie S 7 | Sinnott L 7 | Bower M 1+2 | Verity D —+1 | Grant G 1+2 | Match No. |
|---|---|---|---|---|---|---|---|---|---|---|---|---|---|---|---|---|---|---|---|---|---|---|---|---|---|---|---|---|---|---|---|---|
| 1 | 2 | 3 | 4 | 5 | 6 | 7 | 8 | $9^1$ | 10 | $11^2$ | 12 | 13 |  |  |  |  |  |  |  |  |  |  |  |  |  |  |  |  |  |  |  | 1 |
| 1 | 2 | 3 |  | 5 | 6 | $7^1$ | 8 | 12 | $10^2$ | 11 | $9^1$ | 4 | 14 | 13 |  |  |  |  |  |  |  |  |  |  |  |  |  |  |  |  |  | 2 |
| 1 | 2 | 3 |  | 5 | 6 | $7^1$ | 8 | 12 | 10 | 11 | $9^2$ | 4 |  | 13 |  |  |  |  |  |  |  |  |  |  |  |  |  |  |  |  |  | 3 |
|  | 2 | 3 | 12 | 5 | 6 | 7 | 8 | 13 | $10^3$ | 11 | $9^2$ | $4^1$ | 14 |  | 1 |  |  |  |  |  |  |  |  |  |  |  |  |  |  |  |  | 4 |
|  | 2 | 3 | 12 | 5 | 6 | 7 | 8 | 13 | $10^3$ | 11 | $9^2$ | $4^1$ | 14 |  | 1 |  |  |  |  |  |  |  |  |  |  |  |  |  |  |  |  | 5 |
|  | 2 | 3 | 12 | 5 | 6 | 7 | $8^1$ | 13 | 10 | 11 | $9^2$ | $4^3$ | 14 |  | 1 |  |  |  |  |  |  |  |  |  |  |  |  |  |  |  |  | 6 |
| 1 | 2 | 3 |  | 5 | 6 | 7 |  |  | 10 | 11 | 9 | 4 | 8 |  |  |  |  |  |  |  |  |  |  |  |  |  |  |  |  |  |  | 7 |
| 1 | 2 | 3 |  | 5 | 6 | $7^1$ | 12 | $9^2$ | 10 | 11 |  | 4 | $8^3$ | 13 |  | 14 |  |  |  |  |  |  |  |  |  |  |  |  |  |  |  | 8 |
|  | 2 | 3 | 7 | $5^1$ | 12 |  |  | 10² | 11 | 9 | 4 | 8 | 13 |  |  |  | 1 | 6 |  |  |  |  |  |  |  |  |  |  |  |  |  | 9 |
|  | 2 | 3 | 7 | $5^2$ |  | 13 |  | 12 | 10 | 11 | 9 | $4^1$ | 8 |  |  |  | 1 | 6 |  |  |  |  |  |  |  |  |  |  |  |  |  | 10 |
| 12 |  | 3 | 4 | 5 | $2^1$ | $7^3$ | 11 |  | 10 | 13 | 9 | $8^2$ | 14 |  |  |  | 1 | 6 |  |  |  |  |  |  |  |  |  |  |  |  |  | 11 |
|  | 2 | 3 | 7 | 5 |  | 12 | 8 |  | 10 | 11 | $9^1$ | 4 |  |  |  |  | 1 | 6 |  |  |  |  |  |  |  |  |  |  |  |  |  | 12 |
|  | 2 | 3 | 7 | 5 | 12 | 13 | $8^3$ |  | 10 | 11 | $9^2$ | 4 | 14 |  |  |  | 1 | $6^1$ |  |  |  |  |  |  |  |  |  |  |  |  |  | 13 |
|  |  | 3 | 7 | 5 |  | 12 |  |  | 10 | 11 | $9^1$ | 4 | 8 |  |  |  | 1 | 6 | 2 |  |  |  |  |  |  |  |  |  |  |  |  | 14 |
| 13 |  | 3 |  | 5 | 9 | $7^2$ |  |  | 10 | $11^1$ | 12 | 4 | 8 |  |  |  | 1 | 6 | 2 |  |  |  |  |  |  |  |  |  |  |  |  | 15 |
|  |  | 3 | 11 | 5 |  | 7 |  |  | $10^1$ | 13 | 12 | 4 | $8^2$ |  |  |  | 1 | 6 | 2 | 9 |  |  |  |  |  |  |  |  |  |  |  | 16 |
|  | $2^1$ |  | 7 | 5 | $3^2$ | 13 |  | 14 | $10^3$ | 11 | 12 | 4 |  |  |  |  | 1 | 6 | 8 | 9 |  |  |  |  |  |  |  |  |  |  |  | 17 |
|  | 2 |  | 4 | 5 |  | 7 | 9 |  | $10^1$ | 12 |  | 11 |  |  |  |  | 1 | 6 | 3 | 8 |  |  |  |  |  |  |  |  |  |  |  | 18 |
|  |  |  | 4 | 5 | 2 | $7^3$ | 9 |  | $10^1$ | 13 | 12 | $11^2$ |  |  |  | 14 | 1 | 6 | 3 | 8 |  |  |  |  |  |  |  |  |  |  |  | 19 |
|  |  |  | 4 | 5 | 2 | 7 | 8 |  |  | 11 | 9 |  |  |  |  |  | 1 | 6 | 3 | 10 |  |  |  |  |  |  |  |  |  |  |  | 20 |
| 14 |  |  | 4 | 5 | 2 | 7 | 8 | $13^3$ |  | 11 | 9 | 12 |  |  |  | $3^1$ | 1 | 6 |  | $10^2$ |  |  |  |  |  |  |  |  |  |  |  | 21 |
| 2 |  |  | 4 | 5 | $3^1$ | 7 | 8 | 12 | 13 | 9 | $11^3$ | 14 |  |  |  |  | 1 | 6 |  | $10^2$ |  |  |  |  |  |  |  |  |  |  |  | 22 |
| 2 |  |  | 5 |  | $7^3$ | 8 | 12 | 13 | 4 | $9^2$ | 11 | 14 |  |  |  | 6 | 1 |  |  | $10^1$ | 3 |  |  |  |  |  |  |  |  |  |  | 23 |
| 12 |  |  | 5 |  | 2 | 7 | 13 | 10 | 11 | $9^2$ | $4^3$ | $8^1$ |  |  |  | 6 | 1 |  |  | 14 | 3 |  |  |  |  |  |  |  |  |  |  | 24 |
| 2 |  |  | 5 |  | 7 | 8 | 10 |  | 4 | $9^1$ | 11 |  |  |  |  | 6 | 1 |  |  | 12 | 3 |  |  |  |  |  |  |  |  |  |  | 25 |
| 1 | 2 | 9 | 5 |  | 7 |  | 10 |  | 4 |  | 11 |  |  |  |  | 6 |  |  |  |  | 3 |  |  | $8^1$ | 3 | 12 |  |  |  |  |  | 26 |
|  | 2 | 9 | 5 |  | $7^1$ |  | 10 | 12 | 4 |  | 11 |  |  |  |  | 6 | 1 |  |  |  |  |  |  | 8 | $3^2$ | 13 |  |  |  |  |  | 27 |
|  | 2 | 3 |  | 5 |  | $7^3$ | 8 | 10 | $9^1$ | 11 | 12 |  |  |  |  | 4 | 1 | $6^2$ |  | 13 | 14 |  |  |  |  |  |  |  |  |  |  | 28 |
|  | 2 | 3 |  | 5 |  | 7 | 8 | 10 | $9^1$ | 11 | 12 |  |  |  |  | 4 | 1 | $6^2$ |  | 13 |  |  |  |  |  |  |  |  |  |  |  | 29 |
|  | $2^2$ | 3 |  | 5 |  | 7 | 8 | 10 | $9^1$ | 11 | 12 | 13 |  |  |  | 4 | 1 | $6^3$ |  | 14 |  |  |  |  |  |  |  |  |  |  |  | 30 |
|  | 2 | 3 |  | 5 |  | 7 | 8 | 10 | $9^1$ | 12 |  | 11 |  |  |  | 4 | 1 | 6 |  |  |  |  |  |  |  |  |  |  |  |  |  | 31 |
| 2 |  | 3 |  | 5 |  | 7 |  | $10^1$ | 9 | 6 | 12 | 11 |  |  |  | 4 | 1 |  |  |  |  |  |  | $8^2$ |  |  |  | 5 | 13 |  |  | 32 |
|  | 2 | 3 |  | 5 |  | 7 |  | 10 | $9^1$ | 8 | 11 |  |  |  |  | 4 | 1 |  |  | 12 |  |  |  | 6 |  |  |  |  |  |  |  | 33 |
|  | 2 | 3 |  | 5 |  | $7^1$ | 8 | 10 | $9^2$ |  | 11 | 12 |  |  |  | 4 | 1 |  |  | 13 |  |  |  | 6 |  |  |  |  |  |  |  | 34 |
|  | 2 | 3 |  | $5^2$ |  |  | 8 | $10^1$ | 12 | 13 | 11 | 9 |  |  |  | 4 | 1 |  |  | 7 |  |  |  | 6 |  |  |  |  |  |  |  | 35 |
|  | 2 | 3 |  | 5 |  | $7^1$ | 8 | 10 | $9^2$ |  | 13 | 11 | 4 |  |  | 12 | 1 |  |  |  |  |  |  | 6 |  |  |  |  |  |  |  | 36 |
|  | 2 | 3 |  | 5 |  | 7 | 8 | 10 | 12 |  | $9^1$ | 11 | 4 |  |  | 1 |  |  |  |  |  |  |  | 6 |  |  |  |  |  |  |  | 37 |
| 1 | 2 | 3 |  | 5 |  | 7 | 8 | $10^2$ | 12 | 9 | $11^3$ | $4^1$ |  |  |  | 6 |  |  |  |  |  | 13 |  |  |  |  | 14 |  |  |  |  | 38 |
| 1 | 2 | 3 |  | 5 |  | $7^3$ | 8 | 10 | $11^1$ | 9 | $4^2$ |  |  |  |  | 6 |  |  |  | 12 |  |  |  |  |  | 13 | 14 |  |  |  |  | 39 |
|  |  | 3 |  |  |  | 7 | 8 | 11 | 12 | $9^2$ | 4 |  |  |  |  | 6 | 1 |  |  | $10^1$ |  |  |  |  |  | 13 | 2 | 5 |  |  |  | 40 |
|  |  | $3^2$ |  |  |  | 7 |  | 11 | 10 |  | 4 |  |  |  |  | 8 | 1 | 6 |  | 12 |  |  |  |  |  | $9^1$ | 2 | 5 | 13 |  |  | 41 |
|  |  | 3 |  |  |  | 7 |  | 11 | 10 | 9 | 4 |  |  |  |  | 8 | 1 | 6 |  |  |  |  |  |  |  |  | 2 | 5 |  |  |  | 42 |
|  |  |  |  |  |  | 7 | 8 | 11 | $10^1$ | 12 | 9 | $4^2$ |  |  |  | 6 | 1 |  |  | 13 |  |  |  |  |  |  | 2 | $5^3$ | 3 | 14 |  | 43 |
|  |  | 3 |  |  |  | 7 | $8^1$ | 11 | 10 | 12 | $9^2$ | 4 |  |  |  | 6 | 1 |  |  |  |  |  |  |  |  |  | 2 | 5 | 13 |  |  | 44 |
|  |  | 3 |  |  |  | 7 |  | 11 | $10^1$ | $8^2$ | $9^3$ | 4 |  |  |  | 6 | 1 |  |  | 13 |  |  |  |  |  | 12 | 2 | 5 | 14 |  |  | 45 |
|  |  | 3 |  |  |  |  |  | 11 | 12 | 10 | 13 | 4 |  |  |  | 8 | 1 | $6^3$ |  | 7 |  |  |  |  |  |  | $2^1$ | 5 | 14 |  | $9^2$ | 46 |

**Coca-Cola Cup**
First Round   Huddersfield T   (a) 1-2
                               (h) 1-1

**FA Cup**
Third Round   Manchester C   (a) 0-2

BRENTFORD 1997–98    *Back row (left to right):* Marcus Bent, David McGhee, Richard Goddard, Robert Taylor, Jamie Bates, Carl Hutchings, Gus Hurdle.
*Middle row:* Joe Omigie, Gary Duffy, Lee Harvey, Tamer Fernandes, Kevin Dearden, Graham Benstead, Stuart Myall, Kevin Dennis.
*Front row:* Ryan Denys, Simon Spencer, Ijah Anderson, Charlie Oatway, Scott Canham, Simon Wormull, Kevin Rapley, Paul Barrowcliff.

# Division 3 **BRENTFORD**

*Griffin Park, Braemar Rd, Brentford, Middlesex TW8 0NT.* Telephone: (0181) 847 2511. Fax: (0181) 568 9940. Commercial Dept: (0181) 560 6062. Press Office: (0181) 847 2511. Clubcall: 0891 121108.

*Ground capacity:* 12,763.

*Record attendance:* 38,678 v Leicester C, FA Cup 6th rd, 20 February 1949.

*Record receipts:* £111,804 v Manchester C, FA Cup 3rd rd, 25 January 1997.

*Pitch measurements:* 111yd × 74yd.

*Chairman:* Ron Noades.

*President:* E. J. Radley-Smith. *Managing Director:* G. Hargraves.

*Directors:* T. Swaisland, D. Miller, J. Herting, M. Lange, D. Webb, D. Tana.

*Manager:* Ron Noades. *Assistant Manager:* Glenn Cockerill.

*Youth Team Manager:* Bob Booker.

*Football Co-ordinator:* Kevin Lock

*Community Officer:* Lee Doyle.

*Secretary:* Polly Kates. *Physio:*

*Safety Officer:* Jill Dawson. *Marketing Manager:* Peter Gilham. *Commercial Manager:* Samantha Marmara.

*Year Formed:* 1889. *Turned Professional:* 1899. *Ltd Co.:* 1901.

*Club Nickname:* 'The Bees'.

*Previous Grounds:* 1889–91, Clifden Road; 1891–95, Benns Fields, Little Ealing; 1895–98, Shotters Field; 1898–1900, Cross Road, S. Ealing; 1900–04, Boston Park; 1904, Griffin Park.

*Foundation:* Formed as a small amateur concern in 1889 they were very successful in local circles. They won the championship of the West London Alliance in 1893 and a year later the West Middlesex Junior Cup before carrying off the Senior Cup in 1895. After winning both the London Senior Amateur Cup and the Middlesex Senior Cup in 1898 they were admitted to the Second Division of the Southern League.

*First Football League game:* 28 August 1920, Division 3, v Exeter C (a), L 0-3 – Young; Hodson, Rosier, Elliott J, Levitt, Amos, Smith, Thompson, Spreadbury, Morley, Henery.

*Record League Victory:* 9–0 v Wrexham, Division 3, 15 October 1963 – Cakebread; Coote, Jones; Slater, Scott, Higginson; Summers (1), Brooks (2), McAdams (2), Ward (2), Hales (1). (1 og).

*Record Cup Victory:* 7–0 v Windsor & Eton (away), FA Cup 1st rd, 20 November 1982 – Roche; Rowe, Harris (Booker), McNichol (1), Whitehead, Hurlock (2), Kamara, Joseph (1), Mahoney (3), Bowles, Roberts.

*Record Defeat:* 0–7 v Swansea T, Division 3 (S), 8 November 1924 and v Walsall, Division 3 (S), 19 January 1957.

*Most League Points (2 for a win):* 62, Division 3 (S), 1932–33 and Division 4, 1962–63.

*Most League Points (3 for a win):* 85, Division 2, 1994–95.

*Most League Goals:* 98, Division 4, 1962–63.

*Highest League Scorer in Season:* Jack Holliday, 38, Division 3 (S), 1932–33.

*Most League Goals in Total Aggregate:* Jim Towers, 153, 1954–61.

*Most Capped Player:* John Buttigieg, (63), Malta.

*Most League Appearances:* Ken Coote, 514, 1949–64.

*Record Transfer Fee Received:* £720,000 from Wimbledon for Dean Holdsworth, August 1992.

*Record Transfer Fee Paid:* £275,000 to Chelsea for Joe Allon, November 1992.

*Football League Record:* 1920 Original Member of Division 3; 1921–33 Division 3 (S); 1933–35 Division 2; 1935–47 Division 1; 1947–54 Division 2; 1954–62 Division 3 (S); 1962–63 Division 4; 1963–66 Division 3; 1966–72 Division 4; 1972–73 Division 3; 1973–78 Division 4; 1978–92 Division 3; 1992–93 Division 1; 1993–98 Division 2; 1998 – Division 3.

*Honours: Football League:* Division 1 best season: 5th, 1935–36; Division 2 – Champions 1934–35; Division 3 – Champions 1991–92; Division 3 (S) – Champions 1932–33; Runners-up 1929–30, 1957–58; Division 4 – Champions 1962–63. *FA Cup:* best season: 6th rd, 1938, 1946, 1949, 1989. *Football League Cup:* best season: 4th rd, 1983. *Freight Rover Trophy;* Runners-up 1985.

*Colours:* Red and white vertical striped shirts, black shorts, black stockings. *Change colours:* Blue and yellow shirts, blue shorts, yellow stockings.

**Did you know?**
Goalkeeper Jack Durston dashed from Lords Cricket Ground after taking five Surrey wickets for Middlesex to play in Brentford's opening home game against Millwall on 30 August 1920. Brentford won 1-0.

## BRENTFORD 1997–98 LEAGUE RECORD

| Match No. | Date | Venue | Opponents | Result | H/T Score | Lg. Pos. | Goalscorers | Atten-dance |
|---|---|---|---|---|---|---|---|---|
| 1 | Aug 9 | A | Millwall | L | 0-3 | 0-1 | — | 8951 |
| 2 | 16 | H | Chesterfield | D | 0-0 | 0-0 | 22 | 4000 |
| 3 | 23 | A | Watford | L | 1-3 | 0-2 | 23 | 10,125 |
| 4 | 30 | A | Grimsby T | W | 3-1 | 2-0 | 17 | Rapley [12], Taylor 2 [25, 71] | 3875 |
| 5 | Sept 2 | H | Gillingham | W | 2-0 | 0-0 | — | Bent [73], Taylor (pen) [79] | 4903 |
| 6 | 5 | A | Southend U | L | 1-3 | 1-3 | — | Rapley [2] | 3458 |
| 7 | 13 | A | Plymouth Arg | D | 0-0 | 0-0 | 15 | | 4394 |
| 8 | 19 | H | Wycombe W | D | 1-1 | 1-1 | — | Taylor [31] | 3695 |
| 9 | 27 | H | Burnley | W | 2-1 | 1-0 | 13 | Hutchings [2], Rapley [89] | 4548 |
| 10 | Oct 4 | A | Preston NE | L | 1-2 | 1-0 | 16 | Bent [35] | 8804 |
| 11 | 11 | A | York C | L | 1-3 | 0-1 | 18 | Taylor [75] | 2831 |
| 12 | 18 | H | Walsall | W | 3-0 | 0-0 | 16 | Taylor [49], Denys [56], Bent [90] | 4874 |
| 13 | 21 | H | Bristol R | L | 2-3 | 1-2 | — | Bent [7], Rapley [46] | 3967 |
| 14 | 25 | A | Luton T | L | 0-2 | 0-1 | 20 | | 5972 |
| 15 | Nov 1 | A | Bournemouth | D | 0-0 | 0-0 | 19 | | 4772 |
| 16 | 4 | H | Carlisle U | L | 0-1 | 0-1 | — | | 3424 |
| 17 | 8 | H | Bristol C | L | 1-4 | 0-2 | 24 | Reina [84] | 6183 |
| 18 | 18 | A | Northampton T | L | 0-4 | 0-4 | — | | 5277 |
| 19 | 22 | A | Oldham Ath | D | 1-1 | 0-0 | 22 | Scott [80] | 5012 |
| 20 | 29 | H | Wrexham | D | 1-1 | 0-0 | 23 | Aspinall [80] | 3748 |
| 21 | Dec 2 | A | Fulham | D | 1-1 | 1-0 | — | Gleghorn [35] | 10,767 |
| 22 | 13 | H | Blackpool | W | 3-1 | 1-1 | 21 | Taylor [32], Townley 2 [62, 78] | 3725 |
| 23 | 20 | A | Wigan Ath | L | 0-4 | 0-2 | 21 | | 3301 |
| 24 | 26 | H | Southend U | D | 1-1 | 1-0 | 22 | Taylor [42] | 5341 |
| 25 | 29 | A | Gillingham | L | 1-3 | 0-2 | — | Taylor [81] | 5908 |
| 26 | Jan 3 | A | Chesterfield | D | 0-0 | 0-0 | 22 | | 4049 |
| 27 | 10 | H | Millwall | W | 2-1 | 1-1 | 21 | Taylor [44], Aspinall [59] | 5529 |
| 28 | 17 | A | Grimsby T | L | 0-4 | 0-2 | 21 | | 4624 |
| 29 | 24 | H | Watford | L | 1-2 | 1-1 | 23 | Rapley [21] | 6969 |
| 30 | 31 | H | Plymouth Arg | W | 3-1 | 0-1 | 22 | Bates [62], Scott [66], Hogg [88] | 4783 |
| 31 | Feb 7 | A | Wycombe W | D | 0-0 | 0-0 | 22 | | 6328 |
| 32 | 14 | H | Preston NE | D | 0-0 | 0-0 | 22 | | 4952 |
| 33 | 21 | A | Burnley | D | 1-1 | 0-0 | 22 | Taylor [50] | 10,097 |
| 34 | 24 | A | Walsall | D | 0-0 | 0-0 | — | | 3166 |
| 35 | 28 | H | York C | L | 1-2 | 0-0 | 24 | McGhee [75] | 4490 |
| 36 | Mar 3 | A | Bristol C | D | 2-2 | 1-0 | — | Bryan [44], Rapley [79] | 10,398 |
| 37 | 7 | H | Bournemouth | W | 3-2 | 2-2 | 22 | Hutchings [3], Bryan [44], Rapley [81] | 4973 |
| 38 | 14 | H | Carlisle U | W | 2-1 | 0-1 | 20 | Hogg [62], Scott [72] | 6021 |
| 39 | 21 | H | Northampton T | D | 0-0 | 0-0 | 20 | | 5746 |
| 40 | 28 | H | Oldham Ath | W | 2-1 | 2-0 | 20 | Scott [38], Taylor [44] | 4547 |
| 41 | Apr 4 | A | Wrexham | D | 2-2 | 1-0 | 20 | Rapley [9], Hutchings [68] | 4132 |
| 42 | 11 | H | Fulham | L | 0-2 | 0-1 | 21 | | 10,510 |
| 43 | 13 | A | Blackpool | W | 2-1 | 2-0 | 21 | Hutchings [3], Aspinall (pen) [13] | 3926 |
| 44 | 18 | H | Wigan Ath | L | 0-2 | 0-0 | 21 | | 4480 |
| 45 | 25 | A | Luton T | D | 2-2 | 1-1 | 20 | Scott [22], Hutchings [80] | 6598 |
| 46 | May 2 | A | Bristol R | L | 1-2 | 0-0 | 21 | Rapley [79] | 9043 |

**Final League Position: 21**      1996–97 DIV2 4

### GOALSCORERS

*League (50):* Taylor 13 (2 pens), Rapley 9, Hutchings 5, Scott 5, Bent 4, Aspinall 3 (1 pen), Bryan 2, Hogg 2, Townley 2, Bates 1, Denys 1, Gleghorn 1, McGhee 1, Reina 1.
*Coca-Cola Cup (7):* Taylor 3, Rapley 2, Bent 1, Denys 1.
*FA Cup (2):* Taylor 2.

| Dearden K 35 | Hurdle G 17 | Anderson I 17 | Hutchings C 43 | Bates J 40 | McGhee D 19+10 | Spencer S 1 | Wormull S 3+2 | Bent M 19+5 | Barrowcliff P 5+6 | Taylor R 39+1 | Denys R 12+7 | Canham S 11+11 | Rapley K 23+14 | Onigie J —+1 | Oatway C 30+3 | Bryan D 2+9 | Townley L 15+1 | Hall S 6 | Reina R 2+4 | Benstead G 1 | Colgan N 5 | Myall S 2 | Cockerill G 23 | Gleghorn N 11 | Scott A 24+2 | Aspinall W 24 | McPherson M 7+2 | Watson P 25 | Pollitt M 5 | Hogg G 17 | Dennis K —+5 | Clark D —+4 | Cullip D 13 | Thompson N 6+2 | Blaney S 4+1 | Match No. |
|---|---|---|---|---|---|---|---|---|---|---|---|---|---|---|---|---|---|---|---|---|---|---|---|---|---|---|---|---|---|---|---|---|---|---|---|---|
| 1 | 2 | 3 | 4 | 5 | 6 | 7 | 8 | 9¹ | 10 | 11 | 12 | | | | | | | | | | | | | | | | | | | | | | | | | 1 |
| 1 | 2 | 3 | 4 | 5 | | | 7¹ | 10 | 6 | 11 | 9² | 8 | 12 | 13 | | | | | | | | | | | | | | | | | | | | | | 2 |
| 1 | 2 | 3 | 4 | 5 | | | | 10 | 6¹ | 11 | 9 | 8 | 12 | | | | | | | | | | | | | | | | | | | | | | | 3 |
| 1 | 2 | 3 | 4 | 5 | | | | 9 | | 11 | 7 | 8 | 10 | | 6 | | | | | | | | | | | | | | | | | | | | | 4 |
| 1 | 2 | 3 | 4 | 5 | | | | 9 | | 11 | 7 | 8 | 10 | | 6 | | | | | | | | | | | | | | | | | | | | | 5 |
| 1 | 2 | 3 | 4 | 5 | 12 | | | 9 | | 11 | 7 | 8¹ | 10 | | 6 | | | | | | | | | | | | | | | | | | | | | 6 |
| 1 | 2 | 3 | 4 | 5 | | | | 9 | | 11 | 7¹ | 8 | 10 | | 6 | 12 | | | | | | | | | | | | | | | | | | | | 7 |
| 1 | 2 | 3 | 4 | 5 | 12 | | | 9 | | 11 | 7¹ | | 10 | | 8 | 6 | | | | | | | | | | | | | | | | | | | | 8 |
| 1 | 2 | 3 | 4 | 5 | 12 | | | 9 | | 11 | 7² | 13 | 10 | | 8 | 6¹ | | | | | | | | | | | | | | | | | | | | 9 |
| 1 | 2 | 3 | 4 | 5 | 12 | | | 9² | | 11 | | | 10 | | 8 | 6¹ | 7 | 13 | | | | | | | | | | | | | | | | | | 10 |
| | 2¹ | 3 | 4 | 5 | 6 | | | 9 | | 11 | | 12 | 10² | | 8 | | 7 | 13 | | 1 | | | | | | | | | | | | | | | | 11 |
| | | 3 | 4 | 5 | 12 | | | 9 | | 11 | 7¹ | | 10² | | 8 | 13 | 2 | 6 | | | 1 | | | | | | | | | | | | | | | 12 |
| | | 3 | 4 | 5 | 12 | | | 9 | | 11 | 7² | | 10 | | 8 | 13 | 2¹ | 6 | | | 1 | | | | | | | | | | | | | | | 13 |
| | | 3 | 4 | 5 | 2 | | | 9¹ | | 11 | 7 | 12 | 10 | | 8 | | | 6 | | | 1 | | | | | | | | | | | | | | | 14 |
| | | 3 | 4 | 5 | 6 | | | 9 | | 11 | | | 10 | | 8 | | 2 | | | | 1 | 7 | | | | | | | | | | | | | | 15 |
| | 2¹ | 3 | 4 | 5 | 6 | | | 9 | | 11 | | 13 | 12 | | 10 | | 8 | | | | 1 | 7² | | | | | | | | | | | | | | 16 |
| 1 | 2 | 3 | 4 | 5 | 7 | | | 9 | | 11 | | 12 | | | 6 | | | | 10 | | | | 8¹ | | | | | | | | | | | | | 17 |
| 1 | 2 | | 4 | 5 | 7¹ | | | 9 | | 11 | 12 | 13 | 14 | | 6 | | | | 10³ | | | | 8² | 3 | | | | | | | | | | | | 18 |
| 1 | 2³ | | 4 | 5 | | | | | | 11 | 12 | | | | 6 | | 7 | | 13 | | | | 8² | 3 | 9¹ | 10 | 14 | | | | | | | | | 19 |
| 1 | | | 4 | 5 | | | | | | 11³ | 12 | 13 | 14 | | 6¹ | | 7 | | | | | | 8² | 3 | 9 | 10 | | 2 | | | | | | | | 20 |
| 1 | | | 4 | 5 | | | | | | 11 | 12 | | | | 6 | | 7 | | 13 | | | | 8¹ | 3 | 9² | 10 | | 2 | | | | | | | | 21 |
| 1 | | | 4 | 5 | | | | | | 11¹ | 12 | 13 | | | 6² | 14 | 7 | | | | | | 8 | | 9 | 10 | 2 | 3² | | | | | | | | 22 |
| 1 | | | 4 | 5³ | | | | | | | 12 | 13 | 10 | | 6 | 14 | 7 | | | | | | 8¹ | 11 | 9 | | 3 | 2² | | | | | | | | 23 |
| 1 | | | 4 | 5 | | | | | | 11 | 12 | 13 | | | 6 | 14 | 7 | | | | | | 8 | | 9¹ | 10 | 3² | 2³ | | | | | | | | 24 |
| 1 | | | 4 | 5 | | | | | | 11 | 12 | 2² | | | 6³ | 14 | 7 | | | | | | 8 | | 9 | 10 | | 3 | | | | | 13 | | | 25 |
| 1 | | | 4 | 5 | | | | | | 11 | | | | | 6 | | 7 | | | | | | 8 | | 9 | 10 | 2 | 3 | | | | | | | | 26 |
| 1 | | | 4¹ | 5 | | | | | | 11 | 12 | | | | 6 | | 7 | | 13 | | | | 8² | | 9 | 10 | 2 | 3 | | | | | | | | 27 |
| 1 | | | 4³ | 5 | | | | 12 | 8 | 11 | | 13 | | | 6 | | 7¹ | | | | | | | | 9² | 10 | 2 | 3 | | | | | | | | 28 |
| 1 | 2 | | 4 | 5 | | | | | | 11 | | | | | | | 7 | | | | | | 8 | | 9 | 10 | | 3 | 1 | 6 | | | | | | 29 |
| 1 | 2 | | 4 | 5 | | | | | | 11 | 12 | | | | | | 7³ | | | | | | 8 | | 9 | 10² | | 3¹ | 1 | 6 | 14 | | 13 | | | 30 |
| 1 | 2 | | 4¹ | 5 | | | | | | 11 | 12 | 13 | | | | | 7 | | | | | | 8 | | 9² | 10 | | 3 | 1 | 6 | | | | | | 31 |
| 1 | 2 | | 4² | 5 | | | | | | 11 | 12 | | | | | | 7¹ | | | | | | 8 | | 9 | 10 | | 3 | 1 | 6 | | | 13 | | | 32 |
| 1 | 2 | | 4 | 5 | | | | | | 11 | | | | | | | 7 | | | | | | 8 | | 9¹ | 10 | 12 | 3 | 1 | 6 | | | | | | 33 |
| 1 | 2 | | 4 | 5 | | | | | | 11 | | | | | | | 7 | | | | | | 8 | | 9¹ | 10 | 12 | 3 | | 6 | | | | | | 34 |
| 1 | 2 | | | 5 | | | | | | 11 | 12 | 13 | | | | | 7³ | | | | | | 8¹ | | 9² | 10 | | 3 | | 6 | 14 | | 4 | | | 35 |
| 1 | 2 | | | | | | | | | 11 | 12 | 13 | | | | | 7² | | | | | | 8 | 5¹ | 9³ | 10 | | 3 | | 6 | 14 | | 4 | | | 36 |
| 1 | 2 | | | 5 | | | | | | 11 | 12 | 13 | | | | | 7³ | | | | | | 8 | | 9² | 10 | 14 | 3 | | 6¹ | | | 4 | | | 37 |
| 1 | 2 | | 4¹ | 5 | | | | | | 11 | 12 | 13 | | | | | 7³ | | | | | | 8² | | 9 | 10 | 14 | 3 | | 6 | | | | | | 38 |
| 1 | 2 | | 4 | 5 | | | | | | 11 | 12 | 13 | | | | | 7² | | | | | | 8¹ | | 9³ | 10 | | 3 | | 6 | 14 | | | | | 39 |
| 1 | 2 | | 4 | 5 | | | | | | 11 | 12 | | | | | | 7 | | | | | | 8¹ | | 9 | 10 | | 3 | | 6 | | | | | | 40 |
| 1 | 2 | | 4 | 5 | | | | | | 11¹ | | | | | | | 7 | | | | | | 8³ | | 9² | 10 | 12 | 3 | | 6 | 13 | 14 | | | | 41 |
| 1 | 2 | | 4 | 5 | | | | | | 11¹ | 12 | 13 | | | | | 7 | | | | | | 8² | | 9 | 10 | 14 | 3 | | 6³ | | | | | | 42 |
| 1 | 2 | | 4 | 5 | | | | | | | | 13 | 12² | | | | | | | | | | 8 | | 9¹ | 10 | | 3 | | 6 | | | | 11 | 7 | 43 |
| 1 | 2 | | 4² | 5 | | | | | | | | | | | | | 7 | | | | | | 8¹ | | 9 | 10 | 12 | 3 | | 6 | 13 | | | 11 | | 44 |
| 1 | 2 | | 4 | 5 | | | | | | | 12 | 13 | | | | | | | | | | | 8³ | | 9 | 10² | | 3 | | 6 | 14 | | | 11¹ | 7 | 45 |
| 1 | 2 | | 4 | 5² | | | | | | 11 | | 13 | | | | | | | | | | | 8¹ | | 9 | 10 | 12 | 3 | | 6 | 14 | | | | 7³ | 46 |

**Coca-Cola Cup**
First Round — Shrewsbury T — (h) 1-1 / (a) 5-3
Second Round — Southampton — (a) 1-3 / (h) 0-2

**FA Cup**
First Round — Colchester U — (h) 2-2 / (a) 0-0

BRIGHTON & HOVE ALBION 1997–98   *Back row (left to right):* John Jackson (Youth Development Officer), Robbie Reinelt, Ross McNally, Peter Smith, Mark Morris, John Humphrey, Stuart Tuck, Malcolm Stuart (Physio).

*Middle row:* Kerry Mayo, Craig Maskell, James Rowlands, Mark Ormerod, Stuart Storer, Ross Johnson, Nicky Rust, Derek Allan, Denny Mundee, Paul Armstrong.

*Front row:* Jock Riddell (Kit Man), Gary Hobson, Ian Baird, Paul McDonald, Steve Gritt (Manager), Jeff Minton, Eric Saul, John Westcott, Jeff Wood (Assistant Manager).

# Division 3    **BRIGHTON & HOVE ALBION**

*Offices:* Fifth floor, Hanover House, 118 Queens Road, Brighton BN1 3XG. Telephone: (01273) 778855. Fax: (01273) 321095. Ground address (Match days only): *The Priestfield Stadium (Gillingham FC), Redfern Avenue, Gillingham, Kent. Telephone: (01634) 851854. Albion Clubline: 0891 800609.

*Ground capacity:* 10,952.

*Record attendance:* 36,747 v Fulham, Division 2, 27 December 1958.

*Record receipts:* £109,615.65 v Crawley T, FA Cup 3rd rd, 4 January 1992.

*Pitch measurements:* 114yd × 77yd (at Gillingham).

*Directors:* H. R. Knight (Chairman), W. E. Archer, M. J. Perry, R. L. Pinnock FCA.

*Non-Executive Directors:* R. O. Faulkner, Sir John Smith QPM.

*Manager:* Brian Horton. *Assistant Manager:* Jeff Wood. *General Manager:* Nick Rowe.

*Secretary:* Derek Allan.

*Physio:* Malcolm Stuart. *Youth Development Officer:* Martin Hinshelwood. *Youth Team Coach:* Dean Wilkins.

*Year Formed:* 1901. *Turned Professional:* 1901. *Ltd Co.:* 1904.

*Previous Grounds:* 1901, County Ground; 1902, Goldstone Ground.

*Club Nickname:* 'The Seagulls'.

*Foundation:* A professional club Brighton United was formed in November 1897 at the Imperial Hotel, Queen's Road, but folded in March 1900 after less than two seasons in the Southern League at the County Ground. An amateur team, Brighton & Hove Rangers was then formed by some prominent United supporters and after one season at Withdean, decided to turn semi-professional and play at the County Ground. Rangers were accepted into the Southern League but then also folded June 1901. John Jackson the former United manager organised a meeting at the Seven Stars public house, Ship Street on 24 June 1901 at which a new third club Brighton & Hove United was formed. They took over Rangers' place in the Southern League and pitch at County Ground. The name was changed to Brighton & Hove Albion before a match was played because of objections by Hove FC.

*First Football League game:* 28 August 1920, Division 3, v Southend U (a), L 0-2 – Hayes; Woodhouse, Little; Hall, Comber, Bentley; Longstaff, Ritchie, Doran, Rodgerson, March.

*Record League Victory:* 9–1 v Newport Co, Division 3 (S), 18 April 1951 – Ball; Tennant (1p), Mansell (1p); Willard, McCoy, Wilson; Reed, McNichol (4), Garbutt, Bennett (2), Keene (1). 9–1 v Southend U, Division 3, 27 November 1965 – Powney; Magill, Baxter; Leck, Gall, Turner; Gould (1), Collins (1), Livesey (2), Smith (3), Goodchild (2).

*Record Cup Victory:* 10–1 v Wisbech, FA Cup 1st rd, 13 November 1965 – Powney; Magill, Baxter; Collins (1), Gall, Turner; Gould, Smith (2), Livesey (3), Cassidy (2), Goodchild (1). (1 og).

*Record Defeat:* 0–9 v Middlesbrough, Division 2, 23 August 1958.

*Most League Points (2 for a win):* 65, Division 3 (S), 1955–56 and Division 3, 1971–72.

*Most League Points (3 for a win):* 84, Division 3, 1987–88.

*Most League Goals:* 112, Division 3 (S), 1955–56.

*Highest League Scorer in Season:* Peter Ward, 32, Division 3, 1976–77.

*Most League Goals in Total Aggregate:* Tommy Cook, 114, 1922–29.

*Most Capped Player:* Steve Penney, 17, Northern Ireland.

*Most League Appearances:* 'Tug' Wilson, 509, 1922–36.

*Record Transfer Fee Received:* £900,000 from Liverpool for Mark Lawrenson, August 1981.

*Record Transfer Fee Paid:* £500,000 to Manchester U for Andy Ritchie, October 1980.

*Football League Record:* 1920 Original Member of Division 3; 1921–58 Division 3 (S); 1958–62 Division 2; 1962–63 Division 3; 1963–65 Division 4; 1965–72 Division 3; 1972–73 Division 2; 1973–77 Division 3; 1977–79 Division 2; 1979–83 Division 1; 1983–87 Division 2; 1987–88 Division 3; 1988–96 Division 2; 1996– Division 3.

*Honours:* Football League: Division 1 best season: 13th, 1981–82; Division 2 – Runners-up 1978–79; Division 3 (S) – Champions 1957–58; Runners-up 1953–54, 1955–56; Division 3 – Runners-up 1971–72, 1976–77, 1987–88; Division 4 – Champions 1964–65. FA Cup: Runners-up 1983. Football League Cup: best season: 5th rd, 1979.

*Colours:* Blue and white striped shirts, blue shorts, white stockings. *Change colours:* All red.

**Did you know?**
Mark Morris made his 500th career League appearance against Rochdale on 27 September 1997 and scored in a 2-1 win.

*N.B. The club will only be playing at Gillingham until the end of October 1998. It will then return to the Brighton area to play home matches at Withdean Sports Stadium, Tongdean Lane, Brighton. Every home match will then be 'all-ticket'.*

## BRIGHTON & HOVE ALBION 1997–98 LEAGUE RECORD

| Match No. | Date | | Venue | Opponents | Result | | H/T Score | Lg. Pos. | Goalscorers | Attendance |
|---|---|---|---|---|---|---|---|---|---|---|
| 1 | Aug | 9 | A | Swansea C | L | 0-1 | 0-0 | — | | 6800 |
| 2 | | 16 | H | Macclesfield T | D | 1-1 | 0-1 | 19 | McDonald 63 | 2336 |
| 3 | | 22 | A | Scarborough | L | 1-2 | 1-1 | — | Mayo 25 | 2505 |
| 4 | | 30 | H | Leyton Orient | L | 0-1 | 0-0 | 23 | | 2285 |
| 5 | Sept | 3 | H | Peterborough U | D | 2-2 | 1-1 | — | Mayo 14, Maskell 55 | 1215 |
| 6 | | 8 | A | Colchester U | L | 1-3 | 0-1 | — | Baird 47 | 3081 |
| 7 | | 13 | H | Darlington | D | 0-0 | 0-0 | 23 | | 1803 |
| 8 | | 20 | A | Torquay U | L | 0-3 | 0-2 | 23 | | 2110 |
| 9 | | 27 | H | Rochdale | W | 2-1 | 1-1 | 22 | Morris 15, Tuck 73 | 1544 |
| 10 | Oct | 4 | A | Doncaster R | W | 3-1 | 1-0 | 21 | Allan 38, Maskell 66, Pemberton (og) 85 | 2351 |
| 11 | | 11 | A | Chester C | L | 0-2 | 0-1 | 21 | | 2402 |
| 12 | | 18 | H | Exeter C | L | 1-3 | 0-1 | 22 | Reinelt 79 | 2210 |
| 13 | | 22 | H | Lincoln C | L | 0-1 | 0-0 | — | | 1036 |
| 14 | | 25 | A | Hull C | D | 0-0 | 0-0 | 23 | | 5686 |
| 15 | Nov | 1 | A | Hartlepool U | D | 0-0 | 0-0 | 23 | | 2561 |
| 16 | | 5 | H | Barnet | L | 0-3 | 0-1 | — | | 1025 |
| 17 | | 8 | H | Rotherham U | L | 1-2 | 0-1 | 23 | Storer 86 | 1950 |
| 18 | | 18 | A | Cambridge U | D | 1-1 | 0-1 | — | Emblen 73 | 2370 |
| 19 | | 22 | H | Cardiff C | L | 0-1 | 0-1 | 23 | | 2086 |
| 20 | | 29 | A | Scunthorpe U | W | 2-0 | 0-0 | 23 | Storer 47, Ryan 68 | 3187 |
| 21 | Dec | 3 | H | Notts Co | L | 0-1 | 0-1 | — | | 1279 |
| 22 | | 13 | A | Mansfield T | D | 1-1 | 0-1 | 23 | Minton 83 | 2197 |
| 23 | | 20 | H | Shrewsbury T | D | 0-0 | 0-0 | 23 | | 1917 |
| 24 | | 26 | H | Colchester U | D | 4-4 | 0-3 | 23 | Emblen 3 47, 62, 66, Minton (pen) 86 | 2647 |
| 25 | | 28 | A | Peterborough U | W | 2-1 | 1-0 | 23 | Minton 21, Reinelt 54 | 8221 |
| 26 | Jan | 10 | H | Swansea C | L | 0-1 | 0-1 | 23 | | 2997 |
| 27 | | 17 | A | Leyton Orient | L | 1-3 | 0-0 | 23 | Reinelt 53 | 6591 |
| 28 | | 24 | A | Scarborough | D | 1-1 | 1-0 | 23 | Smith 30 | 1988 |
| 29 | | 27 | A | Macclesfield T | L | 0-1 | 0-0 | — | | 2024 |
| 30 | | 31 | A | Darlington | L | 0-1 | 0-0 | 23 | | 2487 |
| 31 | Feb | 7 | H | Torquay U | L | 1-4 | 1-1 | 23 | Smith 24 | 2083 |
| 32 | | 14 | H | Doncaster R | D | 0-0 | 0-0 | 23 | | 6339 |
| 33 | | 21 | A | Rochdale | L | 0-2 | 0-1 | 23 | | 1865 |
| 34 | | 24 | A | Exeter C | L | 1-2 | 1-1 | — | Ansah 33 | 2754 |
| 35 | | 28 | H | Chester C | W | 3-2 | 2-1 | 23 | Mayo 2 30, 60, Ansah 42 | 2510 |
| 36 | Mar | 3 | A | Rotherham U | D | 0-0 | 0-0 | — | | 3724 |
| 37 | | 7 | H | Hartlepool U | D | 0-0 | 0-0 | 23 | | 2811 |
| 38 | | 14 | A | Barnet | L | 0-2 | 0-1 | 23 | | 2845 |
| 39 | | 21 | H | Cambridge U | L | 0-2 | 0-2 | 23 | | 2746 |
| 40 | | 28 | A | Cardiff C | D | 0-0 | 0-0 | 23 | | 3509 |
| 41 | Apr | 4 | H | Scunthorpe U | W | 2-1 | 1-0 | 22 | Minton 2 (1 pen) 28, 87 (p) | 2141 |
| 42 | | 11 | A | Notts Co | D | 2-2 | 1-0 | 23 | Mayo 2 20, 70 | 5344 |
| 43 | | 13 | H | Mansfield T | D | 1-1 | 1-0 | 23 | Reinelt 33 | 2704 |
| 44 | | 18 | A | Shrewsbury T | L | 1-2 | 1-0 | 23 | Minton 29 | 2728 |
| 45 | | 25 | H | Hull C | D | 2-2 | 1-0 | 23 | Ansah 32, Barker 54 | 3888 |
| 46 | May | 2 | A | Lincoln C | L | 1-2 | 0-0 | 23 | Barker 90 | 9890 |

**Final League Position: 23**          1996–97 DIV3 23

### GOALSCORERS
*League (38):* Mayo 6, Minton 6 (2 pens), Emblen 4, Reinelt 4, Ansah 3, Barker 2, Maskell 2, Smith 2, Storer 2, Allan 1, Baird 1, McDonald 1, Morris 1, Ryan 1, Tuck 1, own goal 1.
*Coca-Cola Cup (2):* Maskell 1, Minton 1 (pen).
*FA Cup (1):* Storer 1.

| Ormerod M 30 | Humphrey J 11 | Hobson G 30+3 | Minton J 36 | Morris M 19 | Johnson R 38 | Storer S 33+4 | Mayo K 43+1 | Reinelt R 25+7 | Maskell C 16+1 | McDonald P 7+4 | Westcott J 19+15 | Armstrong P 12+8 | Allan D 17+2 | Baird I 9 | Smith P 25+2 | Tuck S 19+3 | Gislason V 7 | Emblen P 15 | Ryan D 1+3 | Rust N 16 | Ansah A 7+7 | Saul E —+4 | Barker R 15+2 | Linger P 17+2 | Barnes S 12 | McNally R 1+1 | Mahoney-Johnson M 3+1 | Atkinson G 9 | Hilton D 4+1 | Andrews B 2+1 | Thomas S 7 | Woolsey J 1+2 | Streeter T —+2 | Match No. |
|---|---|---|---|---|---|---|---|---|---|---|---|---|---|---|---|---|---|---|---|---|---|---|---|---|---|---|---|---|---|---|---|---|---|---|
| 1 | 2 | 3 | 4 | 5 | 6 | 7 | 8 | 9 | 10 | 11¹ | 12 | | | | | | | | | | | | | | | | | | | | | | | 1 |
| 1 | 2 | 3 | 4² | 5 | 6 | 7 | 8¹ | 9 | 10 | 11 | 12 | 13 | | | | | | | | | | | | | | | | | | | | | | 2 |
| 1 | 2² | 3 | 4 | 5 | 6 | 7 | 8 | 11 | 9 | 10¹ | 12 | | | 13 | | | | | | | | | | | | | | | | | | | | 3 |
| 1 | 2 | 3 | 4 | 5 | 6 | 7² | 8 | 12 | 10 | 11¹ | 13 | | | | 9 | | | | | | | | | | | | | | | | | | | 4 |
| 1 | 2² | 3 | 4¹ | 5 | 6 | 7 | 8 | 11 | 10 | | 12 | | | | 9 | 13 | | | | | | | | | | | | | | | | | | 5 |
| 1 | | 3 | | 5 | 6 | 7 | 8 | 11 | 10¹ | | 13 | 12 | 4² | | 9 | 2 | | | | | | | | | | | | | | | | | | 6 |
| 1 | | | | 5 | 6² | 7 | 8 | 11 | 10 | | 13 | 12 | 4 | | 9 | 2 | 3¹ | | | | | | | | | | | | | | | | | 7 |
| 1 | | | | 5 | 6 | 7 | 3 | 8¹ | | | 11 | 10 | 12 | 14 | 4 | 9 | 2² | 13³ | | | | | | | | | | | | | | | | 8 |
| 1 | 2 | | 4 | 5 | | | 12 | 8 | 10 | | | | 7¹ | 11 | 6 | 9 | | 3 | | | | | | | | | | | | | | | | 9 |
| 1 | 2 | | 4 | 5 | | | 12 | 8 | 13 | | 10² | | 7¹ | 11 | 6 | 9 | | 3 | | | | | | | | | | | | | | | | 10 |
| 1 | 2 | | 4 | 5 | | | 12 | 8 | 10 | | | | 7¹ | | 6 | 9 | | 3 | 11 | | | | | | | | | | | | | | | 11 |
| 1 | 2 | | 4 | 5 | | | 8 | 12 | 10 | | | | 7 | | 6 | 9 | | 3 | 11¹ | | | | | | | | | | | | | | | 12 |
| 1 | 2 | | 4 | 5 | | | 8 | 9 | 10 | | | | 7 | | 6 | | | 3 | 11 | | | | | | | | | | | | | | | 13 |
| 1 | 2 | | 4 | 5 | | | 8 | 9 | 10 | | | | 7 | | 6 | | | 3 | 11 | | | | | | | | | | | | | | | 14 |
| 1 | 12 | | 5 | 2 | | | 4 | 8 | 9 | | 10 | | 7¹ | | 11 | 6 | 9 | 3 | | | | | | | | | | | | | | | | 15 |
| 1 | 3 | | 5 | 2 | | | 4 | 8 | 10¹ | | 12 | | 7 | 13 | 6 | 11² | 9 | | | | | | | | | | | | | | | | | 16 |
| 1 | 3 | | 5 | 2³ | | | 4 | 8 | 10 | | 12 | | 7¹ | 13 | 6 | 14 | 11² | 9 | | | | | | | | | | | | | | | | 17 |
| | | | 4 | | 6 | 7 | | 9 | | | 11 | | | | 8 | 5 | | 2 | 3 | 10 | 1 | | | | | | | | | | | | | 18 |
| | | | 4 | | 6 | 7 | | 9 | | | 12 | | | | 8² | 5 | | 2 | 3 | 10 | 11¹ | 1 | 13 | | | | | | | | | | | 19 |
| | | | 4 | 5 | 6 | 7 | 8 | 9 | | | 11¹ | | | | | | | 2 | 3 | 10 | 12 | 1 | | | | | | | | | | | | 20 |
| 12 | | | 4 | 5¹ | 6 | 7 | 8 | 9 | | | 11 | | | | | | | 2 | 3 | 10 | | 1 | | | | | | | | | | | | 21 |
| | | | 4 | 5 | 6² | 7 | 8 | 9 | | | 11 | | | | | | | 2 | 3¹ | 10 | 12 | 1 | 13 | | | | | | | | | | | 22 |
| | | | 4 | 5 | 6 | 7¹ | 8² | 12 | | | | | | | | | | 2 | 3 | 10 | 1 | 13 | 9 | 11 | | | | | | | | | | 23 |
| | | | 4 | 5 | 6 | 7 | 8 | 12 | | | | | | | | | | 2 | 3¹ | 10 | 1 | | 9 | 11 | | | | | | | | | | 24 |
| | | | 4 | 5 | 6 | 7¹ | 3 | 12 | | | 8² | | 14 | | | | | 2 | | 10 | 13³ | 1 | 9 | 11 | | | | | | | | | | 25 |
| | | | 4 | 5 | 6 | 3 | 7 | 8² | | | 12 | | | | | | | 2 | | 10 | 1 | 13 | 9 | 11¹ | | | | | | | | | | 26 |
| | | | 4 | | 6 | 7 | 8 | 12 | | | | | 5 | | | | | 2 | 3¹ | 10 | 1 | | 9 | 11 | | | | | | | | | | 27 |
| | | | 4 | | 6 | 3 | 7 | | | | | | 5 | | | | | 2 | | 10 | 1 | | 9 | 8 | 11 | | | | | | | | | 28 |
| 12 | | | 4 | | 6 | 3 | 7 | 13 | | | | | 5¹ | | | | | 2 | 14 | 10 | 1 | | 9² | 8¹ | 11 | | | | | | | | | 29 |
| | | | 4 | 5 | 6² | 8 | 7 | 12 | | | | | | | | | | 2 | 3 | 10 | 1 | | 9¹ | 11 | 13 | | | | | | | | | 30 |
| | | | 4 | 5 | | 8 | 10 | 7¹ | | | | | | | | | | 2 | 3² | | 1 | 14 | 12 | 9³ | 13 | 11 | 6 | | | | | | | 31 |
| | | | 4 | 5 | | 6 | 7 | 3 | 10¹ | | | | | | | | | 2 | | | 1 | | 12 | 8 | 11 | 9 | | | | | | | | 32 |
| | | | 4 | 5 | | 6 | 7 | 3 | 10² | | 12 | | | | | | | 2 | 14 | | 1 | 13 | | 8¹ | 11 | 9¹ | | | | | | | | 33 |
| 1 | | | 4¹ | 5 | 6 | 7 | 8 | 9 | | | | | | | | | | 2 | 3 | | 10² | | 13 | 12 | 11 | | | | | | | | | 34 |
| 1 | | | | 5 | 6 | 7 | 8 | 9 | | | | | | | | | | 2 | 3 | | 10 | | 4 | 11 | | | | | | | | | | 35 |
| 1 | | | | 5 | 6 | 7 | 8 | 9 | | | | | | | | | | 2 | | | 10 | | 4 | 11 | 3 | | | | | | | | | 36 |
| 1 | | | | 5 | 6 | 7 | 8 | 9¹ | 12 | | | | | | | | | 2 | | | 10² | | 4 | 11 | 13 | 3 | | | | | | | | 37 |
| 1 | | | | 5 | 6 | 7 | 8 | 9¹ | 12 | | | | | | | | | 2 | | | | 13 | 4² | 11 | | 3 | 10 | | | | | | | 38 |
| 1 | | | 4 | 5 | 6 | 7¹ | 8 | 12 | 9 | | | | | | | | | 2 | | | 13 | | | 11 | | 3 | 10² | | | | | | | 39 |
| 1 | | | 4 | 5 | 6 | 7 | 8 | 12 | | | | | | | | | | 2 | | | 13 | | 10¹ | | | 11 | 10¹ | 3 | 9² | | | | | 40 |
| 1 | | | 4 | 5 | 6 | 7 | 8³ | 12² | | | | | | | | | | 2 | | | 10¹ | | 9 | | | 3 | 13 | 14 | 11 | | | | | 41 |
| 1 | | | 4 | 5¹ | 6 | 7 | 8 | | | | | | | | | | | 2 | | | | | 9 | 2 | | 3 | 10² | | 11 | 12 | 13 | | | 42 |
| 1 | | | 4 | 5 | 6 | 7 | 8 | 10 | | | | | | | | | | 2 | | | | | 9 | 2 | | 3 | | | 11¹ | 12 | | | | 43 |
| 1 | | | 4 | 5 | 6 | 7 | 8 | 10¹ | | | | | | | | | | 12 | | | | | 9 | 2 | | 3 | | | 11 | | | | | 44 |
| 1 | | | 4 | 5 | | 7 | 12 | 13 | | | 8 | | | | | | | 10 | | | | | 9 | 2¹ | | 3 | | | 11¹ | 6 | | | | 45 |
| 1 | | | 4 | 5 | | 6 | 12² | 8 | 14 | | | | | | | 8 | | 2¹ | 3 | | 10 | | 9 | | | | | | 11 | 7³ | 13 | | | 46 |

**Coca-Cola Cup**
First Round    Leyton Orient    (h)  1-1
                               (a)  1-3

**FA Cup**
First Round    Hereford U    (a)  1-2

BRISTOL CITY 1997–98   *Back row (left to right):* Louis Carey, Matthew Hale, Gregory Goodridge, Paul Tisdale, Steve Phillips, Keith Welch, Stuart Naylor, Jim Brennan, Mickey Bell, Steve Torpey, Adam Locke.

*Middle row:* Tony Fawthrop (Chief Scout), Dr Dasgupta (Club Doctor), Rob Edwards, Brian Tinnion, Shaun Goater, Shaun Taylor, Matthew Hewlett, Scott Paterson, Mark Shail, Colin Cramb, Darren Hobbs, Peter Amos (Youth Team Coach), Mike Gibson (Goalkeeping Coach).

*Front row:* Michael Vanes, Kevin Langan, Tom Docherty, Dwayne Plummer, Terry Connor (Coach), John Ward (Manager), Buster Footman (Physio), Sean Dyche, Dominic Barclay, Mommainais Bokoto, Gary Owers.

# Division 1            **BRISTOL CITY**

*Ashton Gate, Bristol BS3 2EJ.* Telephone: (0117) 9630630 (5 lines). Fax: (0117) 9630400. Commercial: (0117) 9630600. Shop: (0117) 9538566. Clubcall: 0891 121176. Supporters Club: (0117) 9665554. Community Dept: (0117) 9664685.

*Ground capacity:* 21,479.

*Record attendance:* 43,335 v Preston NE, FA Cup 5th rd, 16 February 1935.

*Record receipts:* £148,282 v Everton, FA Cup 4th rd, 29 January 1995.

*Pitch measurements:* 115yd × 75yd.

*Chairman:* S. Davidson.

*Directors:* J. Laycock, J. Clapp, R. Neale, S. Lansdowne, K. Dawe, A. Gooch. *Sales Manager:* Shaun Parker.

*General Manager:* Ian Wilson. *Secretary:* Eddie Harrison.

*Manager:* John Ward. *Coach:* Terry Connor.

*Physio:* H. Footman. *Stadium Manager:* D. Lewis. *Safety Officer:* Keith Draisey.

*Year Formed:* 1894. *Turned Professional:* 1897. *Ltd Co.:* 1897. BCFC (1982) Plc.

*Previous Name:* Bristol South End 1894–97.

*Club Nickname:* 'Robins'.

*Previous Grounds:* 1894, St John's Lane; 1904, Ashton Gate.

*Foundation:* The name Bristol City came into being in 1897 when the Bristol South End club, formed three years earlier, decided to adopt professionalism and apply for admission to the Southern League after competing in the Western League. The historic meeting was held at The Albert Hall, Bedminster. Bristol City employed Sam Hollis from Woolwich Arsenal as manager and gave him £40 to buy players. In 1901 they merged with Bedminster, another leading Bristol club.

*First Football League game:* 7 September 1901, Division 2, v Blackpool (a) W 2-0 – Moles; Tuft, Davies; Jones, McLean, Chambers; Bradbury, Connor, Boucher, O'Brien (2), Flynn.

*Record League Victory:* 9–0 v Aldershot, Division 3 (S), 28 December 1946 – Eddols; Morgan, Fox; Peacock, Roberts, Jones (1); Chilcott, Thomas, Clark (4 incl. 1p), Cyril Williams (1), Hargreaves (3).

*Record Cup Victory:* 11–0 v Chichester C, FA Cup 1st rd, 5 November 1960 – Cook; Collinson, Thresher; Connor, Alan Williams, Etheridge; Tait (1), Bobby Williams (1), Atyeo (5), Adrian Williams (3), Derrick. (1 og).

*Record Defeat:* 0–9 v Coventry C, Division 3 (S), 28 April 1934.

*Most League Points (2 for a win):* 70, Division 3 (S), 1954–55.

*Most League Points (3 for a win):* 91, Division 3, 1989–90.

*Most League Goals:* 104, Division 3 (S), 1926–27.

*Highest League Scorer in Season:* Don Clark, 36, Division 3 (S), 1946–47.

*Most League Goals in Total Aggregate:* John Atyeo, 314, 1951–66.

*Most Capped Player:* Billy Wedlock, 26, England.

*Most League Appearances:* John Atyeo, 597, 1951–66.

*Record Transfer Fee Received:* £1,750,000 from Newcastle U for Andy Cole, March 1993.

*Record Transfer Fee Paid:* £1,200,000 to Gillingham for Ade Akinbiyi, May 1998.

*Football League Record:* 1901 Elected to Division 2; 1906–11 Division 1; 1911–22 Division 2; 1922–23 Division 3 (S); 1923–24 Division 2; 1924–27 Division 3 (S); 1927–32 Division 2; 1932–55 Division 3 (S); 1955–60 Division 2; 1960–65 Division 3; 1965–76 Division 2; 1976–80 Division 1; 1980–81 Division 2; 1981–82 Division 3; 1982–84 Division 4; 1984–90 Division 3; 1990–92 Division 2; 1992–95 Division 1; 1995–98 Division 2; 1998– Division 1.

*Honours: Football League:* Division 1 – Runners-up 1906–07; Division 2 – Champions 1905–06; Runners-up 1975–76, 1997–98; Division 3 (S) – Champions 1922–23, 1926–27, 1954–55; Runners-up 1937–38; Division 3 – Runners-up 1964–65, 1989–90. *FA Cup:* Runners-up 1909. *Football League Cup:* Semi-final 1971, 1989. *Welsh Cup:* Winners 1934. *Anglo-Scottish Cup:* Winners 1978. *Freight Rover Trophy:* Winners 1986; Runners-up 1987.

*Colours:* Red shirts, white shorts, red stockings. *Change colours:* Yellow shirts, green shorts, black and green stockings.

**Did you know?**
When Bristol City beat Grimsby Town 4-1 on 10 January 1998, Colin Cramb scored the opening goal after only 17 seconds.

1897 1997

## BRISTOL CITY 1997–98 LEAGUE RECORD

| Match No. | Date | Venue | Opponents | Result | Score | H/T Score | Lg. Pos. | Goalscorers | Atten- dance |
|---|---|---|---|---|---|---|---|---|---|
| 1 | Aug 9 | A | Grimsby T | D | 1-1 | 1-0 | — | Torpey [27] | 6220 |
| 2 | 16 | H | Blackpool | W | 2-0 | 0-0 | 3 | Cramb [48], Goater [87] | 9043 |
| 3 | 23 | A | Northampton T | L | 1-2 | 1-2 | 10 | Cramb [5] | 6217 |
| 4 | 30 | H | Wigan Ath | W | 3-0 | 3-0 | 6 | Goater 3 (1 pen) [26, 37, 39 (p)] | 9255 |
| 5 | Sept 2 | H | Fulham | L | 0-2 | 0-1 | — | | 10,293 |
| 6 | 13 | A | Wrexham | L | 1-2 | 0-1 | 17 | Goater [68] | 3251 |
| 7 | 20 | H | Bournemouth | D | 1-1 | 1-0 | 19 | Goater [26] | 8330 |
| 8 | 27 | A | Luton T | W | 3-0 | 3-0 | 15 | Bell (pen) [5], Torpey 2 [27, 31] | 8509 |
| 9 | Oct 4 | A | Gillingham | L | 0-2 | 0-2 | 19 | | 6277 |
| 10 | 11 | A | Southend U | W | 2-0 | 1-0 | 15 | Bell [34], Hails (og) [56] | 3273 |
| 11 | 17 | H | York C | W | 2-1 | 0-1 | — | Cramb [68], Torpey [82] | 9568 |
| 12 | 21 | H | Preston NE | W | 2-1 | 0-0 | — | Bell (pen) [64], Goodridge [89] | 9039 |
| 13 | 25 | A | Walsall | D | 0-0 | 0-0 | 7 | | 4618 |
| 14 | 29 | A | Millwall | W | 2-0 | 1-0 | — | Torpey [9], Locke [54] | 7026 |
| 15 | Nov 1 | H | Oldham Ath | W | 1-0 | 0-0 | 2 | Bell (pen) [61] | 10,221 |
| 16 | 4 | A | Bristol R | W | 2-1 | 1-0 | — | Goater 2 [27, 49] | 7552 |
| 17 | 8 | A | Brentford | W | 4-1 | 2-0 | 2 | Torpey [31], Goater 2 [32, 67], Doherty [77] | 6183 |
| 18 | 18 | H | Plymouth Arg | W | 2-1 | 2-0 | 2 | Bell 2 [33, 34] | 10,867 |
| 19 | 22 | H | Wycombe W | W | 3-1 | 1-0 | 2 | Hewlett 2 [38, 59], Torpey [67] | 11,129 |
| 20 | 29 | A | Carlisle U | W | 3-0 | 1-0 | 2 | Goater 2 [19, 53], Goodridge [59] | 5044 |
| 21 | Dec 2 | H | Burnley | W | 3-1 | 0-1 | — | Goodridge 2 [48, 83], Bell (pen) [71] | 11,136 |
| 22 | 13 | H | Watford | D | 1-1 | 0-0 | 2 | Goater [54] | 16,072 |
| 23 | 20 | A | Chesterfield | W | 1-0 | 1-0 | 2 | Bell (pen) [13] | 11,791 |
| 24 | 26 | H | Millwall | W | 4-1 | 2-0 | 2 | Cramb [10], Edwards [17], Tinnion [59], Taylor [68] | 16,128 |
| 25 | 28 | A | Fulham | L | 0-1 | 0-0 | 2 | | 13,273 |
| 26 | Jan 10 | A | Grimsby T | W | 4-1 | 3-0 | 1 | Cramb 2 [1, 39], Taylor [5], Goater [47] | 12,567 |
| 27 | 17 | A | Wigan Ath | W | 3-0 | 2-0 | 1 | Doherty [3], Tinnion [24], Goater [71] | 5078 |
| 28 | 24 | H | Northampton T | D | 0-0 | 0-0 | 2 | | 14,753 |
| 29 | 31 | H | Wrexham | D | 1-1 | 1-0 | 2 | Goater [5] | 11,741 |
| 30 | Feb 3 | A | Blackpool | D | 2-2 | 0-0 | — | Hewlett 2 [66, 76] | 3724 |
| 31 | 7 | A | Bournemouth | L | 0-1 | 0-1 | 2 | | 6623 |
| 32 | 14 | H | Gillingham | L | 0-2 | 0-0 | 2 | | 11,781 |
| 33 | 21 | A | Luton T | D | 0-0 | 0-0 | 2 | | 6405 |
| 34 | 24 | H | York C | W | 1-0 | 0-0 | — | Bell (pen) [65] | 3770 |
| 35 | 28 | H | Southend U | W | 1-0 | 1-0 | 2 | Cramb [44] | 12,049 |
| 36 | Mar 3 | A | Brentford | D | 2-2 | 0-1 | — | Torpey [55], Cockerill (og) [61] | 10,398 |
| 37 | 14 | H | Bristol R | W | 2-0 | 1-0 | 1 | Bell (pen) [35], Goater [59] | 17,086 |
| 38 | 21 | A | Plymouth Arg | L | 0-2 | 0-0 | 2 | | 7622 |
| 39 | 28 | A | Wycombe W | W | 2-1 | 1-0 | 2 | Cramb 2 [41, 84] | 6326 |
| 40 | 31 | A | Oldham Ath | W | 2-1 | 0-1 | — | Goodridge [53], Roberts [54] | 4543 |
| 41 | Apr 4 | H | Carlisle U | W | 1-0 | 0-0 | 1 | Goodridge [53] | 12,578 |
| 42 | 11 | A | Burnley | L | 0-1 | 0-1 | 1 | | 10,600 |
| 43 | 13 | H | Watford | D | 1-1 | 0-0 | 1 | Edwards [68] | 19,141 |
| 44 | 18 | A | Chesterfield | L | 0-1 | 0-1 | 1 | | 5085 |
| 45 | 25 | H | Walsall | W | 2-1 | 1-1 | 1 | Owers [3], Tinnion [80] | 15,059 |
| 46 | May 2 | A | Preston NE | L | 1-2 | 1-2 | 2 | McCarthy [9] | 12,067 |

**Final League Position: 2**   1996–97 DIV2 5

## GOALSCORERS

*League (69):* Goater 17 (1 pen), Bell 10 (7 pens), Cramb 9, Torpey 8, Goodridge 6, Hewlett 4, Tinnion 3, Doherty 2, Edwards 2, Taylor 2, Locke 1, McCarthy 1, Owers 1, Roberts 1, own goals 2.
*Coca-Cola Cup (5):* Taylor 2, Bent 1, Goater 1, Goodridge 1.
*FA Cup (2):* Cramb 1, Taylor 1.

| Welch K 44 | Carey L 37 + 1 | Bell M 44 | Paterson S 7 + 3 | Taylor S 43 | Edwards R 34 + 3 | Hewlett M 27 + 7 | Owers G 20 + 2 | Goater S 28 + 5 | Torpey S 19 + 10 | Tinnion B 44 | Cramb C 34 + 6 | Barclay D — + 8 | Locke A 35 + 2 | Bent J — + 2 | Tisdale P 2 + 3 | Langan K — + 3 | Goodridge G 28 + 3 | Dyche S 10 + 1 | Doherty T 22 + 8 | Shail M 2 | Plummer D — + 1 | Brennan J 4 + 2 | Murray S 10 + 13 | Johansen S 2 + 1 | McCarthy S 7 | Roberts J 1 + 2 | Naylor S 2 | Match No. |
|---|---|---|---|---|---|---|---|---|---|---|---|---|---|---|---|---|---|---|---|---|---|---|---|---|---|---|---|---|
| 1 | 2 | 3 | 4 | 5 | 6 | 7 | 8 | 9 | 10¹ | 11 | 12² | 13 | | | | | | | | | | | | | | | | 1 |
| 1 | | 3 | 4 | 5 | 6 | 7 | 8 | 9 | | 11¹ | 10² | | 2 | | 12 | 13 | | | | | | | | | | | | 2 |
| 1 | 2 | 3 | 4³ | 5 | 6 | 7² | 8 | 9 | 12 | 11 | 10¹ | | | | | 14 | 13 | | | | | | | | | | | 3 |
| 1 | 2 | 3 | 4 | 5 | 6³ | 7 | 8 | 9² | | 11¹ | 10 | 13 | | | 12 | 14 | | | | | | | | | | | | 4 |
| 1 | 2 | 3 | 4¹ | 5 | 6 | 7² | 8 | 9 | | 11 | 10 | 13 | 12 | | | | | | | | | | | | | | | 5 |
| 1 | 12 | 3 | 4 | 5 | 6³ | 7¹ | 8 | 9 | 13 | 11 | 10² | | 2 | | | | 14 | | | | | | | | | | | 6 |
| 1 | 2 | 3 | | 5 | 6 | 7 | 8 | 9 | 10 | 11 | | | 4 | | | | | | | | | | | | | | | 7 |
| 1 | | 3 | | 5 | | 6 | 8 | | 10 | 11 | 9¹ | 12 | 2 | | | | 7² | | 4 | 13 | | | | | | | | 8 |
| 1 | | 3 | | 5 | 6 | | 8 | 12 | 9 | 11 | | | 2 | | | | 7 | | 4 | 10¹ | | | | | | | | 9 |
| 1 | | 3 | | 5 | | | 8 | 12 | 9 | 11 | 10¹ | | 2 | | | | 4 | 7² | 6 | 13 | | | | | | | | 10 |
| 1 | | 3 | | 5 | 12 | | 8 | | 9 | 11 | 10 | | 2 | | | | 13 | 4 | 7¹ | 6² | | | | | | | | 11 |
| 1 | | 3 | | 5 | 6 | | | | 9 | 11 | 10 | | 2 | | | | 7 | 4 | 8 | | | | | | | | | 12 |
| 1 | | 3 | | 5 | 6 | 12 | | 13 | 9 | 11 | 10² | | 2 | | | | 7¹ | 4 | 8 | | | | | | | | | 13 |
| 1 | 8 | 3 | | 5 | 6 | 7 | | | 9 | 11 | 10 | | 2 | | | | 4 | | | | | | | | | | | 14 |
| 1 | 8 | 3² | | 5 | 6 | 7 | | 12 | 9 | 11 | 10¹ | | 2 | | | | 4 | 13 | | | | | | | | | | 15 |
| 1 | 8 | | 3 | 5 | 6 | 7 | | 10¹ | 9 | 11 | 12 | | 2 | | | | 4 | | | | | 3 | | | | | | 16 |
| 1 | 8 | 3 | | 5 | 6¹ | 7 | | 10 | 9 | 11 | | | 2 | | | | 4 | 12 | | | | | | | | | | 17 |
| 1 | 6 | 3 | | 5 | | 7 | | 10 | 9 | 11² | | | 2 | | | 12 | 4¹ | | 8 | | | | 13 | | | | | 18 |
| 1 | 6 | 3 | | 5 | 7 | | | 10¹ | 9 | | 12 | | 2² | | | 13 | 4 | | 8 | | | | 11 | | | | | 19 |
| 1 | 6 | 3 | | 5 | 12 | 7 | | 9 | | 11² | 10 | 14 | 2 | | | | 4³ | | 8¹ | | | | 13 | | | | | 20 |
| 1 | 6 | 3 | | 5 | 7 | | | 9 | | | 10¹ | 12 | 2 | | | | 4 | | 8 | | | | 11 | | | | | 21 |
| 1 | 6 | 3 | | 5 | 7 | | | 9 | | 11 | 10¹ | | 2 | | | | 4 | 12 | 8 | | | | | | | | | 22 |
| 1 | 8 | 3 | 12 | 5 | 6 | 7 | | 9 | | 11 | 10² | | 2 | | | | 4¹ | | | | | | 13 | | | | | 23 |
| 1 | 8 | 3 | | 5 | 6 | | | 9¹ | 12 | 11 | 10 | | 2 | | | | 4² | | 7 | | | | 13 | | | | | 24 |
| 1 | 6 | 3 | | 5 | 7 | | | 9 | 12 | 11 | 10 | 2¹ | | | | | 4 | | 8² | | | | 13 | | | | | 25 |
| 1 | 6 | 3 | | 5 | 7 | 12 | | 9² | 13 | 11 | 10 | 2³ | | | | | 4 | | 8¹ | | | | 14 | | | | | 26 |
| 1 | 6 | 3 | | 5 | 7 | 12 | | 9 | 13 | 11 | 10² | | | | | | 4¹ | | 8 | | | | 2 | | | | | 27 |
| 1 | 6 | 3 | | 5 | | 7 | | 9 | 12 | 11 | 10¹ | | | | | | 4 | | 8 | | | | 2 | | | | | 28 |
| 1 | 6 | 3 | | 5 | 7 | 12 | | 9 | 13 | 11 | 10² | | | | | | 4 | | 8¹ | | | | 2 | | | | | 29 |
| 1 | 6 | 3 | | 5 | 7 | 8 | | 9 | 12 | 11 | 10¹ | | | | | | 4 | | | | | | 2 | | | | | 30 |
| 1 | 6 | 3 | | 5 | 7 | 8 | | 9 | 10² | 11 | | 13 | 12 | | | | 4¹ | | | | | | 2 | | | | | 31 |
| 1 | | 3 | | 5 | 7 | 8 | 6 | 9 | 12 | 11 | | | 2² | | | | 4 | | | | | | 13 | 10¹ | | | | 32 |
| 1 | 6 | 3 | | 5 | 7 | 8 | | 9 | | 11 | 12 | | 2 | | | | 4² | | | | | | 13 | 10¹ | | | | 33 |
| 1 | 6 | 3 | | 5 | 7 | 8¹ | 12 | 9² | 10 | 11 | 13 | | 2 | | | | | | 8¹ | | | | 4 | | | | | 34 |
| 1 | 6 | 3 | | 5 | 7 | | 12 | | 9 | 11 | 10² | | 2 | | | | | | 8¹ | | | | 4 | 13 | | | | 35 |
| 1 | 6 | 3 | | 5 | 7 | | | 12 | 9 | 11 | 10¹ | | 2 | | | | | | 8 | | | | 4 | | | | | 36 |
| 1 | 6 | 3 | | 5 | 7 | 8 | 10 | 9¹ | 11 | 12 | | | 2 | | | | 13 | | | | | | 4² | | | | | 37 |
| 1 | 6 | 3 | | 5 | 7¹ | 8 | | 9 | 11² | 10 | 13 | 2 | | | | | | | 12 | | | | 4 | | | | | 38 |
| 1 | 6 | 3 | | 5 | | 8¹ | 7 | | 11 | 10³ | | 2 | | | | 4² | | 12 | | | | 13 | | | 9 | 14 | | 39 |
| 1 | 6 | 12 | 5 | | 8¹ | 7 | | | 11 | 10³ | | 2 | | | | 4 | | 13 | | | | 3² | 14 | | 9¹ | | | 40 |
| 1 | 6 | 3 | | 5 | | 8¹ | 7 | | 11 | 10² | | 2 | | | | 4 | | 12 | | | | 13 | 9² | | | | | 41 |
| 1 | 6 | 3 | | 5 | | 8¹ | 7 | | 11 | 10 | | 2 | | | | 4 | | 12 | | | | 13 | 9² | | | | | 42 |
| 1 | 6 | 3 | | 5¹ | 12 | 13 | 7 | | 11 | 10 | | 2 | | | | 4³ | | 8² | | | | 14 | 9 | | | | | 43 |
| 1¹ | 6 | 3 | 12 | 5 | | 7 | | | 11 | 10 | | 2 | | | | 4 | | 8² | | | | 13 | 9 | | | | | 44 |
| | 6 | 3 | 5 | | 12 | 7 | | | 11 | 10² | | 2 | | | | 4¹ | | 8 | | | | 13 | 9 | | 1 | | 45 |
| | 6 | 3 | | 5 | 12 | 7 | | | 11 | 10¹ | | 2 | | | | 4 | | 8 | | | | 13 | 9² | | 1 | | 46 |

**Coca-Cola Cup**

| | | | |
|---|---|---|---|
| First Round | Bristol R | (h) | 0-0 |
| | | (a) | 2-1 |
| Second Round | Leeds U | (a) | 1-3 |
| | | (h) | 2-1 |

**FA Cup**

| | | | |
|---|---|---|---|
| First Round | Millwall | (h) | 1-0 |
| Second Round | Bournemouth | (a) | 1-3 |

BRISTOL ROVERS 1997–98 *Back row (left to right):* Steve Foster, Billy Clark, Peter Beadle, Jason Perry, Andy Collett, Julian Alsop, Shane Higgs, Lee Martin, Joshua Low, Tom Ramasut, Andy Tillson.

*Middle row:* Tom White, Justin Skinner, Matthew Hayfield, Dave Pritchard, Barry Hayles, Steve Parmenter, Frankie Bennett, Lee Zabek, Jonathan French, Graeme Power, Matthew Lockwood, Brian Gayle.

*Front row:* Gary Penrice, Jamie Cureton, John Trollope (Centre of Excellence Director), Roy Dolling (Youth Development Manager), Ian Holloway (Player/Manager), Phil Bater (First Team Coach), Phil Kite (Physio), Ray Kendall (Kit Manager), Justin Brown, Simon Teague.

# Division 2     **BRISTOL ROVERS**

*Registered Offices:* The Beeches, Broomhill Road, Brislington, Bristol BS4 5BF. (0117) 9772000. *Ground:* The Memorial Ground, Filton Avenue, Horfield, Bristol, BS7 0AQ. Training Ground: (0117) 9772000. Matchday Ticket Office: (0117) 9098848. Pirates Hotline: 0891 664422. Fax: (0117) 9773888. Community Office: (0117) 9773111. Additional Ticket Office: (0117) 924 3200.

*Ground capacity:* 9173.

*Record attendance:* 9173 v Northampton T, play-off semi-final, 1st leg, 10 May 1998 (Memorial Ground). 9464 v Liverpool, FA Cup 4th rd, 8 February 1992 (Twerton Park). 38,472 v Preston NE, FA Cup 4th rd, 30 January 1960 (Eastville).

*Record receipts:* £74,952 v Northampton T, play-off semi-final 1st leg, 10 May 1998.

*Pitch measurements:* 101m × 68m.

*President:* Marquis of Worcester.

*Vice-Presidents:* Dr W. T. Cussen, A. I. Seager, R. Redmond.

*Chairman:* D. H. A. Dunford. *Vice-Chairman:* G. M. H. Dunford.

*Directors:* R. Craig, B. Andrews, V. Stokes, B. Bradshaw, C. Jelf.

*Player/Manager:* Ian Holloway. *Player-coach:* Gary Penrice.

*Physio:* Phil Kite. *Director of Youth:* Rod Wesson. *Community Scheme Organiser:* Alan Walsh.

*Chief Administrator/Club Secretary:* Roger Brinsford. *Office Manager:* Mrs Angela Mann.

*Year Formed:* 1883. *Turned Professional:* 1897. *Ltd Co.:* 1896.

*Previous Names:* 1883, Black Arabs; 1884, Eastville Rovers; 1897, Bristol Eastville Rovers; 1898, Bristol Rovers.

*Club Nickname:* 'Pirates'.

*Previous Grounds:* 1883, Purdown; Three Acres, Ashley Hill; Rudgeway, Fishponds; 1897, Eastville; 1986, Twerton Park; 1996, The Memorial Ground.

*Foundation:* Bristol Rovers were formed at a meeting in Stapleton Road, Eastville, in 1883. However, they first went under the name of the Black Arabs (wearing black shirts). Changing their name to Eastville Rovers in their second season, they won the Gloucestershire Senior Cup in 1888–89. Original members of the Bristol & District League in 1892, this eventually became the Western League and Eastville Rovers adopted professionalism in 1897.

*First Football League game:* 28 August 1920, Division 3, v Millwall (a) L 0-2 – Stansfield; Bethune, Panes; Boxley, Kenny, Steele; Chance, Bird, Sims, Bell, Palmer.

*Record League Victory:* 7–0 v Brighton & HA, Division 3 (S), 29 November 1952 – Hoyle; Bamford, Geoff Fox; Pitt, Warren, Sampson; McIlvenny, Roost (2), Lambden (1), Bradford (1), Petherbridge (2). (1 og). 7–0 v Swansea T, Division 2, 2 October 1954 – Radford; Bamford, Watkins; Pitt, Muir, Anderson; Petherbridge, Bradford (2), Meyer, Roost (1), Hooper (2). (2 og). 7–0 v Shrewsbury T, Division 3, 21 March 1964 – Hall; Hillard, Gwyn Jones; Oldfield, Stone (1), Mabbutt; Jarman (2), Brown (1), Biggs (1p), Hamilton, Bobby Jones (2).

*Record Cup Victory:* 6–0 v Merthyr Tydfil, FA Cup 1st rd, 14 November 1987 – Martyn; Alexander (Dryden), Tanner, Hibbitt, Twentyman, Jones, Holloway, Meacham (1), White (2), Penrice (3) (Reece), Purnell.

*Record Defeat:* 0–12 v Luton T, Division 3 (S), 13 April 1936.

*Most League Points (2 for a win):* 64, Division 3 (S), 1952–53.

*Most League Points (3 for a win):* 93, Division 3, 1989–90.

*Most League Goals:* 92, Division 3 (S), 1952–53.

*Highest League Scorer in Season:* Geoff Bradford, 33, Division 3 (S), 1952–53.

*Most League Goals in Total Aggregate:* Geoff Bradford, 242, 1949–64.

*Most Capped Player:* Neil Slatter, 10 (22), Wales.

*Most League Appearances:* Stuart Taylor, 546, 1966–80.

*Record Transfer Fee Received:* £1,200,000 from Huddersfield T for Marcus Stewart, July 1996.

*Record Transfer Fee Paid:* £370,000 to QPR for Andy Tillson, November 1992.

*Football League Record:* 1920 Original Member of Division 3; 1921–53 Division 3 (S); 1953–62 Division 2; 1962–74 Division 3; 1974–81 Division 2; 1981–90 Division 3; 1990–92 Division 2. 1992–93 Division 1; 1993– Division 2.

*Honours: Football League:* Division 2 best season: 4th, 1994–95; Division 3 (S) – Champions 1952–53; Division 3 – Champions 1989–90; Runners-up 1973–74. *FA Cup:* best season: 6th rd, 1951, 1958. *Football League Cup:* best season: 5th rd, 1971, 1972.

*Colours:* Blue and white quartered shirts, white shorts, blue stockings. *Change colours:* Yellow shirts, black shorts, black stockings.

**Did you know?**
Bristol Rovers beat a Manchester United team of the Busby Babes era, lacking only Duncan Edwards, 4-0 in the FA Cup Third Round on 7 January 1956, watched by a crowd of 35,872.

## BRISTOL ROVERS 1997–98 LEAGUE RECORD

| Match No. | Date | Venue | Opponents | Result | | H/T Score | Lg. Pos. | Goalscorers | Attendance |
|---|---|---|---|---|---|---|---|---|---|
| 1 | Aug 9 | H | Plymouth Arg | D | 1-1 | 1-0 | — | Hayles [41] | 7386 |
| 2 | 16 | A | York C | W | 1-0 | 0-0 | 5 | Hayles [56] | 3307 |
| 3 | 23 | H | Carlisle U | W | 3-1 | 2-1 | 3 | Bennett [9], Hayles [20], Penrice [46] | 6044 |
| 4 | 30 | A | Burnley | D | 0-0 | 0-0 | 4 | | 9887 |
| 5 | Sept 2 | A | Bournemouth | D | 1-1 | 1-1 | — | Cureton (pen) [29] | 5550 |
| 6 | 9 | H | Walsall | W | 2-0 | 1-0 | — | Ramasut [21], Hayles [65] | 6225 |
| 7 | 13 | H | Gillingham | L | 1-2 | 0-0 | 5 | Hayles [52] | 6572 |
| 8 | 20 | A | Chesterfield | D | 0-0 | 0-0 | 5 | | 5309 |
| 9 | 27 | H | Oldham Ath | D | 4-4 | 2-3 | 5 | Beadle 2 [30, 33], Hayles [45], Cureton (pen) [87] | 5990 |
| 10 | Oct 4 | H | Wrexham | W | 1-0 | 0-0 | 3 | Ramasut [55] | 6829 |
| 11 | 14 | H | Watford | L | 1-2 | 0-0 | — | Penrice [83] | 8110 |
| 12 | 18 | A | Wycombe W | L | 0-1 | 0-0 | 10 | | 5836 |
| 13 | 21 | A | Brentford | W | 3-2 | 2-1 | — | Hayles 2 [12, 71], Beadle [17] | 3967 |
| 14 | 25 | H | Blackpool | L | 0-3 | 0-1 | 10 | | 6183 |
| 15 | Nov 1 | A | Northampton T | D | 1-1 | 0-0 | 9 | Cureton [79] | 7264 |
| 16 | 4 | H | Bristol C | L | 1-2 | 0-1 | — | Tillson [85] | 7552 |
| 17 | 8 | H | Fulham | L | 2-3 | 0-1 | 14 | Penrice 2 [61, 78] | 6166 |
| 18 | 18 | A | Preston NE | W | 2-1 | 1-0 | — | Penrice [10], Alsop [57] | 7798 |
| 19 | 22 | A | Southend U | D | 1-1 | 0-1 | 13 | Beadle (pen) [85] | 3653 |
| 20 | 29 | H | Millwall | W | 2-1 | 1-0 | 10 | Beadle [10], Hayles [80] | 5542 |
| 21 | Dec 2 | A | Wigan Ath | L | 0-3 | 0-1 | — | | 2738 |
| 22 | 12 | H | Grimsby T | L | 0-4 | 0-2 | — | | 4801 |
| 23 | 20 | A | Luton T | W | 4-2 | 4-2 | 10 | Cureton [13], Hayles 2 [22, 38], Beadle [32] | 5266 |
| 24 | 26 | A | Walsall | W | 1-0 | 0-0 | 9 | Beadle [48] | 6634 |
| 25 | 28 | H | Bournemouth | W | 5-3 | 4-1 | 5 | Beadle 3 [15, 26, 44], Hayles 2 [28, 76] | 7256 |
| 26 | Jan 10 | A | Plymouth Arg | W | 2-1 | 2-0 | 3 | Cureton [23], Hayles [27] | 6850 |
| 27 | 17 | H | Burnley | W | 1-0 | 0-0 | 3 | Cureton [50] | 7208 |
| 28 | 24 | A | Carlisle U | L | 1-3 | 0-2 | 4 | Cureton [55] | 5725 |
| 29 | 31 | A | Gillingham | D | 1-1 | 1-1 | 5 | Cureton (pen) [38] | 5593 |
| 30 | Feb 7 | H | Chesterfield | W | 3-1 | 1-1 | 4 | Bennett [13], Cureton 2 [66, 88] | 5481 |
| 31 | 14 | A | Wrexham | L | 0-1 | 0-1 | 7 | | 3716 |
| 32 | 21 | H | Oldham Ath | W | 3-1 | 2-0 | 6 | Hayles 2 [43, 79], Ramasut [44] | 5789 |
| 33 | 24 | H | Wycombe W | W | 3-1 | 0-0 | — | Hayles [51], Beadle [57], Ramasut [81] | 5805 |
| 34 | 28 | A | Watford | L | 2-3 | 0-2 | 5 | White [51], Cureton [81] | 12,186 |
| 35 | Mar 3 | A | Fulham | L | 0-1 | 0-0 | — | | 6843 |
| 36 | 7 | H | Northampton T | L | 0-2 | 0-1 | 8 | | 6535 |
| 37 | 10 | A | York C | L | 1-2 | 0-1 | — | Ramasut [52] | 4289 |
| 38 | 14 | A | Bristol C | L | 0-2 | 0-1 | 8 | | 17,086 |
| 39 | 21 | H | Preston NE | D | 2-2 | 0-1 | 8 | Cureton (pen) [71], Hayles [75] | 5278 |
| 40 | 27 | H | Southend U | W | 2-0 | 0-0 | — | Tillson [62], Hayles [89] | 5323 |
| 41 | Apr 4 | A | Millwall | D | 1-1 | 0-0 | 8 | Zabek [88] | 5635 |
| 42 | 10 | H | Wigan Ath | W | 5-0 | 3-0 | — | Hayles [25], Ramasut [31], Beadle 3 [45, 51, 56] | 6038 |
| 43 | 13 | A | Grimsby T | W | 2-1 | 2-1 | 7 | Hayles 2 [39, 42] | 5484 |
| 44 | 18 | H | Luton T | W | 2-1 | 2-0 | 5 | Beadle [5], Tillson [32] | 8038 |
| 45 | 25 | A | Blackpool | L | 0-1 | 0-0 | 7 | | 7057 |
| 46 | May 2 | H | Brentford | W | 2-1 | 0-0 | 5 | Cureton [51], Hayles [84] | 9043 |

**Final League Position: 5**　　　　1996–97 DIV2 17

### GOALSCORERS

*League (70):* Hayles 23, Beadle 15 (1 pen), Cureton 13 (4 pens), Ramasut 6, Penrice 5, Tillson 3, Bennett 2, Alsop 1, White 1, Zabek 1.
*Coca-Cola Cup (1):* Alsop 1.
*FA Cup (7):* Beadle 2, Hayles 2, Alsop 1, Holloway 1, Penrice 1.

| Collett A 30 | Perry J 24+1 | Power G 9+1 | Parmenter S 1+3 | Gayle B 16 | Tillson A 32+1 | Holloway I 34+5 | Penrice G 38+2 | Alsop J 10+7 | Cureton J 39+4 | Hayles B 45 | Foster S 32+2 | Ramasut T 25+6 | Beadle P 36+4 | White T 22+2 | Bennett F 8+11 | Pritchard D 32+1 | Higgs S 8 | Zabek L 9+4 | Lockwood M 22+2 | French J 2+1 | Low J 6+4 | Hayfield M 9+9 | Basford L 5+2 | Whyte D —+4 | Skinner J 4 | Jones L 8 | Match No. |
|---|---|---|---|---|---|---|---|---|---|---|---|---|---|---|---|---|---|---|---|---|---|---|---|---|---|---|---|
| 1 | 2 | $3^1$ | $4^2$ | 5 | 6 | 7 | 8 | $9^3$ | 10 | 11 | 12 | 13 | 14 | | | | | | | | | | | | | | 1 |
| 1 | 2 | | | 5 | 6 | 7 | 8 | 9 | 10 | 11 | 12 | | | | | 3 | $4^1$ | | | | | | | | | | 2 |
| 1 | 2 | | | 5 | 6 | 7 | 8 | 9 | $10^1$ | 11 | 12 | | | | | 3 | 4 | | | | | | | | | | 3 |
| 1 | 2 | | | 5 | 6 | 7 | 4 | 9 | 10 | 11 | 12 | | | $8^1$ | | 3 | | | | | | | | | | | 4 |
| 1 | 2 | | | 5 | | 7 | 4 | $9^2$ | 10 | 11 | 12 | 13 | | 6 | $8^1$ | 3 | | | | | | | | | | | 5 |
| 1 | 2 | | | 5 | 6 | 7 | 4 | | 10 | 11 | | | | 8 | 9 | 3 | | | | | | | | | | | 6 |
| 1 | 2 | | | 5 | 6 | 7 | 4 | 12 | $10^1$ | 11 | | | | 8 | $9^1$ | 13 | 3 | | | | | | | | | | 7 |
| 1 | 2 | | | 5 | 6 | 7 | 4 | | $10^1$ | 11 | | | | 8 | 9 | 12 | 3 | | | | | | | | | | 8 |
| | 2 | | | 5 | 6 | 7 | $4^2$ | | 10 | 11 | 13 | | | $8^1$ | 9 | 12 | 3 | 1 | | | | | | | | | 9 |
| 1 | 2 | | | 5 | 6 | 7 | 4 | | $10^2$ | 11 | 3 | | | 8 | $9^1$ | 12 | | 13 | | | | | | | | | 10 |
| 1 | 2 | | | 5 | 6 | 7 | 4 | 8 | $10^1$ | 11 | 3 | | | | 9 | 12 | | | | | | | | | | | 11 |
| 1 | 2 | | | 5 | 6 | | 4 | $8^1$ | 10 | 11 | 3 | | | | 9 | | | | | 7 | 12 | | | | | | 12 |
| 1 | 2 | | | 5 | 6 | 7 | 4 | | | 11 | 3 | | | 8 | 9 | 10 | | | | | | | | | | | 13 |
| 1 | 2 | | | $5^1$ | 6 | 7 | 4 | 12 | 13 | 11 | 3 | | | $8^2$ | 9 | | | $10^3$ | 14 | | | | | | | | 14 |
| 1 | | | | 5 | 6 | 7 | 4 | 12 | 11 | | $3^1$ | | 9 | | | 2 | | 10 | 8 | | | | | | | | 15 |
| 1 | | | | $5^2$ | 6 | 7 | 4 | 12 | 10 | 11 | | 9 | 13 | | | 2 | | 3 | $8^1$ | | | | | | | | 16 |
| 1 | | | | | 6 | 7 | 4 | 9 | 8 | 11 | 3 | 12 | | 5 | | 2 | | $10^1$ | | | | | | | | | 17 |
| 1 | | 12 | | | 6 | | 4 | $9^1$ | 13 | 11 | $3^2$ | | | 5 | | 2 | | 10 | | 7 | 8 | | | | | | 18 |
| 1 | 12 | 13 | | | 6 | | 4 | $9^3$ | $10^1$ | 11 | | 14 | | 5 | | 2 | | 3 | | $7^2$ | 8 | | | | | | 19 |
| 1 | 3 | | | | 6 | 12 | $4^2$ | 13 | | 11 | | | | 9 | | 5 | | 2 | | $7^1$ | 8 | | | | | | 20 |
| 1 | 3 | 12 | | | 6 | 13 | $4^3$ | 14 | | 11 | | | | 9 | | 5 | | $10^2$ | | 7 | $8^1$ | | | | | | 21 |
| 1 | | | | | 6 | 12 | $4^3$ | 14 | 13 | 11 | | | | 9 | | 5 | | 2 | | 10 | $7^1$ | $8^2$ | 3 | | | | 22 |
| 1 | | | | | | 7 | 4 | | 10 | 11 | 6 | | | $8^1$ | 9 | 5 | | | | 3 | | $2$ | 12 | | | | 23 |
| 1 | | | | | | 7 | 4 | | $10^1$ | 11 | 6 | | | 8 | 9 | 5 | | 2 | | 3 | | 12 | | | | | 24 |
| 1 | | | | | | $7^2$ | 4 | 12 | 10 | $11^1$ | 6 | | | 8 | 9 | 5 | | 2 | | 3 | | | 13 | | | | 25 |
| 1 | | 12 | | | | $7^2$ | 4 | | $10^1$ | 11 | 6 | | | $8^2$ | 9 | 5 | 13 | 2 | 14 | 3 | | | | | | | 26 |
| 1 | 2 | | | | | 7 | 4 | | 10 | $11^2$ | 6 | | | | 9 | 5 | 12 | | | 3 | | 13 | $8^1$ | | | | 27 |
| 1 | 2 | | | | | 7 | 4 | | 10 | 11 | 6 | | | | 9 | 5 | 12 | | | $3^2$ | | 13 | $8^1$ | | | | 28 |
| | 2 | | | | | 7 | | | 10 | $11^1$ | 6 | | | | 9 | 5 | 12 | 1 | 4 | 13 | | $8^2$ | 3 | | | | 29 |
| | 2 | | | | | 7 | 12 | | 10 | 11 | 6 | | | | 9 | 5 | $8^3$ | 13 | 1 | $4^1$ | | 14 | $3^2$ | | | | 30 |
| | $2^1$ | 12 | | | | | 4 | | 10 | 11 | 6 | | | | 5 | $9^3$ | 3 | 1 | $7^2$ | 13 | | 8 | | 14 | | | 31 |
| | | 3 | | | | $4^1$ | | | 10 | 11 | 6 | 9 | | | 5 | $8^2$ | 2 | 1 | 12 | | | 13 | | | 7 | | 32 |
| | | 3 | | | 12 | $4^1$ | | | 10 | 11 | 6 | 8 | 9 | 5 | | 2 | 1 | | | | | | 13 | $7^2$ | | | 33 |
| | | 3 | | | 12 | $4^1$ | | | 10 | 11 | 6 | $8^2$ | 9 | 5 | | 2 | 1 | | | | | | 13 | 7 | | | 34 |
| | | 3 | | | | 4 | | | 10 | 11 | 6 | $8^2$ | 9 | $5^1$ | | 2 | 1 | | 12 | | | | 13 | 7 | | | 35 |
| | | 3 | | | 6 | 4 | | | 10 | 11 | 5 | $8^2$ | 9 | | $7^1$ | 2 | 13 | | 12 | | | | | | | 1 | 36 |
| 1 | 2 | $3^1$ | | | 6 | 7 | 4 | | 10 | 11 | 5 | 8 | 9 | | | | | | 12 | | | | | | | | 37 |
| 1 | | $3^2$ | | | 6 | 7 | 4 | | 10 | | 5 | 8 | 9 | 12 | 2 | | | | $11^1$ | 13 | | | | | | | 38 |
| 1 | | 3 | | | 6 | 7 | 4 | | 10 | 11 | 5 | 12 | 9 | | 2 | | | | $8^1$ | | | | | | | | 39 |
| | 2 | | | | 6 | 7 | 4 | | $10^2$ | 11 | 5 | $8^1$ | 9 | 13 | | 3 | | | 12 | | | | | | | 1 | 40 |
| | 2 | | | | 6 | 7 | 4 | | 10 | 11 | 5 | $8^1$ | 9 | 12 | 3 | | 7 | | | | | | | | | 1 | 41 |
| | | | | | 6 | 4 | | | 10 | 11 | 5 | 8 | 9 | | | 2 | | | 7 | 3 | | | | | | 1 | 42 |
| | | | | | 6 | 4 | | | 10 | 11 | 5 | 8 | 9 | | | 2 | | | 7 | 3 | | | | | | 1 | 43 |
| | | | | | 6 | 4 | | | 10 | 11 | 5 | 8 | 9 | | | 2 | | | 7 | 3 | | | | | | 1 | 44 |
| | | | | | 6 | $4^1$ | 12 | | 10 | 11 | 5 | 8 | 9 | | | 2 | | | 7 | 3 | | | | | | 1 | 45 |
| | | | | | 6 | 4 | | | $10^1$ | 11 | 5 | $8^2$ | 9 | 12 | | 2 | | | 7 | 3 | | 13 | | | | 1 | 46 |

**Coca-Cola Cup**

| First Round | Bristol C | (a) | 0-0 |
|---|---|---|---|
| | | (h) | 1-2 |

**FA Cup**

| First Round | Gillingham | (h) | 2-2 |
|---|---|---|---|
| | | (a) | 2-0 |
| Second Round | Wisbech T | (a) | 2-0 |
| Third Round | Ipswich T | (h) | 1-1 |
| | | (a) | 0-1 |

BURNLEY 1997–98　*Back row (left to right):* Glen Little, Ian Helliwell, Vince Overson, Mark Winstanley, Marlon Beresford, Chris Woods, Craig Mawson, Steve Blatherwick, Marco Gentile, Ian Duerden, Phil Eastwood.
*Middle row:* Nigel Gleghorn, Gerry Harrison, Jamie Hoyland, Andy Cooke, Richard Huxford, Colin Carr-Lawton, Paul Smith, Mark Ford, Damian Matthew.
*Front row:* Michael Williams, Paul Barnes, Chris Brass, Chris Vinnicombe, Gordon Cowans (Reserve Team Coach), Chris Waddle (Manager), Glen Roeder (Assistant Manager), David Eyres, Jason Heffernan, Paul Weller, Garth West.

# Division 2     **BURNLEY**

*Turf Moor, Burnley BB10 4BX.* Telephone: (01282) 700000. Fax: (01282) 700014. Clubcall: 0891 121153.
Ticket Office: (01282) 70010. Community Programme: (01282) 70011. Commercial Department: (01282) 70007.

*Ground capacity:* 22,546.

*Record attendance:* 54,775 v Huddersfield T, FA Cup 3rd rd, 23 February 1924.

*Record receipts;* £150,000 v Liverpool, FA Cup 4th rd, 28 January 1995.

*Pitch measurements:* 114yd × 72yd.

*Chairman:* F. J. Teasdale.

*Vice-Chairman:* Dr R. D. Iven MRCS (Eng), LRCP (Lond), MRCGP.

*Directors:* B. Rothwell JP, C. Holt, R. Blakeborough.

*Manager:* Stan Ternent.

*Secretary:* John Howarth.

*Coaches:* Terry Pashley, Alan Harper, Gordon Cowans, Chris Woods.

*Commercial Manager:* Peter Davis.

*Year Formed:* 1882. *Turned Professional:* 1883. *Ltd Co.:* 1897.

*Previous Name:* 1881–82, Burnley Rovers.

*Club Nickname:* 'The Clarets'.

*Previous Grounds:* 1881, Calder Vale; 1882, Turf Moor.

*Foundation:* The majority of those responsible for the formation of the Burnley club in 1881 were from the defunct rugby club Burnley Rovers. Indeed, they continued to play rugby for a year before changing to soccer and dropping "Rovers" from their name. The changes were decided at a meeting held in May 1882 at the Bull Hotel.

*First Football League game:* 8 September 1888, Football League, v Preston NE (a), L 2-5 – Smith; Lang, Bury, Abrams, Friel, Keenan, Brady, Tait, Poland (1), Gallocher (1), Yates.

*Record League Victory:* 9–0 v Darwen, Division 1, 9 January 1892 – Hillman; Walker, McFettridge, Lang, Matthews, Keenan, Nicol (3), Bowes, Espie (1), McLardie (3), Hill (2).

*Record Cup Victory:* 9–0 v Crystal Palace, FA Cup 2nd rd (replay), 10 February 1909 – Dawson; Barron, McLean; Cretney (2), Leake, Moffat; Morley, Ogden, Smith (3), Abbott (2), Smethams (1). 9–0 v New Brighton, FA Cup 4th rd, 26 January 1957 – Blacklaw; Angus, Winton; Seith, Adamson, Miller; Newlands (1), McIlroy (3), Lawson (3), Cheesebrough (1), Pilkington (1). 9–0 v Penrith, FA Cup 1st rd, 17 November 1984 – Hansbury; Miller, Hampton, Phelan, Overson (Kennedy), Hird (3 incl. 1p), Grewcock (1), Powell (2), Taylor (3), Biggins, Hutchison.

*Record Defeat:* 0–10 v Aston Villa, Division 1, 29 August 1925 and v Sheffield U, Division 1, 19 January 1929.

*Most League Points (2 for a win):* 62, Division 2, 1972–73.

*Most League Points (3 for a win):* 83, Division 4, 1991–92.

*Most League Goals:* 102, Division 1, 1960–61.

*Highest League Scorer in Season:* George Beel, 35, Division 1, 1927–28.

*Most League Goals in Total Aggregate:* George Beel, 178, 1923–32.

*Most Capped Player:* Jimmy McIlroy, 51 (55), Northern Ireland.

*Most League Appearances:* Jerry Dawson, 522, 1907–28.

*Record Transfer Fee Received:* £750,000 from Luton T for Steve Davis, August 1995.

*Record Transfer Fee Paid:* £350,000 to Birmingham C for Paul Barnes, September 1996.

*Football League Record:* 1888 Original Member of the Football League; 1897–98 Division 2; 1898–1900 Division 1; 1900–13 Division 2; 1913–30 Division 1; 1930–47 Division 2; 1947–71 Division 1; 1971–73 Division 2; 1973–76 Division 1; 1976–80 Division 2; 1980–82 Division 3; 1982–83 Division 2; 1983–85 Division 3; 1985–92 Division 4; 1992–94 Division 2; 1994–95 Division 1; 1995– Division 2.

*Honours: Football League:* Division 1 – Champions 1920–21, 1959–60; Runners-up 1919–20, 1961–62; Division 2 – Champions 1897–98, 1972–73; Runners-up 1912–13, 1946–47; Promoted from Division 2, 1993–94 (play-offs); Division 3 – Champions 1981–82; Division 4 – Champions 1991–92. Record 30 consecutive Division 1 games without defeat 1920–21. *FA Cup:* Winners 1914; Runners-up 1947, 1962. *Football League Cup:* semi-final 1961, 1969, 1983. *Anglo–Scottish Cup:* Winners 1979. *Sherpa Van Trophy:* Runners-up 1988. **European Competitions;** *European Cup:* 1960–61. *European Fairs Cup:* 1966–67.

*Colours:* Claret body with blue sleeves, claret shorts, blue stockings. *Change colours:* Navy and yellow shirts, yellow shorts, yellow stockings.

**Did you know?**
George Beel was top scorer for Burnley in six out of nine seasons from 1923-24 to 1931-32.

## BURNLEY 1997–98 LEAGUE RECORD

| Match No. | Date | | Venue | Opponents | Result | | H/T Score | Lg. Pos. | Goalscorers | Attendance |
|---|---|---|---|---|---|---|---|---|---|---|
| 1 | Aug | 9 | A | Watford | L | 0-1 | 0-1 | — | | 11,155 |
| 2 | | 16 | H | Gillingham | D | 0-0 | 0-0 | 20 | | 11,811 |
| 3 | | 23 | A | Southend U | L | 0-1 | 0-1 | 24 | | 4218 |
| 4 | | 30 | H | Bristol R | D | 0-0 | 0-0 | 23 | | 9887 |
| 5 | Sept | 2 | H | Oldham Ath | D | 0-0 | 0-0 | — | | 11,189 |
| 6 | | 7 | A | Chesterfield | L | 0-1 | 0-1 | 24 | | 7406 |
| 7 | | 13 | A | York C | L | 1-3 | 1-0 | 24 | Barnes [12] | 5424 |
| 8 | | 20 | H | Preston NE | D | 1-1 | 0-1 | 24 | Cooke [80] | 13,809 |
| 9 | | 27 | A | Brentford | L | 1-2 | 0-1 | 24 | Ford [57] | 4548 |
| 10 | Oct | 4 | H | Wycombe W | D | 2-2 | 1-1 | 24 | Creaney 2 [3, 73] | 9057 |
| 11 | | 11 | H | Carlisle U | W | 3-1 | 1-0 | 24 | Barnes [18], Creaney 2 [67, 71] | 10,687 |
| 12 | | 18 | A | Wrexham | D | 0-0 | 0-0 | 24 | | 5132 |
| 13 | | 21 | A | Plymouth Arg | D | 2-2 | 1-1 | — | Eyres (pen) [8], Creaney [58] | 3006 |
| 14 | | 25 | H | Bournemouth | D | 2-2 | 1-0 | 23 | Waddle [45], Creaney [65] | 9501 |
| 15 | Nov | 1 | H | Walsall | W | 2-1 | 1-0 | 22 | Barnes [27], Cooke [80] | 9293 |
| 16 | | 4 | A | Luton T | W | 3-2 | 1-2 | — | Williams [25], Creaney [62], Barnes [65] | 5315 |
| 17 | | 8 | A | Blackpool | L | 1-2 | 1-1 | 20 | Creaney [14] | 7429 |
| 18 | | 18 | A | Millwall | L | 1-2 | 1-1 | — | Cooke [29] | 8834 |
| 19 | | 22 | A | Grimsby T | L | 1-4 | 1-1 | 21 | Weller [16] | 4829 |
| 20 | | 29 | H | Northampton T | W | 2-1 | 0-0 | 19 | Moore [76], Barnes [82] | 8369 |
| 21 | Dec | 2 | A | Bristol C | L | 1-3 | 1-0 | — | Barnes [29] | 11,136 |
| 22 | | 13 | H | Wigan Ath | L | 0-2 | 0-2 | 23 | | 9520 |
| 23 | | 19 | A | Fulham | L | 0-1 | 0-0 | — | | 5096 |
| 24 | | 26 | H | Chesterfield | D | 0-0 | 0-0 | 23 | | 10,861 |
| 25 | Jan | 3 | A | Gillingham | L | 0-2 | 0-1 | 24 | | 5886 |
| 26 | | 10 | H | Watford | W | 2-0 | 2-0 | 24 | Cooke 2 [13, 35] | 9551 |
| 27 | | 17 | A | Bristol R | L | 0-1 | 0-0 | 24 | | 7208 |
| 28 | | 24 | H | Southend U | W | 1-0 | 1-0 | 24 | Payton [43] | 9386 |
| 29 | | 31 | H | York C | W | 7-2 | 2-1 | 21 | Moore [40], Barras (og) [43], Brass [46], Cooke 3 [49, 58, 88], Payton [81] | 9975 |
| 30 | Feb | 7 | A | Preston NE | W | 3-2 | 0-1 | 19 | Payton [48], Cooke [57], Moore [90] | 12,263 |
| 31 | | 14 | A | Wycombe W | L | 1-2 | 0-1 | 19 | Cooke [88] | 5926 |
| 32 | | 21 | H | Brentford | D | 1-1 | 0-0 | 20 | Little [77] | 10,097 |
| 33 | | 24 | A | Wrexham | L | 1-2 | 1-1 | — | Cooke [30] | 8576 |
| 34 | | 28 | A | Carlisle U | L | 1-2 | 0-1 | 22 | Cooke [50] | 7192 |
| 35 | Mar | 7 | A | Walsall | D | 0-0 | 0-0 | 23 | | 5212 |
| 36 | | 14 | H | Luton T | D | 1-1 | 0-0 | 23 | Payton [60] | 9656 |
| 37 | | 21 | A | Millwall | L | 0-1 | 0-1 | 24 | | 7582 |
| 38 | | 28 | H | Grimsby T | W | 2-1 | 1-1 | 24 | Little [12], Payton [80] | 8256 |
| 39 | Apr | 4 | A | Northampton T | W | 1-0 | 1-0 | 22 | Payton [16] | 7264 |
| 40 | | 7 | H | Blackpool | L | 1-2 | 1-1 | — | Payton [13] | 13,413 |
| 41 | | 11 | H | Bristol C | W | 1-0 | 0-0 | 22 | Payton (pen) [7] | 10,600 |
| 42 | | 13 | A | Wigan Ath | L | 1-5 | 0-2 | 22 | Little [47] | 4926 |
| 43 | | 18 | H | Fulham | W | 2-1 | 1-1 | 22 | Cooke [2], Payton [83] | 9745 |
| 44 | | 25 | A | Bournemouth | L | 1-2 | 0-0 | 22 | Matthew (pen) [72] | 6527 |
| 45 | | 28 | A | Oldham Ath | D | 3-3 | 3-1 | — | Cooke [26], Weller [32], Little [38] | 9781 |
| 46 | May | 2 | H | Plymouth Arg | W | 2-1 | 2-1 | 20 | Cooke 2 [12, 41] | 18,811 |

**Final League Position: 20**          1996–97 DIV2 9

### GOALSCORERS

**League (55):** Cooke 16, Payton 9 (1 pen), Creaney 8, Barnes 6, Little 4, Moore 3, Weller 2, Brass 1, Eyres 1 (pen), Ford 1, Matthew 1 (pen), Waddle 1, Williams 1, own goal 1.
**Coca-Cola Cup (3):** Cook 1, Eyres 1 (pen), Howey 1.
**FA Cup (3):** Cook 1, Moore 1, Weller 1.

| Beresford M 34 | Huxford R 4 | Winstanley M 27 | Williams M 13 + 1 | Blatherwick S 13 + 8 | Brass C 37 + 3 | Waddle C 26 + 5 | Ford M 32 + 4 | Eastwood P 1 + 2 | Barnes P 24 + 1 | Eyres D 13 | Hoyland J 2 + 7 | Matthew D 21 + 6 | Vinnicombe C 20 + 3 | Howey L 21 + 2 | Weller P 32 + 7 | Cooke A 26 + 8 | Duerden I 1 | Gleghorn N 1 | Moore N 38 + 2 | Kiwomya A 1 + 2 | Little G 19 + 5 | Smith P 8 + 6 | Harrison G 33 + 2 | Creaney G 9 + 1 | Cowans G 5 + 1 | Carr-Lawton C —+ 1 | Payton A 19 | Robertson M 8 + 3 | Henderson K —+ 7 | Woods C 12 | Smith C —+ 1 | Mullin J 6 | Match No. |
|---|---|---|---|---|---|---|---|---|---|---|---|---|---|---|---|---|---|---|---|---|---|---|---|---|---|---|---|---|---|---|---|---|---|
| 1 | 2 | 3 | 4¹ | 5 | 6 | 7 | 8 | 9² | 10 | 11 | 12 | 13 | | | | | | | | | | | | | | | | | | | | | 1 |
| 1 | 2 | 7 | 4 | 5 | 6² | 12 | 8 | | 10¹ | 11 | | 13 | 3³ | 9 | 14 | | | | | | | | | | | | | | | | | | 2 |
| 1 | 2 | 3 | 4² | 5 | | 12 | 8 | | 10¹ | 11 | | 13 | | | 6 | 7 | | | 9 | | | | | | | | | | | | | | 3 |
| 1 | 2 | 3 | 4 | 5 | | 12 | 8 | | 10 | 11¹ | | 13 | | | 6 | 7 | | | 9² | | | | | | | | | | | | | | 4 |
| 1 | | 3 | 4 | 5 | 2 | 7¹ | 8 | | 10 | 11 | 12 | 13 | | | 6 | | | | 9² | | | | | | | | | | | | | | 5 |
| 1 | | 5 | 3 | | 2 | 7¹ | 8 | | 10 | 11 | | 4 | | | 6 | 2 | | | 9 | | | | | | | | | | | 12 | | | 6 |
| 1 | | 4 | 5 | 3 | | | 8 | | 10 | 11 | | 7² | | | 6 | 2 | | | 9¹ | | 12 | 13 | | | | | | | | | | | 7 |
| 1 | | | 2 | 12 | 8³ | | 10 | 11² | | 4 | 3 | | | 7 | 9 | | | | 6 | 13 | | | 5¹ | 14 | | | | | | | | | 8 |
| 1 | | | 2 | 7 | 8 | | 10¹ | 11 | | | 3 | 5 | | | 6 | | | | | | | 4 | 9 | 12 | | | | | | | | | 9 |
| 1 | | | 2¹ | 7 | 8 | | 10 | 11 | | | 3 | 5 | 12 | | 6 | | | | | | | 4 | 9 | | | | | | | | | | 10 |
| 1 | 5 | | 2 | 7¹ | 8 | | 10 | 11 | | | 3 | | 12 | 13 | 6 | | | | | | | 4 | 9² | | | | | | | | | | 11 |
| 1 | 14 | | 2 | 7¹ | 8 | | 10² | 11 | | | 3 | 5 | 12 | 13 | 6 | | | | | | | 4 | 9 | | | | | | | | | | 12 |
| 1 | | | 2 | 7 | 8 | | 10 | 11 | | | 3¹ | 5 | 12 | | 6 | | | | | | | 4 | 9 | | | | | | | | | | 13 |
| 1 | 8³ | | 2 | 7 | | | 10 | 11 | | | 3¹ | 6 | 12 | 13 | 5 | | | | 14 | | | 4 | 9² | | | | | | | | | | 14 |
| 1 | | 8 | 12 | 2 | | 7³ | | 10² | | | 3 | 5 | 11 | 13 | 6 | | | | | 14 | | | 9¹ | 4 | | | | | | | | | 15 |
| 1 | | 8 | 14 | 2 | | 7² | | 10 | | | 3 | 5 | 11 | 12 | 6 | | | | | 13 | | | 9¹ | 4³ | | | | | | | | | 16 |
| 1 | | 8 | 12 | 2² | | 7 | | 10 | | | 3¹ | 5 | 11 | 13 | 6 | | | | | | | | 9 | 4 | | | | | | | | | 17 |
| 1 | | 8 | 12 | 2² | | | | 10 | | | 3¹ | 5 | 11 | 9 | 6 | | | | | | 7 | 13 | | 4 | | | | | | | | | 18 |
| 1 | | 8 | 5 | 2 | | 7² | 12 | 10 | | | | | 3 | 9 | 6 | | | | | | 11³ | 13 | | 4¹ | 14 | | | | | | | | 19 |
| 1 | | | 5 | 2 | | 7 | 8 | 10 | | | 12 | 3 | 9 | 11² | 13 | 6 | | | | | | 4 | | | | | | | | | | | 20 |
| 1 | | | 5 | 2 | | 7⁴ | 8 | 10 | | | 13 | 3¹ | 9 | 11 | 12 | 6 | | | | | | 4 | | | | | | | | | | | 21 |
| 1 | | | 5¹ | 2 | | 7 | 8 | 10 | | | 12 | 3² | 6 | 11 | 9 | | | | | | 13 | 4 | | | | | | | | | | | 22 |
| 1 | | 7² | | 2 | 12 | 8 | | 10 | | | 11¹ | | 6 | 3 | 9 | | | | 5 | 13 | | 4 | | | | | | | | | | | 23 |
| 1 | | 7¹ | | 2 | | 8 | | 10 | | | 11 | 3² | 5 | | 9 | | | | 6 | 12 | 13 | 4 | | | | | | | | | | | 24 |
| 1 | | 7² | | 2 | 12 | 8¹ | | 10 | | | 11 | 3³ | 5 | | 9 | | | | 6 | 13 | 14 | 4 | | | | | | | | | | | 25 |
| 1 | 3 | | 12 | 2 | 7¹ | 8 | | | | | 11 | | | | 9 | | | | 5 | | 6 | 10 | 4 | | | | | | | | | | 26 |
| 1 | 3 | | | 2 | 7 | 8 | | 12 | | | 11² | | | | | | | | 5 | | 6¹ | 10 | 4 | | | | 9 | 13 | | | | | 27 |
| 1 | 3 | | 12 | 2² | 7 | 8 | | | | | 11 | | | 9¹ | | | | | 5 | | 6 | | 4 | | | | 10 | 13 | | | | | 28 |
| 1 | 3 | | | 2 | | | | 12 | | | 11 | | | 7¹ | 9 | | | | 5 | | 6 | | 4 | | | | 10 | 8 | | | | | 29 |
| 1 | 3 | | | 2 | | | | | | | 11 | | | 7 | 9 | | | | 5 | | 6 | | 4 | | | | 10¹ | 8 | 12 | | | | 30 |
| 1 | 3 | | 12 | 2 | | | | | | | 11 | | | 7¹ | 9 | | | | 5 | | 6 | | 4 | | | | 10 | 8² | 13 | | | | 31 |
| 1 | 3 | | 7 | 2 | | | 12 | | | | 11¹ | | | | | | | | 5 | | 6 | | 4 | | | | 10 | 8 | | | | | 32 |
| 1 | 3 | | 7 | 2 | | | 12 | | | | | 11¹ | | | 13 | 9 | | | 5 | | 6 | | 4 | | | | 10 | 8² | | | | | 33 |
| 1 | 3 | | 12 | 2 | | | 7² | | | | | 13 | | | 11¹ | 9 | | | 5 | | 6 | | 4 | | | | 10 | 8³ | 14 | | | | 34 |
| | 3 | | | 2 | | | 8 | | | | | | | | 7 | 11¹ | | | 5 | | 6 | | | | | | 10 | 12 | | 1 | | | 35 |
| | 3 | | | 2 | | | 8 | | | | | | | 7² | 12 | 6 | | | 5 | | | | 13 | 4¹ | | | 10 | 11 | | 1 | | | 36 |
| | 3¹ | | | | | | 7 | 8 | | | | | | | 6 | 12 | | | 2 | | 9 | | 5 | | | | 10² | | 13 | 1 | | | 37 |
| | 3 | | | | | | 7¹ | 8 | | | | | 12 | | 13 | 2 | | | 5 | | 6³ | | 11² | 4 | | | 10 | | 14 | 1 | | 9 | 38 |
| | 3 | | | | | | 7 | 8 | | | | | | | | 2 | | | 5 | | 6 | | 11 | 4 | | | 10 | | | 1 | | 9 | 39 |
| | 3 | | | | | | 7 | 8¹ | | | | | | | | 2 | | | 5 | | 6 | | 11 | 4 | | | 10 | | 12 | 1 | | 9 | 40 |
| | 3 | | 12 | | | | 7² | | | | | | | | 13 | 11 | 14 | | 2 | | 9 | | 6¹ | 4 | | | 10³ | | | 1 | | 8 | 41 |
| | 3 | | 12 | | | | | | | | | | | | 7 | 11¹ | | | 2 | | 9 | | 6 | 4 | | | 10² | 13 | | 1 | | 8 | 42 |
| | 3 | | 12 | | | | 8 | | | | | | | | 11 | 13 | | | 2 | | 9 | | 6¹ | 4 | | | 10² | | | 1 | | 7 | 43 |
| | 3 | | 4 | | | | 7 | 8 | 12 | | | | | | 11 | | | | 2 | | 9 | | 5 | 6 | | | 10¹ | | | 1 | | | 44 |
| | 3 | | 2 | | | | 8 | 12 | | | | | 13 | | 11² | | | | 7 | | 9 | | 5 | 6 | | | 10¹ | | | 1 | | | 45 |
| | 3 | | 2 | | | | 8 | | | | | | | | 11 | | | | 7 | | 9 | | 5 | 6 | | | 10 | | | 1 | | | 46 |

**Coca-Cola Cup**

| | | | | |
|---|---|---|---|---|
| First Round | Lincoln C | (a) | 1-1 | |
| | | (h) | 2-1 | |
| Second Round | Stoke | (h) | 0-4 | |
| | | (a) | 0-2 | |

**FA Cup**

| | | | |
|---|---|---|---|
| First Round | Rotherham U | (a) | 3-3 |
| | | (h) | 0-3 |

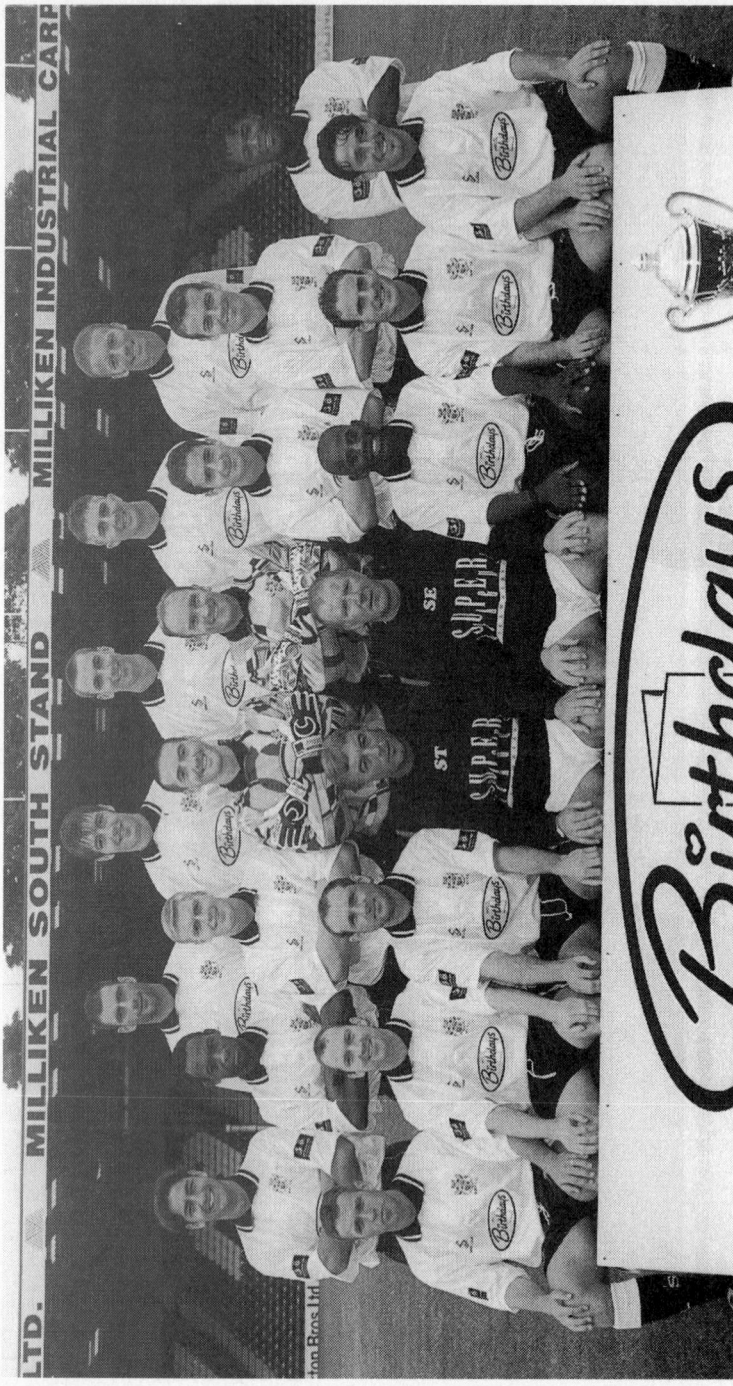

BURY 1997–98 *Back row (left to right):* Adrian Randall, Paul Butler, Brian Linighan, Chris Lucketti, Ronnie Jepson.
*Middle row:* Andy Woodward, Andy Gray, Tony Battersby, Dean Kiely, Lee Bracey, Ian Hughes, Gordon Armstrong, David Johnson.
*Front row:* Nick Daws, Rob Matthews, David Pugh, Stan Ternent (Manager), Sam Ellis (Assistant Manager), Lennie Johnrose, Dean West, Tony Rigby.

# Division 1 **BURY**

*Gigg Lane, Bury BL9 9HR.* Telephone: (0161) 764 4881. Fax: (0161) 764 5521. Commercial Dept: (0161) 705 2144. Fax: (0161) 763 3103. Clubcall: 0891 121197. Community Programme: (0161) 797 5423. Social Club: (0161) 764 6771.

*Ground capacity:* 11,841.

*Record attendance:* 35,000 v Bolton W, FA Cup 3rd rd, 9 January 1960.

*Record receipts:* £86,000 v Manchester C, Division 1, 12 September 1997.

*Pitch measurements:* 112yd × 72yd.

*Chairman:* T. Robinson.

*Directors:* C. H. Eaves, J. Smith, F. Mason.

*Manager:* Neil Warnock. *Assistant Manager:* Sam Ellis. *Coach:* Cliff Roberts. *Physio:* Peter Hampton.

*Youth Development:* Geoff Lutley. *Stadium Manager:* Wilf Linton.

*Secretary:* J. Neville. *Commercial Manager:* Neville Neville.

*Year Formed:* 1885. *Turned professional:* 1885. *Ltd Co.:* 1897. *Club Nickname:* 'Shakers'.

*Club Sponsors:* Birthdays.

*Foundation:* A meeting at the Waggon & Horses Hotel, attended largely by members of Bury Wesleyans and Bury Unitarians football clubs, decided to form a new Bury club. This was officially formed at a subsequent gathering at the Old White Horse Hotel, Fleet Street, Bury on 24 April 1885.

*First Football League game:* 1 September 1894, Division 2, v Manchester C (h) W 4-2 – Lowe; Gillespie, Davies; White, Clegg, Ross; Wylie, Barbour (2), Millar (1), Ostler (1), Plant.

*Record League Victory:* 8–0 v Tranmere R, Division 3, 10 January 1970 – Forrest; Tinney, Saile; Anderson, Turner, McDermott; Hince (1), Arrowsmith (1), Jones (4), Kerr (1), Grundy. (1 og).

*Record Cup Victory:* 12–1 v Stockton, FA Cup 1st rd (replay), 2 February 1897 – Montgomery; Darroch, Barbour; Hendry (1), Clegg, Ross (1); Wylie (3), Pangbourn, Millar (4), Henderson (2), Plant. (1 og).

*Record Defeat:* 0–10 v Blackburn R, FA Cup preliminary round, 1 October 1887 and v West Ham U, Milk Cup 2nd rd 2nd leg, 25 October 1983.

*Most League Points (2 for a win):* 68, Division 3, 1960–61.

*Most League Points (3 for a win):* 84, Division 4, 1984–85 and Division 2, 1996–97.

*Most League Goals:* 108, Division 3, 1960–61.

*Highest League Scorer in Season:* Craig Madden, 35, Division 4, 1981–82.

*Most League Goals in Total Aggregate:* Craig Madden, 129, 1978–86.

*Most Capped Player:* Bill Gorman, 11 (13), Republic of Ireland and (4), Northern Ireland.

*Most League Appearances:* Norman Bullock, 506, 1920–35.

*Record Transfer Fee Received:* £1,100,000 from Ipswich T for David Johnson, November 1997.

*Record Transfer Fee Paid:* £200,000 to Ipswich T for Chris Swailes, November 1997.

*Football League Record:* 1894 Elected to Division 2; 1895–1912 Division 1; 1912–24 Division 2; 1924–29 Division 1; 1929–57 Division 2; 1957–61 Division 3; 1961–67 Division 2; 1967–68 Division 3; 1968–69 Division 2; 1969–71 Division 2; 1971–74 Division 4; 1974–80 Division 3; 1980–85 Division 4; 1985–96 Division 3; 1996–97 Division 2; 1997– Division 1.

*Honours: Football League:* Division 1 best season: 4th, 1925–26; Division 2 – Champions 1894–95, 1996–97; Runners-up 1923–24; Division 3 – Champions 1960–61; Runners-up 1967–68; Promoted from Division 3 (3rd) 1995–96. *FA Cup:* Winners 1900, 1903. *Football League Cup:* Semi-final 1963.

*Colours:* White shirts, royal blue shorts, royal blue stockings. *Change colours:* Royal blue shirts, white shorts, royal blue stockings.

**Did you know?**
Up to 27 September 1997, Bury completed a club record 29 unbeaten home League games.

## BURY 1997–98 LEAGUE RECORD

| Match No. | Date | Venue | Opponents | Result | H/T Score | Lg. Pos. | Goalscorers | Attendance |
|---|---|---|---|---|---|---|---|---|
| 1 | Aug 9 | H | Reading | D | 1-1 | 0-1 | — | Armstrong [52] | 5065 |
| 2 | 16 | A | Stockport Co | D | 0-0 | 0-0 | 14 | | 7260 |
| 3 | 23 | H | Charlton Ath | D | 0-0 | 0-0 | 18 | | 4657 |
| 4 | 30 | A | Wolverhampton W | L | 2-4 | 1-2 | 18 | Battersby [19], Johnson [61] | 21,141 |
| 5 | Sept 2 | A | Crewe Alex | W | 2-1 | 1-1 | — | Johnson [14], Swan [63] | 4447 |
| 6 | 7 | H | Tranmere R | W | 1-0 | 1-0 | 7 | Swan [42] | 5073 |
| 7 | 12 | H | Manchester C | D | 1-1 | 0-0 | — | Johnson [65] | 11,216 |
| 8 | 20 | A | Port Vale | D | 1-1 | 0-1 | 13 | Swan [82] | 6781 |
| 9 | 27 | H | WBA | L | 1-3 | 0-2 | 14 | Lucketti [90] | 6439 |
| 10 | Oct 4 | A | Stoke C | L | 2-3 | 0-0 | 17 | Swan [70], Gray Andy (pen) [85] | 11,760 |
| 11 | 11 | A | Swindon T | L | 1-3 | 1-2 | 18 | Battersby [41] | 7640 |
| 12 | 18 | H | Birmingham C | W | 2-1 | 2-0 | 16 | Johnson [19], Swan [28] | 5700 |
| 13 | 21 | H | QPR | D | 1-1 | 0-0 | — | Battersby [57] | 4602 |
| 14 | 25 | A | Ipswich T | L | 0-2 | 0-0 | 16 | | 10,478 |
| 15 | Nov 1 | A | Norwich C | D | 2-2 | 1-2 | 15 | Battersby [40], Johnrose [90] | 14,419 |
| 16 | 4 | H | Nottingham F | W | 2-0 | 1-0 | — | Swan [16], Johnson [63] | 6137 |
| 17 | 8 | H | Portsmouth | L | 0-2 | 0-0 | 15 | | 5065 |
| 18 | 15 | A | Oxford U | D | 1-1 | 1-1 | 15 | Swailes [43] | 5811 |
| 19 | 22 | H | Sunderland | D | 1-1 | 1-1 | 17 | Lucketti [9] | 7790 |
| 20 | 29 | A | Huddersfield T | L | 0-2 | 0-1 | 17 | | 11,929 |
| 21 | Dec 6 | H | Middlesbrough | L | 0-1 | 0-0 | 20 | | 8016 |
| 22 | 13 | A | Bradford C | L | 0-1 | 0-1 | 22 | | 15,812 |
| 23 | 20 | A | Sheffield U | D | 1-1 | 1-0 | 22 | Johnrose [18] | 6012 |
| 24 | 26 | A | Tranmere R | D | 0-0 | 0-0 | 24 | | 9146 |
| 25 | 28 | H | Crewe Alex | D | 1-1 | 0-0 | 23 | Patterson [62] | 5661 |
| 26 | Jan 10 | A | Reading | D | 1-1 | 0-1 | 23 | Gray Andrew [87] | 7499 |
| 27 | 18 | H | Stockport Co | L | 0-1 | 0-1 | 23 | | 5699 |
| 28 | 27 | A | Wolverhampton W | L | 1-3 | 1-1 | — | Battersby [43] | 6134 |
| 29 | 31 | A | Charlton Ath | D | 0-0 | 0-0 | 23 | | 15,312 |
| 30 | Feb 7 | H | Port Vale | D | 2-2 | 1-2 | 23 | Battersby [30], Ellis [60] | 5285 |
| 31 | 14 | A | Manchester C | W | 1-0 | 0-0 | 23 | Butler [52] | 28,885 |
| 32 | 17 | H | Stoke C | D | 0-0 | 0-0 | — | | 5802 |
| 33 | 21 | A | WBA | D | 1-1 | 0-1 | 23 | Ellis [57] | 15,840 |
| 34 | 25 | A | Birmingham C | W | 3-1 | 1-0 | — | Rigby [32], Patterson [53], Ellis [75] | 20,021 |
| 35 | 28 | H | Swindon T | W | 1-0 | 1-0 | 18 | Daws [39] | 5002 |
| 36 | Mar 3 | A | Portsmouth | D | 1-1 | 1-0 | — | Johnrose [21] | 12,462 |
| 37 | 7 | H | Norwich C | W | 1-0 | 0-0 | 17 | Jemson (pen) [60] | 5154 |
| 38 | 14 | A | Nottingham F | L | 0-3 | 0-0 | 18 | | 18,846 |
| 39 | 21 | H | Oxford U | W | 1-0 | 0-0 | 17 | Ellis [68] | 5159 |
| 40 | 28 | A | Sunderland | L | 1-2 | 1-1 | 17 | Small [28] | 37,425 |
| 41 | Apr 4 | H | Huddersfield T | D | 2-2 | 1-1 | 17 | Butler [33], Ellis [47] | 8042 |
| 42 | 11 | A | Middlesbrough | L | 0-4 | 0-1 | 20 | | 30,218 |
| 43 | 13 | H | Bradford C | W | 2-0 | 1-0 | 18 | Ellis [41], Daws [53] | 6570 |
| 44 | 18 | A | Sheffield U | L | 0-3 | 0-1 | 18 | | 16,056 |
| 45 | 25 | H | Ipswich T | L | 0-1 | 0-0 | 19 | | 7830 |
| 46 | May 3 | A | QPR | W | 1-0 | 1-0 | 17 | Armstrong [22] | 15,210 |

**Final League Position: 17**     1996–97 DIV2 1

### GOALSCORERS

*League (42):* Battersby 6, Ellis 6, Swan 6, Johnson 5, Johnrose 3, Armstrong 2, Butler 2, Daws 2, Lucketti 2, Patterson 2, Andrew Gray 1, Andy Gray 1 (pen), Jemson 1 (pen), Rigby 1, Small 1, Swailes 1.
*Coca-Cola Cup (8):* Johnson 3, Armstrong 1, Battersby 1 (pen), Daws 1, Andy Gray 1, Jepson 1 (pen).
*FA Cup (2):* Andy Gray 2.

| Kiely D 46 | West D 4 | Pugh D 1 | Daws N 46 | Lucketti C 46 | Butler P 43 | Gray Andy 21 | Johnson D 17 | Jepson R 7 + 9 | Johnrose L 44 | Battersby T 28 + 9 | Armstrong G 33 + 4 | Randall A 2 + 13 | Swan P 26 + 11 | Hughes I 12 + 1 | Woodward A 20 + 12 | Morgan S 5 | Peake J 3 + 3 | Rigby T 8 + 16 | Swailes C 12 + 1 | Dalgish P 1 + 11 | Gray Andrew 4 + 2 | Ellis T 21 + 1 | Paterson M 18 | Small B 18 | Matthews R 9 + 6 | Jemson N 11 + 4 | Match No. |
|---|---|---|---|---|---|---|---|---|---|---|---|---|---|---|---|---|---|---|---|---|---|---|---|---|---|---|---|
| 1 | 2 | $3^1$ | 4 | 5 | 6 | 7 | $8^2$ | $9^2$ | 10 | 11 | 12 | 13 | 14 | | | | | | | | | | | | | | 1 |
| 1 | $2^1$ | | 4 | 5 | 6 | 7 | 8 | $9^2$ | 10 | 11 | 3 | 13 | 12 | | | | | | | | | | | | | | 2 |
| 1 | 2 | | 4 | 5 | 6 | 7 | 8 | 9 | 10 | | 3 | | 11 | | | | | | | | | | | | | | 3 |
| 1 | $2^2$ | | $4^1$ | 5 | 6 | $7^3$ | 8 | 12 | 10 | 11 | 3 | 13 | 9 | 14 | | | | | | | | | | | | | 4 |
| 1 | | | 4 | 5 | 6 | 7 | $8^1$ | 12 | 10 | $11^2$ | 3 | | 9 | 2 | 13 | | | | | | | | | | | | 5 |
| 1 | | | 4 | 5 | 6 | 7 | $8^1$ | 12 | 10 | $11^2$ | 3 | 13 | 9 | 2 | | | | | | | | | | | | | 6 |
| 1 | | | 4 | 5 | 6 | 7 | $8^1$ | 12 | 10 | $11^2$ | 3 | | 9 | 2 | 13 | | | | | | | | | | | | 7 |
| 1 | | | 4 | 5 | 6 | 7 | 8 | 12 | 10 | $11^2$ | | 13 | 9 | $2^1$ | 3 | | | | | | | | | | | | 8 |
| 1 | | | 4 | 5 | 6 | $7^2$ | 8 | | $10^1$ | 11 | | 12 | 9 | 2 | 13 | 3 | | | | | | | | | | | 9 |
| 1 | | | 4 | 5 | 6 | 7 | 8 | | 10 | $11^1$ | | 12 | 9 | $2^2$ | 13 | 3 | | | | | | | | | | | 10 |
| 1 | | | $4^1$ | 5 | 6 | 7 | 8 | | $10^3$ | 11 | | | 9 | $2^2$ | 12 | 3 | 13 | 14 | | | | | | | | | 11 |
| 1 | | | 4 | 5 | 6 | $7^2$ | 8 | | 10 | $11^1$ | | | 9 | 2 | 12 | 3 | 13 | | | | | | | | | | 12 |
| 1 | | | 4 | 5 | 6 | 7 | 8 | | 10 | 11 | | | $9^2$ | 2 | | $3^1$ | 12 | 13 | | | | | | | | | 13 |
| 1 | | | 4 | 5 | 6 | 7 | 8 | | $10^2$ | 11 | | 12 | | 2 | 9 | $3^1$ | 13 | | | | | | | | | | 14 |
| 1 | | | 4 | 5 | 6 | 7 | 8 | 12 | 10 | $11^1$ | | 13 | 14 | $2^2$ | 9 | | $3^3$ | | | | | | | | | | 15 |
| 1 | | | 4 | 5 | 6 | 7 | $8^1$ | 12 | 10 | $11^2$ | | 13 | 9 | 2 | 3 | | | | | | | | | | | | 16 |
| 1 | | | 4 | 5 | 6 | | 8 | 12 | 10 | $11^1$ | 7 | 13 | 9 | | $3^3$ | $2^2$ | 14 | | | | | | | | | | 17 |
| 1 | | | 4 | 5 | 6 | | 8 | | 10 | $11^2$ | 3 | 12 | 9 | | $2^1$ | | 13 | 7 | | | | | | | | | 18 |
| 1 | | | 4 | 5 | 6 | | 8 | | 10 | $11^2$ | 3 | $2^1$ | 9 | | 12 | | | 7 | 13 | | | | | | | | 19 |
| 1 | | | 4 | 5 | 6 | | 8 | | 10 | $11^3$ | 3 | $2^1$ | 9 | | $12^2$ | | | 13 | 7 | 14 | | | | | | | 20 |
| 1 | | | 4 | 5 | 6 | | 8 | | 10 | $11^2$ | 3 | | 9 | | $2^1$ | | | 7 | 12 | 13 | | | | | | | 21 |
| 1 | | | 4 | 5 | 6 | | | | 10 | | 3 | 12 | 9 | $2^2$ | $13^3$ | | | $7^1$ | 14 | 11 | | | 8 | | | | 22 |
| 1 | | | 4 | 5 | 6 | 11 | | | 10 | $9^1$ | 3 | | | | 2 | | | 7 | 12 | | | | 8 | | | | 23 |
| 1 | | | 4 | 5 | 6 | $11^1$ | | | 10 | 9 | 3 | | | | 12 | | | 7 | | | | | 8 | 2 | | | 24 |
| 1 | | | 4 | 5 | | 7 | | | 10 | $9^2$ | 3 | | | | 12 | | | 6 | 13 | 2 | | $8^1$ | $11^1$ | | | | 25 |
| 1 | | | 4 | 5 | 6 | 2 | | | 12 | 10 | $9^2$ | 3 | | | | | | $7^1$ | | 13 | | | 8 | 11 | | | 26 |
| 1 | | | 4 | 5 | 6 | 2 | | | $10^2$ | 12 | 3 | | 9 | | | | | 13 | | $7^1$ | | | 8 | 11 | | | 27 |
| 1 | | | 4 | 5 | 6 | | | | 10 | $11^2$ | | $12^2$ | $9^1$ | | 2 | | | 3 | $7^1$ | 13 | 2 | | 8 | | | | 28 |
| 1 | | | 4 | 5 | 6 | | | | 10 | $11^3$ | | | 2 | | | | | 13 | | 7 | | 8 | | 3 | 14 | | 29 |
| 1 | | | 4 | 5 | 6 | | | | 10 | $9^2$ | 12 | | 13 | | 2 | | | | | 11 | $8^1$ | 3 | 13 | 7 | | | 30 |
| 1 | | | 4 | 5 | 6 | | | | $10^1$ | $11^2$ | 9 | | 13 | | 2 | | | | | $11^1$ | 8 | 3 | | $7^2$ | | | 31 |
| 1 | | | 4 | 5 | 6 | | | | $10^1$ | $11^2$ | 9 | | 12 | | 2 | | | 13 | | | 8 | 3 | 14 | $7^3$ | | | 32 |
| 1 | | | 4 | 5 | 6 | | | | | 9 | | | 12 | | $2^2$ | | | 7 | | | 8 | $13^3$ | $10^1$ | | | | 33 |
| 1 | | | 4 | 5 | 6 | | | | 10 | | 9 | | 12 | | | | | 2 | | 14 | $11^1$ | 8 | 3 | $13^3$ | $7^2$ | | 34 |
| 1 | | | 4 | 5 | 6 | | | | 10 | 12 | 9 | | | | | | | 2 | | 13 | | 8 | 3 | $11^2$ | $7^1$ | | 35 |
| 1 | | | 4 | 5 | 6 | | | | 10 | 12 | 9 | | | | | | | 2 | | | | 8 | 3 | $11^1$ | 7 | | 36 |
| 1 | | | 4 | 5 | 6 | | | | $10^2$ | 12 | 9 | | | | 13 | | | 2 | | 14 | | 8 | 3 | $11^3$ | $7^1$ | | 37 |
| 1 | | | 4 | 5 | | | | | | 12 | 9 | | 13 | | 2 | | | $7^3$ | 6 | 14 | | $8^1$ | $11^1$ | 3 | | $10^2$ | 38 |
| 1 | | | 4 | 5 | | | | | 10 | 12 | 9 | | 13 | | | | | $2^1$ | 6 | | | $7^1$ | 11 | 3 | 14 | $8^2$ | 39 |
| 1 | | | 4 | 5 | 6 | | | | 10 | | 2 | | 12 | | 13 | | | 14 | | | | $7^1$ | $11^2$ | 3 | $9^1$ | $8^3$ | 40 |
| 1 | | | 4 | 5 | 6 | | | | 10 | | 2 | | $8^2$ | | | | | 12 | | | | $7^1$ | 11 | 3 | $9^1$ | 13 | 41 |
| 1 | | | 4 | 5 | 6 | | | | 10 | | $9^2$ | | 12 | | 2 | | | 13 | | | | $7^3$ | 11 | 3 | $8^1$ | 14 | 42 |
| 1 | | | 4 | 5 | 6 | | | | 10 | | 9 | | 11 | | 2 | | | 7 | | | | | | 3 | 8 | | 43 |
| 1 | | | 4 | 5 | 6 | | | | 10 | 12 | 11 | | 9 | | $2^2$ | | | 13 | | | | 7 | | 3 | $8^1$ | | 44 |
| 1 | | | 4 | 5 | 6 | | | | 10 | | 11 | | $9^3$ | | 2 | | | 12 | 13 | | | 7 | | $3^2$ | $8^1$ | 14 | 45 |
| 1 | | | 4 | 5 | 6 | | | | 10 | 12 | 8 | | $9^3$ | | 2 | | | 13 | | | | $7^1$ | $11^2$ | 3 | | 14 | 46 |

**Coca-Cola Cup**
First Round    Crewe Alex    (a) 3-2   (h) 3-3
Second Round    Sunderland    (a) 1-2   (h) 1-2

**FA Cup**
Third Round    Sheffield U    (a) 1-1   (h) 1-2

CAMBRIDGE UNITED 1997–98 *Back row (left to right):* Paul Wilson, Marc Joseph, Jamie Campbell, Dave Thompson, John Taylor, Ian Ashbee, Paul Wanless.
*Middle row:* Michael Kyd, Adie Hayes, Ben Chenery, Shaun Marshall, Scott Barrett, Trevor Benjamin, Jamie Barnwell-Edinboro, Ken Steggles (Physio).
*Front row:* David Williamson, Jason Rees, David Preece (Player/Coach), Roy McFarland (Team Manager), Billy Beall, Adam Wilde, Matthew Joseph.

# Division 3     **CAMBRIDGE UNITED**

*Abbey Stadium, Newmarket Rd, Cambridge, CB5 8LN.* Telephone: (01223) 566500. Fax: (01223) 566502. Abbey Update: 0891 555885. Website: www.cambridgeunited.com.

*Ground capacity:* 9617.

*Record attendance:* 14,000 v Chelsea, Friendly, 1 May 1970.

*Record receipts:* £86,308 v Manchester U, Rumbelows Cup 2nd rd 2nd leg, 9 October 1991.

*Pitch measurements:* 110yd × 74yd.

*Chairman:* R. H. Smart. *Vice-Chairman:* R. F. Hunt. *Directors:* G. Harwood, J. Howard, R. Hunt, G. Lowe, R. Summerfield.

*Manager:* Roy McFarland. *Player/coach:* David Preece. *Youth Manager:* David Batch.

*Physio:* Ken Steggles.

*Secretary:* Steve Greenall. *Commercial Manager:* Carla Frediani. *Stadium Manager:* Ian Darler.

*Year Formed:* 1919. *Turned Professional:* 1946. *Ltd Co.:* 1948.

*Club Nickname:* The 'U's'.

*Previous Name:* Abbey United until 1949.

*Foundation:* The football revival in Cambridge began soon after World War II when the Abbey United club (formed 1919) decided to turn professional and in 1949 changed their name to Cambridge United. They were competing in the United Counties League before graduating to the Eastern Counties League in 1951 and the Southern League in 1958.

*First Football League game:* 15 August 1970, Division 4, v Lincoln C (h) D 1-1 – Roberts; Thompson, Meldrum (1), Slack, Eades, Hardy, Leggett, Cassidy, Lindsey, McKinven, Harris.

*Record League Victory:* 6–0 v Darlington, Division 4, 18 September 1971 – Roberts; Thompson, Akers, Guild, Eades, Foote, Collins (1p), Horrey, Hollett, Greenhalgh (4), Phillips. (1 og). 6–0 v Hartlepool U, Division 4, 11 February 1989 – Vaughan; Beck, Kimble, Turner, Chapple (1), Daish, Clayton, Holmes, Taylor (3 incl. 1p), Bull (1), Leadbitter (1).

*Record Cup Victory:* 5–1 v Bristol C, FA Cup 5th rd second replay, 27 February 1990 – Vaughan; Fensome, Kimble, Bailie (O'Shea), Chapple, Daish, Cheetham (Robinson), Leadbitter (1), Dublin (2), Taylor (1), Philpott (1).

*Record Defeat:* 0–6 v Aldershot, Division 3, 13 April 1974; v Darlington, Division 4, 28 September 1974; v Chelsea, Division 2, 15 January 1983 and v Brentford, Division 2, 28 January 1995.

*Most League Points (2 for a win):* 65, Division 4, 1976–77.

*Most League Points (3 for a win):* 86, Division 3, 1990–91.

*Most League Goals:* 87, Division 4, 1976–77.

*Highest League Scorer in Season:* David Crown, 24, Division 4, 1985–86.

*Most League Goals in Total Aggregate:* Alan Biley, 74, 1975–80.

*Most Capped Player:* Tom Finney, 7 (15), Northern Ireland.

*Most League Appearances:* Steve Spriggs, 416, 1975–87.

*Record Transfer Fee Received:* £1,000,000 from Manchester U for Dion Dublin, August 1992.

*Record Transfer Fee Paid:* £190,000 to Luton T for Steve Claridge, November 1992.

*Football League Record:* 1970 Elected to Division 4; 1973–74 Division 3; 1974–77 Division 4; 1977–78 Division 3; 1978–84 Division 2; 1984–85 Division 3; 1985–90 Division 4; 1990–91 Division 3; 1991–92 Division 2; 1992–93 Division 1; 1993–95 Division 2; 1995– Division 3.

*Honours: Football League:* Division 2 best season: 5th, 1991–92; Division 3 – Champions 1990–91; Runners-up 1977–78; Division 4 – Champions 1976–77; Promoted from Division 4 1989–90 (play-offs). *FA Cup:* best season: 6th rd, 1990 (shared record for Fourth Division club), 1991. *Football League Cup:* 5th rd, 1993.

*Colours:* Amber shirts with black trim, black shorts, black stockings. *Change colours:* Light and dark blue halved shirts, dark blue shorts, dark blue stockings.

**Did you know?**
Cambridge United were voted 'Best Ground for Away Supporters' by Total Football magazine in September 1997 and 'Best Football Food' by Colman's in February 1998.

## CAMBRIDGE UNITED 1997–98 LEAGUE RECORD

| Match No. | Date | | Venue | Opponents | Result | | H/T Score | Lg. Pos. | Goalscorers | Atten-dance |
|---|---|---|---|---|---|---|---|---|---|---|
| 1 | Aug | 9 | A | Scarborough | L | 0-1 | 0-0 | — | | 2225 |
| 2 | | 16 | H | Rotherham U | W | 2-1 | 0-0 | 11 | Kyd 46, Taylor 82 | 2725 |
| 3 | | 23 | A | Chester C | D | 1-1 | 1-0 | 15 | Kyd 7 | 2167 |
| 4 | | 30 | H | Shrewsbury T | W | 4-3 | 1-1 | 7 | Wanless 2 10, 61, Butler 57, Kyd 71 | 2585 |
| 5 | Sept | 2 | H | Colchester U | W | 4-1 | 1-1 | — | Butler 2 6, 47, Taylor 2 62, 69 | 3264 |
| 6 | | 5 | A | Leyton Orient | W | 2-0 | 1-0 | — | Kyd 34, Foster 72 | 4638 |
| 7 | | 13 | H | Barnet | L | 1-3 | 0-1 | 5 | Taylor 84 | 3395 |
| 8 | | 20 | A | Doncaster R | D | 0-0 | 0-0 | 5 | | 1258 |
| 9 | | 27 | H | Cardiff C | D | 2-2 | 0-1 | 5 | Barnwell-Edinboro 2 50, 79 | 2728 |
| 10 | Oct | 4 | A | Lincoln C | D | 0-0 | 0-0 | 5 | | 3397 |
| 11 | | 11 | A | Mansfield T | L | 2-3 | 1-2 | 7 | Finney 35, Wanless 77 | 2239 |
| 12 | | 18 | H | Rochdale | D | 1-1 | 1-0 | 10 | Finney 16 | 2703 |
| 13 | | 21 | H | Hull C | L | 0-1 | 0-0 | — | | 2388 |
| 14 | | 25 | A | Notts Co | L | 0-1 | 0-0 | 15 | | 4279 |
| 15 | Nov | 1 | H | Torquay U | D | 1-1 | 1-0 | 14 | Butler 24 | 2314 |
| 16 | | 4 | H | Scunthorpe U | D | 3-3 | 2-0 | — | Wilson 10, Butler 17, Wanless 76 | 2417 |
| 17 | | 8 | A | Macclesfield T | L | 1-3 | 0-2 | 18 | Campbell 60 | 2337 |
| 18 | | 18 | H | Brighton & HA | D | 1-1 | 1-0 | — | Wilson (pen) 23 | 2370 |
| 19 | | 22 | A | Darlington | D | 1-1 | 1-1 | 19 | Taylor 7 | 2221 |
| 20 | | 29 | H | Hartlepool U | W | 2-0 | 1-0 | 17 | Kyd 2, Campbell 47 | 2513 |
| 21 | Dec | 2 | A | Peterborough U | L | 0-1 | 0-0 | — | | 10,791 |
| 22 | | 12 | H | Exeter C | W | 2-1 | 1-1 | — | Taylor 2 16, 79 | 2224 |
| 23 | | 20 | A | Swansea C | D | 1-1 | 0-1 | 15 | Wilson (pen) 59 | 2605 |
| 24 | | 26 | A | Leyton Orient | W | 1-0 | 0-0 | 15 | Wanless 47 | 4808 |
| 25 | | 29 | A | Colchester U | L | 2-3 | 1-1 | — | Barnwell-Edinboro 2 6, 69 | 4518 |
| 26 | Jan | 10 | H | Scarborough | L | 2-3 | 1-1 | 16 | Brebner 21, Wilson 54 | 2636 |
| 27 | | 17 | A | Shrewsbury T | D | 1-1 | 1-1 | 16 | Taylor 9 | 2210 |
| 28 | | 24 | A | Chester C | L | 1-2 | 0-0 | 16 | Wilson (pen) 81 | 2473 |
| 29 | | 27 | A | Rotherham U | D | 2-2 | 0-0 | — | Kyd 59, Chenery 72 | 3096 |
| 30 | | 31 | A | Barnet | L | 0-2 | 0-1 | 18 | | 2455 |
| 31 | Feb | 7 | H | Doncaster R | W | 2-1 | 0-1 | 16 | Taylor 54, Wanless 82 | 2478 |
| 32 | | 13 | H | Lincoln C | D | 1-1 | 1-0 | — | Chenery 25 | 3891 |
| 33 | | 21 | A | Cardiff C | D | 0-0 | 0-0 | 18 | | 2681 |
| 34 | | 24 | A | Rochdale | L | 0-2 | 0-1 | — | | 1192 |
| 35 | | 28 | H | Mansfield T | W | 2-0 | 0-0 | 17 | Charles 71, Ashbee 78 | 2303 |
| 36 | Mar | 3 | H | Macclesfield T | D | 0-0 | 0-0 | — | | 2012 |
| 37 | | 7 | A | Torquay U | W | 3-0 | 1-0 | 17 | Kyd 42, Benjamin 55, Wanless 79 | 3809 |
| 38 | | 14 | H | Scunthorpe U | D | 2-2 | 2-0 | 17 | Benjamin 2 24, 41 | 2423 |
| 39 | | 21 | A | Brighton & HA | W | 2-0 | 2-0 | 16 | Kyd 30, Benjamin 37 | 2746 |
| 40 | | 28 | H | Darlington | W | 1-0 | 0-0 | 15 | Taylor 90 | 2649 |
| 41 | Apr | 4 | A | Hartlepool U | D | 3-3 | 1-1 | 15 | Butler 2 17, 54, Wanless 53 | 1867 |
| 42 | | 11 | H | Peterborough U | W | 1-0 | 0-0 | 15 | Kyd 81 | 5445 |
| 43 | | 13 | A | Exeter C | L | 0-1 | 0-1 | 16 | | 3527 |
| 44 | | 18 | A | Swansea C | W | 4-1 | 2-1 | 15 | Butler 2 17, 38, Kyd 2 56, 81 | 2336 |
| 45 | | 25 | H | Notts Co | D | 2-2 | 2-1 | 15 | Butler 19, Beall 29 | 4009 |
| 46 | May | 2 | A | Hull C | L | 0-1 | 0-1 | 16 | | 4930 |

**Final League Position: 16**      1996–97 DIV3 10

### GOALSCORERS

League (63): Kyd 11, Butler 10, Taylor 10, Wanless 8, Wilson 5 (3 pens), Barnwell-Edinboro 4, Benjamin 4, Campbell 2, Chenery 2, Finney 2, Ashbee 1, Beall 1, Brebner 1, Charles 1, Foster 1.
Coca-Cola Cup (2): Butler 1, Kyd 1.
FA Cup (5): Butler 2, Beall 1, Benjamin 1, Wilson 1 (pen).

| Barrett S 43 | Chenery B 36 | Wilson P 31 | Joseph M 37 + 4 | Foster C 26 | Campbell J 46 | Wanless P 42 | Rees J 17 + 3 | Kyd M 36 + 2 | Butler M 28 + 3 | Preece D 15 + 7 | Taylor J 19 + 15 | Williamson D 2 + 4 | Joseph M 5 + 2 | Youngs T 1 + 3 | Benjamin T 16 + 9 | Barnwell-Edinboro J 11 + 5 | Hayes A 5 + 3 | Finney S 4 + 3 | Rodosthenous M — + 2 | Marshall S 2 | Beall B 25 + 5 | Ashbee I 27 | Brebner G 6 | Duncan A 18 + 1 | Larkin J 1 | Charles L 7 | Wilde A — + 2 | Moore M — + 1 | McCammon M — + 2 | Smith T — + 1 | Match No. |
|---|---|---|---|---|---|---|---|---|---|---|---|---|---|---|---|---|---|---|---|---|---|---|---|---|---|---|---|---|---|---|---|
| 1 | 2 | 3 | 4 | 5 | 6 | 7 | $8^1$ | $9^2$ | 10 | 11 | 12 | 13 | | | | | | | | | | | | | | | | | | | 1 |
| 1 | 2 | 3 | 4 | 5 | 6 | $7^1$ | 8 | 9 | 10 | $11^2$ | 12 | 13 | | | | | | | | | | | | | | | | | | | 2 |
| 1 | 2 | 3 | 4 | 5 | 6 | $7^1$ | 8 | 9 | 10 | 11 | 12 | | | | | | | | | | | | | | | | | | | | 3 |
| 1 | $3^3$ | 2 | 4 | 5 | 6 | 7 | $8^1$ | 9 | 10 | 12 | 13 | $11^2$ | 14 | | | | | | | | | | | | | | | | | | 4 |
| 1 | 2 | 3 | 4 | 5 | 6 | 7 | $8^1$ | $9^2$ | 10 | 12 | 11 | | | | 13 | | | | | | | | | | | | | | | | 5 |
| 1 | 2 | 3 | 4 | 5 | 6 | 7 | 8 | 9 | 10 | 12 | $11^1$ | | | | | | | | | | | | | | | | | | | | 6 |
| 1 | 2 | 3 | 4 | $5^1$ | 6 | 7 | 8 | $9^2$ | 10 | 12 | 11 | 13 | | | | | | | | | | | | | | | | | | | 7 |
| 1 | 2 | 3 | 4 | 5 | 6 | 7 | 8 | | 10 | | 12 | $11^2$ | | | $9^1$ | 13 | | | | | | | | | | | | | | | 8 |
| 1 | $2^1$ | 3 | 4 | 5 | 6 | 7 | 8 | | | $11^2$ | 9 | | | | 12 | 10 | 13 | | | | | | | | | | | | | | 9 |
| 1 | | 3 | 4 | 5 | 6 | 7 | | | 10 | 11 | $9^1$ | | | | 12 | 8 | 2 | | | | | | | | | | | | | | 10 |
| 1 | | 3 | 4 | 5 | 6 | 7 | $8^1$ | | $10^2$ | $11^1$ | | 12 | | | 13 | | 2 | 9 | 14 | | | | | | | | | | | | 11 |
| 1 | | 3 | 4 | 5 | 6 | 7 | 10 | | 9 | $8^1$ | | 2 | | | 12 | 11 | | | | | | | | | | | | | | | 12 |
| | | 3 | 4 | 5 | 6 | 7 | $11^1$ | 9 | 10 | 12 | | 2 | | | 13 | 8 | | | | 1 | | | | | | | | | | | 13 |
| | | 3 | 4 | 5 | 6 | $7^2$ | 11 | $9^1$ | 10 | 12 | | $2^2$ | | | 13 | 8 | | | | 1 | 14 | | | | | | | | | | 14 |
| | | 3 | 4 | 5 | 6 | 7 | 8 | $9^1$ | 11 | | | 2 | | | 10 | 12 | | | | | | | | | | | | | | | 15 |
| | | 3 | 4 | 5 | 6 | 7 | 8 | $9^1$ | 10 | | | 2 | | | $11^1$ | 13 | | | | | 12 | | | | | | | | | | 16 |
| | | 3 | 4 | 5 | 6 | 7 | $8^1$ | $9^1$ | 10 | 12 | | | | | 11 | 13 | | | | | 14 | $2^3$ | | | | | | | | | 17 |
| 1 | 2 | 3 | | 5 | 6 | 7 | | $9^1$ | 10 | 8 | 12 | | | | | | | | | | 11 | 4 | | | | | | | | | 18 |
| 1 | 2 | 3 | | 5 | 6 | 7 | 12 | | 10 | $8^1$ | $9^2$ | | | | 13 | | | | | | 11 | 4 | | | | | | | | | 19 |
| 1 | 2 | 3 | | 5 | 6 | 7 | | 10 | | 9 | | | | | 8 | | | | | | 11 | 4 | | | | | | | | | 20 |
| 1 | 2 | 3 | | 5 | 6 | 7 | | $10^1$ | 12 | 9 | | | | | 8 | | | | | | 11 | 4 | | | | | | | | | 21 |
| 1 | $2^1$ | 3 | 12 | 5 | 6 | 7 | | | 10 | 9 | | | | | 8 | | | | | | 11 | 4 | | | | | | | | | 22 |
| 1 | $2^2$ | 3 | 12 | 5 | 6 | 7 | 13 | 14 | 10 | 9 | | | | | $8^3$ | | | | | | $11^1$ | 4 | | | | | | | | | 23 |
| 1 | 2 | 3 | | 5 | 6 | 7 | | 8 | 10 | 9 | | | | | | | | | | | 11 | 4 | | | | | | | | | 24 |
| 1 | $2^3$ | 3 | 12 | $5^1$ | 6 | 7 | 8 | | | $9^2$ | | | | | 13 | 10 | | | 14 | | 11 | 4 | | | | | | | | | 25 |
| 1 | 2 | $3^3$ | 12 | $5^1$ | 6 | | 14 | 13 | | $9^2$ | | | | | 8 | 10 | | | | | 11 | 4 | 7 | | | | | | | | 26 |
| 1 | 2 | 3 | | 5 | 6 | | | $10^1$ | | 8 | 9 | | | | 12 | | | | | | 11 | 4 | 7 | 13 | | | | | | | 27 |
| 1 | | 3 | | 5 | 6 | 7 | | 10 | | 9 | | | | | 12 | | | | | | $11^1$ | 4 | 8 | 2 | | | | | | | 28 |
| | 2 | 3 | | 5 | 6 | $7^1$ | | 10 | | 12 | | | | | 9 | | | | | | 11 | 8 | | 4 | 1 | | | | | | 29 |
| 1 | 2 | $3^1$ | | 5 | 6 | 7 | | $10^2$ | | 12 | | 13 | | | 9 | | | | | | 11 | 8 | | 4 | | | | | | | 30 |
| 1 | | 3 | | 5 | 6 | 7 | | 10 | | $2^2$ | 9 | | | | $11^1$ | 12 | 13 | | | | | 8 | | 4 | | | | | | | 31 |
| 1 | 2 | | | 5 | 6 | 7 | | 10 | | 8 | $9^1$ | 13 | | | 12 | $11^2$ | | | | | | 3 | | 4 | | | | | | | 32 |
| 1 | 2 | | | 5 | 6 | 7 | | 10 | | $8^2$ | | | | | | 11 | | | | | 12 | 3 | | 4 | | 9 | | | 13 | | 33 |
| 1 | 2 | | | 5 | 6 | 7 | | 10 | | $8^2$ | | | | | | 11 | | | | | 12 | 3 | | 4 | | 9 | | | 13 | | 34 |
| 1 | 2 | | | 5 | 6 | $7^1$ | | 10 | | 8 | | | | | | 11 | | | | | 12 | 3 | | 4 | | 9 | | | | | 35 |
| 1 | 2 | | | 5 | 6 | 7 | | 10 | | | | | | | 12 | $11^1$ | | | | | 8 | 3 | | 4 | | 9 | | | | | 36 |
| 1 | 2 | | | 5 | 6 | 7 | | 10 | | | | | | | | 11 | | | | | 8 | 3 | | 4 | | 9 | | | | | 37 |
| 1 | 2 | | | 5 | 6 | 7 | | | $10^1$ | 12 | 13 | | | | | 11 | | | | | 8 | 3 | | 4 | | $9^2$ | | | | | 38 |
| 1 | 2 | | | 5 | 6 | 7 | | | 10 | 12 | | | | | | 11 | | | | | 8 | 3 | | 4 | | $9^1$ | | | | | 39 |
| 1 | 2 | | | 5 | 6 | 7 | | | 10 | 9 | 12 | | | | 11 | | | | | 8$^1$ | 3 | | 4 | | | | | | | | 40 |
| 1 | 2 | | | 5 | 6 | 7 | | | $10^1$ | 9 | 13 | 12 | | | | 11 | | | | | $8^2$ | 3 | | 4 | | | | | | | 41 |
| 1 | 2 | | | 5 | 6 | 7 | | | 10 | 9 | 7 | 12 | | | | 11 | | | | | $8^1$ | 3 | | 4 | | | | | | | 42 |
| 1 | 2 | | | 5 | 6 | 7 | | | 10 | 9 | 12 | | | | | 11 | | | | | $8^1$ | 3 | | 4 | | | | | | | 43 |
| 1 | 2 | | | 5 | 6 | $7^1$ | | | 10 | 9 | | | | | | 11 | | | | | $8^2$ | 3 | | 4 | | | | | 12 | 13 | 44 |
| 1 | 2 | | | 5 | 6 | 7 | | | 10 | $9^1$ | 12 | | | | | 11 | | | | | 8 | 3 | | 4 | | | | | | | 45 |
| 1 | 2 | | | 5 | 6 | 7 | | | $10^2$ | 9 | | | | | 12 | 11 | | | | | $8^3$ | $3^3$ | | 4 | | | | | 13 | 14 | 46 |

**Coca-Cola Cup**
First Round    WBA      (h)   1-1
                                       (a)   1-2

**FA Cup**
First Round    Plymouth Arg    (a)   0-0
                                            (h)   3-2
Second Round    Stevenage B    (h)   1-1
                                            (a)   1-2

CARDIFF CITY 1997–98 *Back row (left to right)*: Jeff Eckhardt, Scott Young, Jason Fowler, Mark Harris, Lee Jarman, Kevin Nugent, Kevin Lloyd, Lee Phillips. *Middle row*: John Cross, Jimmy Rollo, John Rendall, Jon Hallworth, Tony Elliott, Steve White, Carl Dale. *Front row*: Chris Beech, Gareth Stoker, Scott Partridge, David Penney, Anthony Carss, Wayne O'Sullivan, Craig Middleton.

# Division 3 **CARDIFF CITY**

*Ninian Park, Cardiff CF1 8SX.* Telephone: (01222) 398636. Fax: (01222) 341148. Newsline: 0891 888603.

*Ground capacity:* 14,660.

*Record attendance:* 61,566, Wales v England, 14 October 1961.

*Club record:* 57,893 v Arsenal, Division 1, 22 April 1953.

*Record receipts:* £141,756 v Manchester C, FA Cup 4th rd, 29 January 1994.

*Pitch measurements:* 100yd × 70yd.

*Directors:* S. Kumar (Chairman), R. East, J. Hill, P. Guy, R. Phillips, S. Borley, D. Temme.

*Director of Football Development:* Kenny Hibbitt.

*Chief Executive Director:* Joan Hill.

*Secretary:* Ceri Whitehead.

*Manager:* Frank Burrows.

*Physio:* Jimmy Goodfellow.

*Year Formed:* 1899. *Turned Professional:* 1910. *Ltd Co.:* 1910.

*Previous Names:* 1899–1902, Riverside; 1902–08, Riverside Albion; 1908, Cardiff City.

*Club Nickname:* 'Bluebirds'.

*Previous Grounds:* Riverside, Sophia Gardens, Old Park and Fir Gardens. Moved to Ninian Park, 1910.

*Foundation:* Credit for the establishment of a first class professional football club in such a rugby stronghold as Cardiff, is due to members of the Riverside club formed in 1899 out of a cricket club of that name. Cardiff became a city in 1905 and in 1908 the local FA granted Riverside permission to call themselves Cardiff City.

*First Football League game:* 28 August 1920, Division 2, v Stockport Co (a) W 5-2 – Kneeshaw; Brittain, Leyton; Keenor (1), Smith, Hardy; Grimshaw (1), Gill (2), Cashmore, West, Evans (1).

*Record League Victory:* 9–2 v Thames, Division 3 (S), 6 February 1932 – Farquharson; E. L. Morris, Roberts; Galbraith, Harris, Ronan; Emmerson (1), Keating (1), Jones (1), McCambridge (1), Robbins (5).

*Record Cup Victory:* 8–0 v Enfield, FA Cup 1st rd, 28 November 1931 – Farquharson; Smith, Roberts; Harris (1), Galbraith, Ronan; Emmerson (2), Keating (3); O'Neill (2), Robbins, McCambridge.

*Record Defeat:* 2–11 v Sheffield U, Division 1, 1 January 1926.

*Most League Points (2 for a win):* 66, Division 3 (S), 1946–47.

*Most League Points (3 for a win):* 86, Division 3, 1982–83.

*Most League Goals:* 93, Division 3 (S), 1946–47.

*Highest League Scorer in Season:* Stan Richards, 30, Division 3 (S), 1946–47.

*Most League Goals in Total Aggregate:* Len Davies, 128, 1920–31.

*Most Capped Player:* Alf Sherwood, 39 (41), Wales.

*Most League Appearances:* Phil Dwyer, 471, 1972–85.

*Record Transfer Fee Received:* £300,000 from Sheffield U for Nathan Blake, February 1994.

*Record Transfer Fee Paid:* £180,000 to San Jose Earthquakes for Godfrey Ingram, September 1982.

*Football League Record:* 1920 Elected to Division 2; 1921–29 Division 1; 1929–31 Division 2; 1931–47 Division 3 (S); 1947–52 Division 2; 1952–57 Division 1; 1957–60 Division 2; 1960–62 Division 1; 1962–75 Division 2; 1975–76 Division 3; 1976–82 Division 2; 1982–83 Division 3; 1983–85 Division 2; 1985–86 Division 3; 1986–88 Division 4; 1988–90 Division 3; 1990–92 Division 4; 1992–93 Division 3; 1993–95 Division 2; 1995– Division 3.

*Honours: Football League:* Division 1 – Runners-up 1923–24; Division 2 – Runners-up 1920–21, 1951–52, 1959–60; Division 3 (S) – Champions 1946–47; Division 3 – Champions 1992–93. Runners-up 1975–76, 1982–83; Division 4 – Runners-up 1987–88. *FA Cup:* Winners 1927 (only occasion the Cup has been won by a club outside England); Runners-up 1925. *Football League Cup:* Semi-final 1966. *Welsh Cup:* Winners 21 times. *Charity Shield:* 1927. **European Competitions:** *European Cup-Winners' Cup:* 1964–65, 1965–66, 1967–68, 1968–69, 1969–70, 1970–71, 1971–72, 1973–74, 1974–75, 1976–77, 1977–78, 1988–89, 1991–92, 1992–93, 1993–94.

*Colours:* Blue shirts, white shorts, white stockings. *Change colours:* Yellow shirts, black shorts, yellow stockings.

**Did you know?**
Fred Keenor's last goal for Cardiff City enabled them to win 1-0 at Southampton on 1 November 1930. He served the club for 20 years.

## CARDIFF CITY 1997–98 LEAGUE RECORD

| Match No. | Date | Venue | Opponents | Result | H/T Score | Lg. Pos. | Goalscorers | Attendance |
|---|---|---|---|---|---|---|---|---|
| 1 | Aug 9 | A | Leyton Orient | W 1-0 | 0-0 | — | Dale [64] | 5414 |
| 2 | 23 | A | Mansfield T | W 2-1 | 1-0 | 7 | Partridge [7], Greenacre [69] | 2743 |
| 3 | 30 | H | Notts Co | D 1-1 | 1-1 | 11 | Young [36] | 6191 |
| 4 | Sept 2 | H | Shrewsbury T | D 2-2 | 0-1 | — | Partridge [56], O'Sullivan [79] | 4271 |
| 5 | 9 | A | Exeter C | D 1-1 | 0-0 | — | Fowler [73] | 4843 |
| 6 | 13 | H | Rochdale | W 2-1 | 1-1 | 8 | White [40], Eckhardt [87] | 4306 |
| 7 | 16 | H | Chester C | L 0-2 | 0-2 | — | | 3949 |
| 8 | 20 | A | Lincoln C | L 0-1 | 0-1 | 12 | | 3130 |
| 9 | 27 | A | Cambridge U | D 2-2 | 1-0 | 13 | Greenacre [31], Eckhardt [90] | 2728 |
| 10 | Oct 4 | H | Barnet | D 1-1 | 1-0 | 14 | Eckhardt [22] | 3938 |
| 11 | 18 | A | Rotherham U | D 1-1 | 1-1 | 17 | Penney (pen) [21] | 3197 |
| 12 | 21 | A | Darlington | D 0-0 | 0-0 | — | | 2278 |
| 13 | 25 | H | Hartlepool U | D 1-1 | 0-1 | 16 | Crowe [73] | 3383 |
| 14 | Nov 2 | H | Swansea C | L 0-1 | 0-1 | 17 | | 6459 |
| 15 | 4 | A | Doncaster R | D 1-1 | 0-0 | — | Saville [59] | 1004 |
| 16 | 8 | H | Torquay U | D 1-1 | 0-0 | 19 | Stoker [70] | 2797 |
| 17 | 11 | H | Scunthorpe U | D 0-0 | 0-0 | — | | 2340 |
| 18 | 18 | H | Hull C | W 2-1 | 2-0 | — | Saville [2], Penney [19] | 2504 |
| 19 | 22 | A | Brighton & HA | W 1-0 | 1-0 | 14 | Allan (og) [20] | 2086 |
| 20 | 29 | H | Scarborough | D 1-1 | 0-1 | 14 | Dale [69] | 2593 |
| 21 | Dec 13 | H | Peterborough U | D 0-0 | 0-0 | 14 | | 3401 |
| 22 | 20 | A | Macclesfield T | L 0-1 | 0-0 | 16 | | 2398 |
| 23 | 26 | H | Exeter C | D 1-1 | 1-0 | 17 | Dale [10] | 6623 |
| 24 | 28 | A | Shrewsbury T | L 2-3 | 0-1 | 18 | Fowler [69], Young [78] | 3238 |
| 25 | Jan 10 | H | Leyton Orient | W 1-0 | 1-0 | 15 | Penney (pen) [19] | 4335 |
| 26 | 17 | A | Notts Co | L 1-3 | 1-1 | 17 | Harris [31] | 6448 |
| 27 | 20 | A | Colchester U | L 1-2 | 0-0 | — | Dale [85] | 1929 |
| 28 | 27 | A | Chester C | D 0-0 | 0-0 | — | | 1757 |
| 29 | 31 | A | Rochdale | D 0-0 | 0-0 | 17 | | 1445 |
| 30 | Feb 7 | H | Lincoln C | L 0-1 | 0-0 | 19 | | 2896 |
| 31 | 14 | A | Barnet | D 2-2 | 2-1 | 20 | Saville [4], Fowler [16] | 2406 |
| 32 | 17 | H | Mansfield T | W 4-1 | 1-0 | — | Saville (pen) [42], Fowler [46], Carss [53], Penney [78] | 2451 |
| 33 | 21 | H | Cambridge U | D 0-0 | 0-0 | 17 | | 2681 |
| 34 | 24 | H | Rotherham U | D 2-2 | 1-1 | — | Saville [17], White [68] | 2731 |
| 35 | 28 | A | Scunthorpe U | D 3-3 | 1-2 | 18 | Saville 3 [29, 52, 88] | 2135 |
| 36 | Mar 3 | A | Torquay U | L 0-1 | 0-1 | — | | 3358 |
| 37 | 8 | A | Swansea C | D 1-1 | 0-0 | 19 | Fowler [58] | 5621 |
| 38 | 14 | H | Doncaster R | W 7-1 | 2-0 | 19 | Saville 2 [27, 84], O'Sullivan [45], Roberts [55], Beech [68], Penney [76], Young [78] | 2931 |
| 39 | 21 | A | Hull C | W 1-0 | 0-0 | 17 | Roberts [57] | 3408 |
| 40 | 28 | H | Brighton & HA | D 0-0 | 0-0 | 17 | | 3509 |
| 41 | Apr 3 | A | Scarborough | L 1-3 | 0-3 | — | Saville [51] | 2905 |
| 42 | 11 | H | Colchester U | L 0-2 | 0-0 | 20 | | 2809 |
| 43 | 13 | A | Peterborough U | L 0-2 | 0-0 | 21 | | 4756 |
| 44 | 18 | H | Macclesfield T | L 1-2 | 1-0 | 21 | Roberts [25] | 2497 |
| 45 | 25 | A | Hartlepool U | L 0-2 | 0-1 | 21 | | 2817 |
| 46 | May 2 | H | Darlington | D 0-0 | 0-0 | 21 | | 2610 |

**Final League Position: 21**        1996–97 DIV3 7

### GOALSCORERS

*League (48):* Saville 11 (1 pen), Fowler 5, Penney 5 (2 pens), Dale 4, Eckhardt 3, Roberts 3, Young 3, Greenacre 2, O'Sullivan 2, Partridge 2, White 2, Beech 1, Carss 1, Crowe 1, Harris 1, Stoker 1, own goal 1.
*Coca-Cola Cup (2):* Fowler 1, Rollo 1.
*FA Cup (10):* Dale 4, Saville 2, Fowler 1, Nugent 1, O'Sullivan 1, White 1.

| Hallworth J 43 | Young S 31 | Beech C 46 | Jarman L 18+5 | Harris M 38 | Fowler J 38 | Partridge S 15+7 | Middleton C 28+5 | Nugent K 2+2 | Dale C 16+9 | Carss A 36+6 | White S 12+17 | Stoker G 12+8 | Penney D 32+2 | Greenacre C 11 | O'Sullivan W 40+3 | Eckhardt J 19+2 | Roberts C 5+6 | Elliott T 2+1 | Rollo J 3+2 | Phillips L 7+1 | Crowe G 7+1 | Saville A 32+1 | Paterson S 5 | Hill D 7 | Zois P 1 | Earnshaw R —+5 | Cadette N —+4 | Lloyd K —+2 | Match No. |
|---|---|---|---|---|---|---|---|---|---|---|---|---|---|---|---|---|---|---|---|---|---|---|---|---|---|---|---|---|---|
| 1 | 2 | 3 | 4 | 5 | 6 | 7 | 8 | 9¹ | 10² | 11 | 12 | 13 | | | | | | | | | | | | | | | | | 1 |
| 1 | | 3 | 4 | 5 | 6 | 7 | 2 | | | 11 | 12 | 8² | 9¹ | 10 | 13 | | | | | | | | | | | | | | 2 |
| 1 | 4 | 3 | 12 | 5 | 6 | 7 | 2¹ | | | 11 | 13 | 8² | | | 9 | 10 | | | | | | | | | | | | | 3 |
| 1 | 4 | 3 | 2 | 5 | 6 | 7 | | | | 11 | 12 | 8¹ | | | 9 | 10 | | | | | | | | | | | | | 4 |
| 1 | 4 | 3 | 2 | 5 | 6¹ | 11 | 12 | | 10³ | 13 | 8² | | 9 | | 7 | 14 | | | | | | | | | | | | | 5 |
| 1 | 4 | 3 | 2¹ | 5 | 6 | 11 | | | 10 | | | 8 | 9² | | 7 | 12 | 13 | | | | | | | | | | | | 6 |
| 1 | 4 | 3 | | 5 | 6 | 11¹ | 12 | | 10 | | | 8 | 9 | | 7 | 2 | | | | | | | | | | | | | 7 |
| 1 | 4 | 3 | 12 | 5 | 6 | 11³ | | | 10 | 14 | 8² | 13 | 9 | | 7 | 2¹ | | | | | | | | | | | | | 8 |
| 1¹ | 4 | 3 | | 5 | 6 | 12 | 13 | | 11 | | 10¹ | 8² | 9 | | 7 | 2 | 15 | | | | | | | | | | | | 9 |
| 1 | 4 | 3 | 10 | 5 | 6 | 12 | | | | 11² | 14 | 13 | 8¹ | 9³ | 7 | 2 | | | | | | | | | | | | | 10 |
| 1 | | 3 | 4 | 5 | 6¹ | | | | 10 | 11 | 12 | 8 | 9 | | 7 | | | | | | 2 | | | | | | | | 11 |
| 1 | | 3 | | 5 | 6 | | | | 12 | 11 | 10¹ | 8 | 9 | | 7 | | | | | | 2 | 4 | | | | | | | 12 |
| 1 | | 3 | | 5 | 6 | | | | 10 | 12 | 11 | 8 | 7 | | | | | | | | 2 | 4¹ | 9 | | | | | | 13 |
| 1 | 4 | 3 | | 5 | 6¹ | 13 | 2³ | | | 11² | 12 | 14 | 8 | | 7 | | | | | | 10 | 9 | | | | | | | 14 |
| 1 | 4³ | 3 | | 5 | 6 | 14 | 2 | | | 12 | 13 | 11² | 8 | | 7 | | | | | | 10¹ | 9 | | | | | | | 15 |
| 1 | | 3 | | 5¹ | 6 | | 2 | | | 12 | 11 | | 8 | | 7 | | | | | | 10 | 9 | 4 | | | | | | 16 |
| 1 | | 3 | | 5 | 6¹ | | 2² | | | 13 | 12 | 11 | 8 | | 7 | | | | | | 10 | 9 | 4 | | | | | | 17 |
| 1 | | 3 | | 5 | 6 | | 2 | | | 12 | 11 | 8 | | | 7 | | | | | | 10¹ | 9 | 4 | | | | | | 18 |
| | 2 | 3 | | 5 | 6 | | | | | 12 | 11 | 13 | 8 | | 7 | | | | 1 | | 10¹ | 9² | 4 | | | | | | 19 |
| | | 3 | 12 | 5¹ | 6² | | 2 | | 10 | 11 | | 8 | | | 7 | | | | 1 | | 13 | 9 | 4 | | | | | | 20 |
| 1 | 4 | 3 | | 5 | 6 | | 2 | | 10 | 11 | | 8 | | | 7 | | | | | | | 9 | | | | | | | 21 |
| 1 | 4 | 3 | 12 | 5 | 6³ | | 2¹ | | 10² | 11 | 13 | 14 | 8 | | 7 | | | | | | | 9 | | | | | | | 22 |
| 1 | 4 | 3 | | 5 | 6 | | 2 | | 10 | 11 | | 8 | | | 7 | | | | | | | 9 | | | | | | | 23 |
| 1 | 4 | 3 | | 5 | 6¹ | | 2² | | 10 | 11 | 12 | 13 | 8 | | 7 | | | | | | | 9² | | | | | | | 24 |
| 1 | 4 | 3 | | 5 | 6¹ | | 2 | | 10 | 11 | 12 | 13 | 8 | | 7 | | | | | | | 9² | | | | | | | 25 |
| 1 | 4 | 3 | | 5 | 6 | | | | 10 | 11² | 12 | 13 | 8 | | 7¹ | 2³ | 14 | | | | | 9 | | | | | | | 26 |
| 1 | 4 | 3 | 12 | 5 | 6 | 13 | | 9 | 10 | 11¹ | | | 8 | | 7 | 2² | | | | | | 14 | | | | | | | 27 |
| 1 | 4 | 3 | | 5 | | | | | | 11 | 12 | 8 | 10¹ | | 7 | | | | | | 6 | 9 | | | | | | | 28 |
| 1 | | 3 | | 5 | | | 2 | | 10 | 11² | 12 | | 4 | 8 | 7 | | | | | | 6 | 9 | | | | | | | 29 |
| 1 | | 3 | 4 | 5 | 6² | 13³ | 2¹ | | 10 | 11 | 12 | | 8 | | 7 | | | | 14 | | | 9 | | | | | | | 30 |
| 1 | 4 | 3 | | 5 | 6 | | 2 | | 10 | 11 | 12 | 13 | | | 7² | | | | | | | 9 | 8 | | | | | | 31 |
| 1 | 4 | 3 | | | 6 | 7 | 2 | | 10¹ | 11 | 12 | | | | | 5² | 13 | | | | | 9 | | | | | | | 32 |
| 1 | 4 | 3 | | | 6 | 7 | 2 | | 10¹ | 11³ | 12² | 13 | 14 | | | 5 | | | | | | 9 | 8 | | | | | | 33 |
| | | 3 | | 5 | 6 | 7 | 2 | | 10 | 11 | 12 | | | | | 4 | | | | | | 9 | 8 | 1 | | | | | 34 |
| | | 3 | | 5 | | 7 | 2 | | 10 | 11 | | | | | | 4 | | | | | | 9 | 8 | | | | | | 35 |
| 1 | 5 | 3 | | | | 7 | 2 | | 10 | 11¹ | 12 | | | | | 4 | | | | | | 9 | 8 | | | | | | 36 |
| 1 | 5 | 3 | 2 | | | | | | 10¹ | 11 | 12 | | | | 7 | 4 | | | | | 6 | 9 | 8 | | | | | | 37 |
| 1 | 5 | 3 | 2 | | | | | | | 11 | 12 | 13 | 10² | | 7 | 4 | | | | | 6 | 9 | 8 | | | | | | 38 |
| 1 | 5 | 3 | 2 | | | | | | | 11 | 12 | | 10¹ | | 7 | 4 | | | | | | 9 | 8 | | | | | | 39 |
| 1 | 5 | 3 | 2 | | | | | | | 11² | 12 | | 10¹ | | 7 | | | | | | | 9 | 8 | 4 | | 13 | | | 40 |
| 1 | 5 | 3² | 2 | | 6 | | | | | 11 | | | 10² | | 7 | | | | | | | 9 | 8 | 4³ | | 13 | 14 | | 41 |
| 1 | 5 | 3 | 2 | | 6 | | | | 10¹ | 11 | 12 | | | | 7² | | | | | | | 9 | 8 | 4¹ | | 13 | 14 | | 42 |
| 1 | 5¹ | 3 | 2 | | 6³ | | | | 10² | 11 | 12 | | | | 7 | | | | | | | 9 | 8 | 4 | | 13 | 14 | | 43 |
| 1 | | 3 | | 5³ | 6 | | 2 | | 10¹ | 11 | | | 8 | | 7² | | | | | | | 9 | | 4 | | 12 | 13 | 14 | 44 |
| 1 | | 3 | | 5¹ | 6 | | 2 | | 10 | 11² | 12 | | | | 7 | | | | | | | 9 | | 4¹ | | 13 | | 14 | 45 |
| 1 | | 3² | | 5 | 6 | | 2 | | 10² | 11 | 12 | | | | 7 | | | | | | | 9 | | 4 | | 13 | | | 46 |

**Coca-Cola Cup**
First Round · Southend U · (h) 1-1 · (a) 1-3

**FA Cup**
First Round · Slough T · (a) 1-1 · (h) 3-2
Second Round · Hendon · (h) 3-1
Third Round · Oldham Ath · (h) 1-0
Fourth Round · Reading · (h) 1-1 · (a) 1-1

CARLISLE UNITED 1997-98  *Back row (left to right)*: James Hampton, Lee Taylor, Paul Boertien, Ross Milligan, Kevin Sandwith, Jeff Thorpe, Tommy Harrison.
*Third row*: Paul Devlin (Community Officer), Jon-Karl Benson, Kevin Swanson, Billy Barr, Tony Hopper, Rob Bowman, Stephane Pounewatchy, Michael Swann, Tony Caig, George Dixon, Will
Varty, Rory Delap, Matthew Jansen, Edward Harrison, Liam Bell, Neil Dalton (Physio).
*Second row*: Gareth McAlindon, Andrew Couzens, Owen Archdeacon, David Wilkes (Coach), Michael Knighton (Chairman), John Halpin (Coach), Warren Aspinall, Ian Stevens, Richard Prokas.
*Front row*: Stuart Miller, Lee Burton, Barry Stevens, Jamie Howe, Andrew Douglas, Christopher Barton, Mark Jones, Craig Thompson, Jamie Heath, Alan Hodgson, Michael Irving, Gavin Skelton.

# Division 3      **CARLISLE UNITED**

*Brunton Park, Carlisle CA1 1LL.* Telephone: (01228) 526237. Fax: (01228) 530138. Commercial Dept: (01228) 524014. Information Line: 0891 230011.

*Record attendance:* 27,500 v Birmingham C, FA Cup 3rd rd, 5 January 1957 and v Middlesbrough, FA Cup 5th rd, 7 February 1970.

*Record receipts:* £146,000 v Tottenham H, Coca-Cola Cup 2nd rd, 30 September 1997.

*Ground capacity:* 16,651.

*Pitch measurements:* 117yd × 72yd.

*Directors:* M Knighton (Chairman), J. T. T. Fuller (Managing), B. Chaytow, R. McKnight, A. Doweck, H. A. Jenkins.

*Directors of Coaching:* David Wilkes and John Halpin.

*Physio:* Neil Dalton.

*Commercial Manager:* Daphne Tweddle.

*Secretary:* Angela Ritchie.

*Year Formed:* 1903. *Ltd Co.:* 1921.

*Previous Grounds:* 1903–05, Milholme Bank; 1905–09, Devonshire Park; 1909, Brunton Park.

*Previous Name:* Shaddongate United.

*Club Nickname:* 'Cumbrians' or 'The Blues'.

*Foundation:* Carlisle United came into being in 1903 through the amalgamation of Shaddongate United and Carlisle Red Rose. The new club was admitted to the Second Division of the Lancashire Combination in 1905–06, winning promotion the following season.

*First Football League game:* 25 August 1928, Division 3 (N), v Accrington S (a) W 3-2 – Prout; Coulthard, Cook; Harrison, Ross, Pigg; Agar, Hutchison, McConnell (1), Ward (1), Watson (1) o.g.

*Record League Victory:* 8–0 v Hartlepool U, Division 3 (N), 1 September 1928 – Prout; Smiles, Cook; Robinson (1) Ross, Pigg; Agar (1), Hutchison (1), McConnell (4), Ward (1), Watson. 8–0 v Scunthorpe U, Division 3 (N), 25 December 1952 – MacLaren; Hill, Scott; Stokoe, Twentyman, Waters; Harrison (1), Whitehouse (5), Ashman (2), Duffett, Bond.

*Record Cup Victory:* 6–0 v Shepshed Dynamo, FA Cup 1st rd, 16 November 1996 – Caig; Hopper, Archdeacon (pen), Walling, Robinson, Pounewatchy, Peacock (1), Conway (1) (Jansen), Smart (McAlindon (1)), Hayward, Aspinall (Thorpe) (2og).

*Record Defeat:* 1–11 v Hull C, Division 3 (N), 14 January 1939.

*Most League Points (2 for a win):* 62, Division 3 (N), 1950–51.

*Most League Points (3 for a win):* 91, Division 3, 1994–95.

*Most League Goals:* 113, Division 4, 1963–64.

*Highest League Scorer in Season:* Jimmy McConnell, 42, Division 3 (N), 1928–29.

*Most League Goals in Total Aggregate:* Jimmy McConnell, 126, 1928–32.

*Most Capped Player:* Eric Welsh, 4, Northern Ireland.

*Most League Appearances:* Allan Ross, 466, 1963–79.

*Record Transfer Fee Received:* £1,500,000 from Crystal Palace for Matt Jansen, February 1998.

*Record Transfer Fee Paid:* £121,000 to Notts Co for David Reeves, December 1993.

*Football League Record:* 1928 Elected to Division 3 (N); 1958–62 Division 4; 1962–63 Division 3; 1963–64 Division 4; 1964–65 Division 3; 1965–74 Division 2; 1974–75 Division 1; 1975–77 Division 2; 1977–82 Division 3; 1982–86 Division 2; 1986–87 Division 3; 1987–92 Division 4; 1992–95 Division 3; 1995–96 Division 2; 1996–97 Division 3; 1997–98 Division 2; 1998– Division 3.

*Honours: Football League:* Division 1 best season: 22nd, 1974–75; Promoted from Division 2 (3rd) 1973–74; Division 3 – Champions 1964–65, 1994–95; Runners-up 1981–82; Promoted from Division 3 1996–97; Division 4 – Runners-up 1963–64. *FA Cup:* 6th rd 1975. *Football League Cup:* Semi-final 1970. *Auto Windscreens Shield:* Winners 1997, Runners-up 1995.

*Colours:* Blue shirts, white shorts, white stockings. *Change colours:* All gold with red, white and green trim.

**Did you know?**
Gareth McAlindon scored an injury time winning goal against Wigan Athletic on 2 September 1997. He was only included in the team because of an injury crisis.

## CARLISLE UNITED 1997–98 LEAGUE RECORD

| Match No. | Date | | Venue | Opponents | Result | H/T Score | Lg. Pos. | Goalscorers | Atten- dance |
|---|---|---|---|---|---|---|---|---|---|
| 1 | Aug | 9 | A | Southend U | D | 1-1 | 0-1 | — | Smart [51] | 4507 |
| 2 | | 16 | H | Watford | L | 0-2 | 0-0 | 19 | | 7395 |
| 3 | | 23 | A | Bristol R | L | 1-3 | 1-2 | 22 | Jansen [38] | 6044 |
| 4 | | 30 | H | Northampton T | L | 0-2 | 0-2 | 24 | | 6307 |
| 5 | Sept | 2 | H | Wigan Ath | W | 1-0 | 0-0 | — | McAlindon [90] | 5352 |
| 6 | | 7 | A | Blackpool | L | 1-2 | 0-1 | 22 | Archdeacon (pen) [89] | 7259 |
| 7 | | 13 | A | Wycombe W | W | 4-1 | 2-1 | 18 | Couzens [4], Jansen 2 [39, 90], Archdeacon (pen) [78] | 6018 |
| 8 | | 20 | H | Plymouth Arg | D | 2-2 | 2-1 | 18 | Jansen 2 [2, 45] | 5667 |
| 9 | | 27 | H | Gillingham | W | 2-1 | 0-0 | 16 | Archdeacon [48], Pounewatchy [63] | 5063 |
| 10 | Oct | 4 | A | Walsall | L | 1-3 | 0-1 | 18 | Archdeacon (pen) [82] | 3957 |
| 11 | | 11 | H | Burnley | L | 1-3 | 0-1 | 20 | Couzens [82] | 10,687 |
| 12 | | 17 | H | Preston NE | L | 0-2 | 0-1 | — | | 6541 |
| 13 | | 21 | H | Luton T | L | 0-1 | 0-0 | — | | 4341 |
| 14 | | 25 | A | York C | L | 3-4 | 2-1 | 22 | Pounewatchy [25], Barr [35], McAlindon [78] | 3700 |
| 15 | Nov | 1 | H | Wrexham | D | 2-2 | 2-2 | 24 | Stevens [12], Bowman [17] | 4464 |
| 16 | | 4 | A | Brentford | W | 1-0 | 1-0 | — | Jansen [45] | 3424 |
| 17 | | 8 | A | Millwall | D | 1-1 | 0-1 | 23 | Jansen [85] | 6959 |
| 18 | | 18 | H | Chesterfield | L | 0-2 | 0-0 | — | | 3591 |
| 19 | | 22 | A | Bournemouth | L | 2-3 | 1-2 | 24 | Barr [24], Stevens [61] | 3709 |
| 20 | | 29 | H | Bristol C | L | 0-3 | 0-1 | 24 | | 5044 |
| 21 | Dec | 2 | A | Oldham Ath | L | 1-3 | 1-2 | — | Anthony [9] | 4449 |
| 22 | | 13 | H | Fulham | W | 2-0 | 0-0 | 24 | Stevens 2 [60, 84] | 4574 |
| 23 | | 20 | A | Grimsby T | L | 0-1 | 0-0 | 24 | | 6222 |
| 24 | | 26 | H | Blackpool | D | 1-1 | 1-0 | 24 | Stevens [15] | 8010 |
| 25 | | 28 | A | Wigan Ath | W | 2-0 | 1-0 | 22 | Stevens [4], McAlindon [88] | 4511 |
| 26 | Jan | 10 | A | Southend U | W | 5-0 | 1-0 | 22 | Wright [42], Jansen 2 [52, 65], Stevens [81], Wallwork [85] | 5389 |
| 27 | | 17 | H | Northampton T | L | 1-2 | 1-0 | 22 | Stevens [37] | 6327 |
| 28 | | 24 | H | Bristol R | W | 3-1 | 2-0 | 20 | Stevens 3 [3, 44, 86] | 5725 |
| 29 | | 31 | H | Wycombe W | D | 0-0 | 0-0 | 20 | | 6220 |
| 30 | Feb | 7 | A | Plymouth Arg | L | 1-2 | 0-1 | 23 | Stevens (pen) [51] | 4540 |
| 31 | | 14 | H | Walsall | D | 1-1 | 0-0 | 23 | Varty [89] | 4530 |
| 32 | | 21 | A | Gillingham | L | 0-1 | 0-0 | 23 | | 6270 |
| 33 | | 24 | A | Preston NE | W | 3-0 | 2-0 | — | Barr [10], Wright 2 [26, 62] | 8985 |
| 34 | | 28 | H | Burnley | W | 2-1 | 1-0 | 20 | Stevens [18], Smart [88] | 7192 |
| 35 | Mar | 3 | H | Millwall | W | 1-0 | 0-0 | — | Smart [52] | 5217 |
| 36 | | 7 | A | Wrexham | D | 2-2 | 1-1 | 18 | Wright [37], Stevens [83] | 4242 |
| 37 | | 14 | H | Brentford | L | 1-2 | 1-0 | 19 | Stevens [40] | 6021 |
| 38 | | 17 | H | Watford | L | 1-2 | 0-1 | — | Stevens [69] | 7274 |
| 39 | | 21 | A | Chesterfield | L | 1-2 | 1-0 | 21 | Smart [40] | 3967 |
| 40 | | 28 | H | Bournemouth | L | 0-1 | 0-1 | 22 | | 4951 |
| 41 | Apr | 4 | A | Bristol C | L | 0-1 | 0-0 | 23 | | 12,578 |
| 42 | | 11 | H | Oldham Ath | W | 3-1 | 2-1 | 23 | Stevens [7], Anthony [12], Smart [90] | 4594 |
| 43 | | 13 | A | Fulham | L | 0-5 | 0-2 | 23 | | 9243 |
| 44 | | 21 | A | Grimsby T | L | 0-1 | 0-1 | — | | 3956 |
| 45 | | 25 | H | York C | L | 1-2 | 1-0 | 23 | Smart [36] | 3897 |
| 46 | May | 2 | A | Luton T | L | 2-3 | 0-1 | 23 | Anthony [53], Wright [82] | 6729 |
| **Final League Position: 23** | | | | | 1996–97 DIV3 3 | | | | |

### GOALSCORERS

*League (57):* Stevens 17 (1 pen), Jansen 9, Smart 6, Wright 5, Archdeacon 4 (3 pens), Anthony 3, Barr 3, McAlindon 3, Couzens 2, Pounewatchy 2, Bowman 1, Varty 1, Wallwork 1.
*Coca-Cola Cup (7):* Jansen 3, Aspinall 1, Couzens 1, Smart 1, Walling 1.
*FA Cup (0).*

| Caig T 46 | Delap R 8+1 | Archdeacon O 18 | Walling D 6 | Varty W 43+1 | Pounewatchy S 39 | Barr B 39 | Prokas R 33+1 | Smart A 16 | Aspinall W 18 | Peacock L 1+1 | Thorpe J 12+2 | Jansen M 22+1 | Milligan R 2+5 | Dobie S 9+14 | Couzens A 18+9 | McAlindon G 16+12 | Harrison E 6+4 | Holloway D 5 | Stevens I 33+4 | Boertien P 8+1 | Sandwith K 2+1 | Bowman R 6+1 | Croci L 1 | Hoyland J 5 | Hopper T 16+3 | Anthony N 25 | Wright N 25 | Wallwork R 10 | Gray A —+1 | Pagal J 1 | Liburd R 9 | Hughes D 1 | Foster J 7 | Match No. |
|---|---|---|---|---|---|---|---|---|---|---|---|---|---|---|---|---|---|---|---|---|---|---|---|---|---|---|---|---|---|---|---|---|---|---|
| 1 | 2 | 3 | 4 | 5 | 6 | 7 | 8 | 9¹ | 10 | 11² | 12 | 13 | | | | | | | | | | | | | | | | | | | | | | 1 |
| 1 | 2 | 3 | 4 | 5 | | 7 | 8 | 9 | 10 | | | | | 6¹ | 11² | 12 | 13 | | | | | | | | | | | | | | | | | 2 |
| 1 | | 3 | 4 | 5 | | 7 | 8 | | 10 | | | | | 6² | 11 | 2¹ | 12 | 9 | 13 | | | | | | | | | | | | | | | 3 |
| 1 | | 3 | 4 | 5² | 6 | 7 | 8¹ | | 10 | | | | | | 11 | 9 | 2 | 12 | 13 | | | | | | | | | | | | | | | 4 |
| 1 | | 3 | 4 | 5 | 6 | 10 | | | 11 | | | | | | 8 | 9 | 7 | 2 | | | | | | | | | | | | | | | | 5 |
| 1 | | 3 | 4 | 5 | 6 | 10 | | | 11 | | | | 9 | | 8 | 12 | 7¹ | 2 | | | | | | | | | | | | | | | | 6 |
| 1 | | 3 | | 5 | 6 | 7 | 4 | | 11 | | | | 10 | | 8¹ | 9 | 12 | 2 | | | | | | | | | | | | | | | | 7 |
| 1 | | 3 | | 5 | 6 | 7² | 4 | | 11 | | | | 10 | | 8¹ | 9 | 12 | 2 | 13 | | | | | | | | | | | | | | | 8 |
| 1 | | 3 | | 5 | 6 | 7 | 4 | | 11¹ | | 12 | | 10 | | 8 | 9 | | 2 | | | | | | | | | | | | | | | | 9 |
| 1 | | 3 | | 5 | 6 | 2 | 4 | | 11 | | | | 10 | | 12 | 8² | 9 | | | 7¹ | 13 | | | | | | | | | | | | | 10 |
| 1 | | 3 | | 5 | 6 | 7 | 4 | | 11 | | | | 10 | | 8 | 9¹ | | 12 | | | 2 | | | | | | | | | | | | | 11 |
| 1 | | 3 | | 5 | 6 | 7¹ | | | 11³ | | | | 10 | | 9² | 12 | 13 | 8 | 14 | | 2 | 4 | | | | | | | | | | | | 12 |
| 1 | | 3 | | 5 | 6 | 7 | | | 11¹ | | | | 10 | | 9⁴ | 8 | 12 | 4 | 13 | | 2 | | | | | | | | | | | | | 13 |
| 1 | | 3 | | 5 | 6 | | 4 | | 11 | | | | 10 | | 12 | 8 | 7 | | 9¹ | | 2 | | | | | | | | | | | | | 14 |
| 1 | | 3 | | 5 | 6 | | 4 | | 11 | | | | 10 | | 8 | 7 | 12 | | 9² | 13 | 2¹ | | | | | | | | | | | | | 15 |
| 1 | | 3 | | 5 | 6 | | 4¹ | | 11 | | | | 10 | | 12 | 13 | 8 | 7 | 9² | | 2 | | | | | | | | | | | | | 16 |
| 1 | | 3 | | 5 | 6 | | 4 | 8 | 11 | | | | 10 | | 12 | | 7 | | 9¹ | | 2 | | | | | | | | | | | | | 17 |
| 1 | | 3 | | 5 | 6 | | 4 | 8 | 11 | | | | 10¹ | | 7 | 12 | 13 | | 9 | | 2² | | | | | | | | | | | | | 18 |
| 1 | | | | 5 | 6 | 2 | | | 11 | | | | | 10 | 8¹ | | 7 | | 9 | 3 | | | | | 4 | 12 | | | | | | | | 19 |
| 1 | | | | | 6 | 2 | | 5 | | | | | | 10 | | 12 | 7¹ | | 9 | 3 | | | | | 4 | | 8 | 11 | | | | | | 20 |
| 1 | | | | | 6 | 2 | | | | | | | | 10 | 12 | 13 | 7² | | 9 | 3 | | | | | 4 | 5 | 8¹ | 11 | | | | | | 21 |
| 1 | | 12 | | 5 | | | 4 | 8 | | | | | | 10 | | | | | 9 | 3³ | | | | 6 | 2 | 7 | 11 | | | | | | | 22 |
| 1 | | 3 | | 5 | | | 4 | 8 | | | | | 12 | 10 | | | | | 9 | | | | | 6 | 2¹ | 7 | 11 | | | | | | | 23 |
| 1 | | 3 | | 5 | | | 4 | 8 | | | | | | 10 | | | | | 9 | | | | | | 2 | 7 | 11 | | | | 6 | | | 24 |
| 1 | | | | 5 | 8 | | 4 | 3 | | | | | | 10 | | | 7 | 12 | 9¹ | | | 2² | | | 13 | | 11 | | | | 6 | | | 25 |
| 1 | 2 | | | 5 | 8 | | 4 | 3 | | | | | | 10 | | | | | 9 | | | | | | | 7 | 11 | | | | 6 | | | 26 |
| 1 | 2 | | | 5 | 8 | | 4 | 3 | | | | | | | | 12 | 10¹ | | 9 | | | | | | | 7 | 11 | | | | 6 | | | 27 |
| 1 | 2 | | | 5 | 8 | | 4 | 12 | | | | | | 3¹ | 10 | | | 13 | 9 | | | | | | | 7 | 11² | | | | 6 | | | 28 |
| 1 | 2 | | | 5 | 8 | | 4 | | | | | | | 3 | 10 | 12 | 11¹ | | 9 | | | | | | | 7 | | | | | 6 | | | 29 |
| 1 | | | | 5¹ | 8 | | 4 | | 11 | | | | | | | 12 | | | 9 | 3² | | | | | 2 | 7 | 10 | | | | 6 | 13 | | 30 |
| 1 | | | | 5 | 8 | | 4 | 3 | | | | | | | | 12 | 13 | 11¹ | 9 | | | | | | 2 | 7² | 10 | | | | 6 | | | 31 |
| 1 | | | | 5 | 8 | | 4 | 3 | | | | | | | | 12 | | | 9 | | | | | | 2 | 7 | 10 | | | 11¹ | 6 | | | 32 |
| 1 | | | | 5 | 8 | | 4 | 3 | 11² | | | | | | | | 13 | 12 | 9 | | | | | | 2 | 7¹ | 10 | | | | 6 | | | 33 |
| 1 | | | | 5 | 8 | | 4 | 3 | 11 | | | | | | | | | | 9 | | | | | | 2 | 7 | 10 | | | | | | 6 | 34 |
| 1 | | | | 5 | 8 | | 4 | 3 | 11¹ | | | | | | | 12 | | | 9 | | | | | | 2 | 7 | 10 | | | | | | 6 | 35 |
| 1 | | | | 5 | 8 | | 4 | 3 | 11² | | | | | | | | 13 | 12 | 9 | | | | | | 2 | 7 | 10¹ | | | | | | 6 | 36 |
| 1 | | | | 5² | 8 | | 4 | 3 | 11 | | | 2 | | | | | 13 | 12 | 9 | | | | | | 14 | 7¹ | 10 | | | | 6³ | | | 37 |
| 1 | | | | 5 | 8 | | 4 | 3 | 11 | | | 2 | | | | | | | 9 | | | | | 6 | | 7 | 10 | | | | | | | 38 |
| 1 | | | | 5 | 8 | | 4 | 3 | 11 | | | 2¹ | | | 6 | | | | 9 | | | 12 | | | | 7 | 10 | | | | | | | 39 |
| 1 | | | | 12 | 8 | 4² | 3 | | 11 | | | | | | 13 | | | | 9 | | | | | | 2 | 7 | 10 | | | | | 5¹ | 6 | 40 |
| 1 | | | | 5 | 8 | | 3 | | 11 | | | 4 | | | 12 | | | | 9 | | | | | | | 7 | 10 | | | | 2¹ | | 6 | 41 |
| 1 | | | | 5 | 8 | | 3 | | 11 | | | 4 | | | | | | | 9 | | | | | | | 7 | 10 | | | | 2 | | 6 | 42 |
| 1 | | | | 5 | 8 | | 4 | | 11 | | | | 12 | | | 2 | | | 9¹ | | | | | 3 | | 7 | 10 | | | | | | 6 | 43 |
| 1 | | | | 5 | 8 | | | 10 | | | | 4 | 12 | 2¹ | 11 | | | | 9 | | | | | 3 | | 7 | | | | | | | 6 | 44 |
| 1 | | | | 5 | | | 4 | 10 | | | | 12 | | 8² | | | 13 | | 9 | | | | | 3¹ | 7 | 11 | | | | | 2 | | 6 | 45 |
| 1 | | | | 5 | | | 4 | 11 | | | | | | 8 | | | | | 9 | 3 | | | | | | 7 | 10 | | | | 2 | | 6 | 46 |

**Coca-Cola Cup**

First Round  Chester C  (a) 2-1  
  (h) 3-0  
Second Round  Tottenham H  (a) 2-3  
  (h) 0-2  

**FA Cup**

First Round  Wigan Ath  (h) 0-1

CHARLTON ATHLETIC 1997–98    *Back row (left to right):* Kevin Lisbie, Steve Jones, Gary Poole, Mike Salmon, Phil Chapple, Andy Petterson, Carl Leaburn, Matt Lee, Jason Tindall.
*Middle row:* Keith Peacock (Reserve Team Coach), Steve Watts (Youth Development Officer), Dwayne Minors, Jamie Stuart, Brendan O'Connell, Kevin Nicholls, Paul Emblen, Matt Holmes,
Shaun Newton, Terry Westley (Youth Team Coach), Jimmy Hendry (Physio).
*Front row:* Mark Kinsella, Clive Mendonca, Anthony Barness, Paul Mortimer, Stuart Balmer, Alan Curbishley (Manager), Les Reed (First Team Coach), Keith Jones, Richard Rufus, Bradley Allen,
Steve Brown, John Robinson.
(Photograph: Tom Morris)

# FA Premiership CHARLTON ATHLETIC

*The Valley, Floyd Road, Charlton, London SE7 8BL.* Telephone: (0181) 333 4000. Fax: (0181) 333 4001. Box Office: (0181) 33 4010. Clubcall 0891 121146.

*Ground capacity:* 20,000.

*Record attendance:* 75,031 v Aston Villa, FA Cup 5th rd, 12 February 1938 (at The Valley).

*Record receipts:* £163,864 v Newcastle United, FA Cup 3rd rd, 5 January 1997.

*Pitch measurements:* 111yd × 73yd.

*Managing Director:* P. D. Varney.

*Chairman:* M. A. Simons. *Vice-Chairman:* R. A. Murray.

*Directors:* R. N. Alwen, G. P. Bone, R. D. Collins, D. J. Hughes, R. D. King, M. C. Stevens, D. G. Ufton, R. C. Whitehand, D. C. Sumners, N. E. Capelin, M. A. Gebbett.

*Manager:* Alan Curbishley.

*Reserve Team Manager:* Keith Peacock. *Youth Team Manager:* Terry Westley.

*Youth Development Officer:* Steve Watts. *Physio:* Jimmy Hendry. *Coach:* Les Reed.

*Secretary:* Chris Parkes.

*Marketing Manager:* Steve Dixon. *Safety Officer:* John Little.

*Media and P. R.:* Mick Everett. *Hospitality and Banqueting:* Dave Archer.

*Year Formed:* 1905. *Turned Professional:* 1920. *Ltd Co.:* 1919.

*Club Nickname:* 'Addicks'.

*Previous Grounds:* 1906, Siemen's Meadow; 1907, Woolwich Common; 1909, Pound Park; 1913, Horn Lane; 1920, The Valley; 1923, Catford (The Mount); 1924, The Valley; 1985, Selhurst Park; 1991, Upton Park; 1992, The Valley.

*Foundation:* The club was formed on 9 June 1905, by a group of 14 and 15-year-old youths living in streets by the Thames in the area which now borders the Thames Barrier. The club's progress through local leagues was so rapid that after the First World War they joined the Kent League where they spent a season before turning professional and joining the Southern League in 1920. A year later they were elected to the Football League's Division 3 (South).

*First Football League game:* 27 August 1921, Division 3 (S), v Exeter C (h) W 1-0 – Hughes; Mitchell, Goodman; Dowling (1), Hampson, Dunn; Castle, Bailey, Halse, Green, Wilson.

*Record League Victory:* 8–1 v Middlesbrough, Division 1, 12 September 1953 – Bartram; Campbell, Ellis; Fenton, Ufton, Hammond; Hurst (2), O'Linn (2), Leary (1), Firmani (3), Kiernan.

*Record Cup Victory:* 7–0 v Burton A, FA Cup 3rd rd, 7 January 1956 – Bartram; Campbell, Townsend; Hewie, Ufton, Hammond; Hurst (1), Gauld (1), Leary (3), White, Kiernan (2).

*Record Defeat:* 1–11 v Aston Villa, Division 2, 14 November 1959.

*Most League Points (2 for a win):* 61, Division 3 (S), 1934–35.

*Most League Points (3 for a win):* 88, Division 1, 1997–98.

*Most League Goals:* 107, Division 2, 1957–58.

*Highest League Scorer in Season:* Ralph Allen, 32, Division 3 (S), 1934–35.

*Most League Goals in Total Aggregate:* Stuart Leary, 153, 1953–62.

*Most Capped Player:* John Hewie, 19, Scotland.

*Most League Appearances:* Sam Bartram, 583, 1934–56.

*Record Transfer Fee Received:* £2,800,000 from Leeds United for Lee Bowyer, July 1996.

*Record Transfer Fee Paid:* £700,000 to Grimsby T for Clive Mendonca, June 1997.

*Football League Record:* 1921 Elected to Division 3 (S); 1929–33 Division 2; 1933–35 Division 3 (S); 1935–36 Division 2; 1936–57 Division 1; 1957–72 Division 2; 1972–75 Division 3; 1975–80 Division 2; 1980–81 Division 3; 1981–86 Division 2; 1986–90 Division 1; 1990–92 Division 2; 1992–98 Division 1; 1998– FA Premier League.

*Honours: Football League: Division 1* – Runners-up 1936–37; Promoted from Division 1, 1997–98 (play-offs); Division 2 – Runners-up 1935–36, 1985–86; Division 3 (S) – Champions 1928–29, 1934–35; Promoted from Division 3 (3rd) 1974–75, 1980–81. *FA Cup:* Winners 1947; Runners-up 1946. *Football League Cup:* best season: 4th rd, 1963, 1966, 1979. *Full Members Cup:* Runners-up 1987.

*Colours:* Red shirts, white shorts, red stockings. *Change colours:* White shirts, green shorts, white stockings.

**Did you know?**
Paul Konchesky at 16 years 92 days became the youngest player to make his Football League debut for the club v Oxford United on 16 August 1997. Charlton won 3-2.

## CHARLTON ATHLETIC 1997–98 LEAGUE RECORD

| Match No. | Date | Venue | Opponents | Result | H/T Score | Lg. Pos. | Goalscorers | Attendance |
|---|---|---|---|---|---|---|---|---|
| 1 | Aug 9 | A | Middlesbrough | L | 1-2 | 1-0 | — | Jones S [8] | 29,414 |
| 2 | 16 | H | Oxford U | W | 3-2 | 1-0 | 9 | Jones S [20], Mendonca [57], Lisbie [90] | 10,230 |
| 3 | 23 | A | Bury | D | 0-0 | 0-0 | 8 | | 4657 |
| 4 | 30 | H | Manchester C | W | 2-1 | 0-1 | 9 | Van Blerk (og) [67], Jones K [69] | 14,009 |
| 5 | Sept 13 | A | Wolverhampton W | L | 1-3 | 0-3 | 14 | Chapple [72] | 22,683 |
| 6 | 17 | A | Norwich C | W | 4-0 | 3-0 | — | Mendonca 3 [7, 22, 28], Chapple [84] | 10,157 |
| 7 | 21 | H | Bradford C | W | 4-1 | 3-1 | 6 | Mendonca 2 [8, 69], Mortimer [18], Brown [23] | 11,583 |
| 8 | 27 | H | Stockport Co | L | 1-3 | 1-0 | 10 | Mortimer [40] | 12,083 |
| 9 | Oct 4 | A | QPR | W | 4-2 | 2-1 | 6 | Robinson 2 [16, 58], Jones S [42], Chapple [62] | 14,825 |
| 10 | 14 | A | Huddersfield T | W | 3-0 | 1-0 | — | Mendonca [15], Brown [69], Robinson [75] | 9596 |
| 11 | 19 | H | Stoke C | D | 1-1 | 0-0 | 4 | Kinsella [79] | 12,345 |
| 12 | 22 | H | Birmingham C | D | 1-1 | 0-0 | — | Mendonca [62] | 10,072 |
| 13 | 25 | A | Tranmere R | D | 2-2 | 0-1 | 5 | Kinsella [57], Leaburn [59] | 5911 |
| 14 | Nov 1 | H | Ipswich T | W | 3-0 | 2-0 | 3 | Mendonca [10], Chapple [34], Leaburn [90] | 12,627 |
| 15 | 4 | A | Sunderland | D | 0-0 | 0-0 | — | | 25,455 |
| 16 | 8 | A | WBA | L | 0-1 | 0-1 | 6 | | 16,124 |
| 17 | 15 | H | Crewe Alex | W | 3-2 | 2-1 | 6 | Jones K [6], Allen [27], Holmes [76] | 14,091 |
| 18 | 22 | A | Nottingham F | L | 2-5 | 0-1 | 6 | Allen [58], Woan (og) [79] | 18,532 |
| 19 | 28 | H | Swindon T | W | 3-0 | 2-0 | — | Jones K [9], Mendonca 2 (1 pen) [42 (p), 57] | 13,769 |
| 20 | Dec 6 | A | Reading | L | 0-2 | 0-2 | 7 | | 8076 |
| 21 | 9 | H | Sheffield U | W | 2-1 | 1-0 | — | Mendonca 2 (1 pen) [44 (p), 75] | 9868 |
| 22 | 13 | H | Port Vale | W | 1-0 | 0-0 | 5 | Newton [84] | 11,077 |
| 23 | 20 | A | Portsmouth | W | 2-0 | 1-0 | 4 | Robinson [44], Leaburn [52] | 8581 |
| 24 | 26 | H | Norwich C | W | 2-1 | 0-0 | 3 | Kinsella [59], Robinson [62] | 14,472 |
| 25 | 28 | A | Sheffield U | L | 1-4 | 0-2 | 4 | Bright [89] | 18,677 |
| 26 | Jan 10 | H | Middlesbrough | W | 3-0 | 2-0 | 3 | Newton 2 [20, 59], Bright [36] | 15,742 |
| 27 | 17 | A | Oxford U | W | 2-1 | 0-1 | 3 | Mendonca [81], Robinson [87] | 7234 |
| 28 | 28 | A | Manchester C | D | 2-2 | 0-1 | — | Jones S 2 [74, 90] | 24,058 |
| 29 | 31 | H | Bury | D | 0-0 | 0-0 | 3 | | 15,312 |
| 30 | Feb 7 | A | Bradford C | L | 0-1 | 0-1 | 5 | | 14,851 |
| 31 | 17 | H | QPR | D | 1-1 | 1-1 | — | Robinson [42] | 15,555 |
| 32 | 21 | A | Stockport Co | L | 0-3 | 0-1 | 5 | | 7705 |
| 33 | 25 | A | Stoke C | W | 2-1 | 1-1 | — | Robinson [17], Barness [73] | 10,027 |
| 34 | 28 | H | Huddersfield T | W | 1-0 | 0-0 | 4 | Bright [79] | 12,908 |
| 35 | Mar 3 | H | WBA | W | 5-0 | 1-0 | — | Bright [44], Newton [53], Mendonca 2 (1 pen) [70 (p), 79], Kinsella [73] | 10,893 |
| 36 | 7 | A | Ipswich T | L | 1-3 | 1-0 | 4 | Mendonca [22] | 19,831 |
| 37 | 15 | H | Sunderland | D | 1-1 | 0-1 | 4 | Bright [55] | 15,355 |
| 38 | 21 | A | Crewe Alex | W | 3-0 | 2-0 | 4 | Mills [3], Newton [44], Kinsella [77] | 5252 |
| 39 | 28 | H | Nottingham F | W | 4-2 | 1-1 | 4 | Bright [14], Mortimer [60], Mendonca (pen) [88], Kinsella [89] | 15,815 |
| 40 | Apr 4 | A | Swindon T | W | 1-0 | 0-0 | 4 | Jones S [80] | 7845 |
| 41 | 7 | H | Wolverhampton W | W | 1-0 | 1-0 | — | Mendonca [8] | 13,743 |
| 42 | 10 | H | Reading | W | 3-0 | 2-0 | — | Mendonca [6], Mortimer [44], Bright [79] | 14,220 |
| 43 | 13 | A | Port Vale | W | 1-0 | 0-0 | 3 | Mendonca (pen) [73] | 9973 |
| 44 | 18 | H | Portsmouth | W | 1-0 | 0-0 | 3 | Jones S [57] | 14,082 |
| 45 | 25 | H | Tranmere R | W | 2-0 | 1-0 | 3 | Mendonca 2 (2 pens) [11, 63] | 15,393 |
| 46 | May 3 | A | Birmingham C | D | 0-0 | 0-0 | 4 | | 25,877 |

**Final League Position: 4**     1996–97 DIV1 15

### GOALSCORERS
*League (80):* Mendonca 23 (7 pens), Robinson 8, Bright 7, Jones S 7, Kinsella 6, Newton 5, Chapple 4, Mortimer 4, Jones K 3, Leaburn 3, Allen 2, Brown 2, Barness 1, Holmes 1, Lisbie 1, Mills 1, own goals 2.
*Coca-Cola Cup (1):* Mendonca 1.
*FA Cup (5):* Brown 1, Jones K 1, Leaburn 1, Mendonca 1, Robinson 1.

Superscript figures (shown as [n]) indicate goals scored.

| Match No | Petterson A 23 | Brown S 27+7 | Barness A 21+8 | Jones K 44 | Rufus R 42 | Balmer S 13+3 | Newton S 33+8 | Kinsella M 46 | Robinson J 37+1 | Mendonca C 40 | Jones S 18+5 | Nicholls K 1+5 | Bright M 13+3 | Konchesky P 2+1 | Lisbie K 1+16 | Chapple P 29+6 | Parker S —+3 | Mortimer P 8+5 | Leaburn C 13+1 | Bowen M 34+2 | Emben P —+4 | Holmes M 10+6 | Allen B 7+5 | Stuart J —+1 | Salmon M 9 | Ilic S 14 | Mills D 9 | Youds E 8 | Heaney N 4+2 |
|---|---|---|---|---|---|---|---|---|---|---|---|---|---|---|---|---|---|---|---|---|---|---|---|---|---|---|---|---|---|
| 1 | 1 | 2 | 3 | 4[1] | 5 | 6 | 7 | 8 | 9 | 10 | 11[2] | 12 | 13 | | | | | | | | | | | | | | | | |
| 2 | 1 | 2[1] | | 4 | 5 | 6 | 7 | 8 | 9[1] | 10 | 11 | 12[2] | | | | 3 | | 13 | 14 | | | | | | | | | | |
| 3 | 1 | 2 | | | 5[2] | 6 | 7 | 8 | 9 | 10 | 11[1] | 4 | | | | 3[2] | | 12 | 13 | 14 | | | | | | | | | |
| 4 | 1 | 2 | 3 | 4 | 5 | | 7 | 8 | 9 | 10 | 11 | | | | | 6 | | | | | | | | | | | | | |
| 5 | 1 | 2 | 3 | 4[2] | | 6 | | 8 | 9 | 10 | 11[3] | 13 | 12 | | | 5 | | | 7[1] | 14 | | | | | | | | | |
| 6 | 1 | 2 | 3 | 4 | | 6 | | 8[1] | 9 | 10[2] | 11 | 12 | 13 | | | 5[3] | | | 7 | 14 | | | | | | | | | |
| 7 | 1 | 2 | 3 | 4[2] | 5[1] | 6 | | 8 | 9 | 10 | 11 | 13 | 12 | | | | | | 7 | | | | | | | | | | |
| 8 | 1 | 2 | 3[3] | 4 | 5[2] | 6 | 12 | 8 | 9 | 10 | 11 | | 13 | | | | | | 7[1] | 14 | | | | | | | | | |
| 9 | 1 | 2[3] | 3 | 4 | 5 | 6[1] | 7[2] | 8 | 9 | 10 | 11 | 13 | 12 | | | | | | 14 | | | | | | | | | | |
| 10 | 1 | 2 | 3 | 4 | 5 | | 7[2] | 8 | 9[1] | 10 | 11 | 12 | | | | 6 | | | | | | 13 | | | | | | | |
| 11 | 1 | | 3 | 4 | 5 | | 7[1] | 8 | 9 | 10 | 11[2] | | | | | 6 | | | | 2 | | 12 | 13 | | | | | | |
| 12 | 1 | | 3 | 4 | 5[2] | | 7[1] | 8 | 9 | 10 | 11 | | | | | 6 | | | | 2 | | 12 | 13 | | | | | | |
| 13 | 1 | | 3 | 4 | 5 | | 7 | 8 | 9 | 10 | | | | | | 6 | | 11 | | 2 | | | | | | | | | |
| 14 | 1 | 2 | | 4 | 5 | | 7[1] | 8 | 9 | 10 | | | | | | 6 | | 11 | | 3 | | 12 | | | | | | | |
| 15 | 1 | 2[1] | 12 | 4 | 5 | 13 | | 8 | 9 | 10 | | | | | | 6 | | 11 | 7[2] | 3 | | | | | | | | | |
| 16 | 1 | 2 | | 4 | 5 | 12 | | 8 | 9 | 13 | | | | | | 6 | | 11 | 7[1] | 3 | | 10[2] | | | | | | | |
| 17 | 1 | 2 | | 4 | 5 | 12 | | 8 | 9[1] | | | | | | | 6 | | 11 | 7 | 3 | | 10 | | | | | | | |
| 18 | 1 | 2 | 12 | 4[2] | 5 | | 14 | 8 | 9 | 13 | | | | | | 6 | | 11 | 7[3] | 3[1] | | 10 | | | | | | | |
| 19 | 1 | 2[1] | 12 | 4 | 5 | | | 8 | 9 | 10 | | | | | | 6 | | 11 | 7 | 3 | | | | | | | | | |
| 20 | | 2[3] | | 4 | 5[1] | 12 | 13 | 8 | 9 | 10 | | | | | | 6 | | 11[2] | 7 | 3 | | 14 | | | 1 | | | | |
| 21 | | 2 | | 4 | 5 | | | 8 | 9 | 10 | | | | | | 6 | | 11 | 7 | 3 | | | | | 1 | | | | |
| 22 | | 2 | | 4 | 5 | | 12 | 8 | 9 | 10 | | | | | | 6 | | 11 | 7[1] | 3 | | | | | 1 | | | | |
| 23 | | 2 | | 4 | 5 | | 7 | 8 | 9[1] | 10 | | | | | 12 | 6 | | 11 | | 3 | | | | | 1 | | | | |
| 24 | | 2 | | 4 | 5 | | 7 | 8 | 9 | 10 | | | | | | 6 | | 11 | | 3 | | | | | 1 | | | | |
| 25 | | 2 | 12 | 4 | 5 | | 7 | 8[3] | 9[1] | 10 | | | | | 13 | 6 | | 11[2] | 14 | 3 | | | | | 1 | | | | |
| 26 | | 2 | | 4 | 5 | | 7[1] | 8 | 9 | 10 | 11[2] | | | | | 6 | | | | 3 | | 12 | 13 | | 1 | | | | |
| 27 | | 2 | 12 | 4[2] | 5 | | 7[3] | 8 | 9 | 10 | 11[1] | | | | | 6 | | | | 3 | | 13 | 14 | | 1 | | | | |
| 28 | | 2 | 12 | 4 | 5 | | 7[1] | 8 | | | | | 13 | | | 6 | | 11 | | 3 | | 9 | 10 | | 1 | | | | |
| 29 | 1 | 2 | | 4 | 5 | | 7 | 8 | | | 11 | 12 | 13 | | | 6 | | | | 3 | | 9[1] | 10[4] | | | | | | |
| 30 | 1 | 2[1] | 12 | 4 | 5 | | 7 | 8 | 9 | 10 | 11 | | | | 13 | 6 | | 4[2] | | 3[3] | | 14 | | | | | | | |
| 31 | 1 | 2 | | 4[1] | 5 | | 7 | 8 | 9 | 10 | | | | | 13 | 6 | | 11[2] | 12 | 3 | | | | | | | | | |
| 32 | 1 | 2[3] | 12 | 4 | 5 | 13 | 7 | 8 | 9 | 10 | | | | | 14 | 6 | | 11[1] | | 3[2] | | | | | | | | | |
| 33 | | 2 | 7 | 4 | | 6 | 12 | 8 | 9 | 10 | 11[1] | | | | | 5 | | | | 3 | | | | | | 1 | | | |
| 34 | | 12 | 2 | 4 | 5 | 6 | 7 | 8 | 9 | 10[2] | 11 | | | | 13 | | | | | 3[1] | | | | | | 1 | | | |
| 35 | | 12 | 2 | 4 | 5[2] | 6 | 7 | 8 | 9[1] | 10 | 11[3] | | | | 14 | 13 | | | | 3 | | | | | | 1 | | | |
| 36 | | 2[1] | | 4 | 5 | 6 | 7 | 8 | 9 | 10 | 11 | | | | 12 | | | | | 3 | | | | | | 1 | | | |
| 37 | | 2[1] | | 4 | 5 | 6 | 7 | 8 | 9[2] | 10 | 11 | | | | 13 | 12 | | | | 3 | | | | | | 1 | | | |
| 38 | | | | 4[2] | | 6 | 7 | 8 | 9[1] | 10 | 11 | | | | 14 | 5 | 13 | | | 3 | | 12 | | | | 1 | 2[1] | | |
| 39 | | | | 4 | 5 | | 7[1] | 8 | 9[2] | 10 | 11 | | | | 12 | | 13 | | | 3 | | | | | | 1 | 2 | 6 | |
| 40 | | | | 4 | 5 | | 7 | 8 | 9 | 10 | 11 | | | | | | | | | 3 | | | | | | 1 | 2 | 6 | |
| 41 | | 12 | | 4 | 5 | | 7 | 8 | 9[2] | 10 | 11[3] | | | | 13 | | | | | 3[1] | | | | | | 1 | 2 | 6 | 14 |
| 42 | | 12 | 3 | 4 | 5 | | 7 | 8[1] | 9 | | 11[3] | | | | 13 | | | | | | | 10 | | | | 1 | 2 | 6 | 14 |
| 43 | | 12 | 3 | 4 | 5[1] | | 7 | 8 | 9 | | | | | | 13[3] | | 14 | | | | | 10 | | | | 1 | 2 | 6 | 11[2] |
| 44 | | 12 | | 4 | 5 | | 7 | 8 | 9[1] | | | | | | | | | | | 3 | | 10 | | | | 1 | 2 | 6 | 11 |
| 45 | | 12 | | 4[1] | 5 | 13 | 7[3] | 8 | 9 | | | | | | | | 14 | | | 3 | | 10 | | | | 1 | 2 | 6 | 11[2] |
| 46 | | | | 4 | 5 | | 7 | 8 | 9[2] | | | | | | 13 | | | | | 3 | | 10 | 12 | | | 1 | 2 | 6 | 11[1] |

**Coca-Cola Cup**

| | | | |
|---|---|---|---|
| First Round | Ipswich T | (h) | 0-1 |
| | | (a) | 1-3 |

**FA Cup**

| | | | |
|---|---|---|---|
| Third Round | Nottingham F | (h) | 4-1 |
| Fourth Round | Wolverhampton W | (h) | 1-1 |
| | | (a) | 0-3 |

CHELSEA 1997-98 *Back row (left to right):* Dave Collyer (Youth Development Officer), Bernie Dixson (Youth Development Officer), Jon Harley, Steve Hampshire, Paul Hughes, Neil Clement, Nick Colgan, Tore Andre Flo, Kevin Hitchcock, Michael Duberry, Joe Sheerin, Danny Granville, Mark Nicolls, Bob Orsborn (Kit Manager), Ted Dale (Youth Team Manager).
*Middle row:* George Price (Reserve Team Physio), Mick McGiven (Reserve Team Manager), Mark Stein, Celestine Babayaro, Andy Myers, Bernard Lambourde, David Lee, Frode Grodas, Ed De Goey, Dmitri Kharine, Gustavo Poyet, Frank Leboeuf, Steve Clark, David Rocastle, Nick Crittenden, Mike Banks (Physio), Terry Byrne (Assistant Physio).
*Front row:* Eddie Niedzwiecki (Goalkeeping Coach), Graeme Le Saux, Dan Petrescu, Eddie Newton, Gianluca Vialli, Dennis Wise, Gwyn Williams (Assistant Manager), Ruud Gullit (Player/Manager), Graham Rix (First Team Coach), Roberto Di Matteo, Mark Hughes, Frank Sinclair, Gianfranco Zola, Jody Morris, Ade Mafe (Fitness Trainer).
(Photograph: Action Images)

# FA Premiership

# CHELSEA

*Stamford Bridge, London SW6 1HS.* Telephone: (0171) 385 5545. Fax: (0171) 381 4831. Clubcall: 0891 121159. Ticket News and Promotions: 0891 121011. Ticket Credit Card Service: (0171) 386 7799.

*Ground capacity:* 31,791 (during ground development); 41,000 (eventually).

*Record attendance:* 82,905 v Arsenal, Division 1, 12 October 1935.

*Record receipts:* £488,960 v Liverpool, FA Premier League, 30 December 1995.

*Pitch measurements:* 113yd × 74yd.

*Chairman:* K. W. Bates.

*Directors:* C. Hutchinson (Managing), Ms Y. S. Todd.

*Player/Manager:* Gianluca Vialli. *Assistant Manager:* Gwyn Williams. *Coach:* Graham Rix.

*Physio:* Michael Banks. *Reserve Team Manager:* Mick McGiven.

*Company Secretary:* Alan Shaw. *Match Secretary:* Keith Lacy.

*Commercial Manager:* Carole Phair. *Safety Officer:* David Lowery.

*Year Formed:* 1905. *Turned Professional:* 1905. *Ltd Co.:* 1905.

*Club Nickname:* 'The Blues'.

*Foundation:* Chelsea may never have existed but for the fact that Fulham rejected an offer to rent the Stamford Bridge ground from Mr. H. A. Mears who had owned it since 1904. Fortunately he was determined to develop it as a football stadium rather than sell it to the Great Western Railway and got together with Frederick Parker, who persuaded Mears of the financial advantages of developing a major sporting venue. Chelsea FC was formed in 1905, and when admission to the Southern League was denied, they immediately gained admission to the Second Division of the Football League.

*First Football League game:* 2 September 1905, Division 2, v Stockport Co (a) L 0-1 – Foulke; Mackie, McEwan; Key, Harris, Miller; Moran, J.T. Robertson, Copeland, Windridge, Kirwan.

*Record League Victory:* 9–2 v Glossop N E, Division 2, 1 September 1906 – Byrne; Walton, Miller; Key (1), McRoberts, Henderson; Moran, McDermott (1), Hilsdon (5), Copeland (1), Kirwan (1).

*Record Cup Victory:* 13–0 v Jeunesse Hautcharage, ECWC, 1st rd 2nd leg, 29 September 1971 – Bonetti; Boyle, Harris (1), Hollins (1p), Webb (1), Hinton, Cooke, Baldwin (3), Osgood (5), Hudson (1), Houseman (1).

*Record Defeat:* 1–8 v Wolverhampton W, Division 1, 26 September 1953.

*Most League Points (2 for a win):* 57, Division 2, 1906–07.

*Most League Points (3 for a win):* 99, Division 2, 1988–89.

*Most League Goals:* 98, Division 1, 1960–61.

*Highest League Scorer in Season:* Jimmy Greaves, 41, 1960–61.

*Most League Goals in Total Aggregate:* Bobby Tambling, 164, 1958–70.

*Most Capped Player:* Ray Wilkins, 24 (84), England.

*Most League Appearances:* Ron Harris, 655, 1962–80.

*Record Transfer Fee Received:* £2,200,000 from Tottenham H for Gordon Durie, July 1991.

*Record Transfer Fee Paid:* £5,400,000 to Lazio for Pierluigi Casiraghi, July 1998.

*Football League Record:* 1905 Elected to Division 2; 1907–10 Division 1; 1910–12 Division 2; 1912–24 Division 1; 1924–30 Division 2; 1930–62 Division 1; 1962–63 Division 2; 1963–75 Division 1; 1975–77 Division 2; 1977–79 Division 1; 1979–84 Division 2; 1984–88 Division 1; 1988–89 Division 2; 1989–92 Division 1; 1992– FA Premier League.

*Honours: Football League:* Division 1 – Champions 1954–55; Division 2 – Champions 1983–84, 1988–89; Runners-up 1906–07, 1911–12, 1929–30, 1962–63, 1976–77. *FA Cup:* Winners 1970, 1997; Runners-up 1915, 1967, 1994. *Football League Cup:* Winners 1965, 1998; Runners-up 1972. *Full Members' Cup:* Winners 1986. *Zenith Data Systems Cup:* Winners 1990. **European Competitions:** *European Fairs Cup:* 1958–60, 1965–66, 1968–69; *European Cup-Winners' Cup:* 1970–71, 1971–72, 1994–95, 1997–98 (winners).

*Colours:* Royal blue with white and amber trim shirts and shorts, white stockings with royal blue and amber trim. *Change colours:* White shirts and shorts with royal blue/yellow trim, white stockings with royal blue/ yellow trim on turnover.

**Did you know?**
On 27 October 1975 Chelsea drew 0-0 with the Italian Under-23 team for the Prince Philip Cup at Stamford Bridge, watched by a crowd of 9061.

## CHELSEA 1997–98 LEAGUE RECORD

| Match No. | Date | Venue | Opponents | Result | H/T Score | Lg. Pos. | Goalscorers | Attendance |
|---|---|---|---|---|---|---|---|---|
| 1 | Aug 9 | A | Coventry C | L | 2-3 | 1-1 | — | Sinclair [39], Flo [71] | 22,691 |
| 2 | 24 | A | Barnsley | W | 6-0 | 3-0 | 11 | Petrescu [25], Poyet [38], Vialli 4 [44, 57, 65, 82] | 18,177 |
| 3 | 27 | A | Wimbledon | W | 2-0 | 0-0 | — | Di Matteo [60], Petrescu [64] | 22,237 |
| 4 | 30 | H | Southampton | W | 4-2 | 4-1 | 4 | Petrescu [7], Leboeuf [28], Hughes M [31], Wise [33] | 28,832 |
| 5 | Sept 13 | A | Crystal Palace | W | 3-0 | 2-0 | 3 | Hughes M [20], Leboeuf (pen) [26], Le Saux [90] | 26,186 |
| 6 | 21 | H | Arsenal | L | 2-3 | 1-1 | 5 | Poyet [40], Zola [60] | 31,290 |
| 7 | 24 | A | Manchester U | D | 2-2 | 1-1 | — | Berg (og) [25], Hughes M [68] | 55,163 |
| 8 | 27 | H | Newcastle U | W | 1-0 | 0-0 | 4 | Poyet [75] | 31,050 |
| 9 | Oct 5 | A | Liverpool | L | 2-4 | 1-2 | 5 | Zola [22], Poyet (pen) [85] | 36,647 |
| 10 | 18 | H | Leicester C | W | 1-0 | 0-0 | 4 | Leboeuf [88] | 33,356 |
| 11 | 26 | A | Bolton W | L | 0-1 | 0-0 | 4 | | 24,080 |
| 12 | Nov 1 | A | Aston Villa | W | 2-0 | 1-0 | 4 | Hughes M [38], Flo [82] | 39,372 |
| 13 | 9 | H | West Ham U | W | 2-1 | 0-0 | 4 | Ferdinand (og) [57], Zola [83] | 33,256 |
| 14 | 22 | A | Blackburn R | L | 0-1 | 0-1 | 5 | | 27,683 |
| 15 | 26 | H | Everton | W | 2-0 | 0-0 | — | Wise (pen) [80], Zola (pen) [90] | 32,736 |
| 16 | 29 | H | Derby Co | W | 4-0 | 2-0 | 2 | Zola 3 [12, 66, 77], Hughes M [35] | 33,837 |
| 17 | Dec 1 | A | Tottenham H | W | 6-1 | 1-1 | 2 | Flo 3 [40, 63, 90], Di Matteo [48], Petrescu [59], Nicholls [78] | 28,476 |
| 18 | 13 | H | Leeds U | D | 0-0 | 0-0 | 3 | | 34,779 |
| 19 | 20 | A | Sheffield W | W | 4-1 | 1-0 | 3 | Petrescu [30], Vialli [56], Leboeuf (pen) [65], Flo [84] | 28,334 |
| 20 | 26 | H | Wimbledon | D | 1-1 | 1-1 | 3 | Vialli [8] | 32,754 |
| 21 | 29 | A | Southampton | L | 0-1 | 0-1 | — | | 15,237 |
| 22 | Jan 10 | H | Coventry C | W | 3-1 | 0-1 | 2 | Nicholls 2 [65, 70], Di Matteo [78] | 33,395 |
| 23 | 18 | A | Everton | L | 1-3 | 1-1 | 3 | Flo [37] | 32,355 |
| 24 | 31 | H | Barnsley | W | 2-0 | 1-0 | 2 | Vialli [23], Hughes M [47] | 34,442 |
| 25 | Feb 8 | A | Arsenal | L | 0-2 | 0-2 | 2 | | 38,083 |
| 26 | 21 | A | Leicester C | L | 0-2 | 0-1 | 4 | | 21,335 |
| 27 | 28 | H | Manchester U | L | 0-1 | 0-1 | 5 | | 34,517 |
| 28 | Mar 8 | H | Aston Villa | L | 0-1 | 0-0 | 5 | | 33,018 |
| 29 | 11 | A | Crystal Palace | W | 6-2 | 3-1 | — | Vialli 2 [15, 44], Zola [17], Wise [84], Flo 2 [89, 90] | 31,844 |
| 30 | 14 | A | West Ham U | L | 1-2 | 0-0 | 4 | Charvet [54] | 25,829 |
| 31 | Apr 5 | A | Derby Co | W | 1-0 | 1-0 | 4 | Hughes M [37] | 30,062 |
| 32 | 8 | H | Leeds U | L | 1-3 | 1-2 | — | Charvet [11] | 37,246 |
| 33 | 11 | H | Tottenham H | W | 2-0 | 0-0 | 4 | Flo [75], Vialli [88] | 34,149 |
| 34 | 19 | A | Sheffield W | W | 1-0 | 1-0 | 4 | Leboeuf (pen) [23] | 29,075 |
| 35 | 25 | H | Liverpool | W | 4-1 | 1-1 | 3 | Hughes M 2 [11, 78], Clarke [67], Flo [72] | 34,639 |
| 36 | 29 | H | Blackburn R | L | 0-1 | 0-0 | — | | 33,311 |
| 37 | May 2 | A | Newcastle U | L | 1-3 | 0-2 | 4 | Di Matteo [77] | 36,710 |
| 38 | 10 | H | Bolton W | W | 2-0 | 0-0 | 4 | Vialli [73], Morris [90] | 34,845 |

**Final League Position: 4**     1996–97 PREM 6

### GOALSCORERS

*League (71):* Flo 11, Vialli 11, Hughes M 9, Zola 8 (1 pen), Leboeuf 5 (3 pens), Petrescu 5, Di Matteo 4, Poyet 4 (1 pen), Nicholls 3, Wise 3 (1 pen), Charvet 2, Clarke 1, Le Saux 1, Morris 1, Sinclair 1, own goals 2.
*Coca-Cola Cup (11):* Di Matteo 3, Flo 2, Hughes M 2, Le Saux 1, Morris 1, Petrescu 1, Sinclair 1.
*FA Cup (3):* Vialli 2, Le Saux 1.

| De Goey E 28 | Petrescu D 31 | Le Saux G 26 | Sinclair F 20+2 | Leboeuf F 32 | Clarke S 22+4 | Poyet G 11+3 | Di Matteo R 28+2 | Zola G 23+4 | Hughes M 25+4 | Wise D 26 | Morris J 9+3 | Flo T 16+18 | Myers A 11+1 | Vialli G 14+7 | Granville D 9+4 | Nicholls M 8+11 | Duberry M 23 | Hughes P 5+4 | Lambourde B 5+2 | Gullit R —+6 | Babayaro C 8 | Newton E 17+1 | Crittenden N —+2 | Charvet L 7+4 | Kharine D 10 | Harley J 3 | Lee D 1 | Match No. |
|---|---|---|---|---|---|---|---|---|---|---|---|---|---|---|---|---|---|---|---|---|---|---|---|---|---|---|---|---|
| 1 | 2 | 3 | 4 | 5 | 6 | 7 | 8[1] | 9 | 10[2] | 11 | 12 | 13 | | | | | | | | | | | | | | | | 1 |
| 1 | 2[2] | 3 | 4 | | 6 | 7[3] | 8 | | 10[1] | 11 | | 12 | 5 | 9 | 13 | 14 | | | | | | | | | | | | 2 |
| 1 | 2 | 3 | 4 | | 6 | 7 | 8 | | | 11 | | 10 | | 9 | | | 5 | | | | | | | | | | | 3 |
| 1 | 2[1] | 3 | 4 | 5 | 12 | 7 | 8[2] | 9[3] | 10 | 11 | | | | 14 | 13 | | 6 | | | | | | | | | | | 4 |
| 1 | 2 | 3 | | 5 | | 7 | 10 | 11 | 9 | 8 | | | | | 4 | | 6 | | | | | | | | | | | 5 |
| 1 | 2[2] | 3 | | 5 | | 7 | 8[3] | | 10 | 12 | | 11 | | 14 | 9[1] | 13 | 4 | 6 | | | | | | | | | | 6 |
| 1 | 2 | 3 | | 5 | | 7 | | 9[1] | 10 | 11 | | 12 | | | 4 | | 6 | | 8 | | | | | | | | | 7 |
| 1 | | 3 | 12 | 5 | | 7 | 8[2] | | 10 | 13 | | 11 | | 9 | | | 4 | | 6[1] | | | 2 | | | | | | 8 |
| 1 | 2[1] | 3 | 4 | 5 | | 7 | 8 | 9 | 10 | 11 | | 12 | | | | | 6 | | 13 | | | | | | | | | 9 |
| 1 | 2 | 3[2] | 4 | 5 | 6 | | 8[1] | | | 11 | | 12 | | 9[2] | 13 | 14 | | | | | | 7 | 10 | | | | | 10 |
| 1 | 2 | | 4 | 5 | 3 | | | | 10 | 9 | | | | | 6 | | | | 8[1] | | | 12 | 7 | 11 | | | | 11 |
| 1 | 2[2] | | 4 | 5 | 13 | | 12 | 9[3] | 10 | 8[1] | | | | 14 | | | 6 | | | | 3 | | 7 | 11 | | | | 12 |
| 1 | 2[1] | | 4 | 5[2] | | | 8 | 9 | 10 | 11 | | 12 | | | | | 6 | | 13 | | 3 | 7 | | | | | | 13 |
| 1 | 2[1] | | 4 | 5[2] | 6 | | 8 | 9 | 10 | 11 | | 12 | | | | | 13 | | | | 3 | 7 | | | | | | 14 |
| 1 | 2 | | 4 | | 6[3] | | 8 | 7 | 12 | 11 | | 13 | | 9[2] | 14 | 10[1] | 5 | | 3 | | | | | | | | | 15 |
| 1 | 2 | 3 | 4 | 5 | | | 8 | 9[2] | 10[1] | 11 | | 12 | | | 6 | | | | 7 | | | 13 | | | | | | 16 |
| 1 | 2 | 3 | 4 | 5 | | | 8 | 10 | 11 | 9 | | 12 | | | 6 | | | | 7[1] | | | | | | | | | 17 |
| 1 | 2[2] | 3 | 4 | 5 | | | 8 | 10 | 11 | 9 | | 12 | | | 7[1] | 6 | | | | | | 13 | | | | | | 18 |
| 1 | 2 | 3 | 4[1] | 5 | 12 | | 8 | 7[2] | | 11 | | 13 | | 9 | 10 | | 6 | | | | | | | | | | | 19 |
| 1 | 2 | 11 | 4[1] | 5 | 12 | | 8 | 13 | | 7 | | 10 | | 9[2] | 3 | | 6 | | | | | | | | | | | 20 |
| 1 | 2[2] | 11 | 4 | 5 | | | 8 | 9 | 10 | 13 | | 12 | | 3[3] | 14 | 6 | 7[1] | | | | | | | | | | | 21 |
| 1 | 11 | | 5 | 6 | | | 8 | 9[1] | 10 | 7 | | 3[2] | 13 | 4 | | | | | 2 | 12 | | | | | | | | 22 |
| 1 | 2 | 11 | 4[2] | 5 | 3 | | | 10 | 11[1] | 12 | | | | 9 | | | | | 6 | 7 | 13 | 8 | | | | | | 23 |
| 1 | 2 | 3 | 12 | 5 | 6 | | | 10 | 11[1] | | | 9 | | | 13 | 4 | | | 8[2] | | | 7 | | | | | | 24 |
| 1 | 2[3] | 3 | | 5 | | | 8 | 12 | 10 | 11 | | 13 | | 9[1] | 14 | 6 | | | | | | 7[2] | 4 | | | | | 25 |
| | 2 | 3 | | 5 | 6 | | 8 | 7[1] | 10 | 11 | | 12 | | 9 | | | 4 | | | | | | | | | 1 | | 26 |
| | 2 | 3 | | 5 | 6 | | 8 | 7 | 10 | 11 | | 12 | | 9[1] | | | 4 | | | | | | | | | 1 | | 27 |
| 1 | | 2 | 5 | | | | 8[1] | 12 | | | | 4 | 10 | 3[2] | 9 | | 7 | 6 | | | | 11 | 13 | | | | | 28 |
| | 2 | 4[3] | 5 | 6 | | 7 | | 11 | 10[2] | 12 | | 9[1] | 3 | | | | | 13 | 14 | | | 8 | | | | 1 | | 29 |
| | | | | 5 | | | 8 | 12 | 10 | 11[1] | | 9 | 6 | | 3 | | 4 | | | | | 7 | | 2 | | 1 | | 30 |
| | 2 | | 5 | 6[3] | 8 | | 10 | 7 | 9[2] | 4 | | 3 | 13 | | | | 12 | | | | | 14 | 1 | 11[1] | | | | 31 |
| | | 3 | | | | | 9[1] | 10 | 11 | 7[2] | 12 | 6 | | | 4 | 13 | 14 | | | | | 8[3] | 2 | 1 | | | 5 | 32 |
| 1 | 2 | 3 | | 5 | 6 | 12 | | 11 | 7[2] | 10 | 13 | 9 | | | 4 | | | | | | | | | | 8[1] | | | 33 |
| | | | | 5[1] | 6 | 8 | | 10 | 13 | 9[2] | | 3 | 14 | 4 | 12 | | | | | | | 7 | | 2 | 1 | 11[2] | | 34 |
| | 2[3] | 3 | | 5 | 6 | 7 | 8 | 9[1] | 10[2] | | | 12 | 13 | | | | 4 | | | | | 11 | 14 | | 1 | | | 35 |
| | 2[3] | 3 | | 5 | 6 | 7 | 8 | | 10 | 12 | | 9[2] | 4 | 13 | | | | | | | | 11[1] | 14 | 1 | | | | 36 |
| | | | | 5[1] | 6 | 12 | 8 | | 10[2] | 4 | 13 | 9 | | | 3 | 7 | | 14 | | | | 11[3] | 2 | 1 | | | | 37 |
| 1 | 2[1] | | | 5 | 6 | 12 | 13 | 10 | 11[2] | 4 | | 9[3] | 14 | 3 | | | | | | | | 8 | 7 | | | | | 38 |

**Coca-Cola Cup**

|  |  | |  |
|---|---|---|---|
| Third Round | Blackburn R | (h) | 1-1 |
| Fourth Round | Southampton | (h) | 2-1 |
| Fifth Round | Ipswich T | (a) | 2-2 |
| Semi-Final | Arsenal | (a) | 1-2 |
| | | (h) | 3-1 |
| Final | Middlesbrough (at Wembley) | | 2-0 |

**FA Cup**

|  |  | |  |
|---|---|---|---|
| Third Round | Manchester U | (h) | 3-5 |

CHESTER CITY 1997-98    *Back row (left to right):* Craig Warrington, Philip Clench, Matty Woods, Nick Richardson, Spencer Whelan, Andy Milner, John Jones, Gary Bennett, Chris Priest.
*Middle row:* Stuart Walker (Physio), John Murphy, Julian Alsford, Ronnie Sinclair, David Flitcroft, Wayne Brown, Shaun Reid, Rod Thomas, Dave Fogg (Youth Team Coach).
*Front row:* Ryan Dobson, Rod McDonald, Neil Fisher, Gary Shelton (Assistant Manager), Iain Jenkins, Kevin Ratcliffe (Manager), Stuart Rimmer, Ross Davison, Martin Giles.
(Photograph: Andrew R. Price)

## CHESTER CITY 1997–98 LEAGUE RECORD

| Match No. | Date | Venue | Opponents | Result | H/T Score | Lg. Pos. | Goalscorers | Attendance |
|---|---|---|---|---|---|---|---|---|
| 1 | Aug 9 | H | Lincoln C | W 2-0 | 0-0 | — | Flitcroft [64], Bennett [85] | 2478 |
| 2 | 23 | H | Cambridge U | D 1-1 | 0-1 | 14 | Bennett [68] | 2167 |
| 3 | 30 | A | Barnet | L 1-2 | 0-0 | 17 | Simpson (og) [61] | 1790 |
| 4 | Sept 2 | A | Scunthorpe U | L 1-2 | 1-0 | — | Bennett [23] | 2633 |
| 5 | 5 | H | Hull C | W 1-0 | 1-0 | — | Bennett [42] | 2271 |
| 6 | 13 | H | Shrewsbury T | W 2-0 | 1-0 | 14 | Bennett 2 [21, 66] | 2853 |
| 7 | 16 | A | Cardiff C | W 2-0 | 2-0 | — | Alsford [11], Bennett (pen) [32] | 3949 |
| 8 | 20 | A | Mansfield T | L 1-4 | 1-3 | 10 | Davidson (pen) [18] | 2183 |
| 9 | 27 | A | Rotherham U | L 2-4 | 0-3 | 12 | Alsford [69], Priest [75] | 3061 |
| 10 | Oct 4 | H | Hartlepool U | W 3-1 | 2-1 | 6 | Whelan [34], Bennett [38], Murphy [73] | 2163 |
| 11 | 11 | H | Brighton & HA | W 2-0 | 1-0 | 4 | Bennett 2 [39, 50] | 2402 |
| 12 | 18 | A | Torquay U | L 1-3 | 0-3 | 5 | Richardson [90] | 2047 |
| 13 | 21 | A | Scarborough | L 1-4 | 0-2 | — | Thomas [47] | 1451 |
| 14 | 25 | H | Macclesfield T | D 1-1 | 0-0 | 11 | Priest [78] | 3245 |
| 15 | Nov 1 | H | Rochdale | W 4-0 | 1-0 | 8 | McDonald [10], Bennett [69], Rimmer 2 [72, 79] | 2431 |
| 16 | 4 | A | Notts Co | W 2-1 | 0-0 | — | McDonald [60], Bennett [87] | 3104 |
| 17 | 8 | A | Leyton Orient | L 0-1 | 0-1 | 6 | | 3894 |
| 18 | 18 | H | Peterborough U | D 0-0 | 0-0 | — | | 2612 |
| 19 | 26 | H | Swansea C | W 2-0 | 1-0 | — | Flitcroft (pen) [33], Thomas [53] | 1510 |
| 20 | 29 | H | Exeter C | D 1-1 | 0-1 | 8 | Rimmer [66] | 2288 |
| 21 | Dec 2 | A | Doncaster R | L 1-2 | 1-1 | — | Jones [13] | 864 |
| 22 | 13 | H | Darlington | W 2-1 | 0-0 | 7 | McDonald [74], Alsford [80] | 1812 |
| 23 | 19 | A | Colchester U | L 0-2 | 0-1 | — | | 1867 |
| 24 | 26 | A | Hull C | W 2-1 | 0-0 | 9 | Whelan [82], Thomas [87] | 6807 |
| 25 | 28 | H | Scunthorpe U | W 1-0 | 0-0 | 7 | Priest [63] | 2263 |
| 26 | Jan 10 | A | Lincoln C | W 3-1 | 2-0 | 4 | Priest [37], Jenkins [44], Rimmer [73] | 2913 |
| 27 | 17 | H | Barnet | L 0-1 | 0-0 | 7 | | 2479 |
| 28 | 24 | A | Cambridge U | W 2-1 | 0-0 | 6 | Rimmer [53], McDonald [90] | 2473 |
| 29 | 27 | H | Cardiff C | D 0-0 | 0-0 | — | | 1757 |
| 30 | 31 | A | Shrewsbury T | D 1-1 | 0-1 | 6 | Woods [70] | 3002 |
| 31 | Feb 7 | H | Mansfield T | L 0-1 | 0-0 | 9 | | 2055 |
| 32 | 14 | A | Hartlepool U | D 0-0 | 0-0 | 9 | | 2186 |
| 33 | 21 | H | Rotherham U | W 4-0 | 0-0 | 8 | Murphy [47], Alsford [50], Priest 2 [71, 87] | 2432 |
| 34 | 24 | H | Torquay U | L 1-3 | 0-2 | — | Woods [46] | 2163 |
| 35 | 28 | A | Brighton & HA | L 2-3 | 1-2 | 10 | Flitcroft [8], Murphy [78] | 2510 |
| 36 | Mar 3 | H | Leyton Orient | D 1-1 | 0-1 | — | Richardson [65] | 1650 |
| 37 | 7 | A | Rochdale | D 1-1 | 0-0 | 11 | Murphy [85] | 1955 |
| 38 | 14 | H | Notts Co | L 0-1 | 0-0 | 11 | | 2753 |
| 39 | 21 | A | Peterborough U | L 1-2 | 1-1 | 11 | McDonald [43] | 4817 |
| 40 | 28 | A | Swansea C | L 0-2 | 0-1 | 14 | | 2500 |
| 41 | Apr 4 | A | Exeter C | L 0-5 | 0-3 | 14 | | 2965 |
| 42 | 11 | H | Doncaster R | W 2-1 | 2-1 | 14 | Flitcroft (pen) [8], Rimmer [35] | 1593 |
| 43 | 13 | A | Darlington | L 0-1 | 0-0 | 15 | | 1901 |
| 44 | 18 | H | Colchester U | W 3-1 | 0-0 | 13 | Whelan [19], Fisher [34], Rimmer [36] | 1780 |
| 45 | 25 | A | Macclesfield T | L 2-3 | 0-1 | 16 | Whelan [52], Thomas [79] | 5982 |
| 46 | May 2 | H | Scarborough | D 1-1 | 0-0 | 14 | Rimmer [86] | 2719 |

**Final League Position: 14**     1996–97 DIV3 6

### GOALSCORERS
League (60): Bennett 12 (1 pen), Rimmer 8, Priest 6, McDonald 5, Alsford 4, Flitcroft 4 (2 pens), Murphy 4, Thomas 4, Whelan 4, Richardson 2, Woods 2, Davidson 1 (pen), Fisher 1, Jenkins 1, Jones 1, own goal 1.
Coca-Cola Cup (1): Woods 1.
FA Cup (2): Priest 1, Richardson 1.

# Division 3 CHESTER CITY

*The Deva Stadium, Bumpers Lane, Chester CH1 4LT.* Telephone: (01244) 371376, 371809. Fax: (01244) 390265. Commercial: (01244) 390243.

*Ground capacity:* 6000.

*Record attendance:* 20,500 v Chelsea, FA Cup 3rd rd (replay), 16 January 1952 (at Sealand Road).

*Record receipts:* £30,609 v Sheffield W, FA Cup 4th rd, 31 January 1987.

*Pitch measurements:* 115yd × 75yd.

*Club Patron:* Duke of Westminster. *Honorary President:* C. Thompson.

*Chairman:* M. S. Guterman. *Manager:* Kevin Ratcliffe.

*Honorary Vice-Presidents:* J. F. Kane, L. Lloyd, Dr. M. D. Swallow.

*Assistant Secretary:* Gill Dugan. *Physio:* Stuart Walker.

*Year Formed:* 1885. *Turned Professional:* 1902. *Ltd Co.:* 1909.

*Previous Name:* Chester until 1983.

*Club Nickname:* 'Blues' and 'City'.

*Previous Grounds:* 1885, Faulkner Street; 1898, The Old Showground; 1901, Whipcord Lane; 1906, Sealand Road; 1990, Moss Rose Ground, Macclesfield; 1992, Deva Stadium, Bumpers Lane.

*Foundation:* All students of soccer history have read about the medieval games of football in Chester, but the present club was not formed until 1884 through the amalgamation of King's School Old Boys with Chester Rovers. For many years Chester were overshadowed in Cheshire by Northwich Victoria and Crewe Alexandra who had both won the Senior Cup several times before Chester's first success in 1894–95.

*First Football League game:* 2 September 1931, Division 3 (N), v Wrexham (a) D 1-1 – Johnson; Herod, Jones; Keeley, Skitt, Reilly; Thompson, Ranson, Jennings (1), Cresswell, Hedley.

*Record League Victory:* 12–0 v York C, Division 3 (N), 1 February 1936 – Middleton; Common, Hall; Wharton, Wilson, Howarth; Horsman (2), Hughes, Wrightson (4), Cresswell (2), Sargeant (4).

*Record Cup Victory:* 6–1 v Darlington, FA Cup 1st rd, 25 November 1933 – Burke; Bennett, Little; Pitcairn, Skitt, Duckworth; Armes (3), Whittam, Mantle (2), Cresswell (1), McLachlan.

*Record Defeat:* 2–11 v Oldham Ath, Division 3 (N), 19 January 1952.

*Most League Points (2 for a win):* 56, Division 3 (N), 1946–47 and Division 4, 1964–65.

*Most League Points (3 for a win):* 84, Division 4, 1985–86.

*Most League Goals:* 119, Division 4, 1964–65.

*Highest League Scorer in Season:* Dick Yates, 36, Division 3 (N), 1946–47.

*Most League Goals in Total Aggregate:* Stuart Rimmer, 135, 1985–88, 1991–98.

*Most Capped Player:* Bill Lewis, 13 (27), Wales.

*Most League Appearances:* Ray Gill, 406, 1951–62.

*Record Transfer Fee Received:* £300,000 from Liverpool for Ian Rush, May 1980.

*Record Transfer Fee Paid:* £94,000 to Barnsley for Stuart Rimmer, August 1991.

*Football League Record:* 1931 Elected Division 3 (N); 1958–75 Division 4; 1975–82 Division 3; 1982–86 Division 4; 1986–92 Division 3; 1992–93 Division 2; 1993–94 Division 3; 1994–95 Division 2; 1995– Division 3.

*Honours: Football League:* Division 3 – Runners-up 1993–94; Division 3 (N) – Runners-up 1935–36; Division 4 – Runners-up 1985–86. *FA Cup:* best season: 5th rd, 1977, 1980. *Football League Cup:* Semi-final 1975. *Welsh Cup:* Winners 1908, 1933, 1947. *Debenhams Cup:* Winners 1977.

*Colours:* Blue and white striped shirts, white shorts, blue and white stockings. *Change colours:* Claret and white.

**Did you know?**
In the season before they were elected to the Football League in 1931-32, Chester scored an incredible 1 goals in the Cheshire County League. No fewer than 73 of these came from Arthur Gale, a schoolmaster.

## CHESTER CITY 1997–98 LEAGUE RECORD

| Match No. | Date | | Venue | Opponents | Result | H/T Score | Lg. Pos. | Goalscorers | Attendance |
|---|---|---|---|---|---|---|---|---|---|
| 1 | Aug | 9 | H | Lincoln C | W 2-0 | 0-0 | — | Flitcroft [64], Bennett [85] | 2478 |
| 2 | | 23 | H | Cambridge U | D 1-1 | 0-1 | 14 | Bennett [68] | 2167 |
| 3 | | 30 | A | Barnet | L 1-2 | 0-0 | 17 | Simpson (og) [61] | 1790 |
| 4 | Sept | 2 | A | Scunthorpe U | L 1-2 | 1-0 | — | Bennett [23] | 2633 |
| 5 | | 5 | H | Hull C | W 1-0 | 1-0 | — | Bennett [42] | 2271 |
| 6 | | 13 | H | Shrewsbury T | W 2-0 | 1-0 | 14 | Bennett 2 [21, 66] | 2853 |
| 7 | | 16 | A | Cardiff C | W 2-0 | 2-0 | — | Alsford [11], Bennett (pen) [32] | 3949 |
| 8 | | 20 | A | Mansfield T | L 1-4 | 1-3 | 10 | Davidson (pen) [18] | 2183 |
| 9 | | 27 | A | Rotherham U | L 2-4 | 0-3 | 12 | Alsford [69], Priest [75] | 3061 |
| 10 | Oct | 4 | H | Hartlepool U | W 3-1 | 2-1 | 6 | Whelan [34], Bennett [38], Murphy [73] | 2163 |
| 11 | | 11 | H | Brighton & HA | W 2-0 | 1-0 | 4 | Bennett 2 [39, 50] | 2402 |
| 12 | | 18 | A | Torquay U | L 1-3 | 0-3 | 5 | Richardson [90] | 2047 |
| 13 | | 21 | A | Scarborough | L 1-4 | 0-2 | — | Thomas [47] | 1451 |
| 14 | | 25 | H | Macclesfield T | D 1-1 | 0-0 | 11 | Priest [78] | 3245 |
| 15 | Nov | 1 | H | Rochdale | W 4-0 | 1-0 | 8 | McDonald [10], Bennett [69], Rimmer 2 [72, 79] | 2431 |
| 16 | | 4 | A | Notts Co | W 2-1 | 0-0 | — | McDonald [60], Bennett [87] | 3104 |
| 17 | | 8 | A | Leyton Orient | L 0-1 | 0-1 | 6 | | 3894 |
| 18 | | 18 | H | Peterborough U | D 0-0 | 0-0 | — | | 2612 |
| 19 | | 26 | H | Swansea C | W 2-0 | 1-0 | — | Flitcroft (pen) [33], Thomas [53] | 1510 |
| 20 | | 29 | H | Exeter C | D 1-1 | 0-1 | 8 | Rimmer [66] | 2288 |
| 21 | Dec | 2 | A | Doncaster R | L 1-2 | 1-1 | — | Jones [13] | 864 |
| 22 | | 13 | H | Darlington | W 2-1 | 0-0 | 7 | McDonald [74], Alsford [80] | 1812 |
| 23 | | 19 | A | Colchester U | L 0-2 | 0-1 | — | | 1867 |
| 24 | | 26 | A | Hull C | W 2-1 | 0-0 | 9 | Whelan [82], Thomas [87] | 6807 |
| 25 | | 28 | H | Scunthorpe U | W 1-0 | 0-0 | 7 | Priest [63] | 2263 |
| 26 | Jan | 10 | A | Lincoln C | W 3-1 | 2-0 | 4 | Priest [37], Jenkins [44], Rimmer [73] | 2913 |
| 27 | | 17 | H | Barnet | L 0-1 | 0-0 | 7 | | 2479 |
| 28 | | 24 | A | Cambridge U | W 2-1 | 0-0 | 6 | Rimmer [53], McDonald [90] | 2473 |
| 29 | | 27 | H | Cardiff C | D 0-0 | 0-0 | — | | 1757 |
| 30 | | 31 | A | Shrewsbury T | D 1-1 | 0-1 | 6 | Woods [70] | 3002 |
| 31 | Feb | 7 | A | Mansfield T | L 0-1 | 0-0 | 9 | | 2055 |
| 32 | | 14 | A | Hartlepool U | D 0-0 | 0-0 | 9 | | 2186 |
| 33 | | 21 | H | Rotherham U | W 4-0 | 0-0 | 8 | Murphy [47], Alsford [50], Priest 2 [71, 87] | 2432 |
| 34 | | 24 | H | Torquay U | L 1-3 | 0-2 | — | Woods [46] | 2163 |
| 35 | | 28 | A | Brighton & HA | L 2-3 | 1-2 | 10 | Flitcroft [8], Murphy [78] | 2510 |
| 36 | Mar | 3 | H | Leyton Orient | D 1-1 | 0-1 | — | Richardson [65] | 1650 |
| 37 | | 7 | A | Rochdale | D 1-1 | 0-0 | 11 | Murphy [85] | 1955 |
| 38 | | 14 | H | Notts Co | L 0-1 | 0-0 | 11 | | 2753 |
| 39 | | 21 | A | Peterborough U | L 1-2 | 1-1 | 11 | McDonald [43] | 4817 |
| 40 | | 28 | A | Swansea C | L 0-2 | 0-1 | 14 | | 2500 |
| 41 | Apr | 4 | A | Exeter C | L 0-5 | 0-3 | 14 | | 2965 |
| 42 | | 11 | H | Doncaster R | W 2-1 | 2-1 | 14 | Flitcroft (pen) [8], Rimmer [35] | 1593 |
| 43 | | 13 | A | Darlington | L 0-1 | 0-0 | 15 | | 1901 |
| 44 | | 18 | A | Colchester U | W 3-1 | 3-0 | 13 | Whelan [19], Fisher [34], Rimmer [36] | 1780 |
| 45 | | 25 | A | Macclesfield T | L 2-3 | 0-1 | 16 | Whelan [52], Thomas [79] | 5982 |
| 46 | May | 2 | H | Scarborough | D 1-1 | 0-0 | 14 | Rimmer [86] | 2719 |

**Final League Position: 14**      1996–97 DIV3 6

### GOALSCORERS

*League (60):* Bennett 12 (1 pen), Rimmer 8, Priest 6, McDonald 5, Alsford 4, Flitcroft 4 (2 pens), Murphy 4, Thomas 4, Whelan 4, Richardson 2, Woods 2, Davidson 1 (pen), Fisher 1, Jenkins 1, Jones 1, own goal 1.
*Coca-Cola Cup (1):* Woods 1.
*FA Cup (2):* Priest 1, Richardson 1.

# Division 3     **CHESTER CITY**

*The Deva Stadium, Bumpers Lane, Chester CH1 4LT.* Telephone: (01244) 371376, 371809. Fax: (01244) 390265. Commercial: (01244) 390243.

*Ground capacity:* 6000.

*Record attendance:* 20,500 v Chelsea, FA Cup 3rd rd (replay), 16 January 1952 (at Sealand Road).

*Record receipts:* £30,609 v Sheffield W, FA Cup 4th rd, 31 January 1987.

*Pitch measurements:* 115yd × 75yd.

*Club Patron:* Duke of Westminster. *Honorary President:* C. Thompson.

*Chairman:* M. S. Guterman. *Manager:* Kevin Ratcliffe.

*Honorary Vice-Presidents:* J. F. Kane, L. Lloyd, Dr. M. D. Swallow.

*Assistant Secretary:* Gill Dugan. *Physio:* Stuart Walker.

*Year Formed:* 1885. *Turned Professional:* 1902. *Ltd Co.:* 1909.

*Previous Name:* Chester until 1983.

*Club Nickname:* 'Blues' and 'City'.

*Previous Grounds:* 1885, Faulkner Street; 1898, The Old Showground; 1901, Whipcord Lane; 1906, Sealand Road; 1990, Moss Rose Ground, Macclesfield; 1992, Deva Stadium, Bumpers Lane.

*Foundation:* All students of soccer history have read about the medieval games of football in Chester, but the present club was not formed until 1884 through the amalgamation of King's School Old Boys with Chester Rovers. For many years Chester were overshadowed in Cheshire by Northwich Victoria and Crewe Alexandra who had both won the Senior Cup several times before Chester's first success in 1894–95.

*First Football League game:* 2 September 1931, Division 3 (N), v Wrexham (a) D 1-1 – Johnson; Herod, Jones; Keeley, Skitt, Reilly; Thompson, Ranson, Jennings (1), Cresswell, Hedley.

*Record League Victory:* 12–0 v York C, Division 3 (N), 1 February 1936 – Middleton; Common, Hall; Wharton, Wilson, Howarth; Horsman (2), Hughes, Wrightson (4), Cresswell (2), Sargeant (4).

*Record Cup Victory:* 6–1 v Darlington, FA Cup 1st rd, 25 November 1933 – Burke; Bennett, Little; Pitcairn, Skitt, Duckworth; Armes (3), Whittam, Mantle (2), Cresswell (1), McLachlan.

*Record Defeat:* 2–11 v Oldham Ath, Division 3 (N), 19 January 1952.

*Most League Points (2 for a win):* 56, Division 3 (N), 1946–47 and Division 4, 1964–65.

*Most League Points (3 for a win):* 84, Division 4, 1985–86.

*Most League Goals:* 119, Division 4, 1964–65.

*Highest League Scorer in Season:* Dick Yates, 36, Division 3 (N), 1946–47.

*Most League Goals in Total Aggregate:* Stuart Rimmer, 135, 1985–88, 1991–98.

*Most Capped Player:* Bill Lewis, 13 (27), Wales.

*Most League Appearances:* Ray Gill, 406, 1951–62.

*Record Transfer Fee Received:* £300,000 from Liverpool for Ian Rush, May 1980.

*Record Transfer Fee Paid:* £94,000 to Barnsley for Stuart Rimmer, August 1991.

*Football League Record:* 1931 Elected Division 3 (N); 1958–75 Division 4; 1975–82 Division 3; 1982–86 Division 4; 1986–92 Division 3; 1992–93 Division 2; 1993–94 Division 3; 1994–95 Division 2; 1995– Division 3.

*Honours: Football League:* Division 3 – Runners-up 1993–94; Division 3 (N) – Runners-up 1935–36; Division 4 – Runners-up 1985–86. *FA Cup:* best season: 5th rd, 1977, 1980. *Football League Cup:* Semi-final 1975. *Welsh Cup:* Winners 1908, 1933, 1947. *Debenhams Cup:* Winners 1977.

*Colours:* Blue and white striped shirts, white shorts, blue and white stockings. *Change colours:* Claret and white.

**Did you know?**
In the season before they were elected to the Football League in 1931-32, Chester scored an incredible 170 goals in the Cheshire County League. No fewer than 73 of these came from Arthur Gale, a schoolmaster.

| Sinclair R 33 | Davidson R 24 | Jenkins I 34 | Fisher N 29+6 | Whelan S 35 | Alsford J 39 | Bennett G 37+4 | Richardson N 41+3 | Rimmer S 26+8 | Flitcroft D 43+1 | Thomas R 25+13 | Murphy J 19+8 | Woods M 24+5 | Milner A 1 | McDonald R 21+10 | Priest C 37 | Jones J 2+5 | Shelton G 3 | Brown W 13 | Dobson R 6 | Giles M 8+2 | McKay M 3+2 | Wright D 3+2 | Shelton A —+2 | Match No. |
|---|---|---|---|---|---|---|---|---|---|---|---|---|---|---|---|---|---|---|---|---|---|---|---|---|
| 1 | 2 | 3 | 4 | 5 | 6 | $7^1$ | 8 | 9 | 10 | $11^2$ | 12 | 13 | | | | | | | | | | | | 1 |
| 1 | 2 | 3 | 4 | 5 | 6 | 7 | $8^1$ | | 10 | 11 | | 12 | | $9^2$ | 13 | | | | | | | | | 2 |
| 1 | 2 | 3 | 4 | 5 | 6 | 7 | 8 | | 10 | | | 12 | | 9 | $11^1$ | | | | | | | | | 3 |
| 1 | 2 | 3 | $4^3$ | 5 | 6 | 7 | $8^1$ | | 10 | 14 | 13 | 12 | | $9^2$ | 11 | | | | | | | | | 4 |
| 1 | 2 | 3 | 11 | 5 | 6 | 7 | 12 | | $10^1$ | 13 | | 4 | | $9^2$ | 8 | | | | | | | | | 5 |
| 1 | 2 | 3 | 11 | 5 | 6 | 7 | 12 | | 10 | 13 | | $4^1$ | | $9^2$ | 8 | | | | | | | | | 6 |
| 1 | 2 | 3 | $11^1$ | 5 | 6 | $7^1$ | 13 | | 10 | 12 | 9 | $4^2$ | | 8 | 14 | | | | | | | | | 7 |
| 1 | 2 | 3 | $11^1$ | 5 | 6 | 7 | 4 | | 10 | 12 | | | | 9 | 8 | | | | | | | | | 8 |
| 1 | $2^2$ | 3 | $11^1$ | 5 | 6 | 7 | 4 | | 10 | 12 | 13 | | | 9 | 8 | | | | | | | | | 9 |
| 1 | $2^1$ | $3^2$ | 12 | 5 | 6 | 7 | 4 | 13 | 10 | $11^1$ | 9 | | | 14 | 8 | | | | | | | | | 10 |
| 1 | | 3 | | 5 | 6 | $7^1$ | 2 | 12 | 10 | $11^2$ | 9 | | | 13 | 8 | 4 | | | | | | | | 11 |
| 1 | | 3 | 12 | 5 | 6 | $7^3$ | 2 | 13 | 10 | 11 | $9^2$ | | | 14 | $8^1$ | 4 | | | | | | | | 12 |
| 1 | | 3 | 4 | 5 | 6 | $7^1$ | 2 | 12 | $10^2$ | 11 | 9 | | | 13 | 8 | | | | | | | | | 13 |
| 1 | | 3 | 4 | 5 | 6 | 7 | 2 | 12 | 10 | $11^1$ | | | | 9 | 8 | | | | | | | | | 14 |
| | | 5 | 3 | | 6 | $7^2$ | 4 | 12 | 10 | $11^1$ | | | | 9 | 8 | 13 | 1 | 2 | | | | | | 15 |
| | | 5 | | | 6 | 7 | 4 | 11 | 10 | | 12 | | | 9 | 8 | | 1 | 2 | 3 | | | | | 16 |
| | | 5 | | | 6 | $7^1$ | 4 | 11 | 10 | 13 | 12 | | | 9 | 8 | | 1 | $2^2$ | 3 | | | | | 17 |
| | 2 | 3 | | 5 | 6 | 7 | 4 | | 9 | 10 | $11^1$ | | | 12 | 8 | | 1 | | | | | | | 18 |
| | 2 | 3 | | 5 | 6 | $7^2$ | 4 | | 9 | 10 | 11 | | | 12 | $8^1$ | 13 | 1 | | | | | | | 19 |
| | 2 | 3 | | 5 | 6 | 7 | 4 | | 9 | 10 | 11 | | | | 8 | | 1 | | | | | | | 20 |
| | 2 | 3 | | 5 | 6 | | 4 | | 10 | 11 | | | | 9 | 8 | 7 | 1 | | | | | | | 21 |
| | 2 | 3 | $8^1$ | 5 | 6 | | 4 | | 9 | $10^2$ | 11 | | | 12 | | 7 | 1 | | | | 13 | | | 22 |
| 1 | 2 | 3 | | 5 | 6 | 7 | 4 | | 9 | 10 | $11^1$ | 12 | | | 8 | | | | | | | | | 23 |
| 1 | 2 | 3 | | 5 | 6 | 7 | 4 | | 9 | 10 | 12 | $8^2$ | | $11^1$ | | 13 | | | | | | | | 24 |
| 1 | 2 | 3 | 12 | 5 | 6 | 7 | 4 | | 9 | 10 | $11^1$ | | | | 8 | | | | | | | | | 25 |
| 1 | $2^1$ | 3 | | 5 | 6 | 7 | 4 | | 9 | 10 | 12 | 11 | | | 8 | | | | | | | | | 26 |
| 1 | | 3 | 2 | | 6 | 7 | 4 | | 9 | $10^1$ | 11 | $5^2$ | | 12 | 8 | | | | | | 13 | | | 27 |
| 1 | 2 | 3 | | | 6 | 7 | 4 | | 9 | 10 | | 5 | | 11 | 8 | | | | | | | | | 28 |
| 1 | 2 | | | | 6 | $7^1$ | 4 | | 9 | 10 | 11 | 5 | | 12 | 8 | | | | 3 | | | | | 29 |
| 1 | | 3 | | 5 | 6 | 7 | 4 | | 9 | 10 | 12 | 2 | | $11^1$ | 8 | | | | 3 | | | | | 30 |
| 1 | 2 | | | | 6 | $7^1$ | 4 | | 9 | 10 | $11^1$ | 12 | | 5 | 13 | 8 | | | 3 | | | | | 31 |
| 1 | 2 | | | | 6 | | 4 | | 9 | 10 | | 5 | | 11 | 8 | 7 | | | 3 | | | | | 32 |
| 1 | $2^1$ | 12 | 5 | 6 | 13 | | $9^2$ | | 7 | 10 | 4 | | | 11 | 8 | | | | 3 | | | | | 33 |
| 1 | 2 | 12 | 5 | 6 | 13 | | $9^2$ | 14 | 7 | 10 | 4 | | | $11^3$ | 8 | | | | $3^1$ | | | | | 34 |
| 1 | 2 | $3^2$ | 5 | 6 | 12 | | 4 | | $9^1$ | 7 | 13 | 10 | | 11 | 8 | | | | | | | | | 35 |
| 1 | 2 | 3 | 12 | | 6 | 7 | 4 | | 10 | $11^1$ | 9 | 5 | | | 8 | | | | | | | | | 36 |
| 1 | 2 | 3 | | | 6 | 7 | 4 | | 10 | | 9 | 5 | | 11 | | | | | | | 8 | | | 37 |
| 1 | 2 | 3 | | | 6 | 7 | 4 | | 10 | 11 | 9 | 5 | | | | | | | | | 8 | | | 38 |
| 1 | 2 | 3 | | 5 | 6 | $7^1$ | 4 | 13 | 10 | $12^2$ | 9 | | | 11 | | | | | | | 8 | | | 39 |
| 1 | 2 | 8 | | 5 | | $7^2$ | 4 | 12 | 10 | | 9 | 6 | | $11^1$ | 13 | | | | 3 | | | | | 40 |
| 1 | 2 | 3 | | 5 | | 7 | 4 | $11^2$ | 10 | 12 | 9 | $6^1$ | | | 8 | | | | | | | 13 | | 41 |
| | | 3 | | 5 | | $7^1$ | 2 | 4 | 10 | 11 | 9 | 6 | | | 8 | | 1 | | | | | 12 | | 42 |
| | | 3 | | 5 | | 12 | 2 | 4 | 10 | $11^2$ | 9 | 6 | | | 8 | | 1 | | 13 | | | $7^1$ | | 43 |
| | | 3 | | 5 | | $7^1$ | 4 | 11 | 10 | | | 6 | | | 8 | | 1 | | $2^2$ | 12 | | 9 | 13 | 44 |
| | | 3 | | 5 | | | 4 | 11 | 10 | 12 | 9 | 6 | | | 8 | | 1 | | 2 | | | $7^1$ | | 45 |
| | | 3 | | 5 | | | 4 | 10 | 7 | 11 | 9 | 6 | | | 8 | | 1 | | $2^1$ | | | | 12 | 46 |

**Coca-Cola Cup**
First Round    Carlisle U    (h) 1-2
                             (a) 0-3

**FA Cup**
First Round    Winsford U    (h) 2-1
Second Round   Wrexham       (h) 0-2

CHESTERFIELD 1997–98   *Back row (left to right):* James Lomas, Tony Lormor, Andy Leaning, Billy Mercer, Darren Carr, Jamie Hewitt.
*Middle row:* Adrian Shaw (Youth Development Officer), Iain Dunn, Mark Williams, Steve Wilkinson, Ian Breckin, Andrew Morris, Steve Gaughan, Chris Beaumont, Roger Willis, Lee Rogers, Dave Rushbury (Physio).
*Front row:* Mark Jules, Tom Curtis, Chris Perkins, Chris Perkins, Kevin Randall (Assistant Manager), John Duncan (Manager), Jonathan Howard, Paul Holland, Marcus Ebdon.

# Division 2      **CHESTERFIELD**

*Recreation Ground, Chesterfield S40 4SX.* Telephone: (01246) 209765. Fax: (01246) 556799. Commercial Dept: (01246) 231535. Spireites Hotline: (0891) 555818.

*Ground capacity:* 8880.

*Record attendance:* 30,968 v Newcastle U, Division 2, 7 April 1939.

*Record receipts:* £45,000 v Mansfield T, Division 3 play-off semi-final, 17 May 1995.

*Pitch measurements:* 113yd × 71yd.

*President:* His Grace the Duke of Devonshire MC, DL, JP.

*Chairman:* J. Norton Lea. *Vice-Chairman:* B. W. Hubbard.

*Directors:* R. F. Pepper, M. L. Warner.

*Manager:* John Duncan.

*Assistant Manager:* Kevin Randall. *Physio:* Dave Rushbury.

*Secretary/General Manager:* Phil Hough. *Commercial Manager:* Jim Brown.

*Stadium Manager:* W. W. Kenworthy.

*Year Formed:* 1866. *Turned Professional:* 1891. *Ltd Co:* 1871.

*Previous Names:* Chesterfield Town.

*Club Nickname:* 'Blues' or 'Spireites'.

*Foundation:* Chesterfield are fourth only to Stoke, Notts County and Nottingham Forest in age for they can trace their existence as far back as 1866, although it is fair to say that they were somewhat casual in the first few years of their history playing only a few friendlies a year. However, their rules of 1871 are still in existence showing an annual membership of 2s (10p), but it was not until 1891 that they won a trophy (the Barnes Cup) and followed this a year later by winning the Sheffield Cup, Barnes Cup and the Derbyshire Junior Cup.

*First Football League game:* 2 September 1899, Division 2, v Sheffield W (a) L 1-5 – Hancock; Pilgrim, Fletcher; Ballantyne, Bell, Downie; Morley, Thacker, Gooing, Munday (1), Geary.

*Record League Victory:* 10–0 v Glossop NE, Division 2, 17 January 1903 – Clutterbuck; Thorpe, Lerper; Haig, Banner, Thacker; Tomlinson (2), Newton (1), Milward (3), Munday (2), Steel (2).

*Record Cup Victory:* 5–0 v Wath Ath (away), FA Cup 1st rd, 28 November 1925 – Birch; Saxby, Dennis; Wass, Abbott, Thompson; Fisher (1), Roseboom (1), Cookson (2), Whitfield (1), Hopkinson.

*Record Defeat:* 0–10 v Gillingham, Division 3, 5 September 1987.

*Most League Points (2 for a win):* 64, Division 4, 1969–70.

*Most League Points (3 for a win):* 91, Division 4, 1984–85.

*Most League Goals:* 102, Division 3 (N), 1930–31.

*Highest League Scorer in Season:* Jimmy Cookson, 44, Division 3 (N), 1925–26.

*Most League Goals in Total Aggregate:* Ernie Moss, 161, 1969–76, 1979–81 and 1984–86.

*Most Capped Player:* Walter McMillen, 4 (7), Northern Ireland.

*Most League Appearances:* Dave Blakey, 613, 1948–67.

*Record Transfer Fee Received:* £200,000 from Wolverhampton W for Alan Birch, August 1981.

*Record Transfer Fee Paid:* £150,000 to Carlisle U for Phil Bonnyman, March 1980.

*Football League Record:* 1899 Elected to Division 2; 1909 failed re-election; 1921–31 Division 3 (N); 1931–33 Division 2; 1933–36 Division 3 (N); 1936–51 Division 2; 1951–58 Division 3 (N); 1958–61 Division 3; 1961–70 Division 4; 1970–83 Division 3; 1983–85 Division 4; 1985–89 Division 3; 1989–92 Division 4; 1992–95 Division 3; 1995– Division 2.

*Honours: Football League:* Division 2 best season: 4th, 1946–47; Division 3 (N) – Champions 1930–31, 1935–36; Runners-up 1933–34; Division 4 – Champions 1969–70, 1984–85. *FA Cup:* Semi-final 1997. *Football League Cup:* best season: 4th rd, 1965. *Anglo-Scottish Cup:* Winners 1981.

*Colours:* Blue shirts, white shorts, blue stockings. *Change colours:* White shirts, blue shorts, white stockings.

**Did you know?**
Chesterfield scored in a Football League record 46 consecutive League games from 25th December 1929 to the 26th December 1930 and finished as champions of Divison 3 North.

## CHESTERFIELD 1997–98 LEAGUE RECORD

| Match No. | Date | Venue | Opponents | Result | H/T Score | Lg. Pos. | Goalscorers | Attendance |
|---|---|---|---|---|---|---|---|---|
| 1 | Aug 9 | H | Walsall | W 3-1 | 1-0 | — | Willis [8], Perkins [81], Lormor [85] | 5193 |
| 2 | 16 | A | Brentford | D 0-0 | 0-0 | 4 | | 4000 |
| 3 | 23 | H | Preston NE | W 3-2 | 3-0 | 2 | Ebdon [31], Jules [35], Hewitt [41] | 6288 |
| 4 | 30 | A | Plymouth Arg | D 1-1 | 0-1 | 3 | Lormor (pen) [85] | 5284 |
| 5 | Sept 2 | A | York C | W 1-0 | 1-0 | — | Morris [42] | 3284 |
| 6 | 7 | H | Burnley | W 1-0 | 1-0 | 2 | Lormor [3] | 7406 |
| 7 | 13 | A | Watford | L 1-2 | 0-1 | 2 | Willis [82] | 11,204 |
| 8 | 20 | H | Bristol R | D 0-0 | 0-0 | 3 | | 5309 |
| 9 | 27 | A | Wrexham | D 0-0 | 0-0 | 3 | | 3921 |
| 10 | Oct 4 | H | Bournemouth | D 1-1 | 0-1 | 4 | Carr [77] | 4482 |
| 11 | 11 | H | Wigan Ath | L 1-2 | 1-1 | 7 | Lormor (pen) [11], Wilkinson [57] | 4673 |
| 12 | 18 | A | Oldham Ath | L 0-2 | 0-0 | 12 | | 5777 |
| 13 | 21 | A | Blackpool | L 1-2 | 0-1 | — | Curtis [61] | 3682 |
| 14 | 25 | H | Wycombe W | W 1-0 | 0-0 | 11 | Holland [48] | 4119 |
| 15 | Nov 1 | A | Fulham | D 1-1 | 0-1 | 10 | Holland [51] | 7998 |
| 16 | 4 | H | Gillingham | D 1-1 | 0-0 | — | Wilkinson [47] | 3420 |
| 17 | 8 | H | Grimsby T | W 1-0 | 0-0 | 9 | Reeves [77] | 5004 |
| 18 | 18 | A | Carlisle U | W 2-0 | 0-0 | — | Ebdon [47], Beaumont [90] | 3591 |
| 19 | 22 | A | Millwall | D 1-1 | 0-0 | 6 | Perkins [68] | 6556 |
| 20 | 29 | H | Southend U | W 1-0 | 0-0 | 4 | Willis [57] | 4101 |
| 21 | Dec 2 | A | Northampton T | D 0-0 | 0-0 | — | | 4824 |
| 22 | 13 | H | Luton T | D 0-0 | 0-0 | 4 | | 4358 |
| 23 | 20 | A | Bristol C | L 0-1 | 0-1 | 8 | | 11,791 |
| 24 | 26 | A | Burnley | D 0-0 | 0-0 | 8 | | 10,861 |
| 25 | 28 | H | York C | D 1-1 | 0-0 | 9 | Reeves [57] | 5320 |
| 26 | Jan 3 | H | Brentford | D 0-0 | 0-0 | 7 | | 4049 |
| 27 | 10 | A | Walsall | L 2-3 | 1-0 | 10 | Reeves [2], Howard [90] | 4042 |
| 28 | 17 | A | Plymouth Arg | W 2-1 | 1-1 | 8 | Wilkinson 2 [12, 47] | 3879 |
| 29 | 24 | A | Preston NE | D 0-0 | 0-0 | 8 | | 8233 |
| 30 | 31 | H | Watford | L 0-1 | 0-0 | 8 | | 5975 |
| 31 | Feb 7 | A | Bristol R | L 1-3 | 1-1 | 12 | Wilkinson [42] | 5481 |
| 32 | 14 | A | Bournemouth | L 0-2 | 0-2 | 13 | | 4271 |
| 33 | 21 | H | Wrexham | W 3-1 | 2-0 | 11 | Howard 2 [12, 45], Reeves [64] | 3919 |
| 34 | 24 | H | Oldham Ath | W 2-1 | 1-0 | — | Howard [44], Williams [63] | 4077 |
| 35 | 28 | A | Wigan Ath | L 1-2 | 1-2 | 11 | Wilkinson [7] | 3017 |
| 36 | Mar 3 | A | Grimsby T | D 0-0 | 0-0 | — | | 4940 |
| 37 | 7 | H | Fulham | L 0-2 | 0-0 | 11 | | 5129 |
| 38 | 14 | A | Gillingham | L 0-1 | 0-0 | 14 | | 5672 |
| 39 | 21 | H | Carlisle U | W 2-1 | 0-1 | 10 | Willis [54], Holland [82] | 3967 |
| 40 | 28 | H | Millwall | W 3-1 | 2-0 | 9 | Willis 2 [20, 55], Howard [23] | 3952 |
| 41 | Apr 3 | A | Southend U | W 2-0 | 1-0 | — | Reeves [25], Willis [88] | 5425 |
| 42 | 11 | H | Northampton T | W 2-1 | 0-1 | 9 | Breckin [48], Williams [71] | 5064 |
| 43 | 14 | A | Luton T | L 0-3 | 0-1 | — | | 5884 |
| 44 | 18 | H | Bristol C | W 1-0 | 1-0 | 9 | Williams [44] | 5085 |
| 45 | 25 | A | Wycombe W | D 1-1 | 1-1 | 9 | Willis [19] | 5113 |
| 46 | May 2 | H | Blackpool | D 1-1 | 0-0 | 10 | Howard [49] | 4462 |

**Final League Position: 10**          1996–97 DIV2 10

## GOALSCORERS

*League (46):* Willis 8, Howard 6, Wilkinson 6, Reeves 5, Lormor 4 (2 pens), Holland 3, Williams 3, Ebdon 2, Perkins 2, Beaumont 1, Breckin 1, Carr 1, Curtis 1, Hewitt 1, Jules 1, Morris 1.
*Coca-Cola Cup (5):* Lormor 3 (2 pens), Willis 2.
*FA Cup (3):* Breckin 1, Reeves 1, Willis 1.

| Mercer B 36 | Hewitt J 44 | Holland P 32+3 | Curtis T 34+2 | Williams M 44 | Carr D 8+2 | Willis R 19+15 | Gaughan S 2 | Lormor T 11+2 | Ebdon M 29+4 | Perkins C 43 | Wilkinson S 24+6 | Dunn I —+7 | Jules M 29+4 | Beaumont C 32+7 | Breckin I 40+3 | Morris A 3+1 | Jackson K —+3 | Howard J 30+5 | Leaning A 5 | Rogers L 2+1 | Garvey S 2+1 | Gayle M 5 | Reeves D 26 | Creaney G 3+1 | Lomas J 2+2 | Misse-Misse J 1 | Lenagh S —+3 | Allardyce C —+1 | Match No. |
|---|---|---|---|---|---|---|---|---|---|---|---|---|---|---|---|---|---|---|---|---|---|---|---|---|---|---|---|---|---|
| 1 | 2 | $3^1$ | 4 | 5 | 6 | 7 | $8^2$ | 9 | $10^3$ | 11 | 12 | 13 | 14 | | | | | | | | | | | | | | | | 1 |
| 1 | 2 | 3 | 4 | 5 | 6 | 7 | | 9 | 10 | 11 | | | | $8^1$ | 12 | | | | | | | | | | | | | | 2 |
| 1 | 2 | 8 | 4 | 5 | 6 | 7 | | 9 | $10^1$ | 11 | | 3 | | | | 12 | | | | | | | | | | | | | 3 |
| 1 | 2 | 8 | 4 | 5 | $6^1$ | | | 9 | $10^3$ | 11 | | | $3^2$ | 13 | 12 | | 7 | 14 | | | | | | | | | | | 4 |
| 1 | 2 | 8 | 4 | 5 | | | | 9 | 10 | 11 | | | 3 | 12 | 6 | | 7 | | | | | | | | | | | | 5 |
| 1 | 2 | 8 | 4 | 5 | | | | 9 | | 11 | | | 3 | $10^5$ | 6 | | 7 | 12 | | | | | | | | | | | 6 |
| 1 | 2 | 8 | 4 | 5 | | 7 | | 9 | | 11 | 12 | | $3^2$ | 13 | 6 | | | $10^1$ | | | | | | | | | | | 7 |
| 1 | 2 | $8^3$ | 4 | 5 | | 7 | | $9^1$ | 13 | 3 | 12 | | 14 | 11 | 6 | | | $10^2$ | | | | | | | | | | | 8 |
| 1 | 2 | | 4 | 5 | | 7 | $9^1$ | 8 | | 11 | 12 | 3 | | | 6 | | | 10 | | | | | | | | | | | 9 |
| 1 | 2 | | 4 | 5 | 12 | $7^2$ | 13 | 10 | $11^1$ | $8^3$ | 14 | 3 | | | 6 | | | 9 | | | | | | | | | | | 10 |
| 1 | 2 | | 4 | 5 | | | | 9 | 10 | 11 | 8 | $12^2$ | 3 | | 6 | | 7 | 13 | | | | | | | | | | | 11 |
| | | | 4 | 5 | | | | 9 | 10 | 11 | 8 | 3 | | 7 | 6 | | | | 1 | $2^5$ | 12 | | | | | | | | 12 |
| | | 8 | 4 | 5 | 12 | | | | $10^2$ | 13 | 11 | 9 | 3 | | 6 | 14 | | | 1 | $2^1$ | $7^3$ | | | | | | | | 13 |
| | 2 | 8 | 4 | 5 | | | | 9 | $10^2$ | 11 | 12 | 3 | 13 | | 6 | | | $7^1$ | 1 | | | | | | | | | | 14 |
| | 2 | 8 | | 5 | | 10 | | $9^1$ | | 11 | | 3 | | 4 | 6 | | 7 | | 1 | | 12 | | | | | | | | 15 |
| | 2 | 8 | 4 | 5 | | 10 | | | | 11 | | 3 | | $7^1$ | 6 | | | 9 | 1 | | 12 | | | | | | | | 16 |
| | 2 | 8 | 4 | 5 | | 10 | | | | 11 | | 3 | | 7 | 6 | | | | | | | 1 | 9 | | | | | | 17 |
| | 2 | 8 | 4 | 5 | | 10 | | | | 11 | 12 | 3 | | 7 | 6 | | | | | | | 1 | $9^1$ | | | | | | 18 |
| | 2 | 8 | 4 | 5 | | 10 | | | | 11 | 12 | 3 | | $7^1$ | 6 | | | | | | | 1 | 9 | | | | | | 19 |
| | 2 | 8 | 4 | 5 | | 10 | | | | 11 | 12 | 3 | | $7^1$ | 6 | | | | | | | 1 | 9 | | | | | | 20 |
| | 2 | 8 | 4 | 5 | | 10 | | | | 11 | | 3 | | 7 | 6 | | | | | | | 1 | 9 | | | | | | 21 |
| 1 | 2 | 8 | 4 | 5 | | 10 | | | | 11 | | 3 | | 7 | 6 | | | | | | | | 9 | | | | | | 22 |
| 1 | 2 | 8 | 4 | 5 | 12 | 10 | | | 13 | 11 | | 3 | $3^1$ | $7^2$ | 6 | | | | | | | | 9 | | | | | | 23 |
| 1 | 2 | 8 | 4 | 5 | 12 | 10 | | | | 11 | | 3 | | 7 | 6 | | | $7^1$ | | | | | 9 | | | | | | 24 |
| 1 | 2 | $8^1$ | 4 | 5 | 12 | 10 | | | | 11 | | 3 | | 7 | 6 | | | 7 | | | | | 9 | | | | | | 25 |
| 1 | 2 | 12 | 4 | 5 | | $10^1$ | | | 13 | 11 | 14 | 3 | | | 6 | | | $7^2$ | | | | | 9 | $8^3$ | | | | | 26 |
| 1 | $2^2$ | 8 | 4 | 5 | 12 | $10^1$ | | | 13 | 11 | | $3^3$ | | | 6 | | | 7 | | | | | 9 | 14 | | | | | 27 |
| 1 | 2 | 8 | 4 | 5 | 12 | 10 | | | | 11 | | 3 | | | 6 | | | 7 | | | | | $9^1$ | | | | | | 28 |
| 1 | 2 | 8 | 4 | 5 | 12 | 10 | | | 13 | $11^2$ | | 3 | | | 6 | | | $7^1$ | | | | | 9 | | | | | | 29 |
| 1 | 2 | 8 | 4 | 5 | 12 | $10^2$ | | | $13^3$ | 11 | 14 | $3^1$ | | | 6 | | | 7 | | | | | 9 | | | | | | 30 |
| 1 | 2 | $8^1$ | 4 | 5 | | 10 | | | 13 | $11^3$ | 12 | $3^2$ | 14 | | 6 | | | 7 | | | | | 9 | | | | | | 31 |
| 1 | 2 | $8^1$ | 4 | 5 | 12 | 10 | | | 13 | $11^2$ | | 3 | | | 6 | | | 7 | | | | | 9 | | | | | | 32 |
| 1 | 2 | $8^5$ | 4 | 5 | 12 | 10 | | | | 11 | | 3 | | | 6 | | | 7 | | | | | 9 | | | | | | 33 |
| 1 | 2 | $8^5$ | 4 | 5 | 12 | 10 | | | | 11 | | 3 | | | 6 | | | 7 | | | | | 9 | | | | | | 34 |
| 1 | 2 | 8 | $4^1$ | 5 | 12 | 10 | | | 13 | 11 | | $3^2$ | | | 6 | | | 7 | | | | | 9 | | | | | | 35 |
| 1 | 2 | 8 | 4 | 5 | 12 | 10 | | | | $11^1$ | | 3 | | | 6 | | | 7 | | | | | 9 | | | | | | 36 |
| 1 | 2 | 8 | 4 | $5^5$ | | 10 | | | | 11 | | 3 | | | 6 | | | 7 | | | | | 9 | | 12 | | | | 37 |
| 1 | 2 | 8 | $4^2$ | 5 | 12 | $10^1$ | | | 13 | | | 3 | | | 6 | | | 7 | | | | | 9 | | $11^{12}$ | 14 | | | 38 |
| 1 | 2 | 8 | 4 | 5 | | 10 | | | | 11 | | 3 | | | 6 | | | 7 | | | | | 9 | | | | | | 39 |
| 1 | 2 | 8 | | 5 | 12 | $10^1$ | | | | 11 | | 3 | | | 6 | | 7 | | | | | | 9 | | | | | | 40 |
| 1 | 2 | $8^1$ | 12 | 5 | | $10^1$ | | | 13 | 11 | | 3 | | | 6 | | 7 | | | | | | 9 | | | | | | 41 |
| 1 | 2 | | 4 | 5 | | 10 | | | | 11 | | 3 | | | 6 | | 7 | 8 | | | | | 9 | | | | | | 42 |
| 1 | 2 | | 4 | 5 | 6 | 7 | | | 10 | 11 | 12 | $3^1$ | | | | | | 8 | | | | | 9 | | | | | | 43 |
| 1 | 2 | | 4 | 5 | $6^1$ | 7 | | | $10^2$ | 11 | 12 | 3 | | | | | | 8 | | | | | 9 | | 13 | | | | 44 |
| 1 | 2 | | 4 | 5 | $6^1$ | 7 | | | $10^2$ | 11 | 12 | 3 | | | | | | $8^1$ | | | | | $9^3$ | | | | 13 | 14 | 45 |
| 1 | 2 | | 4 | 5 | $6^1$ | 7 | | | $10^2$ | 11 | 12 | 3 | | | | | | 8 | | | | | 9 | | | | 13 | | 46 |

**Coca-Cola Cup**
| | | |
|---|---|---|
| First Round | Wigan Ath | (a) 2-1 |
| | | (h) 1-0 |
| Second Round | Barnsley | (h) 1-2 |
| | | (a) 1-4 |

**FA Cup**
| | | |
|---|---|---|
| First Round | Northwich Vic | (h) 1-0 |
| Second Round | Grimsby T | (a) 2-2 |
| | | (h) 0-2 |

COLCHESTER UNITED 1997–98  *Back row (left to right):* Robert Bates, Nicky Haydon, David Rainford, Gavin Armitage.

*Middle row:* Paul Dyer (Reserves Manager), Richard Wilkins, Aaron Skelton, Steve Forbes, Garrett Caldwell, Mark Sale, Carl Emberson, Peter Cawley, David Gregory, Paul Abrahams, Brian Owen (Physio), Geoff Harrop (Youth Development Officer).

*Front row:* Emma-Jane Barrett (Sponsor), Dave Barrett (Sponsor), Joe Dunne, Tony Adcock, Simon Betts, Tony Lock, Micky Cook (Youth Team Manager), Steve Wignall (Manager), Steve Whitton (Assistant Manager), Karl Duguid, Paul Buckle, Scott Stamps, Ian Hathaway, David Greene, Steve Adams (Sponsor).

# Division 2    **COLCHESTER UNITED**

*Layer Rd Ground, Colchester, Essex CO2 7JJ.* Telephone: (01206) 508800. Fax: (01206) 508803. Club Shop: (01206) 561180. Soccer Centre: (01206) 571581. Lottery: (01206) 508820.

*Ground capacity:* 7556.

*Record attendance:* 19,072 v Reading, FA Cup 1st rd, 27 November 1948.

*Record receipts:* £26,330 v Barrow, GM Vauxhall Conference, 2 May 1992.

*Pitch measurements:* 110yd × 71yd.

*Patron:* The Mayor of Colchester.

*Chairman:* Peter Heard. *Directors:* Gordon Parker, John Worsp, Peter Powell.

*Managing Director:* Stephen Gage.

*Manager:* Steve Wignall. *Assistant Manager/Coach:* Steve Whitton. *Youth Coach:* Micky Cook.

*Physio:* Brian Owen. *Consultant Physio:* Ray Cole.

*Secretary:* Mrs Marie Partner. *Marketing Manager:* John Schultz.

*Commercial Manager:* Brian Wheeler. *Lottery Manager:* John Cross. *Stadium Manager:* David Blacknall.

*Year Formed:* 1937. *Turned Professional:* 1937. *Ltd Co.:* 1937.

*Club Nickname:* 'The U's'.

*Foundation:* Colchester United was formed in 1937 when a number of enthusiasts of the much older Colchester Town club decided to establish a professional concern as a limited liability company. The new club continued at Layer Road which had been the amateur club's home since 1909.

*First Football League game:* 19 August 1950, Division 3 (S), v Gillingham (a) D 0-0 – Wright; Kettle, Allen; Bearryman, Stewart, Elder; Jones, Curry, Turner, McKim, Church.

*Record League Victory:* 9–1 v Bradford C, Division 4, 30 December 1961 – Ames; Millar, Fowler; Harris, Abrey, Ron Hunt; Foster, Bobby Hunt (4), King (4), Hill (1), Wright.

*Record Cup Victory:* 7–1 v Yeovil T (away), FA Cup 2nd rd (replay), 11 December 1958 – Ames; Fisher, Fowler; Parker, Milligan, Hammond; Williams (1), McLeod (2), Langman (4), Evans, Wright and 7–1 v Yeading, FA Cup 1st rd (replay), 22 November 1994 – Cheesewright; Betts, English, Cawley, Caesar, Locke (Dennis), Fry, Brown (2), Whitton (2) (Thompson), Kinsella (1), Abrahams (2).

*Record Defeat:* 0–8 v Leyton Orient, Division 4, 15 October 1989.

*Most League Points (2 for a win):* 60, Division 4, 1973–74.

*Most League Points (3 for a win):* 81, Division 4, 1982–83.

*Most League Goals:* 104, Division 4, 1961–62.

*Highest League Scorer in Season:* Bobby Hunt, 38, Division 4, 1961–62.

*Most League Goals in Total Aggregate:* Martyn King, 130, 1956–64.

*Most Capped Player:* None.

*Most League Appearances:* Micky Cook, 613, 1969–84.

*Record Transfer Fee Received:* £100,000 from Birmingham C for Steve McGavin, January 1994.

*Record Transfer Fee Paid:* £40,000 to Lokeren for Dale Tempest, August 1987.

*Football League Record:* 1950 Elected to Division 3 (S); 1958–61 Division 3; 1961–62 Division 4; 1962–65 Division 3; 1965–66 Division 4; 1966–68 Division 3; 1968–74 Division 4; 1974–76 Division 3, 1976–77 Division 4; 1977–81 Division 3; 1981–90 Division 4; 1990–92 GM Vauxhall Conference; 1992–98 Division 3; 1998– Division 2.

*Honours: Football League:* Promoted from Division 3 – 1997–98 (play-offs); Division 4 – Runners-up 1961–62. *FA Cup:* best season: 1971, 6th rd. *Football League Cup:* best season: 5th rd, 1975. *Auto Windscreens Shield:* Runners-up: 1997. *GM Vauxhall Conference:* Winners: 1991–92. *FA Trophy:* Winners: 1992.

*Colours:* Blue and white striped shirts, white shorts, white stockings. *Change colours:* Black/red shirts, black shorts, black stockings with red trim.

**Did you know?**
Neil and David Gregory became the first brothers to appear in the same starting line-up at a Wembley play-offs final for Colchester United against Torquay United on 22 May 1998.

COLCHESTER UNITED FC

## COLCHESTER UNITED 1997–98 LEAGUE RECORD

| Match No. | Date | | Venue | Opponents | Result | H/T Score | Lg. Pos. | Goalscorers | Attendance |
|---|---|---|---|---|---|---|---|---|---|
| 1 | Aug | 9 | H | Darlington | W 2-1 | 1-0 | — | Abrahams 32, Buckle (pen) 60 | 2958 |
| 2 | | 16 | A | Hartlepool U | L 2-3 | 1-1 | 8 | Buckle (pen) 38, Abrahams 60 | 2174 |
| 3 | | 22 | H | Barnet | D 1-1 | 0-0 | — | Wilkins 72 | 3286 |
| 4 | | 30 | A | Torquay U | D 1-1 | 0-0 | 14 | Wilkins 65 | 2081 |
| 5 | Sept | 2 | A | Cambridge U | L 1-4 | 1-1 | — | Gregory D 37 | 3264 |
| 6 | | 8 | H | Brighton & HA | W 3-1 | 1-0 | — | Greene 2 4, 57, Abrahams 49 | 3081 |
| 7 | | 12 | H | Scarborough | W 1-0 | 0-0 | — | Lock 87 | 2756 |
| 8 | | 20 | A | Swansea C | W 1-0 | 0-0 | 7 | Greene 48 | 3414 |
| 9 | | 27 | H | Exeter C | L 1-2 | 0-1 | 9 | Abrahams 52 | 3175 |
| 10 | Oct | 4 | A | Mansfield T | D 1-1 | 1-1 | 9 | Greene 12 | 2341 |
| 11 | | 11 | A | Peterborough U | L 2-3 | 1-0 | 11 | Rankin 32, Adcock 82 | 6277 |
| 12 | | 18 | A | Shrewsbury T | D 1-1 | 0-1 | 13 | Skelton 51 | 2977 |
| 13 | | 21 | H | Doncaster R | W 2-1 | 2-1 | — | Sale 6, Skelton 8 | 2588 |
| 14 | | 25 | A | Leyton Orient | W 2-0 | 1-0 | 7 | Adcock 4, Forbes 77 | 4592 |
| 15 | | 31 | H | Scunthorpe U | D 3-3 | 3-0 | — | Rankin 2, Buckle 35, Sale 40 | 3134 |
| 16 | Nov | 4 | A | Macclesfield T | D 0-0 | 0-0 | — | | 1577 |
| 17 | | 8 | A | Rochdale | L 1-2 | 0-1 | 12 | Duguid 60 | 1702 |
| 18 | | 18 | H | Notts Co | W 2-0 | 0-0 | — | Sale 67, Rankin 86 | 2643 |
| 19 | | 22 | H | Lincoln C | L 0-1 | 0-0 | 12 | | 2932 |
| 20 | | 29 | A | Rotherham U | L 2-3 | 0-1 | 13 | Skelton 48, Sale 61 | 3259 |
| 21 | Dec | 13 | A | Hull C | L 1-3 | 0-0 | 16 | Adcock 89 | 3896 |
| 22 | | 19 | H | Chester C | W 2-0 | 1-0 | — | Adcock 13, Duguid 75 | 1867 |
| 23 | | 26 | A | Brighton & HA | D 4-4 | 3-0 | 14 | Rankin 2 15, 28, Adcock 23, Stamps 73 | 2647 |
| 24 | | 29 | H | Cambridge U | W 3-2 | 1-1 | — | Wilkins 2 45, 48, Skelton 67 | 4518 |
| 25 | Jan | 3 | H | Hartlepool U | L 1-2 | 0-1 | 13 | Buckle 82 | 2885 |
| 26 | | 10 | A | Darlington | L 2-4 | 0-1 | 13 | Gregory N 2 68, 79 | 2170 |
| 27 | | 16 | H | Torquay U | W 1-0 | 0-0 | — | Lock 86 | 2776 |
| 28 | | 20 | H | Cardiff C | W 2-1 | 0-0 | — | Gregory N 69, Buckle 79 | 1929 |
| 29 | | 24 | A | Barnet | L 2-3 | 1-1 | 13 | Skelton 4, Wilkins 83 | 2471 |
| 30 | | 31 | A | Scarborough | D 1-1 | 0-0 | 13 | Whitton 46 | 2219 |
| 31 | Feb | 6 | H | Swansea C | L 1-2 | 1-0 | — | Gregory N 27 | 2789 |
| 32 | | 13 | H | Mansfield T | W 2-0 | 1-0 | — | Lock 30, Gregory D 68 | 2320 |
| 33 | | 21 | A | Exeter C | W 1-0 | 0-0 | 11 | Lock 69 | 3346 |
| 34 | | 24 | A | Shrewsbury T | W 2-0 | 1-0 | — | Gregory N 7, Gregory D 68 | 1972 |
| 35 | | 27 | H | Peterborough U | W 1-0 | 0-0 | — | Branston 61 | 4117 |
| 36 | Mar | 3 | H | Rochdale | D 0-0 | 0-0 | — | | 2112 |
| 37 | | 7 | A | Scunthorpe U | L 0-1 | 0-1 | 10 | | 2143 |
| 38 | | 14 | H | Macclesfield T | W 5-1 | 1-1 | 7 | Sale 2 36, 57, Skelton 76, Abrahams 79, Lock 88 | 2760 |
| 39 | | 21 | A | Notts Co | D 0-0 | 0-0 | 8 | | 6284 |
| 40 | | 28 | A | Lincoln C | W 1-0 | 1-0 | 7 | Dunne 29 | 4040 |
| 41 | Apr | 3 | H | Rotherham U | W 2-1 | 1-1 | — | Skelton 11, Sale 55 | 3824 |
| 42 | | 11 | A | Cardiff C | W 2-0 | 0-0 | 6 | Abrahams 48, Gregory D 59 | 2809 |
| 43 | | 13 | H | Hull C | W 4-3 | 2-1 | 4 | Gregory D 6, Lock 13, Dunne 79, Duguid 90 | 4700 |
| 44 | | 18 | A | Chester C | L 1-3 | 0-3 | 4 | Abrahams 74 | 1780 |
| 45 | | 25 | H | Leyton Orient | D 1-1 | 1-1 | 5 | Gregory N 44 | 6220 |
| 46 | May | 2 | A | Doncaster R | W 1-0 | 0-0 | 4 | Gregory N 57 | 3572 |

**Final League Position: 4**          1996–97 DIV3 8

### GOALSCORERS
*League (72):* Abrahams 7, Gregory N 7, Sale 7, Skelton 7, Lock 6, Adcock 5, Buckle 5 (2 pens), Gregory D 5, Rankin 5, Wilkins 5, Greene 4, Duguid 3, Dunne 2, Branston 1, Forbes 1, Stamps 1, Whitton 1.
*Coca-Cola Cup (1):* Hathaway 1.
*FA Cup (4):* Gregory D 2, Forbes 1, Sale 1.

| Emberson C 46 | Gregory D 42 + 2 | Stamps S 26 + 1 | Skelton A 37 + 2 | Greene D 38 | Cawley P 27 | Wilkins R 37 | Buckle P 33 + 5 | Sale M 38 + 1 | Abrahams P 16 + 9 | Hathaway I 5 + 7 | Forbes S 25 + 10 | Adcock T 19 + 6 | Lock T 14 + 18 | Haydon N 9 + 8 | Whitton S 15 + 6 | Rankin I 10 + 1 | Duguid K 6 + 15 | Brown W —+ 2 | Dunne J 22 + 3 | Betts S 17 | Gregory N 12 + 3 | Branston G 12 | Match No. |
|---|---|---|---|---|---|---|---|---|---|---|---|---|---|---|---|---|---|---|---|---|---|---|---|
| 1 | 2 | 3 | $4^1$ | 5 | 6 | 7 | 8 | $9^2$ | 10 | 11 | 12 | 13 | | | | | | | | | | | 1 |
| 1 | 2 | 3 | $4^1$ | 5 | 6 | 7 | 8 | $9^2$ | 10 | $11^3$ | 12 | 13 | 14 | | | | | | | | | | 2 |
| 1 | 2 | 3 | $4^2$ | 5 | $6^1$ | 7 | 8 | 9 | 10 | $11^3$ | 13 | 12 | 14 | | | | | | | | | | 3 |
| 1 | 2 | 3 | | 5 | 6 | 7 | 8 | 9 | 10 | 11 | 4 | | | | | | | | | | | | 4 |
| 1 | 2 | 3 | | 5 | 6 | 7 | $8^2$ | 9 | 11 | | | $4^1$ | $10^3$ | 14 | 12 | 13 | | | | | | | 5 |
| 1 | 2 | $3^2$ | | 5 | 6 | 7 | 8 | 9 | 11 | | | 4 | $10^1$ | | 12 | 13 | | | | | | | 6 |
| 1 | 2 | 3 | | 5 | 6 | 7 | 8 | 9 | 11 | | 13 | $4^2$ | $10^1$ | | 12 | | | | | | | | 7 |
| 1 | 2 | 3 | | 5 | 6 | 7 | 8 | 9 | 11 | | | $4^2$ | $10^1$ | | 12 | | 13 | | | | | | 8 |
| 1 | 2 | 3 | $4^2$ | 5 | 6 | 7 | 8 | $9^1$ | 11 | | 12 | 13 | | | | 10 | | | | | | | 9 |
| 1 | 2 | 3 | 4 | 5 | 6 | $7^1$ | 8 | 9 | 11 | | 12 | | 10 | | | | | | | | | | 10 |
| 1 | 2 | 3 | 4 | | 6 | 7 | | $9^2$ | 12 | | | $8^1$ | 10 | | 5 | 11 | 13 | | | | | | 11 |
| 1 | | 3 | 4 | | 6 | | 7 | $9^2$ | 12 | | | $8^1$ | 10 | 2 | $5^3$ | 11 | 13 | 14 | | | | | 12 |
| 1 | $2^1$ | 3 | 4 | | 6 | | 7 | 9 | 11 | | | 8 | 10 | 5 | 12 | | | | | | | | 13 |
| 1 | 2 | 3 | 4 | 5 | 6 | | 7 | 9 | 12 | | | 8 | $10^2$ | $11^1$ | 13 | | | | | | | | 14 |
| 1 | 2 | $3^2$ | 4 | 5 | $6^2$ | 7 | 9 | | 8 | | $10^1$ | 12 | | 13 | 11 | | 14 | | | | | | 15 |
| 1 | 2 | 3 | 4 | 5 | 6 | | 12 | 9 | | 8 | $10^1$ | | 7 | $11^3$ | 13 | | | | | | | | 16 |
| 1 | $2^2$ | 3 | 4 | 5 | 6 | | 9 | | 8 | $10^1$ | 12 | | 7 | | 11 | 13 | | | | | | | 17 |
| 1 | 4 | $3^2$ | | 5 | 6 | | 9 | 7 | 12 | 13 | | 10 | 8 | $11^1$ | | 2 | | | | | | | 18 |
| 1 | 4 | | | 5 | 6 | 9 | 7 | 12 | | 13 | 10 | 8 | $11^1$ | | 2 | $3^2$ | | | | | | | 19 |
| 1 | 4 | $8^1$ | | 5 | 6 | 9 | 7 | | 10 | 12 | | 11 | | | 2 | 3 | | | | | | | 20 |
| 1 | 3 | $11^1$ | 4 | 5 | 6 | $7^2$ | 13 | | 12 | $9^3$ | 10 | 14 | 8 | | 2 | | | | | | | | 21 |
| 1 | $3^1$ | 11 | 4 | 5 | 6 | 7 | | 9 | 10 | | 8 | 12 | | | 2 | | | | | | | | 22 |
| 1 | 3 | 11 | $4^1$ | 5 | 6 | 7 | 12 | $9^2$ | 10 | | 8 | 13 | | | 2 | | | | | | | | 23 |
| 1 | 3 | 14 | 4 | 5 | 6 | 7 | | $9^2$ | $10^1$ | 12 | 13 | 8 | $11^1$ | | 2 | | | | | | | | 24 |
| 1 | $3^3$ | 4 | 5 | 6 | 7 | 12 | 9 | | $10^2$ | 13 | 14 | $8^1$ | 2 | 11 | | | | | | | | | 25 |
| 1 | 12 | $3^1$ | $4^2$ | 5 | 6 | 7 | 11 | 10 | | 14 | 13 | 2 | $8^3$ | 9 | | | | | | | | | 26 |
| 1 | 12 | $3^2$ | 4 | 5 | $6^1$ | 7 | 11 | 10 | 8 | 13 | 2 | 9 | | | | | | | | | | | 27 |
| 1 | 6 | 3 | $4^1$ | 5 | 7 | 11 | $10^2$ | 8 | 13 | $2^3$ | 12 | 14 | 9 | | | | | | | | | | 28 |
| 1 | 6 | $3^3$ | 4 | 5 | 7 | $11^1$ | 10 | $8^2$ | 13 | 14 | 12 | 2 | 9 | | | | | | | | | | 29 |
| 1 | 6 | 4 | 5 | 7 | 10 | 8 | 3 | 11 | | | | 2 | 9 | | | | | | | | | | 30 |
| 1 | 6 | 4 | 5 | 7 | 12 | $10^2$ | 8 | 13 | $3^3$ | $11^1$ | 14 | 2 | 9 | | | | | | | | | | 31 |
| 1 | 2 | 12 | $5^2$ | 7 | 6 | $8^1$ | 10 | 11 | 13 | 3 | 9 | 4 | | | | | | | | | | | 32 |
| 1 | 2 | 4 | 7 | 6 | 8 | 10 | 11 | 3 | 9 | 5 | | | | | | | | | | | | | 33 |
| 1 | 2 | 11 | 4 | 7 | 6 | 8 | 12 | $10^1$ | 3 | 9 | 5 | | | | | | | | | | | | 34 |
| 1 | $2^2$ | 4 | 7 | 6 | $8^1$ | 9 | 10 | 11 | 12 | 13 | 3 | 5 | | | | | | | | | | | 35 |
| 1 | 4 | 7 | 6 | $11^1$ | 12 | 8 | 9 | 10 | 2 | 3 | 5 | | | | | | | | | | | | 36 |
| 1 | $11^1$ | 4 | 7 | 6 | 13 | 12 | $9^2$ | 10 | 8 | 2 | 3 | 5 | | | | | | | | | | | 37 |
| 1 | 6 | 4 | $5^3$ | 7 | 8 | 9 | 12 | 13 | $10^2$ | 14 | $11^1$ | 2 | 3 | | | | | | | | | | 38 |
| 1 | 6 | $4^1$ | 5 | 7 | 8 | $9^2$ | $11^3$ | 13 | 10 | 12 | 14 | 2 | 3 | | | | | | | | | | 39 |
| 1 | 11 | 4 | 5 | 7 | 8 | 9 | 12 | 13 | $10^1$ | $2^2$ | 3 | 6 | | | | | | | | | | | 40 |
| 1 | 11 | 4 | 5 | 7 | 8 | $9^1$ | 12 | $10^2$ | 2 | 3 | 13 | 6 | | | | | | | | | | | 41 |
| 1 | 11 | 4 | 5 | 7 | 8 | $9^3$ | 12 | $10^2$ | 13 | 2 | 3 | 14 | $6^1$ | | | | | | | | | | 42 |
| 1 | $11^1$ | 4 | 5 | 7 | 8 | $9^3$ | 12 | $10^2$ | 13 | 2 | 3 | 14 | 6 | | | | | | | | | | 43 |
| 1 | 11 | $4^2$ | 5 | 7 | $8^1$ | $9^3$ | 12 | 13 | 10 | 14 | 2 | 3 | 6 | | | | | | | | | | 44 |
| 1 | 4 | 12 | $5^1$ | 7 | 8 | $9^3$ | $11^2$ | 13 | 14 | 2 | 3 | 10 | 6 | | | | | | | | | | 45 |
| 1 | 4 | 6 | 5 | $7^2$ | 8 | $9^1$ | $11^3$ | 13 | 12 | 14 | 2 | 3 | 10 | | | | | | | | | | 46 |

**Coca-Cola Cup**
First Round  Luton T  (h) 0-1
                      (a) 1-1

**FA Cup**
First Round  Brentford  (a) 2-2
                        (h) 0-0
Second Round  Hereford U  (h) 1-1
                          (a) 1-1

COVENTRY CITY 1997–98 *Back row (left to right):* Andrew Ducros, Chris Barnett, Scott Goodwin, Gavin Strachan, George Dalton (Physio), Garry Pendrey (Reserve Team Manager), Jim Blyth (Goalkeeping Coach), Alec Miller (Assistant Team Manager), Roger Spry (Conditioning Coach), Craig Faulconbridge, John Andrews, Barry Prenderville, Barry Quinn.
*Middle row:* Adam Willis, Paul Telfer, Brian Borrows, Michael O'Niell, Noel Whelan, Marcus Hall, Magnus Hedman, Steve Ogrizovic, Gary Breen, Liam Daish, Simon Haworth, Richard Shaw, Willie Boland, Kevin Richardson, Sam Shilton.
*Front row:* John Salako, Martin Johansen, Kyle Lightbourne, Trond Egil Soltvedt, Dion Dublin, Gordon Strachan (Manager), Gary McAllister, Paul Williams, Roland Nilsson, David Burrows, Darren Huckerby.

# FA Premiership     **COVENTRY CITY**

*Highfield Road Stadium, King Richard Street, Coventry CV2 4FW.* Telephone: (01203) 234000. Fax: (01203) 234099. Ticket Office: (01203) 234020. Ticket Office Fax: (01203) 234023. Sales & Marketing: (01203) 234010. Clubcall: 0891 121166. Internet: http://www.ccfc.co.uk. Email: chris.m@ccfc.co.uk

*Ground capacity:* 23,611.

*Record attendance:* 51,455 v Wolverhampton W, Division 2, 29 April 1967.

*Record receipts:* £375,510 v Sheffield U, FA Cup 6th Rd, 7 March 1998.

*Pitch measurements:* 110yd × 75yd.

*President:* E. W. Grove.

*Chairman:* B. A. Richardson. *Deputy Chairman:* M. C. McGinnity.

*Directors:* A. M. Jepson, J. F. W Reason, D. A. Higgs, Miss B. Price.

*Secretary:* Graham Hover.

*Manager:* Gordon Strachan. *Coaches:* Garry Pendrey and Trevor Peake.

*Physio:* George Dalton.

*Director of Sales & Marketing :* Mark Jones. *Stadium Manager:* Don Blair.

*Club Statistician:* Jim Brown.

*Year Formed:* 1883. *Turned Professional:* 1893. *Ltd Co.:* 1907.

*Previous Names:* 1883–98, Singers FC; 1898, Coventry City FC.

*Club Nickname:* 'Sky Blues'.

*Previous Grounds:* Binley Road, 1883–87; Stoke Road, 1887–99; Highfield Road, 1899–.

*Foundation:* Workers at Singers' cycle factory formed a club in 1883. The first success of Singers' FC was to win the Birmingham Junior Cup in 1891 and this led in 1894 to their election to the Birmingham and District League. Four years later they changed their name to Coventry City and joined the Southern League in 1908 at which time they were playing in blue and white quarters.

*First Football League game:* 30 August 1919, Division 2, v Tottenham H (h) L 0-5 – Lindon; Roberts, Chaplin, Allan, Hawley, Clarke, Sheldon, Mercer, Sambrooke, Lowes, Gibson.

*Record League Victory:* 9–0 v Bristol C, Division 3 (S), 28 April 1934 – Pearson; Brown, Bisby; Perry, Davidson, Frith; White (2), Lauderdale, Bourton (5), Jones (2), Lake.

*Record Cup Victory:* 7–0 v Scunthorpe U, FA Cup 1st rd, 24 November 1934 – Pearson; Brown, Bisby; Mason, Davidson, Boileau; Birtley (2), Lauderdale (2), Bourton (1), Jones (1), Liddle (1).

*Record Defeat:* 2–10 v Norwich C, Division 3 (S), 15 March 1930.

*Most League Points (2 for a win):* 60, Division 4, 1958–59 and Division 3, 1963–64.

*Most League Points (3 for a win):* 63, Division 1, 1986–87.

*Most League Goals:* 108, Division 3 (S), 1931–32.

*Highest League Scorer in Season:* Clarrie Bourton, 49, Division 3 (S), 1931–32.

*Most League Goals in Total Aggregate:* Clarrie Bourton, 171, 1931–37.

*Most Capped Player:* Roland Nilsson, 94, Sweden.

*Most League Appearances:* Steve Ogrizovic, 502, 1984–98.

*Record Transfer Fee Received:* £3,750,000 from Liverpool for Phil Babb, September 1994.

*Record Transfer Fee Paid:* £3,500,000 to Grasshoppers for Viorel Moldovan, December 1997.

*Football League Record:* 1919 Elected to Division 2; 1925–26 Division 3 (N); 1926–36 Division 3 (S); 1936–52 Division 2; 1952–58 Division 3 (S); 1958–59 Division 4; 1959–64 Division 3; 1964–67 Division 2; 1967–92 Division 1; 1992– FA Premier League.

*Honours: Football League:* Division 1 best season: 6th, 1969–70; Division 2 – Champions 1966–67; Division 3 – Champions 1963–64; Division 3 (S) – Champions 1935–36; Runners-up 1933–34; Division 4 – Runners-up 1958–59. *FA Cup:* Winners 1987. *Football League Cup:* best season: Semi-final 1981, 1990. **European Competitions:** *European Fairs Cup:* 1970–71.

*Colours:* Sky blue and navy stripes with white side stripes, sky blue shorts and stockings. *Change colours:* Purple and gold.

**Did you know?**
On 19 February 1910 Coventry City, then a Southern League club, beat First Division Nottingham Forest 3-1 in a Third Round FA Cup tie. Coventry had trained all week at Droitwich with walks and brine baths.

## COVENTRY CITY 1997–98 LEAGUE RECORD

| Match No. | Date | Venue | Opponents | Result | H/T Score | Lg. Pos. | Goalscorers | Attendance |
|---|---|---|---|---|---|---|---|---|
| 1 | Aug 9 | H | Chelsea | W 3-2 | 1-1 | — | Dublin 3 [41, 82, 88] | 22,691 |
| 2 | 11 | A | Arsenal | L 0-2 | 0-1 | — | | 37,324 |
| 3 | 23 | H | Bolton W | D 2-2 | 2-0 | 10 | Telfer [8], Huckerby [20] | 16,640 |
| 4 | 27 | H | West Ham U | D 1-1 | 1-0 | — | Huckerby [38] | 18,291 |
| 5 | 30 | A | Manchester U | L 0-3 | 0-1 | 12 | | 55,074 |
| 6 | Sept 13 | H | Southampton | W 1-0 | 0-0 | 8 | Soltvedt [65] | 18,666 |
| 7 | 20 | A | Sheffield W | D 0-0 | 0-0 | 11 | | 21,087 |
| 8 | 24 | H | Crystal Palace | D 1-1 | 1-1 | — | Dublin [8] | 15,910 |
| 9 | 28 | A | Blackburn R | D 0-0 | 0-0 | 12 | | 19,086 |
| 10 | Oct 4 | H | Leeds U | D 0-0 | 0-0 | 12 | | 17,771 |
| 11 | 20 | A | Barnsley | L 0-2 | 0-1 | — | | 17,476 |
| 12 | 25 | H | Everton | D 0-0 | 0-0 | 15 | | 18,755 |
| 13 | Nov 1 | A | Wimbledon | W 2-1 | 2-1 | 12 | Huckerby [17], Dublin [22] | 11,201 |
| 14 | 8 | H | Newcastle U | D 2-2 | 1-1 | 10 | Dublin 2 [4, 82] | 22,670 |
| 15 | 22 | A | Derby Co | L 1-3 | 0-3 | 12 | Huckerby [71] | 29,351 |
| 16 | 29 | H | Leicester C | L 0-2 | 0-1 | 15 | | 18,332 |
| 17 | Dec 6 | A | Aston Villa | L 0-3 | 0-1 | 16 | | 33,250 |
| 18 | 13 | H | Tottenham H | W 4-0 | 1-0 | 14 | Huckerby 2 [42, 84], Breen [63], Hall [87] | 19,490 |
| 19 | 20 | A | Liverpool | L 0-1 | 0-1 | 16 | | 39,707 |
| 20 | 26 | A | West Ham U | L 0-1 | 0-1 | 17 | | 22,477 |
| 21 | 28 | H | Manchester U | W 3-2 | 1-1 | 14 | Whelan [12], Dublin (pen) [86], Huckerby [88] | 23,055 |
| 22 | Jan 10 | A | Chelsea | L 1-3 | 1-0 | 17 | Telfer [30] | 33,395 |
| 23 | 17 | H | Arsenal | D 2-2 | 1-0 | 16 | Whelan [21], Dublin (pen) [66] | 22,777 |
| 24 | 31 | A | Bolton W | W 5-1 | 1-1 | 13 | Whelan [26], Huckerby 2 [58, 65], Dublin 2 [73, 79] | 25,000 |
| 25 | Feb 7 | A | Sheffield W | W 1-0 | 0-0 | 12 | Dublin (pen) [74] | 18,371 |
| 26 | 18 | A | Southampton | W 2-1 | 2-0 | — | Whelan [14], Huckerby [29] | 15,091 |
| 27 | 21 | H | Barnsley | W 1-0 | 0-0 | 10 | Dublin (pen) [89] | 20,262 |
| 28 | 28 | A | Crystal Palace | W 3-0 | 2-0 | 10 | Telfer [1], Moldovan [40], Dublin [77] | 21,810 |
| 29 | Mar 14 | A | Newcastle U | D 0-0 | 0-0 | 10 | | 36,762 |
| 30 | 28 | H | Derby Co | W 1-0 | 1-0 | 9 | Huckerby [44] | 18,700 |
| 31 | Apr 4 | A | Leicester C | D 1-1 | 0-0 | 10 | Whelan [80] | 21,137 |
| 32 | 11 | H | Aston Villa | L 1-2 | 0-1 | 11 | Whelan [59] | 22,790 |
| 33 | 13 | A | Tottenham H | D 1-1 | 0-0 | 10 | Dublin [86] | 33,463 |
| 34 | 19 | H | Liverpool | D 1-1 | 0-1 | 11 | Dublin (pen) [47] | 22,724 |
| 35 | 25 | A | Leeds U | D 3-3 | 2-2 | 11 | Huckerby 3 [20, 34, 62] | 36,868 |
| 36 | 29 | H | Wimbledon | D 0-0 | 0-0 | — | | 17,947 |
| 37 | May 2 | H | Blackburn R | W 2-0 | 2-0 | 11 | Dublin (pen) [19], Boateng [34] | 18,792 |
| 38 | 10 | A | Everton | D 1-1 | 0-1 | 11 | Dublin [89] | 40,109 |

**Final League Position: 11**     1996–97 PREM 17

### GOALSCORERS

*League (46):* Dublin 18 (6 pens), Huckerby 14, Whelan 6, Telfer 3, Boateng 1, Breen 1, Hall 1, Moldovan 1, Soltvedt 1.
*Coca-Cola Cup (7):* McAllister 2 (2 pens), Salako 2, Dublin 1, Hall 1, Haworth 1.
*FA Cup (8):* Dublin 4 (1 pen), Telfer 2, Huckerby 1, Moldovan 1.

| Ogrizovic S 24 | Telfer P 33 | Burrows D 33 | Williams P 17 + 3 | Shaw G 33 | Breen G 30 | Huckerby D 32 + 2 | Solvedt T 26 + 4 | Dublin D 36 | McAllister G 14 | Salako J 11 | Boland W 8 + 11 | Lightbourne K 1 + 6 | Richardson K 3 | Nilsson R 32 | Hall M 20 + 5 | Ducros A 1 + 2 | Shilton S 2 | O'Neill M 2 + 2 | Haworth S 4 + 6 | Johansen M — + 2 | Whelan N 21 | Strachan G 2 + 7 | Hedman M 14 | Boateng G 14 | Moldovan V 5 + 5 | Match No. |
|---|---|---|---|---|---|---|---|---|---|---|---|---|---|---|---|---|---|---|---|---|---|---|---|---|---|---|
| 1 | 2 | 3 | 4 | 5 | $6^1$ | $7^2$ | 8 | 9 | 10 | 11 | 12 | 13 | | | | | | | | | | | | | | 1 |
| 1 | 2 | 3 | 4 | 5 | 6 | $7^2$ | $8^1$ | 9 | 10 | 11 | 12 | 13 | | | | | | | | | | | | | | 2 |
| 1 | 2 | 3 | 4 | 5 | 6 | 7 | $8^1$ | 9 | | 11 | 12 | | | 10 | | | | | | | | | | | | 3 |
| 1 | 2 | 3 | 4 | 5 | 6 | $7^2$ | $8^1$ | 9 | | 11 | 12 | 13 | | 10 | | | | | | | | | | | | 4 |
| 1 | 7 | 3 | 4 | 5 | | 8 | | 9 | | 11 | | | 6 | 2 | 10 | | | | | | | | | | | 5 |
| 1 | 7 | 3 | 4 | 5 | | 8 | 6 | 9 | 10 | 11 | | | | 2 | | | | | | | | | | | | 6 |
| 1 | 7 | 3 | 4 | 5 | | | $6^1$ | 9 | 10 | 11 | 12 | | | 2 | 8 | | | | | | | | | | | 7 |
| 1 | 7 | 3 | 4 | 5 | | | | 9 | 10 | | 12 | 13 | | 2 | 6 | $8^2$ | $11^1$ | | | | | | | | | 8 |
| 1 | $7^2$ | 3 | | 5 | 6 | $8^1$ | | 9 | 10 | 11 | 12 | | | 2 | 4 | | | 13 | | | | | | | | 9 |
| 1 | | 3 | | 5 | 6 | | 8 | 9 | 10 | 11 | 7 | | | 2 | $12^2$ | | | $4^1$ | 13 | | | | | | | 10 |
| 1 | | 3 | | 5 | 6 | | | 10 | 11 | 7 | | $9^1$ | | 2 | 4 | | | | | | 8 | 12 | | | | 11 |
| 1 | | 3 | 4 | 5 | | 7 | 8 | | 10 | $11^1$ | | | | 2 | 6 | | | | | | 9 | 12 | | | | 12 |
| 1 | 2 | 3 | 4 | 5 | 6 | 7 | 8 | 9 | 10 | | | | | 11 | | | | | | | | | | | | 13 |
| 1 | 7 | 3 | 4 | 5 | 6 | $11^1$ | | 9 | 10 | | | | | 2 | 8 | | | | | | 12 | | | | | 14 |
| 1 | 7 | 3 | $4^2$ | 5 | 6 | 12 | | 9 | 10 | | | 13 | | 2 | 8 | | | | | | $11^1$ | | | | | 15 |
| 1 | 7 | | 4 | 5 | 6 | 8 | 12 | 9 | $10^1$ | | | $11^2$ | | 2 | 3 | | | | | | 13 | | | | | 16 |
| 1 | $7^2$ | 3 | 4 | 5 | 6 | $11^2$ | 8 | 9 | | | | | | 2 | 12 | | | | 13 | | $10^1$ | 14 | | | | 17 |
| | 7 | 3 | | 5 | 6 | 11 | 12 | 9 | $10^1$ | | | | | 2 | 4 | | | | 13 | | $8^2$ | | 1 | | | 18 |
| | 7 | | | 5 | | 11 | $8^2$ | 6 | | | 12 | | | 2 | 3 | 12 | | $9^1$ | | | 10 | 13 | 1 | 4 | | 19 |
| | 7 | | | 5 | | 9 | | 4 | | | 12 | | | 2 | 6 | 3 | $11^1$ | | | | 8 | | 1 | 10 | | 20 |
| | 7 | 3 | 4 | 5 | | 11 | 12 | 9 | | | 13 | | | 2 | $6^1$ | | | | | | 8 | | 1 | $10^2$ | | 21 |
| | 2 | 3 | 4 | 5 | 6 | 10 | | 9 | | $11^1$ | 7 | | | 2 | | | | | | | 8 | | 1 | | 12 | 22 |
| | 7 | 3 | 4 | | 5 | 11 | 8 | 9 | | | | | | 2 | | | | | | | 10 | | 1 | 6 | | 23 |
| | 7 | 3 | | $5^1$ | 6 | $11^3$ | 8 | 9 | | | | | | 2 | 12 | | | | | | 10 | 13 | 1 | $4^2$ | 14 | 24 |
| | 7 | 3 | | 5 | 6 | 11 | $8^1$ | 9 | | | | | | 2 | 10 | | | | | | 12 | 1 | | 4 | | 25 |
| | | 3 | | | 6 | 11 | 8 | 5 | | | 12 | | | 2 | 4 | | | | | | 9 | $7^1$ | 1 | | 10 | 26 |
| | 7 | 3 | | | 6 | 11 | $8^1$ | 5 | | | | | | 2 | 13 | | | | | | 9 | 12 | 1 | 4 | $10^2$ | 27 |
| | 7 | | | | 6 | 11 | $8^1$ | 5 | | | | | | 2 | 3 | | | | | | 9 | 12 | 1 | 4 | 10 | 28 |
| 1 | $7^1$ | 3 | | | 6 | 11 | 8 | 5 | | | | | | 2 | | | | | | | 13 | 9 | 12 | 4 | $10^2$ | 29 |
| 1 | 7 | 3 | | | 5 | 6 | 11 | 8 | 9 | | | | | 2 | | | | | | | 10 | | | 4 | | 30 |
| 1 | 7 | 3 | | | 5 | 6 | 11 | 8 | 9 | | | | | 2 | | | | | | | 10 | | | 4 | | 31 |
| 1 | 7 | 3 | | | 5 | 6 | 11 | $8^2$ | 9 | | | | | 2 | 12 | | | | | | 10 | | | $4^1$ | 13 | 32 |
| 1 | 7 | 3 | | | 5 | 6 | 12 | 13 | 9 | | | 14 | | 2 | $4^2$ | | | | | | 8 | $11^3$ | | | $10^1$ | 33 |
| 1 | | 3 | 12 | 5 | 6 | 11 | 8 | 9 | | | $7^1$ | | | 2 | 4 | | | | | | 10 | | | | | 34 |
| 1 | 7 | | 12 | 5 | 6 | 8 | 4 | 9 | | 11 | | | | 2 | $3^1$ | | | | | | 10 | | | | | 35 |
| | 7 | 3 | | | 5 | 6 | 11 | $8^1$ | 9 | | | 4 | | 2 | | | | | | | 10 | 1 | | | 12 | 36 |
| | 7 | 3 | | | 5 | 6 | $11^2$ | 8 | 9 | | | 12 | | 2 | | | | | | | 10 | 1 | | $4^1$ | 13 | 37 |
| | $7^2$ | 3 | 12 | 5 | 6 | $11^3$ | 8 | 9 | | | | | | 2 | 13 | | | | | 14 | 10 | 1 | 4 | | | 38 |

**Coca-Cola Cup**

| | | | | |
|---|---|---|---|---|
| Second Round | Blackpool | (a) | 0-1 | |
| | | (h) | 3-1 | |
| Third Round | Everton | (h) | 4-1 | |
| Fourth Round | Arsenal | (a) | 0-1 | |

**FA Cup**

| | | | | |
|---|---|---|---|---|
| Third Round | Liverpool | (a) | 3-1 | |
| Fourth Round | Derby Co | (h) | 2-0 | |
| Fifth Round | Aston Villa | (a) | 1-0 | |
| Sixth Round | Sheffield U | (h) | 1-1 | |
| | | (a) | 1-1 | |

CREWE ALEXANDRA 1997–98    *Back row (left to right):* Jamie Moralee, Phil Charnock, Steve Pope, Steve Anthrobus, Dele Adebola, Chris Lightfoot, Ashley Westwood, Francis Tierney.
*Middle row:* Terry McPhillips (Assistant Youth Coach), John Fleet (Kit Man), Steve Holland (Youth Coach), Richard Norris, Lee Unsworth, Neil Cutler, Jason Kearton, Mark Rivers, Peter Smith, Neil Baker (Assistant Manager), Dario Gradi (Manager).
*Front row:* Kevin Street, Kenny Lunt, David Wright, Shaun Smith, Steve Macauley, Seth Johnson, Colin Little, James Collins, Steve Garvey.

# Division 1      **CREWE ALEXANDRA**

*Football Ground, Gresty Rd, Crewe CW2 6EB.* Telephone: (01270) 213014.

*Ground capacity:* 6000.

*Record attendance:* 20,000 v Tottenham H, FA Cup 4th rd, 30 January 1960.

*Record receipts:* £41,093 v Liverpool, FA Cup 3rd rd, 6 January 1992.

*Pitch measurements:* 112yd × 74yd.

*President:* N. Rowlinson.

*Chairman:* J. Bowler. *Vice-Chairman:* N. Hassall.

*Directors:* D. Rowlinson, R. Clayton, J. McMillan, D. Gradi.

*Manager:* Dario Gradi MBE.

*Secretary:* Mrs Gill Palin. *Marketing Manager:* Alison Bowler.

*Year Formed:* 1877. *Turned Professional:* 1893. *Ltd Co.:* 1892.

*Club Nickname:* 'Railwaymen'.

*Foundation:* Crewe Alexandra played cricket before they decided to form a football club in 1877. They took the name "Alexandra" after Princess Alexandra. Crewe's first trophy was the Crewe and District Cup in 1887 and it is worth noting that they reached the semi-finals of the FA Cup the following year.

*First Football League game:* 3 September 1892, Division 2, v Burton Swifts (a) L 1-7 – Hickton; Moore, Cope; Linnell, Johnson, Osborne; Bennett, Pearson (1), Bailey, Barnett, Roberts.

*Record League Victory:* 8–0 v Rotherham U, Division 3 (N), 1 October 1932 – Foster; Pringle, Dawson; Ward, Keenor (1), Turner (1); Gillespie, Swindells (1), McConnell (2), Deacon (2), Weale (1).

*Record Cup Victory:* 8–0 v Hartlepool U, Auto Windscreens Shield 1st rd, 17 October 1995 – Gayle; Collins (1), Booty, Westwood (Unsworth), Macauley (1), Whalley (1), Garvey (1), Murphy (1), Savage (1) (Rivers (pen)), Lennon, Edwards (1 og).

*Record Defeat:* 2–13 v Tottenham H, FA Cup 4th rd replay, 3 February 1960.

*Most League Points (2 for a win):* 59, Division 4, 1962–63.

*Most League Points (3 for a win):* 83, Division 2, 1994–95.

*Most League Goals:* 95, Division 3 (N), 1931–32.

*Highest League Scorer in Season:* Terry Harkin, 35, Division 4, 1964–65.

*Most League Goals in Total Aggregate:* Bert Swindells, 126, 1928–37.

*Most Capped Player:* Bill Lewis, 9 (27), Wales.

*Most League Appearances:* Tommy Lowry, 436, 1966–78.

*Record Transfer Fee Received:* £1,500,000 from Liverpool for Danny Murphy, July 1997.

*Record Transfer Fee Paid:* £500,000 to Shrewsbury for Dave Walton, October 1997.

*Football League Record:* 1892 Original Member of Division 2; 1896 Failed re-election; 1921 Re-entered Division 3 (N); 1958–63 Division 4; 1963–64 Division 3; 1964–68 Division 4; 1968–69 Division 3; 1969–89 Division 4; 1989–91 Division 3; 1991–92 Division 4; 1992–94 Division 3; 1994–97 Division 2; 1997– Division 1.

*Honours: Football League:* Promoted from Division 2 1996–97 (play-offs). *FA Cup:* best season: semi-final 1888. *Football League Cup:* best season: 3rd rd, 1975, 1976, 1979, 1993. *Welsh Cup:* Winners 1936, 1937.

*Colours:* Red shirts, white shorts, red stockings. *Change colours:* White shirts with gold and navy trim, white shorts, white stockings.

**Did you know?**
When Crewe Alexandra visited Sunderland on 18 April 1998, the crowd of 40,441 was the highest attendance they had played in front of.

## CREWE ALEXANDRA 1997–98 LEAGUE RECORD

| Match No. | Date | Venue | Opponents | Result | H/T Score | Lg. Pos. | Goalscorers | Attendance |
|---|---|---|---|---|---|---|---|---|
| 1 | Aug 9 | A | Swindon T | L | 0-2 | 0-1 | — | 8334 |
| 2 | 16 | H | WBA | L | 2-3 | 1-1 | 21 | Adebola [35], Rivers [63] | 5234 |
| 3 | 23 | A | Norwich C | W | 2-0 | 1-0 | 14 | Rivers [29], Smith S [60] | 11,821 |
| 4 | Sept 2 | H | Bury | L | 1-2 | 1-1 | — | Smith S (pen) [43] | 4447 |
| 5 | 13 | A | Portsmouth | W | 3-2 | 1-0 | 19 | Rivers [1], Anthrobus [57], Adebola [85] | 9505 |
| 6 | 16 | H | Port Vale | L | 0-1 | 0-0 | — | | 5519 |
| 7 | 20 | H | QPR | L | 2-3 | 0-2 | 21 | Lunt [53], Adebola [76] | 5348 |
| 8 | 27 | H | Tranmere R | W | 2-1 | 1-0 | 18 | Anthrobus [27], Street [89] | 4845 |
| 9 | Oct 4 | A | Birmingham C | W | 1-0 | 0-0 | 16 | Rivers [58] | 16,548 |
| 10 | 11 | A | Reading | D | 3-3 | 3-2 | 13 | Westwood [13], Little [20], Adebola [31] | 6685 |
| 11 | 18 | H | Middlesbrough | D | 1-1 | 0-0 | 15 | Adebola [55] | 5759 |
| 12 | 21 | H | Ipswich T | D | 0-0 | 0-0 | — | | 4730 |
| 13 | 25 | A | Bradford C | L | 0-1 | 0-0 | 15 | | 15,333 |
| 14 | 29 | A | Manchester C | L | 0-1 | 0-1 | — | | 27,384 |
| 15 | Nov 1 | A | Nottingham F | L | 1-3 | 1-1 | 17 | Little [15] | 18,268 |
| 16 | 4 | H | Wolverhampton W | L | 0-2 | 0-1 | — | | 5743 |
| 17 | 8 | H | Oxford U | W | 2-1 | 2-1 | 17 | Westwood [31], Anthrobus [41] | 4524 |
| 18 | 15 | A | Charlton Ath | L | 2-3 | 1-2 | 18 | Street [45], Smith S [64] | 14,091 |
| 19 | 22 | H | Stockport Co | L | 0-1 | 0-1 | 19 | | 5231 |
| 20 | 29 | A | Sheffield U | L | 0-1 | 0-0 | 22 | | 16,973 |
| 21 | Dec 6 | H | Huddersfield T | L | 2-5 | 1-2 | 23 | Charnock [41], Adebola [47] | 4861 |
| 22 | 13 | A | Stoke C | W | 2-0 | 1-0 | 20 | Smith S [11], Little [75] | 14,623 |
| 23 | 20 | H | Sunderland | L | 0-3 | 0-2 | 23 | | 5404 |
| 24 | 26 | H | Manchester C | W | 1-0 | 1-0 | 19 | Holsgrove [19] | 5759 |
| 25 | 28 | A | Bury | D | 1-1 | 0-0 | 19 | Adebola [81] | 5661 |
| 26 | Jan 11 | H | Swindon T | W | 2-0 | 0-0 | 17 | Little [46], Street [84] | 4176 |
| 27 | 17 | A | WBA | W | 1-0 | 1-0 | 17 | Little [22] | 15,257 |
| 28 | 24 | A | Port Vale | W | 3-2 | 3-1 | 13 | Smith S (pen) [2], Whalley [33], Foran [41] | 10,571 |
| 29 | 31 | H | Norwich C | W | 1-0 | 0-0 | 14 | Fuglestad (og) [62] | 5559 |
| 30 | Feb 7 | A | QPR | L | 2-3 | 0-1 | 14 | Anthrobus [62], Johnson [72] | 13,429 |
| 31 | 14 | H | Portsmouth | W | 3-1 | 0-0 | 14 | Little [49], Garvey [58], Lunt [73] | 5114 |
| 32 | 17 | H | Birmingham C | L | 0-2 | 0-2 | — | | 5559 |
| 33 | 21 | A | Tranmere R | W | 3-0 | 1-0 | 13 | Rivers [45], Little 2 [64, 70] | 7534 |
| 34 | 25 | A | Middlesbrough | L | 0-1 | 0-0 | — | | 29,936 |
| 35 | 28 | H | Reading | W | 1-0 | 1-0 | 12 | Rivers [11] | 5202 |
| 36 | Mar 3 | A | Oxford U | D | 0-0 | 0-0 | — | | 6069 |
| 37 | 7 | H | Nottingham F | L | 1-4 | 1-4 | 12 | Little [29] | 5759 |
| 38 | 14 | A | Wolverhampton W | L | 0-1 | 0-1 | 14 | | 24,272 |
| 39 | 21 | H | Charlton Ath | L | 0-3 | 0-2 | 14 | | 5252 |
| 40 | 28 | A | Stockport Co | W | 1-0 | 0-0 | 14 | Smith S (pen) [89] | 8370 |
| 41 | Apr 11 | A | Huddersfield T | L | 0-2 | 0-2 | 15 | | 11,263 |
| 42 | 13 | H | Stoke C | W | 2-0 | 1-0 | 13 | Westwood [16], Lightfoot [48] | 5759 |
| 43 | 18 | A | Sunderland | L | 1-2 | 1-2 | 14 | Charnock [30] | 40,441 |
| 44 | 25 | H | Bradford C | W | 5-0 | 4-0 | 13 | Anthrobus [20], Street [26], Little 3 [30, 39, 65] | 5054 |
| 45 | 30 | H | Sheffield U | W | 2-1 | 0-0 | — | Little [80], Anthrobus [82] | 5759 |
| 46 | May 3 | A | Ipswich T | L | 2-3 | 1-1 | 11 | Charnock [40], Garvey [60] | 19,105 |

**Final League Position: 11**     1996–97 DIV2 6

### GOALSCORERS

*League (58):* Little 13, Adebola 7, Anthrobus 6, Rivers 6, Smith S 6 (3 pens), Street 4, Charnock 3, Westwood 3, Garvey 2, Lunt 2, Foran 1, Holsgrove 1, Johnson 1, Lightfoot 1, Whalley 1, own goal 1.
*Coca-Cola Cup (5):* Smith S 2, Lunt 1, Rivers 1, own goal 1.
*FA Cup (1):* Rivers 1.

| Kearton J 43 | Unsworth L 31 + 5 | Smith S 43 | Westwood A 19 + 2 | Lightfoot C 7 + 6 | Pemberton J 1 | Rivers M 31 + 4 | Lunt K 29 + 12 | Adebola D 26 + 1 | Johnson S 39 + 1 | Charnock P 33 | Pope S 2 + 4 | Garvey S 8 + 5 | Moralee J 3 + 6 | Whalley G 18 | Wright D — + 3 | Anthrobus S 27 + 3 | Bignot M 42 | Watts J 5 | Little C 29 + 11 | Smith P 1 + 5 | Collins J — + 1 | Street K 15 + 17 | Walton D 27 | Holsgrove P 7 + 1 | Foran M 10 + 2 | Tierney F 1 + 3 | Guinan S 3 | Wright J 3 + 2 | Bankole A 3 | Match No. |
|---|---|---|---|---|---|---|---|---|---|---|---|---|---|---|---|---|---|---|---|---|---|---|---|---|---|---|---|---|---|---|
| 1 | 2[1] | 3 | 4 | 5 | 6[2] | 7 | 8 | 9[3] | 10 | 11 | 12 | 13 | 14 |  |  |  |  |  |  |  |  |  |  |  |  |  |  |  |  | 1 |
| 1 | 2 | 3 | 4 | 5 |  | 7 | 8 | 9 | 10 | 6 |  | 11 |  |  |  |  |  |  |  |  |  |  |  |  |  |  |  |  |  | 2 |
| 1 |  | 3 | 4 | 5 |  | 2[1] | 8[2] | 9 | 10 | 6 |  | 12 | 11[3] | 7 |  | 13 | 14 |  |  |  |  |  |  |  |  |  |  |  |  | 3 |
| 1 | 12 | 3 | 4[1] |  |  | 7 | 8 | 9 | 10[3] | 6 |  |  |  | 11[2] |  | 14 | 2 |  | 5 | 13 |  |  |  |  |  |  |  |  |  | 4 |
| 1 | 4 | 3 | 13 |  |  | 7[1] | 8 | 9 | 10 | 6 |  |  |  |  |  | 11[3] | 2 |  | 5 | 12[2] | 14 |  |  |  |  |  |  |  |  | 5 |
| 1 | 4 | 3 |  |  |  |  | 8 | 9 | 10 | 6 |  |  |  |  |  | 11[2] | 2 |  | 5 | 7[1] | 13 | 12 |  |  |  |  |  |  |  | 6 |
| 1 | 4 | 3 |  |  |  | 7 | 8 | 9 | 10 | 6 |  |  |  |  |  | 11[1] | 2 |  | 5 | 12 |  |  |  |  |  |  |  |  |  | 7 |
| 1 | 4 | 3 | 14 |  |  | 7[2] | 8 | 9 | 10[1] | 6 |  |  |  |  |  | 11 | 2 |  | 5 | 12 |  |  | 13[3] |  |  |  |  |  |  | 8 |
| 1 | 4 | 3 | 5 |  |  | 7 | 8 | 9 | 12 | 6 |  |  |  |  | 10[1] | 11 | 2 |  |  |  |  |  |  |  |  |  |  |  |  | 9 |
| 1 | 5 | 3 | 4 |  |  | 7 | 8 | 9[1] |  | 6 |  |  |  |  |  | 11 | 2 |  | 10 | 12[2] |  |  | 13 |  |  |  |  |  |  | 10 |
| 1 | 5 | 3 | 4 |  |  | 7[2] | 8[3] | 9 |  | 6 |  | 13 |  |  |  | 11[1] | 2 |  | 12 | 14 |  |  |  |  |  |  |  |  |  | 11 |
| 1 | 5 | 3 | 4 |  |  | 7[1] | 8 | 9 | 10 | 6 |  |  |  |  |  | 11 | 2 |  | 12 |  |  |  |  |  |  |  |  |  |  | 12 |
| 1 | 5[1] | 3 | 4 |  |  |  | 8 | 9 |  | 6 |  | 12 |  |  |  | 11[2] | 2 |  | 10 |  |  | 13 | 7 |  |  |  |  |  |  | 13 |
| 1 |  | 3 | 4 |  |  | 7 | 8 | 9[2] | 10 | 6 |  |  |  |  |  | 12 | 2[1] |  | 11 |  |  | 13 | 5 |  |  |  |  |  |  | 14 |
| 1 |  | 3 | 4 |  |  | 7[1] | 8 | 9 |  | 6 |  |  |  |  |  | 11 | 2 |  | 10 |  |  | 12 | 5 |  |  |  |  |  |  | 15 |
| 1 |  | 3 | 4 |  |  | 7 | 8 |  |  | 6 |  |  |  |  |  | 11[1] | 2 |  | 10 | 12 |  | 9 | 5 |  |  |  |  |  |  | 16 |
| 1 | 12 | 3 | 4 |  |  | 7[1] | 8 |  |  | 6 |  |  | 13 |  |  | 11[2] | 2 |  | 10 |  |  | 9 | 5 |  |  |  |  |  |  | 17 |
| 1 | 12 | 3 | 4 |  |  | 7[2] | 8 | 13 |  | 6 |  |  |  |  |  | 11 | 2 |  | 10[1] |  |  | 9 | 5 |  |  |  |  |  |  | 18 |
| 1 | 4 | 3 |  |  |  | 7 | 12 | 9 | 10[2] | 6 | 14 | 13 |  |  |  |  | 2 |  | 11 |  |  | 5[3] | 8[1] |  |  |  |  |  |  | 19 |
| 1 | 4 | 3 |  |  |  |  | 12 | 9 | 10[2] | 6 | 5 |  | 7[1] |  |  |  | 2 |  | 13 |  |  | 11 | 8 |  |  |  |  |  |  | 20 |
| 1 | 4 | 3 |  |  |  | 7 | 12 | 9 | 10[2] | 6 | 5 | 13 |  |  |  |  | 2 |  | 14 |  |  | 11[3] | 8[1] |  |  |  |  |  |  | 21 |
| 1 | 4 | 3 |  |  |  | 7 | 6[1] | 9[2] | 10 |  |  |  | 12 |  |  |  | 2 |  | 13 |  |  | 11 | 8 | 5 |  |  |  |  |  | 22 |
| 1 | 4 | 3 |  |  |  | 7 | 6 | 9 | 10 |  |  |  | 12 |  |  |  | 2 |  | 13 |  |  | 11[2] | 8 | 5 |  |  |  |  |  | 23 |
| 1 | 5 | 3 | 4 |  |  | 7 | 12 | 9 | 10[1] | 6 |  | 13 |  |  |  |  | 2 |  | 11[2] |  |  |  | 8 |  |  |  |  |  |  | 24 |
| 1 | 5 | 3 |  |  |  | 7[2] | 12 | 9 | 10 | 6 |  |  |  |  |  |  | 2 |  | 11 |  |  | 13 | 8[1] | 4 |  |  |  |  |  | 25 |
| 1 |  | 3 | 4 |  |  | 7[1] |  | 9 | 10 | 6 |  |  |  |  | 8[2] |  | 2 |  | 11 |  |  | 12 | 5 | 13 |  |  |  |  |  | 26 |
| 1 |  | 3 | 4[2] |  |  | 7 | 12 | 9 | 10 | 6[1] |  |  |  |  | 8 |  | 2 |  | 11 |  |  | 5 |  | 13 |  |  |  |  |  | 27 |
| 1 | 12 | 3 |  |  |  | 7[2] | 6 | 9 | 10 |  |  |  |  | 8 |  |  | 2 |  | 11[1] |  |  | 13 | 5 | 4 |  |  |  |  |  | 28 |
| 1 |  | 3 | 12 |  |  | 7 | 6 | 9 | 10 |  |  |  |  | 8 |  |  | 2 |  | 11 |  |  | 8 | 5 | 4[1] |  |  |  |  |  | 29 |
| 1 |  | 3[2] | 12 |  |  |  |  |  |  | 6 |  |  | 7 | 8 |  | 9[1] | 2 |  | 11 |  |  | 13 | 5 | 4 |  |  |  |  |  | 30 |
| 1 | 4 | 3 |  |  |  | 7 |  |  |  | 6 |  |  |  | 8 |  | 9 | 2[1] |  | 11 |  |  | 12 | 5 |  |  |  |  |  |  | 31 |
| 1 | 4 | 3 |  |  |  | 7[1] |  |  |  | 6 |  |  |  | 8 |  | 9 | 2 |  | 11 |  |  | 12 | 5 |  |  |  |  |  |  | 32 |
| 1 | 4 | 3 | 12 |  |  | 7[2] | 6[1] |  | 10 |  |  |  |  | 8 |  | 9 | 2 |  | 11 |  |  | 13 | 5 |  |  |  |  | 11[3] |  | 33 |
| 1 | 4 | 3 | 12 |  |  | 7 | 6[1] |  | 10[2] |  |  |  |  | 8 |  | 9 | 2 |  | 11 |  |  | 13 | 5 |  |  |  |  |  |  | 34 |
| 1 | 4 | 3 | 6 |  |  | 7[3] | 12 |  | 10 |  |  | 13 |  | 8 |  | 9[2] | 2 |  | 11[1] |  |  | 14 | 5 |  |  | 7 |  |  |  | 35 |
| 1 | 4 | 3 | 6[1] |  |  |  | 12 |  | 10 |  |  |  |  | 8 |  | 9 | 2 |  | 11 |  |  | 13 | 5 |  |  |  | 7 |  |  | 36 |
| 1 | 4 | 3 |  |  |  |  | 12 |  | 10 | 6 |  |  |  | 8 |  | 9[1] | 2 |  | 11 | 13 |  | 7 | 5 |  |  | 7[4] |  |  |  | 37 |
| 1 | 4 | 3 |  |  |  |  | 12 |  | 10 | 6[1] |  |  |  | 8 |  | 9[2] | 2 |  | 11 | 13 |  | 7 | 5 |  |  |  |  |  |  | 38 |
| 1 |  | 3 | 12 |  |  |  |  |  | 10 | 6 |  |  |  | 8 |  |  | 2 |  | 11 |  |  | 5 | 4 | 9 | 7[1] |  |  |  |  | 39 |
| 1 |  | 3 | 12 |  |  | 7[2] |  |  | 10 | 6 |  |  |  |  |  |  | 2 |  | 11 |  |  | 8 | 5 | 4 | 13 | 9[1] |  |  |  | 40 |
| 1 |  | 3 | 4 |  |  | 7[2] |  |  | 10 | 6[1] |  |  |  | 8 |  |  | 2 |  | 11 |  |  | 12 | 5 | 13 | 14 | 9[3] |  |  |  | 41 |
| 1 | 12 | 3 | 4[1] | 6 |  | 13 |  |  |  |  |  |  |  | 8 |  | 9[3] | 2 |  | 11 |  |  | 7[2] | 5 | 14 |  |  |  |  |  | 42 |
| 1 |  |  | 12 |  |  | 13 |  |  | 3 | 6 |  | 7 | 8[2] | 9 | 2 |  | 10[3] |  | 11 | 5 |  | 4[1] |  | 14 |  |  |  |  |  | 43 |
|  | 2 | 3 |  | 4[3] |  | 12 | 13 | 8 | 6 | 7 |  | 14 | 9 |  |  | 10[1] |  |  | 11[2] | 5 |  |  |  |  |  |  | 1 |  |  | 44 |
|  | 4 | 3 |  |  |  | 12 |  | 8 | 6 | 7 |  |  | 9 | 2 |  | 10[1] |  |  | 11 | 5 |  |  |  |  |  |  | 1 |  |  | 45 |
|  | 4 | 3 |  |  |  | 12 | 11 | 8 | 6 | 7 |  | 13 | 9 | 2[2] |  | 10[1] |  |  |  | 5[3] |  |  |  | 14 | 1 |  |  |  |  | 46 |

**Coca-Cola Cup**
First Round  Bury  (h) 2-3
          (a) 3-3

**FA Cup**
Third Round  Birmingham C  (h) 1-2

CRYSTAL PALACE 1997-98    *Back row (left to right):* Steve Kember (Reserve Team Coach), Sagi Burton, Andy Linighan, David Tuttle, Carlo Nash, Gareth Ormshaw, Kevin Miller, Herman Hreidarsson, Neil Emblen, George Ndah, Gary Sadley (Physio).

*Middle row:* Ray Wilkins (Assistant Coach), Danny Boxall, Jamie Fullarton, Kevin Muscat, Neil Shipperley, Carl Veart, Paul Warhurst, Gareth Davies, Ray Lewington (First Team Coach).

*Front row:* Dougie Freedman, Dean Gordon, Marc Edworthy, Andy Roberts, Steve Coppell (Manager), Attilio Lombardo, Simon Rodger, Bruce Dyer, Leon McKenzie.

# Division 1     **CRYSTAL PALACE**

*Selhurst Park, London SE25 6PU.* Telephone: (0181) 768 6000. Fax: (0181) 771 5311. Lottery Office: (0181) 768 6094. Club Shop: (0181) 768 6100. Dial-A-Seat Ticketline: (0181) 771 8841. Palace Publications: (0181) 768 6093. Fax: (0181) 653 6312. Palace Clubline: 0891 400 333. Palace Ticket Line: 0891 400 334 (normal 0891 charges apply for these services). Press Office: (0181) 768 6020. Fax: (01702) 511 343.

*Ground capacity:* 26,400.

*Record attendance:* 51,482 v Burnley, Division 2, 11 May 1979.

*Record receipts:* £327,124 v Manchester U, FA Premier League, 21 April 1993 (League); £336,583 v Chelsea, Coca-Cola Cup 5th rd, 6 January 1993.

*Pitch measurements:* 110yd × 74yd.

*Chairman:* M. Goldberg.

*Directors:* P. J. Alexander (Managing), R. E. Anderson, P. Barnes, S. J. Coppell, L. W. Grimes, S. Hume-Kendall, J. McAvoy, P. L. Morley CBE, JP. V. E. Murphy, G. Wilder.

*Head Coach:* Terry Venables. *First Team Coach:* Terry Fenwick.

*Physio:* Gary Sadler. *Stadium Manager:* Vic Worrall.

*Company Secretary:* Gary Witney. *Club Secretary:* Mike Hurst. *PR and Media Manager:* Terry Byfield.

*Year Formed:* 1905. *Turned Professional:* 1905. *Ltd Co.:* 1905.

*Club Nickname:* 'The Eagles'.

*Club Sponsor:* TDK.

*Previous Grounds:* 1905, Crystal Palace; 1915, Herne Hill; 1918, The Nest; 1924, Selhurst Park.

*Foundation:* There was a Crystal Palace club as early as 1861 but the present organisation was born in 1905 after the formation of a club by the company that controlled the Crystal Palace (building), had been rejected by the FA who did not like the idea of the Cup Final hosts running their own club. A separate company had to be formed and they had their home on the old Cup Final ground until 1915.

*First Football League game:* 28 August 1920, Division 3, v Merthyr T (a) L 1-2 – Alderson; Little, Rhodes; McCracken, Jones, Feebury; Bateman, Conner, Smith, Milligan (1), Whibley.

*Record League Victory:* 9–0 v Barrow, Division 4, 10 October 1959 – Rouse; Long, Noakes; Truett, Evans, McNichol; Gavin (1), Summersby (4 incl. 1p), Sexton, Byrne (2), Colfar (2).

*Record Cup Victory:* 8–0 v Southend U, Rumbelows League Cup 2nd rd (1st leg), 25 September 1989 – Martyn; Humphrey (Thompson (1)), Shaw, Pardew, Young, Thorn, McGoldrick, Thomas, Bright (3), Wright (3), Barber (Hodges (1)).

*Record Defeat:* 0–9 v Burnley, FA Cup 2nd rd replay, 10 February 1909 and 0–9 v Liverpool, Division 1, 12 September 1990.

*Most League Points (2 for a win):* 64, Division 4, 1960–61.

*Most League Points (3 for a win):* 90, Division 1, 1993–94.

*Most League Goals:* 110, Division 4, 1960–61.

*Highest League Scorer in Season:* Peter Simpson, 46, Division 3 (S), 1930–31.

*Most League Goals in Total Aggregate:* Peter Simpson, 153, 1930–36.

*Most Capped Player:* Eric Young, 19 (21), Wales.

*Most League Appearances:* Jim Cannon, 571, 1973–88.

*Record Transfer Fee Received:* £4,500,000 from Tottenham H for Chris Armstrong, June 1995.

*Record Transfer Fee Paid:* £2,750,000 to RC Strasbourg for Valerien Ismael, January 1998.

*Football League Record:* 1920 Original Members of Division 3; 1921–25 Division 2; 1925–58 Division 3 (S); 1958–61 Division 4; 1961–64 Division 3; 1964–69 Division 2; 1969–73 Division 1; 1973–74 Division 2; 1974–77 Division 3; 1977–79 Division 2; 1979–81 Division 1; 1981–89 Division 2; 1989–92 Division 1; 1992–93 FA Premier League; 1993–94 Division 1; 1994–95 FA Premier League; 1995–97 Division 1; 1997–98 FA Premier League; 1998– Division 1.

*Honours: Football League:* Division 1 – Champions 1993–94; 3rd 1990–91; Promoted from Division 1, 1996–97 (play-offs); Division 2 – Champions 1978–79; Runners-up 1968–69; Division 3 – Runners-up 1963–64; Division 3 (S) – Champions 1920–21; Runners-up 1928–29, 1930–31, 1938–39; Division 4 – Runners-up 1960–61. *FA Cup:* best season: Runners-up 1990. *Football League Cup:* best season; semi-final 1993, 1995. *Zenith Data Systems Cup:* Winners: 1991.

*Colours:* Red shirts with blue trim, red shorts with blue and white trim, red stockings. *Change colours:* White shirts with red and blue trim, white shorts with blue trim, white stockings.

**Did you know?**
Commentator Stuart Hall, best known for BBC TV's It's a Knockout played for Crystal Palace reserves in 1953.

## CRYSTAL PALACE 1997–98 LEAGUE RECORD

| Match No. | Date | Venue | Opponents | Result | H/T Score | Lg. Pos. | Goalscorers | Attendance |
|---|---|---|---|---|---|---|---|---|
| 1 | Aug 9 | A | Everton | W 2-1 | 1-0 | — | Lombardo [36], Dyer (pen) [77] | 35,716 |
| 2 | 12 | H | Barnsley | L 0-1 | 0-0 | — | | 21,547 |
| 3 | 23 | A | Leeds U | W 2-0 | 1-0 | 5 | Warhurst [22], Lombardo [51] | 29,108 |
| 4 | 27 | A | Southampton | L 0-1 | 0-0 | — | | 15,032 |
| 5 | 30 | H | Blackburn R | L 1-2 | 0-2 | 9 | Dyer [51] | 20,849 |
| 6 | Sept 13 | H | Chelsea | L 0-3 | 0-2 | 14 | | 26,186 |
| 7 | 20 | A | Wimbledon | W 1-0 | 0-0 | 10 | Lombardo [80] | 16,747 |
| 8 | 24 | H | Coventry C | D 1-1 | 1-1 | — | Fullarton [9] | 15,910 |
| 9 | 27 | H | Bolton W | D 2-2 | 2-1 | 11 | Warhurst [9], Gordon [19] | 17,134 |
| 10 | Oct 4 | A | Manchester U | L 0-2 | 0-2 | 13 | | 55,143 |
| 11 | 18 | H | Arsenal | D 0-0 | 0-0 | 15 | | 26,180 |
| 12 | 25 | A | Sheffield W | W 3-1 | 1-0 | 12 | Hreidarsson [27], Rodger [52], Shipperley [60] | 22,072 |
| 13 | Nov 8 | A | Aston Villa | D 1-1 | 1-0 | 12 | Shipperley [42] | 21,097 |
| 14 | 24 | A | Tottenham H | W 1-0 | 0-0 | — | Shipperley [57] | 25,634 |
| 15 | 29 | H | Newcastle U | L 1-2 | 0-1 | 10 | Shipperley [67] | 26,085 |
| 16 | Dec 3 | A | West Ham U | L 1-4 | 1-2 | — | Shipperley [42] | 23,335 |
| 17 | 6 | A | Leicester C | D 1-1 | 1-0 | 13 | Padovano [43] | 19,191 |
| 18 | 13 | H | Liverpool | L 0-3 | 0-1 | 15 | | 25,790 |
| 19 | 20 | A | Derby Co | D 0-0 | 0-0 | 13 | | 26,590 |
| 20 | 26 | H | Southampton | D 1-1 | 0-1 | 13 | Shipperley [62] | 22,853 |
| 21 | 28 | A | Blackburn R | D 2-2 | 1-1 | 13 | Dyer [12], Warhurst [48] | 23,872 |
| 22 | Jan 10 | A | Everton | L 1-3 | 1-3 | 16 | Dyer (pen) [17] | 23,311 |
| 23 | 17 | A | Barnsley | L 0-1 | 0-1 | 17 | | 17,831 |
| 24 | 31 | H | Leeds U | L 0-2 | 0-2 | 17 | | 25,248 |
| 25 | Feb 9 | H | Wimbledon | L 0-3 | 0-0 | — | | 14,410 |
| 26 | 21 | A | Arsenal | L 0-1 | 0-0 | 19 | | 38,094 |
| 27 | 28 | H | Coventry C | L 0-3 | 0-2 | 20 | | 21,810 |
| 28 | Mar 11 | A | Chelsea | L 2-6 | 1-3 | — | Hreidarsson [7], Bent [87] | 31,844 |
| 29 | 14 | A | Aston Villa | L 1-3 | 0-3 | 20 | Jansen [62] | 33,781 |
| 30 | 18 | A | Newcastle U | W 2-1 | 2-0 | — | Lombardo [14], Jansen [23] | 36,565 |
| 31 | 28 | H | Tottenham H | L 1-3 | 0-0 | 20 | Shipperley [82] | 26,116 |
| 32 | Apr 11 | H | Leicester C | L 0-3 | 0-1 | 20 | | 18,771 |
| 33 | 13 | A | Liverpool | L 1-2 | 0-1 | 20 | Bent [72] | 43,007 |
| 34 | 18 | H | Derby Co | W 3-1 | 0-0 | 20 | Jansen [73], Curcic [80], Bent [90] | 18,101 |
| 35 | 27 | H | Manchester U | L 0-3 | 0-2 | — | | 26,180 |
| 36 | May 2 | A | Bolton W | L 2-5 | 2-3 | 20 | Gordon [8], Bent [16] | 24,449 |
| 37 | 5 | H | West Ham U | D 3-3 | 1-1 | — | Bent [44], Rodger [48], Lombardo [63] | 19,129 |
| 38 | 10 | H | Sheffield W | W 1-0 | 0-0 | 20 | Morrison [90] | 16,878 |

**Final League Position: 20**          1996–97 DIV1 6

### GOALSCORERS

*League (37):* Shipperley 7, Bent 5, Lombardo 5, Dyer 4 (2 pens), Jansen 3, Warhurst 3, Gordon 2, Hreidarsson 2, Rodger 2, Curcic 1, Fullarton 1, Morrison 1, Padovano 1.
*Coca-Cola Cup (2):* Ndah 1, Veart 1.
*FA Cup (6):* Dyer 4, Emblen 2.

| Miller K 38 | Edworthy M 33 + 1 | Gordon D 36 + 1 | Roberts A 25 | Tuttle D 8 + 1 | Linighan A 26 | Muscat K 9 | Warhurst P 22 | Dyer B 21 + 3 | Rodger S 27 + 2 | Lombardo A 21 + 3 | Fullarton J 19 + 6 | Shipperley N 17 + 9 | Veart C 1 + 5 | Freedman D 2 + 5 | Hreidarsson H 26 + 4 | Emblen N 8 + 5 | Zohar I 2 + 4 | McKenzie L — + 3 | Quinn R — + 1 | Ndah G 2 + 1 | Bonetti I — + 2 | Smith J 16 + 2 | Padovano M 8 + 2 | Davies G — + 1 | Ginty R 2 + 3 | Burton S 1 + 1 | Brolin T 13 | Boxall D — + 1 | Bent M 10 + 6 | Ismael V 13 | Jansen M 5 + 3 | Bilic P 1 + 2 | Curcic S 6 + 2 | Folan A — + 1 | Morrison C — + 1 | Match No. |
|---|---|---|---|---|---|---|---|---|---|---|---|---|---|---|---|---|---|---|---|---|---|---|---|---|---|---|---|---|---|---|---|---|---|---|---|---|
| 1 | 2 | 3 | 4 | 5 | 6 | 7 | $8^1$ | $9^2$ | 10 | $11^3$ | 12 | 13 | 14 | | | | | | | | | | | | | | | | | | | | | | | 1 |
| 1 | 2 | 3 | 4 | 5 | 6 | 7 | $8^2$ | 9 | $10^1$ | 11 | 12 | 13 | | | | | | | | | | | | | | | | | | | | | | | | 2 |
| 1 | 2 | 3 | 4 | 5 | 6 | 7 | $8^1$ | $9^3$ | 10 | $11^2$ | 13 | 12 | | 14 | | | | | | | | | | | | | | | | | | | | | | 3 |
| 1 | 2 | 3 | 4 | 5 | 6 | $7^2$ | $8^1$ | 9 | 10 | 11 | | 12 | | 13 | | | | | | | | | | | | | | | | | | | | | | 4 |
| 1 | 2 | 3 | 4 | $5^1$ | $6^2$ | $7^3$ | 8 | 9 | 10 | 11 | | 12 | | | 13 | 14 | | | | | | | | | | | | | | | | | | | | 5 |
| 1 | | 3 | 4 | 5 | 6 | $2^2$ | | $9^2$ | | 11 | 7 | 10 | 12 | 13 | | $8^1$ | 14 | | | | | | | | | | | | | | | | | | | 6 |
| 1 | 12 | 3 | 4 | $5^1$ | 6 | 7 | $8^2$ | $9^2$ | | 11 | 10 | 13 | | | | 14 | 2 | | | | | | | | | | | | | | | | | | | 7 |
| 1 | 5 | 3 | 4 | | 6 | 2 | | | | $11^2$ | 7 | 9 | 12 | $10^1$ | | 8 | | | 13 | | | | | | | | | | | | | | | | | 8 |
| 1 | 5 | 3 | 4 | | 6 | $7^3$ | $8^1$ | | | 11 | 10 | 13 | 12 | $9^2$ | | 2 | | 14 | | | | | | | | | | | | | | | | | | 9 |
| 1 | 2 | 3 | 4 | | $6^1$ | | 8 | | 10 | $11^2$ | 7 | | 12 | | 5 | | 13 | | | 9 | | | | | | | | | | | | | | | | 10 |
| 1 | 2 | 3 | 4 | | 6 | | $8^1$ | | 10 | $11^2$ | 7 | 9 | | | 5 | | | 12 | 13 | | | | | | | | | | | | | | | | | 11 |
| 1 | 5 | 3 | 4 | | 6 | | | | | $11^1$ | | 10 | | 9 | 7 | 12 | | | | $8^2$ | 13 | 2 | | | | | | | | | | | | | | 12 |
| 1 | 6 | 3 | 4 | 5 | | | | $9^1$ | 10 | 11 | | | | 8 | 7 | 12 | | | | | | 2 | | | | | | | | | | | | | | 13 |
| 1 | 2 | 3 | 4 | | 6 | | | 8 | 10 | 11 | | 9 | | 12 | 5 | | | | | | | | | | | | $7^1$ | | | | | | | | | 14 |
| 1 | 2 | 3 | $4^1$ | | 6 | | | 8 | | $10^2$ | | 11 | | 9 | 5 | 14 | 12 | | | | | 13 | $7^3$ | | | | | | | | | | | | | 15 |
| 1 | 4 | 3 | | | 6 | | | | | | | 11 | | 9 | 5 | 10 | 7 | | | | | $2^1$ | 12 | | | | | | | | | | | | | 16 |
| 1 | 2 | 3 | | | 6 | | | 4 | | 11 | | 12 | 9 | 8 | 5 | $10^2$ | | | | | | | $7^1$ | | | | 13 | | | | | | | | | 17 |
| 1 | 2 | 3 | | | 6 | | | 8 | | | $7^2$ | 10 | | 9 | 5 | 12 | | | | | | | $11^1$ | | | | 13 | | | | | | | | | 18 |
| 1 | | 3 | 4 | | 6 | | | | | | | 9 | 12 | 10 | 7 | 5 | 8 | | | | | | $11^1$ | | | | 2 | | | | | | | | | 19 |
| 1 | | 3 | 4 | | 6 | | | | | | | 5 | 8 | 10 | $7^2$ | $9^1$ | 11 | 12 | | | | | | | | | | | 2 | 13 | | | | | | 20 |
| 1 | | 3 | 4 | | 6 | | | | | | | 8 | 9 | 10 | 5 | 11 | 12 | | | | | 2 | 7 | | | | | | | | | | | | | 21 |
| 1 | 2 | 3 | 4 | | 6 | | | | | | | 9 | $10^2$ | 7 | 5 | $11^1$ | | | | | | | | | | | 8 | | 12 | 13 | | | | | | 22 |
| 1 | 8 | 3 | 4 | | $6^1$ | | | | | | | 9 | | 7 | 5 | | | | | | | 2 | | | | | 12 | | 11 | 10 | | | | | | 23 |
| 1 | 7 | 3 | 8 | | 6 | | | | | | | 9 | | | 5 | | | | | | | 2 | | | | | 11 | | 10 | | 8 | | | | | 24 |
| 1 | 7 | 3 | 8 | | 6 | | | | | | | 9 | 12 | | 5 | | | | | | | 2 | $7^2$ | | | 13 | 11 | | $10^2$ | | $4^1$ | | | | | 25 |
| 1 | 6 | 3 | 8 | | | | | | 12 | | | $9^1$ | 10 | 7 | 5 | | | | | | | $2^2$ | | | | | 11 | | | 13 | 4 | | | | | 26 |
| 1 | 6 | 3 | 8 | | | | | | | | | $9^2$ | $10^3$ | 7 | 5 | 12 | | | | | | 2 | | | | | $11^1$ | | | 13 | 4 | 14 | | | | 27 |
| 1 | 6 | $5^2$ | | | | | | $9^2$ | $10^2$ | 12 | 7 | | | | | 3 | $8^1$ | | | | | 2 | | | | | 11 | | $10^2$ | | 4 | 14 | | | | 28 |
| 1 | 6 | 3 | | | | | | 9 | 12 | 13 | 7 | | | | | $8^1$ | $5^1$ | | | | | 2 | | | | | 11 | | $10^2$ | | 4 | 14 | | | | 29 |
| 1 | 6 | 3 | | | | | | | | | | | $10^3$ | $7^1$ | 5 | | | 12 | | | | 2 | 13 | | | | | | $9^2$ | 4 | 8 | 14 | | | | 30 |
| 1 | 6 | 3 | | | | | | | | | | 5 | 7 | | | 12 | 13 | | | | | 2 | $9^1$ | | | | | | $11^3$ | 4 | 10 | 14 | $8^2$ | | | 31 |
| 1 | 5 | 3 | | | | | | | | $9^2$ | 12 | 10 | 7 | 6 | | | | | | | | 2 | $11^1$ | | | | | | | 13 | 4 | | $8^2$ | 14 | | 32 |
| 1 | 4 | 12 | | | 6 | | | | 3 | 2 | $7^1$ | 9 | | | 5 | | | | | | | | | | | | $11^2$ | 8 | | 10 | | 13 | | | | 33 |
| 1 | 5 | 3 | | | 6 | | | | 12 | | | 9 | | | | 2 | $7^1$ | | | | | 11 | 13 | | 4 | | $10^2$ | | 8 | | | | 6 | | | 34 |
| 1 | 5 | 3 | | | | | 12 | | | | $7^3$ | 13 | 9 | 14 | 5 | | | | | | | 2 | $8^1$ | | | | $11^2$ | 10 | 4 | | | 6 | | | | 35 |
| 1 | 2 | 3 | | | | | 5 | | | | | $7^1$ | 8 | 12 | 6 | | | | | | | | | | | | 9 | 4 | 10 | 11 | | | | | | 36 |
| 1 | 2 | 3 | | | | | 6 | | 10 | 7 | 12 | 9 | | | 5 | | | | | | | 13 | | | | | 8 | $4^2$ | $11^1$ | | | | | | | 37 |
| 1 | 2 | 3 | | 4 | | | 6 | | 10 | 7 | | $9^2$ | | | 5 | | | | | | | | | | | | 8 | | | | | $11^1$ | 12 | 13 | | 38 |

**Coca-Cola Cup**
Second Round    Hull C    (a) 0-1
                         (h) 2-1

**FA Cup**
Third Round     Scunthorpe U    (h) 2-0
Fourth Round    Leicester C     (h) 3-0
Fifth Round     Arsenal         (a) 0-0
                               (h) 1-2

DARLINGTON 1997–98 *Back row (left to right):* Carl Shutt, Darren Roberts, Simon Shaw, Richard Hope, Jason Devos, Lee Turnbull, Kenny Lowe, Michael Oliver, Brian Atkinson.
*Middle row:* Peter Darke (Kit Manager), Paul Robinson, Lee Brydon, Loukas Papaconstantinou, Andy Crosby, David Preece, Phil Brumwell, Glen Naylor, Mark Barnard, Andrew Thompson (Groundsman).
*Front row:* Will Guimmarra, Mark Riley (Physio), Gary Bannister (Assistant Director of Coaching), David Hodgson (Director of Coaching), Capt J Wood (Physical Training Advisor), Stuart Gibson (Youth Team Coach), Iain Leckie (Centre of Excellence), Neil Tarrant.

# Division 3 **DARLINGTON**

*Feethams Ground, Darlington DL1 5JB.* Telephone: (01325) 465097. Fax: (01325) 381377.

*Ground capacity:* 8500.

*Record attendance:* 21,023 v Bolton W, League Cup 3rd rd, 14 November 1960.

*Record receipts:* £32,300 v Rochdale, Division 4, 11 May 1991.

*Pitch measurements:* 110yd × 74yd.

*President:* A. Noble.

*Chairman:* B. Lowery. *Vice-Chairman:* G. Hodgson.

*Manager:* David Hodgson. *Coach:* Gary Bannister.

*Chief Executive:* M. J. Peden. *Secretary:* K. J. Lavery.

*Year Formed:* 1883. *Turned Professional:* 1908. *Ltd Co.:* 1891.

*Club Nickname:* 'The Quakers'.

*Foundation:* A football club was formed in Darlington as early as 1861 but the present club began in 1883 and reached the final of the Durham Senior Cup in their first season, losing to Sunderland in a replay after complaining that they had suffered from intimidation in the first. The following season Darlington won this trophy and for many years were one of the leading amateur clubs in their area.

*First Football League game:* 27 August 1921, Division 3 (N), v Halifax T (h) W 2-0 – Ward; Greaves, Barbour; Dickson (1), Sutcliffe, Malcolm; Dolphin, Hooper (1), Edmunds, Wolstenholme, Winship.

*Record League Victory:* 9–2 v Lincoln C, Division 3 (N), 7 January 1928 – Archibald; Brooks, Mellen; Kelly, Waugh, McKinnell; Cochrane (1), Gregg (1), Ruddy (3), Lees (3), McGiffen (1).

*Record Cup Victory:* 7–2 v Evenwood T, FA Cup 1st rd, 17 November 1956 – Ward; Devlin, Henderson; Bell (1p), Greener, Furphy; Forster (1), Morton (3), Tulip (2), Davis, Moran.

*Record Defeat:* 0–10 v Doncaster R, Division 4, 25 January 1964.

*Most League Points (2 for a win):* 59, Division 4, 1965–66.

*Most League Points (3 for a win):* 85, Division 4, 1984–85.

*Most League Goals:* 108, Division 3 (N), 1929–30.

*Highest League Scorer in Season:* David Brown, 39, Division 3 (N), 1924–25.

*Most League Goals in Total Aggregate:* Alan Walsh, 90, 1978–84.

*Most Capped Player:* Jason Devos, 3, Canada.

*Most League Appearances:* Ron Greener, 442, 1955–68.

*Record Transfer Fee Received:* £250,000 from Preston NE for Sean Gregan, November 1996.

*Record Transfer Fee Paid:* £95,000 to Motherwell for Nick Cusack, January 1992.

*Football League Record:* 1921 Original Member Division 3 (N); 1925–27 Division 2; 1927–58 Division 3 (N); 1958–66 Division 4; 1966–67 Division 3; 1967–85 Division 4; 1985–87 Division 3; 1987–89 Division 4; 1989–90 GM Vauxhall Conference; 1990–91 Division 4; 1991– Division 3.

*Honours: Football League:* Division 2 best season: 15th, 1925–26; Division 3 (N) – Champions 1924–25; Runners-up 1921–22; Division 4 – Champions 1990–91; Runners-up 1965–66. *FA Cup:* best season: 3rd rd, 1911, 5th rd, 1958. *Football League Cup:* best season: 5th rd, 1968. *GM Vauxhall Conference:* Champions 1989–90.

*Colours:* Black and white. *Change colours:* All green.

**Did you know?**
Darlington beat Chelsea 4-1 in an FA Cup fourth round replay on 29 January 1958, having drawn 3-3 at Stamford Bridge after leading 3-0.

## DARLINGTON 1997–98 LEAGUE RECORD

| Match No. | Date | | Venue | Opponents | Result | | H/T Score | Lg. Pos. | Goalscorers | Attendance |
|---|---|---|---|---|---|---|---|---|---|---|
| 1 | Aug | 9 | A | Colchester U | L | 1-2 | 0-1 | — | Oliver (pen) [75] | 2958 |
| 2 | | 23 | A | Exeter C | L | 0-1 | 0-0 | 22 | | 3334 |
| 3 | | 30 | H | Rotherham U | D | 1-1 | 0-0 | 22 | Roberts [60] | 2613 |
| 4 | Sept | 2 | A | Scarborough | L | 1-2 | 1-2 | — | Roberts (pen) [36] | 2417 |
| 5 | | 5 | A | Macclesfield T | L | 1-2 | 1-0 | — | Roberts [26] | 2459 |
| 6 | | 9 | H | Swansea C | W | 3-2 | 0-2 | — | Roberts (pen) [52], Naylor 2 [88, 90] | 2150 |
| 7 | | 13 | A | Brighton & HA | D | 0-0 | 0-0 | 21 | | 1803 |
| 8 | | 20 | H | Hartlepool U | D | 1-1 | 1-1 | 21 | Naylor [21] | 3169 |
| 9 | | 27 | H | Mansfield T | D | 0-0 | 0-0 | 21 | | 2596 |
| 10 | Oct | 4 | A | Notts Co | D | 1-1 | 1-1 | 22 | Roberts [2] | 4428 |
| 11 | | 11 | A | Rochdale | L | 0-5 | 0-2 | 23 | | 2134 |
| 12 | | 18 | A | Doncaster R | W | 5-1 | 1-1 | 20 | Naylor [42], Devos 2 [50, 70], Shutt [85], Shaw [90] | 2451 |
| 13 | | 21 | H | Cardiff C | D | 0-0 | 0-0 | — | | 2278 |
| 14 | | 25 | A | Lincoln C | L | 1-3 | 0-3 | 21 | Roberts [82] | 3384 |
| 15 | Nov | 1 | H | Hull C | W | 4-3 | 1-1 | 21 | Shaw [10], Dorner [56], Devos [67], Roberts [87] | 2893 |
| 16 | | 4 | A | Torquay U | L | 1-2 | 0-1 | — | Roberts [67] | 1411 |
| 17 | | 8 | A | Peterborough U | D | 1-1 | 0-1 | 21 | Roberts [49] | 6207 |
| 18 | | 18 | H | Leyton Orient | W | 1-0 | 1-0 | — | Dorner [28] | 1703 |
| 19 | | 22 | H | Cambridge U | D | 1-1 | 1-1 | 20 | Shutt [6] | 2221 |
| 20 | | 29 | A | Barnet | L | 0-2 | 0-2 | 20 | | 1726 |
| 21 | Dec | 13 | A | Chester C | L | 1-2 | 0-0 | 22 | Davidson (og) [89] | 1812 |
| 22 | | 20 | H | Scunthorpe U | W | 1-0 | 0-0 | 20 | Crosby [54] | 2267 |
| 23 | | 26 | H | Macclesfield T | W | 4-2 | 1-0 | 20 | Naylor [45], Oliver [55], Dorner 2 [65, 73] | 3042 |
| 24 | Jan | 6 | A | Scarborough | L | 1-2 | 0-1 | — | Atkinson [60] | 1751 |
| 25 | | 10 | H | Colchester U | W | 4-2 | 1-0 | 19 | Gaughan [40], Roberts [58], Haydon (og) [84], Dorner [86] | 2170 |
| 26 | | 17 | A | Rotherham U | L | 0-3 | 0-2 | 19 | | 3877 |
| 27 | | 24 | H | Exeter C | W | 3-2 | 1-1 | 17 | Dorner [38], Naylor 2 [51, 60] | 1917 |
| 28 | | 27 | A | Swansea C | L | 0-4 | 0-2 | — | | 2128 |
| 29 | | 31 | H | Brighton & HA | W | 1-0 | 0-0 | 15 | Dorner [52] | 2487 |
| 30 | Feb | 7 | A | Hartlepool U | D | 2-2 | 0-2 | 17 | Roberts 2 [62, 88] | 3212 |
| 31 | | 14 | H | Notts Co | L | 0-2 | 0-2 | 18 | | 2781 |
| 32 | | 21 | A | Mansfield T | L | 0-4 | 0-0 | 19 | | 2071 |
| 33 | | 24 | A | Doncaster R | W | 2-0 | 1-0 | — | Dorner [41], Robinson [85] | 1342 |
| 34 | | 28 | H | Rochdale | W | 1-0 | 0-0 | 16 | Robinson [54] | 2181 |
| 35 | Mar | 3 | H | Peterborough U | W | 3-1 | 1-0 | — | Robinson [35], Resch [59], Shutt [85] | 1939 |
| 36 | | 7 | A | Hull C | D | 1-1 | 1-0 | 16 | Dorner [33] | 3616 |
| 37 | | 14 | A | Torquay U | L | 1-2 | 1-1 | 18 | Naylor [21] | 2386 |
| 38 | | 21 | A | Leyton Orient | L | 0-2 | 0-1 | 19 | | 4752 |
| 39 | | 28 | A | Cambridge U | L | 0-1 | 0-0 | 20 | | 2649 |
| 40 | | 31 | H | Shrewsbury T | W | 3-1 | 1-1 | — | Shutt 2 [35, 85], Ellison [83] | 1816 |
| 41 | Apr | 4 | H | Barnet | L | 2-3 | 0-2 | 18 | Campbell [46], Dorner [82] | 1880 |
| 42 | | 11 | A | Shrewsbury T | L | 0-3 | 0-0 | 19 | | 1942 |
| 43 | | 13 | H | Chester C | W | 1-0 | 0-0 | 18 | Ellison [65] | 1901 |
| 44 | | 18 | A | Scunthorpe U | L | 0-1 | 0-0 | 19 | | 2267 |
| 45 | | 25 | H | Lincoln C | D | 2-2 | 1-1 | 19 | Hope [34], Ellison [62] | 3160 |
| 46 | May | 2 | A | Cardiff C | D | 0-0 | 0-0 | 19 | | 2610 |

**Final League Position: 19**　　　　1996–97 DIV3 18

### GOALSCORERS

*League (56):* Roberts 12 (2 pens), Dorner 10, Naylor 8, Shutt 5, Devos 3, Ellison 3, Robinson 3, Oliver 2 (1 pen), Shaw 2, Atkinson 1, Campbell 1, Crosby 1, Gaughan 1, Hope 1, Resch 1, own goals 2.
*Coca-Cola Cup (2):* Naylor 1, Roberts 1.
*FA Cup (5):* Atkinson 1 (pen), Dorner 1, Naylor 1, Roberts 1 (pen), Robinson 1.

| Preece D 45 | Shaw S 28 + 3 | Barnard M 30 + 6 | Devos J 24 | Crosby A 32 + 2 | Hope R 34 + 1 | Oliver M 33 + 6 | Lowe K 5 + 2 | Roberts D 24 + 4 | Shutt C 15 + 18 | Naylor G 38 + 4 | Turnbull L 4 + 5 | Robinson P 7 + 12 | Brydon L 11 + 4 | Gray A 6 | Atkinson B 29 + 3 | Hilton D — + 1 | Brumwell P 26 + 9 | Guimarra W — + 4 | Davey S 10 + 1 | Papaconstantinou L 1 | Dorner M 25 + 2 | Resch F 15 + 2 | Gaughan S 23 + 1 | Davies L 2 | Di Lella G — + 5 | Midgley C 1 | Liddle C 15 | Tutill S 7 | Fickling A 8 | Ellison L 4 + 4 | Campbell P 4 + 2 | Match No. |
|---|---|---|---|---|---|---|---|---|---|---|---|---|---|---|---|---|---|---|---|---|---|---|---|---|---|---|---|---|---|---|---|---|
| 1 | 2 | 3 | 4 | 5 | 6¹ | 7 | 8 | 9² | 10 | 11³ | 12 | 13 | 14 |  |  |  |  |  |  |  |  |  |  |  |  |  |  |  |  |  |  | 1 |
| 1 |  | 3 | 4 | 5 | 6¹ | 7 | 13 | 9 | 10³ | 14 | 11¹² | 12 |  | 2 | 8 |  |  |  |  |  |  |  |  |  |  |  |  |  |  |  |  | 2 |
| 1 |  | 3¹ | 4 | 5 | 6 | 7 | 11 | 9 | 10 |  |  | 12 |  | 2 | 8¹ | 13 |  |  |  |  |  |  |  |  |  |  |  |  |  |  |  | 3 |
| 1 |  | 3 |  | 5 | 6 | 7¹ |  | 9 | 10³ | 11 | 12 |  | 4 | 2 | 8² |  | 13 | 14 |  |  |  |  |  |  |  |  |  |  |  |  |  | 4 |
| 1 | 12 |  |  |  | 5¹ | 7³ |  | 9 | 13 | 11 | 4 | 10² |  |  | 8 |  | 2 |  | 6 |  | 14 | 3 |  |  |  |  |  |  |  |  |  | 5 |
| 1 |  | 3 | 6 |  | 6 | 7 |  | 9 | 12 | 10 | 5¹ | 13 | 4 |  | 2³ |  | 8² |  | 11 |  | 14 |  |  |  |  |  |  |  |  |  |  | 6 |
| 1 |  | 3 |  |  | 6 | 7 |  | 9² | 12 | 10¹ | 5 | 13³ | 4 |  | 2 |  | 11 |  | 14 |  |  |  | 8 |  |  |  |  |  |  |  |  | 7 |
| 1 | 2 | 3 |  | 5 | 6 | 7 |  | 9¹ | 12 | 10 |  |  | 4 |  |  |  | 11 |  |  |  |  |  | 8 |  |  |  |  |  |  |  |  | 8 |
|  | 2 | 3 |  | 5 | 6 | 7 | 12 | 9 | 13 | 10² |  |  | 4 |  |  |  | 11¹ |  |  | 1 |  |  | 8 |  |  |  |  |  |  |  |  | 9 |
| 1 |  | 3 | 6 | 5 | 4 | 7¹ |  | 9 | 12 | 10 |  | 11 |  |  | 2 |  | 8 |  |  |  |  |  |  |  |  |  |  |  |  |  |  | 10 |
| 1 | 2 | 3 | 6 | 5 |  | 7¹ |  | 9 | 10 | 11 | 12 |  | 4² |  | 13 |  | 8 |  |  |  |  |  |  |  |  |  |  |  |  |  |  | 11 |
| 1 | 2 | 3¹ | 4 | 5 | 6 |  |  | 8² | 9³ | 10 | 11 |  |  |  | 12 |  | 13 |  | 7 |  | 14 |  |  |  |  |  |  |  |  |  |  | 12 |
| 1 | 2 |  | 4 | 5 | 6 |  |  | 8² | 12 | 10¹ | 11 |  |  |  | 13 |  |  |  | 7 |  | 9 | 3 |  |  |  |  |  |  |  |  |  | 13 |
| 1 | 2 | 12 | 4³ | 5 | 6 |  |  | 8² | 9 |  | 11 |  |  |  |  |  | 13 | 14 | 7 |  | 10 | 3¹ |  |  |  |  |  |  |  |  |  | 14 |
| 1 | 2 | 11 | 4 | 5 | 6¹ |  | 13 | 9 | 12 |  |  |  |  |  |  |  |  |  | 7 |  | 10 | 3² | 8 |  |  |  |  |  |  |  |  | 15 |
| 1 | 2 | 8¹ | 5 | 4 |  |  | 12 | 9 | 11² |  |  | 13 |  |  |  |  |  |  | 7³ |  | 14 | 3 | 6 |  | 10 |  |  |  |  |  |  | 16 |
| 1 | 2 | 11 |  | 5 | 6 | 7 |  | 9 | 12 |  |  | 4 |  |  |  |  |  |  |  |  | 10¹ | 3² | 8 |  | 13 |  |  |  |  |  |  | 17 |
| 1 | 2 | 3 | 4 | 5 |  | 7 |  | 9 |  | 11 | 8 |  |  |  | 6¹ |  | 12 |  |  |  | 10 |  |  |  |  |  |  |  |  |  |  | 18 |
| 1 | 2 | 3 | 4 | 5 |  | 7 |  | 9 |  | 11 | 8 |  |  |  |  |  | 12 |  |  |  | 10¹ | 6 |  |  |  |  |  |  |  |  |  | 19 |
| 1 | 2 | 3¹ | 4 | 5 |  | 7 |  |  | 10¹ | 12 | 11 |  |  |  | 6 |  | 13 |  |  |  | 9² | 14 | 8 |  |  |  |  |  |  |  |  | 20 |
| 1 | 2 | 3 | 4 | 5 |  | 7 |  | 9 |  | 12 | 11¹ |  |  |  | 6 |  |  |  |  |  |  |  | 8 |  | 10² |  | 13 |  |  |  |  | 21 |
| 1 | 2 | 3 | 4 | 5 |  |  |  | 9 |  | 11 |  |  |  |  | 6 |  |  |  |  |  |  |  | 8 |  | 10 |  | 12 | 7¹ |  |  |  | 22 |
| 1 | 2 | 3 | 4 |  |  | 7 |  | 9² |  | 11 | 12 |  |  |  | 6 |  |  |  |  |  | 10¹ | 5 | 8 |  | 13 |  |  |  |  |  |  | 23 |
| 1 | 2 | 3³ |  | 5 |  | 7 |  |  | 12 |  | 11¹ | 13 |  |  | 6 |  |  |  |  |  | 9² | 4 | 8 |  | 10 |  | 14 |  |  |  |  | 24 |
| 1 | 2 | 3 |  | 5 | 4 | 7 |  | 9 | 12 |  |  | 13 |  |  | 6³ |  |  |  |  |  | 10² |  | 8 |  | 14 |  | 11¹ |  |  |  |  | 25 |
| 1 | 2 | 3 | 4 | 5 |  | 7 |  | 9¹ |  | 11 |  |  |  |  | 6 |  |  |  |  |  | 10 |  | 8 |  | 12 |  |  |  |  |  |  | 26 |
| 1¹ | 2 | 3 | 4 | 5 |  | 7 |  |  |  | 12 | 10 |  |  |  | 6 |  |  |  |  |  | 9 | 11 | 8 |  |  |  |  |  |  |  |  | 27 |
| 1 | 2 | 3¹ | 4 | 5 |  | 7² |  |  | 14 | 13 | 10 |  |  |  | 6³ |  | 12 |  |  |  | 9 | 11 | 8 |  |  |  |  |  |  |  |  | 28 |
| 1 | 2 | 3 | 4 |  |  | 7 |  |  |  |  | 10 |  |  |  | 6 |  |  |  |  |  | 9 | 5 | 11 |  | 8 |  |  |  |  |  |  | 29 |
| 1 | 2 | 3 | 4 |  |  | 7² | 12 | 9 | 13 | 10³ |  | 14 |  |  | 6 |  |  |  |  |  |  | 5 | 11¹ |  | 8 |  |  |  |  |  |  | 30 |
| 1 | 11 | 3 | 4 | 5 |  | 7² |  |  | 12 | 13 | 10 |  |  |  | 6 |  |  |  |  |  | 9 | 2¹ | 8 |  |  |  |  |  |  |  |  | 31 |
| 1 | 2 | 11¹ |  | 12 | 3 | 7 |  |  | 13 | 10 |  |  |  |  | 6 |  | 14 |  |  |  | 9² |  | 8³ |  |  |  | 4 | 5 |  |  |  | 32 |
| 1 |  | 12 |  | 4 | 13 |  |  |  | 10³ | 11 |  | 14 |  |  | 7² |  | 2 |  |  |  | 9 | 3¹ | 8 |  |  |  | 6 | 5 |  |  |  | 33 |
| 1 | 2 |  |  | 4 |  |  |  |  | 11 | 10 |  | 12 |  |  | 7 |  |  |  |  |  | 9 | 3¹ | 8 |  |  |  | 6 | 5 |  |  |  | 34 |
| 1 | 2 |  |  | 4 |  |  |  |  | 12 | 11 |  | 10¹ |  |  | 7 |  |  |  |  |  | 9 | 3 | 8 |  |  |  | 6 | 5 |  |  |  | 35 |
| 1 | 12 |  | 2 | 4¹ |  |  |  | 13 | 14 | 11 |  | 10³ |  |  | 7 |  |  |  |  |  | 9 | 3² | 8 |  |  |  | 6 | 5 |  |  |  | 36 |
| 1 | 2 |  |  | 4 |  |  |  |  | 12 | 13 | 11 | 10 |  |  | 7² |  |  |  |  |  | 9 | 3¹ | 8 |  |  |  | 6 | 5 |  |  |  | 37 |
| 1 | 2 | 3 | 12 |  |  |  |  |  | 13 | 11 | 10 | 14 |  |  | 6 |  | 7 |  |  |  | 9² |  | 8¹ |  |  |  | 4 |  | 5³ |  |  | 38 |
| 1 | 12 |  |  | 5 | 3 | 7 |  | 9² |  | 10 |  |  |  |  | 6 |  | 11 |  |  |  |  | 8¹ |  |  |  |  | 4 |  | 2 | 13 |  | 39 |
| 1 | 12 |  |  | 5 | 3 | 7 |  | 9 |  | 10² |  |  |  |  | 6¹ |  | 11 |  |  |  |  | 8³ |  |  |  |  | 4 |  | 2 | 13 | 14 | 40 |
| 1 | 12 |  |  | 5 | 3¹ | 7 |  | 9 |  | 10³ |  |  |  |  | 6 |  | 11¹² |  |  |  |  |  | 13 |  |  |  | 4 |  | 2 | 10 | 11² | 41 |
| 1 |  |  |  | 5 | 3 | 7 |  | 12 |  | 13 |  |  |  |  | 6 |  | 8 |  |  |  | 9¹ |  |  |  |  |  | 4 |  | 2 | 10 | 11² | 42 |
| 1 | 12 |  |  | 5 | 3 | 7 |  | 13³ |  | 10 |  |  |  |  | 6¹ |  | 8 |  |  |  | 9² |  |  |  |  |  | 4 |  | 2 | 14 | 11 | 43 |
| 1 | 12 |  | 6 | 5 | 3 |  |  |  |  | 10 |  | 11 |  |  | 8 |  |  |  |  |  |  |  |  |  | 7² |  | 4 |  | 2 | 9¹ | 13 | 44 |
| 1 |  |  | 6 | 5 | 3 | 7 |  |  |  | 10 |  | 11 |  |  | 8 |  |  |  |  |  |  |  |  |  |  |  | 4 |  | 2 | 9 |  | 45 |
| 1 | 12 |  | 6 | 5 | 3 | 7 |  |  | 13 | 10¹ |  |  |  |  | 8 |  |  |  |  |  |  |  |  |  | 14 |  | 4 |  | 2 | 2² 9 | 11³ | 46 |

**Coca-Cola Cup**
First Round    Notts Co    (h) 1-1    (a) 1-2

**FA Cup**
First Round    Solihull B    (h) 1-1    (a) 3-3
Second Round    Hednesford T    (a) 1-0
Third Round    Wolverhampton W    (h) 0-4

DERBY COUNTY 1997–98    *Back row (left to right):* Gordon Guthrie (Assistant Physio), Dane Farrell (Fitness Coach), Gary Rowett, Paulo Wanchope, Matt Carbon, Dean Yates, Darryl Powell, Ashley Ward, Christian Dailly, Jacob Laursen, Eric Steele (Goalkeeping Coach), Billy McEwan (Reserve Team Coach).
*Second row:* Steve McLaren (First Team Coach), Wayne Sutton, Stefano Eranio, Lee Carsley, Jonathan Hunt, Russell Hoult, Mart Poom, Ron Willems, Aljosa Asanovic, Paul Trollope, Peter Melville (Physio).
*Third row:* Francesco Baiano, Chris Powell, Mauricio Solis, Igor Stimac, Jim Smith (Manager), Robin van der Laan, Paul Simpson, Dean Sturridge, Sean Flynn.
*Front row:* Chris Boden, Nick Wright, Rob Kozluk, Kevin Cooper.
(Photograph: Raymonds Press Agency)

# FA Premiership

# DERBY COUNTY

*Pride Park Stadium, Derby DE24 8XL.* Telephone: (01332) 667503. Fax: (01332) 667519. Clubcall: 0891 121187.

*Ground capacity:* 30,000 (33,000 by November 1998).

*Record attendance:* 41,826 v Tottenham H, Division 1, 20 September 1969.

*Record receipts:* £265,162 v Coventry C, FA Cup 5th rd, 26 February 1997.

*Pitch measurements:* 115yd × 75yd.

*Chairman:* L. V. Pickering. *Vice-Chairman:* P. J. Gadsby.

*Directors:* J. N. Kirkland, A. S. Webb, R. Clarke.

*Manager:* Jim Smith. *Chief Scout:* Bobby Roberts.

*First Team Coach:* Steve McClaren. *Physio:* Peter Melville. *Stadium Manager:* David Goodwin.

*Chief Executive:* Keith Loring. *Secretary:* Keith Pearson ACIS. *Commercial Consultant:* Colin Tunnicliffe.

*Year Formed:* 1884. *Turned Professional:* 1884. *Ltd Co.:* 1896.

*Club Nickname:* 'The Rams'.

*Previous Grounds:* 1884–95, Racecourse Ground; 1895–1997, Baseball Ground.

*Foundation:* Derby County was formed by members of the Derbyshire County Cricket Club in 1884, when football was booming in the area and the cricketers thought that a football club would help boost finances for the summer game. To begin with, they sported the cricket club's colours of amber, chocolate and pale blue, and went into the game at the top immediately entering the FA Cup.

*First Football League game:* 8 September 1888, Football League, v Bolton W (a) W 6-3 – Marshall; Latham, Ferguson, Williamson; Monks, W. Roulstone; Bakewell (2), Cooper (2), Higgins, H. Plackett, L. Plackett (2).

*Record League Victory:* 9–0 v Wolverhampton W, Division 1, 10 January 1891 – Bunyan; Archie Goodall, Roberts; Walker, Chalmers, Roulston (1); Bakewell, McLachlan, Johnny Goodall (1), Holmes (2), McMillan (5). 9–0 v Sheffield W, Division 1, 21 January 1899 – Fryer; Methven, Staley; Cox, Archie Goodall, May; Oakden (1), Bloomer (6), Boag, McDonald (1), Allen. (1 og).

*Record Cup Victory:* 12–0 v Finn Harps, UEFA Cup 1st rd 1st leg, 15 September 1976 – Moseley; Thomas, Nish, Rioch (1), McFarland, Todd (King), Macken, Gemmill, Hector (5), George (3), James (3).

*Record Defeat:* 2–11 v Everton, FA Cup 1st rd, 1889–90.

*Most League Points (2 for a win):* 63, Division 2, 1968–69 and Division 3 (N), 1955–56 and 1956–57.

*Most League Points (3 for a win):* 84, Division 1, 1985–86 and Division 3, 1986–87.

*Most League Goals:* 111, Division 3 (N), 1956–57.

*Highest League Scorer in Season:* Jack Bowers, 37, Division 1, 1930–31 and Ray Straw, 37 Division 3 (N), 1956–57.

*Most League Goals in Total Aggregate:* Steve Bloomer, 292, 1892–1906 and 1910–14.

*Most Capped Player:* Peter Shilton, 34 (125), England.

*Most League Appearances:* Kevin Hector, 486, 1966–78 and 1980–82.

*Record Transfer Fee Received:* £2,900,000 from Liverpool for Dean Saunders, July 1991.

*Record Transfer Fee Paid:* £2,700,000 to Rosario Central for Horacio Angel Carbonari, May 1998.

*Football League Record:* 1888 Founder Member of the Football League; 1907–12 Division 2; 1912–14 Division 1; 1914–15 Division 2; 1915–21 Division 1; 1921–26 Division 2; 1926–53 Division 1; 1953–55 Division 2; 1955–57 Division 3 (N); 1957–69 Division 2; 1969–80 Division 1; 1980–84 Division 2; 1984–86 Division 3; 1986–87 Division 2; 1987–91 Division 1; 1991–92 Division 2; 1992–96 Division 1; 1996– FA Premier League.

*Honours: Football League:* Division 1 – Champions 1971–72, 1974–75; Runners-up 1895–96, 1929–30, 1935–36, 1995–96; Division 2 – Champions 1911–12, 1914–15, 1968–69, 1986–87; Runners-up 1925–26; Division 3 (N) Champions 1956–57; Runners-up 1955–56. *FA Cup:* Winners 1946; Runners-up 1898, 1899, 1903. *Football League Cup:* Semi-final 1968. *Texaco Cup:* 1972. **European Competitions:** *European Cup:* 1972–73, 1975–76; UEFA Cup: 1974–75, 1976–77. *Anglo-Italian Cup:* Runners-up 1993.

*Colours:* Black shirts with white trim, black shorts with white stripes, white stockings. *Change colours:* Yellow shirts, blue trim on sleeves, royal blue shorts with white trim, yellow stockings with blue and white trim turnover.

**Did you know?**
In less than three seasons, Dai Astley scored 49 goals in 98 League and Cup matches for Derby County from November 1936 to January 1939, including 29 in his first 30 matches.

## DERBY COUNTY 1997–98 LEAGUE RECORD

| Match No. | Date | Venue | Opponents | Result | H/T Score | Lg. Pos. | Goalscorers | Atten- dance |
|---|---|---|---|---|---|---|---|---|
| 1 | Aug 9 | A | Blackburn R | L 0-1 | 0-1 | — | | 23,557 |
| 2 | 23 | A | Tottenham H | L 0-1 | 0-1 | 18 | | 25,886 |
| 3 | 30 | H | Barnsley | W 1-0 | 1-0 | 16 | Eranio (pen) 43 | 27,232 |
| 4 | Sept 13 | H | Everton | W 3-1 | 2-1 | 11 | Hunt 23, Powell C 33, Sturridge 66 | 27,828 |
| 5 | 20 | A | Aston Villa | L 1-2 | 1-0 | 15 | Baiano 15 | 35,444 |
| 6 | 24 | A | Sheffield W | W 5-2 | 3-2 | — | Baiano 2 7, 48, Laursen 26, Wanchope 33, Burton 75 | 22,437 |
| 7 | 27 | H | Southampton | W 4-0 | 0-0 | 8 | Eranio (pen) 76, Wanchope 79, Baiano 82, Carsley 83 | 25,625 |
| 8 | Oct 6 | A | Leicester C | W 2-1 | 1-0 | — | Baiano 2 21, 62 | 19,585 |
| 9 | 18 | H | Manchester U | D 2-2 | 2-0 | 7 | Baiano 24, Wanchope 39 | 30,014 |
| 10 | 22 | H | Wimbledon | D 1-1 | 0-0 | — | Baiano 53 | 28,595 |
| 11 | 25 | A | Liverpool | L 0-4 | 0-1 | 7 | | 38,017 |
| 12 | Nov 1 | H | Arsenal | W 3-0 | 0-0 | 6 | Wanchope 2 46, 65, Sturridge 82 | 30,004 |
| 13 | 8 | A | Leeds U | L 3-4 | 3-2 | 8 | Sturridge 2 4, 11, Asanovic (pen) 33 | 33,572 |
| 14 | 22 | H | Coventry C | W 3-1 | 3-0 | 6 | Baiano 3, Eranio (pen) 30, Wanchope 39 | 29,351 |
| 15 | 29 | A | Chelsea | L 0-4 | 0-2 | 9 | | 33,837 |
| 16 | Dec 6 | A | West Ham U | W 2-0 | 1-0 | 7 | Miklosko (og) 10, Sturridge 49 | 29,300 |
| 17 | 14 | A | Bolton W | D 3-3 | 0-0 | 7 | Eranio 55, Baiano 2 64, 69 | 23,027 |
| 18 | 17 | A | Newcastle U | D 0-0 | 0-0 | — | | 36,289 |
| 19 | 20 | H | Crystal Palace | D 0-0 | 0-0 | 7 | | 26,590 |
| 20 | 26 | H | Newcastle U | W 1-0 | 1-0 | 7 | Eranio (pen) 4 | 30,232 |
| 21 | 28 | A | Barnsley | L 0-1 | 0-0 | 7 | | 18,686 |
| 22 | Jan 11 | H | Blackburn R | W 3-1 | 2-0 | 6 | Sturridge 2 15, 40, Wanchope 88 | 27,823 |
| 23 | 17 | A | Wimbledon | D 0-0 | 0-0 | 6 | | 13,031 |
| 24 | 31 | H | Tottenham H | W 2-1 | 1-0 | 6 | Sturridge 25, Wanchope 77 | 30,187 |
| 25 | Feb 7 | A | Aston Villa | L 1-1 | 0-0 | 6 | | 30,251 |
| 26 | 14 | A | Everton | W 2-1 | 1-0 | 6 | Stimac 21, Wanchope 50 | 34,876 |
| 27 | 21 | A | Manchester U | L 0-2 | 0-1 | 6 | | 55,170 |
| 28 | 28 | H | Sheffield W | W 3-0 | 1-0 | 6 | Wanchope 2 3, 49, Rowett 67 | 30,203 |
| 29 | Mar 15 | H | Leeds U | L 0-5 | 0-3 | 7 | | 30,217 |
| 30 | 28 | A | Coventry C | L 0-1 | 0-1 | 7 | | 18,700 |
| 31 | Apr 5 | H | Chelsea | L 0-1 | 0-1 | 8 | | 30,062 |
| 32 | 11 | A | West Ham U | D 0-0 | 0-0 | 9 | | 25,155 |
| 33 | 13 | H | Bolton W | W 4-0 | 4-0 | 7 | Wanchope 27, Burton 2 37, 40, Baiano 45 | 29,126 |
| 34 | 18 | A | Crystal Palace | L 1-3 | 0-0 | 9 | Bohinen 85 | 18,101 |
| 35 | 26 | H | Leicester C | L 0-4 | 0-4 | 10 | | 29,855 |
| 36 | 29 | A | Arsenal | L 0-1 | 0-1 | — | | 38,121 |
| 37 | May 2 | A | Southampton | W 2-0 | 0-0 | 9 | Dailly 50, Sturridge 88 | 15,202 |
| 38 | 10 | H | Liverpool | W 1-0 | 0-0 | 9 | Wanchope 63 | 30,492 |

**Final League Position: 9**          1996–97 PREM 12

### GOALSCORERS
*League (52):* Wanchope 13, Baiano 12, Sturridge 9, Eranio 5 (4 pens), Burton 3, Asanovic 1 (pen), Bohinen 1, Carsley 1, Dailly 1, Hunt 1, Laursen 1, Powell C 1, Rowett 1, Stimac 1, own goal 1.
*Coca-Cola Cup (8):* Wanchope 4, Rowett 2, Sturridge 1, Trollope 1.
*FA Cup (2):* Baiano 1 (pen), Powell C 1.

| Poom M 36 | Eranio S 23 | Powell C 35+2 | Laursen J 27+1 | Stimac I 22 | Dailly C 30 | Simpson P 1 | Van der Laan R 7+3 | Carbon M 3+1 | Hunt J 7+12 | Carsley L 34 | Ward A 2+1 | Powell D 12+11 | Burton D 12+17 | Sturridge D 24+6 | Solis M 3+6 | Baiano F 30+3 | Rowett G 32+3 | Trollope P 4+6 | Asanovic A 3+1 | Wanchope P 30+2 | Kozluk R 6+3 | Yates D 8+1 | Elliott S 3 | Willems R 3+7 | Delap R 10+3 | Hoult R 2 | Bohinen L 9 | Match No. |
|---|---|---|---|---|---|---|---|---|---|---|---|---|---|---|---|---|---|---|---|---|---|---|---|---|---|---|---|---|
| 1 | 2 | 3 | 4 | 5 | 6 | 7¹ | 8² | 9¹ | 10 | 11 | 12 | 13 | 14 | | | | | | | | | | | | | | | 1 |
| 1 | 2 | 3 | 4 | 5 | 6 | | 8¹ | | 10³ | 11 | 9 | 12 | 7² | 13 | 14 | | | | | | | | | | | | | 2 |
| 1 | 2² | 3 | 4 | 5¹ | 6 | 7 | 8 | 9 | 10¹ | 11 | 12 | 13 | 14 | | | | | | | | | | | | | | | 3 |
| 1 | | 3 | 4¹ | 5 | 6 | 7 | | | 10² | | 12 | | 13 | 8 | 14 | 9 | | 2 | 11³ | | | | | | | | | 4 |
| 1 | 2 | 3 | 4 | 5 | | 7 | | | 10² | 11 | 12 | 13 | 14 | 8¹ | | 9³ | 6 | | | | | | | | | | | 5 |
| 1 | 2 | 3 | 4 | 5 | 6 | 7 | 8 | | 10 | 11 | 12 | | | | | 9¹ | | | | | | | | | | | | 6 |
| 1 | 2 | 3 | 4 | 5 | 6 | 7 | 8¹ | | 10 | 11 | 12 | | | | | 9 | | | | | | | | | | | | 7 |
| 1 | 2² | 3 | 4 | 5 | 6 | 7 | 8 | | 10³ | 11 | 12 | | 13 | | 14 | 9¹ | | | | | | | | | | | | 8 |
| 1 | 2 | 3 | 4 | 5 | 6 | 7 | | | 10 | | 12 | | 13 | 8¹ | | 9² | | | 11 | | | | | | | | | 9 |
| 1 | 2 | 3 | 4 | 5 | | 7 | | | | | 12 | | 13 | 8² | | 9 | 6 | | 11¹ | 10 | | | | | | | | 10 |
| 1 | 2 | 3 | 4 | 5 | | 7 | | | | | 12 | | 13 | 8² | | 9 | 6 | | 11¹ | 10 | | | | | | | | 11 |
| 1 | 2 | 3 | 4 | 5 | | 7 | | | | | 12 | | 13 | 8¹ | 14 | 9² | 6 | | 11³ | 10 | | | | | | | | 12 |
| 1 | 2³ | 3 | 4 | 5 | | 7 | | | | | 12 | | 13 | 8 | 14 | 9 | 6 | | 11² | 10¹ | | | | | | | | 13 |
| 1 | 2 | 3 | 4¹ | 5 | | 7 | | | | 11 | 12 | | 13 | 8 | | 9² | 6 | | | 10 | | | | | | | | 14 |
| 1 | 7¹ | 3 | | 5 | | | | | | 4² | 12 | | 13 | 8 | 14 | 9¹ | 6 | | 11 | 10³ | 2 | | | | | | | 15 |
| 1 | 7¹ | 3 | | 5 | 6 | | | | | 4 | 12 | | 13 | 8 | | 9¹ | | | 11 | 10 | 2 | | | | | | | 16 |
| 1 | 7 | 3 | | 5 | 6 | | | | | 4 | 12 | | 13 | 8 | | 9 | | | 11 | 10² | 2¹ | | | | | | | 17 |
| 1 | 7 | 3 | | 5 | | | | | | 4 | 12 | | 13 | 8² | 14 | 9³ | 6 | | 11 | 10¹ | 2 | | | | | | | 18 |
| 1 | 7 | 3 | | 5 | | | | | | 4 | 12 | | 13 | 8² | | 9 | 6 | | 11 | 10 | 2¹ | | | | | | | 19 |
| 1 | 2¹ | 3 | | 5 | | | | | | 4 | 12 | | 13 | 8⁴ | 14 | 9 | 6 | | 11 | 10 | | | | | | | 7 | 20 |
| 1 | 2 | 3³ | 4³ | 5 | | | | | | | 12 | | 13 | 8 | 14 | 9 | 6 | | 11 | 10¹ | | | | | | | 7 | 21 |
| 1 | | 3 | 4 | 5 | | | | | | | 12 | | 13 | 8¹ | | 9 | 6 | | 11 | 10 | 2 | | | 7² | | | | 22 |
| 1 | | 3 | 4 | 5 | | | | | | | | | | 8 | | 9 | 6 | | 11 | 10 | 2 | | | 7 | | | | 23 |
| 1 | 2 | 3 | 4 | 5 | | | | | | | | | 13 | 8 | | 9² | 6 | | 11 | 10 | | | 12 | 7¹ | | | | 24 |
| 1 | 2 | 3 | 4 | 5 | 6 | | | | | | | | 13 | 8 | | 9¹ | | | 11 | 10² | | | 12 | 7 | | | | 25 |
| 1 | 7 | 3 | | 5 | 6 | | | | | 4 | | | | 8 | | 9¹ | | | 11 | 10 | 2 | | 12 | | | | | 26 |
| 1 | 7 | 3 | | 5 | 6 | | | | | 4 | | | | 8 | | 9 | | | 11 | 10 | 2¹ | | | 12 | | | | 27 |
| 1 | 2¹ | | 4 | 5 | 6 | | | | | | | | 13 | 8² | | 9 | | | 11 | 10 | | | 12 | | 3 | | 7 | 28 |
| 1 | 2² | | 4³ | 5 | 6 | | | | | | | | 13 | 8 | 14 | 9 | | | 11 | 10 | | | 12 | | 3¹ | | 7 | 29 |
| | | 3 | 4 | 5¹ | 6 | | | | | | | | 13 | | 14 | 9¹ | | | 11 | 10 | | | 12 | 7² | 2 | 1 | 8 | 30 |
| | | 3 | 4¹ | 5 | | | | | | | | | 13 | 8 | 14 | 9² | 6 | | 11 | 10 | | | 12 | | 2 | 1 | 7³ | 31 |
| 1 | 7 | 3 | | 5 | 6 | | | | | 4 | | | 13 | | | 9² | | | 11 | 10¹ | | | 12 | | 2 | | 8 | 32 |
| 1 | 7² | 3 | | 5 | | | | | | 4 | | | 13 | 8¹ | | 9 | 6 | | 11 | 10 | | | 12 | 14 | 2³ | | | 33 |
| 1 | | 3 | | 5 | 6 | | | | | 4 | | | 13 | 8² | | 9³ | | | 11 | 10 | | | 12 | 14 | 2¹ | | 7 | 34 |
| 1 | | 3 | 4 | 5 | | | | | | | | | 13 | 8 | 14 | 9³ | 6 | | 11 | 10 | | | 12 | 7² | 2 | | | 35 |
| 1 | | 3 | 4 | 5 | | | | | | | | | 13 | 8 | | 9² | 6 | | 11 | 10 | | | 12 | 7¹ | 2 | | | 36 |
| 1 | | 3 | 4 | 5 | | | | | | | | | 13 | 8 | 14 | | 6 | | 11 | 10³ | | | 12 | 7¹ | 2² | | 9 | 37 |
| 1 | | 3 | 4 | 5 | | | | | | | | | 13 | 8 | | 9 | 6 | | 11 | 10² | | | 12 | | 2 | | 7¹ | 38 |

**Coca-Cola Cup**

| | | | | |
|---|---|---|---|---|
| Second Round | Southend U | (a) | 1-0 | |
| | | (h) | 5-0 | |
| Third Round | Tottenham H | (a) | 2-1 | |
| Fourth Round | Newcastle U | (h) | 0-1 | |

**FA Cup**

| | | | |
|---|---|---|---|
| Third Round | Southampton | (h) | 2-0 |
| Fourth Round | Coventry C | (a) | 0-2 |

**Doncaster Rovers
Football Club Ltd.**
(Founded 1879)

## DONCASTER ROVERS 1997–98 LEAGUE RECORD

| Match No. | Date | | Venue | Opponents | Result | | H/T Score | Lg. Pos. | Goalscorers | Atten- dance |
|---|---|---|---|---|---|---|---|---|---|---|
| 1 | Aug | 9 | A | Shrewsbury T | L | 1-2 | 0-1 | — | Conlon [77] | 3029 |
| 2 | | 16 | H | Peterborough U | L | 0-5 | 0-1 | 22 | | 1920 |
| 3 | | 23 | A | Macclesfield T | L | 0-3 | 0-1 | 23 | | 2635 |
| 4 | | 30 | H | Exeter C | L | 0-1 | 0-1 | 24 | | 1186 |
| 5 | Sept | 2 | H | Leyton Orient | L | 1-4 | 1-0 | — | Moncrieffe [18] | 1098 |
| 6 | | 5 | A | Mansfield T | D | 1-1 | 0-1 | — | Moncrieffe [75] | 2874 |
| 7 | | 13 | A | Scunthorpe U | D | 1-1 | 1-1 | 24 | McDonald [17] | 3378 |
| 8 | | 20 | H | Cambridge U | D | 0-0 | 0-0 | 24 | | 1258 |
| 9 | | 27 | A | Torquay U | L | 0-2 | 0-1 | 24 | | 1650 |
| 10 | Oct | 4 | H | Brighton & HA | L | 1-3 | 0-1 | 24 | Cunningham [68] | 2351 |
| 11 | | 11 | H | Hartlepool U | D | 2-2 | 1-0 | 24 | Moncrieffe 2 [19, 53] | 1526 |
| 12 | | 18 | A | Darlington | L | 1-5 | 1-1 | 24 | Moncrieffe [45] | 2451 |
| 13 | | 21 | A | Colchester U | L | 1-2 | 1-2 | — | McDonald [31] | 2588 |
| 14 | | 24 | H | Swansea C | L | 0-3 | 0-2 | — | | 1170 |
| 15 | Nov | 1 | A | Scarborough | L | 0-4 | 0-0 | 24 | | 2345 |
| 16 | | 4 | H | Cardiff C | D | 1-1 | 0-0 | — | Moncrieffe [54] | 1004 |
| 17 | | 8 | A | Barnet | D | 1-1 | 0-1 | 24 | Warren [78] | 2015 |
| 18 | | 18 | A | Lincoln C | L | 1-2 | 0-1 | — | Moncrieffe [57] | 2957 |
| 19 | | 22 | H | Rochdale | L | 0-3 | 0-1 | 24 | | 1503 |
| 20 | | 29 | A | Hull C | L | 0-3 | 0-0 | 24 | | 4721 |
| 21 | Dec | 2 | H | Chester C | W | 2-1 | 1-1 | — | Helliwell [14], Smith M [83] | 864 |
| 22 | | 13 | A | Notts Co | L | 2-5 | 1-3 | 24 | Pell [28], Smith M (pen) [87] | 4024 |
| 23 | | 19 | H | Rotherham U | L | 0-3 | 0-1 | — | | 3533 |
| 24 | | 28 | A | Leyton Orient | L | 0-8 | 0-4 | 24 | | 4437 |
| 25 | Jan | 10 | H | Shrewsbury T | W | 1-0 | 0-0 | 24 | Moncrieffe [75] | 1116 |
| 26 | | 17 | A | Exeter C | L | 1-5 | 0-2 | 24 | Pemberton [58] | 4145 |
| 27 | | 24 | H | Macclesfield T | L | 0-3 | 0-1 | 24 | | 1707 |
| 28 | | 30 | H | Scunthorpe U | L | 1-2 | 1-1 | — | Mike [19] | 2036 |
| 29 | Feb | 3 | H | Mansfield T | L | 0-3 | 0-1 | — | | 1538 |
| 30 | | 7 | A | Cambridge U | L | 1-2 | 1-0 | 24 | Wilson [44] | 2478 |
| 31 | | 10 | A | Peterborough U | W | 1-0 | 0-0 | — | Smith M [90] | 4577 |
| 32 | | 14 | A | Brighton & HA | D | 0-0 | 0-0 | 24 | | 6339 |
| 33 | | 21 | H | Torquay U | L | 0-1 | 0-0 | 24 | | 1424 |
| 34 | | 24 | H | Darlington | L | 0-2 | 0-1 | — | | 1342 |
| 35 | | 28 | A | Hartlepool U | L | 1-3 | 0-1 | 24 | Rowe [83] | 1920 |
| 36 | Mar | 3 | H | Barnet | L | 0-2 | 0-0 | — | | 739 |
| 37 | | 10 | H | Scarborough | L | 1-2 | 0-1 | — | Rowe [58] | 1129 |
| 38 | | 14 | A | Cardiff C | L | 1-7 | 0-2 | 24 | Mike [89] | 2931 |
| 39 | | 21 | H | Lincoln C | L | 2-4 | 2-2 | 24 | George [35], Donnelly [37] | 2357 |
| 40 | | 28 | A | Rochdale | L | 1-4 | 0-2 | 24 | Tedaldi [80] | 1858 |
| 41 | Apr | 4 | H | Hull C | W | 1-0 | 0-0 | 24 | Mike [90] | 2597 |
| 42 | | 11 | A | Chester C | L | 1-2 | 1-2 | 24 | Mike [19] | 1593 |
| 43 | | 13 | H | Notts Co | L | 1-2 | 0-0 | 24 | Messer [90] | 2485 |
| 44 | | 18 | A | Rotherham U | L | 0-3 | 0-0 | 24 | | 4328 |
| 45 | | 25 | A | Swansea C | D | 0-0 | 0-0 | 24 | | 3661 |
| 46 | May | 2 | H | Colchester U | L | 0-1 | 0-0 | 24 | | 3572 |

**Final League Position: 24**   1996–97 DIV3 22

### GOALSCORERS
*League (30):* Moncrieffe 8, Mike 4, Smith M 3 (1 pen), McDonald 2, Rowe 2, Conlon 1, Cunningham 1, Donnelly 1, George 1, Helliwell 1, Messer 1, Pell 1, Pemberton 1, Tedaldi 1, Warren 1, Wilson 1.
*Coca-Cola Cup (1):* own goal 1.
*FA Cup (2):* Hammond 1, Mike 1.

| Ingham G 10 | Esdaille D 21+1 | Dowell W 1 | Warren L 44 | Gore I 25 | Brookes D 9+2 | Cunningham H 32+1 | McDonald M 15 | Mike A 42 | Pemberton M 24+2 | Ireland S 34 | Sanders S 19+6 | Parks T 6 | Conlon P 4+10 | Esdaille D 10+3 | Donnelly M 8+1 | Moncrieffe P 30+8 | Rowe Z 6 | Utley D 2+2 | Debenham R 4+2 | Dobbin J 28+3 | Clark I 1+1 | Borg J 1 | Finley G 6+1 | Ramsay J 2+8 | Russell M 4+1 | Thorpe A 2 | Hawes S 8+3 | Smith D 1 | Tedaldi D –+2 | Thornley R 1 | Williams D 6 | Messer G 4+9 | Smith M 9+10 | Betts R 2+1 | Helliwell I 8 | Hoggett G 8 | Hilton M 9+1 | Pell R 6+4 | Hammond A 1 | Davis C 15 | Hawthorne M 7+1 | George D 16+2 | Wilson P 10 | Edwards P 5+4 | Match No |
|---|---|---|---|---|---|---|---|---|---|---|---|---|---|---|---|---|---|---|---|---|---|---|---|---|---|---|---|---|---|---|---|---|---|---|---|---|---|---|---|---|---|---|---|---|---|
| 1 | 2 | 3¹ | 4 | 5 | 6 | 7² | 8 | 9 | 10³ | 11 | 12 | 13 | 14 | | | | | | | | | | | | | | | | | | | | | | | | | | | | | | | | 1 |
| 1 | 2 | | 4 | 5 | 6¹ | 7 | 8 | 9 | 10² | 11 | 3 | 13³ | | 12 | 14 | | | | | | | | | | | | | | | | | | | | | | | | | | | | | | 2 |
| 1 | | | 4¹ | 5 | 6 | 12 | 8 | 9 | 13 | 11 | 3 | | 10² | | | | | | | 2³ | 7 | | 14 | | | | | | | | | | | | | | | | | | | | | | 3 |
| 1 | | | | 5 | | 7 | 8³ | 9 | 10² | 11 | 3 | 12 | 4¹ | | | 13 | | 6 | | 2 | | | 14 | | | | | | | | | | | | | | | | | | | | | | 4 |
| 1 | | | 4 | | | 7 | 8 | | 10 | 5 | 3 | | 12 | | | 9 | | 13 | | 14 | 11¹ | | 6¹ | 2² | | | | | | | | | | | | | | | | | | | | | 5 |
| 1 | 3 | | 4 | | 6¹ | 7 | 8 | | 10 | 2 | 12 | 13 | | | | 9 | | | | | 14 | | 11² | 5³ | | | | | | | | | | | | | | | | | | | | | 6 |
| 1 | 3 | | 4 | 5 | | 7 | 8 | 11 | 10 | 2 | 6¹ | | | | | 9 | | | | 12 | | | | | | | | | | | | | | | | | | | | | | | | | 7 |
| 1 | 3 | | 4 | 5² | | 7 | | 11 | 10 | | 2 | | 12 | | | 9 | | | | 13 | 6 | | 8¹ | | | | | | | | | | | | | | | | | | | | | | 8 |
| 1 | 3² | | 4 | | | 7 | | 11 | 10³ | | 2 | | 8 | 14 | | 9 | | 12 | | 5 | 13 | | 6¹ | | | | | | | | | | | | | | | | | | | | | | 9 |
| | | | 4 | | 6 | 7 | | 11 | | 2 | 3 | | 10 | | | 12 | | | | 5 | | | | | | | 8 | 1 | | | | 9¹ | | | | | | | | | | | | | 10 |
| 1 | | | 4 | 5 | | 7 | 8¹ | 9 | | | 3 | | 2 | 6² | | 10 | | 12 | 13 | 11 | | | | | | | | | | | | | | | | | | | | | | | | | 11 |
| 2 | | | 4 | 5 | | | | 9 | | 3 | | | 12 | 8¹ | | 10 | | 6 | | 11 | | | | | | | | 1 | | | | | | | | | | | | | | | | | 12 |
| | | | 4 | 5 | | 7 | 8 | 9 | | 3 | 10 | | 2 | | | 12 | | 6 | | 11¹ | | | | | | | | 1 | | | | | | | | | | | | | | | | | 13 |
| | | | 4 | 5 | | 7² | 8 | 9 | | 3 | 10 | | 12 | | | 11³ | | 6 | | 13 | 2¹ | | | | | 1 | 14 | | | | | | | | | | | | | | | | | | 14 |
| 2 | | | | 6 | 5 | 7¹ | 8 | 9 | 11² | 3 | | | 12 | | | 10 | | 4 | | | | | | | | | 1 | | | | | 13 | | | | | | | | | | | | | 15 |
| 2¹ | | | | 5 | 6 | 7 | 8 | | 11 | 3 | | | | | | 10² | | 4 | | 12 | | | | | | | | | | | | 13 | 9 | | | | | | | | | | | | 16 |
| 2 | | | | 5 | 6 | 7 | 8 | | 13 | | | | | | | 10 | | 4 | | 11 | | | | | | | 1 | | | | | 12² | 3 | | | | | | | | 9¹ | | | | 17 |
| 8 | | 2 | | 5 | 6 | 7 | | | | | | | | | | 10 | | 4 | | 11 | | | | | | | 12 | | | | | | | | | | 1 | 3 | | | 9¹ | | | | 18 |
| 8 | | 2¹ | | 5 | 6 | 7 | | | 13 | | | | | | | 10 | | 4 | | 11 | | | | | | | 12² | | | | | | | | | | 1 | 3 | 6 | | | | | | 19 |
| | | | | 5 | 12 | 4¹ | | 11 | | | | | | | | 10 | | 6 | | 7 | 2 | | | | | | 8 | | | | | 3 | 9 | | | | 1 | | | | | | | | 20 |
| | | | 4 | 5 | | | | 11 | | | | | | | | 10 | | 6 | | 7 | 2 | | | | | | 8 | | | | | 3 | 9 | | | | | | | 1 | | | | | 21 |
| | | | 4 | | 12 | | | 2 | 11 | | | | | | | 13 | | 10 | | 5 | | | | | | | 8 | | | | | 3 | 9 | | | | 1¹ | | 6² | | | | | | 22 |
| | | | 4 | 5 | | 8¹ | | 6 | | | 7 | | 2 | 12 | | 10² | | 13 | | 11 | | | | | | | | | | | | 3 | 9 | | | | | | | 1 | | | | | 23 |
| 7 | | | 8 | 5 | | | | 6 | | | 12 | | | | | 10³ | | 11 | | | 2¹ | | 13 | | | | | | | | | 14 | 3 | 9² | | | 1 | | | | | 4 | | | 24 |
| 8 | | | 4 | 5 | 6 | | | 9 | 10¹ | 2 | | | 12 | | | 7 | | | | 11 | | | | | | | | | | | | | | | | 3 | | | | 1 | | | | | 25 |
| 8 | | | 4 | 5 | 6¹ | | | 9 | 10 | 2 | | | | | | 7 | | | | 11 | | | | | | | | | | | | | | | | 3 | | | | 1 | | 12 | | | 26 |
| | | | 4 | 5 | 6 | | | 10 | | 2 | | | | | | 7 | | | | | | | | | | | | | | | | | | | 9¹ | 3 | 12 | | | 1 | | 13 | 11² | | 27 |
| 10 | | | 4 | 5 | | | | 9 | | 3 | | | 2 | | | 11¹ | | 7 | | | | | | | | | | | | | | 12 | | | | | | | | 1 | 8¹ | 6 | 5 | 11 | 28 |
| | | | 4 | | | | | 9 | | 3 | | | 2 | | | 10² | | 6 | | | 12 | | | | | | | | | | | | 13 | | | | | | | 1 | | 5 | 11 | 8¹ | 29 |
| | | | 4 | 5 | | 7 | | 9 | | 3 | | | 2¹ | | | 10² | | 12 | | | | | | | | | 8 | | | | | | 13 | | | | | | | 1 | | 6 | 11 | | 30 |
| 7 | | | 4 | | | 5¹ | | 9 | | 3 | | | 2 | | | 10 | | 8 | | | | | | | | | | | | | | | 12 | | | | | | | 1 | | 6 | 11 | | 31 |
| 9 | | | 4 | | | 7 | | 5 | | 3 | | | 2 | | | 10¹ | | 8 | | | | | | | | | | | | | | | 12 | | | | | | | | | 6 | 11 | | 32 |
| 9¹ | | | 4 | | | 7 | | 5 | | 3 | | | 2 | | 6 | 10 | 1 | 8 | | | | | | | | | | | | | | | 12 | | | | | | | | | | | 11 | 33 |
| 11 | | | 4 | | | 7¹ | | 5 | | | | | 2 | 3 | 1 | | 10³ | | 9 | 8 | | | | | | | | | | | | 12 | 14 | 13 | | | | | | | | 6² | | | 34 |
| 11¹ | | | 4 | | | 7 | | 5 | | | | | 2 | | 6 | | 10³ | | 9 | 8 | | | | | | | | | | | | 12 | 13 | 3² | | | | | | | | | 14 | | 35 |
| 2 | | | 4 | | | 7 | | 5 | | | | | 3 | | 6 | | 10¹ | | 9 | 8 | | | | | | | | | | | | 12 | | | | | | | | | | | 11 | | 36 |
| | | | 4 | 5 | | 7 | | | | | | | 2 | | 1 | | 10¹ | 9 | 8 | | | | | | | | | | | | | 11 | 3 | | | | | | | | | 6 | 12 | | 37 |
| 2³ | | | 4 | | | 7 | | 5 | | | | | | | | 10² | 9¹ | 11 | 8 | | | | | | | | | | | | | 12 | 3 | | | | | | | 13 | | 6 | 14 | | 38 |
| 7 | | | 4 | | | | | 5 | | | | | | | | 11 | 8 | 12 | | | | | | 2 | | | | | | | | 10 | | | | | | | | 9 | | 6 | | 3¹ | 39 |
| | | | 4 | | | | | 6 | | | | | | | | 11² | 8 | | 2¹ | | | 7 | | | | | 13 | | 14 | | | 10³ | | | | | 1 | 9 | | 12 | | 5 | 3 | | 40 |
| | | | 4 | | | 7 | | | 10 | | | | | | | 8 | | | 2 | | | | | | | | 11 | | 13 | | | 12 | | | | | 1 | 3² | 9¹ | | | 5 | 6 | | 41 |
| 13 | | | 4 | | | 7 | | | 10 | | | | | | | 8 | | 12 | | | 2¹ | | | | | | 11 | | | | | | | | | | 1 | 3³ | 9² | | | 5 | 6 | 14 | 42 |
| 2¹ | | | 4 | | | 7 | | | 10 | | | | | | | 8 | | 12 | | | | | 14 | | | | 11 | | | | | 9 | | | | | | | | 13 | | 5² | 6 | 3³ | 43 |
| | | | 4 | | | 7 | | | 9 | | | | | | | 8² | | 2 | | | | | | | | | 11 | | | | | | | | 13 | 12 | | | | 1 | | 5 | 6 | 10 | 44 |
| | | | 4 | | | 7 | | | 10 | | | | 12 | | | 8² | | 2¹ | | | | 13 | | | | | | | | | | | | | 9 | | | 3 | | | | 3 | 12 | | 45 |
| | | | 4 | | | 7 | | | 10 | | | | | | | 2¹ | | 8 | | | | | | | | | | | | | | | | | 11 | | 3 | 12 | | 1 | | 6 | 5 | 9 | 46 |

EVERTON 1997–98    *Back row (left to right):* Phil Jevons, Slaven Bilic, Graham Allen, Claus Thomsen, Paul Gerrard, Neville Southall, John O'Toole, Joe Parkinson, Andy Hinchliffe, Richard Dunne, Gareth Farrelly.

*Middle row:* Jimmy Martin (Kit Manager), Adrian Heath (First Team Coach), John Hills, Michael Branch, John O'Connor, Gavin McCann, Craig Short, John Oster, Mark Quayle, Nick Barmby, Viv Busby, Les Helm (Physio).

*Front row:* Tony Grant, Graham Stuart, Gary Speed, Terry Phelan, Earl Barrett, Howard Kendall (Manager), Dave Watson, Michael Ball, David Unsworth, Duncan Ferguson, Chris Lane.

# FA Premiership

## EVERTON

*Goodison Park, Liverpool L4 4EL.* Telephone: (0151) 330 2200. Fax: (0151) 286 9112. Ticket Infoline: 0891 121599. Clubcall 0891 121199. Dial-A-Seat Service: (0151) 471 8000.

*Ground capacity:* 40,200.

*Record attendance:* 78,299 v Liverpool, Division 1, 18 September 1948.

*Record receipts:* £450,000 v Liverpool, FA Premier League, 16 April 1996.

*Pitch measurements:* 112yd × 78yd.

*Chairman:* Peter R. Johnson.

*Directors:* Sir Desmond Pitcher, Clifford Finch, Sir Philip Carter CBE, Keith Tamlin, Bill Kenwright, Arthur Abercromby, Lord Grantchester.

*Manager:* Walter Smith OBE. *First Team Coach:* Archie Knox.

*Physio:* A. Jones.

*Secretary:* Michael J. Dunford.

*Commercial Manager:* Andrew Watson. *Sales Promotion Manager:* Graham Cass.

*Stadium Manager:* A. Bowen. *Media and Public Relations Executive:* Alan Myers.

*Year Formed:* 1878. *Turned Professional:* 1885. *Ltd Co.:* 1892.

*Previous Name:* St Domingo FC, 1878–79.

*Club Nickname:* 'The Toffees'.

*Previous Grounds:* 1878, Stanley Park; 1882, Priory Road; 1884, Anfield Road; 1892, Goodison Park.

*Foundation:* St. Domingo Church Sunday School formed a football club in 1878 which played at Stanley Park. Enthusiasm was so great that in November 1879 they decided to expand membership and changed the name to Everton playing in black shirts with a white sash and nicknamed the "Black Watch". After wearing several other colours, royal blue was adopted in 1901.

*First Football League game:* 8 September 1888, Football League, v Accrington (h) W 2-1 – Smalley; Dick, Ross; Holt, Jones, Dobson; Fleming (2), Waugh, Lewis, E. Chadwick, Farmer.

*Record League Victory:* 9–1 v Manchester C, Division 1, 3 September 1906 – Scott; Balmer, Crelley; Booth, Taylor (1), Abbott (1); Sharp, Bolton (1), Young (4), Settle (2), George Wilson. 9–1 v Plymouth Arg, Division 2, 27 December 1930 – Coggins; Williams, Cresswell; McPherson, Griffiths, Thomson; Critchley, Dunn, Dean (4), Johnson (1), Stein (4).

*Record Cup Victory:* 11–2 v Derby Co, FA Cup 1st rd, 18 January 1890 – Smalley; Hannah, Doyle (1); Kirkwood, Holt (1), Parry; Latta, Brady (3), Geary (3), Chadwick, Millward (3).

*Record Defeat:* 4–10 v Tottenham H, Division 1, 11 October 1958.

*Most League Points (2 for a win):* 66, Division 1, 1969–70.

*Most League Points (3 for a win):* 90, Division 1, 1984–85.

*Most League Goals:* 121, Division 2, 1930–31.

*Highest League Scorer in Season:* William Ralph 'Dixie' Dean, 60, Division 1, 1927–28 (All-time League record).

*Most League Goals in Total Aggregate:* William Ralph 'Dixie' Dean, 349, 1925–37.

*Most Capped Player:* Neville Southall, 92, Wales.

*Most League Appearances:* Neville Southall, 578, 1981–98.

*Record Transfer Fee Received:* £8,000,000 from Fiorentina for Andrei Kanchelskis, February 1997.

*Record Transfer Fee Paid:* £5,750,000 to Middlesbrough for Nick Barmby, October 1996.

*Football League Record:* 1888 Founder Member of the Football League; 1930–31 Division 2; 1931–51 Division 1; 1951–54 Division 2; 1954–92 Division 1; 1992– FA Premier League.

*Honours: Football League:* Division 1 – Champions 1890–91, 1914–15, 1927–28, 1931–32, 1938–39, 1962–63, 1969–70, 1984–85, 1986–87; Runners-up 1889–90, 1894–95, 1901–02, 1904–05, 1908–09, 1911–12, 1985–86; Division 2 – Champions 1930–31; Runners-up 1953–54. *FA Cup:* Winners 1906, 1933, 1966, 1984, 1995; Runners-up 1893, 1897, 1907, 1968, 1985, 1986, 1989. *Football League Cup:* Runners-up 1977, 1984. *League Super Cup:* Runners-up 1986. *Simod Cup:* Runners-up 1989. *Zenith Data Systems Cup:* Runners-up 1991. **European Competitions:** *European Cup:* 1963–64, 1970–71. *European Cup-Winners' Cup:* 1966–67, 1984–85 (winners), 1995–96. *European Fairs Cup:* 1962–63, 1964–65, 1965–66. *UEFA Cup:* 1975–76, 1978–79, 1979–80.

*Colours:* Royal blue shirts with white and black trim, white shorts with blue and black trim, blue stockings with black rings. *Change colours:* Amber shirts with black stripes, black shorts, amber stockings.

**Did you know?**
In 1984-85, Everton set a club record of 28 consecutive games without defeat. These comprised 18 League, six FA Cup, four European Cup-Winners' Cup matches.

## EVERTON 1997–98 LEAGUE RECORD

| Match No. | Date | Venue | Opponents | Result | H/T Score | Lg. Pos. | Goalscorers | Atten- dance |
|---|---|---|---|---|---|---|---|---|
| 1 | Aug 9 | H | Crystal Palace | L 1-2 | 0-1 | — | Ferguson [85] | 35,716 |
| 2 | 23 | H | West Ham U | W 2-1 | 0-1 | 12 | Speed [67], Stuart [83] | 34,356 |
| 3 | 27 | H | Manchester U | L 0-2 | 0-1 | — | | 40,479 |
| 4 | Sept 1 | A | Bolton W | D 0-0 | 0-0 | — | | 23,131 |
| 5 | 13 | A | Derby Co | L 1-3 | 1-2 | 18 | Stuart [28] | 27,828 |
| 6 | 20 | H | Barnsley | W 4-2 | 2-1 | 13 | Speed 2 (1 pen) [12, 77 (p)], Cadamarteri [42], Oster [84] | 32,659 |
| 7 | 24 | A | Newcastle U | L 0-1 | 0-0 | — | | 36,705 |
| 8 | 27 | H | Arsenal | D 2-2 | 0-2 | 16 | Ball [49], Cadamarteri [56] | 35,457 |
| 9 | Oct 4 | A | Sheffield W | L 1-3 | 0-0 | 18 | Cadamarteri [84] | 24,483 |
| 10 | 18 | H | Liverpool | W 2-0 | 1-0 | 16 | Ruddock (og) [45], Cadamarteri [75] | 40,112 |
| 11 | 25 | A | Coventry C | D 0-0 | 0-0 | 16 | | 18,755 |
| 12 | Nov 2 | H | Southampton | L 0-2 | 0-1 | 17 | | 29,565 |
| 13 | 8 | A | Blackburn R | L 2-3 | 1-1 | 17 | Speed [7], Ferguson [55] | 25,397 |
| 14 | 22 | A | Aston Villa | L 1-2 | 1-1 | 20 | Speed (pen) [12] | 36,389 |
| 15 | 26 | A | Chelsea | L 0-2 | 0-0 | — | | 32,736 |
| 16 | 29 | H | Tottenham H | L 0-2 | 0-0 | 20 | | 36,670 |
| 17 | Dec 6 | A | Leeds U | D 0-0 | 0-0 | 19 | | 34,872 |
| 18 | 13 | H | Wimbledon | D 0-0 | 0-0 | 19 | | 28,533 |
| 19 | 20 | A | Leicester C | W 1-0 | 0-0 | 19 | Speed (pen) [89] | 20,628 |
| 20 | 26 | A | Manchester U | L 0-2 | 0-2 | 19 | | 55,167 |
| 21 | 28 | H | Bolton W | W 3-2 | 2-2 | 18 | Ferguson 3 [17, 41, 67] | 37,149 |
| 22 | Jan 10 | A | Crystal Palace | W 3-1 | 3-1 | 15 | Barmby [3], Ferguson [12], Madar [34] | 23,311 |
| 23 | 18 | A | Chelsea | W 3-1 | 1-1 | 13 | Speed [39], Ferguson [62], Duberry (og) [83] | 32,355 |
| 24 | 31 | A | West Ham U | D 2-2 | 1-1 | 14 | Barmby [25], Madar [60] | 25,905 |
| 25 | Feb 7 | A | Barnsley | D 2-2 | 1-1 | 15 | Ferguson [40], Grant [50] | 18,654 |
| 26 | 14 | H | Derby Co | L 1-2 | 0-1 | 16 | Thomsen [85] | 34,876 |
| 27 | 23 | H | Liverpool | D 1-1 | 0-0 | — | Ferguson [58] | 44,501 |
| 28 | 28 | H | Newcastle U | D 0-0 | 0-0 | 16 | | 37,972 |
| 29 | Mar 7 | A | Southampton | L 1-2 | 0-0 | 16 | Tiler [89] | 15,102 |
| 30 | 14 | H | Blackburn R | W 1-0 | 0-0 | 16 | Madar [62] | 33,423 |
| 31 | 28 | H | Aston Villa | L 1-4 | 1-1 | 17 | Madar [38] | 36,471 |
| 32 | Apr 4 | A | Tottenham H | D 1-1 | 1-0 | 17 | Madar [24] | 35,624 |
| 33 | 11 | H | Leeds U | W 2-0 | 2-0 | 15 | Hutchison [10], Ferguson [38] | 37,099 |
| 34 | 13 | A | Wimbledon | D 0-0 | 0-0 | 16 | | 15,131 |
| 35 | 18 | H | Leicester C | D 1-1 | 1-1 | 16 | Madar [2] | 33,642 |
| 36 | 25 | H | Sheffield W | L 1-3 | 0-2 | 17 | Ferguson [72] | 35,497 |
| 37 | May 3 | A | Arsenal | L 0-4 | 0-2 | 18 | | 38,269 |
| 38 | 10 | H | Coventry C | D 1-1 | 1-0 | 17 | Farrelly [7] | 40,109 |
| **Final League Position: 17** | | | | 1996–97 PREM 15 | | | | |

## GOALSCORERS

*League (41):* Ferguson 11, Speed 7 (3 pens), Madar 6, Cadamarteri 4, Barmby 2, Stuart 2, Ball 1, Farrelly 1, Grant 1, Hutchison 1, Oster 1, Thomsen 1, Tiler 1, own goals 2.
*Coca-Cola Cup (7):* Barmby 2, Oster 2, Cadamateri 1, Farrelly 1, Stuart 1.
*FA Cup (0).*

Note: cells give the shirt number each player wore; a bracketed figure indicates goals scored (e.g. 2[1] = shirt 2, 1 goal).

| Southall N 12 | Thomas T 6+1 | Phelan T 8+1 | Thomsen C 2+6 | Watson D 25+1 | Bilic S 22+2 | Stuart G 14 | Farrelly G 18+8 | Ferguson D 28+1 | Oster J 16+15 | Speed G 21 | Branch M 1+5 | Barmby N 26+4 | Short C 27+4 | Williamson D 15 | Barrett E 12+1 | Hinchcliffe A 15+2 | Cadamarteri D 15+11 | Gerrard P 4 | Grant T 7 | McCann G 5+6 | Ball M 21+4 | O'Connor J —+1 | Ward M 8 | Tiler C 19 | Myhre T 22 | Allen G 2+3 | Jeffers F —+1 | Dunne R 2+1 | Madar M 15+2 | O'Kane J 12 | Hutchison D 11 | Spencer J 3+3 | Beagrie P 4+2 | Match No. |
|---|---|---|---|---|---|---|---|---|---|---|---|---|---|---|---|---|---|---|---|---|---|---|---|---|---|---|---|---|---|---|---|---|---|---|
| 1 | 2[1] | 3 | 4[2] | 5 | 6 | 7 | 8 | 9 | 10[3] | 11 | 12 | 13 | 14 | | | | | | | | | | | | | | | | | | | | | 1 |
| 1 | | 3 | | 5 | 6 | 7 | 10[2] | 9 | 13 | 11 | | | 8 | 12 | 4[1] | 2 | | | | | | | | | | | | | | | | | | 2 |
| 1 | 12 | 3 | | 5 | 6 | 7 | | 9 | 13 | 11 | 14 | 8[2] | 4[3] | 10 | 2[1] | | | | | | | | | | | | | | | | | | | 3 |
| 1 | 2[3] | 3 | | 5[1] | 6 | 7 | | 9 | 10 | 11 | 13 | 8[2] | 12 | 4 | | | 14 | | | | | | | | | | | | | | | | | 4 |
| 1 | | | | | 6 | 7 | | 9 | 10 | 11 | | 8[2] | 12 | 5 | 4 | 2[1] | 3 | 13 | | | | | | | | | | | | | | | | 5 |
| | | | | 5 | 6 | 7 | 12 | 9 | 13 | 11 | | 8 | 2 | 4[1] | | 3 | 10[2] | 1 | | | | | | | | | | | | | | | | 6 |
| | | | | 5 | 6 | 7 | 12 | | 10 | 11 | | 8[3] | | | 2 | 3 | 9[1] | 1 | | 4[2] | 13 | 14 | | | | | | | | | | | | 7 |
| | | 3 | | 5 | 6 | 7 | | | 10 | 11 | | | | | 2 | | 9 | 1 | | 8[1] | 12 | 4 | | | | | | | | | | | | 8 |
| | 2[2] | | | 5 | 6 | 7 | | | 10 | 11 | 12 | | 13 | | 4 | 3 | 9[1] | 1 | | 8[1] | | | | | | | | | | | | | | 9 |
| 1 | | | | 5 | | 7 | | 9 | 10[1] | 11 | | | 6 | 4 | 2 | 3 | 8[2] | | | 12 | 13 | | | | | | | | | | | | | 10 |
| 1 | | | | 5 | | 7 | | 9 | 10 | 11 | 12 | | 6 | 4 | 2 | 3 | 8[1] | | | | | | | | | | | | | | | | | 11 |
| 1 | 12 | | | 5 | | 7 | | 9 | 10 | 11 | 13 | | 6 | 4 | 2[1] | 3 | 8[2] | | | | | | | | | | | | | | | | | 12 |
| 1 | | 3 | | | 6 | 7[3] | 12 | 9 | 13 | 10 | 14 | | 5 | 4[1] | 2 | 11 | 8[2] | | | | | | | | | | | | | | | | | 13 |
| 1 | | | | | 6 | 7 | 12 | 9 | 13 | 11 | | 8 | 5 | 4[1] | 2[3] | 3 | 10[2] | | | | | | | | | | | | | | | | | 14 |
| 1 | 3[3] | | | | 6 | | 10[2] | 9 | 12 | 11 | | 8 | | 4 | 7 | 5[1] | 13 | | | 14 | | | | | | 2 | | | | | | | | 15 |
| 1 | 3[2] | | | | 6 | | 10[1] | 9 | 12 | 11 | | 8 | | 4[3] | 7 | 13 | 14 | | | | | | | | | 2 | 5 | | | | | | | 16 |
| | | | | 5 | | 7 | | 9 | | 11 | | 8 | 4 | | 10 | | 3 | | | | 2 | | | 6 | 1 | | | | | | | | | 17 |
| | | | | 5 | | 7 | 12 | | | 11 | | 8 | 4 | | 10[1] | 13 | 3 | | 9 | | 2[2] | | | 6 | 1 | | | | | | | | | 18 |
| | | | | 5 | | 7 | | | | 11 | | | 10[1] | 8 | 4 | 2 | 3 | | 9 | | | | 12 | 6 | 1 | | | | | | | | | 19 |
| | | | 12 | 5[1] | | 7 | | | 10 | | | 8 | | 4 | 2[2] | | 3 | | 9 | 11[1] | | | | 6 | 1 | 13 | 14 | | | | | | | 20 |
| 2 | 12 | | | | | 7 | | 9 | 10[1] | | | 8 | | | 3 | | | | | 11 | | | | 6 | 1 | 4 | 5 | | | | | | | 21 |
| 2 | 14 | | | | 6 | | 12 | 9 | | 11 | | 8 | | 4 | | | 13[3] | | | 10[1] | 3 | | | 5 | 1 | | | | 7[2] | | | | | 22 |
| | 12 | | | | 6 | | 13 | 9 | | 11 | | 8 | | 4[1] | | | | | | 10 | 3 | | | 5 | 1 | 2 | | | 7[2] | | | | | 23 |
| | | | | 5 | 6 | 7 | | 9 | | | | | 8 | | | | 12 | | | 10 | 4 | | | | | 2 | | 1 | 13 | 11[1] | 3[3] | | | 24 |
| | 12 | | | 5 | | 7 | | 9 | 13 | | | 8[1] | 4 | | | | 14 | | | 10 | 3 | | | | | 2 | | 1 | 11[3] | 6[2] | | | | 25 |
| 2 | 12 | | 5 | | 13 | 7 | | 9 | 10 | | | | 4[2] | | | | 14 | | | 8[1] | 3 | | | | 1 | | | | 11[3] | | | | | 26 |
| | 8 | | 5 | 6 | | 7 | | 9 | 12 | | | | | | | | 10[1] | | | 13 | 3 | | 2 | 4 | 1 | | | | 11[2] | | | | | 27 |
| | | | | 5 | | 7 | | | 12 | | | | 4 | | | | 9 | | | | 3 | | | | | 2[2] | 6 | 1 | | 11 | 8[1] | 10 | | 28 |
| | | | | 5 | 6 | | | | | | | 7[1] | 10 | | 8 | | 12 | | | | 3 | | | 4 | 1 | | | | 9[1] | 2 | 11 | | | 29 |
| | | | | 5 | 6 | | | | | | | | 10 | 8[2] | | | 12 | | | 13 | 3 | | | 4 | 1 | | | | 9[1] | 2 | 11 | 7 | | 30 |
| | | | | 5 | | | | | | | | 7[1] | 10[3] | | 8 | 4[2] | 12 | | | | 2 | | | | 1 | | | 13 | 9 | 3 | 6 | 11 | 14 | 31 |
| | | | | 5 | | | | | | | | 9 | | | 8 | 4 | | | | 10 | 3 | | | | 1 | | 6 | 7[1] | 2 | 11 | 12 | | | 32 |
| | | | | | | | 12 | 9[2] | | | | 8[1] | 4 | | | | | | | 7 | 3 | | | 5 | 1 | | | 13 | 2 | 6 | 10 | 11 | | 33 |
| | | | | | | | 12 | 9 | 13 | | | 8[2] | 4 | | | | | | | 6 | 3 | | | 5 | 1 | | | 10[1] | 2 | 7 | 14 | 11[3] | | 34 |
| | | | | | | | 12 | 7 | 9 | 13 | | | 4 | | | | | | | 6[2] | 3 | | | 5 | 1 | | | 10[2] | 2 | 8 | 14 | 11[3] | | 35 |
| | | | | | | | 12 | 6 | | 9 | | 13 | | | | | 8 | 4[2] | | 7 | 3 | | | 5[1] | 1 | 2[3] | | | 10 | | 11 | | 14 | 36 |
| | | | | 5 | 6[1] | | 12 | 9 | 13 | | | 8 | 4 | | | | | | | | 3 | | | 7 | 1 | | | 14 | 2[2] | 10 | | 11[3] | | 37 |
| | | | | | | | | 5 | 7[2] | 9 | | 8 | 4 | | | | | | | 12 | | | | 13 | 3 | | | 6 | 1 | 11[1] | 2 | 10 | | 38 |

**Coca-Cola Cup**

| | | | | |
|---|---|---|---|---|
| Second Round | Scunthorpe U | (a) | 1-0 | |
| | | (h) | 5-0 | |
| Third Round | Coventry C | (a) | 1-4 | |

**FA Cup**

| | | | |
|---|---|---|---|
| Third Round | Newcastle U | (h) | 0-1 |

EXETER CITY 1997-98    *Back row (left to right):* Steve Flack, Jimmy Gardner, Shaun Gale, Ashley Bayes, Matthew Hare, Leon Braithwaite, John Williams.
*Middle row:* Micky Chapman (Physio), Peter Fox (Manager), Chris Curran, Lee Baddeley, Barry McConnell, Mark Devlin, Chris Fry, Jason Minett, Billy Clark, Mike Radford (Youth Development Officer), Noel Blake (Assistant Manager/Coach).
*Front row:* Paul Birch, Sufyan Ghazghazi, Jon Richardson, Ivor Doble (Chairman), Darran Rowbotham, Nicky Medlin, Andy Cyrus.

# Division 3        **EXETER CITY**

*St James Park, Exeter EX4 6PX.* Telephone: (01392) 254073. Fax: (01392) 425885. Training Ground: (01395) 232784.

*Ground capacity:* 10,570.

*Record attendance:* 20,984 v Sunderland, FA Cup 6th rd (replay), 4 March 1931.

*Record receipts:* £59,862.98 v Aston Villa, FA Cup 3rd rd, 8 January 1994.

*Pitch measurements:* 114yd × 73yd.

*Honorary President:* W. C. Hill.

*Chairman:* A. I. Doble.

*Directors:* P. Carter, I. M. Couch, S. W. Dawe, L. G. Vallance, M. Shelbourne.

*Manager:* Peter Fox. *Assistant Manager/Coach:* Noel Blake. *Physio:* Simon Shakeshaft.

*Chief Executive:* Bernard Frowd OBE.

*Secretary:* Margaret Bond. *Company Secretary:* P. Carter.

*Commercial Manager:* Keith Hartshorn.

*Year Formed:* 1904. *Turned Professional:* 1908. *Ltd Co.:* 1908.

*Club Nickname:* 'The Grecians'.

*Foundation:* Exeter City was formed in 1904 by the amalgamation of St. Sidwell's United and Exeter United. The club first played in the East Devon League and then the Plymouth & District League. After an exhibition match between West Bromwich Albion and Woolwich Arsenal was held to test interest as Exeter was then a rugby stronghold, Exeter City decided at a meeting at the Red Lion Hotel to turn professional in 1908.

*First Football League game:* 28 August 1920, Division 3, v Brentford (h) W 3-0 – Pym; Coleburne, Feebury (1p); Crawshaw, Carrick, Mitton; Appleton, Makin, Wright (1), Vowles (1), Dockray.

*Record League Victory:* 8–1 v Coventry C, Division 3 (S), 4 December 1926 – Bailey; Pollard, Charlton; Pullen, Pool, Garrett; Purcell (2), McDevitt, Blackmore (2), Dent (2), Compton (2). 8–1 v Aldershot, Division 3 (S), 4 May 1935 – Chesters; Gray, Miller; Risdon, Webb, Angus; Jack Scott (1), Wrightson (1), Poulter (3), McArthur (1), Dryden (1). (1 og).

*Record Cup Victory:* 9–1 v Aberdare, FA Cup 1st rd, 26 November 1927 – Holland; Pollard, Charlton; Phoenix, Pool, Gee; Purcell (2), McDevitt, Dent (4), Vaughan (2), Compton (1).

*Record Defeat:* 0–9 v Notts Co, Division 3 (S), 16 October 1948 and v Northampton T, Division 3 (S), 12 April 1958.

*Most League Points (2 for a win):* 62, Division 4, 1976–77.

*Most League Points (3 for a win):* 89, Division 4, 1989–90.

*Most League Goals:* 88, Division 3 (S), 1932–33.

*Highest League Scorer in Season:* Fred Whitlow, 33, Division 3 (S), 1932–33.

*Most League Goals in Total Aggregate:* Tony Kellow, 129, 1976–78, 1980–83, 1985–88.

*Most Capped Player:* Dermot Curtis, 1 (17), Eire.

*Most League Appearances:* Arnold Mitchell, 495, 1952–66.

*Record Transfer Fee Received:* £500,000 from Rangers for Chris Vinnicombe, November 1989 and £500,000 from Manchester C for Martin Phillips, November 1995.

*Record Transfer Fee Paid:* £65,000 to Blackpool for Tony Kellow, March 1980.

*Football League Record:* 1920 Elected Division 3; 1921–58 Division 3 (S); 1958–64 Division 4; 1964–66 Division 3; 1966–77 Division 4; 1977–84 Division 3; 1984–90 Division 4; 1990–92 Division 3; 1992–94 Division 2; 1994– Division 3.

*Honours: Football League:* Division 3 best season: 8th, 1979–80; Division 3 (S) – Runners-up 1932–33; Division 4 – Champions 1989–90; Runners-up 1976–77. *FA Cup:* best season: 6th rd replay, 1931, 6th rd 1981. *Football League Cup:* never beyond 4th rd. *Division 3 (S) Cup:* Winners 1934.

*Colours:* Red and white striped shirts, black shorts, red stockings. *Change colours:* Blue and white striped shirts, blue shorts, blue stockings.

**Did you know?**
Stanley Rous, later Sir Stanley, secretary of the Football Association and president of FIFA, made several appearances as a goalkeeper for Exeter City reserves in 1919 while studying at St Luke's training college.

## EXETER CITY 1997–98 LEAGUE RECORD

| Match No. | Date | Venue | Opponents | Result | H/T Score | Lg. Pos. | Goalscorers | Attendance |
|---|---|---|---|---|---|---|---|---|
| 1 | Aug 9 | H | Hartlepool U | D 1-1 | 0-1 | — | Flack [85] | 3409 |
| 2 | 16 | A | Barnet | W 2-1 | 2-0 | 4 | Flack [15], Birch [43] | 2137 |
| 3 | 23 | H | Darlington | W 1-0 | 0-0 | 2 | Rowbotham (pen) [70] | 3334 |
| 4 | 30 | A | Doncaster R | W 1-0 | 1-0 | 1 | Rowbotham [26] | 1186 |
| 5 | Sept 2 | A | Torquay U | W 2-1 | 0-0 | — | Rowbotham 2 [48, 84] | 4217 |
| 6 | 9 | H | Cardiff C | D 1-1 | 0-0 | — | Flack [90] | 4843 |
| 7 | 13 | A | Leyton Orient | L 0-1 | 0-1 | 4 | | 4036 |
| 8 | 20 | H | Rotherham U | W 3-1 | 1-0 | 3 | Gardner [22], Gale [60], Braithwaite [74] | 3420 |
| 9 | 27 | A | Colchester U | W 2-1 | 1-0 | 2 | Rowbotham [28], Flack [56] | 3175 |
| 10 | Oct 4 | H | Scarborough | D 1-1 | 1-1 | 3 | Flack [23] | 4464 |
| 11 | 11 | H | Swansea C | W 1-0 | 1-0 | 2 | Birch [32] | 3909 |
| 12 | 18 | A | Brighton & HA | W 3-1 | 1-0 | 2 | Rowbotham 2 (1 pen) [22, 48 (p)], Gale [66] | 2210 |
| 13 | 21 | A | Macclesfield T | D 2-2 | 2-0 | — | Flack [24], Rowbotham [44] | 2286 |
| 14 | 25 | H | Scunthorpe U | L 2-3 | 1-1 | 3 | Williams 2 [25, 55] | 4552 |
| 15 | Nov 1 | H | Peterborough U | D 0-0 | 0-0 | 3 | | 5984 |
| 16 | 4 | A | Hull C | L 2-3 | 0-1 | — | Flack [66], Gale [90] | 3837 |
| 17 | 8 | A | Notts Co | D 1-1 | 1-0 | 3 | Rowbotham [3] | 5107 |
| 18 | 18 | H | Mansfield T | W 1-0 | 1-0 | — | Devlin [32] | 2888 |
| 19 | 22 | H | Shrewsbury T | D 2-2 | 1-1 | 3 | Rowbotham [1], Flack [69] | 4041 |
| 20 | 29 | A | Chester C | D 1-1 | 1-0 | 3 | Rowbotham [45] | 2288 |
| 21 | Dec 2 | H | Lincoln C | L 1-2 | 1-0 | — | Williams [11] | 4224 |
| 22 | 12 | A | Cambridge U | L 1-2 | 1-1 | — | Blake [19] | 2224 |
| 23 | 20 | H | Rochdale | W 3-0 | 3-0 | 4 | Tisdale [30], Devlin [38], Richardson (pen) [44] | 33378 |
| 24 | 26 | A | Cardiff C | D 1-1 | 0-1 | 4 | Illman [82] | 6623 |
| 25 | 28 | H | Torquay U | D 1-1 | 1-1 | 6 | Rowbotham (pen) [12] | 8350 |
| 26 | Jan 10 | A | Hartlepool U | D 1-1 | 1-0 | 9 | Flack [38] | 2507 |
| 27 | 17 | H | Doncaster R | W 5-1 | 2-0 | 6 | Rowbotham 2 [15, 45], Flack [50], Illman [62], Fry [80] | 4145 |
| 28 | 20 | H | Barnet | D 0-0 | 0-0 | — | | 3697 |
| 29 | 24 | A | Darlington | L 2-3 | 1-1 | 7 | Flack 2 [44, 81] | 1917 |
| 30 | 31 | H | Leyton Orient | D 2-2 | 1-1 | 9 | Rowbotham [21], Birch [79] | 4023 |
| 31 | Feb 7 | A | Rotherham U | L 0-1 | 0-0 | 11 | | 4158 |
| 32 | 14 | A | Scarborough | L 1-4 | 0-2 | 11 | Rowbotham (pen) [62] | 2078 |
| 33 | 21 | H | Colchester U | L 0-1 | 0-0 | 12 | | 3346 |
| 34 | 24 | A | Brighton & HA | W 2-1 | 1-1 | — | Williams [36], McConnell (pen) [90] | 2754 |
| 35 | 28 | A | Swansea C | L 1-2 | 0-0 | 12 | McConnell (pen) [87] | 3323 |
| 36 | Mar 3 | H | Notts Co | L 2-5 | 1-3 | — | Rowbotham [42], Clark [59] | 2966 |
| 37 | 7 | A | Peterborough U | D 1-1 | 1-0 | 13 | Clark [32] | 4888 |
| 38 | 14 | H | Hull C | W 3-0 | 2-0 | 12 | McConnell 2 [16, 58], Baddeley [38] | 3052 |
| 39 | 21 | A | Mansfield T | L 2-3 | 1-1 | 12 | Richardson [45], Gale [61] | 2033 |
| 40 | 28 | A | Shrewsbury T | D 1-1 | 0-1 | 13 | Flack [54] | 2251 |
| 41 | Apr 4 | H | Chester C | W 5-0 | 3-0 | 11 | Rowbotham [6], McConnell 2 [12, 63], Clark [45], Flack [82] | 2965 |
| 42 | 13 | A | Cambridge U | W 1-0 | 1-0 | 11 | Birch [13] | 3527 |
| 43 | 18 | A | Rochdale | L 0-3 | 0-0 | 11 | | 1850 |
| 44 | 21 | A | Lincoln C | L 1-2 | 0-1 | — | Rowbotham (pen) [64] | 4284 |
| 45 | 25 | A | Scunthorpe U | L 1-2 | 1-2 | 14 | Rowbotham (pen) [38] | 2024 |
| 46 | May 2 | H | Macclesfield T | L 1-3 | 0-1 | 15 | Birch [46] | 4499 |

**Final League Position: 15**   1996–97 DIV3 22

## GOALSCORERS

*League (68):* Rowbotham 20 (6 pens), Flack 14, McConnell 6 (2 pens), Birch 5, Gale 4, Williams 4, Clark 3, Devlin 2, Illman 2, Richardson 2 (1 pen), Baddeley 1, Blake 1, Braithwaite 1, Fry 1, Gardner 1, Tisdale 1.
*Coca-Cola Cup (0).*
*FA Cup (2):* Clark 1, Rowbotham 1.

| Bayes A 45 | Gale S 42 + 1 | Cyrus A 17 + 4 | Minett J 6 | Curran C 9 | Richardson J 41 | Rowbotham D 42 + 1 | Medlin N 11 + 9 | Flack S 37 + 4 | Gardner J 19 + 4 | Hara M 5 + 2 | Ghazghazi S 1 + 8 | Fry C 16 + 12 | Birch P 31 + 2 | Baddeley L 29 + 3 | Braithwaite L — + 5 | Blake N 36 + 2 | Holcroft P 3 + 3 | Williams J 16 + 20 | Devlin M 31 + 2 | Clark B 31 | McConnell B 10 + 6 | Dungey J 1 | Illman N 6 + 2 | Tisdale P 10 | Holloway C 4 + 2 | Phillips M 7 + 1 | Wilkinson J — + 1 | Breslan G — + 1 | Match No. |
|---|---|---|---|---|---|---|---|---|---|---|---|---|---|---|---|---|---|---|---|---|---|---|---|---|---|---|---|---|---|
| 1 | 2 | 3¹ | 4 | 5 | 6 | 7 | 8² | 9 | 10 | 11 | 12 | 13 | | | | | | | | | | | | | | | | | 1 |
| 1 | 2 | | 4 | 5 | 6 | 7³ | 13 | 9 | 10² | 12 | | | 3¹ | 8 | 11 | 14 | | | | | | | | | | | | | 2 |
| 1 | 2 | | 4 | 5 | 6 | 7 | | 9 | 10 | | | 12 | 3¹ | 8 | 11² | 13 | | | | | | | | | | | | | 3 |
| 1 | | 3¹ | 8 | 5 | 6 | 7 | 12 | 9 | 10 | | | 2³ | | | 13 | 4 | | 11² | 14 | | | | | | | | | | 4 |
| 1 | 2 | 3 | 8 | 5¹ | 6 | 7 | | 9 | 10 | | | 12 | | | | 4 | | 11² | 13 | | | | | | | | | | 5 |
| 1 | 2 | 3 | | 5 | 6 | 7 | 11¹ | 9 | 10 | | | 12 | | | | 4 | | 8² | 13 | | | | | | | | | | 6 |
| 1 | 2² | 3¹ | 8 | 5 | 6 | 7 | | 9 | 10 | | | 11 | | | | 4 | | 12 | 13 | | | | | | | | | | 7 |
| 1 | 2 | | | 5 | 6 | 7 | | 9 | 10 | | | | 3 | 8² | 12 | 4 | | 13 | 11¹ | | | | | | | | | | 8 |
| 1 | 2 | | 5² | | 6 | 7 | | 9 | 10 | | | | 3 | 8 | 13³ | 4 | | 12 | 14 | 11¹ | | | | | | | | | 9 |
| 1 | 2 | 12 | | | 6 | 7 | | 9 | 10 | | | | 3¹ | 8 | 5 | 4 | | 13 | 11² | | | | | | | | | | 10 |
| 1 | 2 | | | | 6 | 7² | | 9 | 10 | | | | 3 | 8 | 5 | 4 | | 11¹ | 13 | | | | | | | | | | 11 |
| 1 | 2 | | | | 6 | 7 | | 9 | 10 | | | | 3 | | 5 | 4 | | 11 | 8 | | | | | | | | | | 12 |
| 1 | 2 | | | | 6 | 7¹ | | 9 | 10 | | | | 3 | 12 | 5 | 4 | | 11 | 8 | | | | | | | | | | 13 |
| 1 | 2 | 12 | | | 6 | 7 | | 9² | 10¹ | | | | 3 | 8 | 5 | 4 | | 11 | 13 | | | | | | | | | | 14 |
| 1 | 2 | 9 | | | 6 | 7 | | 12 | | | | | 3¹ | 8 | 5 | 4 | | 11 | 10 | | | | | | | | | | 15 |
| 1 | 2 | 3¹ | | | 6 | 7 | | 9 | 12 | | | | | 8 | 5² | 13 | | 11³ | 10 | 4 | 14 | | | | | | | | 16 |
| 1 | 2 | | | | 6 | 7 | | 9¹ | | | | | 3 | 8 | 5 | 4 | | 12 | 10 | 11 | | | | | | | | | 17 |
| 1 | | 3 | | | 6 | 7 | 11 | | | | | 9¹ | 2 | 8 | | 4 | | | 10 | 5 | 12 | | | | | | | | 18 |
| 1 | 2 | 3 | | | 6 | 7 | 11¹ | 9² | | | | | 13 | 12 | 8 | 4 | | | 10 | 5 | | | | | | | | | 19 |
| 1 | 2 | 3 | | | 6 | 7² | | 9¹ | 11 | | | | 12 | | 8 | 4 | | 13 | 10 | 5 | | | | | | | | | 20 |
| 1 | 2 | | | | 6 | 7 | 12 | 9 | 10¹ | | | | 13 | | 3 | 4 | | 11² | 8 | 5 | | | | | | | | | 21 |
| | 2 | | | | 6 | 7 | 10¹ | 9 | 12 | | | | 3² | | 11 | 4 | | 13 | 8 | 5 | 1 | | | | | | | | 22 |
| 1 | 2 | 3 | | | 6 | 7² | 10 | 9 | | | | | 12 | | 11¹ | 4 | | 8 | 5 | | | | 13 | 4 | | | | | 23 |
| 1 | 2 | 3² | | | 6 | 7 | 10¹ | 11 | | | | | 12 | | 4 | | | 8 | 5 | | | | 13 | 9 | | | | | 24 |
| 1 | 2 | 12 | | | 6 | 7¹ | 3 | 9 | | | | | 13 | | 4 | | | 10 | 5 | | | | 11² | 8 | | | | | 25 |
| 1 | 2 | | | | 6 | | | 9 | | | | 12 | 3 | | 11 | 4 | | 8 | 5 | | | | 7¹ | 10 | | | | | 26 |
| 1 | 2¹ | 12 | | | 6 | 7 | | 9 | | | | 13 | 4² | 11 | | 4 | | 8 | 5 | | | | 3³ | 10 | | | | | 27 |
| 1 | 2 | | | | 6 | 7 | | 9 | | | | | 4 | 11 | | 12 | | 8 | 5 | | | | 3¹ | 10 | | | | | 28 |
| 1 | 2 | | | | 6 | 7 | | 9 | | | | 12 | 11¹ | 4 | | | | 13 | 8 | 5 | | | | 3¹ | 10 | | | | 29 |
| 1 | 2 | | | | 6² | 7 | 13 | 9 | | | | | 4 | 11 | 12 | | | 8 | 5 | | | | 3¹ | 10 | | | | | 30 |
| 1 | 2 | 3 | | | | 7 | 12 | 9 | | | | | 4 | | | 6² | | 11¹ | 8 | 5 | 13 | | | 10 | | | | | 31 |
| 1 | 2 | 3² | | | | 7 | 12 | 9 | 13 | | | | 4 | | | 6 | | 11¹ | 8 | 5¹ | 14 | | | 10 | | | | | 32 |
| 1 | 2 | 3 | | | | 7¹ | 11³ | 9² | | 6 | 12 | | 10 | | | 4 | | 13 | 8 | 5 | 14 | | | | | | | | 33 |
| 1 | 2 | 3 | | | | 11 | | 9¹ | 6² | | | 12 | 10 | | | 4 | | 8 | | 5 | 7 | | | | 13 | | | | 34 |
| 1 | 2 | | | | | 11¹ | | 9 | | | | 12 | 10 | 6 | | 4 | | 8 | 3 | 5 | 7 | | | | | | | | 35 |
| 1 | 2 | | | | 11 | 7 | 12 | 9¹ | | | | 13 | 10 | 6 | | 8² | | 4³ | 5 | 3 | | | 14 | | | | | | 36 |
| 1 | 12 | | | | 11 | 7² | | | 3¹ | | | | 10 | 6 | | 4 | | 13 | 2 | 5 | 9 | | | 8 | | | | | 37 |
| | 3 | | | | 11 | 7 | 12 | | 13 | | | | 10³ | 6² | | 4 | | 14 | 2 | 5 | 9 | | | 8¹ | | | | | 38 |
| 1 | 3 | | | | 11 | 7 | | | | | | | 10 | 6 | | 4 | | 12 | 2 | 5 | 9¹ | | | | | 8² | 13 | | 39 |
| 1 | 3 | | | | 11 | 7 | 12 | | | | | | 10 | 6 | | 4 | | 13 | 2 | 5 | 9¹ | | | | | 8² | | | 40 |
| 1 | 3 | | | | 11 | 7¹ | 12 | | | | | 13 | 10 | 6 | | 4 | | 14 | 2² | 5 | 9³ | | | | | 8 | | | 41 |
| 1 | 3 | | | | 11 | 12 | | 7 | | | | | 10 | 6 | | 4 | | 13 | 2 | 5 | 9¹ | | | | | 8² | | | 42 |
| 1 | 3 | | | | 11 | 7³ | 12 | 9 | 13 | | | | 10 | 6 | | 4¹ | | 14 | 2² | 5 | | | | | | 8 | | | 43 |
| 1 | 3 | | | | 11 | 7 | | 9 | | | | | 10 | 6 | | 4 | | 12 | 2¹ | 5 | | | | | | 8 | | | 44 |
| 1 | 3 | 2 | | | | 7 | 12 | 9² | 11 | | | | 13 | 10 | 6 | 4¹ | | | | 5 | 14 | | | | | 8³ | | | 45 |
| 1 | 3 | 2 | | | | 7 | | 6¹ | 4 | | | 12 | 10 | | | | | | | 5 | 9² | | | | | 11³ | 8 | 13 14 | 46 |

**Coca-Cola Cup**
First Round    Walsall    (a)  0-2
    (h)  0-1

**FA Cup**
First Round    Northampton T    (h)  1-1
    (a)  1-2

FULHAM 1997-98     *Back row (left to right):* Darren Freeman, Chris Coleman, Matthew Lawrence, Ian McGuckin, Jimmy Aggrey, Paul Moody, Rob Scott, Tony Thorpe, Simon Morgan.
*Middle row:* John Marshall (Youth Team Coach), Alan Smith (Director of Youth), Ian Selley, Richard Carpenter, Andy Arnott, Andre Arendse, Mark Walton, Mike Conroy, Simon Stewart, Mark Blake, Chris Smith (Physio), John Nolan (Kit Manager).
*Front row:* Rod McAree, Paul Brooker, Paul Trollope, Martin Thomas, Ray Wilkins (Manager), Paul Bracewell (Manager), Frank Sibley (Assistant Manager), Paul Peschisolido, Robbie Herrera, Neil Smith, Steve Hayward.

# Division 2 **FULHAM**

*Craven Cottage, Stevenage Rd, Fulham, London SW6 6HH.* Telephone: (0171) 384 4700. Fax: (0171) 384 4715. Call Line: 0891 440044.

*Ground capacity:* 19,250.

*Record attendance:* 49,335 v Millwall, Division 2, 8 October 1938.

*Record receipts:* £139,235 v Watford, Division 2, 2 May 1998.

*Pitch measurements:* 110yd × 75yd.

*Chairman:* M. Al Fayed.

*Directors:* W. F. Muddyman (Vice-Chairman), Stuart Benson, Mark Griffiths, Andy Muddyman.

*Advisory Board Directors:* David Shrimpton, Brian Basham, Alex Carlile, Robert Fallowfield, Mark Collins, Tim Delaney, Joe Newman, John McNamara, Bob Nobay, Cyril Swain.

*Chief Operating Officer:* Kevin Keegan OBE. *Assistant Manager:* Frank Sibley. *Player-Coach:* Paul Bracewell.

*Chief Scout:* Arthur Cox. *Director of Youth:* Alan Smith. *Youth Team Coach:* John Marshall.

*Community Officer:* Gary Mulcahey (0171) 384 4759. *Stadium Manager:* Kevin Moore.

*Club Secretary:* Etain McKinney. *Marketing Director:* Annie Bassett.

*Year Formed:* 1879. *Turned Professional:* 1898. *Ltd Co.:* 1903. *Reformed:* 1987.

*Club Nickname:* 'Cottagers'.

*Previous Name:* 1879–88, Fulham St Andrew's.

*Previous Grounds:* 1879 Star Road, Fulham; c.1883 Eel Brook Common, 1884 Lillie Road; 1885 Putney Lower Common; 1886 Ranelagh House, Fulham; 1888 Barn Elms, Castelnau; 1889 Purser's Cross (Roskell's Field), Parsons Green Lane; 1891 Eel Brook Common; 1891 Half Moon, Putney; 1895 Captain James Field, West Brompton; 1896 Craven Cottage.

*Foundation:* Churchgoers were responsible for the foundation of Fulham, which first saw the light of day as Fulham St. Andrew's Church Sunday School FC in 1879. They won the West London Amateur Cup in 1887 and the championship of the West London League in its initial season of 1892–93. The name Fulham had been adopted in 1888.

*First Football League game:* 3 September 1907, Division 2, v Hull C (h) L 0-1 – Skene; Ross, Lindsay; Collins, Morrison, Goldie; Dalrymple, Freeman, Bevan, Hubbard, Threlfall.

*Record League Victory:* 10–1 v Ipswich T, Division 1, 26 December 1963 – Macedo; Cohen, Langley; Mullery (1), Keetch, Robson (1); Key, Cook (1), Leggat (4), Haynes, Howfield (3).

*Record Cup Victory:* 7–0 v Swansea C, FA Cup 1st rd, 11 November 1995 – Lange; Jupp (1), Herrera, Barkus (Brooker (1)), Moore, Angus, Thomas (1), Morgan, Brazil (Hamill), Conroy (3) (Bolt), Cusack (1).

*Record Defeat:* 0–10 v Liverpool, League Cup 2nd rd 1st leg, 23 September 1986.

*Most League Points (2 for a win):* 60, Division 2, 1958–59 and Division 3, 1970–71.

*Most League Points (3 for a win):* 87, Division 3, 1996–97.

*Most League Goals:* 111, Division 3 (S), 1931–32.

*Highest League Scorer in Season:* Frank Newton, 43, Division 3 (S), 1931–32.

*Most League Goals in Total Aggregate:* Gordon Davies, 159, 1978–84, 1986–91.

*Most Capped Player:* Johnny Haynes, 56, England.

*Most League Appearances:* Johnny Haynes, 594, 1952–70.

*Record Transfer Fee Received:* £333,333 from Liverpool for Richard Money, May 1980.

*Record Transfer Fee Paid:* £2,100,000 to Blackburn R for Chris Coleman, December 1997.

*Football League Record:* 1907 Elected to Division 2; 1928–32 Division 3 (S); 1932–49 Division 2; 1949–52 Division 1; 1952–59 Division 2; 1959–68 Division 1; 1968–69 Division 2; 1969–71 Division 3; 1971–80 Division 2; 1980–82 Division 3; 1982–86 Division 2; 1986–92 Division 3; 1992–94 Division 2; 1994–97 Division 3; 1997– Division 2.

*Honours: Football League:* Division 1 best season: 10th, 1959–60; Division 2 – Champions 1948–49; Runners-up 1958–59; Division 3 (S) – Champions 1931–32; Division 3 – Runners-up 1970–71, 1996–97. *FA Cup:* Runners-up 1975. *Football League Cup:* best season: 5th rd, 1968, 1971.

*Colours:* White shirts, red and black trim, black shorts, white stockings red and black trim.
*Change colours:* Yellow shirts with black trim, black shorts, yellow stockings.

**Did you know?**
Jim Hammond was known to Fulham supporters of the late 1920's and 30's as the 'Galloping Hairpin'. At six foot two inches tall, he was an accomplished goalscorer and the first Fulham player to complete a century of goals. He was also an all-rounder with Sussex CCC.

## FULHAM 1997–98 LEAGUE RECORD

| Match No. | Date | Venue | Opponents | Result | H/T Score | Lg. Pos. | Goalscorers | Attendance |
|---|---|---|---|---|---|---|---|---|
| 1 | Aug 9 | H | Wrexham | W 1-0 | 1-0 | — | Conroy [39] | 8789 |
| 2 | 16 | A | Walsall | D 1-1 | 0-0 | 6 | Keister (og) [53] | 4418 |
| 3 | 23 | H | Luton T | D 0-0 | 0-0 | 6 | | 8142 |
| 4 | 30 | A | Wycombe W | L 0-2 | 0-1 | 13 | | 6278 |
| 5 | Sept 2 | A | Bristol C | W 2-0 | 1-0 | — | Newhouse [14], Carpenter [79] | 10,293 |
| 6 | 9 | H | Plymouth Arg | W 2-0 | 0-0 | — | Moody 2 [57, 77] | 8961 |
| 7 | 13 | H | Grimsby T | L 0-2 | 0-1 | 9 | | 6874 |
| 8 | 20 | A | Southend U | L 0-1 | 0-1 | 11 | | 5026 |
| 9 | 27 | A | Wigan Ath | L 1-2 | 1-1 | 18 | Hayward [19] | 4951 |
| 10 | Oct 4 | H | Oldham Ath | W 3-1 | 1-0 | 10 | Moody 2 [11, 53], Sinnott (og) [65] | 8805 |
| 11 | 11 | H | Blackpool | W 1-0 | 1-0 | 8 | Conroy [35] | 7760 |
| 12 | 18 | A | Bournemouth | L 1-2 | 0-1 | 13 | Vincent (og) [72] | 7606 |
| 13 | 21 | A | Watford | L 0-2 | 0-1 | — | | 11,486 |
| 14 | 25 | H | Northampton T | D 1-1 | 1-0 | 16 | Peschisolido [43] | 9848 |
| 15 | Nov 1 | H | Chesterfield | D 1-1 | 1-0 | 17 | Blake [39] | 7998 |
| 16 | 4 | A | Millwall | D 1-1 | 0-0 | — | Peschisolido [54] | 10,291 |
| 17 | 8 | A | Bristol R | W 3-2 | 1-0 | 11 | Carpenter [37], Scott 2 [83, 89] | 6166 |
| 18 | 18 | H | York C | D 1-1 | 0-1 | — | Peschisolido [57] | 5521 |
| 19 | 21 | H | Gillingham | W 3-0 | 1-0 | — | Peschisolido 2 [10, 86], Watson [60] | 8274 |
| 20 | 29 | A | Preston NE | L 1-3 | 1-1 | 14 | Scott [6] | 9723 |
| 21 | Dec 2 | H | Brentford | D 1-1 | 0-1 | — | Peschisolido [66] | 10,767 |
| 22 | 13 | A | Carlisle U | L 0-2 | 0-0 | 15 | | 4574 |
| 23 | 19 | H | Burnley | W 1-0 | 0-0 | — | Cullip [89] | 5096 |
| 24 | 26 | A | Plymouth Arg | W 4-1 | 1-1 | 10 | Moody 2 [18, 80], Hayward [63], Trollope [75] | 9469 |
| 25 | 28 | H | Bristol C | W 1-0 | 0-0 | 6 | Moody [55] | 13,273 |
| 26 | Jan 10 | H | Wrexham | W 3-0 | 1-0 | 4 | Moody [38], Peschisolido [56], Trollope [85] | 5338 |
| 27 | 17 | H | Wycombe W | D 0-0 | 0-0 | 6 | | 10,468 |
| 28 | 24 | A | Luton T | W 4-1 | 2-1 | 3 | Moody 3 (1 pen) [1, 37, 56 (p)], Hayward [61] | 8366 |
| 29 | 31 | A | Grimsby T | D 1-1 | 0-0 | 4 | Lightbourne [56] | 6785 |
| 30 | Feb 7 | H | Southend U | W 2-0 | 1-0 | 3 | Peschisolido [25], Lightbourne [56] | 9122 |
| 31 | 14 | A | Oldham Ath | L 0-1 | 0-0 | 6 | | 6063 |
| 32 | 21 | H | Wigan Ath | W 2-0 | 0-0 | 5 | Hayward [56], Peschisolido [89] | 7791 |
| 33 | 24 | H | Bournemouth | L 0-1 | 0-1 | — | | 7708 |
| 34 | 28 | A | Blackpool | L 1-2 | 1-0 | 6 | Coleman [24] | 5183 |
| 35 | Mar 3 | H | Bristol R | W 1-0 | 0-0 | — | Thorpe [75] | 6843 |
| 36 | 7 | A | Chesterfield | W 2-0 | 0-0 | 5 | Morgan [50], Blake [76] | 5129 |
| 37 | 14 | H | Millwall | L 1-2 | 1-0 | 5 | Thorpe [26] | 12,318 |
| 38 | 21 | A | York C | W 1-0 | 0-0 | 6 | Peschisolido [75] | 4871 |
| 39 | 28 | A | Gillingham | L 0-2 | 0-1 | 6 | | 10,507 |
| 40 | Apr 4 | H | Preston NE | W 2-1 | 0-1 | 5 | Brazier [68], Collins [77] | 8814 |
| 41 | 7 | H | Walsall | D 1-1 | 0-1 | — | Trollope [87] | 6733 |
| 42 | 11 | A | Brentford | W 2-0 | 1-0 | 4 | Moody 2 [21, 77] | 10,510 |
| 43 | 13 | H | Carlisle U | W 5-0 | 2-0 | 3 | Peschisolido 3 [8, 43, 50], Moody (pen) [72], Thorpe [76] | 9243 |
| 44 | 18 | A | Burnley | L 1-2 | 1-1 | 3 | Moody [35] | 9745 |
| 45 | 25 | A | Northampton T | L 0-1 | 0-0 | 4 | | 7443 |
| 46 | May 2 | H | Watford | L 1-2 | 0-1 | 6 | Beardsley [61] | 17,114 |

**Final League Position: 6**   1996–97 DIV3 2

### GOALSCORERS

*League (60):* Moody 15 (2 pens), Peschisolido 13, Hayward 4, Scott 3, Thorpe 3, Trollope 3, Blake 2, Carpenter 2, Conroy 2, Lightbourne 2, Beardsley 1, Brazier 1, Coleman 1, Collins 1, Cullip 1, Morgan 1, Newhouse 1, Watson 1, own goals 3.
*Coca-Cola Cup (6):* Newhouse 3, Conroy 2, Carpenter 1.
*FA Cup (4):* Blake 1 (pen), Carpenter 1, Scott 1, Smith 1.

| Walton M 12 | Watson P 4 + 2 | Herrera R 26 | Cullip D 18 + 3 | Smith N 42 + 2 | Blake M 24 + 2 | Newhouse A 7 + 1 | Hayward S 32 + 3 | Conroy M 10 + 1 | Morgan S 18 + 1 | Carpenter R 15 + 9 | Scott R 6 + 11 | Moody P 27 + 6 | Cockerill G 5 + 3 | Lawrence M 43 | Brooker P 4 + 5 | McAree R 1 + 1 | Thomas M — + 4 | Arendse A 6 | Cusack N 1 + 1 | McKenzie L 1 + 2 | Bracewell P 36 | Selley 13 | Freeman D — + 7 | Peschisolido P 32 | Taylor M 28 | McAnespie S 2 + 2 | Coleman C 26 | Neilson A 17 | Trollope P 19 + 5 | Lightbourne K 4 | Collins W 10 + 3 | Brevett R 11 | Arnott A — + 1 | Thorpe T 5 + 8 | Brazier M 3 + 4 | Beardsley P 8 | Match No. |
|---|---|---|---|---|---|---|---|---|---|---|---|---|---|---|---|---|---|---|---|---|---|---|---|---|---|---|---|---|---|---|---|---|---|---|---|---|---|
| 1 | 2 | 3 | 4 | 5 | 6 | 7¹ | 8 | 9² | 10 | 11¹³ | 12 | 13 | 14 | | | | | | | | | | | | | | | | | | | | | | | | 1 |
| 1 | | 3 | 4 | 5 | | 7¹ | 8² | 9 | 10 | 11¹² | 12 | | | 6 | 2 | 13 | 14 | | | | | | | | | | | | | | | | | | | | 2 |
| 1 | | 3 | 4 | 5 | | 7 | 8 | 9¹ | 10 | 11¹² | 12 | | | 13 | 2 | 6 | | | | | | | | | | | | | | | | | | | | | 3 |
| 1 | | 3 | 4 | 5¹ | 6 | 7 | 8 | | 10 | | 12 | 13 | | 11¹ | 2 | 14 | | | | | | | | | | | | | | | | | | | | | 4 |
| 1 | | 3 | 4 | 5 | 6 | 7² | 8 | | 10 | | 12 | 13 | 9¹ | 11¹ | 2 | 14 | | | | | | | | | | | | | | | | | | | | | 5 |
| 1 | | 3 | 4 | 5¹ | 6 | 7² | 8 | | 10 | | 12 | 13 | 9 | 14 | 2 | 11³ | | | | | | | | | | | | | | | | | | | | | 6 |
| 1 | | 3 | 4 | 5 | 6² | 7² | 8 | | 10 | | 12 | | 9 | 2 | 11 | | | 13 | | | | | | | | | | | | | | | | | | | 7 |
| | | 3¹ | 4 | 5 | | | | 13 | 8 | 12 | 10 | 11³ | 7 | 9² | 2 | 14 | | 1 | 6 | | | | | | | | | | | | | | | | | | 8 |
| | | 3 | 5 | 12 | | | 8 | | 9 | 10 | 2 | 13 | 11² | 7 | 6 | | | 4¹ | 1 | | | | | | | | | | | | | | | | | | 9 |
| | | 3 | 2 | 7 | 5 | | 11 | 10¹ | | 4 | | 9 | 8 | 6 | | | | 1 | | 12 | | | | | | | | | | | | | | | | | 10 |
| 1 | | 3 | 2 | 7¹ | 5 | | 11 | 10³ | | 4 | 12 | 9² | | 6 | | | | | | 13 | 14 | 8 | | | | | | | | | | | | | | | 11 |
| 1 | | 3 | 2 | 7³ | 5 | | 11 | 10 | 12 | 13 | | | 6 | | | | | | | 9 | 8² | 4¹ | 14 | | | | | | | | | | | | | | 12 |
| 1 | | 3 | 2 | 7 | | | 11 | 10 | 5 | | 12 | 9 | | 6 | | | | | | 8 | 4¹ | | | | | | | | | | | | | | | | 13 |
| 1 | 12 | 3¹ | 2 | 7 | | | 11 | | 5 | 13 | | 9 | | 6 | | | | | | 8 | 4² | | 10 | | | | | | | | | | | | | | 14 |
| 1 | | 3 | | 7 | 2 | | 11 | | 5 | 4 | | 9 | | 6 | | | | | | 8 | | | 10 | | | | | | | | | | | | | | 15 |
| | | 3 | | 7 | 2 | | 9¹ | 5 | 4 | 12 | | | 6 | | | 1 | | | | 8 | | | 10 | | | | | | | | | | | | | | 16 |
| 12 | | 3 | | 7 | 2 | | 11¹ | | 5 | 4 | 13 | 9 | | 6 | | 1 | | | | 8 | | | 10² | | | | | | | | | | | | | | 17 |
| 11² | | 3 | 12 | 7 | 2 | | | | 5¹ | 4 | 9 | | | 6 | | | | | | 8 | | | 10 | | 1 | | | | | | | | | | | | 18 |
| 11 | | 3 | 5 | 7 | 2 | | | | | 4 | 9 | | | 6 | | | | | | 8 | | | 10 | | 1 | | | | | | | | | | | | 19 |
| 11 | | 3 | 5 | 7 | 2 | 6 | | | | 4¹ | 9 | 12 | | 6 | | | | | | 8 | | | 10 | | 1 | | | | | | | | | | | | 20 |
| | | 3 | 4¹ | 7 | | | | | | 9 | 12 | | | 6 | | | | | | 8 | | | 10 | 1 | | 2 | 5 | 6 | 11 | | | | | | | | 21 |
| | | 3 | 4 | 7 | | | | | | 12 | 9² | 13 | | 2³ | | | | | | 8¹ | | | 10 | 1 | 14 | 5 | 6 | 11 | | | | | | | | 22 |
| | | 3 | 12 | 7 | | | 11 | | | 4² | | 9 | | 2² | 13 | | | | | 8¹ | | | 10 | 1 | 14 | 5 | 6 | | | | | | | | | 23 |
| | | 3 | | 7 | | | 11 | | | | 13 | | | 9 | 2 | | | | | 8 | | | 10 | 1 | | 5 | 6 | 4 | | | | | | | | 24 |
| | | 3¹ | 12 | 7² | | | 11 | | | 13 | | | | 9 | 2 | | | | | 8 | | | 10 | 1 | | 5 | 6 | 4 | | | | | | | | 25 |
| | | 3 | | 7 | | | 11 | | | 12 | | 9 | | 2 | | | | | | 8¹ | | 13 | 10² | 1 | | 5 | 6 | 4 | | | | | | | | 26 |
| | | 7¹ | | 11 | | | | | | | | 3 | | | | | | | | 8 | | 12 | 10 | 1 | 2 | 5 | 6 | 4 | 9 | | | | | | | 27 |
| | | 2 | | 11 | | | | | | 7 | | 3 | | | | | | | | 8 | | 12 | 10² | 1 | | 5 | 6 | 4 | 9¹ | 13 | | | | | | 28 |
| | | 7 | | 11 | | | | | | 9 | | 2¹ | | | | | | | | 8 | | | 10 | 1 | | 5 | 6 | 4 | 10 | 12 | 3 | | | | | 29 |
| | | 7 | | | | | | | | 9¹ | | 2 | 12 | | | | | | | 8 | | | 10 | 1 | | 5 | 6 | 4 | 11² | 13 | 3 | | | | | 30 |
| | | 7 | | 12 | | | | | | 9¹ | | 2 | | | | | | | | 8 | | | 10 | 1 | | 5 | 6 | 4 | | 11 | 3 | | | | | 31 |
| | | | | 11 | | | | | | 12 | | 2 | 7¹ | | | | | | | 8 | | | 10 | 1 | | 5 | 6 | 4 | | 9 | 3 | | | | | 32 |
| | | 12 | | 11 | | | | | | 7¹ | | 2 | | 13 | | | | | | 8 | | | 10¹ | 1 | | 5 | 6 | 4³ | | 9 | 3 | 14 | | | | 33 |
| | | 7 | 12 | 11 | | | | | | | | 2 | | | | | | | | 8 | | 13 | 10 | 1 | | 5 | 6¹ | 4 | | | 3 | | 9² | | | 34 |
| | | 7 | 6 | 12 | | | | | | | | 2 | | 1 | | | | | | 8 | | 13 | 10 | | | 5 | | 4 | 11² | 3 | | | 9¹ | | | 35 |
| | | 7 | 6 | 11 | | | 3 | | | | | 2 | | | | | | | | 8 | | | 9 | 1 | | 5 | | 4 | | | | | 10 | | | 36 |
| | | 11 | 6¹ | 10 | | | 3 | | | | | 2 | | | | | | | | 7 | | 12 | 8 | 1 | | 5 | | 4 | | | | | 9 | | | 37 |
| | | 7 | 6 | 11 | | | | | | | 12 | 2 | | | | | | | | 8² | | | 9 | 1 | | 5 | 3 | 4 | | | | | 10¹ | 13 | | 38 |
| | | 2² | | 11 | | | | | | | | 9 | | 3 | 12 | | | | | 8 | | | 10³ | 1 | | 5 | 6 | 4¹ | | | | 14 | 13 | 7 | | 39 |
| | | 12 | | | | | | | | | | 9² | | 2 | | | | | | 8 | | | 10 | 1 | | 5 | 6 | 4¹ | 11 | | | 13 | 3 | 7 | | 40 |
| | | | 4 | 6 | | | | | | | | 9² | | 2 | | | | | | 8 | | | 10 | 1 | | 5 | | 12 | 11¹ | | | 13 | 3 | 7 | | 41 |
| | | | 4 | 6 | | | | | | | | 9 | | 2 | | | | | | 8 | | | 10² | 1 | | 5 | | 12 | 11¹ | 3 | | 13 | | 7 | | 42 |
| | | | 4 | 6 | | | | | | | | 9 | | 2 | | | | | | 8¹ | | | 10³ | 1 | | 5 | | 12 | 11² | 3 | | 14 | 13 | 7 | | 43 |
| | | | 4 | 6 | | | | | | | | 9 | | 2 | | | | | | 8 | | | 10² | 1 | | 5 | | 12 | | 3 | | 13 | 11¹ | 7 | | 44 |
| | | | 4 | 6 | | | | | | | 3 | 9 | | 2 | | | | | | 8 | | | 10² | 1 | | 5 | | | 11 | | | 13 | 12 | 7¹ | | 45 |
| | | | 4¹ | 6 | | | | | | | | 9 | | 2 | | | | | | 8 | | | 10² | 1 | | 5 | | 12 | | 11 | 3 | | 13 | 7 | | 46 |

**Coca-Cola Cup**

| | | | | |
|---|---|---|---|---|
| First Round | Wycombe W | (a) | 2-1 | |
| | | (h) | 4-4 | |
| Second Round | Wolverhampton W | (h) | 0-1 | |
| | | (a) | 0-1 | |

**FA Cup**

| | | | |
|---|---|---|---|
| First Round | Margate | (a) | 2-1 |
| Second Round | Southend U | (h) | 1-0 |
| Third Round | Tottenham H | (a) | 1-3 |

GILLINGHAM 1997–98   *Back row (left to right):* Wayne Jones (Physio) Paul Smith, Sam Tydeman, Leo Fortune-West, Roland Edge, Ian Chapman, Kevin Bremner (Youth Team Manager).
*Second row:* Tony Pulis (Manager) Neil Masters, Simon Ratcliffe, Guy Butters, Richard Green, Jim Stannard, Steve Butler, Glen Thomas, Adrian Pennock, Matthew Bryant, Lindsay Parsons (Assistant Manager).
*Third row:* Lennie Piper, Mark O'Connor, Dennis Bailey, Andy Hessenthaler, Paul Scally (Chairman & Chief Executive), Mick Galloway, Ade Akinbiyi, James Pinnock, Steve Norman.
*Front row:* Barry Sinclair, Danny Bovis, Paul Hobbs, Jim Corbett, Richard Radbourne, Tommy Osborne.

# Division 2      **GILLINGHAM**

*Priestfield Stadium, Gillingham, ME7 4DD.* Telephone: (01634) 851854/576828. Fax: (01634) 850986.

*Ground capacity:* 10,600.

*Record attendance:* 23,002 v QPR, FA Cup 3rd rd, 10 January 1948.

*Record receipts:* £80,184 v Sheffield W, FA Cup 3rd rd, 7 January 1995.

*Pitch measurements:* 114yd × 75yd.

*Chairman/Chief Executive:* P. D. P. Scally.

*Director:* P. A. Spokes. *Associate Director:* Yvonne Paulley.

*Manager:* Tony Pulis. *Assistant Manager:* Lindsay Parsons.

*Physio:* W. Jones.

*Secretary:* Mrs G. E. Poynter. *Sales and Marketing Manager:* M. Sullivan.

*Year Formed:* 1893. *Turned Professional:* 1894. *Ltd Co.:* 1893.

*Club Nickname:* 'The Gills'.

*Previous Name:* New Brompton, 1893–1913.

*Foundation:* The success of the pioneering Royal Engineers of Chatham excited the interest of the residents of the Medway Towns and led to the formation of many clubs including Excelsior. After winning the Kent Junior Cup and the Chatham District League in 1893, Excelsior decided to go for bigger things and it was at a meeting in the Napier Arms, Brompton, in 1893 that New Brompton FC came into being, buying and developing the ground which is now Priestfield Stadium.

*First Football League game:* 28 August 1920, Division 3, v Southampton (h) D 1-1 – Branfield; Robertson, Sissons; Battiste, Baxter, Wigmore; Holt, Hall, Gilbey (1), Roe, Gore.

*Record League Victory:* 10–0 v Chesterfield, Division 3, 5 September 1987 – Kite; Haylock, Pearce, Shipley (2) (Lillis), West, Greenall (1), Pritchard (2), Shearer (2), Lovell, Elsey (2), David Smith (1).

*Record Cup Victory:* 10–1 v Gorleston, FA Cup 1st rd, 16 November 1957 – Brodie; Parry, Hannaway; Riggs, Boswell, Laing; Payne, Fletcher (2), Saunders (5), Morgan (1), Clark (2).

*Record Defeat:* 2–9 v Nottingham F, Division 3 (S), 18 November 1950.

*Most League Points (2 for a win):* 62, Division 4, 1973–74.

*Most League Points (3 for a win):* 83, Division 3, 1984–85 and Division 3, 1995–96.

*Most League Goals:* 90, Division 4, 1973–74.

*Highest League Scorer in Season:* Ernie Morgan, 31, Division 3 (S), 1954–55 and Brian Yeo, 31, Division 4, 1973–74.

*Most League Goals in Total Aggregate:* Brian Yeo, 135, 1963–75.

*Most Capped Player:* Tony Cascarino, 3 (76), Republic of Ireland.

*Most League Appearances:* John Simpson, 571, 1957–72.

*Record Transfer Fee Received:* £1,200,000 from Bristol C for Ade Akinbiyi, May 1998.

*Record Transfer Fee Paid:* £250,000 to Norwich C for Ade Akinbiyi, January 1997.

*Football League Record:* 1920 Original Member of Division 3; 1921 Division 3 (S); 1938 Failed re-election; Southern League 1938–44; Kent League 1944–46; Southern League 1946–50; 1950 Re-elected to Division 3 (S); 1958–64 Division 4; 1964–71 Division 3; 1971–74 Division 4; 1974–89 Division 3; 1989–92 Division 4; 1992–96; Division 3; 1996– Division 2.

*Honours: Football League:* Division 3: Runners-up 1995-96; Division 4 – Champions 1963–64; Runners-up 1973–74. *FA Cup:* best season: 5th rd, 1970. *Football League Cup:* best season: 4th rd, 1964, 1997.

*Colours:* Blue and black. *Change colours:* Red and black.

**Did you know?**
On 13 January 1987 Mark Weatherly the Gillingham captain, walked six miles through snow to reach the game v Wigan Athletic, only to discover the match was postponed.

## GILLINGHAM 1997–98 LEAGUE RECORD

| Match No. | Date | Venue | Opponents | Result | | H/T Score | Lg. Pos. | Goalscorers | Attendance |
|---|---|---|---|---|---|---|---|---|---|
| 1 | Aug 9 | H | Preston NE | D | 0-0 | 0-0 | — | | 6562 |
| 2 | 16 | A | Burnley | D | 0-0 | 0-0 | 15 | | 11,811 |
| 3 | 23 | H | Walsall | W | 2-1 | 0-0 | 7 | Smith [49], Akinbiyi [68] | 5083 |
| 4 | 30 | A | York C | L | 1-2 | 0-0 | 11 | Bailey [84] | 2853 |
| 5 | Sept 2 | A | Brentford | L | 0-2 | 0-0 | — | | 4903 |
| 6 | 5 | H | Bournemouth | W | 2-1 | 0-1 | — | Butters (pen) [48], Butler [76] | 5168 |
| 7 | 13 | A | Bristol R | W | 2-1 | 0-0 | 8 | Butler [77], Akinbiyi [80] | 6572 |
| 8 | 20 | H | Watford | D | 2-2 | 1-0 | 9 | Butters [36], Butler [58] | 7780 |
| 9 | 27 | A | Carlisle U | L | 1-2 | 0-0 | 12 | Butters (pen) [90] | 5063 |
| 10 | Oct 4 | H | Bristol C | W | 2-0 | 2-0 | 7 | Akinbiyi 2 [6, 44] | 6277 |
| 11 | 11 | H | Wycombe W | W | 1-0 | 0-0 | 4 | Akinbiyi [78] | 5545 |
| 12 | 18 | A | Northampton T | L | 1-2 | 0-2 | 6 | Akinbiyi [53] | 7191 |
| 13 | 21 | A | Wigan Ath | W | 4-1 | 1-0 | — | Akinbiyi [31], Ratcliffe [47], Butler (pen) [71], Fortune-West [79] | 3214 |
| 14 | 25 | H | Plymouth Arg | W | 2-1 | 1-1 | 3 | Akinbiyi [32], Fortune-West [87] | 6679 |
| 15 | Nov 1 | H | Millwall | L | 1-3 | 0-1 | 5 | Fortune-West [67] | 8383 |
| 16 | 4 | A | Chesterfield | D | 1-1 | 0-0 | — | Akinbiyi [73] | 3420 |
| 17 | 7 | A | Oldham Ath | L | 1-3 | 0-2 | — | Butters [49] | 5338 |
| 18 | 18 | H | Blackpool | D | 1-1 | 1-0 | — | Butters (pen) [32] | 5045 |
| 19 | 21 | A | Fulham | L | 0-3 | 0-1 | — | | 8274 |
| 20 | 29 | H | Grimsby T | L | 0-2 | 0-1 | 15 | | 4855 |
| 21 | Dec 2 | A | Luton T | D | 2-2 | 1-1 | — | Akinbiyi 2 [27, 57] | 4408 |
| 22 | 13 | A | Southend U | L | 1-2 | 1-0 | 16 | Southall [4] | 4774 |
| 23 | 20 | A | Wrexham | D | 0-0 | 0-0 | 17 | | 2834 |
| 24 | 26 | A | Bournemouth | L | 0-4 | 0-1 | 17 | | 5672 |
| 25 | 29 | H | Brentford | W | 3-1 | 2-0 | — | Aspinall (og) [10], Akinbiyi 2 [45, 80] | 5908 |
| 26 | Jan 3 | A | Burnley | W | 2-0 | 1-0 | 11 | Butler [10], Smith [68] | 5886 |
| 27 | 10 | A | Preston NE | W | 3-1 | 2-0 | 8 | Butters [7], Galloway [45], Onuora [51] | 7776 |
| 28 | 17 | H | York C | D | 0-0 | 0-0 | 9 | | 5891 |
| 29 | 31 | H | Bristol R | D | 1-1 | 1-1 | 10 | Onuora [1] | 5593 |
| 30 | Feb 8 | A | Watford | W | 2-0 | 1-0 | 9 | Akinbiyi 2 [21, 90] | 10,498 |
| 31 | 14 | A | Bristol C | W | 2-0 | 0-0 | 9 | Corbett [48], Southall [71] | 11,781 |
| 32 | 21 | H | Carlisle U | W | 1-0 | 0-0 | 8 | Butler [71] | 6270 |
| 33 | 24 | H | Northampton T | W | 1-0 | 0-0 | — | Butters (pen) [69] | 6463 |
| 34 | 28 | A | Wycombe W | L | 0-1 | 0-1 | 7 | | 5583 |
| 35 | Mar 3 | H | Oldham Ath | W | 2-1 | 1-1 | — | Kelly (og) [35], Akinbiyi [50] | 5254 |
| 36 | 7 | A | Millwall | L | 0-1 | 0-0 | 6 | | 8241 |
| 37 | 14 | H | Chesterfield | W | 1-0 | 0-0 | 6 | Corbett [83] | 5672 |
| 38 | 21 | H | Blackpool | L | 1-2 | 0-0 | 7 | Fortune-West [88] | 4165 |
| 39 | 28 | H | Fulham | W | 2-0 | 1-0 | 7 | Akinbiyi 2 [32, 90] | 10,507 |
| 40 | 31 | A | Walsall | L | 0-1 | 0-0 | — | | 3117 |
| 41 | Apr 4 | A | Grimsby T | D | 0-0 | 0-0 | 7 | | 5190 |
| 42 | 11 | H | Luton T | W | 2-1 | 1-1 | 6 | Akinbiyi 2 [29, 49] | 6846 |
| 43 | 13 | A | Southend U | D | 0-0 | 0-0 | 6 | | 6151 |
| 44 | 18 | H | Wrexham | D | 1-1 | 1-1 | 8 | Akinbiyi [44] | 7869 |
| 45 | 25 | A | Plymouth Arg | W | 1-0 | 0-0 | 6 | Smith [90] | 7941 |
| 46 | May 2 | H | Wigan Ath | D | 0-0 | 0-0 | 8 | | 10,361 |

**Final League Position: 8**　　　　1996–97 DIV2 11

### GOALSCORERS

*League (52):* Akinbiyi 21, Butters 7 (4 pens), Butler 6 (1 pen), Fortune-West 4, Smith 3, Corbett 2, Onuora 2, Southall 2, Bailey 1, Galloway 1, Ratcliffe 1, own goals 2.
*Coca-Cola Cup (0).*
*FA Cup (2):* Akinbiyi 1, Onuora 1.

| Moss N 10 | Ratcliffe S 16+5 | Butters G 31 | Smith P 46 | Ashby B 43 | Bryant M 25+10 | Hessenthaler A 42 | Galloway M 32+7 | Butler S 30+13 | Akinbiyi A 44 | Masters N 11 | Green R 17+8 | Bailey D 7+6 | Fortune-West L 5+15 | Corbett J 8+8 | Statham B 16+4 | Piper L —+1 | Ndah G 4 | Onuora I 16+6 | Stannard J 20 | Patterson M 23 | Pennock A 20 | Pollitt M 6 | Southall N 22+1 | Thomas G 2+1 | Walton M 1 | Bartram V 9 | Pinnock J —+1 | Match No. |
|---|---|---|---|---|---|---|---|---|---|---|---|---|---|---|---|---|---|---|---|---|---|---|---|---|---|---|---|---|
| 1 | 2 | 3 | 4 | 5¹ | 6 | 7 | 8² | 9³ | 10 | 11 | 12 | 13 | 14 | | | | | | | | | | | | | | | 1 |
| 1 | 2 | 3 | 4 | 5 | 6 | 7 | 8 | 9³ | 10² | 11¹ | 12 | 14 | 13 | | | | | | | | | | | | | | | 2 |
| 1 | 2² | 3 | 4 | 5 | 6 | 7 | 8 | 9¹ | 10³ | | 12 | 13 | | 11 | 14 | | | | | | | | | | | | | 3 |
| 1 | 2 | 3 | 4 | 5 | 6 | 7 | | 9 | 10 | | 12 | | | | | | 8 | 11 | | | | | | | | | | 4 |
| 1 | 2 | 3 | 4 | 5 | 6 | 7 | 8¹ | 12 | 10 | | 9 | | | | | | | 11 | | | | | | | | | | 5 |
| 1 | 2 | 3 | 4 | 5 | | 7 | 6 | 11 | 10 | | 12 | 9¹ | | | | | | 8 | | | | | | | | | | 6 |
| 1 | 2 | 3 | 4 | 5 | 6¹ | 7 | | 9 | 10 | | 12 | 13 | | | | | | 8 | | 11² | | | | | | | | 7 |
| 1 | 8 | 3 | 4 | 5 | 6 | 7 | 12 | 9² | 10³ | 2 | | 14 | 13 | | | | | | | 11¹ | | | | | | | | 8 |
| 1 | | 3 | 4 | 5 | 6 | 7 | 8 | 9 | 10 | 2 | | | | | | | | | | 11 | | | | | | | | 9 |
| 1 | 8 | 3 | 4 | 5 | 6¹ | 7 | 12 | 9⁴ | 10 | 2 | | 13 | 11² | | | | | | | 14 | | | | | | | | 10 |
| | 8 | 3 | 4 | 5 | | 7 | 12 | 9¹ | 10 | 11 | 6² | 13 | | | | | | | 1 | 2 | | | | | | | | 11 |
| | 8 | | 4 | 5 | | 7 | 3 | 9 | 10 | | 6 | 11 | | | | | | | 1 | 2 | | | | | | | | 12 |
| | 8 | | 4 | 5 | | 7 | 3 | 9¹ | 10 | | 6 | 11 | 12 | | | | | | 1 | 2 | | | | | | | | 13 |
| | 8 | | 4 | 5 | | 7 | 3 | 9¹ | 10 | | 6 | 11² | 13 | 12 | | | | | 1 | 2 | | | | | | | | 14 |
| | 12 | 3 | 4 | 5 | | 7 | | 13 | 10 | | 6 | 8² | | | 2 | | | 9¹ | 1 | 11 | | | | | | | | 15 |
| | 12 | 3 | 4 | 5 | | 7 | | 13 | 10 | 14 | | 8² | | | 2 | | | 9¹ | 1 | 11 | 6³ | | | | | | | 16 |
| | | 3 | 4 | 5 | 12 | 7 | | 8 | 10 | | 6² | 13 | | | 2 | | | 9 | 1 | 11¹ | | | | | | | | 17 |
| 8¹ | 6 | 4 | 5 | 13 | | 7 | 11 | 9⁴ | 10 | | 2 | | | | 12 | 1 | | | | 3 | | | | | | | | 18 |
| 12 | 3 | 4 | 5 | 6¹ | | 7 | 9 | 13 | 10 | | 11 | | | | 8² | 1 | | | | 2 | | | | | | | | 19 |
| 6² | | 4 | 5 | 13 | | 7 | 11 | 12 | 10 | 3 | 9¹ | | | | 2 | | | | 8 | 1 | | | | | | | | 20 |
| 8 | | 4 | 5 | 6 | | 7 | 11¹ | | 10 | 3 | 12 | | | | 2 | | | | 9 | 1 | | | | | | | | 21 |
| | 4 | 5 | 6 | 7 | | 11¹ | 12 | 10 | 3 | 13 | | | | | 14 | | | 9³ | | 2⁴ | | | 1 | 8 | | | | 22 |
| 12 | 6 | 4 | | 7 | | 11 | | 10 | 3 | 2 | | | | | | | | 9 | | | | | 1 | 8 | 5¹ | | | 23 |
| 11¹ | 6 | 4 | | 12 | | 7² | 14 | 13 | 10 | 3 | 5³ | | | | | | | 9 | | | 2 | | 1 | 8 | | | | 24 |
| | 6 | 4 | 5 | 12 | | 7 | | 9 | 10 | 3¹ | | | | | | | | | | 2 | | | 8 | 1 | 11 | | | 25 |
| | 6 | 4 | 5 | 2 | | | | 11 | 9 | 10 | | | | | | | | | | 3¹ | 8 | 1 | 7 | | | | | 26 |
| | 6 | 4 | 5 | 2 | | | 8 | 9 | | 3 | | 11 | 10 | | | | | | | | | | 1 | 7 | | | | 27 |
| | 6 | 4 | 5 | 2 | 7 | | 11 | 9 | | 3¹ | 12 | | | | | | | | | 10 | 1 | | 8 | | | | | 28 |
| | 6 | 4 | 5 | 12 | 7 | | 11 | 9 | 10² | 3³ | | 13 | 14 | | | | | | | 8¹ | 1 | | 2 | | | | | 29 |
| | 6 | 4 | 5 | 12 | 7 | | 11² | 9¹ | 10 | | | 14 | | | | | | | | 13 | 2 | 3 | 8³ | 1 | | | | 30 |
| 13 | 6 | 4 | 5 | 12² | 7 | | 11¹ | 9³ | 10 | | | 2 | | | | | | | | 14 | 1 | 3 | 8 | | | | | 31 |
| | 6 | 4 | 5 | | 7 | 12 | 13 | 10 | 11² | | | | | | | | | 9¹ | 1 | 2 | 3 | | 8 | | | | | 32 |
| | 6 | 4 | 5 | | 7 | | | 9 | 10 | | | | | | | | | 11 | 1 | 2 | 3 | | 8 | | | | | 33 |
| | 6 | 4 | 5 | | 7 | 11¹ | | 9 | 10 | | 12 | | | | | | | | 1 | 2 | 3 | | 8 | | | | | 34 |
| | 6 | 4 | 5 | 12 | 7³ | | 13 | 9¹ | 10 | | | | | | | | | 11 | 1 | 2 | 3 | | 8 | | | | | 35 |
| | 6² | 4 | 5 | 12 | 7 | | 13 | 9¹ | 10 | | | | | | | | | 11 | 1 | 2 | 3 | | 8 | | | | | 36 |
| | | 4 | 5 | 6¹ | 7 | | 8⁰ | 9 | 10 | 11² | 12 | | 13 | 14 | | | | | 1 | 2 | 3 | | | | | | | 37 |
| | | 4 | 5 | 6 | | | 8 | 9¹ | 10 | | 12 | 11 | | | | | | | | 2 | 3 | | 7 | | | 1 | | 38 |
| | | 4 | 5 | 6 | | | 8 | 12 | 10 | | 9 | 11¹ | | | | | | | | 2 | 3 | | 7 | | | 1 | | 39 |
| | | 4 | 5 | 6 | 7 | | 8¹ | 12 | 10 | | 9 | 13 | | | | | | | | 2 | 3 | | 7 | | | 1 | | 40 |
| | | 9 | 5 | 6 | 7 | | 8 | 12 | 10 | | | | | | | | | | | 2 | 3 | | 11¹ | 4 | | 1 | | 41 |
| | | 4 | 5 | 6 | 7 | | 8 | 9² | 10¹ | | 12 | 13 | | | | | | | | 2 | 3 | | 11² | 14 | | 1 | | 42 |
| | | 4 | 5 | 6 | 7 | | 8 | | 10 | | 12 | 11 | | | | | | | | 2 | 3 | | 9¹ | | | 1 | | 43 |
| | | 4 | 5 | 6 | 7 | | 8 | 9¹ | 10 | | 12 | 13 | | | | | | | | 2 | 3 | | 11² | | | 1 | | 44 |
| | | 4 | 5¹ | 6 | 7 | | 11 | 12 | 10 | | 3² | | | | | | | 9¹ | 13 | 2 | 8 | | | | | 1 | 14 | 45 |
| | | 4 | | 6² | 7 | | 8⁰ | 12 | 10 | 3 | 5 | | | | | | | 9¹ | 11 | 13 | 2 | | | 14 | | 1 | | 46 |

**Coca-Cola Cup**  
First Round    Birmingham C    (h)   0-1  
                                          (a)   0-3

**FA Cup**  
First Round    Bristol R    (a)   2-2  
                                   (h)   0-2

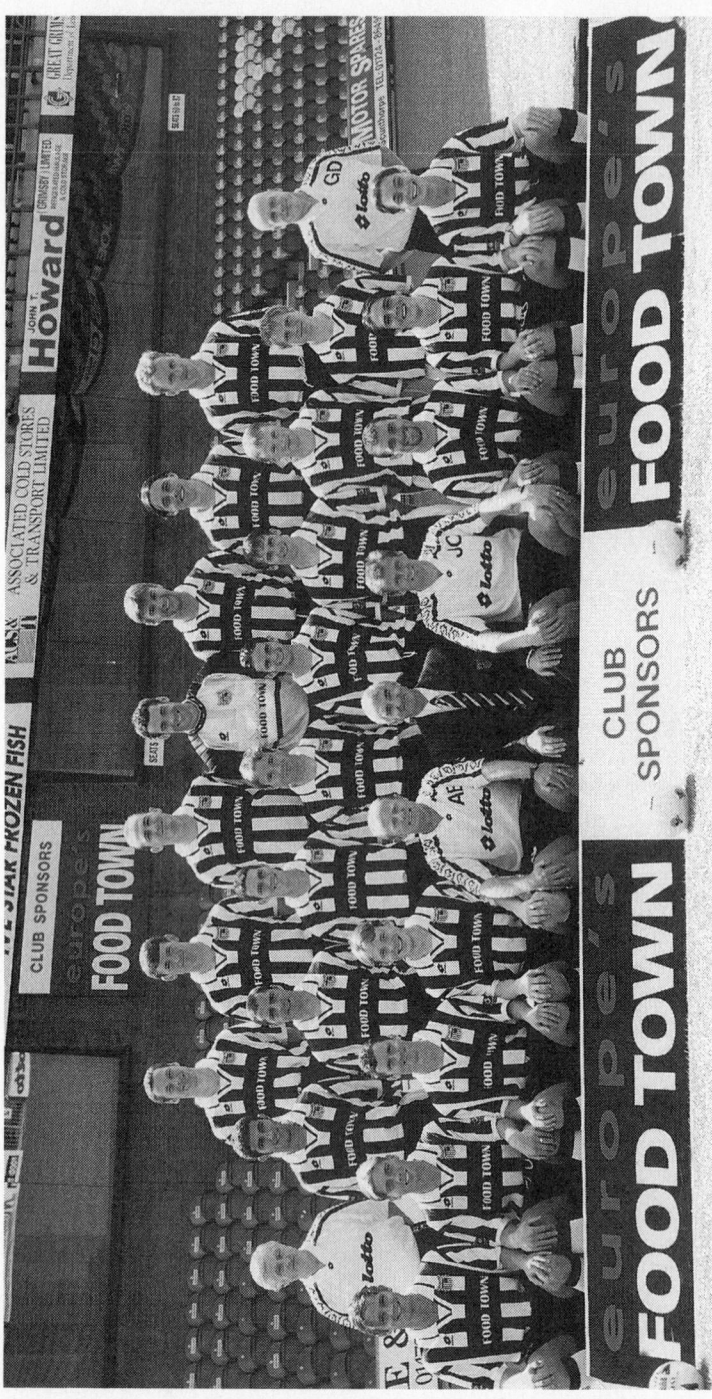

GRIMSBY TOWN 1997-98    *Back row (left to right):* Paul Groves, Neil Woods, Graham Rodger, Aidan Davison, Mark Lever, Peter Handyside, Steve Livingstone.
*Middle row:* Mike Bielby (Kit Manager), Jack Lester, Kevin Jobling, Ashley Fickling, Kingsley Black, James Brown, Jimmy Neil, Lee Stevenson, Ben Chapman, Gerry Delahunt (Physio).
*Front row:* Tony Gallimore, Nicky Southall, John McDermott, Darren Wrack, Alan Buckley (Manager), Bill Carr (Chairman), John Cockerill (Assistant Manager), Tommy Widdrington, Daryl Clare, Matthew Bloomer.

# Division 1     **GRIMSBY TOWN**

*Blundell Park, Cleethorpes, North East Lincolnshire DN35 7PY.* Telephone: (01472) 697111. Fax: (01472) 693665. Mariners Hotline: 0891 555 855.

*Ground capacity:* 8870.

*Record attendance:* 31,657 v Wolverhampton W, FA Cup 5th rd, 20 February 1937.

*Record receipts:* £119,799 v Aston Villa, FA Cup 4th rd, 29 January 1994.

*Pitch measurements:* 111yd × 75yd.

*President:* T. J. Lindley.

*Chairman:* W. H. Carr. *Vice-Chairman:* T. Aspinall.

*Directors:* G. Lamming, J. Mager, J. Teanby, C. Aspinall.

*Manager:* Alan Buckley.

*Assistant Manager:* John Cockerill.

*Chief Executive/Company Secretary:* Ian Fleming. *Commercial Manager:* Tony Richardson.

*Assistant Commercial Manager/Lottery Manager:* Tim Harvey.

*Physio:* Paul Mitchell.

*Year Formed.* 1878. *Turned Professional:* 1890. *Ltd Co.:* 1890.

*Previous Name:* Grimsby Pelham.

*Club Nickname:* 'The Mariners'.

*Previous Grounds:* Clee Park; Abbey Park.

*Foundation:* Grimsby Pelham FC as they were first known, came into being at a meeting held at the Wellington Arms in September 1878. Pelham is the family name of big landowners in the area, the Earls of Yarborough. The receipts for their first game amounted to 6s. 9d. (approx. 39p). After a year, the club name was changed to Grimsby Town.

*First Football League game:* 3 September 1892, Division 2, v Northwich Victoria (h) W 2-1 – Whitehouse; Lundie, T. Frith; C. Frith, Walker, Murrell; Higgins, Henderson, Brayshaw, Riddoch (2), Ackroyd.

*Record League Victory:* 9–2 v Darwen, Division 2, 15 April 1899 – Bagshaw; Lockie, Nidd; Griffiths, Bell (1), Nelmes; Jenkinson (3), Richards (1), Cockshutt (3), Robinson, Chadburn (1).

*Record Cup Victory:* 8–0 v Darlington, FA Cup 2nd rd, 21 November 1885 – G. Atkinson; J. H. Taylor, H. Taylor; Hall, Kimpson, Hopewell; H. Atkinson (1), Garnham, Seal (3), Sharman, Monument (4).

*Record Defeat:* 1–9 v Arsenal, Division 1, 28 January 1931.

*Most League Points (2 for a win):* 68, Division 3 (N), 1955–56.

*Most League Points (3 for a win):* 83, Division 3, 1990–91.

*Most League Goals:* 103, Division 2, 1933–34.

*Highest League Scorer in Season:* Pat Glover, 42, Division 2, 1933–34.

*Most League Goals in Total Aggregate:* Pat Glover, 180, 1930–39.

*Most Capped Player:* Pat Glover, 7, Wales.

*Most League Appearances:* Keith Jobling, 448, 1953–69.

*Record Transfer Fee Received:* £1,500,000 from Everton for John Oster, July 1997.

*Record Transfer Fee Paid:* £300,000 to Southampton for Tommy Widdrington, July 1996 and £300,000 to WBA for Kevin Donovan, July 1997.

*Football League Record:* 1892 Original Member Division 2; 1901–03 Division 1; 1903 Division 2; 1910 Failed re-election; 1911 re-elected Division 2; 1920–21 Division 3; 1921–26 Division 3 (N); 1926–29 Division 2; 1929–32 Division 1; 1932–34 Division 2; 1934–48 Division 1; 1948–51 Division 2; 1951–56 Division 3 (N); 1956–59 Division 2; 1959–62 Division 3; 1962–64 Division 2; 1964–68 Division 3; 1968–72 Division 4; 1972–77 Division 3; 1977–79 Division 4; 1979–80 Division 3; 1980–87 Division 2; 1987–88 Division 3; 1988–90 Division 4; 1990–91 Division 3; 1991–92 Division 2; 1992–97 Division 1; 1997–98 Division 2; 1998– Division 1.

*Honours: Football League:* Division 1 best season: 5th, 1934–35; Division 2 – Champions 1900–01, 1933–34; Runners-up 1928–29, Promoted from Division 2 1997–98 (play-offs); Division 3 (N) – Champions 1925–26, 1955–56; Runners-up 1951–52; Division 3 – Champions 1979–80; Runners-up 1961–62; Division 4 – Champions 1971–72; Runners-up 1978–79; 1989–90. *FA Cup:* Semi-finals, 1936, 1939. *Football League Cup:* best season: 5th rd, 1980, 1985. *League Group Cup:* Winners 1982. *Auto Windscreen Shield:* Winners 1998.

*Colours:* Black and white striped shirts, black shorts, black stockings. *Change colours:* Blue shirts, white shorts, blue stockings.

**Did you know?**
Tommy McCairns scored six goals for Grimsby Town v Leicester Fosse on 11 April 1896 in a 7-1 win.

## GRIMSBY TOWN 1997–98 LEAGUE RECORD

| Match No. | Date | | Venue | Opponents | Result | H/T Score | Lg. Pos. | Goalscorers | Attendance |
|---|---|---|---|---|---|---|---|---|---|
| 1 | Aug | 9 | H | Bristol C | D 1-1 | 0-1 | — | Widdrington [75] | 6220 |
| 2 | | 16 | A | Plymouth Arg | D 2-2 | 0-2 | 13 | Donovan (pen) [66], Nogan [73] | 6002 |
| 3 | | 23 | H | Wrexham | D 0-0 | 0-0 | 19 | | 4404 |
| 4 | | 30 | A | Brentford | L 1-3 | 0-2 | 21 | Nogan [66] | 3875 |
| 5 | Sept | 2 | A | Preston NE | L 0-2 | 0-0 | — | | 9489 |
| 6 | | 9 | H | York C | D 0-0 | 0-0 | — | | 5308 |
| 7 | | 13 | H | Fulham | W 2-0 | 1-0 | 20 | Livingstone 2 [23, 86] | 6874 |
| 8 | | 20 | H | Millwall | L 0-1 | 0-0 | 21 | | 4267 |
| 9 | | 27 | A | Bournemouth | W 1-0 | 0-0 | 20 | Groves [57] | 3712 |
| 10 | Oct | 4 | H | Wigan Ath | W 2-1 | 1-0 | 15 | Donovan 2 (2 pens) [2, 79] | 4623 |
| 11 | | 11 | H | Northampton T | W 1-0 | 1-0 | 12 | Donovan [44] | 4778 |
| 12 | | 18 | A | Blackpool | D 2-2 | 1-1 | 14 | Nogan [7], Donovan (pen) [85] | 5234 |
| 13 | | 21 | A | Oldham Ath | L 0-2 | 0-0 | — | | 4520 |
| 14 | | 25 | H | Watford | L 0-1 | 0-1 | 17 | | 5699 |
| 15 | Nov | 1 | H | Southend U | W 5-1 | 3-0 | 13 | Nogan 2 [3, 62], Lester [16], Groves [19], Widdrington [53] | 4501 |
| 16 | | 4 | A | Walsall | D 0-0 | 0-0 | — | | 2599 |
| 17 | | 8 | A | Chesterfield | L 0-1 | 0-0 | 15 | | 5004 |
| 18 | | 22 | H | Burnley | W 4-1 | 1-1 | 15 | Groves [19], Widdrington [59], Lester [73], Nogan [78] | 4829 |
| 19 | | 29 | A | Gillingham | W 2-0 | 1-0 | 13 | Jobling [35], Black [76] | 4855 |
| 20 | Dec | 2 | H | Wycombe W | D 0-0 | 0-0 | — | | 4160 |
| 21 | | 12 | A | Bristol R | W 4-0 | 2-0 | — | Gallimore [23], Livingstone 2 [26, 84], Donovan [82] | 4801 |
| 22 | | 20 | H | Carlisle U | W 1-0 | 0-0 | 7 | McDermott [58] | 6222 |
| 23 | | 26 | A | York C | D 0-0 | 0-0 | 7 | | 7093 |
| 24 | | 28 | H | Preston NE | W 3-1 | 3-0 | 4 | Donovan 2 [11, 36], Black [20] | 6725 |
| 25 | Jan | 10 | A | Bristol C | L 1-4 | 0-3 | 6 | Groves [82] | 12,567 |
| 26 | | 17 | H | Brentford | W 4-0 | 2-0 | 5 | Groves [10], Smith [18], Donovan [58], Clare [85] | 4624 |
| 27 | | 31 | H | Fulham | D 1-1 | 0-0 | 7 | Burnett [88] | 6785 |
| 28 | Feb | 7 | A | Millwall | W 1-0 | 1-0 | 6 | Livingstone [23] | 6020 |
| 29 | | 14 | A | Wigan Ath | W 2-0 | 0-0 | 5 | Nogan [51], Donovan [86] | 3548 |
| 30 | | 21 | H | Bournemouth | W 2-1 | 0-1 | 4 | O'Neill (og) [66], Groves [79] | 5456 |
| 31 | | 24 | H | Blackpool | W 1-0 | 0-0 | — | Clare [60] | 4924 |
| 32 | | 28 | A | Northampton T | L 1-2 | 1-0 | 6 | Donovan [17] | 6932 |
| 33 | Mar | 3 | H | Chesterfield | D 0-0 | 0-0 | — | | 4940 |
| 34 | | 7 | A | Southend U | W 1-0 | 0-0 | 3 | Clare [58] | 4829 |
| 35 | | 14 | H | Walsall | W 3-0 | 0-0 | 3 | Nogan [59], Donovan 2 [67, 89] | 4916 |
| 36 | | 21 | A | Luton T | D 2-2 | 0-0 | 4 | Gallimore [54], Donovan [64] | 5700 |
| 37 | | 24 | A | Plymouth Arg | W 1-0 | 0-0 | — | Groves [78] | 4661 |
| 38 | | 28 | A | Burnley | L 1-2 | 1-1 | 3 | Lester [16] | 8256 |
| 39 | | 31 | A | Wrexham | D 0-0 | 0-0 | — | | 5421 |
| 40 | Apr | 4 | H | Gillingham | D 0-0 | 0-0 | 3 | | 5190 |
| 41 | | 7 | H | Luton T | L 0-1 | 0-0 | — | | 4455 |
| 42 | | 10 | A | Wycombe W | D 1-1 | 0-1 | — | Lester [90] | 5846 |
| 43 | | 13 | H | Bristol R | L 1-2 | 1-2 | 4 | Donovan (pen) [13] | 5484 |
| 44 | | 21 | A | Carlisle U | W 1-0 | 1-0 | — | Donovan (pen) [28] | 3956 |
| 45 | | 25 | H | Watford | D 0-0 | 0-0 | — | | 14,002 |
| 46 | May | 2 | H | Oldham Ath | L 0-2 | 0-0 | 3 | | 8054 |

**Final League Position: 3**    1996–97 DIV2 22

### GOALSCORERS

*League (55):* Donovan 16 (6 pens), Nogan 8, Groves 7, Livingstone 5, Lester 4, Clare 3, Widdrington 3, Black 2, Gallimore 2, Burnett 1, Jobling 1, McDermott 1, Smith 1, own goal 1.
*Coca-Cola Cup (12):* Livingstone 4, Lester 3, Groves 2, Donovan 1, Jobling 1, Nogan 1.
*FA Cup (12):* Lester 2, Nogan 2, Donovan 1, Groves 1, Jobling 1, McDermott 1, Rodger 1, Southall 1, Woods 1, own goal 1.

| Davison A 42 | McDermott J 40 + 1 | Gallimore T 34 + 1 | Handyside P 40 + 2 | Lever M 37 + 1 | Widdrington T 15 + 6 | Donovan K 46 | Black K 24 + 15 | Livingstone S 28 + 13 | Nogan L 33 + 3 | Groves P 46 | Jobling K 17 + 13 | Woods N 1 + 9 | Southall N 4 + 1 | Gilbert D 5 | Lester J 27 + 13 | Pearcey J 4 | Butterfield D 4 + 3 | Holsgrove P 3 + 7 | Rodger G 10 + 1 | Clare D 8 + 14 | Burnett W 20 + 1 | Smith D 17 | Wrack D —+ 1 | Dobbin J 1 + 1 | Match No |
|---|---|---|---|---|---|---|---|---|---|---|---|---|---|---|---|---|---|---|---|---|---|---|---|---|---|
| 1 | 2 | $3^1$ | 4 | 5 | 6 | 7 | $8^2$ | 9 | 10 | 11 | 12 | 13 | | | | | | | | | | | | | 1 |
| 1 | 2 | $3^1$ | 4 | 5 | | 7 | | $9^2$ | 10 | 11 | 12 | | 6 | 8 | 13 | | | | | | | | | | 2 |
| 1 | 2 | | 4 | 5 | | 7 | | 12 | 10 | 11 | 3 | | 6 | $8^1$ | 9 | | | | | | | | | | 3 |
| 1 | 2 | 12 | 4 | 5 | 13 | 7 | 14 | 9 | 11 | 3 | | | $6^1$ | $8^2$ | $10^3$ | | | | | | | | | | 4 |
| 1 | $2^1$ | | 4 | 5 | 12 | 7 | 13 | 9 | 11 | 3 | 14 | | 6 | $8^2$ | $10^3$ | | | | | | | | | | 5 |
| | 3 | 4 | 5 | 6 | 7 | 12 | $10^2$ | 9 | 11 | 14 | | | | $8^1$ | 13 | 1 | $2^3$ | | | | | | | | 6 |
| | 12 | 3 | 4 | 5 | 7 | 8 | 10 | $9^2$ | 11 | 13 | | | | | | 1 | $2^1$ | 6 | | | | | | | 7 |
| | 2 | $3^1$ | 4 | 5 | 12 | 7 | $8^2$ | 10 | $9^3$ | 11 | 13 | 14 | | | | 1 | | 6 | | | | | | | 8 |
| 1 | $2^1$ | 3 | 4 | 5 | 12 | 7 | 8 | 10 | 13 | 11 | $9^2$ | | | | | | | 6 | | | | | | | 9 |
| 1 | 2 | 3 | 4 | 5 | 6 | 7 | $8^3$ | 12 | $9^1$ | 11 | 13 | | | | $10^2$ | | 14 | | | | | | | | 10 |
| | 3 | 4 | | $6^3$ | 7 | 8 | 12 | 9 | 11 | 13 | | | | | $10^1$ | 1 | $2^3$ | 14 | 5 | | | | | | 11 |
| | $3^2$ | $4^3$ | 5 | 6 | 7 | $8^1$ | 10 | 9 | 11 | 2 | | | | | 12 | | | 13 | 14 | | | | | | 12 |
| 1 | | | 4 | 5 | 6 | 7 | $8^1$ | $10^2$ | 9 | 11 | 3 | | | | 12 | | | 13 | 14 | $2^3$ | | | | | 13 |
| 1 | 2 | 3 | $4^1$ | 5 | 6 | 7 | $8^2$ | 12 | 9 | 11 | 13 | | | | 10 | | | | | | | | | | 14 |
| 1 | 2 | | 4 | 5 | $6^2$ | 7 | 8 | $9^1$ | 11 | 3 | 12 | | | | $10^3$ | | 13 | 14 | | | | | | | 15 |
| 1 | 2 | | 4 | 5 | $6^3$ | 7 | $8^2$ | 12 | 9 | 11 | 3 | | | | $10^1$ | | 13 | 14 | | | | | | | 16 |
| 1 | 2 | | 4 | 5 | $6^3$ | 7 | $8^1$ | 10 | $9^2$ | 11 | 3 | 12 | | | 13 | | 14 | | | | | | | | 17 |
| 1 | 2 | 3 | 4 | | 6 | 7 | 8 | 12 | $9^2$ | 11 | 13 | | | | $10^1$ | | | | 5 | | | | | | 18 |
| 1 | 2 | 3 | 4 | | | 7 | 8 | 12 | 9 | 11 | 6 | | | | $10^1$ | | | | 5 | | | | | | 19 |
| 1 | 2 | 3 | 4 | | 12 | 7 | $8^2$ | 13 | 9 | 11 | 6 | | | | $10^1$ | | | | $5^3$ | 14 | | | | | 20 |
| 1 | 2 | 3 | 4 | | 6 | 7 | 12 | 9¹ | 11 | 8 | | | | | $10^2$ | | 13 | | $5^3$ | 14 | | | | | 21 |
| 1 | 2 | 3 | 4 | | $8^1$ | 7 | 12 | 9 | 11 | 6 | | | | | | | 13 | | 5 | $10^2$ | | | | | 22 |
| 1 | 2 | 3 | 4 | | 8 | 7 | 10 | 9 | 11 | $6^1$ | | | | | | | | | 5 | 12 | | | | | 23 |
| 1 | 2 | 3 | 4 | 12 | $6^2$ | 7 | 8 | 9 | 11 | 13 | | | | | 14 | | | | $5^1$ | $10^3$ | | | | | 24 |
| 1 | 2 | 3 | | 5 | | 7 | 8 | 9 | 11 | 6 | 12 | | | | $4^2$ | | | | $10^1$ | 13 | | | | | 25 |
| 1 | 2 | $3^3$ | | 5 | 12 | 7 | 13 | 9 | 11 | 14 | $4^2$ | | | | 10 | | | | $6^1$ | 8 | | | | | 26 |
| 1 | 2 | $3^2$ | 4 | $5^1$ | | 7 | 12 | 9 | 11 | 13 | | | | | $10^3$ | | | | 14 | 6 | 8 | | | | 27 |
| 1 | 2 | 3 | 4 | $5^2$ | | 7 | 12 | 9 | 13 | 11 | | | | | $10^1$ | | | | | 6 | 8 | | | | 28 |
| 1 | 2 | 3 | 4 | 5 | | 7 | | 10 | $9^1$ | 11 | 12 | | | | | | | | | 6 | 8 | | | | 29 |
| 1 | 2 | 3 | 4 | $5^2$ | | 7 | 12 | 10 | $9^3$ | 11 | 13 | | | | | | | | 14 | 6 | $8^1$ | | | | 30 |
| 1 | 2 | | 5 | | | 7 | 8 | 4 | $9^1$ | 11 | 3 | | | | 10 | | | | 12 | 6 | | | | | 31 |
| 1 | 2 | | 5 | | | 7 | $8^2$ | 4 | 9 | 11 | 3 | | | | $10^1$ | | | | 12 | 6 | | 13 | | | 32 |
| 1 | 2 | 12 | 5 | | | 7 | $8^1$ | 4 | $9^2$ | 11 | 3 | | | | 13 | | | | 10 | 6 | | | | | 33 |
| 1 | 2 | 3 | 12 | 5 | | 7 | $8^1$ | 4 | $9^2$ | 11 | | | | | 13 | | | | 10 | 6 | | | | | 34 |
| 1 | 2 | $3^1$ | 4 | 5 | | 7 | 12 | | $9^2$ | 11 | 13 | | | | 14 | | | | $10^3$ | 6 | 8 | | | | 35 |
| 1 | 2 | 3 | 4 | 5 | | 7 | | 12 | $9^1$ | 11 | | | | | 10 | | | | | 6 | 8 | | | | 36 |
| 1 | 2 | $3^1$ | 4 | 5 | | 7 | 12 | 13 | $9^2$ | 11 | | | | | 10 | | | | | 6 | 8 | | | | 37 |
| 1 | 2 | | 4 | 5 | | 7 | $8^2$ | 9 | 12 | 11 | 13 | | | | $10^1$ | | 14 | | | | 3 | | $6^3$ | | 38 |
| 1 | 2 | 3 | 4 | 5 | | 7 | | 12 | 9 | 11 | | | | | $10^1$ | | | | | 6 | 8 | | | | 39 |
| 1 | $2^1$ | 3 | 4 | 5 | | 7 | 12 | $9^2$ | 11 | | | | | | 10 | | | | 13 | 6 | 8 | | | | 40 |
| | 3 | 4 | $5^3$ | | | 7 | 12 | | 11 | | | 13 | | | $10^1$ | 2 | | | 9 | 6 | $8^2$ | 14 | | | 41 |
| 1 | 2 | $3^1$ | 4 | 5 | | 7 | 12 | | 9 | 11 | | | | | 10 | | | | | 6 | 8 | | | | 42 |
| 1 | 2 | $3^1$ | 4 | 5 | | 7 | 12 | | $9^1$ | 11 | 13 | | | | 10 | | | | 14 | $6^2$ | 8 | | | | 43 |
| 1 | 2 | | 4 | | | 7 | 8 | 5 | 9 | 11 | | | | | $10^1$ | | | | 12 | 6 | 3 | | | | 44 |
| 1 | 2 | 3 | 4 | 5 | | $7^1$ | 12 | $10^2$ | $9^3$ | 11 | 14 | | | | 13 | | | | | 6 | 8 | | | | 45 |
| 1 | 2 | $3^1$ | $4^2$ | 5 | | 7 | 12 | 10 | | 11 | 13 | | | | $9^3$ | | 14 | | | 6 | 8 | | | | 46 |

**Coca-Cola Cup**

| | | | |
|---|---|---|---|
| First Round | Oldham Ath | (a) | 0-1 |
| | | (h) | 5-0 |
| Second Round | Sheffield W | (h) | 2-0 |
| | | (a) | 2-3 |
| Third Round | Leicester C | (h) | 3-1 |
| Fourth Round | Liverpool | (a) | 0-3 |

**FA Cup**

| | | | |
|---|---|---|---|
| First Round | Shrewsbury T | (a) | 1-1 |
| | | (h) | 4-0 |
| Second Round | Chesterfield | (h) | 2-2 |
| | | (a) | 2-0 |
| Third Round | Norwich C | (h) | 3-0 |
| Fourth Round | Leeds U | (a) | 0-2 |

HALIFAX TOWN 1997–98     *Back row (left to right):* Paul Hand, Darren Lyons, Peter Jackson, Lee Williams, Paul Stoneman, Noel Horner, Geoff Horsfield, Andy Thackeray, Mark Bradshaw.
*Middle row:* A. Russell-Cox (Physio), Martin Ayscough, Chris Newton, Gareth Hamlet, Paul Trudgill, Michael Rosser, Karl Cochrane, Phil McDonald, Ryan Gonzalves, Billy Callaghan, Dave Worthington (Reserve Team Manager).
*Front row:* Damian Place, Willie Griffiths, Kieran O'Regan, George Mulhall (Manager), Jamie Paterson, Jon Brown, Gary Brook, Kevin Hulme.

# Division 3        **HALIFAX TOWN**

*The Shay Stadium, Shaw Hill, Halifax HX1 2YS.* Telephone Halifax (01422) 345543. Fax (01422) 349487. Souvenir Shop (01422) 353423. Info Line 0891 227328.

*Ground capacity:* 7449

*Record attendance:* 36,885 v Tottenham H, FA Cup 5th rd, 15 February 1953.

*Record receipts:* £27,000 v Manchester U, League Cup, 2nd rd, 1st leg, 26 September 1990.

*Pitch measurements:* 110yd × 70yd.

*President:* Robert Holmes. *Vice-Presidents:* Dr M. Choucri, J. Haymer.

*Chairman:* J. C. Stockwell.

*Directors:* D. C. Greenwood, A. Hall, D. Cairns, S. J. Brown, M. Hitchen.

*Manager:* George Mulhall. *Coach:* K. O'Regan. *Physio:* A. Russell-Cox.

*Youth Team Coach:* B. Ellison.

*Club Secretary:* Derek A. Newiss.

*Year Formed:* 1911. *Turned Professional:* 1911. *Ltd Co.:* 1911.

*Club Nickname:* 'The Shaymen'.

*Previous Grounds:* Sandhall and Exley.

*Club Sponsors:* Nationwide.

*Foundation:* The real pioneer behind the setting up of the club was Mr A. E. Jones, who, using the *non de plume* 'Old Sport', wrote to the *The Halifax Evening Courier*. His letter suggesting a club be set up and inviting public opinion was published on 20 April 1911. A public meeting was held at the Saddle Hotel on 23 May 1911, whereafter Dr A. H. Muir became the club's first president and Joe McClelland its first secretary.

*First Football League game:* 27 August 1921, Division 3 (N), v Darlington (a) L 0-2 – Haldane; Hawley, Mackrill; Hall, Wellock, Challinor; Pinkey, Hetherington, Woods, Dent, Phipps.

*Record League Victory:* 6–0 v Bradford PA, Division 3 (N), 3 December 1955 – Johnson; Griffiths, Ferguson; Watson, Harris, Bell; Hampson (2), Baker (3), Watkinson (1), Capel, Lonsdale. 6–0 v Doncaster R, Division 4, 2 November 1976 – Gennoe; Trainer, Loska (Bradley), McGill, Dunleavy (1), Phelan, Hoy (2), Carroll (1), Bullock (1), Lawson (1), Johnston.

*Record Cup Victory:* 7–0 v Bishop Auckland, FA Cup 2nd rd (replay), 10 January 1967 – White; Russell, Bodell; Smith, Holt, Jeff Lee; Taylor (2), Hutchison (2), Parks (2), Atkins (1), McCarthy.

*Record Defeat:* 0–13 v Stockport Co, Division 3 (N), 6 January 1934.

*Most League Points (2 for a win):* 57, Division 4, 1968–69.

*Most League Points (3 for a win):* 60, Division 4, 1982–83.

*Most League Goals:* 83, Division 3 (N), 1957–58.

*Highest League Scorer in Season:* Albert Valentine, 34, Division 3 (N), 1934–35.

*Most League Goals in Total Aggregate:* Ernest Dixon, 129, 1922–30.

*Most Capped Player:* None.

*Most League Appearances:* John Pickering, 367, 1965–74.

*Record Transfer Fee Received:* £250,000 from Watford for Wayne Allison, July 1989.

*Record Transfer Fee Paid:* £50,000 to Hereford U for Ian Juryeff, September 1990.

*Football League Record:* 1921 Original Member of Division 3 (N); 1958–63 Division 3; 1963–69 Division 4; 1969–76 Division 3; 1976–92 Division 4; 1992–93 Division 3; 1993–98 Vauxhall Conference; 1998– Division 3.

*Honours: Football League:* Division 3 best season: 3rd, 1970–71; Division 3 (N)—Runners-up 1934–35; Division 4: Runners-up 1968–69. *FA Cup:* best season: 5th rd, 1932–33, 1952–53. *Football League Cup:* best season: 4th rd, 1964. *Vauxhall Conference:* Champions 1997–98.

*Colours:* Blue shirts, white trim, blue shorts, white trim, white stockings.

**Did you know?**
Halifax Town defeated a Manchester United team, which included Bobby Charlton, Denis Law and George Best, 2-1 in a pre-season Watney Cup match on 31 July 1971, watched by a home crowd of 19,765.

HARTLEPOOL UNITED 1997–98   *Back row (left to right):* Chris Beech, Marc Nash, Joe Allon, Graeme Lee, Denny Ingram, Jon Cullen, Ian Gallagher, Paul Baker (Player/Coach), Darren Knowles. *Middle row:* Gary Hinchley (Physio), Jan Ove Pederson, Tommy Miller, Steve Hutt, Stephen Howard, Warren Dobson, Martin Hollund, Glen Davies, Glen Downey, Richard Lucas, Tommy Miller (Chief Scout), Billy Horner (Youth Team Coach). *Front row:* Ian Clark, Michael Barron, Stephen Halliday, Brian Honour (Coach), Russell Bradley, Mick Tait (Manger), Chris McDonald, Stuart Irvine, Paul Walton.

# Division 3 **HARTLEPOOL UNITED**

*Victoria Park, Clarence Road, Hartlepool TS24 8BZ.* Telephone: (01429) 272584. Commercial Dept: (01429) 272584. Fax: (01429) 863007. Football in the Community: (01429) 862595.

*Ground capacity:* 7229.

*Record attendance:* 17,426 v Manchester U, FA Cup 3rd rd, 5 January 1957.

*Record receipts:* £42,300 v Tottenham H, Rumbelows Cup 2nd rd 2nd leg, 9 October 1990.

*Pitch measurements:* 110yd × 75yd.

*Chairman:* K. Hodcroft.

*Directors:* H. Hornsey, I. Prescott, M. Downey.

*Manager:* Mick Tait. *Player/Coach:* Paul Baker.

*Youth Coach:* Billy Horner. *Physio:* Gary Hinchley. *Commercial Manager:* Frank Baggs.

*Secretary:* Maureen Smith. *Football in the Community Officer:* Mick Smith. *Safety Officer:* Maurice Russell.

*Year Formed:* 1908. *Turned Professional:* 1908. *Ltd Co.:* 1908.

*Club Nickname:* 'The Pool'.

*Previous Names:* Hartlepools United until 1968; Hartlepool until 1977.

*Foundation:* The inspiration for the launching of Hartlepool United was the West Hartlepool club which won the FA Amateur Cup in 1904–05. They had been in existence since 1881 and their Cup success led in 1908 to the formation of the new professional concern which first joined the North-Eastern League. In those days they were Hartlepools United and won the Durham Senior Cup in their first two seasons.

*First Football League game:* 27 August 1921, Division 3 (N), v Wrexham (a) W 2-0 – Gill; Thomas, Crilly; Dougherty, Hopkins, Short; Kessler, Mulholland (1), Lister (1), Robertson, Donald.

*Record League Victory:* 10–1 v Barrow, Division 4, 4 April 1959 – Oakley; Cameron, Waugh; Johnson, Moore, Anderson; Scott (1), Langland (1), Smith (3), Clark (2), Luke (2). (1 og).

*Record Cup Victory:* 6–0 v North Shields, FA Cup 1st rd, 30 November 1946 – Heywood; Brown, Gregory; Spelman, Lambert, Jones; Price, Scott (2), Sloan (4), Moses, McMahon.

*Record Defeat:* 1–10 v Wrexham, Division 4, 3 March 1962.

*Most League Points (2 for a win):* 60, Division 4, 1967–68.

*Most League Points (3 for a win):* 82, Division 4, 1990–91.

*Most League Goals:* 90, Division 3 (N), 1956–57.

*Highest League Scorer in Season:* William Robinson, 28, Division 3 (N), 1927–28 and Joe Allon, 28, Division 4, 1990–91.

*Most League Goals in Total Aggregate:* Ken Johnson, 98, 1949–64.

*Most Capped Player:* Ambrose Fogarty, 1 (11), Republic of Ireland.

*Most League Appearances:* Wattie Moore, 447, 1948–64.

*Record Transfer Fee Received:* £300,000 from Chelsea for Joe Allon, August 1991.

*Record Transfer Fee Paid:* £60,000 to Barnsley for Andy Saville, March 1992.

*Football League Record:* 1921 Original Member of Division 3 (N); 1958–68 Division 4; 1968–69 Division 3; 1969–91 Division 4; 1991–92 Division 3; 1992–94 Division 2; 1994– Division 3.

*Honours: Football League:* Division 3 (N) – Runners-up 1956–57. *FA Cup:* best season: 4th rd, 1955, 1978, 1989, 1993. *Football League Cup,* best season: 4th rd, 1975.

*Colours:* Royal blue and white striped shirts. *Change colours:* Grey shirts with navy trim.

**Did you know?**
Tewfik Abdallah, an Egyptian, played 11 times at inside-right for Hartlepools United during 1923-24. Previously with International SC (Cairo), Derby County and Cowdenbeath, he later coached in the USA.

## HARTLEPOOL UNITED 1997–98 LEAGUE RECORD

| Match No. | Date | Venue | Opponents | Result | H/T Score | Lg. Pos. | Goalscorers | Attendance |
|---|---|---|---|---|---|---|---|---|
| 1 | Aug 9 | A | Exeter C | D | 1-1 | 1-0 | — | Cullen 38 | 3409 |
| 2 | 16 | H | Colchester U | W | 3-2 | 1-1 | 3 | Baker 3, Allon 2 55, 63 | 2174 |
| 3 | 23 | A | Rotherham U | L | 1-2 | 0-2 | 13 | Cullen 86 | 3086 |
| 4 | 30 | H | Macclesfield T | D | 0-0 | 0-0 | 15 | | 2283 |
| 5 | Sept 2 | H | Notts Co | D | 1-1 | 0-0 | — | Howard 68 | 2010 |
| 6 | 7 | A | Scarborough | D | 1-1 | 0-0 | 12 | Cullen 61 | 3027 |
| 7 | 13 | H | Torquay U | W | 3-0 | 1-0 | 12 | Baker 45, Cullen 48, Lee 55 | 1927 |
| 8 | 20 | A | Darlington | D | 1-1 | 1-1 | 14 | Cullen 20 | 3169 |
| 9 | 27 | H | Shrewsbury T | W | 2-1 | 2-0 | 7 | Ingram (pen) 2, Cullen 11 | 2253 |
| 10 | Oct 4 | A | Chester C | L | 1-3 | 1-2 | 12 | Baker 29 | 2163 |
| 11 | 11 | A | Doncaster R | D | 2-2 | 0-1 | 10 | Cullen 83, Lucas 89 | 1526 |
| 12 | 18 | A | Leyton Orient | D | 2-2 | 2-1 | 12 | Howard 4, Ingram 32 | 2108 |
| 13 | 21 | H | Peterborough U | W | 2-1 | 1-0 | — | Howard 2 12, 78 | 1990 |
| 14 | 25 | A | Cardiff C | D | 1-1 | 1-0 | 10 | Baker 21 | 3383 |
| 15 | Nov 1 | H | Brighton & HA | D | 0-0 | 0-0 | 12 | | 2561 |
| 16 | 4 | A | Swansea C | W | 2-0 | 0-0 | — | Cullen 76, Baker 89 | 2949 |
| 17 | 8 | A | Scunthorpe U | D | 1-1 | 0-1 | 10 | Knowles 65 | 3272 |
| 18 | 18 | H | Rochdale | W | 2-0 | 1-0 | — | Beech 36, Halliday 67 | 1666 |
| 19 | 22 | H | Barnet | W | 2-0 | 1-0 | 6 | Cullen 2 25, 76 | 2225 |
| 20 | 29 | A | Cambridge U | L | 0-2 | 0-1 | 9 | | 2513 |
| 21 | Dec 2 | H | Hull C | D | 2-2 | 1-0 | — | Beech 30, Lucas 90 | 1933 |
| 22 | 13 | A | Lincoln C | D | 1-1 | 0-1 | 9 | Cullen 90 | 2849 |
| 23 | 20 | H | Mansfield T | D | 2-2 | 1-0 | 8 | Halliday 24, Howard 90 | 2309 |
| 24 | 26 | H | Scarborough | W | 3-0 | 1-0 | 7 | Halliday 2 4, 68, Clark 87 | 3905 |
| 25 | 28 | A | Notts Co | L | 0-2 | 0-1 | 9 | | 6073 |
| 26 | Jan 3 | A | Colchester U | W | 2-1 | 1-0 | 6 | Clark 13, Howard 74 | 2885 |
| 27 | 10 | H | Exeter C | D | 1-1 | 0-1 | 8 | Clark 50 | 2507 |
| 28 | 17 | A | Macclesfield T | L | 1-2 | 0-0 | 9 | Cullen 53 | 2334 |
| 29 | 24 | H | Rotherham U | D | 0-0 | 0-0 | 12 | | 2375 |
| 30 | 31 | A | Torquay U | L | 0-1 | 0-0 | 12 | | 2238 |
| 31 | Feb 7 | H | Darlington | D | 2-2 | 2-0 | 12 | Pedersen 15, Clark 42 | 3212 |
| 32 | 14 | A | Chester C | D | 0-0 | 0-0 | 13 | | 2186 |
| 33 | 21 | A | Shrewsbury T | L | 0-1 | 0-0 | 13 | | 2160 |
| 34 | 24 | A | Leyton Orient | L | 1-2 | 1-1 | — | Clark 42 | 3713 |
| 35 | 28 | H | Doncaster R | W | 3-1 | 1-0 | 13 | Clark 17, Bradley 80, Howard 82 | 1920 |
| 36 | Mar 3 | H | Scunthorpe U | L | 0-1 | 0-1 | — | | 1588 |
| 37 | 7 | A | Brighton & HA | D | 0-0 | 0-0 | 15 | | 2811 |
| 38 | 14 | H | Swansea C | W | 4-2 | 1-1 | 14 | Halliday 44, Lee 2 47, 54, Beech 63 | 1727 |
| 39 | 21 | A | Rochdale | L | 1-2 | 0-0 | 15 | Clark 83 | 1395 |
| 40 | 28 | A | Barnet | D | 1-1 | 0-1 | 16 | Midgley 67 | 2344 |
| 41 | Apr 4 | H | Cambridge U | D | 3-3 | 1-1 | 16 | Miller 4, Di Lella 2 71, 88 | 1867 |
| 42 | 11 | A | Hull C | L | 1-2 | 1-0 | 17 | Midgley 35 | 3343 |
| 43 | 13 | H | Lincoln C | D | 1-1 | 1-1 | 17 | Beech 22 | 1997 |
| 44 | 18 | A | Mansfield T | D | 2-2 | 2-1 | 17 | Beech 2 39, 41 | 2047 |
| 45 | 25 | H | Cardiff C | W | 2-0 | 1-0 | 17 | Midgley 3, Ingram (pen) 54 | 2817 |
| 46 | May 2 | A | Peterborough U | D | 0-0 | 0-0 | 17 | | 4727 |

**Final League Position: 17**  1996–97 DIV3 20

## GOALSCORERS

*League (61):* Cullen 12, Clark 7, Howard 7, Beech 6, Baker 5, Halliday 5, Ingram 3 (2 pens), Lee 3, Midgley 3, Allon 2, Di Lella 2, Lucas 2, Bradley 1, Knowles 1, Miller 1, Pedersen 1.
*Coca-Cola Cup (3):* Baker 1, Howard 1, Lee 1.
*FA Cup (2):* Beech 1, Pedersen 1.

| Davis K 2 | Knowles D 46 | Lucas R 42 | Ingram D 35 + 1 | Davies G 18 + 2 | Bradley R 43 | Allon J 3 + 1 | Cullen J 28 | Baker P 16 | Beech C 34 + 2 | Howard S 34 + 9 | Halliday S 21 + 10 | Barron M 32 + 1 | Dobson W 1 | Lee G 35 + 2 | Harper S 15 | Elliott A — + 4 | McDonald C 4 + 2 | Gavin M — + 3 | Miller T 11 + 2 | Irvine S 1 + 8 | Clark I 19 + 5 | Pedersen J 17 | Hollund M 28 | Larsen S — + 4 | Connor P 4 + 1 | Hutt S 4 | Nash M — + 1 | Midgley C 9 | Di Lella G 1 + 4 | Stephenson P 3 | Match No. |
|---|---|---|---|---|---|---|---|---|---|---|---|---|---|---|---|---|---|---|---|---|---|---|---|---|---|---|---|---|---|---|---|
| 1 | 2 | 3 | 4 | 5 | 6 | 7 | $8^1$ | 9 | 10 | 11 | 12 | | | | | | | | | | | | | | | | | | | | 1 |
| 1 | 2 | 3 | 4 | 5 | 6 | $7^1$ | 8 | 9 | | 11 | 12 | 10 | | | | | | | | | | | | | | | | | | | 2 |
| | 2 | 3 | 4 | $5^3$ | 6 | $7^1$ | 8 | $9^2$ | | 11 | 13 | 12 | 10 | 1 | 14 | | | | | | | | | | | | | | | | 3 |
| | 2 | 3 | 4 | 12 | 6 | | 8 | 9 | 7 | 11 | | 10 | | 1 | $5^1$ | | | | | | | | | | | | | | | | 4 |
| | 2 | 3 | 4 | | 6 | | $8^1$ | 9 | 7 | 11 | 12 | 10 | | 1 | 5 | | | | | | | | | | | | | | | | 5 |
| | 2 | 3 | 4 | | 6 | | 8 | $9^5$ | 7 | 11 | 12 | $10^2$ | 13 | 1 | 5 | | | | | | | | | | | | | | | | 6 |
| | 2 | 3 | $4^1$ | | 6 | | 8 | 9 | 7 | 11 | 12 | $10^2$ | 13 | 1 | 5 | | | | | | | | | | | | | | | | 7 |
| | 2 | 3 | 4 | | 6 | | 8 | $9^5$ | $7^3$ | 11 | 12 | $10^2$ | 14 | 1 | 5 | | 13 | | | | | | | | | | | | | | 8 |
| | 2 | 3 | 4 | | 6 | | 8 | 9 | 7 | 11 | | 10 | | 1 | 5 | | | | | | | | | | | | | | | | 9 |
| | 2 | 3 | 4 | | 6 | | 8 | 9 | $7^1$ | 11 | 12 | $10^2$ | 13 | 1 | 5 | | | | | | | | | | | | | | | | 10 |
| | 2 | 3 | 4 | 12 | 6 | | 8 | 9 | 7 | $11^2$ | 13 | $10^3$ | 14 | 1 | $5^1$ | | | | | | | | | | | | | | | | 11 |
| | 2 | 3 | 4 | | 6 | | 8 | $9^5$ | 7 | 11 | 12 | 10 | | 1 | 5 | | | | | | | | | | | | | | | | 12 |
| | $2^1$ | 3 | 4 | | 6 | | 8 | 9 | 7 | 11 | 12 | 10 | | 1 | 5 | | | | | | | | | | | | | | | | 13 |
| | 2 | 3 | 4 | | 6 | | 8 | 9 | 7 | 11 | | 10 | | 1 | 5 | | | | | | | | | | | | | | | | 14 |
| | 2 | 3 | 4 | | 6 | | 8 | $9^5$ | 7 | 11 | 13 | $10^2$ | 12 | 1 | 5 | | | | | | | | | | | | | | | | 15 |
| | 2 | 3 | 4 | | 6 | | 8 | 9 | 7 | 11 | | 10 | | 1 | 5 | | | | | | | | | | | | | | | | 16 |
| | 2 | 3 | 4 | | $6^3$ | | $8^2$ | $9^5$ | 7 | 13 | 14 | 10 | 12 | 1 | 5 | | 11 | | | | | | | | | | | | | | 17 |
| | 2 | 3 | 4 | | 6 | | 8 | | 7 | 11 | | 10 | | 1 | 5 | | | | | | | | 9 | | | | | | | | 18 |
| | 2 | 3 | 4 | | 6 | | 8 | | 7 | 11 | | 10 | | | 5 | | | | | | | | 9 | | 1 | | | | | | 19 |
| | 2 | 3 | | 4 | 6 | | $8^2$ | | 7 | 11 | | $10^1$ | | | 5 | | | | 13 | | | | 9 | | 1 | | | | | | 20 |
| | 2 | 3 | | | 6 | | 8 | | 7 | 11 | | 10 | | | 5 | | $4^1$ | | | | | | 9 | | 1 | | | | | | 21 |
| | 2 | 3 | | | 6 | | 8 | | 7 | 11 | | 10 | 4 | | 5 | | | | | | | | 9 | | 1 | | | | | | 22 |
| | 2 | 3 | 12 | | $6^1$ | | 8 | | 7 | 11 | | 10 | $4^2$ | | 5 | | | | | | | | 9 | | 1 | | 13 | | | | 23 |
| | 2 | 3 | | | 6 | | 8 | | 7 | $11^1$ | | 10 | 4 | | | | | | | | | 12 | 9 | 5 | 1 | | | | | | 24 |
| | $2^1$ | 3 | | | 6 | | 8 | | 7 | $11^3$ | | $10^2$ | 4 | | | | 12 | | | | | 13 | $9^2$ | 5 | 1 | 14 | | | | | 25 |
| | 2 | $3^1$ | | | 6 | | 8 | | 7 | 11 | | | 4 | | 5 | | | | | | | 10 | 9 | | 1 | | 12 | | | | 26 |
| | 2 | 3 | 4 | | 6 | | 8 | | 7 | 11 | 12 | | | | 5 | | | | | | | $10^1$ | 9 | | 1 | | | | | | 27 |
| | 2 | 3 | 4 | | 6 | | 8 | | 7 | 12 | | $10^1$ | | | 5 | | | | | | | $11^2$ | 9 | | 1 | 13 | | | | | 28 |
| | 2 | 3 | 8 | | 6 | | | | 7 | 11 | | | 4 | | 5 | | | | | | | 10 | 9 | | 1 | | | | | | 29 |
| | 2 | 3 | 8 | | 6 | | | | | 11 | | $10^1$ | 4 | | 5 | | | | 12 | | 7 | | 9 | | 1 | | | | | | 30 |
| | 2 | 3 | 8 | 5 | 6 | | | | | 11 | 12 | | 4 | | | | | | | | $7^1$ | | 9 | | 1 | | | 10 | | | 31 |
| | 2 | 3 | | 5 | 6 | | 8 | | | 11 | | | 4 | | | | | | 12 | | 7 | | 9 | | 1 | | | $10^1$ | | | 32 |
| | 2 | 3 | $4^3$ | | 6 | | | | 9 | 11 | | | 5 | | | 14 | | 12 | | 7² | | | | | 1 | $10^1$ | | 8 | 13 | | 33 |
| | 2 | 3 | 8 | | 6 | | | | 9 | 12 | | | 4 | | 5 | | | | | | 7 | | | | 1 | $10^1$ | | | 11 | | 34 |
| | 2 | 3 | 8 | | 6 | | | | 10 | 9 | | | 4 | | 5 | | | | | | 7 | | | | 1 | | | | 11 | | 35 |
| | 2 | 3 | 8 | 12 | $6^3$ | | | | 10 | 9 | 13 | | 4 | | $5^1$ | | | | | | 7 | | | | 1 | | | 14 | $11^2$ | | 36 |
| | 2 | 3 | | 5 | 6 | | | | 11 | 9 | | 10 | 4 | | | | | | | | | 8 | | | 7 | | | | 1 | | 37 |
| | 2 | 3 | | 5 | 6 | | | | 11 | | 10 | $4^1$ | | | | 7 | | 12 | | | | 8 | | | | | | 9 | 1 | | 38 |
| | 2 | 3 | | 5 | 6 | | | | 11 | 12 | 10 | 4 | | | | $7^1$ | | | | | | $8^3$ | 13 | | | | | $9^2$ | 14 | 1 | 39 |
| | 2 | 3 | | | 6 | | | | 11 | 10 | | 4 | | | 5 | | | | 12 | | 8 | 13 | $7^3$ | | | | | $9^2$ | 14 | 1 | 41 |
| | 2 | 3 | 7 | | 6 | | | | 12 | 10 | | 4 | | | 5 | | | | | | | 8 | | | | | | 9 | $11^1$ | 1 | 42 |
| | 2 | | 3 | | 6 | | | | 11 | 10 | | 4 | | | $5^1$ | | | | | | | 8 | 7 | | | | | 9 | 12 | 1 | 43 |
| | 2 | | | 4 | 5 | 6 | | | 7 | 10 | | | 8 | | | | | | | | | | 12 | 3 | | | | $9^1$ | | 11 | 44 |
| | 2 | | | $4^2$ | 5 | 6 | | | 7 | 10 | | | 8 | | | | | | | | | | 12 | 3 | | | | 9 | 13 | $11^1$ | 45 |
| | 2 | | | 4 | | 6 | | | 7 | 10 | | 5 | 8 | | | | | | | | | | 12 | 3 | | | | $9^1$ | | 11 | 46 |

**Coca-Cola Cup**
First Round     Tranmere R     (a) 1-3    (h) 2-1

**FA Cup**
First Round     Macclesfield T     (h) 2-4

HUDDERSFIELD TOWN 1997-98    *Back row (left to right):* Rob Edwards, Simon Baldry, Jeremy Illingworth, Ian Lawson, Jon Dyson, Paul Dalton, Robbie Ryan, Delroy Facey, Tom Cowan.
*Middle row:* Les Chapman (Youth Team Coach), Gerry Murphy (Youth Development Officer), Kevin Gray, Marcus Browning, Derek O'Connor, Sam Collins, Steve Francis, Wayne Burnett, Darren Edmondson, John Dickens (Physio).
*Front row:* David Moss (Coach), David Beresford, Marcus Stewart, Andy Morrison, Brian Horton (Team Manager), Steve Jenkins, Andy Payton, Lee Makel, Dennis Booth (First Team Coach).

# Division 1     HUDDERSFIELD TOWN

*The Alfred McAlpine Stadium, Leeds Rd, Huddersfield HD1 6PX.* Telephone: (01484) 484100. Fax: (01484) 484101. Ticket Office: (01484) 484123. Club Shop: (01484) 484144. Recorded Information: 0891 121635.

*Ground capacity:* 24,000.

*Record attendance:* 67,037 v Arsenal, FA Cup 6th rd, 27 February 1932 (at old ground): 18,820 v Middlesbrough, Division 1, 26 December 1997 (at new ground).

*Record receipts:* £155,149 v Wimbledon, FA Cup 5th rd, 17 February 1996.

*Pitch measurements:* 115yd × 76yd.

*President:* Lawrence Batley OBE. *Chairman:* J. M. Asquith.

*Directors:* D. A. Taylor, E. R. Whiteley, D. G. Headey.

*Associate Director:* T. J. Cherry.

*Manager:* Peter Jackson. *First Team Coach:* Terry Yorath. *Coach:* Terry Dolan.

*Secretary:* Alan D. Sykes. *Assistant Secretary:* Ann Hough. *Commercial Manager:* Alan Stevenson.

*Physio:* John Dickens. *Stadium Manager:* Brian Buckley.

*Year Formed:* 1908. *Turned Professional:* 1908. *Ltd Co.:* 1908.

*Club Nickname:* 'The Terriers'.

*Foundation:* A meeting, attended largely by members of the Huddersfield & District FA, was held at the Imperial Hotel in 1906 to discuss the feasibility of establishing a football club in this rugby stronghold. However, it was not until a man with both the enthusiasm and the money to back the scheme came on the scene, that real progress was made. This benefactor was Mr Hilton Crowther and it was at a meeting at the Albert Hotel in 1908, that the club formally came into existence with a capital of £2,000 and joined the North-Eastern League.

*First Football League game:* 3 September 1910, Division 2, v Bradford PA (a) W 1-0 – Mutch; Taylor, Morris; Beaton, Hall, Bartlett; Blackburn, Wood, Hamilton (1), McCubbin, Jee.

*Record League Victory:* 10–1 v Blackpool, Division 1, 13 December 1930 – Turner; Goodall, Spencer; Redfern, Wilson, Campbell; Bob Kelly (1), McLean (4), Robson (3), Davies (1), Smailes (1).

*Record Cup Victory:* 7–0 v Lincoln U, FA Cup 1st rd, 16 November 1991 – Clarke; Trevitt, Charlton, Donovan (2), Mitchell, Doherty, O'Regan (1), Stapleton (1) (Wright), Roberts (2), Onuora (1), Barnett (Ireland).

*Record Defeat:* 1–10 v Manchester C, Division 2, 7 November 1987.

*Most League Points (2 for a win):* 66, Division 4, 1979–80.

*Most League Points (3 for a win):* 82, Division 3, 1982–83.

*Most League Goals:* 101, Division 4, 1979–80.

*Highest League Scorer in Season:* Sam Taylor, 35, Division 2, 1919–20; George Brown, 35, Division 1, 1925–26.

*Most League Goals in Total Aggregate:* George Brown, 142, 1921–29 and Jimmy Glazzard, 142, 1946–56.

*Most Capped Player:* Jimmy Nicholson, 31 (41), Northern Ireland.

*Most League Appearances:* Billy Smith, 520, 1914–34.

*Record Transfer Fee Received:* £2,700,000 from Sheffield W for Andy Booth, July 1996.

*Record Transfer Fee Paid:* £1,200,000 to Bristol R for Marcus Stewart, July 1996.

*Football League Record:* 1910 Elected to Division 2; 1920–52 Division 1; 1952–53 Division 2; 1953–56 Division 1; 1956–70 Division 2; 1970–72 Division 1; 1972–73 Division 2; 1973–75 Division 3; 1975–80 Division 4; 1980–83 Division 3; 1983–88 Division 2; 1988–92 Division 3; 1992–95 Division 2; 1995– Division 1.

*Honours: Football League:* Division 1 – Champions 1923–24, 1924–25, 1925–26; Runners-up 1926–27, 1927–28, 1933–34; Division 2 – Champions 1969–70; Runners-up 1919–20, 1952–53; Promoted from Division 2 1994–95 (play-offs); Division 4 – Champions 1979–80. *FA Cup:* Winners 1922; Runners-up 1920, 1928, 1930, 1938. *Football League Cup:* Semi-final 1968. *Autoglass Trophy:* Runners-up 1994.

*Colours:* Blue and white striped shirts, white shorts, white stockings with single navy hoop.
*Change colours:* Ecru shirt with single jade and navy band and jade and navy sleeves, ecru shorts with jade and navy trim, ecru, jade and navy hooped stockings.

**Did you know?**
When Peter Jackson took over as manager of Huddersfield Town in 1997-98 they had achieved only four points from 15 games. By the time the club had avoided relegation, he had collected a Vauxhall Conference Championship medal as a Halifax Town player.

## HUDDERSFIELD TOWN 1997–98 LEAGUE RECORD

| Match No. | Date | | Venue | Opponents | Result | | H/T Score | Lg. Pos. | Goalscorers | Attendance |
|---|---|---|---|---|---|---|---|---|---|---|
| 1 | Aug | 9 | A | Oxford U | L | 0-2 | 0-0 | — | | 7085 |
| 2 | | 23 | A | Swindon T | D | 1-1 | 1-1 | 22 | Stewart 43 | 7683 |
| 3 | | 30 | H | Sheffield U | D | 0-0 | 0-0 | 23 | | 14,268 |
| 4 | Sept | 2 | H | Bradford C | L | 1-2 | 0-1 | — | Stewart 75 | 13,159 |
| 5 | | 9 | H | Birmingham C | L | 0-1 | 0-0 | — | | 9477 |
| 6 | | 13 | H | Ipswich T | D | 2-2 | 1-0 | 24 | Jenkins 41, Dyer 88 | 9313 |
| 7 | | 20 | A | Stockport Co | L | 0-3 | 0-2 | 24 | | 6995 |
| 8 | | 27 | A | Wolverhampton W | D | 1-1 | 1-1 | 24 | Stewart 32 | 21,723 |
| 9 | Oct | 3 | H | Nottingham F | L | 0-2 | 0-0 | — | | 11,258 |
| 10 | | 14 | H | Charlton Ath | L | 0-3 | 0-1 | — | | 9596 |
| 11 | | 18 | A | Sunderland | L | 1-3 | 1-1 | 24 | Dalton 45 | 24,782 |
| 12 | | 21 | A | Port Vale | L | 1-4 | 0-1 | — | Stewart 86 | 5244 |
| 13 | | 25 | A | Portsmouth | D | 1-1 | 0-1 | 24 | Dalton 80 | 8985 |
| 14 | | 28 | A | Middlesbrough | L | 0-3 | 0-2 | — | | 29,965 |
| 15 | Nov | 1 | H | Stoke C | W | 3-1 | 0-0 | 24 | Richardson 46, Stewart 80, Dalton 90 | 10,916 |
| 16 | | 4 | A | Tranmere R | L | 0-1 | 0-1 | — | | 5127 |
| 17 | | 7 | A | Manchester C | W | 1-0 | 0-0 | — | Edwards 76 | 24,425 |
| 18 | | 15 | H | Reading | W | 1-0 | 0-0 | 24 | Dalton 73 | 12,617 |
| 19 | | 22 | A | QPR | L | 1-2 | 0-1 | 24 | Morrison 89 | 16,066 |
| 20 | | 29 | H | Bury | W | 2-0 | 1-0 | 23 | Dalton 2 7, 83 | 11,929 |
| 21 | Dec | 6 | A | Crewe Alex | W | 5-2 | 2-1 | 22 | Stewart 2 24, 70, Dalton 2 (1 pen) 40, 83 (p), Allison 89 | 4861 |
| 22 | | 13 | H | Norwich C | L | 1-3 | 0-2 | 24 | Stewart 58 | 11,436 |
| 23 | | 20 | A | WBA | W | 2-0 | 0-0 | 20 | Dalton 2 51, 72 | 14,619 |
| 24 | | 26 | H | Middlesbrough | L | 0-1 | 0-0 | 23 | | 18,820 |
| 25 | | 28 | A | Bradford C | D | 1-1 | 1-1 | 22 | Dalton 34 | 17,842 |
| 26 | Jan | 10 | H | Oxford U | W | 5-1 | 3-0 | 20 | Gray (og) 21, Phillips 30, Stewart 2 41, 55, Allison 59 | 10,378 |
| 27 | | 17 | A | Birmingham C | D | 0-0 | 0-0 | 19 | | 17,850 |
| 28 | | 27 | A | Sheffield U | D | 1-1 | 1-1 | — | Dalton 24 | 16,535 |
| 29 | | 31 | H | Swindon T | D | 0-0 | 0-0 | 19 | | 10,028 |
| 30 | Feb | 7 | H | Stockport Co | W | 1-0 | 0-0 | 18 | Allison 53 | 11,121 |
| 31 | | 14 | A | Ipswich T | L | 1-5 | 1-1 | 19 | Stewart 37 | 10,509 |
| 32 | | 17 | A | Nottingham F | L | 0-3 | 0-1 | — | | 18,231 |
| 33 | | 21 | H | Wolverhampton W | W | 1-0 | 0-0 | 18 | Dyson 90 | 12,663 |
| 34 | | 24 | H | Sunderland | L | 2-3 | 0-3 | — | Allison 51, Phillips 57 | 14,615 |
| 35 | | 28 | A | Charlton Ath | L | 0-1 | 0-0 | 22 | | 12,908 |
| 36 | Mar | 3 | H | Manchester C | L | 1-3 | 1-2 | — | Dalton (pen) 38 | 15,694 |
| 37 | | 7 | A | Stoke C | W | 2-1 | 2-0 | 21 | Barnes 15, Stewart 18 | 12,594 |
| 38 | | 14 | H | Tranmere R | W | 3-0 | 1-0 | 17 | Allison 10, Stewart 67, Hill (og) 77 | 10,844 |
| 39 | | 21 | A | Reading | W | 2-0 | 0-0 | 15 | Stewart 2 73, 88 | 8593 |
| 40 | | 28 | H | QPR | D | 1-1 | 0-0 | 15 | Gray 59 | 13,681 |
| 41 | Apr | 4 | A | Bury | D | 2-2 | 1-1 | 15 | Richardson 2 (1 pen) 34 (p), 71 | 8042 |
| 42 | | 11 | H | Crewe Alex | W | 2-0 | 2-0 | 14 | Allison 42, Johnson 44 | 11,263 |
| 43 | | 13 | A | Norwich C | L | 0-5 | 0-2 | 16 | | 16,550 |
| 44 | | 18 | H | WBA | W | 1-0 | 1-0 | 13 | Baldry 12 | 11,704 |
| 45 | | 25 | A | Portsmouth | L | 0-3 | 0-1 | 14 | | 14,013 |
| 46 | May | 3 | H | Port Vale | L | 0-4 | 0-2 | 16 | | 15,610 |

**Final League Position: 16**      1996–97 DIV1 20

## GOALSCORERS

*League (50):* Stewart 15, Dalton 13 (2 pens), Allison 6, Richardson 3 (1 pen), Phillips 2, Baldry 1, Barnes 1, Dyer 1, Dyson 1, Edwards 1, Gray 1, Jenkins 1, Johnson 1, Morrison 1, own goals 2.
*Coca-Cola Cup (4):* Burnett 1, Dyer 1, Payton 1, own goal 1.
*FA Cup (1):* Stewart 1.

| Francis S 9 | Dyson J 35 + 1 | Ryan R 10 | Heary T 2 + 1 | Morrison A 22 + 1 | Gray K 34 + 1 | Beresford D 5 + 3 | Makel L 10 + 3 | Stewart M 38 + 3 | Payton A 4 + 1 | Burnett W 11 + 4 | Midwood M — + 1 | Edwards R 26 + 12 | Jenkins S 28 + 1 | Dyer A 8 + 4 | Baldry S 8 + 3 | Browning M 10 + 4 | Hurst C 1 + 2 | Lawson I 3 + 15 | Martin L 2 + 1 | Facey D 1 + 2 | Edmondson D 15 + 4 | Dalton P 26 + 5 | Collins S 9 + 1 | O'Connor D 1 | Bartram V 12 | Horne B 29 + 1 | Richardson L 16 + 5 | Allison W 27 | Phillips D 29 | Johnson G 28 + 1 | Harper S 24 | Barnes P 11 + 4 | Watts J 8 | Smith S 4 + 2 | Nielsen M — + 3 | Hessey S — + 1 | Match No. |
|---|---|---|---|---|---|---|---|---|---|---|---|---|---|---|---|---|---|---|---|---|---|---|---|---|---|---|---|---|---|---|---|---|---|---|---|---|---|
| 1 | 2 | 3 | 4¹ | 5 | 6 | 7² | 8 | 9 | 10 | 11 | 12 | 13 | | | | | | | | | | | | | | | | | | | | | | | | | 1 |
| 1 | 4 | 3 | | 5 | | 7¹ | 8² | 9 | | 11 | | 6 | 2 | 10 | 12 | 13 | | | | | | | | | | | | | | | | | | | | | 2 |
| 1 | 4 | 3 | | 5¹ | | | 8 | 9 | | 11 | | 12 | 2 | 10³ | 7 | 6³ | 13 | 14 | | | | | | | | | | | | | | | | | | | 3 |
| 1 | 4 | 3 | | | | 12 | 8 | 9 | | 11 | | 5² | 2 | 10 | 7¹ | 6³ | 13 | 14 | | | | | | | | | | | | | | | | | | | 4 |
| 1 | 4² | | | 5 | | 12 | 8 | 9 | | 11 | | 13 | 2 | 10¹ | 7 | 6³ | | | | 3 | 14 | | | | | | | | | | | | | | | | 5 |
| 1 | 4 | | | 5² | | 6³ | 8 | 9 | | 11 | | | 2 | 12 | 7 | | | | | 3 | 10¹ | 13 | 14 | | | | | | | | | | | | | | 6 |
| 1 | 4 | 3 | | 5 | | 12 | 8 | 9 | | 11² | | 13 | 2 | 10 | | | | 14 | | | 6³ | 7¹ | | | | | | | | | | | | | | | 7 |
| 1 | 4² | | 6 | 5 | | | 8 | 9 | 10 | | | 12 | 2 | | | 14 | 11¹ | 7³ | | | 3 | | 13 | | | | | | | | | | | | | | 8 |
| | 4² | | 7¹ | 5 | 6 | | 8 | 9 | 10 | 11 | | 12 | 2 | | 8 | | | | | | 3 | 13 | | 1 | | | | | | | | | | | | | 9 |
| 1 | 4 | 3 | | 5 | | | 8¹ | 9 | | 11² | | 13 | 2 | 12 | | | | | | | 10 | 7 | | | | | 6 | | | | | | | | | | 10 |
| | 4 | 3 | | 5 | | | | 9 | | 11 | | 6¹ | 2 | 10² | | | | 13 | | | 12 | 7 | | | 1 | | 8 | | | | | | | | | | 11 |
| | 4 | 3 | | 5 | 14 | | | 9 | | 11² | | 6¹ | 2 | 10 | | | | 13³ | | | 12 | 7 | | | 1 | | 8 | | | | | | | | | | 12 |
| | 4 | 3¹ | | 5 | 6 | | | 9 | | | | | 2 | 12 | | | 11² | | | | 13 | 7 | | | 1 | | 8 | | 10 | | | | | | | | 13 |
| | 4 | 3¹ | | 5 | 6 | | | 9 | | | | 13 | 2 | 12 | | | 11² | | | | | 7 | | | 1 | | 8 | | 10 | | | | | | | | 14 |
| | 4 | | | 5 | 6 | | | 9 | | | | 11¹ | 2 | 12 | | | | | | | 3 | 7 | | | 1 | | 8 | | 10 | | | | | | | | 15 |
| | 4 | | | 5 | 6 | | | 9 | | | | 13 | 2 | 12 | | | 11² | | | | 3¹ | 7 | | | 1 | | 8 | | 10 | | | | | | | | 16 |
| | 4 | | | 5 | 6 | | | 9¹ | | | | 11 | 2 | 12 | | | | | | | 3 | 7 | | | 1 | | 8 | | 10 | | | | | | | | 17 |
| | 4 | | | 5 | 6 | | | | | | | 11 | 2 | 12 | | | | | | | 3² | 7¹ | | | 1 | | 8 | 9 | 10 | 13 | | | | | | | 18 |
| | 4¹ | | | 5 | 6 | | | | | | | 13 | | 12 | | | 11² | | | | 3 | 7 | | | 1 | | 8 | | 10 | 2 | 9 | | | | | | 19 |
| | 4 | | | 5 | 6 | | | 9¹ | | | | | | 12 | | | | | | | 3 | 7 | | | 1 | | 8 | | 10 | 2 | | 11 | | | | | 20 |
| | 4 | | | 5 | 6 | | | 9 | | | | | | | | | | | | | 3¹ | 7 | | | 1 | | 8 | 12 | 10 | 2 | | 11 | | | | | 21 |
| | 4 | | | 5 | 6 | | | 9 | | | | | | 12 | | | | | | | 3¹ | 7 | | | 1 | | 8 | 13 | 10 | 2 | | 11² | | | | | 22 |
| | 4 | | | 5 | 6 | | | 9² | | | | 13 | | 12 | | | | | | | 3 | | | | | 7¹ | 8 | | 10 | 2 | 1 | 11 | | | | | 23 |
| | 4 | | | 5 | 6 | | | 9² | | | | | | 12 | | | | | | | 3 | | | | | 7 | 8¹ | 13 | 10 | 2 | 1 | 11 | | | | | 24 |
| | 4 | | | | 6 | | | 9² | | | | | | 12 | | | | | | | 3 | | | | | 7 | 8 | 13 | 10 | 2¹ | 5 | 11 | 1 | | | | 25 |
| | 4 | | | | 6 | | | 9 | | | | | 2 | 12 | | | | | | | 3 | | | | | 7² | 8 | 13 | 10 | 5 | 1 | 11¹ | | | | | 26 |
| | 4 | | | 5 | 6 | | | 9 | | | | | 2 | | | | | | | | 3 | | | | | 7¹ | 8 | | 10 | 5 | 1 | 11 | 12 | | | | 27 |
| | 4 | | | | 6 | | | 9 | | | | | 2 | 12 | | | | | | | 3 | | | | | 7¹ | 8 | | 10 | 5 | 1 | 11 | | | | | 28 |
| | 4 | | | | 6¹ | | | 9 | | | | | 2³ | 12² | | | | | | | 3 | | | | | 7 | 8 | 13 | 10 | 5 | 1 | 11 | 14 | | | | 29 |
| | 4 | | | | 6 | | | 9¹ | | | | | 2 | | | | | | | | 3 | | | | | 7 | 8 | | 10 | 5 | 1 | 11 | 12 | | | | 30 |
| | 4 | | | | 6 | | | 9 | | | | | 2 | | | | | | | | 3² | | | | | 7¹ | 8 | | 10 | 5 | 1 | 11 | 12 | 13 | | | 31 |
| | 4 | | | | 6 | | | 9¹ | | | | | 2 | 12 | | | | | | | 3 | | | | | 7 | 8 | | 10 | 5 | 1 | 11 | | | | | 32 |
| | 4 | | | | 6 | | | 9¹ | | | | | | 12 | | | | | | | 3 | | | | | 7 | 8 | | 10 | 5 | 1 | 11 | | | | | 33 |
| | 4 | | | | 6 | | | 9² | | | | | | 12 | | | | | | | 3 | | | | | 7 | 8 | 13 | 10 | 2 | 1 | 11 | 9¹ | 5 | | | 34 |
| | 4² | | | | 6 | | | | | | | | 2¹ | 12 | | | | | | | 3 | | | | | | 8 | 13 | 10 | 9 | 1 | 11 | | 5 | 7 | | 35 |
| | 4 | | | | 6 | | | | | | | | 2² | 12 | | | | | | | 3³ | 7¹ | | | | | 8 | 13 | 10 | 9 | 1 | 11 | | 5 | 14 | | 36 |
| | 4 | | | | 6 | | | 9 | | | | | 2 | 12 | | | | 13 | | | 3 | 7¹ | | | | | 8 | | 10 | 2 | 1 | 11 | 8¹ | 5 | | | 37 |
| | 4¹ | | | | 6 | | | 9 | | | | | 2 | 12 | | | | | | | 3 | 7 | | | | | | | 10 | 5 | 1 | 11 | 8 | | | | 38 |
| | 4¹ | | | | 6 | | | 9 | | | | | | | | | | | | | 3 | 7 | | | | | 8² | | 10 | 5 | 1 | 11 | | | 12 | 13 | 39 |
| | 4 | | | | 6 | | | 9 | | | | | | 12 | | | | | | | 3 | 7 | | | | | | | 10 | 5 | 1 | 11 | 8¹ | | | | 40 |
| | 4² | | | | 6 | 9¹ | | | | | | 13 | | 12 | | | | | | | 3 | 7 | | | | | 8 | | 10 | 5 | 1 | 11 | | | | | 41 |
| | 4¹ | | | | 6 | | | 9 | | | | | | 12 | | | | | | | 3 | 7 | | | | | | | 10 | 5 | 1 | 11 | 8² | | 13 | | 42 |
| | 4 | | | | 6 | | | 9¹ | | | | | | 12 | | | | | | | 3 | 7 | | | | | 8 | | 10 | 5 | 1 | 11 | | | | | 43 |
| 12 | | | | | 6 | | | 9 | | | | | | | | | | | | | 3 | 7¹ | | | | | 8 | | 10 | 5 | 1 | 11 | | | | | 44 |
| 4 | 12 | | | | | | | 9 | | | | | | | | | | 7² | | | 13 | | | | | 6¹ | 8 | | 10 | 3 | 1 | 11³ | | | 14 | 5 | 45 |
| 4¹ | 2 | 13 | | | | | | 9 | | | | | | | | | | 7 | | | 3 | | | | | 6 | 8 | 14 | 10² | 12 | 1 | 11³ | | | | 5 | 46 |

**Coca-Cola Cup**

| First Round | Bradford C | (h) | 2-1 |
| Second Round | West Ham U | (a) | 1-1 |
| | | (h) | 1-0 |
| | | (a) | 0-3 |

**FA Cup**

| Third Round | Bournemouth | (a) | 1-0 |
| Fourth Round | Wimbledon | (h) | 0-1 |

HULL CITY 1997–98    *Back row (left to right):* Gavin Gordon, Ian Wright, Rob Dewhurst, Andy Brown, Scott Thomson, Tony Brien, Mark Greaves, Richard Peacock, Paul Fewings.
*Middle row:* Mike McGurn (Fitness Coach), Billy Kirkwood (Assistant Manager), Sam Sharman, Simon Trevitt, Gregor Rioch, Steve Wilson, Antonio Doncel, Jamie Marks, Duane Darby, Jeff Radcliffe (Physio), Rod Arnold (Goalkeeping Coach/Youth Team Manager).
*Front row:* Patrick Dickinson, Neil Mann, Scott Maxfield, Adam Lowthorpe, Mark Hateley (Player Manager), Michael Quigley, Paul Wharton, Craig Baxter, Warren Joyce.

# Division 3      **HULL CITY**

*Boothferry Park, Hull HU4 6EU.* Telephone: (01482) 327200. Fax: (01482) 565752. Sales/Marketing Manager: (01482) 327200. Football in the Community Office: (01482) 568088. Club Shop: 01482 327200.

*Ground capacity:* 12,996.

*Record attendance:* 55,019 v Manchester U, FA Cup 6th rd, 26 February 1949.

*Record receipts:* £79,604 v Liverpool, FA Cup 5th rd, 18 February 1989.

*Pitch measurements:* 115yd × 75yd.

*Honorary Vice-President:* H. Bermitz.

*Vice-Presidents:* R. Booth, A. Fetiveau, W. Law.

*Chairman:* David Lloyd.

*Director:* Albert Harrison.

*Manager:* Mark Hateley. *Assistant Manager:* Billy Kirkwood.

*Secretary:* Brian Johnson. *Physio:* Keith Warner.

*Sales/Marketing Manager:* Frank Killen. *Stadium Manager:* Gary Scaife.

*Ticket Office Manager:* Carol Taylor. *Hon. Medical Officers:* Mr F. R. Howell MA, FRCS, Dr B. Kell MBBS.

*Year Formed:* 1904. *Turned Professional:* 1905. *Ltd Co.:* 1905.

*Club Nickname:* 'The Tigers'.

*Previous Grounds:* 1904, Boulevard Ground (Hull RFC); 1905, Anlaby Road (Hull CC); 1944–45, Boulevard Ground; 1946, Boothferry Park.

*Foundation:* The enthusiasts who formed Hull City in 1904 were brave men indeed. More than that they were audacious for they immediately put the club on the map in this Rugby League fortress by obtaining a three-year agreement with the Hull Rugby League club to rent their ground! They had obtained quite a number of conversions to the dribbling code, before the Rugby League forbade the use of any of their club grounds by Association Football clubs. By that time, Hull City were well away having entered the FA Cup in their initial season and the Football League, Second Division after only a year.

*First Football League game:* 2 September 1905, Division 2, v Barnsley (h) W 4-1 – Spendiff; Langley, Jones; Martin, Robinson, Gordon (2); Rushton, Spence (1), Wilson (1), Howe, Raisbeck.

*Record League Victory:* 11–1 v Carlisle U, Division 3 (N), 14 January 1939 – Ellis; Woodhead, Dowen; Robinson (1), Blyth, Hardy; Hubbard (2), Richardson (2), Dickinson (2), Davies (2), Cunliffe (2).

*Record Cup Victory:* 8–2 v Stalybridge Celtic (away), FA Cup 1st rd, 26 November 1932 – Maddison; Goldsmith, Woodhead; Gardner, Hill (1), Denby; Forward (1), Duncan, McNaughton (1), Wainscoat (4), Sargeant (1).

*Record Defeat:* 0–8 v Wolverhampton W, Division 2, 4 November 1911.

*Most League Points (2 for a win):* 69, Division 3, 1965–66.

*Most League Points (3 for a win):* 90, Division 4, 1982–83.

*Most League Goals:* 109, Division 3, 1965–66.

*Highest League Scorer in Season:* Bill McNaughton, 39, Division 3 (N), 1932–33.

*Most League Goals in Total Aggregate:* Chris Chilton, 195, 1960–71.

*Most Capped Player:* Terry Neill, 15 (59), Northern Ireland.

*Most League Appearances:* Andy Davidson, 520, 1952–67.

*Record Transfer Fee Received:* £750,000 from Middlesbrough for Andy Payton, November 1991.

*Record Transfer Fee Paid:* £200,000 to Leeds U for Peter Swan, March 1989.

*Football League Record:* 1905 Elected to Division 2; 1930–33 Division 3 (N); 1933–36 Division 2; 1936–49 Division 3 (N); 1949–56 Division 2; 1956–58 Division 3 (N); 1958–59 Division 3; 1959–60 Division 2; 1960–66 Division 3; 1966–78 Division 2; 1978–81 Division 3; 1981–83 Division 4; 1983–85 Division 3; 1985–91 Division 2; 1991–92 Division 3; 1992–96 Division 2; 1996– Division 3.

*Honours: Football League:* Division 2 best season: 3rd, 1909–10; Division 3 (N) – Champions 1932–33, 1948–49; Division 3 – Champions 1965–66; Runners-up 1958–59; Division 4 – Runners-up 1982–83. *FA Cup:* best season: Semi-final 1930. *Football League Cup:* best season: 4th, 1974, 1976, 1978. *Associate Members' Cup:* Runners-up 1984.

*Colours:* Amber shirts, black shorts, amber stockings. *Change colours:* All white.

**Did you know?**
On 6 December 1913 Billy Halligan, who once had scored a hat-trick for Wolves against Hull City, scored four as Hull beat Wolverhampton Wanderers 7-1.

## HULL CITY 1997–98 LEAGUE RECORD

| Match No. | Date | Venue | Opponents | Result | | H/T Score | Lg. Pos. | Goalscorers | Attendance |
|---|---|---|---|---|---|---|---|---|---|
| 1 | Aug 9 | A | Mansfield T | L | 0-2 | 0-1 | — | | 4627 |
| 2 | 16 | H | Notts Co | L | 0-3 | 0-1 | 24 | | 7412 |
| 3 | 23 | A | Peterborough U | L | 0-2 | 0-1 | 24 | | 5701 |
| 4 | 30 | H | Swansea C | W | 7-4 | 2-1 | 18 | Darby 3 [13, 62, 82], Rioch [36], Hodges [54], Mann 2 [69, 73] | 5198 |
| 5 | Sept 2 | H | Rotherham U | D | 0-0 | 0-0 | — | | 6127 |
| 6 | 5 | A | Chester C | L | 0-1 | 0-1 | — | | 2271 |
| 7 | 13 | H | Lincoln C | L | 0-2 | 0-1 | 22 | | 4736 |
| 8 | 20 | H | Rochdale | L | 1-2 | 1-1 | 22 | Lowthorpe [38] | 2085 |
| 9 | 27 | A | Scunthorpe U | L | 0-2 | 0-1 | 23 | | 4905 |
| 10 | Oct 4 | H | Torquay U | D | 3-3 | 1-0 | 23 | Peacock [18], Gordon [66], Greaves [72] | 5139 |
| 11 | 11 | H | Scarborough | W | 3-0 | 2-0 | 22 | Peacock [7], Rocastle [20], Quigley [65] | 5315 |
| 12 | 18 | A | Barnet | L | 0-2 | 0-1 | 23 | | 2315 |
| 13 | 21 | A | Cambridge U | W | 1-0 | 0-0 | — | Greaves [88] | 2388 |
| 14 | 25 | H | Brighton & HA | D | 0-0 | 0-0 | 22 | | 5686 |
| 15 | Nov 1 | A | Darlington | L | 3-4 | 1-1 | 22 | Joyce [28], Rioch [54], Gordon [81] | 2893 |
| 16 | 4 | H | Exeter C | W | 3-2 | 1-0 | — | Joyce [5], Ellington 2 [65, 84] | 3837 |
| 17 | 8 | H | Shrewsbury T | L | 1-4 | 0-2 | 22 | Rioch [76] | 4758 |
| 18 | 18 | A | Cardiff C | L | 1-2 | 0-2 | — | Darby [64] | 2504 |
| 19 | 22 | A | Macclesfield T | L | 0-2 | 0-1 | 22 | | 2508 |
| 20 | 29 | H | Doncaster R | W | 3-0 | 0-0 | 22 | Gore (og) [48], Rioch (pen) [58], Hocking [83] | 4721 |
| 21 | Dec 2 | A | Hartlepool U | D | 2-2 | 0-1 | — | Joyce [52], Hodges [73] | 1933 |
| 22 | 13 | H | Colchester U | W | 3-1 | 0-0 | 20 | Dewhurst [55], Rioch (pen) [58], Darby [84] | 3896 |
| 23 | 20 | A | Leyton Orient | L | 1-2 | 0-1 | 21 | Wright [83] | 4013 |
| 24 | 26 | H | Chester C | L | 1-2 | 0-0 | 21 | Dewhurst [68] | 6807 |
| 25 | 28 | A | Rotherham U | L | 4-5 | 1-2 | 21 | Darby 2 [32, 72], Hodges 2 [66, 70] | 5995 |
| 26 | Jan 10 | H | Mansfield T | D | 0-0 | 0-0 | 22 | | 4440 |
| 27 | 17 | A | Swansea C | L | 0-2 | 0-0 | 22 | | 2899 |
| 28 | 20 | A | Notts Co | L | 0-1 | 0-0 | — | | 4017 |
| 29 | 24 | H | Peterborough U | W | 3-1 | 0-0 | 22 | Joyce [49], Darby 2 [67, 74] | 4669 |
| 30 | 31 | A | Lincoln C | L | 0-1 | 0-1 | 22 | | 4067 |
| 31 | Feb 7 | H | Rochdale | L | 0-2 | 0-1 | 22 | | 4031 |
| 32 | 14 | A | Torquay U | L | 1-5 | 1-3 | 22 | Bettney [16] | 2793 |
| 33 | 21 | H | Scunthorpe U | W | 2-1 | 2-1 | 22 | Dewhurst [15], McGinty [37] | 4904 |
| 34 | 24 | H | Barnet | L | 0-2 | 0-1 | — | | 3296 |
| 35 | 28 | A | Scarborough | L | 1-2 | 0-2 | 22 | Boyack [61] | 3831 |
| 36 | Mar 3 | A | Shrewsbury T | L | 0-2 | 0-0 | — | | 1523 |
| 37 | 7 | H | Darlington | D | 1-1 | 0-1 | 22 | Wright [79] | 3616 |
| 38 | 14 | A | Exeter C | L | 0-3 | 0-2 | 22 | | 3052 |
| 39 | 21 | H | Cardiff C | L | 0-1 | 0-0 | 22 | | 3408 |
| 40 | 28 | H | Macclesfield T | D | 0-0 | 0-0 | 22 | | 3677 |
| 41 | Apr 4 | A | Doncaster R | L | 0-1 | 0-0 | 23 | | 2597 |
| 42 | 11 | H | Hartlepool U | W | 2-1 | 0-1 | 22 | Brown D 2 [48, 72] | 3343 |
| 43 | 13 | A | Colchester U | L | 3-4 | 1-2 | 22 | Boyack [24], McGinty [48], Darby [71] | 4700 |
| 44 | 18 | H | Leyton Orient | W | 3-2 | 1-0 | 22 | Mann [32], Lowthorpe [46], Boyack [48] | 3744 |
| 45 | 25 | A | Brighton & HA | D | 2-2 | 0-1 | 22 | Darby 2 [51, 61] | 3888 |
| 46 | May 2 | H | Cambridge U | W | 1-0 | 1-0 | 22 | Darby [32] | 4930 |

**Final League Position: 22**       1996–97 DIV3 17

### GOALSCORERS

*League (56):* Darby 13, Rioch 5 (2 pens), Hodges 4, Joyce 4, Boyack 3, Dewhurst 3, Mann 3, Brown D 2, Ellington 2, Gordon 2, Greaves 2, Lowthorpe 2, McGinty 2, Peacock 2, Wright 2, Bettney 1, Hocking 1, Quigley 1, Rocastle 1, own goal 1.
*Coca-Cola Cup (4):* Darby 1, Joyce 1, Peacock 1, Wright 1.
*FA Cup (0).*

| Thomson S 9 | Trevitt S 4 | Mann N 20+14 | Wright I 25+8 | Brien T 14+1 | Dewhurst R 24 | Joyce W 45 | Rioch G 38+1 | Peacock R 26+1 | Hateley M 4+5 | Quigley M 4+5 | Greaves M 17+8 | Brown A —+3 | Darby D 27+2 | Dickinson P 2+1 | Hodges G 13+5 | Doncel A 8+4 | Lowthorpe A 18+5 | Fewings P 13+5 | Gage K 8+2 | Wilson S 37 | Hocking M 31 | Bettney C 28+2 | Gordon G —+5 | Rocastle D 10 | Ellington L 4+3 | Maxfield S 10+4 | McGinty B 21 | Edwards M 20+1 | Tucker D 1+6 | Morley B 5+3 | Wharton P 1 | Boyack S 12 | Brown D 7 | Match No. |
|---|---|---|---|---|---|---|---|---|---|---|---|---|---|---|---|---|---|---|---|---|---|---|---|---|---|---|---|---|---|---|---|---|---|---|
| 1 | 2 | 3 | 4 | 5 | 6 | 7 | 8 | 9 | 10¹ | 11² | 12 | 13 |  |  |  |  |  |  |  |  |  |  |  |  |  |  |  |  |  |  |  |  |  | 1 |
| 1 | 2 | 3 | 4 | 5 | 6 | 7 | 8 | 11 | 10 |  |  |  | 9 |  |  |  |  |  |  |  |  |  |  |  |  |  |  |  |  |  |  |  |  | 2 |
| 1 |  | 12 | 4 | 5 | 6 | 8 | 3 | 7 |  |  | 13 |  | 9 |  | 2² | 10¹ | 11 |  |  |  |  |  |  |  |  |  |  |  |  |  |  |  |  | 3 |
| 1 |  | 11 | 4 | 5 | 6 | 8 | 3 | 7 |  |  | 12 |  | 9 |  | 2² | 10¹ | 13 |  |  |  |  |  |  |  |  |  |  |  |  |  |  |  |  | 4 |
| 1 |  | 11 | 4 | 5 | 6 | 7 | 3 | 8 |  |  | 12 | 2² | 9 |  |  | 10¹ | 13 |  |  |  |  |  |  |  |  |  |  |  |  |  |  |  |  | 5 |
| 1 | 2¹ | 11² | 4 | 5 | 6 | 7 | 3 | 8 | 10 |  | 12 |  | 9 |  |  |  | 13 |  |  |  |  |  |  |  |  |  |  |  |  |  |  |  |  | 6 |
| 1 | 3¹ |  | 4 | 5 | 6 | 7 |  | 8 |  | 10 |  |  | 9 | 12 |  |  |  | 2 | 11 |  |  |  |  |  |  |  |  |  |  |  |  |  |  | 7 |
| 1 |  | 11 | 2 | 4 | 3 | 8 | 7 | 10 |  |  |  |  |  | 9¹ | 5² | 6 | 12 | 13 |  |  |  |  |  |  |  |  |  |  |  |  |  |  |  | 8 |
|  |  | 4¹ | 5 |  | 8 | 3 | 7 |  |  |  | 12 | 2 |  |  | 11² | 10 |  |  |  | 1 | 6 | 9 | 13 |  |  |  |  |  |  |  |  |  |  | 9 |
|  |  | 5 | 6 |  | 8 | 3 | 7 |  |  |  |  | 2 |  |  | 12 | 10 | 11¹ |  |  | 1 | 4 | 9² | 13 |  |  |  |  |  |  |  |  |  |  | 10 |
|  |  | 5² | 6 |  |  | 3 | 7¹ |  |  |  | 12 | 13 | 4 |  | 11 | 8 |  |  |  | 1 | 2 | 9 |  | 10 |  |  |  |  |  |  |  |  |  | 11 |
|  |  | 5 | 8¹ |  |  | 3 | 7 |  |  |  | 12 | 13 | 4 |  | 11 | 6 |  |  |  | 1 | 2² | 9³ | 14 | 10 |  |  |  |  |  |  |  |  |  | 12 |
|  |  | 4 |  |  | 8 | 7 | 3 |  |  |  |  | 2 |  |  | 5 | 11 |  |  |  | 1 | 6 | 9 |  | 10 |  |  |  |  |  |  |  |  |  | 13 |
|  |  | 4 |  |  | 8 | 7² | 3 |  |  |  | 12 | 13 |  |  | 5¹ | 11 |  | 2³ |  | 1 | 6 | 9 | 14 | 10 |  |  |  |  |  |  |  |  |  | 14 |
|  |  | 4 |  |  |  | 7 | 3 | 8 |  |  | 12 |  |  |  | 5 | 2² | 11 |  |  | 1 | 6 | 9 | 13 | 10¹ |  |  |  |  |  |  |  |  |  | 15 |
|  |  | 4 | 6 |  | 8 | 3 | 7 |  |  |  |  |  |  |  | 5 | 10² | 11 |  |  | 1 | 2 | 9¹ |  |  |  | 12 | 13 |  |  |  |  |  |  | 16 |
|  |  | 4 | 6¹ |  | 8 | 3 | 7 |  |  |  |  |  |  | 12 | 5 | 10 | 11 |  |  | 1 | 2 | 9 |  |  |  |  |  |  |  |  |  |  |  | 17 |
|  |  | 4 |  |  | 8 | 3 | 7 |  |  |  | 12 | 13 | 14 |  | 5² | 11¹ | 10³ | 9 | 2 | 1 | 6 |  |  |  |  |  |  |  |  |  |  |  |  | 18 |
|  |  | 12 | 4 |  | 6 | 3 | 7 | 8² |  |  |  | 2³ |  |  |  |  | 11¹ | 9 |  | 1 | 5 | 13 | 14 | 10 |  |  |  |  |  |  |  |  |  | 19 |
|  |  | 12 | 4 |  | 6 | 3 |  |  |  |  |  |  |  |  |  |  | 11³ | 2 |  | 1 | 5 | 9 | 14 | 10 |  | 7² |  | 13 | 8¹ |  |  |  |  | 20 |
|  |  | 11² | 4 |  | 6 | 3 |  |  |  |  | 12 |  |  |  |  |  | 14 | 13 |  | 1 | 5 | 9 |  | 10 |  | 7³ |  | 8¹ |  |  |  |  |  | 21 |
|  |  | 11 | 4 |  | 6 | 3 |  |  |  |  |  | 2 |  |  |  |  |  |  |  | 1 | 5 | 9 |  | 10 | 8 | 7 |  |  |  |  |  |  |  | 22 |
|  |  | 11¹ | 4 |  | 6 | 3 | 13 |  |  |  |  | 2 |  |  |  |  |  |  |  | 1 | 5² | 9 |  | 10 | 8 | 7 | 12 |  |  |  |  |  |  | 23 |
|  |  | 10 | 4 |  | 6 | 3 |  |  |  |  | 12 | 2 |  |  |  |  |  |  |  | 1 | 5 | 9 |  |  | 8 | 7 | 11¹ |  |  |  |  |  |  | 24 |
|  |  | 11 | 4 |  | 6 | 8¹ |  |  |  |  |  | 2 |  |  |  |  |  |  |  | 1 | 5 | 9 |  | 10 |  | 7 | 13 | 12 | 3² |  |  |  |  | 25 |
|  |  | 10 | 5¹ |  | 4 | 6 | 11² |  |  |  | 12 |  |  |  |  |  |  |  |  | 1 | 2 | 9 |  | 7 |  | 8 | 3 | 13 |  |  |  |  |  | 26 |
|  |  | 10 | 5 |  | 4 | 6 |  |  |  |  | 12 |  |  |  |  |  | 13 |  |  | 1 | 2 | 9 |  | 7 |  | 8 | 3¹ | 11² |  |  |  |  |  | 27 |
|  |  | 11² | 4 |  | 8 | 5 |  |  |  |  | 12 | 2³ |  |  |  |  |  |  |  | 1 | 6 | 9 |  | 7¹ | 3 | 10 | 13 | 14 |  |  |  |  |  | 28 |
|  | 3 |  | 4 |  | 7 | 9 |  |  |  |  | 11 |  |  |  |  |  |  |  |  | 1 | 5 | 10 |  | 8 | 6 | 2 |  |  |  |  |  |  |  | 29 |
|  | 3 |  | 4 |  | 7 | 9 | 11¹ |  |  |  |  |  |  |  |  |  |  |  |  | 1 | 5 | 10 |  | 8 | 6 | 12 | 2 |  |  |  |  |  |  | 30 |
|  | 3³ | 12 | 4 |  | 7 | 13 | 9 |  |  |  |  |  |  |  |  |  |  |  |  | 1 | 5 | 11 | 14 | 8 | 6 | 2¹ | 10² |  |  |  |  |  |  | 31 |
| 1 |  | 11 | 12 |  | 4 | 7 | 3² | 9 |  |  |  |  |  | 2¹ |  |  |  |  |  | 5 | 10 | 13 | 8 | 6³ | 14 |  |  |  |  |  |  |  |  | 32 |
|  |  | 12 | 2 |  | 4 | 6 | 10¹ | 9² |  |  |  |  |  | 13 |  |  |  |  |  | 1 | 5 | 7 |  | 8 | 3 | 14 | 11³ |  |  |  |  |  |  | 33 |
|  |  | 12 | 2² |  | 4 | 6 | 11 |  |  |  | 13 |  |  | 9³ |  |  |  |  |  | 1 | 5 | 10 |  | 8 | 3 | 14 | 7¹ |  |  |  |  |  |  | 34 |
|  |  | 12 |  |  | 4 | 6¹ | 3 |  |  |  |  | 2 |  | 11² |  |  |  |  |  | 1 | 5 | 9 |  | 10 | 8 | 13 | 7 |  |  |  |  |  |  | 35 |
|  |  | 11 | 4¹ |  | 6 |  |  | 12 |  |  |  | 13 |  |  |  |  |  |  |  | 1 | 5 | 7 | 9 | 3 | 8² | 2 |  | 10 |  |  |  |  |  | 36 |
|  |  | 4 |  |  | 6 | 11 |  | 12 |  |  |  | 13 |  |  |  |  |  |  |  | 1 | 5¹ | 7 | 9² | 3 | 8 | 2 |  | 10 |  |  |  |  |  | 37 |
|  |  | 12 | 4 | 5 | 6 | 7 |  | 13 |  |  |  |  |  |  |  |  |  |  |  | 1 | 2 | 10 | 9 | 11 | 3¹ | 8 |  |  |  |  |  |  |  | 38 |
|  |  | 12 |  |  | 6 | 11 | 7 | 5 |  |  |  |  |  |  |  |  |  |  |  | 1 | 4² | 9¹ | 3 | 8 | 2 | 13 | 10 |  |  |  |  |  |  | 39 |
|  |  | 12 |  |  | 6 | 11 | 7¹ | 5 |  |  |  |  | 2 |  |  |  |  |  |  | 1 |  | 3 | 8 | 4 | 10 | 9 |  |  |  |  |  |  |  | 40 |
|  |  | 12 |  |  | 6 | 11 | 7² | 5 |  |  |  | 13 | 2 |  |  |  |  |  |  | 1 | 3 | 10¹ | 4 | 8 | 9 |  |  |  |  |  |  |  |  | 41 |
|  |  | 12 | 13 |  | 6 | 11 | 7 | 5 |  |  |  | 14 | 2 |  |  |  |  |  |  | 1 | 3² | 10² | 4 | 8 | 9¹ |  |  |  |  |  |  |  |  | 42 |
|  |  | 12 | 13 |  | 6 | 3 | 7 | 10¹ |  |  |  |  | 5 | 2² |  |  |  |  |  | 1 | 8 | 4 | 11 | 9 |  |  |  |  |  |  |  |  |  | 43 |
|  |  | 11¹ | 12 |  | 6 | 3 | 7³ | 13 |  |  |  |  | 10 | 5 |  |  |  |  |  | 1 | 4 | 14 | 8 | 9² |  |  |  |  |  |  |  |  |  | 44 |
|  |  | 12 | 13 |  | 6 | 3 | 7 | 14 |  |  |  |  | 10³ | 5 |  |  |  |  |  | 1 | 8¹ | 4 | 11 | 9² |  |  |  |  |  |  |  |  |  | 45 |
|  |  | 12 | 13 |  | 6 | 3 | 7¹ | 14 |  |  |  |  | 10 | 5 |  |  | 2² |  |  | 1 | 8 | 4 | 11 | 9³ |  |  |  |  |  |  |  |  |  | 46 |

**Coca-Cola Cup**

| First Round | Macclesfield T | (a) | 0-0 |
| | | (h) | 2-1 |
| Second Round | Crystal Palace | (h) | 1-0 |
| | | (a) | 1-2 |
| Third Round | Newcastle U | (a) | 0-2 |

**FA Cup**

| First Round | Hednesford T | (h) | 0-2 |

IPSWICH TOWN 1997-98    *Back row (left to right):* Leon Bell, Neil Gregory, Mark Venus, Dave Williams (Physio), Kevin Ellis, Stuart Niven, Mark Burgess.

*Middle row:* Bryan Klug, John Kennedy, Tony Mowbray, Jason Cundy, James Scowcroft, Craig Forrest, Richard Wright, Danny Sonner, Adam Tanner, Richard Naylor, Chris Swailes, Wayne Brown, Dale Roberts (First Team Coach).

*Front row:* Simon Milton, Mick Stockwell, Mauricio Taricco, Paul Mason, Alex Mathie, Geraint Williams, George Burley (Manager), Kevin Gaughan, Chris Keeble, David Theobold, Kieron Dyer, Gus Uhlenbeek, Bobby Petta.

(Photograph: Allsport)

# Division 1     **IPSWICH TOWN**

*Portman Road, Ipswich, Suffolk IP1 2DA.* Telephone: (01473) 400500 (4 lines). Fax: (01473) 400040. Ticket Office: (01473) 400555. Sales & Marketing Dept: (01473) 400523.

*Ground capacity:* 22,600.

*Record attendance:* 38,010 v Leeds U, FA Cup 6th rd, 8 March 1975.

*Record receipts:* £105,952 v AZ 67 Alkmaar, UEFA Cup Final 1st leg, 6 May 1981.

*Pitch measurements:* 112yd × 82yd.

*Chairman:* David Sheepshanks.

*Vice-Presidents:* Kenneth H. Brightwell, Harold R. Smith.

*Directors:* P. Hope-Cobbold, J. Kerridge, R. Moore, John Kerr MBE, R. J. Finbow.

*Manager:* George Burley. *Assistant Manager:* Dale Roberts. *Reserve Team Coach:* Bryan Klug.

*Youth Team Coach:* Paul Goddard. *Chief Scout:* Charlie Woods. *Director of Coaching:* Colin Suggett.

*Physio:* Dave Williams.

*Secretary:* David C. Rose.

*Sales & Promotions Manager:* Mike Noye.

*Year Formed:* 1878. *Turned Professional:* 1936. *Ltd Co.:* 1936.

*Club Nickname:* 'Blues' or 'Town'.

*Foundation:* Considering that Ipswich Town only reached the Football League in 1938, many people outside of East Anglia may be surprised to learn that this club was formed at a meeting held in the Town Hall as far back as 1878 when Mr T. C. Cobbold, MP, was voted president. Originally it was the Ipswich Association FC to distinguish it from the older Ipswich Football Club which played rugby. These two amalgamated in 1888 and the handling game was dropped in 1893.

*First Football League game:* 27 August 1938, Division 3 (S), v Southend U (h) W 4-2 – Burns; Dale, Parry; Perrett, Fillingham, McLuckie; Williams, Davies (1), Jones (2), Alsop (1), Little.

*Record League Victory:* 7–0 v Portsmouth, Division 2, 7 November 1964 – Thorburn; Smith, McNeil; Baxter, Bolton, Thompson; Broadfoot (1), Hegan (2), Baker (1), Leadbetter, Brogan (3). 7–0 v Southampton, Division 1, 2 February 1974 – Sivell; Burley, Mills (1), Morris, Hunter, Beattie (1), Hamilton (2), Viljoen, Johnson, Whymark (2), Lambert (1) (Woods). 7–0 v WBA, Division 1, 6 November 1976 – Sivell; Burley, Mills, Talbot, Hunter, Beattie (1), Osborne, Wark (1), Mariner (1) (Bertschin), Whymark (4), Woods.

*Record Cup Victory:* 10–0 v Floriana, European Cup Prel. rd, 25 September 1962 – Bailey; Malcolm, Compton; Baxter, Laurel, Elsworthy (1); Stephenson, Moran (2), Crawford (5), Phillips (2), Blackwood.

*Record Defeat:* 1–10 v Fulham, Division 1, 26 December 1963.

*Most League Points (2 for a win):* 64, Division 3 (S), 1953–54 and 1955–56.

*Most League Points (3 for a win):* 84, Division 1, 1991–92.

*Most League Goals:* 106, Division 3 (S), 1955–56.

*Highest League Scorer in Season:* Ted Phillips, 41, Division 3 (S), 1956–57.

*Most League Goals in Total Aggregate:* Ray Crawford, 203, 1958–63 and 1966–69.

*Most Capped Player:* Allan Hunter, 47 (53), Northern Ireland.

*Most League Appearances:* Mick Mills, 591, 1966–82.

*Record Transfer Fee Received:* £1,900,000 from Tottenham H for Jason Dozzell, August 1993.

*Record Transfer Fee Paid:* £1,100,000 to Bury for David Johnson, November 1997.

*Football League Record:* 1938 Elected to Division 3 (S); 1954–55 Division 2; 1955–57 Division 3 (S); 1957–61 Division 2; 1961–64 Division 1; 1964–68 Division 2; 1968–86 Division 1; 1986–92 Division 2; 1992–95 FA Premier League; 1995– Division 1.

*Honours: Football League:* Division 1 – Champions 1961–62; Runners-up 1980–81, 1981–82; Division 2 – Champions 1960–61, 1967–68, 1991–92; Division 3 (S) – Champions 1953–54, 1956–57. *FA Cup:* Winners 1978. *Football League Cup:* best season: Semi-final 1982, 1985. *Texaco Cup:* 1973. **European Competitions:** *European Cup:* 1962–63. *European Cup-Winners' Cup:* 1978–79. *UEFA Cup:* 1973–74, 1974–75, 1975–76, 1977–78, 1979–80, 1980–81 (winners), 1981–82, 1982–83.

*Colours:* Blue shirts, white shorts, blue stockings. *Change colours:* Orange shirts, navy shorts, orange stockings.

**Did you know?**
The youngest team fielded by Ipswich Town was on 21 August 1976 v Tottenham Hotspur. Their average age was 22 years 9 months and they won 3-1.

## IPSWICH TOWN 1997–98 LEAGUE RECORD

| Match No. | Date | | Venue | Opponents | Result | | H/T Score | Lg. Pos. | Goalscorers | Attendance |
|---|---|---|---|---|---|---|---|---|---|---|
| 1 | Aug | 9 | A | QPR | D | 0-0 | 0-0 | — | | 17,614 |
| 2 | | 23 | A | Bradford C | L | 1-2 | 0-1 | 21 | Dyer 74 | 13,913 |
| 3 | | 30 | H | WBA | D | 1-1 | 1-0 | 22 | Stein 40 | 13,508 |
| 4 | Sept | 2 | H | Swindon T | W | 2-1 | 1-1 | — | Venus 36, Sonner 82 | 11,246 |
| 5 | | 13 | A | Huddersfield T | D | 2-2 | 0-1 | 20 | Edmondson (og) 65, Dyer 90 | 9313 |
| 6 | | 20 | H | Stoke C | L | 2-3 | 0-2 | 22 | Scowcroft 48, Holland 67 | 10,665 |
| 7 | | 26 | A | Norwich C | L | 1-2 | 0-1 | — | Stein 73 | 18,911 |
| 8 | Oct | 4 | H | Manchester C | W | 1-0 | 0-0 | 22 | Mathie 63 | 14,322 |
| 9 | | 18 | A | Oxford U | L | 0-1 | 0-0 | 22 | | 7594 |
| 10 | | 21 | A | Crewe Alex | D | 0-0 | 0-0 | — | | 4730 |
| 11 | | 25 | H | Bury | W | 2-0 | 0-0 | 20 | Tanner (pen) 80, Dozzell 86 | 10,478 |
| 12 | | 28 | A | Birmingham C | D | 1-1 | 1-0 | — | Holland 34 | 16,778 |
| 13 | Nov | 1 | A | Charlton Ath | L | 0-3 | 0-2 | 21 | | 12,627 |
| 14 | | 4 | H | Stockport Co | L | 0-2 | 0-0 | — | | 8938 |
| 15 | | 9 | H | Sheffield U | D | 2-2 | 0-1 | 21 | Legg 50, Gregory 87 | 9695 |
| 16 | | 15 | A | Wolverhampton W | D | 1-1 | 1-1 | 21 | Johnson 44 | 21,937 |
| 17 | | 22 | A | Reading | W | 4-0 | 2-0 | 18 | Holland 26, Johnson 30, Scowcroft 49, Naylor 87 | 9400 |
| 18 | | 29 | H | Nottingham F | L | 0-1 | 0-0 | 20 | | 17,580 |
| 19 | Dec | 2 | H | Middlesbrough | D | 1-1 | 0-1 | — | Johnson 90 | 13,619 |
| 20 | | 6 | A | Tranmere R | D | 1-1 | 1-0 | 19 | Johnson 27 | 5720 |
| 21 | | 13 | A | Portsmouth | W | 2-0 | 1-0 | 16 | Cundy 30, Johnson 68 | 11,641 |
| 22 | | 20 | A | Port Vale | W | 3-1 | 3-0 | 14 | Mathie 2 10, 22, Johnson 43 | 5784 |
| 23 | | 26 | H | Birmingham C | L | 0-1 | 0-0 | 16 | | 17,459 |
| 24 | | 28 | A | Swindon T | W | 2-0 | 0-0 | 13 | Johnson (pen) 49, Petta 79 | 10,609 |
| 25 | Jan | 10 | H | QPR | D | 0-0 | 0-0 | 14 | | 12,672 |
| 26 | | 17 | A | Middlesbrough | D | 1-1 | 0-0 | 15 | Johnson 76 | 30,081 |
| 27 | | 27 | A | WBA | W | 3-2 | 0-0 | — | Holland 57, Scowcroft 75, Cundy 89 | 12,403 |
| 28 | | 31 | H | Bradford C | W | 2-1 | 0-0 | 13 | Mathie 2 72, 86 | 11,864 |
| 29 | Feb | 7 | A | Stoke C | D | 1-1 | 0-0 | 13 | Holland 78 | 11,416 |
| 30 | | 14 | H | Huddersfield T | W | 5-1 | 1-1 | 12 | Holland 42, Johnson 2 54, 61, Mathie 69, Naylor 89 | 10,509 |
| 31 | | 18 | H | Manchester C | W | 2-1 | 0-1 | — | Petta 63, Dyer 90 | 27,156 |
| 32 | | 21 | H | Norwich C | W | 5-0 | 3-0 | 10 | Mathie 3 2, 27, 42, Petta 2 56, 81 | 21,858 |
| 33 | | 24 | A | Oxford U | W | 5-2 | 3-1 | — | Mathie 28, Johnson 3 (1 pen) 35, 38, 85 (p), Holland 56 | 11,824 |
| 34 | | 28 | A | Sunderland | D | 2-2 | 2-1 | 7 | Petta 11, Dyer 28 | 35,114 |
| 35 | Mar | 3 | A | Sheffield U | W | 1-0 | 1-0 | — | Holland 18 | 14,120 |
| 36 | | 7 | H | Charlton Ath | W | 3-1 | 0-1 | 5 | Stockwell 53, Cundy 76, Johnson 88 | 19,831 |
| 37 | | 14 | A | Stockport Co | W | 1-0 | 0-0 | 5 | Johnson 55 | 8939 |
| 38 | | 21 | H | Wolverhampton W | W | 3-0 | 1-0 | 5 | Johnson 3, Holland 57, Scowcroft 74 | 21,510 |
| 39 | | 28 | H | Reading | W | 1-0 | 1-0 | 5 | Scowcroft 39 | 19,075 |
| 40 | Apr | 5 | A | Nottingham F | L | 1-2 | 0-0 | 5 | Scowcroft 46 | 22,292 |
| 41 | | 11 | H | Tranmere R | D | 0-0 | 0-0 | 6 | | 18,039 |
| 42 | | 13 | A | Portsmouth | W | 1-0 | 1-0 | 5 | Johnson 8 | 15,040 |
| 43 | | 18 | H | Port Vale | W | 5-1 | 3-0 | 5 | Johnson 2 4, 58, Petta 2 27, 29, Mathie 56 | 16,205 |
| 44 | | 25 | A | Bury | W | 1-0 | 0-0 | 5 | Stockwell 75 | 7830 |
| 45 | | 28 | H | Sunderland | W | 2-0 | 0-0 | — | Holland 48, Mathie 61 | 20,902 |
| 46 | May | 3 | H | Crewe Alex | W | 3-2 | 1-1 | 5 | Johnson 33, Stockwell 53, Mathie 55 | 19,105 |

**Final League Position: 5** 　　　1996–97 DIV1 4

### GOALSCORERS

*League (77):* Johnson 20 (2 pens), Mathie 13, Holland 10, Petta 7, Scowcroft 6, Dyer 4, Cundy 3, Stockwell 3, Naylor 2, Stein 2, Dozzell 1, Gregory 1, Legg 1, Sonner 1, Tanner 1 (pen), Venus 1, own goal 1.
*Coca-Cola Cup (14):* Holland 2, Mathie 2, Taricco 2, Dozzell 1, Dyer 1, Mowbray 1, Scowcroft 1, Stein 1, Stockwell 1, Venus 1, own goal 1.
*FA Cup (3):* Johnson 2, Stockwell 1.

| Wright R 46 | Stockwell M 46 | Taricco M 41 | Williams G 23 | Venus M 12+2 | Cundy J 40+1 | Dyer K 41 | Holland M 46 | Petta B 28+4 | Scowcroft J 19+12 | Mason P 1 | Gregory N 2+6 | Swailes C 3+2 | Milton S 7+13 | Stein M 6+1 | Kerslake D 2+5 | Mathie A 25+12 | Sonner D 6+17 | Mowbray T 23+2 | Dozzell J 8 | Tanner A 14+4 | Whyte D 2 | Legg A 6 | Johnson D 30+1 | Naylor R —+5 | Kennedy J —+1 | Keeble C —+1 | Clapham J 22 | Brown W 1 | Uhlenbeek G 6+5 | Match No. |
|---|---|---|---|---|---|---|---|---|---|---|---|---|---|---|---|---|---|---|---|---|---|---|---|---|---|---|---|---|---|---|
| 1 | 2 | 3 | 4 | $5^1$ | 6 | 7 | 8 | $9^2$ | 10 | $11^3$ | 12 | 13 | 14 |  |  |  |  |  |  |  |  |  |  |  |  |  |  |  |  | 1 |
| 1 | 2 | 3 | 4 | 5 | $6^1$ |  | 8 | $11^2$ | 10 |  |  |  |  | 12 | 9 | 13 |  |  |  |  |  |  |  |  |  |  |  |  |  | 2 |
| 1 | 2 | 3 | 4 | 5 | 6 |  | 8 |  | 10 |  |  |  |  | $11^1$ | 9 | 12 |  |  |  |  |  |  |  |  |  |  |  |  |  | 3 |
| 1 | 2 | 3 | 4 | 5 |  | 7 | 8 | $10^1$ |  |  |  |  |  |  | 6 | $11^2$ | 9 | 12 | 13 |  |  |  |  |  |  |  |  |  |  | 4 |
| 1 | 2 | 3 | 4 | 5 |  | 7 | 8 | 12 |  |  |  |  |  |  | 6 | 9 |  | $10^1$ | 11 |  |  |  |  |  |  |  |  |  |  | 5 |
| 1 | 2 | 3 | 4 | 5 | 12 | 7 | 8 |  | 10 |  |  |  |  |  | 6 | 9 |  | $11^1$ |  |  |  |  |  |  |  |  |  |  |  | 6 |
| 1 | 2 |  | 4 | $3^2$ | 6 | 7 | 8 | 11 | $10^1$ |  |  |  |  |  | 9 | 13 | 12 |  |  | 5 |  |  |  |  |  |  |  |  |  | 7 |
| 1 | 2 |  | $4^1$ |  |  | 7 | 8 | 11 |  |  | $10^2$ |  |  |  |  | 12 |  | 3 | 9 | 5 | 6 | 13 |  |  |  |  |  |  |  | 8 |
| 1 | 2 | 3 |  |  | 6 | 7 | 8 | $11^1$ |  |  |  |  |  |  |  | 13 | 12 | 9 | $5^2$ | 10 | 4 |  |  |  |  |  |  |  |  | 9 |
| 1 | 2 | 3 |  |  | 6 | 7 | 8 | 11 |  |  |  |  |  |  |  | 5 |  | 9 |  | 10 | 4 |  |  |  |  |  |  |  |  | 10 |
| 1 | 2 | 3 | 4 |  | 6 | $7^1$ | 8 | 11 |  |  |  | 13 |  |  |  | 12 |  | $9^2$ |  | 10 | 5 |  |  |  |  |  |  |  |  | 11 |
| 1 | $2^1$ | 3 | 4 |  | 6 | 7 | 8 | $11^3$ |  |  |  | 13 |  |  |  | 12 | 14 | 9 |  | $10^2$ | 5 |  |  |  |  |  |  |  |  | 12 |
| 1 | 2 | 3 | $4^1$ |  | 6 | $7^2$ | 8 |  |  |  |  |  | 9 | 14 | 12 | 5 | 13 | $10^3$ | 11 |  |  |  |  |  |  |  |  |  |  | 13 |
| 1 | 2 | $3^1$ |  |  | 6 |  | 8 |  |  |  |  |  | 12 |  | 7 | 13 | $9^2$ | 4 | 5 | 10 | 11 |  |  |  |  |  |  |  |  | 14 |
| 1 | 2 |  | 4 |  | 6 | 7 | 8 |  |  |  |  |  | 12 |  |  | $9^1$ | 13 | 5 | 10 | $3^2$ | 11 |  |  |  |  |  |  |  |  | 15 |
| 1 | 2 | 3 | 4 |  | 6 | 7 | 8 |  |  |  |  |  | 12 |  |  | 13 |  | 10 | 5 | $11^2$ | $9^1$ |  |  |  |  |  |  |  |  | 16 |
| 1 | 2 | 3 | $4^1$ |  | 6 | 7 | 8 | $10^3$ |  |  |  |  | 12 |  |  | 13 |  | 5 |  | 11 | $9^2$ | 14 |  |  |  |  |  |  |  | 17 |
| 1 | 2 | 3 |  |  | 6 | 7 | 8 | 10 |  |  |  |  |  |  |  | 5 |  |  |  | 11 | $9^1$ | 12 |  |  |  |  |  |  |  | 18 |
| 1 | 2 | 3 |  |  | 6 | 7 | 8 | 10 |  |  |  |  |  |  | $4^1$ | 12 |  | $5^3$ |  | 14 | $11^3$ | 9 | 13 |  |  |  |  |  |  | 19 |
| 1 | 2 | 3 | 4 |  | 6 | $7^1$ | 8 | 11 | 10 |  |  |  | 12 |  |  | 5 |  |  |  |  |  |  | 9 |  |  |  |  |  |  | 20 |
| 1 | 2 | 3 | 4 |  | 6 | $7^2$ | 8 | $11^1$ | $10^3$ |  |  |  | 13 |  |  | 5 |  |  |  |  |  |  | 9 |  |  |  |  |  |  | 21 |
| 1 | $2^2$ | 3 | 4 |  | 6 |  | 8 | $11^3$ |  |  |  |  |  |  |  | 10 | $7^1$ | 12 | 5 |  |  |  | 9 |  |  | 13 | 14 |  |  | 22 |
| 1 | 2 | 3 | 4 |  | 6 |  | 8 | 11 |  |  |  |  |  |  |  | 10 | 7 | 12 | $5^1$ |  |  |  | 9 |  |  |  |  |  |  | 23 |
| 1 | 2 | 3 | 4 |  | 6 | $7^1$ | 8 | 11 |  |  |  |  | 12 |  |  | 10 |  | 5 |  |  |  |  | 9 |  |  |  |  |  |  | 24 |
| 1 | $2^1$ | 3 | 4 |  | 6 |  | 8 | 11 | $10^2$ |  |  |  | 12 |  |  | 13 |  | 5 |  |  |  |  | 9 |  |  |  | 7 |  |  | 25 |
| 1 | 2 | 3 | 4 |  |  |  | 8 |  | 10 |  |  |  |  |  |  | 12 | 7 | 5 |  |  |  |  | 9 |  |  |  | 11 |  | $6^1$ | 26 |
| 1 | 2 | 3 |  |  | 6 | 4 | 8 |  | 10 |  |  |  |  |  |  | 12 |  | 5 |  |  |  |  | 9 |  |  |  | $11^1$ |  | 7 | 27 |
| 1 | 2 | 3 |  |  | 6 | 4 | 8 | 12 | 10 |  |  |  |  |  |  | 13 | 14 | $5^2$ |  |  |  |  | 9 |  |  |  | $11^3$ |  | $7^1$ | 28 |
| 1 | 2 | 3 | $4^2$ |  | 6 | 11 | 8 | 10 |  |  |  |  |  |  |  | 9 | 12 | 5 |  |  |  |  | 13 |  |  |  | $7^1$ |  |  | 29 |
| 1 | 2 | 3 |  |  | 6 | 11 | 8 | 12 |  |  |  |  |  |  |  | 10 | $4^1$ | 5 |  |  |  |  | $9^2$ | 13 |  |  | $7^2$ |  | 14 | 30 |
| 1 | 2 | 3 |  |  | 6 | 4 | 8 | 12 |  |  |  |  |  |  |  | 10 |  | 5 |  |  |  |  | $9^2$ | 13 |  |  | $11^1$ |  | 7 | 31 |
| 1 | $2^3$ |  |  |  | 6 | 4 | 8 | 11 | 12 |  |  |  |  |  |  | $10^1$ | 13 | 5 |  |  |  |  | 9 |  |  |  | 3 |  | 7 | 32 |
| 1 | $2^3$ | 3 |  |  | 6 | 4 | 8 | $11^2$ | 12 |  |  |  |  |  |  | $10^1$ | 13 | 5 |  |  |  |  | 9 |  |  |  | 7 |  | 14 | 33 |
| 1 | 2 | 3 |  |  | 6 | 4 | 8 | $11^1$ | 12 |  |  |  |  |  |  | 10 | 13 | 5 |  |  |  |  | $9^2$ |  |  |  | 7 |  |  | 34 |
| 1 | 2 | 3 |  |  | 6 | 4 | 8 | $11^2$ | 12 |  |  |  |  |  |  | 10 | 13 | 5 |  |  |  |  | 9 |  |  |  | 7 |  |  | 35 |
| 1 | 2 | 3 |  |  | 6 | 4 | 8 | 11 | 12 |  |  |  |  |  |  | $10^1$ |  | 5 |  |  |  |  | 9 |  |  |  | 7 |  |  | 36 |
| 1 | 2 | 3 |  |  | 6 | 4 | 8 | 11 | 12 |  |  |  |  |  |  | $10^1$ |  | 5 |  |  |  |  | 9 |  |  |  | 7 |  |  | 37 |
| 1 | 2 |  |  |  | 6 | $4^2$ | 8 | $11^3$ | 12 |  |  |  |  |  |  | $10^1$ | 13 | 5 |  | 14 |  |  | 9 |  |  |  | 3 |  | 7 | 38 |
| 1 | 2 | 3 |  |  | 6 | 4 | 8 | $11^1$ | 10 |  |  |  |  |  |  | 12 | 13 | 5 |  |  |  |  | 9 |  |  |  | 7 |  |  | 39 |
| 1 | 2 | 3 |  |  | 6 | 4 | 8 | $11^2$ | 10 |  |  |  |  |  |  | 12 |  | $5^1$ |  |  |  |  | 9 |  |  |  | 7 |  | 13 | 40 |
| 1 | 2 | 3 |  | 12 | 6 | 4 | 8 | $11^3$ | 10 |  |  |  |  |  |  | 13 | 14 | $5^1$ |  |  |  |  | $9^2$ |  |  |  | 7 |  |  | 41 |
| 1 | 2 | 3 |  | 12 | 6 | 4 | 8 | 11 | 13 |  |  |  |  |  |  | $10^2$ |  | $5^1$ |  |  |  |  | 9 |  |  |  | 7 |  |  | 42 |
| 1 | 2 | $3^3$ |  | 5 | 6 | 4 | 8 | $11^2$ | 12 |  |  |  |  |  |  | 10 | 13 |  |  | 14 |  |  | $9^1$ |  |  |  | 7 |  |  | 43 |
| 1 | 2 | 3 |  | 5 | 6 | 4 | 8 | $11^1$ | 12 |  |  |  |  |  |  | $10^2$ | 13 |  |  |  |  |  | 9 |  |  |  | 7 |  |  | 44 |
| 1 | 2 | 3 |  | 5 | 6 | $4^2$ | 8 | $11^3$ | 12 |  |  |  |  |  |  | 10 | 13 |  |  |  |  |  | $9^1$ |  |  |  | 7 |  | 14 | 45 |
| 1 | $2^2$ | $3^3$ |  | 5 | 6 | 4 | 8 | 11 | 12 |  |  |  |  |  |  | $10^1$ | 13 |  |  |  |  |  | 9 |  |  |  | 7 |  | 14 | 46 |

**Coca-Cola Cup**

| | | | |
|---|---|---|---|
| First Round | Charlton Ath | (a) | 1-0 |
| | | (h) | 3-1 |
| Second Round | Torquay U | (h) | 1-1 |
| | | (a) | 3-0 |
| Third Round | Manchester U | (h) | 2-0 |
| Fourth Round | Oxford U | (a) | 2-1 |
| Fifth Round | Chelsea | (h) | 2-2 |

**FA Cup**

| | | | |
|---|---|---|---|
| Third Round | Bristol R | (a) | 1-1 |
| | | (h) | 1-0 |
| Fourth Round | Sheffield U | (h) | 1-1 |
| | | (a) | 0-1 |

LEEDS UNITED 1997-98    *Back row (left to right):* Bruno Ribeiro, Richard Jobson, David Wetherall, Mark Beeney, Nigel Martyn, Robert Molenaar, Gunnar Halle, Lee Bowyer.
*Middle row:* David O'Leary (Assistant Manager), David Swift (Senior Physio), Pierre Laurent, Jimmy Floyd Hasselbaink, Lee Sharpe, David Hopkin, Harry Kewell, Andy Gray, Rod Wallace, David Williams (First Team Coach).
*Front row:* Ian Harte, Alfie Haaland, Lucas Radebe, George Graham (Manger), David Robertson, Derek Lilley, Gary Kelly.

# FA Premiership     **LEEDS UNITED**

*Elland Road, Leeds LS11 0ES.* Telephone: (0113) 2266000. Fax: (0113) 2266050. Ticket Information: 0891 121680. Clubcall: 0891 121180.

*Ground capacity:* 40,000.

*Record attendance:* 57,892 v Sunderland, FA Cup 5th rd (replay), 15 March 1967.

*Record receipts:* £314,063 v Oldham Ath, FA Cup 4th rd, 28 January 1995.

*Pitch measurements:* 105m × 65m.

*President:* The Right Hon The Earl of Harewood LL.D.

*Chairman:* Peter Ridsdale.

*Directors:* R. Barker, A. Hudson, J. W. G. Marjason, P. D. G. McCormick, L. H. Silver OBE.

*Chief Executive:* R. P. Launders.

*Manager:* George Graham. *Assistant Manager:* David O'Leary.

*Company/Club Secretary:* Nigel Pleasants.

*Coach:* Eddie Gray.

*Physio:* David Swift.

*Commercial Manager:* Keith Hanvey. *Stadium Manager:* Harry Stokey.

*Year Formed:* 1919, as Leeds United after disbandment (by FA order) of Leeds City (formed in 1904).

*Turned Professional:* 1920. *Ltd Co.:* 1920.

*Club Nickname:* 'United'.

*Foundation:* Immediately the Leeds City club (founded in 1904) was wound up by the FA in October 1919, following allegations of illegal payments to players, a meeting was called by a Leeds solicitor, Mr. Alf Masser, at which Leeds United was formed. They joined the Midland League playing their first game in that competition in November 1919. It was in this same month that the new club had discussions with the directors of a virtually bankrupt Huddersfield Town who wanted to move to Leeds in an amalgamation. But Huddersfield survived even that crisis.

*First Football League game:* 28 August 1920, Division 2, v Port Vale (a) L 0-2 – Down; Duffield, Tillotson; Musgrove, Baker, Walton; Mason, Goldthorpe, Thompson, Lyon, Best.

*Record League Victory:* 8–0 v Leicester C, Division 1, 7 April 1934 – Moore; George Milburn, Jack Milburn; Edwards, Hart, Copping; Mahon (2), Firth (2), Duggan (2), Furness (2), Cochrane.

*Record Cup Victory:* 10–0 v Lyn (Oslo), European Cup 1st rd 1st leg, 17 September 1969 – Sprake; Reaney, Cooper, Bremner (2), Charlton, Hunter, Madeley, Clarke (2), Jones (3), Giles (2) (Bates), O'Grady (1).

*Record Defeat:* 1–8 v Stoke C, Division 1, 27 August 1934.

*Most League Points (2 for a win):* 67, Division 1, 1968–69.

*Most League Points (3 for a win):* 85, Division 2, 1989–90.

*Most League Goals:* 98, Division 2, 1927–28.

*Highest League Scorer in Season:* John Charles, 42, Division 2, 1953–54.

*Most League Goals in Total Aggregate:* Peter Lorimer, 168, 1965–79 and 1983–86.

*Most Capped Player:* Billy Bremner, 54, Scotland.

*Most League Appearances:* Jack Charlton, 629, 1953–73.

*Record Transfer Fee Received:* £3,500,000 from Everton for Gary Speed, June 1996.

*Record Transfer Fee Paid:* £4,500,000 to Parma for Tomas Brolin, 23 November 1995.

*Football League Record:* 1920 Elected to Division 2; 1924–27 Division 1; 1927–28 Division 2; 1928–31 Division 1; 1931–32 Division 2; 1932–47 Division 1; 1947–56 Division 2; 1956–60 Division 1; 1960–64 Division 2; 1964–82 Division 1; 1982–90 Division 2; 1990–92 Division 1; 1992– FA Premier League.

*Honours: Football League:* Division 1 – Champions 1968–69, 1973–74, 1991–92; Runners-up 1964–65, 1965–66, 1969–70, 1970–71, 1971–72; Division 2 – Champions 1923–24, 1963–64, 1989–90; Runners-up 1927–28, 1931–32, 1955–56. *FA Cup:* Winners 1972; Runners-up 1965, 1970, 1973. *Football League Cup:* Winners 1968; Runners-up 1996. **European Competitions:** *European Cup:* 1969–70, 1974–75 (runners-up), 1992–93. *European Cup-Winners' Cup:* 1972–73 (runners-up). *European Fairs Cup:* 1965–66, 1966–67 (runners-up), 1967–68 (winners), 1968–69, 1970–71 (winners). *UEFA Cup:* 1971–72, 1973–74, 1979–80, 1995–96.

*Colours:* White with yellow and blue trim. *Change colours:* Yellow with white and blue trim.

**Did you know?**
John Charles scored five hat-tricks in the 1953-54 season and 11 in his career with Leeds United during which he scored 157 League and Cup goals.

## LEEDS UNITED 1997–98 LEAGUE RECORD

| Match No. | Date | Venue | Opponents | Result | H/T Score | Lg. Pos. | Goalscorers | Atten-dance |
|---|---|---|---|---|---|---|---|---|
| 1 | Aug 9 | H | Arsenal | D 1-1 | 1-1 | — | Hasselbaink [42] | 37,993 |
| 2 | 13 | A | Sheffield W | W 3-1 | 2-0 | — | Wallace 2 [7, 62], Ribeiro [36] | 31,520 |
| 3 | 23 | H | Crystal Palace | L 0-2 | 0-1 | 9 | | 29,108 |
| 4 | 26 | H | Liverpool | L 0-2 | 0-1 | — | | 39,878 |
| 5 | 30 | A | Aston Villa | L 0-1 | 0-0 | 14 | | 39,027 |
| 6 | Sept 14 | A | Blackburn R | W 4-3 | 4-3 | 9 | Wallace 2 [3, 17], Molenaar [6], Hopkin [23] | 21,956 |
| 7 | 20 | H | Leicester C | L 0-1 | 0-1 | 14 | | 29,442 |
| 8 | 24 | A | Southampton | W 2-0 | 1-0 | — | Molenaar [36], Wallace [55] | 15,102 |
| 9 | 27 | H | Manchester U | W 1-0 | 1-0 | 6 | Wetherall [34] | 39,943 |
| 10 | Oct 4 | A | Coventry C | D 0-0 | 0-0 | 8 | | 17,771 |
| 11 | 18 | H | Newcastle U | W 4-1 | 3-0 | 6 | Ribeiro [30], Kewell [38], Beresford (og) [43], Wetherall [47] | 39,865 |
| 12 | 25 | A | Wimbledon | L 0-1 | 0-1 | 8 | | 15,718 |
| 13 | Nov 1 | A | Tottenham H | W 1-0 | 1-0 | 7 | Wallace [20] | 26,441 |
| 14 | 8 | H | Derby Co | W 4-3 | 2-3 | 5 | Wallace [37], Kewell [40], Hasselbaink (pen) [82], Bowyer [90] | 33,572 |
| 15 | 23 | H | West Ham U | W 3-1 | 0-0 | 4 | Hasselbaink 2 [76, 90], Haaland [88] | 29,447 |
| 16 | 29 | A | Barnsley | W 3-2 | 1-2 | 4 | Haaland [35], Wallace [79], Lilley [82] | 18,690 |
| 17 | Dec 6 | H | Everton | D 0-0 | 0-0 | 5 | | 34,872 |
| 18 | 13 | A | Chelsea | D 0-0 | 0-0 | 4 | | 34,779 |
| 19 | 20 | H | Bolton W | W 2-0 | 0-0 | 4 | Ribeiro [68], Hasselbaink [81] | 31,184 |
| 20 | 26 | A | Liverpool | L 1-3 | 0-0 | 5 | Haaland [84] | 43,854 |
| 21 | 28 | H | Aston Villa | D 1-1 | 0-0 | 5 | Hasselbaink [79] | 36,909 |
| 22 | Jan 10 | A | Arsenal | L 1-2 | 0-0 | 7 | Hasselbaink [69] | 38,018 |
| 23 | 17 | H | Sheffield W | L 1-2 | 0-0 | 7 | Pembridge (og) [63] | 33,596 |
| 24 | 31 | A | Crystal Palace | W 2-0 | 2-0 | 7 | Wallace [7], Hasselbaink [13] | 25,248 |
| 25 | Feb 7 | A | Leicester C | L 0-1 | 0-1 | 7 | | 21,244 |
| 26 | 22 | H | Newcastle U | D 1-1 | 0-0 | 8 | Wallace [62] | 36,511 |
| 27 | 28 | H | Southampton | L 0-1 | 0-0 | 8 | | 28,926 |
| 28 | Mar 4 | H | Tottenham H | W 1-0 | 1-0 | — | Kewell [45] | 31,802 |
| 29 | 11 | H | Blackburn R | W 4-0 | 0-0 | — | Bowyer [48], Hasselbaink [53], Haaland 2 [56, 89] | 32,935 |
| 30 | 15 | A | Derby Co | W 5-0 | 3-0 | 5 | Laursen (og) [8], Halle [36], Bowyer [42], Kewell [59], Hasselbaink [72] | 30,217 |
| 31 | 30 | A | West Ham U | L 0-3 | 0-2 | — | | 24,107 |
| 32 | Apr 4 | H | Barnsley | W 2-1 | 1-1 | 5 | Hasselbaink [20], Moses (og) [80] | 37,749 |
| 33 | 8 | H | Chelsea | W 3-1 | 2-1 | — | Hasselbaink 2 [7, 47], Wetherall [22] | 37,246 |
| 34 | 11 | A | Everton | L 0-2 | 0-2 | 5 | | 37,099 |
| 35 | 18 | A | Bolton W | W 3-2 | 2-0 | 5 | Haaland [16], Halle [34], Hasselbaink [85] | 25,000 |
| 36 | 25 | H | Coventry C | D 3-3 | 2-2 | 5 | Hasselbaink 2 [16, 28], Kewell [75] | 36,868 |
| 37 | May 4 | A | Manchester U | L 0-3 | 0-2 | — | | 55,167 |
| 38 | 10 | H | Wimbledon | D 1-1 | 0-0 | 5 | Haaland [81] | 38,445 |

**Final League Position: 5**     1996–97 PREM 11

### GOALSCORERS

*League (57):* Hasselbaink 16 (1 pen), Wallace 10, Haaland 7, Kewell 5, Bowyer 3, Ribeiro 3, Wetherall 3, Halle 2, Molenaar 2, Hopkin 1, Lilley 1, own goals 4.
*Coca-Cola Cup (9):* Hasselbaink 2 (1 pen), Wallace 2, Wetherall 2, Bowyer 1, Kewell 1, Ribeiro 1.
*FA Cup (9):* Hasselbaink 4 (1 pen), Kewell 2, Molenaar 1, Radebe 1, Wallace 1.

| Martyn N 37 | Halle G 31 + 2 | Robertson D 24 + 2 | Kelly G 34 | Radebe L 26 + 1 | Wetherall D 33 + 1 | Hopkin D 22 + 3 | Wallace R 29 + 2 | Hasselbaink J 30 + 3 | Ribeiro B 28 + 1 | Bowyer L 21 + 4 | Haaland A 26 + 6 | Kewell H 26 + 3 | Molenaar R 18 + 4 | Lilley D — + 13 | Maybury A 9 + 3 | Beeney M 1 | Matthews L — + 3 | McPhail S — + 4 | Harte I 12 | Hiden M 11 | Jackson M — + 1 | Match No. |
|---|---|---|---|---|---|---|---|---|---|---|---|---|---|---|---|---|---|---|---|---|---|---|
| 1 | 2 | 3 | 4 | 5 | 6 | $7^1$ | 8 | 9 | $10^2$ | 11 | 12 | 13 | | | | | | | | | | 1 |
| 1 | 2 | 3 | 4 | | 6 | 7 | 8 | $9^1$ | 10 | $11^1$ | 12 | | | 5 | 13 | | | | | | | 2 |
| 1 | $2^1$ | 3 | 4 | 12 | 6 | 7 | 8 | 9 | $10^2$ | $11^3$ | 14 | 13 | 5 | | | | | | | | | 3 |
| 1 | 4 | 3 | 2 | 5 | | 7 | 8 | 9 | 10 | | 11 | | 6 | | | | | | | | | 4 |
| 1 | 12 | 3 | 2 | 5 | 6 | $7^1$ | 8 | $9^2$ | 10 | | 4 | 11 | | 13 | | | | | | | | 5 |
| 1 | 2 | 3 | 4 | 5 | 6 | 7 | 8 | $9^2$ | 12 | | 10 | $11^1$ | 13 | | | | | | | | | 6 |
| 1 | 2 | 3 | 4 | $5^1$ | 6 | | $8^3$ | $9^2$ | 10 | 11 | 7 | 13 | 12 | 14 | | | | | | | | 7 |
| 1 | 2 | 3 | 4 | | 6 | $7^1$ | 8 | | 10 | 12 | 11 | 9 | 5 | | | | | | | | | 8 |
| 1 | 2 | 3 | 4 | 5 | 6 | $7^1$ | 8 | | 10 | 11 | 9 | 12 | | | | | | | | | | 9 |
| 1 | 2 | 3 | 4 | 5 | 6 | 7 | 8 | $9^1$ | 10 | | 11 | | 12 | | | | | | | | | 10 |
| 1 | 2 | 3 | 4 | 5 | 6 | $7^1$ | 8 | | 10 | 12 | 11 | 9 | | | | | | | | | | 11 |
| 1 | $2^2$ | 3 | | 5 | 6 | $7^1$ | 8 | | 10 | 11 | 4 | 9 | | 12 | 13 | | | | | | | 12 |
| 1 | | 3 | 4 | 5 | 6 | 7 | 8 | | 10 | 11 | 9 | | | | 2 | | | | | | | 13 |
| 1 | | 3 | 4 | 5 | 6 | $7^1$ | 8 | 12 | 10 | 13 | 11 | 9 | | | $2^2$ | | | | | | | 14 |
| 1 | 2 | 3 | 4 | 5 | 6 | | 8 | 9 | 10 | 7 | 11 | | | | | | | | | | | 15 |
| 1 | $2^3$ | 3 | 4 | 5 | 6 | | 8 | 9 | 10 | $7^2$ | $11^1$ | 12 | 13 | 14 | | | | | | | | 16 |
| 1 | 2 | 3 | 4 | 5 | 6 | | 8 | 12 | 10 | $7^1$ | 11 | 9 | | | | | | | | | | 17 |
| 1 | 2 | 3 | 4 | 5 | 6 | 7 | 8 | $9^1$ | 10 | | 11 | | 12 | | | | | | | | | 18 |
| 1 | 2 | 3 | 4 | | 6 | $7^1$ | 8 | 9 | 10 | 12 | 11 | | 5 | | | | | | | | | 19 |
| 1 | 2 | 3 | 4 | | 6 | 7 | 8 | 9 | 10 | | 11 | | 5 | | | | | | | | | 20 |
| 1 | | 3 | | 5 | 6 | | 8 | 9 | $10^1$ | 11 | | 7 | 4 | 12 | 2 | | | | | | | 21 |
| 1 | 3 | | 4 | 5 | 6 | | $8^3$ | 12 | 10 | $7^1$ | $11^2$ | 9 | 13 | 14 | 2 | | | | | | | 22 |
| 1 | 12 | 3 | 4 | 8 | 6 | 7 | 13 | 9 | $10^3$ | | 11 | $5^1$ | 14 | $2^2$ | 1 | | | | | | | 23 |
| 1 | | 3 | 2 | 5 | 6 | 7 | 8 | $9^2$ | 10 | 12 | 11 | $4^1$ | | 13 | | | | | | | | 24 |
| 1 | 2 | 3 | 4 | | 6 | 7 | $8^1$ | 9 | $10^2$ | 5 | 11 | 12 | | 13 | | | | | | | | 25 |
| 1 | 3 | | 4 | | 6 | | 8 | 9 | 10 | 7 | 11 | 5 | 2 | | | | | | | | | 26 |
| 1 | 4 | | | | | 7 | 8 | 9 | 10 | | 11 | 5 | $2^1$ | | 12 | | | | 3 | 6 | | 27 |
| 1 | 4 | | | | | 7 | $8^2$ | $9^1$ | 11 | | 10 | 5 | 2 | | 12 | 13 | | | 3 | | | 28 |
| 1 | | 2 | 5 | 6 | 7 | | 9 | | 11 | 8 | 10 | | | | | | | | 3 | 4 | | 29 |
| 1 | 4 | | 2 | 8 | | | 9 | | 11 | 7 | $10^1$ | 5 | | | | | | 12 | 3 | 6 | | 30 |
| 1 | 8 | | 4 | 12 | | 13 | 9 | 10 | $11^2$ | 7 | | 5 | $2^1$ | | | | | | 3 | 6 | | 31 |
| 1 | 7 | | 2 | 4 | | | 9 | $10^1$ | 11 | | 8 | 5 | | | | | | 12 | 3 | 6 | | 32 |
| 1 | 7 | | 2 | 8 | 6 | | 9 | | 11 | 12 | 10 | $5^1$ | | | | | | | 3 | 4 | | 33 |
| 1 | 7 | | 2 | 8 | 6 | | 9 | | 11 | 12 | $10^2$ | $5^1$ | 13 | | | | | | 3 | 4 | | 34 |
| 1 | 7 | | 2 | 5 | 6 | | 9 | | 11 | 8 | 10 | | | | | | | | 3 | 4 | | 35 |
| 1 | 7 | 12 | 2 | | 6 | 13 | $8^2$ | 9 | | 11 | 4 | 10 | | | | | | | $3^1$ | 5 | | 36 |
| 1 | 7 | 12 | 2 | 5 | 6 | 13 | | 9 | | 11 | 8 | 10 | | | | | | | $3^1$ | $4^2$ | | 37 |
| 1 | 4 | | 2 | $5^1$ | 6 | 12 | $8^2$ | 9 | | 11 | 7 | $10^1$ | 13 | | | | | | 3 | | 14 | 38 |

**Coca-Cola Cup**

| Second Round | Bristol C | (h) | 3-1 |
| | | (a) | 1-2 |
| Third Round | Stoke C | (a) | 3-1 |
| Fourth Round | Reading | (h) | 2-3 |

**FA Cup**

| Third Round | Oxford U | (h) | 4-0 |
| Fourth Round | Grimsby T | (h) | 2-0 |
| Fifth Round | Birmingham C | (h) | 3-2 |
| Sixth Round | Wolverhampton W | (h) | 0-1 |

LEICESTER CITY 1997-98 *Back row (left to right):* David Nish (Youth Team Coach), Neville Hamilton (Head Coach of Youth Development), Emile Heskey, Michael Whitlow, Paul Emerson, Garry Parker, Stevie Wilson, Kasey Keller, Spencer Prior, Julian Watts, Matt Elliott, Steve Walsh, Steve Claridge, Seamus McDonagh (Goalkeeping Coach), Alan Smith (Physio).
*Middle row:* Steve Sims (Youth Development Officer), Mick Yeoman (Physio), Paul McAndrew (Kit Manager), Robbie Savage, Gary Neil, Martin Fox, Miguel Arcos-Diaz, Mark Robins, Guy Branston, Stefan Oakes, John Robertson (Assistant Manager), Steve Walford (First Team Coach), Paul Franklin (Reserve Team Coach).
*Front row:* Graeme Jaffa, Stephen Wenlock, Stuart Wilson, Sam McMahon, Stuart Campbell, Kevin Skeldon, Tom Smeaton (Chairman), Martin O'Neill (Manager), Neil Lennon, Mustafa Izzet, Scott Taylor, Ian Marshall, Steve Guppy, Rob Ullathorne.

# FA Premiership LEICESTER CITY

*City Stadium, Filbert St, Leicester LE2 7FL.* Telephone: (0116) 2915000. Fax: (0116) 2470585. Ticket Office: (0116) 2915232. Clubcall: 0891 121185.

*Ground capacity:* 22,000.

*Record attendance:* 47,298 v Tottenham H, FA Cup 5th rd, 18 February 1928.

*Record receipts:* £302,714 v Northampton T, FA Cup 3rd rd, 3 January 1998.

*Pitch measurements:* 110yd × 76yd.

*President:* K. R. Brigstock.

*Chairman:* T. Smeaton. *Vice-Chairman:* John Elsom FCA.

*Managing Director:* Barrie Pierpoint.

*Directors:* R. W. Parker, T. W. Shipman, M. F. George, S. A. Kind.

*Manager:* Martin O'Neill. *Assistant Manager:* John Robertson. *First Team Coach:* Steve Walford.

*Youth Team Coach:* David Nish. *Physio:* Alan Smith.

*Finance Director and Company Secretary:* Steve Kind. *Deputy Managing Director:* Charles Rayner.

*Press Officer:* Paul Mace. *Head of Communications:* Paul Barker.

*Football Secretary:* Ian Silvester. *Stadium Manager:* John Petherick.

*Year Formed:* 1884.

*Club Nickname:* 'Filberts' or 'Foxes'.

*Previous Grounds:* 1884, Victoria Park; 1887, Belgrave Road; 1888, Victoria Park; 1891, Filbert Street.

*Previous Name:* 1884–1919, Leicester Fosse.

*Foundation:* In 1884 a number of young footballers who were mostly old boys of Wyggeston School, held a meeting at a house on the Roman Fosse Way and formed Leicester Fosse FC. They collected 9d (less than 4p) towards the cost of a ball, plus the same amount for membership. Their first professional, Harry Webb from Stafford Rangers, was signed in 1888 for 2s 6d (12p) per week, plus travelling expenses.

*First Football League game:* 1 September 1894, Division 2, v Grimsby T (a) L 3-4 – Thraves; Smith, Bailey; Seymour, Brown, Henrys; Hill, Hughes, McArthur (1), Skea (2), Priestman.

*Record League Victory:* 10–0 v Portsmouth, Division 1, 20 October 1928 – McLaren; Black, Brown; Findlay, Carr, Watson; Adcock, Hine (3), Chandler (6), Lochhead, Barry (1).

*Record Cup Victory:* 8–1 v Coventry C (away), League Cup 5th rd, 1 December 1964 – Banks; Sjoberg, Norman (2); Roberts, King, McDerment; Hodgson (2), Cross, Goodfellow, Gibson (1), Stringfellow (2). (1 og).

*Record Defeat:* 0–12 (as Leicester Fosse) v Nottingham F, Division 1, 21 April 1909.

*Most League Points (2 for a win):* 61, Division 2, 1956–57.

*Most League Points (3 for a win):* 77, Division 2, 1991–92.

*Most League Goals:* 109, Division 2, 1956–57.

*Highest League Scorer in Season:* Arthur Rowley, 44, Division 2, 1956–57.

*Most League Goals in Total Aggregate:* Arthur Chandler, 259, 1923–35.

*Most Capped Player:* John O'Neill, 39, Northern Ireland.

*Most League Appearances:* Adam Black, 528, 1920–35.

*Record Transfer Fee Received:* £3,250,000 from Aston Villa for Mark Draper, July 1995.

*Record Transfer Fee Paid:* £1,600,000 to Oxford U for Matt Elliott, January 1997.

*Football League Record:* 1894 Elected to Division 2; 1908–09 Division 1; 1909–25 Division 2; 1925–35 Division 1; 1935–37 Division 2; 1937–39 Division 1; 1946–54 Division 2; 1954–55 Division 1; 1955–57 Division 2; 1957–69 Division 1; 1969–71 Division 2; 1971–78 Division 1; 1978–80 Division 2; 1980–81 Division 1; 1981–83 Division 2; 1983–87 Division 1; 1987–92 Division 2; 1992–94 Division 1; 1994–95 FA Premier League; 1995–96 Division 1; 1996– FA Premier League.

*Honours: Football League:* Division 1 – Runners-up 1928–29; Promoted from Division 1 1993–94 (play-offs) and 1995–96 (play-offs) Division 2 – Champions 1924–25, 1936–37, 1953–54, 1956–57, 1970–71, 1979–80; Runners-up 1907–08. *FA Cup:* Runners-up 1949, 1961, 1963, 1969. *Football League Cup:* Winners 1964, 1997; Runners-up 1965. **European Competitions:** *European Cup-Winners' Cup:* 1961–62. *UEFA Cup:* 1997–98.

*Colours:* Royal blue shirts, white shorts, blue stockings. *Change colours:* White shirts, royal blue shorts, white stockings.

**Did you know?**
Goalkeeper Mark Wallington was an ever-present for Leicester City from 1975-76 to 1980-81 and again in 1982-83.

## LEICESTER CITY 1997–98 LEAGUE RECORD

| Match No. | Date | Venue | Opponents | Result | H/T Score | Lg. Pos. | Goalscorers | Atten- dance |
|---|---|---|---|---|---|---|---|---|
| 1 | Aug 9 | H | Aston Villa | W 1-0 | 1-0 | — | Marshall 37 | 20,304 |
| 2 | 13 | A | Liverpool | W 2-1 | 1-0 | — | Elliott 1, Fenton 83 | 35,007 |
| 3 | 23 | H | Manchester U | D 0-0 | 0-0 | 4 | | 21,221 |
| 4 | 27 | H | Arsenal | D 3-3 | 0-1 | — | Heskey 84, Elliott 90, Walsh 90 | 21,089 |
| 5 | 30 | A | Sheffield W | L 0-1 | 0-0 | 6 | | 24,851 |
| 6 | Sept 13 | H | Tottenham H | W 3-0 | 0-0 | 5 | Walsh 55, Guppy 68, Heskey 77 | 20,683 |
| 7 | 20 | A | Leeds U | W 1-0 | 1-0 | 4 | Walsh 32 | 29,442 |
| 8 | 24 | H | Blackburn R | D 1-1 | 1-1 | — | Izzet 43 | 19,921 |
| 9 | 27 | A | Barnsley | W 2-0 | 0-0 | 3 | Marshall 55, Fenton 63 | 18,660 |
| 10 | Oct 6 | H | Derby Co | L 1-2 | 0-1 | — | Elliott 67 | 19,585 |
| 11 | 18 | A | Chelsea | L 0-1 | 0-0 | 5 | | 33,356 |
| 12 | 27 | H | West Ham U | W 2-1 | 1-0 | — | Heskey 16, Marshall 82 | 20,201 |
| 13 | Nov 1 | A | Newcastle U | D 3-3 | 2-2 | 5 | Marshall 2 12, 32, Elliott 54 | 36,754 |
| 14 | 10 | H | Wimbledon | L 0-1 | 0-0 | — | | 18,553 |
| 15 | 22 | H | Bolton W | D 0-0 | 0-0 | 7 | | 20,464 |
| 16 | 29 | A | Coventry C | W 2-0 | 1-0 | 6 | Fenton 32, Elliott (pen) 75 | 18,332 |
| 17 | Dec 6 | H | Crystal Palace | D 1-1 | 0-1 | 6 | Izzet 90 | 19,191 |
| 18 | 13 | A | Southampton | L 1-2 | 0-1 | 8 | Savage 84 | 15,121 |
| 19 | 20 | H | Everton | L 0-1 | 0-0 | 8 | | 20,628 |
| 20 | 26 | A | Arsenal | L 1-2 | 0-1 | 9 | Lennon 77 | 38,023 |
| 21 | 28 | H | Sheffield W | D 1-1 | 1-0 | 9 | Guppy 28 | 20,800 |
| 22 | Jan 10 | A | Aston Villa | D 1-1 | 0-0 | 9 | Parker (pen) 53 | 36,429 |
| 23 | 17 | H | Liverpool | D 0-0 | 0-0 | 9 | | 21,633 |
| 24 | 31 | A | Manchester U | W 1-0 | 1-0 | 9 | Cottee 30 | 55,156 |
| 25 | Feb 7 | H | Leeds U | W 1-0 | 1-0 | 9 | Parker (pen) 44 | 21,244 |
| 26 | 14 | A | Tottenham H | D 1-1 | 1-0 | 9 | Cottee 34 | 28,355 |
| 27 | 21 | H | Chelsea | W 2-0 | 1-0 | 7 | Heskey 2 3, 89 | 21,335 |
| 28 | 28 | A | Blackburn R | L 3-5 | 0-3 | 7 | Wilson 68, Izzet 80, Ullathorne 81 | 24,854 |
| 29 | Mar 14 | A | Wimbledon | L 1-2 | 0-1 | 9 | Savage 57 | 13,229 |
| 30 | 28 | A | Bolton W | L 0-2 | 0-0 | 12 | | 25,000 |
| 31 | Apr 4 | H | Coventry C | D 1-1 | 0-0 | 12 | Wilson 78 | 21,137 |
| 32 | 11 | A | Crystal Palace | W 3-0 | 1-0 | 12 | Heskey 2 45, 60, Elliott 74 | 18,771 |
| 33 | 14 | H | Southampton | D 3-3 | 1-2 | — | Lennon 18, Elliott 52, Parker (pen) 90 | 20,708 |
| 34 | 18 | A | Everton | D 1-1 | 1-1 | 10 | Marshall 38 | 33,642 |
| 35 | 26 | A | Derby Co | W 4-0 | 4-0 | 9 | Heskey 2 1, 8, Izzet 2, Marshall 15 | 29,855 |
| 36 | 29 | A | Newcastle U | D 0-0 | 0-0 | — | | 21,699 |
| 37 | May 2 | H | Barnsley | W 1-0 | 0-0 | 8 | Zagorakis 57 | 21,293 |
| 38 | 10 | A | West Ham U | L 3-4 | 0-2 | 10 | Cottee 2 59, 83, Heskey 66 | 25,781 |

**Final League Position: 10**　　　1996–97 PREM 9

## GOALSCORERS

*League (51):* Heskey 10, Elliott 7 (1 pen), Marshall 7, Cottee 4, Izzet 4, Fenton 3, Parker 3 (3 pens), Walsh 3, Guppy 2, Lennon 2, Savage 2, Wilson 2, Ullathorne 1, Zagorakis 1.
*Coca-Cola Cup (1):* Marshall 1.
*FA Cup (4):* Cottee 1, Marshall 1, Parker 1 (pen), Savage 1.

| Keller K 32 | Kamark P 35 | Guppy S 37 | Elliott M 37 | Walsh S 23 + 3 | Prior S 28 + 2 | Lennon N 37 | Izzet M 36 | Campbell S 6 + 5 | Marshall I 22 + 2 | Heskey E 35 | Savage R 28 + 7 | Claridge S 10 + 7 | Fenton G 9 + 14 | Parker G 15 + 7 | Cottee T 7 + 12 | Arphexad P 6 | Watts J — + 3 | Wilson S — + 11 | Ullathorne R 3 + 3 | McMahon S — + 1 | Zagorakis T 12 + 2 | Match No. |
|---|---|---|---|---|---|---|---|---|---|---|---|---|---|---|---|---|---|---|---|---|---|---|
| 1 | 2 | 3 | 4 | 5 | 6 | 7 | 8 | $9^1$ | $10^2$ | 11 | 12 | 13 | | | | | | | | | | 1 |
| 1 | 2 | 3 | 4 | 5 | 6 | 7 | $8^1$ | 9 | $10^2$ | 12 | | | 13 | | | | | | | | | 2 |
| 1 | 2 | 3 | 4 | 5 | 6 | 7 | 8 | 9 | $10^1$ | 11 | 13 | 12 | | | | | | | | | | 3 |
| 1 | 2 | 3 | 4 | 5 | 6 | 7 | $8^2$ | | | 11 | $10^3$ | 9 | 12 | 13 | 14 | | | | | | | 4 |
| 1 | 2 | 3 | 4 | 5 | $6^2$ | 7 | 8 | | | 11 | $10^3$ | $9^1$ | 12 | 14 | 13 | | | | | | | 5 |
| 1 | $2^1$ | $3^3$ | 4 | 5 | 6 | 7 | 8 | $9^2$ | 11 | | | 13 | 12 | 10 | 14 | | | | | | | 6 |
| 1 | 2 | 3 | 4 | $5^1$ | 6 | 7 | 8 | 13 | 9 | 11 | | | 12 | $10^2$ | | | | | | | | 7 |
| 1 | 2 | 3 | 4 | | 6 | 7 | 8 | | | 5 | 11 | 12 | | $9^2$ | $10^1$ | 13 | | | | | | 8 |
| 1 | 2 | 3 | 4 | | 6 | 7 | 8 | | | 5 | 11 | 10 | 12 | $9^2$ | | 13 | | | | | | 9 |
| 1 | 2 | 3 | 4 | | 6 | 7 | $8^2$ | 12 | $5^3$ | 11 | 13 | | 14 | $10^1$ | 9 | | | | | | | 10 |
| | 2 | 3 | 4 | | 6 | 7 | 8 | $5^2$ | | 11 | 10 | $9^1$ | 12 | | | 1 | 13 | | | | | 11 |
| | $2^1$ | 3 | 4 | | 6 | 7 | 8 | 12 | 5 | 11 | $10^2$ | 9 | 13 | | | 1 | | | | | | 12 |
| | 2 | 3 | 4 | | 6 | 7 | 8 | | | 5 | 11 | 12 | $9^2$ | 13 | $10^1$ | 1 | | | | | | 13 |
| | 2 | 3 | 4 | 12 | 6 | 7 | 8 | | | 5 | 11 | 13 | $9^1$ | | $10^2$ | 1 | | | | | | 14 |
| | 2 | 3 | 4 | 5 | 6 | 7 | 8 | | 10 | | | | $9^1$ | 12 | $11^2$ | | 13 | | | | | 15 |
| | 2 | 3 | 4 | 5 | 6 | 7 | 8 | | 9 | | | 10 | | | 11 | | | | | | | 16 |
| 1 | 5 | | 4 | | 6 | 7 | 8 | $10^4$ | | 2 | | $9^1$ | 11 | | | | 12 | 13 | $3^2$ | 14 | | 17 |
| 1 | 2 | 3 | 4 | 5 | $6^1$ | 7 | 8 | | | 11 | 10 | 12 | $9^2$ | | | | | 13 | | | | 18 |
| 1 | $2^2$ | 3 | 4 | 5 | 6 | 7 | 8 | | | 11 | 10 | 12 | $9^1$ | | | | | 13 | | | | 19 |
| 1 | 6 | 3 | 4 | 5 | | | 8 | $10^1$ | | 11 | 2 | $9^4$ | 12 | 13 | | | | | | | | 20 |
| 1 | 6 | 3 | 4 | $5^1$ | 12 | 7 | 8 | $9^2$ | | 11 | 2 | 13 | 10 | | | | | | | | | 21 |
| 1 | 6 | 3 | 4 | 5 | | 7 | 8 | $9^1$ | | 11 | 2 | 10 | 12 | | | | | | | | | 22 |
| 1 | 6 | 3 | 4 | 5 | | 7 | 8 | 9 | | $11^1$ | 2 | 10 | 12 | | | | | | | | | 23 |
| 1 | 6 | 3 | 4 | $5^1$ | 12 | 7 | 8 | 13 | | 11 | 2 | $10^2$ | $9^3$ | 14 | | | | | | | | 24 |
| 1 | 5 | 3 | 4 | | 6 | 7 | 8 | | | 11 | $2^1$ | 10 | 9 | | | | | 12 | | | | 25 |
| | 5 | 3 | 4 | | 6 | 7 | 8 | | | 11 | 2 | $10^1$ | 9 | | | 1 | | 12 | | | | 26 |
| | $5^3$ | 3 | 4 | 12 | 6 | 7 | 8 | 14 | | 11 | $2^1$ | 13 | $9^2$ | | | 1 | | 10 | | | | 27 |
| 1 | | 3 | 4 | 5 | $6^2$ | 7 | 8 | | | 11 | 2 | $9^1$ | | | | | 12 | 13 | | | 10 | 28 |
| 1 | | 3 | | $5^1$ | 6 | 7 | | | $4^1$ | 11 | 2 | 9 | | | | | 13 | 12 | | 8 | 10 | 29 |
| 1 | 5 | 3 | 4 | | 6 | $7^1$ | | | | 11 | 2 | 12 | 10 | | | | 13 | | | 8 | $9^2$ | 30 |
| 1 | 5 | 3 | 4 | | $6^2$ | 7 | 8 | | | 11 | 2 | 12 | $9^1$ | | | | 13 | | | | 10 | 31 |
| 1 | 5 | 3 | 4 | | 6 | 7 | 8 | 12 | | 11 | $2^3$ | $9^1$ | 13 | | | | 14 | | | | $10^2$ | 32 |
| 1 | 5 | 3 | 4 | 12 | $6^1$ | 7 | 8 | 13 | | 11 | 2 | $9^2$ | | | | | 14 | | | | $10^3$ | 33 |
| 1 | 6 | 3 | 4 | 5 | | | 8 | 9 | | 11 | 2 | | 7 | 12 | | | | | | | $10^1$ | 34 |
| 1 | 6 | $3^3$ | 4 | $5^2$ | | 7 | 8 | 9 | | 11 | 2 | | 12 | 13 | | | | | 14 | | $10^1$ | 35 |
| 1 | 6 | 3 | 4 | 5 | | 7 | 8 | $9^1$ | | 11 | 2 | | 12 | | | | | | 13 | | $10^2$ | 36 |
| 1 | | 3 | 4 | 5 | | 7 | 8 | 6 | | 11 | 2 | | 12 | $9^1$ | | | | | | | 10 | 37 |
| 1 | 6 | 3 | 4 | $5^1$ | | 7 | 8 | $9^3$ | | 11 | 2 | | 13 | 12 | | | | | 14 | | $10^2$ | 38 |

**Coca-Cola Cup**
Third Round      Grimsby T          (a)   1-3

**FA Cup**
Third Round      Northampton T      (h)   4-0
Fourth Round     Crystal Palace     (a)   0-3

LEYTON ORIENT 1997–98 *Back row (left to right):* Roger Joseph, Shaun Howes, Justin Channing, Mark Warren, David Morrison, Danny Brown, David Hanson.
*Middle row:* Simon Clark, Colin West, Stuart Hicks, Paul Hyde, Luke Weaver, Lee Shearer, Dean Smith, Tony Richards.
*Front row:* Sam Winston, Scott McGleish, Alex Inglethorpe, Dominic Naylor, Martin Ling, Carl Griffiths, Joe Baker.

# Division 3 **LEYTON ORIENT**

*Leyton Stadium, Brisbane Road, Leyton, London E10 5NE.* Telephone: (0181) 926 1111. Fax: (0181) 926 1110. Clubcall: 0891 121150.

*Ground capacity:* 13,842.

*Record attendance:* 34,345 v West Ham U, FA Cup 4th rd, 25 January 1964.

*Record receipts:* £87,867.92 v West Ham U, FA Cup 3rd rd, 10 January 1987.

*Pitch measurements:* 110yd × 80yd.

*Chairman:* Barry Hearn.

*Chief Executive:* Bernard Goodall. *Financial Director:* Steve Dawson.

*Directors:* Tony Wood OBE, John Goldsmith FRIBA, Rod Cousens, David Dodd, Steve Davis.

*Team Manager:* Tommy Taylor. *First Team Coach:* Paul Clark. *Physio:* Tony Flynn.

*Secretary:* Frank Woolf. *Commercial Manager:* Lyn Newman.

*Stadium Manager:* Janet Hasler.

*Year Formed:* 1881. *Turned Professional:* 1903. *Ltd Co.:* 1906.

*Club Nickname:* 'The O's'.

*Previous Names:* 1881–86, Glyn Cricket and Football Club; 1886–88, Eagle Football Club; 1888–98, Orient Football Club; 1898–1946, Clapton Orient; 1946–66, Leyton Orient; 1966–87, Orient.

*Previous Grounds:* Glyn Road, 1884–96; Whittles Athletic Ground, 1896–1900; Millfields Road, 1900–30; Lea Bridge Road, 1930–37.

*Foundation:* There is some doubt about the foundation of Leyton Orient, and, indeed, some confusion with clubs like Leyton and Clapton over their early history. As regards the foundation, the most favoured version is that Leyton Orient was formed originally by members of Homerton Theological College who established Glyn Cricket Club in 1881 and then carried on through the following winter playing football. Eventually many employees of the Orient Shipping Line became involved and so the name Orient was chosen in 1888.

*First Football League game:* 2 September 1905, Division 2, v Leicester Fosse (a) L 1-2 – Butler; Holmes, Codling; Lamberton, Boden, Boyle; Kingaby (1), Wootten, Leigh, Evenson, Bourne.

*Record League Victory:* 8–0 v Crystal Palace, Division 3 (S), 12 November 1955 – Welton; Lee, Earl; Blizzard, Aldous, McKnight; White (1), Facey (3), Burgess (2), Heckman, Hartburn (2). 8–0 v Rochdale, Division 4, 20 October 1987 – Wells; Howard, Dickenson (1), Smalley (1), Day, Hull, Hales (2), Castle (Sussex), Shinners (2), Godfrey (Harvey), Comfort (2). 8–0 v Colchester U, Division 4, 15 October 1988 – Wells; Howard, Dickenson, Hales (1p), Day (1). Sitton (1), Baker (1), Ward, Hull (3). Juryeff, Comfort (1). 8–0 v Doncaster R, Division 3, 28 December 1997 – Hyde; Channing, Naylor, Smith (pen), Hicks, Clark, Ling, Joseph R, Griffiths (3) (Harris), Richards (2) (Baker (1)), Inglethorpe (1) (Simpson).

*Record Cup Victory:* 9–2 v Chester, League Cup 3rd rd, 15 October 1962 – Robertson; Charlton, Taylor; Gibbs, Bishop, Lea; Deeley (1), Waites (3), Dunmore (2), Graham (3), Wedge.

*Record Defeat:* 0–8 v Aston Villa, FA Cup 4th rd, 30 January 1929.

*Most League Points (2 for a win):* 66, Division 3 (S), 1955–56.

*Most League Points (3 for a win):* 75, Division 4, 1988–89.

*Most League Goals:* 106, Division 3 (S), 1955–56.

*Highest League Scorer in Season:* Tom Johnston, 35, Division 2, 1957–58.

*Most League Goals in Total Aggregate:* Tom Johnston, 121, 1956–58, 1959–61.

*Most Capped Player:* John Chiedozie, 8 (10), Nigeria.

*Most League Appearances:* Peter Allen, 432, 1965–78.

*Record Transfer Fee Received:* £600,000 from Notts Co for John Chiedozie, August 1981.

*Record Transfer Fee Paid:* £175,000 to Wigan Ath for Paul Beesley, October 1989.

*Football League Record:* 1905 Elected to Division 2; 1929–56 Division 3 (S); 1956–62 Division 2; 1962–63 Division 1; 1963–66 Division 2; 1966–70 Division 3; 1970–82 Division 2; 1982–85 Division 3; 1985–89 Division 4; 1989–92 Division 3; 1992–95 Division 3; 1995– Division 3.

*Honours:* Football League: Division 1 best season: 22nd, 1962–63; Division 2 – Runners-up 1961–62; Division 3 – Champions 1969–70; Division 3 (S) – Champions 1955–56; Runners-up 1954–55; Promoted from Division 4 1988–89 (play-offs). *FA Cup:* Semi-final 1978. *Football League Cup:* best season: 5th rd, 1963.

*Colours:* White shirts with red V, black shorts, red stockings. *Change colours:* Blue and yellow.

**Did you know?**
Colin Simpson scored two goals for Hendon against Leyton Orient in the FA Cup in 1997-98 and subsequently joined the East London club.

## LEYTON ORIENT 1997–98 LEAGUE RECORD

| Match No. | Date | | Venue | Opponents | Result | | H/T Score | Lg. Pos. | Goalscorers | Atten- dance |
|---|---|---|---|---|---|---|---|---|---|---|
| 1 | Aug | 9 | H | Cardiff C | L | 0-1 | 0-0 | — | | 5414 |
| 2 | | 16 | A | Scunthorpe U | L | 0-1 | 0-1 | 23 | | 3068 |
| 3 | | 23 | H | Rochdale | W | 2-0 | 1-0 | 20 | Smith 2 (2 pens) [1, 85] | 3463 |
| 4 | | 30 | A | Brighton & HA | W | 1-0 | 0-0 | 13 | Griffiths [66] | 2285 |
| 5 | Sept | 2 | A | Doncaster R | W | 4-1 | 0-1 | — | Hicks [47], Griffiths [58], Clark 2 [69, 71] | 1098 |
| 6 | | 5 | H | Cambridge U | L | 0-2 | 0-1 | — | | 4638 |
| 7 | | 13 | H | Exeter C | W | 1-0 | 1-0 | 9 | Griffiths [22] | 4036 |
| 8 | | 20 | A | Peterborough U | L | 0-2 | 0-2 | 13 | | 6629 |
| 9 | | 27 | A | Swansea C | D | 1-1 | 0-0 | 15 | Clark [71] | 3494 |
| 10 | Oct | 4 | H | Macclesfield T | D | 1-1 | 1-0 | 15 | Griffiths [26] | 4522 |
| 11 | | 11 | H | Rotherham U | D | 1-1 | 0-0 | 16 | Griffiths [90] | 3658 |
| 12 | | 18 | A | Hartlepool U | D | 2-2 | 1-2 | 14 | Inglethorpe [44], Griffiths [82] | 2108 |
| 13 | | 21 | A | Torquay U | D | 1-1 | 1-0 | — | Harris [6] | 1702 |
| 14 | | 25 | H | Colchester U | L | 0-2 | 0-1 | 17 | | 4592 |
| 15 | Nov | 1 | A | Lincoln C | L | 0-1 | 0-0 | 18 | | 4129 |
| 16 | | 4 | H | Scarborough | W | 3-1 | 2-1 | — | Inglethorpe 2 [21, 33], Harris [88] | 2480 |
| 17 | | 8 | H | Chester C | W | 1-0 | 1-0 | 14 | Smith [24] | 3894 |
| 18 | | 18 | A | Darlington | L | 0-1 | 0-1 | — | | 1703 |
| 19 | | 22 | H | Notts Co | D | 1-1 | 0-0 | 16 | Harris [70] | 4372 |
| 20 | | 29 | A | Mansfield T | D | 0-0 | 0-0 | 16 | | 2086 |
| 21 | Dec | 2 | H | Barnet | W | 2-0 | 1-0 | — | Smith [42], Hanson [88] | 2598 |
| 22 | | 13 | A | Shrewsbury T | W | 2-1 | 2-0 | 12 | Simpson [21], Smith [38] | 2137 |
| 23 | | 20 | H | Hull C | W | 2-1 | 1-0 | 11 | Smith (pen) [44], Harris [52] | 4013 |
| 24 | | 26 | A | Cambridge U | L | 0-1 | 0-0 | 11 | | 4808 |
| 25 | | 28 | H | Doncaster R | W | 8-0 | 4-0 | 11 | Griffiths 3 [20, 48, 55], Inglethorpe [40], Smith (pen) [43], Richards 2 [45, 59], Baker [64] | 4437 |
| 26 | Jan | 10 | A | Cardiff C | L | 0-1 | 0-1 | 11 | | 4335 |
| 27 | | 17 | H | Brighton & HA | W | 3-1 | 0-0 | 11 | Griffiths [56], Simpson 2 [80, 83] | 6591 |
| 28 | | 24 | A | Rochdale | W | 2-0 | 0-0 | 10 | Inglethorpe [66], Griffiths [69] | 1774 |
| 29 | | 31 | A | Exeter C | D | 2-2 | 1-1 | 11 | Ling [32], Clark [85] | 4023 |
| 30 | Feb | 6 | H | Peterborough U | W | 1-0 | 0-0 | — | Baker [83] | 5991 |
| 31 | | 14 | A | Macclesfield T | L | 0-1 | 0-1 | 10 | | 2725 |
| 32 | | 21 | A | Swansea C | D | 2-2 | 1-1 | 10 | Griffiths [43], Harris [65] | 4261 |
| 33 | | 24 | H | Hartlepool U | W | 2-1 | 1-1 | — | Joseph M [21], Harris [69] | 3713 |
| 34 | | 28 | A | Rotherham U | L | 1-2 | 1-0 | 11 | Griffiths [43] | 3542 |
| 35 | Mar | 3 | A | Chester C | D | 1-1 | 1-0 | — | Smith [27] | 1650 |
| 36 | | 7 | H | Lincoln C | W | 1-0 | 0-0 | 8 | Inglethorpe [76] | 4745 |
| 37 | | 14 | A | Scarborough | L | 0-2 | 0-1 | 10 | | 2655 |
| 38 | | 21 | H | Darlington | W | 2-0 | 1-0 | 10 | Naylor [37], Inglethorpe [74] | 4752 |
| 39 | | 28 | A | Notts Co | L | 0-1 | 0-0 | 10 | | 8383 |
| 40 | Apr | 4 | H | Mansfield T | D | 2-2 | 1-2 | 10 | Griffiths 2 [43, 69] | 4081 |
| 41 | | 11 | A | Barnet | W | 2-1 | 0-0 | 9 | Baker [83], Griffiths [90] | 3437 |
| 42 | | 13 | H | Shrewsbury T | L | 2-3 | 1-0 | 9 | Maskell [31], Griffiths [53] | 4956 |
| 43 | | 18 | A | Hull C | L | 2-3 | 0-1 | 16 | Inglethorpe [47], Griffiths [52] | 3744 |
| 44 | | 21 | H | Scunthorpe U | W | 1-0 | 0-0 | — | Ling [74] | 2735 |
| 45 | | 25 | A | Colchester U | D | 1-1 | 1-1 | 11 | Inglethorpe [43] | 6220 |
| 46 | May | 2 | H | Torquay U | W | 2-1 | 2-0 | 11 | Smith (pen) [6], Maskell [24] | 6545 |

**Final League Position: 11**       1996–97 DIV3 16

### GOALSCORERS

*League (62):* Griffiths 18, Inglethorpe 9, Smith 9 (5 pens), Harris 6, Clark 4, Baker 3, Simpson 3, Ling 2, Maskell 2, Richards 2, Hanson 1, Hicks 1, Joseph M 1, Naylor 1.
*Coca-Cola Cup (9):* Griffiths 3, Baker 2, Inglethorpe 2, McGleish 1, Warren 1.
*FA Cup (2):* Harris 1, Smith 1.

| Hyde P 28 | Channing J 29 + 5 | Naylor D 43 | Smith D 43 | Hicks S 35 | Clark S 39 | Ling M 46 | Warren M 41 | McGleish S 8 | West C 2 + 5 | Morrison D 1 + 1 | Richards T 10 + 7 | Hanson D 4 + 8 | Joseph R 13 + 12 | Hodge S 1 | Baker J 4 + 27 | Griffiths C 31 + 2 | Richardson C 1 | Cotkin L 5 + 6 | Inglethorpe A 38 | Harris J 21 + 14 | Williams M — + 1 | Linger P 1 + 2 | Regis D 4 | MacKenzie C 4 | Simpson C 9 + 5 | Pitcher D 1 | Cooper M — + 1 | Joseph M 14 | Bennett M 1 + 1 | Fenn N 3 | Turley B 14 | Raynor P 5 + 5 | Maskell C 7 + 1 | Martin J — + 1 | Match No. |
|---|---|---|---|---|---|---|---|---|---|---|---|---|---|---|---|---|---|---|---|---|---|---|---|---|---|---|---|---|---|---|---|---|---|---|---|
| 1 | 2 | 3 | 4 | $5^1$ | 6 | 7 | 8 | 9 | $10^2$ | $11^3$ | 12 | 13 | 14 | | | | | | | | | | | | | | | | | | | | | | 1 |
| 1 | $2^2$ | 3 | 4 | 5 | | 7 | 8 | 9 | $10^1$ | | 11 | 13 | 14 | | $6^2$ | 12 | | | | | | | | | | | | | | | | | | | 2 |
| 1 | | 3 | 4 | 5 | 6 | 7 | $8^1$ | $10^2$ | 13 | | 12 | | | | | 2 | | 14 | 9 | $11^3$ | | | | | | | | | | | | | | | 3 |
| 1 | | 3 | 4 | 5 | 6 | $7^1$ | 8 | 10 | $11^2$ | | | | | | | 2 | | 12 | 9 | 13 | | | | | | | | | | | | | | | 4 |
| 1 | | 3 | 4 | 5 | 6 | 7 | 8 | $10^1$ | 12 | $11^2$ | | | | | | 2 | | 13 | $9^3$ | 14 | | | | | | | | | | | | | | | 5 |
| 1 | | 3 | 4 | $5^1$ | 6 | 7 | 8 | 10 | 12 | 11 | | | | | | 2 | | 13 | $9^2$ | 2 | | | | | | | | | | | | | | | 6 |
| 1 | 11 | 3 | 4 | 5 | 6 | 7 | | $10^1$ | 12 | | | | | | | 13 | | 14 | $9^3$ | 2 | $8^2$ | | | | | | | | | | | | | | 7 |
| 1 | $2^2$ | 3 | 4 | | 6 | 7 | 8 | 10 | $5^1$ | 13 | 12 | | 9 | | | | | | 11 | | | | | | | | | | | | | | | | 8 |
| 1 | $2^1$ | 3 | 4 | 5 | 6 | 7 | 8 | | | | | | 12 | | 9 | | | 13 | 11 | $10^2$ | | | | | | | | | | | | | | | 9 |
| 1 | 12 | 3 | 4 | $5^1$ | 6 | 7 | 2 | | | | | | 8 | | 9 | | | 13 | 11 | $10^2$ | | | | | | | | | | | | | | | 10 |
| 1 | 5 | $3^1$ | 4 | | 6 | 7 | 2 | | | | | 13 | | | 12 | 9 | | $8^3$ | 11 | $10^2$ | 14 | | | | | | | | | | | | | | 11 |
| 1 | $5^3$ | 3 | 4 | | 6 | 7 | 2 | | | | | $11^1$ | | | 12 | 9 | | 13 | 8 | $10^2$ | 14 | | | | | | | | | | | | | | 12 |
| 1 | 5 | 3 | 4 | | 6 | 7 | 2 | | | | | 12 | | | 13 | $9^1$ | | 11 | 8 | $10^2$ | | | | | | | | | | | | | | | 13 |
| 1 | $6^2$ | 3 | 4 | 5 | | 7 | 2 | 12 | | | | | | | 10 | 9 | | $11^1$ | 8 | 13 | | | | | | | | | | | | | | | 14 |
| 1 | $2^1$ | 3 | 4 | 5 | 6 | 7 | 8 | | 10 | | | | | | 12 | $11^2$ | 13 | | 9 | | | | | | | | | | | | | | | | 15 |
| 1 | $2^1$ | 3 | 4 | 5 | 6 | 7 | 8 | | $10^2$ | 12 | | | | | 11 | 13 | | 9 | | | | | | | | | | | | | | | | | 16 |
| 1 | 2 | 3 | 4 | $5^1$ | 6 | 7 | 8 | | 10 | 12 | | | | | 11 | 13 | | $9^2$ | | | | | | | | | | | | | | | | | 17 |
| 1 | 2 | 3 | | 5 | 6 | 7 | 8 | | 10 | | | 9 | | | $4^1$ | 12 | 11 | | | | | | | | | | | | | | | | | | 18 |
| 1 | 2 | 3 | 4 | 5 | 6 | 7 | 8 | | | | 12 | 11 | 9 | | $10^1$ | $11^1$ | | | | | | | | | | | | | | | | | | | 19 |
| 1 | 2 | 3 | 4 | 5 | 6 | 7 | 8 | | 12 | | 11 | 9 | | | $10^1$ | | | | | | | | | | | | | | | | | | | | 20 |
| 1 | 2 | 3 | 4 | 5 | 6 | 7 | 8 | | 12 | 13 | $11^2$ | 9 | | | $10^1$ | | | | | | | | | | | | | | | | | | | | 21 |
| | 2 | 3 | 4 | 5 | 6 | 7 | 8 | | $12^2$ | 14 | 13 | | 11 | $10^3$ | | | | | | 1 | $9^1$ | | | | | | | | | | | | | | 22 |
| | 2 | 3 | 4 | 5 | | 7 | 8 | | 12 | 6 | | 13 | 11 | $10^1$ | | | | | | $9^2$ | | | | | | | | | | | | | | | 23 |
| | 2 | 3 | 4 | $5^2$ | | 7 | 8 | | 14 | 12 | 6 | | 13 | $11^1$ | 10 | | | | | $9^3$ | | | | | | | | | | | | | | | 24 |
| 1 | 2 | 3 | 4 | 5 | 6 | 7 | | $10^2$ | | 8 | | 13 | $9^1$ | $11^3$ | 12 | | | | 14 | | | | | | | | | | | | | | | | 25 |
| 1 | $2^2$ | 3 | $4^3$ | 5 | 6 | 7 | 8 | | 13 | | | 9 | | | 11 | 12 | | | | | | | | $10^1$ | 14 | | | | | | | | | | 26 |
| 1 | $2^2$ | 3 | 4 | | 6 | 7 | 8 | | $11^1$ | | | 12 | 9 | | 5 | 10 | | 13 | | | | | | | | | | | | | | | | | 27 |
| 1 | 2 | 3 | 4 | | 6 | 7 | 8 | | | | | | 9 | | 5 | 12 | | $11^1$ | | 10 | | | | | | | | | | | | | | | 28 |
| $1^1$ | | 3 | 4 | | 6 | 7 | 11 | | 13 | 12 | | | 8 | | $5^2$ | 14 | | | | | | | | 9 | $2^3$ | 10 | | | | | | | | | 29 |
| | 3 | 4 | | 6 | 7 | 8 | | | | $2^1$ | 12 | 9 | | $5^2$ | 13 | | | | | | | | | 10 | 11 | 1 | | | | | | | | | 30 |
| | 3 | | | 6 | 7 | 8 | | 4 | | $2^1$ | 12 | | 5 | 9 | | | | | | | | | | 10 | 13 | $11^2$ | 1 | | | | | | | | 31 |
| | 3 | | $5^1$ | 6 | 7 | 8 | | | $11^2$ | 2 | 12 | 9 | | 4 | 13 | | | | | | | | | 10 | | 1 | | | | | | | | | 32 |
| | 3 | 4 | $5^1$ | 6 | 7 | 8 | | | | | 12 | $9^2$ | | 11 | 10 | | | | 13 | | | | | 2 | | 1 | | | | | | | | | 33 |
| 12 | 3 | 4 | 5 | 6 | 7 | 8 | | | 13 | | | $9^1$ | | 11 | 14 | | | | | | | | | $2^1$ | | 1 | | $10^3$ | | | | | | | 34 |
| 12 | 3 | 4 | 5 | 6 | 7 | 8 | | | | | | 9 | | 11 | | | | | | | | | | 2 | | 1 | | $10^1$ | | | | | | | 35 |
| 12 | 3 | 4 | $5^1$ | 6 | $7^1$ | 8 | | | | | 13 | 9 | | 11 | 14 | | | | | | | | | 2 | | 1 | | $10^3$ | | | | | | | 36 |
| 12 | 3 | 4 | $5^1$ | 6 | 7 | 8 | | 9 | | | 13 | | | 11 | 10 | | | | | | | | | $2^1$ | | 1 | | | | | | | | | 37 |
| | 2 | 3 | 4 | 5 | 6 | 7 | 8 | | 12 | | | | | 11 | $10^2$ | | | | $9^1$ | | | | | | | | | 1 | 13 | | | | | | 38 |
| | 2 | 3 | $4^1$ | 5 | 6 | 7 | | | 12 | | | | 9 | 11 | $10^3$ | | | | $8^2$ | | | | | | | | 1 | 13 | 14 | | | | | | 39 |
| | 2 | 3 | 4 | 5 | 6 | 7 | | | | | | 12 | 9 | $11^2$ | 13 | | | | 8 | | | | | | | | 1 | $10^1$ | | | | | | 40 |
| | 2 | 3 | 4 | $5^1$ | 6 | 7 | | | | | | 12 | 9 | 11 | 8 | | | | | | | | | | | | 1 | 13 | $10^1$ | | | | | | 41 |
| | $2^2$ | 3 | 4 | 5 | | 7 | 6 | | | | | 12 | 9 | 11 | 8 | | | | | | | | | | | | 1 | 13 | $10^1$ | | | | | | 42 |
| $8^1$ | 3 | 4 | $5^1$ | | 7 | 6 | | | | | | 12 | | 11 | | | | 13 | | | | 2 | | | 1 | | 10 | | | | | | | | 43 |
| | 4 | 5 | | 7 | 6 | | | | $8^1$ | | 12 | | | 11 | 13 | | 1 | $9^2$ | 2 | | | | | | | | | | | $3^1$ | 10 | 14 | | 44 |
| | 4 | | 5 | 7 | 6 | | | | | | 2 | 12 | | 11 | 9 | | 1 | 13 | | | | | 8 | | | | | | | $3^1$ | $10^1$ | | | 45 |
| | 4 | | 6 | 7 | 5 | | 12 | | | | | 2 | 13 | 11 | $9^2$ | | 1 | $8^3$ | | | | | 3 | | | | | | | 14 | $10^1$ | | | 46 |

**Coca-Cola Cup**

| | | | | |
|---|---|---|---|---|
| First Round | Brighton & HA | (a) | 1-1 | |
| | | (h) | 3-1 | |
| Second Round | Bolton W | (h) | 1-3 | |
| | | (a) | 4-4 | |

**FA Cup**

| | | | |
|---|---|---|---|
| First Round | Hendon | (a) | 2-2 |
| | | (h) | 0-1 |

LINCOLN CITY 1997–98    *Back row (left to right):* Steve Holmes, John Robertson, Barry Richardson, John Vaughan, Mark Hone, Colin Alcide.
*Middle row:* Stuart Bimson, Paul Miller, Joby Gowshall, Jon Whitney, Craig Stones, Kevin Austin, Dean Chandler, Lee Thorpe, Keith Oakes (Physio).
*Front row:* Jason Barnett, Terry Fleming, Gareth Ainsworth, John Beck (Manager), Shane Westley (Assistant Manager), Steve Brown, Jae Martin, Phil Stant.

# Division 2          **LINCOLN CITY**

***Sincil Bank, Lincoln LN5 8LD.*** Telephone: (01522) 880011. Fax: (01522) 880020.

***Ground capacity:*** 10,918.

***Record attendance:*** 23,196 v Derby Co, League Cup 4th rd, 15 November 1967.

***Record receipts:*** £44,184.46 v Everton, Coca-Cola Cup 2nd rd 1st leg, 21 September 1993.

***Pitch measurements:*** 110yd × 71yd.

***Hon. Life Presidents:*** V. C. Withers, D. W. L. Bocock.

***Chairman:*** K. J. Reames. ***Vice-Chairman:*** H. C. Sills.

***Directors:*** J. Hicks, N. Woolsey, P. Jackson.

***Hon. Consultant Surgeon:*** Mr Brian Smith. ***Hon. Club Doctor:*** Chris Batty.

***Company Secretary:*** H. C. Sills.

***Manager:*** Shane Westley. ***Assistants:*** Phil Stant, Keith Oakes. ***Physio:*** Keith Oakes.

***Commercial Manager:*** Jerry Lonsdale. ***Stadium Manager:*** Nigel Dennis.

***Year Formed:*** 1884. ***Turned Professional:*** 1892. ***Ltd Co.:*** 1895.

***Club Nickname:*** 'The Red Imps'.

***Previous Grounds:*** 1883, John O'Gaunt's; 1894, Sincil Bank.

***Foundation:*** Although there was a Lincoln club as far back as 1861, the present organisation was formed in 1884 winning the Lincolnshire Senior Cup in only their fourth season. They were founder members of the Midland League in 1889 and that competition's first champions.

***First Football League game:*** 3 September 1892, Division 2, v Sheffield U (a) L 2-4 – W. Gresham; Coulton, Neill; Shaw, Mettam, Moore; Smallman, Irving (1), Cameron (1), Kelly, J. Gresham.

***Record League Victory:*** 11–1 v Crewe Alex, Division 3 (N), 29 September 1951 – Jones; Green (1p), Varney; Wright, Emery, Grummett (1); Troops (1), Garvey, Graver (6), Whittle (1), Johnson (1).

***Record Cup Victory:*** 8–1 v Bromley, FA Cup 2nd rd, 10 December 1938 – McPhail; Hartshorne, Corbett; Bean, Leach, Whyte (1); Hancock, Wilson (1), Ponting (3), Deacon (1), Clare (2).

***Record Defeat:*** 3–11 v Manchester C, Division 2, 23 March 1895.

***Most League Points (2 for a win):*** 74, Division 4, 1975–76.

***Most League Points (3 for a win):*** 77, Division 3, 1981–82.

***Most League Goals:*** 121, Division 3 (N), 1951–52.

***Highest League Scorer in Season:*** Allan Hall, 42, Division 3 (N), 1931–32.

***Most League Goals in Total Aggregate:*** Andy Graver, 144, 1950–55 and 1958–61.

***Most Capped Player:*** David Pugh, 3 (7), Wales and George Moulson, 3, Republic of Ireland.

***Most League Appearances:*** Tony Emery, 402, 1946–59.

***Record Transfer Fee Received:*** £500,000 from Port Vale for Gareth Ainsworth, September 1997.

***Record Transfer Fee Paid:*** £75,000 to Carlisle U for Dean Walling, September 1997.

***Football League Record:*** 1892 Founder member of Division 2. Remained in Division 2 until 1920 when they failed re-election but also missed seasons 1908–09 and 1911–12 when not re-elected. 1921–32 Division 3 (N); 1932–34 Division 2; 1934–48 Division 3 (N); 1948–49 Division 2; 1949–52 Division 3 (N); 1952–61 Division 2; 1961–62 Division 3; 1962–76 Division 4; 1976–79 Division 3; 1979–81 Division 4; 1981–86 Division 3; 1986–87 Division 4; 1987–88 GM Vauxhall Conference; 1988–92 Division 4; 1992–98 Division 3; 1998– Division 2.

***Honours:*** *Football League:* Division 2 best season: 5th, 1901–02; Promotion from Division 3, 1997–98; Division 3 (N) – Champions 1931–32, 1947–48, 1951–52; Runners-up 1927–28, 1930–31, 1936–37; Division 4 – Champions 1975–76; Runners-up 1980–81. *FA Cup:* best season: 1st rd of Second Series (5th rd equivalent), 1887, 2nd rd (5th rd equivalent), 1890, 1902. *Football League Cup:* best season: 4th rd, 1968. *GM Vauxhall Conference:* Champions 1987–88.

***Colours:*** Red and white striped shirts, white shorts, white stockings with red trim. ***Change colours:*** All blue.

**Did you know?**

Lincoln City's first nickname was the 'Citizens', often shortened to 'Cits'. They were also referred to as the 'Window Blinds' as their red and white striped shirts were similar to those of shops.

## LINCOLN CITY 1997–98 LEAGUE RECORD

| Match No. | Date | Venue | Opponents | Result | H/T Score | Lg. Pos. | Goalscorers | Atten-dance |
|---|---|---|---|---|---|---|---|---|
| 1 | Aug 9 | A | Chester C | L 0-2 | 0-0 | — | | 2478 |
| 2 | 16 | H | Shrewsbury T | W 1-0 | 0-0 | 18 | Miller [53] | 3019 |
| 3 | 23 | A | Notts Co | W 2-1 | 1-0 | 9 | Alcide [26], Stant [75] | 5707 |
| 4 | 30 | H | Scarborough | D 3-3 | 2-1 | 9 | Ainsworth 3 [35, 42, 70] | 3162 |
| 5 | Sept 2 | H | Mansfield T | L 0-2 | 0-1 | — | | 3539 |
| 6 | 10 | A | Rotherham U | L 1-3 | 0-0 | — | Miller [88] | 2871 |
| 7 | 13 | A | Hull C | W 2-0 | 1-0 | 13 | Thorpe [23], Fleming [76] | 4736 |
| 8 | 20 | H | Cardiff C | W 1-0 | 1-0 | 11 | Thorpe [5] | 3130 |
| 9 | 27 | A | Barnet | D 0-0 | 0-0 | 11 | | 1734 |
| 10 | Oct 4 | H | Cambridge U | D 0-0 | 0-0 | 11 | | 3397 |
| 11 | 11 | H | Torquay U | D 1-1 | 0-1 | 8 | Fleming [48] | 2462 |
| 12 | 18 | A | Scunthorpe U | W 1-0 | 0-0 | 6 | Walling [72] | 4152 |
| 13 | 22 | A | Brighton & HA | W 1-0 | 0-0 | — | Thorpe [64] | 1036 |
| 14 | 25 | H | Darlington | W 3-1 | 3-0 | 4 | Thorpe 2 [2, 44], Whitney [33] | 3384 |
| 15 | Nov 1 | H | Leyton Orient | W 1-0 | 0-0 | 4 | Walling [59] | 4129 |
| 16 | 4 | A | Rochdale | D 0-0 | 0-0 | — | | 1537 |
| 17 | 8 | A | Swansea C | D 0-0 | 0-0 | 4 | | 2871 |
| 18 | 18 | A | Doncaster R | W 2-1 | 1-0 | — | Walling [14], Holmes [66] | 2957 |
| 19 | 22 | A | Colchester U | W 1-0 | 0-0 | 1 | Gordon [61] | 2932 |
| 20 | 29 | H | Macclesfield T | D 1-1 | 0-1 | 1 | Gordon [59] | 3402 |
| 21 | Dec 2 | A | Exeter C | W 2-1 | 0-1 | — | Thorpe [47], Brown Steve [80] | 4224 |
| 22 | 13 | H | Hartlepool U | W 2-1 | 1-0 | 2 | Cullen (og) [14] | 2849 |
| 23 | 20 | A | Peterborough U | L 1-5 | 1-4 | 3 | Thorpe [2] | 8771 |
| 24 | 26 | H | Rotherham U | L 0-1 | 0-0 | 3 | | 6350 |
| 25 | 28 | A | Mansfield T | D 2-2 | 0-1 | 3 | Alcide [55], Smith [83] | 3449 |
| 26 | Jan 10 | A | Chester C | L 1-3 | 0-2 | 7 | Brown Steve [48] | 2913 |
| 27 | 17 | A | Scarborough | D 2-2 | 1-0 | 8 | Thorpe [10], Walling [90] | 2905 |
| 28 | 24 | H | Notts Co | L 3-5 | 0-3 | 11 | Smith [48], Hone [52], Brown Steve [61] | 5911 |
| 29 | 31 | H | Hull C | W 1-0 | 1-0 | 10 | Walling [21] | 4067 |
| 30 | Feb 7 | A | Cardiff C | W 1-0 | 0-0 | 8 | Alcide [51] | 2896 |
| 31 | 13 | A | Cambridge U | D 1-1 | 0-1 | — | Alcide [57] | 3891 |
| 32 | 21 | H | Barnet | W 2-0 | 0-0 | 6 | Hone [54], Gordon [89] | 2945 |
| 33 | 24 | H | Scunthorpe U | D 1-1 | 1-0 | — | Alcide [20] | 3407 |
| 34 | 28 | A | Torquay U | L 2-3 | 1-2 | 8 | Thorpe [41], Alcide [67] | 3540 |
| 35 | Mar 3 | H | Swansea C | D 1-1 | 0-0 | — | Thorpe [80] | 2281 |
| 36 | 7 | A | Leyton Orient | L 0-1 | 0-0 | 9 | | 4745 |
| 37 | 14 | H | Rochdale | W 2-0 | 1-0 | 6 | Thorpe [14], Alcide [82] | 2992 |
| 38 | 21 | A | Doncaster R | W 4-2 | 2-2 | 6 | Stant [8], Thorpe [10], Martin [72], Alcide [84] | 2357 |
| 39 | 24 | A | Shrewsbury T | W 2-0 | 1-0 | — | Alcide [13], Thorpe [73] | 1877 |
| 40 | 28 | H | Colchester U | L 0-1 | 0-1 | 6 | | 4040 |
| 41 | Apr 4 | A | Macclesfield T | L 0-1 | 0-0 | 7 | | 3278 |
| 42 | 13 | A | Hartlepool U | D 1-1 | 1-1 | 8 | Alcide [30] | 1997 |
| 43 | 18 | H | Peterborough U | W 3-0 | 3-0 | 7 | Alcide 2 [2, 44], Smith [6] | 6748 |
| 44 | 21 | H | Exeter C | W 2-1 | 1-0 | — | Holmes 2 [30, 80] | 4284 |
| 45 | 25 | A | Darlington | D 2-2 | 1-1 | 4 | Holmes (pen) [21], Bailey [90] | 3160 |
| 46 | May 2 | H | Brighton & HA | W 2-1 | 0-0 | 3 | Fleming [55], Thorpe [58] | 9890 |

**Final League Position: 3**        1996–97 DIV3 9

### GOALSCORERS

*League (60):* Thorpe 14, Alcide 12, Walling 5, Holmes 4 (1 pen), Ainsworth 3, Steve Brown 3, Fleming 3, Gordon 3, Smith 3, Hone 2, Miller 2, Stant 2, Bailey 1, Martin 1, Whitney 1, own goal 1.
*Coca-Cola Cup (2):* Ainsworth 1, Stant 1.
*FA Cup (9):* Walling 3, Fleming 2, Whitney 2, Alcide 1, Hone 1.

| Vaughan J 19 | Barnett J 33 | Whitney J 42 + 2 | Hone M 22 + 2 | Holmes S 46 | Austin K 46 | Ainsworth G 6 | Miller P 20 + 4 | Stant P 17 + 4 | Thorpe L 44 | Fleming T 40 | Brown Steve 16 + 15 | Stones C 10 + 5 | Alcide C 25 + 4 | Harris J — + 1 | Robertson J 2 | Bimson S 7 + 5 | Wilkins 11 + 1 | Richardson B 26 | Walling D 35 | Flash R 2 + 3 | Martin J — + 7 | Smith P 15 + 2 | Gordon G 9 + 4 | Brown Simon 1 | Regis D — + 1 | Brown G 15 | Bailey D 1 + 4 | Finnigan J 6 | Match No. |
|---|---|---|---|---|---|---|---|---|---|---|---|---|---|---|---|---|---|---|---|---|---|---|---|---|---|---|---|---|---|
| 1 | 2 | 3 | 4 | 5 | 6 | 7 | 8 | 9 | 10 | 11 | | | | | | | | | | | | | | | | | | | 1 |
| 1 | 2 | 3 | 4 | 5 | 6 | 7 | 8 | 9 | $10^1$ | $11^1$ | 12 | 13 | | | | | | | | | | | | | | | | | 2 |
| 1 | 2 | 3 | 4 | 5 | 6 | 7 | 8 | 9 | 10 | | | | 11 | | | | | | | | | | | | | | | | 3 |
| 1 | 2 | 3 | 4 | 5 | 6 | 7 | 8 | 9 | 10 | | | | 11 | | | | | | | | | | | | | | | | 4 |
| 1 | 2 | 3 | 4 | 5 | 6 | 7 | 8 | 9 | 10 | | | | $11^1$ | 12 | | | | | | | | | | | | | | | 5 |
| 1 | 2 | 3 | | 5 | 6 | 7 | 8 | $9^1$ | 10 | 4 | 12 | | 11 | | | | | | | | | | | | | | | | 6 |
| 1 | 2 | 3 | | 5 | 6 | | 8 | 9 | 7 | 4 | 10 | | 11 | | | | | | | | | | | | | | | | 7 |
| 1 | 2 | 3 | | 5 | 6 | | 8 | $9^1$ | 7 | 4 | $10^2$ | 12 | | | | 11 | 13 | | | | | | | | | | | | 8 |
| 1 | 2 | 3 | | 5 | 6 | | 8 | 9 | 7 | 4 | 10 | $11^1$ | | | | | 12 | | | | | | | | | | | | 9 |
| | 2 | 3 | | 5 | 6 | | $8^1$ | 9 | 10 | 4 | 12 | | | | | | | 1 | 7 | | | 11 | | | | | | | 10 |
| | 2 | 3 | | 5 | 6 | | | $9^2$ | 10 | 4 | 8 | 12 | | | | | | 1 | 7 | | | $11^1$ | 13 | | | | | | 11 |
| | 2 | 3 | | 5 | 6 | | 8 | 9 | 10 | 4 | | | $11^1$ | | | | | 1 | 7 | | | 12 | | | | | | | 12 |
| | 2 | 3 | | 5 | 6 | | 8 | $9^2$ | 10 | 4 | 12 | | $11^1$ | | | | | 1 | 7 | | | 13 | | | | | | | 13 |
| | 2 | 3 | | 5 | 6 | | $8^1$ | $9^2$ | 10 | 4 | 12 | | $11^2$ | | | | | 1 | 7 | | | 13 | 14 | | | | | | 14 |
| | 2 | 3 | 12 | 5 | 6 | | 8 | $9^2$ | 10 | 4 | | 13 | $11^1$ | | | | | 1 | 7 | | | | | | | | | | 15 |
| | 2 | 3 | 12 | 5 | 6 | | $8^2$ | 13 | 10 | 4 | $9^2$ | | $11^1$ | | | | | 1 | 7 | | | 14 | | | | | | | 16 |
| | 2 | 3 | 11 | 5 | 6 | | 8 | | 10 | 4 | $9^1$ | | | | | | | 1 | 7 | | | 12 | | | | | | | 17 |
| | 2 | 3 | 11 | 5 | 6 | | | 9 | 10 | 4 | 12 | | | | | | | 1 | 7 | | | $8^1$ | | | | | | | 18 |
| | 2 | 3 | 11 | 5 | 6 | | 8 | | | 4 | | | | | | | | 1 | 7 | | | 10 | 9 | | | | | | 19 |
| | 2 | 3 | | 5 | 6 | | 12 | 8 | | 4 | | 13 | 11 | | | | | 1 | 7 | | | $10^2$ | $9^1$ | | | | | | 20 |
| | 2 | $3^2$ | | 5 | 6 | | | 8 | | 4 | 12 | | 11 | | | 13 | | 1 | 7 | | | 10 | $9^1$ | | | | | | 21 |
| 1 | 2 | $3^2$ | 8 | 5 | 6 | | 10 | | | 4 | 12 | 13 | | | | | | | 7 | | | $11^1$ | $9^2$ | | | | | | 22 |
| | | 3 | 8 | 5 | 6 | $6^3$ | 10 | | | 4 | 12 | 13 | 11 | | $2^1$ | | | | 7 | | | $9^2$ | 14 | 1 | | | | | 23 |
| 1 | | 3 | 8 | 5 | 6 | | 12 | | | 4 | $10^1$ | | 11 | | 2 | 13 | | | 7 | | | | $9^2$ | | | | | | 24 |
| 1 | 2 | 3 | 8 | 5 | 6 | | 12 | | | 4 | $10^2$ | 13 | | | | | | | 7 | | | 11 | $9^1$ | | | | | | 25 |
| 1 | 2 | 3 | | 5 | 6 | | 10 | | | 4 | 12 | $8^2$ | $9^1$ | | | 13 | | | 7 | | | 11 | | | | | | | 26 |
| 1 | 2 | 12 | | 5 | 6 | | 14 | | 10 | 4 | $9^1$ | 3 | 8 | | | | | | 7 | | | $13^3$ | $11^2$ | | | | | | 27 |
| 1 | 2 | 3 | 8 | 5 | 6 | | 10 | | | 4 | 12 | | | | | | | | 7 | | | 11 | $9^1$ | | | | | | 28 |
| | 2 | 3 | | 5 | 6 | | 10 | | | 4 | 9 | 12 | 13 | | | $8^1$ | | 1 | 7 | | | $11^2$ | | | | | | | 29 |
| | | 3 | 8 | 5 | 6 | | 10 | | | 4 | 9 | | 11 | | $2^1$ | | 12 | 1 | 7 | | | | | | | | | | 30 |
| | | 3 | 8 | 5 | 6 | | 10 | | | 4 | 9 | | 11 | | 2 | | | 1 | 7 | | | | | | | | | | 31 |
| | | 3 | 8 | 5 | 6 | | 10 | | | | 9 | | $11^1$ | | 2 | | | 1 | 7 | | | 12 | 4 | | | | | | 32 |
| | | 3 | 8 | 5 | 6 | 12 | 10 | | | | 9 | | 11 | | $2^1$ | | | 1 | 7 | | | | 4 | | | | | | 33 |
| | | 3 | 8 | 5 | 6 | | $10^2$ | | | | 9 | | 11 | | 2 | | | 1 | 7 | | | | 4 | | | | | | 34 |
| | | 3 | 8 | 5 | 6 | 12 | 10 | | | 4 | | $13^3$ | 11 | | | | | 1 | 7 | | | 14 | $9^1$ | | | $2^2$ | | | 35 |
| | | 3 | 8 | 5 | 6 | | $10^2$ | | | 4 | $9^1$ | | $11^3$ | | | 12 | | 1 | 7 | | | 13 | 14 | | | 2 | | | 36 |
| | | 3 | | 5 | 6 | | | 9 | 10 | 4 | 12 | | 11 | | | $8^1$ | | 1 | 7 | | | | | | | 2 | | | 37 |
| | | 3 | | 5 | 6 | | 8 | $9^1$ | 10 | 4 | | | 11 | | | | | 1 | 7 | | | 12 | | | | 2 | | | 38 |
| | | 3 | 9 | 5 | 6 | | 8 | | 10 | 4 | | | 11 | | | | | 1 | 7 | | | | | | | 2 | | | 39 |
| | | 3 | $9^1$ | $5^2$ | 6 | | 8 | | 10 | 4 | | | 11 | | | | | 1 | 7 | | | 12 | | | | 2 | 13 | | 40 |
| | 8 | 3 | | 5 | 6 | 12 | 10 | | | 4 | | | 11 | | | | | 1 | | | | | | | | 2 | $9^1$ | 7 | 41 |
| | 8 | 3 | | 5 | 6 | | $10^1$ | | | 4 | | | 11 | | | | | 1 | 7 | | | 12 | | | | 2 | | 9 | 42 |
| 1 | | 3 | | 5 | 6 | | 10 | | | 4 | | | 11 | | | | | | 7 | | | | $9^1$ | | | 2 | 12 | 8 | 43 |
| 1 | | 3 | | 5 | 6 | | 10 | | | $4^1$ | | | 11 | | | | | | 7 | | | 12 | 9 | | | 2 | | 8 | 44 |
| 1 | | 3 | 12 | $5^2$ | 6 | | 10 | | | 4 | | | 11 | | | | | | $7^1$ | | | | 9 | | | 2 | 13 | 8 | 45 |
| 1 | | 3 | 7 | 5 | 6 | | | $9^1$ | 10 | 4 | | | 11 | | | | | | | | | | | | | 2 | 12 | 8 | 46 |

**Coca-Cola Cup**
First Round　　　Burnley　　　　　　　(h)　1-1
　　　　　　　　　　　　　　　　　　　　(a)　1-2

**FA Cup**
First Round　　　Gainsborough T　　　(h)　1-1
　　　　　　　　　　　　　　　　　　　　(a)　3-2
Second Round　　Emley　　　　　　　 (h)　2-2
　　　　　　　　　　　　　　　　　　　　(a)　3-3

LIVERPOOL 1997–98  *Back row (left to right):* Mark Leather (Physio), Dominic Matteo, Paul Ince, Mark Wright, Tony Warner, Jorgen Nielsen, David James, Rob Jones, Jamie Redknapp, Neil Ruddock, Sammy Lee (Reserve Team Coach).

*Middle row:* Joe Corrigan (Goalkeeping Coach), Jamie Carragher, Phil Babb, Jason McAteer, Patrik Berger, Bjorn Tore Kvarme, Stig Inge Bjornebye, Karlheinz Riedle, David Thompson, Michael Owen, Ronnie Moran (Chief Coach).

*Front row:* Michael Thomas, Mark Kennedy, Oyvind Leonhardsen, John Barnes, Roy Evans (Manager), Doug Livermore (Assistant Manager), Steve Harkness, Steve McManaman, Robbie Fowler, Danny Murphy.

# FA Premiership                                   **LIVERPOOL**

*Anfield Road, Liverpool L4 0TH.* Telephone: (0151) 263 2361. Fax: (0151) 260 8813. Clubcall: 0891 121184. Ticket and Match Information: (0151) 260 9999 (24-hour service) or (0151) 260 8680 (office hours) Credit Card Bookings: 0151-263 5727. International Supporters Club: (0151) 261 1444. Museum and Stadium Tours: (0151) 260 6677. LFC Direct Mail Order: (0990) 532532.

*Ground Capacity:* 45,362

*Record attendance:* 61,905 v Wolverhampton W, FA Cup 4th rd, 2 February 1952.

*Record receipts:* £496,000 v Newcastle U, Coca-Cola Cup 4th rd, 29 November 1995.

*Pitch measurements:* 111yd × 74yd.

*Chairman:* D. R. Moores.

*Executive Vice-Chairman:* Peter B. Robinson. *Chief Executive:* Rick Parry BSC, FCA. *Finance Director:* David Chestnutt FCA. *Directors:* J. T. Cross, N. White FSCA, T. D. Smith, T. W. Saunders, K. E. B. Clayton FCA.

*Vice-President:* H. E. Roberts.

*Joint Managers:* Roy Evans and Gerard Houllier. *Assistant Manager:* Doug Livermore.

*Physio:* Mark Leather.

*Secretary:* Bryce Morrison.

*Year Formed:* 1892. *Turned Professional:* 1892. *Ltd Co.:* 1892.

*Club Nickname:* 'Reds' or 'Pool'.

*Foundation:* But for a dispute between Everton FC and their landlord at Anfield in 1892, there may never have been a Liverpool club. This dispute persuaded the majority of Evertonians to quit Anfield for Goodison Park, leaving the landlord, Mr. John Houlding, to form a new club. He originally tried to retain the name "Everton" but when this failed, he founded Liverpool Association FC on 15 March 1892.

*First Football League game:* 2 September 1893, Division 2, v Middlesbrough Ironopolis (a) W 2-0 – McOwen; Hannah, McLean; Henderson, McQue (1), McBride; Gordon, McVean (1), M. McQueen, Stott, H. McQueen.

*Record League Victory:* 10–1 v Rotherham T, Division 2, 18 February 1896 – Storer; Goldie, Wilkie; McCarthy, McQueen, Holmes; McVean (3), Ross (2), Allan (4), Becton (1), Bradshaw.

*Record Cup Victory:* 11–0 v Stromsgodset Drammen, ECWC 1st rd 1st leg, 17 September 1974 – Clemence; Smith (1), Lindsay (1p), Thompson (2), Cormack (1), Hughes (1), Boersma (2), Hall, Heighway (1), Kennedy (1), Callaghan (1).

*Record Defeat:* 1–9 v Birmingham C, Division 2, 11 December 1954.

*Most League Points (2 for a win):* 68, Division 1, 1978–79.

*Most League Points (3 for a win):* 90, Division 1, 1987–88.

*Most League Goals:* 106, Division 2, 1895–96.

*Highest League Scorer in Season:* Roger Hunt, 41, Division 2, 1961–62.

*Most League Goals in Total Aggregate:* Roger Hunt, 245, 1959–69.

*Most Capped Player:* Ian Rush, 67 (73), Wales.

*Most League Appearances:* Ian Callaghan, 640, 1960–78.

*Record Transfer Fee Received:* £7,000,000 from Aston Villa for Stan Collymore, May 1997.

*Record Transfer Fee Paid:* £8,500,000 to Nottingham F for Stan Collymore, June 1995.

*Football League Record:* 1893 Elected to Division 2; 1894–95 Division 1; 1895–96 Division 2; 1896–1904 Division 1; 1904–05 Division 2; 1905–54 Division 1; 1954–62 Division 2; 1962–92 Division 1; 1992– FA Premier League.

*Honours: Football League:* Division 1 – Champions 1900–01, 1905–06, 1921–22, 1922–23, 1946–47, 1963–64, 1965–66, 1972–73, 1975–76, 1976–77, 1978–79, 1979–80, 1981–82, 1982–83, 1983–84, 1985–86, 1987–88, 1989–90 (Liverpool have a record number of 18 League Championship wins); Runners-up 1898–99, 1909–10, 1968–69, 1973–74, 1974–75, 1977–78, 1984–85, 1986–87, 1988–89, 1990–91; Division 2 – Champions 1893–94, 1895–96, 1904–05, 1961–62. *FA Cup:* Winners 1965, 1974, 1986, 1989, 1992; Runners-up 1914, 1950, 1971, 1977, 1988, 1996; *Football League Cup:* Winners 1981, 1982, 1983, 1984, 1995; Runners-up 1978, 1987. *League Super Cup:* Winners 1986. **European Competitions:** *European Cup:* 1964–65, 1966–67, 1973–74, 1976–77 (winners), 1977–78 (winners), 1978–79, 1979–80, 1980–81 (winners), 1981–82, 1982–83, 1983–84 (winners), 1984–85 (runners-up); *European Cup-Winners' Cup:* 1965–66 (runners-up), 1971–72, 1974–75, 1992–93, 1996–97 (sf); *European Fairs Cup:* 1967–68, 1968–69, 1969–70, 1970–71; *UEFA Cup:* 1972–73 (winners), 1975–76 (winners), 1991–92, 1995–96, 1997–98; *Super Cup:* 1977 (winners), 1978, 1984; *World Club Championship:* 1981 (runners-up).

*Colours:* All red. *Change colours:* All yellow.

**Did you know?**
When Liverpool beat Strasbourg 2-0 last season, it was their 100th victory in one of the major European competitions.

## LIVERPOOL 1997–98 LEAGUE RECORD

| Match No. | Date | Venue | Opponents | Result | | H/T Score | Lg. Pos. | Goalscorers | Attendance |
|---|---|---|---|---|---|---|---|---|---|
| 1 | Aug 9 | A | Wimbledon | D | 1-1 | 0-0 | — | Owen (pen) [71] | 26,106 |
| 2 | 13 | H | Leicester C | L | 1-2 | 0-1 | — | Ince [85] | 35,007 |
| 3 | 23 | A | Blackburn R | D | 1-1 | 0-0 | 16 | Owen [52] | 30,187 |
| 4 | 26 | A | Leeds U | W | 2-0 | 1-0 | — | McManaman [23], Riedle [75] | 39,878 |
| 5 | Sept 13 | H | Sheffield W | W | 2-1 | 0-0 | 7 | Ince [55], Thomas [68] | 34,705 |
| 6 | 20 | A | Southampton | D | 1-1 | 1-0 | 7 | Riedle [37] | 15,242 |
| 7 | 22 | H | Aston Villa | W | 3-0 | 0-0 | — | Fowler (pen) [56], McManaman [79], Riedle [90] | 34,843 |
| 8 | 27 | A | West Ham U | L | 1-2 | 0-1 | 9 | Fowler [52] | 25,908 |
| 9 | Oct 5 | H | Chelsea | W | 4-2 | 2-1 | 6 | Berger 3 [20, 35, 57], Fowler [64] | 36,647 |
| 10 | 18 | A | Everton | L | 0-2 | 0-1 | 9 | | 40,112 |
| 11 | 25 | H | Derby Co | W | 4-0 | 1-0 | 5 | Fowler 2 [27, 84], Leonhardsen [65], McManaman [88] | 38,017 |
| 12 | Nov 1 | A | Bolton W | D | 1-1 | 1-0 | 8 | Fowler [1] | 25,000 |
| 13 | 8 | H | Tottenham H | W | 4-0 | 0-0 | 6 | McManaman [48], Leonhardsen [50], Redknapp [65], Owen [86] | 38,006 |
| 14 | 22 | H | Barnsley | L | 0-1 | 0-1 | 8 | | 41,011 |
| 15 | 30 | A | Arsenal | W | 1-0 | 0-0 | 7 | McManaman [55] | 38,094 |
| 16 | Dec 6 | H | Manchester U | L | 1-3 | 0-0 | 8 | Fowler (pen) [60] | 41,027 |
| 17 | 13 | A | Crystal Palace | W | 3-0 | 1-0 | 6 | McManaman [39], Owen [56], Leonhardsen [61] | 25,790 |
| 18 | 20 | H | Coventry C | W | 1-0 | 1-0 | 5 | Owen [14] | 39,707 |
| 19 | 26 | H | Leeds U | W | 3-1 | 0-0 | 4 | Owen [46], Fowler 2 [79, 83] | 43,854 |
| 20 | 28 | A | Newcastle U | W | 2-1 | 2-1 | 4 | McManaman 2 [31, 43] | 36,702 |
| 21 | Jan 10 | A | Wimbledon | W | 2-0 | 0-0 | 4 | Redknapp 2 [71, 84] | 38,011 |
| 22 | 17 | A | Leicester C | D | 0-0 | 0-0 | 4 | | 21,633 |
| 23 | 20 | H | Newcastle U | W | 1-0 | 1-0 | — | Owen [17] | 42,791 |
| 24 | 31 | H | Blackburn R | D | 0-0 | 0-0 | 4 | | 43,890 |
| 25 | Feb 7 | A | Southampton | L | 2-3 | 1-1 | 3 | Owen 2 [24, 90] | 43,550 |
| 26 | 14 | A | Sheffield W | D | 3-3 | 1-1 | 2 | Owen 3 [27, 73, 78] | 35,405 |
| 27 | 23 | H | Everton | D | 1-1 | 0-0 | — | Ince [68] | 44,501 |
| 28 | 28 | A | Aston Villa | L | 1-2 | 1-1 | 4 | Owen (pen) [6] | 39,372 |
| 29 | Mar 7 | H | Bolton W | W | 2-1 | 0-1 | 2 | Ince [58], Owen [65] | 44,532 |
| 30 | 14 | A | Tottenham H | D | 3-3 | 1-1 | 3 | McManaman 2 [21, 89], Ince [64] | 30,245 |
| 31 | 28 | A | Barnsley | W | 3-2 | 1-1 | 3 | Riedle 2 [44, 59], McManaman [90] | 18,687 |
| 32 | Apr 10 | A | Manchester U | D | 1-1 | 1-1 | — | Owen [36] | 55,171 |
| 33 | 13 | H | Crystal Palace | W | 2-1 | 1-0 | 3 | Leonhardsen [29], Thompson [85] | 43,007 |
| 34 | 19 | A | Coventry C | D | 1-1 | 1-0 | 3 | Owen [33] | 22,724 |
| 35 | 25 | A | Chelsea | L | 1-4 | 1-1 | 4 | Riedle [45] | 34,639 |
| 36 | May 2 | H | West Ham U | W | 5-0 | 4-0 | 3 | Owen [4], McAteer 2 [21, 25], Leonhardsen [45], Ince [61] | 44,414 |
| 37 | 6 | A | Arsenal | W | 4-0 | 3-0 | — | Ince 2 [28, 30], Owen [40], Leonhardsen [86] | 44,417 |
| 38 | 10 | A | Derby Co | L | 0-1 | 0-0 | 3 | | 30,492 |

**Final League Position: 3**　　　　1996–97 PREM 4

### GOALSCORERS

*League (68):* Owen 18 (2 pens), McManaman 11, Fowler 9 (2 pens), Ince 8, Leonhardsen 6, Riedle 6, Berger 3, Redknapp 3, McAteer 2, Thomas 1, Thompson 1.
*Coca-Cola Cup (9):* Owen 4 (1 pen), Fowler 3, Berger 1, Redknapp 1.
*FA Cup (1):* Redknapp 1.

| James D 27 | Jones R 20 + 1 | Bjornebye S 24 + 1 | Babb P 18 + 1 | Wright M 6 | Ruddock N 2 | McManaman S 36 | Ince P 31 | Owen M 34 + 2 | Riedle K 18 + 7 | Thomas M 10 + 1 | McAteer J 15 + 6 | Murphy D 6 + 10 | Harkness S 24 + 1 | Matteo D 24 + 2 | Carragher J 17 + 3 | Kvarme B 22 + 1 | Berger P 6 + 16 | Fowler R 19 + 1 | Thompson D 1 + 4 | Leonhardsen O 27 + 1 | Redknapp J 20 | Friedel B 11 | Kennedy M — + 1 | Match No. |
|---|---|---|---|---|---|---|---|---|---|---|---|---|---|---|---|---|---|---|---|---|---|---|---|---|
| 1 | $2^1$ | $3^2$ | 4 | 5 | $6^3$ | 7 | 8 | 9 | 10 | 11 | 12 | 13 | 14 | | | | | | | | | | | 1 |
| 1 | 2 | $3^2$ | $4^1$ | 5 | | 7 | 8 | 9 | 10 | $11^3$ | | 13 | 6 | 12 | 14 | | | | | | | | | 2 |
| 1 | 2 | 3 | | 5 | | 7 | 8 | 9 | $10^1$ | 11 | | | 6 | | | 4 | 12 | | | | | | | 3 |
| 1 | 2 | 3 | | 5 | | 7 | 8 | 9 | $10^1$ | 11 | | | 6 | | | 4 | 12 | | | | | | | 4 |
| 1 | $2^2$ | 3 | | 5 | | 7 | 8 | 9 | $10^1$ | 11 | | 13 | $6^3$ | 14 | | 4 | 12 | | | | | | | 5 |
| 1 | | 3 | | 5 | | 7 | 8 | $9^2$ | $10^1$ | 11 | | | 6 | 2 | | 4 | 12 | 13 | | | | | | 6 |
| 1 | | 3 | | | | 7 | | | 10 | 11 | 12 | | 6 | 2 | $4^2$ | 5 | 13 | $9^1$ | | 8 | | | | 7 |
| 1 | | 3 | | | | 7 | 8 | | 10 | $11^2$ | 12 | 13 | 6 | $2^1$ | $4^3$ | 5 | | 9 | | 14 | | | | 8 |
| 1 | $2^1$ | 3 | | | | 7 | 8 | 9 | 10 | | 12 | | 6 | | 4 | 5 | 11 | | | | | | | 9 |
| 1 | | 3 | | | | 7 | 8 | 9 | $10^1$ | | 12 | 13 | 6 | 2 | 4 | 5 | $11^2$ | | | | | | | 10 |
| 1 | 2 | 3 | | | | 7 | 8 | 9 | 10 | | | | | | 4 | 5 | 11 | | | | 6 | | | 11 |
| 1 | 2 | 3 | | | | 7 | 8 | 9 | $10^1$ | | 12 | | | | 4 | 5 | 11 | | | | 6 | | | 12 |
| 1 | $2^2$ | 3 | | | | $7^3$ | 8 | 9 | $10^1$ | | 12 | 13 | | 14 | 4 | 5 | 11 | | | | 6 | | | 13 |
| 1 | | $3^1$ | | | | 7 | | 9 | 10 | | 12 | | | 2 | 4 | 5 | 11 | | | 8 | 6 | | | 14 |
| 1 | | 3 | | | | 7 | | $9^1$ | 10 | | 12 | | | 2 | 4 | 5 | 11 | | | 8 | 6 | | | 15 |
| 1 | | $3^1$ | | | | 7 | | 9 | 10 | | 12 | 13 | | 2 | $4^2$ | 5 | 11 | | | 8 | 6 | | | 16 |
| 1 | | $3^1$ | | | | 7 | | 9 | 10 | | 12 | 13 | | 2 | 4 | 5 | 11 | | | 8 | $6^2$ | | | 17 |
| 1 | | 3 | | | | 7 | | 9 | 10 | | | | | 2 | 4 | 5 | 11 | | | 8 | 6 | | | 18 |
| 1 | | 3 | | | | 7 | $8^3$ | $9^1$ | 10 | | 12 | 13 | | 2 | 4 | 5 | $11^2$ | | | 14 | 6 | | | 19 |
| 1 | | 3 | | | | 7 | 8 | $9^1$ | 10 | | 12 | | | 2 | 4 | 5 | 11 | | | | 6 | | | 20 |
| 1 | | 3 | 4 | | | 7 | 8 | 9 | 10 | | 12 | | | 2 | | 5 | 11 | | | | $6^1$ | | | 21 |
| 1 | | 3 | 4 | | | 7 | 8 | 9 | $10^1$ | | 12 | | | 2 | | 5 | 11 | | | | 6 | | | 22 |
| 1 | | 3 | 4 | | | 7 | 8 | 9 | 10 | | | | | 2 | | 5 | 11 | | | | 6 | | | 23 |
| 1 | | 3 | 4 | | | $7^2$ | 8 | 9 | 10 | | 12 | 13 | | $2^1$ | | 5 | 11 | | | | 6 | | | 24 |
| 1 | 2 | 3 | 4 | | | 7 | 8 | 9 | 10 | | 12 | 13 | | | | 5 | $11^1$ | | | | $6^2$ | | | 25 |
| 1 | $2^2$ | 3 | | | | 7 | 8 | 9 | 10 | | 12 | 13 | | | $4^1$ | 5 | 11 | | | | 6 | | | 26 |
| 1 | 2 | 3 | | | | 7 | 8 | $9^1$ | 10 | | 12 | | | | 4 | 5 | 11 | | | | 6 | | | 27 |
| | $2^1$ | 3 | | | | 7 | 8 | 9 | 10 | | 12 | 13 | | | 4 | 5 | 11 | | | | $6^2$ | 1 | | 28 |
| | 2 | 3 | | | | 7 | 8 | 9 | $10^1$ | | | | | | 4 | 5 | 11 | | | | 6 | 1 | 12 | 29 |
| | 2 | 3 | | | | 7 | 8 | 9 | $10^2$ | | 12 | 13 | | | 4 | 5 | 11 | | | | $6^1$ | 1 | | 30 |
| | 2 | 3 | 4 | | | 7 | 8 | 9 | 10 | | 12 | | | | | 5 | 11 | | | | 6 | 1 | | 31 |
| | 2 | 3 | 4 | | | 7 | 8 | 9 | $10^1$ | | 12 | | | | | 5 | 11 | | | | 6 | 1 | | 32 |
| | 2 | $3^1$ | 4 | | | 7 | 8 | 9 | $10^2$ | | 12 | 13 | | | | 5 | 11 | | | | 6 | 1 | | 33 |
| | 2 | 3 | 4 | | | 7 | 8 | 9 | 10 | | 12 | | | | | 5 | $11^1$ | | | | 6 | 1 | | 34 |
| | 2 | 3 | 4 | | | 7 | 8 | $9^3$ | $10^2$ | | 12 | 13 | | | | 5 | 11 | | | 14 | $6^1$ | 1 | | 35 |
| | | 3 | 4 | | | 7 | 8 | 9 | 10 | | | | | 2 | | 5 | 11 | | | | 6 | 1 | | 36 |
| | | 3 | 4 | | | 7 | 8 | 9 | $10^2$ | | 12 | 13 | | $2^1$ | | 5 | 11 | | | | 6 | 1 | | 37 |
| | | 3 | 4 | | | 7 | 8 | 9 | 10 | | | | | 2 | | 5 | 11 | | | | 6 | 1 | | 38 |

**Coca-Cola Cup**

| | | | |
|---|---|---|---|
| Third Round | WBA | (a) | 2-0 |
| Fourth Round | Grimsby T | (h) | 3-0 |
| Fifth Round | Newcastle U | (a) | 2-0 |
| Semi-Final | Middlesbrough | (h) | 2-1 |
| | | (a) | 0-2 |

**FA Cup**

| | | | |
|---|---|---|---|
| Third Round | Coventry C | (h) | 1-3 |

LUTON TOWN 1997–98  *Back row (left to right)*: Robert Kean, Sean Evers, Stuart Douglas, Steve Augustine, Andrew Barr, Paul McLaren, Simon Davies, Gary Doherty, Matthew Spring, Ian Jones, Andrew Fotiadis, Richard Harvey, Dwight Marshall.

*Second row*: Bob Bird (Financial Controller), Cherry Newbery (Club Secretary), Clive Goodyear (Physio), Paul Lowe (Youth Development Officer), Wayne Turner (First Team Coach), Paul Showler, David Oldfield, Mitchell Thomas, Nathan Abbey, Ian Feuer, Kelvin Davis, Marvin Johnson, Chris Willmott, Graham Alexander, John Moore (Youth Team Coach), Trevor Peake (Reserve Team Coach), Kathy Leather (Commercial Manager), Les Shannon (Scouting Co-ordinator).

*Third row*: Liam George, Tony Thorpe, Steve Davis, Nigel Terry (Director), David Kohler (Chairman), Lennie Lawrence (Manager), Cliff Bassett (Director), Chris Green (Director), Gary Waddock, Julian James, Terry Sweeney.

*Front row*: Jimmy Cox, Russell Lawes, Stuart Fraser, Darren Howe, James Ayres, Daniel Tate, Nick Webb, Emerson Boyce, Moses Jerry, Michael McIndoe, Andre Scarlett, Delroy McKoy.

# Division 2       **LUTON TOWN**

*Kenilworth Road Stadium, 1 Maple Rd, Luton, Beds LU4 8AW.* Telephone: (01582) 411622. Ticket Office: (01582) 416976. Credit Hotline: (01582) 30748 (24 hrs). Clubcall: 0891 121123.

*Ground capacity:* 9975.

*Record attendance:* 30,069 v Blackpool, FA Cup 6th rd replay, 4 March 1959.

*Record receipts:* £115,541.20 v West Ham U, FA Cup 6th rd, 23 March 1994.

*Pitch measurements:* 110yd × 72yd.

*Chairman & Managing Director:* D. A. Kohler BSC (HONS), ARICS.

*Directors:* C. S. Bassett, C. T. F. Green, N. S. Terry.

*Secretary:* Cherry Newbery.

*Commercial Manager:* Kathy Leather.

*Stadium Manager:* Geoff Lovell.

*Manager:* Lennie Lawrence. *Coach:* John Moore.

*Physio:* Clive Goodyear.

*Year Formed:* 1885. *Turned Professional:* 1890. *Ltd Co.:* 1897.

*Club Nickname:* 'The Hatters'.

*Previous Grounds:* 1885, Excelsior, Dallow Lane; 1897, Dunstable Road; 1905, Kenilworth Road.

*Foundation:* Formed by an amalgamation of two leading local clubs, Wanderers and Excelsior a works team, at a meeting in Luton Town Hall in April 1885. The Wanderers had three months earlier changed their name to Luton Town Wanderers and did not take too kindly to the formation of another Town club but were talked around at this meeting. Wanderers had already appeared in the FA Cup and the new club entered in its inaugural season.

*First Football League game:* 4 September 1897, Division 2, v Leicester Fosse (a) D 1-1 – Williams; McCartney, McEwen; Davies, Stewart, Docherty; Gallacher, Coupar, Birch, McInnes, Ekins (1).

*Record League Victory:* 12–0 v Bristol R, Division 3 (S), 13 April 1936 – Dolman; Mackey, Smith; Finlayson, Nelson, Godfrey; Rich, Martin (1), Payne (10), Roberts (1), Stephenson.

*Record Cup Victory:* 9–0 v Clapton, FA Cup 1st rd (replay after abandoned game), 30 November 1927 – Abbott; Kingham, Graham; Black, Rennie, Fraser; Pointon, Yardley (4), Reid (2), Woods (1), Dennis (2).

*Record Defeat:* 0–9 v Small Heath, Division 2, 12 November 1898.

*Most League Points (2 for a win):* 66, Division 4, 1967–68.

*Most League Points (3 for a win):* 88, Division 2, 1981–82.

*Most League Goals:* 103, Division 3 (S), 1936–37.

*Highest League Scorer in Season:* Joe Payne, 55, Division 3 (S), 1936–37.

*Most League Goals in Total Aggregate:* Gordon Turner, 243, 1949–64.

*Most Capped Player:* Mal Donaghy, 58 (91), Northern Ireland.

*Most League Appearances:* Bob Morton, 494, 1948–64.

*Record Transfer Fee Received:* £2,500,000 from Arsenal for John Hartson, January 1995.

*Record Transfer Fee Paid:* £850,000 to Odense for Lars Elstrup, August 1989.

*Football League Record:* 1897 Elected to Division 2; 1900 Failed re-election; 1920 Division 3; 1921–37 Division 3 (S); 1937–55 Division 2; 1955–60 Division 1; 1960–63 Division 2; 1963–65 Division 3; 1965–68 Division 4; 1968–70 Division 3; 1970–74 Division 2; 1974–75 Division 1; 1975–82 Division 2; 1982–96 Division 1; 1996– Division 2.

*Honours: Football League:* Division 1 best season: 7th, 1986–87; Division 2 – Champions 1981–82; Runners-up 1954–55, 1973–74; Division 3 – Runners-up 1969–70; Division 4 – Champions 1967–68; Division 3 (S) – Champions 1936–37; Runners-up 1935–36. *FA Cup:* Runners-up 1959. *Football League Cup:* Winners 1988; Runners-up 1989. *Simod Cup:* Runners-up 1988.

*Colours:* White shirts with blue shoulder bar, blue shorts with white trim, blue stockings with orange and white trim. *Change colours:* Orange shirts and shorts with blue sides and white trim, yellow stockings.

**Did you know?**
After Joe Payne's 10-goal achievement for Luton Town v Bristol Rovers watched by a crowd of 13,962, the attendance increased to 23,142 for the next home game v Coventry City when Payne scored again in a 1-1 draw.

## LUTON TOWN 1997–98 LEAGUE RECORD

| Match No. | Date | Venue | Opponents | Result | H/T Score | Lg. Pos. | Goalscorers | Attendance |
|---|---|---|---|---|---|---|---|---|
| 1 | Aug 9 | A | Blackpool | L 0-1 | 0-1 | — | | 6547 |
| 2 | 18 | H | Southend U | W 1-0 | 0-0 | — | Douglas 76 | 5140 |
| 3 | 23 | A | Fulham | D 0-0 | 0-0 | 15 | | 8142 |
| 4 | 30 | H | Oldham Ath | D 1-1 | 0-0 | 12 | Thorpe 60 | 5404 |
| 5 | Sept 2 | H | Millwall | L 0-2 | 0-0 | — | | 5781 |
| 6 | 9 | A | Northampton T | L 0-1 | 0-1 | — | | 7246 |
| 7 | 13 | A | Bournemouth | D 1-1 | 1-0 | 21 | Marshall 43 | 4561 |
| 8 | 20 | H | Wrexham | L 2-5 | 1-2 | 23 | Davis S 42, Gray 50 | 5241 |
| 9 | 27 | A | Bristol C | L 0-3 | 0-3 | 23 | | 8509 |
| 10 | Oct 4 | H | Watford | L 0-4 | 0-4 | 23 | | 9041 |
| 11 | 11 | H | Plymouth Arg | W 3-0 | 1-0 | 23 | Thorpe 2 36, 58, Davies 82 | 4931 |
| 12 | 18 | A | Wigan Ath | D 1-1 | 0-0 | 22 | Oldfield 68 | 4466 |
| 13 | 21 | A | Carlisle U | W 1-0 | 0-0 | — | White 87 | 4341 |
| 14 | 25 | H | Brentford | W 2-0 | 1-0 | 18 | Alexander 20, Thorpe 59 | 5972 |
| 15 | Nov 1 | A | Wycombe W | D 2-2 | 1-1 | 18 | Oldfield 45, Thorpe 74 | 6219 |
| 16 | 4 | H | Burnley | L 2-3 | 2-1 | — | Alexander 2 32, 35 | 5315 |
| 17 | 8 | H | Preston NE | L 1-3 | 1-2 | 22 | Thorpe 25 | 5767 |
| 18 | 22 | H | Walsall | L 0-1 | 0-0 | 23 | | 4726 |
| 19 | 29 | A | York C | W 2-1 | 1-0 | 20 | Alexander 13, Thorpe 72 | 3636 |
| 20 | Dec 2 | H | Gillingham | D 2-2 | 1-1 | — | Davis S 26, Thorpe 78 | 4408 |
| 21 | 13 | A | Chesterfield | D 0-0 | 0-0 | 22 | | 4358 |
| 22 | 20 | H | Bristol R | L 2-4 | 2-4 | 22 | Allen C 9, Oldfield 26 | 5266 |
| 23 | 26 | H | Northampton T | D 2-2 | 0-2 | 21 | Oldfield 67, Thorpe 85 | 8035 |
| 24 | 28 | A | Millwall | W 2-0 | 0-0 | 20 | Davis S 89, Thorpe 90 | 7461 |
| 25 | Jan 3 | A | Southend U | W 2-1 | 1-1 | 19 | Alexander 2 2, 61 | 5056 |
| 26 | 10 | A | Blackpool | W 3-0 | 1-0 | 18 | Thorpe 3 33, 74, 75 | 5574 |
| 27 | 17 | A | Oldham Ath | L 1-2 | 0-0 | 18 | Alexander 78 | 6057 |
| 28 | 24 | H | Fulham | L 1-4 | 1-2 | 19 | Thorpe 43 | 8366 |
| 29 | 31 | H | Bournemouth | L 1-2 | 0-1 | 19 | Johnson 72 | 5466 |
| 30 | Feb 7 | A | Wrexham | L 1-2 | 0-0 | 20 | Davis S 89 | 3527 |
| 31 | 14 | A | Watford | D 1-1 | 0-0 | 20 | Johnson 81 | 15,182 |
| 32 | 21 | H | Bristol C | D 0-0 | 0-0 | 21 | | 6405 |
| 33 | 24 | H | Wigan Ath | D 1-1 | 1-1 | — | Oldfield 29 | 4403 |
| 34 | 28 | A | Plymouth Arg | W 2-0 | 0-0 | 19 | Fotiadis 80, Evers 88 | 4846 |
| 35 | Mar 3 | A | Preston NE | L 0-1 | 0-0 | — | | 6992 |
| 36 | 7 | H | Wycombe W | D 0-0 | 0-0 | 21 | | 6114 |
| 37 | 14 | A | Burnley | D 1-1 | 0-0 | 21 | Thomas 79 | 9656 |
| 38 | 21 | H | Grimsby T | D 2-2 | 0-0 | 23 | Evers 67, Davis S 85 | 5700 |
| 39 | 28 | A | Walsall | W 3-2 | 1-0 | 21 | Oldfield 35, Allen R 58, Marshall 73 | 3922 |
| 40 | Apr 4 | H | York C | W 3-0 | 2-0 | 19 | Alexander (pen) 35, Oldfield 45, Gray 85 | 5541 |
| 41 | 7 | A | Grimsby T | W 1-0 | 0-0 | — | Allen R 54 | 4455 |
| 42 | 11 | A | Gillingham | L 1-2 | 1-1 | 19 | Allen R 45 | 6846 |
| 43 | 14 | H | Chesterfield | W 3-0 | 1-0 | — | Williams (og) 24, Allen R 49, Oldfield 64 | 5884 |
| 44 | 18 | A | Bristol R | L 1-2 | 0-2 | 19 | Oldfield 75 | 8038 |
| 45 | 25 | A | Brentford | D 2-2 | 1-1 | 18 | Marshall 13, Allen R 59 | 6598 |
| 46 | May 2 | H | Carlisle U | W 3-2 | 1-0 | 17 | Evers 26, Oldfield 84, Allen R 90 | 6729 |

**Final League Position: 17** 1996–97 DIV2 3

### GOALSCORERS

*League (60):* Thorpe 14, Oldfield 10, Alexander 8 (1 pen), Allen R 6, Davis S 5, Evers 3, Marshall 3, Gray 2, Johnson 2, Allen C 1, Davies 1, Douglas 1, Fotiadis 1, Thomas 1, White 1, own goal 1.
*Coca-Cola Cup (5):* Thorpe 3, Davis S 1, Douglas 1.
*FA Cup (0).*

| Feuer I 13 | McGowan G 6 + 2 | Thomas M 27 + 1 | Waddock G 36 + 2 | Davis S 38 | Johnson M 13 + 1 | McLaren P 41 + 2 | Alexander G 39 | Oldfield D 45 | Thorpe T 27 + 1 | Davies S 8 + 12 | Douglas S 5 + 12 | James J 23 + 1 | Fotiadis A 5 + 10 | Marshall D 19 + 10 | Davis K 32 | Harvey R 5 + 1 | Showler P — + 1 | Evers S 14 + 9 | Doherty G 1 + 9 | Small B 15 | Dibble A 1 | Gray P 14 + 3 | Peake T — + 1 | White A 26 + 2 | George L 1 | Spring M 6 + 6 | Keen R — + 1 | Allen C 14 | Patterson D 23 | Allen R 8 | Fraser S 1 | Match No. |
|---|---|---|---|---|---|---|---|---|---|---|---|---|---|---|---|---|---|---|---|---|---|---|---|---|---|---|---|---|---|---|---|---|
| 1 | 2 | 3 | 4 | 5 | 6 | 7 | 8 | 9 | 10 | 11¹ | 12 | | | | | | | | | | | | | | | | | | | | | 1 |
| 1 | | 3 | 4 | 5 | 6 | 12 | 8 | | 10¹ | 7 | 13 | 2 | 9² | 11 | | | | | | | | | | | | | | | | | | 2 |
| | 12 | 3 | 4 | 5¹ | 6 | 13 | 8² | 9 | | 7 | 10¹ | 2 | | 11 | 1 | 14 | | | | | | | | | | | | | | | | 3 |
| | 12 | 3 | 4 | 5 | 6 | | 8 | 9 | 10 | 7² | 13 | 2¹ | | 11³ | 1 | 14 | | | | | | | | | | | | | | | | 4 |
| | | 3 | 4 | 5 | 6 | 7 | 8³ | 9 | 10 | | 12 | 2² | | 11¹ | 1 | 13 | | | 14 | | | | | | | | | | | | | 5 |
| | 2 | | 4 | 5 | 6 | 7 | 8² | 9 | 10 | | 12 | | | 11¹ | 1 | | | | 13 | | | 3 | | | | | | | | | | 6 |
| | 2 | | 4 | 5 | 6 | 8 | | 9 | 7² | 10¹ | | 11 | | | 1 | 13 | | | 12 | 3 | | | | | | | | | | | | 7 |
| | 2 | | 4¹ | 5 | | 8 | | 9 | 12 | 10 | | 11² | 3³ | 13 | 6 | 1 | 7 | 14 | | | | | | | | | | | | | | 8 |
| | 7¹ | | | 6 | | 11 | 10 | 8 | | | | | | | 1 | 5 | | 2 | | | | 3 | | 4 | | 9² | | 13 | 12 | | | 9 |
| | 2¹ | | 4 | | | 8 | 9 | 10 | 11² | 13 | 12 | | | | 1 | | | | 3 | | | | | 5 | | 7 | | | 6 | | | 10 |
| | | | 4 | | 8 | | 9 | 10² | | | 12 | 2 | | 11¹ | 1 | 5 | | | 13 | | | 3 | | 6 | | 7 | | | | | | 11 |
| | | | | 5 | | 8 | 11 | 9 | 10 | | 12 | 2 | | 13 | 1 | | | | | | | 3 | | 6 | | 7² | | 4¹ | | | | 12 |
| | 12 | | | 5 | | 8 | 11 | 9 | 10 | | | 2 | | 13 | 1 | | | | | | | 3 | | 6 | | 7² | | 4¹ | | | | 13 |
| | | | 4 | 5 | 12 | 8 | 11 | 9 | 10² | | | 2¹ | | 13 | 1 | | | | | | | 3 | | 6 | | 7 | | | | | | 14 |
| | | | 4 | 5 | 6 | 8 | 11 | 9 | 10 | | | 2 | | | 1 | | | | | | | 3 | | | | 7 | | | | | | 15 |
| | | | 4¹ | 5 | 6 | 8 | 11 | 9 | 10 | | | 2 | 12 | | 1 | | | | | | | 3 | | | | 7 | | | | | | 16 |
| | | | 4² | | 6 | 8 | 11 | 9 | 10 | 12 | | 2 | 14 | 13 | 1 | | | | | | | 3¹ | | 7³ | | 5 | | | | | | 17 |
| 1 | | | 4² | | | 8 | 11 | 9 | 10 | 6¹ | 12 | 2 | 7 | | | | | | | | | 3 | | 5 | | 13 | | | | | | 18 |
| 1 | | | 4 | 5 | | 8 | 11 | 9 | 10 | | | 2 | | | | | | | | | | 3 | | 6 | | | | | 7 | | | 19 |
| 1 | 12 | | 4² | 5 | | 8 | 11 | 9 | 10 | | | 2 | | 13 | | | | | | | | 3 | | 6¹ | | | | | 7 | | | 20 |
| 1 | | 3 | 4 | 5 | | 8 | 11 | 9 | 10 | | 12 | 2¹ | | | | | | | | | | | | 6 | | | | | 7 | | | 21 |
| 1 | | 3 | | 5 | | 4¹ | 11 | 9 | 10 | 12 | 8² | 13 | | | | | | | | | | | | 6 | | | | 7 | 2 | | | 22 |
| 1 | | 3 | 4 | 5 | | 8 | 11¹ | 9 | 10 | | 12 | | | | | | | | | | | | | 6 | | | | 7 | 2 | | | 23 |
| 1 | | 3 | 4 | 5 | | 8 | 11 | 9 | 10 | | | | | | | | | | | | | | | 6 | | | | 7 | 2 | | | 24 |
| 1 | | 3 | 4 | 5 | | 8 | 11 | 9 | 10 | | | | | | | | | | | | | | | 6 | | | | 7 | 2 | | | 25 |
| 1 | | 3 | 4 | 5 | | 8 | 11 | 9 | 10 | | | | | | | | | | | | | | | 6 | | | | 7 | 2 | | | 26 |
| 1 | | 3 | 4² | 5 | | | 11 | 9 | 10 | 12 | | 13 | | | | | | | | | | | | 6 | | 8¹ | | 7 | 2 | | | 27 |
| 1 | | 3 | 4 | 5 | | 8 | 11 | 9 | 10 | 12 | | | | | | | | | | | | | | 6¹ | | | | 7 | 2 | | | 28 |
| | | | 4¹ | 5 | 6 | 8² | 11 | 9 | 10 | 12 | | 13 | | | 1 | | | 3 | 14 | | | | | | | | | 7³ | 2 | | | 29 |
| | | | 4¹ | 5 | 6 | 8 | 11 | 9 | 10 | 12 | | | | | 1 | | | 3 | | | | | | | | | | 7 | 2 | | | 30 |
| | | 3 | 4² | | 6¹ | 8 | 11 | 9 | 10 | 12 | | 13 | | | 1 | | | 14 | | | | | | 5 | | | | 7³ | 2 | | | 31 |
| | | 3 | | 5 | | 8 | 11 | 9 | | | 12 | 13 | | | 1 | | | 4² | | | | | | 10 | | 6 | | 7¹ | 2 | | | 32 |
| | | 3 | | 5 | | 8 | 11 | 9 | | | 12 | 7¹ | | | 1 | | | 4 | | | | | | 10 | | 6 | | | 2 | | | 33 |
| | | 3 | 4 | 5 | | 8 | 2 | 9 | | 12² | 11¹ | | | | 1 | | | 7 | 13 | | | | | 10 | | | | 6 | | | | 34 |
| | | 3 | 4 | 5¹ | | 8 | 2 | 9 | | 12 | 13 | 11² | | | 1 | | | 7³ | | | | | | 10 | | | 14 | 6 | | | | 35 |
| | | 3 | | 5 | | 8 | 2 | 9 | | 12 | 13 | 11² | | | 1 | | | 7 | | | | | | 10 | | | 4¹ | 6 | | | | 36 |
| | | 3 | 4¹ | 5 | | 8 | | 9 | | 12 | | 2 | 11² | 13 | 1 | | | 7 | | | | | | 10 | | | | 6 | | | | 37 |
| | | 3 | | 5 | | 8 | 11 | 9 | | 12 | | 2 | 7¹ | 10 | 1 | | | 4 | | | | | | 6 | | | | | | | | 38 |
| | | 3 | 4 | 5 | | 8² | 11 | 9¹ | | | | 2 | 7 | | 1 | | | 13 | 12 | | | 6 | | | | | | | 10 | | | 39 |
| | | 3 | | 5² | | 8 | 11 | 9 | | | | 2 | 7¹ | | 1 | | | 4 | | | | 12 | 13 | 6 | | | | | 10 | | | 40 |
| | | 3 | 4 | | | 8 | 11 | 9¹ | | | | 2 | 7³ | | 1 | | | 14 | 13 | | | 12 | 6 | | | | | 5 | 10² | | | 41 |
| | | 3 | 4² | | | 8 | 11 | 9 | | | | 2³ | 7¹ | | 1 | | | 14 | 13 | | | 12 | 6 | | | | | 5 | 10 | | | 42 |
| | | 3 | 12 | 5 | | | 11 | 9 | | 13 | | 2 | 7 | | 1 | | | 4 | | | | | | | | | | | 6 | 8¹ | 10² | 43 |
| | | 3 | 4³ | 5 | | | 11 | 9 | | 12 | | 2² | 7¹ | | 1 | | | 8 | | | | 13 | 14 | 6 | | | | | 10 | | | 44 |
| | | 3 | 4 | 5 | | 8¹ | 2 | 9 | | 12² | | 11¹ | | | 1 | | | 7 | 13 | | | 6 | | 14 | | | | | 10 | | | 45 |
| | | | | 5 | | 8² | 2 | 9 | | 12 | | 11¹ | | | 1 | | | 7 | 13 | | | 6² | 14 | | | | | 4 | 10 | 3 | | 46 |

**Coca-Cola Cup**

| First Round | Colchester U | (a) | 1-0 |
|---|---|---|---|
| | | (h) | 1-1 |
| Second Round | WBA | (h) | 1-1 |
| | | (a) | 2-4 |

**FA Cup**

| First Round | Torquay U | (h) | 0-1 |
|---|---|---|---|

MACCLESFIELD TOWN 1997–98　*Back row (left to right):* Pete Everson (Fitness Coach), David Gardner, Stuart Whittaker, Richard Landon, Steve Payne, Efetobore Sodje, Steve Hitchen, Andy Mason, Mark Gardiner, Peter Davenport (Player/Coach).

*Middle row:* Steve Wade (Physio), Dennis Ohandjanian, Colin Rose, Steve Wood, Glyn Clyde, Ryan Price, Nathan Peel, Neil Sorvel, Andy Levendis, Eric Campbell (Assistant Physio).

*Front row:* Darren Tinson, Neil Mitchell, Sammy McIlroy (Manager), Neil Howarth, Gil Prescott (Assistant Manager), Phil Power, John Askey.

# Division 2 **MACCLESFIELD TOWN**

*The Moss Rose Ground, London Road, Macclesfield, Cheshire SK11 7SP.* Telephone: (01625) 264686. Fax: (01625) 264692. Commercial Office: (01625) 264693. Social Club: (01625) 424324. Press Box: (01625) 264690/1. Club Call Line: 0930 555835.

*Ground Capacity:* 6028 (seated 1053, standing 4975).

*Record attendance:* 9008 v Winsford U, Cheshire Senior Cup 2nd rd, 4 February 1948.

*Pitch measurements:* 100m × 66m.

*Chairman:* Alan Cash.

*Directors:* Harry Armstrong, John Brooks, Alan Cash, Reg Flowers, Colin Garlick, Roy Higginbotham, John Chesworth.

*Manager:* Sammy McIlroy.

*Secretary:* Colin Garlick.

*Administration Manager:* Dianne Hehir.

*Commercial Manager:* Jackie Birks.

*Club Doctor:* Dr Mike Whiteside.

*Year formed:* 1874.

*Club Nickname:* 'The Silkmen'.

*Foundation:* From the mid-19th Century until 1874, Macclesfield Town FC played under rugby rules. In 1891 they moved to the Moss Rose and finished champions of the Manchester & District League in 1906 and 1908. By 1911, they had carried off the Cheshire Senior Cup five times. Macclesfield were founder members of the Cheshire County League in 1919.

*Record Win:* 15-0 v Chester St Marys, Cheshire Senior Cup, 2nd rd, 16 February 1886.

*Record Defeat:* 1-13 v Tranmere R reserves, 3 May 1929.

*Most League Points (3 for a win):* 82, Division 3, 1997–98.

*Most League Goals:* 63, Division 3, 1997–98.

*Highest League Scorer in Season:* Steve Wood, 13, Division 3, 1997–98.

*Most League Appearances:* Ryan Price, 46, 1997–98.

*Record Transfer Fee Received:* £40,000 from Sheffield U for Mike Lake, 1988.

*Record Transfer Fee Paid:* £30,000 to Stevenage Borough for Efetobore Sodje, August 1997.

*Honours: Football League:* Division 3 – Runners-up 1997–98. *Vauxhall Conference:* Champions 1994–95, 1996–97. *FA Trophy:* Winners 1969–70, 1995–96; Runners-up 1988–89. *Bob Lord Trophy:* Winners 1993–94; Runners-up 1995–96, 1996–97. *Vauxhall Conference Championship Shield:* Winners 1996, 1997, 1998. *Northern Premier League:* Winners 1968–69, 1969–70, 1986–87; Runners-up 1984–85. *Northern Premier League Challenge Cup:* Winners 1986–87; Runners-up 1969–70, 1970–71, 1982–83. *Northern Premier League Presidents Cup:* Winners 1986–87; Runners-up 1984–85. *Cheshire Senior Cup:* Winners 19 times; Runners-up 11.

*Colours:* Royal blue shirts, white shorts, blue stockings. *Change Colours:* White shirts, royal blue shorts, white stockings.

**Did you know?**
Goalkeeper Ryan Price rushed from hospital following the birth of his first child to become Man of the Match in the 1-0 win over Leyton Orient on 14 February 1998.

## MACCLESFIELD TOWN 1997–98 LEAGUE RECORD

| Match No. | Date | | Venue | Opponents | Result | | H/T Score | Lg. Pos. | Goalscorers | Attendance |
|---|---|---|---|---|---|---|---|---|---|---|
| 1 | Aug | 9 | H | Torquay U | W | 2-1 | 1-1 | — | Sodje 7, Landon 59 | 3379 |
| 2 | | 16 | A | Brighton & HA | D | 1-1 | 1-0 | 5 | Landon 38 | 2336 |
| 3 | | 23 | H | Doncaster R | W | 3-0 | 1-0 | 1 | Brookes (og) 44, Askey 72, Landon (pen) 90 | 2635 |
| 4 | | 30 | A | Hartlepool U | D | 0-0 | 0-0 | 4 | | 2283 |
| 5 | Sept | 2 | A | Rochdale | L | 0-2 | 0-0 | — | | 2197 |
| 6 | | 5 | H | Darlington | W | 2-1 | 0-1 | — | Power 2 50, 88 | 2459 |
| 7 | | 13 | H | Swansea C | W | 3-0 | 1-0 | 2 | Gardiner 42, Peel 63, Askey 66 | 2479 |
| 8 | | 20 | A | Scarborough | L | 1-2 | 1-1 | 6 | Peel 38 | 2256 |
| 9 | | 27 | H | Peterborough U | D | 1-1 | 0-0 | 6 | Landon (pen) 87 | 3079 |
| 10 | Oct | 4 | A | Leyton Orient | D | 1-1 | 0-1 | 7 | Landon 90 | 4522 |
| 11 | | 11 | A | Notts Co | D | 1-1 | 0-1 | 6 | Wood 74 | 4871 |
| 12 | | 18 | H | Mansfield T | W | 1-0 | 0-0 | 4 | Cooper 59 | 3277 |
| 13 | | 21 | H | Exeter C | D | 2-2 | 0-2 | — | Whittaker 69, Cooper 73 | 2286 |
| 14 | | 25 | A | Chester C | D | 1-1 | 0-0 | 8 | Landon 51 | 3245 |
| 15 | Nov | 1 | A | Rotherham U | L | 0-1 | 0-0 | 10 | | 3649 |
| 16 | | 4 | H | Colchester U | D | 0-0 | 0-0 | — | | 1577 |
| 17 | | 8 | H | Cambridge U | W | 3-1 | 2-0 | 7 | Gardiner 21, Power 2 23, 88 | 2337 |
| 18 | | 18 | A | Shrewsbury T | L | 3-4 | 2-1 | — | Griffiths (og) 35, Wood 39, Power 74 | 2600 |
| 19 | | 22 | H | Hull C | W | 2-0 | 1-0 | 8 | Peel 37, Landon 87 | 2508 |
| 20 | | 29 | A | Lincoln C | D | 1-1 | 1-0 | 10 | Whittaker 14 | 3402 |
| 21 | Dec | 13 | A | Barnet | L | 1-3 | 0-0 | 13 | Wood 68 | 1710 |
| 22 | | 20 | H | Cardiff C | W | 1-0 | 0-0 | 12 | Wood 95 | 2398 |
| 23 | | 26 | A | Darlington | L | 2-4 | 0-1 | 12 | Devos (og) 48, Askey 90 | 3042 |
| 24 | | 28 | H | Rochdale | W | 1-0 | 0-0 | 12 | Howarth (pen) 52 | 2666 |
| 25 | Jan | 10 | A | Torquay U | L | 0-2 | 0-1 | 12 | | 2428 |
| 26 | | 17 | H | Hartlepool U | W | 2-1 | 0-0 | 12 | Chambers 52, Wood 72 | 2334 |
| 27 | | 20 | H | Scunthorpe U | W | 2-0 | 2-0 | — | Chambers 2 7, 37 | 1450 |
| 28 | | 24 | A | Doncaster R | W | 3-0 | 1-0 | 8 | Sorvel 10, Wood 2 54, 81 | 1707 |
| 29 | | 27 | H | Brighton & HA | W | 1-0 | 0-0 | — | Whittaker 53 | 2024 |
| 30 | | 31 | A | Swansea C | D | 1-1 | 1-1 | 5 | Howarth 8 | 3293 |
| 31 | Feb | 7 | H | Scarborough | W | 3-3 | 3-0 | 4 | Askey 14, Wood 15, Howarth 44 | 2488 |
| 32 | | 14 | H | Leyton Orient | W | 1-0 | 1-0 | 3 | McDonald 14 | 2725 |
| 33 | | 21 | A | Peterborough U | W | 1-0 | 0-0 | 2 | Askey 70 | 6224 |
| 34 | | 24 | A | Mansfield T | L | 0-1 | 0-0 | — | | 2683 |
| 35 | | 28 | H | Notts Co | W | 2-0 | 0-0 | 3 | Askey 50, Wood 70 | 5122 |
| 36 | Mar | 3 | A | Cambridge U | D | 0-0 | 0-0 | — | | 2012 |
| 37 | | 7 | H | Rotherham U | D | 0-0 | 0-0 | 3 | | 3156 |
| 38 | | 14 | A | Colchester U | L | 1-5 | 1-1 | 5 | Whittaker 38 | 2760 |
| 39 | | 21 | H | Shrewsbury T | W | 2-0 | 0-0 | 3 | Chambers 49, Wood 81 | 3013 |
| 40 | | 28 | A | Hull C | D | 0-0 | 0-0 | 3 | | 3677 |
| 41 | Apr | 4 | H | Lincoln C | W | 1-0 | 0-0 | 3 | Wood 88 | 3278 |
| 42 | | 11 | A | Scunthorpe U | L | 0-1 | 0-1 | 3 | | 2949 |
| 43 | | 13 | H | Barnet | W | 2-0 | 2-0 | 2 | Sodje 10, Power 25 | 4171 |
| 44 | | 18 | A | Cardiff C | W | 2-1 | 0-1 | 2 | Sodje 58, Sorvel 79 | 2497 |
| 45 | | 25 | H | Chester C | W | 3-2 | 1-0 | 2 | Wood 14, Sorvel 49, Power 59 | 5982 |
| 46 | May | 2 | A | Exeter C | W | 3-1 | 1-0 | 2 | Wood 12, Davenport 51, Philliskirk 59 | 4499 |

**Final League Position: 2**        1996–97 VAUXHALL CONFERENCE 1

### GOALSCORERS
*League (63):* Wood 13, Landon 7 (2 pens), Power 7, Askey 6, Chambers 4, Whittaker 4, Howarth 3 (1 pen), Peel 3, Sodje 3, Sorvel 3, Cooper 2, Gardiner 2, Davenport 1, McDonald 1, Philliskirk 1, own goals 3.
*Coca-Cola Cup (1):* Mason 1.
*FA Cup (4):* Whittaker 2, Wood 2.

| Price R 46 | Tinson D 44 | Rose C 15+4 | Payne S 39 | Howarth N 38+3 | Sodje E 41 | Askey J 37+2 | Wood S 43 | Landon R 6+12 | Mason A 7+5 | Sorvel N 41+4 | Edey C 9+4 | Power P 21+17 | Mitchell N 2+4 | Peel N 10+4 | Gardiner M 7 | Hitchen S 1+1 | Davenport P 2+2 | Cooper M 8 | Whittaker S 29+2 | Irving R 6+3 | McDonald M 22 | Brown G 2 | Chambers L 17+4 | Phillskirk T 1+9 | Ingram R 5 | Sedgemore B 5 | Durkan K 2+2 | Match No. |
|---|---|---|---|---|---|---|---|---|---|---|---|---|---|---|---|---|---|---|---|---|---|---|---|---|---|---|---|---|
| 1 | 2 | 3 | 4¹ | 5 | 6 | 7 | 8 | 9² | 10 | 11 | 12 | 13 | | | | | | | | | | | | | | | | 1 |
| 1 | 2 | 3 | 4 | 5 | 6 | 7 | 8 | 9¹ | 10 | 11 | | 12 | | | | | | | | | | | | | | | | 2 |
| 1 | 2 | 3 | 4 | 5 | 6 | 7¹ | 8 | 9 | 10¹ | 11 | | 12 | 13 | | | | | | | | | | | | | | | 3 |
| 1 | 2 | 3 | 4 | 5 | 6 | 7² | 8 | 9 | 10¹ | 11 | | 12 | 13 | | | | | | | | | | | | | | | 4 |
| 1 | 2 | 3 | 4 | 5 | 6 | 7¹ | 8 | 12 | 9 | 11² | | 10 | 13 | | | | | | | | | | | | | | | 5 |
| 1 | 2 | 3 | 4 | 5 | 6 | 12 | 8¹ | | 13 | 11 | | 10 | 7 | 9² | | | | | | | | | | | | | | 6 |
| 1 | 2 | 3 | 4³ | 5 | 6 | 12 | | | 13 | 11 | | 10² | 7¹ | 9 | 8 | 14 | | | | | | | | | | | | 7 |
| 1 | 2 | 3 | | 5 | 6 | 7 | | 12 | 13 | 11 | | 10¹ | | 9 | 8 | 4² | 14 | | | | | | | | | | | 8 |
| 1 | 2 | 3 | | 5 | 6 | 7 | | | 12 | 11 | | 10¹ | | 9 | 4 | | | 8 | | | | | | | | | | 9 |
| 1 | 2² | 3¹ | | 5 | 6 | 7 | 8 | 12 | | 11 | 13 | | 9¹ | 4 | | | | 10 | 14 | | | | | | | | | 10 |
| 1 | 2 | | | 5 | 6 | 7 | 8 | | | 11 | 3 | 10 | | | | | | 4 | 9 | | | | | | | | | 11 |
| 1 | 2 | 12 | | 5 | 6 | 7² | 8¹ | 13 | | 11 | 3 | 10¹ | | | | | | 4 | 9 | 14 | | | | | | | | 12 |
| 1 | 2 | | | 5 | 6 | 7 | 8 | | | 11 | 3 | 12 | | | | | | 4 | 9 | 10¹ | | | | | | | | 13 |
| 1 | 2 | | 4 | 5 | 6 | 7¹ | 8 | 12 | | 11 | | 13 | | | | | | 3 | 9 | 10² | | | | | | | | 14 |
| 1 | 2 | 3 | 4 | 5 | 6 | | 8 | 9¹ | | 11 | | 12 | 13 | | | | | 7² | | 10 | | | | | | | | 15 |
| 1 | 2 | | 4 | | 6 | | 8 | 9² | | 11 | 12 | 13 | | | | | | 3 | 7 | 5 | 10¹ | | | | | | | 16 |
| 1 | 2 | 5 | 4 | 12 | 6 | | 8 | | 13 | 11 | | 10 | 9² | | | | | 3¹ | | | 7 | | | | | | | 17 |
| 1 | 2 | 3¹ | 5 | | 6 | | 8 | 12 | | 11 | | 10 | 9² | | | | | 4 | | | 7 | | 13 | | | | | 18 |
| 1 | 2 | 5 | 4 | 3 | 6 | | 8 | 12 | | 11 | | 10 | 9¹ | | | | | | | | 7² | | 13 | | | | | 19 |
| 1 | 2 | 5 | 4 | 3 | 6 | | 8² | 12 | | 11 | | 10 | 13 | 9¹ | | | | | | | 7 | | | | | | | 20 |
| 1 | 2 | | 4 | 3 | 6 | 7 | 8 | 12 | | 11 | | 10 | 9¹ | | | | | | | | | 5 | | | | | | 21 |
| 1 | 2 | 12 | 4 | 5 | | 7 | 8¹ | | | 11 | 3 | 10 | 13 | | | | | | | | 9² | 6 | | | | | | 22 |
| 1 | 2¹ | 12 | 4 | 5 | | 7 | 8 | | | 11 | 3 | 10 | 13 | | | | | | | | 9² | 6 | | | | | | 23 |
| 1 | | | 4 | 5 | | 7 | 8 | 12 | | 11 | | 10 | 9¹ | | | | | | | | 6 | 3 | | | | | | 24 |
| 1 | 12 | | 5 | 6 | 7³ | 8 | 13 | | | 11 | 2 | 10² | 14 | | | | | | 4¹ | | 3 | | 9 | | | | | 25 |
| 1 | 2 | 4 | 3 | | 6 | 7 | 8 | | | 10 | | | | | | | | | 11 | | 5 | | 9 | | | | | 26 |
| 1 | 2 | 4 | 3 | | 6 | 7¹ | 8 | | | 10 | | 12 | | | | | | | 11 | | 5 | | 9 | | | | | 27 |
| 1 | 2 | 4 | 3¹ | | 6 | 7⁴ | 8 | | | 10 | | 12 | 13 | | | | | | 11 | | 5 | | 9 | | | | | 28 |
| 1 | 2 | 4 | 3 | | 6 | 7 | 8 | | | 10 | | 12 | | | | | | | 11 | | 5 | | 9¹ | | | | | 29 |
| 1 | 2 | 4 | 3 | | 6 | 7 | 8 | | | 10 | | | | | | | | | 11 | | 5 | | 9 | | | | | 30 |
| 1 | 2 | 4 | 3 | | 6 | 7¹ | 8 | | | 10 | | 12 | | | | | | | 11 | | 5 | | 9 | | | | | 31 |
| 1 | 2 | 4 | 5 | | 6 | 7² | 8 | | | 10 | | 12 | | | | | | | 11¹ | | 3 | | 9 | 13 | | | | 32 |
| 1 | 2 | 4 | 5 | | 6 | 7 | 8 | | | 10 | | | | | | | | | 11 | | 3 | | 9 | | | | | 33 |
| 1 | 2 | 4 | 5 | | 6 | 7 | 8 | | | 10 | | 12 | | | | | | | 11 | | | | 9¹ | 3 | | | | 34 |
| 1 | 2 | 4 | 3 | | 6 | 7 | 8 | | | 10 | | 5 | | | | | | | 11 | | | | 9¹ | 12 | | | | 35 |
| 1 | 2 | 4 | 5 | | 6 | 7¹ | 8 | | | 10 | | 12 | | | | | | | 11 | | 3 | | 9² | 13 | | | | 36 |
| 1 | 2 | 4 | 5 | | | 7² | 8 | | | 10 | | 6 | | 12 | | | | | 11 | | | | 9¹ | 13 | | | | 37 |
| 1 | 2 | 4 | 5 | | | 7 | 8 | | | 10 | | 6 | | 12 | | | | | 11² | | 3 | | 9¹ | 13 | | | | 38 |
| 1 | 2 | 4 | | | 6 | 7 | 8 | | | 10 | | 11¹ | | | | | | | 3 | | | | 9 | 12 | 5 | 10 | | 39 |
| 1 | 2 | 4 | | | 6 | 7 | 8 | | 12 | | | 11 | | | | | | | | | 9² | 13 | | | 5 | 10 | 3¹ | 40 |
| 1 | 2 | 4 | 12 | | 6 | 7¹ | 8 | 9² | 13 | | | 11² | | | | | | | 3 | | 14 | | | | 5 | 10 | | 41 |
| 1 | 2 | 4 | 12 | | 6 | | 8² | 9¹ | 13 | | | 11³ | | | | | | | 3 | | 7 | | 14 | | 5 | 10 | | 42 |
| 1 | 2 | | 4 | 5 | 6 | 7² | 8 | | | 12 | | 10¹ | | | | | | | 11³ | | 3 | | 13 | | 9 | 14 | | 43 |
| 1 | 2 | | 4 | 5 | 6 | 7² | 8 | 9 | | 10 | 12 | | | | | | | | 12 | | 3 | | 13 | | | 11¹ | | 44 |
| 1 | 2 | | 4 | | 6 | 7¹ | 8 | 9 | | 10 | | 11² | | | | | | | | | 3 | | 12 | | 5 | 13 | | 45 |
| 1 | 2¹ | | 4 | 5 | 6 | 7³ | 8 | | 13 | 9 | 12 | 10 | | | | | 3² | | 11 | | | | 14 | | | | | 46 |

**Coca-Cola Cup**
First Round    Hull C    (h)  0-0
                         (a)  1-2

**FA Cup**
First Round    Hartlepool U    (a)  4-2
Second Round   Walsall         (h)  0-7

MANCHESTER CITY 1997–98    Back row (left to right): Ian Brightwell, Alan Kernaghan, Kevin Horlock, Uwe Rosler, Nick Summerbee, Lee Crooks, John Foster, Lee Bradbury, Tony Vaughan, Paul Beesley.

Middle row: Roy Bailey (Physio), Ronnie Evans (Assistant Physio), Richard Money (First Team Coach), Eddie McGoldrick, Neil Heaney, Ged Brannan, Martyn Margetson, Tommy Wright, Gerard Wiekens, Rae Ingram, Chris Greenacre, George Smith (Director of School of Excellence), Alex Stepney (Goalkeeping Coach), Ian Miller (Youth Team Coach).

Front row: Peter Edwards (Fitness Trainer), Nigel Clough, Gerry Creaney, Paul Dickov, Scott Thomas, Georgi Kinkladze, Frank Clark (Manager), Alan Hill (Assistant Manager), Kit Symons, Scott Hiley, Richard Edghill, Michael Brown, Martin Phillips, Asa Hartford (Coach).

(Photograph: Professional Sport International)

# Division 2 **MANCHESTER CITY**

*Maine Road, Moss Side, Manchester M14 7WN.* Telephone: (0161) 224 5000. Fax: (0161) 248 8449. Ticket Office: (0161) 226 2224. Dial-A-Seat: (0161) 227 9229. Development Office: (0161) 226 3143. Clubcall: 0891 121191. Ticketcall: 0891 121591.

*Ground capacity:* 31,458.

*Record attendance:* 84,569 v Stoke C, FA Cup 6th rd, 3 March 1934 (British record for any game outside London or Glasgow).

*Record receipts:* £512,235 Manchester U v Oldham Ath, FA Cup semi-final replay, 13 April 1994.

*Pitch measurements:* 117yd × 78yd.

*Chairman:* D. A. Bernstein. *Chief Executive:* M. Turner.

*Directors:* J. Wardle, D. Tueart, A. Lewis, A. Thomas, M. Turner.

*General Secretary:* J. B. Halford. *Commercial Manager:* Geoff Durbin.

*Manager:* Joe Royle. *Assistant Manager:* Alan Hill. *First Team Coaches:* Willie Donachie, Asa Hartford. *Physio:* Roy Bailey. *Youth Team Coach:* Neil McNab.

*Year Formed:* 1887 as Ardwick FC; 1894 as Manchester City.

*Turned Professional:* 1887 as Ardwick FC. *Ltd Co.:* 1894. *Club Nickname:* 'Blues' The Citizens.

*Previous Names:* 1887–94, Ardwick FC (formed through the amalgamation of West Gorton and Gorton Athletic, the latter having been formed in 1880).

*Previous Grounds:* 1880–81, Clowes Street; 1881–82, Kirkmanshulme Cricket Ground; 1882–84, Queens Road; 1884–87, Pink Bank Lane; 1887–1923, Hyde Road (1894–1923, as City); 1923, Maine Road.

*Foundation:* Manchester City was formed as a Limited Company in 1894 after their predecessors Ardwick had been forced into bankruptcy. However, many historians like to trace the club's lineage as far back as 1880 when St. Mark's Church, West Gorton added a football section to their cricket club. They amalgamated with Gorton Athletic in 1884 as Gorton FC. Because of a change of ground they became Ardwick in 1887.

*First Football League game:* 3 September 1892, Division 2, v Bootle (h) W 7-0 – Douglas; McVickers, Robson; Middleton, Russell, Hopkins; Davies (3), Morris (2), Angus (1), Weir (1), Milarvie.

*Record League Victory:* 10–1 v Huddersfield T, Division 2, 7 November 1987 – Nixon; Gidman, Hinchcliffe, Clements, Lake, Redmond, White (3), Stewart (3), Adcock (3), McNab (1) Simpson.

*Record Cup Victory:* 10–1 v Swindon T, FA Cup 4th rd, 29 January 1930 – Barber; Felton, McCloy; Barrass, Cowan, Heinemann; Toseland, Marshall (5), Tait (3), Johnson (1), Brook (1).

*Record Defeat:* 1–9 v Everton, Division 1, 3 September 1906.

*Most League Points (2 for a win):* 62, Division 2, 1946–47.

*Most League Points (3 for a win):* 82, Division 2, 1988–89.

*Most League Goals:* 108, Division 2, 1926–27.

*Highest League Scorer in Season:* Tommy Johnson, 38, Division 1, 1928–29.

*Most League Goals in Total Aggregate:* Tommy Johnson, 158, 1919–30.

*Most Capped Player:* Colin Bell, 48, England.

*Most League Appearances:* Alan Oakes, 565, 1959–76.

*Record Transfer Fee Received:* £4,925,000 from Ajax for Georgi Kinkladze, May 1998.

*Record Transfer Fee Paid:* £3,000,000 to Portsmouth for Lee Bradbury, July 1997.

*Football League Record:* 1892 Ardwick elected founder member of Division 2; 1894 Newly-formed Manchester C elected to Division 2; Division 1 1899–1902, 1903–09, 1910–26, 1928–38, 1947–50, 1951–63, 1966–83, 1985–87, 1989–92; Division 2 1902–03, 1909–10, 1926–28, 1938–47, 1950–51, 1963–66, 1983–85, 1987–96 FA Premier League; 1992–96 Division 1; 1998– Division 2.

*Honours: Football League:* Division 1 – Champions 1936–37, 1967–68; Runners-up 1903–04, 1920–21, 1976–77; Division 2 – Champions 1898–99, 1902–03, 1909–10, 1927–28, 1946–47, 1965–66; Runners-up 1895–96, 1950–51, 1987–88. *FA Cup:* Winners 1904, 1934, 1956, 1969; Runners-up 1926, 1933, 1955, 1981. *Football League Cup:* Winners 1970, 1976; Runners-up 1974. **European Competitions:** *European Cup:* 1968–69. *European Cup-Winners' Cup:* 1969–70 (winners), 1970–71. *UEFA Cup:* 1972–73, 1976–77, 1977–78, 1978–79.

*Colours:* Lazer blue shirts, white shorts, navy stockings. *Change colours:* Yellow and navy shirts, navy shorts, navy stockings.

**Did you know?**
In 1946-47 Manchester City's Maine Road ground saw 2.2 million people pass through its turnstiles. The FA Cup semi-final replay between Liverpool and Burnley and the Rugby League Challenge Cup Final were both played there.

## MANCHESTER CITY 1997–98 LEAGUE RECORD

| Match No. | Date | Venue | Opponents | Result | H/T Score | Lg. Pos. | Goalscorers | Attendance |
|---|---|---|---|---|---|---|---|---|
| 1 | Aug 9 | H | Portsmouth | D 2-2 | 1-1 | — | Rosler [16], Wiekens [55] | 30,474 |
| 2 | 15 | A | Sunderland | L 1-3 | 0-1 | — | Kinkladze (pen) [76] | 38,894 |
| 3 | 22 | H | Tranmere R | D 1-1 | 0-0 | — | Horlock [46] | 26,336 |
| 4 | 30 | A | Charlton Ath | L 1-2 | 1-0 | 20 | Wiekens [20] | 14,009 |
| 5 | Sept 3 | A | Nottingham F | W 3-1 | 1-0 | — | Brannan 2 [20, 71], Dickov [88] | 23,681 |
| 6 | 12 | A | Bury | D 1-1 | 0-0 | — | Morley [81] | 11,216 |
| 7 | 20 | H | Norwich C | L 1-2 | 1-1 | 20 | Bradbury [27] | 27,258 |
| 8 | 27 | H | Swindon T | W 6-0 | 3-0 | 16 | Kinkladze [7], Casper (og) [17], Horlock [37], Dickov 2 [50, 59], Bradbury [80] | 26,646 |
| 9 | Oct 4 | A | Ipswich T | L 0-1 | 0-0 | 21 | | 14,322 |
| 10 | 18 | H | Reading | D 0-0 | 0-0 | 21 | | 26,488 |
| 11 | 22 | H | Stoke C | L 0-1 | 0-0 | — | | 25,333 |
| 12 | 26 | A | QPR | L 0-2 | 0-2 | 22 | | 14,451 |
| 13 | 29 | H | Crewe Alex | W 1-0 | 1-0 | — | Greenacre [44] | 27,384 |
| 14 | Nov 1 | A | Oxford U | D 0-0 | 0-0 | 20 | | 8592 |
| 15 | 4 | H | Port Vale | L 2-3 | 2-2 | — | Wiekens [15], Dickov [41] | 24,554 |
| 16 | 7 | H | Huddersfield T | L 0-1 | 0-0 | — | | 24,425 |
| 17 | 15 | A | Sheffield U | D 1-1 | 0-1 | 22 | Horlock [90] | 23,780 |
| 18 | 22 | H | Bradford C | W 1-0 | 0-0 | 20 | Vaughan [90] | 29,746 |
| 19 | 29 | A | Stockport Co | L 1-3 | 0-3 | 21 | Brannan [49] | 11,351 |
| 20 | Dec 2 | A | WBA | W 1-0 | 0-0 | — | Dickov [55] | 17,904 |
| 21 | 6 | H | Wolverhampton W | L 0-1 | 0-1 | 18 | | 28,999 |
| 22 | 13 | A | Birmingham C | L 1-2 | 0-0 | 21 | Shelia [88] | 21,014 |
| 23 | 20 | H | Middlesbrough | W 2-0 | 2-0 | 19 | Rosler (pen) [17], Dickov [32] | 28,097 |
| 24 | 26 | A | Crewe Alex | L 0-1 | 0-1 | 20 | | 5759 |
| 25 | 28 | H | Nottingham F | L 2-3 | 0-1 | 20 | Shelia [56], Dickov [77] | 31,839 |
| 26 | Jan 10 | A | Portsmouth | W 3-0 | 1-0 | 18 | Russell [44], Kinkladze [51], Rosler [89] | 13,512 |
| 27 | 17 | H | Sunderland | L 0-1 | 0-0 | 21 | | 31,715 |
| 28 | 28 | A | Charlton Ath | D 2-2 | 1-0 | — | Dickov (pen) [7], Symons [88] | 24,058 |
| 29 | 31 | A | Tranmere R | D 0-0 | 0-0 | 20 | | 12,830 |
| 30 | Feb 7 | A | Norwich C | D 0-0 | 0-0 | 21 | | 15,274 |
| 31 | 14 | H | Bury | L 0-1 | 0-0 | 22 | | 28,885 |
| 32 | 18 | H | Ipswich T | L 1-2 | 1-0 | — | Symons [5] | 27,156 |
| 33 | 21 | A | Swindon T | W 3-1 | 1-0 | 22 | Rosler 2 [22, 77], Bradbury [83] | 12,280 |
| 34 | 24 | A | Reading | L 0-3 | 0-2 | — | | 11,513 |
| 35 | 28 | H | WBA | W 1-0 | 1-0 | 20 | Rosler [43] | 28,460 |
| 36 | Mar 3 | A | Huddersfield T | W 3-1 | 2-1 | — | Wiekens [10], Briscoe [45], Tskhadadze [65] | 15,694 |
| 37 | 7 | A | Oxford U | L 0-2 | 0-1 | 20 | | 28,720 |
| 38 | 14 | H | Port Vale | L 1-2 | 0-1 | 22 | Wiekens [61] | 13,122 |
| 39 | 21 | H | Sheffield U | D 0-0 | 0-0 | 22 | | 28,496 |
| 40 | 28 | A | Bradford C | L 1-2 | 1-0 | 22 | Whitley Jeffrey [24] | 17,099 |
| 41 | Apr 4 | A | Stockport Co | W 4-1 | 3-1 | 21 | Goater [5], Jobson [32], Bradbury 2 [37, 57] | 31,855 |
| 42 | 11 | A | Wolverhampton W | D 2-2 | 1-1 | 21 | Pollock [13], Horlock [63] | 24,458 |
| 43 | 13 | H | Birmingham C | L 0-1 | 0-0 | 21 | | 29,569 |
| 44 | 17 | A | Middlesbrough | L 0-1 | 0-1 | — | | 30,182 |
| 45 | 25 | H | QPR | D 2-2 | 1-2 | 23 | Kinkladze [1], Bradbury [48] | 32,040 |
| 46 | May 3 | A | Stoke C | W 5-2 | 1-0 | 22 | Goater 2 [32, 71], Dickov [49], Bradbury [64], Horlock [90] | 26,664 |

**Final League Position: 22**    1996–97 DIV1 14

### GOALSCORERS
*League (56):* Dickov 9 (1 pen), Bradbury 7, Horlock 5, Wiekens 5, Kinkladze 4 (1 pen), Brannan 3, Goater 3, Shelia 2, Symons 2, Briscoe 1, Greenacre 1, Jobson 1, Morley 1, Pollock 1, Russell 1, Tskhadadze 1, Vaughan 1, Jeff Whitley 1, own goal 1.
*Coca-Cola Cup (1):* Horlock 1.
*FA Cup (3):* Brown 1, Kinkladze 1, Rosler 1.

| Margetson M 28 | Brightwell I 19+2 | Vaughan T 19 | Wiekens G 35+2 | Symons K 42 | Beesley P 4+3 | Brannan G 27+5 | Horlock K 25 | Bradbury L 23+4 | Kinkladze G 29+1 | Rosler U 23+6 | Summerbee N 4+5 | Dickov P 21+9 | Kernaghan A 1 | Van Blerk J 10+9 | McGoldrick E 6+1 | Scully T 1+8 | Edghill R 36 | Morley D 1+2 | Conlon B 1+6 | Heaney N 3 | Wright T 18 | Whitley Jeff 14+3 | Greenacre C 2+1 | Brown M 18+8 | Kelly R 1 | Creaney G 1 | Russell C 17+7 | Shelia M 12 | Whitley Jim 17+2 | Crooks L 3+2 | Tskhadadze K 10 | Beardsley P 5+1 | Briscoe L 5 | Jobson R 6 | Pollock J 8 | Goater S 7 | Bishop I 4+2 | Match No. |
|---|---|---|---|---|---|---|---|---|---|---|---|---|---|---|---|---|---|---|---|---|---|---|---|---|---|---|---|---|---|---|---|---|---|---|---|---|---|---|
| 1 | 2 | 3 | 4 | 5 | 6¹ | 7 | 8 | 9 | 10 | 11¹² | 12 | 13 |  |  |  |  |  |  |  |  |  |  |  |  |  |  |  |  |  |  |  |  |  |  |  |  |  | 1 |
| 1 | 2 | 3 | 4 | 5 |  | 7¹ | 8 | 9 | 10 | 11¹² | 12 |  |  |  | 6 | 13 |  |  |  |  |  |  |  |  |  |  |  |  |  |  |  |  |  |  |  |  |  | 2 |
| 1 | 2 | 3 | 4 | 5 | 6 | 7 | 8 | 9 | 10 | 11¹² | 12 |  |  |  |  |  |  |  |  |  |  |  |  |  |  |  |  |  |  |  |  |  |  |  |  |  |  | 3 |
| 1 | 2 |  | 4 | 5 |  | 7 | 8 | 9 |  | 11 |  | 10 |  | 3 | 6¹ | 12 |  |  |  |  |  |  |  |  |  |  |  |  |  |  |  |  |  |  |  |  |  | 4 |
| 1 | 2 |  | 4 | 5 |  | 7 | 8 | 9 | 10¹ |  | 11 | 12 |  | 3 |  |  | 6 |  |  |  |  |  |  |  |  |  |  |  |  |  |  |  |  |  |  |  |  | 5 |
| 1 |  |  | 4 | 5 | 11 |  | 8 | 9 | 10 | 7 |  |  |  | 3¹ |  | 12 | 6 | 2 |  |  |  |  |  |  |  |  |  |  |  |  |  |  |  |  |  |  |  | 6 |
| 1 | 2 |  | 4 | 5 | 11¹ |  | 8 | 9 | 10 | 7 | 12 |  |  | 3² |  | 13 | 6 |  |  |  |  |  |  |  |  |  |  |  |  |  |  |  |  |  |  |  |  | 7 |
| 1 | 2 |  | 4 | 5 | 3 | 11 | 8 | 9 | 10² |  |  | 7¹ |  |  | 12 |  | 6 |  | 13 |  |  |  |  |  |  |  |  |  |  |  |  |  |  |  |  |  |  | 8 |
| 1 | 2 |  | 4 | 5² | 3 | 11 | 8 | 9 | 10 |  | 12 | 7¹ |  |  | 13 |  | 6 |  |  |  |  |  |  |  |  |  |  |  |  |  |  |  |  |  |  |  |  | 9 |
| 1 | 2 | 4² |  | 5 |  | 7¹ | 8 |  | 10 |  | 12 | 11 |  | 3 | 13 |  | 6 |  |  | 9 |  |  |  |  |  |  |  |  |  |  |  |  |  |  |  |  |  | 10 |
| 1 | 2 |  |  | 5 |  | 7¹ | 8 |  | 10 |  | 12 | 11 |  | 3 | 4 |  | 6 |  | 13 | 9² |  |  |  |  |  |  |  |  |  |  |  |  |  |  |  |  |  | 11 |
| 1 | 2¹ |  | 3 | 5 |  | 7 | 8 |  | 10 |  |  | 11 |  |  | 4² |  | 6 |  |  |  | 12 | 13 | 9 |  |  |  |  |  |  |  |  |  |  |  |  |  |  | 12 |
|  | 2 | 3 |  | 5 |  | 7 | 8 |  |  | 11 |  |  |  |  | 13 | 14 | 6 |  | 12 |  | 1 | 4¹ | 10³ | 9² |  |  |  |  |  |  |  |  |  |  |  |  |  | 13 |
|  | 2 | 3 |  | 5 |  | 7 | 8 |  |  | 11 |  |  |  |  |  | 6 | 12 |  | 1 |  |  | 4 | 10¹ | 9 |  |  |  |  |  |  |  |  |  |  |  |  |  | 14 |
|  | 2 | 3 |  | 5 |  | 7 | 8 |  |  | 11 |  |  |  |  | 4 | 6¹ |  |  | 12 |  | 1 |  |  | 9 |  |  |  |  |  |  |  |  |  |  |  |  |  | 15 |
| 1 |  | 2 | 3 | 5 |  | 7 | 8 |  |  | 11 |  |  |  |  | 12 | 6³ |  | 13 |  |  |  | 4³ |  | 14 | 9⁷ |  |  |  |  |  |  |  |  |  |  |  |  | 16 |
| 1 |  | 5 | 4 | 3 |  | 6¹ | 7 |  | 10 |  | 12 |  |  |  | 8 |  | 2 |  |  |  |  |  |  | 13 |  |  | 9² | 11 |  |  |  |  |  |  |  |  |  | 17 |
| 1 |  | 3 | 6 | 5 |  | 7 | 8 |  | 10 |  | 9 |  |  |  | 4¹ |  | 2 |  |  |  |  |  |  | 12 |  |  | 11 |  |  |  |  |  |  |  |  |  |  | 18 |
| 1 |  | 3 | 6 | 5 |  | 7 | 8 |  | 10 |  | 9 |  |  |  | 4¹ |  | 2 |  |  |  |  |  |  | 12 |  |  | 11 |  |  |  |  |  |  |  |  |  |  | 19 |
| 1 |  | 3 | 6 | 5 |  | 7 | 8² |  | 10¹ | 12 | 9 |  | 13 |  |  | 2 |  |  | 4 |  |  |  |  |  |  |  | 11 |  |  |  |  |  |  |  |  |  |  | 20 |
| 1 |  | 3 | 6 | 5 |  | 7 |  |  | 12 |  | 9 | 10¹ |  |  |  | 2 |  | 8 |  | 4 |  |  |  |  |  |  | 11 |  |  |  |  |  |  |  |  |  |  | 21 |
| 1 | 12 |  | 6 | 5 |  | 7 |  |  |  | 11 | 9 | 10 |  |  |  | 2 |  |  | 4¹ |  | 8 | 3 |  |  |  |  |  |  |  |  |  |  |  |  |  |  |  | 22 |
| 1 |  |  | 6 | 5 |  | 7 |  |  | 10 | 11 | 9 |  |  |  |  | 2 |  | 1 |  | 4 |  | 8 | 3 |  |  |  |  |  |  |  |  |  |  |  |  |  |  | 23 |
| 1 |  | 12 |  | 6 | 5¹ |  | 7 |  |  | 10 | 11 | 9 |  | 13 |  |  | 2 |  |  | 4² |  | 8 | 3 |  |  |  |  |  |  |  |  |  |  |  |  |  |  | 24 |
|  | 2 | 5² | 6 |  |  | 7 |  |  | 10 | 11 | 9 |  | 13 | 12 |  | 1 |  | 4¹ |  | 8 | 3 |  |  |  |  |  |  |  |  |  |  |  |  |  |  |  |  | 25 |
|  | 2 |  |  | 5 |  |  |  |  | 10 | 11 | 9 |  |  |  | 6 |  | 1 |  | 4 |  | 8 | 3 | 7 |  |  |  |  |  |  |  |  |  |  |  |  |  |  | 26 |
|  | 2 | 7¹ |  | 5 |  |  | 12 |  | 10³ | 11 | 9 |  | 13 |  | 6 | 14 |  | 1 |  | 4 |  | 8 | 3² |  |  |  |  |  |  |  |  |  |  |  |  |  |  | 27 |
|  | 2 |  |  | 5 |  |  |  |  | 12 | 10 | 11¹ |  | 9³ |  | 13 |  |  | 1 |  | 4 |  | 8² | 3 | 7 | 14 |  |  |  |  |  |  |  |  |  |  |  |  | 28 |
|  | 2 |  |  | 5 |  |  |  |  | 9¹ | 10 | 11 |  | 12 |  | 6 |  |  | 1 |  | 4 |  | 8 | 3 |  | 7 |  |  |  |  |  |  |  |  |  |  |  |  | 29 |
|  | 2 |  |  | 5 |  |  |  |  | 9 | 10¹ | 11 |  | 12 |  | 6 |  |  | 1 |  | 4² |  | 8 |  | 13 | 7 | 3 |  |  |  |  |  |  |  |  |  |  |  | 30 |
|  | 2¹ |  |  | 5 | 12 |  |  |  | 9 |  | 11 |  | 10 |  | 6 |  | 13 | 1 |  | 8 |  | 4² | 7 | 3 |  |  |  |  |  |  |  |  |  |  |  |  |  | 31 |
|  |  |  | 5 | 14 |  |  |  |  | 12 | 10 | 11 |  |  |  | 2² |  |  | 1 | 7 |  |  | 8 | 4 | 6 | 13³ | 3 | 9¹ |  |  |  |  |  |  |  |  |  |  | 32 |
|  | 12 |  | 5 |  |  |  |  |  | 13 | 10³ | 11 |  |  |  |  |  | 1 | 2 |  | 8 |  | 9² | 4¹ | 7 |  | 6 | 14 | 3 |  |  |  |  |  |  |  |  |  | 33 |
|  | 2² |  | 4 | 5 |  |  |  |  | 9 |  | 11 | 12 |  |  |  |  | 1 | 13 |  | 8 |  | 14 | 7³ |  | 6 | 10¹ | 3 |  |  |  |  |  |  |  |  |  |  | 34 |
|  |  |  | 4 | 5 | 12 |  |  |  | 9 |  | 11 |  |  |  |  |  | 1 | 2 |  | 8 |  |  | 6 | 10 | 3 |  |  |  |  |  |  |  |  |  |  |  |  | 35 |
|  |  |  | 7 | 5 |  |  |  |  | 9² |  | 11 |  |  |  |  |  | 1 | 2 |  | 8¹ |  | 13 | 4 | 12 | 6 | 10 | 3 |  |  |  |  |  |  |  |  |  |  | 36 |
|  |  |  | 7 | 5 |  |  |  |  | 9¹ |  | 11 | 12 |  |  |  |  | 1 | 2 |  | 13 |  | 14 | 4³ | 8 | 6 | 10 | 3² |  |  |  |  |  |  |  |  |  |  | 37 |
| 1 |  |  | 4 | 5 |  |  | 8² |  |  | 10 | 11 | 12 |  |  |  |  | 3 |  | 9³ | 2 | 13 |  | 14 | 7¹ |  |  |  |  |  |  |  |  |  |  |  |  | 6 | 38 |
| 1 |  | 10¹ | 5 |  | 12 |  |  |  | 9² |  | 11 | 13 |  |  |  |  | 3 |  |  | 2 |  |  |  | 7 | 6 |  | 4 | 8 |  |  |  |  |  |  |  |  |  | 39 |
| 1 |  | 12 | 5 |  |  |  | 13 |  |  | 11² |  |  |  |  | 3 |  | 2 |  |  | 14 |  | 7 | 6³ |  | 4 | 8 | 9 | 10¹ |  |  |  |  |  |  |  |  |  | 40 |
| 1 |  | 6 | 5 |  |  |  |  |  | 11 |  |  |  |  |  | 3 |  | 2 |  |  | 7 |  |  |  | 4 | 8 | 9 | 10 |  |  |  |  |  |  |  |  |  |  | 41 |
| 1 |  | 6 | 5 |  |  | 3 | 11¹ |  | 12 |  |  |  |  |  | 2 |  |  | 13 |  | 7 |  |  |  | 4 | 8³ | 9 | 10² |  |  |  |  |  |  |  |  |  |  | 42 |
| 1 |  | 6 | 5 |  |  | 12 | 3 | 11² |  | 13 |  |  |  |  | 2 |  |  | 14 |  | 7 |  |  | 4¹ | 8 | 9 | 10³ |  |  |  |  |  |  |  |  |  |  |  | 43 |
| 1 |  | 6 |  | 5 |  | 12 | 3 | 11 | 13⁴ |  |  |  |  |  | 2 |  |  | 4² | 10¹ |  | 7 |  |  |  | 8 | 9 | 14 |  |  |  |  |  |  |  |  |  |  | 44 |
| 1 |  | 6 |  | 5 |  | 4² | 3 | 11 | 10¹ |  |  | 12 |  |  | 2 |  |  |  |  | 13 | 7 |  |  |  | 8³ | 9 | 14 |  |  |  |  |  |  |  |  |  |  | 45 |
| 1 |  | 6 | 4 | 5 |  | 12 | 3 | 11 | 13 |  |  | 10³ |  |  | 2 |  |  |  |  |  | 7¹ |  |  |  | 8 | 9² | 14 |  |  |  |  |  |  |  |  |  |  | 46 |

**Coca-Cola Cup**

| | | | | |
|---|---|---|---|---|
| First Round | Blackpool | (a) | 0-1 | |
| | | (h) | 1-0 | |

**FA Cup**

| | | | |
|---|---|---|---|
| Third Round | Bradford C | (h) | 2-0 |
| Fourth Round | West Ham U | (h) | 1-2 |

MANCHESTER UNITED 1997–98 *Back row (left to right):* Michael Appleton, Philip Mulryne, Brian McClair, Nicky Butt, Andy Cole, Chris Casper, Phil Neville, Ryan Giggs, John O'Kane, Gary Neville.

*Middle row:* Albert Morgan (Kit Manager), David Beckham, Jordi Cruyff, Teddy Sheringham, Raimond van der Gouw, Peter Schmeichel, Gary Pallister, Ronny Johnsen, David May, David Fevre (Physio).

*Front row:* Terry Cooke, Karel Poborsky, Ole Gunnar Solskjaer, Graeme Tomlinson, Alex Ferguson (Manager), Roy Keane (Manager), Brian Kidd (Assistant Manager), Michael Clegg, Denis Irwin, Ben Thornley, Paul Scholes.

# FA Premiership  **MANCHESTER UNITED**

*Sir Matt Busby Way, Old Trafford, Manchester M16 0RA.* Telephone: (0161) 872 1661, (0161) 930 1968. Fax: (0161) 876 5502. Ticket and Match Information: (0161) 872 0199. Membership Enquiries and Supporters Club: (0161) 872 5208. Clubcall: 0891 121161.

*Ground capacity:* 56,387.

*Record attendance:* 76,962 Wolverhampton W v Grimsby T, FA Cup semi-final, 25 March 1939.

*Club record:* 70,504 v Aston Villa, Division 1, 27 December 1920.

*Record receipts:* £779,631 v Barnsley, FA Cup 5th rnd, 15 February 1998.

*Pitch measurements:* 116yd × 76yd.

*Chairman/Chief Executive:* C. M. Edwards.

*Directors:* J. M. Edelson, Sir Bobby Charlton CBE, E. M. Watkins LL.M., R. L. Olive, P. F. Kenyon, D. A. Gill.

*Manager:* Alex Ferguson CBE. *Assistant Manager:* Brian Kidd. *Physio:* D. Fevre MCSP, SRP.

*Secretary:* Kenneth Merrett. *Commercial Manager:* Danny McGregor. *Stadium Manager:* E. Cassin.

*Year Formed:* 1878 as Newton Heath LYR; 1902, Manchester United.

*Turned Professional:* 1885. *Ltd Co.:* 1907.

*Previous Name:* Newton Heath, 1880–1902. *Club Nickname:* 'Red Devils'.

*Previous Grounds:* 1880–93, North Road, Monsall Road; 1893, Bank Street; 1910, Old Trafford (played at Maine Road 1941–49).

*Foundation:* Manchester United was formed as comparatively recently as 1902 after their predecessors, Newton Heath, went bankrupt. However, it is usual to give the date of the club's foundation as 1878 when the dining room committee of the carriage and waggon works of the Lancashire and Yorkshire Railway Company formed Newton Heath L and YR Cricket and Football Club. They won the Manchester Cup in 1886 and as Newton Heath FC were admitted to the Second Division in 1892.

*First Football League game:* 3 September 1892, Division 1, v Blackburn R (a) L 3-4 – Warner; Clements, Brown; Perrins, Stewart, Erentz; Farman (1), Coupar (1), Donaldson (1), Carson, Mathieson.

*Record League Victory (as Newton Heath):* 10–1 v Wolverhampton W, Division 1, 15 October 1892 – Warner; Mitchell, Clements; Perrins, Stewart (3), Erentz; Farman (1), Hood (1), Donaldson (3), Carson (1), Hendry (1).

*Record League Victory (as Manchester U):* 9–0 v Ipswich T, FA Premier League, 4 March 1995 – Schmeichel; Keane (1) (Sharpe), Irwin, Bruce (Butt), Kanchelskis, Pallister, Cole (5), Ince (1), McClair, Hughes (2), Giggs.

*Record Cup Victory:* 10–0 v RSC Anderlecht, European Cup Prel. rd (2nd leg), 26 September 1956 – Wood; Foulkes, Byrne; Colman, Jones, Edwards; Berry (1), Whelan (2), Taylor (3), Viollet (4), Pegg.

*Record Defeat:* 0–7 v Blackburn R, Division 1, 10 April 1926 and v Aston Villa, Division 1, 27 December 1930 and v Wolverhampton W, Division 2, 26 December 1931.

*Most League Points (2 for a win):* 64, Division 1, 1956–57.

*Most League Points (3 for a win):* 92, FA Premier League, 1993–94.

*Most League Goals:* 103, Division 1, 1956–57 and 1958–59.

*Highest League Scorer in Season:* Dennis Viollet, 32, 1959–60.

*Most League Goals in Total Aggregate:* Bobby Charlton, 199, 1956–73.

*Most Capped Player:* Bobby Charlton, 106, England.

*Most League Appearances:* Bobby Charlton, 606, 1956–73.

*Record Transfer Fee Received:* £7,000,000 from Internazionale for Paul Ince, June 1995.

*Record Transfer Fee Paid:* £10,500,000 to PSV Eindhoven for Jaap Stam, July 1998.

*Football League Record:* 1892 Newton Heath elected to Division 1; 1894–1906 Division 2; 1906–22 Division 1; 1922–25 Division 2; 1925–31 Division 1; 1931–36 Division 2; 1936–37 Division 1; 1937–38 Division 2; 1938–74 Division 1; 1974–75 Division 2; 1975–92 Division 1; 1992– FA Premier League.

*Honours:* FA Premier League: – Champions 1992–93, 1993–94, 1995–96, 1996–97; Runners-up 1994–95, 1997–98. *Football League:* Division 1 – Champions 1907–08, 1910–11, 1951–52, 1955–56, 1956–57, 1964–65, 1966–67; Runners-up 1946–47, 1947–48, 1948–49, 1950–51, 1958–59, 1963–64, 1967–68, 1979–80, 1987–88, 1991–92. Division 2 – Champions 1935–36, 1974–75; Runners-up 1896–97, 1905–06, 1924–25, 1937–38. *FA Cup:* Winners 1909, 1948, 1963, 1977, 1983, 1985, 1990, 1994; Runners-up 1957, 1958, 1976, 1979, 1995. *Football League Cup:* Winners 1992, 1983 (Runners-up), 1991 (Runners-up), 1994 (Runners-up). **European Competitions:** *European Cup:* 1956–57 (s-f), 1957–58 (s-f), 1965–66 (s-f), 1967–68 (winners), 1968–69 (s-f), 1993–94, 1994–95, 1996–97 (s-f), 1997–98. *European Cup-Winners' Cup:* 1963–64, 1977–78, 1983–84, 1990–91 (winners). 1991–92. *European Fairs Cup:* 1964–65. *UEFA Cup:* 1976–77, 1980–81, 1982–83, 1984–85, 1992–93, 1995–96. *World Club Championship:* 1968. *Super Cup:* 1991 (winners).

*Colours:* Red shirts, white shorts, black stockings. *Change colours:* All white.

**Did you know?**
While still known as Newton Heath, the club's first League goal was scored by Robert Donaldson against Blackburn Rovers on 3 September 1892. Later that season, he also achieved the first hat-trick for them.

## MANCHESTER UNITED 1997–98 LEAGUE RECORD

| Match No. | Date | Venue | Opponents | Result | H/T Score | Lg. Pos. | Goalscorers | Attendance |
|---|---|---|---|---|---|---|---|---|
| 1 | Aug 10 | A | Tottenham H | W 2-0 | 0-0 | — | Butt [82], Vega (og) [83] | 26,359 |
| 2 | 13 | H | Southampton | W 1-0 | 0-0 | — | Beckham [78] | 55,008 |
| 3 | 23 | A | Leicester C | D 0-0 | 0-0 | 3 | | 21,221 |
| 4 | 27 | A | Everton | W 2-0 | 1-0 | — | Beckham [29], Sheringham [51] | 40,479 |
| 5 | 30 | H | Coventry C | W 3-0 | 1-0 | 2 | Cole [2], Keane [72], Poborsky [90] | 55,074 |
| 6 | Sept 13 | H | West Ham U | W 2-1 | 1-1 | 1 | Keane [21], Scholes [76] | 55,068 |
| 7 | 20 | A | Bolton W | D 0-0 | 0-0 | 1 | | 25,000 |
| 8 | 24 | H | Chelsea | D 2-2 | 1-1 | — | Scholes [36], Solskjaer [86] | 55,163 |
| 9 | 27 | A | Leeds U | L 0-1 | 0-1 | 2 | | 39,943 |
| 10 | Oct 4 | H | Crystal Palace | W 2-0 | 2-0 | 2 | Sheringham [17], Hreidarsson (og) [30] | 55,143 |
| 11 | 18 | A | Derby Co | D 2-2 | 0-2 | 3 | Sheringham [51], Cole [84] | 30,014 |
| 12 | 25 | H | Barnsley | W 7-0 | 4-0 | 1 | Cole 3 [17, 19, 45], Giggs 2 [43, 56], Scholes [59], Poborsky [90] | 55,142 |
| 13 | Nov 1 | H | Sheffield W | W 6-1 | 4-0 | 1 | Sheringham 2 [13, 63], Cole 2 [20,38], Solskjaer 2 [41, 75] | 55,295 |
| 14 | 9 | A | Arsenal | L 2-3 | 2-2 | 1 | Sheringham 2 [33, 41] | 38,205 |
| 15 | 22 | A | Wimbledon | W 5-2 | 0-0 | 1 | Butt [48], Beckham 2 [66, 76], Scholes [81], Cole [87] | 26,309 |
| 16 | 30 | H | Blackburn R | W 4-0 | 1-0 | 1 | Solskjaer 2 [18, 53], Henchoz (og) [60], Kenna (og) [85] | 55,175 |
| 17 | Dec 6 | A | Liverpool | W 3-1 | 0-0 | 1 | Cole 2 [51, 74], Beckham [70] | 41,027 |
| 18 | 15 | H | Aston Villa | W 1-0 | 0-0 | — | Giggs [52] | 55,175 |
| 19 | 21 | A | Newcastle U | W 1-0 | 0-0 | 1 | Cole [66] | 36,763 |
| 20 | 26 | H | Everton | W 2-0 | 2-0 | 1 | Berg [14], Cole [35] | 55,167 |
| 21 | 28 | A | Coventry C | L 2-3 | 1-1 | 1 | Solskjaer [30], Sheringham [47] | 23,055 |
| 22 | Jan 10 | H | Tottenham H | W 2-0 | 1-0 | 1 | Giggs 2 [44, 67] | 55,281 |
| 23 | 19 | A | Southampton | L 0-1 | 0-1 | — | | 15,241 |
| 24 | 31 | H | Leicester C | L 0-1 | 0-1 | 1 | | 55,156 |
| 25 | Feb 7 | H | Bolton W | D 1-1 | 0-0 | 1 | Cole [85] | 55,156 |
| 26 | 18 | A | Aston Villa | W 2-0 | 0-0 | — | Beckham [82], Giggs [89] | 39,372 |
| 27 | 21 | H | Derby Co | W 2-0 | 1-0 | 1 | Giggs [18], Irwin (pen) [71] | 55,170 |
| 28 | 28 | A | Chelsea | W 1-0 | 1-0 | 1 | Neville P [31] | 34,517 |
| 29 | Mar 7 | A | Sheffield W | L 0-2 | 0-1 | 1 | | 39,427 |
| 30 | 11 | A | West Ham U | D 1-1 | 0-1 | — | Scholes [66] | 25,892 |
| 31 | 14 | H | Arsenal | L 0-1 | 0-0 | 1 | | 55,174 |
| 32 | 28 | H | Wimbledon | W 2-0 | 0-0 | 1 | Johnsen [83], Scholes [90] | 55,306 |
| 33 | Apr 6 | A | Blackburn R | W 3-1 | 0-1 | — | Cole [56], Scholes [73], Beckham [89] | 30,547 |
| 34 | 10 | H | Liverpool | D 1-1 | 1-1 | — | Johnsen [12] | 55,171 |
| 35 | 18 | H | Newcastle U | D 1-1 | 1-1 | 2 | Beckham [38] | 55,194 |
| 36 | 27 | A | Crystal Palace | W 3-0 | 2-0 | — | Scholes [5], Butt [21], Cole [84] | 26,180 |
| 37 | May 4 | H | Leeds U | W 3-0 | 2-0 | — | Giggs [6], Irwin (pen) [31], Beckham [58] | 55,167 |
| 38 | 10 | A | Barnsley | W 2-0 | 1-0 | 2 | Cole [5], Sheringham [67] | 18,694 |

**Final League Position: 2**  1996–97 PREM 1

### GOALSCORERS
*League (73):* Cole 16, Beckham 9, Sheringham 9, Giggs 8, Scholes 8, Solskjaer 6, Butt 3, Irwin 2 (2 pens), Johnsen 2, Keane 2, Poborsky 2, Berg 1, Neville P 1, own goals 4.
*Coca-Cola Cup (0):*
*FA Cup (13):* Cole 5, Sheringham 3, Beckham 2, Solskjaer 2, Johnsen 1.

| Schmeichel P 32 | Irwin D 23 + 2 | Neville P 24 + 6 | Johnsen R 18 + 4 | Keane R 9 | Pallister G 33 | Scholes P 28 + 3 | Butt N 31 + 2 | Cruyff J 3 + 2 | Sheringham T 28 + 3 | Giggs R 28 + 1 | Beckham D 34 + 3 | Berg H 23 + 4 | Neville G 34 | Cole A 31 + 2 | Poborsky K 3 + 7 | McClair B 2 + 11 | Solskjaer O 15 + 7 | Thornley B — + 5 | Curtis J 3 + 5 | Wallwork R — + 1 | Pilkington K 2 | Nevland E — + 1 | Clegg M 1 + 2 | Van der Gouw R 4 + 1 | May D 7 + 2 | Brown W 1 + 1 | Mulryne P 1 | Higginbotham D — + 1 | Match No. |
|---|---|---|---|---|---|---|---|---|---|---|---|---|---|---|---|---|---|---|---|---|---|---|---|---|---|---|---|---|---|
| 1 | 2 | 3 | 4 | 5 | 6 | 7¹ | 8 | 9 | 10 | 11 | 12 | | | | | | | | | | | | | | | | | | 1 |
| 1 | 2 | 3 | 4² | 5 | 6 | 7¹ | 8 | 9 | 10 | 11 | 12 | 13 | | | | | | | | | | | | | | | | | 2 |
| 1 | 3 | | | 5 | 6 | 12 | 8 | 9¹ | 10 | 11 | 7 | 4 | 2 | | | | | | | | | | | | | | | | 3 |
| 1 | 3 | | | 5 | 6 | 9 | 8 | | 10¹ | 11 | 7 | 4 | 2 | 12 | | | | | | | | | | | | | | | 4 |
| 1 | 12 | 3¹ | | 5 | 6 | | 8 | | 10 | 11 | 7 | 4 | 2 | 9² | 13 | | | | | | | | | | | | | | 5 |
| 1 | 3 | | | 5 | 6 | 10 | 8 | | | 11¹ | 7 | 4 | 2 | 9² | 12 | 13 | | | | | | | | | | | | | 6 |
| 1 | 3 | 12 | | 5 | 6 | 10 | 8 | | | 11¹ | 7 | 4 | 2 | 9 | | 13 | | | | | | | | | | | | | 7 |
| 1 | 3 | | | 5 | 6 | 10³ | 8 | 12 | 13 | | 7 | 4 | 2² | 9 | 11¹ | 14 | | | | | | | | | | | | | 8 |
| 1 | 3 | 12 | 13 | 5 | 6 | | 8² | | 10 | 11³ | 7 | 4 | 2¹ | 9 | | 14 | | | | | | | | | | | | | 9 |
| 1 | 12 | 3¹ | 5² | | 6 | 9 | 8 | | 10 | 11 | 7 | 4 | 2 | | 13 | | | | | | | | | | | | | | 10 |
| 1 | 3¹ | 12 | 13 | | 6 | 5³ | 8² | | 10 | 11 | 7 | 4 | 2 | 14 | 9 | | | | | | | | | | | | | | 11 |
| 1 | 3 | | | | 6³ | 5¹ | 8 | 12 | | 11 | 7² | 4 | 9 | 13 | 10 | | 2 | 14 | | | | | | | | | | | 12 |
| 1 | 3 | | | | 6 | 5¹ | 8² | | 10 | | 7 | 4³ | 2 | 9 | 12 | 13 | 11 | 14 | | | | | | | | | | | 13 |
| 1 | 3 | 12 | | | 6¹ | 5 | 8 | | 10 | 11² | 7 | 4 | 2 | 9 | | 13 | | | | | | | | | | | | | 14 |
| 1 | 3 | 5 | | | 6 | 7 | 8 | | 10 | 11 | 12 | 4 | 2¹ | 9 | | | | | | | | | | | | | | | 15 |
| 1 | 3 | 12 | | | 6² | | 8¹ | | 10³ | 11 | 7 | 4 | 2 | 9 | 13 | 14 | 5 | | | | | | | | | | | | 16 |
| 1 | 3 | 5 | | | 6 | | 8 | | 10 | 11 | 7 | 4 | 2 | 9 | | | | | | | | | | | | | | | 17 |
| 1 | 3 | 4 | | | 6 | | 5 | | 10 | 11 | 7 | | 2 | 9 | 12 | 8¹ | | | | | | | | | | | | | 18 |
| 1 | 3 | 4 | | | 6 | 5² | 8 | | 10¹ | 11 | 7 | | 2 | 9 | 12 | 13 | | | | | | | | | | | | | 19 |
| | 3³ | 5 | | | 6² | 11 | 8 | | | 7¹ | 4 | 2 | 9 | 12 | 13 | 10 | | 14 | | 1 | | | | | | | | 20 |
| | 3² | | | | 6 | 5 | 12 | | 10 | 11 | 7 | 4 | 2 | 9 | | 8¹ | 13 | | 1 | | | | | | | | | 21 |
| 1 | 3 | 4 | | | 6 | 5 | | | 10 | 11 | 7 | | 2 | 9 | | 8 | | | | | | | | | | | | | 22 |
| 1 | 3 | 4 | | | 6 | 5 | 8¹ | | | 11 | 7 | | 2² | 9 | 12 | 10 | | 13 | | | | | | | | | | | 23 |
| 1 | 3 | 12 | 4² | | 6 | 5¹ | 8 | | 14 | 11 | 7 | 13³ | 2 | 9 | | 10 | | | | | | | | | | | | | 24 |
| 1 | 3 | 2 | | | 6 | 5 | | | 10¹ | 11 | 7 | 12 | 4 | 9 | | 8 | | | | | | | | | | | | | 25 |
| 1 | 3 | 12 | | | 6 | | 8 | | 10 | 11 | 7 | 4 | 2 | 9 | 5¹ | | | | | | | | | | | | | | 26 |
| 1 | 3³ | 5 | | | 6 | | 8 | 12 | 10 | 11² | 7 | 4 | 2 | 9¹ | 13 | | | | | | | | | | 14 | | | | 27 |
| 1 | 3 | 5 | 4 | | 6¹ | 11 | 8 | | 10 | | 7 | 12 | 2 | 9 | | | | | | | | | | | | | | | 28 |
| | | 5¹ | 6¹ | | | 12 | | | 10 | | 7 | 3 | 2 | 9² | 13 | 11 | | | 14 | | | | | 1 | 4 | | | | 29 |
| 1 | 3 | | | | | 11 | 8³ | | 10 | | 7 | 6 | 2 | 9¹ | 5² | 12 | 13 | | 14 | | | | | | 4 | | | | 30 |
| 1 | 3 | 8¹ | 5² | | | 11 | | | 10 | | 7 | 6 | 4 | 9 | | 12 | 14 | 2¹ | | | | | | | 13 | | | | 31 |
| | 3 | 8 | 5 | | | 11 | | | | | 7 | 6 | 2 | 9¹ | | 12 | 10² | 13 | | | | | | | 4 | | | | 32 |
| 1 | 3 | 5 | 4 | | 6 | 8 | | 12 | | | 7 | | 2 | 9 | | 10¹ | | | | | | | | | | | | | 33 |
| 1 | 3 | 5¹ | 4² | | 6 | 10 | 8 | | 12 | 11³ | 7 | | 2 | 9 | | | | | 14 | | | | | | 13 | | | | 34 |
| 1⁹ | 3 | 5 | | | 6 | 12 | 8¹ | | 10 | 11 | 7 | | 2² | 9 | | 13 | | | | | | | 15 | | 4 | | | | 35 |
| 1 | 3¹ | 2 | | | 6 | 5 | 8 | | 10 | 11 | 7 | | | 9 | | | | | | | | 12 | | | 4 | | | | 36 |
| | 3¹ | 12 | | | 6 | 5 | 8 | | 10² | 11 | 7 | | 2 | 9 | 13 | | | | | | | | | | 1 | 4³ | 14 | | 37 |
| | | | | | | | 8 | | 10 | 11 | | | 2 | 9 | | | 3 | | | | | | | 6¹ | 1 | 4 | 5 | 7  12 | 38 |

**Coca-Cola Cup**
Third Round    Ipswich T                          (a)   0-2

**FA Cup**
Third Round    Chelsea    (a)   5-3
Fourth Round   Walsall    (h)   5-1
Fifth Round    Barnsley   (h)   1-1
                          (a)   2-3

MANSFIELD TOWN 1997–98 *Back row (left to right):* Bob Shaw (Scout), Steven Harper, Michael Sissons, Mark Peters, John Doolan, Stewart Hadley, Darrell Clarke, Iyseden Christie, David Kerr, Ivan Hollett (Assistant Youth Team Manager).
*Middle row:* Lee Williams, Steve Whitehall, Ben Sedgemore, Duncan Roberts, Scott Eustace, Stuart Watkiss, Ian Bowling, John Schofield, Leigh Holbrook, Johnny Walker.
*Front row:* Tony Ford (Assistant Manager/Youth Team Manager), Alan Meale MP, Keith Haslam (Chairman), Steve Parkin (Manager), Tony Hewson (Director), Barry Statham (Physio).

# Division 3     **MANSFIELD TOWN**

*Field Mill Ground, Quarry Lane, Mansfield NG18 5DA.* Telephone: (01623) 623567. Fax: (01623) 625014. Marketing: (01623) 658070. Football in the Community: (01623) 25197.

*Ground capacity:* 6905.

*Record attendance:* 24,467 v Nottingham F, FA Cup 3rd rd, 10 January 1953.

*Record receipts:* £46,915 v Sheffield W, FA Cup 3rd rd, 5 January 1991.

*Pitch measurements:* 115yd × 70yd.

*Chairman/Chief Executive:* Keith Haslam.

*Director:* Mrs M. Haslam. *Associate Directors:* T. Hewson, K. Woodcock, S. Whetton, M. Murphy.

*Manager:* Steve Parkin.

*Physio:* Barry Statham.

*Community Scheme Organiser:* D. Bentley Tel: (01623) 625197.

*Secretary:* Christine Reynolds. *Marketing:* Nicola Wilcockson.

*Year Formed:* 1897. *Turned Professional:* 1906. *Ltd Co.:* 1922.

*Previous Name:* Mansfield Wesleyans 1897–1906; Mansfield Wesley 1906–10.

*Club Nickname:* 'The Stags'.

*Foundation:* The club was formed as Mansfield Wesleyans in 1897, and changed their name to Mansfield Wesley in 1906 and Mansfield Town in 1910.

*First Football League game:* 29 August 1931, Division 3 (S), v Swindon T (h) W 3-2 – Wilson; Clifford, England; Wake, Davis, Blackburn; Gilhespy, Readman (1), Johnson, Broom (2), Baxter.

*Record League Victory:* 9–2 v Rotherham U, Division 3 (N), 27 December 1932 – Wilson; Anthony, England; Davies, S. Robinson, Slack; Prior, Broom, Readman (3), Hoyland (3), Bowater (3).

*Record Cup Victory:* 8–0 v Scarborough (away), FA Cup 1st rd, 22 November 1952 – Bramley; Chessell, Bradley; Field, Plummer, Lewis; Scott, Fox (3), Marron (2), Sid Watson (1), Adam (2).

*Record Defeat:* 1–8 v Walsall, Division 3 (N), 19 January 1933.

*Most League Points (2 for a win):* 68, Division 4, 1974–75.

*Most League Points (3 for a win):* 81, Division 4, 1985–86.

*Most League Goals:* 108, Division 4, 1962–63.

*Highest League Scorer in Season:* Ted Harston, 55, Division 3 (N), 1936–37.

*Most League Goals in Total Aggregate:* Harry Johnson, 104, 1931–36.

*Most Capped Player:* John McClelland, 6 (53), Northern Ireland.

*Most League Appearances:* Rod Arnold, 440, 1970–83.

*Record Transfer Fee Received:* £655,000 from Tottenham H for Colin Calderwood, July 1993.

*Record Transfer Fee Paid:* £80,000 to Leicester C for Steve Wilkinson, September 1989 and £80,000 to Notts Co for Wayne Fairclough, March 1990.

*Football League Record:* 1931 Elected to Division 3 (S); 1932–37 Division 3 (N); 1937–47 Division 3 (S); 1947–58 Division 3 (N); 1958–60 Division 3; 1960–63 Division 4; 1963–72 Division 3; 1972–75 Division 4; 1975–77 Division 3; 1977–78 Division 2; 1978–80 Division 3; 1980–86 Division 4; 1986–91 Division 3; 1991–92 Division 4; 1992–93 Division 2; 1993– Division 3.

*Honours: Football League:* Division 2 best season: 21st, 1977–78; Division 3 – Champions 1976–77; Division 4 – Champions 1974–75; Division 3 (N) – Runners-up 1950–51. *FA Cup:* best season: 6th rd, 1969. *Football League Cup:* best season: 5th rd, 1976. *Freight Rover Trophy:* Winners 1987.

*Colours:* Amber shirts with royal blue stripe down side, royal blue collar, amber shorts with royal blue stripe down sides, royal blue stockings with amber trim. *Change colours:* White shirts and shorts with thin blue stripe, white stockings with blue stripe.

**Did you know?**
On 23 August 1997, Jonathan Milner at 16 years 146 days became the club's youngest debutant; on 13 December 1997 Tony Ford at 38 years 212 days, the club's oldest first team player.

## MANSFIELD TOWN 1997–98 LEAGUE RECORD

| Match No. | Date | | Venue | Opponents | Result | | H/T Score | Lg. Pos. | Goalscorers | Attendance |
|---|---|---|---|---|---|---|---|---|---|---|
| 1 | Aug | 9 | H | Hull C | W | 2-0 | 1-0 | — | Christie [38], Clarke [54] | 4627 |
| 2 | | 16 | A | Rochdale | L | 0-2 | 0-2 | 12 | | 2133 |
| 3 | | 23 | H | Cardiff C | L | 1-2 | 0-1 | 17 | Doolan (pen) [88] | 2743 |
| 4 | | 30 | A | Scunthorpe U | L | 0-1 | 0-0 | 21 | | 3414 |
| 5 | Sept | 2 | A | Lincoln C | W | 2-0 | 1-0 | — | Whitehall [16], Christie [84] | 3539 |
| 6 | | 5 | H | Doncaster R | D | 1-1 | 1-0 | — | Christie [43] | 2874 |
| 7 | | 13 | A | Notts Co | L | 0-1 | 0-1 | 18 | | 6706 |
| 8 | | 20 | H | Chester C | W | 4-1 | 3-1 | 15 | Whitehall 2 [26, 38], Ford [28], Christie [85] | 2183 |
| 9 | | 27 | A | Darlington | D | 0-0 | 0-0 | 17 | | 2596 |
| 10 | Oct | 4 | H | Colchester U | D | 1-1 | 1-1 | 18 | Whitehall [6] | 2341 |
| 11 | | 11 | H | Cambridge U | W | 3-2 | 2-1 | 13 | Christie [11], Whitehall 2 [17, 62] | 2239 |
| 12 | | 18 | A | Macclesfield T | L | 0-1 | 0-0 | 15 | | 3277 |
| 13 | | 21 | A | Swansea C | W | 1-0 | 0-0 | — | Clarke [66] | 2589 |
| 14 | | 25 | H | Barnet | L | 1-2 | 1-1 | 14 | Hackett [20] | 2340 |
| 15 | Nov | 1 | A | Shrewsbury T | L | 2-3 | 1-1 | 16 | Whitehall [45], Christie [88] | 2338 |
| 16 | | 4 | H | Rotherham U | D | 3-3 | 1-2 | — | Whitehall 2 [15, 48], Christie [74] | 2927 |
| 17 | | 8 | H | Scarborough | W | 3-2 | 2-2 | 16 | Peacock [30], Whitehall [38], Harper [90] | 2134 |
| 18 | | 18 | A | Exeter C | L | 0-1 | 0-1 | — | | 2888 |
| 19 | | 22 | A | Peterborough U | D | 1-1 | 0-1 | 17 | Peacock [57] | 6202 |
| 20 | | 29 | H | Leyton Orient | D | 0-0 | 0-0 | 18 | | 2086 |
| 21 | Dec | 2 | A | Torquay U | L | 1-2 | 1-0 | — | Peacock [45] | 1440 |
| 22 | | 13 | A | Brighton & HA | D | 1-1 | 1-0 | 19 | Whitehall [1] | 2197 |
| 23 | | 20 | A | Hartlepool U | D | 2-2 | 0-1 | 18 | Christie [68], Sedgemore [71] | 2309 |
| 24 | | 28 | H | Lincoln C | D | 2-2 | 1-0 | 19 | Whitehall 2 [43, 58] | 3449 |
| 25 | Jan | 3 | H | Rochdale | W | 3-0 | 0-0 | 17 | Williams 2 [70, 78], Whitehall [86] | 2303 |
| 26 | | 10 | A | Hull C | D | 0-0 | 0-0 | 17 | | 4440 |
| 27 | | 17 | H | Scunthorpe U | W | 1-0 | 1-0 | 14 | Kerr [5] | 2375 |
| 28 | | 31 | H | Notts Co | L | 0-2 | 0-2 | 16 | | 6786 |
| 29 | Feb | 3 | A | Doncaster R | W | 3-0 | 1-0 | — | Eustace [20], Whitehall [49], Harper [64] | 1538 |
| 30 | | 7 | A | Chester C | W | 1-0 | 0-0 | 14 | Whitehall (pen) [55] | 2055 |
| 31 | | 13 | A | Colchester U | L | 0-2 | 0-1 | — | | 2320 |
| 32 | | 17 | A | Cardiff C | L | 1-4 | 0-1 | — | Williams [74] | 2451 |
| 33 | | 21 | H | Darlington | W | 4-0 | 0-0 | 14 | Harper 3 [47, 48, 64], Sedgemore [67] | 2071 |
| 34 | | 24 | H | Macclesfield T | W | 1-0 | 0-0 | — | Peters [73] | 2683 |
| 35 | | 28 | A | Cambridge U | L | 0-2 | 0-0 | 14 | | 2303 |
| 36 | Mar | 3 | A | Scarborough | D | 2-2 | 0-1 | — | Christie [66], Clarke [90] | 2019 |
| 37 | | 7 | H | Shrewsbury T | D | 1-1 | 0-1 | 14 | Peacock [48] | 2219 |
| 38 | | 14 | A | Rotherham U | D | 2-2 | 2-2 | 15 | Whitehall 2 [13, 28] | 4054 |
| 39 | | 21 | H | Exeter C | W | 3-2 | 1-1 | 14 | Ford 2 [39, 67], Peters [65] | 2033 |
| 40 | | 28 | H | Peterborough U | W | 2-0 | 2-0 | 12 | Whitehall [15], Tallon [45] | 2760 |
| 41 | Apr | 4 | A | Leyton Orient | D | 2-2 | 2-1 | 12 | Whitehall [8], Clarke [33] | 4081 |
| 42 | | 11 | H | Torquay U | D | 2-2 | 0-1 | 13 | Whitehall [52], Peacock [76] | 2282 |
| 43 | | 13 | A | Brighton & HA | D | 1-1 | 0-1 | 13 | Christie [83] | 2704 |
| 44 | | 18 | H | Hartlepool U | D | 2-2 | 1-2 | 14 | Whitehall 2 (1 pen) [22 (p), 60] | 2047 |
| 45 | | 25 | A | Barnet | W | 1-0 | 0-0 | 12 | Whitehall (pen) [52] | 2792 |
| 46 | May | 2 | H | Swansea C | W | 1-0 | 0-0 | 12 | Kerr [52] | 2867 |

**Final League Position: 12**        1996–97 DIV3 11

### GOALSCORERS

*League (64):* Whitehall 24 (3 pens), Christie 10, Harper 5, Peacock 5, Clarke 4, Ford 3, Williams 3, Kerr 2, Peters 2, Sedgemore 2, Doolan 1 (pen), Eustace 1, Hackett 1, Tallon 1.
*Coca-Cola Cup (7):* Christie 4, Doolan 1, Ford 1, own goal 1.
*FA Cup (1):* Whitehall 1.

| Bowling I 33 | Ford T 33+1 | Harper S 46 | Watkiss S 10 | Eustace S 24+5 | Jones S 6 | Schofield J 44 | Clarke D 26+9 | Christie I 26+13 | Whitehall S 42+1 | Doolan J 24 | Sedgemore B 21+7 | Williams L 33+5 | Kerr D 7+11 | Squires J 1 | Milner J 1+6 | Hackett W 23 | Hassell B 8+1 | Hadley S —+2 | Peacock L 25+7 | Gibson P 13 | Peters M 24 | Tallon G 26 | Thorn S 5 | Walker J —+1 | Sisson M —+1 | Woods N 5+1 | Sedlan J —+1 | Match No. |
|---|---|---|---|---|---|---|---|---|---|---|---|---|---|---|---|---|---|---|---|---|---|---|---|---|---|---|---|---|
| 1 | 2 | 3 | 4 | 5 | 6 | 7 | 8 | 9 | 10 | 11 | | | | | | | | | | | | | | | | | | 1 |
| 1 | 2 | 3 | 4¹ | 5 | 6 | 7 | | 9 | 10 | 11 | 8² | 12 | 13 | | | | | | | | | | | | | | | 2 |
| 1 | 2 | 3 | | 5 | 6 | 7 | | | 10 | 11 | 8¹ | 9² | 12 | 4 | 13 | | | | | | | | | | | | | 3 |
| 1 | 2 | 3 | 4 | 5 | 6 | 7 | 8 | 9 | 10² | 11¹ | 12 | | | | 13 | | | | | | | | | | | | | 4 |
| 1 | 2 | 3 | 4 | 5 | 6 | 7 | 8 | 9 | 10 | 11 | | | | | | | | | | | | | | | | | | 5 |
| 1 | 2 | 3 | 4 | 5 | 6 | 7 | 8¹ | 9 | 10 | 11 | 12 | | | | | | | | | | | | | | | | | 6 |
| 1 | 2 | 3 | 4¹ | 5 | | 7 | 12 | 9² | 10³ | 11 | 8 | 13 | | | 14 | 6 | | | | | | | | | | | | 7 |
| 1 | 2 | 3¹ | | 5 | | 7 | 8² | 9² | 10 | 11 | 4 | 12 | | | 13 | 6 | 14 | | | | | | | | | | | 8 |
| 1 | 2 | 3 | | 5 | | 7 | | 9 | 10 | 11 | 8 | | | | | 6 | 4 | | | | | | | | | | | 9 |
| 1 | 2 | 3 | | 5 | | 7 | | 9 | 10¹ | 11 | 8 | | | | | 6 | 4 | 12 | | | | | | | | | | 10 |
| 1 | 2 | 3 | | 5 | | 7 | 8 | 9¹ | 10 | 11 | 4 | | | | | 6 | | | 12 | | | | | | | | | 11 |
| 1 | 2² | 3 | | 5 | | 7 | 8 | 9¹ | 10 | 11 | 4 | 13 | | | | 6 | | | 12 | | | | | | | | | 12 |
| | | 3 | | 5 | | 7 | 8 | 9¹ | 10 | 11 | 4 | 2 | | | | 6 | | | 12 | 1 | | | | | | | | 13 |
| | | 3 | | 5 | | 7 | 8 | 9 | 10¹ | 11 | 4 | 2 | | | | 6 | | | 12 | 1 | | | | | | | | 14 |
| | | 3 | | 5 | | 7¹ | 8 | 12 | 10¹ | 11 | | 2 | 13 | | | 6 | | | 9 | 1 | 4 | | | | | | | 15 |
| | | 3 | 12 | | | 7¹ | 8 | 13 | 10 | 11 | | 2 | | | | 6 | 5¹ | | 9 | 1 | 4 | | | | | | | 16 |
| | | 3 | | 5 | | 7 | 8 | 12 | 10 | 11 | | 2 | | | | 6 | | | 9¹ | 1 | 4 | | | | | | | 17 |
| | | 3 | | 5 | | 7 | | 12 | 10¹ | 11 | 8 | 2 | | | | 6 | | | 9 | 1 | 4 | | | | | | | 18 |
| | | 3 | | 5 | | 7 | | 12 | 10¹ | 11 | 8 | 2 | | | | 6 | | | 9 | 1 | 4 | | | | | | | 19 |
| | | 3 | | 5 | | 7 | 8 | 9 | 10 | 11 | | 2 | | | | 6 | | | | 1 | 4 | | | | | | | 20 |
| | | 3 | | | | 7 | 12 | 13 | 10 | 11 | 14 | 2 | 8¹ | | | 6 | | | 9 | 1 | 4³ | 5² | | | | | | 21 |
| | 6² | 3 | | | | 7 | 8 | 12 | 10 | 11 | | 2 | 13 | | | 4 | | | 9¹ | 1 | | 5 | | | | | | 22 |
| | 7 | 3² | 5 | | | 12 | | 9 | 10¹ | 11 | | 2 | 13 | | 14 | 4 | | | 8³ | 1 | | 6 | | | | | | 23 |
| | 7 | 3¹ | | | | | | 9 | 10 | 11 | | 2 | | | 12 | 4 | | | 8 | 1 | | 6 | 5 | | | | | 24 |
| | 6 | 3 | | | | 7 | | 9¹ | 10 | | 12 | 2 | 13 | | | | 5 | | 8 | 1² | 11 | 4 | | | | | | 25 |
| 1 | 6 | 3 | | | | 7 | | 9 | 10 | | 12 | 2 | 5² | | | | | | 8¹ | | 11 | 4 | | 13 | | | | 26 |
| 1 | 6 | 3 | 12 | | | 7 | 13 | | 10 | | 8 | 2 | 5¹ | | | | | | 9² | | 11 | 4 | | | | | | 27 |
| 1 | 6² | 3 | 12 | | | 7 | 13 | 9 | 10 | | 8 | 2 | 5³ | | | | | | 14 | | | 11 | 4¹ | | | | | 28 |
| 1 | 6¹ | 3 | 5 | | | 7 | 12 | 9 | 10² | | 8 | 2³ | 14 | | 13 | | | | | | 4 | 11 | | | | | | 29 |
| 1 | 6 | 3 | | 5 | | 7 | | 9 | 10 | | 8 | 2 | | | | | | | | | 4 | 11 | | | | | | 30 |
| 1 | 6 | 3 | | 5 | | 7 | | 9 | 10² | | 8³ | 2 | 13 | | | | | | 12 | | 4 | 11¹ | | 14 | | | | 31 |
| 1 | 6 | 3¹ | | 5 | | 7 | 8¹ | | 10 | | | 2 | 13 | | | | | | 12 | | 4 | 11 | | 9 | | | | 32 |
| 1 | 5¹ | 3 | | | | 7 | 8 | | 10 | | | 2 | | | | 6 | | | 12 | | 4 | 11 | | 9 | | | | 33 |
| 1 | | 3 | | | | 7 | 8 | 12 | 10 | | | 2 | | | | 6 | 5 | | | | 4 | 11 | | 9¹ | | | | 34 |
| 1 | 12 | 3 | | | | 7 | 13 | | 10² | | 8² | 2 | 5¹ | | 14 | 6 | | | | | 4 | 11 | | 9 | | | | 35 |
| 1 | 5 | 3 | | | | 7 | 8 | 9 | | | | 2 | | | | 6 | | | 12 | | 4 | 11 | | 10¹ | | | | 36 |
| 1 | 5 | 3 | | | | 7 | 8² | 9¹ | 12 | | | 2 | | | | 6 | | | 10 | | 4 | 11 | | 13 | | | | 37 |
| 1 | 5 | 3 | | | | 7 | 8 | | 10 | | | 2 | | | | 6 | | | 9 | | 4 | 11 | | | | | | 38 |
| 1 | 5 | 3 | | 6 | | 7 | 8 | 12 | 10 | | | 2 | | | | | | | 9¹ | | 4 | 11 | | | | | | 39 |
| 1 | 5 | 3 | | 6 | | 7 | 8 | 12 | 10 | | | 2 | | | | | | | 9¹ | | 4 | 11 | | | | | | 40 |
| 1 | 5 | 3 | | 6 | | 7 | 8 | 12 | 10 | | | 2 | | | | | | | 9¹ | | 4 | 11 | | | | | | 41 |
| 1 | 5 | 3 | | 6 | | 7 | 8 | 12 | 10 | | | 2 | | | | | | | 9 | | 4 | 11¹ | | | | | | 42 |
| 1 | 5 | 3 | | | | 7 | 8 | 12 | 10 | | | 2 | 13 | | | 6 | | | 9¹ | | 4 | 11² | | | | | | 43 |
| 1 | 5 | 3 | 12 | | | 7 | 8² | 13 | 10 | | | 2 | | | | 6 | | | 9 | | 4¹ | 11 | | | | | | 44 |
| 1 | | 3 | 12 | | | 7 | 13 | 9 | 10 | | | 2 | 5² | | | 6 | | | 8 | | 4¹ | 11 | | | | | | 45 |
| 1 | | 3 | 5 | | | 7 | 12 | 9¹ | 10 | | | 2 | 4² | | | 6 | | | 8 | | | 11 | | | | | 13 | 46 |

**Coca-Cola Cup**
First Round     Stockport Co     (h) 4-2    (a) 3-6

**FA Cup**
First Round     Oldham Ath     (a) 1-1    (h) 0-1

MIDDLESBROUGH 1997-98 *Back row (left to right):* Derek Whyte, Paul Merson, Fabio Moreira, Mark Schwarzer, Ben Roberts, Gary Walsh, Gianluca Festa, Fabrizio Ravanelli, Alan White.
*Middle row:* John Pickering (First Team Coach), David Geddis (Youth Team Coach), Gordon McQueen (Reserve Team Coach), Bob Ward (Senior Physio), Steven Baker, Paul Connor, Robbie Mustoe, Steve Vickers, Mikkel Beck, Philip Stamp, Chris Freestone, Craig Liddle, Mark Summerbell, Craig Harrison, Michael Cummins, Andrew Campbell, Vladimir Kinder, Kenny Wharton (Youth Coach), Ron Bone (Youth Development Officer), Alex Smith (Kit Manager).
*Front row:* Gary Henderson (Physio), David French (Masseur), Craig Hignett, Curtis Fleming, Viv Anderson (Assistant Manager), Nigel Pearson, Bryan Robson (Manager), Clayton Blackmore, Alan Moore, Stan Nixon (Youth Technical Director), John Emmett (Fitness Coach).

# FA Premiership     **MIDDLESBROUGH**

*Cellnet Riverside Stadium, Middlesbrough, Cleveland TS3 6RS.* Telephone: (01642) 877700. Fax: (01642) 877840. Boro Livewire: 0891 424200. Ticket Office: (01642) 877745. Stadium Shop (01642) 877720. Town Centre Shop: (01642) 877849. Tour Booking Line: (01642) 877730.

*Ground capacity:* 35,000.

*Record attendance:* Ayresome Park: 53,596 v Newcastle U, Division 1, 27 December 1949. Cellnet Riverside Stadium: 30,228 v Oxford U, Division 1, 3 May 1998.

*Record receipts:* £361, 444 v Liverpool, Coca-Cola Cup semi-final 2nd leg, 18 February 1998.

*Pitch measurements:* 115yd × 74yd.

*Chairman:* Steve Gibson.

*Director:* George Cooke.

*Chief Executive:* Keith Lamb. *Secretary:* Karen Nelson.

*Manager:* Bryan Robson. *Assistant Manager:* Viv Anderson.

*Physio:* Bob Ward. *First Team Coach:* Gordon McQueen. *Reserve Team Coach:* David Geddis. *Youth Academy Head Coach:* John Pickering. *Youth Team Coach:* Kenny Wharton. *Chief Scout:* Ray Train.

*Head of Marketing and Commercial:* John Knox. *General Manager Business Operations:* Reg Corbidge. *Commercial Manager:* Graham Fordy.

*Youth Development Officer:* Ron Bone. *Public Relations Manager:* Dave Allan.

*Stadium Manager:* Terry Tasker.

*Year Formed:* 1876; re-formed 1986. *Turned Professional:* 1889; became amateur 1892, and professional again, 1899. *Ltd Co:* 1892.

*Club Nickname:* 'Boro'.

*Previous Grounds:* 1877, Old Archery Ground, Albert Park; 1879, Breckon Hill; 1882, Linthorpe Road Ground; 1903, Ayresome Park; 1995, Cellnet Riverside Stadium.

*Foundation:* A previous belief that Middlesbrough Football Club was founded at a tripe supper at the Corporation Hotel has proved to be erroneous. In fact, members of Middlesbrough Cricket Club were responsible for forming it at a meeting in the gymnasium of the Albert Park Hotel in 1875.

*First Football League game:* 2 September 1899, Division 2, v Lincoln C (a) L 0-3 – Smith; Shaw, Ramsey; Allport, McNally, McCracken; Wanless, Longstaffe, Gettins, Page, Pugh.

*Record League Victory:* 9–0 v Brighton & HA, Division 2, 23 August 1958 – Taylor; Bilcliff, Robinson; Harris (2 p), Phillips, Walley; Day, McLean, Clough (5), Peacock (2), Holliday.

*Record Cup Victory:* 7–0 v Hereford U, Coca-Cola Cup 2nd rd, 1st leg, 18 September 1996 – Miller; Fleming (1), Branco (1), Whyte, Vickers, Whelan, Emerson (1), Mustoe, Stamp, Juninho, Ravanelli (4).

*Record Defeat:* 0–9 v Blackburn R, Division 2, 6 November 1954.

*Most League Points (2 for a win):* 65, Division 2, 1973–74.

*Most League Points (3 for a win):* 94, Division 3, 1986–87.

*Most League Goals:* 122, Division 2, 1926–27.

*Highest League Scorer in Season:* George Camsell, 59, Division 2, 1926–27 (Second Division record).

*Most League Goals in Total Aggregate:* George Camsell, 326, 1925–39.

*Most Capped Player:* Wilf Mannion, 26, England.

*Most League Appearances:* Tim Williamson, 563, 1902–23.

*Record Transfer Fee Received:* £12,000,000 from Atletico Madrid for Juninho, July 1997.

*Record Transfer Fee Paid:* £7,000,000 to Juventus for Fabrizio Ravanelli, August 1996.

*Football League Record:* 1899 Elected to Division 2; 1902–24 Division 1; 1924–27 Division 2; 1927–28 Division 1; 1928–29 Division 2; 1929–54 Division 1; 1954–66 Division 2; 1966–67 Division 3; 1967–74 Division 2; 1974–82 Division 1; 1982–86 Division 2; 1986–87 Division 3; 1987–88 Division 2; 1988–89 Division 1; 1989–92 Division 2; 1992–93 FA Premier League; 1993–95 Division 1; 1995–97 FA Premier League; 1997–98 Division 1; 1998– FA Premier League.

*Honours: Football League:* Division 1 – Champions 1994–95; Runners-up 1997–98. Division 2 – Champions 1926–27, 1928–29, 1973–74; Runners-up 1901–02, 1991–92. Division 3 – Runners-up 1966–67, 1986–87. *FA Cup:* Runners-up 1997. *Football League Cup:* Runners-up 1997, 1998. *Amateur Cup:* Winners 1895, 1898, *Anglo-Scottish Cup:* Winners 1976.

*Colours:* Red and white. *Change colours:* White and royal blue.

**Did you know?**
Middlesbrough broke two post-war club records during the 1997-98 season. They fielded 36 players and 20 of them scored goals.

## MIDDLESBROUGH 1997–98 LEAGUE RECORD

| Match No. | Date | Venue | Opponents | Result | H/T Score | Lg. Pos. | Goalscorers | Attendance |
|---|---|---|---|---|---|---|---|---|
| 1 | Aug 9 | H | Charlton Ath | W 2-1 | 0-1 | — | Festa [80], Ravanelli [90] | 29,414 |
| 2 | 23 | H | Stoke C | L 0-1 | 0-0 | 17 | | 30,122 |
| 3 | 30 | A | Tranmere R | W 2-0 | 1-0 | 10 | Mustoe [25], Beck [54] | 12,095 |
| 4 | Sept 2 | A | Stockport Co | D 1-1 | 1-0 | — | Emerson [6] | 8257 |
| 5 | 13 | A | Bradford C | D 2-2 | 1-1 | 12 | Kinder [42], Ormerod [77] | 17,767 |
| 6 | 20 | H | Birmingham C | W 3-1 | 3-0 | 11 | Kinder [23], Beck [41], Emerson [43] | 30,125 |
| 7 | 28 | A | Sunderland | W 2-1 | 0-0 | 8 | Emerson [68], Mustoe [79] | 35,384 |
| 8 | Oct 5 | H | Sheffield U | L 1-2 | 1-1 | 8 | Beck [19] | 30,000 |
| 9 | 18 | A | Crewe Alex | D 1-1 | 0-0 | 13 | Townsend [48] | 5759 |
| 10 | 21 | A | Oxford U | W 4-1 | 1-0 | — | Emerson [36], Mustoe [79], Fleming [81], Merson [90] | 8306 |
| 11 | 25 | H | Port Vale | W 2-1 | 1-0 | 7 | Merson 2 (2 pens) [11, 68] | 30,096 |
| 12 | 28 | H | Huddersfield T | W 3-0 | 2-0 | — | Merson [13], Beck 2 [18, 58] | 29,965 |
| 13 | Nov 1 | A | Wolverhampton W | L 0-1 | 0-0 | 6 | | 26,896 |
| 14 | 5 | H | Portsmouth | D 1-1 | 0-0 | — | Townsend [65] | 29,724 |
| 15 | 8 | H | QPR | W 3-0 | 2-0 | 5 | Beck [22], Merson [37], Ormerod [90] | 30,067 |
| 16 | 15 | A | Norwich C | W 3-1 | 1-1 | 4 | Beck [39], Merson [52], Ormerod [55] | 16,011 |
| 17 | 22 | A | Swindon T | W 2-1 | 1-1 | 3 | Merson [22], Emerson [75] | 15,228 |
| 18 | 26 | H | Nottingham F | D 0-0 | 0-0 | — | | 30,143 |
| 19 | 29 | H | WBA | W 1-0 | 1-0 | 2 | Beck [34] | 30,164 |
| 20 | Dec 2 | A | Ipswich T | D 1-1 | 1-0 | 2 | Merson [33] | 13,619 |
| 21 | 6 | A | Bury | W 1-0 | 0-0 | 1 | Beck [60] | 8016 |
| 22 | 13 | H | Reading | W 4-0 | 0-0 | 1 | Hignett 2 [77, 90], Beck 2 [79, 84] | 29,876 |
| 23 | 20 | A | Manchester C | L 0-2 | 0-2 | 1 | | 28,097 |
| 24 | 26 | A | Huddersfield T | W 1-0 | 0-0 | 1 | Gray (og) [76] | 18,820 |
| 25 | 28 | H | Stockport Co | W 3-1 | 1-1 | 1 | Hignett [10], Beck 2 [66, 89] | 30,166 |
| 26 | Jan 10 | A | Charlton Ath | L 0-3 | 0-2 | 2 | | 15,742 |
| 27 | 17 | H | Ipswich T | D 1-1 | 0-0 | 2 | Pearson [63] | 30,081 |
| 28 | Feb 1 | A | Stoke C | W 2-1 | 1-1 | 2 | Pearson [17], Moreno [81] | 13,242 |
| 29 | 4 | H | Tranmere R | W 3-0 | 2-0 | — | Hignett [31], Merson 2 [38, 65] | 29,540 |
| 30 | 7 | A | Birmingham C | D 1-1 | 1-1 | 2 | Festa [38] | 20,639 |
| 31 | 14 | H | Bradford C | W 1-0 | 0-0 | 1 | Hignett [49] | 30,165 |
| 32 | 21 | H | Sunderland | W 3-1 | 1-0 | 1 | Branca 2 [31, 68], Armstrong [87] | 30,227 |
| 33 | 25 | H | Crewe Alex | W 1-0 | 0-0 | — | Maddison [80] | 29,936 |
| 34 | Mar 1 | A | Nottingham F | L 0-4 | 0-2 | 2 | | 25,286 |
| 35 | 4 | A | QPR | L 0-5 | 0-4 | — | | 11,580 |
| 36 | 11 | H | Swindon T | W 6-0 | 2-0 | — | Branca 2 [16, 88], Maddison 2 [22, 55], Armstrong 2 [50, 73] | 29,581 |
| 37 | 14 | A | Portsmouth | D 0-0 | 0-0 | 2 | | 17,003 |
| 38 | 22 | H | Norwich C | W 3-0 | 1-0 | 2 | Maddison [22], Armstrong [71], Beck [90] | 30,040 |
| 39 | Apr 4 | A | WBA | L 1-2 | 0-1 | 3 | Branca [75] | 20,620 |
| 40 | 7 | A | Sheffield U | L 0-1 | 0-0 | — | | 18,421 |
| 41 | 11 | H | Bury | W 4-0 | 1-0 | 4 | Ricard [29], Branca 3 [63, 73, 83] | 30,218 |
| 42 | 13 | A | Reading | W 1-0 | 1-0 | 4 | Branca [8] | 14,501 |
| 43 | 17 | H | Manchester C | W 1-0 | 1-0 | — | Armstrong [43] | 30,182 |
| 44 | 24 | A | Port Vale | W 1-0 | 1-0 | — | Merson [2] | 12,096 |
| 45 | 29 | H | Wolverhampton W | D 1-1 | 1-1 | — | Ricard [12] | 29,878 |
| 46 | May 3 | H | Oxford U | W 4-1 | 0-0 | 2 | Armstrong 2 [47, 48], Hignett 2 [57, 63] | 30,228 |

**Final League Position: 2**          1996–97 PREM 19

### GOALSCORERS
*League (77):* Beck 14, Merson 11 (2 pens), Branca 9, Armstrong 7, Hignett 7, Emerson 5, Maddison 4, Mustoe 3, Ormerod 3, Festa 2, Kinder 2, Pearson 2, Ricard 2, Townsend 2, Fleming 1, Moreno 1, Ravanelli 1, own goal 1.
*Coca-Cola Cup (11):* Hignett 3, Merson 3 (2 pens), Beck 1, Branca 1, Campbell 1, Freestone 1, Summerbell 1.
*FA Cup (5):* Mustoe 2, Campbell 1, Hignett 1, Merson 1.

| Roberts B 6 | Fleming C 28+3 | Kinder V 25+1 | Vickers S 30+3 | Festa G 38 | Emerson 21 | Blackmore C 1+1 | Mustoe R 31+1 | Beck M 31+8 | Merson P 45 | Ravanelli F 2 | Hignett C 28+8 | Stamp P 8+2 | Liddle C 2+4 | Moore A 3+1 | Freestone C —+2 | Townsend A 35+2 | Ormerod A 8+10 | Campbell A 5+2 | Pearson N 29 | Schwarzer M 35 | Whyte D 4+4 | Baker S 5+1 | Harrison C 16+4 | Summerbell M 7+4 | Maddison N 16+6 | Moreira F 1 | Moreno J 1+4 | Thomas M 10 | Stockdale R 1 | Branca M 11 | Armstrong A 7+4 | Dibble A 2 | Beresford M 3 | Ricard H 4+5 | Gascoigne P 7 | Match No. |
|---|---|---|---|---|---|---|---|---|---|---|---|---|---|---|---|---|---|---|---|---|---|---|---|---|---|---|---|---|---|---|---|---|---|---|---|---|
| 1 | 2 | 3 | 4 | 5 | 6 | $7^1$ | 8 | $9^2$ | 10 | 11 | 12 | 13 | | | | | | | | | | | | | | | | | | | | | | | | 1 |
| 1 | 3 | | 4 | 5 | | | 8 | 12 | 10 | 11 | $7^2$ | 6 | 2 | $9^1$ | 13 | | | | | | | | | | | | | | | | | | | | | 2 |
| 1 | 2 | 3 | 4 | 5 | $6^2$ | | 8 | $9^1$ | 10 | | 7 | 12 | 11 | | | 13 | | | | | | | | | | | | | | | | | | | | 3 |
| 1 | 2 | 3 | 4 | 5 | 6 | | 8 | 9 | 10 | | 7 | | | | $11^1$ | 12 | | | | | | | | | | | | | | | | | | | | 4 |
| 1 | 2 | 3 | 4 | | $6^1$ | | 8 | 12 | 10 | | | | | 5 | | 11 | 7 | 9 | | | | | | | | | | | | | | | | | | 5 |
| 1 | 3 | $4^1$ | 2 | | $6^2$ | | 8 | $9^3$ | 10 | | 12 | | | | 14 | 11 | 7 | 13 | 5 | | | | | | | | | | | | | | | | | 6 |
| | 2 | 3 | 4 | | 6 | | 8 | 9 | 10 | | 12 | | | | | 11 | $7^1$ | | 5 | 1 | | | | | | | | | | | | | | | | 7 |
| | 2 | 3 | 4 | | 6 | | 8 | 9 | 10 | | $7^1$ | | | | | 11 | 12 | | 5 | 1 | | | | | | | | | | | | | | | | 8 |
| | 2 | 3 | 4 | | 6 | | 8 | 12 | 10 | | | 13 | | | | 11 | $7^1$ | $9^2$ | 5 | 1 | | | | | | | | | | | | | | | | 9 |
| | 2 | $3^2$ | 4 | | 6 | | 8 | 9 | 10 | | $7^1$ | | | | | 11 | 12 | | 5 | 1 | 13 | | | | | | | | | | | | | | | 10 |
| | | | 4 | | 6 | | $8^1$ | 9 | 10 | | 7 | | | | | | | | 5 | 1 | 3 | 2 | 11 | 12 | | | | | | | | | | | | 11 |
| | | | 4 | | 6 | | | 9 | 10 | | 7 | | | | | 12 | | | $5^1$ | 1 | 2 | 3 | 8 | | 11 | | | | | | | | | | | 12 |
| | 2 | | | | 6 | | | 9 | 10 | 12 | 7 | | | | | 11 | | | 5 | 1 | 4 | 3 | 8 | $7^1$ | | | | | | | | | | | | 13 |
| | 2 | $3^2$ | 4 | | 6 | | | $9^1$ | 10 | | 7 | | | | | 11 | 12 | | 5 | 1 | 13 | | | | 8 | | | | | | | | | | | 14 |
| | | | 4 | | 6 | | | 9 | 10 | | 7 | | | | | 8 | 12 | $11^1$ | 5 | 1 | 3 | | | | 2 | | | | | | | | | | | 15 |
| | | 3 | 4 | | 6 | | | 9 | 10 | | 7 | | | | | 11 | | | 5 | 1 | | | | $2^1$ | 12 | 8 | | | | | | | | | | 16 |
| | 12 | | 4 | | 6 | | | 9 | $10^1$ | | 7 | | | | | 8 | 11 | | 5 | 1 | 3 | | | | 2 | | | | | | | | | | | 17 |
| | | $3^2$ | 4 | | 6 | | | 9 | 10 | | $7^1$ | | | | | 11 | 12 | | 5 | 1 | | | 13 | 8 | 2 | | | | | | | | | | | 18 |
| | | $5^2$ | 4 | | 6 | | | 9 | 10 | | 7 | | | | | 8 | 11 | | | 1 | 12 | | 3 | 13 | $2^1$ | | | | | | | | | | | 19 |
| | 2 | | 4 | | 6 | | | 9 | $10^1$ | | $7^2$ | | | | | 11 | 12 | | 5 | 1 | 13 | | 3 | 8 | | | | | | | | | | | | 20 |
| | 2 | | 4 | | 6 | | | 9 | 10 | | 7 | | | | | 8 | 11 | | 5 | 1 | | | 3 | | | | | | | | | | | | | 21 |
| | 2 | | 4 | | 6 | | | 9 | 10 | | 7 | $11^3$ | | | | $8^1$ | | | $5^2$ | 1 | 3 | 13 | | 12 | | | 14 | | | | | | | | | 22 |
| | 2 | 12 | 4 | | | | 13 | 9 | 10 | | $7^3$ | 11 | | | | 8 | | | 5 | 1 | | | $3^1$ | $6^2$ | | | 14 | | | | | | | | | 23 |
| | 2 | $3^1$ | 4 | | | | 6 | $9^2$ | 10 | | 7 | 11 | | | | 8 | | | 5 | 1 | | | | | 12 | | 13 | | | | | | | | | 24 |
| | 2 | 3 | 4 | | | | 6 | 9 | 10 | | 7 | 11 | | | | 8 | | | 5 | 1 | | | | | | | | | | | | | | | | 25 |
| | | 3 | 4 | | 6 | | | $9^2$ | 10 | | 7 | | 12 | | | $8^1$ | 13 | | 5 | 1 | | | 14 | | 2 | | $11^2$ | | | | | | | | | 26 |
| | 12 | 3 | 4 | | 6 | | | 9 | 10 | | 7 | | | | | 8 | | | 5 | 1 | | | | | 2 | | | | | | | | | | | 27 |
| | | 3 | 4 | | 6 | | | 12 | 10 | | 7 | | | | | 8 | | $9^2$ | 5 | 1 | 2 | | $11^1$ | | 13 | | | | | | | | | | | 28 |
| | | 3 | 4 | | $6^2$ | | | 9 | 10 | | 7 | | 12 | | | 8 | | | $5^1$ | 1 | | | | | 13 | | | | | 11 | 2 | | | | | 29 |
| | | 3 | 4 | 5 | | | | 9 | 10 | | 7 | | | | | 8 | | | | 1 | | | | $2^1$ | 12 | | | | | 11 | | | | | | 30 |
| | 2 | | 4 | 5 | 6 | | | $9^1$ | 10 | | 7 | | 12 | | | 8 | 13 | | | 1 | | | 3 | | | | | | | $11^2$ | | | | | | 31 |
| | 12 | 3 | 4 | 2 | 6 | | | 13 | 10 | | $7^3$ | | | | | $8^2$ | | | 5 | 1 | | | $11^1$ | | | | | | | 9 | 14 | | | | | 32 |
| | 2 | 3 | $4^2$ | 5 | 6 | | $8^1$ | | 10 | | 7 | | | | | | | | | 1 | | | | | 13 | | | 11 | | | 9 | 12 | | | | 33 |
| | $2^2$ | 3 | 4 | | 6 | | | | 10 | | 7 | | | | | 12 | | | 5 | | | | | | 8 | | | 11 | | | $9^1$ | 13 | | 1 | | 34 |
| | 2 | 3 | 4 | | 6 | | | 12 | 10 | | $7^1$ | | | | | 8 | | | $5^2$ | | | | 13 | | | | | $11^3$ | | | 9 | 14 | | 1 | | 35 |
| | 12 | 3 | 4 | 2 | 6 | | | 13 | $10^1$ | | | | 14 | | | $8^3$ | | | | | | | 3 | | $6^1$ | | | 11 | | | 9 | 7 | | 1 | | 36 |
| | 2 | | 4 | 5 | 6 | | | | 10 | | | | | | | 8 | | | | | | | 3 | | $6^1$ | | | 11 | | | 9 | 7 | | 1 | | 37 |
| | 2 | | 4 | $6^1$ | | | 13 | | | | | 12 | | | | | | | 5 | | | | 3 | | 10 | | | 11 | | | $9^2$ | 8 | | 1 | 7 | 38 |
| | 12 | 3 | 4 | 2 | | | 7 | $11^1$ | $10^3$ | | | | | | | $6^2$ | | | 5 | 1 | | | 13 | | | | | 9 | | | | 14 | | 8 | 39 |
| | 2 | | 4 | 5 | | | 6 | | 10 | | | | | | | 12 | | | | 1 | | | 3 | | 7 | | | 9 | | | | 11 | | $8^1$ | 40 |
| | 2 | | 4 | 5 | | | 7 | | 10 | | 12 | | | | | $6^2$ | | | | 1 | | | 3 | | 13 | | | 9 | | | | $11^3$ | | 8 | 41 |
| | 2 | | 4 | 5 | | | 7 | | $10^2$ | | 12 | | | | | 6 | | | | 1 | | | 3 | | 13 | | | $9^1$ | | | | $11^3$ | 14 | $8^1$ | 42 |
| | 3 | | 4 | 5 | | 14 | 7 | | 10 | | 12 | | | | | 6 | | | | 1 | | | 2 | | | | | $9^2$ | 11 | | | $13^3$ | | $8^1$ | 43 |
| | 2 | 3 | 4 | 5 | | | 7 | 9 | 10 | | $11^1$ | | | | | 6 | | | | 1 | | | | | 8 | | | | | | | | 12 | | | 44 |
| | 3 | 12 | 4 | 5 | | | 7 | 9 | 10 | | | | | | | 6 | | | | 1 | | | | | $2^1$ | | | | | | | 11 | | 8 | 45 |
| | 2 | | | 4 | | | 7 | | 10 | 11 | | | | | | 6 | | | 5 | 1 | | | 3 | | | | | | | | $9^1$ | | | 12 | 8 | 46 |

**Coca-Cola Cup**

| Second Round | Barnet | (h) | 1-0 |
|---|---|---|---|
| | | (a) | 2-0 |
| Third Round | Sunderland | (h) | 2-0 |
| Fourth Round | Bolton W | (h) | 2-1 |
| Fifth Round | Reading | (a) | 1-0 |
| Semi-Final | Liverpool | (a) | 1-2 |
| | | (h) | 2-0 |
| Final | Chelsea | | 0-2 |
| | (at Wembley) | | |

**FA Cup**

| Third Round | QPR | (a) | 2-2 |
|---|---|---|---|
| | | (h) | 2-0 |
| Fourth Round | Arsenal | (h) | 1-2 |

MILLWALL 1997-98 *Back row (left to right):* Steve Aris, Dave Savage, Alan McLeary, Brian Law, Tony Witter, Damian Webber, Keith Stevens, Scott Fitzgerald, Paul Sturgess, Danny Hockton. *Middle row:* Gill Chapman (Reserve Physio), Kenny Brown, Ricky Newman, Graham Robertson, Tim Carter, James Connor, David Nurse, Dean Canoville, Lee McRobert, Bobby Bowry, Gerry Docherty (Physio). *Front row:* Marc Bircham, Lucas Neill, Jason Dair, Paul Hartley, Kevin O'Callaghan (Youth Team Coach), Billy Bonds (Manager), Pat Holland (Assistant Manager), Maurice Doyle, Brendan Markey, Gerard Lavin, Paul Allan.

# Division 2     **MILLWALL**

*Millwall Football & Athletic Company (1985) plc, The Den, Zampa Road, Bermondsey SE16 3LN.*
Telephone: (0171) 232 1222. Ticket Office: (0171) 231 9999. Club Shop: (0171) 231 9845. Fax: (0171) 231 3663.
*Ground capacity:* 20,146 (all-seater).

*Record Attendance:* 20,093 v Arsenal, FA Cup 3rd rd, 10 January 1994.

*Pitch measurements:* 100m × 68m.

*Life President:* Reg Burr.

*Chairman:* Theo Paphitis. *Directors:* Reg Burr, Peter Mead, Steven Ring, Doug Woodward, David Sullivan.

*Secretary:* Yvonne Haines.

*Manager:* Keith Stevens. *Assistant Manager:* Alan McLeary. *Reserve Team Coach:* Steve Gritt.

*Chief Scout:* Ronnie Boyce. *Youth Development Officer and Senior Scout:* Bob Pearson. *Assistant Youth Development Officer:* Mick Beard. *Physio:* Gerry Docherty. *Hon. Medical Officer:* Dr. Charlotte Cowie.

*Stadium Manager:* Colin Sayer. *Sales and Promotions Manager:* Mark Cole.

*Year Formed:* 1885. *Turned Professional:* 1893. *Ltd Co.:* 1894.

*Previous Names:* 1885, Millwall Rovers; 1889, Millwall Athletic.

*Club Nickname:* 'The Lions'.

*Previous Grounds:* 1885, Glengall Road, Millwall; 1886, Back of 'Lord Nelson'; 1890, East Ferry Road; 1901, North Greenwich; 1910, The Den, Cold Blow Lane; 1993, The Den, Bermondsey.

*Foundation:* Formed in 1885 as Millwall Rovers by employees of Morton & Co, a jam and marmalade factory in West Ferry Road. The founders were predominantly Scotsmen. Their first headquarters was The Islanders pub in Tooke Street, Millwall. Their first trophy was the East End Cup in 1887.

*First Football League game:* 28 August 1920, Division 3, v Bristol R (h) W 2-0 – Lansdale; Fort, Hodge; Voisey (1), Riddell, McAlpine; Waterall, Travers, Broad (1), Sutherland, Dempsey.

*Record League Victory:* 9–1 v Torquay U, Division 3 (S), 29 August 1927 – Lansdale; Tilling, Hill; Amos, Bryant (3), Graham; Chance, Hawkins (3), Landells (1), Phillips (2), Black. 9–1 v Coventry C, Division 3 (S), 19 November 1927 – Lansdale; Fort, Hill; Amos, Collins (1), Graham; Chance, Landells (4), Cock (2), Phillips (2), Black.

*Record Cup Victory:* 7–0 v Gateshead, FA Cup 2nd rd, 12 December 1936 – Yuill; Ted Smith, Inns; Brolly, Hancock, Forsyth; Thomas (1), Mangnall (1), Ken Burditt (2), McCartney (2), Thorogood (1).

*Record Defeat:* 1–9 v Aston Villa, FA Cup 4th rd, 28 January 1946.

*Most League Points (2 for a win):* 65, Division 3 (S), 1927–28 and Division 3, 1965–66.

*Most League Points (3 for a win):* 90, Division 3, 1984–85.

*Most League Goals:* 127, Division 3 (S), 1927–28.

*Highest League Scorer in Season:* Richard Parker, 37, Division 3 (S), 1926–27.

*Most League Goals in Total Aggregate:* Teddy Sheringham, 93, 1984–91.

*Most Capped Player:* Eamonn Dunphy, 22 (23), Republic of Ireland.

*Most League Appearances:* Barry Kitchener, 523, 1967–82.

*Record Transfer Fee Received:* £2,300,000 from Liverpool for Mark Kennedy, March 1995.

*Record Transfer Fee Paid:* £800,000 to Derby Co for Paul Goddard, December 1989.

*Football League Record:* 1920 Original Members of Division 3; 1921 Division 3 (S); 1928–34 Division 2; 1934–38 Division 3 (S); 1938–48 Division 2; 1948–58 Division 3 (S); 1958–62 Division 4; 1962–64 Division 3; 1964–65 Division 4; 1965–66 Division 3; 1966–75 Division 2; 1975–76 Division 3; 1976–79 Division 2; 1979–85 Division 3; 1985–88 Division 2; 1988–90 Division 1; 1990–92 Division 2; 1992–96 Division 1; 1996– Division 2.

*Honours: Football League:* Division 1 best season: 7th 1992–93; Division 2 – Champions 1987–88; Division 3 (S) – Champions 1927–28, 1937–38; Runners-up 1952–53; Division 3 – Runners–up 1965–66, 1984–85; Division 4 – Champions 1961–62; Runners-up 1964–65. *FA Cup:* Semi-final 1900, 1903, 1937 (first Division 3 side to reach semi-final). *Football League Cup:* best season: 5th rd, 1974, 1977, 1995. *Football League Trophy:* Winners 1983.

*Colours:* Blue shirts, white shorts, blue stockings. *Change colours:* White shirts, black shorts.

**Did you know?**
Millwall is the only Football League club to have been unbeaten at home in a full season in four different divisions.

## MILLWALL 1997–98 LEAGUE RECORD

| Match No. | Date | | Venue | Opponents | Result | | H/T Score | Lg. Pos. | Goalscorers | Attendance |
|---|---|---|---|---|---|---|---|---|---|---|
| 1 | Aug | 9 | H | Brentford | W | 3-0 | 1-0 | — | Bates (og) [22], Sadlier [50], Grant [61] | 8951 |
| 2 | | 16 | A | Preston NE | L | 1-2 | 1-1 | 9 | Sadlier [6] | 11,486 |
| 3 | | 23 | H | York C | L | 2-3 | 1-1 | 16 | Grant 2 [21, 71] | 6583 |
| 4 | Sept | 2 | A | Luton T | W | 2-0 | 0-0 | — | Law [68], Hockton [72] | 5781 |
| 5 | | 13 | H | Southend U | W | 3-1 | 0-1 | 13 | Newman [54], Sadlier [68], Hockton [90] | 8606 |
| 6 | | 20 | A | Grimsby T | W | 1-0 | 0-0 | 6 | Wilkinson [79] | 4267 |
| 7 | | 27 | A | Northampton T | L | 0-2 | 0-0 | 10 | | 6578 |
| 8 | Oct | 4 | H | Blackpool | W | 2-1 | 0-0 | 6 | Wilkinson [48], Grant [65] | 7042 |
| 9 | | 11 | H | Oldham Ath | W | 2-1 | 0-1 | 3 | Law [58], Black [66] | 7906 |
| 10 | | 18 | A | Watford | W | 1-0 | 1-0 | 3 | Shaw [37] | 12,530 |
| 11 | | 21 | A | Bournemouth | D | 0-0 | 0-0 | — | | 4752 |
| 12 | | 25 | A | Wigan Ath | D | 1-1 | 0-0 | 4 | Bowry [90] | 7986 |
| 13 | | 29 | H | Bristol C | L | 0-2 | 0-1 | — | | 7026 |
| 14 | Nov | 1 | A | Gillingham | W | 3-1 | 1-0 | 4 | Black [34], Shaw [83], Wilkinson [89] | 8383 |
| 15 | | 4 | H | Fulham | D | 1-1 | 0-0 | — | Shaw [84] | 10,291 |
| 16 | | 8 | H | Carlisle U | D | 1-1 | 1-0 | 4 | Law [2] | 6959 |
| 17 | | 18 | A | Burnley | W | 2-1 | 1-1 | — | Bowry [2], Savage [63] | 8834 |
| 18 | | 22 | H | Chesterfield | D | 1-1 | 0-0 | 3 | Shaw [61] | 6556 |
| 19 | | 29 | A | Bristol R | L | 1-2 | 0-1 | 3 | Shaw [60] | 5542 |
| 20 | Dec | 3 | A | Walsall | L | 0-1 | 0-0 | — | | 4647 |
| 21 | | 13 | A | Plymouth Arg | L | 0-3 | 0-2 | 6 | | 4460 |
| 22 | | 20 | H | Wycombe W | W | 1-0 | 0-0 | 4 | Shaw [48] | 6092 |
| 23 | | 26 | A | Bristol C | L | 1-4 | 0-2 | 6 | Veart [53] | 16,128 |
| 24 | | 28 | H | Luton T | L | 0-2 | 0-0 | 10 | | 7461 |
| 25 | Jan | 10 | A | Brentford | L | 1-2 | 1-1 | 12 | Grant [20] | 5529 |
| 26 | | 17 | H | Wrexham | L | 0-1 | 0-0 | 15 | | 5550 |
| 27 | | 24 | A | York C | W | 3-2 | 0-1 | 11 | Grant [48], Shaw 2 [63, 90] | 3508 |
| 28 | | 31 | A | Southend U | D | 0-0 | 0-0 | 11 | | 5705 |
| 29 | Feb | 7 | H | Grimsby T | L | 0-1 | 0-1 | 14 | | 6020 |
| 30 | | 14 | A | Blackpool | L | 0-3 | 0-3 | 15 | | 4455 |
| 31 | | 21 | H | Northampton T | D | 0-0 | 0-0 | 15 | | 6007 |
| 32 | | 25 | H | Watford | D | 1-1 | 1-0 | — | Shaw [26] | 7126 |
| 33 | | 28 | A | Oldham Ath | D | 1-1 | 0-0 | 15 | McNiven S (og) [68] | 4805 |
| 34 | Mar | 3 | A | Carlisle U | L | 0-1 | 0-0 | — | | 5217 |
| 35 | | 7 | H | Gillingham | W | 1-0 | 0-0 | 15 | Law [47] | 8241 |
| 36 | | 14 | A | Fulham | W | 2-1 | 0-1 | 13 | Shaw [48], Gray [77] | 12,318 |
| 37 | | 17 | A | Wrexham | L | 0-1 | 0-1 | — | | 4167 |
| 38 | | 21 | H | Burnley | W | 1-0 | 1-0 | 9 | Grant [21] | 7582 |
| 39 | | 25 | H | Preston NE | L | 0-1 | 0-1 | — | | 5888 |
| 40 | | 28 | A | Chesterfield | L | 1-3 | 0-2 | 13 | Tomlinson [60] | 3952 |
| 41 | Apr | 4 | H | Bristol R | D | 1-1 | 0-0 | 13 | Shaw [89] | 5635 |
| 42 | | 11 | A | Walsall | L | 0-2 | 0-1 | 16 | | 3307 |
| 43 | | 13 | H | Plymouth Arg | D | 1-1 | 1-1 | 18 | Hockton [4] | 5496 |
| 44 | | 18 | A | Wycombe W | D | 0-0 | 0-0 | 18 | | 5371 |
| 45 | | 24 | H | Wigan Ath | D | 0-0 | 0-0 | — | | 4045 |
| 46 | May | 2 | H | Bournemouth | L | 1-2 | 1-2 | 18 | Grant (pen) [25] | 7872 |

**Final League Position: 18**          1996–97 DIV2 14

### GOALSCORERS

*League (43):* Shaw 11, Grant 8 (1 pen), Law 4, Hockton 3, Sadlier 3, Wilkinson 3, Black 2, Bowry 2, Gray 1, Newman 1, Savage 1, Tomlinson 1, Veart 1, own goals 2.
*Coca-Cola Cup (5):* Hockton 2, Grant 1, Savage 1, Shaw 1 (pen).
*FA Cup (0).*

| Carter T 12 | Brown R 45 | Sturgess P 12+2 | McLeary A 19 | Law B 40 | Fitzgerald S 16+2 | Allen P 21+7 | Savage D 24+7 | Sadlier R 3+1 | Grant K 31+8 | Newman R 35 | Roche S —+1 | Hockton D 10+16 | Bowry B 41+2 | Robertson G —+1 | Bircham M 3+1 | Doyle M 8+12 | Wilkinson P 22+8 | Shaw P 40 | Spink N 21 | Webber D —+1 | Black M 13 | Neill L 3+3 | Veart C 7+1 | Witter T 10+1 | Stevens K 3+1 | Cook A 3 | Nethercott S 10 | Gray A 12 | McRobert L 4+1 | Ryan R 16 | Crossley M 13 | Tomlinson G 2+1 | Lavin G 4+3 | Harris N 2+1 | Cahill T 1 | Reid S —+1 | Match No. |
|---|---|---|---|---|---|---|---|---|---|---|---|---|---|---|---|---|---|---|---|---|---|---|---|---|---|---|---|---|---|---|---|---|---|---|---|---|---|
| 1 | 2 | 3 | $4^1$ | 5 | 6 | 7 | 8 | $9^2$ | 10 | 11 | 12 | 13 |  |  |  |  |  |  |  |  |  |  |  |  |  |  |  |  |  |  |  |  |  |  |  |  | 1 |
| 1 | 2 | 3 | 4 | 5 | 6 | 7 | $8^1$ | 9 | $10^2$ | 11 |  | 12 | 13 |  |  |  |  |  |  |  |  |  |  |  |  |  |  |  |  |  |  |  |  |  |  |  | 2 |
| 1 | 2 | 3 | 4 | 5 | 6 | 7 | $8^3$ | $9^1$ | 10 | $11^2$ |  | 12 | 13 | 14 |  |  |  |  |  |  |  |  |  |  |  |  |  |  |  |  |  |  |  |  |  |  | 3 |
| 1 | 2 | 3 | 6 | 5 |  | 7 |  |  | $10^1$ | 11 |  | 8 | 4 |  |  | 12 |  | 9 |  |  |  |  |  |  |  |  |  |  |  |  |  |  |  |  |  |  | 4 |
| 1 | 2 | 3 | 6 | 5 |  | 7 | $11^1$ |  | $10^2$ | 8 |  | 9 | 4 |  |  | 13 |  |  |  |  |  |  |  |  |  |  |  |  |  |  |  |  |  |  |  |  | 5 |
| 1 | 2 | 3 | 6 | 5 |  | $7^1$ | 11 |  |  | 8 |  | 12 | 4 |  |  |  |  | 9 | 10 |  |  |  |  |  |  |  |  |  |  |  |  |  |  |  |  |  | 6 |
|  | 2 | 3 | $6^2$ | 5 |  | 7 | $11^1$ |  | 12 | 8 |  |  | 4 |  |  |  |  | 9 | 10 | 1 | 13 |  |  |  |  |  |  |  |  |  |  |  |  |  |  |  | 7 |
|  | 2 | 12 | $6^2$ | 5 | 13 | 11 |  |  | $10^3$ | 3 |  | 14 | $4^1$ |  |  |  |  | 9 | 8 | 1 |  |  | 7 |  |  |  |  |  |  |  |  |  |  |  |  |  | 8 |
|  | 2 |  | 6 | 5 | 11 | 12 |  |  | $10^1$ | 3 |  |  | 4 |  |  |  |  | 9 | 8 | 1 |  |  | 7 |  |  |  |  |  |  |  |  |  |  |  |  |  | 9 |
|  | 2 |  | 6 | 5 |  | 7 | 12 |  | $10^1$ | 3 |  | 13 | 4 |  |  |  |  | 9 | 8 | 1 | $11^2$ |  |  |  |  |  |  |  |  |  |  |  |  |  |  |  | 10 |
|  | 2 |  | 6 | 5 |  | 7 | $12^2$ |  | $10^1$ | 3 |  | 13 | 4 |  |  |  |  | 9 | 8 | 1 | 11 |  |  |  |  |  |  |  |  |  |  |  |  |  |  |  | 11 |
|  | 2 |  | 6 | 5 |  | 7 |  |  | $10^1$ | 3 |  | 12 | 4 |  |  |  |  | 9 | 8 | 1 | 11 |  |  |  |  |  |  |  |  |  |  |  |  |  |  |  | 12 |
|  | 2 |  | 6 | 5 | $11^2$ | 12 |  |  | $10^1$ | 3 |  | 13 | 4 |  |  |  |  | 9 | 8 | 1 | 7 |  |  |  |  |  |  |  |  |  |  |  |  |  |  |  | 13 |
|  | 2 |  | 6 | 5 |  | 10 |  |  |  | 11 |  |  | 4 | 3 |  |  |  | 9 | 8 | 1 | 7 |  |  |  |  |  |  |  |  |  |  |  |  |  |  |  | 14 |
| 1 | 2 |  | 6 | 5 |  | 10 |  |  |  | 11 |  | 12 | 4 | $3^1$ |  |  |  | 9 | 8 |  | 7 |  |  |  |  |  |  |  |  |  |  |  |  |  |  |  | 15 |
|  | 2 |  | 6 | 5 | 12 | 10 |  |  | 3 |  |  | 13 | 4 |  |  | 11 |  | 9 | $8^1$ | 1 | $7^1$ |  |  |  |  |  |  |  |  |  |  |  |  |  |  |  | 16 |
|  | 2 | 3 | 6 | 5 |  | 11 |  |  | 12 | 8 |  |  | $4^1$ |  |  |  |  | 9 | 10 | 1 | 7 |  |  |  |  |  |  |  |  |  |  |  |  |  |  |  | 17 |
|  | 2 | 3 | 6 | 5 | 12 | $11^1$ |  |  | 13 | 10 |  |  | 4 |  |  |  |  | 9 | 8 | 1 | $7^2$ |  |  |  |  |  |  |  |  |  |  |  |  |  |  |  | 18 |
|  | 2 | $3^1$ | $6^2$ | 5 | 13 | 11 |  |  | 12 | 8 |  |  | 4 |  |  | 9 | 10 | 1 |  |  | $7^3$ | 14 |  |  |  |  |  |  |  |  |  |  |  |  |  |  | 19 |
|  | 2 | 3 |  | 5 | 6 | $7^2$ | 11 |  | 12 | 8 |  |  | 4 |  |  | $9^1$ | 10 | 1 |  | 13 |  |  |  |  |  |  |  |  |  |  |  |  |  |  |  |  | 20 |
|  | 2 |  |  |  | 6 | 12 | 9 |  | $8^2$ |  |  | 13 | 11 |  |  | $3^0$ |  |  | 10 | 1 |  | $7^1$ | 14 | 4 | 5 |  |  |  |  |  |  |  |  |  |  |  | 21 |
|  | 2 |  | 4 | 5 | 12 | $6^1$ |  |  | 13 | 11 |  |  | 3 |  |  | $8^2$ | 9 | 1 |  |  | 10 | 7 |  |  |  |  |  |  |  |  |  |  |  |  |  |  | 22 |
|  | 2 | 12 |  | 3 | 5 |  | 6 |  | 10 | 7 |  |  | 4 |  |  |  | 9 | 1 |  |  | $8^1$ | 11 |  |  |  |  |  |  |  |  |  |  |  |  |  |  | 23 |
|  | 2 | 3 |  | 5 | 6 | 12 |  |  | 8 | 7 |  |  | 4 |  |  |  | 10 | 1 |  |  | $9^1$ |  | 11 |  |  |  |  |  |  |  |  |  |  |  |  |  | 24 |
|  |  |  | 5 | 6 | 2 |  |  |  | 8 |  |  | 12 | 7 |  |  | $9^1$ | 10 | 1 |  |  | 11 | 4 | 3 |  |  |  |  |  |  |  |  |  |  |  |  |  | 25 |
| 1 | 2 |  | 5 | $6^3$ | 7 |  |  |  | $9^1$ | 11 |  | 4 | 13 | $12^2$ | 10 |  |  |  |  |  | 8 | 14 | 3 |  |  |  |  |  |  |  |  |  |  |  |  |  | 26 |
| 1 | 2 |  | 5 |  | 7 |  |  |  | $8^1$ | 3 |  | 4 | 12 | 10 |  |  |  |  |  |  | 6 | 9 | 11 |  |  |  |  |  |  |  |  |  |  |  |  |  | 27 |
| 1 | 2 |  | 5 |  | 7 |  |  |  | 8 | 4 |  | 10 |  |  |  |  |  |  |  |  | 6 | 9 | 11 | 3 |  |  |  |  |  |  |  |  |  |  |  |  | 28 |
| 1 | 2 |  | 5 |  | 7 |  |  |  | 8 | 12 | 4 | 10 | 13 |  |  |  |  |  |  |  | 6 | $9^2$ | $11^1$ | 3 |  |  |  |  |  |  |  |  |  |  |  |  | 29 |
| 1 | 2 |  | 5 | $7^1$ |  |  |  |  | 12 | 4 | 13 | 9 | 10 |  |  | $11^2$ | 8 |  |  |  | 6 | 3 |  |  |  |  |  |  |  |  |  |  |  |  |  |  | 30 |
|  | 2 |  | 5 | $7^2$ |  |  |  |  | 8 | 12 | 4 | 13 | 9 | 10 |  |  |  |  |  |  | 6 | $11^1$ | 3 | 1 |  |  |  |  |  |  |  |  |  |  |  |  | 31 |
|  | 2 |  | 5 |  | 7 |  |  |  | 8 | 4 |  | 9 | 10 |  |  |  |  |  |  |  | 6 | 11 | 3 | 1 |  |  |  |  |  |  |  |  |  |  |  |  | 32 |
|  | 2 |  | 5 |  | 7 | 12 | $8^1$ |  | 13 | 4 | 14 | $9^2$ | 10 |  |  |  |  |  |  |  | 6 | $11^3$ | 3 | 1 |  |  |  |  |  |  |  |  |  |  |  |  | 33 |
|  | 2 |  | 5 | 12 | $7^1$ | $11^2$ | 8 |  | 13 | 4 |  | 9 | 10 |  |  |  |  |  |  |  | 6 | 3 | 1 |  |  |  |  |  |  |  |  |  |  |  |  |  | 34 |
|  | 2 |  | 5 |  |  | 9 | 8 |  | 7 | $4^1$ |  | 12 | 10 |  |  |  |  |  |  |  | 6 | 11 | 3 | 1 |  |  |  |  |  |  |  |  |  |  |  |  | 35 |
|  | 2 |  | 5 | 12 |  | $9^1$ | 8 |  | $7^2$ | 4 |  | 13 | 10 |  |  | 14 |  |  |  |  | $6^3$ | 11 | 3 | 1 |  |  |  |  |  |  |  |  |  |  |  |  | 36 |
|  | 2 |  |  |  | $7^1$ | 9 | 8 |  |  | 4 |  | 6 | 12 | 10 |  |  |  |  |  |  | 5 | 11 | 3 | 1 |  |  |  |  |  |  |  |  |  |  |  |  | 37 |
|  | 2 |  | 5 |  |  | 9 | 8 |  | $7^1$ | 4 |  | 12 | 10 |  |  |  |  |  |  |  | 6 | 11 | 3 | 1 |  |  |  |  |  |  |  |  |  |  |  |  | 38 |
|  | 2 |  | 5 | 12 |  | 9 | $8^2$ |  | $7^1$ | $4^1$ |  | 13 | 14 | 10 |  |  |  |  |  |  | 6 | 11 | 3 | 1 |  |  |  |  |  |  |  |  |  |  |  |  | 39 |
|  | 2 |  | 5 | 6 | $7^1$ | 9 |  |  |  | 4 |  | 12 | 10 |  |  |  |  |  |  |  |  | 11 | $3^2$ | 1 |  | 8 | 13 |  |  |  |  |  |  |  |  |  | 40 |
|  | 2 |  | 5 |  |  |  | 8 |  | 12 | 4 |  | 13 | 9 | 10 |  |  |  |  |  |  | 6 | 11 | 13 | 1 | $9^1$ | 3 | $7^2$ |  |  |  |  |  |  |  |  |  | 41 |
|  | 2 |  | 5 |  | 7 | $11^2$ |  |  | $8^1$ | 12 | 10 |  |  |  |  |  |  |  |  |  | 6 |  | 1 | 13 | 3 |  |  |  |  |  |  |  |  |  |  |  | 42 |
|  | 2 |  | $7^2$ | 12 |  |  | 9 | $8^1$ | $11^1$ | 4 |  | 10 |  |  |  |  |  |  |  |  | 6 |  | 3 |  |  |  | 13 | 14 |  |  |  |  |  |  |  |  | 43 |
|  | 2 |  | 5 | 12 |  | $9^1$ |  |  | $11^2$ | 4 |  | 8 | 13 | 10 | 1 |  |  |  |  |  | 6 |  | 3 |  |  | 7 |  |  |  |  |  |  |  |  |  |  | 44 |
|  | 2 |  | 5 |  |  | 9 |  |  | $11^1$ | 4 |  | 8 | 12 | 10 | 1 |  |  |  |  |  | 6 |  | 3 |  |  | 7 |  |  |  |  |  |  |  |  |  |  | 45 |
|  | 2 |  | 6 |  |  | 9 |  |  | 12 | 4 |  | 8 |  | 1 |  |  | $7^2$ | 5 | $3^2$ |  |  |  |  |  |  | 13 | $10^1$ | 11 | 14 |  |  |  |  |  |  |  | 46 |

**Coca-Cola Cup**

| | | | | |
|---|---|---|---|---|
| First Round | Northampton T | (a) | 1-2 | |
| | | (h) | 2-1 | |
| Second Round | Wimbledon | (a) | 1-5 | |
| | | (h) | 1-4 | |

**FA Cup**

| | | | |
|---|---|---|---|
| First Round | Bristol C | (a) | 0-1 |

NEWCASTLE UNITED 1997–98  *Back row (left to right):* Paul Brayson, David Burt, Stuart Elliott, Pavel Srnicek, Shaka Hislop, Shay Given, Stephen Harper, Brian Pinas, Bjarni Gudjonsson, Jimmy Crawford, Patrick Kelly.

*Middle row:* Terry Gennoe (Goalkeeping Coach), Paul Ferris (Physio), Keith Gillespie, John Beresford, Temuri Ketsbaia, Philippe Albert, Des Hamilton, Aaron Hughes, Darren Peacock, Alessandro Pistone, Chris McMenemy (Coach), Tommy Burns (Coach).

*Front row:* Alan Irvine (Coach), Derek Wright (Physio), Warren Barton, Steve Watson, Stuart Pearce, Jon Dahl Tomasson, Terry McDermott (Assistant Manager), Kenny Dalglish (Manager), Alan Shearer, Robert Lee, David Batty, Faustino Asprilla, John Carver (Youth Team Coach), John Murray (Youth Development Officer).

# FA Premiership  NEWCASTLE UNITED

*St James' Park, Newcastle-upon-Tyne NE1 4ST.* Telephone: (0191) 201 8400. Club Fax: (0191) 201 8600. Lottery Office: (0191) 201 8502. Commercial Department: (0191) 201 8422. Ticket Office Hotline: (0191) 261 1571. Mail Order: (0990) 501892. Football in the Community Scheme: (0191) 261 9715. Clubcall: 0891 121590. Clubcall Main Line: 0891 121190. Ticket Line: 0891 121590. Club Shop numbers: St James' Park Club Shop: (0191) 201 8426. Garden Walk, Metro Centre: (0191) 461 0000; Russell Way, Metro Centre: (0191) 460 3509; Within Asda, Metro Centre (0191) 460 3974; Asda, Gosforth (0191) 213 0638; Asda, Blyth (01670) 351653; Newcastle Airport: (0191) 271 2631. Monument Mall: (0191) 232 4488. Eldon Way, Eldon Square: (0191) 230 2303. Whitecross Way, Eldon Square: (0191) 230 0808. Travel Club: (0191) 201 8550. Junior Magpies: (0191) 201 8472. Corporate Hospitality: (0191) 201 8424. Photographic Dept: (0191) 235 3906.

*Ground capacity:* 36,834.

*Record attendance:* 68,386 v Chelsea, Division 1, 3 September 1930.

*Record receipts:* £744,544 v Monaco, UEFA Cup quarter-final, 4 March 1997.

*Pitch measurements:* 105m × 68m.

*Chairman:* D. Cassidy.

*Chief Executive:* A. O. Fletcher.

*Directors:* A. O. Fletcher, R. Jones, A. M. Wilson.

*Manager:* Kenny Dalglish. *Assistant Manager:* Terry McDermott.

*Coaches:* Alan Irvine, John Carver, Tommy Craig, Terry Gennoe. *Physios:* Derek Wright, Paul Ferris.

*Director of Football Administration:* Russell Cushing. *Director of Marketing:* Alec King. *Operations Manager:* P. W. Stevens.

*Assistant Secretary:* Tony Toward. *Youth Development Officer:* John Murray.

*Year Formed:* 1881. *Turned Professional:* 1889. *Ltd Co.:* 1890.

*Club Nickname:* 'Magpies'.

*Previous Names:* Stanley 1881; Newcastle East End 1882–92.

*Previous Grounds:* South Byker, 1881; Chillingham Road, Heaton, 1886–92.

*Foundation:* It stemmed from a newly formed club called Stanley in 1881. In October 1882 they changed their name to Newcastle East End to avoid confusion with two other local clubs, Stanley Nops and Stanley Albion. Shortly afterwards another club Rosewood merged with them. Newcastle West End had been formed in August 1882 and they played on a pitch which was part of the Town Moor. Moved to Brandling Park 1885 and St James' Park 1886 (home of Newcastle Rangers). West End went out of existence after a bad run and the remaining committee men invited East End to move to St James' Park. They accepted and, at a meeting in Bath Lane Hall in 1892, changed their name to Newcastle United.

*First Football League game:* 2 September 1893, Division 2, v Royal Arsenal (a) D 2-2 – Ramsay; Jeffery, Miller; Crielly, Graham, McKane; Bowman, Crate (1), Thompson, Sorley (1), Wallace. Graham and not Crate scored according to some reports.

*Record League Victory:* 13–0 v Newport Co, Division 2, 5 October 1946 – Garbutt; Cowell, Graham; Harvey, Brennan, Wright; Milburn (2), Bentley (1), Wayman (4), Shackleton (6), Pearson.

*Record Cup Victory:* 9–0 v Southport (at Hillsborough) FA Cup 4th rd, 1 February 1932 – McInroy; Nelson, Fairhurst; McKenzie, Davidson, Weaver (1); Boyd (1), Jimmy Richardson (3), Cape (2), McMenemy (1), Lang (1).

*Record Defeat:* 0–9 v Burton Wanderers, Division 2, 15 April 1895.

*Most League Points (2 for a win):* 57, Division 2, 1964–65.

*Most League Points (3 for a win):* 96, Division 1, 1992–93.

*Most League Goals:* 98, Division 1, 1951–52.

*Highest League Scorer in Season:* Hughie Gallacher, 36, Division 1, 1926–27.

*Most League Goals in Total Aggregate:* Jackie Milburn, 177, 1946–57.

*Most Capped Player:* Alf McMichael, 40, Northern Ireland.

*Most League Appearances:* Jim Lawrence, 432, 1904–22.

*Record Transfer Fee Received:* £6,250,000 from Manchester U for Andy Cole, January 1995.

*Record Transfer Fee Paid:* £15,000,000 to Blackburn R for Alan Shearer, July 1996.

*Football League Record:* 1893 Elected to Division 2; 1898–1934 Division 1; 1934–48 Division 2; 1948–61 Division 1; 1961–65 Division 2; 1965–78 Division 1; 1978–84 Division 2; 1984–89 Division 1; 1989–92 Division 2; 1992–93 Division 1; 1993– FA Premier League.

*Honours:* FA Premier League: Runners-up 1995–96, 1996–97. *Football League:* Division 1 – Champions 1904–05, 1906–07, 1908–09, 1926–27, 1992–93; Division 2 – Champions 1964–65; Runners-up 1897–98, 1947–48. *FA Cup:* Winners 1910, 1924, 1932, 1951, 1952, 1955; Runners-up 1905, 1906, 1908, 1911, 1974, 1998. *Football League Cup:* Runners-up 1976. *Texaco Cup:* Winners 1974, 1975. **European Competitions:** *European Cup:* 1997–98. *European Fairs Cup:* 1968–69 (winners), 1969–70, 1970–71. *UEFA Cup:* 1977–78, 1994–95, 1996–97. *Anglo-Italian Cup:* Winners 1972–73.

*Colours:* Black and white striped shirts, black shorts, black stockings. *Change colours:* Italian blue.

**Did you know?**
In 1950-51 when Newcastle United reached the FA Cup semi-final, they had to play 13 games in seven weeks and 11 in four weeks after the 1955 semi-final. Both years they were successful in the Final.

## NEWCASTLE UNITED 1997–98 LEAGUE RECORD

| Match No. | Date | Venue | Opponents | Result | H/T Score | Lg. Pos. | Goalscorers | Attendance |
|---|---|---|---|---|---|---|---|---|
| 1 | Aug 9 | H | Sheffield W | W 2-1 | 1-1 | — | Asprilla 2 [2, 72] | 36,711 |
| 2 | 23 | H | Aston Villa | W 1-0 | 1-0 | 6 | Beresford [13] | 36,783 |
| 3 | Sept 13 | H | Wimbledon | L 1-3 | 1-1 | 12 | Barton [32] | 36,692 |
| 4 | 20 | A | West Ham U | W 1-0 | 1-0 | 8 | Barnes [44] | 25,884 |
| 5 | 24 | H | Everton | W 1-0 | 0-0 | — | Lee [87] | 36,705 |
| 6 | 27 | A | Chelsea | L 0-1 | 0-0 | 10 | | 31,050 |
| 7 | Oct 4 | H | Tottenham H | W 1-0 | 0-0 | 7 | Barton [89] | 36,708 |
| 8 | 18 | A | Leeds U | L 1-4 | 0-3 | 10 | Gillespie [62] | 39,865 |
| 9 | 25 | H | Blackburn R | D 1-1 | 1-0 | 10 | Gillespie [27] | 36,716 |
| 10 | Nov 1 | H | Leicester C | D 3-3 | 2-2 | 9 | Barnes (pen) [4], Tomasson [45], Beresford [90] | 36,754 |
| 11 | 8 | A | Coventry C | D 2-2 | 1-1 | 9 | Barnes [31], Lee [87] | 22,670 |
| 12 | 22 | H | Southampton | W 2-1 | 0-1 | 9 | Barnes 2 [55, 75] | 36,769 |
| 13 | 29 | A | Crystal Palace | W 2-1 | 1-0 | 8 | Ketsbaia [45], Tomasson [63] | 26,085 |
| 14 | Dec 1 | A | Bolton W | L 0-1 | 0-1 | — | | 24,494 |
| 15 | 6 | H | Arsenal | L 0-1 | 0-1 | 9 | | 36,751 |
| 16 | 13 | H | Barnsley | D 2-2 | 1-1 | 9 | Gillespie 2 [44, 49] | 18,694 |
| 17 | 17 | H | Derby Co | D 0-0 | 0-0 | — | | 36,289 |
| 18 | 21 | H | Manchester U | L 0-1 | 0-0 | 9 | | 36,763 |
| 19 | 26 | A | Derby Co | L 0-1 | 0-1 | 10 | | 30,232 |
| 20 | 28 | H | Liverpool | L 1-2 | 1-2 | 11 | Watson [16] | 36,702 |
| 21 | Jan 10 | A | Sheffield W | L 1-2 | 1-1 | 11 | Tomasson [20] | 29,446 |
| 22 | 17 | H | Bolton W | W 2-1 | 1-0 | 10 | Barnes [7], Ketsbaia [90] | 36,767 |
| 23 | 20 | A | Liverpool | L 0-1 | 0-1 | — | | 42,791 |
| 24 | Feb 1 | A | Aston Villa | W 1-0 | 0-0 | 10 | Batty [58] | 38,266 |
| 25 | 7 | H | West Ham U | L 0-1 | 0-1 | 10 | | 36,736 |
| 26 | 22 | H | Leeds U | D 1-1 | 0-0 | 13 | Ketsbaia [87] | 36,511 |
| 27 | 28 | A | Everton | D 0-0 | 0-0 | 12 | | 37,972 |
| 28 | Mar 14 | H | Coventry C | D 0-0 | 0-0 | 15 | | 36,762 |
| 29 | 18 | H | Crystal Palace | L 1-2 | 0-2 | — | Shearer [77] | 36,565 |
| 30 | 28 | A | Southampton | L 1-2 | 0-0 | 15 | Lee [46] | 15,251 |
| 31 | 31 | A | Wimbledon | D 0-0 | 0-0 | — | | 15,478 |
| 32 | Apr 11 | H | Arsenal | L 1-3 | 1-0 | 16 | Barton [79] | 38,102 |
| 33 | 13 | H | Barnsley | W 2-1 | 1-0 | 15 | Andersson [40], Shearer [86] | 36,534 |
| 34 | 18 | A | Manchester U | D 1-1 | 1-1 | 15 | Andersson [11] | 55,194 |
| 35 | 25 | A | Tottenham H | L 0-2 | 0-1 | 15 | | 35,847 |
| 36 | 29 | A | Leicester C | D 0-0 | 0-0 | — | | 21,699 |
| 37 | May 2 | H | Chelsea | W 3-1 | 2-0 | 13 | Dabizas [39], Lee [42], Speed [59] | 36,710 |
| 38 | 10 | A | Blackburn R | L 0-1 | 0-0 | 13 | | 29,300 |

**Final League Position: 13**   1996–97 PREM 2

## GOALSCORERS

*League (35):* Barnes 6 (1 pen), Gillespie 4, Lee 4, Barton 3, Ketsbaia 3, Tomasson 3, Andersson 2, Asprilla 2, Beresford 2, Shearer 2, Batty 1, Dabizas 1, Speed 1, Watson 1.
*Coca-Cola Cup (3):* Hamilton 1, Rush 1, Tomasson 1.
*FA Cup (9):* Shearer 5, Batty 1, Ketsbaia 1, Rush 1, Speed 1.

| Given S 24 | Watson S 27+2 | Beresford J 17+1 | Albert P 21+2 | Pistone A 28 | Pearce S 25 | Lee R 26+2 | Batty D 32 | Asprilla F 8+2 | Ketsbaia T 16+15 | Tomasson J 17+6 | Rush I 6+4 | Gillespie K 25+4 | Barton W 17+6 | Barnes J 22+4 | Peacock D 19+1 | Howey S 11+3 | Smicek P 1 | Hamilton D 7+5 | Hislop S 13 | Hughes A 4 | Shearer A 15+2 | Griffin A 4 | Andersson A 10+2 | Speed G 13 | Dabizas N 10+1 | Match No. |
|---|---|---|---|---|---|---|---|---|---|---|---|---|---|---|---|---|---|---|---|---|---|---|---|---|---|---|
| 1 | 2 | 3 | 4 | 5 | 6 | 7 | 8 | 9 | 10 | 11 | | | | | | | | | | | | | | | | 1 |
| 1 | 2 | 3 | 4 | 5 | 6 | 7 | 8 | | 11² | 12 | 9¹ | 10 | 13 | | | | | | | | | | | | | 2 |
| 1 | 2 | 3 | 4 | 5 | | 7 | | | 12 | 13 | 11 | 9 | 8¹ | 6² | 10 | | | | | | | | | | | 3 |
| 1 | 2 | 3 | | 6 | | 7 | 8 | 9 | | | 11 | 4 | 10¹ | 5 | 12 | | | | | | | | | | | 4 |
| 1 | 2 | 12 | 6 | 3 | | 7¹ | 4 | 9 | 11² | 13 | 8³ | 14 | 10 | 5 | | | | | | | | | | | | 5 |
| 1 | 2 | 3¹ | 4 | 5 | | 8 | | 12 | 11¹ | 9 | 13 | 7 | 10² | 6 | 14 | | | | | | | | | | | 6 |
| 1 | 2 | 3 | | | | 4 | | 7 | 11 | 9 | | 8 | 10 | 5 | 6 | | | | | | | | | | | 7 |
| 1 | 4 | 3 | | | | 7 | 8 | 11¹ | 12 | 9 | 13 | 2 | 10² | 5 | 6 | | | | | | | | | | | 8 |
| | 2 | 3 | 6 | | | 12 | 4 | 11 | 9 | | 8² | | 10 | 5 | 13 | 1 | | 7¹ | | | | | | | | 9 |
| 1 | 2 | 3 | 4 | | | 7 | 8 | 11 | 9¹ | 12 | | 10 | 5 | 6² | 13 | | | | | | | | | | | 10 |
| 1 | 2 | 3 | 4 | 5 | | 7 | 8¹ | 9 | | 11 | 12 | 10 | 6 | | | | | | | | | | | | | 11 |
| | 2 | | 6 | 3 | | 7 | 4 | 8 | 9 | 11 | | 10 | 5 | | 1 | | | | | | | | | | | 12 |
| | 2 | | 5 | 3 | 12 | 4 | 8 | 9 | 11 | 10¹ | 6 | | 7 | 1 | | | | | | | | | | | | 13 |
| | 2 | | 5 | 3 | 7 | 4 | 9 | 10 | 11 | 12 | 6 | 8¹ | 1 | | | | | | | | | | | | | 14 |
| | 2 | 12 | 5 | 3 | 7 | 4 | 9¹ | 13 | 8² | 11 | 10 | 6 | 1 | | | | | | | | | | | | | 15 |
| | 2 | 4 | 5 | 3 | 7 | 8 | 9¹ | 12 | 11 | 10 | 6 | 1 | | | | | | | | | | | | | | 16 |
| | 2 | 6 | 5 | 3 | 4 | 9¹ | 8 | 11 | 12 | 7 | 10 | 1 | | | | | | | | | | | | | | 17 |
| | 2 | 11¹ | 4² | 3 | 6 | 8 | 9 | 12 | 7 | 13 | 10 | 5 | 1 | | | | | | | | | | | | | 18 |
| | 2 | 11 | 3 | 6 | 4 | 12 | 13 | 10² | 9¹ | 7 | 14 | 5¹ | 8 | 1 | | | | | | | | | | | | 19 |
| | 4 | 3 | 5 | 6 | 7 | 8 | 9 | 11 | 2¹ | 10 | 12 | 1 | | | | | | | | | | | | | | 20 |
| | 6 | 11 | 4 | | 12 | 9 | 13 | 7 | 2¹ | 10 | 5 | 8² | 1 | 3 | | | | | | | | | | | | 21 |
| | 4 | 11 | 3 | 6 | 7 | 12 | 9¹ | 8 | 2 | 10² | 5 | 1 | 13 | | | | | | | | | | | | | 22 |
| | 4 | 11¹ | 3 | 6 | 7 | 12 | 9 | 8 | 2 | 10² | 1 | 5 | 13 | | | | | | | | | | | | | 23 |
| | 2 | 3 | 4 | 6 | 7 | 8 | 12 | 11 | 5 | 1 | 9 | 3¹ | 10 | 11 | | | | | | | | | | | | 24 |
| 1 | | | 2 | 6 | 7 | 4 | 12 | 8 | 5 | | 9 | 3¹ | 10 | 11 | | | | | | | | | | | | 25 |
| 1 | | 12 | 3 | 6 | 7 | 4 | 13 | 8¹ | 5 | | 2⁴ | 9 | 10 | 11 | | | | | | | | | | | | 26 |
| 1 | | 6 | 3 | 7 | 4 | 12 | 8¹ | 2 | 5 | | 9 | 10 | 11 | | | | | | | | | | | | | 27 |
| 1 | | 6¹ | 2 | 3² | 7 | 4 | 8 | 12 | 5 | 9 | 10 | 11 | 13 | | | | | | | | | | | | | 28 |
| 1 | | 3 | 4 | 8¹ | 12 | 7 | 2 | 13 | 14 | 5³ | 9 | 10² | 11 | 6 | | | | | | | | | | | | 29 |
| 1 | | 3 | 6 | 7² | 12 | 8 | 11¹ | 10 | 5 | 13 | 2 | 9 | 4 | | | | | | | | | | | | | 30 |
| 1 | 2 | 4 | 3 | 8 | 12 | 13 | 5² | 7 | 9 | 6¹ | 11 | 10 | | | | | | | | | | | | | | 31 |
| 1 | 6 | 3 | 4 | 12 | 7 | 10² | 8¹ | 9 | 2 | 13 | 11 | 5 | | | | | | | | | | | | | | 32 |
| 1 | 12 | 6 | 3 | 7 | 4 | 13 | 8² | 2 | 9 | 10¹ | 11 | 5 | | | | | | | | | | | | | | 33 |
| 1 | 4 | 3 | 6 | 7 | 8 | 12 | 2 | 9 | 10¹ | 11 | 5 | | | | | | | | | | | | | | | 34 |
| 1 | 2 | 4¹ | 3 | 6 | 8 | 13 | 12² | 7 | 9 | 10 | 11 | 5 | | | | | | | | | | | | | | 35 |
| 1 | | 3 | 6 | 7 | 8 | 10 | 2 | 5 | 9 | 11 | 4 | | | | | | | | | | | | | | | 36 |
| 1 | 12 | 3 | 6 | 7³ | 8 | 2 | 13 | 5¹ | 14 | 9 | 10² | 11 | 4 | | | | | | | | | | | | | 37 |
| 1 | 4 | 6 | 3 | 8 | 7¹ | 10² | 12 | 9 | 2 | 13 | 11 | 5 | | | | | | | | | | | | | | 38 |

**Coca-Cola Cup**

| | | | |
|---|---|---|---|
| Third Round | Hull C | (h) | 2-0 |
| Fourth Round | Derby Co | (a) | 1-0 |
| Fifth Round | Liverpool | (h) | 0-2 |

**FA Cup**

| | | | |
|---|---|---|---|
| Third Round | Everton | (a) | 1-0 |
| Fourth Round | Stevenage B | (a) | 1-1 |
| | | (h) | 2-1 |
| Fifth Round | Tranmere R | (h) | 1-0 |
| Sixth Round | Barnsley | (h) | 3-1 |
| Semi Final | Sheffield U | | 1-0 |
| | (at Old Trafford) | | |
| Final | Arsenal | | 0-2 |
| | (at Wembley) | | |

NORTHAMPTON TOWN 1997–98    *Back row (left to right):* Denis Casey (Physio), Claudio DeVito, James Hunt, Chris Lee, Tony Godden (Goalkeeping Coach), Lee Colkin, Jason White, Ian Clarkson, Garry Thompson (Coach).
*Middle row:* Carl Heggs, Dean Peer, David Brightwell, Billy Turley, Ian Sampson, Andy Woodman, David Martin, David Rennie, John Gayle.
*Front row:* Ian Atkins (Manager), Ali Gibb, Roy Hunter, Michael Warner, Ray Warburton, Paul Conway, Sean Parrish, John Frain, Kevin Wilson (Assistant Manager).
(Photograph: Pete Norton)

# Division 2 NORTHAMPTON TOWN

*Sixfields Stadium, Upton Way, Northampton NN5 5QA.* Telephone: (01604) 757773. Fax: (01604) 751613/754960. Ticket Office: (01604) 588338. Soccer Line: 0930 555970.

*Ground capacity:* 7653 (all seating).

*Record attendance (at County Ground):* 24,523 v Fulham, Division 1, 23 April 1966. (Sixfields Stadium): 7461 v Barnet, Division 3, 15 October 1994.

*Record receipts (at Sixfields):* £68,616 v Bristol R, Division 2 play-off, 2nd leg, 13 May 1998.

*Pitch measurements:* 116yd × 72yd.

*Chairman:* B. J. Ward.

*Directors:* B. Stonhill, B. Hancock, M. Church, D. Kerr, B. Collins, B. Lomax, C. Smith.

*Secretary:* Mrs Rebecca Kerr. *Company Secretary:* Barry W. Collins.

*Manager:* Ian Atkins. *Coach:* Kevin Wilson.

*Physio:* Dennis Casey. *Commercial Manager:* Jenny Ball. *Stadium Manager:* Martin Girvan (ACMS Ltd).

*Year Formed:* 1897. *Turned Professional:* 1901. *Ltd Co.:* 1901.

*Previous Ground:* County Ground.

*Club Nickname:* 'The Cobblers'.

*Foundation:* Formed in 1897 by school teachers connected with the Northampton and District Elementary Schools' Association, they survived a financial crisis at the end of their first year when they were £675 in the red and became members of the Midland League – a fast move indeed for a new club. They achieved Southern League membership in 1901.

*First Football League game:* 28 August 1920, Division 3, v Grimsby T (a) L 0-2 – Thorpe; Sproston, Hewison; Jobey, Tomkins, Pease; Whitworth, Lockett, Thomas, Freeman, MacKechnie.

*Record League Victory:* 10–0 v Walsall, Division 3 (S), 5 November 1927 – Hammond; Watson, Jeffs; Allen, Brett, Odell; Daley, Smith (3), Loasby (3), Hoten (1), Wells (3).

*Record Cup Victory:* 10–0 v Sutton T, FA Cup Prel rd, 7 December 1907 – Cooch; Drennan, Lloyd Davies, Tirrell (1), McCartney, Hickleton, Badenock (3), Platt (3), Lowe (1), Chapman (2), McDiarmid.

*Record Defeat:* 0–11 v Southampton, Southern League, 28 December 1901.

*Most League Points (2 for a win):* 68, Division 4, 1975–76.

*Most League Points (3 for a win):* 99, Division 4, 1986–87.

*Most League Goals:* 109, Division 3, 1962–63 and Division 3 (S), 1952–53.

*Highest League Scorer in Season:* Cliff Holton, 36, Division 3, 1961–62.

*Most League Goals in Total Aggregate:* Jack English, 135, 1947–60.

*Most Capped Player:* E. Lloyd Davies, 12 (16), Wales.

*Most League Appearances:* Tommy Fowler, 521, 1946–61.

*Record Transfer Fee Received:* £265,000 from Watford for Richard Hill, July 1987.

*Record Transfer Fee Paid:* £90,000 to Bristol City for David Seal, September 1997.

*Football League Record:* 1920 Original Member of Division 3; 1921 Division 3 (S); 1958–61 Division 4; 1961–63 Division 3; 1963–65 Division 2; 1965–66 Division 1; 1966–67 Division 2; 1967–69 Division 3; 1969–76 Division 4; 1976–77 Division 3; 1977–87 Division 4; 1987–90 Division 3; 1990–92 Division 4; 1992–97 Division 3; 1997– Division 2.

*Honours: Football League:* Division 1 best season: 21st, 1965–66; Division 2 – Runners-up 1964–65; Division 3 – Champions 1962–63; Promoted from Division 3 1996–97 (play-offs); Division 3 (S) – Runners-up 1927–28, 1949–50; Division 4 – Champions 1986–87; Runners-up 1975–76. *FA Cup:* best season: 5th rd, 1934, 1950, 1970. *Football League Cup:* best season: 5th rd, 1965, 1967.

*Colours:* Claret with white shirts, white shorts, white stockings. *Change colours:* Orange and black shirts, black shorts, black stockings.

**Did you know?**
Ralph Hoten scored five goals for Northampton Town in their 8-1 win over Crystal Palace on 27 October 1928.

## NORTHAMPTON TOWN 1997–98 LEAGUE RECORD

| Match No. | Date | | Venue | Opponents | Result | H/T Score | Lg. Pos. | Goalscorers | Attendance |
|---|---|---|---|---|---|---|---|---|---|
| 1 | Aug | 9 | H | Bournemouth | L | 0-2 | 0-0 | — | 6384 |
| 2 | | 16 | A | Wycombe W | D | 0-0 | 0-0 | 21 | 5130 |
| 3 | | 23 | H | Bristol C | W | 2-1 | 2-1 | 14 | Seal [23], Gayle [45] | 6217 |
| 4 | | 30 | A | Carlisle U | W | 2-0 | 2-0 | 9 | Seal 2 [16, 33] | 6307 |
| 5 | Sept | 2 | A | Walsall | W | 2-0 | 1-0 | — | Seal [30], Gayle [80] | 4435 |
| 6 | | 9 | H | Luton T | W | 1-0 | 1-0 | — | Parrish [2] | 7246 |
| 7 | | 13 | A | Oldham Ath | D | 2-2 | 1-2 | 3 | Seal [1], Hunter (pen) [65] | 5829 |
| 8 | | 20 | A | Wigan Ath | W | 1-0 | 0-0 | 2 | Seal [54] | 6570 |
| 9 | | 27 | H | Millwall | W | 2-0 | 0-0 | 2 | Sampson [53], Hunter (pen) [65] | 6578 |
| 10 | Oct | 4 | A | Southend U | D | 0-0 | 0-0 | 2 | | 4300 |
| 11 | | 11 | A | Grimsby T | L | 0-1 | 0-1 | 2 | | 4778 |
| 12 | | 18 | H | Gillingham | W | 2-1 | 2-0 | 2 | Gayle [35], Heggs [39] | 7191 |
| 13 | | 21 | H | York C | D | 1-1 | 1-0 | — | Hunter (pen) [6] | 6059 |
| 14 | | 25 | A | Fulham | D | 1-1 | 0-1 | 2 | Gayle [50] | 9848 |
| 15 | Nov | 1 | H | Bristol R | D | 1-1 | 0-0 | 3 | Gayle [57] | 7264 |
| 16 | | 4 | A | Blackpool | D | 1-1 | 0-1 | — | Sampson [75] | 3685 |
| 17 | | 8 | A | Wrexham | L | 0-1 | 0-0 | 5 | | 3766 |
| 18 | | 18 | H | Brentford | W | 4-0 | 4-0 | — | Heggs [4], Gayle [10], Seal 2 [40, 43] | 5277 |
| 19 | | 22 | H | Watford | L | 0-1 | 0-0 | 4 | | 7373 |
| 20 | | 29 | A | Burnley | L | 1-2 | 0-0 | 6 | Gibb [49] | 8369 |
| 21 | Dec | 2 | H | Chesterfield | D | 0-0 | 0-0 | — | | 4824 |
| 22 | | 13 | A | Preston NE | L | 0-1 | 0-0 | 7 | | 7448 |
| 23 | | 20 | H | Plymouth Arg | W | 2-1 | 0-1 | 5 | Freestone 2 [66, 71] | 5546 |
| 24 | | 26 | A | Luton T | D | 2-2 | 2-0 | 4 | Dozzell (pen) [8], White (og) [13] | 8035 |
| 25 | | 28 | H | Walsall | W | 3-2 | 1-1 | 3 | Seal [31], Freestone [48], Dozzell [54] | 7094 |
| 26 | Jan | 10 | A | Bournemouth | L | 0-3 | 0-0 | 5 | | 4257 |
| 27 | | 17 | H | Carlisle U | W | 2-1 | 0-1 | 4 | Heggs [54], Dozzell [77] | 6327 |
| 28 | | 24 | A | Bristol C | D | 0-0 | 0-0 | 5 | | 14,753 |
| 29 | | 31 | H | Oldham Ath | D | 0-0 | 0-0 | 6 | | 6559 |
| 30 | Feb | 7 | A | Wigan Ath | D | 1-1 | 0-0 | 7 | Freestone [68] | 3579 |
| 31 | | 10 | H | Wycombe W | W | 2-0 | 0-0 | — | Seal (pen) [59], Freestone [69] | 5302 |
| 32 | | 14 | H | Southend U | W | 3-1 | 2-1 | 3 | Freestone [30], Brightwell [41], Frain [55] | 6147 |
| 33 | | 21 | A | Millwall | D | 0-0 | 0-0 | 3 | | 6007 |
| 34 | | 24 | A | Gillingham | L | 0-1 | 0-0 | — | | 6463 |
| 35 | | 28 | H | Grimsby T | W | 2-1 | 0-1 | 3 | Seal (pen) [59], Gleghorn [64] | 6932 |
| 36 | Mar | 3 | H | Wrexham | L | 0-1 | 0-1 | — | | 5183 |
| 37 | | 7 | A | Bristol R | W | 2-0 | 1-0 | 4 | Freestone [34], Dozzell (pen) [61] | 6535 |
| 38 | | 14 | H | Blackpool | W | 2-0 | 1-0 | 4 | Freestone [27], Heggs [73] | 6586 |
| 39 | | 21 | A | Brentford | D | 0-0 | 0-0 | 5 | | 5746 |
| 40 | | 28 | A | Watford | D | 1-1 | 0-0 | 5 | Peer [84] | 14,268 |
| 41 | Apr | 4 | H | Burnley | L | 0-1 | 0-1 | 6 | | 7264 |
| 42 | | 11 | A | Chesterfield | L | 1-2 | 1-0 | 7 | Clarkson [9] | 5064 |
| 43 | | 13 | H | Preston NE | D | 2-2 | 0-1 | 8 | Sampson [78], Seal [82] | 5664 |
| 44 | | 18 | A | Plymouth Arg | W | 3-1 | 1-1 | 6 | Freestone 3 [8, 47, 90] | 6389 |
| 45 | | 25 | H | Fulham | W | 1-0 | 0-0 | 6 | Peer [58] | 7443 |
| 46 | May | 2 | A | York C | D | 0-0 | 0-0 | 4 | | 6688 |

**Final League Position: 4**     1996–97 DIV3 4

### GOALSCORERS
League (52): Seal 12 (2 pens), Freestone 11, Gayle 6, Dozzell 4 (2 pens), Heggs 4, Hunter 3 (3 pens), Sampson 3, Peer 2, Brightwell 1, Clarkson 1, Frain 1, Gibb 1, Gleghorn 1, Parrish 1, own goal 1.
Coca-Cola Cup (3): Gayle 2, Seal 1.
FA Cup (4): Hunter 2, Heggs 1, Seal 1.

| Woodman A 46 | Clarkson I 42 | Frain J 45 | Sampson I 39 | Warburton R 39 | Brightwell D 34+1 | Parrish S 12 | Heggs C 21+12 | Gayle J 26+9 | Lee C 3+3 | Hunter R 28 | Gibb A 6+29 | Van Dullemen R —+1 | Seal D 30+7 | Conway P 2+1 | Peer D 26+4 | Wilson K 1+8 | Rennie D 3+2 | West C 1+1 | Hunt J 14+7 | Potter G 4 | Warner M 3+7 | Hill C 27 | Bishop C 7 | Freestone C 23+2 | Dozzell J 18+3 | Tait P 2+1 | Gleghorn N 3+5 | Drysdale J 1 | Match No. |
|---|---|---|---|---|---|---|---|---|---|---|---|---|---|---|---|---|---|---|---|---|---|---|---|---|---|---|---|---|---|
| 1 | 2 | 3 | 4 | 5 | $6^1$ | 7 | 8 | $9^2$ | $10^3$ | 11 | 12 | 13 | 14 | | | | | | | | | | | | | | | | 1 |
| 1 | 2 | 3 | 4 | 5 | 6 | 7 | 12 | 10 | | 11 | | | $9^1$ | 8 | | | | | | | | | | | | | | | 2 |
| 1 | 2 | 3 | 4 | 5 | 6 | 7 | 12 | 10 | | 11 | | | $9^1$ | $8^2$ | 13 | | | | | | | | | | | | | | 3 |
| 1 | 2 | 3 | 4 | 5 | 6 | 7 | 12 | $10^2$ | | 11 | | | $9^1$ | 13 | 8 | | | | | | | | | | | | | | 4 |
| 1 | 2 | 3 | 4 | 5 | 6 | 7 | 12 | 10 | | 11 | | | $9^2$ | $8^1$ | 13 | | | | | | | | | | | | | | 5 |
| 1 | 2 | 3 | 4 | 5 | 6 | 7 | | 10 | | 11 | | | $9^1$ | 8 | 12 | | | | | | | | | | | | | | 6 |
| 1 | 2 | 3 | 4 | 5 | 6 | 7 | 12 | 10 | | 11 | | | $9^2$ | $8^1$ | 13 | | | | | | | | | | | | | | 7 |
| 1 | 2 | 3 | 4 | 5 | 6 | 7 | $8^1$ | 10 | | 11 | 13 | | $9^2$ | 12 | | | | | | | | | | | | | | | 8 |
| 1 | 2 | 3 | 4 | 5 | 6 | 7 | 12 | 10 | | 11 | 13 | | $9^2$ | $8^1$ | | | | | | | | | | | | | | | 9 |
| 1 | 2 | 3 | 4 | 5 | 6 | 7 | 12 | | | 11 | 13 | | $9^2$ | 8 | $10^1$ | | | | | | | | | | | | | | 10 |
| 1 | 2 | 3 | 4 | $5^2$ | 6 | $7^1$ | $8^3$ | 10 | | 11 | 12 | | 9 | 14 | | | | | | | | | | | | | | | 11 |
| 1 | 2 | 3 | 4 | 5 | 6 | $7^1$ | $8^3$ | 10 | | 11 | 12 | | $9^2$ | 13 | 14 | | | | | | | | | | | | | | 12 |
| 1 | 2 | 3 | 4 | 5 | 6 | | $8^1$ | 10 | | 11 | 12 | | 9 | | 13 | | | | $7^2$ | | | | | | | | | | 13 |
| 1 | 2 | 3 | 4 | $5^1$ | 6 | 13 | 10 | | | 11 | 12 | | $9^2$ | 8 | 14 | | | | $7^2$ | | | | | | | | | | 14 |
| 1 | 2 | 3 | 4 | 5 | 6 | | 8 | 10 | | 11 | 12 | | $9^1$ | | | | | | 7 | | | | | | | | | | 15 |
| 1 | 2 | 3 | 4 | 5 | 6 | | $8^1$ | 10 | 13 | 11 | 12 | | $9^2$ | 14 | | | | | $7^3$ | | | | | | | | | | 16 |
| 1 | 2 | 3 | 4 | 5 | 6 | | 12 | 10 | | 11 | 13 | | $9^1$ | $8^3$ | 14 | | | | $7^2$ | | | | | | | | | | 17 |
| 1 | 2 | 3 | 4 | 5 | $6^1$ | | 8 | $10^2$ | 13 | 11 | 12 | | $9^3$ | 7 | 14 | | | | | | | | | | | | | | 18 |
| 1 | $2^1$ | 3 | 4 | 5 | | | 8 | $10^2$ | | 11 | 12 | | 9 | 7 | 13 | | | | | | 6 | | | | | | | | 19 |
| 1 | $2^2$ | 3 | $4^1$ | 5 | 6 | | 8 | 10 | | 11 | 7 | | 12 | | | | | | | | 13 | 9 | | | | | | | 20 |
| 1 | 2 | 3 | | 5 | 6 | | 8 | 10 | | 11 | 12 | | $9^2$ | | 13 | | | | $7^1$ | | | 4 | | | | | | | 21 |
| 1 | 2 | | | | 6 | | 8 | 10 | | 11 | 12 | | $9^2$ | | | | 5 | | $7^1$ | | | 4 | 3 | 13 | | | | | 22 |
| 1 | 2 | 3 | | | 6 | | $8^2$ | | | $11^3$ | 12 | | 13 | 7 | | | | 14 | | | 4 | $5^1$ | 9 | 10 | | | | | 23 |
| 1 | 2 | 3 | | | 6 | | 8 | | | 5 | | | 7 | | | | | 11 | 12 | | 4 | | | $9^2$ | $10^1$ | 13 | | | 24 |
| 1 | 2 | 3 | | | 6 | | 12 | $10^3$ | | 5 | | | $9^1$ | 7 | | | | 11 | 13 | | 4 | | | $9^2$ | $8^2$ | 4 | | | 25 |
| 1 | 2 | 3 | | | 6 | | 12 | 13 | | 11 | 5 | | 14 | $7^1$ | | | | | 4 | | | | | $9^2$ | $10^3$ | 8 | | | 26 |
| 1 | | 3 | | 5 | | | $10^1$ | 12 | 13 | 11 | | | 6 | | | | | 7 | 2 | | 4 | | | $9^1$ | 8 | | | | 27 |
| 1 | | 3 | 4 | 5 | 6 | | | 10 | | 11 | 12 | | | | | | | 7 | | | 2 | | | $9^1$ | 8 | | | | 28 |
| 1 | 2 | 3 | 4 | | 6 | | | 12 | | 11 | | | | $9^1$ | | | | 7 | | | 5 | | | 10 | 8 | | | | 29 |
| 1 | 2 | 3 | 4 | | 6 | | | $10^1$ | | $11^2$ | | | 12 | | | | | 7 | 13 | | | 9 | | 8 | | | | | 30 |
| 1 | | 3 | 4 | 5 | 6 | | | | | 12 | | | $9^1$ | | $13^3$ | | | 7 | | | 14 | 11 | | 10 | $8^2$ | | | | 31 |
| 1 | | 3 | 4 | 5 | 6 | | | | | 8 | | | $9^2$ | 2 | 12 | | | | | | $7^1$ | 11 | | 10 | | | 13 | | 32 |
| 1 | 2 | 3 | 4 | 5 | 6 | | | | | 12 | | | $8^2$ | 11 | 13 | | | | | | 10 | | | 9 | $7^1$ | | | | 33 |
| 1 | $2^1$ | 3 | 4 | 5 | $6^3$ | | 9 | | | 12 | | | 13 | 7 | | | | | | | 11 | | | 10 | $8^2$ | | 14 | | 34 |
| 1 | $2^1$ | 3 | 4 | 5 | | | | | | 12 | | | $9^2$ | 7 | | | | | | | 13 | 11 | $6^3$ | 10 | 14 | | 8 | | 35 |
| 1 | | 3 | 4 | 5 | | | 12 | | | | | | 2 | $9^1$ | 7 | | | | 13 | | | 11 | 6 | $9^2$ | $6^2$ | | 8 | | 36 |
| 1 | 2 | 3 | 4 | 5 | | | $10^3$ | 12 | | 13 | | | | 7 | | | | | | | 11 | 6 | $9^2$ | $8^1$ | | | 14 | | 37 |
| 1 | 2 | 3 | 4 | 5 | | | $9^1$ | 12 | | 13 | | | | 7 | | | | 14 | | | 11 | 6 | $10^2$ | $8^1$ | | | | | 38 |
| 1 | 2 | 3 | 4 | 5 | 6 | | $9^1$ | 12 | | | | | | 7 | | | | | | | 11 | | | 10 | $8^2$ | | 13 | | 39 |
| 1 | $2^1$ | 3 | 4 | 5 | $6^3$ | | 9 | | | 12 | | | | 7 | $8^2$ | | | | | | 11 | | | 10 | 13 | | 14 | | 40 |
| 1 | 2 | 3 | 4 | 5 | | | 9 | | | 12 | | | | 7 | | | 13 | | | | $11^2$ | | | 10 | 14 | | $8^1$ | $6^3$ | 41 |
| 1 | 2 | 3 | 4 | $5^1$ | | | 9 | 8 | | 12 | | | | 7 | | | | | | | 11 | | | 10 | | | | | 42 |
| 1 | 2 | 3 | 4 | 5 | | | 9 | $8^1$ | | 13 | | | 12 | 14 | | | | | | | 6 | $11^2$ | | 10 | $7^2$ | | | | 43 |
| 1 | 2 | 3 | 4 | 5 | | | 12 | | | $9^1$ | | | | 7 | | | | | | | 6 | 11 | 8 | 10 | | | | | 44 |
| 1 | 2 | 3 | 4 | 5 | | | 12 | | | | | | $9^1$ | 7 | | | | | | | 6 | 11 | | 10 | 8 | | | | 45 |
| 1 | $2^2$ | 3 | 4 | 5 | 12 | | 14 | | | 13 | | | $9^3$ | 7 | | | | | | | 6 | 11 | | 10 | $8^1$ | | | | 46 |

**Coca-Cola Cup**
First Round    Millwall     (h) 2-1   (a) 1-2

**FA Cup**
First Round    Exeter C     (a) 1-1   (h) 2-1
Second Round    Basingstoke T     (h) 1-1   (a) 0-0
Third Round    Leicester C     (a) 0-4

NORWICH CITY 1997–98 *Back row (left to right):* Damian Hilton, John Polston, Keith O'Neill, Rob Newman, Kevin Scott, Drewe Broughton, Iwan Roberts, Matthew Jackson, Joe Green, Adrian Coote.

*Middle row:* Steve Foley (Reserve Team Coach), Lee Marshall, Danny Mills, Gaven Tipple, Che Wilson, Andy Marshall, Robert Green, Bryan Gunn, Kori Davis, Darren Kenton, Daryl Sutch, Karl Simpson, Tim Sheppard (Physio).

*Front row:* Jamie Shore, Adrian Forbes, Shaun Carey, Neil Adams, Robert Fleck, John Faulkner (Assistant Manager), Mike Walker (Manager), Craig Fleming, Mike Milligan, Darren Eadie, Victor Segura, Craig Bellamy.

# Division 1           NORWICH CITY

*Carrow Road, Norwich NR1 1JE.* Telephone: (01603) 760760. Fax: (01603) 613886. Box Office: (01603) 761661. Clubcall: 0891 121144.

*Ground capacity:* 21,994.

*Record attendance:* 43,984 v Leicester C, FA Cup 6th rd, 30 March 1963.

*Record receipts:* £261,918 v Internazionale, UEFA Cup 3rd rd 1st leg, 24 November 1993.

*Pitch measurements:* 114yd × 74yd.

*President:* G. C. Watling.

*Chairman:* Barry Lockwood. *Joint Vice-Chairmen:* R. J. Munby, M. L. Armstrong.

*Company Secretary:* N. A. Doncaster.

*Directors:* M. M. Foulger, B. J. Skipper, M. Wynn Jones, Delia Smith.

*Director of Football:* Bryan Hamilton.

*First Team Coach:* Bruce Rioch.

*Assistant Manager:* John Faulkner.

*Youth Team Coach:* Keith Webb.

*Physio:* Tim Sheppard MCSP, SRP.

*Secretary:* A. R. W. Neville.

*Year Formed:* 1902. *Turned Professional:* 1905. *Ltd Co.:* 1905.

*Club Nickname:* 'The Canaries'.

*Previous Grounds:* 1902, Newmarket Road; 1908–35, The Nest, Rosary Road; 1935, Carrow Road.

*Foundation:* Formed in 1902, largely through the initiative of two local schoolmasters who called a meeting at the Criterion Cafe, they were shocked by an FA Commission which in 1904 declared the club professional and ejected them from the FA Amateur Cup. However, this only served to strengthen their determination. New officials were appointed and a professional club established at a meeting in the Agricultural Hall in March 1905.

*First Football League game:* 28 August 1920, Division 3, v Plymouth Arg (a) D 1-1 – Skermer; Gray, Gadsden; Wilkinson, Addy, Martin; Laxton, Kidger, Parker, Whitham (1), Dobson.

*Record League Victory:* 10–2 v Coventry C, Division 3 (S), 15 March 1930 – Jarvie; Hannah, Graham; Brown, O'Brien, Lochhead (1); Porter (1), Anderson, Hunt (5), Scott (2), Slicer (1).

*Record Cup Victory:* 8–0 v Sutton U, FA Cup 4th rd, 28 January 1989 – Gunn; Culverhouse, Bowen, Butterworth, Linighan, Townsend (Crook), Gordon, Fleck (3), Allen (4), Phelan, Putney (1).

*Record Defeat:* 2–10 v Swindon T, Southern League, 5 September 1908.

*Most League Points (2 for a win):* 64, Division 3 (S), 1950–51.

*Most League Points (3 for a win):* 84, Division 2, 1985–86.

*Most League Goals:* 99, Division 3 (S), 1952–53.

*Highest League Scorer in Season:* Ralph Hunt, 31. Division 3 (S), 1955–56.

*Most League Goals in Total Aggregate:* Johnny Gavin, 122, 1945–54, 1955–58.

*Most Capped Player:* Mark Bowen, 35 (41), Wales.

*Most League Appearances:* Ron Ashman, 592, 1947–64.

*Record Transfer Fee Received:* £5,000,000 from Blackburn R for Chris Sutton, July 1994.

*Record Transfer Fee Paid:* £1,000,000 to Leeds U for Jon Newsome, June 1994.

*Football League Record:* 1920 Original Member of Division 3; 1921 Division 3 (S): 1934–39 Division 2; 1946–58 Division 3 (S); 1958–60 Division 3; 1960–72 Division 2; 1972–74 Division 1; 1974–75 Division 2; 1975–81 Division 1; 1981–82 Division 2; 1982–85 Division 1; 1985–86 Division 2; 1986–92 Division 1; 1992–95 FA Premier League; 1995– Division 1.

*Honours: FA Premier League:* best season: 3rd 1992–93. *Football League:* Division 2 – Champions 1971–72, 1985–86. Division 3 (S) – Champions 1933–34; Division 3 – Runners-up 1959–60. *FA Cup:* Semi-finals 1959, 1989, 1992. *Football League Cup:* Winners 1962, 1985; Runners-up 1973, 1975. **European Competitions:** *UEFA Cup:* 1993–94.

*Colours:* Yellow shirts, yellow shorts, yellow stockings. *Change colours:* All green.

**Did you know?**
Norwich City's Carrow Road ground was constructed in just 82 days during the summer of 1935. It was the largest work carried out in the city since the building of Norwich Castle.

**NORWICH CITY FC**

## NORWICH CITY 1997–98 LEAGUE RECORD

| Match No. | Date | Venue | Opponents | Result | H/T Score | Lg. Pos. | Goalscorers | Attendance |
|---|---|---|---|---|---|---|---|---|
| 1 | Aug 9 | H | Wolverhampton W | L | 0-2 | 0-1 | — | 17,230 |
| 2 | 15 | A | Nottingham F | L | 1-4 | 1-1 | — | O'Neill [7] | 16,524 |
| 3 | 23 | H | Crewe Alex | L | 0-2 | 0-1 | 24 | | 11,821 |
| 4 | 30 | A | Sunderland | W | 1-0 | 0-0 | 19 | Sutch [76] | 29,204 |
| 5 | Sept 2 | A | Portsmouth | D | 1-1 | 0-0 | — | Adams (pen) [89] | 10,577 |
| 6 | 13 | H | Port Vale | W | 1-0 | 0-0 | 16 | Fleck [59] | 11,269 |
| 7 | 17 | H | Charlton Ath | L | 0-4 | 0-3 | — | | 10,157 |
| 8 | 20 | A | Manchester C | W | 2-1 | 1-1 | 15 | Adams [38], Coote [64] | 27,258 |
| 9 | 26 | H | Ipswich T | W | 2-1 | 1-0 | — | Eadie [8], Cundy (og) [59] | 18,911 |
| 10 | Oct 4 | A | Tranmere R | L | 0-2 | 0-1 | 14 | | 6674 |
| 11 | 18 | H | Stockport Co | D | 1-1 | 0-1 | 17 | Eadie [73] | 12,689 |
| 12 | 21 | H | Reading | D | 0-0 | 0-0 | — | | 17,781 |
| 13 | 25 | A | Swindon T | L | 0-1 | 0-0 | 17 | | 9256 |
| 14 | Nov 1 | H | Bury | D | 2-2 | 2-1 | 16 | Bellamy [2], Adams [23] | 14,419 |
| 15 | 4 | A | WBA | L | 0-1 | 0-0 | — | | 13,949 |
| 16 | 8 | A | Birmingham C | W | 2-1 | 2-1 | 16 | Forbes 2 [23, 36] | 16,464 |
| 17 | 15 | H | Middlesbrough | L | 1-3 | 1-1 | 16 | Roberts [32] | 16,011 |
| 18 | 22 | H | Oxford U | W | 2-1 | 1-0 | 15 | Fleck [31], Bellamy [61] | 11,241 |
| 19 | 29 | A | Bradford C | L | 1-2 | 0-1 | 15 | Bellamy [75] | 16,637 |
| 20 | Dec 3 | A | QPR | D | 1-1 | 0-0 | — | Forbes [51] | 10,141 |
| 21 | 6 | H | Sheffield U | W | 2-1 | 0-0 | 15 | Vonk (og) [61], Fuglestad [84] | 11,745 |
| 22 | 13 | A | Huddersfield T | W | 3-1 | 2-0 | 12 | Forbes [3], Bellamy [40], Grant [90] | 11,436 |
| 23 | 20 | H | Stoke C | D | 0-0 | 0-0 | 13 | | 12,265 |
| 24 | 26 | A | Charlton Ath | L | 1-2 | 0-0 | 13 | Bellamy (pen) [81] | 14,472 |
| 25 | 30 | H | Portsmouth | W | 2-0 | 1-0 | — | Jackson [14], Bellamy [66] | 16,441 |
| 26 | Jan 10 | A | Wolverhampton W | L | 0-5 | 0-4 | 12 | | 23,703 |
| 27 | 17 | H | Nottingham F | W | 1-0 | 0-0 | 12 | Roberts [46] | 17,059 |
| 28 | 28 | H | Sunderland | W | 2-1 | 1-0 | — | Eadie [32], Craddock (og) [62] | 15,940 |
| 29 | 31 | A | Crewe Alex | L | 0-1 | 0-0 | 12 | | 5559 |
| 30 | Feb 7 | H | Manchester C | D | 0-0 | 0-0 | 12 | | 15,274 |
| 31 | 14 | A | Port Vale | D | 2-2 | 0-1 | 13 | Grant [64], Jackson [68] | 6664 |
| 32 | 18 | H | Tranmere R | L | 0-2 | 0-0 | 14 | | 12,105 |
| 33 | 21 | A | Ipswich T | L | 0-5 | 0-3 | 14 | | 21,858 |
| 34 | 24 | A | Stockport Co | D | 2-2 | 0-1 | — | Grant [56], Coote [89] | 7471 |
| 35 | 28 | H | QPR | D | 0-0 | 0-0 | 14 | | 12,730 |
| 36 | Mar 4 | H | Birmingham C | D | 3-3 | 0-2 | — | Bellamy 2 [47, 66], Llewellyn [58] | 9819 |
| 37 | 7 | A | Bury | L | 0-1 | 0-0 | 15 | | 5154 |
| 38 | 14 | H | WBA | D | 1-1 | 1-0 | 15 | Bellamy [5] | 19,069 |
| 39 | 22 | A | Middlesbrough | L | 0-3 | 0-1 | 16 | | 30,040 |
| 40 | 28 | A | Oxford U | L | 0-2 | 0-0 | 18 | | 7869 |
| 41 | Apr 4 | H | Bradford C | L | 2-3 | 0-1 | 20 | Llewellyn [64], Bellamy [89] | 13,260 |
| 42 | 11 | A | Sheffield U | D | 2-2 | 0-2 | 19 | Bellamy [72], Llewellyn [78] | 16,915 |
| 43 | 13 | H | Huddersfield T | W | 5-0 | 2-0 | 17 | Fleming [12], Adams (pen) [30], Roberts 2 [57, 67], Fuglestad [90] | 16,550 |
| 44 | 18 | A | Stoke C | L | 0-2 | 0-1 | 17 | | 13,098 |
| 45 | 25 | H | Swindon T | W | 5-0 | 2-0 | 15 | Llewellyn [16], Jackson [34], Roberts [51], Bellamy [66], Fenn [76] | 18,443 |
| 46 | May 3 | A | Reading | W | 1-0 | 0-0 | 15 | Bellamy [57] | 14,817 |

**Final League Position: 15** 　　　1996–97 DIV1 13

### GOALSCORERS

**League (52):** Bellamy 13 (1 pen), Roberts 5, Adams 4 (2 pens), Forbes 4, Llewellyn 4, Eadie 3, Grant 3, Jackson 3, Coote 2, Fleck 2, Fuglestad 2, Fenn 1, Fleming 1, O'Neill 1, Sutch 1, own goals 3.
*Coca-Cola Cup (3):* Roberts 2, Adams 1.
*FA Cup (0).*

Player appearances and goals grid (shirt number worn; superscript = goals). Column headers show each player with total appearances (starts + substitute):

| Marshall A 42 | Fleming C 20 + 2 | Newman R 10 + 5 | Sutch D 40 | Segura V 22 + 3 | Polston J 7 + 5 | Adams N 30 | Mills D 11 + 9 | Roberts I 29 + 2 | Eadie D 18 + 1 | O'Neill K 5 + 4 | Bellamy C 30 + 6 | Fleck R 23 + 4 | Scott K 22 + 2 | Bradshaw C 1 | Grant P 33 + 2 | Milligan M 20 | Forbes A 28 + 5 | Jackson M 39 + 2 | Coote A 11 + 12 | Kenton D 7 + 4 | Simpson K 2 + 4 | Marshall L 2 + 2 | Broughton D — + 1 | Fuglestad E 23 + 1 | Carey S 11 + 3 | Gunn B 4 | Llewellyn C 10 + 5 | Fenn N 6 + 1 | Russell D — + 1 | Match No. |
|---|---|---|---|---|---|---|---|---|---|---|---|---|---|---|---|---|---|---|---|---|---|---|---|---|---|---|---|---|---|---|
| 1 | 2 | 3¹ | 4 | 5 | 6 | 7 | 8 | 9² | 10 | 11 | 12 | 13 | | | | | | | | | | | | | | | | | | 1 |
| 1 | 2 | | 8 | 5 | 6 | 7 | 13 | 9 | 10 | 11 | 12 | | 3² | 4¹ | | | | | | | | | | | | | | | | 2 |
| 1 | | 3 | 5 | 12 | 6 | 7 | 2¹ | 9 | 11 | | 8 | | | | 4² | 10 | 13 | | | | | | | | | | | | | 3 |
| 1 | | 3 | 5 | 2 | 6 | 7 | | 9 | 11 | 12 | | 8¹ | | | 4 | 10² | 13 | | | | | | | | | | | | | 4 |
| 1 | | 3 | 5 | 2¹ | 6 | 7 | | 9 | 11 | 12² | | 8¹ | 13 | | 4 | 10 | 14 | | | | | | | | | | | | | 5 |
| 1 | | 3 | 5 | | 6 | 7 | | 9² | | | 12 | 8¹ | | | 4 | 10 | 11 | 2 | 13 | | | | | | | | | | | 6 |
| 1 | 12 | 3 | 5 | | 6¹ | 7 | | | | | 13 | 8 | | | 4 | 10² | 11 | 2 | 9 | | | | | | | | | | | 7 |
| 1 | 2 | 12 | 3 | | 13 | 7 | 14 | | 10³ | | 8¹ | | 5 | | 4 | 11 | 6 | 9² | | | | | | | | | | | | 8 |
| 1 | 2 | 3 | | | | 7 | | 9 | | | 12 | 8 | 5 | | 4 | 10¹ | 11² | 6 | 13 | | | | | | | | | | | 9 |
| 1 | | 5 | 3 | | | 7 | 2 | 9 | | | 8¹ | | | | 4 | 10 | 11² | 6 | 12 | 13 | | | | | | | | | | 10 |
| 1 | 2³ | 3 | | | | 7 | 12 | 9¹ | 10 | | | 8 | 5 | | 4 | 11² | 6 | | 13 | 14 | | | | | | | | | | 11 |
| 1 | 12 | 3 | | | | 7 | | 9 | 10 | | | 8 | 5 | | 4 | 11 | 6 | 2² | 13 | | | | | | | | | | | 12 |
| 1 | 12 | 3¹ | | | | 7 | 13 | 9 | 10 | | | 8³ | 5 | | 4 | 11² | 6 | 2 | 14 | | | | | | | | | | | 13 |
| 1 | | 3 | | | | 7 | | 9 | 10 | | | 8² | 5 | | 4 | 11¹ | 6 | 2 | 12 | | 13 | | | | | | | | | 14 |
| 1 | 12 | 3 | | | | 7 | | 9 | 10 | | | 8² | 5 | | 4 | 11 | 6¹ | 2 | 14 | | 2³ | | | | | | | | | 15 |
| 1 | 6 | 3 | 2² | | | 7 | 4 | 9 | | | | | 5 | | 10 | 11 | | | 12 | | | | | | | | | | | 16 |
| 1 | 6 | 3 | 2 | | | 7 | 12² | 9 | | | | 14 | 8³ | 5 | 4¹ | 10 | 11 | | | | | | | 13 | | | | | | 17 |
| 1 | | | 2 | | | 7 | | 9 | | | | | 4 | 8 | 5 | 10 | 11 | 6 | | | | | | 3 | | | | | | 18 |
| 1 | | 3 | 2 | | | 7 | | 9 | | | | | 4 | 8 | 5 | 10 | 12 | 6 | | | | | | 11 | | | | | | 19 |
| 1 | 12 | 3² | 2 | | | 7 | | 9 | | | | | 4 | 8 | 5 | 10¹ | 13 | 6 | | | | | | 11 | | | | | | 20 |
| 1 | | | 2 | | | 7 | 3 | 9 | | | | | 4 | 8 | 5 | | 10 | 6 | | | | | | 11 | | | | | | 21 |
| 1 | | | 2 | | | 7 | 3 | 9 | | | | | 4 | 8¹ | 5 | 12 | 10² | 6 | | | | | | 11 | 13 | | | | | 22 |
| 1 | | | 2 | | | | 3 | 9 | | | 12 | 10 | 4 | 11 | 5 | | 7¹ | 6 | | | | | | 8 | | | | | | 23 |
| 1 | | | 2 | | | | 3 | 9¹ | | | 12 | 10 | 4 | 11 | 5 | | 7¹ | 6 | | | | | | 8 | | | | | | 24 |
| 1 | | | 2 | | | | 3 | | | | 11 | 10 | 12 | 5 | 4 | 9 | 7¹ | 6 | | | | | | 8 | | | | | | 25 |
| | 12 | | 7 | | | | | 3 | 9 | | 11 | 10 | | 5¹ | 4 | | 6 | | | | | | | 2 | 8² | 1 | 13 | | | 26 |
| | 5 | 2 | | | | | | | 9 | 10 | 11 | | | | 4 | | 7 | 6 | 8 | | | | | 3 | | 1 | | | | 27 |
| | 5 | 2 | 12 | | | | | 13 | 9 | 11 | | | | | 4 | 10¹ | 7 | 6 | 8 | | | | | 3 | | 1 | | | | 28 |
| | 5 | 2 | | | | | | | 9 | 11 | | 10 | | | 4 | | 7 | 6 | 8 | | | | | 3 | | 1 | | | | 29 |
| 1 | | 2 | 5 | | | | | 12 | 9 | 11² | | 10 | | | 4 | 13 | 6 | 8 | 7 | | | | | 3¹ | | | | | | 30 |
| 1 | 3 | 2 | 5 | | | | | 9¹ | | | 10 | 12 | | | 4 | | 6 | 8 | 7² | | | | | 11 | | | 13 | | | 31 |
| 1 | 5 | 2 | 3 | | | 7¹ | | 11 | 10 | 8² | | | | | 4² | | 6 | 9 | 12 | | | | | 13 | 14 | | | | | 32 |
| 1 | 5 | 2 | 3² | | | 12 | | 11 | | 8¹ | | | | | 4 | 7³ | 6 | 9 | 13 | | | | | 10 | 14 | | | | | 33 |
| 1 | 5 | 2 | 3 | | | | | 11 | | | | | | | 4 | 7¹ | 6 | 12 | 8 | | | | | 10 | 9 | | | | | 34 |
| 1 | 5 | 2 | 3 | | | | | 11² | | | | 12 | | | 4 | 7¹ | 6 | 13 | 8 | | | | | 10 | 9 | | | | | 35 |
| 1 | 5 | 2 | 3² | | | | | | | 11 | | 8¹ | | | 4 | 7 | 6 | 12 | 13 | | | | | 10 | 9 | | | | | 36 |
| 1 | 5 | 2 | | | | 12 | | 11 | 8¹ | | | | | | 4² | 7³ | 6 | 13 | 3 | 14 | | | | 10 | 9 | | | | | 37 |
| 1 | 5 | 2 | | | | | | 12 | 9 | 8¹ | | | | | 4 | 7² | 6 | | 3 | 13 | | | | 11¹ | 10 | 14 | | | | 38 |
| 1 | 5 | 2 | | | | 7 | | 9 | 8 | | | | | | 4 | 12 | 6 | 3¹ | | | | | | 11 | 10 | | | | | 39 |
| 1 | 5 | 2 | | 12 | 7 | | | 9 | 8 | | | | | | 4 | 11¹ | 6 | | | | | | | 3 | 10² | | | | 13 | 40 |
| 1 | 5 | 2 | | | 7 | | | 9 | 12 | 8 | | | | | 4¹ | | 6 | | | | | | | 3 | 11 | 10 | | | | 41 |
| 1 | 5 | 2 | | | 7 | | | 9 | 4 | 8 | | | | | | | 6 | | | | | | | 3 | 11 | 10 | | | | 42 |
| 1 | 5² | 2 | 12 | | 7 | | | 9 | 4¹ | 8 | | | 13 | | | | 6 | | | | | | | 3 | 11 | 10 | | | | 43 |
| 1 | | 2 | 4¹ | 12 | 7 | | | 9 | | 8 | | | 5 | | 14 | | 6 | 13 | | | | | | 3¹ | 11 | 10³ | | | | 44 |
| 1 | | 2 | | 12 | 7 | | | 9 | | 8² | | | 5 | | | 4³ | 6 | 13 | | | | | 14 | 3 | 11¹ | 10 | | | | 45 |
| 1 | | 2 | | 12 | 7 | | | 9¹ | | 8 | | | 5 | | | | 6 | | | | | | 4 | 3 | 11 | 10² | 13 | | | 46 |

**Coca-Cola Cup**
First Round    Barnet    (h)  2-1
                         (a)  1-3

**FA Cup**
Third Round    Grimsby T    (a)  0-3

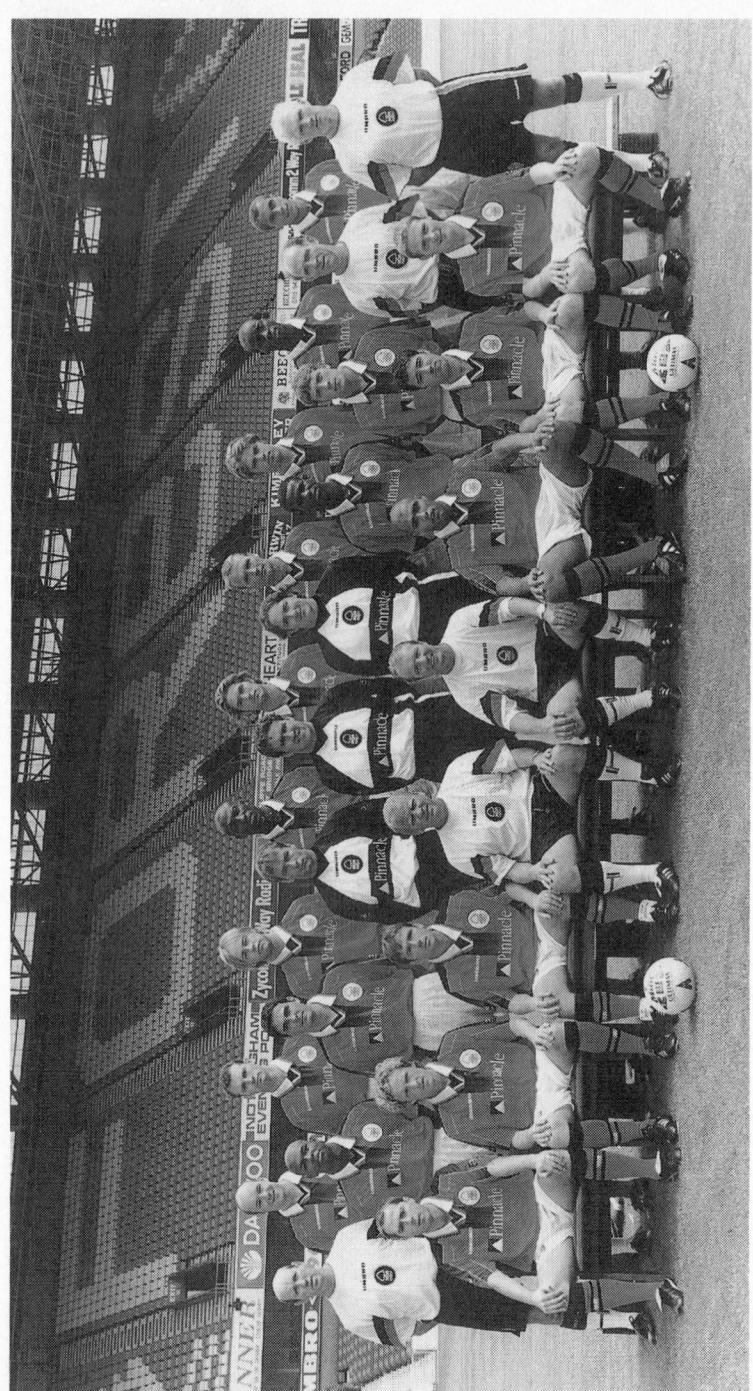

NOTTINGHAM FOREST 1997–98 *Back row (left to right):* Steve Stone, Colin Cooper, Paul McGregor, Kevin Campbell, Andy Johnson, Geoff Thomas, Paul Smith, Chris Allen, Thierry Bonalair. *Middle row:* Liam O'Kane (Coach), Des Lyttle, Steve Chettle, Marco Pascolo, Alan Fettis, Chris Bart-Williams, Alan Rogers, John Haselden (Physio), Mike Kelly (Coach). *Front row:* Ian Woan, Scot Gemmill, David Phillips, Bobby Houghton (Assistant Manager), Dave Bassett (Manager), Pierre Van Hooijdonk, Dean Saunders, Ian Moore.

# FA Premiership   **NOTTINGHAM FOREST**

*City Ground, Nottingham NG2 5FJ.* Telephone: (0115) 982 4444. Fax: (0115) 982 4455. Information Desk: (0115) 982 4446. Commercial Office: (0115) 982 4450. Commercial Office Fax: (0115) 982 4410. Ticket Office: (0115) 982 4445. Souvenir Shop: (0115) 982 4447. Junior Reds: (0115) 982 4454. Clubcall: 0891 121174.

*Ground capacity:* 30,602.

*Record attendance:* 49,946 v Manchester U, Division 1, 28 October 1967.

*Record receipts:* £499,099 v Bayern Munich, UEFA Cup quarter-final 2nd leg, 19 March 1996.

*Pitch measurements:* 116yd × 76yd.

*Deputy Chairman/Chief Executive:* P. W. Soar.

*Directors:* R. W. Dove, R. A. Fairhall, P. R. Markham, T. H. Farr, K. J. Eggleston, I. I. Korn.

*Manager:* Dave Bassett. *Assistant Manager:* Micky Adams.

*Secretary:* Paul White. *Commercial Director:* D. Clayton.

*Coach:* Liam O'Kane. *Physio:* John Haselden.

*Year Formed:* 1865. *Turned Professional:* 1889. *Ltd Co.:* 1982.

*Club Nickname:* 'Reds'.

*Previous Grounds:* 1865, Forest Racecourse; 1879, The Meadows; 1880, Trent Bridge Cricket Ground; 1882, Parkside, Lenton; 1885, Gregory, Lenton; 1890, Town Ground; 1898, City Ground.

*Foundation:* One of the oldest football clubs in the world, Nottingham Forest was formed at a meeting in the Clinton Arms in 1865. Known originally as the Forest Football Club, the game which first drew the founders together was "shinney" a form of hockey. When they determined to change to football in 1865, one of their first moves was to buy a set of red caps to wear on the field.

*First Football League game:* 3 September 1892, Division 1, v Everton (a) D 2-2 – Brown; Earp, Scott; Hamilton, A. Smith, McCracken; McCallum, W. Smith, Higgins (2), Pike, McInnes.

*Record League Victory:* 12–0 v Leicester Fosse, Division 1, 12 April 1909 – Iremonger; Dudley, Maltby; Hughes (1), Needham, Armstrong; Hooper (3), Marrison; Hooper (3), Spouncer (3 incl. 1p).

*Record Cup Victory:* 14–0 v Clapton (away), FA Cup 1st rd, 17 January 1891 – Brown; Earp, Scott; A. Smith, Russell, Jeacock; McCallum (2), 'Tich' Smith (1), Higgins (5), Lindley (4), Shaw (2).

*Record Defeat:* 1–9 v Blackburn R, Division 2, 10 April 1937.

*Most League Points (2 for a win):* 70, Division 3 (S), 1950–51.

*Most League Points (3 for a win):* 94, Division 1, 1997–98.

*Most League Goals:* 110, Division 3 (S), 1950–51.

*Highest League Scorer in Season:* Wally Ardron, 36, Division 3 (S), 1950–51.

*Most League Goals in Total Aggregate:* Grenville Morris, 199, 1898–1913.

*Most Capped Player:* Stuart Pearce, 76, England.

*Most League Appearances:* Bob McKinlay, 614, 1951–70.

*Record Transfer Fee Received:* £8,500,000 from Liverpool for Stan Collymore, June 1995.

*Record Transfer Fee Paid:* £3,500,000 to Celtic for Pierre van Hooijdonk, March 1997.

*Football League Record:* 1892 Elected to Division 1; 1906–07 Division 2; 1907–11 Division 1; 1911–22 Division 2; 1922–25 Division 1; 1925–49 Division 2; 1949–51 Division 3 (S); 1951–57 Division 2; 1957–72 Division 1; 1972–77 Division 2; 1977–92 Division 1; 1992–93 FA Premier League; 1993–94 Division 1; 1994–97 FA Premier League; 1997–98 Division 1; 1998– FA Premier League.

*Honours: Football League:* Division 1 – Champions 1977–78, 1997–98; Runners-up 1966–67, 1978–79; Division 2 – Champions 1906–07, 1921–22; Runners-up 1956–57; Division 3 (S) – Champions 1950–51. *FA Cup:* Winners 1898, 1959; Runners-up 1991. *Anglo-Scottish Cup:* Winners 1977; *Football League Cup:* Winners 1978, 1979, 1989, 1990; Runners-up 1980, 1992. *Simod Cup:* Winners 1989. *Zenith Data Systems Cup:* Winners: 1992. **European Competitions:** *Fairs Cup:* 1961–62, 1967–68. *European Cup:* 1978–79 (winners), 1979–80 (winners), 1980–81. *Super Cup:* 1979–80 (winners), 1980–81 (runners-up). *World Club Championship:* 1980. *UEFA Cup:* 1983–84, 1984–85, 1995–96.

*Colours:* Red shirts with black shoulders, white shorts, red stockings. *Change colours:* Yellow and navy.

**Did you know?**
Dave 'Boy' Martin scored in eight consecutive League games for Nottingham Forest in the 1936-37 season. He hit 29 of their 68 goals.

## NOTTINGHAM FOREST 1997–98 LEAGUE RECORD

| Match No. | Date | Venue | Opponents | Result | H/T Score | Lg. Pos. | Goalscorers | Attendance |
|---|---|---|---|---|---|---|---|---|
| 1 | Aug 9 | A | Port Vale | W 1-0 | 1-0 | — | Campbell [39] | 12,533 |
| 2 | 15 | H | Norwich C | W 4-1 | 1-1 | — | Van Hooijdonk [22], Thomas 2 [57, 61], Campbell [59] | 16,524 |
| 3 | 23 | A | Oxford U | W 1-0 | 0-0 | 1 | Bart-Williams [71] | 9486 |
| 4 | 30 | H | QPR | W 4-0 | 1-0 | 1 | Van Hooijdonk 3 [44, 50, 88], Saunders [79] | 18,804 |
| 5 | Sept 3 | H | Manchester C | L 1-3 | 0-1 | — | Campbell [81] | 23,681 |
| 6 | 7 | A | Swindon T | D 0-0 | 0-0 | 2 | | 13,051 |
| 7 | 13 | A | Sheffield U | L 0-1 | 0-0 | 5 | | 24,536 |
| 8 | 20 | H | Portsmouth | W 1-0 | 1-0 | 1 | Van Hooijdonk [34] | 17,292 |
| 9 | 27 | H | Stoke C | W 1-0 | 0-0 | 1 | Campbell [67] | 19,018 |
| 10 | Oct 3 | A | Huddersfield T | W 2-0 | 0-0 | — | Cooper [67], Saunders [73] | 11,258 |
| 11 | 18 | H | Tranmere R | D 2-2 | 2-1 | 1 | Van Hooijdonk [19], Gemmill [41] | 17,009 |
| 12 | 21 | H | WBA | W 1-0 | 0-0 | — | Campbell [74] | 19,243 |
| 13 | 24 | A | Reading | D 3-3 | 1-0 | — | Van Hooijdonk 2 (1 pen) [3, 48 (p)], Campbell [65] | 12,610 |
| 14 | Nov 1 | H | Crewe Alex | W 3-1 | 1-1 | 1 | Campbell [10], Van Hooijdonk 2 [53, 86] | 18,268 |
| 15 | 4 | A | Bury | L 0-2 | 0-1 | — | | 6137 |
| 16 | 8 | A | Sunderland | D 1-1 | 1-1 | 2 | Hjelde [25] | 33,160 |
| 17 | 15 | H | Birmingham C | W 1-0 | 1-0 | 1 | Campbell [17] | 19,610 |
| 18 | 22 | H | Charlton Ath | W 5-2 | 1-0 | 1 | Van Hooijdonk 3 [21, 50, 56], Woan [75], Campbell [85] | 18,532 |
| 19 | 26 | A | Middlesbrough | D 0-0 | 0-0 | — | | 30,143 |
| 20 | 29 | A | Ipswich T | W 1-0 | 0-0 | 1 | Campbell [65] | 17,580 |
| 21 | Dec 6 | H | Bradford C | D 2-2 | 1-0 | 2 | Cooper [13], Bonalair [63] | 17,943 |
| 22 | 14 | A | Wolverhampton W | L 1-2 | 0-1 | 2 | Johnson A [84] | 24,635 |
| 23 | 20 | H | Stockport Co | W 2-1 | 0-1 | 2 | Van Hooijdonk (pen) [81], Stone [85] | 16,701 |
| 24 | 26 | H | Swindon T | W 3-0 | 3-0 | 2 | Campbell 2 [10, 22], Johnson A [29] | 26,500 |
| 25 | 28 | A | Manchester C | W 3-2 | 1-0 | 2 | Van Hooijdonk 2 (2 pens) [31, 53], Campbell [50] | 31,839 |
| 26 | Jan 10 | H | Port Vale | W 2-1 | 1-1 | 1 | Van Hooijdonk 2 [27, 83] | 17,639 |
| 27 | 17 | A | Norwich C | L 0-1 | 0-0 | 1 | | 17,059 |
| 28 | 24 | A | QPR | W 1-0 | 0-0 | 1 | Cooper [84] | 13,220 |
| 29 | 31 | H | Oxford U | L 1-3 | 1-1 | 1 | Van Hooijdonk (pen) [28] | 18,392 |
| 30 | Feb 7 | A | Portsmouth | W 1-0 | 0-0 | 1 | Chettle [52] | 15,033 |
| 31 | 17 | H | Huddersfield T | W 3-0 | 1-0 | — | Van Hooijdonk 2 [36, 80], Bonalair [67] | 18,231 |
| 32 | 21 | A | Stoke C | D 1-1 | 0-1 | 2 | Moore [87] | 16,899 |
| 33 | 24 | A | Tranmere R | D 0-0 | 0-0 | — | | 7377 |
| 34 | Mar 1 | H | Middlesbrough | W 4-0 | 0-0 | 1 | Van Hooijdonk 2 (1 pen) [53, 85 (p)], Campbell [55], Cooper [75] | 25,286 |
| 35 | 4 | A | Sunderland | L 0-3 | 0-1 | — | | 29,009 |
| 36 | 7 | A | Crewe Alex | W 4-1 | 4-1 | 1 | Bart-Williams [10], Campbell 3 [15, 25, 30] | 5759 |
| 37 | 14 | H | Bury | W 3-0 | 0-0 | 1 | Armstrong (og) [63], Van Hooijdonk [69], Rogers [82] | 18,846 |
| 38 | 21 | H | Birmingham C | W 2-1 | 0-0 | 1 | Van Hooijdonk 2 [84, 88] | 24,663 |
| 39 | 28 | A | Charlton Ath | L 2-4 | 1-1 | 1 | Campbell 2 [16, 90] | 15,815 |
| 40 | Apr 1 | H | Sheffield U | W 3-0 | 2-0 | — | Thomas [20], Campbell 2 [26, 81] | 21,512 |
| 41 | 5 | H | Ipswich T | W 2-1 | 0-0 | 1 | Cooper [53], Van Hooijdonk [58] | 22,292 |
| 42 | 11 | A | Bradford C | W 3-0 | 1-0 | 1 | Campbell [38], Gemmill [63], Bart-Williams [63] | 17,248 |
| 43 | 13 | H | Wolverhampton W | W 3-0 | 2-0 | 1 | Johnson A [32], Van Hooijdonk [39], Campbell [90] | 22,863 |
| 44 | 18 | A | Stockport Co | D 2-2 | 1-1 | 1 | Van Hooijdonk [26], Johnson A [67] | 9892 |
| 45 | 26 | H | Reading | W 1-0 | 0-0 | 1 | Bart-Williams [87] | 29,302 |
| 46 | May 3 | A | WBA | D 1-1 | 1-0 | 1 | Stone [18] | 23,013 |

**Final League Position: 1**   1996–97 PREM 20

### GOALSCORERS

*League (82):* Van Hooijdonk 29 (6 pens), Campbell 23, Cooper 5, Bart-Williams 4, Johnson A 4, Thomas 3, Bonalair 2, Gemmill 2, Saunders 2, Stone 2, Chettle 1, Hjelde 1, Moore 1, Rogers 1, Woan 1, own goal 1.
*Coca-Cola Cup (12):* Van Hooijdonk 4, Hjelde 2, Saunders 2, Allen 1, Armstrong 1, Guinan 1, Thomas 1.
*FA Cup (1):* Van Hooijdonk 1.

| Pascolo M 5 | Lyttle D 35 | Rogers A 46 | Hjelde J 23 + 5 | Chettle S 45 | Thomas G 13 + 7 | Stone S 27 + 2 | Johnson A 24 + 10 | Van Hooijdonk P 41 + 1 | Campbell K 42 | Bonalair T 24 + 7 | Armstrong C 4 + 14 | Gemmill S 43 + 1 | Saunders D 6 + 3 | Beasant D 41 | Allen C 1 | Guinan S 1 + 1 | Bart-Williams C 30 + 3 | Moore I 2 + 8 | Cooper C 35 | Woan I 12 + 9 | Johnson D 5 + 1 | Harewood M 1 | Match No. |
|---|---|---|---|---|---|---|---|---|---|---|---|---|---|---|---|---|---|---|---|---|---|---|---|
| 1 | 2 | 3 | 4 | 5 | 6 | 7[1] | 8 | 9 | 10 | 11[2] |  | 13 | 12 |  |  |  |  |  |  |  |  |  | 1 |
| 1 | 2 | 3 | 4 | 5 | 6[2] | 7[1] | 12 | 9 | 10 | 11 |  | 8 | 13 |  |  |  |  |  |  |  |  |  | 2 |
|  | 2 | 3 | 4 | 5 | 6 |  | 8 | 9 |  | 11[2] |  | 7 |  | 1 |  |  | 10[1] | 12 | 13 |  |  |  | 3 |
|  | 2 | 3 | 4 | 5 | 6 |  |  | 9 |  | 7 |  | 8 | 10 | 1 |  |  | 11 |  |  |  |  |  | 4 |
| 1 | 2[2] | 3 | 4 | 5 | 6 |  | 12 |  | 10 | 7[1] |  | 8 | 9 |  |  |  | 11 | 13 |  |  |  |  | 5 |
|  | 2 | 3[2] | 4 | 5 | 6 |  | 7 | 12 | 10 | 13 |  | 8 | 9[1] | 1 |  |  | 11 |  |  |  |  |  | 6 |
|  | 2[2] | 3 | 4 | 5 | 6[1] |  | 7 | 9 | 10 | 12 |  | 8 | 13 | 1 |  |  | 11 |  |  |  |  |  | 7 |
|  | 2 | 3 | 6[1] | 5 |  |  | 12 | 9 | 10 |  |  | 8 | 7 | 1 |  |  | 11 |  | 4 |  |  |  | 8 |
|  | 2 | 3 |  | 5 |  |  | 12 | 9 | 10 | 6 |  | 8 | 7 | 1 |  |  | 11 |  | 4[1] |  |  |  | 9 |
|  | 2 | 3[1] |  | 5 |  |  | 12 | 9 | 10 | 6 |  | 8 | 7 | 1 |  |  | 11 |  | 4 |  |  |  | 10 |
|  | 2 | 3 | 6 | 5 |  |  | 12 | 9 | 10 |  |  | 8 |  | 1 |  |  | 7 |  | 4 | 11[1] |  |  | 11 |
|  | 2 | 3 | 6[1] | 5 | 13 |  | 12 | 9 | 10 |  |  | 8 |  | 1 |  |  | 11 |  | 4 | 7[2] |  |  | 12 |
|  | 2 | 3 |  | 5 |  | 7 |  | 9 | 10 | 6 |  | 8 |  | 1 |  |  | 11 |  | 4 |  |  |  | 13 |
|  | 2 | 3 | 12 | 5 |  | 7 |  | 9 | 10 | 6[1] |  | 8 |  | 1 |  |  | 11 |  | 4 |  |  |  | 14 |
|  | 2 | 3[1] | 6 | 5 |  | 7 |  | 9 | 10 |  |  | 8 |  | 1 |  |  | 11 |  | 4 | 12 |  |  | 15 |
|  | 2 | 3 | 6 | 5 |  | 7 |  | 9 | 10 |  |  | 8 |  | 1 |  |  | 11 |  | 4 |  |  |  | 16 |
|  | 2 | 3[1] | 6 | 5 |  | 7 |  | 9 | 10 | 12 |  | 8 |  | 1 |  |  | 11[2] |  | 4 | 13 |  |  | 17 |
|  | 2 | 3 | 6 | 5 |  | 7 |  | 9 | 10 |  |  | 8 |  | 1 |  |  | 12 |  | 4 | 11[1] |  |  | 18 |
|  | 2 | 3 | 6 | 5 |  | 7 |  | 9 | 10 |  |  | 8 |  | 1 |  |  | 11 |  | 4 |  |  |  | 19 |
|  | 2 | 3 | 6 | 5 |  | 7 |  | 9 | 10 |  |  | 8 |  | 1 |  |  | 11 |  | 4 |  |  |  | 20 |
|  | 2[2] | 3 | 6 | 5 |  | 7 |  | 9 | 10 | 13 | 12 | 8 |  | 1 |  |  |  |  | 4 | 11[1] |  |  | 21 |
| 1 | 2[2] | 3[3] | 6[1] | 5 |  |  | 14 | 9 | 10 | 7 | 12 | 8 |  | 1 |  |  | 13 |  | 4 | 11 |  |  | 22 |
| 1 | 2[1] | 3[2] |  | 5 |  | 7 | 6 | 9 |  | 12 | 13 | 8 |  |  |  |  | 10[3] | 14 | 4 | 11 |  |  | 23 |
|  | 2 | 3 |  | 5 |  | 7[2] | 6 | 9 | 10 | 12 | 13 | 8[1] |  | 1 |  |  | 14 |  | 4 | 11[2] |  |  | 24 |
|  | 2 | 3 |  | 5 |  | 7 | 6[2] | 9 | 10 | 12 | 13 | 8 |  | 1 |  |  |  |  | 4 | 11[1] |  |  | 25 |
|  | 2 | 3 |  | 5[1] |  | 7 | 6 | 9 | 10 | 12 |  | 8 |  | 1 |  |  | 11 |  | 4 |  |  |  | 26 |
|  | 2 | 3 |  | 5 | 12 |  | 6 | 9 | 10 | 7[2] |  | 8 |  | 1 |  |  | 13 |  | 4 | 11[1] |  |  | 27 |
|  | 2 | 3 |  | 5 | 12 |  | 6 | 9 | 10 | 7 | 13 | 8[2] |  | 1 |  |  |  |  | 4 | 11[1] |  |  | 28 |
|  | 2 | 3 |  | 5 | 8 |  | 6 | 9 | 10 | 11[2] | 12 |  |  | 1 |  |  | 13 |  | 4 |  | 7[1] |  | 29 |
|  | 2 | 3 |  | 5 | 8 |  | 6 | 9 | 10 | 11 |  |  |  | 1 |  |  |  |  | 4 |  | 7 |  | 30 |
|  | 2 | 3[2] |  | 5 | 12 |  | 6[1] | 9[2] | 10 | 11 | 13 | 8 |  | 1 |  |  | 14 |  | 4 |  | 7 |  | 31 |
|  | 2 | 3 |  | 5[2] | 12 |  | 6[1] |  | 10 | 11 | 13 | 8 |  | 1 |  |  | 14 | 9 | 4 |  | 7[3] |  | 32 |
|  | 2 | 3 |  | 5 | 12 |  | 6 |  | 10 | 7 |  | 8[1] |  | 1 |  |  | 11 | 9 | 4 |  |  |  | 33 |
|  | 2 | 3 |  | 5 |  | 7[1] | 6 | 9 | 10 | 12 |  | 8 |  | 1 |  |  | 11 |  | 4 |  |  |  | 34 |
|  | 2[1] | 3 |  | 5 | 13 |  | 6 | 9 | 10 | 12 |  | 8 |  | 1 |  |  | 11 |  | 4 |  | 7[2] |  | 35 |
|  |  | 3 | 4 | 5 | 6 | 7 | 12 |  | 10[3] | 2 | 13 | 8[1] |  | 1 |  |  | 9 | 14 |  | 11[2] |  |  | 36 |
|  |  | 3 | 4 | 5 | 6 | 7[2] | 12 | 9 | 10 | 2 |  | 8[1] |  | 1 |  |  | 11 |  |  |  | 13 |  | 37 |
|  |  | 3 |  | 5 | 12 | 7 | 6[1] | 9 | 10 | 2 |  | 8[2] |  | 1 |  |  | 11 |  | 4 | 13 |  |  | 38 |
|  |  | 3 |  | 5 | 6 | 7 |  | 9 | 10 | 2 |  | 8[1] |  | 1 |  |  | 11 |  | 4 | 12 |  |  | 39 |
|  |  | 3[2] |  | 5 | 6[1] | 7 | 12 | 9 | 10 | 2 | 13 | 8 |  | 1 |  |  | 11[3] |  | 4 | 14 |  |  | 40 |
|  |  | 3 | 12 | 5 |  | 7 | 6[1] | 9 | 10 | 2 |  | 8 |  | 1 |  |  | 11 |  | 4 |  |  |  | 41 |
|  |  | 3 | 12 | 5 |  | 7 | 6 | 9 | 10[2] | 2 |  | 8 |  | 1 |  |  | 11 |  | 4[1] | 13 |  |  | 42 |
|  |  | 3 | 4 | 5 |  | 7 | 6 | 9 | 10 | 2 |  | 8 |  | 1 |  |  | 11 |  |  |  |  |  | 43 |
|  |  | 3 | 4 | 5 |  | 7 | 6 | 9 | 10[1] | 2 |  | 8 |  | 1 |  |  | 11 | 12 |  |  |  |  | 44 |
|  |  | 3 | 12 | 5[1] |  | 7 | 6 | 9 | 10[2] | 2 |  | 8 |  | 1 |  |  | 11 |  | 4 | 13 |  |  | 45 |
|  |  | 3 | 12 | 5 |  | 7 | 6[1] | 9 |  | 2 |  | 8[2] |  | 1 |  |  | 11 |  | 4 | 13 |  | 10 | 46 |

**Coca-Cola Cup**

|  |  | |  |
|---|---|---|---|
| First Round | Doncaster R | (a) | 8-0 |
| | | (h) | 2-1 |
| Second Round | Walsall | (h) | 0-1 |
| | | (a) | 2-2 |

**FA Cup**

|  |  | |  |
|---|---|---|---|
| Third Round | Charlton Ath | (a) | 1-4 |

NOTTS COUNTY 1997–98. *Back row (left to right):* Ben Marshall, Paul Mitchell, Craig Dudley, Gary Jones, Ian Baraclough, Phil Robinson, Dennis Pearce, Mark Robson, Steve Finnan. *Middle row:* Roger Cleary (Physio), Shaun Cunnington, Ian Hendon, Darren Ward, Mike Pollitt, Shaun Derry, Ian Richardson, Alan Young (Youth Team Coach). *Front row:* Dean Randall, Gary Strodder, Matthew Redmile, Mark Smith (Assistant Manager), Derek Pavis (Chairman), Sam Allardyce (Manager), Devon White, Graeme Hogg, Sean Farrell.

# Division 2 NOTTS COUNTY

*County Ground, Meadow Lane, Nottingham NG2 3HJ.* Telephone: (0115) 9529000. Fax: (0115) 9553994. Ticket Office: (0115) 9557210. Clubline: 0891 888684. Football in the Community: (0115) 955 7215. Supporters Club: (0115) 9557255.

*Ground capacity:* 20,300.

*Record attendance:* 47,310 v York C, FA Cup 6th rd, 12 March 1955.

*Record receipts:* £124,539.10 v Manchester C, FA Cup 6th rd, 16 February 1991.

*Pitch measurements:* 114yd × 74yd.

*Chairman:* D. C. Pavis. *Vice-Chairman:* J. Mounteney.

*Directors:* W. Barrowcliffe, Mrs V. Pavis, M. Youdell MBE, G. Davey (Managing).

*Manager:* Sam Allardyce. *Assistant Manager:* Mark Smith. *Youth Coach:* Gary Brazil.

*Secretary:* Ian Moat.

*Commercial Manager:* Clair Finnigan. *Conference & Banqueting Manager:* Matthew Foote.

*Physio:* Roger Cleary. *Stadium Manager:* Bob Davy.

*Year Formed:* 1862 *(see Foundation).* **Turned Professional:** 1885. *Ltd Co.:* 1888.

*Club Nickname:* 'Magpies'.

*Previous Grounds:* 1862, The Park; 1864, The Meadows; 1877, Beeston Cricket Ground; 1880, Castle Ground; 1883, Trent Bridge; 1910, Meadow Lane.

*Foundation:* For many years the foundation date of the Football League's oldest club was given as 1862 and the club celebrated its centenary in 1962. However, the researches of Keith Warsop have since shown that the club was on a very haphazard basis at that time, playing little more than practice matches. The meeting which put it on a firm footing was held at the George IV Hotel in December 1864, when they became known as the Notts Football Club.

*First Football League game:* 15 September 1888, Football League, v Everton (a) L 1-2 – Holland; Guttridge, McLean; Brown, Warburton, Shelton; Hodder, Harker, Jardine, Moore (1), Wardle.

*Record League Victory:* 11–1 v Newport Co, Division 3 (S), 15 January 1949 – Smith; Southwell, Purvis; Gannon, Baxter, Adamson; Houghton (1), Sewell (4), Lawton (4), Pimbley, Johnston (2).

*Record Cup Victory:* 15–0 v Rotherham T (at Trent Bridge), FA Cup 1st rd, 24 October 1885 – Sherwin; Snook, H. T. Moore; Dobson (1), Emmett (1), Chapman; Gunn (1), Albert Moore (2), Jackson (3), Daft (2), Cursham (4). (1 og).

*Record Defeat:* 1–9 v Blackburn R, Division 1, 16 November 1889 and v Aston Villa, Division 1, 29 September 1888 and v Portsmouth, Division 2, 9 April 1927.

*Most League Points (2 for a win):* 69, Division 4, 1970–71.

*Most League Points (3 for a win):* 99, Division 3, 1997–98.

*Most League Goals:* 107, Division 4, 1959–60.

*Highest League Scorer in Season:* Tom Keetley, 39, Division 3 (S), 1930–31.

*Most League Goals in Total Aggregate:* Les Bradd, 124, 1967–78.

*Most Capped Player:* Kevin Wilson, 15 (42), Northern Ireland.

*Most League Appearances:* Albert Iremonger, 564, 1904–26.

*Record Transfer Fee Received:* £2,500,000 from Derby Co for Craig Short, September 1992.

*Record Transfer Fee Paid:* £685,000 to Sheffield U for Tony Agana, November 1991.

*Football League Record:* 1888 Founder Member of the Football League; 1893–97 Division 2; 1897–1913 Division 1; 1913–14 Division 2; 1914–20 Division 1; 1920–23 Division 2; 1923–26 Division 1; 1926–30 Division 2; 1930–31 Division 3 (S); 1931–35 Division 2; 1935–50 Division 3 (S); 1950–58 Division 2; 1958–59 Division 3; 1959–60 Division 4; 1960–64 Division 2; 1964–71 Division 4; 1971–73 Division 3; 1973–81 Division 2; 1981–84 Division 1; 1984–85 Division 2; 1985–90 Division 3; 1990–91 Division 2; 1991–95 Division 1; 1995–97 Division 2; 1997–98 Division 3; 1998– Division 2.

*Honours: Football League:* Division 1 best season: 3rd, 1890–91, 1900–01; Division 2 – Champions 1896–97, 1913–14, 1922–23; Runners-up 1894–95, 1980–81; Promoted from Division 2 1990–91 (play-offs); Division 3 (S) – Champions 1930–31, 1949–50; Runners-up 1936–37; Division 3 – Champions 1997–98; Runners-up 1972–73; Promoted from Division 3 1989–90 (play-offs); Division 4 – Champions 1970–71; Runners-up 1959–60. *FA Cup:* Winners 1894; Runners-up 1891. *Football League Cup:* best season: 5th rd, 1964, 1973, 1976. *Anglo-Italian Cup:* Winners 1995; Runners-up 1994.

*Colours:* Black and white striped shirts, white shorts, black stockings. *Change colours:* Tartan shirts, black shorts, tartan stockings.

**Did you know?**
On 10 January 1998 Notts County celebrated their 4000th Football League game with a 2-1 win at Rochdale.

## NOTTS COUNTY 1997–98 LEAGUE RECORD

| Match No. | Date | Venue | Opponents | Result | H/T Score | Lg. Pos. | Goalscorers | Attendance |
|---|---|---|---|---|---|---|---|---|
| 1 | Aug 9 | H | Rochdale | W 2-1 | 1-0 | — | Robson (pen) [45], Redmile [89] | 4173 |
| 2 | 16 | A | Hull C | W 3-0 | 1-0 | 1 | Redmile [31], White [70], Jones [72] | 7412 |
| 3 | 23 | H | Lincoln C | L 1-2 | 0-1 | 4 | White [64] | 5707 |
| 4 | 30 | A | Cardiff C | D 1-1 | 1-1 | 5 | Finnan [10] | 6191 |
| 5 | Sept 2 | A | Hartlepool U | D 1-1 | 0-0 | — | Baraclough (pen) [53] | 2010 |
| 6 | 7 | H | Scunthorpe U | W 2-1 | 1-0 | 5 | Redmile [6], Derry [86] | 5009 |
| 7 | 13 | H | Mansfield T | W 1-0 | 1-0 | 3 | Martindale [23] | 6706 |
| 8 | 20 | A | Shrewsbury T | W 2-1 | 0-0 | 2 | Jones [71], Finnan [82] | 2532 |
| 9 | 27 | A | Scarborough | W 2-1 | 1-1 | 1 | Baraclough (pen) [3], Farrell [75] | 2751 |
| 10 | Oct 4 | H | Darlington | D 1-1 | 1-1 | 2 | Dudley [4] | 4428 |
| 11 | 11 | H | Macclesfield T | D 1-1 | 1-0 | 3 | Richardson [43] | 4871 |
| 12 | 18 | A | Swansea C | W 2-1 | 0-1 | 3 | Jones [57], Jackson [77] | 3668 |
| 13 | 21 | A | Rotherham U | D 1-1 | 1-0 | — | Farrell [40] | 3161 |
| 14 | 25 | H | Cambridge U | W 1-0 | 0-0 | 2 | Jones [49] | 4279 |
| 15 | Nov 1 | A | Barnet | W 2-1 | 0-0 | 1 | Baraclough [64], Derry [83] | 2530 |
| 16 | 4 | H | Chester C | L 1-2 | 0-0 | — | Strodder [59] | 3104 |
| 17 | 8 | H | Exeter C | D 1-1 | 0-1 | 2 | Strodder [57] | 5107 |
| 18 | 18 | A | Colchester U | L 0-2 | 0-0 | — | | 2643 |
| 19 | 22 | A | Leyton Orient | D 1-1 | 0-0 | 4 | Farrell [66] | 4372 |
| 20 | 29 | H | Peterborough U | D 2-2 | 2-1 | 4 | Jones [27], Robson [39] | 8006 |
| 21 | Dec 3 | A | Brighton & HA | W 1-0 | 1-0 | — | Farrell [7] | 1279 |
| 22 | 13 | H | Doncaster R | W 5-2 | 3-1 | 1 | Baraclough 2 (1 pen) [2, 8 (p)], Utley (og) [20], Finnan [74], Farrell [84] | 4024 |
| 23 | 20 | A | Torquay U | W 2-0 | 1-0 | 1 | Farrell 2 [9, 72] | 2536 |
| 24 | 26 | A | Scunthorpe U | W 2-1 | 1-1 | 1 | Jones 2 [6, 48] | 4781 |
| 25 | 28 | H | Hartlepool U | W 2-0 | 1-0 | 1 | Farrell 2 [13, 87] | 6073 |
| 26 | Jan 10 | A | Rochdale | W 2-1 | 0-0 | 1 | Jones [68], Robinson [78] | 2387 |
| 27 | 17 | H | Cardiff C | W 3-1 | 1-1 | 1 | Robinson [19], Jones 2 [76, 79] | 6448 |
| 28 | 20 | H | Hull C | W 1-0 | 0-0 | 1 | Richardson [54] | 4017 |
| 29 | 24 | A | Lincoln C | W 5-3 | 3-0 | 1 | Farrell 2 [5, 72], Baraclough [25], Strodder [36], Jones [62] | 5911 |
| 30 | 31 | A | Mansfield T | W 2-0 | 2-0 | 1 | Jones 2 [16, 30] | 6786 |
| 31 | Feb 7 | H | Shrewsbury T | D 1-1 | 0-1 | 1 | Jones [90] | 5789 |
| 32 | 14 | A | Darlington | W 2-0 | 2-0 | 1 | Jones [16], Finnan [24] | 2781 |
| 33 | 21 | H | Scarborough | W 1-0 | 1-0 | 1 | Farrell [6] | 5645 |
| 34 | 24 | H | Swansea C | W 2-1 | 2-1 | 1 | Jones 2 [11, 40] | 4484 |
| 35 | 28 | A | Macclesfield T | L 0-2 | 0-0 | 1 | | 5122 |
| 36 | Mar 3 | A | Exeter C | W 5-2 | 3-1 | 1 | Robson [7], Farrell 2 [10, 35], Jones 2 [48, 77] | 2966 |
| 37 | 7 | H | Barnet | W 2-0 | 1-0 | 1 | Jones [33], Hughes [85] | 6180 |
| 38 | 14 | A | Chester C | W 1-0 | 0-0 | 1 | Jones [85] | 2753 |
| 39 | 21 | H | Colchester U | D 0-0 | 0-0 | 1 | | 6284 |
| 40 | 28 | H | Leyton Orient | W 1-0 | 0-0 | 1 | Robson [50] | 8383 |
| 41 | Apr 3 | A | Peterborough U | L 0-1 | 0-0 | — | | 6498 |
| 42 | 11 | H | Brighton & HA | D 2-2 | 0-1 | 1 | Hughes [61], Jones [74] | 5344 |
| 43 | 13 | A | Doncaster R | W 2-1 | 0-0 | 1 | Strodder [56], Finnan [64] | 2485 |
| 44 | 18 | H | Torquay U | W 3-0 | 1-0 | 1 | Pearce [1], Jones 2 [74, 78] | 5183 |
| 45 | 25 | A | Cambridge U | D 2-2 | 1-2 | 1 | Jones 2 [26, 75] | 4009 |
| 46 | May 2 | H | Rotherham U | W 5-2 | 1-1 | 1 | Jones 2 [31, 73], Pearce [51], Farrell [75], Robinson [89] | 12,430 |

**Final League Position: 1**        1996–97 DIV2 24

### GOALSCORERS

*League (82):* Jones 28, Farrell 15, Baraclough 6 (3 pens), Finnan 5, Robson 4 (1 pen), Strodder 4, Redmile 3, Robinson 3, Derry 2, Hughes 2, Pearce 2, Richardson 2, White 2, Dudley 1, Jackson 1, Martindale 1, own goal 1.
*Coca-Cola Cup (4):* Baraclough 1 (pen), Dudley 1, Hendon 1, White 1.
*FA Cup (5):* Derry 1, Farrell 1, Finnan 1, Hogg 1, Richardson 1.

| Ward D 44 | Hendon I 38 | Pearce D 37+1 | Redmile M 32+2 | Strodder G 37+2 | Derry S 27+1 | Finnan S 41+3 | Robinson P 30+10 | Dudley C 5+12 | Jones G 43+1 | Robson M 26+2 | Baraclough I 36+2 | Richardson I 25+5 | White D 4+2 | Cunnington S 3+6 | Hogg G 4 | Martindale G 5+17 | Otto R 4 | Farrell S 32+3 | Jackson J 4+11 | Kiwomya A —+2 | Hughes A 12+3 | Lormor T 2+5 | Pollitt M 2 | Dyer A 10 | Poric A 3+1 | Mitchell P —+1 | Diuk W —+1 | Match No. |
|---|---|---|---|---|---|---|---|---|---|---|---|---|---|---|---|---|---|---|---|---|---|---|---|---|---|---|---|---|
| 1 | 2 | 3 | 4 | 5 | 6 | 7 | $8^2$ | 9 | 10 | 11 | 12 | 13 | 14 | | | | | | | | | | | | | | | 1 |
| 1 | 2 | 3 | 4 | 5 | 6 | 7 | 8 | | $10^1$ | | 12 | 13 | | 9 | | $11^2$ | | | | | | | | | | | | 2 |
| 1 | 2 | 3 | 4 | | | $7^2$ | 8 | 12 | 10 | | $11^1$ | 6 | | 9 | 5 | 13 | | | | | | | | | | | | 3 |
| 1 | 2 | 3 | 4 | | | 7 | 8 | 12 | $10^2$ | | 11 | 6 | | $9^1$ | 5 | 13 | | | | | | | | | | | | 4 |
| 1 | 2 | 3 | 4 | | 6 | 7 | 8 | | $10^1$ | 11 | 12 | | | 9 | 5 | | | | | | | | | | | | | 5 |
| 1 | 2 | 3 | 4 | 5 | | 7 | 8 | 12 | 10 | | | 6 | | $9^1$ | | 11 | | | | | | | | | | | | 6 |
| 1 | 2 | 3 | 4 | 5 | | $7^1$ | 12 | 8 | 13 | $10^3$ | 6 | | 14 | $9^2$ | | 11 | | | | | | | | | | | | 7 |
| 1 | 2 | 3 | 4 | 5 | | 7 | 12 | 13 | $10^3$ | 6 | 14 | $8^1$ | | $9^2$ | | 11 | | | | | | | | | | | | 8 |
| 1 | 2 | 3 | 4 | 5 | | 7 | 11 | 12 | $9^3$ | $10^1$ | 6 | 8 | | | | | | 13 | | | | | | | | | | 9 |
| 1 | 2 | 3 | 4 | 5 | | 7 | 11 | $9^3$ | $10^1$ | 6 | 8 | | | | | 12 | | 13 | | | | | | | | | | 10 |
| 1 | 2 | 3 | 4 | 5 | | $7^1$ | 12 | $9^2$ | $10^3$ | 6 | 8 | | | | | 11 | 13 | 14 | | | | | | | | | | 11 |
| 1 | 2 | 12 | $4^2$ | 5 | | 7 | 11 | | 10 | $8^1$ | 3 | 6 | | | | | | 9 | 13 | | | | | | | | | 12 |
| 1 | 2 | 3 | | 5 | 6 | 7 | 8 | | 10 | $11^1$ | 4 | | | 13 | | | | 9 | $12^2$ | | | | | | | | | 13 |
| 1 | 2 | 3 | | 5 | | 7 | 11 | 8 | 10 | $6^1$ | 4 | | | 12 | | | | 9 | | | | | | | | | | 14 |
| 1 | 2 | 3 | | 5 | 8 | 7 | 12 | $10^2$ | $11^1$ | 6 | 4 | | | 13 | | | | 9 | | | | | | | | | | 15 |
| 1 | 2 | 3 | | 5 | 8 | 7 | 13 | $10^1$ | 11 | 6 | 4 | | | $12^2$ | | | | 9 | | | | | | | | | | 16 |
| 1 | 2 | 3 | 12 | 5 | 8 | 7 | | 10 | 13 | $11^2$ | 6 | $4^1$ | | | | | | 9 | | | | | | | | | | 17 |
| 1 | 2 | 3 | 4 | 5 | 8 | 7 | | 9 | $11^1$ | 13 | | $6^2$ | 12 | | | 10 | | | | | | | | | | | | 18 |
| 1 | 2 | | 4 | 5 | 8 | 7 | 13 | | 11 | 6 | 3 | | | $10^1$ | | | | 9 | $12^2$ | | | | | | | | | 19 |
| 1 | 2 | | 4 | 5 | 8 | $7^2$ | 12 | 13 | 10 | $11^1$ | 6 | 3 | | | | | | 9 | | | | | | | | | | 20 |
| 1 | 2 | | 4 | 5 | 8 | 7 | 6 | 12 | 10 | $11^1$ | 3 | | | 13 | | | | $9^2$ | | | | | | | | | | 21 |
| 1 | 2 | 3 | 4 | 5 | 7 | 11 | 12 | 9 | $10^1$ | $6^3$ | | | | 13 | | | | $8^2$ | 14 | | | | | | | | | 22 |
| 1 | 2 | 3 | 4 | 5 | 8 | 7 | 12 | $10^2$ | $11^3$ | 6 | | | | 13 | | | | $9^1$ | 14 | | | | | | | | | 23 |
| 1 | 2 | 3 | 4 | 5 | 8 | 7 | 12 | 10 | $11^2$ | $6^1$ | | | | 13 | | | | 9 | | | | | | | | | | 24 |
| 1 | 2 | 3 | 4 | 5 | 8 | 7 | 12 | 10 | $11^1$ | 6 | | | | | | | | 9 | | | | | | | | | | 25 |
| 1 | 2 | 3 | | | 8 | 7 | 5 | 10 | $11^1$ | 6 | 4 | | | 12 | | | | 9 | | | | | | | | | | 26 |
| 1 | $2^1$ | 3 | | | 8 | 7 | 5 | 10 | $11^2$ | 6 | 4 | 13 | | 12 | | | | 9 | | | | | | | | | | 27 |
| 1 | | 3 | 2 | 5 | 8 | 7 | 5 | 10 | 11 | 6 | 4 | | | | | | | 9 | | | | | | | | | | 28 |
| 1 | | 3 | 2 | 5 | 11 | 7 | 8 | 10 | | 6 | 4 | | | 12 | | | | $9^1$ | | | | | | | | | | 29 |
| 1 | $2^1$ | 3 | 11 | 5 | | 7 | 8 | 10 | | 6 | 4 | | | | | | | 9 | 12 | | | | | | | | | 30 |
| 1 | $2^2$ | 3 | $11^1$ | 5 | | 7 | 8 | 12 | 10 | 6 | 4 | | | 14 | | | | 9 | $13^3$ | | | | | | | | | 31 |
| 1 | 2 | 3 | 11 | 5 | | 7 | 8 | 10 | | 6 | 4 | 12 | | | | | | $9^1$ | | | | | | | | | | 32 |
| 1 | 2 | $3^1$ | $11^1$ | 5 | | 7 | 8 | | 6 | 4 | 12 | 13 | | | | | | $9^2$ | 14 | 10 | | | | | | | | 33 |
| 1 | $2^1$ | | 11 | 5 | | 7 | 8 | 10 | 3 | 4 | 6 | 12 | | | | | | $9^2$ | 13 | | | | | | | | | 34 |
| 1 | | 11 | | | | 7 | 8 | 12 | 10 | 13 | 6 | 4 | | | | | $3^1$ | 9 | | | 5 | $2^4$ | 1 | | | | | 35 |
| | 2 | | | | | 7 | $8^2$ | 12 | $10^1$ | 11 | 6 | 4 | | | | | | 9 | | | 5 | 13 | 1 | 3 | | | | 36 |
| 1 | 2 | | 12 | | | 7 | 8 | 10 | $11^1$ | 6 | 4 | | | | | | | $9^2$ | | | 5 | 13 | | 3 | | | | 37 |
| 1 | 2 | | 12 | | | 7 | 8 | $10^2$ | $11^1$ | 6 | 4 | | | | | | | $9^2$ | 13 | | 5 | 14 | | 3 | | | | 38 |
| 1 | 2 | 3 | | 5 | | 7 | 8 | $10^3$ | 11 | | | 12 | | | | | | $9^2$ | 13 | | $4^1$ | 14 | | 6 | | | | 39 |
| 1 | 2 | 3 | | 5 | | 7 | 8 | 10 | $11^2$ | | | | | | | | | $9^1$ | 12 | | 4 | | | 6 | 13 | | | 40 |
| 1 | 2 | 3 | 12 | 5 | | 7 | 8 | 10 | | | 4 | | | | | | | $9^2$ | 13 | $11^1$ | 6 | | | | | | | 41 |
| 1 | | 3 | 4 | 5 | | 7 | 8 | 12 | 10 | 13 | | | | | | | | $9^1$ | 11 | | 6 | | | $2^2$ | | | | 42 |
| 1 | | 3 | 4 | 5 | | 7 | $8^2$ | 12 | 10 | 11 | | 13 | | | | | | $9^1$ | 6 | | 2 | | | | | | | 43 |
| 1 | | 3 | 4 | 5 | | 7 | 8 | 12 | 10 | $11^2$ | | 13 | | | | | | $2^3$ | $9^1$ | 6 | | | | | | 14 | | 44 |
| 1 | | 3 | 4 | 5 | | $7^3$ | 12 | | 10 | $11^2$ | | | | | | | | 9 | 13 | 8 | | | 6 | $2^1$ | | 14 | | 45 |
| 1 | | 3 | 4 | 5 | | | 8 | | 10 | 11 | | | | | | | | 9 | 12 | 6 | | | | 2 | $7^1$ | | | 46 |

**Coca-Cola Cup**

| | | | | |
|---|---|---|---|---|
| First Round | Darlington | (a) | 1-1 |
| | | (h) | 2-1 |
| Second Round | Tranmere R | (h) | 0-2 |
| | | (a) | 1-0 |

**FA Cup**

| | | | | |
|---|---|---|---|---|
| First Round | Colwyn Bay | (h) | 2-0 |
| Second Round | Preston NE | (a) | 2-2 |
| | | (h) | 1-2 |

OLDHAM ATHLETIC 1997–98      *Back row (left to right):* Steve Redmond, Richard Graham, Doug Hodgson, Shaun Garnett, Ian Ormondroyd, Lee Sinnott, Sean McCarthy, Barrie Hart, Carl Serrant.
*Middle row:* Bill Urmson (Chief Youth Coach), Toddy Orlygsson, Mark Allott, Matthew Rush, Ian Ironside, Gary Kelly, Andrew Holt, Lloyd Richardson, David McNiven, Alex Moreno (Physio).
*Front row:* Andy Ritchie (Player/Coach), Scott McNiven, Stuart Barlow, Lee Duxbury, Neil Warnock (Manager), Paul Reid, Paul Rickers, Andrew Hughes, Ron Reid (Manager's Assistant).
(Photograph: Action Images)

# Division 2 **OLDHAM ATHLETIC**

*Boundary Park, Oldham OL1 2PA.* Telephone: (0161) 624 4972. Fax: (0161) 627 5915. Ticket Call: 0891 121582. Commercial Office: (0161) 627 1802 Fax: (0161) 652 6501. Clubcall: 0891 121142.

*Ground capacity:* 13,559.

*Record attendance:* 47,671 v Sheffield W, FA Cup 4th rd, 25 January 1930.

*Record receipts:* £138,680 v Manchester U, FA Premier League, 29 December 1993.

*Pitch measurements:* 110yd × 74yd.

*Chairman & Managing Director:* I. H. Stott, *Vice-Chairman:* D. A. Brierley.

*Directors:* G. T. Butterworth, D. R. Taylor, P. Chadwick, J. Slevin, N. Holden.

*Manager:* Andy Ritchie.

*Chief Executive/Secretary:* Alan Hardy. *Commercial Manager:* Bob Gorrill. *Public Relations Office:* Gordon A. Lawton.

*Stadium Manager:* Stuart Oddie. *Safety Officer:* Frank Carlisle.

*Senior Coach:* Bill Urmson. *Physio:* Alex Moreno MCSP SRP.

*Year Formed:* 1895. *Turned Professional:* 1899. *Ltd Co.:* 1906.

*Previous Name:* 1895, Pine Villa; 1899, Oldham Athletic.

*Club Nickname:* 'The Latics'.

*Previous Ground:* Sheepfoot Lane; 1905, Boundary Park.

*Foundation:* It was in 1895 that John Garland, the landlord of the Featherstall and Junction Hotel, decided to form a football club. As Pine Villa they played in the Oldham Junior League. In 1899 the local professional club Oldham County, went out of existence and one of the liquidators persuaded Pine Villa to take over their ground at Sheepfoot Lane and change their name to Oldham Athletic.

*First Football League game:* 9 September 1907, Division 2, v Stoke (a) W 3-1 – Hewitson; Hodson, Hamilton; Fay, Walders, Wilson; Ward, W. Dodds (1), Newton (1), Hancock, Swarbrick (1).

*Record League Victory:* 11-0 v Southport, Division 4, 26 December 1962 – Hollands; Branagan, Marshall; McCall, Williams, Scott; Ledger (1), Johnstone, Lister (6), Colquhoun (1), Whitaker (3).

*Record Cup Victory:* 10-1 v Lytham, FA Cup 1st rd, 28 November 1925 – Gray; Wynne, Grundy; Adlam, Heaton, Naylor (1), Douglas, Pynegar (2), Ormston (2), Barnes (3), Watson (2).

*Record Defeat:* 4–13 v Tranmere R, Division 3 (N), 26 December 1935.

*Most League Points (2 for a win):* 62, Division 3, 1973–74.

*Most League Points (3 for a win):* 88, Division 2, 1990–91.

*Most League Goals:* 95, Division 4, 1962–63.

*Highest League Scorer in Season:* Tom Davis, 33, Division 3 (N), 1936–37.

*Most League Goals in Total Aggregate:* Roger Palmer, 141, 1980–94.

*Most Capped Player:* Gunnar Halle, (61), Norway.

*Most League Appearances:* Ian Wood, 525, 1966–80.

*Record Transfer Fee Received:* £1,700,000 from Aston Villa for Earl Barrett, February 1992.

*Record Transfer Fee Paid:* £750,000 to Aston Villa for Ian Olney, June 1992.

*Football League Record:* 1907 Elected to Division 2; 1910–23 Division 1; 1923–35 Division 2; 1935–53 Division 3 (N); 1953–54 Division 2; 1954–58 Division 3 (N); 1958–63 Division 4; 1963–69 Division 3; 1969–71 Division 4; 1971–74 Division 3; 1974–91 Division 2; 1991–92 Division 1; 1992–94 FA Premier League; 1994–97 Division 1; 1997– Division 2.

*Honours: Football League:* Division 1 – Runners-up 1914–15; Division 2 – Champions 1990–91; Runners-up 1909–10; Division 3 (N) – Champions 1952–53; Division 3 – Champions 1973–74; Division 4 – Runners-up 1962–63. *FA Cup:* Semi-final 1913, 1990, 1994. *Football League Cup:* Runners-up 1990.

*Colours:* All blue. *Change colours:* White shirts, claret shorts, claret stockings.

**Did you know?**
When Oldham Athletic beat Newton-le-Willows 11-0 on 7 January 1905, Plumpton scored the first five, Sheridan the last six goals.

## OLDHAM ATHLETIC 1997–98 LEAGUE RECORD

| Match No. | Date | Venue | Opponents | Result | H/T Score | Lg. Pos. | Goalscorers | Attendance |
|---|---|---|---|---|---|---|---|---|
| 1 | Aug 9 | H | York C | W 3-1 | 1-0 | — | Garnett [12], Barlow [46], Reid [90] | 6474 |
| 2 | 16 | A | Wrexham | L 1-3 | 0-2 | 10 | McCarthy [54] | 4429 |
| 3 | 23 | H | Bournemouth | W 2-1 | 1-0 | 4 | McCarthy 2 [17, 76] | 4986 |
| 4 | 30 | A | Luton T | D 1-1 | 0-0 | 7 | Barlow [53] | 5404 |
| 5 | Sept 2 | A | Burnley | D 0-0 | 0-0 | — | | 11,189 |
| 6 | 9 | H | Preston NE | W 1-0 | 0-0 | — | Wright [76] | 8732 |
| 7 | 13 | H | Northampton T | D 2-2 | 2-1 | 4 | Graham [8], McNiven S [35] | 5829 |
| 8 | 20 | A | Blackpool | D 2-2 | 1-1 | 4 | Barlow 2 [43, 68] | 7174 |
| 9 | 27 | A | Bristol R | D 4-4 | 3-3 | 4 | Barlow 2 [8, 23], McCarthy [25], Garnett [59] | 5990 |
| 10 | Oct 4 | A | Fulham | L 1-3 | 0-1 | 8 | Hodgson [72] | 8805 |
| 11 | 11 | A | Millwall | L 1-2 | 1-0 | 13 | Hodgson [25] | 7906 |
| 12 | 18 | H | Chesterfield | W 2-0 | 0-0 | 7 | Ritchie [61], Barlow [73] | 5777 |
| 13 | 21 | H | Grimsby T | W 2-0 | 0-0 | — | Wright [48], Duxbury [90] | 4520 |
| 14 | 25 | A | Southend U | D 1-1 | 1-1 | 5 | Barlow [34] | 3595 |
| 15 | Nov 1 | A | Bristol C | L 0-1 | 0-0 | 8 | | 10,221 |
| 16 | 4 | H | Wigan Ath | W 3-1 | 2-1 | — | McCarthy 2 [6, 62], Graham [24] | 5446 |
| 17 | 7 | H | Gillingham | W 3-1 | 2-0 | — | Reid 2 (1 pen) [26 (p), 54], Barlow [37] | 5338 |
| 18 | 18 | A | Watford | L 1-2 | 0-1 | — | Duxbury [58] | 8397 |
| 19 | 22 | H | Brentford | D 1-1 | 0-0 | 7 | McCarthy [66] | 5012 |
| 20 | 29 | A | Plymouth Arg | W 2-0 | 1-0 | 5 | Mauge (og) [9], Rickers [90] | 5452 |
| 21 | Dec 2 | H | Carlisle U | W 3-1 | 2-1 | — | Rickers [43], Barlow [45], Duxbury [49] | 4449 |
| 22 | 13 | A | Wycombe W | L 1-2 | 0-0 | 3 | Barlow [72] | 5327 |
| 23 | 19 | A | Walsall | D 0-0 | 0-0 | — | | 4677 |
| 24 | 26 | A | Preston NE | D 1-1 | 1-0 | 3 | Hodgson [32] | 13,441 |
| 25 | Jan 10 | A | York C | D 0-0 | 0-0 | 7 | | 4454 |
| 26 | 17 | H | Luton T | W 2-1 | 0-0 | 7 | Graham 2 [55, 65] | 6057 |
| 27 | 24 | A | Bournemouth | D 0-0 | 0-0 | 6 | | 4079 |
| 28 | 27 | H | Wrexham | W 3-0 | 2-0 | — | Rickers [30], Duxbury [45], Ritchie [85] | 4680 |
| 29 | 31 | A | Northampton T | D 0-0 | 0-0 | 3 | | 6559 |
| 30 | Feb 7 | A | Blackpool | L 0-1 | 0-0 | 5 | | 6576 |
| 31 | 14 | H | Fulham | W 1-0 | 0-0 | 4 | Duxbury [82] | 6063 |
| 32 | 21 | A | Bristol R | L 1-3 | 0-2 | 7 | Starbuck (pen) [60] | 5789 |
| 33 | 24 | A | Chesterfield | L 1-2 | 0-1 | — | Garnett [82] | 4077 |
| 34 | 28 | H | Millwall | D 1-1 | 0-0 | 9 | Barlow [56] | 4805 |
| 35 | Mar 3 | A | Gillingham | L 1-2 | 1-1 | — | Holt [27] | 5254 |
| 36 | 14 | A | Wigan Ath | L 0-1 | 0-0 | 12 | | 4277 |
| 37 | 21 | H | Watford | D 2-2 | 0-1 | 11 | Littlejohn [53], Allott [90] | 5744 |
| 38 | 28 | A | Brentford | L 1-2 | 0-2 | 14 | Reid [67] | 4547 |
| 39 | 31 | A | Bristol C | L 1-2 | 1-0 | — | Rush [23] | 4543 |
| 40 | Apr 4 | H | Plymouth Arg | W 2-0 | 1-0 | 12 | Littlejohn 2 [43, 54] | 4244 |
| 41 | 11 | A | Carlisle U | L 1-3 | 1-2 | 12 | Hodgson [41] | 4594 |
| 42 | 13 | H | Wycombe W | L 0-1 | 0-0 | 16 | | 4305 |
| 43 | 18 | A | Walsall | D 0-0 | 0-0 | 16 | | 3562 |
| 44 | 25 | H | Southend U | W 2-0 | 0-0 | 14 | Jepson [68], McNiven D [87] | 4485 |
| 45 | 28 | H | Burnley | D 3-3 | 1-3 | — | Jepson [27], Rickers [76], Allott [77] | 9781 |
| 46 | May 2 | A | Grimsby T | W 2-0 | 0-0 | 13 | Jepson 2 [67, 71] | 8054 |

**Final League Position: 13**　　1996–97 DIV1 23

### GOALSCORERS

League (62): Barlow 12, McCarthy 7, Duxbury 5, Graham 4, Hodgson 4, Jepson 4, Reid 4 (1 pen), Rickers 4, Garnett 3, Littlejohn 3, Allott 2, Ritchie 2, Wright 2, Holt 1, McNiven D 1, McNiven S 1, Rush 1, Starbuck 1 (pen), own goal 1.
Coca-Cola Cup (1): Ritchie 1.
FA Cup (4): Barlow 1, Graham 1, McCarthy 1, Serrant 1.

| Kelly G 26 | Redmond S 32+2 | Serrant C 30 | Rickers P 35+5 | Hodgson D 22+6 | Garnett S 32+2 | Orlygsson T 8+3 | McCarthy S 16+9 | Barlow S 31+1 | Reid P 44 | Graham R 34 | Sinnott L 11+2 | Allott M 10+12 | Hughes A 1+9 | McNiven S 25+7 | Pollitt M 16 | Wright T 10+2 | Ormondroyd I —+1 | Innes M 2+2 | Salt P 1+1 | Kyratzoglou A —+1 | Ritchie A 10+5 | Rush M 11+5 | Boxall D 18 | Thompson N 8 | Jepson R 9 | Starbuck P 7+2 | Holt A 7+7 | Tipton M 1+2 | McNiven D 2+6 | Hotte M —+1 | Littlejohn A 5 | Clitheroe L 1+2 | Grobbelaar B 4 | Match No. |
|---|---|---|---|---|---|---|---|---|---|---|---|---|---|---|---|---|---|---|---|---|---|---|---|---|---|---|---|---|---|---|---|---|---|---|
| 1 | 2 | 3 | 4 | 5 | 6 | 7 | 8 | 9 | 10 | 11 | | | | | | | | | | | | | | | | | | | | | | | | 1 |
| 1 | 2 | 3 | | 12 | 6 | $7^1$ | 8 | $9^2$ | 10 | 11 | 4 | 5 | 13 | | | | | | | | | | | | | | | | | | | | | 2 |
| 1 | $2^2$ | 3 | | 12 | 6 | | 8 | 9 | $10^1$ | 11 | 4 | 5 | $7^3$ | 13 | 14 | | | | | | | | | | | | | | | | | | | 3 |
| | $2^1$ | 3 | | 5 | 6 | | 8 | $9^2$ | 10 | 11 | 4 | | | 7 | 1 | 12 | 13 | | | | | | | | | | | | | | | | | 4 |
| | 2 | 3 | | $5^1$ | 6 | | 12 | 9 | 10 | 11 | 4 | | | 7 | 1 | 8 | | | | | | | | | | | | | | | | | | 5 |
| | 2 | 3 | | | 6 | | 12 | 9 | 10 | 11 | 4 | 5 | | 7 | 1 | $8^1$ | | | | | | | | | | | | | | | | | | 6 |
| | 2 | 3 | | | 6 | | 12 | 9 | $10^2$ | 11 | 4 | 5 | 13 | $7^1$ | 1 | 8 | | | | | | | | | | | | | | | | | | 7 |
| | $2^1$ | 3 | 13 | | 6 | | 12 | 9 | 10 | $11^2$ | 4 | 5 | | 7 | 1 | 8 | | | | | | | | | | | | | | | | | | 8 |
| | $2^1$ | 3 | 13 | 14 | 6 | | 12 | 9 | 10 | $11^3$ | 4 | $5^2$ | | 7 | 1 | 8 | | | | | | | | | | | | | | | | | | 9 |
| | 2 | $3^3$ | | 12 | 6 | | $8^2$ | 9 | 10 | 11 | 4 | 5 | | $7^1$ | 1 | | 13 | 14 | | | | | | | | | | | | | | | | 10 |
| | 6 | 3 | 7 | 9 | 12 | | 8 | | $10^3$ | 11 | $4^2$ | 5 | 13 | $2^1$ | 1 | 14 | | | | | | | | | | | | | | | | | | 11 |
| | 6 | 3 | 7 | 9 | | $2^2$ | 8 | | $10^1$ | 11 | 4 | $5^3$ | | 12 | 1 | 13 | 14 | | | | | | | | | | | | | | | | | 12 |
| | 2 | 3 | | 5 | 6 | | 8 | | 10 | 11 | 4 | | 13 | 12 | 1 | $7^2$ | | | | | $9^1$ | | | | | | | | | | | | | 13 |
| | 2 | 3 | | 5 | 6 | | 8 | 9 | 10 | $11^2$ | 4 | | 13 | 12 | 1 | $7^1$ | | | | | | | | | | | | | | | | | | 14 |
| | 2 | 3 | 10 | 5 | $6^1$ | | 8 | $9^2$ | | 11 | 4 | | 13 | 12 | 1 | $7^3$ | | 14 | | | | | | | | | | | | | | | | 15 |
| | 2 | 3 | | 5 | 6 | | 8 | 9 | $10^2$ | 11 | 4 | | 13 | 12 | 1 | $7^1$ | | | | | | | | | | | | | | | | | | 16 |
| | 2 | 3 | | 5 | 6 | | 8 | 9 | 10 | 11 | 4 | | | 12 | 1 | $7^1$ | | | | | | | | | | | | | | | | | | 17 |
| | $2^1$ | 3 | | | 6 | | 8 | 9 | $10^2$ | 11 | 4 | 7 | 13 | | 1 | | | | | | 12 | | 5 | | | | | | | | | | | 18 |
| | 2 | 3 | | | 6 | | 8 | 9 | $10^2$ | 11 | 4 | 5 | 13 | 12 | 1 | $7^1$ | | | | | 2 | | | | | | | | | | | | | 19 |
| 1 | 6 | 3 | 2 | 5 | | | 8 | 9 | 7 | 11 | | | | | | | | | | | 10 | | 4 | | | | | | | | | | | 20 |
| 1 | 6 | 3 | 7 | 5 | | | 8 | 9 | | 11 | 4 | | 13 | 12 | | | | | | | $10^2$ | | $2^1$ | | | | | | | | | | | 21 |
| 1 | 6 | 3 | 7 | 5 | | | $8^2$ | 9 | | 11 | 4 | | 13 | 12 | | | | | | | $10^1$ | | 2 | | | | | | | | | | | 22 |
| 1 | 6 | 3 | 2 | 5 | | | 8 | 9 | | 11 | 4 | | | 12 | | 7 | | | | | $10^1$ | | | | | | | | | | | | | 23 |
| 1 | 6 | 3 | 2 | $5^2$ | | | 8 | 9 | 10 | 11 | 4 | | 13 | | | $7^1$ | | | | | 12 | | 3 | | | | | | | | | | | 24 |
| 1 | 6 | 3 | 7 | 5 | | | 8 | 9 | | 11 | 4 | | | $2^2$ | | | | | | | $10^1$ | | 13 | 3 | | | | | | | | | | 25 |
| 1 | 6 | 3 | 2 | 5 | | | 8 | | $10^1$ | 11 | 4 | | 13 | | | | | | | | $7^2$ | | 3 | | 9 | | | | | | | | | 26 |
| 1 | 6 | 3 | 2 | 5 | | | 8 | 9 | | 11 | 4 | | | 12 | | | | | | | $7^1$ | | 3 | | 10 | | | | | | | | | 27 |
| 1 | 6 | 3 | | 4 | | | 8 | 9 | 10 | 11 | 5 | | | 2 | | | | | | | 7 | | 3 | | 10 | | | | | | | | | 28 |
| 1 | 6 | 3 | 4 | | | 11 | 12 | | 10 | | 5 | | | 2 | | | | | | | 8 | | | | $9^1$ | 7 | | | | | | | | 29 |
| 1 | $6^1$ | 3 | 4 | $8^3$ | | | | | 10 | 11 | 5 | | | 2 | | $7^2$ | | | | | 12 | | | | 9 | 13 | 14 | | | | | | | 30 |
| 1 | 6 | 2 | 4 | 8 | | | 7 | | 10 | 11 | 5 | | | | | | | | | | 10 | | 3 | | $9^1$ | 12 | | | | | | | | 31 |
| 1 | 6 | 5 | $12^4$ | 4 | | | 8 | 9 | $10^1$ | $11^3$ | 2 | | | | | | | | | | | | 3 | | | 7 | 13 | 14 | | | | | | 32 |
| 1 | 12 | 13 | $5^1$ | 4 | | | 8 | $9^2$ | | 11 | 14 | | | 2 | | 3 | | | | | | | | | 7 | $10^3$ | 6 | | | | | | | 33 |
| 1 | 6 | | $9^4$ | 4 | | | 8 | $9^2$ | | 11 | 2 | | | 7 | | 5 | | | | | | | 3 | | | $10^1$ | 13 | | | | | | | 34 |
| 1 | 6 | $9^4$ | 4 | 8 | | | 12 | 10 | | 11 | 7 | | 13 | | | 5 | | | | | | | $2^1$ | | | 3 | | | | | | | | 35 |
| 1 | 2 | | 4 | 8 | | | 12 | $10^1$ | | 11 | $6^2$ | | 7 | | | 5 | | | | | | | 9 | | | 3 | 13 | | | | | | | 36 |
| 1 | 6 | | 4 | 8 | | | | 11 | 13 | 14 | 2 | | | | | | | | | | $12^2$ | $7^3$ | 5 | | $9^1$ | 3 | | | | | 10 | | | 37 |
| 1 | $6^2$ | $3^1$ | 7 | 12 | 4 | | 8 | 11 | | | | | | $9^3$ | | 13 | | | | | 14 | 2 | | | 5 | | | | | | 10 | | | 38 |
| 1 | 12 | 6 | 9 | 4 | | | 8 | 11 | | 13 | | | | $2^1$ | | $7^2$ | | | | | | 5 | 3 | | 14 | | | | $10^1$ | | | | | 39 |
| 1 | 3 | 6 | $9^4$ | 4 | | | 8 | 11 | | 12 | | | | 2 | | 7 | | | | | | 5 | 13 | | | | | | $10^1$ | | | | | 40 |
| 1 | 3 | 6 | 12 | 4 | | | 9 | 8 | | 13 | | | | 2 | | $7^2$ | | | | | $5^1$ | 11 | | | | | 14 | | $10^3$ | | | | | 41 |
| 1 | 3 | $6^3$ | $9^1$ | 4 | 7 | | 8 | 11 | | | | | | $10^2$ | | 2 | | | | | | 5 | | | | 12 | 13 | | | 14 | | | | 42 |
| | 6 | 3 | 12 | | 4 | | 7 | | 10 | | 5 | $8^1$ | | 11 | | | | | $9^2$ | | 2 | | | | | $13$ | | | | | | 1 | | 43 |
| | 6 | 3 | 8 | | 4 | | $7^3$ | | 10 | | 12 | | | 11 | | $5^1$ | | | | | 2 | | | | 9 | 13 | 14 | | | | | 1 | | 44 |
| | 6 | 3 | 8 | | 4 | | | | 10 | $10^2$ | 12 | | | 11 | | 5 | | | | | $2^1$ | | 9 | | 13 | $7^3$ | | | 14 | | | 1 | | 45 |
| | 6 | 3 | 8 | | 12 | | | | | 11 | 5 | | | 10 | | 2 | | | | | $4^2$ | | | | $9^1$ | 13 | 14 | | $7^3$ | | | 1 | | 46 |

**Coca-Cola Cup**

| First Round | Grimsby T | (h) | 1-0 |
|---|---|---|---|
| | | (a) | 0-5 |

**FA Cup**

| First Round | Mansfield T | (h) | 1-1 |
|---|---|---|---|
| | | (a) | 1-0 |
| Second Round | Blackpool | (h) | 2-1 |
| Third Round | Cardiff C | (a) | 0-1 |

OXFORD UNITED 1997–98    *Back row (left to right):* Ken Ridley (Kit Man), Malcolm Crosby (Assistant Manager), John Clinkard (Physio), Gerald Sacks (Club Doctor), Peter Rhoades-Brown (Football Community Officer), Maurice Evans (Chief Scout).
*Second row:* Les Robinson, Mark Angel, Andrew Rose, Jamie Cook, Mark Harrison (Reserve Team Coach), Paul Powell, Nicky Banger, Christophe Remy, Martin Gray.
*Third row:* Phil Whitehead, Bobby Ford, Dave Smith, Joey Beauchamp, Simon Marsh, Martin Aldridge, Nigel Jemson, Simon Weatherstone, Nigel Emsden, Elliott Jackson.
*Front row:* Phil Gilchrist, Brian Wilsterman, Phil Whelan, Stuart Massey, Denis Smith (Manager/Director of Football), Mike Ford, Mark Stevens, Matt Murphy, Darren Purse.

# Division 1     **OXFORD UNITED**

*Manor Ground, Headington, Oxford OX3 7RS.* Telephone: (01865) 761503. Fax: (01865) 741820. Supporters Club: (01865) 763063. Clubline: 0891 440055.

*Ground capacity:* 9572.

*Record attendance:* 22,750 v Preston NE, FA Cup 6th rd, 29 February 1964.

*Record receipts:* £103,411 v Leeds U, FA Cup 4th rd, 29 January 1994.

*Pitch measurements:* 110yd × 75yd.

*President:* The Duke of Marlborough.

*Directors:* G. E. Coppock, N. J. W. Harris, M. G. Evans.

*Managing Director:* K. A. Cox.

*Manager:* Malcolm Shotton. *Coach:* Mark Harrison. *Physio:* John Clinkard.

*Secretary:* Mick Brown. *Commercial Manager:* Trevor Baxter. *Stadium Manager:* Mick Moore.

*Year Formed:* 1893. *Turned Professional:* 1949. *Ltd Co.:* 1949.

*Club Nickname:* 'The U's'.

*Previous Names:* 1893, Headington; 1894, Headington United; 1960, Oxford United.

*Previous Grounds:* 1893–94 Headington Quarry; 1894–98 Wootten's Field; 1898–1902 Sandy Lane Ground; 1902–09 Britannia Field; 1909–10 Sandy Lane; 1910–14 Quarry Recreation Ground; 1914–22 Sandy Lane; 1922–25 The Paddock Manor Road; 1925, Manor Ground.

*Foundation:* There had been an Oxford United club around the time of World War I but only in the Oxfordshire Thursday League and there is no connection with the modern club which began as Headington in 1893, adding "United" a year later. Playing first on Quarry Fields and subsequently Wootten's Fields, they owe much to a Dr. Hitchings for their early development.

*First Football League game:* 18 August 1962, Division 4, v Barrow (a) L 2-3 – Medlock; Beavon, Quartermain; R. Atkinson, Kyle, Jones; Knight, G. Atkinson (1), Houghton (1), Cornwell, Colfar.

*Record League Victory:* 7–0 v Barrow, Division 4, 19 December 1964 – Fearnley; Beavon, Quartermain; R. Atkinson (1), Kyle, Jones; Morris, Booth (3), Willey (1), G. Atkinson (1), Harrington (1).

*Record Cup Victory:* 9–1 v Dorchester T, FA Cup 1st rd, 11 November 1995 – Whitehead; Wood (2), Ford M (1), Smith, Elliott, Gilchrist, Rush (1), Massey (Murphy), Moody (3), Ford R (1), Angel (Beauchamp (1)).

*Record Defeat:* 0–6 v Liverpool, Division 1, 22 March 1986.

*Most League Points (2 for a win):* 61, Division 4, 1964–65.

*Most League Points (3 for a win):* 95, Division 3, 1983–84.

*Most League Goals:* 91, Division 3, 1983–84.

*Highest League Scorer in Season:* John Aldridge, 30, Division 2, 1984–85.

*Most League Goals in Total Aggregate:* Graham Atkinson, 77, 1962–73.

*Most Capped Player:* Jim Magilton, 18 (39), Northern Ireland.

*Most League Appearances:* John Shuker, 478, 1962–77.

*Record Transfer Fee Received:* £1,600,000 from Leicester C for Matt Elliott, January 1997.

*Record Transfer Fee Paid:* £285,000 to Gillingham for Colin Greenall, February 1988.

*Football League Record:* 1962 Elected to Division 4; 1965–68 Division 3; 1968–76 Division 2; 1976–84 Division 3; 1984–85 Division 2; 1985–88 Division 1; 1988–92 Division 2; 1992–94 Division 1; 1994–96 Division 2; 1996– Division 1.

*Honours: Football League:* Division 1 best season: 12th, 1997–98; Division 2 – Champions 1984–85; Runners-up 1995–96; Division 3 – Champions 1967–68, 1983–84; Division 4 – Promoted 1964–65 (4th). *FA Cup:* best season: 6th rd, 1964 (shared record for 4th Division club). *Football League Cup:* Winners 1986.

*Colours:* Yellow shirts with navy trim, navy shorts, navy stockings. *Change colours:* All white.

**Did you know?**
While still known as Headington United, the club's first floodlit match at the Manor Ground was on 18 December 1950 and resulted in a 3-0 win over Banbury Spencer, watched by a crowd of 2603.

## OXFORD UNITED 1997–98 LEAGUE RECORD

| Match No. | Date | Venue | Opponents | Result | H/T Score | Lg. Pos. | Goalscorers | Attendance |
|---|---|---|---|---|---|---|---|---|
| 1 | Aug 9 | H | Huddersfield T | W 2-0 | 0-0 | — | Jemson (pen) [69], Aldridge [77] | 7085 |
| 2 | 16 | A | Charlton Ath | L 2-3 | 0-1 | 8 | Purse [85], Jemson (pen) [90] | 10,230 |
| 3 | 23 | H | Nottingham F | L 0-1 | 0-0 | 13 | | 9486 |
| 4 | 30 | A | Portsmouth | L 1-2 | 1-1 | 14 | Ford B [36] | 10,209 |
| 5 | Sept 2 | A | Sunderland | L 1-3 | 1-2 | — | Angel [20] | 27,643 |
| 6 | 7 | H | Wolverhampton W | W 3-0 | 2-0 | 14 | Beauchamp 2 [17, 71], Ford B [23] | 6921 |
| 7 | 13 | A | Reading | L 1-2 | 1-1 | 17 | Jemson [2] | 9003 |
| 8 | 20 | H | Sheffield U | L 2-4 | 1-2 | 18 | Jemson 2 [25, 76] | 7514 |
| 9 | 27 | H | Bradford C | D 0-0 | 0-0 | 21 | | 6468 |
| 10 | Oct 4 | A | WBA | W 2-1 | 1-1 | 19 | Banger [13], Purse [53] | 15,819 |
| 11 | 11 | A | Stockport Co | L 2-3 | 0-0 | 19 | Purse [84], Aldridge [88] | 7333 |
| 12 | 18 | H | Ipswich T | W 1-0 | 0-0 | 18 | Smith [64] | 7594 |
| 13 | 21 | H | Middlesbrough | L 1-4 | 0-1 | — | Purse [51] | 8306 |
| 14 | 25 | A | Birmingham C | D 0-0 | 0-0 | 18 | | 16,352 |
| 15 | Nov 1 | H | Manchester C | D 0-0 | 0-0 | 18 | | 8592 |
| 16 | 4 | A | Stoke C | D 0-0 | 0-0 | — | | 8423 |
| 17 | 8 | A | Crewe Alex | L 1-2 | 1-2 | 19 | Ford M [14] | 4524 |
| 18 | 15 | H | Bury | D 1-1 | 1-1 | 20 | Banger [30] | 5811 |
| 19 | 22 | A | Norwich C | L 1-2 | 0-1 | 22 | Powell [80] | 11,241 |
| 20 | 29 | H | Port Vale | W 2-0 | 1-0 | 19 | Beauchamp [32], Jemson [57] | 5762 |
| 21 | Dec 6 | A | Swindon T | L 1-4 | 1-2 | 21 | Ford M [24] | 10,902 |
| 22 | 12 | H | QPR | W 3-1 | 2-1 | — | Jemson [3], Beauchamp 2 [36, 49] | 6664 |
| 23 | 20 | A | Tranmere R | W 2-0 | 0-0 | 16 | Massey [54], Robinson [87] | 5181 |
| 24 | 26 | A | Wolverhampton W | L 0-1 | 0-1 | 17 | | 26,238 |
| 25 | 28 | H | Sunderland | D 1-1 | 1-1 | 17 | Jemson (pen) [27] | 8659 |
| 26 | Jan 10 | A | Huddersfield T | L 1-5 | 0-3 | 19 | Gray [74] | 10,378 |
| 27 | 17 | H | Charlton Ath | L 1-2 | 1-0 | 20 | Jemson [6] | 7234 |
| 28 | 24 | H | Portsmouth | W 1-0 | 0-0 | 18 | Beauchamp [90] | 7402 |
| 29 | 31 | A | Nottingham F | W 3-1 | 1-1 | 16 | Beauchamp 2 [8, 49], Weatherstone [90] | 18,392 |
| 30 | Feb 7 | A | Sheffield U | L 0-1 | 0-1 | 17 | | 16,881 |
| 31 | 17 | H | WBA | W 2-1 | 1-0 | — | Gilchrist [15], Francis [81] | 9412 |
| 32 | 21 | H | Bradford C | D 0-0 | 0-0 | 16 | | 14,190 |
| 33 | 24 | A | Ipswich T | L 2-5 | 1-3 | — | Francis [11], Donaldson (pen) [59] | 11,824 |
| 34 | 28 | H | Stockport Co | W 3-0 | 1-0 | 15 | Davis [5], Donaldson [65], Francis [80] | 6650 |
| 35 | Mar 3 | H | Crewe Alex | D 0-0 | 0-0 | — | | 6069 |
| 36 | 7 | A | Manchester C | W 2-0 | 1-0 | 14 | Beauchamp [44], Cook [81] | 28,720 |
| 37 | 14 | A | Stoke C | W 5-1 | 1-0 | 13 | Murphy 2 [45, 61], Francis 2 [65, 68], Beauchamp [87] | 7300 |
| 38 | 17 | H | Reading | W 3-0 | 1-0 | — | Beauchamp 2 [44, 70], Gray [77] | 8103 |
| 39 | 21 | A | Bury | L 0-1 | 0-0 | 12 | | 5159 |
| 40 | 28 | H | Norwich C | W 2-0 | 0-0 | 10 | Francis [64], Beauchamp (pen) [80] | 7869 |
| 41 | Apr 4 | A | Port Vale | L 0-3 | 0-2 | 12 | | 6524 |
| 42 | 11 | H | Swindon T | W 2-1 | 2-0 | 10 | Francis [28], Gilchrist [37] | 8005 |
| 43 | 14 | A | QPR | D 1-1 | 1-0 | — | Davis [24] | 12,859 |
| 44 | 18 | H | Tranmere R | D 1-1 | 1-0 | 10 | Cook [22] | 6489 |
| 45 | 25 | H | Birmingham C | L 0-2 | 0-0 | 11 | | 8818 |
| 46 | May 3 | A | Middlesbrough | L 1-4 | 0-0 | 12 | Banger [70] | 30,228 |

**Final League Position: 12**      1996–97 DIV1 17

### GOALSCORERS

*League (60):* Beauchamp 13 (1 pen), Jemson 9 (3 pens), Francis 7, Purse 4, Banger 3, Aldridge 2, Cook 2, Davis 2, Donaldson 2 (1 pen), Ford B 2, Ford M 2, Gilchrist 2, Gray 2, Murphy 2, Angel 1, Massey 1, Powell 1, Robinson 1, Smith 1, Weatherstone 1.
*Coca-Cola Cup (15):* Beauchamp 6, Aldridge 2, Purse 2, Banger 1, Jemson 1, Murphy 1, Robinson 1, own goal 1.
*FA Cup (0).*

| Whitehead P 32 | Remy C 13 + 3 | Ford M 22 | Robinson L 46 | Whelan P 6 + 2 | Gilchrist P 35 + 4 | Ford B 17 + 1 | Smith D 43 + 1 | Banger N 18 + 10 | Jemson N 24 | Beauchamp J 44 | Purse D 27 + 1 | Angel M 9 + 13 | Aldridge M 13 + 11 | Massey S 14 + 3 | Gray M 28 + 3 | Jackson E 3 | Marsh S 13 + 1 | Wilsterman B 15 + 9 | Murphy M 15 + 14 | Stevens M — + 1 | Cook J 9 + 11 | Powell P 11 + 10 | Van Heusden A 11 | Folland R — + 2 | Weatherstone S 2 + 9 | Donaldson O 6 | Davis S 15 | Francis K 15 | Rose A — + 1 | Wright T — + 1 | Match No. |
|---|---|---|---|---|---|---|---|---|---|---|---|---|---|---|---|---|---|---|---|---|---|---|---|---|---|---|---|---|---|---|---|
| 1 | 2 | 3 | 4 | $5^1$ | 6 | $7^2$ | 8 | $9^3$ | 10 | 11 | 12 | 13 | 14 | | | | | | | | | | | | | | | | | | 1 |
| 1 | | $3^3$ | 4 | | 6 | 7 | 8 | $9^1$ | 10 | 11 | 5 | | 12 | | 2 | 13 | | | | | | | | | | | | | | | 2 |
| | $2^2$ | | 4 | | | 7 | 8 | | 10 | 11 | 5 | 12 | | | | 1 | $3^1$ | 6 | $9^3$ | 13 | 14 | | | | | | | | | | 3 |
| 1 | 2 | | 4 | 12 | | 7 | 8 | | 10 | 11 | 5 | | | | | | $3^2$ | $6^3$ | $9^1$ | 13 | 14 | | | | | | | | | | 4 |
| 1 | $2^3$ | | 4 | | 6 | 7 | 8 | $9^2$ | $10^1$ | 11 | 5 | 3 | 12 | | | | | | | | 13 | | | | | | | | | | 5 |
| 1 | $2^1$ | | 4 | 12 | $6^2$ | 7 | 8 | 9 | $10^3$ | 11 | 5 | 3 | | | | | 13 | | | | 14 | | | | | | | | | | 6 |
| | 2 | | 4 | $5^3$ | 6 | 7 | 8 | 12 | 10 | $11^2$ | | 3 | | | | | 13 | | $9^1$ | | 14 | | 1 | | | | | | | | 7 |
| | 2 | | 4 | 12 | 6 | 7 | $8^3$ | 13 | 10 | 11 | 5 | $3^1$ | | | | | | | $9^2$ | | 14 | | 1 | | | | | | | | 8 |
| | $2^2$ | 3 | 4 | | 6 | 14 | 7 | 8 | 9 | $10^1$ | 11 | $5^2$ | 12 | | | | | 13 | | | | | 1 | | | | | | | | 9 |
| | 2 | 3 | 4 | $5^2$ | 6 | 7 | 8 | $9^1$ | 10 | 11 | 12 | | | | | | | 13 | | | | | 1 | | | | | | | | 10 |
| | 2 | $3^1$ | 4 | | 6 | 13 | 8 | $9^3$ | 10 | 11 | 5 | $12^2$ | | | | | | 7 | | | 14 | | 1 | | | | | | | | 11 |
| | 2 | | 4 | | 6 | 7 | 8 | $9^1$ | $10^2$ | 11 | 5 | 3 | 12 | | | | | | | | | | 1 | | | 13 | | | | | 12 |
| | $2^1$ | | 4 | | 6 | 7 | 8 | 9 | $10^2$ | 11 | 5 | $3^1$ | 12 | | | | | 13 | | | 14 | | 1 | | | | | | | | 13 |
| | 2 | | $4^1$ | | 6 | 7 | 8 | $9^1$ | $10^2$ | 11 | 5 | 3 | 12 | | | | | 13 | | | 14 | | 1 | | | | | | | | 14 |
| | 2 | 3 | 4 | | 6 | 7 | 8 | $9^1$ | $10^2$ | 11 | 5 | 12 | | | | | | 13 | | | | | 1 | | | | | | | | 15 |
| | 2 | 3 | 4 | | 6 | 7 | 8 | 9 | $10^1$ | 11 | $5^2$ | 12 | | | | | | 13 | | | | | 1 | | | | | | | | 16 |
| | 2 | 3 | 4 | | 6 | 7 | 8 | $9^2$ | $10^1$ | 11 | | 12 | $5^3$ | | | | | 13 | | | 14 | | 1 | | | | | | | | 17 |
| | 2 | 3 | 4 | | $6^2$ | 7 | $8^1$ | 9 | 10 | 11 | 5 | | 12 | | | | | 13 | | | | | 1 | | | | | | | | 18 |
| | 2 | 3 | 4 | | 6 | 7 | $8^2$ | $9^1$ | 10 | 11 | 5 | | 12 | | | | | 13 | | | | | 1 | | | | | | | | 19 |
| 1 | | 3 | 4 | | 6 | 7 | 8 | 12 | $10^3$ | 11 | 5 | | 14 | | 2 | | | 13 | $9^2$ | | | $7^1$ | | | | | | | | | 20 |
| 1 | | $4^2$ | | 12 | $6^1$ | 7 | 8 | 9 | 10 | 11 | 5 | | | | $2^3$ | | | 13 | 14 | | | 7 | | | | | | | | | 21 |
| 1 | 12 | 3 | $4^1$ | | 6 | 7 | 8 | $9^2$ | 10 | 11 | 5 | | | | 2 | | | 13 | | | | | | | | | | | | | 22 |
| 1 | | 3 | 4 | | 6 | 7 | 8 | 9 | 10 | 11 | 5 | | | | 2 | | | | | | | | | | | | | | | | 23 |
| 1 | 12 | 3 | 4 | | 6 | 7 | $8^3$ | $9^2$ | 10 | 11 | 5 | | 14 | | 2 | | | 13 | | | | $7^1$ | | | | | | | | | 24 |
| 1 | | 3 | 4 | | 6 | 7 | 8 | $9^1$ | 10 | 11 | 5 | | 12 | | 2 | | | | | | | | | | | | | | | | 25 |
| 1 | | 3 | 4 | | 6 | 7 | $8^1$ | 9 | 10 | 11 | 5 | | | | $3^2$ | | | 13 | | | | | | | 12 | | | | | | 26 |
| 1 | | | 4 | | 6 | 7 | 8 | $9^3$ | 10 | 11 | 5 | | 12 | | $2^1$ | | $3^2$ | | | | | | | | | | | | | | 27 |
| 1 | 2 | | | | 6 | $7^1$ | 8 | $9^3$ | 10 | 11 | 5 | | 12 | | 4 | | $3^2$ | | 13 | | | | | | 14 | | | | | | 28 |
| 1 | 2 | | | | 6 | $7^2$ | 8 | $9^1$ | $10^1$ | 11 | 5 | | | | 4 | | 3 | | 13 | | | 12 | | | 14 | | | | | | 29 |
| 1 | 2 | | | | 6 | 7 | 8 | $9^1$ | $10^2$ | 11 | 5 | | | | 4 | | $3^2$ | 13 | | | | 12 | | | 14 | | | | | | 30 |
| 1 | 3 | 2 | | | 6 | $7^1$ | 8 | 9 | $10^3$ | 11 | | | | | 4 | | | 13 | | | | | | | 14 | | $5^2$ | 9 | | | 31 |
| 1 | $3^1$ | 2 | | | 6 | 7 | 8 | 9 | $10^2$ | 11 | | | | | 4 | | | 13 | | | | 5 | | | | | | 9 | | | 32 |
| 1 | 3 | 2 | | | 6 | $7^1$ | 8 | 9 | $10^3$ | 11 | 12 | | | | 4 | | | 13 | | | | | | | | | 5 | 9 | | | 33 |
| 1 | $3^1$ | 2 | | | 6 | 7 | 8 | 12 | 10 | 11 | | | | | 4 | | | | | | | | | | | | 5 | 9 | | | 34 |
| 1 | | 2 | | | 6 | $7^1$ | 8 | 12 | $10^2$ | 11 | | | | | 4 | | 3 | 13 | | | | | | | | | 5 | 9 | | | 35 |
| 1 | | 2 | | | 6 | $7^1$ | 8 | 12 | $10^2$ | 11 | | | | | 4 | | 3 | 13 | | | | | | | | | 5 | 9 | | | 36 |
| 1 | | 2 | | | 6 | $7^1$ | 8 | 12 | $10^2$ | 11 | | | | | 4 | | 3 | 13 | | | | | | | | | 5 | 9 | | | 37 |
| 1 | | 2 | | | 6 | 7 | 8 | 12 | $10^3$ | 11 | | | | | 4 | | 3 | 13 | | | | | | | 14 | | $5^2$ | $9^1$ | | | 38 |
| 1 | | 2 | | | 6 | $7^1$ | 8 | 12 | $10^2$ | 11 | | | | | 4 | | 3 | 13 | | | | | | | | | 5 | 9 | | | 39 |
| 1 | | 2 | | | 6 | $7^1$ | 8 | 12 | $10^2$ | 11 | | | | | 4 | | 3 | 13 | | | | | | | | | 5 | 9 | | | 40 |
| 1 | | 2 | | | 6 | $7^2$ | $8^3$ | 9 | $10^1$ | 11 | 12 | | | | 4 | | 3 | 13 | | | | | | | | | 5 | 9 | 14 | | 41 |
| 1 | | 2 | | | 6 | 7 | $8^2$ | 12 | $10^1$ | 11 | | | | | 4 | | 3 | 13 | | | | | | | | | 5 | 9 | | | 42 |
| 1 | | 2 | | | $6^2$ | 7 | 8 | 12 | 10 | $11^1$ | | | | | 4 | | 3 | 13 | | | | | | | | | 5 | 9 | | | 43 |
| 1 | 6 | 2 | | | | 7 | $8^1$ | 12 | 10 | 11 | | $3^2$ | | | 4 | | | 13 | | | | | | | | | 5 | 9 | | | 44 |
| 1 | 6 | 2 | | | | 7 | 8 | 12 | $10^2$ | 11 | | | | | 4 | | 3 | 13 | | | | | | | | | 5 | 9 | | | 45 |
| 1 | 12 | 2 | | | 6 | $7^2$ | 8 | | $10^1$ | 11 | | | | | 4 | | 3 | 13 | | | | | | | 14 | | 5 | $9^3$ | | | 46 |

**Coca-Cola Cup**

| First Round | Plymouth Arg | (h) | 2-0 |
|---|---|---|---|
| | | (a) | 5-3 |
| Second Round | York C | (h) | 4-1 |
| | | (a) | 2-1 |
| Third Round | Tranmere R | (h) | 1-1 |
| Fourth Round | Ipswich T | (h) | 1-2 |

**FA Cup**

| Third Round | Leeds U | (a) | 0-4 |
|---|---|---|---|

PETERBOROUGH UNITED 1997–98    *Back row (left to right):* Simon Davies, Anders Koogi; Greg Heald, Mark Foran, Mark Tyler, Bart Griemink, Jimmy Quinn, Ashley Neal, David Farrell, Chris McMenamin.

*Middle row:* Gordon Ogbourne (Kit Manager), Neil Lewis, Adrian Boothroyd, Martin Carruthers, Mick Bodley, Andy Edwards, Miguel De Souza, Des Linton, Zeke Rowe, Adam Drury, Niall Inman.

*Front row:* Chris Turner (Football Co-ordinator), Giuliano Grazioli, Derek Payne, Steve Castle, Barry Fry (Football Manager), Peter Boizot (Chairman), Peter Boizot (Chairman), Phil Neal (Assistant Manager), Wayne Bullimore, Chris Cleaver, Scott Houghton, Roy Johnson (Physio).

# Division 3   **PETERBOROUGH UNITED**

*London Road Ground, Peterborough PE2 8AL.* Telephone: (01733) 563947. Fax: (01733) 557210.

*Ground capacity:* 15,314.

*Record attendance:* 30,096 v Swansea T, FA Cup 5th rd, 20 February 1965.

*Record receipts:* £51,315 v Brighton & HA, FA Cup 5th rd, 15 February 1986.

*Pitch measurements:* 112yd × 75yd.

*Chairman:* Peter Boizot MBE. *Vice-Chairman:* Roger Terrell.

*Directors:* A. Hand, N. Hards, P. Sagar. *Company Secretary:* Timothy Warren. *Club Secretary:* Caroline Hand.

*Chief Executive:* Richard Maxwell.

*First Team Manager:* Barry Fry. *Assistant Manager:* Jimmy Quinn. *Youth Academy Director:* Kit Carson.

*Physio:* Phil McLoughlin.

*Year Formed:* 1934. *Turned Professional:* 1934. *Ltd Co.:* 1934.

*Club Nickname:* 'The Posh'.

*Foundation:* The old Peterborough & Fletton club, founded in 1923, was suspended by the FA during season 1932–33 and disbanded. Local enthusiasts determined to carry on and in 1934 a new professional club Peterborough United was formed and entered the Midland League the following year.

*First Football League game:* 20 August 1960, Division 4, v Wrexham (h) W 3-0 – Walls; Stafford, Walker; Rayner, Rigby, Norris; Hails, Emery (1), Bly (1), Smith, McNamee (1).

*Record League Victory:* 8–1 v Oldham Ath, Division 4, 26 November 1969 – Drewery; Potts, Noble; Conmy, Wile, Wright; Moss (1), Price (3), Hall (4), Halliday, Robson.

*Record Cup Victory:* 7–0 v Harlow T, FA Cup 1st rd, 16 November 1991 – Barber; Luke, Johnson, Halsall (1), Robinson D, Welsh, Sterling (1) (Butterworth), Cooper G (2 (1 pen)), Riley (1) (Culpin (1)), Charlery (1), Kimble.

*Record Defeat:* 1–8 v Northampton T, FA Cup 2nd rd (2nd replay), 18 December 1946.

*Most League Points (2 for a win):* 66, Division 4, 1960–61.

*Most League Points (3 for a win):* 82, Division 4, 1981–82.

*Most League Goals:* 134, Division 4, 1960–61.

*Highest League Scorer in Season:* Terry Bly, 52, Division 4, 1960–61.

*Most League Goals in Total Aggregate:* Jim Hall, 122, 1967–75.

*Most Capped Player:* Tony Millington, 8 (21), Wales.

*Most League Appearances:* Tommy Robson, 482, 1968–81.

*Record Transfer Fee Received:* £350,000 from Walsall for Martin O'Connor, July 1996.

*Record Transfer Fee Paid:* £450,000 to Birmingham C for Martin O'Connor, November 1996.

*Football League Record:* 1960 Elected to Division 4; 1961–68 Division 3, when they were demoted for financial irregularities; 1968–74 Division 4; 1974–79 Division 3; 1979–91 Division 4; 1991–92 Division 3; 1992–94 Division 1; 1994–97 Division 2; 1997– Division 3.

*Honours: Football League:* Division 1 best season: 10th Division 1 1992–93; Division 4 – Champions 1960–61, 1973–74. *FA Cup:* best season: 6th rd, 1965. *Football League Cup:* Semi-final 1966.

*Colours:* Royal blue shirts, white shorts, white stockings. *Change colours:* All red.

**Did you know?**
On 28 May 1960 at the AGM of the Football League, Peterborough United were elected to the competition. Peterborough with 35 votes, Oldham Athletic 39, Southport 29 and Hartlepool United 34 were the successful clubs, the initials of these clubs spelling the word 'Posh'.

## PETERBOROUGH UNITED 1997–98 LEAGUE RECORD

| Match No. | Date | | Venue | Opponents | Result | H/T Score | Lg. Pos. | Goalscorers | Attendance |
|---|---|---|---|---|---|---|---|---|---|
| 1 | Aug | 9 | H | Scunthorpe U | L 0-1 | 0-0 | — | | 5761 |
| 2 | | 16 | A | Doncaster R | W 5-0 | 1-0 | 6 | Edwards [31], Payne [56], Carruthers 2 [67, 88], Quinn [69] | 1920 |
| 3 | | 23 | H | Hull C | W 2-0 | 1-0 | 3 | Carruthers [30], Quinn [88] | 5701 |
| 4 | | 30 | A | Rochdale | W 2-1 | 1-1 | 2 | Carruthers [13], Farrell [56] | 2104 |
| 5 | Sept | 3 | A | Brighton & HA | D 2-2 | 1-1 | — | Carruthers [20], Payne [85] | 1215 |
| 6 | | 7 | H | Barnet | W 5-1 | 2-0 | 1 | Quinn 3 (1 pen) [25, 39 (pl), 52], Farrell [56], Carruthers [60] | 7243 |
| 7 | | 13 | A | Rotherham U | D 2-2 | 1-2 | 1 | Carruthers 2 [20, 72] | 3859 |
| 8 | | 20 | H | Leyton Orient | W 2-0 | 2-0 | 1 | Castle [3], Quinn [21] | 6629 |
| 9 | | 27 | A | Macclesfield T | D 1-1 | 0-0 | 4 | Houghton [80] | 3079 |
| 10 | Oct | 4 | H | Swansea C | W 3-1 | 2-0 | 1 | Quinn 2 [19, 85], Houghton [23] | 5849 |
| 11 | | 11 | H | Colchester U | W 3-2 | 0-1 | 1 | Carruthers [54], Houghton [60], Quinn [77] | 6277 |
| 12 | | 18 | A | Scarborough | W 3-1 | 3-0 | 1 | Bullimore [16], Farrell [20], Quinn [27] | 2565 |
| 13 | | 21 | A | Hartlepool U | L 1-2 | 0-1 | — | De Souza [89] | 1990 |
| 14 | | 25 | H | Torquay U | W 2-0 | 1-0 | 1 | Carruthers [38], Quinn [64] | 6325 |
| 15 | Nov | 1 | A | Exeter C | D 0-0 | 0-0 | 2 | | 5984 |
| 16 | | 4 | H | Shrewsbury T | D 1-1 | 1-0 | — | Houghton [9] | 4727 |
| 17 | | 8 | H | Darlington | D 1-1 | 1-0 | 1 | Quinn [41] | 6207 |
| 18 | | 18 | A | Chester C | D 0-0 | 0-0 | — | | 2612 |
| 19 | | 22 | H | Mansfield T | D 1-1 | 1-0 | 2 | Quinn [4] | 6202 |
| 20 | | 29 | A | Notts Co | D 2-2 | 1-2 | 2 | Gregory [6], Quinn (pen) [58] | 8006 |
| 21 | Dec | 2 | A | Cambridge U | W 1-0 | 0-0 | — | Quinn [85] | 10,791 |
| 22 | | 13 | A | Cardiff C | D 0-0 | 0-0 | 3 | | 3401 |
| 23 | | 20 | H | Lincoln C | W 5-1 | 4-1 | 2 | Carruthers 2 [12, 14], Farrell 2 [24, 80], Thorpe (og) [45] | 8771 |
| 24 | | 26 | A | Barnet | L 0-2 | 0-0 | 2 | | 3449 |
| 25 | | 28 | H | Brighton & HA | L 1-2 | 0-1 | 2 | Quinn [85] | 8221 |
| 26 | Jan | 10 | A | Scunthorpe U | W 3-1 | 2-1 | 2 | Carruthers [18], Bodley [26], Quinn [63] | 3584 |
| 27 | | 17 | H | Rochdale | W 3-1 | 2-1 | 2 | Cleaver [24], Quinn 2 [44, 73] | 5676 |
| 28 | | 24 | A | Hull C | L 1-3 | 0-0 | 2 | Edwards [84] | 4669 |
| 29 | | 31 | H | Rotherham U | W 1-0 | 0-0 | 2 | Quinn [65] | 7165 |
| 30 | Feb | 6 | A | Leyton Orient | L 0-1 | 0-0 | — | | 5991 |
| 31 | | 10 | H | Doncaster R | L 0-1 | 0-0 | — | | 4577 |
| 32 | | 14 | A | Swansea C | W 1-0 | 0-0 | 2 | De Souza [75] | 3737 |
| 33 | | 21 | H | Macclesfield T | L 0-1 | 0-0 | 4 | | 6224 |
| 34 | | 24 | H | Scarborough | D 0-0 | 0-0 | — | | 4208 |
| 35 | | 27 | A | Colchester U | L 0-1 | 0-0 | — | | 4117 |
| 36 | Mar | 3 | A | Darlington | L 1-3 | 0-1 | — | De Souza [67] | 1939 |
| 37 | | 7 | H | Exeter C | D 1-1 | 0-1 | 6 | Cleaver [53] | 4888 |
| 38 | | 14 | A | Shrewsbury T | L 1-4 | 0-3 | 8 | Carruthers [48] | 2421 |
| 39 | | 21 | H | Chester C | W 2-1 | 1-1 | 7 | Carruthers [7], Farrell [56] | 4817 |
| 40 | | 28 | A | Mansfield T | L 0-2 | 0-2 | 8 | | 2760 |
| 41 | Apr | 3 | H | Notts Co | W 1-0 | 0-0 | — | Castle [78] | 6498 |
| 42 | | 11 | A | Cambridge U | L 0-1 | 0-0 | 8 | | 5445 |
| 43 | | 13 | H | Cardiff C | W 2-0 | 0-0 | 7 | Castle [48], Inman [67] | 4756 |
| 44 | | 18 | A | Lincoln C | L 0-3 | 0-3 | 9 | | 6748 |
| 45 | | 25 | A | Torquay U | L 1-3 | 1-2 | 9 | Green [5] | 4472 |
| 46 | May | 2 | H | Hartlepool U | D 0-0 | 0-0 | 10 | | 4727 |

**Final League Position: 10**      1996–97 DIV2 21

### GOALSCORERS

*League (63):* Quinn 20 (2 pens), Carruthers 15, Farrell 6, Houghton 4, Castle 3, De Souza 3, Cleaver 2, Edwards 2, Payne 2, Bodley 1, Bullimore 1, Green 1, Gregory 1, Inman 1, own goal 1.
*Coca-Cola Cup (4):* Carruthers 1, Farrell 1, Quinn 1, own goal 1.
*FA Cup (7):* Quinn 3, Carruthers 2, Castle 2.

| Tyler M 46 | Linton D 25 + 5 | Lewis N 31 + 3 | Payne D 35 + 2 | Edwards A 46 | Bodley M 31 | Farrell D 40 + 2 | Castle S 34 + 3 | De Souza M 8 + 16 | Quinn J 40 + 2 | Houghton S 24 + 6 | Bullimore W 8 + 7 | Cleaver C 4 + 10 | Carruthers M 37 + 2 | McMenamin C 25 + 3 | Drury A 24 + 7 | Foran M 3 + 1 | Rowe Z 3 + 3 | Gregory N 2 + 1 | Rennie D 18 | Neal A 2 + 2 | Vickers A 1 | Davies S 4 + 2 | Comforth J 3 + 1 | Roberts D 2 + 1 | Green F 2 + 2 | Inman N 4 | Gill M 2 | Etherington M 2 | Shields A — + 1 | Match No. |
|---|---|---|---|---|---|---|---|---|---|---|---|---|---|---|---|---|---|---|---|---|---|---|---|---|---|---|---|---|---|---|
| 1 | 2 | 3 | $4^1$ | 5 | 6 | 7 | | 8 | $9^2$ | 10 | $11^3$ | 12 | 13 | 14 | | | | | | | | | | | | | | | | 1 |
| 1 | 5 | 3 | 7 | 6 | | $11^1$ | 8 | | 10 | 12 | | | 13 | 9 | 2 | $4^2$ | | | | | | | | | | | | | | 2 |
| 1 | 2 | 3 | 7 | 6 | 5 | 11 | 8 | | 10 | | | | 9 | | 4 | | | | | | | | | | | | | | | 3 |
| 1 | $2^2$ | $3^1$ | 7 | 6 | 5 | 11 | 8 | | 10 | | | 12 | 9 | | 4 | 13 | | | | | | | | | | | | | | 4 |
| 1 | | 3 | 7 | 6 | 5 | 11 | $8^2$ | | 10 | 12 | 13 | 14 | $9^1$ | | $4^3$ | 2 | | | | | | | | | | | | | | 5 |
| 1 | 2 | 3 | 4 | 6 | 5 | 7 | 8 | | 10 | 11 | | | 9 | | | | | | | | | | | | | | | | | 6 |
| 1 | 2 | 3 | 4 | 6 | 5 | 7 | 8 | | 10 | 11 | | | 9 | | | | | | | | | | | | | | | | | 7 |
| 1 | | 3 | 4 | 6 | 5 | 7 | 8 | | $10^1$ | $11^2$ | 13 | 12 | 9 | 2 | | | | | | | | | | | | | | | | 8 |
| 1 | 12 | 3 | | 6 | 5 | 7 | 8 | 13 | $10^2$ | 11 | | $4^1$ | 9 | 2 | | | | | | | | | | | | | | | | 9 |
| 1 | 12 | $3^1$ | | 6 | 5 | $7^2$ | 8 | 13 | 10 | 11 | | $4^1$ | 9 | 2 | 14 | | | | | | | | | | | | | | | 10 |
| 1 | | 3 | | 6 | 5 | 7 | 8 | 12 | 10 | 11 | | 4 | $9^1$ | 2 | | | | | | | | | | | | | | | | 11 |
| 1 | | 3 | | 6 | 5 | 7 | 8 | 12 | 10 | 11 | | 4 | $9^1$ | 2 | | | | | | | | | | | | | | | | 12 |
| 1 | 12 | 3 | 13 | 6 | 5 | 7 | $8^1$ | 14 | $10^2$ | 11 | | $4^3$ | 9 | 2 | | | | | | | | | | | | | | | | 13 |
| 1 | 12 | | 8 | 6 | 5 | 7 | | 13 | 10 | $11^2$ | | $4^1$ | 9 | 2 | 3 | | | | | | | | | | | | | | | 14 |
| 1 | 5 | 3 | 8 | 6 | | 7 | 4 | 12 | 10 | 11 | | | $9^1$ | 2 | | | | | | | | | | | | | | | | 15 |
| 1 | 12 | 3 | 8 | 6 | 5 | 7 | $4^1$ | 13 | 10 | 11 | | | $9^2$ | 2 | | | | | | | | | | | | | | | | 16 |
| 1 | | $3^1$ | 8 | 6 | 5 | 7 | 4 | 13 | 10 | $11^2$ | | | 9 | 2 | 12 | | | | | | | | | | | | | | | 17 |
| 1 | 4 | 3 | 8 | 6 | 5 | 7 | | | 10 | 11 | | | 9 | 2 | | | | | | | | | | | | | | | | 18 |
| 1 | 4 | 3 | 8 | 6 | 5 | | | 12 | $10^1$ | $11^3$ | $7^2$ | | 9 | 2 | 13 | | 14 | | | | | | | | | | | | | 19 |
| 1 | 2 | $7^1$ | 8 | 6 | | | | | 10 | | 12 | | 9 | 4 | 3 | 5 | | 11 | | | | | | | | | | | | 20 |
| 1 | 2 | $3^1$ | 8 | 6 | | | | | 10 | | 12 | | 9 | $4^2$ | 13 | 5 | 14 | $11^3$ | 7 | | | | | | | | | | | 21 |
| 1 | 2 | | 8 | 6 | | 11 | 4 | | 10 | | | | 9 | | 3 | | $7^1$ | 12 | 5 | | | | | | | | | | | 22 |
| 1 | 2 | 12 | 8 | 6 | | 11 | 4 | | 10 | $7^1$ | | | 9 | | 3 | | | | 5 | | | | | | | | | | | 23 |
| 1 | $2^3$ | 12 | 8 | 6 | | 11 | $4^1$ | | 10 | 7 | | | $9^2$ | | 3 | | 13 | | 5 | 14 | | | | | | | | | | 24 |
| 1 | 2 | 3 | 8 | $6^2$ | | 11 | 13 | | 10 | 12 | | 14 | $9^3$ | | $7^1$ | | | | 4 | | 5 | | | | | | | | | 25 |
| 1 | | $3^1$ | 8 | 6 | 5 | 11 | | | 10 | 7 | | | 9 | 2 | 12 | | | | 4 | | | | | | | | | | | 26 |
| 1 | $7^2$ | $3^3$ | $8^1$ | 6 | 5 | 11 | 12 | | 10 | | | 13 | 9 | 2 | 14 | | | | 4 | | | | | | | | | | | 27 |
| 1 | | 3 | $8^2$ | 6 | 5 | 11 | 12 | | 10 | | | 7 | $9^3$ | 2 | 13 | | | | $4^1$ | | | 14 | | | | | | | | 28 |
| 1 | | | 11 | 6 | 5 | 7 | 8 | | 10 | | | | 9 | 2 | 3 | | | | 4 | | | | | | | | | | | 29 |
| 1 | 2 | $11^1$ | 8 | 6 | 5 | 7 | | | 12 | 10 | | | 9 | | 3 | | | | 4 | | | | | | | | | | | 30 |
| 1 | $2^1$ | | 8 | 6 | 5 | 7 | | | 13 | $10^3$ | | | 14 | $9^2$ | 12 | 3 | | | 4 | | | 11 | | | | | | | | 31 |
| 1 | 2 | | | 6 | 5 | 11 | | | 9 | $10^1$ | 13 | | | 12 | | 3 | | | 4 | | | $7^2$ | 8 | | | | | | | 32 |
| 1 | $7^1$ | | | 6 | 5 | 11 | 2 | | $9^2$ | 13 | 12 | | | | 3 | | | | 4 | | | | 8 | 10 | | | | | | 33 |
| 1 | | 12 | | 6 | 5 | 13 | 8 | | 9 | $10^2$ | 14 | | | 2 | 3 | | | | $4^3$ | | | | | $7^1$ | 11 | | | | | 34 |
| 1 | | 12 | 4 | 6 | 5 | 7 | 8 | 9 | | $11^1$ | | $10^2$ | | 2 | 3 | | | | | | | 13 | | | | | | | | 35 |
| 1 | | $4^2$ | 6 | 5 | 7 | 8 | 9 | | 11 | | | $10^1$ | | 2 | 3 | | | | | | | | 12 | 13 | | | | | | 36 |
| 1 | | 4 | 6 | 5 | 7 | 8 | 9 | | 11 | | | 10 | | 2 | 3 | | | | | | | | | | | | | | | 37 |
| 1 | | 4 | 6 | 5 | 7 | 8 | 12 | | 10 | $11^1$ | | 13 | 9 | $2^2$ | 3 | | | | | | | | | | | | | | | 38 |
| 1 | | 4 | 6 | $5^1$ | 7 | 8 | 12 | | 10 | 11 | | | 9 | 2 | 3 | | | | | | | | | | | | | | | 39 |
| 1 | | 2 | 4 | 6 | | 7 | 8 | 5 | 10 | 11 | | | 9 | 12 | $3^1$ | | | | | | | | | | | | | | | 40 |
| 1 | 2 | | 4 | 6 | | 7 | 8 | | 10 | | | | 9 | | 3 | | | | 5 | | | | | | | | | 11 | | 41 |
| 1 | 2 | | 4 | 6 | | 7 | 8 | 12 | 10 | | | | $9^3$ | 13 | $3^2$ | | | | 5 | | | | | | 14 | $11^1$ | | | | 42 |
| 1 | 2 | 3 | 4 | 6 | | 7 | 8 | | 10 | | | | 9 | | 3 | | | | 5 | | | | | | | 11 | | | | 43 |
| 1 | 2 | 3 | | 6 | | 7 | 8 | 12 | $10^3$ | | 4 | | $9^1$ | | | | | $5^2$ | 13 | | | | | 14 | | 11 | | | | 44 |
| 1 | 2 | 3 | | 6 | | | 8 | | 12 | | 13 | 14 | | | 10 | | | | 5 | | | $7^3$ | | | 9 | | | $4^2$ | $11^1$ | 45 |
| 1 | 2 | 3 | | 6 | | 12 | 8 | | | 13 | | | | | 10 | | | | 5 | | | $7^1$ | | | $9^3$ | | | 4 | $11^2$ 14 | 46 |

**Coca-Cola Cup**

| | | | |
|---|---|---|---|
| First Round | Portsmouth | (h) | 2-2 |
| | | (a) | 2-1 |
| Second Round | Reading | (a) | 0-0 |
| | | (h) | 0-2 |

**FA Cup**

| | | | |
|---|---|---|---|
| First Round | Swansea C | (a) | 4-1 |
| Second Round | Dagenham & R | (h) | 3-2 |
| Third Round | Walsall | (h) | 0-2 |

PLYMOUTH ARGYLE 1997–98    *Back row (left to right):* Gary Clayton, Jon Ashton, Paul Wotton, Steve Perkins, Mick Heathcote, Tony James, Simon Collins, Jon Beswetherick, Kevin Summerfield (Youth Team).

*Middle row:* Norman Medhurst (Physio), Graham Anthony, Jason Rowbottom, Mark Patterson, Chris Billy, Jon Sheffield, James Dungey, Mark Saunders, Ronnie Mauge, Ryan Bushby, Chris Leadbitter, Kevin Blackwell (Assistant Manager).

*Front row:* Kevin Francis, Carlo Corrazin, Earl Jean, Neil Illman, Mick Jones (Manager), Dan McCauley (Chairman), Adrian Littlejohn, Paul Williams, Martin Barlow, Andrew Sargent.

# Division 3     **PLYMOUTH ARGYLE**

*Home Park, Plymouth, Devon PL2 3DQ.* Telephone: (01752) 562561. Fax: (01752) 606167. Pilgrim Shop: (01752) 558292.

*Ground capacity:* 19,630.

*Record attendance:* 43,596 v Aston Villa, Division 2, 10 October 1936.

*Record receipts:* £128,000 v Burnley, Division 2 play-off, 18 May 1994.

*Pitch measurements:* 110yd × 72yd.

*President:* S. J. Rendell.

*Chairman:* D. McCauley. *Vice-Chairman:* P. Bloom.

*Director:* Paul Stapleton.

*Manager:* Kevin Hodges. *Assistant Manager:* Kevin Blackwell. *Physio:* Norman Medhurst.

*Secretary/Chief Executive:* Roger Matthews.

*Year Formed:* 1886. *Turned Professional:* 1903. *Ltd Co.:* 1903.

*Club Nickname:* 'The Pilgrims'.

*Previous Name:* 1886–1903, Argyle Athletic Club.

*Foundation:* The club was formed in September 1886 as the Argyle Football Club by former public and private school pupils who wanted to continue playing the game. The meeting was held in a room above the Borough Arms (a Coffee House), Bedford Street, Plymouth. It was common then to choose a local street/terrace as a club name and Argyle or Argyll was a fashionable name throughout the land due to Queen Victoria's great interest in Scotland.

*First Football League game:* 28 August 1920, Division 3, v Norwich C (h) D 1-1 – Craig; Russell, Atterbury; Logan, Dickinson, Forbes; Kirkpatrick, Jack, Bowler, Heeps (1), Dixon.

*Record League Victory:* 8–1 v Millwall, Division 2, 16 January 1932 – Harper; Roberts, Titmuss; Mackay, Pullan, Reed; Grozier, Bowden (2), Vidler (3), Leslie (1), Black (1). (1 og). 8–1 v Hartlepool U (a), Division 2, 7 May 1994 – Nicholls; Patterson (Naylor), Hill, Burrows, Comyn, McCall (1), Barlow, Castle (1), Landon (3), Marshall (1), Dalton (2).

*Record Cup Victory:* 6–0 v Corby T, FA Cup 3rd rd, 22 January 1966 – Leiper; Book, Baird; Williams, Nelson, Newman; Jones (1), Jackson (1), Bickle (3), Piper (1), Jennings.

*Record Defeat:* 0–9 v Stoke C, Division 2, 17 December 1960.

*Most League Points (2 for a win):* 68, Division 3 (S), 1929–30.

*Most League Points (3 for a win):* 87, Division 3, 1985–86.

*Most League Goals:* 107, Division 3 (S), 1925–26 and 1951–52.

*Highest League Scorer in Season:* Jack Cock, 32, Division 3 (S), 1925–26.

*Most League Goals in Total Aggregate:* Sammy Black, 180, 1924–38.

*Most Capped Player:* Moses Russell, 20 (23), Wales.

*Most League Appearances:* Kevin Hodges, 530, 1978–92.

*Record Transfer Fee Received:* £750,000 from Southampton for Mickey Evans, March 1997.

*Record Transfer Fee Paid:* £250,000 to Hartlepool U for Paul Dalton, June 1992.

*Football League Record:* 1920 Original Member of Division 3; 1921–30 Division 3 (S); 1930–50 Division 2; 1950–52 Division 3 (S); 1952–56 Division 2; 1956–58 Division 3 (S); 1958–59 Division 2; 1959–68 Division 2; 1968–75 Division 3; 1975–77 Division 2; 1977–86 Division 3; 1986–95 Division 2; 1995–96 Division 3; 1996–98 Division 2; 1998– Division 3.

*Honours: Football League:* Division 2 best season: 4th, 1931–32, 1952–53; Division 3 (S) – Champions 1929–30, 1951–52; Runners-up 1921–22, 1922–23, 1923–24, 1924–25, 1925–26, 1926–27 (record of six consecutive years); Division 3 – Champions 1958–59; Runners-up 1974–75, 1985–86, Promoted 1995–96 (play-offs). *FA Cup:* best season: Semi-final 1984. *Football League Cup:* Semi-final 1965, 1974.

*Colours:* Green and black shirts, black shorts, green, black and white stockings. *Change colours:* All white.

**Did you know?**
Frank Richardson scored a hat-trick on his League debut against Bristol Rovers on 27 August 1921, achieved two more trebles that season and four goals in an FA Cup tie the following season.

## PLYMOUTH ARGYLE 1997–98 LEAGUE RECORD

| Match No. | Date | | Venue | Opponents | Result | | H/T Score | Lg. Pos. | Goalscorers | Attendance |
|---|---|---|---|---|---|---|---|---|---|---|
| 1 | Aug | 9 | A | Bristol R | D | 1-1 | 0-1 | — | Heathcote 58 | 7386 |
| 2 | | 16 | H | Grimsby T | D | 2-2 | 2-0 | 14 | Logan 28, Littlejohn 42 | 6002 |
| 3 | | 23 | A | Wigan Ath | D | 1-1 | 0-1 | 17 | Logan 84 | 3761 |
| 4 | | 30 | H | Chesterfield | D | 1-1 | 1-0 | 16 | Jean 31 | 5284 |
| 5 | Sept | 2 | H | Watford | L | 0-1 | 0-0 | — | | 5141 |
| 6 | | 9 | A | Fulham | L | 0-2 | 0-0 | — | | 8961 |
| 7 | | 13 | H | Brentford | D | 0-0 | 0-0 | 23 | | 4394 |
| 8 | | 20 | A | Carlisle U | D | 2-2 | 1-2 | 22 | Littlejohn 6, Wilson 74 | 5667 |
| 9 | | 27 | H | Walsall | W | 2-1 | 1-1 | 21 | Barlow 2 34, 70 | 6207 |
| 10 | Oct | 4 | A | York C | L | 0-1 | 0-1 | 22 | | 2894 |
| 11 | | 11 | A | Luton T | L | 0-3 | 0-1 | 22 | | 4931 |
| 12 | | 18 | A | Southend U | L | 2-3 | 2-2 | 23 | Littlejohn 30, Corazzin 31 | 3430 |
| 13 | | 21 | H | Burnley | D | 2-2 | 1-1 | — | Jean 40, Heathcote 47 | 3006 |
| 14 | | 25 | A | Gillingham | L | 1-2 | 1-1 | 23 | Jean 4 | 6679 |
| 15 | Nov | 1 | A | Preston NE | W | 1-0 | 0-0 | 23 | Corazzin 65 | 8405 |
| 16 | | 4 | H | Wycombe W | W | 4-2 | 2-1 | — | Corazzin 2 (1 pen) 17 (p), 18, Littlejohn 54, Mauge 57 | 2993 |
| 17 | | 8 | H | Bournemouth | W | 3-0 | 2-0 | 18 | Jean 10, Littlejohn 2 15, 85 | 5067 |
| 18 | | 18 | A | Bristol C | L | 1-2 | 0-2 | — | Corazzin 83 | 10,867 |
| 19 | | 22 | H | Wrexham | D | 1-1 | 0-0 | 17 | Billy 58 | 3641 |
| 20 | | 29 | H | Oldham Ath | L | 0-2 | 0-1 | 18 | | 5452 |
| 21 | Dec | 2 | A | Blackpool | D | 0-0 | 0-0 | — | | 3281 |
| 22 | | 13 | H | Millwall | W | 3-0 | 2-0 | 20 | Collins 23, Billy 43, Corazzin (pen) 78 | 4460 |
| 23 | | 20 | A | Northampton T | L | 1-2 | 1-0 | 20 | Corazzin 45 | 5546 |
| 24 | | 26 | H | Fulham | L | 1-4 | 1-1 | 20 | Barlow 5 | 9469 |
| 25 | | 28 | A | Watford | D | 1-1 | 0-0 | 21 | Saunders 86 | 11,594 |
| 26 | Jan | 10 | H | Bristol R | L | 1-2 | 0-2 | 23 | Corazzin 50 | 6850 |
| 27 | | 17 | A | Chesterfield | L | 1-2 | 1-1 | 23 | Corazzin (pen) 33 | 3879 |
| 28 | | 24 | H | Wigan Ath | W | 3-2 | 0-2 | 21 | Saunders 52, Barlow 77, Collins 86 | 4345 |
| 29 | | 31 | A | Brentford | L | 1-3 | 1-0 | 23 | Corazzin 27 | 4783 |
| 30 | Feb | 7 | H | Carlisle U | W | 2-1 | 1-0 | 21 | Heathcote 45, Corazzin 68 | 4540 |
| 31 | | 14 | H | York C | D | 0-0 | 0-0 | 21 | | 4382 |
| 32 | | 21 | A | Walsall | W | 1-0 | 1-0 | 19 | Heathcote 15 | 4612 |
| 33 | | 24 | A | Southend U | L | 0-3 | 0-1 | — | | 4363 |
| 34 | | 28 | H | Luton T | L | 0-2 | 0-0 | 21 | | 4846 |
| 35 | Mar | 3 | A | Bournemouth | D | 3-3 | 2-1 | — | Saunders 31, Logan 40, Corazzin 89 | 3545 |
| 36 | | 7 | H | Preston NE | W | 2-0 | 1-0 | 20 | Wotton 36, Conlon 65 | 4201 |
| 37 | | 14 | A | Wycombe W | L | 1-5 | 1-1 | 22 | Corazzin 44 | 5508 |
| 38 | | 21 | H | Bristol C | W | 2-0 | 0-0 | 19 | Saunders 50, Conlon 77 | 7622 |
| 39 | | 24 | A | Grimsby T | L | 0-1 | 0-0 | — | | 4661 |
| 40 | | 28 | A | Wrexham | W | 2-0 | 1-0 | 19 | Corazzin 31, Saunders 79 | 4749 |
| 41 | Apr | 4 | A | Oldham Ath | L | 0-2 | 0-1 | 21 | | 4244 |
| 42 | | 11 | H | Blackpool | W | 3-1 | 0-1 | 20 | Butler (og) 57, Logan 78, Corazzin (pen) 90 | 5655 |
| 43 | | 13 | A | Millwall | D | 1-1 | 1-1 | 20 | Corazzin 25 | 5496 |
| 44 | | 18 | H | Northampton T | L | 1-3 | 0-1 | 20 | Saunders 45 | 6389 |
| 45 | | 25 | H | Gillingham | L | 0-1 | 0-0 | 21 | | 7941 |
| 46 | May | 2 | A | Burnley | L | 1-2 | 1-2 | 22 | Saunders 25 | 18,811 |

**Final League Position: 22**     1996–97 DIV2 19

### GOALSCORERS
League (55): Corazzin 16 (4 pens), Saunders 7, Littlejohn 6, Barlow 4, Heathcote 4, Jean 4, Logan 4, Billy 2, Collins 2, Conlon 2, Mauge 1, Wilson 1, Wotton 1, own goal 1.
Coca-Cola Cup (3): Logan 1, Wilson 1, own goal 1.
FA Cup (2): Jean 1, Mauge 1.

| Sheffield J 46 | Collins S 30 + 2 | Williams P 39 | Rowbotham J 23 + 2 | Heathcote M 36 | Wotton P 31 + 3 | Billy C 41 | Logan R 23 + 4 | Littlejohn A 27 + 4 | Corazzin C 38 | Anthony G 5 | Jean E 16 + 20 | Mauge R 23 + 8 | Clayton G — + 1 | Wilson P 7 + 4 | Illman N 1 + 5 | Barlow M 41 + 1 | Saunders M 34 + 3 | Beswetherick J — + 2 | Hodges L 9 | O'Hagan D 5 + 4 | Phillips L 3 + 7 | Conlon B 13 | Starbuck P 6 + 1 | Woods S 4 + 1 | Currie D 5 + 2 | Match No. |
|---|---|---|---|---|---|---|---|---|---|---|---|---|---|---|---|---|---|---|---|---|---|---|---|---|---|---|
| 1 | 2 | 3 | 4 | 5 | 6 | $7^1$ | 8 | 9 | 10 | 11 | 12 | | | | | | | | | | | | | | | 1 |
| 1 | 3 | 7 | 5 | 6 | 2 | $8^1$ | 9 | 10 | 11 | 12 | | $4^2$ | 13 | | | | | | | | | | | | | 2 |
| 1 | 3 | 7 | 5 | 6 | 2 | 8 | 9 | $11^1$ | 10 | | | 4 | | | | | | | | | | | | | | 3 |
| 1 | 3 | | 5 | 6 | 2 | 8 | 9 | 7 | $10^1$ | | | 4 | | 11 | 12 | | | | | | | | | | | 4 |
| 1 | 3 | | 5 | 6 | 2 | 8 | 9 | $7^1$ | $10^2$ | | | 4 | | 11 | 13 | 12 | | | | | | | | | | 5 |
| 1 | 12 | 3 | 5 | 6 | 2 | 8 | 9 | | $10^2$ | | | 4 | | 13 | $11^1$ | 7 | | | | | | | | | | 6 |
| 1 | 3 | | 5 | 6 | 2 | 8 | 9 | | $10^1$ | | | 4 | | 11 | 12 | 7 | | | | | | | | | | 7 |
| 1 | 3 | | 5 | 6 | 2 | 8 | 9 | $10^1$ | | | | 4 | | 11 | | 7 | 12 | | | | | | | | | 8 |
| 1 | 3 | | 5 | 6 | 2 | | 9 | 10 | | | | 4 | | 11 | | 7 | 8 | | | | | | | | | 9 |
| 1 | 3 | | 5 | 6 | 2 | | 9 | $10^1$ | | | 12 | 4 | | 11 | | 7 | 8 | | | | | | | | | 10 |
| 1 | 2 | 3 | | 5 | 6 | 10 | | 9 | | | | 12 | 4 | $11^1$ | | 7 | 8 | | | | | | | | | 11 |
| 1 | 2 | 3 | | 5 | $6^1$ | 11 | | 9 | 10 | | | 12 | 4 | | | 7 | 8 | | | | | | | | | 12 |
| 1 | 2 | 3 | | 5 | 6 | 11 | | 9 | 10 | | | 8 | 4 | | | 7 | | | | | | | | | | 13 |
| 1 | 2 | 3 | | $5^2$ | 6 | $11^3$ | | 9 | 10 | | | $8^1$ | 4 | 13 | 12 | 7 | | 14 | | | | | | | | 14 |
| 1 | 2 | 3 | | | 6 | 11 | | 9 | 10 | | | 8 | 4 | | | 7 | 5 | | | | | | | | | 15 |
| 1 | 2 | 3 | | | 6 | 11 | | 9 | 10 | | | 8 | $4^1$ | | 12 | 7 | 5 | | | | | | | | | 16 |
| 1 | 2 | 3 | | | 6 | 11 | | 9 | | | | 8 | | | | 7 | 5 | | 4 | 10 | | | | | | 17 |
| 1 | | 3 | | | $6^1$ | 11 | 2 | 9 | 10 | | | $8^2$ | 5 | 13 | | 7 | 12 | | 4 | | | | | | | 18 |
| 1 | | 3 | | | 6 | 11 | 2 | 9 | 10 | | | $8^1$ | | | | 7 | 5 | | 4 | 12 | | | | | | 19 |
| 1 | | 3 | | | $6^2$ | 11 | 2 | 9 | 10 | | | 8 | $4^1$ | | | 7 | 12 | | 5 | 13 | | | | | | 20 |
| 1 | 6 | 3 | 2 | | | 11 | 8 | $9^1$ | 10 | | | | | | | 7 | 5 | | 4 | 12 | | | | | | 21 |
| 1 | 6 | 3 | 2 | | 12 | 11 | 8 | | $10^1$ | | 13 | | | | | 7 | 5 | 14 | $4^2$ | $9^1$ | | | | | | 22 |
| 1 | 6 | 3 | 2 | | | 11 | $8^1$ | | 10 | | 12 | | | | | 7 | 5 | | 4 | 9 | | | | | | 23 |
| 1 | 6 | 3 | 2 | | | $11^1$ | 8 | 12 | 10 | | 13 | 14 | | | | 7 | $5^3$ | | 4 | $9^2$ | | | | | | 24 |
| 1 | 2 | 3 | | 5 | | 11 | | | 9 | 10 | 12 | 4 | | | | 7 | 6 | | | $8^1$ | | | | | | 25 |
| 1 | 2 | $3^1$ | 11 | 5 | | | | | 9 | 10 | $8^2$ | 4 | | | | 7 | 6 | | | | 12 | 13 | | | | 26 |
| 1 | 2 | 3 | 11 | 5 | $8^1$ | | 12 | | 10 | 13 | | 4 | | | | 7 | 6 | | | $9^2$ | | | | | | 27 |
| 1 | 2 | 3 | $6^1$ | 5 | | 11 | 12 | $9^1$ | 10 | 13 | | 4 | | | | 7 | 8 | | | | | | | | | 28 |
| 1 | 2 | 3 | $6^1$ | 5 | | 11 | 12 | 9 | 10 | 13 | | $4^2$ | | | | 7 | $8^3$ | | | | 14 | | | | | 29 |
| 1 | 2 | 3 | 6 | 5 | | 11 | 12 | $10^1$ | | | $9^2$ | 4 | | | | 7 | 8 | | | | 13 | | | | | 30 |
| 1 | 2 | 3 | 6 | 5 | | 11 | $4^1$ | | 10 | | | 12 | | | | 7 | 8 | | | | 9 | | | | | 31 |
| 1 | 2 | 3 | 6 | 5 | | 11 | | | 9 | 10 | 12 | | | | | 7 | 4 | | | | $8^1$ | | | | | 32 |
| 1 | 2 | 3 | $6^1$ | 5 | 13 | 11 | 12 | | 10 | | 9 | | | | | 7 | 4 | | | | $8^2$ | | | | | 33 |
| 1 | 2 | 3 | $6^1$ | 5 | 12 | 11 | | | 9 | 10 | | | | | | 7 | 4 | | | | | 8 | | | | 34 |
| 1 | 2 | $3^1$ | 12 | 5 | 6 | 11 | | 8 | 13 | 10 | | | | | | 7 | 4 | | | | | $9^2$ | | | | 35 |
| 1 | 2 | | 3 | 5 | 6 | 11 | 8 | | 10 | | | | | | | 7 | 4 | | | | | 9 | | | | 36 |
| 1 | 2 | | 3 | 5 | 6 | 11 | 8 | 12 | 10 | | 13 | | | | | $7^1$ | 4 | | | | | $9^2$ | | | | 37 |
| 1 | 2 | $3^1$ | 12 | 5 | 6 | 11 | | | $10^2$ | | | | | | | 7 | 4 | | | | 13 | 9 | 8 | | | 38 |
| 1 | 2 | 3 | | 5 | 6 | $11^1$ | | | $10^2$ | 12 | | | | | | 7 | 4 | | | | 13 | 9 | 8 | | | 39 |
| 1 | | 3 | | 5 | 6 | 11 | | | $10^1$ | | | | | | | 7 | 4 | | | | 12 | 9 | $8^2$ | 2 | 13 | 40 |
| 1 | 11 | 3 | | 5 | $6^3$ | | | | 10 | | 12 | | | | | 7 | 4 | | | | 13 | $9^2$ | $8^1$ | 2 | 14 | 41 |
| 1 | 2 | | 3 | 5 | | | 6 | | 10 | | 12 | 13 | | | | 7 | 4 | | | | | $9^1$ | $8^2$ | | 11 | 42 |
| 1 | | | 3 | 5 | 2 | $11^2$ | 6 | | 10 | | 12 | 13 | | | | 7 | 4 | | | | | $9^1$ | 14 | | $8^3$ | 43 |
| 1 | | | 3 | 5 | $2^2$ | 11 | 6 | | 10 | | 12 | 13 | | | | 7 | $4^3$ | | | | | $9^1$ | 14 | | | 44 |
| 1 | 2 | $3^2$ | | 5 | | 11 | | | 10 | | 12 | 13 | | | | 7 | 4 | | | | | $9^1$ | | 6 | 8 | 45 |
| 1 | 12 | $3^3$ | | 5 | 2 | | | | 10 | | 13 | 14 | | | | $7^2$ | 4 | | | | | 9 | $8^1$ | 6 | 11 | 46 |

**Coca-Cola Cup**  
First Round    Oxford U    (a) 0-2  
                                 (h) 3-5

**FA Cup**  
First Round    Cambridge U    (h) 0-0  
                                         (a) 2-3

PORTSMOUTH 1997–98    *Back row (left to right):* Deon Burton, Jimmy Carter, Ashkan Karimzadeh, Mark Thompson, Hamilton Thorp, Keith Waldon (Assistant Manager), Andy Thomson, Martin Hinshelwood (Youth Team Manager), Mathias Svensson, Martin Allen, Nathan Jukes, Alan McLoughlin, Fitzroy Simpson.

*Middle row:* Gordon Neave (Kit Manager), Neil Sillett (Physio) Danny Hinshelwood, Gavin Rees, Jon Hawley, Aaron Flahavan, Alan Knight, Russell Perrett, John Durnin, Adam Williams, Ian McDonald (Reserve Team Manager), Shaun North (Youth Team Coach).

*Front row:* Sam Igoe, Andy Cook, Paul Hall, Robbie Pethick, David Waterman, Adrian Whitbread, Terry Fenwick (Manager), David Hillier, Scott Bundy, Lee Russell, Robert Simpson, Andy Awford, Andy Turner.

# Division 1 **PORTSMOUTH**

*Fratton Park, Frogmore Rd, Portsmouth PO4 8RA.* Telephone: (01705) 731204. Fax: (01705) 734129. Commercial Dept: (01705) 731204. Ticket Office: (01705) 618777. Membership Office: (01705) 825016. Clubcall: 0891 121182.

*Ground capacity:* 19,179.

*Record attendance:* 51,385 v Derby Co, FA Cup 6th rd, 26 February 1949.

*Record receipts:* £233,000 v Chelsea, FA Cup 6th rd, 9 March 1997.

*Pitch measurements:* 110yd × 72yd.

*Chairman:* Martin Gregory.

*Directors:* F. Dinenage, G. P. Hinkinson FIMI. M. INST. PET., B. A. V. Henson FCA.

*Manager:* Alan Ball. *First Team Coach:* Kevin Bond.

*Secretary:* Paul Weld. *Marketing Manager:* Julie Baker.

*Reserve Team Coach:* Neil McNab. *Youth Team Coach:* Martin Allen.

*Physio:* Jonathon Trigg.

*Year Formed:* 1898. *Turned Professional:* 1898. *Ltd Co.:* 1898.

*Club Nickname:* 'Pompey'.

*Foundation:* At a meeting held in his High Street, Portsmouth offices in 1898, solicitor Alderman J. E. Pink and five other business and professional men agreed to buy some ground close to Goldsmith Avenue for £4,950 which they developed into Fratton Park in record breaking time. A team of professionals was signed up by manager Frank Brettell and entry to the Southern League obtained for the new club's September 1899 kick-off.

*First Football League game:* 28 August 1920, Division 3, v Swansea T (h) W 3-0 – Robson; Probert, Potts; Abbott, Harwood, Turner; Thompson, Stringfellow (1), Reid (1), James (1), Beedie.

*Record League Victory:* 9–1 v Notts Co, Division 2, 9 April 1927 – McPhail; Clifford, Ted Smith; Reg Davies (1), Foxall, Moffat; Forward (1), Mackie (2), Haines (3), Watson, Cook (2).

*Record Cup Victory:* 7–0 v Stockport Co, FA Cup 3rd rd, 8 January 1949 – Butler; Rookes, Ferrier; Scoular, Flewin, Dickinson; Harris (3), Barlow, Clarke (2), Phillips (2), Froggatt.

*Record Defeat:* 0–10 v Leicester C, Division 1, 20 October 1928.

*Most League Points (2 for a win):* 65, Division 3, 1961–62.

*Most League Points (3 for a win):* 91, Division 3, 1982–83.

*Most League Goals:* 91, Division 4, 1979–80.

*Highest League Scorer in Season:* Guy Whittingham, 42, Division 1, 1992–93.

*Most League Goals in Total Aggregate:* Peter Harris, 194, 1946–60.

*Most Capped Player:* Jimmy Dickinson, 48, England.

*Most League Appearances:* Jimmy Dickinson, 764, 1946–65.

*Record Transfer Fee Received:* £3,500,000 from Manchester C for Lee Bradbury, August 1997.

*Record Transfer Fee Paid:* £650,000 to Celtic for Gerry Creaney, January 1994.

*Football League Record:* 1920 Original Member of Division 3; 1921 Division 3 (S); 1924–27 Division 2; 1927–59 Division 1; 1959–61 Division 2; 1961–62 Division 3; 1962–76 Division 2; 1976–78 Division 3; 1978–80 Division 4; 1980–83 Division 3; 1983–87 Division 2; 1987–88 Division 1; 1988–92 Division 2; 1992– Division 1.

*Honours: Football League:* Division 1 – Champions 1948–49, 1949–50; Division 2 – Runners-up 1926–27, 1986–87; Division 3 (S) – Champions 1923–24; Division 3 – Champions 1961–62, 1982–83. *FA Cup:* Winners 1939; Runners-up 1929, 1934. *Football League Cup:* best season: 5th rd, 1961, 1986.

*Colours:* Blue shirts, white shorts, red stockings. *Change colours:* White shirts, navy shorts, white stockings.

**Did you know?**
On 4 April 1998 Portsmouth celebrated their 100th birthday with an injury time equaliser against Birmingham City.

## PORTSMOUTH 1997–98 LEAGUE RECORD

| Match No. | Date | | Venue | Opponents | Result | | H/T Score | Lg. Pos. | Goalscorers | Attendance |
|---|---|---|---|---|---|---|---|---|---|---|
| 1 | Aug | 9 | A | Manchester C | D | 2-2 | 1-1 | — | Aloisi [5], Hall [80] | 30,474 |
| 2 | | 16 | H | Port Vale | W | 3-1 | 2-1 | 4 | Aloisi [24], Svensson 2 [38, 47] | 10,605 |
| 3 | | 23 | A | Sheffield U | L | 1-2 | 0-2 | 7 | Perrett [57] | 15,895 |
| 4 | | 30 | H | Oxford U | W | 2-1 | 1-1 | 6 | Aloisi [4], Svensson [66] | 10,209 |
| 5 | Sept | 2 | H | Norwich C | D | 1-1 | 0-0 | — | Turner [65] | 10,577 |
| 6 | | 13 | H | Crewe Alex | L | 2-3 | 0-1 | 11 | Aloisi 2 [70, 73] | 9505 |
| 7 | | 20 | A | Nottingham F | L | 0-1 | 0-1 | 16 | | 17,292 |
| 8 | | 24 | A | QPR | L | 0-1 | 0-1 | — | | 12,620 |
| 9 | | 27 | H | Reading | L | 0-2 | 0-1 | 19 | | 9593 |
| 10 | Oct | 4 | A | Stockport Co | L | 1-3 | 0-2 | 23 | Aloisi [73] | 7824 |
| 11 | | 18 | H | WBA | L | 2-3 | 0-1 | 23 | McLoughlin [78], Foster [85] | 9158 |
| 12 | | 21 | H | Bradford C | D | 1-1 | 1-1 | — | McLoughlin (pen) [17] | 6827 |
| 13 | | 25 | H | Huddersfield T | D | 1-1 | 1-0 | 23 | Igoe [37] | 8985 |
| 14 | | 31 | H | Swindon T | L | 0-1 | 0-1 | — | | 8707 |
| 15 | Nov | 5 | A | Middlesbrough | D | 1-1 | 0-0 | — | Igoe [85] | 29,724 |
| 16 | | 8 | A | Bury | W | 2-0 | 0-0 | 23 | Aloisi [53], Durnin [90] | 5065 |
| 17 | | 15 | H | Sunderland | L | 1-4 | 1-3 | 23 | Aloisi [7] | 10,702 |
| 18 | | 29 | A | Birmingham C | L | 1-2 | 1-1 | 24 | Hall [35] | 17,738 |
| 19 | Dec | 6 | H | Stoke C | W | 2-0 | 2-0 | 24 | Aloisi [31], Svensson [43] | 7072 |
| 20 | | 9 | H | Wolverhampton W | W | 3-2 | 1-0 | — | Durnin 2 [14, 47], Hillier [74] | 8042 |
| 21 | | 13 | A | Ipswich T | L | 0-2 | 0-1 | 23 | | 11,641 |
| 22 | | 20 | A | Charlton Ath | L | 0-2 | 0-1 | 24 | | 8581 |
| 23 | | 26 | H | QPR | W | 3-1 | 1-1 | 21 | Pethick [35], McLoughlin (pen) [62], Hall [80] | 12,314 |
| 24 | | 30 | A | Norwich C | L | 0-2 | 0-1 | — | | 16,441 |
| 25 | Jan | 10 | A | Manchester C | L | 0-3 | 0-1 | 24 | | 13,512 |
| 26 | | 17 | A | Port Vale | L | 1-2 | 1-1 | 24 | Durnin [36] | 6028 |
| 27 | | 24 | A | Oxford U | L | 0-1 | 0-0 | 24 | | 7402 |
| 28 | | 31 | H | Sheffield U | D | 1-1 | 1-1 | 24 | Foster [18] | 12,003 |
| 29 | Feb | 7 | H | Nottingham F | L | 0-1 | 0-0 | 24 | | 15,033 |
| 30 | | 14 | A | Crewe Alex | L | 1-3 | 0-0 | 24 | Aloisi [81] | 5114 |
| 31 | | 17 | H | Stockport Co | W | 1-0 | 1-0 | — | Claridge [15] | 8622 |
| 32 | | 21 | A | Reading | W | 1-0 | 0-0 | 24 | Whitbread [83] | 9928 |
| 33 | | 24 | A | WBA | W | 3-0 | 2-0 | — | Hillier [12], Claridge [33], McLoughlin [86] | 12,757 |
| 34 | | 28 | H | Tranmere R | W | 1-0 | 1-0 | 21 | Aloisi [37] | 12,250 |
| 35 | Mar | 3 | H | Bury | D | 1-1 | 0-1 | — | Aloisi [68] | 12,462 |
| 36 | | 7 | A | Swindon T | W | 1-0 | 0-0 | 18 | Durnin [89] | 9100 |
| 37 | | 14 | H | Middlesbrough | D | 0-0 | 0-0 | 20 | | 17,003 |
| 38 | | 21 | A | Sunderland | L | 1-2 | 0-1 | 21 | Hall [73] | 38,134 |
| 39 | | 29 | A | Wolverhampton W | L | 0-2 | 0-1 | 21 | | 20,718 |
| 40 | Apr | 4 | H | Birmingham C | D | 1-1 | 0-0 | 22 | Thomson [89] | 14,591 |
| 41 | | 7 | A | Tranmere R | D | 2-2 | 1-1 | — | Durnin [21], Hall [81] | 8020 |
| 42 | | 11 | A | Stoke C | L | 1-2 | 0-0 | 22 | Durnin [69] | 15,569 |
| 43 | | 13 | H | Ipswich T | L | 0-1 | 0-1 | 22 | | 15,040 |
| 44 | | 18 | A | Charlton Ath | L | 0-1 | 0-0 | 23 | | 14,082 |
| 45 | | 25 | H | Huddersfield T | W | 3-0 | 1-0 | 21 | Pethick [27], Thomson [60], Durnin [70] | 14,013 |
| 46 | May | 3 | A | Bradford C | W | 3-1 | 1-0 | 20 | Durnin 2 [36, 74], Igoe [65] | 15,890 |

**Final League Position: 20**     1996–97 DIV1 7

### GOALSCORERS

*League (51):* Aloisi 12, Durnin 10, Hall 5, McLoughlin 4 (2 pens), Svensson 4, Igoe 3, Claridge 2, Foster 2, Hillier 2, Pethick 2, Thomson 2, Perrett 1, Turner 1, Whitbread 1.
*Coca-Cola Cup (3):* Hillier 1, Svensson 1, Thorp 1.
*FA Cup (2):* Foster 2.

| Knight A 20 | Waterman D 11+4 | Thomson A 34+1 | McLoughlin A 34+3 | Whitbread A 38 | Hillier D 30 | Hall P 22+7 | Simpson F 17+2 | Aloisi J 33+5 | Svensson M 17+9 | Igoe S 21+10 | Awford A 36+3 | Pethick R 43+1 | Thorp H —+7 | Flahavan A 26 | Perrett R 15+1 | Russell L 8 | Turner A 12+4 | Allen M 4+10 | Durnin J 23+11 | Foster C 13+3 | Cook A 1 | Carter J 6+4 | Harries P —+1 | Enes R 1+4 | Claridge S 10 | Vlachos M 15 | Robinson M 15 | Cook A 1 | Simpson R —+2 | Match No. |
|---|---|---|---|---|---|---|---|---|---|---|---|---|---|---|---|---|---|---|---|---|---|---|---|---|---|---|---|---|---|---|
|  | 2 | 3 | 4 | 5 | 6 | 7 | 8¹ | 9² | 10³ | 11 | 12 | 13 | 14 |  |  |  |  |  |  |  |  |  |  |  |  |  |  |  |  | 1 |
|  | 2 | 3 |  | 5 | 6 | 7 | 8 | 9 | 10¹ | 11 |  | 4 | 12 | 1 |  |  |  |  |  |  |  |  |  |  |  |  |  |  |  | 2 |
|  |  | 3 |  | 5 | 6 | 7 |  | 9 | 10¹ | 11² |  | 4 | 12 | 1 | 2 | 8 | 13 |  |  |  |  |  |  |  |  |  |  |  |  | 3 |
|  |  |  | 4 | 5 |  |  |  | 9² | 10¹ | 11 |  | 2 | 12 | 1 | 6 | 3 | 8 | 7 | 13 |  |  |  |  |  |  |  |  |  |  | 4 |
|  |  |  | 4 | 5 |  |  |  | 9¹ | 10² | 11 |  | 2 | 12 | 1 | 6 | 3 | 8 | 7 | 13 |  |  |  |  |  |  |  |  |  |  | 5 |
|  | 12 |  | 4¹ | 5 |  | 7 |  | 9 | 10³ | 11² |  | 2 |  | 1 | 6 | 3 | 8 | 13 | 14 |  |  |  |  |  |  |  |  |  |  | 6 |
|  | 12 |  | 5¹ | 4² |  | 7 |  | 9 |  | 11 |  | 2 |  | 1 | 6 | 3 | 8 |  | 10 | 13 |  |  |  |  |  |  |  |  |  | 7 |
|  | 8 |  |  | 4 |  | 7 | 12 | 9 |  | 11 | 5² | 2 |  | 1 | 6 | 3 |  | 13 | 10¹ |  |  |  |  |  |  |  |  |  |  | 8 |
|  | 5 |  | 12 |  |  | 4² | 7 | 8 | 9 | 11 | 13 | 2³ |  | 1 | 6 | 3 |  | 14 | 10¹ |  |  |  |  |  |  |  |  |  |  | 9 |
|  |  | 7 | 4 |  | 8 |  |  | 9 |  |  | 5¹ | 2 |  | 1 | 6 | 11² |  |  | 10 | 3 |  | 12 | 13 |  |  |  |  |  |  | 10 |
|  |  | 3 | 12 | 5 |  | 7 | 8² | 9 |  | 11 | 6 | 2 | 13 | 1 |  |  |  |  | 10 |  |  |  |  |  | 4¹ |  |  |  |  | 11 |
| 1 |  | 3 | 4 | 5 |  | 7 | 8 | 9¹ |  | 11² | 13 | 2 | 12 |  | 6 |  |  |  | 10 |  |  |  |  |  |  |  |  |  |  | 12 |
| 1 |  | 3 |  | 5 |  | 7 | 8 | 9 |  | 11 | 4 | 2 |  |  | 6 |  |  |  | 10 |  |  |  |  |  |  |  |  |  |  | 13 |
| 1 |  | 3 | 12 | 5 |  | 7 | 8 | 9 |  | 11² | 4 | 2 |  |  | 6 |  | 13 |  | 10¹ |  |  |  |  |  |  |  |  |  |  | 14 |
| 1 |  |  | 4 | 5 | 8 |  |  | 9² |  | 12 |  | 3 | 2 | 6³ | 11 | 7 |  |  | 10¹ | 13 | 14 |  |  |  |  |  |  |  |  | 15 |
| 1 |  | 3 | 4¹ | 5 | 8 |  |  | 9 |  |  | 10 | 2 |  |  | 6 | 11 | 7 |  | 12 |  |  |  |  |  |  |  |  |  |  | 16 |
| 1 |  | 3 |  | 5 | 8 |  |  | 9 |  |  | 4² | 2 |  |  | 6¹ | 11 | 7 |  | 10 | 12 | 13 |  |  |  |  |  |  |  |  | 17 |
| 1 |  | 3 | 4 | 5 | 9² |  | 7 | 8¹ |  | 12 | 13 | 2 |  |  | 6 | 14 | 11³ | 10 |  |  |  |  |  |  |  |  |  |  |  | 18 |
| 1 |  | 3 | 4 | 5 | 11 | 7 |  | 9² | 10 | 12 | 6 | 2 | 13 |  |  | 8¹ |  |  |  |  |  |  |  |  |  |  |  |  |  | 19 |
| 1 | 12 | 3 | 4 | 5 | 11 | 7¹ |  | 9 | 10 | 13 | 6 | 2 | 8² |  |  |  |  |  |  |  |  |  |  |  |  |  |  |  |  | 20 |
| 1 | 12 | 3 | 4 | 5 | 11² | 7 | 8¹ | 9 | 10 | 13 | 6³ | 2 | 14 |  |  |  |  |  |  |  |  |  |  |  |  |  |  |  |  | 21 |
| 1 |  | 3 | 4 | 5 | 11¹ | 7 | 8² | 9 | 10 | 12 | 6 | 2 | 13 |  |  |  |  |  |  |  |  |  |  |  |  |  |  |  |  | 22 |
| 1 | 5 | 3 | 4 |  |  | 7¹ |  | 9² | 10 | 12 | 6 | 2 | 11 | 13 | 8 |  |  |  |  |  |  |  |  |  |  |  |  |  |  | 23 |
| 1 | 5³ | 3 | 4 |  |  | 7 |  | 9² | 10 | 12 | 6 | 2 | 11¹ | 13 | 8 | 14 |  |  |  |  |  |  |  |  |  |  |  |  |  | 24 |
| 1 | 5 | 3 | 4 |  |  | 7 |  | 9¹ | 10 | 11 | 6 | 2 | 13 | 8 | 12² |  |  |  |  |  |  |  |  |  |  |  |  |  |  | 25 |
| 1 | 2² | 3 | 4 | 5 |  | 7 | 8 | 12 | 6 | 11 | 9 | 10¹ | 13 |  |  |  |  |  |  |  |  |  |  |  |  |  |  |  |  | 26 |
| 1 | 2¹ | 3 | 4 | 5 |  | 7 | 8 | 12 | 6 | 9 | 11 | 10 |  |  |  |  |  |  |  |  |  |  |  |  |  |  |  |  |  | 27 |
| 1 |  | 4 | 5 |  | 12 | 7¹ | 6 | 2 | 9 |  |  | 8 | 11 |  |  | 10 | 3 |  |  |  |  |  |  |  |  |  |  |  |  | 28 |
| 1 |  | 4 | 5 | 7¹ | 13 | 12 | 6 | 2 | 9² |  |  | 8 | 11 |  |  | 10 | 3 |  |  |  |  |  |  |  |  |  |  |  |  | 29 |
| 1 |  | 4 | 5 | 12 | 10² | 13 | 6 | 2 | 9¹ |  |  | 7 | 11 |  |  | 8 | 3 |  |  |  |  |  |  |  |  |  |  |  |  | 30 |
|  |  | 4 | 5 | 9¹ | 12 | 8 | 6 | 2 | 1 |  | 13 | 11 | 10 | 7 | 3⁴ |  |  |  |  |  |  |  |  |  |  |  |  |  |  | 31 |
|  | 12 | 4² | 5 | 9 | 13 | 10¹ | 6 | 2 | 1 |  | 14 | 11³ | 8 | 7 | 3 |  |  |  |  |  |  |  |  |  |  |  |  |  |  | 32 |
|  | 11 | 4 | 5 | 10² | 9¹ | 12 | 6 | 2 | 1 |  | 13 | 8 | 7 | 3 |  |  |  |  |  |  |  |  |  |  |  |  |  |  |  | 33 |
|  | 11 | 4¹ | 5 | 10³ | 13 | 12 | 9² | 6 | 2 | 1 | 14 |  | 8 | 7 | 3 |  |  |  |  |  |  |  |  |  |  |  |  |  |  | 34 |
|  | 11 | 4 | 5 | 10 | 12 | 9 | 6 | 2 | 1 |  |  | 8 | 7 | 3¹ |  |  |  |  |  |  |  |  |  |  |  |  |  |  |  | 35 |
|  | 11 | 4 | 5 | 10 |  | 9¹ | 6 | 2 | 1 | 12 |  | 8 | 7 | 3 |  |  |  |  |  |  |  |  |  |  |  |  |  |  |  | 36 |
|  | 11 | 4² | 5 | 10 | 12 | 9³ | 8¹ | 6 | 2 | 1 | 13 | 14 | 7 | 3 |  |  |  |  |  |  |  |  |  |  |  |  |  |  |  | 37 |
| 8² | 11 | 4 | 5 | 10 | 9 | 12 | 6 | 2 | 1 |  | 13 |  | 7¹ | 3 |  |  |  |  |  |  |  |  |  |  |  |  |  |  |  | 38 |
|  | 11 | 4² | 5 | 10 | 7¹ | 8³ | 9 | 12 | 6 | 2 | 1 | 14 | 13 | 3 |  |  |  |  |  |  |  |  |  |  |  |  |  |  |  | 39 |
|  | 11 | 4 | 5 | 8 | 9¹ | 12 | 6 | 2 | 1 |  | 7 | 10² | 3 |  | 13 |  |  |  |  |  |  |  |  |  |  |  |  |  |  | 40 |
|  | 11 | 4¹ | 5 | 7 | 12 | 8 | 9 | 6 | 2 | 1 |  | 10 | 3 |  |  |  |  |  |  |  |  |  |  |  |  |  |  |  |  | 41 |
|  | 11 | 4¹ | 5 | 7 | 12 | 8 | 9 | 13 | 6 | 2 | 1 | 14 | 10² | 3 |  |  |  |  |  |  |  |  |  |  |  |  |  |  |  | 42 |
|  | 11¹ | 5 | 4 | 12 | 8 | 9² | 6 | 2 | 1 |  | 10 | 7 | 3 |  | 13 |  |  |  |  |  |  |  |  |  |  |  |  |  |  | 43 |
|  | 11 | 4 | 5 | 12 | 9¹ | 13 | 8² | 6 | 2 | 1 |  | 10 | 7 | 3 |  |  |  |  |  |  |  |  |  |  |  |  |  |  |  | 44 |
|  | 11 | 5 | 4 |  | 9 | 8 | 6 | 2 | 1 | 12 | 10 | 7¹ | 3 |  |  |  |  |  |  |  |  |  |  |  |  |  |  |  |  | 45 |
| 5 | 11 | 4 |  |  | 9 | 8 | 6 | 2 | 1 |  | 10 | 7 | 3 |  |  |  |  |  |  |  |  |  |  |  |  |  |  |  |  | 46 |

**Coca-Cola Cup**
First Round    Peterborough U    (a) 2-2
                                 (h) 1-2

**FA Cup**
Third Round    Aston Villa    (h) 2-2
                              (a) 0-1

PORT VALE 1997–98 *Back row (left to right)*: Jan Jansson, Allen Tankard, Simon Armstrong, Neil Aspin, Steve Williams, Lee Mills, Gareth Griffiths, Jermaine Holwyn, Justin O'Reilly, Rogier Koordes, Liam Burns, Stewart Talbot, Dean Glover.

*Middle row*: Stan Nicholls (Kit Man), Mark Grew (Youth Team Coach), Martin Foyle, Wayne Corden, Matthew Boswell, Paul Musselwhite, Arjan van Heusden, Andy Hill, Richard Eyre, Rick Carter (Physio), Jim Cooper (Community Officer).

*Front row*: Matthew Carragher, Ian Bogie, Tony Naylor, John Rudge (Manager), Andy Porter, Bill Dearden (Coach), Tony McShane, Jon McCarthy, Dean Stokes.
(Photograph: Bill Bache)

# Division 1 PORT VALE

*Vale Park, Burslem, Stoke-on-Trent ST6 1AW.* Telephone: (01782) 814134. Fax: (01782) 834981. Marketing Dept: (01782) 835524. Clubcall: 0891 121636. Marketing Fax: (01782) 836875. Valiant Leisure Shop: (01782) 833545. Community: (01782) 575594

*Ground capacity:* 22,356.

*Record attendance:* 49,768 v Aston Villa, FA Cup 5th rd, 20 February 1960.

*Record receipts:* £170,349 v Everton, FA Cup 4th rd, 14 February 1996.

*Pitch measurements:* 114yd × 77yd.

*President:* J. Burgess.

*Chairman:* W. T. Bell LAE, TECH. ENG, MIMI.

*Directors:* A. Belfield, I. McPherson, S. Plant (Associate Director), N. Hughes (Marketing Director).

*Manager:* John Rudge. *Secretary:* F. W. Lodey.

*Coach:* Bill Dearden. *Physio:* Rick Carter. *Medical Officer:* Dr. D. Phillips. *Safety Officer:* W. Stevenson. *Groundsman:* S. Speed. *Community Scheme Officer:* Jim Cooper (01782 575594).

*Year Formed:* 1876. *Turned Professional:* 1885. *Ltd Co.:* 1911.

*Club Nickname:* 'Valiants'.

*Previous Name:* Burslem Port Vale; became Port Vale, 1909.

*Previous Grounds:* 1876, Limekin Lane, Longport; 1881, Westport; 1884, Moorland Road, Burslem; 1886, Athletic Ground, Cobridge; 1913, Recreation Ground, Hanley; 1950, Vale Park.

*Foundation:* Formed in 1876 as Port Vale, adopting the prefix 'Burslem' in 1884 upon moving to that part of the city. It was dropped in 1909.

*First Football League game:* 3 September 1892, Division 2, v Small Heath (a) L 1-5 – Frail; Clutton, Elson; Farrington, McCrindle, Delves; Walker, Scarratt, Bliss (1), Jones. (Only 10 men).

*Record League Victory:* 9–1 v Chesterfield, Division 2, 24 September 1932 – Leckie; Shenton, Poyser; Sherlock, Round, Jones; McGrath, Mills, Littlewood (6), Kirkham (2), Morton (1).

*Record Cup Victory:* 7–1 v Irthlingborough, FA Cup 1st rd, 12 January 1907 – Matthews; Dunn, Hamilton; Eardley, Baddeley, Holyhead; Carter, Dodds (2), Beats, Mountford (2), Coxon (3).

*Record Defeat:* 0–10 v Sheffield U, Division 2, 10 December 1892 and v Notts Co, Division 2, 26 February 1895.

*Most League Points (2 for a win):* 69, Division 3 (N), 1953–54.

*Most League Points (3 for a win):* 89, Division 2, 1992–93.

*Most League Goals:* 110, Division 4, 1958–59.

*Highest League Scorer in Season:* Wilf Kirkham 38, Division 2, 1926–27.

*Most League Goals in Total Aggregate:* Wilf Kirkham, 154, 1923–29, 1931–33.

*Most Capped Player:* Sammy Morgan, 7 (18), Northern Ireland.

*Most League Appearances:* Roy Sproson, 761, 1950–72.

*Record Transfer Fee Received:* £1,000,000 from Sheffield W for Ian Taylor, August 1994.

*Record Transfer Fee Paid:* £450,000 to York C for Jon McCarthy, July 1995.

*Football League Record:* 1892 Original Member of Division 2. Failed re-election in 1896; Re-elected 1898; Resigned 1907; Returned in Oct, 1919, when they took over the fixtures of Leeds City; 1929–30 Division 3 (N); 1930–36 Division 2; 1936–38 Division 3 (N); 1938–52 Division 3 (S); 1952–54 Division 3 (N); 1954–57 Division 2; 1957–58 Division 3 (S); 1958–59 Division 4; 1959–65 Division 3; 1965–70 Division 4; 1970–78 Division 3; 1978–83 Division 4; 1983–84 Division 3; 1984–86 Division 4; 1986–89 Division 3; 1989–94 Division 2; 1994– Division 1.

*Honours: Football League:* Division 2 – Runners-up 1993–94; Division 3 (N) – Champions 1929–30, 1953–54; Runners-up 1952–53; Division 4 – Champions 1958–59; Promoted 1969–70 (4th). *FA Cup:* Semi-final 1954, when in Division 3. *Football League Cup:* 3rd rd 1992, 1997. *Autoglass Trophy:* Winners: 1993. *Anglo-Italian Cup:* Runners-up: 1996.

*Colours:* White shirts, black shorts, black and white stockings. *Change colours:* All yellow.

**Did you know?**
Chris Young scored seven of Port Vale's goals in a 14-1 win over Burton Rangers in the Birmingham Cup on 21 September 1914.

## PORT VALE 1997–98 LEAGUE RECORD

| Match No. | Date | Venue | Opponents | Result | H/T Score | Lg. Pos. | Goalscorers | Attendance |
|---|---|---|---|---|---|---|---|---|
| 1 | Aug 9 | H | Nottingham F | L | 0-1 | 0-1 | — | 12,533 |
| 2 | 16 | A | Portsmouth | L | 1-3 | 1-2 | 22 | Talbot [43] | 10,605 |
| 3 | 23 | H | Sunderland | W | 3-1 | 2-0 | 15 | Mills [3], Naylor 2 [39, 72] | 8290 |
| 4 | Sept 3 | A | Wolverhampton W | D | 1-1 | 0-0 | — | Foyle [82] | 21,524 |
| 5 | 9 | H | Stockport Co | W | 2-1 | 2-1 | — | Mills 2 [1, 36] | 6615 |
| 6 | 13 | A | Norwich C | L | 0-1 | 0-0 | 15 | | 11,269 |
| 7 | 16 | A | Crewe Alex | W | 1-0 | 0-0 | — | Mills [55] | 5519 |
| 8 | 20 | H | Bury | D | 1-1 | 1-0 | 12 | Ainsworth [7] | 6781 |
| 9 | 27 | H | QPR | W | 2-0 | 2-0 | 9 | Snijders [17], Naylor [20] | 7197 |
| 10 | Oct 4 | A | Swindon T | L | 2-4 | 1-0 | 9 | Glover [36], Foyle [86] | 8048 |
| 11 | 12 | A | Stoke C | L | 1-2 | 1-2 | 11 | Naylor [21] | 20,125 |
| 12 | 18 | H | Bradford C | D | 0-0 | 0-0 | 14 | | 7148 |
| 13 | 21 | H | Huddersfield T | W | 4-1 | 1-0 | — | Horne (og) [26], Talbot [47], Ainsworth [73], Naylor [83] | 5244 |
| 14 | 25 | A | Middlesbrough | L | 1-2 | 0-1 | 14 | Foyle [90] | 30,096 |
| 15 | Nov 1 | H | Reading | D | 0-0 | 0-0 | 14 | | 6569 |
| 16 | 4 | A | Manchester C | W | 3-2 | 2-2 | — | Snijders [17], Talbot [45], Naylor [50] | 24,554 |
| 17 | 8 | A | Tranmere R | W | 2-1 | 1-0 | 7 | Naylor 2 [14, 67] | 7063 |
| 18 | 15 | H | WBA | L | 1-2 | 0-0 | 11 | Mills [48] | 11,124 |
| 19 | 22 | H | Sheffield U | D | 0-0 | 0-0 | 9 | | 8017 |
| 20 | 29 | A | Oxford U | L | 0-2 | 0-1 | 11 | | 5762 |
| 21 | Dec 6 | A | Birmingham C | L | 0-1 | 0-1 | 13 | | 7509 |
| 22 | 13 | A | Charlton Ath | L | 0-1 | 0-0 | 14 | | 11,077 |
| 23 | 20 | H | Ipswich T | L | 1-3 | 0-3 | 17 | Foyle [50] | 5784 |
| 24 | 26 | A | Stockport Co | L | 0-3 | 0-0 | 18 | | 10,003 |
| 25 | 28 | H | Wolverhampton W | L | 0-2 | 0-1 | 18 | | 10,898 |
| 26 | Jan 10 | A | Nottingham F | L | 1-2 | 1-1 | 21 | Mills [16] | 17,639 |
| 27 | 17 | H | Portsmouth | W | 2-1 | 1-1 | 18 | Talbot [29], Mills [56] | 6028 |
| 28 | 24 | H | Crewe Alex | L | 2-3 | 1-3 | 19 | Naylor [1], Porter (pen) [74] | 10,571 |
| 29 | 31 | A | Sunderland | L | 2-4 | 1-3 | 21 | Talbot [37], Jansson [90] | 39,258 |
| 30 | Feb 7 | A | Bury | D | 2-2 | 2-1 | 20 | Mills [10], Bogie [17] | 5285 |
| 31 | 14 | H | Norwich C | D | 2-2 | 1-0 | 21 | Mills 2 [34, 85] | 6664 |
| 32 | 17 | H | Swindon T | L | 0-1 | 0-1 | — | | 5925 |
| 33 | 21 | A | QPR | W | 1-0 | 1-0 | 21 | Mills [24] | 14,198 |
| 34 | 24 | A | Bradford C | L | 1-2 | 1-1 | — | Foyle [29] | 13,293 |
| 35 | Mar 1 | H | Stoke C | D | 0-0 | 0-0 | 24 | | 13,853 |
| 36 | 4 | H | Tranmere R | L | 0-1 | 0-0 | — | | 5465 |
| 37 | 7 | A | Reading | W | 3-0 | 2-0 | 23 | Mills [7], Talbot [19], Jansson [82] | 7139 |
| 38 | 14 | H | Manchester C | W | 2-1 | 1-0 | 19 | Foyle [13], Ainsworth [73] | 13,122 |
| 39 | 21 | A | WBA | D | 2-2 | 0-1 | 20 | Jansson [69], Foyle [90] | 14,242 |
| 40 | 28 | A | Sheffield U | L | 1-2 | 0-0 | 20 | Corden [90] | 15,860 |
| 41 | Apr 4 | H | Oxford U | W | 3-0 | 2-0 | 18 | Mills [29], Naylor [42], Ainsworth [84] | 6524 |
| 42 | 11 | A | Birmingham C | D | 1-1 | 0-0 | 17 | Ainsworth [58] | 17,193 |
| 43 | 13 | H | Charlton Ath | L | 0-1 | 0-0 | 19 | | 9973 |
| 44 | 18 | A | Ipswich T | L | 1-5 | 0-3 | 20 | Barnett [65] | 16,205 |
| 45 | 24 | H | Middlesbrough | L | 0-1 | 0-1 | — | | 12,096 |
| 46 | May 3 | A | Huddersfield T | W | 4-0 | 2-0 | 19 | Foyle [2], Jansson 2 [25, 60], Mills [79] | 15,610 |

**Final League Position: 19**      1996–97 DIV1 8

### GOALSCORERS

League (56): Mills 14, Naylor 10, Foyle 8, Talbot 6, Ainsworth 5, Jansson 5, Snijders 2, Barnett 1, Bogie 1, Corden 1, Glover 1, Porter 1 (pen), own goal 1.
Coca-Cola Cup (2): Mills 2.
FA Cup (1): Corden 1.

| Musselwhite P 41 | Hill A 25+2 | Tankard A 39 | Talbot S 42 | Aspin N 26 | Glover D 21+4 | McCarthy J 4 | Porter A 28+13 | Mills L 39+3 | Naylor T 28+10 | Corden W 19+14 | Jansson J 22+11 | Foyle M 19+20 | Koordes R 9+1 | Stokes D 5+3 | Bogie I 32+6 | Snijders M 22+2 | Ainsworth G 38+2 | Carragher M 26 | Griffiths G 3 | Eyre R —+1 | Beesley P 5 | Burns L —+1 | Van Heusden A 5 | Barnett D 8+1 | Mahorn P —+1 | Match No. |
|---|---|---|---|---|---|---|---|---|---|---|---|---|---|---|---|---|---|---|---|---|---|---|---|---|---|---|
| 1 | 2 | 3 | 4 | 5 | 6 | 7 | 8 | 9 | 10¹ | 11² | 12 | 13 | | | | | | | | | | | | | | 1 |
| 1 | 2 | 3 | 10 | 5 | 6² | | 8 | 9 | 12 | 7 | 4¹ | 11 | 13 | | | | | | | | | | | | | 2 |
| 1 | 2 | 3 | 4³ | 5 | 6 | 7 | 8 | 9 | 10¹ | 11² | 12 | | | | 13 | 14 | | | | | | | | | | 3 |
| 1 | 2 | 3 | 4 | 5 | 6 | 7 | 8² | 9 | 10 | 11¹ | 13 | 12 | | | | | | | | | | | | | | 4 |
| 1 | 2 | 3 | 4 | 5 | | 7 | 8 | 9 | | 11¹ | 12 | 10 | | | 6 | | | | | | | | | | | 5 |
| 1 | 2 | 3 | 4 | 5 | | | 8 | 9 | 10 | 7¹ | 11 | | | | 6 | 12 | | | | | | | | | | 6 |
| 1 | 2 | 3 | 4 | 5 | | | 12 | 9 | | 11 | 13 | 10 | | | 8² | 6¹ | 7 | | | | | | | | | 7 |
| 1 | 2 | 3 | 4 | 5 | | | 8 | 9 | | 11 | 10 | | | | | 6 | 7 | | | | | | | | | 8 |
| 1 | 2³ | 3 | 4² | 5 | 13 | | 12 | 9 | 10¹ | | | 11 | 14 | | 8 | 6 | 7 | | | | | | | | | 9 |
| 1 | | 3¹ | 4 | 5 | 2 | | 12 | 9 | 10 | 13 | 14 | 11³ | | | 8 | 6 | 7² | | | | | | | | | 10 |
| 1 | 2² | 3 | 4 | 5 | | | 8 | 9¹ | 10 | 14 | 12 | 11³ | | | 13 | 6 | 7 | | | | | | | | | 11 |
| 1 | | 3 | 4 | 5 | | | 12 | 9² | 10 | 11 | | 13 | | | 8¹ | 6 | 7 | 2 | | | | | | | | 12 |
| 1 | | 3 | 4 | 5 | | | | 9 | 10 | 11 | | | | | 8 | 6 | 7 | 2 | | | | | | | | 13 |
| 1 | | 3 | 9¹ | 5 | 4 | | | | 10 | 11 | 12 | 13 | 14 | | 8² | 6 | 7 | 2¹ | | | | | | | | 14 |
| 1 | | 3 | 4 | 5 | | | | 9 | 12 | 11 | 13 | 10¹ | | | 8² | 6 | 7 | 2 | | | | | | | | 15 |
| 1 | | 3 | 9³ | 5 | | | 8 | 12 | 10¹ | 11² | 4 | 13 | 14 | | | 6 | 7 | 2 | | | | | | | | 16 |
| 1 | 13 | 3 | | 5 | | | 8 | 12 | 10¹ | 4 | 11 | 9 | | | | 6² | 7 | 2 | | | | | | | | 17 |
| 1 | | 3 | 8¹ | 5 | | | 12 | 9 | 10 | 13 | 4³ | 11 | | | | 6² | 7 | 2 | | | | | | | | 18 |
| 1 | | 3 | 8¹ | 5 | | | 12 | 9 | 10³ | 13 | 14 | 11² | 4 | | | 6 | 7 | 2 | | | | | | | | 19 |
| 1 | 12 | 3 | 10 | 5¹ | | | 8² | 9 | | 11 | | 13 | | | 4 | 6 | 7 | 2 | | | | | | | | 20 |
| 1 | | 3 | 8 | | | | 12 | 9 | 10 | 11² | | 13 | | | 4 | 6 | 7¹ | 2 | 5 | | | | | | | 21 |
| 1 | | 3 | 8 | | | | | | 10 | 12 | 9 | 11 | | | 4 | 6 | 7 | 2¹ | 5 | | | | | | | 22 |
| 1 | | 3³ | 8 | | | | 12 | 9 | 10 | 11 | | 13 | 14 | 5² | 4 | 6¹ | 7 | 2 | | | | | | | | 23 |
| 1 | 5 | 3 | 8 | | | | 2 | 9 | 10¹ | | 12 | 13 | | | 4 | | 7 | 6 | | | | | | | | 24 |
| 1 | 5 | 3 | 2 | | | | 8 | 9 | 10¹ | 11² | 12 | 13 | | | 4 | | 7 | 6 | | | | | | | | 25 |
| 1 | 2 | 3 | 7 | 5 | | | 8 | 9 | 10² | | 12 | 13 | | | 4¹ | 6³ | 14 | 11 | | | | | | | | 26 |
| 1 | 2 | 3 | 4 | 5 | | | 8 | 9 | 10¹ | 11 | 12 | | | | | | 7 | 6 | | | | | | | | 27 |
| 1 | 2 | | 4 | 5 | 12 | | 8 | 9¹ | 10 | 11³ | | 13 | | | 3¹ | 14 | 7 | 6 | | | | | | | | 28 |
| 1 | | | 4 | 5 | 3 | | 8 | | 10 | 11² | 12 | 13 | | | 9¹ | | 7 | 2 | 6³ | 14 | | | | | | 29 |
| 1 | | 3 | | 5 | 12 | | 8 | 9 | 10 | | | 4¹ | | | 11 | 6 | 7 | 2 | | | | | | | | 30 |
| 1 | 2 | 3 | 5¹ | | 12 | | 8 | 9 | 10³ | 13 | 11 | 14 | | | 4² | 6 | 7 | | | | | | | | | 31 |
| | 2 | 3² | 4 | 5 | | | 8 | 9 | 12 | 13 | 11³ | 10¹ | | | 14 | 6 | 7 | | | | | | 1 | | | 32 |
| | 2 | 3 | 4 | 5 | | | 8 | 9 | | 11 | | 10 | | | | 6 | 7 | | | | | | 1 | | | 33 |
| | 2 | 3 | 4³ | 5 | | | 8 | 9 | 12 | 13 | 11² | 10 | | | 14 | 6 | 7 | | | | | | 1 | | | 34 |
| | 2 | 3² | | 5 | | | 8 | 9¹ | 12 | | 11 | 10 | | | 4 | 13 | 7 | 6 | | | | | 1 | | | 35 |
| | 2 | | 3 | | 5 | | 8 | 9 | 12 | | 11 | 10 | | | 4 | | 7 | 6¹ | | | | | 1 | | | 36 |
| 1 | 2 | | 3 | | 5 | | 8 | 9 | 12² | 11 | | 10¹ | | | 4 | 13 | 7 | 6 | | | | | | | | 37 |
| 1 | 2 | 3 | | | | | 8 | 9 | 12 | 11 | | 10 | | | 4 | | 7 | 6 | | | | | 13 | | | 38 |
| 1 | 2² | | 8 | | 5 | | | 9 | | 12 | 11 | 10 | | | 3 | 4 | 7¹ | | | | | | 6 | 13 | | 39 |
| 1 | 2 | | 8¹ | 5 | | | 12² | 9 | 13 | 14 | 11 | 10 | | 3³ | 4 | | 7 | | | | | | 6 | | | 40 |
| 1 | | 3 | 8¹ | 5 | | | 12 | 9 | 10 | | | 11 | | | 4 | | 7 | 2 | | | | | 6 | | | 41 |
| 1 | | 3 | 8 | 5 | | | 12 | 9 | 10² | | 11¹ | 13 | | | 4 | | 7 | 2 | | | | | 6 | | | 42 |
| 1 | | 3 | 8 | 5 | | | | 9 | 10² | 12 | 11 | 13 | | | 4 | | 7 | 2¹ | | | | | 6 | | | 43 |
| 1 | | 3 | 8 | 5 | | | 12 | 9 | 10² | | 11¹ | 13 | | | 4 | | 7 | 2 | | | | | 6 | | | 44 |
| 1 | | 3¹ | 8 | 5 | | | 11² | 9 | 12 | | | 13 | 10 | | 4 | | 7 | 2 | | | | | 6 | | | 45 |
| 1 | | 3 | 8¹ | 5 | | | 12 | 9 | | | 11 | 10 | | | 4 | | 7 | 2 | | | | | 6 | | | 46 |

**Coca-Cola Cup**  
First Round    York C    (h) 1-2  
                         (a) 1-1

**FA Cup**  
Third Round    Arsenal    (a) 0-0  
                          (h) 1-1

PRESTON NORTH END 1997–98    *Back row (left to right):* Simon Davey, Paul Sparrow, David Reeves, Jamie Squires, David Lucas, Teuvo Moilanen, Colin Murdock, Sean Gregan, Ryan Kidd, Julian Darby.

*Middle row:* Mick Rathbone (Physio), Lee Cartwright, Kurt Nogan, Paul Morgan, Michael Jackson, Gary Parkinson, Jonathan Macken, Lee Ashcroft, Michael Appleton, Dean Barrick, Brian Hickson (Kit Manager).

*Front row:* Paul McKenna, Graeme Atkinson, Neil McDonald (Youth Team Coach), David Moyes (Manager), Bryan Gray (Chairman), Gary Peters (Director of School of Excellence), Derek Shaw (Deputy Chairman), Steve Harrison, Kelham O'Hanlon (Coach), Mark Rankine, Michael Holt.

# Division 2     **PRESTON NORTH END**

*Deepdale, Preston PR1 6RU.* Telephone: (01772) 902020. Fax: (01772) 653266. Ticket Enquiries: (01772) 902000. Ticket Office Credit Card Bookings: (01772) 902222. Corporate Hospitality: (01772) 902048. Publishing: (01772) 902046. Community: (01772) 902030. Kit 1 Shop at Deepdale: (01772) 902040. Kit 2 Shop, Preston Town Centre: (01772) 887088. Kit 3 Shop, Leyland: (01772) 624600.

*Ground capacity:* 21,412.

*Record attendance:* 42,684 v Arsenal, Division 1, 23 April 1938.

*Record receipts:* £68,650 v Sheffield W, FA Cup 3rd rd, 4 January 1992.

*Pitch measurements:* 110yd × 77yd.

*President:* Sir Tom Finney OBE, JP.

*Chairman:* Bryan M. Gray.

*Directors:* K. W. Leeming and M. J. Woodhouse (snr) (Vice-Chairmen), D. Shaw (Non-Executive), T. Scholes (Finance Director/Company Secretary).

*Chief Executive:* P. Church

*Manager:* David Moyes. *Coach/Goalkeeping Coach:* Kelham O'Hanlon.

*Secretary:* M. Wearmouth.

*Year Formed:* 1881. *Turned Professional:* 1885. *Ltd Co.:* 1893.

*Club Nicknames:* 'The Lilywhites' or 'North End'.

*Foundation:* North End Cricket and Rugby Club which was formed in 1863, indulged in most sports before taking up soccer in about 1879. In 1881 they decided to stick to football to the exclusion of other sports and even a 16–0 drubbing by Blackburn Rovers in an invitation game at Deepdale, a few weeks after taking this decision, did not deter them for they immediately became affiliated to the Lancashire FA.

*First Football League game:* 8 September 1888, Football League, v Burnley (h) W 5-2 – Trainer; Howarth, Holmes; Robertson, W. Graham, J. Graham; Gordon (1), Ross (2), Goodall, Dewhurst (2), Drummond.

*Record League Victory:* 10–0 v Stoke, Division 1, 14 September 1889 – Trainer; Howarth, Holmes; Kelso, Russell (1), Graham; Gordon, Jimmy Ross (2), Nick Ross (3), Thomson (2), Drummond (2).

*Record Cup Victory:* 26–0 v Hyde, FA Cup 1st rd, 15 October 1887 – Addison; Howarth, Nick Ross; Russell (1), Thomson (5), Graham (1); Gordon (5), Jimmy Ross (8), John Goodall (1), Dewhurst (3), Drummond (2).

*Record Defeat:* 0–7 v Blackpool, Division 1, 1 May 1948.

*Most League Points (2 for a win):* 61, Division 3, 1970–71.

*Most League Points (3 for a win):* 90, Division 4, 1986–87.

*Most League Goals:* 100, Division 2, 1927–28 and Division 1, 1957–58.

*Highest League Scorer in Season:* Ted Harper, 37, Division 2, 1932–33.

*Most League Goals in Total Aggregate:* Tom Finney, 187, 1946–60.

*Most Capped Player:* Tom Finney, 76, England.

*Most League Appearances:* Alan Kelly, 447, 1961–75.

*Record Transfer Fee Received:* £765,000 from Manchester C for Michael Robinson, June 1979.

*Record Transfer Fee Paid:* £500,000 to Manchester U for Michael Appleton, August 1997.

*Football League Record:* 1888 Founder Member of League; 1901–04 Division 2; 1904–12 Division 1; 1912–13 Division 2; 1913–14 Division 1; 1914–15 Division 2; 1919–25 Division 1; 1925–34 Division 2; 1934–49 Division 1; 1949–51 Division 2; 1951–61 Division 1; 1961–70 Division 2; 1970–71 Division 3; 1971–74 Division 2; 1974–78 Division 3; 1978–81 Division 2; 1981–85 Division 3; 1985–87 Division 4; 1987–92 Division 2; 1992–93 Division 2; 1993–96 Division 3; 1996– Division 2.

*Honours: Football League:* Division 1 – Champions 1888–89 (first champions), 1889–90; Runners-up 1890–91, 1891–92, 1892–93, 1905–06, 1952–53, 1957–58; Division 2 – Champions 1903–04, 1912–13, 1950–51; Runners-up 1914–15, 1933–34; Division 3 – Champions 1970–71, 1995–96; Division 4 – Runners-up 1986–87. *FA Cup:* Winners 1889, 1938; Runners-up 1888, 1922, 1937, 1954, 1964. *Double Performed:* 1888–89. *Football League Cup:* best season: 4th rd, 1963, 1966, 1972, 1981.

*Colours:* White shirts, navy shorts, white stockings. *Change colours:* All Royal blue.

**Did you know?**
Preston North End have completed a 6000 seater Bill Shankly Kop named after their former player from 1933 to 1949.

**PRESTON NORTH END FC**

## PRESTON NORTH END 1997–98 LEAGUE RECORD

| Match No. | Date | | Venue | Opponents | Result | H/T Score | Lg. Pos. | Goalscorers | Attendance |
|---|---|---|---|---|---|---|---|---|---|
| 1 | Aug | 9 | A | Gillingham | D 0-0 | 0-0 | — | | 6562 |
| 2 | | 16 | H | Millwall | W 2-1 | 1-1 | 7 | Macken [43], Ashcroft [51] | 11,486 |
| 3 | | 23 | A | Chesterfield | L 2-3 | 0-3 | 11 | Rankine [63], Barrick [88] | 6288 |
| 4 | | 30 | H | Watford | W 2-0 | 1-0 | 8 | Nogan 2 [38, 67] | 11,042 |
| 5 | Sept | 2 | H | Grimsby T | W 2-0 | 0-0 | — | Reeves [67], Ashcroft [74] | 9489 |
| 6 | | 9 | A | Oldham Ath | L 0-1 | 0-0 | — | | 8732 |
| 7 | | 13 | H | Walsall | D 0-0 | 0-0 | 7 | | 9092 |
| 8 | | 20 | A | Burnley | D 1-1 | 1-0 | 8 | Nogan [19] | 13,809 |
| 9 | | 27 | A | Wycombe W | D 0-0 | 0-0 | 8 | | 4838 |
| 10 | Oct | 4 | H | Brentford | W 2-1 | 0-1 | 5 | Ashcroft [50], Murdock [84] | 8804 |
| 11 | | 11 | H | Bournemouth | L 0-1 | 0-0 | 11 | | 8531 |
| 12 | | 17 | A | Carlisle U | W 2-0 | 1-0 | — | Parkinson [22], Ashcroft [47] | 6541 |
| 13 | | 21 | A | Bristol C | L 1-2 | 0-0 | — | Dyche (og) [68] | 9039 |
| 14 | | 25 | H | Wrexham | L 0-1 | 0-0 | 13 | | 9098 |
| 15 | Nov | 1 | H | Plymouth Arg | L 0-1 | 0-0 | 16 | | 8405 |
| 16 | | 4 | A | York C | L 0-1 | 0-0 | — | | 3370 |
| 17 | | 8 | A | Luton T | W 3-1 | 2-1 | 12 | Lormor [16], Eyres [45], Ashcroft [90] | 5767 |
| 18 | | 18 | A | Bristol R | L 1-2 | 0-1 | — | Jackson [53] | 7798 |
| 19 | | 22 | A | Wigan Ath | W 4-1 | 1-0 | 14 | Cartwright 2 [21, 53], Ashcroft [71], Kidd [73] | 5649 |
| 20 | | 29 | H | Fulham | W 3-1 | 1-1 | 12 | Ashcroft 3 (1 pen) [11, 69 (p), 83] | 9723 |
| 21 | Dec | 2 | A | Southend U | L 2-3 | 2-3 | — | Lormor 2 [6, 11] | 2307 |
| 22 | | 13 | H | Northampton T | W 1-0 | 0-0 | 8 | Macken [56] | 7448 |
| 23 | | 20 | A | Blackpool | L 1-2 | 0-2 | 11 | Holt [51] | 8342 |
| 24 | | 26 | H | Oldham Ath | D 1-1 | 0-1 | 13 | Holt [51] | 13,441 |
| 25 | | 28 | A | Grimsby T | L 1-3 | 0-3 | 14 | Gregan [88] | 6725 |
| 26 | Jan | 10 | H | Gillingham | L 1-3 | 0-2 | 17 | Gregan [76] | 7776 |
| 27 | | 17 | A | Watford | L 1-3 | 0-2 | 17 | Parkinson [56] | 10,182 |
| 28 | | 24 | H | Chesterfield | D 0-0 | 0-0 | 17 | | 8233 |
| 29 | | 31 | A | Walsall | D 1-1 | 0-0 | 18 | Nogan (pen) [89] | 5377 |
| 30 | Feb | 7 | H | Burnley | L 2-3 | 1-0 | 18 | Nogan [34], Jackson [61] | 12,263 |
| 31 | | 14 | A | Brentford | D 0-0 | 0-0 | 18 | | 4952 |
| 32 | | 21 | H | Wycombe W | D 1-1 | 0-0 | 18 | Macken [64] | 7665 |
| 33 | | 24 | H | Carlisle U | L 0-3 | 0-2 | — | | 8985 |
| 34 | | 28 | A | Bournemouth | W 2-0 | 2-0 | 17 | Davey [16], Appleton [22] | 5009 |
| 35 | Mar | 3 | H | Luton T | W 1-0 | 0-0 | — | Kidd [64] | 6992 |
| 36 | | 7 | A | Plymouth Arg | L 0-2 | 0-1 | 17 | | 4201 |
| 37 | | 14 | H | York C | W 3-2 | 0-1 | 16 | Eyres [47], Appleton [82], Parkinson [87] | 7664 |
| 38 | | 21 | A | Bristol R | D 2-2 | 1-0 | 16 | Davey [23], Ashcroft [83] | 5278 |
| 39 | | 25 | A | Millwall | W 1-0 | 1-0 | — | Ashcroft [33] | 5888 |
| 40 | | 28 | H | Wigan Ath | D 1-1 | 1-0 | 15 | Ashcroft [33] | 10,171 |
| 41 | Apr | 4 | A | Fulham | L 1-2 | 1-0 | 16 | Macken [33] | 8814 |
| 42 | | 11 | H | Southend U | W 1-0 | 0-0 | 13 | Parkinson [63] | 8096 |
| 43 | | 13 | A | Northampton T | D 2-2 | 1-0 | 14 | Ashcroft [45], Macken [90] | 5664 |
| 44 | | 18 | H | Blackpool | D 3-3 | 1-2 | 14 | Eyres [23], Parkinson [50], Macken [60] | 13,500 |
| 45 | | 25 | A | Wrexham | D 0-0 | 0-0 | 16 | | 7302 |
| 46 | May | 2 | H | Bristol C | W 2-1 | 2-1 | 15 | Ashcroft [5], Eyres [10] | 12,067 |

**Final League Position: 15**  1996–97 DIV2 15

### GOALSCORERS

*League (56):* Ashcroft 14 (1 pen), Macken 6, Nogan 5 (1 pen), Parkinson 5, Eyres 4, Lormor 3, Appleton 2, Cartwright 2, Davey 2, Gregan 2, Holt 2, Jackson 2, Kidd 2, Barrick 1, Murdock 1, Rankine 1, Reeves 1, own goal 1.
*Coca-Cola Cup (6):* Reeves 3, Macken 2, Barrick 1.
*FA Cup (8):* Ashcroft 2 (1 pen), Eyres 2, Gregan 2, Moyes 1, Parkinson 1.

| Moilanen T 40 | Parkinson G 44+1 | Kidd R 32+1 | Murdock C 27 | Jackson M 39+1 | Gregan S 33+2 | Cartwright L 24+12 | Ashcroft L 37 | Reeves D 12+1 | Macken J 20+9 | Rankine M 34+1 | Nogan K 14+8 | Barrick D 29+4 | Appleton M 31+7 | Derby J 6+6 | Atkinson G 1+2 | Holt M 4+10 | Lucas D 6 | Moyes D 8+1 | Eyres D 26+2 | Lormor T 9+3 | Davey S 17+1 | Mullin J 4+3 | Sissoko H 4+3 | McKenna P 4+1 | Sparrow P 1 | Match No. |
|---|---|---|---|---|---|---|---|---|---|---|---|---|---|---|---|---|---|---|---|---|---|---|---|---|---|---|
| 1 | 2 | 3 | 4 | 5 | 6 | 7 | 8 | 9 | 10[1] | 11 | 12 | | | | | | | | | | | | | | | 1 |
| 1 | 2 | 3 | 4[1] | 5 | 6[2] | 7 | 8 | 9 | 10 | 11 | | 12 | 13 | | | | | | | | | | | | | 2 |
| 1 | 2 | | 4 | 5 | 6[3] | 7[1] | 8 | 9 | 10[2] | 11 | 12 | 3 | 13 | 14 | | | | | | | | | | | | 3 |
| 1 | 2 | 6 | | 5 | | 7[2] | 8 | 9 | 12 | 11 | 10[1] | 3 | 4 | 13 | | | | | | | | | | | | 4 |
| 1 | 2 | 6[1] | | 5 | 12 | 7[2] | 8 | 9 | | 11 | 10 | 3 | 4 | 13 | | | | | | | | | | | | 5 |
| 1 | 2 | | | 5 | 6 | 7 | 8 | 9 | 12 | 11 | 10[1] | 3 | 4 | | | | | | | | | | | | | 6 |
| 1 | 2 | 12 | | 5 | 6 | 7 | 8 | 9[1] | 13 | 11 | 10[2] | 3 | 4 | | | | | | | | | | | | | 7 |
| 1 | 2 | | 4 | 5 | 6 | 7 | 8 | 9 | | 11 | 10[1] | 3 | 12 | | | | | | | | | | | | | 8 |
| 1 | 2 | 3 | 4 | 5 | 6[2] | | 8 | 12 | 9 | 10 | | 11[1] | 7 | | 13 | | | | | | | | | | | 9 |
| 1 | 2 | 3[1] | 4 | 5 | 6 | 12 | 8 | | 9[2] | 10 | | 11 | 7 | | 13 | | | | | | | | | | | 10 |
| | 2 | 3 | 4 | 5[1] | | 7 | 8 | | 10 | 13 | | 11 | 6 | | 12[2] | | 1 | 9 | | | | | | | | 11 |
| 1 | 2 | 3 | 4 | | | 7 | 8 | | 9 | 10 | | | 11 | | | 6 | | 5 | | | | | | | | 12 |
| 1 | 2 | 3 | 4 | | | 7 | 8 | | 9 | 10 | | | 11 | | | 6 | | 5 | | | | | | | | 13 |
| 1 | 2 | 3 | 4 | | | 7[2] | 8 | | 9 | 10 | | 6 | 13 | | 11[1] | 12 | | 5 | | | | | | | | 14 |
| 1 | 2[1] | 3 | 4 | | 13 | 12 | 8 | 7[2] | 10 | 9[3] | | 6 | 14 | | | | | 5 | 11 | | | | | | | 15 |
| 1 | 2 | 3 | 4[1] | | 6 | 13 | 8 | 7[3] | 10 | 9[2] | | 12 | 14 | | | | | 5 | 11 | | | | | | | 16 |
| 1 | 2 | | 4 | 5 | 6 | | 8[1] | 12 | 10 | | | 3 | 7 | | | | | | 11 | 9 | | | | | | 17 |
| 1 | 2 | 3[1] | 4 | 5 | 6 | | 8[2] | | 10 | | 12 | | 7 | 13 | | | | | 11 | 9 | | | | | | 18 |
| 1 | 2 | | 4 | 5 | 6 | 11[1] | 8 | | 10 | | | 3 | 7 | | 12 | | | | 9 | | | | | | | 19 |
| 1 | 2 | | 4 | 5 | 6 | 11 | 8[1] | | 10 | | | 3 | 7 | | 12 | | | | 9 | | | | | | | 20 |
| 1 | 2 | | 4 | 5 | 6 | 11[1] | 8 | | 10 | | | 3 | 7 | 10 | 12 | | | | 9 | | | | | | | 21 |
| 1 | 2 | | 4 | 5 | 6 | | | | 10[1] | | | 3 | 7 | | 12 | 8 | | | 11 | 9 | | | | | | 22 |
| 1 | 2 | | 4 | 5 | 6 | 12 | | | 10 | | | 3[2] | 7 | | 14 | 8[1] | | 13 | 11 | 9[3] | | | | | | 23 |
| 1 | 2[2] | | 4 | 12 | 6 | | 8 | | 10[3] | | | 3[1] | 7 | | 13 | 9 | | 5 | 11 | 14 | | | | | | 24 |
| 1 | 12 | | 4 | 2 | 6 | | 8 | | | | 13 | 3 | 7 | | 10[2] | 9[3] | | 5[1] | 11 | 14 | | | | | | 25 |
| | 2[1] | 3 | 4 | 5 | 6 | 12 | 8 | | 9 | 10[2] | | 7 | 13 | | | | 1 | | 11 | | | | | | | 26 |
| | 2 | 6 | | 5 | | 7 | 8 | 12 | 10 | | | 3[1] | | | | | 1 | | 11 | 9 | 4 | | | | | 27 |
| | 2 | 3 | | 5 | 6 | 7 | 8 | 12 | 10 | | | | | | | | 1 | | 11 | 9[1] | 4 | | | | | 28 |
| | 2 | 3 | | 5 | 6 | 7 | 8 | 9[2] | 10 | | 12 | | | | | | 1 | | 11[1] | | 4 | 13 | | | | 29 |
| | 2 | 3 | | 5 | 6 | 7 | 8 | 9 | 10 | | 12 | | | | | | 1 | | 11[1] | | 4 | | | | | 30 |
| 1 | 2 | 3[1] | 4 | 5 | 6 | 7 | 8 | | 10 | | | | 12 | | | | | | 11 | | 13 | | 9[2] | | | 31 |
| 1 | 2 | | 4 | 5 | 6 | 7 | 8 | 12 | 10[1] | | | 3 | | | | | | | 11 | | 9[2] | 13 | | | | 32 |
| 1 | 2 | | | 5 | 6 | 7[3] | 8[2] | 12 | 10 | | | 3 | | | | | | 4 | 13 | 14 | 9[1] | 11 | | | | 33 |
| 1 | 2 | 3 | 4 | 5 | 6 | | | | 9[1] | | | | 7 | | | | | | 11 | | 8 | 12 | 10 | | | 34 |
| 1 | 2 | 3 | 4 | 5 | 6 | | | | 9 | | | | 7 | | | | | | 11 | | 8 | 12 | 10[1] | | | 35 |
| 1 | 2 | 3[1] | 4 | 5 | 6 | | | 12 | 9 | | | | 7 | | | | | | 11 | | 8 | 13 | 10[2] | | | 36 |
| 1 | 2 | | 4 | 5 | 6 | | | 12 | 9 | | | 3 | 7 | | | | | | 11 | | 8[2] | 10[1] | 13 | | | 37 |
| 1 | 2 | 3 | 4 | 5 | | | | | 9 | 10[2] | 12 | 6[1] | 7 | 13 | | | | | 11 | | 8 | | | | | 38 |
| 1 | 2 | 3[1] | 4 | 5 | | | | | 9[3] | 10[2] | 13 | 6 | 7 | 14 | 12 | | | | 11 | | 8 | | | | | 39 |
| 1 | 2 | | 4 | 5 | | | | | 9 | 10[2] | 12 | 3 | 7 | | | | | | 11[1] | | 8 | 13 | | | | 40 |
| 1 | 2 | | 4 | 5 | | | | | 9 | 10[2] | 12 | 3 | 7[1] | | 13 | | | | 11 | | 8 | | | | | 41 |
| 1 | 2 | | 4 | 5 | 6[1] | 12 | | | 9 | 10 | | 3 | 7[2] | | | | | | 11 | | 8 | | 13 | | | 42 |
| 1 | 2 | | 4 | 5 | | 12 | | | 9 | 10 | | 3 | 7 | | 13 | | | | 11[2] | | 8[1] | | | 6 | | 43 |
| 1 | 2 | | 4 | | 6 | | | | 9 | 10 | | 3 | 7 | | 12 | | | | 11[1] | | 8 | | | 5 | | 44 |
| 1 | 2 | | | 5 | 6 | | | | 9 | 10 | | | 7 | | 12 | | | | 11[1] | | 8 | | | 4 | 3 | 45 |
| 1 | 2 | | | 5 | 6 | | | | 9 | 10 | | 3 | 7 | | | | | | 11[1] | | 8 | | | 4 | | 46 |

**Coca-Cola Cup**

| | | | |
|---|---|---|---|
| First Round | Rotherham U | (a) | 3-1 |
| | | (h) | 2-0 |
| Second Round | Blackburn R | (a) | 0-6 |
| | | (h) | 1-0 |

**FA Cup**

| | | | |
|---|---|---|---|
| First Round | Doncaster R | (h) | 3-2 |
| Second Round | Notts Co | (h) | 2-2 |
| | | (a) | 2-1 |
| Third Round | Stockport Co | (h) | 1-2 |

QUEENS PARK RANGERS 1997-98 *Back row (left to right):* Trevor Challis, Lee Charles, Nigel Quashie, Chris Plummer, Karl Ready, Michael Mahoney-Johnson, Stephen Morrow, Steve Slade, Paul Murray, Kevin Gallen, Paul Bruce.

*Middle row:* Bob Oteng (Kit Manager), Steve Burtenshaw (Chief Scout), Mark Browse (Physio), Craig Hamilton (Masseur), Mike Sheron, Mark Perry, Paul Hart, Richard Hurst, Tony Roberts, Lee Harper, Steve Yates, Simon Barker, Brian Morris (Physio), Warren Neill (Youth Team Manager), Gary Micklewhite (Youth Team Coach).

*Front row:* John Hollins (Reserve Team Manager), Matthew Rose, Danny Maddix, Matthew Brazier, Mark Graham, Stewart Houston (Manager), Gavin Peacock, Rufus Brevett, Trevor Sinclair, John Spencer, Bruce Rioch (Assistant Manager).

(Photograph: Action Images)

# Division 1 QUEENS PARK RANGERS

*South Africa Road, London W12 7PA.* Telephone: (0181) 743 0262. Fax: (0181) 749 0994. Box office: (0181) 740 0503. Supporters Club: (0181) 740 2534. Club Shop: (0181) 749 6862. Marketing: (0181) 740 2514. Ticket Master: (0171) 344 9494.

*Ground capacity:* 19,148.

*Record attendance:* 35,353 v Leeds U, Division 1, 27 April 1974.

*Record receipts:* £218,475 v Manchester U, FA Premier League, 5 February 1994.

*Pitch measurements:* 112yd × 72yd.

*Chairman:* Chris Wright. *Chief Executive:* Clive Berlin.

*Executive Directors:* Nick Blackburn, Paul Hart, Alan Hedges, Stephen Oakley.

*Non-Executive Directors:* Sir Terence Burns GCB, Peter Ellis, David Hudd, Charles Levison.

*Associate Directors:* Andrew Ellis, Tony Ingham, Chris O'Donnell, Keith Westcott.

*Manager:* Ray Harford.

*Secretary:* Sheila Marson. *Sales and Marketing Executive:* Brian Rowe.

*Physio:* Brian Morris.

*Year Formed:* 1885 *(see Foundation).* *Turned Professional:* 1898. *Ltd Co.:* 1899.

*Club Nicknames:* 'Rangers' or 'Rs'. *Previous Name:* 1885–87, St Jude's.

*Previous Grounds:* 1885 *(see Foundation);* Welford's Fields; 1888–99; London Scottish Ground, Brondesbury, Home Farm, Kensal Rise Green, Gun Club Wormwood Scrubs, Kilburn Cricket Ground; 1899, Kensal Rise Athletic Ground; 1901, Latimer Road, Notting Hill; 1904, Agricultural Society, Park Royal; 1907, Park Royal Ground; 1917, Loftus Road; 1931, White City; 1933, Loftus Road; 1962, White City; 1963, Loftus Road.

*Foundation:* There is an element of doubt about the date of the foundation of this club, but it is believed that in either 1885 or 1886 it was formed through the amalgamation of Christchurch Rangers and St Jude's Institute FC. The leading light was George Wodehouse, whose family maintained a connection with the club until comparatively recent times. Most of the players came from the Queen's Park district so this name was adopted after a year as St Jude's Institute.

*First Football League game:* 28 August 1920, Division 3, v Watford (h) L 1-2 – Price; Blackman, Wingrove; McGovern, Grant, O'Brien; Faulkner, Birch (1), Smith, Gregory, Middlemiss.

*Record League Victory:* 9–2 v Tranmere R, Division 3, 3 December 1960 – Drinkwater; Woods, Ingham; Keen, Rutter, Angell; Lazarus (2), Bedford (2), Evans (2), Andrews (1), Clark (2).

*Record Cup Victory:* 8–1 v Bristol R (away), FA Cup 1st rd, 27 November 1937 – Gilfillan; Smith, Jefferson; Lowe, James, March; Cape, Mallett, Cheetham (3), Fitzgerald (3) Bott (2). 8–1 v Crewe Alex, Milk Cup 1st rd, 3 October 1983 – Hucker; Neill, Dawes, Waddock (1), McDonald (1), Fenwick, Micklewhite (1), Stewart (1), Allen (1), Stainrod (3), Gregory.

*Record Defeat:* 1–8 v Mansfield T, Division 3, 15 March 1965 and v Manchester U, Division 1, 19 March 1969.

*Most League Points (2 for a win):* 67, Division 3, 1966–67.

*Most League Points (3 for a win):* 85, Division 2, 1982–83.

*Most League Goals:* 111, Division 3, 1961–62.

*Highest League Scorer in Season:* George Goddard, 37, Division 3 (S), 1929–30.

*Most League Goals in Total Aggregate:* George Goddard, 172, 1926–34.

*Most Capped Player:* Alan McDonald, 52, Northern Ireland.

*Most League Appearances:* Tony Ingham, 519, 1950–63.

*Record Transfer Fee Received:* £6,000,000 from Newcastle U for Les Ferdinand, June 1995.

*Record Transfer Fee Paid:* £2,350,000 to Chelsea for John Spencer, November 1996.

*Football League Record:* 1920 Original Members of Division 3; 1921–48 Division 3 (S); 1948–52 Division 2; 1952–58 Division 3 (S); 1958–67 Division 3; 1967–68 Division 2; 1968–69 Division 1; 1969–73 Division 2; 1973–79 Division 1; 1979–83 Division 2; 1983–92 Division 1; 1992–96 FA Premier League; 1996– Division 1.

*Honours: Football League:* Division 1 – Runners-up 1975–76; Division 2 – Champions 1982–83; Runners-up 1967–68, 1972–73; Division 3 (S) – Champions 1947–48; Runners-up 1946–47; Division 3 – Champions 1966–67. *FA Cup:* Runners-up 1982. *Football League Cup:* Winners 1967; Runners-up 1986. (In 1966–67 won Division 3 and Football League Cup). **European Competitions:** *UEFA Cup:* 1976–77, 1984–85.

*Colours:* Blue and white hooped shirts, white shorts, white stockings. *Change colours:* All red with black trim.

**Did you know?**
Stan Bowles scored in five consecutive UEFA Cup matches in 1976-77 including two hat-tricks. His total in that competition was 11.

## QUEENS PARK RANGERS 1997–98 LEAGUE RECORD

| Match No. | Date | Venue | Opponents | Result | H/T Score | Lg. Pos. | Goalscorers | Attendance |
|---|---|---|---|---|---|---|---|---|
| 1 | Aug 9 | H | Ipswich T | D | 0-0 | 0-0 | — | 17,614 |
| 2 | 15 | A | Tranmere R | L | 1-2 | 0-1 | — | Peacock 90 | 7467 |
| 3 | 23 | H | Stockport Co | W | 2-1 | 1-1 | 10 | Sinclair 2 23, 66 | 11,108 |
| 4 | 30 | A | Nottingham F | L | 0-4 | 0-1 | 12 | | 18,804 |
| 5 | Sept 2 | A | Reading | W | 2-1 | 0-1 | — | Spencer 71, Swailes (og) 72 | 10,203 |
| 6 | 13 | H | WBA | W | 2-0 | 1-0 | 10 | Sheron 15, Peacock 75 | 14,399 |
| 7 | 20 | A | Crewe Alex | W | 3-2 | 2-0 | 9 | Spencer 4, Maddix 8, Sinclair 47 | 5348 |
| 8 | 24 | H | Portsmouth | W | 1-0 | 1-0 | — | Spencer 44 | 12,620 |
| 9 | 27 | A | Port Vale | L | 0-2 | 0-2 | 3 | | 7197 |
| 10 | Oct 4 | H | Charlton Ath | L | 2-4 | 1-2 | 7 | Sheron 2 24, 80 | 14,825 |
| 11 | 18 | A | Sheffield U | D | 2-2 | 0-1 | 8 | Murray 58, Morrow 90 | 18,006 |
| 12 | 21 | A | Bury | D | 1-1 | 0-0 | — | Spencer 82 | 4602 |
| 13 | 26 | H | Manchester C | W | 2-0 | 2-0 | 8 | Ready 13, Peacock (pen) 33 | 14,451 |
| 14 | Nov 1 | H | Birmingham C | D | 1-1 | 1-1 | 8 | Barker 36 | 12,715 |
| 15 | 5 | A | Swindon T | L | 1-3 | 1-0 | — | Peacock 14 | 10,132 |
| 16 | 8 | A | Middlesbrough | L | 0-3 | 0-2 | 13 | | 30,067 |
| 17 | 15 | H | Stoke C | D | 1-1 | 0-1 | 13 | Barker (pen) 61 | 11,923 |
| 18 | 22 | H | Huddersfield T | W | 2-1 | 1-0 | 10 | Quashie 2 25, 79 | 16,066 |
| 19 | 29 | A | Wolverhampton W | L | 2-3 | 0-1 | 12 | Sheron 61, Peacock 85 | 23,645 |
| 20 | Dec 3 | H | Norwich C | D | 1-1 | 0-0 | — | Peacock 71 | 10,141 |
| 21 | 6 | H | Sunderland | L | 0-1 | 0-0 | 12 | | 15,266 |
| 22 | 12 | A | Oxford U | L | 1-3 | 1-2 | — | Peacock 19 | 6664 |
| 23 | 21 | H | Bradford C | W | 1-0 | 1-0 | 12 | Peacock (pen) 27 | 8853 |
| 24 | 26 | A | Portsmouth | L | 1-3 | 1-1 | 12 | Sheron 31 | 12,314 |
| 25 | 28 | H | Reading | D | 1-1 | 1-0 | 12 | Spencer 15 | 13,015 |
| 26 | Jan 10 | A | Ipswich T | D | 0-0 | 0-0 | 13 | | 12,672 |
| 27 | 17 | H | Tranmere R | D | 0-0 | 0-0 | 13 | | 12,033 |
| 28 | 24 | H | Nottingham F | L | 0-1 | 0-0 | 14 | | 13,220 |
| 29 | 31 | A | Stockport Co | L | 0-2 | 0-1 | 17 | | 7958 |
| 30 | Feb 7 | H | Crewe Alex | W | 3-2 | 1-0 | 15 | Kennedy 2 43, 59, Ready 78 | 13,429 |
| 31 | 14 | A | WBA | D | 1-1 | 1-0 | 15 | Dowie 26 | 19,143 |
| 32 | 17 | A | Charlton Ath | D | 1-1 | 1-1 | — | Peacock (pen) 22 | 15,555 |
| 33 | 21 | H | Port Vale | L | 0-1 | 0-1 | 15 | | 14,198 |
| 34 | 25 | H | Sheffield U | D | 2-2 | 1-1 | — | Sheron 4, Ready 53 | 9560 |
| 35 | 28 | A | Norwich C | D | 0-0 | 0-0 | 16 | | 12,730 |
| 36 | Mar 4 | H | Middlesbrough | W | 5-0 | 4-0 | — | Vickers (og) 32, Bruce 37, Gallen 38, Sheron 2 45, 53 | 11,580 |
| 37 | 7 | A | Birmingham C | L | 0-1 | 0-1 | 16 | | 18,298 |
| 38 | 14 | H | Swindon T | L | 1-2 | 1-2 | 16 | Quashie 8 | 13,486 |
| 39 | 21 | A | Stoke C | L | 1-2 | 0-1 | 18 | Barker (pen) 90 | 11,051 |
| 40 | 28 | A | Huddersfield T | D | 1-1 | 0-0 | 19 | Jones 55 | 13,681 |
| 41 | Apr 1 | H | Wolverhampton W | D | 0-0 | 0-0 | — | | 12,337 |
| 42 | 10 | A | Sunderland | D | 2-2 | 0-1 | — | Sheron 2 75, 83 | 40,014 |
| 43 | 14 | H | Oxford U | D | 1-1 | 0-1 | — | Gallen 80 | 12,859 |
| 44 | 19 | A | Bradford C | D | 1-1 | 0-1 | 19 | Gallen 48 | 14,871 |
| 45 | 25 | A | Manchester C | D | 2-2 | 2-1 | 18 | Sheron 8, Pollock (og) 21 | 32,040 |
| 46 | May 3 | H | Bury | L | 0-1 | 0-1 | 21 | | 15,210 |

**Final League Position: 21**     1996–97 DIV1 9

### GOALSCORERS

*League (51):* Sheron 11, Peacock 9 (3 pens), Spencer 5, Barker 3 (2 pens), Gallen 3, Quashie 3, Ready 3, Sinclair 3, Kennedy 2, Bruce 1, Dowie 1, Jones 1, Maddix 1, Morrow 1, Murray 1, own goals 3.
*Coca-Cola Cup (2):* Murray 1, Peacock 1.
*FA Cup (2):* Gallen 1, Spencer 1.

| Harper L 36 | Rose M 13+3 | Brevett R 20+3 | Barker S 20+3 | Maddix D 23+2 | Morrow S 31 | Spencer J 22+1 | Peacock G 38+1 | Brazier M 8+3 | Gallen K 19+8 | Murray P 31+1 | Perry M 6+2 | Sinclair T 24+2 | Slade S 3+19 | Yates S 21+9 | Quashie N 30+3 | Sheron M 36+4 | Ready K 38+1 | Roberts T 10 | Mahoney-Johnson M —+1 | Kulcsar G 11+1 | Bruce P 1+4 | Heinola A —+10 | Rowland K 7 | Dowie I 9+2 | Kennedy M 8 | Bardsley D 12 | Baraclough 18 | Scully T 7 | Jones V 7 | Ruddock N 7 | Match No. |
|---|---|---|---|---|---|---|---|---|---|---|---|---|---|---|---|---|---|---|---|---|---|---|---|---|---|---|---|---|---|---|---|
| 1 | 2 | 3 | 4 | $5^1$ | 6 | 7 | 8 | $9^2$ | $10^3$ | 11 | 12 | 13 | 14 | | | | | | | | | | | | | | | | | | 1 |
| 1 | 5 | 3 | 4 | | 6 | 7 | 8 | 13 | $10^1$ | 9 | 2 | $11^2$ | 12 | | | | | | | | | | | | | | | | | | 2 |
| 1 | 2 | 3 | 4 | 5 | 6 | $7^2$ | 8 | $9^1$ | $10^2$ | 11 | 12 | 13 | 14 | | | | | | | | | | | | | | | | | | 3 |
| 1 | 2 | 3 | $4^3$ | 5 | 6 | 12 | 8 | 13 | 9 | 7 | $11^1$ | $10^2$ | 14 | | | | | | | | | | | | | | | | | | 4 |
| 1 | 2 | 3 | | 5 | 6 | 7 | 8 | | 9 | | | 11 | | | 4 | 10 | | | | | | | | | | | | | | | 5 |
| 1 | $2^1$ | 3 | | 5 | 6 | 7 | 8 | | 9 | | | 11 | | | 4 | 10 | 12 | | | | | | | | | | | | | | 6 |
| 1 | | 3 | | 5 | 6 | 7 | 8 | | 9 | | | 11 | 12 | | 4 | $10^1$ | 2 | | | | | | | | | | | | | | 7 |
| 1 | 12 | 3 | | 5 | $6^1$ | 7 | 8 | | 9 | | | 11 | | | 4 | 10 | 2 | | | | | | | | | | | | | | 8 |
| 1 | 2 | 3 | 12 | 5 | | 7 | 8 | | $9^1$ | | | 11 | 13 | | $4^2$ | 10 | 6 | | | | | | | | | | | | | | 9 |
| 1 | 2 | 3 | 12 | 5 | 6 | $7^2$ | 8 | | 9 | | | 11 | 13 | | $4^1$ | 10 | | | | | | | | | | | | | | | 10 |
| 1 | $2^1$ | 3 | $11^3$ | 5 | 6 | 7 | 8 | | 9 | 12 | | 13 | 14 | | 4 | $10^2$ | | | | | | | | | | | | | | | 11 |
| 1 | | 3 | 2 | 5 | 6 | 7 | 8 | | 9 | | | 11 | | | 4 | 10 | | | | | | | | | | | | | | | 12 |
| 1 | $2^3$ | 3 | 12 | 5 | 6 | 7 | 8 | | $9^1$ | | | 11 | 13 | 14 | 4 | $10^2$ | | | | | | | | | | | | | | | 13 |
| 1 | 2 | 3 | 9 | 5 | 6 | $7^1$ | 8 | 12 | | 11 | | 13 | | | $4^2$ | 10 | | | | | | | | | | | | | | | 14 |
| 1 | 2 | $7^3$ | | 5 | 6 | 8 | 3 | | $9^1$ | | | 11 | | $12^2$ | 4 | 10 | 13 | 14 | | | | | | | | | | | | | 15 |
| 1 | 2 | $7^1$ | | 5 | 6 | 8 | 3 | | 9 | | | 11 | 12 | | 4 | 10 | | | | | | | | | | | | | | | 16 |
| | | | 4 | | | 7 | 8 | 3 | $9^1$ | | 2 | 11 | | 6 | 12 | 10 | 5 | 1 | | | | | | | | | | | | | 17 |
| | 12 | | 4 | | | | 8 | $3^1$ | 9 | | 2 | 11 | | 6 | 7 | 10 | 5 | 1 | | | | | | | | | | | | | 18 |
| | 12 | | 4 | | 6 | | 8 | 3 | 9 | | | 11 | | $2^1$ | 7 | 10 | 5 | 1 | | | | | | | | | | | | | 19 |
| | 12 | | $4^1$ | | 6 | | 8 | 3 | 9 | | 2 | 11 | | | 7 | 10 | 5 | 1 | | | | | | | | | | | | | 20 |
| | | | 4 | | | 7 | 8 | 3 | 9 | | $2^1$ | 11 | | 6 | $10^2$ | | 5 | 1 | | | | 13 | | | | | | | | | 21 |
| | $3^1$ | | | | | 7 | 8 | 13 | 9 | | $2^2$ | 11 | | 6 | 10 | | 5 | 1 | | $4^2$ | | | | | | | | | | | 22 |
| | | | | | | 7 | 8 | 12 | 9 | | 2 | 11 | | 6 | $10^1$ | | 5 | 1 | | $4^2$ | | 13 | | | | | | | | | 23 |
| | | | | | 6 | $7^1$ | 8 | 3 | 9 | | 2 | 11 | | | 10 | | 5 | 1 | | 4 | | 12 | | | | | | | | | 24 |
| | | | | | 6 | 7 | 8 | | 9 | | 2 | 11 | | | 10 | | 5 | 1 | | 4 | | | | | | | | | | | 25 |
| | | | | | 6 | $7^1$ | 8 | | 9 | | 2 | 11 | | | 10 | | 5 | 1 | | 4 | | 12 | | | | | | | | | 26 |
| 1 | | 3 | | | 6 | $11^2$ | 8 | | 9 | | 7 | 12 | | 2 | $10^1$ | | 5 | | | 4 | | 13 | | | | | | | | | 27 |
| 1 | | 3 | | | 6 | $11^1$ | 8 | | $10^2$ | | 7 | 12 | | 2 | 9 | | 5 | | | 4 | | 13 | | | | | | | | | 28 |
| 1 | | | | | 6 | 7 | 8 | | $10^1$ | | 2 | | | 12 | 4 | | 5 | | | | | | 3 | | | | 9 | 11 | | | 29 |
| 1 | | | | | 6 | | 8 | | $10^1$ | $7^2$ | 2 | | | 12 | 4 | | 5 | | | | | | 3 | | | | 9 | 11 | | | 30 |
| 1 | | | | | 6 | | 8 | | $10^1$ | 7 | 2 | | | 12 | | | 5 | | | 4 | | | 3 | | | | 9 | 11 | | | 31 |
| 1 | $4^2$ | | | | 6 | | 8 | 12 | | 7 | 2 | | | | $10^1$ | | 5 | | | | | 13 | 3 | | | | 9 | 11 | | | 32 |
| 1 | $4^1$ | | | | 6 | | 8 | $10^2$ | | 7 | 14 | | | $2^1$ | 12 | | 5 | | | | | 13 | 3 | | | | 9 | 11 | | | 33 |
| 1 | | | | | $6^2$ | | 8 | 12 | | 7 | | 13 | | | 10 | | 5 | | | 4 | | | 3 | | 2 | | $9^1$ | 11 | | | 34 |
| 1 | | | | | 6 | | 8 | | | $7^2$ | | 12 | | | 10 | | 5 | | | 4 | | 13 | 3 | | 2 | | $9^1$ | 11 | | | 35 |
| 1 | | 3 | | | | | $8^3$ | $10^1$ | $7^2$ | | 12 | | 6 | | 9 | | 5 | | | 4 | | $13^1$ | | | | 2 | | 11 | | | 36 |
| 1 | 12 | $3^3$ | | | | | | 10 | | | 13 | | $6^1$ | 7 | 9 | | 5 | | | 4 | | $11^2$ | | | | 2 | | 14 | | | 37 |
| 1 | | 6 | | | | | $8^1$ | 9 | | | 13 | | 3 | 7 | 10 | | 5 | | | 4 | | $12^2$ | | | | 2 | | 14 | 11 | | 38 |
| 1 | | 8 | 6 | | | | 3 | 12 | | | 13 | | $2^4$ | | 10 | | 5 | | | $4^2$ | | 14 | | | | $9^1$ | | 7 | 11 | | 39 |
| 1 | 7 | | | | | | 8 | $10^1$ | | 9 | | | | | | | 5 | | | 12 | | | | | | 2 | 3 | 11 | 4 | 6 | 40 |
| 1 | | $3^1$ | | | | | 8 | $10^1$ | | 9 | | | | | | | 5 | | | 12 | | | 7 | | 2 | | 11 | 4 | 6 | | 41 |
| 1 | 12 | | | | | | 8 | $10^1$ | 13 | | | | | | | | 5 | | | 7 | | | | | | 2 | 3 | 11 | $4^2$ | 6 | 42 |
| 1 | | | | | | | $8^2$ | 10 | 12 | | | | | | | | 5 | | | $7^1$ | | 13 | | | | 2 | 3 | 11 | 4 | 6 | 43 |
| 1 | | | | | | | 8 | 10 | 12 | | | | | | | | 5 | | | $7^1$ | | | | | | 2 | 3 | 11 | 4 | 6 | 44 |
| 1 | 12 | | | 5 | | | 8 | $9^1$ | | | | 13 | | | $11^2$ | 7 | | | | | | 14 | | | | 2 | 3 | | 4 | $6^8$ | 45 |
| 1 | | | | | | | 8 | 9 | | | | 13 | | | $11^2$ | 7 | 5 | | | | | 12 | | | | 2 | 3 | 11 | $4^2$ | $6^1$ | 46 |

**Coca-Cola Cup**
First Round — Wolverhampton W — (h) 0-2 / (a) 2-1

**FA Cup**
Third Round — Middlesbrough — (h) 2-2 / (a) 0-2

READING 1997–98    *Back row (left to right):* Ron Grant (Kit Manager), Steve Swales, Andy Bernal, Phil Parkinson, Michael Thorp, Barry Hunter, Lee Hodges, Trevor Morley, Dariusz Wdowczyk, Alan Pardew (Reserve Team Coach).

*Middle row:* Paul Turner (Physio), Keith McPherson, Carl Asaba, Stuart Lovell, Sal Bibbo, Steve Mautone, Nicky Hammond, Michael Meaker, Linvoy Primus, Darren Caskey, Kevin Dillon (Youth Development).

*Front row:* Allan Harris (Assistant Manager), Ray Houghton, Martyn Booty, Byron Glasgow, Ben Smith, Terry Bullivant (Manager), Neville Roach, Andy Freeman, James Lambert, Martin Williams, Steve Kean (Youth Team Coach).

# Division 2       **READING**

*Elm Park, Norfolk Road, Reading RG30 2EF.* Telephone: (01189) 507878. Fax: (01189) 566628. Community Office: (01189) 560898. Promotions Office: (01189) 464008. *Moving to Madejski Stadium, Junction 11, M4, Reading, Berks RG2 0FL (August 22).* Telephone: (0118) 9681100. Ticket Office: (0118) 9681000. Fax: (0118) 9681101. Ticket Office Fax: (0118) 9681001.

*Ground capacity:* 15,000.

*Record attendance:* 33,042 v Brentford, FA Cup 5th rd, 19 February 1927.

*Record receipts:* £110,741 v Manchester U, FA Cup 4th rd, 27 January 1996.

*Pitch measurements:* 112yd × 77yd.

*President:* F. Orton.

*Chairman:* John Madejski.

*Director:* I. Wood-Smith.

*Manager:* Tommy Burns.

*Chief Executive:* Nigel Howe.

*Physio:* Paul Turner.

*Commercial Manager:* Kevin Girdler.

*Secretary:* Ms Andrea Barker.

*Year Formed:* 1871. *Turned Professional:* 1895. *Ltd Co.:* 1895.

*Club Nickname:* 'The Royals'.

*Previous Grounds:* 1871, Reading Recreation; Reading Cricket Ground; 1882, Coley Park; 1889, Caversham Cricket Ground; 1896, Elm Park.

*Foundation:* Reading was formed as far back as 1871 at a public meeting held at the Bridge Street Rooms. They first entered the FA Cup as early as 1877 when they amalgamated with the Reading Hornets. The club was further strengthened in 1889 when Earley FC joined them. They were the first winners of the Berks and Bucks Cup in 1878–79.

*First Football League game:* 28 August 1920, Division 3, v Newport Co (a) W 1-0 – Crawford; Smith, Horler; Christie, Mavin, Getgood; Spence, Weston, Yarnell, Bailey (1), Andrews.

*Record League Victory:* 10–2 v Crystal Palace, Division 3 (S), 4 September 1946 – Groves; Glidden, Gulliver; McKenna, Ratcliffe, Young; Chitty, Maurice Edelston (3), McPhee (4), Barney (1), Deverell (2).

*Record Cup Victory:* 6–0 v Leyton, FA Cup 2nd rd, 12 December 1925 – Duckworth; Eggo, McConnell; Wilson, Messer, Evans; Smith (2), Braithwaite (1), Davey (1), Tinsley, Robson (2).

*Record Defeat:* 0–18 v Preston NE, FA Cup 1st rd, 1893–94.

*Most League Points (2 for a win):* 65, Division 4, 1978–79.

*Most League Points (3 for a win):* 94, Division 3, 1985–86.

*Most League Goals:* 112, Division 3 (S), 1951–52.

*Highest League Scorer in Season:* Ronnie Blackman, 39, Division 3 (S), 1951–52.

*Most League Goals in Total Aggregate:* Ronnie Blackman, 158, 1947–54.

*Most Capped Player:* Jimmy Quinn, 17 (46), Northern Ireland.

*Most League Appearances:* Martin Hicks, 500, 1978–91.

*Record Transfer Fee Received:* £1,575,000 from Newcastle U for Shaka Hislop, August 1995.

*Record Transfer Fee Paid:* £800,000 to Brentford for Carl Asaba, August 1997.

*Football League Record:* 1920 Original Member of Division 3; 1921–26 Division 3 (S); 1926–31 Division 2; 1931–58 Division 3 (S); 1958–71 Division 3; 1971–76 Division 4; 1976–77 Division 3; 1977–79 Division 4; 1979–83 Division 3; 1983–84 Division 4; 1984–86 Division 3; 1986–88 Division 2; 1988–92 Division 3; 1992–94 Division 2; 1994–98 Division 1; 1998– Division 2.

*Honours: Football League:* Division 1 – Runners-up 1994–95; Division 2 – Champions 1993–94; Division 3 – Champions 1985–86. Division 3 (S) – Champions 1925–26; Runners-up 1931–32, 1934–35, 1948–49, 1951–52; Division 4 – Champions 1978–79. *FA Cup:* Semi-final 1927. *Football League Cup:* best season: 5th rd. 1996. *Simod Cup:* Winners 1988.

*Colours:* Royal blue and white hooped shirts, white shorts, white and blue hooped stockings.

*Change colours:* Toro red and white shirts, Toro red shorts, Toro red/white stockings.

**Did you know?**
Reading reached the last 16 of the FA Cup for the first time in 63 years against Cardiff City on 3 February 1998. After a 1-1 draw, goalkeeper Nicky Hammond saved three penalties in the resulting shoot-out, as Reading won 4-1 on penalties.

## READING 1997–98 LEAGUE RECORD

| Match No. | Date | Venue | Opponents | Result | H/T Score | Lg. Pos. | Goalscorers | Attendance |
|---|---|---|---|---|---|---|---|---|
| 1 | Aug 9 | A | Bury | D | 1-1 | 1-0 | — | Swales [13] | 5065 |
| 2 | 16 | H | Swindon T | L | 0-1 | 0-1 | 17 | | 9338 |
| 3 | 23 | A | Birmingham C | L | 0-3 | 0-1 | 23 | | 16,495 |
| 4 | 30 | H | Bradford C | L | 0-3 | 0-2 | 24 | | 7163 |
| 5 | Sept 2 | H | QPR | L | 1-2 | 1-0 | — | Hodges [10] | 10,203 |
| 6 | 7 | A | WBA | L | 0-1 | 0-0 | 24 | | 15,966 |
| 7 | 13 | H | Oxford U | W | 2-1 | 1-1 | 22 | Asaba [21], Hodges [61] | 9003 |
| 8 | 20 | A | Tranmere R | L | 0-6 | 0-5 | 23 | | 5565 |
| 9 | 27 | A | Portsmouth | W | 2-0 | 1-0 | 22 | Hodges [15], Williams [88] | 9593 |
| 10 | Oct 4 | H | Sunderland | W | 4-0 | 2-0 | 20 | Asaba 2 [16, 26], Williams [60], Lambert [64] | 10,795 |
| 11 | 11 | H | Crewe Alex | D | 3-3 | 2-3 | 17 | Asaba 2 [35, 60], Westwood (og) [43] | 6685 |
| 12 | 18 | A | Manchester C | D | 0-0 | 0-0 | 19 | | 26,488 |
| 13 | 21 | A | Norwich C | D | 0-0 | 0-0 | — | | 17,781 |
| 14 | 24 | H | Nottingham F | D | 3-3 | 0-1 | — | Williams (pen) [57], Lambert [73], Primus [78] | 12,610 |
| 15 | Nov 1 | A | Port Vale | D | 0-0 | 0-0 | 19 | | 6569 |
| 16 | 4 | H | Sheffield U | L | 0-1 | 0-0 | — | | 8132 |
| 17 | 8 | H | Stockport Co | W | 1-0 | 1-0 | 18 | Morley (pen) [42] | 7444 |
| 18 | 15 | A | Huddersfield T | L | 0-1 | 0-0 | 19 | | 12,617 |
| 19 | 22 | H | Ipswich T | L | 0-4 | 0-2 | 21 | | 9400 |
| 20 | 29 | A | Stoke C | W | 2-1 | 1-0 | 18 | Morley 2 (1 pen) [32 (p), 59] | 11,103 |
| 21 | Dec 6 | A | Charlton Ath | W | 2-0 | 2-0 | 16 | Hodges [9], Morley (pen) [36] | 8076 |
| 22 | 13 | A | Middlesbrough | L | 0-4 | 0-0 | 17 | | 29,876 |
| 23 | 20 | H | Wolverhampton W | D | 0-0 | 0-0 | 18 | | 11,715 |
| 24 | 26 | H | WBA | W | 2-1 | 2-0 | 15 | McDermott (og) [1], Williams [27] | 10,154 |
| 25 | 28 | A | QPR | D | 1-1 | 0-1 | 16 | Morley [64] | 13,015 |
| 26 | Jan 10 | H | Bury | D | 1-1 | 1-0 | 15 | Lucketti (og) [29] | 7499 |
| 27 | 17 | A | Swindon T | W | 2-0 | 2-0 | 14 | Lovell [9], Lambert [14] | 9500 |
| 28 | 27 | A | Bradford C | L | 1-4 | 1-2 | — | Asaba [2] | 13,021 |
| 29 | 31 | H | Birmingham C | W | 2-0 | 0-0 | 15 | Hodges [74], Asaba [83] | 10,315 |
| 30 | Feb 7 | H | Tranmere R | L | 1-3 | 0-1 | 16 | Williams [75] | 7069 |
| 31 | 17 | A | Sunderland | L | 1-4 | 0-2 | — | Bowen [53] | 40,579 |
| 32 | 21 | H | Portsmouth | L | 0-1 | 0-0 | 19 | | 9928 |
| 33 | 24 | H | Manchester C | W | 3-0 | 2-0 | — | Hodges [8], Houghton [29], Asaba [89] | 11,513 |
| 34 | 28 | A | Crewe Alex | L | 0-1 | 0-1 | 17 | | 5202 |
| 35 | Mar 3 | A | Stockport Co | L | 1-5 | 0-4 | — | Williams (pen) [80] | 6148 |
| 36 | 7 | H | Port Vale | L | 0-3 | 0-2 | 22 | | 7139 |
| 37 | 14 | A | Sheffield U | L | 0-4 | 0-1 | 23 | | 15,473 |
| 38 | 17 | A | Oxford U | L | 0-3 | 0-1 | — | | 8103 |
| 39 | 21 | H | Huddersfield T | L | 0-2 | 0-0 | 24 | | 8593 |
| 40 | 28 | A | Ipswich T | L | 0-1 | 0-1 | 24 | | 19,075 |
| 41 | Apr 4 | H | Stoke C | W | 2-0 | 1-0 | 23 | O'Neill [32], Meaker [48] | 10,448 |
| 42 | 10 | A | Charlton Ath | L | 0-3 | 0-2 | — | | 14,220 |
| 43 | 13 | H | Middlesbrough | L | 0-1 | 0-1 | 24 | | 14,501 |
| 44 | 18 | A | Wolverhampton W | L | 1-3 | 1-1 | 24 | Brayson [44] | 19,785 |
| 45 | 26 | A | Nottingham F | L | 0-1 | 0-0 | 24 | | 29,302 |
| 46 | May 3 | H | Norwich C | L | 0-1 | 0-0 | 24 | | 14,817 |

**Final League Position: 24**          1996–97 DIV1 18

### GOALSCORERS

*League (39):* Asaba 8, Hodges 6, Williams 6 (2 pens), Morley 5 (3 pens), Lambert 3, Bowen 1, Brayson 1, Houghton 1, Lovell 1, Meaker 1, O'Neill 1, Primus 1, Swales 1, own goals 3.
*Coca-Cola Cup (12):* Asaba 3, Williams 2, Lambert 1, McPherson 1, Meaker 1, Morley 1, Parkinson 1, Roach 1, own goal 1.
*FA Cup (5):* Morley 3, Asaba 1, Booty 1.

| Mautone S 14 | Booty M 24+1 | Swales S 26+5 | Widowczyk D 3+3 | McPherson K 24 | Primus L 36 | Bernal A 34 | Houghton R 20+5 | Asaba C 31+1 | Hodges L 20+4 | Lambert J 33+1 | Roach N —+8 | Holsgrove P 1+1 | Meaker M 16+5 | Glasgow B 1+2 | Bodin P 3+1 | Robins M 5 | Parkinson P 36+1 | Williams M 25+4 | Sandford L 5 | Caskey D 19+4 | Hammond N 18 | Morley T 17+6 | Thorp M —+3 | Lovell S 8+7 | Davies G 17+1 | Bowen J 11+3 | Bibbo S 2 | Legg A 10 | Colgan N 5 | O'Neill M 9 | Howie S 7 | Kelly P 3 | Fleck R 3+2 | Gray S 7 | McIntyre J 6 | Crawford J 5+1 | Brayson P 2+4 | Match No. |
|---|---|---|---|---|---|---|---|---|---|---|---|---|---|---|---|---|---|---|---|---|---|---|---|---|---|---|---|---|---|---|---|---|---|---|---|---|---|---|
| 1 | 2 | 3 | 4 | 5 | 6 | 7 | 8 | 9 | $10^1$ | $11^2$ | 12 | 13 | | | | | | | | | | | | | | | | | | | | | | | | | | 1 |
| 1 | $2^2$ | 3 | 4 | 5 | 6 | 7 | | 9 | $10^1$ | 11 | 12 | | $8^3$ | 13 | 14 | | | | | | | | | | | | | | | | | | | | | | | 2 |
| 1 | 2 | $3^2$ | $4^1$ | 5 | 6 | 7 | 8 | 9 | 10 | 11 | 12 | | | | 13 | | | | | | | | | | | | | | | | | | | | | | | 3 |
| 1 | $2^1$ | | | 5 | 6 | 7 | 8 | 9 | $10^2$ | 11 | | | | | 3 | | 4 | 12 | 13 | | | | | | | | | | | | | | | | | | | 4 |
| 1 | 2 | 3 | | 5 | 6 | 7 | 8 | $9^1$ | 10 | 11 | 12 | | | | | | 4 | | | | | | | | | | | | | | | | | | | | | 5 |
| 1 | 2 | | | 5 | 6 | | 8 | $9^1$ | 10 | $11^2$ | 12 | | | | 3 | | 4 | 7 | | | | | | | | | | | | | | | | | | | | 6 |
| 1 | 13 | | | 5 | 6 | 2 | 8 | $9^1$ | 10 | $11^2$ | 12 | | | | 3 | | 4 | 7 | | | | | | | | | | | | | | | | | | | | 7 |
| 1 | 2 | 12 | | 5 | 6 | 10 | 8 | 9 | | $11^1$ | 13 | | | | 3 | | $4^2$ | 7 | | | | | | | | | | | | | | | | | | | | 8 |
| 1 | 12 | | | 5 | 6 | 2 | 10 | 9 | $8^1$ | 11 | | | | | 3 | | 7 | 4 | | | | | | | | | | | | | | | | | | | | 9 |
| 1 | 12 | 13 | | 5 | 6 | $2^1$ | 10 | 9 | | 8 | | | | | $3^2$ | | 7 | 4 | | | | | | | | | | | | | | | | | | | | 10 |
| 1 | 3 | 12 | | 5 | $6^1$ | 2 | | 9 | $10^2$ | 8 | 13 | | | | | | 7 | 4 | | | | | | | | | | | | | | | | | | | | 11 |
| 1 | 3 | 12 | | 5 | $6^1$ | 2 | 10 | 9 | | 8 | | | | | | | 7 | 4 | | | | | | | | | | | | | | | | | | | | 12 |
| 1 | 3 | | | 5 | 6 | 2 | 10 | 9 | | 8 | 12 | | | | | | 7 | $4^1$ | | | | | | | | | | | | | | | | | | | | 13 |
| 1 | 3 | | | 5 | 6 | 2 | 10 | 9 | | 8 | | | | | | | 7 | 4 | | | | | | | | | | | | | | | | | | | | 14 |
| | 3 | | | 5 | 6 | 2 | | $8^1$ | | 10 | | | 11 | | | | 7 | 4 | | 9 | 1 | 12 | | | | | | | | | | | | | | | | 15 |
| | 3 | | | 5 | 6 | 2 | | 8 | | 11 | | | | | | | 7 | 4 | | 9 | 1 | 10 | | | | | | | | | | | | | | | | 16 |
| | 3 | | | 5 | 6 | 2 | 12 | 9 | | $8^1$ | | | 11 | | | | 7 | 13 | | 4 | 1 | $10^2$ | | | | | | | | | | | | | | | | 17 |
| | 3 | | | 5 | 6 | 2 | | 9 | 12 | $8^1$ | | | 11 | | | | 7 | 11 | | 4 | 1 | 10 | | | | | | | | | | | | | | | | 18 |
| 12 | 3 | | | 5 | 6 | $2^1$ | 8 | 9 | 13 | | | | | | | | 7 | 11 | | $4^2$ | 1 | 10 | | | | | | | | | | | | | | | | 19 |
| | 2 | 3 | | 5 | 6 | | 8 | $9^3$ | 12 | $4^1$ | | | | | | | 7 | $11^2$ | | 13 | 1 | 10 | 14 | | | | | | | | | | | | | | | 20 |
| | 2 | 3 | | 5 | 6 | | | 9 | $8^1$ | $4^2$ | | | | | | | 7 | 11 | | 12 | 1 | 10 | 13 | | | | | | | | | | | | | | | 21 |
| | 2 | 3 | | 5 | | | | 9 | 8 | $4^1$ | | | | | | | 7 | 11 | | 12 | 1 | 10 | | 6 | | | | | | | | | | | | | | 22 |
| | 2 | | | 5 | | | | 9 | $8^1$ | 4 | | | | | | | 7 | 11 | | 1 | | $10^2$ | 12 | 13 | 6 | | | | | | | | | | | | | 23 |
| | 2 | 3 | | 5 | | | | 9 | 8 | $4^2$ | | | | | | | 7 | 11 | | 1 | | 10 | | 12 | 6 | 13 | | | | | | | | | | | | 24 |
| | 2 | 3 | | 5 | | | | 9 | 8 | | | | | | | | 11 | | | 4 | 1 | 10 | | $7^1$ | 6 | 12 | | | | | | | | | | | | 25 |
| | 2 | 3 | | 5 | | | | 9 | 8 | 7 | | | | | | | | | | 4 | 1 | 10 | | | 6 | 11 | | | | | | | | | | | | 26 |
| | 2 | 3 | | 4 | 12 | | | $8^1$ | 11 | | | 13 | | | | | 6 | | | 1 | 9 | | | $10^2$ | 5 | 7 | | | | | | | | | | | | 27 |
| | 2 | 3 | | 4 | 12 | 10 | 8 | $11^1$ | | | | | | $5^2$ | | | 6 | | | 1 | 9 | 13 | | | | 7 | | | | | | | | | | | | 28 |
| | 2 | 3 | | 4 | 8 | 10 | 12 | | | | | | | | | | 6 | $11^1$ | | 1 | $9^2$ | | | 13 | 5 | 7 | | | | | | | | | | | | 29 |
| | 2 | 3 | | 4 | 8 | $10^2$ | $11^1$ | | | | | | | | | | 6 | 12 | | | 9 | | | 13 | 5 | 7 | 1 | | | | | | | | | | | 30 |
| | 2 | 3 | | 5 | 8 | 10 | 11 | | | | | | | | | | 6 | | | | 9 | | | | 4 | 7 | 1 | | | | | | | | | | | 31 |
| | 2 | | | 5 | 8 | 10 | | | | | | | | | | | 6 | $11^1$ | | 1 | 9 | 12 | | 4 | | 7 | | 3 | | | | | | | | | | 32 |
| | 2 | | | 5 | 8 | 10 | $11^1$ | | | | | | | | | | 6 | 9 | | 1 | | 12 | | 4 | | 7 | | 3 | | | | | | | | | | 33 |
| | 2 | | 6 | 5 | 8 | $10^1$ | | | | | | | | | | | 9 | | 11 | 12 | | | | | 4 | 7 | | 3 | 1 | | | | | | | | | 34 |
| | 2 | | 6 | 5 | 8 | 10 | | | | | | | | | | | 9 | 12 | | | | | | | $4^1$ | 7 | | 3 | 1 | 11 | | | | | | | | 35 |
| | $2^1$ | 12 | | 5 | 6 | 8 | $10^2$ | | | | | 13 | | | | | $9^2$ | | | 14 | | | | | 4 | 7 | | 3 | 1 | 11 | | | | | | | | 36 |
| | 2 | | | 5 | 6 | 12 | | 11 | | 8 | | | | | | | $7^1$ | | | 9 | | 4 | | | | | | 3 | 1 | 10 | | | | | | | | 37 |
| | 2 | | | 5 | 6 | 12 | | 11 | | 8 | | | | | | | 7 | | | 9 | | 4 | | | | | | 3 | 1 | $10^1$ | | | | | | | | 38 |
| | | | | 5 | 2 | $7^1$ | | | 11 | 12 | $7^2$ | | | | | | 8 | 10 | | 6 | 1 | | | 9 | | 4 | 13 | $3^1$ | | | | | | | | | | 39 |
| | | | | 5 | 2 | $7^1$ | | | | | | | | | | | 6 | | | 8 | | | | | | 3 | | | | 1 | 4 | 9 | 10 | $11^2$ | 12 | 13 | | 40 |
| | | | | 5 | 2 | | | 12 | | 11 | | | $7^1$ | | | | 4 | | | 8 | | | | | | | | | | 10 | 1 | | 13 | 3 | $9^2$ | 6 | | 41 |
| | | | | | 2 | | | 11 | | 12 | | | | | | | 5 | | | 8 | 13 | | | | | | | $3^1$ | | 10 | 1 | | $7^2$ | 6 | $9^3$ | 4 | 14 | 42 |
| | | | | $2^3$ | | | | 11 | | 12 | | | | | | | 3 | | | 8 | 13 | | 14 | | | | | | | $10^1$ | 1 | 5 | | 6 | $9^2$ | 4 | 7 | 43 |
| | | | | 5 | | | | 11 | | $7^1$ | | | | | | | 6 | | | 8 | 12 | 4 | | | | | | | | 1 | | | 3 | 10 | 2 | 9 | | 44 |
| | | | | 5 | 2 | | | 11 | | | | | | | | | 4 | | | 8 | | | | | | | | | | 6 | 1 | | $12^2$ | 3 | $9^1$ | $10^1$ | 13 | 45 |
| | | | | 5 | 2 | | | 12 | | $7^1$ | | | | | | | 4 | | | 8 | | 11 | | | | | | | | 10 | 1 | | $6^2$ | 9 | 3 | | 13 | 46 |

## Coca-Cola Cup

| | | | |
|---|---|---|---|
| First Round | Swansea C | (h) | 2-0 |
| | | (a) | 1-1 |
| Second Round | Peterborough U | (h) | 0-0 |
| | | (a) | 2-0 |
| Third Round | Wolverhampton W | (h) | 4-2 |
| Fourth Round | Leeds U | (a) | 3-2 |
| Fifth Round | Middlesbrough | (h) | 0-1 |

## FA Cup

| | | | |
|---|---|---|---|
| Third Round | Cheltenham T | (a) | 1-1 |
| | | (h) | 2-1 |
| Fourth Round | Cardiff C | (a) | 1-1 |
| | | (h) | 1-1 |
| Fifth Round | Sheffield U | (a) | 0-1 |

ROCHDALE 1997–98 *Back row (left to right):* Nick Irwin, Ian Bryson, Robbie Painter, Andy Farrell, Mark Stuart, Alex Russell, Glen Robson, Neil Taylor.
*Middle row:* Keith Hicks (Centre of Excellence Director), Jimmy Robson (Youth Team Coach), John Pender, Mark Leonard, Steven Bywater, Ian Gray, Keith Hill, Dave Bayliss, David Bywater
(Centre of Excellence), Joe Hinnigan (First Team Coach/Physio).
*Front row:* Andy Fensome, Andy Barlow, Mark Bailey, Graham Barrow (Manager), Andy Gouck, Steve Whitehall, Mark Carter.
(Photograph: Alpha Photography)

# Division 3     **ROCHDALE**

*Spotland, Sandy Lane, Rochdale OL11 5DS.* Telephone: (01706) 644648. Fax: (01706) 648466. Commercial: (01706) 647521.

*Ground capacity:* 9195.

*Record attendance:* 24,231 v Notts Co, FA Cup 2nd rd, 10 December 1949.

*Record receipts:* £46,000 v Burnley, Division 4, 5 May 1992.

*Pitch measurements:* 114yd × 76yd.

*President:* Mrs L. Stoney.

*Chairman:* D. F. Kilpatrick.

*Directors:* G. R. Brierley, C. Dunphy, J. Marsh, G. Morris, K. Clegg.

*Manager:* Graham Barrow.

*Secretary:* Mrs Karen Jagger. *Coach:* Jimmy Robson. *Lottery and Merchandising Managers:* F. Collins, R. Wild.

*Advertising & Sponsorship Manager:* L. Duckworth. *Stadium Manager:* Ronnie Cowgill.

*Physio:* J. Hinnigan.

*Year Formed:* 1907. *Turned Professional:* 1907. *Ltd Co.:* 1910.

*Club Nickname:* 'The Dale'. ·

*Foundation:* Considering the love of rugby in their area, it is not surprising that Rochdale had difficulty in establishing an Association Football club. The earlier Rochdale Town club formed in 1900 went out of existence in 1907 when the present club was immediately established and joined the Manchester League, before graduating to the Lancashire Combination in 1908.

*First Football League game:* 27 August 1921, Division 3 (N), v Accrington Stanley (h) W 6-3 – Crabtree; Nuttall, Sheehan; Hill, Farrer, Yarwood; Hoad, Sandiford, Dennison (2), Owens (3), Carney (1).

*Record League Victory:* 8–1 v Chesterfield, Division 3 (N), 18 December 1926 – Hill; Brown, Ward; Hillhouse, Parkes, Braidwood; Hughes, Bertram, Whitehurst (5), Schofield (2), Martin (1).

*Record Cup Victory:* 8–2 v Crook T, FA Cup 1st rd, 26 November 1927 – Moody; Hopkins, Ward; Braidwood, Parkes, Barker; Tompkinson, Clennell (3) Whitehurst (4), Hall, Martin (1).

*Record Defeat:* 1–9 v Tranmere R, Division 3 (N), 25 December 1931.

*Most League Points (2 for a win):* 62, Division 3 (N), 1923–24.

*Most League Points (3 for a win):* 67, Division 4, 1991–92.

*Most League Goals:* 105, Division 3 (N), 1926–27.

*Highest League Scorer in Season:* Albert Whitehurst, 44, Division 3 (N), 1926–27.

*Most League Goals in Total Aggregate:* Reg Jenkins, 119, 1964–73.

*Most Capped Player:* None.

*Most League Appearances:* Graham Smith, 317, 1966–74.

*Record Transfer Fee Received:* £300,000 from Wimbledon for Alan Reeves, September 1994.

*Record Transfer Fee Paid:* £80,000 to Scunthorpe U for Andy Flounders, August 1991.

*Football League Record:* 1921 Elected to Division 3 (N); 1958–59 Division 3; 1959–69 Division 4; 1969–74 Division 3; 1974–92 Division 4; 1992– Division 3.

*Football League:* Division 3 best season: 9th, 1969–70; Division 3 (N) – Runners-up 1923–24, 1926–27. *FA Cup:* best season: 5th rd, 1990. *Football League Cup:* Runners-up 1962 (record for 4th Division club).

*Colours:* Blue shirts with white trim, blue shorts, blue stockings with white hoop on turnover.
*Change colours:* Yellow shirts, black shorts, black stockings.

**Did you know?**
Jimmy Wynn scored 64 goals in only 86 League games for Rochdale between 1936 and 1938.

## ROCHDALE 1997–98 LEAGUE RECORD

| Match No. | Date | Venue | Opponents | Result | H/T Score | Lg. Pos. | Goalscorers | Attendance |
|---|---|---|---|---|---|---|---|---|
| 1 | Aug 9 | A | Notts Co | L | 1-2 | 0-1 | — | Painter [69] | 4173 |
| 2 | 16 | H | Mansfield T | W | 2-0 | 2-0 | 9 | Russell [11], Painter [22] | 2133 |
| 3 | 23 | A | Leyton Orient | L | 0-2 | 0-1 | 18 | | 3463 |
| 4 | 30 | H | Peterborough U | L | 1-2 | 1-1 | 20 | Painter [19] | 2104 |
| 5 | Sept 2 | H | Macclesfield T | W | 2-0 | 0-0 | — | Carter [47], Hill [73] | 2197 |
| 6 | 9 | A | Shrewsbury T | L | 0-1 | 0-0 | — | | 2410 |
| 7 | 13 | A | Cardiff C | L | 1-2 | 1-1 | 20 | Carter (pen) [10] | 4306 |
| 8 | 20 | H | Hull C | W | 2-1 | 1-1 | 19 | Hill [13], Stuart [78] | 2085 |
| 9 | 27 | A | Brighton & HA | L | 1-2 | 1-1 | 19 | Bayliss [33] | 1544 |
| 10 | Oct 4 | H | Scunthorpe U | W | 2-0 | 1-0 | 17 | Russell [4], Painter (pen) [58] | 2087 |
| 11 | 11 | H | Darlington | W | 5-0 | 2-0 | 9 | Painter 2 (1 pen) [4 (p), 71], Lancashire 2 [10, 89], Russell [86] | 2134 |
| 12 | 18 | A | Cambridge U | D | 1-1 | 0-1 | 11 | Gouck [64] | 2703 |
| 13 | 21 | A | Barnet | L | 1-3 | 0-1 | — | Leonard [60] | 1310 |
| 14 | 25 | H | Rotherham U | L | 0-1 | 0-1 | 18 | | 2267 |
| 15 | Nov 1 | A | Chester C | L | 0-4 | 0-1 | 19 | | 2431 |
| 16 | 4 | H | Lincoln C | D | 0-0 | 0-0 | — | | 1537 |
| 17 | 8 | H | Colchester U | W | 2-1 | 1-0 | 17 | Stuart [44], Painter (pen) [63] | 1702 |
| 18 | 18 | A | Hartlepool U | L | 0-2 | 0-1 | — | | 1666 |
| 19 | 22 | A | Doncaster R | W | 3-0 | 1-0 | 18 | Stuart 2 [42, 56], Lancashire [69] | 1503 |
| 20 | 29 | H | Torquay U | L | 0-1 | 0-0 | 19 | | 1729 |
| 21 | Dec 6 | A | Scarborough | L | 0-1 | 0-1 | 19 | | 1705 |
| 22 | 13 | H | Swansea C | W | 3-0 | 2-0 | 18 | Painter 2 [26, 37], Leonard [62] | 1482 |
| 23 | 20 | A | Exeter C | L | 0-3 | 0-3 | 19 | | 33378 |
| 24 | 26 | H | Shrewsbury T | W | 3-1 | 1-1 | 16 | Lancashire [40], Painter [71], Bryson [90] | 2247 |
| 25 | 28 | A | Macclesfield T | L | 0-1 | 0-0 | 17 | | 2666 |
| 26 | Jan 3 | A | Mansfield T | L | 0-3 | 0-0 | 18 | | 2303 |
| 27 | 10 | H | Notts Co | L | 1-2 | 0-0 | 20 | Farrell [81] | 2387 |
| 28 | 17 | A | Peterborough U | L | 1-3 | 1-2 | 20 | Farrell [30] | 5676 |
| 29 | 24 | H | Leyton Orient | L | 0-2 | 0-0 | 20 | | 1774 |
| 30 | 31 | H | Cardiff C | D | 0-0 | 0-0 | 21 | | 1445 |
| 31 | Feb 7 | H | Hull C | W | 2-0 | 1-0 | 21 | Russell [4], Stuart [64] | 4031 |
| 32 | 14 | A | Scunthorpe U | L | 0-2 | 0-1 | 21 | | 2284 |
| 33 | 21 | H | Brighton & HA | W | 2-0 | 1-0 | 20 | Jones [37], Gouck [54] | 1865 |
| 34 | 24 | H | Cambridge U | W | 2-0 | 1-0 | — | Gouck 2 [28, 77] | 1192 |
| 35 | 28 | A | Darlington | L | 0-1 | 0-0 | 20 | | 2181 |
| 36 | Mar 3 | A | Colchester U | D | 0-0 | 0-0 | — | | 2112 |
| 37 | 7 | H | Chester C | D | 1-1 | 0-0 | 21 | Lancashire [68] | 1955 |
| 38 | 14 | A | Lincoln C | L | 0-2 | 0-1 | 21 | | 2992 |
| 39 | 21 | H | Hartlepool U | W | 2-1 | 0-0 | 20 | Painter (pen) [75], Farrell [88] | 1395 |
| 40 | 28 | A | Doncaster R | W | 4-1 | 2-0 | 19 | Painter 2 [18, 58], Stuart [42], Lancashire [59] | 1858 |
| 41 | Apr 4 | A | Torquay U | D | 0-0 | 0-0 | 20 | | 2796 |
| 42 | 11 | H | Scarborough | W | 4-0 | 1-0 | 18 | Painter 2 [17, 58], Lancashire [76], Farrell [90] | 1795 |
| 43 | 13 | A | Swansea C | L | 0-3 | 0-0 | 19 | | 2854 |
| 44 | 18 | H | Exeter C | W | 3-0 | 0-0 | 18 | Bayliss [50], Lancashire 2 [60, 62] | 1850 |
| 45 | 25 | A | Rotherham U | D | 2-2 | 2-0 | 18 | Jones [32], Painter (pen) [44] | 3463 |
| 46 | May 2 | H | Barnet | W | 2-1 | 2-0 | 18 | Gouck [22], Painter [45] | 2102 |

**Final League Position: 18**      1996–97 DIV3 14

### GOALSCORERS

*League (56):* Painter 17 (5 pens), Lancashire 9, Stuart 6, Gouck 5, Farrell 4, Russell 4, Bayliss 2, Carter 2 (1 pen), Hill 2, Jones 2, Leonard 2, Bryson 1.
*Coca-Cola Cup (2):* Painter 1, Russell 1.
*FA Cup (0).*

| Key L 19 | Fensome A 42 | Barlow A 35 + 3 | Hill K 36 + 1 | Farrell A 40 | Gouck A 36 + 2 | Bailey M 24 + 9 | Painter R 45 | Leonard M 33 | Russell A 26 + 5 | Stuart M 30 + 15 | Scott A 1 + 2 | Bayliss D 23 + 6 | Carter M 7 + 4 | Smith C 1 + 2 | Bryson I 12 + 3 | Lancashire G 20 + 7 | Edwards N 27 | Pender J 14 | Robson G — + 7 | Reed A 10 | Atkinson G 5 + 1 | Jones G 17 | Carden P 3 + 4 | Match No. |
|---|---|---|---|---|---|---|---|---|---|---|---|---|---|---|---|---|---|---|---|---|---|---|---|---|
| 1 | 2 | 3 | 4[1] | 5[2] | 6[3] | 7 | 8 | 9 | 10 | 11 | 12 | 13 | 14 | | | | | | | | | | | 1 |
| 1 | 2 | 3 | 4 | 5 | 6 | 12 | 8 | 9 | 7 | 11 | | | 10[1] | | | | | | | | | | | 2 |
| 1 | 2 | 3 | 4 | 5 | 6 | 13 | 8 | 9 | 7 | 11 | | | 10[1] | 12[2] | | | | | | | | | | 3 |
| 1 | 2 | 3 | 4 | 5 | 6 | 12 | 8 | 9 | 7 | 11[2] | | 13 | 10[1] | | | | | | | | | | | 4 |
| 1 | 2 | 3 | 4 | 5 | 6 | 7 | 8 | 9 | 11 | 12 | | | 10[1] | | | | | | | | | | | 5 |
| 1 | 2 | 3 | | 5 | 6 | 7 | 8 | | 10 | 11 | 4 | 9[1] | 12 | | | | | | | | | | | 6 |
| 1 | 2 | 3 | 4 | | 6 | 7 | 8 | 9 | 11 | 12 | | 5 | 10[1] | | | | | | | | | | | 7 |
| 1 | 2 | 3 | 4 | | 6 | 7 | 8 | 9 | 11 | 12 | | 5 | 10[1] | | | | | | | | | | | 8 |
| 1 | 2 | 3[1] | 4 | | 6 | 7 | 8 | 9 | 11 | 12 | | 5 | 10 | | | | | | | | | | | 9 |
| 1 | 2 | | 4 | 5 | | 7 | 8 | 9 | 11[1] | 12 | | 3 | | | 6 | 10 | | | | | | | | 10 |
| 1 | 2 | 12 | 4 | 5 | | 7 | 8 | 9 | | | | 3[1] | | | 6 | 10 | | | | | | | | 11 |
| 1 | 2[1] | 3 | 4 | 5 | 6 | 7 | 8[3] | 9 | 11[2] | 12 | | 13 | 14 | | | 10 | | | | | | | | 12 |
| 1 | 2[2] | 3 | 4 | 5 | 6[1] | 7 | 8 | 9 | 11 | 12 | | 13 | | | | 10 | | | | | | | | 13 |
| 1 | 2 | 3 | 4 | 5 | 6 | 7[1] | 8 | 9 | 11 | 12 | | | 13 | | | 10[2] | | | | | | | | 14 |
| 1 | 2 | 3 | 4 | 5 | 6 | | 8 | 9 | 10 | 11 | | | | | 7 | | | | | | | | | 15 |
| | 2 | 3 | 4 | 5 | 6 | 12 | 8 | 9 | 10[1] | 11 | | | | | 7 | | 1 | | | | | | | 16 |
| | 2 | 3 | 4 | 5 | 6 | | 8 | 9 | 10 | 11 | | | | | 7 | | 1 | | | | | | | 17 |
| | 2 | 3[1] | 4 | 7 | 6 | 12 | 8 | 9 | | 11 | | | | | | 10 | 1 | 5 | | | | | | 18 |
| | | 3 | 4 | | | 7 | 8 | 9 | | 11 | | 2 | | | 6 | 10[1] | 1 | 5 | 12 | | | | | 19 |
| | | 3[1] | 4 | | 12 | 7 | 8 | 9 | | 11 | | 2 | | | 6[2] | 10 | 1 | 5 | 13 | | | | | 20 |
| | 2[1] | | | | 6 | 7 | 8 | 9 | | 12 | | 3 | | | 11 | 10[2] | 1 | 5 | 13 | 4 | | | | 21 |
| | 2 | | | | 10 | 6 | 7[1] | 8 | 9[3] | 13 | | 3 | | | 12 | | 1 | 5 | 14 | 4 | 11[2] | | | 22 |
| | | 3 | | | 10 | 6[2] | 2 | 8 | 9 | 12 | | 13 | | | 7[1] | | 1 | 5 | | 4 | 11 | | | 23 |
| | 2 | 3 | | | 10 | 6 | 7[2] | 8 | 9 | 12 | | 13 | | | 14 | | 1 | 5[3] | | 4 | 11[1] | | | 24 |
| 1 | 2 | 3[1] | | 5 | 6 | | 8 | 9 | | 12 | | | | | 7 | 10 | | | | 4 | 11 | | | 25 |
| 1 | 2 | 3 | | | | | 8 | 9 | 6[2] | 12 | | 13 | 14 | | 7[1] | 10 | | | | 4 | 11[3] | | | 26 |
| | | 3 | | | 10 | 6 | 7[2] | 8 | 9[1] | 11 | | 2 | | | 12 | | 1 | 5 | 13 | 4 | | | | 27 |
| | | 3[1] | | | 12 | | 7[2] | 8 | 9 | 11 | | 2 | | | 13 | 10 | 1 | 5 | | 4 | | 6 | | 28 |
| | 2 | 6[1] | | | 12 | | 8 | | 10 | 11 | 3 | | | | | 9[2] | 1 | 5 | 13 | 4 | | 7 | | 29 |
| | 2 | 3 | 4 | | 6 | | 8 | | | 11 | | 12 | | | | 9 | 1 | 5 | | 10[1] | | 7 | | 30 |
| | 2 | 3 | 4 | | 6 | | 8 | | 10 | 11 | | | | | | 12 | 1 | 5 | | | | | | 31 |
| | 2 | 3 | 4 | | 6 | 7[2] | 8 | | 10 | 11 | | | | 12 | | 13 | 1 | 5[1] | | | | | | 32 |
| | 2 | | 4 | 9 | 6 | | 8 | | | 11 | 3 | 5 | | 12 | | 10[1] | 1 | | | | | 7 | | 33 |
| | 2 | | 4 | 9 | 6 | | 8 | | | 11 | 3 | 5 | | | | 10 | 1 | | | | | 7 | | 34 |
| | 2 | 12 | 4 | 9 | 6 | | 8 | | | 11 | 3[1] | 5 | | | | 10[2] | 1 | | | | | 7 | | 35 |
| | 2 | 12 | 4 | 9 | 6 | | 8 | | | 11 | 3[1] | 5 | | | | 10 | 1 | | | | | 7 | | 36 |
| | 2 | 3 | 4 | 10 | 6 | | 8 | | | 11 | | 5 | | | | 9 | 1 | | | | | 7 | | 37 |
| 1 | 2 | 3 | 4 | | 6 | 7[2] | 8 | | | 11 | | 5 | | 12 | 13 | | | | 14 | | | 9[2] | 10[1] | 38 |
| 1 | 2 | 3 | 4 | | 6 | 7 | 8 | | | 11 | | 5 | | 12 | | | | | | | | 9[1] | 10 | 39 |
| | 2[2] | 3 | 4 | 10 | 6 | | 8 | 9 | | 11 | | 5 | | 12 | 13 | | 1 | | | | | 7[1] | | 40 |
| | 2 | 3 | 4 | 10 | 6 | | 8 | | | 11 | | 5 | | 12 | | 9[2] | 1 | | | | | 7[1] | 13 | 41 |
| | 2 | 3 | 4 | 10 | 6 | 12 | 8[1] | | | 11 | | 5 | | | | 9[2] | 1 | | | | | 7 | 13 | 42 |
| | 2 | 3 | 4 | 10 | 6[1] | | 8 | | | 11 | | 5 | | | | 9 | 1 | | | | | 7 | 12 | 43 |
| | 2 | 3 | 4 | 10 | 6 | | 8 | | | 11 | | 5 | | | | 9 | 1 | | | | | 7[1] | 12 | 44 |
| | 2 | 3 | 4[1] | 10 | 6 | 12 | 8 | | | 11 | | 5 | | 13 | | | 1 | | | | | 7 | 9[2] | 45 |
| | 2 | 3 | 4 | | 6[1] | 12 | 8 | | | 11 | | 5 | | | | 9[2] | 1 | | 13 | | | 7 | 10 | 46 |

**Coca-Cola Cup**

| | | | | |
|---|---|---|---|---|
| First Round | Stoke C | | (h) | 1-3 |
| | | | (a) | 1-1 |

**FA Cup**

| | | | | |
|---|---|---|---|---|
| First Round | Wrexham | | (h) | 0-2 |

ROTHERHAM UNITED 1997-98    *Back row (left to right):* Steve Thompson, Andy Hayward, Mark Monington, Gijsbert Bos, Paul Pettinger, Bobby Mimms, Alan Knill, Robert Pell, Andrew Brownrigg, Lee Glover.
*Middle row:* Billy Russell, Danny Hudson, David Bass, Mark Druce, Neil Richardson, John Taylor, Steven Heath, Rob McKenzie, Barry Shuttleworth, Ian Bailey.
*Front row:* Gary Scott, Trevor Berry, Paul Hurst, Paul Dillon, John Breckin (Assistant Manager), Ronnie Moore (Manager), Andy Roscoe, Shaun Goodwin, Martin Clark, Darren Garner.

# Division 3    **ROTHERHAM UNITED**

*Millmoor Ground, Rotherham S60 1HR.* Telephone: (01709) 512434. Fax: (01709) 512762. Commercial Dept: (01709) 512760. Fax: (01709) 512763. Football in the Community: (01709) 512761.

*Ground Capacity:* 11,514.

*Record attendance:* 25,170 v Sheffield U, Division 2, 13 December 1952 and v Sheffield W, Division 2, 26 January 1952.

*Record receipts:* £79,155 v Newcastle U, FA Cup 4th rd, 23 January 1993.

*Pitch measurements.* 115yd × 75yd.

*Chairman:* K. F. Booth.

*Directors:* R. Hull (Vice-Chairman), C. A. Luckock, J. A. Webb, N. Freeman. *Chief Executive:* Phil Henson.

*Manager:* Ronnie Moore. *Assistant Manager:* John Breckin. *Youth Development Officer:* Fraser Foster.

*Physio:* Ian Bailey. *Coach:* Billy Russell.

*Stadium Manager/Safety Officer:* David Sumner.

*Commercial Manager:* D. Nicholls.

*Year Formed:* 1870. *Turned Professional:* 1905. *Ltd Co.:* 1920.

*Club Nickname:* 'The Merry Millers'.

*Previous Names:* 1877, Thornhill United; 1905, Rotherham County; 1925, amalgamated with Rotherham Town under Rotherham United.

*Previous Ground:* Red House Ground; 1907, Millmoor.

*Foundation:* Rotherham were formed in 1870 before becoming Town in the late 1880s. Thornhill United were founded in 1877 and changed their name to Rotherham County in 1905. The Town amalgamated with Rotherham County to form Rotherham United in 1925.

*First Football League game:* 2 September 1893, Division 2, Rotherham T v Lincoln C (a) D 1-1 – McKay; Thickett, Watson; Barr, Brown, Broadhead; Longden, Cutts, Leatherbarrow, McCormick, Pickering. (1 og) 30 August 1919, Division 2, Rotherham Co v Nottingham F (h) W 2-0 – Branston; Alton, Baines; Bailey, Coe, Stanton; Lee (1), Cawley (1), Glennon, Lees, Lamb.

*Record League Victory:* 8–0 v Oldham Ath, Division 3 (N), 26 May 1947 – Warnes; Selkirk, Ibbotson; Edwards, Horace Williams, Danny Williams; Wilson (2), Shaw (1), Ardron (3), Guest (1), Hainsworth (1).

*Record Cup Victory:* 6–0 v Spennymoor U, FA Cup 2nd rd, 17 December 1977 – McAlister; Forrest, Breckin, Womble, Stancliffe, Green, Finney, Phillips (3), Gwyther (2) (Smith), Goodfellow, Crawford (1). 6–0 v Wolverhampton W, FA Cup 1st rd, 16 November 1985 – O'Hanlon; Forrest, Dungworth, Gooding (1), Smith (1), Pickering, Birch (2), Emerson, Tynan (1), Simmons (1), Pugh.

*Record Defeat:* 1–11 v Bradford C, Division 3 (N), 25 August 1928.

*Most League Points (2 for a win):* 71, Division 3 (N), 1950–51.

*Most League Points (3 for a win):* 82, Division 4, 1988–89.

*Most League Goals:* 114, Division 3 (N), 1946–47.

*Highest League Scorer in Season:* Wally Ardron, 38, Division 3 (N), 1946–47.

*Most League Goals in Total Aggregate:* Gladstone Guest, 130, 1946–56.

*Most Capped Player:* Shaun Goater, 18, Bermuda.

*Most League Appearances:* Danny Williams, 459, 1946–62.

*Record Transfer Fee Received:* £255,000 from Fortuna Sittard for Mike Jeffrey, January 1996.

*Record Transfer Fee Paid:* £150,000 to Millwall for Tony Towner, August 1980.

*Football League Record:* 1893 Rotherham Town elected to Division 2; 1896 Failed re-election; 1919 Rotherham County elected to Division 2; 1923–51 Division 3 (N); 1951–68 Division 2; 1968–73 Division 3; 1973–75 Division 4; 1975–81 Division 3; 1981–83 Division 2; 1983–88 Division 3; 1988–89 Division 4; 1989–91 Division 3; 1991–92 Division 4; 1992–97 Division 2; 1997– Division 3.

*Honours: Football League:* Division 2 best season: 3rd, 1954–55 (equal points with champions and runners-up); Division 3 – Champions 1980–81; Division 3 (N) – Champions 1950–51; Runners-up 1946–47, 1947–48, 1948–49; Division 4 – Champions 1988–89; Runners-up 1991–92. *FA Cup:* best season: 5th rd, 1953, 1968. *Football League Cup:* Runners-up 1961. *Auto Windscreens Shield:* Winners 1996.

*Colours:* Red and white. *Change colours:* White shirts, black shorts, black stockings.

**Did you know?**
Vic Wright scored four goals for Rotherham United in an 8-1 win over Accrington Stanley on 4 October 1930, but was transferred to Sheffield Wednesday ten days later, for a then undisclosed record fee for the club.

## ROTHERHAM UNITED 1997–98 LEAGUE RECORD

| Match No. | Date | | Venue | Opponents | Result | | H/T Score | Lg. Pos. | Goalscorers | Attendance |
|---|---|---|---|---|---|---|---|---|---|---|
| 1 | Aug | 9 | H | Barnet | L | 2-3 | 1-1 | — | Roscoe [29], Goodwin (pen) [61] | 4220 |
| 2 | | 16 | A | Cambridge U | L | 1-2 | 0-0 | 20 | Bos [51] | 2725 |
| 3 | | 23 | H | Hartlepool U | W | 2-1 | 2-0 | 16 | Berry [28], Hayward [40] | 3086 |
| 4 | | 30 | A | Darlington | D | 1-1 | 0-0 | 16 | Glover [75] | 2613 |
| 5 | Sept | 2 | A | Hull C | D | 0-0 | 0-0 | — | | 6127 |
| 6 | | 10 | H | Lincoln C | W | 3-1 | 0-0 | — | Roscoe [69], Glover [75], White [81] | 2871 |
| 7 | | 13 | H | Peterborough U | D | 2-2 | 2-1 | 15 | White [41], Thompson [45] | 3859 |
| 8 | | 20 | A | Exeter C | L | 1-3 | 0-1 | 17 | Bos [88] | 3420 |
| 9 | | 27 | A | Chester C | W | 4-2 | 3-0 | 16 | White [16], Bos 2 [38, 41], Glover [47] | 3061 |
| 10 | Oct | 4 | A | Shrewsbury T | L | 1-2 | 0-1 | 16 | White [89] | 2432 |
| 11 | | 11 | A | Leyton Orient | D | 1-1 | 0-0 | 18 | White [51] | 3658 |
| 12 | | 18 | H | Cardiff C | D | 1-1 | 1-1 | 18 | Thompson (pen) [3] | 3197 |
| 13 | | 21 | H | Notts Co | D | 1-1 | 0-1 | — | Hayward [90] | 3161 |
| 14 | | 25 | A | Rochdale | W | 1-0 | 1-0 | 13 | Garner [5] | 2267 |
| 15 | Nov | 1 | H | Macclesfield T | W | 1-0 | 0-0 | 11 | Hayward [69] | 3649 |
| 16 | | 4 | A | Mansfield T | D | 3-3 | 2-1 | — | White [22], Glover [27], Garner [49] | 2927 |
| 17 | | 8 | A | Brighton & HA | W | 2-1 | 1-0 | 9 | Richardson [3], Glover [49] | 1950 |
| 18 | | 18 | H | Scunthorpe U | L | 1-3 | 0-1 | — | Roscoe [60] | 3355 |
| 19 | | 22 | A | Scarborough | W | 2-1 | 0-1 | 9 | Roscoe [52], Thompson [77] | 3317 |
| 20 | | 29 | H | Colchester U | W | 3-2 | 1-0 | 7 | Glover 2 [11, 62], Knill [73] | 3259 |
| 21 | Dec | 2 | A | Swansea C | D | 1-1 | 0-0 | — | Garner [80] | 2463 |
| 22 | | 13 | H | Torquay U | L | 0-1 | 0-0 | 11 | | 3636 |
| 23 | | 19 | A | Doncaster R | W | 3-0 | 1-0 | — | Roscoe [37], Glover [69], Taylor [70] | 3533 |
| 24 | | 26 | A | Lincoln C | W | 1-0 | 0-0 | 5 | White [82] | 6350 |
| 25 | | 28 | H | Hull C | W | 5-4 | 2-1 | 4 | Glover 4 [21, 50, 54, 62], Taylor [25] | 5995 |
| 26 | Jan | 10 | H | Barnet | D | 0-0 | 0-0 | 5 | | 2558 |
| 27 | | 17 | A | Darlington | W | 3-0 | 2-0 | 3 | Goodwin [5], White 2 [39, 89] | 3877 |
| 28 | | 24 | A | Hartlepool U | D | 0-0 | 0-0 | 5 | | 2375 |
| 29 | | 27 | A | Cambridge U | D | 2-2 | 0-0 | — | Richardson [89], Taylor [90] | 3096 |
| 30 | | 31 | H | Peterborough U | L | 0-1 | 0-0 | 7 | | 7165 |
| 31 | Feb | 7 | H | Exeter C | W | 1-0 | 0-0 | 5 | Glover [64] | 4158 |
| 32 | | 14 | H | Shrewsbury T | L | 0-1 | 0-0 | 6 | | 3603 |
| 33 | | 21 | A | Chester C | L | 0-4 | 0-0 | 9 | | 2432 |
| 34 | | 24 | H | Cardiff C | D | 2-2 | 1-1 | — | Middleton (og) [11], Glover [61] | 2731 |
| 35 | | 28 | H | Leyton Orient | W | 2-1 | 0-1 | 7 | Roscoe [89], Monington [90] | 3542 |
| 36 | Mar | 3 | H | Brighton & HA | D | 0-0 | 0-0 | — | | 3724 |
| 37 | | 7 | A | Macclesfield T | D | 0-0 | 0-0 | 7 | | 3156 |
| 38 | | 14 | H | Mansfield T | D | 2-2 | 2-2 | 9 | Knill 2 [32, 35] | 4054 |
| 39 | | 21 | H | Scunthorpe U | D | 1-1 | 0-0 | 9 | Glover [52] | 4011 |
| 40 | | 28 | H | Scarborough | D | 0-0 | 0-0 | 9 | | 3836 |
| 41 | Apr | 3 | A | Colchester U | L | 1-2 | 1-1 | — | Martindale [12] | 3824 |
| 42 | | 11 | H | Swansea C | D | 1-1 | 1-1 | 10 | Martindale [41] | 2942 |
| 43 | | 13 | A | Torquay U | W | 2-1 | 1-0 | 9 | White [31], Roscoe [50] | 3963 |
| 44 | | 18 | H | Doncaster R | W | 3-0 | 0-0 | 8 | Berry 2 [76, 90], White [84] | 4328 |
| 45 | | 25 | H | Rochdale | D | 2-2 | 0-2 | 8 | White [69], Glover [90] | 3463 |
| 46 | May | 2 | A | Notts Co | L | 2-5 | 1-1 | 9 | White [11], Glover [65] | 12,430 |

**Final League Position: 9**　　　1996–97 DIV3 23

## GOALSCORERS

*League (67):* Glover 17, White 13, Roscoe 7, Bos 4, Berry 3, Garner 3, Hayward 3, Knill 3, Taylor 3, Thompson 3 (1 pen), Goodwin 2 (1 pen), Martindale 2, Richardson 2, Monington 1, own goal 1.
*Coca-Cola Cup (1):* Richardson 1.
*FA Cup (13):* Garner 3, Berry 2, Roscoe 2, Druce 1, Glover 1, Hudson 1, Knill 1, Richardson 1, White 1.

| Mimms B 43 | Clark M 28 | Hurst P 19+11 | Thompson S 32+7 | Knill A 38 | Monington M 15 | Berry T 40+2 | Goodwin S 8+5 | Druce M 5+9 | Glover L 36+1 | Roscoe A 43+2 | Bos G 6+10 | Bass D 13+5 | Sedgwick C —+4 | Richardson N 37+1 | Hayward A 6+7 | Garner D 37+3 | Scott G 6+1 | Warner V 21 | White J 26+1 | Pettinger P 3 | Dillon P 14+2 | Hudson D 6+4 | Taylor S 10 | Poric A 4 | Martindale G 7+1 | Darby J 3 | Match No. |
|---|---|---|---|---|---|---|---|---|---|---|---|---|---|---|---|---|---|---|---|---|---|---|---|---|---|---|---|
| 1 | 2 | 3 | 4 | 5[1] | 6[2] | 7 | 8 | 9[3] | 10 | 11 | 12 | 13 | 14 | | | | | | | | | | | | | | 1 |
| 1 | 2[1] | 3 | 4 | 5 | | 7 | 8[2] | 12 | | 11 | 9 | 10 | | 6 | 13 | | | | | | | | | | | | 2 |
| 1 | 2 | 3 | | 5 | | 7 | | | 11 | 9 | 4 | | | 6 | 10 | 8 | | | | | | | | | | | 3 |
| 1 | | 5 | 3 | | | 7[2] | 12 | 9[3] | 10 | 11 | 14 | 8[1] | 13 | 6 | | 4 | | 2 | | | | | | | | | 4 |
| 1 | 2 | 3 | | 5 | | 7 | 8 | 9 | 10 | 11[1] | 12 | | | 6 | 13 | 4[2] | | | | | | | | | | | 5 |
| 1 | 2 | 3 | 12 | | | 7 | 8 | | 10 | 11 | | 13 | 14 | 6[3] | | 4[1] | | 9[2] | 5 | | | | | | | | 6 |
| 1 | 2 | 3 | 4[1] | 5 | | 7 | 8 | | 10 | 11[2] | 12 | 13 | | 6 | | 9 | | | | | | | | | | | 7 |
| 1 | 2 | 3 | 4[2] | | | 7[1] | 8 | | 10 | 11 | 12 | 13 | | 6 | | 9 | | | | | | | | | | | 8 |
| 1 | 2 | 12 | 4[1] | 5 | | 7 | 8 | | 10 | 11 | | | | 6 | | 9 | 3 | | | | | | | | | | 9 |
| 1[2] | | | 4 | 5 | | 7[1] | 8 | | 10 | 11 | 12 | 13 | | 6 | | 9 | 3 | 2 | | | | | | | | | 10 |
| | | | 4 | 5 | | 7 | 8 | | 10 | 11 | | | | 6 | | 9 | 3 | 2 | | 1 | | | | | | | 11 |
| | 2 | 12 | 4 | 5 | | 7 | 8 | | 10[2] | 11 | | 13 | | 6 | | 9 | | | | 1 | 3[1] | | | | | | 12 |
| 1 | 2 | 12 | | 5 | | 7[2] | 8[2] | | 10 | 11 | | 13 | 14 | 6 | | 4 | | 9 | | | 3[1] | | | | | | 13 |
| 1 | 2 | 3 | | 5 | | 7[2] | 8[2] | | 10[1] | 11 | 12 | 13 | 14 | 6 | | 4 | | 9 | | | | | | | | | 14 |
| 1 | 2 | | | 5 | | 7 | 8 | | 10 | 11 | 12 | | | 6 | | 4 | 3 | 9[1] | | | | | | | | | 15 |
| 1 | 2 | 12 | | 5 | | 7 | 8[2] | | 10 | 11[1] | | 13 | | 6 | | 4 | 3 | 9 | | | | | | | | | 16 |
| 1 | 2 | | | 5 | | 7 | 8[1] | | 10 | 11 | 12 | | | 6 | | 4 | 3 | 9 | | | | | | | | | 17 |
| 1 | 2[1] | 12 | | 5 | | 7 | 8 | | 10 | 11[3] | | 13 | | 6[2] | 9 | 4 | 3 | | | | 14 | | | | | | 18 |
| 1 | 2 | 3 | | 5 | | 7 | 8 | | 10 | 11 | | | | 6 | 9 | 4 | | | | | | | | | | | 19 |
| 1 | 2 | 3 | | 5 | | 7 | 8 | | 10 | 11 | 12 | | | 6 | | 4 | | 9[1] | | | | | | | | | 20 |
| 1 | 2 | 3 | | | | 7[2] | 8 | | 10 | 11 | 12 | 13 | | 6 | 9[1] | 4 | | | | | 5 | | | | | | 21 |
| 1 | 2[1] | | | | 6 | 7 | 8 | | 10 | 11 | 12 | | | | 9 | 4 | 3 | 2 | | | | | | | | | 22 |
| 1 | | | | | | 7 | 8 | | 10 | 11 | 12 | | | 6 | | 4 | 3 | 2 | 9[1] | | 5 | | | | | | 23 |
| 1 | | | | | | 7 | 8[1] | | 10 | 11 | 12 | | | 6 | | 4 | 3 | 2 | 9 | | 5 | | | | | | 24 |
| 1 | | 12 | | | | 7 | 8[1] | | 10 | 11 | | | | 6 | | 4 | 3 | 2 | 9 | | 5 | | | | | | 25 |
| 1 | | | | | | 7 | 8 | | 10 | 11 | | | | 6 | | 4 | 3 | 2 | 9 | | 5 | | | | | | 26 |
| 1 | | 12[2] | | | | 7[1] | 8 | | 10 | 11 | | 13 | | 6 | | 4 | 3 | 2 | 9 | | 5 | | | | | | 27 |
| 1 | | | | | | 7 | 8[2] | | 10 | 11 | 12 | 13 | | 6 | | 4 | 3 | 2 | 9[1] | | 5 | | | | | | 28 |
| 1 | | | | | | 7 | 8[1] | | 10 | 11 | 12 | 13 | | 6 | | 4 | 3[2] | 2 | 9 | | 5 | | | | | | 29 |
| 1 | | | | | | 7 | 8 | | 10 | 11[2] | 12 | 13 | | 6[1] | | 4 | 3 | 2 | 9 | | 5 | | | | | | 30 |
| 1 | | | | | | 7 | 8[1] | | 10 | 11 | 12 | | | 6 | | 4 | 3 | 2 | 9 | | 5 | | | | | | 31 |
| 1 | | 3 | | | | 7 | 8 | | 10 | 11 | 12 | | | 6 | | 4 | | 2[1] | 9 | | 5 | | | | | | 32 |
| 1 | | 3 | | | | 7 | 8 | | 10 | 11 | 12 | 13 | | 6 | | 4[1] | | 2[3] | 9[2] | | 5 | | | | 14 | | 33 |
| 1 | 2 | | | | | 7 | 8 | | 10 | 11 | 12 | | | 6 | | 4[1] | 3 | | 9 | | 5 | | | | | | 34 |
| 1 | 2 | 12 | | | | 7 | 8[2] | | 10 | 11 | | 13 | | 6 | | 4 | 3[1] | | 9[3] | | 5 | | | | 14 | | 35 |
| 1 | 2 | 12 | | | | 7 | 8[1] | | 10 | 11 | | | | 6 | | 4 | 3 | | 9 | | 5 | | | | | | 36 |
| | 2[1] | 12 | | | | 7 | 8 | | 10 | 11 | | 13 | | 6 | | 4 | 3[2] | | 9[2] | 1 | 5 | | | | 14 | | 37 |
| 1 | 2 | | | | | 7 | 8 | | 10 | 11 | | | | 6 | | 4 | 3 | | 9 | | 5 | | | | | | 38 |
| 1 | | 12 | | | | 7[2] | 8[1] | | 10 | 11 | | 13 | | 6 | | 4 | 3 | 2 | 9 | | 5 | | | | | | 39 |
| 1 | | 12 | | | | 7 | | | 10 | 11[1] | | 13 | | 6 | | 4 | 3 | 2[2] | 9 | | 5 | | | | | 8 | 40 |
| 1 | | 12 | | | | 7[2] | 8 | | 10 | 11[3] | | 13 | | 6 | | 4 | 3 | 2 | 9 | | 5[1] | | | | 14 | | 41 |
| 1 | | 12 | | | | 7 | 8[2] | | 10 | 11 | | 13 | | 6 | | 4[1] | 3 | 2 | 9 | | 5 | | | | | | 42 |
| 1 | | | | | | 7 | 8 | | 10 | 11 | | | | | | 4 | 3 | 2 | 9 | | 5 | 6 | | | | | 43 |
| 1 | | | | | | 7 | 8 | | 10[1] | 11 | 12 | | | | | 4 | 3 | 2 | 9 | | 5 | 6 | | | | | 44 |
| 1 | | | | | | 7[2] | 8 | | 10 | 11 | | 13 | | | | 4[1] | 3 | 2 | 9 | | 5 | 6 | 12 | | | | 45 |
| 1 | | | | | | 7 | 8 | | 10 | 11 | 12 | | | | | 4 | 3 | 2[1] | 9 | | 5 | 6 | | | | | 46 |

**Coca-Cola Cup**

| | | | | |
|---|---|---|---|---|
| First Round | Preston NE | | (h) | 1-3 |
| | | | (a) | 0-2 |

**FA Cup**

| | | | | |
|---|---|---|---|---|
| First Round | Burnley | | (h) | 3-3 |
| | | | (a) | 3-0 |
| Second Round | Kings Lynn | | (h) | 6-0 |
| Third Round | Sunderland | | (h) | 1-5 |

SCARBOROUGH 1997–98   *Back row (left to right):* Chris Tate, Scott Boys, John Kay, John Murray (Physio), Matthew Russell, Troy Bennett, Steve Brodie.
*Middle row:* Simon Bochenski, Carel Van der Velden, Paul Atkin, Jason Rockett, Kevin Martin, Gary Bennett, Gareth Williams, Michael McElhatton, Jamie Mitchell.
*Front row:* Mark Lee, Colin Sutherland, Liam Robinson, Mick Wadsworth (Manager), John Russell (Chairman), Ray McHale (Assistant Manager), Eamon Bazelya, Graham Carr, Ben Worrall.

# Division 3     SCARBOROUGH

*The McCain Stadium, Seamer Road, Scarborough YO12 4HF.* Telephone: (01723) 375094. Fax: (01723) 378733.

*Ground capacity:* 6899.

*Record Attendance:* 11,130 v Luton T, FA Cup 3rd rd, 8 January 1938. Football League: 7314 v Wolverhampton W, Division 4, 15 August 1987.

*Record receipts:* £37,609.50 v Arsenal, Coca-Cola Cup 4th rd, 6 January 1993.

*Pitch measurements:* 114yd × 74yd.

*President:* John Birley.

*Chairman:* K. Ferrie.

*Directors:* J. Russell, T. Milton, R. Robinson, R. Kemp, R. Green, Mrs G. Russell.

*Manager:* Mick Wadsworth. *Assistant Manager:* Ray McHale.

*Secretary:* Mrs Gillian Russell. *Physio:* J. Murray.

*Year Formed:* 1879. *Turned Professional:* 1926. *Ltd Co.:* 1933.

*Club Nickname:* 'The Boro'.

*Previous Grounds:* 1879–87, Scarborough Cricket Ground; 1887–98, Recreation Ground; 1898– Athletic Ground.

*Foundation:* Scarborough came into being as early as 1879 when they were formed by members of the town's cricket club and went under the name of Scarborough Cricketers' FC with home games played on the North Marine Road Cricket Ground.

*First Football League game:* 15 August 1987, Division 4, v Wolverhampton W (h) D 2-2 – Blackwell; McJannet, Thompson, Bennyworth, Richards, Kendall, Hamill, Moss, McHale (1), Mell (1), Graham.

*Record League Victory:* 4–0 v Bolton W, Division 4, 29 August 1987 – Blackwell; McJannet, Thompson, Bennyworth (Walker), Richards (1) (Cook), Kendall, Hamill (1), Moss, McHale, Mell (1), Graham. (1 og). 4–0 v Newport Co (away), Division 4, 12 April 1988 – Ironside; McJannet, Thompson, Kamara, Richards (1), Short (1), Adams (Cook 1), Brook, Outhart (1), Russell, Graham. 4–0 v Doncaster R, Division 3, 1 November 1997 – Martin; Jackson, Heckingbottom, Snodin, Atkin, Bennett G (1), Williams (2), McElhatton (1), Robinson, Brodie, Bennett T.

*Record Cup Victory:* 6–0 v Rhyl Ath, FA Cup 1st rd, 29 November 1930 – Turner; Severn, Belton; Maskell, Robinson, Wallis; Small (1), Rand (2), Palfreman (2), A. D. Hill (1), Mickman.

*Record Defeat:* 1–7 v Wigan Ath, Division 3, 11 March 1997.

*Most League Points (3 for a win):* 77, Division 4, 1988–89.

*Most League Goals:* 69, Division 4, 1990–91.

*Highest League Scorer in Season:* Darren Foreman, 27, Division 4, 1992–93.

*Most League Goals in Total Aggregate:* Darren Foreman, 35, 1991–95.

*Most Capped Player:* None.

*Most League Appearances:* Ian Ironside, 183, 1988–91, 1992, 1994–97.

*Record Transfer Fee Received:* £240,000 from Notts Co for Chris Short, September 1990.

*Record Transfer Fee Paid:* £102,000 to Leicester C for Martin Russell, March 1989.

*Football League Record:* Promoted to Division 4 1987; 1992– Division 3.

*Honours: Football League:* Division 3 best season: 6th, 1997–98. *FA Cup:* best seasons: 3rd rd, 1931, 1938, 1976, 1978, 1995. *Football League Cup:* best season: 4th rd 1993. *FA Trophy:* Winners 1973, 1976, 1977. *GM Vauxhall Conference:* Winners 1986–87.

*Colours:* White shirts and shorts with red and green trim, red and white hooped stockings.
*Change colours:* Fluorescent lime shirts with black trim, lime shorts, black and lime stockings.

**Did you know?**
In 1929-30 Scarborough dropped only one point at home when winning the Midland League six points ahead of Barnsley reserves.

## SCARBOROUGH 1997–98 LEAGUE RECORD

| Match No. | Date | Venue | Opponents | Result | H/T Score | Lg. Pos. | Goalscorers | Atten-dance |
|---|---|---|---|---|---|---|---|---|
| 1 | Aug 9 | H | Cambridge U | W 1-0 | 0-0 | — | Williams [71] | 2225 |
| 2 | 16 | A | Torquay U | L 0-1 | 0-0 | 17 | | 1863 |
| 3 | 22 | H | Brighton & HA | W 2-1 | 1-1 | — | Bennett G [43], Robinson [60] | 2505 |
| 4 | 30 | A | Lincoln C | D 3-3 | 1-2 | 8 | Brown [21], Bennett T [54], Van der Velden [69] | 3162 |
| 5 | Sept 2 | A | Darlington | W 2-1 | 2-1 | — | Rockett [13], Bennett G [43] | 2417 |
| 6 | 7 | H | Hartlepool U | D 1-1 | 0-0 | 6 | Bennett T [66] | 3027 |
| 7 | 12 | A | Colchester U | L 0-1 | 0-0 | — | | 2756 |
| 8 | 20 | H | Macclesfield T | W 2-1 | 1-1 | 8 | Williams 2 [14, 53] | 2256 |
| 9 | 27 | H | Notts Co | L 1-2 | 1-1 | 10 | Campbell [12] | 2751 |
| 10 | Oct 4 | A | Exeter C | D 1-1 | 1-1 | 10 | Brodie [6] | 4464 |
| 11 | 11 | A | Hull C | L 0-3 | 0-2 | 15 | | 5315 |
| 12 | 18 | H | Peterborough U | L 1-3 | 0-3 | 16 | Brodie [64] | 2565 |
| 13 | 21 | H | Chester C | W 4-1 | 2-0 | — | Robinson [28], Atkin [42], Williams 2 [48, 71] | 1451 |
| 14 | 25 | A | Shrewsbury T | W 1-0 | 0-0 | 9 | Bennett G [51] | 2395 |
| 15 | Nov 1 | H | Doncaster R | W 4-0 | 0-0 | 5 | McElhatton [52], Bennett G [67], Williams 2 [76, 87] | 2345 |
| 16 | 4 | A | Leyton Orient | L 1-3 | 1-2 | — | Williams [3] | 2480 |
| 17 | 8 | A | Mansfield T | L 2-3 | 2-2 | 11 | Robinson [19], Mitchell [35] | 2134 |
| 18 | 18 | H | Swansea C | W 3-2 | 1-1 | — | McElhatton 2 [38, 65], Williams [70] | 1408 |
| 19 | 22 | H | Rotherham U | L 1-2 | 1-0 | 10 | Mitchell [45] | 3317 |
| 20 | 29 | A | Cardiff C | D 1-1 | 1-0 | 11 | McElhatton [41] | 2593 |
| 21 | Dec 6 | H | Rochdale | W 1-0 | 1-0 | 9 | Campbell [44] | 1705 |
| 22 | 13 | A | Scunthorpe U | W 3-1 | 2-1 | 6 | Williams 2 (1 pen) [20, 35 (p)], Conway [59] | 2535 |
| 23 | 19 | H | Barnet | W 1-0 | 1-0 | — | Brodie [3] | 1714 |
| 24 | 26 | A | Hartlepool U | L 0-3 | 0-1 | 8 | | 3905 |
| 25 | Jan 6 | H | Darlington | W 2-1 | 1-0 | — | Williams (pen) [43], Robinson [87] | 1751 |
| 26 | 10 | A | Cambridge U | W 3-2 | 1-1 | 3 | Bennett G [18], Brodie 2 [70, 81] | 2636 |
| 27 | 17 | H | Lincoln C | D 2-2 | 0-1 | 5 | Bennett G [54], Campbell [78] | 2905 |
| 28 | 20 | H | Torquay U | W 4-1 | 1-0 | — | Bennett G [42], Campbell [55], McElhatton [66], Brodie [81] | 2467 |
| 29 | 24 | A | Brighton & HA | D 1-1 | 0-1 | 4 | Mitchell [86] | 1988 |
| 30 | 31 | H | Colchester U | D 1-1 | 0-0 | 4 | Campbell [88] | 2219 |
| 31 | Feb 7 | A | Macclesfield T | L 1-3 | 0-3 | 7 | Williams (pen) [73] | 2488 |
| 32 | 14 | H | Exeter C | W 4-1 | 2-0 | 5 | McElhatton [7], Brodie 2 [35, 53], Williams [57] | 2078 |
| 33 | 21 | H | Notts Co | L 0-1 | 0-1 | 7 | | 5645 |
| 34 | 24 | A | Peterborough U | D 0-0 | 0-0 | — | | 4208 |
| 35 | 28 | H | Hull C | W 2-1 | 2-0 | 5 | Brodie [2], Conway (pen) [28] | 3831 |
| 36 | Mar 3 | H | Mansfield T | D 2-2 | 1-0 | — | Tate [13], Brodie [82] | 2019 |
| 37 | 10 | A | Doncaster R | W 2-1 | 1-0 | — | Campbell [37], Rockett [84] | 1129 |
| 38 | 14 | H | Leyton Orient | W 2-0 | 1-0 | 4 | Williams (pen) [36], Campbell [73] | 2655 |
| 39 | 21 | A | Swansea C | D 0-0 | 0-0 | 5 | | 2797 |
| 40 | 28 | A | Rotherham U | D 0-0 | 0-0 | 5 | | 3836 |
| 41 | Apr 3 | H | Cardiff C | W 3-1 | 3-0 | — | Worrall 2 [8, 15], Bennett G [44] | 2905 |
| 42 | 11 | A | Rochdale | L 0-4 | 0-1 | 5 | | 1795 |
| 43 | 13 | H | Scunthorpe U | D 0-0 | 0-0 | 5 | | 3427 |
| 44 | 18 | A | Barnet | D 1-1 | 1-1 | 5 | Bennett G [34] | 2353 |
| 45 | 25 | H | Shrewsbury T | D 0-0 | 0-0 | 6 | | 3712 |
| 46 | May 2 | A | Chester C | D 1-1 | 0-0 | 6 | Flitcroft (og) [82] | 2719 |

**Final League Position: 6**     1996–97 DIV3 12

### GOALSCORERS

*League (67):* Williams 15 (4 pens), Brodie 10, Bennett G 9, Campbell 7, McElhatton 6, Robinson 4, Mitchell 3, Bennett T 2, Conway 2 (1 pen), Rockett 2, Worrall 2, Atkin 1, Brown 1, Tate 1, Van der Velden 1, own goal 1.
*Coca-Cola Cup (1):* Bennett G 1.
*FA Cup (1):* Robinson 1.

| Martin K 17 | Kay J 40 | Sutherland C 18+4 | Bennett G 40+2 | McElhatton M 38+4 | Rockett J 32 | Van der Velden C 5+3 | Worrall B 14+7 | Mitchell J 8+27 | Brodie S 43+1 | Williams G 40+3 | Bennett T 24+10 | Snodin I 33+2 | Atkin P 26+8 | Robinson L 28+8 | Brown L 4 | Campbell N 20+14 | Tate C 3+21 | Heckingbottom P 28+1 | Jackson R 2 | Buxton N 3 | Rhodes A 11 | Conway P 13 | Elliott T 15 | Russell M —+2 | Dobbin J 1 | Match No. |
|---|---|---|---|---|---|---|---|---|---|---|---|---|---|---|---|---|---|---|---|---|---|---|---|---|---|---|
| 1 | 2 | 3 | 4[1] | 5 | 6 | 7 | 8 | 9[2] | 10[3] | 11 | 12 | 13 | 14 | | | | | | | | | | | | | 1 |
| 1 | 2 | 3[1] | 12 | 5 | | | 7[2] | 13 | 14 | 10[3] | 11 | 8 | 4 | 6 | | 9 | | | | | | | | | | 2 |
| 1 | 2[2] | 3 | 7 | 5 | 6 | | 12 | | 10 | 11 | 8 | 4 | 13 | | | 9[1] | | | | | | | | | | 3 |
| 1 | 2 | 12 | 7 | 8 | 6 | | 13 | 14 | 10[3] | 11 | 4 | 5[1] | 9 | 3[2] | | | | | | | | | | | | 4 |
| 1 | 2 | 3 | 7 | 5[1] | 6 | | 13 | | 10 | 12 | 11 | 4[3] | 14 | 9 | | 8[2] | | | | | | | | | | 5 |
| 1 | 2 | 3[1] | | 5 | 6 | | 12 | | 10 | 7 | 11 | 4 | | 9 | | 8[2] | 13 | | | | | | | | | 6 |
| 1 | 2 | 3 | 5 | 12 | 6 | | 8[2] | | 10 | 7 | 11[1] | 4 | | 9 | | 13 | | | | | | | | | | 7 |
| 1 | 2 | 3 | 12 | 6 | | 8[2] | 14 | 13 | 7 | 11 | 4 | 5 | 10[1] | 9[3] | | | | | | | | | | | | 8 |
| 1 | 2 | 3 | 12 | 6 | | 8[1] | 13 | 10 | 7 | 11[2] | 4 | 5 | 14 | 9[3] | | | | | | | | | | | | 9 |
| 1 | 2 | 3 | 8[1] | 12 | 6 | | 10[2] | 7 | 11 | 4 | 5 | 13 | 9[3] | 14 | | | | | | | | | | | | 10 |
| 1 | 2 | 3[3] | 8 | 6[1] | 12 | | 10 | 7 | 11 | 4 | 5 | 9[2] | 14 | 13 | | | | | | | | | | | | 11 |
| 1 | 2 | 12 | 6 | 8[3] | | | 10 | 7 | 11[2] | 4 | 5 | 9 | 13 | 14 | 3[1] | | | | | | | | | | | 12 |
| 1 | 2 | | 6 | 8 | 12 | | 10[2] | 7 | 11 | 4 | 5 | 9[1] | 13[3] | 14 | 3 | | | | | | | | | | | 13 |
| 1 | 2 | | 6 | 8 | 12 | | 10[1] | 7 | 11 | 4 | 5 | 9[2] | 13 | 3 | | | | | | | | | | | | 14 |
| 1 | | | 6 | 8 | 12 | | 10 | 7 | 11 | 4 | 5 | 9[1] | 13 | 3 | 2[2] | | | | | | | | | | | 15 |
| 1 | | 2 | 8 | 6 | 12 | | 10[1] | 7 | 11 | 4 | 5 | 9[2] | 13 | 14 | 3[3] | | | | | | | | | | | 16 |
| 1 | | 2 | 8 | 6 | 10[2] | | 12 | 7 | 11[1] | 4 | 5 | 9[3] | 13 | 14 | 3 | | | | | | | | | | | 17 |
| | | 3 | 2 | 8 | 6 | | 10[2] | 11 | 7 | | 4 | 5 | 9[1] | 12 | 13 | | | | | 1 | | | | | | 18 |
| | | 2 | 4 | 8[1] | 6 | | 10[2] | 11 | 7 | 12 | | 5 | 9 | 13 | 3 | | | | | 1 | | | | | | 19 |
| | 2 | 5[1] | 4 | 8 | 6 | | 10 | 7 | 11 | | 9 | 12 | | 3 | | | | 1 | | | | | | | | 20 |
| | 2 | | 4 | 8 | 6 | | 12 | 7 | 10[1] | 5 | 9 | 11[2] | 13 | 3 | | | | 1 | | | | | | | | 21 |
| | 2 | | | 8 | 6 | | 12 | 10[1] | 7 | 5 | 9 | 11[2] | 13 | 3 | | | | 1 | | | | 4 | | | | 22 |
| | 2 | 12 | | 8 | 6 | | 10 | 7[1] | 13 | 5 | 9[2] | 11[3] | 14 | 3 | | | | 1 | | | | 4 | | | | 23 |
| | 2 | | 12 | 8[3] | 6 | | 10 | 7 | 13 | 11[2] | 5 | 9[1] | 14 | 3 | | | | 1 | | | | 4 | | | | 24 |
| | 2 | 5 | 8 | 6 | | | 12 | 10[1] | 7[3] | 13 | 11 | 14 | 9[1] | 3 | | | | 1 | | | | 4 | | | | 25 |
| | 2 | 5 | 8 | 6 | | | 12 | 10[1] | 7 | 11 | 13 | 9[2] | 3 | | | | | 1 | | | | 4 | | | | 26 |
| | 2 | 5 | 8 | 6 | | | 10 | 7 | 12 | 11 | 13 | 9 | 3[2] | | | | | 1 | | | | 4[1] | | | | 27 |
| | 2 | 5 | 8 | 6 | | | 12 | 10 | 7[1] | 13 | 4[2] | 14 | 11[3] | 9 | | | | 3 | | | | 1 | | | | 28 |
| | 2 | 5 | 8 | 6 | | | 12 | 10 | 7[1] | 13 | 4 | 11[2] | 9 | 3 | | | | 1 | | | | | | | | 29 |
| | 2 | 6[1] | 5 | 13 | 8[3] | | 10 | 7 | 4 | 12 | 11 | 9 | 14 | 3[1] | | | | 1 | | | | | | | | 30 |
| | 2 | 5 | 6 | 12 | | | 10 | 7 | 3 | 4[2] | 13 | 11[1] | 9[3] | 14 | | | | | 1 | | | 8 | | | | 31 |
| | 2 | 5 | 9 | 6 | 4 | | 12 | 10 | 7[2] | 11[1] | 13 | 3 | | | | | | | | | | 8 | 1 | | | 32 |
| | 2 | 5 | 9 | 11[1] | 12 | | 10 | 7[2] | 4 | 6 | 13 | 3 | | | | | | | | | | 8[3] | 1 | 14 | | 33 |
| | 2[1] | 5 | 7 | 6 | 11 | 12 | 10[3] | | 4[2] | 13 | 9 | 3 | | | | | | | | | | 8 | 1 | 14 | | 34 |
| | 2 | 5 | 7 | 6 | 11 | 12 | 10 | | 4[1] | | 9 | 3 | | | | | | | | | | 8 | 1 | | | 35 |
| | 2 | 5 | 7 | | 12 | 10 | 13 | 11[3] | 6 | 4[2] | 14 | 9[1] | 3 | | | | | | | | | 8 | 1 | | | 36 |
| | 2 | 5 | 11 | 6 | 4[2] | | 10[3] | 7 | 3 | 14 | 9[1] | 13 | | | | | | | | | | 8 | 1 | | | 37 |
| | 2 | 5 | 8[3] | 4 | 12 | | 10[2] | 7 | 11 | 6 | 14 | 9[1] | 13 | 3 | | | | | | | | 1 | | | | 38 |
| | 2 | 5 | 11 | 8 | 12 | | 10[1] | 7 | 6 | 9[2] | 13 | 3 | | | | | | | | | | 1 | | 4 | | 39 |
| | 2 | 12 | 5 | 8 | 6 | | 11 | 13 | 10 | 7 | 4[1] | 9[2] | 3 | | | | | | | | | 1 | | | | 40 |
| | 2 | 5 | 8 | 6 | 11 | 12 | 10[1] | 7 | 13 | 4[2] | 9[3] | 14 | 3 | | | | | | | | | 1 | | | | 41 |
| | 2 | 5 | 8 | 6 | 11 | 12 | 10 | 7 | 13 | 4[1] | 9[3] | 14 | 3[2] | | | | | | | | | 1 | | | | 42 |
| | 2 | 3 | 5 | 8 | 11 | 12 | 10[1] | 7 | 4 | 6 | 9[2] | 13 | | | | | | | | | | 1 | | | | 43 |
| | 2 | 3 | 9 | 8 | 6 | 11 | 12 | 10[2] | 7[1] | 4 | 5 | 13 | | | | | | | | | | 1 | | | | 44 |
| | | 3 | 6 | 8 | 11[2] | 9[1] | 10 | 7[3] | 12 | 4 | 5 | 13 | 14 | | | | 2 | | | | | 1 | | | | 45 |
| | 2 | 3 | 6 | 8 | 12 | 11[2] | 10 | 13 | 7[3] | 4 | 5 | 14 | 9[1] | | | | | | | | | 1 | | | | 46 |

**Coca-Cola Cup**
First Round    Scunthorpe U    (h)   0-2
                                        (a)   1-2

**FA Cup**
First Round    Scunthorpe U    (a)   1-2

SCUNTHORPE UNITED 1997–98   *Back row (left to right):* David D'Auria, Craig Shakespeare, Sean McAuley, John Eyre, Steve Housham, Paul Harsley.
*Middle row:* Nigel Adkins (Physio), Mark Gavin, Russ Wilcox, Mark Sertori, Tim Clark, Darryn Stamp, Chris Hope, Michael Walsh, Paul Wilson (Youth Development Officer).
*Front row:* Jamie Forrester, Alex Calvo-Garcia, Mark Lillis (Assistant Manager), Don Rowing (Chief Executive), Keith Wagstaff (Chairman), Brian Laws (Manager), Lee Marshall, Justin Walker.

# Division 3     **SCUNTHORPE UNITED**

*Glanford Park, Scunthorpe, South Humberside DN15 8TD.* Telephone: (01724) 848077. Fax: (01724) 857986.

*Ground capacity:* 9183.

*Record attendance:* Old Showground: 23,935 v Portsmouth, FA Cup 4th rd, 30 January 1954. Glanford Park: 8775 v Rotherham U, Division 4, 1 May 1989.

*Record receipts:* £44,481.50 v Leeds U, Rumbelows Cup 2nd rd lst leg, 24 September 1991.

*Pitch measurements:* 110yd × 71yd.

*Vice-Presidents:* I. T. Botham, G. Johnson, A. Harvey, R. Ashman, K. Waters, J. Brownsword, B. Heywood, Dr. J. Zacarias.

*Chairman:* K. Wagstaff.

*Vice-Chairman:* R. Garton.

*Directors:* J. B. Borrill, J. S. Wharton, B. Collen, J. A. C. Godfrey.

*Team Manager:* Brian Laws.

*Chief Executive/Secretary:* A. D. Rowing. *Commercial Manager:* A. D. Rowing.

*Year Formed:*1899. *Turned Professional:* 1912. *Ltd Co.:* 1912.

*Club Nickname:* 'The Iron'.

*Previous Names:* Amalgamated first with Brumby Hall then North Lindsey United to become Scunthorpe & Lindsey United, 1910; dropped '& Lindsey' in 1958.

*Previous ground:* Old Showground to 1988.

*Foundation:* The year of foundation for Scunthorpe United has often been quoted as 1910, but the club can trace its history back to 1899 when Brumby Hall FC, who played on the Old Showground, consolidated their position by amalgamating with some other clubs and changing their name to Scunthorpe United. The year 1910 was when that club amalgamated with North Lindsey United as Scunthorpe and Lindsey United. The link is Mr W. T. Lockwood whose chairmanship covers both years.

*First Football League game:* 19 August 1950, Division 3 (N), v Shrewsbury T (h) D 0-0 – Thompson; Barker, Brownsword; Allen, Taylor, McCormick; Mosby, Payne, Gorin, Rees, Boyes.

*Record League Victory:* 8–1 v Luton T, Division 3, 24 April 1965 – Sidebottom; Horstead, Hemstead; Smith, Neale, Lindsey; Bramley (1), Scott, Thomas (5), Mahy (1), Wilson (1) and 8–1 v Torquay U (away), Division 3, 28 October 1995 – Samways; Housham, Wilson, Ford (1), Knill (1), Hope (Nicholson), Thornber, Bullimore (Walsh), McFarlane (4) (Young), Eyre (2), Paterson.

*Record Cup Victory:* 9–0 v Boston U, FA Cup 1st rd, 21 November 1953 – Malan; Hubbard, Brownsword; Sharpe, White, Bushby; Mosby (1), Haigh (3), Whitfield (2), Gregory (1), Mervyn Jones (2).

*Record Defeat:* 0–8 v Carlisle U, Division 3 (N), 25 December 1952.

*Most League Points (2 for a win):* 66, Division 3 (N), 1956–57, 1957–58.

*Most League Points (3 for a win):* 83, Division 4, 1982–83.

*Most League Goals:* 88, Division 3 (N), 1957–58.

*Highest League Scorer in Season:* Barrie Thomas, 31, Division 2, 1961–62.

*Most League Goals in Total Aggregate:* Steve Cammack, 110, 1979–81, 1981–86.

*Most Capped Player:* None.

*Most League Appearances:* Jack Brownsword, 595, 1950–65.

*Record Transfer Fee Received:* £350,000 from Aston Villa for Neil Cox, February 1991.

*Record Transfer Fee Paid:* £80,000 to York C for Ian Helliwell, August 1991.

*Football League Record:* 1950 Elected to Division 3 (N); 1958–64 Division 2; 1964–68 Division 3; 1968–72 Division 4; 1972–73 Division 3; 1973–83 Division 4; 1983–84 Division 3; 1984–92 Division 4; 1992– Division 3.

*Honours: Football League:* Division 2 best season: 4th, 1961–62; Division 3 (N) – Champions 1957–58. *FA Cup:* best season: 5th rd, 1958, 1970. *Football League Cup:* never past 3rd rd.

*Colours:* Sky blue and claret halved shirts, white shorts, white stockings with claret trim. *Change colours:* Navy and yellow shirts, navy shorts, navy and yellow stockings.

**Did you know?**
Harry Johnson scored 51 for Scunthorpe United's 133 Midland League goals in 1938-39. He scored one 6, one 5, a four and three hat-tricks.

## SCUNTHORPE UNITED 1997–98 LEAGUE RECORD

| Match No. | Date | | Venue | Opponents | Result | | H/T Score | Lg. Pos. | Goalscorers | Attendance |
|---|---|---|---|---|---|---|---|---|---|---|
| 1 | Aug | 9 | A | Peterborough U | W | 1-0 | 0-0 | — | Forrester [62] | 5761 |
| 2 | | 16 | H | Leyton Orient | W | 1-0 | 1-0 | 2 | Forrester [19] | 3068 |
| 3 | | 23 | A | Swansea C | L | 0-2 | 0-1 | 10 | | 4895 |
| 4 | | 30 | H | Mansfield T | W | 1-0 | 0-0 | 3 | Calvo-Garcia [73] | 3414 |
| 5 | Sept | 2 | H | Chester C | W | 2-1 | 0-1 | — | Eyre 2 (1 pen) [72 (pl. 86] | 2633 |
| 6 | | 7 | A | Notts Co | L | 1-2 | 0-1 | 4 | Strodder (og) [90] | 5009 |
| 7 | | 13 | H | Doncaster R | D | 1-1 | 1-1 | 7 | Eyre [23] | 3378 |
| 8 | | 20 | A | Barnet | W | 1-0 | 1-0 | 4 | Eyre (pen) [28] | 1951 |
| 9 | | 27 | H | Hull C | W | 2-0 | 1-0 | 3 | Forrester [4], Calvo-Garcia [60] | 4905 |
| 10 | Oct | 4 | A | Rochdale | L | 0-2 | 0-1 | 4 | | 2087 |
| 11 | | 18 | H | Lincoln C | L | 0-1 | 0-0 | 7 | | 4152 |
| 12 | | 21 | H | Shrewsbury T | D | 1-1 | 1-1 | — | Forrester [20] | 2303 |
| 13 | | 25 | A | Exeter C | W | 3-2 | 1-1 | 6 | Walsh [43], Hope [47], D'Auria [82] | 4552 |
| 14 | | 31 | A | Colchester U | D | 3-3 | 0-3 | — | Hope [52], D'Auria 2 [61, 63] | 3134 |
| 15 | Nov | 4 | H | Cambridge U | D | 3-3 | 0-2 | — | Forrester [59], Eyre [62], D'Auria [67] | 2417 |
| 16 | | 8 | H | Hartlepool U | D | 1-1 | 1-0 | 8 | Hope [38] | 3272 |
| 17 | | 11 | A | Cardiff C | D | 0-0 | 0-0 | — | | 2340 |
| 18 | | 18 | A | Rotherham U | W | 3-1 | 1-0 | — | Eyre 2 [36, 50], Forrester [61] | 3355 |
| 19 | | 22 | A | Torquay U | W | 4-2 | 2-1 | 5 | Calvo-Garcia 2 [11, 78], D'Auria [45], Wilcox [71] | 2152 |
| 20 | | 29 | H | Brighton & HA | L | 0-2 | 0-0 | 5 | | 3187 |
| 21 | Dec | 13 | H | Scarborough | L | 1-3 | 1-2 | 10 | D'Auria [10] | 2535 |
| 22 | | 20 | A | Darlington | L | 0-1 | 0-0 | 13 | | 2267 |
| 23 | | 26 | H | Notts Co | L | 1-2 | 1-1 | 13 | Hendon (og) [3] | 4781 |
| 24 | | 28 | A | Chester C | L | 0-1 | 0-0 | 13 | | 2263 |
| 25 | Jan | 10 | H | Peterborough U | L | 1-3 | 1-2 | 14 | Forrester [23] | 3584 |
| 26 | | 17 | A | Mansfield T | L | 0-1 | 0-1 | 15 | | 2375 |
| 27 | | 20 | A | Macclesfield T | L | 0-2 | 0-2 | — | | 1450 |
| 28 | | 24 | H | Swansea C | W | 1-0 | 1-0 | 14 | D'Auria [21] | 2123 |
| 29 | | 30 | A | Doncaster R | W | 2-1 | 1-1 | — | D'Auria [23], Housham [82] | 2036 |
| 30 | Feb | 7 | H | Barnet | D | 1-1 | 0-0 | 15 | Walker [51] | 2313 |
| 31 | | 14 | H | Rochdale | W | 2-0 | 0-0 | 14 | Regis [16], Eyre [75] | 2284 |
| 32 | | 21 | A | Hull C | L | 1-2 | 1-2 | 15 | Regis [36] | 4904 |
| 33 | | 24 | A | Lincoln C | D | 1-1 | 0-1 | — | Forrester [61] | 3407 |
| 34 | | 28 | H | Cardiff C | D | 3-3 | 2-1 | 15 | Eyre (pen) [14], Forrester [32], Calvo-Garcia [86] | 2135 |
| 35 | Mar | 3 | A | Hartlepool U | W | 1-0 | 1-0 | — | Wilcox [23] | 1588 |
| 36 | | 7 | H | Colchester U | W | 1-0 | 1-0 | 12 | McAuley [17] | 2143 |
| 37 | | 14 | A | Cambridge U | D | 2-2 | 0-2 | 13 | Forrester [52], Stamp [77] | 2423 |
| 38 | | 21 | H | Rotherham U | D | 1-1 | 0-0 | 13 | Eyre [77] | 4011 |
| 39 | | 28 | H | Torquay U | W | 2-0 | 0-0 | 11 | Hope [69], Calvo-Garcia [85] | 3264 |
| 40 | Apr | 4 | A | Brighton & HA | L | 1-2 | 0-1 | 13 | Hope [66] | 2141 |
| 41 | | 11 | H | Macclesfield T | W | 1-0 | 1-0 | 11 | D'Auria [9] | 2949 |
| 42 | | 13 | A | Scarborough | D | 0-0 | 0-0 | 12 | | 3427 |
| 43 | | 18 | H | Darlington | W | 1-0 | 0-0 | 10 | Sertori [49] | 2267 |
| 44 | | 21 | A | Leyton Orient | L | 0-1 | 0-0 | — | | 2735 |
| 45 | | 25 | H | Exeter C | W | 2-1 | 2-1 | 10 | D'Auria [7], Harsley [43] | 2024 |
| 46 | May | 2 | A | Shrewsbury T | W | 2-0 | 1-0 | 8 | Marshall [21], Forrester [60] | 2704 |

**Final League Position: 8**      1996–97 DIV3 13

## GOALSCORERS
*League (56):* Forrester 11, D'Auria 10, Eyre 10 (3 pens), Calvo-Garcia 6, Hope 5, Regis 2, Wilcox 2, Harsley 1, Housham 1, Marshall 1, McAuley 1, Sertori 1, Stamp 1, Walker 1, Walsh 1, own goals 2.
*Coca-Cola Cup (4):* Calvo-Garcia 4.
*FA Cup (5):* Forrester 2, Wilcox 2, Calvo-Garcia 1.

| Clarke T 41 | Walsh M 37 + 2 | Neil J 6 + 1 | Sertori M 40 + 1 | Wilcox R 30 + 1 | Hope C 46 | Walker J 38 + 2 | D'Auria D 37 + 4 | Regis D 9 | Forrester J 43 + 2 | Calvo-Garcia A 39 + 5 | Eyre J 33 + 9 | Housham S 17 + 7 | McAuley S 30 + 5 | Shakespeare C 3 + 1 | Ormondroyd I 7 + 13 | Laws B 9 + 5 | Harsley P 11 + 4 | Marshall L 12 + 9 | Stamp D 4 + 6 | Murphy M 1 + 2 | Phillips M 2 + 1 | Woods N 2 | Evans T 5 | Pemberton M 3 + 3 | Graves W — + 3 | Stanton N — + 1 | Featherstone J — + 1 | Nottingham S 1 | Sheldon G — + 1 | Match No. |
|---|---|---|---|---|---|---|---|---|---|---|---|---|---|---|---|---|---|---|---|---|---|---|---|---|---|---|---|---|---|---|
| 1 | 2 | 3 | 4 | 5 | 6 | 7 | 8 | 9 | 10 | 11 |  |  |  |  |  |  |  |  |  |  |  |  |  |  |  |  |  |  |  | 1 |
| 1 | 2 | 3 | 4 | 5 | 6 | 7 | 8 | 9 | $10^1$ | $11^2$ | 12 | 13 |  |  |  |  |  |  |  |  |  |  |  |  |  |  |  |  |  | 2 |
| 1 | 2 | $3^1$ | $4^2$ | 5 | 6 | 7 | $8^3$ | 9 | 10 | 11 | 12 |  | 13 | 14 |  |  |  |  |  |  |  |  |  |  |  |  |  |  |  | 3 |
| 1 | 2 | 12 | 4 |  | 6 | 7 | 8 | 5 | 10 | 11 | $9^2$ | 13 | $3^1$ |  |  |  |  |  |  |  |  |  |  |  |  |  |  |  |  | 4 |
| 1 | 2 |  | 4 |  | 6 | 7 | 8 | 9 | $10^1$ | 11 | 12 | 5 | 3 |  |  |  |  |  |  |  |  |  |  |  |  |  |  |  |  | 5 |
| 1 |  | $3^1$ | 4 |  | 6 | 7 | 8 |  | 10 | $11^2$ | 12 | 5 | 2 |  | 9 | 13 |  |  |  |  |  |  |  |  |  |  |  |  |  | 6 |
| 1 | 12 |  | 4 |  | 6 | 7 | 8 |  | 10 | $11^1$ | 5 | 2 | 3 |  | $9^1$ | 13 |  |  |  |  |  |  |  |  |  |  |  |  |  | 7 |
| 1 |  |  | 4 |  | 6 | 7 |  |  | 10 | $11^1$ | 9 | 2 | 3 | 8 |  | 5 | 12 |  |  |  |  |  |  |  |  |  |  |  |  | 8 |
| $1^1$ |  |  | 4 |  | 6 | 7 | 5 |  | 10 | 11 | $9^2$ | 2 | 3 | 8 |  |  |  | 12 | 13 |  |  |  |  |  |  |  |  |  |  | 9 |
| 1 | 5 |  | 4 |  | 6 | 7 |  |  | $10^2$ | 11 | 9 | $2^3$ | 3 | $8^1$ | 13 | 12 |  | 14 |  |  |  |  |  |  |  |  |  |  |  | 10 |
| 1 |  |  | 4 |  | 6 | 7 | 12 |  | 10 | 11 | 9 |  | 3 |  | $8^2$ | 5 |  | $2^1$ | 13 |  |  |  |  |  |  |  |  |  |  | 11 |
| 1 | 2 |  | 4 |  | 6 | 7 | 12 |  | 10 | 11 | 9 | 13 | $3^2$ |  |  | 5 |  |  | $8^1$ |  |  |  |  |  |  |  |  |  |  | 12 |
| 1 | 2 |  | 4 |  | 6 | 7 | 8 |  | 10 |  | 9 |  | 3 |  |  | 5 |  | 11 |  |  |  |  |  |  |  |  |  |  |  | 13 |
| 1 | 2 |  | 4 |  | 6 | 7 | 8 |  | 10 | 12 | 9 |  | 3 |  |  | 5 |  | $11^1$ |  |  |  |  |  |  |  |  |  |  |  | 14 |
| 1 | 2 |  | 4 |  | 6 | 7 | 8 |  | 10 | 11 | 9 | 12 | $3^1$ |  |  | 5 |  |  |  |  |  |  |  |  |  |  |  |  |  | 15 |
| 1 | 2 |  | 4 | 5 | 6 | 7 | 8 |  | 10 | 11 | 9 |  | 3 |  |  |  |  |  |  |  |  |  |  |  |  |  |  |  |  | 16 |
| 1 | $2^1$ |  | 4 | 5 | 6 | 7 | 8 |  | 10 | 11 | 9 |  | 3 |  |  |  |  | 12 |  |  |  |  |  |  |  |  |  |  |  | 17 |
| 1 | 2 |  | 4 | 5 | 6 | 7 | 8 |  | 10 | 11 | 9 |  | $3^1$ | 12 |  |  |  |  |  |  |  |  |  |  |  |  |  |  |  | 18 |
| 1 | 2 |  | 4 | 5 | 6 |  | 8 |  | 10 | 11 | 9 |  | 3 |  |  |  | 7 |  |  |  |  |  |  |  |  |  |  |  |  | 19 |
| 1 | 2 |  | 4 | 5 | 6 |  | 8 |  | 10 | 11 | 9 |  | $3^2$ |  | 13 | 12 | $7^1$ |  |  |  |  |  |  |  |  |  |  |  |  | 20 |
| 1 | $2^1$ |  | 4 | $5^2$ | 6 | 7 | 8 |  | 10 | 11 |  | 12 | 3 |  | 13 |  |  |  | 9 |  |  |  |  |  |  |  |  |  |  | 21 |
| 1 | 2 |  | 4 | $5^1$ | 6 | 7 | 8 |  | $10^2$ | $11^3$ | 9 | 12 | 3 |  | 13 |  |  |  |  | 14 |  |  |  |  |  |  |  |  |  | 22 |
| 1 | $2^1$ | 5 | 4 | 12 | 6 | 7 | $8^2$ |  | 10 | 13 | 9 | 11 | $3^3$ |  | 14 |  |  |  |  |  |  |  |  |  |  |  |  |  |  | 23 |
| 1 |  | $2^4$ | 4 | 5 | 6 | $7^1$ | 8 |  | $10^3$ | 12 | 9 | 11 | 13 |  | 3 |  |  |  |  | 14 |  |  |  |  |  |  |  |  |  | 24 |
| 1 | 2 |  | 4 | 5 | 6 | 7 | $8^2$ |  | $10^1$ | 11 | 9 |  | 3 |  | 12 |  |  |  |  |  |  | 13 |  |  |  |  |  |  |  | 25 |
| 1 | 2 |  | 4 |  | 6 | 7 |  |  | 10 | 11 | 9 |  | $3^1$ |  | $8^2$ |  | 13 | 12 | 5 |  |  |  |  |  |  |  |  |  |  | 26 |
| 1 | 2 |  | 4 | 5 | 6 | 7 | 12 |  | 10 | 11 | 13 |  | $3^2$ |  | 14 |  |  |  | $8^1$ | $9^3$ |  |  |  |  |  |  |  |  |  | 27 |
|  | 2 |  | 4 | 5 | 6 | 7 | 8 |  | 10 | 11 | 12 |  | $3^1$ |  |  |  |  | 9 |  |  |  |  | 1 |  |  |  |  |  |  | 28 |
| 1 | 2 |  | 4 | 5 | 6 | $7^2$ | 8 |  | $10^1$ | 11 | 12 | 13 |  |  | 14 |  |  | 3 |  |  |  |  |  | $9^3$ |  |  |  |  |  | 29 |
| 1 | $2^1$ |  | 4 | 5 | 6 | 7 | 8 | 10 |  | 11 | 9 |  | 3 |  | 13 |  |  |  | $12^2$ |  |  |  |  |  |  |  |  |  |  | 30 |
| 1 | 12 |  | 4 | 5 | 6 | 7 | $8^2$ | $10^3$ | 2 | 11 | 9 |  | $3^1$ |  | 14 | 13 |  |  |  |  |  |  |  |  |  |  |  |  |  | 31 |
| 1 |  |  | 4 | 5 | 6 | 7 | 8 | 10 | 2 | $11^2$ | $9^1$ |  | 3 |  | 12 | 13 |  |  |  |  |  |  |  |  |  |  |  |  |  | 32 |
| 1 |  | 4 | $5^1$ | 6 | 7 | 8 | $10^2$ | 11 |  | 13 |  | 12 |  | 9 | 2 | 3 |  |  |  |  |  |  |  |  |  |  |  |  |  | 33 |
| 1 | 5 |  | 4 |  | 6 | 7 | $8^2$ |  | $11^1$ | 12 | 10 |  | 13 |  | $9^3$ | 2 | 3 | 14 |  |  |  |  |  |  |  |  |  |  |  | 34 |
| 1 | 2 |  | 4 | 5 | 6 | 7 | 12 |  | 13 | 11 | $9^2$ |  | 3 |  |  |  | $8^1$ | 10 |  |  |  |  |  |  |  |  |  |  |  | 35 |
| 1 | 2 | $4^2$ | 5 |  | 6 | 7 |  |  | 12 | 11 | 9 |  | 3 |  | 13 |  | 8 | $10^1$ |  |  |  |  |  |  |  |  |  |  |  | 36 |
| 1 | 2 |  |  |  | 5 | 6 | 7 |  | $4^1$ | 11 | 9 |  | 3 |  | $10^2$ |  | 8 | 12 | 13 |  |  |  |  |  |  |  |  |  |  | 37 |
| 1 | 2 |  |  |  | 5 | 6 | 7 | 8 | $4^1$ | 11 | 9 |  | 3 |  | 12 |  |  | 10 |  |  |  |  |  |  |  |  |  |  |  | 38 |
| 1 | 2 |  |  |  | 5 | 6 | 7 | 8 | $4^1$ | 11 | 9 |  | 3 |  |  |  |  | 10 |  |  |  |  |  | 12 |  |  |  |  |  | 39 |
| 1 | 2 | 12 |  |  | 5 | 6 |  | 8 | 4 | 11 | $9^3$ |  | 3 |  |  | 13 | $7^2$ | $10^1$ |  |  |  |  |  | 14 |  |  |  |  |  | 40 |
| 1 | 2 |  | 4 |  | 5 | 6 |  | 8 | $10^1$ | 11 |  |  | 3 |  |  | $7^3$ | 12 | 13 |  |  |  |  |  | $9^2$ | 14 |  |  |  |  | 41 |
|  | 2 |  | 4 |  | 5 | 6 |  | 8 | $10^2$ | 11 |  |  | 3 |  |  | 7 | 12 |  |  |  |  |  | 1 |  | $9^1$ | 13 |  |  |  | 42 |
|  | 2 |  | 4 |  | 5 | 6 |  | 8 | 10 | $11^2$ | 12 |  | 3 |  |  | 7 | 13 |  |  |  |  |  | 1 |  | $9^1$ |  |  |  |  | 43 |
|  | 2 |  | 4 |  | 5 | 6 | 12 | 8 | $10^2$ | $11^1$ | 9 |  | $3^3$ |  |  | 7 | 13 |  |  |  |  |  | 1 |  |  |  | 14 |  |  | 44 |
|  | 2 |  |  |  | 5 | 6 | 12 | 8 | $10^3$ | $11^3$ | 9 |  | 3 |  |  | 7 | $4^1$ |  |  |  |  |  | 1 |  |  | 13 | 14 |  |  | 45 |
| 1 | 2 |  |  |  | 6 | 7 | $8^1$ |  | $10^3$ | 12 | 9 |  | 3 |  |  | 11 | 4 |  |  |  |  |  |  |  |  | 13 |  | $5^2$ | 14 | 46 |

**Coca-Cola Cup**

| | | | | |
|---|---|---|---|---|
| First Round | Scarborough | (a) | 2-0 | |
| | | (h) | 2-1 | |
| Second Round | Everton | (h) | 0-1 | |
| | | (a) | 0-5 | |

**FA Cup**

| | | | |
|---|---|---|---|
| First Round | Scarborough | (h) | 2-1 |
| Second Round | Ilkeston T | (h) | 1-1 |
| | | (a) | 2-1 |
| Third Round | Crystal Palace | (a) | 0-2 |

SHEFFIELD UNITED 1997–98 *Back row (left to right):* Don Hutchison, Carl Tiler, Alan Kelly, Gareth Taylor, Brian Deane, Jan Age Fjortoft, Simon Tracey, Michael Vonk, Andy Scott. *Middle row:* Vassilis Borbokis, Chris Short, Roger Nilsen, David Holdsworth, Willie Donachie (Coach), David White, Petr Katchuro, Paul McGrath, Nicky Marker. *Front row:* Nick Henry, Mark Beard, Dane Whitehouse, Andy Walker, Nigel Spackman (Manager), Wayne Quinn, John Ebbrell, Mitch Ward, Mark Patterson.

# Division 1     **SHEFFIELD UNITED**

*Bramall Lane Ground, Sheffield S2 4SU.* Telephone: (0114) 221 5757. Fax: (0114) 272 3030. Ticket Office: (0114) 221 1889. Pools Office: (0114) 221 3131. Club Shop: (0114) 221 3132. Executive Suite: (0114) 221 3195. Football in the Community: (0114) 221 3134. Ticket info line: (0891) 332 950. Clubcall: (0891) 888 650.

*Ground capacity:* 30,370.

*Record attendance:* 68,287 v Leeds U, FA Cup 5th rd, 15 February 1936.

*Record receipts:* £298,364 v Coventry C, FA Cup 6th rd replay, 17 March 1998.

*Pitch measurements:* 112yd × 72yd.

*Vice-Chairman:* F. Pye.

*Directors:* B. Proctor, K. C. McCabe, S. White.

*Manager:* Steve Bruce. *Youth Team Managers:* Russell Slade, Steve Myles.

*Physios:* Denis Pettitt, Stuart Pavely. *Secretary:* D. Capper AFA.

*Commercial Manager:* Andy R. Daykin. *Stadium Manager:* Roy Mitchell.

*Community Programme Organiser:* Tony Currie, Tel: (0114) 2769314.

*Year Formed:* 1889. *Turned Professional:* 1889. *Ltd Co.:* 1899.

*Club Nickname:* 'The Blades'.

*Foundation:* In March 1889, Yorkshire County Cricket Club formed Sheffield United six days after an FA Cup semi-final between Preston North End and West Bromwich Albion had finally convinced Charles Stokes, a member of the cricket club, that the formation of a professional football club would prove successful at Bramall Lane. The United's first secretary, Mr. J. B. Wostinholm was also secretary of the cricket club.

*First Football League game:* 3 September 1892, Division 2, v Lincoln C (h) W 4-2 – Lilley; Witham, Cain; Howell, Hendry, Needham (1); Wallace, Dobson, Hammond (3), Davies, Drummond.

*Record League Victory:* 10–0 v Burslem Port Vale (away), Division 2, 10 December 1892 – Howlett; Witham, Lilley; Howell, Hendry, Needham; Drummond (1), Wallace (1), Hammond (4), Davies (2), Watson (2).

*Record Cup Victory:* 5–0 v Newcastle U (away), FA Cup 1st rd, 10 January 1914 – Gough; Cook, English; Brelsford, Howley, Sturgess; Simmons (2), Gillespie (1), Kitchen (1), Fazackerley, Revill (1). 5–0 v Corinthians, FA Cup 1st rd, 10 January 1925 – Sutcliffe; Cook, Milton; Longworth, King, Green; Partridge, Boyle (1), Johnson (4), Gillespie, Tunstall. 5–0 v Barrow, FA Cup 3rd rd, 7 January 1956 – Burgin; Coldwell, Mason; Fountain, Johnson, Iley; Hawksworth (1), Hoyland (2), Howitt, Wragg (1), Grainger (1).

*Record Defeat:* 0–13 v Bolton W, FA Cup 2nd rd, 1 February 1890.

*Most League Points (2 for a win):* 60, Division 2, 1952–53.

*Most League Points (3 for a win):* 96, Division 4, 1981–82.

*Most League Goals:* 102, Division 1, 1925–26.

*Highest League Scorer in Season:* Jimmy Dunne, 41, Division 1, 1930–31.

*Most League Goals in Total Aggregate:* Harry Johnson, 205, 1919–30.

*Most Capped Player:* Billy Gillespie, 25, Northern Ireland.

*Most League Appearances:* Joe Shaw, 629, 1948–66.

*Record Transfer Fee Received:* £2,700,000 from Leeds U for Brian Deane, July 1993.

*Record Transfer Fee Paid:* £1,200,000 to West Ham U for Don Hutchison, January 1996.

*Football League Record:* 1892 Elected to Division 2; 1893–1934 Division 1; 1934–39 Division 2; 1946–49 Division 1; 1949–53 Division 2; 1953–56 Division 1; 1956–61 Division 2; 1961–68 Division 1; 1968–71 Division 2; 1971–76 Division 1; 1976–79 Division 2; 1979–81 Division 3; 1981–82 Division 4; 1982–84 Division 3; 1984–88 Division 2; 1988–89 Division 3; 1989–90 Division 2; 1990–92 Division 1; 1992–94 FA Premier League; 1994– Division 1.

*Honours: Football League:* Division 1 – Champions 1897–98; Runners-up 1896–97, 1899–1900; Division 2 – Champions 1952–53; Runners-up 1892–93, 1938–39, 1960–61, 1970–71, 1989–90; Division 4 – Champions 1981–82. *FA Cup:* Winners 1899, 1902, 1915, 1925; Runners-up 1901, 1936. *Football League Cup:* best season: 5th rd, 1962, 1967, 1972.

*Colours:* Red and white striped shirts with black trim, black shorts and stockings with red trim.
*Change colours:* All white with black trim.

**Did you know?**
Sheffield United met Celtic in the unofficial Championship of Great Britain over two games in 1898. United won 1-0 at home on 12 March, courtesy of a Ralph Gaudie goal and in Glasgow on 16 April, equalised in the last minute through Jack Almond.

## SHEFFIELD UNITED 1997–98 LEAGUE RECORD

| Match No. | Date | Venue | Opponents | Result | | H/T Score | Lg. Pos. | Goalscorers | Attendance |
|---|---|---|---|---|---|---|---|---|---|
| 1 | Aug 10 | H | Sunderland | W | 2-0 | 2-0 | — | Fjortoft [33], Borbokis [42] | 17,324 |
| 2 | 16 | A | Wolverhampton W | D | 0-0 | 0-0 | 5 | | 23,102 |
| 3 | 23 | H | Portsmouth | W | 2-1 | 2-0 | 3 | Fjortoft 2 [4, 15] | 15,895 |
| 4 | 30 | A | Huddersfield T | D | 0-0 | 0-0 | 5 | | 14,268 |
| 5 | Sept 13 | H | Nottingham F | W | 1-0 | 0-0 | 8 | Taylor [78] | 24,536 |
| 6 | 20 | A | Oxford U | W | 4-2 | 2-1 | 5 | Deane [1], Fjortoft (pen) [39], Holdsworth [67], Whitehouse [80] | 7514 |
| 7 | 27 | H | Birmingham C | D | 0-0 | 0-0 | 5 | | 20,553 |
| 8 | Oct 5 | A | Middlesbrough | W | 2-1 | 1-1 | 5 | Deane [23], Whitehouse [59] | 30,000 |
| 9 | 18 | H | QPR | D | 2-2 | 1-0 | 6 | Deane [31], Marcello [73] | 18,006 |
| 10 | 21 | H | Stockport Co | W | 5-1 | 2-1 | — | Whitehouse [6], Fjortoft 3 [21, 49, 90], Deane [55] | 16,241 |
| 11 | 25 | H | WBA | L | 0-2 | 0-1 | 6 | | 17,311 |
| 12 | Nov 1 | H | Tranmere R | W | 2-1 | 0-0 | 4 | Tiler [83], Taylor [85] | 16,578 |
| 13 | 4 | A | Reading | W | 1-0 | 0-0 | — | Patterson [52] | 8132 |
| 14 | 9 | A | Ipswich T | D | 2-2 | 1-1 | 4 | Taylor [9], Ward [79] | 9695 |
| 15 | 15 | H | Manchester C | D | 1-1 | 1-0 | 5 | Deane [21] | 23,780 |
| 16 | 18 | A | Bradford C | D | 1-1 | 0-0 | — | Deane [63] | 16,127 |
| 17 | 22 | A | Port Vale | D | 0-0 | 0-0 | 5 | | 8017 |
| 18 | 29 | H | Crewe Alex | W | 1-0 | 0-0 | 4 | Fjortoft [47] | 16,973 |
| 19 | Dec 2 | H | Stoke C | W | 3-2 | 0-1 | — | Taylor [46], Fjortoft [64], Deane [80] | 14,347 |
| 20 | 6 | A | Norwich C | L | 1-2 | 0-0 | 4 | Deane [51] | 11,745 |
| 21 | 9 | A | Charlton Ath | L | 1-2 | 0-1 | — | Marker [90] | 9868 |
| 22 | 13 | H | Swindon T | W | 2-1 | 1-1 | 3 | Holdsworth [45], Saunders [81] | 18,115 |
| 23 | 20 | A | Bury | D | 1-1 | 0-1 | 3 | Deane [79] | 6012 |
| 24 | 26 | A | Stoke C | D | 2-2 | 0-0 | 4 | Taylor [59], Deane [90] | 19,723 |
| 25 | 28 | H | Charlton Ath | W | 4-1 | 2-0 | 3 | Taylor [8], Saunders [32], Deane [57], Marker [64] | 18,677 |
| 26 | Jan 10 | A | Sunderland | L | 2-4 | 1-1 | 5 | Saunders [17], Taylor [82] | 36,391 |
| 27 | 17 | H | Wolverhampton W | W | 1-0 | 0-0 | 5 | Marcello [39] | 22,144 |
| 28 | 27 | H | Huddersfield T | D | 1-1 | 1-1 | — | Saunders [28] | 16,535 |
| 29 | 31 | A | Portsmouth | D | 1-1 | 1-1 | 5 | Knight (og) [32] | 12,003 |
| 30 | Feb 7 | H | Oxford U | W | 1-0 | 1-0 | 4 | Ford [43] | 16,881 |
| 31 | 22 | A | Birmingham C | L | 0-2 | 0-1 | 4 | | 17,965 |
| 32 | 25 | A | QPR | D | 2-2 | 1-1 | — | Saunders [8], Stuart [69] | 9560 |
| 33 | 28 | H | Bradford C | W | 2-1 | 1-0 | 5 | Taylor 2 [34, 79] | 17,848 |
| 34 | Mar 3 | H | Ipswich T | L | 0-1 | 0-1 | — | | 14,120 |
| 35 | 14 | A | Reading | W | 4-0 | 1-0 | 6 | Stuart [44], Marcello [46], Taylor [54], Quinn [90] | 15,473 |
| 36 | 21 | A | Manchester C | D | 0-0 | 0-0 | 6 | | 28,496 |
| 37 | 28 | H | Port Vale | W | 2-1 | 0-0 | 6 | Marcello [83], Saunders [89] | 15,860 |
| 38 | Apr 1 | A | Nottingham F | L | 0-3 | 0-2 | — | | 21,512 |
| 39 | 7 | A | Middlesbrough | W | 1-0 | 0-0 | — | Saunders [52] | 18,421 |
| 40 | 11 | H | Norwich C | D | 2-2 | 2-0 | 5 | Stuart [28], Borbokis [33] | 16,915 |
| 41 | 13 | A | Swindon T | D | 1-1 | 0-1 | 6 | Marcello [81] | 5956 |
| 42 | 18 | H | Bury | W | 3-0 | 1-0 | 6 | Stuart (pen) [29], Saunders 2 [76, 85] | 16,056 |
| 43 | 25 | H | WBA | L | 2-4 | 1-1 | 6 | Stuart (pen) [9], Marcello [69] | 21,248 |
| 44 | 28 | A | Tranmere R | D | 3-3 | 0-1 | — | Quinn [52], Saunders [78], Devlin [90] | 7526 |
| 45 | 30 | A | Crewe Alex | L | 1-2 | 0-0 | — | Hamilton [90] | 5759 |
| 46 | May 3 | A | Stockport Co | L | 0-1 | 0-0 | 6 | | 9683 |

**Final League Position: 6**      1996–97 DIV1 5

### GOALSCORERS

*League (69):* Deane 11, Saunders 10, Taylor 10, Fjortoft 9 (1 pen), Marcello 6, Stuart 5 (2 pens), Whitehouse 3, Borbokis 2, Holdsworth 2, Marker 2, Quinn 2, Devlin 1, Ford 1, Hamilton 1, Patterson 1, Tiler 1, Ward 1, own goal 1.
*Coca-Cola Cup (10):* Whitehouse 3, Borbokis 2, Deane 2, Fjortoft 1, Scott 1, own goal 1.
*FA Cup (8):* Fjortoft 2, Saunders 2, Holdsworth 1, Hutchison 1 (pen), Marcello 1, Sandford 1.

| Tracey S 27 | Borbokis V 36 | Quinn W 28 | McGrath P 12 | Tiler C 17 | Devlin P 4 + 6 | Holdsworth D 40 | Wilder C 7 + 1 | Patterson M 17 + 1 | Marker N 43 | Hamilton I 8 | Fjortoft J 15 + 2 | Deane B 24 | Whitehouse D 17 | Nilsen R 18 + 4 | Katchuro P 6 + 10 | Scott A 1 - 5 | Hutchison D 14 + 4 | White D — + 1 | Taylor G 13 + 15 | Walker A — + 1 | Ward M 3 + 3 | Marcello 12 + 9 | Dellas T 5 + 4 | Woodhouse C 4 + 5 | Ford B 20 + 3 | Stuart G 27 + 1 | Vonk M 3 | Saunders D 23 + 1 | Kelly A 19 | Henry N 1 | Lee D 5 | Barrett E 5 | Morris L — + 5 | Beard M — + 2 | Sandford L 15 | Derry S 8 + 4 | Cullen J — + 2 | Short C 5 | Rush I 4 | O'Connor J — + 2 | Match No. |
|---|---|---|---|---|---|---|---|---|---|---|---|---|---|---|---|---|---|---|---|---|---|---|---|---|---|---|---|---|---|---|---|---|---|---|---|---|---|---|---|---|---|
| 1 | 2 | 3¹ | 4 | 5 | 6 | 7 | 8 | 9² | 10 | 11 | 12 | 13 |  |  |  |  |  |  |  |  |  |  |  |  |  |  |  |  |  |  |  |  |  |  |  |  |  |  |  |  | 1 |
| 1 | 2 | 3 | 4 | 5 | 6 | 7 | 8 |  | 10 | 11 |  |  | 9¹ | 12 |  |  |  |  |  |  |  |  |  |  |  |  |  |  |  |  |  |  |  |  |  |  |  |  |  |  | 2 |
| 1 | 2 | 3 | 4 | 5 | 6 | 7 | 8 | 9¹ | 10 | 11 |  |  |  |  | 12 | 13 |  |  |  |  |  |  |  |  |  |  |  |  |  |  |  |  |  |  |  |  |  |  |  |  | 3 |
| 1 | 2 | 3 | 4 | 5 | 6 | 7 | 8 | 9² | 10¹ | 11 |  |  | 12 |  |  |  | 13 |  |  |  |  |  |  |  |  |  |  |  |  |  |  |  |  |  |  |  |  |  |  |  | 4 |
| 1 | 2 | 3 | 4 | 5 | 6 | 7 | 8¹ | 9³ |  | 11 | 12 |  | 10² |  |  |  | 13 | 14 |  |  |  |  |  |  |  |  |  |  |  |  |  |  |  |  |  |  |  |  |  |  | 5 |
| 1 | 2 | 3¹ | 4 | 5 | 6 | 7 | 8 | 9¹ | 10 | 11 | 13³ | 12 | 14 |  |  |  |  |  |  |  |  |  |  |  |  |  |  |  |  |  |  |  |  |  |  |  |  |  |  |  | 6 |
| 1 | 2 | 3¹ | 4 | 5 | 6 | 7 | 8 |  | 10 | 11 |  |  | 9¹ | 12 | 13 |  |  |  |  |  |  |  |  |  |  |  |  |  |  |  |  |  |  |  |  |  |  |  |  |  | 7 |
| 1 | 2 | 3 | 4 | 5 | 6 | 7 | 8 |  | 10 | 11² |  |  | 9¹ | 12 |  |  |  |  |  |  | 13 |  |  |  |  |  |  |  |  |  |  |  |  |  |  |  |  |  |  |  | 8 |
| 1 | 2 | 3 | 4 | 5 | 6 | 7 | 8 | 9¹ | 10 | 11 |  |  |  |  |  |  |  |  | 12 |  |  |  |  |  |  |  |  |  |  |  |  |  |  |  |  |  |  |  |  |  | 9 |
| 1 | 2¹ | 3 | 4 | 5 | 6 | 7² | 8 | 9 | 10³ | 11 |  | 13 |  |  |  |  |  |  | 12 |  | 14 |  |  |  |  |  |  |  |  |  |  |  |  |  |  |  |  |  |  |  | 10 |
| 1 | 2³ | 3 | 4 | 5 | 6 | 7 | 8 | 9 | 11 | 12 | 13 |  |  |  |  |  |  |  | 10¹ |  |  |  |  |  |  |  |  |  |  |  |  |  |  |  |  |  |  |  |  |  | 11 |
| 1 | 2 | 3 |  | 5 | 6 | 7¹ | 8 | 9² | 10 | 11 |  |  |  |  | 4 |  | 12 |  | 13 |  |  |  |  |  |  |  |  |  |  |  |  |  |  |  |  |  |  |  |  |  | 12 |
| 1 | 2 |  |  | 5 | 6 | 7 | 8 |  | 10 | 11 |  |  | 3 |  | 4 |  | 9 |  |  |  |  |  |  |  |  |  |  |  |  |  |  |  |  |  |  |  |  |  |  |  | 13 |
| 1¹ | 2 |  | 4 | 5 | 6 | 7 | 8 |  | 10 | 11 |  |  | 3 |  | 9 |  | 12 |  |  |  |  |  |  |  |  |  |  |  |  |  |  |  |  |  |  |  |  |  |  |  | 14 |
| 1 | 2 |  |  | 5 | 6 | 7² | 8 | 12 | 10 | 11 | 13 |  | 4 |  | 9¹ | 3 |  |  |  |  |  |  |  |  |  |  |  |  |  |  |  |  |  |  |  |  |  |  |  |  | 15 |
| 1 | 2 |  |  | 5 | 6 |  | 8 | 9 | 10 | 11 |  |  | 3 |  | 4 |  | 7 |  |  |  |  |  |  |  |  |  |  |  |  |  |  |  |  |  |  |  |  |  |  |  | 16 |
| 1 | 2 |  |  | 5 | 6 | 12 | 8 |  | 10 | 11³ |  |  | 3 |  | 4 |  | 9 |  | 7² | 13 |  |  |  |  |  |  |  |  |  |  |  |  |  |  |  |  |  |  |  |  | 17 |
| 1 | 2³ |  |  |  | 6 | 7² | 8 | 9¹ | 10 |  |  |  | 3 |  | 4 |  | 12 |  |  |  |  |  |  | 5 | 13 | 14 | 11 |  |  |  |  |  |  |  |  |  |  |  |  |  | 18 |
| 1 | 2 |  |  |  | 6 | 7³ | 8 | 9 | 10 |  |  |  | 3² | 4¹ |  |  | 12 |  |  |  |  |  |  | 5 | 13 | 14 | 11 |  |  |  |  |  |  |  |  |  |  |  |  |  | 19 |
| 1 | 2 |  |  |  | 6 |  | 8 | 9¹ | 10 |  |  |  | 12 |  |  |  |  |  |  |  | 3 | 4 | 11 | 5 | 7 |  |  |  |  |  |  |  |  |  |  |  |  |  |  |  | 20 |
|  | 2 |  |  |  | 6 |  | 8 | 12 | 10 |  |  |  | 3³ |  | 13 |  |  |  |  |  | 14 | 4 | 7¹ | 5 | 9 |  | 1 | 11² |  |  |  |  |  |  |  |  |  |  |  |  | 21 |
|  | 2 |  |  |  | 6 |  | 8 | 9¹ | 10 |  |  |  | 3 |  |  |  |  |  | 12 |  | 13 | 4 | 11² | 5 | 7 |  | 1 |  |  |  |  |  |  |  |  |  |  |  |  |  | 22 |
|  |  |  |  |  |  |  | 8 | 9¹ | 10 |  |  |  | 5 |  | 6 |  | 12 |  |  |  | 3 | 4 | 11 | 7 |  | 1 |  |  |  |  |  |  |  |  |  |  |  |  | 2 |  | 23 |
|  | 2² |  |  |  |  |  | 8 |  | 10 |  |  |  | 6 | 12 | 13 |  | 9 |  | 3¹ |  | 4 | 11 | 7 |  | 1 |  |  |  | 5 |  |  |  |  |  |  |  |  |  |  |  | 24 |
|  | 2² |  |  |  |  |  | 8 | 10¹ |  |  |  |  | 6 | 12 | 11 |  | 9 |  | 3 |  | 4 | 13 | 7 |  | 1 |  |  |  | 5 |  |  |  |  |  |  |  |  |  |  |  | 25 |
|  | 2 |  |  |  | 6 |  | 8 |  | 10 |  |  |  | 3 |  | 11 |  | 12 |  | 4 |  | 9 |  | 7 |  | 1 |  |  |  | 5¹ |  |  |  |  |  |  |  |  |  |  |  | 26 |
|  |  |  |  |  | 6 | 7 |  | 3² | 10 |  |  |  |  |  | 8¹ |  | 4 |  | 9 |  | 11 |  | 1 |  | 5 |  |  |  | 2 |  |  |  |  |  | 13 | 12 |  |  |  |  | 27 |
| 1 |  |  |  |  | 6 |  | 8 |  | 11² |  |  |  | 5¹ |  | 9 |  | 10 |  | 7 |  |  |  | 2 |  | 12 | 3 | 4 | 13 |  |  |  |  |  |  |  |  |  |  |  |  | 28 |
| 1 |  |  |  |  | 6 |  | 8 |  | 11 |  |  |  |  |  | 9 |  | 10 |  | 7 |  |  |  | 5 |  | 3 | 4 |  |  |  |  |  |  |  |  |  |  |  | 2 |  |  | 29 |
| 1 |  |  |  |  | 6 |  | 8 |  | 5² |  |  |  | 11 |  | 9 | 12 |  |  | 4 |  | 10¹ |  | 7 |  | 2 | 3 |  |  | 13 |  |  |  |  |  |  |  |  |  |  |  | 30 |
|  | 2³ | 3² |  |  | 6 |  | 8 |  | 12 |  |  |  |  |  | 9¹ | 13 |  |  | 10 |  | 11 |  | 7 | 1 |  |  | 4 |  |  |  |  | 5 | 14 |  |  |  |  |  |  |  | 31 |
|  | 4¹ | 3 |  |  | 6 |  | 8 |  |  |  |  |  |  |  | 12 |  |  |  |  |  |  |  | 10 | 11 | 7 | 1 |  |  |  |  |  | 5 |  |  |  | 2 | 9 |  |  | 32 |
|  | 4² | 3 |  |  | 6 |  | 8 |  |  |  |  |  |  |  | 12 |  |  |  |  |  |  |  | 10 | 11 | 7¹ | 1 |  |  |  |  |  | 5 |  |  |  | 2 | 9 | 13 | 33 |
|  | 4² | 3 |  |  | 6 |  | 8 |  |  |  |  |  |  |  |  | 10 |  |  | 12 |  |  |  | 7 | 11 |  | 1 |  |  |  |  |  | 13 | 5¹ |  |  | 2 | 9 |  | 34 |
|  | 4 | 3 | 14 | 6 |  | 8 |  |  |  |  |  |  | 12 |  |  |  |  |  |  |  |  | 9¹ | 10³ | 7 | 11² | 1 |  |  |  |  |  |  |  | 5 | 2 | 13 |  |  | 35 |
|  | 4³ | 3 | 14 | 6 |  | 8 |  |  |  |  |  |  | 12 |  |  |  |  |  |  |  |  | 10¹ | 13 | 7 | 11² | 1 |  |  |  |  |  |  |  | 5 | 2 |  | 9 | 36 |
|  |  | 3 |  |  |  | 6 | 2 | 8 |  |  | 4³ |  |  |  |  |  |  |  |  |  |  | 9² | 10 | 12 | 7¹ | 11 | 13 | 1 |  |  |  |  |  |  | 5 | 14 |  |  | 37 |
| 1 |  | 3 |  | 14 |  |  | 2 | 8⁸ |  | 4 |  |  |  |  |  |  |  |  |  |  | 12 | 10¹ | 6 | 13¹¹ | 9² |  | 1 |  |  |  |  |  | 5 | 7 |  |  |  |  | 38 |
|  | 2 | 4 | 13 | 6 |  |  |  | 8 |  |  |  | 3 |  |  |  |  |  |  | 9¹ |  | 12 | 10 | 11 | 7² | 1 |  |  |  |  |  |  |  | 5 |  |  |  |  |  | 39 |
|  | 2 | 4 | 13 | 6 |  |  |  | 8¹ |  |  |  | 3 |  |  |  |  |  |  | 9² |  |  | 10 | 11 | 7 | 1 |  |  |  |  |  |  |  | 5 |  |  |  |  |  | 40 |
|  | 3 |  |  |  | 9 | 6 |  | 2 | 8² |  |  |  |  |  |  |  |  |  | 10 |  | 12 | 4¹ | 11 | 7 | 1 |  |  |  |  |  |  |  | 5 | 13 |  |  |  | 41 |
|  | 2 | 3 |  |  | 6 | 13 | 8 |  |  |  |  |  | 12 |  |  |  |  |  | 10¹ |  | 9 | 4² | 11 | 7 | 1 |  |  |  |  |  |  |  | 5 |  |  |  |  |  | 42 |
|  | 2 | 3 | 13 |  | 4 | 8 | 6 |  |  |  |  | 5² |  |  |  |  |  |  | 10 | 9¹ | 12 | 11 | 7 | 1 |  |  |  |  |  |  |  | 5 |  |  |  |  |  |  | 43 |
| 1 |  | 3 |  |  | 9 | 6 | 2¹ | 8¹ |  |  |  |  |  |  |  | 10 |  |  | 4 |  | 12 | 11 | 7 |  |  |  |  |  |  |  |  |  | 13 | 5 |  |  |  |  | 44 |
| 1 | 2 | 3 |  |  | 9 | 6 |  | 8 |  |  |  |  |  |  | 4³ |  | 12 |  | 10¹ |  | 11² | 7 |  |  |  |  |  |  |  |  |  |  | 13 | 5 | 14 |  |  |  |  | 45 |
| 1 |  | 3 |  |  | 9 | 6 | 4 | 8² |  | 10 | 11¹ |  |  |  |  |  | 12 |  |  |  |  | 7 |  |  |  |  |  |  |  |  |  |  | 13 | 5 |  |  | 2 |  | 46 |

**Coca-Cola Cup**

| First Round | Wrexham | (a) | 1-1 |
|---|---|---|---|
|  |  | (h) | 3-1 |
| Second Round | Watford | (a) | 1-1 |
|  |  | (h) | 4-0 |
| Third Round | Walsall | (a) | 1-2 |

**FA Cup**

| Third Round | Bury | (h) | 1-1 |
|---|---|---|---|
|  |  | (a) | 2-1 |
| Fourth Round | Ipswich T | (a) | 1-1 |
|  |  | (h) | 1-0 |
| Fifth Round | Reading | (h) | 1-0 |
| Sixth Round | Coventry C | (a) | 1-1 |
|  |  | (h) | 1-1 |
| Semi Final | Newcastle U (at Old Trafford) |  | 0-1 |

SHEFFIELD WEDNESDAY 1997-98    *Back row (left to right):* Dejan Stefanovic, Orlando Trustfull, Lee Briscoe, Kevin Pressman, Jon Newsome, Matt Clarke, Andy Booth, Wayne Collins, O'Neill Donaldson.
*Middle row:* Peter Shreeves (Assistant Manager), Ian Nolan, Guy Whittingham, Scott Oakes, Patrick Blondeau, Ritchie Humphreys, Adem Poric, David Galley (Physio).
*Front row:* Mark Pembridge, Benito Carbone, Regi Blinker, Des Walker, David Pleat (Manager), Peter Atherton, Graham Hyde, Steve Nicol, David Hirst.

# FA Premiership **SHEFFIELD WEDNESDAY**

*Hillsborough, Sheffield S6 1SW.* Telephone: (0114) 2212121. Fax: (0114) 2212122. Ticket Office: (0114) 2212400. Clubcall: 0891 121186.

*Ground capacity:* 39,859.

*Record attendance:* 72,841 v Manchester C, FA Cup 5th rd, 17 February 1934.

*Record receipts:* £533,918 Sunderland v Norwich C, FA Cup semi-final, 5 April 1992.

*Pitch measurements:* 115yd × 74yd.

*President:* K. T. Addy.

*Chairman:* D. G. Richards. *Vice-Chairman:* K. T. Addy.

*Directors:* G. K. Hulley, R. M. Grierson FCA, J. Ashton MP, G. A. Thorpe, H. E. Culley.

*Manager:* Danny Wilson. *Assistant Manager:* Peter Shreeves.

*Physio:* David Galley.

*Secretary:* Graham Mackrell FCCA. *Commercial Manager:* Sean O'Toole. *Stadium Manager:* Trevor Grayson.

*Year Formed:* 1867 (fifth oldest League club).

*Turned Professional:* 1887. *Ltd Co.:* 1899.

*Former Names:* The Wednesday until 1929.

*Club Nickname:* 'The Owls'.

*Previous Grounds:* 1867, Highfield; 1869, Myrtle Road; 1877, Sheaf House; 1887, Olive Grove; 1899, Owlerton (since 1912 known as Hillsborough). Some games were played at Endcliffe in the 1880s. Until 1895 Bramall Lane was used for some games.

*Foundation:* Sheffield, being one of the principal centres of early Association Football, this club was formed as long ago as 1867 by the Sheffield Wednesday Cricket Club (formed 1825) and their colours from the start were blue and white. The inaugural meeting was held at the Adelphi Hotel and the original committee included Charles Stokes who was subsequently a founder member of Sheffield United.

*First Football League game:* 3 September 1892, Division 1, v Notts Co (a) W 1-0 – Allan; Tom Brandon (1), Mumford; Hall, Betts, Harry Brandon; Spiksley, Brady, Davis, R.N. Brown, Dunlop.

*Record League Victory:* 9–1 v Birmingham, Division 1, 13 December 1930 – Brown; Walker, Blenkinsop; Strange, Leach, Wilson; Hooper (3), Seed (2), Ball (2), Burgess (1), Rimmer (1).

*Record Cup Victory:* 12–0 v Halliwell, FA Cup 1st rd, 17 January 1891 – Smith; Thompson, Brayshaw; Harry Brandon (1), Betts, Cawley (2); Winterbottom, Mumford (2), Bob Brandon (1), Woolhouse (5), Ingram (1).

*Record Defeat:* 0–10 v Aston Villa, Division 1, 5 October 1912.

*Most League Points (2 for a win):* 62, Division 2, 1958–59.

*Most League Points (3 for a win):* 88, Division 2, 1983–84.

*Most League Goals:* 106, Division 2, 1958–59.

*Highest League Scorer in Season:* Derek Dooley, 46, Division 2, 1951–52.

*Most League Goals in Total Aggregate:* Andy Wilson, 199, 1900–20.

*Most Capped Player:* Nigel Worthington, 50 (66), Northern Ireland.

*Most League Appearances:* Andy Wilson, 502, 1900–20.

*Record Transfer Fee Received:* £2,650,000 from Blackburn R for Paul Warhurst, September 1993.

*Record Transfer Fee Paid:* £4,700,000 to Celtic for Paolo Di Canio, August 1997.

*Football League Record:* 1892 Elected to Division 1; 1899–1900 Division 2; 1900–20 Division 1; 1920–26 Division 2; 1926–37 Division 1; 1937–50 Division 2; 1950–51 Division 1; 1951–52 Division 2; 1952–55 Division 1; 1955–56 Division 2; 1956–58 Division 1; 1958–59 Division 2; 1959–70 Division 1; 1970–75 Division 1; 1975–80 Division 3; 1980–84 Division 2; 1984–90 Division 1; 1990–91 Division 2; 1991–92 Division 1; 1992– FA Premier League.

*Honours:* Football League: Division 1 – Champions 1902–03, 1903–04, 1928–29, 1929–30; Runners-up 1960–61; Division 2 – Champions 1899–1900, 1925–26, 1951–52, 1955–56, 1958–59; Runners-up 1949–50, 1983–84. *FA Cup:* Winners 1896, 1907, 1935; Runners-up 1890, 1966, 1993. *Football League Cup:* Winners 1991; Runners-up 1993. **European Competitions:** *Fairs Cup:* 1961–62, 1963–64, *UEFA Cup:* 1992–93.

*Colours:* Blue and white striped shirts, black shorts, black stockings. *Change colours:* Yellow shirts, navy shorts, yellow/navy stockings.

**Did you know?**
On 26 December 1911 Sheffield Wednesday defeated Sunderland 8-0, scoring seven goals in the first half. David McLean scored four goals but Sunderland had a player injured and off the field early in the match.

## SHEFFIELD WEDNESDAY 1997–98 LEAGUE RECORD

| Match No. | Date | Venue | Opponents | Result | | H/T Score | Lg. Pos. | Goalscorers | Atten-dance |
|---|---|---|---|---|---|---|---|---|---|
| 1 | Aug 9 | A | Newcastle U | L | 1-2 | 1-1 | — | Carbone [8] | 36,711 |
| 2 | 13 | H | Leeds U | L | 1-3 | 0-2 | — | Hyde [70] | 31,520 |
| 3 | 23 | A | Wimbledon | D | 1-1 | 0-1 | 17 | Di Canio [75] | 11,503 |
| 4 | 25 | A | Blackburn R | L | 2-7 | 1-5 | — | Carbone 2 [8, 47] | 19,618 |
| 5 | 30 | H | Leicester C | W | 1-0 | 0-0 | 15 | Carbone (pen) [56] | 24,851 |
| 6 | Sept 13 | A | Liverpool | L | 1-2 | 0-0 | 19 | Collins [80] | 34,705 |
| 7 | 20 | H | Coventry C | D | 0-0 | 0-0 | 19 | | 21,087 |
| 8 | 24 | H | Derby Co | L | 2-5 | 2-3 | — | Di Canio [9], Carbone (pen) [12] | 22,437 |
| 9 | 27 | A | Aston Villa | D | 2-2 | 2-1 | 18 | Collins [26], Whittingham [42] | 32,044 |
| 10 | Oct 4 | H | Everton | W | 3-1 | 0-0 | 16 | Carbone 2 (1 pen) [78, 82 (p)], Di Canio [89] | 24,483 |
| 11 | 19 | A | Tottenham H | L | 2-3 | 0-3 | 17 | Collins [72], Di Canio [85] | 25,097 |
| 12 | 25 | H | Crystal Palace | L | 1-3 | 0-1 | 19 | Collins [57] | 22,072 |
| 13 | Nov 1 | A | Manchester U | L | 1-6 | 0-4 | 20 | Whittingham [69] | 55,295 |
| 14 | 8 | H | Bolton W | W | 5-0 | 5-0 | 19 | Di Canio [20], Whittingham [26], Booth 3 [29, 33, 44] | 25,027 |
| 15 | 22 | H | Arsenal | W | 2-0 | 1-0 | 16 | Booth [42], Whittingham [86] | 34,373 |
| 16 | 29 | A | Southampton | W | 3-2 | 1-0 | 14 | Atherton [28], Collins [69], Di Canio [84] | 15,244 |
| 17 | Dec 8 | H | Barnsley | W | 2-1 | 1-1 | — | Stefanovic [19], Di Canio [89] | 29,086 |
| 18 | 13 | A | West Ham U | L | 0-1 | 0-0 | 13 | | 24,344 |
| 19 | 20 | H | Chelsea | L | 1-4 | 0-1 | 14 | Pembridge [71] | 28,334 |
| 20 | 26 | H | Blackburn R | D | 0-0 | 0-0 | 14 | | 33,502 |
| 21 | 28 | A | Leicester C | D | 1-1 | 0-1 | 15 | Booth [85] | 20,800 |
| 22 | Jan 10 | H | Newcastle U | W | 2-1 | 1-1 | 12 | Di Canio [1], Newsome [51] | 29,446 |
| 23 | 17 | A | Leeds U | W | 2-1 | 0-0 | 11 | Newsome [51], Booth [83] | 33,596 |
| 24 | 31 | H | Wimbledon | D | 1-1 | 1-1 | 11 | Pembridge [14] | 22,655 |
| 25 | Feb 7 | A | Coventry C | L | 0-1 | 0-0 | 14 | | 18,371 |
| 26 | 14 | H | Liverpool | D | 3-3 | 1-1 | 12 | Carbone [7], Di Canio [63], Hinchcliffe [69] | 35,405 |
| 27 | 21 | H | Tottenham H | W | 1-0 | 1-0 | 12 | Di Canio [33] | 29,871 |
| 28 | 28 | A | Derby Co | L | 0-3 | 0-1 | 13 | | 30,203 |
| 29 | Mar 7 | H | Manchester U | W | 2-0 | 1-0 | 12 | Atherton [26], Di Canio [88] | 39,427 |
| 30 | 14 | A | Bolton W | L | 2-3 | 1-1 | 13 | Booth [26], Atherton [59] | 24,847 |
| 31 | 28 | A | Arsenal | L | 0-1 | 0-1 | 13 | | 38,087 |
| 32 | Apr 4 | H | Southampton | W | 1-0 | 0-0 | 13 | Carbone [78] | 29,677 |
| 33 | 11 | A | Barnsley | L | 1-2 | 0-0 | 14 | Stefanovic [86] | 18,692 |
| 34 | 13 | H | West Ham U | D | 1-1 | 0-1 | 14 | Magilton [59] | 28,036 |
| 35 | 19 | A | Chelsea | L | 0-1 | 0-1 | 14 | | 29,075 |
| 36 | 25 | H | Everton | W | 3-1 | 2-0 | 13 | Pembridge 2 [6, 41], Di Canio [90] | 35,497 |
| 37 | May 2 | H | Aston Villa | L | 1-3 | 0-2 | 14 | Sanetti [89] | 34,177 |
| 38 | 10 | A | Crystal Palace | L | 0-1 | 0-0 | 16 | | 16,878 |

**Final League Position: 16**　　　1996–97 PREM 7

### GOALSCORERS

*League (52):* Di Canio 12, Carbone 9 (3 pens), Booth 7, Collins 5, Pembridge 4, Whittingham 4, Atherton 3, Newsome 2, Stefanovic 2, Hinchcliffe 1, Hyde 1, Magilton 1, Sanetti 1.
*Coca-Cola Cup (3):* Di Canio 2, own goal 1.
*FA Cup (1):* Alexandersson 1.

| Pressman K 36 | Blondeau P 5 + 1 | Nolan I 27 | Atherton P 27 | Stefanovic D 19 + 1 | Walker D 38 | Pembridge M 31 + 3 | Hyde G 14 + 8 | Donaldson O 1 + 4 | Carbone B 28 + 5 | Whittingham G 17 + 11 | Collins W 8 + 11 | Di Canio P 34 + 1 | Agogo M — + 1 | Booth A 21 + 2 | Humphreys R 2 + 5 | Oakes S — + 4 | Newsome J 25 | Hirst D 3 + 3 | Nicol S 4 + 3 | Briscoe L 3 + 4 | Magilton J 13 + 8 | Clarke M 2 + 1 | Poric A — + 4 | Clough N 1 | Rudi P 19 + 3 | Alexandersson N 5 + 1 | Hinchcliffe A 15 | Mayrleb C — + 3 | Barrett E 10 | Sedloski G 3 + 1 | Emerson 6 | Quinn A — + 1 | Sanetti F 1 + 1 | Match No. |
|---|---|---|---|---|---|---|---|---|---|---|---|---|---|---|---|---|---|---|---|---|---|---|---|---|---|---|---|---|---|---|---|---|---|---|
| 1 | 2 | 3 | 4 | 5 | 6 | 7 | 8¹ | 9² | 10 | 11¹ | 12 | 13 | 14 | | | | | | | | | | | | | | | | | | | | | 1 |
| 1 | 2 | 3 | 4 | 5 | 6 | | | 12 | 13 | 10² | | 7¹ | | 11 | | | 9 | 8³ | 14 | | | | | | | | | | | | | | | 2 |
| 1 | 2 | 3 | 4 | | 6 | 7¹ | 8 | | 10 | 12 | 11 | 9 | | | | | 5 | | | | | | | | | | | | | | | | | 3 |
| 1 | 2 | 3 | 4 | | 6¹ | | 8 | | 10 | 7¹² | 12 | 11 | | 9³ | | | 5 | 13 | 14 | | | | | | | | | | | | | | | 4 |
| 1 | 3³ | 2 | | | 6 | | 8¹ | | 10 | 13 | 12 | 11 | | 7² | | | 5 | 9 | 4 | 14 | | | | | | | | | | | | | | 5 |
| 1 | 3 | 2 | | | 6 | 10¹ | 7 | | 12 | 11 | | | | | | | 5 | 9 | 4² | 13 | 8 | | | | | | | | | | | | | 6 |
| 1⁶ | 2 | 4¹ | | | 6 | 10 | 7 | | 12 | 11 | 13 | 5 | | 9 | | | 3 | 8² | 15 | | | | | | | | | | | | | | | 7 |
| | 2 | 3 | 6 | | 4 | 10 | 7¹ | | 12 | 11 | 5² | 14 | | 13 | | | 8 | 1 | 9¹ | | | | | | | | | | | | | | | 8 |
| | 2 | | | 5 | 6 | 4¹ | | | 10 | 7 | 11 | 9 | | 3 | | | 8 | 1 | 12 | | | | | | | | | | | | | | | 9 |
| 1 | 3 | | | 5 | 6 | 4¹ | | | 10 | 7 | 11 | 9 | | 12 | | | 2² | 13 | 8³ | 14 | | | | | | | | | | | | | | 10 |
| 1 | 2 | | | 5² | 6 | 7 | | 12 | 10 | 14 | 13 | 9 | | 4 | | | 3¹ | 8 | 11³ | | | | | | | | | | | | | | | 11 |
| 1 | 2 | | | 6 | 4 | 12 | 10 | 7¹ | 11² | 9 | | | | | | | 5 | 3⁸ | 8 | 13 | 14 | | | | | | | | | | | | | 12 |
| 1 | 2 | | | 6 | 3 | 10¹ | 7 | 11³ | 9² | | 12 | | | | | | 5 | 13 | 8 | 14 | 4 | | | | | | | | | | | | | 13 |
| 1 | 12 | 3 | 2² | | 6 | 4 | 13 | 14 | 7 | 11¹ | | 9³ | | | | | 5 | 8 | 10 | | | | | | | | | | | | | | | 14 |
| 1 | | 3 | 2 | | 6 | 4 | 12 | 13 | 7 | 11² | | 9 | | | | | 5 | 8¹ | 10 | | | | | | | | | | | | | | | 15 |
| 1 | | 3 | 2 | | 6 | 4 | 12 | 7 | 13 | 11 | | 9¹ | | | | | 5 | 8² | 10 | | | | | | | | | | | | | | | 16 |
| 1 | | 2 | | 5 | 6 | 3 | 12 | | 8¹ | 7 | 10 | 11 | | 9 | | | 4 | | | | | | | | | | | | | | | | | 17 |
| 1 | | 2 | | 3 | 6 | 12 | 8¹ | | 13 | 7² | 10 | 11 | | 9³ | 14 | | 5 | | 4 | | | | | | | | | | | | | | | 18 |
| 1 | | 2 | | 3 | 6 | 4 | 13 | | 12 | 7³ | 8² | 11¹ | | 9 | | | 5 | | | | 10 | 14 | | | | | | | | | | | | 19 |
| 1 | | 2 | 4 | 3² | 6 | 11 | | | 10¹ | 12 | 13 | | | 9 | | | 5 | | | | 8 | 7 | | | | | | | | | | | | 20 |
| 1 | | 2 | 4 | 3 | 6 | 11² | 12 | | 10 | 13³ | | | | 9 | 14 | | 5 | | | | 8¹ | 7 | | | | | | | | | | | | 21 |
| 1 | | 2 | 4 | | 6 | 3 | 8² | | 10 | | | 9¹ | | 12 | 13 | | 5 | | | | 11 | 7 | | | | | | | | | | | | 22 |
| 1 | | 2 | 4 | | 6 | 3 | 8³ | | 12 | | | 11² | | 9 | 13 | | 5 | | | | 14 | 10 | 7¹ | | | | | | | | | | | 23 |
| 1 | | 2 | 4 | | 6 | 11 | | | 10² | 12 | | 9 | | | | | 5 | | | | 8 | 7¹ | 3 | 13 | | | | | | | | | | 24 |
| 1 | | 2 | 4 | | 6 | 11³ | 8² | | 10 | 12 | | 9 | | | | | 5 | | | | 13 | 7¹ | 3 | 14 | | | | | | | | | | 25 |
| 1 | | 2 | 4 | | 6 | 11¹ | 8² | | 10 | 12 | | 9 | | | | | 5 | | | | 13 | 7 | 3 | | | | | | | | | | | 26 |
| 1 | | 2¹ | 4 | 13 | 6 | 11² | 8³ | | 10 | | | 9 | | | | | 12 | 5 | | | 14 | 7 | 3 | | | | | | | | | | | 27 |
| 1 | | | 4 | | 6 | 11² | 8¹ | | 10 | | | 9¹ | | 12 | | | 5 | 13 | | | | 7 | 3 | | 14 | 2 | | | | | | | | 28 |
| 1 | | | 4 | 8 | 6 | 7¹ | | | 10 | 12 | | 11² | | 9 | | | 13 | 5 | | | | | 3 | | | 2 | | | | | | | | 29 |
| 1 | | | 4 | 8 | 6 | 7¹ | | | 10 | 11 | | 9 | | 5² | | | | | | | 12 | | 3 | | | 2 | 13 | | | | | | | 30 |
| 1 | | | 8 | 4 | 6 | 7¹ | 12 | | 10¹ | 13 | | 11 | | 9 | | | | | | | | | 3 | | | 2 | 5 | | | | | | | 31 |
| 1 | | | 4 | 8 | 6 | 7¹ | | | 10 | 12 | | 11 | | 9 | | | | | | | | | 3 | | | 2 | 5 | | | | | | | 32 |
| 1 | | | 8 | 6 | | 4² | 12 | | 13 | 7 | | 11 | | 9 | | | | | | | | | 3 | | | 2 | 5¹ | 10 | | | | | | 33 |
| 1 | | | 4 | | 6 | 12 | | | 10 | | | 11 | | 9 | | | 8 | | | | | | 7¹ | | | 3 | 2 | 5 | | | | | | 34 |
| 1 | | | 4 | 8 | 6 | 12 | | | 10 | | | 11 | | 9 | | | 13 | | | | | | 7¹ | | | 3 | 2² | 5 | | | | | | 35 |
| 1 | | 2 | | | 6 | 10 | 8² | | 7 | | | 11 | | 9 | | | 12 | | | | 4¹ | | 3 | | | | 5 | 13 | | | | | | 36 |
| 1 | | 7 | 4 | | 6 | 11³ | 8 | | 10 | 12 | | 9 | | | | | 13 | | | | | | 3 | | | | 2² | 5¹ | | | | 14 | | 37 |
| 1 | | 7 | 4 | | 6 | | 8¹ | | 10² | | | 9 | | 12 | | | | | | | | | 13 | | | 3 | 2 | 5 | | | | | 11 | 38 |

**Coca-Cola Cup**
Second Round     Grimsby T     (a) 0-2     (h) 3-2

**FA Cup**
Third Round     Watford     (a) 1-1     (h) 0-0
Fourth Round     Blackburn R     (h) 0-3

SHREWSBURY TOWN 1997-98　Back row (left to right): James Cope, Richard Scott, Mark Dempsey, Peter Wilding, Nick Ward, Mark Taylor, Kevin Seabury, Shaun Wray, Lee Taylor.
Third row: Scott Laydon, Jes Hardon, Mark Kearney (Assistant Manager), Malcolm Musgrove (Physio), Anthony Briscoe, Emeka Nwadike, Benny Gall, Paul Edwards, Mark Williams, Nathan Blaney, Roger Preece (Player/Coach), Charlie Walker (Chief Scout), Scott Rose.
Second row: Martyn Naylor, Ian Reed, Darran Currie, David Walton Jake King (Manager), Paul Evans, Michael Brown, Austin Berkley, Gareth Hamner, Craig Taite.
Front row: Anthony Ashton, Leon Drysdale, Mathew Jones, Joe Williams, John Newman, Glyn Thompson, Craig Poutney, Sean Northwood, Lee Bell, Paul Greenway, Matthew Neville.

# Division 3     **SHREWSBURY TOWN**

*Gay Meadow, Shrewsbury SY2 6AB.* Telephone: (01743) 360111. Fax: (01743) 236384. Commercial Dept: (01743) 356316. Clubcall: 0891 121194. Community Officer: Derek Mann (01743) 356623.

*Ground capacity:* 8000.

*Record attendance:* 18,917 v Walsall, Division 3, 26 April 1961.

*Record receipts:* £80,610 v Arsenal, FA Cup 5th rd, 27 February 1991.

*Pitch measurements:* 114yd × 74yd.

*President:* F. C. G. Fry. *Vice-President:* Dr J. Millard Bryson.

*Chairman:* R. Wycherley.

*Directors:* R. Bailey, A. Hopkins, M. J. Starkey, K. R. Woodhouse.

*Associate Directors:* M. R. Ashton, H. J. Wilson, K. J. Sayfritz.

*Manager:* Jake King. *Commercial Manager:* M. Thomas.

*Physio:* Malcolm Musgrove. *Coaches:* Mark Kearney, Roger Preece.

*Secretary:* M. J. Starkey. *Operations Manager:* M. R. Ashton.

*Club Nickname:* 'Town' or 'Blues'.

*Year Formed:* 1886. *Turned Professional:* 1896. *Ltd Co.:* 1936.

*Previous Ground:* Old Shrewsbury Racecourse.

*Foundation:* Shrewsbury School having provided a number of the early England and Wales international players it is not surprising that there was a Town club as early as 1876 which won the Birmingham Senior Cup in 1879. However, the present Shrewsbury Town club was formed in 1886 and won the Welsh FA Cup as early as 1891.

*First Football League game:* 19 August 1950, Division 3 (N), v Scunthorpe U (a) D 0-0 – Egglestone; Fisher, Lewis; Wheatley, Depear, Robinson; Griffin, Hope, Jackson, Brown, Barker.

*Record League Victory:* 7–0 v Swindon T, Division 3 (S), 6 May 1955 – McBride; Bannister, Skeech; Wallace, Maloney, Candlin; Price, O'Donnell (1), Weigh (4), Russell, McCue (2).

*Record Cup Victory:* 11–2 v Marine, FA Cup 1st rd, 11 November 1995 – Edwards, Seabury (Dempsey (1)), Withe (1), Evans (1), Whiston (2), Scott (1), Woods, Stevens (1), Spink (3) (Anthrobus), Walton, Berkley. (1 og).

*Record Defeat:* 1–8 v Norwich C, Division 3 (S), 13 September 1952 and v Coventry C, Division 3, 22 October 1963.

*Most League Points (2 for a win):* 62, Division 4, 1974–75.

*Most League Points (3 for a win):* 79, Division 3, 1993–94.

*Most League Goals:* 101, Division 4, 1958–59.

*Highest League Scorer in Season:* Arthur Rowley, 38, Division 4, 1958–59.

*Most League Goals in Total Aggregate:* Arthur Rowley, 152, 1958–65 (thus completing his League record of 434 goals).

*Most Capped Player:* Jimmy McLaughlin, 5 (12), Northern Ireland and Bernard McNally, 5, Northern Ireland.

*Most League Appearances:* Colin Griffin, 406, 1975–89.

*Record Transfer Fee Received:* £385,000 from WBA for Bernard McNally, July 1989.

*Record Transfer Fee Paid:* £100,000 to Aldershot for John Dungworth, November 1979 and £100,000 to Southampton for Mark Blake, August 1990.

*Football League Record:* 1950 Elected to Division 3 (N); 1951–58 Division 3 (S); 1958–59 Division 4; 1959–74 Division 3; 1974–75 Division 4; 1975–79 Division 3; 1979–89 Division 2; 1989–94 Division 3; 1994– Division 2.

*Honours: Football League:* Division 2 best season: 8th, 1983–84, 1984–85; Division 3 – Champions 1978–79, 1993–94; Division 4 – Runners-up 1974–75. *FA Cup:* best season: 6th rd, 1979, 1982. *Football League Cup:* Semi-final 1961. *Welsh Cup:* Winners 1891, 1938, 1977, 1979, 1984, 1985; Runners-up 1931, 1948, 1980. *Auto Windscreens Shield:* Runners-up 1996.

*Colours:* Blue shirts with white trim, blue shorts, blue stockings with white trim. *Change colours:* Yellow shirts, navy blue sleeves, yellow shorts, yellow stockings with navy blue tops.

**Did you know?**
In a first round Welsh Cup tie against Mold Alyn on 27 October 1894, Shrewsbury Town won 21-0 with Alf Ellis scoring seven times.

## SHREWSBURY TOWN 1997–98 LEAGUE RECORD

| Match No. | Date | | Venue | Opponents | Result | | H/T Score | Lg. Pos. | Goalscorers | Attendance |
|---|---|---|---|---|---|---|---|---|---|---|
| 1 | Aug | 9 | H | Doncaster R | W | 2-1 | 1-0 | — | Walton [15], Currie [55] | 3029 |
| 2 | | 16 | A | Lincoln C | L | 0-1 | 0-0 | 13 | | 3019 |
| 3 | | 23 | H | Torquay U | L | 1-2 | 0-0 | 19 | Evans [82] | 2556 |
| 4 | | 30 | A | Cambridge U | L | 3-4 | 1-1 | 19 | Evans [19], Scott [52], Dempsey [88] | 2585 |
| 5 | Sept | 2 | A | Cardiff C | D | 2-2 | 1-0 | — | Berkley [39], Steele [52] | 4271 |
| 6 | | 9 | H | Rochdale | W | 1-0 | 0-0 | — | Evans (pen) [78] | 2410 |
| 7 | | 13 | A | Chester C | L | 0-2 | 0-1 | 17 | | 2853 |
| 8 | | 20 | H | Notts Co | L | 1-2 | 0-0 | 20 | Blamey [51] | 2532 |
| 9 | | 27 | A | Hartlepool U | L | 1-2 | 0-2 | 20 | Evans (pen) [78] | 2253 |
| 10 | Oct | 4 | H | Rotherham U | W | 2-1 | 1-0 | 19 | White [13], Currie (pen) [83] | 2432 |
| 11 | | 11 | H | Barnet | W | 2-0 | 1-0 | 19 | Steele [29], Currie [76] | 2112 |
| 12 | | 18 | A | Colchester U | D | 1-1 | 1-0 | 19 | Seabury [25] | 2977 |
| 13 | | 21 | A | Scunthorpe U | D | 1-1 | 1-1 | — | Currie (pen) [39] | 2303 |
| 14 | | 25 | H | Scarborough | L | 0-1 | 0-0 | 19 | | 2395 |
| 15 | Nov | 1 | H | Mansfield T | W | 3-2 | 1-1 | 15 | White [43], Scott 2 [66, 78] | 2338 |
| 16 | | 4 | A | Peterborough U | D | 1-1 | 0-1 | — | White [65] | 4727 |
| 17 | | 8 | A | Hull C | W | 4-1 | 2-0 | 15 | Steele [17], White 2 [45, 52], Scott [69] | 4758 |
| 18 | | 18 | H | Macclesfield T | W | 4-3 | 1-2 | — | White 3 [27, 57, 84], Scott [58] | 2600 |
| 19 | | 22 | A | Exeter C | D | 2-2 | 1-1 | 13 | Scott 2 [17, 79] | 4041 |
| 20 | | 29 | H | Swansea C | L | 0-1 | 0-0 | 15 | | 2697 |
| 21 | Dec | 13 | H | Leyton Orient | L | 1-2 | 0-2 | 17 | Steele [90] | 2137 |
| 22 | | 20 | A | Brighton & HA | D | 0-0 | 0-0 | 17 | | 1917 |
| 23 | | 26 | A | Rochdale | L | 1-3 | 1-1 | 18 | Wilding [45] | 2247 |
| 24 | | 28 | H | Cardiff C | W | 3-2 | 1-0 | 16 | Brown [37], White [53], Preece [86] | 3238 |
| 25 | Jan | 10 | A | Doncaster R | L | 0-1 | 0-0 | 18 | | 1116 |
| 26 | | 17 | H | Cambridge U | D | 1-1 | 1-1 | 18 | Taylor (og) [1] | 2210 |
| 27 | | 24 | A | Torquay U | L | 0-3 | 0-2 | 19 | | 1996 |
| 28 | | 31 | A | Chester C | D | 1-1 | 1-0 | 19 | Steele [7] | 3002 |
| 29 | Feb | 7 | A | Notts Co | D | 1-1 | 1-0 | 20 | Hanmer [16] | 5789 |
| 30 | | 14 | A | Rotherham U | W | 1-0 | 0-0 | 17 | Steele [62] | 3603 |
| 31 | | 21 | H | Hartlepool U | W | 1-0 | 0-0 | 16 | Evans (pen) [90] | 2160 |
| 32 | | 24 | A | Colchester U | L | 0-2 | 0-1 | — | | 1972 |
| 33 | | 28 | A | Barnet | D | 1-1 | 1-1 | 19 | Tretton [25] | 2322 |
| 34 | Mar | 3 | H | Hull C | W | 2-0 | 0-0 | — | Evans [79], Kerrigan [90] | 1523 |
| 35 | | 7 | A | Mansfield T | D | 1-1 | 1-0 | 18 | Seabury [18] | 2219 |
| 36 | | 14 | H | Peterborough U | W | 4-1 | 3-0 | 16 | White [29], Steele 2 [36, 57], Scott [42] | 2421 |
| 37 | | 21 | A | Macclesfield T | L | 1-2 | 0-0 | 18 | Brown [47] | 3013 |
| 38 | | 24 | H | Lincoln C | L | 0-2 | 0-1 | — | | 1877 |
| 39 | | 28 | H | Exeter C | D | 1-1 | 1-0 | 18 | Steele [26] | 2251 |
| 40 | | 31 | A | Darlington | L | 1-3 | 1-1 | — | Scott [42] | 1816 |
| 41 | Apr | 4 | A | Swansea C | W | 1-0 | 1-0 | 17 | Berkley [40] | 2623 |
| 42 | | 11 | H | Darlington | W | 3-0 | 0-0 | 16 | Scott [52], Steele [57], Berkley [78] | 1942 |
| 43 | | 13 | A | Leyton Orient | W | 3-2 | 0-1 | 14 | Steele 3 [55, 67, 81] | 4956 |
| 44 | | 18 | H | Brighton & HA | W | 2-1 | 0-1 | 12 | Kerrigan [83], Jagielka [84] | 2728 |
| 45 | | 25 | A | Scarborough | D | 0-0 | 0-0 | 13 | | 3712 |
| 46 | May | 2 | H | Scunthorpe U | L | 0-2 | 0-1 | 13 | | 2704 |

**Final League Position: 13**       1996–97 DIV2 22

### GOALSCORERS

**League (61):** Steele 13, Scott 10, White 10, Evans 6 (3 pens), Currie 4 (2 pens), Berkley 3, Brown 2, Kerrigan 2, Seabury 2, Blamey 1, Dempsey 1, Hanmer 1, Jagielka 1, Preece 1, Tretton 1, Walton 1, Wilding 1, own goal 1.
**Coca-Cola Cup (4):** Steele 3 (1 pen), Currie 1.
**FA Cup (1):** Herbert 1.

| Edwards P 34 | Naylor M 2 | Dempsey M 8+4 | Wilding P 33+1 | Walton D 6 | Herbert C 23+1 | Currie D 10+6 | Brown M 24+6 | Steele L 37+1 | Evans P 37+2 | Taylor M 17+1 | Jagielka S 4+12 | Blamey N 9 | Seabury K 35+4 | Ward N 3+3 | Berkley A 28+8 | Scott R 28+6 | Hanmer G 39 | Nwadike E 1 | Taylor L 1 | Overson V 2 | Gall B 11 | White D 30+2 | Preece R 25+2 | Griffiths G 6 | Gayle B 23 | Tretton A 14 | Germaine G 1 | Dudley C 3+1 | Kerrigan S 11+3 | Williams M —+5 | Craven D 1 | Pountney C —+1 | Match No. |
|---|---|---|---|---|---|---|---|---|---|---|---|---|---|---|---|---|---|---|---|---|---|---|---|---|---|---|---|---|---|---|---|---|---|
| 1 | 2 | 3 | 4 | 5 | 6 | 7 | 8¹ | 9 | 10 | 11 | 12 | | | | | | | | | | | | | | | | | | | | | | 1 |
| 1 | | 3 | 4 | 5 | 6 | 7 | 8 | 9¹ | 10 | 11 | 12 | 2 | | | | | | | | | | | | | | | | | | | | | 2 |
| 1 | | 3 | 4 | | 6 | 7¹ | 12 | 9 | 10 | 11 | | | 2² | 5 | 8¹ | 14 | 13 | | | | | | | | | | | | | | | | 3 |
| 1 | 2 | 12 | | | 6 | | 13 | 9 | 10 | | | | 8² | 5 | 11 | 7 | 3¹ | 4 | | | | | | | | | | | | | | | 4 |
| 1 | | 3 | | | 6 | | 11 | 9 | 10 | | | 2 | 8¹ | | 12 | 7 | 4 | | | 5 | | | | | | | | | | | | | 5 |
| 1 | | 3 | 5 | | 6 | 7¹ | | 9 | 10 | | | 2 | 8² | 12 | 13 | 11 | 4 | | | | | | | | | | | | | | | | 6 |
| 1 | | 3 | 5 | | 6 | 12 | 7¹ | 9 | 10 | | | | 2² | | 13 | 8 | 11 | 4 | | | | | | | | | | | | | | | 7 |
| 1 | | 5¹ | 4 | | 12 | 13 | | 9 | 10 | 8² | | 2 | 11³ | 14 | | 7 | | | | | 6 | | | | | | | | | | | | 8 |
| | | 5 | 4 | 12 | | | | 9 | 10 | | | 2 | 13 | 7¹ | 3 | | | | | | 6 | 1 | 8 | 11² | | | | | | | | | 9 |
| | | 5 | 4 | 7 | 6 | | | 9 | 10¹ | | | 2 | | | 12 | | 3 | | | | 1 | 8 | 11 | | | | | | | | | | 10 |
| | | 12 | 5 | 4 | 7 | 8 | 9 | | | | | 2² | | 13 | 11¹ | 3 | | | | | 1 | 10 | 6 | | | | | | | | | | 11 |
| | | 12 | 4 | | 5 | 10 | 8 | | | | | 2 | | 6 | 7¹ | 3 | | | | | 1 | 9 | 11 | | | | | | | | | | 12 |
| | | 12 | 4 | | 5 | 10 | 8² | | 13 | | | 2³ | 6 | | 7¹ | 14 | 3 | | | | 1 | 9 | 11 | | | | | | | | | | 13 |
| | | | 4 | | 5 | 10¹ | 8 | | 12 | | 13 | 2² | 6 | | 7 | 3 | | | | | 1 | 9 | 11 | | | | | | | | | | 14 |
| | 2¹ | 4 | | | 6 | 7 | 9² | 10 | 13 | 14 | 12 | | 3 | | 1 | 8 | 11² | 5 | | | | | | | | | | | | | | | 15 |
| | | 6 | | 4 | | | | 9 | 10 | | | 2 | | 11 | 3 | | | | | 1 | 8 | 7 | 5 | | | | | | | | | | 16 |
| | | 6 | | 4 | | | | 9 | 10 | | | 2 | | 11 | 3 | | | | | 1 | 8 | 7 | 5 | | | | | | | | | | 17 |
| | | 6 | | 4 | | | | 9 | 10 | | | 2 | | 11 | 3 | | | | | 1 | 8 | 7 | 5 | | | | | | | | | | 18 |
| | | 6 | | 4 | 12 | 13 | | 9 | 10 | | | 2² | | 11 | 3 | | | | | 1 | 8 | 7¹ | 5 | | | | | | | | | | 19 |
| 1 | | 6 | | 4 | 12 | | 10 | 13 | | | | 2² | 9¹ | 14 | 11 | 3 | | | | | 8 | 7³ | 5 | | | | | | | | | | 20 |
| 1 | | 4 | | | 7 | | 9 | | 2 | | | | 12 | 11¹ | 3 | | | | | 8 | 10 | 5 | 6 | | | | | | | | | | 21 |
| 1 | | 6 | | | 10 | | 9¹ | | 2 | 12 | | | 11 | 3 | | | | | | 8 | 4 | 5 | 7 | | | | | | | | | | 22 |
| 1 | | 6¹ | 12 | 13 | | 9 | | 2³ | 14 | 10 | | | 11¹ | 3 | | | | | | 8 | 4 | 5 | 7 | | | | | | | | | | 23 |
| 1 | | | 10¹ | 9 | | 6 | | 2 | 11 | 12 | | | 3 | | | | | | | 8 | 4 | 5 | 7 | | | | | | | | | | 24 |
| | | | 11 | | 10 | | 2 | 7 | 12 | | | 3 | | | | | | | 8 | 4¹ | 5 | 6 | 1 | 9 | | | | | | | | | 25 |
| 1 | 4 | 5² | 12 | | 10 | 7 | 2 | 13 | 11¹ | | 3 | | | | | | | | | 9 | | 6 | 8 | | | | | | | | | | 26 |
| 1 | 6 | | 9 | 10 | 4 | 2 | 12 | 11¹ | 3 | | | | | | | | | 8 | | | 5 | 13 | 7² | | | | | | | | | | 27 |
| 1 | | 9 | 10 | 4 | 2 | 11 | 3 | 12 | 7 | | | | | | | | | 6 | 5 | 8¹ | | | | | | | | | | | | | 28 |
| 1 | | 9 | 10 | 4 | 2 | 11 | 3 | 8 | 11 | | | | | | | | | 6 | 5 | | | | | | | | | | | | | | 29 |
| 1 | 12 | 9² | 10 | 4¹ | 2 | 7 | 3 | 8 | 11 | | | | | | | | | 6 | 5 | 13 | | | | | | | | | | | | | 30 |
| 1 | | 9 | 10 | 4¹ | 2 | 7 | 12 | 3 | 8 | 11 | | | | | | | | 6 | 5 | | | | | | | | | | | | | | 31 |
| 1 | | 9² | 10 | 12 | 2 | 7 | 6¹ | 3 | 8 | 11 | 4 | 5 | | | | | | | | 13 | | | | | | | | | | | | | 32 |
| 1 | 4 | 10 | 2 | 7 | 3 | 8 | 11 | 6 | 5 | 9 | | | | | | | | | | | | | | | | | | | | | | | 33 |
| 1 | 4 | 12 | 10 | 2 | 7 | 3 | 8 | 11 | 6 | 5¹ | 9 | | | | | | | | | | | | | | | | | | | | | | 34 |
| 1 | 4 | 5 | 12 | 10 | 2 | 7 | 3 | 8¹ | 11 | 6 | 9 | | | | | | | | | | | | | | | | | | | | | | 35 |
| 1 | 4 | 11 | 9 | 10 | 2 | 7 | 5 | 3 | 8¹ | 6 | 12 | | | | | | | | | | | | | | | | | | | | | | 36 |
| 1 | 4 | 6 | 11¹ | 9 | 10 | 2 | 7 | 5 | 3 | 8 | 12 | | | | | | | | | | | | | | | | | | | | | | 37 |
| 1 | 4 | 11 | 9 | 10 | 2 | 7 | 5 | 3 | 8¹ | 6 | 12 | | | | | | | | | | | | | | | | | | | | | | 38 |
| 1 | 4 | 11¹ | 9 | 10 | 2 | 7 | 5 | 3 | 12 | 6 | 8 | | | | | | | | | | | | | | | | | | | | | | 39 |
| 1 | 4 | 11³ | 9¹ | 10² | 12 | 2 | 7 | 5 | 3 | 13 | 6 | 8 | 14 | | | | | | | | | | | | | | | | | | | | 40 |
| 1 | 4 | 11¹ | 9 | 10 | 2 | 7 | 5 | 3 | 6 | 8 | | | | | | | | | | | | | | | | | | | | | | | 41 |
| 1 | 4 | 11¹ | 9 | 10 | 12 | 2 | 7² | 5 | 3 | 13 | 6 | 8 | | | | | | | | | | | | | | | | | | | | | 42 |
| 1 | 4 | 11¹ | 9 | 10 | 12 | 2 | 7 | 5 | 3 | 6 | 8 | | | | | | | | | | | | | | | | | | | | | | 43 |
| 1 | 4 | 11¹ | 9 | 10 | 12 | 2 | 7 | 5 | 3 | 6 | 8 | | | | | | | | | | | | | | | | | | | | | | 44 |
| 1 | 4 | 11 | 9 | 10 | 12 | 2 | 7¹ | 5 | 3 | 8² | 6 | 13 | | | | | | | | | | | | | | | | | | | | | 45 |
| 1 | 4 | 11³ | 9 | 10¹ | 12 | 2 | 5 | 3 | 6 | 8² | 13 | 7 | 14 | | | | | | | | | | | | | | | | | | | | 46 |

**Coca-Cola Cup**  
First Round   Brentford   (a) 1-1  
   (h) 3-5

**FA Cup**  
First Round   Grimsby T   (h) 1-1  
   (a) 0-4

SOUTHAMPTON 1997–98   *Back row (left to right):* Malcolm Taylor (Kit Manager), Andrew Catley, Garry Monk, Philip Warner, Russ Watkinson, Chris Deegan, David Piper, Stewart Henderson (Youth Development Officer).

*Third row:* Lee Todd, Simon Charlton, Christer Warren, Adam Batchelor, Matthew Robinson, Neil Moss, Steve Basham, Duncan Spedding, Darryl Flahavan, Kevin Davies, Matthew Oakley, Andy Williams, Alan Neilson, Robbie Slater.

*Second row:* Stuart Gray (Reserve Team Manager), Jim Magilton, Egil Ostenstad, Neil Maddison, Ulrich Van Gobbel, Paul Jones, Dave Beasant, Maik Taylor, Ken Monkou, Claus Lundekvam, Michael Evans, Richard Dryden, Joe Jakub (Youth Team Manager).

*Front row:* Jim Joyce (Physio), Jason Dodd, Matthew Le Tissier, Terry Cooper (Assistant Manager), David Jones (Manager), Rupert Lowe (Chairman), John Sainty (Assistant Manager), John Mortimore (Assistant Manager), Barry Venison, Francis Benali, Don Taylor (Physio).

# FA Premiership　　　　　　SOUTHAMPTON

*The Dell, Milton Road, Southampton SO15 2XH.* Telephone: (01703) 220505. Fax: (01703) 330360. Recorded Ticket Information: (01703) 228575. Clubcall: 0891 121178.

*Ground capacity:* 15,000.

*Record attendance:* 31,044 v Manchester U, Division 1, 8 October 1969.

*Record receipts:* £215,450 v Portsmouth, FA Cup 3rd rd, 7 January 1996.

*Pitch measurements:* 110yd × 72yd.

*Chairman:* R. J. G. Lowe.

*Vice-Chairman:* B. H. D. Hunt.

*Directors:* I. L. Gordon, K. St. J. Wiseman, M. R. Richards FCA, A. Cowen.

*President:* E. T. Bates. *Manager:* Dave Jones.

*Joint Assistant Managers:* John Sainty, John Mortimore, Terry Cooper.

*Physios:* Don Taylor, Jim Joyce.

*Secretary:* Brian Truscott.

*Year Formed:* 1885. *Turned Professional:* 1894. *Ltd Co.:* 1897.

*Club Nickname:* 'The Saints'.

*Previous Name:* Southampton St Mary's until 1885.

*Previous Grounds:* 1885, Antelope Ground; 1897, County Cricket Ground; 1898, The Dell.

*Foundation:* Formed largely by players from the Deanery FC, which had been established by school teachers in 1880. Most of the founders were connected with the young men's association of St. Mary's Church. At the inaugural meeting held in November 1885 the club was named Southampton St. Mary's and the church's curate was elected president.

*First Football League game:* 28 August 1920, Division 3, v Gillingham (a) D 1-1 – Allen; Parker, Titmuss; Shelley, Campbell, Turner; Barratt, Dominy (1), Rawlings, Moore, Foxall.

*Record League Victory:* 9–3 v Wolverhampton W, Division 2, 18 September 1965 – Godfrey; Jones, Williams; Walker, Knapp, Huxford; Paine (2), O'Brien (1), Melia, Chivers (4), Sydenham (2).

*Record Cup Victory:* 7–1 v Ipswich T, FA Cup 3rd rd, 7 January 1961 – Reynolds; Davies, Traynor; Conner, Page, Huxford; Paine (1), O'Brien (3 incl. 1p), Reeves, Mulgrew (2), Penk (1).

*Record Defeat:* 0–8 v Tottenham H, Division 2, 28 March 1936 and v Everton, Division 1, 20 November 1971.

*Most League Points (2 for a win):* 61, Division 3 (S), 1921–22 and Division 3, 1959–60.

*Most League Points (3 for a win):* 77, Division 1, 1983–84.

*Most League Goals:* 112, Division 3 (S), 1957–58.

*Highest League Scorer in Season:* Derek Reeves, 39, Division 3, 1959–60.

*Most League Goals in Total Aggregate:* Mike Channon, 185, 1966–77, 1979–82.

*Most Capped Player:* Peter Shilton, 49 (125), England.

*Most League Appearances:* Terry Paine, 713, 1956–74.

*Record Transfer Fee Received:* £3,300,000 from Blackburn R for Alan Shearer, July 1992.

*Record Transfer Fee Paid:* £2,000,000 to Sheffield Wednesday for David Hirst, October 1997.

*Football League Record:* 1920 Original Member of Division 3; 1921–22 Division 3 (S); 1922–53 Division 2; 1953–58 Division 3 (S); 1958–60 Division 3; 1960–66 Division 2; 1966–74 Division 1; 1974–78 Division 2; 1978–92 Division 1; 1992– FA Premier League.

*Honours: Football League:* Division 1 – Runners-up 1983–84; Division 2 – Runners-up 1965–66, 1977–78; Division 3 (S) – Champions 1921–22; Runners-up 1920–21; Division 3 – Champions 1959–60. *FA Cup:* Winners 1976; Runners-up 1900, 1902. *Football League Cup:* Runners-up 1979. *Zenith Data Systems Cup:* Runners-up 1992. **European Competitions:** *European Fairs Cup:* 1969–70. *UEFA Cup:* 1971–72, 1981–82, 1982–83, 1984–85. *European Cup-Winners' Cup:* 1976–77.

*Colours:* Red and white striped shirts, black shorts, red and white hooped stockings. *Change colours:* Yellow shirts with blue trim, blue shorts, yellow stockings with blue trim.

**Did you know?**
Between 15 April 1922 and 28 August 1922 Southampton played 845 minutes without their opponents scoring. The 21 goals they conceded in 1921-22 was then a Football League record.

## SOUTHAMPTON 1997–98 LEAGUE RECORD

| Match No. | Date | Venue | Opponents | | Result | H/T Score | Lg. Pos. | Goalscorers | Attendance |
|---|---|---|---|---|---|---|---|---|---|
| 1 | Aug 9 | H | Bolton W | L | 0-1 | 0-1 | — | | 15,206 |
| 2 | 13 | A | Manchester U | L | 0-1 | 0-0 | — | | 55,008 |
| 3 | 23 | H | Arsenal | L | 1-3 | 1-1 | 19 | Maddison 25 | 15,246 |
| 4 | 27 | H | Crystal Palace | W | 1-0 | 0-0 | — | Davies 57 | 15,032 |
| 5 | 30 | A | Chelsea | L | 2-4 | 1-4 | 18 | Davies 25, Monkou 59 | 28,832 |
| 6 | Sept 13 | A | Coventry C | L | 0-1 | 0-0 | 20 | | 18,666 |
| 7 | 20 | H | Liverpool | D | 1-1 | 0-1 | 20 | Davies 48 | 15,242 |
| 8 | 24 | H | Leeds U | L | 0-2 | 0-1 | — | | 15,102 |
| 9 | 27 | A | Derby Co | L | 0-4 | 0-0 | 20 | | 25,625 |
| 10 | Oct 4 | H | West Ham U | W | 3-0 | 0-0 | 19 | Ostenstad 54, Davies 65, Dodd 68 | 15,212 |
| 11 | 18 | A | Blackburn R | L | 0-1 | 0-1 | 19 | | 24,130 |
| 12 | 25 | H | Tottenham H | W | 3-2 | 0-1 | 18 | Campbell (og) 54, Hirst 2 67, 80 | 15,255 |
| 13 | Nov 2 | A | Everton | W | 2-0 | 1-0 | 16 | Le Tissier 24, Davies 54 | 29,565 |
| 14 | 8 | H | Barnsley | W | 4-1 | 3-1 | 13 | Le Tissier (pen) 3, Palmer 5, Davies 35, Hirst 54 | 15,018 |
| 15 | 22 | A | Newcastle U | L | 1-2 | 1-0 | 14 | Davies 5 | 36,769 |
| 16 | 29 | H | Sheffield W | L | 2-3 | 0-1 | 16 | Hirst 48, Palmer 55 | 15,244 |
| 17 | Dec 7 | A | Wimbledon | L | 0-1 | 0-1 | 17 | | 12,009 |
| 18 | 13 | H | Leicester C | W | 2-1 | 1-0 | 17 | Le Tissier 2, Benali 54 | 15,121 |
| 19 | 20 | A | Aston Villa | D | 1-1 | 0-0 | 15 | Ostenstad 72 | 29,343 |
| 20 | 26 | A | Crystal Palace | D | 1-1 | 1-0 | 15 | Oakley 39 | 22,853 |
| 21 | 29 | H | Chelsea | W | 1-0 | 1-0 | — | Davies 16 | 15,237 |
| 22 | Jan 10 | A | Bolton W | D | 0-0 | 0-0 | 13 | | 23,333 |
| 23 | 19 | H | Manchester U | W | 1-0 | 1-0 | — | Davies 3 | 15,241 |
| 24 | 31 | A | Arsenal | L | 0-3 | 0-0 | 12 | | 38,056 |
| 25 | Feb 7 | A | Liverpool | W | 3-2 | 1-1 | 11 | Hirst 2 (1 pen) 8 (p), 89, Ostenstad 85 | 43,550 |
| 26 | 18 | H | Coventry C | L | 1-2 | 0-2 | — | Le Tissier (pen) 79 | 15,091 |
| 27 | 21 | H | Blackburn R | W | 3-0 | 1-0 | 11 | Ostenstad 2 19, 88, Hirst 78 | 15,162 |
| 28 | 28 | A | Leeds U | W | 1-0 | 0-0 | 11 | Hirst 54 | 28,926 |
| 29 | Mar 7 | A | Everton | W | 2-1 | 0-0 | 10 | Le Tissier (pen) 69, Ostenstad 86 | 15,102 |
| 30 | 14 | A | Barnsley | L | 3-4 | 2-3 | 11 | Ostenstad 25, Le Tissier 2 41, 71 | 18,366 |
| 31 | 28 | H | Newcastle U | W | 2-1 | 0-0 | 10 | Pearce (og) 69, Le Tissier (pen) 85 | 15,251 |
| 32 | Apr 4 | A | Sheffield W | L | 0-1 | 0-0 | 11 | | 29,677 |
| 33 | 11 | H | Wimbledon | L | 0-1 | 0-1 | 12 | | 14,815 |
| 34 | 14 | A | Leicester C | D | 3-3 | 2-1 | — | Ostenstad 2 17, 27, Hirst 49 | 20,708 |
| 35 | 18 | H | Aston Villa | L | 1-2 | 1-1 | 12 | Le Tissier 19 | 15,238 |
| 36 | 25 | A | West Ham U | W | 4-2 | 1-1 | 12 | Le Tissier 40, Ostenstad 2 63, 86, Palmer 80 | 25,878 |
| 37 | May 2 | H | Derby Co | L | 0-2 | 0-0 | 12 | | 15,202 |
| 38 | 10 | A | Tottenham H | D | 1-1 | 1-1 | 12 | Le Tissier 21 | 35,995 |

**Final League Position: 12**     1996–97 PREM 16

### GOALSCORERS

*League (50):* Le Tissier 11 (4 pens), Ostenstad 11, Davies 9, Hirst 9 (1 pen), Palmer 3, Benali 1, Dodd 1, Maddison 1, Monkou 1, Oakley 1, own goals 2.
*Coca-Cola Cup (8):* Davies 3, Le Tissier 3, Evans 1, Monkou 1.
*FA Cup (0).*

| Jones P 38 | Oakley M 32 + 1 | Todd L 9 + 1 | Magilton J 5 | Monkou K 30 + 2 | Dryden R 11 + 2 | Slater R 3 + 8 | Maddison N 5 + 1 | Ostenstad E 21 + 8 | Evans M 6 + 4 | Williams A 3 + 17 | Van Gobbel U 1 + 1 | Johansen S 3 + 3 | Davies K 20 + 5 | Benali F 32 + 1 | Robinson M — + 1 | Dodd J 36 | Spedding D 4 + 3 | Hughes D 6 + 8 | Neilson A 3 + 5 | Lundekvam C 31 | Richardson K 25 + 3 | Bowen J 1 + 2 | Le Tissier M 25 + 1 | Palmer C 26 | Charlton S 2 + 1 | Hirst D 28 | Basham S — + 9 | Beresford J 10 | Gibbens K 2 | Warner P — + 1 | Match No. |
|---|---|---|---|---|---|---|---|---|---|---|---|---|---|---|---|---|---|---|---|---|---|---|---|---|---|---|---|---|---|---|---|
| 1 | 2 | 3 | 4 | 5 | 6 | $7^{1}$ | 8 | 9 | $10^{2}$ | $11^{3}$ | 12 | 13 | 14 | | | | | | | | | | | | | | | | | | 1 |
| 1 | 7 | 3 | 4 | 5 | $11^{3}$ | | 8 | 9 | 12 | 13 | $2^{2}$ | $10^{1}$ | | 6 | 14 | | | | | | | | | | | | | | | | 2 |
| 1 | $7^{2}$ | 3 | 4 | 5 | | | 8 | $9^{3}$ | 12 | | | 14 | 10 | 6 | | 2 | $11^{1}$ | 13 | | | | | | | | | | | | | 3 |
| 1 | | 3 | 4 | 5 | | | $8^{2}$ | | 12 | | | $10^{1}$ | 9 | 6 | | 2 | 11 | 7 | 13 | | | | | | | | | | | | 4 |
| 1 | | 3 | 4 | 5 | | | $8^{3}$ | 9 | 12 | 13 | | $10^{1}$ | | 6 | | 2 | $11^{2}$ | 7 | 14 | | | | | | | | | | | | 5 |
| 1 | 7 | 3 | | | 6 | | | $9^{2}$ | 10 | | | 12 | 13 | | | 2 | $8^{2}$ | 14 | | 5 | 4 | | $11^{1}$ | | | | | | | | 6 |
| 1 | 11 | | | | 6 | | | | 10 | 13 | | 9 | 3 | | | 2 | | | | 8 | 5 | | 4 | $12^{2}$ | $7^{1}$ | | | | | | 7 |
| 1 | $7^{2}$ | | | | $6^{1}$ | | | | 12 | 10 | 11 | 9 | 3 | | | 2 | | | | 8 | 5 | | 4 | 13 | | | | | | | 8 |
| 1 | | | | | 6 | | | | 10 | 12 | | $7^{1}$ | 9 | 3 | | $2^{2}$ | | 13 | 11 | 5 | 4 | | | 8 | | | | | | | 9 |
| 1 | $11^{3}$ | | | 14 | 6 | | | 12 | $10^{1}$ | | | 9 | 13 | | | 2 | | | | 5 | 4 | | 7 | 8 | $3^{2}$ | | | | | | 10 |
| 1 | 12 | | | | 6 | $7^{1}$ | | | 13 | | | 10 | 3 | | | 2 | | | | 5 | 4 | | 8 | $11^{2}$ | 9 | | | | | | 11 |
| 1 | $11^{1}$ | | | | 6 | | 13 | | 12 | | | 10 | $3^{3}$ | | | 2 | | | | 5 | 4 | | $7^{2}$ | 8 | 14 | 9 | | | | | 12 |
| 1 | $11^{2}$ | | | | 6 | | 12 | | 10 | | | 3 | 2 | | | 13 | | | | 5 | 4 | | $7^{1}$ | 8 | | $9^{1}$ | 14 | | | | 13 |
| 1 | 11 | | | | 6 | | 12 | | 10 | | | 3 | 2 | | | | | | | 5 | 4 | | $7^{1}$ | 8 | | $9^{2}$ | 13 | | | | 14 |
| 1 | $11^{1}$ | 12 | | | 6 | | | | 10 | | | 3 | 2 | | | 13 | | | | 5 | 4 | | $7^{2}$ | 8 | | $9^{1}$ | 14 | | | | 15 |
| 1 | 11 | | | | 6 | | 12 | | 10 | | | 3 | 2 | | | | | | | 5 | $4^{2}$ | | 7 | 8 | | $9^{1}$ | 13 | | | | 16 |
| 1 | 11 | | | | 6 | | 12 | 13 | 10 | | | 3 | 2 | | | | | | | 5 | $4^{1}$ | | $7^{2}$ | 8 | | 9 | | | | | 17 |
| 1 | $11^{2}$ | | | | 6 | | 12 | 13 | 10 | | | 3 | 2 | | | 14 | | | | 5 | $4^{3}$ | | $7^{1}$ | 8 | | 9 | | | | | 18 |
| 1 | 11 | | | | 6 | | 12 | | $10^{1}$ | | | 3 | 2 | | | | | | | 5 | 4 | | 7 | 8 | | 9 | | | | | 19 |
| 1 | $11^{1}$ | | | | 6 | | 12 | | $10^{3}$ | 13 | | 14 | 3 | | | 2 | | | | 5 | 4 | | $7^{2}$ | 8 | | 9 | | | | | 20 |
| 1 | 11 | | | | 6 | | 12 | 13 | 10 | | | 3 | 2 | | | | | | | 5 | 4 | | $7^{2}$ | 8 | | $9^{1}$ | | | | | 21 |
| 1 | 11 | | | 5 | 6 | $7^{2}$ | 12 | 13 | 10 | | | 3 | 2 | | | | | | | | 4 | | | 8 | | $9^{1}$ | | | | | 22 |
| 1 | 11 | | | | 6 | | 12 | 13 | $10^{2}$ | | | 3 | 2 | | | 14 | | | | 5 | $4^{3}$ | | $7^{1}$ | 8 | | 9 | | | | | 23 |
| 1 | 11 | 3 | | | 6 | | | | 10 | 12 | | 2 | $8^{1}$ | | | 13 | | | | 5 | 4 | | $7^{2}$ | | | 9 | | | | | 24 |
| 1 | $7^{2}$ | 3 | | | 6 | 12 | | | 14 | 13 | | $10^{3}$ | 2 | | | 8 | | | | $5^{1}$ | 4 | | | | | 9 | | 11 | | | 25 |
| 1 | 11 | $3^{2}$ | | | 6 | | | | 10 | $7^{3}$ | | 2 | 13 | | | 12 | | | | 5 | $4^{1}$ | | 14 | 8 | | 9 | | | | | 26 |
| 1 | 11 | | | | 6 | | | | 10 | | | 3 | 2 | | | 12 | | | | 5 | $4^{1}$ | | 7 | 8 | | 9 | | | | | 27 |
| 1 | 8 | | | | 6 | | | | 10 | 12 | | 3 | 2 | | | 13 | | | | $5^{2}$ | 14 | | $7^{3}$ | 4 | | $9^{1}$ | | 11 | | | 28 |
| 1 | 8 | | | | 6 | | 12 | | 10 | | | 3 | 2 | | | | | | | 5 | | | $7^{1}$ | 4 | | 9 | | 11 | | | 29 |
| 1 | 8 | | | | 6 | | | | 10 | 12 | | 3 | 2 | | | | | | | 5 | $4^{1}$ | | 7 | | | 9 | | 11 | | | 30 |
| 1 | $8^{1}$ | | | | 6 | | | | 10 | | | 3 | 2 | | | 5 | 12 | | | $7^{2}$ | 4 | | | | | 9 | 13 | 11 | | | 31 |
| 1 | | | | | 6 | | | | 10 | 12 | | 13 | 3 | | | 2 | 8 | | | 5 | $4^{1}$ | | $7^{2}$ | | | 9 | | 11 | | | 32 |
| 1 | | | | 12 | 6 | | | | 10 | 13 | | 14 | $3^{1}$ | | | 2 | 7 | | | 5 | $4^{2}$ | | | 8 | | $9^{2}$ | | 11 | | | 33 |
| 1 | 8 | | | 12 | 6 | | | | 10 | | | 3 | 2 | | | 13 | | | | $5^{1}$ | | | 7 | 4 | | $9^{2}$ | | 11 | | | 34 |
| 1 | 8 | | | 5 | $6^{1}$ | | | | 10 | | | 3 | 2 | | | 12 | | | | | | | 7 | 4 | | $9^{2}$ | 13 | 11 | | | 35 |
| 1 | 8 | | | | 6 | | | | 10 | | | 3 | 2 | | | 5 | | | | | | | 7 | 4 | | $9^{1}$ | 12 | 11 | | | 36 |
| 1 | 8 | | | | 6 | | | | 10 | 12 | | 3 | 2 | | | 5 | | | | | | | 7 | 4 | | $9^{2}$ | 13 | $11^{1}$ | | | 37 |
| 1 | 8 | | | | 6 | | | | 10 | | | 3 | $2^{2}$ | | | 5 | 12 | | | | | | 7 | 4 | | $9^{2}$ | 13 | $11^{1}$ | | 14 | 38 |

**Coca-Cola Cup**

| Second Round | Brentford | (h) | 3-1 |
| | | (a) | 2-0 |
| Third Round | Barnsley | (a) | 2-1 |
| Fourth Round | Chelsea | (a) | 1-2 |

**FA Cup**

| Third Round | Derby Co | (a) | 0-2 |

SOUTHEND UNITED 1997-98 *Back row (left to right):* Mark Jones, Paul Taylor, Chris Perkins, Simon Royce, Andy Rammell, Tony Henriksen, Jeroen Boere, Nathan Jones, John Nielsen. *Middle row:* Spencer Barham (Physio), John Gowens (Physio), Adrian Clarke, Paul Williams, Andy Harris, Mark Stimson, Phil Leggatt (Youth Team Manager), Peter Johnson. *Front row:* Leo Roget, Paul Byrne, Peter Trevivian (Assistant Manager), Alvin Martin (Manager), Mike Marsh, Andy Thomson, Phil Gridelet.

# Division 3　　　　　　　SOUTHEND UNITED

*Roots Hall Football Ground, Victoria Avenue, Southend-on-Sea SS2 6NQ.* Telephone: (01702) 304050. Fax: (01702) 330164. Commercial: (01702) 304050. Soccerline: 0839 664444. Ticket Office: (01702) 304090. Infoline: 0839 664443.

*Ground capacity:* 12,306.

*Record attendance:* 31,090 v Liverpool, FA Cup 3rd rd, 10 January 1979.

*Record receipts:* £83,999 v West Ham U, Division 1, 7 April 1993.

*Pitch measurements:* 110yd × 74yd.

*President:* N. J. Woodcock.

*Chairman and Managing Director:* V. T. Jobson. *Vice-Chairman and Chief Executive:* J. W. Adams.

*Secretary:* Miss H. Giles.

*Directors:* J. A. Bridge, B. R. Gunner, W. R. Kelleway, D. M. Markscheffel, R. J. Osborne.

*Associate Directors:* A. W. Jobson, W. E. Parsons.

*Manager:* Alvin Martin. *Assistant Manager:* Peter Trevivian.

*Physio:* John Gowens. *Commercial Manager:* Jacqueline Parker. *Safety Officer:* George Wright.

*Club Nickname:* 'The Blues' or 'The Shrimpers'.

*Year Formed:* 1906. *Turned Professional:* 1906. *Ltd Co.:* 1919.

*Previous Grounds:* 1906, Roots Hall, Prittlewell; 1920, Kursaal; 1934, Southend Stadium; 1955, Roots Hall Football Ground.

*Foundation:* The leading club in Southend around the turn of the century was Southend Athletic, but they were an amateur concern. Southend United was a more ambitious professional club when they were founded in 1906, employing Bob Jack as secretary-manager and immediately joining the Second Division of the Southern League.

*First Football League game:* 28 August 1920, Division 3, v Brighton & HA (a) W 2-0 – Capper; Reid, Newton; Wileman, Henderson, Martin; Nicholls, Nuttall, Fairclough (2), Myers, Dorsett.

*Record League Victory:* 9–2 v Newport Co, Division 3 (S), 5 September 1936 – McKenzie; Nelson, Everest (1); Deacon, Turner, Carr; Bolan, Lane (1), Goddard (4), Dickinson (2), Oswald (1).

*Record Cup Victory:* 10–1 v Golders Green, FA Cup 1st rd, 24 November 1934 – Moore; Morfitt, Kelly; Mackay, Joe Wilson, Carr (1); Lane (1), Johnson (5), Cheesmuir (2), Deacon (1), Oswald. 10–1 v Brentwood, FA Cup 2nd rd, 7 December 1968 – Roberts; Bentley, Birks; McMillan (1) Beesley, Kurila; Clayton, Chisnall, Moore (4), Best (5), Hamilton. 10–1 v Aldershot, Leyland Daf Cup Prel rd, 6 November 1990 – Sansome; Austin, Powell, Cornwell, Prior (1), Tilson (3), Cawley, Butler, Ansah (1), Benjamin (1), Angell (4).

*Record Defeat:* 1–9 v Brighton & HA, Division 3, 27 November 1965.

*Most League Points (2 for a win):* 67, Division 4, 1980–81.

*Most League Points (3 for a win):* 85, Division 3, 1990–91.

*Most League Goals:* 92, Division 3 (S), 1950–51.

*Highest League Scorer in Season:* Jim Shankly, 31, 1928–29 and Sammy McCrory, 1957–58, both in Division 3 (S).

*Most League Goals in Total Aggregate:* Roy Hollis, 122, 1953–60.

*Most Capped Player:* George Mackenzie, 9, Eire.

*Most League Appearances:* Sandy Anderson, 451, 1950–63.

*Record Transfer Fee Received:* £3,570,000 from Nottingham F for Stan Collymore, June 1993.

*Record Transfer Fee Paid:* £750,000 to Crystal Palace for Stan Collymore, November 1992.

*Football League Record:* 1920 Original Member of Division 3; 1921–58 Division 3 (S); 1958–66 Division 3; 1966–72 Division 4; 1972–76 Division 3; 1976–78 Division 4; 1978–80 Division 3; 1980–81 Division 4; 1981–84 Division 3; 1984–87 Division 4; 1987–89 Division 3; 1989–90 Division 4; 1990–91 Division 3; 1991–92 Division 2; 1992–97 Division 1; 1997–98 Division 2; 1998– Division 3.

*Honours: Football League:* Best season: 13th, Division 1, 1994–95. Division 3 – Runners-up 1990–91; Division 4 – Champions 1980–81; Runners-up 1971–72, 1977–78. *FA Cup:* best season: old 3rd rd, 1921, 5th rd, 1926, 1952, 1976, 1993. *Football League Cup:* never past 3rd rd.

*Colours:* Royal blue/yellow. *Change colours:* All red.

**Did you know?**
Sam McCrory scored Southend United's fastest goal ten seconds after the start of the game v Crystal Palace at Selhurst Park on 10 March 1956. United won 2-1.

## SOUTHEND UNITED 1997–98 LEAGUE RECORD

| Match No. | Date | Venue | Opponents | Result | | H/T Score | Lg. Pos. | Goalscorers | Attendance |
|---|---|---|---|---|---|---|---|---|---|
| 1 | Aug 9 | H | Carlisle U | D | 1-1 | 1-0 | — | Boere [25] | 4507 |
| 2 | 18 | A | Luton T | L | 0-1 | 0-0 | — | | 5140 |
| 3 | 23 | H | Burnley | W | 1-0 | 1-0 | 13 | Boere [6] | 4218 |
| 4 | 30 | A | Walsall | L | 1-3 | 1-2 | 19 | Williams [22] | 3304 |
| 5 | Sept 2 | A | Wycombe W | L | 1-4 | 1-2 | — | Boere [43] | 4528 |
| 6 | 5 | H | Brentford | W | 3-1 | 3-1 | — | Marsh [3], Boere [25], Clarke [43] | 3458 |
| 7 | 13 | A | Millwall | L | 1-3 | 1-0 | 19 | Boere [18] | 8606 |
| 8 | 20 | H | Fulham | W | 1-0 | 1-0 | 16 | Lewis [16] | 5026 |
| 9 | 27 | A | Blackpool | L | 0-3 | 0-1 | 19 | | 4542 |
| 10 | Oct 4 | H | Northampton T | D | 0-0 | 0-0 | 21 | | 4300 |
| 11 | 11 | H | Bristol C | L | 0-2 | 0-1 | 21 | | 3273 |
| 12 | 18 | A | Plymouth Arg | W | 3-2 | 2-2 | 19 | Wotton (og) [4], Clarke [20], N'Diaye [75] | 3430 |
| 13 | 21 | A | Wrexham | L | 1-3 | 1-0 | — | Rammell [22] | 2039 |
| 14 | 25 | H | Oldham Ath | D | 1-1 | 1-1 | 21 | Coulbault [13] | 3595 |
| 15 | Nov 1 | A | Grimsby T | L | 1-5 | 0-3 | 21 | Coulbault [64] | 4501 |
| 16 | 4 | H | Watford | L | 0-3 | 0-2 | — | | 4001 |
| 17 | 8 | H | Wigan Ath | W | 1-0 | 0-0 | 19 | Boere [71] | 2716 |
| 18 | 18 | A | Bournemouth | L | 1-2 | 1-1 | — | Dublin [5] | 3019 |
| 19 | 22 | H | Bristol R | D | 1-1 | 1-0 | 20 | N'Diaye [40] | 3653 |
| 20 | 29 | A | Chesterfield | L | 0-1 | 0-0 | 22 | | 4101 |
| 21 | Dec 2 | H | Preston NE | W | 3-2 | 3-2 | — | Boere (pen) [25], Gridelet 2 [42, 45] | 2307 |
| 22 | 13 | A | Gillingham | W | 2-1 | 0-1 | 19 | Coulbault [89], Boere [90] | 4774 |
| 23 | 19 | H | York C | D | 4-4 | 2-2 | — | Clarke 2 [28, 42], Dublin 2 [52, 82] | 3215 |
| 24 | 26 | A | Brentford | D | 1-1 | 0-1 | 19 | Coulbault [80] | 5341 |
| 25 | 28 | H | Wycombe W | L | 1-2 | 0-1 | 19 | Thomson [47] | 5162 |
| 26 | Jan 3 | A | Luton T | L | 1-2 | 1-1 | 20 | Thomson [19] | 5056 |
| 27 | 10 | A | Carlisle U | L | 0-5 | 0-1 | 20 | | 5389 |
| 28 | 17 | H | Walsall | L | 0-1 | 0-0 | 20 | | 3310 |
| 29 | 24 | A | Burnley | L | 0-1 | 0-1 | 22 | | 9386 |
| 30 | 31 | H | Millwall | D | 0-0 | 0-0 | 24 | | 5705 |
| 31 | Feb 7 | A | Fulham | L | 0-2 | 0-1 | 24 | | 9122 |
| 32 | 14 | A | Northampton T | L | 1-3 | 1-2 | 24 | Boere [34] | 6147 |
| 33 | 21 | H | Blackpool | W | 2-1 | 2-0 | 24 | Dublin [9], Boere [12] | 3340 |
| 34 | 24 | H | Plymouth Arg | W | 3-0 | 1-0 | — | Aldridge [40], Maher [62], Jobson [73] | 4363 |
| 35 | 28 | A | Bristol C | L | 0-1 | 0-1 | 23 | | 12,049 |
| 36 | Mar 7 | H | Grimsby T | L | 0-1 | 0-0 | 24 | | 4829 |
| 37 | 14 | A | Watford | D | 1-1 | 0-1 | 24 | Thomson [66] | 10,750 |
| 38 | 17 | A | Wigan Ath | W | 3-1 | 2-0 | — | Thomson [32], Rammell [33], Whyte [87] | 2616 |
| 39 | 21 | H | Bournemouth | W | 5-3 | 0-0 | 22 | Boere 2 (1 pen) [59 (p), 66], Thomson 2 [62, 65], Clarke [88] | 4823 |
| 40 | 27 | A | Bristol R | L | 0-2 | 0-0 | — | | 5323 |
| 41 | Apr 3 | H | Chesterfield | L | 0-2 | 0-1 | — | | 5425 |
| 42 | 11 | A | Preston NE | L | 0-1 | 0-0 | 24 | | 8096 |
| 43 | 13 | H | Gillingham | D | 0-0 | 0-0 | 24 | | 6151 |
| 44 | 18 | A | York C | D | 1-1 | 1-0 | 24 | Boere [30] | 2850 |
| 45 | 25 | A | Oldham Ath | L | 0-2 | 0-0 | 24 | | 4485 |
| 46 | May 2 | H | Wrexham | L | 1-3 | 1-1 | 24 | Boere [12] | 4220 |

**Final League Position: 24**  1996–97 DIV1 24

### GOALSCORERS

*League (47):* Boere 14 (2 pens), Thomson 6, Clarke 5, Coulbault 4, Dublin 4, Gridelet 2, N'Diaye 2, Rammell 2, Aldridge 1, Jobson 1, Lewis 1, Maher 1, Marsh 1, Whyte 1, Williams 1, own goal 1.
*Coca-Cola Cup (4):* Williams 2, Byrne 1, Marsh 1.
*FA Cup (2):* Gridelet 1, Jones 1.

| Royce S 37 | Harris A 26 + 1 | Stimson M 17 + 3 | Marsh M 9 | Roget L 11 | Dublin K 41 | Byrne P 9 + 1 | Beeston C 5 + 1 | Boere J 28 + 3 | Thomson A 16 + 17 | Jones N 34 + 5 | Clarke A 42 + 3 | Rammell A 18 + 8 | Williams P 6 | Hails J 41 + 3 | Parris G 1 | Gridelet P 31 + 6 | Nielsen J 1 + 4 | Lewis B 14 | Nzamba G — + 1 | Allen M 5 | Perkins C 3 + 2 | Coulbault R 30 + 4 | N'Diaye S 15 + 2 | Beard M 6 + 2 | Southall N 9 | Fitzpatrick T 1 + 2 | Jobson R 8 | Maher K 18 | Coleman S 14 | Aldridge M 7 + 4 | Whyte D 3 + 5 | Match No. |
|---|---|---|---|---|---|---|---|---|---|---|---|---|---|---|---|---|---|---|---|---|---|---|---|---|---|---|---|---|---|---|---|---|
| 1 | 2 | $3^1$ | 4 | 5 | 6 | 7 | 8 | $9^2$ | 10 | 11 | 12 | 13 | | | | | | | | | | | | | | | | | | | | 1 |
| 1 | 2 | | 4 | 5 | 6 | 7 | 8 | $9^1$ | 10 | 3 | 11 | 12 | | | | | | | | | | | | | | | | | | | | 2 |
| 1 | 2 | | 4 | 5 | 6 | 7 | 8 | 9 | 12 | 3 | $11^2$ | | | | | $10^1$ | 13 | | | | | | | | | | | | | | | 3 |
| | | | | 5 | 6 | $7^2$ | 8 | 9 | | 3 | 11 | 12 | | | | $10^1$ | 13 | $4^3$ | 14 | | | | | | | | | | | | | 4 |
| 1 | 2 | | | 5 | 6 | $7^1$ | $8^2$ | 9 | | 3 | 11 | 10 | | | | 12 | 4 | 13 | | | | | | | | | | | | | | 5 |
| 1 | 2 | | 4 | 5 | 6 | | | 9 | | 7 | 11 | 12 | $10^1$ | 3 | | 8 | | | | | | | | | | | | | | | | 6 |
| 1 | 2 | | 4 | 5 | $6^1$ | 12 | | $9^2$ | | 7 | 11 | 13 | 10 | 3 | | 8 | | | | | | | | | | | | | | | | 7 |
| 1 | 6 | | 4 | | | | $7^1$ | 14 | 9 | | 3 | 11 | 12 | $10^2$ | 2 | 8 | 5 | $13^3$ | | | | | | | | | | | | | | 8 |
| 1 | | | 4 | | 7 | | | 9 | 12 | 3 | $11^2$ | 10 | | 2 | | $8^1$ | | 5 | | 6 | 13 | | | | | | | | | | | 9 |
| 1 | | | 4 | 3 | 8 | | | $10^1$ | 11 | | 9 | | | 2 | | 12 | | 5 | | 7 | 6 | | | | | | | | | | | 10 |
| 1 | | | $4^1$ | 10 | $8^3$ | | | 13 | | 3 | 11 | 9 | | $2^2$ | | 12 | | 5 | | 7 | 6 | 14 | | | | | | | | | | 11 |
| 1 | 6 | | | | | | | 3 | | | 11 | 9 | | 2 | | 8 | | 5 | | 7 | | 4 | 10 | | | | | | | | | 12 |
| 1 | 6 | | | | | | | 12 | | 3 | 11 | 9 | | 2 | | 8 | | $5^2$ | | 7 | 13 | 4 | 10 | | | | | | | | | 13 |
| 1 | 6 | | 3 | | | | | 12 | 13 | 7 | $11^2$ | 9 | | $2^1$ | | | 13 | 5 | | | | 4 | 10 | | 8 | | | | | | | 14 |
| 1 | 6 | | 3 | | | | | 12 | | 7 | 11 | 9 | | 2 | | | | $5^1$ | | | | 4 | 10 | | 8 | | | | | | | 15 |
| 1 | 6 | | 5 | | | | | 12 | | 7 | 11 | 9 | | 2 | | | | | | 4 | | $3^1$ | 10 | | 8 | | | | | | | 16 |
| 1 | 6 | | 3 | | | | | 12 | 13 | 7 | 11 | $9^1$ | | 2 | | | | | | | | 4 | $10^2$ | | 8 | | | | | | | 17 |
| 1 | 5 | | 4 | | | | | 9 | $10^2$ | 3 | $11^1$ | | | 2 | | 8 | | 6 | | | | 7 | 13 | 12 | | | | | | | | 18 |
| 1 | 5 | | 4 | | | | | 9 | | 3 | 11 | | | 2 | | 8 | | 6 | | | | 7 | 10 | | | | | | | | | 19 |
| 1 | 5 | | 4 | | | | | 9 | 12 | 3 | 13 | | | $2^2$ | | 8 | | 6 | | | | 7 | $10^1$ | 11 | | | | | | | | 20 |
| 1 | 5 | | 4 | | | | | 9 | 12 | 3 | $11^1$ | | | 2 | | 8 | | 6 | | | | 7 | 10 | | | | | | | | | 21 |
| 1 | 5 | | 6 | | | | | 9 | 10 | 3 | 11 | | | 2 | | 8 | | 12 | | | | 4 | $7^1$ | | | | | | | | | 22 |
| 1 | 5 | | 6 | | | | | 9 | 10 | 3 | 11 | | | 2 | | 8 | | | | | | 4 | $7^1$ | 12 | | | | | | | | 23 |
| | 5 | | 6 | | | | | 9 | | 3 | 11 | | | 2 | | 8 | | | | | | 4 | 10 | | 1 | | | 7 | | | | 24 |
| | 5 | 12 | 6 | | | | | 9 | 13 | 3 | 11 | | | 2 | | 8 | | | | | | 4 | $7^2$ | $10^1$ | 1 | | | | | | | 25 |
| | 5 | 3 | 6 | | | | | 9 | | | 7 | 11 | | 2 | | 8 | | | | | | 4 | $10^1$ | | 1 | | 12 | | | | | 26 |
| | 5 | 3 | | | | | | 9 | | | 7 | 11 | | 2 | | 8 | | 6 | | | | 4 | | | 1 | | | 10 | | | | 27 |
| | 5 | 3 | 6 | | 10 | | | 9 | | | $7^2$ | 11 | | 2 | | 8 | | | | | | $4^1$ | 12 | 13 | 1 | | | | | | | 28 |
| | | 3 | 6 | | 12 | | | $9^1$ | 10 | | 13 | 11 | | 2 | | 8 | | | | | | $4^2$ | | | 1 | | 5 | 7 | | | | 29 |
| | | 3 | 6 | | 9 | | | | $10^2$ | | 12 | 11 | | 2 | | 8 | | | | | | $4^1$ | 13 | | 1 | | 5 | 7 | | | | 30 |
| | | 3 | 6 | | 9 | | | | 12 | | 13 | 11 | | 2 | | 8 | | | | | | $4^2$ | $10^1$ | | 1 | | 5 | 7 | | | | 31 |
| | 2 | 3 | 6 | | 9 | | | | 12 | 10 | 13 | $11^2$ | | | | $8^1$ | | | | | | 4 | | | 1 | | 5 | 7 | | | | 32 |
| 1 | | 3 | | | $9^1$ | | | 12 | | 10 | $8^2$ | 11 | | 2 | | 13 | | | | | | 4 | | | | | 5 | 7 | 6 | | | 33 |
| 1 | | 3 | | | $9^1$ | | | 13 | | 12 | 8 | $11^2$ | 12 | 2 | | 14 | | | 14 | | | $4^3$ | | | | | 5 | 7 | 6 | 10 | | 34 |
| 1 | 12 | 3 | | | | | | 13 | | 9 | 8 | 11 | | 2 | | | | | | | | $4^1$ | | | | | 5 | 7 | 6 | $10^2$ | | 35 |
| 1 | 12 | 3 | | | | | | 13 | | $9^1$ | $8^3$ | 11 | 14 | 2 | | | | | | | | 4 | | | | | 5 | 7 | 6 | $10^2$ | | 36 |
| 1 | | 3 | 6 | | 10 | | | | | 9 | 11 | | | 2 | | 8 | | | | | | 4 | | | | | 5 | 7 | | | | 37 |
| 1 | | 3 | 6 | 12 | 10 | | | $9^1$ | | | $11^2$ | | | 2 | | 8 | | | | | | 4 | | | | | 5 | 7 | | | 13 | 38 |
| 1 | | 3 | 6 | | $9^1$ | | | | 10 | | $8^3$ | $11^2$ | 12 | 2 | | | | | | | | 4 | | | | | 5 | 7 | 14 | | 13 | 39 |
| 1 | | 3 | 6 | | 9 | | | | 10 | | $11^2$ | | | 2 | | $8^1$ | | | | | | 4 | | | | | 5 | 7 | 12 | | 13 | 40 |
| 1 | | 3 | 6 | | 9 | | | | $10^2$ | | 11 | | | 2 | | $8^1$ | | | | | | 4 | | | | | 5 | 7 | 12 | | 13 | 41 |
| 1 | | 3 | 6 | | 12 | | | 9 | | | 11 | | | 2 | | 8 | | | | | | $4^1$ | | | | | 5 | 7 | | 10 | | 42 |
| 1 | | 3 | 4 | | 6 | | | 9 | | | 11 | | | 2 | | $8^1$ | | | | | | 12 | | | | | 5 | 7 | | 10 | | 43 |
| 1 | | $3^1$ | 4 | | 6 | | | 9 | 12 | | 11 | | | 2 | | $8^2$ | 13 | | | | | 4 | | | | | 5 | 7 | | 10 | | 44 |
| 1 | | 3 | 4 | | 6 | | | 9 | | | $11^1$ | | | 2 | | 8 | | | | | | | | | | | 5 | 7 | 12 | 10 | | 45 |
| 1 | 12 | | $4^1$ | 3 | | | | 9 | | | $8^2$ | $11^3$ | | 2 | | | 13 | 6 | | | | | | | | | 5 | 7 | 14 | 10 | | 46 |

**Coca-Cola Cup**

| | | | |
|---|---|---|---|
| First Round | Cardiff C | (a) | 1-1 |
| | | (h) | 3-1 |
| Second Round | Derby Co | (h) | 0-1 |
| | | (a) | 0-5 |

**FA Cup**

| | | | |
|---|---|---|---|
| First Round | Woking | (a) | 2-0 |
| Second Round | Fulham | (a) | 0-1 |

STOCKPORT COUNTY 1997–98  *Back row (left to right):* Matthew Bound, Brett Angell, Ian Gray, Neil Edwards, Colin Woodthorpe, Lea Jones.
*Third row:* Gary Lewis, Simon Carden, James Gannon, Andy Mutch, Danny Kilduff, Gary Ansell.
*Second row:* John Paul King, Kiko Charana, Tom Bennett, Sean Connelly, Damon Searle, Nelson De Costa, Luis Cavaco, Lee Shearer, Kevin Cooper.
*Front row:* Alun Armstrong, Martin Nash, Mike Flynn, Gary Megson (Manager), Chris Marsden, Kieron Durkan, Tony Dinning.

# Division 1 **STOCKPORT COUNTY**

*Edgeley Park, Hardcastle Road, Stockport, Cheshire SK3 9DD.* Telephone: (0161) 286 8888. Fax: (0161) 286 8900. Club Shop: (0161) 286 8899. Clubcall: 0891 121638.

*Ground capacity:* 11,540

*Record attendance:* 27,833 v Liverpool, FA Cup 5th rd, 11 February 1950.

*Record receipts:* £181,449 v Middlesbrough, Coca-Cola Cup Semi-final 1st leg, 26 February 1997.

*Pitch measurements:* 111yd × 72yd.

*Hon. Vice-Presidents:* Mike Yarwood OBE, Freddie Pye, Andrew Barlow.

*Chairman:* Brendan Elwood. *Vice-Chairman:* Grahame White.

*Directors:* Mike Baker, Michael Rains, Brian Taylor, David Jolley.

*Secretary:* Gary Glendenning BA (HONS), FCCA.

*Manager:* Gary Megson. *Assistant Manager:* Mike Phelan.

*Physio:* Rodger Wylde.

*Assistant Secretary:* Andrea Dawson. *Commercial Manager:* John Rutter.

*Marketing Manager and Programme Editor:* Steve Bellis.

*Year Formed:* 1883. *Turned Professional:* 1891. *Ltd Co.:* 1908.

*Club Nicknames:* 'County' or 'Hatters'.

*Previous Names:* Heaton Norris Rovers, 1883–88; Heaton Norris, 1888–90.

*Previous Grounds:* 1883 Heaton Norris Recreation Ground; 1884 Heaton Norris Wanderers Cricket Ground; 1885 Chorlton's Farm, Chorlton's Lane; 1886 Heaton Norris Cricket Ground; 1887 Wilkes' Field, Belmont Street; 1889 Nursery Inn, Green Lane; 1902 Edgeley Park.

*Foundation:* Formed at a meeting held at Wellington Road South by members of Wycliffe Congregational Chapel in 1883, they called themselves Heaton Norris Rovers until changing to Stockport County in 1890, a year before joining the Football Combination.

*First Football League game:* 1 September 1900, Division 2, v Leicester Fosse (a) D 2-2 – Moores; Earp, Wainwright; Pickford, Limond, Harvey; Stansfield, Smith (1), Patterson, Foster, Betteley (1).

*Record League Victory:* 13–0 v Halifax T, Division 3 (N), 6 January 1934 – McGann; Vincent (1p), Jenkinson; Robinson, Stevens, Len Jones; Foulkes (1), Hill (3), Lythgoe (2), Stevenson (2), Downes (4).

*Record Cup Victory:* 5–0 v Lincoln C, FA Cup 1st rd, 11 November 1995 – Edwards; Connelly, Todd, Bennett, Flynn, Gannon (Dinning), Beaumont, Oliver, Ware, Eckhardt (3), Armstrong (1) (Mike), Chalk (1 og).

*Record Defeat:* 1–8 v Chesterfield, Division 2, 19 April 1902.

*Most League Points (2 for a win):* 64, Division 4, 1966–67.

*Most League Points (3 for a win):* 85, Division 2, 1993–94.

*Most League Goals:* 115, Division 3 (N), 1933–34.

*Highest League Scorer in Season:* Alf Lythgoe, 46, Division 3 (N), 1933–34.

*Most League Goals in Total Aggregate:* Jack Connor, 132, 1951–56.

*Most Capped Player:* Martin Nash, 8, Canada.

*Most League Appearances:* Andy Thorpe, 489, 1978–86, 1988–92.

*Record Transfer Fee Received:* £1,600,000 from Middlesbrough for Alun Armstrong, February 1998.

*Record Transfer Fee Paid:* £250,000 to Tranmere R for Paul Cook, October 1997.

*Football League Record:* 1900 Elected to Division 2; 1904 Failed re-election; 1905–21 Division 2; 1921–22 Division 3 (N); 1922–26 Division 2; 1926–37 Division 3 (N); 1937–38 Division 2; 1938–58 Division 3 (N); 1958–59 Division 3; 1959–67 Division 4; 1967–70 Division 3; 1970–91 Division 4; 1991–92 Division 3; 1992–97 Division 2; 1997– Division 1.

*Honours: Football League:* Division 1 best season: 8th, 1997–98; Division 2 – Runners-up 1996–97; Division 3 (N) – Champions 1921–22, 1936–37; Runners-up 1928–29, 1929-30; Division 4 – Champions 1966–67; Runners-up 1990–91. *FA Cup:* best season: 5th rd, 1935, 1950. *Football League Cup:* Semi-final 1997. *Autoglass Trophy:* Runners-up 1992, 1993.

*Colours:* Blue and white striped shirts, blue shorts and stockings with white trim. *Change colours:* Sunshine yellow shirts with vertical green chestband, green shorts and stockings with yellow trim.

**Did you know?**
On 11 October 1997 in Stockport County's 3-2 win over Oxford United, Brett Angell scored his 50th club goal and the 100th of his career.

## STOCKPORT COUNTY 1997–98 LEAGUE RECORD

| Match No. | Date | Venue | Opponents | Result | H/T Score | Lg. Pos. | Goalscorers | Attendance |
|---|---|---|---|---|---|---|---|---|
| 1 | Aug 9 | A | Bradford C | L 1-2 | 0-1 | — | Durkan [69] | 14,312 |
| 2 | 16 | H | Bury | D 0-0 | 0-0 | 18 | | 7260 |
| 3 | 23 | A | QPR | L 1-2 | 1-1 | 20 | Armstrong [28] | 11,108 |
| 4 | 29 | H | Birmingham C | D 2-2 | 1-0 | — | Armstrong [6], Angell [48] | 6260 |
| 5 | Sept 2 | H | Middlesbrough | D 1-1 | 0-1 | — | Connelly [60] | 8257 |
| 6 | 9 | A | Port Vale | L 1-2 | 1-2 | — | Dinning (pen) [43] | 6615 |
| 7 | 13 | A | Stoke C | L 1-2 | 0-1 | 23 | Mutch [48] | 11,743 |
| 8 | 20 | H | Huddersfield T | W 3-0 | 2-0 | 19 | Angell 2 [6, 18], Armstrong [63] | 6995 |
| 9 | 27 | A | Charlton Ath | W 3-1 | 0-1 | 17 | Armstrong [69], Angell [71], Rufus (og) [78] | 12,083 |
| 10 | Oct 4 | A | Portsmouth | W 3-1 | 2-0 | 15 | Cook (og) [7], Angell 2 [45, 90] | 7824 |
| 11 | 11 | H | Oxford U | W 3-2 | 0-0 | 10 | Angell [47], Dinning [71], Armstrong [75] | 7333 |
| 12 | 18 | A | Norwich C | D 1-1 | 1-0 | 10 | Angell [34] | 12,689 |
| 13 | 21 | A | Sheffield U | L 1-5 | 1-2 | — | McIntosh [23] | 16,241 |
| 14 | 25 | H | Wolverhampton W | W 1-0 | 1-0 | 11 | Cook [20] | 9804 |
| 15 | Nov 1 | H | Sunderland | D 1-1 | 1-0 | 13 | Gannon [79] | 9473 |
| 16 | 4 | A | Ipswich T | W 2-0 | 0-0 | — | Angell 2 [70, 81] | 8938 |
| 17 | 8 | A | Reading | L 0-1 | 0-1 | 11 | | 7444 |
| 18 | 15 | H | Swindon T | W 4-2 | 2-1 | 7 | Cook [8], McIntosh [33], Armstrong 2 [79, 87] | 7694 |
| 19 | 22 | A | Crewe Alex | W 1-0 | 1-0 | 7 | Cooper [24] | 5231 |
| 20 | 29 | H | Manchester C | W 3-1 | 3-0 | 7 | Cook [6], Armstrong [8], Angell [30] | 11,351 |
| 21 | Dec 6 | A | WBA | L 2-3 | 0-1 | 8 | Armstrong [60], Byrne [90] | 13,957 |
| 22 | 13 | H | Tranmere R | W 3-1 | 1-1 | 8 | Byrne [45], Cooper [47], Angell [90] | 7903 |
| 23 | 20 | A | Nottingham F | L 1-2 | 1-0 | 9 | Armstrong [14] | 16,701 |
| 24 | 26 | H | Port Vale | W 3-0 | 0-0 | 8 | Travis 2 [66, 80], Bennett [71] | 10,003 |
| 25 | 28 | A | Middlesbrough | L 1-3 | 1-1 | 8 | Flynn [30] | 30,166 |
| 26 | Jan 10 | H | Bradford C | L 1-2 | 0-2 | 9 | Armstrong [84] | 8460 |
| 27 | 18 | A | Bury | W 1-0 | 1-0 | 8 | Angell [17] | 5699 |
| 28 | 27 | A | Birmingham C | L 1-4 | 0-3 | — | Connelly [79] | 17,118 |
| 29 | 31 | H | QPR | W 2-0 | 1-0 | 8 | Armstrong [14], Dinning (pen) [58] | 7958 |
| 30 | Feb 7 | A | Huddersfield T | L 0-1 | 0-0 | 8 | | 11,121 |
| 31 | 14 | H | Stoke C | W 1-0 | 0-0 | 8 | Grant [82] | 8701 |
| 32 | 17 | A | Portsmouth | L 0-1 | 0-1 | — | | 8622 |
| 33 | 21 | H | Charlton Ath | W 3-0 | 1-0 | 7 | Cooper 2 [12, 53], Mutch [66] | 7705 |
| 34 | 24 | A | Norwich C | D 2-2 | 1-0 | — | Dinning [19], Grant [46] | 7471 |
| 35 | 28 | A | Oxford U | L 0-3 | 0-3 | 8 | | 6650 |
| 36 | Mar 3 | H | Reading | W 5-1 | 4-0 | — | Byrne 2 [10, 32], Angell 2 [11, 70], Grant [23] | 6148 |
| 37 | 7 | A | Sunderland | L 1-4 | 0-1 | 8 | Angell [61] | 34,870 |
| 38 | 14 | H | Ipswich T | L 0-1 | 0-0 | 9 | | 8939 |
| 39 | 21 | H | Swindon T | D 1-1 | 0-0 | 9 | Woodthorpe [86] | 6684 |
| 40 | 28 | H | Crewe Alex | L 0-1 | 0-0 | 9 | | 8370 |
| 41 | Apr 4 | A | Manchester C | L 1-4 | 1-3 | 11 | Wilbraham [6] | 31,855 |
| 42 | 11 | H | WBA | W 2-1 | 1-1 | 9 | Cooper (pen) [29], Byrne [66] | 7943 |
| 43 | 13 | A | Tranmere R | L 0-3 | 0-2 | 9 | | 8070 |
| 44 | 18 | H | Nottingham F | D 2-2 | 1-1 | 9 | Angell 2 [29, 67] | 9892 |
| 45 | 25 | A | Wolverhampton W | W 4-3 | 1-2 | 9 | Cooper 2 (2 pens) [40, 83], Byrne 2 [57, 86] | 22,452 |
| 46 | May 3 | H | Sheffield U | W 1-0 | 0-0 | 8 | Cooper [62] | 9683 |

**Final League Position: 8**        1996–97 DIV2 2

### GOALSCORERS
*League (71):* Angell 18, Armstrong 12, Cooper 8 (3 pens), Byrne 7, Dinning 4 (2 pens), Cook 3, Grant 3, Connelly 2, McIntosh 2, Mutch 2, Travis 2, Bennett 1, Durkan 1, Flynn 1, Gannon 1, Wilbraham 1, Woodthorpe 1, own goals 2.
*Coca-Cola Cup (11):* Angell 3, Armstrong 2, Mutch 2, Cooper 1, Dinning 1 (pen), Flynn 1, Woodthorpe 1.
*FA Cup (3):* Angell 2, Armstrong 1.

| Gray I 3 | Connelly S 45 | Searle D 27+4 | Bennett T 27 | Flynn M 34 | Gannon J 31+5 | Durkan K 5+2 | Marsden C 10 | Angell B 45 | Armstrong A 29 | Cooper K 30+8 | Nash M —+8 | Kalogeracus V —+2 | Woodthorpe C 29+3 | Dinning T 24+6 | Mutch A 2+18 | Richardson L 4+2 | Nixon E 43 | McIntosh M 38 | Grant S 9+7 | Cook P 25 | Travis S 3+10 | Byrne C 21+5 | Aunger G —+1 | Phillips W 7+6 | Wallwork R 7 | Cavaco L —+2 | McGoldrick E 2 | Wilbraham A 6+1 | Match No |
|---|---|---|---|---|---|---|---|---|---|---|---|---|---|---|---|---|---|---|---|---|---|---|---|---|---|---|---|---|---|
| 1 | 2 | 3 | 4 | 5 | 6 | 7 | 8 | 9¹ | 10 | 11² | 12 | 13 |  |  |  |  |  |  |  |  |  |  |  |  |  |  |  |  | 1 |
| 1 | 2 |  | 4 | 5 | 6 | 7 | 8 | 9 | 10¹ |  |  |  | 3 | 11² | 12 | 13 |  |  |  |  |  |  |  |  |  |  |  |  | 2 |
| 1 | 2 |  | 4² | 5 | 6 | 7 | 8 | 9 | 10 | 12 |  | 14 | 3 | 13 |  | 11¹ |  |  |  |  |  |  |  |  |  |  |  |  | 3 |
|  | 2 |  | 4 | 5¹ | 6² | 12 | 8 | 9 | 10 | 11 |  |  | 3 | 14 | 13 | 7¹ | 1 |  |  |  |  |  |  |  |  |  |  |  | 4 |
|  | 2 | 7 | 4 |  |  |  | 8 | 9 | 10 |  |  |  | 3 | 6 | 12 | 11¹ | 1 | 5 |  |  |  |  |  |  |  |  |  |  | 5 |
|  | 2 | 6¹ | 4 |  |  | 12 | 8 | 9² | 10 |  |  | 14 | 3 | 11³ | 13 | 7 | 1 | 5 |  |  |  |  |  |  |  |  |  |  | 6 |
|  | 2 |  | 4 |  | 6 | 7¹ | 8 | 9² |  | 11 |  |  | 3 | 10 | 12 |  | 1 | 5 | 13 |  |  |  |  |  |  |  |  |  | 7 |
|  | 2 | 12 | 4 |  |  | 7 | 8 | 9 | 10 | 11 |  |  | 3¹ | 6 |  |  | 1 | 5 |  |  |  |  |  |  |  |  |  |  | 8 |
|  | 2 |  | 4¹ |  |  | 7 | 8 | 9 | 10 | 11 | 12 |  | 3 | 6 |  |  | 1 | 5 |  |  |  |  |  |  |  |  |  |  | 9 |
|  | 2 |  | 4¹ |  |  | 7 | 8 | 9 | 10 | 11 | 12 |  | 3 | 6 |  |  | 1 | 5 |  |  |  |  |  |  |  |  |  |  | 10 |
|  | 2 | 8 | 4 |  |  | 7 |  | 9 | 10¹ | 11 |  |  | 3 | 6 | 12 |  | 1 | 5 |  |  |  |  |  |  |  |  |  |  | 11 |
|  | 2 | 8 | 4² |  |  | 7 |  | 9 | 10¹ | 11 |  | 13 | 3 | 6 | 12 |  | 1 | 5 |  |  |  |  |  |  |  |  |  |  | 12 |
|  | 2 | 8 | 4 |  |  | 7 |  | 9 | 10¹ | 11 |  |  | 3 | 6 | 12 |  | 1 | 5 |  |  |  |  |  |  |  |  |  |  | 13 |
|  | 2 |  | 4 |  |  | 7 |  | 9 | 10¹ | 11 |  |  | 3 | 6 | 12 |  | 1 | 5 | 8 |  |  |  |  |  |  |  |  |  | 14 |
|  | 2 |  | 4 |  |  | 7 |  | 9 | 10 | 11 |  |  | 3 | 6 |  |  | 1 | 5 | 8 |  |  |  |  |  |  |  |  |  | 15 |
|  | 2 | 12 | 4 |  | 6 | 7 |  | 9 | 10 | 11 |  |  | 3¹ |  |  |  | 1 | 5 | 8 |  |  |  |  |  |  |  |  |  | 16 |
|  | 2 | 12 | 4 |  | 6 | 7 |  | 9 | 10³ | 11³ |  |  | 3¹ |  |  |  | 1 | 5 | 8 |  |  | 14 |  |  |  |  |  |  | 17 |
|  | 2 | 3 | 4 | 5 |  | 7 |  | 9¹ | 10 | 11² |  |  |  |  | 12 |  | 1 | 6 | 8 | 13 |  |  |  |  |  |  |  |  | 18 |
|  | 2² | 3 | 4 | 5 |  | 7 |  | 9 | 10¹ | 11³ |  |  |  | 12 | 13 |  | 1 | 6 | 8 |  |  | 14 |  |  |  |  |  |  | 19 |
|  | 2 | 3 | 4 | 5 |  | 7 |  | 9 | 10 | 11 |  |  |  |  |  |  | 1 | 6 | 8¹ | 12 |  |  |  |  |  |  |  |  | 20 |
|  | 2 | 3¹ | 4 | 5 |  | 7 |  | 9 | 10 |  | 12 | 14 |  |  | 13 |  | 1 | 6¹ | 8² |  |  | 11 |  |  |  |  |  |  | 21 |
|  | 2 | 3 | 4 | 5 |  | 7 |  | 9 | 10 |  |  |  |  | 8² | 12 |  | 1 | 6 |  | 13 |  | 11¹ |  |  |  |  |  |  | 22 |
|  |  | 3² | 4 | 5 |  | 7¹ |  | 9 | 10 | 11³ | 12 | 13 |  |  |  |  | 1 | 6 | 8 |  | 2 | 14 |  |  |  |  |  |  | 23 |
|  | 2 | 3 | 4 | 5 |  | 7 |  | 9 | 10 | 11 |  |  |  |  |  |  | 1 | 6 | 8¹ | 12 |  |  |  |  |  |  |  |  | 24 |
|  | 2 | 3¹ | 4 | 5¹ |  |  |  | 9 | 10 | 11 | 12 | 13 |  |  |  | 7 | 1 | 6 | 8³ |  |  | 14 |  |  |  |  |  |  | 25 |
|  | 2 | 3 | 4 |  |  | 7¹ |  | 9 | 10 | 11 | 12 |  |  | 5 |  |  | 1 | 6 | 8 |  |  |  |  |  |  |  |  |  | 26 |
|  | 2 | 3 | 4 | 5 |  | 7 |  | 9 | 10 | 11¹ |  |  |  |  | 12 |  | 1 | 6 | 8² | 13² |  | 14 |  |  |  |  |  |  | 27 |
|  | 2 | 3¹ | 4² | 5 |  | 7³ |  | 9 | 10 | 11 |  |  |  |  | 12 |  | 1 | 6 | 8 | 13 |  | 14 |  |  |  |  |  |  | 28 |
|  | 2 | 3 | 4 | 5 |  | 7 |  | 9 | 10 | 11¹ | 12 |  |  |  |  |  | 1 | 6 | 8 |  |  |  |  |  |  |  |  |  | 29 |
|  | 2 | 3² | 4 | 5 |  | 7 |  | 9² | 10 | 11 | 12 | 14 |  |  | 13 |  | 1 | 6¹ | 8 |  |  |  |  |  |  |  |  |  | 30 |
|  | 2 |  | 4² | 5 |  | 7 |  | 9 |  | 11 | 12 | 14 | 3 | 6 | 10² |  | 1 | 13 | 8¹ | 12 |  |  |  |  |  |  |  |  | 31 |
|  | 2 |  | 4 | 5 |  | 7¹ |  | 9 |  | 11² | 12 |  | 3 | 6 |  |  | 1 | 10 | 8 | 13 |  |  |  |  |  |  |  |  | 32 |
|  | 2 |  |  | 5 |  |  |  | 9 |  | 11 | 12 |  | 3 | 4¹ | 13 |  | 1 | 6 | 8 | 10² |  |  |  | 7 |  |  |  |  | 33 |
|  | 2 |  |  | 5 |  |  |  | 9 |  | 11 | 12 |  | 3 | 4 | 13 |  | 1 | 6 | 8 | 10² |  |  |  | 7 |  |  |  |  | 34 |
|  | 2 |  |  | 5 |  |  |  | 9 |  | 11¹ | 12 |  | 3 | 4 | 13 |  | 1 | 6 | 8 | 10² |  | 14 |  | 7³ |  |  |  |  | 35 |
|  | 2 |  |  | 5 |  | 7 |  | 9¹ |  | 11 | 12 |  | 3 | 4² |  |  | 1 | 6 | 8 | 10 |  | 13 |  |  |  |  |  |  | 36 |
|  | 2 |  |  | 5 |  | 7 |  | 9 |  | 11 | 12 |  | 3 | 4² |  |  | 1 | 6 | 8 | 10¹ |  | 13 |  |  |  |  |  |  | 37 |
|  | 2 |  |  | 5 |  | 7 |  | 9 |  | 11 | 12 |  | 3¹ | 4² |  |  | 1 | 6 | 8 | 10 |  | 13 |  |  |  |  |  |  | 38 |
|  | 2 |  |  | 5 |  | 7 |  | 9 |  | 11 | 12 |  | 3 | 4 |  |  | 1 | 6 | 8 | 10¹ |  |  |  |  |  |  |  |  | 39 |
|  | 2 |  |  | 5 |  | 7¹ |  | 9 |  | 11 | 12 |  | 3² | 4³ |  |  | 1 | 6 | 8 | 10 |  | 13 | 14 |  |  |  | 6 | 14 | 40 |
|  | 2 |  |  | 5 |  |  |  | 9 |  | 11 | 12 |  | 3 | 4 |  |  | 1 | 6 | 8¹ | 10 |  |  |  | 7 |  |  |  |  | 41 |
|  | 2 |  |  | 5 |  |  |  | 9 |  | 11 | 12 |  | 3 | 4 |  |  | 1 | 6 | 8 | 10¹ |  |  |  | 7 |  |  |  |  | 42 |
|  | 2 |  |  | 5 |  |  |  | 9² |  | 11 | 12 |  | 3 | 4¹ |  |  | 1 | 6 | 8 | 10 |  | 13 |  | 7 |  |  |  |  | 43 |
|  | 2 |  |  | 5 |  |  |  | 9 |  | 11 | 12 |  | 3 | 4 |  |  | 1 | 6 | 8² | 10¹ |  | 13 |  | 7 |  |  |  |  | 44 |
|  | 2 |  |  | 5 |  |  |  | 9 |  | 11 | 12 |  | 3¹ | 4 |  |  | 1 | 6 | 8 | 10² |  | 13 | 14 | 7³ |  |  |  |  | 45 |
|  | 2 |  |  | 5 |  |  |  | 9 |  | 11¹ | 12 |  | 3 | 4 |  |  | 1 | 6 | 8 | 10² |  | 13 |  | 7 |  |  |  |  | 46 |

**Coca-Cola Cup**

| | | | | |
|---|---|---|---|---|
| First Round | Mansfield T | (a) | 2-4 | |
| | | (h) | 6-3 | |
| Second Round | Birmingham C | (a) | 1-4 | |
| | | (h) | 2-1 | |

**FA Cup**

| | | | |
|---|---|---|---|
| Third Round | Preston NE | (a) | 2-1 |
| Fourth Round | Birmingham C | (a) | 1-2 |

STOKE CITY 1997–98 *Back row (left to right)*: Simon Sturridge, Ray Wallace, Peter Thorne, Justin Whittle, Carl Muggleton, Steven Tweed, Jose Andrade, Paul Stewart, Mark McNally.
*Middle row*: Ashley Grimes (Coach), Mark Birch, Graham Stokoe, Richard Burgess, Gerry McMahon, Mark Devlin, Phil Morgan, Stuart Fraser, Kofi Nyamah, Mike Macari, Paul Macari, David Talbot, Steve Woods, Ian Liversedge (Physio).
*Front row*: Robert Heath, Jan Schreuder, Graham Kavanagh, Ally Pickering, Larus Sigurdsson, Mike Pejic (Coach), Chic Bates (Manager), Andrew Griffin, Kevin Keen, Neil Mackenzie, Richard Forsyth, Dean Crowe.

# Division 2     STOKE CITY

***Britannia Stadium, Stoke-on-Trent ST4 4EG.*** Telephone: (01782) 592222. Fax: (01782) 592221. Commercial Dept: (01782) 592211. Soccerline Information: 0891 121040. Football in the Community: (01782) 592255.

***Ground capacity:*** 24,054.

***Record attendance:*** 51,380 v Arsenal, Division 1, 29 March 1937.

***Record receipts:*** £160,000 v Newcastle U, Coca-Cola Cup 3rd rd, 25 October 1995.

***Pitch measurements:*** 116yd × 72yd.

***Vice-President:*** J. A. M. Humphries.

***Vice-Chairman:*** K. A. Humphreys.

***Directors:*** D. J. Edwards, P. E. Doona BA, FCA, P. Coates

***Manager:*** Brian Little.

***Physio:*** R. Ryles

***Stadium Manager/Safety Officer:*** J. Alcock.

***Chief Executive:*** J. Moxey F. INST SMM.

***Year Formed:*** 1863*(*see Foundation*).*

***Turned Professional:*** 1885. ***Ltd Co.:*** 1908.

***Club Nickname:*** 'The Potters'.

***Previous Name:*** Stoke.

***Previous Grounds:*** 1875, Sweeting's Field; 1878–1997, Victoria Ground (previously known as the Athletic Club Ground).

***Foundation:*** The date of the formation of this club has long been in doubt. The year 1863 was claimed, but more recent research by Wade Martin has uncovered nothing earlier than 1868, when a couple of Old Carthusians, who were apprentices at the local works of the old North Staffordshire Railway Company, met with some others from that works, to form Stoke Ramblers. It should also be noted that the old Stoke club went bankrupt in 1908 when a new club was formed.

***First Football League game:*** 8 September 1888, Football League, v WBA (h) L 0-2 – Rowley; Clare, Underwood; Ramsey, Shutt, Smith; Sayer, McSkimming, Staton, Edge, Tunnicliffe.

***Record League Victory:*** 10–3 v WBA, Division 1, 4 February 1937 – Doug Westland; Brigham, Harbot; Tutin, Turner (1p), Kirton; Matthews, Antonio (2), Freddie Steele (5), Jimmy Westland, Johnson (2).

***Record Cup Victory:*** 7–1 v Burnley, FA Cup 2nd rd (replay), 20 February 1896 – Clawley; Clare, Eccles; Turner, Grewe, Robertson; Willie Maxwell, Dickson, A. Maxwell (3), Hyslop (4), Schofield.

***Record Defeat:*** 0–10 v Preston NE, Division 1, 14 September 1889.

***Most League Points (2 for a win):*** 63, Division 3 (N), 1926–27.

***Most League Points (3 for a win):*** 93, Division 2, 1992–93.

***Most League Goals:*** 92, Division 3 (N), 1926–27.

***Highest League Scorer in Season:*** Freddie Steele, 33, Division 1, 1936–37.

***Most League Goals in Total Aggregate:*** Freddie Steele, 142, 1934–49.

***Most Capped Player:*** Gordon Banks, 36 (73), England.

***Most League Appearances:*** Eric Skeels, 506, 1958–76.

***Record Transfer Fee Received:*** £1,500,000 from Chelsea for Mark Stein, October 1993.

***Record Transfer Fee Paid:*** £580,000 to Birmingham C for Paul Peschisolido, July 1994.

***Football League Record:*** 1888 Founder Member of Football League; 1890 Not re-elected; 1891 Re-elected; relegated in 1907, and after one year in Division 2, resigned for financial reasons; 1919 re-elected to Division 2; 1922–23 Division 1; 1923–26 Division 2; 1926–27 Division 3 (N); 1927–33 Division 2; 1933–53 Division 1; 1953–63 Division 2; 1963–77 Division 1; 1977–79 Division 2; 1979–85 Division 1; 1985–90 Division 2; 1990–92 Division 3; 1992–93 Division 2; 1993–98 Division 1; 1998– Division 2.

***Honours:*** *Football League:* Division 1 best season: 4th, 1935–36, 1946–47; Division 2 – Champions 1932–33, 1962–63, 1992–93; Runners-up 1921–22; Promoted 1978–79 (3rd); Division 3 (N) – Champions 1926–27. *FA Cup:* Semi-finals 1899, 1971, 1972. *Football League Cup:* Winners 1972. *Autoglass Trophy:* Winners: 1992. **European Competitions:** *UEFA Cup:* 1972–73, 1974–75.

***Colours:*** Red and white striped shirts, white shorts, red and white hooped stockings.
***Change colours:*** White and royal blue shirts, blue shorts, blue stockings.

**Did you know?**
The fewest number of players used in a season by Stoke City was 19 in 1935-36.

## STOKE CITY 1997–98 LEAGUE RECORD

| Match No. | Date | | Venue | Opponents | Result | H/T Score | Lg. Pos. | Goalscorers | Attendance |
|---|---|---|---|---|---|---|---|---|---|
| 1 | Aug | 9 | A | Birmingham C | L | 0-2 | 0-1 | — | 20,608 |
| 2 | | 15 | A | Bradford C | D | 0-0 | 0-0 | — | 13,823 |
| 3 | | 23 | A | Middlesbrough | W | 1-0 | 0-0 | 12 | Stewart [60] | 30,122 |
| 4 | | 30 | H | Swindon T | L | 1-2 | 1-0 | 13 | Forsyth [34] | 23,000 |
| 5 | Sept | 3 | H | WBA | D | 0-0 | 0-0 | — | 17,500 |
| 6 | | 13 | H | Stockport Co | W | 2-1 | 1-0 | 13 | Wallace [28], Thorne [50] | 11,743 |
| 7 | | 20 | A | Ipswich T | W | 3-2 | 2-0 | 14 | Thorne 2 [13, 30], Stewart [55] | 10,665 |
| 8 | | 27 | A | Nottingham F | L | 0-1 | 0-0 | 15 | | 19,018 |
| 9 | Oct | 4 | H | Bury | W | 3-2 | 0-0 | 11 | Andrade [63], Forsyth [69], Thorne [73] | 11,760 |
| 10 | | 12 | H | Port Vale | W | 2-1 | 2-1 | 7 | Forsyth [5], Keen [34] | 20,125 |
| 11 | | 19 | A | Charlton Ath | D | 1-1 | 0-0 | 7 | Wallace [51] | 12,345 |
| 12 | | 22 | A | Manchester C | W | 1-0 | 0-0 | — | Wallace [63] | 25,333 |
| 13 | | 25 | H | Sunderland | L | 1-2 | 0-1 | 9 | Stewart [81] | 14,587 |
| 14 | Nov | 1 | A | Huddersfield T | L | 1-3 | 0-0 | 12 | Griffin [79] | 10,916 |
| 15 | | 4 | H | Oxford U | D | 0-0 | 0-0 | — | | 8423 |
| 16 | | 8 | H | Wolverhampton W | W | 3-0 | 2-0 | 9 | Kavanagh 2 (1 pen) [8, 23 (p)], Forsyth [60] | 18,490 |
| 17 | | 15 | A | QPR | D | 1-1 | 1-0 | 10 | Forsyth [4] | 11,923 |
| 18 | | 22 | A | Tranmere R | L | 1-3 | 1-1 | 12 | Kavanagh (pen) [35] | 8009 |
| 19 | | 29 | H | Reading | L | 1-2 | 0-1 | 13 | Thorne [81] | 11,103 |
| 20 | Dec | 2 | A | Sheffield U | L | 2-3 | 1-0 | — | Thorne 2 [8, 63] | 14,347 |
| 21 | | 6 | A | Portsmouth | L | 0-2 | 0-2 | 14 | | 7072 |
| 22 | | 13 | H | Crewe Alex | L | 0-2 | 0-1 | 15 | | 14,623 |
| 23 | | 20 | A | Norwich C | D | 0-0 | 0-0 | 15 | | 12,265 |
| 24 | | 26 | H | Sheffield U | D | 2-2 | 0-0 | 14 | Forsyth [66], Thorne [86] | 19,723 |
| 25 | | 28 | A | WBA | L | 1-2 | 0-0 | 15 | Thorne [47] | 17,690 |
| 26 | Jan | 10 | H | Birmingham C | L | 0-7 | 0-3 | 16 | | 14,940 |
| 27 | | 16 | H | Bradford C | W | 2-1 | 2-1 | — | Forsyth (pen) [35], Thorne [42] | 10,459 |
| 28 | | 28 | H | Swindon T | L | 0-1 | 0-0 | — | | 6683 |
| 29 | Feb | 1 | H | Middlesbrough | L | 1-2 | 1-1 | 18 | Kavanagh (pen) [36] | 13,242 |
| 30 | | 7 | A | Ipswich T | D | 1-1 | 1-0 | 19 | Holsgrove [15] | 11,416 |
| 31 | | 14 | A | Stockport Co | L | 0-1 | 0-0 | 20 | | 8701 |
| 32 | | 17 | A | Bury | D | 0-0 | 0-0 | — | | 5802 |
| 33 | | 21 | H | Nottingham F | D | 1-1 | 0-0 | 20 | Crowe [32] | 16,899 |
| 34 | | 25 | H | Charlton Ath | L | 1-2 | 1-1 | — | Kavanagh [42] | 10,027 |
| 35 | Mar | 1 | A | Port Vale | D | 0-0 | 0-0 | 23 | | 13,853 |
| 36 | | 4 | A | Wolverhampton W | D | 1-1 | 0-1 | — | Crowe [89] | 21,058 |
| 37 | | 7 | H | Huddersfield T | L | 1-2 | 0-2 | 24 | Tiatto [90] | 12,594 |
| 38 | | 14 | A | Oxford U | L | 1-5 | 0-1 | 24 | Crowe [69] | 7300 |
| 39 | | 21 | H | QPR | W | 2-1 | 1-0 | 23 | Dowie (og) [21], Crowe [51] | 11,051 |
| 40 | | 28 | H | Tranmere R | L | 0-3 | 0-2 | 23 | | 16,692 |
| 41 | Apr | 4 | A | Reading | L | 0-2 | 0-1 | 24 | | 10,448 |
| 42 | | 11 | A | Portsmouth | W | 2-1 | 0-0 | 23 | Pickering [78], Lightbourne [90] | 15,569 |
| 43 | | 13 | A | Crewe Alex | L | 0-2 | 0-1 | 23 | | 5759 |
| 44 | | 18 | H | Norwich C | W | 2-0 | 1-0 | 21 | Sigurdsson [19], Lightbourne [50] | 13,098 |
| 45 | | 25 | A | Sunderland | L | 0-3 | 0-1 | 22 | | 41,214 |
| 46 | May | 3 | H | Manchester C | L | 2-5 | 0-1 | 23 | Thorne 2 [62, 87] | 26,664 |

**Final League Position: 23**      1996–97 DIV1 12

### GOALSCORERS

*League (44):* Thorne 12, Forsyth 7 (1 pen), Kavanagh 5 (3 pens), Crowe 4, Stewart 3, Wallace 3, Lightbourne 2, Andrade 1, Griffin 1, Holsgrove 1, Keen 1, Pickering 1, Sigurdsson 1, Tiatto 1, own goal 1.
*Coca-Cola Cup (11):* Kavanagh 5 (1 pen), Thorne 4, Forsyth 1, Keen 1.
*FA Cup (1):* Gabbiadini 1.

| Muggleton C 34 | Pickering A 42 | Nyamah K 9+1 | Sigurdsson L 43 | Whittle J 15+5 | Keen K 37+3 | Forsyth R 37 | Wallace R 36+3 | Thorne P 33+3 | Stewart P 22 | Kavanagh G 44 | Sturridge S —+1 | Tweed S 35+3 | Griffin A 23 | McMahon G 7+10 | Andrade J 4+8 | Crowe D 10+6 | Mackenzie N 7+5 | Macari P —+3 | Tiatto D 11+4 | Gabbiadini M 2+6 | Holsgrove P 11+1 | Scully T 7 | McKinlay T 3 | Xausa D 1 | Lightbourne K 9+4 | Southall N 12 | McNally M 3+1 | Woods S —+1 | Heath R 4+2 | Donaldson O 2 | Sobiech J 3 | Taaffe S —+3 | Match No. |
|---|---|---|---|---|---|---|---|---|---|---|---|---|---|---|---|---|---|---|---|---|---|---|---|---|---|---|---|---|---|---|---|---|---|
| 1 | 2 | 3 | 4 | 5 | 6¹ | 7 | 8 | 9 | 10 | 11 | 12 | | | | | | | | | | | | | | | | | | | | | | 1 |
| 1 | 2 | 3 | 4 | | 6 | 7 | 8 | 9 | 10 | 11 | | 5 | | | | | | | | | | | | | | | | | | | | | 2 |
| 1 | 2 | | 4 | | 6 | 7 | 8 | 9¹ | 10² | 11 | | 5 | 3 | 12 | 13 | | | | | | | | | | | | | | | | | | 3 |
| 1 | 2 | | 4 | | 6 | 7 | 8 | 9 | 10¹ | 11 | | 5 | 3 | 12 | | | | | | | | | | | | | | | | | | | 4 |
| 1 | 2 | | | 4 | 6 | 7 | 8 | 9¹ | 10 | 11 | | 5 | 3 | 12 | | | | | | | | | | | | | | | | | | | 5 |
| 1 | 2 | | 4 | | 6 | 7 | 8 | 9 | 10² | 11¹ | | 5 | 3 | 12 | 13 | | | | | | | | | | | | | | | | | | 6 |
| 1 | 2 | | 4 | | 6 | 7 | 8 | 9 | 10 | 11 | | 5 | 3 | | | | | | | | | | | | | | | | | | | | 7 |
| 1 | 2 | | 4 | | 6 | 7¹ | 8 | 9 | | 11 | | 5 | 3 | 10² | | 12 | 13 | | | | | | | | | | | | | | | | 8 |
| 1 | 2 | | 4 | | 6 | 7 | 8 | 9 | | 11 | | 5 | 3 | 12 | | 10¹ | | | | | | | | | | | | | | | | | 9 |
| 1 | 2 | | 4 | | 6 | 7 | 8 | 9 | | 11 | | 5 | 3 | | | 10¹ | 12 | | | | | | | | | | | | | | | | 10 |
| 1 | 2 | | 4 | 12 | 6 | 7 | 8 | | 11 | | | 5 | 3 | | | 9¹ | 10² | | 13 | | | | | | | | | | | | | | 11 |
| 1 | 2 | 12 | 4 | | 6 | 7 | 8 | | 10¹ | 11 | | 5 | 3 | | | 9 | | | | | | | | | | | | | | | | | 12 |
| 1 | 2² | 3 | 4 | 12 | 6 | 7 | 8 | | 10 | 11¹ | | 5 | | | | 9 | 13 | | | | | | | | | | | | | | | | 13 |
| 1 | 2 | | 4 | | 6 | 7 | 8¹ | 9² | 10 | 11 | | 5 | 3 | | | 13 | 12 | | | | | | | | | | | | | | | | 14 |
| 1 | 2 | | 4 | | 6² | 7 | 8 | 9 | 10¹ | 11 | | 5 | 3 | | | 13 | 12 | | | | | | | | | | | | | | | | 15 |
| 1 | 2 | | 4 | | 6 | 7 | 8 | 9 | 10¹ | 11 | | 5 | 3 | | | 12 | | | | | | | | | | | | | | | | | 16 |
| 1 | 2 | 3 | 4 | | 6 | 7 | 8 | 9 | 10 | 11 | | 5 | 3 | | | | | | | | | | | | | | | | | | | | 17 |
| 1 | 2 | | 4 | | 6 | 7 | 8¹ | 9 | 10 | 11 | | 5 | 3 | | | 12 | | | | | | | | | | | | | | | | | 18 |
| 1 | 2 | | 4 | | 6 | 7 | | 9 | 10¹ | 11 | | 5 | 3 | 8² | | | | 12 | 13 | | | | | | | | | | | | | | 19 |
| 1 | 2 | | 4 | | 6 | 7 | | 9 | | 11 | | 5 | 3 | 12 | | | | 8 | 10¹ | | | | | | | | | | | | | | 20 |
| 1 | 2 | | 4 | | 6 | 7 | | 9 | | 11 | | 5 | 3 | 12 | | | | 8¹ | 10 | | | | | | | | | | | | | | 21 |
| 1 | 2 | | 4 | | 6 | 7 | | 9 | 10 | 11 | | 5 | 3¹ | | | | | 8 | 12 | | | | | | | | | | | | | | 22 |
| 1 | 2 | | 4 | | 6 | 7 | | 9 | 10 | 11 | | 5 | 3 | | | | | 8 | | | | | | | | | | | | | | | 23 |
| 1 | 2 | | 4 | | 6 | 7 | | 9¹ | 10² | 11 | | 5 | 3 | | | | | 8 | 12 | 13 | | | | | | | | | | | | | 24 |
| 1 | 3¹ | | 4 | 12 | 6 | 7 | 13 | 9 | 10³ | 11 | | 5 | 2 | 8² | | | | 14 | | | | | | | | | | | | | | | 25 |
| 1 | 3¹ | | 4 | | 6 | 7 | 12 | 9 | 10² | 11 | | 5 | 2 | 8 | | | | 13 | | | | | | | | | | | | | | | 26 |
| 1 | 2 | | 4 | 11 | 6 | 7 | 8 | 9 | | | | 5 | 3 | 12 | | | | | | | 10¹ | | | | | | | | | | | | 27 |
| 1 | 2 | 3 | 4 | | 6 | | 8 | 9 | | 11² | | 5 | | 12 | | | | | | | 13 | 7 | | | 10¹ | | | | | | | | 28 |
| 1 | 2 | | 4 | | 6 | | 8 | | | 11 | | 5¹ | | 9 | | | | | | | 12 | 7 | | | 10 | | 3 | | | | | | 29 |
| 1 | 2 | | 4 | 5 | 6 | | 8 | | | 11¹ | | | | 9² | | | | | 12 | | 13 | 7 | | | 10 | | 3 | | | | | | 30 |
| 1 | 2 | | 4 | 5 | | | 8 | | | 11 | | 12 | | 9² | | 14 | 13 | | | 6² | | 7 | | | 10 | | 3¹ | | | | | | 31 |
| 1 | 2 | | 4 | 5 | | | 8 | | | 11 | | | | | | | 6 | | | | 3 | 7 | | | 10 | | 9 | | | | | | 32 |
| 1 | 2 | | 4 | 5 | 12 | | 8 | | | 11² | | | | 9 | | | 13 | | | | 3 | 7 | 6¹ | | 10 | | | | | | | | 33 |
| 1 | 2¹ | | 4 | 5 | | 7² | 8 | 13 | | 11 | | 12 | | 9 | | | | | | | 3 | | 6 | | 10 | | | | | | | | 34 |
| | 2 | | 4 | 5 | | 7 | 8 | 9 | | 11 | | | | 6¹ | | | | | 12 | | 3 | | | | 10 | 1 | | | | | | | 35 |
| | 2¹ | | 4 | 5 | | 7 | 8 | 9 | | 11 | | | | 12 | | | | | | | 3 | | 6² | | 10 | 1 | 13 | | | | | | 36 |
| | 2³ | | 4 | 5 | 12 | 7 | 8 | 9 | | 11³ | | | | 13 | | | | | | | 3 | | 6 | | 10¹ | 1 | 14 | | | | | | 37 |
| | 2 | | 4 | | 6¹ | 7 | 8 | 9 | | 11 | | 5 | | 12 | | | | | | | 3² | | | | | 1 | | | 13 | 10 | | | 38 |
| | | | 4 | 5 | | 7 | 12 | | 10² | 11 | | | | 8 | | | | | 6 | | | | | | 13 | 1 | 2 | | 9¹ | 3 | | | 39 |
| | | | 4 | 5 | | 7 | | 9 | 10² | 11 | | | | 8 | | | | | 12 | 6¹ | | | | | 13 | 1 | 2³ | | | 3 | | 14 | 40 |
| | 2 | | 4 | | 12 | 7 | 8¹ | 9 | | 11³ | | | | | | | 14 | | 10 | 6² | | | | | 13 | 1 | 5 | | | 3 | | | 41 |
| | 2 | 3 | 4 | 12 | 6 | 7³ | 8 | 9² | | 11 | | 5 | | 10¹ | | | | | | | | | | | 13 | 1 | 14 | | | | | | 42 |
| | 2 | 3⁴ | 4 | | 6 | | 8 | | | 11¹ | | 5 | | 10 | | 12 | | | | | | | | | 9 | 1 | | | 7 | | 13 | | 43 |
| | 2 | | 4 | | 6 | | 8 | | 12 | 11 | | 5 | | 10 | | | | | | | 3 | | | | 9¹ | 1 | | | 7 | | | | 44 |
| | 2 | | 4 | 12 | 6 | 7¹ | 8 | 13 | | | | 5 | | 10 | | | | | | | 3³ | | 14 | | 9² | 1 | | 11 | | | | | 45 |
| | 2 | | 4 | | 6 | 7 | 8 | 9 | | 11 | | 5 | | 10¹ | | | | | | | | | | | | 1 | 3 | | | 12 | | | 46 |

**Coca-Cola Cup**

| First Round | Rochdale | (a) | 3-1 |
| | | (h) | 1-1 |
| Second Round | Burnley | (a) | 4-0 |
| | | (h) | 2-0 |
| Third Round | Leeds U | (h) | 1-3 |

**FA Cup**

| Third Round | WBA | (a) | 1-3 |

SUNDERLAND 1997–98    Back row (left to right): Kevin Phillips, Paul Heckingbottom, Michael Bridges, Jan Eriksson, Niall Quinn, Richard Ord, Jody Craddock, Darren Holloway, Lee Clark, Michael Gray.
Middle row: Kim Heiselberg, John Mullin, Chris Makin, Lionel Perez, Tony Coton, Edwin Zoetebier, Sam Aiston, Andy Melville, Gareth Hall.
Front row: Darren Williams, Craig Russell, Martin Smith, Steve Agnew, Alex Rae, Kevin Ball, Martin Scott, Chris Byrne, Alan Johnston, Paul Bracewell.

# Division 1     **SUNDERLAND**

*Sunderland Stadium of Light, Sunderland, Tyne and Wear SR5 1SU.* Telephone: (0191) 551 5000. Fax: (0191) 551 5123.

*Ground capacity:* 41,590.

*Record attendance:* 40,579 v Reading, Division 1, 17 February 1998. 75,118 v Derby Co, FA Cup 6th rd replay, 8 March 1933 (Roker Park).

*Record receipts:* £605,310 v Sheffield U, Division 1 play-off semi-final, 13 May 1998.

*Pitch measurements:* 115yd × 75yd.

*Chairman:* R. S. Murray.

*Chief Executive:* John Fickling.

*Directors:* G. McDonnell, D. C. Stonehouse. *Associate Directors:* J. R. Featherstone, G. S. Wood, J. G. Wood.

*Manager:* Peter Reid. *Assistant Manager:* Bobby Saxton. *Physio:* Neil Metcalfe.

*Youth Team Coach:* Bryan Robson. *Director of Youth:* Bob Oates. *Academy Director:* Ian Branfoot.

*Secretary:* Mark Blackbourne. *Commercial Director:* Grahame McDonnell.

*Stadium Manager:* Dave Nicholson. *Safety Officer:* John Davidson.

*Year Formed:* 1879. *Turned Professional:* 1886. *Ltd Co.:* 1906.

*Previous Name:* 1879–80, Sunderland and District Teacher's AFC.

*Previous Grounds:* 1879, Blue House Field, Hendon; 1882, Groves Field, Ashbrooke; 1883, Horatio Street; 1884, Abbs Field, Fulwell; 1886, Newcastle Road; 1898–1997, Roker Park.

*Foundation:* A Scottish schoolmaster named James Allan, working at Hendon Boarding School, took the initiative in the foundation of Sunderland in 1879 when they were formed as The Sunderland and District Teachers' Association FC at a meeting in the Adults School, Norfolk Street. Due to financial difficulties, they quickly allowed members from outside the teaching profession and so became Sunderland AFC in October 1880.

*First Football League game:* 13 September 1890, Football League, v Burnley (h) L 2-3 – Kirtley; Porteous, Oliver; Wilson, Auld, Gibson; Spence (1), Miller, Campbell (1), Scott, D. Hannah.

*Record League Victory:* 9–1 v Newcastle U (away), Division 1, 5 December 1908 – Roose; Forster, Melton; Daykin, Thomson, Low; Mordue, Hogg (4), Brown, Holley (3), Bridgett (2).

*Record Cup Victory:* 11–1 v Fairfield, FA Cup 1st rd, 2 February 1895 – Doig; McNeill, Johnston; Dunlop, McCreadie (1), Wilson; Gillespie (1), Millar (5), Campbell, Hannah (3), Scott (1).

*Record Defeat:* 0–8 v West Ham U, Division 1, 19 October 1968 and v Watford, Division 1, 25 September 1982.

*Most League Points (2 for a win):* 61, Division 2, 1963–64.

*Most League Points (3 for a win):* 93, Division 3, 1987–88.

*Most League Goals:* 109, Division 1, 1935–36.

*Highest League Scorer in Season:* Dave Halliday, 43, Division 1, 1928–29.

*Most League Goals in Total Aggregate:* Charlie Buchan, 209, 1911–25.

*Most Capped Player:* Charlie Hurley, 38 (40), Republic of Ireland.

*Most League Appearances:* Jim Montgomery, 537, 1962–77.

*Record Transfer Fee Received:* £1,500,000 from Crystal Palace for Marco Gabbiadini, September 1991.

*Record Transfer Fee Paid:* £2,500,000 to Newcastle U for Lee Clark, June 1997.

*Football League Record:* 1890 Elected to Division 1; 1958–64 Division 2; 1964–70 Division 1; 1970–76 Division 2; 1976–77 Division 1; 1977–80 Division 2; 1980–85 Division 1; 1985–87 Division 2; 1987–88 Division 3; 1988–90 Division 2; 1990–91 Division 1; 1991–92 Division 2; 1992–96 Division 1; 1996–97 FA Premier League; 1997– Division 1.

*Honours:* *Football League:* Division 1 – Champions 1891–92, 1892–93, 1894–95, 1901–02, 1912–13, 1935–36, 1995–96; Runners-up 1893–94; 1897–98, 1900–01, 1922–23, 1934–35; Division 2 – Champions 1975–76; Runners-up 1963–64, 1979–80; Division 3 – Champions 1987–88. *FA Cup:* Winners 1937, 1973; Runners-up 1913, 1992. *Football League Cup:* Runners-up 1985. **European Competitions:** *Cup-Winners' Cup:* 1973–74.

*Colours:* Red and white striped shirts, black shorts, black stockings, red turnover. *Change colours:* Navy blue shirts with red and white hoop across chest, navy shorts and stockings with red and white trim.

**Did you know?**
Kevin Phillips became the first Sunderland player since Bobby Gurney to score in seven consecutive games; he achieved this feat on 17 January 1998 v Manchester City.

## SUNDERLAND 1997–98 LEAGUE RECORD

| Match No. | Date | Venue | Opponents | Result | H/T Score | Lg. Pos. | Goalscorers | Attendance |
|---|---|---|---|---|---|---|---|---|
| 1 | Aug 10 | A | Sheffield U | L | 0-2 | 0-2 | — | 17,324 |
| 2 | 15 | H | Manchester C | W | 3-1 | 1-0 | — | Quinn 17, Phillips 84, Clark 89 | 38,894 |
| 3 | 23 | A | Port Vale | L | 1-3 | 0-2 | 16 | Phillips 76 | 8290 |
| 4 | 30 | H | Norwich C | L | 0-1 | 0-0 | 17 | | 29,204 |
| 5 | Sept 2 | H | Oxford U | W | 3-1 | 2-1 | — | Phillips 40, Beauchamp (og) 44, Melville 49 | 27,643 |
| 6 | 5 | A | Bradford C | W | 4-0 | 4-0 | — | Gray 5, Clark 30, Phillips 33, Johnston 37 | 16,484 |
| 7 | 14 | A | Birmingham C | W | 1-0 | 0-0 | 6 | Gray 72 | 17,478 |
| 8 | 20 | H | Wolverhampton W | D | 1-1 | 1-1 | 7 | Smith 17 | 30,682 |
| 9 | 28 | H | Middlesbrough | L | 1-2 | 0-0 | 11 | Ball 90 | 35,384 |
| 10 | Oct 4 | A | Reading | L | 0-4 | 0-2 | 12 | | 10,795 |
| 11 | 18 | H | Huddersfield T | W | 3-1 | 1-1 | 11 | Smith 41, Bridges 68, Clark 74 | 24,782 |
| 12 | 21 | H | Swindon T | D | 0-0 | 0-0 | — | | 27,553 |
| 13 | 25 | A | Stoke C | W | 2-1 | 1-0 | 10 | Clark 2 40, 70 | 14,587 |
| 14 | Nov 1 | A | Stockport Co | D | 1-1 | 0-0 | 10 | Clark 90 | 9473 |
| 15 | 4 | H | Charlton Ath | D | 0-0 | 0-0 | — | | 25,455 |
| 16 | 8 | H | Nottingham F | D | 1-1 | 1-1 | 12 | Phillips 2 | 33,160 |
| 17 | 15 | A | Portsmouth | W | 4-1 | 3-1 | 8 | Quinn 11, Clark 14, Johnston 33, Summerbee 65 | 10,702 |
| 18 | 22 | A | Bury | D | 1-1 | 1-1 | 8 | Phillips 32 | 7790 |
| 19 | 29 | H | Tranmere R | W | 3-0 | 3-0 | 8 | Clark 2 12, 14, Phillips 42 | 26,674 |
| 20 | Dec 6 | A | QPR | W | 1-0 | 0-0 | 6 | Quinn 84 | 15,266 |
| 21 | 13 | H | WBA | W | 2-0 | 1-0 | 7 | Phillips 40, Johnston 53 | 29,231 |
| 22 | 20 | A | Crewe Alex | W | 3-0 | 2-0 | 6 | Phillips 2, Summerbee 37, Quinn 82 | 5404 |
| 23 | 26 | H | Bradford C | W | 2-0 | 1-0 | 5 | Phillips 11, Johnston 58 | 40,055 |
| 24 | 28 | A | Oxford U | D | 1-1 | 1-1 | 5 | Phillips 14 | 8659 |
| 25 | Jan 10 | H | Sheffield U | W | 4-2 | 1-1 | 4 | Quinn 21, Rae 66, Phillips 2 81, 90 | 36,391 |
| 26 | 17 | A | Manchester C | W | 1-0 | 0-0 | 4 | Phillips 55 | 31,715 |
| 27 | 28 | A | Norwich C | L | 1-2 | 0-1 | — | Clark 84 | 15,940 |
| 28 | 31 | H | Port Vale | W | 4-2 | 3-1 | 4 | Johnston 12, Phillips 13, Quinn 20, Carragher (og) 87 | 39,258 |
| 29 | Feb 7 | A | Wolverhampton W | W | 1-0 | 0-0 | 3 | Ball 88 | 27,502 |
| 30 | 17 | H | Reading | W | 4-1 | 2-0 | — | Quinn 21, Rae 22, Phillips 2 46, 61 | 40,579 |
| 31 | 21 | A | Middlesbrough | L | 1-3 | 0-1 | 3 | Clark 90 | 30,227 |
| 32 | 24 | A | Huddersfield T | W | 3-2 | 3-0 | — | Johnston 3 (1 pen) 17, 24, 39 (p) | 14,615 |
| 33 | 28 | H | Ipswich T | D | 2-2 | 1-2 | 3 | Williams 13, Phillips 51 | 35,114 |
| 34 | Mar 4 | A | Nottingham F | W | 3-0 | 1-0 | — | Rae 31, Johnston 65, Phillips 80 | 29,009 |
| 35 | 7 | H | Stockport Co | W | 4-1 | 1-0 | 2 | Quinn 3 42, 54, 63, Phillips 86 | 34,870 |
| 36 | 10 | H | Birmingham C | D | 1-1 | 0-0 | 3 | Johnston 90 | 37,602 |
| 37 | 15 | A | Charlton Ath | D | 1-1 | 1-0 | 3 | Phillips 37 | 15,355 |
| 38 | 21 | H | Portsmouth | W | 2-1 | 1-0 | 3 | Phillips 16, Johnston 85 | 38,134 |
| 39 | 28 | H | Bury | W | 2-1 | 1-1 | 2 | Clark 43, Phillips (pen) 70 | 37,425 |
| 40 | Apr 3 | A | Tranmere R | W | 2-0 | 2-0 | — | Phillips 6, Summerbee 12 | 14,116 |
| 41 | 10 | H | QPR | D | 2-2 | 1-0 | 2 | Quinn 2 28, 55 | 40,014 |
| 42 | 13 | A | WBA | D | 3-3 | 2-2 | 2 | Quinn 2 17, 50, Phillips 28 | 20,181 |
| 43 | 18 | H | Crewe Alex | W | 2-1 | 2-1 | 2 | Ball 4, Clark 22 | 40,441 |
| 44 | 25 | H | Stoke C | W | 3-0 | 1-0 | 2 | Williams 6, Phillips 2 54, 88 | 41,214 |
| 45 | 28 | A | Ipswich T | L | 0-2 | 0-0 | — | | 20,902 |
| 46 | May 3 | H | Swindon T | W | 2-1 | 2-0 | 3 | Phillips 2 21, 44 | 14,868 |

**Final League Position: 3**        1996–97 PREM 18

### GOALSCORERS
*League (86):* Phillips 29 (1 pen), Quinn 14, Clark 13, Johnston 11 (1 pen), Ball 3, Rae 3, Summerbee 3, Gray 2, Smith 2, Williams 2, Bridges 1, Melville 1, own goals 2.
*Coca-Cola Cup (4):* Bridges 1, Rae 1, Smith 1, Williams 1.
*FA Cup (5):* Phillips 4 (1 pen), Quinn 1.

| Perez L 46 | Makin C 23 + 2 | Scott M 8 | Clark L 46 | Ball K 29 + 2 | Melville A 10 | Agnew S 3 | Ord R 13 + 1 | Quinn N 33 + 2 | Rae A 24 + 5 | Gray M 44 | Bridges M 6 + 3 | Byrne C 4 + 4 | Phillips K 42 + 1 | Aiston S 1 + 2 | Williams D 35 + 1 | Mullin J 1 + 5 | Smith M 11 + 5 | Johnston A 38 + 2 | Bracewell P — + 1 | Russell C — + 3 | Craddock J 31 + 1 | Holloway D 32 | Summerbee N 22 + 3 | Hall G 1 + 1 | Dichio D 2 + 11 | Lumsdon C 1 | Match No. |
|---|---|---|---|---|---|---|---|---|---|---|---|---|---|---|---|---|---|---|---|---|---|---|---|---|---|---|---|
| 1 | 2 | 3 | 4 | 5¹ | 6 | 7 | 8 | 9 | 10² | 11 | 12 | 13 | | | | | | | | | | | | | | | 1 |
| 1 | 2 | | 4 | 5 | 6 | 7² | 8² | 9 | 10 | 3 | | | 11 | | 10 | | 12 | 13 | | | | | | | | | 2 |
| 1 | 2 | | 4 | 5 | 6 | | 8 | 9 | 10 | 3 | | 13 | 11² | | | | 12 | 7¹ | | | | | | | | | 3 |
| 1 | 2 | 3 | 4 | 5¹ | 6 | 7² | 8 | 9 | 10 | 11 | | 13 | 12 | | | | | | | | | | | | | | 4 |
| 1 | 2 | 3 | 4 | 5 | 6 | | 8 | 9² | 10 | 11 | | | 12 | | | | 13 | 7¹ | | | | | | | | | 5 |
| 1 | 2 | 3 | 4² | 5 | 6 | | 8 | 9¹ | 10 | 11 | | | 12 | | | | 13 | 7 | | | | | | | | | 6 |
| 1 | 2 | | 4 | 5 | 6 | | 8 | 9¹ | 10² | 3 | 12 | | 11 | | | | 13 | 7 | | | | | | | | | 7 |
| 1 | 2 | 3 | 4¹ | 5 | 6 | | 8 | 9 | 10² | 11 | | | 12 | | | | 13 | 7 | | | | | | | | | 8 |
| 1 | 2 | 3 | 4 | 5 | 6 | | 8 | 9¹ | 10 | 11 | | | 12 | | | | | 7 | | | | | | | | | 9 |
| 1 | 2 | 3 | 4 | 5 | 6 | | 8 | 9¹ | 10² | 11 | | | 12 | | | | 13 | 7 | | | | | | | | | 10 |
| 1 | 2 | 3 | 4 | 5 | | | 8 | 9¹ | 10 | | 12 | | 11² | | | | 13 | 7 | | | 6 | | | | | | 11 |
| 1 | 2¹ | | 4 | 5 | | | 8 | 9 | 10 | 3 | 12 | | 11 | | | | | 7 | | | 6 | | | | | | 12 |
| 1 | | | 4 | 5 | | | | 9¹ | | 3 | | 13 | 10 | | 8 | | 12 | 11² | | | 6 | 2 | | | | | 13 |
| 1 | | | 4 | 5 | | | | 9² | | 3 | 12 | | 10 | | 8¹ | | 13 | 11 | | | 6 | 2 | 7 | | | | 14 |
| 1 | | | 4 | 5 | | | | 9 | | 3 | | | 10 | | 8 | | | 11 | | | 6 | 2 | 7 | | | | 15 |
| 1 | | | 4 | 5 | | | | 9¹ | | 3 | 12 | | 10 | | 8 | | | 11 | | | 6 | 2 | 7 | | | | 16 |
| 1 | | | 4 | 5 | | | | 9 | | 3 | | | 10 | | 8 | | 12 | 11¹ | | | 6 | 2 | 7 | | | | 17 |
| 1 | | | 4 | 5 | | | | 9 | | 3 | | 13 | 10 | | 8 | | 12 | 11¹ | | | 6² | 2 | 7 | | | | 18 |
| 1 | | | 4 | 5 | | | | 9 | | 3 | | | 10 | | 8 | | | 11 | | | 6 | 2 | 7 | | | | 19 |
| 1 | | | 4 | 5 | | | | 9 | | 3 | | | 10 | | 8 | | | 11 | | | 6 | 2 | 7 | | | | 20 |
| 1 | | | 4 | 5 | | | | 9 | | 3 | | | 10 | | 8 | | | 11 | | | 6 | 2 | 7 | | | | 21 |
| 1 | | | 4 | 5 | | | | 9 | | 3 | | | 10 | | 8 | | 12 | 11¹ | | | 6 | 2 | 7 | | | | 22 |
| 1 | | | 4 | 5 | | | | 9 | | 3 | | | 10 | | 8 | | | 11 | | | 6 | 2 | 7 | | | | 23 |
| 1 | | | 4 | 5 | | | | 9 | | 3 | | | 10 | | 8 | | 12 | 11¹ | | | 6 | 2 | 7 | | | | 24 |
| 1 | | | 4 | 5 | | | | 9 | | 3 | | | 10 | | 8 | | | 11 | | | 6 | 2 | 7 | | | | 25 |
| 1 | 12 | | 4 | 5 | | | | 9 | | 3 | | | 10 | | 8 | | | 11 | | | 6¹ | 2 | 7 | | | | 26 |
| 1 | | | 4 | 5 | | | | 9¹ | | 3 | | | 10 | | 8 | | 12 | 11 | | | 6 | 2 | 7 | | | | 27 |
| 1 | 2 | | 4 | 5 | | | | 9 | | 3 | 12 | | 10 | | 8 | | | 11 | | | 6¹ | | 7 | | | | 28 |
| 1 | | | 4 | 5 | | | | 9 | | 3 | | | 10 | | 8 | | 12 | 11 | | | 6 | 2 | 7¹ | | | | 29 |
| 1 | | | 4 | 5 | | | | 9¹ | | 3 | | | 10 | | 8 | | 12 | 11 | | | 6 | 2 | 7 | | | | 30 |
| 1 | 2 | | 4 | 5 | | | | 9 | | 3 | | | 10 | | 8 | | 12 | 11¹ | | | 6 | | 7 | | | | 31 |
| 1 | 2 | | 4 | 5 | | | | 9 | | 3 | 12 | | 10² | | 8 | | 13 | 11 | | | 6 | | 7¹ | | | | 32 |
| 1 | | | 4 | 5 | | | | 9 | | 3 | 12 | | 10 | | 8 | | | 11 | | | 6 | 2 | 7¹ | | | | 33 |
| 1 | | | 4 | 5 | | | | 9 | | 3 | | | 10 | | 8 | | | 11 | | | 6 | 2 | 7 | | | | 34 |
| 1 | | | 4 | 5 | | | | 9¹ | | 3 | | | 10 | | 8 | | 12 | 11 | | | 6 | 2 | 7 | | | | 35 |
| 1 | | | 4 | 5 | | | | 9¹ | | 3 | 12 | | 10 | | 8 | | 13 | 11 | | | 6 | 2² | 7 | | | | 36 |
| 1 | 12 | | 4 | 5¹ | | | | 9² | | 3 | | | 10 | | 8 | | 13 | 11 | | | 6 | 2 | 7 | | | | 37 |
| 1 | 2 | | 4 | 5 | | | | 9² | | 3 | | 13 | 10 | | 8¹ | | 12 | 11 | | | 6 | | 7 | | | | 38 |
| 1 | 2 | | 4 | 5 | | | | 9 | | 3 | | | 10 | | 8 | | | 11 | | | 6 | | 7 | | | | 39 |
| 1 | 2 | | 4 | 5 | | | | 9 | | 3 | | | 10 | | 8 | | | 11 | | | 6 | | 7 | | | | 40 |
| 1 | 2 | | 4 | 5 | | | | 9 | | 3 | | | 10 | | 8 | | | 11 | | | 6 | | 7 | | | | 41 |
| 1 | 2 | | 4¹ | 5² | | | | 9² | | 3 | 12 | | 10 | | 8 | | | 11 | | 13 | 6 | | 7 | | 14 | | 42 |
| 1 | | | 4 | 5 | | | | 9 | | 3 | | | 10 | | 8 | | | 11 | | | 6 | 2 | 7 | | | | 43 |
| 1 | | | 4 | 5 | | | | 9¹ | | 3 | | | 10 | | 8 | | 12 | 11 | | | 6 | 2 | 7 | | | | 44 |
| 1 | | | 4¹ | 5 | | | | 9 | | 3 | 12 | | 10 | | 8 | | 13 | 11 | | | 6 | 2 | 7 | | | | 45 |
| 1 | | | 4 | 5 | | | | 9¹ | | 3 | 12 | | 10 | | 8 | | | 11 | | | 6 | 2 | 7 | | | | 46 |

**Coca-Cola Cup**

| Second Round | Bury | (h) | 2-1 |
|---|---|---|---|
| | | (a) | 2-1 |
| Third Round | Middlesbrough | (a) | 0-2 |

**FA Cup**

| Third Round | Rotherham U | (a) | 5-1 |
|---|---|---|---|
| Fourth Round | Tranmere R | (a) | 0-1 |

SWANSEA CITY 1997–98 *Back row (left to right):* Jamie Harris, Christian Edwards, Jason Jones, Roger Freestone, Lee Jones, Aidan Newhouse, Jason Price.
*Middle row:* Paul Morgan (Kit Man), Joao Moreira, Jonathan Coates, Mark Clode, Kwame Ampadu, Steve Watkin, Richard Appleby, Tony Bird, Kristian O'Leary, Ron Walton (Youth Team Coach), Nick Cusack, Alan Curtis (First Team Coach).
*Front row:* Ryan Casey, Steve Jones, Damian Lacey, David O'Gorman, Keith Walker, Alan Cork (Manager), Gary Jones, Lee Jenkins, Linton Brown, Robert King.
(Photograph: Reg Pike)

# Division 3 **SWANSEA CITY**

*Vetch Field, Swansea SA1 3SU.* Telephone: (01792) 474114. Fax: (01792) 646120. Club Shop: 33 William St, Swansea SA1 3QS. Telephone: (01792) 462584. Ticket Hotline: 0845 6040189

*Ground capacity:* 11,477.

*Record attendance:* 32,796 v Arsenal, FA Cup 4th rd, 17 February 1968.

*Record receipts:* £36,477.42 v Liverpool, Division 1, 18 September 1982.

*Pitch measurements:* 112yd × 74yd.

*President:* I. C. Pursey MBE.

*Chairman:* Steve Hamer. *Vice-Chairman:* N. J. McClure.

*Directors:* Professor D. H. Farmer, R. G. Hamill.

*Chief Executive:* Peter Day.

*Manager:* John Hollins MBE. *Assistant Manager:* Alan Curtis. *Youth Development Officer:* Malcolm Elias.

*Physio:* Mike Davenport. *Football Development Officers:* Jeremy Charles, Lyndon Jones.

*Club Secretary:* Vicki Townsend. *Commercial Manager:* Mike Lewis. *Safety Officer:* Don Goss.

*Programme Editor:* Major Reg Pike (01792) 474114.

*Year Formed:* 1912. *Turned Professional:* 1912. *Ltd Co.:* 1912.

*Previous Name:* Swansea Town until February 1970.

*Club Nickname:* 'The Swans'.

*Foundation:* The earliest Association Football in Wales was played in the Northern part of the country and no international took place in the South until 1894, when a local paper still thought it necessary to publish an outline of the rules and an illustration of the pitch markings. There had been an earlier Swansea club, but this has no connection with Swansea Town (now City) formed at a public meeting in June 1912.

*First Football League game:* 28 August 1920, Division 3, v Portsmouth (a) L 0-3 – Crumley; Robson, Evans; Smith, Holdsworth, Williams; Hole, I. Jones, Edmundson, Rigsby, Spottiswood.

*Record League Victory:* 8–0 v Hartlepool U, Division 4, 1 April 1978 – Barber; Evans, Bartley, Lally (1) (Morris), May, Bruton, Kevin Moore, Robbie James (3 incl. 1p), Curtis (3), Toshack (1), Chappell.

*Record Cup Victory:* 12–0 v Sliema W (Malta), ECWC 1st rd 1st leg, 15 September 1982 – Davies; Marustik, Hadziabdic (1), Irwin (1), Kennedy, Rajkovic (1), Loveridge (2) (Leighton James), Robbie James, Charles (2), Stevenson (1), Latchford (1) (Walsh (3)).

*Record Defeat:* 0–8 v Liverpool, FA Cup 3rd rd, 9 January 1990; 0–8 v Monaco, European Cup Winners' Cup, 1 October 1991.

*Most League Points (2 for a win):* 62, Division 3 (S), 1948–49.

*Most League Points (3 for a win):* 73, Division 2, 1992–93.

*Most League Goals:* 90, Division 2, 1956–57.

*Highest League Scorer in Season:* Cyril Pearce, 35, Division 2, 1931–32.

*Most League Goals in Total Aggregate:* Ivor Allchurch, 166, 1949–58, 1965–68.

*Most Capped Player:* Ivor Allchurch, 42 (68), Wales.

*Most League Appearances:* Wilfred Milne, 585, 1919–37.

*Record Transfer Fee Received:* £375,000 from Nottingham F for Des Lyttle, July 1993.

*Record Transfer Fee Paid:* £340,000 to Liverpool for Colin Irwin, August 1981.

*Football League Record:* 1920 Original Member of Division 3; 1921–25 Division 3 (S); 1925–47 Division 2; 1947–49 Division 3 (S); 1949–65 Division 2; 1965–67 Division 3; 1967–70 Division 4; 1970–73 Division 3; 1973–78 Division 4; 1978–79 Division 3; 1979–81 Division 2; 1981–83 Division 1; 1983–84 Division 2; 1984–86 Division 3; 1986–88 Division 4; 1988–92 Division 3; 1992–96 Division 2; 1996– Division 3.

*Honours: Football League:* Division 1 best season: 6th, 1981–82; Division 2 – Promoted 1980–81 (3rd); Division 3 (S) – Champions 1924–25, 1948–49; Division 3 – Promoted 1978–79 (3rd); Division 4 – Promoted 1969–70 (3rd), 1977–78 (3rd), 1987–88 (play-offs). *FA Cup:* Semi-finals 1926, 1964. *Football League Cup:* best season: 4th rd, 1965, 1977. *Welsh Cup:* Winners 9 times; Runners-up 8 times. *Autoglass Trophy:* Winners 1994. **European Competitions:** *European Cup-Winners' Cup:* 1961–62, 1966–67, 1981–82, 1982–83, 1983–84, 1989–90, 1991–92.

*Colours:* White shirts with maroon and black facing, white shorts with maroon and black trim, white stockings with maroon ring top. *Change colours:* Maroon shirts with black and white facings, maroon shorts with black and white trim, maroon stockings with white band.

**Did you know?**
Goalkeeper Alex Ferguson made a then club record 108 consecutive League appearances from 29 September 1928 to 7 March 1931.

## SWANSEA CITY 1997–98 LEAGUE RECORD

| Match No. | Date | | Venue | Opponents | Result | | H/T Score | Lg. Pos. | Goalscorers | Attendance |
|---|---|---|---|---|---|---|---|---|---|---|
| 1 | Aug | 9 | H | Brighton & HA | W | 1-0 | 0-0 | — | Bird [80] | 6800 |
| 2 | | 23 | H | Scunthorpe U | W | 2-0 | 1-0 | 6 | Hills [11], Bird (pen) [47] | 4895 |
| 3 | | 30 | A | Hull C | L | 4-7 | 1-2 | 12 | Coates [14], Bird [53], Price [65], Dewhurst (og) [77] | 5198 |
| 4 | Sept | 2 | A | Barnet | L | 0-2 | 0-2 | — | | 1946 |
| 5 | | 5 | H | Torquay U | W | 2-0 | 0-0 | — | O'Gorman [63], Bird [90] | 4135 |
| 6 | | 9 | A | Darlington | L | 2-3 | 2-0 | — | Bird [13], O'Gorman [36] | 2150 |
| 7 | | 13 | A | Macclesfield T | L | 0-3 | 0-1 | 16 | | 2479 |
| 8 | | 20 | H | Colchester U | L | 0-1 | 0-0 | 18 | | 3414 |
| 9 | | 27 | H | Leyton Orient | D | 1-1 | 0-0 | 18 | Bird [58] | 3494 |
| 10 | Oct | 4 | A | Peterborough U | L | 1-3 | 0-2 | 20 | Bird [80] | 5849 |
| 11 | | 11 | A | Exeter C | L | 0-1 | 0-1 | 20 | | 3909 |
| 12 | | 18 | H | Notts Co | L | 1-2 | 1-0 | 21 | Edwards [5] | 3668 |
| 13 | | 21 | H | Mansfield T | L | 0-1 | 0-0 | — | | 2589 |
| 14 | | 24 | A | Doncaster R | W | 3-0 | 2-0 | — | Bird [9], O'Gorman [12], Lacey [80] | 1170 |
| 15 | Nov | 2 | A | Cardiff C | W | 1-0 | 1-0 | 20 | Walker [11] | 6459 |
| 16 | | 4 | H | Hartlepool U | L | 0-2 | 0-0 | — | | 2949 |
| 17 | | 8 | H | Lincoln C | D | 0-0 | 0-0 | 20 | | 2871 |
| 18 | | 18 | A | Scarborough | L | 2-3 | 1-1 | — | Bird 2 (1 pen) [2, 76 (p)] | 1408 |
| 19 | | 26 | A | Chester C | L | 0-2 | 0-1 | — | | 1510 |
| 20 | | 29 | A | Shrewsbury T | W | 1-0 | 0-0 | 21 | Coates [73] | 2697 |
| 21 | Dec | 2 | H | Rotherham U | D | 1-1 | 0-0 | — | Coates [49] | 2463 |
| 22 | | 13 | A | Rochdale | L | 0-3 | 0-2 | 21 | | 1482 |
| 23 | | 20 | H | Cambridge U | D | 1-1 | 1-0 | 22 | Watkin [11] | 2605 |
| 24 | | 26 | A | Torquay U | L | 0-2 | 0-0 | 22 | | 2998 |
| 25 | | 28 | H | Barnet | L | 0-2 | 0-1 | 22 | | 3987 |
| 26 | Jan | 10 | A | Brighton & HA | W | 1-0 | 1-0 | 21 | Bird [37] | 2997 |
| 27 | | 17 | H | Hull C | W | 2-0 | 0-0 | 21 | Bird [47], Coates [89] | 2899 |
| 28 | | 24 | A | Scunthorpe U | L | 0-1 | 0-1 | 21 | | 2123 |
| 29 | | 27 | H | Darlington | W | 4-0 | 2-0 | — | Edwards [13], Alsop [20], Appleby [49], O'Gorman [89] | 2128 |
| 30 | | 31 | H | Macclesfield T | D | 1-1 | 1-1 | 20 | Alsop [10] | 3293 |
| 31 | Feb | 6 | A | Colchester U | W | 2-1 | 0-1 | — | Coates [52], Price [78] | 2789 |
| 32 | | 14 | H | Peterborough U | L | 0-1 | 0-0 | 19 | | 3737 |
| 33 | | 21 | A | Leyton Orient | D | 2-2 | 1-1 | 21 | Coates [33], O'Gorman [75] | 4261 |
| 34 | | 24 | A | Notts Co | L | 1-2 | 1-2 | — | Hartfield [19] | 4484 |
| 35 | | 28 | H | Exeter C | W | 2-1 | 0-0 | 21 | Hartfield [80], Bird [81] | 3323 |
| 36 | Mar | 3 | H | Lincoln C | D | 1-1 | 0-0 | — | Price [69] | 2281 |
| 37 | | 8 | H | Cardiff C | D | 1-1 | 0-0 | 20 | Coates [84] | 5621 |
| 38 | | 14 | A | Hartlepool U | L | 2-4 | 1-1 | 20 | Watkin [11], Walker [49] | 1727 |
| 39 | | 21 | H | Scarborough | D | 0-0 | 0-0 | 21 | | 2797 |
| 40 | | 28 | H | Chester C | W | 2-0 | 1-0 | 21 | Barwood [14], Watkin [87] | 2500 |
| 41 | Apr | 4 | H | Shrewsbury T | L | 0-1 | 0-1 | 21 | | 2623 |
| 42 | | 11 | A | Rotherham U | D | 1-1 | 1-1 | 21 | Alsop [17] | 2942 |
| 43 | | 13 | H | Rochdale | W | 3-0 | 0-0 | 20 | Appleby 2 [61, 65], Walker [74] | 2854 |
| 44 | | 18 | A | Cambridge U | L | 1-4 | 1-2 | 20 | Bird [22] | 2336 |
| 45 | | 25 | H | Doncaster R | D | 0-0 | 0-0 | 20 | | 3661 |
| 46 | May | 2 | A | Mansfield T | L | 0-1 | 0-0 | 20 | | 2867 |

**Final League Position: 20**   1996–97 DIV3 5

### GOALSCORERS
*League (49):* Bird 14 (2 pens), Coates 7, O'Gorman 5, Alsop 3, Appleby 3, Price 3, Walker 3, Watkin 3, Edwards 2, Hartfield 2, Barwood 1, Hills 1, Lacey 1, own goal 1.
*Coca-Cola Cup (1):* Coates 1.
*FA Cup (1):* Appleby 1.

| Freestone R 43 | Price J 31+3 | Moreira J 5 | Walker K 39 | Edwards C 32 | Coates J 42+2 | Lacey D 16+6 | O'Gorman D 11+23 | Bird T 35+6 | Ampadu K 16+2 | Putnam D 4 | Hills J 7 | Jones G 3+5 | Chapple S 3+1 | Appleby R 33+2 | O'Leary K 25+4 | Harris J —+6 | Jones L 2 | Agnew P 7 | Jenkins L 14+7 | Watkin S 24+8 | Molby J 1 | Casey R 2+4 | Phillips G —+6 | Clode M 7+1 | Cusack N 32 | Newhouse A 3+5 | Bound M 28 | Mainwaring C 2+1 | Hartfield C 22 | Trevitt S 1 | Brown L —+2 | Barwood D 1+2 | Alsop J 12 | Howard M 2+1 | Munroe K —+1 | Jones J 1 | Match No. |
|---|---|---|---|---|---|---|---|---|---|---|---|---|---|---|---|---|---|---|---|---|---|---|---|---|---|---|---|---|---|---|---|---|---|---|---|---|---|
| 1 | 2 | 3 | 4 | 5 | 6 | 7 | 8 | 9 | 10 | 11 | | | | | | | | | | | | | | | | | | | | | | | | | | | 1 |
| 1 | 2 | | 4 | 5 | 6 | | $8^2$ | 9 | 10 | 11 | | 3 | $7^1$ | 12 | 13 | | | | | | | | | | | | | | | | | | | | | | 2 |
| 1 | 2 | | 4 | 5 | 6 | | 8 | 9 | 10 | 11 | | 3 | 7 | | | | | | | | | | | | | | | | | | | | | | | 3 |
| 1 | 2 | | 4 | | 6 | | 8 | 9 | 10 | $11^1$ | 3 | | 7 | 5 | 12 | | | | | | | | | | | | | | | | | | | | | 4 |
| 1 | 2 | | 4 | | 6 | | 8 | 9 | 10 | $11^1$ | 3 | 12 | | 7 | 5 | | | | | | | | | | | | | | | | | | | | | 5 |
| 1 | 2 | | 4 | | 6 | | 8 | 9 | 10 | 11 | 3 | | 7 | 5 | | | | | | | | | | | | | | | | | | | | | | 6 |
| | 2 | | 4 | 5 | 12 | | $8^2$ | 9 | 10 | 11 | $3^1$ | | 7 | 13 | 1 | 6 | | | | | | | | | | | | | | | | | | | | 7 |
| 1 | 2 | | 4 | 5 | 6 | | 8 | 9 | $10^1$ | $11^2$ | 12 | 7 | 13 | 3 | | | | | | | | | | | | | | | | | | | | | | 8 |
| 1 | 2 | 3 | 4 | 5 | 6 | | $8^2$ | 9 | | 11 | $7^1$ | 12 | 13 | 10 | | | | | | | | | | | | | | | | | | | | | | 9 |
| 1 | 2 | | | 5 | 11 | | | 9 | | | $8^1$ | 6 | $7^1$ | 4 | 3 | | | 10 | 12 | | | | | | | | | | | | | | | | | 10 |
| 1 | 2 | | 4 | 5 | $6^1$ | $7^2$ | | 9 | | | 13 | 8 | 12 | 14 | 3 | $10^3$ | 11 | | | | | | | | | | | | | | | | | | | 11 |
| 1 | 2 | 6 | 4 | 5 | | 7 | | 12 | 9 | | | $10^3$ | $11^2$ | 13 | 3 | $8^1$ | | 14 | | | | | | | | | | | | | | | | | | 12 |
| 1 | $2^3$ | 6 | 4 | 5 | | $7^2$ | | 12 | 9 | | 13 | $10^1$ | 11 | 3 | 8 | | 14 | | | | | | | | | | | | | | | | | | | 13 |
| 1 | 12 | $6^1$ | 4 | 5 | | 7 | 13 | $11^2$ | 9 | | | $10^3$ | 2 | 3 | 8 | | 14 | | | | | | | | | | | | | | | | | | | 14 |
| 1 | 2 | | 4 | 5 | 6 | | | $9^1$ | | | | 10 | 11 | 8 | | | | 3 | 7 | 12 | | | | | | | | | | | | | | | | 15 |
| 1 | 2 | | 4 | 5 | 6 | 12 | | 9 | | | | $10^1$ | 11 | 13 | | | | 3 | 7 | $8^2$ | | | | | | | | | | | | | | | | 16 |
| 1 | $2^1$ | | 4 | 5 | 6 | | | $9^2$ | | | 12 | 10 | 11 | 13 | | | | 3 | 7 | 8 | | | | | | | | | | | | | | | | 17 |
| | 2 | | 4 | 5 | 3 | 12 | | $9^1$ | $7^1$ | | | 10 | $11^2$ | 1 | | 14 | | | 13 | 6 | $8^3$ | | | | | | | | | | | | | | | 18 |
| 1 | | | 4 | 5 | 11 | | | 9 | 7 | | | 8 | | | | | | 3 | 6 | | 2 | 10 | | | | | | | | | | | | | | 19 |
| 1 | 2 | | 4 | 5 | 11 | | | 12 | 9 | 10 | | | | $8^1$ | | | | 7 | 6 | 3 | | | | | | | | | | | | | | | | 20 |
| 1 | 2 | | 4 | 5 | 11 | | | 12 | $9^1$ | 10 | | | | 8 | | | | 7 | 6 | 3 | | | | | | | | | | | | | | | | 21 |
| 1 | 12 | | 4 | 5 | $11^2$ | | | 13 | 9 | 10 | | | | 14 | | | | 8 | 7 | 6 | $3^3$ | $2^1$ | | | | | | | | | | | | | | 22 |
| 1 | 2 | | 4 | 5 | 11 | | | 12 | 13 | 10 | | | | 9 | | | | $8^1$ | 7 | 6 | $3^2$ | | | | | | | | | | | | | | | 23 |
| 1 | 2 | | 4 | 5 | 11 | | | 12 | 13 | 10 | | | | $9^2$ | | | | 14 | $8^1$ | 7 | 6 | $3^2$ | | | | | | | | | | | | | | 24 |
| 1 | | | 4 | | | | 2 | 12 | 9 | | | | | 10 | 5 | | | | 8 | 13 | | | $11^2$ | 7 | 6 | $3^1$ | | | | | | | | | | 25 |
| 1 | | | | | 8 | 3 | $11^2$ | 7 | 12 | | | | | 5 | | | | | 9 | 13 | | | | 10 | 6 | 4 | $2^1$ | | | | | | | | | 26 |
| 1 | | | 5 | | 3 | 2 | 12 | $9^1$ | | | | | | 4 | | | | | 8 | $10^3$ | | | $11^1$ | 7 | 13 | | | | 14 | | | | | | | 27 |
| 1 | | | 4 | 5 | 3 | 2 | 12 | $9^2$ | | | | | $11^1$ | | | | | | 8 | 13 | | | | 7 | 6 | | 10 | | | | | | | | | 28 |
| 1 | 8 | | 4 | 5 | 3 | | 12 | $9^1$ | | | | | 11 | | | | | | | 13 | | | | 7 | 6 | 2 | $10^2$ | | | | | | | | | 29 |
| 1 | 8 | | 4 | 5 | 3 | | 12 | $9^2$ | | | | | 11 | | | | | | 14 | 13 | | 13 | | 7 | 6 | 2 | 10 | | | | | | | | | 30 |
| 1 | 8 | | 4 | 5 | 3 | | | $9^2$ | | | | | $11^2$ | 14 | | | | | 13 | | | | | 7 | 6 | 2 | $10^1$ | | | | | | | | | 31 |
| 1 | $8^2$ | | | 4 | 3 | | 12 | 13 | | | | | 5 | | | | | | 9 | | | | $11^1$ | 7 | 6 | $2^3$ | 10 | | | | | | | | | 32 |
| 1 | 8 | | | 4 | $3^1$ | 12 | 13 | 9 | 14 | | | | $11^2$ | | | | | | 5 | | | | | 10 | 7 | 6 | $2^3$ | | | | | | | | | 33 |
| 1 | $8^1$ | | $4^2$ | 11 | 12 | | | 9 | 3 | | | | 5 | | | | | | 13 | 10 | | | | 7 | 6 | $2^3$ | | | 14 | | | | | | | 34 |
| 1 | 12 | | 5 | 4 | 11 | | $8^1$ | 9 | | | | | 13 | | | | | | $10^2$ | | | | | 7 | 6 | 2 | 14 | $3^2$ | | | | | | | | 35 |
| 1 | 8 | | 4 | 5 | 11 | $2^1$ | | 9 | | | | | 12 | | | | | | 10 | | | | | 7 | 6 | 13 | $3^2$ | | | | | | | | | 36 |
| 1 | 8 | | 4 | 5 | 11 | $3^2$ | 12 | 9 | | | | | $10^1$ | 13 | | | | | 14 | | | | | 7 | 6 | $2^2$ | | | | | | | | | | 37 |
| 1 | $8^1$ | | 4 | 5 | $11^3$ | 12 | | | | | | | 10 | 13 | | | | | $3^2$ | 2 | | | | 7 | 6 | 14 | | | 9 | | | | | | | 38 |
| 1 | | | 5 | | 3 | 2 | 12 | | | | | | 10 | 4 | | | | | $8^1$ | | | | | 7 | 6 | 11 | | | 9 | | | | | | | 39 |
| 1 | | | 3 | 2 | 12 | | | | | | | | $10^1$ | 4 | | | | | $8^2$ | 9 | 13 | 14 | | 5 | 6 | 7 | | | $11^2$ | | | | | | | 40 |
| 1 | | | 3 | $2^1$ | 12 | 13 | | | | | | | 11 | $4^3$ | | | | | 8 | $10^2$ | | | | 5 | 14 | 6 | 7 | | | 9 | | | | | | | 41 |
| 1 | | | 5 | $3^3$ | 2 | 12 | 13 | | | | | | $10^2$ | 4 | | | | | 14 | 8 | | | | | 7 | 6 | 11 | | | $9^1$ | | | | | | | 42 |
| 1 | | | 5 | 2 | 12 | 13 | | 10 | | | | | 4 | $3^1$ | | | | | $8^2$ | | | | | 7 | 14 | 6 | 11 | | | $9^3$ | | | | | | | 43 |
| 1 | | | 5 | 12 | 2 | 13 | 9 | | | | | | $10^2$ | 4 | | | | | 3 | $8^3$ | | | | | 7 | 14 | 6 | | | $11^1$ | | | | | | | 44 |
| 1 | $2^1$ | | 5 | 11 | $3^2$ | 12 | | | | | | | 4 | | | | | | 8 | $10^2$ | | 14 | | 7 | 13 | 6 | | | 9 | | | | | | | 45 |
| | $5^3$ | | 3 | 11 | 4 | | 2 | 12 | 13 | | | | 7 | | | | | | 6 | $10^2$ | 8 | | | | $9^1$ | 14 | 1 | | | | | | | | | | 46 |

**Coca-Cola Cup**

| First Round | Reading | (a) | 0-2 |
|---|---|---|---|
| | | (h) | 1-1 |

**FA Cup**

| First Round | Peterborough U | (h) | 1-4 |

SWINDON TOWN 1997–98    *Back row (left to right):* Wayne Allison, Mark Seagraves, Fraser Digby, Steve Mildenhall, Frank Talia, Steve Finney, Kevin Watson.
*Third row:* Alan McDonald, Mark Walters, Craig Taylor, Gary Elkins, Mark Robinson, Scott Leitch, Ian Culverhouse, Frederic Darras, Alex Finlayson.
*Second row:* Lee Collins, Peter Holcroft, Phil King, Darren Bullock, Wayne O'Sullivan, Ty Godden, Steve Cowe.
*Front row:* Jason Drysdale, Jonathan Trigg (Physio), Ross MacLaren (Reserve Team Coach), Steve McMahon (Manager), Mike Walsh (First Team Coach), Les O'Neill (Chief Scout), Alex Smith.

# Division 1 SWINDON TOWN

*County Ground, Swindon, Wiltshire SN1 2ED.* Telephone: (01793) 430430. Fax: (01793) 536170. Marketing: (01793) 532121. Marketing Fax: (01793) 423771. Superstore: (01793) 423030. Community Office: (01793) 421303. Clubcall: 0891 121640.

*Ground capacity:* 15,728.

*Record attendance:* 32,000 v Arsenal, FA Cup 3rd rd, 15 January 1972.

*Record receipts:* £149,371 v Bolton W, Coca-Cola Cup semi-final 1st leg, 12 February 1995.

*Pitch measurements:* 110yd × 70yd.

*President:* C. J. Green.

*Chairman:* Rikki Hunt. *Vice-Chairman:* Cliff Puffett.

*Directors:* Sir Seton Wills Bt, P. R. Godwin CBE, J. M. Spearman, P. T. Archer, W. Carson OBE (Associate).

*Manager:* Steve McMahon. *Assistant Manager:* Mike Walsh.

*Coach:* Ross MacLaren. *Physios:* Dave Moore and Dick Mackey.

*Chief Executive/Secretary:* Steve Jones.

*Youth Team Manager:* Thomas Wheeldon.

*Head of Sales and Marketing:* Julian Wetherall.

*Community Officers:* Clive Maguire and Jon Holloway.

*Year Formed:* 1881*(see Foundation). *Turned Professional:* 1894. *Ltd Co.:* 1894.

*Club Nickname:* 'Robins'.

*Previous Ground:* 1881–96, The Croft.

*Foundation:* It is generally accepted that Swindon Town came into being in 1881, although there is no firm evidence that the club's founder, Rev. William Pitt, captain of the Spartans (an offshoot of a cricket club) changed his club's name to Swindon Town before 1883, when the Spartans amalgamated with St. Mark's Young Men's Friendly Society.

*First Football League game:* 28 August 1920, Division 3, v Luton T (h) W 9-1 – Nash; Kay, Macconachie; Langford, Hawley, Wareing; Jefferson (1), Fleming (4), Rogers, Batty (2), Davies (1). (1 og).

*Record League Victory:* 9–1 v Luton T, Division 3 (S), 28 August 1920 – Nash; Kay, Macconachie; Langford, Hawley, Wareing; Jefferson (1), Fleming (4), Rogers, Batty (2), Davies (1). (1 og).

*Record Cup Victory:* 10–1 v Farnham U Breweries (away), FA Cup 1st rd (replay), 28 November 1925 – Nash; Dickenson, Weston, Archer, Bew, Adey; Denyer (2), Wall (1), Richardson (4), Johnson (3), Davies.

*Record Defeat:* 1–10 v Manchester C, FA Cup 4th rd (replay), 25 January 1930.

*Most League Points (2 for a win):* 64, Division 3, 1968–69.

*Most League Points (3 for a win):* 102, Division 4, 1985–86 (League record).

*Most League Goals:* 100, Division 3 (S), 1926–27.

*Highest League Scorer in Season:* Harry Morris, 47, Division 3 (S), 1926–27.

*Most League Goals in Total Aggregate:* Harry Morris, 216, 1926–33.

*Most Capped Player:* Rod Thomas, 30 (50), Wales.

*Most League Appearances:* John Trollope, 770, 1960–80.

*Record Transfer Fee Received:* £1,500,000 from Manchester C for Kevin Horlock, January 1997.

*Record Transfer Fee Paid:* £800,000 to West Ham U for Joey Beauchamp, August 1994.

*Football League Record:* 1920 Original Member of Division 3; 1921–58 Division 3 (S); 1958–63 Division 3; 1963–65 Division 2; 1965–69 Division 3; 1969–74 Division 2; 1974–82 Division 3; 1982–86 Division 4; 1986–87 Division 3; 1987–92 Division 2; 1992–93 Division 1; 1993–94 FA Premier League; 1994–95 Division 1; 1995–96 Division 2; 1996– Division 1.

*Honours: FA Premier League:* best season: 22nd 1993–94; *Football League:* Division 2 – Champions 1995–96. Division 3 – Runners-up 1962–63, 1968–69; Division 4 – Champions 1985–86 (with record 102 points). *FA Cup:* Semi-finals 1910, 1912. *Football League Cup:* Winners 1969. *Anglo-Italian Cup:* Winners 1970.

*Colours:* All red. *Change colours:* Black/blue shirts, blue shorts, blue stockings.

**Did you know?**
In August 1948 the Swindon Town pre-season trial match attracted an incredible crowd of 11,882 to the County Ground.

**SWINDON TOWN FC**

## SWINDON TOWN 1997–98 LEAGUE RECORD

| Match No. | Date | Venue | Opponents | Result | | H/T Score | Lg. Pos. | Goalscorers | Attendance |
|---|---|---|---|---|---|---|---|---|---|
| 1 | Aug 9 | H | Crewe Alex | W | 2-0 | 1-0 | — | Allison [43], Finney (pen) [88] | 8334 |
| 2 | 16 | A | Reading | W | 1-0 | 1-0 | 3 | Hay [18] | 9338 |
| 3 | 23 | H | Huddersfield T | D | 1-1 | 1-1 | 4 | Hay [26] | 7683 |
| 4 | 30 | A | Stoke C | W | 2-1 | 0-1 | 4 | Allison [78], Hay [80] | 23,000 |
| 5 | Sept 2 | A | Ipswich T | L | 1-2 | 1-1 | — | Allison [23] | 11,246 |
| 6 | 7 | H | Nottingham F | D | 0-0 | 0-0 | 4 | | 13,051 |
| 7 | 13 | H | Tranmere R | W | 2-1 | 1-1 | 2 | Walters [14], Casper [64] | 6811 |
| 8 | 20 | A | WBA | D | 0-0 | 0-0 | 2 | | 16,237 |
| 9 | 27 | A | Manchester C | L | 0-6 | 0-3 | 6 | | 26,646 |
| 10 | Oct 4 | H | Port Vale | W | 4-2 | 0-1 | 3 | Hay 3 [49, 81, 85], Taylor [67] | 8048 |
| 11 | 11 | H | Bury | W | 3-1 | 2-1 | 2 | Hay 2 [4, 15], Gooden [79] | 7640 |
| 12 | 18 | A | Wolverhampton W | L | 1-3 | 1-1 | 2 | Hay (pen) [24] | 21,794 |
| 13 | 21 | A | Sunderland | D | 0-0 | 0-0 | — | | 27,553 |
| 14 | 25 | H | Norwich C | W | 1-0 | 0-0 | 2 | Hay [84] | 9256 |
| 15 | 31 | A | Portsmouth | W | 1-0 | 1-0 | — | Hay [24] | 8707 |
| 16 | Nov 5 | H | QPR | W | 3-1 | 0-1 | — | Walters [66], Taylor [84], Hay [87] | 10,132 |
| 17 | 8 | H | Bradford C | W | 1-0 | 1-0 | 1 | Cowe [24] | 10,029 |
| 18 | 15 | A | Stockport Co | L | 2-4 | 1-2 | 2 | Hay [20], Leitch [85] | 7694 |
| 19 | 22 | H | Middlesbrough | L | 1-2 | 1-1 | 4 | Ndah [12] | 15,228 |
| 20 | 28 | A | Charlton Ath | L | 0-3 | 0-2 | — | | 13,769 |
| 21 | Dec 6 | H | Oxford U | W | 4-1 | 2-1 | 5 | Wilsterman (og) [28], Walters (pen) [34], Finney [56], Gooden [86] | 10,902 |
| 22 | 13 | A | Sheffield U | L | 1-2 | 1-1 | 6 | Finney [24] | 18,115 |
| 23 | 20 | H | Birmingham C | D | 1-1 | 1-1 | 7 | Finney [11] | 10,334 |
| 24 | 26 | A | Nottingham F | L | 0-3 | 0-3 | 9 | | 26,500 |
| 25 | 28 | H | Ipswich T | L | 0-2 | 0-0 | 9 | | 10,609 |
| 26 | Jan 11 | A | Crewe Alex | L | 0-2 | 0-0 | 10 | | 4176 |
| 27 | 17 | H | Reading | L | 0-2 | 0-2 | 10 | | 9500 |
| 28 | 24 | A | Bradford C | D | 1-1 | 0-1 | 10 | Hay [90] | 15,130 |
| 29 | 28 | H | Stoke C | W | 1-0 | 0-0 | — | Robinson [71] | 6683 |
| 30 | 31 | A | Huddersfield T | D | 0-0 | 0-0 | 10 | | 10,028 |
| 31 | Feb 7 | H | WBA | L | 0-2 | 0-1 | 11 | | 9861 |
| 32 | 10 | A | Tranmere R | L | 0-3 | 0-2 | — | | 5288 |
| 33 | 17 | A | Port Vale | W | 1-0 | 1-0 | — | Collins [4] | 5925 |
| 34 | 21 | H | Manchester C | L | 1-3 | 0-1 | 11 | Cowe [71] | 12,280 |
| 35 | 28 | A | Bury | L | 0-1 | 0-1 | 13 | | 5002 |
| 36 | Mar 7 | H | Portsmouth | L | 0-1 | 0-0 | 13 | | 9100 |
| 37 | 11 | A | Middlesbrough | L | 0-6 | 0-2 | — | | 29,581 |
| 38 | 14 | A | QPR | W | 2-1 | 2-1 | 12 | Walters (pen) [16], Onuora [45] | 13,486 |
| 39 | 18 | H | Wolverhampton W | D | 0-0 | 0-0 | — | | 7770 |
| 40 | 21 | H | Stockport Co | D | 1-1 | 0-0 | 11 | McDonald [76] | 6684 |
| 41 | Apr 4 | H | Charlton Ath | L | 0-1 | 0-0 | 13 | | 7845 |
| 42 | 11 | A | Oxford U | L | 1-2 | 0-2 | 13 | Ndah (pen) [64] | 8005 |
| 43 | 13 | H | Sheffield U | D | 1-1 | 1-0 | 14 | Walters [33] | 5956 |
| 44 | 18 | A | Birmingham C | L | 0-3 | 0-2 | 16 | | 17,016 |
| 45 | 25 | H | Norwich C | L | 0-5 | 0-2 | 17 | | 18,443 |
| 46 | May 3 | H | Sunderland | L | 1-2 | 0-2 | 18 | Walters [86] | 14,868 |

**Final League Position: 18**     1996–97 DIV1 19

### GOALSCORERS
*League (42):* Hay 14 (1 pen), Walters 6 (2 pens), Finney 4 (1 pen), Allison 3, Cowe 2, Gooden 2, Ndah 2 (1 pen), Taylor 2, Casper 1, Collins 1, Leitch 1, McDonald 1, Onuora 1, Robinson 1, own goal 1.
*Coca-Cola Cup (1):* Leitch 1.
*FA Cup (1):* Walters 1.

| Digby F 38 | Darras F 12 + 2 | Drysdale J 11 + 3 | Leitch S 25 + 1 | Seagraves M 5 | McDonald A 30 + 3 | Robinson M 26 + 1 | Cuervo P 14 + 9 | Hay C 30 + 6 | Allison W 16 | Gooden T 38 + 1 | Bullock D 26 + 5 | Finney S 17 + 6 | Walters M 25 + 9 | McMahon S — + 1 | Cowe S 8 + 9 | Smith A 2 + 3 | Borrows B 40 | Casper C 8 + 1 | Watson K 13 + 5 | Taylor C 28 + 4 | Collins L 22 + 4 | Culverhouse I 9 + 2 | Hulbert R — + 1 | Meechan A — + 1 | Mildenhall S 4 | Davis S 5 + 1 | Pattimore M — + 2 | Warner T 2 | Thompson D 10 | Ndah G 14 | Howe S 9 + 1 | Elliott S 1 + 1 | Talia F 2 | Kerslake D 10 | Onuora I 6 | McAreavey P — + 1 | Match No. |
|---|---|---|---|---|---|---|---|---|---|---|---|---|---|---|---|---|---|---|---|---|---|---|---|---|---|---|---|---|---|---|---|---|---|---|---|---|---|
| 1 | 2 | 3 | 4 | 5 | 6 | 7 | $8^1$ | $9^2$ | 10 | 11 | 12 | 13 | | | | | | | | | | | | | | | | | | | | | | | | | 1 |
| 1 | 2 | 3 | 4 | 5 | 6 | 7 | $8^1$ | $9^2$ | 10 | 11 | 12 | $13^3$ | 14 | | | | | | | | | | | | | | | | | | | | | | | | 2 |
| 1 | 2 | | 4 | 5 | 6 | | 8 | $9^2$ | 10 | 11 | $3^1$ | | 7 | | 12 | | 13 | | | | | | | | | | | | | | | | | | | | 3 |
| 1 | 2 | $3^1$ | $4^2$ | 5 | 6 | | 8 | 9 | 10 | 11 | 12 | | 7 | | | | 13 | | | | | | | | | | | | | | | | | | | | 4 |
| 1 | 2 | 3 | $4^1$ | $5^2$ | 6 | | 8 | 9 | 10 | 11 | 12 | | 7 | | | | 13 | | | | | | | | | | | | | | | | | | | | 5 |
| 1 | 2 | | | | 6 | | 8 | 9 | 10 | 11 | 4 | | 7 | | | | 3 | 5 | | | | | | | | | | | | | | | | | | | 6 |
| 1 | 2 | 8 | | | 6 | | | $9^1$ | 10 | 11 | 4 | 12 | $7^2$ | | | | 3 | 5 | 13 | | | | | | | | | | | | | | | | | | 7 |
| 1 | 2 | 8 | | | 6 | | | | 10 | 11 | 4 | | | | 9 | 7 | 3 | 5 | | | | | | | | | | | | | | | | | | | 8 |
| 1 | $2^1$ | 12 | 4 | | 6 | | | 13 | 10 | 11 | 8 | | | 14 | $9^3$ | $7^2$ | 3 | 5 | | | | | | | | | | | | | | | | | | | 9 |
| 1 | 12 | $2^1$ | 4 | | 6 | | | 9 | 10 | 11 | | | 7 | | | | 3 | | $8^2$ | 5 | 13 | | | | | | | | | | | | | | | | 10 |
| 1 | 12 | | 4 | | $6^2$ | | | 9 | 10 | 11 | | | $7^1$ | | | | 2 | 13 | 8 | 5 | 3 | | | | | | | | | | | | | | | | 11 |
| 1 | | $4^1$ | | | | | | 9 | 10 | 11 | | | $7^2$ | | | | 2 | 6 | | 5 | 8 | 3 | 12 | 13 | | | | | | | | | | | | | 12 |
| 1 | | | | | | | | 9 | 10 | 11 | 4 | 12 | | | | | 2 | 6 | $7^1$ | 5 | 8 | 3 | | | | | | | | | | | | | | | 13 |
| 1 | | | | | | | | 9 | 10 | 11 | 4 | | | | 8 | $8^1$ | | 12 | 2 | 6 | 7 | 5 | | 3 | | | | | | | | | | | | | 14 |
| | | | | | | | | 9 | 10 | 11 | 4 | | | | 8 | | 2 | 6 | 7 | 5 | | 3 | | | 1 | | | | | | | | | | | | 15 |
| 1 | | | | 6 | | | | 9 | 10 | 11 | 4 | | | | | $8^2$ | 2 | | 7 | 5 | | $3^1$ | | | | | | | 12 | 13 | | | | | | | 16 |
| 1 | 8 | $4^1$ | | 6 | | | | 9 | | 11 | | | | 10 | | | 2 | | 7 | 5 | | $3^1$ | | | | | | 12 | 1 | | | | | | | | 17 |
| | | | 4 | | 6 | 12 | | $9^2$ | | 11 | | 13 | 8 | | | 10 | 2 | | 7 | 5 | | $3^1$ | | | | | 1 | | | | | | | | | | 18 |
| 1 | | | 4 | | 6 | 3 | | | | 11 | | 9 | 12 | | | | 2 | | 8 | 5 | | | | | | | | | | 7 | $10^1$ | | | | | | 19 |
| 1 | | $4^3$ | | | 6 | 3 | | | | 11 | 12 | $9^2$ | | | | 13 | 2 | | $8^1$ | 5 | | 14 | | | | | | | | 7 | 10 | | | | | | 20 |
| 1 | 5 | | | | 6 | 3 | 12 | | | 11 | $4^1$ | 9 | $8^2$ | | | | 2 | | 13 | | | | | | | | | | | 7 | 10 | | | | | | 21 |
| 1 | $5^1$ | | | | 6 | 3 | | | | 11 | 4 | | 9 | | | | 2 | | 12 | 8 | | | | | | | | | | 7 | 10 | | | | | | 22 |
| 1 | 12 | | | | 6 | 3 | 13 | | | 11 | 4 | | $9^2$ | | $8^3$ | | 2 | | | 5 | 14 | | | | | | | | | 7 | $10^1$ | | | | | | 23 |
| 1 | 13 | 4 | | | 6 | 3 | 12 | | | 11 | | | $9^1$ | | | | $2^2$ | | | 5 | 8 | | | | | | | | | 7 | 10 | | | | | | 24 |
| 1 | $5^3$ | $4^2$ | | | 6 | 3 | | 9 | | 11 | 12 | | $8^1$ | | | | | | 14 | 13 | 2 | | | | | | | | | 7 | 10 | | | | | | 25 |
| 1 | | | | | $6^2$ | 3 | 12 | 9 | | 11 | | $7^1$ | 13 | | | | 2 | | 4 | 5 | 8 | | | | | | | | | | 10 | | | | | | 26 |
| 1 | | | | | $6^1$ | 3 | 7 | 9 | | 11 | $4^2$ | 10 | | | | | 2 | 13 | 5 | 12 | | | | | | | | | | | 8 | | | | | | 27 |
| 1 | | | | | 12 | 3 | $7^2$ | 9 | | 11 | | 10 | | | | | 2 | | 5 | $6^1$ | | 4 | | | | | | | | | 8 | | | | | | 28 |
| | $11^1$ | 12 | | | | 3 | 7 | 9 | | | | 10 | | | | | 2 | | 5 | 6 | | | | | | 1 | | | 4 | | 8 | | | | | | 29 |
| | $11^2$ | 4 | 13 | | | 3 | 12 | 9 | | | | $10^1$ | | | | | 2 | | 5 | 6 | | | | | | 1 | | | 7 | | 8 | | | | | | 30 |
| 1 | | | 4 | | | 3 | $7^2$ | $9^1$ | | $11^3$ | | 10 | | 12 | | | 2 | 13 | 5 | 6 | 14 | | | | | | | | | | 8 | | | | | | 31 |
| 1 | | | 4 | | | 3 | $11^3$ | $9^2$ | | 10 | | | | 12 | | | 2 | 14 | 5 | 6 | $7^1$ | | | | | | | | | | 8 | | | | | | 32 |
| $1^2$ | $11^1$ | | 4 | | | 2 | 12 | $9^3$ | | | | 7 | 10 | | 13 | | 3 | | | 5 | 6 | | | | | | | | | | 8 | | | | | | 33 |
| 1 | | | 4 | 12 | | 2 | | $9^1$ | | | | 7 | $10^3$ | 13 | | | 3 | | | 5 | 6 | | | | | 1 | | | | | 8 | | | | $11^2$ | | 34 |
| | | | 4 | 2 | | 12 | | | | 11 | 7 | | $10^2$ | 13 | 9 | | 3 | | | 5 | 6 | | | | | | | | | | $8^1$ | | 1 | | | | 35 |
| | | | 4 | 2 | | 8 | | | | 11 | | 9 | 7 | | | | 3 | | | 5 | 6 | | | | | | | | | | | | 1 | | | | 36 |
| 1 | | | 4 | 2 | | | | 9 | | 11 | | | 8 | | | | 3 | | | 5 | 6 | | | | | | | | | | | | | | 7 | | 37 |
| 1 | 8 | | 4 | | | | | | | 11 | 5 | | $7^1$ | | | | 3 | | | | 6 | | | | | | | | | $10^2$ | 12 | 13 | | 2 | 9 | | 38 |
| 1 | $8^1$ | | 4 | | | | 12 | 13 | | 11 | 5 | | 7 | | | | 3 | | | | 6 | | | | | | | | | $10^2$ | | | | 2 | 9 | | 39 |
| 1 | | | 4 | | | 8 | 10 | | | 11 | 5 | | 7 | | | | 3 | | | | 6 | | | | | | | | | | | | | 2 | 9 | | 40 |
| 1 | 8 | | 4 | | $6^1$ | 12 | | | | 11 | 5 | | 7 | | | | 3 | | | | | | | | | | | | | 10 | | | | 2 | 9 | | 41 |
| 1 | | $4^1$ | $7^2$ | | | 13 | | | | 11 | 5 | | 14 | | | | 6 | | $8^3$ | 12 | 9 | | | | | | 3 | | | 10 | | | | 2 | | | 42 |
| 1 | | | 12 | | | 9 | | | | 11 | 5 | | 7 | | | | 6 | | | 4 | $8^1$ | | | | | | 3 | | | 10 | | | | 2 | | | 43 |
| 1 | 11 | | 12 | | | $9^1$ | | | | 13 | 5 | | $10^3$ | 7 | | | 6 | | | 4 | $8^2$ | | | | | | 3 | | | | | | | 2 | | | 44 |
| 1 | $11^2$ | | | | | | | | | | 5 | | 7 | 12 | | | 6 | | 8 | 4 | | | | | | | 3 | | | $10^1$ | | | | 2 | 9 | 13 | 45 |
| 1 | | | 4 | 11 | | $8^1$ | 12 | | | | $5^2$ | | 7 | | | | 10 | | 6 | | 13 | | | | | | 3 | | | | | | | 2 | 9 | | 46 |

**Coca-Cola Cup**
First Round    Watford     (h)   0-2
                                         (a)   1-1

**FA Cup**
Third Round    Stevenage B     (h)   1-2

TORQUAY UNITED 1997–98 *Back row (left to right):* Lee Barrow, Jon Gittens, Alex Watson, Andy McFarlane, Jamie Robinson, Wayne Thomas, Paul Mitchell.
*Middle row:* Ian Pearce (Youth Team Physio), Damien Davey (Physio), Charlie Oatway, Andy Gurney, Matthew Gregg, Paul Gibbs, Wayne Hockley, Phil Lloyd (Youth Coach), Peter Distin (Assistant Youth Manager).
*Front row:* Leon Hapgood, Rodney Jack, Kevin Hodges (Head Coach), Mervyn Benney (Chairman), Steve McCall (Assistant Coach/Youth Development Officer), Tony Bedeau, Michael Preston.

# Division 3     **TORQUAY UNITED**

*Plainmoor Ground, Torquay, Devon TQ1 3PS.* Telephone: (01803) 328666. Fax: (01803) 323976.

*Ground capacity:* 6003.

*Record attendance:* 21,908 v Huddersfield T, FA Cup 4th rd, 29 January 1955.

*Record receipts:* £26,205 v Exeter C, Division 3, 1 January 1992.

*Pitch measurements:* 112yd × 74yd.

*Chairman:* M. Benney. *Managing Director:* Miss H. Kindeleit. *Directors:* M. Bateson, Mrs S. Bateson, I. Hayman, B. Palk.

*Manager:* Wes Saunders. *Physio:* D. Davey.

*Company Secretary:* Miss H. Kindeleit.

*Year Formed:* 1899. *Turned Professional:* 1921. *Ltd Co.:* 1921.

*Previous Name:* 1910, Torquay Town; 1921, Torquay United.

*Nickname:* 'The Gulls'.

*Previous Grounds:* 1899, Teignmouth Road; 1900, Torquay Recreation Ground; 1904, Cricket Field Road; 1906–10, Torquay Cricket Ground; Plainmoor Ground.

*Foundation:* The idea of establishing a Torquay club was agreed by old boys of Torquay College and Torbay College, while sitting in Princess Gardens listening to the band. A proper meeting was subsequently held at Tor Abbey Hotel at which officers were elected. This was on 1 May 1899 and the club's first competition was the Eastern League (later known as the East Devon League).

*First Football League game:* 27 August 1927, Division 3 (S), v Exeter C (h) D 1-1 – Millsom; Cook, Smith; Wellock, Wragg, Connor, Mackey, Turner (1), Jones, McGovern, Thomson.

*Record League Victory:* 9–0 v Swindon T, Division 3 (S), 8 March 1952 – George Webber; Topping, Ralph Calland; Brown, Eric Webber, Towers; Shaw (1), Marchant (1), Northcott (2), Collins (3), Edds (2).

*Record Cup Victory:* 7–1 v Northampton T, FA Cup 1st rd, 14 November 1959 – Gill; Penford, Downs; Bettany, George Northcott, Rawson; Baxter, Cox, Tommy Northcott (1), Bond (3), Pym (3).

*Record Defeat:* 2–10 v Fulham, Division 3 (S), 7 September 1931 and v Luton T, Division 3 (S), 2 September 1933.

*Most League Points (2 for a win):* 60, Division 4, 1959–60.

*Most League Points (3 for a win):* 77, Division 4, 1987–88.

*Most League Goals:* 89, Division 3 (S), 1956–57.

*Highest League Scorer in Season:* Sammy Collins, 40, Division 3 (S), 1955–56.

*Most League Goals in Total Aggregate:* Sammy Collins, 204, 1948–58.

*Most Capped Player:* Rodney Jack, St Vincent.

*Most League Appearances:* Dennis Lewis, 443, 1947–59.

*Record Transfer Fee Received:* £180,000 from Manchester U for Lee Sharpe, May 1988.

*Record Transfer Fee Paid:* £60,000 to Dundee for Wes Saunders, July 1990.

*Football League Record:* 1927 Elected to Division 3 (S); 1958–60 Division 4; 1960–62 Division 3; 1962–66 Division 4; 1966–72 Division 3; 1972–91 Division 4; 1991– Division 3.

*Honours: Football League:* Division 3 best season: 4th, 1967–68; Division 3 (S) – Runners-up 1956–57; Division 4 – Promoted 1959–60 (3rd), 1965–66 (3rd), 1990–91 (play-offs). *FA Cup:* best season: 4th rd, 1949, 1955, 1971, 1983, 1990. *Football League Cup:* never past 3rd rd. *Sherpa Van Trophy:* Runners-up 1989.

*Colours:* Yellow and navy striped shirts, navy shorts, yellow stockings. *Change colours:* White shirts, white shorts, white stockings.

**Did you know?**
Torquay United's 1-0 win over Cardiff City on 3 March 1998 represented a club record 8th successive victory.

## TORQUAY UNITED 1997–98 LEAGUE RECORD

| Match No. | Date | Venue | Opponents | Result | H/T Score | Lg. Pos. | Goalscorers | Attendance |
|---|---|---|---|---|---|---|---|---|
| 1 | Aug 9 | A | Macclesfield T | L 1-2 | 1-1 | — | Gurney [9] | 3379 |
| 2 | 16 | H | Scarborough | W 1-0 | 0-0 | 14 | Gittens [73] | 1863 |
| 3 | 23 | A | Shrewsbury T | W 2-1 | 0-0 | 5 | Jack 2 [57, 64] | 2556 |
| 4 | 30 | H | Colchester U | D 1-1 | 0-0 | 10 | Gittens [85] | 2081 |
| 5 | Sept 2 | H | Exeter C | L 1-2 | 0-0 | — | Gurney [66] | 4217 |
| 6 | 5 | A | Swansea C | L 0-2 | 0-0 | — | | 4135 |
| 7 | 13 | A | Hartlepool U | L 0-3 | 0-1 | 19 | | 1927 |
| 8 | 20 | H | Brighton & HA | W 3-0 | 2-0 | 16 | Gittens [16], Hapgood [45], Hill [69] | 2110 |
| 9 | 27 | H | Doncaster R | W 2-0 | 1-0 | 14 | Hill [1], Hapgood [48] | 1650 |
| 10 | Oct 4 | A | Hull C | D 3-3 | 0-1 | 13 | Bedeau [73], Gittens [90], McFarlane [90] | 5139 |
| 11 | 11 | A | Lincoln C | D 1-1 | 1-0 | 12 | Watson [12] | 2462 |
| 12 | 18 | H | Chester C | W 3-1 | 3-0 | 8 | McCall [14], Jack [21], McFarlane [26] | 2047 |
| 13 | 21 | H | Leyton Orient | D 1-1 | 0-1 | — | Gibbs [90] | 1702 |
| 14 | 25 | A | Peterborough U | L 0-2 | 0-1 | 12 | | 6325 |
| 15 | Nov 1 | A | Cambridge U | D 1-1 | 0-1 | 13 | Gibbs (pen) [73] | 2314 |
| 16 | 4 | H | Darlington | W 2-1 | 1-0 | — | Jack [25], Bedeau [52] | 1411 |
| 17 | 8 | A | Cardiff C | D 1-1 | 0-0 | 13 | McFarlane [51] | 2797 |
| 18 | 18 | A | Barnet | D 3-3 | 1-1 | — | Gibbs (pen) [19], Jack [57], Gittens [87] | 1246 |
| 19 | 22 | H | Scunthorpe U | L 2-4 | 1-2 | 15 | Gibbs [34], Gurney [79] | 2152 |
| 20 | 29 | A | Rochdale | W 1-0 | 0-0 | 12 | Jack [51] | 1729 |
| 21 | Dec 2 | H | Mansfield T | W 2-1 | 0-1 | — | Gurney [74], Thomas [85] | 1440 |
| 22 | 13 | A | Rotherham U | W 1-0 | 0-0 | 8 | Gibbs (pen) [59] | 3636 |
| 23 | 20 | H | Notts Co | L 0-2 | 0-1 | 10 | | 2536 |
| 24 | 26 | H | Swansea C | W 2-0 | 0-0 | 10 | Hill [52], Roberts [80] | 2998 |
| 25 | 28 | A | Exeter C | D 1-1 | 1-1 | 8 | Leadbitter [6] | 8350 |
| 26 | Jan 10 | H | Macclesfield T | W 2-0 | 1-0 | 10 | Mitchell [21], Roberts [60] | 2428 |
| 27 | 16 | A | Colchester U | L 0-1 | 0-0 | — | | 2776 |
| 28 | 20 | A | Scarborough | L 1-4 | 0-1 | — | Heckingbottom (og) [70] | 2467 |
| 29 | 24 | H | Shrewsbury T | W 3-0 | 2-0 | 9 | Gurney [27], Gittens [45], Roberts [61] | 1996 |
| 30 | 31 | H | Hartlepool U | W 1-0 | 0-0 | 8 | Gibbs [76] | 2238 |
| 31 | Feb 7 | A | Brighton & HA | W 4-1 | 1-1 | 6 | Roberts 2 [37, 66], Gurney [52], Jack [90] | 2083 |
| 32 | 14 | H | Hull C | W 5-1 | 3-1 | 7 | Clayton [14], Hill 2 [27, 43], Hapgood [58], Jack [72] | 2793 |
| 33 | 21 | A | Doncaster R | W 1-0 | 0-0 | 3 | Bedeau [87] | 1424 |
| 34 | 24 | A | Chester C | W 3-1 | 2-0 | — | Gurney [13], Roberts [33], Jack [83] | 2163 |
| 35 | 28 | H | Lincoln C | W 3-2 | 2-1 | 2 | Jack [31], Gurney [36], Gibbs (pen) [68] | 3540 |
| 36 | Mar 3 | H | Cardiff C | W 1-0 | 1-0 | — | Hill [45] | 3358 |
| 37 | 7 | A | Cambridge U | L 0-3 | 0-1 | 2 | | 3809 |
| 38 | 14 | A | Darlington | W 2-1 | 1-1 | 2 | Bedeau [28], Jack [90] | 2386 |
| 39 | 21 | H | Barnet | D 0-0 | 0-0 | 2 | | 4020 |
| 40 | 28 | A | Scunthorpe U | L 0-2 | 0-0 | 2 | | 3264 |
| 41 | Apr 4 | H | Rochdale | D 0-0 | 0-0 | 2 | | 2796 |
| 42 | 11 | A | Mansfield T | D 2-2 | 1-0 | 2 | Hill [43], Gurney [81] | 2282 |
| 43 | 13 | H | Rotherham U | L 1-2 | 0-1 | 3 | Bedeau [67] | 3963 |
| 44 | 18 | A | Notts Co | L 0-3 | 0-1 | 3 | | 5183 |
| 45 | 25 | H | Peterborough U | W 3-1 | 2-1 | 3 | Clayton [16], McFarlane [45], Jack [63] | 4472 |
| 46 | May 2 | A | Leyton Orient | L 1-2 | 0-2 | 5 | McFarlane [77] | 6545 |

**Final League Position: 5**        1996–97 DIV3 21

### GOALSCORERS

*League (68):* Jack 12, Gurney 9, Gibbs 7 (4 pens), Hill 7, Gittens 6, Roberts 6, Bedeau 5, McFarlane 5, Hapgood 3, Clayton 2, Leadbitter 1, McCall 1, Mitchell 1, Thomas 1, Watson 1, own goal 1.
*Coca-Cola Cup (3):* Gibbs 1 (pen), Jack 1, McFarlane 1.
*FA Cup (3):* Clayton 1, Gibbs 1 (pen), Gurney 1.

| Gragg M 19 | Gurney A 44 | Gibbs P 40+1 | Robinson J 46 | Gittens J 45 | Watson A 46 | Oatway C 2 | Mitchell P 11+3 | McFarlane A 18+4 | Jack R 40 | McCall S 20+7 | Bedeau A 14+20 | Hill K 31+6 | Clayton G 41 | Barrow L —+2 | Veysey K 27 | Thomas W 5+16 | Hapgood L 15+7 | Newell J —+1 | Tully S 4+5 | Leadbitter C 21+5 | Roberts J 13+1 | Partridge S 4+1 | Match No. |
|---|---|---|---|---|---|---|---|---|---|---|---|---|---|---|---|---|---|---|---|---|---|---|---|
| 1 | 2 | $3^1$ | 4 | 5 | 6 | 7 | 8 | 9 | 10 | $11^2$ | 12 | 13 | | | | | | | | | | | 1 |
| 1 | 2 | 3 | 4 | 5 | 6 | 7 | $8^1$ | 12 | 9 | 13 | 10 | $11^2$ | | | | | | | | | | | 2 |
| 1 | 2 | 3 | 4 | 5 | $6^2$ | | 8 | 10 | $9^1$ | 11 | 12 | | 7 | | | 13 | | | | | | | 3 |
| 1 | 2 | 3 | 4 | 5 | 6 | | $8^1$ | $10^2$ | 9 | $11^3$ | 13 | 12 | 7 | 14 | | | | | | | | | 4 |
| 1 | 2 | 3 | 4 | 5 | 6 | | 8 | | 9 | 11 | 10 | | 7 | | | | | | | | | | 5 |
| | 2 | 3 | 4 | 5 | 6 | | 8 | 12 | 9 | $11^1$ | 10 | | 7 | | 1 | | | | | | | | 6 |
| | 2 | 3 | 4 | 5 | 6 | | $8^1$ | | 9 | 11 | 12 | | 7 | | 1 | 10 | | | | | | | 7 |
| 1 | 2 | $3^1$ | 4 | 5 | 6 | | 8 | 10 | $9^1$ | $11^3$ | 12 | | 7 | | | 13 | 14 | | | | | | 8 |
| 1 | 2 | 3 | 4 | 5 | 6 | | 8 | 10 | $9^1$ | 11 | 12 | | 7 | | | | | | | | | | 9 |
| 1 | 2 | 3 | 4 | 5 | 6 | | 8 | 10 | 12 | $9^2$ | $11^1$ | 13 | 7 | | | | | | | | | | 10 |
| 1 | 2 | 3 | 4 | 5 | 6 | | 8 | 10 | 11 | 9 | | | 7 | | | | | | | | | | 11 |
| 1 | 2 | $3^2$ | $4^1$ | 5 | 6 | | 8 | 10 | 9 | 11 | 12 | 13 | 7 | | | | | | | | | | 12 |
| 1 | 2 | 3 | 4 | 5 | 6 | | $8^1$ | 10 | 9 | 11 | 12 | | 7 | | | | | | | | | | 13 |
| 1 | $2^1$ | $3^2$ | 4 | 5 | 6 | | 8 | 10 | 9 | 11 | 12 | 13 | 7 | | | | | | | | | | 14 |
| 1 | 2 | 3 | 4 | 5 | 6 | | 8 | 10 | $9^1$ | 11 | 12 | 13 | $7^2$ | | | | | | | | | | 15 |
| 1 | 2 | 3 | 4 | 5 | 6 | | 8 | $10^1$ | 9 | 11 | 12 | | 7 | | | | | | | | | | 16 |
| 1 | 2 | 3 | 4 | 5 | 6 | | 8 | $10^1$ | 9 | $11^2$ | 12 | 13 | 7 | | | | | | | | | | 17 |
| 1 | 2 | 3 | 4 | 5 | 6 | | | 9 | 10 | $8^1$ | | | 7 | | | 12 | $11^2$ | | | 13 | | | 18 |
| 1 | 2 | 3 | 4 | 5 | 6 | | | 9 | 10 | $8^2$ | 12 | | 7 | | | | $11^1$ | | | 13 | | | 19 |
| | 2 | $3^1$ | 4 | 5 | 6 | | | 9 | 10 | 8 | | | 7 | | 1 | 12 | 11 | | | | | | 20 |
| | 2 | 3 | 4 | 5 | 6 | | | 9 | $10^1$ | 8 | | | $7^3$ | 14 | 1 | 12 | $11^2$ | | | 13 | | | 21 |
| | 2 | 3 | 4 | 5 | 6 | | | 9 | 10 | $8^1$ | | | 7 | | 1 | 12 | 11 | | | | | | 22 |
| | 2 | | 4 | 5 | 6 | | 3 | 9 | 10 | $8^2$ | | | 7 | | 1 | 12 | $11^1$ | | | 13 | | | 23 |
| | 2 | | 4 | 5 | 6 | | 3 | 9 | 10 | 8 | | | 7 | | 1 | | 11 | | | | | | 24 |
| 1 | 2 | 3 | 4 | 5 | 6 | | | 9 | 10 | 8 | | | 7 | | | | 11 | | | | | | 25 |
| | | 3 | 4 | 5 | 6 | | 2 | 9 | 10 | 8 | 12 | | 7 | | 1 | | $11^1$ | | | | | | 26 |
| | 2 | 3 | 4 | 5 | 6 | | | 9 | 10 | 8 | 12 | | $7^1$ | | 1 | 13 | $11^2$ | | | | | | 27 |
| | 2 | 3 | 4 | 5 | 6 | | | 9 | $10^1$ | 8 | 12 | | 7 | | 1 | 13 | $11^2$ | | | | | | 28 |
| | 2 | $3^1$ | 4 | 5 | 6 | | | $9^3$ | $10^2$ | 8 | | | 7 | 14 | 1 | 12 | 11 | | | 13 | | | 29 |
| 1 | $2^3$ | 3 | 4 | 5 | 6 | | | $9^2$ | 10 | 8 | | | 7 | 14 | | 12 | $11^1$ | | | 13 | | | 30 |
| | 2 | | 4 | 5 | 6 | | | 9 | 10 | 8 | 12 | | 7 | | 1 | | $11^1$ | | | | 3 | | 31 |
| | $2^1$ | | 4 | 5 | 6 | | | 9 | $10^2$ | 8 | 12 | | 7 | | 1 | 13 | 11 | | | | 3 | | 32 |
| | 2 | 12 | 4 | 5 | 6 | | | 9 | $10^1$ | $8^2$ | | | 7 | | 1 | | $11^1$ | | | 13 | 3 | | 33 |
| | 2 | 3 | 4 | 5 | 6 | | | 9 | 10 | 8 | | | 7 | | 1 | | 11 | | | | | | 34 |
| | 2 | 3 | 4 | 5 | 6 | | | $9^1$ | 10 | 8 | | | 7 | | 1 | 12 | 11 | | | | | | 35 |
| | 2 | 3 | 4 | 5 | 6 | | | $9^2$ | 10 | 8 | | | 7 | | 1 | 12 | $11^1$ | | | 13 | | | 36 |
| | 2 | $3^1$ | 4 | 5 | 6 | | | 9 | 10 | 8 | | | 7 | | 1 | 12 | $11^2$ | | | 13 | | | 37 |
| | | | 4 | 5 | 6 | | | 9 | $10^1$ | 8 | 12 | | 7 | | | 12 | 11 | 1 | 2 | | 3 | | 38 |
| | 2 | 3 | 4 | 5 | 6 | | | 9 | $10^3$ | $8^2$ | | | 7 | 14 | 1 | 12 | $11^1$ | | | 13 | | | 39 |
| | 2 | $3^1$ | 4 | 5 | 6 | | | 9 | $10^2$ | $8^2$ | | | 7 | 14 | 1 | 12 | 11 | | | 13 | | | 40 |
| | 2 | 3 | 4 | 5 | 6 | | | 9 | $10^2$ | $8^1$ | 12 | | 7 | 14 | 1 | 13 | $11^3$ | | | | | | 41 |
| | 2 | 3 | 4 | 5 | 6 | | | 9 | 10 | 8 | 12 | | $7^1$ | | 1 | 12 | 11 | | | | | | 42 |
| | 2 | 3 | 4 | 5 | 6 | | | 9 | $10^2$ | $8^1$ | | | 7 | | 1 | 12 | 11 | | | 13 | | | 43 |
| | 2 | 3 | 4 | 5 | 6 | | | $9^3$ | $10^2$ | 8 | 13 | | $7^1$ | 14 | 1 | 12 | 11 | | | | | | 44 |
| | 2 | 3 | 4 | 5 | 6 | | | $10^1$ | 9 | 11 | 12 | 8 | $7^2$ | | 1 | | | | | 13 | | | 45 |
| | 2 | 3 | 4 | 5 | 6 | | | 10 | 9 | $11^2$ | 12 | $8^1$ | 7 | | 1 | | | | | 13 | | | 46 |

**Coca-Cola Cup**

| | | | | |
|---|---|---|---|---|
| First Round | Bournemouth | (a) | 1-0 | |
| | | (h) | 1-1 | |
| Second Round | Ipswich T | (a) | 1-1 | |
| | | (h) | 0-3 | |

**FA Cup**

| | | | | |
|---|---|---|---|---|
| First Round | Luton T | (a) | 1-0 | |
| | | (h) | 1-1 | |
| Second Round | Watford | (a) | 1-2 | |

TOTTENHAM HOTSPUR 1997–98　Back row (left to right): Chris Hughton (Reserve Team Manager), Danny Hill, Rory Allen, Darren Anderton, Ramon Vega, John Scales, Jason Dozzell, Stuart Nethercott, Steffen Iversen, Colin Calderwood, Pat Jennings (Goalkeeping Coach).

Middle row: Tony Lenaghan (Physio), Jamie Clapham, Neale Fenn, Allan Nielsen, Sol Campbell, Espen Baardsen, Ian Walker, Paul Mahorn, David Howells, Steve Carr, Paul McVeigh, Roy Reyland (Kit Manager).

Front row: Ruel Fox, David Ginola, Justin Edinburgh, Chris Armstrong, Roger Cross (Assistant Manager), Gary Mabbutt, Gary Francis (Manager), Les Ferdinand, Dean Austin, Andy Sinton, Clive Wilson.

(Photograph: Action Images)

# FA Premiership **TOTTENHAM HOTSPUR**

**748 High Rd, Tottenham, London N17 0AP.** Telephone: (0181) 365 5000. Fax: (0181) 365 5005. Commercial Dept: (0181) 365 5010. Ticketline: 0891 335566. Telephone Bookings: (0171) 396 4567. Ticket Office: (0181) 365 5050. Spurs Line: 0891 335555. Members Ticketline: (0181) 365 5100.

**Ground capacity:** 36,200.

**Record attendance:** 75,038 v Sunderland, FA Cup 6th rd, 5 March 1938.

**Record receipts:** £336,702 v Manchester U, Division 1, 28 September 1991.

**Pitch measurements:** 110yd × 73yd.

**Directors:** A. M. Sugar (Chairman), C. M. Littner (Chief Executive), J. Sedgwick (Finance Director). **Non-Executive:** A. G. Berry (Deputy Chairman), D. A. Alexiou, I. Yawetz, C. T. Sandy, J. Ireland (Company Secretary), David Pleat (Director of Football).

**President:** W. E. Nicholson OBE. **Vice-President:** N. Solomon.

**Head Coach:** Christian Gross. **Assistant Head Coach:** Chris Hughton. **Reserve Team Manager:** Bob Arber. **Physio:** Tony Lenaghan. **Club Secretary:** Peter Barnes. **Commercial Manager:** Mike Rollo. **PRO:** John Fennelly.

**Year Formed:** 1882. **Turned Professional:** 1895. **Ltd Co.:** 1898.

**Club Nickname:** 'Spurs'.

**Previous Name:** 1882–85, Hotspur Football Club.

**Previous Grounds:** 1882, Tottenham Marshes; 1885, Northumberland Park; 1898, White Hart Lane.

**Foundation:** The Hotspur Football Club was formed from an older cricket club in 1882. Most of the founders were old boys of St. John's Presbyterian School and Tottenham Grammar School. The Casey brothers were well to the fore as the family provided the club's first goalposts (painted blue and white) and their first ball. They soon adopted the local YMCA as their meeting place, but after a couple of moves settled at the Red House, which is still their headquarters, although now known simply as 748 High Road.

**First Football League game:** 1 September 1908, Division 2, v Wolverhampton W (h) W 3-0 – Hewitson; Coquet, Burton; Morris (1), D. Steel, Darnell; Walton, Woodward (2), Macfarlane, R. Steel, Middlemiss.

**Record League Victory:** 9–0 v Bristol R, Division 2, 22 October 1977 – Daines; Naylor, Holmes, Hoddle (1), McAllister, Perryman, Pratt, McNab, Moores (3), Lee (4), Taylor (1).

**Record Cup Victory:** 13–2 v Crewe Alex, FA Cup 4th rd (replay), 3 February 1960 – Brown; Hills, Henry; Blanchflower, Norman, Mackay; White, Harmer (1), Smith (4), Allen (5), Jones (3 incl. 1p).

**Record Defeat:** 0–8 v Cologne, UEFA Inter Toto Cup, 22 July 1995.

**Most League Points (2 for a win):** 70, Division 2, 1919–20.

**Most League Points (3 for a win):** 77, Division 1, 1984–85.

**Most League Goals:** 115, Division 1, 1960–61.

**Highest League Scorer in Season:** Jimmy Greaves, 37, Division 1, 1962–63.

**Most League Goals in Total Aggregate:** Jimmy Greaves, 220, 1961–70.

**Most Capped Player:** Pat Jennings, 74 (119), Northern Ireland.

**Most League Appearances:** Steve Perryman, 655, 1969–86.

**Record Transfer Fee Received:** £5,500,000 from Lazio for Paul Gascoigne, May 1992.

**Record Transfer Fee Paid:** £6,000,000 to Newcastle U for Les Ferdinand, July 1997.

**Football League Record:** 1908 Elected to Division 2; 1909–15 Division 1; 1919–20 Division 2; 1920–28 Division 1; 1928–33 Division 2; 1933–35 Division 1; 1935–50 Division 2; 1950–77 Division 1; 1977–78 Division 2; 1978–92 Division 1; 1992– FA Premier League.

**Honours:** Football League: Division 1 – Champions 1950–51, 1960–61; Runners-up 1921–22, 1951–52, 1956–57, 1962–63; Division 2 – Champions 1919–20, 1949–50; Runners-up 1908–09, 1932–33; Promoted 1977–78 (3rd). FA Cup: Winners 1901 (as non-League club), 1921, 1961, 1962, 1967, 1981, 1982, 1991; Runners-up 1987. Football League Cup: Winners 1971, 1973; Runners-up 1982. **European Competitions:** European Cup: 1961–62. European Cup-Winners' Cup: 1962–63 (winners), 1963–64, 1967–68, 1981–82, 1982–83, 1991–92. UEFA Cup: 1971–72 (winners), 1972–73, 1973–74 (runners-up), 1983–84 (winners), 1984–85.

**Colours:** White shirts, navy blue shorts, white stockings. **Change colours:** French navy shirts, ecru shorts, French navy stockings.

**Did you know?**
On 8 January 1901, Tottenham Hotspur played a German Association team from Berlin and won 9-6 on a snow-covered pitch at White Hart Lane.

## TOTTENHAM HOTSPUR 1997–98 LEAGUE RECORD

| Match No. | Date | Venue | Opponents | Result | H/T Score | Lg. Pos. | Goalscorers | Atten-dance |
|---|---|---|---|---|---|---|---|---|
| 1 | Aug 10 | H | Manchester U | L 0-2 | 0-0 | — | | 26,359 |
| 2 | 13 | A | West Ham U | L 1-2 | 0-1 | — | Ferdinand [83] | 25,354 |
| 3 | 23 | H | Derby Co | W 1-0 | 1-0 | 13 | Calderwood [45] | 25,886 |
| 4 | 27 | H | Aston Villa | W 3-2 | 1-1 | — | Ferdinand 2 [6, 66], Fox [77] | 26,316 |
| 5 | 30 | A | Arsenal | D 0-0 | 0-0 | 7 | | 38,102 |
| 6 | Sept 13 | A | Leicester C | L 0-3 | 0-0 | 10 | | 20,683 |
| 7 | 20 | H | Blackburn R | D 0-0 | 0-0 | 12 | | 26,573 |
| 8 | 23 | A | Bolton W | D 1-1 | 0-1 | — | Armstrong [71] | 23,433 |
| 9 | 27 | H | Wimbledon | D 0-0 | 0-0 | 13 | | 26,261 |
| 10 | Oct 4 | A | Newcastle U | L 0-1 | 0-0 | 14 | | 36,708 |
| 11 | 19 | H | Sheffield W | W 3-2 | 3-0 | 11 | Dominguez [6], Armstrong [40], Ginola [45] | 25,097 |
| 12 | 25 | A | Southampton | L 2-3 | 1-0 | 14 | Dominguez [42], Ginola [65] | 15,255 |
| 13 | Nov 1 | H | Leeds U | L 0-1 | 0-1 | 15 | | 26,441 |
| 14 | 8 | A | Liverpool | L 0-4 | 0-0 | 16 | | 38,006 |
| 15 | 24 | H | Crystal Palace | L 0-1 | 0-0 | — | | 25,634 |
| 16 | 29 | A | Everton | W 2-0 | 0-0 | 17 | Vega [72], Ginola [76] | 36,670 |
| 17 | Dec 6 | H | Chelsea | L 1-6 | 1-1 | 18 | Vega [43] | 28,476 |
| 18 | 13 | A | Coventry C | L 0-4 | 0-1 | 18 | | 19,490 |
| 19 | 20 | H | Barnsley | W 3-0 | 3-0 | 18 | Nielsen [6], Ginola 2 [12, 18] | 28,232 |
| 20 | 26 | A | Aston Villa | L 1-4 | 0-1 | 18 | Calderwood [59] | 38,644 |
| 21 | 28 | H | Arsenal | D 1-1 | 1-0 | 19 | Nielsen [28] | 29,601 |
| 22 | Jan 10 | A | Manchester U | L 0-2 | 0-1 | 19 | | 55,281 |
| 23 | 17 | H | West Ham U | W 1-0 | 1-0 | 18 | Klinsmann [7] | 30,284 |
| 24 | 31 | A | Derby Co | L 1-2 | 0-1 | 18 | Fox [46] | 30,187 |
| 25 | Feb 7 | A | Blackburn R | W 3-0 | 1-0 | 17 | Berti [37], Armstrong [89], Fox [90] | 30,388 |
| 26 | 14 | H | Leicester C | D 1-1 | 0-1 | 17 | Calderwood [51] | 28,355 |
| 27 | 21 | A | Sheffield W | L 0-1 | 0-1 | 17 | | 29,871 |
| 28 | Mar 1 | H | Bolton W | W 1-0 | 1-0 | 17 | Nielsen [45] | 29,032 |
| 29 | 4 | A | Leeds U | L 0-1 | 0-1 | — | | 31,802 |
| 30 | 14 | H | Liverpool | D 3-3 | 1-1 | 17 | Klinsmann [13], Ginola [49], Vega [80] | 30,245 |
| 31 | 28 | A | Crystal Palace | W 3-1 | 0-0 | 16 | Berti [55], Armstrong [72], Klinsmann [77] | 26,116 |
| 32 | Apr 4 | H | Everton | D 1-1 | 0-1 | 16 | Armstrong [74] | 35,624 |
| 33 | 11 | A | Chelsea | L 0-2 | 0-0 | 17 | | 34,149 |
| 34 | 13 | H | Coventry C | D 1-1 | 0-0 | 17 | Berti [68] | 33,463 |
| 35 | 18 | A | Barnsley | D 1-1 | 0-1 | 17 | Calderwood [47] | 18,692 |
| 36 | 25 | H | Newcastle U | W 2-0 | 1-0 | 16 | Klinsmann [31], Ferdinand [73] | 35,847 |
| 37 | May 2 | A | Wimbledon | W 6-2 | 2-2 | 15 | Ferdinand [18], Klinsmann 4 [41, 54, 58, 60], Saib [79] | 25,972 |
| 38 | 10 | H | Southampton | D 1-1 | 1-1 | 14 | Klinsmann [27] | 35,995 |

**Final League Position: 14**    1996–97 PREM 10

## GOALSCORERS

*League (44):* Klinsmann 9, Ginola 6, Armstrong 5, Ferdinand 5, Calderwood 4, Berti 3, Fox 3, Nielsen 3, Vega 3, Dominguez 2, Saib 1.
*Coca-Cola Cup (6):* Ginola 2 (1 pen), Armstrong 1, Fenn 1, Fox 1, Mahorn 1.
*FA Cup (5):* Calderwood 1, Campbell 1, Clemence 1, Ginola 1, own goal 1.

| Walker I 29 | Carr S 37+1 | Edinburgh J 13+3 | Clemence S 12+5 | Vega R 22+3 | Campbell S 34 | Ginola D 34 | Nielsen A 21+5 | Iversen S 8+5 | Ferdinand L 19+2 | Howells D 14+6 | Sinton A 14+5 | Scales J 9+1 | Dominguez J 8+10 | Calderwood C 21+5 | Fox R 32 | Mabbutt G 8+3 | Fenn N —+4 | Armstrong C 13+6 | Mahorn P 2 | Anderton D 7+8 | Allen R 1+3 | Wilson C 16 | Klinsmann J 15 | Baardsen E 9 | Berti N 17 | Brady G —+9 | Saib M 3+6 | Match No. |
|---|---|---|---|---|---|---|---|---|---|---|---|---|---|---|---|---|---|---|---|---|---|---|---|---|---|---|---|---|
| 1 | 2 | 3 | 4¹ | 5 | 6 | 7 | 8 | 9 | 10 | 11 | 12 | | | | | | | | | | | | | | | | | 1 |
| 1 | 2 | 3 | 13 | 5 | 6² | 7 | 8¹ | 9 | 10 | 11 | 12 | 4 | | | | | | | | | | | | | | | | 2 |
| 1 | 2 | 3 | | | 6 | 7² | 12 | 9 | 10 | 8 | 11¹ | 4 | 13 | 5 | | | | | | | | | | | | | | 3 |
| 1 | 2 | 3¹ | | | 6 | | | 9 | 10² | 8 | 11 | 4 | | 5 | 7 | 12 | 13 | | | | | | | | | | | 4 |
| 1 | 2 | 3 | | 6 | | 5 | 12 | 9¹ | 10 | 8 | 11² | 4 | 13 | | 7¹ | 14 | | | | | | | | | | | | 5 |
| 1 | 2 | | 3 | | | 5 | 7 | 8 | 10¹ | 9 | | 4 | 11 | 6 | | 12 | | | | | | | | | | | | 6 |
| 1 | 2 | 3 | 4 | 12 | 5 | 7 | | | 8 | | | 11 | | 10 | 6 | | | 9¹ | | | | | | | | | | 7 |
| 1 | 2 | 3² | 8 | 13 | 4 | 7 | 12 | | | | | 11 | 5¹ | 10 | 6 | | 14 | 9³ | | | | | | | | | | 8 |
| 1 | 2 | | 3 | 4 | 5 | 7 | 12 | | 10 | | | 11 | 8¹ | 6 | 9 | | | | | | | | | | | | | 9 |
| 1 | 2 | | 8¹ | 4 | 3 | 11² | | | 10 | | 12 | 13 | 5 | 7 | 6 | | 9 | | | | | | | | | | | 10 |
| 1 | 2¹ | 3 | | 5 | 6 | 7 | | | 4 | 10 | | 11²12 | 8 | 13³ | 9 | | 14 | | | | | | | | | | | 11 |
| 1 | 2 | 3² | | 5 | 6 | 7 | | | 4 | 10 | | 11 | 13³ | 8¹ | 14 | 9 | 12 | | | | | | | | | | | 12 |
| 1 | 12 | 2 | | 5 | 7 | | 13 | | 8³ | 3 | 4 | 11² | 10 | 6¹ | 9 | | 14 | | | | | | | | | | | 13 |
| 1 | 2 | 3 | | 6 | 11 | | 9 | | 8 | 13 | 4 | 14 | 5² | | 12 | 7³ | 10¹ | | | | | | | | | | | 14 |
| 1 | 2 | 3¹ | 6 | 12 | 5 | 11 | 13 | 9² | 10 | 8 | 4 | | | | | | 7³ | 14 | | | | | | | | | | 15 |
| 1 | 2 | | 4 | 6¹ | 7 | 8³ | 13 | 10² | | 11 | 12 | | 5 | 9 | | | 14 | 3 | | | | | | | | | | 16 |
| 1 | 2 | 12 | | 6 | | 7 | 8² | 10 | | 11¹ | 4³ | | 5 | 9 | | | 13 | 14 | 3 | | | | | | | | | 17 |
| 1 | 2 | 12 | 13 | | 11 | | 4 | 14 | 9 | 10² | | | 5 | 8 | 6 | | 7³ | 3¹ | | | | | | | | | | 18 |
| 1 | 2 | 12 | | 6 | 11¹ | 4 | 13 | 9² | 10 | | 14 | 5 | 8 | | 7³ | 3 | | | | | | | | | | | | 19 |
| 1 | 2 | 12 | | 4 | 7 | 8 | 9 | | 11¹ | | | 5 | 10 | 6² | | | 13 | 14 | 3³ | | | | | | | | | 20 |
| 1 | 2 | 10 | 4 | 6 | 11³ | 8 | 12 | | | | | 13 | 5 | 7² | | | | | 3 | 9 | | | | | | | | 21 |
| | 2 | 8¹ | 4 | 6 | | | | | 12 | | | 11 | 5 | 7² | | | | | 3 | 9 | 1 | 10 | 13 | | | | | 22 |
| | 2 | | 4 | 6 | 7² | | | 12 | 11 | | | 13 | 5¹ | 10³ | | | | | 3 | 9 | 1 | 8 | 14 | | | | | 23 |
| | 2 | | 4 | 5 | 7 | | | 10 | 12 | 11¹ | | 13 | | 8 | | | | | 3² | 9 | 1 | 6 | | | | | | 24 |
| | 2 | 12 | 4 | 5 | 11 | 8¹ | | 9² | 10 | | | | 7 | | | 13 | | | 3³ | | 1 | 6 | 14 | | | | | 25 |
| | 2 | 12 | | 4 | 6 | 11 | 8 | | | | | | 5² | 7 | | 9 | | | 3¹ | | 1 | 10 | 13 | | | | | 26 |
| | 2 | 3¹ | | 6 | 11 | 8 | | | 4 | | | 12 | 5 | 7 | | 9 | | | | | 1 | 10² | 13 | | | | | 27 |
| | 2 | | | 6 | 11³ | 8 | | | 12 | | | | 5 | 7² | | 9¹ | | | 3 | 10 | 1 | 4 | 13 | 14 | | | | 28 |
| | 2 | | 5 | 6 | 11 | 8 | | 4³ | | | | | | 7 | 12 | | | | 3¹ | 9 | 1 | 10² | 13 | 14 | | | | 29 |
| | 2 | | 5 | 6 | 11² | 8 | | | 12 | | | | | 7 | | | | | 9¹ | | 1 | 4 | 13 | | | | | 30 |
| 1 | 2¹ | | 4 | 6 | | | | | 12 | | | | 13 | 5 | 7³ | | | 9² | | | 3 | 10 | | 8 | 14 | 11 | | 31 |
| 1 | 2¹ | | 5 | 6 | 11 | 8 | | | 12 | | | | | 13 | 7 | | | 9 | | | 3² | 10 | | 4³ | 14 | | | 32 |
| 1 | 2 | | 5 | 6 | 11 | 3 | | | 12 | | | | | 13 | 7 | | | 9¹ | 14 | | | 10² | | 4³ | | 8 | | 33 |
| 1 | 2 | | 5 | 6 | 11 | 3 | | | 12 | | | | | 13 | 7 | | | 9¹ | | | | 10 | | 4 | | 8² | | 34 |
| 1 | 2 | | 4 | 6 | 11 | 3 | | | 10¹ | | | | | 5 | 7 | | | 13 | 12 | | | 9² | | 8 | | | | 35 |
| 1 | 2 | | 5 | 6 | 11 | | | | 10 | | | | | 3 | 8 | | | | | 7¹ | | 9 | | 4 | | 12 | | 36 |
| 1 | 2 | | | 6 | 11 | 3 | | | 10¹ | | | | | 5 | 8² | | | 12 | | 7 | | 9 | | 4 | | 13 | | 37 |
| 1 | 2 | | | 6 | 11 | 3 | | | 10 | | | | | 5¹ | 8 | 12 | | | | 7 | | 9 | | 4² | | 13 | | 38 |

**Coca-Cola Cup**

| | | | |
|---|---|---|---|
| Second Round | Carlisle U | (h) | 3-2 |
| | | (a) | 2-0 |
| Third Round | Derby Co | (h) | 1-2 |

**FA Cup**

| | | | |
|---|---|---|---|
| Third Round | Fulham | (h) | 3-1 |
| Fourth Round | Barnsley | (h) | 1-1 |
| | | (a) | 1-3 |

TRANMERE ROVERS 1997–98   *Back row (left to right):* Alan Morgan, Kevin McIntyre, Dave Challinor, Graham Branch, Gary Jones, Mauro Pereira, Liam O'Brien, Kenny Irons, John Morrissey. *Middle row:* Warwick Rimmer (Youth Development Officer), Dave Philpotts (Chief Scout/Coach) Les Parry (Physio), Andy Parkinson, Steve Simonsen, Clint Hill, Eric Nixon, Alan Mahon, Danny Coyne, Mike Howard, Steve Mungall (Kit Man), Ray Mathias (Assistant Manager/Coach), Kevin Sheedy (Reserves Manager/Coach). *Front row:* Andy Thompson, Stuart Connolly, Ryan Williams, Gary Stevens, John McGreal, John Aldridge (Player/Manager), Lee Jones, Paul Cook, Dave Kelly, Andy Thorn.

# Division 1 **TRANMERE ROVERS**

*Prenton Park, Prenton Road West, Birkenhead L42 9PN.* Telephone: (0151) 608 4194. Fax: (0151) 608 4385. Commercial: (0151) 608 0371. Shop: (0151) 608 0438. Ticket Office: (0151) 609 0137.

*Ground capacity:* 16,789 (all seated).

*Record attendance:* 24,424 v Stoke C, FA Cup 4th rd, 5 February 1972.

*Record receipts:* £130,541 v Sunderland, FA Cup 4th rd, 24 January 1998.

*Pitch measurements:* 110yd × 70yd.

*President:* H. B. Thomas.

*Chairman and Chief Executive:* F. D. Corfe.

*Directors:* Norman Wilson FAAI, A. J. Adams BDS, G. E. H. Jones LLB, F. J. Williams, J. J. Holsgrove FCA.

*Secretary:* Mick Horton. *General Manager:* Janet Ratcliffe.

*Manager:* John Aldridge. *Assistant Manager:* Kevin Sheedy.

*Youth Development Officer:* Warwick Rimmer.

*Reserve Team Manager:* Ray Mathias. *Physio:* Les Parry.

*Year Formed:* 1884. *Turned Professional:* 1912. *Ltd Co.:* 1920.

*Previous Name:* Belmont AFC, 1884–85.

*Club Nickname:* 'The Rovers'.

*Previous Grounds:* 1884, Steeles Field; 1887, Ravenshaws Field/Old Prenton Park; 1912, Prenton Park.

*Foundation:* Formed in 1884 as Belmont they adopted their present title the following year and eventually joined their first league, the West Lancashire League in 1889–90, the same year as their first success in the Wirral Challenge Cup. The club almost folded in 1899–1900 when all the players left en bloc to join a rival club, but they survived the crisis and went from strength to strength winning the 'Combination' title in 1907–08 and the Lancashire Combination in 1913–14. They joined the Football League in 1921 from the Central League.

*First Football League game:* 27 August 1921, Division 3 (N), v Crewe Alex (h) W 4-1 – Bradshaw; Grainger, Stuart (1); Campbell, Milnes (1), Heslop; Moreton, Groves (1), Hyam, Ford (1), Hughes.

*Record League Victory:* 13–4 v Oldham Ath, Division 3 (N), 26 December 1935 – Gray; Platt, Fairhurst; McLaren, Newton, Spencer; Eden, MacDonald (1), Bell (9), Woodward (2), Urmson (1).

*Record Cup Victory:* 13–0 v Oswestry U, FA Cup 2nd prel rd, 10 October 1914 – Ashcroft; Stevenson, Bullough, Hancock, Taylor, Holden (1), Moreton (1), Cunningham (2), Smith (5), Leck (3), Gould (1).

*Record Defeat:* 1–9 v Tottenham H, FA Cup 3rd rd (replay), 14 January 1953.

*Most League Points (2 for a win):* 60, Division 4, 1964–65.

*Most League Points (3 for a win):* 80, Division 4, 1988–89 and Division 3, 1989–90.

*Most League Goals:* 111, Division 3 (N), 1930–31.

*Highest League Scorer in Season:* Bunny Bell, 35, Division 3 (N), 1933–34.

*Most League Goals in Total Aggregate:* Ian Muir, 142, 1985–95.

*Most Capped Player:* John Aldridge, 30 (69), Republic of Ireland.

*Most League Appearances:* Harold Bell, 595, 1946–64 (incl. League record 401 consecutive appearances).

*Record Transfer Fee Received:* £2,000,000 from Nottingham F for Alan Rogers, July 1997.

*Record Transfer Fee Paid:* £450,000 to Aston Villa for Shaun Teale, August 1995.

*Football League Record:* 1921 Original Member of Division 3 (N): 1938–39 Division 2; 1946–58 Division 3 (N); 1958–61 Division 3; 1961–67 Division 4; 1967–75 Division 3; 1975–76 Division 4; 1976–79 Division 3; 1979–89 Division 4; 1989–91 Division 3; 1991–92 Division 2; 1992– Division 1.

*Honours: Football League* Division 1 best season: 4th, 1992–93; Promoted from Division 3 1990–91 (play-offs); Division 3 (N) – Champions 1937–38; Promotion to 3rd Division: 1966–67, 1975–76; Division 4 – Runners-up 1988–89. *FA Cup:* best season: 5th rd, 1968. *Football League Cup:* semi-final 1994. *Welsh Cup:* Winners 1935; Runners-up 1934. *Leyland Daf Cup:* Winners 1990; Runners-up 1991.

*Colours:* White shirts, blue shorts. *Change colours:* Orange, green and white.

**Did you know?**
Ray Mathias holds the League and Cup record of appearances for Tranmere Rovers completing 637 (567 League and 70 Cup) from 1967-68 to 1984-85.

## TRANMERE ROVERS 1997–98 LEAGUE RECORD

| Match No. | Date | Venue | Opponents | Result | H/T Score | Lg. Pos. | Goalscorers | Atten-dance |
|---|---|---|---|---|---|---|---|---|
| 1 | Aug 9 | A | WBA | L | 1-2 | 0-2 | — | Kelly [74] | 16,727 |
| 2 | 15 | H | QPR | W | 2-1 | 1-0 | — | Kelly [40], Jones L [72] | 7467 |
| 3 | 22 | A | Manchester C | D | 1-1 | 0-0 | — | Jones L [60] | 26,336 |
| 4 | 30 | H | Middlesbrough | L | 0-2 | 0-1 | 11 | | 12,095 |
| 5 | Sept 2 | H | Birmingham C | L | 0-3 | 0-2 | — | | 6620 |
| 6 | 7 | A | Bury | L | 0-1 | 0-1 | 19 | | 5073 |
| 7 | 13 | A | Swindon T | L | 1-2 | 1-1 | 21 | Jones L [43] | 6811 |
| 8 | 20 | H | Reading | W | 6-0 | 5-0 | 17 | Morrissey [4], Kelly 2 [10, 41], Jones L [20], Jones G [38], Thompson [59] | 5565 |
| 9 | 27 | A | Crewe Alex | L | 1-2 | 0-1 | 20 | Stevens [60] | 4845 |
| 10 | Oct 4 | H | Norwich C | W | 2-0 | 1-0 | 18 | Kelly [12], Jones L [68] | 6674 |
| 11 | 18 | A | Nottingham F | D | 2-2 | 1-2 | 20 | Jones L [5], Thompson [59] | 17,009 |
| 12 | 22 | A | Wolverhampton W | L | 1-2 | 0-2 | — | Jones G [65] | 20,841 |
| 13 | 25 | H | Charlton Ath | D | 2-2 | 1-0 | 21 | Branch [13], Jones L [66] | 5911 |
| 14 | Nov 1 | A | Sheffield U | L | 1-2 | 0-0 | 22 | Kelly [69] | 16,578 |
| 15 | 4 | H | Huddersfield T | W | 1-0 | 1-0 | — | Irons [3] | 5127 |
| 16 | 8 | H | Port Vale | L | 1-2 | 0-1 | 20 | Irons [51] | 7063 |
| 17 | 15 | A | Bradford C | W | 1-0 | 0-0 | 17 | Aldridge [61] | 16,494 |
| 18 | 22 | H | Stoke C | W | 3-1 | 1-1 | 16 | Jones L [9], Aldridge [66], O'Brien [87] | 8009 |
| 19 | 29 | A | Sunderland | L | 0-3 | 0-3 | 16 | | 26,674 |
| 20 | Dec 6 | H | Ipswich T | D | 1-1 | 0-1 | 17 | Jones L [73] | 5720 |
| 21 | 13 | A | Stockport Co | L | 1-3 | 1-1 | 19 | Aldridge [33] | 7903 |
| 22 | 20 | H | Oxford U | L | 0-2 | 0-0 | 21 | | 5181 |
| 23 | 26 | H | Bury | D | 0-0 | 0-0 | 22 | | 9146 |
| 24 | 28 | A | Birmingham C | D | 0-0 | 0-0 | 21 | | 19,533 |
| 25 | Jan 9 | A | WBA | D | 0-0 | 0-0 | — | | 8058 |
| 26 | 17 | A | QPR | D | 0-0 | 0-0 | 22 | | 12,033 |
| 27 | 31 | H | Manchester C | D | 0-0 | 0-0 | 22 | | 12,830 |
| 28 | Feb 4 | A | Middlesbrough | L | 0-3 | 0-2 | — | | 29,540 |
| 29 | 7 | A | Reading | W | 3-1 | 1-0 | 22 | Irons [10], Kelly [65], Branch [72] | 7069 |
| 30 | 10 | H | Swindon T | W | 3-0 | 2-0 | — | Thompson [35], Branch [39], Morrissey [70] | 5288 |
| 31 | 18 | A | Norwich C | W | 2-0 | 0-0 | — | O'Brien [66], Kelly [75] | 12,105 |
| 32 | 21 | H | Crewe Alex | L | 0-3 | 0-1 | 17 | | 7534 |
| 33 | 24 | H | Nottingham F | D | 0-0 | 0-0 | — | | 7377 |
| 34 | 28 | A | Portsmouth | L | 0-1 | 0-1 | 19 | | 12,250 |
| 35 | Mar 4 | A | Port Vale | W | 1-0 | 0-0 | — | Kelly [47] | 5465 |
| 36 | 14 | A | Huddersfield T | L | 0-3 | 0-1 | 21 | | 10,844 |
| 37 | 21 | H | Bradford C | W | 3-1 | 0-1 | 19 | Irons [56], Jones G [66], Kelly [81] | 9463 |
| 38 | 28 | A | Stoke C | W | 3-0 | 2-0 | 16 | Jones G [26], Mellon [39], Kelly [60] | 16,692 |
| 39 | Apr 3 | H | Sunderland | L | 0-2 | 0-2 | — | | 14,116 |
| 40 | 7 | H | Portsmouth | D | 2-2 | 1-1 | — | Jones G [14], Challinor [53] | 8020 |
| 41 | 11 | H | Ipswich T | D | 0-0 | 0-0 | 16 | | 18,039 |
| 42 | 13 | H | Stockport Co | W | 3-0 | 2-0 | 15 | Jones G 2 [7, 42], Mellon [51] | 8070 |
| 43 | 18 | A | Oxford U | D | 1-1 | 0-1 | 15 | Mahon [69] | 6489 |
| 44 | 25 | A | Charlton Ath | L | 0-2 | 0-1 | 16 | | 15,393 |
| 45 | 28 | H | Sheffield U | D | 3-3 | 1-0 | — | O'Brien [10], Jones G [64], Parkinson [66] | 7526 |
| 46 | May 3 | H | Wolverhampton W | W | 2-1 | 1-0 | 14 | Aldridge 2 (1 pen) [34 (p), 75] | 11,144 |

**Final League Position: 14**   1996–97 DIV1 11

### GOALSCORERS

*League (54):* Kelly 11, Jones L 9, Jones G 8, Aldridge 5 (1 pen), Irons 4, Branch 3, O'Brien 3, Thompson 3, Mellon 2, Morrissey 2, Challinor 1, Mahon 1, Parkinson 1, Stevens 1.
*Coca-Cola Cup (7):* Kelly 3, Jones G 1, Jones L 1, Morrissey 1, O'Brien 1.
*FA Cup (4):* Jones G 2, Hill 1, Parkinson 1.

| Coyne D 16 | Stevens G 25 | Thompson A 44 | McGreal J 42 | Thorn A 17 | O'Brien L 37 + 3 | Branch G 16 + 9 | Cook P 9 | Kelly D 28 + 1 | Jones G 37 + 6 | Jones L 29 + 5 | Aldridge J 7 + 7 | Morrissey J 27 + 10 | Irons K 36 + 7 | Challinor D 28 + 4 | Morgan A 14 + 5 | Mahon A 3 + 15 | Hill C 13 + 1 | McIntyre K — + 2 | Parkinson A 8 + 10 | Mellon M 24 + 9 | Simonsen S 30 | Frail S 4 + 2 | Kubicki D 12 | Match No. |
|---|---|---|---|---|---|---|---|---|---|---|---|---|---|---|---|---|---|---|---|---|---|---|---|---|
| 1 | 2 | 3 | 4 | 5 | 6¹ | 7² | 8³ | 9 | 10 | 11 | 12 | 13 | 14 |  |  |  |  |  |  |  |  |  |  | 1 |
| 1 | 2 | 3 | 4 | 5 | 6³ | 13 | 8 | 9¹ | 10 | 11 | 12 | 7⁴ | 14 |  |  |  |  |  |  |  |  |  |  | 2 |
| 1 | 2 | 3 | 4 | 5 | 6 | 12 | 8 | 9 | 10 | 11¹ |  |  | 7² | 13 |  |  |  |  |  |  |  |  |  | 3 |
| 1 | 2 | 3 | 4 | 5² | 6 | 12 | 8 | 9³ | 10 | 11 |  | 14 | 7² | 13 |  |  |  |  |  |  |  |  |  | 4 |
| 1 | 2² | 3 |  | 5 | 6¹ | 7 | 8 | 9 |  | 11 | 12 | 13 |  |  | 4 | 10 |  |  |  |  |  |  |  | 5 |
| 1 | 2³ | 3 | 4 | 5 |  | 12 | 7 | 8 | 9 | 11 |  | 13 |  | 6² | 14 | 10¹ |  |  |  |  |  |  |  | 6 |
| 1 | 2 | 3 | 4 | 5 | 6 | 12 | 8 | 9 | 10 | 11 |  |  | 7¹ |  |  |  |  |  |  |  |  |  |  | 7 |
| 1 | 2² | 3 | 4 |  | 6 | 12 | 8³ | 9 | 10 | 11 |  |  | 7¹ | 5 | 13 | 14 |  |  |  |  |  |  |  | 8 |
| 1 | 2² | 3 | 4 |  | 6¹ | 11 | 8 | 9 | 10 |  |  |  | 7 | 12 | 5 |  | 13 |  |  |  |  |  |  | 9 |
| 1 | 2 | 3 | 4 |  |  |  | 8² | 9 | 10 | 11¹ | 12 |  | 7 | 6 | 5³ | 14 | 13 |  |  |  |  |  |  | 10 |
| 1 | 2 | 3 |  |  |  | 12 |  | 9¹ | 10 | 11 |  |  | 7 | 6 | 5 |  | 13 |  | 8² |  |  | 4 |  | 11 |
| 1 | 2 | 3 |  |  |  | 12 |  | 9 | 10 | 11 |  |  | 7² | 6 | 5 | 4 | 13 |  | 8¹ |  |  |  |  | 12 |
| 1 | 2 | 3² |  |  |  |  | 8 | 9 | 10 | 11 | 12 |  | 7¹ | 6 | 5 | 4 | 13 |  |  |  |  |  |  | 13 |
| 1 | 2 | 3 | 4 | 5 |  |  | 8 | 9 | 10 | 11 | 12 |  | 7 | 6¹ |  |  |  |  |  |  |  |  |  | 14 |
| 1 | 2 | 3 | 4 | 5 |  |  | 8 | 9 | 10 | 11 |  |  | 7 | 6 |  |  |  |  |  |  |  |  |  | 15 |
| 1 | 2 | 3 | 4 | 5³ |  |  | 8¹ | 9 | 10² | 11 | 12 |  | 7 | 6 | 14 | 13 |  |  |  |  |  |  |  | 16 |
|  | 2 | 3 | 4 | 5 | 10 |  |  | 9 |  | 11 |  |  | 7 | 6² |  | 8¹ |  |  | 13 | 12 | 1 |  |  | 17 |
|  | 2 | 3 | 4² | 5 | 10 |  |  | 9 |  | 11³ | 12 | 13 | 7 | 6 | 14 | 8¹ |  |  | 14 |  | 1 |  |  | 18 |
|  | 2 | 3 | 4 | 5³ | 10 |  |  | 9 |  | 11 | 12 | 13 | 7 | 6¹ | 14 | 8² |  |  |  |  | 1 |  |  | 19 |
|  | 2¹ |  | 4 |  | 10 |  |  | 9 |  | 11² | 12 | 13 | 7 | 6 | 5 | 3 |  |  | 8 |  | 1 |  |  | 20 |
|  | 2 |  | 4 |  | 10¹ |  |  | 9 |  | 11 | 12 |  | 7 | 6 | 5 | 3 |  |  | 8 |  | 1 |  |  | 21 |
|  | 2 | 3 | 4 | 5² | 10¹ |  |  | 9 |  | 11 | 12 | 13 | 7 | 6 |  | 8 |  |  |  |  | 1 |  |  | 22 |
|  | 2 | 3 | 4 | 5 | 10 |  |  | 9 |  | 11 | 12 |  | 7 | 6¹ |  | 8 |  |  |  |  | 1 |  |  | 23 |
|  | 2 | 3 | 4 | 5 | 10 |  |  | 9 |  | 11 |  |  | 7 | 6 |  |  |  |  | 8 |  | 1 |  |  | 24 |
|  | 2¹ | 3 | 4 | 5 | 10 |  |  | 9 |  | 11 | 12 | 13 | 7 | 6 |  | 8² |  |  |  |  | 1 |  |  | 25 |
|  | 2 | 3 | 4 |  | 10 |  |  | 9 |  | 11 | 12 |  | 7 | 6 | 5 |  |  |  | 8¹ |  | 1 |  |  | 26 |
|  |  | 3 | 4 |  | 10 | 12 |  |  | 9 | 11¹ |  |  | 7 |  | 5 | 8³ |  |  | 13 | 14 | 1 | 6 | 2² | 27 |
|  |  | 3 | 4 |  | 10 | 12 |  |  | 9 | 11 |  |  | 7² | 6 | 5 | 8¹ |  |  | 13 | 14 | 1 |  | 2² | 28 |
|  |  | 3 | 4¹ |  | 10² | 12 |  |  | 9 | 11 |  |  | 7 | 6 | 5 |  |  |  | 8 |  | 1 |  | 2 | 29 |
|  |  | 3 | 4 |  | 10¹ | 12 |  |  | 9 | 11² |  |  | 7 | 6 | 5 |  |  |  | 8 | 14 | 1 |  | 2³ | 30 |
|  |  | 3 | 4 |  | 10 | 12 |  |  | 9 |  |  |  | 7 | 6 | 5 |  | 13 |  | 8 | 11¹ | 1 |  | 2² | 31 |
|  |  | 3 | 4 |  | 10 | 12 |  |  | 9 |  |  |  | 7 | 6 | 5 |  |  |  | 8 | 11¹ | 1 |  | 2 | 32 |
|  |  | 3 | 4 |  | 10 | 12 |  |  | 9¹ | 11 |  |  | 7 | 6 | 5 |  |  |  | 8 |  | 1 |  | 2 | 33 |
|  |  | 3 | 4 |  | 10 | 12 |  |  | 9 | 11 |  |  | 7 | 6¹ | 5 |  |  |  | 8 | 14 | 1 | 13³ | 2² | 34 |
|  |  | 3 | 4 |  | 10 | 12 |  |  | 9 | 11³ |  |  | 7² | 6 | 5 |  | 13 |  | 8 |  | 1 |  | 2 | 35 |
|  |  | 3 | 4 |  | 10¹ | 12 |  |  | 9² | 11 |  |  | 7² | 6 | 5 |  | 13 |  | 8 | 14 | 1 |  | 2 | 36 |
|  |  | 3 | 4 |  | 10¹ | 12 |  |  | 9 | 11² |  |  | 7³ | 6 | 5 |  | 13 |  | 8 | 14 | 1 |  | 2 | 37 |
|  |  | 3 | 4 |  | 10 | 12 |  |  | 9 | 11 |  |  | 7 | 6 | 5 |  |  |  | 8 |  | 1 |  | 2¹ | 38 |
|  |  | 3 | 4 |  | 10 | 12 |  |  | 9 | 11¹ |  |  | 7 | 6² | 5 |  | 13 |  | 8 |  | 1 |  | 2 | 39 |
|  |  | 3 | 4 |  | 10 | 12 |  |  | 9 | 11² |  |  | 7¹ | 6 | 5 |  | 13 |  | 8 |  | 1 |  | 2 | 40 |
|  |  | 3 | 4 |  | 10 | 12 |  |  | 9¹ | 11 |  |  | 7² | 6 | 5 |  | 13 |  | 8 |  | 1 |  | 2 | 41 |
|  |  | 3 | 4 |  | 10¹ | 12 |  |  | 9 | 11² |  |  | 7 | 6 | 5 |  | 13 |  | 8 |  | 1 |  | 2 | 42 |
|  |  | 3 | 4 |  | 10 | 12 |  |  | 9 | 11² |  |  | 7¹ | 6 | 5 |  | 13 |  | 8 |  | 1 |  | 2 | 43 |
|  |  | 3 | 4 |  | 10 | 12 |  |  | 9 | 11 |  |  | 7¹ | 6² | 5 |  | 13 |  | 8 |  | 1 |  | 2 | 44 |
|  |  | 3 | 4 |  | 10 | 12 |  |  | 9 | 11¹ |  |  | 7 | 6 | 5² |  | 13 |  | 8 |  | 1 |  | 2 | 45 |
|  |  | 3 | 4 |  | 10 | 12 |  |  | 9 | 11 |  |  | 7² | 6¹ | 5 |  | 13 |  | 8 | 14 | 1 |  | 2³ | 46 |

**Coca-Cola Cup**

| First Round | Hartlepool U | (h) | 3-1 |
|---|---|---|---|
|  |  | (a) | 1-2 |
| Second Round | Notts Co | (a) | 2-0 |
|  |  | (h) | 0-1 |
| Third Round | Oxford U | (a) | 1-1 |

**FA Cup**

| Third Round | Hereford U | (a) | 3-0 |
|---|---|---|---|
| Fourth Round | Sunderland | (h) | 1-0 |
| Fifth Round | Newcastle U | (a) | 0-1 |

WALSALL 1997-98  *Back row (left to right)*: Tom Bradley (Physio), Darren Rogers, Ian Roper, Mark Perry, Clive Platt, Mark Smith, Danny Naisbitt, James Walker, Michael Ricketts, John Williams, Stuart Ryder, Mark Blake, Eric McManus (Youth Development Officer).
*Front row*: John Keister, Wayne Evans, Dean Keates, Gary Porter, John Hodge, Adrian Viveash, Jan Sorensen (Manager), Roger Boli, Louie Donowa, Wayne Thomas, Andy Watson, Derek Mountfield (Coach), Darren Beckford.

# Division 2 **WALSALL**

*Bescot Stadium, Bescot Crescent, Walsall WS1 4SA.* Telephone: (01922) 622791. Fax: (01922) 613202. Commercial Dept: (01922) 651412. Saddlers Hotline: 0891 555800.

*Ground capacity:* 9000.

*Record attendance:* 10,628 B International, England v Switzerland, 20 May 1991.

*Record receipts:* £98,828 v Leeds U, FA Cup 3rd rd, 7 January 1995.

*Pitch measurements:* 110yd × 73yd.

*Chairman:*

*Directors:* M. N. Lloyd (Acting Chairman), K. R. Whalley, C. Welch, R. M. Tisdale, S. A. Joesbury.

*Manager:* Ray Graydon. *General Manager:* Paul Taylor. *Physio:* Tom Bradley.

*Secretary/Commercial Manager:* Roy Whalley.

*Year Formed:* 1888. *Turned Professional:* 1888. *Ltd Co.:* 1921.

*Club Nickname:* 'The Saddlers'.

*Previous Names:* Walsall Swifts (founded 1877) and Walsall Town (founded 1879) amalgamated in 1888 and were known as Walsall Town Swifts until 1895.

*Previous Grounds:* Fellows Park to 1990.

*Foundation:* Two of the leading clubs around Walsall in the 1880s were Walsall Swifts (formed 1877) and Walsall Town (formed 1879). The Swifts were winners of the Birmingham Senior Cup in 1881, while the Town reached the 4th round (5th round modern equivalent) of the FA Cup in 1883. These clubs amalgamated as Walsall Town Swifts in 1888, becoming simply Walsall in 1895.

*First Football League game:* 3 September 1892, Division 2, v Darwen (h) L 1-2 – Hawkins; Withington, Pinches; Robinson, Whitrick, Forsyth; Marshall, Holmes, Turner, Gray (1), Pangbourn.

*Record League Victory:* 10–0 v Darwen, Division 2, 4 March 1899 – Tennent; E. Peers (1), Davies; Hickinbotham, Jenkyns, Taggart; Dean (3), Vail (2), Aston (4), Martin, Griffin.

*Record Cup Victory:* 7-0 v Macclesfield T (away), FA Cup 2nd rd, 6 December 1997 – Walker; Evans, Marsh, Viveash (1), Ryder, Peron, Boli (2, 1 pen) (Ricketts), Porter (2), Keates, Watson (Platt), Hodge (2, 1 pen).

*Record Defeat:* 0–12 v Small Heath, 17 December 1892 and v Darwen, 26 December 1896, both Division 2.

*Most League Points (2 for a win):* 65, Division 4, 1959–60.

*Most League Points (3 for a win):* 83, Division 3, 1994–95.

*Most League Goals:* 102, Division 4, 1959–60.

*Highest League Scorer in Season:* Gilbert Alsop, 40, Division 3 (N), 1933–34 and 1934–35.

*Most League Goals in Total Aggregate:* Tony Richards, 184, 1954–63, and Colin Taylor, 184, 1958–63, 1964–68, 1969–73.

*Most Capped Player:* Mick Kearns, 15 (18), Republic of Ireland.

*Most League Appearances:* Colin Harrison, 467, 1964–82.

*Record Transfer Fee Received:* £600,000 from West Ham U for David Kelly, July 1988.

*Record Transfer Fee Paid:* £175,000 to Birmingham C for Alan Buckley, June 1979.

*Football League Record:* 1892 Elected to Division 2; 1895 Failed re-election; 1896–1901 Division 2; 1901 Failed re-election; 1921 Original Member of Division 3 (N); 1927–31 Division 3 (S); 1931–36 Division 3 (N); 1936–58 Division 3 (S); 1958–60 Division 4; 1960–61 Division 3; 1961–63 Division 4; 1963–79 Division 3; 1979–80 Division 4; 1980–88 Division 3; 1988–89 Division 2; 1989–90 Division 3; 1990–92 Division 4; 1992–95 Division 3; 1995– Division 2.

*Honours: Football League:* Division 2 best season: 6th, 1898–99; Division 3 – Runners-up 1960–61, 1994–95; Division 4 – Champions 1959–60; Runners-up 1979–80. *FA Cup:* best season: 5th rd, 1939, 1975, 1978, 1987 and last 16 1889. *Football League Cup:* Semi-final 1984.

*Colours:* Red shirts with black trim, red shorts with black trim, red stockings with black turnover. *Change colours:* Green shirts with white trim, green shorts with white trim, green stockings with white turnover.

**Did you know?**
When Walsall beat Macclesfield Town 7-0 away in a FA Cup second round tie on 6 December 1997, it was their biggest away win for 50 years.

## WALSALL 1997–98 LEAGUE RECORD

| Match No. | Date | | Venue | Opponents | Result | H/T Score | Lg. Pos. | Goalscorers | Atten- dance |
|---|---|---|---|---|---|---|---|---|---|
| 1 | Aug | 9 | A | Chesterfield | L | 1-3 | 0-1 | — | Platt [78] | 5193 |
| 2 | | 16 | H | Fulham | D | 1-1 | 0-0 | 16 | Mountfield [87] | 4418 |
| 3 | | 23 | A | Gillingham | L | 1-2 | 0-0 | 21 | Boli [90] | 5083 |
| 4 | | 30 | H | Southend U | W | 3-1 | 2-1 | 14 | Boli 3 [11, 25, 90] | 3304 |
| 5 | Sept | 2 | H | Northampton T | L | 0-2 | 0-1 | — | | 4435 |
| 6 | | 9 | A | Bristol R | L | 0-2 | 0-1 | — | | 6225 |
| 7 | | 13 | A | Preston NE | D | 0-0 | 0-0 | 22 | | 9092 |
| 8 | | 20 | H | York C | W | 2-0 | 0-0 | 20 | Boli [49], Hodge [90] | 2972 |
| 9 | | 27 | A | Plymouth Arg | L | 1-2 | 1-1 | 22 | Boli [31] | 6207 |
| 10 | Oct | 4 | A | Carlisle U | W | 3-1 | 1-0 | 20 | Boli 2 [16, 60], Watson [74] | 3957 |
| 11 | | 11 | H | Wrexham | W | 3-0 | 0-0 | 14 | Boli [16], Hodge (pen) [19], Watson [82] | 4042 |
| 12 | | 18 | A | Brentford | L | 0-3 | 0-0 | 18 | | 4874 |
| 13 | | 21 | A | Wycombe W | L | 2-4 | 2-3 | — | Viveash [29], Watson [39] | 3884 |
| 14 | | 25 | H | Bristol C | D | 0-0 | 0-0 | 19 | | 4618 |
| 15 | Nov | 1 | A | Burnley | L | 1-2 | 0-1 | 20 | Viveash [79] | 9293 |
| 16 | | 4 | H | Grimsby T | D | 0-0 | 0-0 | — | | 2599 |
| 17 | | 8 | H | Watford | D | 0-0 | 0-0 | 21 | | 5077 |
| 18 | | 22 | A | Luton T | W | 1-0 | 0-0 | 18 | Hodge [60] | 4726 |
| 19 | | 29 | H | Blackpool | W | 2-1 | 0-1 | 16 | Watson [64], Boli [86] | 3933 |
| 20 | Dec | 3 | A | Millwall | W | 1-0 | 0-0 | — | Keates [78] | 4647 |
| 21 | | 13 | H | Bournemouth | W | 2-1 | 0-0 | 13 | Boli [60], Hodge [66] | 3548 |
| 22 | | 19 | A | Oldham Ath | D | 0-0 | 0-0 | — | | 4677 |
| 23 | | 26 | H | Bristol R | L | 0-1 | 0-0 | 15 | | 6634 |
| 24 | | 28 | A | Northampton T | L | 2-3 | 1-1 | 16 | Porter [40], Hodge [61] | 7094 |
| 25 | Jan | 10 | H | Chesterfield | W | 3-2 | 0-1 | 15 | Reeves (og) [55], Watson 2 [79, 82] | 4042 |
| 26 | | 17 | A | Southend U | W | 1-0 | 0-0 | 14 | Watson [53] | 3310 |
| 27 | | 31 | H | Preston NE | D | 1-1 | 0-0 | 14 | Hodge (pen) [90] | 5377 |
| 28 | Feb | 7 | A | York C | L | 0-1 | 0-1 | 15 | | 2959 |
| 29 | | 14 | A | Carlisle U | D | 1-1 | 0-0 | 16 | Hodge [47] | 4530 |
| 30 | | 21 | H | Plymouth Arg | L | 0-1 | 0-1 | 16 | | 4612 |
| 31 | | 24 | H | Brentford | D | 0-0 | 0-0 | — | | 3166 |
| 32 | | 28 | A | Wrexham | L | 1-2 | 1-2 | 18 | Ricketts [44] | 3622 |
| 33 | Mar | 3 | A | Watford | W | 2-1 | 1-0 | — | Tholot [9], Blake [73] | 8096 |
| 34 | | 7 | H | Burnley | D | 0-0 | 0-0 | 16 | | 5212 |
| 35 | | 14 | A | Grimsby T | L | 0-3 | 0-0 | 18 | | 4916 |
| 36 | | 21 | H | Wigan Ath | W | 1-0 | 0-0 | 17 | Peron [57] | 3169 |
| 37 | | 28 | A | Luton T | L | 2-3 | 0-1 | 17 | Viveash [52], Tholot [74] | 3922 |
| 38 | | 31 | H | Gillingham | W | 1-0 | 0-0 | — | Evans [71] | 3117 |
| 39 | Apr | 4 | A | Blackpool | L | 0-1 | 0-0 | 17 | | 4451 |
| 40 | | 7 | A | Fulham | D | 1-1 | 1-0 | — | Boli [30] | 6733 |
| 41 | | 11 | H | Millwall | W | 2-0 | 1-0 | 14 | Tholot [1], Hodge (pen) [59] | 3307 |
| 42 | | 14 | A | Bournemouth | L | 0-1 | 0-0 | — | | 3404 |
| 43 | | 18 | H | Oldham Ath | D | 0-0 | 0-0 | 17 | | 3562 |
| 44 | | 21 | A | Wigan Ath | L | 0-2 | 0-0 | — | | 2725 |
| 45 | | 25 | A | Bristol C | L | 1-2 | 1-1 | 19 | Tholot [23] | 15,059 |
| 46 | May | 2 | H | Wycombe W | L | 0-1 | 0-1 | 19 | | 4412 |

**Final League Position: 19**          1996–97 DIV2 12

### GOALSCORERS

*League (43):* Boli 12, Hodge 8 (3 pens), Watson 7, Tholot 4, Viveash 3, Blake 1, Evans 1, Keates 1, Mountfield 1, Peron 1, Platt 1, Porter 1, Ricketts 1, own goal 1.
*Coca-Cola Cup (9):* Watson 4, Boli 2, Platt 1, Skinner 1, own goal 1.
*FA Cup (12):* Boli 4 (1 pen), Watson 3, Hodge 2 (1 pen), Porter 2, Viveash 1.

| Walker J 46 | Evans W 43 | Rogers D 4 | Viveash A 42 | Ryder S 11+2 | Donowa L 5+1 | Boli R 41 | Keister J 11+2 | Platt C 12+8 | Porter G 25+4 | Hodge J 35+4 | Williams J —+1 | Keates D 32+1 | Mountfield D 26+1 | Watson A 23+4 | Peron J 38 | Roper I 18+3 | Blake M 16+7 | Ricketts M 6+18 | Skinner J 10 | Marsh C 36 | Thomas W 3+2 | Eydelie J 10+1 | Tholot D 13+1 | Gadsby M —+1 | Match No. |
|---|---|---|---|---|---|---|---|---|---|---|---|---|---|---|---|---|---|---|---|---|---|---|---|---|---|
| 1 | 2 | 3 | 4 | 5 | 6¹ | 7 | 8 | 9 | 10 | 11 | 12 | | | | | | | | | | | | | | 1 |
| 1 | 2 | | 4 | | 6 | 7 | 8 | 9 | 10¹ | 11 | | 3 | 5 | 12 | | | | | | | | | | | 2 |
| 1 | 2 | | 4 | 12 | | 7 | 8 | 9 | 10² | 11 | | 3¹ | 5 | 13 | 6 | | | | | | | | | | 3 |
| 1 | 2 | | 4 | | 3 | 7 | 8 | 12 | 10 | | | | | | 9¹ | 6 | 5 | 11 | | | | | | | 4 |
| 1 | 2 | | 4 | 3¹ | 8 | 7 | | 12 | 10² | 13 | | | | | 9 | 6 | 5 | 11³ | 14 | | | | | | 5 |
| 1 | 3 | | 4 | 10² | | 7 | | 9 | | 11 | | 12 | 5 | 13 | 6 | 2 | 8¹ | | | | | | | | 6 |
| 1 | 2 | 3 | 4 | | | 7 | | 9³ | | 11 | | 10 | 5 | | 6 | | 12 | | 8 | | | | | | 7 |
| 1 | 2 | 3 | 4 | | | 7 | | 12 | | 11 | | 9 | | 10¹ | 6 | 5 | 8 | | | | | | | | 8 |
| 1 | 2 | 3¹ | 4 | | | 7 | | 12 | | 13 | | 11 | | 9² | 5 | 10 | 8 | | | | | | | | 9 |
| 1 | 2 | | 4 | | | 7 | | | 12 | 11¹ | | 9 | 5 | 10 | 6 | | 8 | | | 3 | | | | | 10 |
| 1 | 2 | | 4 | | | 7 | | | | 11 | | 9 | 5 | 10 | 6 | | 8 | | | 3 | | | | | 11 |
| 1 | 2 | | 4 | | | 7 | | 12 | 9¹ | 11¹ | | | 5 | 10 | 6 | | 13 | | 8 | 3 | | | | | 12 |
| 1 | 2 | | 4² | | | 7 | | 12 | | 13 | | 9 | 5³ | 10 | 6 | 14 | 11¹ | | 8 | 3 | | | | | 13 |
| 1 | 3 | | 4 | | | 7¹ | | | | 11 | | 9 | 5 | 10 | 6 | | 12 | | 8 | 2 | | | | | 14 |
| 1 | 2 | | 4 | | | 7 | | | | 11¹ | | 9 | 5 | 10 | 6 | | 12 | | 8 | 3 | | | | | 15 |
| 1 | 2 | | 4 | | | 7 | | | | 11¹ | | 9 | | 10 | 6 | 5 | 13 | 12 | 8² | 3 | | | | | 16 |
| 1 | 2 | | 4 | 11 | | 7 | 8 | | | | | 9 | | 12 | 6 | 5 | | 10¹ | | 3 | | | | | 17 |
| 1 | 2 | | 4 | | | 7¹ | | 8 | | 11 | | 9 | 5 | 10 | 6 | | 12 | | | 3 | | | | | 18 |
| 1 | 2 | | 4 | | | 7 | | 8 | | 11 | | 9¹ | 5 | 10 | 6 | | 12 | | | 3 | | | | | 19 |
| 1 | 2 | | 4 | | | 7 | | 8 | | 11¹ | | 9 | 5 | 10 | 6 | | 12 | | | 3 | | | | | 20 |
| 1 | | | 4 | | | 7 | 8 | | | 11 | | 9¹ | 5 | 10 | 6 | 2 | 12 | | | 3 | | | | | 21 |
| 1 | | | 4 | | | 7 | 8 | | | 11 | | 9 | 5 | 10 | 6 | 2 | | | | 3 | | | | | 22 |
| 1 | | | 4 | | | 7 | 8¹ | 12 | | 11 | | 9 | 5 | 10 | 6 | 2 | | | | 3 | | | | | 23 |
| 1¹ | 2 | | 4 | 5 | | 7 | | 8 | | 11 | | 9 | | 10 | 6 | | 12 | | | 3 | | | | | 24 |
| 1 | 2 | | 4 | | | 7 | | 8 | | 11 | | 9 | 5¹ | 10 | 6 | 12 | | | | 3 | | | | | 25 |
| 1 | 2 | | 4 | | | 7 | | 8 | | 11 | | 9 | 5¹ | 10 | | 12 | 6 | | | 3 | | | | | 26 |
| 1 | 2 | | 4 | 12 | | 7 | | 8² | | 11 | | 9 | 5¹ | 10 | 6 | | 13 | | | 3 | | | | | 27 |
| 1 | 2 | | 4 | 5 | | 7 | | | | 11¹ | | 9² | | 10 | 6 | 5 | 8 | 12 | | 3 | 13 | | | | 28 |
| 1 | 2 | | 4 | | | 7¹ | | | | 11 | | 9 | | 10 | 6 | 5 | 8 | 12 | | 3 | | | | | 29 |
| 1 | 2 | | 4 | | | 7 | | 12 | | 11 | | 9 | | | 6 | 5 | 8¹ | 10 | | 3 | | | | | 30 |
| 1 | 2 | | 4 | | | 7 | | 10 | | 11 | | 9 | | | 6 | 5 | 8 | | | 3 | | | | | 31 |
| 1 | 2 | | 4 | | | 7 | 11 | 10 | | | | 9 | | | 6¹ | 5 | 8 | 12 | | 3 | | | | | 32 |
| 1 | 2 | | 4 | | | 7¹ | 12 | | | | | 9 | | | | 5 | 8 | 11 | | 3 | | 6 | 10 | | 33 |
| 1 | 2 | | 4 | | | 7 | | 12 | | 11 | | | | | | 5 | 8¹ | 9 | | 3 | | 6 | 10 | | 34 |
| 1 | 2 | 4¹ | | | | | | 9 | 8 | 11 | | 3 | 12 | | | 5 | 7 | 13 | | | 14 | 6² | 10² | | 35 |
| 1 | 2 | | 4 | | | 7 | | 9¹ | 10 | | | 8 | | | 6 | 5 | 11 | | | 3 | | | 12 | | 36 |
| 1 | 2 | | 4 | | | 7 | | 9¹ | 10 | | | 8² | | | 6 | 5 | 12 | | | 3 | | 13 | 11 | | 37 |
| 1 | 2 | | 4 | | | | | | 10 | 11¹ | | 9 | 5 | | 6 | | 12 | | | 3 | | 7 | 8 | | 38 |
| 1 | 2 | | 4² | | | 7 | 12 | | 10 | 11 | | 5 | | | 6 | | 13 | | | 3 | | 8¹ | 9 | | 39 |
| 1 | 2 | | 4 | 8 | | 7² | | | 10 | 12 | | 5 | | | 6 | | 13 | | | 3 | | 11 | 9¹ | | 40 |
| 1 | 2 | | 4 | | | 7 | | | 10 | 11 | | 5 | | | 6 | | | | | 3 | | 8 | 9 | | 41 |
| 1 | 2 | | 4 | | | 7 | | | 10 | 11 | | 5¹ | | | 6 | | 12 | | | 3 | | 8 | 9 | | 42 |
| 1 | 2 | | 4 | 12 | | 7 | | | 10 | 11 | | 5¹ | | | 6² | | 13 | | | 3 | | 8 | 9 | | 43 |
| 1 | 2 | | 4 | 6² | | 7 | | | 10 | 12 | | | | | 5 | | 13 | | | 3 | 11¹ | 8 | 9 | | 44 |
| 1 | 2 | | 4 | | | | 8 | 12 | 10 | 11 | | | | | | | | | | 3 | 7 | 6¹ | | 9 | 45 |
| 1 | 2 | | 4² | | | | 8 | 7 | 10 | | | | | | 6 | 5 | 12 | | | 3 | 11¹ | | 9 | 13 | 46 |

**Coca-Cola Cup**

|  |  | |  |
|---|---|---|---|
| First Round | Exeter C | (h) | 2-0 |
| | | (a) | 1-0 |
| Second Round | Nottingham F | (a) | 1-0 |
| | | (h) | 2-2 |
| Third Round | Sheffield U | (h) | 2-1 |
| Fourth Round | West Ham U | (a) | 1-4 |

**FA Cup**

|  |  | |  |
|---|---|---|---|
| First Round | Lincoln U | (h) | 2-0 |
| Second Round | Macclesfield T | (a) | 7-0 |
| Third Round | Peterborough U | (a) | 2-0 |
| Fourth Round | Manchester U | (a) | 1-5 |

WATFORD 1997–98 *Back row (left to right):* Kirk Wheeler (Football in the Community Officer), Daniel Grieves, Nathan Lowndes, Robert Page, Keith Millen, Jason Lee, Darren Ward, Gifton Noel-Williams, Lars Melvang, Colin Pluck, David Perpetuini, Dominic Ludden, Roy Clare (Kit Manager).

*Middle row:* Jimmy Gilligan (Youth Team Manager), Gary Johnson (Youth Development Officer), Vince Cave, Steve Talboys, David Thomas, Tommy Mooney, Alec Chamberlain, Chris Day, Steve Palmer, Peter Kennedy, Micah Hyde, Mark Rooney, Tom Walley (Reserve Team Manager), Phil Edwards (Physio).

*Front row:* Chris Johnson, Richard Johnson, Wayne Andrews, Paul Robinson, Clint Easton, Kenny Jackett (First Team Coach), Graham Taylor (First Team Manager), Luther Blissett (Coach), Stuart Slater, Nigel Gibbs, Richard Flash, Darren Bazeley, Andy Johnson.

# Division 1     **WATFORD**

*Vicarage Road Stadium, Watford WD1 8ER.* Telephone: (01923) 496000. Fax: (01923) 496001. Hornet Hotline: 0891 104104. Ticket Office: (01923) 496010. Club Shop: (01923) 496005. Catering: (01923) 252323. Football in the Community: (01923) 440449. Junior Hornets Club: (01923) 496256. Marketing: (01923) 496006. Press Office: (01923) 496234.

*Ground capacity:* 22,000.

*Record attendance:* 34,099 v Manchester U, FA Cup 4th rd (replay), 3 February 1969.

*Record receipts:* £189,799.13 v Sheffield W, FA Cup 3rd rd, 3 January 1998.

*Pitch measurements:* 113yd × 73yd.

*Life Presidents:* Sir Elton John CBE, Geoff Smith.

*Chairman:* Sir Elton John CBE.

*Directors:* B. Anderson, C. Lissack, D. Meller, H. Oundjian.

*Secretary:* John Alexander.

*General Manager:* Graham Taylor. *First Team Coach:* Kenny Jackett.

*Head of Youth Football:* Gary Johnson. *Youth Development Officer:* Jimmy Gilligan.

*Press and Publications Officer:* Andrew French.

*Safety Officer:* Mick Buttle.

*Year Formed:* 1881. *Turned Professional:* 1897. *Ltd Co.:* 1909.

*Club Nickname:* 'The Hornets'.

*Previous Names:* Watford Rovers, West Herts.

*Previous Grounds:* 1883, Vicarage Meadow, Rose and Crown Meadow; 1889, Colney Butts; 1890, Cassio Road; 1922, Vicarage Road.

*Foundation:* The club was formed as Watford Rovers in 1881. The name was changed to West Herts in 1893 and then the name Watford was adopted after rival club Watford St Mary's was absorbed in 1898.

*First Football League game:* 28 August 1920, Division 3, v QPR (a) W 2-1 – Williams; Horseman, F. Gregory; Bacon, Toone, Wilkinson; Bassett, Ronald (1), Hoddinott, White (1), Waterall.

*Record League Victory:* 8–0 v Sunderland, Division 1, 25 September 1982 – Sherwood; Rice, Rostron, Taylor, Terry, Bolton, Callaghan (2), Blissett (4), Jenkins (2), Jackett, Barnes.

*Record Cup Victory:* 10–1 v Lowestoft T, FA Cup 1st rd, 27 November 1926 – Yates; Prior, Fletcher (1); F. Smith, 'Bert' Smith, Strain; Stephenson, Warner (3), Edmonds (3), Swan (1), Daniels (1). (1 og).

*Record Defeat:* 0–10 v Wolverhampton W, FA Cup 1st rd (replay), 24 January 1912.

*Most League Points (2 for a win):* 71, Division 4, 1977–78.

*Most League Points (3 for a win):* 88, Division 2, 1997–98.

*Most League Goals:* 92, Division 4, 1959–60.

*Highest League Scorer in Season:* Cliff Holton, 42, Division 4, 1959–60.

*Most League Goals in Total Aggregate:* Luther Blissett, 148, 1976–83, 1984–88, 1991–92.

*Most Capped Player:* John Barnes, 31 (79), England and Kenny Jackett, 31, Wales.

*Most League Appearances:* Luther Blissett, 415, 1976–83, 1984–88, 1991–92.

*Record Transfer Fee Received:* £2,300,000 from Chelsea for Paul Furlong, May 1994.

*Record Transfer Fee Paid:* £550,000 to AC Milan for Luther Blissett, August 1984.

*Football League Record:* 1920 Original Member of Division 3; 1921–58 Division 3 (S); 1958–60 Division 4; 1960–69 Division 3; 1969–72 Division 2; 1972–75 Division 3; 1975–78 Division 4; 1978–79 Division 3; 1979–82 Division 2; 1982–88 Division 1; 1988–92 Division 2; 1992–96 Division 1; 1996–98 Division 2; 1998– Division 1.

*Honours: Football League:* Division 1 – Runners-up 1982–83; Division 2 – Champions 1997–98; Runners-up 1981–82; Division 3 – Champions 1968–69; Runners-up 1978–79; Division 4 – Champions 1977–78; Promoted 1959–60 (4th). *FA Cup:* Runners-up 1984. *Football League Cup:* Semi- final 1979. **European Competitions:** *UEFA Cup:* 1983–84.

*Colours:* Yellow shirts with red sleeves and black collar and cuffs, red shorts, red stockings with yellow tops and two black hoops. *Change colours:* Blue and silver striped shirts with red pinstripes, blue shorts, blue stockings with red tops and two black hoops.

**Did you know?**
On 10 April 1937 Watford won 7-4 at Torquay United, having led 5-2 at half-time and played most of the second half minus the injured Ralph Reed.

## WATFORD 1997–98 LEAGUE RECORD

| Match No. | Date | | Venue | Opponents | Result | | H/T Score | Lg. Pos. | Goalscorers | Attendance |
|---|---|---|---|---|---|---|---|---|---|---|
| 1 | Aug | 9 | H | Burnley | W | 1-0 | 1-0 | — | Lee [30] | 11,155 |
| 2 | | 16 | A | Carlisle U | W | 2-0 | 0-0 | 2 | Kennedy [60], Johnson [78] | 7395 |
| 3 | | 23 | H | Brentford | W | 3-1 | 2-0 | 1 | Millen [4], Melvang [11], Johnson [90] | 10,125 |
| 4 | | 30 | A | Preston NE | L | 0-2 | 0-1 | 2 | | 11,042 |
| 5 | Sept | 2 | A | Plymouth Arg | W | 1-0 | 0-0 | — | Noel-Williams [71] | 5141 |
| 6 | | 7 | H | Wycombe W | W | 2-1 | 1-0 | 1 | Hyde [6], Lee [62] | 12,100 |
| 7 | | 13 | H | Chesterfield | W | 2-1 | 1-0 | 1 | Rosenthal [44], Lee [62] | 11,204 |
| 8 | | 20 | A | Gillingham | D | 2-2 | 0-1 | 1 | Rosenthal (pen) [50], Johnson [72] | 7780 |
| 9 | | 27 | H | York C | D | 1-1 | 0-1 | 1 | Lee [72] | 13,812 |
| 10 | Oct | 4 | A | Luton T | W | 4-0 | 4-0 | 1 | Johnson [5], Thomas [19], Kennedy 2 [27, 29] | 9041 |
| 11 | | 14 | A | Bristol R | W | 2-1 | 0-0 | — | Kennedy [62], Rosenthal (pen) [80] | 8110 |
| 12 | | 18 | H | Millwall | L | 0-1 | 0-1 | 1 | | 12,530 |
| 13 | | 21 | H | Fulham | W | 2-0 | 1-0 | — | Rosenthal [42], Robinson [88] | 11,486 |
| 14 | | 25 | A | Grimsby T | W | 1-0 | 1-0 | 1 | Rosenthal [1] | 5699 |
| 15 | Nov | 1 | H | Blackpool | W | 4-1 | 1-0 | 1 | Lee 2 [36, 53], Johnson [64], Rosenthal [70] | 9723 |
| 16 | | 4 | A | Southend U | W | 3-0 | 2-0 | — | Kennedy 3 [14, 37, 67] | 4001 |
| 17 | | 8 | A | Walsall | D | 0-0 | 0-0 | 1 | | 5077 |
| 18 | | 18 | H | Oldham Ath | W | 2-1 | 1-0 | — | Thomas [5], Mooney [83] | 8397 |
| 19 | | 22 | A | Northampton T | W | 1-0 | 0-0 | 1 | Kennedy [57] | 7373 |
| 20 | | 29 | H | Wigan Ath | W | 2-1 | 2-1 | 1 | Thomas [12], Mooney [45] | 9455 |
| 21 | Dec | 2 | A | Wrexham | D | 1-1 | 0-0 | — | Rosenthal [72] | 3702 |
| 22 | | 13 | H | Bristol C | D | 1-1 | 0-0 | 1 | Noel-Williams [85] | 16,072 |
| 23 | | 20 | A | Bournemouth | W | 1-0 | 0-0 | 1 | Kennedy [57] | 6081 |
| 24 | | 26 | A | Wycombe W | D | 0-0 | 0-0 | 1 | | 8090 |
| 25 | | 28 | H | Plymouth Arg | D | 1-1 | 0-0 | 1 | Mooney [90] | 11,594 |
| 26 | Jan | 10 | A | Burnley | L | 0-2 | 0-2 | 2 | | 9551 |
| 27 | | 17 | H | Preston NE | W | 3-1 | 2-0 | 2 | Kennedy 2 [17, 60], Hyde [29] | 10,182 |
| 28 | | 24 | A | Brentford | W | 2-1 | 1-1 | 1 | Mooney [7], Johnson [71] | 6969 |
| 29 | | 31 | A | Chesterfield | W | 1-0 | 0-0 | 1 | Noel-Williams [87] | 5975 |
| 30 | Feb | 8 | H | Gillingham | L | 0-2 | 0-1 | 1 | | 10,498 |
| 31 | | 14 | H | Luton T | D | 1-1 | 0-0 | 1 | Robinson [52] | 15,182 |
| 32 | | 21 | A | York C | D | 1-1 | 0-1 | 1 | Palmer [90] | 4890 |
| 33 | | 25 | A | Millwall | D | 1-1 | 0-1 | — | Mooney [49] | 7126 |
| 34 | | 28 | H | Bristol R | W | 3-2 | 2-0 | 1 | Noel-Williams [18], Rosenthal [24], Mooney [88] | 12,186 |
| 35 | Mar | 3 | H | Walsall | L | 1-2 | 0-1 | — | Noel-Williams [57] | 8096 |
| 36 | | 7 | A | Blackpool | D | 1-1 | 0-0 | 1 | Bazeley [53] | 5237 |
| 37 | | 14 | H | Southend U | D | 1-1 | 1-0 | 2 | Hyde [45] | 10,750 |
| 38 | | 17 | H | Carlisle U | W | 2-1 | 1-0 | — | Palmer [5], Bazeley [59] | 7274 |
| 39 | | 21 | A | Oldham Ath | D | 2-2 | 1-0 | 1 | Bazeley [8], Gibbs [61] | 5744 |
| 40 | | 28 | H | Northampton T | D | 1-1 | 0-0 | 1 | Johnson [57] | 14,268 |
| 41 | Apr | 4 | A | Wigan Ath | L | 2-3 | 0-3 | 2 | Foley [54], Hyde [80] | 4262 |
| 42 | | 11 | A | Wrexham | W | 1-0 | 1-0 | 2 | Lee [9] | 12,340 |
| 43 | | 13 | A | Bristol C | D | 1-1 | 0-0 | 2 | Lee [64] | 19,141 |
| 44 | | 25 | H | Grimsby T | D | 0-0 | 0-0 | 2 | | 14,002 |
| 45 | | 28 | A | Bournemouth | W | 2-1 | 0-1 | — | Lee [47], Noel-Williams [69] | 12,834 |
| 46 | May | 2 | A | Fulham | W | 2-1 | 1-0 | 1 | Noel-Williams [35], Lee [71] | 17,114 |

**Final League Position: 1**      1996–97 DIV2 13

### GOALSCORERS
League (67): Kennedy 11, Lee 10, Rosenthal 8 (2 pens), Johnson 7, Noel-Williams 7, Mooney 6, Hyde 4, Bazeley 3, Thomas 3, Palmer 2, Robinson 2, Foley 1, Gibbs 1, Melvang 1, Millen 1.
Coca-Cola Cup (4): Hyde 1, Kennedy 1, Noel-Williams 1, Rosenthal 1.
FA Cup (6): Noel-Williams 3, Rosenthal 2, Kennedy 1.

| Chamberlain A 46 | Gibbs N 34 + 4 | Kennedy P 34 | Page R 41 | Millen K 38 | Mooney T 45 | Noel-Williams G 27 + 11 | Hyde M 40 | Lee J 35 + 1 | Johnson R 42 | Slater S 9 + 5 | Talboys S — + 2 | Palmer S 32 + 9 | Rosenthal R 24 + 1 | Melvang L 4 | Thomas D 8 + 8 | Andrews W — + 2 | Easton C 8 + 4 | Pluck K 1 | Bazeley D 14 + 2 | Robinson P 14 + 8 | Smith T — + 1 | Lowndes N 1 + 3 | Hazan A 7 + 3 | Foley D 2 + 6 | Match No. |
|---|---|---|---|---|---|---|---|---|---|---|---|---|---|---|---|---|---|---|---|---|---|---|---|---|---|
| 1 | 2 | 3 | 4 | 5 | 6 | 7 | 8 | 9 | 10 | 11 | | | | | | | | | | | | | | | 1 |
| 1 | $2^1$ | 3 | $4^2$ | 5 | 6 | 7 | 8 | $9^2$ | 10 | 11 | 12 | 13 | 14 | | | | | | | | | | | | 2 |
| 1 | | 3 | 4 | 5 | 6 | | 8 | | 10 | 11 | | 12 | 7 | $2^1$ | $9^2$ | 13 | | | | | | | | | 3 |
| 1 | 2 | 3 | 4 | | 6 | 7 | $8^2$ | | 10 | $11^3$ | 13 | 5 | $9^1$ | 14 | 12 | | | | | | | | | | 4 |
| 1 | | 3 | 4 | | 6 | 7 | 8 | 9 | 10 | | | 5 | 11 | 2 | | | | | | | | | | | 5 |
| 1 | 12 | 3 | 4 | | 6 | 7 | 8 | 9 | 10 | | | 5 | $11^2$ | $2^1$ | 13 | | | | | | | | | | 6 |
| 1 | 2 | 3 | 4 | | 6 | 7 | 8 | 9 | 10 | | | 5 | 11 | | | | | | | | | | | | 7 |
| 1 | 12 | 3 | 4 | | | 7 | | 9 | 10 | 13 | | 5 | 11 | $2^2$ | | | $6^1$ | | | | | | | | 8 |
| 1 | $2^1$ | 3 | 4 | 5 | 6 | $7^2$ | 8 | 9 | 10 | 13 | | 12 | 11 | | | | | | | | | | | | 9 |
| 1 | 2 | 3 | 4 | 5 | 6 | 12 | | | 10 | 7 | | 8 | $11^1$ | | 9 | | | | | | | | | | 10 |
| 1 | | 3 | 4 | 5 | 6 | | 8 | | 10 | 11 | | 2 | 7 | | 9 | | | | | | | | | | 11 |
| 1 | $2^3$ | 3 | 4 | 5 | $6^2$ | 12 | 8 | 9 | 10 | $7^1$ | | 13 | 11 | | 14 | | | | | | | | | | 12 |
| 1 | | | 4 | 5 | 6 | 7 | 8 | 9 | 10 | | | | 11 | | | | | | 2 | 3 | | | | | 13 |
| 1 | | | $4^1$ | 5 | 6 | 7 | 8 | 9 | 10 | | | 12 | 11 | | | | | | 2 | 3 | | | | | 14 |
| 1 | | 3 | 4 | 5 | 6 | 7 | 8 | $9^2$ | $10^3$ | | | 12 | 11 | | 13 | | 14 | $2^1$ | 2 | 3 | | | | | 15 |
| 1 | 2 | 3 | 4 | 5 | 6 | $7^1$ | | 9 | 10 | | | 8 | 11 | | 12 | | | | | | | | | | 16 |
| 1 | 2 | 3 | 4 | 5 | 6 | $7^1$ | | 9 | 10 | | | 8 | 11 | | 12 | | | | | | | | | | 17 |
| 1 | 2 | 3 | 4 | | 6 | $7^1$ | 8 | | 10 | | | 5 | $11^2$ | | 9 | | | | 12 | 13 | | | | | 18 |
| 1 | 2 | 3 | 4 | | 6 | 7 | 8 | | 10 | | | 5 | | | 9 | | | | 11 | | | | | | 19 |
| 1 | 2 | 3 | 4 | | 6 | 7 | 8 | | 10 | | | 5 | 11 | | 9 | | | | | | | | | | 20 |
| 1 | 12 | 3 | 4 | 5 | 6 | 7 | 8 | | 10 | | | $2^1$ | 11 | | $9^2$ | | | | 13 | | | | | | 21 |
| 1 | 2 | 3 | 4 | 5 | 7 | 12 | 8 | 9 | 10 | | | 6 | $11^1$ | | | | | | | | | | | | 22 |
| 1 | 2 | 3 | 4 | 5 | 6 | 7 | 8 | 9 | 10 | | | | | | | | | | 11 | | | | | | 23 |
| 1 | 2 | 3 | 4 | 5 | 6 | 7 | 8 | 9 | 10 | | | | | | | | | | 11 | | | | | | 24 |
| 1 | 2 | 3 | 4 | 5 | 6 | 7 | 8 | 9 | 10 | | | | | | | | | | $11^1$ | 12 | | | | | 25 |
| 1 | 2 | 3 | | 5 | 6 | 12 | 8 | 9 | 10 | | | 4 | | | $11^1$ | | | | 13 | $7^2$ | | | | | 26 |
| 1 | 2 | 3 | 4 | 5 | 6 | | 8 | 9 | 10 | | | 12 | | | | | | | 11 | | $7^1$ | | | | 27 |
| 1 | 2 | 3 | 4 | 5 | 6 | | 8 | 9 | 10 | | | $11^1$ | 13 | | | | | | 12 | | $7^2$ | | | | 28 |
| 1 | 2 | | 4 | 5 | 6 | 12 | 8 | 9 | 10 | | | 3 | $7^1$ | | | | | | 11 | | | | | | 29 |
| 1 | 2 | 3 | 4 | 5 | 6 | $7^1$ | 8 | $9^2$ | 10 | | | 12 | 13 | | | | | | 11 | | | | | | 30 |
| 1 | 2 | | 4 | 5 | 6 | 12 | 8 | 9 | 10 | $7^1$ | | 3 | | | | | | | 11 | | | | | | 31 |
| 1 | 2 | | 4 | 5 | 6 | | $8^3$ | 9 | 10 | $7^1$ | | 12 | 11 | | 13 | | $3^2$ | | 14 | | | | 12 | | 32 |
| 1 | 2 | | 4 | 5 | 6 | 7 | 8 | $9^1$ | 10 | | | 3 | 11 | | | | | | | | | | 12 | | 33 |
| 1 | 2 | | 4 | 5 | 6 | 7 | | | 10 | 12 | | 8 | 11 | | | | $3^2$ | | 13 | | | | $9^4$ | | 34 |
| 1 | 2 | | 4 | 5 | 6 | $7^1$ | | | 10 | 13 | | 8 | 11 | | 12 | | $3^2$ | | 14 | | | | $9^3$ | | 35 |
| 1 | 2 | | 4 | 5 | 6 | 12 | | 9 | 10 | | | 8 | $11^1$ | | | | 3 | | 7 | | | | | | 36 |
| 1 | 2 | | 4 | 5 | 6 | 9 | 8 | 12 | $10^2$ | | | 11 | | | | | $3^3$ | | 7 | 14 | 13 | | | | 37 |
| 1 | 2 | | 4 | 5 | 6 | | 8 | 9 | | | | 10 | | | 11 | | $7^1$ | | 3 | | | | 12 | | 38 |
| 1 | 2 | | 4 | 5 | 6 | | 8 | 9 | | | | 10 | $11^1$ | | | | 7 | | $3^2$ | | | | 12 | 13 | 39 |
| 1 | $2^1$ | $3^2$ | 4 | 5 | 6 | | 8 | 9 | | | | 10 | | | 11 | | | | 7 | | | | 12 | 13 | 40 |
| 1 | | 3 | 4 | $5^1$ | 6 | 12 | 8 | $9^1$ | 10 | | | 7 | | | | | 2 | | $11^2$ | | | 13 | 14 | | 41 |
| 1 | 2 | $3^2$ | | 5 | 6 | 12 | 8 | $9^1$ | 10 | | | 4 | | | 13 | | 7 | | 14 | | | | $11^3$ | | 42 |
| 1 | 2 | 3 | 4 | 5 | 6 | 12 | 8 | 9 | | | | 10 | | | | | | | 7 | | | | $11^1$ | | 43 |
| 1 | 2 | 3 | | 5 | 6 | 12 | 8 | $9^2$ | | | | 4 | | | 10 | | | | 7 | | | | $11^1$ | 13 | 44 |
| 1 | | 3 | | 5 | 6 | $7^1$ | 8 | 9 | 10 | 13 | | 4 | | | | | 2 | | 12 | | | | $11^2$ | | 45 |
| 1 | 12 | 3 | | 5 | 6 | $7^1$ | 8 | 9 | 10 | | | $4^1$ | | | | | 2 | | 13 | | | | 11 | | 46 |

**Coca-Cola Cup**

| | | | |
|---|---|---|---|
| First Round | Swindon T | (a) | 2-0 |
| | | (h) | 1-1 |
| Second Round | Sheffield U | (h) | 1-1 |
| | | (a) | 0-4 |

**FA Cup**

| | | | |
|---|---|---|---|
| First Round | Barnet | (a) | 2-1 |
| Second Round | Torquay U | (a) | 1-1 |
| | | (h) | 2-1 |
| Third Round | Sheffield W | (h) | 1-1 |
| | | (a) | 0-0 |

WEST BROMWICH ALBION 1997–98     *Back row (left to right):* Shane Nicholson, Dean Bennett, Lee Hughes, Paul Raven, Chris Adamson, Gary Germaine, Paul Crichton, Shaun Murphy, Graham Potter, Tony Dobson, Michael Rodosthenous.

*Middle row:* John Trewick (First Team Coach), Cyrille Regis (Coach), Dean Craven, Andy McDermott, Carl Tranter, Paul Mardon, Nigel Spink, Alan Miller, Kevin Kilbane, Anthony James, Darren Bowman, David Gilbert, Paul Mitchell (Physio), Richard O'Kelly (Youth Team Coach).

*Front row:* Stacy Coldicott, Daryl Burgess, Richard Sneekes, Andy Hunt, Paul Holmes, Ray Harford (Manager), David Smith, Ian Hamilton, Paul Peschisolido, Peter Butler, Bob Taylor.

# Division 1   WEST BROMWICH ALBION

*The Hawthorns, West Bromwich B71 4LF.* Telephone: (0121) 525 8888 (all Depts). Fax: (0121) 553 6634.
Registered Office: 'The Tom Silk Building', Halfords Lane, West Bromwich, West Midlands B71 4BR.
*Ground capacity:* 25,396 (all seated).

*Record attendance:* 64,815 v Arsenal, FA Cup 6th rd, 6 March 1937.

*Record receipts:* £270,000 v Nottingham F, Div 1, 3 May 1998.

*Pitch measurements:* 115yd × 75yd.

*President:* Sir F. A. Millichip. *Vice-President:* John G. Silk ᴌᴌ.ʙ (Lond).

*Chairman:* A. B. Hale. *Vice-Chairman:* C. M. Stapleton.

*Directors:* P. Thompson, J. W. Brandrick, B. Hurst, R. E. McGing, J. D. Wile (Chief Executive).

*Manager:* Denis Smith. *First Team Coach:* Malcolm Crosby.

*Coaches:* John Trewick, Cyrille Regis, Richard O'Kelly.

*Secretary:* Dr John J. Evans ʙᴀ, ᴘʜᴅ. (Wales).

*Club Statistician:* Tony Matthews. *Commercial Executive:* Tom Cardall.

*Year Formed:* 1878. *Turned Professional:* 1885. *Ltd Co.:* 1892. *plc:* 1996.

*Previous Name:* 1878–81, West Bromwich Strollers.

*Club Nicknames:* 'Throstles', 'Baggies', 'Albion'.

*Previous Grounds:* 1878, Coopers Hill; 1879, Dartmouth Park; 1881, Bunns Field, Walsall Street; 1882, Four Acres (Dartmouth Cricket Club); 1885, Stoney Lane; 1900, The Hawthorns.

*Foundation:* There is a well known story that when employees of Salter's Spring Works in West Bromwich decided to form a football club, they had to send someone to the nearby Association Football stronghold of Wednesbury to purchase a football. A weekly subscription of 2d (less than 1p) was imposed and the name of the new club was West Bromwich Strollers.

*First Football League game:* 8 September 1888, Football League, v Stoke (a) W 2-0 – Roberts; J. Horton, Green; E. Horton, Perry, Bayliss; Bassett, Woodhall (1), Hendry, Pearson, Wilson (1).

*Record League Victory:* 12–0 v Darwen, Division 1, 4 April 1892 – Reader; J. Horton, McCulloch; Reynolds (2), Perry, Groves; Bassett (3), McLeod, Nicholls (1), Pearson (4), Geddes (1). (1 og).

*Record Cup Victory:* 10–1 v Chatham (away), FA Cup 3rd rd, 2 March 1889 – Roberts; J. Horton, Green; Timmins (1), Charles Perry, E. Horton; Bassett (2), Perry (1), Bayliss (2), Pearson, Wilson (3). (1 og).

*Record Defeat:* 3–10 v Stoke C, Division 1, 4 February 1937.

*Most League Points (2 for a win):* 60, Division 1, 1919–20.

*Most League Points (3 for a win):* 85, Division 2, 1992–93.

*Most League Goals:* 105, Division 2, 1929–30.

*Highest League Scorer in Season:* William 'Ginger' Richardson, 39, Division 1, 1935–36.

*Most League Goals in Total Aggregate:* Tony Brown, 218, 1963–79.

*Most Capped Player:* Stuart Williams, 33 (43), Wales.

*Most League Appearances:* Tony Brown, 574, 1963–80.

*Record Transfer Fee Received:* £1,500,000 from Manchester U for Bryan Robson, October 1981.

*Record Transfer Fee Paid:* £1,250,000 to Preston NE for Kevin Kilbane, June 1997.

*Football League Record:* 1888 Founder Member of Football League; 1901–02 Division 2; 1902–04 Division 1; 1904–11 Division 2; 1911–27 Division 1; 1927–31 Division 2; 1931–38 Division 1; 1938–49 Division 2; 1949–73 Division 1; 1973–76 Division 2; 1976–86 Division 1; 1986–91 Division 2; 1991–92 Division 3; 1992–93 Division 2; 1993– Division 1.

*Honours: Football League:* Division 1 – Champions 1919–20; Runners-up 1924–25, 1953–54; Division 2 – Champions 1901–02, 1910–11; Runners-up 1930–31, 1948–49; Promoted to Division 1 1975–76 (3rd). *FA Cup:* Winners 1888, 1892, 1931, 1954, 1968; Runners-up 1886, 1887, 1895, 1912, 1935. *Football League Cup:* Winners 1966; Runners-up 1967, 1970. *European Competitions: European Cup-Winners' Cup:* 1968–69; *European Fairs Cup:* 1966–67; *UEFA Cup:* 1978–79, 1979–80, 1981–82.

*Colours:* Navy blue and white striped shirts, white shorts, blue and white stockings. *Change colours:* Red shirts with navy blue sleeves, white shorts with navy blue trim, red and navy blue hooped stockings.

**Did you know?**
West Bromwich Albion were the first to score over 100 First Division goals in a season. They achieved this feat in 1919-20 with 104.

## WEST BROMWICH ALBION 1997–98 LEAGUE RECORD

| Match No. | Date | | Venue | Opponents | Result | | H/T Score | Lg. Pos. | Goalscorers | Atten- dance |
|---|---|---|---|---|---|---|---|---|---|---|
| 1 | Aug | 9 | H | Tranmere R | W | 2-1 | 2-0 | — | Kilbane [37], Hunt [39] | 16,727 |
| 2 | | 16 | A | Crewe Alex | W | 3-2 | 1-1 | 2 | Hunt (pen) [25], Hughes 2 [85, 90] | 5234 |
| 3 | | 24 | H | Wolverhampton W | W | 1-0 | 1-0 | 2 | Curle (og) [16] | 21,511 |
| 4 | | 30 | A | Ipswich T | D | 1-1 | 0-1 | 3 | Sneekes [58] | 13,508 |
| 5 | Sept | 3 | A | Stoke C | D | 0-0 | 0-0 | — | | 17,500 |
| 6 | | 7 | H | Reading | W | 1-0 | 0-0 | 1 | Hunt [79] | 15,966 |
| 7 | | 13 | A | QPR | L | 0-2 | 0-1 | 3 | | 14,399 |
| 8 | | 20 | H | Swindon T | D | 0-0 | 0-0 | 3 | | 16,237 |
| 9 | | 27 | A | Bury | W | 3-1 | 2-0 | 2 | Peschisolido 3 [10, 45, 61] | 6439 |
| 10 | Oct | 4 | H | Oxford U | L | 1-2 | 1-1 | 4 | Hunt [7] | 15,819 |
| 11 | | 18 | A | Portsmouth | W | 3-2 | 1-0 | 3 | Mardon [7], Hunt 2 [49, 51] | 9158 |
| 12 | | 21 | A | Nottingham F | L | 0-1 | 0-0 | — | | 19,243 |
| 13 | | 25 | H | Sheffield U | W | 2-0 | 1-0 | 3 | Hunt [7], Hughes [87] | 17,311 |
| 14 | Nov | 1 | A | Bradford C | D | 0-0 | 0-0 | 5 | | 16,212 |
| 15 | | 4 | H | Norwich C | W | 1-0 | 0-0 | — | Hughes [85] | 13,949 |
| 16 | | 8 | H | Charlton Ath | W | 1-0 | 1-0 | 3 | Hunt [34] | 16,124 |
| 17 | | 15 | A | Port Vale | W | 2-1 | 0-0 | 3 | Hunt [57], Hamilton [68] | 11,124 |
| 18 | | 23 | H | Birmingham C | W | 1-0 | 0-0 | 2 | Sneekes [83] | 18,444 |
| 19 | | 29 | A | Middlesbrough | L | 0-1 | 0-1 | 3 | | 30,164 |
| 20 | Dec | 2 | H | Manchester C | L | 0-1 | 0-0 | — | | 17,904 |
| 21 | | 6 | H | Stockport Co | W | 3-2 | 1-0 | 3 | Sneekes [17], Hughes [78], Hunt [85] | 13,957 |
| 22 | | 13 | A | Sunderland | L | 0-2 | 0-1 | 4 | | 29,231 |
| 23 | | 20 | H | Huddersfield T | L | 0-2 | 0-0 | 5 | | 14,619 |
| 24 | | 26 | A | Reading | L | 1-2 | 0-2 | 6 | Kilbane [77] | 10,154 |
| 25 | | 28 | H | Stoke C | D | 1-1 | 0-0 | 7 | Hunt [62] | 17,690 |
| 26 | Jan | 9 | H | Tranmere R | D | 0-0 | 0-0 | — | | 8058 |
| 27 | | 17 | H | Crewe Alex | L | 0-1 | 0-1 | 7 | | 15,257 |
| 28 | | 27 | H | Ipswich T | L | 2-3 | 0-0 | — | Murphy [70], Flynn [72] | 12,403 |
| 29 | | 31 | A | Wolverhampton W | W | 1-0 | 0-0 | 7 | Hunt [72] | 28,244 |
| 30 | Feb | 7 | A | Swindon T | W | 2-0 | 1-0 | 7 | Carbon [40], Evans [81] | 9861 |
| 31 | | 14 | H | QPR | D | 1-1 | 0-1 | 6 | Hughes [75] | 19,143 |
| 32 | | 17 | A | Oxford U | L | 1-2 | 0-1 | — | Taylor [63] | 9412 |
| 33 | | 21 | H | Bury | D | 1-1 | 1-0 | 9 | Hughes [45] | 15,840 |
| 34 | | 24 | H | Portsmouth | L | 0-3 | 0-2 | — | | 12,757 |
| 35 | | 28 | A | Manchester C | L | 0-1 | 0-1 | 10 | | 28,460 |
| 36 | Mar | 3 | A | Charlton Ath | L | 0-5 | 0-1 | — | | 10,893 |
| 37 | | 7 | H | Bradford C | D | 1-1 | 0-1 | 10 | Burgess [90] | 13,281 |
| 38 | | 14 | A | Norwich C | D | 1-1 | 0-1 | 10 | Hughes [50] | 19,069 |
| 39 | | 21 | H | Port Vale | D | 2-2 | 1-0 | 10 | Flynn [24], Taylor [83] | 14,242 |
| 40 | | 28 | A | Birmingham C | L | 0-1 | 0-0 | 12 | | 23,260 |
| 41 | Apr | 4 | H | Middlesbrough | W | 2-1 | 1-0 | 10 | Quinn 2 (1 pen) [22 (p), 47] | 20,620 |
| 42 | | 11 | A | Stockport Co | L | 1-2 | 1-1 | 12 | Hughes [20] | 7943 |
| 43 | | 13 | H | Sunderland | D | 3-3 | 2-2 | 10 | Hughes 2 [2, 89], Kilbane [11] | 20,181 |
| 44 | | 18 | A | Huddersfield T | L | 0-1 | 0-1 | 12 | | 11,704 |
| 45 | | 25 | A | Sheffield U | W | 4-2 | 1-1 | 10 | Hunt [30], Hughes 2 [65, 78], Kilbane [72] | 21,248 |
| 46 | May | 3 | H | Nottingham F | D | 1-1 | 0-1 | 10 | Hughes (pen) [88] | 23,013 |

**Final League Position: 10**       1996–97 DIV1 16

## GOALSCORERS

*League (50):* Hughes 14 (1 pen), Hunt 13 (1 pen), Kilbane 4, Peschisolido 3, Sneekes 3, Flynn 2, Quinn 2 (1 pen), Taylor 2, Burgess 1, Carbon 1, Evans 1, Hamilton 1, Mardon 1, Murphy 1, own goal 1.
*Coca-Cola Cup (8):* Peschisolido 3, Hunt 1, McDermott 1, Raven 1, Sneekes 1 (pen), Taylor 1.
*FA Cup (3):* Sneekes 2, Kilbane 1.

| Miller A 41 | McDermott A 13 | Nicholson S 16 | Sneekes R 37+5 | Mardon P 18 | Murphy S 14+3 | Flynn S 30+5 | Butler P 31+3 | Peschisolido P 6+2 | Hunt A 38 | Kibane K 42+1 | Hamilton I 29+8 | Hughes L 18+19 | Coldicott S 7+15 | Holmes P 30 | Smith D 18+4 | Raven P 8 | Taylor B 11+4 | Burgess D 27 | Thomas J 1+2 | Dobson T 6+5 | Evans M 2+8 | Carbon M 16 | Carr F 1+3 | Quinn J 12+1 | Potter G 4+1 | Qualley B —+5 | Gilbert D —+4 | Van Blerk J 8 | Beesley P 8 | Nicol S 9 | Adamson C 3 | Crichton P 2 | Match No. |
|---|---|---|---|---|---|---|---|---|---|---|---|---|---|---|---|---|---|---|---|---|---|---|---|---|---|---|---|---|---|---|---|---|---|
| 1 | 2 | 3 | 4¹ | 5 | 6 | 7 | 8 | 9² | 10 | 11³ | 12 | 13 | 14 | | | | | | | | | | | | | | | | | | | | 1 |
| 1 | | 3 | 4¹ | 5 | 6 | 7³ | 8 | 9² | 10 | 11 | 12 | 13 | | 2 | | 14 | | | | | | | | | | | | | | | | | 2 |
| 1 | | 3 | 4 | 5 | | 7 | 8 | 9² | 10 | 11 | 12 | 13 | | 2 | | | | 6 | | | | | | | | | | | | | | | 3 |
| 1 | | 3 | 4² | 5 | | 7 | 8 | | 10¹ | 11³ | 12 | | 13 | 2 | | 14 | | 6 | 9 | | | | | | | | | | | | | | 4 |
| 1 | | 3 | 4 | | | 7 | 8 | | 10¹ | | 12 | | | 2 | 11 | | | 6 | 9² | 5 | 13 | | | | | | | | | | | | 5 |
| 1 | | 3 | 4¹ | | | 7 | 8 | | 10 | | 12 | | | 2 | 11 | | | 6 | 9² | 5 | 13 | | | | | | | | | | | | 6 |
| 1 | | 3 | 4 | | | 7¹ | 8³ | | 10 | 13 | 12 | | | 2 | 11 | | | 6 | | 5 | 9² | 14 | | | | | | | | | | | 7 |
| 1 | 2 | | 4 | | | 7 | | 12 | 10 | 11² | | 8 | 13 | | | | 3 | 6 | 9¹ | 5 | | | | | | | | | | | | | 8 |
| 1 | 2 | | 4 | | | 7 | | 9¹ | 10 | 11 | 8 | 12 | | | | | 3 | 6 | | 5 | | | | | | | | | | | | | 9 |
| 1 | 2¹ | | 4 | | | 7 | | 9 | 10 | 11³ | 12 | 8 | 13 | | | | 3 | 6 | | 5 | | | | | | | | | | | | | 10 |
| 1 | | | 4 | | 6 | 7¹ | 12 | 9² | 10 | 11³ | | 8 | 13 | 2 | | | 3 | | | 5 | | | | | | | | | | | | | 11 |
| 1 | | | 4² | | 6 | | | 9 | 10 | 11³ | 12 | 8¹ | 13 | 7 | | | 3 | 2 | | 5 | 14 | | | | | | | | | | | | 12 |
| 1 | | | 4¹ | | 6 | 7 | 9 | | 10 | 11² | 12 | 8 | 13 | 2 | | | 3 | | | 5 | | | | | | | | | | | | | 13 |
| 1 | | | 4 | | 6 | 7¹ | 9 | | 10² | 11³ | 12 | 8 | 13 | 2 | | | 3 | | | 5 | 14 | | | | | | | | | | | | 14 |
| 1 | | | 4 | | 6 | 7¹ | 9 | | 10 | 11² | 12 | 8 | 13 | 2 | | | 3 | | | | | 5 | | | | | | | | | | | 15 |
| 1 | | | 4² | | 6 | 7¹ | 9 | | 10 | 11 | 12 | 8 | 13 | 2 | | | 3 | | | 5 | | | | | | | | | | | | | 16 |
| 1 | | | 4 | | 6¹ | 7 | 9 | | 10 | | | 8 | 11 | 2 | | | 3 | | | 5 | 12 | | | | | | | | | | | | 17 |
| 1 | | | 4 | | 6 | 7¹ | 9 | | 10 | 11 | 12 | 8 | | 2 | | | 3 | | | 5 | | | | | | | | | | | | | 18 |
| 1 | | | 4¹ | | 6 | 7 | 9 | | 10 | 11 | 12 | 8 | | 2¹ | | | 3 | | | 5 | 13 | | | | | | | | | | | | 19 |
| 1 | | | 4² | | 6 | 7 | 9 | | 10 | 11 | 12 | 8 | | 2¹ | | | 3 | | | 5 | 13 | | | | | | | | | | | | 20 |
| 1 | | | 4¹ | | 6 | 7 | 12 | | 10 | 11³ | | 8 | 13 | 2 | | 14 | 3 | | | 5 | 9² | | | | | | | | | | | | 21 |
| 1 | 3 | | 4¹ | | 6 | 7² | 9 | | 10 | 11 | 12 | 8 | 13 | 2 | | | 3 | | | 5 | | | | | | | | | | | | | 22 |
| 1 | 2 | | 4 | | 6 | 7 | | | 10 | 11¹ | 12 | 8 | 13 | | | | | 9² | | 5 | 3³ | 14 | | | | | | | | | | | 23 |
| 1 | 2 | | 4 | | 6² | 7¹ | 9³ | | 10 | 11 | 12 | 8 | | | | | 3 | | | 5 | 13 | 14 | | | | | | | | | | | 24 |
| 1 | 2 | | 4 | | 6 | 7 | | | 10 | 11 | 8¹ | 9 | 12² | | | | 3 | | | 5 | 13 | | | | | | | | | | | | 25 |
| 1 | 3 | | 4 | 5 | 12 | 7 | | | 10 | 11¹ | 8 | 9² | | 2 | | | | 6 | | 13 | | | | | | | | | | | | | 26 |
| 1 | 3 | | 4 | 5 | 12 | 9² | | | 10 | 11 | 8¹ | 13 | | 2 | | | | 6 | 7 | | | | | | | | | | | | | | 27 |
| 1 | 3 | | 4 | 5 | 7¹ | 12 | | | 10 | 11 | 8 | 9 | | 2 | | | | 6 | | | | | | | | | | | | | | | 28 |
| 1 | 3 | | 4¹ | 5 | | 7 | | | 10 | 11 | 8 | 9² | 12 | 2 | | | | 6 | | 13 | | | | | | | | | | | | | 29 |
| 1 | 3 | | 4 | 5 | | 7 | | | 10¹ | 11 | 8 | 9 | | 2 | | | | 6 | | 12 | | | | | | | | | | | | | 30 |
| 1 | 3 | | 4 | 5 | | 7 | | | 10 | 11 | | 9 | | 2 | | | | 6 | 8¹ | 12 | | | | | | | | | | | | | 31 |
| 1 | 3 | | 4 | 5 | | 7¹ | | | 10² | 11 | | 9 | 12 | 2 | | | | 6 | 13 | 8 | | | | | | | | | | | | | 32 |
| 1 | 3 | | 4² | 5 | | 7¹ | | | 11 | | 8 | 9 | 12 | 2 | | | | 6 | 13 | | | 10 | | | | | | | | | | | 33 |
| 1 | | | 5 | | | 7 | | | 11 | 10² | 9¹ | 12 | | 2 | | | | 8 | | | | | 6 | 13 | 4 | 3 | | | | | | | 34 |
| 1 | | | 12 | | | 7 | | | 11 | 10³ | 8¹ | | | 2 | | | | 9 | | 5 | | | 6 | | 4² | 3 | 13 | 14 | | | | | 35 |
| 1 | | | 12 | | | 7³ | | | 11² | 10 | 8 | | | 2 | | | | 9 | | 5 | | | 6 | 13 | 4¹ | 3 | 14 | | | | | | 36 |
| 1 | | | 7 | | | | | | 11 | 8 | 10 | 4¹ | | 2 | | | | 9 | | 5 | | | 6² | | | 3 | 12 | 13 | | | | | 37 |
| 1 | 4 | | 7 | | | | | | 11 | 12 | 9 | | | 2¹ | | 13 | | 5 | | | | | 10² | | | 3 | | 6 | 8 | | | | 38 |
| 1 | 4 | | 7 | | | | 12 | | 11³ | 2¹ | 9 | | | 13 | | | | 6 | | | | | 10² | 14 | | 3 | | 5 | 8 | | | | 39 |
| 1 | 4 | 3 | 7¹ | | | 9² | | | 11 | 12 | | | | 2 | | | | 6 | | | | | 10 | 13 | | | | 5 | 8 | | | | 40 |
| 1 | 2 | 12 | 4 | | | 9¹ | 11 | | 10² | 13 | | | | | | | | 6 | | | | | 7 | | | | | 3 | 5 | 8 | | | 41 |
| | 2 | 12 | 4 | | | 9¹ | 11 | | 10 | | | | | | | | | 6 | | | | | 7 | | | | | 3 | 5 | 8 | | 1 | 42 |
| | 2 | 12 | 13 | 4 | | 9¹ | 11 | | 10 | | | | | | | | | 6 | | | | | 7 | | | | | 3 | 5 | 8 | 1 | | 43 |
| | 2 | 12 | 13 | 4 | | 9 | 11 | | 10 | | | | | | | | | 6² | | | | | 7 | | | | | 3 | 5 | 8¹ | 1 | | 44 |
| | 2 | 12 | 5 | 4 | | 9 | 11² | | 10³ | | | | | | | | | 6 | | | | | 7¹ | 13 | 14 | | | 3 | | 8 | 1 | | 45 |
| | 2 | 9 | 12 | 4² | | | 11 | | 10 | | | | | | | | | 6 | | | | | 7 | 13 | | | | 3 | 5¹ | 8 | 1 | | 46 |

**Coca-Cola Cup**

| First Round | Cambridge U | (a) | 1-1 |
| | | (h) | 2-1 |
| Second Round | Luton T | (a) | 1-1 |
| | | (h) | 4-2 |
| Third Round | Liverpool | (h) | 0-2 |

**FA Cup**

| Third Round | Stoke C | (h) | 3-1 |
| Fourth Round | Aston Villa | (a) | 0-4 |

WEST HAM UNITED 1997-98 *Back row (left to right):* Tim Breacker, Ian Pearce, Iain Dowie, Ludek Miklosko, Les Sealey, Craig Forrest, John Hartson, Richard Hall. *Middle row:* Eyal Berkovic, Keith Rowland, Andrew Impey, Samassi Abou, David Terrier, Paul Kitson, Steve Potts, Stan Lazaridis, Scott Mean. *Front row:* Frank Lampard, Rio Ferdinand, John Moncur, Julian Dicks, Steve Lomas, Ian Bishop, David Unsworth.

# FA Premiership    **WEST HAM UNITED**

*Boleyn Ground, Green Street, Upton Park, London E13 9AZ.* Telephone General Office: (0181) 548 2748. Ticket Office: (0181) 548 2700. Merchandise Shop: (0181) 548 2722. Fax: (0181) 548 2758. Membership Office: (0181) 548 2727. Promotions: (0181) 548 2777. Dial-a-seat: (0181) 548 2700. Football in the Community: (0181) 548 2707. Clubcall: 0891 121165.

*Ground capacity:* 26,012.

*Record attendance:* 42,322 v Tottenham H, Division 1, 17 October 1970.

*Record receipts:* £339,420 gross v Liverpool, FA Premier League, 22 November 1995.

*Pitch measurements:* 112yd × 72yd.

*Chairman:* T. W. Brown FCIS, AII, FCCA. *Vice-Chairman:* M. W. Cearns ACIB.

*Directors:* C. J. Warner, P. J. Storrie, N. Igoe, P. Aldridge.

*Manager:* Harry Redknapp. *Assistant Manager:* Frank Lampard. *Coaches:* Roger Cross, Tony Carr.

*Physio:* John Green BSC, MCSP, SRP.

*Football Secretary:* Neil Harrison. *Stadium Manager:* John Ball.

*Year Formed:* 1895. *Turned Professional:* 1900. *Ltd Co.:* 1900.

*Previous Name:* Thames Ironworks FC, 1895–1900.

*Club Nickname:* 'The Hammers'.

*Previous Ground:* Memorial Recreation Ground, Canning Town: 1904 Boleyn Ground.

*Foundation:* Thames Ironworks FC was formed by employees of this shipbuilding yard in 1895 and entered the FA Cup in their initial season at Chatham and the London League in their second. Short of funds, the club was wound up in June 1900 and relaunched a month later as West Ham United. Connection with the Ironworks was not finally broken until four years later.

*First Football League game:* 30 August 1919, Division 2, v Lincoln C (h) D 1-1 – Hufton; Cope, Lee; Lane, Fenwick, McCrae; D. Smith, Moyes (1), Puddefoot, Morris, Bradshaw.

*Record League Victory:* 8–0 v Rotherham U, Division 2, 8 March 1958 – Gregory; Bond, Wright; Malcolm, Brown, Lansdowne; Grice, Smith (2), Keeble (2), Dick (4), Musgrove. 8–0 v Sunderland, Division 1, 19 October 1968 – Ferguson; Bonds, Charles; Peters, Stephenson, Moore (1); Redknapp, Boyce, Brooking (1), Hurst (6), Sissons.

*Record Cup Victory:* 10–0 v Bury, League Cup 2nd rd (2nd leg), 25 October 1983 – Parkes; Stewart (1), Walford, Bonds (Orr), Martin (1), Devonshire (2), Allen, Cottee (4), Swindlehurst, Brooking (2), Pike.

*Record Defeat:* 2–8 v Blackburn R, Division 1, 26 December 1963.

*Most League Points (2 for a win):* 66, Division 2, 1980–81.

*Most League Points (3 for a win):* 88, Division 1, 1992–93.

*Most League Goals:* 101, Division 2, 1957–58.

*Highest League Scorer in Season:* Vic Watson, 42, Division 1, 1929–30.

*Most League Goals in Total Aggregate:* Vic Watson, 298, 1920–35.

*Most Capped Player:* Bobby Moore, 108, England.

*Most League Appearances:* Billy Bonds, 663, 1967–88.

*Record Transfer Fee Received:* £4,250,000 from Everton for Slaven Bilic, May 1997.

*Record Transfer Fee Paid:* £3,200,000 to Arsenal for John Hartson, February 1997.

*Football League Record:* 1919 Elected to Division 2; 1923–32 Division 1; 1932–58 Division 2; 1958–78 Division 1; 1978–81 Division 2; 1981–89 Division 1; 1989–91 Division 2; 1991–93 Division 1; 1993– FA Premier League.

*Honours: Football League:* Division 1 best season: 3rd, 1985–86; Division 2 – Champions 1957–58, 1980–81; Runners-up 1922–23, 1990–91. *FA Cup:* Winners 1964, 1975, 1980; Runners-up 1923. *Football League Cup:* Runners-up 1966, 1981. **European Competitions:** *European Cup-Winners' Cup:* 1964–65 (winners), 1965–66, 1975–76 (runners-up), 1980–81.

*Colours:* Claret shirts with blue sleeves, white shorts, light blue with claret hooped stockings. *Change colours:* All white.

**Did you know?**
In the 1972-73 season Bryan 'Pop' Robson scored two goals in a match eight times, all on Saturdays. He did manage one hat-trick against Southampton on Good Friday.

## WEST HAM UNITED 1997–98 LEAGUE RECORD

| Match No. | Date | Venue | Opponents | Result | H/T Score | Lg. Pos. | Goalscorers | Attendance |
|---|---|---|---|---|---|---|---|---|
| 1 | Aug 9 | A | Barnsley | W 2-1 | 0-1 | — | Hartson [53], Lampard [76] | 18,667 |
| 2 | 13 | H | Tottenham H | W 2-1 | 1-0 | — | Hartson [4], Berkovic [70] | 25,354 |
| 3 | 23 | A | Everton | L 1-2 | 1-0 | 7 | Watson (og) [23] | 34,356 |
| 4 | 27 | A | Coventry C | D 1-1 | 0-1 | — | Kitson [64] | 18,291 |
| 5 | 30 | H | Wimbledon | W 3-1 | 0-0 | 3 | Hartson [48], Rieper [54], Berkovic [55] | 24,516 |
| 6 | Sept 13 | A | Manchester U | L 1-2 | 1-1 | 6 | Hartson [14] | 55,068 |
| 7 | 20 | H | Newcastle U | L 0-1 | 0-1 | 6 | | 25,884 |
| 8 | 24 | A | Arsenal | L 0-4 | 0-4 | — | | 38,012 |
| 9 | 27 | H | Liverpool | W 2-1 | 1-0 | 7 | Hartson [15], Berkovic [65] | 25,908 |
| 10 | Oct 4 | A | Southampton | L 0-3 | 0-0 | 10 | | 15,212 |
| 11 | 18 | H | Bolton W | W 3-0 | 0-0 | 8 | Berkovic [67], Hartson 2 [77, 90] | 24,864 |
| 12 | 27 | A | Leicester C | L 1-2 | 0-1 | — | Berkovic [58] | 20,201 |
| 13 | Nov 9 | H | Chelsea | L 1-2 | 0-0 | 14 | Hartson (pen) [85] | 33,256 |
| 14 | 23 | A | Leeds U | L 1-3 | 0-0 | 15 | Lampard [65] | 29,447 |
| 15 | 29 | H | Aston Villa | W 2-1 | 1-0 | 12 | Hartson 2 [18, 48] | 24,976 |
| 16 | Dec 3 | H | Crystal Palace | W 4-1 | 2-1 | — | Hartson [31], Berkovic [45], Unsworth [48], Lomas [71] | 23,335 |
| 17 | 6 | A | Derby Co | L 0-2 | 0-1 | 11 | | 29,300 |
| 18 | 13 | H | Sheffield W | W 1-0 | 0-0 | 10 | Kitson [68] | 24,344 |
| 19 | 20 | A | Blackburn R | L 0-3 | 0-1 | 10 | | 21,653 |
| 20 | 26 | H | Coventry C | W 1-0 | 1-0 | 8 | Kitson [17] | 22,477 |
| 21 | 28 | A | Wimbledon | W 2-1 | 1-0 | 8 | Kimble (og) [31], Kitson [54] | 22,087 |
| 22 | Jan 10 | H | Barnsley | W 6-0 | 2-0 | 8 | Lampard [5], Abou 2 [31, 52], Moncur [57], Hartson [67], Lazaridis [90] | 23,714 |
| 23 | 17 | A | Tottenham H | L 0-1 | 0-1 | 8 | | 30,284 |
| 24 | 31 | H | Everton | D 2-2 | 1-1 | 8 | Sinclair 2 [10, 48] | 25,905 |
| 25 | Feb 7 | A | Newcastle U | W 1-0 | 1-0 | 8 | Lazaridis [16] | 36,736 |
| 26 | 21 | A | Bolton W | D 1-1 | 0-0 | 9 | Sinclair [65] | 25,000 |
| 27 | Mar 2 | H | Arsenal | D 0-0 | 0-0 | — | | 25,717 |
| 28 | 11 | H | Manchester U | D 1-1 | 1-0 | — | Sinclair [6] | 25,892 |
| 29 | 14 | H | Chelsea | W 2-1 | 0-0 | 8 | Sinclair [69], Unsworth [75] | 25,829 |
| 30 | 30 | H | Leeds U | W 3-0 | 2-0 | — | Hartson [8], Abou [23], Pearce [68] | 24,107 |
| 31 | Apr 4 | A | Aston Villa | L 0-2 | 0-0 | 7 | | 39,372 |
| 32 | 11 | H | Derby Co | D 0-0 | 0-0 | 7 | | 25,155 |
| 33 | 13 | A | Sheffield W | D 1-1 | 1-0 | 8 | Berkovic [7] | 28,036 |
| 34 | 18 | H | Blackburn R | W 2-1 | 2-1 | 6 | Hartson 2 [7, 28] | 24,733 |
| 35 | 25 | A | Southampton | L 2-4 | 1-1 | 7 | Sinclair [42], Lomas [82] | 25,878 |
| 36 | May 2 | A | Liverpool | L 0-5 | 0-4 | 10 | | 44,414 |
| 37 | 5 | A | Crystal Palace | D 3-3 | 1-1 | — | Curcic (og) [4], Omoyimni 2 [68, 89] | 19,129 |
| 38 | 10 | H | Leicester C | W 4-3 | 2-0 | 8 | Lampard [15], Abou 2 [31, 74], Sinclair [65] | 25,781 |
| **Final League Position: 8** | | | | 1996–97 PREM 14 | | | | |

### GOALSCORERS

*League (56):* Hartson 15 (1 pen), Berkovic 7, Sinclair 7, Abou 5, Kitson 4, Lampard 4, Lazaridis 2, Lomas 2, Omoyimni 2, Unsworth 2, Moncur 1, Pearce 1, Rieper 1, own goals 3.
*Coca-Cola Cup (11):* Hartson 6, Lampard 4, Abou 1.
*FA Cup (9):* Hartson 3, Berkovic 2, Kitson 1, Lampard 1, Lomas 1, Pearce 1.

| Miklosko L 13 | Breacker T 18+1 | Hughes M 2+3 | Potts S 14+9 | Ferdinand R 35 | Rieper M 5 | Moncur J 17+3 | Berkovic E 34+1 | Kitson P 12+1 | Hartson J 32 | Lomas S 33 | Lazaridis S 27+1 | Lampard F 27+4 | Terrier D —+1 | Dowie I 7+5 | Unsworth D 32 | Pearce I 30 | Bishop I 3 | Impey A 19 | Moore I —+1 | Forrest C 13 | Rowland K 6+1 | Abou S 12+7 | Alves P —+4 | Hodges L —+2 | Sinclair T 14 | Lama B 12 | Mean S —+3 | Omoyinmi E 1+4 | Match No. |
|---|---|---|---|---|---|---|---|---|---|---|---|---|---|---|---|---|---|---|---|---|---|---|---|---|---|---|---|---|---|
| 1 | $2^1$ | 3 | 4 | 5 | 6 | 7 | $8^2$ | $9^1$ | 10 | 11 | 12 | 13 | 14 | | | | | | | | | | | | | | | | 1 |
| 1 | 2 | 12 | 4 | 5 | 6 | $7^2$ | 8 | $9^1$ | $10^2$ | 11 | | 3 | 13 | | 14 | | | | | | | | | | | | | | 2 |
| 1 | $2^3$ | 12 | | 5 | 6 | $7^1$ | $8^2$ | 9 | 10 | 11 | | 3 | 13 | | 14 | 4 | | | | | | | | | | | | | 3 |
| 1 | 2 | | | 5 | 6 | 7 | 8 | $9^1$ | 10 | 11 | | 3 | | | 12 | 4 | | | | | | | | | | | | | 4 |
| 1 | 2 | | | 5 | 6 | 7 | 10 | | 9 | 11 | 3 | | | | 8 | 4 | | | | | | | | | | | | | 5 |
| 1 | 2 | 3 | 4 | 5 | | $7^1$ | 8 | 9 | 10 | 11 | | 12 | | | 6 | | | | | | | | | | | | | | 6 |
| 1 | $2^1$ | 12 | 13 | 5 | | $10^2$ | | | 9 | 11 | 3 | 7 | | | 8 | 4 | 6 | | | | | | | | | | | | 7 |
| 1 | 2 | | 12 | $5^1$ | | | | | 9 | 11 | 3 | 7 | | | 8 | 4 | 6 | 10 | | | | | | | | | | | 8 |
| 1 | 2 | | 5 | | | 10 | | | 9 | 11 | | 7 | | | 8 | 4 | 6 | 3 | | | | | | | | | | | 9 |
| 1 | 2 | | 5 | | | 10 | | | 9 | 11 | | | | | $8^1$ | 4 | 6 | 7 | 3 | 12 | | | | | | | | | 10 |
| | 2 | | | 5 | | 7 | 10 | | 9 | 6 | | 11 | | | 8 | 4 | | | | 1 | 3 | | | | | | | | 11 |
| | 2 | | | 5 | | 7 | 10 | | 9 | 6 | | 11 | | | 8 | 4 | | | | 1 | 3 | | | | | | | | 12 |
| | | 12 | | 5 | | $7^2$ | 10 | | 9 | 11 | | 8 | | | $4^1$ | 6 | | 2 | | 1 | 3 | 13 | | | | | | | 13 |
| 1 | 2 | | | 5 | | | | | 9 | 11 | 12 | $10^1$ | 7 | 13 | 4 | 6 | | 3 | | | | $8^2$ | | | | | | | 14 |
| 1 | 2 | | | 5 | | 7 | 10 | | 9 | 11 | | | | | 4 | 6 | | 3 | | | | $8^1$ | 12 | | | | | | 15 |
| | 2 | | | 5 | | 7 | 10 | | 9 | 11 | | $3^1$ | | | 4 | 6 | | | | 1 | 12 | $8^1$ | 13 | | | | | | 16 |
| 1 | $2^1$ | | | 5 | | 7 | 10 | | 9 | 11 | | $3^2$ | | 8 | 4 | 6 | | | | | | 12 | 13 | | | | | | 17 |
| | | | 12 | 5 | | | 8 | $9^2$ | 10 | 11 | | 7 | | | 4 | 6 | | $2^1$ | | 1 | 3 | 13 | | | | | | | 18 |
| | | | | 5 | | | 8 | $9^1$ | 10 | 11 | | 7 | | | 4 | 6 | | 2 | | 1 | 3 | 12 | | | | | | | 19 |
| | | | 12 | 5 | | | $8^1$ | 9 | 10 | 11 | 3 | 7 | | | 4 | 6 | | 2 | | 1 | | | | | | | | | 20 |
| | 2 | | | 5 | | | 10 | 9 | | 11 | 3 | 8 | | | 4 | 6 | | 7 | | 1 | | | | | | | | | 21 |
| | 2 | | | 5 | | | 12 | $10^2$ | 9 | | 3 | 8 | | | 4 | 6 | | $7^1$ | | 1 | | | | | 11 | 13 | | | 22 |
| | 2 | | | 5 | | 7 | $10^2$ | | 9 | | $3^1$ | 8 | | 12 | 4 | 6 | | | | 1 | | | | | 11 | 13 | | | 23 |
| | 2 | 4 | | 5 | | 7 | 10 | | 9 | | 3 | | | 8 | | 6 | | | | | | | 12 | | $11^1$ | | | | 24 |
| | 2 | | 12 | 5 | | $7^1$ | 8 | 9 | $9^1$ | | 3 | | | 13 | 4 | 6 | | | | 1 | | | | | 11 | | | | 25 |
| | | | | 5 | | 7 | 10 | | 9 | | 3 | 8 | | | 4 | 6 | | 2 | | 1 | | | | | 11 | | | | 26 |
| | $2^1$ | | 12 | | | | 10 | | 9 | | 4 | 3 | | | 8 | 6 | 5 | 7 | | | | | | | 11 | 1 | | | 27 |
| | | 4 | | 5 | | | 10 | | | | 3 | 7 | | | 8 | 6 | | 2 | | | | 9 | | | 11 | 1 | | | 28 |
| | | | 12 | 5 | | | 10 | | | | 3 | 8 | | 7 | 4 | 6 | | $2^1$ | | | | 9 | | | 11 | 1 | | | 29 |
| | 2 | | | 5 | | 7 | 10 | | | | 3 | $8^1$ | | | 4 | 6 | | | | | | $9^2$ | | | 11 | 1 | 12 | 13 | 30 |
| | $2^1$ | | | 5 | | 7 | 10 | 9 | | | 3 | 8 | | | 4 | 6 | | | | 1 | | 12 | | | 11 | | | | 31 |
| | | | 12 | 5 | | 7 | $10^2$ | 8 | 9 | | 3 | | | 13 | 4 | $6^1$ | | | | 1 | | $2^3$ | | 14 | 11 | | | | 32 |
| | | | | 5 | | 7 | 10 | | 9 | 11 | 3 | | | | 4 | 6 | | 2 | | | | $8^1$ | | | | 1 | 12 | | 33 |
| | | | 12 | 5 | | 7 | $10^1$ | | 9 | | 3 | | | | 4 | 6 | | 2 | | | | | | | 11 | 1 | | | 34 |
| | | | $4^1$ | 5 | | 7 | 10 | 12 | | | 3 | | | | | 6 | | 2 | | | | 9 | | | 11 | 1 | | | 35 |
| | | | | 5 | | $7^1$ | $10^1$ | | $9^2$ | 6 | 3 | 8 | | | 4 | 2 | | | | | | 12 | | | 11 | 1 | 13 | 14 | 36 |
| | | | | 5 | | 7 | 10 | | 9 | 6 | 3 | | | | 4 | 2 | | | | | | $8^1$ | | | 11 | 1 | 12 | | 37 |
| | | | | 5 | | 7 | $10^1$ | | 9 | | 3 | | | | 4 | 6 | | | | | | | | | 11 | 1 | 12 | 2 | 38 |

| Coca-Cola Cup | | | | | FA Cup | | | | |
|---|---|---|---|---|---|---|---|---|---|
| Second Round | Huddersfield T | (a) | 0-1 | | Third Round | Emley | (h) | 2-1 | |
| | | (h) | 3-0 | | Fourth Round | Manchester C | (a) | 2-1 | |
| Third Round | Aston Villa | (h) | 3-0 | | Fifth Round | Blackburn R | (h) | 2-2 | |
| Fourth Round | Walsall | (h) | 4-1 | | | | (a) | 1-1 | |
| Fifth Round | Arsenal | (h) | 1-2 | | Sixth Round | Arsenal | (a) | 1-1 | |
| | | | | | | | (h) | 1-1 | |

WIGAN ATHLETIC 1997–98  *Back row (left to right):* Tony Black, David Lowe, Charlie Bishop, Ian Kilford, Pat McGibbon, Neil Fitzhenry, Gavin Johnson, Brendan O'Connell. *Middle row:* Simon Farnworth (Physio), Steve Morgan, Graeme Jones, Lee Butler, Andy Saville, Roy Carroll, Paul Rogers, Scott Green, John Benson (Assistant Manager). *Front row:* Paul Warne, David Lee, Kevin Sharp, John Deehan (Manager), Colin Greenall, Roberto Martinez, Graham Lancashire.

# Division 2     **WIGAN ATHLETIC**

***Springfield Park, Wigan WN6 7BA.*** Telephone: (01942) 244433. Fax: (01942) 494654. Commercial Dept: (01942) 243067. Latics Clubcall: 0891 121655. Football in the Community: (01942) 824599.

***Ground capacity:*** 7290.

***Record attendance:*** 27,526 v Hereford U, 12 December 1953.

***Record receipts:*** £40,577 v Leeds U, FA Cup 6th rd, 15 March 1987.

***Pitch measurements:*** 114yd × 72yd.

***President:*** S. Jackson.

***Chairman:*** David Whelan.

***Directors:*** D. Whelan, J. Winstanley, D. Sharpe, P. Williams, B. Ashcroft.

***Chief Executive/Secretary:*** Mrs Brenda Spencer. ***Assistant Secretary:*** Stuart Hayton.

***Football Co-Ordinator:*** Frank Lord.

***Manager:***     ***Assistant Manager:*** John Benson. ***Coach:*** Alex Cribley. ***Safety Officer:*** David Johnson. ***Groundsman:*** David Pinch.

***Year Formed:*** 1932.

***Club Nickname:*** 'The Latics'.

***Foundation:*** Following the demise of Wigan Borough and their resignation from the Football League in 1931, a public meeting was called in Wigan at the Queen's Hall in May 1932 at which a new club Wigan Athletic, was founded in the hope of carrying on in the Football League. With this in mind, they bought Springfield Park for £2,250, but failed to gain admission to the Football League until 46 years later.

***First Football League game:*** 19 August 1978, Division 4, v Hereford U (a) D 0-0 – Brown; Hinnigan, Gore, Gillibrand, Ward, Davids, Corrigan, Purdie, Houghton, Wilkie, Wright.

***Record League Victory:*** 7–1 v Scarborough, Division 3, 11 March 1997 – Butler L, Butler J, Sharp (Morgan), Greenall, McGibbon (Biggins (1)), Martinez (1), Diaz (2), Jones (Lancashire (1)), Lowe (2), Rogers, Kilford.

***Record Cup Victory:*** 6–0 v Carlisle U (away), FA Cup 1st rd, 24 November 1934 – Caunce; Robinson, Talbot; Paterson, Watson, Tufnell; Armes (2), Robson (1), Roberts (2), Felton, Scott (1).

***Record Defeat:*** 1–6 v Bristol R, Division 3, 3 March 1990.

***Most League Points (2 for a win):*** 55, Division 4, 1978–79 and 1979–80.

***Most League Points (3 for a win):*** 91, Division 4, 1981–82.

***Most League Goals:*** 84, Division 3, 1996–97.

***Highest League Scorer in Season:*** Graeme Jones, 31, Division 3, 1996–97.

***Most League Goals in Total Aggregate:*** David Lowe, 65, 1982–87; 1995–98.

***Most Capped Player:*** Roy Carroll, 1, Northern Ireland, Pat McGibbon, 1, Northern Ireland.

***Most League Appearances:*** Kevin Langley, 317, 1981–86, 1990–94.

***Record Transfer Fee Received:*** £329,000 from Coventry C for Peter Atherton, August 1991.

***Record Transfer Fee Paid:*** £350,000 to Hull C for Roy Carroll, April 1997.

***Football League Record:*** 1978 Elected to Division 4; 1982–92 Division 3; 1992–93 Division 2; 1993–97 Division 3; 1997– Division 2.

***Honours:*** *Football League:* Division 3 Champions, 1996–97; Division 4 – Promoted (3rd) 1981–82. *FA Cup:* 6th rd 1987. *Football League Cup:* best season: 4th rd, 1982. *Freight Rover Trophy:* Winners 1985.

***Colours:*** Blue shirts with white side panel, blue shorts and stockings. ***Change colours:*** White shirts with green side panel, white shorts and stockings.

**Did you know?**
Jorg Smeets, who joined Wigan Athletic from Dutch football in 1997-98 wore boots size only three and a half.

## WIGAN ATHLETIC 1997–98 LEAGUE RECORD

| Match No. | Date | | Venue | Opponents | Result | H/T Score | Lg. Pos. | Goalscorers | Atten-dance |
|---|---|---|---|---|---|---|---|---|---|
| 1 | Aug | 9 | H | Wycombe W | W 5-2 | 4-0 | — | O'Connell 3 5, 27, 90, Green 28, Kilford 42 | 4706 |
| 2 | | 16 | A | Bournemouth | L 0-1 | 0-0 | 8 | | 3799 |
| 3 | | 23 | H | Plymouth Arg | D 1-1 | 1-0 | 8 | Lowe 25 | 3761 |
| 4 | | 30 | A | Bristol C | L 0-3 | 0-3 | 15 | | 9255 |
| 5 | Sept | 2 | A | Carlisle U | L 0-1 | 0-0 | — | | 5352 |
| 6 | | 8 | H | Wrexham | W 3-2 | 1-0 | — | O'Connell 36, Lowe 72, Jones (pen) 78 | 3872 |
| 7 | | 13 | H | Blackpool | W 3-0 | 0-0 | 11 | Johnson 48, Lowe 2 62, 82 | 5517 |
| 8 | | 20 | A | Northampton T | L 0-1 | 0-0 | 13 | | 6570 |
| 9 | | 27 | H | Fulham | W 2-1 | 1-1 | 6 | Johnson 26, Greenall 89 | 4951 |
| 10 | Oct | 4 | A | Grimsby T | L 1-2 | 0-1 | 12 | Lowe 52 | 4623 |
| 11 | | 11 | A | Chesterfield | W 3-2 | 1-1 | 9 | O'Connell 13, Greenall 62, Lowe 67 | 4673 |
| 12 | | 18 | H | Luton T | D 1-1 | 0-0 | 8 | Jones (pen) 72 | 4466 |
| 13 | | 21 | H | Gillingham | L 1-4 | 0-1 | — | Lee 69 | 3214 |
| 14 | | 25 | A | Millwall | D 1-1 | 0-0 | 14 | Jones 86 | 7986 |
| 15 | Nov | 1 | H | York C | D 1-1 | 0-0 | 14 | Greenall 90 | 3701 |
| 16 | | 4 | A | Oldham Ath | L 1-3 | 1-2 | — | Lowe 14 | 5446 |
| 17 | | 8 | A | Southend U | L 0-1 | 0-0 | 17 | | 2716 |
| 18 | | 22 | H | Preston NE | L 1-4 | 0-1 | 19 | Kilford 59 | 5649 |
| 19 | | 29 | A | Watford | L 1-2 | 1-2 | 21 | Jones 11 | 9455 |
| 20 | Dec | 2 | A | Bristol R | W 3-0 | 1-0 | — | Kilford 20, Lowe 2 78, 85 | 2738 |
| 21 | | 13 | A | Burnley | W 2-0 | 2-0 | 18 | Lee 13, Jones 44 | 9520 |
| 22 | | 20 | H | Brentford | W 4-0 | 2-0 | 16 | Lowe 24, Smeets 2 34, 82, Kilford 88 | 3301 |
| 23 | | 26 | A | Wrexham | D 2-2 | 1-1 | 16 | Smeets 22, Kilford 71 | 4577 |
| 24 | | 28 | H | Carlisle U | L 0-2 | 0-1 | 17 | | 4511 |
| 25 | Jan | 10 | H | Wycombe W | W 2-1 | 1-0 | 16 | Martinez 20, Lee 81 | 5549 |
| 26 | | 17 | H | Bristol C | L 0-3 | 0-2 | 16 | | 5078 |
| 27 | | 24 | A | Plymouth Arg | L 2-3 | 2-0 | 18 | Kilford 37, Lee 41 | 4345 |
| 28 | | 31 | A | Blackpool | W 2-0 | 2-0 | 16 | Warne 8, Lydiate (og) 15 | 5288 |
| 29 | Feb | 7 | A | Northampton T | D 1-1 | 0-0 | 16 | Morgan 60 | 3579 |
| 30 | | 14 | H | Grimsby T | L 0-2 | 0-0 | 17 | | 3548 |
| 31 | | 21 | A | Fulham | L 0-2 | 0-0 | 17 | | 7791 |
| 32 | | 24 | A | Luton T | D 1-1 | 1-1 | — | Jones 16 | 4403 |
| 33 | | 28 | H | Chesterfield | W 2-1 | 2-1 | 16 | Lowe 16, Jones (pen) 37 | 3017 |
| 34 | Mar | 7 | A | York C | D 2-2 | 1-0 | 19 | Greenall 45, Jones 72 | 3536 |
| 35 | | 14 | H | Oldham Ath | W 1-0 | 0-0 | 17 | Kilford 64 | 4277 |
| 36 | | 17 | H | Southend U | L 1-3 | 0-2 | — | Lowe 84 | 2616 |
| 37 | | 21 | A | Walsall | L 0-1 | 0-0 | 18 | | 3169 |
| 38 | | 28 | A | Preston NE | D 1-1 | 0-1 | 18 | Lowe 57 | 10,171 |
| 39 | Apr | 4 | H | Watford | W 3-2 | 3-0 | 18 | Barlow 12, Lowe 25, Kilford 40 | 4262 |
| 40 | | 7 | H | Bournemouth | W 1-0 | 0-0 | — | Lee 80 | 2798 |
| 41 | | 10 | A | Bristol R | L 0-5 | 0-3 | — | | 6038 |
| 42 | | 13 | H | Burnley | W 5-1 | 0-0 | 13 | Barlow 31, Lowe 2 43, 87, Warne 77, Kilford 80 | 4926 |
| 43 | | 18 | A | Brentford | W 2-0 | 0-0 | 12 | Bradshaw (pen) 54, Kilford 68 | 4480 |
| 44 | | 21 | H | Walsall | W 2-0 | 0-0 | — | Barlow 47, Jones 69 | 2725 |
| 45 | | 24 | H | Millwall | D 0-0 | 0-0 | — | | 4045 |
| 46 | May | 2 | A | Gillingham | D 0-0 | 0-0 | 11 | | 10,361 |

**Final League Position: 11**     1996–97 DIV3 1

### GOALSCORERS

League (64): Lowe 16, Kilford 10, Jones 9 (3 pens), Lee 5, O'Connell 5, Greenall 4, Barlow 3, Smeets 3, Johnson 2, Warne 2, Bradshaw 1 (pen), Green 1, Martinez 1, Morgan 1, own goal 1.
Coca-Cola Cup (1): Lee 1.
FA Cup (5): Lee 2, Jones 1, Lowe 1, Martinez 1.

| Butler L 17 | Green S 37+1 | Johnson G 18+2 | Greenall C 39 | Bishop C 7 | Sharp K 34+4 | Lee D 41+2 | Lowe D 42+1 | O'Connell B 17 | Rogers P 32+6 | Kilford J 29+1 | McGibbon P 32+3 | Broughton D 1+3 | Black T —+1 | Lancashire G —+1 | Fitzhenry N 1+2 | Carroll R 29 | Martinez R 26+7 | Jones G 28+5 | Warne P 3+22 | Saville A —+5 | Smeets J 10+13 | Bradshaw C 27+1 | Woods N 1 | Diaz I 1+1 | Morgan S 13 | Branch G 2+1 | Bruno P 1 | Whitworth N 1+3 | Newman R 8 | Barlow S 9 | Match No. |
|---|---|---|---|---|---|---|---|---|---|---|---|---|---|---|---|---|---|---|---|---|---|---|---|---|---|---|---|---|---|---|---|
| 1 | 2 | 3 | 4 | 5 | $6^1$ | 7 | 8 | 9 | 10 | 11 | 12 | | | | | | | | | | | | | | | | | | | | 1 |
| 1 | 2 | $3^1$ | 4 | | 6 | 7 | 8 | 9 | 5 | 10 | $11^2$ | 12 | $13^3$ | 14 | | | | | | | | | | | | | | | | | 2 |
| 1 | 2 | 3 | 4 | | 6 | 7 | 8 | 9 | 10 | $11^1$ | 5 | 12 | | | | | | | | | | | | | | | | | | | 3 |
| | 2 | 3 | 4 | 12 | | 7 | $11^3$ | $9^2$ | 10 | 5 | | | | | | 1 | 6 | $8^1$ | 13 | 14 | | | | | | | | | | | 4 |
| | 2 | 3 | 4 | | $6^2$ | 7 | | 9 | 10 | 5 | | 12 | | | | 1 | 11 | $8^1$ | 13 | | | | | | | | | | | | 5 |
| | 2 | 3 | 4 | | 10 | 7 | 11 | 9 | | 5 | | 12 | | | | 1 | 6 | $8^1$ | | | | | | | | | | | | | 6 |
| 1 | 2 | 3 | 4 | | 10 | 7 | 11 | 9 | 12 | 5 | | | | | | | $6^1$ | $8^2$ | 13 | | | | | | | | | | | | 7 |
| 1 | 2 | $3^1$ | 4 | | 10 | 7 | 11 | 9 | 6 | 5 | | | | | | | 12 | $8^2$ | 13 | | | | | | | | | | | | 8 |
| 1 | 2 | 3 | 4 | | $10^1$ | 7 | 11 | 9 | 12 | 5 | | | | | | | 6 | $8^2$ | 13 | | | | | | | | | | | | 9 |
| 1 | 2 | 12 | 4 | | $3^2$ | 7 | 11 | 9 | | 5 | | | | | | | 6 | 8 | 13 | | $10^1$ | | | | | | | | | | 10 |
| 1 | 2 | | 4 | 5 | 3 | $7^1$ | 11 | 8 | 12 | | | | | | | | 6 | 9 | | | 10 | | | | | | | | | | 11 |
| 1 | | 12 | 4 | 5 | 3 | 7 | $11^3$ | 8 | | | | 13 | | | | | 6 | 9 | 14 | | $10^2$ | 2 | | | | | | | | | 12 |
| 1 | | 3 | 4 | 5 | | 7 | 11 | 8 | 9 | | | | | | | | $6^1$ | 12 | | | 10 | 2 | | | | | | | | | 13 |
| 1 | | | 4 | 6 | 3 | 7 | 11 | 10 | 8 | 5 | | | | | | | | 9 | | | | 2 | | | | | | | | | 14 |
| 1 | 2 | | 4 | | 3 | 7 | 11 | $10^1$ | $8^2$ | 5 | | | | | | | 12 | 9 | 13 | | | 6 | | | | | | | | | 15 |
| 1 | 2 | | 4 | 5 | 3 | $7^1$ | 11 | $10^2$ | | | | | | | | | 6 | 9 | 12 | | 13 | 8 | | | | | | | | | 16 |
| 1 | 2 | | 4 | $5^2$ | 3 | 12 | 11 | 7 | $10^3$ | | | | | | | | 8 | 13 | 14 | | | 6 | $9^1$ | | | | | | | | 17 |
| 1 | 2 | | 4 | | 3 | 7 | 11 | 10 | 8 | 5 | | | | | | | | 9 | | | | 6 | | | | | | | | | 18 |
| | 2 | | 4 | | 3 | 11 | 8 | $12^2$ | 7 | 5 | | | | | | 1 | 6 | 9 | | | 13 | $10^1$ | | | | | | | | | 19 |
| | 2 | | 4 | | $3^2$ | 7 | 11 | 8 | 12 | 10 | 5 | | | | | 1 | $6^1$ | 9 | | | 13 | | | | | | | | | | 20 |
| | 2 | | 4 | | 3 | 7 | 11 | 10 | $8^2$ | 5 | | | | | | 1 | 6 | $9^1$ | 12 | | 13 | | | | | | | | | | 21 |
| | 2 | | 4 | | 3 | $7^3$ | $11^2$ | 10 | 8 | $5^1$ | | | | | 12 | 1 | | 13 | 9 | | | | 14 | 6 | | | | | | | 22 |
| | 2 | | 4 | | 3 | 7 | $11^2$ | 10 | 8 | 5 | | | | | | 1 | | 12 | $9^1$ | | | | 6 | 13 | | | | | | | 23 |
| | 2 | | $4^1$ | | $3^3$ | 7 | 11 | 10 | 8 | 5 | | | | | | 1 | 12 | 13 | 14 | | | | 6 | $9^2$ | | | | | | | 24 |
| | 2 | | 4 | | | 7 | 11 | 8 | 12 | 5 | | | | | | $1^1$ | 6 | | | | $10^2$ | 9 | | 3 | | | | | | | 25 |
| 1 | | | 4 | 12 | | 7 | 11 | 8 | | $5^1$ | | | | | $10^3$ | | 6 | 9 | 13 | | | 14 | $2^2$ | 3 | | | | | | | 26 |
| 1 | 2 | | 4 | 11 | | 7 | | $8^2$ | 5 | | | | | | | | 6 | 9 | 12 | | | 13 | | | 3 | $10^1$ | | | | | 27 |
| | 2 | | 4 | | 3 | 11 | | | 5 | | | | | | | 1 | 6 | 9 | | | | 10 | 7 | 8 | | | | | | | 28 |
| | 2 | | 4 | | 12 | 7 | 11 | | 5 | | | | | | | 1 | 6 | 9 | | | | $10^1$ | 3 | 8 | | | | | | | 29 |
| | 2 | $3^2$ | | 12 | | 7 | 11 | 8 | 5 | | | | | | | 1 | 6 | 9 | | | 13 | 10 | | | | $4^1$ | | | | | 30 |
| | | | 4 | | | 7 | 12 | 8 | 11 | 5 | | | | | | 1 | $6^1$ | 9 | 10 | | | 2 | | 3 | | | | | | | 31 |
| | 2 | | 4 | | 3 | $7^1$ | 11 | 12 | 10 | 5 | | | | | | 1 | | $9^2$ | 13 | | 6 | 8 | | | | | | | | | 32 |
| | 2 | | 4 | | 3 | $7^2$ | 11 | 10 | 5 | | | | | | | 1 | 12 | 9 | 13 | | $6^1$ | 8 | | | | | | | | | 33 |
| | 2 | | 4 | | 3 | 7 | 11 | 6 | 10 | 5 | | | | | | 1 | 12 | 9 | | | | $8^1$ | | | | | | | | | 34 |
| | 2 | | 4 | | $3^1$ | 7 | 11 | 6 | 10 | 5 | | | | | | 1 | | 9 | | | | 8 | | | 12 | | | | | | 35 |
| | $2^2$ | $3^1$ | 4 | | | 7 | 11 | 8 | 10 | 5 | | | | | | 1 | 12 | 9 | 13 | | | 6 | | | | | | | | | 36 |
| | 2 | | $4^2$ | | 3 | 12 | 11 | 8 | 10 | $5^1$ | | | | | | 1 | | 9 | 13 | | | 6 | | | | 7 | | | | | 37 |
| | $2^1$ | 3 | | | | 7 | 11 | 8 | 10 | 5 | | | | | | 1 | 12 | | 13 | | | 6 | | | | | | 4 | | $9^4$ | 38 |
| | | 3 | | | 2 | 7 | 11 | 8 | 10 | 5 | | | | | | 1 | 12 | | | | | 6 | | | | | | 4 | | $9^1$ | 39 |
| | 12 | 3 | | | 2 | 7 | 11 | 8 | 10 | $5^1$ | | | | | | 1 | 13 | | | | | 6 | | | | | | 4 | | $9^2$ | 40 |
| | $2^3$ | | | | 3 | | | | $11^1$ | | | | | | | 1 | 7 | $10^2$ | 13 | | 12 | 8 | 6 | 5 | | 14 | | 4 | | 9 | 41 |
| | | 4 | | | 3 | 7 | 11 | 8 | 10 | | | | | | | 1 | 12 | 13 | | | $2^1$ | 6 | | | | | | 5 | | $9^2$ | 42 |
| | | 4 | | | 3 | 7 | 11 | 8 | $10^1$ | 12 | | | | | | 1 | $2^3$ | 13 | | | 14 | 6 | | | | | | 5 | | $9^2$ | 43 |
| | 2 | 3 | $4^3$ | | | 7 | $11^1$ | 8 | 5 | | | | | | | 1 | 6 | 10 | 13 | | 12 | | | | | 14 | | | | $9^2$ | 44 |
| | 10 | 3 | | | | 7 | 11 | 8 | $5^1$ | | | | | | | 1 | 6 | 12 | 13 | | | 2 | | | | | | 4 | | $9^2$ | 45 |
| | 10 | 3 | | | | 7 | 11 | 8 | 5 | | | | | | | 1 | 6 | 12 | | | | 2 | | | | | | 4 | | $9^1$ | 46 |

**Coca-Cola Cup**

| First Round | Chesterfield | (h) | 1-2 |
|---|---|---|---|
| | | (a) | 0-1 |

**FA Cup**

| First Round | Carlisle U | (a) | 1-0 |
|---|---|---|---|
| Second Round | York C | (h) | 2-1 |
| Third Round | Blackburn R | (a) | 2-4 |

WIMBLEDON 1997–98 *Back row (left to right):* Kenny Cunningham, Stewart Castledine, Paul Heald, Lawrie Sanchez (Coach), Neil Sullivan, Brian McAllister, Jon Goodman. *Middle row:* Steve Allen (Physio), Neal Ardley, Peter Fear, Efan Ekoku, Alan Reeves, Mick Harford, Dean Blackwell, Dean Holdsworth, David Kemp (Coach). *Front row:* Ben Thatcher, Jason Euell, Chris Perry, Marcus Gayle, Joe Kinnear (Manager), Vinnie Jones, Ceri Hughes, Andy Clarke, Duncan Jupp. *Inset:* Robbie Earle (left), Alan Kimble (right).

# FA Premiership

# WIMBLEDON

*Selhurst Park, South Norwood, London SE25 6PY.* Telephone: (0181) 771 2233. Fax: (0181) 768 0641. Box Office: (0181) 771 8841.

*Ground capacity:* 26,309.

*Record attendance:* 30,115 v Manchester U, FA Premier League, 9 May 1993.

*Record receipts:* £398,422 v Manchester U, FA Cup 4th rd replay, 4 February 1997.

*Pitch measurements:* 110yd × 74yd.

*Chairman:* S. G. Reed. *Deputy Chairman:* J. H. Lelliott.

*Directors:* S. G. N. Hammam, K. I. Røkke, B. R. Gjelsten, J. P. Storetvedt, P. Cork, P. R. Lloyd Cooper, N. N. Hammam, P. Miller.

*Chief Executive:* David Barnard.

*Manager:* Joe Kinnear. *Coaches:* Lawrie Sanchez, David Kemp, Mick Harford. *Chief Scout:* Ron Suart.

*Physio:* Steve Allen. *Stadium Manager:* Vic Worrall. *Safety Officer:* George Crawford, QPM.

*Club Secretary:* Steve Rooke. *Marketing Manager:* Sharon Sillitoe. *Press and PR Manager:* Reg Davis.

*Academy Director:* Terry Burton.

*Year Formed:* 1889. *Turned Professional:* 1964. *Ltd Co.:* 1964.

*Previous Name:* Wimbledon Old Centrals, 1899–1905.

*Previous Ground:* Plough Lane.

*Club Nickname:* 'The Dons', 'The Crazy Gang'.

*Foundation:* Old boys from Central School formed this club as Wimbledon Old Centrals in 1889. Their earliest successes were in the Clapham League before switching to the Southern Suburban League in 1902.

*First Football League game:* 20 August 1977, Division 4, v Halifax T (h) D 3-3 – Guy; Bryant (1), Galvin, Donaldson, Aitken, Davies, Galliers, Smith, Connell (1), Holmes, Leslie (1).

*Record League Victory:* 6–0 v Newport Co, Division 3, 3 September 1983 – Beasant; Peters, Winterburn, Galliers, Morris, Hatter, Evans (2), Ketteridge (1), Cork (3 incl. 1p), Downes, Hodges (Driver).

*Record Cup Victory:* 7–2 v Windsor & Eton, FA Cup 1st rd, 22 November 1980 – Beasant; Jones, Armstrong, Galliers, Mick Smith (2), Cunningham (1), Ketteridge, Hodges, Leslie, Cork (1), Hubbick (3).

*Record Defeat:* 0–8 v Everton, League Cup 2nd rd, 29 August 1978.

*Most League Points (2 for a win):* 61, Division 4, 1978–79.

*Most League Points (3 for a win):* 98, Division 4, 1982–83.

*Most League Goals:* 97, Division 3, 1983–84.

*Highest League Scorer in Season:* Alan Cork, 29, 1983–84.

*Most League Goals in Total Aggregate:* Alan Cork, 145, 1977–92.

*Most Capped Player:* Kenny Cunningham, 16, Republic of Ireland.

*Most League Appearances:* Alan Cork, 430, 1977–92.

*Record Transfer Fee Received:* £4,000,000 from Newcastle U for Warren Barton, June 1995.

*Record Transfer Fee Paid:* £2,000,000 to Liverpool for Mark Kennedy, March 1998, £2,000,000 to Crystal Palace for Andy Roberts, March 1998.

*Football League Record:* 1977 Elected to Division 4; 1979–80 Division 3; 1980–81 Division 4; 1981–82 Division 3; 1982–83 Division 4; 1983–84 Division 3; 1984–86 Division 2; 1986–92 Division 1; 1992– FA Premier League.

*Honours: FA Premier League* : best season: 6th, 1993–94; *Football League:* Division 3 – Runners-up 1983–84; Division 4 – Champions 1982–83. *FA Cup:* Winners 1988. *Football League Cup:* Semi-final 1996–97. *League Group Cup:* Runners-up 1982. *Amateur Cup:* Winners 1963; Runners-up 1935, 1947.

*Colours:* All navy blue with yellow trim. *Change colours:* Red shirts with black trim, red shorts, red stockings with black trim.

**Did you know?**
When Wimbledon beat Sutton United 4-2 in the FA Amateur Cup Final at Wembley on 4 May 1963, Eddie Reynolds scored all their goals with his head.

## WIMBLEDON 1997–98 LEAGUE RECORD

| Match No. | Date | | Venue | Opponents | Result | H/T Score | Lg. Pos. | Goalscorers | Attendance |
|---|---|---|---|---|---|---|---|---|---|
| 1 | Aug | 9 | H | Liverpool | D 1-1 | 0-0 | — | Gayle 55 | 26,106 |
| 2 | | 23 | H | Sheffield W | D 1-1 | 1-0 | 15 | Euell 17 | 11,503 |
| 3 | | 27 | H | Chelsea | L 0-2 | 0-0 | — | | 22,237 |
| 4 | | 30 | A | West Ham U | L 1-3 | 0-0 | 20 | Ekoku 81 | 24,516 |
| 5 | Sept | 13 | A | Newcastle U | W 3-1 | 1-1 | 16 | Cort 2, Perry 59, Ekoku 75 | 36,692 |
| 6 | | 20 | H | Crystal Palace | L 0-1 | 0-0 | 18 | | 16,747 |
| 7 | | 23 | H | Barnsley | W 4-1 | 0-1 | — | Cort 49, Earle 65, Hughes C 68, Ekoku 84 | 7688 |
| 8 | | 27 | A | Tottenham H | D 0-0 | 0-0 | 15 | | 26,261 |
| 9 | Oct | 4 | A | Blackburn R | L 0-1 | 0-1 | 15 | | 15,600 |
| 10 | | 18 | A | Aston Villa | W 2-1 | 1-1 | 13 | Earle 39, Cort 61 | 32,087 |
| 11 | | 22 | A | Derby Co | D 1-1 | 0-0 | — | Dailly (og) 70 | 28,595 |
| 12 | | 25 | H | Leeds U | W 1-0 | 1-0 | 9 | Ardley (pen) 29 | 15,718 |
| 13 | Nov | 1 | H | Coventry C | L 1-2 | 1-2 | 10 | Cort 28 | 11,201 |
| 14 | | 10 | A | Leicester C | W 1-0 | 0-0 | — | Gayle 50 | 18,553 |
| 15 | | 22 | H | Manchester U | L 2-5 | 0-0 | 10 | Ardley 68, Hughes M 70 | 26,309 |
| 16 | | 29 | A | Bolton W | L 0-1 | 0-0 | 11 | | 22,703 |
| 17 | Dec | 7 | H | Southampton | W 1-0 | 1-0 | 10 | Earle 18 | 12,009 |
| 18 | | 13 | A | Everton | D 0-0 | 0-0 | 11 | | 28,533 |
| 19 | | 26 | A | Chelsea | D 1-1 | 1-1 | 12 | Hughes M 28 | 32,754 |
| 20 | | 28 | H | West Ham U | L 1-2 | 0-1 | 12 | Solbakken 90 | 22,087 |
| 21 | Jan | 10 | A | Liverpool | L 0-2 | 0-0 | 14 | | 38,011 |
| 22 | | 17 | H | Derby Co | D 0-0 | 0-0 | 15 | | 13,031 |
| 23 | | 31 | A | Sheffield W | D 1-1 | 1-1 | 16 | Hughes M 21 | 22,655 |
| 24 | Feb | 9 | A | Crystal Palace | W 3-0 | 0-0 | — | Leaburn 2 47, 51, Euell 57 | 14,410 |
| 25 | | 21 | H | Aston Villa | W 2-1 | 2-1 | 14 | Euell 10, Leaburn 39 | 13,131 |
| 26 | | 28 | A | Barnsley | L 1-2 | 0-1 | 15 | Euell 71 | 17,172 |
| 27 | Mar | 11 | H | Arsenal | L 0-1 | 0-1 | — | | 22,291 |
| 28 | | 14 | H | Leicester C | W 2-1 | 1-0 | 14 | Roberts 14, Hughes M 62 | 13,229 |
| 29 | | 28 | A | Manchester U | L 0-2 | 0-0 | 14 | | 55,306 |
| 30 | | 31 | H | Newcastle U | D 0-0 | 0-0 | — | | 15,478 |
| 31 | Apr | 4 | H | Bolton W | D 0-0 | 0-0 | 14 | | 11,356 |
| 32 | | 11 | A | Southampton | W 1-0 | 1-0 | 13 | Leaburn 38 | 14,815 |
| 33 | | 13 | H | Everton | D 0-0 | 0-0 | 13 | | 15,131 |
| 34 | | 18 | A | Arsenal | L 0-5 | 0-3 | 13 | | 38,024 |
| 35 | | 25 | A | Blackburn R | D 0-0 | 0-0 | 14 | | 24,848 |
| 36 | | 29 | H | Coventry C | D 0-0 | 0-0 | — | | 17,947 |
| 37 | May | 2 | H | Tottenham H | L 2-6 | 2-2 | 16 | Fear 2 21, 30 | 25,972 |
| 38 | | 10 | A | Leeds U | D 1-1 | 0-0 | 15 | Ekoku 88 | 38,445 |

**Final League Position: 15** 1996–97 PREM 8

### GOALSCORERS

*League (34):* Cort 4, Ekoku 4, Euell 4, Hughes M 4, Leaburn 4, Earle 3, Ardley 2 (1 pen), Fear 2, Gayle 2, Hughes C 1, Perry 1, Roberts 1, Solbakken 1, own goal 1.
*Coca-Cola Cup (9):* Euell 3, Castledine 2, Cort 2 (1 pen), Clarke 1, Gayle 1.
*FA Cup (6):* Hughes M 2, Ardley 1, Euell 1, Gayle 1, Jones 1.

| Sullivan N 38 | Cunningham K 32 | Kimble A 23 + 2 | Jones V 22 + 2 | Blackwell D 35 | Perry C 35 | Ardley N 31 + 3 | Earle R 20 + 2 | Ekoku E 11 + 5 | Holdsworth D 4 + 1 | Gayle M 21 + 9 | Castledine S 3 + 3 | Hughes C 13 + 4 | Clarke A 1 + 13 | Euell J 14 + 5 | McAllister B 4 + 3 | Jupp D 3 | Cort C 16 + 6 | Thatcher B 23 + 3 | Hughes M 29 | Solbakken S 4 + 2 | Leaburn C 15 + 1 | Fear P 5 + 3 | Roberts A 12 | Francis D — + 2 | Kennedy M 4 | Match No. |
|---|---|---|---|---|---|---|---|---|---|---|---|---|---|---|---|---|---|---|---|---|---|---|---|---|---|---|
| 1 | 2 | 3 | $4^1$ | 5 | 6 | 7 | 8 |  | 9 | $10^2$ | $11^3$ | 12 | 13 | 14 |  |  |  |  |  |  |  |  |  |  |  | 1 |
| 1 | 2 | 3 | 4 | 5 | 6 | 7 | $8^3$ | 12 | $10^2$ | $11^1$ |  |  | 14 | 13 | 9 |  |  |  |  |  |  |  |  |  |  | 2 |
| 1 | 2 | 3 |  | 5 | 6 | 7 | 8 | $9^2$ | $10^1$ | 11 |  | 12 | 13 |  | 4 |  |  |  |  |  |  |  |  |  |  | 3 |
| 1 | 11 | 3 |  | 5 | 6 | 7 | 8 | 12 | $10^1$ | 13 |  |  | 14 | $9^2$ | $4^3$ | 2 |  |  |  |  |  |  |  |  |  | 4 |
| 1 | 2 | 3 | 4 | 5 | 6 | $7^2$ |  | 9 |  | $11^1$ | 13 | 8 |  |  |  |  | 10 | 12 |  |  |  |  |  |  |  | 5 |
| 1 | 2 | 3 | 4 | 5 | 6 |  |  | $9^2$ | 12 | $11^3$ | 8 | 7 | 13 |  |  |  | $10^1$ | 14 |  |  |  |  |  |  |  | 6 |
| 1 | 2 | 3 | 4 | 5 | 6 |  | 8 | 9 |  |  |  |  | 7 |  | 11 |  | 10 |  |  |  |  |  |  |  |  | 7 |
| 1 | 2 | 3 | $4^2$ | 5 | 6 |  | 8 | $9^1$ |  |  |  |  | 7 |  | 12 |  | 10 | 13 | 11 |  |  |  |  |  |  | 8 |
| 1 | 2 | 3 | 4 | 5 | 6 | $7^1$ |  | 9 |  | 12 |  | 8 | 13 |  |  |  | 10 | $11^2$ |  |  |  |  |  |  |  | 9 |
| 1 | 2 |  | 4 | 5 | 6 | 12 | $8^1$ | 9 |  |  |  | 7 |  |  |  |  | 10 | 3 | 11 |  |  |  |  |  |  | 10 |
| 1 | 2 |  | 4 | 5 | 6 | 12 | 8 | 9 |  |  |  |  | $7^1$ |  | 13 |  | 10 | $3^2$ | 11 |  |  |  |  |  |  | 11 |
| 1 |  |  | 4 | 5 | 6 | 7 | 8 | 9 |  |  | 12 |  |  |  |  | 2 | $10^1$ | 3 | 11 |  |  |  |  |  |  | 12 |
| 1 | $2^1$ |  | 4 | 5 | 6 | 12 | 8 | $9^2$ |  |  | 13 |  | $7^3$ | 14 |  |  | 10 | 3 | 11 |  |  |  |  |  |  | 13 |
| 1 | 2 |  | 4 | 5 | 6 | 7 |  | 9 |  |  |  | 8 |  |  |  |  | 10 | 3 | 11 |  |  |  |  |  |  | 14 |
| 1 | 2 |  | $4^3$ | 5 | 6 | $7^2$ | 12 | 9 |  |  |  | $8^1$ | 13 |  |  |  | 10 | 3 | 11 | 14 |  |  |  |  |  | 15 |
| 1 | 2 |  | 4 | 5 | 6 | 7 |  | 9 |  |  |  | 8 |  |  |  |  | 10 | 3 | 11 |  |  |  |  |  |  | 16 |
| 1 | 2 | 12 | 13 | 5 | 6 | 7 | 8 | $9^2$ |  |  |  |  |  |  |  |  | $10^1$ | 3 | 11 | 4 |  |  |  |  |  | 17 |
| 1 | 2 | 3 | 12 | 5 |  | 7 | 8 | $9^1$ |  |  |  |  | 13 |  |  |  | $10^2$ | 6 | 11 | 4 |  |  |  |  |  | 18 |
| 1 | 2 | 3 | 4 | 5 |  | 7 | 8 | $9^1$ |  |  |  |  |  |  |  |  | 12 | 6 | 11 | 10 |  |  |  |  |  | 19 |
| 1 | 2 | 3 | $4^2$ | 5 |  | 7 | 8 | $9^1$ |  |  |  |  | 12 |  |  |  | 13 | 6 | 11 | 10 |  |  |  |  |  | 20 |
| 1 | 2 | 3 | 4 | 5 | 6 | 7 | 8 | $9^1$ |  |  |  |  | 12 |  |  |  | $10^2$ |  | 11 |  | 13 |  |  |  |  | 21 |
| 1 | 2 | 3 | 4 | 5 | 6 | 7 | 8 | $9^1$ |  |  |  |  |  |  |  |  | 12 |  | 11 |  | 10 |  |  |  |  | 22 |
| 1 | 2 | 3 |  | 5 | 6 | 7 |  |  | 12 | 10 |  |  | $9^1$ |  |  |  |  |  | 11 |  | 8 | 4 |  |  |  | 23 |
| 1 | 2 |  | 4 | 5 | 6 | $7^2$ |  |  |  |  |  |  | 13 | 12 | $10^1$ |  |  |  | 11 |  | 9 | 8 |  |  |  | 24 |
| 1 |  |  | 4 | 5 | 6 | 7 |  |  |  |  | $11^2$ |  |  | 10 |  | $2^1$ | 13 | 3 |  | 12 | 9 | 8 |  |  |  | 25 |
| 1 | 2 |  | 4 | 5 | 6 | 7 |  |  |  |  | 12 | $8^1$ |  | 10 |  |  |  | 3 | 11 |  | 9 |  |  |  |  | 26 |
| 1 | 2 | 12 | $4^2$ | 5 | 6 | 7 |  |  |  |  | 13 |  |  | $10^3$ |  | 14 | $3^1$ | 11 |  |  | 9 |  | 8 |  |  | 27 |
| 1 | 2 | 3 |  | 5 | 6 | 7 |  |  | 12 |  | 9 |  |  | $10^1$ |  |  |  | 11 |  |  | 8 |  | 4 |  |  | 28 |
| 1 | 2 | 3 |  |  | 6 | 7 | 8 |  |  |  | $9^1$ |  | 12 |  |  |  | 5 | 11 |  |  | 10 |  | 4 |  |  | 29 |
| 1 | 2 | 3 |  | 5 | 6 | 7 | 8 |  |  |  | 9 |  |  |  |  |  |  | 11 |  |  | 10 |  | 4 |  |  | 30 |
| 1 | 2 | 3 |  | 5 | 6 | $7^3$ | 8 |  |  |  | 12 |  | 13 | $10^2$ |  |  |  | 11 |  |  | $9^1$ | 14 | 4 |  |  | 31 |
| 1 | 2 |  |  | 5 | 6 | 7 | 8 |  |  |  | $9^1$ |  | 12 |  |  |  |  | 3 | 11 |  | 10 |  | 4 |  |  | 32 |
| 1 |  | 3 |  | 5 | 6 | 7 |  |  |  |  | 9 |  | $8^2$ | 12 | 13 |  |  | 2 | 11 |  | $10^1$ |  | 4 |  |  | 33 |
| 1 | 2 |  |  | $5^2$ | 6 | $7^3$ |  |  |  |  | 9 |  | $8^1$ | 10 | 13 |  | 12 | 3 | 11 |  |  | 4 |  | 14 |  | 34 |
| 1 | 2 |  |  | 5 | 6 | 7 | 12 |  |  |  |  |  | $9^1$ |  |  |  | 10 | 3 | $11^2$ |  | 13 | 4 |  | 8 |  | 35 |
| 1 |  | 3 |  | $5^2$ | 6 | 7 | 12 |  |  |  |  |  | $10^1$ | 13 |  |  | 2 |  | 11 | 9 | 14 | 4 |  | $8^3$ |  | 36 |
| 1 |  | 3 |  |  | 6 |  |  | 12 |  |  | 13 |  | $10^3$ | 5 |  |  | 2 |  | 11 | $9^1$ | 4 | 8 | 14 | $7^2$ |  | 37 |
| 1 |  | 3 |  |  | 6 | 7 | 12 |  |  |  |  |  | $10^1$ | 5 |  |  | 2 |  |  | 9 | 4 | 8 |  |  | 11 | 38 |

**Coca-Cola Cup**

| | | | |
|---|---|---|---|
| Second Round | Millwall | (h) | 5-1 |
| | | (a) | 4-1 |
| Third Round | Bolton W | (a) | 0-2 |

**FA Cup**

| | | | |
|---|---|---|---|
| Third Round | Wrexham | (h) | 0-0 |
| | | (a) | 3-2 |
| Fourth Round | Huddersfield T | (a) | 1-0 |
| Fifth Round | Wolverhampton W | (h) | 1-1 |
| | | (a) | 1-2 |

WOLVERHAMPTON WANDERERS 1997–98 *Back row (left to right):* Mark Jones, Darren Ferguson, Carl Robinson, Simon Osborn, Glen Crowe, Jermaine Wright, Michael Gilkes.
*Middle row:* Colin Lee (Assistant Manager), Don Goodman, Neil Emblen, Steve Sedgley, Dean Richards, Justin Bray, Mike Stowell, Adrian Williams, Dominic Foley, Richard Leadbeater, Jamie Smith, Mark McGhee (Manager).
*Front row:* Mike Hickman (Coach), Dave Hancock (Physio), Robbie Keane, Steve Froggatt, Mark Atkins, Steve Bull, Keith Curle, Steve Corica, Chris Westwood, Tony Daley, Barry Holmes (Physio), Taff Davies (Kit Manager).
(Photograph: Action Images)

# Division 1 WOLVERHAMPTON WANDERERS

*Molineux Grounds, Wolverhampton WV1 4QR.* Telephone: (01902) 655000; Fax: (01902) 687006.
*Ground capacity:* 28,525.

*Record attendance:* 63,315 v Liverpool, FA Cup 5th rd, 11 February 1939.

*Record receipts:* £276,168 v Tottenham H, FA Cup 4th rd, 7 February 1996.

*Pitch measurements:* 110yd × 75yd.

*President:* Sir Jack Hayward.

*Chairman:* Sir Jack Hayward.

*Managing Director:* John Richards.

*Directors:* Jack Harris, John Harris, Rachael Heyhoe Flint, Rick Hayward.

*Manager:* Mark McGhee. *Assistant Manager:* Colin Lee. *Stadium Manager:* Clive Mountford.

*Coach:* Mike Hickman. *Physio:* Barry Holmes.

*Secretary:* Richard Skirrow.

*Year Formed:* 1877*(see Foundation). Turned Professional:* 1888. *Ltd Co.:* 1982.

*Club Nickname:* 'Wolves'.

*Previous Grounds:* 1877, Goldthorn Hill; 1879, John Harper's Field; 1881, Dudley Road; 1889, Molineux.

*Previous Names:* 1880, St Luke's, Blakenhall combined with Blakenhall Wanderers to become Wolverhampton Wanderers (1923) Ltd until 1982.

*Foundation:* Another club where precise details of information are confused, due in part to the existence of an earlier Wolverhampton club which played rugby. However, it is now considered likely that it came into being in 1879 when players from St. Luke's (founded 1877) and Goldthorn (founded 1876) broke away to form Wolverhampton Wanderers Association FC.

*First Football League game:* 8 September 1888, Football League, v Aston Villa (h) D 1-1 – Baynton; Baugh, Mason; Fletcher, Allen, Lowder; Hunter, Cooper, Anderson, White, Cannon. Scorer – Cox (og).

*Record League Victory:* 10–1 v Leicester C, Division 1, 15 April 1938 – Sidlow; Morris, Dowen; Galley, Cullis, Gardiner; Maguire (1), Horace Wright, Westcott (4), Jones (1), Dorsett (4).

*Record Cup Victory:* 14–0 v Cresswell's Brewery, FA Cup 2nd rd, 13 November 1886 – I. Griffiths; Baugh, Mason; Pearson, Allen (1), Lowder; Hunter (4), Knight (2), Brodie (4), B. Griffiths (2), Wood. Plus one goal 'scrambled through'.

*Record Defeat:* 1–10 v Newton Heath, Division 1, 15 October 1892.

*Most League Points (2 for a win):* 64, Division 1, 1957–58.

*Most League Points (3 for a win):* 92, Division 4, 1988–89.

*Most League Goals:* 115, Division 2, 1931–32.

*Highest League Scorer in Season:* Dennis Westcott, 38, Division 1, 1946–47.

*Most League Goals in Total Aggregate:* Steve Bull, 247, 1986–98.

*Most Capped Player:* Billy Wright, 105, England (70 consecutive).

*Most League Appearances:* Derek Parkin, 501, 1967–82.

*Record Transfer Fee Received:* £1,150,000 from Manchester C for Steve Daley, September 1979.

*Record Transfer Fee Paid:* £1,850,000 to Bradford C for Dean Richards, May 1995.

*Football League Record:* 1888 Founder Member of Football League: 1906–23 Division 2; 1923–24 Division 3 (N); 1924–32 Division 2; 1932–65 Division 1; 1965–67 Division 2; 1967–76 Division 1; 1976–77 Division 2; 1977–82 Division 1; 1982–83 Division 2; 1983–84 Division 3; 1984–85 Division 2; 1985–86 Division 3; 1986–88 Division 4; 1988–89 Division 3; 1989–92 Division 2; 1992– Division 1.

*Honours: Football League:* Division 1 – Champions 1953–54, 1957–58, 1958–59; Runners-up 1937–38, 1938–39, 1949–50, 1954–55, 1959–60; Division 2 – Champions 1931–32, 1976–77; Runners-up 1966–67, 1982–83; Division 3 (N) – Champions 1923–24; Division 3 – Champions 1988–89; Division 4 – Champions 1987–88. *FA Cup:* Winners 1893, 1908, 1949, 1960; Runners-up 1889, 1896, 1921, 1939. *Football League Cup:* Winners 1974, 1980. *Texaco Cup:* Winners: 1971. *Sherpa Van Trophy:* Winners 1988. **European Competitions:** *European Cup:* 1958–59, 1959–60. *European Cup-Winners' Cup:* 1960–61. *UEFA Cup:* 1971–72 (runners-up), 1973–74, 1974–75, 1980–81.

*Colours:* Gold shirts, black shorts, gold stockings. *Change colours:* White shirts, teal shorts.

**Did you know?**
When Steve Bull scored against Bradford City on 18 February 1998 it was his 300th goal in all competitions for Wolverhampton Wanderers.

**Wolverhampton
Wanderers FC**

## WOLVERHAMPTON WANDERERS 1997–98 LEAGUE RECORD

| Match No. | Date | | Venue | Opponents | Result | H/T Score | Lg. Pos. | Goalscorers | Atten- dance |
|---|---|---|---|---|---|---|---|---|---|
| 1 | Aug | 9 | A | Norwich C | W 2-0 | 1-0 | — | Keane 2 [34, 64] | 17,230 |
| 2 | | 16 | H | Sheffield U | D 0-0 | 0-0 | 6 | | 23,102 |
| 3 | | 24 | A | WBA | L 0-1 | 0-1 | 11 | | 21,511 |
| 4 | | 30 | H | Bury | W 4-2 | 2-1 | 8 | Keane 2 [5, 86], Bull 2 [42, 51] | 21,141 |
| 5 | Sept | 3 | H | Port Vale | D 1-1 | 0-0 | — | Bull [74] | 21,524 |
| 6 | | 7 | A | Oxford U | L 0-3 | 0-2 | 9 | | 6921 |
| 7 | | 13 | H | Charlton Ath | W 3-1 | 3-0 | 7 | Bull 2 [9, 35], Froggatt [26] | 22,683 |
| 8 | | 20 | A | Sunderland | D 1-1 | 1-1 | 10 | Melville (og) [34] | 30,682 |
| 9 | | 27 | H | Huddersfield T | D 1-1 | 1-1 | 12 | Bull [1] | 21,723 |
| 10 | Oct | 4 | A | Bradford C | L 0-2 | 0-2 | 13 | | 15,236 |
| 11 | | 12 | A | Birmingham C | L 0-1 | 0-1 | 15 | | 17,822 |
| 12 | | 18 | H | Swindon T | W 3-1 | 1-1 | 12 | Freedman [11], Curle [78], Simpson [80] | 21,794 |
| 13 | | 22 | H | Tranmere R | W 2-1 | 2-0 | — | Robinson [15], Freedman [16] | 20,841 |
| 14 | | 25 | A | Stockport Co | L 0-1 | 0-1 | 12 | | 9804 |
| 15 | Nov | 1 | H | Middlesbrough | W 1-0 | 0-0 | 9 | Keane [82] | 26,896 |
| 16 | | 4 | A | Crewe Alex | W 2-0 | 1-0 | — | Freedman [14], Muscat [63] | 5743 |
| 17 | | 8 | A | Stoke C | L 0-3 | 0-2 | 8 | | 18,490 |
| 18 | | 15 | H | Ipswich T | D 1-1 | 1-1 | 9 | Keane [27] | 21,937 |
| 19 | | 29 | H | QPR | W 3-2 | 1-0 | 9 | Osborn [44], Goodman 2 [67, 77] | 23,645 |
| 20 | Dec | 6 | A | Manchester C | W 1-0 | 1-0 | 9 | Symons (og) [42] | 28,999 |
| 21 | | 9 | A | Portsmouth | L 2-3 | 0-1 | — | Westwood [76], Froggatt [87] | 8042 |
| 22 | | 14 | H | Nottingham F | W 2-1 | 1-0 | 9 | Freedman [20], Robinson [66] | 24,635 |
| 23 | | 20 | A | Reading | D 0-0 | 0-0 | 8 | | 11,715 |
| 24 | | 26 | H | Oxford U | W 1-0 | 1-0 | 7 | Goodman [19] | 26,238 |
| 25 | | 28 | A | Port Vale | W 2-0 | 1-0 | 6 | Muscat [45], Freedman [87] | 10,898 |
| 26 | Jan | 10 | H | Norwich C | W 5-0 | 4-0 | 6 | Keane [22], Goodman [24], Freedman 3 [43, 45, 77] | 23,703 |
| 27 | | 17 | A | Sheffield U | L 0-1 | 0-0 | 6 | | 22,144 |
| 28 | | 27 | A | Bury | W 3-1 | 1-1 | — | Keane [22], Simpson 2 [55, 62] | 6134 |
| 29 | | 31 | H | WBA | L 0-1 | 0-0 | 6 | | 28,244 |
| 30 | Feb | 7 | H | Sunderland | L 0-1 | 0-0 | 6 | | 27,502 |
| 31 | | 18 | H | Bradford C | W 2-1 | 1-0 | — | Robinson [43], Bull [89] | 21,510 |
| 32 | | 21 | A | Huddersfield T | L 0-1 | 0-0 | 6 | | 12,663 |
| 33 | | 28 | H | Birmingham C | L 1-3 | 1-1 | 9 | Freedman [13] | 25,591 |
| 34 | Mar | 4 | H | Stoke C | D 1-1 | 1-0 | — | Freedman [22] | 21,058 |
| 35 | | 14 | H | Crewe Alex | W 1-0 | 1-0 | 8 | Keane [35] | 24,272 |
| 36 | | 18 | A | Swindon T | D 0-0 | 0-0 | — | | 7770 |
| 37 | | 21 | A | Ipswich T | L 0-3 | 0-1 | 8 | | 21,510 |
| 38 | | 29 | H | Portsmouth | W 2-0 | 1-0 | 8 | Goodman [44], Osborn [90] | 20,718 |
| 39 | Apr | 1 | A | QPR | D 0-0 | 0-0 | — | | 12,337 |
| 40 | | 7 | A | Charlton Ath | L 0-1 | 0-1 | — | | 13,743 |
| 41 | | 11 | H | Manchester C | D 2-2 | 1-1 | 8 | Margetson (og) [34], Simpson [85] | 24,458 |
| 42 | | 13 | A | Nottingham F | L 0-3 | 0-2 | 8 | | 22,863 |
| 43 | | 18 | H | Reading | W 3-1 | 1-1 | 8 | Muscat [9], Goodman 2 [69, 90] | 19,785 |
| 44 | | 25 | H | Stockport Co | L 3-4 | 2-1 | 8 | Keane 2 [5, 59], Atkins [45] | 22,452 |
| 45 | | 29 | A | Middlesbrough | D 1-1 | 1-1 | — | Atkins [10] | 29,878 |
| 46 | May | 3 | A | Tranmere R | L 1-2 | 0-1 | 9 | Goodman [51] | 11,144 |

**Final League Position: 9**     1996–97 DIV1 3

### GOALSCORERS

*League (57):* Keane 11, Freedman 10, Goodman 8, Bull 7, Simpson 4, Muscat 3, Robinson 3, Atkins 2, Froggatt 2, Osborn 2, Curle 1, Westwood 1, own goals 3.
*Coca-Cola Cup (7):* Bull 2, Ferguson 1 (pen), Froggatt 1, Garcia Sanjuan 1, Goodman 1, Paatelainen 1.
*FA Cup (12):* Paatelainen 4, Freedman 2, Curle 1 (pen), Ferguson 1, Goodman 1, Naylor 1, Richards 1, Robinson 1.

| Stowell M 35 | Smith J 11 | Kubicki D 12 | Atkins M 30 + 4 | Sedgley S 18 + 1 | Curle K 40 | Keane R 34 + 4 | Ferguson D 22 + 4 | Bull S 24 + 7 | Goodman D 29 + 1 | Froggatt S 31 + 2 | Wright J — + 4 | Paatelainen M 10 + 13 | Robinson C 27 + 5 | Coleman S 3 + 1 | Crowe G — + 2 | Diaz I 1 | Williams A 20 | Garcia Senjuan J 4 | Westwood C 3 + 1 | Foley D 1 + 4 | Freedman D 25 + 4 | Simpson P 23 + 5 | Naylor L 14 + 2 | Muscat K 22 + 2 | Corica S — + 1 | Gilkes M 3 | Osborn S 23 + 1 | Richards D 13 | Daley T — + 2 | Segers H 11 | Slater R 4 + 2 | Emblen N 6 + 1 | Claridge S 4 + 1 | Wright S 3 | Match No. |
|---|---|---|---|---|---|---|---|---|---|---|---|---|---|---|---|---|---|---|---|---|---|---|---|---|---|---|---|---|---|---|---|---|---|---|---|
| 1 | 2 | 3 | 4 | 5 | 6 | 7 | 8 | 9 | 10 | 11 | | | | | | | | | | | | | | | | | | | | | | | | | 1 |
| 1 | 2[1] | 3 | 4 | 5 | 6 | 7 | 8 | 9[2] | 10 | 11 | 12 | 13 | | | | | | | | | | | | | | | | | | | | | | | 2 |
| 1 | 2 | 3 | 4 | 5 | 6 | 7[1] | 8 | 9 | 10 | 11 | | | 12 | | | | | | | | | | | | | | | | | | | | | | 3 |
| 1 | 2 | 3 | 4 | 5[1] | | 7 | 8 | 9 | 10 | 11 | 12 | | | | | | 6 | | | | | | | | | | | | | | | | | | 4 |
| 1 | 2 | 3 | 4 | | | 7 | 8 | 9 | 10[1] | 11 | | | | | | | 6 | 5 | 12 | | | | | | | | | | | | | | | | 5 |
| 1 | 2[1] | 3 | 4 | | | 7 | 8 | 9 | | 11 | 12 | 13 | | | | | 6 | 5 | | 10[2] | | | | | | | | | | | | | | | 6 |
| 1 | 2 | 3[1] | 4 | | | 7 | 8 | 9 | | 11 | 12 | 10 | | | | | 6 | 5 | | | | | | | | | | | | | | | | | 7 |
| 1 | 2 | 3 | 4 | | | 7[2] | 8 | 9 | | | | | 10 | 6 | 12 | | | 5[1] | 11 | 13 | | | | | | | | | | | | | | | 8 |
| 1 | 2 | 3 | | | 6 | 7 | 8 | 9[1] | 12 | | | | 10 | 4[2] | | | 5 | 11 | | 13 | | | | | | | | | | | | | | | 9 |
| 1 | 2 | 3 | 4 | | 6 | 7 | 8 | 9 | 10 | | | | 12 | | | | 5 | 11[1] | | | | | | | | | | | | | | | | | 10 |
| 1 | 2 | | 4 | | 6 | 7[2] | 8 | 9 | | | | | 12 | | | | 5 | 10[1] | | 13 | | 11 | 3 | | | | | | | | | | | | 11 |
| 1 | 3[2] | 2 | | | 6 | 7[1] | 8 | 9 | | | | | 4 | | | | 5 | | | | 12 | 10 | 11 | 13 | | | | | | | | | | | 12 |
| 1 | | 3 | | | 6 | | 8 | 9 | | | | | 4 | | | | 5 | | | | 7 | 10 | 11 | | 2 | | | | | | | | | | 13 |
| 1 | | 3[2] | | | 6 | | 8 | 9 | | 7[1] | | | 4 | | | | 5 | | | | 12 | 10 | 11 | | 2 | 13 | | | | | | | | | 14 |
| 1 | | | | | 6 | 7 | 8 | 9 | | 3 | | | 4 | | | | 5 | | | | | 10 | 11 | | 2 | | | | | | | | | | 15 |
| 1 | | | | | 6 | 7 | 8 | 9 | | 3 | | | 4 | | | | 5 | | | | | 10 | 11 | | 2 | | | | | | | | | | 16 |
| 1 | | | | | 6 | 7 | 8 | 9 | | 3 | | | 4[1] | | | | 5 | | | | | 10 | 11 | 12 | 2 | | | | | | | | | | 17 |
| 1 | | 2 | | | 6 | 9 | 8[2] | | | | | 7 | 12 | 4 | | | 5 | | | | | 10 | 11[1] | | | | 3 | 13 | | | | | | | 18 |
| 1 | | 8 | | | 6 | 9 | 12 | | | | | 7 | 3 | 13 | | | | | 5 | 4 | 10[2] | | | | | | 2 | 11[1] | | | | | | | 19 |
| 1 | | 8 | 4 | 6 | 9 | | | | | | | 7 | 3 | 12 | | | | | | 5 | 10 | | | | | | 2[1] | 11 | | | | | | | 20 |
| 1 | 2[1] | 8 | 4 | 6 | 9[2] | | | | | | | 7 | 3 | 13 | | | | | | 5 | 10 | 14 | | | | | | 11[3] | | | | | | | 21 |
| 1 | | 2 | 4 | | 6 | 9 | 12 | | | | | 7 | 3 | | | | 5 | | | | 10[1] | 8 | | | | | 11 | | | | | | | | 22 |
| 1 | | 2 | 4 | | 6 | 9[1] | 12 | | | | | 7 | 3 | | | | 5 | | | | 10 | 8 | | | | | 11 | | | | | | | | 23 |
| 1 | | 2 | | | 6 | 9 | | | | | | 7 | 3 | | | | 4 | | | | 10[1] | 8 | | 12 | | | 11 | 5 | | | | | | | 24 |
| 1 | | 4 | | | 6 | 9[1] | | | | | | 7[2] | 3 | 13 | 12 | | | | | | 10 | 8 | | 2 | | | 11 | 5 | | | | | | | 25 |
| 1 | | 4 | | | 6 | 9[3] | 8 | | | | | 7[2] | 3 | 13 | 12 | | | | | | 10 | | | 2 | | | 11[1] | 5 | 14 | | | | | | 26 |
| 1 | | 4[2] | 11 | | 6 | 9[1] | 8 | | | | | 7 | 3 | 12 | 13 | | | | | | 10[3] | | | 2 | | | | 5 | 14 | | | | | | 27 |
| 1 | | 12 | 4 | | 6 | 9[1] | | | | | | 7 | 3 | | | | 8 | | | | 10 | 11 | | 2 | | | 5 | | | | | | | | 28 |
| 1 | | 12 | 4 | | 6 | 9[2] | | | | | | 7 | 3[1] | 13 | 8 | | | | | | 10 | 11 | | 2 | | | 5 | | | | | | | | 29 |
| | | | 4 | | 6 | 9 | 8 | | | | | 7 | | | 11 | | | | | | 10 | | 3 | 2 | | | 5 | | | 1 | | | | | 30 |
| | | 2 | | | 6 | | | 12 | | 7[1] | | | 9[2] | 4 | | 13 | | | | | 10 | 8 | 3 | | | | 11 | 5 | | 1 | | | | | 31 |
| | | 8 | | | 6 | | | 12 | | | | | 9 | 7 | | | 4 | | | | 10[1] | | 3 | 2 | | | 11 | 5 | | 1 | | | | | 32 |
| | | 4 | | | 6 | 9[1] | | | | | | 12 | | | 7 | 8 | | | | | 10 | 13 | 3 | 2[2] | | | 11 | 5 | | 1 | | | | | 33 |
| | | 2 | | | 6 | 7[2] | | | 9 | | | | | 12 | 8 | | | | | | 10[1] | 4 | 3 | 13 | | | 11 | 5 | | 1 | | | | | 34 |
| | | | | | 6 | 9 | | 12 | 7 | 4[2] | | | | 8 | | | 5 | | | | 10[1] | 13 | 3 | 2 | | | 11 | | | | | 1 | | | 35 |
| | | | | | 6 | | | 12 | 7 | 4 | | | 9 | 8 | | | 5 | | | | 10[1] | | 3 | 2 | | | 11 | | | | | 1 | | | 36 |
| | | 12 | | | 6 | 13 | | 9 | | 7 | | | 10[1] | 8 | | | 5 | | | | 14 | 3[1] | | | | | 11 | 4[2] | 1 | | | 7[1] | 8 | 9 | 37 |
| | | | | | 4[2] | 6 | 12 | | 13 | 10[2] | 3 | | | | | | 5 | | | | | 14 | | | | | 11 | | | 1 | 7[1] | 8 | 9 | 2 | 38 |
| | | | | | 4 | | 12 | | | 9[2] | 3 | | | | | | 5 | | | | 13 | 7 | 2 | | | | 11[1] | 6 | 1 | | 8 | 10 | | 39 |
| | | | | | 4 | 6 | | | | 9[2] | 7 | | | | | | 5 | | | | 13 | 12 | 3[1] | 2 | | | 11[3] | | | 1 | 14 | 8 | 10 | 40 |
| | | | | | 5 | 6 | 10[1] | | 9 | 7 | 3 | | | | | | | | | | 4 | | | 2 | | | 11 | | | 1 | 8 | 12 | | 2 | 41 |
| | | | | | 4 | 6 | | | 9[1] | 7 | 3 | | | | | | 5 | | | | 12 | 10 | 2 | | | | 11 | | | 1 | 8 | | | | 42 |
| | | 12 | | | 5 | 6 | 13 | | 14 | 9 | | | 8[1] | | | | | | | | | 7 | 3 | 2 | | | 11 | | | 1 | 4[3] | 10[2] | | | 43 |
| | | 4 | | | 6[2] | 10 | | | 9 | 7 | | | 12 | | | | | | | | | 8[1] | 3 | 2 | | | 11 | 13 | 5 | 1 | | | | | 44 |
| 1 | | 4 | | 6 | 10[1] | | | | 7 | 12 | | 9 | | | | | | | | | | 8 | 3 | 2 | | | 11 | | | | | | 5 | | 45 |
| 1 | | 4 | 12 | 6 | | 8[1] | 10[2] | 7 | 13 | 9 | | | | | | | | | | | | 11[3] | 3 | 2 | | | | | | | | | 5 | 14 | 46 |

**Coca-Cola Cup**

| | | | |
|---|---|---|---|
| First Round | QPR | (a) | 2-0 |
| | | (h) | 1-2 |
| Second Round | Fulham | (a) | 1-0 |
| | | (h) | 1-0 |
| Third Round | Reading | (a) | 2-4 |

**FA Cup**

| | | | |
|---|---|---|---|
| Third Round | Darlington | (a) | 4-0 |
| Fourth Round | Charlton Ath | (a) | 1-1 |
| | | (h) | 3-0 |
| Fifth Round | Wimbledon | (a) | 1-1 |
| | | (h) | 2-1 |
| Sixth Round | Leeds U | (a) | 1-0 |

WREXHAM 1997–98  *Back row (left to right):* Tony Humes, Karl Connolly, Leigh Edwards, Andy Marriott, Mark Cartwright, David Walsh, Barry Jones, Mark McGregor.
*Second row:* Steve Weaver (Schoolboy Development Officer), Cliff Sear (Youth Development Officer), Gareth Shone, Steve Watkin, David Ridler, Brian Carey, Dean Spink, Scott Williams, David Brammer, Kevin Russell, Brian Prandle (Coach), Mel Pejic (Physio).
*Third row:* Steve Hughes (Community Officer), Wayne Phillips, Gareth Owen, Neil Roberts, Craig Skinner, Joey Jones (Coach), Brian Flynn (Manager), Kevin Reeves (Assistant Manager), Phil Hardy, Peter Ward, Paul Roberts, Jonathan Cross, Dudley Hall (Assistant Physio).
*Front row:* Deryn Brace, Martyn Chalk, Neil Wainwright, Andy Griffiths, Stephen Thomas, Robert Morris.

# Division 2     **WREXHAM**

*Racecourse Ground, Mold Road, Wrexham LL11 2AH.* Telephone: (01978) 262129. Fax: (01978) 357821.
Commercial Dept: (01978) 352536. Community Office: (01978) 358545. Clubcall: 0891 121642.

*Ground capacity:* 9200.

*Record attendance:* 34,445 v Manchester U, FA Cup 4th rd, 26 January 1957.

*Record receipts:* £126,012 v West Ham U, FA Cup 4th rd, 4 February 1992.

*Pitch measurements:* 111yd × 71yd.

*Chairman:* W. P. Griffiths.

*Managing Director:* D. L. Rhodes.

*Directors:* C. Griffiths, S. Mackreth, G. Paletta, B. Williams (Vice-Chairman), P. Griffiths, Mrs B. Derosa.

*Manager:* Brian Flynn. *Assistant Manager:* Kevin Reeves.

*Secretary:* D. L. Rhodes. *Player-Coach:* Joey Jones.

*Commercial Manager:* Allan Thomas. *Physio:* Mel Pejic.

*Year Formed:* 1873 (oldest club in Wales).

*Turned Professional:* 1912. *Ltd Co.:* 1912.

*Previous Ground:* Acton Park.

*Club Nickname:* 'Robins'.

*Foundation:* The oldest club still in existence in Wales, Wrexham was founded in 1873 by a group of local businessmen initially to play a 17-a-side game against the Provincial Insurance team. By 1875 their team formation was reduced to 11 men and a year later they were among the founders of the Welsh FA.

*First Football League game:* 27 August 1921, Division 3 (N), v Hartlepools U (h) L 0-2 – Godding; Ellis, Simpson; Matthias, Foster, Griffiths; Burton, Goode, Cotton, Edwards, Lloyd.

*Record League Victory:* 10–1 v Hartlepool U, Division 4, 3 March 1962 – Keelan; Peter Jones, McGavan; Tecwyn Jones, Fox, Ken Barnes; Ron Barnes (3), Bennion (1), Davies (3), Ambler (3), Ron Roberts.

*Record Cup Victory:* 6–0 v Gateshead, FA Cup 1st rd, 20 November 1976 – Lloyd; Evans, Whittle, Davis, Roberts, Thomas (Hill), Shinton (3 incl. 1p), Sutton, Ashcroft (2), Lee (1), Griffiths. 6–0 v Charlton Ath, FA Cup 3rd rd, 5 January 1980 – Davies; Darracott, Kenworthy, Davis, Jones (Hill), Fox, Vinter (3), Sutton, Edwards (1), McNeil (2), Carrodus.

*Record Defeat:* 0–9 v Brentford, Division 3, 15 October 1963.

*Most League Points (2 for a win):* 61, Division 4, 1969–70 and Division 3, 1977–78.

*Most League Points (3 for a win):* 80, Division 3, 1992–93.

*Most League Goals:* 106, Division 3 (N), 1932–33.

*Highest League Scorer in Season:* Tom Bamford, 44, Division 3 (N), 1933–34.

*Most League Goals in Total Aggregate:* Tom Bamford, 175, 1928–34.

*Most Capped Player:* Dai Davies, 28 (51), Wales.

*Most League Appearances:* Arfon Griffiths, 592, 1959–61, 1962–79.

*Record Transfer Fee Received:* £800,000 from Birmingham C for Bryan Hughes, March 1997.

*Record Transfer Fee Paid:* £210,000 to Liverpool for Joey Jones, October 1978.

*Football League Record:* 1921 Original Member of Division 3 (N); 1958–60 Division 3; 1960–62 Division 4; 1962–64 Division 3; 1964–70 Division 4; 1970–78 Division 3; 1978–82 Division 2; 1982–83 Division 3; 1983–92 Division 4; 1992–93 Division 3; 1993– Division 2.

*Honours: Football League:* Division 2 best season: 7th, 1997–98; Division 3 – Champions 1977–78, Runners-up 1992–93; Division 3 (N) – Runners-up 1932–33; Division 4 – Runners-up 1969–70. *FA Cup:* best season: 6th rd, 1974, 1978, 1997. *Football League Cup:* best season: 5th rd, 1961, 1978. *Welsh Cup:* Winners 23 times (record); Runners-up 22 times (record). **European Competition:** *European Cup-Winners' Cup:* 1972–73, 1975–76, 1978–79, 1979–80, 1984–85, 1986–87, 1990–91, 1995–96.

*Colours:* Red shirts, white shorts, red stockings. *Change colours:* Gold shirts, navy blue shorts, navy blue stockings.

**Did you know?**
Ted Regan scored twice on his League debut for Wrexham on 29 October 1921 against Accrington Stanley and a hat-trick the following week against Chesterfield.

## WREXHAM 1997–98 LEAGUE RECORD

| Match No. | Date | | Venue | Opponents | Result | | H/T Score | Lg. Pos. | Goalscorers | Attendance |
|---|---|---|---|---|---|---|---|---|---|---|
| 1 | Aug | 9 | A | Fulham | L | 0-1 | 0-1 | — | | 8789 |
| 2 | | 16 | H | Oldham Ath | W | 3-1 | 2-0 | 11 | Jones [8], Carey [44], Ward [77] | 4429 |
| 3 | | 23 | A | Grimsby T | D | 0-0 | 0-0 | 12 | | 4404 |
| 4 | Sept | 2 | H | Blackpool | L | 3-4 | 2-0 | — | Owen [22], Phillips [39], Spink [51] | 3763 |
| 5 | | 8 | A | Wigan Ath | L | 2-3 | 0-1 | — | Spink 2 [57, 82] | 3872 |
| 6 | | 13 | H | Bristol C | W | 2-1 | 1-0 | 16 | Spink [13], Watkin [60] | 3251 |
| 7 | | 20 | A | Luton T | W | 5-2 | 2-1 | 12 | Brammer [10], Connolly 3 [26, 63, 73], Skinner (pen) [62] | 5241 |
| 8 | | 27 | H | Chesterfield | D | 0-0 | 0-0 | 14 | | 3921 |
| 9 | Oct | 4 | A | Bristol R | L | 0-1 | 0-0 | 17 | | 6829 |
| 10 | | 11 | A | Walsall | L | 0-3 | 0-2 | 19 | | 4042 |
| 11 | | 18 | H | Burnley | D | 0-0 | 0-0 | 20 | | 5132 |
| 12 | | 21 | H | Southend U | W | 3-1 | 0-1 | — | McGregor [60], Kelly [65], Connolly (pen) [87] | 2039 |
| 13 | | 25 | A | Preston NE | W | 1-0 | 0-0 | 15 | Chalk [50] | 9098 |
| 14 | Nov | 1 | A | Carlisle U | D | 2-2 | 2-2 | 15 | Roberts 2 [20, 33] | 4464 |
| 15 | | 4 | H | Bournemouth | W | 2-1 | 2-0 | — | Roberts [12], Spink [15] | 2462 |
| 16 | | 8 | H | Northampton T | W | 1-0 | 0-0 | 7 | Roberts [48] | 3766 |
| 17 | | 18 | A | Wycombe W | D | 0-0 | 0-0 | — | | 3635 |
| 18 | | 22 | H | Plymouth Arg | D | 1-1 | 0-0 | 10 | Ward [71] | 3641 |
| 19 | | 29 | A | Brentford | D | 1-1 | 0-0 | 11 | Owen [62] | 3748 |
| 20 | Dec | 2 | H | Watford | D | 1-1 | 0-0 | — | McGregor [89] | 3702 |
| 21 | | 13 | A | York C | L | 0-1 | 0-0 | 12 | | 2871 |
| 22 | | 20 | H | Gillingham | D | 0-0 | 0-0 | 13 | | 2834 |
| 23 | | 26 | H | Wigan Ath | D | 2-2 | 1-1 | 14 | Owen [39], Connolly [65] | 4577 |
| 24 | | 28 | A | Blackpool | W | 2-1 | 0-1 | 11 | Owen [85], Wainwright [88] | 5424 |
| 25 | Jan | 10 | H | Fulham | L | 0-3 | 0-1 | 13 | | 5338 |
| 26 | | 17 | A | Millwall | W | 1-0 | 0-0 | 11 | Wainwright [76] | 5550 |
| 27 | | 27 | A | Oldham Ath | L | 0-3 | 0-2 | — | | 4680 |
| 28 | | 31 | A | Bristol C | D | 1-1 | 0-1 | 13 | Roberts [48] | 11,741 |
| 29 | Feb | 7 | H | Luton T | W | 2-1 | 0-0 | 11 | Brammer [66], Roberts [88] | 3527 |
| 30 | | 14 | H | Bristol R | W | 1-0 | 1-0 | 10 | Owen [26] | 3716 |
| 31 | | 21 | A | Chesterfield | L | 1-3 | 0-2 | 10 | Owen [76] | 3919 |
| 32 | | 24 | A | Burnley | W | 2-1 | 1-1 | — | Roberts [11], Wilson [64] | 8576 |
| 33 | | 28 | H | Walsall | W | 2-1 | 2-1 | 8 | Brammer [6], Wainwright [29] | 3622 |
| 34 | Mar | 3 | A | Northampton T | W | 1-0 | 1-0 | — | Spink [39] | 5183 |
| 35 | | 7 | H | Carlisle U | D | 2-2 | 1-1 | 7 | Ward [45], Connolly [78] | 4242 |
| 36 | | 14 | A | Bournemouth | W | 1-0 | 0-0 | 7 | Owen [52] | 5512 |
| 37 | | 17 | H | Millwall | W | 1-0 | 1-0 | — | Roberts [6] | 4167 |
| 38 | | 21 | H | Wycombe W | W | 2-0 | 1-0 | 3 | Kavanagh (og) [42], Brammer [90] | 4290 |
| 39 | | 28 | A | Plymouth Arg | L | 0-2 | 0-1 | 4 | | 4749 |
| 40 | | 31 | H | Grimsby T | D | 0-0 | 0-0 | — | | 5421 |
| 41 | Apr | 4 | H | Brentford | D | 2-2 | 0-1 | 4 | Wilson [60], Ward [63] | 4132 |
| 42 | | 11 | A | Watford | L | 0-1 | 0-1 | 5 | | 12,340 |
| 43 | | 13 | H | York C | L | 1-2 | 0-0 | 5 | Wilson [65] | 5231 |
| 44 | | 18 | A | Gillingham | D | 1-1 | 1-1 | 7 | Wilson [16] | 7869 |
| 45 | | 25 | H | Preston NE | D | 0-0 | 0-0 | 8 | | 7302 |
| 46 | May | 2 | A | Southend U | W | 3-1 | 1-1 | 7 | Ward 2 [43, 86], Connolly [72] | 4220 |

**Final League Position: 7**　　　1996–97 DIV2 8

### GOALSCORERS

*League (55):* Roberts 8, Connolly 7 (1 pen), Owen 7, Spink 6, Ward 6, Brammer 4, Wilson 4, Wainwright 3, McGregor 2, Carey 1, Chalk 1, Jones 1, Kelly 1, Phillips 1, Skinner 1 (pen), Watkin 1, own goal 1.
*Coca-Cola Cup (2):* Connolly 1 (pen), Spink 1.
*FA Cup (6):* Connolly 5, Roberts 1.

| Marriott A 42 | McGregor M 41+1 | Brace D 8 | Phillips W 14+6 | Jones B 12+2 | Carey B 43 | Chalk M 15+11 | Russell K 11+5 | Connolly K 31+4 | Skinner C 16+9 | Ward P 35+2 | Watkin S —+3 | Brammer D 29+4 | Spink D 33+3 | Cross J 2 | Owen G 36+4 | Hardy P 34 | Humes T 22+2 | Roberts N 29+5 | Kelly R 5+5 | Cartwright M 4 | Ridler D 18+2 | Wainwright N 7+4 | Basham S 4+1 | Wilson M 12+1 | Williams S 3 | Match No. |
|---|---|---|---|---|---|---|---|---|---|---|---|---|---|---|---|---|---|---|---|---|---|---|---|---|---|---|
| 1 | 2 | 3 | 4 | 5 | 6 | $7^1$ | 8 | 9 | 10 | $11^2$ | 12 | 13 | | | | | | | | | | | | | | 1 |
| 1 | 2 | 3 | $4^1$ | 5 | 6 | | 8 | 9 | 7 | 11 | | 12 | 10 | | | | | | | | | | | | | 2 |
| 1 | 2 | 3 | 4 | 5 | 6 | 12 | | 9 | $7^1$ | 11 | | 8 | 10 | | | | | | | | | | | | | 3 |
| 1 | 2 | | 4 | 5 | 6 | 12 | | 9 | $7^1$ | | | 11 | 10 | 3 | 8 | | | | | | | | | | | 4 |
| 1 | 2 | | $4^1$ | 5 | 6 | 7 | 12 | 9 | | | | 11 | 10 | 3 | 8 | | | | | | | | | | | 5 |
| 1 | 2 | | 4 | 12 | 6 | | | 9 | 7 | 11 | | 13 | $10^2$ | | 8 | 3 | $5^1$ | | | | | | | | | 6 |
| 1 | 2 | | 4 | 5 | 6 | | | $9^1$ | 7 | 11 | | 12 | 10 | | 8 | 3 | | | | | | | | | | 7 |
| 1 | 2 | | $4^2$ | 5 | 6 | 12 | | $9^3$ | $7^1$ | 11 | | 13 | 10 | | 8 | 3 | | 14 | | | | | | | | 8 |
| 1 | 2 | | $4^1$ | 5 | 6 | $7^2$ | 12 | | | 11 | | 13 | 10 | | 8 | 3 | | 9 | | | | | | | | 9 |
| | 2 | | | 12 | 6 | $7^1$ | | 9 | | 11 | | 4 | 10 | | 8 | 3 | $5^1$ | 13 | | | | | | | 1 | 10 |
| 1 | 2 | | | 12 | 6 | 13 | | 9 | | $11^1$ | | 4 | 10 | | 8 | 3 | 5 | $7^2$ | | | | | | | | 11 |
| 1 | 2 | | | | 6 | | | 9 | | 11 | | 4 | 10 | | 8 | 3 | 5 | 7 | | | | | | | | 12 |
| 1 | 2 | | | 12 | 6 | 13 | | $9^2$ | | 11 | | $4^1$ | 10 | | 8 | 3 | 5 | 7 | | | | | | | | 13 |
| 1 | 2 | | | 12 | 6 | 13 | | 9 | | 11 | | $4^1$ | | | 8 | 3 | 5 | 10 | $7^2$ | | | | | | | 14 |
| 1 | $2^1$ | | | 12 | 6 | | | | 7 | 11 | | 4 | 10 | | 8 | 3 | 5 | 9 | | | | | | | | 15 |
| 1 | 2 | | | | 6 | | | | 7 | 11 | | 4 | 10 | | 8 | 3 | 5 | 9 | | | | | | | | 16 |
| 1 | 2 | | 4 | 12 | | | | $9^1$ | 7 | 11 | | | | | 8 | 3 | 5 | 10 | 6 | | | | | | | 17 |
| 1 | 2 | | 4 | 12 | | 13 | | 9 | $7^1$ | 11 | | | | | $8^2$ | 3 | 5 | 10 | 6 | | | | | | | 18 |
| 1 | $2^1$ | | | 12 | 6 | | | 9 | 7 | 11 | | 4 | | | 8 | 3 | 5 | 10 | | | | | | | | 19 |
| 1 | 2 | | | | 6 | | | 9 | $7^1$ | 11 | 12 | 4 | | | 8 | 3 | 5 | 10 | | | | | | | | 20 |
| 1 | 2 | | | 12 | 6 | | | 9 | 7 | 11 | | 4 | $10^2$ | | 8 | $3^1$ | 5 | 13 | | | | | | | | 21 |
| 1 | 2 | | | 12 | 6 | | | 9 | 7 | 11 | | 4 | $10^2$ | | $8^1$ | 3 | 5 | 13 | | | | | | | | 22 |
| 1 | 2 | | | | 6 | 12 | | 9 | $7^1$ | 11 | | 4 | $10^2$ | | 8 | 3 | $5^3$ | 13 | 14 | | | | | | | 23 |
| 1 | 2 | | | 12 | 6 | | | 9 | 7 | $11^1$ | | $4^2$ | | | 8 | 3 | 5 | 10 | 13 | | | | | | | 24 |
| 1 | 2 | | | 12 | 6 | | | 9 | | $11^1$ | | 4 | $10^2$ | | 8 | 3 | 5 | 13 | 7 | | | | | | | 25 |
| 1 | 2 | | | | 6 | | | 9 | | 11 | | 4 | | | 8 | 3 | 5 | 10 | 7 | | | | | | | 26 |
| 1 | 2 | | | 12 | 6 | | | 9 | | 11 | 13 | $4^1$ | | | 8 | 3 | 5 | $10^2$ | 7 | | | | | | | 27 |
| 1 | 2 | | | 12 | 6 | | | $9^1$ | 7 | 11 | | 4 | | | 8 | 3 | 5 | 10 | | | | | | | | 28 |
| 1 | 2 | | | | 6 | | | $9^2$ | $7^1$ | 11 | | 4 | | | 8 | 3 | 5 | 10 | 12 | 13 | | | | | | 29 |
| | 2 | 3 | | | 6 | | | | | 11 | | 4 | | | 8 | | | 10 | | 1 | 5 | 7 | 9 | | | 30 |
| | 2 | 3 | | 12 | 6 | | | | | $11^1$ | 13 | 4 | | | 8 | | 14 | 10 | | 1 | $5^3$ | 7 | $9^2$ | | | 31 |
| | 2 | 3 | | 12 | 6 | | | | | 11 | | 4 | | | 8 | | | 10 | 13 | $1^2$ | 5 | 7 | $9^1$ | | | 32 |
| 1 | 2 | $3^1$ | | 12 | 6 | | | | | 11 | 13 | 4 | | | 8 | | 5 | 10 | $7^2$ | | | | 9 | | | 33 |
| 1 | 2 | | | | 6 | | | 9 | 7 | 11 | | 4 | | | 8 | 3 | 5 | 10 | | | | | | | | 34 |
| 1 | 2 | | | 12 | 6 | | | 9 | $7^1$ | 11 | | 4 | | | 8 | 3 | 5 | 10 | | | | | | | | 35 |
| 1 | 2 | | | 12 | 6 | | | 9 | $7^1$ | 11 | 13 | $4^2$ | | | 8 | | 5 | 10 | | | | | 3 | | | 36 |
| 1 | 2 | | | 12 | 6 | | | $9^1$ | 7 | 11 | 13 | 4 | | | $8^2$ | | 5 | 10 | | | | | 3 | | | 37 |
| 1 | 2 | | | 12 | 6 | | | 9 | $7^1$ | 11 | | 4 | | | | 3 | 5 | 10 | | | | | | 8 | | 38 |
| 1 | 2 | | | 12 | 6 | | | $9^2$ | 7 | $11^1$ | | 4 | | | | 3 | | 10 | | | 5 | 13 | | 8 | | 39 |
| 1 | 2 | | | 12 | 6 | | | 9 | 7 | 11 | | 4 | | | | 3 | | 10 | | | $5^2$ | 13 | | $8^1$ | | 40 |
| 1 | 2 | | | 12 | 6 | | | $9^2$ | 7 | $11^1$ | | 4 | | | | 3 | | 10 | | | 5 | 13 | | 8 | | 41 |
| 1 | 2 | | | 12 | 6 | | | $9^1$ | 7 | $11^2$ | 13 | 4 | | | | 3 | | $10^3$ | | | 5 | 14 | | 8 | | 42 |
| 1 | 2 | | | 12 | 6 | | | $9^1$ | $7^2$ | 11 | 13 | 4 | | | | 3 | | 10 | | | $5^3$ | 14 | | 8 | | 43 |
| 1 | 2 | | | | 6 | | | 9 | 7 | 11 | | 4 | | | | 3 | | 10 | | | 5 | | | 8 | | 44 |
| 1 | 2 | | | 12 | 6 | | | $9^2$ | 7 | 11 | | $4^1$ | | | | 3 | | 10 | | | 5 | 13 | | 8 | | 45 |
| 1 | 2 | | | 12 | 6 | | | 9 | $7^3$ | 11 | 13 | $4^2$ | | | | 3 | | $10^1$ | | | 5 | 14 | | 8 | | 46 |

**Coca-Cola Cup**

| First Round | Sheffield U | (h) | 1-1 |
|---|---|---|---|
| | | (a) | 1-3 |

**FA Cup**

| First Round | Rochdale | (a) | 2-0 |
|---|---|---|---|
| Second Round | Chester C | (a) | 2-0 |
| Third Round | Wimbledon | (a) | 0-0 |
| | | (h) | 2-3 |

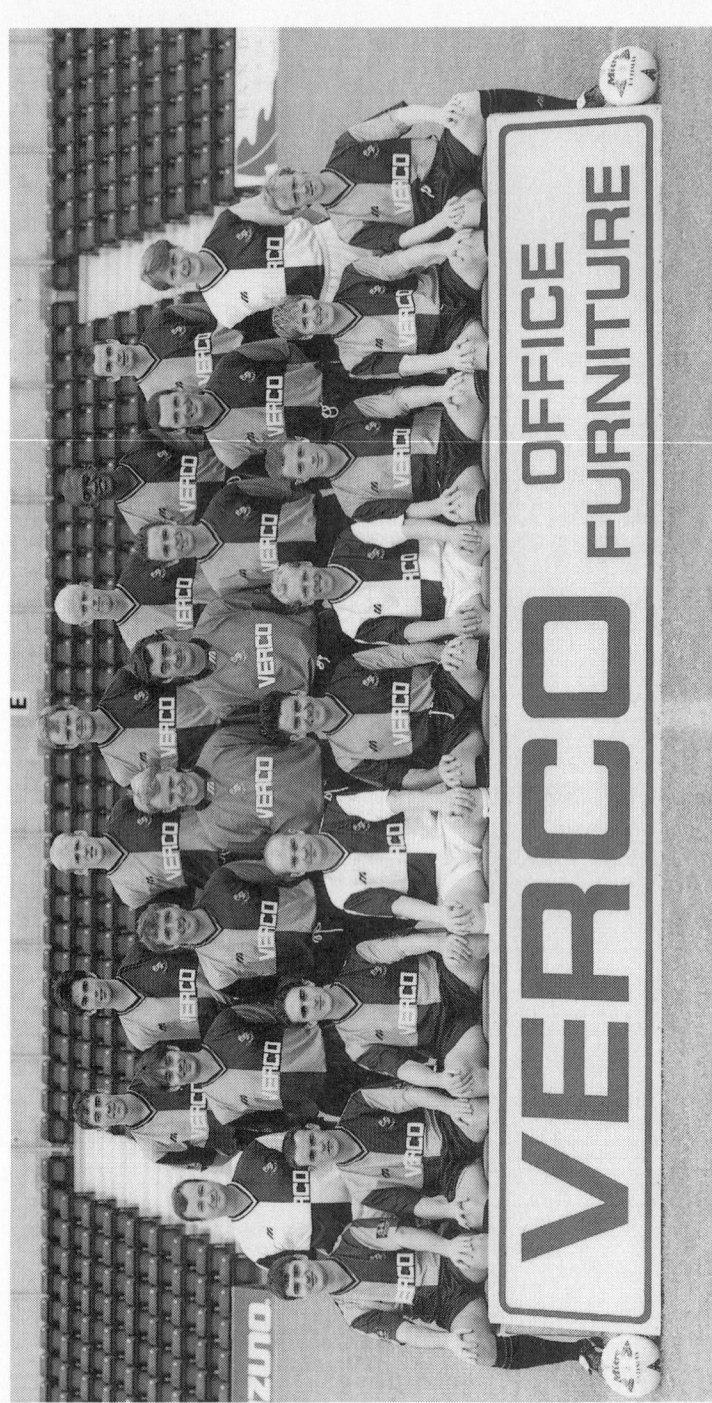

WYCOMBE WANDERERS 1997–98   *Back row (left to right):* Gary Wraight, Maurice Harkin, Keith Ryan, Keith Scott, Alan Beeton, Steve Brown, Aaron Patton.
*Middle row:* Adrian Cole (Youth Development Officer), Jason Kavanagh, Paul McCarthy, Martin Taylor, Brian Parkin, Michael Forsyth, John Cornforth, David Jones (Physio).
*Front row:* Jason Cousins, Michael Simpson, Mark Stallard, Richard Hill (Assistant Manager), John Gregory (Manager), Neil Smillie (Youth Team Manager), Paul Read, Steve McGavin, Dave Carroll.

# Division 2    **WYCOMBE WANDERERS**

***Adams Park, Hillbottom Road, Sands, High Wycombe HP12 4HJ.*** Telephone (01494) 472100. Fax: (01494) 527633. Credit Card Hotline: (01494) 441118. Information Line 0891 446855.

***Ground Capacity:*** 10,000 new stand; now seats 7250.

***Record attendance:*** 9007 v West Ham U, FA Cup 3rd rd, 7 January 1995.

***Record receipts:*** £61,221 (net of VAT) v West Ham U, FA Cup 3rd rd, 7 January 1995.

***Pitch measurements:*** 115yd × 75yd.

***Patron:*** J. Adams.

***President:*** M. E. Seymour.

***Chairman:*** I. L. Beeks.

***Directors:*** G. Peart (Financial), G. Richards, B. R. Lee, A. Parry, A. Thibault, G. Cox.

***Associate Director:*** J. Goldsworthy.

***Manager:*** Neil Smillie. ***Assistant Manager:*** Wayne Turner.

***Physio:*** David Jones. ***Marketing Manager:*** Mark Austin. ***Promotions Manager:*** Mike Phillips.

***Year Formed:*** 1884. ***Turned Professional:*** 1974. ***Club Nicknames:*** 'Chairboys' (after High Wycombe's tradition of furniture making), 'The Blues'.

***Previous Ground:*** 1887 The Rye; 1893 Spring Meadow; 1895 Loakes Park, 1899 Daws Hill Park; 1901 Loakes Park; 1990 Adams Park.

***Foundation:*** In 1884 a group of young furniture trade workers started playing together informally under the name of North Town Wanderers, the area of the town where they lived. They decided to better themselves by entering junior football and in 1887 Jim Ray, secretary, and Datchett Webb, captain, called a meeting at the Steam Engine public house. Wycombe Wanderers FC was formed and probably named after the famous FA Cup winners, The Wanderers, who had visited the town in 1877 for a tie with the original High Wycombe club.

***First Football League Game:*** 14 August 1993, Division 3 v Carlisle U (a), D 2-2: Hyde; Cousins, Horton (Langford), Kerr, Crossley, Ryan, Carroll, Stapleton, Thompson, Scott, Guppy (1) (Hutchinson). Wycombe's first goal was an own goal by Chris Curran.

***Record League Victory:*** 5–0 v Burnley (h), Division 2, 15 April 1997 – Parkin; Cousins, Bell, Kavanagh, McCarthy, Forsyth, Carroll (2 pens) (Simpson), Scott (Farrell), Stallard (1), McGavin (1) (Read (1)), Brown.

***Record Cup Victory:*** 5–0 v Hitchin T (away), FA Cup 2nd rd, 3 December 1994 – Hyde; Cousins, Brown, Crossley, Evans, Ryan (1), Carroll, Bell (1), Thompson, Garner (3) (Hemmings), Stapleton (Langford).

***Record Defeat:*** 0–5 v Walsall, Auto Windscreens Shield 1st rd, 7 November 1995.

***Most League Points:*** 70, Division 3, 1993–94.

***Most League Goals:*** 66, Division 3, 1993–94.

***Highest League Goalscorer in Season:*** Miguel De Souza 18, 1995–96.

***Most League Goals in Total Aggregate:*** Dave Carroll, 31, 1993–98.

***Most League Appearances:*** Dave Carroll, 210, 1993–98.

***Record Transfer Fee Received:*** £375,000 from Swindon T for Keith Scott, November 1993.

***Record Transfer Fee Paid:*** £140,000 to Birmingham C for Steve McGavin, March 1995.

***Football League Record:*** Promoted to Division 3 from GMVC in 1993; 1993–94 Division 3; 1994– Division 2.

***Honours:*** *Football League:* Division 2 best season: 6th, 1994–95; *FA Amateur Cup:* Winners 1931; *FA Trophy:* Winners 1991, 1993; *GM Vauxhall Conference:* Winners 1992–93; *FA Cup:* best season: 3rd rd 1975, 1986, 1994, 1995; *Football League Cup:* never beyond 2nd rd.

***Colours:*** Light & dark blue striped quartered shirts, light blue shorts, light blue stockings.
***Change colours:*** Dark blue and yellow quartered shirts, yellow shorts, yellow stockings.

**Did you know?**
Reggie Boreham was the first Wycombe Wanderers player to earn an amateur international cap when he played for England v Ireland in 1921. He later had three years with Arsenal.

**Founded 1884**

## WYCOMBE WANDERERS 1997–98 LEAGUE RECORD

| Match No. | Date | Venue | Opponents | Result | | H/T Score | Lg. Pos. | Goalscorers | Attendance |
|---|---|---|---|---|---|---|---|---|---|
| 1 | Aug 9 | A | Wigan Ath | L | 2-5 | 0-4 | — | Scott 2 [66, 69] | 4706 |
| 2 | 16 | H | Northampton T | D | 0-0 | 0-0 | 17 | | 5130 |
| 3 | 23 | A | Blackpool | W | 4-2 | 2-1 | 9 | Stallard 2 [36, 50], Kavanagh [38], Cornforth [62] | 4733 |
| 4 | 30 | H | Fulham | W | 2-0 | 1-0 | 5 | Cornforth [8], Stallard [60] | 6278 |
| 5 | Sept 2 | H | Southend U | W | 4-1 | 2-1 | — | Stallard 2 [10, 90], Cornforth [44], Read [59] | 4528 |
| 6 | 7 | A | Watford | L | 1-2 | 0-1 | 3 | Read [70] | 12,100 |
| 7 | 13 | H | Carlisle U | L | 1-4 | 1-2 | 10 | Cornforth (pen) [11] | 6018 |
| 8 | 19 | A | Brentford | D | 1-1 | 1-1 | — | Stallard [3] | 3695 |
| 9 | 27 | H | Preston NE | D | 0-0 | 0-0 | 9 | | 4838 |
| 10 | Oct 4 | A | Burnley | D | 2-2 | 1-1 | 11 | Cornforth (pen) [12], Scott [54] | 9057 |
| 11 | 11 | A | Gillingham | L | 0-1 | 0-0 | 16 | | 5545 |
| 12 | 18 | H | Bristol R | W | 1-0 | 0-0 | 15 | Stallard [71] | 5836 |
| 13 | 21 | H | Walsall | W | 4-2 | 3-2 | — | Stallard 3 [11, 22, 47], Read [27] | 3884 |
| 14 | 25 | A | Chesterfield | L | 1-2 | 0-0 | 12 | | 4119 |
| 15 | Nov 1 | H | Luton T | D | 2-2 | 1-1 | 11 | Stallard [12], McGavin [62] | 6219 |
| 16 | 4 | A | Plymouth Arg | L | 2-4 | 1-2 | — | Collins (og) [5], Scott [52] | 2993 |
| 17 | 8 | A | York C | L | 0-2 | 0-1 | 16 | | 3343 |
| 18 | 18 | H | Wrexham | D | 0-0 | 0-0 | — | | 3635 |
| 19 | 22 | A | Bristol C | L | 1-3 | 0-1 | 16 | Scott (pen) [82] | 11,129 |
| 20 | 29 | H | Bournemouth | D | 1-1 | 0-0 | 17 | Stallard [52] | 4340 |
| 21 | Dec 2 | A | Grimsby T | D | 0-0 | 0-0 | — | | 4160 |
| 22 | 13 | H | Oldham Ath | W | 2-1 | 0-0 | 17 | Scott [53], McGavin [83] | 5327 |
| 23 | 20 | A | Millwall | L | 0-1 | 0-0 | 18 | | 6092 |
| 24 | 26 | H | Watford | D | 0-0 | 0-0 | 18 | | 8090 |
| 25 | 28 | A | Southend U | W | 2-1 | 1-0 | 15 | Scott 2 [6, 84] | 5162 |
| 26 | Jan 10 | H | Wigan Ath | L | 1-2 | 0-1 | 19 | Brown [89] | 5549 |
| 27 | 17 | A | Fulham | D | 0-0 | 0-0 | 19 | | 10,468 |
| 28 | 24 | H | Blackpool | W | 2-1 | 1-1 | 16 | Harkin [8], Stallard [67] | 5073 |
| 29 | 31 | A | Carlisle U | D | 0-0 | 0-0 | 17 | | 6220 |
| 30 | Feb 7 | H | Brentford | D | 0-0 | 0-0 | 17 | | 6328 |
| 31 | 10 | A | Northampton T | L | 0-2 | 0-0 | — | | 5302 |
| 32 | 14 | H | Burnley | W | 2-1 | 1-0 | 14 | Brown [32], McCarthy [57] | 5926 |
| 33 | 21 | A | Preston NE | D | 1-1 | 0-0 | 14 | Brown [60] | 7665 |
| 34 | 24 | A | Bristol R | L | 1-3 | 0-0 | — | Scott [70] | 5805 |
| 35 | 28 | H | Gillingham | W | 1-0 | 1-0 | 14 | Ryan [29] | 5583 |
| 36 | Mar 3 | H | York C | W | 1-0 | 0-0 | — | Ryan [71] | 3768 |
| 37 | 7 | A | Luton T | D | 0-0 | 0-0 | 14 | | 6114 |
| 38 | 14 | H | Plymouth Arg | W | 5-1 | 1-1 | 10 | Ryan [23], Scott [47], Stallard 2 [52, 75], Carroll [83] | 5508 |
| 39 | 21 | A | Wrexham | L | 0-2 | 0-1 | 14 | | 4290 |
| 40 | 28 | H | Bristol C | L | 1-2 | 0-1 | 16 | Harkin [57] | 6326 |
| 41 | Apr 4 | A | Bournemouth | D | 0-0 | 0-0 | 14 | | 4271 |
| 42 | 10 | H | Grimsby T | D | 1-1 | 1-0 | — | Scott [17] | 5846 |
| 43 | 13 | A | Oldham Ath | W | 1-0 | 0-0 | 12 | Stallard [66] | 4305 |
| 44 | 18 | H | Millwall | D | 0-0 | 0-0 | 13 | | 5371 |
| 45 | 25 | H | Chesterfield | D | 1-1 | 1-1 | 15 | Stallard [26] | 5113 |
| 46 | May 2 | A | Walsall | W | 1-0 | 1-0 | 14 | Read [18] | 4412 |

**Final League Position: 14**          1996–97 DIV2 18

## GOALSCORERS

**League (51):** Stallard 17, Scott 11 (1 pen), Cornforth 5 (2 pens), Read 4, Brown 3, Ryan 3, Harkin 2, McGavin 2, Carroll 1, Kavanagh 1, McCarthy 1, own goal 1.
*Coca-Cola Cup (5):* Scott 2, Harkin 1, Read 1, Ryan 1.
*FA Cup (4):* Cornforth 2 (1 pen), McGavin 2.

| Taylor M 45 | Ryan K 40 | Brown S 40 | Kavanagh J 43 + 2 | McCarthy P 28 + 3 | Forsyth M 25 | Carroll D 35 + 4 | Scott K 28 + 1 | Stallard M 43 | McGavin S 35 + 2 | Simpson M 10 + 11 | Cornforth J 18 + 6 | Beeton A 15 + 5 | Read P 14 + 14 | Mohan N 33 | Harkin M 13 + 22 | Cousins J 25 + 4 | Bodin P 5 | Parkin B 1 | Kerslake D 9 + 1 | Wraight G 1 | Baird A — + 2 | Patton A — + 1 | Match No. |
|---|---|---|---|---|---|---|---|---|---|---|---|---|---|---|---|---|---|---|---|---|---|---|---|
| 1 | 2¹ | 3 | 4 | 5 | 6 | 7 | 8² | 9¹ | 10 | 11 | 12 | 13 | 14 | | | | | | | | | | 1 |
| 1 | | 3 | | 5 | 6 | 7 | 8¹ | 9 | 10 | 11 | 2 | 12 | | 4 | | | | | | | | | 2 |
| 1 | | 2 | | 5 | 6 | 12 | 8³ | 9² | 10¹ | 11 | 7 | 3 | 13 | 4 | 14 | | | | | | | | 3 |
| 1 | 11 | 2 | | 5 | 6 | | 8¹ | 9² | 10² | 13 | 7 | 3 | 12 | 4 | 14 | | | | | | | | 4 |
| 1 | 11³ | 2 | | 5 | 6 | 12 | | 9 | 13 | 14 | 7¹ | 3 | 8 | 4 | 10² | | | | | | | | 5 |
| 1 | 11² | 2 | | 5 | 6¹ | | | 9 | 10 | 12 | 7 | 3 | 8 | 4 | 13 | | | | | | | | 6 |
| 1 | 11¹ | 2 | | 5 | | 12 | | 9 | 10² | 13 | 7 | 3³ | 8 | 4 | 6 | 14 | | | | | | | 7 |
| 1 | 6 | 11 | 4 | 5 | | 12 | | 9 | 10 | 7¹ | 8 | | | | | 2 | 3 | | | | | | 8 |
| 1 | 4 | 11 | 12 | 5 | 6 | 10 | 13 | 9⁴ | 7¹ | 8² | | | | | 14 | 2 | 3 | | | | | | 9 |
| 1 | 4 | 11 | 12 | 5 | 6 | 10 | 8 | 9⁴ | 7 | | | | | | 13 | 2¹ | 3 | | | | | | 10 |
| 1 | 4 | 11 | 2 | | 6 | 10 | 8 | 9 | 7¹ | | | | | 5 | 12 | | 3 | | | | | | 11 |
| 1 | 4 | 11 | 2 | 5 | 6 | 10³ | | 9 | 12 | 7¹ | 8² | | | | 13 | 14 | 3 | | | | | | 12 |
| 1 | 4 | 11 | 3 | 5 | 6 | 7 | | 9 | 10¹ | 12 | 13 | 8³ | | | 14 | 2² | | | | | | | 13 |
| 1 | 4 | 11 | 3 | 5 | 6 | 7 | | 9 | 10 | 12 | 8¹ | | | | 13 | 2² | | | | | | | 14 |
| 1 | 4 | 11¹ | 3 | | 6 | 7 | 8 | 9² | 10 | 12 | | | | 5 | 13 | 2 | | | | | | | 15 |
| 1 | 4 | 3 | 12 | | 6¹ | 7 | 8 | 9 | 10 | 11² | | | 13 | 5 | | 2 | | | | | | | 16 |
| | 4 | 3 | | | 6 | 7 | 8 | 9 | 10² | 11¹ | 12 | | | 5 | 13 | 2 | | 1 | | | | | 17 |
| 1 | 4 | 11 | 7 | 12 | 8 | 10² | 13 | 9³ | 6 | 3 | | | | 5¹ | 14 | 2 | | | | | | | 18 |
| 1 | 4 | 11 | 7 | 12 | 8 | 10 | | 9² | | | 6¹ | 3 | | 5 | 13 | 2 | | | | | | | 19 |
| 1 | 4 | 11 | 3 | 7 | 6 | | | 9 | 10 | 8 | | | | 5 | | 2 | | | | | | | 20 |
| 1 | 4 | 11 | 3 | 7 | 6 | | | 9 | 10 | 8 | | | | 5 | | 2 | | | | | | | 21 |
| 1 | 4 | 11 | 3 | 5 | 6 | 7 | 8 | 9 | 10 | | 12 | | | | | 2 | | | | | | | 22 |
| 1 | 4 | 11 | 3² | 5 | 6 | 7 | 8¹ | 9 | 10 | | 12 | | | | 13 | 2 | | | | | | | 23 |
| 1 | 4 | 11 | 3 | 5 | 6 | 7 | 8 | 9 | 10 | | | | | | | 2 | | | | | | | 24 |
| 1 | 4 | 11 | 3 | 5 | 6 | 7 | 8 | 9² | 10¹ | | 12 | | | | 13 | 2 | | | | | | | 25 |
| 1 | 4 | 11 | 3 | | | 7 | | 9 | 10 | 12 | 8² | | | 5 | 13 | 2 | | | 6¹ | | | | 26 |
| 1 | 4 | 11 | 3 | 5 | 6 | 7 | | 9 | 10 | | 8 | | | | | 2 | | | | | | | 27 |
| 1 | 4 | | 3 | 5 | 6 | 7 | | 9 | 10 | 11 | 8 | | | | | 2 | | | | | | | 28 |
| 1 | 4 | 2 | 3 | 5 | 6² | 7 | 8 | 9 | 10¹ | 11 | | 13 | | | 12 | | | | | | | | 29 |
| 1 | 4 | 11 | 2 | 5 | | 7 | | 9 | 10 | 3¹ | 12 | | | 8 | | 6 | | | | | | | 30 |
| 1 | 4 | 11 | 2 | 5 | | 7 | | 9 | 10² | 3¹ | 12 | 13 | | 8 | | 6 | | | | | | | 31 |
| 1 | 4 | 11 | 3 | 5 | | 7 | 8² | 9¹ | 10 | | 12 | | | | 13 | 6 | | | 2 | | | | 32 |
| 1 | 4 | 11 | 3 | 5 | | 7 | 8 | 9 | 10 | | 12 | | | | | 6 | | | 2 | | | | 33 |
| 1 | 4 | 11¹ | 3 | 5³ | | 7 | 8 | 9 | 10² | | 12 | | | | 13 | 6 | | | 2 | | 14 | | 34 |
| 1 | 4 | 11 | 3 | | | 7 | 8 | 9 | 10 | | | | | 5 | | 6 | | | 2 | | | | 35 |
| 1 | 4 | 11 | 3 | | | 7 | 8 | 9¹ | 10 | | 12 | | | 5 | | 6 | | | 2 | | | | 36 |
| 1 | 4 | 11 | 3 | | | 7 | 8 | 9¹ | 10 | | 12 | | | 5 | | 6 | | | 2 | | | | 37 |
| 1 | 4 | 11 | 2³ | | 3 | 7 | 8² | 9 | 10¹ | 12 | | 13 | | 5 | 14 | 6 | | | | | | | 38 |
| 1 | 4 | 11 | 2 | | 3² | 7 | 8 | 9 | 10¹ | 12 | | 13 | | 5 | | 6 | | | | | | | 39 |
| 1 | 4 | 11 | 2 | | 3 | 7¹ | 8 | 9 | 10² | 12 | | | | 5 | 13 | 6 | | | | | | | 40 |
| 1 | 4 | 11 | 2 | | 3 | 7 | 8 | 9 | 10 | | | | | 5 | | 6 | | | | | | | 41 |
| 1 | 4 | 11 | 2 | | 3 | 7 | 8 | 9¹ | 10 | | | | | 5 | | 6 | | | | | | | 42 |
| 1 | 4 | 11 | 2 | | 3 | 7 | 8 | 9 | 10 | | | | | 5 | | 6 | | | | | | | 43 |
| 1 | 4 | 11¹ | 2 | | 3 | 7 | 8 | 9 | 10 | 12 | | | | 5 | | 6 | | | | | | | 44 |
| 1 | 4 | 11 | 2 | | 3 | 7 | 8¹ | 9³ | 10² | 12 | | 13 | | 5 | | 6 | | | | | 14 | | 45 |
| 1 | 4 | 2 | 3 | | | 7 | 8³ | 9² | 10¹ | 12 | | | 11 | 5 | | 6 | | | | | 13 | 14 | 46 |

**Coca-Cola Cup**
First Round    Fulham    (h) 1-2   (a) 4-4

**FA Cup**
First Round    Basingstoke T    (h) 2-2   (a) 2-2

YORK CITY 1997–98    *Back row (left to right):* Mark Tinkler, Martin Reed, John Sharples, Tony Barras, Andy Warrington, Mark Samways, Neil Tolson, Steve Tutill, Alan Pouton, Neil Campbell. *Middle row:* Derek Bell (First Team Coach), Steve Bushell, Richard Cresswell, David Rush, Alan Little (Manager), Andy McMillan, Jonathan Greening, Wayne Hall, Jeff Miller (Physiol). *Front row:* Gary Himsworth, Gary Bull, Paddy Atkinson, Rodney Rowe, Graeme Murty, Scott Jordan, Paul Stephenson.

# Division 2 YORK CITY

*Bootham Crescent, York YO3 7AQ.* Telephone: (01904) 624447. Fax: (01904) 631457.

*Ground capacity:* 9534.

*Record attendance:* 28,123 v Huddersfield T, FA Cup 6th rd, 5 March 1938.

*Record receipts:* £63,680 v Manchester U, Coca-Cola Cup 2nd rd 2nd leg, 3 October 1995.

*Pitch measurements:* 115yd × 74yd.

*Chairman:* D. M. Craig OBE, JP, BSC, FICE, FI, MUN E, FCI ARB, M CONS E.

*Directors:* B. A. Houghton, C. Webb, E. B. Swallow, J. E. H. Quickfall FCA.

*Manager:* Alan Little. *First Team Coach:* Derek Bell.

*Secretary:* Keith Usher. *Commercial Manager:* Mrs Maureen Leslie.

*Physio:* Jeff Miller.

*Hon. Orthopaedic Surgeon:* Mr Peter De Boer MA, FRCS. *Medical Officer:* Dr R. Porter.

*Year Formed:* 1922. *Turned Professional:* 1922. *Ltd Co.:* 1922.

*Club Nickname:* 'Minstermen'.

*Previous Ground:* 1922, Fulfordgate; 1932, Bootham Crescent.

*Foundation:* Although there was a York City club formed in 1903 by a soccer enthusiast from Darlington, this has no connection with the modern club because it went out of existence during World War I. Unlike many others of that period who restarted in 1919, York City did not re-form until 1922 and the tendency now is to ignore the modern club's pre-1922 existence.

*First Football League game:* 31 August 1929, Division 3 (N), v Wigan Borough (a) W 2-0 – Farmery; Archibald, Johnson; Beck, Davis, Thompson; Evans, Gardner, Cowie (1), Smailes, Stockhill (1).

*Record League Victory:* 9–1 v Southport, Division 3 (N), 2 February 1957 – Forgan; Phillips, Howe; Brown (1), Cairney, Mollatt; Hill, Bottom (4 incl. 1p), Wilkinson (2), Wragg (1), Fenton (1).

*Record Cup Victory:* 6–0 v South Shields (away), FA Cup 1st rd, 16 November 1968 – Widdowson; Baker (1p), Richardson; Carr, Jackson, Burrows; Taylor, Ross (3), MacDougall (2), Hodgson, Boyer.

*Record Defeat:* 0–12 v Chester, Division 3 (N), 1 February 1936.

*Most League Points (2 for a win):* 62, Division 4, 1964–65.

*Most League Points (3 for a win):* 101, Division 4, 1983–84.

*Most League Goals:* 96, Division 4, 1983–84.

*Highest League Scorer in Season:* Bill Fenton, 31, Division 3 (N), 1951–52; Arthur Bottom, 31, Division 3 (N), 1954–55 and 1955–56.

*Most League Goals in Total Aggregate:* Norman Wilkinson, 125, 1954–66.

*Most Capped Player:* Peter Scott, 7 (10), Northern Ireland.

*Most League Appearances:* Barry Jackson, 481, 1958–70.

*Record Transfer Fee Received:* £450,000 from Port Vale for Jon McCarthy, July 1995.

*Record Transfer Fee Paid:* £140,000 to Burnley for Adrian Randall, December 1995.

*Football League Record:* 1929 Elected to Division 3 (N); 1958–59 Division 4; 1959–60 Division 3; 1960–65 Division 4; 1965–66 Division 3; 1966–71 Division 4; 1971–74 Division 3; 1974–76 Division 2; 1976–77 Division 3; 1977–84 Division 4; 1984–88 Division 3; 1988–92 Division 4; 1992–93 Division 3; 1993– Division 2.

*Honours: Football League:* Division 3 – Promoted 1973–74 (3rd); Division 4 – Champions 1983–84. *FA Cup:* Semi-finals 1955, when in Division 3. *Football League Cup:* best season: 5th rd, 1962.

*Colours:* Red shirts and shorts with white and navy contoured lines, red stockings with 4 blue bands. *Change colours:* All blue.

*Did you know?*
Alf Patrick was the first York City player to score as many as four and five goals in League games in 1947 and 1948.

## YORK CITY 1997–98 LEAGUE RECORD

| Match No. | Date | Venue | Opponents | Result | H/T Score | Lg. Pos. | Goalscorers | Atten-dance |
|---|---|---|---|---|---|---|---|---|
| 1 | Aug 9 | A | Oldham Ath | L | 1-3 | 0-1 | 23 | Bushell [65] | 6474 |
| 2 | 16 | H | Bristol R | L | 0-1 | 0-0 | 23 | | 3307 |
| 3 | 23 | A | Millwall | W | 3-2 | 1-1 | 18 | Tinkler [45], Pouton [63], Stephenson [86] | 6583 |
| 4 | 30 | H | Gillingham | W | 2-1 | 0-0 | 10 | Rowe [60], Greening [88] | 2853 |
| 5 | Sept 2 | H | Chesterfield | L | 0-1 | 0-1 | — | | 3284 |
| 6 | 9 | A | Grimsby T | D | 0-0 | 0-0 | — | | 5308 |
| 7 | 13 | H | Burnley | W | 3-1 | 0-1 | 12 | Davis [62], Rowe [64], Tolson [82] | 5424 |
| 8 | 20 | A | Walsall | L | 0-2 | 0-0 | 15 | | 2972 |
| 9 | 27 | A | Watford | D | 1-1 | 1-0 | 17 | Tolson [34] | 13,812 |
| 10 | Oct 4 | H | Plymouth Arg | W | 1-0 | 1-0 | 9 | Rowe [8] | 2894 |
| 11 | 11 | H | Brentford | W | 3-1 | 1-0 | 6 | Stephenson [17], Tinkler [51], Murty [66] | 2831 |
| 12 | 17 | A | Bristol C | L | 1-2 | 1-0 | — | Rowe [37] | 9568 |
| 13 | 21 | A | Northampton T | D | 1-1 | 0-1 | — | Rowe [48] | 6059 |
| 14 | 25 | H | Carlisle U | W | 4-3 | 1-2 | 6 | Rowe [14], Stephenson 2 [82, 85], Bushell [87] | 3700 |
| 15 | Nov 1 | A | Wigan Ath | D | 1-1 | 0-0 | 6 | Rowe [76] | 3701 |
| 16 | 4 | H | Preston NE | W | 1-0 | 0-0 | — | Tinkler [61] | 3370 |
| 17 | 8 | H | Wycombe W | W | 2-0 | 1-0 | 3 | Barras (pen) [45], Rowe [56] | 3343 |
| 18 | 18 | A | Fulham | D | 1-1 | 1-0 | — | Barras (pen) [19] | 5521 |
| 19 | 22 | A | Blackpool | L | 0-1 | 0-0 | 5 | | 4508 |
| 20 | 29 | H | Luton T | L | 1-2 | 0-1 | 7 | Cresswell [87] | 3636 |
| 21 | Dec 2 | A | Bournemouth | D | 0-0 | 0-0 | — | | 3365 |
| 22 | 13 | H | Wrexham | W | 1-0 | 0-0 | 5 | Barras [62] | 2871 |
| 23 | 19 | A | Southend U | D | 4-4 | 2-2 | — | Pouton 2 [22, 66], Barras (pen) [45], Tinkler [88] | 3215 |
| 24 | 26 | H | Grimsby T | D | 0-0 | 0-0 | 5 | | 7093 |
| 25 | 28 | A | Chesterfield | D | 1-1 | 0-0 | 8 | Greening [90] | 5320 |
| 26 | Jan 10 | H | Oldham Ath | D | 0-0 | 0-0 | 9 | | 4454 |
| 27 | 17 | A | Gillingham | D | 0-0 | 0-0 | 10 | | 5891 |
| 28 | 24 | H | Millwall | L | 2-3 | 1-0 | 10 | Stephenson [11], Bull [89] | 3508 |
| 29 | 31 | A | Burnley | L | 2-7 | 1-2 | 12 | Pouton [34], Barras [76] | 9975 |
| 30 | Feb 7 | H | Walsall | W | 1-0 | 1-0 | 10 | Tinkler [27] | 2959 |
| 31 | 14 | A | Plymouth Arg | D | 0-0 | 0-0 | 12 | | 4382 |
| 32 | 21 | H | Watford | D | 1-1 | 1-0 | 13 | Barras (pen) [26] | 4890 |
| 33 | 24 | H | Bristol C | L | 0-1 | 0-0 | — | | 3770 |
| 34 | 28 | A | Brentford | W | 2-1 | 0-0 | 13 | Gabbiadini [50], Jones [70] | 4490 |
| 35 | Mar 3 | A | Wycombe W | L | 0-1 | 0-0 | — | | 3768 |
| 36 | 7 | H | Wigan Ath | D | 2-2 | 0-1 | 13 | Thompson [46], McGibbon (og) [53] | 3536 |
| 37 | 10 | A | Bristol R | W | 2-1 | 1-0 | — | Jones [34], Cresswell [72] | 4289 |
| 38 | 14 | A | Preston NE | L | 2-3 | 1-0 | 11 | Rowe 2 [2, 77] | 7664 |
| 39 | 21 | H | Fulham | L | 0-1 | 0-0 | 15 | | 4871 |
| 40 | 28 | H | Blackpool | D | 1-1 | 0-1 | 12 | Cresswell [90] | 3650 |
| 41 | Apr 4 | A | Luton T | L | 0-3 | 0-2 | 15 | | 5541 |
| 42 | 11 | H | Bournemouth | L | 0-1 | 0-1 | 18 | | 2840 |
| 43 | 13 | A | Wrexham | W | 2-1 | 0-0 | 15 | Thompson (pen) [67], Cresswell [81] | 5231 |
| 44 | 18 | A | Southend U | D | 1-1 | 0-1 | 15 | Tolson [74] | 2850 |
| 45 | 25 | A | Carlisle U | W | 2-1 | 0-1 | 13 | Pouton [63], McMillan [84] | 3897 |
| 46 | May 2 | H | Northampton T | D | 0-0 | 0-0 | 16 | | 6688 |

**Final League Position: 16**　　　　1996–97 DIV2 20

### GOALSCORERS

*League (52):* Rowe 10, Barras 6 (4 pens), Pouton 5, Stephenson 5, Tinkler 5, Cresswell 4, Tolson 3, Bushell 2, Greening 2, Jones 2, Thompson 2 (1 pen), Bull 1, Davis 1, Gabbiadini 1, McMillan 1, Murty 1, own goal 1.
*Coca-Cola Cup (5):* Barras 1, Bull 1, Bushell 1, Murty 1, Rowe 1.
*FA Cup (5):* Rowe 3, Pouton 1, own goal 1.

| Samways M 29 | McMillan A 30 | Atkinson P 3+2 | Bushell S 40 | Tutill S 2 | Barras T 38 | Stephenson P 34+1 | Tinkler M 43+1 | Tolson N 10+6 | Bull G 18+9 | Pouton A 37+4 | Rowe R 38+3 | Hall W 31+1 | Campbell N 1 | Jordan S 6+10 | Rush D 1+2 | Reed M 21+1 | Cresswell R 18+8 | Greening J 5+15 | Murty G 32+2 | Davis S 2 | Himsworth G 9+6 | Warrington A 17 | Jones B 23 | Gabbiadin M 5+2 | Thompson N 12 | Rennison G 1 | Alderson R —+1 | Match No. |
|---|---|---|---|---|---|---|---|---|---|---|---|---|---|---|---|---|---|---|---|---|---|---|---|---|---|---|---|---|
| 1 | 2 | 3 | 4 | 5 | 6 | 7¹ | 8 | 9 | 10 | 11 | 12 | | | | | | | | | | | | | | | | | 1 |
| 1 | 2 | | 4 | 5² | 6 | 12 | 8 | | 10 | 11 | 9 | 3 | 7¹ | 13³ | 14 | | | | | | | | | | | | | 2 |
| 1 | 2 | | 4 | | 6 | 7 | 8 | | 12 | 11 | 9² | 3 | | 10¹ | | 5 | 13 | | | | | | | | | | | 3 |
| 1 | 2 | 12 | 4 | | 6³ | 7 | 8 | | 10² | 11¹ | 9 | 3 | | | | 5 | 13 | 14 | | | | | | | | | | 4 |
| 1 | 2 | | 4 | | | 7 | 6 | | | 8 | 9 | 3 | | | | 5 | 10 | 11¹ | 12 | | | | | | | | | 5 |
| 1 | 2 | | 4 | | 6 | 11 | 5 | | 12 | 8 | 9 | 3 | | | | 10¹ | | | 7 | | | | | | | | | 6 |
| 1 | 2 | | 4 | | 6 | 11 | 8 | 9 | 12 | | 13 | 3 | | 10¹ | | | | | | | 7² | 5 | | | | | | 7 |
| 1 | 2 | | 4 | | 6 | 11¹ | 8 | 9² | 12 | 10 | | 3 | | 13 | | | | | | | 7 | 5 | | | | | | 8 |
| 1 | 2 | | 4 | | 6 | | 8 | 9¹ | 12 | 11 | 10 | 3 | | | | 5 | | | | | 7 | | | | | | | 9 |
| 1 | | | 4 | | 6 | 7 | 8 | 9 | 12 | 11² | 10 | 3 | | | | 5 | | | 2 | | 13 | | | | | | | 10 |
| 1 | 2 | | 4 | | 6 | 11³ | 8 | 9² | 12 | | 10¹ | 3 | | | | 5 | 13 | 14 | | | 7 | | | | | | | 11 |
| 1 | 2 | | 4 | | 6 | 11 | 8 | 9 | | | 10 | 3 | | | | 5 | | | | | 7 | | | | | | | 12 |
| 1 | 2 | | 4 | | 6 | 11 | 8 | 9 | | | 10 | 3 | | | | 5 | | | | | 7 | | | | | | | 13 |
| 1 | 2³ | | 4 | | 6 | 11 | 8 | | 12 | 10 | 9² | 3 | | | | 5¹ | 13 | 14 | | | 7 | | | | | | | 14 |
| 1 | | | 4 | | 6 | 11 | 8 | 9 | | 7 | 10 | 3 | | | | 5 | | | 2 | | 12 | | | | | | | 15 |
| 1 | | | 4 | | 6 | 11 | 8¹ | 9 | | 7 | 10 | 3 | | 12 | | 5 | | | 2 | | | | | | | | | 16 |
| 1 | | | 4 | | 6 | 11 | 8 | | | 7 | 10² | 3 | | 12 | | 5¹ | 13 | | 2 | | 14 | | | | | | | 17 |
| 1 | | | 4 | | 6 | | 8 | 9¹ | | 7 | 10 | 3 | | | | 5 | 12 | | 2 | | 11 | | | | | | | 18 |
| 1 | | 12 | 4 | | 6 | | 8 | | | 7 | 10 | 3 | | | | 5 | 9² | 13 | 2 | | 11¹ | | | | | | | 19 |
| | | 3 | 4 | | 6 | 11 | 8 | 9¹ | | 7 | 10 | | | | | 5 | 12 | | 2 | | | 1 | | | | | | 20 |
| | | | 4 | | 6 | 11 | 8 | | 12 | 7 | 10¹ | | | | | 5 | 9 | | 2 | | 3 | 1 | | | | | | 21 |
| | | | 4 | | 6 | 7 | 8 | | 12 | | 10² | 3 | | | 14 | 5² | 9¹ | 13 | 2 | | 11 | 1 | | | | | | 22 |
| | | | 4 | | 6 | 11 | 8 | | 12 | | 10¹ | 3 | | | | | 9 | 13 | 2 | | 7² | 1 | 5 | | | | | 23 |
| | | | 4 | | 6 | 11 | 8 | | | | 10 | 3 | | | | | 9 | | 2 | | 7 | 1 | 5 | | | | | 24 |
| | | | 4 | | 6 | 11 | 8 | | | | 10 | 3 | | 12 | | | 9² | 13 | 2 | | 7¹ | 1 | 5 | | | | | 25 |
| | | | 4 | | 6 | 11 | 8 | | | 5 | 10 | 3 | | | | | 9¹ | 12 | | | 7 | 1 | 2 | | | | | 26 |
| | 2 | | 4 | | 6 | 11¹ | 8 | | | | 10 | 3 | | 12 | | | 9 | | | | 7 | 1 | 5 | | | | | 27 |
| | 2² | | 4 | | 6 | 11 | 8 | | 12 | 13 | 10¹ | 3 | | | | | 9³ | 14 | | | 7 | 1 | 5 | | | | | 28 |
| | | 3 | 4 | | 6 | 11³ | 5 | 9 | 8 | | 10¹ | | | 13 | | | 12² | 14 | | | 7 | 1 | 2 | | | | | 29 |
| 1 | | | 4 | | 6 | 11¹ | 8 | 9² | | 7 | | 3 | | 12 | 13 | | 10 | | 2 | | | | 5 | | | | | 30 |
| 1 | | | 4 | | 6 | 11 | 8 | 9 | | 7² | 12 | 3³ | | | 14 | 13 | 10¹ | | 2 | | | | 5 | | | | | 31 |
| 1 | 2 | | 4 | | 6 | 11 | 8 | 9 | | 7 | | 3 | | | | | | | | | | | 5 | | 10 | | | 32 |
| 1 | 2 | | 4 | | 6 | 11 | 8 | 9¹ | | 7 | 10 | | | | | | | | | | 12 | | 3 | | 5 | | | 33 |
| 1 | 2 | | 4 | | 6 | 11 | 8 | | | 7 | 9¹ | | | | | | | | | | 12 | | 3 | | 5 | 10 | | 34 |
| 1 | 2 | | 4 | | 6 | 11 | 8 | | | 7 | 9 | | | | | | | | | | | | 5 | | 10 | 3 | | 35 |
| 1 | 2 | | 4 | | 6 | 11 | 8¹ | | | 12 | 9 | | | | | | 13 | | | | 7 | | 5 | | 10² | 3 | | 36 |
| 1 | 2 | | 4 | | 6 | 11 | 8 | | | 9 | | | | | | | 10 | | | | 7 | | 5 | | | 3 | | 37 |
| 1 | 2 | | 4 | | 6¹ | 11 | 12 | | | 8 | 9 | | | 13 | | | 10³ | 14 | | | 7² | | 5 | | | 3 | | 38 |
| 1 | 2 | | 4 | | | | 8 | | 12 | 10 | 9 | 7 | | 13 | | 6 | | | | | 11¹ | | 5 | | | 3 | | 39 |
| | 2 | | 4 | | | | 8 | | 12 | 10 | 9² | | | | | 6 | 13 | | | | | 1 | 5 | | 11¹ | 3 | | 40 |
| | 2 | | | 11 | | | 8 | | 12 | | 9¹ | | | | 4 | | 10² | | | | | 1 | 5 | 13 | 3 | | 6 | 41 |
| | 2 | | 4 | | 6¹ | | 8 | 9³ | 12 | 7 | | | | 13 | | | 10 | 11² | | | | 1 | 5 | 14 | 3 | | | 42 |
| | 2 | | 4 | | | | 8 | 9 | | 7 | | 3 | | | | | 10 | 11 | | | | 1 | 5 | | | 6 | | 43 |
| | 2 | | 4 | | | | 8 | | 12 | 7 | 9 | 3 | | | | | 10 | | | | 11¹ | 1 | 5 | | | 6 | | 44 |
| | 2 | | 4² | | 6 | | 8 | | 12 | 7 | 9 | | | | | | 10¹ | 11 | | | | 1 | 5 | 13 | 3 | | | 45 |
| | 2 | | 4 | | 6 | | 8 | 9² | 10 | 7 | | | | | | 5¹ | | 11 | | | | 1 | 12 | | 3 | | 13 | 46 |

**Coca-Cola Cup**

| First Round | Port Vale | (a) | 2-1 |
| | | (h) | 1-1 |
| Second Round | Oxford U | (a) | 1-4 |
| | | (h) | 1-2 |

**FA Cup**

| First Round | Southport | (a) | 4-0 |
| Second Round | Wigan Ath | (a) | 1-2 |

# ENGLISH LEAGUE PLAYERS DIRECTORY

*Free transfer, †Non-contract, ‡Registration cancelled, §Trainee/Schoolboy
#Players over age 24, out of contract but who have been made an offer of re-engagement

| Player | Ht | Wt | Pos | Birth Date | Place | Source | Clubs | League App | Gls |
|---|---|---|---|---|---|---|---|---|---|
| | | | | | | | **ARSENAL** | | |
| **Adams** Tony | 6 3 | 13 11 | D | 10 10 66 | London | Apprentice | Arsenal | 421 | 30 |
| **Anelka** Nicolas | 5 11 | 12 03 | F | 14 3 79 | Versailles | | Paris St Germain | 10 | 1 |
| | | | | | | | Arsenal | 30 | 6 |
| **Bergkamp** Dennis | 6 0 | 12 05 | F | 18 5 69 | Amsterdam | | Ajax | 185 | 103 |
| | | | | | | | Internazionale | 52 | 11 |
| | | | | | | | Arsenal | 90 | 39 |
| **Black** Michael | 5 8 | 11 08 | M | 6 10 76 | Chigwell | Trainee | Arsenal | — | — |
| | | | | | | | Millwall (loan) | 13 | 2 |
| **Boa Morte** Luis | 5 10 | 11 05 | F | 4 8 77 | Lisbon | Sporting Lisbon | Arsenal | 15 | — |
| **Bould** Steve | 6 4 | 14 02 | D | 16 11 62 | Stoke | Apprentice | Stoke C | 183 | 6 |
| | | | | | | | Torquay U (loan) | 9 | — |
| | | | | | | | Arsenal | 268 | 5 |
| **Crowe** Jason | 5 9 | 10 09 | D | 30 9 78 | Sidcup | Trainee | Arsenal | — | — |
| **Day** Jamie | 5 7 | 10 09 | M | 13 9 79 | Bexley | Trainee | Arsenal | — | — |
| **Dixon** Lee | 5 8 | 11 08 | D | 17 3 64 | Manchester | Local | Burnley | 4 | — |
| | | | | | | | Chester C | 16 | 1 |
| | | | | | | | Chester | 41 | — |
| | | | | | | | Bury | 45 | 5 |
| | | | | | | | Stoke C | 71 | 5 |
| | | | | | | | Arsenal | 352 | 20 |
| **Garde** Remi* | 5 9 | 11 07 | M | 3 4 66 | L'Arbresle | | Lyon | 81 | 13 |
| | | | | | | | Strasbourg | 68 | 3 |
| | | | | | | | Arsenal | 21 | — |
| **Gislason** Valur‡ | 6 1 | 11 12 | M | 8 9 77 | Reykjavik | | Fram | 30 | 2 |
| | | | | | | | Arsenal | — | — |
| | | | | | | | Brighton & HA (loan) | 7 | — |
| **Grimandi** Gilles | 6 0 | 12 07 | D | 11 11 70 | Gap | FC Gap | Monaco | 90 | 3 |
| | | | | | | | Arsenal | 22 | 1 |
| **Helder** Glenn | 5 11 | 11 07 | F | 28 10 68 | Leiden | | Sparta | 93 | 9 |
| *(Transferred to NAC Breda, October 1997)* | | | | | | | Vitesse | 52 | 12 |
| | | | | | | | Arsenal | 39 | 1 |
| **Hughes** Richard | 5 9 | 9 12 | D | 25 6 79 | Glasgow | Atalanta | Arsenal | — | — |
| **Hughes** Stephen | 6 0 | 12 05 | M | 18 9 76 | Wokingham | Trainee | Arsenal | 33 | 3 |
| **Keown** Martin | 6 1 | 12 04 | D | 24 7 66 | Oxford | Apprentice | Arsenal | 22 | — |
| | | | | | | | Brighton & HA (loan) | 16 | — |
| | | | | | | | Brighton & HA (loan) | 7 | 1 |
| | | | | | | | Aston Villa | 112 | 3 |
| | | | | | | | Everton | 96 | — |
| | | | | | | | Arsenal | 165 | 2 |
| **Kiwomya** Chris* | 5 9 | 10 07 | F | 2 12 69 | Huddersfield | Trainee | Ipswich T | 225 | 51 |
| | | | | | | | Arsenal | 14 | 3 |
| | | | | | | | Le Havre (loan) | 7 | — |
| **Lukic** John* | 6 4 | 13 07 | G | 11 12 60 | Chesterfield | Apprentice | Leeds U | 146 | — |
| | | | | | | | Arsenal | 223 | — |
| | | | | | | | Leeds U | 209 | — |
| | | | | | | | Arsenal | 15 | — |
| **Macdonald** James | 6 0 | 12 05 | M | 21 2 79 | Inverness | Trainee | Arsenal | — | — |
| **Manninger** Alex | 6 2 | 13 03 | G | 4 6 77 | Salzburg | | Vorwaerts Steyr | 5 | — |
| | | | | | | | Salzburg | 1 | — |
| | | | | | | | Graz | 23 | — |
| | | | | | | | Arsenal | 7 | — |
| **Marshall** Scott | 6 1 | 12 05 | D | 1 5 73 | Edinburgh | Trainee | Arsenal | 24 | 1 |
| | | | | | | | Rotherham U (loan) | 10 | 1 |
| | | | | | | | Oxford U (loan) | — | — |
| | | | | | | | Sheffield U (loan) | 17 | — |
| **McGovern** Brian | | | D | 23 4 80 | Dublin | | Arsenal | — | — |
| **McGowan** Gavin* | 5 8 | 11 07 | D | 16 1 76 | Blackheath | Trainee | Arsenal | 6 | — |
| | | | | | | | Luton T (loan) | 2 | — |
| | | | | | | | Luton T (loan) | 8 | — |
| **McNevin** Alan* | | | F | 10 1 80 | Dublin | | Arsenal | — | — |
| **Mendez** Alberto | 5 11 | 11 09 | M | 24 10 74 | Nuremberg | FC Feucht | Arsenal | 3 | — |
| **Overmars** Marc | 5 8 | 11 04 | F | 29 3 73 | Emst | | Go Ahead | 11 | 1 |
| | | | | | | | Willem II | 31 | 1 |
| | | | | | | | Ajax | 135 | 36 |
| | | | | | | | Arsenal | 32 | 12 |
| **Parlour** Ray | 5 10 | 11 12 | M | 7 3 73 | Romford | Trainee | Arsenal | 170 | 11 |
| **Petit** Emmanuel | 6 1 | 12 07 | M | 22 9 70 | Dieppe | ES Arques | Monaco | 222 | 4 |
| | | | | | | | Arsenal | 32 | 2 |

| Name | Ht | Wt | Pos | DOB | Birthplace | Source | Club | Apps | Gls |
|---|---|---|---|---|---|---|---|---|---|
| **Platt** David | 5 10 | 11 12 | M | 10 6 66 | Chadderton | Chadderton | Manchester U | — | — |
| | | | | | | | Crewe Alex | 134 | 55 |
| | | | | | | | Aston Villa | 121 | 50 |
| | | | | | | | Bari | 29 | 11 |
| | | | | | | | Juventus | 16 | 3 |
| | | | | | | | Sampdoria | 55 | 17 |
| | | | | | | | Arsenal | 88 | 13 |
| **Rankin** Isiah | 5 10 | 11 00 | F | 22 5 78 | London | Trainee | Arsenal | 1 | — |
| | | | | | | | Colchester U (loan) | 11 | 5 |
| **Seaman** David | 6 4 | 14 10 | G | 19 9 63 | Rotherham | Apprentice | Leeds U | — | — |
| | | | | | | | Peterborough U | 91 | — |
| | | | | | | | Birmingham C | 75 | — |
| | | | | | | | QPR | 141 | — |
| | | | | | | | Arsenal | 280 | — |
| **Taylor** Ross* | 5 10 | 11 12 | D | 14 1 77 | Southend | Trainee | Arsenal | — | — |
| **Thorogood** Marc‡ | | | F | 13 1 79 | Waltham Abbey | Trainee | Arsenal | — | — |
| **Upson** Matthew | 6 1 | 11 05 | D | 18 4 79 | Eye | Trainee | Luton T | 1 | — |
| | | | | | | | Arsenal | 5 | — |
| **Vernazza** Paulo | | | M | 1 11 79 | Islington | Trainee | Arsenal | 1 | — |
| **Vieira** Patrick | 6 4 | 13 00 | M | 23 6 76 | Dakar | | Cannes | 49 | 2 |
| | | | | | | | AC Milan | 2 | — |
| | | | | | | | Arsenal | 64 | 4 |
| **Wicks** Matthew | 6 2 | 13 05 | D | 8 9 78 | Reading | Manchester U | Arsenal | — | — |
| **Winterburn** Nigel | 5 8 | 11 04 | D | 11 12 63 | Coventry | Local | Birmingham C | — | — |
| | | | | | | | Oxford U | — | — |
| | | | | | | | Wimbledon | 165 | 8 |
| | | | | | | | Arsenal | 382 | 8 |
| **Wreh** Christopher | 5 8 | 11 13 | F | 14 5 75 | Liberia | | Monaco | 13 | 3 |
| | | | | | | | Guincamp | 33 | 10 |
| | | | | | | | Arsenal | 16 | 3 |
| **Wright** Ian | 5 9 | 11 08 | F | 3 11 63 | Woolwich | Greenwich Bor | Crystal Palace | 225 | 89 |
| | | | | | | | Arsenal | 221 | 128 |

**Trainees**
Barrett, Graham; Beale, David; Black, Thomas R; Boeteng, Daniel; Bowes, Terence D; Canoville, Lee; Clark, Peter J; Cole, Ashley; Cowell, Clayden; Doherty, Lee J; Douglas, Andrew R; Gray, Julian R; Harper, James A J; Lincoln, Greg D; Livermore, David; McLeod, Allan J; Norbert, Guillaume; Perna, Ferdinando; Riza, Omer K; Taylor, Stuart J; Weston, Rhys D.

**Associated Schoolboys**
Britton, Leon; Brown, Jermaine A; Chorley, Benjamin F; Itonga, Carlin D; Palmer, Marc K; Ricketts, Rowan A; Santry, Steven; Sidwell, Steven J; Solkhon, Brett M.

**Associated Schoolboys who have accepted the club's offer of a Traineeship/Contract**
Bothroyd, Jay; Chilvers, Liam C; Halls, John; Noble, David J; Stack, Graham.

# ASTON VILLA

| Name | Ht | Wt | Pos | DOB | Birthplace | Source | Club | Apps | Gls |
|---|---|---|---|---|---|---|---|---|---|
| **Barry** Gareth | | | D | 23 2 81 | Hastings | Trainee | Aston Villa | 2 | — |
| **Blackwood** Michael | | | F | 30 9 79 | Birmingham | Trainee | Aston Villa | — | — |
| **Bosnich** Mark | 6 1 | 14 07 | G | 13 1 72 | Fairfield | Croatia Sydney | Manchester U | 3 | — |
| | | | | | | | Aston Villa | 164 | 1 |
| **Byfield** Darren | 5 11 | 11 11 | F | 29 9 76 | Sutton Coldfield | Trainee | Aston Villa | 7 | — |
| **Charles** Gary | 5 9 | 11 03 | D | 13 4 70 | London | Trainee | Nottingham F | 56 | 1 |
| | | | | | | | Leicester C (loan) | 8 | — |
| | | | | | | | Derby Co | 61 | 3 |
| | | | | | | | Aston Villa | 68 | 2 |
| **Collins** Lee | 6 1 | 12 06 | D | 10 9 77 | Birmingham | Trainee | Aston Villa | — | — |
| **Collymore** Stan | 6 2 | 12 02 | F | 22 1 71 | Stone | Stafford R | Crystal Palace | 20 | 1 |
| | | | | | | | Southend U | 30 | 15 |
| | | | | | | | Nottingham F | 65 | 41 |
| | | | | | | | Liverpool | 61 | 26 |
| | | | | | | | Aston Villa | 25 | 6 |
| **Curtolo** David | | | M | 30 9 80 | Stockholm | | Aston Villa | — | — |
| **Davis** Neil* | 5 10 | 11 07 | F | 15 8 73 | Bloxwich | Redditch U | Aston Villa | 2 | — |
| | | | | | | | Wycombe W (loan) | 13 | — |
| **Draper** Mark | 5 10 | 12 04 | M | 11 11 70 | Long Eaton | Trainee | Notts Co | 222 | 40 |
| | | | | | | | Leicester C | 39 | 5 |
| | | | | | | | Aston Villa | 96 | 5 |
| **Ehiogu** Ugo | 6 2 | 14 10 | D | 3 11 72 | Hackney | Trainee | WBA | 2 | — |
| | | | | | | | Aston Villa | 179 | 9 |
| **Ghent** Matthew | | | G | 5 10 80 | Burton | Trainee | Aston Villa | — | — |
| **Grayson** Simon | 6 0 | 13 07 | D | 16 12 69 | Ripon | Trainee | Leeds U | 2 | — |
| | | | | | | | Leicester C | 188 | 4 |
| | | | | | | | Aston Villa | 33 | — |
| **Hadland** Guy* | 6 1 | 12 11 | D | 23 1 79 | Nuneaton | Trainee | Aston Villa | — | — |
| **Hazell** Reuben | 5 11 | 11 12 | D | 24 4 79 | Birmingham | Trainee | Aston Villa | — | — |
| **Hendrie** Lee | 5 10 | 10 02 | F | 18 5 77 | Birmingham | Trainee | Aston Villa | 24 | 3 |
| **Hines** Leslie* | 5 7 | 9 10 | D | 7 1 77 | Iserlohn | Trainee | Aston Villa | — | — |
| **Hughes** David | 6 4 | 13 06 | D | 1 2 78 | Wrexham | Trainee | Aston Villa | 7 | — |
| | | | | | | | Carlisle U (loan) | 1 | — |
| **Jaszczun** Tommy | 5 10 | 10 10 | D | 16 9 77 | Kettering | Trainee | Aston Villa | — | — |

| | | | | | | | | | |
|---|---|---|---|---|---|---|---|---|---|
| **Joachim** Julian | 5 6 | 12 00 | F | 20 9 74 | Boston | Trainee | Leicester C | 99 | 25 |
| | | | | | | | Aston Villa | 52 | 12 |
| **Kirby** Alan* | 5 7 | 10 06 | M | 8 9 77 | Waterford | Trainee | Aston Villa | — | — |
| **Lee** Alan | 6 2 | 13 09 | F | 21 8 78 | Galway | Trainee | Aston Villa | — | — |
| **Lescott** Aaron | 5 8 | 10 09 | M | 2 12 78 | Birmingham | Trainee | Aston Villa | — | — |
| **Middleton** Darren | 6 0 | 11 05 | F | 28 12 78 | Lichfield | Trainee | Aston Villa | — | — |
| **Milosevic** Savo | 6 1 | 13 08 | F | 2 9 73 | Bijelina | | Partizan Belgrade | 98 | 64 |
| | | | | | | | Aston Villa | 90 | 28 |
| **Nelson** Fernando | 5 11 | 11 08 | D | 5 11 71 | Oporto | | Sporting | 115 | 3 |
| | | | | | | | Aston Villa | 59 | — |
| **Oakes** Michael | 6 2 | 14 07 | G | 30 10 73 | Northwich | Trainee | Aston Villa | 28 | — |
| | | | | | | | Scarborough (loan) | 1 | — |
| | | | | | | | Tranmere R (loan) | — | — |
| **Petty** Ben | 6 0 | 12 05 | D | 22 3 77 | Solihull | Trainee | Aston Villa | — | — |
| **Rachel** Adam | 5 11 | 12 08 | G | 10 12 76 | Birmingham | Trainee | Aston Villa | — | — |
| **Ridley** Martin | | | D | 30 3 80 | Leicester | Trainee | Aston Villa | — | — |
| **Scimeca** Riccardo | 6 0 | 13 03 | D | 13 6 75 | Leamington Spa | Trainee | Aston Villa | 55 | — |
| **Sheridan** Darragh* | 5 11 | 11 01 | M | 11 1 79 | Galway | Trainee | Aston Villa | — | — |
| **Southgate** Gareth | 6 0 | 12 03 | D | 3 9 70 | Watford | Trainee | Crystal Palace | 152 | 15 |
| | | | | | | | Aston Villa | 91 | 2 |
| **Standing** Michael | | | M | 20 3 81 | Shoreham | Trainee | Aston Villa | — | — |
| **Staunton** Steve | 6 1 | 12 11 | D | 19 1 69 | Drogheda | Dundalk | Liverpool | 65 | — |
| | | | | | | | Bradford C (loan) | 8 | — |
| | | | | | | | Aston Villa | 208 | 16 |
| **Taylor** Ian | 6 1 | 12 00 | M | 4 6 68 | Birmingham | Moor Green | Port Vale | 83 | 28 |
| | | | | | | | Sheffield W | 14 | 1 |
| | | | | | | | Aston Villa | 113 | 12 |
| **Vassell** Darius | | | F | 13 6 80 | Birmingham | Trainee | Aston Villa | — | — |
| **Walker** Richard | 6 0 | 12 00 | F | 8 11 77 | Sutton Coldfield | Trainee | Aston Villa | 1 | — |
| **Wright** Alan | 5 4 | 9 09 | D | 28 9 71 | Ashton-under-Lyme | Trainee | Blackpool | 98 | — |
| | | | | | | | Blackburn R | 74 | 1 |
| | | | | | | | Aston Villa | 121 | 3 |
| **Yorke** Dwight | 5 9 | 12 03 | F | 3 11 71 | Tobago | St Clair's | Aston Villa | 230 | 73 |

**Trainees**
Evans, Stephen G; Harding, David M; Kearns, James; Melaugh, Gavin M J; Meredith, Alex D; Mulholland, Brian; Price, Michael; Prince, Luke; Pulisciano, Nathan I; Reece, Dominic M A; Samuel, J Lloyd; Thornley, Stuart; Tongue, Philip G.

**Associated Schoolboys**
Amoo, Ryan L; Andrewartha, David P; Bell, Liam M; Bewers, Jonathan; Brooker, Matthew A; Davenport, Calum R; De Bolla, Mark; Edwards, Jamie; Edwards, Robert O; Husbands, Michael P; Hylton, Leon D; Jackman, Daniel J; Jackson, Ben P; McConnell, Peter M; Moore, Stefan; Myhill, Boaz G O; Rhule, Jonathan; Roberts, Matthew; Rollins, Mark A; Ryan, Jordan C; Smith, Adam A; Tranter, Martin; Wells, Andrew M.

**Associated Schoolboys who have accepted the club's offer of a Traineeship/Contract**
Berks, David; Bull, Nikki; Folds, Liam J.

# BARNET

| | | | | | | | | | |
|---|---|---|---|---|---|---|---|---|---|
| **Adams** Kieran | 5 11 | 11 03 | M | 20 10 77 | St Ives | Trainee | Barnet | 19 | 1 |
| **Basham** Mike | 6 2 | 13 02 | D | 27 9 73 | Barking | Trainee | West Ham U | — | — |
| | | | | | | | Colchester U (loan) | 1 | — |
| | | | | | | | Swansea C | 29 | 1 |
| | | | | | | | Peterborough U | 19 | 1 |
| | | | | | | | Barnet | 20 | 1 |
| **Brady** Matthew | 5 11 | 11 01 | M | 27 10 77 | London | Trainee | Barnet | 10 | — |
| **Charlery** Ken | 6 0 | 12 00 | F | 28 11 64 | Stepney | Beckton U | Maidstone U | 59 | 11 |
| | | | | | | | Peterborough U | 51 | 19 |
| | | | | | | | Watford | 48 | 13 |
| | | | | | | | Peterborough U | 70 | 24 |
| | | | | | | | Birmingham C | 17 | 4 |
| | | | | | | | Southend U (loan) | 3 | — |
| | | | | | | | Peterborough U | 56 | 12 |
| | | | | | | | Stockport Co | 10 | — |
| | | | | | | | Barnet | 32 | 5 |
| **Devine** Sean | 6 0 | 13 08 | F | 6 9 72 | Lewisham | Omonia | Barnet | 106 | 46 |
| **Devito** Claudio† | 6 1 | 12 02 | F | 21 7 78 | Peterborough | Trainee | Northampton T | — | — |
| | | | | | | | Barnet | 1 | — |
| **Doolan** John | 6 1 | 13 01 | M | 7 5 74 | Liverpool | Trainee | Everton | — | — |
| | | | | | | | Mansfield T | 131 | 10 |
| | | | | | | | Barnet | 17 | — |
| **Ford** John | 6 0 | 13 12 | D | 12 4 68 | Birmingham | Cradley T | Swansea C | 160 | 7 |
| | | | | | | | Bradford C | 19 | — |
| | | | | | | | Gillingham | 4 | — |
| | | | | | | | Barnet | 32 | 1 |
| **Goodhind** Warren | 5 11 | 11 02 | D | 16 8 77 | Johannesburg | Trainee | Barnet | 38 | 1 |
| **Harle** Mike | 6 0 | 12 06 | D | 31 10 72 | Lewisham | Sittingbourne | Millwall | 21 | 1 |
| | | | | | | | Bury (loan) | 1 | — |
| | | | | | | | Barnet | 43 | 2 |

| Harrison Lee | 6 2 | 12 08 | G | 12 9 71 | Billericay | Trainee | Charlton Ath | — | — |
|---|---|---|---|---|---|---|---|---|
| | | | | | | | Fulham (loan) | — | — |
| | | | | | | | Gillingham (loan) | 2 | — |
| | | | | | | | Fulham (loan) | — | — |
| | | | | | | | Fulham | 12 | — |
| | | | | | | | Barnet | 67 | — |
| Heald Greg | 6 2 | 13 01 | D | 26 9 71 | Enfield | Enfield | Peterborough U | 105 | 6 |
| | | | | | | | Barnet | 43 | 3 |
| Howarth Lee# | 6 3 | 13 09 | D | 3 1 68 | Bolton | Chorley | Peterborough U | 62 | — |
| | | | | | | | Mansfield T | 57 | 2 |
| | | | | | | | Barnet | 102 | 5 |
| Manuel Billy | 5 9 | 11 10 | M | 28 6 69 | Hackney | Apprentice | Tottenham H | — | — |
| | | | | | | | Gillingham | 87 | 5 |
| | | | | | | | Brentford | 94 | 1 |
| | | | | | | | Cambridge U | 10 | — |
| | | | | | | | Peterborough U | 27 | 2 |
| | | | | | | | Gillingham | 21 | — |
| | | | | | | | Barnet | 17 | — |
| McDonald David* | 5 10 | 12 11 | D | 2 1 71 | Dublin | Trainee | Tottenham H | 2 | — |
| | | | | | | | Gillingham (loan) | 10 | — |
| | | | | | | | Bradford C (loan) | 7 | — |
| | | | | | | | Reading (loan) | 11 | — |
| | | | | | | | Peterborough U | 29 | — |
| | | | | | | | Barnet | 96 | — |
| McGleish Scott | 5 9 | 11 00 | F | 10 2 74 | Camden Town | Edgware T | Charlton Ath | 6 | — |
| | | | | | | | Leyton Orient (loan) | 6 | 1 |
| | | | | | | | Peterborough U | 13 | — |
| | | | | | | | Colchester U (loan) | 15 | 6 |
| | | | | | | | Cambridge U (loan) | 10 | 7 |
| | | | | | | | Leyton Orient | 36 | 7 |
| | | | | | | | Barnet | 37 | 13 |
| McMenemy Tom‡ | 5 11 | 11 01 | M | 3 3 79 | Southampton | Trainee | Barnet | — | — |
| Mills Danny* | 5 11 | 11 07 | M | 13 2 75 | Sidcup | Trainee | Charlton Ath | — | — |
| | | | | | | | Barnet | 27 | — |
| Mustafa Tarkan | 5 10 | 11 07 | M | 28 8 73 | London | Kettering T | Barnet | 11 | — |
| Onwere Udo | 6 0 | 11 07 | M | 9 11 72 | Hammersmith | Trainee | Fulham | 85 | 7 |
| | | | | | | | Lincoln C | 43 | 4 |
| | | | | | | | Blackpool | 9 | — |
| | | | | | | | Barnet | 17 | — |
| Rattray Kevin‡ | 5 11 | 11 02 | M | 6 10 68 | London | Woking | Gillingham | 26 | 3 |
| | | | | | | | Barnet | 9 | — |
| Samuels Dean | 5 10 | 12 06 | F | 29 3 73 | Hackney | Boreham Wood | Barnet | 39 | 4 |
| Sawyers Robert | 5 10 | 11 03 | D | 20 11 78 | Dudley | Wolverhampton W | Barnet | 1 | — |
| Searle Stevie | 5 10 | 11 04 | M | 7 3 77 | Lambeth | Sittingbourne | Barnet | 30 | 2 |
| Simpson Phil | 5 9 | 11 01 | M | 18 10 69 | London | Stevenage Bor | Barnet | 87 | 7 |
| Stockley Sam | 5 8 | 11 00 | D | 5 9 77 | Tiverton | Trainee | Southampton | — | — |
| | | | | | | | Barnet | 62 | — |
| Tomlinson Micky‡ | 5 8 | 11 00 | F | 15 9 72 | Lambeth | Trainee | Leyton Orient | 14 | 1 |
| | | | | | | | Barnet | 93 | 4 |
| Wilson Paul | 5 10 | 11 02 | M | 26 9 64 | London | Barking | Barnet | 213 | 21 |

**Trainees**
Bell, Leon E; Beverstock, Paul R; Butterfield, John P; Chapman, Danny P; Coggon, Simon J; Galloway, Neil J; Gledhill, Lee; Keilty, Paul R; King, Marlon F; Luscombe, Billy; Osbourne, Dion R; Rollins, Lee; Webb, Adam J.

**Non-Contract**
Cheesewright, John; De Vito, Claudio G.

## BARNSLEY

| Appleby Matty | 5 7 | 12 01 | D | 16 4 72 | Middlesbrough | Trainee | Newcastle U | 20 | — |
|---|---|---|---|---|---|---|---|---|
| | | | | | | | Darlington (loan) | 10 | 1 |
| | | | | | | | Darlington | 79 | 7 |
| | | | | | | | Barnsley | 50 | — |
| Bagshaw Paul | 5 7 | 12 02 | F | 29 5 79 | Sheffield | Trainee | Barnsley | — | — |
| Barnard Darren | 5 6 | 12 00 | D | 30 11 71 | Rinteln | Wokingham T | Chelsea | 29 | 2 |
| | | | | | | | Reading (loan) | 4 | — |
| | | | | | | | Bristol C | 78 | 15 |
| | | | | | | | Barnsley | 35 | 2 |
| Bassinder Gavin§ | 6 0 | 12 02 | D | 24 9 79 | Mexborough | Trainee | Barnsley | — | — |
| Beckett Duane* | 5 8 | 11 06 | M | 31 1 78 | Sheffield | Trainee | Barnsley | — | — |
| Beckett Luke | 5 11 | 11 06 | F | 25 11 76 | Sheffield | Trainee | Barnsley | — | — |
| Bernard Curtis§ | 5 7 | 12 00 | F | 3 7 80 | Leeds | Trainee | Barnsley | — | — |
| Bosancic Jovo* | 5 11 | 13 00 | M | 7 8 70 | Novi Sad | Uniao Madeira | Barnsley | 42 | 3 |
| Bullock Martin | 5 4 | 10 00 | M | 5 3 75 | Derby | Eastwood T | Barnsley | 131 | 1 |
| Bullock Tony | 6 1 | 12 13 | G | 18 2 72 | Warrington | Leek T | Barnsley | — | — |
| Butler Ian§ | 5 8 | 11 05 | D | 9 11 79 | Barnsley | Trainee | Barnsley | — | — |
| Cataroche David§ | 5 7 | 11 07 | M | 13 12 80 | Leeds | Trainee | Barnsley | — | — |
| Coleano Rudi§ | 5 8 | 13 02 | G | 27 5 79 | Leeds | Trainee | Barnsley | — | — |
| Crookes Dale§ | 5 7 | 12 03 | M | 10 3 80 | Sheffield | Trainee | Barnsley | — | — |
| Cross Matthew§ | 5 6 | 12 03 | D | 25 3 80 | Bury | Trainee | Barnsley | — | — |

| | | | | | | | | | |
|---|---|---|---|---|---|---|---|---|---|
| **De Zeeuw** Arjan | 6 1 | 13 04 | D | 16 4 70 | Castricum | Vitesse 22 | Telstar | 102 | 5 |
| | | | | | | | Barnsley | 100 | 3 |
| **Eaden** Nicky | 5 8 | 12 08 | D | 12 12 72 | Sheffield | Trainee | Barnsley | 211 | 8 |
| **Fjortoft** Jan-Aage | 6 2 | 14 00 | F | 10 1 67 | Aalesund | | Hamar | 22 | 10 |
| | | | | | | | Lillestrom | 35 | 20 |
| | | | | | | | Rapid Vienna | 128 | 62 |
| | | | | | | | Swindon T | 72 | 28 |
| | | | | | | | Middlesbrough | 41 | 9 |
| | | | | | | | Sheffield U | 34 | 19 |
| | | | | | | | Barnsley | 15 | 6 |
| **Goodyear** Craig§ | 5 7 | 12 01 | M | 7 11 80 | Barnsley | Trainee | Barnsley | — | — |
| **Gregory** Andrew | 5 8 | 11 06 | M | 8 10 76 | Barnsley | Trainee | Barnsley | — | — |
| **Hendrie** John | 5 7 | 12 08 | F | 24 10 63 | Lennoxtown | Apprentice | Coventry C | 21 | 2 |
| | | | | | | | Hereford U (loan) | 6 | — |
| | | | | | | | Bradford C | 173 | 46 |
| | | | | | | | Newcastle U | 34 | 4 |
| | | | | | | | Leeds U | 27 | 5 |
| | | | | | | | Middlesbrough | 192 | 44 |
| | | | | | | | Barnsley | 56 | 16 |
| **Heritage** Paul* | 6 2 | 12 11 | G | 17 4 79 | Sheffield | Trainee | Sheffield U | — | — |
| | | | | | | | Barnsley | — | — |
| **Hristov** Georgi | 6 0 | 12 03 | F | 30 1 76 | Bitola | | Partizan Belgrade | 37 | 12 |
| | | | | | | | Barnsley | 23 | 4 |
| **Hulson** Shane* | 5 9 | 11 06 | D | 17 12 78 | Barnsley | Trainee | Barnsley | — | — |
| **Hume** Mark* | 6 2 | 13 04 | D | 21 5 78 | Barnsley | Trainee | Barnsley | — | — |
| **Jackson** Chris* | 5 9 | 11 06 | F | 16 1 76 | Barnsley | Trainee | Barnsley | 23 | 2 |
| **Jones** Dean* | 6 1 | 12 05 | D | 12 10 77 | Barnsley | Trainee | Barnsley | — | — |
| **Jones** Scott | 5 10 | 12 08 | D | 1 5 75 | Sheffield | Trainee | Barnsley | 34 | 1 |
| | | | | | | | Mansfield T (loan) | 6 | — |
| | | | | | | | Notts Co (loan) | — | — |
| **Krizan** Ales | 5 8 | 12 12 | D | 25 7 71 | Maribor | | Branik Maribor | 159 | — |
| | | | | | | | Barnsley | 12 | — |
| **Leese** Lars | 6 3 | 14 07 | G | 18 8 69 | Cologne | Leverkusen | Barnsley | 9 | — |
| **Liddell** Andrew | 5 6 | 11 06 | F | 28 6 73 | Leeds | Trainee | Barnsley | 190 | 34 |
| **Marcelle** Clint | 5 4 | 10 00 | M | 9 11 68 | Port of Spain | | Falgueiras | 21 | — |
| | | | | | | | Barnsley | 60 | 8 |
| **Markstedt** Peter | 5 9 | 14 00 | D | 11 1 72 | Vasteras | | Vasteras | 23 | 4 |
| | | | | | | | Barnsley | 7 | — |
| **Massey** Miles* | | | M | 21 4 79 | York | | Barnsley | — | — |
| **McClare** Sean | 5 9 | 11 06 | M | 12 1 78 | Rotherham | Trainee | Barnsley | — | — |
| **Morgan** Chris | 5 10 | 12 09 | D | 9 11 77 | Barnsley | Trainee | Barnsley | 11 | — |
| **Moses** Adrian | 5 10 | 12 02 | D | 4 5 75 | Doncaster | School | Barnsley | 91 | 3 |
| **Perry** Jonathan‡ | 6 0 | 12 06 | D | 22 11 76 | Hamilton | Trainee | Barnsley | — | — |
| **Prendergast** Rory* | 5 8 | 11 13 | M | 6 4 78 | Pontefract | Rochdale | Barnsley | — | — |
| **Redfearn** Neil | 5 8 | 13 07 | M | 20 6 65 | Bradford | Nottingham F | Bolton W | 35 | 1 |
| | | | | | | | Lincoln C (loan) | 10 | 1 |
| | | | | | | | Lincoln C | 90 | 12 |
| | | | | | | | Doncaster R | 46 | 14 |
| | | | | | | | Crystal Palace | 57 | 10 |
| | | | | | | | Watford | 24 | 3 |
| | | | | | | | Oldham Ath | 62 | 16 |
| | | | | | | | Barnsley | 292 | 71 |
| **Rose** Karl | 5 8 | 11 04 | F | 12 10 78 | Barnsley | | Barnsley | — | — |
| **Shenton** Daniel* | 5 11 | 12 07 | M | 29 9 78 | Sheffield | Trainee | Barnsley | — | — |
| **Sheridan** Darren | 5 4 | 11 05 | M | 8 12 67 | Manchester | Winsford U | Barnsley | 146 | 4 |
| **Shirtliff** Peter† | 6 1 | 12 02 | D | 6 4 61 | Sheffield | Apprentice | Sheffield W | 188 | 4 |
| | | | | | | | Charlton Ath | 103 | 7 |
| | | | | | | | Sheffield W | 104 | 4 |
| | | | | | | | Wolverhampton W | 69 | — |
| | | | | | | | Barnsley | 49 | — |
| | | | | | | | Carlisle U (loan) | 5 | — |
| **Ten Heuvel** Laurens* | 6 0 | 12 01 | F | 6 6 76 | Duivendrecht | Den Bosch | Barnsley | 8 | — |
| | | | | | | | Northampton (loan) | — | — |
| **Tinkler** Eric | 6 2 | 12 03 | M | 30 7 70 | Roodepoort | | Vitoria Setubal | 57 | 1 |
| | | | | | | | Cagliari | 20 | — |
| | | | | | | | Barnsley | 25 | 2 |
| **Ward** Ashley | 6 2 | 13 09 | F | 24 11 70 | Manchester | Trainee | Manchester C | 1 | — |
| | | | | | | | Wrexham (loan) | 4 | 2 |
| | | | | | | | Leicester C | 10 | — |
| | | | | | | | Blackpool (loan) | 2 | 1 |
| | | | | | | | Crewe Alex | 61 | 25 |
| | | | | | | | Norwich C | 53 | 18 |
| | | | | | | | Derby Co | 40 | 9 |
| | | | | | | | Barnsley | 29 | 8 |
| **Watson** David | 5 11 | 12 12 | G | 10 11 73 | Barnsley | Trainee | Barnsley | 172 | — |

**Trainees**
Bassinder, Gavin D; Bernard, Curtis J; Butler, Ian M; Cataroche, David; Crookes, Dale W; Cross, Matthew F; Dudgeon, James F; Goodyear, Craig; Heckingbottom, Marc; Kennedy, Paul J; O'Carroll, Ryan P; Ravenhill, Richard J; Sidebottom, Frazer; Smith, Andrew A; Taylor, David J; Wood, James.

**Non-Contract**
Shirtliff, Peter A.

**Associated Schoolboys**
Austin, Neil J; Jackson, Paul S; Kay, Anthony R; Marsh, Adam; Reece, Gary L; Wilkinson, Craig.

**Associated Schoolboys who have accepted the club's offer of a Traineeship/Contract**
Barraclough, Carl; Richards, Duncan.

# BIRMINGHAM CITY

| | | | | | | | | | |
|---|---|---|---|---|---|---|---|---|---|
| **Ablett** Gary | 6 0 | 11 04 | D | 19 11 65 | Liverpool | Apprentice | Liverpool | 109 | 1 |
| | | | | | | | Derby Co (loan) | 6 | — |
| | | | | | | | Hull C (loan) | 5 | — |
| | | | | | | | Everton | 128 | 5 |
| | | | | | | | Sheffield U (loan) | 12 | — |
| | | | | | | | Birmingham C | 78 | 1 |
| **Adebola** Dele | 6 3 | 12 08 | F | 23 6 75 | Lagos | Trainee | Crewe Alex | 124 | 39 |
| | | | | | | | Birmingham C | 17 | 7 |
| **Barnes** Steve | 5 4 | 10 05 | F | 5 1 76 | Wembley | Welling U | Birmingham C | 3 | — |
| | | | | | | | Brighton & HA (loan) | 12 | — |
| **Bass** Jonathan | 6 0 | 12 02 | D | 1 1 76 | Weston-Super-Mare | Trainee | Birmingham C | 48 | — |
| | | | | | | | Carlisle U (loan) | 3 | — |
| **Bennett** Ian | 6 0 | 12 10 | G | 10 10 70 | Worksop | Newcastle U | Peterborough U | 72 | — |
| | | | | | | | Birmingham C | 177 | — |
| **Bruce** Steve | 6 0 | 12 06 | D | 31 12 60 | Corbridge | Apprentice | Gillingham | 205 | 29 |
| | | | | | | | Norwich C | 141 | 14 |
| | | | | | | | Manchester U | 309 | 36 |
| | | | | | | | Birmingham C | 72 | 2 |
| **Charlton** Simon | 5 8 | 11 10 | D | 25 10 71 | Huddersfield | Trainee | Huddersfield T | 124 | 1 |
| | | | | | | | Southampton | 114 | 2 |
| | | | | | | | Birmingham C | 24 | — |
| **Dukes** Lee* | 5 9 | 11 06 | D | 24 10 79 | Walsall | Trainee | Birmingham C | — | — |
| **Dyson** James | 6 2 | 12 00 | D | 20 4 79 | Wordsley | Trainee | Birmingham C | — | — |
| **Forinton** Howard | 5 11 | 11 00 | F | 18 9 75 | Boston | Yeovil T | Birmingham C | 1 | — |
| **Forster** Nicky | 5 9 | 11 05 | F | 8 9 73 | Caterham | Horley T | Gillingham | 67 | 24 |
| | | | | | | | Brentford | 109 | 39 |
| | | | | | | | Birmingham C | 35 | 6 |
| **Furlong** Paul | 6 0 | 11 00 | F | 1 10 68 | London | Enfield | Coventry C | 37 | 4 |
| | | | | | | | Watford | 79 | 37 |
| | | | | | | | Chelsea | 64 | 13 |
| | | | | | | | Birmingham C | 68 | 25 |
| **Gardner** Lee | | | D | 18 5 78 | Doncaster | | Birmingham C | — | — |
| **Gill** Jeremy | 5 8 | 11 00 | D | 8 9 70 | Clevedon | Yeovil T | Birmingham C | 3 | — |
| **Grainger** Martin | 5 10 | 11 07 | D | 23 8 72 | Enfield | Trainee | Colchester U | 46 | 7 |
| | | | | | | | Brentford | 101 | 12 |
| | | | | | | | Birmingham C | 64 | 5 |
| **Hatton** Paul‡ | 6 0 | 11 00 | F | 2 11 78 | Kidderminster | Trainee | Birmingham C | — | — |
| **Hey** Tony | 5 9 | 11 07 | M | 19 9 70 | Berlin | | Fortuna Cologne | 32 | 9 |
| | | | | | | | Birmingham C | 9 | — |
| **Hinton** Craig‡ | 5 11 | 11 00 | D | 26 11 77 | Wolverhampton | Trainee | Birmingham C | — | — |
| **Holland** Chris | 5 9 | 11 05 | M | 11 9 75 | Whalley | Trainee | Preston NE | 1 | — |
| | | | | | | | Newcastle U | 3 | — |
| | | | | | | | Birmingham C | 42 | — |
| **Hughes** Bryan | 5 9 | 10 00 | M | 19 6 76 | Liverpool | Trainee | Wrexham | 94 | 12 |
| | | | | | | | Birmingham C | 51 | 5 |
| **Johnson** Andrew | | | F | 10 2 81 | Bedford | Trainee | Birmingham C | — | — |
| **Johnson** Michael | 5 11 | 11 00 | D | 4 7 73 | Nottingham | Trainee | Notts Co | 107 | — |
| | | | | | | | Birmingham C | 106 | 3 |
| **Marsden** Chris | 5 11 | 10 12 | M | 3 1 69 | Sheffield | Trainee | Sheffield U | 16 | 1 |
| | | | | | | | Huddersfield T | 121 | 9 |
| | | | | | | | Coventry C (loan) | 7 | — |
| | | | | | | | Wolverhampton W | 8 | — |
| | | | | | | | Notts Co | 10 | — |
| | | | | | | | Stockport Co | 65 | 3 |
| | | | | | | | Birmingham C | 32 | 1 |
| **McCarthy** Jon | 5 9 | 11 05 | M | 18 8 70 | Middlesbrough | | Hartlepool U | 1 | — |
| | | | | | | Shepshed | York C | 199 | 31 |
| | | | | | | | Port Vale | 94 | 11 |
| | | | | | | | Birmingham C | 41 | 4 |
| **Moore** Richard‡ | | | M | 2 9 77 | Scunthorpe | | Birmingham C | — | — |
| **Ndlovu** Peter | 5 8 | 10 02 | F | 25 2 73 | Zimbabwe | Highlanders | Coventry C | 177 | 37 |
| | | | | | | | Birmingham C | 39 | 9 |

| Name | ht | wt | Pos | DOB | Birthplace | Signed from | Club | Apps | Gls |
|---|---|---|---|---|---|---|---|---|---|
| **Newell** Mike *(Transferred to Aberdeen, July 1997)* | 6 0 | 13 00 | F | 27 1 65 | Liverpool | Liverpool | Crewe Alex | 3 | — |
| | | | | | | | Wigan Ath | 72 | 25 |
| | | | | | | | Luton T | 63 | 18 |
| | | | | | | | Leicester C | 81 | 21 |
| | | | | | | | Everton | 68 | 15 |
| | | | | | | | Blackburn R | 130 | 28 |
| | | | | | | | Birmingham C | 15 | 1 |
| | | | | | | | West Ham U (loan) | 7 | — |
| | | | | | | | Bradford C (loan) | 7 | — |
| | | | | | | | Aberdeen | 21 | 4 |
| **O'Connor** Martin | 5 8 | 10 08 | M | 10 12 67 | Walsall | Bromsgrove R | Crystal Palace | 2 | — |
| | | | | | | | Walsall (loan) | 10 | 1 |
| | | | | | | | Walsall | 94 | 21 |
| | | | | | | | Peterborough U | 18 | 3 |
| | | | | | | | Birmingham C | 57 | 5 |
| **Otto** Ricky‡ | 5 10 | 11 00 | M | 9 11 67 | Hackney | Dartford | Leyton Orient | 56 | 13 |
| | | | | | | | Southend U | 64 | 17 |
| | | | | | | | Birmingham C | 46 | 6 |
| | | | | | | | Charlton Ath (loan) | 7 | — |
| | | | | | | | Peterborough U (loan) | 15 | 4 |
| | | | | | | | Notts Co (loan) | 4 | — |
| **Poole** Kevin | 5 10 | 11 11 | G | 21 7 63 | Bromsgrove | Apprentice | Aston Villa | 28 | — |
| | | | | | | | Northampton T (loan) | 3 | — |
| | | | | | | | Middlesbrough | 34 | — |
| | | | | | | | Hartlepool U (loan) | 12 | — |
| | | | | | | | Leicester C | 163 | — |
| | | | | | | | Birmingham C | 1 | — |
| **Purse** Darren | 6 2 | 12 08 | D | 14 2 77 | Stepney | Trainee | Leyton Orient | 55 | 3 |
| | | | | | | | Oxford U | 59 | 5 |
| | | | | | | | Birmingham C | 8 | — |
| **Rea** Simon | 6 1 | 13 00 | D | 20 9 76 | Coventry | Trainee | Birmingham C | 1 | — |
| **Robinson** Steve | 5 9 | 11 00 | M | 17 10 75 | Nottingham | Trainee | Birmingham C | 40 | — |
| | | | | | | | Peterborough U (loan) | 5 | — |
| **Tait** Paul | 6 1 | 10 07 | M | 31 7 71 | Sutton Coldfield | Trainee | Birmingham C | 170 | 14 |
| | | | | | | | Millwall (loan) | — | — |
| | | | | | | | Northampton T (loan) | 3 | — |
| **Wassall** Darren | 6 0 | 12 07 | D | 27 6 68 | Edgbaston | | Nottingham F | 27 | — |
| | | | | | | | Hereford U (loan) | 5 | — |
| | | | | | | | Bury (loan) | 7 | 1 |
| | | | | | | | Derby Co | 98 | — |
| | | | | | | | Manchester C (loan) | 15 | — |
| | | | | | | | Birmingham C (loan) | 8 | — |
| | | | | | | | Birmingham C | 14 | — |

**Trainees**
Burns, Robert J; Capaldi, Anthony C; Haarhoff, James P; Higgs, Andrew I; Powell, Jason D; Scheppel, Daniel J.

**Associated Schoolboys**
Allinson, Christopher; Bowater, David W; Chisholm, Kelvin S; Collins, Adam; Eskauriatza, Javier S; Evans, Stephen; Fagan, Craig A; Goodison, Anthony; Harris, Matthew G; Hipkiss, Robert J; Holyoak, Daniel; Jones, Ben; Kavanagh, Christopher D; King, Kieran; Marson, Matthew J; McGettrick, James M; Montgomery, Gary S; Morgan, Scott J; Onions, Lee S; Parker, Sonny; Philips, Gary; Pinkney, Grant E; Pitt, Adam L; Richards, Barry; Richards, Elliott C; Robertson, Daniel; Shannon, Ian.

## BLACKBURN ROVERS

| Name | ht | wt | Pos | DOB | Birthplace | Signed from | Club | Apps | Gls |
|---|---|---|---|---|---|---|---|---|---|
| **Andersson** Anders | 5 9 | 11 09 | M | 15 3 74 | Tomelilla | | Malmo | 126 | 19 |
| | | | | | | | Blackburn R | 4 | — |
| **Beattie** James | 6 1 | 12 00 | F | 27 2 78 | Lancaster | Trainee | Blackburn R | 4 | — |
| **Benson** Mark‡ | 5 5 | 10 05 | D | 7 8 78 | Dublin | Trainee | Blackburn R | — | — |
| **Brewer** Ben‡ | | | D | 6 10 78 | Pontypool | Trainee | Blackburn R | — | — |
| **Broomes** Marlon | 6 0 | 12 12 | D | 28 11 77 | Birmingham | Trainee | Blackburn R | 4 | — |
| | | | | | | | Swindon T (loan) | 12 | 1 |
| **Brown** Keith | 6 0 | 11 00 | D | 24 12 79 | Edinburgh | | Blackburn R | — | — |
| **Cassin** Graham* | 5 10 | 11 07 | F | 24 3 78 | Dublin | Belvedere | Blackburn R | — | — |
| **Connolly** Patrick | | | M | 3 3 80 | Preston | Trainee | Blackburn R | — | — |
| **Coughlan** Graham | 6 3 | 14 00 | D | 18 11 74 | Dublin | Bray Wanderers | Blackburn R | — | — |
| | | | | | | | Swindon T (loan) | 3 | — |
| **Croft** Gary | 5 8 | 10 08 | D | 17 2 74 | Burton | Trainee | Grimsby T | 149 | 3 |
| | | | | | | | Blackburn R | 28 | 1 |
| **Dahlin** Martin | 6 1 | 13 03 | F | 16 4 68 | Lund | Lund BK | Malmo | 79 | 39 |
| | | | | | | | Moenchengladbach | 106 | 50 |
| | | | | | | | Roma | 3 | — |
| | | | | | | | Blackburn R | 21 | 4 |
| **Davidson** Callum | 5 10 | 11 00 | D | 25 6 76 | Stirling | | St Johnstone | 44 | 4 |
| | | | | | | | Blackburn R | 1 | — |
| **Donis** George‡ | 6 0 | 12 00 | M | 29 10 69 | Greece | | Yannina | 22 | 3 |
| | | | | | | | Panathinaikos | 136 | 34 |
| | | | | | | | Blackburn R | 22 | 2 |
| **Duff** Damien | 5 10 | 9 07 | F | 2 3 79 | Ballyboden | | Blackburn R | 27 | 4 |
| **Dunn** David | | | M | 27 12 79 | Blackburn | Trainee | Blackburn R | — | — |

| Player | | | | | | | Club | Apps | Goals |
|---|---|---|---|---|---|---|---|---|---|
| **Fettis** Alan | 6 2 | 13 00 | G | 1 2 71 | Belfast | Ards | Hull C | 135 | 2 |
| | | | | | | | WBA (loan) | 3 | — |
| | | | | | | | Nottingham F | 4 | — |
| | | | | | | | Blackburn R | 8 | — |
| **Filan** John | 5 11 | 13 02 | G | 8 2 70 | Sydney | Budapest St George | Cambridge U | 68 | |
| | | | | | | | Nottingham F (loan) | — | — |
| | | | | | | | Coventry C | 16 | — |
| | | | | | | | Blackburn R | 7 | — |
| **Fitzpatrick** Lee | 5 10 | 11 07 | M | 31 10 78 | Manchester | Trainee | Blackburn R | — | — |
| **Flitcroft** Garry | 6 0 | 11 08 | M | 6 11 72 | Bolton | Trainee | Manchester C | 115 | 13 |
| | | | | | | | Bury (loan) | 12 | — |
| | | | | | | | Blackburn R | 64 | 3 |
| **Flowers** Tim | 6 3 | 14 04 | G | 3 2 67 | Kenilworth | Apprentice | Wolverhampton W | 63 | — |
| | | | | | | | Southampton (loan) | — | — |
| | | | | | | | Southampton | 192 | — |
| | | | | | | | Swindon T (loan) | 2 | — |
| | | | | | | | Swindon T (loan) | 5 | — |
| | | | | | | | Blackburn R | 166 | — |
| **Gallacher** Kevin | 5 8 | 11 03 | F | 23 11 66 | Clydebank | Duntocher BC | Dundee U | 131 | 27 |
| | | | | | | | Coventry C | 100 | 28 |
| | | | | | | | Blackburn R | 123 | 41 |
| **Gill** Wayne *(On loan to Dundee U)* | 5 9 | 11 00 | M | 28 11 75 | Chorley | Trainee | Blackburn R | — | — |
| | | | | | | | Dundee U | 2 | — |
| **Hamilton** Gary | | | F | 6 10 80 | Bambridge | Trainee | Blackburn R | — | — |
| **Hawe** Steven | | | F | 23 12 80 | Machbrafelt | Trainee | Blackburn R | — | — |
| **Henchoz** Stephane | 6 1 | 12 08 | D | 7 9 74 | Billens | Bulle | Neuchatel Xamax | 91 | 1 |
| | | | | | | | Hamburg | 49 | 2 |
| | | | | | | | Blackburn R | 36 | — |
| **Hendry** Colin | 6 1 | 12 07 | D | 7 12 65 | Keith | Islavale | Dundee | 41 | 2 |
| | | | | | | | Blackburn R | 102 | 22 |
| | | | | | | | Manchester C | 63 | 5 |
| | | | | | | | Blackburn R | 234 | 12 |
| **Johnson** Damien | 5 8 | 11 02 | M | 18 11 78 | Blackburn | Trainee | Blackburn R | — | — |
| | | | | | | | Nottingham F (loan) | 6 | — |
| **Kenna** Jeff | 5 11 | 12 03 | D | 28 8 70 | Dublin | Trainee | Southampton | 114 | 4 |
| | | | | | | | Blackburn R | 115 | 1 |
| **McAvoy** Andy | 6 0 | 12 00 | M | 28 8 79 | Middlesbrough | Trainee | Blackburn R | — | — |
| **McCallion** Edward* | | | D | 25 1 79 | Derry | | Blackburn R | — | — |
| **McKinlay** Billy | 5 8 | 11 06 | M | 22 4 69 | Glasgow | Hamilton Th | Dundee U | 222 | 23 |
| | | | | | | | Blackburn R | 74 | 3 |
| **Pedersen** Per | 5 11 | 13 00 | F | 30 3 69 | Aalborg | | Odense | 44 | 16 |
| | | | | | | | Lyngby | 96 | 38 |
| | | | | | | | Odense | 49 | 27 |
| | | | | | | | Blackburn R | 11 | 1 |
| **Pedersen** Tore | | | D | 29 9 69 | Fredrikstad | Fredrikstad | IFK Gothenburg | 64 | — |
| | | | | | | | Brann | 22 | — |
| | | | | | | | Oldham Ath | 10 | — |
| | | | | | | | Brann | 1 | — |
| | | | | | | Sanfrecce | St Pauli | 37 | — |
| | | | | | | | Blackburn R | 5 | — |
| **Reed** Adam* | 6 2 | 11 00 | D | 18 2 75 | Bishop Auckland | Trainee | Darlington | 52 | 1 |
| | | | | | | | Blackburn R | — | — |
| | | | | | | | Darlington (loan) | 14 | — |
| | | | | | | | Rochdale (loan) | 10 | — |
| **Richards** Ian | 5 8 | 11 04 | D | 5 10 79 | Barnsley | Trainee | Blackburn R | — | — |
| **Richardson** Leam | | | D | 19 11 79 | Leeds | Trainee | Blackburn R | — | — |
| **Ripley** Stuart | 6 0 | 13 00 | F | 20 11 67 | Middlesbrough | Apprentice | Middlesbrough | 249 | 26 |
| | | | | | | | Bolton W (loan) | 5 | 1 |
| | | | | | | | Blackburn R | 187 | 13 |
| **Ryan** Ciaran | 5 8 | 11 00 | D | 3 9 79 | Dublin | Trainee | Blackburn R | — | — |
| **Scates** Garth | | | M | 27 8 79 | Dundonald | Trainee | Blackburn R | — | — |
| **Sherwood** Tim | 6 1 | 12 09 | M | 2 2 69 | St Albans | Trainee | Watford | 32 | 2 |
| | | | | | | | Norwich C | 71 | 10 |
| | | | | | | | Blackburn R | 227 | 22 |
| **Staton** Luke | 5 7 | 10 07 | M | 10 3 79 | Doncaster | Trainee | Blackburn R | — | — |
| **Stewart** Gareth | 6 0 | 12 08 | G | 3 2 80 | Preston | Trainee | Blackburn R | — | — |
| **Sutton** Chris | 6 3 | 13 07 | F | 10 3 73 | Nottingham | Trainee | Norwich C | 102 | 35 |
| | | | | | | | Blackburn R | 113 | 44 |
| **Taylor** Martin | | | D | 9 11 79 | Northumberland | Trainee | Blackburn R | — | — |
| **Thomas** James | | | F | 16 1 79 | Swansea | Trainee | Blackburn R | — | — |
| | | | | | | | WBA (loan) | 3 | — |
| **Topley** Jonathan | | | F | 12 7 80 | Craigavon | Trainee | Blackburn R | — | — |
| **Valery** Patrick | 5 8 | 13 04 | D | 3 7 69 | Brignoles | AS Brignoles | Monaco | 210 | — |
| | | | | | | | Blackburn R | 15 | — |
| **Watt** Michael‡ | 6 1 | 11 10 | G | 27 11 70 | Aberdeen | | Aberdeen | 79 | — |
| | | | | | | | Blackburn R | — | — |
| **Whealing** Anthony* | 5 9 | 10 02 | D | 3 9 76 | Manchester | Trainee | Blackburn R | — | — |
| **Wilcox** Jason | 6 0 | 11 00 | F | 15 7 71 | Bolton | Trainee | Blackburn R | 219 | 28 |
| **Williams** Anthony | | | G | 20 9 77 | Ogwr | Trainee | Blackburn R | — | — |
| | | | | | | | QPR (loan) | — | — |

**Woodfield** Craig             M   4 9 79   Coventry   Trainee   Blackburn R   —   —
**Worrell** David    6 0   12 04   D   12 1 78   Dublin   Trainee   Blackburn R   —   —

**Trainees**
Baldocchino, Ryan L; Berry, Adam; Bingham, Michael J; Dunning, Darren; Dunning, Richard; Forsyth, Paul J; Harding, John M; Lawless, Michael;
Lomax, Michael J; Murphy, Peter; Whittle, Christopher T.

**Associated Schoolboys**
Emmerson, Scott; Green, Daniel; Hevicon, Ryan; Hill, David J P; McLean, Matthew; Stainsby, James H; Webb, Mark A; Woodhead, Robert A.

**Associated Schoolboys who have accepted the club's offer of a Traineeship/Contract**
Hardy, Lee; Howson, Stuart L.

# BLACKPOOL

| Name | Ht | Wt | Pos | Born date | Born place | Source | Club | Apps | Gls |
|---|---|---|---|---|---|---|---|---|---|
| **Banks** Steve | 6 0 | 13 02 | G | 9 2 72 | Hillingdon | Trainee | West Ham U | — | — |
| | | | | | | | Gillingham | 67 | — |
| | | | | | | | Blackpool | 115 | — |
| **Barnes** Phil | 6 1 | 11 01 | G | 2 3 79 | Rotherham | Trainee | Rotherham U | 2 | — |
| | | | | | | | Blackpool | 1 | — |
| **Bent** Junior | 5 5 | 10 06 | F | 1 3 70 | Huddersfield | Trainee | Huddersfield T | 36 | 6 |
| | | | | | | | Burnley (loan) | 9 | 3 |
| | | | | | | | Bristol C | 183 | 20 |
| | | | | | | | Stoke C (loan) | 1 | — |
| | | | | | | | Shrewsbury T (loan) | 6 | — |
| | | | | | | | Blackpool | 36 | 3 |
| **Bonner** Mark# | 5 10 | 11 00 | M | 7 6 74 | Ormskirk | Trainee | Blackpool | 178 | 14 |
| **Brabin** Gary | 5 11 | 14 08 | M | 9 2 70 | Liverpool | Trainee | Stockport Co | 2 | — |
| | | | | | | Runcorn | Doncaster R | 59 | 11 |
| | | | | | | | Bury | 5 | — |
| | | | | | | | Blackpool | 56 | 5 |
| **Bradshaw** Darren‡ | 5 11 | 11 03 | D | 19 3 67 | Sheffield | Matlock T | Chesterfield | 18 | — |
| | | | | | | | York C | 59 | 3 |
| | | | | | | | Newcastle U | 38 | — |
| | | | | | | | Peterborough U | 73 | 1 |
| | | | | | | | Plymouth Arg (loan) | 6 | 1 |
| | | | | | | | Blackpool | 67 | 1 |
| **Bryan** Marvin | 6 0 | 12 02 | D | 2 8 75 | Paddington | Trainee | QPR | — | — |
| | | | | | | | Doncaster R (loan) | 5 | 1 |
| | | | | | | | Blackpool | 123 | 3 |
| **Butler** Tony | 6 2 | 12 00 | D | 28 9 72 | Stockport | Trainee | Gillingham | 148 | 5 |
| | | | | | | | Blackpool | 79 | — |
| **Carlisle** Clarke | 6 1 | 12 07 | D | 14 10 79 | Preston | Trainee | Blackpool | 11 | 2 |
| **Clarkson** Phil | 5 10 | 12 05 | M | 13 11 68 | Garstang | Fleetwood T | Crewe Alex | 98 | 27 |
| | | | | | | | Scunthorpe U | 52 | 19 |
| | | | | | | | Blackpool | 62 | 18 |
| **Conroy** Mike | 6 0 | 13 04 | F | 31 12 65 | Glasgow | Apprentice | Coventry C | — | — |
| | | | | | | | Clydebank | 114 | 38 |
| | | | | | | | St Mirren | 10 | 1 |
| | | | | | | | Reading | 80 | 7 |
| | | | | | | | Burnley | 77 | 30 |
| | | | | | | | Preston NE | 57 | 22 |
| | | | | | | | Fulham | 94 | 32 |
| | | | | | | | Blackpool | 6 | — |
| **Cross** Jamie* | 5 10 | 12 02 | D | 29 8 79 | Blackpool | Trainee | Blackpool | — | — |
| **Dixon** Ben* | 6 1 | 11 00 | D | 16 9 74 | Lincoln | Trainee | Lincoln C | 43 | — |
| | | | | | | | Blackpool | 18 | — |
| **Haddow** Paul* | 5 8 | 10 10 | M | 11 10 78 | Fleetwood | Trainee | Blackpool | 1 | — |
| **Heighton** Henry* | 6 0 | 13 02 | G | 27 11 78 | Sunderland | Trainee | Blackpool | — | — |
| **Hills** John | 5 9 | 10 08 | D | 21 4 78 | St Annes-on-Sea | Trainee | Blackpool | — | — |
| | | | | | | | Everton | 3 | — |
| | | | | | | | Swansea C (loan) | 11 | — |
| | | | | | | | Swansea C (loan) | 7 | 1 |
| | | | | | | | Blackpool | 19 | 1 |
| **Hughes** Ian | 5 11 | 12 00 | D | 2 8 74 | Bangor | Trainee | Bury | 175 | 1 |
| | | | | | | | Blackpool | 21 | — |
| **Jones** David | 5 7 | 9 10 | M | 17 11 78 | Goole | Goole T | Blackpool | — | — |
| **Linighan** David* | 6 2 | 12 06 | D | 9 1 65 | Hartlepool | Local | Hartlepool U | 91 | 5 |
| | | | | | | | Leeds U (loan) | — | — |
| | | | | | | | Derby Co | — | — |
| | | | | | | | Shrewsbury T | 65 | 1 |
| | | | | | | | Ipswich T | 277 | 12 |
| | | | | | | | Blackpool | 100 | 5 |
| **Longworth** Steve§ | 5 9 | 11 00 | F | 6 2 80 | Leyland | Trainee | Blackpool | 2 | — |
| **Lydiate** Jason* | 5 11 | 12 03 | D | 29 10 71 | Manchester | Trainee | Manchester U | — | — |
| | | | | | | | Bolton W | 30 | — |
| | | | | | | | Blackpool | 86 | 2 |
| **Malkin** Chris | 6 3 | 12 09 | F | 4 6 67 | Hoylake | Overpool | Tranmere R | 232 | 60 |
| | | | | | | | Millwall | 52 | 14 |
| | | | | | | | Blackpool | 35 | 5 |
| **Nowland** Adam§ | 5 11 | 11 06 | F | 6 7 81 | Preston | Trainee | Blackpool | 1 | — |
| **Ormerod** Brett | 5 11 | 11 04 | F | 18 10 76 | Blackburn | Accrington S | Blackpool | 13 | 2 |

| | | | | | | | | | |
|---|---|---|---|---|---|---|---|---|---|
| **Philpott** Lee# | 5 9 | 11 08 | M | 21 2 70 | Barnet | Trainee | Peterborough U | 4 | — |
| | | | | | | | Cambridge U | 134 | 17 |
| | | | | | | | Leicester C | 75 | 3 |
| | | | | | | | Blackpool | 71 | 5 |
| **Preece** Andy* | 6 1 | 12 00 | F | 27 3 67 | Evesham | Evesham U | Northampton T | 1 | — |
| | | | | | | Worcester C | Wrexham | 51 | 7 |
| | | | | | | | Stockport Co | 97 | 42 |
| | | | | | | | Crystal Palace | 20 | 4 |
| | | | | | | | Blackpool | 126 | 35 |
| **Reed** John* | 5 10 | 10 11 | M | 27 8 72 | Rotherham | Trainee | Sheffield U | 15 | 2 |
| | | | | | | | Scarborough (loan) | 14 | 6 |
| | | | | | | | Scarborough (loan) | 6 | — |
| | | | | | | | Darlington (loan) | 10 | 2 |
| | | | | | | | Mansfield T (loan) | 13 | 2 |
| | | | | | | | Blackpool | 3 | — |
| **Rogan** Anton | 6 0 | 13 00 | D | 25 3 66 | Belfast | Distillery | Celtic | 127 | 4 |
| | | | | | | | Sunderland | 46 | 1 |
| | | | | | | | Oxford U | 58 | 3 |
| | | | | | | | Millwall | 36 | 8 |
| | | | | | | | Blackpool | 1 | — |
| **Russell** Keith‡ | 5 10 | 12 00 | M | 31 1 74 | Aldridge | Hednesford T | Blackpool | 1 | — |
| **Thompson** Phil§ | 5 11 | 12 00 | D | 1 4 81 | Blackpool | Trainee | Blackpool | 1 | — |
| **Worthington** Nigel | 5 11 | 12 06 | D | 4 11 61 | Ballymena | Ballymena U | Notts Co | 67 | 4 |
| | | | | | | | Sheffield W | 338 | 12 |
| | | | | | | | Leeds U | 43 | 1 |
| | | | | | | | Stoke C | 12 | — |
| | | | | | | | Blackpool | 9 | — |

**Trainees**
Bamber, Michael J; Byrne, Tamas; Dickinson, Ian J; Ellis, Christopher A; Jarrett, Jason L M; Lazenby, Mark; Longworth, Steven P; Nowland, Adam C; Robinson, Philip D; Seaton, Simon J; Shockledge, Lee S; Skeoch, Jamie A; Sugden, Scott I; Talbot, Robert T; Thompson, Philip P.

**Associated Schoolboys**
Beavers, Terry J; Blinkhorn, Craig L; Bridges, Simon; Carroll, John D; Connors, John J; Dodd, Alexander P; Edwards, Michael L; Faber, Carl B; Grand, Simon; Greco, Nicki; Heatley, Anthony G; Holden, Wesley J; Holmes, Karl; Hone, James; Maden, Wayne T; Mallard, Simon J; Morgan, Nicholas S; Newby, Craig C; Nicholson, Kevin J; Richards, David J; Smyth, Marc; Watson, David L; Zammit, Daniel S R.

**Associated Schoolboys who have accepted the club's offer of a Traineeship/Contract**
Coid, Daniel J; Connell, Darren; Ellison, Gavin; Fahey, Mark A; Lambert, Rickie L; Lynch, Patrick A; Manchester, Brian N; Sidebotham, Paul; Smith, Robert.

## BOLTON WANDERERS

| | | | | | | | | | |
|---|---|---|---|---|---|---|---|---|---|
| **Aljofree** Hasney | 6 0 | 12 03 | D | 11 7 78 | Manchester | Trainee | Bolton W | 2 | — |
| **Beardsley** Peter | 5 8 | 11 07 | F | 18 1 61 | Newcastle | Wallsend BC | Carlisle U | 104 | 22 |
| | | | | | | Vancouver Whitecaps | Manchester U | — | — |
| | | | | | | Vancouver Whitecaps | Newcastle U | 147 | 61 |
| | | | | | | | Liverpool | 131 | 46 |
| | | | | | | | Everton | 81 | 25 |
| | | | | | | | Newcastle U | 129 | 46 |
| | | | | | | | Bolton W | 17 | 2 |
| | | | | | | | Manchester C (loan) | 6 | — |
| | | | | | | | Fulham (loan) | 8 | 1 |
| **Bergsson** Gudni | 6 1 | 12 03 | D | 21 7 65 | Reykjavik | Valur | Tottenham H | 71 | 2 |
| | | | | | | | Bolton W | 110 | 9 |
| **Blake** Nathan | 5 11 | 12 08 | F | 27 1 72 | Cardiff | Chelsea | Cardiff C | 131 | 35 |
| | | | | | | | Sheffield U | 69 | 34 |
| | | | | | | | Bolton W | 95 | 32 |
| **Branagan** Keith | 6 0 | 13 02 | G | 10 7 66 | Fulham | | Cambridge U | 110 | — |
| | | | | | | | Millwall | 46 | — |
| | | | | | | | Brentford (loan) | 2 | — |
| | | | | | | | Gillingham (loan) | 1 | — |
| | | | | | | | Fulham (loan) | — | — |
| | | | | | | | Bolton W | 200 | — |
| **Buggie** Lee | | | F | 11 2 81 | Bury | Trainee | | — | — |
| **Cox** Neil | 6 0 | 13 07 | D | 8 10 71 | Scunthorpe | Trainee | Scunthorpe U | 17 | 1 |
| | | | | | | | Aston Villa | 42 | 3 |
| | | | | | | | Middlesbrough | 106 | 3 |
| | | | | | | | Bolton W | 21 | 1 |
| **Doherty** Martin | 6 1 | 12 02 | M | 17 10 78 | Urmston | Trainee | Bolton W | — | — |
| **Elliott** Robbie | 5 10 | 10 13 | D | 25 12 73 | Gosforth | Trainee | Newcastle U | 79 | 9 |
| | | | | | | | Bolton W | 4 | — |
| **Fairclough** Chris* | 5 11 | 11 00 | D | 12 4 64 | Nottingham | Apprentice | Nottingham F | 107 | 1 |
| | | | | | | | Tottenham H | 60 | 5 |
| | | | | | | | Leeds U | 193 | 21 |
| | | | | | | | Bolton W | 90 | 8 |
| **Fish** Mark | 6 4 | 12 11 | D | 14 3 74 | Cape Town | Orlando Pirates | Lazio | 15 | 1 |
| | | | | | | | Bolton W | 22 | 2 |
| **Frandsen** Per | 6 1 | 12 06 | M | 6 2 70 | Copenhagen | B 1903 | Lille | 109 | 19 |
| | | | | | | | FC Copenhagen | 55 | 19 |
| | | | | | | | Bolton W | 79 | 7 |
| **Giallanza** Gaetano | 6 0 | 11 03 | F | 6 6 74 | Dornach | | Basle | 32 | 19 |
| | | | | | | | Nantes | 12 | 2 |
| | | | | | | | Bolton W | 3 | — |

| | | | | | | | | | |
|---|---|---|---|---|---|---|---|---|---|
| **Glennon** Matthew | 6 2 | 13 11 | G | 8 10 78 | Stockport | Trainee | Bolton W | — | — |
| **Gunnlaugsson** Arnar | 5 11 | 11 04 | F | 6 3 73 | Akranes | | IA Akranes | 18 | 15 |
| | | | | | | | Feyenoord | 9 | — |
| | | | | | | | Nuremberg | 28 | 8 |
| | | | | | | | IA Akranes | 9 | 16 |
| | | | | | | | Bolton W | 15 | — |
| **Holden** Dean | | | D | 15 9 79 | Salford | | Bolton W | — | — |
| **Holdsworth** Dean | 5 11 | 11 13 | F | 8 11 68 | Walthamstow | Trainee | Watford | 16 | 3 |
| | | | | | | | Carlisle U (loan) | 4 | 1 |
| | | | | | | | Port Vale (loan) | 6 | 2 |
| | | | | | | | Swansea C (loan) | 5 | 1 |
| | | | | | | | Brentford (loan) | 7 | 1 |
| | | | | | | | Brentford | 110 | 53 |
| | | | | | | | Wimbledon | 169 | 58 |
| | | | | | | | Bolton W | 20 | 3 |
| **Jaaskelainen** Jussi | 6 4 | 12 10 | G | 17 4 75 | Vaasa | | MP | 64 | — |
| | | | | | | | VPS | 54 | — |
| | | | | | | | Bolton W | — | — |
| **Johansen** Michael | 5 6 | 10 05 | M | 22 7 72 | Glostrup | | KB Copenhagen | 15 | 1 |
| | | | | | | | B 1903 | 26 | 1 |
| | | | | | | | FC Copenhagen | 114 | 17 |
| | | | | | | | Bolton W | 49 | 6 |
| **Phillips** Jimmy | 6 0 | 12 07 | D | 8 2 66 | Bolton | Apprentice | Bolton W | 108 | 2 |
| | | | | | | | Rangers | 25 | — |
| | | | | | | | Oxford U | 79 | 8 |
| | | | | | | | Middlesbrough | 139 | 6 |
| | | | | | | | Bolton W | 183 | 2 |
| **Potter** Lee | 5 11 | 12 10 | F | 3 9 78 | Salford | Trainee | Bolton W | — | — |
| **Salako** John* | 5 9 | 12 03 | M | 11 2 69 | Nigeria | Trainee | Crystal Palace | 215 | 22 |
| | | | | | | | Swansea C (loan) | 13 | 3 |
| | | | | | | | Coventry C | 72 | 4 |
| | | | | | | | Bolton W | 7 | — |
| **Sellars** Scott | 5 8 | 10 00 | M | 27 11 65 | Sheffield | Apprentice | Leeds U | 76 | 12 |
| | | | | | | | Blackburn R | 202 | 35 |
| | | | | | | | Leeds U | 7 | — |
| | | | | | | | Newcastle U | 61 | 5 |
| | | | | | | | Bolton W | 86 | 13 |
| **Sheridan** John* | 5 10 | 12 01 | M | 1 10 64 | Stretford | Local | Leeds U | 230 | 47 |
| | | | | | | | Nottingham F | — | — |
| | | | | | | | Sheffield W | 197 | 25 |
| | | | | | | | Birmingham C (loan) | 2 | — |
| | | | | | | | Bolton W | 32 | 2 |
| **Smith** Gordon | | | M | 18 12 80 | Glasgow | Trainee | Bolton W | — | — |
| **Spooner** Nicky | 5 10 | 11 09 | D | 5 6 71 | Manchester | Trainee | Bolton W | 23 | 2 |
| **Strong** Greg | 6 2 | 11 12 | D | 5 9 75 | Bolton | Trainee | Wigan Ath | 35 | 3 |
| | | | | | | | Bolton W | 1 | — |
| | | | | | | | Blackpool (loan) | 11 | 1 |
| **Taggart** Gerry | 6 1 | 12 00 | D | 18 10 70 | Belfast | Trainee | Manchester C | 12 | 1 |
| | | | | | | | Barnsley | 212 | 16 |
| | | | | | | | Bolton W | 69 | 4 |
| **Taylor** Scott | 5 10 | 11 04 | F | 5 5 76 | Chertsey | Staines | Millwall | 28 | — |
| | | | | | | | Bolton W | 12 | 1 |
| | | | | | | | Rotherham U (loan) | 10 | 3 |
| | | | | | | | Blackpool (loan) | 5 | 1 |
| **Thompson** Alan | 6 0 | 12 08 | M | 22 12 73 | Newcastle | Trainee | Newcastle U | 16 | — |
| | | | | | | | Bolton W | 157 | 33 |
| **Todd** Andy | 5 10 | 10 11 | D | 21 9 74 | Derby | Trainee | Middlesbrough | 8 | — |
| | | | | | | | Swindon T (loan) | 13 | — |
| | | | | | | | Bolton W | 52 | 2 |
| **Ward** Gavin | 6 2 | 12 12 | G | 30 6 70 | Sutton Coldfield | Aston Villa | Shrewsbury T | — | — |
| | | | | | | | WBA | — | — |
| | | | | | | | Cardiff C | 59 | — |
| | | | | | | | Leicester C | 38 | — |
| | | | | | | | Bradford C | 36 | — |
| | | | | | | | Bolton W | 22 | — |
| **Whitehead** Stuart* | 5 11 | 12 04 | M | 17 7 76 | Bromsgrove | Bromsgrove R | Bolton W | — | — |
| **Whitlow** Mike | 6 0 | 13 03 | D | 13 1 68 | Northwich | Witton Alb | Leeds U | 77 | 4 |
| | | | | | | | Leicester C | 147 | 8 |
| | | | | | | | Bolton W | 13 | — |
| **Xiourouppa** Costas | | | F | 11 9 79 | Dudley | Trainee | Bolton W | — | — |

**Trainees**
Bell, Phillip S; Corrigan, Noel P; Dawson, Christopher J; Fagan, Steven J; Morrison, Peter A; O'Malley, Carl; Power, Alan M; Pryers, Lee M; Trueman, Kevin.

**Associated Schoolboys**
Bassett, Shaun P; Bohannon, Paul W; Cordingley, Matthew W; Downey, Christopher A; Drew, Mark S; Flanagan, Daniel J; Greenhalgh, Christopher J; Hammond, Samuel J M; Lindsay, Allistair W; Lyons, Bradley J; Marshall, Craig L; Morris, Jonathan P; Robinson, Michael J; Salt, Graeme D; Trevett, Barry R; Turner, Daniel R; Watson, Andrew; Whiting, Ashley.

**Associated Schoolboys who have accepted the club's offer of a Traineeship/Contract**
Astle, Brook M; Laidlaw, Simon G; O'Connor, Kieran J; Tagoe, Darrel J.

## BOURNEMOUTH

| | | | | | | | | | |
|---|---|---|---|---|---|---|---|---|---|
| **Bailey** John | 5 8 | 10 02 | M | 6 5 69 | London | Enfield | Bournemouth | 116 | 6 |
| **Beardsmore** Russell | 5 8 | 10 04 | M | 28 9 68 | Wigan | Apprentice | Manchester U | 56 | 4 |
| | | | | | | | Blackburn R (loan) | 2 | — |
| | | | | | | | Bournemouth | 178 | 4 |
| **Brissett** Jason | 5 9 | 12 00 | M | 7 9 74 | Redbridge | Arsenal | Peterborough U | 35 | — |
| | | | | | | | Bournemouth | 124 | 8 |
| **Coll** Owen* | 6 0 | 11 07 | D | 9 4 76 | Donegal | Amateur | Tottenham H | — | — |
| | | | | | | | Bournemouth | 24 | — |
| **Cotterell** Leo‡ | 5 9 | 10 00 | D | 2 9 74 | Cambridge | Trainee | Ipswich T | 2 | — |
| | | | | | | | Bournemouth | 9 | — |
| **Cox** Ian | 6 0 | 12 00 | M | 25 3 71 | Croydon | Carshalton Ath | Crystal Palace | 15 | — |
| | | | | | | | Bournemouth | 98 | 11 |
| **Dean** Michael | 5 9 | 11 10 | M | 9 3 78 | Weymouth | Trainee | Bournemouth | 25 | — |
| **Fletcher** Carl§ | | | | 7 4 80 | Surrey Heath | Trainee | Bournemouth | 1 | — |
| **Fletcher** Steve | 6 2 | 14 09 | F | 26 6 72 | Hartlepool | Trainee | Hartlepool U | 32 | 4 |
| | | | | | | | Bournemouth | 191 | 36 |
| **Glass** Jimmy* | 6 1 | 13 04 | G | 1 8 73 | Epsom | Trainee | Crystal Palace | — | — |
| | | | | | | | Portsmouth (loan) | 3 | — |
| | | | | | | | Bournemouth | 94 | — |
| **Griffin** Anthony | 5 11 | 11 02 | D | 22 3 79 | Bournemouth | Trainee | Bournemouth | — | — |
| **Harrington** Justin* | 5 9 | 10 09 | F | 18 6 75 | Truro | Trainee | Norwich C | — | — |
| | | | | | | | Leicester C | — | — |
| | | | | | | | Bournemouth | 8 | — |
| **Hayter** James | 5 9 | 10 13 | F | 9 4 79 | Newport (IW) | Trainee | Bournemouth | 7 | — |
| **Howe** Eddie | 5 9 | 11 02 | D | 29 11 77 | Amersham | Trainee | Bournemouth | 58 | 1 |
| **Jenkins** Jamie | 5 8 | 10 07 | D | 1 1 79 | Pontypool | Trainee | Bournemouth | — | — |
| **Murray** Robert* | 5 11 | 12 07 | M | 31 10 74 | Hammersmith | Trainee | Bournemouth | 147 | 12 |
| **O'Neill** Jon* | 5 11 | 12 00 | F | 2 1 74 | Glasgow | Queen's Park BC | Queen's Park | 91 | 30 |
| | | | | | | | Celtic | 1 | — |
| | | | | | | | Bournemouth | 67 | 4 |
| **Ovendale** Mark | 6 2 | 13 02 | G | 22 11 73 | Leicester | Wisbech T | Northampton T | 6 | — |
| | | | | | | Barry T | Bournemouth | — | — |
| **Rawlinson** Mark | 5 10 | 11 04 | M | 9 6 75 | Bolton | Trainee | Manchester U | — | — |
| | | | | | | | Bournemouth | 69 | 2 |
| **Robinson** Steve | 5 9 | 11 02 | F | 10 12 74 | Lisburn | Trainee | Tottenham H | 2 | — |
| | | | | | | | Leyton Orient (loan) | — | — |
| | | | | | | | Bournemouth | 158 | 29 |
| **Rolling** Frank | 6 2 | 13 00 | D | 23 8 68 | Colmar | FC Pau | Ayr U | 35 | 2 |
| | | | | | | | Leicester C | 18 | — |
| | | | | | | | Bournemouth | 30 | 4 |
| **Town** David | 5 7 | 11 13 | F | 9 12 76 | Bournemouth | Trainee | Bournemouth | 46 | 2 |
| **Vincent** Jamie | 5 10 | 11 09 | D | 18 6 75 | London | Trainee | Crystal Palace | 25 | — |
| | | | | | | | Bournemouth (loan) | 8 | — |
| | | | | | | | Bournemouth | 73 | 3 |
| **Warren** Christer | 5 10 | 11 12 | F | 10 10 74 | Poole | Cheltenham T | Southampton | 8 | — |
| | | | | | | | Brighton & HA (loan) | 3 | — |
| | | | | | | | Fulham (loan) | 11 | 1 |
| | | | | | | | Bournemouth | 30 | 6 |
| **Wells** David* | 6 2 | 12 07 | G | 29 12 77 | Portsmouth | Trainee | Bournemouth | 1 | — |
| **Young** Neil | 5 9 | 12 00 | D | 31 8 73 | Harlow | Trainee | Tottenham H | — | — |
| | | | | | | | Bournemouth | 161 | 2 |

**Trainees**
Birmingham, David P; Broadhurst, Karl M; Chavez-Munoz, Adrian M; Davey, Benjamin A; Dodds, Ishmael J L; Fernandez, Ricky J; Fletcher, Carl N; Jenkins, Jody D; Johnson, Robert N; Mitchell, Robert S; Nash, Adam D; Saunders, Steele; Williams, John.

**Associated Schoolboys**
Curtis, Christopher; Hart, Thomas; Nunn, Anthony D; Palmer, Paul; Tchupan, Daniel; Trickey, Steven I; Watts, Darren.

**Associated Schoolboys who have accepted the club's offer of a Traineeship/Contract**
Ford, James A; Holland, Christopher J; Lattimer, James D; Leach, Graham M.

## BRADFORD CITY

| | | | | | | | | | |
|---|---|---|---|---|---|---|---|---|---|
| **Beagrie** Peter | 5 8 | 12 00 | M | 28 11 65 | Middlesbrough | Local | Middlesbrough | 33 | 2 |
| | | | | | | | Sheffield U | 84 | 11 |
| | | | | | | | Stoke C | 54 | 7 |
| | | | | | | | Everton | 114 | 11 |
| | | | | | | | Sunderland (loan) | 5 | 1 |
| | | | | | | | Manchester C | 52 | 3 |
| | | | | | | | Bradford C | 34 | — |
| | | | | | | | Everton (loan) | 6 | — |
| **Blake** Robbie | 5 8 | 11 00 | F | 4 3 76 | Middlesbrough | Trainee | Darlington | 68 | 21 |
| | | | | | | | Bradford C | 39 | 8 |
| **Bolland** Paul | 5 10 | 10 12 | M | 23 12 79 | Bradford | Trainee | Bradford C | 10 | — |
| **Bower** Mark | 5 10 | 10 11 | D | 23 1 80 | Bradford | Trainee | Bradford C | 3 | — |

| Name | | | | | Birthplace | From | Club | Apps | Goals |
|---|---|---|---|---|---|---|---|---|---|
| **Davies** Lawrence | 6 1 | 11 11 | F | 3 9 77 | Abergavenny | Trainee | Leeds U | — | — |
| | | | | | | | Bradford C | 4 | — |
| | | | | | | | Darlington (loan) | 2 | — |
| **Donaldson** David | 5 7 | 9 08 | M | 17 12 78 | Gravesend | Arsenal | Bradford C | — | — |
| **Dreyer** John# | 6 1 | 13 02 | D | 11 6 63 | Alnwick | Wallingford T | Oxford U | 60 | 2 |
| | | | | | | | Torquay U (loan) | 5 | — |
| | | | | | | | Fulham (loan) | 12 | 2 |
| | | | | | | | Luton T | 214 | 13 |
| | | | | | | | Stoke C | 49 | 3 |
| | | | | | | | Bolton W (loan) | 2 | — |
| | | | | | | | Bradford C | 45 | 1 |
| **Edinho** | 5 8 | 12 12 | F | 21 2 67 | Brazil | | Chaves | 32 | 14 |
| | | | | | | | Guimaraes | 32 | 15 |
| | | | | | | | Bradford C | 56 | 15 |
| **Grant** Gareth | | | F | 6 9 80 | Leeds | Trainee | Bradford C | 3 | — |
| **Jacobs** Wayne | 5 8 | 11 02 | D | 3 2 69 | Sheffield | Apprentice | Sheffield W | 6 | — |
| | | | | | | | Hull C | 129 | 4 |
| | | | | | | | Rotherham U | 42 | 2 |
| | | | | | | | Bradford C | 141 | 6 |
| **Jewell** Paul† | 5 8 | 12 01 | F | 28 9 64 | Liverpool | Apprentice | Liverpool | — | — |
| | | | | | | | Wigan Ath | 137 | 35 |
| | | | | | | | Bradford C | 269 | 56 |
| | | | | | | | Grimsby T (loan) | 5 | 1 |
| **Lawrence** Jamie | 6 0 | 12 06 | M | 8 3 70 | Balham | Cowes | Sunderland | 4 | — |
| | | | | | | | Doncaster R | 25 | 3 |
| | | | | | | | Leicester C | 47 | 1 |
| | | | | | | | Bradford C | 43 | 3 |
| **McGinlay** John | 5 9 | 11 04 | F | 8 4 64 | Inverness | Elgin C | Shrewsbury T | 60 | 27 |
| | | | | | | | Bury | 25 | 9 |
| | | | | | | | Millwall | 34 | 10 |
| | | | | | | | Bolton W | 192 | 87 |
| | | | | | | | Bradford C | 17 | 3 |
| **McLean** Ian* | 5 10 | 11 04 | D | 13 9 78 | Leeds | Trainee | Bradford C | — | — |
| **Moore** Darren | 6 3 | 15 08 | D | 22 4 74 | Birmingham | Trainee | Torquay U | 103 | 8 |
| | | | | | | | Doncaster R | 76 | 7 |
| | | | | | | | Bradford C | 18 | — |
| **Murray** Shaun* | 5 7 | 10 10 | M | 7 2 70 | Newcastle | Trainee | Tottenham H | — | — |
| | | | | | | | Portsmouth | 34 | 1 |
| | | | | | | | Millwall (loan) | — | — |
| | | | | | | | Scarborough | 29 | 5 |
| | | | | | | | Bradford C | 130 | 8 |
| **O'Brien** Andrew | 5 10 | 10 06 | D | 29 6 79 | Harrogate | Trainee | Bradford C | 48 | 2 |
| **Patterson** Andrew | | | M | 26 11 80 | Kirkaldy | | Bradford C | — | — |
| **Pepper** Nigel | 5 10 | 11 13 | M | 25 4 68 | Rotherham | Apprentice | Rotherham U | 45 | 1 |
| | | | | | | | York C | 235 | 39 |
| | | | | | | | Bradford C | 43 | 10 |
| **Prudhoe** Mark | 6 0 | 14 00 | G | 8 11 63 | Washington | Apprentice | Sunderland | 7 | — |
| | | | | | | | Hartlepool U (loan) | 3 | — |
| | | | | | | | Birmingham C | 1 | — |
| | | | | | | | Walsall | 26 | — |
| | | | | | | | Doncaster R (loan) | 5 | — |
| | | | | | | | Sheffield W (loan) | — | — |
| | | | | | | | Grimsby T (loan) | 8 | — |
| | | | | | | | Hartlepool U (loan) | 13 | — |
| | | | | | | | Bristol C (loan) | 3 | — |
| | | | | | | | Carlisle U | 34 | — |
| | | | | | | | Darlington | 146 | — |
| | | | | | | | Stoke C | 82 | — |
| | | | | | | | Peterborough U (loan) | 6 | — |
| | | | | | | | Liverpool (loan) | — | — |
| | | | | | | | York C (loan) | 2 | — |
| | | | | | | | Bradford C | 8 | — |
| **Ramage** Craig | 5 9 | 11 08 | M | 30 3 70 | Derby | Trainee | Derby Co | 42 | 4 |
| | | | | | | | Wigan Ath (loan) | 10 | 2 |
| | | | | | | | Watford | 104 | 27 |
| | | | | | | | Peterborough U (loan) | 7 | — |
| | | | | | | | Bradford C | 32 | 1 |
| **Sepp** Dennis‡ | 5 9 | 11 04 | F | 5 6 73 | Apeldoorn | HSC 21 | Bradford C | 3 | — |
| **Steiner** Rob | 6 2 | 13 00 | F | 20 6 73 | Finsprong | | Norrkoping | 41 | 14 |
| | | | | | | | Bradford C | 15 | 4 |
| | | | | | | | Norrkoping | 6 | 1 |
| | | | | | | | Bradford C | 37 | 10 |
| **Sundgot** Ole | 6 1 | 11 04 | F | 21 3 72 | Olsumd | | Molde | 69 | 30 |
| *(Transferred to Molde, November 1997)* | | | | | | | Oldham Ath | — | — |
| | | | | | | | Bradford C | 25 | 6 |
| **Verity** Daniel | 5 11 | 10 12 | D | 19 4 80 | Bradford | Trainee | Bradford C | 1 | — |
| **Walsh** Gary | 6 3 | 14 11 | G | 21 3 68 | Wigan | Apprentice | Manchester U | 50 | — |
| | | | | | | | Airdrieonians (loan) | 3 | — |
| | | | | | | | Oldham Ath (loan) | 6 | — |
| | | | | | | | Middlesbrough | 44 | — |
| | | | | | | | Bradford C | 35 | — |

| **Watson** Gordon | 5 10 | 12 08 | F | 20 3 71 | Sidcup | Trainee | Charlton Ath | 31 | 7 |
|---|---|---|---|---|---|---|---|---|---|
| | | | | | | | Sheffield W | 66 | 15 |
| | | | | | | | Southampton | 52 | 8 |
| | | | | | | | Bradford C | 3 | 1 |
| **Wright** Tommy | 5 7 | 11 05 | F | 10 1 66 | Dunfermline | Apprentice | Leeds U | 81 | 24 |
| *(Transferred to St. Johnstone, December 1997)* | | | | | | | Oldham Ath | 112 | 23 |
| | | | | | | | Leicester C | 129 | 22 |
| | | | | | | | Middlesbrough | 53 | 5 |
| | | | | | | | Bradford C | 45 | 5 |
| | | | | | | | Oldham Ath | 12 | 2 |
| | | | | | | | St Johnstone | 5 | — |
| **Zabica** Robert‡ | 6 2 | 13 01 | G | 9 4 64 | Perth | Spearwood | Bradford C | 3 | — |

**Trainees**
Airdrie, Stewart W; Bates, Craig A; Brown, Liam M; Hamilton, James; Lee, Damien A; Meehan, Mark; Nettleton, James D; Smith, Steven L; Stevenson, Matthew J; Walker, Lee.

**Non-Contract**
Jewell, Paul.

**Associated Schoolboys**
Clark, Gareth A; Dufton, Jack P; Emanuel, Lewis J; Fishlock, Craig C; Hatton, Damian; Heap, Alex J; Jones, Benjamin; Lee, Andrew J; Lloyd, Matthew; Loftus, Lewis P; Lopiccolo, Giuseppe M W; McGinty, Dean; Rutherford, James; Sayers, Joseph J; Tyson, Gary W; Worshop, Jon.

**Associated Schoolboys who have accepted the club's offer of a Traineeship/Contract**
Kerr, Scott A.

**Players who do not hold a current contract but their registration has been retained by the club**
Hutton, Peter; Holmes, Richard M; Sas, Marco; Tomlinson, Paul.

# BRENTFORD

| **Adams** Micky‡ | 5 8 | 11 11 | D | 8 11 61 | Sheffield | Apprentice | Gillingham | 92 | 5 |
|---|---|---|---|---|---|---|---|---|---|
| | | | | | | | Coventry C | 90 | 9 |
| | | | | | | | Leeds U | 73 | 2 |
| | | | | | | | Southampton | 144 | 7 |
| | | | | | | | Stoke C | 10 | 3 |
| | | | | | | | Fulham | 29 | 9 |
| | | | | | | | Swansea C | — | — |
| | | | | | | | Brentford | — | — |
| **Anderson** Ijah | 5 8 | 10 03 | M | 30 12 75 | Hackney | Tottenham H | Southend U | — | — |
| | | | | | | | Brentford | 88 | 3 |
| **Aspinall** Warren | 5 9 | 11 12 | M | 13 9 67 | Wigan | Apprentice | Wigan Ath | 10 | 1 |
| | | | | | | | Everton | 7 | — |
| | | | | | | | Wigan Ath (loan) | 41 | 21 |
| | | | | | | | Aston Villa | 44 | 14 |
| | | | | | | | Portsmouth | 132 | 21 |
| | | | | | | | Swansea C (loan) | 5 | — |
| | | | | | | | Bournemouth | 33 | 9 |
| | | | | | | | Carlisle U (loan) | 7 | 1 |
| | | | | | | | Carlisle U | 100 | 11 |
| | | | | | | | Brentford | 24 | 3 |
| **Barrowcliff** Paul‡ | 5 7 | 11 03 | M | 15 6 69 | Hillingdon | Stevenage Bor | Brentford | 11 | — |
| **Bates** Jamie | 6 1 | 12 12 | D | 24 2 68 | London | Trainee | Brentford | 392 | 17 |
| **Benstead** Graham‡ | 6 2 | 14 00 | G | 20 8 63 | Aldershot | | QPR | — | — |
| | | | | | | | Norwich C (loan) | 1 | — |
| | | | | | | | Norwich C | 15 | — |
| | | | | | | | Colchester U (loan) | 18 | — |
| | | | | | | | Sheffield U (loan) | 8 | — |
| | | | | | | | Sheffield U | 39 | — |
| | | | | | | | Brentford | 113 | — |
| **Blaney** Steven‡ | 6 0 | 13 00 | D | 24 3 77 | Orsett | Trainee | West Ham U | — | — |
| | | | | | | | Brentford | 5 | — |
| **Bryan** Derek | 5 10 | 11 05 | F | 11 11 74 | London | Hampton | Brentford | 11 | 2 |
| **Canham** Scott‡ | 5 10 | 11 08 | M | 5 11 74 | London | Trainee | West Ham U | — | — |
| | | | | | | | Torquay U (loan) | 3 | — |
| | | | | | | | Brentford (loan) | 14 | — |
| | | | | | | | Brentford | 35 | 1 |
| **Clark** Dean | | | M | 31 3 80 | Hillingdon | Trainee | Brentford | 4 | — |
| **Cockerill** Glenn† | 5 10 | 12 08 | M | 25 8 59 | Grimsby | Louth U | Lincoln C | 71 | 10 |
| | | | | | | | Swindon T | 26 | 1 |
| | | | | | | | Lincoln C | 115 | 25 |
| | | | | | | | Sheffield U | 62 | 10 |
| | | | | | | | Southampton | 287 | 32 |
| | | | | | | | Leyton Orient | 90 | 7 |
| | | | | | | | Fulham | 40 | 1 |
| | | | | | | | Brentford | 23 | — |
| **Cullip** Danny | 6 0 | 12 07 | D | 17 9 76 | Bracknell | Trainee | Oxford U | — | — |
| | | | | | | | Fulham | 50 | 2 |
| | | | | | | | Brentford | 13 | — |

| Name | Ht | Wt | Pos | Born | Birthplace | From | Club | Apps | Gls |
|---|---|---|---|---|---|---|---|---|---|
| **Dearden** Kevin | 5 11 | 12 06 | G | 8 3 70 | Luton | Trainee | Tottenham H | 1 | — |
| | | | | | | | Cambridge U (loan) | 15 | — |
| | | | | | | | Hartlepool U (loan) | 10 | — |
| | | | | | | | Oxford U (loan) | — | — |
| | | | | | | | Swindon T (loan) | 1 | — |
| | | | | | | | Peterborough U (loan) | 7 | — |
| | | | | | | | Hull C (loan) | 3 | — |
| | | | | | | | Rochdale (loan) | 2 | — |
| | | | | | | | Birmingham C (loan) | 12 | — |
| | | | | | | | Portsmouth (loan) | — | — |
| | | | | | | | Brentford | 198 | — |
| **Dennis** Kevin | 5 10 | 12 00 | M | 14 12 76 | Islington | Arsenal | Brentford | 17 | — |
| **Denys** Ryan | | | F | 16 8 78 | Brentford | Trainee | Brentford | 19 | 1 |
| **Duffy** Gary‡ | | | M | 10 2 79 | Kingston | Trainee | Brentford | — | — |
| **Goddard-Crawley** Richard‡ | 6 3 | 14 00 | M | 31 3 78 | Burnt Oak | Arsenal | Brentford | 1 | — |
| **Hogg** Graeme‡ | 6 1 | 12 04 | D | 17 6 64 | Aberdeen | Apprentice | Manchester U | 83 | 1 |
| | | | | | | | WBA (loan) | 7 | — |
| | | | | | | | Portsmouth | 100 | 2 |
| | | | | | | | Hearts | 58 | 3 |
| | | | | | | | Notts Co | 66 | — |
| | | | | | | | Brentford | 17 | 2 |
| **Hurdle** Gus‡ | 6 0 | 11 04 | D | 14 10 73 | London | Fulham | Brentford | 71 | — |
| **Hutchings** Carl | 5 11 | 11 00 | M | 24 9 74 | London | Trainee | Brentford | 162 | 7 |
| **McGhee** David | 5 11 | 12 05 | D | 19 6 76 | Sussex | Trainee | Brentford | 117 | 8 |
| **McPherson** Malcolm‡ | 6 1 | 12 00 | F | 19 12 74 | Glasgow | Yeovil T | West Ham U | — | — |
| | | | | | | | Brentford | 12 | — |
| **Myall** Stuart‡ | 5 10 | 13 07 | M | 12 11 74 | Eastbourne | Trainee | Brighton & HA | 80 | 4 |
| | | | | | | | Brentford | 2 | — |
| **Oatway** Charlie | 5 7 | 10 10 | M | 28 11 73 | Hammersmith | Yeading | Cardiff C | 32 | — |
| | | | | | | | Torquay U | 67 | 1 |
| | | | | | | | Brentford | 33 | — |
| **Omigie** Joe‡ | 6 2 | 13 00 | F | 13 6 72 | Hammersmith | Donna | Brentford | 24 | 1 |
| **Rapley** Kevin | 5 9 | 10 08 | F | 21 9 77 | Reading | Trainee | Brentford | 39 | 9 |
| **Reina** Ricky‡ | 6 0 | 13 05 | F | 2 10 71 | Folkestone | Dover Ath | Brentford | 6 | 1 |
| **Scott** Andy | 6 1 | 11 05 | F | 2 8 72 | Epsom | Sutton U | Sheffield U | 75 | 6 |
| | | | | | | | Chesterfield (loan) | 5 | 3 |
| | | | | | | | Bury (loan) | 8 | — |
| | | | | | | | Brentford | 26 | 5 |
| **Spencer** Simon‡ | 5 9 | 10 04 | M | 10 9 76 | Islington | Trainee | Tottenham H | — | — |
| | | | | | | | Brentford | 1 | — |
| **Taylor** Robert | 6 1 | 13 06 | F | 30 4 71 | Norwich | Trainee | Norwich C | — | — |
| | | | | | | | Leyton Orient (loan) | 3 | 1 |
| | | | | | | | Birmingham C | — | — |
| | | | | | | | Leyton Orient | 73 | 20 |
| | | | | | | | Brentford | 173 | 56 |
| **Thompson** Niall | 5 11 | 11 00 | F | 16 4 74 | Birmingham | Trainee | Crystal Palace | — | — |
| | | | | | | | Colchester U | 13 | 5 |
| | | | | | | Zulte VV | Brentford | 8 | — |
| **Townley** Leon | 6 2 | 13 11 | D | 16 2 76 | Loughton | Trainee | Tottenham H | — | — |
| | | | | | | | Brentford | 16 | 2 |
| **Watson** Paul | 5 8 | 10 09 | D | 4 1 75 | Hastings | Trainee | Gillingham | 62 | 2 |
| | | | | | | | Fulham | 50 | 4 |
| | | | | | | | Brentford | 25 | — |
| **Wormull** Simon‡ | 5 10 | 12 03 | M | 1 12 76 | Crawley | Trainee | Tottenham H | — | — |
| | | | | | | | Brentford | 5 | — |
| | | | | | | | Brighton & HA | — | — |

**Trainees**
Brooks, Leyton C C; Courtnage, James M; Dobson, Michael W; James, Clement J; Muldowney, Jamie J; Patel, Neerav R; Procter, Sebastian M; Saroya, Nevin; Tunnell, Lee F.

**Non-Contract**
Cockerill, Glenn.

**Associated Schoolboys**
Gallagher, Kane; Johnson, Lee; Owens, Christopher; Windell, Gavin.

**Associated Schoolboys who have accepted the club's offer of a Traineeship/Contract**
King, Daryl; O'Connor, Kevin; Smith, Jay; Taggart, Anthony C; Williams, Mark.

## BRIGHTON & HOVE ALBION

| Name | Ht | Wt | Pos | Born | Birthplace | From | Club | Apps | Gls |
|---|---|---|---|---|---|---|---|---|---|
| **Allan** Derek | 5 11 | 12 05 | D | 24 12 74 | Irvine | Ayr U BC | Ayr U | 5 | — |
| | | | | | | | Southampton | 1 | — |
| | | | | | | | Brighton & HA (loan) | 8 | — |
| | | | | | | | Brighton & HA | 50 | 1 |
| **Andrews** Ben | 6 0 | 12 10 | D | 18 11 80 | Burton-on-Trent | Trainee | Brighton & HA | 3 | — |

| | | | | | | | | | |
|---|---|---|---|---|---|---|---|---|---|
| **Ansah** Andy† | 5 7 | 10 07 | F | 19 3 69 | Lewisham | Crystal Palace | Brentford | 8 | 2 |
| | | | | | | | Southend U | 157 | 33 |
| | | | | | | | Brentford (loan) | 3 | 1 |
| | | | | | | | Brentford (loan) | 6 | 1 |
| | | | | | | | Peterborough U | 2 | 1 |
| | | | | | | | Gillingham | 2 | — |
| | | | | | | | Leyton Orient | 2 | — |
| | | | | | | | Brighton & HA | 14 | 3 |
| **Armstrong** Paul | 5 10 | 10 09 | M | 5 10 78 | Dublin | Trainee | Brighton & HA | 20 | — |
| **Atkinson** Graeme* | 5 8 | 11 05 | D | 11 11 71 | Hull | Trainee | Hull C | 149 | 23 |
| | | | | | | | Preston NE | 79 | 6 |
| | | | | | | | Rochdale (loan) | 6 | — |
| | | | | | | | Brighton & HA | 9 | — |
| **Baird** Ian‡ | 6 0 | 12 00 | F | 1 4 64 | Rotherham | Apprentice | Southampton | 22 | 5 |
| | | | | | | | Cardiff C (loan) | 12 | 6 |
| | | | | | | | Newcastle U (loan) | 5 | 1 |
| | | | | | | | Leeds U | 85 | 33 |
| | | | | | | | Portsmouth | 20 | 1 |
| | | | | | | | Leeds U | 77 | 17 |
| | | | | | | | Middlesbrough | 63 | 19 |
| | | | | | | | Hearts | 64 | 15 |
| | | | | | | | Bristol C | 57 | 11 |
| | | | | | | | Plymouth Arg | 27 | 5 |
| | | | | | | | Brighton & HA | 44 | 14 |
| **Barker** Richard‡ | 6 0 | 14 03 | F | 30 5 75 | Sheffield | Trainee | Sheffield W | — | — |
| | | | | | | | Doncaster R (loan) | 6 | — |
| | | | | | | Linfield | Brighton & HA | 17 | 2 |
| **Hilton** Damien‡ | 6 2 | 12 06 | F | 6 9 77 | Norwich | Trainee | Norwich C | — | — |
| | | | | | | | Brighton & HA | 5 | — |
| **Hobson** Gary | 6 1 | 13 05 | D | 12 11 72 | North Ferriby | Trainee | Hull C | 142 | — |
| | | | | | | | Brighton & HA | 79 | 1 |
| **Humphrey** John‡ | 5 10 | 11 11 | D | 31 1 61 | Paddington | Apprentice | Wolverhampton W | 149 | 3 |
| | | | | | | | Charlton Ath | 194 | 3 |
| | | | | | | | Crystal Palace | 160 | 2 |
| | | | | | | | Reading (loan) | 8 | — |
| | | | | | | | Charlton Ath | 28 | — |
| | | | | | | | Gillingham | 9 | — |
| | | | | | | | Brighton & HA | 22 | — |
| **Johnson** Ross | 6 0 | 13 00 | D | 2 1 76 | Brighton | Trainee | Brighton & HA | 89 | — |
| **Linger** Paul* | 5 6 | 10 03 | M | 20 12 74 | Stepney | Trainee | Charlton Ath | 23 | 1 |
| | | | | | | | Leyton Orient | 3 | — |
| | | | | | | | Brighton & HA | 19 | — |
| **Mayo** Kerry | 5 10 | 13 02 | M | 21 9 77 | Cuckfield | Trainee | Brighton & HA | 68 | 6 |
| **McDonald** Paul | 5 6 | 10 00 | F | 20 4 68 | Motherwell | Merry Street BC | Hamilton A | 215 | 26 |
| *(Transferred to Dunfermline Ath, January 1998)* | | | | | | | Southampton | 3 | — |
| | | | | | | | Burnley (loan) | 9 | 1 |
| | | | | | | | Brighton & HA | 61 | 5 |
| | | | | | | | Dunfermline Ath | 3 | — |
| **McNally** Ross* | 6 1 | 12 05 | D | 6 9 78 | Dublin | Trainee | Brighton & HA | 2 | — |
| **Minton** Jeffrey# | 5 6 | 11 11 | M | 28 12 73 | Hackney | Trainee | Tottenham H | 2 | 1 |
| | | | | | | | Brighton & HA | 139 | 22 |
| **Morris** Mark‡ | 6 2 | 14 00 | D | 26 9 62 | Carshalton | Apprentice | Wimbledon | 168 | 9 |
| | | | | | | | Aldershot (loan) | 14 | — |
| | | | | | | | Watford | 41 | 1 |
| | | | | | | | Sheffield U | 56 | 3 |
| | | | | | | | Bournemouth | 194 | 8 |
| | | | | | | | Gillingham (loan) | 6 | — |
| | | | | | | | Brighton & HA | 31 | 2 |
| **Mundee** Denny‡ | 5 10 | 13 00 | M | 10 10 68 | Swindon | Apprentice | QPR | — | — |
| | | | | | | | Swindon T | — | — |
| | | | | | | | Bournemouth | 100 | 6 |
| | | | | | | | Torquay U (loan) | 9 | — |
| | | | | | | | Brentford | 84 | 16 |
| | | | | | | | Brighton & HA | 61 | 7 |
| **Ormerod** Mark | 6 0 | 12 08 | G | 5 2 76 | Bournemouth | Trainee | Brighton & HA | 51 | — |
| **Reinelt** Robbie* | 5 11 | 11 11 | F | 11 3 74 | Epping | Trainee | Aldershot | 5 | — |
| | | | | | | | Gillingham | 52 | 5 |
| | | | | | | | Colchester U | 48 | 10 |
| | | | | | | | Brighton & HA | 44 | 7 |
| **Rowlands** James‡ | 5 9 | 10 07 | F | 31 5 79 | Aberdare | Trainee | Brighton & HA | — | — |
| **Rust** Nicky* | 6 0 | 13 02 | G | 25 9 74 | Ely | Arsenal | Brighton & HA | 177 | — |
| **Ryan** Darragh | 5 10 | 10 10 | F | 21 5 80 | Cuckfield | Trainee | Brighton & HA | 4 | 1 |
| **Saul** Eric* | 5 7 | 10 10 | D | 28 10 78 | Dublin | Trainee | Brighton & HA | 4 | — |
| **Smith** Peter | 6 2 | 12 10 | D | 12 7 69 | Stone | Alma Swanley | Brighton & HA | 126 | 5 |
| **Storer** Stuart | 5 11 | 12 12 | F | 16 1 67 | Rugby | Local | Mansfield T | 1 | — |
| | | | | | | | Birmingham C | 8 | — |
| | | | | | | | Everton | — | — |
| | | | | | | | Wigan Ath (loan) | 12 | — |
| | | | | | | | Bolton W | 123 | 12 |
| | | | | | | | Exeter C | 77 | 8 |
| | | | | | | | Brighton & HA | 119 | 11 |
| **Streeter** Terry§ | | | M | 26 10 79 | Brighton | Trainee | Brighton & HA | 2 | — |
| **Tuck** Stuart | 5 10 | 11 10 | D | 1 10 74 | Brighton | Trainee | Brighton & HA | 91 | 1 |

| | | | | | | | | | |
|---|---|---|---|---|---|---|---|---|---|
| **Westcott** John | 5 6 | 10 04 | F | 31 5 79 | Eastbourne | Trainee | Brighton & HA | 34 | — |
| **Woolsey** Jeff | 5 11 | 12 03 | D | 8 11 77 | Upminster | Trainee | Arsenal | — | — |
| | | | | | | | QPR | — | — |
| | | | | | | | Brighton & HA | 3 | — |

**Trainees**
Burke, Alan P; Carey, John R; Davis, Daniel J S; Francis, Neil G; McArthur, Duncan E; Ottley, Matthew J; Packham, William J; Ramsay, Scott A; Streeter, Terry S; Winter, Neil D.

**Non-Contract**
Ansah, Andrew; Wood, Jeffrey R.

**Associated Schoolboy**
Vanson, Lloyd D.

# BRISTOL CITY

| | | | | | | | | | |
|---|---|---|---|---|---|---|---|---|---|
| **Barclay** Dominic | 5 10 | 11 07 | F | 5 9 76 | Bristol | Trainee | Bristol C | 12 | — |
| **Bell** Mickey | 5 8 | 10 04 | D | 15 11 71 | Newcastle | Trainee | Northampton T | 153 | 10 |
| | | | | | | | Wycombe W | 118 | 6 |
| | | | | | | | Bristol C | 44 | 10 |
| **Bokoto** Mommainais* | 5 11 | 11 13 | F | 20 10 74 | France | Maria Aalter | Bristol C | — | — |
| **Brennan** Jim | 5 9 | 11 06 | D | 8 5 77 | Toronto | Sora Lazio | Bristol C | 14 | — |
| **Brown** Aaron | | | F | 14 3 80 | Bristol | Trainee | Bristol C | — | — |
| **Carey** Louis | 5 10 | 11 10 | M | 22 1 77 | Bristol | Trainee | Bristol C | 103 | — |
| **Cramb** Colin | 6 0 | 11 09 | F | 23 6 74 | Lanark | Hamilton A BC | Hamilton A | 48 | 10 |
| | | | | | | | Southampton | 1 | — |
| | | | | | | | Falkirk | 8 | 1 |
| | | | | | | | Hearts | 6 | 1 |
| | | | | | | | Doncaster R | 62 | 25 |
| | | | | | | | Bristol C | 40 | 9 |
| **Doherty** Tom | 5 8 | 9 13 | M | 17 3 79 | Bristol | Trainee | Bristol C | 30 | 2 |
| **Dyche** Sean | 6 0 | 13 07 | D | 28 6 71 | Kettering | Trainee | Nottingham F | — | — |
| | | | | | | | Chesterfield | 231 | 8 |
| | | | | | | | Bristol C | 11 | — |
| **Edwards** Robert | 6 0 | 11 01 | D | 1 7 73 | Kendal | Trainee | Carlisle U | 48 | 5 |
| | | | | | | | Bristol C | 193 | 5 |
| **Goodridge** Greg | 5 6 | 10 00 | F | 10 2 75 | Barbados | Lambada | Torquay U | 38 | 4 |
| | | | | | | | QPR | 7 | 1 |
| | | | | | | | Bristol C | 59 | 12 |
| **Hale** Matthew | 5 6 | 10 00 | M | 2 2 79 | Bristol | Trainee | Bristol C | — | — |
| **Hewlett** Matthew | 6 2 | 10 11 | M | 25 2 76 | Bristol | Trainee | Bristol C | 110 | 8 |
| **Hobbs** Darren‡ | 6 2 | 13 00 | D | 18 1 79 | Bristol | Trainee | Bristol C | — | — |
| **Jordan** Andrew | | | D | 14 12 79 | Manchester | Trainee | Bristol C | — | — |
| **Langan** Kevin | 5 11 | 11 02 | D | 7 4 78 | Jersey | Trainee | Bristol C | 3 | — |
| **Locke** Adam | 6 0 | 12 07 | D | 20 8 70 | Croydon | Trainee | Crystal Palace | — | — |
| | | | | | | | Southend U | 73 | 4 |
| | | | | | | | Colchester U (loan) | 4 | — |
| | | | | | | | Colchester U | 79 | 8 |
| | | | | | | | Bristol C | 37 | 1 |
| **Muntasser** Jehad | 5 11 | 12 05 | M | 26 7 78 | Tripoli | Prosesto | Arsenal | — | — |
| | | | | | | | Bristol C | — | — |
| **Murray** Scott | 5 9 | 11 00 | M | 26 5 74 | Aberdeen | Fraserburgh | Aston Villa | 4 | — |
| | | | | | | | Bristol C | 23 | — |
| **Naylor** Stuart# | 6 4 | 11 03 | G | 6 12 62 | Wetherby | Yorkshire Amat | Lincoln C | 49 | — |
| | | | | | | | Peterborough U (loan) | 8 | — |
| | | | | | | | Crewe Alex (loan) | 38 | — |
| | | | | | | | Crewe Alex (loan) | 17 | — |
| | | | | | | | WBA | 355 | — |
| | | | | | | | Bristol C | 37 | — |
| **Owers** Gary | 5 11 | 11 01 | M | 3 10 68 | Newcastle | Apprentice | Sunderland | 268 | 25 |
| | | | | | | | Bristol C | 126 | 9 |
| **Paterson** Scott* | 5 11 | 11 09 | D | 13 5 72 | Aberdeen | Cove Rangers | Liverpool | — | — |
| | | | | | | | Bristol C | 50 | 1 |
| | | | | | | | Cardiff C (loan) | 5 | — |
| **Phillips** Steve | 6 1 | 11 10 | G | 6 5 78 | Bath | Paulton R | Bristol C | — | — |
| **Plummer** Dwayne | 5 9 | 11 06 | F | 12 10 76 | Bristol | Trainee | Bristol C | 14 | — |
| **Shail** Mark | 6 1 | 13 03 | D | 15 10 66 | Sweden | Yeovil T | Bristol C | 103 | 4 |
| **Taylor** Shaun# | 6 1 | 12 08 | D | 26 2 63 | Plymouth | Bideford | Exeter C | 200 | 16 |
| | | | | | | | Swindon T | 212 | 30 |
| | | | | | | | Bristol C | 72 | 3 |
| **Tinnion** Brian# | 5 11 | 11 05 | M | 23 2 68 | Stanley | Apprentice | Newcastle U | 32 | 2 |
| | | | | | | | Bradford C | 145 | 22 |
| | | | | | | | Bristol C | 193 | 16 |
| **Tisdale** Paul | 5 9 | 10 09 | M | 14 1 73 | Malta | School | Southampton | 16 | 1 |
| | | | | | | | Northampton T (loan) | 5 | — |
| | | | | | | | Huddersfield T (loan) | 2 | — |
| | | | | | | | Bristol C | 5 | — |
| | | | | | | | Exeter C (loan) | 10 | 1 |

| Name | | | | | | | Club | App | Gls |
|---|---|---|---|---|---|---|---|---|---|
| **Torpey** Steve | 6 3 | 13 03 | F | 8 12 70 | Islington | Trainee | Millwall | 7 | — |
| | | | | | | | Bradford C | 96 | 22 |
| | | | | | | | Swansea C | 162 | 44 |
| | | | | | | | Bristol C | 29 | 8 |
| **Vanes** Michael‡ | 5 6 | 10 00 | M | 16 3 79 | Cayman Islands | Trainee | Bristol C | — | — |
| **Welch** Keith | 6 2 | 12 05 | G | 3 10 68 | Bolton | Trainee | Bolton W | — | — |
| | | | | | | | Rochdale | 205 | — |
| | | | | | | | Bristol C | 250 | — |

**Trainees**
Ashton, Lee; Badman, Mark; Ball, Alex I; Betterton, Anthony G; Burnell, Joseph M; Farmer, Christopher; Hill, Matthew C; Morrison, Scott E; Rai, Adam K B; Ridge, Neil A; Sammut, Benjamin A; Sloan, Christopher J; Spiller, Richard B; Thompson, Phillip W; Watts, Leigh G; Whittington, Geoffrey; Wilmot, Ellis J.

**Associated Schoolboys**
Anyinsah, David; Blake, David J; Brown, Marvin R; Dew, Simon J; Douglas, Chris; Ganfield, Ian J; Gibbs, Stuart J; Harrty, Nick; Havard, Ryan L; Horseman, David J; Jones, Darren; Lokton, Dean; Lowe, David J; Lowe, Oliver; Missiato, Adamo; Pedley, Neil R; Platt, Daniel; Reid, Andrew K; Sandell, Andrew; Sheppard, Peter K; Stickland, Ross; Turner, Michael J; Walters, James; Woodman, Craig A; Young, Daniel J.

**Associated Schoolboys who have accepted the club's offer of a Traineeship/Contract**
Claridge, Jamie; Coles, Daniel; Harrison, Jamie; Jordan, Thomas; King, Rohan; McLay, Steven; Reynolds, Nicholas; Shorey, Adam; Spencer, Damian M.

**Player who does not hold a current contract but his registration has been retained by the club**
Stewart, Christopher A.

# BRISTOL ROVERS

| Name | | | | | | | Club | App | Gls |
|---|---|---|---|---|---|---|---|---|---|
| **Archer** Lee‡ | 5 6 | 9 06 | M | 6 11 72 | Bristol | Trainee | Bristol R | 126 | 15 |
| **Basford** Luke§ | 5 6 | 8 07 | D | 6 1 80 | Lambeth | Trainee | Bristol R | 7 | — |
| **Beadle** Peter | 6 2 | 13 07 | F | 13 5 72 | London | Trainee | Gillingham | 67 | 14 |
| | | | | | | | Tottenham H | — | — |
| | | | | | | | Bournemouth (loan) | 9 | 2 |
| | | | | | | | Southend U (loan) | 8 | 1 |
| | | | | | | | Watford | 23 | 1 |
| | | | | | | | Bristol R | 109 | 39 |
| **Bennett** Frankie | 5 7 | 12 01 | F | 13 1 69 | Birmingham | Halesowen T | Southampton | 19 | 1 |
| | | | | | | | Shrewsbury T (loan) | 4 | 3 |
| | | | | | | | Bristol R | 30 | 3 |
| **Brown** Justin‡ | 5 11 | 10 06 | M | 9 11 78 | Leeds | Trainee | Bristol R | — | — |
| **Collett** Andy | 6 0 | 12 10 | G | 28 10 73 | Middlesbrough | Trainee | Middlesbrough | 2 | — |
| | | | | | | | Bristol R | 104 | — |
| **Cureton** Jamie | 5 7 | 10 07 | F | 28 8 75 | Bristol | Trainee | Norwich C | 29 | 6 |
| | | | | | | | Bournemouth (loan) | 5 | — |
| | | | | | | | Bristol R | 81 | 24 |
| **Foster** Stephen | 6 1 | 12 00 | D | 3 12 74 | Mansfield | Trainee | Mansfield T | 5 | — |
| | | | | | | | Woking | | |
| | | | | | | | Bristol R | 34 | — |
| **French** Jon* | 5 10 | 10 10 | M | 25 9 76 | Bristol | Trainee | Bristol R | 17 | 1 |
| **Hayfield** Matt | 5 10 | 11 07 | M | 8 8 75 | Bristol | Trainee | Bristol R | 41 | — |
| **Hayles** Barry | 5 9 | 13 00 | F | 17 4 72 | London | Stevenage Bor | Bristol R | 45 | 23 |
| **Higgs** Shane* | 6 2 | 12 12 | G | 13 5 77 | Oxford | Trainee | Bristol R | 10 | — |
| **Holloway** Ian | 5 7 | 10 10 | M | 12 3 63 | Kingswood | Apprentice | Bristol R | 111 | 14 |
| | | | | | | | Wimbledon | 19 | 2 |
| | | | | | | | Brentford (loan) | 13 | 2 |
| | | | | | | | Brentford | 17 | — |
| | | | | | | | Torquay U (loan) | 5 | — |
| | | | | | | | Bristol R | 179 | 26 |
| | | | | | | | QPR | 147 | 4 |
| | | | | | | | Bristol R | 70 | 1 |
| **Jones** Lee | 6 3 | 14 07 | G | 9 8 70 | Pontypridd | Porth | Swansea C | 6 | — |
| | | | | | | | Crewe Alex (loan) | — | — |
| | | | | | | | Bristol R | 8 | — |
| **Kite** Phil | 6 2 | 15 04 | G | 26 10 62 | Bristol | Apprentice | Bristol R | 96 | — |
| | | | | | | | Tottenham H (loan) | — | — |
| | | | | | | | Southampton | 4 | — |
| | | | | | | | Middlesbrough (loan) | 2 | — |
| | | | | | | | Gillingham | 70 | — |
| | | | | | | | Bournemouth | 7 | — |
| | | | | | | | Sheffield U | 11 | — |
| | | | | | | | Mansfield T (loan) | 11 | — |
| | | | | | | | Plymouth Arg (loan) | 2 | — |
| | | | | | | | Rotherham U (loan) | 1 | — |
| | | | | | | | Crewe Alex (loan) | 5 | — |
| | | | | | | | Stockport Co (loan) | 5 | — |
| | | | | | | | Cardiff C | 18 | — |
| | | | | | | | Bristol C | 6 | — |
| | | | | | | | Bristol R | — | — |
| **Lockwood** Matt | 5 9 | 10 12 | M | 17 10 76 | Rochford | Trainee | QPR | — | — |
| | | | | | | | Bristol R | 63 | 1 |
| **Low** Josh | 6 0 | 11 12 | F | 15 12 79 | Bristol | Trainee | Bristol R | 14 | — |
| **Martin** Lee* | 6 0 | 12 08 | D | 5 2 68 | Hyde | | Manchester U | 73 | 1 |
| | | | | | | | Celtic | 19 | — |
| | | | | | | | Bristol R | 25 | — |
| | | | | | | | Huddersfield T (loan) | 3 | — |
| **Morgan** Ryan‡ | 6 1 | 12 07 | M | 12 7 78 | Bristol | Trainee | Bristol R | 1 | — |

| | Ht | Wt | Pos | | DOB | Birthplace | Source | Club | Apps | Gls |
|---|---|---|---|---|---|---|---|---|---|---|
| **Parmenter** Steve‡ | 5 9 | 11 00 | F | 22 | 1 77 | Chelmsford | Trainee | QPR | — | — |
| | | | | | | | | Bristol R | 18 | 2 |
| **Penrice** Gary | 5 8 | 11 07 | M | 23 | 3 64 | Bristol | Bristol C | Bristol R | 188 | 54 |
| | | | | | | | | Watford | 43 | 18 |
| | | | | | | | | Aston Villa | 20 | 1 |
| | | | | | | | | QPR | 82 | 20 |
| | | | | | | | | Watford | 39 | 2 |
| | | | | | | | | Bristol R | 40 | 5 |
| **Perry** Jason* | 6 1 | 11 12 | D | 2 | 4 70 | Caerphilly | Trainee | Cardiff C | 281 | 5 |
| | | | | | | | | Bristol R | 25 | — |
| **Perry** Richard‡ | 5 11 | 11 04 | M | 24 | 8 78 | Darlington | Trainee | Bristol C | — | — |
| | | | | | | | | Bristol R | — | — |
| **Power** Graeme* | 5 11 | 10 10 | D | 7 | 3 77 | Northwick Park | Trainee | QPR | — | — |
| | | | | | | | | Bristol R | 26 | — |
| **Pritchard** David | 5 7 | 11 04 | D | 27 | 5 72 | Wolverhampton | Telford U | WBA | 5 | — |
| | | | | | | | Telford U | Bristol R | 125 | — |
| **Ramasut** Tom | 5 10 | 11 00 | M | 30 | 8 77 | Cardiff | | Norwich C | — | — |
| | | | | | | | | Bristol R | 42 | 6 |
| **Skinner** Justin | 6 0 | 11 03 | M | 30 | 1 69 | Hounslow | Apprentice | Fulham | 135 | 23 |
| *(Transferred to Hibernian, March 1998)* | | | | | | | | Bristol R | 187 | 12 |
| | | | | | | | | Walsall (loan) | 10 | — |
| | | | | | | | | Hibernian | 6 | — |
| **Teague** Simon‡ | 5 6 | 10 00 | F | 23 | 2 79 | Henley | Trainee | Bristol R | — | — |
| **Tillson** Andrew | 6 2 | 12 10 | D | 30 | 6 66 | Huntingdon | Kettering T | Grimsby T | 105 | 5 |
| | | | | | | | | QPR | 29 | 2 |
| | | | | | | | | Grimsby T (loan) | 4 | — |
| | | | | | | | | Bristol R | 191 | 8 |
| **White** Tom | 5 11 | 12 02 | D | 26 | 1 76 | Bristol | Trainee | Bristol R | 51 | 1 |
| **Zabek** Lee | 6 0 | 12 00 | M | 13 | 10 78 | Bristol | Trainee | Bristol R | 14 | 1 |

**Trainees**
Adams, Michael J; Basford, Luke W B; Claridge, Robert R; Coles, Kevin J; Court, Anthony M; Edwards, Christian M S; French, James R; Hines, Alistair; Johnston, Ray; Jones, Guy A; Lloyd, Andrew P; Pendry, Dean; Smith, Mark J W; Trought, Michael; White, Daniel A J; White, Jonathan W; Williams, Luke; Zamora, Bobby.

**Associated Schoolboys**
Aylott, James S; Bright, Jarrod S; Bryant, Simon; Chambers, Andrew J; Clarke, Thomas W; Cleverley, Daniel J; Davis, Anthony; French, Steven D; Gilroy, David; Gosling, Ian J; Graydon, Neil; Hardcastle, Kevin J; Hardcastle, Mark; Hogg, Lewis J; Ingram, Simon; Newell, Michael W; Price, Oliver; Scott, Robert T; Taylor, Matthew A; Winter, Hadleigh.

**Associated Schoolboys who have accepted the club's offer of a Traineeship/Contract**
Pope, Mark; Powell, Gary N; Shore, Andrew J; Watts, David J; Williamson, Matthew J; Zabek, James K.

# BURNLEY

| | Ht | Wt | Pos | | DOB | Birthplace | Source | Club | Apps | Gls |
|---|---|---|---|---|---|---|---|---|---|---|
| **Blatherwick** Steve | 6 1 | 15 00 | D | 20 | 9 73 | Nottingham | Notts Co | Nottingham F | 10 | — |
| | | | | | | | | Wycombe W (loan) | 2 | — |
| | | | | | | | | Hereford U (loan) | 10 | 1 |
| | | | | | | | | Reading (loan) | 7 | — |
| | | | | | | | | Burnley | 21 | — |
| **Brass** Chris | 5 9 | 12 06 | D | 24 | 7 75 | Easington | Trainee | Burnley | 93 | 1 |
| | | | | | | | | Torquay U (loan) | 7 | — |
| **Carr-Lawton** Colin | | | F | 5 | 9 78 | South Shields | Trainee | Burnley | 1 | — |
| **Cooke** Andy | 5 11 | 12 08 | F | 20 | 1 74 | Stoke | Newtown | Burnley | 88 | 34 |
| **Cowans** Gordon† | 5 7 | 9 07 | M | 27 | 10 58 | Durham | Apprentice | Aston Villa | 286 | 42 |
| | | | | | | | | Bari | 94 | 3 |
| | | | | | | | | Aston Villa | 117 | 7 |
| | | | | | | | | Blackburn R | 50 | 2 |
| | | | | | | | | Aston Villa | 11 | — |
| | | | | | | | | Derby Co | 36 | — |
| | | | | | | | | Wolverhampton W | 37 | — |
| | | | | | | | | Sheffield U | 20 | — |
| | | | | | | | | Bradford C | 24 | — |
| | | | | | | | | Stockport Co | 7 | — |
| | | | | | | | | Burnley | 6 | — |
| **Duerden** Ian* | 5 10 | 12 07 | F | 27 | 3 78 | Burnley | Trainee | Burnley | 1 | — |
| **Eastwood** Philip | 5 10 | 12 02 | F | 6 | 4 78 | Blackburn | Trainee | Burnley | 3 | — |
| **Ford** Mark | 5 7 | 10 08 | M | 10 | 10 75 | Pontefract | Trainee | Leeds U | 29 | 1 |
| | | | | | | | | Burnley | 36 | 1 |
| **Gentile** Marco‡ | | | M | 24 | 8 68 | Den Haag | MVV | Burnley | — | — |
| **Gleghorn** Nigel* | 6 0 | 13 07 | M | 12 | 8 62 | Seaham | Seaham Red Star | Ipswich T | 66 | 11 |
| | | | | | | | | Manchester C | 34 | 7 |
| | | | | | | | | Birmingham C | 142 | 33 |
| | | | | | | | | Stoke C | 166 | 26 |
| | | | | | | | | Burnley | 34 | 4 |
| | | | | | | | | Brentford (loan) | 11 | 1 |
| | | | | | | | | Northampton T (loan) | 8 | 1 |

| | | | | | | | | | |
|---|---|---|---|---|---|---|---|---|---|
| **Harrison** Gerry# | 5 9 | 12 03 | M | 15 4 72 | Lambeth | Trainee | Watford | 9 | — |
| | | | | | | | Bristol C | 38 | 1 |
| | | | | | | | Cardiff C (loan) | 10 | 1 |
| | | | | | | | Hereford U (loan) | 6 | — |
| | | | | | | | Huddersfield T | — | — |
| | | | | | | | Burnley | 124 | 3 |
| **Heffernan** Jason* | | | D | 1 6 79 | Burnley | Trainee | Burnley | — | — |
| **Helliwell** Ian* | 6 4 | 14 08 | F | 7 11 62 | Rotherham | Matlock T | York C | 160 | 40 |
| | | | | | | | Scunthorpe U | 80 | 22 |
| | | | | | | | Rotherham U | 52 | 4 |
| | | | | | | | Stockport Co | 39 | 13 |
| | | | | | | | Burnley | 4 | — |
| | | | | | | | Mansfield T (loan) | 5 | 1 |
| | | | | | | | Chester C (loan) | 9 | 1 |
| | | | | | | | Doncaster R (loan) | 8 | 1 |
| **Henderson** Kevin | | | F | 8 6 74 | Ashington | Morpeth T | Burnley | 7 | — |
| **Howey** Lee | 6 3 | 14 05 | F | 1 4 69 | Sunderland | AC Hemptinne | Sunderland | 69 | 8 |
| | | | | | | | Burnley | 23 | — |
| **Hoyland** Jamie | 6 0 | 12 08 | D | 23 1 66 | Sheffield | Apprentice | Manchester C | 2 | — |
| | | | | | | | Bury | 172 | 35 |
| | | | | | | | Sheffield U | 89 | 6 |
| | | | | | | | Bristol C (loan) | 6 | — |
| | | | | | | | Burnley | 87 | 3 |
| | | | | | | | Carlisle U (loan) | 5 | — |
| **Huxford** Richard* | 5 10 | 11 06 | D | 25 7 69 | Scunthorpe | Kettering T | Barnet | 33 | 1 |
| | | | | | | | Millwall | 32 | — |
| | | | | | | | Birmingham C (loan) | 5 | — |
| | | | | | | | Bradford C | 61 | 2 |
| | | | | | | | Peterborough U (loan) | 7 | — |
| | | | | | | | Burnley | 13 | — |
| | | | | | | | Dunfermline Ath (loan) | 10 | — |
| **Little** Glen | 6 3 | 13 00 | M | 15 10 75 | Wimbledon | Trainee | Crystal Palace | — | — |
| | | | | | | | Glentoran | 6 | 2 |
| | | | | | | | Burnley | 33 | 4 |
| **Matthew** Damian# | 5 11 | 10 10 | M | 23 9 70 | Islington | Trainee | Chelsea | 21 | — |
| | | | | | | | Luton T (loan) | 5 | — |
| | | | | | | | Crystal Palace | 24 | 1 |
| | | | | | | | Bristol R (loan) | 8 | — |
| | | | | | | | Burnley | 59 | 7 |
| **Mawson** Craig | | | G | 16 5 79 | Keighley | Trainee | Burnley | — | — |
| **Moore** Neil | 6 1 | 12 07 | D | 21 9 72 | Liverpool | Trainee | Everton | 5 | — |
| | | | | | | | Blackpool (loan) | 7 | — |
| | | | | | | | Oldham Ath (loan) | 5 | — |
| | | | | | | | Carlisle U (loan) | 13 | — |
| | | | | | | | Rotherham U (loan) | 11 | — |
| | | | | | | | Norwich C | 2 | — |
| | | | | | | | Burnley | 40 | 3 |
| **Overson** Vince* | 6 2 | 14 13 | D | 15 5 62 | Kettering | Apprentice | Burnley | 211 | 6 |
| | | | | | | | Birmingham C | 182 | 3 |
| | | | | | | | Stoke C | 170 | 6 |
| | | | | | | | Burnley | 8 | — |
| | | | | | | | Shrewsbury T (loan) | 2 | — |
| **Parks** Tony# | 5 10 | 11 05 | G | 28 1 63 | Hackney | | Tottenham H | 37 | — |
| | | | | | | | Oxford U (loan) | 5 | — |
| | | | | | | | Gillingham (loan) | 2 | — |
| | | | | | | | Brentford | 71 | — |
| | | | | | | | QPR (loan) | — | — |
| | | | | | | | Fulham | 2 | — |
| | | | | | | | West Ham U | 6 | — |
| | | | | | | | Stoke C | 2 | — |
| | | | | | | | Falkirk | 112 | — |
| | | | | | | | Blackpool | — | — |
| | | | | | | | Burnley | — | — |
| | | | | | | | Doncaster R (loan) | 6 | — |
| **Payton** Andy | 5 9 | 11 13 | F | 23 10 67 | Burnley | Apprentice | Hull C | 144 | 55 |
| | | | | | | | Middlesbrough | 19 | 3 |
| | | | | | | | Celtic | 36 | 15 |
| | | | | | | | Barnsley | 108 | 41 |
| | | | | | | | Huddersfield T | 43 | 17 |
| | | | | | | | Burnley | 19 | 9 |
| **Robertson** Mark | | | M | 6 4 77 | Sydney | Marconi | Burnley | 11 | — |
| **Smith** Carl | 5 8 | 11 00 | M | 15 1 79 | Sheffield | Trainee | Burnley | 1 | — |
| **Smith** Paul | 6 0 | 13 03 | F | 22 1 76 | Leeds | Trainee | Burnley | 62 | 4 |
| **Vinnicombe** Chris# | 5 8 | 10 12 | D | 20 10 70 | Exeter | | Exeter C | 39 | 1 |
| | | | | | | | Rangers | 23 | 1 |
| | | | | | | | Burnley | 95 | 3 |
| **Waddle** Chris‡ | 6 1 | 13 03 | F | 14 12 60 | Hedworth | Tow Law T | Newcastle U | 170 | 46 |
| | | | | | | | Tottenham H | 138 | 33 |
| | | | | | | | Marseille | 107 | 22 |
| | | | | | | | Sheffield W | 109 | 10 |
| | | | | | | | Falkirk | 4 | 1 |
| | | | | | | | Bradford C | 25 | 5 |
| | | | | | | | Sunderland | 7 | 1 |
| | | | | | | | Burnley | 31 | 1 |
| **Weller** Paul | 5 8 | 11 02 | M | 6 3 75 | Brighton | Trainee | Burnley | 95 | 5 |

| Name | | | | | | | Club | Apps | Gls |
|---|---|---|---|---|---|---|---|---|---|
| **West** Gareth | 6 1 | 11 10 | D | 1 8 78 | Oldham | Trainee | Burnley | — | — |
| **Williams** Michael | 5 11 | 11 04 | F | 21 11 69 | Bradford | Maltby MW | Sheffield W | 23 | 1 |
| | | | | | | | Halifax T (loan) | 9 | 1 |
| | | | | | | | Huddersfield T (loan) | 2 | — |
| | | | | | | | Peterborough U (loan) | 6 | — |
| | | | | | | | Burnley | 14 | 1 |
| **Winstanley** Mark# | 6 1 | 12 08 | D | 22 1 68 | St Helens | Trainee | Bolton W | 220 | 3 |
| | | | | | | | Burnley | 151 | 5 |
| **Woods** Chris# | 6 2 | 14 12 | G | 14 11 59 | Boston | Apprentice | Nottingham F | — | — |
| | | | | | | | QPR | 63 | — |
| | | | | | | | Norwich C (loan) | 10 | — |
| | | | | | | | Norwich C | 206 | — |
| | | | | | | | Rangers | 173 | — |
| | | | | | | | Sheffield W | 107 | — |
| | | | | | | | Reading (loan) | 5 | — |
| | | | | | | Colorado R | Southampton | 4 | — |
| | | | | | | USSF | Sunderland | — | — |
| | | | | | | | Burnley | 12 | — |

**Trainees**
Berry, Shaun D; Collins, David W; Devenney, Michael P; Gardiner, Marc A; Graham, Paul D; Gregson, Gareth C; Henry, David; Heywood, Matthew S; Kelly, Eamonn P; Kevan, Alexander; Maylett, Bradley; McCoy, James J; McDonald, Christopher N; Murphy, Terence P; Pates, Bradley J; Scott, Christopher J; Williamson, John B; Woods, Ben.

**Non-Contract**
Cowans, Gordon S.

**Associated Schoolboys**
Airey, Benjamin R; Akbar, Ali; Barrett, Paul J; Billinge, Neil A; Brennan, Aneurin J; Claffey, Patrick J; Collins, David; Davis, Earl A; Fagan, John P; Hartigan, Trevor P; Ingham, Gary E; Kielthy, Anthony A T; Licastri, Dominic; Park, Deon S; Peel, Ryan A; Tempest, Adam J; Waine, Andrew P.

# BURY

| Name | | | | | | | Club | Apps | Gls |
|---|---|---|---|---|---|---|---|---|---|
| **Armstrong** Gordon | 6 0 | 12 11 | M | 15 7 67 | Newcastle | Apprentice | Sunderland | 349 | 50 |
| | | | | | | | Bristol C (loan) | 6 | — |
| | | | | | | | Northampton T (loan) | 4 | 1 |
| | | | | | | | Bury | 69 | 4 |
| **Battersby** Tony | 6 0 | 12 09 | F | 30 8 75 | Doncaster | Trainee | Sheffield U | 10 | 1 |
| | | | | | | | Southend U (loan) | 8 | 1 |
| | | | | | | | Notts Co | 39 | 8 |
| | | | | | | | Bury (loan) | 11 | 2 |
| | | | | | | | Bury | 37 | 6 |
| **Beckford** Darren‡ | 6 1 | 11 01 | F | 12 5 67 | Manchester | Apprentice | Manchester C | 11 | — |
| | | | | | | | Bury (loan) | 12 | 5 |
| | | | | | | | Port Vale (loan) | 11 | 4 |
| | | | | | | | Port Vale | 167 | 68 |
| | | | | | | | Norwich C | 38 | 8 |
| | | | | | | | Oldham Ath | 52 | 11 |
| | | | | | | | Hearts | 8 | — |
| | | | | | | | Preston NE | 2 | — |
| | | | | | | | Fulham | — | — |
| | | | | | | | Walsall | 8 | — |
| **Butler** Paul | 6 2 | 13 00 | D | 2 11 72 | Manchester | Trainee | Rochdale | 158 | 10 |
| | | | | | | | Bury | 84 | 4 |
| **Crossland** Mark | 5 11 | 12 02 | M | 14 12 78 | Ashton-under-Lyne | Lincoln C | Bury | — | — |
| **Daws** Nick | 5 11 | 13 06 | M | 15 3 70 | Salford | Altrincham | Bury | 236 | 9 |
| **Ellis** Tony | 5 11 | 11 00 | F | 20 10 64 | Salford | Northwich Vic | Oldham Ath | 8 | — |
| | | | | | | | Preston NE | 86 | 26 |
| | | | | | | | Stoke C | 77 | 19 |
| | | | | | | | Preston NE | 72 | 48 |
| | | | | | | | Blackpool | 146 | 54 |
| | | | | | | | Bury | 22 | 6 |
| **Forrest** Martyn | 5 10 | 12 02 | M | 2 1 79 | Bury | Trainee | Bury | — | — |
| **Hirst** Matthew‡ | 6 4 | 12 05 | D | 14 11 77 | St Albans | Millwall | Bury | — | — |
| **Jemson** Nigel | 5 11 | 13 03 | F | 10 8 69 | Preston | Trainee | Preston NE | 32 | 8 |
| | | | | | | | Nottingham F | 47 | 13 |
| | | | | | | | Bolton W (loan) | 5 | — |
| | | | | | | | Preston NE (loan) | 9 | 2 |
| | | | | | | | Sheffield W | 51 | 9 |
| | | | | | | | Grimsby T (loan) | 6 | 2 |
| | | | | | | | Notts Co | 14 | 1 |
| | | | | | | | Watford (loan) | 4 | — |
| | | | | | | | Coventry C (loan) | — | — |
| | | | | | | | Rotherham U (loan) | 16 | 5 |
| | | | | | | | Oxford U | 68 | 27 |
| | | | | | | | Bury | 15 | 1 |
| **Johnrose** Lenny | 5 11 | 12 06 | M | 27 11 69 | Preston | Trainee | Blackburn R | 42 | 11 |
| | | | | | | | Preston NE (loan) | 3 | 1 |
| | | | | | | | Hartlepool U | 66 | 11 |
| | | | | | | | Bury | 161 | 17 |
| **Kiely** Dean | 6 0 | 12 13 | G | 10 10 70 | Salford | WBA | Coventry C | — | — |
| | | | | | | | Ipswich T (loan) | — | — |
| | | | | | | | York C (loan) | — | — |
| | | | | | | | York C | 210 | — |
| | | | | | | | Bury | 92 | — |
| **Linighan** Brian | 6 4 | 11 04 | D | 2 11 73 | Hartlepool | Trainee | Sheffield W | 1 | — |
| | | | | | | | Bury | — | — |

| | | | | | | | | | |
|---|---|---|---|---|---|---|---|---|---|
| **Lonergan** Darren‡ | 6 0 | 13 01 | D | 28 1 74 | Waterford | Waterford | Oldham Ath | 2 | — |
| | | | | | | | Bury | — | — |
| **Lucketti** Chris | 6 0 | 13 06 | D | 28 9 71 | Littleborough | Trainee | Rochdale | 1 | — |
| | | | | | | | Stockport Co | | |
| | | | | | | | Halifax T | 78 | 2 |
| | | | | | | | Bury | 192 | 7 |
| **Matthews** Rob | 6 0 | 12 05 | M | 14 10 70 | Slough | Loughborough | Notts Co | 43 | 11 |
| | | | | | | Univ | Luton T | 11 | — |
| | | | | | | | York C | 17 | 1 |
| | | | | | | | Bury | 58 | 9 |
| **Patterson** Mark | 5 8 | 11 12 | F | 24 5 65 | Darwen | Apprentice | Blackburn R | 101 | 20 |
| | | | | | | | Preston NE | 55 | 19 |
| | | | | | | | Bury | 42 | 10 |
| | | | | | | | Bolton W | 169 | 11 |
| | | | | | | | Sheffield U | 74 | 4 |
| | | | | | | | Southend U (loan) | 4 | — |
| | | | | | | | Bury | 18 | 2 |
| **Peake** Jason | 5 10 | 13 00 | M | 29 9 71 | Leicester | Trainee | Leicester C | 8 | 1 |
| | | | | | | | Hartlepool U (loan) | 6 | 1 |
| | | | | | | | Halifax T | 33 | 1 |
| | | | | | | | Rochdale | 95 | 6 |
| | | | | | | | Brighton & HA | 30 | 1 |
| | | | | | | | Bury | 6 | — |
| **Phillips** Paul* | 5 8 | 12 01 | G | 15 11 78 | Manchester | Trainee | Bury | — | — |
| **Pugh** David* | 6 2 | 13 00 | F | 19 9 64 | Liverpool | Runcorn | Chester C | 179 | 23 |
| | | | | | | | Bury | 103 | 28 |
| **Randall** Adrian | 5 11 | 12 04 | M | 10 11 68 | Salisbury | Apprentice | Bournemouth | 3 | — |
| | | | | | | | Aldershot | 107 | 12 |
| | | | | | | | Burnley | 125 | 8 |
| | | | | | | | York C | 32 | 2 |
| | | | | | | | Bury | 34 | 3 |
| **Rigby** Tony | 5 10 | 12 12 | M | 10 8 72 | Ormskirk | Barrow | Bury | 164 | 19 |
| | | | | | | | Scarborough (loan) | 5 | 1 |
| **Small** Bryan# | 5 9 | 11 09 | D | 15 11 71 | Birmingham | Trainee | Aston Villa | 36 | — |
| | | | | | | | Birmingham C (loan) | 3 | — |
| | | | | | | | Bolton W | 12 | — |
| | | | | | | | Luton T (loan) | 15 | — |
| | | | | | | | Bradford C (loan) | 5 | — |
| | | | | | | | Bury | 18 | 1 |
| **Swailes** Chris | 6 2 | 12 07 | D | 19 10 70 | Gateshead | Bridlington T | Doncaster R | 49 | — |
| | | | | | | | Ipswich T | 33 | 1 |
| | | | | | | | Bury | 13 | 1 |
| **Swailes** Daniel | 6 3 | 12 06 | D | 1 4 79 | Bolton | Trainee | Bury | — | — |
| **Swan** Peter | 6 2 | 14 12 | F | 28 9 66 | Leeds | Local | Leeds U | 49 | 11 |
| | | | | | | | Hull C | 80 | 24 |
| | | | | | | | Port Vale | 111 | 5 |
| | | | | | | | Plymouth Arg | 27 | 2 |
| | | | | | | | Burnley | 49 | 7 |
| | | | | | | | Bury | 37 | 6 |
| **Watson** Richard‡ | 5 10 | 11 10 | M | 2 11 78 | Salford | Trainee | Bury | — | — |
| **West** Dean | 5 10 | 11 07 | D | 5 12 72 | Wakefield | Leeds U | Lincoln C | 119 | 20 |
| | | | | | | | Bury | 87 | 5 |
| **Winrow** Brian‡ | 5 9 | 10 00 | D | 19 5 79 | Oldham | Trainee | Bury | — | — |
| **Woodward** Andy | 5 10 | 10 12 | D | 23 9 73 | Stockport | Trainee | Crewe Alex | 20 | — |
| | | | | | | | Bury | 64 | — |

**Trainees**
Ball, Nicholas C; Barrass, Matthew R; Beal, Philip L; Bury, Daniel J; Connell, Lee A; Denney, Philip M; Green, Alexander J; Hackett, Kristian S; Halford, Stephen P; Hill, Nicholas D; Hutchinson, Ian P A; Joyce, Wayne E; McPadden, Ian J; Messer, Gary M; Smith, Paul A; Sturtivant, David M; Tedaldi, Dominico A; Wardle, Darren C; Wilkinson, Steven D; Willcox, Robert; Wright, Gary J; Young, Ian T.

**Non-Contract**
Radcliffe, Matthew S.

**Associated Schoolboys**
Boulton, Matthew J; Chapman, Neil D; Collis, Paul A; Gidley, Stuart; Johnson, Anthony M; Law, Philip J; Lee, Matthew A; McGill, John S; Menzies, Anton M; Rezai, Carl; Robinson, Christopher J; Scholes, Neil A.

**Associated Schoolboys who have accepted the club's offer of a Traineeship/Contract**
Gaynor, John; Gleaves, Carl M; Martin, Adam T; Oshaughnesy, Paul J; Thompson, Nicholas A.

## CAMBRIDGE UNITED

| | | | | | | | | | |
|---|---|---|---|---|---|---|---|---|---|
| **Armstrong** Dean | | | M | 7 9 79 | Chiswick | | Cambridge U | — | — |
| **Ashbee** Ian | 6 1 | 13 04 | D | 6 9 76 | Birmingham | Trainee | Derby Co | 1 | — |
| | | | | | | | Cambridge U | 45 | 1 |
| **Barnwell-Edinboro** Jamie* | 5 11 | 11 10 | F | 26 12 75 | Hull | Trainee | Coventry C | 1 | — |
| | | | | | | | Swansea C (loan) | 4 | — |
| | | | | | | | Wigan Ath (loan) | 10 | 1 |
| | | | | | | | Cambridge U | 63 | 12 |

| Name | Ht | Wt | Pos | DOB | Birthplace | Source | Club | Apps | Gls |
|---|---|---|---|---|---|---|---|---|---|
| **Barrett** Scott | 6 0 | 14 05 | G | 2 4 63 | Ilkeston | Ilkeston T | Wolverhampton W | 30 | — |
| | | | | | | | Stoke C | 51 | — |
| | | | | | | | Colchester U (loan) | 13 | — |
| | | | | | | | Stockport Co (loan) | 10 | — |
| | | | | | | | Colchester U | — | — |
| | | | | | | | Gillingham | 51 | — |
| | | | | | | | Cambridge U | 119 | — |
| **Beall** Billy | 5 8 | 10 11 | M | 4 12 77 | Enfield | Trainee | Cambridge U | 81 | 7 |
| **Benjamin** Trevor | 6 3 | 13 05 | M | 8 2 79 | Wellingborough | Trainee | Cambridge U | 37 | 5 |
| **Butler** Martin | 5 11 | 12 00 | F | 15 9 74 | Wordsley | Trainee | Walsall | 74 | 8 |
| | | | | | | | Cambridge U | 31 | 10 |
| **Campbell** Jamie | 6 1 | 12 06 | M | 21 10 72 | Birmingham | Trainee | Luton T | 36 | 1 |
| | | | | | | | Mansfield T (loan) | 3 | 1 |
| | | | | | | | Cambridge U (loan) | 12 | — |
| | | | | | | | Barnet | 67 | 5 |
| | | | | | | | Cambridge U | 46 | 2 |
| **Chenery** Ben | 5 11 | 11 10 | D | 28 1 77 | Ipswich | Trainee | Luton T | 2 | — |
| | | | | | | | Cambridge U | 36 | 2 |
| **Cockrill** Darren | | | F | 28 2 80 | Great Yarmouth | Trainee | Cambridge U | — | — |
| **Duncan** Andrew | 5 11 | 13 04 | D | 20 10 77 | Hexham | Trainee | Manchester U | — | — |
| | | | | | | | Cambridge U | 19 | — |
| **Finlayson** Alex‡ | 6 0 | 12 02 | F | 30 1 79 | Edinburgh | Trainee | Swindon T | — | — |
| | | | | | | | Cambridge U | — | — |
| **Foster** Colin* | 6 4 | 15 02 | D | 16 7 64 | Chislehurst | Apprentice | Orient | 174 | 10 |
| | | | | | | | Nottingham F | 72 | 5 |
| | | | | | | | West Ham U | 93 | 5 |
| | | | | | | | Notts Co (loan) | 9 | — |
| | | | | | | | Watford | 66 | 8 |
| | | | | | | | Cambridge U (loan) | 7 | — |
| | | | | | | | Cambridge U | 26 | 1 |
| **Gibson** Mark§ | | | M | 24 8 81 | Hitchin | Trainee | Cambridge U | — | — |
| **Gutzmore** Leon‡ | | | F | 30 10 76 | London | Trainee | Cambridge U | 2 | — |
| **Hayes** Adie* | 6 0 | 11 09 | M | 22 5 78 | Norwich | Trainee | Cambridge U | 34 | — |
| **Ingham** Andrew§ | | | M | 21 8 81 | Leeds | Trainee | Cambridge U | — | — |
| **Joseph** Marc | 6 1 | 12 09 | D | 10 11 76 | Leicester | Trainee | Cambridge U | 61 | — |
| **Kyd** Michael | 5 9 | 12 10 | F | 21 5 77 | Hackney | Trainee | Cambridge U | 94 | 20 |
| **Marshall** Shaun | 6 1 | 12 11 | G | 3 10 78 | Fakenham | Trainee | Cambridge U | 3 | — |
| **McAvoy** Lawrence | | | D | 7 9 79 | Lambeth | Trainee | — | — | — |
| **McCammon** Mark† | | | F | 7 8 78 | Barnet | | Cambridge U | 2 | — |
| **Moore** Mark‡ | | | M | 9 7 72 | Bradford | | Cambridge U | 1 | — |
| **Murphy** Jamie‡ | 6 1 | 13 00 | D | 25 2 73 | Manchester | Trainee | Blackpool | 55 | 1 |
| | | | | | | | Doncaster R | 54 | — |
| | | | | | | | Cambridge U | — | — |
| **Preece** David | 5 6 | 10 12 | M | 28 5 63 | Bridgnorth | Apprentice | Walsall | 111 | 5 |
| | | | | | | | Luton T | 336 | 21 |
| | | | | | | | Derby Co | 13 | 1 |
| | | | | | | | Birmingham C (loan) | 6 | — |
| | | | | | | | Swindon T (loan) | 7 | 1 |
| | | | | | | | Cambridge U | 47 | — |
| **Rees** Jason‡ | 5 5 | 10 00 | F | 22 12 69 | Aberdare | Trainee | Luton T | 82 | — |
| | | | | | | | Mansfield T (loan) | 15 | 1 |
| | | | | | | | Portsmouth | 43 | 3 |
| | | | | | | | Exeter C (loan) | 7 | — |
| | | | | | | | Cambridge U | 20 | — |
| **Rodosthenous** Michael‡ | 5 11 | 11 02 | F | 25 8 76 | Islington | Trainee | WBA | 1 | — |
| | | | | | | | Cambridge U | 2 | — |
| **Smith** Tommy† | 5 9 | 13 00 | M | 25 11 77 | Northampton | Trainee | Manchester U | — | — |
| | | | | | | | Cambridge U | 1 | — |
| **Sumner** Jed* | | | G | 1 8 79 | Basildon | Coventry C | Cambridge U | — | — |
| **Taylor** John# | 6 1 | 14 00 | F | 24 10 64 | Norwich | Local Sudbury T | Colchester U | — | — |
| | | | | | | | Cambridge U | 160 | 46 |
| | | | | | | | Bristol R | 95 | 44 |
| | | | | | | | Bradford C | 36 | 11 |
| | | | | | | | Luton T | 37 | 3 |
| | | | | | | | Lincoln C (loan) | 5 | 2 |
| | | | | | | | Colchester U (loan) | 8 | 5 |
| | | | | | | | Cambridge U | 55 | 14 |
| **Thompson** David‡ | 6 2 | 12 11 | D | 20 11 68 | Ashington | Trainee | Millwall | 92 | 6 |
| | | | | | | | Bristol C | 17 | — |
| | | | | | | | Brentford | 10 | 1 |
| | | | | | | | Blackpool | 17 | — |
| | | | | | | | Cambridge U | 44 | 2 |
| **Wanless** Paul | 6 1 | 13 11 | M | 14 12 73 | Banbury | Trainee | Oxford U | 32 | — |
| | | | | | | | Lincoln C | 8 | — |
| | | | | | | | Cambridge U (loan) | 14 | 1 |
| | | | | | | | Cambridge U | 72 | 11 |
| **Webb** Darren | | | M | 24 10 79 | Brighton | Trainee | Cambridge U | — | — |
| **Wilde** Adam† | 5 10 | 11 09 | D | 22 5 79 | Southampton | Trainee | Cambridge U | 3 | — |
| **Williamson** Davey‡ | 5 6 | 10 06 | D | 15 12 75 | Hong Kong | Irvine Vics | Motherwell | — | — |
| | | | | | | | Cambridge U | 6 | — |

| | | | | | | | | | |
|---|---|---|---|---|---|---|---|---|---|
| **Wilson** Paul* | 5 11 | 11 10 | D | 2 8 68 | Bradford | Trainee | Huddersfield T | 15 | — |
| | | | | | | | Norwich C | — | — |
| | | | | | | | Northampton T | 141 | 6 |
| | | | | | | | Halifax T | 45 | 7 |
| | | | | | | | Burnley | 31 | — |
| | | | | | | | York C | 22 | — |
| | | | | | | | Scunthorpe U | 77 | 2 |
| | | | | | | | Cambridge U (loan) | 7 | — |
| | | | | | | | Cambridge U | 31 | 5 |
| **Youngs** Tom | 5 8 | 10 08 | F | 31 8 79 | Bury St Edmunds | Trainee | Cambridge U | 4 | — |

**Trainees**
Barrows, Michael R D; Beadell, Scott S; Dolby, Lee R; Fox, Karl; Gibson, Mark A; Ingham, Andrew J; King, Stuart; Mason, Terry S; McNeil, Martin J; Mills, Jonathan; Newby, Keith; Scales, Jamie; Steward, Michael J.

**Non-Contract**
McCammon, Mark J; Smith, Thomas E; Wilde, Adam.

**Associated Schoolboys**
Armes, Henry W; Bennett, Lee; Bridges, David; Fordham, William; Franklin, Mark; Galea, Joseph; George, Rikki; Heathcote, Jonathan; Lockhart, Duncan; Moody, Philip; Nacca, Francesco; Norman, Edward J; Paynter, Owen; White, Daniel R; Winkworth, Kevin

**Associated Schoolboys who have accepted the club's offer of a Traineeship/Contract**
Chillingworth, Daniel T; Haniver, Matthew G.

# CARDIFF CITY

| | | | | | | | | | |
|---|---|---|---|---|---|---|---|---|---|
| **Beech** Chris* | 5 9 | 11 06 | D | 5 11 75 | Congleton | Trainee | Manchester C | — | — |
| | | | | | | | Cardiff C | 46 | 1 |
| **Cadette** Nathan§ | | | M | 6 1 80 | Cardiff | Trainee | Cardiff C | 4 | — |
| **Carss** Anthony* | 5 10 | 11 08 | M | 31 3 76 | Alnwick | Bradford C | Blackburn R | — | — |
| | | | | | | | Darlington | 57 | 2 |
| | | | | | | | Cardiff C | 42 | 1 |
| **Cross** John‡ | 5 9 | 13 00 | M | 6 4 76 | Barking | Trainee | QPR | — | — |
| | | | | | | | Cardiff C | — | — |
| **Dale** Carl* | 5 7 | 12 01 | F | 29 4 66 | Colwyn Bay | Bangor C | Chester C | 116 | 41 |
| | | | | | | | Cardiff C | 213 | 71 |
| **Earnshaw** Robert§ | | | F | 6 4 81 | Zambia | Trainee | Cardiff C | 5 | — |
| **Eckhardt** Jeff | 5 11 | 12 00 | D | 7 10 65 | Sheffield | | Sheffield U | 74 | 2 |
| | | | | | | | Fulham | 249 | 25 |
| | | | | | | | Stockport Co | 62 | 7 |
| | | | | | | | Cardiff C | 56 | 8 |
| **Fowler** Jason | 6 2 | 11 11 | M | 20 8 74 | Bristol | Trainee | Bristol C | 25 | — |
| | | | | | | | Cardiff C | 75 | 10 |
| **Hallworth** Jon | 6 2 | 14 09 | G | 26 10 65 | Stockport | School | Ipswich T | 45 | — |
| | | | | | | | Swindon T (loan) | — | — |
| | | | | | | | Fulham (loan) | — | — |
| | | | | | | | Bristol R (loan) | 2 | — |
| | | | | | | | Oldham Ath | 174 | — |
| | | | | | | | Cardiff C | 43 | — |
| **Harris** Mark* | 6 3 | 14 08 | D | 15 7 63 | Reading | Wokingham T | Crystal Palace | 2 | — |
| | | | | | | | Burnley (loan) | 4 | — |
| | | | | | | | Swansea C | 228 | 14 |
| | | | | | | | Gillingham | 65 | 3 |
| | | | | | | | Cardiff C | 38 | 1 |
| **Jarman** Lee | 6 3 | 13 05 | D | 16 12 77 | Cardiff | Trainee | Cardiff C | 87 | — |
| **Lloyd** Kevin* | 6 0 | 12 03 | D | 26 9 70 | Llanidloes | Caersws | Hereford U | 51 | 3 |
| | | | | | | | Cardiff C | 33 | 1 |
| **Middleton** Craig# | 5 10 | 11 10 | M | 10 9 70 | Nuneaton | Trainee | Coventry C | 3 | — |
| | | | | | | | Cambridge U | 59 | 10 |
| | | | | | | | Cardiff C | 74 | 4 |
| **Nugent** Kevin | 6 2 | 13 04 | F | 10 4 69 | Edmonton | Trainee | Leyton Orient | 94 | 20 |
| | | | | | | | Plymouth Arg | 131 | 32 |
| | | | | | | | Bristol C | 70 | 14 |
| | | | | | | | Cardiff C | 4 | — |
| **O'Sullivan** Wayne | 5 8 | 10 12 | M | 25 2 74 | Akrotiri | Trainee | Swindon T | 89 | 3 |
| | | | | | | | Cardiff C | 43 | 2 |
| **Osman** Russell‡ | 5 11 | 12 01 | D | 14 2 59 | Repton | Apprentice | Ipswich T | 294 | 17 |
| | | | | | | | Leicester C | 108 | 8 |
| | | | | | | | Southampton | 96 | 6 |
| | | | | | | | Bristol C | 70 | 3 |
| | | | | | | | Plymouth Arg | — | — |
| | | | | | | | Brighton & HA | 12 | — |
| | | | | | | | Cardiff C | 15 | — |
| **Penney** David | 5 9 | 12 04 | M | 17 8 64 | Wakefield | Pontefract | Derby Co | 19 | — |
| | | | | | | | Oxford U | 110 | 15 |
| | | | | | | | Swansea C (loan) | 12 | 3 |
| | | | | | | | Swansea C (loan) | 11 | 2 |
| | | | | | | | Swansea C | 108 | 18 |
| | | | | | | | Cardiff C | 34 | 5 |
| **Phillips** Lee | 6 1 | 12 03 | D | 18 3 79 | Aberdare | Trainee | Cardiff C | 11 | — |

| **Philliskirk** Tony* | 6 2 | 12 12 | F | 10 2 65 | Sunderland | Amateur | Sheffield U | 80 | 20 |
| | | | | | | | Rotherham U (loan) | 6 | 1 |
| | | | | | | | Oldham Ath | 10 | 1 |
| | | | | | | | Preston NE | 14 | 6 |
| | | | | | | | Bolton W | 141 | 51 |
| | | | | | | | Peterborough U | 43 | 15 |
| | | | | | | | Burnley | 40 | 9 |
| | | | | | | | Carlisle U (loan) | 3 | 1 |
| | | | | | | | Cardiff C | 61 | 5 |
| | | | | | | | Macclesfield T (loan) | 10 | 1 |
| **Rendell** John‡ | 6 1 | 12 00 | M | 8 8 78 | Bristol | Trainee | Cardiff C | — | — |
| **Roberts** Chris | 5 11 | 11 12 | F | 22 10 79 | Cardiff | Trainee | Cardiff C | 11 | 3 |
| **Rollo** Jimmy* | 6 0 | 11 00 | M | 22 5 76 | Wisbech | Trainee | Walsall | — | — |
| | | | | | | | Cardiff C | 15 | — |
| **Saville** Andy | 6 1 | 12 10 | F | 12 12 64 | Hull | Local | Hull C | 100 | 18 |
| | | | | | | | Walsall | 38 | 5 |
| | | | | | | | Barnsley | 82 | 21 |
| | | | | | | | Hartlepool U | 37 | 13 |
| | | | | | | | Birmingham C | 59 | 17 |
| | | | | | | | Burnley (loan) | 4 | 1 |
| | | | | | | | Preston NE | 56 | 30 |
| | | | | | | | Wigan Ath | 25 | 4 |
| | | | | | | | Cardiff C | 33 | 11 |
| **Stoker** Gareth | 5 9 | 11 04 | M | 22 2 73 | Bishop Auckland | Leeds U | Hull C | 30 | 2 |
| | | | | | | | Hereford U | 70 | 6 |
| | | | | | | | Cardiff C | 37 | 4 |
| **White** Steve* | 5 10 | 12 08 | F | 2 1 59 | Chipping Sodbury | Mangotsfield U | Bristol R | 50 | 20 |
| | | | | | | | Luton T | 72 | 25 |
| | | | | | | | Charlton Ath | 29 | 12 |
| | | | | | | | Lincoln C (loan) | 3 | — |
| | | | | | | | Luton T (loan) | 4 | — |
| | | | | | | | Bristol R | 101 | 24 |
| | | | | | | | Swindon T | 244 | 83 |
| | | | | | | | Hereford U | 76 | 44 |
| | | | | | | | Cardiff C | 67 | 15 |
| **Young** Scott | 6 1 | 12 00 | M | 14 1 76 | Tonypandy | Trainee | Cardiff C | 132 | 4 |
| **Zois** Peter‡ | | | G | 21 4 78 | Australia | | Cardiff C | 1 | — |

**Trainees**
Cadette, Nathan D; Clarke, Daniel P; Earnshaw, Robert; George, Stephen A; Kelly, Philip J; Loveless, Ian C; Owen, Philip N R; Parnell, Blake L; Smith, Gavin J; Stevens, Daniel; Vaughan, Ian D.

**Associated Schoolboys**
Harris, Adrian E; Howse, Ian J; Maye, Adam; Peters, Gareth J; Pratt, Leigh; Roberts, Anthony D; Slade-Jones, Daryl; Watts, Leigh T.

**Associated Schoolboys who have accepted the club's offer of a Traineeship/Contract**
Phillips, Darryl J; Skelly, Lee.

# CARLISLE UNITED

| **Anthony** Graham | 5 7 | 10 09 | M | 9 8 75 | South Shields | Trainee | Sheffield U | 3 | — |
| | | | | | | | Scarborough (loan) | 2 | — |
| | | | | | | | Swindon T | 3 | — |
| | | | | | | | Plymouth Arg | 5 | — |
| | | | | | | | Carlisle U | 25 | 3 |
| **Archdeacon** Owen (*Transferred to Morton, November 1997*) | 5 7 | 11 00 | D | 4 3 66 | Greenock | Gourock U | Celtic | 76 | 7 |
| | | | | | | | Barnsley | 233 | 23 |
| | | | | | | | Carlisle U | 64 | 10 |
| **Barr** Billy | 5 11 | 10 08 | M | 21 1 69 | Halifax | Trainee / Halifax T | Halifax T | 196 | 13 |
| | | | | | | | Crewe Alex | 85 | 7 |
| | | | | | | | Carlisle U | 39 | 3 |
| **Boertien** Paul | 5 10 | 11 00 | D | 20 1 79 | Haltwhistle | Trainee | Carlisle U | 9 | — |
| **Bowman** Rob | 6 0 | 12 10 | D | 21 11 75 | Durham | Trainee | Leeds U | 7 | — |
| | | | | | | | Rotherham U | 13 | — |
| | | | | | | | Carlisle U | 7 | 1 |
| **Caig** Tony | 6 1 | 12 00 | G | 11 4 74 | Whitehaven | Trainee | Carlisle U | 186 | — |
| **Couzens** Andy | 5 10 | 11 11 | M | 4 6 75 | Shipley | Trainee | Leeds U | 28 | 1 |
| | | | | | | | Carlisle U | 27 | 2 |
| **Croci** Laurent‡ | | | M | 8 12 64 | Montbeliard | Bordeaux | Carlisle U | 1 | — |
| **Day** Richard* | 6 2 | 13 10 | G | 25 1 79 | Chelmsford | Trainee | Carlisle U | — | — |
| **Dixon** George | 6 0 | 14 02 | G | 24 10 78 | Whitehaven | Trainee | Carlisle U | — | — |
| **Dobie** Scott | 6 1 | 12 12 | F | 10 10 78 | Workington | Trainee | Carlisle U | 25 | 1 |
| **Foster** John# | 5 11 | 13 02 | D | 19 9 73 | Blackley | Trainee | Manchester C | 19 | — |
| | | | | | | | Carlisle U | 7 | — |
| **Gray** Alan‡ | 5 10 | 12 04 | D | 2 5 74 | Carlisle | US Colleges | Doncaster R | 1 | — |
| | | | | | | | Darlington | 6 | — |
| | | | | | | | Carlisle U | 1 | — |
| **Harrison** Edward§ | | | M | 14 2 80 | Carlisle | Trainee | Carlisle U | 10 | — |
| **Hopper** Tony | 5 10 | 12 08 | D | 31 5 76 | Carlisle | Trainee | Carlisle U | 50 | 1 |

| Name | Ht | Wt | Pos | Date | Birthplace | Source | Club | Apps | Gls |
|---|---|---|---|---|---|---|---|---|---|
| Joyce Joe* | 5 9 | 11 01 | D | 18 3 61 | Consett | School | Barnsley | 334 | 4 |
| | | | | | | | Scunthorpe U | 91 | 2 |
| | | | | | | | Carlisle U | 50 | — |
| | | | | | | | Darlington (loan) | 4 | — |
| Liburd Richard# | 5 9 | 11 01 | D | 26 9 73 | Nottingham | Forest Ath | Middlesbrough | 41 | 1 |
| | | | | | | | Bradford C | 78 | 3 |
| | | | | | | | Carlisle U | 9 | — |
| McAlindon Gareth | 5 9 | 11 10 | F | 6 4 77 | Hexham | Newcastle U | Carlisle U | 43 | 5 |
| Milligan Ross* | 5 11 | 12 10 | D | 2 6 78 | Dumfries | | Rangers | — | — |
| | | | | | | Maxwelton T | Carlisle U | 7 | — |
| Pagal John‡ | 5 11 | 12 04 | D | 15 9 64 | Cameroon | | Carlisle U | 1 | — |
| Pounewatchy Stephane* | 6 0 | 15 00 | D | 10 2 68 | Paris | | Martigues | 44 | 2 |
| | | | | | | | Gueugnon | 30 | — |
| | | | | | | | Carlisle U | 81 | 3 |
| Prokas Richard | 5 8 | 11 04 | M | 22 1 76 | Penrith | Trainee | Carlisle U | 106 | 2 |
| Sandwith Kevin | 5 11 | 12 05 | D | 30 4 78 | Workington | Trainee | Carlisle U | 3 | — |
| Smart Allan | 6 2 | 12 07 | F | 8 7 74 | Perth | | Caledonian Th | 4 | — |
| | | | | | | | Preston NE | 21 | 6 |
| | | | | | | | Carlisle U (loan) | 4 | — |
| | | | | | | | Northampton T (loan) | 1 | — |
| | | | | | | | Carlisle U | 44 | 16 |
| Stevens Ian | 5 10 | 12 07 | F | 21 10 66 | Malta | Trainee | Preston NE | 11 | 2 |
| | | | | | | | Stockport Co | 2 | — |
| | | | | | | Lancaster C | Bolton W | 47 | 7 |
| | | | | | | | Bury | 110 | 38 |
| | | | | | | | Shrewsbury T | 111 | 37 |
| | | | | | | | Carlisle U | 37 | 17 |
| Taylor Lee* | 6 0 | 12 13 | D | 12 9 77 | Whitehaven | Trainee | Carlisle U | — | — |
| Thorpe Jeff# | 5 11 | 12 08 | D | 17 11 72 | Cockermouth | Trainee | Carlisle U | 150 | 6 |
| Varty Will | 6 0 | 12 04 | D | 1 10 76 | Workington | Trainee | Carlisle U | 76 | 1 |
| Wright Nick | 5 11 | 11 02 | F | 15 10 75 | Derby | Trainee | Derby Co | — | — |
| | | | | | | | Carlisle U | 25 | 5 |

**Trainees**
Barton, Christopher; Bell, Liam R; Benson, Jon K; Burton, Lee R; Douglas, Andrew S; Harrison, Edward W; Heath, Jamie; Hodgson, Alan; Howe, Jamie I; Irving, Michael J; Jones, Mark A; Millar, Stuart J; Skelton, Gavin R; Stevens, Barry J; Swann, Michael; Swanson, Kevin; Thompson, Craig; Thornthwaite, Scott A.

**Non-Contract**
Dalton, Neil J; Wilkes, David A.

**Associated Schoolboys**
Allan, Jonathan M; Andrews, Lee; Brain, Jonathan R; Foster, Craig; Hewson, David L; Higginson, Andrew J; Hoolikin, Lee; Jack, Michael L; Johnston, Craig; Jones, Andrew D; Lewis, Craig; May, Kyle; Rooke, Steven; Rustico, Andrea; Yallop, James T.

**Associated Schoolboys who have accepted the club's offer of a Traineeship/Contract**
Antony, Paul M; Ballantyne, Paul; Clark, Barry J; Graham, Ricky; Heggie, John A; Hetherington, Philip M; Hore, John; Reid, Paul M; Thurston, Mark R; Thwaites, Adam.

## CHARLTON ATHLETIC

| Name | Ht | Wt | Pos | Date | Birthplace | Source | Club | Apps | Gls |
|---|---|---|---|---|---|---|---|---|---|
| Allen Bradley | 5 8 | 11 00 | F | 13 9 71 | Harold Wood | School | QPR | 81 | 27 |
| | | | | | | | Charlton Ath | 40 | 9 |
| Allman Anthony | | | M | 14 12 80 | Sidcup | Trainee | Charlton Ath | — | — |
| Balmer Stuart | 6 0 | 12 11 | D | 20 9 69 | Falkirk | Celtic BC | Celtic | — | — |
| | | | | | | | Charlton Ath | 227 | 8 |
| Barness Anthony | 5 10 | 11 11 | D | 25 2 73 | Lewisham | Trainee | Charlton Ath | 27 | 1 |
| | | | | | | | Chelsea | 14 | — |
| | | | | | | | Middlesbrough (loan) | — | — |
| | | | | | | | Southend U (loan) | 5 | — |
| | | | | | | | Charlton Ath | 74 | 3 |
| Bowen Mark# | 5 8 | 11 07 | D | 7 12 63 | Neath | Apprentice | Tottenham H | 17 | 2 |
| | | | | | | | Norwich C | 320 | 24 |
| | | | | | | | West Ham U | 17 | 1 |
| | | | | | | Shimizu | Charlton Ath | 36 | — |
| Bright Mark# | 6 0 | 13 04 | F | 6 6 62 | Stoke | Leek T | Port Vale | 29 | 10 |
| | | | | | | | Leicester C | 42 | 6 |
| | | | | | | | Crystal Palace | 227 | 92 |
| | | | | | | | Sheffield W | 133 | 48 |
| | | | | | | | Millwall (loan) | 3 | 1 |
| | | | | | | | Sion | — | — |
| | | | | | | | Charlton Ath | 22 | 9 |
| Brown Steve | 6 1 | 14 03 | D | 13 5 72 | Brighton | Trainee | Charlton Ath | 142 | 5 |
| Chapple Phil* | 6 2 | 13 01 | D | 26 11 66 | Norwich | Apprentice | Norwich C | — | — |
| | | | | | | | Cambridge U | 187 | 19 |
| | | | | | | | Charlton Ath | 142 | 15 |
| Curbishley Alan | 5 10 | 11 07 | M | 8 11 57 | Forest Gate | Apprentice | West Ham U | 85 | 5 |
| | | | | | | | Birmingham C | 130 | 11 |
| | | | | | | | Aston Villa | 36 | 1 |
| | | | | | | | Charlton Ath | 63 | 6 |
| | | | | | | | Brighton & HA | 116 | 13 |
| | | | | | | | Charlton Ath | 28 | — |

| Name | | | Pos | DOB | Birthplace | Source | Club | Apps | Gls |
|---|---|---|---|---|---|---|---|---|---|
| Emblen Paul | 5 11 | 12 05 | F | 3 4 76 | Bromley | Tonbridge A | Charlton Ath | 4 | — |
| | | | | | | | Brighton & HA (loan) | 15 | 4 |
| Holmes Matt | 5 7 | 11 00 | M | 1 8 69 | Luton | Trainee | Bournemouth | 114 | 8 |
| | | | | | | | Cardiff C (loan) | 1 | — |
| | | | | | | | West Ham U | 76 | 4 |
| | | | | | | | Blackburn R | 9 | 1 |
| | | | | | | | Charlton Ath | 16 | 1 |
| Ilic Sasa | 6 4 | 14 00 | G | 18 7 72 | Melbourne | St Leonards Stamcrof | Charlton Ath | 14 | — |
| Jones Keith | 5 7 | 11 02 | M | 14 10 65 | Dulwich | Apprentice | Chelsea | 52 | 7 |
| | | | | | | | Brentford | 169 | 13 |
| | | | | | | | Southend U | 90 | 11 |
| | | | | | | | Charlton Ath | 119 | 4 |
| Jones Steve | 6 1 | 13 03 | F | 17 3 70 | Cambridge | Billericay T | West Ham U | 16 | 4 |
| | | | | | | | Bournemouth | 74 | 26 |
| | | | | | | | West Ham U | 8 | — |
| | | | | | | | Charlton Ath | 25 | 7 |
| | | | | | | | Bournemouth (loan) | 5 | 4 |
| Kearley Dean‡ | | | D | 11 10 77 | Greenwich | Trainee | Charlton Ath | — | — |
| Kinsella Mark | 5 8 | 11 04 | M | 12 8 72 | Dublin | Home Farm | Colchester U | 180 | 27 |
| | | | | | | | Charlton Ath | 83 | 12 |
| Konchesky Paul§ | | | M | 15 5 81 | Barking | Trainee | Charlton Ath | 3 | — |
| Lee Matt | 5 11 | 11 00 | D | 13 5 79 | Farnborough | Trainee | Charlton Ath | — | — |
| Lisbie Kevin | 5 8 | 10 12 | F | 17 10 78 | Hackney | Trainee | Charlton Ath | 42 | 2 |
| Mendonca Clive | 5 10 | 12 05 | F | 9 9 68 | Islington | Apprentice | Sheffield U | 13 | 4 |
| | | | | | | | Doncaster R (loan) | 2 | — |
| | | | | | | | Rotherham U | 84 | 27 |
| | | | | | | | Sheffield U | 10 | 1 |
| | | | | | | | Grimsby T (loan) | 10 | 3 |
| | | | | | | | Grimsby T | 156 | 56 |
| | | | | | | | Charlton Ath | 40 | 23 |
| Mills Danny | 5 10 | 11 11 | D | 18 5 77 | Norwich | Trainee | Norwich C | 66 | — |
| | | | | | | | Charlton Ath | 9 | 1 |
| Minors Dwayne‡ | | | F | 6 9 78 | Hackney | Trainee | Charlton Ath | — | — |
| Mortimer Paul# | 5 11 | 12 07 | M | 8 5 68 | Kensington | Fulham | Charlton Ath | 113 | 17 |
| | | | | | | | Aston Villa | 12 | 1 |
| | | | | | | | Crystal Palace | 22 | 2 |
| | | | | | | | Brentford (loan) | 6 | — |
| | | | | | | | Charlton Ath | 69 | 14 |
| Newton Shaun | 5 8 | 11 07 | M | 20 8 75 | Camberwell | Trainee | Charlton Ath | 172 | 15 |
| Nicholls Kevin | 6 0 | 11 00 | M | 2 1 79 | Newham | Trainee | Charlton Ath | 12 | 1 |
| Parker Scott | 5 9 | 11 00 | M | 13 10 80 | Lambeth | Trainee | Charlton Ath | 3 | — |
| Petterson Andy | 6 2 | 14 07 | G | 26 9 69 | Fremantle | | Luton T | 19 | — |
| | | | | | | | Swindon T (loan) | — | — |
| | | | | | | | Ipswich T (loan) | — | — |
| | | | | | | | Ipswich T (loan) | 1 | — |
| | | | | | | | Charlton Ath | 62 | — |
| | | | | | | | Bradford C (loan) | 3 | — |
| | | | | | | | Ipswich T (loan) | 1 | — |
| | | | | | | | Plymouth Arg (loan) | 6 | — |
| | | | | | | | Colchester U (loan) | 5 | — |
| Poole Gary | 6 0 | 12 08 | D | 11 9 67 | Stratford | Arsenal | Tottenham H | — | — |
| | | | | | | | Cambridge U | 43 | — |
| | | | | | | Barnet | Barnet | 40 | 2 |
| | | | | | | | Plymouth Arg | 39 | 5 |
| | | | | | | | Southend U | 44 | 2 |
| | | | | | | | Birmingham C | 72 | — |
| | | | | | | | Charlton Ath | 16 | 1 |
| Robinson John | 5 10 | 11 07 | M | 29 8 71 | Bulawayo | Apprentice | Brighton & HA | 62 | 6 |
| | | | | | | | Charlton Ath | 187 | 23 |
| Rufus Richard | 6 1 | 11 10 | D | 12 1 75 | Lewisham | Trainee | Charlton Ath | 145 | — |
| Salmon Mike# | 6 2 | 14 00 | G | 14 7 64 | Leyland | Local | Blackburn R | 1 | — |
| | | | | | | | Chester C (loan) | 16 | — |
| | | | | | | | Stockport Co | 118 | — |
| | | | | | | | Bolton W | 26 | — |
| | | | | | | | Wrexham (loan) | 17 | — |
| | | | | | | | Wrexham | 83 | — |
| | | | | | | | Charlton Ath | 148 | — |
| Stuart Jamie‡ | 5 10 | 11 00 | D | 15 10 76 | Southwark | Trainee | Charlton Ath | 50 | 3 |
| Tindall Jason* | 6 1 | 11 10 | D | 15 11 77 | Mile End | Trainee | Charlton Ath | — | — |
| Youds Eddie | 6 3 | 14 00 | D | 3 5 70 | Liverpool | Trainee | Everton | 8 | — |
| | | | | | | | Cardiff C (loan) | 1 | — |
| | | | | | | | Wrexham (loan) | 20 | 2 |
| | | | | | | | Ipswich T | 50 | 1 |
| | | | | | | | Bradford C | 85 | 8 |
| | | | | | | | Charlton Ath | 8 | — |

**Trainees**
Ali, Sharmarke; Beale, Michael W; Day, Aaron A; Fortune, Jonathan J; Goldup, Robert J; Hales, Leigh R; Hawkins, John A; Hockley, David C E; Izzet, Kemal; James, Kevin E; Kessell, Anthony L; Konchesky, Paul M; Macdonald, Charles L; Neufville, Marvin C; Nwanokwu, Uchenna J N; Toms, Frazer P; Turner, John S; Watson, Kevin M.

**Associated Schoolboys**
Allman, Jonathan L; Ashman, Kacey P; Barrie, Hamed; Bolangi, Pierre; Chambers, Tristan; Collis, David J; Creasey, Joseph; Defoe, Jermain; Duffy, Robert J; Durrant, George; Lewis, Yohance; Martin, Alex; Rolle, Junior J; Simpson, James W; Smith, Martyn D; Smith, Richard; Szeller, Adam C; Taylor, Kris J; Turner, Michael.

# CHELSEA

| Player | | | | | | | Club | Apps | Gls |
|---|---|---|---|---|---|---|---|---|---|
| **Babayaro** Celestine | 5 9 | 10 12 | D | 29 8 78 | Kaduna | | Anderlecht | 75 | 8 |
| | | | | | | | Chelsea | 8 | — |
| **Broad** Stephen | | | D | 10 6 80 | Epsom | Trainee | Chelsea | — | — |
| **Burley** Craig | 6 1 | 12 13 | M | 24 9 71 | Ayr | Trainee | Chelsea | 113 | 7 |
| *(Transferred to Celtic, July 1997)* | | | | | | | Celtic | 35 | 10 |
| **Charvet** Laurent* | | | M | 8 5 73 | Beziers | | Cannes | 99 | 19 |
| | | | | | | | Chelsea | 11 | 2 |
| **Clarke** Steve | 5 10 | 12 07 | D | 29 8 63 | Saltcoats | Beith Jun | St Mirren | 151 | 6 |
| | | | | | | | Chelsea | 330 | 7 |
| **Clement** Neil | 6 0 | 12 03 | D | 3 10 78 | Reading | Trainee | Chelsea | 1 | — |
| **Colgan** Nick* | 6 1 | 13 06 | G | 19 9 73 | Eire | Drogheda | Chelsea | 1 | — |
| | | | | | | | Crewe Alex (loan) | — | — |
| | | | | | | | Grimsby T (loan) | — | — |
| | | | | | | | Millwall (loan) | — | — |
| | | | | | | | Brentford (loan) | 5 | — |
| | | | | | | | Reading (loan) | 5 | — |
| **Crittenden** Nick | 5 8 | 10 07 | M | 11 11 78 | Bracknell | Trainee | Chelsea | 2 | — |
| **De Goey** Ed | 6 6 | 15 04 | G | 20 12 66 | Gouda | | Sparta | 145 | — |
| | | | | | | | Feyenoord | 201 | — |
| | | | | | | | Chelsea | 28 | — |
| **Di Matteo** Roberto | 5 10 | 12 00 | M | 29 5 70 | Schaffhausen | | Schaffhausen | 50 | 2 |
| | | | | | | | Zurich | 34 | 6 |
| | | | | | | | Aarau | 32 | 1 |
| | | | | | | | Lazio | 88 | 7 |
| | | | | | | | Chelsea | 64 | 11 |
| **Duberry** Michael | 6 1 | 14 00 | D | 14 10 75 | Enfield | Trainee | Chelsea | 61 | 1 |
| | | | | | | | Bournemouth (loan) | 7 | — |
| **Flo** Tor Andre | 6 4 | 13 08 | F | 15 6 73 | Strin | | Sogndal | 22 | 5 |
| | | | | | | | Tromso | 26 | 18 |
| | | | | | | | Brann | 40 | 28 |
| | | | | | | | Chelsea | 34 | 11 |
| **Granville** Danny | 5 11 | 12 01 | D | 19 1 75 | Islington | Trainee | Cambridge U | 99 | 7 |
| | | | | | | | Chelsea | 18 | — |
| **Gullit** Ruud* | 6 3 | 13 12 | F | 1 9 62 | Surinam | DWS Amsterdam | Haarlem | 91 | 32 |
| | | | | | | | Feyenoord | 85 | 30 |
| | | | | | | | PSV Eindhoven | 68 | 46 |
| | | | | | | | AC Milan | 117 | 35 |
| | | | | | | | Sampdoria | 31 | 15 |
| | | | | | | | AC Milan | 8 | 3 |
| | | | | | | | Sampdoria | 22 | 9 |
| | | | | | | | Chelsea | 49 | 4 |
| **Hampshire** Steve | 5 10 | 10 10 | F | 17 10 79 | Edinburgh | Trainee | Chelsea | — | — |
| **Harley** Jon | 5 8 | 10 03 | M | 26 9 79 | Maidstone | Trainee | Chelsea | 3 | — |
| **Hitchcock** Kevin | 6 1 | 13 00 | G | 5 10 62 | Custom House | Barking | Nottingham F | — | — |
| | | | | | | | Mansfield T (loan) | 14 | — |
| | | | | | | | Mansfield T | 168 | — |
| | | | | | | | Chelsea | 93 | — |
| | | | | | | | Northampton T (loan) | 17 | — |
| | | | | | | | West Ham U (loan) | — | — |
| **Hughes** Mark | 5 10 | 13 03 | F | 1 11 63 | Wrexham | Apprentice | Manchester U | 89 | 37 |
| | | | | | | | Barcelona | 28 | 4 |
| | | | | | | | Bayern Munich (loan) | 18 | 6 |
| | | | | | | | Manchester U | 256 | 82 |
| | | | | | | | Chelsea | 95 | 25 |
| **Hughes** Paul | 6 0 | 12 06 | M | 19 4 76 | Hammersmith | Trainee | Chelsea | 21 | 2 |
| **Kharine** Dmitri | 6 2 | 13 11 | G | 16 8 68 | Moscow | | Torpedo Moscow | 63 | — |
| | | | | | | | Dynamo Moscow | 40 | — |
| | | | | | | | CSKA Moscow | 34 | — |
| | | | | | | | Chelsea | 117 | — |
| **Lambourde** Bernard | 6 2 | 12 02 | D | 11 5 71 | Pointe-A-Pitre | Cannes | Bordeaux | 28 | 1 |
| | | | | | | | Chelsea | 7 | — |
| **Le Saux** Graeme | 5 10 | 11 09 | D | 17 10 68 | Jersey | St Pauls | Chelsea | 90 | 8 |
| | | | | | | | Blackburn R | 129 | 7 |
| | | | | | | | Chelsea | 26 | 1 |
| **Leboeuf** Franck | 6 0 | 12 00 | D | 22 1 68 | Marseille | Laval | Strasbourg | 172 | 40 |
| | | | | | | | Chelsea | 58 | 11 |
| **Lee** David | 6 3 | 15 00 | D | 26 11 69 | Kingswood | Trainee | Chelsea | 151 | 11 |
| | | | | | | | Reading (loan) | 5 | 5 |
| | | | | | | | Plymouth Arg (loan) | 9 | 1 |
| | | | | | | | Portsmouth (loan) | 5 | — |
| | | | | | | | Sheffield U (loan) | 5 | — |
| **Morris** Jody | 5 5 | 10 11 | M | 22 12 78 | Hammersmith | Trainee | Chelsea | 25 | 1 |
| **Myers** Andy | 5 10 | 13 11 | M | 3 11 73 | Isleworth | Trainee | Chelsea | 83 | 2 |
| **Newton** Eddie | 6 0 | 12 11 | F | 13 12 71 | Hammersmith | Trainee | Chelsea | 158 | 8 |
| | | | | | | | Cardiff C (loan) | 18 | 4 |
| **Nicholls** Mark | 5 10 | 10 04 | F | 30 5 77 | Hillingdon | Trainee | Chelsea | 27 | 3 |

| Petrescu Dan | 5 10 | 11 07 | M | 22 12 67 | Bucharest | | Steaua | 95 | 26 |
|---|---|---|---|---|---|---|---|---|---|
| | | | | | | | FC Olt (loan) | 24 | — |
| | | | | | | | Foggia | 55 | 7 |
| | | | | | | | Genoa | 24 | 1 |
| | | | | | | | Sheffield W | 37 | 3 |
| | | | | | | | Chelsea | 89 | 10 |
| Poyet Gustavo | 6 1 | 13 01 | M | 15 11 67 | Montevideo | Bella Vista | Zaragoza | 239 | 63 |
| | | | | | | | Chelsea | 14 | 4 |
| Richardson Jay | | | M | 14 11 79 | Keston | Trainee | Chelsea | — | — |
| Rix Graham‡ | 5 9 | 11 00 | F | 23 10 57 | Doncaster | Apprentice | Arsenal | 351 | 41 |
| | | | | | | | Brentford (loan) | 6 | — |
| | | | | | Caen, Le Havre | | Dundee | 14 | 2 |
| | | | | | | | Chelsea | 1 | — |
| Rocastle David‡ | 5 9 | 12 07 | F | 2 5 67 | Lewisham | Apprentice | Arsenal | 218 | 24 |
| | | | | | | | Leeds U | 25 | 2 |
| | | | | | | | Manchester C | 21 | 2 |
| | | | | | | | Chelsea | 29 | — |
| | | | | | | | Norwich C (loan) | 11 | — |
| | | | | | | | Hull C (loan) | 10 | 1 |
| Sheerin Joe | 6 1 | 13 09 | F | 1 2 79 | Hammersmith | Trainee | Chelsea | 1 | — |
| Sinclair Frank | 5 9 | 12 07 | D | 3 12 71 | Lambeth | Trainee | Chelsea | 169 | 7 |
| | | | | | | | WBA (loan) | 6 | 1 |
| Slatter Danny | | | M | 15 11 80 | Cardiff | Trainee | Chelsea | — | — |
| Stein Mark‡ | 5 6 | 11 07 | F | 29 1 66 | S. Africa | | Luton T | 54 | 19 |
| | | | | | | | Aldershot (loan) | 2 | 1 |
| | | | | | | | QPR | 33 | 4 |
| | | | | | | | Oxford U | 82 | 18 |
| | | | | | | | Stoke C | 94 | 50 |
| | | | | | | | Chelsea | 50 | 21 |
| | | | | | | | Stoke C (loan) | 11 | 4 |
| | | | | | | | Ipswich T (loan) | 7 | 2 |
| | | | | | | | Bournemouth (loan) | 11 | 4 |
| Terry John | | | D | 7 12 80 | London | Trainee | Chelsea | — | — |
| Vialli Gianluca | 5 10 | 13 06 | F | 9 7 64 | Cremona | | Cremonese | 105 | 23 |
| | | | | | | | Sampdoria | 223 | 85 |
| | | | | | | | Juventus | 102 | 38 |
| | | | | | | | Chelsea | 49 | 20 |
| Wise Dennis | 5 6 | 10 11 | F | 16 12 66 | Kensington | Southampton | Wimbledon | 135 | 27 |
| | | | | | | | Chelsea | 244 | 46 |
| Zola Gianfranco | 5 6 | 10 10 | F | 5 7 66 | Oliena | | Nuorese | 31 | 10 |
| | | | | | | | Torres | 88 | 21 |
| | | | | | | | Napoli | 105 | 32 |
| | | | | | | | Parma | 102 | 49 |
| | | | | | | | Chelsea | 50 | 16 |

**Trainees**
Cummings, Warren; Davies, Stephen T; Demetrious, Shayne; Hook, Mark; King, John S; Nicholls, Paul D; Osborne, Steven J; Rattray, John W; Wolleaston, Robert A.

**Associated Schoolboys**
Baldwin, Patrick M; Cole, Carlton; Girvan, Ronnie D; Harpur, Chad L; Ives, Nicky; Keenan, Jospeh J; Knight, Leon L; Nichols, Glen; Parkin, Sam; Pidgeley, Leonard J; Ross, Andrew; Thornton, Paul E; Wolton, Lee; Woodards, Daniel; Woolford, Scott.

**Associated Schoolboys who have accepted the club's offer of a Traineeship/Contract**
Barrett, Neil W; Baxter, Darren L; Evans, Rhys K; Hajgato, Geza; Pitt, Courtney; Royal, Mark.

# CHESTER CITY

| Alsford Julian | 6 2 | 13 01 | D | 24 12 72 | Poole | Trainee | Watford | 13 | 1 |
|---|---|---|---|---|---|---|---|---|---|
| *(Transferred to Dundee U, April 1998)* | | | | | | | Chester C | 141 | 6 |
| | | | | | | | Dundee U | 3 | — |
| Bennett Gary | 5 10 | 12 00 | F | 20 9 63 | Kirby | Kirby T | Wigan Ath | 20 | 3 |
| | | | | | | | Chester C | 126 | 36 |
| | | | | | | | Southend U | 42 | 6 |
| | | | | | | | Chester C | 80 | 15 |
| | | | | | | | Wrexham | 121 | 77 |
| | | | | | | | Tranmere R | 29 | 9 |
| | | | | | | | Preston NE | 24 | 4 |
| | | | | | | | Wrexham | 15 | 5 |
| | | | | | | | Chester C | 41 | 12 |
| Brown Wayne | 6 0 | 11 12 | G | 14 1 77 | Southampton | Trainee | Bristol C | 1 | — |
| | | | | | | Weston-Super-Mare | Chester C | 15 | — |
| Clench Philip | | | M | 23 3 79 | Chester | Trainee | Chester C | — | — |
| Davidson Ross | 5 9 | 11 06 | D | 13 11 73 | Chertsey | Walton & Hersham | Sheffield U | 2 | — |
| | | | | | | | Chester C | 83 | 4 |
| Dobson Ryan* | | | D | 24 9 78 | Wellington | Trainee | Chester C | 6 | — |
| Fisher Neil* | 5 10 | 10 09 | M | 7 11 70 | St Helens | Trainee | Bolton W | 24 | 1 |
| | | | | | | | Chester C | 108 | 4 |
| Flitcroft David | 5 10 | 13 05 | M | 14 1 74 | Bolton | Trainee | Preston NE | 8 | 2 |
| | | | | | | | Lincoln C (loan) | 2 | — |
| | | | | | | | Chester C | 125 | 12 |
| Giles Martin* | | | D | 1 1 79 | Shrewsbury | Trainee | Chester C | 10 | — |

| | | | | | | | | | |
|---|---|---|---|---|---|---|---|---|---|
| **Jenkins** Iain | 5 9 | 11 10 | D | 24 12 72 | Whiston | Trainee | Everton | 5 | — |
| *(Transferred to Dundee U, April 1998)* | | | | | | | Bradford C (loan) | 6 | — |
| | | | | | | | Chester C | 160 | 1 |
| | | | | | | | Dundee U | 7 | — |
| **Jones** Jon | 5 9 | 11 05 | F | 27 10 78 | Wrexham | Trainee | Chester C | 24 | 2 |
| **McDonald** Rod* | 5 10 | 12 06 | F | 20 3 67 | London | Colne D | Walsall | 149 | 41 |
| | | | | | | | Partick T | 41 | 10 |
| | | | | | | | Chester C | 53 | 11 |
| **Milner** Andy‡ | 6 0 | 11 00 | F | 10 2 67 | Kendal | Netherfield | Manchester C | — | — |
| | | | | | | | Rochdale | 127 | 25 |
| | | | | | | | Chester C | 125 | 24 |
| **Murphy** John | 6 3 | 14 00 | F | 18 10 76 | Whiston | Trainee | Chester C | 61 | 8 |
| **Priest** Chris | 5 8 | 10 10 | M | 18 10 73 | Leigh | Trainee | Everton | — | — |
| | | | | | | | Chester C | 132 | 22 |
| **Ratcliffe** Kevin# | 6 1 | 13 06 | D | 12 11 60 | Mancot | Apprentice | Everton | 359 | 2 |
| | | | | | | | Dundee | 4 | — |
| | | | | | | | Everton | — | — |
| | | | | | | | Cardiff C | 25 | 1 |
| | | | | | | | Nottingham F | — | — |
| | | | | | | | Derby Co | 6 | — |
| | | | | | | | Chester C | 23 | — |
| **Reid** Shaun | 5 8 | 12 10 | M | 13 10 65 | Huyton | Local | Rochdale | 133 | 4 |
| | | | | | | | Preston NE (loan) | 3 | — |
| | | | | | | | York C | 106 | 7 |
| | | | | | | | Rochdale | 107 | 10 |
| | | | | | | | Bury | 21 | — |
| | | | | | | | Chester C | 27 | 1 |
| **Richardson** Nick# | 6 0 | 12 06 | M | 11 4 67 | Halifax | Local | Halifax T | 101 | 17 |
| | | | | | | | Cardiff C | 111 | 13 |
| | | | | | | | Wrexham (loan) | 4 | 2 |
| | | | | | | | Chester C (loan) | 6 | 1 |
| | | | | | | | Bury | 5 | — |
| | | | | | | | Chester C | 90 | 6 |
| **Rimmer** Stuart* | 5 7 | 11 00 | F | 12 10 64 | Southport | Apprentice | Everton | 3 | — |
| | | | | | | | Chester C | 114 | 67 |
| | | | | | | | Watford | 10 | 1 |
| | | | | | | | Notts Co | 4 | 2 |
| | | | | | | | Walsall | 88 | 31 |
| | | | | | | | Barnsley | 15 | 1 |
| | | | | | | | Chester C | 247 | 68 |
| | | | | | | | Rochdale (loan) | 3 | — |
| | | | | | | | Preston NE (loan) | 2 | — |
| **Shelton** Andrew§ | 6 0 | 12 00 | M | 19 6 80 | Sutton Coldfield | Trainee | Chester C | 2 | — |
| **Shelton** Gary | 5 7 | 10 12 | M | 21 3 58 | Nottingham | Apprentice | Walsall | 24 | — |
| | | | | | | | Aston Villa | 24 | 7 |
| | | | | | | | Notts Co (loan) | 8 | — |
| | | | | | | | Sheffield W | 198 | 18 |
| | | | | | | | Oxford U | 65 | 1 |
| | | | | | | | Bristol C | 150 | 24 |
| | | | | | | | Rochdale (loan) | 3 | — |
| | | | | | | | Chester C | 69 | 5 |
| **Sinclair** Ronnie* | 5 11 | 12 09 | G | 19 11 64 | Stirling | Apprentice | Nottingham F | — | — |
| | | | | | | | Wrexham (loan) | 11 | — |
| | | | | | | | Derby Co (loan) | — | — |
| | | | | | | | Sheffield U (loan) | — | — |
| | | | | | | | Leeds U (loan) | — | — |
| | | | | | | | Leeds U | 8 | — |
| | | | | | | | Halifax T (loan) | 4 | — |
| | | | | | | | Halifax T (loan) | 10 | — |
| | | | | | | | Bristol C | 44 | — |
| | | | | | | | Walsall (loan) | 10 | — |
| | | | | | | | Stoke C | 80 | — |
| | | | | | | | Bradford C (loan) | — | — |
| | | | | | | | Chester C | 70 | — |
| **Thomas** Rod | 5 4 | 11 02 | F | 10 10 70 | London | Trainee | Watford | 84 | 9 |
| | | | | | | | Gillingham (loan) | 8 | 1 |
| | | | | | | | Carlisle U | 146 | 16 |
| | | | | | | | Chester C | 38 | 4 |
| **Warrington** Craig* | | | M | 20 6 79 | Chester | Trainee | Chester C | — | — |
| **Whelan** Spencer | 6 2 | 11 00 | D | 17 9 71 | Liverpool | Liverpool | Chester C | 215 | 8 |
| **Woods** Mattie | 6 0 | 12 13 | D | 9 9 76 | Gosport | Trainee | Everton | — | — |
| | | | | | | | Chester C | 50 | 3 |
| **Wright** Darren§ | 5 8 | 11 00 | F | 7 9 79 | Warrington | Trainee | Chester C | 5 | — |

**Trainees**
Carson, Daniel; Conkie, Matthew J; Lancaster, Martin N; Lloyd, David; Moss, Darren M; Patterson, Phillip M; Pendleton, David J; Rendell, Carl; Shelton, Andrew M; Thompson, Scott R; Whitehead, Stephen J; Williams, Scott J; Wright, Darren.

**Associated Schoolboys**
Brown, Martin T; Cooper, Joseph D; Cross, Michael S; Davies, Michael B; Hopwood, Christopher P; Moore, James; Shelton, Gary P; Williams, Michael A.

**Associated Schoolboys who have accepted the club's offer of a Traineeship/Contract**
Doughty, Matthew L; Kilgannon, Wesley M; Lloyd-Hughes, Lee A.

## CHESTERFIELD

| Player | Ht | Wt | Pos | DOB | Birthplace | Source | Clubs | Apps | Gls |
|---|---|---|---|---|---|---|---|---|---|
| **Allardyce** Craig‡ | 6 2 | 12 05 | D | 9 6 75 | Bolton | Trainee | Preston NE | 1 | — |
| | | | | | | | Blackpool | 1 | — |
| | | | | | | Chorley | Chesterfield | 1 | — |
| **Beaumont** Chris# | 5 11 | 11 12 | M | 5 12 65 | Sheffield | Denaby U | Rochdale | 34 | 7 |
| | | | | | | | Stockport Co | 258 | 39 |
| | | | | | | | Chesterfield | 72 | 2 |
| **Breckin** Ian | 5 11 | 11 07 | D | 24 2 75 | Rotherham | Trainee | Rotherham U | 132 | 6 |
| | | | | | | | Chesterfield | 43 | 1 |
| **Carr** Darren# | 6 2 | 13 07 | D | 4 9 68 | Bristol | Trainee | Bristol R | 30 | — |
| | | | | | | | Newport Co | 9 | — |
| | | | | | | | Sheffield U | 13 | 1 |
| | | | | | | | Crewe Alex | 104 | 5 |
| | | | | | | | Chesterfield | 86 | 4 |
| **Curtis** Tom | 5 8 | 10 08 | M | 1 3 73 | Exeter | School | Derby Co | — | — |
| | | | | | | | Chesterfield | 198 | 9 |
| **Dunn** Iain | 5 10 | 10 07 | M | 1 4 70 | Derwent | School | York C | 77 | 11 |
| | | | | | | | Chesterfield | 13 | 1 |
| | | | | | | Goole T | Huddersfield T | 120 | 14 |
| | | | | | | | Scunthorpe U (loan) | 3 | — |
| | | | | | | | Chesterfield | 18 | — |
| **Ebdon** Marcus | 5 10 | 11 02 | M | 17 10 70 | Pontypool | Trainee | Everton | — | — |
| | | | | | | | Peterborough U | 147 | 15 |
| | | | | | | | Chesterfield | 45 | 3 |
| **Hewitt** Jamie | 5 10 | 10 08 | M | 17 5 68 | Chesterfield | School | Chesterfield | 249 | 14 |
| | | | | | | | Doncaster R | 33 | — |
| | | | | | | | Chesterfield | 176 | 10 |
| **Holland** Paul | 5 11 | 12 10 | M | 8 7 73 | Lincoln | School | Mansfield T | 149 | 25 |
| | | | | | | | Sheffield U | 18 | 1 |
| | | | | | | | Chesterfield | 77 | 8 |
| **Howard** Jonathan | 5 11 | 11 07 | F | 7 10 71 | Sheffield | Trainee | Rotherham U | 36 | 5 |
| | | | | | | | Chesterfield | 112 | 18 |
| **Jackson** Kirk* | 5 10 | 11 07 | F | 16 10 76 | Barnsley | Trainee | Sheffield W | — | — |
| | | | | | | | Scunthorpe U | 4 | 1 |
| | | | | | | | Chesterfield | 3 | — |
| **Jules** Mark | 5 7 | 10 09 | D | 5 9 71 | Bradford | Trainee | Bradford C | — | — |
| | | | | | | | Scarborough | 77 | 16 |
| | | | | | | | Chesterfield | 163 | 4 |
| **Leaning** Andy# | 6 2 | 13 00 | G | 18 5 63 | York | Rowntree Mackintosh | York C | 69 | — |
| | | | | | | | Sheffield U | 21 | — |
| | | | | | | | Bristol C | 75 | — |
| | | | | | | | Lincoln C | 36 | — |
| | | | | | | | Chesterfield | 14 | — |
| **Lenagh** Steven | 5 11 | 10 09 | D | 21 3 79 | Durham | Sheffield W | Chesterfield | 3 | — |
| **Lomas** Jamie | 5 11 | 10 09 | M | 18 10 77 | Chesterfield | Trainee | Chesterfield | 6 | — |
| **Mercer** Billy | 6 1 | 11 00 | G | 22 5 69 | Liverpool | Trainee | Liverpool | — | — |
| | | | | | | | Rotherham U | 104 | — |
| | | | | | | | Sheffield U | 4 | — |
| | | | | | | | Nottingham F (loan) | — | — |
| | | | | | | | Chesterfield | 105 | — |
| **Misse-Misse** ‡ Jean-Jacques | 5 10 | 11 00 | F | 7 8 68 | Yaounde | | Charleroi | 93 | 37 |
| | | | | | | | Sporting Lisbon | 4 | — |
| | | | | | | Trabzonspor | Dundee U | 4 | — |
| | | | | | | | Chesterfield | 1 | — |
| **Morris** Andy* | 6 4 | 14 07 | F | 17 11 67 | Sheffield | School | Rotherham U | 7 | — |
| | | | | | | | Chesterfield | 265 | 56 |
| | | | | | | | Exeter C (loan) | 7 | 2 |
| **Pearce** Greg | 5 9 | 10 09 | M | 26 5 80 | Bolton | Trainee | Chesterfield | — | — |
| **Perkins** Chris | 5 11 | 10 09 | M | 9 1 74 | Nottingham | Trainee | Mansfield T | 8 | — |
| | | | | | | | Chesterfield | 113 | 2 |
| **Reeves** David | 6 0 | 12 06 | F | 19 11 67 | Birkenhead | Heswall | Sheffield W | 17 | 2 |
| | | | | | | | Scunthorpe U (loan) | 4 | 2 |
| | | | | | | | Scunthorpe U (loan) | 6 | 4 |
| | | | | | | | Burnley (loan) | 16 | 8 |
| | | | | | | | Bolton W | 134 | 29 |
| | | | | | | | Notts Co | 13 | 2 |
| | | | | | | | Carlisle U | 127 | 48 |
| | | | | | | | Preston NE | 47 | 12 |
| | | | | | | | Chesterfield | 26 | 5 |
| **Rogers** Lee* | 5 11 | 12 01 | D | 28 10 66 | Doncaster | Doncaster R | Chesterfield | 334 | 1 |
| **Simpkins** James† | | | M | 28 11 78 | Sheffield | Trainee | Sheffield W | — | — |
| | | | | | | | Chesterfield | — | — |
| **Simpkins** Michael† | 6 0 | 11 11 | D | 28 11 78 | Sheffield | Trainee | Sheffield W | — | — |
| | | | | | | | Chesterfield | — | — |
| **Todd** Luke‡ | | | M | 26 12 78 | Doncaster | Sheffield W | Chesterfield | — | — |

| | | | | | | | | | |
|---|---|---|---|---|---|---|---|---|---|
| **Wilkinson** Steve | 5 11 | 11 11 | F | 1 9 68 | Lincoln | Apprentice | Leicester C | 9 | 1 |
| | | | | | | | Rochdale (loan) | — | — |
| | | | | | | | Crewe Alex (loan) | 5 | 2 |
| | | | | | | | Mansfield T | 232 | 83 |
| | | | | | | | Preston NE | 52 | 13 |
| | | | | | | | Chesterfield | 30 | 6 |
| **Williams** Mark | 6 0 | 12 04 | D | 28 9 70 | Stalybridge | Newtown | Shrewsbury T | 102 | 3 |
| | | | | | | | Chesterfield | 128 | 9 |
| **Willis** Roger | 6 0 | 12 00 | M | 17 6 67 | Islington | | Grimsby T | 9 | — |
| | | | | | | Barnet | Barnet | 44 | 13 |
| | | | | | | | Watford | 36 | 2 |
| | | | | | | | Birmingham C | 19 | 5 |
| | | | | | | | Southend U | 31 | 7 |
| | | | | | | | Peterborough U | 40 | 6 |
| | | | | | | | Chesterfield | 34 | 8 |

**Trainees**
Barrett, Daniel T; Bowler, Paul S; Clark, Damian M; Danysz, Lee J; Dooley, James; Hawke, Richard J; Henshaw, Carl H; Newton, Lee R; Reynolds, Steven J; Robinson, Scott A; Spencer, Matthew; Williams, Daniel J; Wilson, Jonathan S.

**Non-Contract**
Brown, James G; Simpkins, James M; Simpkins, Michael J.

# COLCHESTER UNITED

| | | | | | | | | | |
|---|---|---|---|---|---|---|---|---|---|
| **Abrahams** Paul | 5 10 | 11 00 | F | 31 10 73 | Colchester | Trainee | Colchester U | 55 | 8 |
| | | | | | | | Brentford | 35 | 8 |
| | | | | | | | Colchester U (loan) | 8 | 2 |
| | | | | | | | Colchester U | 54 | 14 |
| **Adcock** Tony* | 5 11 | 11 05 | F | 27 3 63 | Bethnal Green | Apprentice | Colchester U | 210 | 98 |
| | | | | | | | Manchester C | 15 | 5 |
| | | | | | | | Northampton T | 72 | 30 |
| | | | | | | | Bradford C | 38 | 6 |
| | | | | | | | Northampton T | 35 | 10 |
| | | | | | | | Peterborough U | 111 | 35 |
| | | | | | | | Luton T | 2 | — |
| | | | | | | | Colchester U | 102 | 28 |
| **Armitage** Gavin‡ | 5 10 | 12 06 | M | 2 9 78 | Maldon | Trainee | Colchester U | — | — |
| **Bates** Robert‡ | 5 9 | 12 00 | F | 27 2 78 | Redbridge | Trainee | Colchester U | — | — |
| **Betts** Simon* | 5 6 | 11 06 | D | 3 5 73 | Middlesbrough | Trainee | Ipswich T | — | — |
| | | | | | | | Scarborough | — | — |
| | | | | | | | Colchester U | 163 | 9 |
| **Buckle** Paul# | 5 9 | 11 07 | M | 16 12 70 | Welwyn | Trainee | Brentford | 57 | 1 |
| | | | | | | | Torquay U | 59 | 9 |
| | | | | | | | Exeter C | 22 | 2 |
| | | | | | | | Northampton T | — | — |
| | | | | | | | Wycombe W | — | — |
| | | | | | | | Colchester U | 62 | 5 |
| **Caldwell** Garrett* | 6 1 | 13 00 | G | 6 11 73 | Princeton | | Colchester U | 6 | — |
| **Cawley** Peter* | 6 4 | 15 10 | D | 15 9 65 | London | Chertsey T | Wimbledon | 1 | — |
| | | | | | | | Bristol R (loan) | 10 | — |
| | | | | | | | Fulham (loan) | 5 | — |
| | | | | | | | Bristol R | 3 | — |
| | | | | | | | Southend U | 7 | 1 |
| | | | | | | | Exeter C | 7 | — |
| | | | | | | | Barnet | 3 | — |
| | | | | | | | Colchester U | 180 | 8 |
| **Duguid** Karl | 5 11 | 11 00 | M | 21 3 78 | Hitchin | Trainee | Colchester U | 57 | 7 |
| **Dunne** Joe* | 5 9 | 11 06 | D | 25 5 73 | Dublin | Trainee | Gillingham | 115 | 1 |
| | | | | | | | Colchester U | 65 | 3 |
| **Emberson** Carl# | 6 2 | 14 05 | G | 13 7 73 | Epsom | Trainee | Millwall | — | — |
| | | | | | | | Colchester U (loan) | 13 | — |
| | | | | | | | Colchester U | 142 | — |
| **Fernandes** Tamer | 6 2 | 13 08 | G | 7 12 74 | London | Trainee | Brentford | 12 | — |
| | | | | | | | Peterborough U (loan) | — | — |
| | | | | | | | Colchester U | — | — |
| **Forbes** Steve | 6 1 | 13 03 | M | 24 12 75 | Hackney | Sittingbourne | Millwall | 5 | — |
| | | | | | | | Colchester U | 36 | 2 |
| **Goss** Jeremy† | 5 9 | 11 08 | M | 11 5 65 | Oekolia | Amateur | Norwich C | 188 | 14 |
| | | | | | | | Hearts | 10 | — |
| | | | | | | | Colchester U | — | — |
| **Greene** David | 6 3 | 14 02 | M | 26 10 73 | Luton | Trainee | Luton T | 19 | — |
| | | | | | | | Colchester U (loan) | 14 | 1 |
| | | | | | | | Brentford (loan) | 11 | — |
| | | | | | | | Colchester U | 82 | 6 |
| **Gregory** David# | 5 11 | 12 03 | M | 23 1 70 | Polstead | Trainee | Ipswich T | 32 | 2 |
| | | | | | | | Hereford U (loan) | 2 | — |
| | | | | | | | Peterborough U | 3 | — |
| | | | | | | | Colchester U | 92 | 6 |
| **Gregory** Neil | 6 0 | 12 03 | F | 7 10 72 | Zambia | Trainee | Ipswich T | 45 | 9 |
| | | | | | | | Chesterfield (loan) | 3 | 1 |
| | | | | | | | Scunthorpe U (loan) | 10 | 7 |
| | | | | | | | Torquay U (loan) | 5 | — |
| | | | | | | | Peterborough U (loan) | 3 | 1 |
| | | | | | | | Colchester U | 15 | 7 |

| | | | | | | | | | |
|---|---|---|---|---|---|---|---|---|---|
| **Hathaway** Ian | 5 4 | 10 12 | M | 22 8 68 | Wordsley | Bedworth U | Mansfield T | 44 | 2 |
| | | | | | | | Rotherham U | 13 | 1 |
| | | | | | | | Torquay U | 140 | 14 |
| | | | | | | | Colchester U | 12 | — |
| **Haydon** Nicky | 5 9 | 11 07 | M | 10 8 78 | Barking | Trainee | Colchester U | 18 | 1 |
| **Lock** Tony | 5 10 | 12 08 | F | 3 9 76 | Harlow | Trainee | Colchester U | 41 | 8 |
| **Potter** Daniel* | | | G | 18 3 79 | Ipswich | Chelsea | Colchester U | — | — |
| **Rainford** David | 6 0 | 11 11 | M | 21 4 79 | Stepney | Trainee | Colchester U | — | — |
| **Sale** Mark | 6 5 | 14 07 | F | 27 2 72 | Burton-on-Trent | Trainee | Stoke C | 2 | — |
| | | | | | | | Cambridge U | — | — |
| | | | | | | | Birmingham C | 21 | — |
| | | | | | | | Torquay U | 44 | 8 |
| | | | | | | | Preston NE | 13 | 7 |
| | | | | | | | Mansfield T | 45 | 12 |
| | | | | | | | Colchester U | 49 | 10 |
| **Skelton** Aaron | 6 0 | 12 01 | D | 22 11 74 | Welwyn | Trainee | Luton T | 8 | — |
| | | | | | | | Colchester U | 39 | 7 |
| **Stamps** Scott | 5 9 | 11 07 | D | 20 3 75 | Edgbaston | Trainee | Torquay U | 86 | 5 |
| | | | | | | | Colchester U | 35 | 1 |
| **Whitton** Steve* | 6 0 | 11 08 | F | 4 12 60 | East Ham | Apprentice | Coventry C | 74 | 21 |
| | | | | | | | West Ham U | 39 | 6 |
| | | | | | | | Birmingham C (loan) | 8 | 2 |
| | | | | | | | Birmingham C | 95 | 28 |
| | | | | | | | Sheffield W | 32 | 4 |
| | | | | | | | Ipswich T | 88 | 15 |
| | | | | | | | Colchester U | 116 | 21 |
| **Wilkins** Richard | 6 0 | 11 08 | M | 28 5 65 | Streatham | Haverhill R | Colchester U | 152 | 22 |
| | | | | | | | Cambridge U | 81 | 7 |
| | | | | | | | Hereford U | 77 | 5 |
| | | | | | | | Colchester U | 77 | 7 |

**Trainees**
Burch, Michael; Cook, Meyrick D; Cooksey, Ernest G; Gallant, Paul K; Grace, Daniel J; King, Aaron S; Newman, Robert D; Rogers, Joel H; Taylor, Andrew D; Terry, Simon J; Watkins, John; Wiles, Ian R; Willis, David A.

**Non-Contract**
Goss, Jeremy.

**Associated Schoolboys who have accepted the club's offer of a Traineeship/Contract**
Delaney, Paul M; Gyoury, Nicky D; Opara, Chris-Santos; Taylor, Andrew C.

# COVENTRY CITY

| | | | | | | | | | |
|---|---|---|---|---|---|---|---|---|---|
| **Andrews** John* | 6 1 | 13 00 | D | 27 9 78 | Cork | Trainee | Coventry C | — | — |
| **Barnett** Christopher | 5 11 | 12 00 | M | 20 12 78 | Derby | Trainee | Coventry C | — | — |
| **Blake** Aslam‡ | 6 0 | 11 12 | F | 19 10 79 | Birmingham | Trainee | Coventry C | — | — |
| **Boateng** George | 5 9 | 10 12 | M | 5 9 75 | Nkawkaw | | Excelsior | 9 | — |
| | | | | | | | Feyenoord | 68 | 1 |
| | | | | | | | Coventry C | 14 | 1 |
| **Boland** Willie | 5 9 | 11 02 | M | 6 8 75 | Ennis | Trainee | Coventry C | 63 | — |
| **Breen** Gary | 6 1 | 11 12 | D | 12 12 73 | London | Charlton Ath | Maidstone U | 19 | — |
| | | | | | | | Gillingham | 51 | — |
| | | | | | | | Peterborough U | 69 | 1 |
| | | | | | | | Birmingham C | 40 | 2 |
| | | | | | | | Coventry C | 39 | 1 |
| **Burrows** David | 5 8 | 11 08 | D | 25 10 68 | Dudley | Apprentice | WBA | 46 | 1 |
| | | | | | | | Liverpool | 146 | 3 |
| | | | | | | | West Ham U | 29 | 1 |
| | | | | | | | Everton | 19 | — |
| | | | | | | | Coventry C | 73 | — |
| **Burrows** Mark | 6 3 | 12 08 | D | 14 8 80 | Kettering | Trainee | Coventry C | — | — |
| **Colwell** Richard | 5 9 | 11 02 | D | 2 9 79 | Wordsley | Trainee | Coventry C | — | — |
| **Daish** Liam | 6 2 | 13 05 | D | 23 9 68 | Portsmouth | Apprentice | Portsmouth | 1 | — |
| | | | | | | | Cambridge U | 139 | 4 |
| | | | | | | | Birmingham C | 73 | 3 |
| | | | | | | | Coventry C | 31 | 2 |
| **Devaney** Martin | 5 10 | 11 12 | M | 1 6 80 | Cheltenham | Trainee | Coventry C | — | — |
| **Donlevy** Andrew | 5 11 | 10 12 | D | 13 4 81 | Hong Kong | Trainee | Coventry C | — | — |
| **Dublin** Dion | 6 0 | 12 04 | F | 22 4 69 | Leicester | | Norwich C | — | — |
| | | | | | | | Cambridge U | 156 | 52 |
| | | | | | | | Manchester U | 12 | 2 |
| | | | | | | | Coventry C | 135 | 58 |
| **Ducros** Andrew | 5 6 | 9 08 | F | 16 9 77 | Evesham | Trainee | Coventry C | 8 | — |
| **Eribenne** Chukkie | 5 10 | 11 12 | F | 2 11 80 | London | Trainee | Coventry C | — | — |
| **Eustace** John | 5 11 | 11 12 | M | 3 11 79 | Solihull | Trainee | Coventry C | — | — |
| **Faulconbridge** Craig | 6 1 | 13 00 | F | 20 4 78 | Nuneaton | Trainee | Coventry C | — | — |
| *(Transferred to Dunfermline Ath, March 1998)* | | | | | | | Dunfermline Ath | 7 | 1 |
| **Genaux** Regis‡ | 5 11 | 12 06 | D | 31 8 73 | Belgium | | Standard Liege | 151 | 1 |
| | | | | | | | Coventry C | 4 | — |
| **Goodwin** Scott* | 5 9 | 11 08 | D | 13 9 78 | Hull | Trainee | Coventry C | — | — |
| **Hall** Marcus | 6 1 | 12 02 | D | 24 3 76 | Coventry | Trainee | Coventry C | 68 | 1 |

| Player | Ht | Wt | Pos | DOB | Birthplace | Source | Club | Apps | Gls |
|---|---|---|---|---|---|---|---|---|---|
| **Haworth** Simon | 6 1 | 13 01 | F | 30 3 77 | Cardiff | Trainee | Cardiff C | 37 | 9 |
| | | | | | | | Coventry C | 10 | — |
| **Hedman** Magnus | 6 3 | 14 00 | G | 19 3 73 | Stockholm | | AIK Stockholm | 127 | — |
| | | | | | | | Coventry C | 14 | — |
| **Huckerby** Darren | 5 11 | 11 04 | F | 23 4 76 | Nottingham | Trainee | Lincoln C | 28 | 5 |
| | | | | | | | Newcastle U | 1 | — |
| | | | | | | | Millwall (loan) | 6 | 3 |
| | | | | | | | Coventry C | 59 | 19 |
| **Jess** Eoin | 5 10 | 11 07 | F | 13 12 70 | Aberdeen | Rangers | Aberdeen | 201 | 50 |
| *(Transferred to Aberdeen, July 1997)* | | | | | | | Coventry C | 39 | 1 |
| | | | | | | | Aberdeen | 34 | 9 |
| **Johansen** Martin | 5 8 | 11 01 | M | 22 7 72 | Glostrup | | KB Copenhagen | 20 | 4 |
| | | | | | | | B1903 | 25 | 8 |
| | | | | | | | FC Copenhagen | 116 | 31 |
| | | | | | | | Coventry C | 2 | — |
| **Kadi** Junior* | | | M | 16 8 79 | London | Trainee | Coventry C | — | — |
| **Kirkland** Christopher | 6 3 | 11 07 | G | 2 5 81 | Leicester | Trainee | Coventry C | — | — |
| **McAllister** Gary | 6 1 | 11 11 | M | 25 12 64 | Motherwell | Fir Park BC | Motherwell | 59 | 6 |
| | | | | | | | Leicester C | 201 | 47 |
| | | | | | | | Leeds U | 231 | 31 |
| | | | | | | | Coventry C | 52 | 6 |
| **Moldovan** Viorel | 5 9 | 11 08 | F | 8 7 72 | Bistrita | | Gloria | 84 | 22 |
| | | | | | | | Dynamo Bucharest | 60 | 19 |
| | | | | | | | Neuchatel Xamax | 32 | 19 |
| | | | | | | | Grasshoppers | 51 | 44 |
| | | | | | | | Coventry C | 10 | 1 |
| **Mooney** Gerard | 5 9 | 11 00 | D | 28 8 80 | Glasgow | Trainee | Coventry C | — | — |
| **Nilsson** Roland | 5 10 | 11 10 | D | 27 11 63 | Helsingborg | IFK Gothenburg | Sheffield W | 151 | 2 |
| | | | | | | | Helsingborg | 64 | 6 |
| | | | | | | | Coventry C | 32 | — |
| **O'Neill** Michael | 5 11 | 10 10 | F | 5 7 69 | Portadown | Coleraine | Newcastle U | 48 | 15 |
| | | | | | | | Dundee U | 64 | 11 |
| | | | | | | | Hibernian | 98 | 19 |
| | | | | | | | Coventry C | 5 | — |
| | | | | | | | Reading (loan) | 9 | 1 |
| **Ogrizovic** Steve | 6 3 | 15 00 | G | 12 9 57 | Mansfield | ONRYC | Chesterfield | 16 | — |
| | | | | | | | Liverpool | 4 | — |
| | | | | | | | Shrewsbury T | 84 | — |
| | | | | | | | Coventry C | 502 | 1 |
| **Prenderville** Barry | 6 0 | 12 08 | D | 16 10 76 | Dublin | Trainee | Coventry C | — | — |
| **Quinn** Barry | 6 0 | 12 02 | M | 9 5 79 | Dublin | Trainee | Coventry C | — | — |
| **Scope** Tynan | 6 2 | 13 09 | G | 30 7 79 | Sydney | | Coventry C | — | — |
| **Shaw** Richard | 5 9 | 12 08 | D | 11 9 68 | Brentford | Apprentice | Crystal Palace | 207 | 3 |
| | | | | | | | Hull C (loan) | 4 | — |
| | | | | | | | Coventry C | 89 | — |
| **Shilton** Sam | 5 11 | 11 06 | M | 21 7 78 | Nottingham | Schoolboy | Plymouth Arg | 3 | — |
| | | | | | | | Coventry C | 2 | — |
| **Soltvedt** Trond Egil | 6 1 | 12 08 | M | 15 2 67 | Voss | | Viking | 33 | 4 |
| | | | | | | | Brann | 64 | 34 |
| | | | | | | | Rosenborg | 60 | 18 |
| | | | | | | | Coventry C | 30 | 1 |
| **Strachan** Gavin | 5 10 | 11 07 | M | 23 12 78 | Aberdeen | Trainee | Coventry C | 9 | — |
| **Strachan** Gordon* | 5 6 | 10 06 | M | 9 2 57 | Edinburgh | | Dundee | 60 | 13 |
| | | | | | | | Aberdeen | 183 | 55 |
| | | | | | | | Manchester U | 160 | 33 |
| | | | | | | | Leeds U | 197 | 37 |
| | | | | | | | Coventry C | 26 | — |
| **Telfer** Paul | 5 9 | 11 06 | M | 21 10 71 | Edinburgh | Trainee | Luton T | 144 | 19 |
| | | | | | | | Coventry C | 98 | 4 |
| **Whelan** Noel | 6 2 | 12 03 | F | 30 12 74 | Leeds | Trainee | Leeds U | 48 | 7 |
| | | | | | | | Coventry C | 77 | 20 |
| **Williams** Jamie | 5 9 | 12 00 | D | 3 1 80 | Bedworth | Trainee | Coventry C | — | — |
| **Williams** Paul | 5 11 | 12 10 | D | 26 3 71 | Burton | Trainee | Derby Co | 160 | 26 |
| | | | | | | | Lincoln C (loan) | 3 | — |
| | | | | | | | Coventry C | 84 | 4 |

**Trainees**
Anderson, Ross; Beech, Sean P; Bindley, Christopher J; Castro-Pearson, David; Hegley, Nicholas J; Mullen, Nicky R; Vincent, Luke R; Watson, Steven.

**Associated Schoolboys**
Ashby, Jason; Brush, David J; Cook, Matthew; Forsdick, Simon D; Hidle, Robert E; Joseph, Daniel; Miller, Kirk; Noon, Mark; Shanahan, Aaron; Stanley, Craig; Whittingham, James.

**Associated Schoolboys who have accepted the club's offer of a Traineeship/Contract**
Cudworth, Thomas J S; Graham, Mark A; Hall, Daniel; Lewis, David M J; McSheffrey, Gary; Muir, Richard A D; Parkinson, Simon A; Pead, Craig G; Strachan, Craig; Thompson, Nathan.

# CREWE ALEXANDRA

| | | | | | | | | | |
|---|---|---|---|---|---|---|---|---|---|
| **Anthrobus** Steve | 6 2 | 12 06 | F | 10 11 68 | Lewisham | | Millwall | 21 | 4 |
| | | | | | | | Southend U (loan) | — | — |
| | | | | | | | Wimbledon | 28 | — |
| | | | | | | | Peterborough U (loan) | 2 | — |
| | | | | | | | Chester C (loan) | 7 | — |
| | | | | | | | Shrewsbury T | 72 | 16 |
| | | | | | | | Crewe Alex | 40 | 6 |
| **Bankole** Ademola# | 6 3 | 12 08 | G | 9 9 69 | Lagos | Leyton Orient | Crewe Alex | 6 | — |
| **Bignot** Marcus | 5 9 | 11 00 | D | 22 8 74 | Birmingham | Kidderminster H | Crewe Alex | 42 | — |
| **Charnock** Phil | 5 10 | 11 03 | M | 14 2 75 | Southport | Trainee | Liverpool | — | — |
| | | | | | | | Blackpool (loan) | 4 | — |
| | | | | | | | Crewe Alex | 65 | 4 |
| **Collins** James | 5 8 | 10 00 | M | 28 5 78 | Liverpool | Trainee | Crewe Alex | 1 | — |
| **Cox** Lee* | | | M | 16 10 78 | Liverpool | Trainee | Crewe Alex | — | — |
| **Critchley** Neil | | | M | 18 10 78 | Crewe | Trainee | Crewe Alex | — | — |
| **Cutler** Neil* | 6 1 | 12 00 | G | 3 9 76 | Birmingham | Trainee | WBA | — | — |
| | | | | | | | Coventry C (loan) | — | — |
| | | | | | | | Chester C (loan) | 1 | — |
| | | | | | | | Crewe Alex | — | — |
| | | | | | | | Chester C (loan) | 5 | — |
| **Flood** Colin‡ | | | M | 29 10 79 | Liverpool | Stantondale | Crewe Alex | — | — |
| **Foran** Mark | 6 3 | 13 04 | D | 30 10 73 | Aldershot | Trainee | Millwall | — | — |
| | | | | | | | Sheffield U | 11 | 1 |
| | | | | | | | Rotherham U (loan) | 3 | — |
| | | | | | | | Wycombe W (loan) | 5 | — |
| | | | | | | | Peterborough U | 25 | 1 |
| | | | | | | | Lincoln C (loan) | 2 | — |
| | | | | | | | Oldham Ath (loan) | 1 | — |
| | | | | | | | Crewe Alex | 12 | 1 |
| **Garvey** Steve* | 5 9 | 10 09 | F | 22 11 73 | Stalybridge | Trainee | Crewe Alex | 108 | 8 |
| | | | | | | | Chesterfield (loan) | 3 | — |
| **Gayle** Mark* | 6 2 | 12 03 | G | 21 10 69 | Bromsgrove | Trainee | Leicester C | — | — |
| | | | | | | | Blackpool | — | — |
| | | | | | | Worcester C | Walsall | 75 | — |
| | | | | | | | Crewe Alex | 83 | — |
| | | | | | | | Liverpool (loan) | — | — |
| | | | | | | | Birmingham C (loan) | — | — |
| | | | | | | | Chesterfield (loan) | 5 | — |
| | | | | | | | Luton T (loan) | — | — |
| **Johnson** Seth | 5 10 | 11 00 | M | 12 3 79 | Birmingham | Trainee | Crewe Alex | 51 | 2 |
| **Kearton** Jason | 6 1 | 12 03 | G | 9 7 69 | Ipswich (Aus) | Brisbane Lions | Everton | 6 | — |
| | | | | | | | Stoke C (loan) | 16 | — |
| | | | | | | | Blackpool (loan) | 14 | — |
| | | | | | | | Notts Co (loan) | 10 | — |
| | | | | | | | Preston NE (loan) | — | — |
| | | | | | | | Crewe Alex | 73 | — |
| **Lightfoot** Chris | 6 1 | 12 00 | D | 1 4 70 | Penketh | Trainee | Chester C | 277 | 32 |
| | | | | | | | Wigan Ath | 14 | 1 |
| | | | | | | | Crewe Alex | 44 | 1 |
| **Little** Colin | 5 10 | 11 00 | F | 4 11 72 | Wythenshaw | Hyde U | Crewe Alex | 69 | 14 |
| **Lunt** Kenny | 5 10 | 10 00 | M | 20 11 79 | Runcorn | Trainee | Crewe Alex | 41 | 2 |
| **Macauley** Steve | 6 1 | 12 00 | D | 4 3 69 | Lytham | Fleetwood T | Crewe Alex | 165 | 20 |
| **Moralee** Jamie‡ | 5 11 | 11 00 | F | 2 12 71 | Wandsworth | Trainee | Crystal Palace | 6 | — |
| | | | | | | | Millwall | 67 | 19 |
| | | | | | | | Watford | 49 | 7 |
| | | | | | | | Crewe Alex | 16 | — |
| **Morse** Peter | | | M | 5 3 79 | Stoke | Trainee | Crewe Alex | — | — |
| **Norris** Richard | | | M | 5 1 78 | Birkenhead | Marine | Crewe Alex | — | — |
| **Pemberton** John | 5 11 | 11 09 | D | 18 11 64 | Oldham | Chadderton | Rochdale | 1 | — |
| | | | | | | | Crewe Alex | 121 | 1 |
| | | | | | | | Crystal Palace | 78 | 2 |
| | | | | | | | Sheffield U | 68 | — |
| | | | | | | | Leeds U | 53 | — |
| | | | | | | | Crewe Alex | 1 | — |
| **Pope** Steven‡ | 5 11 | 11 00 | D | 8 9 76 | Stoke | Trainee | Crewe Alex | 6 | — |
| **Richardson** Paul* | | | M | 7 12 78 | Oldham | Trainee | Crewe Alex | — | — |
| **Rivers** Mark | 5 10 | 11 00 | F | 26 11 75 | Crewe | Trainee | Crewe Alex | 95 | 22 |
| **Smith** Peter | 5 10 | 10 00 | F | 15 9 78 | Rhuddlan | Trainee | Crewe Alex | 7 | — |
| **Smith** Shaun | 5 10 | 11 00 | D | 9 4 71 | Leeds | Trainee | Halifax T | 7 | — |
| | | | | | | | Crewe Alex | 238 | 30 |
| **Street** Kevin | 5 10 | 10 08 | F | 25 11 77 | Crewe | Trainee | Crewe Alex | 32 | 4 |
| **Tierney** Fran* | 5 10 | 11 00 | F | 10 9 75 | Liverpool | Trainee | Crewe Alex | 87 | 10 |
| **Unsworth** Lee | 5 11 | 11 02 | D | 25 2 73 | Eccles | Ashton U | Crewe Alex | 94 | — |
| **Walton** David | 6 2 | 14 07 | D | 10 4 73 | Bedlingham | Trainee | Sheffield U | — | — |
| | | | | | | | Shrewsbury T | 128 | 10 |
| | | | | | | | Crewe Alex | 27 | — |
| **Westwood** Ashley | 5 11 | 11 02 | D | 31 8 76 | Bridgnorth | Trainee | Manchester U | — | — |
| | | | | | | | Crewe Alex | 98 | 9 |

| Whalley Gareth | 5 10 | 11 06 | M | 19 12 73 | Manchester | Trainee | Crewe Alex | 180 | 9 |
| Whittaker David | | | M | 13 8 78 | Stockport | Trainee | Crewe Alex | — | — |
| Williamson Michael | | | M | 29 12 78 | Liverpool | | Crewe Alex | — | — |
| Wright David | 5 11 | 10 08 | D | 1 5 80 | Warrington | Trainee | Crewe Alex | 3 | — |
| Wright Jermaine | 5 10 | 11 09 | M | 21 10 75 | Greenwich | Trainee | Millwall | — | — |
| | | | | | | | Wolverhampton W | 20 | — |
| | | | | | | | Doncaster R (loan) | 13 | — |
| | | | | | | | Crewe Alex | 5 | — |

**Trainees**
Allen, Christopher D; Arrowsmith, Paul; Beeston, Mark A; Brown, Christopher M; Chadwick, Gareth P; Foster, Stephen J; Grant, John A C; Hill, Sammy G; Hoult, Stephen R; Hulse, Robert W; Jones, Andrew J; Knight, Darren P; Laurie, Carl A; Walker, Richard S; Webster, Colin J L; Welsby, Kevin J.

**Associated Schoolboys**
Ashton, Dean; Bell, Lee; Betts, Thomas G; Booth, Martin T; Davies, Clark W; Eaton, George; Edwards, Paul; Frost, Carl R; Higdon, Michael; Jeffs, Ian D; Jenkins, Byron L; Johnson, Mark E; Jones, Robert A; Malbon, Craig D; Malpass, John; McKenzie, Andrew; Mead, John M; Morris, Alexander S; Platt, Matthew; Rix, Benjamin; Roberts, Mark A; Robinson, James G; Spooner, Mark S; Vaughan, David O; Westwood, Lee K; Wilcock, James W; Yates, Adam P.

**Associated Schoolboys who have accepted the club's offer of a Traineeship/Contract**
Baylis, Philip; Blake, Mathew L; Bostock, Andrew M; Harris, Paul J; Liddle, Gareth J C; Lunt, Gary T; Marrow, James F J; Marsh, Nicholas J; McCready, Christopher J.

# CRYSTAL PALACE

| Bent Marcus | 6 3 | 11 13 | F | 19 5 78 | Hammersmith | Trainee | Brentford | 70 | 8 |
| | | | | | | | Crystal Palace | 16 | 5 |
| Billio Patrizio‡ | 5 8 | 11 00 | M | 19 4 74 | Treviso | | Crystal Palace | 3 | — |
| Bonetti Ivano | 5 9 | 11 05 | M | 1 8 64 | Brescia | Torino | Grimsby T | 19 | 3 |
| (Transferred to Genoa, October 1997) | | | | | | | Tranmere R | 13 | 1 |
| | | | | | | | Crystal Palace | 2 | — |
| Boxall Danny | 5 8 | 10 05 | D | 24 8 77 | Croydon | Trainee | Crystal Palace | 8 | — |
| | | | | | | | Oldham Ath (loan) | 18 | — |
| Brolin Tomas* | 5 8 | 13 00 | M | 29 11 69 | Hudiksvall | | Sundsvall | 54 | 13 |
| | | | | | | | Norrkoping | 11 | 7 |
| | | | | | | | Parma | 133 | 20 |
| | | | | | | | Leeds U | 19 | 4 |
| | | | | | | | Zurich (loan) | 3 | — |
| | | | | | | | Parma (loan) | 11 | — |
| | | | | | | | Crystal Palace | 13 | — |
| Burton Sagi | 6 2 | 13 06 | D | 25 11 77 | Birmingham | Trainee | Crystal Palace | 2 | — |
| Carlisle Wayne* | 6 0 | 11 06 | M | 9 9 79 | Lisburn | Trainee | Crystal Palace | — | — |
| Clarke Jonathan‡ | | | M | 4 9 78 | Drogheda | Trainee | Crystal Palace | — | — |
| Curcic Sasa | 5 9 | 11 00 | M | 14 2 72 | Belgrade | | OFK Belgrade | 49 | 5 |
| | | | | | | | Partizan Belgrade | 74 | 16 |
| | | | | | | | Bolton W | 28 | 4 |
| | | | | | | | Aston Villa | 29 | — |
| | | | | | | | Crystal Palace | 8 | 1 |
| Dyer Bruce | 5 11 | 11 03 | F | 13 4 75 | Ilford | Trainee | Watford | 31 | 6 |
| | | | | | | | Crystal Palace | 129 | 35 |
| Edworthy Marc | 5 8 | 10 03 | D | 24 12 72 | Barnstaple | Trainee | Plymouth Arg | 69 | 1 |
| | | | | | | | Crystal Palace | 123 | — |
| Folan Tony | 5 10 | 10 08 | D | 18 9 78 | Lewisham | Trainee | Crystal Palace | 1 | — |
| Frampton Andrew | | | M | 3 9 79 | Wimbledon | Trainee | Crystal Palace | — | — |
| Fullarton Jamie | 5 9 | 10 09 | M | 20 7 74 | Bellshill | | St Mirren | 102 | 3 |
| | | | | | | | Bastia | 17 | — |
| | | | | | | | Crystal Palace | 25 | 1 |
| Ginty Rory* | 5 9 | 11 00 | M | 23 1 77 | Galway | Trainee | Crystal Palace | 5 | — |
| Gordon Dean | 6 0 | 13 04 | D | 10 2 73 | Thornton Heath | Trainee | Crystal Palace | 201 | 20 |
| Graham Gareth | 5 7 | 10 02 | M | 6 12 78 | Belfast | Trainee | Crystal Palace | — | — |
| Harris Richard | | | M | 23 10 80 | Croydon | Trainee | Crystal Palace | — | — |
| Hibburt James | 6 0 | 12 08 | D | 30 10 79 | Ashford | Trainee | Crystal Palace | — | — |
| Hreidarsson Hermann | 6 1 | 12 12 | D | 11 7 74 | Iceland | | IBV | 66 | 5 |
| | | | | | | | Crystal Palace | 30 | 2 |
| Ismael Valerien | 6 2 | 13 01 | D | 28 9 75 | Strasbourg | | Strasbourg | 85 | 1 |
| | | | | | | | Crystal Palace | 13 | — |
| Jansen Matt | 5 11 | 11 03 | F | 20 10 77 | Carlisle | Trainee | Carlisle U | 42 | 10 |
| | | | | | | | Crystal Palace | 8 | 3 |
| Kendall Lee | | | G | 8 1 81 | Newport | Trainee | Crystal Palace | — | — |
| Kennedy Richard* | 5 10 | 10 05 | M | 28 8 78 | Waterford | Trainee | Crystal Palace | — | — |
| Linighan Andy | 6 4 | 13 10 | D | 18 6 62 | Hartlepool | Smiths BC | Hartlepool U | 110 | 4 |
| | | | | | | | Leeds U | 66 | 3 |
| | | | | | | | Oldham Ath | 87 | 6 |
| | | | | | | | Norwich C | 86 | 8 |
| | | | | | | | Arsenal | 118 | 5 |
| | | | | | | | Crystal Palace | 45 | 2 |

| Lombardo Attilio | 5 11 | 11 07 | M | 6 1 66 | St. Maria | | Pergocrema | 38 | 9 |
| | | | | | La Fossa | | Cremonese | 141 | 17 |
| | | | | | | | Sampdoria | 201 | 34 |
| | | | | | | | Juventus | 35 | 2 |
| | | | | | | | Crystal Palace | 24 | 5 |
| Martin Andrew | 6 0 | 10 12 | F | 28 2 80 | Cardiff | Trainee | Crystal Palace | — | — |
| McKenzie Leon | 5 10 | 10 03 | F | 17 5 78 | Croydon | Trainee | Crystal Palace | 36 | 2 |
| | | | | | | | Fulham (loan) | 3 | — |
| Miller Kevin | 6 1 | 13 00 | G | 15 3 69 | Falmouth | Newquay | Exeter C | 163 | — |
| | | | | | | | Birmingham C | 24 | — |
| | | | | | | | Watford | 128 | — |
| | | | | | | | Crystal Palace | 38 | — |
| Morrison Clinton | 6 1 | 11 02 | F | 14 5 79 | Tooting | Trainee | Crystal Palace | 1 | 1 |
| Mullins Hayden | 6 0 | 11 12 | D | 27 3 79 | Reading | Trainee | Crystal Palace | — | — |
| Nash Carlo | 6 5 | 14 01 | G | 13 9 73 | Bolton | Clitheroe | Crystal Palace | 21 | — |
| Ormshaw Gareth | 6 0 | 12 10 | G | 8 7 79 | Durban | Ramblers | Crystal Palace | — | — |
| Padovano Michele | 5 10 | 11 00 | F | 28 8 66 | Turin | | Asti | 24 | 5 |
| | | | | | | | Cosenza | 103 | 25 |
| | | | | | | | Pisa | 30 | 11 |
| | | | | | | | Napoli | 27 | 7 |
| | | | | | | | Genoa | 27 | 9 |
| | | | | | | | Reggiana | 29 | 10 |
| | | | | | | | Genoa | 2 | — |
| | | | | | | | Reggiana | 19 | 7 |
| | | | | | | | Juventus | 42 | 12 |
| | | | | | | | Crystal Palace | 10 | 1 |
| Pitcher Darren‡ | 5 9 | 12 02 | M | 12 10 69 | London | Trainee | Charlton Ath | 173 | 8 |
| | | | | | | | Crystal Palace | 64 | — |
| | | | | | | | Leyton Orient (loan) | 1 | — |
| Quinn Robert | 5 11 | 11 02 | D | 8 11 76 | Sidcup | Trainee | Crystal Palace | 23 | 1 |
| Rodger Simon | 5 9 | 11 09 | M | 3 10 71 | Shoreham | Trainee | Crystal Palace | 155 | 7 |
| | | | | | | | Manchester C (loan) | 8 | 1 |
| | | | | | | | Stoke C (loan) | 5 | — |
| Shipperley Neil | 6 1 | 13 11 | F | 30 10 74 | Chatham | Trainee | Chelsea | 37 | 7 |
| | | | | | | | Watford (loan) | 6 | 1 |
| | | | | | | | Southampton | 66 | 12 |
| | | | | | | | Crystal Palace | 58 | 19 |
| Smith Jamie | 5 8 | 11 02 | D | 17 9 74 | Birmingham | Trainee | Wolverhampton W | 87 | — |
| | | | | | | | Crystal Palace | 18 | — |
| Stevens David* | 5 10 | 11 04 | F | 29 4 79 | Ashford | Trainee | Crystal Palace | — | — |
| Thomson Steve* | 5 8 | 10 04 | M | 23 1 78 | Glasgow | Trainee | Crystal Palace | — | — |
| Tuttle David | 6 2 | 12 10 | D | 6 2 72 | Reading | Trainee | Tottenham H | 13 | — |
| | | | | | | | Peterborough U (loan) | 7 | — |
| | | | | | | | Sheffield U | 63 | 1 |
| | | | | | | | Crystal Palace | 58 | 3 |
| Warhurst Paul | 6 1 | 13 08 | D | 26 6 69 | Stockport | Trainee | Manchester C | — | — |
| | | | | | | | Oldham Ath | 67 | 2 |
| | | | | | | | Sheffield W | 66 | 6 |
| | | | | | | | Blackburn R | 57 | 4 |
| | | | | | | | Crystal Palace | 22 | 3 |
| Woozley David | 6 0 | 12 10 | D | 6 12 79 | Berkshire | Trainee | Crystal Palace | — | — |
| Wordsworth Dean‡ | 6 2 | 13 00 | F | 2 7 72 | London | Bromley | Crystal Palace | — | — |
| Zohar Itzhak | 6 1 | 12 08 | M | 31 10 70 | Tel Aviv | Antwerp | Crystal Palace | 6 | — |

*(Transferred to Maccabi Haifa, January 1998)*

**Trainees**
Bibby, Matthew; Boardman, Jonathan G; Dsane, Roscoe; Evans, Stephen J; Fowler, Michael; Hankin, Sean A; Harney, Michael; Hunt, Stephen; Kabba, Steven; Loughran, Kieran; Sears, Paul; Wilde, Bobby.

**Associated Schoolboys**
Allen-Page, Danny L; Awbery, Jason; Blackman, Lloyd J; Coles, Ricky A; Dimond, Kristian; Elsegood, Christopher J; Fieldwick, Lee P; Garlick, Malcolm L; Hibburt, Matthew D; Hunt, David; Phelps, Craig C; Smith, Robert; Stratton, Robert K; Surey, Ben; Warren, Neil P.

**Associated Schoolboys who have accepted the club's offer of a Traineeship/Contract**
Gooding, Scott; Lock, Christopher; Tabb, Jay A.

# DARLINGTON

| Atkinson Brian | 5 10 | 12 10 | M | 19 1 71 | Darlington | Trainee | Sunderland | 141 | 4 |
| | | | | | | | Carlisle U (loan) | 2 | — |
| | | | | | | | Darlington | 62 | 4 |
| Barnard Mark | 5 11 | 11 10 | D | 27 11 75 | Sheffield | Trainee | Rotherham U | — | — |
| | | | | | | | Darlington | 110 | 3 |
| Brumwell Phil | 5 8 | 11 00 | M | 8 8 75 | Darlington | Trainee | Sunderland | — | — |
| | | | | | | | Darlington | 101 | 1 |
| Brydon Lee* | 5 11 | 13 00 | D | 15 11 74 | Stockton | Trainee | Liverpool | — | — |
| | | | | | | | Darlington | 40 | — |
| Campbell Paul§ | 6 1 | 11 00 | M | 29 1 80 | Middlesbrough | Trainee | Darlington | 6 | 1 |
| Crosby Andy* | 6 2 | 13 06 | D | 3 3 73 | Rotherham | Leeds U | Doncaster R | 51 | — |
| | | | | | | | Darlington | 181 | 3 |
| Devos Jason | 6 4 | 13 07 | D | 2 1 74 | Ontario | Montreal Impact | Darlington | 32 | 3 |

|  | | | | | | | | | |
|---|---|---|---|---|---|---|---|---|---|
| **Dorner** Mario | 5 10 | 13 02 | F | 21 3 70 | Baden | Modling | Motherwell | 2 | — |
| | | | | | | | Darlington | 27 | 10 |
| **Ellison** Lee# | 5 11 | 12 06 | F | 13 1 73 | Darlington | Trainee | Darlington | 72 | 17 |
| | | | | | | | Hartlepool U (loan) | 4 | 1 |
| | | | | | | | Leicester C | — | — |
| | | | | | | | Crewe Alex | 4 | 2 |
| | | | | | | | Hereford U | 1 | — |
| | | | | | | | Mansfield T | — | — |
| | | | | | | Bishop Auckland | Darlington | 8 | 3 |
| **Gaughan** Steve | 5 11 | 11 04 | M | 14 4 70 | Doncaster | Hatfield Main | Doncaster R | 67 | 3 |
| | | | | | | | Sunderland | — | — |
| | | | | | | | Darlington | 171 | 15 |
| | | | | | | | Chesterfield | 20 | — |
| | | | | | | | Darlington | 24 | 1 |
| **Guimarra** Willy‡ | | | | 26 8 71 | Ontario | Montreal Impact | Darlington | 4 | — |
| **Hilton** David‡ | 5 11 | 10 10 | D | 10 11 77 | Barnsley | Trainee | Manchester U | — | — |
| | | | | | | | Darlington | 1 | — |
| **Hope** Richard | 6 2 | 12 06 | D | 28 8 78 | Stockton | Trainee | Blackburn R | — | — |
| | | | | | | | Darlington | 55 | 1 |
| **Hunt** David§ | | | D | 5 3 80 | Durham | Trainee | Darlington | 1 | — |
| **Lowe** Kenny‡ | 6 1 | 11 13 | M | 6 11 64 | Sedgefield | Apprentice | Hartlepool U | 54 | 3 |
| | | | | | | Barrow | Scarborough | 4 | — |
| | | | | | | Barrow | Barnet | 72 | 5 |
| | | | | | | | Stoke C | 9 | — |
| | | | | | | | Birmingham C | 21 | 3 |
| | | | | | | | Carlisle U (loan) | 2 | — |
| | | | | | | | Hartlepool U (loan) | 13 | 3 |
| | | | | | | | Darlington | 14 | — |
| **Naylor** Glenn# | 5 10 | 11 10 | F | 11 8 72 | York | Trainee | York C | 111 | 30 |
| | | | | | | | Darlington (loan) | 4 | 1 |
| | | | | | | | Darlington | 79 | 19 |
| **Oliver** Michael | 5 10 | 11 04 | M | 2 8 75 | Middlesbrough | Trainee | Middlesbrough | — | — |
| | | | | | | | Stockport Co | 22 | 1 |
| | | | | | | | Darlington | 78 | 11 |
| **Papaconstantinou**‡ Loukas | 6 4 | 14 00 | G | 10 5 74 | Toronto | Alabama Saints | Darlington | 1 | — |
| **Preece** David | 6 2 | 11 11 | G | 26 8 76 | Sunderland | Trainee | Sunderland | — | — |
| | | | | | | | Darlington | 45 | — |
| **Resch** Franz* | 6 0 | 12 00 | M | 4 5 69 | Vienna | Modling | Motherwell | 3 | — |
| | | | | | | | Darlington | 17 | 1 |
| **Roberts** Darren | 6 0 | 12 04 | F | 12 10 69 | Birmingham | Burton Alb | Wolverhampton W | 21 | 5 |
| | | | | | | | Hereford U (loan) | 6 | 5 |
| | | | | | | | Doncaster R | — | — |
| | | | | | | | Chesterfield | 25 | 1 |
| | | | | | | | Darlington | 72 | 28 |
| | | | | | | | Peterborough U (loan) | 3 | — |
| **Shaw** Simon* | 6 0 | 12 00 | M | 21 9 73 | Middlesbrough | Trainee | Darlington | 176 | 12 |
| **Shutt** Carl | 5 10 | 12 10 | F | 10 10 61 | Sheffield | Spalding U | Sheffield W | 40 | 16 |
| | | | | | | | Bristol C | 46 | 10 |
| | | | | | | | Leeds U | 79 | 17 |
| | | | | | | | Birmingham C | 26 | 4 |
| | | | | | | | Manchester C (loan) | 6 | — |
| | | | | | | | Bradford C | 88 | 15 |
| | | | | | | | Darlington | 39 | 7 |
| **Stephenson** Ashlyn | 6 2 | 11 05 | G | 6 7 74 | Manchester | | Birmingham C | — | — |
| | | | | | | | Darlington | 1 | — |
| **Tarrant** Neil‡ | 6 0 | 12 00 | M | 24 6 79 | Darlington | Trainee | Darlington | — | — |
| **Turnbull** Lee* | 6 0 | 13 04 | D | 27 9 67 | Stockton | Local | Middlesbrough | 16 | 4 |
| | | | | | | | Aston Villa | — | — |
| | | | | | | | Doncaster R | 123 | 21 |
| | | | | | | | Chesterfield | 87 | 26 |
| | | | | | | | Doncaster R | 11 | 1 |
| | | | | | | | Wycombe W | 11 | 1 |
| | | | | | | | Scunthorpe U (loan) | 10 | 3 |
| | | | | | | | Scunthorpe U | 37 | 4 |
| | | | | | | | Darlington | 9 | — |
| **Tutill** Steve | 5 10 | 12 06 | D | 1 10 69 | Derwent | Trainee | York C | 301 | 6 |
| | | | | | | | Darlington | 7 | — |

**Trainees**
Campbell, Paul A; Carter, Michael D; Christie, David; Hunt, David; Keegan, Justin; Kilty, Mark T; Pepper, Carl; Pomford, Paul J; Skelton, Craig E; Smith, Martin; Stokoe, Dennis M; Wells, David J.

**Non-Contract**
Hodgson, David J.

**Associated Schoolboys**
Ellenden, John; Foster, Stephen M; Gillan, Terry L; Gordon, Steven M; Reay, Andrew D; Stonehouse, John P; Thompson, Gavin L; Windrass, Andrew J.

**Associated Schoolboys who have accepted the club's offer of a Traineeship/Contract**
Bowes, Michael G; Finch, Keith J; Jackson, Neil P; Liddle, Graham B; Scroggins, Lee P; Williamson, Garry.

# DERBY COUNTY

| Player | Ht | Wt | Pos | Born | Birthplace | Source | Club | Apps | Gls |
|---|---|---|---|---|---|---|---|---|---|
| **Asanovic** Aljosa | 6 1 | 11 12 | M | 14 12 65 | Split | | Hajduk Split | 116 | 28 |
| *(Transferred to Napoli, January 1998)* | | | | | | | Metz | 35 | 13 |
| | | | | | | | Cannes | 28 | 7 |
| | | | | | | | Montpellier | 43 | 10 |
| | | | | | | | Hajduk Split | 33 | 8 |
| | | | | | | | Derby Co | 38 | 7 |
| **Baiano** Francesco | 5 6 | 10 07 | F | 24 2 68 | Naples | | Napoli | 4 | — |
| | | | | | | | Empoli | 26 | 2 |
| | | | | | | | Napoli | 1 | — |
| | | | | | | | Parma | 25 | 4 |
| | | | | | | | Empoli | 38 | 14 |
| | | | | | | | Avellino | 32 | 6 |
| | | | | | | | Foggia | 69 | 38 |
| | | | | | | | Fiorentina | 118 | 29 |
| | | | | | | | Derby Co | 33 | 12 |
| **Boden** Chris‡ | 5 9 | 11 12 | D | 13 10 73 | Wolverhampton | Trainee | Aston Villa | 1 | — |
| | | | | | | | Barnsley (loan) | 4 | — |
| | | | | | | | Derby Co | 10 | — |
| | | | | | | | Shrewsbury T (loan) | 5 | — |
| **Bohinen** Lars | 6 1 | 13 00 | M | 8 9 69 | Vadso | | Valerengen | 33 | 5 |
| | | | | | | | Viking | 10 | — |
| | | | | | | | Young Boys | 58 | 6 |
| | | | | | | | Nottingham F | 64 | 7 |
| | | | | | | | Blackburn R | 58 | 7 |
| | | | | | | | Derby Co | 9 | 1 |
| **Burton** Deon | 5 9 | 11 10 | F | 25 10 76 | Reading | Trainee | Portsmouth | 62 | 10 |
| | | | | | | | Cardiff C (loan) | 5 | 2 |
| | | | | | | | Derby Co | 29 | 3 |
| **Carsley** Lee | 5 9 | 12 00 | D | 28 2 74 | Birmingham | Trainee | Derby Co | 116 | 4 |
| **Dailly** Christian | 6 0 | 12 05 | D | 23 10 73 | Dundee | | Dundee U | 141 | 18 |
| | | | | | | | Derby Co | 66 | 4 |
| **Delap** Rory | 6 0 | 13 00 | M | 6 7 76 | Sutton Coldfield | Trainee | Carlisle U | 65 | 7 |
| | | | | | | | Derby Co | 13 | — |
| **Elliott** Steve | 6 1 | 13 12 | D | 29 10 78 | Swadlincote | Trainee | Derby Co | 3 | — |
| **Eranio** Stefano | 5 10 | 12 00 | M | 29 12 68 | Genoa | | Genoa | 213 | 13 |
| | | | | | | | AC Milan | 98 | 6 |
| | | | | | | | Derby Co | 23 | 5 |
| **Hoult** Russell | 6 4 | 14 07 | G | 22 11 72 | Ashby | Trainee | Leicester C | 10 | — |
| | | | | | | | Lincoln C (loan) | 2 | — |
| | | | | | | | Blackpool (loan) | — | — |
| | | | | | | | Bolton W (loan) | 4 | — |
| | | | | | | | Lincoln C (loan) | 15 | — |
| | | | | | | | Derby Co (loan) | 15 | — |
| | | | | | | | Derby Co | 75 | — |
| **Hunt** Jonathan | 5 10 | 11 13 | F | 2 11 71 | London | Slough T | Barnet | 33 | — |
| | | | | | | | Southend U | 49 | 6 |
| | | | | | | | Birmingham C | 77 | 18 |
| | | | | | | | Derby Co | 19 | 1 |
| **Knight** Richard | 6 1 | 14 00 | G | 3 8 79 | Burton | Burton Alb | Derby Co | — | — |
| **Kozluk** Robert | 5 7 | 10 12 | D | 5 8 77 | Sutton-in-Ashfield | Trainee | Derby Co | 9 | — |
| **Laursen** Jacob | 5 11 | 12 01 | D | 6 10 71 | Vejle | | Silkeborg | 125 | 8 |
| | | | | | | | Derby Co | 64 | 2 |
| **McDonald** Jamie | | | M | 29 1 80 | Luton | Trainee | Derby Co | — | — |
| **Murphy** Leroy | | | M | 26 12 78 | Birmingham | Trainee | Derby Co | — | — |
| **Poom** Mart | 6 5 | 13 05 | G | 3 2 72 | Tallinn | FC Wil<br>Flora Tallinn | Portsmouth | 4 | — |
| | | | | | | | Derby Co | 40 | — |
| **Porter** Daniel | | | M | 23 1 79 | Portsmouth | | Derby Co | — | — |
| **Powell** Chris | 5 10 | 11 07 | D | 8 6 69 | Lambeth | Trainee | Crystal Palace | 3 | — |
| | | | | | | | Aldershot (loan) | 11 | — |
| | | | | | | | Southend U | 248 | 3 |
| | | | | | | | Derby Co | 91 | 1 |
| **Powell** Darryl | 6 0 | 13 00 | M | 15 11 70 | Lambeth | Trainee | Portsmouth | 132 | 16 |
| | | | | | | | Derby Co | 93 | 6 |
| **Radzki** Lee | | | M | 14 11 78 | Mansfield | Trainee | Derby Co | — | — |
| **Rowett** Gary | 6 0 | 12 07 | D | 6 3 74 | Bromsgrove | Trainee | Cambridge U | 63 | 9 |
| | | | | | | | Everton | 4 | — |
| | | | | | | | Blackpool (loan) | 17 | — |
| | | | | | | | Derby Co | 105 | 2 |
| **Smith** Craig‡ | 6 1 | 13 07 | D | 2 8 76 | Mansfield | Trainee | Derby Co | — | — |
| | | | | | | | Rochdale (loan) | 3 | — |
| **Solis** Mauricio | 5 8 | 12 00 | M | 13 12 72 | Costa Rica | Herediano | Derby Co | 11 | — |
| **Stimac** Igor | 6 2 | 13 00 | D | 6 9 67 | Metkovic | Hajduk Split | Cadiz | 62 | 4 |
| | | | | | | | Hajduk Split | 21 | 2 |
| | | | | | | | Derby Co | 70 | 3 |
| **Sturridge** Dean | 5 8 | 12 06 | F | 27 7 73 | Birmingham | Trainee | Derby Co | 122 | 41 |
| | | | | | | | Torquay U (loan) | 10 | 5 |
| **Sutton** Wayne‡ | 6 0 | 13 09 | D | 1 10 75 | Derby | Trainee | Derby Co | 7 | — |
| | | | | | | | Hereford U (loan) | 4 | — |

| Van der Laan Robin | 6 0 | 13 08 | M | 5 9 68 | Schiedam | Wageningen | Port Vale | 176 | 24 |
| | | | | | | | Derby Co | 65 | 8 |
| | | | | | | | Wolverhampton W (loan) | 7 | — |
| Wanchope Paulo | 6 4 | 12 05 | F | 31 7 76 | Costa Rica | Herediano | Derby Co | 37 | 14 |
| Wilkinson Mark | 5 6 | 10 08 | M | 16 3 79 | Nuneaton | Trainee | Derby Co | — | — |
| Willems Ron | 6 1 | 12 05 | F | 20 9 66 | Epe | | PEC Zwolle | 43 | 7 |
| | | | | | | | Twente | 85 | 16 |
| | | | | | | | Ajax | 47 | 15 |
| | | | | | | | Grasshoppers | 56 | 18 |
| | | | | | | | Derby Co | 59 | 13 |
| Yates Dean* | 6 1 | 12 08 | D | 26 10 67 | Leicester | Apprentice | Notts Co | 314 | 33 |
| | | | | | | | Derby Co | 68 | 3 |

**Trainees**
Bate, Christopher T; Betteridge, Thomas D; Greenhill, Ross F; Gummer, Sean M; Hanson, Craig P; Lyons, Michael A; McBride, Liam; Messina, Robert; Morton, Colin; Phillips, Thomas G; Riggott, Christopher M; Thornhill, Wayne; Wall, James.

**Associated Schoolboys**
Adams, Wayne A; Alexander, Earl; Bailey, Richard W; Clare, Robert; Dixon, Christopher; Kellogg, Sam; Kilmartin, Joseph T; Lambert, Jordon K; Stevens, Paul; Turner, James J.

**Associated Schoolboys who have accepted the club's offer of a Traineeship/Contract**
Evatt, Ian R; Murray, Adam D; Rickards, Scott; Robinson, Marvin L S C; Sidhu, Amrit S.

# DONCASTER ROVERS

| Betts Robert§ | 5 10 | 11 00 | M | 21 12 81 | Doncaster | School | Doncaster R | 3 | — |
| Borg John§ | 5 7 | 10 07 | M | 22 2 80 | Salford | Trainee | Doncaster R | 1 | — |
| Brookes Darren | 6 3 | 14 00 | D | 7 7 78 | Sheffield | Worksop T | Doncaster R | 11 | — |
| Conlon Paul‡ | 5 8 | 12 00 | F | 5 1 78 | Sunderland | Trainee | Hartlepool U | 15 | 4 |
| | | | | | | | Sunderland | — | — |
| | | | | | | | Doncaster R | 14 | 1 |
| Cunningham Harvey | 5 9 | 11 05 | D | 11 9 68 | Manchester | Trafford Barons | Doncaster R | 44 | 1 |
| Davis Craig‡ | 6 2 | 12 00 | G | 12 10 77 | Rotherham | Trainee | Rotherham U | — | — |
| | | | | | | | Doncaster R | 15 | — |
| Debenham Rob§ | 5 8 | 10 09 | D | 28 11 79 | Doncaster | Trainee | Doncaster R | 6 | — |
| Dixon Kerry‡ | 6 1 | 13 10 | F | 24 7 61 | Luton | Dunstable | Reading | 116 | 51 |
| | | | | | | | Chelsea | 335 | 147 |
| | | | | | | | Southampton | 9 | 2 |
| | | | | | | | Luton T (loan) | 17 | 3 |
| | | | | | | | Luton T | 58 | 16 |
| | | | | | | | Millwall | 31 | 9 |
| | | | | | | | Watford | 11 | — |
| | | | | | | | Doncaster R | 16 | 3 |
| Donnelly Mark§ | 6 0 | 11 02 | M | 22 12 79 | Leeds | Trainee | Doncaster R | 11 | 1 |
| Dowell Wayne‡ | 5 10 | 11 13 | D | 28 12 73 | Co Durham | Trainee | Burnley | 6 | — |
| | | | | | | | Carlisle U (loan) | 7 | — |
| | | | | | | | Rochdale | 7 | — |
| | | | | | | | Doncaster R | 1 | — |
| Edwards Paul‡ | 5 10 | 11 08 | D | 1 1 80 | Manchester | Ashton U | Doncaster R | 9 | — |
| Esdaille Darren‡ | 5 8 | 10 07 | D | 4 11 74 | Manchester | Hyde U | Doncaster R | 40 | 1 |
| Esdaille David‡ | 5 9 | 12 01 | M | 22 7 63 | Manchester | Droylsden | Doncaster R | 13 | — |
| Finley Gary‡ | 6 0 | 12 12 | D | 14 11 70 | Liverpool | Netherfield | Doncaster R | 7 | — |
| George Danny | 6 1 | 12 01 | D | 22 10 78 | Lincoln | Trainee | Nottingham F | — | — |
| | | | | | | | Doncaster R | 18 | 1 |
| Gore Ian‡ | 6 0 | 12 07 | D | 10 1 68 | Liverpool | | Birmingham C | — | — |
| | | | | | | Southport | Blackpool | 200 | — |
| | | | | | | | Torquay U | 25 | 2 |
| | | | | | | | Doncaster R | 66 | 1 |
| Hammond Andy‡ | 6 0 | 12 00 | F | 21 11 78 | Rotherham | Trainee | Doncaster R | 1 | — |
| Hawthorne Mark* | 6 0 | 12 10 | D | 21 8 79 | Sunderland | Trainee | Doncaster R | 8 | — |
| Hilton Maurice‡ | 5 11 | 11 10 | D | 14 3 79 | Sunderland | Trainee | Doncaster R | 10 | — |
| Hoggeth Gary§ | 6 1 | 12 07 | G | 7 10 79 | South Shields | Trainee | Doncaster R | 8 | — |
| Ingham Gary‡ | 6 1 | 12 10 | G | 9 10 64 | Rotherham | Rotherham U | Doncaster R | 11 | — |
| Ireland Simon‡ | 5 10 | 11 10 | M | 23 11 71 | Halifax | School | Huddersfield T | 19 | — |
| | | | | | | | Wrexham (loan) | 5 | — |
| | | | | | | | Blackburn R | 1 | — |
| | | | | | | | Mansfield T (loan) | 9 | 1 |
| | | | | | | | Mansfield T | 85 | 10 |
| | | | | | | | Doncaster R | 61 | 2 |
| Messer Gary‡ | 6 1 | 13 00 | F | 22 9 79 | Consett | Trainee | Doncaster R | 14 | 1 |

| Name | Ht | Wt | Pos | Born | Birthplace | From | Club | Apps | Gls |
|---|---|---|---|---|---|---|---|---|---|
| **Mike** Adie‡ | 6 0 | 12 10 | F | 16 11 73 | Manchester | Trainee | Manchester C | 16 | 2 |
| | | | | | | | Bury (loan) | 7 | 1 |
| | | | | | | | Stockport Co | 9 | — |
| | | | | | | | Hartlepool U (loan) | 7 | 1 |
| | | | | | | | Doncaster R (loan) | 5 | 1 |
| | | | | | | | Doncaster R | 42 | 4 |
| **Moncrieffe** Prince | 5 9 | 11 00 | F | 27 2 77 | Manchester | Hyde U | Doncaster R | 38 | 8 |
| **Ohandjianian** Dmis‡ | | | F | 1 5 78 | Manchester | Curzon Ashton | Doncaster R | 1 | — |
| **Ramsay** John‡ | 5 8 | 9 10 | M | 25 1 79 | Sunderland | Trainee | Doncaster R | 10 | — |
| **Smith** David‡ | 6 0 | 14 07 | G | 2 5 73 | Stockport | Bramhall | Doncaster R | 1 | — |
| **Smith** Mike* | 5 9 | 11 01 | F | 28 9 73 | Liverpool | Runcorn | Doncaster R | 50 | 5 |
| **Tedaldi** Dino‡ | 5 11 | 11 10 | F | 12 8 80 | Aberystwyth | Trainee | Doncaster R | 2 | 1 |
| **Thornley** Rob‡ | 5 9 | 11 05 | F | 2 8 77 | Bury | Warrington T | Doncaster R | 1 | — |
| **Thorpe** Andy‡ | 5 11 | 12 02 | D | 15 9 60 | Stockport | Amateur | Stockport Co | 314 | 3 |
| | | | | | | | Tranmere R | 53 | — |
| | | | | | | | Stockport Co | 175 | — |
| | | | | | Chorley | | Doncaster R | 2 | — |
| **Utley** Darren‡ | 6 1 | 12 11 | D | 28 9 77 | Barnsley | Trainee | Doncaster R | 28 | 1 |
| **Warren** Lee | 6 1 | 12 11 | M | 28 2 69 | Manchester | Trainee | Leeds U | — | — |
| | | | | | | | Rochdale | 31 | 1 |
| | | | | | | | Hull C | 153 | 1 |
| | | | | | | | Lincoln C (loan) | 3 | 1 |
| | | | | | | | Doncaster R | 125 | 3 |
| **Williams** Dean‡ | 6 0 | 12 07 | G | 5 1 72 | Lichfield | Tamworth | Brentford | 7 | — |
| | | | | | | | Doncaster R | 85 | — |
| | | | | | | | Huddersfield T (loan) | — | — |
| **Wilson** Padi‡ | 5 8 | 10 10 | M | 9 11 71 | Manchester | Ashton U | Plymouth Arg | 11 | 1 |
| | | | | | | | Doncaster R | 10 | 1 |

**Trainees**
Borg, John C A; Combellack, Brian; Crosby, Marc H R; Debenham, Robert K; Donnelly, Mark P; Hoggeth, Gary D; McDonald, Anthony; Powell, Richard J; Reeve, David T; Wild, Robert F.

**Associated Schoolboy**
Betts, Robert.

# EVERTON

| Name | Ht | Wt | Pos | Born | Birthplace | From | Club | Apps | Gls |
|---|---|---|---|---|---|---|---|---|---|
| **Allen** Graham | 6 1 | 12 00 | D | 8 4 77 | Bolton | Trainee | Everton | 6 | — |
| **Ball** Michael | | | M | 2 10 79 | Liverpool | Trainee | Everton | 30 | 1 |
| **Barmby** Nick | 5 6 | 11 00 | F | 11 2 74 | Hull | Trainee | Tottenham H | 87 | 20 |
| | | | | | | | Middlesbrough | 42 | 8 |
| | | | | | | | Everton | 55 | 6 |
| **Bilic** Slaven | 6 2 | 13 02 | D | 11 9 68 | Split | | Hajduk Split | 109 | 13 |
| | | | | | | | Karlsruhe | 54 | 5 |
| | | | | | | | West Ham U | 48 | 2 |
| | | | | | | | Everton | 24 | — |
| **Branch** Michael | 5 10 | 11 00 | F | 18 10 78 | Liverpool | Trainee | Everton | 34 | 3 |
| **Cadamarteri** Danny | | | F | 12 10 79 | Bradford | Trainee | Everton | 27 | 4 |
| **Delany** Dean | | | G | 15 9 80 | Dublin | | Everton | — | — |
| **Dempsey** Gary | | | M | 15 1 81 | Wexford | Trainee | Everton | — | — |
| **Drew** Padraig* | | | F | 7 6 80 | Dublin | Trainee | Everton | — | — |
| **Dunne** Richard | 6 0 | 13 00 | D | 21 9 79 | Dublin | Trainee | Everton | 10 | — |
| **Eaton** Adam | | | D | 2 5 80 | Wigan | Trainee | Everton | — | — |
| **Farley** Adam | | | D | 12 1 80 | Liverpool | Trainee | Everton | — | — |
| **Farrelly** Gareth | 6 0 | 12 13 | M | 28 8 75 | Dublin | Home Farm | Aston Villa | 8 | — |
| | | | | | | | Rotherham U (loan) | 10 | 2 |
| | | | | | | | Everton | 26 | 1 |
| **Ferguson** Duncan | 6 4 | 14 06 | F | 27 12 71 | Stirling | Carse T | Dundee U | 77 | 28 |
| | | | | | | | Rangers | 14 | 2 |
| | | | | | | | Everton | 103 | 33 |
| **Gerrard** Paul | 6 2 | 13 01 | G | 22 1 73 | Heywood | Trainee | Oldham Ath | 119 | 1 |
| | | | | | | | Everton | 9 | — |
| **Grant** Tony | 5 10 | 10 02 | M | 14 11 74 | Liverpool | Trainee | Everton | 43 | 2 |
| | | | | | | | Swindon T (loan) | 3 | 1 |
| **Hutchison** Don | 6 1 | 11 11 | M | 9 5 71 | Gateshead | Trainee | Hartlepool U | 24 | 2 |
| | | | | | | | Liverpool | 45 | 7 |
| | | | | | | | West Ham U | 35 | 11 |
| | | | | | | | Sheffield U | 78 | 5 |
| | | | | | | | Everton | 11 | 1 |
| **Jeffers** Francis | | | F | 25 1 81 | Merseyside | Trainee | Everton | 1 | — |
| **Jevons** Phillip | | | M | 1 8 79 | Liverpool | Trainee | Everton | — | — |
| **Lane** Christopher* | | | D | 24 5 79 | Liverpool | Trainee | Everton | — | — |

| Name | | | Pos | DOB | Birthplace | Source | Club | Apps | Goals |
|------|---|---|-----|-----|-----------|--------|------|------|-------|
| **Madar** Mikael | 6 1 | 12 06 | F | 8 5 68 | Paris | | Sochaux | 46 | 6 |
| | | | | | | | Cannes | 54 | 26 |
| | | | | | | | Monaco | 52 | 14 |
| | | | | | | | La Coruna | 24 | 4 |
| | | | | | | | Everton | 17 | 6 |
| **McAlpine** Joseph† | | | D | 12 9 81 | Glasgow | | Everton | — | — |
| **McCann** Gavin | 5 11 | 11 00 | M | 10 1 78 | Blackpool | Trainee | Everton | 11 | — |
| **McKay** Matthew | | | M | 21 1 81 | Warrington | Trainee | Chester C | 5 | — |
| | | | | | | | Everton | — | — |
| **Milligan** Jamie | | | F | 3 1 80 | Blackpool | Trainee | Everton | — | — |
| **Myhre** Thomas | | | G | 16 10 73 | Sarpsborg | | Viking | 94 | — |
| | | | | | | | Everton | 22 | — |
| **O'Brien** Michael | | | M | 25 9 79 | Liverpool | Trainee | Everton | — | — |
| **O'Kane** John | 5 10 | 12 04 | D | 15 11 74 | Nottingham | Trainee | Manchester U | 2 | — |
| | | | | | | | Wimbledon (loan) | — | — |
| | | | | | | | Bury (loan) | 13 | 3 |
| | | | | | | | Bradford C (loan) | 7 | — |
| | | | | | | | Everton | 12 | — |
| **O'Toole** John* | | | G | 23 2 79 | Merseyside | Trainee | Everton | — | — |
| **Oster** John | 5 8 | 10 08 | F | 8 12 78 | Boston | Trainee | Grimsby T | 24 | 3 |
| | | | | | | | Everton | 31 | 1 |
| **Parkinson** Joe | 5 8 | 12 02 | M | 11 6 71 | Eccles | Trainee | Wigan Ath | 119 | 6 |
| | | | | | | | Bournemouth | 30 | 1 |
| | | | | | | | Everton | 90 | 3 |
| **Phelan** Terry | 5 8 | 10 00 | D | 16 3 67 | Manchester | Trainee | Leeds U | 14 | — |
| | | | | | | | Swansea C | 45 | — |
| | | | | | | | Wimbledon | 159 | 1 |
| | | | | | | | Manchester C | 103 | 1 |
| | | | | | | | Chelsea | 15 | — |
| | | | | | | | Everton | 24 | — |
| **Poppleton** David | | | M | 19 12 79 | Doncaster | Trainee | Everton | — | — |
| **Quayle** Mark‡ | 5 9 | 10 02 | F | 2 10 78 | Liverpool | Trainee | Everton | — | — |
| **Regan** Carl | | | D | 9 9 80 | Liverpool | Trainee | Everton | — | — |
| **Short** Craig | 6 0 | 11 04 | D | 25 6 68 | Bridlington | Pickering T | Scarborough | 63 | 7 |
| | | | | | | | Notts Co | 128 | 6 |
| | | | | | | | Derby Co | 118 | 9 |
| | | | | | | | Everton | 77 | 4 |
| **Spencer** John | 5 7 | 11 05 | F | 11 9 70 | Glasgow | Rangers BC | Rangers | 13 | 2 |
| | | | | | | | Morton (loan) | 4 | 1 |
| | | | | | | | Chelsea | 103 | 36 |
| | | | | | | | QPR | 48 | 22 |
| | | | | | | | Everton | 6 | — |
| **Thomas** Tony | 5 11 | 12 05 | D | 12 7 71 | Liverpool | Trainee | Tranmere R | 257 | 12 |
| | | | | | | | Everton | 7 | — |
| **Thomsen** Claus‡ | 6 3 | 11 06 | M | 31 5 70 | Aarhus | Aarhus | Ipswich T | 81 | 7 |
| | | | | | | | Everton | 24 | 1 |
| **Tiler** Carl | 6 2 | 13 10 | D | 11 2 70 | Sheffield | Trainee | Barnsley | 71 | 3 |
| | | | | | | | Nottingham F | 69 | 1 |
| | | | | | | | Swindon T (loan) | 2 | — |
| | | | | | | | Aston Villa | 12 | 1 |
| | | | | | | | Sheffield U | 23 | 2 |
| | | | | | | | Everton | 19 | 1 |
| **Ward** Mitch | 5 9 | 11 07 | M | 19 6 71 | Sheffield | Trainee | Sheffield U | 154 | 11 |
| | | | | | | | Crewe Alex (loan) | 4 | 1 |
| | | | | | | | Everton | 8 | — |
| **Watson** Dave | 5 11 | 11 12 | D | 20 11 61 | Liverpool | Amateur | Liverpool | — | — |
| | | | | | | | Norwich C | 212 | 11 |
| | | | | | | | Everton | 395 | 23 |
| **Williamson** Danny | 5 10 | 11 06 | M | 5 12 73 | West Ham | Trainee | West Ham U | 51 | 5 |
| | | | | | | | Doncaster R (loan) | 13 | 1 |
| | | | | | | | Everton | 15 | — |

**Trainees**
Hibbert, Anthony J; Holmes, Neil; Howarth, Carl J; Knowles, David J; Logan, Damian G; McDermott, Wayne; McLeod, Kevin A; O'Brien, Edward; Osman, Leon; Southern, Keith W; Williams, David P; Wright, John G.

**Non-Contract**
McAlpine, Joseph C.

**Associated Schoolboys**
Borrows, Matthew; Burgess, Benjamin K; Chadwick, Nicholas G; Clitheroe, Peter C; Doforo, Liam; Evans, Richard G; Hussey, Stephen J; Machin, Jonathan P; McDonald, Colin G; McGuire, Liam J; Miles, Robin; O'Hanlon, Sean P; Pike, James A; Ralph, Andrew O; Stapleton-Smith, Matthew K; Symes, Michael; Willetts, Benjamin S; Williams, Christopher.

**Associated Schoolboys who have accepted the club's offer of a Traineeship/Contract**
Clarke, Peter M; Curran, Damien M; Hogg, Craig A; Kearney, Thomas J; Pilkington, George E; Price, Michael D; Tuft, Dean K; Valentine, Ryan D; Woodstock, Colin.

## EXETER CITY

| Player | Ht | DOB | Pos | Birthplace | Source | Club | Apps | Gls |
|---|---|---|---|---|---|---|---|---|
| **Baddeley** Lee | 6 1 | 12 07 | D | 2 7 74 | Cardiff | Trainee | Cardiff C | 133 | 1 |
| | | | | | | | Exeter C | 43 | 1 |
| **Bailey** Danny‡ | 5 8 | 12 11 | M | 21 5 64 | Leyton | Apprentice | Bournemouth | 2 | — |
| | | | | | | Dagenham | Torquay U | 1 | — |
| | | | | | | Wealdstone | Exeter C | 64 | 2 |
| | | | | | | | Reading | 50 | 2 |
| | | | | | | | Fulham (loan) | 3 | — |
| | | | | | | | Exeter C | 152 | 4 |
| **Bayes** Ashley# | 6 1 | 13 05 | G | 19 4 72 | Lincoln | Trainee | Brentford | 4 | — |
| | | | | | | | Torquay U | 97 | — |
| | | | | | | | Exeter C | 86 | — |
| **Birch** Paul | 5 6 | 10 04 | M | 20 11 62 | West Bromwich | Apprentice | Aston Villa | 173 | 16 |
| | | | | | | | Wolverhampton W | 142 | 15 |
| | | | | | | | Preston NE (loan) | 11 | 2 |
| | | | | | | | Doncaster R | 27 | 2 |
| | | | | | | | Exeter C | 35 | 5 |
| **Blake** Noel | 6 2 | 14 02 | D | 12 1 62 | Jamaica | Sutton Coldfield T | Aston Villa | 4 | — |
| | | | | | | | Shrewsbury T (loan) | 6 | — |
| | | | | | | | Birmingham C | 76 | 5 |
| | | | | | | | Portsmouth | 144 | 10 |
| | | | | | | | Leeds U | 51 | 4 |
| | | | | | | | Stoke C | 75 | 3 |
| | | | | | | | Bradford C (loan) | 6 | — |
| | | | | | | | Bradford C | 39 | 3 |
| | | | | | | | Dundee | 54 | 2 |
| | | | | | | | Exeter C | 128 | 9 |
| **Braithwaite** Leon‡ | 6 0 | 12 00 | F | 17 12 72 | Hackney | Bishops Stortford | Exeter C | 66 | 9 |
| **Breslan** Geoff§ | | | F | 4 6 80 | Torbay | Trainee | Exeter C | 1 | — |
| **Clark** Billy | 6 0 | 12 03 | D | 19 5 67 | Christchurch | Trainee | Bournemouth | 4 | — |
| | | | | | | | Bristol R | 248 | 14 |
| | | | | | | | Exeter C | 31 | 3 |
| **Curran** Chris | 5 11 | 11 09 | D | 17 9 71 | Birmingham | Trainee | Torquay U | 152 | 4 |
| | | | | | | | Plymouth Arg | 30 | — |
| | | | | | | | Exeter C | 9 | — |
| **Cyrus** Andy* | 5 8 | 9 03 | D | 30 9 76 | Lambeth | Trainee | Crystal Palace | 1 | — |
| | | | | | | | Exeter C | 21 | — |
| **Devlin** Mark* | 5 10 | 11 13 | M | 8 1 73 | Irvine | Trainee | Stoke C | 55 | 2 |
| | | | | | | | Exeter C | 33 | 2 |
| **Dungey** James‡ | 5 9 | 11 08 | G | 7 2 78 | Plymouth | Trainee | Plymouth Arg | 10 | — |
| | | | | | | | Exeter C | 1 | — |
| **Flack** Steve | 6 1 | 11 04 | F | 29 5 71 | Cambridge | Cambridge C | Cardiff C | 11 | 1 |
| | | | | | | | Exeter C | 68 | 18 |
| **Fox** Peter# | 5 11 | 13 10 | G | 5 7 57 | Scunthorpe | Apprentice | Sheffield W | 49 | — |
| | | | | | | | West Ham U (loan) | — | — |
| | | | | | | | Barnsley (loan) | 1 | — |
| | | | | | | | Stoke C | 409 | — |
| | | | | | | | Wrexham (loan) | — | — |
| | | | | | | | Exeter C | 108 | — |
| **Fry** Chris | 5 10 | 10 07 | F | 23 10 69 | Cardiff | Trainee | Cardiff C | 55 | 1 |
| | | | | | | | Hereford U | 90 | 10 |
| | | | | | | | Colchester U | 130 | 16 |
| | | | | | | | Exeter C | 28 | 1 |
| **Gale** Shaun | 6 1 | 12 02 | D | 8 10 69 | Reading | Trainee | Portsmouth | 3 | — |
| | | | | | | | Barnet | 114 | 5 |
| | | | | | | | Exeter C | 43 | 4 |
| **Gardner** Jimmy | 5 11 | 11 08 | F | 27 9 67 | Dunfermline | Ayresome North | Queen's Park | 2 | — |
| | | | | | | | Motherwell | 16 | — |
| | | | | | | | St Mirren | 41 | 1 |
| | | | | | | | Scarborough | 6 | 1 |
| | | | | | | | Cardiff C | 63 | 5 |
| | | | | | | | Exeter C | 23 | 1 |
| **Ghazghazi** Sufyan* | 5 7 | 11 00 | F | 24 8 77 | Honiton | Trainee | Exeter C | 15 | — |
| **Hare** Matthew* | 6 2 | 13 00 | D | 26 12 76 | Barnstaple | Trainee | Exeter C | 45 | 1 |
| **Holloway** Christopher§ | | | M | 5 2 80 | Swansea | Trainee | Exeter C | 6 | — |
| **Hughes** Darren‡ | 5 11 | 13 01 | D | 6 10 65 | Prescot | Apprentice | Everton | 3 | — |
| | | | | | | | Shrewsbury T | 37 | 1 |
| | | | | | | | Brighton & HA | 26 | 2 |
| | | | | | | | Port Vale | 184 | 4 |
| | | | | | | | Northampton T | 21 | — |
| | | | | | | | Exeter C | 62 | 1 |
| **Illman** Neil‡ | 5 7 | 10 07 | F | 29 9 75 | Doncaster | Trainee | Middlesbrough | 1 | — |
| | | | | | | Eastwood T | Plymouth Arg | 31 | 4 |
| | | | | | | | Cambridge U (loan) | 5 | — |
| | | | | | | | Exeter C | 8 | 2 |
| **McConnell** Barry | 5 11 | 10 03 | F | 1 1 77 | Exeter | Trainee | Exeter C | 58 | 6 |
| **Medlin** Nicky* | 5 7 | 10 01 | M | 23 11 76 | Camborne | Trainee | Exeter C | 37 | 1 |

| | | | | | | | | | |
|---|---|---|---|---|---|---|---|---|---|
| **Minett** Jason* | 5 9 | 10 04 | M | 12 8 71 | Peterborough | Trainee | Norwich C | 3 | — |
| | | | | | | | Exeter C (loan) | 12 | — |
| | | | | | | | Exeter C | 76 | 3 |
| | | | | | | | Lincoln C | 46 | 5 |
| | | | | | | | Exeter C | 19 | — |
| **Rice** Gary‡ | 5 9 | 11 10 | D | 29 9 75 | Zambia | Trainee | Exeter C | 44 | — |
| **Richardson** Jon | 6 1 | 12 05 | D | 29 8 75 | Nottingham | Trainee | Exeter C | 172 | 5 |
| **Rowbotham** Darren | 5 10 | 12 13 | F | 22 10 66 | Cardiff | Trainee | Plymouth Arg | 46 | 2 |
| | | | | | | | Exeter C | 118 | 47 |
| | | | | | | | Torquay U | 14 | 3 |
| | | | | | | | Birmingham C | 36 | 6 |
| | | | | | | | Hereford U (loan) | 8 | 2 |
| | | | | | | | Mansfield T (loan) | 4 | — |
| | | | | | | | Crewe Alex | 61 | 21 |
| | | | | | | | Shrewsbury T | 40 | 9 |
| | | | | | | | Exeter C | 68 | 29 |
| **Wilkinson** John§ | | | M | 24 8 79 | Exeter | Trainee | Exeter C | 1 | — |
| **Williams** John* | 6 1 | 13 12 | M | 11 5 68 | Birmingham | Cradley T | Swansea C | 39 | 11 |
| | | | | | | | Coventry C | 80 | 11 |
| | | | | | | | Notts Co (loan) | 5 | — |
| | | | | | | | Stoke C (loan) | 4 | — |
| | | | | | | | Swansea C (loan) | 7 | 2 |
| | | | | | | | Wycombe W | 48 | 8 |
| | | | | | | | Hereford U | 11 | 3 |
| | | | | | | | Walsall | 1 | — |
| | | | | | | | Exeter C | 36 | 4 |

**Trainees**
Breslan, Geoffrey F; Chesterfield, Gavin A; Cowan, Gavin P; Harris, Daniel; Hillson, Bradley; Holloway, Christopher D; Rendle, Daniel L; Smith, Peter E; Vinnicombe, Luke; Walker, Scott; Watts, Shaun S; Waugh, Warren A; Whitmore, Jake; Wilkinson, John C.

**Associated Schoolboys**
Ash, Jacob W H; Breslan, Gavin A C; Carpenter, Perry S; Casey, Ross E; Clemoes, Joseph G; Conibere, Brett D; Fox, Robert A; Gross, Marcus J; Hallam, Robin S; Hayes, Gary J; Hensor, Stephen J; Mudge, James R M; Orchard, Jack F; Ovey, Simon F; Rampaul, Steven R; Schamroth, Daniel S; Wainwright, Thomas W; Walker, David.

**Associated Schoolboys who have accepted the club's offer of a Traineeship/Contract**
Jee, Russell; Pointing, Neil T.

# FULHAM

| | | | | | | | | | |
|---|---|---|---|---|---|---|---|---|---|
| **Aggrey** Jimmy* | 6 3 | 13 06 | D | 26 10 78 | London | Chelsea | Fulham | — | — |
| **Arendse** Andre | 6 4 | 11 05 | G | 27 6 67 | Cape Town | Cape Town S | Fulham | 6 | — |
| **Arnott** Andy | 6 0 | 13 03 | D | 18 10 73 | Chatham | Trainee | Gillingham | 73 | 12 |
| | | | | | | | Manchester U (loan) | — | — |
| | | | | | | | Leyton Orient | 50 | 6 |
| | | | | | | | Fulham | 1 | — |
| **Blake** Mark | 6 0 | 12 06 | D | 17 12 67 | Portsmouth | Apprentice | Southampton | 18 | 2 |
| | | | | | | | Colchester U (loan) | 4 | 1 |
| | | | | | | | Shrewsbury T (loan) | 10 | — |
| | | | | | | | Shrewsbury T | 132 | 3 |
| | | | | | | | Fulham | 140 | 17 |
| **Bracewell** Paul | 5 9 | 12 03 | M | 19 7 62 | Heswall | Apprentice | Stoke C | 129 | 5 |
| | | | | | | | Sunderland | 38 | 4 |
| | | | | | | | Everton | 95 | 7 |
| | | | | | | | Sunderland | 113 | 2 |
| | | | | | | | Newcastle U | 73 | 3 |
| | | | | | | | Sunderland | 77 | — |
| | | | | | | | Fulham | 36 | — |
| **Brazier** Matthew | 5 8 | 11 08 | M | 2 7 76 | Whipps Cross | Trainee | QPR | 49 | 2 |
| | | | | | | | Fulham | 7 | 1 |
| **Brevett** Rufus | 5 8 | 11 08 | D | 24 9 69 | Derby | Trainee | Doncaster R | 109 | 3 |
| | | | | | | | QPR | 152 | 1 |
| | | | | | | | Fulham | 11 | — |
| **Brooker** Paul | 5 8 | 10 01 | F | 25 11 76 | Hammersmith | Trainee | Fulham | 55 | 4 |
| **Carpenter** Richard | 5 11 | 13 00 | M | 30 9 72 | Sheppey | Trainee | Gillingham | 122 | 4 |
| | | | | | | | Fulham | 58 | 7 |
| **Coleman** Chris | 6 2 | 14 04 | D | 10 6 70 | Swansea | Apprentice | Swansea C | 160 | 2 |
| | | | | | | | Crystal Palace | 154 | 13 |
| | | | | | | | Blackburn R | 28 | — |
| | | | | | | | Fulham | 26 | 1 |
| **Collins** Wayne | 6 0 | 11 07 | M | 4 3 69 | Manchester | Winsford U | Crewe Alex | 117 | 14 |
| | | | | | | | Sheffield W | 31 | 6 |
| | | | | | | | Fulham | 13 | 1 |
| **Freeman** Darren* | 5 11 | 13 00 | F | 22 8 73 | Brighton | Horsham T | Gillingham | 12 | — |
| | | | | | | | Fulham | 46 | 9 |
| **Hayward** Steve | 5 11 | 12 07 | M | 8 9 71 | Walsall | Trainee | Derby Co | 26 | 1 |
| | | | | | | | Carlisle U | 90 | 13 |
| | | | | | | | Fulham | 35 | 4 |
| **Herrera** Robbie | 5 6 | 10 08 | D | 12 6 70 | Torbay | Trainee | QPR | 6 | — |
| | | | | | | | Torquay U (loan) | 11 | — |
| | | | | | | | Torquay U (loan) | 5 | — |
| | | | | | | | Fulham | 145 | 1 |
| **Lawrence** Matthew | 6 1 | 12 05 | D | 19 6 74 | Northampton | Grays Ath | Wycombe W | 16 | 1 |
| | | | | | | | Fulham | 58 | — |
| **Maher** Shaun | 6 2 | 12 03 | D | 10 6 78 | Dublin | Bohemians | Fulham | — | — |

| Name | Ht | Wt | Pos | DOB | Birthplace | Source | Club | Apps | Gls |
|---|---|---|---|---|---|---|---|---|---|
| **Marshall** John† | 5 10 | 12 04 | D | 18 8 64 | Surrey | Apprentice | Fulham | 411 | 28 |
| **McAnespie** Steve | 5 9 | 10 08 | D | 1 2 72 | Kilmarnock | Vasterhauringe | Raith R | 40 | — |
| | | | | | | | Bolton W | 24 | — |
| | | | | | | | Fulham | 4 | — |
| | | | | | | | Bradford C (loan) | 7 | — |
| **McAree** Rod | 5 7 | 11 00 | M | 10 8 74 | Dungannon | Trainee | Liverpool | — | — |
| | | | | | | | Bristol C | 6 | — |
| | | | | | | | Fulham | 28 | 3 |
| **McGuckin** Ian | 6 2 | 14 02 | D | 24 4 73 | Middlesbrough | Trainee | Hartlepool U | 152 | 8 |
| | | | | | | | Fulham | — | — |
| **Moody** Paul | 6 3 | 14 08 | F | 13 6 67 | Portsmouth | Waterlooville | Southampton | 12 | — |
| | | | | | | | Reading (loan) | 5 | 1 |
| | | | | | | | Oxford U | 136 | 49 |
| | | | | | | | Fulham | 33 | 15 |
| **Morgan** Simon | 5 10 | 12 05 | D | 5 9 66 | Birmingham | Trainee | Leicester C | 160 | 3 |
| | | | | | | | Fulham | 290 | 43 |
| **Neilson** Alan | 5 11 | 12 08 | D | 26 9 72 | Wegburg | Trainee | Newcastle U | 42 | 1 |
| | | | | | | | Southampton | 55 | — |
| | | | | | | | Fulham | 17 | — |
| **Peschisolido** Paul | 5 7 | 11 02 | F | 25 5 71 | Canada | Toronto Blizzard | Birmingham C | 43 | 16 |
| | | | | | | | Stoke C | 66 | 19 |
| | | | | | | | Birmingham C | 9 | 1 |
| | | | | | | | WBA | 45 | 18 |
| | | | | | | | Fulham | 32 | 13 |
| **Scott** Rob | 6 1 | 12 02 | F | 15 8 73 | Epsom | Sutton U | Sheffield U | 6 | 1 |
| | | | | | | | Scarborough (loan) | 8 | 3 |
| | | | | | | | Northampton T (loan) | 5 | — |
| | | | | | | | Fulham | 81 | 17 |
| **Selley** Ian | 5 9 | 11 05 | M | 14 6 74 | Chertsey | Trainee | Arsenal | 41 | — |
| | | | | | | | Southend U (loan) | 4 | — |
| | | | | | | | Fulham | 3 | — |
| **Smith** Neil | 5 8 | 12 02 | M | 30 9 71 | Lambeth | Trainee | Tottenham H | — | — |
| | | | | | | | Gillingham | 212 | 10 |
| | | | | | | | Fulham | 44 | — |
| **Stewart** Simon* | 6 2 | 13 09 | D | 1 11 73 | Leeds | | Sheffield W | 6 | — |
| | | | | | | | Shrewsbury T (loan) | 4 | — |
| | | | | | | Trainee | Fulham | 3 | — |
| **Taylor** Maik | 6 3 | 13 09 | G | 4 9 71 | Hildeshein | Farnborough T | Barnet | 70 | — |
| | | | | | | | Southampton | 18 | — |
| | | | | | | | Fulham | 28 | — |
| **Thomas** Martin* | 5 8 | 12 04 | M | 12 9 73 | Lyndhurst | Trainee | Southampton | — | — |
| | | | | | | | Leyton Orient | 5 | 2 |
| | | | | | | | Fulham | 90 | 8 |
| **Thorpe** Tony | 5 9 | 12 03 | F | 10 4 74 | Leicester | Leicester C | Luton T | 120 | 50 |
| | | | | | | | Fulham | 13 | 3 |
| **Trollope** Paul | 6 0 | 12 01 | M | 3 6 72 | Swindon | Trainee | Swindon T | — | — |
| | | | | | | | Torquay U (loan) | 10 | — |
| | | | | | | | Torquay U | 96 | 16 |
| | | | | | | | Derby Co | 65 | 5 |
| | | | | | | | Grimsby T (loan) | 7 | 1 |
| | | | | | | | Crystal Palace (loan) | 9 | — |
| | | | | | | | Fulham | 24 | 3 |
| **Walton** Mark | 6 4 | 16 00 | G | 1 6 69 | Merthyr | Swansea C | Luton T | — | — |
| | | | | | | | Colchester U | 40 | — |
| | | | | | | | Norwich C | 22 | — |
| | | | | | | | Wrexham (loan) | 6 | — |
| | | | | | | | Dundee | — | — |
| | | | | | | | Bolton W | 3 | — |
| | | | | | | Fakenham T | Fulham | 40 | — |
| | | | | | | | Gillingham (loan) | 1 | — |
| | | | | | | | Norwich C (loan) | — | — |

**Trainees**
Cornwall, Lucas C; Curtis, Darren D; Davis, Sean; Donnelly, Paul A; Edwards, Ashley T; Gray, Ryan; Hammond, Elvis Z; Henderson, Kevin; Hughes, Robert A; Keevill, Sam A; Morse, Richard; Oram, Christopher J A; Palmer, Ryan W J; Roome, Stephen; Smith, Duncan M; Wilkinson, James S; Willis, Jonathan M.

**Non-Contract**
Marshall, John P.

**Associated Schoolboy**
Lee, Andrew J.

**Associated Schoolboys who have accepted the club's offer of a Traineeship/Contract**
Hudson, Mark; Hunter, Jermaine A; Johnson, Michael; Lampton, Neil J; Pomroy, John S; Upsher, Tom P.

# GILLINGHAM

| Name | Ht | Wt | Pos | DOB | Birthplace | Source | Club | Apps | Gls |
|---|---|---|---|---|---|---|---|---|---|
| **Akinbiyi** Ade | 6 0 | 12 05 | F | 10 10 74 | Greenwich | Trainee | Norwich C | 49 | 3 |
| | | | | | | | Hereford U (loan) | 4 | 2 |
| | | | | | | | Brighton & HA (loan) | 7 | 4 |
| | | | | | | | Gillingham | 63 | 28 |
| **Ashby** Barry | 6 1 | 13 02 | D | 2 11 70 | London | Trainee | Watford | 114 | 3 |
| | | | | | | | Brentford | 121 | 4 |
| | | | | | | | Gillingham | 43 | — |

| | | | | | | | | | |
|---|---|---|---|---|---|---|---|---|---|
| **Bartram** Vince* | 6 2 | 13 07 | G | 7 8 68 | Birmingham | Local | Wolverhampton W | 5 | — |
| | | | | | | | Blackpool (loan) | 9 | — |
| | | | | | | | WBA (loan) | — | — |
| | | | | | | | Bournemouth | 132 | — |
| | | | | | | | Arsenal | 11 | — |
| | | | | | | | Wolverhampton W (loan) | — | — |
| | | | | | | | Huddersfield T (loan) | 12 | — |
| | | | | | | | Gillingham | 9 | — |
| **Bryant** Matthew | 6 0 | 12 06 | D | 21 9 70 | Bristol | Trainee | Bristol C | 203 | 7 |
| | | | | | | | Walsall (loan) | 13 | — |
| | | | | | | | Gillingham | 74 | — |
| **Butler** Steve# | 6 1 | 12 02 | F | 27 1 62 | Birmingham | Wokingham T | Brentford | 21 | 3 |
| | | | | | | Maidstone U | Maidstone U | 76 | 41 |
| | | | | | | | Watford | 62 | 9 |
| | | | | | | | Bournemouth (loan) | 1 | — |
| | | | | | | | Cambridge U | 109 | 51 |
| | | | | | | | Gillingham | 101 | 20 |
| **Butters** Guy | 6 2 | 14 01 | D | 30 10 69 | Hillingdon | Trainee | Tottenham H | 35 | 1 |
| | | | | | | | Southend U (loan) | 16 | 3 |
| | | | | | | | Portsmouth | 154 | 6 |
| | | | | | | | Oxford U (loan) | 3 | 1 |
| | | | | | | | Gillingham | 61 | 7 |
| **Chapman** Ian* | 5 8 | 12 07 | D | 31 5 70 | Brighton | Trainee | Brighton & HA | 281 | 14 |
| | | | | | | | Gillingham | 23 | 1 |
| **Corbett** James | 5 9 | 10 12 | F | 6 7 80 | London | Trainee | Gillingham | 16 | 2 |
| **Edge** Roland | 5 9 | 11 06 | D | 25 11 78 | Gillingham | Trainee | Gillingham | | |
| **Fortune-West** Leo# | 6 4 | 13 11 | F | 9 4 71 | Stratford | Stevenage Bor | Gillingham | 67 | 18 |
| | | | | | | | Leyton Orient (loan) | 5 | — |
| **Galloway** Mick | 5 10 | 12 05 | M | 13 10 74 | Nottingham | Trainee | Notts Co | 21 | — |
| | | | | | | | Gillingham (loan) | 9 | 1 |
| | | | | | | | Gillingham | 39 | 1 |
| **Green** Richard | 6 0 | 12 00 | D | 22 11 67 | Wolverhampton | Apprentice | Shrewsbury T | 125 | 5 |
| | | | | | | | Swindon T | — | — |
| | | | | | | | Gillingham | 216 | 16 |
| **Hessenthaler** Andy | 5 7 | 11 06 | M | 17 6 65 | Gravesend | Redbridge Forest | Watford | 195 | 11 |
| | | | | | | | Gillingham | 80 | 2 |
| **Masters** Neil | 6 0 | 13 05 | D | 25 5 72 | Lisburn | Trainee | Bournemouth | 38 | 2 |
| | | | | | | | Wolverhampton W | 12 | — |
| | | | | | | | Gillingham | 11 | — |
| **Norman** Steven‡ | | | M | 30 1 79 | Harold Wood | Trainee | Gillingham | — | — |
| **O'Connor** Mark | 5 8 | 11 03 | M | 10 3 63 | Rochdale | Apprentice | QPR | 3 | — |
| | | | | | | | Exeter C (loan) | 38 | 1 |
| | | | | | | | Bristol R | 80 | 10 |
| | | | | | | | Bournemouth | 128 | 12 |
| | | | | | | | Gillingham | 116 | 8 |
| | | | | | | | Bournemouth | 58 | 3 |
| | | | | | | | Gillingham | 40 | 1 |
| **Patterson** Mark | 5 9 | 11 10 | D | 13 9 68 | Leeds | Trainee | Carlisle U | 22 | — |
| | | | | | | | Derby Co | 51 | 3 |
| | | | | | | | Plymouth Arg | 134 | 3 |
| | | | | | | | Gillingham | 23 | — |
| **Pennock** Adrian# | 6 0 | 12 12 | M | 27 3 71 | Ipswich | Trainee | Norwich C | 1 | — |
| | | | | | | | Bournemouth | 131 | 9 |
| | | | | | | | Gillingham | 46 | 2 |
| **Pinnock** James | 5 8 | 11 11 | F | 1 8 78 | Dartford | Trainee | Gillingham | 3 | — |
| **Piper** Lennie* | 5 8 | 11 06 | F | 8 8 77 | London | Trainee | Wimbledon | — | — |
| | | | | | | | Gillingham | 20 | 1 |
| **Ratcliffe** Simon | 6 0 | 12 13 | M | 6 2 67 | Davyhulme | Apprentice | Manchester U | — | — |
| | | | | | | | Norwich C | 9 | — |
| | | | | | | | Brentford | 214 | 14 |
| | | | | | | | Gillingham | 105 | 10 |
| **Sambrook** Andrew† | | | M | 13 7 79 | Chatham | Trainee | Gillingham | 1 | — |
| **Smith** Paul | 5 10 | 12 05 | M | 18 9 71 | East Ham | Trainee | Southend U | 20 | 1 |
| | | | | | | | Brentford | 159 | 11 |
| | | | | | | | Gillingham | 46 | 3 |
| **Southall** Nicky | 5 9 | 12 00 | M | 28 1 72 | Middlesbrough | Trainee | Hartlepool U | 138 | 24 |
| | | | | | | | Grimsby T | 72 | 5 |
| | | | | | | | Gillingham | 23 | 2 |
| **Stannard** Jim* | 6 2 | 16 07 | G | 16 10 62 | London | Local | Fulham | 41 | — |
| | | | | | | | Charlton Ath (loan) | 1 | — |
| | | | | | | | Southend U (loan) | 17 | — |
| | | | | | | | Southend U | 92 | — |
| | | | | | | | Fulham | 348 | 1 |
| | | | | | | | Gillingham | 104 | — |
| **Statham** Brian | 5 7 | 11 06 | D | 21 5 69 | Zimbabwe | Apprentice | Tottenham H | 24 | — |
| | | | | | | | Reading (loan) | 8 | — |
| | | | | | | | Bournemouth (loan) | 2 | — |
| | | | | | | | Brentford (loan) | 18 | — |
| | | | | | | | Brentford | 148 | 1 |
| | | | | | | | Gillingham | 20 | — |

| Thomas Glen* | 6 0 | 14 00 | D | 6 10 67 | Hackney | Apprentice | Fulham | 251 | 6 |
| | | | | | | | Peterborough U | 8 | — |
| | | | | | | | Barnet | 23 | — |
| | | | | | | | Gillingham | 28 | — |
| Tydeman Sam* | 5 11 | 11 05 | M | 14 12 78 | Chatham | Trainee | Gillingham | — | — |

**Trainees**
Ampofo, Russell S; Bovis, Danny S; Carter, James F W; Hobbs, Paul M; Osborne, Tommy P; Radbourne, Richard J; Sinclair, Barry.
**Non-Contract**
Bremner, Kevin J; Sambrook, Andrew J; Scally, Paul D P.

## GRIMSBY TOWN

| Black Kingsley# | 5 8 | 12 03 | M | 22 6 68 | Luton | School | Luton T | 127 | 26 |
| | | | | | | | Nottingham F | 98 | 14 |
| | | | | | | | Sheffield U (loan) | 11 | 2 |
| | | | | | | | Millwall (loan) | 3 | 1 |
| | | | | | | | Grimsby T | 63 | 2 |
| Bloomer Matthew | 6 1 | 13 00 | D | 3 11 78 | Grimsby | Trainee | Grimsby T | — | — |
| Brown James* | 5 10 | 11 00 | M | 13 9 78 | Grantham | Trainee | Grimsby T | — | — |
| Buckley Adam | | | M | 2 8 79 | Nottingham | | Grimsby T | — | — |
| Burnett Wayne | 5 10 | 12 00 | M | 4 9 71 | Lambeth | Trainee | Leyton Orient | 40 | — |
| | | | | | | | Blackburn R | — | — |
| | | | | | | | Plymouth Arg | 70 | 3 |
| | | | | | | | Bolton W | 2 | — |
| | | | | | | | Huddersfield T | 50 | — |
| | | | | | | | Grimsby T | 21 | 1 |
| Butterfield Danny | 5 9 | 11 08 | D | 21 11 79 | Boston | Trainee | Grimsby T | 7 | — |
| Chapman Ben | 5 7 | 10 12 | D | 2 3 79 | Scunthorpe | Trainee | Grimsby T | — | — |
| Clare Daryl | 5 9 | 12 00 | F | 1 8 78 | Jersey | Trainee | Grimsby T | 23 | 3 |
| Davison Aidan | 6 1 | 13 12 | G | 11 5 68 | Sedgefield | Billingham Syn | Notts Co | 1 | — |
| | | | | | | | Leyton Orient (loan) | — | — |
| | | | | | | | Bury | — | — |
| | | | | | | | Chester C (loan) | — | — |
| | | | | | | | Blackpool (loan) | — | — |
| | | | | | | | Millwall | 34 | — |
| | | | | | | | Bolton W | 37 | — |
| | | | | | | | Ipswich T (loan) | — | — |
| | | | | | | | Hull C (loan) | 9 | — |
| | | | | | | | Bradford C | 10 | — |
| | | | | | | | Grimsby T | 42 | — |
| Dobbin Jim* | 5 9 | 10 07 | M | 17 9 63 | Dunfermline | Whitburn BC | Celtic | 2 | — |
| | | | | | | | Motherwell (loan) | 2 | — |
| | | | | | | | Doncaster R | 64 | 13 |
| | | | | | | | Barnsley | 129 | 12 |
| | | | | | | | Grimsby T | 164 | 21 |
| | | | | | | | Rotherham U | 19 | — |
| | | | | | | | Doncaster R | 31 | — |
| | | | | | | | Scarborough | 1 | — |
| | | | | | | | Grimsby T | 2 | — |
| Donovan Kevin | 5 8 | 11 02 | F | 17 12 71 | Halifax | Trainee | Huddersfield T | 20 | 1 |
| | | | | | | | Halifax T (loan) | 6 | — |
| | | | | | | | WBA | 168 | 19 |
| | | | | | | | Grimsby T | 46 | 16 |
| Fickling Ashley* | 5 10 | 11 08 | D | 15 11 72 | Sheffield | Trainee | Sheffield U | — | — |
| | | | | | | | Darlington (loan) | 14 | — |
| | | | | | | | Darlington (loan) | 1 | — |
| | | | | | | | Grimsby T | 39 | 2 |
| | | | | | | | Darlington (loan) | 8 | — |
| Gallimore Tony | 5 11 | 12 05 | D | 21 2 72 | Crewe | Trainee | Stoke C | 11 | — |
| | | | | | | | Carlisle U (loan) | 16 | — |
| | | | | | | | Carlisle U (loan) | 8 | 1 |
| | | | | | | | Carlisle U | 116 | 8 |
| | | | | | | | Grimsby T | 87 | 4 |
| Groves Paul | 5 11 | 11 05 | M | 28 2 66 | Derby | Burton Alb | Leicester C | 16 | 1 |
| | | | | | | | Lincoln C (loan) | 8 | 1 |
| | | | | | | | Blackpool | 107 | 21 |
| | | | | | | | Grimsby T | 184 | 38 |
| | | | | | | | WBA | 29 | 4 |
| | | | | | | | Grimsby T | 46 | 7 |
| Handyside Peter | 6 1 | 13 07 | D | 31 7 74 | Dumfries | Trainee | Grimsby T | 140 | 1 |
| Jobling Kevin* | 5 9 | 12 02 | D | 1 1 68 | Sunderland | Apprentice | Leicester C | 9 | — |
| | | | | | | | Grimsby T | 285 | 10 |
| | | | | | | | Scunthorpe U (loan) | — | — |
| Lester Jack | 5 10 | 12 00 | F | 8 10 75 | Sheffield | Trainee | Grimsby T | 74 | 9 |
| | | | | | | | Doncaster R (loan) | 11 | 1 |
| Lever Mark# | 6 3 | 13 06 | D | 29 3 70 | Beverley | Trainee | Grimsby T | 302 | 8 |
| Livingstone Steve# | 6 1 | 13 07 | F | 8 9 68 | Middlesbrough | Trainee | Coventry C | 31 | 5 |
| | | | | | | | Blackburn R | 30 | 10 |
| | | | | | | | Chelsea | 1 | — |
| | | | | | | | Port Vale (loan) | 5 | — |
| | | | | | | | Grimsby T | 172 | 33 |
| Love Andrew | 6 2 | 13 10 | G | 28 3 79 | Grimsby | Trainee | Grimsby T | 3 | — |
| McDermott John# | 5 7 | 10 13 | D | 3 2 69 | Middlesbrough | Trainee | Grimsby T | 374 | 7 |

| | | | | | | | | | |
|---|---|---|---|---|---|---|---|---|---|
| **Nogan** Lee | 5 8 | 11 01 | F | 21 5 69 | Cardiff | Apprentice | Oxford U | 64 | 10 |
| | | | | | | | Brentford (loan) | 11 | 2 |
| | | | | | | | Southend U (loan) | 6 | 1 |
| | | | | | | | Watford | 105 | 26 |
| | | | | | | | Southend U (loan) | 5 | — |
| | | | | | | | Reading | 91 | 26 |
| | | | | | | | Notts Co (loan) | 6 | — |
| | | | | | | | Grimsby T | 36 | 8 |
| **Pearcey** Jason* | 6 1 | 14 00 | G | 23 7 71 | Leamington Spa | Trainee | Mansfield T | 77 | — |
| | | | | | | | Grimsby T | 49 | — |
| **Rodger** Graham* | 6 2 | 13 08 | D | 1 4 67 | Glasgow | Apprentice | Wolverhampton W | 1 | — |
| | | | | | | | Coventry C | 36 | 2 |
| | | | | | | | Luton T | 28 | 2 |
| | | | | | | | Grimsby T | 146 | 11 |
| **Smith** David | 5 8 | 10 08 | M | 29 3 68 | Stonehouse | | Coventry C | 154 | 19 |
| | | | | | | | Bournemouth (loan) | 1 | — |
| | | | | | | | Birmingham C | 38 | 3 |
| | | | | | | | WBA | 102 | 2 |
| | | | | | | | Grimsby T | 17 | 1 |
| **Smith** Richard# | 6 0 | 13 05 | D | 3 10 70 | Lutterworth | Trainee | Leicester C | 98 | 1 |
| | | | | | | | Cambridge U (loan) | 4 | — |
| | | | | | | | Grimsby T | 32 | — |
| **Stephenson** Lee* | 5 11 | 13 00 | F | 18 8 78 | Grimsby | Trainee | Grimsby T | — | — |
| **Widdrington** Tommy | 5 8 | 11 01 | M | 1 10 71 | Newcastle | Trainee | Southampton | 75 | 3 |
| | | | | | | | Wigan Ath (loan) | 6 | — |
| | | | | | | | Grimsby T | 63 | 7 |
| **Woods** Neil* | 6 0 | 13 00 | F | 30 7 66 | York | Apprentice | Doncaster R | 65 | 16 |
| | | | | | | | Rangers | 3 | — |
| | | | | | | | Ipswich T | 27 | 5 |
| | | | | | | | Bradford C | 14 | 2 |
| | | | | | | | Grimsby T | 226 | 42 |
| | | | | | | | Wigan Ath (loan) | 1 | — |
| | | | | | | | Scunthorpe U (loan) | 2 | — |
| | | | | | | | Mansfield T (loan) | 6 | — |
| **Wrack** Darren | 5 9 | 12 07 | F | 5 5 76 | Cleethorpes | Trainee | Derby Co | 26 | 1 |
| | | | | | | | Grimsby T | 13 | 1 |
| | | | | | | | Shrewsbury T (loan) | 4 | — |

**Trainees**
Blake, Kirk A; Crew, Lee N; Croudson, Steven D; Dimech, Mark; Goodhand, Paul A; Hanslip, Nicholas; Melbourne, James; Oakes, Andrew; Oswin, Matthew S W; Rockhill, Antony J; Soley, Martin R; Steadman, Daniel M; Taylor, Jonathan F; Teanby, Jonathan H; Young, James R.

**Non-Contract**
Turner, Barry.

**Associated Schoolboys**
Beacock, Carl J; Carr, Philip A; Cartwright, Timothy A; Davy, Michael J; Gibson, Thomas W; Hutchinson, Philip G; Lawrence, Jamie D; Martin, Carl A; Nilsson, Steven; Peterson, Daniel; Richmond, Paul J; Smith, Philip J; Smithson, Luke R; Stiff, Gareth T; Tatari, Yaman; Ward, Iain.

**Associated Schoolboys who have accepted the club's offer of a Traineeship/Contract**
Chapman, Benjamin C R; Cocksworth, Matthew R; Pritchard, Gareth J; Rowan, Jonathan R; Thompson, Mark S.

## HALIFAX TOWN

| | | | | | | | | | | |
|---|---|---|---|---|---|---|---|---|---|---|
| **Boardman** Craig | 5 10 | 11 12 | D | 30 11 70 | Barnsley | | | Nottingham F | — | — |
| | | | | | | | | Peterborough U | — | — |
| | | | | | | | Halifax T | Scarborough | 9 | — |
| | | | | | | | Stalybridge C | Halifax T | 4 | — |
| **Bradshaw** Mark | 5 11 | 11 00 | D | 7 9 69 | Ashton-under-Lyne | | | Blackpool | 42 | 1 |
| | | | | | | | | York C (loan) | 1 | — |
| | | | | | | | Macclesfield T | Halifax T | 42 | 5 |
| **Brook** Gary | 5 10 | 11 07 | F | 9 5 64 | Dewsbury | | | Newport Co | 14 | 2 |
| | | | | | | | | Scarborough | 64 | 15 |
| | | | | | | | | Blackpool | 29 | 6 |
| | | | | | | | | Notts Co (loan) | 1 | — |
| | | | | | | | | Scarborough | 8 | — |
| | | | | | | | | Blackpool | 1 | — |
| | | | | | | | Boston U | Halifax T | 22 | 3 |
| **Brown** Jon | 5 10 | 11 03 | D | 8 9 66 | Barnsley | | | Exeter C | 164 | 3 |
| | | | | | | | | Halifax T | 37 | — |
| **Griffiths** Willie | 5 8 | 9 07 | F | 20 5 79 | Manchester | | | Halifax T | 2 | — |
| **Mand** Paul | 5 8 | 10 00 | D | 18 7 79 | Halifax | | | Halifax T | — | — |
| **Horner** Noel | 5 10 | 11 07 | M | 18 2 78 | Halifax | | | Halifax T | 18 | — |
| **Horsfield** Geoff | 6 0 | 11 07 | F | 1 11 73 | Barnsley | | | Scarborough | 12 | 1 |
| | | | | | | | Witton Alb | Halifax T | 40 | 30 |
| **Hulme** Kevin | 5 10 | 11 07 | M | 7 12 67 | Farnworth | | | Bury | 110 | 21 |
| | | | | | | | | Chester C (loan) | 4 | — |
| | | | | | | | | Doncaster R | 34 | 8 |
| | | | | | | | | Bury | 29 | — |
| | | | | | | | | Lincoln C | 5 | — |
| | | | | | | | Macclesfield T | Halifax T | 30 | 7 |
| **Lyons** Darren | 6 1 | 11 07 | M | 9 11 67 | Manchester | | | Bury | 36 | 7 |
| | | | | | | | Winsford U | Halifax T | 24 | 3 |
| **Martin** Lee | 6 0 | 13 00 | G | 9 9 68 | Huddersfield | Trainee | | Huddersfield T | 54 | — |
| | | | | | | | | Blackpool | 98 | — |
| | | | | | | | | Bradford C (loan) | — | — |
| | | | | | | | | Rochdale | — | — |
| | | | | | | | | Halifax T | 32 | — |

| Player | Ht | Wt | Pos | Born | Birthplace | Source | Club | Apps | Gls |
|---|---|---|---|---|---|---|---|---|---|
| **Midwood** Michael | 5 10 | 11 07 | F | 19 4 76 | Huddersfield | | Huddersfield T | — | — |
| | | | | | | | Halifax T | 5 | — |
| **O'Regan** Kieran | 5 9 | 10 12 | M | 9 11 63 | Cork | | Brighton & HA | 86 | 2 |
| | | | | | | | Swindon T | 26 | 1 |
| | | | | | | | Huddersfield T | 199 | 25 |
| | | | | | | | WBA | 25 | 2 |
| | | | | | | | Halifax T | 37 | 1 |
| **Paterson** Jamie‡ | 5 3 | 10 02 | F | 26 4 73 | Dumfries | Trainee | Halifax T | 86 | 18 |
| | | | | | | | Falkirk | 4 | — |
| | | | | | | | Scunthorpe U | 55 | 2 |
| | | | | | | | Halifax T | 36 | 14 |
| **Place** Damien | 5 9 | 10 07 | M | 31 12 78 | Halifax | | Halifax T | 1 | — |
| **Rosser** Michael | | | D | | | | Halifax T | — | — |
| **Stoneman** Paul | 6 1 | 12 07 | D | 26 2 73 | Whitley Bay | | Blackpool | 43 | — |
| | | | | | | | Colchester U (loan) | 3 | 1 |
| | | | | | | | Halifax T | 38 | 2 |
| **Thackeray** Andy | 5 9 | 11 00 | M | 13 2 68 | Huddersfield | School | Manchester C | — | — |
| | | | | | | | Huddersfield T | 2 | — |
| | | | | | | | Newport Co | 54 | 4 |
| | | | | | | | Wrexham | 152 | 14 |
| | | | | | | | Rochdale | 165 | 13 |
| | | | | | | | Halifax T | 1 | — |
| **Woods** Andy | 6 0 | 11 00 | G | 15 1 76 | Colchester | | Oldham Ath | — | — |
| | | | | | | | Halifax T | 41 | 2 |

Appearances and goals for Halifax Town players are from the 1997–98 season in the Football Conference.

## HARTLEPOOL UNITED

| Player | Ht | Wt | Pos | Born | Birthplace | Source | Club | Apps | Gls |
|---|---|---|---|---|---|---|---|---|---|
| **Allon** Joe‡ | 5 11 | 13 00 | F | 12 11 66 | Gateshead | Trainee | Newcastle U | 9 | 2 |
| | | | | | | | Swansea C | 34 | 11 |
| | | | | | | | Hartlepool U | 112 | 50 |
| | | | | | | | Chelsea | 14 | 2 |
| | | | | | | | Port Vale (loan) | 6 | — |
| | | | | | | | Brentford | 45 | 19 |
| | | | | | | | Southend U (loan) | 3 | — |
| | | | | | | | Port Vale | 23 | 9 |
| | | | | | | | Lincoln C | 4 | — |
| | | | | | | | Hartlepool U | 56 | 19 |
| **Baker** Paul# | 6 2 | 14 07 | F | 5 1 63 | Newcastle | Bishop Auckland | Southampton | — | — |
| | | | | | | | Carlisle U | 71 | 11 |
| | | | | | | | Hartlepool U | 197 | 67 |
| | | | | | | | Motherwell | 9 | 1 |
| | | | | | | | Gillingham | 62 | 16 |
| | | | | | | | York C | 48 | 18 |
| | | | | | | | Torquay U | 30 | 8 |
| | | | | | | | Scunthorpe U | 21 | 9 |
| | | | | | | | Hartlepool U | 22 | 7 |
| **Barron** Michael | 5 11 | 11 12 | D | 22 12 74 | Lumley | Trainee | Middlesbrough | 3 | — |
| | | | | | | | Hartlepool U (loan) | 16 | — |
| | | | | | | | Hartlepool U | 33 | — |
| **Beech** Chris | 5 10 | 11 13 | M | 16 9 74 | Blackpool | Trainee | Blackpool | 82 | 4 |
| | | | | | | | Hartlepool U | 78 | 13 |
| **Bradley** Russell | 6 2 | 13 02 | D | 28 3 66 | Birmingham | Dudley T | Nottingham F | — | — |
| | | | | | | | Hereford U (loan) | 12 | 1 |
| | | | | | | | Hereford U | 77 | 3 |
| | | | | | | | Halifax T | 56 | 3 |
| | | | | | | | Scunthorpe U | 119 | 5 |
| | | | | | | | Hartlepool U (loan) | 12 | 1 |
| | | | | | | | Hartlepool U | 43 | 1 |
| **Clark** Ian | 5 10 | 11 05 | M | 23 10 74 | Stockton | Stockton | Doncaster R | 45 | 3 |
| | | | | | | | Hartlepool U | 24 | 7 |
| **Davies** Glen* | 6 2 | 13 08 | D | 20 7 76 | Brighton | Trainee | Burnley | — | — |
| | | | | | | | Hartlepool U | 52 | 1 |
| **Di Lella** Gustavo | | | M | 6 10 73 | Buenos Aires | | Darlington | 5 | — |
| | | | | | | Blyth S | Hartlepool U | 5 | 2 |
| **Dixon** Andy‡ | 5 9 | 10 00 | F | 5 8 68 | Hartlepool | Mons | Hartlepool U | 3 | — |
| **Dobson** Warren* | 6 1 | 13 08 | G | 5 11 78 | North Shields | QPR | Hartlepool U | 1 | — |
| **Downey** Glen | 6 1 | 11 13 | D | 20 9 78 | Newcastle | | Hartlepool U | — | — |
| **Elliott** Andy* | 5 9 | 11 07 | F | 2 5 74 | Newcastle | | Hartlepool U | 8 | — |
| **Gallagher** Ian‡ | 5 10 | 11 07 | M | 13 5 78 | Hartlepool | Trainee | Hartlepool U | 1 | — |
| **Gavin** Mark‡ | 5 7 | 11 02 | F | 10 2 63 | Holytown | Apprentice | Leeds U | 30 | 3 |
| | | | | | | | Hartlepool U (loan) | 7 | — |
| | | | | | | | Carlisle U | 13 | 1 |
| | | | | | | | Bolton W | 49 | 3 |
| | | | | | | | Rochdale | 23 | 6 |
| | | | | | | | Hearts | 9 | — |
| | | | | | | | Bristol C | 69 | 6 |
| | | | | | | | Watford | 13 | — |
| | | | | | | | Bristol C | 41 | 2 |
| | | | | | | | Exeter C | 77 | 4 |
| | | | | | | | Scunthorpe U | 11 | — |
| | | | | | | | Hartlepool U | 3 | — |
| **Halliday** Stephen | 5 10 | 12 07 | F | 3 5 76 | Sunderland | Charlton Ath | Hartlepool U | 140 | 25 |

| | | | | | | | | | |
|---|---|---|---|---|---|---|---|---|---|
| **Hollund** Martin | 6 0 | 12 13 | G | 11 8 74 | Stord | | Brann | 24 | — |
| | | | | | | | Hartlepool U | 28 | — |
| **Howard** Steve | 6 2 | 14 12 | M | 10 5 76 | Durham | Tow Law T | Hartlepool U | 114 | 22 |
| **Hutt** Stephen | 6 2 | 11 07 | M | 19 2 79 | Middlesbrough | Trainee | Hartlepool U | 5 | — |
| **Ingram** Denny | 5 11 | 12 01 | D | 27 6 76 | Sunderland | Trainee | Hartlepool U | 154 | 6 |
| **Irvine** Stuart | 5 9 | 11 06 | F | 1 3 79 | Hartlepool | Trainee | Hartlepool U | 13 | 1 |
| **Knowles** Darren | 5 6 | 11 05 | D | 8 10 70 | Sheffield | Trainee | Sheffield U | — | — |
| | | | | | | | Stockport Co | 63 | — |
| | | | | | | | Scarborough | 144 | 2 |
| | | | | | | | Hartlepool U | 53 | 1 |
| **Larsen** Stig‡ | 6 1 | 13 04 | F | 29 9 73 | Bergen | Fana | Hartlepool U | 4 | — |
| **Lee** Graeme | 6 2 | 13 07 | D | 31 5 78 | Middlesbrough | Trainee | Hartlepool U | 67 | 3 |
| **Lucas** Richard* | 5 10 | 12 10 | D | 22 9 70 | Chapeltown | Trainee | Sheffield U | 10 | — |
| | | | | | | | Preston NE | 50 | — |
| | | | | | | | Lincoln C (loan) | 4 | — |
| | | | | | | | Scarborough | 72 | — |
| | | | | | | | Hartlepool U | 49 | 2 |
| **McDonald** Chris | 6 0 | 13 04 | D | 14 10 75 | Edinburgh | Trainee | Arsenal | — | — |
| | | | | | | | Hartlepool U | 15 | — |
| **Midgley** Craig | 5 7 | 11 07 | F | 24 5 76 | Bradford | Trainee | Bradford C | 11 | 1 |
| | | | | | | | Scarborough (loan) | 16 | 1 |
| | | | | | | | Scarborough (loan) | 6 | 2 |
| | | | | | | | Darlington (loan) | 1 | — |
| | | | | | | | Hartlepool U | 9 | 3 |
| **Miller** Thomas | 6 1 | 11 12 | D | 8 1 79 | Easington | Trainee | Hartlepool U | 13 | 1 |
| **Nash** Marc | 5 9 | 11 07 | F | 13 5 78 | Newcastle | Benfield Park | Hartlepool U | 1 | — |
| **Pears** Steve‡ | 6 0 | 14 09 | G | 22 1 62 | Brandon | Apprentice | Manchester U | 4 | — |
| | | | | | | | Middlesbrough (loan) | 12 | — |
| | | | | | | | Middlesbrough | 327 | — |
| | | | | | | | Liverpool | — | — |
| | | | | | | | Hartlepool U | 16 | — |
| **Pedersen** Jan Ove‡ | 5 8 | 11 13 | M | 12 11 68 | Oslo | | Lillestrom | 166 | 15 |
| | | | | | | | Brann | 46 | 4 |
| | | | | | | | Hartlepool U | 17 | 1 |
| **Skedd** Anthony‡ | 5 5 | 10 01 | M | 19 5 75 | Hartlepool | Trainee | Hartlepool U | 46 | — |
| **Stephenson** Paul | 5 10 | 12 07 | F | 2 1 68 | Wallsend | Apprentice | Newcastle U | 61 | 1 |
| | | | | | | | Millwall | 98 | 6 |
| | | | | | | | Gillingham (loan) | 12 | 2 |
| | | | | | | | Brentford | 70 | 2 |
| | | | | | | | York C | 97 | 8 |
| | | | | | | | Hartlepool U | 3 | — |
| **Tait** Mick* | 5 11 | 14 05 | D | 30 9 56 | Wallsend | Apprentice | Oxford U | 64 | 23 |
| | | | | | | | Carlisle U | 106 | 20 |
| | | | | | | | Hull C | 33 | 3 |
| | | | | | | | Portsmouth | 240 | 30 |
| | | | | | | | Reading | 99 | 9 |
| | | | | | | | Darlington | 79 | 2 |
| | | | | | | | Hartlepool U | 139 | 3 |
| **Walton** Paul* | 5 9 | 11 04 | D | 2 7 79 | Sunderland | Trainee | Hartlepool U | 10 | — |

**Trainees**
Briggs, John D; Cooper, Paul; Downey, Gareth; Dunwell, Michael; Evans, Nicholas A; Forster, Alan C; Forster, Richard J; Hay, Andrew J; Jones, Francis; Lake, Craig R; McCabe, Christopher; Moss, Paul W; Nicholson, Mark; Robinson, Mark; Smith, Jeffrey; Sullivan, Wayne A; Timmons, Darren; Walton, Phillip.

**Associated Schoolboys**
Provett, Robert J C; Ross, Brian S; Sheeran, Mark J; Shepherd, Gary J; Skilbeck, Lee R.

**Associated Schoolboys who have accepted the club's offer of a Traineeship/Contract**
Davison, Craig; Hill, Terence; McLean, Stephen.

## HUDDERSFIELD TOWN

| | | | | | | | | | |
|---|---|---|---|---|---|---|---|---|---|
| **Allison** Wayne | 6 0 | 14 00 | F | 16 10 68 | Huddersfield | | Halifax T | 84 | 23 |
| | | | | | | | Watford | 7 | — |
| | | | | | | | Bristol C | 195 | 48 |
| | | | | | | | Swindon T | 101 | 31 |
| | | | | | | | Huddersfield T | 27 | 6 |
| **Baldry** Simon | 5 9 | 11 08 | M | 12 2 76 | Huddersfield | Trainee | Huddersfield T | 53 | 3 |
| **Barnes** Paul | 5 11 | 13 05 | F | 16 11 67 | Leicester | Apprentice | Notts Co | 53 | 14 |
| | | | | | | | Stoke C | 24 | 3 |
| | | | | | | | Chesterfield (loan) | 1 | — |
| | | | | | | | York C | 148 | 76 |
| | | | | | | | Birmingham C | 15 | 7 |
| | | | | | | | Burnley | 65 | 30 |
| | | | | | | | Huddersfield T | 15 | 1 |
| **Beresford** David | 5 6 | 10 07 | F | 11 11 76 | Manchester | Trainee | Oldham Ath | 64 | 2 |
| | | | | | | | Swansea C (loan) | 6 | — |
| | | | | | | | Huddersfield T | 14 | 1 |
| **Brennan** Damien | | | D | 30 8 80 | Dublin | Belvedere | Huddersfield T | — | — |
| **Browning** Marcus | 6 0 | 12 08 | M | 22 4 71 | Bristol | Trainee | Bristol R | 174 | 13 |
| | | | | | | | Hereford U (loan) | 7 | 5 |
| | | | | | | | Huddersfield T | 27 | — |
| **Collins** Sam | 6 1 | 14 03 | D | 5 6 77 | Pontefract | Trainee | Huddersfield T | 14 | — |

| Name | | | | | Birthplace | Source | Club | Apps | Gls |
|---|---|---|---|---|---|---|---|---|---|
| **Cowan** Tom | 5 8 | 11 08 | D | 28 8 69 | Bellshill | Netherdale BC | Clyde | 16 | 2 |
| | | | | | | | Rangers | 12 | — |
| | | | | | | | Sheffield U | 45 | — |
| | | | | | | | Stoke C (loan) | 14 | — |
| | | | | | | | Huddersfield T (loan) | 10 | — |
| | | | | | | | Huddersfield T | 122 | 8 |
| **Cuss** Paul | 6 1 | 13 05 | G | 19 4 79 | Hanover | Trainee | Huddersfield T | — | — |
| **Dalton** Paul | 6 0 | 12 07 | M | 25 4 67 | Middlesbrough | Brandon U | Manchester U | — | — |
| | | | | | | | Hartlepool U | 151 | 37 |
| | | | | | | | Plymouth Arg | 98 | 25 |
| | | | | | | | Huddersfield T | 89 | 22 |
| **Dyson** Jon | 6 0 | 12 07 | D | 18 12 71 | Mirfield | School | Huddersfield T | 141 | 3 |
| **Edmondson** Darren | 6 0 | 12 04 | D | 4 11 71 | Coniston | Trainee | Carlisle U | 214 | 9 |
| | | | | | | | Huddersfield T | 29 | — |
| **Edwards** Rob | 5 8 | 11 11 | F | 23 2 70 | Manchester | Trainee | Crewe Alex | 155 | 44 |
| | | | | | | | Huddersfield T | 84 | 11 |
| **Facey** Delroy | 5 11 | 13 07 | F | 22 4 80 | Huddersfield | Trainee | Huddersfield T | 6 | — |
| **Francis** Steve | 6 0 | 13 12 | G | 29 5 64 | Billericay | Apprentice | Chelsea | 71 | — |
| | | | | | | | Reading | 216 | — |
| | | | | | | | Huddersfield T | 183 | — |
| **Gray** Kevin | 5 11 | 13 12 | D | 7 1 72 | Sheffield | Trainee | Mansfield T | 141 | 3 |
| | | | | | | | Huddersfield T | 117 | 2 |
| **Heary** Thomas | 5 9 | 12 03 | M | 14 2 79 | Dublin | Trainee | Huddersfield T | 8 | — |
| **Hessey** Sean | 5 10 | 12 06 | D | 19 9 78 | Whiston | Liverpool | Wigan Ath | — | — |
| | | | | | | | Leeds U | — | — |
| | | | | | | | Huddersfield T | 1 | — |
| **Horne** Barry# | 5 8 | 12 00 | M | 18 5 62 | St Asaph | Rhyl | Wrexham | 136 | 17 |
| | | | | | | | Portsmouth | 70 | 7 |
| | | | | | | | Southampton | 112 | 6 |
| | | | | | | | Everton | 123 | 3 |
| | | | | | | | Birmingham C | 33 | — |
| | | | | | | | Huddersfield T | 30 | — |
| **Hurst** Chris | 5 11 | 11 06 | M | 3 10 73 | Barnsley | Emley | Huddersfield T | 3 | — |
| **Illingworth** Jeremy‡ | 5 10 | 12 01 | M | 20 5 77 | Huddersfield | Trainee | Huddersfield T | 3 | — |
| **Jenkins** Steve | 5 11 | 12 04 | D | 16 7 72 | Merthyr | Trainee | Swansea C | 165 | 1 |
| | | | | | | | Huddersfield T | 93 | 2 |
| **Johnson** Grant | 5 8 | 10 09 | M | 24 3 72 | Dundee | Dundee | Dundee U | 85 | 7 |
| | | | | | | | Huddersfield T | 29 | 1 |
| **Kaye** Peter‡ | 5 7 | 11 00 | F | 30 7 75 | Huddersfield | Trainee | Huddersfield T | 1 | — |
| **Lawson** Ian | 5 11 | 11 00 | F | 4 11 77 | Huddersfield | Trainee | Huddersfield T | 36 | 3 |
| **Makel** Lee | 5 9 | 11 05 | M | 11 1 73 | Sunderland | Trainee | Newcastle U | 12 | 1 |
| *(Transferred to Hearts, March 1998)* | | | | | | | Blackburn R | 6 | — |
| | | | | | | | Huddersfield T | 65 | 5 |
| | | | | | | | Hearts | 5 | — |
| **Midwood** Michael‡ | | | F | 19 4 76 | Huddersfield | Trainee | Huddersfield T | 1 | — |
| **Morrison** Andy | 5 11 | 15 06 | D | 30 7 70 | Inverness | Trainee | Plymouth Arg | 113 | 6 |
| | | | | | | | Blackburn R | 5 | — |
| | | | | | | | Blackpool | 47 | 3 |
| | | | | | | | Huddersfield T | 33 | 2 |
| **Murphy** Stephen* | 5 11 | 11 06 | M | 5 4 78 | Dublin | Belvedere | Huddersfield T | — | — |
| **Nielsen** Martin* | | | F | 24 3 73 | Aarhus | | FC Copenhagen | 59 | 4 |
| | | | | | | | Huddersfield T | 3 | — |
| **O'Connor** Derek* | 5 11 | 12 06 | G | 9 3 78 | Dublin | Crumplin U | Huddersfield T | 1 | — |
| **Phillips** Dave# | 5 9 | 12 03 | D | 29 7 63 | Wegberg | Apprentice | Plymouth Arg | 73 | 15 |
| | | | | | | | Manchester C | 81 | 13 |
| | | | | | | | Coventry C | 100 | 8 |
| | | | | | | | Norwich C | 152 | 18 |
| | | | | | | | Nottingham F | 126 | 5 |
| | | | | | | | Huddersfield T | 29 | 2 |
| **Richardson** Lee J | 5 11 | 11 00 | M | 12 3 69 | Halifax | | Halifax T | 56 | 2 |
| | | | | | | | Watford | 41 | 1 |
| | | | | | | | Blackburn R | 62 | 3 |
| | | | | | | | Aberdeen | 64 | 6 |
| | | | | | | | Oldham Ath | 88 | 21 |
| | | | | | | | Stockport Co (loan) | 6 | — |
| | | | | | | | Huddersfield T | 21 | 3 |
| **Smith** Alex* | 5 6 | 11 10 | D | 15 2 76 | Liverpool | Trainee | Everton | — | — |
| | | | | | | | Swindon T | 31 | 1 |
| | | | | | | | Huddersfield T | — | — |
| **Smith** Steve* | | | M | 13 10 78 | Huddersfield | Trainee | Huddersfield T | 6 | — |
| **Stansfield** James‡ | | | D | 18 9 78 | Dewsbury | Trainee | Huddersfield T | — | — |
| **Stewart** Marcus | 5 10 | 11 00 | F | 7 11 72 | Bristol | Trainee | Bristol R | 171 | 57 |
| | | | | | | | Huddersfield T | 61 | 22 |

**Trainees**
Atkinson, Robert F; Bemrose, Daniel S; Brown, Nathaniel L; Cartwright, Christopher R A; Crossley, Ryan S; Gledhill, James G; Greene, Neil T; Horsley, Jamie L; Mattis, Dwayne; Scott, Paul; Senior, Michael G; Walker, Richard J; Williams, Adam R.

**Associated Schoolboys**
Atkins, Oliver D; Austin, Ben; Baldwin, Nicholas; Batchelor, Alistair A; Bennett, Ric J; Brown, Christopher; Clapham, Daniel D; Clarke, Nathan; Field, Craig A; Gibbons, James M; Greaves, Robert; Jennings, David; Kelly, Gregory; Livingstone, Craig; Lloyd, Anthony F; Oleksewycz, Stephen M; Sanderson, Michael; Sasimowicz, Steven; Senior, Philip A; Smith, Timothy K; Stead, Jonathan; Trueman, Daniel; Wadsworth, Jonathan P; Worthington, Jonathan.

**Associated Schoolboys who have accepted the club's offer of a Traineeship/Contract**
Clarke, Doni J; Derry, John; Fowler, Adam M; Hay, Nathan A; Senior, Christopher M; Simpson, Neil.

# HULL CITY

| | | | | | | | | | |
|---|---|---|---|---|---|---|---|---|---|
| **Baxter** Craig‡ | 6 0 | 11 00 | D | 24 4 79 | Glasgow | Morrison YMCA | Hull C | — | — |
| **Brien** Tony‡ | 6 0 | 13 02 | D | 10 2 69 | Dublin | Apprentice | Leicester C | 16 | 1 |
| | | | | | | | Chesterfield | 204 | 8 |
| | | | | | | | Rotherham U | 43 | 2 |
| | | | | | | | WBA | 2 | — |
| | | | | | | | Mansfield T (loan) | 4 | — |
| | | | | | | | Chester C (loan) | 8 | — |
| | | | | | | | Hull C | 47 | 1 |
| **Brown** Andrew‡ | 6 3 | 13 10 | F | 11 10 76 | Edinburgh | Trainee | Leeds U | — | — |
| | | | | | | | Hull C | 29 | 1 |
| **Darby** Duane# | 5 11 | 12 06 | F | 17 10 73 | Birmingham | Trainee | Torquay U | 108 | 26 |
| | | | | | | | Doncaster R | 17 | 4 |
| | | | | | | | Hull C | 78 | 27 |
| **Dewhurst** Rob | 6 3 | 14 00 | D | 10 9 71 | Keighley | Trainee | Blackburn R | 13 | — |
| | | | | | | | Darlington (loan) | 11 | 1 |
| | | | | | | | Huddersfield T (loan) | 7 | — |
| | | | | | | | Hull C | 130 | 13 |
| **Dickinson** Patrick‡ | 5 10 | 10 08 | M | 6 5 78 | Vancouver | Trainee | Hull C | 4 | — |
| **Doncel** Antonio‡ | 6 0 | 12 01 | D | 31 1 67 | Lugo | Ferrol | Hull C | 38 | 2 |
| **Edwards** Michael§ | | | | 25 4 80 | Beverley | Trainee | Hull C | 21 | — |
| **Ellington** Lee§ | | | D | 3 7 80 | Bradford | Trainee | Hull C | 9 | 2 |
| **Fewings** Paul* | 6 0 | 12 06 | F | 18 2 78 | Hull | Trainee | Hull C | 57 | 2 |
| **Gage** Kevin | 5 10 | 12 05 | D | 21 4 64 | Chiswick | Apprentice | Wimbledon | 168 | 15 |
| | | | | | | | Aston Villa | 115 | 8 |
| | | | | | | | Sheffield U | 112 | 7 |
| | | | | | | | Preston NE | 23 | — |
| | | | | | | | Hull C | 10 | — |
| **Greaves** Mark | 6 1 | 13 00 | D | 22 1 75 | Hull | Brigg Town | Hull C | 55 | 4 |
| **Hateley** Mark | 6 2 | 13 00 | F | 7 11 61 | Liverpool | Apprentice | Coventry C | 93 | 25 |
| | | | | | | | Portsmouth | 38 | 22 |
| | | | | | | | AC Milan | 66 | 17 |
| | | | | | | | Monaco | 59 | 22 |
| | | | | | | | Rangers | 165 | 85 |
| | | | | | | | QPR | 27 | 3 |
| | | | | | | | Leeds U (loan) | 6 | — |
| | | | | | | | Rangers | 4 | 1 |
| | | | | | | | Hull C | 9 | — |
| **Hocking** Matthew | 5 11 | 12 00 | D | 30 1 78 | Boston | Trainee | Sheffield U | — | — |
| | | | | | | | Hull C | 31 | 1 |
| **Joyce** Warren | 5 9 | 12 00 | M | 20 1 65 | Oldham | School | Bolton W | 184 | 17 |
| | | | | | | | Preston NE | 177 | 34 |
| | | | | | | | Plymouth Arg | 30 | 3 |
| | | | | | | | Burnley | 70 | 9 |
| | | | | | | | Hull C (loan) | 9 | 3 |
| | | | | | | | Hull C | 90 | 9 |
| **Lowthorpe** Adam* | 5 7 | 11 03 | D | 7 8 75 | Hull | Trainee | Hull C | 81 | 3 |
| **Mann** Neil | 5 10 | 12 01 | M | 19 11 72 | Nottingham | Grantham T | Hull C | 140 | 8 |
| **Marks** Jamie‡ | 5 9 | 10 13 | D | 18 3 77 | Belfast | Trainee | Leeds U | — | — |
| | | | | | | | Hull C | 15 | — |
| **Maxfield** Scott* | 5 10 | 11 05 | D | 13 7 76 | Doncaster | Trainee | Doncaster R | 29 | 1 |
| | | | | | | | Hull C | 35 | — |
| **McGinty** Brian | 6 1 | 11 04 | M | 10 12 76 | East Kilbride | | Rangers | 3 | — |
| | | | | | | | Hull C | 21 | 2 |
| **Morley** Ben§ | | | D | 20 12 80 | Hull | Trainee | Hull C | 8 | — |
| **Peacock** Richard | 5 10 | 11 05 | F | 29 10 72 | Sheffield | Sheffield FC | Hull C | 160 | 19 |
| **Quigley** Michael‡ | 5 7 | 11 04 | M | 2 10 70 | Manchester | Trainee | Manchester C | 12 | — |
| | | | | | | | Wrexham (loan) | 4 | — |
| | | | | | | | Hull C | 51 | 3 |
| **Rioch** Greg | 5 11 | 12 10 | D | 24 6 75 | Sutton Coldfield | Trainee | Luton T | — | — |
| | | | | | | | Barnet (loan) | 3 | — |
| | | | | | | | Peterborough U | 18 | — |
| | | | | | | | Hull C | 78 | 6 |
| **Sharman** Sam | 5 10 | 12 01 | D | 7 11 77 | Hull | Sheffield W | Hull C | 4 | — |
| **Thomson** Scott Y | 6 0 | 11 09 | G | 8 11 66 | Edinburgh | | Dundee U | 6 | — |
| | | | | | | | Forfar Ath | 88 | — |
| | | | | | | | Raith R | 123 | — |
| | | | | | | | Hull C | 9 | — |
| | | | | | | | Motherwell | 1 | — |
| **Trevitt** Simon‡ | 5 11 | 12 09 | D | 20 12 67 | Dewsbury | Apprentice | Huddersfield T | 229 | 3 |
| | | | | | | | Hull C | 51 | 1 |
| | | | | | | | Swansea C (loan) | 1 | — |
| **Tucker** Dexter§ | | | M | 22 9 79 | Pontefract | Trainee | Hull C | 7 | — |
| **Wharton** Paul‡ | 5 4 | 10 00 | M | 26 6 77 | Newcastle | Trainee | Leeds U | — | — |
| | | | | | | | Hull C | 11 | — |
| **Wilkinson** Ian* | 6 2 | 13 00 | D | 19 9 77 | Ferriby | Trainee | Hull C | 8 | 1 |
| **Wilson** Steve | 5 10 | 10 12 | G | 24 4 74 | Hull | Trainee | Hull C | 131 | — |

| | | | | | | | | | |
|---|---|---|---|---|---|---|---|---|---|
| Wright Ian# | 6 1 | 13 04 | D | 10 3 72 | Lichfield | Trainee | Stoke C | 6 | — |
| | | | | | | | Bristol R | 54 | 1 |
| | | | | | | | Hull C | 73 | 2 |

**Trainees**
Baker, Matthew C; Blythe, Michael; Bolder, Adam P; Bradshaw, Christopher; Brown, Daniel P; Dixon, Steven M; Edwards, Michael; Ellington, Lee S; Flanagan, Lee M; Harvey, Jarred; Heppinstall, Ian D; Morley, Ben; Oakes, Gary C; Thacker, Martin; Tucker, Dexter C; Wilson, Paul A.

**Associated Schoolboys**
Benson, Philip A; Bonsley, Anthony; Burton, Steven; Harrison, Richard C; Leebetter, James E; Macklin, Lee; Marris, Christopher J; Palmer, Craig; Peat, Nathan N M.

**Associated Schoolboys who have accepted the club's offer of a Traineeship/Contract**
Artymiuk, Michael J; Bolder, Christopher; Flower, Clayton J; Lafferty, Mark A; McIntosh, Neil G; Schofield, David P; Waslin, Daniel.

# IPSWICH TOWN

| | | | | | | | | | |
|---|---|---|---|---|---|---|---|---|---|
| Bell Leon* | 5 8 | 11 00 | M | 23 9 77 | Ipswich | Trainee | Ipswich T | — | — |
| Bracey Lee | 6 2 | 13 02 | G | 11 9 68 | Barking | Trainee | West Ham U | — | — |
| | | | | | | | Swansea C | 99 | — |
| | | | | | | | Halifax T | 73 | — |
| | | | | | | | Bury | 67 | — |
| | | | | | | | Ipswich T (loan) | — | — |
| | | | | | | | Ipswich T | — | — |
| Brown Wayne | 6 0 | 12 06 | D | 20 8 77 | Barking | Trainee | Ipswich T | 1 | — |
| | | | | | | | Colchester U (loan) | 2 | — |
| Burgess Mark | 5 10 | 11 09 | D | 3 2 79 | Ipswich | Trainee | Ipswich T | — | — |
| Clapham Jamie | 5 9 | 10 11 | M | 7 12 75 | Lincoln | Trainee | Tottenham H | 1 | — |
| | | | | | | | Leyton Orient (loan) | 6 | — |
| | | | | | | | Bristol R (loan) | 5 | — |
| | | | | | | | Ipswich T | 22 | — |
| Cundy Jason | 6 0 | 13 10 | D | 12 11 69 | Wimbledon | Trainee | Chelsea | 41 | 1 |
| | | | | | | | Tottenham H (loan) | 10 | — |
| | | | | | | | Tottenham H | 16 | 1 |
| | | | | | | | Crystal Palace (loan) | 4 | — |
| | | | | | | | Bristol C (loan) | 6 | 1 |
| | | | | | | | Ipswich T | 54 | 5 |
| Dyer Kieron | 5 7 | 9 07 | M | 29 12 78 | Ipswich | Trainee | Ipswich T | 54 | 4 |
| Ellis Kevin‡ | 6 2 | 12 07 | D | 12 5 77 | Gt Yarmouth | Trainee | Ipswich T | 1 | — |
| Holland Matt | 5 10 | 11 10 | M | 11 4 74 | Bury | Trainee | West Ham U | — | — |
| | | | | | | | Bournemouth | 104 | 18 |
| | | | | | | | Ipswich T | 46 | 10 |
| Johnson David | 5 6 | 12 00 | F | 15 8 76 | Kingston, Jam | Trainee | Manchester U | — | — |
| | | | | | | | Bury | 97 | 18 |
| | | | | | | | Ipswich T | 31 | 20 |
| Keeble Chris | 5 10 | 10 07 | M | 17 9 78 | Colchester | Trainee | Ipswich T | 1 | — |
| Kennedy John | 5 9 | 10 03 | D | 19 8 78 | Cambridge | Trainee | Ipswich T | 1 | — |
| Mason Paul# | 5 9 | 12 01 | M | 3 9 63 | Liverpool | Groningen | Aberdeen | 158 | 27 |
| | | | | | | | Ipswich T | 113 | 25 |
| Mathie Alex | 5 10 | 11 07 | F | 20 12 68 | Bathgate | Celtic BC | Celtic | 11 | — |
| | | | | | | | Morton | 74 | 31 |
| | | | | | | | Port Vale (loan) | 3 | — |
| | | | | | | | Newcastle U | 25 | 4 |
| | | | | | | | Ipswich T | 101 | 37 |
| Midgley Neil | 5 11 | 11 03 | F | 21 10 78 | Cambridge | Trainee | Ipswich T | — | — |
| Milton Simon* | 5 10 | 11 05 | M | 23 8 63 | Fulham | Bury St Edmunds | Ipswich T | 281 | 48 |
| | | | | | | | Exeter C (loan) | 2 | 3 |
| | | | | | | | Torquay U (loan) | 4 | 1 |
| Mowbray Tony# | 6 1 | 13 00 | D | 22 11 63 | Saltburn | Apprentice | Middlesbrough | 348 | 25 |
| | | | | | | | Celtic | 78 | 6 |
| | | | | | | | Ipswich T | 52 | 2 |
| Naylor Richard | 6 1 | 13 07 | F | 28 2 77 | Leeds | Trainee | Ipswich T | 32 | 6 |
| Niven Stuart | 5 11 | 12 08 | M | 24 12 78 | Glasgow | Trainee | Ipswich T | 2 | — |
| Petta Bobby | 5 7 | 11 03 | M | 6 8 74 | Rotterdam | | Ipswich T | 38 | 7 |
| Scowcroft James | 6 1 | 12 02 | F | 15 11 75 | Bury St Edmunds | Trainee | Ipswich T | 95 | 17 |
| Sonner Danny# | 5 11 | 12 08 | M | 9 1 72 | Wigan | Wigan Ath | Burnley | 6 | — |
| | | | | | | | Bury (loan) | 5 | 3 |
| | | | | | | Erzgebirge Aue | Ipswich T | 52 | 3 |
| Stockwell Mick | 5 9 | 11 04 | M | 14 2 65 | Chelmsford | Apprentice | Ipswich T | 441 | 31 |
| Tanner Adam | 6 0 | 12 01 | M | 25 10 73 | Maldon | Trainee | Ipswich T | 54 | 7 |
| Taricco Mauricio | 5 8 | 11 05 | D | 10 3 73 | Buenos Aires | Argentinos Juniors | Ipswich T | 121 | 3 |
| Theobald David | 6 2 | 11 06 | D | 15 12 78 | Cambridge | Trainee | Ipswich T | — | — |
| Uhlenbeek Gus# | 5 10 | 12 06 | M | 20 8 70 | Paramaribo | | Ajax | 2 | — |
| | | | | | | | Cambuur | 39 | — |
| | | | | | | | TOPS SV | 22 | 3 |
| | | | | | | | Ipswich T | 89 | 4 |
| Venus Mark | 6 0 | 12 12 | D | 6 4 67 | Hartlepool | | Hartlepool U | 4 | — |
| | | | | | | | Leicester C | 61 | 1 |
| | | | | | | | Wolverhampton W | 287 | 7 |
| | | | | | | | Ipswich T | 14 | 1 |

| | | | | | | | | | |
|---|---|---|---|---|---|---|---|---|---|
| **Williams** Geraint* | 5 7 | 12 06 | M | 5 1 62 | Cwmpare | Apprentice | Bristol R | 141 | 8 |
| | | | | | | | Derby Co | 277 | 9 |
| | | | | | | | Ipswich T | 217 | 3 |
| **Wright** Richard | 6 2 | 13 00 | G | 5 11 77 | Ipswich | Trainee | Ipswich T | 112 | — |

**Trainees**
Beckham, Michael J; Bramble, Titus M; Campbell, Gavin; Coburn, Neil; Dixon, Matthew F; Farrington, Louie M; Fox, Justin A; Inglis, Kevin; Lowes, Brendan; Stewart, Colin J; Supple, Michael J; White, David W; Woolnough, Benjamin S; Wright, Carl A J.

**Associated Schoolboys**
Ambrose, Darren P F; Artun, Erdem K; Barker, Rory; Byrne, Richard A; Frost, Darren A; Haywood, Jamie B; Hulyer, Lee A; Kinsella, Sean I; Logan, Stewart A; Mayes, Mark D; Senior, James C; Smith, Robert R; Smy, Daniel J; Smythe, Robert A; Snowdon, William R; Tearney, Trevor L; Tunnicliffe, Andrew J; Wands, Ian A; Wasylyczyn, Wayne M; Westlake, Ian J.

**Associated Schoolboys who have accepted the club's offer of a Traineeship/Contract**
Asiamah, Justin; Logan, Richard J; Miller, Adam E; O'Neill, Lee; Riley, Dominic M.

# LEEDS UNITED

| | | | | | | | | | |
|---|---|---|---|---|---|---|---|---|---|
| **Beeney** Mark | 6 4 | 14 07 | G | 30 12 67 | Pembury | | Gillingham | 2 | — |
| | | | | | | | Maidstone U | 50 | — |
| | | | | | | | Aldershot (loan) | 7 | — |
| | | | | | | | Brighton & HA | 69 | — |
| | | | | | | | Leeds U | 35 | — |
| **Blunt** Jason* | 5 9 | 10 10 | M | 16 8 77 | Penzance | Trainee | Leeds U | 4 | — |
| **Bowyer** Lee | 5 9 | 9 09 | M | 3 1 77 | London | Trainee | Charlton Ath | 46 | 8 |
| | | | | | | | Leeds U | 57 | 7 |
| **Boyle** Wesley | | | M | 30 3 79 | Portadown | Trainee | Leeds U | 1 | — |
| **Briggs** Simon* | | | G | 14 10 78 | Sheffield | | Leeds U | — | — |
| **Butler** John* | | | D | 28 10 79 | Dublin | Belvedere | Leeds U | — | — |
| **Dixon** Kevin | 5 10 | 12 11 | M | 27 6 80 | Easington | Trainee | Leeds U | — | — |
| **Donnelly** Paul | | | M | 31 8 79 | Dublin | Trainee | Leeds U | — | — |
| **Dorigo** Tony | 5 10 | 10 10 | D | 31 12 65 | Melbourne | Apprentice | Aston Villa | 111 | 1 |
| *(Transferred to Torino July 1997)* | | | | | | | Chelsea | 146 | 11 |
| | | | | | | | Leeds U | 171 | 5 |
| **Doyle** Kevin | 5 11 | 11 10 | D | 13 10 80 | Wexford | Trainee | Leeds U | — | — |
| **Evans** Gareth | 6 0 | 11 07 | D | 15 2 81 | Leeds | Trainee | Leeds U | — | — |
| **Evans** Kevin | 6 2 | 12 09 | D | 16 12 80 | Carmarthen | Trainee | Leeds U | — | — |
| **Feeney** Warren | 5 9 | 10 06 | F | 17 1 81 | Belfast | Trainee | Leeds U | — | — |
| **Foster** Martin* | 5 5 | 9 10 | M | 29 10 77 | Sheffield | Trainee | Leeds U | — | — |
| | | | | | | | Blackpool (loan) | 1 | — |
| **Gray** Andrew | 6 0 | 13 00 | M | 15 11 77 | Harrogate | Trainee | Leeds U | 22 | — |
| | | | | | | | Bury (loan) | 6 | 1 |
| **Haaland** Alf-Inge | 5 10 | 12 12 | M | 23 11 72 | Stavanger | Bryne | Nottingham F | 75 | 7 |
| | | | | | | | Leeds U | 32 | 7 |
| **Hackworth** Tony | 6 2 | 13 03 | F | 19 5 80 | Durham | Trainee | Leeds U | — | — |
| **Halle** Gunnar | 5 11 | 11 00 | D | 11 8 65 | Larvik | Lillestrom | Oldham Ath | 188 | 17 |
| | | | | | | | Leeds U | 53 | 2 |
| **Harte** Ian | 5 9 | 11 00 | D | 31 8 77 | Drogheda | Trainee | Leeds U | 30 | 2 |
| **Hasselbaink** Jimmy Floyd | 6 2 | 13 05 | F | 27 3 72 | Paramaribo | | Campomairorense | 31 | 12 |
| | | | | | | | Boavista | 29 | 20 |
| | | | | | | | Leeds U | 33 | 16 |
| **Hiden** Martin | 6 1 | 11 06 | D | 11 3 73 | Stainz | Rapid Vienna | Leeds U | 11 | — |
| **Hopkin** David | 5 9 | 10 03 | M | 21 8 70 | Greenock | Pt Glasgow R BC | Morton | 18 | — |
| | | | | | | | Chelsea | 40 | 1 |
| | | | | | | | Crystal Palace | 83 | 21 |
| | | | | | | | Leeds U | 25 | 1 |
| **Jackson** Mark | 5 11 | 12 00 | D | 30 9 77 | Barnsley | Trainee | Leeds U | 19 | — |
| **Jones** Matthew | 5 11 | 11 05 | M | 1 9 80 | Llanelli | Trainee | Leeds U | — | — |
| **Kelly** Gary | 5 8 | 13 03 | D | 9 7 74 | Drogheda | Home Farm | Leeds U | 190 | 2 |
| **Kewell** Harry | 5 11 | 12 00 | M | 22 9 78 | Sydney | NSW Academy | Leeds U | 32 | 5 |
| **Knarvik** Tommy | | | M | 1 11 79 | Bergen | Skjerjard | Leeds U | — | — |
| **Lagan** Brian | 5 5 | 9 10 | M | 3 10 80 | N Ireland | Trainee | Leeds U | — | — |
| **Laurent** Pierre | 5 8 | 10 10 | M | 13 12 70 | Tulle | Tulle | Bastia | 73 | 13 |
| *(Transferred to Bastia, January 1998)* | | | | | | | Leeds U | 4 | — |
| **Lilley** Derek | 5 11 | 12 07 | F | 9 2 74 | Paisley | Everton BC | Morton | 180 | 57 |
| | | | | | | | Leeds U | 19 | 1 |
| **Lynch** Damien | | | D | 31 7 79 | Dublin | | Leeds U | — | — |
| **Martyn** Nigel | 6 1 | 14 07 | G | 11 8 66 | St Austell | St Blazey | Bristol R | 101 | — |
| | | | | | | | Crystal Palace | 272 | — |
| | | | | | | | Leeds U | 74 | — |
| **Matthews** Lee | | | M | 16 1 79 | Middlesbrough | Trainee | Leeds U | 3 | — |
| **Maybury** Alan | | | M | 8 8 78 | Dublin | Trainee | Leeds U | 13 | — |
| **McPhail** Stephen | | | M | 9 12 79 | London | Trainee | Leeds U | 4 | — |
| **Molenaar** Robert | 6 2 | 14 04 | D | 27 2 69 | Zaamdam | | Volendam | 124 | 3 |
| | | | | | | | Leeds U | 34 | 3 |
| **Quinn** Andrew | | | M | 1 9 79 | Halifax | | Leeds U | — | — |
| **Radebe** Lucas | 6 1 | 11 09 | D | 12 4 69 | Johannesburg | Kaiser Chiefs | Leeds U | 84 | — |

| Name | Ht | Wt | Pos | DOB | Birthplace | Source | Club | Apps | Gls |
|---|---|---|---|---|---|---|---|---|---|
| Ribeiro Bruno | 5 9 | 12 03 | M | 22 10 75 | Setubal | | Setubal | 11 | 1 |
| | | | | | | | Setubal* | — | — |
| | | | | | | | Setubal | 20 | 1 |
| | | | | | | | Leeds U | 29 | 3 |
| Robertson David | 5 11 | 12 10 | D | 17 10 68 | Aberdeen | | Aberdeen | 135 | 2 |
| | | | | | | | Rangers | 183 | 15 |
| | | | | | | | Leeds U | 26 | — |
| Robinson Paul | | | G | 15 10 79 | Beverley | Trainee | Leeds U | — | — |
| Sharpe Lee | 6 0 | 12 06 | M | 27 5 71 | Halesowen | Trainee | Torquay U | 14 | 3 |
| | | | | | | | Manchester U | 193 | 21 |
| | | | | | | | Leeds U | 26 | 5 |
| Shepherd Paul | | | F | 17 11 77 | Leeds | Trainee | Leeds U | 1 | — |
| | | | | | | | Ayr U (loan) | 6 | 1 |
| Smith Alan | 5 9 | 10 06 | F | 28 10 80 | Wakefield | Trainee | Leeds U | — | — |
| Wallace Rod* | 5 7 | 11 03 | F | 2 10 69 | Lewisham | Trainee | Southampton | 128 | 45 |
| | | | | | | | Leeds U | 212 | 53 |
| Watson Simon | 5 10 | 12 10 | M | 22 9 80 | Strabane | Trainee | Leeds U | — | — |
| Wetherall David | 6 2 | 13 12 | D | 14 3 71 | Sheffield | School | Sheffield W | — | — |
| | | | | | | | Leeds U | 181 | 12 |
| Woodgate Jonathan | | | D | 22 1 80 | Middlesbrough | | Leeds U | — | — |
| Wright Andrew | | | M | 21 10 78 | Leeds | Trainee | Leeds U | — | — |
| Yeboah Tony | 5 11 | 13 13 | F | 6 6 66 | Kumasi | Okwawu U | Saarbrucken | 65 | 26 |
| *(Transferred to Hamburg, September 1997)* | | | | | | | Eintracht Frankfurt | 123 | 68 |
| | | | | | | | Leeds U | 47 | 24 |

**Trainees**
Jackson, Daniel M D; Keddie, Alexander; Kennedy, Alan R; Martin, Alan; O'Brien, Carl C; Ray, Mark.

**Associated Schoolboys**
Bone, Liam K; Butterwood, Michael S; Cater, Adam S; Crawford, Dale; Folan, Caleb; Hacking, Anthony; Hague, Philip J; Hitchcock, Thomas E; Ibbitson, Liam J; Johnson, Simon; Kilgallon, Matthew; Loughran, Anthony G; McCargo, Gerard; O'Brien, Robert L; Onions, Christopher J; Porter, Graeme; Powell, Graham; Price, Jamie B; Richardson, Frazer; Rimmington, Dale; Ross, Neil J; Singh, Harpal; Vass, Matthew C; Walker, Liam J.

# LEICESTER CITY

| Name | Ht | Wt | Pos | DOB | Birthplace | Source | Club | Apps | Gls |
|---|---|---|---|---|---|---|---|---|---|
| Allen Lee | 5 10 | 12 00 | M | 12 3 79 | Islington | | Leicester C | — | — |
| Andrews Ian | 6 2 | 14 01 | G | 1 12 64 | Nottingham | Apprentice | Leicester C | 126 | — |
| | | | | | | | Swindon T (loan) | 1 | — |
| | | | | | | | Celtic | 5 | — |
| | | | | | | | Leeds U (loan) | 1 | — |
| | | | | | | | Southampton | 10 | — |
| | | | | | | | Bournemouth | 64 | — |
| | | | | | | | Leicester C (loan) | — | — |
| | | | | | | | Leicester C | — | — |
| Arcos-Diaz Miguel* | 5 6 | 9 11 | F | 1 9 78 | Loughborough | Trainee | Leicester C | — | — |
| Arphexad Pegguy | 6 2 | 13 07 | G | 18 5 73 | Abymes | | Lens | 3 | — |
| | | | | | | | Leicester C | 6 | — |
| Ashley Neil | 5 10 | 10 10 | M | 16 9 80 | Chesterfield | Nottingham F | Leicester C | — | — |
| Branston Guy | 6 1 | 14 00 | D | 9 1 79 | Leicester | | Leicester C | — | — |
| | | | | | | Trainee | Colchester U (loan) | 12 | 1 |
| Brennan Karl | | | M | 19 3 81 | Leicester | Trainee | Leicester C | — | — |
| Campbell Stuart | 5 10 | 10 08 | M | 9 12 77 | Corby | Trainee | Leicester C | 21 | — |
| Carlstrand Lars-Gunnar‡ | 6 1 | 12 12 | F | 29 8 73 | Gothenburg | | Vastra Frolunda | 57 | 14 |
| | | | | | | | Vastra Frolunda* | — | — |
| | | | | | | | Vastra Frolunda | 21 | 8 |
| | | | | | | | Leicester C | — | — |
| Cottee Tony | 5 10 | 12 06 | F | 11 7 65 | West Ham | Apprentice | West Ham U | 212 | 92 |
| | | | | | | | Everton | 184 | 72 |
| | | | | | | | West Ham U | 67 | 23 |
| | | | | | | Selangor | Leicester C | 19 | 4 |
| | | | | | | | Birmingham C (loan) | 5 | 1 |
| Dudfield Lawrie | 6 0 | 12 04 | F | 7 5 80 | London | Kettering T | Leicester C | — | — |
| Elliott Matt | 6 3 | 14 05 | D | 1 11 68 | Wandsworth | Epsom & Ewell | Charlton Ath | — | — |
| | | | | | | | Torquay U | 124 | 15 |
| | | | | | | | Scunthorpe U (loan) | 8 | 1 |
| | | | | | | | Scunthorpe U | 53 | 7 |
| | | | | | | | Oxford U | 148 | 21 |
| | | | | | | | Leicester C | 53 | 11 |
| Emerson Paul | 6 1 | 12 00 | D | 29 8 78 | Newtonards | Trainee | Leicester C | — | — |
| Fenton Graham | 5 11 | 12 10 | F | 22 5 74 | Wallsend | Trainee | Aston Villa | 32 | 3 |
| | | | | | | | WBA (loan) | 7 | 3 |
| | | | | | | | Blackburn R | 27 | 7 |
| | | | | | | | Leicester C | 23 | 3 |
| Fox Martin | 5 8 | 11 00 | D | 21 4 79 | Sutton-in-Ashfield | Trainee | Leicester C | — | — |

| Name | | | | | | | Club | Apps | Goals |
|---|---|---|---|---|---|---|---|---|---|
| **Guppy** Steve | 5 11 | 12 00 | M | 29 3 69 | Winchester | Southampton | Wycombe W | 41 | 8 |
| | | | | | | | Newcastle U | — | — |
| | | | | | | | Port Vale | 105 | 12 |
| | | | | | | | Leicester C | 50 | 2 |
| **Harkin** Fergal* | 5 11 | 11 08 | M | 26 11 76 | Derry | Loughborough Univ | Leicester C | — | — |
| **Heskey** Emile | 6 2 | 13 12 | F | 11 1 78 | Leicester | Trainee | Leicester C | 101 | 27 |
| **Izzet** Muzzy | 5 10 | 10 12 | M | 31 10 74 | Mile End | Trainee | Chelsea | — | — |
| | | | | | | | Leicester C (loan) | 9 | 1 |
| | | | | | | | Leicester C | 71 | 7 |
| **Jaffa** Graeme | 5 6 | 9 08 | F | 8 5 79 | Falkirk | Trainee | Leicester C | — | — |
| **Kamark** Pontus | 5 11 | 12 02 | D | 5 4 69 | Fasteras | | IFK Gothenburg | 126 | 1 |
| | | | | | | IFK Gothenburg | Leicester C | 46 | — |
| **Keller** Kasey | 6 2 | 13 12 | G | 27 11 69 | Washington | Portland University | Millwall | 176 | — |
| | | | | | | | Leicester C | 63 | — |
| **Lennon** Neil | 5 9 | 13 02 | M | 25 6 71 | Lurgan | Trainee | Manchester C | 1 | — |
| | | | | | | | Crewe Alex | 147 | 15 |
| | | | | | | | Leicester C | 87 | 4 |
| **Marshall** Ian | 6 2 | 13 09 | F | 20 3 66 | Liverpool | Apprentice | Everton | 15 | 1 |
| | | | | | | | Oldham Ath | 170 | 36 |
| | | | | | | | Ipswich T | 84 | 32 |
| | | | | | | | Leicester C | 52 | 15 |
| **McMahon** Sam | 5 9 | 11 09 | M | 10 2 76 | Newark | Trainee | Leicester C | 5 | 1 |
| **Mitchell** Ross | 5 11 | 10 13 | M | 24 8 78 | Halifax | Trainee | Leicester C | — | — |
| **Neil** Gary | 6 0 | 12 10 | F | 16 8 78 | Glasgow | Trainee | Leicester C | — | — |
| **Oakes** Stefan | 5 11 | 12 04 | M | 6 9 78 | Leicester | Trainee | Leicester C | — | — |
| **Parker** Garry | 6 0 | 13 03 | M | 7 9 65 | Oxford | Apprentice | Luton T | 42 | 3 |
| | | | | | | | Hull C | 84 | 8 |
| | | | | | | | Nottingham F | 103 | 17 |
| | | | | | | | Aston Villa | 95 | 13 |
| | | | | | | | Leicester C | 107 | 10 |
| **Prior** Spencer | 6 3 | 13 04 | D | 22 4 71 | Rochford | Trainee | Southend U | 135 | 3 |
| | | | | | | | Norwich C | 74 | 1 |
| | | | | | | | Leicester C | 64 | — |
| **Robins** Mark | 5 8 | 11 11 | F | 22 12 69 | Ashton-under-Lyne | Apprentice | Manchester U | 48 | 11 |
| *(Transferred to Orense, January 1998)* | | | | | | | Norwich C | 67 | 20 |
| | | | | | | | Leicester C | 56 | 12 |
| | | | | | | | Reading (loan) | 5 | — |
| **Savage** Robbie | 6 2 | 11 11 | F | 18 10 74 | Wrexham | Trainee | Manchester U | — | — |
| | | | | | | | Crewe Alex | 77 | 10 |
| | | | | | | | Leicester C | 35 | 2 |
| **Skeldon** Kevin* | 5 11 | 11 05 | F | 27 4 78 | Edinburgh | Trainee | Leicester C | — | — |
| **Taylor** Scott | 5 9 | 11 05 | M | 23 11 70 | Portsmouth | Trainee | Reading | 207 | 24 |
| | | | | | | | Leicester C | 64 | 6 |
| **Thomas** Danny | | | M | 1 5 81 | Leamington Spa | Trainee | Nottingham F | — | — |
| | | | | | | | Leicester C | — | — |
| **Ullathorne** Robert | 5 8 | 10 10 | M | 11 10 71 | Wakefield | Trainee | Norwich C | 94 | 7 |
| | | | | | | | Osasuna | 18 | — |
| | | | | | | | Leicester C | 6 | 1 |
| **Walsh** Steve | 6 3 | 14 09 | D | 3 11 64 | Fulwood | Local | Wigan Ath | 126 | 4 |
| | | | | | | | Leicester C | 335 | 50 |
| **Watts** Julian* | 6 2 | 13 07 | D | 17 3 71 | Sheffield | Trainee | Rotherham U | 20 | 1 |
| | | | | | | | Sheffield W | 16 | 1 |
| | | | | | | | Shrewsbury T (loan) | 9 | — |
| | | | | | | | Leicester C | 38 | 1 |
| | | | | | | | Crewe Alex (loan) | 5 | — |
| | | | | | | | Huddersfield T (loan) | 8 | — |
| **Wenlock** Stephen | 5 7 | 11 01 | D | 11 3 78 | Peterborough | Trainee | Leicester C | — | — |
| **Wilson** Stevie‡ | 6 0 | 12 07 | G | 28 11 78 | Leicester | Trainee | Leicester C | — | — |
| **Wilson** Stuart | 5 8 | 9 12 | M | 16 9 77 | Leicester | Trainee | Leicester C | 13 | 3 |
| **Zagorakis** Theo | 5 9 | 11 08 | M | 27 10 71 | Kavala | PAOK Salonika | Leicester C | 14 | 1 |

**Trainees**
Bacon, Carl R; Goodwin, Thomas N; Heppell, Stuart E; Hodges, John K; Jackson, Matthew; Jones, Gareth; Magee, Martyn; McCann, Timothy M; Miller, James C; Neckles, Ainsley M B; Noble, Craig P; Orme, Richard P B; Ramm, Daniel A; Ridgway, David J; Saddington, David; Salter, Alex; Weale, Richard J.

**Associated Schoolboys**
Cattell, Stuart J; Cowell, Adam J; Darby, Brett; Dempsey, Reece J; Hallows, Dominic K; Kilby, David P; Noble, Karl N; Pindar, Andrew M; Purdie, Robert J; Smith, Matthew R; Stevenson, Jonathan.

**Associated Schoolboys who have accepted the club's offer of a Traineeship/Contract**
Heath, Matthew P; Nurse, Matthew J; Piper, Matthew J; Savage, Michael J.

## LEYTON ORIENT

| | | | | | | | | | |
|---|---|---|---|---|---|---|---|---|---|
| **Ayorinde** Sam‡ | 6 0 | 12 07 | F | 20 10 74 | Lagos | Sturm Graz | Leyton Orient | 13 | 2 |
| **Baker** Joe | 5 8 | 10 07 | F | 9 4 77 | London | Charlton Ath | Leyton Orient | 71 | 3 |
| **Bennett** Mickey† | 5 10 | 11 11 | M | 22 7 69 | Camberwell | Apprentice | Charlton Ath | 35 | 2 |
| | | | | | | | Wimbledon | 18 | 2 |
| | | | | | | | Brentford | 46 | 4 |
| | | | | | | | Charlton Ath | 24 | 1 |
| | | | | | | | Millwall | 2 | — |
| | | | | | | | Cardiff C | 14 | 1 |
| | | | | | | Cambridge C | Leyton Orient | 2 | — |
| **Brazier** Jeffrey‡ | | | M | 27 5 79 | Ascot | | Leyton Orient | — | — |
| **Brown** Daniel | | | M | 12 9 80 | London | Trainee | Leyton Orient | — | — |
| **Channing** Justin | 5 11 | 11 07 | D | 19 11 68 | Reading | Apprentice | QPR | 55 | 5 |
| | | | | | | | Bristol R | 130 | 10 |
| | | | | | | | Leyton Orient | 74 | 5 |
| **Clark** Simon | 6 0 | 12 12 | D | 12 3 67 | Boston | Stevenage Bor | Peterborough U | 107 | 4 |
| | | | | | | | Leyton Orient | 39 | 4 |
| **Cooper** Mark | 5 10 | 12 10 | M | 18 12 68 | Wakefield | Trainee | Bristol C | | |
| | | | | | | | Exeter C | 50 | 12 |
| | | | | | | | Southend U (loan) | 5 | — |
| | | | | | | | Birmingham C | 39 | 4 |
| | | | | | | | Fulham | 14 | — |
| | | | | | | | Huddersfield T (loan) | 10 | 4 |
| | | | | | | | Wycombe W | 2 | 1 |
| | | | | | | | Exeter C | 88 | 20 |
| | | | | | | | Hartlepool U | 33 | 9 |
| | | | | | | | Macclesfield T (loan) | 8 | 2 |
| | | | | | | | Leyton Orient | 1 | — |
| **Griffiths** Carl | 5 10 | 11 05 | F | 15 7 71 | Oswestry | Trainee | Shrewsbury T | 143 | 54 |
| | | | | | | | Manchester C | 18 | 4 |
| | | | | | | | Portsmouth | 14 | 2 |
| | | | | | | | Peterborough U | 16 | 2 |
| | | | | | | | Leyton Orient | 46 | 24 |
| **Hanson** Dave‡ | 6 1 | 13 01 | F | 19 11 68 | Huddersfield | Farsley Celtic | Bury | 1 | — |
| | | | | | | Hednesford T | Leyton Orient | 48 | 5 |
| | | | | | | | Chesterfield (loan) | 3 | 1 |
| **Harris** Jason | 6 1 | 11 10 | F | 24 11 76 | Sutton | Trainee | Crystal Palace | 2 | — |
| | | | | | | | Bristol R (loan) | 6 | 2 |
| | | | | | | | Lincoln C (loan) | 1 | — |
| | | | | | | | Leyton Orient | 35 | 6 |
| **Hicks** Stuart | 6 1 | 13 03 | D | 30 5 67 | Peterborough | Wisbech T | Colchester U | 64 | — |
| | | | | | | | Scunthorpe U | 67 | 1 |
| | | | | | | | Doncaster R | 36 | — |
| | | | | | | | Huddersfield T | 22 | 1 |
| | | | | | | | Preston NE | 12 | — |
| | | | | | | | Scarborough | 85 | 2 |
| | | | | | | | Leyton Orient | 35 | 1 |
| **Hodge** Steve‡ | 5 8 | 11 03 | M | 25 10 62 | Nottingham | Apprentice | Nottingham F | 123 | 30 |
| | | | | | | | Aston Villa | 53 | 12 |
| | | | | | | | Tottenham H | 45 | 7 |
| | | | | | | | Nottingham F | 82 | 20 |
| | | | | | | | Leeds U | 54 | 10 |
| | | | | | | | Derby Co (loan) | 10 | 2 |
| | | | | | | | QPR | 15 | — |
| | | | | | | | Watford | 2 | — |
| | | | | | | | Leyton Orient | 1 | — |
| **Honeyball** Scott‡ | | | D | 9 3 79 | London | | Leyton Orient | — | — |
| **Howes** Shaun* | 5 10 | 11 07 | M | 7 11 77 | Norwich | Trainee | Cambridge U | 1 | — |
| | | | | | | | Leyton Orient | 5 | — |
| **Hyde** Paul | 6 1 | 14 09 | G | 7 4 63 | Hayes | Hayes | Wycombe W | 105 | — |
| | | | | | | | Leicester C | — | — |
| | | | | | | | Leyton Orient | 41 | — |
| **Inglethorpe** Alex | 5 11 | 11 04 | F | 14 11 71 | Epsom | School | Watford | 12 | 2 |
| | | | | | | | Barnet (loan) | 6 | 3 |
| | | | | | | | Leyton Orient | 84 | 26 |
| **Jones** Anthony‡ | | | M | 28 1 79 | London | Trainee | Leyton Orient | — | — |
| **Joseph** Matt | 5 7 | 10 02 | D | 30 9 72 | Bethnal Green | Trainee | Arsenal | — | — |
| | | | | | | | Gillingham | — | — |
| | | | | | | | Cambridge U | 159 | 6 |
| | | | | | | | Leyton Orient | 14 | 1 |
| **Joseph** Roger | 5 11 | 11 10 | D | 24 12 65 | Paddington | Juniors | Brentford | 104 | 2 |
| | | | | | | | Wimbledon | 162 | — |
| | | | | | | | Millwall (loan) | 5 | — |
| | | | | | | | Leyton Orient | 15 | — |
| | | | | | | | WBA | 2 | — |
| | | | | | | | Leyton Orient | 25 | — |

| Name | Ht | Wt | Pos | DOB | Birthplace | From | | Club | Apps | Gls |
|---|---|---|---|---|---|---|---|---|---|---|
| **Ling** Martin | 5 7 | 10 08 | M | 15 7 66 | West Ham | Apprentice | | Exeter C | 116 | 14 |
| | | | | | | | | Swindon T | 2 | — |
| | | | | | | | | Southend U | 138 | 31 |
| | | | | | | | | Mansfield T (loan) | 3 | — |
| | | | | | | | | Swindon T (loan) | 1 | — |
| | | | | | | | | Swindon T | 149 | 10 |
| | | | | | | | | Leyton Orient | 90 | 3 |
| **MacKenzie** Chris | 6 0 | 12 06 | G | 14 5 72 | Northampton | Corby T | | Hereford U | 60 | 1 |
| | | | | | | | | Leyton Orient | 4 | — |
| **Martin** John§ | | | D | 15 7 81 | London | | | Leyton Orient | 1 | — |
| **Maskell** Craig† | 5 10 | 11 10 | F | 10 4 68 | Aldershot | Apprentice | | Southampton | 6 | 1 |
| | | | | | | | | Swindon T (loan) | — | — |
| | | | | | | | | Huddersfield T | 87 | 43 |
| | | | | | | | | Reading | 72 | 26 |
| | | | | | | | | Swindon T | 47 | 22 |
| | | | | | | | | Southampton | 17 | 1 |
| | | | | | | | | Bristol C (loan) | 5 | 1 |
| | | | | | | | | Brighton & HA | 69 | 20 |
| | | | | | | | Happy Valley | Leyton Orient | 8 | 2 |
| **Morrison** Dave | 5 11 | 12 10 | M | 30 11 74 | Waltham Forest | Chelmsford C | | Peterborough U | 77 | 12 |
| | | | | | | | | Leyton Orient | 10 | — |
| **Naylor** Dominic‡ | 5 9 | 12 01 | D | 12 8 70 | Watford | Trainee | | Watford | — | — |
| | | | | | | | | Halifax T | 6 | 1 |
| | | | | | | Barnet | | Barnet | 51 | — |
| | | | | | | | | Plymouth Arg | 85 | — |
| | | | | | | | | Gillingham | 31 | 1 |
| | | | | | | | | Leyton Orient | 87 | 4 |
| **Raynor** Paul† | 5 11 | 13 03 | M | 29 4 66 | Nottingham | Apprentice | | Nottingham F | 3 | — |
| | | | | | | | | Bristol R (loan) | 8 | — |
| | | | | | | | | Huddersfield T | 50 | 9 |
| | | | | | | | | Swansea C | 191 | 27 |
| | | | | | | | | Wrexham (loan) | 6 | — |
| | | | | | | | | Cambridge U | 49 | 2 |
| | | | | | | | | Preston NE | 80 | 9 |
| | | | | | | | | Cambridge U | 79 | 7 |
| | | | | | | | From Guang Deong | Leyton Orient | 10 | — |
| **Richards** Tony | 5 10 | 13 06 | F | 17 9 73 | Newham | Sudbury T | | Cambridge U | 42 | 5 |
| | | | | | | | | Leyton Orient | 17 | 2 |
| **Richardson** Craig§ | | | D | 8 10 79 | Newham | Trainee | | Leyton Orient | 1 | — |
| **Shearer** Lee‡ | 6 4 | 12 01 | D | 23 10 77 | Rochford | Trainee | | Leyton Orient | 18 | 1 |
| **Simpson** Colin | 6 1 | 11 05 | F | 30 4 76 | Oxford | Trainee | | Watford | 1 | — |
| | | | | | | Hendon | | Leyton Orient | 14 | 3 |
| **Smith** Dean | 6 0 | 13 00 | D | 19 3 71 | West Bromwich | Trainee | | Walsall | 142 | 2 |
| | | | | | | | | Hereford U | 117 | 19 |
| | | | | | | | | Leyton Orient | 43 | 9 |
| **Timons** Chris‡ | 6 1 | 12 07 | D | 8 12 74 | Longworth | Clipstone Welfare | | Mansfield T | 39 | 2 |
| | | | | | | | | Chesterfield | — | — |
| | | | | | | | | Leyton Orient | 6 | 2 |
| **Warren** Mark | 6 0 | 12 02 | D | 12 11 74 | Hackney | Trainee | | Leyton Orient | 142 | 5 |
| | | | | | | | | West Ham U (loan) | — | — |
| **West** Colin‡ | 6 1 | 13 09 | F | 13 11 62 | Wallsend | Apprentice | | Sunderland | 102 | 21 |
| | | | | | | | | Watford | 45 | 20 |
| | | | | | | | | Rangers | 10 | 2 |
| | | | | | | | | Sheffield W | 45 | 8 |
| | | | | | | | | WBA | 73 | 22 |
| | | | | | | | | Port Vale (loan) | 5 | 1 |
| | | | | | | | | Swansea C | 33 | 12 |
| | | | | | | | | Leyton Orient | 142 | 42 |
| | | | | | | | | Northampton T (loan) | 2 | — |
| **Williams** Michael* | | | M | 9 10 78 | Stepney | Trainee | | Leyton Orient | 1 | — |
| **Winston** Sam‡ | | | F | 6 8 78 | London | Norwich C | | Leyton Orient | 11 | 1 |

**Trainees**
Barrett, Adam N; Cockerill, David A; Curran, Danny; Donovan, Anthony; Ellerton, Gary J; Hart, Adam J; Martin, John; Marwa, Ranbir B; McMurtrie, Trevor; Morris, Jamie B; Richardson, Craig T; Rutherford, Westley; Shorey, Nicholas; Taylor, Mark J.

**Non-Contract**
Bennett, Michael R; Kimble, Garry L; Maskell, Craig D; Raynor, Paul J.

**Associated Schoolboys who have accepted the club's offer of a Traineeship/Contract**
Dorrian, Chris S; Gough, Neil; May, Phillip W; McKay, Darren G.

## LINCOLN CITY

| Name | Ht | Wt | Pos | DOB | Birthplace | From | | Club | Apps | Gls |
|---|---|---|---|---|---|---|---|---|---|---|
| **Alcide** Colin | 6 2 | 13 11 | M | 14 4 72 | Huddersfield | Emley | | Lincoln C | 98 | 25 |
| **Austin** Kevin | 6 1 | 14 00 | D | 12 2 73 | Hackney | Saffron Walden | | Leyton Orient | 109 | 3 |
| | | | | | | | | Lincoln C | 90 | 1 |

| Name | | | Pos | DOB | Birthplace | Source | Club | Apps | Gls |
|---|---|---|---|---|---|---|---|---|---|
| **Bailey** Dennis‡ | 5 10 | 11 08 | F | 13 11 65 | Lambeth | Farnborough T | Crystal Palace | 5 | 1 |
| | | | | | | | Bristol R (loan) | 17 | 9 |
| | | | | | | | Birmingham C | 75 | 23 |
| | | | | | | | Bristol R (loan) | 6 | 1 |
| | | | | | | | QPR | 39 | 10 |
| | | | | | | | Charlton Ath (loan) | 4 | — |
| | | | | | | | Watford (loan) | 8 | 4 |
| | | | | | | | Brentford (loan) | 6 | 3 |
| | | | | | | | Gillingham | 88 | 11 |
| | | | | | | | Lincoln C | 5 | 1 |
| **Barnett** Jason | 5 9 | 10 10 | D | 21 4 76 | Shrewsbury | Trainee | Wolverhampton W | — | — |
| | | | | | | | Lincoln C | 101 | 2 |
| **Bimson** Stuart | 5 11 | 11 08 | D | 29 9 69 | Liverpool | Macclesfield T | Bury | 36 | — |
| | | | | | | | Lincoln C | 27 | 1 |
| **Brown** Grant# | 6 0 | 11 12 | D | 19 11 69 | Sunderland | Trainee | Leicester C | 14 | — |
| | | | | | | | Lincoln C | 303 | 12 |
| **Brown** Steve* | 6 0 | 11 06 | F | 6 12 73 | Southend | Trainee | Southend U | 10 | 2 |
| | | | | | | | Scunthorpe U | — | — |
| | | | | | | | Colchester U | 62 | 17 |
| | | | | | | | Gillingham | 9 | 2 |
| | | | | | | | Lincoln C | 72 | 8 |
| **Chandler** Dean* | 6 1 | 11 02 | D | 6 5 76 | Ilford | Trainee | Charlton Ath | 2 | 1 |
| | | | | | | | Torquay U (loan) | 4 | — |
| | | | | | | | Lincoln C | — | — |
| **Fleming** Terry# | 5 9 | 10 01 | M | 5 1 73 | Marston Green | Trainee | Coventry C | 13 | — |
| | | | | | | | Northampton T | 31 | 1 |
| | | | | | | | Preston NE | 32 | 2 |
| | | | | | | | Lincoln C | 99 | 3 |
| **Gordon** Gavin | 6 1 | 12 00 | F | 24 6 79 | Manchester | Trainee | Hull C | 38 | 9 |
| | | | | | | | Lincoln C | 13 | 3 |
| **Gowshall** Joby‡ | 5 10 | 13 00 | D | 7 8 75 | Louth | Trainee | Grimsby T | — | — |
| | | | | | | | Lincoln C | — | — |
| **Holmes** Steve# | 6 2 | 13 00 | D | 13 1 71 | Middlesbrough | Guisborough T | Preston NE | 13 | 1 |
| | | | | | | | Hartlepool U (loan) | 5 | 2 |
| | | | | | | | Lincoln C | 97 | 10 |
| **Hone** Mark* | 6 1 | 12 00 | M | 31 3 68 | Croydon | Trainee Welling U | Crystal Palace | 4 | — |
| | | | | | | | Southend U | 56 | — |
| | | | | | | | Lincoln C | 53 | 2 |
| **Martin** Jae* | 5 11 | 11 00 | F | 5 2 76 | London | Trainee | Southend U | 8 | — |
| | | | | | | | Leyton Orient (loan) | 4 | — |
| | | | | | | | Birmingham C | 7 | — |
| | | | | | | | Lincoln C | 41 | 5 |
| **Miller** Paul | 6 0 | 11 07 | F | 31 1 68 | Bisley | Trainee | Wimbledon | 80 | 10 |
| | | | | | | | Newport Co (loan) | 6 | 2 |
| | | | | | | | Bristol C (loan) | 3 | — |
| | | | | | | | Bristol R | 105 | 22 |
| | | | | | | | Lincoln C | 24 | 2 |
| **Reeson** Nicholas | | | M | 5 5 80 | Boston | Trainee | Lincoln C | — | — |
| **Richardson** Barry# | 6 1 | 12 01 | G | 5 8 69 | Wallsend | Trainee | Sunderland | — | — |
| | | | | | | | Scunthorpe U | — | — |
| | | | | | | | Scarborough | 30 | — |
| | | | | | | | Northampton T | 96 | — |
| | | | | | | | Preston NE | 20 | — |
| | | | | | | | Lincoln C | 96 | — |
| **Robertson** John* | 6 2 | 12 08 | D | 8 1 74 | Liverpool | Trainee | Wigan Ath | 112 | 4 |
| | | | | | | | Lincoln C | 40 | 1 |
| **Sanders** Steve‡ | 5 9 | 11 02 | D | 2 6 78 | Halifax | Trainee | Huddersfield T | — | — |
| | | | | | | | Doncaster R | 25 | — |
| | | | | | | | Lincoln C | — | — |
| **Smith** Paul | 5 11 | 11 07 | M | 25 1 76 | Hastings | Hastings T | Nottingham F | — | — |
| | | | | | | | Lincoln C | 17 | 3 |
| **Stant** Phil | 6 1 | 12 07 | F | 13 10 62 | Bolton | Camberley Army | Reading | 4 | 2 |
| | | | | | | | Hereford U | 89 | 38 |
| | | | | | | | Notts Co | 22 | 6 |
| | | | | | | | Blackpool (loan) | 12 | 5 |
| | | | | | | | Lincoln C (loan) | 4 | — |
| | | | | | | | Huddersfield T (loan) | 5 | 1 |
| | | | | | | | Fulham | 19 | 5 |
| | | | | | | | Mansfield T | 57 | 32 |
| | | | | | | | Cardiff C | 79 | 34 |
| | | | | | | | Mansfield T (loan) | 4 | 1 |
| | | | | | | | Bury | 62 | 23 |
| | | | | | | | Northampton T (loan) | 5 | 2 |
| | | | | | | | Lincoln C | 43 | 17 |
| **Stones** Craig | | | M | 31 5 80 | Scunthorpe | Trainee | Lincoln C | 17 | — |
| **Thorpe** Lee | 6 0 | 11 06 | F | 14 12 75 | Wolverhampton | Trainee | Blackpool | 12 | — |
| | | | | | | | Lincoln C | 44 | 14 |

| Player | Ht | Wt | Pos | DOB | Birthplace | Source | Club | Apps | Gls |
|---|---|---|---|---|---|---|---|---|---|
| **Vaughan** John | 5 10 | 13 01 | G | 26 6 64 | Isleworth | Apprentice | West Ham U | — | — |
| | | | | | | | Charlton Ath (loan) | 6 | — |
| | | | | | | | Bristol R (loan) | 6 | — |
| | | | | | | | Wrexham (loan) | 4 | — |
| | | | | | | | Bristol C (loan) | 2 | — |
| | | | | | | | Fulham | 44 | — |
| | | | | | | | Bristol C (loan) | 3 | — |
| | | | | | | | Cambridge U | 178 | — |
| | | | | | | | Charlton Ath | 6 | — |
| | | | | | | | Preston NE | 66 | — |
| | | | | | | | Lincoln C | 29 | — |
| | | | | | | | Colchester U (loan) | 5 | — |
| **Walling** Dean | 6 0 | 10 08 | D | 17 4 69 | Leeds | Apprentice | Leeds U | — | — |
| | | | | | | | Rochdale | 65 | 8 |
| | | | | | Guiseley | | Carlisle U | 236 | 22 |
| | | | | | | | Lincoln C | 35 | 5 |
| **Westley** Shane‡ | 6 2 | 13 01 | D | 16 6 65 | Canterbury | Apprentice | Charlton Ath | 8 | — |
| | | | | | | | Southend U | 144 | 10 |
| | | | | | | | Norwich C (loan) | — | — |
| | | | | | | | Wolverhampton W | 50 | 2 |
| | | | | | | | Brentford | 64 | 1 |
| | | | | | | | Southend U (loan) | 5 | — |
| | | | | | | | Cambridge U | 3 | — |
| | | | | | | | Lincoln C | 9 | 1 |
| **Whitney** Jon# | 5 11 | 13 08 | D | 23 12 70 | Nantwich | Winsford U | Huddersfield T | 18 | — |
| | | | | | | | Wigan Ath (loan) | 12 | — |
| | | | | | | | Lincoln C | 88 | 6 |
| **Wilkins** Ian | | | D | 3 4 80 | Lincoln | Trainee | Lincoln C | 2 | — |

**Trainees**
Aiken, Christopher A; Bridge James; Carmody, Ryan D; Clarke, Justin A; Crawford, Stuart I; Crowfoot, Benjamin G; Heaton, Matthew P; Nower, Benjamin E; Ridley, Marc D; Vickers, Ross A; Walshe, Liam R.

**Associated Schoolboys**
Bent, Daniel; Chambers, Paul S; Fleming, Ross J; Gray, Darren K; Martin, Darren S; Moore, Dean A; Robinson, Andrew M; Smith, Lee A.

# LIVERPOOL

| Player | Ht | Wt | Pos | DOB | Birthplace | Source | Club | Apps | Gls |
|---|---|---|---|---|---|---|---|---|---|
| **Babb** Phil | 6 0 | 12 03 | D | 30 11 70 | Lambeth | Trainee | Millwall | — | — |
| | | | | | | | Bradford C | 80 | 14 |
| | | | | | | | Coventry C | 77 | 3 |
| | | | | | | | Liverpool | 103 | 1 |
| **Berger** Patrik | 6 1 | 12 06 | M | 10 11 73 | Prague | | Slavia Prague | 89 | 24 |
| | | | | | | | Borussia Dortmund | 25 | 4 |
| | | | | | | | Liverpool | 45 | 9 |
| **Bjornebye** Stig Inge | 5 10 | 11 09 | D | 11 12 69 | Elverum | | Strammen | 19 | — |
| | | | | | | | Kongsvinger | 62 | 3 |
| | | | | | | | Rosenborg | 21 | 3 |
| | | | | | | | Liverpool | 116 | 2 |
| **Brazier** Phil* | 6 0 | 13 00 | D | 3 9 77 | Liverpool | Trainee | Liverpool | — | — |
| **Byrne** Niall | 5 8 | 11 00 | F | 3 9 79 | Dublin | Trainee | Liverpool | — | — |
| **Carragher** Jamie | 6 1 | 13 00 | M | 28 1 78 | Liverpool | Trainee | Liverpool | 22 | 1 |
| **Cassidy** Jamie | 5 9 | 10 08 | M | 21 11 77 | Liverpool | Trainee | Liverpool | — | — |
| **Culshaw** Thomas | 5 10 | 12 02 | D | 10 10 78 | Liverpool | Trainee | Liverpool | 0 | — |
| **Doherty** Kevin | | | M | 18 4 80 | Dublin | | Liverpool | — | — |
| **Fowler** Robbie | 5 11 | 11 10 | F | 9 4 75 | Liverpool | Trainee | Liverpool | 160 | 92 |
| **Friars** Sean* | 5 9 | 11 00 | M | 15 5 79 | Derry | Trainee | Liverpool | — | — |
| **Friedel** Brad | 6 3 | 14 00 | G | 18 5 71 | Lakewood | | Liverpool | 11 | — |
| **Gerrard** Steven | | | M | 30 5 80 | Whiston | Trainee | Liverpool | — | — |
| **Gudnason** Haukar | | | F | 8 9 78 | Keflavik | | Keflavik | 34 | 11 |
| | | | | | | | Liverpool | — | — |
| **Harkness** Steve | 5 10 | 11 02 | D | 27 8 71 | Carlisle | Trainee | Carlisle U | 13 | — |
| | | | | | | | Liverpool | 96 | 2 |
| | | | | | | | Huddersfield T (loan) | 5 | — |
| | | | | | | | Southend U (loan) | 6 | — |
| **Ince** Paul | 5 10 | 12 02 | M | 21 10 67 | Ilford | Trainee | West Ham U | 72 | 7 |
| | | | | | | | Manchester U | 206 | 24 |
| | | | | | | | Internazionale | 54 | 9 |
| | | | | | | | Liverpool | 31 | 8 |
| **James** David | 6 5 | 14 02 | G | 1 8 70 | Welwyn | Trainee | Watford | 89 | — |
| | | | | | | | Liverpool | 188 | — |
| **Jones** Eifion | | | D | 28 9 80 | Llanrug | Trainee | Liverpool | — | — |
| **Jones** Rob | 5 8 | 11 00 | D | 5 11 71 | Wrexham | Trainee | Crewe Alex | 75 | 2 |
| | | | | | | | Liverpool | 183 | — |
| **Kvarme** Bjorn | 5 11 | 12 04 | D | 17 6 72 | Trondheim | | Rosenborg | 88 | 2 |
| | | | | | | | Liverpool | 38 | — |
| **Leonhardsen** Oyvind | 5 10 | 11 02 | M | 17 8 70 | Kristiansund | Clausenengen | Molde | 64 | 9 |
| | | | | | | | Rosenborg | 63 | 20 |
| | | | | | | | Wimbledon | 76 | 13 |
| | | | | | | | Liverpool | 28 | 6 |
| **Matteo** Dominic | 6 1 | 11 10 | D | 24 4 74 | Dumfries | Trainee | Liverpool | 75 | — |
| | | | | | | | Sunderland (loan) | 1 | — |
| **Maxwell** Leyton | 5 8 | 11 00 | M | 3 10 79 | St Asaph | Trainee | Liverpool | — | — |

| Name | Ht | Wt | Pos | DOB | Birthplace | Source | Club | Apps | Gls |
|---|---|---|---|---|---|---|---|---|---|
| **McAteer** Jason | 5 11 | 11 10 | M | 18 6 71 | Birkenhead | Marine | Bolton W | 114 | 8 |
| | | | | | | | Liverpool | 87 | 3 |
| **McManaman** Steve | 6 0 | 10 06 | M | 11 2 72 | Liverpool | School | Liverpool | 244 | 42 |
| **Murphy** Danny | 5 9 | 10 08 | M | 18 3 77 | Chester | Trainee | Crewe Alex | 134 | 27 |
| | | | | | | | Liverpool | 16 | — |
| **Murphy** Neil | | | D | 19 5 80 | Liverpool | Trainee | Liverpool | — | — |
| **Naylor** Roy* | 6 0 | 12 00 | G | 15 9 78 | Liverpool | Trainee | Liverpool | — | — |
| **Newby** John | 6 0 | 12 00 | F | 28 11 78 | Warrington | | Liverpool | — | — |
| **Nielsen** Jorgen | 6 0 | 13 00 | G | 6 5 71 | Nykabing | | Liverpool | — | — |
| **O'Mara** Paul | | | D | 23 11 80 | Dublin | Trainee | Liverpool | — | — |
| **Owen** Michael | 5 8 | 11 00 | F | 14 12 79 | Chester | Trainee | Liverpool | 38 | 19 |
| **Partridge** Richie | | | M | 12 9 80 | Dublin | | Liverpool | — | — |
| **Redknapp** Jamie | 6 0 | 12 10 | M | 25 6 73 | Barton-on-Sea | Trainee | Bournemouth | 13 | — |
| | | | | | | | Liverpool | 177 | 18 |
| **Riedle** Karlheinz | 5 11 | 12 00 | F | 16 9 65 | Weiler | Augsburg | Blau-Weiss 90 | 34 | 10 |
| | | | | | | | Werder Bremen | 86 | 38 |
| | | | | | | | Lazio | 84 | 30 |
| | | | | | | | Borussia Dortmund | 87 | 24 |
| | | | | | | | Liverpool | 25 | 6 |
| **Rizzo** Nicky | 5 10 | 12 00 | M | 9 6 79 | Sydney | Sydney Olympic | Liverpool | — | — |
| **Roberts** Gareth | 5 8 | 11 00 | D | 6 2 78 | Wrexham | Trainee | Liverpool | 0 | — |
| **Ruddock** Neil | 6 2 | 12 12 | D | 9 5 68 | London | Apprentice | Millwall | — | — |
| | | | | | | | Tottenham H | 9 | — |
| | | | | | | | Millwall | 2 | 1 |
| | | | | | | | Southampton | 107 | 9 |
| | | | | | | | Tottenham H | 38 | 3 |
| | | | | | | | Liverpool | 115 | 11 |
| | | | | | | | QPR (loan) | 7 | — |
| **Thomas** Michael | 5 9 | 12 06 | M | 24 8 67 | Lambeth | Apprentice | Arsenal | 163 | 24 |
| | | | | | | | Portsmouth (loan) | 3 | — |
| | | | | | | | Liverpool | 124 | 9 |
| | | | | | | | Middlesbrough (loan) | 10 | — |
| **Thompson** David | 5 7 | 10 00 | M | 12 9 77 | Birkenhead | Trainee | Liverpool | 7 | 1 |
| | | | | | | | Swindon T (loan) | 10 | — |
| **Turkington** Eddie* | 6 1 | 13 00 | M | 15 5 78 | Merseyside | Trainee | Liverpool | — | — |
| **Warner** Tony | 6 4 | 13 09 | G | 11 5 74 | Liverpool | School | Liverpool | — | — |
| | | | | | | | Swindon T (loan) | 2 | — |
| **Williams** Danny | 6 1 | 13 00 | M | 12 7 79 | Wrexham | Trainee | Liverpool | — | — |
| **Wright** Mark | 6 2 | 13 03 | D | 1 8 63 | Dorchester | Amateur | Oxford U | 10 | — |
| | | | | | | | Southampton | 170 | 7 |
| | | | | | | | Derby Co | 144 | 10 |
| | | | | | | | Liverpool | 158 | 5 |
| **Wright** Stephen | | | D | 8 2 80 | Liverpool | Trainee | Liverpool | — | — |

**Trainees**
Bishop, David S; Boardman, John S; Boggan, Jonathan R; Cass, Matthew; Dunbavin, Ian S; Gregson, Neil R; Harkin, Bryan; Navarro, Alan E; Roberts, John P; Yates, Michael A.

**Associated Schoolboys**
Baker, Carl P; Beck, Lee T; Coupe, Alan E; Daniels, David A; Danns, Neil A; De Arostegui, Daniel; Knowles, Gareth J; Madin, Lee P; McIlroy, Brian P; McNulty, Stephen M; Mitchell, Philip S; Morton, Anthony P; Nicholas, Andrew P; Otsemobor, John; Prince, Neil M; Roberts, Karl D; Robinson, Craig; Tamm, Christopher W; Welsh, John J; Wilde, Richard P.

**Associated Schoolboys who have accepted the club's offer of a Traineeship/Contract**
Armstrong, Ian; Cavanagh, Peter J; Crookes, Peter; Culshaw, Paul R; Miles, John F; O'Brien, Christopher M; Olsen, James P; Park, Stephen M; Porter, Stephen; Thompson, Christopher M; Torpey, Stephen R; Warnock, Stephen.

## LUTON TOWN

| Name | Ht | Wt | Pos | DOB | Birthplace | Source | Club | Apps | Gls |
|---|---|---|---|---|---|---|---|---|---|
| **Abbey** Nathan | 6 1 | 11 13 | G | 11 7 78 | Islington | Trainee | Luton T | — | — |
| **Alexander** Graham | 5 11 | 12 02 | M | 10 10 71 | Coventry | Trainee | Scunthorpe U | 159 | 18 |
| | | | | | | | Luton T | 121 | 11 |
| **Augustine** Steve | 6 0 | 13 07 | M | 13 12 78 | Hammersmith | | Luton T | — | — |
| **Barr** Andrew* | 5 11 | 11 12 | F | 21 6 79 | Solihull | Trainee | Luton T | — | — |
| **Boyce** Emmerson | 5 11 | 11 07 | D | 24 9 79 | Aylesbury | Trainee | Luton T | — | — |
| **Cox** Jimmy | 5 6 | 10 07 | F | 11 4 80 | Gloucester | | Luton T | — | — |
| **Davies** Simon | 6 0 | 12 03 | M | 23 4 74 | Winsford | Trainee | Manchester U | 11 | — |
| | | | | | | | Exeter C (loan) | 6 | 1 |
| | | | | | | | Huddersfield T (loan) | 3 | — |
| | | | | | | | Luton T | 20 | 1 |
| **Davis** Kelvin | 6 1 | 14 00 | G | 29 9 76 | Bedford | Trainee | Luton T | 48 | — |
| | | | | | | | Torquay U (loan) | 2 | — |
| | | | | | | | Hartlepool U (loan) | 2 | — |
| **Davis** Steve | 6 2 | 14 07 | D | 30 10 68 | Hexham | Trainee | Southampton | 7 | — |
| | | | | | | | Burnley (loan) | 9 | — |
| | | | | | | | Notts Co (loan) | 2 | — |
| | | | | | | | Burnley | 162 | 22 |
| | | | | | | | Luton T | 118 | 15 |
| **Doherty** Gary | 6 1 | 13 00 | F | 31 1 80 | Donegal | Trainee | Luton T | 10 | — |
| **Douglas** Stuart | 5 8 | 11 05 | F | 9 4 78 | London | Trainee | Luton T | 34 | 2 |
| **Evers** Sean | 5 9 | 9 11 | M | 10 10 77 | Hitchin | Trainee | Luton T | 25 | 3 |

| Name | Ht | Wt | Pos | DOB | Birthplace | Source | Club | Apps | Gls |
|---|---|---|---|---|---|---|---|---|---|
| **Feuer** Ian‡ | 6 7 | 15 06 | G | 20 5 71 | Las Vegas | Los Angeles Salsa | West Ham U | — | — |
| | | | | | | | Peterborough U (loan) | 16 | — |
| | | | | | | | Luton T | 97 | — |
| **Fotiadis** Andrew | 5 11 | 11 00 | F | 6 9 77 | Hitchin | School | Luton T | 32 | 4 |
| **Fraser** Stuart | 5 9 | 11 00 | D | 9 1 80 | Edinburgh | Trainee | Luton T | 1 | — |
| **George** Liam | 5 9 | 11 04 | F | 2 2 79 | Luton | Trainee | Luton T | 1 | — |
| **Gray** Phil | 5 9 | 12 09 | F | 2 10 68 | Belfast | Apprentice | Tottenham H | 9 | — |
| | | | | | | | Barnsley (loan) | 3 | — |
| | | | | | | | Fulham (loan) | 3 | — |
| | | | | | | | Luton T | 59 | 22 |
| | | | | | | | Sunderland | 115 | 34 |
| | | | | | | | Luton T | 17 | 2 |
| **Harvey** Richard* | 5 10 | 11 12 | D | 17 4 69 | Letchworth | Apprentice | Luton T | 161 | 4 |
| | | | | | | | Blackpool (loan) | 5 | — |
| **James** Julian | 5 10 | 12 04 | D | 22 3 70 | Tring | Trainee | Luton T | 282 | 13 |
| | | | | | | | Preston NE (loan) | 6 | — |
| **Johnson** Marvin | 6 1 | 13 06 | D | 29 10 68 | Wembley | Apprentice | Luton T | 260 | 6 |
| **Jones** Ian* | 5 9 | 11 13 | D | 18 11 78 | Merthyr | Trainee | Luton T | — | — |
| **Kean** Robert‡ | 5 7 | 10 00 | M | 3 6 78 | Luton | Trainee | Luton T | 1 | — |
| **Marshall** Dwight* | 6 1 | 11 02 | F | 3 10 65 | Jamaica | Grays Ath | Plymouth Arg | 99 | 27 |
| | | | | | | | Middlesbrough (loan) | 3 | — |
| | | | | | | | Luton T | 124 | 27 |
| **McIndoe** Michael | 5 8 | 11 00 | M | 2 12 79 | Edinburgh | Trainee | Luton T | — | — |
| **McLaren** Paul | 6 1 | 13 04 | M | 17 11 76 | High Wycombe | Trainee | Luton T | 80 | 1 |
| **Oldfield** David* | 6 0 | 13 04 | F | 30 5 68 | Perth (Aus) | Apprentice | Luton T | 29 | 4 |
| | | | | | | | Manchester C | 26 | 6 |
| | | | | | | | Leicester C | 188 | 26 |
| | | | | | | | Millwall (loan) | 17 | 6 |
| | | | | | | | Luton T | 117 | 18 |
| **Omogbehin** Colin‡ | | | D | 10 9 74 | Croydon | | Luton T | — | — |
| **Patterson** Darren* | 6 1 | 12 10 | D | 15 10 69 | Belfast | Trainee | WBA | — | — |
| | | | | | | | Wigan Ath | 97 | 6 |
| | | | | | | | Crystal Palace | 22 | 1 |
| | | | | | | | Luton T | 56 | — |
| | | | | | | | Preston NE (loan) | 2 | — |
| **Peake** Trevor‡ | 6 0 | 12 09 | D | 10 2 57 | Nuneaton | Nuneaton Bor | Lincoln C | 171 | 7 |
| | | | | | | | Coventry C | 278 | 6 |
| | | | | | | | Luton T | 179 | — |
| **Showler** Paul | 5 7 | 11 00 | M | 10 10 66 | Doncaster | Altrincham | Barnet | 71 | 12 |
| | | | | | | | Bradford C | 88 | 15 |
| | | | | | | | Luton T | 24 | 6 |
| **Spring** Matthew | 5 11 | 11 07 | M | 17 11 79 | Harlow | Trainee | Luton T | 12 | — |
| **Sweeney** Terry* | 5 6 | 10 10 | F | 26 1 79 | Paisley | Trainee | Luton T | — | 1 |
| **Thomas** Mitchell | 6 2 | 13 00 | D | 2 10 64 | Luton | Apprentice | Luton T | 107 | 1 |
| | | | | | | | Tottenham H | 157 | 6 |
| | | | | | | | West Ham U | 38 | 3 |
| | | | | | | | Luton T | 153 | 5 |
| **Waddock** Gary* | 5 10 | 12 05 | M | 17 3 62 | Alperton | Apprentice | QPR | 203 | 8 |
| | | | | | | Charleroi | Millwall | 58 | 2 |
| | | | | | | | QPR | — | — |
| | | | | | | | Swindon T (loan) | 6 | — |
| | | | | | | | Bristol R | 71 | 1 |
| | | | | | | | Luton T | 153 | 3 |
| **Webb** Nicholas* | 6 1 | 12 13 | G | 23 2 79 | Hitchin | Trainee | Luton T | — | — |
| **White** Alan | 6 0 | 13 04 | D | 22 3 76 | Darlington | Derby Co | Middlesbrough | — | — |
| | | | | | | | Luton T | 28 | 1 |
| **Willmott** Chris | 6 2 | 11 05 | D | 30 9 77 | Bedford | Trainee | Luton T | — | — |

**Trainees**
Akurang, Cliff D; Ayres, James M; Clarke, Richard J; Howe, Darren M; Kandol, Tresor O; Lawes, Russell I; McKoy, Delroy N B; Moses, Jerry E; Scarlett, Andre P; Tate, Daniel A.

**Associated Schoolboys**
Clarke, Duane; Deller, Christopher J; Dogbe, Steven; James-Barriteau, Rene W; Mansell, Lee R; Mentore, Ezra; Orchard, Lee; Plant, Raith S; Thomas, William J; Wraight, Graham D.

**Associated Schoolboys who have accepted the club's offer of a Traineeship/Contract**
Harrington, Joseph; Minton, Alex; Moran, Ryan J; Robert, Steven; Stirling, Jude B; Ward, Scott.

# MACCLESFIELD TOWN

| Name | Ht | Wt | Pos | DOB | Birthplace | Source | Club | Apps | Gls |
|---|---|---|---|---|---|---|---|---|---|
| **Askey** John# | 6 0 | 12 02 | F | 4 11 64 | Stoke | Port Vale | Macclesfield T | 39 | 6 |
| **Brown** Greg† | 5 10 | 12 04 | D | 31 7 78 | Wythenshawe | Trainee | Chester C | 4 | — |
| | | | | | | | Macclesfield T | 2 | — |
| **Chambers** Leroy | 5 11 | 11 08 | F | 25 10 72 | Sheffield | Trainee | Sheffield W | — | — |
| | | | | | | | Chester C | 21 | 1 |
| | | | | | | | Chesterfield | — | — |
| | | | | | | Boston U | Macclesfield T | 21 | 4 |
| **Clyde** Glynn | 6 2 | 11 07 | G | 16 1 79 | Derry | Barnsley | Macclesfield T | — | — |
| **Da Costa** Nelson† | 5 10 | 12 03 | D | 8 12 78 | Angola | Belenenses | Stockport Co | — | — |
| | | | | | | | Macclesfield T | — | — |

| | | | | | | | | | |
|---|---|---|---|---|---|---|---|---|---|
| **Davenport** Peter# | 5 11 | 12 10 | M | 24 3 61 | Birkenhead | Everton | Nottingham F | 118 | 54 |
| | | | | | | | Manchester U | 92 | 22 |
| | | | | | | | Middlesbrough | 59 | 7 |
| | | | | | | | Sunderland | 99 | 15 |
| | | | | | | | Airdrie | 38 | 9 |
| | | | | | | | St Johnstone | 22 | 4 |
| | | | | | | | Stockport Co | 6 | 1 |
| | | | | | | Southport | Macclesfield T | 4 | 1 |
| **Durkan** Kieron | 5 10 | 12 09 | M | 1 12 73 | Chester | Trainee | Wrexham | 50 | 3 |
| | | | | | | | Stockport Co | 64 | 4 |
| | | | | | | | Macclesfield T | 4 | — |
| **Edey** Cec‡ | 6 1 | 12 00 | D | 12 3 65 | Manchester | Witton A | Macclesfield T | 13 | — |
| **Gardiner** Mark‡ | 5 10 | 11 07 | M | 25 12 66 | Cirencester | Apprentice | Swindon T | 10 | — |
| | | | | | | | Torquay U | 49 | 4 |
| | | | | | | | Crewe Alex | 193 | 33 |
| | | | | | | | Chester C (loan) | 3 | — |
| | | | | | | Fredrikstad | Macclesfield T | 7 | 2 |
| **Hitchen** Steve | 5 8 | 11 07 | D | 28 11 76 | Salford | Trainee | Blackburn R | — | — |
| | | | | | | | Macclesfield T | 2 | — |
| **Howarth** Neil | 6 3 | 13 07 | D | 15 11 71 | Bolton | Trainee | Burnley | 1 | — |
| | | | | | | Macclesfield T | Macclesfield T | 41 | 3 |
| **Irving** Richard‡ | 5 7 | 12 02 | F | 10 9 75 | Halifax | Trainee | Manchester U | — | — |
| | | | | | | | Nottingham F | 1 | — |
| | | | | | | | Macclesfield T | 9 | — |
| **Landon** Richard | 6 2 | 13 10 | F | 22 3 70 | Worthing | Bedworth U | Plymouth Arg | 30 | 12 |
| | | | | | | | Stockport Co | 13 | 5 |
| | | | | | | | Rotherham U (loan) | 8 | — |
| | | | | | | | Macclesfield T | 18 | 7 |
| **Levendis** Andy‡ | 5 8 | 10 12 | M | 4 7 78 | Cheadle | Oldham Ath | Macclesfield T | — | — |
| **Mason** Andy* | 6 0 | 12 02 | F | 22 11 74 | Bolton | Trainee | Bolton W | — | — |
| | | | | | | | Hull C | 26 | 4 |
| | | | | | | | Chesterfield | 2 | — |
| | | | | | | | Macclesfield T | 12 | — |
| **McDonald** Martin | 5 11 | 11 12 | M | 4 12 73 | Irvine | Southport | Doncaster R | 48 | 4 |
| | | | | | | | Macclesfield T | 22 | 1 |
| **Mitchell** Neil‡ | 5 7 | 11 00 | F | 7 11 74 | Lytham | Trainee | Blackpool | 67 | 8 |
| | | | | | | | Rochdale (loan) | 4 | — |
| | | | | | | | Macclesfield T | 6 | — |
| **Payne** Steve | 5 11 | 12 05 | D | 1 8 75 | Castleford | Trainee | Huddersfield T | — | — |
| | | | | | | | Macclesfield T | 39 | — |
| **Peel** Nathan‡ | 6 1 | 13 04 | F | 17 5 72 | Blackburn | Trainee | Preston NE | 10 | 1 |
| | | | | | | | Sheffield U | 1 | — |
| | | | | | | | Halifax T (loan) | 3 | — |
| | | | | | | | Burnley | 16 | 2 |
| | | | | | | | Rotherham U (loan) | 9 | 4 |
| | | | | | | | Mansfield T (loan) | 2 | — |
| | | | | | | | Doncaster R (loan) | 2 | — |
| | | | | | | | Rotherham U | — | — |
| | | | | | | | Macclesfield T | 14 | 3 |
| **Power** Phil# | 5 7 | 11 00 | F | 25 7 67 | Salford | Witton A | Crewe Alex | 11 | 2 |
| | | | | | | Stalybridge C | Macclesfield T | 38 | 7 |
| **Price** Ryan | 6 6 | 14 00 | G | 13 3 70 | Wolverhampton | Stafford R | Birmingham C | — | — |
| | | | | | | | Macclesfield T | 46 | — |
| **Rose** Colin‡ | 5 8 | 11 00 | M | 22 1 72 | Winsford | Trainee | Crewe Alex | 22 | 1 |
| | | | | | | Witton A | Macclesfield T | 19 | — |
| **Sedgemore** Ben | 6 0 | 12 08 | M | 5 8 75 | Wolverhampton | Trainee | Birmingham C | — | — |
| | | | | | | | Northampton T (loan) | 1 | — |
| | | | | | | | Mansfield T (loan) | 9 | — |
| | | | | | | | Peterborough U | 17 | — |
| | | | | | | | Mansfield T | 67 | 6 |
| | | | | | | | Macclesfield T | 5 | — |
| **Sodje** Efetobar | 6 1 | 12 00 | D | 5 10 72 | Greenwich | Stevenage Bor | Macclesfield T | 41 | 3 |
| **Sorvel** Neil | 6 0 | 12 09 | M | 2 3 73 | Whiston | Trainee | Crewe Alex | 9 | — |
| | | | | | | | Macclesfield T | 45 | 3 |
| **Tinson** Darren | 6 0 | 14 04 | D | 15 11 69 | Birmingham | Northwich V | Macclesfield T | 44 | — |
| **Whittaker** Stuart | 5 7 | 10 00 | M | 2 1 75 | Liverpool | Liverpool | Bolton W | 3 | — |
| | | | | | | | Wigan Ath (loan) | 3 | — |
| | | | | | | | Macclesfield T | 31 | 4 |
| **Wood** Steve# | 5 9 | 10 10 | M | 23 6 63 | Oldham | Ashton U | Macclesfield T | 43 | 13 |

**Non-Contract**
Brown, Greg J; Da Costa, Nelson C P; Gee, Daniel; Ohandjianian, Demis.

## MANCHESTER CITY

| | | | | | | | | | |
|---|---|---|---|---|---|---|---|---|---|
| **Bailey** Alan | 5 9 | 11 07 | F | 1 11 78 | Macclesfield | Trainee | Manchester C | — | — |
| **Beesley** Paul | 6 1 | 12 07 | D | 21 9 65 | Wigan | Marine | Wigan Ath | 155 | 3 |
| | | | | | | | Leyton Orient | 32 | 1 |
| | | | | | | | Sheffield U | 168 | 7 |
| | | | | | | | Leeds U | 22 | — |
| | | | | | | | Manchester C | 13 | — |
| | | | | | | | Port Vale (loan) | 5 | — |
| | | | | | | | WBA (loan) | 8 | — |

| Bishop Ian | 5 9 | 10 12 | M | 29 5 65 | Liverpool | Apprentice | Everton | 1 | — |
|---|---|---|---|---|---|---|---|---|---|
| | | | | | | | Crewe Alex (loan) | 4 | — |
| | | | | | | | Carlisle U | 132 | 14 |
| | | | | | | | Bournemouth | 44 | 2 |
| | | | | | | | Manchester C | 19 | 2 |
| | | | | | | | West Ham U | 254 | 12 |
| | | | | | | | Manchester C | 6 | — |
| Bradbury Lee | 6 2 | 13 10 | F | 3 7 75 | Isle of Wight | Cowes | Portsmouth | 54 | 15 |
| | | | | | | | Exeter C (loan) | 14 | 5 |
| | | | | | | | Manchester C | 27 | 7 |
| Brannan Ged | 6 0 | 12 05 | D | 15 1 72 | Liverpool | Trainee | Tranmere R | 238 | 20 |
| | | | | | | | Manchester C | 43 | 4 |
| Brightwell Ian* | 5 10 | 12 05 | D | 9 4 68 | Lutterworth | Congleton T | Manchester C | 321 | 18 |
| Brisco Neil* | 6 0 | 11 05 | M | 26 1 78 | Wigan | Trainee | Manchester C | — | — |
| Brown Michael | 5 9 | 10 07 | G | 6 11 79 | Stranraer | Trainee | Manchester C | — | — |
| Brown Michael R | 5 10 | 11 08 | M | 25 1 77 | Hartlepool | Trainee | Manchester C | 58 | — |
| | | | | | | | Hartlepool U (loan) | 6 | 1 |
| Callaghan Anthony* | 5 7 | 10 00 | D | 11 1 78 | Manchester | Trainee | Manchester C | — | — |
| Clough Nigel | 5 10 | 12 03 | M | 19 3 66 | Sunderland | AC Hunters | Nottingham F | 311 | 101 |
| | | | | | | | Liverpool | 39 | 7 |
| | | | | | | | Manchester C | 38 | 4 |
| | | | | | | | Nottingham F (loan) | 13 | 1 |
| | | | | | | | Sheffield W (loan) | 1 | — |
| Conlon Barry | 6 3 | 14 00 | F | 1 10 78 | Dublin | QPR | Manchester C | 7 | — |
| | | | | | | | Plymouth Arg (loan) | 13 | 2 |
| Creaney Gerry* | 5 10 | 13 06 | F | 13 4 70 | Coatbridge | Celtic BC | Celtic | 113 | 36 |
| | | | | | | | Portsmouth | 60 | 32 |
| | | | | | | | Manchester C | 21 | 4 |
| | | | | | | | Oldham Ath (loan) | 9 | 2 |
| | | | | | | | Ipswich T (loan) | 6 | 1 |
| | | | | | | | Burnley (loan) | 10 | 8 |
| | | | | | | | Chesterfield (loan) | 4 | — |
| Crooks Lee | 6 1 | 12 01 | M | 14 1 78 | Wakefield | Trainee | Manchester C | 20 | — |
| Dickov Paul | 5 5 | 11 09 | F | 1 11 72 | Glasgow | Trainee | Arsenal | 21 | 3 |
| | | | | | | | Luton T (loan) | 15 | 1 |
| | | | | | | | Brighton & HA (loan) | 8 | 5 |
| | | | | | | | Manchester C | 59 | 14 |
| Doherty George* | | | F | 20 2 80 | Derry | Trainee | Manchester C | — | — |
| Edghill Richard | 5 9 | 11 03 | D | 23 9 74 | Oldham | Trainee | Manchester C | 85 | — |
| Fenton Anthony | 5 10 | 10 02 | D | 23 11 79 | Preston | Trainee | Manchester C | — | — |
| Fenton Nicholas | 5 10 | 10 04 | D | 23 11 79 | Preston | Trainee | Manchester C | — | — |
| Gallagher Benn* | 5 8 | 11 00 | D | 12 10 78 | Rugby | Trainee | Manchester C | — | — |
| Goater Shaun | 6 1 | 11 10 | F | 25 2 70 | Bermuda | | Manchester U | — | — |
| | | | | | | | Rotherham U | 209 | 70 |
| | | | | | | | Notts Co (loan) | 1 | — |
| | | | | | | | Bristol C | 75 | 40 |
| | | | | | | | Manchester C | 7 | 3 |
| Greenacre Chris | 5 11 | 12 08 | F | 23 12 77 | Halifax | Trainee | Manchester C | 7 | 1 |
| | | | | | | | Cardiff C (loan) | 11 | 2 |
| | | | | | | | Blackpool (loan) | 4 | — |
| Heaney Neil | 5 9 | 11 07 | F | 3 11 71 | Middlesbrough | Trainee | Arsenal | 7 | — |
| | | | | | | | Hartlepool U (loan) | 3 | — |
| | | | | | | | Cambridge U (loan) | 13 | 4 |
| | | | | | | | Southampton | 61 | 5 |
| | | | | | | | Manchester C | 18 | 1 |
| | | | | | | | Charlton Ath (loan) | 6 | — |
| Hiley Scott | 5 9 | 11 05 | D | 27 9 68 | Plymouth | Trainee | Exeter C | 210 | 12 |
| | | | | | | | Birmingham C | 49 | — |
| | | | | | | | Manchester C | 9 | — |
| Holmes Shaun | | | D | 27 12 80 | Derry | Trainee | Manchester C | — | — |
| Horlock Kevin | 6 0 | 12 00 | M | 1 11 72 | Erith | Trainee | West Ham U | — | — |
| | | | | | | | Swindon T | 163 | 22 |
| | | | | | | | Manchester C | 43 | 9 |
| Ingram Rae* | 5 11 | 12 02 | D | 6 12 74 | Manchester | Trainee | Manchester C | 23 | — |
| | | | | | | | Macclesfield T (loan) | 5 | — |
| Jobson Richard | 6 1 | 13 05 | D | 9 5 63 | Holderness | Burton Alb | Watford | 28 | 4 |
| | | | | | | | Hull C | 221 | 17 |
| | | | | | | | Oldham Ath | 189 | 10 |
| | | | | | | | Leeds U | 22 | 1 |
| | | | | | | | Southend U (loan) | 8 | 1 |
| | | | | | | | Manchester C | 6 | 1 |
| Kavelashvili Mikhail | 5 11 | 12 01 | M | 22 7 71 | Tbilisi | Spartak Vladikavkaz | Manchester C | 28 | 3 |
| Kelly Ray | 5 11 | 12 00 | F | 29 12 76 | Ballinasloe | Athlone T | Manchester C | 1 | — |
| | | | | | | | Wrexham (loan) | 10 | 1 |
| Kinkladze Georgiou | 5 8 | 10 09 | M | 6 7 73 | Tbilisi | Dynamo Tbilisi | Manchester C | 106 | 20 |
| Margetson Martyn* | 6 0 | 14 00 | G | 8 9 71 | West Neath | Trainee | Manchester C | 51 | — |
| | | | | | | | Bristol R (loan) | 3 | — |
| | | | | | | | Bolton W (loan) | — | — |
| | | | | | | | Luton T (loan) | — | — |
| Mason Gary | 5 8 | 10 01 | M | 15 10 79 | Edinburgh | Trainee | Manchester C | — | — |

| | | | | | | | | | |
|---|---|---|---|---|---|---|---|---|---|
| **McGlinchey** Brian* | 5 7 | 10 02 | M | 26 10 77 | Derry | Trainee | Manchester C | — | — |
| **McGoldrick** Eddie | 5 10 | 11 07 | M | 30 4 65 | London | Nuneaton Bor, Kettering T | Northampton T | 107 | 9 |
| | | | | | | | Crystal Palace | 147 | 11 |
| | | | | | | | Arsenal | 38 | — |
| | | | | | | | Manchester C | 40 | — |
| | | | | | | | Stockport Co (loan) | 2 | — |
| **Morley** David | | | D | 25 9 77 | St Helens | Trainee | Manchester C | 3 | 1 |
| | | | | | | | Ayr U (loan) | 4 | — |
| **Morley** Neil | 5 8 | 10 02 | M | 16 11 78 | Warrington | Trainee | Manchester C | — | — |
| **Phillips** Martin | 5 9 | 10 03 | F | 13 3 76 | Exeter | Trainee | Exeter C | 52 | 5 |
| | | | | | | | Manchester C | 15 | — |
| | | | | | | | Scunthorpe U (loan) | 3 | — |
| | | | | | | | Exeter C (loan) | 8 | — |
| **Pollock** Jamie | 5 10 | 14 01 | M | 16 2 74 | Stockton | Trainee | Middlesbrough | 155 | 17 |
| | | | | | | | Osasuna | — | — |
| | | | | | | | Bolton W | 46 | 5 |
| | | | | | | | Manchester C | 8 | 1 |
| **Porteous** Andrew | 5 11 | 10 11 | M | 13 9 79 | Edinburgh | Trainee | Nottingham F | — | — |
| | | | | | | | Manchester C | — | — |
| **Pridham** Christopher* | | | M | 11 8 78 | Neath | Trainee | Manchester C | — | — |
| **Rimmer** Stephen | 6 3 | 13 02 | D | 23 5 79 | Liverpool | Trainee | Manchester C | — | — |
| **Rosler** Uwe* | 6 0 | 12 06 | F | 15 11 68 | Attenburg | Chemie Leipzig | Magdeburg | 62 | 22 |
| | | | | | | | Dynamo Dresden | 33 | 4 |
| | | | | | | | Nuremberg | 28 | — |
| | | | | | | | Dynamo Dresden | 7 | — |
| | | | | | | | Manchester C | 152 | 50 |
| **Rowlands** Aled* | 5 6 | 10 00 | F | 9 6 78 | Bangor | Trainee | Manchester C | — | — |
| **Russell** Craig | 5 9 | 12 00 | F | 4 2 74 | Jarrow | Trainee | Sunderland | 150 | 31 |
| | | | | | | | Manchester C | 24 | 1 |
| **Shelia** Murtaz | 6 1 | 13 00 | D | 25 3 69 | Georgia | | Dynamo Tbilisi | 10 | 2 |
| | | | | | | | Alania | 62 | 9 |
| | | | | | | | Manchester C | 12 | 2 |
| **Symons** Kit# | 6 1 | 13 07 | D | 8 3 71 | Basingstoke | Trainee | Portsmouth | 161 | 10 |
| | | | | | | | Manchester C | 124 | 4 |
| **Thomas** Scott* | 5 9 | 11 02 | M | 30 10 74 | Bury | Trainee | Manchester C | 2 | — |
| | | | | | | | Brighton & HA (loan) | 7 | — |
| **Tskhadadze** Kakhabor | | | D | 7 9 68 | Rustavi | | Dynamo Tbilisi | 41 | 1 |
| | | | | | | | Sundsvall* | — | — |
| | | | | | | | Sundsvall | 4 | — |
| | | | | | | | Spartak Moscow | 7 | — |
| | | | | | | | Eintracht Frankfurt | 64 | 1 |
| | | | | | | | Eintracht Frankfurt* | — | — |
| | | | | | | | Alania | 17 | 1 |
| | | | | | | | Manchester C | 10 | 1 |
| **Vaughan** Tony | 6 0 | 11 02 | D | 11 10 75 | Manchester | Trainee | Ipswich T | 67 | 3 |
| | | | | | | | Manchester C | 19 | 1 |
| **Weaver** Nick | 6 3 | 13 01 | G | 2 3 79 | Sheffield | Trainee | Mansfield T | 1 | — |
| | | | | | | | Manchester C | — | — |
| **Whitley** Jeff | 5 9 | 11 00 | M | 28 1 79 | Zambia | Trainee | Manchester C | 40 | 2 |
| **Whitley** Jim | 5 9 | 11 00 | M | 14 4 75 | Zambia | Trainee | Manchester C | 19 | — |
| **Wiekens** Gerard | 6 1 | 13 00 | D | 25 2 73 | Tolhuiswyk | | Veendam | 33 | 1 |
| | | | | | | | Manchester C | 37 | 5 |
| **Wills** David* | 5 5 | 9 04 | F | 9 3 79 | Manchester | Trainee | Manchester C | — | — |
| **Winters** Kris‡ | | | M | 28 8 79 | Dundalk | Trainee | Nottingham F | — | — |
| | | | | | | | Manchester C | — | — |
| **Wright** Tommy | 6 1 | 14 05 | G | 29 8 63 | Belfast | Linfield | Newcastle U | 73 | — |
| | | | | | | | Hull C (loan) | 6 | — |
| | | | | | | | Nottingham F | 11 | — |
| | | | | | | | Reading (loan) | 17 | — |
| | | | | | | | Manchester C | 31 | — |

**Trainees**
Acton, Richard F; Allcock, Adam M; Daly, Lee C; Duff, Gregory J; Garfield, Darren J S; Julien, Michael F; Kneen, Jason; Laycock, David; McNab, Joe; McNab, Neil; O'Keefe, Gerald J; Reilly, Alan.

**Associated Schoolboys**
Anderson-Hodgson, David; Barton, Joseph; Day, Rhys; Dootson, Shaun; Egerton, Mark; Fenlon, Thomas; Furnival, Gary R; Gray, John; Hockenhull, Darren; Hughes, Lee S; Innes, Matthew K; Knowles, Alexander; Mellor, Neil A; Mitchard, Aaron P; Orr, Adrian; Pheonix, Jamie; Richards, Leonard R.

**Associated Schoolboys who have accepted the club's offer of a Traineeship/Contract**
Dunfield, Terry; Hodgson, Steven G; Mike, Leon J; Parkhouse, Shane.

## MANCHESTER UNITED

| | | | | | | | | | |
|---|---|---|---|---|---|---|---|---|---|
| **Beckham** David | 6 0 | 11 09 | M | 2 5 75 | Leytonstone | Trainee | Manchester U | 110 | 23 |
| | | | | | | | Preston NE (loan) | 5 | 2 |
| **Berg** Henning | 6 0 | 12 01 | D | 1 9 69 | Eidsvoll | Lillestrom | Blackburn R | 159 | 4 |
| | | | | | | | Manchester U | 27 | 1 |
| **Brebner** Grant | 5 10 | 11 11 | M | 6 12 77 | Edinburgh | Trainee | Manchester U | — | — |
| | | | | | | | Cambridge U (loan) | 6 | 1 |
| | | | | | | | Hibernian (loan) | 9 | 1 |
| **Brightwell** Stuart* | 5 6 | 10 11 | M | 31 1 79 | Easington | Trainee | Manchester U | — | — |

| Name | | | | Born | Birthplace | Source | Clubs | Apps | Gls |
|---|---|---|---|---|---|---|---|---|---|
| **Brown** David* | 5 10 | 12 07 | F | 2 10 78 | Bolton | Trainee | Manchester U | — | — |
| | | | | | | | Hull C (loan) | 7 | 2 |
| **Brown** Wes | 6 1 | 11 11 | D | 16 3 79 | Manchester | Trainee | Manchester U | 2 | — |
| **Butt** Nicky | 5 10 | 11 05 | M | 21 1 75 | Manchester | Trainee | Manchester U | 115 | 11 |
| **Casper** Chris | 6 0 | 12 02 | D | 28 4 75 | Burnley | Trainee | Manchester U | 2 | — |
| | | | | | | | Bournemouth (loan) | 16 | 1 |
| | | | | | | | Swindon T (loan) | 9 | 1 |
| **Clegg** Michael | 5 8 | 11 10 | D | 3 7 77 | Ashton-under-Lyne | Trainee | Manchester U | 7 | — |
| **Cole** Andy | 5 10 | 12 04 | F | 15 10 71 | Nottingham | Trainee | Arsenal | 1 | — |
| | | | | | | | Fulham (loan) | 13 | 3 |
| | | | | | | | Bristol C (loan) | 12 | 8 |
| | | | | | | | Bristol C | 29 | 12 |
| | | | | | | | Newcastle U | 70 | 55 |
| | | | | | | | Manchester U | 105 | 46 |
| **Cooke** Terry | 5 7 | 11 00 | F | 5 8 76 | Marston Green | Trainee | Manchester U | 4 | — |
| | | | | | | | Sunderland (loan) | 6 | — |
| | | | | | | | Birmingham C (loan) | 4 | — |
| **Cruyff** Jordi | 6 1 | 10 12 | F | 9 2 74 | Amsterdam | Ajax | Barcelona | 41 | 11 |
| | | | | | | | Manchester U | 21 | 2 |
| **Culkin** Nick | 6 2 | 13 05 | G | 6 7 78 | York | York C | Manchester U | — | — |
| **Curtis** John | 5 10 | 11 07 | D | 3 9 78 | Nuneaton | Trainee | Manchester U | 8 | — |
| **Evans** Wayne | 5 9 | 9 12 | M | 23 10 80 | Carmarthen | Trainee | Manchester U | — | — |
| **Ford** Ryan | 5 9 | 10 04 | M | 3 9 78 | Worksop | Trainee | Manchester U | — | — |
| **Gibson** Paul | 6 2 | 13 06 | G | 1 11 76 | Sheffield | Trainee | Manchester U | — | — |
| | | | | | | | Mansfield T (loan) | 13 | — |
| **Giggs** Ryan | 5 11 | 10 10 | F | 29 11 73 | Cardiff | School | Manchester U | 236 | 50 |
| **Greening** Jonathan | 6 0 | 11 03 | F | 2 1 79 | Scarborough | Trainee | York C | 25 | 2 |
| | | | | | | | Manchester U | — | — |
| **Healy** David | 5 8 | 10 09 | F | 5 8 79 | Downpatrick | Trainee | Manchester U | — | — |
| **Higginbotham** Danny | 6 1 | 12 03 | D | 29 12 78 | Manchester | Trainee | Manchester U | 1 | — |
| **Irwin** Denis | 5 8 | 10 10 | D | 31 10 65 | Cork | Apprentice | Leeds U | 72 | 1 |
| | | | | | | | Oldham Ath | 167 | 4 |
| | | | | | | | Manchester U | 281 | 17 |
| **Johnsen** Ronny | 6 3 | 13 02 | D | 10 6 69 | Sandefjord | Eik | Lyn | 31 | 7 |
| | | | | | | | Lillestrom | 23 | 4 |
| | | | | | | | Besiktas | 22 | 1 |
| | | | | | | | Manchester U | 53 | 2 |
| **Keane** Roy | 5 11 | 12 01 | M | 10 8 71 | Cork | Cobh Ramb | Nottingham F | 114 | 22 |
| | | | | | | | Manchester U | 121 | 17 |
| **May** David | 6 0 | 13 05 | D | 24 6 70 | Oldham | Trainee | Blackburn R | 123 | 3 |
| | | | | | | | Manchester U | 73 | 6 |
| **McClair** Brian* | 5 10 | 12 12 | F | 8 12 63 | Airdrie | Apprentice | Aston Villa | — | — |
| | | | | | | | Motherwell | 39 | 15 |
| | | | | | | | Celtic | 145 | 99 |
| | | | | | | | Manchester U | 355 | 88 |
| **Millard** Ross* | | | D | 1 1 79 | Bristol | Trainee | Manchester U | — | — |
| **Mulryne** Philip | 5 7 | 10 11 | M | 1 6 78 | Belfast | Trainee | Manchester U | 1 | — |
| **Naylor** Gavin* | 5 7 | 11 02 | F | 30 5 79 | North Cleveland | Trainee | Manchester U | — | — |
| **Neville** Gary | 5 11 | 12 07 | D | 18 2 75 | Bury | Trainee | Manchester U | 115 | 1 |
| **Neville** Philip | 5 11 | 11 11 | D | 21 1 77 | Bury | Trainee | Manchester U | 74 | 1 |
| **Nevland** Erik | 5 10 | 11 12 | F | 10 11 77 | Stavanger | | Viking | 14 | 5 |
| | | | | | | | Manchester U | 1 | — |
| **Notman** Alex | 5 7 | 10 11 | F | 10 12 79 | Edinburgh | Trainee | Manchester U | — | — |
| **Pallister** Gary | 6 4 | 14 12 | D | 30 6 65 | Ramsgate | Billingham T | Middlesbrough | 156 | 5 |
| | | | | | | | Darlington (loan) | 7 | — |
| | | | | | | | Manchester U | 317 | 12 |
| **Pilkington** Kevin* | 6 1 | 13 01 | G | 8 3 74 | Hitchin | Trainee | Manchester U | 6 | — |
| | | | | | | | Rochdale (loan) | 6 | — |
| | | | | | | | Rotherham U (loan) | 17 | — |
| **Poborsky** Karel | 5 9 | 11 05 | F | 30 3 72 | Jindinchuv-Hradec | | Ceske Budejovice | 82 | 15 |
| *(Transferred to Benfica, December 1997)* | | | | | | | Viktoria Zizkov | 28 | 10 |
| | | | | | | | Slavia Prague | 26 | 11 |
| | | | | | | | Manchester U | 32 | 5 |
| **Schmeichel** Peter | 6 4 | 16 00 | G | 18 11 63 | Gladsaxe | | Hvidovre | 88 | 6 |
| | | | | | | | Brondby | 119 | 2 |
| | | | | | | | Manchester U | 258 | — |
| **Scholes** Paul | 5 7 | 11 08 | M | 16 11 74 | Salford | Trainee | Manchester U | 98 | 26 |
| **Sheringham** Teddy | 6 0 | 13 00 | F | 2 4 66 | Highams Park | Apprentice | Millwall | 220 | 93 |
| | | | | | | | Aldershot (loan) | 5 | — |
| | | | | | | | Nottingham F | 42 | 14 |
| | | | | | | | Tottenham H | 166 | 76 |
| | | | | | | | Manchester U | 31 | 9 |
| **Solskjaer** Ole Gunnar | 5 10 | 11 06 | F | 26 2 73 | Kristiansund | | Molde | 42 | 31 |
| | | | | | | | Manchester U | 55 | 23 |
| **Stewart** Michael | | | M | 26 2 81 | Edinburgh | Trainee | Manchester U | — | — |
| **Teather** Paul | 6 0 | 11 08 | D | 28 12 77 | Rotherham | Trainee | Manchester U | — | — |
| | | | | | | | Bournemouth (loan) | 10 | — |

| | | | | | | | | |
|---|---|---|---|---|---|---|---|---|
| **Thornley** Ben | 5 9 | 11 07 | F | 21 4 75 | Bury | Trainee | Manchester U | 9 | — |
| | | | | | | | Stockport Co (loan) | 10 | 1 |
| | | | | | | | Huddersfield T (loan) | 12 | 2 |
| **Thorrington** John | 5 7 | 10 05 | F | 17 10 79 | Johannesburg | US College | Manchester U | — | — |
| **Tomlinson** Graeme* | 5 10 | 12 07 | F | 10 12 75 | Watford | Trainee | Bradford C | 17 | 6 |
| | | | | | | | Manchester U | — | — |
| | | | | | | | Luton T (loan) | 7 | — |
| | | | | | | | Bournemouth (loan) | 7 | 1 |
| | | | | | | | Millwall (loan) | 3 | 1 |
| **Twiss** Michael | 5 11 | 12 08 | M | 26 12 77 | Salford | Trainee | Manchester U | — | — |
| **Van der Gouw** Raimond | 6 3 | 13 07 | G | 24 3 63 | Oldenzaal | | Go Ahead | 97 | — |
| | | | | | | | Vitesse | 258 | — |
| | | | | | | | Manchester U | 7 | — |
| **Wallwork** Ronnie | 5 10 | 12 12 | D | 10 9 77 | Manchester | Trainee | Manchester U | 1 | — |
| | | | | | | | Carlisle U (loan) | 10 | 1 |
| | | | | | | | Stockport Co (loan) | 7 | — |
| **Wellens** Richard | 5 9 | 11 05 | M | 26 3 80 | Manchester | Trainee | Manchester U | — | — |
| **Wilson** Mark | 6 0 | 13 02 | M | 9 2 79 | Scunthorpe | Trainee | Manchester U | — | — |
| | | | | | | | Wrexham (loan) | 13 | 4 |
| **Wood** Jamie | 5 10 | 12 11 | F | 21 9 78 | Salford | Trainee | Manchester U | — | — |

**Trainees**
Chadwick, Luke H; Clegg, George G; Cosgrove, Stephen; Fitzpatrick, Ian M; Gaff, Gerard A; Hickson, Jason M; Hilton, Kirk; Howard, Joshua L; Marsh, Allan S; Mills, Leon J; Molloy, Eric; Rachubka, Paul S; Roche, Lee P; Rose, Stephen D; Ryan, Michael S P; Sadler, Adam; Studley, Dominic P; Wheatcroft, Paul M; Whiteley, Lee A.

**Associated Schoolboys**
Albiston, Ryan P; Clark, Benjamin; Clegg, Steven J; Coates, Craig; Cooke, Stephen L; Dickman, Jonjo; Hutchinson, Ryan C; Mortimer, Alexander B; Muirhead, Ben R; Nardiello, Daniel; Sampson, Gary J F; Tate, Alan; Taylor, Andrew J; Tonge, Michael W; Whiteman, Marc C; Williams, Matthew; Wood, Neil A.

**Associated Schoolboys who have accepted the club's offer of a Traineeship/Contract**
Davis, James R; Dodd, Ashley M; Jones, Rhodri G; Rose, Michael; Strange, Gareth A; Studley, Mark L; Szmid, Marek A; Walker, Joshua G; Webber, Daniel V.

# MANSFIELD TOWN

| | | | | | | | | |
|---|---|---|---|---|---|---|---|---|
| **Bowling** Ian# | 6 3 | 13 11 | G | 27 7 65 | Sheffield | Gainsborough T | Lincoln C | 59 | — |
| | | | | | | | Hartlepool U (loan) | 1 | — |
| | | | | | | | Bradford C (loan) | 7 | — |
| | | | | | | | Bradford C | 29 | — |
| | | | | | | | Mansfield T | 123 | — |
| **Christie** Iyseden | 6 0 | 12 02 | F | 14 11 76 | Coventry | Trainee | Coventry C | 1 | — |
| | | | | | | | Bournemouth (loan) | 4 | — |
| | | | | | | | Mansfield T (loan) | 8 | — |
| | | | | | | | Mansfield T | 39 | 10 |
| **Clarke** Darrell | 5 10 | 10 11 | M | 16 12 77 | Mansfield | Trainee | Mansfield T | 57 | 6 |
| **Eustace** Scott | 6 0 | 13 06 | D | 13 6 75 | Leicester | Trainee | Leicester C | 1 | — |
| | | | | | | | Mansfield T | 98 | 6 |
| **Ford** Tony# | 5 9 | 13 00 | M | 14 5 59 | Grimsby | Apprentice | Grimsby T | 355 | 55 |
| | | | | | | | Sunderland (loan) | 9 | 1 |
| | | | | | | | Stoke C | 112 | 13 |
| | | | | | | | WBA | 114 | 14 |
| | | | | | | | Grimsby T | 68 | 3 |
| | | | | | | | Bradford C (loan) | 5 | — |
| | | | | | | | Scunthorpe U | 76 | 9 |
| | | | | | | Barrow | Mansfield T | 61 | 5 |
| **Hackett** Warren | 6 0 | 12 05 | D | 16 12 71 | Plaistow | Tottenham H | Leyton Orient | 72 | 3 |
| | | | | | | | Doncaster R | 46 | 2 |
| | | | | | | | Mansfield T | 91 | 5 |
| **Hadley** Stewart‡ | 5 11 | 13 05 | F | 30 12 73 | Stourbridge | Halesowen T | Derby Co | — | — |
| | | | | | | | Mansfield T | 124 | 31 |
| **Harper** Steve | 5 10 | 11 12 | M | 3 2 69 | Newcastle-under-Lyne | Trainee | Port Vale | 28 | 2 |
| | | | | | | | Preston NE | 77 | 10 |
| | | | | | | | Burnley | 69 | 8 |
| | | | | | | | Doncaster R | 65 | 11 |
| | | | | | | | Mansfield T | 115 | 12 |
| **Hassell** Bobby§ | 5 8 | 12 02 | D | 4 6 80 | Derby | Trainee | Mansfield T | 9 | — |
| **Kerr** David | 5 11 | 12 01 | M | 6 9 74 | Dumfries | Trainee | Manchester C | 6 | — |
| | | | | | | | Mansfield T (loan) | 5 | — |
| | | | | | | | Mansfield T | 27 | 2 |
| **Kilcline** Brian‡ | 6 2 | 14 13 | D | 7 5 62 | Nottingham | Apprentice | Notts Co | 158 | 9 |
| | | | | | | | Coventry C | 173 | 28 |
| | | | | | | | Oldham Ath | 8 | — |
| | | | | | | | Newcastle U | 32 | — |
| | | | | | | | Swindon T | 17 | — |
| | | | | | | | Mansfield T | 50 | 3 |
| **Milner** Jonathan§ | 5 8 | 11 07 | F | 30 3 81 | Mansfield | Trainee | Mansfield T | 7 | — |
| **Parkin** Steve# | 5 6 | 11 01 | D | 7 11 65 | Mansfield | Apprentice | Stoke C | 113 | 5 |
| | | | | | | | WBA | 48 | 2 |
| | | | | | | | Mansfield T | 87 | 3 |
| **Peacock** Lee | 6 0 | 12 08 | F | 9 10 76 | Paisley | Trainee | Carlisle U | 76 | 11 |
| | | | | | | | Mansfield T | 32 | 5 |

| Name | | | | | Birthplace | Source | Club | Apps | Gls |
|---|---|---|---|---|---|---|---|---|---|
| **Peters** Mark | 6 0 | 11 03 | D | 6 7 72 | St Asaph | Trainee | Manchester C | — | — |
| | | | | | | | Norwich C | — | — |
| | | | | | | | Peterborough U | 19 | — |
| | | | | | | | Mansfield T | 71 | 8 |
| **Schofield** Jon | 5 11 | 11 03 | F | 16 5 65 | Barnsley | Gainsborough T | Lincoln C | 231 | 11 |
| | | | | | | | Doncaster R | 110 | 12 |
| | | | | | | | Mansfield T | 44 | — |
| **Sedlan** Jason§ | | | M | 5 8 79 | Peterborough | Trainee | Mansfield T | 1 | — |
| **Sisson** Michael | 5 8 | 10 06 | M | 24 11 78 | Mansfield | Trainee | Mansfield T | 1 | — |
| **Tallon** Gary | 5 7 | 11 07 | M | 5 9 73 | Drogheda | Trainee | Blackburn R | — | — |
| | | | | | | | Kilmarnock | 4 | — |
| | | | | | | | Chester C (loan) | 1 | — |
| | | | | | | | Mansfield T | 26 | 1 |
| **Walker** John | 5 9 | 11 00 | M | 12 12 73 | Glasgow | Clydebank BC | Rangers | — | — |
| | | | | | | | Clydebank | 27 | 2 |
| | | | | | | | Grimsby T | 3 | 1 |
| | | | | | | | Mansfield T | 37 | 3 |
| **Watkiss** Stuart | 6 2 | 13 06 | D | 8 5 66 | Wolverhampton | Apprentice | Wolverhampton W | 2 | — |
| | | | | | | Rushall Olympic | Walsall | 62 | 2 |
| | | | | | | | Hereford U | 19 | — |
| | | | | | | | Mansfield T | 41 | 1 |
| **Whitehall** Steve | 5 10 | 11 00 | F | 8 12 66 | Bromborough | Southport | Rochdale | 238 | 75 |
| | | | | | | | Mansfield T | 43 | 24 |
| **Williams** Lee# | 5 7 | 12 00 | D | 3 2 73 | Edgbaston | Trainee | Aston Villa | — | — |
| | | | | | | | Shrewsbury T (loan) | 3 | — |
| | | | | | | | Peterborough U | 91 | 1 |
| | | | | | | | Tranmere R | — | — |
| | | | | | | | Mansfield T | 44 | 3 |

**Trainees**
Asher, Alistair A; Bacon, Daniel S; Christian, Dale T; Disley, Craig E; Gibbons, Scott P; Hassell, Robert J F; Hudson, Jamie R; Hutchinson, James A A; Leech, James; Milner, Jonathan R; Preston, Richard J; Rankin, Darrel A; Sedlan, Jason M; Wiggington, Mark; Wilkins, Christopher J.

**Associated Schoolboys**
Allen, Scott; Elliott, Dominic S; Gash, Marc; Scott, Steven M; Stringfellow, Daniel J; Swinscoe, Craig A; Williams, Ryan A; Wyld, Mathew A.

**Associated Schoolboys who have accepted the club's offer of a Traineeship/Contract**
Jervis, David J; Lawrence, Liam; Overton, Paul D; Tye, Kevin.

# MIDDLESBROUGH

| Name | | | | | Birthplace | Source | Club | Apps | Gls |
|---|---|---|---|---|---|---|---|---|---|
| **Armstrong** Alun | 6 1 | 12 02 | F | 22 2 75 | Gateshead | School | Newcastle U | — | — |
| | | | | | | | Stockport Co | 159 | 48 |
| | | | | | | | Middlesbrough | 11 | 7 |
| **Baker** Steve | 5 10 | 11 11 | D | 8 9 78 | Pontefract | | Middlesbrough | 6 | — |
| **Beck** Mikkel | 6 2 | 12 09 | F | 12 5 73 | Aarhus | Kolding | B 1909 | 13 | 2 |
| | | | | | | | Fortuna Cologne | 79 | 26 |
| | | | | | | | Middlesbrough | 64 | 19 |
| **Beresford** Marlon | 6 1 | 13 05 | G | 2 6 69 | Lincoln | Trainee | Sheffield W | — | — |
| | | | | | | | Bury (loan) | 1 | — |
| | | | | | | | Ipswich T (loan) | — | — |
| | | | | | | | Northampton T (loan) | 13 | — |
| | | | | | | | Crewe Alex (loan) | 3 | — |
| | | | | | | | Northampton T (loan) | 15 | — |
| | | | | | | | Burnley | 240 | — |
| | | | | | | | Middlesbrough | 3 | — |
| **Blackmore** Clayton | 5 7 | 11 13 | M | 23 9 64 | Neath | Apprentice | Manchester U | 186 | 19 |
| | | | | | | | Middlesbrough | 53 | 4 |
| | | | | | | | Bristol C (loan) | 5 | 1 |
| **Branca** Marco | 6 0 | 11 07 | F | 6 1 65 | Grosseto | | Grosseto | — | — |
| | | | | | | | Cagliari | 52 | 4 |
| | | | | | | | Udinese | 18 | 2 |
| | | | | | | | Sampdoria | 9 | 1 |
| | | | | | | | Udinese | 55 | 13 |
| | | | | | | | Sampdoria | 20 | 5 |
| | | | | | | | Fiorentina | 23 | 5 |
| | | | | | | | Udinese | 58 | 22 |
| | | | | | | | Parma | 25 | 7 |
| | | | | | | | Roma | 7 | 2 |
| | | | | | | | Internazionale | 52 | 23 |
| | | | | | | | Middlesbrough | 11 | 9 |
| **Burdock** Gary | | | F | 9 3 80 | Dublin | Trainee | Middlesbrough | — | — |
| **Campbell** Andy | 6 0 | 10 10 | F | 18 4 79 | Middlesbrough | Trainee | Middlesbrough | 12 | — |
| **Carter** Graeme* | | | D | 21 2 79 | Middlesbrough | Trainee | Middlesbrough | — | — |
| **Connor** Paul | 6 2 | 11 08 | F | 12 1 79 | Bishop Auckland | Trainee | Middlesbrough | — | — |
| | | | | | | | Hartlepool U (loan) | 5 | — |
| **Cronin** Gary | | | M | 16 3 79 | Dublin | Stella Maris | Middlesbrough | — | — |
| **Cummins** Michael | 6 0 | 11 11 | M | 1 6 78 | Dublin | Trainee | Middlesbrough | — | — |

| Player | Ht | Wt | Pos | Born | Birthplace | From | Club | Apps | Gls |
|---|---|---|---|---|---|---|---|---|---|
| **Dibble** Andy* | 6 2 | 16 02 | G | 8 5 65 | Cwmbran | Apprentice | Cardiff C | 62 | — |
| | | | | | | | Luton T | 30 | — |
| | | | | | | | Sunderland (loan) | 12 | — |
| | | | | | | | Huddersfield T (loan) | 5 | — |
| | | | | | | | Manchester C | 115 | — |
| | | | | | | | Aberdeen (loan) | 5 | — |
| | | | | | | | Middlesbrough (loan) | 19 | — |
| | | | | | | | Bolton W (loan) | 13 | — |
| | | | | | | | WBA (loan) | 9 | — |
| | | | | | | | Oldham Ath (loan) | — | — |
| | | | | | | | Rangers | 7 | — |
| | | | | | | | Luton T | 1 | — |
| | | | | | | | Middlesbrough | 2 | — |
| **Emerson** *(Transferred to Tenerife, January 1998)* | 6 0 | 14 05 | M | 12 4 72 | Rio | Curitiba | Belenenses | 55 | 1 |
| | | | | | | | Porto | 60 | 9 |
| | | | | | | | Middlesbrough | 53 | 9 |
| **Festa** Gianluca | 6 0 | 13 02 | D | 15 3 69 | Cagliari | | Cagliari | 156 | — |
| | | | | | | | Fersuicis (loan) | 26 | 2 |
| | | | | | | | Internazionale | 66 | 3 |
| | | | | | | | Roma (loan) | 21 | 1 |
| | | | | | | | Middlesbrough | 51 | 3 |
| **Fleming** Curtis | 5 10 | 12 08 | D | 8 10 68 | Manchester | St Patrick's Ath | Middlesbrough | 187 | 2 |
| **Gascoigne** Paul | 5 10 | 11 10 | M | 27 5 67 | Gateshead | | Newcastle U | 92 | 21 |
| | | | | | | | Tottenham H | 92 | 19 |
| | | | | | | | Lazio | 41 | 6 |
| | | | | | | | Rangers | 74 | 30 |
| | | | | | | | Middlesbrough | 7 | — |
| **Gavin** Jason | | | D | 14 3 80 | Dublin | Trainee | Middlesbrough | — | — |
| **Harrison** Craig | 6 0 | 11 13 | D | 10 11 77 | Gateshead | Trainee | Middlesbrough | 20 | — |
| **Hignett** Craig# | 5 8 | 11 00 | M | 12 1 70 | Whiston | Liverpool | Crewe Alex | 121 | 42 |
| | | | | | | | Middlesbrough | 156 | 33 |
| **Kinder** Vladimir | 5 8 | 12 11 | D | 9 3 69 | Bratislava | Karlovy Vary | Slovan Bratislava | 161 | 22 |
| | | | | | | | Middlesbrough | 32 | 3 |
| **Liddle** Craig | 5 11 | 12 03 | D | 21 10 71 | Chester-le-Street | Blyth Spartans | Middlesbrough | 25 | — |
| | | | | | | | Darlington (loan) | 15 | — |
| **Maddison** Neil | 5 10 | 12 00 | M | 2 10 69 | Darlington | Trainee | Southampton | 169 | 19 |
| | | | | | | | Middlesbrough | 22 | 4 |
| **Merson** Paul | 6 0 | 12 07 | F | 20 3 68 | London | Apprentice | Arsenal | 327 | 78 |
| | | | | | | | Brentford (loan) | 7 | — |
| | | | | | | | Middlesbrough | 45 | 11 |
| **Moore** Alan | 5 9 | 11 06 | M | 25 11 74 | Dublin | Rivermount | Middlesbrough | 114 | 14 |
| **Moreira** Fabio* | 5 10 | 11 06 | D | 14 3 72 | Rio | Chaves | Middlesbrough | 1 | — |
| **Moreno** Jaime‡ | 5 9 | 11 09 | F | 19 1 74 | Bolivia | Blooming | Middlesbrough | 26 | 2 |
| **Mustoe** Robbie | 5 10 | 11 10 | M | 28 8 68 | Oxford | | Oxford U | 91 | 10 |
| | | | | | | | Middlesbrough | 243 | 19 |
| **O'Brien** Ronnie | | | M | 15 1 79 | Dublin | St Joseph's BC | Middlesbrough | — | — |
| **O'Loughlin** John | | | M | 31 1 79 | Letterkenny | Bruncrana Hearts | Middlesbrough | — | — |
| **Ormerod** Anthony | 5 10 | 11 08 | M | 31 3 79 | Middlesbrough | Trainee | Middlesbrough | 18 | 3 |
| **Pearson** Nigel | 6 1 | 14 01 | D | 21 8 63 | Nottingham | Heanor T | Shrewsbury T | 153 | 5 |
| | | | | | | | Sheffield W | 180 | 14 |
| | | | | | | | Middlesbrough | 116 | 5 |
| **Ravanelli** Fabrizio *(Transferred to Marseille, September 1997)* | 6 2 | 13 04 | F | 11 12 68 | Perugia | | Perugia | 90 | 41 |
| | | | | | | | Avellino | 7 | — |
| | | | | | | | Casertana (loan) | 27 | 12 |
| | | | | | | | Reggiana | 66 | 24 |
| | | | | | | | Juventus | 111 | 41 |
| | | | | | | | Middlesbrough | 35 | 17 |
| **Reeve** Chris | | | F | 1 10 79 | Darlington | Trainee | Middlesbrough | — | — |
| **Ricard** Hamilton | 6 2 | 14 05 | F | 12 1 74 | Colombia | Deportivo Cali | Middlesbrough | 9 | 2 |
| **Roberts** Ben | 6 1 | 13 03 | G | 22 6 75 | Bishop Auckland | Trainee | Middlesbrough | 16 | — |
| | | | | | | | Hartlepool U (loan) | 4 | — |
| | | | | | | | Wycombe W (loan) | 15 | — |
| | | | | | | | Bradford C (loan) | 2 | — |
| **Robson** Bryan† | 5 9 | 12 05 | M | 11 1 57 | Witton Gilbert | Apprentice | WBA | 197 | 39 |
| | | | | | | | Manchester U | 345 | 74 |
| | | | | | | | Middlesbrough | 25 | 1 |
| **Schwarzer** Mark | 6 5 | 13 08 | G | 6 10 72 | Sydney | Dynamo Dresden | Kaiserslautern | 4 | — |
| | | | | | | | Bradford C | 13 | — |
| | | | | | | | Middlesbrough | 42 | — |
| **Shilton** Peter† | 6 1 | 14 02 | G | 18 9 49 | Leicester | Apprentice | Leicester C | 286 | 1 |
| | | | | | | | Stoke C | 110 | — |
| | | | | | | | Nottingham F | 202 | — |
| | | | | | | | Southampton | 188 | — |
| | | | | | | | Derby Co | 175 | — |
| | | | | | | | Plymouth Arg | 34 | — |
| | | | | | | | Wimbledon | — | — |
| | | | | | | | Bolton W | 1 | — |
| | | | | | | | Coventry C | — | — |
| | | | | | | | West Ham U | — | — |
| | | | | | | | Leyton Orient | 9 | — |
| | | | | | | | Middlesbrough | — | — |

| | | | | | | | | | |
|---|---|---|---|---|---|---|---|---|---|
| **Stamp** Phil | 5 10 | 13 10 | M | 12 12 75 | Middlesbrough | Trainee | Middlesbrough | 59 | 3 |
| **Stockdale** Robert§ | | | D | 30 11 79 | Redcar | Trainee | Middlesbrough | 1 | — |
| **Summerbell** Mark | 5 8 | 10 06 | M | 30 10 76 | Durham | Trainee | Middlesbrough | 14 | — |
| **Swalwell** Andrew | | | M | 29 3 79 | Middlesbrough | Trainee | Middlesbrough | — | — |
| **Townsend** Andy | 5 11 | 13 06 | M | 27 7 63 | Maidstone | Weymouth | Southampton | 83 | 5 |
| | | | | | | | Norwich C | 71 | 8 |
| | | | | | | | Chelsea | 110 | 12 |
| | | | | | | | Aston Villa | 134 | 8 |
| | | | | | | | Middlesbrough | 37 | 2 |
| **Trevor** Kris | | | F | 15 5 79 | South Shields | Trainee | Middlesbrough | — | — |
| **Vickers** Steve | 6 1 | 13 02 | D | 13 10 67 | Bishop Auckland | Spennymoor U | Tranmere R | 311 | 11 |
| | | | | | | | Middlesbrough | 164 | 7 |
| **White** Darren* | | | D | 13 1 79 | Easington | Trainee | Middlesbrough | — | — |
| **Whyte** Derek | 5 11 | 12 13 | D | 31 8 68 | Glasgow | Celtic BC | Celtic | 216 | 7 |
| *(Transferred to Aberdeen, January 1998)* | | | | | | | Middlesbrough | 167 | 2 |
| | | | | | | | Aberdeen | 19 | — |

**Trainees**
Barnard, Richard M; Bull, Ronnie R; Davies, Robert M; Eagle, Philip D; Fermie, Jason W; Field, Lewis M; Ifill, Paul; Little, Joseph G; Maguire, Patrick; O'Dunsi, Saheed A; Powell, Terry M; Reid, Steven J.

**Non-Contract**
Dolan, Joseph; Mead, Billy; Williams, Leon K.

**Associated Schoolboys**
Bond-Vaughan, Gareth; Booth, Stuart; Brown, Craig; Davies, Alex J; Draper, Craig J E; Honey, Christopher M; Honey, Paul A; Idaewor, Ambrose; Kevin, Joseph S; Lloyd, Marc H; Lombardo, Daniel C R; McManus, Michael T; Murray, Sam; Redmond, Gary; Rees, Matthew R; Ridley, Liam; Taylor, Billy; Thorogood, Asa; Yellop, Darrell R.

**Associated Schoolboys who have accepted the club's offer of a Traineeship/Contract**
Bubb, Byron J; Deegan, Darren S; Dunne, Alan J; Karaiskos, Andreas.

# MILLWALL

| | | | | | | | | | |
|---|---|---|---|---|---|---|---|---|---|
| **Allen** Paul* | 5 7 | 11 02 | M | 28 6 62 | Aveley | Apprentice | West Ham U | 152 | 6 |
| | | | | | | | Tottenham H | 292 | 23 |
| | | | | | | | Southampton | 43 | 1 |
| | | | | | | | Luton T (loan) | 4 | — |
| | | | | | | | Stoke C (loan) | 17 | 1 |
| | | | | | | | Swindon T | 37 | 1 |
| | | | | | | | Bristol C | 14 | — |
| | | | | | | | Millwall | 28 | — |
| **Aris** Steve* | 5 11 | 11 06 | D | 27 7 79 | London | | Millwall | — | — |
| **Bircham** Marc | 5 10 | 12 08 | D | 11 5 78 | Brent | Trainee | Millwall | 10 | — |
| **Bowry** Bobby | 5 8 | 10 08 | M | 19 5 71 | Croydon | | Crystal Palace | 50 | 1 |
| | | | | | | | Millwall | 109 | 5 |
| **Brown** Kenny | 5 8 | 11 06 | D | 11 7 67 | Upminster | Apprentice | Norwich C | 25 | — |
| | | | | | | | Plymouth Arg | 126 | 4 |
| | | | | | | | West Ham U | 63 | 5 |
| | | | | | | | Huddersfield T (loan) | 5 | — |
| | | | | | | | Reading (loan) | 12 | 1 |
| | | | | | | | Southend U (loan) | 6 | — |
| | | | | | | | Crystal Palace (loan) | 6 | 2 |
| | | | | | | | Reading (loan) | 5 | — |
| | | | | | | | Birmingham C | 11 | — |
| | | | | | | | Millwall | 45 | — |
| **Cahill** Tim | 5 10 | 10 11 | M | 6 12 79 | Sydney | Sydney U | Millwall | 1 | — |
| **Canoville** Dean | 5 10 | 11 10 | M | 30 11 78 | Perivale | Trainee | Millwall | 2 | — |
| **Carter** Tim* | 6 2 | 13 00 | G | 5 10 67 | Bristol | Apprentice | Bristol R | 47 | — |
| | | | | | | | Newport Co (loan) | 1 | — |
| | | | | | | | Carlisle U (loan) | 4 | — |
| | | | | | | | Sunderland | 37 | — |
| | | | | | | | Bristol C (loan) | 3 | — |
| | | | | | | | Birmingham C (loan) | 2 | — |
| | | | | | | | Hartlepool U | 18 | — |
| | | | | | | | Millwall | 4 | — |
| | | | | | | | Oxford U | 12 | — |
| | | | | | | | Millwall | 62 | — |
| **Connor** James‡ | 6 0 | 13 00 | M | 22 8 74 | Middlesbrough | Trainee | Millwall | 9 | — |
| **Cook** Andy | 5 9 | 12 00 | M | 10 8 69 | Romsey | Apprentice | Southampton | 16 | 1 |
| | | | | | | | Exeter C | 70 | 1 |
| | | | | | | | Swansea C | 62 | — |
| | | | | | | | Portsmouth | 9 | — |
| | | | | | | | Millwall | 3 | — |
| **Cort** Leon | | | D | 11 9 79 | Southwark | Dulwich H | Millwall | — | — |
| **Crawford** Steve | 5 10 | 10 07 | F | 9 1 74 | Dunfermline | | Raith R | 115 | 22 |
| *(Transferred to Hibernian, July 1997)* | | | | | | | Millwall | 42 | 11 |
| | | | | | | | Hibernian | 35 | 9 |
| **Dair** Jason | 5 11 | 10 08 | M | 15 6 74 | Dunfermline | | Raith R | 94 | 11 |
| *(Transferred to Raith R, September 1997)* | | | | | | | Millwall | 24 | 1 |
| **Doyle** Maurice* | 5 8 | 10 07 | M | 17 10 69 | Ellesmere Port | Trainee | Crewe Alex | 8 | 2 |
| | | | | | | | QPR | 6 | — |
| | | | | | | | Crewe Alex (loan) | 7 | 2 |
| | | | | | | | Wolverhampton W (loan) | | — |
| | | | | | | | Millwall | 66 | 1 |
| **Edwards** Daniel‡ | | | M | 20 12 79 | Greenwich | Trainee | Millwall | — | — |

| | | | | | | | | | |
|---|---|---|---|---|---|---|---|---|---|
| **Fitzgerald** Scott | 6 0 | 12 02 | D | 13 8 69 | London | Trainee | Wimbledon | 106 | 1 |
| | | | | | | | Sheffield U (loan) | 6 | — |
| | | | | | | | Millwall (loan) | 7 | — |
| | | | | | | | Millwall | 18 | — |
| **Grant** Kim | 5 10 | 11 05 | F | 25 7 72 | Ghana | Trainee | Charlton Ath | 123 | 18 |
| | | | | | | | Luton T | 35 | 5 |
| | | | | | | | Millwall | 39 | 8 |
| **Gray** Andy | 5 11 | 14 04 | M | 22 2 64 | Lambeth | | Crystal Palace | 98 | 27 |
| | | | | | | | Aston Villa | 37 | 4 |
| | | | | | | | QPR | 11 | 2 |
| | | | | | | | Crystal Palace | 90 | 12 |
| | | | | | | | Tottenham H (loan) | 14 | 1 |
| | | | | | | | Tottenham H | 19 | 2 |
| | | | | | | | Swindon T (loan) | 3 | — |
| | | | | | | Marbella | Falkirk | 16 | — |
| | | | | | | | Bury | 21 | 1 |
| | | | | | | | Millwall | 12 | 1 |
| **Harris** Neil | 5 11 | 12 08 | F | 12 7 77 | Orsett | Chelmsford C | Millwall | 3 | — |
| **Hockton** Danny | 6 0 | 11 11 | F | 7 2 79 | Barking | Trainee | Millwall | 28 | 3 |
| **Lavin** Gerard | 5 10 | 11 00 | D | 5 2 74 | Corby | Trainee | Watford | 126 | 3 |
| | | | | | | | Millwall | 36 | — |
| **Law** Brian | 6 2 | 11 12 | D | 1 1 70 | Merthyr | Apprentice | QPR | 20 | — |
| | | | | | | | Wolverhampton W | 31 | 1 |
| | | | | | | | Millwall | 40 | 4 |
| **Markey** Brendan | 5 10 | 12 00 | F | 19 5 76 | Dublin | Bohemians | Millwall | — | — |
| **McLeary** Alan | 6 0 | 11 11 | D | 6 10 64 | Lambeth | Apprentice | Millwall | 307 | 5 |
| | | | | | | | Sheffield U (loan) | 3 | — |
| | | | | | | | Wimbledon (loan) | 4 | — |
| | | | | | | | Charlton Ath | 66 | 3 |
| | | | | | | | Bristol C | 34 | — |
| | | | | | | | Millwall | 34 | — |
| **McRobert** Lee* | 5 9 | 10 12 | M | 4 10 72 | Bromley | Sittingbourne | Millwall | 23 | 1 |
| **Neill** Lucas | 6 1 | 12 00 | M | 9 3 78 | Sydney | NSW Academy | Millwall | 58 | 3 |
| **Nethercott** Stuart | 6 1 | 14 00 | D | 21 3 73 | Chadwell Heath | Trainee | Tottenham H | 54 | — |
| | | | | | | | Maidstone U (loan) | 13 | 1 |
| | | | | | | | Barnet (loan) | 3 | — |
| | | | | | | | Millwall | 10 | — |
| **Newman** Ricky | 5 10 | 12 06 | M | 5 8 70 | Guildford | Trainee | Crystal Palace | 48 | 3 |
| | | | | | | | Maidstone U (loan) | 10 | 1 |
| | | | | | | | Millwall | 112 | 5 |
| **Nurse** David* | 6 4 | 12 06 | G | 12 10 76 | Kings Lynn | Trainee | Manchester C | — | — |
| | | | | | | | Millwall | — | — |
| | | | | | | | Brentford (loan) | — | — |
| **Pitwood** Adam‡ | | | M | 24 1 80 | Crawley | School | Millwall | — | — |
| **Reid** Steven§ | 5 11 | 11 10 | M | 10 3 81 | Kingston | Trainee | Millwall | 1 | — |
| **Robertson** Graham | 5 10 | 11 11 | M | 12 11 76 | Edinburgh | Balgorie Colts | Raith R | — | — |
| | | | | | | | Millwall | 2 | — |
| **Roche** Stephen | 6 1 | 11 05 | M | 2 10 78 | Dublin | Belvedere | Millwall | 8 | — |
| **Ryan** Robbie | 5 10 | 11 06 | D | 16 5 77 | Dublin | Belvedere | Huddersfield T | 15 | — |
| | | | | | | | Millwall | 16 | — |
| **Sadlier** Richard | 6 2 | 12 10 | F | 14 1 79 | Dublin | Belvedere | Millwall | 14 | 3 |
| **Savage** Dave | 6 2 | 12 07 | M | 30 7 73 | Dublin | Longford T | Millwall | 130 | 6 |
| **Shaw** Paul | 5 11 | 12 02 | F | 4 9 73 | Burnham | Trainee | Arsenal | 12 | 2 |
| | | | | | | | Burnley (loan) | 9 | 4 |
| | | | | | | | Cardiff C (loan) | 6 | — |
| | | | | | | | Peterborough U (loan) | 12 | 5 |
| | | | | | | | Millwall | 40 | 11 |
| **Smith** Phil | | | G | 14 12 79 | Wembley | Trainee | Millwall | — | — |
| **Spink** Nigel | 6 2 | 14 06 | G | 8 8 58 | Chelmsford | Chelmsford C | Aston Villa | 361 | — |
| | | | | | | | WBA | 19 | — |
| | | | | | | | Millwall | 21 | — |
| **Stevens** Keith* | 6 0 | 12 12 | D | 21 6 64 | Merton | Apprentice | Millwall | 459 | 9 |
| **Stevens** Shaun‡ | 5 10 | 11 07 | D | 8 3 76 | Chertsey | | Wycombe W | — | — |
| | | | | | | | Millwall | — | — |
| **Sturgess** Paul | 5 11 | 12 05 | D | 4 8 75 | Dartford | Trainee | Charlton Ath | 51 | — |
| | | | | | | | Millwall | 14 | — |
| **Veart** Carl | 5 10 | 11 05 | M | 21 5 70 | Whyalla | Adelaide C | Sheffield U | 66 | 15 |
| | | | | | | | Crystal Palace | 57 | 6 |
| | | | | | | | Millwall | 8 | 1 |
| **Watkinson** Russ* | 6 0 | 12 00 | F | 3 12 77 | Epsom | Woking | Southampton | 2 | — |
| | | | | | | | Bristol C | — | — |
| | | | | | | | Millwall | — | — |
| **Webber** Damien* | 6 4 | 14 00 | D | 8 10 68 | Rustington | Bognor Regis T | Millwall | 65 | 4 |

| Wilkinson Paul | 6 1 | 12 06 | F | 30 10 64 | Louth | Apprentice | Grimsby T | 71 | 27 |
|---|---|---|---|---|---|---|---|---|---|
| | | | | | | | Everton | 31 | 7 |
| | | | | | | | Nottingham F | 34 | 5 |
| | | | | | | | Watford | 134 | 52 |
| | | | | | | | Middlesbrough | 166 | 49 |
| | | | | | | | Oldham Ath (loan) | 4 | 1 |
| | | | | | | | Watford (loan) | 4 | — |
| | | | | | | | Luton T (loan) | 3 | — |
| | | | | | | | Barnsley | 49 | 9 |
| | | | | | | | Millwall | 30 | 3 |
| Witter Tony* | 6 2 | 13 02 | D | 12 8 65 | London | Grays Ath | Crystal Palace | — | — |
| | | | | | | | QPR | 1 | — |
| | | | | | | | Millwall (loan) | — | — |
| | | | | | | | Plymouth Arg (loan) | 3 | 1 |
| | | | | | | | Reading (loan) | 4 | — |
| | | | | | | | Millwall | 102 | 2 |

**Trainees**
Allon, Wayne; Bennion, Christopher; Booth, Gregory; Bowes, Martin; Canavan, Michael G; Cuthbertson, Andrew M; Dunn, Thomas; Graham, Christian J; Hanson Christian; Hudson, Mark; Jackson, John; Jones, Thomas A M; Kell, Richard; Kelly, Brian; Kilgannon, Sean; McStea, Anthony C; Middleton, James R; Newham, Stephen J C; Stockdale, Robert; Terrell, Paul A; Walklate, Steven.

**Non-Contract**
Robson, Bryan; Shilton, Peter L.

**Associated Schoolboys**
Boyce, Marvin; Brackstone, Stephen; Brodie, Keith J; Cade, Jamie W; Collinson, Jonathan E; Dove, Craig; Farrell, Craig W; Gulliver, Philip S; Leach, Paul; Mustard, Philip; Russell, Samuel I; Ryan, Leon M; Skirving, Richard M; Smith, Gary S; Smith, Liam.

**Associated Schoolboys who have accepted the club's offer of a Traineeship/Contract**
Greenwood, David; Moat, David J; Taylor, Andrew.

# NEWCASTLE UNITED

| Albert Philippe | 6 3 | 12 04 | D | 10 8 67 | Bouillon | | Charleroi | 65 | 7 |
|---|---|---|---|---|---|---|---|---|---|
| | | | | | | | Mechelen | 87 | 5 |
| | | | | | | | Anderlecht | 50 | 9 |
| | | | | | | | Newcastle U | 90 | 8 |
| Andersson Andreas | 6 1 | 12 01 | F | 10 4 74 | Osterhoninge | Hova | Tidaholm | 9 | 6 |
| | | | | | | | Degerfors | 40 | 16 |
| | | | | | | | IFK Gothenburg | 39 | 32 |
| | | | | | | | AC Milan | 13 | 1 |
| | | | | | | | Newcastle U | 12 | 2 |
| Arnison Paul | 5 10 | 10 12 | D | 18 9 77 | Hartlepool | Trainee | Newcastle U | — | — |
| Asprilla Faustino | 5 9 | 11 03 | F | 10 11 69 | Tulua | | Cucuta | 15 | 7 |
| *(Transferred to Parma, January 1998)* | | | | | | | Nacional | 61 | 25 |
| | | | | | | | Parma | 84 | 25 |
| | | | | | | | Newcastle U | 48 | 9 |
| Barnes John | 5 11 | 12 07 | M | 7 11 63 | Jamaica | Sudbury Court | Watford | 233 | 65 |
| | | | | | | | Liverpool | 314 | 84 |
| | | | | | | | Newcastle U | 26 | 6 |
| Barrett Paul | 5 9 | 10 11 | M | 13 4 78 | Newcastle | Trainee | Newcastle U | — | — |
| Barton Warren | 5 11 | 12 00 | D | 19 3 69 | Stoke Newington | Leytonstone/Ilford | Maidstone U | 42 | — |
| | | | | | | | Wimbledon | 180 | 10 |
| | | | | | | | Newcastle U | 72 | 4 |
| Batty David | 5 8 | 11 10 | M | 2 12 68 | Leeds | Trainee | Leeds U | 211 | 4 |
| | | | | | | | Blackburn R | 54 | 1 |
| | | | | | | | Newcastle U | 75 | 3 |
| Beharall David | 6 0 | 11 07 | D | 8 3 79 | Newcastle | Trainee | Newcastle U | — | — |
| Broadbent David | 5 9 | 10 06 | F | 26 9 79 | Pembury | Trainee | Newcastle U | — | — |
| Burghall Terry | 6 0 | 11 06 | F | 25 9 78 | Liverpool | Liverpool | Newcastle U | — | — |
| Burt David | 5 9 | 10 11 | M | 5 2 78 | Newcastle | Trainee | Newcastle U | — | — |
| Caldwell Stephen | 6 0 | 11 05 | D | 12 9 80 | Stirling | Trainee | Newcastle U | — | — |
| Coppinger James | 5 7 | 10 03 | M | 10 1 81 | Middlesbrough | Darlington | Newcastle U | — | — |
| Dabizas Nikos | 6 0 | 11 11 | D | 3 8 73 | Amypeo | | Olympiakos | 104 | 8 |
| | | | | | | | Newcastle U | 11 | 1 |
| Dalglish Paul | 5 9 | 10 00 | M | 18 2 77 | Glasgow | X Form | Celtic | — | — |
| | | | | | | | Liverpool | — | — |
| | | | | | | | Newcastle U | — | — |
| | | | | | | | Bury (loan) | 12 | — |
| Eatock David* | 5 4 | 10 05 | F | 11 11 76 | Wigan | Chorley | Newcastle U | — | — |
| Elliott Stuart | 5 8 | 11 05 | D | 27 8 77 | London | Trainee | Newcastle U | — | — |
| | | | | | | | Hull C (loan) | 3 | — |
| | | | | | | | Swindon T (loan) | 2 | — |
| Gibson Barry* | 5 10 | 10 12 | F | 30 3 79 | Newcastle | Trainee | Newcastle U | — | — |
| Gillespie Keith | 5 9 | 11 05 | F | 18 2 75 | Larne | Trainee | Manchester U | 9 | 1 |
| | | | | | | | Wigan Ath (loan) | 8 | 4 |
| | | | | | | | Newcastle U | 106 | 11 |
| Given Shay | 6 0 | 11 08 | G | 24 4 76 | Lifford | Celtic | Blackburn R | 2 | — |
| | | | | | | | Swindon T (loan) | — | — |
| | | | | | | | Swindon T (loan) | 5 | — |
| | | | | | | | Sunderland (loan) | 17 | — |
| | | | | | | | Newcastle U | 24 | — |

| | | | | | | | | | |
|---|---|---|---|---|---|---|---|---|---|
| **Griffin** Andrew | 5 8 | 10 10 | D | 17 3 79 | Wigan | Trainee | Stoke C | 57 | 2 |
| | | | | | | | Newcastle U | 4 | — |
| **Gudjonsson** Bjarni | 5 8 | 10 10 | F | 26 2 79 | Akranes | | IA Akranes | 25 | 15 |
| | | | | | | | Newcastle U | — | — |
| **Hamilton** Des | 5 10 | 12 13 | D | 15 8 76 | Bradford | Trainee | Bradford C | 88 | 5 |
| | | | | | | | Newcastle U | 12 | — |
| **Harper** Steve | 6 1 | 13 09 | G | 3 2 74 | Easington | Seaham Red Star | Newcastle U | — | — |
| | | | | | | | Bradford C (loan) | 1 | — |
| | | | | | | | Stockport Co (loan) | — | — |
| | | | | | | | Hartlepool U (loan) | 15 | — |
| | | | | | | | Huddersfield T (loan) | 24 | — |
| **Hislop** Shaka* | 6 3 | 15 00 | G | 22 2 69 | Hackney | Howard Univ | Reading | 104 | — |
| | | | | | | | Newcastle U | 53 | — |
| **Howey** Steve | 6 1 | 11 12 | D | 26 10 71 | Sunderland | Trainee | Newcastle U | 168 | 6 |
| **Hughes** Aaron | 6 0 | 11 02 | D | 8 11 79 | Magherafelt | Trainee | Newcastle U | 4 | — |
| **Keen** Peter | 6 0 | 11 10 | G | 16 11 76 | Middlesbrough | Trainee | Newcastle U | — | — |
| **Keidal** Ralf | 5 8 | 10 12 | M | 6 3 77 | Wurzburg | Schweinfurt | Newcastle U | — | — |
| **Kelly** Paddy | 6 0 | 11 07 | D | 26 4 78 | Kirkcaldy | | Celtic | 1 | — |
| | | | | | | | Newcastle U | — | — |
| | | | | | | | Reading (loan) | 3 | — |
| **Ketsbaia** Temuri | 5 8 | 10 12 | M | 18 3 68 | Gale | Dynamo Sukhumi | Dynamo Tbilisi | 54 | 8 |
| | | | | | | | Anorthosis | 76 | 36 |
| | | | | | | | AEK Athens | 84 | 24 |
| | | | | | | | Newcastle U | 31 | 3 |
| **Knight** Paul | 5 7 | 10 07 | F | 16 10 80 | Dublin | Trainee | Newcastle U | — | — |
| **Lee** Robert | 5 10 | 11 03 | M | 1 2 66 | West Ham | Hornchurch | Charlton Ath | 298 | 59 |
| | | | | | | | Newcastle U | 209 | 43 |
| **Macklin** Gareth | 5 8 | 10 06 | D | 27 8 80 | Belfast | Trainee | Newcastle U | — | — |
| **McClen** Jamie | 5 8 | 10 07 | M | 13 5 79 | Newcastle | Trainee | Newcastle U | — | — |
| **McMahon** David | 6 1 | 11 05 | F | 17 1 81 | Dublin | Trainee | Newcastle U | — | — |
| **Milbourne** Ian* | 5 11 | 11 02 | F | 21 1 79 | Hexham | Trainee | Newcastle U | — | — |
| **Paxton** Graeme* | 6 0 | 11 05 | D | 11 9 77 | Paisley | Spennymoor U | Newcastle U | — | — |
| **Peacock** Darren* | 6 2 | 12 12 | D | 3 2 68 | Bristol | Apprentice | Newport Co | 28 | — |
| | | | | | | | Hereford U | 59 | 4 |
| | | | | | | | QPR | 126 | 6 |
| | | | | | | | Newcastle U | 133 | 2 |
| **Pearce** Stuart | 5 10 | 12 06 | D | 24 4 62 | Shepherds Bush | Wealdstone | Coventry C | 51 | 4 |
| | | | | | | | Nottingham F | 401 | 63 |
| | | | | | | | Newcastle U | 25 | — |
| **Pinas** Brian | 5 8 | 10 12 | M | 29 12 78 | Rotterdam | Feyenoord | Newcastle U | — | — |
| **Pistone** Alessandro | 5 11 | 11 05 | D | 27 7 75 | Milan | | Vicenza | — | 1 |
| | | | | | | | Solbiatese | 20 | 1 |
| | | | | | | | Crevalcore | 29 | 4 |
| | | | | | | | Vicenza | 6 | — |
| | | | | | | | Internazionale | 45 | 1 |
| | | | | | | | Newcastle U | 28 | — |
| **Reed** Matthew | 5 10 | 11 10 | G | 7 4 80 | Stanford-Le-Hope | Trainee | Newcastle U | — | — |
| **Robinson** Paul | 5 10 | 10 12 | F | 20 11 78 | Sunderland | Trainee | Darlington | 26 | 3 |
| | | | | | | | Newcastle U | — | — |
| **Rush** Ian* | 6 0 | 12 06 | F | 20 10 61 | St Asaph | Apprentice | Chester C | 34 | 14 |
| | | | | | | | Liverpool | 224 | 139 |
| | | | | | | | Juventus | 29 | 7 |
| | | | | | | | Liverpool | 245 | 90 |
| | | | | | | | Leeds U | 36 | 3 |
| | | | | | | | Newcastle U | 10 | — |
| | | | | | | | Sheffield U (loan) | 4 | — |
| **Shearer** Alan | 5 11 | 12 06 | F | 13 8 70 | Newcastle | Trainee | Southampton | 118 | 23 |
| | | | | | | | Blackburn R | 138 | 112 |
| | | | | | | | Newcastle U | 48 | 27 |
| **Speed** Gary | 5 11 | 10 12 | M | 8 9 69 | Mancot | Trainee | Leeds U | 248 | 39 |
| | | | | | | | Everton | 58 | 16 |
| | | | | | | | Newcastle U | 13 | 1 |
| **Srnicek** Pavel* | 6 2 | 14 07 | G | 10 3 68 | Ostrava | Banik Ostrava | Newcastle U | 149 | — |
| **Talbot** Paul | 5 10 | 10 09 | D | 11 8 79 | Gateshead | Trainee | Newcastle U | — | — |
| **Terrier** David* | 5 11 | 11 03 | D | 4 8 73 | Verdun | | Metz | 127 | — |
| | | | | | | | West Ham U | 1 | — |
| | | | | | | | Newcastle U | — | — |
| **Tomasson** Jon Dahl | 6 0 | 11 02 | F | 29 8 76 | Copenhagen | Koge | Heerenveen | 78 | 37 |
| | | | | | | | Newcastle U | 23 | 3 |
| **Walker** Kashka‡ | 5 9 | 10 10 | M | 10 11 78 | Toronto | Canada SA | Newcastle U | — | — |
| **Watson** Steve | 6 1 | 12 07 | D | 1 4 74 | North Shields | Trainee | Newcastle U | 201 | 12 |
| **Woodcock** Chris | 5 7 | 10 08 | F | 7 5 80 | Bradford | Trainee | Newcastle U | — | — |

**Trainees**
Barrett, Lee C; Cunningham, David; Green, Stuart; Harris, Michael J; Hogg, Graham; Leighton, Kris; Martin, Ian; Muir, Karl J; Peterson, Owen; Scott, Ryan L; Stanczak, Darius; Tait, Jordan A; Walker, Andrew J; Warwick, Stephen J.

**Associated Schoolboys**
Bradshaw, Gary; Chopra, Michael; Cowie, Oliver J; Heiniger, Carl S; Hogg, Ryan; Kaveney, Glen; Mann, Jonathon; Orr, Bradley J; Pringle, Phillip C; Robson, Damon.

**Associated Schoolboys who have accepted the club's offer of a Traineeship/Contract**
Boyd, Mark E; Charlton, Craig D; Collins, Shaun T; Cowan, David R; Gall, Kevin A; Parry, Anthony; Wealleans, Kevin.

## NORTHAMPTON TOWN

| | | | | | | | | | |
|---|---|---|---|---|---|---|---|---|---|
| **Beckford** Jason‡ | 5 9 | 14 03 | F | 14 2 70 | Manchester | Trainee | Manchester C | 20 | 1 |
| | | | | | | | Blackburn R (loan) | 4 | — |
| | | | | | | | Port Vale (loan) | 5 | 1 |
| | | | | | | | Birmingham C | 7 | 2 |
| | | | | | | | Bury (loan) | 3 | — |
| | | | | | | | Stoke C | 4 | — |
| | | | | | | | Millwall | 9 | — |
| | | | | | | | Northampton T | 1 | — |
| **Bishop** Charlie | 6 0 | 12 11 | D | 16 2 68 | Nottingham | Stoke C | Watford | — | — |
| | | | | | | | Bury | 114 | 6 |
| | | | | | | | Barnsley | 130 | 1 |
| | | | | | | | Preston NE (loan) | 4 | — |
| | | | | | | | Burnley (loan) | 9 | — |
| | | | | | | | Wigan Ath | 28 | — |
| | | | | | | | Northampton T | 7 | — |
| **Brightwell** David# | 6 2 | 13 05 | D | 7 1 71 | Lutterworth | Trainee | Manchester C | 43 | 1 |
| | | | | | | | Chester C (loan) | 6 | — |
| | | | | | | | Lincoln C (loan) | 5 | — |
| | | | | | | | Stoke C (loan) | 1 | — |
| | | | | | | | Bradford C | 24 | — |
| | | | | | | | Blackpool (loan) | 2 | — |
| | | | | | | | Northampton T | 35 | 1 |
| **Clarkson** Ian | 5 11 | 12 00 | D | 4 12 70 | Solihull | Trainee | Birmingham C | 136 | — |
| | | | | | | | Stoke C | 75 | — |
| | | | | | | | Northampton T | 87 | 1 |
| **Colkin** Lee‡ | 5 11 | 12 04 | D | 15 7 74 | Nuneaton | Trainee | Northampton T | 99 | 3 |
| | | | | | | | Leyton Orient (loan) | 11 | — |
| **Conway** Paul‡ | 6 1 | 12 10 | M | 17 4 70 | Wandsworth | Oldham Ath | Carlisle U | 89 | 22 |
| | | | | | | | Northampton T | 3 | — |
| | | | | | | | Scarborough (loan) | 13 | 2 |
| **Dozzell** Jason‡ | 6 1 | 13 08 | M | 9 12 67 | Ipswich | School | Ipswich T | 332 | 52 |
| | | | | | | | Tottenham H | 84 | 13 |
| | | | | | | | Ipswich T | 8 | 1 |
| | | | | | | | Northampton T | 21 | 4 |
| **Drysdale** Jason* | 5 10 | 12 00 | D | 17 11 70 | Bristol | Trainee | Watford | 145 | 11 |
| | | | | | | | Newcastle U | — | — |
| | | | | | | | Swindon T | 42 | — |
| | | | | | | | Northampton T | 1 | — |
| **Frain** John | 5 8 | 11 09 | D | 8 10 68 | Birmingham | Apprentice | Birmingham C | 274 | 23 |
| | | | | | | | Northampton T | 58 | 1 |
| **Freestone** Chris | 5 11 | 11 07 | F | 4 9 71 | Nottingham | Arnold T | Middlesbrough | 9 | 1 |
| | | | | | | | Carlisle U (loan) | 5 | 2 |
| | | | | | | | Northampton T | 25 | 11 |
| **Gayle** John* | 6 2 | 15 04 | F | 30 7 64 | Bromsgrove | Burton Alb | Wimbledon | 20 | 2 |
| | | | | | | | Birmingham C | 44 | 10 |
| | | | | | | | Walsall (loan) | 4 | 1 |
| | | | | | | | Coventry C | 3 | — |
| | | | | | | | Burnley | 14 | 3 |
| | | | | | | | Stoke C | 26 | 4 |
| | | | | | | | Gillingham (loan) | 9 | 3 |
| | | | | | | | Northampton T | 48 | 7 |
| **Gibb** Ali | 5 9 | 11 07 | M | 17 2 76 | Salisbury | Trainee | Norwich C | — | — |
| | | | | | | | Northampton T | 76 | 4 |
| **Heggs** Carl | 6 1 | 12 10 | F | 11 10 70 | Leicester | Paget R | WBA | 40 | 3 |
| | | | | | | | Bristol R (loan) | 5 | 1 |
| | | | | | | | Swansea C | 46 | 7 |
| | | | | | | | Northampton T | 33 | 4 |
| **Hill** Colin | 6 0 | 12 11 | D | 12 11 63 | Uxbridge | Apprentice | Arsenal | 46 | 1 |
| | | | | | | | Brighton & HA (loan) | — | — |
| | | | | | | Maritimo | Colchester U | 69 | — |
| | | | | | | | Sheffield U | 82 | 1 |
| | | | | | | | Leicester C (loan) | 10 | — |
| | | | | | | | Leicester C | 135 | — |
| | | | | | | | Trelleborg | 11 | — |
| | | | | | | | Northampton T | 27 | — |
| **Hunt** James | 5 8 | 10 03 | M | 17 12 76 | Derby | Trainee | Notts Co | 19 | 1 |
| | | | | | | | Northampton T | 21 | — |
| **Hunter** Roy | 5 10 | 12 08 | M | 29 10 73 | Middlesbrough | Trainee | WBA | 9 | 1 |
| | | | | | | | Northampton T | 98 | 9 |
| **Leczynski** Alex‡ | 5 8 | 11 02 | F | 7 6 79 | London | Trainee | Northampton T | — | — |
| **Lee** Christian | 6 2 | 11 07 | F | 8 10 76 | Aylesbury | Doncaster R | Northampton T | 40 | 7 |
| **Martin** Dave‡ | 6 1 | 13 01 | M | 25 4 63 | East Ham | Apprentice | Millwall | 140 | 6 |
| | | | | | | | Wimbledon | 35 | 3 |
| | | | | | | | Southend U | 221 | 19 |
| | | | | | | | Bristol C | 38 | 1 |
| | | | | | | | Northampton T (loan) | 7 | 1 |
| | | | | | | | Gillingham | 31 | 1 |
| | | | | | | | Leyton Orient | 8 | — |
| | | | | | | | Northampton T | 12 | — |
| | | | | | | | Brighton & HA (loan) | 1 | — |

| | | | | | | | | | |
|---|---|---|---|---|---|---|---|---|---|
| **Newell** Pault | 6 1 | 14 07 | G | 23 2 69 | Woolwich | Trainee | Southend U | 15 | — |
| | | | | | | | Leyton Orient | 61 | — |
| | | | | | | | Colchester U (loan) | 14 | — |
| | | | | | | | Barnet | 16 | — |
| | | | | | | | Darlington | 41 | — |
| | | | | | | | Colchester U | — | — |
| | | | | | | | Northampton T | — | — |
| **Parrish** Sean | 5 10 | 11 10 | M | 14 3 72 | Wrexham | Trainee | Shrewsbury T | 3 | — |
| | | | | | | Telford U | Doncaster R | 66 | 8 |
| | | | | | | | Northampton T | 51 | 9 |
| **Peer** Dean# | 6 2 | 12 04 | M | 8 8 69 | Stourbridge | Trainee | Birmingham C | 120 | 8 |
| | | | | | | | Mansfield T (loan) | 10 | — |
| | | | | | | | Walsall | 45 | 8 |
| | | | | | | | Northampton T | 93 | 4 |
| **Sampson** Ian | 6 2 | 13 03 | D | 14 11 68 | Wakefield | Goole T | Sunderland | 17 | 1 |
| | | | | | | | Northampton T (loan) | 8 | — |
| | | | | | | | Northampton T | 157 | 14 |
| **Seal** David | 5 11 | 12 04 | F | 26 1 72 | Penrith | Aalst | Bristol C | 51 | 10 |
| | | | | | | | Northampton T | 37 | 12 |
| **Thompson** Garryt | 6 1 | 14 07 | F | 7 10 59 | Birmingham | Apprentice | Coventry C | 134 | 38 |
| | | | | | | | WBA | 91 | 39 |
| | | | | | | | Sheffield W | 36 | 7 |
| | | | | | | | Aston Villa | 60 | 17 |
| | | | | | | | Watford | 34 | 8 |
| | | | | | | | Crystal Palace | 20 | 3 |
| | | | | | | | QPR | 19 | 1 |
| | | | | | | | Cardiff C | 43 | 5 |
| | | | | | | | Northampton T | 50 | 6 |
| **Turley** Billy | 6 4 | 14 10 | G | 15 7 73 | Wolverhampton | Evesham U | Northampton T | 3 | — |
| | | | | | | | Leyton Orient (loan) | 14 | — |
| **Van Dullemen** Raymond* | 6 2 | 14 00 | F | 6 5 73 | Gravenhag | | Northampton T | 1 | — |
| **Warburton** Ray | 6 0 | 12 13 | D | 7 10 67 | Rotherham | Apprentice | Rotherham U | 4 | — |
| | | | | | | | York C | 90 | 9 |
| | | | | | | | Northampton T (loan) | 17 | 1 |
| | | | | | | | Northampton T | 157 | 10 |
| **Warner** Michael# | 5 9 | 10 10 | M | 17 1 74 | Harrogate | Tamworth | Northampton T | 19 | — |
| **Wilson** Kevin | 5 8 | 11 04 | F | 18 4 61 | Banbury | Banbury U | Derby Co | 122 | 30 |
| | | | | | | | Ipswich T | 98 | 34 |
| | | | | | | | Chelsea | 152 | 42 |
| | | | | | | | Notts Co | 69 | 3 |
| | | | | | | | Bradford C (loan) | 5 | — |
| | | | | | | | Walsall | 125 | 38 |
| | | | | | | | Northampton T | 9 | — |
| **Woodman** Andy | 6 3 | 13 07 | G | 11 8 71 | Camberwell | Apprentice | Crystal Palace | — | — |
| | | | | | | | Exeter C | 6 | — |
| | | | | | | | Northampton T | 145 | — |

**Trainees**
Burt, Ian C J; Butcher, Richard T; Finlay, Mathew D; Hancock, Adam; Hibbert, Michael B; Hough, Paul D; Hughes, Garry; Marlow, Daniel J; McCleary, Kevin D; Morrow, Andrew G; Piercewright, Brad; Santoro, Gianni M; Woods, Scott.

**Non-Contract**
Atkins, Ian L; Newell, Paul C; Thompson, Garry L.

**Associated Schoolboys**
Brydon, Adam T; Carruthers, Chris; Champlovier, Neil M; Charles, Lee; Coppock, Nicholas R; Giddins, Adam; Hateley, Gary J; Jackman, Steven P; Nash, Ryan M; Southgate, Liam; Tschernischow, Joslin M.

**Associated Schoolboys who have accepted the club's offer of a Traineeship/Contract**
Binder, Paul M; Dedman, Adam L; Dickson, Mark S; Gould, James R; Silvestri, Lorenzo; Thompson, Ryan J D.

# NORWICH CITY

| | | | | | | | | | |
|---|---|---|---|---|---|---|---|---|---|
| **Adams** Neil | 5 8 | 10 12 | M | 23 11 65 | Stoke | Local | Stoke C | 32 | 4 |
| | | | | | | | Everton | 20 | — |
| | | | | | | | Oldham Ath (loan) | 9 | — |
| | | | | | | | Oldham Ath | 129 | 23 |
| | | | | | | | Norwich C | 164 | 22 |
| **Allen** Alex | 6 1 | 11 09 | D | 12 2 80 | Mexborough | Trainee | Norwich C | — | — |
| **Bellamy** Craig | 5 8 | 10 10 | F | 13 1 79 | Cardiff | Trainee | Norwich C | 39 | 13 |
| **Broughton** Drewe | 6 3 | 12 01 | F | 25 10 78 | Hitchin | Trainee | Norwich C | 9 | 1 |
| | | | | | | | Wigan Ath (loan) | 4 | — |
| **Carey** Shaun | 5 9 | 10 10 | M | 13 5 76 | Rushden | Trainee | Norwich C | 37 | — |
| **Coote** Adrian | 6 3 | 12 00 | F | 3 9 78 | Gt Yarmouth | Trainee | Norwich C | 23 | 2 |
| **Davis** Kori* | 6 0 | 11 11 | D | 19 2 79 | Wegburg | Trainee | Norwich C | — | — |
| **Eadie** Darren | 5 8 | 11 00 | F | 10 6 75 | Chippenham | Trainee | Norwich C | 133 | 31 |
| **Fleming** Craig | 6 0 | 12 09 | D | 6 10 71 | Calder | Trainee | Halifax T | 57 | — |
| | | | | | | | Oldham Ath | 164 | 1 |
| | | | | | | | Norwich C | 22 | 1 |
| **Forbes** Adrian | 5 8 | 11 04 | F | 23 1 79 | Greenford | Trainee | Norwich C | 43 | 4 |
| **Fuglestad** Erik | 5 11 | 11 03 | D | 13 8 74 | Randaberg | | Viking | 74 | 4 |
| | | | | | | | Norwich C | 24 | 2 |

| | | | | | | | | | |
|---|---|---|---|---|---|---|---|---|---|
| **Grant** Peter | 5 8 | 11 07 | M | 30 8 65 | Bellshill | | Celtic | 363 | 15 |
| | | | | | | | Norwich C | 35 | 3 |
| **Green** Joe* | 6 3 | 12 02 | D | 2 11 78 | Wisbech | Trainee | Norwich C | — | — |
| **Green** Robert | 6 2 | 12 02 | G | 19 1 80 | Chertsey | Trainee | Norwich C | — | — |
| **Gunn** Bryan | 6 2 | 13 08 | G | 22 12 63 | Thurso | Invergordon BC | Aberdeen | 15 | — |
| *(Transferred to Hibernian, February 1998)* | | | | | | | Norwich C | 390 | — |
| | | | | | | | Hibernian | 12 | — |
| **Jackson** Matt | 6 1 | 12 07 | D | 19 10 71 | Leeds | School | Luton T | 9 | — |
| | | | | | | | Preston NE (loan) | 4 | — |
| | | | | | | | Everton | 138 | 4 |
| | | | | | | | Charlton Ath (loan) | 8 | — |
| | | | | | | | QPR (loan) | 7 | — |
| | | | | | | | Birmingham C (loan) | 10 | — |
| | | | | | | | Norwich C | 60 | 5 |
| **Kenton** Darren | 5 9 | 11 02 | D | 13 9 78 | Wandsworth | Trainee | Norwich C | 11 | — |
| **Llewellyn** Chris | 5 11 | 11 06 | F | 28 8 79 | Swansea | Trainee | Norwich C | 15 | 4 |
| **Marshall** Andy | 6 2 | 13 01 | G | 14 4 76 | Bury | Trainee | Norwich C | 73 | — |
| | | | | | | | Bournemouth (loan) | 11 | — |
| | | | | | | | Gillingham (loan) | 5 | — |
| **Marshall** Lee | 6 0 | 11 10 | D | 21 1 79 | Islington | Enfield | Norwich C | 4 | — |
| **Milligan** Mike | 5 8 | 11 00 | M | 20 2 67 | Manchester | Trainee | Oldham Ath | 162 | 17 |
| | | | | | | | Everton | 17 | 1 |
| | | | | | | | Oldham Ath | 117 | 6 |
| | | | | | | | Norwich C | 111 | 5 |
| **Newman** Rob* | 6 2 | 13 00 | D | 13 12 63 | Bradford-on-Avon | Apprentice | Bristol C | 394 | 52 |
| | | | | | | | Norwich C | 205 | 14 |
| | | | | | | | Motherwell (loan) | 11 | — |
| | | | | | | | Wigan Ath (loan) | 8 | — |
| **O'Neill** Keith | 6 1 | 12 04 | F | 16 2 76 | Dublin | Trainee | Norwich C | 55 | 8 |
| **Polston** John* | 5 11 | 11 12 | D | 10 6 68 | Walthamstow | Apprentice | Tottenham H | 24 | 1 |
| | | | | | | | Norwich C | 215 | 8 |
| **Roberts** Iwan | 6 3 | 14 00 | F | 26 6 68 | Bangor | Trainee | Watford | 63 | 9 |
| | | | | | | | Huddersfield T | 142 | 50 |
| | | | | | | | Leicester C | 100 | 41 |
| | | | | | | | Wolverhampton W | 33 | 12 |
| | | | | | | | Norwich C | 31 | 5 |
| **Russell** Darel | 5 10 | 11 01 | M | 22 10 80 | London | Trainee | Norwich C | 1 | — |
| **Scott** Kevin | 6 2 | 14 01 | D | 17 12 66 | Easington | Middlesbrough | Newcastle U | 227 | 8 |
| | | | | | | | Tottenham H | 18 | 1 |
| | | | | | | | Port Vale (loan) | 17 | 1 |
| | | | | | | | Charlton Ath (loan) | 4 | — |
| | | | | | | | Norwich C | 33 | — |
| **Segura** Victor | 5 11 | 11 09 | D | 13 3 73 | Zaragoza | Lleida | Norwich C | 25 | — |
| **Shore** Jamie* | 5 9 | 11 00 | M | 1 9 77 | Bristol | Trainee | Norwich C | — | — |
| **Simpson** Karl* | 5 11 | 11 06 | M | 14 10 76 | Newmarket | Trainee | Norwich C | 10 | — |
| **Sutch** Daryl | 6 0 | 11 10 | D | 11 9 71 | Lowestoft | Trainee | Norwich C | 165 | 7 |
| **Tipple** Gaven* | 5 9 | 11 00 | M | 9 2 79 | Welwyn | Trainee | Norwich C | 0 | — |
| **Wilson** Che | 5 9 | 11 03 | M | 17 1 79 | Ely | Trainee | Norwich C | — | — |

**Trainees**
Abiodun, Ayodeji O; Alexander, Anthony M T; Andrews, Bradley J; Belgrave, Barrington; Carr, Shaun L; Eldridge, Martin; Etunmu, Anayo S; Goreham, Paul M; Hardy, Coren P A; Henderson, Tommy S; Joynson, Matthew; Murray, David S; Parker, Kevin J; Smith, Robert S; Way, Darren.

**Associated Schoolboys**
Baker, Nicky; Edwards, Julian; Field, Lewis; Fortune, Clayton; Gibbs, Dean; Goodchild, Richard; Hume, Ross; McArthey, Sam; Oxby, Andrew; Packard, Callum; Robinson, Lee; Rudd, Bradley; Scullion, Steven; Smith, Glen; Thomson, Alex; Tod, Bradlee; Turner, Terry A; Williams, Matthew.

**Associated Schoolboys who have accepted the club's offer of a Traineeship/Contract**
Bilham, Neil; Blois, Lewis P; Gay, Daniel K; Ngopwani, Pitshou M; Rafis, Daniel; Thompson, Ian R.

## NOTTINGHAM FOREST

| | | | | | | | | | |
|---|---|---|---|---|---|---|---|---|---|
| **Allen** Chris | 5 11 | 12 04 | M | 18 11 72 | Oxford | Trainee | Oxford U | 150 | 12 |
| | | | | | | | Nottingham F (loan) | 3 | 1 |
| | | | | | | | Nottingham F | 25 | — |
| | | | | | | | Luton T (loan) | 14 | 1 |
| **Anderson** Dale‡ | 5 11 | 11 12 | F | 10 11 79 | Birmingham | Trainee | Nottingham F | — | — |
| **Archer** Paul* | 5 8 | 9 07 | M | 25 4 78 | Leicester | Trainee | Nottingham F | — | — |
| **Armstrong** Craig | 5 11 | 12 10 | M | 23 5 75 | South Shields | Trainee | Nottingham F | 18 | — |
| | | | | | | | Burnley (loan) | 4 | — |
| | | | | | | | Bristol R (loan) | 14 | — |
| | | | | | | | Gillingham (loan) | 10 | — |
| | | | | | | | Watford (loan) | 15 | — |
| **Bart-Williams** Chris | 5 11 | 11 00 | M | 16 6 74 | Freetown | Trainee | Leyton Orient | 36 | 2 |
| | | | | | | | Sheffield W | 124 | 16 |
| | | | | | | | Nottingham F | 82 | 5 |

| Beasant Dave | 6 4 | 13 12 | G | 20 | 3 59 | Ealing | Edgware T | Wimbledon | 340 | — |
|---|---|---|---|---|---|---|---|---|---|---|
| | | | | | | | | Newcastle U | 20 | — |
| | | | | | | | | Chelsea | 133 | — |
| | | | | | | | | Grimsby T (loan) | 6 | — |
| | | | | | | | | Wolverhampton W (loan) | 4 | — |
| | | | | | | | | Southampton | 88 | — |
| | | | | | | | | Nottingham F | 41 | — |
| Bonalair Thierry | 5 8 | 10 05 | M | 14 | 6 66 | Paris | | Nantes | 145 | 2 |
| | | | | | | | | Auxerre | 25 | 1 |
| | | | | | | | | Lille | 69 | 5 |
| | | | | | | | | Neuchatel Xamax | 68 | 9 |
| | | | | | | | | Nottingham F | 31 | 2 |
| Burns John | 5 10 | 11 00 | M | 4 | 12 77 | Dublin | Belvedere | Nottingham F | — | — |
| Campbell Kevin | 6 1 | 13 08 | F | 4 | 2 70 | Lambeth | Trainee | Arsenal | 166 | 46 |
| | | | | | | | | Leyton Orient (loan) | 16 | 9 |
| | | | | | | | | Leicester C (loan) | 11 | 5 |
| | | | | | | | | Nottingham F | 80 | 32 |
| Chettle Steve | 6 1 | 13 01 | D | 27 | 9 68 | Nottingham | Apprentice | Nottingham F | 370 | 8 |
| Cooper Colin | 5 9 | 11 09 | D | 28 | 2 67 | Sedgfield | | Middlesbrough | 188 | 6 |
| | | | | | | | | Millwall | 77 | 6 |
| | | | | | | | | Nottingham F | 180 | 20 |
| Cooper Richard | 5 9 | 11 00 | D | 27 | 9 79 | Nottingham | Trainee | Nottingham F | — | — |
| Cowling Lee | 5 9 | 10 03 | M | 22 | 9 77 | Doncaster | Trainee | Nottingham F | — | — |
| Cox Christopher‡ | 5 7 | 10 01 | M | 17 | 9 79 | Sunderland | Trainee | Nottingham F | — | — |
| Crossley Mark | 6 0 | 16 00 | G | 16 | 6 69 | Barnsley | Trainee | Nottingham F | 271 | — |
| | | | | | | | | Manchester U (loan) | — | — |
| | | | | | | | | Millwall (loan) | 13 | — |
| Dawson Andrew | 5 9 | 10 02 | M | 20 | 10 78 | Northallerton | Trainee | Nottingham F | — | — |
| Doig Christopher | 6 2 | 12 06 | D | 13 | 2 81 | Dumfries | Trainee | Nottingham F | — | — |
| Edds Gareth | 5 11 | 10 12 | M | 3 | 2 81 | Sydney | Trainee | Nottingham F | — | — |
| Edwards Christian | 6 2 | 12 11 | D | 23 | 11 75 | Caerphilly | Trainee | Swansea C | 115 | 4 |
| | | | | | | | | Nottingham F | — | — |
| Finnigan John | 5 8 | 10 11 | M | 28 | 3 76 | Wakefield | Trainee | Nottingham F | — | — |
| | | | | | | | | Lincoln C (loan) | 6 | — |
| Fitchett Scott | 5 8 | 9 06 | M | 20 | 1 79 | Manchester | Trainee | Nottingham F | — | — |
| Follett Richard | 5 9 | 10 02 | D | 29 | 8 79 | Leamington Spa | Trainee | Nottingham F | — | — |
| Freeman David | 5 10 | 10 13 | F | 25 | 11 79 | Dublin | Cherry Orchard | Nottingham F | — | — |
| Gemmill Scot | 5 11 | 11 06 | M | 2 | 1 71 | Paisley | School | Nottingham F | 225 | 21 |
| Goodlad Mark | 6 0 | 13 02 | G | 9 | 9 79 | Barnsley | Trainee | Nottingham F | — | — |
| Gough Steven | 5 11 | 11 10 | M | 16 | 9 80 | Burton | Trainee | Nottingham F | — | — |
| Grim Robert‡ | 5 11 | 11 08 | M | 10 | 9 78 | London | Trainee | Nottingham F | — | — |
| Guinan Stephen | 6 1 | 13 07 | F | 24 | 12 75 | Birmingham | Trainee | Nottingham F | 6 | — |
| | | | | | | | | Darlington (loan) | 3 | 1 |
| | | | | | | | | Burnley (loan) | 6 | — |
| | | | | | | | | Crewe Alex (loan) | 3 | — |
| Harewood Marlon | 6 1 | 10 00 | D | 25 | 8 79 | Hampstead | Trainee | Nottingham F | 1 | — |
| Henry David‡ | 6 3 | 14 09 | G | 12 | 11 77 | Belfast | | Nottingham F | — | — |
| Higgins Paul | 5 7 | 10 02 | D | 6 | 1 81 | Ilkeston | Trainee | Nottingham F | — | — |
| Hjelde Jon Olav | 6 0 | 13 07 | D | 30 | 7 72 | Levanger | | Rosenborg | 27 | 1 |
| | | | | | | | | Nottingham F | 28 | 1 |
| Hodges Glyn* | 6 0 | 12 10 | M | 30 | 4 63 | Streatham | Apprentice | Wimbledon | 232 | 49 |
| | | | | | | | | Newcastle U | 7 | — |
| | | | | | | | | Watford | 86 | 15 |
| | | | | | | | | Crystal Palace | 7 | — |
| | | | | | | | | Sheffield U | 147 | 19 |
| | | | | | | | | Derby Co | 9 | — |
| | | | | | | | Sin Tao | Hull C | 18 | 4 |
| | | | | | | | | Nottingham F | — | — |
| Hodgson Richard | 5 10 | 10 11 | F | 1 | 10 79 | Sunderland | Trainee | Nottingham F | — | — |
| Howarth Paul | 5 6 | 10 01 | D | 21 | 11 80 | Nottingham | Trainee | Nottingham F | — | — |
| Jerkan Nikola | 6 2 | 12 07 | D | 8 | 12 64 | Sinj | Hajduk Split | Oviedo | 203 | 1 |
| | | | | | | | | Nottingham F | 14 | — |
| Johnson Andy | 5 11 | 13 03 | M | 2 | 5 74 | Bristol | Trainee | Norwich C | 66 | 13 |
| | | | | | | | | Nottingham F | 34 | 4 |
| Lyttle Des | 5 8 | 12 13 | D | 26 | 9 71 | Wolverhampton | Worcester C | Swansea C | 46 | 1 |
| | | | | | | | | Nottingham F | 175 | 3 |
| Macari Jon | 5 9 | 11 04 | F | 15 | 12 79 | Stoke | Trainee | Nottingham F | — | — |
| McGregor Paul | 5 10 | 11 06 | F | 17 | 12 74 | Liverpool | Trainee | Nottingham F | 30 | 3 |
| Melton Stephen | 5 11 | 10 11 | M | 3 | 10 78 | Lincoln | Trainee | Nottingham F | — | — |
| Merino Carlos | 5 8 | 10 00 | M | 15 | 3 80 | Bilbao | Urdaneta | Nottingham F | — | — |
| Moore Ian | 5 11 | 12 02 | F | 26 | 8 76 | Birkenhead | Trainee | Tranmere R | 58 | 12 |
| | | | | | | | | Bradford C (loan) | 6 | — |
| | | | | | | | | Nottingham F | 15 | 1 |
| | | | | | | | | West Ham U (loan) | 1 | — |

| | | | | | | | | | |
|---|---|---|---|---|---|---|---|---|---|
| **Pascolo** Marco | 6 2 | 14 04 | G | 9 5 66 | Sion | | Sion | 17 | 1 |
| | | | | | | | Neuchatel Xamax | 52 | — |
| | | | | | | | Servette | 163 | — |
| | | | | | | | Cagliari | 14 | — |
| | | | | | | | Nottingham F | 5 | — |
| **Rogers** Alan | 5 7 | 12 07 | D | 3 1 77 | Liverpool | Trainee | Tranmere R | 57 | 2 |
| | | | | | | | Nottingham F | 46 | 1 |
| **Silenzi** Andrea‡ | 6 3 | 11 13 | F | 10 2 66 | Rome | | Lodigiani | 49 | 18 |
| | | | | | | | Arezzo | 19 | — |
| | | | | | | | Reggiana | 67 | 32 |
| | | | | | | | Napoli | 39 | 6 |
| | | | | | | | Torino | 82 | 24 |
| | | | | | | Torino | Nottingham F | 12 | — |
| **Stone** Steve | 5 8 | 12 05 | M | 20 8 71 | Gateshead | Trainee | Nottingham F | 167 | 20 |
| **Thom** Stuart | 6 2 | 11 12 | D | 27 12 76 | Dewsbury | Trainee | Nottingham F | — | — |
| | | | | | | | Mansfield T (loan) | 5 | — |
| **Thomas** Geoff# | 6 1 | 13 02 | M | 5 8 64 | Manchester | Local | Rochdale | 11 | 1 |
| | | | | | | | Crewe Alex | 125 | 20 |
| | | | | | | | Crystal Palace | 195 | 26 |
| | | | | | | | Wolverhampton W | 46 | 8 |
| | | | | | | | Nottingham F | 20 | 3 |
| **Todd** Andrew* | 6 0 | 11 03 | M | 22 2 79 | Nottingham | Trainee | Nottingham F | — | — |
| **Turner** Barry‡ | 5 9 | 10 01 | M | 1 1 78 | Nottingham | Trainee | Nottingham F | — | — |
| **Van Hooijdonk** Pierre | 6 4 | 13 13 | F | 29 11 69 | Steenbergen | NAC Breda | RBC | 69 | 33 |
| | | | | | | | NAC | 99 | 71 |
| | | | | | | | Celtic | 69 | 44 |
| | | | | | | | Nottingham F | 50 | 30 |
| **Woan** Ian | 5 10 | 12 02 | M | 14 12 67 | Wirrall | Runcorn | Nottingham F | 208 | 31 |
| **Wood** Scott‡ | 5 10 | 11 11 | M | 16 11 79 | Nottingham | Trainee | Nottingham F | — | — |

**Trainees**
Browne, Bevan; Dawson, Kevin E; Foy, Keith P; Reid, Andrew M; Williams, Gareth.

**Associated Schoolboys**
Allen, Oliver J; Blakelock, David J; Bodkin, Matthew J; Carchedi, Giovanni R; Davis, Richard L; Dawson, Michael R; Evans, Gary L; Holmes, Gareth P; Jenas, Jermaine A; Masson, Daniel P; Mulchinock, Daniel T; O'Halloran, Matthew V; Parkinson, Steven A; Potter, Aaron M; Robinson, Paul M; Rowlett, Luke P; Trotter, Chris; Wilkins, David G.

**Associated Schoolboys who have accepted the club's offer of a Traineeship/Contract**
Carter, Nicky M; Dell, Richard T; Gill, Robert; Kearney, Martin R; Prutton, David T; Turner, Matthew J.

## NOTTS COUNTY

| | | | | | | | | | |
|---|---|---|---|---|---|---|---|---|---|
| **Cherry** Steve# | 6 1 | 13 00 | G | 5 8 60 | Nottingham | Apprentice | Derby Co | 77 | — |
| | | | | | | | Port Vale (loan) | 4 | — |
| | | | | | | | Walsall | 71 | — |
| | | | | | | | Plymouth Arg | 73 | — |
| | | | | | | | Chesterfield (loan) | 10 | — |
| | | | | | | | Notts Co | 266 | — |
| | | | | | | | Watford | 4 | — |
| | | | | | | | Plymouth Arg (loan) | 16 | — |
| | | | | | | | Rotherham U | 20 | — |
| | | | | | | | Notts Co | — | — |
| **Cunnington** Shaun* | 5 11 | 11 08 | M | 4 1 66 | Bourne | Bourne T | Wrexham | 199 | 12 |
| | | | | | | | Grimsby T | 182 | 13 |
| | | | | | | | Sunderland | 58 | 8 |
| | | | | | | | WBA | 13 | — |
| | | | | | | | Notts Co | 17 | — |
| **Diuk** Wayne§ | 5 9 | 11 00 | M | 26 5 80 | Nottingham | Trainee | Notts Co | 2 | — |
| **Dudley** Craig | 5 10 | 11 04 | F | 12 9 79 | Ollerton | Trainee | Notts Co | 27 | 3 |
| | | | | | | | Shrewsbury T (loan) | 4 | — |
| **Dyer** Alex# | 6 1 | 12 00 | D | 14 11 65 | West Ham | Watford | Blackpool | 108 | 19 |
| | | | | | | | Hull C | 60 | 14 |
| | | | | | | | Crystal Palace | 17 | 2 |
| | | | | | | | Charlton Ath | 78 | 13 |
| | | | | | | | Oxford U | 76 | 6 |
| | | | | | | | Lincoln C | 1 | — |
| | | | | | | | Barnet | 35 | 2 |
| | | | | | | | Huddersfield T | 12 | 1 |
| | | | | | | | Notts Co | 10 | — |
| **Farrell** Sean | 6 1 | 13 03 | F | 28 2 69 | Watford | Apprentice | Luton T | 25 | 1 |
| | | | | | | | Colchester U (loan) | 9 | 1 |
| | | | | | | | Northampton T (loan) | 4 | 1 |
| | | | | | | | Fulham | 94 | 31 |
| | | | | | | | Peterborough U | 66 | 20 |
| | | | | | | | Notts Co | 49 | 16 |
| **Finnan** Steve | 5 9 | 10 09 | F | 20 4 76 | Chelmsford | Welling U | Birmingham C | 15 | 1 |
| | | | | | | | Notts Co (loan) | 17 | 2 |
| | | | | | | | Notts Co | 67 | 5 |

| Name | | | | | | | Club | Apps | Gls |
|---|---|---|---|---|---|---|---|---|---|
| **Hendon** Ian | 5 11 | 11 05 | D | 5 12 71 | Ilford | Trainee | Tottenham H | 4 | — |
| | | | | | | | Portsmouth (loan) | 4 | — |
| | | | | | | | Leyton Orient (loan) | 6 | — |
| | | | | | | | Barnsley (loan) | 6 | — |
| | | | | | | | Leyton Orient | 131 | 5 |
| | | | | | | | Birmingham C (loan) | 4 | — |
| | | | | | | | Notts Co | 50 | — |
| **Hughes** Andy | 6 0 | 11 00 | M | 2 1 78 | Manchester | Trainee | Oldham Ath | 33 | 1 |
| | | | | | | | Notts Co | 15 | 2 |
| **Jackson** Justin | 5 11 | 11 02 | F | 10 12 74 | Nottingham | Woking | Notts Co | 15 | 1 |
| **Jones** Gary | 6 1 | 12 09 | F | 6 4 69 | Huddersfield | Rossington Main | Doncaster R | 20 | 2 |
| | | | | | | Boston U | Southend U | 70 | 16 |
| | | | | | | | Lincoln C (loan) | 4 | 2 |
| | | | | | | | Notts Co | 89 | 36 |
| | | | | | | | Scunthorpe U (loan) | 11 | 5 |
| **Kiwomya** Andy‡ | 5 10 | 10 10 | F | 1 10 67 | Huddersfield | Trainee | Barnsley | 1 | — |
| | | | | | | | Sheffield W | — | — |
| | | | | | | Retired injury | Dundee | 21 | 1 |
| | | | | | | | Rotherham U | 7 | — |
| | | | | | | Halifax T | Scunthorpe U | 9 | 3 |
| | | | | | | | Bradford C | 43 | 3 |
| | | | | | | | Luton T (loan) | 5 | 1 |
| | | | | | | | Burnley (loan) | 3 | — |
| | | | | | | | Notts Co | 2 | — |
| **Marshall** Ben | 6 0 | 12 00 | M | 5 9 79 | Sutton | Trainee | Notts Co | — | — |
| **Mitchell** Paul* | 5 9 | 10 08 | D | 8 11 78 | Nottingham | Trainee | Notts Co | 2 | — |
| **Pearce** Dennis | 5 10 | 11 02 | D | 10 9 74 | Wolverhampton | Trainee | Aston Villa | — | — |
| | | | | | | | Wolverhampton W | 9 | — |
| | | | | | | | Notts Co | 38 | 2 |
| **Poric** Adem‡ | 5 8 | 12 05 | M | 22 4 73 | London | St George's | Sheffield W | 14 | — |
| | | | | | | Budapest | Southend U (loan) | 7 | — |
| | | | | | | | Rotherham U | 4 | — |
| | | | | | | | Notts Co | 4 | — |
| **Randall** Dean* | 6 1 | 12 00 | D | 15 5 79 | Nottingham | Trainee | Notts Co | — | — |
| **Redmile** Matthew | 6 4 | 12 11 | D | 12 11 76 | Nottingham | Trainee | Notts Co | 57 | 5 |
| **Richardson** Ian | 5 10 | 11 01 | M | 22 10 70 | Barking | Dagenham & | Birmingham C | 7 | — |
| | | | | | | Redbridge | Notts Co | 64 | 3 |
| **Robinson** Phil | 5 10 | 11 07 | M | 6 1 67 | Stafford | Apprentice | Aston Villa | 3 | 1 |
| | | | | | | | Wolverhampton W | 71 | 8 |
| | | | | | | | Notts Co | 66 | 5 |
| | | | | | | | Birmingham C (loan) | 9 | — |
| | | | | | | | Huddersfield T | 75 | 5 |
| | | | | | | | Northampton T (loan) | 14 | — |
| | | | | | | | Chesterfield | 61 | 17 |
| | | | | | | | Notts Co | 77 | 5 |
| **Robson** Mark | 5 7 | 10 02 | M | 22 5 69 | Newham | Trainee | Exeter C | 26 | 7 |
| | | | | | | | Tottenham H | 8 | — |
| | | | | | | | Reading (loan) | 7 | — |
| | | | | | | | Watford (loan) | 1 | — |
| | | | | | | | Plymouth Arg (loan) | 7 | — |
| | | | | | | | Exeter C (loan) | 8 | 1 |
| | | | | | | | West Ham U | 47 | 8 |
| | | | | | | | Charlton Ath | 105 | 9 |
| | | | | | | | Notts Co | 28 | 4 |
| **Strodder** Gary# | 6 1 | 13 03 | D | 1 4 65 | Cleckheaton | Apprentice | Lincoln C | 132 | 6 |
| | | | | | | | West Ham U | 65 | 2 |
| | | | | | | | WBA | 140 | 8 |
| | | | | | | | Notts Co | 110 | 9 |
| **Ward** Darren | 5 11 | 12 09 | G | 11 5 74 | Worksop | Trainee | Mansfield T | 81 | — |
| | | | | | | | Notts Co | 128 | — |

**Trainees**
Bateman, Neal S; Best, Russell S; Brough, Michael; Cockerill, Colin P; Cooke, Russell; Diuk, Wayne J; Henshaw, Terrence R; Holmes, Richard; Howell, Dean G; Jones, Kevin P; Lindley, James E; Norwood, Andrew M; Osborne, Matthew A; Smith, Neil S; Wigginton, Steven.

**Non-Contract**
Smith, Mark C.

**Associated Schoolboys**
Atkinson, Joe; Baum, Adam; Blanchard, Daniel T; Clarke, Ryan; Commons, Kristian; Darby, Thomas W; Dixon, John; Ferguson, Alex; Hartshorn, Michael; Hogg, Tim; Holtham, Michael; Jeffries, Alan B; Maine, Justin; McCaul, Matthew; Osborne, Calum; Pennant, Jermaine; Poznanski, Lee; Riley, Paul; Shaw, Michael; Warner, Jonathan; Worthington, Matthew.

**Associated Schoolboys who have accepted the club's offer of a Traineeship/Contract**
Briggs, Andrew; Davies, Andrew; Harrad, Kirk; Housley, Craig; Skevington, Matthew.

# OLDHAM ATHLETIC

| Name | | | | | | | Club | Apps | Gls |
|---|---|---|---|---|---|---|---|---|---|
| **Allott** Mark | 5 11 | 12 05 | F | 16 3 78 | Manchester | Trainee | Oldham Ath | 27 | 3 |
| **Clitheroe** Lee | 5 10 | 10 04 | F | 18 11 78 | Chorley | Trainee | Oldham Ath | 3 | — |
| **Duxbury** Lee | 5 10 | 11 08 | M | 7 10 69 | Keighley | Trainee | Bradford C | 209 | 25 |
| | | | | | | | Rochdale (loan) | 10 | — |
| | | | | | | | Huddersfield T | 29 | 2 |
| | | | | | | | Bradford C | 63 | 7 |
| | | | | | | | Oldham Ath | 50 | 6 |
| **Earnshaw** Mark | | | D | 11 11 78 | Leeds | Trainee | Oldham Ath | — | — |

| Name | | | | DOB | Birthplace | Signed from | Club | Apps | Gls |
|---|---|---|---|---|---|---|---|---|---|
| **Garnett** Shaun | 6 2 | 13 05 | D | 22 11 69 | Wallasey | Trainee | Tranmere R | 112 | 5 |
| | | | | | | | Chester C (loan) | 9 | — |
| | | | | | | | Preston NE (loan) | 10 | 2 |
| | | | | | | | Wigan Ath (loan) | 13 | 1 |
| | | | | | | | Swansea C | 15 | — |
| | | | | | | | Oldham Ath | 57 | 4 |
| **Graham** Richard | 6 2 | 12 08 | D | 28 11 74 | Dewsbury | Trainee | Oldham Ath | 122 | 9 |
| **Grobbelaar** Bruce† | 6 1 | 12 08 | G | 6 10 57 | Durban | Vancouver Whitecaps | Crewe Alex | 24 | 1 |
| | | | | | | | Liverpool | 440 | — |
| | | | | | | | Stoke C (loan) | 4 | — |
| | | | | | | | Southampton | 32 | — |
| | | | | | | | Plymouth Arg | 36 | — |
| | | | | | | | Oxford U | — | — |
| | | | | | | | Oldham Ath | 4 | — |
| **Hart** Barrie* | 6 2 | 12 12 | D | 17 7 77 | Oldham | Trainee | Oldham Ath | — | — |
| **Hodgson** Doug | 6 1 | 12 07 | D | 27 2 69 | Frankston | Heidelberg | Sheffield U | 30 | — |
| | | | | | | | Plymouth Arg (loan) | 5 | — |
| | | | | | | | Burnley (loan) | 1 | — |
| | | | | | | | Oldham Ath | 40 | 4 |
| **Holt** Andy | 6 1 | 12 09 | D | 21 5 78 | Manchester | Trainee | Oldham Ath | 15 | 1 |
| **Hotte** Mark | 5 11 | 11 01 | M | 27 9 78 | Bradford | Trainee | Oldham Ath | 1 | — |
| **Innes** Mark | 5 10 | 12 01 | D | 27 9 78 | Bellshill | Trainee | Oldham Ath | 4 | — |
| **Ironside** Ian* | 6 2 | 12 10 | G | 8 3 64 | Sheffield | N Ferriby U | Scarborough | 88 | — |
| | | | | | | | Middlesbrough | 13 | — |
| | | | | | | | Scarborough (loan) | 7 | — |
| | | | | | | | Stockport Co | 19 | — |
| | | | | | | | Scarborough | 88 | — |
| | | | | | | | Oldham Ath | — | — |
| **Jablonski** Mark* | | | D | 9 1 79 | Oldham | Trainee | Oldham Ath | — | — |
| **Jepson** Ronnie | 6 1 | 13 05 | F | 12 5 63 | Audley | Nantwich T | Port Vale | 22 | — |
| | | | | | | | Peterborough U (loan) | 18 | 5 |
| | | | | | | | Preston NE | 38 | 8 |
| | | | | | | | Exeter C | 54 | 21 |
| | | | | | | | Huddersfield T | 107 | 36 |
| | | | | | | | Bury | 47 | 9 |
| | | | | | | | Oldham Ath | 9 | 4 |
| **Johnson** Alan* | | | G | 10 11 78 | Manchester | Trainee | Oldham Ath | — | — |
| **Kelly** Gary | 5 11 | 12 06 | G | 3 8 66 | Fulwood | Apprentice | Newcastle U | 53 | — |
| | | | | | | | Blackpool (loan) | 5 | — |
| | | | | | | | Bury | 236 | — |
| | | | | | | | West Ham U (loan) | — | — |
| | | | | | | | Oldham Ath | 68 | — |
| **Kyratzoglou** Alex‡ | 5 10 | 12 01 | M | 27 8 74 | Armitale | | Oldham Ath | 1 | — |
| **Littlejohn** Adrian | 5 9 | 10 07 | F | 26 9 70 | Wolverhampton | WBA | Walsall | 44 | 1 |
| | | | | | | | Sheffield U | 69 | 12 |
| | | | | | | | Plymouth Arg | 110 | 29 |
| | | | | | | | Oldham Ath | 5 | 3 |
| **McCarthy** Sean | 6 1 | 11 07 | F | 12 9 67 | Bridgend | Bridgend | Swansea C | 91 | 25 |
| | | | | | | | Plymouth Arg | 70 | 19 |
| | | | | | | | Bradford C | 131 | 60 |
| | | | | | | | Oldham Ath | 140 | 42 |
| | | | | | | | Bristol C (loan) | 7 | 1 |
| **McKechnie** Ewan* | | | D | 27 8 79 | Paisley | Trainee | Oldham Ath | — | — |
| **McNiven** David | 5 11 | 12 00 | F | 27 5 78 | Leeds | Trainee | Oldham Ath | 16 | 1 |
| **McNiven** Scott | 5 11 | 12 01 | D | 27 5 78 | Leeds | Trainee | Oldham Ath | 60 | 1 |
| **Miskelly** David | | | G | 3 9 79 | Ards | Trainee | Oldham Ath | — | — |
| **Murphy** Gerard | | | M | 19 12 78 | Manchester | Trainee | Oldham Ath | — | — |
| **Oldham** Gavin‡ | | | M | 25 12 78 | Manchester | Trainee | Oldham Ath | — | — |
| **Orlygsson** Toddy | 5 11 | 11 07 | M | 2 8 66 | Odense | FC Akureyi | Nottingham F | 37 | 2 |
| | | | | | | | Stoke C | 90 | 16 |
| | | | | | | | Oldham Ath | 54 | 1 |
| **Ramplin** Jamie* | | | M | 14 10 79 | Manchester | Trainee | Oldham Ath | — | — |
| **Redmond** Steve# | 5 10 | 11 07 | D | 2 11 67 | Liverpool | Apprentice | Manchester C | 235 | 7 |
| | | | | | | | Oldham Ath | 205 | 4 |
| **Reid** Paul | 5 9 | 10 07 | M | 19 1 68 | Oldbury | Apprentice | Leicester C | 162 | 21 |
| | | | | | | | Bradford C (loan) | 7 | — |
| | | | | | | | Bradford C | 82 | 15 |
| | | | | | | | Huddersfield T | 77 | 6 |
| | | | | | | | Oldham Ath | 53 | 5 |
| **Richardson** Lloyd M* | 5 11 | 12 02 | M | 7 10 77 | Dewsbury | Trainee | Oldham Ath | 1 | — |
| **Rickers** Paul | 5 10 | 11 02 | M | 9 5 75 | Leeds | Trainee | Oldham Ath | 113 | 9 |
| **Ritchie** Andy | 5 11 | 11 10 | F | 28 11 60 | Manchester | Apprentice | Manchester U | 33 | 13 |
| | | | | | | | Brighton & HA | 89 | 23 |
| | | | | | | | Leeds U | 136 | 40 |
| | | | | | | | Oldham Ath | 217 | 82 |
| | | | | | | | Scarborough | 68 | 17 |
| | | | | | | | Oldham Ath | 25 | 2 |

| Name | Ht | Wt | Pos | DOB | Birthplace | Source | Clubs | Apps | Gls |
|---|---|---|---|---|---|---|---|---|---|
| **Rush** Matthew | 5 11 | 12 05 | F | 6 8 71 | Dalston | Trainee | West Ham U | 48 | 5 |
| | | | | | | | Cambridge U (loan) | 10 | — |
| | | | | | | | Swansea C (loan) | 13 | — |
| | | | | | | | Norwich C | 3 | — |
| | | | | | | | Northampton T (loan) | 14 | 3 |
| | | | | | | | Oldham Ath | 24 | 3 |
| **Salt** Philip | 5 11 | 11 09 | D | 2 3 79 | Huddersfield | Trainee | Oldham Ath | 2 | — |
| **Scargill** Jon‡ | 6 1 | 14 10 | G | 9 4 77 | Dewsbury | Trainee | Sheffield W | — | — |
| | | | | | | | Chesterfield | — | — |
| | | | | | | | Oldham Ath | — | — |
| **Selfe** Oliver | | | D | 1 10 79 | Warrington | Trainee | Oldham Ath | — | — |
| **Serrant** Carl | 6 0 | 11 02 | D | 12 9 75 | Bradford | Trainee | Oldham Ath | 90 | 1 |
| **Sinnott** Lee | 6 2 | 12 10 | D | 12 7 65 | Pelsall | Apprentice | Walsall | 40 | 2 |
| | | | | | | | Watford | 78 | 2 |
| | | | | | | | Bradford C | 173 | 6 |
| | | | | | | | Crystal Palace | 55 | — |
| | | | | | | | Bradford C | 34 | 1 |
| | | | | | | | Huddersfield T | 87 | 1 |
| | | | | | | | Oldham Ath | 13 | — |
| | | | | | | | Bradford C (loan) | 7 | — |
| **Swan** Iain | | | M | 16 10 79 | Glasgow | Trainee | Oldham Ath | — | — |
| **Tipton** Matthew | 5 10 | 10 07 | F | 29 6 80 | Bangor | Trainee | Oldham Ath | 3 | — |
| **Yorke-Robinson** David* | | | F | 21 12 79 | Ratcliffe | Trainee | Oldham Ath | — | — |

**Trainees**
Battersby, Richard J; Boshell, Daniel K; Campbell, Jamie; Fairhurst, Scott; Fielding, Dale A F; Futcher, Benjamin P; Gardiner, Gareth J; Jeffries, Paul M; Johnston, Patrick P; Lush, Simon; McLaughlin, Gerard J; Pashley, Adam C; Roberts, Glen R; Rowlands, Gareth C; Spurr, Jonathan T; Sugden, Ryan S; Walsh, Daniel G; Wharton, Nathan B; Zarac, Neil.

**Non-Contract**
Grobbelaar, Bruce D.

**Associated Schoolboys**
Broughton, Matthew R; Chadderton, Daniel; Colton, Thomas; Cushion, Steven; Dillon, Richard J; Donnelly, Mark; Doran, Joseph; Duncan, Kevin; Fisher, Neil J; Hall, Daniel; Harris, Chad; Holt, Mark; Martin, Ross C; Nugent, Robert; Otto, Alastair; Pressler, Dennis; Robinson, Christopher; Shaw, Gareth L; Sutcliffe, Darren; Thompson, Darren; Toohey, Mark.

**Associated Schoolboys who have accepted the club's offer of a Traineeship/Contract**
Clark, Liam; McLean, Michael J; Saunders, John J; Smith, Benjamin; Wright, Matthew.

# OXFORD UNITED

| Name | Ht | Wt | Pos | DOB | Birthplace | Source | Clubs | Apps | Gls |
|---|---|---|---|---|---|---|---|---|---|
| **Aldridge** Martin* | 5 11 | 12 03 | F | 6 12 74 | Northampton | Trainee | Northampton T | 70 | 17 |
| | | | | | | | Oxford U | 72 | 19 |
| | | | | | | | Southend U (loan) | 11 | 1 |
| **Angel** Mark | 5 10 | 11 07 | M | 23 8 75 | Newcastle | Trainee | Sunderland | — | — |
| | | | | | | | Oxford U | 73 | 4 |
| **Banger** Nicky | 5 8 | 11 11 | F | 25 2 71 | Southampton | Trainee | Southampton | 55 | 8 |
| | | | | | | | Oldham Ath | 64 | 10 |
| | | | | | | | Oxford U | 28 | 3 |
| **Beauchamp** Joey | 5 10 | 12 11 | M | 13 3 71 | Oxford | Trainee | Oxford U | 124 | 20 |
| | | | | | | | Swansea C (loan) | 5 | 2 |
| | | | | | | | West Ham U | — | — |
| | | | | | | | Swindon T | 45 | 3 |
| | | | | | | | Oxford U | 121 | 27 |
| **Cook** Jamie | 5 10 | 10 09 | F | 2 8 79 | Oxford | Trainee | Oxford U | 20 | 2 |
| **Davis** Steve | 6 1 | 13 06 | D | 26 7 65 | Birmingham | Stoke C | Crewe Alex | 145 | 1 |
| | | | | | | | Burnley | 147 | 11 |
| | | | | | | | Barnsley | 107 | 10 |
| | | | | | | | York C (loan) | 2 | 1 |
| | | | | | | | Oxford U | 15 | 2 |
| **Dyer** Wayne‡ | 6 0 | 10 00 | M | 24 11 77 | Birmingham | Trainee / Trainee | Birmingham C | — | — |
| | | | | | | | Oxford U | — | — |
| **Emsden** Nigel‡ | | | M | 15 8 78 | Oxford | Trainee | Oxford U | — | — |
| **Folland** Robert§ | 5 9 | 10 13 | F | 16 9 79 | Swansea | Trainee | Oxford U | 2 | — |
| **Ford** Mike* | 6 0 | 12 07 | D | 9 2 66 | Bristol | Apprentice / Devizes T | Leicester C | — | — |
| | | | | | | | Cardiff C | 145 | 13 |
| | | | | | | | Oxford U | 289 | 18 |
| **Francis** Kevin | 6 7 | 16 09 | F | 6 12 67 | Moseley | Mile Oak R | Derby Co | 10 | — |
| | | | | | | | Stockport Co | 152 | 88 |
| | | | | | | | Birmingham C | 73 | 13 |
| | | | | | | | Oxford U | 15 | 7 |
| **Gilchrist** Phil | 6 0 | 13 03 | D | 25 8 73 | Stockton | Trainee | Nottingham F | — | — |
| | | | | | | | Middlesbrough | — | — |
| | | | | | | | Hartlepool U | 82 | — |
| | | | | | | | Oxford U | 137 | 8 |
| **Gray** Martin | 5 9 | 11 05 | M | 17 8 71 | Stockton | Trainee | Sunderland | 64 | 1 |
| | | | | | | | Aldershot (loan) | 5 | — |
| | | | | | | | Fulham (loan) | 6 | — |
| | | | | | | | Oxford U | 81 | 4 |
| **Jackson** Elliott | 6 2 | 15 02 | G | 27 8 77 | Swindon | Trainee | Oxford U | 6 | — |

| | | | | | | | | | |
|---|---|---|---|---|---|---|---|---|---|
| **Lewis** Mickey | 5 9 | 12 10 | M | 15 2 65 | Birmingham | School | WBA | 24 | — |
| | | | | | | | Derby Co | 43 | 1 |
| | | | | | | | Oxford U | 300 | 7 |
| **Marsh** Simon | 6 0 | 12 00 | D | 29 1 77 | Ealing | Trainee | Oxford U | 35 | 1 |
| **Massey** Stuart* | 5 10 | 13 07 | M | 17 11 64 | Crawley | Sutton U | Crystal Palace | 2 | — |
| | | | | | | | Oxford U | 103 | 8 |
| **Murphy** Matt | 6 0 | 12 01 | F | 20 8 71 | Northampton | Corby T | Oxford U | 117 | 17 |
| | | | | | | | Scunthorpe U (loan) | 3 | — |
| **Powell** Paul | 5 8 | 11 03 | M | 30 6 78 | Wallingford | Trainee | Oxford U | 24 | 1 |
| **Remy** Christophe | 5 9 | 12 01 | D | 6 8 71 | Besancon | | Auxerre | 22 | — |
| | | | | | | | Derby Co | — | — |
| | | | | | | | Oxford U | 16 | — |
| **Robinson** Les | 5 9 | 12 08 | D | 1 3 67 | Shirerook | Local | Mansfield T | 15 | — |
| | | | | | | | Stockport Co | 67 | 3 |
| | | | | | | | Doncaster R | 82 | 12 |
| | | | | | | | Oxford U | 294 | 3 |
| **Rose** Andrew | 5 9 | 10 03 | D | 9 8 78 | Ascot | Trainee | Oxford U | 1 | — |
| **Smith** David | 5 10 | 12 11 | M | 26 12 70 | Liverpool | Trainee | Norwich C | 18 | — |
| | | | | | | | Oxford U | 176 | 2 |
| **Stevens** Mark‡ | 6 5 | 12 07 | F | 3 12 77 | Swindon | School | Oxford U | 1 | — |
| **Weatherstone** Simon | 5 10 | 12 01 | F | 26 1 80 | Reading | Trainee | Oxford U | 12 | 1 |
| **Whelan** Phil | 6 4 | 14 03 | D | 7 3 72 | Stockport | | Ipswich T | 82 | 2 |
| | | | | | | | Middlesbrough | 22 | 1 |
| | | | | | | | Oxford U | 8 | — |
| **Whitehead** Phil | 6 3 | 15 11 | G | 17 12 69 | Halifax | Trainee | Halifax T | 42 | — |
| | | | | | | | Barnsley | 16 | — |
| | | | | | | | Halifax T (loan) | 9 | — |
| | | | | | | | Scunthorpe U (loan) | 8 | — |
| | | | | | | | Scunthorpe U (loan) | 8 | — |
| | | | | | | | Bradford C (loan) | 6 | — |
| | | | | | | | Oxford U | 186 | — |
| **Wilsterman** Brian | 6 1 | 13 09 | D | 19 11 66 | Surinam | Beerschot | Oxford U | 25 | — |
| **Wright** Tony | 5 7 | 10 11 | M | 1 9 79 | Swansea | Trainee | Oxford U | 1 | — |

**Trainees**
Bennett, Oliver J; Best, Gavin; Brennan, Aaron A; Davies, Alex S; Davies, Gary L; Folland, Robert W; Henshaw, Benjamin A; Nix, Lee E; Richards, Andrew K; Shepheard, Jonathan T; Shepherd, Sam R; Simms, Ian M; Townsend, Jon R; Weatherstone, Ross.

**Associated Schoolboys**
Boyce, Jonathon P; Brooks, Jamie P; Costelloe, Michael W; Di Battista, Santino; Hackett, Christopher; Holder, Jorden A; Jones, Brynmor R; Kershaw, Richard J; King, Simon; Lovegrove, Robert T; Meade, Nathan S; Mills, Jonathan P; Silva, Simon; Spence, Brynley J; Wallace, Stuart S; Wilson, Philip; Zappi, Daniel.

**Associated Schoolboys who have accepted the club's offer of a Traineeship/Contract**
Finlayson, Joseph P; Ricketts, Sam D; Whitehead, Dean; Wickens, Gary J.

# PETERBOROUGH UNITED

| | | | | | | | | | |
|---|---|---|---|---|---|---|---|---|---|
| **Bodley** Mike | 6 1 | 13 01 | D | 14 9 67 | Hayes | Apprentice | Chelsea | 6 | 1 |
| | | | | | | | Northampton T | 20 | — |
| | | | | | | | Barnet | 69 | 3 |
| | | | | | | | Southend U | 67 | 2 |
| | | | | | | | Gillingham (loan) | 7 | — |
| | | | | | | | Birmingham C (loan) | 3 | — |
| | | | | | | | Peterborough U | 62 | 1 |
| **Boothroyd** Aidy | 5 9 | 11 07 | D | 8 2 71 | Bradford | Trainee | Huddersfield T | 10 | — |
| | | | | | | | Bristol R | 16 | — |
| | | | | | | | Hearts | 4 | — |
| | | | | | | | Mansfield T | 102 | 3 |
| | | | | | | | Peterborough U | 26 | 1 |
| **Bullimore** Wayne* | 5 9 | 12 01 | M | 12 9 70 | Mansfield | Trainee | Manchester U | — | — |
| | | | | | | | Barnsley | 35 | 1 |
| | | | | | | | Stockport Co | — | — |
| | | | | | | | Scunthorpe U | 67 | 11 |
| | | | | | | | Bradford C | 2 | — |
| | | | | | | | Doncaster R (loan) | 4 | — |
| | | | | | | | Peterborough U | 21 | 1 |
| **Campbell** Sean | | | M | 31 12 74 | Bristol | | Peterborough U | — | — |
| **Carruthers** Martin | 5 11 | 11 07 | F | 7 8 72 | Nottingham | Trainee | Aston Villa | 4 | — |
| | | | | | | | Hull C (loan) | 13 | 6 |
| | | | | | | | Stoke C | 91 | 13 |
| | | | | | | | Peterborough U | 53 | 19 |
| **Castle** Steve | 5 10 | 12 07 | M | 17 5 66 | Ilford | Apprentice | Orient | 243 | 55 |
| | | | | | | | Plymouth Arg | 101 | 35 |
| | | | | | | | Birmingham C | 23 | 1 |
| | | | | | | | Gillingham (loan) | 6 | 1 |
| | | | | | | | Leyton Orient (loan) | 4 | 1 |
| | | | | | | | Peterborough U | 37 | 3 |
| **Cleaver** Christopher | 5 9 | 11 07 | F | 24 3 79 | Hitchin | Trainee | Peterborough U | 27 | 3 |
| **Connor** Daniel | 6 2 | 12 09 | G | 31 1 81 | Dublin | Trainee | Peterborough U | — | — |
| **Davies** Simon | 5 10 | 11 04 | M | 23 10 79 | Haverfordwest | Trainee | Peterborough U | 6 | — |

| Name | | | | | | | Club | Apps | Goals |
|---|---|---|---|---|---|---|---|---|---|
| **De Souza** Miguel | 5 11 | 13 08 | F | 11 2 70 | Newham | Dagenham | Birmingham C | 15 | — |
| | | | | | | | Bury (loan) | 3 | — |
| | | | | | | | Wycombe W | 83 | 30 |
| | | | | | | | Peterborough U | 32 | 5 |
| **Drury** Adam | 5 10 | 11 06 | D | 29 8 78 | Cottenham | Trainee | Peterborough U | 37 | 1 |
| **Edwards** Andy | 6 2 | 12 00 | D | 17 9 71 | Epping | Trainee | Southend U | 147 | 5 |
| | | | | | | | Birmingham C | 40 | 1 |
| | | | | | | | Peterborough U | 71 | 2 |
| **Etherington** Matthew§ | 5 10 | 10 07 | F | 14 8 81 | Truro | School | Peterborough U | 3 | — |
| **Farrell** Dave | 5 9 | 11 07 | F | 11 11 71 | Birmingham | Redditch U | Aston Villa | 6 | — |
| | | | | | | | Scunthorpe U (loan) | 5 | 1 |
| | | | | | | | Wycombe W | 60 | 8 |
| | | | | | | | Peterborough U | 42 | 6 |
| **Gill** Matthew | 5 11 | 12 10 | M | 8 11 80 | Cambridge | Trainee | Peterborough U | 2 | — |
| **Grazioli** Giuliano | 5 11 | 12 00 | F | 23 3 75 | London | Wembley | Peterborough U | 7 | 1 |
| **Green** Francis | 5 9 | 11 04 | F | 23 4 80 | Derby | Ilkeston T | Peterborough U | 4 | 1 |
| **Griemink** Bart# | 6 3 | 15 04 | G | 29 3 72 | Holland | WKE | Birmingham C | 20 | — |
| | | | | | | | Barnsley (loan) | — | — |
| | | | | | | | Peterborough U | 27 | — |
| **Houghton** Scott | 5 6 | 12 01 | F | 22 10 71 | Hitchin | Trainee | Tottenham H | 10 | 2 |
| | | | | | | | Ipswich T (loan) | 8 | 1 |
| | | | | | | | Cambridge U (loan) | — | — |
| | | | | | | | Gillingham (loan) | 3 | — |
| | | | | | | | Charlton Ath (loan) | 6 | — |
| | | | | | | | Luton T | 16 | 1 |
| | | | | | | | Walsall | 78 | 14 |
| | | | | | | | Peterborough U | 62 | 12 |
| **Inman** Niall | 5 9 | 11 06 | M | 6 2 78 | Wakefield | Trainee | Peterborough U | 8 | 1 |
| **Koogi** Anders | 5 10 | 11 01 | D | 8 9 79 | Denmark | Trainee | Peterborough U | — | — |
| **Lewis** Neil | 5 8 | 10 05 | D | 28 6 74 | Wolverhampton | Trainee | Leicester C | 67 | 1 |
| | | | | | | | Peterborough U | 34 | — |
| **Linton** Des | 6 1 | 13 10 | D | 5 9 71 | Birmingham | Trainee | Leicester C | 11 | — |
| | | | | | | | Luton T | 83 | 1 |
| | | | | | | | Peterborough U | 38 | — |
| **McMenamin** Chris | 5 10 | 11 10 | M | 27 12 73 | Donegal | Hitchin T | Coventry C | — | — |
| | | | | | | | Peterborough U | 28 | — |
| **Neal** Ashley | 6 1 | 14 10 | D | 16 12 74 | Northampton | Trainee | Liverpool | — | — |
| | | | | | | | Brighton & HA (loan) | 8 | — |
| | | | | | | | Huddersfield T | — | — |
| | | | | | | | Peterborough U | 8 | — |
| **Payne** Derek | 5 6 | 10 08 | M | 26 4 67 | Edgware | Hayes | Barnet | 51 | 6 |
| | | | | | | | Southend U | 35 | — |
| | | | | | | | Watford | 36 | 1 |
| | | | | | | | Peterborough U | 73 | 4 |
| **Quinn** Jimmy | 6 1 | 13 10 | F | 18 11 59 | Belfast | Oswestry T | Swindon T | 49 | 10 |
| | | | | | | | Blackburn R | 71 | 17 |
| | | | | | | | Swindon T | 64 | 30 |
| | | | | | | | Leicester C | 31 | 6 |
| | | | | | | | Bradford C | 35 | 14 |
| | | | | | | | West Ham U | 47 | 18 |
| | | | | | | | Bournemouth | 43 | 19 |
| | | | | | | | Reading | 182 | 71 |
| | | | | | | | Peterborough U | 42 | 20 |
| **Rennie** David | 6 0 | 13 00 | D | 29 8 64 | Edinburgh | Apprentice | Leicester C | 21 | 1 |
| | | | | | | | Leeds U | 101 | 5 |
| | | | | | | | Bristol C | 104 | 8 |
| | | | | | | | Birmingham C | 35 | 4 |
| | | | | | | | Coventry C | 82 | 3 |
| | | | | | | | Northampton T | 48 | 3 |
| | | | | | | | Peterborough U | 18 | — |
| **Rowe** Zeke# | 5 10 | 11 08 | F | 30 10 73 | Stoke Newington | Trainee | Chelsea | — | — |
| | | | | | | | Barnet (loan) | 10 | 2 |
| | | | | | | | Brighton & HA (loan) | 9 | 3 |
| | | | | | | | Peterborough U | 28 | 3 |
| | | | | | | | Doncaster R (loan) | 6 | 2 |
| **Shearer** Peter | 6 0 | 11 00 | M | 4 2 67 | Birmingham | Apprentice | Birmingham C | 4 | — |
| | | | | | | | Rochdale | 1 | — |
| | | | | | | | Cheltenham T | Bournemouth | 85 | 10 |
| | | | | | | | Birmingham C | 25 | 7 |
| | | | | | | | Peterborough U | — | — |
| **Shields** Anthony§ | | | D | 4 6 80 | Derry | Trainee | Peterborough U | 1 | — |
| **Tyler** Mark | 5 11 | 12 00 | G | 2 4 77 | Norwich | Trainee | Peterborough U | 54 | — |
| **Vickers** Ashley | 6 3 | 13 10 | D | 14 6 72 | Sheffield | Heybridge S | Peterborough U | 1 | — |

**Trainees**
Blowers, Robert; Bratton, Paul A; Cable, Aaron P; Campbell, James R; Etherington, Matthew; Foster, Ozie L; French, Daniel J; Haley, Grant R; Hann, Matthew; Haxthausen, Michael N; Jelleyman, Gareth A; Kenna, Warren J; Pendleton, Matthew; Sadler, Christopher J; Shields, Anthony G.

**Associated Schoolboys**
Earey, Oliver C; Lang, Adam B.

**Associated Schoolboys who have accepted the club's offer of a Traineeship/Contract**
McCormick, Charles; Rusk, Simon; Vaughan, Jonathan R.

## PLYMOUTH ARGYLE

| | | | | | | | | | |
|---|---|---|---|---|---|---|---|---|---|
| **Ashton** Jon | 6 0 | 12 00 | D | 4 8 79 | Plymouth | Trainee | Plymouth Arg | — | — |
| **Barlow** Martin# | 5 7 | 10 03 | M | 25 6 71 | Barnstable | Trainee | Plymouth Arg | 262 | 19 |
| **Beswetherick** John | 5 11 | 11 04 | D | 15 1 78 | Liverpool | Trainee | Plymouth Arg | 2 | — |
| **Billy** Chris# | 5 11 | 11 08 | D | 2 1 73 | Huddersfield | Trainee | Huddersfield T | 94 | 4 |
| | | | | | | | Plymouth Arg | 118 | 9 |
| **Blackwell** Kevin† | 5 11 | 12 10 | G | 21 12 58 | Luton | Barnet | Scarborough | 44 | — |
| | | | | | | | Notts Co | — | — |
| | | | | | | | Torquay U | 18 | — |
| | | | | | | | Huddersfield T | 5 | — |
| | | | | | | | Plymouth Arg | 24 | — |
| **Collins** Simon | 6 0 | 12 05 | M | 16 12 73 | Pontefract | Trainee | Huddersfield T | 52 | 3 |
| | | | | | | | Plymouth Arg | 44 | 3 |
| **Corazzin** Carlo# | 5 9 | 12 05 | F | 25 12 71 | Canada | Vancouver 86ers | Cambridge U | 105 | 39 |
| | | | | | | | Plymouth Arg | 74 | 22 |
| **Currie** Darren† | 5 11 | 12 07 | M | 29 11 74 | Hampstead | Trainee | West Ham U | — | — |
| | | | | | | | Shrewsbury T (loan) | 17 | 2 |
| | | | | | | | Leyton Orient (loan) | 10 | — |
| | | | | | | | Shrewsbury T | 66 | 8 |
| | | | | | | | Plymouth Arg | 7 | — |
| **Heathcote** Mike | 6 2 | 12 08 | D | 10 9 65 | Durham | Spennymoor U | Sunderland | 9 | — |
| | | | | | | | Halifax T (loan) | 7 | 1 |
| | | | | | | | York C (loan) | 3 | — |
| | | | | | | | Shrewsbury T | 44 | 6 |
| | | | | | | | Cambridge U | 128 | 13 |
| | | | | | | | Plymouth Arg | 122 | 9 |
| **James** Tony# | 6 3 | 13 08 | D | 27 6 67 | Sheffield | Gainsborough T | Lincoln C | 29 | — |
| | | | | | | | Leicester C | 107 | 11 |
| | | | | | | | Hereford U | 35 | 4 |
| | | | | | | | Plymouth Arg | 34 | 1 |
| **Jean** Earl | 5 7 | 11 00 | F | 9 10 71 | St Lucia | Felgueiras | Ipswich T | 1 | — |
| | | | | | | | Rotherham U | 18 | 6 |
| | | | | | | | Plymouth Arg | 36 | 4 |
| **Logan** Richard# | 6 0 | 13 03 | D | 24 5 69 | Barnsley | Gainsborough T | Huddersfield T | 45 | 1 |
| | | | | | | | Plymouth Arg | 86 | 12 |
| **Mauge** Ronnie | 5 10 | 10 06 | M | 10 3 69 | Islington | Trainee | Charlton Ath | — | — |
| | | | | | | | Fulham | 50 | 2 |
| | | | | | | | Bury | 108 | 10 |
| | | | | | | | Manchester C (loan) | — | — |
| | | | | | | | Plymouth Arg | 103 | 11 |
| **O'Hagan** Danny‡ | 6 1 | 13 08 | F | 24 4 76 | Padstow | Trainee | Plymouth Arg | 18 | 1 |
| **Phillips** Lee§ | 5 10 | 12 00 | F | 16 9 80 | Penzance | School | Plymouth Arg | 12 | — |
| **Rowbotham** Jason | 5 9 | 11 09 | D | 3 1 69 | Cardiff | Trainee | Plymouth Arg | 9 | — |
| | | | | | | | Shrewsbury T | — | — |
| | | | | | | | Hereford U | 5 | 1 |
| | | | | | | | Raith R | 56 | 1 |
| | | | | | | | Wycombe W | 27 | — |
| | | | | | | | Plymouth Arg | 40 | — |
| **Saunders** Mark‡ | 5 10 | 11 06 | M | 23 7 71 | Reading | Tiverton | Plymouth Arg | 72 | 11 |
| **Sheffield** Jon | 6 0 | 12 08 | G | 1 2 69 | Bedworth | Apprentice | Norwich C | 1 | — |
| | | | | | | | Aldershot (loan) | 11 | — |
| | | | | | | | Ipswich T (loan) | — | — |
| | | | | | | | Aldershot (loan) | 15 | — |
| | | | | | | | Cambridge U (loan) | 2 | — |
| | | | | | | | Cambridge U | 54 | — |
| | | | | | | | Colchester U (loan) | 6 | — |
| | | | | | | | Swindon T (loan) | 2 | — |
| | | | | | | | Hereford U (loan) | 8 | — |
| | | | | | | | Peterborough U | 62 | — |
| | | | | | | | Watford (loan) | — | — |
| | | | | | | | Oldham Ath (loan) | — | — |
| | | | | | | | Plymouth Arg | 46 | — |
| **Starbuck** Phil* | 5 10 | 10 13 | M | 24 11 68 | Nottingham | Apprentice | Nottingham F | 36 | 2 |
| | | | | | | | Birmingham C (loan) | 3 | — |
| | | | | | | | Hereford U (loan) | 6 | — |
| | | | | | | | Blackburn R (loan) | 6 | 1 |
| | | | | | | | Huddersfield T | 137 | 36 |
| | | | | | | | Sheffield U | 36 | 2 |
| | | | | | | | Bristol C (loan) | 5 | 1 |
| | | | | | | | Oldham Ath | 9 | 1 |
| | | | | | | | Plymouth Arg | 7 | — |
| **Williams** Paul# | 5 10 | 11 00 | D | 11 9 69 | Leicester | Trainee | Leicester C | — | — |
| | | | | | | | Stockport Co | 70 | 4 |
| | | | | | | | Coventry C | 14 | — |
| | | | | | | | WBA (loan) | 5 | — |
| | | | | | | | Huddersfield T (loan) | 9 | — |
| | | | | | | | Plymouth Arg | 131 | 4 |
| **Wotton** Paul | 5 11 | 11 08 | M | 17 8 77 | Plymouth | Trainee | Plymouth Arg | 51 | 2 |

**Trainees**
Adams, Stephen M; Beer, Lee; Evans, Jamie M; Fogarty, Shane G; Ford, Liam A; Gill, James O; Hampton, Andrew J; Howell, Peter; Jordan, John E; McGovern, Brendan; Morrison-Hill, Jamie S; Nevin, Fergus P; Parsons, Mathew; Phillips, Lee P; Smith, Benjamin G; Smith, Lee M; Taylor, Matthew A; Wills, Kevin M; Young, Ryan.

**Non-Contract**
Blackwell, Kevin P; Currie, Darren P.

**Associated Schoolboys**
Baker, Paul M; Bance, Daniel; Cook, Matthew A; Curtis, Karl G; Edwards, Darren P; Griffiths, Nicholas A; McGowan, Jamie; McGowan, Matthew; Moore, Jude; Nancarrow, Daniel; Sundercombe, Thomas; Treacy, John.

**Associated Schoolboys who have accepted the club's offer of a Traineeship/Contract**
Bastow, Darren J; Cusack, Aaron; Parnell, Simon R.

# PORTSMOUTH

| Name | | | | | Birthplace | Source | Club | Apps | Gls |
|---|---|---|---|---|---|---|---|---|---|
| **Allen** Martin | 5 10 | 11 00 | M | 14 8 65 | Reading | School | QPR | 136 | 16 |
| | | | | | | | West Ham U | 190 | 25 |
| | | | | | | | Portsmouth | 45 | 4 |
| | | | | | | | Southend U (loan) | 5 | — |
| **Aloisi** John | 6 0 | 12 06 | F | 5 2 76 | Australia | Cremonese | Portsmouth | 38 | 12 |
| **Awford** Andy | 5 9 | 11 09 | D | 14 7 72 | Worcester | Worcester C | Portsmouth | 242 | 1 |
| **Bundy** Scott | 6 3 | 12 00 | F | 20 10 77 | Southampton | Trainee | Portsmouth | — | — |
| **Carter** Jimmy* | 5 10 | 11 02 | F | 9 11 65 | Belgrade | Apprentice | Crystal Palace | — | — |
| | | | | | | | QPR | — | — |
| | | | | | | | Millwall | 110 | 10 |
| | | | | | | | Liverpool | 5 | — |
| | | | | | | | Arsenal | 25 | 2 |
| | | | | | | | Oxford U (loan) | 5 | — |
| | | | | | | | Oxford U (loan) | 4 | — |
| | | | | | | | Portsmouth | 72 | 5 |
| **Cook** Aaron§ | | | D | 6 12 79 | Caerphilly | Trainee | Portsmouth | 1 | — |
| **Durnin** John# | 5 10 | 11 10 | M | 18 8 65 | Bootle | Waterloo Dock | Liverpool | — | — |
| | | | | | | | WBA (loan) | 5 | 2 |
| | | | | | | | Oxford U | 161 | 44 |
| | | | | | | | Portsmouth | 153 | 24 |
| **Enes** Robbie‡ | 5 8 | 11 11 | M | 22 8 75 | Australia | Sydney U | Portsmouth | 5 | — |
| **Flahavan** Aaron | 6 1 | 11 12 | G | 15 12 75 | Southampton | Trainee | Portsmouth | 50 | — |
| **Foster** Craig‡ | 5 11 | 12 00 | M | 15 4 69 | Australia | Marconi | Portsmouth | 16 | 2 |
| **Hall** Paul | 5 9 | 10 02 | F | 3 7 72 | Manchester | Trainee | Torquay U | 93 | 1 |
| | | | | | | | Portsmouth | 188 | 37 |
| **Harries** Paul‡ | 6 1 | 13 00 | F | 20 10 77 | Australia | NSWSF | Portsmouth | 1 | — |
| **Hawley** Jon | 6 1 | 12 08 | D | 23 1 78 | Lincoln | Trainee | Portsmouth | — | — |
| **Hillier** David | 5 10 | 12 00 | M | 19 12 69 | Blackheath | Trainee | Arsenal | 104 | 2 |
| | | | | | | | Portsmouth | 51 | 4 |
| **Hinshelwood** Danny | 5 9 | 11 00 | D | 12 12 75 | Bromley | Trainee | Nottingham F | — | — |
| | | | | | | | Portsmouth | 5 | — |
| | | | | | | | Torquay U (loan) | 9 | — |
| **Igoe** Sammy | 5 6 | 9 07 | M | 30 9 75 | Spelthorne | Trainee | Portsmouth | 94 | 5 |
| **Jukes** Nathan | 5 11 | 11 13 | M | 10 4 79 | Worcester | Trainee | Portsmouth | — | — |
| **Karimzadeh** Ashkan‡ | 5 11 | 11 07 | F | 12 10 78 | Iran | Trainee | Portsmouth | — | — |
| **Knight** Alan# | 6 1 | 13 11 | G | 3 7 61 | Balham | Apprentice | Portsmouth | 662 | — |
| **McLoughlin** Alan# | 5 8 | 10 10 | M | 20 4 67 | Manchester | Local | Manchester U | — | — |
| | | | | | | | Swindon T | 9 | — |
| | | | | | | | Torquay U | 24 | 4 |
| | | | | | | | Swindon T | 97 | 19 |
| | | | | | | | Southampton | 24 | 1 |
| | | | | | | | Aston Villa (loan) | — | — |
| | | | | | | | Portsmouth | 249 | 42 |
| **Perrett** Russell | 6 2 | 13 00 | D | 18 6 73 | Barton-on-Sea | AFC Lymington | Portsmouth | 57 | 2 |
| **Pethick** Robbie | 5 10 | 11 11 | D | 8 9 70 | Weymouth | Weymouth | Portsmouth | 179 | 3 |
| **Rees** Gavin‡ | 6 1 | 12 08 | D | 1 11 78 | Pembroke | Trainee | Portsmouth | — | — |
| **Robinson** Matthew | 5 11 | 11 10 | D | 23 12 74 | Exeter | Trainee | Southampton | 14 | — |
| | | | | | | | Portsmouth | 15 | — |
| **Russell** Lee# | 5 10 | 11 09 | D | 3 9 69 | Southampton | Trainee | Portsmouth | 123 | 3 |
| | | | | | | | Bournemouth (loan) | 3 | — |
| **Simpson** Fitzroy | 5 8 | 12 00 | M | 26 2 70 | Trowbridge | Trainee | Swindon T | 105 | 9 |
| | | | | | | | Manchester C | 71 | 4 |
| | | | | | | | Bristol C (loan) | 4 | — |
| | | | | | | | Portsmouth | 90 | 9 |
| **Simpson** Robbie | 5 10 | 11 06 | F | 3 3 76 | Luton | Trainee | Tottenham H | — | — |
| | | | | | | | Portsmouth | 2 | — |
| **Svensson** Mathias | 6 0 | 12 06 | F | 24 9 74 | Boras | | Elfsborg | 22 | 15 |
| | | | | | | | Portsmouth | 45 | 10 |
| **Thompson** Mark‡ | 6 1 | 11 10 | M | 17 9 77 | Southampton | Trainee | Portsmouth | — | — |
| **Thomson** Andy | 6 3 | 14 00 | D | 28 3 74 | Swindon | Trainee | Swindon T | 22 | — |
| | | | | | | | Portsmouth | 79 | 3 |
| **Thorp** Hamilton‡ | 6 3 | 13 10 | F | 21 8 73 | Australia | West Adelaide | Portsmouth | 7 | — |

| | | | | | | | | | |
|---|---|---|---|---|---|---|---|---|---|
| **Turner** Andy | 5 10 | 11 10 | F | 23  3 75 | Woolwich | Trainee | Tottenham H | 20 | 3 |
| | | | | | | | Wycombe W (loan) | 4 | — |
| | | | | | | | Doncaster R (loan) | 4 | 1 |
| | | | | | | | Huddersfield T (loan) | 5 | 1 |
| | | | | | | | Southend U (loan) | 6 | — |
| | | | | | | | Portsmouth | 40 | 3 |
| **Vlachos** Michalis | 5 10 | 12 00 | M | 20  9 67 | Athens | | Apollon | 80 | 10 |
| | | | | | | | Olympiakos | 47 | 2 |
| | | | | | | | AEK Athens | 105 | 3 |
| | | | | | | | Portsmouth | 15 | — |
| **Walsh** Paul‡ | 5 8 | 10 04 | F | 1 10 62 | Plumstead | Apprentice | Charlton Ath | 87 | 24 |
| | | | | | | | Luton T | 80 | 24 |
| | | | | | | | Liverpool | 77 | 25 |
| | | | | | | | Tottenham H | 128 | 19 |
| | | | | | | | QPR (loan) | 2 | — |
| | | | | | | | Portsmouth | 73 | 14 |
| | | | | | | | Manchester C | 53 | 16 |
| | | | | | | | Portsmouth | 21 | 5 |
| **Waterman** David | 5 10 | 13 02 | D | 16  5 77 | Guernsey | Trainee | Portsmouth | 19 | — |
| **Whitbread** Adrian | 6 1 | 13 00 | D | 22 10 71 | Epping | Trainee | Leyton Orient | 125 | 2 |
| | | | | | | | Swindon T | 36 | 1 |
| | | | | | | | West Ham U | 10 | — |
| | | | | | | | Portsmouth (loan) | 13 | — |
| | | | | | | | Portsmouth | 62 | 1 |

**Trainees**
Connolly, Gary M; Cook, Aaron; Eastman, Wayne; Fisher, Daniel; Goodban, Matthew N; Groves, Matthew; Hannon, Robert J; Hawkins, David J; Holbrook, Adam P; Hussey, Stuart R; Linpow, Steven J; Macdonald, Gary; Nelson, Michael J; Nightingale, Luke R; Pettefer, Carl J; Sargent, Steven; Tardif, Christopher L; Waterman, Lee; Wright, David S; Wyatt, Nicky.

**Associated Schoolboys**
Boyle, Ashley D; Breslin, Neil J; Buxton, Lewis E; Channell, Aaron; Cole, James; Cooper, Shaun D; Cox, James; Cullen, Craig A; Disney, Lee P; Hudson, Ryan J; Linpow, Neil; Molyneaux, Lee A; O'Neil, Gary P; Parker, Terry J; Parodi, Milan; Pook, Robbie J; Smith, Matthew T; Stacey, Daniel L T; Thorogood, Jonathan T; Udy, David R; Wango, Immanuel C.

**Associated Schoolboys who have accepted the club's offer of a Traineeship/Contract**
Barnett, Phillip; Dodd, Jonathon; Griffiths, Ben; Osborne, Benjamin H; White, Thomas; Wilson, Michael A.

# PORT VALE

| | | | | | | | | | |
|---|---|---|---|---|---|---|---|---|---|
| **Ainsworth** Gareth | 5 8 | 13 02 | M | 10  5 73 | Blackburn | Blackburn R | Preston NE | 5 | — |
| | | | | | | | Cambridge U | 4 | 1 |
| | | | | | | | Preston NE | 82 | 12 |
| | | | | | | | Lincoln C | 83 | 37 |
| | | | | | | | Port Vale | 40 | 5 |
| **Armstrong** Simon* | 5 10 | 11 02 | M | 23 11 78 | Skegness | Boston U | Port Vale | — | — |
| **Aspin** Neil | 6 0 | 13 12 | D | 12  4 65 | Gateshead | Apprentice | Leeds U | 207 | 5 |
| | | | | | | | Port Vale | 318 | 3 |
| **Barnett** Dave | 6 1 | 14 06 | D | 16  4 67 | London | Windsor & Eton | Colchester U | 20 | — |
| | | | | | | | WBA | — | — |
| | | | | | | | Walsall | 5 | — |
| | | | | | | Kidderminster H | Barnet | 59 | 3 |
| | | | | | | | Birmingham C | 46 | — |
| | | | | | | | Dunfermline Ath | 21 | 1 |
| | | | | | | | Port Vale | 9 | 1 |
| **Bogie** Ian | 5 9 | 11 10 | M | 6 12 67 | Newcastle | Apprentice | Newcastle U | 14 | — |
| | | | | | | | Preston NE | 79 | 12 |
| | | | | | | | Millwall | 51 | 1 |
| | | | | | | | Leyton Orient | 65 | 5 |
| | | | | | | | Port Vale | 110 | 7 |
| **Boswell** Matthew* | 6 2 | 13 08 | G | 19  8 77 | Shrewsbury | | Port Vale | — | — |
| | | | | | | | Barnet (loan) | — | — |
| **Burns** Liam | 6 1 | 12 09 | D | 30 10 78 | Belfast | Trainee | Port Vale | 1 | — |
| **Carragher** Matthew | 5 10 | 11 02 | D | 14  1 76 | Liverpool | Trainee | Wigan Ath | 119 | — |
| | | | | | | | Port Vale | 26 | — |
| **Corden** Wayne | 5 10 | 11 03 | M | 1 11 75 | Leek | Trainee | Port Vale | 48 | 1 |
| **Eyre** Richard | 5 11 | 11 06 | M | 15  9 76 | Poynton | Trainee | Port Vale | 1 | — |
| **Foyle** Martin# | 5 11 | 12 01 | F | 2  5 63 | Salisbury | Amateur | Southampton | 12 | 1 |
| | | | | | | | Blackburn R (loan) | — | — |
| | | | | | | | Aldershot | 98 | 35 |
| | | | | | | | Oxford U | 126 | 36 |
| | | | | | | | Port Vale | 239 | 68 |
| **Glover** Dean* | 5 11 | 12 02 | D | 29 12 63 | West Bromwich | Apprentice | Aston Villa | 28 | — |
| | | | | | | | Sheffield U (loan) | 5 | — |
| | | | | | | | Middlesbrough | 50 | 5 |
| | | | | | | | Port Vale | 363 | 15 |
| **Griffiths** Gareth# | 6 4 | 14 04 | D | 10  4 70 | Winsford | Rhyl | Port Vale | 94 | 4 |
| | | | | | | | Shrewsbury T (loan) | 6 | — |
| **Hill** Andy* | 6 0 | 13 08 | D | 21  1 65 | Maltby | Apprentice | Manchester U | — | — |
| | | | | | | | Bury | 264 | 10 |
| | | | | | | | Manchester C | 98 | 6 |
| | | | | | | | Port Vale | 100 | 1 |

| | | | | | | | | | |
|---|---|---|---|---|---|---|---|---|---|
| **Holwyn** Jermaine* | 6 2 | 13 01 | D | 16 4 73 | Amsterdam | Ajax | Port Vale | 7 | — |
| **Jansson** Jan | 5 11 | 11 11 | M | 26 1 68 | Kalmar | | Norrkoping | 73 | 9 |
| | | | | | | | Port Vale | 44 | 6 |
| **Koordes** Rogier | 6 1 | 12 11 | M | 13 6 72 | Holland | | Telstar | 12 | — |
| | | | | | | | Port Vale | 23 | — |
| **Mahorn** Paul‡ | 5 10 | 13 01 | F | 13 8 73 | Whipps Cross | Trainee | Tottenham H | 3 | — |
| | | | | | | | Fulham (loan) | 3 | — |
| | | | | | | | Burnley (loan) | 8 | 1 |
| | | | | | | | Brentford (loan) | — | — |
| | | | | | | | Port Vale | 1 | — |
| **McShane** Tony* | 5 9 | 10 07 | M | 29 9 78 | Belfast | Trainee | Port Vale | — | — |
| **Mills** Lee | 6 2 | 12 09 | F | 10 7 70 | Mexborough | Stocksbridge PS | Wolverhampton W | 25 | 2 |
| | | | | | | | Derby Co | 16 | 7 |
| | | | | | | | Port Vale | 109 | 35 |
| **Musselwhite** Paul# | 6 2 | 14 04 | G | 22 12 68 | Portsmouth | | Portsmouth | — | — |
| | | | | | | | Scunthorpe U | 132 | — |
| | | | | | | | Port Vale | 244 | — |
| **Naylor** Tony | 5 7 | 10 06 | F | 29 3 67 | Manchester | Droylsden | Crewe Alex | 122 | 45 |
| | | | | | | | Port Vale | 153 | 47 |
| **O'Reilly** Justin‡ | 6 0 | 13 08 | F | 29 6 73 | Derby | Gresley R | Port Vale | — | — |
| **Porter** Andy# | 5 9 | 12 00 | M | 17 9 68 | Holmes Chapel | Trainee | Port Vale | 357 | 22 |
| **Snijders** Mark | 6 1 | 13 12 | D | 12 3 72 | Alkmaar | | Port Vale | 24 | 2 |
| **Stokes** Dean* | 5 8 | 11 02 | D | 23 5 70 | Birmingham | Halesowen T | Port Vale | 60 | — |
| **Talbot** Stuart | 6 0 | 13 07 | M | 14 6 73 | Birmingham | Moor Green | Port Vale | 98 | 10 |
| **Tankard** Allen | 5 10 | 12 10 | D | 21 5 69 | Islington | Trainee | Southampton | 5 | — |
| | | | | | | | Wigan Ath | 209 | 4 |
| | | | | | | | Port Vale | 170 | 2 |
| **Van Heusden** Arjan* | 6 0 | 13 12 | G | 11 12 72 | Alphen | Noordwijk | Port Vale | 27 | — |
| | | | | | | | Oxford U (loan) | 11 | — |
| **Williams** Steve* | 6 2 | 14 05 | F | 25 9 78 | Liverpool | Trainee | Port Vale | — | — |

**Trainees**
Blount, Ivan G W; Clitheroe, Stewart; Croft, Steven; Donnelly, Paul M; Gardner, Anthony; Green, Christopher R; Humphreys, Jonny J J; Jackson, Leon; O'Callaghan, George; Smolenski, Andrew W; Stanbrook, Clive; Tarr, Lee A; Taylor, Paul S; Wallace, Carl L.

**Associated Schoolboys**
Barker, Philip; Byrne, Paul; Carrigan, Benjamin D; Clewlow, Matthew; Dolapo, Olaoye; Eldershaw, Simon; Fairbrother, Craig; Goldthorpe, Ben; Goodwin, Mark; Hill, Jason M; Jennings, Simon; Jones, Darren P; Kirkham, Shane; Lightfoot, Philip A; Myatt, Andrew; Orme, Matthew J; Parker, Matthew J; Price, Andrew; Price, Garry T; Reid, Levi S J; Roberts, Dafydd; Rowlands, Stephen J; Seward, Adam; Simpson, Benjamin J; Sneade, Adam; Stevenson, Matthew; Taylor, Andrew; Travis, Michael; Whitehead, Kevin I T; Woodward, Karl C.

## PRESTON NORTH END

| | | | | | | | | | |
|---|---|---|---|---|---|---|---|---|---|
| **Appleton** Michael | 5 8 | 11 00 | M | 4 12 75 | Salford | Trainee | Manchester U | — | — |
| | | | | | | | Lincoln C (loan) | 4 | — |
| | | | | | | | Grimsby T (loan) | 10 | 3 |
| | | | | | | | Preston NE | 38 | 2 |
| **Ashcroft** Lee | 5 10 | 11 00 | F | 7 9 72 | Preston | Trainee | Preston NE | 91 | 13 |
| | | | | | | | WBA | 90 | 17 |
| | | | | | | | Notts Co (loan) | 6 | — |
| | | | | | | | Preston NE | 64 | 22 |
| **Barrick** Dean* | 5 8 | 12 00 | D | 30 9 69 | Hemsworth | Trainee | Sheffield W | 11 | 2 |
| | | | | | | | Rotherham U | 99 | 7 |
| | | | | | | | Cambridge U | 91 | 3 |
| | | | | | | | Preston NE | 109 | 1 |
| **Cartwright** Lee | 5 8 | 10 06 | F | 19 9 72 | Rossendale | Trainee | Preston NE | 232 | 16 |
| **Darby** Julian | 6 0 | 11 04 | M | 3 10 67 | Bolton | Trainee | Bolton W | 270 | 36 |
| | | | | | | | Coventry C | 55 | 5 |
| | | | | | | | WBA | 39 | 1 |
| | | | | | | | Preston NE | 12 | — |
| | | | | | | | Rotherham U (loan) | 3 | — |
| **Davey** Simon | 5 10 | 11 02 | M | 1 10 70 | Swansea | Trainee | Swansea C | 49 | 4 |
| | | | | | | | Carlisle U | 105 | 18 |
| | | | | | | | Preston NE | 106 | 21 |
| | | | | | | | Darlington (loan) | 11 | — |
| **Eyres** David | 6 0 | 11 04 | F | 26 2 64 | Liverpool | Rhyl | Blackpool | 158 | 38 |
| | | | | | | | Burnley | 175 | 37 |
| | | | | | | | Preston NE | 28 | 4 |
| **Gregan** Sean | 6 2 | 12 03 | M | 29 3 74 | Stockton | Trainee | Darlington | 136 | 4 |
| | | | | | | | Preston NE | 56 | 3 |
| **Holt** Michael | 5 10 | 11 03 | F | 28 7 77 | Barnoldswick | Trainee | Blackburn R | — | — |
| | | | | | | | Preston NE | 33 | 5 |
| **Jackson** Michael | 5 11 | 11 09 | D | 4 12 73 | Chester | Trainee | Crewe Alex | 5 | — |
| | | | | | | | Bury | 125 | 9 |
| | | | | | | | Preston NE | 47 | 2 |
| **Kidd** Ryan | 5 11 | 10 08 | D | 16 10 71 | Radcliffe | Trainee | Port Vale | 1 | — |
| | | | | | | | Preston NE | 181 | 6 |

| | | | | | | | | | |
|---|---|---|---|---|---|---|---|---|---|
| **Lormor** Tony | 6 1 | 12 06 | F | 29 10 70 | Ashington | Trainee | Newcastle U | 8 | 3 |
| | | | | | | | Norwich C (loan) | — | — |
| | | | | | | | Lincoln C | 100 | 30 |
| | | | | | | | Peterborough U | 5 | — |
| | | | | | | | Chesterfield | 113 | 35 |
| | | | | | | | Preston NE | 12 | 3 |
| | | | | | | | Notts Co (loan) | 7 | — |
| **Lucas** David | 6 1 | 11 06 | G | 23 11 77 | Preston | | Preston NE | 9 | — |
| | | | | | | | Darlington (loan) | 6 | — |
| | | | | | | | Darlington (loan) | 7 | — |
| | | | | | | | Scunthorpe U (loan) | 6 | — |
| **Macken** Jonathan | 5 10 | 12 01 | F | 7 9 77 | Manchester | Trainee | Manchester U | — | — |
| | | | | | | | Preston NE | 29 | 6 |
| **McDonald** Neil* | 6 0 | 13 10 | D | 2 11 65 | Wallsend | Wallsend BC | Newcastle U | 180 | 24 |
| | | | | | | | Everton | 90 | 4 |
| | | | | | | | Oldham Ath | 24 | 1 |
| | | | | | | | Bolton W | 4 | — |
| | | | | | | | Preston NE | 33 | — |
| **McKenna** Paul | 5 8 | 11 11 | M | 20 10 77 | Chorley | Trainee | Preston NE | 10 | 1 |
| **Moilanen** Teuvo | 6 5 | 12 06 | G | 12 12 73 | Oulu | | Ilves | 63 | — |
| | | | | | | | Jaro | 26 | — |
| | | | | | | | Preston NE | 46 | — |
| | | | | | | | Scarborough (loan) | 4 | — |
| | | | | | | | Darlington (loan) | 16 | — |
| **Morgan** Paul | 6 0 | 11 03 | F | 23 10 78 | Belfast | Trainee | Preston NE | — | — |
| **Moyes** David | 6 1 | 12 12 | D | 25 4 63 | Glasgow | Drumchapel Amat | Celtic | 24 | — |
| | | | | | | | Cambridge U | 79 | 1 |
| | | | | | | | Bristol C | 83 | 6 |
| | | | | | | | Shrewsbury T | 96 | 11 |
| | | | | | | | Dunfermline Ath | 105 | 13 |
| | | | | | | | Hamilton A | 5 | — |
| | | | | | | | Preston NE | 143 | 15 |
| **Murdock** Colin | 6 1 | 12 00 | D | 2 7 75 | Ballymena | Trainee | Manchester U | — | — |
| | | | | | | | Preston NE | 27 | 1 |
| **Nogan** Kurt | 5 10 | 11 01 | F | 9 9 70 | Cardiff | Trainee | Luton T | 33 | 3 |
| | | | | | | | Peterborough U | — | — |
| | | | | | | | Brighton & HA | 97 | 49 |
| | | | | | | | Burnley | 92 | 33 |
| | | | | | | | Preston NE | 29 | 5 |
| **O'Hanlon** Kelham* | 6 1 | 13 12 | G | 16 5 62 | Saltburn | | Middlesbrough | 87 | — |
| | | | | | | | Rotherham U | 248 | — |
| | | | | | | | Carlisle U | 83 | — |
| | | | | | | | Preston NE | 23 | — |
| | | | | | | | Dundee U | 30 | — |
| | | | | | | | Preston NE | 13 | — |
| **Parkinson** Gary | 5 10 | 11 06 | D | 10 1 68 | Middlesbrough | Everton | Middlesbrough | 202 | 5 |
| | | | | | | | Southend U (loan) | 6 | — |
| | | | | | | | Bolton W | 3 | — |
| | | | | | | | Burnley | 135 | 4 |
| | | | | | | | Preston NE | 45 | 5 |
| **Rankine** Mark | 5 10 | 11 08 | M | 30 9 69 | Doncaster | Trainee | Doncaster R | 164 | 20 |
| | | | | | | | Wolverhampton W | 132 | 1 |
| | | | | | | | Preston NE | 58 | 1 |
| **Sissoko** Habib‡ | | | F | 24 5 71 | Juvisy Orge | Louhans-C | Preston NE | 7 | — |
| **Sparrow** Paul* | 6 0 | 11 00 | D | 24 3 75 | London | Trainee | Crystal Palace | 1 | — |
| | | | | | | | Preston NE | 20 | — |
| **Squires** Jamie | 6 2 | 13 03 | D | 15 11 75 | Preston | Trainee | Preston NE | 31 | — |
| *(Transferred to Dunfermline Ath, March 1998)* | | | | | | | Mansfield T (loan) | 1 | — |
| | | | | | | | Dunfermline Ath | 5 | — |

**Trainees**
Bates, Gavin R; Beckett, Grant M; Beesley, Mark A; Bradford, Scott C; Bridgwater, David J; Butler, Carl W; Clare, Gregory J; Connolly, James M; Harron, Alexander; Jones, Darren M; King, Stuart S D; Little, Thomas E S; Old, Andrew B; Ollerton, Neil; Rhodes, Tristan M; Turner, John.

**Associated Schoolboys**
Clarkson, Christian; Hallam, Anthony T; Lonergan, Andrew; Maguire, Gary J; Maguire, Martin T; Mercer, Richard M; Porter, Christopher; Procter, Andrew J; Riding, Lee J; Rimmer, Courtney; Sharples, Christopher; Spearritt, Thomas J; Walsh, Matthew; Wright, Mark S; Wright, Ronnie M.

# QUEENS PARK RANGERS

| | | | | | | | | | |
|---|---|---|---|---|---|---|---|---|---|
| **Baraclough** Ian | 6 1 | 12 02 | D | 4 12 70 | Leicester | Trainee | Leicester C | — | — |
| | | | | | | | Wigan Ath (loan) | 9 | 2 |
| | | | | | | | Grimsby T (loan) | 4 | — |
| | | | | | | | Grimsby T | 1 | — |
| | | | | | | | Lincoln C | 73 | 10 |
| | | | | | | | Mansfield T | 47 | 5 |
| | | | | | | | Notts Co | 111 | 10 |
| | | | | | | | QPR | 8 | — |
| **Bardsley** David* | 5 10 | 12 03 | D | 11 9 64 | Manchester | Apprentice | Blackpool | 45 | — |
| | | | | | | | Watford | 100 | 7 |
| | | | | | | | Oxford U | 74 | 7 |
| | | | | | | | QPR | 253 | 4 |
| **Barker** Simon* | 5 9 | 11 07 | M | 4 11 64 | Farnworth | Apprentice | Blackburn R | 182 | 35 |
| | | | | | | | QPR | 315 | 33 |
| **Bruce** Paul | 5 10 | 12 01 | M | 18 2 78 | London | Trainee | QPR | 5 | 1 |

| | | | | | | | | | |
|---|---|---|---|---|---|---|---|---|---|
| **Challis** Trevor | 5 8 | 11 04 | D | 23 10 75 | Paddington | Trainee | QPR | 13 | — |
| **Charles** Lee* | 5 11 | 11 03 | F | 20 8 71 | Hillingdon | Chertsey T | QPR | 16 | 1 |
| | | | | | | | Barnet (loan) | 5 | — |
| | | | | | | | Cambridge U (loan) | 7 | 1 |
| **Currie** Michael | | | M | 19 10 79 | Westminster | Trainee | QPR | — | — |
| **Dowie** Iain | 6 1 | 13 07 | F | 9 1 65 | Hatfield | Hendon | Luton T | 66 | 16 |
| | | | | | | | Fulham (loan) | 5 | 1 |
| | | | | | | | West Ham U | 12 | 4 |
| | | | | | | | Southampton | 122 | 30 |
| | | | | | | | Crystal Palace | 19 | 6 |
| | | | | | | | West Ham U | 68 | 8 |
| | | | | | | | QPR | 11 | 1 |
| **Gallen** Kevin | 5 11 | 12 10 | F | 21 9 75 | Hammersmith | Trainee | QPR | 96 | 24 |
| **Graham** Mark | 5 7 | 10 08 | M | 24 10 74 | Newry | Trainee | QPR | 18 | — |
| **Graham** Richard | 5 8 | 10 06 | M | 5 8 79 | Newry | Trainee | QPR | — | — |
| **Harper** Lee | 6 1 | 13 11 | G | 30 10 71 | Chelsea | Sittingbourne | Arsenal | 1 | — |
| | | | | | | | QPR | 36 | — |
| **Hart** Paul* | 5 11 | 11 07 | G | 16 11 78 | Lewisham | Trainee | QPR | — | — |
| **Heinola** Antti | 5 7 | 10 05 | D | 20 3 73 | Helsinki | | HJK Helsinki | 80 | 5 |
| | | | | | | | Emmen | 19 | — |
| | | | | | | | Heracles | 31 | 3 |
| | | | | | | | QPR | 10 | — |
| **Hurst** Richard | 6 0 | 13 01 | G | 23 12 76 | Hammersmith | Trainee | QPR | — | — |
| **Jeanne** Leon | | | M | 17 11 80 | Cardiff | Trainee | QPR | — | — |
| **Jones** Vinnie | 6 0 | 11 12 | M | 5 1 65 | Watford | Wealdstone | Wimbledon | 77 | 9 |
| | | | | | | | Leeds U | 46 | 5 |
| | | | | | | | Sheffield U | 35 | 2 |
| | | | | | | | Chelsea | 42 | 4 |
| | | | | | | | Wimbledon | 177 | 12 |
| | | | | | | | QPR | 7 | 1 |
| **Kulcsar** George | 6 1 | 13 08 | M | 12 8 67 | Budapest | | Antwerp | 66 | 1 |
| | | | | | | | Bradford C | 26 | 1 |
| | | | | | | | QPR | 12 | — |
| **Langley** Richard | 5 10 | 11 04 | M | 27 12 79 | London | Trainee | QPR | — | — |
| **Lopez** Rik | 5 10 | 11 04 | M | 25 12 79 | Northwick Park | Arsenal | QPR | — | — |
| **Lusardi** Mario | 5 9 | 10 02 | F | 27 9 79 | Islington | Trainee | QPR | — | — |
| **Maddix** Danny | 5 11 | 12 00 | D | 11 10 67 | Ashford | Apprentice | Tottenham H | — | — |
| | | | | | | | Southend U (loan) | 2 | — |
| | | | | | | | QPR | 238 | 8 |
| **Mahoney-Johnson** Michael | 5 10 | 12 10 | M | 6 11 76 | Paddington | Trainee | QPR | 3 | — |
| | | | | | | | Wycombe W (loan) | 4 | 2 |
| | | | | | | | Brighton & HA (loan) | 4 | — |
| **McFlynn** Terry | | | D | 27 3 81 | Magherafelt | Trainee | QPR | — | — |
| **Morrow** Steve | 6 0 | 11 03 | D | 2 7 70 | Bangor | Trainee | Arsenal | 62 | 1 |
| | | | | | | | Reading (loan) | 10 | — |
| | | | | | | | Watford (loan) | 8 | — |
| | | | | | | | Reading (loan) | 3 | — |
| | | | | | | | Barnet (loan) | 1 | — |
| | | | | | | | QPR | 36 | 2 |
| **Murray** Frazer* | 5 8 | 10 10 | M | 24 9 79 | Paisley | Trainee | QPR | — | — |
| **Murray** Paul | 5 8 | 10 05 | M | 31 8 76 | Carlisle | Trainee | Carlisle U | 41 | 1 |
| | | | | | | | QPR | 65 | 6 |
| **Neill** Warren* | 5 9 | 11 05 | M | 21 11 62 | Acton | Apprentice | QPR | 181 | 3 |
| | | | | | | | Portsmouth | 218 | 2 |
| | | | | | | | Watford | 1 | — |
| **Owen** Karl | 5 11 | 12 06 | D | 12 10 79 | Coventry | Trainee | QPR | — | — |
| **Peacock** Gavin | 5 8 | 11 08 | M | 18 11 67 | Eltham | Apprentice | QPR | 17 | 1 |
| | | | | | | | Gillingham | 70 | 11 |
| | | | | | | | Bournemouth | 56 | 8 |
| | | | | | | | Newcastle U | 105 | 35 |
| | | | | | | | Chelsea | 103 | 17 |
| | | | | | | | QPR | 66 | 14 |
| **Perry** Mark | 5 10 | 12 09 | D | 19 10 78 | Perivale | Trainee | QPR | 10 | 1 |
| **Plummer** Chris | 6 2 | 12 12 | D | 12 10 76 | Isleworth | Trainee | QPR | 6 | — |
| **Purser** Wayne | 5 9 | 11 04 | F | 13 4 80 | Basildon | Trainee | QPR | — | — |
| **Quashie** Nigel | 6 0 | 12 04 | M | 20 7 78 | Nunhead | Trainee | QPR | 57 | 3 |
| **Ready** Karl | 6 1 | 12 10 | D | 14 8 72 | Neath | Trainee | QPR | 129 | 6 |
| **Roberts** Tony* | 6 0 | 13 07 | G | 4 8 69 | Bangor | Trainee | QPR | 122 | — |
| **Rose** Matthew | 5 11 | 11 01 | D | 24 9 75 | Dartford | Trainee | Arsenal | 5 | — |
| | | | | | | | QPR | 16 | — |
| **Rowland** Keith | 5 10 | 10 00 | M | 1 9 71 | Portadown | Trainee | Bournemouth | 72 | 2 |
| | | | | | | | Coventry C (loan) | 2 | — |
| | | | | | | | West Ham U | 80 | 1 |
| | | | | | | | QPR | 7 | — |

| | | | | | | | | | |
|---|---|---|---|---|---|---|---|---|---|
| **Scully** Tony | 5 7 | 11 05 | M | 12 6 76 | Dublin | Trainee | Crystal Palace | 3 | — |
| | | | | | | | Bournemouth (loan) | 10 | — |
| | | | | | | | Cardiff C (loan) | 14 | — |
| | | | | | | | Manchester C | 9 | — |
| | | | | | | | Stoke C (loan) | 7 | — |
| | | | | | | | QPR | 7 | — |
| **Sheron** Mike | 5 9 | 11 06 | F | 11 1 72 | Liverpool | Trainee | Manchester C | 100 | 24 |
| | | | | | | | Bury (loan) | 5 | 1 |
| | | | | | | | Norwich C | 28 | 2 |
| | | | | | | | Stoke C | 69 | 34 |
| | | | | | | | QPR | 40 | 11 |
| **Slade** Steve | 6 0 | 10 13 | F | 6 10 75 | Hackney | Trainee | Tottenham H | 5 | — |
| | | | | | | | QPR | 39 | 4 |
| | | | | | | | Brentford (loan) | 4 | — |
| **Sommer** Jurgen | 6 5 | 15 07 | G | 27 2 69 | New York | | Luton T | 82 | — |
| *(Transferred to Columbus Crew, January 1998)* | | | | | | | Brighton & HA (loan) | 1 | — |
| | | | | | | | Torquay U (loan) | 10 | — |
| | | | | | | | QPR | 66 | — |
| **Whittle** David | 5 10 | 12 07 | D | 2 12 78 | Waterford | Trainee | QPR | — | — |
| **Yates** Steve | 5 10 | 12 02 | D | 29 1 70 | Bristol | Trainee | Bristol R | 197 | — |
| | | | | | | | QPR | 128 | 2 |

**Trainees**
Anderson, Peter M; Andrews, Barry D F; Brown, Carlos D; Bugg, Alvin R; Franklin, Damien M; Lione, Angelo M; Meeking, Scott A; Newall, John F; Norman, Perry B; O'Connor, Sean D; Roostan, Benjamin L.

**Associated Schoolboys**
Bean, Marcus; Brady, Richard L; Conneally, Christopher; D'Austin, Ryan A; Daly, Wesley J P; Dick, Alex R; Duncan, Lyndon E; Egan, Richard L; Fitzgerald, Brian M; Gradley, Patrick; Leary, Michael; Mills, Danny W; Murphy, Danny T; Nugent, Marcel; Pacquette, Richard; Pilgrim, Wayne M; Spackman, Perry E; Tumelty, Christopher J R; Walshe, Ben; Wattley, David A.

**Associated Schoolboys who have accepted the club's offer of a Traineeship/Contract**
Browne, Ricky D; Burgess, Oliver D; Cochrane, Justin V; Rustem, Adam R; Wright, Daniel J.

# READING

| | | | | | | | | | |
|---|---|---|---|---|---|---|---|---|---|
| **Asaba** Carl | 6 1 | 13 07 | F | 28 1 73 | London | Dulwich Hamlet | Brentford | 54 | 25 |
| | | | | | | | Colchester U (loan) | 12 | 2 |
| | | | | | | | Reading | 32 | 8 |
| **Bernal** Andy | 5 10 | 12 05 | D | 16 7 66 | Canberra | Sporting Gijon | Ipswich T | 9 | — |
| | | | | | | Sydney Olympic | Reading | 142 | 2 |
| **Bibbo** Sal* | 6 2 | 14 00 | G | 24 8 74 | Basingstoke | Bournemouth | Sheffield U | — | — |
| | | | | | | | Chesterfield (loan) | 1 | — |
| | | | | | | | Reading | 7 | — |
| **Bodin** Paul‡ | 6 0 | 12 06 | D | 13 9 64 | Cardiff | Chelsea | Newport Co | — | — |
| | | | | | | | Cardiff C | 57 | 3 |
| | | | | | | Bath C | Newport Co | 6 | 1 |
| | | | | | | | Swindon T | 93 | 9 |
| | | | | | | | Crystal Palace | 9 | — |
| | | | | | | | Newcastle U (loan) | 6 | — |
| | | | | | | | Swindon T | 146 | 28 |
| | | | | | | | Reading | 41 | 1 |
| | | | | | | | Wycombe W (loan) | 5 | — |
| **Booty** Martyn | 5 8 | 11 02 | D | 30 5 71 | Kirby Muxloe | Trainee | Coventry C | 5 | — |
| | | | | | | | Crewe Alex | 96 | 5 |
| | | | | | | | Reading | 56 | 1 |
| **Bowen** Jason | 5 7 | 11 00 | M | 24 8 72 | Merthyr | Trainee | Swansea C | 124 | 26 |
| | | | | | | | Birmingham C | 48 | 7 |
| | | | | | | | Southampton (loan) | 3 | — |
| | | | | | | | Reading | 14 | 1 |
| **Brayson** Paul | 5 4 | 10 10 | F | 16 9 77 | Newcastle | Trainee | Newcastle U | — | — |
| | | | | | | | Swansea C (loan) | 11 | 5 |
| | | | | | | | Reading | 6 | 1 |
| **Bristow** Jason | | | D | 23 4 80 | Basingstoke | | Reading | — | — |
| **Caskey** Darren | 5 8 | 11 09 | M | 21 8 74 | Basildon | Trainee | Tottenham H | 32 | 4 |
| | | | | | | | Watford (loan) | 6 | 1 |
| | | | | | | | Reading | 73 | 2 |
| **Crawford** Jimmy | 5 11 | 11 06 | M | 1 5 73 | Chicago | Bohemians | Newcastle U | 2 | — |
| | | | | | | | Rotherham U (loan) | 11 | — |
| | | | | | | | Dundee U (loan) | 2 | — |
| | | | | | | | Reading | 6 | — |
| **Davies** Gareth | 6 1 | 11 03 | D | 11 12 73 | Hereford | Trainee | Hereford U | 95 | 1 |
| | | | | | | | Crystal Palace | 27 | 2 |
| | | | | | | | Cardiff C (loan) | 6 | 2 |
| | | | | | | | Reading | 18 | — |
| **Fleck** Robert | 5 7 | 11 09 | F | 11 8 65 | Glasgow | Possil YM | Partick T | 2 | 1 |
| | | | | | | | Rangers | 85 | 29 |
| | | | | | | | Norwich C | 143 | 40 |
| | | | | | | | Chelsea | 40 | 3 |
| | | | | | | | Bolton W (loan) | 7 | 1 |
| | | | | | | | Bristol C (loan) | 10 | 1 |
| | | | | | | | Norwich C | 104 | 16 |
| | | | | | | | Reading | 5 | — |
| **Freeman** Andy* | 5 7 | 9 06 | F | 8 9 77 | Reading | Crystal Palace | Reading | 1 | — |
| **Glasgow** Byron | 5 6 | 10 11 | M | 18 2 79 | London | Trainee | Reading | 7 | — |

| | | | | | | | | | |
|---|---|---|---|---|---|---|---|---|---|
| **Gray** Stuart | 5 11 | 11 00 | D | 18 12 73 | Harrogate | | Celtic | 28 | 1 |
| | | | | | | | Reading | 7 | — |
| **Hammond** Nicky | 6 0 | 11 13 | G | 7 9 67 | Hornchurch | Apprentice | Arsenal | — | — |
| | | | | | | | Bristol R (loan) | 3 | — |
| | | | | | | | Peterborough U (loan) | — | — |
| | | | | | | | Aberdeen (loan) | — | — |
| | | | | | | | Swindon T | 67 | — |
| | | | | | | | Plymouth Arg | 4 | — |
| | | | | | | | Reading | 24 | — |
| **Harrison** Ross | | | F | 28 12 79 | Leamington Spa | | Reading | — | — |
| **Hodges** Lee | 6 0 | 12 00 | F | 4 9 73 | Epping | Trainee | Tottenham H | 4 | — |
| | | | | | | | Plymouth Arg (loan) | 7 | 2 |
| | | | | | | | Wycombe W (loan) | 4 | — |
| | | | | | | | Barnet | 105 | 26 |
| | | | | | | | Reading | 24 | 6 |
| **Houghton** Ray | 5 7 | 10 10 | M | 9 1 62 | Glasgow | Amateur | West Ham U | 1 | — |
| | | | | | | | Fulham | 129 | 16 |
| | | | | | | | Oxford U | 83 | 10 |
| | | | | | | | Liverpool | 153 | 28 |
| | | | | | | | Aston Villa | 95 | 6 |
| | | | | | | | Crystal Palace | 72 | 7 |
| | | | | | | | Reading | 25 | 1 |
| **Howie** Scott | 6 3 | 13 07 | G | 4 1 72 | Motherwell | | Clyde | 55 | — |
| | | | | | | | Norwich C | 2 | — |
| | | | | | | | Motherwell | 69 | — |
| | | | | | | | Reading | 7 | — |
| **Hunter** Barry | 6 3 | 13 02 | D | 18 11 68 | Coleraine | Crusaders | Wrexham | 91 | 4 |
| | | | | | | | Reading | 27 | 2 |
| **Lambert** James | 5 7 | 11 02 | F | 14 9 73 | Henley | School | Reading | 124 | 16 |
| **Legg** Andy | 5 8 | 10 07 | D | 28 7 66 | Neath | Briton Ferry | Swansea C | 163 | 29 |
| | | | | | | | Notts Co | 89 | 9 |
| | | | | | | | Birmingham C | 45 | 5 |
| | | | | | | | Ipswich T (loan) | 6 | 1 |
| | | | | | | | Reading | 10 | |
| **Lovell** Stuart* | 5 10 | 12 03 | F | 9 1 72 | Sydney | Trainee | Reading | 227 | 58 |
| **Mautone** Steve | 6 2 | 13 03 | G | 10 8 70 | Myrtleford | Canberra Cosmos | West Ham U | 1 | — |
| | | | | | | | Crewe Alex (loan) | 3 | — |
| | | | | | | | Reading | 29 | — |
| **McIntyre** Jim | 5 11 | 12 00 | F | 24 5 72 | Alexandria | | Bristol C | 1 | — |
| | | | | | | | Exeter C (loan) | 15 | 3 |
| | | | | | | | Airdrieonians | 54 | 10 |
| | | | | | | | Kilmarnock | 46 | 9 |
| | | | | | | | Reading | 6 | — |
| **McPherson** Keith | 5 10 | 12 00 | D | 11 9 63 | Greenwich | Apprentice | West Ham U | 1 | — |
| | | | | | | | Cambridge U (loan) | 11 | 1 |
| | | | | | | | Northampton T | 182 | 8 |
| | | | | | | | Reading | 256 | 8 |
| **Meaker** Michael* | 5 11 | 12 00 | M | 18 8 71 | Greenford | Trainee | QPR | 34 | 1 |
| | | | | | | | Plymouth Arg (loan) | 4 | — |
| | | | | | | | Reading | 67 | 2 |
| **Morley** Trevor‡ | 5 11 | 12 01 | F | 20 3 61 | Nottingham | Nuneaton Bor | Northampton T | 107 | 39 |
| | | | | | | | Manchester C | 72 | 18 |
| | | | | | | | West Ham U | 81 | 24 |
| | | | | | | | Brann | 8 | 4 |
| | | | | | | | West Ham U | 41 | 20 |
| | | | | | | | Brann | 6 | 1 |
| | | | | | | | West Ham U | 56 | 13 |
| | | | | | | | Brann | 7 | 4 |
| | | | | | | | Reading | 77 | 31 |
| **Parkinson** Phil | 6 0 | 12 09 | M | 1 12 67 | Chorley | Apprentice | Southampton | — | — |
| | | | | | | | Bury | 145 | 5 |
| | | | | | | | Reading | 215 | 8 |
| **Primus** Linvoy | 6 0 | 13 07 | D | 14 9 73 | Stratford | Trainee | Charlton Ath | 4 | — |
| | | | | | | | Barnet | 127 | 7 |
| | | | | | | | Reading | 36 | 1 |
| **Roach** Neville | 5 10 | 11 00 | F | 29 9 78 | Reading | Trainee | Reading | 11 | 1 |
| **Smith** Ben‡ | 5 9 | 11 09 | M | 23 11 78 | Chelmsford | Arsenal | Reading | 1 | — |
| **Swales** Steve | 5 8 | 10 03 | D | 26 12 73 | Whitby | Trainee | Scarborough | 54 | 1 |
| | | | | | | | Reading | 43 | 1 |
| **Thorp** Michael* | 6 0 | 11 07 | D | 5 12 75 | Wallington | Trainee | Reading | 5 | — |
| **Wdowczyk** Dariusz* | 5 11 | 11 11 | D | 21 9 62 | Warsaw | Legia Warsaw | Celtic | 116 | 4 |
| | | | | | | | Reading | 82 | — |
| **Williams** Martin | 5 9 | 11 12 | F | 12 7 73 | Luton | Leicester C | Luton T | 40 | 2 |
| | | | | | | | Colchester U (loan) | 3 | — |
| | | | | | | | Reading | 73 | 10 |

**Trainees**
Arkins, Stephen F; Ashdown, Jamie L; Beasley, Adam; Bicknell, Matthew B; Costick, Paul; Fenner, Greg A; Garton, Wesley A; Hadland, Philip J; Lackford, Stuart P; McDonald, Marcus; Norris, Jordan R; Rodgers, Declan J; Rooke, Maxwell J M; Shaw, Gary M; Smith, Christopher A; Stamp, Neville; Youngs, Kevin.

**Associated Schoolboys**
Allaway, Ricky; Allaway, Shaun; Bradbury, Oliver J; Campion, Adam J; Candish, Thomas; Cobb, Matthew A; Kurton, Stuart; Matthews, Andrew; Williams, Scott; Zalcman, Sam.

**Associated Schoolboys who have accepted the club's offer of a Traineeship/Contract**
Haddow, Alexander; Sumner, Toby.

# ROCHDALE

| | | | | | | | | | |
|---|---|---|---|---|---|---|---|---|---|
| **Bailey** Mark | 5 7 | 10 12 | M | 12 8 76 | Stoke | Trainee | Stoke C | — | — |
| | | | | | | | Rochdale | 48 | — |
| **Barlow** Andy | 5 7 | 11 01 | D | 24 11 65 | Oldham | | Oldham Ath | 261 | 5 |
| | | | | | | | Bradford C (loan) | 2 | — |
| | | | | | | | Blackpool | 80 | 2 |
| | | | | | | | Rochdale | 38 | — |
| **Bayliss** Dave | 6 0 | 11 02 | D | 8 6 76 | Liverpool | Trainee | Rochdale | 82 | 2 |
| **Bryson** Ian | 5 11 | 12 05 | D | 26 11 62 | Kilmarnock | | Kilmarnock | 215 | 40 |
| | | | | | | | Sheffield U | 155 | 36 |
| | | | | | | | Barnsley | 16 | 3 |
| | | | | | | | Preston NE | 151 | 19 |
| | | | | | | | Rochdale | 15 | 1 |
| **Bywater** Steve§ | | | G | 7 6 81 | Manchester | Trainee | Rochdale | — | — |
| **Carden** Paul | 5 8 | 11 02 | D | 29 3 79 | Liverpool | Trainee | Blackpool | 1 | — |
| | | | | | | | Rochdale | 7 | — |
| **Carter** Mark‡ | 5 8 | 12 05 | F | 17 12 60 | Liverpool | Runcorn | Barnet | 82 | 30 |
| | | | | | | | Bury | 134 | 62 |
| | | | | | | | Rochdale | 11 | 2 |
| **Edwards** Neil | 5 8 | 11 02 | G | 5 12 70 | Aberdare | Trainee | Leeds U | — | — |
| | | | | | | | Huddersfield T (loan) | — | — |
| | | | | | | | Stockport Co | 164 | — |
| | | | | | | | Rochdale | 27 | — |
| **Farrell** Andy# | 5 11 | 12 00 | D | 7 10 65 | Colchester | School | Colchester U | 105 | 5 |
| | | | | | | | Burnley | 257 | 19 |
| | | | | | | | Wigan Ath | 54 | 1 |
| | | | | | | | Rochdale | 80 | 6 |
| **Fensome** Andy* | 5 8 | 11 09 | D | 18 2 69 | Northampton | Trainee | Norwich C | — | — |
| | | | | | | | Newcastle U (loan) | — | — |
| | | | | | | | Cambridge U | 126 | 1 |
| | | | | | | | Preston NE | 93 | 1 |
| | | | | | | | Rochdale | 82 | — |
| **Gouck** Andy* | 5 10 | 12 00 | M | 8 6 72 | Blackpool | Trainee | Blackpool | 148 | 12 |
| | | | | | | | Rochdale | 66 | 8 |
| **Hill** Keith# | 6 0 | 12 04 | D | 17 5 69 | Bolton | Apprentice | Blackburn R | 96 | 3 |
| | | | | | | | Plymouth Arg | 123 | 2 |
| | | | | | | | Rochdale | 80 | 5 |
| **Irwin** Nick* | 5 10 | 12 00 | D | 25 12 78 | Salford | | Rochdale | — | — |
| **Johnson** Alan | 6 0 | 14 00 | D | 19 2 71 | Ince | Trainee | Wigan Ath | 180 | 13 |
| | | | | | | | Lincoln C | 63 | — |
| | | | | | | | Preston NE (loan) | 2 | — |
| | | | | | | | Rochdale | 46 | 4 |
| **Jones** Gary | 5 9 | 11 10 | M | 3 6 77 | Birkenhead | Caernarfon Town | Swansea C | 8 | — |
| | | | | | | | Rochdale | 17 | 2 |
| **Key** Lance | 6 3 | 15 00 | G | 13 5 68 | Kettering | Histon | Sheffield W | — | — |
| | | | | | | | York C (loan) | — | — |
| | | | | | | | Oldham Ath (loan) | 2 | — |
| | | | | | | | Portsmouth (loan) | — | — |
| | | | | | | | Oxford U (loan) | 6 | — |
| | | | | | | | Lincoln C (loan) | 5 | — |
| | | | | | | | Hartlepool U (loan) | 1 | — |
| | | | | | | | Rochdale (loan) | 14 | — |
| | | | | | | | Dundee U | 4 | — |
| | | | | | | | Sheffield U | — | — |
| | | | | | | | Rochdale | 19 | — |
| **Lancashire** Graham | 5 10 | 11 12 | F | 19 10 72 | Blackpool | Trainee | Burnley | 31 | 8 |
| | | | | | | | Halifax T (loan) | 2 | — |
| | | | | | | | Chester C (loan) | 11 | 7 |
| | | | | | | | Preston NE | 23 | 2 |
| | | | | | | | Wigan Ath | 30 | 12 |
| | | | | | | | Rochdale | 27 | 9 |
| **Leonard** Mark# | 6 1 | 13 02 | F | 27 9 62 | St Helens | Witton Alb | Everton | — | — |
| | | | | | | | Tranmere R (loan) | 7 | — |
| | | | | | | | Crewe Alex | 54 | 15 |
| | | | | | | | Stockport Co | 73 | 24 |
| | | | | | | | Bradford C | 157 | 29 |
| | | | | | | | Rochdale | 9 | 1 |
| | | | | | | | Preston NE | 22 | 1 |
| | | | | | | | Chester C | 32 | 8 |
| | | | | | | | Wigan Ath | 64 | 12 |
| | | | | | | | Rochdale | 72 | 6 |
| **Painter** Robbie | 5 10 | 12 02 | F | 26 1 71 | Ince | Trainee | Chester C | 84 | 8 |
| | | | | | | | Maidstone U | 30 | 5 |
| | | | | | | | Burnley | 26 | 2 |
| | | | | | | | Darlington | 115 | 28 |
| | | | | | | | Rochdale | 72 | 24 |

| Name | | | Pos | DOB | Birthplace | Signed from | Club | Apps | Gls |
|---|---|---|---|---|---|---|---|---|---|
| **Pender** John | 6 2 | 13 05 | D | 19 11 63 | Luton | Apprentice | Wolverhampton W | 117 | 3 |
| | | | | | | | Charlton Ath | 41 | — |
| | | | | | | | Bristol C | 83 | 3 |
| | | | | | | | Burnley | 171 | 8 |
| | | | | | | | Wigan Ath | 70 | 1 |
| | | | | | | | Rochdale | 14 | — |
| **Robson** Glen | 5 10 | 10 10 | F | 25 9 77 | Sunderland | Murton | Rochdale | 10 | — |
| **Russell** Alex* | 5 10 | 11 00 | M | 17 3 73 | Crosby | Burscough | Rochdale | 102 | 14 |
| **Scott** Andy* | 6 1 | 11 05 | D | 27 6 75 | Manchester | Trainee | Blackburn R | — | — |
| | | | | | | | Cardiff C | 16 | 1 |
| | | | | | | | Rochdale | 3 | — |
| **Stuart** Mark# | 5 9 | 11 09 | M | 15 12 66 | Hammersmith | QPR | Charlton Ath | 107 | 28 |
| | | | | | | | Plymouth Arg | 57 | 11 |
| | | | | | | | Ipswich T (loan) | 5 | 2 |
| | | | | | | | Bradford C | 29 | 5 |
| | | | | | | | Huddersfield T | 15 | 3 |
| | | | | | | | Rochdale | 183 | 41 |

**Trainees**
Attwood, Wayne M; Brannelly, Ashley C; Bywater, Stephen M; Edghill, Philip A; Gray, David; Hicks, Graham; Lambert, Dale L; Litster, Stuart P; Loft. Paul; Stevens, David G; Taylor, Carl D; Thompson, Roy A; Wilkinson, James; Wilson, Scott A.

**Non-Contract**
Westmoreland, Darren P.

**Associated Schoolboys**
Bell, Colin; Fielding, David P; Lewis, David J; Walsh, David.

**Associated Schoolboys who have accepted the club's offer of a Traineeship/Contract**
Cantello, Stuart L; Gilks, Matthew; Rudd, Paul G.

# ROTHERHAM UNITED

| Name | | | Pos | DOB | Birthplace | Signed from | Club | Apps | Gls |
|---|---|---|---|---|---|---|---|---|---|
| **Bain** Kevin‡ | 5 11 | 12 05 | M | 19 9 72 | Kirkcaldy | Abbey Star | Dundee | 74 | 2 |
| | | | | | | | Rotherham U | 12 | — |
| **Bass** David | 5 11 | 12 03 | M | 29 11 74 | Frimley | Trainee | Reading | 11 | — |
| | | | | | | | Rotherham U | 18 | — |
| **Berry** Trevor | 5 6 | 11 00 | M | 1 8 74 | Haslemere | Bournemouth | Aston Villa | — | — |
| | | | | | | | Rotherham U | 108 | 14 |
| **Bos** Gijsbert | 6 4 | 12 09 | F | 22 2 73 | Spakenburg | Ijsselmeervogels | Lincoln C | 34 | 6 |
| | | | | | | | Rotherham U | 16 | 4 |
| | | | | | | | Walsall (loan) | — | — |
| **Brownrigg** Andrew* | 6 0 | 11 11 | D | 2 8 76 | Sheffield | Trainee | Hereford U | 8 | — |
| | | | | | | | Norwich C | — | — |
| | | | | | | | Rotherham U | — | — |
| **Clark** Martin | 5 9 | 10 12 | D | 12 9 70 | Accrington | Accrington S Southport | Crewe Alex | — | — |
| | | | | | | | Rotherham U | 28 | — |
| **Dillon** Paul | 5 9 | 10 11 | D | 22 10 78 | Limerick | Trainee | Rotherham U | 29 | 1 |
| **Druce** Mark* | 6 0 | 12 07 | F | 3 3 74 | Oxford | Trainee | Oxford U | 52 | 4 |
| | | | | | | | Rotherham U | 34 | 4 |
| **Garner** Darren | 5 9 | 12 07 | M | 10 12 71 | Plymouth | Trainee Dorchester T | Plymouth Arg | 27 | 1 |
| | | | | | | | Rotherham U | 101 | 6 |
| **Glover** Lee | 5 11 | 11 09 | F | 24 4 70 | Kettering | Trainee | Nottingham F | 76 | 9 |
| | | | | | | | Leicester C (loan) | 5 | 1 |
| | | | | | | | Barnsley (loan) | 8 | — |
| | | | | | | | Luton T (loan) | 1 | — |
| | | | | | | | Port Vale | 52 | 7 |
| | | | | | | | Rotherham U | 59 | 18 |
| | | | | | | | Huddersfield T (loan) | 11 | — |
| **Goodwin** Shaun‡ | 5 8 | 11 04 | M | 14 4 69 | Rotherham | Trainee | Rotherham U | 280 | 39 |
| **Hayward** Andy* | 6 0 | 11 00 | M | 21 6 70 | Barnsley | Frickley Ath | Rotherham U | 120 | 15 |
| **Heath** Stephen* | 6 0 | 11 08 | D | 15 11 77 | Hull | Trainee | Leeds U | — | — |
| | | | | | | | Carlisle U | 1 | — |
| | | | | | | | Rotherham U | — | — |
| **Hudson** Danny | 5 8 | 10 03 | M | 25 6 79 | Mexborough | Trainee | Rotherham U | 10 | — |
| **Hurst** Paul | 5 4 | 9 0 | D | 25 9 74 | Sheffield | Trainee | Rotherham U | 117 | 4 |
| **Knill** Alan | 6 4 | 13 00 | D | 8 10 64 | Slough | Apprentice | Southampton | — | — |
| | | | | | | | Halifax T | 118 | 6 |
| | | | | | | | Swansea C | 89 | 3 |
| | | | | | | | Bury | 144 | 8 |
| | | | | | | | Cardiff C (loan) | 4 | — |
| | | | | | | | Scunthorpe U | 131 | 8 |
| | | | | | | | Rotherham U | 38 | 3 |
| **Martindale** Gary | 6 1 | 11 13 | F | 24 6 71 | Liverpool | Burscough | Bolton W | — | — |
| | | | | | | | Peterborough U | 31 | 15 |
| | | | | | | | Notts Co | 66 | 13 |
| | | | | | | | Mansfield T (loan) | 5 | 2 |
| | | | | | | | Rotherham U | 8 | 2 |

| Name | | | Pos | Birth date | Birthplace | From | Club | Apps | Gls |
|---|---|---|---|---|---|---|---|---|---|
| **McDougald** Junior‡ | 5 9 | 11 00 | F | 12 1 75 | Big Spring | Trainee | Tottenham H | — | — |
| | | | | | | | Brighton & HA | 78 | 14 |
| | | | | | | | Chesterfield (loan) | 9 | 3 |
| | | | | | | | Rotherham U | 18 | 2 |
| **McKenzie** Robert* | 5 10 | 12 05 | M | 22 3 79 | Hexham | Trainee | Rotherham U | 11 | — |
| **Mimms** Bobby | 6 2 | 14 01 | G | 12 10 63 | York | Halifax T | Rotherham U | 83 | — |
| | | | | | | | Everton | 29 | — |
| | | | | | | | Notts Co (loan) | 2 | — |
| | | | | | | | Sunderland (loan) | 4 | — |
| | | | | | | | Blackburn R (loan) | 6 | — |
| | | | | | | | Manchester C (loan) | 3 | — |
| | | | | | | | Tottenham H | 37 | — |
| | | | | | | | Aberdeen (loan) | 6 | — |
| | | | | | | | Blackburn R | 128 | — |
| | | | | | | | Crystal Palace | 1 | — |
| | | | | | | | Preston NE | 27 | — |
| | | | | | | | Rotherham U | 43 | — |
| **Monington** Mark* | 6 1 | 14 02 | D | 21 10 70 | Bilsthorpe | School | Burnley | 84 | 5 |
| | | | | | | | Rotherham U | 79 | 3 |
| **Pell** Robert* | 6 1 | 12 10 | D | 5 2 79 | Leeds | Trainee | Rotherham U | 2 | — |
| | | | | | | | Doncaster R (loan) | 10 | 1 |
| **Pettinger** Paul | 6 0 | 13 00 | G | 1 10 75 | Sheffield | Barnsley | Leeds U | — | — |
| | | | | | | | Torquay U (loan) | 3 | — |
| | | | | | | | Rotherham U (loan) | 1 | — |
| | | | | | | | Gillingham | — | — |
| | | | | | | | Carlisle U | — | — |
| | | | | | | | Rotherham U | 3 | — |
| **Richardson** Neil# | 6 0 | 13 00 | D | 3 3 68 | Sunderland | Brandon U | Rotherham U | 179 | 9 |
| | | | | | | | Exeter C (loan) | 14 | — |
| **Roscoe** Andy | 5 10 | 11 08 | M | 4 6 73 | Liverpool | Trainee | Liverpool | — | — |
| | | | | | | | Bolton W | 3 | — |
| | | | | | | | Rotherham U | 164 | 13 |
| **Scott** Gary | 5 8 | 10 09 | D | 2 3 78 | Liverpool | Trainee | Tranmere R | — | — |
| | | | | | | | Rotherham U | 7 | — |
| **Sedgwick** Chris | 5 11 | 10 10 | F | 28 4 80 | Sheffield | Trainee | Rotherham U | 4 | — |
| **Shuttleworth** Barry* | 5 8 | 10 00 | D | 9 7 77 | Accrington | Trainee | Bury | — | — |
| | | | | | | | Rotherham U | — | — |
| **Taylor** John‡ | 5 8 | 11 09 | M | 4 12 78 | Liverpool | Tranmere R | Rotherham U | — | — |
| **Thompson** Steve | 5 11 | 13 00 | M | 2 11 64 | Oldham | Apprentice | Bolton W | 335 | 49 |
| | | | | | | | Luton T | 5 | — |
| | | | | | | | Leicester C | 127 | 18 |
| | | | | | | | Burnley | 49 | 1 |
| | | | | | | | Rotherham U | 39 | 3 |
| **Tracey** Richard | 5 11 | 10 12 | M | 9 7 79 | Dewsbury | Trainee | Sheffield U | — | — |
| | | | | | | | Rotherham U | — | — |
| **Warner** Vance | 6 0 | 13 04 | D | 3 9 74 | Leeds | Trainee | Nottingham F | 5 | — |
| | | | | | | | Grimsby T (loan) | 3 | — |
| | | | | | | | Rotherham U | 21 | — |
| **White** Jason | 6 1 | 12 12 | F | 19 10 71 | Meriden | Derby Co | Scunthorpe U | 68 | 16 |
| | | | | | | | Darlington (loan) | 4 | 1 |
| | | | | | | | Scarborough | 63 | 20 |
| | | | | | | | Northampton T | 77 | 18 |
| | | | | | | | Rotherham U | 27 | 13 |

**Trainees**
Allen, Paul C; Artell, David J; Bagshaw, Neil D; Barton, Warren L; Beesley, Darren K; Beeton, Lee J; Hall, Matthew D; Howard, Daniel R; Ingledow, Jamie G; Levers, Roger; Merris, David A; Monkhouse, Andrew W; Nixon, Adam R C; Otter, Simon A; Roden, Craig L; Smith, Jamie M; Towey, Christopher J; Welsh, Ewan J.

**Associated Schoolboys**
Alabi, Stephen; Barker, Damien J; Barraclough, Simon D; Beggs, John A; Boyd, Darren; Colliver, James L; Ferguson, Daniel J; Foster, James W; Gregory, Benjamin C; Hanson, Christopher; Haythorne, Craig A; Hirst, Nicky C; Holmes, Ian; Holyer, Ian D; Johnson, Mark I; Laycock, Joseph; Lees, Scott; Medlock, Michael; Ollivant, Glenn; Parker, Daniel; Pearce, Lewis J; Phillips, Andrew N; Ring, Andrew I; Sandland, Guy; Savage, Shaun B; Slater, Matthew P; Swallow, Ainsley; Thompson, Michael; Wilkinson, Matthew D; Winder, Nathan J.

**Associated Schoolboys who have accepted the club's offer of a Traineeship/Contract**
Capill, Stephen L; Connor, Gareth A; Cunningham, David G F; Hensman, Matthew D; Kangley, Philip.

# SCARBOROUGH

| Name | | | Pos | Birth date | Birthplace | From | Club | Apps | Gls |
|---|---|---|---|---|---|---|---|---|---|
| **Anastasiadis** Konstantinos‡ | | | M | 4 8 78 | Sydney | Univ NSW | Scarborough | — | — |
| **Atkin** Paul* | 6 0 | 13 00 | D | 3 9 69 | Nottingham | Trainee | Notts Co | — | — |
| | | | | | | | Bury | 21 | 1 |
| | | | | | | | York C | 153 | 3 |
| | | | | | | | Leyton Orient (loan) | 5 | — |
| | | | | | | | Scarborough | 34 | 1 |
| **Bazelya** Eammon | 5 9 | 11 00 | F | 25 10 78 | London | Trainee | Scarborough | — | — |

| Name | | | | | | | Club | Apps | Goals |
|---|---|---|---|---|---|---|---|---|---|
| **Bennett** Gary | 6 1 | 12 01 | D | 4 12 61 | Manchester | Amateur | Manchester C | — | — |
| | | | | | | | Cardiff C | 87 | 11 |
| | | | | | | | Sunderland | 369 | 23 |
| | | | | | | | Carlisle U | 26 | 5 |
| | | | | | | | Scarborough | 88 | 18 |
| **Bennett** Troy* | 6 1 | 11 13 | M | 25 12 75 | Barnsley | Trainee | Barnsley | 2 | — |
| | | | | | | | Scarborough (loan) | 5 | 1 |
| | | | | | | | Scarborough | 34 | 2 |
| **Bochenski** Simon* | 5 11 | 11 13 | F | 6 12 75 | Worksop | Trainee | Barnsley | 1 | — |
| | | | | | | | Scarborough | 19 | 1 |
| **Boyes** Scott‡ | 5 10 | 11 06 | D | 7 1 79 | Guisborough | York C | Scarborough | — | — |
| **Brodie** Steve | 5 7 | 10 08 | F | 14 1 73 | Sunderland | Trainee | Sunderland | 12 | — |
| | | | | | | | Doncaster R (loan) | 5 | 1 |
| | | | | | | | Scarborough | 68 | 15 |
| **Buxton** Nick‡ | 6 0 | 13 00 | G | 6 9 76 | Doncaster | | Bury | — | — |
| | | | | | | Goole T | Scarborough | 3 | — |
| **Campbell** Neil | 6 2 | 13 00 | F | 26 1 77 | Middlesbrough | Trainee | York C | 12 | 1 |
| | | | | | | | Scarborough | 34 | 7 |
| **Carr** Graeme‡ | 5 9 | 11 00 | D | 28 10 78 | Chester-le-Street | Trainee | Scarborough | — | — |
| **Elliott** Tony | 6 0 | 13 09 | G | 13 11 69 | Nuneaton | | Birmingham C | — | — |
| | | | | | | | Hereford U | 75 | — |
| | | | | | | | Huddersfield T | 15 | — |
| | | | | | | | Carlisle U | 22 | — |
| | | | | | | | Cardiff C | 39 | — |
| | | | | | | | Scarborough | 15 | — |
| **Jackson** Richard | 5 8 | 10 12 | D | 18 4 80 | Whitby | Trainee | Scarborough | 2 | — |
| **Kay** John | 5 10 | 11 08 | D | 29 1 64 | Sunderland | Apprentice | Arsenal | 14 | — |
| | | | | | | | Wimbledon | 63 | 2 |
| | | | | | | | Middlesbrough (loan) | 8 | — |
| | | | | | | | Sunderland | 199 | — |
| | | | | | | | Shrewsbury T (loan) | 7 | — |
| | | | | | | | Preston NE | 7 | — |
| | | | | | | | Scarborough | 74 | — |
| **Lee** Mark‡ | 6 0 | 13 00 | M | 31 5 79 | Consett | Trainee | Scarborough | — | — |
| **Martin** Kevin* | 6 0 | 12 09 | G | 26 6 76 | Bromsgrove | Trainee | Scarborough | 23 | — |
| **McElhatton** Mike* | 6 1 | 12 08 | M | 16 4 75 | Co. Kerry | Trainee | Bournemouth | 42 | 2 |
| | | | | | | | Scarborough | 70 | 7 |
| **Mitchell** Jamie* | 5 7 | 9 10 | F | 6 11 76 | Glasgow | Trainee | Norwich C | — | — |
| | | | | | | | Scarborough | 78 | 10 |
| **Rhodes** Andy | 6 0 | 13 06 | G | 23 8 64 | Doncaster | Apprentice | Barnsley | 36 | — |
| | | | | | | | Doncaster R | 106 | — |
| | | | | | | | Oldham Ath | 69 | — |
| | | | | | | | Dunfermline Ath | 79 | — |
| | | | | | | | St Johnstone | 107 | — |
| | | | | | | | Bolton W (loan) | — | — |
| | | | | | | | Airdrieonians | 29 | — |
| | | | | | | | Scarborough | 11 | — |
| **Robinson** Liam | 5 8 | 12 07 | F | 26 12 65 | Bradford | Nottingham F | Huddersfield T | 21 | 2 |
| | | | | | | | Tranmere R (loan) | 4 | 3 |
| | | | | | | | Bury | 262 | 89 |
| | | | | | | | Bristol C | 41 | 4 |
| | | | | | | | Burnley | 63 | 9 |
| | | | | | | | Scarborough | 36 | 4 |
| **Rockett** Jason | 6 1 | 13 04 | D | 26 9 69 | London | | Rotherham U | — | — |
| | | | | | | | Scarborough | 172 | 11 |
| **Russell** Matthew | 5 11 | 11 05 | F | 17 1 78 | Dewsbury | Trainee | Scarborough | 7 | — |
| | | | | | | | Doncaster R (loan) | 5 | — |
| **Snodin** Glynn† | 5 6 | 11 00 | D | 14 2 60 | Rotherham | Apprentice | Doncaster R | 309 | 61 |
| | | | | | | | Sheffield W | 59 | 1 |
| | | | | | | | Leeds U | 94 | 10 |
| | | | | | | | Oldham Ath (loan) | 8 | 1 |
| | | | | | | | Rotherham U | 3 | — |
| | | | | | | | Hearts | 34 | — |
| | | | | | | | Barnsley | 25 | — |
| | | | | | | | Carlisle U | — | — |
| | | | | | | | Scarborough | — | — |
| **Snodin** Ian | 5 9 | 11 03 | M | 15 8 63 | Rotherham | Apprentice | Doncaster R | 188 | 25 |
| | | | | | | | Leeds U | 51 | 6 |
| | | | | | | | Everton | 148 | 3 |
| | | | | | | | Sunderland (loan) | 6 | — |
| | | | | | | | Oldham Ath | 57 | — |
| | | | | | | | Scarborough | 35 | — |
| **Sutherland** Colin* | 6 0 | 11 10 | D | 15 3 75 | Glasgow | Kilpatrick Juve | Clydebank | 35 | 2 |
| | | | | | | | Scarborough | 43 | — |
| **Tate** Chris | 6 0 | 12 00 | F | 27 12 77 | York | York C | Sunderland | — | — |
| | | | | | | | Scarborough | 24 | 1 |
| **Van der Velden** Carel‡ | 6 0 | 13 08 | M | 3 8 72 | Arnheim | Den Bosch | Barnsley | 9 | — |
| | | | | | | | Scarborough | 8 | 1 |
| **Williams** Gareth | 5 10 | 12 02 | F | 12 3 67 | Newport | Gosport Bor | Aston Villa | 12 | — |
| | | | | | | | Barnsley | 34 | 6 |
| | | | | | | | Hull C (loan) | 4 | — |
| | | | | | | | Hull C (loan) | 16 | 2 |
| | | | | | | | Bournemouth | 1 | — |
| | | | | | | | Northampton T | 50 | 1 |
| | | | | | | | Scarborough | 88 | 25 |

| Player | Ht | Wt | Pos | Born | Birthplace | From | Club | Apps | Gls |
|---|---|---|---|---|---|---|---|---|---|
| **Worrall** Ben | 5 6 | 11 06 | M | 7 12 75 | Swindon | Trainee | Swindon T | 3 | — |
| | | | | | | | Scarborough | 36 | 3 |

**Trainees**
Bradley, Paul S; Brunton, Daniel J; Darcy, Richard A; Gildea, Alex; Grant, Leigh; Hunter, Darren T; Lowery, Mark; Lynn, Gary; McNaughton, Michael I; Morris, Stewart I; Newton, Paul A; Radigan, Neil; Rennison, Shaun; Stancliffe, Paul J; Tremble, David G; Wadsworth, Gregory I; Wilson, Dean P.

**Non-Contract**
Snodin, Glynn.

**Associated Schoolboys**
Almond, Michael J; Ball, Jason; Baxter, Nicholas P; Beardmore, Peter; Gildea, Daniel; Green, Nicholas J; Hammond, Kevin M; Jowsey, James R; Marley, Karl N; Taylor, Dean R.

**Associated Schoolboys who have accepted the club's offer of a Traineeship/Contract**
Atkinson, Paul R; Brown, James; Pounder, David.

## SCUNTHORPE UNITED

| Player | Ht | Wt | Pos | Born | Birthplace | From | Club | Apps | Gls |
|---|---|---|---|---|---|---|---|---|---|
| **Calvo-Garcia** Alexander# | 5 11 | 11 10 | M | 1 1 72 | Ordizia | Eibar | Scunthorpe U | 57 | 7 |
| **Clarke** Tim# | 6 3 | 15 12 | G | 19 9 68 | Stourbridge | Halesowen T | Coventry C | — | — |
| | | | | | | | Huddersfield T | 70 | — |
| | | | | | | | Rochdale (loan) | 2 | — |
| | | | | | | | Shrewsbury T | 31 | — |
| | | | | | | Witton Alb | York C | 17 | — |
| | | | | | | | Scunthorpe U | 56 | — |
| **D'Auria** David# | 5 10 | 12 05 | M | 26 3 70 | Swansea | Trainee | Swansea C | 45 | 6 |
| | | | | | | Barry T | Scarborough | 52 | 8 |
| | | | | | | | Scunthorpe U | 107 | 18 |
| **Evans** Tom | 6 1 | 13 02 | G | 31 12 76 | Doncaster | Trainee | Sheffield U | — | — |
| | | | | | | | Crystal Palace | — | — |
| | | | | | | | Coventry C (loan) | — | — |
| | | | | | | | Scunthorpe U | 5 | — |
| **Eyre** John | 5 11 | 13 00 | F | 9 10 74 | Hull | Trainee | Oldham Ath | 10 | 1 |
| | | | | | | | Scunthorpe U (loan) | 9 | 8 |
| | | | | | | | Scunthorpe U | 123 | 28 |
| **Featherstone** James | 6 0 | 12 12 | F | 12 11 79 | Wharfedale | Blackburn R | Scunthorpe U | 1 | — |
| **Forrester** Jamie | 5 6 | 10 12 | F | 1 11 74 | Bradford | Auxerre | Leeds U | 9 | — |
| | | | | | | | Southend U (loan) | 5 | — |
| | | | | | | | Grimsby T (loan) | 9 | 1 |
| | | | | | | | Grimsby T | 41 | 6 |
| | | | | | | | Scunthorpe U | 55 | 17 |
| **Graves** Wayne§ | | | M | 18 9 80 | Scunthorpe | Trainee | Scunthorpe U | 3 | — |
| **Harsley** Paul | 5 10 | 11 03 | M | 29 5 78 | Scunthorpe | Trainee | Grimsby T | — | — |
| | | | | | | | Scunthorpe U | 15 | 1 |
| **Hope** Chris | 6 1 | 12 08 | D | 14 11 73 | Sheffield | Darlington | Nottingham F | — | — |
| | | | | | | | Scunthorpe U | 197 | 11 |
| **Housham** Steven | 5 10 | 12 03 | M | 24 2 76 | Gainsborough T | Trainee | Scunthorpe U | 90 | 4 |
| **Laws** Brian | 5 9 | 12 04 | D | 14 10 61 | Wallsend | Apprentice | Burnley | 125 | 12 |
| | | | | | | | Huddersfield T | 56 | 1 |
| | | | | | | | Middlesbrough | 107 | 12 |
| | | | | | | | Nottingham F | 147 | 4 |
| | | | | | | | Grimsby T | 46 | 2 |
| | | | | | | | Darlington | 10 | — |
| | | | | | | | Scunthorpe U | 18 | — |
| **Marshall** Lee | 5 10 | 10 08 | M | 1 8 75 | Nottingham | Trainee | Nottingham F | — | — |
| | | | | | | Grantham T | Stockport Co | 1 | — |
| | | | | | | Eastwood T | Scunthorpe U | 21 | 1 |
| **McAuley** Sean | 5 11 | 12 02 | D | 23 6 72 | Sheffield | Trainee | Manchester U | — | — |
| | | | | | | | St Johnstone | 62 | — |
| | | | | | | | Chesterfield (loan) | 1 | 1 |
| | | | | | | | Hartlepool U | 84 | 1 |
| | | | | | | | Scunthorpe U | 44 | 1 |
| **Neil** Jim | 5 8 | 12 01 | D | 28 2 76 | Bury St Edmunds | Trainee | Grimsby T | 2 | — |
| | | | | | | | Scunthorpe U | 7 | — |
| **Nottingham** Steve§ | | | D | 21 2 80 | Peterborough | Trainee | Scunthorpe U | 1 | — |
| **Ormondroyd** Ian* | 6 5 | 13 09 | F | 22 9 64 | Bradford | Thackley | Bradford C | 87 | 20 |
| | | | | | | | Oldham Ath (loan) | 10 | 1 |
| | | | | | | | Aston Villa | 56 | 6 |
| | | | | | | | Derby Co | 25 | 8 |
| | | | | | | | Leicester C | 77 | 7 |
| | | | | | | | Hull C (loan) | 10 | 6 |
| | | | | | | | Bradford C | 38 | 6 |
| | | | | | | | Oldham Ath | 31 | 8 |
| | | | | | | | Scunthorpe U | 20 | — |
| **Pemberton** Martin‡ | 5 9 | 11 07 | F | 1 2 76 | Bradford | Trainee | Oldham Ath | 5 | — |
| | | | | | | | Doncaster R | 35 | 2 |
| | | | | | | | Scunthorpe U | 6 | — |

| Regis Dave‡ | 6 0 | 13 08 | F | 3 3 64 | Paddington | Barnet | Notts Co | 46 | 15 |
| | | | | | | | Plymouth Arg | 31 | 4 |
| | | | | | | | Bournemouth (loan) | 6 | 2 |
| | | | | | | | Stoke C | 63 | 15 |
| | | | | | | | Birmingham C | 6 | 2 |
| | | | | | | | Southend U | 38 | 9 |
| | | | | | | | Barnsley | 16 | 1 |
| | | | | | | | Peterborough U (loan) | 7 | 1 |
| | | | | | | | Notts Co (loan) | 10 | 2 |
| | | | | | | | Leyton Orient | 4 | — |
| | | | | | | | Lincoln C | 1 | — |
| | | | | | | | Scunthorpe U | 9 | 2 |
| Sertori Mark* | 6 1 | 14 07 | D | 1 9 67 | Manchester | | Stockport Co | 4 | — |
| | | | | | | | Lincoln C | 50 | 9 |
| | | | | | | | Wrexham | 110 | 3 |
| | | | | | | | Bury | 13 | 1 |
| | | | | | | | Scunthorpe U | 83 | 2 |
| Shakespeare Craig | 5 10 | 13 06 | M | 26 10 63 | Birmingham | Apprentice | Walsall | 284 | 45 |
| | | | | | | | Sheffield W | 17 | — |
| | | | | | | | WBA | 112 | 12 |
| | | | | | | | Grimsby T | 106 | 10 |
| | | | | | | | Scunthorpe U | 4 | — |
| Sheldon Gareth§ | | | F | 31 1 80 | Birmingham | Trainee | Scunthorpe U | 1 | — |
| Stamp Darryn | 6 1 | 11 10 | F | 21 9 78 | Beverley | | Scunthorpe U | 10 | 1 |
| Stanton Nathan§ | | | D | 6 5 81 | Nottingham | Trainee | Scunthorpe U | 1 | — |
| Walker Justin | 6 0 | 13 03 | M | 6 9 75 | Nottingham | Trainee | Nottingham F | — | — |
| | | | | | | | Scunthorpe U | 49 | 1 |
| Walsh Michael | 6 0 | 13 01 | D | 5 8 77 | Rotherham | Trainee | Scunthorpe U | 103 | 1 |
| Wilcox Russ | 6 0 | 12 13 | D | 25 3 64 | Hemsworth | Apprentice | Doncaster R | 1 | — |
| | | | | | | Frickley Ath | Northampton T | 138 | 9 |
| | | | | | | | Hull C | 100 | 7 |
| | | | | | | | Doncaster R | 81 | 6 |
| | | | | | | | Preston NE | 62 | 1 |
| | | | | | | | Scunthorpe U | 31 | 2 |

**Trainees**
Corbett, John R; Edmond, Christopher; Fielding, Jonathan; Graves, Wayne A; Handley, Karl G; Harle, Alex G; Hooley, Gareth R; Kitching, Daniel; McCormack, Steven R; Mitchell, Barry S; Nottingham, Steven E; Page, Brian J; Render, Craig; Sheldon, Gareth; Shirtliff, Philip; Stanton, Nathan; Walton, Paul J.

**Non-Contract**
Adkins, Nigel H; Lillis, Mark A; Wilson, Paul D.

**Associated Schoolboys**
Brown, Andrew; Burfield, Richard J; Dobson, Matthew P; McAvoy, Dwayne T; McLean, Kevin; Nedoszytko, Gareth R; Shaw, Mark J; Singh, Sean; Wilson, Timothy.

**Associated Schoolboys who have accepted the club's offer of a Traineeship/Contract**
Anderson, Mark J; Sparrow, Matthew.

# SHEFFIELD UNITED

| Beard Mark* | 5 10 | 10 12 | M | 8 10 74 | Roehampton | Trainee | Millwall | 45 | 2 |
| | | | | | | | Sheffield U | 38 | — |
| | | | | | | | Southend U (loan) | 8 | — |
| Bettney Chris | 5 10 | 11 00 | F | 27 10 77 | Chesterfield | Trainee | Sheffield U | 1 | — |
| | | | | | | | Hull C (loan) | 30 | 1 |
| Borbokis Vassilis | 5 11 | 12 00 | D | 10 2 69 | Serres | | Apollon | 29 | 2 |
| | | | | | | | AEK Athens | 86 | 9 |
| | | | | | | | Sheffield U | 36 | 2 |
| Capper David | 6 0 | 12 00 | D | 8 9 78 | Stoke | Trainee | Sheffield U | — | — |
| Cullen Jon | 6 0 | 11 10 | M | 10 1 73 | Durham | Trainee | Doncaster R | 9 | — |
| | | | | | | Morpeth T | Hartlepool U | 34 | 12 |
| | | | | | | | Sheffield U | 2 | — |
| Davies Kevin | 5 11 | 12 00 | M | 15 11 78 | Sheffield | Trainee | Sheffield U | — | — |
| Deane Brian | 6 3 | 12 07 | F | 7 2 68 | Leeds | Apprentice | Doncaster R | 66 | 12 |
| *(Transferred to Benfica, January 1998)* | | | | | | | Sheffield U | 197 | 82 |
| | | | | | | | Leeds U | 138 | 32 |
| | | | | | | | Sheffield U | 24 | 11 |
| Dellas Traianos | 6 4 | 15 00 | D | 31 1 76 | Salonika | Aris Salonika | Sheffield U | 9 | — |
| Derry Shaun | 5 10 | 10 13 | M | 6 12 77 | Nottingham | Trainee | Notts Co | 79 | 4 |
| | | | | | | | Sheffield U | 12 | — |
| Devlin Paul | 5 8 | 11 05 | M | 14 4 72 | Birmingham | Stafford R | Notts Co | 141 | 25 |
| | | | | | | | Birmingham C | 76 | 28 |
| | | | | | | | Sheffield U | 10 | 1 |
| Ebbrell John | 5 10 | 11 11 | M | 1 10 69 | Bromborough | | Everton | 217 | 13 |
| | | | | | | | Sheffield U | 1 | — |

| Name | | | Pos | DOB | Birthplace | From | Club | Apps | Gls |
|---|---|---|---|---|---|---|---|---|---|
| **Ford** Bobby | 5 8 | 11 00 | M | 22 9 74 | Bristol | Trainee | Oxford U | 116 | 7 |
| | | | | | | | Sheffield U | 23 | 1 |
| **George** Matthew‡ | | | G | 24 4 79 | Melton Mowbray | Aston Villa | Sheffield U | — | — |
| **Hamilton** Ian | 5 10 | 11 03 | M | 14 12 67 | Stevenage | Apprentice | Southampton | — | — |
| | | | | | | | Cambridge U | 24 | 1 |
| | | | | | | | Scunthorpe U | 145 | 18 |
| | | | | | | | WBA | 240 | 23 |
| | | | | | | | Sheffield U | 8 | 1 |
| **Hawes** Steve‡ | 5 8 | 10 12 | M | 17 7 78 | High Wycombe | Trainee | Sheffield U | 4 | — |
| | | | | | | | Doncaster R (loan) | 11 | — |
| **Henry** Nick | 5 6 | 10 12 | M | 21 2 69 | Liverpool | Trainee | Oldham Ath | 273 | 19 |
| | | | | | | | Sheffield U | 10 | — |
| **Holdsworth** David | 6 0 | 12 10 | D | 8 11 68 | Walthamstow | Trainee | Watford | 258 | 10 |
| | | | | | | | Sheffield U | 77 | 3 |
| **Katchuro** Petr | 6 0 | 12 06 | F | 2 8 72 | Minsk | | Dynamo 93 | 15 | 7 |
| | | | | | | | Dynamo Minsk | 60 | 52 |
| | | | | | | | Sheffield U | 56 | 12 |
| **Kelly** Alan | 6 3 | 14 02 | G | 11 8 68 | Preston | Trainee | Preston NE | 142 | — |
| | | | | | | | Sheffield U | 194 | — |
| **Lehtinen** Ville | 5 10 | 11 07 | M | 17 12 78 | Tampere | | JJK | 22 | 1 |
| | | | | | | | HJK Helsinki | 2 | — |
| | | | | | | | Sheffield U | — | — |
| **Ludlam** Ryan | 6 0 | 12 06 | M | 12 5 79 | Carlisle | Trainee | Sheffield U | — | — |
| **Marcello** | 6 0 | 13 08 | F | 11 10 69 | Niteroi | Alaves | Sheffield U | 21 | 6 |
| **Marker** Nicky | 6 0 | 13 00 | D | 3 5 65 | Exeter | Apprentice | Exeter C | 202 | 3 |
| | | | | | | | Plymouth Arg | 202 | 13 |
| | | | | | | | Blackburn R | 54 | 1 |
| | | | | | | | Sheffield U | 43 | 2 |
| **McGrath** Paul* | 6 2 | 14 03 | D | 4 12 59 | Ealing | St Patrick's Ath | Manchester U | 163 | 12 |
| | | | | | | | Aston Villa | 253 | 9 |
| | | | | | | | Derby Co | 24 | — |
| | | | | | | | Sheffield U | 12 | — |
| **Morris** Lee | 5 10 | 10 07 | M | 30 4 80 | Blackpool | Trainee | Sheffield U | 5 | — |
| **Nilsen** Roger | 5 11 | 12 06 | D | 8 8 69 | Tromso | Viking Stavanger | Sheffield U | 149 | — |
| **O'Connor** Jon | 6 0 | 11 10 | D | 29 10 76 | Darlington | Trainee | Everton | 5 | — |
| | | | | | | | Sheffield U | 2 | — |
| **Quinn** Wayne | 5 10 | 11 11 | M | 19 11 76 | Truro | | Sheffield U | 28 | 2 |
| **Sandford** Lee | 6 0 | 13 07 | D | 22 4 68 | Basingstoke | Apprentice | Portsmouth | 72 | 1 |
| | | | | | | | Stoke C | 258 | 8 |
| | | | | | | | Sheffield U | 45 | 2 |
| | | | | | | | Reading (loan) | 5 | — |
| **Saunders** Dean# | 5 8 | 10 06 | F | 21 6 64 | Swansea | Apprentice | Swansea C | 49 | 12 |
| | | | | | | | Cardiff C (loan) | 4 | — |
| | | | | | | | Brighton & HA | 72 | 21 |
| | | | | | | | Oxford U | 59 | 22 |
| | | | | | | | Derby Co | 106 | 42 |
| | | | | | | | Liverpool | 42 | 11 |
| | | | | | | | Aston Villa | 112 | 37 |
| | | | | | | | Galatasaray | 27 | 15 |
| | | | | | | | Nottingham F | 43 | 5 |
| | | | | | | | Sheffield U | 24 | 10 |
| **Short** Chris# | 5 10 | 12 04 | D | 9 5 70 | Munster | Pickering T | Scarborough | 43 | 1 |
| | | | | | | | Manchester U (loan) | — | — |
| | | | | | | | Notts Co | 94 | 2 |
| | | | | | | | Huddersfield T (loan) | 6 | — |
| | | | | | | | Sheffield U | 44 | — |
| **Spackman** Nigel* | 6 1 | 13 02 | M | 2 12 60 | Romsey | Andover | Bournemouth | 119 | 10 |
| | | | | | | | Chelsea | 141 | 12 |
| | | | | | | | Liverpool | 51 | — |
| | | | | | | | QPR | 29 | 1 |
| | | | | | | | Rangers | 100 | 1 |
| | | | | | | | Chelsea | 67 | — |
| | | | | | | | Sheffield U | 23 | — |
| **Stuart** Graham | 5 8 | 11 11 | M | 24 10 70 | Tooting | Trainee | Chelsea | 87 | 14 |
| | | | | | | | Everton | 136 | 22 |
| | | | | | | | Sheffield U | 28 | 5 |
| **Taylor** Gareth | 6 2 | 13 08 | F | 25 2 73 | Weston-Super-Mare | Southampton | Bristol R | 47 | 16 |
| | | | | | | | Crystal Palace | 20 | 1 |
| | | | | | | | Sheffield U | 72 | 24 |
| **Tracey** Simon | 6 0 | 13 12 | G | 9 12 67 | Woolwich | Apprentice | Wimbledon | 1 | — |
| | | | | | | | Sheffield U | 188 | — |
| | | | | | | | Manchester C (loan) | 3 | — |
| | | | | | | | Norwich C (loan) | 1 | — |
| | | | | | | | Wimbledon (loan) | 1 | — |
| **Vonk** Michael | 6 3 | 13 03 | D | 28 10 68 | Alkmaar | | AZ | 112 | 8 |
| | | | | | | | SVV/Dordrecht | 29 | 1 |
| | | | | | | | Manchester C | 91 | 3 |
| | | | | | | | Oldham Ath (loan) | 5 | 1 |
| | | | | | | | Sheffield U | 37 | 2 |

| | | | | | | | | | |
|---|---|---|---|---|---|---|---|---|---|
| **Walker** Andy | 5 8 | 11 05 | F | 6 4 65 | Glasgow | Baillieston Jun | Motherwell | 76 | 17 |
| | | | | | | | Celtic | 108 | 30 |
| | | | | | | | Newcastle U (loan) | 2 | — |
| | | | | | | | Bolton W | 67 | 44 |
| | | | | | | | Celtic | 42 | 9 |
| | | | | | | | Sheffield U | 52 | 20 |
| | | | | | | | Hibernian (loan) | 8 | 3 |
| | | | | | | | Raith R (loan) | 7 | 2 |
| **White** David | 6 1 | 13 09 | M | 30 10 67 | Manchester | | Manchester C | 285 | 79 |
| | | | | | | | Leeds U | 42 | 9 |
| | | | | | | | Sheffield U | 66 | 13 |
| **Whitehouse** Dane | 5 10 | 12 08 | M | 14 10 70 | Sheffield | Trainee | Sheffield U | 231 | 39 |
| **Wilder** Chris | 5 11 | 12 07 | D | 23 9 67 | Stocksbridge | Apprentice | Southampton | — | — |
| | | | | | | | Sheffield U | 93 | 1 |
| | | | | | | | Walsall (loan) | 4 | — |
| | | | | | | | Charlton Ath (loan) | 1 | — |
| | | | | | | | Charlton Ath (loan) | 2 | — |
| | | | | | | | Leyton Orient (loan) | 16 | 1 |
| | | | | | | | Rotherham U | 132 | 11 |
| | | | | | | | Notts Co | 46 | — |
| | | | | | | | Bradford C | 42 | — |
| | | | | | | | Sheffield U | 8 | — |
| **Woodhouse** Curtis | 5 8 | 11 00 | M | 17 4 80 | Driffield | Trainee | Sheffield U | 9 | — |

**Trainees**
Bamforth, Liam A; Burke, Paul; Burley, Adam G; Camm, Mark L; Doane, Ben N D C; Eastwood, Mark; Henderson, Ewan; Johnson, David S M; McAughtrie, Craig J; Mosley, Matthew J; Patterson, Jamie; Strickland, Robert P; Strickland, Steven J.

**Associated Schoolboys**
Adam, Chris; Burrows, Robin J; Featherstone, Lee; Killeen, Lewis K; Mallon, Ryan; Merry, Kevin; Morgan, Robert D; Myers, Peter; Renton, Gavin R; Tuckwood, Stephen; Willey, Edward R; Young, Matthew P.

**Associated Schoolboys who have accepted the club's offer of a Traineeship/Contract**
Adams, Carl; Anderson, Michael; Clarke, Stuart; Crutchley, Wayne; Parkin, Andrew T; Thompson, Tyrone; Thornley, Carl.

**Player who does not hold a current contract but his registration has been retained by the club**
Capper, David A.

# SHEFFIELD WEDNESDAY

| | | | | | | | | | |
|---|---|---|---|---|---|---|---|---|---|
| **Agogo** Manuel | 5 9 | 11 07 | M | 1 8 79 | Accra | | Sheffield W | 1 | — |
| **Alexandersson** Niclas | 6 2 | 11 07 | M | 29 12 71 | Halmstad | | Halmstad | 114 | 18 |
| | | | | | | | IFK Gothenburg | 52 | 13 |
| | | | | | | | Sheffield W | 6 | — |
| **Atherton** Peter | 5 11 | 13 13 | D | 6 4 70 | Wigan | Trainee | Wigan Ath | 149 | 1 |
| | | | | | | | Coventry C | 114 | — |
| | | | | | | | Sheffield W | 141 | 6 |
| **Barrett** Earl | 5 10 | 11 02 | D | 28 4 67 | Rochdale | Apprentice | Manchester C | 3 | — |
| | | | | | | | Chester C (loan) | 12 | — |
| | | | | | | | Oldham Ath | 183 | 7 |
| | | | | | | | Aston Villa | 119 | 1 |
| | | | | | | | Everton | 74 | — |
| | | | | | | | Sheffield U (loan) | 5 | — |
| | | | | | | | Sheffield W | 10 | — |
| **Batty** Mark* | 5 9 | 10 10 | F | 30 1 79 | Nottingham | Trainee | Sheffield W | — | — |
| **Billington** David | 5 7 | 10 07 | D | 15 10 80 | Oxford | Trainee | Peterborough U | 5 | — |
| | | | | | | | Sheffield W | — | — |
| **Blinker** Regi | 5 8 | 11 07 | F | 2 6 69 | Surinam | | Feyenoord | 51 | 3 |
| *(Transferred to Celtic, July 1997)* | | | | | | | Den Bosch | 25 | 6 |
| | | | | | | | Feyenoord | 187 | 42 |
| | | | | | | | Sheffield W | 42 | 3 |
| | | | | | | | Celtic | 16 | 1 |
| **Blondeau** Patrick | 5 9 | 11 13 | D | 27 1 68 | Marseille | Martigues | Monaco | 148 | 2 |
| *(Transferred to Bordeaux, January 1998)* | | | | | | | Sheffield W | 6 | — |
| **Booth** Andy | 6 1 | 13 00 | F | 6 12 73 | Huddersfield | Trainee | Huddersfield T | 123 | 54 |
| | | | | | | | Sheffield W | 58 | 17 |
| **Brennan** Dean | | | M | 17 6 80 | Dublin | | Sheffield W | — | — |
| **Briscoe** Lee | 5 11 | 11 13 | F | 30 9 75 | Pontefract | Trainee | Sheffield W | 46 | — |
| | | | | | | | Manchester C (loan) | 5 | 1 |
| **Carbone** Benito | 5 6 | 10 09 | F | 14 8 71 | Begnara | | Torino | 8 | — |
| | | | | | | | Reggina | 31 | 5 |
| | | | | | | | Casert | 31 | 4 |
| | | | | | | | Ascoli | 28 | 6 |
| | | | | | | | Torino | 28 | 3 |
| | | | | | | | Napoli | 29 | 5 |
| | | | | | | | Internazionale | 32 | 2 |
| | | | | | | | Sheffield W | 58 | 15 |
| **Clarke** Matthew | 6 4 | 13 10 | G | 3 11 73 | Sheffield | Trainee | Rotherham U | 124 | — |
| | | | | | | | Sheffield W | 4 | — |

| | | | | | | | Club | Apps | Goals |
|---|---|---|---|---|---|---|---|---|---|
| **Di Canio** Paolo | 5 9 | 11 09 | M | 9 7 68 | Rome | | Lazio | — | — |
| | | | | | | | Ternana | 27 | 2 |
| | | | | | | | Lazio | 54 | 4 |
| | | | | | | | Juventus | 78 | 6 |
| | | | | | | | Napoli | 26 | 5 |
| | | | | | | | Juventus | — | — |
| | | | | | | | AC Milan | 37 | 6 |
| | | | | | | | Celtic | 26 | 12 |
| | | | | | | | Sheffield W | 35 | 12 |
| **Emerson** | | | D | 30 3 72 | Porto Alegre | Benfica | Sheffield W | 6 | — |
| **Geary** Derek | | | D | 19 6 80 | Dublin | | Sheffield W | | |
| **Harrison** Mark* | | | M | 7 8 79 | Sheffield | Trainee | Sheffield W | — | — |
| **Haslam** Steven | | | M | 6 9 79 | Sheffield | Trainee | Sheffield W | | |
| **Hinchcliffe** Andy | 5 10 | 12 10 | D | 5 2 69 | Manchester | Apprentice | Manchester C | 112 | 8 |
| | | | | | | | Everton | 182 | 7 |
| | | | | | | | Sheffield W | 15 | 1 |
| **Holmes** Peter | | | M | 18 11 80 | Bishop Auckland | Trainee | Sheffield W | — | — |
| **Humphreys** Richie | 5 11 | 14 07 | F | 30 11 77 | Sheffield | Trainee | Sheffield W | 41 | 3 |
| **Hutchinson** Sean* | | | M | 14 4 79 | Bradford | Trainee | Sheffield W | — | — |
| **Hyde** Graham | 5 8 | 12 04 | M | 10 11 70 | Doncaster | Trainee | Sheffield W | 171 | 11 |
| **Jones** Ryan‡ | 6 3 | 14 00 | M | 23 7 73 | Sheffield | Trainee | Sheffield W | 41 | 6 |
| | | | | | | | Scunthorpe U (loan) | 11 | 3 |
| **Jones** Stuart | | | G | 24 10 77 | Bristol | Weston-Super-Mare | Sheffield W | — | — |
| **Kotylo** Krystof | 5 10 | 11 02 | M | 28 9 77 | Sheffield | School | Sheffield W | — | — |
| **Magilton** Jim | 6 0 | 14 00 | M | 6 5 69 | Belfast | Apprentice | Liverpool | — | — |
| | | | | | | | Oxford U | 150 | 34 |
| | | | | | | | Southampton | 130 | 13 |
| | | | | | | | Sheffield W | 21 | 1 |
| **Mayrleb** Christian* | 5 8 | 11 13 | F | 8 6 72 | Leonding | | Admira Wacker | 66 | 15 |
| | | | | | | | Tirol | 53 | 16 |
| | | | | | | | Sheffield W | 3 | — |
| **McKeever** Mark | 5 9 | 11 08 | F | 16 11 78 | Derry | Trainee | Peterborough U | 3 | — |
| | | | | | | | Sheffield W | — | — |
| **Newsome** Jon | 6 3 | 13 10 | D | 6 9 70 | Sheffield | Trainee | Sheffield W | 7 | — |
| | | | | | | | Leeds U | 76 | 3 |
| | | | | | | | Norwich C | 62 | 7 |
| | | | | | | | Sheffield W | 43 | 4 |
| **Nicholson** Kevin | | | M | 2 10 80 | Derby | Trainee | Sheffield W | — | — |
| **Nicol** Steve* | 5 10 | 12 07 | D | 11 12 61 | Irvine | Ayr U BC | Ayr U | 70 | 7 |
| | | | | | | | Liverpool | 343 | 36 |
| | | | | | | | Notts Co | 32 | 2 |
| | | | | | | | Sheffield W | 49 | — |
| | | | | | | | WBA (loan) | 9 | — |
| **Nolan** Ian | 5 11 | 12 02 | D | 9 7 70 | Liverpool | Marine | Tranmere R | 88 | 1 |
| | | | | | | | Sheffield W | 136 | 4 |
| **Oakes** Scott | 5 11 | 11 12 | M | 5 8 72 | Leicester | Trainee | Leicester C | 3 | — |
| | | | | | | | Luton T | 173 | 27 |
| | | | | | | | Sheffield W | 23 | 1 |
| **Pembridge** Mark | 5 7 | 12 03 | M | 28 11 70 | Merthyr Tydfil | Trainee | Luton T | 60 | 6 |
| | | | | | | | Derby Co | 110 | 28 |
| | | | | | | | Sheffield W | 93 | 11 |
| **Platts** Mark | 5 8 | 11 12 | F | 23 5 79 | Sheffield | Trainee | Sheffield W | 2 | — |
| **Pressman** Kevin | 6 1 | 15 05 | G | 6 11 67 | Fareham | Apprentice | Sheffield W | 232 | — |
| | | | | | | | Stoke C (loan) | 4 | — |
| **Pringle** Alan‡ | | | M | 8 3 78 | Sunderland | Trainee | Sheffield W | — | — |
| **Quinn** Alan | | | F | 13 6 79 | Dublin | | Sheffield W | 1 | — |
| **Rudi** Petter | | | D | 17 9 73 | Kristiansund | | Molde | 116 | 7 |
| | | | | | | | Sheffield W | 22 | — |
| **Sanetti** Francesco | | | F | 11 1 79 | Rome | Genoa | Sheffield W | 2 | 1 |
| **Sedloski** Goce | 6 2 | 13 00 | D | 10 4 74 | Golemo Konjari | | Sheffield W | 4 | — |
| **Smith** Gavin* | 5 10 | 10 09 | F | 24 9 77 | Sheffield | Trainee | Sheffield W | — | — |
| **Stefanovic** Dejan | 6 2 | 13 00 | D | 28 10 74 | Yugoslavia | Red Star Belgrade | Sheffield W | 55 | 4 |
| **Walker** Des | 5 11 | 11 12 | D | 26 11 65 | Hackney | Apprentice | Nottingham F | 264 | 1 |
| | | | | | | | Sampdoria | 30 | — |
| | | | | | | | Sheffield W | 190 | — |
| **Weaver** Simon* | 6 1 | 10 07 | D | 20 12 77 | Doncaster | Trainee | Sheffield W | — | — |
| | | | | | | | Doncaster R (loan) | 2 | — |
| **Whittingham** Guy | 5 8 | 12 02 | F | 10 11 64 | Evesham | Yeovil T, Army | Portsmouth | 160 | 88 |
| | | | | | | | Aston Villa | 25 | 5 |
| | | | | | | | Wolverhampton W (loan) | 13 | 8 |
| | | | | | | | Sheffield W | 111 | 22 |
| **Woodward** Jonathan | | | G | 16 6 79 | Sheffield | Trainee | Sheffield W | — | — |

**Trainees**
Bennett, Neil R; Bettney, Scott; Coubrough, James R; Davis, Ryan L; Harkin, Thomas E; Haslam, Nathan L; Hibbins, John J; Higgins, Alex J; Hutton, John; King, Christopher; Powell, Vill W; Siddall, Christopher J; Staniforth, Thomas; Wainwright, Jody.

**Associated Schoolboys**
Crane, Anthony S; Hepworth, Mark W; Hepworth, Stephen M; Strutt, Luke M; Taylor, Robert J; Tevendale, James R; Wood, Daniel G.

**Associated Schoolboys who have accepted the club's offer of a Traineeship/Contract**
Fraser, Andrew J; Hamshaw, Matthew T; Houlahan, Martin J; Jones, Philip; McNutt, Martin P; Morrison, John O; Nelson, Craig M; Rand, Craig.

## SHREWSBURY TOWN

| Player | Ht | Wt | Pos | D.O.B. | Birthplace | Source | Club | Apps | Gls |
|---|---|---|---|---|---|---|---|---|---|
| **Berkley** Austin# | 5 9 | 10 10 | F | 28 1 73 | Gravesend | Trainee | Gillingham | 3 | — |
| | | | | | | | Swindon T | 1 | — |
| | | | | | | | Shrewsbury T | 98 | 4 |
| **Blamey** Nathan | 5 10 | 11 05 | D | 10 6 77 | Plymouth | Trainee | Southampton | — | — |
| | | | | | | | Shrewsbury T | 15 | 1 |
| **Briscoe** Anthony | | | F | 16 8 78 | Birmingham | Trainee | Shrewsbury T | 1 | — |
| **Brown** Mickey | 5 9 | 10 12 | F | 8 2 68 | Birmingham | Apprentice | Shrewsbury T | 190 | 9 |
| | | | | | | | Bolton W | 33 | 3 |
| | | | | | | | Shrewsbury T | 67 | 11 |
| | | | | | | | Preston NE | 16 | 1 |
| | | | | | | | Rochdale (loan) | 5 | — |
| | | | | | | | Shrewsbury T | 49 | 3 |
| **Cope** James* | 6 1 | 11 01 | M | 4 10 77 | Birmingham | Trainee | Shrewsbury T | 4 | — |
| **Craven** Dean | 5 6 | 10 10 | F | 17 2 79 | Shrewsbury | WBA | Shrewsbury T | 1 | — |
| **Dempsey** Mark* | 5 8 | 11 02 | D | 10 12 72 | Dublin | Trainee | Gillingham | 48 | 2 |
| | | | | | | | Leyton Orient | 43 | 1 |
| | | | | | | | Shrewsbury T | 80 | 3 |
| **Edwards** Paul# | 5 11 | 11 05 | G | 22 2 65 | Liverpool | St. Helens T | Crewe Alex | 29 | — |
| | | | | | | | Shrewsbury T | 203 | — |
| **Evans** Paul | 5 8 | 10 08 | M | 1 9 74 | Oswestry | Trainee | Shrewsbury T | 166 | 20 |
| **Gall** Benny‡ | 6 2 | 14 04 | G | 14 3 71 | Copenhagen | Herfolge | Dordrecht | 33 | — |
| | | | | | | | De Graafschap | — | — |
| | | | | | | | Shrewsbury T | 34 | — |
| **Gayle** Brian# | 6 2 | 13 12 | D | 6 3 65 | Kingston | | Wimbledon | 83 | 3 |
| | | | | | | | Manchester C | 55 | 3 |
| | | | | | | | Ipswich T | 58 | 4 |
| | | | | | | | Sheffield U | 117 | 9 |
| | | | | | | | Exeter C | 10 | — |
| | | | | | | | Rotherham U | 20 | — |
| | | | | | | | Bristol R (loan) | 7 | — |
| | | | | | | | Bristol R | 16 | — |
| | | | | | | | Shrewsbury T | 23 | — |
| **Hanmer** Gary | 5 6 | 10 02 | D | 12 10 73 | Shrewsbury | Newtown | WBA | — | — |
| | | | | | | | Shrewsbury T | 39 | 1 |
| **Herbert** Craig | 5 10 | 11 00 | D | 9 11 75 | Coventry | Torquay U | WBA | 8 | — |
| | | | | | | | Shrewsbury T | 24 | — |
| **Jagielka** Steve | 5 8 | 11 03 | F | 10 3 78 | Manchester | Trainee | Stoke C | — | — |
| | | | | | | | Shrewsbury T | 16 | 1 |
| **Kerrigan** Steve | 6 1 | 12 04 | F | 9 10 72 | Bailleston | Newmains J | Albion R | 53 | 14 |
| | | | | | | | Clydebank | 30 | — |
| | | | | | | | Stranraer | 21 | 5 |
| | | | | | | | Ayr U | 33 | 17 |
| | | | | | | | Shrewsbury T | 14 | 2 |
| **Naylor** Martyn | 5 9 | 10 02 | D | 2 8 77 | Walsall | Telford U | Shrewsbury T | 2 | — |
| **Nwadike** Emeka* | 6 0 | 13 00 | D | 9 8 78 | Camberwell | Trainee | Wolverhampton W | — | — |
| | | | | | | | Shrewsbury T | 3 | — |
| **Pountney** Craig | 5 6 | 9 07 | F | 23 11 79 | Bromsgrove | Trainee | Shrewsbury T | 1 | — |
| **Preece** Roger# | 5 8 | 10 13 | M | 9 6 69 | Much Wenlock | Coventry C | Wrexham | 110 | 12 |
| | | | | | | | Chester C | 170 | 4 |
| | | | | | | | Shrewsbury T | 27 | 1 |
| **Reed** Ian‡ | 5 8 | 10 13 | M | 4 9 75 | Lichfield | Trainee | Shrewsbury T | 18 | 2 |
| **Scott** Richard | 5 9 | 10 10 | M | 29 9 74 | Dudley | Trainee | Birmingham C | 12 | — |
| | | | | | | | Shrewsbury T | 105 | 18 |
| **Seabury** Kevin | 5 10 | 11 06 | D | 24 11 73 | Shrewsbury | Trainee | Shrewsbury T | 142 | 2 |
| **Steele** Lee | 5 8 | 12 05 | F | 2 12 73 | Liverpool | Northwich V | Shrewsbury T | 38 | 13 |
| **Taylor** Lee* | 6 0 | 11 05 | D | 24 2 76 | Hammersmith | Faweh | Shrewsbury T | 17 | — |
| **Taylor** Mark* | 5 9 | 11 08 | M | 22 2 66 | Walsall | Local | Walsall | 113 | 4 |
| | | | | | | | Sheffield W | 9 | — |
| | | | | | | | Shrewsbury T (loan) | 19 | 2 |
| | | | | | | | Shrewsbury T | 249 | 13 |
| **Tretton** Andrew | 6 0 | 12 08 | D | 9 10 76 | Derby | Trainee | Derby Co | — | — |
| | | | | | | | Chesterfield | — | — |
| | | | | | | | Shrewsbury T | 14 | 1 |
| **Ward** Nick‡ | 5 10 | 10 09 | F | 30 11 77 | Wrexham | Trainee | Shrewsbury T | 20 | 1 |

| | | | | | | | | | |
|---|---|---|---|---|---|---|---|---|---|
| **White** Devon | 6 3 | 14 00 | F | 2 3 64 | Nottingham | Arnold T | Lincoln C | 29 | 4 |
| | | | | | | Boston U | Bristol R | 202 | 53 |
| | | | | | | | Cambridge U | 22 | 4 |
| | | | | | | | QPR | 26 | 9 |
| | | | | | | | Notts Co | 40 | 15 |
| | | | | | | | Watford | 38 | 7 |
| | | | | | | | Notts Co | 15 | 4 |
| | | | | | | | Shrewsbury T | 32 | 10 |
| **Wilding** Peter | 6 1 | 12 09 | D | 28 11 68 | Shrewsbury | Telford U | Shrewsbury T | 34 | 1 |
| **Williams** Mark | 5 11 | 12 07 | F | 10 12 73 | Bangor | Trainee | Shrewsbury T | 8 | — |
| **Wray** Shaun‡ | 6 1 | 12 10 | F | 14 3 78 | Dudley | Trainee | Shrewsbury T | 4 | — |

**Trainees**
Bell, Lee J; Drysdale, Leon A; Harman, Jeremy P J; Howarth, Paul A; Jones, Matthew N; Leydon, Scott A; Neville, Mark J; Newman, John; Northwood, Sean; Simpson, Aaron D; Thompson, Glyn W; Williams, Joseph S.

**Associated Schoolboys**
Edwards, Daniel J; Murphy, Gareth A.

**Player who does not hold a current contract but his registration has been retained by the club**
Nielsen, Thomas.

# SOUTHAMPTON

| | | | | | | | | | |
|---|---|---|---|---|---|---|---|---|---|
| **Basham** Steve | 5 11 | 11 11 | F | 2 12 77 | Southampton | Trainee | Southampton | 15 | — |
| | | | | | | | Wrexham (loan) | 5 | — |
| **Benali** Francis | 5 9 | 11 02 | M | 30 12 68 | Southampton | Apprentice | Southampton | 253 | 1 |
| **Beresford** John | 5 7 | 12 01 | M | 4 9 66 | Sheffield | Apprentice | Manchester C | — | — |
| | | | | | | | Barnsley | 88 | 5 |
| | | | | | | | Portsmouth | 107 | 8 |
| | | | | | | | Newcastle U | 179 | 3 |
| | | | | | | | Southampton | 10 | — |
| **Bevan** Scott | 6 5 | 16 01 | G | 16 9 79 | Southampton | Trainee | Southampton | — | — |
| **Blake** Dean | 5 8 | 10 01 | M | 20 2 80 | Southampton | Trainee | Southampton | — | — |
| **Bradley** Shayne | 5 11 | 13 02 | F | 8 12 79 | Gloucester | Trainee | Southampton | — | — |
| **Bridge** Wayne | 5 10 | 11 11 | F | 5 8 80 | Southampton | Trainee | Southampton | — | — |
| **Collins** Chris | 6 0 | 12 07 | D | 26 9 79 | Chatham | Trainee | Southampton | — | — |
| **Davies** Kevin | 6 0 | 13 11 | F | 26 3 77 | Sheffield | Trainee | Chesterfield | 129 | 22 |
| | | | | | | | Southampton | 25 | 9 |
| **Dodd** Jason | 5 10 | 12 06 | D | 2 11 70 | Bath | Bath C | Southampton | 231 | 7 |
| **Dryden** Richard | 6 0 | 13 11 | D | 14 6 69 | Stroud | Trainee | Bristol R | 13 | — |
| | | | | | | | Exeter C | 51 | 7 |
| | | | | | | | Manchester C (loan) | — | — |
| | | | | | | | Notts Co | 31 | 1 |
| | | | | | | | Plymouth Arg (loan) | 5 | — |
| | | | | | | | Birmingham C | 48 | — |
| | | | | | | | Bristol C | 37 | 2 |
| | | | | | | | Southampton | 42 | 1 |
| **Flahavan** Darryl* | 5 10 | 12 01 | G | 28 11 78 | Southampton | Trainee | Southampton | — | — |
| **Gibbens** Kevin | 5 10 | 12 13 | M | 4 11 79 | Southampton | Trainee | Southampton | 2 | — |
| **Hirst** David | 6 0 | 13 11 | F | 7 12 67 | Barnsley | Apprentice | Barnsley | 28 | 9 |
| | | | | | | | Sheffield W | 294 | 106 |
| | | | | | | | Southampton | 28 | 9 |
| **Hughes** David | 5 10 | 11 05 | M | 30 12 72 | St Albans | Trainee | Southampton | 45 | 3 |
| **James** Kevin | 5 8 | 10 05 | F | 26 3 80 | Merthyr | Trainee | Southampton | — | — |
| **Jenkins** Steve | 6 1 | 13 00 | D | 2 1 80 | Bristol | Trainee | Southampton | — | — |
| **Johansen** Stig | 5 9 | 12 05 | F | 13 6 72 | Norway | | Bodo Glimt | 70 | 45 |
| | | | | | | | Southampton | 6 | — |
| | | | | | | | Bristol C (loan) | 3 | — |
| **Jones** Paul | 6 2 | 15 02 | G | 18 4 67 | Chirk | Kidderminster H | Wolverhampton W | 33 | — |
| | | | | | | | Stockport Co | 46 | — |
| | | | | | | | Southampton | 38 | — |
| **Le Tissier** Matthew | 6 0 | 13 09 | F | 14 10 68 | Guernsey | Trainee | Southampton | 383 | 151 |
| **Lundekvam** Claus | 6 3 | 12 11 | D | 22 2 73 | Norway | | Brann | 53 | — |
| | | | | | | | Southampton | 60 | — |
| **Monk** Gary | 6 0 | 13 00 | D | 6 3 79 | Bedford | Trainee | Torquay U | 5 | — |
| | | | | | | | Southampton | — | — |
| **Monkou** Ken | 6 3 | 14 07 | D | 29 11 64 | Surinam | Feyenoord | Chelsea | 94 | 2 |
| | | | | | | | Southampton | 176 | 9 |
| **Moss** Neil | 6 2 | 13 00 | G | 10 5 75 | New Milton | Trainee | Bournemouth | 22 | — |
| | | | | | | | Southampton | 3 | — |
| | | | | | | | Gillingham (loan) | 10 | — |
| **Oakley** Matthew | 5 10 | 12 02 | M | 17 8 77 | Peterborough | Trainee | Southampton | 72 | 4 |
| **Ostenstad** Egil | 5 11 | 13 01 | F | 2 1 72 | Haugesund | | Viking | 128 | 54 |
| | | | | | | | Southampton | 59 | 20 |

| Name | | | Pos | Date of birth | Birthplace | Source | Clubs | Apps | Gls |
|---|---|---|---|---|---|---|---|---|---|
| **Palmer** Carlton | 6 2 | 13 03 | D | 5 12 65 | Oldbury | Trainee | WBA | 121 | 4 |
| | | | | | | | Sheffield W | 205 | 14 |
| | | | | | | | Leeds U | 102 | 5 |
| | | | | | | | Southampton | 26 | 3 |
| **Piper** David‡ | 5 8 | 10 00 | D | 31 10 77 | Bournemouth | Trainee | Southampton | — | — |
| **Richardson** Kevin | 5 10 | 12 00 | M | 4 12 62 | Newcastle | Apprentice | Everton | 109 | 16 |
| | | | | | | | Watford | 39 | 2 |
| | | | | | | | Arsenal | 96 | 5 |
| | | | | | | | Real Sociedad | 37 | — |
| | | | | | | | Aston Villa | 143 | 13 |
| | | | | | | | Coventry C | 78 | — |
| | | | | | | | Southampton | 28 | — |
| **Sarli** Cosimo | | | M | 13 3 79 | Italy | | Southampton | — | — |
| **Spedding** Duncan | 6 1 | 11 03 | D | 7 9 77 | Camberley | Trainee | Southampton | 7 | — |
| **Todd** Lee | 5 7 | 11 00 | D | 7 3 72 | Hartlepool | Hartlepool U | Stockport Co | 225 | 2 |
| | | | | | | | Southampton | 10 | — |
| **Van Gobbel** Ulrich | 6 0 | 15 00 | D | 16 1 71 | Surinam | | Willem II | 34 | 3 |
| *(Transferred to Feyenoord, August 1997)* | | | | | | | Feyenoord | 122 | 2 |
| | | | | | | | Galatasaray | 24 | 2 |
| | | | | | | | Southampton | 27 | 1 |
| **Venison** Barry‡ | 5 10 | 11 12 | M | 16 8 64 | Consett | Apprentice | Sunderland | 173 | 2 |
| | | | | | | | Liverpool | 110 | 1 |
| | | | | | | | Newcastle U | 109 | 1 |
| | | | | | | | Galatasaray | 8 | — |
| | | | | | | | Southampton | 24 | — |
| **Warner** Phil | 5 10 | 11 07 | D | 2 2 79 | Southampton | Trainee | Southampton | 1 | — |
| **Williams** Andy | 5 9 | 10 07 | F | 8 10 77 | Bristol | Trainee | Southampton | 20 | — |

**Trainees**
Cleife, Lloyd R; Liddon, Paul G; McCarthy, Craig; Sims, Adam D; Waller, Andrew P; Webber, Lloyd E; Wilson, Richard S.

**Associated Schoolboys**
Benfield, Sean R; Carter, Samuel J; Cleverly, Gareth; Fullam, Craig A; Gordon, Scott; Halliwell, William A; Howard, Brian R W; Lewis, Christopher; McManus, Garry L; Nicholls, Ryan; Peters, Mark W; Robertson, Andrew J; Stallard, Adam J.

**Associated Schoolboys who have accepted the club's offer of a Traineeship/Contract**
Ashford, Ryan M; Blayney, Alan; Grimshaw, Steven; Huxley, Matthew S; Madgwick, Benjamin; Wallace, Adam.

# SOUTHEND UNITED

| Name | | | Pos | Date of birth | Birthplace | Source | Clubs | Apps | Gls |
|---|---|---|---|---|---|---|---|---|---|
| **Beeston** Carl‡ | 5 10 | 12 08 | M | 30 6 67 | Stoke | Apprentice | Stoke C | 236 | 13 |
| | | | | | | | Hereford U (loan) | 9 | 2 |
| | | | | | | | Southend U | 6 | — |
| **Boere** Jeroen | 6 3 | 13 02 | F | 18 11 67 | Arnheim | Go Ahead | West Ham U | 25 | 6 |
| | | | | | | | Portsmouth (loan) | 5 | — |
| | | | | | | | WBA (loan) | 5 | — |
| | | | | | | | Crystal Palace | 8 | 1 |
| | | | | | | | Southend U | 73 | 25 |
| **Byrne** Paul | 5 11 | 13 00 | M | 30 6 72 | Dublin | Trainee | Oxford U | 6 | — |
| | | | | | | Bangor | Celtic | 28 | 4 |
| | | | | | | | Brighton & HA (loan) | 8 | 1 |
| | | | | | | | Southend U | 83 | 6 |
| **Clarke** Adrian | 5 9 | 11 00 | M | 28 9 74 | Cambridge | Trainee | Arsenal | 7 | — |
| | | | | | | | Rotherham U (loan) | 2 | — |
| | | | | | | | Southend U (loan) | 7 | — |
| | | | | | | | Southend U | 45 | 5 |
| **Coleman** Simon# | 6 0 | 10 08 | D | 13 6 68 | Worksop | Apprentice | Mansfield T | 96 | 7 |
| | | | | | | | Middlesbrough | 55 | 2 |
| | | | | | | | Derby Co | 70 | 2 |
| | | | | | | | Sheffield W | 16 | 1 |
| | | | | | | | Bolton W | 34 | 5 |
| | | | | | | | Wolverhampton W (loan) | 4 | — |
| | | | | | | | Southend U | 14 | — |
| **Coulbault** Regis* | 5 9 | 11 03 | M | 12 8 72 | Brignoles | Toulon | Southend U | 34 | 4 |
| **Dublin** Keith | 6 0 | 12 10 | D | 29 1 66 | Brent | Apprentice | Chelsea | 51 | — |
| | | | | | | | Brighton & HA | 132 | 5 |
| | | | | | | | Watford | 168 | 2 |
| | | | | | | | Southend U | 170 | 9 |
| **Fitzpatrick** Trevor§ | 6 1 | 12 10 | F | 19 2 80 | Surrey | Trainee | Southend U | 3 | — |
| **Gridelet** Phil# | 5 11 | 13 00 | M | 30 4 67 | Edgware | Barnet | Barnsley | 6 | — |
| | | | | | | | Rotherham U (loan) | 9 | — |
| | | | | | | | Southend U | 176 | 10 |
| **Hails** Julian# | 5 10 | 11 02 | M | 20 11 67 | Lincoln | Hemel Hempstead | Fulham | 109 | 12 |
| | | | | | | | Southend U | 149 | 6 |
| **Harris** Andrew | 5 10 | 12 02 | D | 26 2 77 | Springs | Trainee | Liverpool | — | — |
| | | | | | | | Southend U | 71 | — |
| **Henriksen** Tony# | 6 3 | 13 09 | G | 25 4 73 | Hammel | Randers Freja | Southend U | — | — |
| **Jones** Mark§ | | | M | 4 8 79 | Havering | Trainee | Southend U | 1 | — |

| Name | Ht | Wt | Pos | Date | Birthplace | From | Club | Apps | Gls |
|---|---|---|---|---|---|---|---|---|---|
| **Jones** Nathan | 5 7 | 10 12 | D | 28 5 73 | Rhondda | Merthyr T Numaicia | Luton T Southend U | — 39 | — — |
| **Lapper** Mike* | 6 0 | 12 02 | D | 28 8 70 | California | USSF | Southend U | 52 | 1 |
| **Lewis** Ben* | 6 0 | 12 10 | D | 22 6 77 | Chelmsford | Trainee | Colchester U Southend U | 2 14 | — 1 |
| **Maher** Kevin | 5 11 | 12 08 | M | 17 10 76 | Ilford | Trainee | Tottenham H Southend U | — 18 | — 1 |
| **Marsh** Mike* | 5 8 | 11 00 | M | 21 7 69 | Liverpool | Kirkby T | Liverpool West Ham U Coventry C Galatasaray Southend U | 69 49 15 3 84 | 2 1 2 — 11 |
| **N'Diaye** Sada* | 5 8 | 11 01 | F | 27 3 75 | Dakar | Troyes | Southend U | 17 | 2 |
| **Nielsen** John | 5 9 | 11 12 | M | 7 4 72 | Aarhus | Ikast | Ikast Southend U | 19 29 | — 3 |
| **Nzamba** Guy† | | | F | 13 7 70 | Gabon | Trieste | Southend U | 1 | — |
| **Parris** George‡ | 5 9 | 12 10 | M | 11 9 64 | Barking | Apprentice | West Ham U Birmingham C Brentford (loan) Bristol C (loan) Brighton & HA (loan) Norrkoping Brighton & HA Southend U | 239 39 5 6 18 4 56 1 | 12 1 — — 2 — 3 — |
| **Perkins** Chris§ | | | D | 1 3 80 | Stepney | Trainee | Southend U | 5 | — |
| **Rammell** Andy* | 6 2 | 13 10 | F | 10 2 67 | Nuneaton | Atherstone U | Manchester U Barnsley Southend U | — 185 69 | — 44 13 |
| **Roget** Leo | 6 1 | 12 02 | D | 1 8 77 | Ilford | Trainee | Southend U | 44 | 1 |
| **Royce** Simon* | 6 2 | 12 10 | G | 9 9 71 | Forest Gate | Heybridge Swifts | Southend U | 149 | |
| **Stimson** Mark | 5 10 | 12 06 | D | 27 12 67 | Plaistow | Trainee | Tottenham H Leyton Orient (loan) Gillingham (loan) Newcastle U Portsmouth (loan) Portsmouth Barnet (loan) Southend U | 2 10 18 86 4 58 5 39 | — — — 2 — 2 — — |
| **Taylor** Paul‡ | | | M | 30 9 78 | Basildon | Trainee | Southend U | — | — |
| **Thomson** Andy* | 5 10 | 10 12 | F | 1 4 71 | Motherwell | Jerviston BC | Q of S Southend U | 175 122 | 93 28 |
| **Whyte** David† | 5 8 | 12 00 | F | 20 4 71 | Greenwich | Greenwich Bor | Crystal Palace Charlton Ath (loan) Charlton Ath Ipswich T Bristol R Southend U | 27 8 85 2 4 8 | 4 2 28 — — 1 |
| **Williams** Paul* | 5 7 | 10 09 | F | 16 8 65 | London | Woodford T | Charlton Ath Brentford (loan) Sheffield W Crystal Palace Sunderland (loan) Birmingham C (loan) Charlton Ath Torquay U (loan) Southend U | 82 7 93 46 3 11 9 9 39 | 23 3 25 7 — — — — 7 |

**Trainees**
Cross, Garry R; Doyle, Jonathan L; Fisher, Matthew J; Fitzpatrick, Trevor J J; Jones, Mark; Kavanagh, Steven; McDonald, Thomas; Morrish, Adam; Perkins, Christopher P; Spittle, Stephen D; Thurley, Westley S.

**Non-Contract**
Johnson, Leon D; Nzamba, Guy R; Whyte, David A.

**Players who do not hold a current contract but their registration has been retained by the club**
Byrne, Paul P; Roche, David.

**Associated Schoolboys**
Arundell, John; Boot, Tony D; Buckley, Christopher; Collins, Nathan; Cumberworth, Peter J; Davey, Thomas; Evans, Michael; Fisher, James; Gibson, James W; Harding, Dean J; Mardle, George; Quincey, Ryan; Simmons, Michael; Watson, John M; Wray, Matthew K.

**Associated Schoolboy who has accepted the club's offer of a Traineeship/Contract**
Hunter, Leon.

# STOCKPORT COUNTY

| Name | Ht | Wt | Pos | Date | Birthplace | From | Club | Apps | Gls |
|---|---|---|---|---|---|---|---|---|---|
| **Angell** Brett | 6 2 | 13 10 | F | 20 8 68 | Marlborough | Cheltenham T | Derby Co Stockport Co Southend U Everton (loan) Everton Sunderland Sheffield U (loan) WBA (loan) Stockport Co | — 70 115 1 19 10 6 3 79 | — 28 47 — 1 — 2 — 33 |
| **Ansell** Gary‡ | 5 10 | 12 00 | M | 8 11 78 | Redbridge | Trainee | Stockport Co | — | — |

| Name | | | | | | | Club | Apps | Goals |
|---|---|---|---|---|---|---|---|---|---|
| **Aunger** Geoff‡ | 5 11 | 11 09 | M | 4 2 68 | Red Deer | Vancouver 86ers | Luton T | 5 | 1 |
| | | | | | | | Chester C | 5 | — |
| | | | | | | Seattle S | Stockport Co | 1 | — |
| **Bennett** Tom | 5 11 | 11 08 | M | 12 12 69 | Falkirk | Trainee | Aston Villa | — | — |
| | | | | | | | Wolverhampton W | 115 | 2 |
| | | | | | | | Stockport Co | 94 | 5 |
| **Byrne** Chris | 5 9 | 10 02 | M | 9 2 75 | Hulme | Macclesfield T | Sunderland | 8 | — |
| | | | | | | | Stockport Co | 26 | 7 |
| **Carden** Simon* | 5 9 | 11 06 | F | 26 10 78 | Urmston | Trainee | Stockport Co | — | — |
| **Cavaco** Luis* | 5 9 | 11 06 | F | 1 3 72 | Portugal | Estoril | Stockport Co | 29 | 5 |
| **Connelly** Sean | 5 10 | 11 10 | D | 26 6 70 | Sheffield | Hallam | Stockport Co | 211 | 2 |
| **Cook** Paul | 5 11 | 11 00 | M | 22 6 67 | Liverpool | Marine | Wigan Ath | 83 | 14 |
| | | | | | | | Norwich C | 6 | — |
| | | | | | | | Wolverhampton W | 193 | 19 |
| | | | | | | | Coventry C | 37 | 3 |
| | | | | | | | Tranmere R | 60 | 4 |
| | | | | | | | Stockport Co | 25 | 3 |
| **Cooper** Kevin | 5 7 | 10 07 | M | 8 2 75 | Derby | Trainee | Derby Co | 2 | — |
| | | | | | | | Stockport Co (loan) | 12 | 3 |
| | | | | | | | Stockport Co | 38 | 8 |
| **Dinning** Tony | 6 0 | 12 00 | D | 12 4 75 | Wallsend | Trainee | Newcastle U | — | — |
| | | | | | | | Stockport Co | 100 | 8 |
| **Flynn** Mike | 6 0 | 11 02 | D | 23 2 69 | Oldham | Trainee | Oldham Ath | 40 | 1 |
| | | | | | | | Norwich C | — | — |
| | | | | | | | Preston NE | 136 | 7 |
| | | | | | | | Stockport Co | 225 | 12 |
| **Gannon** Jim | 6 2 | 13 00 | D | 7 9 68 | Southwark | Dundalk | Sheffield U | — | — |
| | | | | | | | Halifax T (loan) | 2 | — |
| | | | | | | | Stockport Co | 316 | 52 |
| | | | | | | | Notts Co (loan) | 2 | — |
| **Grant** Stephen | 6 1 | 12 00 | F | 14 4 77 | Birr | Athlone T | Sunderland | — | — |
| | | | | | | Shamrock R | Stockport Co | 16 | 3 |
| **Gray** Ian | 6 2 | 12 00 | G | 25 2 75 | Manchester | Trainee | Oldham Ath | — | — |
| | | | | | | | Rochdale (loan) | 12 | — |
| | | | | | | | Rochdale | 66 | — |
| | | | | | | | Stockport Co | 3 | — |
| **Jeffers** John‡ | 5 10 | 11 10 | F | 5 10 68 | Liverpool | Trainee | Liverpool | — | — |
| | | | | | | | Port Vale | 180 | 10 |
| | | | | | | | Shrewsbury T (loan) | 3 | 1 |
| | | | | | | | Stockport Co | 57 | 6 |
| **Jones** Lea‡ | 6 0 | 14 06 | D | 25 9 77 | Southport | Trainee | Stockport Co | — | — |
| **Kalogeracus** Vas‡ | 5 7 | 11 00 | F | 21 3 75 | Perth | Floreat Athena | Birmingham C | — | — |
| | | | | | | Floreat Athena | Stockport Co | 2 | — |
| **Kiko** Manuel‡ | 5 10 | 12 05 | F | 24 10 76 | Portugal | Belenenses | Stockport Co | 3 | — |
| **Kilduff** Danny‡ | 6 1 | 13 00 | D | 27 12 78 | Stockport | Trainee | Stockport Co | — | — |
| **Lewis** Gary* | 5 9 | 10 12 | F | 5 10 78 | Bolton | Trainee | Stockport Co | — | — |
| **Mannion** Sean | | | M | 3 3 80 | Dublin | Stella Maris | Stockport Co | — | — |
| **McIntosh** Martin | 6 3 | 12 05 | D | 19 3 71 | East Kilbride | Tottenham H | St Mirren | 4 | — |
| | | | | | | | Clydebank | 65 | 10 |
| | | | | | | | Hamilton A | 99 | 12 |
| | | | | | | | Stockport Co | 38 | 2 |
| **Mutch** Andy* | 5 10 | 11 00 | F | 28 12 63 | Liverpool | Southport | Wolverhampton W | 289 | 96 |
| | | | | | | | Swindon T | 50 | 6 |
| | | | | | | | Wigan Ath (loan) | 7 | 1 |
| | | | | | | | Stockport Co | 64 | 10 |
| **Nash** Martin* | 5 11 | 12 03 | M | 27 12 75 | Regina | Vancouver | Stockport Co | 11 | — |
| **Nixon** Eric | 6 4 | 14 00 | G | 4 10 62 | Manchester | Curzon Ashton | Manchester C | 58 | — |
| | | | | | | | Wolverhampton W (loan) | 16 | — |
| | | | | | | | Bradford C (loan) | 3 | — |
| | | | | | | | Southampton (loan) | 4 | — |
| | | | | | | | Carlisle U (loan) | 16 | — |
| | | | | | | | Tranmere R (loan) | 8 | — |
| | | | | | | | Tranmere R | 333 | — |
| | | | | | | | Blackpool (loan) | 20 | — |
| | | | | | | | Bradford C (loan) | 12 | — |
| | | | | | | | Stockport Co | 43 | — |
| **Phelan** Mike† | 5 11 | 11 01 | D | 24 9 62 | Nelson | Apprentice | Burnley | 168 | 9 |
| | | | | | | | Norwich C | 156 | 9 |
| | | | | | | | Manchester U | 102 | 2 |
| | | | | | | | WBA | 21 | — |
| | | | | | | | Blackpool | — | — |
| | | | | | | | Stockport Co | — | — |
| **Phillips** Wayne | 5 10 | 11 00 | M | 15 12 70 | Bangor | Trainee | Wrexham | 207 | 16 |
| | | | | | | | Stockport Co | 13 | — |
| **Searle** Damon# | 5 11 | 10 04 | D | 26 10 71 | Cardiff | Trainee | Cardiff C | 234 | 3 |
| | | | | | | | Stockport Co | 41 | — |
| **Shearer** Lee‡ | 5 9 | 11 00 | F | 30 9 78 | Clackmannan | Trainee | Stockport Co | — | — |
| **Travis** Simon | 5 7 | 10 00 | M | 22 3 77 | Preston | Trainee | Torquay U | 8 | — |
| | | | | | | Holywell T | Stockport Co | 13 | 2 |
| **Vaughan** Francis | | | M | 8 9 79 | Salford | Trainee | Stockport Co | — | — |
| **Wilbraham** Aaron | 6 3 | 12 04 | F | 21 10 79 | Knutsford | Trainee | Stockport Co | 7 | 1 |

| **Woodthorpe** Colin | 5 11 | 11 08 | D | 13 1 69 | Ellesmere Pt | | Chester C | 155 | 6 |
|---|---|---|---|---|---|---|---|---|---|
| | | | | | | | Norwich C | 43 | 1 |
| | | | | | | | Aberdeen | 48 | 1 |
| | | | | | | | Stockport Co | 32 | 1 |

**Trainees**
Abel, Graeme F; Dodd, Scott; Fish, David; Flood, James A; Foster, Leroy T; Green, Robert J; Gunn, Martin F; Hussain, Rafaqat; Johnson, Ben; Lillis, Adam D; McConnell, Darren P; Salmons, Adam L; Smythe, Ben; Taylor, Greg; Thomas, Marc; Wright, Paul S.

**Non-Contract**
Megson, Gary J; Phelan, Michael C.

**Associated Schoolboys**
Andrews, Martyn; Briggs, Keith; Cotter, Robert J; Evans, Lee; Hulse, Paul G; Kent, Gareth C; McLachlan, Fraser M; O'Connell, Michael L; Rowley, Paul; Thomas, Andrew; Wild, Peter.

# STOKE CITY

| **Andrade** Jose‡ | 5 11 | 11 07 | F | 1 6 70 | Gaboverde | Academico | Stoke C | 16 | 2 |
|---|---|---|---|---|---|---|---|---|---|
| **Birch** Mark* | 5 11 | 12 02 | D | 5 1 77 | Stoke | Trainee | Stoke C | — | — |
| **Bullock** Matthew | 5 8 | 11 00 | M | 1 11 80 | Stoke | Trainee | Stoke C | — | — |
| **Burgess** Richard | 5 8 | 11 00 | F | 18 8 78 | Bromsgrove | Trainee | Aston Villa | — | — |
| | | | | | | | Stoke C | — | — |
| **Cairns** Kwesi* | 5 5 | 10 00 | M | 5 8 79 | Westminster | | Stoke C | — | — |
| **Cartwright** Jamie | 5 7 | 9 06 | M | 11 10 79 | Lichfield | Trainee | Stoke C | — | — |
| **Clarke** Clive | 6 1 | 12 03 | D | 14 1 80 | Dublin | Trainee | Stoke C | — | — |
| **Crowe** Dean | 5 5 | 11 02 | F | 6 6 79 | Stockport | Trainee | Stoke C | 16 | 4 |
| **Donaldson** O'Neill* | 5 11 | 12 02 | F | 24 11 69 | Birmingham | Hinckley | Shrewsbury T | 28 | 4 |
| | | | | | | | Doncaster R | 9 | 2 |
| | | | | | | | Mansfield T (loan) | 4 | 6 |
| | | | | | | | Sheffield W | 14 | 3 |
| | | | | | | | Oxford U (loan) | 6 | 2 |
| | | | | | | | Stoke C | 2 | — |
| **Forsyth** Richard | 5 11 | 12 12 | M | 3 10 70 | Dudley | Kidderminster H | Birmingham C | 26 | 2 |
| | | | | | | | Stoke C | 77 | 15 |
| **Fraser** Stuart | 6 0 | 12 00 | G | 1 8 78 | Cheltenham | | Stoke C | — | — |
| **Godbold** Jamie | 5 4 | 9 0 | M | 10 1 80 | Great Yarmouth | Trainee | Stoke C | — | — |
| **Heath** Robert | 5 9 | 10 00 | M | 31 8 78 | Stoke | | Stoke C | 6 | — |
| **Holsgrove** Paul# | 6 2 | 13 03 | M | 26 8 69 | Wellington | Trainee | Aldershot | 3 | — |
| | | | | | | | Wimbledon (loan) | — | — |
| | | | | | | | WBA (loan) | — | — |
| | | | | | | Wokingham T | Luton T | 2 | — |
| | | | | | | Heracles | Millwall | 11 | — |
| | | | | | | | Reading | 70 | 6 |
| | | | | | | | Grimsby T (loan) | 10 | — |
| | | | | | | | Crewe Alex | 8 | 1 |
| | | | | | | | Stoke C | 12 | 1 |
| **Kavanagh** Graham | 5 10 | 12 06 | M | 2 12 73 | Dublin | Home Farm | Middlesbrough | 35 | 3 |
| | | | | | | | Darlington (loan) | 5 | — |
| | | | | | | | Stoke C | 82 | 9 |
| **Keen** Kevin | 5 7 | 10 09 | M | 25 2 67 | Amersham | Apprentice | West Ham U | 219 | 21 |
| | | | | | | | Wolverhampton W | 42 | 7 |
| | | | | | | | Stoke C | 110 | 7 |
| **Lightbourne** Kyle | 6 2 | 12 00 | F | 29 9 68 | Bermuda | | Scarborough | 19 | 3 |
| | | | | | | | Walsall | 165 | 65 |
| | | | | | | | Coventry C | 7 | — |
| | | | | | | | Fulham (loan) | 4 | 2 |
| | | | | | | | Stoke C | 13 | 2 |
| **Macari** Mike* | 5 7 | 11 05 | F | 4 2 73 | Kilwinning | Trainee | West Ham U | — | — |
| | | | | | | | Stoke C | 30 | 3 |
| **Macari** Paul* | 5 8 | 11 06 | F | 23 8 76 | Manchester | Trainee | Stoke C | 3 | — |
| **Mackenzie** Neil | 6 2 | 12 05 | M | 15 4 76 | Birmingham | | Stoke C | 34 | 1 |
| **McMahon** Gerry | 5 11 | 11 13 | M | 29 12 73 | Belfast | Glenavon | Tottenham H | 16 | — |
| *(Transferred to St. Johnstone, February 1998)* | | | | | | | Barnet (loan) | 10 | 2 |
| | | | | | | | Stoke C | 52 | 3 |
| | | | | | | | St Johnstone | 10 | — |
| **McNally** Mark | 5 11 | 12 02 | D | 10 3 71 | Bellshill | Celtic BC | Celtic | 123 | 3 |
| | | | | | | | Southend U | 54 | 2 |
| | | | | | | | Stoke C | 7 | — |
| **Morgan** Phil* | 6 2 | 14 01 | G | 18 12 74 | Stoke | Trainee | Ipswich T | 1 | — |
| | | | | | | | Stoke C | — | — |
| | | | | | | | Chesterfield (loan) | 2 | — |

| | | | | | | | | | |
|---|---|---|---|---|---|---|---|---|---|
| **Muggleton** Carl | 6 2 | 13 03 | G | 13 9 68 | Leicester | Apprentice | Leicester C | 46 | — |
| | | | | | | | Chesterfield (loan) | 17 | — |
| | | | | | | | Blackpool (loan) | 2 | — |
| | | | | | | | Hartlepool U (loan) | 8 | — |
| | | | | | | | Stockport Co (loan) | 4 | — |
| | | | | | | | Liverpool (loan) | — | — |
| | | | | | | | Stoke C (loan) | 6 | — |
| | | | | | | | Sheffield U (loan) | — | — |
| | | | | | | | Celtic | 12 | — |
| | | | | | | | Stoke C | 97 | — |
| | | | | | | | Rotherham U (loan) | 6 | — |
| | | | | | | | Sheffield U (loan) | 1 | — |
| **Nyamah** Kofi | 5 10 | 11 07 | D | 20 6 75 | Islington | Trainee | Cambridge U | 23 | 2 |
| | | | | | | Kettering T | Stoke C | 17 | — |
| **O'Connor** James | 5 8 | 11 00 | M | 1 9 79 | Dublin | Trainee | Stoke C | — | — |
| **Pickering** Ally | 5 9 | 11 05 | D | 22 6 67 | Manchester | Buxton | Rotherham U | 88 | 2 |
| | | | | | | | Coventry C | 65 | — |
| | | | | | | | Stoke C | 82 | 1 |
| **Scheuber** Stuart | | | M | 3 4 81 | Rhuddlan | Trainee | Stoke C | — | — |
| **Schreuder** Jan-Dirk* | | | M | 2 8 71 | Barneveld | | PSV Eindhoven | 7 | — |
| | | | | | | | Sparta | 14 | — |
| | | | | | | | Groningen | 29 | 4 |
| | | | | | | | RKC | 42 | 2 |
| | | | | | | | Stoke C | — | — |
| **Sigurdsson** Kris | 5 11 | 11 11 | D | 7 10 80 | Akureyri | | KA | 15 | — |
| | | | | | | | Stoke C | — | — |
| **Sigurdsson** Larus | 6 0 | 13 11 | D | 4 6 73 | Akureyri | Thor | Stoke C | 157 | 2 |
| **Sobiech** Jorg‡ | | | D | 15 1 69 | Gelsenkirchen | | NEC | 44 | 2 |
| | | | | | | | Stoke C | 3 | — |
| **Southall** Neville | 6 1 | 13 00 | G | 16 9 58 | Llandudno | Winsford U | Bury | 39 | — |
| | | | | | | | Everton | 578 | — |
| | | | | | | | Port Vale (loan) | 9 | — |
| | | | | | | | Southend U (loan) | 9 | — |
| | | | | | | | Stoke C | 12 | — |
| **Stewart** Paul | 6 0 | 13 10 | F | 7 10 64 | Manchester | Apprentice | Blackpool | 201 | 56 |
| | | | | | | | Manchester C | 51 | 26 |
| | | | | | | | Tottenham H | 131 | 28 |
| | | | | | | | Liverpool | 32 | 1 |
| | | | | | | | Crystal Palace (loan) | 18 | 3 |
| | | | | | | | Wolverhampton W (loan) | 8 | 2 |
| | | | | | | | Burnley (loan) | 6 | — |
| | | | | | | | Sunderland | 36 | 5 |
| | | | | | | | Stoke C | 22 | 3 |
| **Stokoe** Graham* | 6 1 | 12 13 | M | 17 12 75 | Newcastle | Birmingham C | Stoke C | 2 | — |
| | | | | | | | Hartlepool U (loan) | 8 | — |
| **Sturridge** Simon | 5 6 | 11 10 | F | 9 12 69 | Birmingham | Trainee | Birmingham C | 150 | 30 |
| | | | | | | | Stoke C | 68 | 14 |
| **Taaffe** Steven | 5 7 | 9 0 | F | 10 9 79 | Stoke | Trainee | Stoke C | 3 | — |
| **Thorne** Peter | 6 0 | 13 07 | F | 21 6 73 | Manchester | Trainee | Blackburn R | — | — |
| | | | | | | | Wigan Ath (loan) | 11 | — |
| | | | | | | | Swindon T | 77 | 27 |
| | | | | | | | Stoke C | 36 | 12 |
| **Tiatto** Danny‡ | | | | 22 5 73 | Melbourne | Baden | Stoke C | 15 | 1 |
| **Tweed** Steven | 6 3 | 14 07 | D | 8 8 72 | Edinburgh | | Hibernian | 108 | 3 |
| | | | | | | | Ionikos | 2 | — |
| | | | | | | | Stoke C | 38 | — |
| **Wallace** Ray | 5 7 | 11 02 | M | 2 10 69 | Lewisham | Trainee | Southampton | 35 | — |
| | | | | | | | Leeds U | 7 | — |
| | | | | | | | Swansea C (loan) | 2 | — |
| | | | | | | | Reading (loan) | 3 | — |
| | | | | | | | Stoke C | 148 | 12 |
| | | | | | | | Hull C (loan) | 7 | — |
| **Whittle** Justin | 6 1 | 12 13 | D | 18 3 71 | Derby | Celtic | Stoke C | 65 | — |
| **Woods** Stephen | 5 11 | 11 13 | D | 15 12 76 | Davenham | Trainee | Stoke C | 1 | — |
| | | | | | | | Plymouth Arg (loan) | 5 | — |
| **Wooliscroft** Ashley | 5 10 | 11 02 | D | 28 12 79 | Stoke | Trainee | Stoke C | — | — |
| **Xausa** Davide | | | F | 10 3 76 | Vancouver | Univ of Portland | Port Vale | — | — |
| *(Transferred to St. Johnstone, February 1998)* | | | | | | | Stoke C | 1 | — |
| | | | | | | | St Johnstone | 1 | — |

**Trainees**
Davies, Benjamin J; Dixon, Calvin G; Simon, Courtney.

**Non-Contract**
Neal, Lewis.

**Associated Schoolboys**
Goodfellow, Marc D; Henry, Karl L D; Lovatt, Paul; Owen, Gareth D.

# SUNDERLAND

| | | | | | | | | | |
|---|---|---|---|---|---|---|---|---|---|
| **Agnew** Steve* | 5 9 | 10 06 | M | 9 11 65 | Shipley | Apprentice | Barnsley | 194 | 29 |
| | | | | | | | Blackburn R | 2 | — |
| | | | | | | | Portsmouth (loan) | 5 | — |
| | | | | | | | Leicester C | 56 | 4 |
| | | | | | | | Sunderland | 63 | 9 |
| **Aiston** Sam | 6 0 | 12 01 | M | 21 11 76 | Newcastle | Newcastle U | Sunderland | 19 | — |
| | | | | | | | Chester C (loan) | 14 | — |
| **Ball** Kevin | 5 9 | 11 06 | M | 12 11 64 | Hastings | Apprentice | Portsmouth | 105 | 4 |
| | | | | | | | Sunderland | 286 | 19 |
| **Beavers** Paul | 6 3 | 13 05 | F | 2 10 78 | Blackpool | Trainee | Sunderland | — | — |
| **Bridges** Michael | 6 1 | 10 11 | F | 5 8 78 | North Shields | Trainee | Sunderland | 49 | 8 |
| **Clark** Lee | 5 8 | 11 07 | M | 27 10 72 | Wallsend | Trainee | Newcastle U | 195 | 23 |
| | | | | | | | Sunderland | 46 | 13 |
| **Coton** Tony | 6 2 | 13 07 | G | 19 5 61 | Tamworth | Mile Oak R | Birmingham C | 94 | — |
| | | | | | | | Hereford U (loan) | — | — |
| | | | | | | | Watford | 233 | — |
| | | | | | | | Manchester C | 164 | — |
| | | | | | | | Manchester U | — | — |
| | | | | | | | Sunderland | 10 | — |
| **Craddock** Jody | 6 0 | 11 01 | D | 25 7 75 | Bromsgrove | Christchurch | Cambridge U | 145 | 4 |
| | | | | | | | Sunderland | 32 | — |
| **Dichio** Daniele | 6 3 | 12 03 | F | 19 10 74 | Hammersmith | Trainee | QPR | 75 | 20 |
| | | | | | | | Barnet (loan) | 9 | 2 |
| | | | | | | | Sampdoria | — | — |
| | | | | | | | Lecce | 4 | 1 |
| | | | | | | | Sunderland | 13 | — |
| **Dickman** Elliot | 5 8 | 9 08 | D | 11 10 78 | Hexham | Trainee | Sunderland | — | — |
| **Duke** David | | | M | 7 11 78 | Inverness | Redby CA | Sunderland | — | — |
| **Eriksson** Jan | 6 0 | 12 04 | D | 24 8 67 | Sundsvall | | AIK | 73 | 2 |
| *(Transferred to Tampa Bay Mutiny, January 1998)* | | | | | | | Norrkoping | 39 | 3 |
| | | | | | | | Kaiserslautern | 37 | 4 |
| | | | | | | | AIK | 7 | — |
| | | | | | | | Servette | 6 | — |
| | | | | | | | Helsingborg | 23 | 2 |
| | | | | | | | Sunderland | 1 | — |
| **Gray** Michael | 5 7 | 10 08 | D | 3 8 74 | Sunderland | Trainee | Sunderland | 189 | 12 |
| **Hall** Gareth* | 5 8 | 12 00 | D | 12 3 69 | Croydon | Apprentice | Chelsea | 138 | 4 |
| | | | | | | | Sunderland | 48 | — |
| | | | | | | | Brentford (loan) | 6 | — |
| **Heckingbottom** Paul | 5 11 | 12 00 | D | 17 7 77 | Barnsley | Manchester U | Sunderland | — | — |
| | | | | | | | Scarborough (loan) | 29 | — |
| **Heiselberg** Kim‡ | | | M | 21 9 77 | Tarm | Esbjerg | Sunderland | — | — |
| **Holloway** Darren | 5 10 | 12 06 | D | 3 10 77 | Bishop Auckland | Trainee | Sunderland | 32 | — |
| | | | | | | | Carlisle U (loan) | 5 | — |
| **Johnston** Allan | 5 7 | 9 07 | F | 14 12 73 | Glasgow | | Hearts | 84 | 12 |
| | | | | | | | Rennes | 23 | 2 |
| | | | | | | | Sunderland | 46 | 12 |
| **Lumsdon** Chris | 5 7 | 10 03 | M | 15 12 79 | Newcastle | Trainee | Sunderland | 1 | — |
| **Makin** Chris | 5 10 | 10 06 | D | 8 5 73 | Manchester | Trainee | Oldham Ath | 94 | 4 |
| | | | | | | | Wigan Ath (loan) | 15 | 2 |
| | | | | | | | Marseille | 29 | — |
| | | | | | | | Sunderland | 25 | — |
| **Maley** Mark | 5 9 | 12 03 | D | 26 1 81 | Newcastle | Trainee | Sunderland | — | — |
| **McKeown** Francis* | 5 9 | 11 07 | M | 11 2 81 | Belfast | Trainee | Sunderland | — | — |
| **Melville** Andy | 6 1 | 12 06 | D | 29 11 68 | Swansea | School | Swansea C | 175 | 22 |
| | | | | | | | Oxford U | 135 | 13 |
| | | | | | | | Sunderland | 160 | 12 |
| | | | | | | | Bradford C (loan) | 6 | 1 |
| **Mullin** John | 6 0 | 11 05 | F | 11 8 75 | Bury | School | Burnley | 18 | 2 |
| | | | | | | | Sunderland | 26 | 2 |
| | | | | | | | Preston NE (loan) | 7 | — |
| | | | | | | | Burnley (loan) | 6 | — |
| **Naisbett** Philip* | | | G | 2 1 79 | Easington | Trainee | Sunderland | — | — |
| **Ord** Richard | 6 2 | 12 08 | D | 3 3 70 | Murton | Trainee | Sunderland | 243 | 7 |
| | | | | | | | York C (loan) | 3 | — |
| **Perez** Lionel* | 6 0 | 13 05 | G | 24 4 67 | Bagnois Ceze | | Nimes | 74 | — |
| | | | | | | | Bordeaux | 16 | — |
| | | | | | | | Sunderland | 75 | — |
| **Phillips** Kevin | 5 7 | 11 00 | F | 25 7 73 | Hitchin | Baldock T | Watford | 59 | 24 |
| | | | | | | | Sunderland | 43 | 29 |

| Name | Ht | Wt | Pos | DOB | Birthplace | Source | Club | Apps | Gls |
|---|---|---|---|---|---|---|---|---|---|
| **Pollitt** Michael* | 6 4 | 14 00 | G | 29 2 72 | Farnworth | Trainee | Manchester U | — | — |
| | | | | | | | Oldham Ath (loan) | — | — |
| | | | | | | | Bury | — | — |
| | | | | | | | Lincoln C | 57 | — |
| | | | | | | | Darlington | 55 | — |
| | | | | | | | Notts Co | 10 | — |
| | | | | | | | Oldham Ath (loan) | 16 | — |
| | | | | | | | Gillingham (loan) | 6 | — |
| | | | | | | | Brentford (loan) | 5 | — |
| | | | | | | | Sunderland | — | — |
| **Proctor** Michael | 5 11 | 12 07 | F | 3 10 80 | Sunderland | Trainee | Sunderland | — | — |
| **Quinn** Niall | 6 4 | 12 04 | F | 6 10 66 | Dublin | | Arsenal | 67 | 14 |
| | | | | | | | Manchester C | 203 | 66 |
| | | | | | | | Sunderland | 47 | 16 |
| **Rae** Alex | 5 8 | 11 08 | M | 30 9 69 | Glasgow | Bishopbriggs | Falkirk | 83 | 20 |
| | | | | | | | Millwall | 218 | 63 |
| | | | | | | | Sunderland | 52 | 5 |
| **Scott** Martin | 5 9 | 11 00 | D | 7 1 68 | Sheffield | Apprentice | Rotherham U | 94 | 3 |
| | | | | | | | Nottingham F (loan) | — | — |
| | | | | | | | Bristol C | 171 | 14 |
| | | | | | | | Sunderland | 90 | 7 |
| **Shannon** Greg | 6 1 | 11 04 | G | 15 2 81 | Maghreafelt | Trainee | Sunderland | — | — |
| **Smith** Martin | 5 11 | 12 00 | F | 13 11 74 | Sunderland | Trainee | Sunderland | 111 | 22 |
| **Smyth** Gary‡ | | | M | 21 3 79 | Dublin | St Joseph's BC | Sunderland | — | — |
| **Summerbee** Nicky | 5 8 | 11 08 | F | 26 8 71 | Altrincham | Trainee | Swindon T | 112 | 6 |
| | | | | | | | Manchester C | 131 | 6 |
| | | | | | | | Sunderland | 25 | 3 |
| **Thirlwell** Paul | 5 11 | 11 04 | M | 13 2 79 | Newcastle | Trainee | Sunderland | — | — |
| **Weaver** Luke | 6 2 | 13 02 | G | 26 6 79 | Woolwich | Trainee | Leyton Orient | 9 | — |
| | | | | | | | West Ham U (loan) | — | — |
| | | | | | | | Sunderland | — | — |
| **Williams** Darren | 5 11 | 11 11 | D | 28 4 77 | Middlesbrough | Trainee | York C | 20 | — |
| | | | | | | | Sunderland | 47 | 4 |
| **Zoetebier** Edwin | | | G | 7 5 70 | Purmerend | | Sunderland | — | — |
| *(Transferred to Feyenoord, January 1998)* | | | | | | | | | |

**Trainees**
Butler, Thomas A; Convery, Mark P; Dolan, Glen T; Frampton, Kevin W; Gibson, Daniel; Harte, Shane P; Ingram, Stuart P; Jackson, Dennis; Lamb, Kris A; McCartney, George; Pitts, Matthew; Porter, Christopher I; Rice, Dominic A; Robson, Michael; Wright, Andrew.

**Associated Schoolboys**
Cogdon, Gavin; Cronin, Christopher P; Dowell, Adam; Hand, Mark; Hope, Shaun; James, Craig; Jolly, Nathan; McConville, Christopher; Redford, Lee; Rowland, Nicholas; Straker, Phillip; Taylor, Alan; Turns, Craig; Williamson, Darren.

**Associated Schoolboys who have accepted the club's offer of a Traineeship/Contract**
Marchant, Ross; McGhie, Gareth; Morgan, David; Vickers, Thomas A.

## SWANSEA CITY

| Name | Ht | Wt | Pos | DOB | Birthplace | Source | Club | Apps | Gls |
|---|---|---|---|---|---|---|---|---|---|
| **Agnew** Paul | 5 9 | 10 07 | D | 15 8 65 | Lisburn | Cliftonville | Grimsby T | 241 | 3 |
| | | | | | | | WBA | 39 | 1 |
| | | | | | | | Swansea C | 7 | — |
| **Alsop** Julian | 6 4 | 14 03 | F | 28 5 73 | Nuneaton | Halesowen T | Bristol R | 33 | 4 |
| | | | | | | | Swansea C | 12 | 3 |
| **Ampadu** Kwame* | 5 10 | 11 10 | M | 20 12 70 | Bradford | Belvedere | Arsenal | 2 | — |
| | | | | | | | Plymouth Arg (loan) | 6 | 1 |
| | | | | | | | WBA (loan) | 7 | 1 |
| | | | | | | | WBA | 42 | 3 |
| | | | | | | | Swansea C | 147 | 12 |
| **Appleby** Ritchie | 5 9 | 11 03 | F | 18 9 75 | Stockton | Trainee | Newcastle U | — | — |
| | | | | | | | Darlington (loan) | — | — |
| | | | | | | | Ipswich T | 3 | — |
| | | | | | | | Swansea C | 46 | 4 |
| **Barwood** Danny§ | 5 9 | 11 00 | F | 25 2 81 | Caerphilly | Trainee | Swansea C | 3 | 1 |
| **Bird** Tony | 5 11 | 12 10 | F | 1 9 74 | Cardiff | Trainee / Barry T | Cardiff C | 75 | 13 |
| | | | | | | | Swansea C | 41 | 14 |
| **Bound** Matthew | 6 2 | 14 00 | D | 9 11 72 | Bradford-on-Avon | Trainee | Southampton | 5 | — |
| | | | | | | | Hull C (loan) | 7 | 1 |
| | | | | | | | Stockport Co | 44 | 5 |
| | | | | | | | Lincoln C (loan) | 4 | — |
| | | | | | | | Swansea C | 28 | — |
| **Brown** Linton‡ | 5 10 | 12 07 | F | 12 4 68 | Driffield | Guiseley | Halifax T | 3 | — |
| | | | | | | | Hull C | 121 | 23 |
| | | | | | | | Swansea C | 27 | 3 |
| | | | | | | | Scarborough (loan) | 4 | 1 |
| **Casey** Ryan | 6 0 | 10 12 | F | 3 1 79 | Coventry | Trainee | Swansea C | 16 | — |
| **Chapple** Shaun* | 5 11 | 12 03 | M | 14 2 73 | Swansea | Trainee | Swansea C | 107 | 9 |
| **Clode** Mark | 5 10 | 10 10 | D | 24 2 73 | Plymouth | Trainee | Plymouth Arg | — | — |
| | | | | | | | Swansea C | 117 | 3 |
| **Coates** Jonathan | 5 8 | 10 04 | F | 27 5 75 | Swansea | Trainee | Swansea C | 111 | 11 |

| Cusack Nick | 6 0 | 12 05 | M | 24 12 65 | Rotherham | Alvechurch | Leicester C | 16 | 1 |
| | | | | | | | Peterborough U | 44 | 10 |
| | | | | | | | Motherwell | 77 | 17 |
| | | | | | | | Darlington | 21 | 6 |
| | | | | | | | Oxford U | 61 | 10 |
| | | | | | | | Wycombe W (loan) | 4 | — |
| | | | | | | | Fulham | 116 | 14 |
| | | | | | | | Swansea C | 32 | — |
| Freestone Roger | 6 3 | 14 06 | G | 19 8 68 | Newport | Trainee | Newport Co | 13 | — |
| | | | | | | | Chelsea | 42 | — |
| | | | | | | | Swansea C (loan) | 14 | — |
| | | | | | | | Hereford U (loan) | 8 | — |
| | | | | | | | Swansea C | 312 | 3 |
| Harris Jamie | 6 2 | 13 07 | F | 28 6 79 | Swansea | Mumbles R | Swansea C | 6 | — |
| Hartfield Charlie | 6 0 | 13 08 | M | 4 9 71 | London | Trainee | Arsenal | — | — |
| | | | | | | | Sheffield U | 56 | 1 |
| | | | | | | | Fulham (loan) | 2 | — |
| | | | | | | | Swansea C | 22 | 2 |
| Howard Mike | 5 9 | 11 13 | D | 2 12 78 | Birkenhead | Tranmere R | Swansea C | 3 | — |
| Jenkins Lee | 5 9 | 10 00 | M | 28 6 79 | Pontypool | Trainee | Swansea C | 44 | 2 |
| Jones Jason | | | G | 10 5 79 | Wrexham | Liverpool | Swansea C | 1 | — |
| Jones Steve | 5 10 | 12 02 | D | 25 12 70 | Bristol | Cheltenham T | Swansea C | 63 | 1 |
| King Robert* | 5 8 | 10 06 | D | 2 9 77 | Merthyr | Trainee | Swansea C | 2 | — |
| Lacey Damien | 5 9 | 11 03 | M | 3 8 77 | Bridgend | Trainee | Swansea C | 32 | 1 |
| Mainwaring Carl§ | 5 11 | 12 07 | F | 15 3 80 | Swansea | Trainee | Swansea C | 3 | — |
| Molby Jan* | 6 2 | 15 10 | M | 4 7 63 | Kolding | Ajax | Liverpool | 218 | 44 |
| | | | | | | | Barnsley (loan) | 5 | — |
| | | | | | | | Norwich C (loan) | 3 | — |
| | | | | | | | Swansea C | 41 | 8 |
| Moreira Joao* | 6 2 | 13 00 | D | 30 6 70 | Angola | Benfica | Swansea C | 15 | — |
| Munroe Karl§ | | | M | 23 9 79 | Manchester | Trainee | Swansea C | 1 | — |
| Newhouse Aidan | 6 2 | 13 10 | F | 23 5 72 | Wallasey | Trainee | Chester C | 44 | 6 |
| | | | | | | | Wimbledon | 23 | 2 |
| | | | | | | | Tranmere R (loan) | — | — |
| | | | | | | | Port Vale (loan) | 2 | — |
| | | | | | | | Portsmouth (loan) | 6 | 1 |
| | | | | | | | Torquay U (loan) | 4 | 2 |
| | | | | | | | Fulham | 8 | 1 |
| | | | | | | | Swansea C | 8 | — |
| O'Gorman Dave | 6 0 | 13 00 | F | 20 6 72 | Chester | School Barry T | Wrexham | 17 | — |
| | | | | | | | Swansea C | 34 | 5 |
| O'Leary Kristian | 6 0 | 13 04 | D | 30 8 77 | Port Talbot | Trainee | Swansea C | 42 | 1 |
| Phillips Gareth§ | 5 8 | 9 08 | M | 19 7 79 | Porth | Trainee | Swansea C | 7 | — |
| Price Jason | 6 2 | 11 05 | M | 12 4 77 | Aberdare | Aberaman Ath | Swansea C | 36 | 3 |
| Puttnam Dave‡ | 5 10 | 11 12 | M | 3 2 67 | Leicester | Leicester U | Leicester C | 7 | — |
| | | | | | | | Lincoln C | 177 | 21 |
| | | | | | | | Gillingham | 40 | 2 |
| | | | | | | | Swansea C | 4 | — |
| Walker Keith | 6 0 | 12 08 | D | 17 4 66 | Edinburgh | ICI Juveniles | Stirling Albion | 91 | 17 |
| | | | | | | | St Mirren | 43 | 6 |
| | | | | | | | Swansea C | 269 | 9 |
| Watkin Steve | 5 10 | 11 10 | F | 16 6 71 | Wrexham | School | Wrexham | 200 | 55 |
| | | | | | | | Swansea C | 32 | 3 |

**Trainees**
Barwood, Daniel D; Cleverley, Richard J T; Davies, Jamie; De-Vulgt, Leigh S; Dyer, Steven P; Howard, Martin G; Jones, Dean; Keegan, Michael J; Kissick, Lee P; Mainwaring, Carl A; Morgan, David B R; Munroe, Karl A; Phillips, Gareth R; Roberts, Stuart I; Simon, Neil P; Taylor, James J; Thomas, Carl I; Watkins, David J.

**Non-Contract**
Cork, Alan G.

**Associated Schoolboys**
Berry, James; Crutch, Mark; Davey, Scott R; Davies, Ross D; Galloway, Nicholas; Healey, Stephen; McLachlan, Lee C; Thomas, Jonathan F.

**Associated Schoolboys who have accepted the club's offer of a Traineeship/Contract**
Gregson, Lyndon; James, Robert K; Kern, Jamie T; Morgan, Ian K; Todd, Christopher.

# SWINDON TOWN

| Borrows Brian | 5 10 | 11 12 | D | 20 12 60 | Liverpool | Amateur | Everton | 27 | — |
| | | | | | | | Bolton W | 95 | — |
| | | | | | | | Coventry C | 409 | 11 |
| | | | | | | | Bristol C (loan) | 6 | — |
| | | | | | | | Swindon T | 40 | — |
| Bullock Darren | 5 9 | 13 04 | M | 12 2 69 | Worcester | Nuneaton Bor | Huddersfield T | 128 | 16 |
| | | | | | | | Swindon T | 44 | 1 |
| Collins Lee | 5 9 | 11 02 | M | 3 2 74 | Bellshill | Possil U | Albion R | 45 | 1 |
| | | | | | | | Swindon T | 35 | 1 |

| | | | | | | | | | |
|---|---|---|---|---|---|---|---|---|---|
| **Cowe** Steve | 5 7 | 10 02 | F | 29 9 74 | Gloucester | Trainee | Aston Villa | — | — |
| | | | | | | | Swindon T | 66 | 9 |
| **Cuervo** Philippe | 5 11 | 11 03 | M | 13 8 69 | France | | St Etienne | 21 | — |
| | | | | | | | Swindon T | 23 | — |
| **Culverhouse** Ian* | 5 10 | 11 02 | D | 22 9 64 | Bishop's Stortford | Apprentice | Tottenham H | 2 | — |
| | | | | | | | Norwich C | 296 | — |
| | | | | | | | Swindon T | 97 | — |
| **Darras** Frederic‡ | 5 11 | 11 03 | D | 19 8 66 | Calais | | Auxerre | 27 | — |
| | | | | | | | Sochaux | 54 | — |
| | | | | | | | Bastia | 39 | — |
| | | | | | | | Swindon T | 49 | — |
| **Davis** Sol§ | 5 7 | 11 00 | D | 4 9 79 | Cheltenham | Trainee | Swindon T | 6 | — |
| **Digby** Fraser* | 6 1 | 12 12 | G | 23 4 67 | Sheffield | Apprentice | Manchester U | — | — |
| | | | | | | | Oldham Ath (loan) | — | — |
| | | | | | | | Swindon T (loan) | — | — |
| | | | | | | | Swindon T | 417 | — |
| | | | | | | | Manchester U (loan) | — | — |
| **Elkins** Gary | 5 9 | 13 04 | D | 4 5 66 | Wallingford | Apprentice | Fulham | 104 | 2 |
| | | | | | | | Exeter C (loan) | 5 | — |
| | | | | | | | Wimbledon | 110 | 3 |
| | | | | | | | Swindon T | 23 | 1 |
| **Finney** Steve* | 5 10 | 12 00 | F | 31 10 73 | Hexham | Trainee | Preston NE | 6 | 1 |
| | | | | | | | Manchester C | — | — |
| | | | | | | | Swindon T | 73 | 18 |
| | | | | | | | Cambridge U (loan) | 7 | 2 |
| **Gooden** Ty | 5 8 | 12 06 | M | 23 10 72 | Canvey Island | Wycombe W | Swindon T | 98 | 8 |
| **Hay** Chris | 6 0 | 12 05 | F | 28 8 74 | Glasgow | | Celtic | 25 | 4 |
| | | | | | | | Swindon T | 36 | 14 |
| **Holcroft** Peter | 5 9 | 11 07 | M | 3 1 76 | Liverpool | Trainee | Everton | — | — |
| | | | | | | | Swindon T | 3 | — |
| | | | | | | | Exeter C (loan) | 6 | — |
| **Howe** Stephen | 5 7 | 10 06 | M | 6 1 73 | Annitsford | Trainee | Nottingham F | 14 | 2 |
| | | | | | | | Ipswich T (loan) | 3 | — |
| | | | | | | | Swindon T | 10 | — |
| **Hulbert** Robin | | | M | 14 3 80 | Plymouth | Trainee | Swindon T | 1 | — |
| | | | | | | | Newcastle U (loan) | — | — |
| **Kerslake** David | 5 9 | 12 04 | D | 19 6 66 | Stepney | Apprentice | QPR | 58 | 6 |
| | | | | | | | Swindon T | 135 | 1 |
| | | | | | | | Leeds U | 8 | — |
| | | | | | | | Tottenham H | 37 | — |
| | | | | | | | Swindon T (loan) | 8 | — |
| | | | | | | | Ipswich T | 7 | — |
| | | | | | | | Wycombe W (loan) | 10 | — |
| | | | | | | | Swindon T | 10 | — |
| **King** Phil | 5 11 | 12 07 | D | 28 12 67 | Bristol | Apprentice | Exeter C | 27 | — |
| | | | | | | | Torquay U | 24 | 3 |
| | | | | | | | Swindon T | 116 | 4 |
| | | | | | | | Sheffield W | 129 | 2 |
| | | | | | | | Notts Co (loan) | 6 | — |
| | | | | | | | Aston Villa | 16 | — |
| | | | | | | | WBA (loan) | 4 | — |
| | | | | | | | Swindon T | 5 | — |
| | | | | | | | Blackpool (loan) | 6 | — |
| **Leitch** Scott | 5 10 | 12 00 | M | 6 10 69 | Motherwell | Shettleston Jun | Dunfermline Ath | 89 | 16 |
| | | | | | | | Hearts | 55 | 2 |
| | | | | | | | Swindon T | 69 | 1 |
| **McAreavey** Paul§ | | | M | 3 12 80 | Belfast | Trainee | Swindon T | 1 | — |
| **McDonald** Alan | 6 3 | 13 10 | D | 12 10 63 | Belfast | Apprentice | QPR | 402 | 13 |
| | | | | | | | Charlton Ath (loan) | 9 | — |
| | | | | | | | Swindon T | 33 | 1 |
| **McMahon** Steve‡ | 5 9 | 11 08 | M | 20 8 61 | Liverpool | Apprentice | Everton | 100 | 11 |
| | | | | | | | Aston Villa | 75 | 7 |
| | | | | | | | Liverpool | 204 | 29 |
| | | | | | | | Manchester C | 87 | 1 |
| | | | | | | | Swindon T | 42 | — |
| **Meechan** Alex§ | | | F | 29 1 80 | Plymouth | Trainee | Swindon T | 1 | — |
| **Mildenhall** Steve | 6 4 | 14 01 | G | 13 5 78 | Swindon | Trainee | Swindon T | 5 | — |
| **Ndah** George | 6 1 | 11 04 | F | 23 12 74 | Camberwell | Trainee | Crystal Palace | 78 | 8 |
| | | | | | | | Bournemouth (loan) | 12 | 2 |
| | | | | | | | Gillingham (loan) | 4 | — |
| | | | | | | | Swindon T | 14 | 2 |
| **Onuora** Iffy | 6 0 | 13 01 | F | 28 7 67 | Glasgow | British Univ | Huddersfield T | 165 | 30 |
| | | | | | | | Mansfield T | 28 | 8 |
| | | | | | | | Gillingham | 62 | 23 |
| | | | | | | | Swindon T | 6 | 1 |
| **Pattimore** Michael* | 5 9 | 11 02 | D | 15 3 79 | Newport | Trainee | Swindon T | 3 | — |
| **Robinson** Mark | 5 9 | 12 04 | D | 21 11 68 | Rochdale | Trainee | WBA | 2 | — |
| | | | | | | | Barnsley | 137 | 6 |
| | | | | | | | Newcastle U | 25 | — |
| | | | | | | | Swindon T | 156 | 3 |

| Name | Ht | Wt | Pos | DOB | Birthplace | Source | Club | Apps | Gls |
|------|----|----|-----|-----|-----------|--------|------|------|-----|
| **Seagraves** Mark* | 6 0 | 12 10 | D | 22 10 66 | Bootle | Apprentice | Liverpool | — | — |
| | | | | | | | Norwich C (loan) | 3 | — |
| | | | | | | | Manchester C | 42 | — |
| | | | | | | | Bolton W | 157 | 7 |
| | | | | | | | Swindon T | 61 | — |
| **Talia** Frank | 6 1 | 13 06 | G | 20 7 72 | Melbourne | Sunshine GC | Blackburn R | — | — |
| | | | | | | | Hartlepool U (loan) | 14 | — |
| | | | | | | | Swindon T | 33 | — |
| **Taylor** Craig | 6 1 | 12 03 | D | 24 1 74 | Plymouth | Dorchester T | Exeter C | 5 | — |
| | | | | | | | Swindon T | 32 | 2 |
| **Walters** Mark | 5 9 | 11 05 | M | 2 6 64 | Birmingham | Apprentice | Aston Villa | 181 | 39 |
| | | | | | | | Rangers | 106 | 32 |
| | | | | | | | Liverpool | 94 | 14 |
| | | | | | | | Stoke C (loan) | 9 | 2 |
| | | | | | | | Wolverhampton W (loan) | 11 | 3 |
| | | | | | | | Southampton | 5 | — |
| | | | | | | | Swindon T | 61 | 13 |
| **Watson** Kevin | 5 9 | 12 08 | M | 3 1 74 | Hackney | Trainee | Tottenham H | 5 | — |
| | | | | | | | Brentford (loan) | 3 | — |
| | | | | | | | Bristol C (loan) | 2 | — |
| | | | | | | | Barnet (loan) | 13 | — |
| | | | | | | | Swindon T | 45 | 1 |
| **Willis** Adam | 6 1 | 12 02 | D | 21 9 76 | Nuneaton | Trainee | Coventry C | — | — |
| | | | | | | | Swindon T | — | — |

**Trainees**
Burke, Nicholas P; Cairns, Peter A; Campagna, Sam P P; Culbertson, Richard D J; Davis, Sol S; Donlan, Jason A; Hodson, Stuart M; Macdiarmid, Philip E; McAreavey, Paul; McHugh, Frazer; McSherry, Ian G R; Meechan, Alexander T; Mills, Jamie M; Peters, Bradley S; Robinson, Karl J; Thorne, Wayne P.

**Associated Schoolboys**
Clayton, Daniel P; Collier, Adam; Dix, Neil A; Evans, Keri S; Horrix, Terence; Hughes, Alun T; Kimber, Daniel S; Mackey, Nick; Pottinger, Dale; Sperti, Giovanni.

## TORQUAY UNITED

| Name | Ht | Wt | Pos | DOB | Birthplace | Source | Club | Apps | Gls |
|------|----|----|-----|-----|-----------|--------|------|------|-----|
| **Barrow** Lee‡ | 5 11 | 13 00 | D | 1 5 73 | Belper | Trainee | Notts Co | — | — |
| | | | | | | | Scarborough | 11 | — |
| | | | | | | | Torquay U | 164 | 5 |
| **Bedeau** Anthony | 5 10 | 11 00 | F | 24 3 79 | Hammersmith | Trainee | Torquay U | 46 | 6 |
| **Clayton** Gary# | 5 10 | 12 08 | M | 2 3 63 | Sheffield | Burton Alb | Doncaster R | 35 | 5 |
| | | | | | | | Cambridge U | 179 | 17 |
| | | | | | | | Peterborough U (loan) | 4 | — |
| | | | | | | | Huddersfield T | 19 | 1 |
| | | | | | | | Plymouth Arg | 38 | 2 |
| | | | | | | | Torquay U | 41 | 2 |
| **Gibbs** Paul# | 5 10 | 11 03 | D | 26 10 72 | Gorleston | Diss T | Colchester U | 53 | 3 |
| | | | | | | | Torquay U | 41 | 7 |
| **Gittens** Jon* | 5 11 | 12 10 | D | 22 1 64 | Moseley | Paget R | Southampton | 18 | — |
| | | | | | | | Swindon T | 126 | 8 |
| | | | | | | | Southampton | 19 | — |
| | | | | | | | Middlesbrough (loan) | 12 | 1 |
| | | | | | | | Middlesbrough | 13 | — |
| | | | | | | | Portsmouth | 83 | 2 |
| | | | | | | | Torquay U | 78 | 9 |
| **Gregg** Matt | 5 11 | 12 00 | G | 30 11 78 | Cheltenham | Trainee | Torquay U | 21 | — |
| **Gurney** Andy# | 5 11 | 12 02 | D | 25 1 74 | Bristol | Trainee | Bristol R | 108 | 9 |
| | | | | | | | Torquay U | 44 | 9 |
| **Hapgood** Leon§ | 5 6 | 10 00 | M | 7 8 79 | Torbay | Trainee | Torquay U | 23 | 3 |
| **Hill** Kevin | 5 8 | 9 12 | F | 6 3 76 | Exeter | Torrington | Torquay U | 37 | 7 |
| **Hodges** Kevin# | 5 8 | 11 02 | M | 12 6 60 | Bridport | Apprentice | Plymouth Arg | 530 | 81 |
| | | | | | | | Torquay U (loan) | 3 | — |
| | | | | | | | Torquay U | 68 | 4 |
| **Jack** Rodney | 5 7 | 10 09 | F | 28 9 72 | Kingston, Jamaica | Lambada | Torquay U | 87 | 24 |
| **Leadbitter** Chris# | 5 9 | 10 06 | M | 17 10 67 | Middlesbrough | Apprentice | Grimsby T | — | — |
| | | | | | | | Hereford U | 36 | 1 |
| | | | | | | | Cambridge U | 176 | 18 |
| | | | | | | | Bournemouth | 54 | 3 |
| | | | | | | | Plymouth Arg | 52 | 1 |
| | | | | | | | Torquay U | 26 | 1 |
| **McCall** Steve# | 5 11 | 12 06 | M | 15 10 60 | Carlisle | Apprentice | Ipswich T | 257 | 7 |
| | | | | | | | Sheffield W | 29 | 2 |
| | | | | | | | Carlisle U (loan) | 6 | — |
| | | | | | | | Plymouth Arg | 100 | 5 |
| | | | | | | | Torquay U | 51 | 2 |

| Name | Ht | Wt | Pos | Born | Birthplace | Source | Club | Apps | Gls |
|---|---|---|---|---|---|---|---|---|---|
| **McFarlane** Andy | 6 3 | 13 08 | F | 30 11 66 | Wolverhampton | Cradley T | Portsmouth | 2 | — |
| | | | | | | | Swansea C | 55 | 8 |
| | | | | | | | Scunthorpe U | 60 | 19 |
| | | | | | | | Torquay U | 41 | 8 |
| **Mitchell** Paul‡ | 5 10 | 12 00 | M | 20 10 71 | Bournemouth | Trainee | Bournemouth | 12 | — |
| | | | | | | | West Ham U | 1 | — |
| | | | | | | | Bournemouth | 4 | — |
| | | | | | | | Torquay U | 38 | 1 |
| **Newell** Justin§ | 6 1 | 10 07 | F | 8 2 80 | Germany | Trainee | Torquay U | 1 | — |
| **Partridge** Scott | 5 9 | 11 02 | M | 13 10 74 | Leicester | Trainee | Bradford C | 5 | — |
| | | | | | | | Bristol C | 57 | 7 |
| | | | | | | | Torquay U (loan) | 5 | 2 |
| | | | | | | | Plymouth Arg (loan) | 7 | 2 |
| | | | | | | | Scarborough (loan) | 7 | 2 |
| | | | | | | | Cardiff C | 37 | 2 |
| | | | | | | | Torquay U | 5 | — |
| **Preston** Michael* | 5 7 | 11 00 | M | 22 11 77 | Plymouth | Trainee | Torquay U | 10 | — |
| **Robinson** Jamie# | 6 1 | 12 08 | D | 26 2 72 | Liverpool | Trainee | Liverpool | — | — |
| | | | | | | | Barnsley | 9 | — |
| | | | | | | | Carlisle U | 57 | 4 |
| | | | | | | | Torquay U | 46 | — |
| **Thomas** Wayne | 5 11 | 11 12 | D | 17 5 79 | Gloucester | Trainee | Torquay U | 39 | 1 |
| **Tully** Stephen§ | 5 9 | 11 00 | D | 10 2 80 | Paignton | Trainee | Torquay U | 9 | — |
| **Veysey** Kenneth | 5 10 | 12 07 | G | 8 6 67 | Hackney | Dorchester T | Torquay U | 27 | — |
| **Watson** Alex# | 6 1 | 13 00 | D | 5 4 68 | Liverpool | Apprentice | Liverpool | 4 | — |
| | | | | | | | Derby Co (loan) | 5 | — |
| | | | | | | | Bournemouth | 151 | 5 |
| | | | | | | | Gillingham (loan) | 10 | 1 |
| | | | | | | | Torquay U | 121 | 4 |

**Trainees**
Froude, Paul T; Gomm, Richard A; Hadley, Shaun L; Hall, Jonathan P; Hapgood, Leon D; Jermyn, Mark S; Medlin, Daniel L; Moores, Jamie O O; Newell, Justin J; Nichols, Jonathan A; Northmore, Ryan; Powell, David; Smillie, Duncan; Tully, Stephen R; Worthington, Martin P.

**Non-Contract**
Lynch, Anthony; Wheeldon, Thomas V.

**Associated Schoolboys**
Ashington, Ryan; Benefield, Jimmy.

## TOTTENHAM HOTSPUR

| Name | Ht | Wt | Pos | Born | Birthplace | Source | Club | Apps | Gls |
|---|---|---|---|---|---|---|---|---|---|
| **Allen** Rory | 5 11 | 11 02 | F | 17 10 77 | Beckenham | Trainee | Tottenham H | 16 | 2 |
| | | | | | | | Luton T (loan) | 8 | 6 |
| **Anderton** Darren | 6 1 | 12 05 | F | 3 3 72 | Southampton | Trainee | Portsmouth | 62 | 7 |
| | | | | | | | Tottenham H | 147 | 22 |
| **Arber** Mark | 6 1 | 11 09 | D | 9 10 77 | South Africa | Trainee | Tottenham H | — | — |
| **Armstrong** Chris | 6 0 | 12 10 | F | 19 6 71 | Newcastle | Llay Welfare | Wrexham | 60 | 13 |
| | | | | | | | Millwall | 28 | 5 |
| | | | | | | | Crystal Palace | 118 | 45 |
| | | | | | | | Tottenham H | 67 | 25 |
| **Austin** Dean* | 6 0 | 11 06 | D | 26 4 70 | Hemel Hempstead | St. Albans C | Southend U | 96 | 2 |
| | | | | | | | Tottenham H | 124 | — |
| **Baardsen** Espen | 6 5 | 13 03 | G | 7 12 77 | San Rafael | San Francisco AB | Tottenham H | 11 | — |
| **Berti** Nicola* | 6 1 | 12 02 | M | 14 4 67 | Salsomaggiore Terme | | Parma | 28 | — |
| | | | | | | | Fiorentina | 80 | 8 |
| | | | | | | | Internazionale | 229 | 29 |
| | | | | | | | Tottenham H | 17 | 3 |
| **Brady** Garry | 5 10 | 10 95 | M | 7 9 76 | Glasgow | Trainee | Tottenham H | 9 | — |
| **Brown** Simon | 6 2 | 15 01 | G | 3 12 76 | Chelmsford | Trainee | Tottenham H | — | — |
| | | | | | | | Lincoln C (loan) | 1 | — |
| **Bunn** James | | | F | 12 1 78 | Tottenham | Trainee | Tottenham H | — | — |
| **Calderwood** Colin | 6 0 | 13 00 | D | 20 1 65 | Glasgow | Amateur | Mansfield T | 100 | 1 |
| | | | | | | | Swindon T | 330 | 20 |
| | | | | | | | Tottenham H | 151 | 6 |
| **Campbell** Sol | 6 21 | 14 04 | D | 18 9 74 | Newham | Trainee | Tottenham H | 168 | 2 |
| **Carr** Stephen | 5 9 | 12 04 | D | 29 8 76 | Dublin | Trainee | Tottenham H | 65 | — |
| **Clemence** Stephen | 5 11 | 11 07 | M | 31 3 78 | Liverpool | Trainee | Tottenham H | 17 | — |
| **Darcy** Ross | 6 0 | 12 02 | D | 21 3 78 | Balbriggan | Trainee | Tottenham H | — | — |
| **Davies** Darren* | 5 8 | 11 07 | D | 13 8 78 | Port Talbot | Trainee | Tottenham H | — | — |
| **Dominguez** Jose | 5 3 | 10 00 | F | 16 2 74 | Lisbon | Benfica | Birmingham C | 35 | 3 |
| | | | | | | | Sporting Lisbon | 30 | 1 |
| | | | | | | | Birmingham C | — | — |
| | | | | | | | Tottenham H | 18 | 2 |
| **Edinburgh** Justin | 5 10 | 12 01 | D | 18 12 69 | Basildon | Trainee | Southend U | 37 | — |
| | | | | | | | Tottenham H (loan) | — | — |
| | | | | | | | Tottenham H | 189 | 1 |

| | | | | | | | | | |
|---|---|---|---|---|---|---|---|---|---|
| **Evans** James* | | | M | 3 10 78 | Epsom | Trainee | Tottenham H | — | — |
| **Fenn** Neale | 5 10 | 12 08 | F | 18 1 77 | Edmonton | Trainee | Tottenham H | 8 | — |
| | | | | | | | Leyton Orient (loan) | 3 | — |
| | | | | | | | Norwich C (loan) | 7 | 1 |
| **Ferdinand** Les | 5 11 | 13 05 | F | 18 12 66 | Acton | Hayes | QPR | 163 | 80 |
| | | | | | | | Brentford (loan) | 3 | — |
| | | | | | | | Besiktas (loan) | 24 | 14 |
| | | | | | | | Newcastle U | 68 | 41 |
| | | | | | | | Tottenham H | 21 | 5 |
| **Fox** Ruel | 5 6 | 10 05 | F | 14 1 68 | Ipswich | Apprentice | Norwich C | 172 | 22 |
| | | | | | | | Newcastle U | 58 | 12 |
| | | | | | | | Tottenham H | 83 | 10 |
| **Gain** Peter | 6 1 | 11 00 | M | 11 11 76 | Hammersmith | Trainee | Tottenham H | — | — |
| **Ginola** David | 5 11 | 11 10 | F | 25 1 67 | Gassin | | Toulon | 81 | 4 |
| | | | | | | | Racing Paris | 61 | 8 |
| | | | | | | | Brest | 50 | 10 |
| | | | | | | | Paris St Germain | 115 | 32 |
| | | | | | | | Newcastle U | 58 | 6 |
| | | | | | | | Tottenham H | 34 | 6 |
| **Gower** Mark | | | M | 5 10 78 | Edmonton | Trainee | Tottenham H | — | — |
| **Grodas** Frode | 6 2 | 14 07 | G | 24 10 64 | Volda | | Lillestrom | 182 | 1 |
| | | | | | | | Chelsea | 21 | — |
| | | | | | | | Tottenham H | — | — |
| **Hill** Danny* | 5 9 | 11 12 | M | 1 10 74 | Edmonton | Trainee | Tottenham H | 10 | — |
| | | | | | | | Birmingham C (loan) | 5 | — |
| | | | | | | | Watford (loan) | 1 | — |
| | | | | | | | Cardiff C (loan) | 7 | — |
| **Howells** David* | 6 0 | 12 07 | M | 15 12 67 | Guildford | Trainee | Tottenham H | 277 | 22 |
| **Iversen** Steffen | 6 1 | 11 08 | F | 10 11 76 | Oslo | | Rosenborg | 25 | 10 |
| | | | | | | | Tottenham H | 29 | 6 |
| **Kersey** Lee | | | M | 12 8 79 | Harlow | Trainee | Tottenham H | — | — |
| **Klinsmann** Jurgen* | 6 2 | 12 13 | F | 30 7 64 | Goppingen | Gingen | Stuttgart Kickers | 61 | 22 |
| | | | | | | | Stuttgart | 156 | 79 |
| | | | | | | | Internazionale | 95 | 34 |
| | | | | | | | Monaco | 65 | 29 |
| | | | | | | | Tottenham H | 41 | 20 |
| | | | | | | | Bayern Munich | 65 | 31 |
| | | | | | | | Sampdoria | 8 | 2 |
| | | | | | | | Tottenham H | 15 | 9 |
| **Mabbutt** Gary* | 5 10 | 13 01 | D | 23 8 61 | Bristol | Apprentice | Bristol R | 131 | 10 |
| | | | | | | | Tottenham H | 477 | 27 |
| **Marriott** Alan | | | M | 3 9 78 | Bedford | Trainee | Tottenham H | — | — |
| **McVeigh** Paul | 5 6 | 10 05 | F | 6 12 77 | Belfast | Trainee | Tottenham H | 3 | 1 |
| **Nielsen** Allan | 5 8 | 11 02 | M | 13 3 71 | Esbjerg | Esbjerg | Bayern Munich | 1 | — |
| | | | | | | | Sion | — | — |
| | | | | | | | Odense | 55 | 9 |
| | | | | | | | FC Copenhagen | 26 | 3 |
| | | | | | | | Brondby | 42 | 11 |
| | | | | | | | Tottenham H | 55 | 9 |
| **Saib** Moussa | 5 9 | 11 08 | M | 5 3 69 | Theniet-El-Had | | Auxerre | 134 | 23 |
| | | | | | | | Valencia | 14 | — |
| | | | | | | | Tottenham H | 9 | 1 |
| **Scales** John | 6 2 | 13 05 | D | 4 7 66 | Harrogate | | Leeds U | — | — |
| | | | | | | | Bristol R | 72 | 2 |
| | | | | | | | Wimbledon | 240 | 11 |
| | | | | | | | Liverpool | 65 | 2 |
| | | | | | | | Tottenham H | 22 | — |
| **Sinton** Andy | 5 8 | 11 01 | M | 19 3 66 | Newcastle | Apprentice | Cambridge U | 93 | 13 |
| | | | | | | | Brentford | 149 | 28 |
| | | | | | | | QPR | 160 | 22 |
| | | | | | | | Sheffield W | 60 | 3 |
| | | | | | | | Tottenham H | 61 | 6 |
| **Vaughan** Wayne | | | M | 18 2 80 | Barking | Trainee | Tottenham H | — | — |
| **Vega** Ramon | 6 3 | 13 00 | D | 14 6 71 | Olten | Trimbach | Grasshoppers | 156 | 13 |
| | | | | | | | Cagliari | 14 | — |
| | | | | | | | Tottenham H | 33 | 4 |
| **Walker** Ian | 6 2 | 13 01 | G | 31 10 71 | Watford | Trainee | Tottenham H | 192 | — |
| | | | | | | | Oxford U (loan) | 2 | — |
| | | | | | | | Ipswich T (loan) | — | — |
| **Webb** Simon | 5 11 | 12 03 | M | 19 1 78 | Castle Bar | Trainee | Tottenham H | — | — |
| **Wilson** Clive | 5 7 | 11 04 | D | 13 11 61 | Manchester | Local | Manchester C | 98 | 9 |
| | | | | | | | Chester (loan) | 21 | 2 |
| | | | | | | | Chelsea | 81 | 5 |
| | | | | | | | Manchester C (loan) | 11 | — |
| | | | | | | | QPR | 172 | 12 |
| | | | | | | | Tottenham H | 70 | 1 |
| **Young** Luke | | | M | 19 7 79 | Harlow | Trainee | Tottenham H | — | — |

**Trainees**
Bauckham, Luke; Bernard, Narada M; Clist, Simon J; Crouch, Peter J; Dobson, Stephen G; Dormer, James S; Duffin, Ciaran; Fitzsimon, Ross J; Hillier, Ian M; Hunt, Nicholas G; Kelly, Gavin R; King, Ledley; Lee, David J; Mills, Stephen J; O'Brien, Kevin G; Piercy, John W; Poole, Glenn S; Sinclair, Jamie; Stone, Gavin; Stonebridge, Ian R; Thelwell, Alton A; Toner, Ciaran; Twidell, Daren; Wood, Paul T.

**Associated Schoolboys**
Adams, Terry P; Bowditch, Ben E; Brady, Lee J; Brennan, Martin I; Burke, Andrew J; Burnham, Sean E; Compton, Steven J; Connell, Alan J; Darbo, Roy; Galbraith, David J; Gardner, Lee R J; Gyimah, Edward; Herron, Christopher J; Hooper, Dennis D; Hughes, Mark; Marney, Dean E; Pilka, James J; Purches, John R; Quilter, James E; Suleyman, Sefki; Sutton, John W M; Thomas, Walter; Victory, Kieran; Webb, Daniel J.

**Associated Schoolboys who have accepted the club's offer of a Traineeship/Contract**
Ellis, Paul D; Jackson, Johnnie; Lacy, Neil D; Mapes, Charles E; Morley, Wayne; Saker, Blake M; Tait, Allan D; Thurgood, Stuart.

## TRANMERE ROVERS

| | | | | | | | | | |
|---|---|---|---|---|---|---|---|---|---|
| **Aldridge** John* | 5 11 | 12 03 | F | 18 9 58 | Liverpool | South Liverpool | Newport Co | 170 | 69 |
| | | | | | | | Oxford U | 114 | 72 |
| | | | | | | | Liverpool | 83 | 50 |
| | | | | | | | Real Sociedad | 63 | 33 |
| | | | | | | | Tranmere R | 242 | 138 |
| **Branch** Graham* | 6 2 | 12 02 | F | 12 2 72 | Liverpool | Heswall | Tranmere R | 102 | 10 |
| | | | | | | | Bury (loan) | 4 | 1 |
| | | | | | | | Wigan Ath (loan) | 3 | — |
| **Challinor** Dave | 6 1 | 12 00 | D | 2 10 75 | Chester | Brombrough Pool | Tranmere R | 37 | 1 |
| **Connolly** Stuart* | 5 8 | 10 09 | M | 8 12 77 | Dublin | Stella Maris | Tranmere R | — | — |
| **Coyne** Danny | 5 11 | 12 05 | G | 27 8 73 | Prestatyn | Trainee | Tranmere R | 94 | — |
| **Frail** Stephen | 5 11 | 12 03 | D | 10 8 69 | Glasgow | | Dundee | 101 | 1 |
| | | | | | | | Hearts | 54 | 4 |
| | | | | | | | Tranmere R | 6 | — |
| **Gibson** Neil | 5 11 | 10 08 | M | 11 10 79 | St Asaph | Trainee | Tranmere R | — | — |
| **Hebel** Dirk | 5 10 | 12 01 | M | 24 11 72 | Cologne | Cologne | Tranmere R | — | — |
| **Hill** Clint | 6 0 | 11 06 | D | 19 10 78 | Liverpool | Trainee | Tranmere R | 14 | — |
| **Holmes** Tommy | 6 0 | 12 08 | D | 1 9 79 | Bevington | Trainee | Tranmere R | — | — |
| **Irons** Kenny | 5 10 | 11 02 | M | 4 11 70 | Liverpool | Trainee | Tranmere R | 308 | 39 |
| **Jones** Gary | 6 3 | 13 05 | F | 10 5 75 | Chester | Trainee | Tranmere R | 121 | 20 |
| **Jones** Lee | 5 9 | 10 06 | F | 29 5 73 | Wrexham | Trainee | Wrexham | 39 | 10 |
| | | | | | | | Liverpool | 3 | — |
| | | | | | | | Crewe Alex (loan) | 8 | 1 |
| | | | | | | | Wrexham (loan) | 20 | 9 |
| | | | | | | | Wrexham (loan) | 6 | — |
| | | | | | | | Tranmere R (loan) | 8 | 5 |
| | | | | | | | Tranmere R | 34 | 9 |
| **Kelly** David | 5 11 | 11 10 | F | 25 11 65 | Birmingham | Alvechurch | Walsall | 147 | 63 |
| | | | | | | | West Ham U | 41 | 7 |
| | | | | | | | Leicester C | 66 | 22 |
| | | | | | | | Newcastle U | 70 | 35 |
| | | | | | | | Wolverhampton W | 83 | 26 |
| | | | | | | | Sunderland | 34 | 2 |
| | | | | | | | Tranmere R | 29 | 11 |
| **Koumas** Jason | 5 10 | 11 00 | F | 25 9 79 | Wrexham | Trainee | Tranmere R | — | — |
| **Mahon** Alan | 5 10 | 11 05 | M | 4 4 78 | Dublin | Crumplin U | Tranmere R | 45 | 3 |
| **Mauro** | | | M | 16 6 76 | Lisbon | Casa Pia | Tranmere R | — | — |
| **McGreal** John | 5 11 | 11 00 | D | 2 6 72 | Birkenhead | Trainee | Tranmere R | 159 | 1 |
| **McIntyre** Kevin | 5 10 | 12 00 | M | 23 12 77 | Liverpool | Trainee | Tranmere R | 2 | — |
| **Mellon** Micky | 5 10 | 12 11 | M | 18 3 72 | Paisley | Trainee | Bristol C | 35 | 1 |
| | | | | | | | WBA | 45 | 6 |
| | | | | | | | Blackpool | 124 | 14 |
| | | | | | | | Tranmere R | 33 | 2 |
| **Moran** Andy | 5 11 | 11 03 | F | 7 10 79 | Wigan | Trainee | Tranmere R | — | — |
| **Morgan** Alan | 5 10 | 11 00 | D | 2 11 73 | Aberystwyth | Trainee | Tranmere R | 24 | 1 |
| **Morrissey** John# | 5 8 | 11 09 | F | 8 3 65 | Liverpool | Apprentice | Everton | 1 | — |
| | | | | | | | Wolverhampton W | 10 | 1 |
| | | | | | | | Tranmere R | 446 | 50 |
| **Nevin** Pat | 5 6 | 11 09 | F | 6 9 63 | Glasgow | Gartcosh U | Clyde | 73 | 17 |
| *(Transferred to Kilmarnock, July 1997)* | | | | | | | Chelsea | 193 | 36 |
| | | | | | | | Everton | 109 | 16 |
| | | | | | | | Tranmere R (loan) | 8 | — |
| | | | | | | | Tranmere R | 193 | 30 |
| | | | | | | | Kilmarnock | 31 | 5 |
| **O'Brien** Liam# | 6 1 | 11 10 | M | 5 9 64 | Dublin | Shamrock R | Manchester U | 31 | 2 |
| | | | | | | | Newcastle U | 151 | 19 |
| | | | | | | | Tranmere R | 158 | 10 |
| **Parkinson** Andy | 5 8 | 10 12 | F | 27 6 79 | Liverpool | Liverpool | Tranmere R | 18 | 1 |
| **Simonsen** Steve | 6 3 | 13 02 | G | 3 4 79 | South Shields | Trainee | Tranmere R | 30 | — |
| **Stevens** Gary* | 5 11 | 11 02 | D | 27 3 63 | Barrow | Apprentice | Everton | 208 | 8 |
| | | | | | | | Rangers | 187 | 8 |
| | | | | | | | Tranmere R | 127 | 2 |

| **Teale** Shaun* | 6 0 | 13 07 | D | 10 3 64 | Southport | Weymouth | Bournemouth | 100 | 4 |
| | | | | | | | Aston Villa | 147 | 2 |
| | | | | | | | Tranmere R | 54 | — |
| | | | | | | | Preston NE (loan) | 5 | — |
| **Thompson** Andy | 5 4 | 10 06 | D | 9 11 67 | Cannock | Apprentice | WBA | 24 | 1 |
| | | | | | | | Wolverhampton W | 376 | 43 |
| | | | | | | | Tranmere R | 44 | 3 |
| **Thorn** Andy* | 6 0 | 11 06 | D | 12 11 66 | Carshalton | Apprentice | Wimbledon | 107 | 2 |
| | | | | | | | Newcastle U | 36 | 2 |
| | | | | | | | Crystal Palace | 128 | 3 |
| | | | | | | | Wimbledon | 37 | 1 |
| | | | | | | | Hearts | 1 | — |
| | | | | | | | Tranmere R | 36 | 1 |
| **Williams** Ryan | 5 5 | 11 02 | M | 31 8 78 | Chesterfield | Trainee | Mansfield T | 26 | 3 |
| | | | | | | | Tranmere R | | |

**Trainees**
Crowe, Barry E; Davies, Kevin M; Edge, Christopher; Gibbons, Frank; Graves, Stuart R; Holmes, Jamie; Jones, Darren J; Joy, Ian P; Kelly, Dominic A; Murphy, Joseph; Powell, Gareth F; Rogers, Peter N; Sharps, Ian W; Small, Glenn J; Sutcliffe, Steven O; Taylor, Perry L.

**Associated Schoolboys**
Baker, Phillip; Climo, Daniel; Cole, Lewis; Connolly, Paul; Doyle, Peter A; Dreves, Thomas; Evans, Dylan; Ewers, Delwyn G; Harrison, Daniel; Hinds, Richard P; Linwood, Paul A; Lovell, Darren B; McGregor, Andrew; Mortin, Alan J; Taylor, Michael; Thurston, Dean; Williams, Ashley L; Williams, Stewart J.

**Associated Schoolboys who have accepted the club's offer of a Traineeship/Contract**
Hay, Alexander; Taylor, Craig; Wright, Kevin.

# WALSALL

| **Blake** Mark* | 5 11 | 12 10 | M | 16 12 70 | Nottingham | Trainee | Aston Villa | 31 | 2 |
| | | | | | | | Wolverhampton W (loan) | 2 | — |
| | | | | | | | Portsmouth | 15 | — |
| | | | | | | | Leicester C | 49 | 4 |
| | | | | | | | Walsall | 61 | 5 |
| **Boli** Roger | 5 8 | 10 12 | F | 26 9 65 | Adjame | Lille | Lens | 164 | 40 |
| | | | | | | | Le Havre | 26 | 4 |
| | | | | | | | Walsall | 41 | 12 |
| **Donowa** Lou‡ | 5 9 | 11 00 | M | 24 9 64 | Ipswich | Apprentice | Norwich C | 62 | 11 |
| | | | | | | | Stoke C (loan) | 4 | 1 |
| | | | | | | Coruna, Willem II | Ipswich T | 23 | 1 |
| | | | | | | | Bristol C | 24 | 3 |
| | | | | | | | Birmingham C | 116 | 18 |
| | | | | | | | Crystal Palace (loan) | — | — |
| | | | | | | | Burnley (loan) | 4 | — |
| | | | | | | | Shrewsbury T (loan) | 4 | — |
| | | | | | | | Walsall (loan) | 6 | 1 |
| | | | | | | | Peterborough U | 22 | 1 |
| | | | | | | | Walsall | 6 | — |
| **Evans** Wayne | 5 10 | 12 00 | D | 25 8 71 | Welshpool | Welshpool | Walsall | 172 | 1 |
| **Eydelie** Jean-Jacques# | | | M | 3 2 66 | Angouleme | Sion | Walsall | 11 | — |
| **Gadsby** Matthew | 6 0 | 11 03 | D | 6 9 79 | Sutton Coldfield | Trainee | Walsall | 1 | — |
| **Hodge** John# | 5 7 | 11 13 | F | 1 4 69 | Ormskirk | Exmouth | Exeter C | 65 | 10 |
| | | | | | | | Swansea C | 112 | 10 |
| | | | | | | | Walsall | 76 | 12 |
| **Keates** Dean | 5 6 | 10 08 | M | 30 6 78 | Walsall | Trainee | Walsall | 35 | 1 |
| **Keister** John | 5 8 | 10 10 | M | 11 11 70 | Manchester | Faweh FC | Walsall | 103 | 2 |
| **Larkin** James | | | G | 23 10 75 | Canada | | Cambridge U | 1 | — |
| | | | | | | | Walsall | — | — |
| **Marsh** Chris | 5 11 | 13 05 | D | 14 1 70 | Dudley | Trainee | Walsall | 302 | 21 |
| **Mountfield** Derek* | 6 1 | 13 08 | D | 2 11 62 | Liverpool | Apprentice | Tranmere R | 26 | 1 |
| | | | | | | | Everton | 106 | 19 |
| | | | | | | | Aston Villa | 90 | 9 |
| | | | | | | | Wolverhampton W | 83 | 4 |
| | | | | | | | Carlisle U | 31 | 3 |
| | | | | | | | Northampton T | 4 | — |
| | | | | | | | Walsall | 97 | 2 |
| **Naisbitt** Daniel | 6 1 | 11 13 | G | 21 11 78 | Bishop Auckland | Trainee | Walsall | — | — |
| **Peron** Jean-Francois | 5 8 | 10 10 | M | 11 10 65 | France | | Walsall | 38 | 1 |
| **Platt** Clive | 6 4 | 13 00 | F | 27 10 77 | Wolverhampton | Trainee | Walsall | 25 | 3 |
| **Porter** Gary | 5 7 | 11 00 | M | 6 3 66 | Sunderland | Apprentice | Watford | 400 | 47 |
| | | | | | | | Walsall | 29 | 1 |
| **Ricketts** Michael | 6 3 | 13 01 | F | 4 12 78 | Birmingham | Trainee | Walsall | 36 | 3 |
| **Rogers** Darren‡ | 5 11 | 13 02 | D | 9 4 70 | Birmingham | Trainee | WBA | 14 | 1 |
| | | | | | | | Birmingham C | 18 | — |
| | | | | | | | Wycombe W (loan) | 1 | — |
| | | | | | | | Walsall | 58 | — |
| **Roper** Ian | 6 3 | 13 04 | D | 20 6 77 | Nuneaton | Trainee | Walsall | 37 | — |
| **Ryder** Stuart* | 6 1 | 12 09 | D | 6 11 73 | Sutton Coldfield | Trainee | Walsall | 101 | 5 |

| Name | | | Pos | Birth date | Birthplace | Signed from | Club | Apps | Gls |
|---|---|---|---|---|---|---|---|---|---|
| Smith Mark‡ | 6 1 | 13 09 | G | 2 1 73 | Birmingham | Trainee | Nottingham F | — | — |
| | | | | | | | Crewe Alex | 63 | — |
| | | | | | | | Walsall | — | — |
| Tholot Didier# | | | F | 2 4 64 | Feurs | Sion | Walsall | 14 | 4 |
| Thomas Wayne | 5 9 | 12 07 | M | 28 8 78 | Manchester | Trainee | Walsall | 25 | — |
| Viveash Adrian | 6 2 | 12 12 | D | 30 9 69 | Swindon | Trainee | Swindon T | 54 | 2 |
| | | | | | | | Reading (loan) | 5 | — |
| | | | | | | | Reading (loan) | 6 | — |
| | | | | | | | Barnsley (loan) | 2 | 1 |
| | | | | | | | Walsall | 119 | 12 |
| Walker James | 5 11 | 13 02 | G | 9 7 73 | Nottingham | Trainee | Notts Co | — | — |
| | | | | | | | Walsall | 143 | — |
| Watson Andy# | 5 9 | 12 06 | F | 1 4 67 | Leeds | Harrogate T | Halifax T | 83 | 15 |
| | | | | | | | Swansea C | 14 | 1 |
| | | | | | | | Carlisle U | 56 | 22 |
| | | | | | | | Blackpool | 115 | 43 |
| | | | | | | | Walsall | 63 | 12 |

**Trainees**
Bowen, Adam P; Carter, Alfonso J; Cooper, Ian A; Danks, Paul R; Davies, Thomas D; Edwards, Gary S; Gozzard, Paul J; Osbourne, Lee M; Scott, Dion E; Smith, Richard D L; Southwick, Matthew L; Turner, Andrew J; Ulfig, Steven P; Wood, Richard D.

**Associated Schoolboys**
Bishop, Andrew J; Bissell, James; Ford, Craig; Garbett, Ian J; Hodgetts, Andrew J; Jones, Craig R; Krasnowski, Andrew M; Reid, Warren; Smith, Nicholas A; Whitehouse, Mark T.

**Associated Schoolboys who have accepted the club's offer of a Traineeship/Contract**
Birch, Gary S; Hawley, Carl L.

# WATFORD

| Name | | | Pos | Birth date | Birthplace | Signed from | Club | Apps | Gls |
|---|---|---|---|---|---|---|---|---|---|
| Andrews Wayne | 5 8 | 11 07 | F | 25 11 77 | Paddington | Trainee | Watford | 28 | 4 |
| Bazeley Darren | 5 10 | 11 07 | D | 5 10 72 | Northampton | Trainee | Watford | 200 | 19 |
| Chamberlain Alec | 6 2 | 13 10 | G | 20 6 64 | March | Ramsey T | Ipswich T | — | — |
| | | | | | | | Colchester U | 184 | — |
| | | | | | | | Everton | — | — |
| | | | | | | | Tranmere R (loan) | 15 | — |
| | | | | | | | Luton T | 138 | — |
| | | | | | | | Chelsea (loan) | — | — |
| | | | | | | | Sunderland | 90 | — |
| | | | | | | | Liverpool (loan) | — | — |
| | | | | | | | Watford | 50 | — |
| Day Chris | 6 2 | 13 06 | G | 28 7 75 | Whipps Cross | Trainee | Tottenham H | — | — |
| | | | | | | | Crystal Palace | 24 | — |
| | | | | | | | Watford | — | — |
| Easton Clint | 6 0 | 10 04 | M | 1 10 77 | Barking | Trainee | Watford | 29 | 1 |
| Flash Richard* | 5 9 | 11 08 | M | 8 4 76 | Birmingham | Trainee | Manchester U | — | — |
| | | | | | | | Wolverhampton W | — | — |
| | | | | | | | Watford | 1 | — |
| | | | | | | | Lincoln C (loan) | 5 | — |
| Gibbs Nigel# | 5 6 | 11 06 | D | 20 11 65 | St Albans | Apprentice | Watford | 374 | 5 |
| Grieves Daniel | 5 9 | 10 07 | F | 21 9 78 | Watford | Trainee | Watford | — | — |
| Gudmundsson Johann | 5 9 | 13 00 | M | 7 12 77 | Reykjavik | | Keflavik | 49 | 13 |
| | | | | | | | Watford | — | — |
| Hazan Alon | 6 0 | 13 08 | M | 14 9 67 | Ashdod | Ironi Ashdod | Watford | 10 | — |
| Hyde Micah | 5 9 | 11 07 | M | 10 11 74 | Newham | Trainee | Cambridge U | 107 | 13 |
| | | | | | | | Watford | 40 | 4 |
| Iga Andrew* | | | G | 9 12 77 | Kampala | Trainee | Millwall | 1 | — |
| | | | | | | | Gillingham | — | — |
| | | | | | | | Watford | — | — |
| Johnson Andy‡ | 5 9 | 12 01 | F | 25 1 79 | Brighton | Trainee | Watford | — | — |
| Johnson Chris‡ | 5 9 | 12 03 | M | 25 1 79 | Brighton | Trainee | Watford | 1 | — |
| Johnson Richard | 6 0 | 11 13 | M | 27 4 74 | Kurri Kurri | Trainee | Watford | 164 | 13 |
| Kennedy Peter | 5 8 | 11 11 | M | 10 9 73 | Lisburn | Portadown | Notts Co | 22 | — |
| | | | | | | | Watford | 34 | 11 |
| Lee Jason | 6 3 | 13 03 | F | 9 5 71 | Newham | Trainee | Charlton Ath | 1 | — |
| | | | | | | | Stockport Co (loan) | 2 | — |
| | | | | | | | Lincoln C | 93 | 21 |
| | | | | | | | Southend U | 24 | 3 |
| | | | | | | | Nottingham F | 76 | 14 |
| | | | | | | | Charlton Ath (loan) | 8 | 3 |
| | | | | | | | Grimsby T (loan) | 7 | 1 |
| | | | | | | | Watford | 36 | 10 |
| Ljung Per-Ola‡ | | | M | 7 11 67 | Almhult | Helsingborg | Watford | — | — |
| Lowndes Nathan | 5 11 | 10 04 | F | 2 6 77 | Salford | Trainee | Leeds U | — | — |
| | | | | | | | Watford | 7 | — |
| Ludden Dominic* | 5 7 | 10 09 | D | 30 3 74 | Basildon | Trainee | Leyton Orient | 58 | 1 |
| | | | | | | | Watford | 33 | — |
| Melvang Lars‡ | 5 9 | 11 06 | D | 3 4 69 | Seattle | | Silkeborg | 140 | 6 |
| | | | | | | | Watford | 4 | 1 |

| Player | Ht | Wt | Pos | Born | Birthplace | Source | Club | Apps | Gls |
|---|---|---|---|---|---|---|---|---|---|
| **Millen** Keith | 6 2 | 12 04 | D | 26 9 66 | Croydon | Juniors | Brentford | 305 | 17 |
| | | | | | | | Watford | 154 | 4 |
| **Mooney** Tommy | 5 9 | 12 10 | D | 11 8 71 | Teesside North | Trainee | Aston Villa | — | — |
| | | | | | | | Scarborough | 107 | 30 |
| | | | | | | | Southend U | 14 | 5 |
| | | | | | | | Watford (loan) | 10 | 2 |
| | | | | | | | Watford | 153 | 28 |
| **Noel-Williams** Gifton | 6 1 | 14 06 | F | 21 1 80 | Islington | Trainee | Watford | 63 | 9 |
| **Page** Robert | 6 0 | 12 05 | D | 3 9 74 | Llwynipia | Trainee | Watford | 105 | — |
| **Palmer** Steve# | 6 1 | 12 13 | D | 31 3 68 | Brighton | Cambridge University | Ipswich T | 111 | 2 |
| | | | | | | | Watford | 117 | 5 |
| **Perpetuini** David | 5 8 | 10 00 | M | 26 9 79 | Hitchin | Trainee | Watford | — | — |
| **Pluck** Colin | 6 0 | 12 10 | D | 6 9 78 | London | Trainee | Watford | 1 | — |
| **Robinson** Paul | 5 9 | 12 11 | M | 14 12 78 | Watford | Trainee | Watford | 34 | 2 |
| **Rooney** Mark* | 5 10 | 10 10 | D | 19 5 78 | Lambeth | Trainee | Watford | — | — |
| **Rosenthal** Ronny | 5 11 | 12 13 | F | 4 10 63 | Haifa | Standard Liege | Luton T (loan) | — | — |
| | | | | | | | Liverpool (loan) | 8 | 7 |
| | | | | | | | Liverpool | 66 | 14 |
| | | | | | | | Tottenham H | 88 | 4 |
| | | | | | | | Watford | 25 | 8 |
| **Slater** Stuart | 5 8 | 10 05 | M | 27 3 69 | Sudbury | Apprentice | West Ham U | 141 | 11 |
| | | | | | | | Celtic | 43 | 3 |
| | | | | | | | Ipswich T | 72 | 4 |
| | | | | | | | Leicester C | — | — |
| | | | | | | | Watford | 30 | 1 |
| **Smith** Tommy | 5 8 | 10 00 | M | 22 5 80 | Hemel Hempsted | Trainee | Watford | 1 | — |
| **Squires** Oliver | 5 11 | 12 03 | M | 15 9 80 | Harrow | Trainee | Watford | — | — |
| **Talboys** Steve‡ | 5 11 | 11 10 | M | 18 9 66 | Bristol | Gloucester C | Wimbledon | 26 | 1 |
| | | | | | | | Watford | 5 | — |
| **Thomas** David | 5 11 | 12 07 | F | 26 9 75 | Caerphilly | Trainee | Swansea C | 56 | 10 |
| | | | | | | | Watford | 16 | 3 |
| **Ward** Darran | 6 3 | 12 10 | D | 13 9 78 | Kenton | Trainee | Watford | 8 | — |

**Trainees**
Boyce, Mark D; Brooker, Stephen M L; Collis, Stephen P; Cornock, Grant L W; Farley, Craig; Johnson, Lee D; Langston, Matthew J; Marsh, David K; Maynard, Stuart A C; Murphy, Mitchell E; Ougham, James B; Panayi, Sofroni; Reid, Lewis I; Tipton, Daniel P.

**Associated Schoolboys**
Beadle, Garry P; Buxton, Nicholas J; Coltman, Mark J; Deamer, William D; Doyley, Lloyd; Francis, Anthony N; Goldsmith, Lee F; Gruar, Danny; Hand, Jamie; Leach, Marc T; Lee, Richard A; Lonergan, Sean; Norville, Jason; Saunders, Neil C; Sinclair, Steve; Smith, Jack D; Swannell, Sam A.

**Associated Schoolboys who have accepted the club's offer of a Traineeship/Contract**
Brathwaite, Daniel S; Dickie, James P; Ettienne, Leon A; Fisken, Gary S; Forde, Fabian W; Neill, Thomas E.

# WEST BROMWICH ALBION

| Player | Ht | Wt | Pos | Born | Birthplace | Source | Club | Apps | Gls |
|---|---|---|---|---|---|---|---|---|---|
| **Adamson** Christopher | 5 11 | 11 00 | G | 4 11 78 | Ashington | Trainee | WBA | 3 | — |
| **Bennett** Dean‡ | 5 10 | 11 00 | F | 13 12 77 | Wolverhampton | | WBA | 1 | — |
| **Bowman** Darren* | | | M | 4 11 78 | Abergavenny | Trainee | WBA | — | — |
| **Burgess** Daryl | 5 11 | 12 04 | D | 20 4 71 | Birmingham | Trainee | WBA | 283 | 9 |
| **Butler** Peter | 5 9 | 11 02 | M | 27 8 66 | Halifax | Apprentice | Huddersfield T | 5 | — |
| | | | | | | | Cambridge U (loan) | 14 | 1 |
| | | | | | | | Bury | 11 | — |
| | | | | | | | Cambridge U | 55 | 9 |
| | | | | | | | Southend U | 142 | 9 |
| | | | | | | | Huddersfield T (loan) | 7 | — |
| | | | | | | | West Ham U | 70 | 3 |
| | | | | | | | Notts Co | 20 | — |
| | | | | | | | Grimsby T (loan) | 3 | — |
| | | | | | | | WBA (loan) | 9 | — |
| | | | | | | | WBA | 51 | — |
| **Carbon** Matt | 6 2 | 12 05 | D | 8 6 75 | Nottingham | Trainee | Lincoln C | 69 | 10 |
| | | | | | | | Derby Co | 20 | — |
| | | | | | | | WBA | 16 | 1 |
| **Carr** Franz‡ | 5 6 | 11 10 | F | 24 9 66 | Preston | Apprentice | Blackburn R | — | — |
| | | | | | | | Nottingham F | 131 | 17 |
| | | | | | | | Sheffield W (loan) | 12 | — |
| | | | | | | | West Ham U (loan) | 3 | — |
| | | | | | | | Newcastle U | 25 | 3 |
| | | | | | | | Sheffield U | 18 | 4 |
| | | | | | | | Leicester C (loan) | 13 | 1 |
| | | | | | | | Aston Villa | 3 | — |
| | | | | | | | Reggiana | 6 | — |
| | | | | | | | Bolton W | 5 | — |
| | | | | | | | WBA | 4 | — |

| | | | | | | | | |
|---|---|---|---|---|---|---|---|---|
| **Coldicott** Stacy | 5 8 | 11 04 | M | 29 4 74 | Redditch | Trainee | WBA | 104 | 3 |
| | | | | | | | Cardiff C (loan) | 6 | — |
| **Crichton** Paul | 6 1 | 12 02 | G | 3 10 68 | Pontefract | Apprentice | Nottingham F | — | — |
| | | | | | | | Notts Co (loan) | 5 | — |
| | | | | | | | Darlington (loan) | 5 | — |
| | | | | | | | Peterborough U (loan) | 4 | — |
| | | | | | | | Darlington (loan) | 3 | — |
| | | | | | | | Swindon T (loan) | 4 | — |
| | | | | | | | Rotherham U (loan) | 6 | — |
| | | | | | | | Torquay U (loan) | 13 | — |
| | | | | | | | Peterborough U | 47 | — |
| | | | | | | | Doncaster R | 77 | — |
| | | | | | | | Grimsby T | 133 | — |
| | | | | | | | WBA | 32 | — |
| | | | | | | | Aston Villa (loan) | — | — |
| **Dobson** Tony | 6 1 | 13 07 | D | 5 2 69 | Coventry | Apprentice | Coventry C | 54 | 1 |
| | | | | | | | Blackburn R | 41 | — |
| | | | | | | | Portsmouth | 53 | 2 |
| | | | | | | | Oxford U (loan) | 5 | — |
| | | | | | | | Peterborough U (loan) | 4 | — |
| | | | | | | | WBA | 11 | — |
| **Evans** Michael | 6 0 | 13 05 | F | 1 1 73 | Plymouth | Trainee | Plymouth Arg | 163 | 38 |
| | | | | | | | Blackburn R (loan) | — | — |
| | | | | | | | Southampton | 22 | 4 |
| | | | | | | | WBA | 10 | 1 |
| **Flynn** Sean | 5 8 | 11 08 | M | 13 3 68 | Birmingham | Halesowen T | Coventry C | 97 | 9 |
| | | | | | | | Derby Co | 59 | 3 |
| | | | | | | | Stoke C (loan) | 5 | — |
| | | | | | | | WBA | 35 | 2 |
| **Germaine** Gary* | 6 0 | 11 07 | G | 2 8 76 | Birmingham | Trainee | WBA | — | — |
| | | | | | | | Scunthorpe U (loan) | 11 | — |
| | | | | | | | Shrewsbury T (loan) | 1 | — |
| **Gilbert** Dave* | 5 4 | 10 08 | M | 22 6 63 | Lincoln | Apprentice | Lincoln C | 30 | 1 |
| | | | | | | | Scunthorpe U | 1 | — |
| | | | | | | Boston U | Northampton T | 120 | 21 |
| | | | | | | | Grimsby T | 259 | 41 |
| | | | | | | | WBA | 62 | 6 |
| | | | | | | | York C (loan) | 9 | 1 |
| | | | | | | | Grimsby T (loan) | 5 | — |
| **Holmes** Paul | 5 10 | 11 00 | D | 18 2 68 | Stocksbridge | Apprentice | Doncaster R | 47 | 1 |
| | | | | | | | Torquay U | 138 | 4 |
| | | | | | | | Birmingham C | 12 | — |
| | | | | | | | Everton | 21 | — |
| | | | | | | | WBA | 86 | 1 |
| **Hughes** Lee | 5 10 | 11 06 | F | 22 5 76 | Birmingham | Kidderminster H | WBA | 37 | 14 |
| **Hunt** Andy# | 6 0 | 11 02 | F | 9 6 70 | Thurrock | Kettering T | Newcastle U | 43 | 11 |
| | | | | | | | WBA (loan) | 10 | 9 |
| | | | | | | | WBA | 202 | 67 |
| **James** Anthony* | | | M | 9 10 78 | Pontypool | Trainee | WBA | — | — |
| **Kilbane** Kevin | 6 0 | 12 07 | F | 1 2 77 | Preston | Trainee | Preston NE | 47 | 3 |
| | | | | | | | WBA | 43 | 4 |
| **Mardon** Paul | 6 0 | 11 10 | D | 14 9 69 | Bristol | Trainee | Bristol C | 42 | — |
| | | | | | | | Doncaster R (loan) | 3 | — |
| | | | | | | | Birmingham C | 64 | — |
| | | | | | | | WBA | 121 | 3 |
| **McDermott** Andy | 5 9 | 11 03 | D | 24 3 77 | Sydney | Aust Inst of Sport | QPR | 6 | 2 |
| | | | | | | | WBA | 19 | — |
| **Miller** Alan | 6 3 | 14 06 | G | 29 3 70 | Epping | Trainee | Arsenal | 8 | — |
| | | | | | | | Plymouth Arg (loan) | 13 | — |
| | | | | | | | WBA (loan) | 3 | — |
| | | | | | | | Birmingham C (loan) | 15 | — |
| | | | | | | | Middlesbrough | 57 | — |
| | | | | | | | Huddersfield T (loan) | — | — |
| | | | | | | | Grimsby T (loan) | 3 | — |
| | | | | | | | WBA | 53 | — |
| **Murphy** Shaun | 6 1 | 12 00 | D | 5 11 70 | Sydney | Perth Italia | Notts Co | 109 | 5 |
| | | | | | | | WBA | 34 | 3 |
| **Nicholson** Shane* | 5 10 | 11 10 | D | 3 6 70 | Newark | Trainee | Lincoln C | 133 | 6 |
| | | | | | | | Derby Co | 74 | 1 |
| | | | | | | | WBA | 52 | — |
| **Potter** Graham | 6 1 | 11 12 | D | 20 5 75 | Solihull | Trainee | Birmingham C | 25 | 2 |
| | | | | | | | Wycombe W (loan) | 3 | — |
| | | | | | | | Stoke C | 45 | 1 |
| | | | | | | | Southampton | 8 | — |
| | | | | | | | WBA | 11 | — |
| | | | | | | | Northampton T (loan) | 4 | — |
| **Quailey** Brian | 6 0 | 12 10 | F | 21 3 78 | Leicester | Nuneaton B | WBA | 5 | — |
| **Quinn** James | 6 1 | 12 10 | F | 15 12 74 | Coventry | Trainee | Birmingham C | 4 | — |
| | | | | | | | Blackpool | 151 | 37 |
| | | | | | | | Stockport Co (loan) | 1 | — |
| | | | | | | | WBA | 13 | 2 |
| **Raven** Paul | 6 1 | 12 11 | D | 28 7 70 | Salisbury | School | Doncaster R | 52 | 4 |
| | | | | | | | WBA | 220 | 14 |
| | | | | | | | Doncaster R (loan) | 7 | — |

| Sneekes Richard | 5 11 | 12 03 | M | 30 10 68 | Amsterdam | | Ajax | 3 | — |
|---|---|---|---|---|---|---|---|---|---|
| | | | | | | | Volendam | 31 | 7 |
| | | | | | | | Fortuna Sittard | 126 | 20 |
| | | | | | | Locarno | Bolton W | 55 | 7 |
| | | | | | | | WBA | 100 | 21 |
| Taylor Bob# | 5 10 | 12 12 | F | 3 2 67 | Easington | Horden CW | Leeds U | 42 | 9 |
| | | | | | | | Bristol C | 106 | 50 |
| | | | | | | | WBA | 238 | 96 |
| | | | | | | | Bolton W (loan) | 12 | 3 |
| Van Blerk Jason | 6 1 | 13 00 | D | 16 3 68 | Sydney | Go Ahead | Millwall | 73 | 2 |
| | | | | | | | Manchester C | 19 | — |
| | | | | | | | WBA | 8 | — |

**Trainees**
Abercrombie, Garry B; Ball, Richard; Blake, Marvin A; Chambers, Adam C; Chambers, James A; Cooper, James L; Gabbidon, Daniel L; Garrity, Michael; Heath, Dominic; Ince, James; Joynson, Dean; Lowndes, Jamie A; McNamara, Ricky P; McWilliams, Jamie K; Morris, Elliott J; Oliver, Adam; Porter, Karl; Richards, Justin.

**Associated Schoolboys**
Dudley, Matthew; Evans, Richard; Hadley, Darren; James, Dale J; Orton, Neil S; Pearson, Adam; Reid, Jason; Russell, Christopher M; Showell, Steven J; Smith, Daniel S; Stewart, Craig; Turton, Adam P; Withers, Lee T.

**Associated Schoolboys who have accepted the club's offer of a Traineeship/Contract**
Briggs, Mark; Scott, Mark.

# WEST HAM UNITED

| Abou Samassi | 6 0 | 11 05 | F | 4 8 73 | Gagnoa | | Cannes | 37 | 5 |
|---|---|---|---|---|---|---|---|---|---|
| | | | | | | | West Ham U | 19 | 5 |
| Alves Paolo‡ | 6 1 | 11 07 | F | 10 12 69 | Mateus Villareal | Sporting Lisbon | West Ham U | 4 | — |
| Berkovic Eyal | 5 7 | 10 02 | M | 2 4 72 | Haifa | | Maccabi Haifa | 128 | 25 |
| | | | | | | | Southampton | 28 | 4 |
| | | | | | | | West Ham U | 35 | 7 |
| Berthe Mohamed* | | | M | 12 9 72 | Guyana | Gaz Ajaccio | West Ham U | — | — |
| Boogers Marco* | 6 1 | 12 00 | M | 12 1 67 | Dordrecht | | DS 79 | 60 | 18 |
| | | | | | | | Utrecht | 60 | 15 |
| | | | | | | | RKC | 33 | 14 |
| | | | | | | | Fortuna Sittard | 29 | 13 |
| | | | | | | | RKC | 71 | 32 |
| | | | | | | | Sparta | 25 | 11 |
| | | | | | | | West Ham U | 4 | — |
| Boylan Lee | | | F | 2 9 78 | Chelmsford | Trainee | West Ham U | 1 | — |
| Breacker Tim | 5 11 | 13 00 | D | 2 7 65 | Bicester | Apprentice | Luton T | 210 | 3 |
| | | | | | | | West Ham U | 237 | 8 |
| Coyne Chris | 6 1 | 13 10 | D | 20 12 78 | Brisbane | Perth SC | West Ham U | — | — |
| Dicks Julian | 5 10 | 13 00 | D | 8 8 68 | Bristol | Apprentice | Birmingham C | 89 | 1 |
| | | | | | | | West Ham U | 159 | 29 |
| | | | | | | | Liverpool | 24 | 3 |
| | | | | | | | West Ham U | 94 | 21 |
| Etherington Craig | | | M | 16 9 79 | Essex | Trainee | West Ham U | — | — |
| Ferdinand Rio | 6 2 | 12 00 | D | 7 11 78 | Peckham | Trainee | West Ham U | 51 | 2 |
| | | | | | | | Bournemouth (loan) | 10 | — |
| Finn Neil* | | | G | 29 12 78 | London | Trainee | West Ham U | 1 | — |
| Forrest Craig | 6 5 | 14 00 | G | 20 9 67 | Vancouver | Apprentice | Ipswich T | 263 | — |
| | | | | | | | Colchester U (loan) | 11 | — |
| | | | | | | | Chelsea (loan) | 3 | — |
| | | | | | | | West Ham U | 13 | — |
| Goodwin Lee* | | | M | 5 9 78 | Stepney | Trainee | West Ham U | — | — |
| Hall Richard | 6 2 | 13 11 | D | 14 3 72 | Ipswich | Trainee | Scunthorpe U | 22 | 3 |
| | | | | | | | Southampton | 126 | 12 |
| | | | | | | | West Ham U | 7 | — |
| Hartson John | 6 1 | 14 06 | F | 5 4 75 | Swansea | Trainee | Luton T | 54 | 11 |
| | | | | | | | Arsenal | 53 | 14 |
| | | | | | | | West Ham U | 43 | 20 |
| Henry Anthony | | | D | 13 9 79 | London | Trainee | West Ham U | — | — |
| Hodges Lee | 5 5 | 10 02 | F | 2 3 78 | Newham | Trainee | West Ham U | 2 | — |
| | | | | | | | Exeter C (loan) | 17 | — |
| | | | | | | | Leyton Orient (loan) | 3 | — |
| | | | | | | | Plymouth Arg (loan) | 9 | — |
| Impey Andrew | 5 8 | 11 02 | D | 13 9 71 | Hammersmith | Yeading | QPR | 187 | 13 |
| | | | | | | | West Ham U | 19 | — |
| Keith Joseph | | | D | 1 10 78 | London | Trainee | West Ham U | — | — |
| Kitson Paul | 5 11 | 10 12 | F | 9 1 71 | Murton | Trainee | Leicester C | 50 | 6 |
| | | | | | | | Derby Co | 105 | 36 |
| | | | | | | | Newcastle U | 36 | 10 |
| | | | | | | | West Ham U | 27 | 12 |

| Name | | | | | | | Club | Apps | Gls |
|---|---|---|---|---|---|---|---|---|---|
| **Lama** Bernard* | 6 3 | 12 05 | G | 7 4 63 | St Symphoricu | | Lille | 103 | 1 |
| | | | | | | | Metz | 38 | — |
| | | | | | | | Brest | 38 | — |
| | | | | | | | Lens | 36 | 1 |
| | | | | | | | Paris St Germain | 177 | — |
| | | | | | | | West Ham U | 12 | — |
| **Lampard** Frank | 6 0 | 11 12 | M | 20 6 78 | Romford | Trainee | West Ham U | 46 | 4 |
| | | | | | | | Swansea C (loan) | 9 | 1 |
| **Lazaridis** Stan | 5 9 | 12 00 | D | 16 8 72 | Perth | West Adelaide | West Ham U | 54 | 3 |
| **Lomas** Steve | 6 0 | 12 08 | M | 18 1 74 | Hanover | Trainee | Manchester C | 111 | 8 |
| | | | | | | | West Ham U | 40 | 2 |
| **McFarlane** Anthony* | | | M | 24 3 79 | London | Trainee | West Ham U | — | — |
| **Mean** Scott | 5 11 | 13 08 | M | 13 12 73 | Crawley | Trainee | Bournemouth | 74 | 8 |
| | | | | | | | West Ham U | 3 | — |
| **Miklosko** Ludek | 6 5 | 14 00 | G | 9 12 61 | Protesov | Banik Ostrava | West Ham U | 315 | — |
| **Moncur** John | 5 7 | 9 10 | M | 22 9 66 | Stepney | Apprentice | Tottenham H | 21 | 1 |
| | | | | | | | Cambridge U (loan) | 4 | — |
| | | | | | | | Doncaster R (loan) | 4 | — |
| | | | | | | | Portsmouth (loan) | 7 | — |
| | | | | | | | Brentford (loan) | 5 | 1 |
| | | | | | | | Ipswich T (loan) | 6 | — |
| | | | | | | | Nottingham F (loan) | — | — |
| | | | | | | | Swindon T | 58 | 5 |
| | | | | | | | West Ham U | 97 | 5 |
| **Moore** Jason* | 5 8 | 11 04 | D | 16 2 79 | Dover | Trainee | West Ham U | — | — |
| **Omoyimni** Emmanuel | 5 6 | 10 07 | F | 28 12 77 | Nigeria | Trainee | West Ham U | 6 | 2 |
| | | | | | | | Bournemouth (loan) | 7 | — |
| | | | | | | | Dundee U (loan) | 4 | — |
| **Partridge** David‡ | | | M | 26 11 78 | Westminster | Trainee | West Ham U | — | — |
| **Pearce** Ian | 6 4 | 14 04 | D | 7 5 74 | Bury St Edmunds | Schoolboy | Chelsea | 4 | — |
| | | | | | | | Blackburn R | 62 | 2 |
| | | | | | | | West Ham U | 30 | 1 |
| **Philson** Graeme‡ | 5 10 | 11 00 | D | 24 3 75 | Ireland | Coleraine | West Ham U | — | — |
| **Potts** Steve | 5 7 | 10 11 | D | 7 5 67 | Hartford (USA) | Apprentice | West Ham U | 355 | 1 |
| **Rieper** Marc | 6 3 | 13 10 | D | 5 6 68 | Denmark | Aarhus | Brondby | 81 | 3 |
| *(Transferred to Celtic, September 1997)* | | | | | | | West Ham U | 90 | 5 |
| | | | | | | | Celtic | 30 | 2 |
| **Sealey** Les | 6 1 | 13 06 | G | 29 9 57 | Bethnal Green | Apprentice | Coventry C | 158 | — |
| | | | | | | | Luton T | 207 | — |
| | | | | | | | Plymouth Arg (loan) | 6 | — |
| | | | | | | | Manchester U (loan) | 2 | — |
| | | | | | | | Manchester U | 31 | — |
| | | | | | | | Aston Villa | 18 | — |
| | | | | | | | Coventry C (loan) | 2 | — |
| | | | | | | | Birmingham C (loan) | 12 | — |
| | | | | | | | Manchester U | — | — |
| | | | | | | | Blackpool | 7 | — |
| | | | | | | | West Ham U | 2 | — |
| | | | | | | | Leyton Orient | 12 | — |
| | | | | | | | West Ham U | 2 | — |
| | | | | | | | Bury (loan) | — | — |
| **Sinclair** Trevor | 5 10 | 12 10 | F | 2 3 73 | Dulwich | Trainee | Blackpool | 112 | 15 |
| | | | | | | | QPR | 167 | 16 |
| | | | | | | | West Ham U | 14 | 7 |
| **Unsworth** David | 6 0 | 14 00 | D | 16 10 73 | Chorley | Trainee | Everton | 116 | 11 |
| | | | | | | | West Ham U | 32 | 2 |

**Trainees**
Alexander, Gary G; Angus, Stevland D; Bartley, Daniel R; Briggs, Ryan D; Byrne, Shaun R; Carrick, Michael; Fernley, Daniel P; Forbes, Terrell; Garcia, Richard; Gray, Edward J R; Hudson, Anthony P; McCann, Grant S; Miller, Robert; Newton, Adam L; O'Reilly, Alexander; Purches, Stephen R; Wells, Andrew R.

**Associated Schoolboys**
Abul, Koya; Cleaver, Dean; Kelly, Adam J R; Lee, Philip C; Tobolewski, Ross.

**Associated Schoolboys who have accepted the club's offer of a Traineeship/Contract**
Birch, Francis A; Cole, Joseph J; Cooper, Ashley D; Iriekpen, Ezomo; Richards, Lee J; Taylor, Sam A J.

# WIGAN ATHLETIC

| Name | | | | | | | Club | Apps | Gls |
|---|---|---|---|---|---|---|---|---|---|
| **Barlow** Stuart | 5 10 | 10 12 | F | 16 7 68 | Liverpool | School | Everton | 71 | 10 |
| | | | | | | | Rotherham U (loan) | — | — |
| | | | | | | | Oldham Ath | 93 | 31 |
| | | | | | | | Wigan Ath | 9 | 3 |
| **Black** Tony‡ | 5 8 | 11 01 | F | 15 7 69 | Barrow | Bamber Bridge | Wigan Ath | 31 | 2 |
| **Bradshaw** Carl | 5 10 | 11 11 | D | 2 10 68 | Sheffield | Apprentice | Sheffield W | 32 | 4 |
| | | | | | | | Barnsley (loan) | 6 | 1 |
| | | | | | | | Manchester C | 5 | — |
| | | | | | | | Sheffield U | 147 | 8 |
| | | | | | | | Norwich C | 65 | 2 |
| | | | | | | | Wigan Ath | 28 | 1 |

| Name | | | | | Birthplace | From | Club | Apps | Gls |
|---|---|---|---|---|---|---|---|---|---|
| **Butler** Lee | 6 2 | 13 00 | G | 30 5 66 | Sheffield | Haworth Colliery | Lincoln C | 30 | — |
| | | | | | | | Aston Villa | 8 | — |
| | | | | | | | Hull C (loan) | 4 | — |
| | | | | | | | Barnsley | 120 | — |
| | | | | | | | Scunthorpe U (loan) | 2 | — |
| | | | | | | | Wigan Ath | 63 | — |
| **Carroll** Roy | 6 2 | 11 09 | G | 30 9 77 | Enniskillen | Trainee | Hull C | 46 | — |
| | | | | | | | Wigan Ath | 29 | — |
| **Diaz** Isidro* | 5 7 | 9 04 | M | 15 5 72 | Valencia | Balaguer | Wigan Ath | 76 | 16 |
| | | | | | | | Wolverhampton W | 1 | — |
| | | | | | | | Wigan Ath | 2 | — |
| **Farnworth** Simon* | 5 11 | 13 04 | G | 28 10 63 | Chorley | Apprentice | Bolton W | 113 | — |
| | | | | | | | Stockport Co (loan) | 10 | — |
| | | | | | | | Tranmere R (loan) | 7 | — |
| | | | | | | | Bury | 105 | — |
| | | | | | | | Preston NE | 81 | — |
| | | | | | | | Wigan Ath | 126 | — |
| **Fitzhenry** Neil | 6 0 | 12 00 | D | 24 9 78 | Billinge | Trainee | Wigan Ath | 3 | — |
| **Green** Scott | 5 10 | 12 05 | D | 15 1 70 | Walsall | Trainee | Derby Co | — | — |
| | | | | | | | Bolton W | 220 | 25 |
| | | | | | | | Wigan Ath | 38 | 1 |
| **Greenall** Colin* | 5 11 | 12 12 | D | 30 12 63 | Billinge | Apprentice | Blackpool | 183 | 9 |
| | | | | | | | Gillingham | 62 | 4 |
| | | | | | | | Oxford U | 67 | 2 |
| | | | | | | | Bury (loan) | 3 | — |
| | | | | | | | Bury | 68 | 5 |
| | | | | | | | Preston NE | 29 | 1 |
| | | | | | | | Chester C | 42 | 1 |
| | | | | | | | Lincoln C | 43 | 3 |
| | | | | | | | Wigan Ath | 122 | 8 |
| **Johnson** Gavin‡ | 5 11 | 11 07 | D | 10 10 70 | Eye | Trainee | Ipswich T | 132 | 11 |
| | | | | | | | Luton T | 5 | — |
| | | | | | | | Wigan Ath | 84 | 8 |
| **Jones** Graeme | 6 0 | 12 12 | F | 13 3 70 | Gateshead | Bridlington T | Doncaster R | 92 | 26 |
| | | | | | | | Wigan Ath | 73 | 40 |
| **Kilford** Ian# | 5 10 | 11 00 | M | 6 10 73 | Bristol | Trainee | Nottingham F | 1 | — |
| | | | | | | | Wigan Ath (loan) | 8 | 3 |
| | | | | | | | Wigan Ath | 125 | 26 |
| **Lee** David | 5 7 | 11 00 | F | 5 11 67 | Whitefield | Blackburn Schools | Bury | 208 | 35 |
| | | | | | | | Southampton | 20 | — |
| | | | | | | | Bolton W | 155 | 17 |
| | | | | | | | Wigan Ath | 43 | 5 |
| **Lowe** David | 5 10 | 11 04 | F | 30 8 65 | Liverpool | Apprentice | Wigan Ath | 188 | 40 |
| | | | | | | | Ipswich T | 134 | 37 |
| | | | | | | | Port Vale (loan) | 9 | 2 |
| | | | | | | | Leicester C | 94 | 22 |
| | | | | | | | Port Vale (loan) | 19 | 5 |
| | | | | | | | Wigan Ath | 92 | 25 |
| **Martinez** Roberto | 5 11 | 11 12 | M | 13 7 73 | Balaguer | Balaguer | Wigan Ath | 118 | 14 |
| **McGibbon** Pat | 6 1 | 13 02 | D | 6 9 73 | Lurgan | Portadown | Manchester U | — | — |
| | | | | | | | Swansea C (loan) | 1 | — |
| | | | | | | | Wigan Ath (loan) | 10 | 1 |
| | | | | | | | Wigan Ath | 35 | — |
| **Morgan** Steve | 6 0 | 11 00 | D | 19 9 68 | Oldham | Apprentice | Blackpool | 144 | 10 |
| | | | | | | | Plymouth Arg | 121 | 6 |
| | | | | | | | Coventry C | 68 | 2 |
| | | | | | | | Bristol R (loan) | 5 | — |
| | | | | | | | Wigan Ath | 36 | 2 |
| | | | | | | | Bury (loan) | 5 | — |
| **Mustoe** Neil‡ | 5 8 | 12 13 | M | 5 11 76 | Gloucester | Trainee | Manchester U | — | — |
| | | | | | | | Wigan Ath | — | — |
| **O'Connell** Brendan | 5 9 | 12 01 | M | 12 11 66 | London | | Portsmouth | — | — |
| | | | | | | | Exeter C | 81 | 19 |
| | | | | | | | Burnley | 64 | 17 |
| | | | | | | | Huddersfield T (loan) | 11 | 1 |
| | | | | | | | Barnsley | 240 | 35 |
| | | | | | | | Charlton Ath | 38 | 2 |
| | | | | | | | Wigan Ath | 17 | 5 |
| **Rogers** Paul | 6 0 | 11 13 | M | 21 3 65 | Portsmouth | Sutton U | Sheffield U | 125 | 10 |
| | | | | | | | Notts Co | 22 | 2 |
| | | | | | | | Wigan Ath | 58 | 3 |
| **Sharp** Kevin | 5 9 | 10 07 | D | 19 9 74 | Ontario | Auxerre | Leeds U | 17 | — |
| | | | | | | | Wigan Ath | 93 | 8 |
| **Smeets** Jorg | | | F | 5 11 70 | Bussum | | Heracles | 8 | 2 |
| | | | | | | | Wigan Ath | 23 | 3 |
| **Warne** Paul | 5 9 | 11 02 | F | 8 5 73 | Norwich | Wroxham | Wigan Ath | 25 | 2 |
| **Whitworth** Neil | 6 2 | 12 06 | D | 12 4 72 | Wigan | | Wigan Ath | 2 | — |
| | | | | | | | Manchester U | 1 | — |
| | | | | | | | Preston NE (loan) | 6 | — |
| | | | | | | | Barnsley (loan) | 11 | — |
| | | | | | | | Rotherham U (loan) | 8 | 1 |
| | | | | | | | Blackpool (loan) | 3 | — |
| | | | | | | | Kilmarnock | 76 | 3 |
| | | | | | | | Wigan Ath | 4 | — |

**Trainees**
Alexander, Paul M; Baccino, Stephen D; Birch, Christopher J; Coyne, John; Critchley, Craig J; Crompton, Paul A; Culshaw, Louis; Cunliffe, David A; Dann, John J; Field, Dean T; Gordon, Richard; Hatton, Barry K; Jones, Philip A; Marfleet, Jonathan L; Rhead, Michael; Seddon, Gareth J; Sing, Stephen; Smith, David; Wiswell, Gareth.

**Associated Schoolboys**
Beardall, Dean M; Clegg, Michael J; Duffy, Graham C; Eaves, Paul; Fitzhenry, Paul J; Hart, Matthew; Hughes, Benjamin; Johnson, Ian R; Jones, Richard; Kay, Stephen B; Lee, Michael T; Lee, Paul K; O'Dell, Denis; Oakes, David; Peoples, Victor; Pitts, Douglas J; Robinson, Nigel T; Speakman, Craig; Williams, Matthew.

**Associated Schoolboys who have accepted the club's offer of a Traineeship/Contract**
Court, Mark; Greenwood, Stephen; McMahon, Francis; Morris, Andrew.

# WIMBLEDON

| | | | | | | | | | |
|---|---|---|---|---|---|---|---|---|---|
| **Ardley** Neal | 5 11 | 11 09 | M | 1 9 72 | Epsom | Trainee | Wimbledon | 139 | 10 |
| **Blackwell** Dean | 6 1 | 12 10 | D | 5 12 69 | Camden | Trainee | Wimbledon | 154 | 1 |
| | | | | | | | Plymouth Arg (loan) | 7 | — |
| **Castledine** Stewart | 6 1 | 12 00 | M | 22 1 73 | Wandsworth | Trainee | Wimbledon | 27 | 4 |
| | | | | | | | Wycombe W (loan) | 7 | 3 |
| **Clarke** Andy | 5 10 | 11 07 | F | 22 7 67 | Islington | Barnet | Wimbledon | 170 | 17 |
| **Cort** Carl | 6 4 | 12 07 | F | 1 11 77 | Southwark | | Wimbledon | 23 | 4 |
| | | | | | | | Lincoln C (loan) | 6 | 1 |
| **Cunningham** Kenny | 5 11 | 11 02 | D | 28 6 71 | Dublin | Tolka R | Millwall | 136 | 1 |
| | | | | | | | Wimbledon | 129 | — |
| **Earle** Robbie | 5 9 | 10 10 | M | 27 1 65 | Newcastle-under-Lyme | Stoke C | Port Vale | 294 | 77 |
| | | | | | | | Wimbledon | 224 | 51 |
| **Ekoku** Efan | 6 2 | 12 00 | F | 8 6 67 | Manchester | Sutton U | Bournemouth | 62 | 21 |
| | | | | | | | Norwich C | 37 | 15 |
| | | | | | | | Wimbledon | 101 | 31 |
| **Euell** Jason | 5 11 | 11 02 | F | 6 2 77 | Lambeth | Trainee | Wimbledon | 35 | 8 |
| **Fear** Peter | 5 10 | 11 07 | M | 10 9 73 | Sutton | Trainee | Wimbledon | 71 | 4 |
| **Francis** Damien | 6 0 | 10 10 | M | 27 2 79 | Wandsworth | Trainee | Wimbledon | 2 | — |
| **Futcher** Andy | 5 7 | 10 07 | D | 10 2 78 | Enfield | Trainee | Wimbledon | — | — |
| **Gardner** James* | 5 11 | 10 06 | D | 26 10 78 | Beckenham | Trainee | Wimbledon | 0 | — |
| **Gayle** Marcus | 6 1 | 12 09 | F | 27 9 70 | Hammersmith | Trainee | Brentford | 156 | 22 |
| | | | | | | | Wimbledon | 133 | 17 |
| **Goodman** Jon | 6 0 | 12 03 | F | 2 6 71 | Walthamstow | Bromley | Millwall | 109 | 35 |
| | | | | | | | Wimbledon | 59 | 11 |
| **Harford** Mick* | 6 3 | 14 05 | F | 12 2 59 | Sunderland | Lambton St BC | Lincoln C | 115 | 41 |
| | | | | | | | Newcastle U | 19 | 4 |
| | | | | | | | Bristol C | 30 | 11 |
| | | | | | | | Birmingham C | 92 | 25 |
| | | | | | | | Luton T | 139 | 57 |
| | | | | | | | Derby Co | 58 | 15 |
| | | | | | | | Luton T | 29 | 12 |
| | | | | | | | Chelsea | 28 | 9 |
| | | | | | | | Sunderland | 11 | 2 |
| | | | | | | | Coventry C | 1 | 1 |
| | | | | | | | Wimbledon | 61 | 9 |
| **Hawkins** Peter | 6 0 | 11 04 | D | 19 9 78 | Maidstone | Trainee | Wimbledon | — | — |
| **Heald** Paul | 6 2 | 12 05 | G | 20 9 68 | Wath-on-Dearne | Trainee | Sheffield U | — | — |
| | | | | | | | Leyton Orient | 176 | — |
| | | | | | | | Coventry C (loan) | 2 | — |
| | | | | | | | Crystal Palace (loan) | — | — |
| | | | | | | | Swindon T (loan) | 2 | — |
| | | | | | | | Wimbledon | 20 | — |
| **Hinds** Leigh | 5 8 | 10 10 | F | 17 8 78 | Beckenham | Trainee | Wimbledon | — | — |
| **Hodges** Danny | 6 0 | 12 07 | D | 14 9 76 | Greenwich | Trainee | Wimbledon | — | — |
| **Hughes** Ceri | 5 10 | 12 07 | M | 26 2 71 | Pontypridd | Trainee | Luton T | 175 | 17 |
| | | | | | | | Wimbledon | 17 | 1 |
| **Hughes** Michael | 5 6 | 10 08 | M | 2 8 71 | Larne | Carrick R | Manchester C | 26 | 1 |
| | | | | | | | Strasbourg | 83 | 9 |
| | | | | | | | West Ham U (loan) | 17 | 2 |
| | | | | | | | West Ham U (loan) | 28 | — |
| | | | | | | | West Ham U | 38 | 3 |
| | | | | | | | Wimbledon | 29 | 4 |
| **Jennings** Patrick* | 5 9 | 11 00 | G | 24 9 79 | Herts | | Wimbledon | — | — |
| **Jupp** Duncan | 6 0 | 12 11 | D | 25 1 75 | Guildford | Trainee | Fulham | 105 | 2 |
| | | | | | | | Wimbledon | 9 | — |
| **Kennedy** Mark | 5 11 | 11 00 | F | 15 5 76 | Dublin | Belvedere | Millwall | 43 | 9 |
| | | | | | | | Liverpool | 16 | — |
| | | | | | | | QPR (loan) | 8 | 2 |
| | | | | | | | Wimbledon | 4 | — |
| **Kimble** Alan | 5 10 | 12 04 | D | 6 8 66 | Poole | | Charlton Ath | 6 | — |
| | | | | | | | Exeter C (loan) | 1 | — |
| | | | | | | | Cambridge U | 299 | 24 |
| | | | | | | | Wimbledon | 127 | — |

| Name | | | | DOB | Birthplace | Source | Club | Apps | Gls |
|---|---|---|---|---|---|---|---|---|---|
| **Leaburn** Carl | 6 3 | 13 00 | F | 30 3 69 | Lewisham | Apprentice | Charlton Ath | 322 | 53 |
| | | | | | | | Northampton T (loan) | 9 | — |
| | | | | | | | Wimbledon | 16 | 4 |
| **McAllister** Brian | 5 11 | 12 05 | D | 30 11 70 | Glasgow | Trainee | Wimbledon | 85 | — |
| | | | | | | | Plymouth Arg (loan) | 8 | — |
| | | | | | | | Crewe Alex (loan) | 13 | 1 |
| **Murphy** Brendan | 5 11 | 11 12 | G | 19 8 75 | Wexford | Bradford C | Wimbledon | — | — |
| **O'Connor** Richard | 5 9 | 10 07 | F | 30 8 78 | Wandsworth | Trainee | Wimbledon | — | — |
| **Odlum** Gary | 5 11 | 11 04 | D | 19 10 78 | Beckenham | Trainee | Wimbledon | — | — |
| **Pearce** Andy | 6 4 | 14 11 | D | 20 4 66 | Bradford-on-Avon | Halesowen T | Coventry C | 71 | 4 |
| | | | | | | | Sheffield W | 69 | 3 |
| | | | | | | | Wimbledon | 7 | — |
| **Perry** Chris | 5 8 | 10 08 | D | 26 4 73 | Carshalton | Trainee | Wimbledon | 133 | 2 |
| **Petrovic** Timotije‡ | | | M | 6 12 78 | Essex | Trainee | Wimbledon | — | — |
| **Reeves** Alan* | 6 0 | 12 00 | D | 19 11 67 | Birkenhead | Heswall | Norwich C | — | — |
| | | | | | | | Gillingham (loan) | 18 | — |
| | | | | | | | Chester C | 40 | 2 |
| | | | | | | | Rochdale | 121 | 9 |
| | | | | | | | Wimbledon | 57 | 4 |
| **Renner** Victor | 6 0 | 11 02 | F | 18 4 79 | Sierra Leone | Trainee | Wimbledon | — | — |
| **Reynolds** Paul* | 6 1 | 11 04 | D | 13 9 78 | Widnes | Trainee | Wimbledon | — | — |
| **Roberts** Andy | 5 10 | 13 00 | M | 20 3 74 | Dartford | Trainee | Millwall | 138 | 5 |
| | | | | | | | Crystal Palace | 108 | 2 |
| | | | | | | | Wimbledon | 12 | 1 |
| **Solbakken** Stale‡ | | | M | 27 2 68 | Norway | | Hamark | 39 | 9 |
| | | | | | | | Lillestrom | 99 | 35 |
| | | | | | | | Wimbledon | 6 | 1 |
| **Sullivan** Neil | 6 0 | 12 01 | G | 24 2 70 | Sutton | Trainee | Wimbledon | 106 | — |
| | | | | | | | Crystal Palace (loan) | 1 | — |
| **Thatcher** Ben | 5 11 | 12 07 | D | 30 11 75 | Swindon | Trainee | Millwall | 90 | 1 |
| | | | | | | | Wimbledon | 35 | — |

**Trainees**
Agyemang, Patrick; Correia, Artur B; Daly, Thomas F; Favata, Sebastian; Flinn, Stephen G; Gier, Robert J; Gray, Wayne W; Halliwell, Bryn S; Henty, Gary P; Lake, Stuart L; O'Sullivan, Marcus F; Owusu, Ansah O; Vella, Simon G; Watkins, Drew A; Williamson, Lee A; Williamson, Russell I; Willy, Mark J.

**Associated Schoolboys**
Cook, Paul T; Hillman, Luke H; Innocent, Anton L; Taylor, Glen J.

**Associated Schoolboys who have accepted the club's offer of a Traineeship/Contract**
Jones, Mark C; Okikiolu, Kola S; Tapp, Alex.

# WOLVERHAMPTON WANDERERS

| Name | | | | DOB | Birthplace | Source | Club | Apps | Gls |
|---|---|---|---|---|---|---|---|---|---|
| **Andrews** Keith | | | M | 13 9 80 | Dublin | Trainee | Wolverhampton W | — | — |
| **Atkins** Mark | 6 1 | 12 00 | M | 14 8 68 | Doncaster | | Scunthorpe U | 48 | 2 |
| | | | | | | | Blackburn R | 257 | 35 |
| | | | | | | | Wolverhampton W | 111 | 9 |
| **Bray** Justin | | | G | 1 1 79 | Great Yarmouth | Trainee | Wolverhampton W | — | — |
| **Bull** Steve | 5 11 | 11 04 | F | 28 3 65 | Tipton | Apprentice | WBA | 4 | 2 |
| | | | | | | | Wolverhampton W | 459 | 247 |
| **Claridge** Steve | 5 11 | 11 08 | F | 10 4 66 | Portsmouth | Fareham T | Bournemouth | 7 | 1 |
| | | | | | | Weymouth | Crystal Palace | — | — |
| | | | | | | | Aldershot | 62 | 19 |
| | | | | | | | Cambridge U | 79 | 28 |
| | | | | | | | Luton T | 16 | 2 |
| | | | | | | | Cambridge U | 53 | 18 |
| | | | | | | | Birmingham C | 88 | 35 |
| | | | | | | | Leicester C | 63 | 16 |
| | | | | | | | Portsmouth (loan) | 10 | 2 |
| | | | | | | | Wolverhampton W | 5 | — |
| **Corica** Steve | 5 8 | 10 10 | M | 24 3 73 | Cairns | Marconi | Leicester C | 16 | 2 |
| | | | | | | | Wolverhampton W | 54 | 2 |
| **Crowe** Glen | 5 10 | 13 01 | F | 25 12 77 | Dublin | Trainee | Wolverhampton W | 10 | 1 |
| | | | | | | | Exeter C (loan) | 10 | 5 |
| | | | | | | | Cardiff C (loan) | 8 | 1 |
| **Crowe** Seamie | | | M | 18 11 80 | Galway | Trainee | Wolverhampton W | — | — |
| **Curle** Keith | 6 0 | 12 07 | D | 14 11 63 | Bristol | Apprentice | Bristol R | 32 | 4 |
| | | | | | | | Torquay U | 16 | 5 |
| | | | | | | | Bristol C | 121 | 1 |
| | | | | | | | Reading | 40 | — |
| | | | | | | | Wimbledon | 93 | 3 |
| | | | | | | | Manchester C | 171 | 11 |
| | | | | | | | Wolverhampton W | 61 | 3 |
| **Daley** Tony* | 5 9 | 11 00 | M | 18 11 67 | Birmingham | Apprentice | Aston Villa | 233 | 31 |
| | | | | | | | Wolverhampton W | 21 | 3 |
| **Dixon** Alan | | | M | 9 10 79 | Dublin | Trainee | Wolverhampton W | — | — |
| **Emblen** Neil | 6 1 | 13 03 | D | 19 6 71 | Bromley | Sittingbourne | Millwall | 12 | — |
| | | | | | | | Wolverhampton W | 95 | 9 |
| | | | | | | | Crystal Palace | 13 | — |

| | | | | | | | | | |
|---|---|---|---|---|---|---|---|---|---|
| **Ferguson** Darren | 5 10 | 10 04 | M | 9 2 72 | Glasgow | Trainee | Manchester U | 27 | — |
| | | | | | | | Wolverhampton W | 113 | 4 |
| **Foley** Dominic | 6 1 | 12 08 | F | 7 7 76 | Cork | St James Gate | Wolverhampton W | 15 | 1 |
| | | | | | | | Watford (loan) | 8 | 1 |
| **Freedman** Dougie | 5 9 | 11 02 | F | 25 5 74 | Glasgow | Trainee | QPR | — | — |
| | | | | | | | Barnet | 47 | 27 |
| | | | | | | | Crystal Palace | 90 | 31 |
| | | | | | | | Wolverhampton W | 29 | 10 |
| **Froggatt** Steve | 5 10 | 11 00 | M | 9 3 73 | Lincoln | Trainee | Aston Villa | 35 | 2 |
| | | | | | | | Wolverhampton W | 98 | 7 |
| **Garcia Sanjuan** Jesus‡ | 5 10 | 12 07 | M | 22 8 71 | Zaragoza | Zaragoza | Wolverhampton W | 4 | — |
| **Gilkes** Michael | 5 8 | 10 10 | M | 20 7 65 | Hackney | Leicester C | Reading | 393 | 43 |
| | | | | | | | Chelsea (loan) | 1 | — |
| | | | | | | | Southampton (loan) | 6 | — |
| | | | | | | | Wolverhampton W | 8 | 1 |
| **Goodman** Don* | 5 10 | 12 12 | F | 9 5 66 | Leeds | School | Bradford C | 70 | 14 |
| | | | | | | | WBA | 158 | 60 |
| | | | | | | | Sunderland | 116 | 40 |
| | | | | | | | Wolverhampton W | 125 | 33 |
| **Green** Ryan | | | D | 20 10 80 | Cardiff | Danes Court | Wolverhampton W | — | — |
| **Hackett** Stephen | | | D | 17 9 80 | Dublin | Trainee | Wolverhampton W | — | — |
| **Jones** Mark | | | M | 7 9 79 | Walsall | Trainee | Wolverhampton W | — | — |
| **Keane** Robbie | 5 9 | 11 07 | F | 8 7 80 | Dublin | Trainee | Wolverhampton W | 38 | 11 |
| **Kubicki** Dariusz* | 5 10 | 11 07 | D | 6 6 63 | Kozuchow | Legia Warsaw | Aston Villa | 25 | — |
| | | | | | | | Sunderland (loan) | 15 | — |
| | | | | | | | Sunderland | 121 | — |
| | | | | | | | Wolverhampton W | 12 | — |
| | | | | | | | Tranmere R (loan) | 12 | — |
| **Lamey** Nathan | | | F | 14 10 80 | Leeds | Trainee | Wolverhampton W | — | — |
| **Leadbeater** Richard* | 6 2 | 12 06 | F | 21 10 77 | Dudley | Trainee | Wolverhampton W | 1 | — |
| **Murray** Matthew | | | M | 2 5 81 | Solihull | Trainee | Wolverhampton W | — | — |
| **Muscat** Kevin | 5 11 | 11 07 | D | 7 8 73 | Crawley | South Melbourne | Crystal Palace | 53 | 2 |
| | | | | | | | Wolverhampton W | 24 | 3 |
| **Naylor** Lee | 5 8 | 11 08 | D | 19 3 80 | Bloxwich | Trainee | Wolverhampton W | 16 | — |
| **Osborn** Simon | 5 10 | 11 04 | M | 19 1 72 | New Addington | Apprentice | Crystal Palace | 55 | 5 |
| | | | | | | | Reading | 32 | 5 |
| | | | | | | | QPR | 9 | 1 |
| | | | | | | | Wolverhampton W | 80 | 9 |
| **Paatelainen** Mixu | 6 0 | 13 10 | F | 3 2 67 | Helsinki | Valkeakosken Haka | Dundee U | 133 | 33 |
| | | | | | | | Aberdeen | 75 | 23 |
| | | | | | | | Bolton W | 69 | 15 |
| | | | | | | | Wolverhampton W | 23 | — |
| **Richards** Dean | 6 2 | 13 07 | D | 9 6 74 | Bradford | Trainee | Bradford C | 86 | 4 |
| | | | | | | | Wolverhampton W (loan) | 10 | 2 |
| | | | | | | | Wolverhampton W | 71 | 2 |
| **Roberts** Jason | | | F | 25 1 78 | Middlesex | Hayes | Wolverhampton W | — | — |
| | | | | | | | Torquay U (loan) | 14 | 6 |
| | | | | | | | Bristol C (loan) | 3 | 1 |
| **Robinson** Carl | 5 10 | 11 11 | M | 13 10 76 | Llandrindod Wells | Trainee | Wolverhampton W | 34 | 3 |
| | | | | | | | Shrewsbury T (loan) | 4 | — |
| **Sedgley** Steve | 6 1 | 13 13 | D | 26 5 68 | Enfield | Apprentice | Coventry C | 84 | 3 |
| | | | | | | | Tottenham H | 164 | 8 |
| | | | | | | | Ipswich T | 105 | 15 |
| | | | | | | | Wolverhampton W | 19 | — |
| **Segers** Hans* | 5 11 | 12 12 | G | 30 10 61 | Eindhoven | PSV Eindhoven | Nottingham F | 58 | — |
| | | | | | | | Stoke C (loan) | 1 | — |
| | | | | | | | Sheffield U (loan) | 10 | — |
| | | | | | | | Dunfermline Ath (loan) | 4 | — |
| | | | | | | | Wimbledon | 267 | — |
| | | | | | | | Wolverhampton W | 11 | — |
| **Simms** Gordon | | | M | 23 3 81 | Larne | Trainee | Wolverhampton W | — | — |
| **Simpson** Paul | 5 8 | 11 11 | M | 26 7 66 | Carlisle | Apprentice | Manchester C | 121 | 18 |
| | | | | | | | Oxford U | 144 | 43 |
| | | | | | | | Derby Co | 186 | 48 |
| | | | | | | | Sheffield U (loan) | 6 | — |
| | | | | | | | Wolverhampton W | 28 | 4 |
| **Slater** Robbie | 5 10 | 13 03 | D | 22 11 64 | Ormskirk | Anderlecht | Lens | 81 | 4 |
| | | | | | | | Blackburn R | 18 | — |
| | | | | | | | West Ham U | 25 | 2 |
| | | | | | | | Southampton | 41 | 2 |
| | | | | | | | Wolverhampton W | 6 | — |
| **Stowell** Mike | 6 2 | 13 10 | G | 19 4 65 | Portsmouth | Leyland Motors | Preston NE | — | — |
| | | | | | | | Everton | — | — |
| | | | | | | | Chester C (loan) | 14 | — |
| | | | | | | | York C (loan) | 6 | — |
| | | | | | | | Manchester C (loan) | 14 | — |
| | | | | | | | Port Vale (loan) | 7 | — |
| | | | | | | | Wolverhampton W (loan) | 7 | — |
| | | | | | | | Preston NE (loan) | 2 | — |
| | | | | | | | Wolverhampton W | 313 | — |
| **Westwood** Chris* | 6 0 | 12 02 | D | 13 2 77 | Dudley | Trainee | Wolverhampton W | 4 | 1 |

| Williams Adrian | 6 2 | 12 06 | D | 16 8 71 | Reading | Trainee | Reading | 196 | 14 |
| | | | | | | | Wolverhampton W | 26 | — |

**Trainees**
Clarke, Christopher E; Clarke, Matthew P; D'Amore, David R; Hampton, Richard P; Haverton, Gary S; Hughes, Daniel P; Loughlin, Paul A; Proudlock, Adam D; Turpin, Jamie L; Winstone, Alexander T.

**Associated Schoolboys**
Bampfield, Steve D; Bonser, John; Brown, Leon; Cash, Ryan; Clark, Nicholas; Danks, Mark; Dickson, Andrew; Downes, Lee; Gilmore, Craig C; Jones, Jimmi L; Keith, Daryl G; Kerr, Aaron G; Morrow, Andrew J; Pierce, Mark; Renton, Mitchell J; Rollins, Mark; Slater, Christopher; Solly, Lewis; Taylor, Paul; Tower, Andrew R; Walker, Richard; Webb, Mark; Webster, Andrew J; Wesley, Robert; Willis, James R; Woolerton, Stephen.

**Associated Schoolboys who have accepted the club's offer of a Traineeship/Contract**
Clegg, Dean R; Easter, Jermaine M; Hagan, Conor; Jones, Kenny R; Tudor, Shane.

**Players who do not hold a current contract but their registration has been retained by the club**
Clark, David; Denner, Lee A.

# WREXHAM

| Brace Deryn | 5 7 | 10 12 | D | 15 3 75 | Haverfordwest | Trainee | Norwich C | — | — |
| | | | | | | | Wrexham | 65 | 2 |
| Brammer David | 5 9 | 12 00 | M | 28 2 75 | Bromborough | Trainee | Wrexham | 103 | 10 |
| Carey Brian | 6 3 | 13 12 | D | 31 5 68 | Cork | Cork C | Manchester U | — | — |
| | | | | | | | Wrexham (loan) | 3 | — |
| | | | | | | | Wrexham (loan) | 13 | 1 |
| | | | | | | | Leicester C | 58 | 1 |
| | | | | | | | Wrexham | 81 | 1 |
| Cartwright Mark | 6 2 | 13 06 | G | 13 1 73 | Chester | York C | Wrexham | 7 | — |
| Chalk Martyn | 5 6 | 10 00 | M | 30 8 69 | Swindon | Louth U | Derby Co | 7 | 1 |
| | | | | | | | Stockport Co | 43 | 6 |
| | | | | | | | Wrexham | 88 | 6 |
| Connolly Karl | 5 9 | 11 00 | F | 9 2 70 | Prescot | Napoli (Liverpool) | Wrexham | 273 | 68 |
| Cross Jonathan* | 5 10 | 11 07 | M | 2 3 75 | Wallasey | Trainee | Wrexham | 119 | 12 |
| | | | | | | | Hereford U (loan) | 5 | 1 |
| | | | | | | | Tranmere R (loan) | — | — |
| Edwards Leigh* | 6 1 | 12 00 | G | 19 9 78 | Wrexham | Trainee | Wrexham | — | — |
| Griffiths Andy | 5 11 | 12 00 | M | 21 11 78 | Wirral | Trainee | Wrexham | — | — |
| Hardy Phil | 5 7 | 11 08 | D | 9 4 73 | Chester | Trainee | Wrexham | 265 | — |
| Humes Tony | 6 0 | 12 00 | D | 19 3 66 | Blyth | Apprentice | Ipswich T | 120 | 10 |
| | | | | | | | Wrexham | 187 | 8 |
| Marriott Andy | 6 1 | 12 08 | G | 11 10 70 | Sutton-in-Ashfield | Trainee | Arsenal | — | — |
| | | | | | | | Nottingham F | 11 | — |
| | | | | | | | WBA (loan) | 3 | — |
| | | | | | | | Blackburn R (loan) | 2 | — |
| | | | | | | | Colchester U (loan) | 10 | — |
| | | | | | | | Burnley (loan) | 15 | — |
| | | | | | | | Wrexham | 213 | — |
| McGregor Mark | 5 10 | 11 05 | D | 16 2 77 | Chester | Trainee | Wrexham | 113 | 4 |
| Morris Rob* | 5 10 | 11 12 | D | 4 9 78 | Oswestry | Trainee | Wrexham | — | — |
| Morris Steve‡ | 5 10 | 12 00 | F | 13 5 76 | Liverpool | Liverpool | Wrexham | 42 | 9 |
| | | | | | | | Rochdale (loan) | — | — |
| Owen Gareth | 5 7 | 12 00 | M | 21 10 71 | Chester | Trainee | Wrexham | 254 | 28 |
| Ridler Dave | 6 0 | 12 02 | D | 12 3 76 | Liverpool | Prescot T | Wrexham | 31 | — |
| Roberts Neil | 5 10 | 11 01 | F | 7 4 78 | Wrexham | Trainee | Wrexham | 34 | 8 |
| Roberts Paul | 5 11 | 11 09 | F | 29 7 77 | Bangor | Porthmadog | Wrexham | 1 | — |
| Roberts Stephen | | | M | 24 2 80 | Wrexham | Trainee | Wrexham | — | — |
| Russell Kevin | 5 9 | 10 12 | F | 6 12 66 | Portsmouth | Brighton & HA | Portsmouth | 4 | 1 |
| | | | | | | | Wrexham | 84 | 43 |
| | | | | | | | Leicester C | 43 | 10 |
| | | | | | | | Peterborough U (loan) | 7 | 3 |
| | | | | | | | Cardiff C (loan) | 3 | — |
| | | | | | | | Hereford U (loan) | 3 | 1 |
| | | | | | | | Stoke C (loan) | 5 | 1 |
| | | | | | | | Stoke C | 40 | 5 |
| | | | | | | | Burnley | 28 | 6 |
| | | | | | | | Bournemouth | 30 | 1 |
| | | | | | | | Notts Co | 11 | — |
| | | | | | | | Wrexham | 97 | 7 |
| Shone Gareth* | 6 0 | 13 00 | D | 5 1 79 | Aldershot | Trainee | Wrexham | — | — |
| Skinner Craig | 5 8 | 11 00 | M | 21 10 70 | Bury | Trainee | Blackburn R | 16 | — |
| | | | | | | | Plymouth Arg | 53 | 4 |
| | | | | | | | Wrexham | 75 | 8 |
| Spink Dean | 6 1 | 14 00 | F | 22 1 67 | Halesowen | Halesowen T | Aston Villa | — | — |
| | | | | | | | Scarborough (loan) | 3 | 2 |
| | | | | | | | Bury (loan) | 6 | 1 |
| | | | | | | | Shrewsbury T | 273 | 52 |
| | | | | | | | Wrexham | 36 | 6 |
| Thomas Steve | 5 10 | 11 12 | M | 23 6 79 | Hartlepool | Trainee | Wrexham | — | — |
| Wainwright Neil | 5 11 | 10 02 | M | 4 11 77 | Warrington | Trainee | Wrexham | 11 | 3 |

| | | | | | | | | | |
|---|---|---|---|---|---|---|---|---|---|
| **Walsh** Dave | 6 1 | 12 00 | G | 29 4 79 | Wrexham | Trainee | Wrexham | — | — |
| **Ward** Peter | 6 0 | 11 07 | M | 15 10 64 | Durham | Chester-le-Street | Huddersfield T | 37 | 2 |
| | | | | | | | Rochdale | 84 | 10 |
| | | | | | | | Stockport Co | 142 | 10 |
| | | | | | | | Wrexham | 95 | 12 |
| **Williams** Scott* | 6 0 | 12 00 | M | 7 8 74 | Bangor | Trainee | Wrexham | 32 | — |

**Trainees**
Andrews, Carl; Cooper, Steven D; Gibson, Robin J; Hannon, Kevin M; Hennessey, David J; Hopkins, Stephen A; Hughes, Gareth J; Jones, Craig S; Jones, Phillip B; Jones, Thomas A; Mazzarella, Paul; Owen, Adam L; Whitley, John S; Williams, Daniel F.

**Associated Schoolboys**
Bates, Matthew J; Brand, Benjamin J; Calder, Barry; Campbell, Luke; Cargill, Gary S; Dabbs, Matthew S; Entwistle, Mark R; Graham, Adam; Jones, Adam; Jones, Darren; Jones, Paul D; O'Toole, Dominic; Pejic, Shaun M; Powell, Sean; Renshaw, Jamie L; Rishworth, Stephen P; Sudlow, Gareth; Taylor, Michael J; Watkin, Daniel T; Williams, Craig E; Williams, David P; Williams, Gavin P.

**Associated Schoolboys who have accepted the club's offer of a Traineeship/Contract**
Harrison, David; Horan, George J; Johnson, Darran M; Lee, Kenneth.

## WYCOMBE WANDERERS

| | | | | | | | | | |
|---|---|---|---|---|---|---|---|---|---|
| **Baird** Andrew | | | D | 18 1 79 | East Kilbride | Trainee | Wycombe W | 2 | — |
| **Beeton** Alan | 5 11 | 11 13 | D | 4 10 78 | Watford | Trainee | Wycombe W | 20 | — |
| **Brown** Steve# | 5 11 | 11 12 | M | 6 7 66 | Northampton | | Northampton T | 158 | 19 |
| | | | | | | | Wycombe W | 161 | 11 |
| **Carroll** Dave# | 6 0 | 12 01 | M | 20 9 66 | Paisley | Ruislip Manor | Wycombe W | 210 | 31 |
| **Cornforth** John | 6 1 | 14 07 | M | 7 10 67 | Whitley Bay | Apprentice | Sunderland | 32 | 2 |
| | | | | | | | Doncaster R (loan) | 7 | 3 |
| | | | | | | | Shrewsbury T (loan) | 3 | — |
| | | | | | | | Lincoln C (loan) | 9 | 1 |
| | | | | | | | Swansea C | 149 | 16 |
| | | | | | | | Birmingham C | 8 | — |
| | | | | | | | Wycombe W | 34 | 5 |
| | | | | | | | Peterborough U (loan) | 4 | — |
| **Cousins** Jason | 5 10 | 12 01 | D | 4 10 70 | Hayes | Trainee | Brentford | 21 | — |
| | | | | | | Wycombe W | Wycombe W | 174 | 3 |
| **Forsyth** Mike | 5 11 | 12 04 | D | 20 3 66 | Liverpool | Apprentice | WBA | 29 | — |
| | | | | | | | Northampton T (loan) | — | — |
| | | | | | | | Derby Co | 325 | 8 |
| | | | | | | | Notts Co | 7 | — |
| | | | | | | | Hereford U (loan) | 12 | — |
| | | | | | | | Wycombe W | 48 | 2 |
| **Harkin** Maurice | 5 8 | 11 07 | F | 16 8 79 | Derry | Trainee | Wycombe W | 39 | 2 |
| **Hodson** Ben‡ | 6 2 | 13 08 | F | 25 1 76 | Nottingham | Yeading | Wycombe W | — | — |
| **Hodson** Matthew§ | | | M | 20 9 79 | Derby | Trainee | Wycombe W | — | — |
| **Holsgrove** Lee | 6 2 | 12 05 | D | 13 12 79 | Wendover | Trainee | Millwall | — | — |
| | | | | | | | Wycombe W | — | — |
| **Kavanagh** Jason | 5 9 | 12 01 | D | 23 11 71 | Birmingham | Birmingham C | Derby Co | 99 | 1 |
| | | | | | | | Wycombe W | 72 | 1 |
| **McCarthy** Paul | 5 10 | 13 10 | D | 4 8 71 | Cork | Trainee | Brighton & HA | 181 | 6 |
| | | | | | | | Wycombe W | 71 | 1 |
| **McGavin** Steve | 5 8 | 12 05 | F | 24 1 69 | North Walsham | Sudbury T | Colchester U | 58 | 17 |
| | | | | | | | Birmingham C | 23 | 2 |
| | | | | | | | Wycombe W | 115 | 14 |
| **Mohan** Nicky | 6 1 | 14 00 | D | 6 10 70 | Middlesbrough | Trainee | Middlesbrough | 99 | 4 |
| | | | | | | | Hull C (loan) | 5 | 1 |
| | | | | | | | Leicester C | 23 | — |
| | | | | | | | Bradford C | 83 | 4 |
| | | | | | | | Wycombe W | 33 | — |
| **Parkin** Brian‡ | 6 4 | 14 02 | G | 12 10 65 | Birkenhead | Local | Oldham Ath | 6 | — |
| | | | | | | | Crewe Alex (loan) | 12 | — |
| | | | | | | | Crewe Alex | 86 | — |
| | | | | | | | Crystal Palace (loan) | — | — |
| | | | | | | | Crystal Palace | 20 | — |
| | | | | | | | Bristol R | 241 | — |
| | | | | | | | Wycombe W | 25 | — |
| **Patton** Aaron | 5 6 | 12 01 | M | 27 2 79 | London | Trainee | Wycombe W | 1 | — |
| **Read** Paul | 5 8 | 12 06 | F | 25 9 73 | Harlow | Trainee | Arsenal | — | — |
| | | | | | | | Leyton Orient (loan) | 11 | — |
| | | | | | | | Southend U (loan) | 4 | 1 |
| | | | | | | | Wycombe W | 41 | 8 |
| **Ryan** Keith | 5 11 | 12 05 | M | 25 6 70 | Northampton | Berkhamsted T | Wycombe W | 129 | 12 |
| **Scott** Keith | 6 2 | 14 07 | F | 9 6 67 | Westminster | Leicester U | Lincoln C | 16 | 2 |
| | | | | | | Wycombe W | Wycombe W | 15 | 10 |
| | | | | | | | Swindon T | 51 | 12 |
| | | | | | | | Stoke C | 25 | 3 |
| | | | | | | | Norwich C | 25 | 5 |
| | | | | | | | Bournemouth (loan) | 8 | 1 |
| | | | | | | | Watford (loan) | 6 | 2 |
| | | | | | | | Wycombe W (loan) | 9 | 3 |
| | | | | | | | Wycombe W | 29 | 11 |
| **Simpson** Michael | 5 6 | 11 07 | M | 28 2 74 | Nottingham | Trainee | Notts Co | 49 | 3 |
| | | | | | | | Plymouth Arg (loan) | 12 | — |
| | | | | | | | Wycombe W | 41 | 1 |

| | | | | | | | | | |
|---|---|---|---|---|---|---|---|---|---|
| **Stallard** Mark | 5 11 | 13 08 | F | 24 10 74 | Derby | Trainee | Derby Co | 27 | 2 |
| | | | | | | | Fulham (loan) | 4 | 3 |
| | | | | | | | Bradford C | 43 | 10 |
| | | | | | | | Preston NE (loan) | 4 | 1 |
| | | | | | | | Wycombe W | 55 | 21 |
| **Taylor** Martin | 5 11 | 14 07 | G | 9 12 66 | Tamworth | Mile Oak R | Derby Co | 97 | — |
| | | | | | | | Carlisle U (loan) | 10 | — |
| | | | | | | | Scunthorpe U (loan) | 8 | — |
| | | | | | | | Crewe Alex (loan) | 6 | — |
| | | | | | | | Wycombe W (loan) | 4 | — |
| | | | | | | | Wycombe W | 45 | — |
| **Wraight** Gary | 5 6 | 11 07 | M | 5 3 79 | Epping | Trainee | Wycombe W | 1 | — |

**Trainees**
Copeman, Nathan J; Fitzpatrick, Daniel J; Hendry, Iain K; Hodson, Matthew J; James, Matthew; Johnson, Lee P; Lamb, Jeffrey D; Leach, Nicholas P; Lee, Martyn J; McCoy, Barry J; Osborn, Mark; Smith, Grant G; Teale, Richard J; Williams, Warren R.

**Associated Schoolboys**
Cook, Lewis L; Dixon, Jonathan J; Holsgrove, Peter; Powell, Kevin; Simpemba, Ian F.

**Player who does not hold a current contract but his registration has been retained by the club**
Baker, Neil

# YORK CITY

| | | | | | | | | | |
|---|---|---|---|---|---|---|---|---|---|
| **Alderson** Richard* | 5 11 | 12 00 | F | 27 1 75 | Durham | Spennymoor U | York C | 1 | — |
| **Atkinson** Paddy* | 5 9 | 11 06 | D | 22 5 70 | Singapore | Sheffield U | Hartlepool U | 21 | 3 |
| | | | | | | Workington | York C | 41 | — |
| **Barras** Tony | 6 0 | 13 00 | D | 29 3 71 | Stockton | Trainee | Hartlepool U | 12 | — |
| | | | | | | | Stockport Co | 99 | 5 |
| | | | | | | | Rotherham U (loan) | 5 | 1 |
| | | | | | | | York C | 147 | 11 |
| **Bull** Gary* | 5 10 | 12 02 | F | 12 6 66 | West Bromwich | Swindon T | Southampton | — | — |
| | | | | | | | Cambridge U | 19 | 4 |
| | | | | | | Barnet | Barnet | 83 | 37 |
| | | | | | | | Nottingham F | 12 | 1 |
| | | | | | | | Birmingham C (loan) | 10 | 6 |
| | | | | | | | Brighton & HA (loan) | 10 | 2 |
| | | | | | | | Birmingham C (loan) | 6 | — |
| | | | | | | | York C | 83 | 11 |
| **Bushell** Steve# | 5 9 | 11 05 | M | 28 12 72 | Manchester | Trainee | York C | 174 | 10 |
| **Cresswell** Richard | 5 11 | 11 07 | F | 20 9 77 | Bridlington | Trainee | York C | 59 | 5 |
| | | | | | | | Mansfield T (loan) | 5 | 1 |
| **Gabbiadini** Marco* | 5 10 | 13 04 | F | 20 1 68 | Nottingham | Apprentice | York C | 60 | 14 |
| | | | | | | | Sunderland | 157 | 74 |
| | | | | | | | Crystal Palace | 15 | 5 |
| | | | | | | | Derby Co | 188 | 50 |
| | | | | | | | Birmingham C (loan) | 2 | — |
| | | | | | | | Oxford U (loan) | 5 | 1 |
| | | | | | | | Stoke C | 8 | — |
| | | | | | | | York C | 7 | 1 |
| **Hall** Wayne# | 5 9 | 10 06 | D | 25 10 68 | Rotherham | Darlington | York C | 304 | 8 |
| **Himsworth** Gary# | 5 7 | 9 10 | F | 19 12 69 | Appleton | Trainee | York C | 88 | 8 |
| | | | | | | | Scarborough | 92 | 6 |
| | | | | | | | Darlington | 94 | 8 |
| | | | | | | | York C | 56 | 3 |
| **Jones** Barry | 6 0 | 11 07 | D | 20 6 70 | Prescot | Prescot T | Liverpool | — | — |
| | | | | | | | Wrexham | 195 | 5 |
| | | | | | | | York C | 23 | 2 |
| **Jordan** Scott | 5 9 | 11 05 | M | 19 7 75 | Newcastle | Trainee | York C | 95 | 5 |
| **McMillan** Andy | 5 10 | 11 09 | D | 22 6 68 | Bloemfontein | | York C | 388 | 5 |
| **Murty** Graeme | 5 10 | 11 12 | M | 13 11 74 | Middlesbrough | Trainee | York C | 117 | 7 |
| **Pouton** Alan | 6 0 | 12 02 | M | 1 2 77 | Newcastle | Newcastle U | Oxford U | — | — |
| | | | | | | | York C | 63 | 6 |
| **Reed** Martin | 6 1 | 11 07 | D | 10 1 78 | Scarborough | Trainee | York C | 24 | — |
| **Rennison** Graham§ | | | | 2 10 78 | Northallerton | Trainee | York C | 1 | — |
| **Rowe** Rodney | 5 8 | 12 08 | F | 30 7 75 | Plymouth | Trainee | Huddersfield T | 34 | 2 |
| | | | | | | | Scarborough (loan) | 14 | 1 |
| | | | | | | | Bury (loan) | 3 | — |
| | | | | | | | York C | 51 | 13 |
| **Rush** David‡ | 5 11 | 10 10 | F | 15 5 71 | Sunderland | Trainee | Sunderland | 59 | 12 |
| | | | | | | | Hartlepool U (loan) | 8 | 2 |
| | | | | | | | Peterborough U (loan) | 4 | 1 |
| | | | | | | | Cambridge U (loan) | 2 | — |
| | | | | | | | Oxford U | 92 | 21 |
| | | | | | | | York C | 5 | — |
| **Samways** Mark* | 6 2 | 14 01 | G | 11 11 68 | Doncaster | Trainee | Doncaster R | 121 | — |
| | | | | | | | Scunthorpe U (loan) | 8 | — |
| | | | | | | | Scunthorpe U | 172 | — |
| | | | | | | | York C (loan) | — | — |
| | | | | | | | York C | 29 | — |

| | | | | | | | | | |
|---|---|---|---|---|---|---|---|---|---|
| **Sharples** John | 6 0 | 11 03 | D | 26 1 73 | Bury | Manchester U | Hearts | — | — |
| | | | | | | | Ayr U | 53 | 4 |
| | | | | | | | York C | 38 | 1 |
| **Thompson** Neil | 5 11 | 13 08 | D | 2 10 63 | Beverley | Nottingham F | Hull C | 31 | — |
| | | | | | | Scarborough | Scarborough | 87 | 15 |
| | | | | | | | Ipswich T | 206 | 19 |
| | | | | | | | Barnsley | 27 | 5 |
| | | | | | | | Oldham Ath (loan) | 8 | — |
| | | | | | | | York C | 12 | 2 |
| **Tinkler** Mark | 5 11 | 13 03 | M | 24 10 74 | Bishop Auckland | Trainee | Leeds U | 25 | — |
| | | | | | | | York C | 53 | 6 |
| **Tolson** Neil | 6 3 | 11 05 | F | 25 10 73 | Wordley | Trainee | Walsall | 9 | 1 |
| | | | | | | | Oldham Ath | 3 | — |
| | | | | | | | Bradford C | 63 | 12 |
| | | | | | | | Chester C (loan) | 4 | — |
| | | | | | | | York C | 56 | 15 |
| **Warrington** Andy | 6 3 | 12 11 | G | 10 6 76 | Sheffield | Trainee | York C | 50 | — |

**Trainees**
Abblett, Mark P; Batchelor, Peter J; Bullock, Lee; Cruddas, David A; Dale, Richard B; Dawson, Andrew S; Dibie, Michael; Douglass, Russell B; Dufton, Thomas S; Farley, Michael C; Foreman, John R; Fox, Christian; Garratt, Martin B G; Mohan, John; Norris, Michael; Rennison, Graham L; Siddle, James D; Turley, James; Urwin, Jonathan G; Walters, Steven K.

**Associated Schoolboys**
Barry, Daniel; Darlow, Kieran B; Freary, Paul; Gowen, Christopher J; Hellens, Lee; Hilton, Richard; McDaid, James P; Parton, Matthew J; Paxton, James M; Pearson, Mathew; Pell, Richard M; Rhodes, Benjamin; Russell, Adam J; Vasey, Peter W J; Watt, Neil E; Wood, Leigh.

**Associated Schoolboys who have accepted the club's offer of a Traineeship/Contract**
Fielding, John R; Hakami, Darren R; Howarth, Russell M.

# The FA's Restructured Framework For Coaching in England
## by Ken Goldman

The FA Coaching department has been completely revamped since the departure of Mr Charles Hughes the former Director of Coaching. Many of the old titles and even the incumbents have changed. The current composition comprises:

- Mr Howard Wilkinson the FA Technical Director
- Mr Les Reed – Director of Technical Development
- Mr John McDermott – National Football Development Officer
- Mr Colin Murphy – Research Officer (with particular responsibility for requiring a site for the National Football Control)
- Ms Hope Powell – National Coach for Girls and Women's Football
- Mr Ken Swain – Technical Director of the FA National School

The new Football Development staff, under John McDermott consists of:
- Mr Jeff Davis (South East)
- Mr Graham Keeley (North West)
- Mr Les Howie (Midlands)
- Mr Paul Harrison (North East)
- Mr Andy Mitchell (South West)

The Regional Networks have the following Directors:
- Mr Alex Gibson (North West)
- Mr Martin Hunter (North East)
- Mr Dick Bate (South West)
- Mr Chris Ramsey (South East)
- Mr Ken Swain (West Midlands)

Howard Wilkinson has pioneered an important and far-reaching academic structure entitled the "Charter for Quality" which will have a marked effect on the way the game is to alter over the forthcoming years. Apart from conversion courses for "badge holders" at preliminary, intermediate and full level, to the new UEFA "A" & "B" licences, there will be development to produce a UEFA "Pro Licence" qualification.

Furthermore, the FA have introduced their own compulsory Coaching Association (FACA) for the holders of Coaching Awards and there is a strict regime for attending sessions to obtain the necessary NVQ's and CPD hours, within the context of football. FACA holds an annual conference that incorporates an international flavour.

The teaching of young players has also altered radically since the co-operation "synthesis" of the FA with the English School's FA. The Charter for Quality will see the introduction of licensed Football Academies at professional clubs with the option given to them to create either Acadamies or to enhance their existing Centres of Excellence. However it will be mandatory for every Academy to appoint an "Education and Welfare Officer" with approved qualifications and each one is further required to employ a qualified physiotherapist. The age group for the children attending will start at nine or under, progressing to 13 and from 13 to 16 years of age.

# THE FOREIGN (INTERNATIONAL) LEGION

The following full international players born outside the UK played in the FA Premier League and Nationwide Football League in 1997-98.

| | Player | Club | From | Fee £s |
|---|---|---|---|---|
| **AUSTRALIA** | Paul Agostino | Bristol C | Young Boys Berne | 50,000 |
| | John Aloisi | Portsmouth | Cremonese | 300,000 |
| | Andy Bernal | Reading | Syndey Olympic | 30,000 |
| | Mark Bosnich | Aston Villa | Croatia Sydney | Free |
| | Steve Corica | Wolverhampton W | Leicester C | 1,100,000 |
| | John Filan | Blackburn R | Coventry C | 700,000 |
| | Harry Kewell | Leeds U | NSW Soccer Academy | Free |
| | George Kulcsar | QPR | Bradford C | 250,000 |
| | Stan Lazaridis | West Ham U | West Adelaide | 300,000 |
| | Kevin Muscat | Wolverhampton W | Crystal Palace | exch. |
| | Lucas Neill | Millwall | NSW Soccer Academy | Free |
| | Adem Poric | Notts Co | Rotherham U | Free |
| | Robbie Slater | Wolverhampton W | Southampton | 75,000 |
| | Mark Schwarzer | Middlesbrough | Bradford C | 1,500,000 |
| | Jason Van Blerk | WBA | Manchester C | 50,000 |
| | Carl Veart | Millwall | Crystal Palace | 50,000 |
| **AUSTRIA** | Martin Hiden | Leeds U | Rapid Vienna | 1,300,000 |
| **BARBADOS** | Greg Goodridge | Bristol C | QPR | 50,000 |
| **BELARUS** | Petr Katchuro | Sheffield U | Dynamo Minsk | 650,000 |
| **BELGIUM** | Philippe Albert | Newcastle U | Anderlecht | 2,650,000 |
| **BERMUDA** | Shaun Goater | Manchester C | Bristol C | 500,000 |
| | Kyle Lightbourne | Stoke C | Coventry C | 500,000 |
| **BOLIVIA** | Jaime Moreno | Middlesbrough | Washington D | Loan |
| **BRAZIL** | Emerson | Middlesbrough | Porto | 4,000,000 |
| **CANADA** | Geoff Aunger | Stockport Co | Seattle Sounders | undisclosed |
| | Carlo Corazzin | Plymouth Arg | Cambridge U | 150,000 |
| | Jason Devos | Darlington | Montreal Impact | undisclosed |
| | Craig Forrest | West Ham U | Ipswich T | 500,000 |
| | Martin Nash | Stockport Co | Vancouver | undisclosed |
| | Paul Peschisolido | Fulham | WBA | 1,100,000 |
| **COLOMBIA** | Faustino Asprilla | Newcastle U | Parma | 7,500,000 |
| | Hamilton Ricard | Middlesbrough | Deportivo Cali | 200,000 |
| **COSTA RICA** | Mauricio Solis | Derby Co | Heridiano | 600,000 |
| | Paulo Wanchope | Derby Co | Heridiano | 600,000 |
| **CROATIA** | Alijosa Asanovic | Derby Co | Hajduk Split | 950,000 |
| | Slaven Bilic | Everton | West Ham U | 4,500,000 |
| | Igor Stimac | Derby Co | Hajduk Split | 1,500,000 |
| **CZECH REPUBLIC** | Patrik Berger | Liverpool | Borussia Dortmund | 3,250,000 |
| | Ludek Miklosko | West Ham U | Banik Ostrava | 300,000 |
| | Karel Poborsky | Manchester U | Slavia Prague | 3,500,000 |
| | Pavel Srnicek | Newcastle U | Banik Ostrava | 350,000 |
| **DENMARK** | Mikkel Beck | Middlesbrough | Fortuna Cologne | Free |
| | Per Frandsen | Bolton W | FC Copenhagen | 1,250,000 |
| | Jacob Laursen | Derby Co | Silkeborg | 500,000 |
| | Jan Molby | Swansea C | Liverpool | Free |
| | Allan Nielsen | Tottenham H | Brondby | 1,650,000 |
| | Marc Rieper | West Ham U | Brondby | 1,000,000 |
| | Peter Schmeichel | Manchester U | Brondby | 550,000 |
| | Claus Thomsen | Everton | Ipswich T | 900,000 |
| | Jon Dahl Tomasson | Newcastle U | Heerenveen | 2,200,000 |
| **ESTONIA** | Mart Poom | Derby Co | Flora | 500,000 |
| **FINLAND** | Antti Heinola | QPR | Heracles | 100,000 |
| | Mixu Paatelainen | Wolverhampton W | Bolton W | 250,000 |
| **FRANCE** | Nicolas Anelka | Arsenal | Paris St Germain | 500,000 |
| | Patrick Blondeau | Sheffield W | Monaco | 1,800,000 |
| | Remy Garde | Arsenal | Strasbourg | Free |
| | David Ginola | Tottenham H | Newcastle U | 2,000,000 |
| | Bernard Lama | West Ham U | Paris St Germain | Loan |
| | Frank Leboeuf | Chelsea | Strasbourg | 2,500,000 |
| | Mikael Madar | Everton | La Coruna | Free |
| | Emmanuel Petit | Arsenal | Monaco | 3,500,000 |
| | Patrick Vieira | Arsenal | AC Milan | 3,500,000 |

| | | | |
|---|---|---|---|
| **GEORGIA** | Temuri Ketsbaia | Newcastle U | AEK Athens | Free |
| | Georgi Kinkladze | Manchester | Dynamo Tbilisi | 2,000,000 |
| | Murtaz Shelia | Manchester C | Alania | 500,000 |
| | Kakhabor Tskhadadze | Manchester C | Alania | 300,000 |
| **GERMANY** | Jurgen Klinsmann | Tottenham H | Sampdoria | 175,000 |
| | Karlheinz Riedle | Liverpool | Borussia Dortmund | 1,600,000 |
| | Uwe Rosler | Manchester C | Dynamo Dresden | 750,000 |
| **GHANA** | Kim Grant | Millwall | Luton T | undisclosed |
| **GREECE** | Nikos Dabizas | Newcastle U | Olympiakos | 2,000,000 |
| | Michalis Vlachos | Portsmouth | AEK Athens | |
| | Theo Zagorakis | Leicester C | PAOK Salonika | 750,000 |
| **HOLLAND** | Dennis Bergkamp | Arsenal | Inter Milan | 7,500,000 |
| | Jordi Cruyff | Manchester U | Barcelona | 1,400,000 |
| | Ed De Goey | Chelsea | Feyenoord | 2,250,000 |
| | Ruud Gullit | Chelsea | Sampdoria | Free |
| | Jimmy Hasselbaink | Leeds U | Boavista | 2,000,000 |
| | Marc Overmars | Arsenal | Ajax | 5,000,000 |
| | Ulrich Van Gobbel | Southampton | Galatasaray | 1,300,000 |
| | Pierre Van Hooijdonk | Nottingham F | Celtic | 3,500,000 |
| **ICELAND** | Gudni Bergsson | Bolton W | Tottenham H | 65,000 |
| | Arnar Gunnlaugsson | Bolton W | IA Akranes | 100,000 |
| | Hermann Hreidarsson | Crystal Palace | IBV | undisclosed |
| | Teuvo Molianen | Preston NE | Jaro | undisclosed |
| | Thorvaldur Orlygsson | Oldham Ath | Stoke C | 180,000 |
| | Larus Sigurdsson | Stoke C | Thor | undisclosed |
| **ISRAEL** | Eyal Berkovic | West Ham U | Maccabi Haifa | 1,700,000 |
| | Alon Hazan | Watford | Ironi Ashdod | 200,000 |
| | Ronny Rosenthal | Watford | Tottenham H | undisclosed |
| | Itzhak Zohar | Crystal Palace | Antwerp | 1,000,000 |
| **ITALY** | Nicola Berti | Tottenham H | Internazionale | Free |
| | Roberto Di Matteo | Chelsea | Lazio | 4,900,000 |
| | Stefano Eranio | Derby Co | AC Milan | Free |
| | Attilio Lombardo | Crystal Palace | Juventus | 1,600,000 |
| | Michele Padovano | Crystal Palace | Juventus | 1,700,000 |
| | Fabrizio Ravanelli | Middlesbrough | Juventus | 7,000,000 |
| | Gianluca Vialli | Chelsea | Juventus | Free |
| | Gianfranco Zola | Chelsea | Parma | 4,500,000 |
| **IVORY COAST** | Samassi Abou | West Ham U | Cannes | 300,000 |
| **JAMAICA** | Deon Burton | Derby Co | Portsmouth | 1,500,000 |
| | Robbie Earle | Wimbledon | Port Vale | 775,000 |
| | Marcus Gayle | Wimbledon | Brentford | 250,000 |
| | Paul Hall | Portsmouth | Torquay U | 70,000 |
| | Darryl Powell | Derby Co | Portsmouth | 750,000 |
| | Fitzroy Simpson | Portsmouth | Manchester C | 200,000 |
| | Frank Sinclair | Chelsea | Trainee | |
| **MACEDONIA** | Georgi Hristov | Barnsley | Partizan Belgrade | 1,500,000 |
| | Sasa Ilic | Charlton Ath | St Leonards Stamcroft | undisclosed |
| | Goce Sedloski | Sheffield W | Hajduk Split | 750,000 |
| **NIGERIA** | Celestine Babayaro | Chelsea | Anderlecht | 2,250,000 |
| | Efan Ekoku | Wimbledon | Norwich C | 900,000 |
| **NORWAY** | Espen Baardsen | Tottenham H | San Francisco | Free |
| | Henning Berg | Manchester U | Blackburn R | 5,000,000 |
| | Stig Inge Bjornebye | Liverpool | Rosenborg | 600,000 |
| | Lars Bohinen | Derby Co | Blackburn R | 1,450,000 |
| | Jan-Aage Fjortoft | Barnsley | Sheffield U | 800,000 |
| | Tor Andre Flo | Chelsea | Brann | 300,000 |
| | Froda Grodas | Tottenham H | Chelsea | 250,000 |
| | Alf Inge Haaland | Leeds U | Tottenham H | 1,600,000 |
| | Gunnar Halle | Leeds U | Oldham Ath | 400,000 |
| | Stig Johansen | Southampton | Bodo Glimt | 550,000 |
| | Ronny Johnsen | Manchester U | Besiktas | 1,200,000 |
| | Bjorn Kvarme | Liverpool | Rosenborg | undisclosed |
| | Oyvind Leonhardsen | Liverpool | Wimbledon | 3,500,000 |
| | Claus Lundekvam | Southampton | Brann | 400,000 |
| | Thomas Myhre | Everton | Viking Stavanger | 800,000 |
| | Roger Nilsen | Sheffield U | Viking Stavanger | 550,000 |
| | Egil Ostenstad | Southampton | Viking Stavanger | 800,000 |
| | Jan Ove Pedersen | Brann | Hartlepool U | Free |
| | Tore Pedersen | Blackburn R | St Pauli | 500,000 |
| | Petter Rudi | Sheffield W | Molde | 800,000 |
| | Stale Solbakken | Wimbledon | Lillestrom | 250,000 |
| | Ole Gunnar Solskjaer | Manchester U | Molde | 1,500,000 |
| | Trond Egil Soltvedt | Coventry C | Rosenborg | 500,000 |

| | | | | |
|---|---|---|---|---|
| **POLAND** | Dariusz Kubicki | Wolverhampton W | Sunderland | Free |
| | Dariusz Wdowczyk | Reading | Celtic | Free |
| **PORTUGAL** | Paolo Alves | West Ham U | Sporting Lisbon | Loan |
| | Jose Dominguez | Tottenham H | Sporting Lisbon | 1,600,000 |
| | Fernando Nelson | Aston Villa | Sporting Lisbon | 1,750,000 |
| **ROMANIA** | Viorel Moldovan | Coventry C | Grasshoppers | 3,250,000 |
| | Dan Petrescu | Chelsea | Sheffield W | 2,300,000 |
| **RUSSIA** | Dmitri Kharine | Chelsea | CSKA Moscow | 200,000 |
| **SLOVAKIA** | Vladimir Kinder | Middlesbrough | Slovan Bratislava | 1,000,000 |
| **SLOVENIA** | Ales Krizan | Barnsley | Branik Maribor | 500,000 |
| **SOUTH AFRICA** | Andre Arendse | Fulham | Cape Town Spurs | undisclosed |
| | Mark Fish | Bolton W | Lazio | 2,000,000 |
| | Lucas Radebe | Leeds U | Kaiser Chiefs | 250,000 |
| | Eric Tinkler | Barnsley | Cagliari | 650,000 |
| **ST LUCIA** | Earl Jean | Plymouth Arg | Rotherham U | Free |
| **ST VINCENT** | Rodney Jack | Torquay U | Lambada | Free |
| **SWEDEN** | Niclas Alexandersson | Sheffield W | IFK Gothenburg | 750,000 |
| | Anders Andersson | Blackburn R | Malmo | 500,000 |
| | Andreas Andersson | Newcastle U | AC Milan | 3,600,000 |
| | Tomas Brolin | Crystal Palace | Leeds U | Free |
| | Martin Dahlin | Blackburn R | Roma | 2,500,000 |
| | Magnus Hedman | Coventry C | AIK Stockholm | 500,000 |
| | Jan Jansson | Port Vale | Norrkoping | 200,000 |
| | Pontus Kamark | Leicester C | IFK Gothenburg | 840,000 |
| | Roland Nilsson | Coventry C | Helsingborg | 200,000 |
| | Robert Steiner | Bradford C | Norrkoping | 600,000 |
| | Mathias Svensson | Portsmouth | Elfsborg | 200,000 |
| **SWITZERLAND** | Stephane Henchoz | Blackburn R | Hamburg | 3,000,000 |
| | Marco Pascolo | Cagliari | Nottingham F | 750,000 |
| | Ramon Vega | Tottenham H | Cagliari | 3,750,000 |
| **TRINIDAD & TOBAGO** | Clint Marcelle | Barnsley | Felgueiras | Free |
| | Dwight Yorke | Aston Villa | Signal Hill | 120,000 |
| **URUGUAY** | Gustavo Poyet | Chelsea | Zaragoza | Free |
| **USA** | Ian Feuer | Luton T | West Ham U | 580,000 |
| | Brad Friedel | Liverpool | Columbus Crew | 1,000,000 |
| | Kasey Keller | Leicester C | Millwall | 900,000 |
| **YUGOSLAVIA** | Sasa Curcic | Crystal Palace | Aston Villa | 1,000,000 |
| | Savo Milosevic | Aston Villa | Partizan Belgrade | 3,500,000 |
| | Dejan Stefanovic | Sheffield W | Red Star Belgrade | 2,000,000 |
| **ZIMBABWE** | Bruce Grobbelaar | Oldham Ath | Oxford U | Free |
| | Peter Ndlovu | Birmingham C | Coventry C | 1,600,000 |

# TRANSFERS 1997–98

| JUNE 1997 | From | To | Fee in £s |
|---|---|---|---|
| 19 Arnott, Andrew J. | Leyton Orient | Fulham | undisclosed |
| 16 Christie, Iyseden | Coventry City | Mansfield Town | Free |
| 7 Clark, Lee | Newcastle United | Sunderland | 2,500,000 |
| 16 Clark, Simon | Peterborough United | Leyton Orient | undisclosed |
| 13 Darby, Julian T. | West Bromwich Albion | Preston North End | 150,000 |
| 23 Gale, Shaun M. | Barnet | Exeter City | undisclosed |
| 17 Gavin, Patrick J. | Farnborough Town | Harrow Borough | undisclosed |
| 30 Green, Scott P. | Bolton Wanderers | Wigan Athletic | 300,000 |
| 9 Hallam, Mark J. | Hinckley Town | Worcester City | undisclosed |
| 4 Haworth, Simon O. | Cardiff City | Coventry City | 500,000 |
| 4 Hayles, Barry | Stevenage Borough | Bristol Rovers | undisclosed |
| 23 Hayward, Steve L. | Carlisle United | Fulham | undisclosed |
| 18 Jones, Philip L. | Liverpool | Tranmere Rovers | 100,000 |
| 13 Kilbane, Kevin D. | Preston North End | West Bromwich Albion | 1,250,000 |
| 17 Lawrence, James H. | Leicester City | Bradford City | 50,000 |
| 16 Lee, Jason | Nottingham Forest | Watford | 200,000 |
| 3 Leonhardsen, Oyvind | Wimbledon | Liverpool | 3,500,000 |
| 26 Lewis, Neil A. | Leicester City | Peterborough United | undisclosed |
| 16 McGuckin, Thomas I. | Hartlepool United | Fulham | undisclosed |
| 18 Moore, Darren M. | Doncaster Rovers | Bradford City | undisclosed |
| 18 Newhouse, Aidan R. | Wimbledon | Fulham | Free |
| 23 Robson, Mark A. | Charlton Athletic | Notts County | undisclosed |
| 11 Seal, David | Bristol City | Northampton Town | undisclosed |
| 16 Smith, Dean | Hereford United | Leyton Orient | 42,500 |
| 25 Stewart, Paul A. | Sunderland | Stoke City | undisclosed |
| 5 Street, Tyrone T. | Hednesford Town | Nuneaton Borough | undisclosed |
| 6 Underwood, Paul V. | Enfield | Rushden & Diamonds | undisclosed |
| 10 Wilding, Peter J. | Telford United | Shrewsbury Town | undisclosed |
| **JULY 1997** | | | |
| 22 Barnes, Philip K. | Rotherham United | Blackpool | 100,000 |
| 23 Bashir, Naseem | St Albans City | Hendon | undisclosed |
| 19 Bayliss, Warren L. | Hampton | Windsor & Eton | undisclosed |
| 2 Beagrie, Peter S. | Manchester City | Bradford City | 200,000 |
| 9 Bell, Michael | Wycombe Wanderers | Bristol City | 150,000 |
| 25 Bennett, Gary M. | Wrexham | Chester City | 50,000 |
| 18 Blatherwick, Steven S. | Nottingham Forest | Burnley | 150,000 |
| 5 Blount, Mark | Gresley Rovers | Burton Albion | undisclosed |
| 23 Book, Steven K. | Forest Green Rovers | Cheltenham Town | undisclosed |
| 25 Breckin, Ian | Rotherham United | Chesterfield | 100,000 |
| 31 Brown, Kenneth J. | Birmingham City | Millwall | 40,000 |
| 17 Cooper, Adrian P. | Dudley Town | Halesowen Town | undisclosed |
| 21 Cousens, Andrew J. | Leeds United | Carlisle United | 100,000 |
| 10 Cramb, Colin | Doncaster Rovers | Bristol City | 250,000 |
| 21 Crawford, Stephen | Millwall | Hibernian | 360,000 |
| 31 Curran, Christopher | Plymouth Argyle | Exeter City | 20,000 |
| 18 Day, Christopher M. | Crystal Palace | Watford | exch. |
| 29 Deane, Brian C. | Leeds United | Sheffield United | 1,500,000 |
| 29 Donovan, Kevin | West Bromwich Albion | Grimsby Town | 300,000 |
| 11 Dyche, Sean M. | Chesterfield | Bristol City | 275,000 |
| 2 Elliott, Robert J. | Newcastle United | Bolton Wanderers | 2,200,000 |
| 9 Farrelly, Gareth | Aston Villa | Everton | 700,000 |
| 10 Filan, John R. | Coventry City | Blackburn Rovers | 700,000 |
| 28 Fitzgerald, Scott B. | Wimbledon | Millwall | 50,000 |
| 1 Fleming, Craig | Oldham Athletic | Norwich City | 600,000 |
| 18 Ford, Mark | Leeds United | Burnley | 250,000 |
| 14 Forinton, Howard L. | Yeovil Town | Birmingham City | 50,000 |
| 23 Forrest, Craig L. | Ipswich Town | West Ham United | 500,000 |
| 18 Foster, Adrian M. | Hereford United | Rushden & Diamonds | undisclosed |
| 14 Gill, Jeremy M. | Yeovil Town | Birmingham City | 50,000 |
| 18 Ginola, David | Newcastle United | Tottenham Hotspur | 2,000,000 |
| 14 Given, Seamus J.J. | Blackburn Rovers | Newcastle United | 1,500,000 |
| 30 Gray, Ian J. | Rochdale | Stockport County | Trib |
| 1 Grayson, Simon N. | Leicester City | Aston Villa | 1,350,000 |
| 21 Groves, Paul | West Bromwich Albion | Grimsby Town | 250,000 |
| 17 Haaland, Alf-Inge R. | Nottingham Forest | Leeds United | 1,600,000 |
| 25 Hanmer, Gareth C. | West Bromwich Albion | Shrewsbury Town | 10,000 |
| 16 Harle, Michael J. | Millwall | Barnet | Free |
| 11 Harper, Lee C.P. | Arsenal | Queens Park Rangers | 125,000 |
| 31 Heggs, Carl S. | Swansea City | Northampton Town | 25,000 |
| 29 Hodges, Lee L. | Barnet | Reading | 250,000 |
| 31 Holland, Matthew R. | AFC Bournemouth | Ipswich Town | 800,000 |
| 12 Holmes, David J. | Gloucester City | Burton Albion | undisclosed |
| 29 Holmes, Matthew J. | Blackburn Rovers | Charlton Athletic | 250,000 |
| 23 Hopkin, David | Crystal Palace | Leeds United | 3,250,000 |
| 4 Hughes, Ceri | Luton Town | Wimbledon | 400,000 |
| 21 Hyde, Micah | Cambridge United | Watford | 250,000 |
| 4 Johnson, Andrew J. | Norwich City | Nottingham Forest | 2,200,000 |
| 28 Jones, Paul S. | Stockport County | Southampton | 900,000 |
| 17 Kennedy, Peter H.J. | Notts County | Watford | 130,000 |
| 17 Lamb, Paul | Gravesend & Northfleet | Margate | undisclosed |
| 18 Lee, David M. | Bolton Wanderers | Wigan Athletic | 250,000 |

| | From | To | Fee in £s |
|---|---|---|---|
| 25 Leworthy, David J. | Rushden & Diamonds | Kingstonian | undisclosed |
| 18 Liburd, Marc E. | Boreham Wood | Aylesbury United | undisclosed |
| 18 Lightbourne, Kyle L. | Walsall | Coventry City | 500,000 |
| 31 Mackin, Jonathan P. | Manchester United | Preston North End | 250,000 |
| 29 Marker, Nicholas R.T. | Blackburn Rovers | Sheffield United | 400,000 |
| 5 Marsden, Anthony V. | Gresley Rovers | Burton Albion | undisclosed |
| 30 McGibbon, Patrick | Manchester United | Wigan Athletic | 250,000 |
| 21 Miller, Kevin | Watford | Crystal Palace | 1,000,000 + exch. |
| 17 Moody, Paul | Oxford United | Fulham | 200,000 |
| 17 Murphy, Daniel B. | Crewe Alexandra | Liverpool | 1,500,000 |
| 15 Ndlovu, Peter | Coventry City | Birmingham City | 200,000 |
| 22 Newell, Michael C. | Birmingham City | Aberdeen | 160,000 |
| 29 Nilsson, Roland N.J. | Helsingborg | Coventry City | 200,000 |
| 24 Nogan, Lee M. | Reading | Grimsby Town | 170,000 |
| 21 Oster, John | Grimsby Town | Everton | 1,500,000 |
| 2 Payne, Stephen R. | Sutton United | Hastings Town | undisclosed |
| 22 Pender, John P. | Wigan Athletic | Rochdale | 11,500 |
| 24 Penney, David M. | Swansea City | Cardiff City | 20,000 |
| 17 Phillips, Kevin M. | Watford | Sunderland | 325,000 |
| 9 Pickard, Owen | Dorchester Town | Yeovil Town | undisclosed |
| 29 Primus, Linvoy S. | Barnet | Reading | 250,000 |
| 17 Prudhoe, Mark | Stoke City | Bradford City | 70,000 |
| 10 Rawlins, Matthew | Mangotsfield United | Clevedon Town | undisclosed |
| 24 Richards, Tony S. | Cambridge United | Leyton Orient | 15,000 |
| 9 Roberts, Iwan W. | Wolverhampton Wanderers | Norwich City | 1,000,000 |
| 10 Rogers, Alan | Tranmere Rovers | Nottingham Forest | 2,000,000 |
| 23 Savage, Robert W. | Crewe Alexandra | Leicester City | 400,000 |
| 11 Scott, Keith | Norwich City | Wycombe Wanderers | 55,000 |
| 29 Sedgley, Stephen P. | Ipswich Town | Wolverhampton Wanderers | 500,000 |
| 28 Sheffield, Jonathan | Peterborough United | Plymouth Argyle | 100,000 |
| 1 Sheringham, Edward P. | Tottenham Hotspur | Manchester United | 3,500,000 |
| 2 Sheron, Michael N. | Stoke City | Queens Park Rangers | 2,750,000 |
| 7 Sinnott, Lee | Huddersfield Town | Oldham Athletic | 30,000 |
| 23 Steele, Lee A.J. | Northwich Victoria | Shrewsbury Town | 30,000 |
| 4 Smith, Neil J. | Gillingham | Fulham | Trib |
| 25 Smith, Paul W. | Brentford | Gillingham | Trib |
| 15 Spink, Dean P. | Shrewsbury Town | Wrexham | 65,000 |
| 1 Stewart, Paul A. | Sunderland | Stoke City | Free |
| 17 Thomas, David J. | Swansea City | Watford | 100,000 |
| 25 Thorne, Peter L. | Swindon Town | Stoke City | 350,000 |
| 28 Todd, Lee | Stockport County | Southampton | 500,000 |
| 9 Vaughan, Anthony J. | Ipswich Town | Manchester City | 1,350,000 |
| 29 Venus, Mark | Wolverhampton Wanderers | Ipswich Town | 150,000 |
| 31 Warhurst, Paul | Blackburn Rovers | Crystal Palace | 1,250,000 |
| 28 Watkins, Dale A. | Gloucester City | Cheltenham Town | undisclosed |
| 18 Whelan, Philip J. | Middlesbrough | Oxford United | 170,000 |
| 8 Wilcox, Russell | Preston North End | Scunthorpe United | 15,000 |
| 11 Wilkinson, Stephen J. | Preston North End | Chesterfield | 150,000 |
| 11 Willis, Roger C. | Peterborough United | Chesterfield | 100,000 |
| 29 Woodthorpe, Colin J. | Aberdeen | Stockport County | 200,000 |
| 14 Worthington, Nigel | Stoke City | Blackpool | Free |
| 16 Wright, Evran | Halesowen Town | Telford United | undisclosed |

**TEMPORARY TRANSFERS**

| | | | |
|---|---|---|---|
| 17 McGowan, Gavin G. | Arsenal | Luton Town | |
| 15 Merson, Paul C. | Arsenal | Middlesbrough | |
| 28 Mildenhall, Stephen J. | Swindon Town | Salisbury City | |

**AUGUST 1997**

| | | | |
|---|---|---|---|
| 2 Angus, Terence | Fulham | Slough Town | undisclosed |
| 8 Appleton, Michael A. | Manchester United | Preston North End | 500,000 |
| 7 Asaba, Carl E. | Brentford | Reading | 800,000 |
| 8 Ashby, Barry J. | Brentford | Gillingham | 140,000 |
| 8 Barnard, Darren S. | Bristol City | Barnsley | 750,000 |
| 20 Beardsley, Peter A. | Newcastle United | Bolton Wanderers | 450,000 |
| 29 Bent, Junior A. | Bristol City | Blackpool | undisclosed |
| 12 Berg, Henning | Blackburn Rovers | Manchester United | 5,000,000 |
| 7 Bos, Gijsbert | Lincoln City | Rotherham United | 20,000 |
| 5 Bracey, Lee M.I. | Bury | Ipswich Town | 40,000 |
| 1 Bradbury, Lee M. | Portsmouth | Manchester City | 3,500,000 |
| 8 Brown, Kenneth J. | Birmingham City | Millwall | 40,000 |
| 15 Brownrigg, Andrew D. | Norwich City | Rotherham United | Free |
| 11 Burton, Deon J. | Portsmouth | Derby County | 1,000,000 |
| 8, Butler, Martin N. | Walsall | Cambridge United | undisclosed |
| 7 Charlery, Kenneth L. | Stockport County | Barnet | 80,000 |
| 8 Cooper, Kevin L. | Derby County | Stockport County | 150,000 |
| 29 Costello, Mark B. | Sutton United | Staines Town | undisclosed |
| 4 Craddock, Jody D. | Cambridge United | Sunderland | 300,000 |
| 22 Cuggy, Michael S. | Hastings Town | Folkestone Invicta | undisclosed |
| 7 Curran, Christopher | Plymouth Argyle | Exeter City | 20,000 |
| 5 Davies, Simon I. | Manchester United | Luton Town | 150,000 |
| 8 Dore, Craig A. | Burnham | Witney Town | undisclosed |
| 21 Emblen, Neil R. | Wolverhampton Wanderers | Crystal Palace | 2,000,000 |
| 8 Fenton, Graham A. | Blackburn Rovers | Leicester City | 1,000,000 |
| 8 Ferdinand, Leslie | Newcastle United | Tottenham Hotspur | 6,000,000 |
| 8 Flynn, Sean M. | Derby County | West Bromwich Albion | 260,000 |
| 8 Ford, Mark S. | Leeds United | Burnley | 250,000 |

| | From | To | Fee in £s |
|---|---|---|---|
| 8 Galloway, Michael A. | Notts County | Gillingham | 10,000 |
| 29 Grant, Kim T. | Luton T | Millwall | undisclosed |
| 22 Grant, Peter | Celtic | Norwich City | 200,000 |
| 6 Gray, Ian J. | Rochdale | Stockport County | 200,000 |
| 1 Harle, Michael J.L. | Millwall | Barnet | Free |
| 22 Hartley, Paul | Millwall | Raith Rovers | 150,000 |
| 6 Hay, Christopher | Celtic | Swindon Town | 330,000 |
| 8 Heald, Gregory J. | Peterborough United | Barnet | 130,000 |
| 8 Hill, Kevin | Torrington | Torquay United | Free |
| 5 Holland, Matthew R. | AFC Bournemouth | Ipswich Town | 800,000 |
| 11 Howey, Lee M. | Sunderland | Burnley | 200,000 |
| 29 Hurst, Christopher M. | Emley | Huddersfield Town | undisclosed |
| 29 Jones, Marcus L. | Kingstonian | VS Rugby | undisclosed |
| 5 Kelly, David T. | Sunderland | Tranmere Rovers | 350,000 |
| 9 Kelly, Patrick | Celtic | Newcastle United | Free |
| 8 Kubicki, Darius | Sunderland | Wolverhampton Wanderers | Free |
| 8 Le Saux, Graeme P. | Blackburn Rovers | Chelsea | 5,000,000 |
| 14 McCormack, Joe R. | Newport (IOW) | Fareham Town | undisclosed |
| 15 McIntosh, Martin | Hamilton Academical | Stockport County | undisclosed |
| 15 Merson, Paul C. | Arsenal | Middlesbrough | 4,500,000 |
| 6 Morrisey, Terence | Oxford City | Chesham United | undisclosed |
| 1 Nevin, Patrick K.F. | Tranmere Rovers | Kilmarnock | 60,000 |
| 28 Nixon, Eric W. | Tranmere Rovers | Stockport County | 100,000 |
| 4 Nugent, Kevin P. | Bristol City | Cardiff City | 65,000 |
| 13 Nuttell, Michael J. | Burton Albion | Kettering Town | undisclosed |
| 8 O'Connell, Brendan | Charlton Athletic | Wigan Athletic | 120,000 |
| 15 O'Connell, Iain A. | Dover Athletic | Margate | undisclosed |
| 22 O'Sullivan, Wayne S.J. | Swindon Town | Cardiff City | 75,000 |
| 21 Oatway, Anthony P.D. | Torquay United | Brentford | 10,000 |
| 8 Paatelainen, Mika M.P. | Bolton Wanderers | Wolverhampton Wanderers | 250,000 |
| 22 Parker, Jeffrey S. | Barrow | Runcorn | undisclosed |
| 9 Riley, Andrew | Sutton United | Crawley Town | undisclosed |
| 15 Rush, Ian J. | Leeds United | Newcastle United | Free |
| 8 Schofield, John D. | Doncaster Rovers | Mansfield Town | 10,000 |
| 12 Scully, Anthony D.T. | Crystal Palace | Manchester City | 300,000 |
| 22 Statham, Brian | Brentford | Gillingham | 10,000 |
| 8 Swan, Peter H. | Burnley | Bury | 50,000 |
| 7 Thomas, Tony A. | Tranmere Rovers | Everton | 400,000 |
| 8 Torpey, Stephen D.J. | Swansea City | Bristol City | 400,000 |
| 29 Townsend, Andrew D. | Aston Villa | Middlesbrough | 500,000 |
| 18 Turner, Paul E. | Yeovil Town | St Albans City | undisclosed |
| 18 Unsworth, David G. | Everton | West Ham United | 1,000,000 |
| 22 Whitehall, Steven C. | Rochdale | Mansfield Town | 20,000 |
| 14 Williamson, Daniel A. | West Ham United | Everton | exch. |
| 20 Wilson, Patrick | Ashton United | Plymouth Argyle | 45,000 |

**TEMPORARY TRANSFERS**

| | | |
|---|---|---|
| 22 Beasant, David | Southampton | Nottingham Forest |
| 8 Boswell, Matthew H. | Port Vale | Witton Albion |
| 15 Broughton, Drewe O. | Norwich City | Wigan Athletic |
| 29 Brown, Linton | Swansea City | Scarborough |
| 29 Colkin, Lee | Northampton Town | Leyton Orient |
| 16 Connor, Paul | Middlesbrough | Gateshead |
| 11 Crichton, Paul A. | West Bromwich Albion | Aston Villa |
| 8 Davis, Kelvin G. | Luton Town | Hartlepool United |
| 15 Gilbert, David J. | West Bromwich Albion | Grimsby Town |
| 7 Grant, Kim T. | Luton Town | Millwall |
| 22 Greenacre, Christopher M. | Manchester City | Cardiff City |
| 29 Harper, Stephen A. | Newcastle United | Hartlepool United |
| 11 Harris, Jason A.S. | Crystal Palace | Lincoln City |
| 22 Hills, John D. | Everton | Swansea City |
| 28 Holcroft, Peter I. | Swindon Town | Exeter City |
| 29 Holloway, Darren | Sunderland | Carlisle United |
| 15 Howes, Shaun | Leyton Orient | Purfleet |
| 8 Jones, Scott | Barnsley | Mansfield Town |
| 29 Martin, David | Northampton Town | Welling United |
| 29 Mildenhall, Stephen J. | Swindon Town | Salisbury City |
| 14 Mohan, Nicholas | Bradford City | Wycombe Wanderers |
| 18 Morris, Stephen | Wrexham | Rochdale |
| 8 Moss, Neil G. | Southampton | Gillingham |
| 29 Ndah, George E. | Crystal Palace | Gillingham |
| 29 Pollitt, Michael F. | Notts County | Oldham Athletic |
| 6 Regis, David | Barnsley | Scunthorpe United |
| 15 Richardson, Lee J. | Oldham Athletic | Stockport County |
| 29 Robbins, Mark G. | Leicester City | Reading |
| 8 Seal, David | Bristol City | Northampton Town |
| 15 Simpson, Robert A. | Portsmouth | Stevenage Borough |
| 29 Smith, Craig | Derby County | Rochdale |
| 22 Squires, James A. | Preston North End | Mansfield Town |
| 22 Stein, Mark E.S. | Chelsea | Ipswich Town |
| 22 Stewart, Simon A. | Fulham | Woking |
| 22 Taylor, Paul | Southend United | Purfleet |
| 29 Thomas, James A. | Blackburn Rovers | West Bromwich Albion |
| 8 Tomlinson, Graeme M. | Manchester United | AFC Bournemouth |
| 15 Walker, David J. | Gravesend & Northfleet | Erith & Belvedere |
| 29 Warner, Vance | Nottingham Forest | Rotherham United |
| 29 Watts, Julian | Leicester City | Crewe Alexandra |

| | From | To | Fee in £s |
|---|---|---|---|
| 22 Williams, Dean P. | Doncaster Rovers | Huddersfield Town | |

**SEPTEMBER 1997**

| | From | To | Fee in £s |
|---|---|---|---|
| 12 Ainsworth, Gareth | Lincoln City | Port Vale | 500,000 |
| 1 Bignot, Marcus | Kidderminster Harriers | Crewe Alexandra | undisclosed |
| 19 Brown, Andrew S. | Hull City | Clydebank | Free |
| 5 Campbell, Neil A. | York City | Scarborough | undisclosed |
| 16 Cartwright, Neil A. | Kidderminster Harriers | Telford United | undisclosed |
| 11 Dair, Jason | Millwall | Raith Rovers | Free |
| 4 Danzey, Michael J. | Aylesbury United | Woking | undisclosed |
| 12 Fettis, Alan | Nottingham Forest | Blackburn Rovers | 300,000 |
| 19 Gage, Kevin W. | Preston North End | Hull City | Free |
| 13 Garner, Andrew | Gresley Rovers | Burton Albion | undisclosed |
| 2 Grant, Kim T. | Luton Town | Millwall | undisclosed |
| 3 Grant, Stephen H. | Shamrock Rovers | Stockport County | undisclosed |
| 23 Grobbelaar, Bruce D. | Oxford United | Sheffield Wednesday | undisclosed |
| 23 Harris, Jason A.S. | Crystal Palace | Leyton Orient | 25,000 |
| 26 Hocking, Matthew J. | Sheffield United | Hull City | undisclosed |
| 25 Hughes, Michael E. | West Ham United | Wimbledon | 800,000 |
| 26 Impey, Andrew R. | Queens Park Rangers | West Ham United | 1,300,000 |
| 26 Jackson, Justin J. | Woking | Notts County | 30,000 |
| 25 Jones, David J. | Goole | Blackpool | undisclosed |
| 4 Leaver, David | Morecambe | Accrington Stanley | undisclosed |
| 30 Liddle, Simon M. | Dulwich Hamlet | Canvey Island | undisclosed |
| 24 Linger, Paul H. | Charlton Athletic | Leyton Orient | Free |
| 10 Magilton, James | Southampton | Sheffield Wednesday | 1,600,000 |
| 11 McCarthy, Jonathan D. | Port Vale | Birmingham City | 1,850,000 |
| 19 McCormack, Joe R. | Fareham Town | Salisbury City | undisclosed |
| 9 Milsom, Paul J. | Gloucester City | Trowbridge Town | undisclosed |
| 22 Newson, Mark J. | Aylesbury United | Gravesend & Northfleet United | undisclosed |
| 5 Ormondroyd, Ian | Oldham Athletic | Scunthorpe United | 25,000 |
| 26 Palmer, Carlton L. | Leeds United | Southampton | 1,000,000 |
| 19 Pearce, Ian A. | Blackburn Rovers | West Ham United | 1,600,000 |
| 20 Quailey, Brian S. | Nuneaton Borough | West Bromwich Albion | undisclosed |
| 10 Richardson, Kevin | Coventry City | Southampton | 150,000 |
| 9 Richefond, Gary | Ilkeston Town | Arnold Town | undisclosed |
| 26 Robinson, Mark J. | Gravesend & Northfleet United | Weymouth | undisclosed |
| 8 Seal, David | Bristol City | Northampton Town | 90,000 |
| 15 Shaw, Paul | Arsenal | Millwall | 250,000 |
| 26 Spink, Nigel P. | West Bromwich Albion | Millwall | 50,000 |
| 18 Stott, Steve T.W. | Rushden & Diamonds | Yeovil Town | undisclosed |
| 5 Taylor, Paul | Southend United | Purfleet | undisclosed |
| 18 Townley, Leon | Tottenham Hotspur | Brentford | 50,000 |
| 27 Trundle, Lee C. | Chorley | Stalybridge Celtic | undisclosed |
| 30 Walling, Dean A. | Carlisle United | Lincoln City | 75,000 |
| 5 Ward, Ashley S. | Derby County | Barnsley | 1,300,000 |
| 26 Watkin, Stephen | Wrexham | Swansea City | undisclosed |
| 22 White, Alan | Middlesbrough | Luton Town | 40,000 |
| 23 White, Devon W. | Notts County | Shrewsbury Town | 35,000 |
| 19 Whitlow, Michael W. | Leicester City | Bolton Wanderers | 600,000 |
| 18 Wilkinson, Paul | Barnsley | Millwall | 150,000 |
| 19 Wilkinson, Paul | Dorchester Town | Basingstoke Town | undisclosed |

**TEMPORARY TRANSFERS**

| | From | To | |
|---|---|---|---|
| 5 Adams, Kieran C. | Barnet | St Leonards Stamcroft | |
| 26 Allen, Martin J. | Portsmouth | Southend United | |
| 26 Bettney, Christopher J. | Sheffield United | Hull City | |
| 18 Bodin, Paul J. | Reading | Wycombe Wanderers | |
| 5 Borrows, Brian | Coventry City | Swindon Town | |
| 2 Bowen, Jason P. | Birmingham City | Southampton | |
| 5 Brady, Matthew | Barnet | St Leonards Stamcroft | |
| 5 Casper, Christopher M. | Manchester United | Swindon Town | |
| 15 Clark, William R. | Bristol Rovers | Cheltenham Town | |
| 12 Clough, Nigel H. | Manchester City | Sheffield Wednesday | |
| 2 Coleman, Simon | Bolton Wanderers | Wolverhampton Wanderers | |
| 26 Coles, David A. | Gloucester City | Farnborough Town | |
| 26 Cooper, Mark N. | Hartlepool United | Macclesfield Town | |
| 5 Cotterill, John R. | Hednesford Town | Gresley Rovers | |
| 19 Creaney, Gerard | Manchester City | Burnley | |
| 5 Cretton, Scott | Stevenage Borough | Baldock Town | |
| 11 Davey, Simon | Preston North End | Darlington | |
| 5 Davies, Martin L. | Rushden & Diamonds | Tamworth | |
| 12 Davis, Steven P. | Barnsley | York City | |
| 2 Finlayson, Alexander | Swindon Town | Salisbury City | |
| 26 Gayle, Mark S.R. | Crewe Alexandra | Hereford United | |
| 29 Hanson, David | Leyton Orient | Dover Athletic | |
| 18 Hawes, Steven R. | Sheffield United | Doncaster Rovers | |
| 19 Hayfield, Matthew | Bristol Rovers | Yeovil Town | |
| 12 Holsgrove, Paul | Reading | Grimsby Town | |
| 18 Honeyball, Scott | Leyton Orient | Gravesend & Northfleet United | |
| 8 Hynes, Mark C. | Sutton United | Hendon | |
| 19 Kelly, Warren L. | Stevenage Borough | Rushden & Diamonds | |
| 19 Kernaghan, Alan N. | Manchester City | St Johnstone | |
| 8 Kilner, Aidan | Woking | Yeading | |
| 1 Kiwomya, Andrew D. | Bradford City | Burnley | |
| 1 Martin, Lee A. | Bristol Rovers | Huddersfield Town | |
| 19 McRobert, Lee | Millwall | Dover Athletic | |

| | From | To | Fee in £s |
|---|---|---|---|
| 12 Milner, Andrew J. | Chester City | Hereford United | |
| 26 Moore, Ian R. | Nottingham Forest | West Ham United | |
| 26 Morgan, Stephen A. | Wigan Athletic | Bury | |
| 3 Otto, Ricky | Birmingham City | Notts County | |
| 18 Overson, Vincent D. | Burnley | Shrewsbury Town | |
| 19 Parmenter, Steven J. | Bristol Rovers | Yeovil Town | |
| 12 Pearson, Christopher | Kettering Town | Eastwood Town | |
| 25 Rankin, Isaiah | Arsenal | Colchester United | |
| 5 Rowe, Ezekiel B. | Peterborough United | Kettering Town | |
| 5 Sandford, Lee R. | Sheffield United | Reading | |
| 12 Skinner, Justin | Bristol Rovers | Walsall | |
| 8 Small, Bryan | Bolton Wanderers | Luton Town | |
| 7 Tomlinson, Graham | Manchester United | AFC Bournemouth | |
| 19 Town, David | AFC Bournemouth | Dorchester Town | |
| 26 Van Heusden, Arjan | Port Vale | Oxford United | |
| 26 Walsh, Gary | Middlesbrough | Bradford City | |
| 19 West, Colin | Leyton Orient | Northampton Town | |
| 9 White, Jason G. | Northampton Town | Rotherham United | |
| 10 Whittaker, Stuart | Macclesfield Town | Stalybridge Celtic | |
| 1 Wilkinson, Paul | Dorchester Town | Basingstoke Town | |

**OCTOBER 1997**

| | From | To | Fee in £s |
|---|---|---|---|
| 7 Archer, Lee | Bristol Rovers | Yeovil Town | undisclosed |
| 17 Boothe, Christopher | Farnborough Town | Hayes | undisclosed |
| 10 Bracewell, Paul W. | Sunderland | Fulham | 75,000 |
| 24 Clark, Ian D. | Doncaster Rovers | Hartlepool United | Free |
| 30 Clark, William R. | Bristol Rovers | Exeter City | Free |
| 17 Clarke, Matthew L. | Halesowen Town | Kidderminster Harriers | undisclosed |
| 24 Cook, Paul A. | Tranmere Rovers | Stockport County | 250,000 |
| 25 Cooper, Gary | Kingstonian | Enfield | undisclosed |
| 30 Cusack, Nicholas J. | Fulham | Swansea City | 50,000 |
| 25 Darlington, Steven | Kingstonian | Enfield | undisclosed |
| 17 Deadman, John | Kingstonian | Enfield | undisclosed |
| 27 Evans, Michael J. | Southampton | West Bromwich Albion | 750,000 |
| 29 Eyres, David | Burnley | Preston North End | 80,000 |
| 22 Freedman, Douglas A. | Crystal Palace | Wolverhampton Wanderers | exch. |
| 6 Green, Paul W. | Buxton | Bradford Park Avenue | undisclosed |
| 17 Hirst, David E. | Sheffield Wednesday | Southampton | 2,000,000 |
| 3 Holdsworth, Dean C. | Wimbledon | Bolton Wanderers | 3,500,000 |
| 13 Horne, Barry | Birmingham City | Huddersfield Town | Free |
| 1 Jackson, Mark R. | Whitstable Town | Weymouth | undisclosed |
| 17 Kelly, Warren L. | Stevenage Borough | Rushden & Diamonds | undisclosed |
| 2 Lancashire, Graham | Wigan Athletic | Rochdale | 40,000 |
| 31 Maddison, Neil S. | Southampton | Middlesbrough | 250,000 |
| 9 Marsden, Christopher | Stockport County | Birmingham City | 500,000 |
| 1 McGleish, Scott | Leyton Orient | Barnet | 70,000 |
| 31 Mellon, Michael J. | Blackpool | Tranmere Rovers | 300,000 |
| 10 Mohan, Nicholas | Bradford City | Wycombe Wanderers | 85,000 |
| 22 Muscat, Kevin V. | Crystal Palace | Wolverhampton Wanderers | exch. |
| 7 Newbury, Richard J. | Gravesend & Northfleet | Carshalton Athletic | undisclosed |
| 31 Newhouse, Aidan R. | Fulham | Swansea City | 30,000 |
| 30 Patterson, Mark | Plymouth Argyle | Gillingham | 150,000 |
| 17 Peacock, Lee A. | Carlisle United | Mansfield Town | 150,000 |
| 8 Peake, Jason W. | Brighton & Hove Albion | Bury | Free |
| 24 Peschisolido, Paulo P. | West Bromwich Albion | Fulham | 1,100,000 |
| 10 Rattray, Kevin | Barnet | Kingstonian | undisclosed |
| 24 Richardson, Lee J. | Oldham Athletic | Huddersfield Town | 65,000 |
| 10 Rodosthenous, Michael | West Bromwich Albion | Cambridge United | Free |
| 31 Saville, Andrew V. | Wigan Athletic | Cardiff City | 60,000 |
| 17 Selley, Ian | Arsenal | Fulham | 500,000 |
| 11 Shepherd, Mark | Kidderminster Harriers | Moor Green | undisclosed |
| 22 Smith, James J.A. | Wolverhampton Wanderers | Crystal Palace | exch. |
| 24 Sutton, Wayne F. | Derby County | Woking | Free |
| 18 Taylor, Stephen C. | Bromsgrove Rovers | Telford United | undisclosed |
| 23 Terry, Peter E. | Basingstoke Town | Maidenhead United | undisclosed |
| 31 Thomas, Anton | Worcester City | Nuneaton Borough | undisclosed |
| 31 Walsh, Gary | Middlesbrough | Bradford City | 300,000 |
| 20 Walton, David L. | Shrewsbury Town | Crewe Alexandra | 500,000 |
| 8 Warren, Christer | Southampton | AFC Bournemouth | 50,000 |
| 10 White, Jason G. | Northampton Town | Rotherham United | 25,000 |

**TEMPORARY TRANSFERS**

| | From | To | |
|---|---|---|---|
| 31 Ayorinde, Samuel T. | Leyton Orient | Dover Athletic | |
| 31 Barnwell-Edinboro, Jamie | Cambridge United | Rushden & Diamonds | |
| 9 Barrowcliff, Paul J. | Brentford | Stevenage Borough | |
| 17 Bartram, Vincent L. | Arsenal | Huddersfield Town | |
| 24 Beard, Mark | Sheffield United | Southend United | |
| 3 Black, Michael J. | Arsenal | Millwall | |
| 10 Bochenski, Simon | Scarborough | Gateshead | |
| 27 Bonfield, Darren | Wealdstone | Wembley | |
| 9 Borrows, Brian | Coventry City | Swindon Town | |
| 10 Brady, Matthew | Barnet | Aylesbury United | |
| 10 Branston, Guy | Leicester City | Rushden & Diamonds | |
| 16 Brown, Wayne L. | Ipswich Town | Colchester United | |
| 17 Bundy, Scott D. | Portsmouth | Dorchester Town | |
| 18 Carden, Paul A. | Blackpool | Marine | |
| 5 Casper, Christopher M. | Manchester United | Swindon Town | |

| | From | To | Fee in £s |
|---|---|---|---|
| 3 Clyde, Darron E.J. | Gateshead | Emley | |
| 16 Colgan, Nicholas V. | Chelsea | Brentford | |
| 6 Colkin, Lee | Northampton Town | Leyton Orient | |
| 25 Constantinou, Anthony | Billericay Town | Witham Town | |
| 24 Cope, James A. | Shrewsbury Town | Stafford Rangers | |
| 9 Cross, John R. | Cardiff City | Inter Cable-Tel | |
| 24 Crowe, Glen N. | Wolverhampton Wanderers | Cardiff City | |
| 10 Cutler, Neil A. | Crewe Alexandra | Leek Town | |
| 10 Devlin, Mark A. | Stoke City | Exeter City | |
| 3 Fernandes, Tamer H. | Brentford | Peterborough United | |
| 10 Finney, Stephen K. | Swindon Town | Cambridge United | |
| 2 Flash, Richard G. | Watford | Lincoln City | |
| 17 Freedman, Douglas A. | Crystal Palace | Wolverhampton Wanderers | |
| 31 Freeman, Andrew J. | Reading | Kingstonian | |
| 17 Garvey, Stephen H. | Crewe Alexandra | Chesterfield | |
| 20 Gayle, Mark S.R. | Crewe Alexandra | Chesterfield | |
| 20 Gibson, Paul R. | Manchester United | Mansfield Town | |
| 8 Gislason, Valur | Arsenal | Brighton & Hove Albion | |
| 16 Goddard-Crawley, Richard L. | Brentford | Woking | |
| 31 Griffiths, Gareth J. | Port Vale | Shrewsbury Town | |
| 3 Hall, Gareth D. | Sunderland | Brentford | |
| 17 Heckingbottom, Paul | Sunderland | Scarborough | |
| 27 Hurst, Christopher M. | Huddersfield Town | Halifax Town | |
| 24 Jones, Scott | Barnsley | Notts County | |
| 13 Joyce, Anthony J. | Boreham Wood | Aylesbury United | |
| 3 Kearns, Andrew S. | Gravesend & Northfleet | Tonbridge | |
| 3 Kelly, Raymond | Manchester City | Wrexham | |
| 20 King, Philip G. | Swindon Town | Blackpool | |
| 23 Laker, Barry J. | Sutton United | Dulwich Hamlet | |
| 4 McDonnell, Matthew T. | Oxford City | Witney Town | |
| 3 McKenzie, Leon M. | Crystal Palace | Fulham | |
| 24 Markey, Brendan | Millwall | Bohemians | |
| 14 Milner, Andrew J. | Chester City | Hereford United | |
| 14 Minors, Dwayne J. | Charlton Athletic | Bromley | |
| 27 Morgan, Stephen A. | Wigan Athletic | Bury | |
| 8 Murphy, Dean K. | Hendon | Chesham United | |
| 31 O'Kane, John A. | Manchester United | Bradford City | |
| 31 Phillips, Steven | Bristol City | Evesham United | |
| 24 Potter, Graham S. | West Bromwich Albion | Northampton Town | |
| 8 Richardson, John P. | Hendon | Chesham United | |
| 9 Rocastle, David C. | Chelsea | Hull City | |
| 3 Russell, Keith D. | Blackpool | Altrincham | |
| 10 Simpson, Paul D. | Derby County | Wolverhampton Wanderers | |
| 9 Small, Bryan | Bolton Wanderers | Luton Town | |
| 17 Smith, Paul A. | Nottingham Forest | Lincoln City | |
| 3 Ward, Nicholas J. | Shrewsbury Town | Telford United | |
| 15 Warrilow, Thomas E. | Dartford | Gravesend & Northfleet | |
| 10 West, Gareth | Burnley | Gateshead | |
| 10 Williams, Carwyn | Stalybridge Celtic | Northwich Victoria | |
| 24 Wray, Shaun | Shrewsbury Town | Stafford Rangers | |
| 3 Wright, Evran | Telford United | Bilston Town | |

**NOVEMBER 1997**

| | | | |
|---|---|---|---|
| 11 Allison, Wayne A. | Swindon Town | Huddersfield Town | 800,000 |
| 14 Arter, David J. | Gravesend & Northfleet | Folkestone Invicta | undisclosed |
| 21 Aspinall, Warren | Carlisle United | Brentford | 50,000 |
| 11 Beasant, David | Southampton | Nottingham Forest | Free |
| 21 Bignall, Michael G. | Morecambe | Kidderminster Harriers | undisclosed |
| 14 Borrows, Brian | Coventry City | Swindon Town | Free |
| 21 Bound, Matthew T. | Stockport County | Swansea City | undisclosed |
| 21 Byrne, Christopher T. | Sunderland | Stockport County | 200,000 |
| 12 Cotterill, John R. | Hednesford Town | Gresley Rovers | undisclosed |
| 3 Edwards, Neil R. | Stockport County | Rochdale | 25,000 |
| 28 Ford, Robert J. | Oxford United | Sheffield United | 400,000 |
| 22 Gaughan, Steven E. | Chesterfield | Darlington | undisclosed |
| 7 Gordon, Kenyatta G. | Hull City | Lincoln City | undisclosed |
| 21 Harding, Paul J. | Worcester City | Halesowen Town | undisclosed |
| 14 Johnson, David A. | Bury | Ipswich Town | 1,100,000 |
| 14 Johnson, Ian G. | Dundee United | Huddersfield Town | 90,000 |
| 5 Lormor, Anthony | Chesterfield | Preston North End | 130,000 |
| 28 McAnespie, Stephen | Bolton Wanderers | Fulham | 100,000 |
| 7 McCue, James G. | Kidderminster Harriers | Hereford United | undisclosed |
| 15 McDonnell, Matthew T. | Oxford City | Witney Town | undisclosed |
| 6 McGinlay, John | Bolton Wanderers | Bradford City | 625,000 |
| 14 Murphy, Dean K. | Hendon | Chesham United | undisclosed |
| 21 Ndah, George E. | Crystal Palace | Swindon Town | 500,000 |
| 28 Neilson, Alan B. | Southampton | Fulham | 250,000 |
| 14 Phillips, David O. | Nottingham Forest | Huddersfield Town | Free |
| 6 Reeves, David | Preston North End | Chesterfield | exch. |
| 14 Russell, Craig S. | Sunderland | Manchester City | 1,000,000 |
| 21 Scott, Andrew | Sheffield United | Brentford | 75,000 |
| 13 Simpson, Paul D. | Derby County | Wolverhampton Wanderers | 75,000 |
| 28 Stuart, Graham C. | Everton | Sheffield United | 500,000 |
| 14 Summerbee, Nicholas J. | Manchester City | Sunderland | 1,000,000 |
| 14 Swailes, Christopher W. | Ipswich Town | Bury | 200,000 |
| 17 Taylor, Maik S. | Southampton | Fulham | 700,000 |
| 28 Tiler, Carl | Sheffield United | Everton | exch. |

|  |  | *From* | *To* | *Fee in £s* |
|---|---|---|---|---|
| 28 | Trollope, Paul J. | Derby County | Fulham | 600,000 |
| 28 | Ward, Mitchum D. | Sheffield United | Everton | exch. |
| 7 | Warner, Vance | Nottingham Forest | Rotherham United | undisclosed |
| 27 | Whitmarsh, Paul | Dulwich Hamlet | Hendon | undisclosed |
| 15 | Wray, Shaun | Shrewsbury Town | Stafford Rangers | undisclosed |

**TEMPORARY TRANSFERS**

|  |  | | | |
|---|---|---|---|---|
| 18 | Adamson, Christopher | West Bromwich Albion | Moor Green | |
| 28 | Allen, Christopher A. | Nottingham Forest | Luton Town | |
| 10 | Barr, Andrew R. | Luton Town | Hitchin Town | |
| 18 | Bartram, Vincent L. | Arsenal | Huddersfield Town | |
| 25 | Beard, Mark | Sheffield United | Southend United | |
| 9 | Bettney, Christopher J. | Sheffield United | Hull City | |
| 14 | Birkby, Dean | Yeovil Town | Forest Green Rovers | |
| 28 | Bonfield, Darren | Wealdstone | Wembley | |
| 21 | Boxall, Daniel J. | Crystal Palace | Oldham Athletic | |
| 14 | Bradford, Lee T. | Weymouth | Salisbury City | |
| 11 | Brady, Matthew | Barnet | Aylesbury United | |
| 7 | Carroll, Stephen A. | Altrincham | Droylsden | |
| 22 | Carter, Mark C. | Rochdale | Gateshead | |
| 28 | Chandler, Dean A. | Lincoln City | Yeovil Town | |
| 24 | Collins, James I. | Crewe Alexandra | Northwich Victoria | |
| 25 | Cope, James A. | Shrewsbury Town | Stafford Rangers | |
| 14 | Cottee, Antony R. | Leicester City | Birmingham City | |
| 21 | Dalglish, Paul | Liverpool | Bury | |
| 4 | Emblen, Paul D. | Charlton Athletic | Brighton & Hove Albion | |
| 15 | Fearon, Ronald T. | Dover Athletic | Hastings Town | |
| 1 | Ford, Richard J. | Forest Green Rovers | Yate Town | |
| 30 | Freeman, Andrew J. | Reading | Kingstonian | |
| 21 | Gibson, Paul R. | Manchester United | Mansfield Town | |
| 17 | Gleghorn, Nigel W. | Burnley | Brentford | |
| 27 | Gregory, Neil R. | Ipswich Town | Peterborough United | |
| 25 | Hart, Barrie R. | Oldham Athletic | Radcliffe Borough | |
| 25 | Heckingbottom, Paul | Sunderland | Scarborough | |
| 3 | Helliwell, Ian | Burnley | Doncaster Rovers | |
| 7 | Hercock, David | Ilkeston Town | Nuneaton Borough | |
| 6 | Hodges, Lee L. | West Ham United | Plymouth Argyle | |
| 14 | Housley, Neil | Weymouth | Salisbury City | |
| 21 | Hoyland, Jamie W. | Burnley | Carlisle United | |
| 12 | Jones, Ian | Luton Town | Hitchin Town | |
| 20 | Karimzadeh, Ashkan | Portsmouth | Bognor Regis Town | |
| 3 | Legg, Andrew | Birmingham City | Ipswich Town | |
| 21 | O'Hagan, Daniel A.N. | Weston-Super-Mare | Plymouth Argyle | |
| 7 | Paterson, Scott | Bristol City | Cardiff City | |
| 21 | Pell, Robert A. | Rotherham United | Doncaster Rovers | |
| 2 | Pollitt, Michael F. | Notts County | Oldham Athletic | |
| 28 | Potter, Graham S. | West Bromwich Albion | Northampton Town | |
| 14 | Reed, Ian P. | Shrewsbury Town | Halesowen Town | |
| 27 | Rhodes, Andrew C. | Airdrieonians | Scarborough | |
| 9 | Rocastle, David C. | Chelsea | Hull City | |
| 21 | Sharpe, Robert L. | Aylesbury United | Berkhamsted Town | |
| 21 | Strong, Greg | Bolton Wanderers | Blackpool | |
| 14 | Thomas, Wayne | Walsall | Kidderminster Harriers | |
| 21 | Thompson, David A. | Liverpool | Swindon Town | |
| 17 | Tracey, Richard | Sheffield United | Matlock Town | |
| 7 | Utley, Darren | Doncaster Rovers | Stalybridge Celtic | |
| 25 | Ward, Mitcham D. | Sheffield United | Everton | |
| 5 | Warner, Anthony R. | Liverpool | Swindon Town | |
| 28 | West, Colin | Leyton Orient | Rushden & Diamonds | |
| 6 | Woods, Neil S. | Grimsby Town | Wigan Athletic | |
| 28 | Wright, Nicholas J. | Derby County | Carlisle United | |

**DECEMBER 1997**

|  |  | | | |
|---|---|---|---|---|
| 2 | Ayorinde, Samuel T. | Leyton Orient | Dover Athletic | undisclosed |
| 12 | Bishop, Charles D. | Wigan Athletic | Northampton Town | 20,000 |
| 24 | Bowen, Jason | Birmingham City | Reading | 200,000 |
| 1 | Coleman, Christopher | Blackburn Rovers | Fulham | 2,100,000 |
| 31 | Coppin, Matthew | Redditch United | Stourbridge | undisclosed |
| 12 | Davies, Gareth M. | Crystal Palace | Reading | 175,000 |
| 12 | Ellis, Anthony J. | Blackpool | Bury | 70,000 |
| 12 | Foran, Mark J. | Peterborough United | Crewe Alexandra | 45,000 |
| 24 | Freestone, Christopher M. | Middlesbrough | Northampton Town | 75,000 |
| 5 | Furnell, Andrew P. | Rushden & Diamonds | Nuneaton Borough | undisclosed |
| 1 | Gray, Andrew | Wokingham Town | Hampton | undisclosed |
| 24 | Grazioli, Giuliano | Peterborough United | Stevenage Borough | Free |
| 19 | Honeyball, Scott | Leyton Orient | Gravesend & Northfleet | undisclosed |
| 12 | Hughes, Ian | Bury | Blackpool | 200,000 |
| 24 | Inman, Niall E. | Peterborough United | Stevenage Borough | Free |
| 12 | Johnson, David D. | Gloucester City | Raunds Town | undisclosed |
| 19 | Kulcsar, George | Bradford City | Queens Park Rangers | 250,000 |
| 17 | Linger, Paul H. | Leyton Orient | Brighton & Hove Albion | Free |
| 6 | Magee, Jonathan P. | St Leonards Stamcroft | Margate | undisclosed |
| 19 | Mainwaring, Andrew | Bromsgrove Rovers | Gloucester City | undisclosed |
| 10 | McDonald, Martin J. | Doncaster Rovers | Macclesfield Town | undisclosed |
| 12 | Murray, Scott G. | Aston Villa | Bristol City | 150,000 |
| 11 | Patterson, Mark A. | Sheffield United | Bury | 125,000 |
| 1 | Rennie, David | Northampton Town | Peterborough United | Free |

| | | From | To | Fee in £s |
|---|---|---|---|---|
| 20 | Smith, Paul A. | Nottingham Forest | Lincoln City | 20,000 |
| 9 | Southall, Leslie N. | Grimsby Town | Gillingham | Free |
| 11 | Veart, Thomas C. | Crystal Palace | Millwall | 50,000 |
| 18 | Watson, Paul D. | Fulham | Brentford | 50,000 |
| 8 | Wilkins, Craig | Tonbridge | Gravesend & Northfleet | undisclosed |

**TEMPORARY TRANSFERS**

| | | | | |
|---|---|---|---|---|
| 12 | Anderson, Simon P. | Witney Town | Thame United | |
| 22 | Anthony, Marc | Celtic | Tranmere Rovers | |
| 23 | Armstrong, Simon | Port Vale | Boston United | |
| 12 | Atkinson, Graeme | Preston North End | Rochdale | |
| 18 | Barker, Richard I. | Linfield | Brighton & Hove Albion | |
| 24 | Beesley, Paul | Manchester City | Port Vale | |
| 18 | Braithwaite, Leon | Exeter City | Welling United | |
| 24 | Branch, Graham | Tranmere Rovers | Wigan Athletic | |
| 20 | Brockie, Vincent | Hyde United | Farsley Celtic | |
| 19 | Brown, Simon J. | Tottenham Hotspur | Lincoln City | |
| 24 | Brownrigg, Andrew D. | Rotherham United | Stalybridge Celtic | |
| 12 | Catlin, Neil | Stevenage Borough | Marlow | |
| 5 | Charlton, Simon T. | Southampton | Birmingham City | |
| 11 | Conway, Paul J. | Northampton Town | Scarborough | |
| 1 | Davies, Lawrence | Bradford City | Darlington | |
| 15 | Dempsey, Mark A.P. | Shrewsbury Town | Dover Athletic | |
| 6 | Dillnutt, James | Stevenage Borough | Bishops Stortford | |
| 19 | Dobson, Warren E. | Hartlepool United | Bishop Auckland | |
| 24 | Finlayson, Alexander J. | Swindon Town | Worcester City | |
| 4 | Foster, Martin | Leeds United | Blackpool | |
| 31 | Freeman, Andrew J. | Reading | Yeovil Town | |
| 8 | Freestone, Christopher M. | Middlesbrough | Northampton Town | |
| 13 | Gallagher, Benn S. | Manchester City | Stafford Rangers | |
| 11 | Gray, Andrew D. | Leeds United | Bury | |
| 30 | Green, Joseph A. | Norwich City | Wisbech Town | |
| 19 | Hale, Matthew | Bristol City | Weymouth | |
| 18 | Harper, Stephen A. | Newcastle United | Huddersfield Town | |
| 12 | Hercock, David | Ilkeston Town | Rothwell Town | |
| 12 | Hodges, Tristan J. | Gravesend & Northfleet | Erith & Belvedere | |
| 5 | Hodson, Simeon P. | Rushden & Diamonds | Telford United | |
| 19 | Howell, Ian R. | Gloucester City | Newport (IOW) | |
| 24 | Huckerby, Scott | Ilkeston Town | VS Rugby | |
| 17 | Jones, Barry | Wrexham | York City | |
| 24 | Jones, Stephen G. | Charlton Athletic | AFC Bournemouth | |
| 20 | Joyce, Anthony J. | Boreham Wood | Aylesbury United | |
| 12 | Kerslake, David | Ipswich Town | Wycombe Wanderers | |
| 24 | Leadbeater, Richard P. | Wolverhampton Wanderers | Hereford United | |
| 19 | Lee, David J. | Chelsea | Sheffield United | |
| 12 | Lilwall, Stephen | Kidderminster Harriers | Solihull Borough | |
| 5 | Marshall, Robert J. | Stevenage Borough | Harrow Borough | |
| 1 | Midgley, Craig S. | Bradford City | Darlington | |
| 19 | Moran, Stephen | Southport | Barrow | |
| 12 | Murphy, Matthew S. | Oxford United | Scunthorpe United | |
| 12 | Newman, Robert | Norwich City | Motherwell | |
| 19 | O'Shea, Daniel E. | Rushden & Diamonds | Aylesbury United | |
| 23 | Palmer, Charles A. | Burton Albion | Moor Green | |
| 12 | Parker, Jeffrey S. | Runcorn | Leek Town | |
| 5 | Parsons, John | Sutton Coldfield Town | Bromsgrove Rovers | |
| 5 | Peaks, Andrew M. | Rushden & Diamonds | Nuneaton Borough | |
| 13 | Phillips, Gary C. | Aylesbury United | Aldershot Town | |
| 12 | Pollitt, Michael F. | Notts County | Gillingham | |
| 12 | Rainford, David J. | Colchester United | Wivenhoe Town | |
| 5 | Reed, Adam M. | Blackburn Rovers | Rochdale | |
| 19 | Roberts, Jason A.D. | Wolverhampton Wanderers | Torquay United | |
| 12 | Rowlands, Aled J.R. | Manchester City | Sligo Rovers | |
| 19 | Small, Bryan | Bolton Wanderers | Bradford City | |
| 12 | Smith, Steven P. | Gravesend & Northfleet | Erith & Belvedere | |
| 24 | Southall, Neville | Everton | Southend United | |
| 24 | Tait, Paul | Birmingham City | Northampton Town | |
| 12 | Taylor, Scott J. | Bolton Wanderers | Rotherham United | |
| 19 | Teather, Paul | Manchester United | AFC Bournemouth | |
| 24 | Thom, Stuart P. | Nottingham Forest | Mansfield Town | |
| 24 | Thompson, Neil | Barnsley | Oldham Athletic | |
| 23 | Tisdale, Paul R. | Bristol City | Exeter City | |
| 12 | Trevitt, Simon | Hull City | Swansea City | |
| 19 | Van Dullemen, Raymond V. | Northampton Town | Kettering Town | |
| 12 | Walker, Andrew | Sheffield United | Hibernian | |
| 22 | Wallwork, Ronald | Manchester United | Carlisle United | |
| 12 | Watson, Paul D. | Fulham | Brentford | |
| 5 | Whittle, Simon M. | Radcliffe Borough | Congleton Town | |

**JANUARY 1998**

| | | | | |
|---|---|---|---|---|
| 16 | Barnes, Paul L. | Burnley | Huddersfield Town | exch. |
| 8 | Bent, Marcus N. | Brentford | Crystal Palace | 150,000 |
| 28 | Brevett, Rufus E. | Queens Park Rangers | Fulham | 375,000 |
| 12 | Brindley, Christopher | Kidderminster Harriers | Hednesford Town | undisclosed |
| 26 | Carbon, Matthew P. | Derby County | West Bromwich Albion | 800,000 |
| 8 | Charlton, Simon T. | Southampton | Birmingham City | 250,000 |
| 23 | Collins, Wayne A. | Sheffield Wednesday | Fulham | 400,000 |
| 8 | Cook, Andrew C. | Portsmouth | Millwall | 50,000 |

| | From | To | Fee in £s |
|---|---|---|---|
| 26 Cullen, David J. | Hartlepool United | Sheffield United | 250,000 |
| 26 Derry, Shaun P. | Notts County | Sheffield United | 500,000 |
| 9 Devlin, Mark A. | Stoke City | Exeter City | Free |
| 13 Doolan, John | Mansfield Town | Barnet | 60,000 |
| 30 Dowie, Iain | West Ham United | Queens Park Rangers | exch. |
| 16 Fjortoft, Jan-Age | Sheffield United | Barnsley | 800,000 |
| 30 Frail, Stephen | Heart of Midlothian | Tranmere Rovers | 90,000 |
| 21 Gray, Andrew A. | Bury | Millwall | undisclosed |
| 30 Griffin, Andrew | Stoke City | Newcastle United | 1,500,000 |
| 30 Grodas, Frode | Chelsea | Tottenham Hotspur | 250,000 |
| 23 Hanson, David | Leyton Orient | Halifax Town | Free |
| 22 Haynes, Junior L.A. | Hayes | Sutton United | undisclosed |
| 30 Hinchcliffe, Andrew G. | Everton | Sheffield Wednesday | 3,000,000 |
| 17 Hodson, Simeon P. | Rushden & Diamonds | Telford United | undisclosed |
| 23 Hogg, Graeme J. | Notts County | Brentford | Free |
| 16 Howe, Stephen R. | Nottingham Forest | Swindon Town | 30,000 |
| 16 Jepson, Ronald F. | Bury | Oldham Athletic | 30,000 |
| 20 Jones, Barry | Wrexham | York City | 35,000 |
| 22 Joseph, Matthew N.A. | Cambridge United | Leyton Orient | 10,000 |
| 9 Leaburn, Carl W. | Charlton Athletic | Wimbledon | 300,000 |
| 23 Maher, Kevin A. | Tottenham Hotspur | Southend United | Free |
| 23 Metcalfe, Christian W. | Harrow Borough | Hayes | undisclosed |
| 30 Muntasser, Jehad | Arsenal | Bristol City | Free |
| 7 Mustoe, Neil J. | Manchester United | Wigan Athletic | undisclosed |
| 14 Niblett, Nigel | Hednesford Town | Kidderminster Harriers | undisclosed |
| 30 O'Kane, John A. | Manchester United | Everton | 250,000 |
| 16 Parker, Jeffrey S. | Runcorn | Leek Town | undisclosed |
| 16 Payton, Andrew P. | Huddersfield Town | Burnley | exch. |
| 30 Rowland, Keith | West Ham United | Queens Park Rangers | exch. |
| 30 Ryan, Robert P. | Huddersfield Town | Millwall | 10,000 |
| 30 Sinclair, Trevor L. | Queens Park Rangers | West Ham United | 2,300,000 |
| 16 Smith, David | West Bromwich Albion | Grimsby Town | 200,000 |
| 9 Weaver, Luke D.S. | Leyton Orient | Sunderland | 250,000 |
| 22 Wilson, Patrick | Plymouth Argyle | Doncaster Rovers | Free |

**TEMPORARY TRANSFERS**

| | From | To |
|---|---|---|
| 20 Alsop, Julian | Bristol Rovers | Swansea City |
| 16 Anderson, Simon P. | Witney Town | Thame United |
| 23 Barnes, Steven L. | Birmingham City | Brighton & Hove Albion |
| 16 Barrett, Earl D. | Everton | Sheffield United |
| 9 Brebner, Grant I. | Manchester United | Cambridge United |
| 15 Briscoe, Anthony M. | Shrewsbury Town | Weymouth |
| 27 Brownrigg, Andrew D. | Rotherham United | Stalybridge Celtic |
| 9 Burnett, Wayne | Huddersfield Town | Grimsby Town |
| 9 Clapham, James R. | Tottenham Hotspur | Ipswich Town |
| 23 Claridge, Stephen E. | Leicester City | Portsmouth |
| 30 Clark, Richard | Evesham United | Salisbury City |
| 27 Clyde, Darron E.J. | Gateshead | Bradford Park Avenue |
| 2 Creaney, Gerard | Manchester City | Chesterfield |
| 30 Denys, Ryan H. | Brentford | Yeovil Town |
| 30 Donaldson, O'Neill M. | Sheffield Wednesday | Oxford United |
| 8 Dudley, Craig B. | Notts County | Shrewsbury Town |
| 9 Duncan, Andrew | Manchester United | Cambridge United |
| 16 Eaton, Grant A. | Slough Town | Wokingham Town |
| 8 Falana, Wade R. | Romford | Harlow Town |
| 30 Fenn, Neale M.C. | Tottenham Hotspur | Leyton Orient |
| 16 George, Daniel S. | Nottingham Forest | Doncaster Rovers |
| 2 Germaine, Gary | West Bromwich Albion | Shrewsbury Town |
| 2 Gregory, Neil R. | Ipswich Town | Colchester United |
| 2 Harries, Paul G. | Portsmouth | Basingstoke Town |
| 14 Hart, Barry R. | Oldham Athletic | Radcliffe Borough |
| 16 Hills, John D. | Everton | Blackpool |
| 30 Hitchen, Steven J. | Macclesfield Town | Flixton |
| 6 Hodges, Lee L. | West Ham United | Plymouth Argyle |
| 28 Howie, Scott | Motherwell | Coventry City |
| 29 Hughes, Andrew J. | Oldham Athletic | Notts County |
| 16 Hunter, Colin | Guiseley | Harrogate Town |
| 29 Irving, Richard J. | Macclesfield Town | Runcorn |
| 16 Jackson, Kirk S. | Chesterfield | Gainsborough Trinity |
| 23 Jobson, Richard I. | Leeds United | Southend United |
| 29 Johnson, Damien M. | Blackburn Rovers | Nottingham Forest |
| 15 Jones, Gary | Swansea City | Rochdale |
| 30 Jones, Lee | Swansea City | Bristol Rovers |
| 27 Kennedy, Mark | Liverpool | Queens Park Rangers |
| 16 Lightbourne, Kyle L. | Coventry City | Fulham |
| 2 MacKenzie, Stuart M. | Farnborough Town | Kingstonian |
| 28 McKinlay, Thomas V. | Celtic | Stoke City |
| 23 Mason, Andrew J. | Macclesfield Town | Boston United |
| 16 McLeary, Stewart | Oxford City | Abingdon Town |
| 29 Murray, Robert J. | AFC Bournemouth | Dorchester Town |
| 22 Nethercott, Stuart | Tottenham Hotspur | Millwall |
| 24 Perry, Mark | Walsall | Stafford Rangers |
| 5 Phillips, Martin J. | Manchester City | Scunthorpe United |
| 22 Phillips, Steven J. | Bristol City | Clevedon Town |
| 5 Pitcher, Darren E.J. | Crystal Palace | Leyton Orient |
| 22 Pollitt, Michael F. | Notts County | Brentford |
| 2 Rees, Gavin R. | Portsmouth | Basingstoke Town |

| | From | To | Fee in £s |
|---|---|---|---|
| 2 Roach, Neville | Reading | Kingstonian | |
| 27 Scully, Anthony D.T. | Manchester City | Stoke City | |
| 30 Small, Bryan | Bolton Wanderers | Bury | |
| 30 Street, Tyrone T. | Nuneaton Borough | Blakenall | |
| 8 Taylor, Robert | West Bromwich Albion | Bolton Wanderers | |
| 23 Thompson, Mark | Portsmouth | Bognor Regis Town | |
| 25 Thom, Stuart | Nottingham Forest | Mansfield Town | |
| 20 Tisdale, Paul R. | Bristol City | Exeter City | |
| 23 Watts, Kirk | Gravesend & Northfleet | Croydon | |
| 12 West, Colin | Leyton Orient | Rushden & Diamonds | |
| 23 Whittaker, David A. | Crewe Alexandra | Witton Albion | |
| 23 Williams, Paul A. | Southend United | Canvey Island | |
| 30 Williams, Stephen | Port Vale | Witton Albion | |
| 19 Woods, Neil S. | Grimsby Town | Scunthorpe United | |

**FEBRUARY 1998**

| | From | To | Fee in £s |
|---|---|---|---|
| 6 Adebola, Bamberdele | Crewe Alexandra | Birmingham City | 1,000,000 |
| 16 Armstrong, Alun | Stockport County | Middlesbrough | 1,600,000 |
| 25 Barrett, Earl D. | Everton | Sheffield Wednesday | Free |
| 13 Burnett, Wayne | Huddersfield Town | Grimsby Town | 100,000 |
| 20 Coleman, Simon | Bolton Wanderers | Southend United | Free |
| 17 Cullip, Daniel | Fulham | Brentford | 75,000 |
| 6 Delap, Rory J. | Carlisle United | Derby County | 500,000 |
| 12 Elliott, Anthony R. | Cardiff City | Scarborough | Free |
| 17 Francis, Kevin D.M. | Birmingham City | Oxford United | 100,000 |
| 20 George, Daniel | Nottingham Forest | Doncaster Rovers | Free |
| 14 Grocutt, Darren | Bromsgrove Rovers | Burton Albion | undisclosed |
| 20 Gunn, Bryan | Norwich City | Hibernian | undisclosed |
| 13 Hills, John D. | Everton | Blackpool | 75,000 |
| 27 Hutchison, Donald | Sheffield United | Everton | 1,000,000 |
| 12 Jansen, Matthew B. | Carlisle United | Crystal Palace | 1,500,000 |
| 5 Jemson, Nigel B. | Oxford United | Bury | 100,000 |
| 20 Legg, Andrew | Birmingham City | Reading | 75,000 |
| 16 Lightbourne, Kyle L. | Coventry City | Stoke City | 500,000 |
| 27 McMahon, Gerard J. | Stoke City | St Johnstone | 85,000 |
| 4 Muntasser, Jehad | Arsenal | Bristol City | Free |
| 27 Nethercott, Stuart | Tottenham Hotspur | Millwall | undisclosed |
| 27 O'Connor, Jonathan | Everton | Sheffield United | exch. |
| 27 Payne, Stuart | Halesowen Harriers | Bromsgrove Rovers | undisclosed |
| 20 Phillips, Wayne | Wrexham | Stockport County | undisclosed |
| 17 Purse, Darren J. | Oxford United | Birmingham City | 600,000 |
| 20 Quinn, Stephen J. | Blackpool | West Bromwich Albion | 500,000 |
| 20 Robinson, Matthew R. | Southampton | Portsmouth | 50,000 |
| 6 Smith, Alexander P. | Swindon Town | Huddersfield Town | Free |
| 6 Speed, Gary A. | Everton | Newcastle United | 5,500,000 |
| 27 Taylor, Stephen C. | Telford United | Bromsgrove Rovers | undisclosed |
| 26 Thorpe, Anthony L. | Luton Town | Fulham | 800,000 |
| 4 West, Colin | Leyton Orient | Rushden & Diamonds | undisclosed |
| 19 Wright, Jermaine M. | Wolverhampton Wanderers | Crewe Alexandra | 25,000 |
| 19 Wright, Nicholas J. | Derby County | Carlisle United | 35,000 |
| 13 Yates, Luke | Halesowen Town | Nuneaton Borough | undisclosed |

**TEMPORARY TRANSFERS**

| | From | To | |
|---|---|---|---|
| 20 Abbey, Nathanael | Luton Town | Woking | |
| 23 Aldridge, Martin J. | Oxford United | Southend United | |
| 12 Alford, Carl P. | Rushden & Diamonds | Dover Athletic | |
| 11 Allen, Eben | Yeading | Molesey | |
| 6 Basham, Steven | Southampton | Wrexham | |
| 17 Beardsley, Peter A. | Bolton Wanderers | Manchester City | |
| 13 Birch, Mark | Stoke City | Leek Town | |
| 27 Boxall, Daniel J. | Crystal Palace | Oldham Athletic | |
| 27 Boyack, Steven | Rangers | Hull City | |
| 9 Branston, Guy P.B. | Leicester City | Colchester United | |
| 20 Briscoe, Lee S. | Sheffield Wednesday | Manchester City | |
| 12 Brown, Derek | Nuneaton Borough | Rothwell Town | |
| 10 Bullen, Michael | Aldershot Town | Yeading | |
| 17 Carroll, Lee G. | Northwood | Wokingham Town | |
| 20 Charles, Lee M. | Queens Park Rangers | Cambridge United | |
| 10 Clyde, Glynn N. | Macclesfield Town | Winsford United | |
| 27 Colgan, Nicholas V. | Chelsea | Reading | |
| 27 Conlon, Barry J. | Manchester City | Plymouth Argyle | |
| 6 Connor, Paul | Middlesbrough | Hartlepool United | |
| 12 Constantinou, Anthony | Billericay Town | Witham Town | |
| 2 Cope, James A. | Shrewsbury Town | Redditch United | |
| 13 Cornforth, John M. | Wycombe Wanderers | Peterborough United | |
| 20 Crossley, Mark G. | Nottingham Forest | Millwall | |
| 13 Daley, Ryan S. | Telford United | Bromsgrove Rovers | |
| 16 Davis, Steven P. | Barnsley | Oxford United | |
| 12 Dixon, Gary J. | Stevenage Borough | Hemel Hempstead | |
| 5 Dudley, Derek A. | Telford United | Bilston Town | |
| 6 Duerden, Ian C. | Burnley | Telford United | |
| 6 Eastwood, Phillip | Burnley | Telford United | |
| 20 Elliott, Stuart T. | Newcastle United | Swindon Town | |
| 13 Fearon, Ronald T. | Dover Athletic | Gravesend & Northfleet | |
| 28 Finch, Busbie D. | Enfield | Grays Athletic | |
| 24 Foley, Dominic J. | Wolverhampton Wanderers | Watford | |
| 13 Gleghorn, Nigel W. | Burnley | Northampton Town | |

| | From | To | Fee in £s |
|---|---|---|---|
| 11 Hazle, Daniel | Dagenham & Redbridge | Billericay Town | |
| 19 Hill, Daniel R.L. | Tottenham Hotspur | Cardiff City | |
| 10 Hirst, Lee | Alfreton Town | Worksop Town | |
| 10 Huxford, Richard J. | Burnley | Dunfermline Athletic | |
| 19 Jackson, Adam | Stevenage Borough | Tring Town | |
| 12 Johansen, Stig | Southampton | Bristol City | |
| 12 Jones, David | Billericay Town | Witham Town | |
| 6 Joyce, Anthony J. | Boreham Wood | Bishops Stortford | |
| 16 Kean, Robert S. | Luton Town | Boreham Wood | |
| 23 Landon, Richard J. | Macclesfield Town | Hednesford Town | |
| 20 Liddle, Craig G. | Middlesbrough | Darlington | |
| 20 Lormor, Anthony | Preston North End | Notts County | |
| 13 Mahoney-Johnson, Michael | Queens Park Rangers | Brighton & Hove Albion | |
| 19 Marshall, Robert J. | Stevenage Borough | St Albans City | |
| 20 Mason, Andrew J. | Macclesfield Town | Boston United | |
| 13 McCleary, Stuart | Oxford City | Abingdon Town | |
| 13 Melville, Andrew R. | Sunderland | Bradford City | |
| 6 Mills, Daniel R. | Barnet | Sutton United | |
| 13 Mullin, John | Sunderland | Preston North End | |
| 27 Ndekine, Malcolm S. | Rushden & Diamonds | Aylesbury United | |
| 10 O'Connor, Jonathan | Everton | Sheffield United | |
| 20 O'Hagan, Daniel A. | Weston-Super-Mare | Dorchester Town | |
| 13 Parks, Anthony | Burnley | Doncaster Rovers | |
| 27 Pattullo, David | Sutton United | Molesey | |
| 24 Perry, Mark | Walsall | Stafford Rangers | |
| 6 Peverell, Nicholas J. | Bishop Auckland | Gateshead | |
| 13 Phillips, Wayne | Wrexham | Stockport County | |
| 12 Philliskirk, Anthony | Cardiff City | Macclesfield Town | |
| 23 Pollitt, Michael F. | Notts County | Sunderland | |
| 6 Pope, Steven A. | Crewe Alexandra | Kidderminster Harriers | |
| 3 Roach, Neville | Reading | Kingstonian | |
| 20 Roberts, Darren A. | Darlington | Peterborough United | |
| 20 Rose, Colin J. | Macclesfield Town | Winsford United | |
| 20 Rowe, Ezekiel B. | Peterborough United | Doncaster Rovers | |
| 23 Rush, Ian J. | Newcastle United | Sheffield United | |
| 6 Smith, Craig | Derby County | Rushden & Diamonds | |
| 13 Smith, Nicholas L. | Cambridge City | Braintree Town | |
| 27 Southall, Neville | Everton | Stoke City | |
| 6 Stephenson, David | Dulwich Hamlet | Aldershot Town | |
| 6 Ten Heuvel, Laurens | Barnsley | Northampton Town | |
| 3 Thomas, Michael L. | Liverpool | Middlesbrough | |
| 12 Thorp, Michael S. | Reading | Cheltenham Town | |
| 5 Turley, William L. | Northampton Town | Leyton Orient | |
| 20 Tutill, Stephen A. | York City | Darlington | |
| 6 Walton, Mark A. | Fulham | Gillingham | |
| 5 Watts, Julian | Leicester City | Huddersfield Town | |
| 5 Williams, Anthony S. | Blackburn Rovers | Queens Park Rangers | |
| 23 Wilson, Mark A. | Manchester United | Wrexham | |
| 16 Woods, Neil S. | Grimsby Town | Mansfield Town | |
| 19 Young, Martin | Stevenage Borough | Tring Town | |

## MARCH 1998

| | From | To | Fee in £s |
|---|---|---|---|
| 20 Allsop, Kevin D. | Gresley Rovers | Ilkeston Town | undisclosed |
| 12 Alsop, Julian | Bristol Rovers | Swansea City | 15,000 |
| 6 Anderson, Simon P. | Witney Town | Thame United | undisclosed |
| 5 Atkinson, Graeme | Preston North End | Brighton & Hove Albion | Free |
| 19 Baraclough, Ian R. | Notts County | Queens Park Rangers | 50,000 |
| 26 Barlow, Stuart | Oldham Athletic | Wigan Athletic | 45,000 |
| 20 Bartram, Vincent L. | Arsenal | Gillingham | Free |
| 10 Beresford, Marlon | Burnley | Middlesbrough | 500,000 |
| 26 Bishop, Ian W. | West Ham United | Manchester City | Free |
| 27 Bohinen, Lars | Blackburn Rovers | Derby County | 1,450,000 |
| 26 Brayson, Paul | Newcastle United | Reading | 100,000 |
| 20 Brazier, Matthew R. | Queens Park Rangers | Fulham | 65,000 |
| 9 Brown, Kevan B. | Woking | Yeovil Town | undisclosed |
| 13 Clapham, James R. | Tottenham Hotspur | Ipswich Town | 300,000 |
| 26 Claridge, Stephen E. | Leicester City | Wolverhampton Wanderers | 350,000 |
| 26 Conroy, Michael K. | Fulham | Blackpool | 50,000 |
| 26 Crawford, James | Newcastle United | Reading | 50,000 |
| 26 Curcic, Sasa | Aston Villa | Crystal Palace | 1,000,000 |
| 17 Davis, Steven P. | Barnsley | Oxford United | 75,000 |
| 13 Devlin, Paul J. | Birmingham City | Sheffield United | 200,000 |
| 25 Durkan, Kieron J. | Stockport County | Macclesfield Town | undisclosed |
| 2 Dyer, Alexander C. | Huddersfield Town | Notts County | Free |
| 26 Edwards, Christian N.H. | Swansea City | Nottingham Forest | 175,000 |
| 26 Emblen, Neil R. | Crystal Palace | Wolverhampton Wanderers | 900,000 |
| 26 Fleck, Robert | Norwich City | Reading | 50,000 |
| 26 Foster, John C. | Manchester City | Carlisle United | Free |
| 26 Gascoigne, Paul J. | Rangers | Middlesbrough | 3,450,000 |
| 26 Goater, Leonard S. | Bristol City | Manchester City | 500,000 |
| 9 Goddard-Crawley, Richard | Brentford | Woking | 7,500 |
| 26 Gray, Stuart | Celtic | Reading | 100,000 |
| 5 Grayson, Neil | Hereford United | Cheltenham Town | undisclosed |
| 2 Green, Francis | Ilkeston Town | Peterborough United | 11,000 |
| 25 Greening, Jonathan | York City | Manchester United | 1,000,000 |
| 26 Gregory, Neil R. | Ipswich Town | Colchester United | 50,000 |
| 26 Hamilton, Ian R. | West Bromwich Albion | Sheffield United | 325,000 |

| | From | To | Fee in £s |
|---|---|---|---|
| 26 Harris, Neil | Cambridge City | Millwall | undisclosed |
| 13 Hilton, Damien A. | Norwich City | Brighton & Hove Albion | Free |
| 24 Holsgrove, Lee | Millwall | Wycombe Wanderers | Free |
| 26 Howie, Scott | Motherwell | Reading | 30,000 |
| 25 Hughes, Andrew J. | Oldham Athletic | Notts County | 150,000 |
| 5 Inman, Niall E. | Stevenage Borough | Peterborough United | undisclosed |
| 12 Jobson, Richard I. | Leeds United | Manchester City | Free |
| 26 Jones, Vincent P. | Wimbledon | Queens Park Rangers | 500,000 |
| 27 Keeble, Shaun R. | Rounds Town | Wisbech Town | undisclosed |
| 27 Kennedy, Mark | Liverpool | Wimbledon | 2,000,000 |
| 11 Kerslake, David | Ipswich Town | Swindon Town | Free |
| 20 Littlejohn, Adrian S. | Plymouth Argyle | Oldham Athletic | exch. |
| 12 Martindale, Gary | Notts County | Rotherham United | undisclosed |
| 26 McIntyre, James | Kilmarnock | Reading | 420,000 |
| 13 Mehew, David S. | Farnborough Town | Rushden & Diamonds | undisclosed |
| 13 Midgley, Craig S. | Bradford City | Hartlepool United | 10,000 |
| 19 Mills, Daniel | Norwich City | Charlton Athletic | 350,000 |
| 26 Nartey, Joseph H. | Chertsey Town | Aldershot Town | 4,000 |
| 7 Norbury, Michael S. | Hednesford Town | Telford United | 120,000 |
| 13 Onuora, Ifem | Gillingham | Swindon Town | undisclosed |
| 26 O'Reilly, Justin | Port Vale | Southport | Free |
| 26 Partridge, Scott M. | Cardiff City | Torquay United | undisclosed |
| 24 Pollitt, Michael F. | Notts County | Sunderland | 75,000 |
| 20 Pollock, Jamie | Bolton Wanderers | Manchester City | 1,000,000 |
| 10 Roberts, Andrew J. | Crystal Palace | Wimbledon | 2,000,000 |
| 26 Robinson, David | Gresley Rovers | Grantham Town | undisclosed |
| 27 Robinson, Paul D. | Darlington | Newcastle United | 250,000 |
| 17 Russell, Keith D. | Blackpool | Altrincham | undisclosed |
| 26 Salako, John A. | Coventry City | Bolton Wanderers | Free |
| 18 Scully, Anthony D.T. | Manchester City | Queens Park Rangers | 155,000 |
| 20 Sedgemore, Benjamin R. | Mansfield Town | Macclesfield Town | 25,000 |
| 26 Slater, Robert D. | Southampton | Wolverhampton Wanderers | 75,000 |
| 2 Small, Bryan | Bolton Wanderers | Bury | undisclosed |
| 17 Southall, Neville | Everton | Stoke City | Free |
| 20 Starbuck, Philip M. | Oldham Athletic | Plymouth Argyle | exch. |
| 20 Stephenson, Paul | York City | Hartlepool United | Free |
| 6 Street, Tyrone T. | Nuneaton Borough | Stourbridge | undisclosed |
| 13 Thompson, Steven | Woking | Yeovil Town | undisclosed |
| 25 Titterton, David S. | Burton Albion | Stourbridge | undisclosed |
| 20 Tutill, Stephen A. | York City | Darlington | Free |
| 13 Van Blerk, Jason C. | Manchester City | West Bromwich Albion | 50,000 |
| 26 Wilder, Christopher J. | Bradford City | Sheffield United | 150,000 |
| 26 Youds, Edward P. | Bradford City | Charlton Athletic | 550,000 |

## TEMPORARY TRANSFERS

| | | |
|---|---|---|
| 31 Adcock, Paul | Gloucester City | Weymouth |
| 16 Alford, Carl P. | Rushden & Diamonds | Dover Athletic |
| 26 Allen, Rory W. | Tottenham Hotspur | Luton Town |
| 21 Anderson, Luke | Dulwich Hamlet | Crawley Town |
| 6 Armstrong, Simon | Port Vale | Boston United |
| 2 Barnes, Steven L. | Birmingham City | Brighton & Hove Albion |
| 13 Barnett, David | Dunfermline Athletic | Port Vale |
| 26 Beagrie, Peter S. | Bradford City | Everton |
| 26 Beardsley, Peter A. | Bolton Wanderers | Fulham |
| 12 Beesley, Paul | Manchester City | West Bromwich Albion |
| 11 Billing, Peter G. | Northwich Victoria | Bamber Bridge |
| 31 Bonfield, Darren | Wealdstone | Hitchin Town |
| 26 Bos, Gijsbert | Rotherham United | Walsall |
| 25 Boswell, Matthew H. | Port Vale | Barnet |
| 30 Boxall, Daniel J. | Crystal Palace | Oldham Athletic |
| 2 Boyle, Martin A. | Forest Green Rovers | Weston-Super-Mare |
| 10 Branston, Guy | Leicester City | Colchester United |
| 21 Brisco, Neil A. | Manchester City | Stafford Rangers |
| 26 Brown, David A. | Manchester United | Hull City |
| 17 Bullen, Michael | Aldershot Town | Gravesend & Northfleet |
| 31 Cartwright, Neil A. | Telford United | Stafford Rangers |
| 31 Celaire, Mario | Wealdstone | Chesham United |
| 27 Clarke, Christopher | Chorley | Barrow |
| 26 Conlon, Barry J. | Manchester City | Plymouth Argyle |
| 26 Cross, Jonathan N. | Wrexham | Tranmere Rovers |
| 25 Cutler, Neil | Crewe Alexandra | Stalybridge Celtic |
| 26 Darby, Julian T. | Preston North End | Rotherham United |
| 16 Davis, Kori M. | Norwich City | Kings Lynn |
| 9 Duncan, Andrew | Manchester United | Cambridge United |
| 27 Falana, Wade R. | Romford | Harlow Town |
| 26 Fenn, Neale M.C. | Tottenham Hotspur | Norwich City |
| 26 Fickling, Ashley | Grimsby Town | Darlington |
| 26 Finnigan, John | Nottingham Forest | Lincoln City |
| 27 Finn, Neil E. | West Ham United | Dorchester Town |
| 25 Gallagher, Kieran | Aylesbury United | Hayes |
| 26 Gayle, Mark S.R. | Crewe Alexandra | Luton Town |
| 6 Green, Joseph A. | Norwich City | Wisbech Town |
| 5 Greenacre, Christopher M. | Manchester City | Blackpool |
| 19 Guinan, Stephen | Nottingham Forest | Crewe Alexandra |
| 30 Hale, Matthew | Bristol City | Weymouth |
| 31 Hammatt, Bryan | Hayes | Enfield |
| 20 Hart, Barrie R. | Oldham Athletic | Radcliffe Borough |

| | From | To | Fee in £s |
|---|---|---|---|
| 16 Hayward, Andrew | Rotherham United | Woking | |
| 24 Heaney, Neil A. | Manchester City | Charlton Athletic | |
| 26 Heath, Stephen D. | Rotherham United | Stalybridge Celtic | |
| 2 Henriksen, Tony T. | Southend United | Purfleet | |
| 27 Henriksen, Tony T. | Southend United | Witham Town | |
| 6 Hitchen, Steven J. | Macclesfield Town | Flixton | |
| 4 Hodges, Tristan J. | Gravesend & Northfleet | Erith & Belvedere | |
| 23 Holden, Steven A. | Stevenage Borough | Cambridge City | |
| 20 Hughes, Andrew J. | Oldham Athletic | Notts County | |
| 26 Hughes, Robert D. | Aston Villa | Carlisle United | |
| 19 Hulbert, Robin J. | Swindon Town | Newcastle United | |
| 6 Imber, Noel S.P. | Wealdstone | Harrow Borough | |
| 19 Ingram, Rae | Manchester City | Macclesfield Town | |
| 2 Johnson, Damien M. | Blackburn Rovers | Nottingham Forest | |
| 26 Kelly, Patrick | Newcastle United | Reading | |
| 26 Kelly, Raymond | Manchester City | Wrexham | |
| 3 Kubicki, Dariusz | Wolverhampton Wanderers | Tranmere Rovers | |
| 2 Leadbeater, Richard P. | Wolverhampton Wanderers | Hereford United | |
| 20 Lewis, Ben | Southend United | Rushden & Diamonds | |
| 30 Lovell, Jason P. | Waterlooville | Fisher Athletic | |
| 26 McAnespie, Stephen | Fulham | Bradford City | |
| 6 McAree, Rodney J. | Fulham | Woking | |
| 26 McCarthy, Sean C. | Oldham Athletic | Bristol City | |
| 8 McCleary, Stuart | Oxford City | Abingdon Town | |
| 26 McGoldrick, Eddie J.P. | Manchester City | Stockport County | |
| 3 McKenzie, Christy G. | Hednesford Town | Redditch United | |
| 11 Milligan, Mark | Bamber Bridge | Northwich Victoria | |
| 20 Morgan, Philip J. | Stoke City | Halifax Town | |
| 14 Morley, David T. | Manchester City | Ayr United | |
| 26 Mullin, John | Sunderland | Burnley | |
| 26 Newman, Robert N. | Norwich City | Wigan Athletic | |
| 12 Nicol, Stephen | Sheffield Wednesday | West Bromwich Albion | |
| 26 Nurse, David J. | Millwall | Brentford | |
| 2 O'Neill, Michael A. | Coventry City | Reading | |
| 30 Peaks, Andrew M. | Rushden & Diamonds | Wealdstone | |
| 19 Phillips, Martin J. | Manchester City | Exeter City | |
| 23 Pierce, David E. | Ashton United | Barrow | |
| 24 Pridham, Christopher | Manchester City | Altrincham | |
| 9 Randall, Dean | Notts County | Ilkeston Town | |
| 26 Roberts, Jason A.D. | Wolverhampton Wanderers | Bristol City | |
| 26 Ruddock, Neil | Liverpool | Queens Park Rangers | |
| 26 Russell, Matthew L. | Scarborough | Doncaster Rovers | |
| 26 Sealey, Leslie J. | West Ham United | Bury | |
| 26 Shakespeare, Craig R. | Scunthorpe United | Telford United | |
| 26 Sinnott, Lee | Oldham Athletic | Bradford City | |
| 4 Smith, Steven P. | Gravesend & Northfleet | Erith & Belvedere | |
| 10 Spencer, John | Queens Park Rangers | Everton | |
| 4 Stein, Earl M.S. | Chelsea | AFC Bournemouth | |
| 26 Taylor, Robert | West Bromwich Albion | Bolton Wanderers | |
| 26 Taylor, Scott J. | Bolton Wanderers | Blackpool | |
| 9 Thomas, Michael I. | Liverpool | Middlesbrough | |
| 25 Thomas, Scott L. | Manchester City | Brighton & Hove Albion | |
| 2 Thompson, Neil | Barnsley | York City | |
| 10 Tipple, Gaven L. | Norwich City | Wisbech Town | |
| 26 Tomlinson, Graeme M. | Manchester United | Millwall | |
| 13 Vickers, Ashley J. | Peterborough United | St Albans City | |
| 13 Walker, Andrew F. | Sheffield United | Raith Rovers | |
| 18 Wallwork, Ronald | Manchester United | Stockport County | |
| 26 Walton, Mark A. | Fulham | Norwich City | |
| 3 Watson, Mark L. | Welling United | Sutton United | |
| 26 Woods, Stephen J. | Stoke City | Plymouth Argyle | |
| 20 Wright, Stephen | Rangers | Wolverhampton Wanderers | |

**APRIL 1998**

| | From | To | Fee in £s |
|---|---|---|---|
| 7 Duncan, Andrew | Manchester United | Cambridge United | undisclosed |
| 4 Perry, Mark | Walsall | Stafford Rangers | undisclosed |

**TEMPORARY TRANSFERS**

| | From | To | Fee in £s |
|---|---|---|---|
| 2 Aldridge, Martin J. | Oxford United | Southend United | |
| 15 Archer, Paul | Nottingham Forest | Chesham United | |

**MAY 1998**

| | From | To | Fee in £s |
|---|---|---|---|
| 22 Akinbiyi, Adeola P. | Gillingham | Bristol City | 1,200,000 |
| 30 Beckett, Luke J. | Barnsley | Chester City | undisclosed |
| 22 Brown, Derek | Nuneaton Borough | Rothwell Town | undisclosed |
| 23 Bulman, Dannie | Ashford Town | Wycombe Wanderers | undisclosed |
| 22 Hall, Gareth D. | Sunderland | Swindon Town | undisclosed |
| 8 O'Hagan, Daniel A. | Weston-Super-Mare | Dorchester Town | undisclosed |
| 6 Spencer, John | Queens Park Rangers | Everton | undisclosed |

**TEMPORARY TRANSFERS**

| | From | To | Fee in £s |
|---|---|---|---|
| 3 Boswell, Matthew H. | Port Vale | Barnet | |
| 6 McAree, Rodney J. | Fulham | Woking | |

# ENGLISH LEAGUE MANAGERS

GM General Manager,   CC Chief Coach,   HC Head Coach,   DoC Director of Coaching,   DoF Director of Football,
* Secretary-Manager,   MD Managing Director,   TM Team Manager,   TD Technical Director,   CE Chief Executive.

## ARSENAL
Sam Hollis 1894–97, Tom Mitchell 1897–98, George Elcoat 1898–99, Harry Bradshaw 1899–1904, Phil Kelso 1904–08,
George Morrell 1908–15, Leslie Knighton 1919–25, Herbert Chapman 1925–34, George Allison 1934–47, Tom
Whittaker 1947–56, Jack Crayston 1956–58, George Swindin 1958–62, Billy Wright 1962–66, Bertie Mee 1966–76, Terry
Neill 1976–83, Don Howe 1984–86, George Graham 1986–95, Bruce Rioch 1995–96, Arsène Wenger September 1996– .

## ASTON VILLA
George Ramsay 1884–1926*, W. J. Smith 1926–34*, Jimmy McMullan 1934–35, Jimmy Hogan 1936–44, Alex Massie
1945–50, George Martin 1950–53, Eric Houghton 1953–58, Joe Mercer 1958–64, Dick Taylor 1965–67, Tommy
Cummings 1967–68, Tommy Docherty 1968–70, Vic Crowe 1970–74, Ron Saunders 1974–82, Tony Barton 1982–84,
Graham Turner 1984–86, Billy McNeill 1986–87, Graham Taylor 1987–90, Dr. Jozef Venglos 1990–91, Ron Atkinson
1991–94, Brian Little 1994–1998, John Gregory February 1998– .

## BARNET
Lester Finch, George Wheeler, Dexter Adams, Tommy Coleman, Gerry Ward, Gordon Ferry, Brian Kelly, Bill
Meadows, Barry Fry, Roger Thompson, Don McAllister, Barry Fry, Edwin Stein, Gary Phillips (player-manager)
1993–94, Ray Clemence 1994–96, Alan Mullery (DoF) 1996–97, Terry Bullivant 1997, John Still June 1997– .

## BARNSLEY
Arthur Fairclough 1898–1901*, John McCartney 1901–04*, Arthur Fairclough 1904–12, John Hastie 1912–14, Percy
Lewis 1914–19, Peter Sant 1919–26, John Commins 1926–29, Arthur Fairclough 1929–30, Brough Fletcher 1930–37,
Angus Seed 1937–53, Tim Ward 1953–60, Johnny Steele 1960–71 (continued as GM), John McSeveney 1971–72, Johnny
Steele (GM) 1972–73, Jim Iley 1973–78, Allan Clarke 1978–80, Norman Hunter 1980–84, Bobby Collins 1984–85, Allan
Clarke 1985–89, Mel Machin 1989–93, Viv Anderson 1993–94, Danny Wilson 1994–98, John Hendrie July 1998– .

## BIRMINGHAM CITY
Alfred Jones 1892–1908*, Alec Watson 1908–10, Bob McRoberts 1910–15, Frank Richards 1915–23, Billy Beer 1923–27,
Leslie Knighton 1928–33, George Liddell 1933–39, Harry Storer 1945–48, Bob Brocklebank 1949–54, Arthur Turner
1954–58, Pat Beasley 1959–60, Gil Merrick 1960–64, Joe Mallett 1965, Stan Cullis 1965–70, Fred Goodwin 1970–75,
Willie Bell 1975–77, Jim Smith 1978–82, Ron Saunders 1982–86, John Bond 1986–87, Garry Pendrey 1987–89, Dave
Mackay 1989–1991, Lou Macari 1991, Terry Cooper 1991–93, Barry Fry 1993–96, Trevor Francis May 1996– .

## BLACKBURN ROVERS
Thomas Mitchell 1884–96*, J. Walmsley 1896–1903*, R. B. Middleton 1903–25, Jack Carr 1922–26 (TM under
Middleton to 1925), Bob Crompton 1926–30 (Hon. TM), Arthur Barritt 1931–36 (had been Sec. from 1927), Reg Taylor
1936–38, Bob Crompton 1938–41, Eddie Hapgood 1944–47, Will Scott 1947, Jack Bruton 1947–49, Jackie Bestall
1949–53, Johnny Carey 1953–58, Dally Duncan 1958–60, Jack Marshall 1960–67, Eddie Quigley 1967–70, Johnny Carey
1970–71, Ken Furphy 1971–73, Gordon Lee 1974–75, Jim Smith 1975–78, Jim Iley 1978, John Pickering 1978–79,
Howard Kendall 1979–81, Bobby Saxton 1981–86, Don Mackay 1987–91, Kenny Dalglish 1991–95, Ray Harford
1995–97, Roy Hodgson June 1997– .

## BLACKPOOL
Tom Barcroft 1903–33* (Hon. Sec.), John Cox 1909–11, Bill Norman 1919–23, Maj. Frank Buckley 1923–27, Sid
Beaumont 1927–28, Harry Evans 1928–33 (Hon. TM), Alex "Sandy" Macfarlane 1933–35, Joe Smith 1935–58, Ronnie
Suart 1958–67, Stan Mortensen 1967–69, Les Shannon 1969–70, Bob Stokoe 1970–72, Harry Potts 1972–76, Allan
Brown 1976–78, Bob Stokoe 1978–79, Stan Ternent 1979–80, Alan Ball 1980–81, Allan Brown 1981–82, Sam Ellis
1982–89, Jimmy Mullen 1989–90, Graham Carr 1990, Bill Ayre 1990–94, Sam Allardyce 1994–96, Gary Megson 1996–97,
Nigel Worthington July 1997– .

## BOLTON WANDERERS
Tom Rawthorne 1874–85*, J. J. Bentley 1885–86*, W. G. Struthers 1886–87*, Fitzroy Norris 1887*, J. J. Bentley
1887–95*, Harry Downs 1895–96*, Frank Brettell 1896–98*, John Somerville 1898–1910, Will Settle 1910–15, Tom
Mather 1915–19, Charles Foweraker 1919–44, Walter Rowley 1944–50, Bill Ridding 1951–68, Nat Lofthouse 1968–70,
Jimmy McIlroy 1970, Jimmy Meadows 1971, Nat Lofthouse 1971 (then admin. man. to 1972), Jimmy Armfield 1971–74,
Ian Greaves 1974–80, Stan Anderson 1980–81, George Mulhall 1981–82, John McGovern 1982–85, Charlie Wright 1985,
Phil Neal 1985–92, Bruce Rioch 1992–95, Roy McFarland 1995–96, Colin Todd January 1996– .

## AFC BOURNEMOUTH
Vincent Kitcher 1914–23*, Harry Kinghorn 1923–25, Leslie Knighton 1925–28, Frank Richards 1928–30, Billy Birrell
1930–35, Bob Crompton 1935–36, Charlie Bell 1936–39, Harry Kinghorn 1939–47, Harry Lowe 1947–50, Jack Bruton
1950–56, Fred Cox 1956–58, Don Welsh 1958–61, Bill McGarry 1961–63, Reg Flewin 1963–65, Fred Cox 1965–70, John
Bond 1970–73, Trevor Hartley 1974–75, John Benson 1975–78, Alec Stock 1979–80, David Webb 1980–82, Don Megson
1983, Harry Redknapp 1983–92, Tony Pulis 1992–94, Mel Machin August 1994– .

## BRADFORD CITY
Robert Campbell 1903–05, Peter O'Rourke 1905–21, David Menzies 1921–26, Colin Veitch 1926–28, Peter O'Rourke
1928–30, Jack Peart 1930–35, Dick Ray 1935–37, Fred Westgarth 1938–43, Bob Sharp 1943–46, Jack Barker 1946–47,
John Milburn 1947–48, David Steele 1948–52, Albert Harris 1952, Ivor Powell 1952–55, Peter Jackson 1955–61,

Bob Brocklebank 1961–64, Bill Harris 1965–66, Willie Watson 1966–69, Grenville Hair 1967–68, Jimmy Wheeler 1968–71, Bryan Edwards 1971–75, Bobby Kennedy 1975–78, John Napier 1978, George Mulhall 1978–81, Roy McFarland 1981–82, Trevor Cherry 1982–87, Terry Dolan 1987–89, Terry Yorath 1989–90, John Docherty 1990–91, Frank Stapleton 1991–94, Lennie Lawrence 1994–95, Chris Kamara 1995–98, Paul Jewell May 1998– .

## BRENTFORD
Will Lewis 1900–03*, Dick Molyneux 1903–06, W. G. Brown 1906–08, Fred Halliday 1908–26 (only secretary to 1922), Ephraim Rhodes 1912–15, Archie Mitchell 1921–22, Harry Curtis 1926–49, Jackie Gibbons 1949–52, Jimmy Blain 1952–53, Tommy Lawton 1953, Bill Dodgin Snr 1953–57, Malcolm Macdonald 1957–65, Tommy Cavanagh 1965–66, Billy Gray 1966–67, Jimmy Sirrel 1967–69, Frank Blunstone 1969–73, Mike Everitt 1973–75, John Docherty 1975–76, Bill Dodgin Jnr 1976–80, Fred Callaghan 1980–84, Frank McLintock 1984–87, Steve Perryman 1987–90, Phil Holder 1990–93, David Webb 1993–97, Micky Adams 1997–98, Ron Noades July 1998– .

## BRIGHTON & HOVE ALBION
John Jackson 1901–05, Frank Scott-Walford 1905–08, John Robson 1908–14, Charles Webb 1919–47, Tommy Cook 1947, Don Welsh 1947–51, Billy Lane 1951–61, George Curtis 1961–63, Archie Macaulay 1963–68, Fred Goodwin 1968–70, Pat Saward 1970–73, Brian Clough 1973–74, Peter Taylor 1974–76, Alan Mullery 1976–81, Mike Bailey 1981–82, Jimmy Melia 1982–83, Chris Cattlin 1983–86, Alan Mullery 1986–87, Barry Lloyd 1987–93, Liam Brady 1993–95, Jimmy Case 1995–96, Steve Gritt 1996–98, Brian Horton February 1998– .

## BRISTOL CITY
Sam Hollis 1897–99, Bob Campbell 1899–1901, Sam Hollis 1901–05, Harry Thickett 1905–10, Sam Hollis 1911–13, George Hedley 1913–15, Jack Hamilton 1915–19, Joe Palmer 1919–21, Alex Raisbeck 1921–29, Joe Bradshaw 1929–32, Bob Hewison 1932–49 (under suspension 1938–39), Bob Wright 1949–50, Pat Beasley 1950–58, Peter Doherty 1958–60, Fred Ford 1960–67, Alan Dicks 1967–80, Bobby Houghton 1980–82, Roy Hodgson 1982, Terry Cooper 1982–88 (Director from 1983), Joe Jordan 1988–90, Jimmy Lumsden 1990–92, Denis Smith 1992–93, Russell Osman 1993–94, Joe Jordan 1994–97, John Ward March 1997– .

## BRISTOL ROVERS
Alfred Homer 1899–1920 (continued as secretary to 1928), Ben Hall 1920–21, Andy Wilson 1921–26, Joe Palmer 1926–29, Dave McLean 1929–30, Albert Prince-Cox 1930–36, Percy Smith 1936–37, Brough Fletcher 1938–49, Bert Tann 1950–68 (continued as GM to 1972), Fred Ford 1968–69, Bill Dodgin Snr 1969–72, Don Megson 1972–77, Bobby Campbell 1978–79, Harold Jarman 1979–80, Terry Cooper 1980–81, Bobby Gould 1981–83, David Williams 1983–85, Bobby Gould 1985–87, Gerry Francis 1987–91, Martin Dobson 1991, Dennis Rofe 1992, Malcolm Allison 1992–93, John Ward 1993–96, Ian Holloway May 1996– .

## BURNLEY
Arthur F. Sutcliffe 1893–96*, Harry Bradshaw 1896–99*, Ernest Magnall 1899–1903*, Spen Whittaker 1903–10, R. H. Wadge 1910–11*, John Haworth 1911–25, Albert Pickles 1925–32, Tom Bromilow 1932–35, Alf Boland 1935–39*, Cliff Britton 1945–48, Frank Hill 1948–54, Alan Brown 1954–57, Billy Dougall 1957–58, Harry Potts 1958–70 (GM to 1972), Jimmy Adamson 1970–76, Joe Brown 1976–77, Harry Potts 1977–79, Brian Miller 1979–83, John Bond 1983–84, John Benson 1984–85, Martin Buchan 1985, Tommy Cavanagh 1985–86, Brian Miller 1986–89, Frank Casper 1989–91, Jimmy Mullen 1991–96, Adrian Heath 1996–97, Chris Waddle 1997–98, Stan Ternent June 1998– .

## BURY
T. Hargreaves 1887*, H. S. Hamer 1887–1907*, Archie Montgomery 1907–15, William Cameron 1919–23, James Hunter Thompson 1923–27, Percy Smith 1927–30, Arthur Paine 1930–34, Norman Bullock 1934–38, Jim Porter 1944–45, Norman Bullock 1945–49, John McNeil 1950–53, Dave Russell 1953–61, Bob Stokoe 1961–65, Bert Head 1965–66, Les Shannon 1966–69, Jack Marshall 1969, Les Hart 1970, Tommy McAnearney 1970–72, Alan Brown 1972–73, Bobby Smith 1973–77, Bob Stokoe 1977–78, David Hatton 1978–79, Dave Connor 1979–80, Jim Iley 1980–84, Martin Dobson 1984–89, Sam Ellis 1989–90, Mike Walsh 1990–95, Stan Ternent 1995–98, Neil Warnock June 1998– .

## CAMBRIDGE UNITED
Bill Whittaker 1949–55, Gerald Williams 1955, Bert Johnson 1955–59, Bill Craig 1959–60, Alan Moore 1960–63, Roy Kirk 1964–66, Bill Leivers 1967–74, Ron Atkinson 1974–78, John Docherty 1978–83, John Ryan 1984–85, Ken Shellito 1985, Chris Turner 1985–90, John Beck 1990–1992, Ian Atkins 1992–93, Gary Johnson 1993–95, Tommy Taylor 1995–96, Roy McFarland November 1996– .

## CARDIFF CITY
Davy McDougall 1910–11, Fred Stewart 1911–33, Bartley Wilson 1933–34, B. Watts-Jones 1934–37, Bill Jennings 1937–39, Cyril Spiers 1939–46, Billy McCandless 1946–48, Cyril Spiers 1948–54, Trevor Morris 1954–58, Bill Jones 1958–62, George Swindin 1962–64, Jimmy Scoular 1964–73, Frank O'Farrell 1973–74, Jimmy Andrews 1974–78, Richie Morgan 1978–82, Len Ashurst 1982–84, Jimmy Goodfellow 1984, Alan Durban 1984–86, Frank Burrows 1986–89, Len Ashurst 1989–91, Eddie May 1991–94, Terry Yorath 1994–95, Eddie May 1995, Kenny Hibbitt (CC) 1995, Phil Neal 1996, Russell Osman 1996–97, Kenny Hibbitt 1996–98, Frank Burrows February 1998– .

## CARLISLE UNITED
Harry Kirkbride 1904–05*, McCumiskey 1905–06*, Jack Houston 1906–08*, Bert Stansfield 1908–10, Jack Houston 1910–12, Davie Graham 1912–13, George Bristow 1913–30, Billy Hampson 1930–33, Bill Clarke 1933–35, Robert Kelly 1935–36, Fred Westgarth 1936–38, David Taylor 1938–40, Howard Harkness 1940–45, Bill Clark 1945–46*, Ivor Broadis 1946–49, Bill Shankly 1949–51, Fred Emery 1951–58, Andy Beattie 1958–60, Ivor Powell 1960–63, Alan Ashman 1963–67, Tim Ward 1967–68, Bob Stokoe 1968–70, Ian MacFarlane 1970–72, Alan Ashman 1972–75, Dick Young

1975–76, Bobby Moncur 1976–80, Martin Harvey 1980, Bob Stokoe 1980–85, Bryan "Pop" Robson 1985, Bob Stokoe 1985–86, Harry Gregg 1986–87, Cliff Middlemass 1987–91, Aidan McCaffery 1991–92, David McCreery 1992–93, Mick Wadsworth (DoC) 1993–96, Mervyn Day 1996–97, David Wilkes, John Halpin, Michael Knighton 1997– .

## CHARLTON ATHLETIC
Bill Rayner 1920–25, Alex McFarlane 1925–27, Albert Lindon 1928, Alex McFarlane 1928–32, Jimmy Seed 1933–56, Jimmy Trotter 1956–61, Frank Hill 1961–65, Bob Stokoe 1965–67, Eddie Firmani 1967–70, Theo Foley 1970–74, Andy Nelson 1974–79, Mike Bailey 1979–81, Alan Mullery 1981–82, Ken Craggs 1982, Lennie Lawrence 1982–91, Steve Gritt/Alan Curbishley 1991–95, Alan Curbishley June 1995– .

## CHELSEA
John Tait Robertson 1905–07, David Calderhead 1907–33, Leslie Knighton 1933–39, Billy Birrell 1939–52, Ted Drake 1952–61, Tommy Docherty 1962–67, Dave Sexton 1967–74, Ron Suart 1974–75, Eddie McCreadie 1975–77, Ken Shellito 1977–78, Danny Blanchflower 1978–79, Geoff Hurst 1979–81, John Neal 1981–85 (Director to 1986), John Hollins 1985–88, Bobby Campbell 1988–91, Ian Porterfield 1991–93, David Webb 1993, Glenn Hoddle 1993–96, Ruud Gullit 1996–98, Gianluca Vialli February 1998– .

## CHESTER CITY
Charlie Hewitt 1930–36, Alex Raisbeck 1936–38, Frank Brown 1938–53, Louis Page 1953–56, John Harris 1956–59, Stan Pearson 1959–61, Bill Lambton 1962–63, Peter Hauser 1963–68, Ken Roberts 1968–76, Alan Oakes 1976–82, Cliff Sear 1982, John Sainty 1982–83, John McGrath 1984, Harry McNally 1985–92, Graham Barrow 1992–94, Mike Pejic 1994–95, Derek Mann 1995, Kevin Ratcliffe April 1995– .

## CHESTERFIELD
E. Russell Timmeus 1891–95*, Gilbert Gillies 1895–1901, E. F. Hind 1901–02, Jack Hoskin 1902–06, W. Furness 1906–07, George Swift 1907–10, G. H. Jones 1911–13, R. L. Weston 1913–17, T. Callaghan 1919, J. J. Caffrey 1920–22, Harry Hadley 1922, Harry Parkes 1922–27, Alec Campbell 1927, Ted Davison 1927–32, Bill Harvey 1932–38, Norman Bullock 1938–45, Bob Brocklebank 1945–48, Bobby Marshall 1948–52, Ted Davison 1952–58, Duggie Livingstone 1958–62, Tony McShane 1962–67, Jimmy McGuigan 1967–73, Joe Shaw 1973–76, Arthur Cox 1976–80, Frank Barlow 1980–83, John Duncan 1983–87, Kevin Randall 1987–88, Paul Hart 1988–91, Chris McMenemy 1991–93, John Duncan February 1993– .

## COLCHESTER UNITED
Ted Fenton 1946–48, Jimmy Allen 1948–53, Jack Butler 1953–55, Benny Fenton 1955–63, Neil Franklin 1963–68, Dick Graham 1968–72, Jim Smith 1972–75, Bobby Roberts 1975–82, Allan Hunter 1982–83, Cyril Lea 1983–86, Mike Walker 1986–87, Roger Brown 1987–88, Jock Wallace 1989, Mick Mills 1990. Ian Atkins 1990–91, Roy McDonough 1991–94, George Burley 1994, Steve Wignall January 1995– .

## COVENTRY CITY
H. R. Buckle 1909–10, Robert Wallace 1910–13*, Frank Scott-Walford 1913–15, William Clayton 1917–19, H. Pollitt 1919–20, Albert Evans 1920–24, Jimmy Kerr 1924–28, James McIntyre 1928–31, Harry Storer 1931–45, Dick Bayliss 1945–47, Billy Frith 1947–48, Harry Storer 1948–53, Jack Fairbrother 1953–54, Charlie Elliott 1954–55, Jesse Carver 1955–56, Harry Warren 1956–57, Billy Frith 1957–61, Jimmy Hill 1961–67, Noel Cantwell 1967–72, Bob Dennison 1972, Joe Mercer 1972–75, Gordon Milne 1972–81, Dave Sexton 1981–83, Bobby Gould 1983–84, Don Mackay 1985–86, George Curtis 1986–87 (became MD), John Sillett 1987–90, Terry Butcher 1990–92, Don Howe 1992, Bobby Gould 1992–93, Phil Neal 1993–95, Ron Atkinson 1995–96 (became DoF), Gordon Strachan (player-manager) November 1996– .

## CREWE ALEXANDRA
W. C. McNeill 1892–94*, J. G. Hall 1895–96*, R. Roberts* (1st team sec.) 1897, J. B. Bromerley 1898–1911* (continued as Hon. Sec. to 1925), Tom Bailey 1925–38, George Lillicrop 1938–44, Frank Hill 1944–48, Arthur Turner 1948–51, Harry Catterick 1951–53, Ralph Ward 1953–55, Maurice Lindley 1955–58, Harry Ware 1958–60, Jimmy McGuigan 1960–64, Ernie Tagg 1964–71 (continued as secretary to 1972), Dennis Viollet 1971, Jimmy Melia 1972–73, Ernie Tagg 1974, Harry Gregg 1975–78, Warwick Rimmer 1978–79, Tony Waddington 1979–81, Arfon Griffiths 1981–82, Peter Morris 1982–83, Dario Gradi June 1983– .

## CRYSTAL PALACE
John T. Robson 1905–07, Edmund Goodman 1907–25 (had been secretary since 1905 and afterwards continued in this position to 1933). Alec Maley 1925–27, Fred Mavin 1927–30, Jack Tresadern 1930–35, Tom Bromilow 1935–36, R. S. Moyes 1936, Tom Bromilow 1936–39, George Irwin 1939–47, Jack Butler 1947–49, Ronnie Rooke 1949–50, Charlie Slade and Fred Dawes (joint managers) 1950–51, Laurie Scott 1951–54, Cyril Spiers 1954–58, George Smith 1958–60, Arthur Rowe 1960–62, Dick Graham 1962–66, Bert Head 1966–72 (continued as GM to 1973), Malcolm Allison 1973–76, Terry Venables 1976–80, Ernie Walley 1980, Malcolm Allison 1980–81, Dario Gradi 1981, Steve Kember 1981–82, Alan Mullery 1982–84, Steve Coppell 1984–93, Alan Smith 1993–95, Steve Coppell (TD) 1995–96, Dave Bassett 1996–97, Steve Coppell 1997–98, Attillio Lombardo 1998, Terry Venables (HC) June 1998– .

## DARLINGTON
Tom McIntosh 1902–11, W. L. Lane 1911–12*, Dick Jackson 1912–19, Jack English 1919–28, Jack Fairless 1928–33, George Collins 1933–36, George Brown 1936–38, Jackie Carr 1938–42, Jack Surtees 1942, Jack English 1945–46, Bill Forrest 1946–50, George Irwin 1950–52, Bob Gurney 1952–57, Dick Duckworth 1957–60, Eddie Carr 1960–64, Lol Morgan 1964–66, Jimmy Greenhalgh 1966–68, Ray Yeoman 1968–70, Len Richley 1970–71, Frank Brennan 1971, Ken Hale 1971–72, Allan Jones 1972, Ralph Brand 1972–73, Dick Conner 1973–74, Billy Horner 1974–76, Peter Madden 1976–78, Len Walker 1978–79, Billy Elliott 1979–83, Cyril Knowles 1983–87, Dave Booth 1987–89, Brian Little 1989–91, Frank Gray 1991–92, Ray Hankin 1992, Billy McEwan 1992–93, Alan Murray 1993–95, Paul Futcher 1995, David Hodgson/ Jim Platt (DoC) 1995, Jim Platt 1995–96, David Hodgson November 1996– .

## DERBY COUNTY

Harry Newbould 1896–1906, Jimmy Methven 1906–22, Cecil Potter 1922–25, George Jobey 1925–41, Ted Magner 1944–46, Stuart McMillan 1946–53, Jack Barker 1953–55, Harry Storer 1955–62, Tim Ward 1962–67, Brian Clough 1967–73, Dave Mackay 1973–76, Colin Murphy 1977, Tommy Docherty 1977–79, Colin Addison 1979–82, Johnny Newman 1982, Peter Taylor 1982–84, Roy McFarland 1984, Arthur Cox 1984–93, Roy McFarland 1993–95, Jim Smith June 1995– .

## DONCASTER ROVERS

Arthur Porter 1920–21*, Harry Tufnell 1921–22, Arthur Porter 1922–23, Dick Ray 1923–27, David Menzies 1928–36, Fred Emery 1936–40, Bill Marsden 1944–46, Jackie Bestall 1946–49, Peter Doherty 1949–58, Jack Hodgson and Sid Bycroft (joint managers) 1958, Jack Crayston 1958–59 (continued as Sec-Man to 1961), Jackie Bestall (TM) 1959–60, Norman Curtis 1960–61, Danny Malloy 1961–62, Oscar Hold 1962–64, Bill Leivers 1964–66, Keith Kettleborough 1966–67, George Raynor 1967–68, Lawrie McMenemy 1968–71, Maurice Setters 1971–74, Stan Anderson 1975–78, Billy Bremner 1978–85, Dave Cusack 1985–87, Dave Mackay 1987–89, Billy Bremner 1989–91, Steve Beaglehole 1991–93, Ian Atkins 1994, Sammy Chung 1994–96, Kerry Dixon (player-manager) 1996–97, Dave Cowling 1997, Mark Weaver December 1997– .

## EVERTON

W. E. Barclay 1888–89*, Dick Molyneux 1889–1901*, William C. Cuff 1901–18*, W. J. Sawyer 1918–19*, Thomas H. McIntosh 1919–35*, Theo Kelly 1936–48, Cliff Britton 1948–56, Ian Buchan 1956–58, Johnny Carey 1958–61, Harry Catterick 1961–73, Billy Bingham 1973–77, Gordon Lee 1977–81, Howard Kendall 1981–87, Colin Harvey 1987–90, Howard Kendall 1990–93, Mike Walker 1994, Joe Royle 1994–97, Howard Kendall 1997–98, Walter Smith July 1998– .

## EXETER CITY

Arthur Chadwick 1910–22, Fred Mavin 1923–27, Dave Wilson 1928–29, Billy McDevitt 1929–35, Jack English 1935–39, George Roughton 1945–52, Norman Kirkman 1952–53, Norman Dodgin 1953–57, Bill Thompson 1957–58, Frank Broome 1958–60, Glen Wilson 1960–62, Cyril Spiers 1962–63, Jack Edwards 1963–65, Ellis Stuttard 1965–66, Jock Basford 1966–67, Frank Broome 1967–69, Johnny Newman 1969–76, Bobby Saxton 1977–79, Brian Godfrey 1979–83, Gerry Francis 1983–84, Jim Iley 1984–85, Colin Appleton 1985–87, Terry Cooper 1988–91, Alan Ball 1991–94, Terry Cooper 1994–95, Peter Fox June 1995– .

## FULHAM

Harry Bradshaw 1904–09, Phil Kelso 1909–24, Andy Ducat 1924–26, Joe Bradshaw 1926–29, Ned Liddell 1929–31, Jim MacIntyre 1931–34, Jimmy Hogan 1934–35, Jack Peart 1935–48, Frank Osborne 1948–64 (was secretary-manager or GM for most of this period), Bill Dodgin Snr 1949–53, Duggie Livingstone 1956–58, Bedford Jezzard 1958–64 (GM for last two months), Vic Buckingham 1965–68, Bobby Robson 1968, Bill Dodgin Jnr 1969–72, John Haynes 1972, Alec Stock 1972–76, Bobby Campbell 1976–80, Malcolm Macdonald 1980–84, Ray Harford 1984–96, Ray Lewington 1986–90, Alan Dicks 1990–91, Don Mackay 1991–94, Ian Branfoot 1994–96 (continued as GM), Micky Adams 1996–97, Ray Wilkins 1997–98, Kevin Keegan May 1998– .

## GILLINGHAM

W. Ironside Groombridge 1896–1906* (previously financial secretary), Steve Smith 1906–08, W. I. Groombridge 1908–19*, George Collins 1919–20, John McMillan 1920–23, Harry Curtis 1923–26, Albert Hoskins 1926–29, Dick Hendrie 1929–31, Fred Mavin 1932–37, Alan Ure 1937–38, Bill Harvey 1938–39, Archie Clark 1939–58, Harry Barratt 1958–62, Freddie Cox 1962–65, Basil Hayward 1966–71, Andy Nelson 1971–74, Len Ashurst 1974–75, Gerry Summers 1975–81, Keith Peacock 1981–87, Paul Taylor 1988, Keith Burkinshaw 1988–89, Damien Richardson 1989–93, Mike Flanagan 1993–95, Neil Smillie 1995, Tony Pulis June 1995– .

## GRIMSBY TOWN

H. N. Hickson 1902–20*, Haydn Price 1920, George Fraser 1921–24, Wilf Gillow 1924–32, Frank Womack 1932–36, Charles Spencer 1937–51, Bill Shankly 1951–53, Billy Walsh 1954–55, Allenby Chilton 1955–59, Tim Ward 1960–62, Tom Johnston 1962–64, Jimmy McGuigan 1964–67, Don McEvoy 1967–68, Bill Harvey 1968–69, Bobby Kennedy 1969–71, Lawrie McMenemy 1971–73, Ron Ashman 1973–75, Tom Casey 1975–76, Johnny Newman 1976–79, George Kerr 1979–82, David Booth 1982–85, Mike Lyons 1985–87, Bobby Roberts 1987–88, Alan Buckley 1988–94, Brian Laws 1994–96, Kenny Swain 1997, Alan Buckley May 1997– .

## HALIFAX TOWN

A. M. Ricketts 1911–12*, Joe McClelland 1912–30, Alec Raisbeck 1930–36, Jimmy Thomson 1936–47, Jack Breedon 1947–50, William Wootton 1951–52, Gerald Henry 1952–54, Willie Watson 1954–56, Billy Burnikell 1956, Harry Hooper 1957–62, Willie Watson 1964–66, Vic Metcalfe 1966–67, Alan Ball Snr 1967–70, George Kirby 1970–71, Ray Henderson 1971–72, George Mulhall 1972–74, Johnny Quinn 1974–76, Alan Ball Snr 1976–77, Jimmy Lawson 1977–78, George Kirby 1978–81, Mick Bullock 1981–84, Mick Jones 1984–86, Bill Ayre 1986–90, Jim McCalliog 1990–91, John McGrath 1991–92, Peter Wragg 1992–93, John Bird 1993–95, John Carroll 1996, George Mulhall 1996– .

## HARTLEPOOL UNITED

Alfred Priest 1908–12, Percy Humphreys 1912–13, Jack Manners 1913–20, Cecil Potter 1920–22, David Gordon 1922–24, Jack Manners 1924–27, Bill Norman 1927–31, Jack Carr 1932–35 (had been player-coach since 1931), Jimmy Hamilton 1935–43, Fred Westgarth 1943–57, Ray Middleton 1957–59, Bill Robinson 1959–62, Allenby Chilton 1962–63, Bob Gurney 1963–64, Alvan Williams 1964–66, Geoff Twentyman 1965, Brian Clough 1965–67, Angus McLean 1967–70, John Simpson 1970–71, Len Ashurst 1971–74, Ken Hale 1974–76, Billy Horner 1976–83, Johnny Duncan 1983, Mike Docherty 1983, Billy Horner 1984–86, John Bird 1986–88, Bobby Moncur 1988–89, Cyril Knowles 1989–91, Alan Murray 1991–93, Viv Busby 1993, John MacPhail 1993–94, David McCreery 1994–95, Keith Houchen 1995–96, Mick Tait December 1996– .

## HUDDERSFIELD TOWN

Fred Walker 1908–10, Richard Pudan 1910–12, Arthur Fairclough 1912–19, Ambrose Langley 1919–21, Herbert Chapman 1921–25, Cecil Potter 1925–26, Jack Chaplin 1926–29, Clem Stephenson 1929–42, David Steele 1943–47, George Stephenson 1947–52, Andy Beattie 1952–56, Bill Shankly 1956–59, Eddie Boot 1960–64, Tom Johnston 1964–68, Ian Greaves 1968–74, Bobby Collins 1974, Tom Johnston 1975–78 (had been GM since 1975), Mike Buxton 1978–86, Steve Smith 1986–87, Malcolm Macdonald 1987–88, Eoin Hand 1988–92, Ian Ross 1992–93, Neil Warnock 1993–95, Brian Horton 1995–97, Peter Jackson October 1997– .

## HULL CITY

James Ramster 1904–05*, Ambrose Langley 1905–13, Harry Chapman 1913–14, Fred Stringer 1914–16, David Menzies 1916–21, Percy Lewis 1921–23, Bill McCracken 1923–31, Haydn Green 1931–34, John Hill 1934–36, David Menzies 1936, Ernest Blackburn 1936–46, Major Frank Buckley 1946–48, Raich Carter 1948–51, Bob Jackson 1952–55, Bob Brocklebank 1955–61, Cliff Britton 1961–70 (continued as GM to 1971), Terry Neill 1970–74, John Kaye 1974–77, Bobby Collins 1977–78, Ken Houghton 1978–79, Mike Smith 1979–82, Bobby Brown 1982, Colin Appleton 1982–84, Brian Horton 1984–88, Eddie Gray 1988–89, Colin Appleton 1989, Stan Ternent 1989–91, Terry Dolan 1991–97, Mark Hateley July 1997– .

## IPSWICH TOWN

Mick O'Brien 1936–37, Scott Duncan 1937–55 (continued as secretary), Alf Ramsey 1955–63, Jackie Milburn 1963–64, Bill McGarry 1964–68, Bobby Robson 1969–82, Bobby Ferguson 1982–87, Johnny Duncan 1987–90, John Lyall 1990–94, George Burley December 1994– .

## LEEDS UNITED

Dick Ray 1919–20, Arthur Fairclough 1920–27, Dick Ray 1927–35, Bill Hampson 1935–47, Willis Edwards 1947–48, Major Frank Buckley 1948–53, Raich Carter 1953–58, Bill Lambton 1958–59, Jack Taylor 1959–61, Don Revie 1961–74, Brian Clough 1974, Jimmy Armfield 1974–78, Jock Stein 1978, Jimmy Adamson 1978–80, Allan Clarke 1980–82, Eddie Gray 1982–85, Billy Bremner 1985–88, Howard Wilkinson 1988–96, George Graham September 1996– .

## LEICESTER CITY

William Clark 1896–97, George Johnson 1898–1907*, James Blessington 1907–09, Andy Aitken 1909–11, John William Bartlett 1912–14, Peter Hodge 1919–26, William Orr 1926–32, Peter Hodge 1932–34, Andy Lochhead 1934–36, Frank Womack 1936–39, Tom Bromilow 1939–45, Tom Mather 1945–46, Johnny Duncan 1946–49, Norman Bullock 1949–55, David Halliday 1955–58, Matt Gillies 1959–68, Frank O'Farrell 1968–71, Jimmy Bloomfield 1971–77, Frank McLintock 1977–78, Jock Wallace 1978–82, Gordon Milne 1982–86, Bryan Hamilton 1986–87, David Pleat 1987–91, Brian Little 1991–94, Mark McGhee 1994–95, Martin O'Neill December 1995– .

## LEYTON ORIENT

Sam Omerod 1905–06, Ike Ivenson 1906, Billy Holmes 1907–22, Peter Proudfoot 1922–29, Arthur Grimsdell 1929–30, Peter Proudfoot 1930–31, Jimmy Seed 1931–33, David Pratt 1933–34, Peter Proudfoot 1935–39, Tom Halsey 1939, Bill Wright 1939–45, Willie Hall 1945, Bill Wright 1945–46, Charlie Hewitt 1946–48, Neil McBain 1948–49, Alec Stock 1949–56, 1956–57, 1958–59, Johnny Carey 1961–63, Benny Fenton 1963–64, Dave Sexton 1965, Dick Graham 1966–68, Jimmy Bloomfield 1968–71, George Petchey 1971–77, Jimmy Bloomfield 1977–81, Paul Went 1981, Ken Knighton 1981, Frank Clark 1982–91 (MD), Peter Eustace 1991–94, Chris Turner/John Sitton 1994–95, Pat Holland 1995–96, Tommy Taylor November 1996– .

## LINCOLN CITY

David Calderhead 1900–07, John Henry Strawson 1907–14 (had been secretary), George Fraser 1919–21, David Calderhead Jnr. 1921–24, Horace Henshall 1924–27, Harry Parkes 1927–36, Joe McClelland 1936–46, Bill Anderson 1946–65 (GM to 1966), Roy Chapman 1965–66, Ron Gray 1966–70, Bert Loxley 1970–71, David Herd 1971–72, Graham Taylor 1972–77, George Kerr 1977–78, Willie Bell 1977–78, Colin Murphy 1978–85, John Pickering 1985, George Kerr 1985–87, Peter Daniel 1987, Colin Murphy 1987–90, Allan Clarke 1990, Steve Thompson 1990–93, Keith Alexander 1993–94, Sam Ellis 1994–95, Steve Wicks (HC) 1995, John Beck 1995–98, Shane Westley June 1998– .

## LIVERPOOL

W. E. Barclay 1892–96, Tom Watson 1896–1915, David Ashworth 1920–22, Matt McQueen 1923–28, George Patterson 1928–36 (continued as secretary), George Kay 1936–51, Don Welsh 1951–56, Phil Taylor 1956–59, Bill Shankly 1959–74, Bob Paisley 1974–83, Joe Fagan 1983–85, Kenny Dalglish 1985–91, Graeme Souness 1991–94, Roy Evans January 1994– 98 (then joint manager) Gerard Houllier July 1998– .

## LUTON TOWN

Charlie Green 1901–28*, George Thomson 1925, John McCartney 1927–29, George Kay 1929–31, Harold Wightman 1931–35, Ted Liddell 1935–38, Neil McBain 1938–39, George Martin 1939–47, Dally Duncan 1947–58, Syd Owen 1959–60, Sam Bartram 1960–62, Bill Harvey 1962–64, George Martin 1965–66, Allan Brown 1966–68, Alec Stock 1968–72, Harry Haslam 1972–78, David Pleat 1978–86, John Moore 1986–87, Ray Harford 1987–89, Jim Ryan 1900–91, David Pleat 1991–95, Terry Westley 1995, Lennie Lawrence December 1995– .

## MANCHESTER CITY

Joshua Parlby 1893–95*, Sam Omerod 1895–1902, Tom Maley 1902–06, Harry Newbould 1906–12, Ernest Magnall 1912–24, David Ashworth 1924–25, Peter Hodge 1926–32, Wilf Wild 1932–46 (continued as secretary to 1950), Sam Cowan 1946–47, John "Jock" Thomson 1947–50, Leslie McDowall 1950–63, George Poyser 1963–65, Joe Mercer 1965–71 (continued as GM to 1972), Malcolm Allison 1972–73, Johnny Hart 1973, Ron Saunders 1973–74, Tony Book 1974–79, Malcolm Allison 1979–80, John Bond 1980–83, John Benson 1983, Billy McNeill 1983–86, Jimmy Frizzell 1986–87 (continued as GM), Mel Machin 1987–89, Howard Kendall 1990, Peter Reid 1990–93, Brian Horton 1993–95, Alan Ball 1995–96, Steve Coppell 1996, Frank Clark 1996–98, Joe Royle February 1998– .

## MANCHESTER UNITED

J. Ernest Mangnall 1903–12, John Bentley 1912–14, John Robson 1914–21 (SM from 1916), John Chapman 1921–26, Clarence Hilditch 1926–27, Herbert Bamlett 1927–31, Walter Crickmer 1931–32, Scott Duncan 1932–37, Walter Crickmer 1937–45*, Matt Busby 1945–69 (continued as GM then Director), Wilf McGuinness 1969–70, Sir Matt Busby 1970–71, Frank O'Farrell 1971–72, Tommy Docherty 1972–77, Dave Sexton 1977–81, Ron Atkinson 1981–86, Alex Ferguson November 1986– .

## MANSFIELD TOWN

John Baynes 1922–25, Ted Davison 1926–28, Jack Hickling 1928–33, Henry Martin 1933–35, Charlie Bell 1935, Harold Wightman 1936, Harold Parkes 1936–38, Jack Poole 1938–44, Lloyd Barke 1944–45, Roy Goodall 1945–49, Freddie Steele 1949–51, George Jobey 1952–53, Stan Mercer 1953–55, Charlie Mitten 1956–58, Sam Weaver 1958–60, Raich Carter 1960–63, Tommy Cummings 1963–67, Tommy Eggleston 1967–70, Jock Basford 1970–71, Danny Williams 1971–74, Dave Smith 1974–76, Peter Morris 1976–78, Billy Bingham 1978–79, Mick Jones 1979–81, Stuart Boam 1981–83, Ian Greaves 1983–89, George Foster 1989–93, Andy King 1993–96, Steve Parkin October 1996– .

## MIDDLESBROUGH

John Robson 1899–1905, Alex Mackie 1905–06, Andy Aitken 1906–09, J. Gunter 1908–10*, Andy Walker 1910–11, Tom McIntosh 1911–19, Jimmy Howie 1920–23, Herbert Bamlett 1923–26, Peter McWilliam 1927–34, Wilf Gillow 1934–44, David Jack 1944–52, Walter Rowley 1952–54, Bob Dennison 1954–63, Raich Carter 1963–66, Stan Anderson 1966–73, Jack Charlton 1973–77, John Neal 1977–81, Bobby Murdoch 1981–82, Malcolm Allison 1982–84, Willie Maddren 1984–86, Bruce Rioch 1986–90, Colin Todd 1990–91, Lennie Lawrence 1991–94, Bryan Robson May 1994– .

## MILLWALL

William Henderson 1894–99*, E. R. Stopher 1899–1900, George Saunders 1900–11, Herbert Lipsham 1911–19, Robert Hunter 1919–33, Bill McCracken 1933–36, Charlie Hewitt 1936–40, Bill Voisey 1940–44, Jack Cock 1944–48, Charlie Hewitt 1948–56, Ron Gray 1956–57, Jimmy Seed 1958–59, Reg Smith 1959–61, Ron Gray 1961–63, Billy Gray 1963–66, Benny Fenton 1966–74, Gordon Jago 1974–77, George Petchey 1978–80, Peter Anderson 1980–82, George Graham 1982–86, John Docherty 1986–90, Bob Pearson 1990, Bruce Rioch 1990–92, Mick McCarthy 1992–96, Jimmy Nicholl 1996–97, John Docherty 1997, Billy Bonds 1997–98, Keith Stevens May 1998– .

## NEWCASTLE UNITED

Frank Watt 1895–32*, Andy Cunningham 1930–35, Tom Mather 1935–39, Stan Seymour 1939–47 (Hon-manager), George Martin 1947–50, Stan Seymour 1950–54 (Hon-manager), Duggie Livingstone 1954–56, Stan Seymour 1956–58 (Hon-manager), Charlie Mitten 1958–61, Norman Smith 1961–62, Joe Harvey 1962–75, Gordon Lee 1975–77, Richard Dinnis 1977, Bill McGarry 1977–80, Arthur Cox 1980–84, Jack Charlton 1984, Willie McFaul 1985–88, Jim Smith 1988–91, Ossie Ardiles 1991–92, Kevin Keegan 1992–97, Kenny Dalglish January 1997– .

## NORTHAMPTON TOWN

Arthur Jones 1897–1907*, Herbert Chapman 1907–12, Walter Bull 1912–13, Fred Lessons 1913–19, Bob Hewison 1920–25, Jack Tresadern 1925–30, Jack English 1931–35, Syd Puddefoot 1935–37, Warney Cresswell 1937–39, Tom Smith 1939–49, Bob Dennison 1949–54, Dave Smith 1954–59, David Bowen 1959–67, Tony Marchi 1967–68, Ron Flowers 1968–69, Dave Bowen 1969–72 (continued as GM and secretary to 1985 when joined the board), Billy Baxter 1972–73, Bill Dodgin Jnr 1973–76, Pat Crerand 1976–77, Bill Dodgin Jnr 1977, John Petts 1977–78, Mike Keen 1978–79, Clive Walker 1979–80, Bill Dodgin Jnr 1980–82, Clive Walker 1982–84, Tony Barton 1984–85, Graham Carr 1985–90, Theo Foley 1990–92, Phil Chard 1992–93, John Barnwell 1993–95, Ian Atkins January 1995– .

## NORWICH CITY

John Bowman 1905–07, James McEwen 1907–08, Arthur Turner 1909–10, Bert Stansfield 1910–15, Major Frank Buckley 1919–20, Charles O'Hagan 1920–21, Albert Gosnell 1921–26, Bert Stansfield 1926, Cecil Potter 1926–29, James Kerr 1929–33, Tom Parker 1933–37, Bob Young 1937–39, Jimmy Jewell 1939, Bob Young 1939–45, Cyril Spiers 1946–47, Duggie Lochhead 1947–50, Norman Low 1950–55, Tom Parker 1955–57, Archie Macaulay 1957–61, Willie Reid 1961–62, George Swindin 1962, Ron Ashman 1962–66, Lol Morgan 1966–69, Ron Saunders 1969–73, John Bond 1973–80, Ken Brown 1980–87, Dave Stringer 1987–92, Mike Walker 1992–94, John Deehan 1994–95, Martin O'Neill 1995, Gary Megson 1995–96, Mike Walker 1996–98, Bruce Rioch (FTM) July 1998– .

## NOTTINGHAM FOREST

Harry Radford 1889–97*, Harry Haslam 1897–1909*, Fred Earp 1909–12, Bob Masters 1912–25, John Baynes 1925–29, Stan Hardy 1930–31, Noel Watson 1931–36, Harold Wightman 1936–39, Billy Walker 1939–60, Andy Beattie 1960–63, Johnny Carey 1963–68, Matt Gillies 1969–72, Dave Mackay 1972, Allan Brown 1973–75, Brian Clough 1975–93, Frank Clark 1993–96, Stuart Pearce 1996–97, Dave Bassett May 1997– (previously GM from February).

## NOTTS COUNTY

Edwin Browne 1883–93*, Tom Featherstone 1893*, Tom Harris 1893–1913*, Albert Fisher 1913–27, Horace Henshall 1927–34, Charlie Jones 1934–35, David Pratt 1935, Percy Smith 1935–36, Jimmy McMullan 1936–37, Harry Parkes 1938–39, Tony Towers 1939–42, Frank Womack 1942–43, Major Frank Buckley 1944–46, Arthur Stollery 1946–49, Eric Houghton 1949–53, George Poyser 1953–57, Tommy Lawton 1957–58, Frank Hill 1958–61, Tim Coleman 1961–63, Eddie Lowe 1963–65, Tim Coleman 1965–66, Jack Burkitt 1966–67, Andy Beattie (GM 1967), Billy Gray 1967–68, Jimmy Sirrel 1969–75, Ron Fenton 1975–77, Jimmy Sirrel 1978–82 (continued as GM to 1984), Howard Wilkinson 1982–83, Larry Lloyd 1983–84, Richie Barker 1984–85, Jimmy Sirrel 1985–87, John Barnwell 1987–88, Neil Warnock 1989–93, Mick Walker 1993–94, Russell Slade 1994–95, Howard Kendall 1995, Colin Murphy June 1995 (continued as GM to 1996), Steve Thompson 1996, Sam Allardyce January 1997– .

## OLDHAM ATHLETIC
David Ashworth 1906–14, Herbert Bamlett 1914–21, Charlie Roberts 1921–22, David Ashworth 1923–24, Bob Mellor 1924–27, Andy Wilson 1927–32, Jimmy McMullan 1933–34, Bob Mellor 1934–45 (continued as secretary to 1953), Frank Womack 1945–47, Billy Wootton 1947–50, George Hardwick 1950–56, Ted Goodier 1956–58, Norman Dodgin 1958–60, Jack Rowley 1960–63, Les McDowall 1963–65, Gordon Hurst 1965–66, Jimmy McIlroy 1966–68, Jack Rowley 1968–69, Jimmy Frizzell 1970–82, Joe Royle 1982–94, Graeme Sharp 1994–97, Neil Warnock 1997–98, Andy Ritchie May 1998– .

## OXFORD UNITED
Harry Thompson 1949–58 (Player-Manager 1949-51), Arthur Turner 1959–69 (continued as GM to 1972), Ron Saunders 1969, George Summers 1969–75, Mike Brown 1975–79, Bill Asprey 1979–80, Ian Greaves 1980–82, Jim Smith 1982–85, Maurice Evans 1985–88, Mark Lawrenson 1988, Brian Horton 1988–93, Denis Smith 1993–97, Malcolm Crosby 1997, Malcolm Shotton January 1998– .

## PETERBOROUGH UNITED
Jock Porter 1934–36, Fred Taylor 1936–37, Vic Poulter 1937–38, Sam Madden 1938–48, Jack Blood 1948–50, Bob Gurney 1950–52, Jack Fairbrother 1952–54, George Swindin 1954–58, Jimmy Hagan 1958–62, Jack Fairbrother 1962–64, Gordon Clark 1964–67, Norman Rigby 1967–69, Jim Iley 1969–72, Noel Cantwell 1972–77, John Barnwell 1977–78, Billy Hails 1978–79, Peter Morris 1979–82, Martin Wilkinson 1982–83, John Wile 1983–86, Noel Cantwell 1986–88 (continued as GM), Mick Jones 1988–89, Mark Lawrenson 1989–90, Chris Turner 1991–92, Lil Fuccillo 1992–93, John Still 1994–95, Mick Halsall 1995–96, Barry Fry May 1996– .

## PLYMOUTH ARGYLE
Frank Brettell 1903–05, Bob Jack 1905–06, Bill Fullerton 1906–07, Bob Jack 1910–38, Jack Tresadern 1938–47, Jimmy Rae 1948–55, Jack Rowley 1955–60, Neil Dougall 1961, Ellis Stuttard 1961–63, Andy Beattie 1963–64, Malcolm Allison 1964–65, Derek Ufton 1965–68, Billy Bingham 1968–70, Ellis Stuttard 1970–72, Tony Waiters 1972–77, Mike Kelly 1977–78, Malcolm Allison 1978–79, Bobby Saxton 1979–81, Bobby Moncur 1981–83, Johnny Hore 1983–84, Dave Smith 1984–88, Ken Brown 1988–90, David Kemp 1990–92, Peter Shilton 1992–95, Steve McCall 1995, Neil Warnock 1995–97, Mick Jones 1997– 98, Kevin Hodges June 1998– .

## PORTSMOUTH
Frank Brettell 1898–1901, Bob Blyth 1901–04, Richard Bonney 1905–08, Bob Brown 1911–20, John McCartney 1920–27, Jack Tinn 1927–47, Bob Jackson 1947–52, Eddie Lever 1952–58, Freddie Cox 1958–61, George Smith 1961–70, Ron Tindall 1970–73 (GM to 1974), John Mortimore 1973–74, Ian St. John 1974–77, Jimmy Dickinson 1977–79, Frank Burrows 1979–82, Bobby Campbell 1982–84, Alan Ball 1984–89, John Gregory 1989–90, Frank Burrows 1990–1991, Jim Smith 1991–95, Terry Fenwick 1995–98, Alan Ball January 1998– .

## PORT VALE
Sam Gleaves 1896–1905*, Tom Clare 1905–11, A. S. Walker 1911–12, H. Myatt 1912–14, Tom Holford 1919–24 (continued as trainer), Joe Schofield 1924–30, Tom Morgan 1930–32, Tom Holford 1932–35, Warney Cresswell 1936–37, Tom Morgan 1937–38, Billy Frith 1945–46, Gordon Hodgson 1946–51, Ivor Powell 1951, Freddie Steele 1951–57, Norman Low 1957–62, Freddie Steele 1962–65, Jackie Mudie 1965–67, Sir Stanley Matthews (GM) 1965–68, Gordon Lee 1968–74, Roy Sproson 1974–77, Colin Harper 1977, Bobby Smith 1977–78, Dennis Butler 1978–79, Alan Bloor 1979, John McGrath 1980–83, John Rudge March 1984– .

## PRESTON NORTH END
Charlie Parker 1906–15, Vincent Hayes 1919–23, Jim Lawrence 1923–25, Frank Richards 1925–27, Alex Gibson 1927–31, Lincoln Hayes 1931–1932, (run by committee 1932–36), Tommy Muirhead 1936–37, (run by committee 1937–49), Will Scott 1949–53, Scot Symon 1953–54, Frank Hill 1954–56, Cliff Britton 1956–61, Jimmy Milne 1961–68, Bobby Seith 1968–70, Alan Ball Sr 1970–73, Bobby Charlton 1973–75, Harry Catterick 1975–77, Nobby Stiles 1977–81, Tommy Docherty 1981, Gordon Lee 1981–83, Alan Kelly 1983–85, Tommy Booth 1985–86, Brian Kidd 1986, John McGrath 1986–90, Les Chapman 1990–92, John Beck 1992–94, Gary Peters 1994–98, David Moyes January 1998– .

## QUEENS PARK RANGERS
James Cowan 1906–13, Jimmy Howie 1913–20, Ted Liddell 1920–24, Will Wood 1924–25 (had been secretary since 1903), Bob Hewison 1925–30, John Bowman 1930–31, Archie Mitchell 1931–33, Mick O'Brien 1933–35, Billy Birrell 1935–39, Ted Vizard 1939–44, Dave Mangnall 1944–52, Jack Taylor 1952–59, Alec Stock 1959–65 (GM to 1968), Bill Dodgin Jnr 1968, Tommy Docherty 1968, Les Allen 1968–71, Gordon Jago 1971–74, Dave Sexton 1974–77, Frank Sibley 1977–78, Steve Burtenshaw 1978–79, Tommy Docherty 1979–80, Terry Venables 1980–84, Gordon Jago 1984, Alan Mullery 1984, Frank Sibley 1984–85, Jim Smith 1985–88, Trevor Francis 1988–90, Don Howe 1990–91, Gerry Francis 1991–94, Ray Wilkins 1994–96, Stewart Houston 1996–97, Ray Harford December 1997– .

## READING
Thomas Sefton 1897–1901*, James Sharp 1901–02, Harry Matthews 1902–20, Harry Marshall 1920–22, Arthur Chadwick 1923–25, H. S. Bray 1925–26 (secretary only since 1922 and 1926-35), Andrew Wylie 1926–31, Joe Smith 1931–35, Billy Butler 1935–39, John Cochrane 1939, Joe Edelston 1939–47, Ted Drake 1947–52, Jack Smith 1952–55, Harry Johnston 1955–63, Roy Bentley 1963–69, Jack Mansell 1969–71, Charlie Hurley 1972–77, Maurice Evans 1977–84, Ian Branfoot 1984–89, Ian Porterfield 1989–91, Mark McGhee 1991–94, Jimmy Quinn/Mick Gooding 1994–97, Terry Bullivant 1997–98, Tommy Burns March 1998– .

## ROCHDALE
Billy Bradshaw 1920, (run by committee 1920–22), Tom Wilson 1922–23, Jack Peart 1923–30, Will Cameron 1930–31, Herbert Hopkinson 1932–34, Billy Smith 1934–35, Ernest Nixon 1935–37, Sam Jennings 1937–38, Ted Goodier 1938–52,

Jack Warner 1952–53, Harry Catterick 1953–58, Jack Marshall 1958–60, Tony Collins 1960–68, Bob Stokoe 1967–68, Len Richley 1968–70, Dick Conner 1970–73, Walter Joyce 1973–76, Brian Green 1976–77, Mike Ferguson 1977–78, Doug Collins 1979, Bob Stokoe 1979–80, Peter Madden 1980–83, Jimmy Greenhoff 1983–84, Vic Halom 1984–86, Eddie Gray 1986–88, Danny Bergara 1988–89, Terry Dolan 1989–91, Dave Sutton 1991–94, Mick Docherty 1995–96, Graham Barrow May 1996– .

## ROTHERHAM UNITED
Billy Heald 1925–29 (secretary only for long spell), Stanley Davies 1929–30, Billy Heald 1930–33, Reg Freeman 1934–52, Andy Smailes 1952–58, Tom Johnston 1958–62, Danny Williams 1962–65, Jack Mansell 1965–67, Tommy Docherty 1967–68, Jimmy McAnearney 1968–73, Jimmy McGuigan 1973–79, Ian Porterfield 1979–81, Emlyn Hughes 1981–83, George Kerr 1983–85, Norman Hunter 1985–87, Dave Cusack 1987–88, Billy McEwan 1988–91, Phil Henson 1991–94, Archie Gemmill/ John McGovern 1994–96, Danny Bergara 1996–97, Ronnie Moore May 1997– .

## SCARBOROUGH
B. Chapman 1945–47*, George Hall 1946–47, Harold Taylor 1947–48, Frank Taylor 1948–50, A. C. Bell (Director & Hon. TM) 1950–53, Reg Halton 1953–54, Charles Robson (Hon. TM) 1954–57, George Higgins 1957–58, Andy Smailes 1959–61, Eddie Brown 1961–64, Albert Franks 1964–65, Stuart Myers 1965–66, Graham Shaw 1968–69, Colin Appleton 1969–73, Ken Houghton 1974–75, Colin Appleton 1975–81, Jimmy McAnearney 1981–82, John Cottam 1982–84, Harry Dunn 1984–86, Neil Warnock 1986–88, Colin Morris 1989, Ray McHale 1989–93, Phil Chambers 1993, Steve Wicks 1993–94, Billy Ayre 1994, Ray McHale 1994–96, Mitch Cook (DoC) 1996, Mick Wadsworth June 1996– .

## SCUNTHORPE UNITED
Harry Allcock 1915–53*, Tom Crilly 1936–37, Bernard Harper 1946–48, Leslie Jones 1950–51, Bill Corkhill 1952–56, Ron Suart 1956–58, Tony McShane 1959, Bill Lambton 1959, Frank Soo 1959–60, Dick Duckworth 1960–64, Fred Goodwin 1964–66, Ron Ashman 1967–73, Ron Bradley 1973–74, Dick Rooks 1974–76, Ron Ashman 1976–81, John Duncan 1981–83, Allan Clarke 1983–84, Frank Barlow 1984–87, Mick Buxton 1987–91, Bill Green 1991–93, Richard Money 1993–94, David Moore 1994–96, Mick Buxton 1996–97, Brian Laws February 1997– .

## SHEFFIELD UNITED
J. B. Wostinholm 1889–1899*, John Nicholson 1899–1932, Ted Davison 1932–52, Reg Freeman 1952–55, Joe Mercer 1955–58, Johnny Harris 1959–68 (continued as GM to 1970), Arthur Rowley 1968–69, Johnny Harris (GM resumed TM duties) 1969–73, Ken Furphy 1973–75, Jimmy Sirrel 1975–77, Harry Haslam 1978–81, Martin Peters 1981, Ian Porterfield 1981–86, Billy McEwan 1986–88, Dave Bassett 1988–95, Howard Kendall 1995–97, Nigel Spackman 1997–98, Steve Bruce July 1998– .

## SHEFFIELD WEDNESDAY
Arthur Dickinson 1891–1920*, Robert Brown 1920–33, Billy Walker 1933–37, Jimmy McMullan 1937–42, Eric Taylor 1942–58 (continued as GM to 1974), Harry Catterick 1958–61, Vic Buckingham 1961–64, Alan Brown 1964–68, Jack Marshall 1968–69, Danny Williams 1969–71, Derek Dooley 1971–73, Steve Burtenshaw 1974–75, Len Ashurst 1975–77, Jackie Charlton 1977–83, Howard Wilkinson 1983–88, Peter Eustace 1988–89, Ron Atkinson 1989–91, Trevor Francis 1991–95, David Pleat 1995–97, Ron Atkinson 1997–98, Danny Wilson July 1998– .

## SHREWSBURY TOWN
W. Adams 1905–12*, A. Weston 1912–34*, Jack Roscamp 1934–35, Sam Ramsey 1935–36, Ted Bousted 1936–40, Leslie Knighton 1945–49, Harry Chapman 1949–50, Sammy Crooks 1950–54, Walter Rowley 1955–57, Harry Potts 1957–58, Johnny Spuhler 1958, Arthur Rowley 1958–68, Harry Gregg 1968–72, Maurice Evans 1972–73, Alan Durban 1974–78, Richie Barker 1978, Graham Turner 1978–84, Chic Bates 1984–87, Ian McNeill 1987–90, Asa Hartford 1990–91, John Bond 1991–93, Fred Davies 1994 (previously caretaker-manager from 1993)–97, Jake King May 1997– .

## SOUTHAMPTON
Cecil Knight 1894–95*, Charles Robson 1895–97, E. Arnfield 1897–1911* (continued as secretary), George Swift 1911–12, Ernest Arnfield 1912–19, Jimmy McIntyre 1919–24, Arthur Chadwick 1925–31, George Kay 1931–36, George Gross 1936–37, Tom Parker 1937–43, J. R. Sarjantson stepped down from the board to act as secretary-manager 1943–47 with the next two listed being team managers during this period, Arthur Dominy 1943–46, Bill Dodgin Snr 1946–49, Sid Cann 1949–51, George Roughton 1952–55, Ted Bates 1955–73, Lawrie McMenemy 1973–85, Chris Nicholl 1985–91, Ian Branfoot 1991–94, Alan Ball 1994–95, Dave Merrington 1995–96, Graeme Souness 1996–97, Dave Jones June 1997– .

## SOUTHEND UNITED
Bob Jack 1906–10, George Molyneux 1910–11, O. M. Howard 1911–12, Joe Bradshaw 1912–19, Ned Liddell 1919–20, Tom Mather 1920–21, Ted Birnie 1921–34, David Jack 1934–40, Harry Warren 1946–56, Eddie Perry 1956–60, Frank Broome 1960, Ted Fenton 1961–65, Alvan Williams 1965–67, Ernie Shepherd 1967–69, Geoff Hudson 1969–70, Arthur Rowley 1970–76, Dave Smith 1976–83, Peter Morris 1983–84, Bobby Moore 1984–86, Dave Webb 1986–87, Dick Bate 1987, Paul Clark 1987–88, Dave Webb (GM) 1988–92, Colin Murphy 1992–93, Barry Fry 1993, Peter Taylor 1993–95, Steve Thompson 1995, Ronnie Whelan 1995–97, Alvin Martin July 1997–.

## STOCKPORT COUNTY
Fred Stewart 1894–1911, Harry Lewis 1911–14, David Ashworth 1914–19, Albert Williams 1919–24, Fred Scotchbrook 1924–26, Lincoln Hyde 1926–31, Andrew Wilson 1932–33, Fred Westgarth 1934–36, Bob Kelly 1936–38, George Hunt 1938–39, Bob Marshall 1939–49, Andy Beattie 1949–52, Dick Duckworth 1952–56, Billy Moir 1956–60, Reg Flewin 1960–63, Trevor Porteous 1963–65, Bert Trautmann (GM) 1965–66, Eddie Quigley (TM) 1965–66, Jimmy Meadows 1966–69, Wally Galbraith 1969–70, Matt Woods 1970–71, Brian Doyle 1972–74, Jimmy Meadows 1974–75, Roy Chapman 1975–76, Eddie Quigley 1976–77, Alan Thompson 1977–78, Mike Summerbee 1978–79, Jimmy McGuigan 1979–82, Eric Webster 1982–85, Colin Murphy 1985, Les Chapman 1985–86, Jimmy Melia 1986, Colin Murphy 1986–87, Asa Hartford 1987–89, Danny Bergara 1989–95, Dave Jones 1995–97, Gary Megson July 1997– .

## STOKE CITY

Tom Slaney 1874–83*, Walter Cox 1883–84*, Harry Lockett 1884–90, Joseph Bradshaw 1890–92, Arthur Reeves 1892–95, William Rowley 1895–97, H. D. Austerberry 1897–1908, A. J. Barker 1908–14, Peter Hodge 1914–15, Joe Schofield 1915–19, Arthur Shallcross 1919–23, John "Jock" Rutherford 1923, Tom Mather 1923–35, Bob McGrory 1935–52, Frank Taylor 1952–60, Tony Waddington 1960–77, George Eastham 1977–78, Alan A'Court 1978, Alan Durban 1978–81, Richie Barker 1981–83, Bill Asprey 1984–85, Mick Mills 1985–89, Alan Ball 1989–91, Lou Macari 1991–93, Joe Jordan 1993–94, Lou Macari 1994–97, Chic Bates 1997–98, Chris Kamara 1998, Brian Little May 1998– .

## SUNDERLAND

Tom Watson 1888–96, Bob Campbell 1896–99, Alex Mackie 1899–1905, Bob Kyle 1905–28, Johnny Cochrane 1928–39, Bill Murray 1939–57, Alan Brown 1957–64, George Hardwick 1964–65, Ian McColl 1965–68, Alan Brown 1968–72, Bob Stokoe 1972–76, Jimmy Adamson 1976–78, Ken Knighton 1979–81, Alan Durban 1981–84, Len Ashurst 1984–85, Lawrie McMenemy 1985–87, Denis Smith 1987–91, Malcolm Crosby 1992–93, Terry Butcher 1993, Mick Buxton 1993–95, Peter Reid March 1995– .

## SWANSEA CITY

Walter Whittaker 1912–14, William Bartlett 1914–15, Joe Bradshaw 1919–26, Jimmy Thomson 1927–31, Neil Harris 1934–39, Haydn Green 1939–47, Bill McCandless 1947–55, Ron Burgess 1955–58, Trevor Morris 1958–65, Glyn Davies 1965–66, Billy Lucas 1967–69, Roy Bentley 1969–72, Harry Gregg 1972–75, Harry Griffiths 1975–77, John Toshack 1978–83 (resigned October re-appointed in December) 1983–84, Colin Appleton 1984, John Bond 1984–85, Tommy Hutchison 1985–86, Terry Yorath 1986–89, Ian Evans 1989–90, Terry Yorath 1990–91, Frank Burrows 1991–95, Kevin Cullis 1996, Jan Molby 1996–97, Micky Adams 1997, Alan Cork 1997–98, John Hollins July 1998– .

## SWINDON TOWN

Sam Allen 1902–33, Ted Vizard 1933–39, Neil Harris 1939–41, Louis Page 1945–53, Maurice Lindley 1953–55, Bert Head 1956–65, Danny Williams 1965–69, Fred Ford 1969–71, Dave Mackay 1971–72, Les Allen 1972–74, Danny Williams 1974–78, Bobby Smith 1978–80, John Trollope 1980–83, Ken Beamish 1983–84, Lou Macari 1984–89, Ossie Ardiles 1989–91, Glenn Hoddle 1991–93, John Gorman 1993–94, Steve McMahon November 1994– .

## TORQUAY UNITED

Percy Mackrill 1927–29, A. H. Hoskins 1929*, Frank Womack 1929–32, Frank Brown 1932–38, Alf Steward 1938–40, Billy Butler 1945–46, Jack Butler 1946–47, John McNeil 1947–50, Bob John 1950, Alex Massie 1950–51, Eric Webber 1951–65, Frank O'Farrell 1965–68, Alan Brown 1969–71, Jack Edwards 1971–73, Malcolm Musgrove 1973–76, Mike Green 1977–81, Frank O'Farrell 1981–82 (continued as GM to 1983), Bruce Rioch 1982–84, Dave Webb 1984–85, John Sims 1985, Stuart Morgan 1985–87, Cyril Knowles 1987–89, Dave Smith 1989–91, John Impey 1991–92, Ivan Golac 1992, Paul Compton 1992–93, Don O'Riordan 1993–95, Eddie May 1995–96, Kevin Hodges (HC) 1996–98, Wes Saunders July 1998– .

## TOTTENHAM HOTSPUR

Frank Brettell 1898–99, John Cameron 1899–1906, Fred Kirkham 1907–08, Peter McWilliam 1912–27, Billy Minter 1927–29, Percy Smith 1930–35, Jack Tresadern 1935–38, Peter McWilliam 1938–42, Arthur Turner 1942–46, Joe Hulme 1946–49, Arthur Rowe 1949–55, Jimmy Anderson 1955–58, Bill Nicholson 1958–74, Terry Neill 1974–76, Keith Burkinshaw 1976–84, Peter Shreeves 1984–86, David Pleat 1986–87, Terry Venables 1987–91, Peter Shreeves 1991–92, Ossie Ardiles 1993–94, Gerry Francis 1994–97, Christian Gross (HC) November 1997– .

## TRANMERE ROVERS

Bert Cooke 1912–35, Jackie Carr 1935–36, Jim Knowles 1936–39, Bill Ridding 1939–45, Ernie Blackburn 1946–55, Noel Kelly 1955–57, Peter Farrell 1957–60, Walter Galbraith 1961, Dave Russell 1961–69, Jackie Wright 1969–72, Ron Yeats 1972–75, John King 1975–80, Bryan Hamilton 1980–85, Frank Worthington 1985–87, Ronnie Moore 1987, John King 1987–96, John Aldridge April 1996– .

## WALSALL

H. Smallwood 1888–91*, A. G. Burton 1891–93, J. H. Robinson 1893–95, C. H. Ailso 1895–96*, A. E. Parsloe 1896–97*, L. Ford 1897–98*, G. Hughes 1898–99*, L. Ford 1899–1901*, J. E. Shutt 1908–13*, Haydn Price 1914–20, Joe Burchell 1920–26, David Ashworth 1926–27, Jack Torrance 1927–28, James Kerr 1928–29, Sid Scholey 1929–30, Peter O'Rourke 1930–32, Bill Slade 1932–34, Andy Wilson 1934–37, Tommy Lowes 1937–44, Harry Hibbs 1944–51, Tony McPhee 1951, Brough Fletcher 1952–53, Major Frank Buckley 1953–55, John Love 1955–57, Billy Moore 1957–64, Alf Wood 1964, Reg Shaw 1964–68, Dick Graham 1968, Ron Lewin 1968–69, Billy Moore 1969–72, John Smith 1972–73, Doug Fraser 1973–77, Dave Mackay 1977–78, Alan Ashman 1978, Frank Sibley 1979, Alan Buckley 1979–86, Neil Martin (joint manager with Buckley) 1981–82, Tommy Coakley 1986–88, John Barnwell 1989–90, Kenny Hibbitt 1990–94, Chris Nicholl 1994–97, Jan Sorensen 1997–98, Ray Graydon 1998– .

## WATFORD

John Goodall 1903–10, Harry Kent 1910–26, Fred Pagnam 1926–29, Neil McBain 1929–37, Bill Findlay 1938–47, Jack Bray 1947–48, Eddie Hapgood 1948–50, Ron Gray 1950–51, Haydn Green 1951–52, Len Goulden 1952–55 (GM to 1956), Johnny Paton 1955–56, Neil McBain 1956–59, Ron Burgess 1959–63, Bill McGarry 1963–64, Ken Furphy 1964–71, George Kirby 1971–73, Mike Keen 1973–77, Graham Taylor 1977–87, Dave Bassett 1987–88, Steve Harrison 1988–90, Colin Lee 1990, Steve Perryman 1990–93, Glenn Roeder 1993–96, Kenny Jackett 1996–97, Graham Taylor May 1997– (GM since February 1996).

## WEST BROMWICH ALBION

Louis Ford 1890–92*, Henry Jackson 1892–94*, Edward Stephenson 1894–95*, Clement Keys 1895–96*, Frank Heaven 1896–1902*, Fred Everiss 1902–48, Jack Smith 1948–52, Jesse Carver 1952, Vic Buckingham 1953–59, Gordon Clark

1959–61, Archie Macaulay 1961–63, Jimmy Hagan 1963–67, Alan Ashman 1967–71, Don Howe 1971–75, Johnny Giles 1975–77, Ronnie Allen 1977, Ron Atkinson 1978–81, Ronnie Allen 1981–82, Ron Wylie 1982–84, Johnny Giles 1984–85, Ron Saunders 1986–87, Ron Atkinson 1987–88, Brian Talbot 1988–91, Bobby Gould 1991–92, Ossie Ardiles 1992–93, Keith Burkinshaw 1993–94, Alan Buckley 1994–97, Ray Harford 1997, Denis Smith December 1997– .

## WEST HAM UNITED

Syd King 1902–32, Charlie Paynter 1932–50, Ted Fenton 1950–61, Ron Greenwood 1961–74 (continued as GM to 1977), John Lyall 1974–89, Lou Macari 1989–90, Billy Bonds 1990–94, Harry Redknapp August 1994– .

## WIGAN ATHLETIC

Charlie Spencer 1932–37, Jimmy Milne 1946–47, Bob Pryde 1949–52, Ted Goodier 1952–54, Walter Crook 1954–55, Ron Suart 1955–56, Billy Cooke 1956, Sam Barkas 1957, Trevor Hitchen 1957–58, Malcolm Barrass 1958–59, Jimmy Shirley 1959, Pat Murphy 1959–60, Allenby Chilton 1960, Johnny Ball 1961–63, Allan Brown 1963–66, Alf Craig 1966–67, Harry Leyland 1967–68, Alan Saunders 1968, Ian McNeill 1968–70, Gordon Milne 1970–72, Les Rigby 1972–74, Brian Tiler 1974–76, Ian McNeill 1976–81, Larry Lloyd 1981–83, Harry McNally 1983–85, Bryan Hamilton 1985–86, Ray Mathias 1986–89, Bryan Hamilton 1989–93, Dave Philpotts 1993, Kenny Swain 1993–94, Graham Barrow 1994–95, John Deehan 1995–98.

## WIMBLEDON

Les Henley 1955–71, Mike Everitt 1971–73, Dick Graham 1973–74, Allen Batsford 1974–78, Dario Gradi 1978–81, Dave Bassett 1981–87, Bobby Gould 1987–90, Ray Harford 1990–91, Peter Withe 1991, Joe Kinnear January 1992– .

## WOLVERHAMPTON WANDERERS

George Worrall 1877–85*, John Addenbrooke 1885–1922, George Jobey 1922–24, Albert Hoskins 1924–26 (had been secretary since 1922), Fred Scotchbrook 1926–27, Major Frank Buckley 1927–44, Ted Vizard 1944–48, Stan Cullis 1948–64, Andy Beattie 1964–65, Ronnie Allen 1966–68, Bill McGarry 1968–76, Sammy Chung 1976–78, John Barnwell 1978–81, Ian Greaves 1982, Graham Hawkins 1982–84, Tommy Docherty 1984–85, Bill McGarry 1985, Sammy Chapman 1985–86, Brian Little 1986, Graham Turner 1986–94, Graham Taylor 1994–95, Mark McGhee December 1995– .

## WREXHAM

Ted Robinson 1912–25* (continued as secretary to 1930), Charlie Hewitt 1925–29, Jack Baynes 1929–31, Ernest Blackburn 1932–36, Jimmy Logan 1937–38, Arthur Cowell 1938, Tom Morgan 1938–40, Tom Williams 1940–49, Les McDowall 1949–50, Peter Jackson 1951–54, Cliff Lloyd 1954–57, John Love 1957–59, Billy Morris 1960–61, Ken Barnes 1961–65, Billy Morris 1965, Jack Rowley 1966–67, Alvan Williams 1967–68, John Neal 1968–77, Arfon Griffiths 1977–81, Mel Sutton 1981–82, Bobby Roberts 1982–85, Dixie McNeil 1985–89, Brian Flynn November 1989– .

## WYCOMBE WANDERERS

First coach appointed 1951. Prior to Brian Lee's appointment in 1969, the team was selected by a Match Committee which met every Monday evening. James McCormack 1951–52, Sid Cann 1952–61, Graham Adams 1961–62, Don Welsh 1962–64, Barry Darvill 1964–68, Brian Lee 1969–76, Ted Powell 1976–77, John Reardon 1977–78, Andy Williams 1978–80, Mike Keen 1980–84, Paul Bence 1984–86, Alan Gane 1986–87, Peter Suddaby 1987–88, Jim Kelman 1988–90, Martin O'Neill 1990–95, Alan Smith 1995–96, John Gregory 1996–98, Neil Smillie February 1998– .

## YORK CITY

Bill Sherrington 1924–60 (was secretary for most of this time but virtually secretary-manager for a long pre-war spell), John Collier 1929–36, Tom Mitchell 1936–50, Dick Duckworth 1950–52, Charlie Spencer 1952–53, Jimmy McCormick 1953–54, Sam Bartram 1956–60, Tom Lockie 1960–67, Joe Shaw 1967–68, Tom Johnston 1968–75, Wilf McGuinness 1975–77, Charlie Wright 1977–80, Barry Lyons 1980–81, Denis Smith 1982–87, Bobby Saxton 1987–88, John Bird 1988–91, John Ward 1991–93, Alan Little March 1993– .

# THE THINGS THEY SAID ...

**Dutch star Bryan Roy, on leaving relegated Forest for Hertha Berlin:**
*"Nottingham does not have much life at all. They have Robin Hood, but he is dead. Berlin has everything, and the people are not as narrow-minded as in Nottingham."*

**Chelsea chairman Ken Bates, at the Rothmans launch, when asked about reducing the size of the Premiership:**
*"It ain't going to happen. When was the last time turkeys voted for Christmas?"*

**Ken Bates, on the influx of foreign players:**
*"There is a suggestion that so-called foreign mercenaries are driving out English footballers, destroying the grass roots. What actually happens is that the foreign players bring new ideas, new ways of living and new attitudes to training which brush off on the youngsters."*

**PFA chief executive Gordon Taylor, on the same influx:**
*"It's grown from a trickle to a stream, and I wouldn't want it to become a torrent."*

**Newcastle manager Kenny Dalglish, after adding Ian Rush (35) to his recent signings of Stuart Pearce (35) and John Barnes (33):**
*"We are developing our youth policy."*

**Barnsley-based Premier League referee Steve Lodge, after seeing a video of an over-the-line incident he had not given as a goal:**
*"I am of the opinion [as I expressed last season when witnessing the Chesterfield v Middlesbrough semi-final with 'the goal that never was'] that possibly the time has come for some kind of electronic aid.... In the meantime, perhaps I shall go for another eye test and change my contact lenses."*

**Carlton TV traffic news:**
*"... and Wimbledon play Barnsley, so Plough Lane will be very busy."*

**Man Utd manager Alex Ferguson, speaking at the Birmingham launch of the FA's Coaches Association:**
*"Since Eric Cantona came to United, I've learnt that practice is so important. After the first day's training Eric said 'Can I have two players?' I asked him what for and he said he wanted them to practise with. For half-an-hour he practised volleys and finishing, and it was marvellous to watch. Such was the impact, that all the players wanted to come back. It was the same every day. To get to the very top, the Cantona level, you have to practise."*

**FIFA secretary Sepp Blatter, interviewed by a German magazine:**
*"We must outlaw the tackle in the football of the future. We have to combat aggression, especially in matches where the stakes are high. Players such as Ronaldo are being literally kicked to pieces."*

**FIFA's director of communications Keith Cooper, explaining the above:**
*"There is something of a misinterpretation here.... Tackle means something more sinister in their language [German]. We are not trying to outlaw tackling, but the slide-tackle is under review."*

**Spurs chairman Alan Sugar, answering questions at the Oxford Union from an audience that included a number of Tottenham fans:**
*"The problem with fans is that they apply pressure, which forces you to bring in some other idiot who is going to ruin the team more than the professional you already have in place."*

**Sugar on the FA:**
*"They are more interested in their white jackets and match tickets. They haven't got a clue what's going on in the outside world.... They are totally out to lunch. The FA is like going into Madame Tussaud's. It's hard to tell the difference between the dummies and the real people."*

**Wimbledon captain Vinnie Jones:**
*"Referees should start thinking about how a massive talent like Dennis Bergkamp can be encouraged and how the game here can grow to new heights."*

**Former Sheffield Wed manager Ron Atkinson on their search for a new manager:**
*"I have had no contact with anyone from Sheffield Wednesday, and I will not become their next manager."*

**Ron Atkinson 4 days later, on signing as new Sheff Wed boss to the end of the season, having rejected a 3-year contract:**
*"I would be very happy to be with the club in some sort of capacity for three years. What capacity I don't know, but I know that if we get relegated it will be as a distant relative."*

**Express Sport headline when an unconvincing Chelsea scrape a 2-0 win over Everton at Stamford Bridge with two late penalties:**
*"Chelsea third after double penalty glory."*

**Spurs shareholder at AGM:**
*"There is a company in another part of North London that treats its customers with respect and behaves with decorum. There is another company which treats its customers with contempt, offers an inferior product, invests unwisely and squanders its assets. It also demotivates its employees, exploits its customers and insults their intelligence. I have to say Tottenham is in that latter category."*

**Football coach Vanessa Hardwick, after winning her case against the FA for deliberately failing her on an advanced course because of her sex:**
*"The course was a world run by men for men.... They were demoralising and excluding me from the group. As a result of being failed, I lost the opportunity to coach at a high level."*

**Australia striker Graham Arnold, who retired after their failure to qualify for the World Cup, on the proposed retention of Terry Venables as coach when his contract expires in the summer:**
*"If we do that, we'd be the only country in the world prepared to put up with that situation [part-time coaching]. I've been in four World Cup campaigns, and the preparation we had this time was the worst. We failed badly. We should have been going to the World Cup, and it wasn't all about bad luck."*

**Spurs chairman Alan Sugar eats his words ("I wouldn't wash my car with Klinsmann's shirt now ...", 1995) as the German striker returns:**
*"It was a long time ago and it is all water under the bridge now. It was all down to my naïvety at the time. In other businesses I've been involved with we don't have contracts on things like that, we have handshakes.... I was wrong, but I can't keep continually eating humble pie."*

**Former referee Clive Thomas, who was castigated for blowing for time to deny Brazil a headed winner from a corner against Sweden in the 1978 World Cup, after Steve Dunn does the same thing to deny Wimbledon a winner against Wrexham in the 3rd round of the FA Cup:**
*"I've been waiting 20 years for someone else to do that. I have been praying, every Cup tie. The law is there. Time should only be extended for a penalty kick."*

**Barnsley's Macedonian international striker Georgi Hristov, 21, complaining it was difficult to find a girl-friend:**
*"The local girls are far uglier than the ones back in Belgrade or Skopje [the capital of Macedonia]. Our women are far prettier. Besides, they don't drink as much beer as the Barnsley girls, which is something I don't like at all."*

**Arsenal manager Arsène Wenger on why he blocked Ian Wright's lucrative transfer to Benfica:**
*"It took Arsenal 40 years to find a goalscorer like him, and maybe there will never be a true replacement."*

**Leeds manager George Graham on Alan Shearer after their 1-1 draw at Newcastle:**
*"Every time we had a corner there was almost an assault on Hasselbaink. It was embarrassing, and how the referee didn't see it I don't know. I can't believe it. Shearer wasn't watching the ball, just the man. We should have had three or four penalties. I don't know what the referee was thinking about."*

**Liverpool manager Roy Evans after his former striker Stan Collymore scores twice in their 2-1 defeat at Villa:**
*"Having been booked, he [Collymore] then committed a series of fouls, eight or ten. He was allowed to do what he wanted."*

**A German federation official, on retiring FIFA president João Havelange's stated support, when visiting PM Tony Blair in London, for England's bid for the 2006 World Cup:**
*"You cannot take him seriously any longer. I don't know where he's going next, but if it's Malta – then he'll say Malta should stage the World Cup."*

**Distraught Spurs stalwart David Howells after being dropped from the 18-man squad for the important relegation battle at Barnsley:**
*"I don't know if that's the way he always treats players, but while Christian Gross is manager I can't see a future for me.... The only time I've spoken to Christian since he's been at the club about being dropped, he refused to give me a reason. So that was that. He told me I had to accept it. End of conversation."*

**Man U sub Ole Gunnar Solskjaer, after being sent off for a 'professional foul' that possibly saved a point against Newcastle and might just have swung the title United's way:**
*"I've got no regrets because I did it for the team. I thought I had no other option and I don't feel the need to apologise."*

**A philosophical Kenny Dalglish, on the Solskjaer foul that possibly cost his relegation-threatened side a win:**
*"It isn't a pleasant side of football to see, although it is a professional thing – the guy's got to do what he's got to do."*

**Leicester manager Martin O'Neill after Newcastle's Alan Shearer apparently kicks Neil Lennon in the face and escapes without even a yellow card:**
*"I don't care whether you are Alan Shearer or the Pope, you don't do that. It isn't in the game. He [Lennon] got kicked in the face and rules are rules – the same for everybody. Of course it was deliberate – he [Shearer] should have been sent off the field."*

**Alan Shearer in his defence:**
*"I have now seen the television pictures of the incident and I am amazed how bad it looks by comparison to what actually happened. I was brought down by Neil Lennon over by the touchline and we both fell clumsily. As I tried to get to my feet, I had to really tug my left foot free, and the momentum of doing this looked on television like a kick. It certainly wasn't, and the fact that Neil is virtually unmarked confirms this."*

**England coach Glenn Hoddle explaining to the press why he gave his blessing to Paul Gascoigne's 20-a-day smoking habit:**
*"If I stop him for three weeks, it could have an adverse affect coming out of his system. He's been smoking since he went to Rome with Lazio, but if you think it's a major issue write about it.... Ossie Ardiles was on 40 a day when he won the World Cup."*

**England manager Glenn Hoddle, outlining his beliefs in spiritual reincarnation in a radio interview:**
*"The spirit comes back. This physical body is just an overcoat. Take it away and your spirit goes into another life in the spirit dimension."*

**Extracts from FIFA secretary Sepp Blatter's presidential election 'manifesto', a glossy multi-language brochure outlining his visions for the future:**
*"I shall put in place a modern structure of leadership which will facilitate a more efficient decision-making*

*process.... I shall cultivate an open dialogue with our partners on the social, economic and political planes."*

**Paul Gascoigne, in a newspaper interview:**
*"I'll tell you what my real dream is. I mean my absolute No.1 dream that [will mean] I will die happy if it happens. I want to see a UFO. They're real. I don't care if you look at me like that. UFOs are a definite fact and I've got to see one soon."*

**A (sober) Paul Gascoigne on his obsession with numbers:**
*"Numbers are the thing with me. I have this thing about 4. I don't know why 4 – my favourite used to be 5 and then 7. Then I got into this thing about 13, where nothing would be done in 4s because 4 and 9 are 13. I don't know where 9 comes from. I got it into my head because 4 and 9 are 13. That's like 6 and 7. I can't bear to see them together, because that's 13 again. So, when I go out onto the park, I won't go out in 6th or 7th. Nor 4th. It'll be either 5th or 8th."*

**Glenn Hoddle on why he controversially omitted Paul Gascoigne from England's World Cup 22:**
*"... the reasons why Paul Gascoigne is not going to the World Cup come down purely to his fitness levels. Physically and mentally he hasn't been right. Mentally, he has always had a few problems, and I've seen them over the last week or so."*

**Paul Gascoigne, confessing that he was drunk at a karaoke party the night (and early morning) before he got the chop:**
*"Yes, I was drunk. I got drunk quite quickly. I hadn't had a drink in nine days."*

**An anonymous 'eyewitness':**
*"He [Gascoigne] staggered out of the bar around 2.30 am and virtually tripped over Glenn [Hoddle]. It was very embarrassing."*

**A *Daily Express* piece suggesting that 'player power' helped force Glenn Hoddle's decision to axe Paul Gascoigne from the World Cup squad, quoting one of the senior players in the England party who were apparently angered by Gascoigne's behaviour at the team's hotel in Spain:**
*"The players could not believe the way Gazza was acting. He didn't seem to be taking his problems seriously and it was affecting squad morale."*

***Daily Telegraph* columnist Michael Parkinson on Paul Gascoigne:**
*"He [Gascoigne] is yesterday's man, whose only contribution to the future of the game is as an example of the dangers of drinking on an empty head."*

**FIFA presidential candidate Sepp Blatter, campaigning in Liberia:**
*"I will not give you all my programmes for Africa, but what I can promise, which will be a reality, is that if I am elected president of FIFA, I will give the 2006 World Cup to Africa.... UEFA were wrong to declare themselves in favour of Germany's candidature. This was undemocratic. The English bid is a very professional one and they are, after all, the motherland of football."*

**An angry Sir Bobby Charlton, a Man Utd director, on hearing about the behaviour of Teddy Sheringham, a Man Utd player, in a Portuguese night club just days before the World Cup finals:**
*"If the players don't have the common sense to behave themselves and act in a reasonably proper manner, then it's absolutely nonsensical to think that we have a chance of winning the World Cup.... I hope he [Sheringham] feels suitably embarrassed."*

**Former England supremo and successful European coach Bobby Robson, asked in his role as TV pundit by Jim Rosenthal whether he would have taken Paul Gascoigne to France:**
*"Oh yes. We're not talking about taking 14 players. We're taking 22 to Italy, sorry, to Spain.... Where are we, Jim?"*

# FA CHARITY SHIELD WINNERS 1908-97

| | | | | | | |
|---|---|---|---|---|---|---|
| 1908 | Manchester U v QPR | 4-0 after 1-1 draw | 1960 | Burnley v Wolverhampton W | | 2-2* |
| 1909 | Newcastle U v Northampton T | 2-0 | 1961 | Tottenham H v FA XI | | 3-2 |
| 1910 | Brighton v Aston Villa | 1-0 | 1962 | Tottenham H v Ipswich T | | 5-1 |
| 1911 | Manchester U v Swindon T | 8-4 | 1963 | Everton v Manchester U | | 4-0 |
| 1912 | Blackburn R v QPR | 2-1 | 1964 | Liverpool v West Ham U | | 2-2* |
| 1913 | Professionals v Amateurs | 7-2 | 1965 | Manchester U v Liverpool | | 2-2* |
| 1920 | WBA v Tottenham H | 2-0 | 1966 | Liverpool v Everton | | 1-0 |
| 1921 | Tottenham H v Burnley | 2-0 | 1967 | Manchester U v Tottenham H | | 3-3* |
| 1922 | Huddersfield T v Liverpool | 1-0 | 1968 | Manchester C v WBA | | 6-1 |
| 1923 | Professionals v Amateurs | 2-0 | 1969 | Leeds U v Manchester C | | 2-1 |
| 1924 | Professionals v Amateurs | 3-1 | 1970 | Everton v Chelsea | | 2-1 |
| 1925 | Amateurs v Professionals | 6-1 | 1971 | Leicester C v Liverpool | | 1-0 |
| 1926 | Amateurs v Professionals | 6-3 | 1972 | Manchester C v Aston Villa | | 1-0 |
| 1927 | Cardiff C v Corinthians | 2-1 | 1973 | Burnley v Manchester C | | 1-0 |
| 1928 | Everton v Blackburn R | 2-1 | 1974 | Liverpool† v Leeds U | | 1-1 |
| 1929 | Professionals v Amateurs | 3-0 | 1975 | Derby Co v West Ham U | | 2-0 |
| 1930 | Arsenal v Sheffield W | 2-1 | 1976 | Liverpool v Southampton | | 1-0 |
| 1931 | Arsenal v WBA | 1-0 | 1977 | Liverpool v Manchester U | | 0-0* |
| 1932 | Everton v Newcastle U | 5-3 | 1978 | Nottingham F v Ipswich T | | 5-0 |
| 1933 | Arsenal v Everton | 3-0 | 1979 | Liverpool v Arsenal | | 3-1 |
| 1934 | Arsenal v Manchester C | 4-0 | 1980 | Liverpool v West Ham U | | 1-0 |
| 1935 | Sheffield W v Arsenal | 1-0 | 1981 | Aston Villa v Tottenham H | | 2-2* |
| 1936 | Sunderland v Arsenal | 2-1 | 1982 | Liverpool v Tottenham H | | 1-0 |
| 1937 | Manchester C v Sunderland | 2-0 | 1983 | Manchester U v Liverpool | | 2-0 |
| 1938 | Arsenal v Preston NE | 2-1 | 1984 | Everton v Liverpool | | 1-0 |
| 1948 | Arsenal v Manchester U | 4-3 | 1985 | Everton v Manchester U | | 2-0 |
| 1949 | Portsmouth v Wolverhampton W | 1-1* | 1986 | Everton v Liverpool | | 1-1* |
| 1950 | World Cup Team v Canadian Touring Team | 4-2 | 1987 | Everton v Coventry C | | 1-0 |
| 1951 | Tottenham H v Newcastle U | 2-1 | 1988 | Liverpool v Wimbledon | | 2-1 |
| 1952 | Manchester U v Newcastle U | 4-2 | 1989 | Liverpool v Arsenal | | 1-0 |
| 1953 | Arsenal v Blackpool | 3-1 | 1990 | Liverpool v Manchester U | | 1-1* |
| 1954 | Wolverhampton W v WBA | 4-4* | 1991 | Arsenal v Tottenham H | | 0-0* |
| 1955 | Chelsea v Newcastle U | 3-0 | 1992 | Leeds U v Liverpool | | 4-3 |
| 1956 | Manchester U v Manchester C | 1-0 | 1993 | Manchester U† v Arsenal | | 1-1 |
| 1957 | Manchester U v Aston Villa | 4-0 | 1994 | Manchester U v Blackburn R | | 2-0 |
| 1958 | Bolton W v Wolverhampton W | 4-1 | 1995 | Everton v Blackburn R | | 1-0 |
| 1959 | Wolverhampton W v Nottingham F | 3-1 | 1996 | Manchester U v Newcastle U | | 4-0 |

*Each club retained shield for six months.    † Won on penalties.*

## FA CHARITY SHIELD 1997

**Manchester U (0) 1, Chelsea (0) 1**

At Wembley, 3 August 1997, attendance 73,636
*Manchester U won 4-2 on penalties.*

*Manchester U:* Schmeichel; Irwin, Neville P, Johnsen, Keane, Pallister, Scholes, Butt, Cole, Sheringham (Cruyff), Giggs (Beckham).

*Scorer:* Johnsen 57.

*Chelsea:* De Goey; Sinclair, Granville, Morris (Petrescu), Leboeuf, Clarke, Poyet, Di Matteo, Zola, Hughes M (Vialli), Wise.

*Scorer:* Hughes M 52.

*Referee:* P. Jones (Loughborough).

# ENGLISH LEAGUE HONOURS 1888–89 to 1997–98

## FA PREMIER LEAGUE
Maximum points: a 126; b 114.

| | First | Pts | Second | Pts | Third | Pts |
|---|---|---|---|---|---|---|
| 1992–93a | Manchester U | 84 | Aston Villa | 74 | Norwich C | 72 |
| 1993–94a | Manchester U | 92 | Blackburn R | 84 | Newcastle U | 77 |
| 1994–95a | Blackburn R | 89 | Manchester U | 88 | Nottingham F | 77 |
| 1995–96a | Manchester U | 82 | Newcastle U | 78 | Liverpool | 71 |
| 1996–97b | Manchester U | 75 | Newcastle U* | 68 | Arsenal* | 68 |
| 1997–98b | Arsenal | 78 | Manchester U | 77 | Liverpool | 65 |

## FIRST DIVISION
Maximum points: 138

| | | | | | | |
|---|---|---|---|---|---|---|
| 1992–93 | Newcastle U | 96 | West Ham U* | 88 | Portsmouth†† | 88 |
| 1993–94 | Crystal Palace | 90 | Nottingham F | 83 | Millwall†† | 74 |
| 1994–95 | Middlesbrough | 82 | Reading†† | 79 | Bolton W | 77 |
| 1995–96 | Sunderland | 83 | Derby Co | 79 | Crystal Palace†† | 75 |
| 1996–97 | Bolton W | 98 | Barnsley | 80 | Wolverhampton W | 76 |
| 1997–98 | Nottingham F | 94 | Middlesbrough | 91 | Sunderland†† | 90 |

## SECOND DIVISION
Maximum points: 138

| | | | | | | |
|---|---|---|---|---|---|---|
| 1992–93 | Stoke C | 93 | Bolton W | 90 | Port Vale†† | 89 |
| 1993–94 | Reading | 89 | Port Vale | 88 | Plymouth Arg*†† | 85 |
| 1994–95 | Birmingham C | 89 | Brentford†† | 85 | Crewe Alex†† | 83 |
| 1995–96 | Swindon T | 92 | Oxford U | 83 | Blackpool†† | 82 |
| 1996–97 | Bury | 84 | Stockport Co | 82 | Luton T | 78 |
| 1997–98 | Watford | 88 | Bristol C | 85 | Grimsby T | 72 |

## THIRD DIVISION
Maximum points: a 126; b 138.

| | | | | | | |
|---|---|---|---|---|---|---|
| 1992–93a | Cardiff C | 83 | Wrexham | 80 | Barnet | 79 |
| 1993–94a | Shrewsbury T | 79 | Chester C | 74 | Crewe Alex | 73 |
| 1994–95a | Carlisle U | 91 | Walsall | 83 | Chesterfield | 81 |
| 1995–96a | Preston NE | 86 | Gillingham | 83 | Bury | 79 |
| 1996–97b | Wigan Ath* | 87 | Fulham | 87 | Carlisle U | 84 |
| 1997–98b | Notts Co | 99 | Macclesfield T | 82 | Lincoln C | 72 |

††Not promoted after play-offs.

## FOOTBALL LEAGUE
Maximum points: a 44; b 60

| | First | Pts | Second | Pts | Third | Pts |
|---|---|---|---|---|---|---|
| 1888–89a | Preston NE | 40 | Aston Villa | 29 | Wolverhampton W | 28 |
| 1889–90a | Preston NE | 33 | Everton | 31 | Blackburn R | 27 |
| 1890–91a | Everton | 29 | Preston NE | 27 | Notts Co | 26 |
| 1891–92b | Sunderland | 42 | Preston NE | 37 | Bolton W | 36 |

## FIRST DIVISION to 1991–92
Maximum points: a 44; b 52; c 60; d 68; e 76; f 84; g 126; h 120; k 114.

| | | | | | | |
|---|---|---|---|---|---|---|
| 1892–93c | Sunderland | 48 | Preston NE | 37 | Everton | 36 |
| 1893–94c | Aston Villa | 44 | Sunderland | 38 | Derby Co | 36 |
| 1894–95c | Sunderland | 47 | Everton | 42 | Aston Villa | 39 |
| 1895–96c | Aston Villa | 45 | Derby Co | 41 | Everton | 39 |
| 1896–97c | Aston Villa | 47 | Sheffield U* | 36 | Derby Co | 36 |
| 1897–98c | Sheffield U | 42 | Sunderland | 37 | Wolverhampton W* | 35 |
| 1898–99d | Aston Villa | 45 | Liverpool | 43 | Burnley | 39 |
| 1899–1900d | Aston Villa | 50 | Sheffield U | 48 | Sunderland | 41 |
| 1900–01d | Liverpool | 45 | Sunderland | 43 | Notts Co | 40 |
| 1901–02d | Sunderland | 44 | Everton | 41 | Newcastle U | 37 |
| 1902–03d | The Wednesday | 42 | Aston Villa* | 41 | Sunderland | 41 |
| 1903–04d | The Wednesday | 47 | Manchester C | 44 | Everton | 43 |
| 1904–05d | Newcastle U | 48 | Everton | 47 | Manchester C | 46 |
| 1905–06e | Liverpool | 51 | Preston NE | 47 | The Wednesday | 44 |
| 1906–07e | Newcastle U | 51 | Bristol C | 48 | Everton* | 45 |
| 1907–08e | Manchester U | 52 | Aston Villa* | 43 | Manchester C | 43 |
| 1908–09e | Newcastle U | 53 | Everton | 46 | Sunderland | 44 |
| 1909–10e | Aston Villa | 53 | Liverpool | 48 | Blackburn R* | 45 |
| 1910–11e | Manchester U | 52 | Aston Villa | 51 | Sunderland* | 45 |
| 1911–12e | Blackburn R | 49 | Everton | 46 | Newcastle U | 44 |
| 1912–13e | Sunderland | 54 | Aston Villa | 50 | Sheffield W | 49 |
| 1913–14e | Blackburn R | 51 | Aston Villa | 44 | Middlesbrough* | 43 |
| 1914–15e | Everton | 46 | Oldham Ath | 45 | Blackburn R* | 43 |
| 1919–20f | WBA | 60 | Burnley | 51 | Chelsea | 49 |
| 1920–21f | Burnley | 59 | Manchester C | 54 | Bolton W | 52 |
| 1921–22f | Liverpool | 57 | Tottenham H | 51 | Burnley | 49 |
| 1922–23f | Liverpool | 60 | Sunderland | 54 | Huddersfield T | 53 |
| 1923–24f | Huddersfield T* | 57 | Cardiff C | 57 | Sunderland | 53 |
| 1924–25f | Huddersfield T | 58 | WBA | 56 | Bolton W | 55 |
| 1925–26f | Huddersfield T | 57 | Arsenal | 52 | Sunderland | 48 |
| 1926–27f | Newcastle U | 56 | Huddersfield T | 51 | Sunderland | 49 |
| 1927–28f | Everton | 53 | Huddersfield T | 51 | Leicester C | 48 |
| 1928–29f | Sheffield W | 52 | Leicester C | 51 | Aston Villa | 50 |
| 1929–30f | Sheffield W | 60 | Derby Co | 50 | Manchester C* | 47 |
| 1930–31f | Arsenal | 66 | Aston Villa | 59 | Sheffield W | 52 |
| 1931–32f | Everton | 56 | Arsenal | 54 | Sheffield W | 50 |
| 1932–33f | Arsenal | 58 | Aston Villa | 54 | Sheffield W | 51 |

*Won or placed on goal average, goal difference or most goals scored.

| | First | Pts | Second | Pts | Third | Pts |
|---|---|---|---|---|---|---|
| 1933–34f | Arsenal | 59 | Huddersfield T | 56 | Tottenham H | 49 |
| 1934–35f | Arsenal | 58 | Sunderland | 54 | Sheffield W | 49 |
| 1935–36f | Sunderland | 56 | Derby Co* | 48 | Huddersfield T | 48 |
| 1936–37f | Manchester C | 57 | Charlton Ath | 54 | Arsenal | 52 |
| 1937–38f | Arsenal | 52 | Wolverhampton W | 51 | Preston NE | 49 |
| 1938–39f | Everton | 59 | Wolverhampton W | 55 | Charlton Ath | 50 |
| 1946–47f | Liverpool | 57 | Manchester U* | 56 | Wolverhampton W | 56 |
| 1947–48f | Arsenal | 59 | Manchester U* | 52 | Burnley | 52 |
| 1948–49f | Portsmouth | 58 | Manchester U* | 53 | Derby Co | 53 |
| 1949–50f | Portsmouth* | 53 | Wolverhampton W | 53 | Sunderland | 52 |
| 1950–51f | Tottenham H | 60 | Manchester U | 56 | Blackpool | 50 |
| 1951–52f | Manchester U | 57 | Tottenham H* | 53 | Arsenal | 53 |
| 1952–53f | Arsenal* | 54 | Preston NE | 54 | Wolverhampton W | 51 |
| 1953–54f | Wolverhampton W | 57 | WBA | 53 | Huddersfield T | 51 |
| 1954–55f | Chelsea | 52 | Wolverhampton W* | 48 | Portsmouth* | 48 |
| 1955–56f | Manchester U | 60 | Blackpool* | 49 | Wolverhampton W | 49 |
| 1956–57f | Manchester U | 64 | Tottenham H* | 56 | Preston NE | 56 |
| 1957–58f | Wolverhampton W | 64 | Preston NE | 59 | Tottenham H | 51 |
| 1958–59f | Wolverhampton W | 61 | Manchester U | 55 | Arsenal* | 50 |
| 1959–60f | Burnley | 55 | Wolverhampton W | 54 | Tottenham H | 53 |
| 1960–61f | Tottenham H | 66 | Sheffield W | 58 | Wolverhampton W | 57 |
| 1961–62f | Ipswich T | 56 | Burnley | 53 | Tottenham H | 52 |
| 1962–63f | Everton | 61 | Tottenham H | 55 | Burnley | 54 |
| 1963–64f | Liverpool | 57 | Manchester U | 53 | Everton | 52 |
| 1964–65f | Manchester U* | 61 | Leeds U | 61 | Chelsea | 56 |
| 1965–66f | Liverpool | 61 | Leeds U* | 55 | Burnley | 55 |
| 1966–67f | Manchester U | 60 | Nottingham F* | 56 | Tottenham H | 56 |
| 1967–68f | Manchester C | 58 | Manchester U | 56 | Liverpool | 55 |
| 1968–69f | Leeds U | 67 | Liverpool | 61 | Everton | 57 |
| 1969–70f | Everton | 66 | Leeds U | 57 | Chelsea | 55 |
| 1970–71f | Arsenal | 65 | Leeds U | 64 | Tottenham H* | 52 |
| 1971–72f | Derby Co | 58 | Leeds U* | 57 | Liverpool* | 57 |
| 1972–73f | Liverpool | 60 | Arsenal | 57 | Leeds U | 53 |
| 1973–74f | Leeds U | 62 | Liverpool | 57 | Derby Co | 48 |
| 1974–75f | Derby Co | 53 | Liverpool* | 51 | Ipswich T | 51 |
| 1975–76f | Liverpool | 60 | QPR | 59 | Manchester U | 56 |
| 1976–77f | Liverpool | 57 | Manchester C | 56 | Ipswich T | 52 |
| 1977–78f | Nottingham F | 64 | Liverpool | 57 | Everton | 55 |
| 1978–79f | Liverpool | 68 | Nottingham F | 60 | WBA | 59 |
| 1979–80f | Liverpool | 60 | Manchester U | 58 | Ipswich T | 52 |
| 1980–81f | Aston Villa | 60 | Ipswich T | 56 | Arsenal | 53 |
| 1981–82g | Liverpool | 87 | Ipswich T | 83 | Manchester U | 78 |
| 1982–83g | Liverpool | 82 | Watford | 71 | Manchester U | 70 |
| 1983–84g | Liverpool | 80 | Southampton | 77 | Nottingham F* | 74 |
| 1984–85g | Everton | 90 | Liverpool* | 77 | Tottenham H | 77 |
| 1985–86g | Liverpool | 88 | Everton | 86 | West Ham U | 84 |
| 1986–87g | Everton | 86 | Liverpool | 77 | Tottenham H | 71 |
| 1987–88h | Liverpool | 90 | Manchester U | 81 | Nottingham F | 73 |
| 1988–89k | Arsenal* | 76 | Liverpool | 76 | Nottingham F | 64 |
| 1989–90k | Liverpool | 79 | Aston Villa | 70 | Tottenham H | 63 |
| 1990–91k | Arsenal† | 83 | Liverpool | 76 | Crystal Palace | 69 |
| 1991–92g | Leeds U | 82 | Manchester U | 78 | Sheffield W | 75 |

*No official competition during 1915–19 and 1939–46; Regional Leagues operated.*
†2 pts deducted

SECOND DIVISION to 1991–92
*Maximum points: a 44; b 56; c 60; d 68; e 76; f 84; g 126; h 132; k 138.*

| | First | Pts | Second | Pts | Third | Pts |
|---|---|---|---|---|---|---|
| 1892–93a | Small Heath | 36 | Sheffield U | 35 | Darwen | 30 |
| 1893–94b | Liverpool | 50 | Small Heath | 42 | Notts Co | 39 |
| 1894–95c | Bury | 48 | Notts Co | 39 | Newton Heath* | 38 |
| 1895–96c | Liverpool* | 46 | Manchester C | 46 | Grimsby T* | 42 |
| 1896–97c | Notts Co | 42 | Newton Heath | 39 | Grimsby T | 38 |
| 1897–98c | Burnley | 48 | Newcastle U | 45 | Manchester C | 39 |
| 1898–99d | Manchester C | 52 | Glossop NE | 46 | Leicester Fosse | 45 |
| 1899–1900d | The Wednesday | 54 | Bolton W | 52 | Small Heath | 46 |
| 1900–01d | Grimsby T | 49 | Small Heath | 48 | Burnley | 44 |
| 1901–02d | WBA | 55 | Middlesbrough | 51 | Preston NE* | 42 |
| 1902–03d | Manchester C | 54 | Small Heath | 51 | Woolwich A | 48 |
| 1903–04d | Preston NE | 50 | Woolwich A | 49 | Manchester U | 48 |
| 1904–05d | Liverpool | 58 | Bolton W | 56 | Manchester U | 53 |
| 1905–06e | Bristol C | 66 | Manchester U | 62 | Chelsea | 53 |
| 1906–07e | Nottingham F | 60 | Chelsea | 57 | Leicester Fosse | 48 |
| 1907–08e | Bradford C | 54 | Leicester Fosse | 52 | Oldham Ath | 50 |
| 1908–09e | Bolton W | 52 | Tottenham H* | 51 | WBA | 51 |
| 1909–10e | Manchester C | 54 | Oldham Ath* | 53 | Hull C* | 53 |
| 1910–11e | WBA | 53 | Bolton W | 51 | Chelsea | 49 |
| 1911–12e | Derby Co* | 54 | Chelsea | 54 | Burnley | 52 |
| 1912–13e | Preston NE | 53 | Burnley | 50 | Birmingham | 46 |
| 1913–14e | Notts Co | 53 | Bradford PA* | 49 | Woolwich A | 49 |
| 1914–15e | Derby Co | 53 | Preston NE | 50 | Barnsley | 47 |
| 1919–20f | Tottenham H | 70 | Huddersfield T | 64 | Birmingham | 56 |
| 1920–21f | Birmingham* | 58 | Cardiff C | 58 | Bristol C | 51 |
| 1921–22f | Nottingham F | 56 | Stoke C* | 52 | Barnsley | 52 |

*Won or placed on goal average/goal difference.*

| | First | Pts | Second | Pts | Third | Pts |
|---|---|---|---|---|---|---|
| 1922–23*f* | Notts Co | 53 | West Ham U* | 51 | Leicester C | 51 |
| 1923–24*f* | Leeds U | 54 | Bury* | 51 | Derby Co | 51 |
| 1924–25*f* | Leicester C | 59 | Manchester U | 57 | Derby Co | 55 |
| 1925–26*f* | Sheffield W | 60 | Derby Co | 57 | Chelsea | 52 |
| 1926–27*f* | Middlesbrough | 62 | Portsmouth* | 54 | Manchester C | 54 |
| 1927–28*f* | Manchester C | 59 | Leeds U | 57 | Chelsea | 54 |
| 1928–29*f* | Middlesbrough | 55 | Grimsby T | 53 | Bradford PA* | 48 |
| 1929–30*f* | Blackpool | 58 | Chelsea | 55 | Oldham Ath | 53 |
| 1930–31*f* | Everton | 61 | WBA | 54 | Tottenham H | 51 |
| 1931–32*f* | Wolverhampton W | 56 | Leeds U | 54 | Stoke C | 52 |
| 1932–33*f* | Stoke C | 56 | Tottenham H | 55 | Fulham | 50 |
| 1933–34*f* | Grimsby T | 59 | Preston NE | 52 | Bolton W* | 51 |
| 1934–35*f* | Brentford | 61 | Bolton W* | 56 | West Ham U | 56 |
| 1935–36*f* | Manchester U | 56 | Charlton Ath | 55 | Sheffield U* | 52 |
| 1936–37*f* | Leicester C | 56 | Blackpool | 55 | Bury | 52 |
| 1937–38*f* | Aston Villa | 57 | Manchester U* | 53 | Sheffield U | 53 |
| 1938–39*f* | Blackburn R | 55 | Sheffield U | 54 | Sheffield W | 53 |
| 1946–47*f* | Manchester C | 62 | Burnley | 58 | Birmingham C | 55 |
| 1947–48*f* | Birmingham C | 59 | Newcastle U | 56 | Southampton | 52 |
| 1948–49*f* | Fulham | 57 | WBA | 56 | Southampton | 55 |
| 1949–50*f* | Tottenham H | 61 | Sheffield W* | 52 | Sheffield U* | 52 |
| 1950–51*f* | Preston NE | 57 | Manchester C | 52 | Cardiff C | 50 |
| 1951–52*f* | Sheffield W | 53 | Cardiff C* | 51 | Birmingham C | 51 |
| 1952–53*f* | Sheffield U | 60 | Huddersfield T | 58 | Luton T | 52 |
| 1953–54*f* | Leicester C* | 56 | Everton | 56 | Blackburn R | 55 |
| 1954–55*f* | Birmingham C* | 54 | Luton T* | 54 | Rotherham U | 54 |
| 1955–56*f* | Sheffield W | 55 | Leeds U | 52 | Liverpool* | 48 |
| 1956–57*f* | Leicester C | 61 | Nottingham F | 54 | Liverpool | 53 |
| 1957–58*f* | West Ham U | 57 | Blackburn R | 56 | Charlton Ath | 55 |
| 1958–59*f* | Sheffield W | 62 | Fulham | 60 | Sheffield U* | 53 |
| 1959–60*f* | Aston Villa | 59 | Cardiff C | 58 | Liverpool* | 50 |
| 1960–61*f* | Ipswich T | 59 | Sheffield U | 58 | Liverpool | 52 |
| 1961–62*f* | Liverpool | 62 | Leyton Orient | 54 | Sunderland | 53 |
| 1962–63*f* | Stoke C | 53 | Chelsea* | 52 | Sunderland | 52 |
| 1963–64*f* | Leeds U | 63 | Sunderland | 61 | Preston NE | 56 |
| 1964–65*f* | Newcastle U | 57 | Northampton T | 56 | Bolton W | 50 |
| 1965–66*f* | Manchester C | 59 | Southampton | 54 | Coventry C | 53 |
| 1966–67*f* | Coventry C | 59 | Wolverhampton W | 58 | Carlisle U | 52 |
| 1967–68*f* | Ipswich T | 59 | QPR* | 58 | Blackpool | 58 |
| 1968–69*f* | Derby Co | 63 | Crystal Palace | 56 | Charlton Ath | 50 |
| 1969–70*f* | Huddersfield T | 60 | Blackpool | 53 | Leicester C | 51 |
| 1970–71*f* | Leicester C | 59 | Sheffield U | 56 | Cardiff C* | 53 |
| 1971–72*f* | Norwich C | 57 | Birmingham C | 56 | Millwall | 55 |
| 1972–73*f* | Burnley | 62 | QPR | 61 | Aston Villa | 50 |
| 1973–74*f* | Middlesbrough | 65 | Luton T | 50 | Carlisle U | 49 |
| 1974–75*f* | Manchester U | 61 | Aston Villa | 58 | Norwich C | 53 |
| 1975–76*f* | Sunderland | 56 | Bristol C* | 53 | WBA | 53 |
| 1976–77*f* | Wolverhampton W | 57 | Chelsea | 55 | Nottingham F | 52 |
| 1977–78*f* | Bolton W | 58 | Southampton | 57 | Tottenham H* | 56 |
| 1978–79*f* | Crystal Palace | 57 | Brighton & HA* | 56 | Stoke C | 56 |
| 1979–80*f* | Leicester C | 55 | Sunderland | 54 | Birmingham C* | 53 |
| 1980–81*f* | West Ham U | 66 | Notts Co | 53 | Swansea C* | 50 |
| 1981–82*g* | Luton T | 88 | Watford | 80 | Norwich C | 71 |
| 1982–83*g* | QPR | 85 | Wolverhampton W | 75 | Leicester C | 70 |
| 1983–84*g* | Chelsea* | 88 | Sheffield W | 88 | Newcastle U | 80 |
| 1984–85*g* | Oxford U | 84 | Birmingham C | 82 | Manchester C | 74 |
| 1985–86*g* | Norwich C | 84 | Charlton Ath | 77 | Wimbledon | 76 |
| 1986–87*g* | Derby Co | 84 | Portsmouth | 78 | Oldham Ath†† | 75 |
| 1987–88*h* | Millwall | 82 | Aston Villa* | 78 | Middlesbrough | 78 |
| 1988–89*k* | Chelsea | 99 | Manchester C | 82 | Crystal Palace | 81 |
| 1989–90*k* | Leeds U* | 85 | Sheffield U | 85 | Newcastle U†† | 80 |
| 1990–91*k* | Oldham Ath | 88 | West Ham U | 87 | Sheffield W | 82 |
| 1991–92*k* | Ipswich T | 84 | Middlesbrough | 80 | Derby Co | 78 |

*No official competition during 1915–19 and 1939–46; Regional Leagues operated.*
*††Not promoted after play-offs.*

THIRD DIVISION to 1991–92
*Maximum points: 92; 138 from 1981–82.*

| | First | Pts | Second | Pts | Third | Pts |
|---|---|---|---|---|---|---|
| 1958–59 | Plymouth Arg | 62 | Hull C | 61 | Brentford* | 57 |
| 1959–60 | Southampton | 61 | Norwich C | 59 | Shrewsbury T* | 52 |
| 1960–61 | Bury | 68 | Walsall | 62 | QPR | 60 |
| 1961–62 | Portsmouth | 65 | Grimsby T | 62 | Bournemouth* | 59 |
| 1962–63 | Northampton T | 62 | Swindon T | 58 | Port Vale | 54 |
| 1963–64 | Coventry C* | 60 | Crystal Palace | 60 | Watford | 58 |
| 1964–65 | Carlisle U | 60 | Bristol C* | 59 | Mansfield T | 59 |
| 1965–66 | Hull C | 69 | Millwall | 65 | QPR | 57 |
| 1966–67 | QPR | 67 | Middlesbrough | 55 | Watford | 54 |
| 1967–68 | Oxford U | 57 | Bury | 56 | Shrewsbury T | 55 |
| 1968–69 | Watford* | 64 | Swindon T | 64 | Luton T | 61 |
| 1969–70 | Orient | 62 | Luton T | 60 | Bristol R | 56 |
| 1970–71 | Preston NE | 61 | Fulham | 60 | Halifax T | 56 |
| 1971–72 | Aston Villa | 70 | Brighton & HA | 65 | Bournemouth* | 62 |
| 1972–73 | Bolton W | 61 | Notts Co | 57 | Blackburn R | 55 |

*Won or placed on goal average/goal difference.*

| | First | Pts | Second | Pts | Third | Pts |
|---|---|---|---|---|---|---|
| 1973–74 | Oldham Ath | 62 | Bristol R* | 61 | York C | 61 |
| 1974–75 | Blackburn R | 60 | Plymouth Arg | 59 | Charlton Ath | 55 |
| 1975–76 | Hereford U | 63 | Cardiff C | 57 | Millwall | 56 |
| 1976–77 | Mansfield T | 64 | Brighton & HA | 61 | Crystal Palace* | 59 |
| 1977–78 | Wrexham | 61 | Cambridge U | 58 | Preston NE* | 56 |
| 1978–79 | Shrewsbury T | 61 | Watford* | 60 | Swansea C | 60 |
| 1979–80 | Grimsby T | 62 | Blackburn R | 59 | Sheffield W | 58 |
| 1980–81 | Rotherham U | 61 | Barnsley* | 59 | Charlton Ath | 59 |
| 1981–82 | Burnley* | 80 | Carlisle U | 80 | Fulham | 78 |
| 1982–83 | Portsmouth | 91 | Cardiff C | 86 | Huddersfield T | 82 |
| 1983–84 | Oxford U | 95 | Wimbledon | 87 | Sheffield U* | 83 |
| 1984–85 | Bradford C | 94 | Millwall | 90 | Hull C | 87 |
| 1985–86 | Reading | 94 | Plymouth Arg | 87 | Derby Co | 84 |
| 1986–87 | Bournemouth | 97 | Middlesbrough | 94 | Swindon T | 87 |
| 1987–88 | Sunderland | 93 | Brighton & HA | 84 | Walsall | 82 |
| 1988–89 | Wolverhampton W | 92 | Sheffield U* | 84 | Port Vale | 84 |
| 1989–90 | Bristol R | 93 | Bristol C | 91 | Notts Co | 87 |
| 1990–91 | Cambridge U | 86 | Southend U | 85 | Grimsby T* | 83 |
| 1991–92 | Brentford | 82 | Birmingham C | 81 | Huddersfield T | 78 |

### FOURTH DIVISION (1958–1992)
*Maximum points: 92; 138 from 1981–82.*

| | First | Pts | Second | Pts | Third | Pts | Fourth | Pts |
|---|---|---|---|---|---|---|---|---|
| 1958–59 | Port Vale | 64 | Coventry C* | 60 | York C | 60 | Shrewsbury T | 58 |
| 1959–60 | Walsall | 65 | Notts Co* | 60 | Torquay U | 60 | Watford | 57 |
| 1960–61 | Peterborough U | 66 | Crystal Palace | 64 | Northampton T* | 60 | Bradford PA | 60 |
| 1961–62† | Millwall | 56 | Colchester U | 55 | Wrexham | 53 | Carlisle U | 52 |
| 1962–63 | Brentford | 62 | Oldham Ath* | 59 | Crewe Alex | 59 | Mansfield T* | 57 |
| 1963–64 | Gillingham* | 60 | Carlisle U | 60 | Workington | 59 | Exeter C | 58 |
| 1964–65 | Brighton & HA | 63 | Millwall* | 62 | York C | 62 | Oxford U | 61 |
| 1965–66 | Doncaster R* | 59 | Darlington | 59 | Torquay U | 58 | Colchester U* | 56 |
| 1966–67 | Stockport Co | 64 | Southport* | 59 | Barrow | 59 | Tranmere R | 58 |
| 1967–68 | Luton T | 66 | Barnsley | 61 | Hartlepools U | 60 | Crewe Alex | 58 |
| 1968–69 | Doncaster R | 59 | Halifax T | 57 | Rochdale* | 56 | Bradford C | 56 |
| 1969–70 | Chesterfield | 64 | Wrexham | 61 | Swansea C | 60 | Port Vale | 59 |
| 1970–71 | Notts Co | 69 | Bournemouth | 60 | Oldham Ath | 59 | York C | 56 |
| 1971–72 | Grimsby T | 63 | Southend U | 60 | Brentford | 59 | Scunthorpe U | 57 |
| 1972–73 | Southport | 62 | Hereford U | 58 | Cambridge U | 57 | Aldershot* | 56 |
| 1973–74 | Peterborough U | 65 | Gillingham | 62 | Colchester U | 60 | Bury | 59 |
| 1974–75 | Mansfield T | 68 | Shrewsbury T | 62 | Rotherham U | 59 | Chester* | 57 |
| 1975–76 | Lincoln C | 74 | Northampton T | 68 | Reading | 60 | Tranmere R | 58 |
| 1976–77 | Cambridge U | 65 | Exeter C | 62 | Colchester U* | 59 | Bradford C | 59 |
| 1977–78 | Watford | 71 | Southend U | 60 | Swansea C* | 56 | Brentford | 56 |
| 1978–79 | Reading | 65 | Grimsby T* | 61 | Wimbledon* | 61 | Barnsley | 61 |
| 1979–80 | Huddersfield T | 66 | Walsall | 64 | Newport Co | 61 | Portsmouth* | 60 |
| 1980–81 | Southend U | 67 | Lincoln C | 65 | Doncaster R | 56 | Wimbledon | 55 |
| 1981–82 | Sheffield U | 96 | Bradford C* | 91 | Wigan Ath | 91 | Bournemouth | 88 |
| 1982–83 | Wimbledon | 98 | Hull C | 90 | Port Vale | 88 | Scunthorpe U | 83 |
| 1983–84 | York C | 101 | Doncaster R | 85 | Reading* | 82 | Bristol C | 82 |
| 1984–85 | Chesterfield | 91 | Blackpool | 86 | Darlington | 85 | Bury | 84 |
| 1985–86 | Swindon T | 102 | Chester C | 84 | Mansfield T | 81 | Port Vale | 79 |
| 1986–87 | Northampton T | 99 | Preston NE | 90 | Southend U | 80 | Wolverhampton W†† | 79 |
| 1987–88 | Wolverhampton W | 90 | Cardiff C | 85 | Bolton W | 78 | Scunthorpe U†† | 77 |
| 1988–89 | Rotherham U | 82 | Tranmere R | 80 | Crewe Alex | 78 | Scunthorpe U†† | 77 |
| 1989–90 | Exeter C | 89 | Grimsby T | 79 | Southend U | 75 | Stockport Co†† | 74 |
| 1990–91 | Darlington | 83 | Stockport Co* | 82 | Hartlepool U | 82 | Peterborough U | 80 |
| 1991–92†* | Burnley | 83 | Rotherham U* | 77 | Mansfield T | 77 | Blackpool | 76 |

†*Maximum points:* 88 owing to Accrington Stanley's resignation.    ††*Not promoted after play-offs.*
†*Maximum points:* 126 owing to Aldershot being expelled.

### THIRD DIVISION—SOUTH (1920–1958)
*Maximum points: a 84; b 92.*

| | First | Pts | Second | Pts | Third | Pts |
|---|---|---|---|---|---|---|
| 1920–21a | Crystal Palace | 59 | Southampton | 54 | QPR | 53 |
| 1921–22a | Southampton* | 61 | Plymouth Arg | 61 | Portsmouth | 53 |
| 1922–23a | Bristol C | 59 | Plymouth Arg* | 53 | Swansea T | 53 |
| 1923–24a | Portsmouth | 59 | Plymouth Arg | 55 | Millwall | 54 |
| 1924–25a | Swansea T | 57 | Plymouth Arg | 56 | Bristol C | 53 |
| 1925–26a | Reading | 57 | Plymouth Arg | 56 | Millwall | 53 |
| 1926–27a | Bristol C | 62 | Plymouth Arg | 60 | Millwall | 56 |
| 1927–28a | Millwall | 65 | Northampton T | 55 | Plymouth Arg | 53 |
| 1928–29a | Charlton Ath* | 54 | Crystal Palace | 54 | Northampton T* | 52 |
| 1929–30a | Plymouth Arg | 68 | Brentford | 61 | QPR | 51 |
| 1930–31a | Notts Co | 59 | Crystal Palace | 51 | Brentford | 50 |
| 1931–32a | Fulham | 57 | Reading | 55 | Southend U | 53 |
| 1932–33a | Brentford | 62 | Exeter C | 58 | Norwich C | 57 |
| 1933–34a | Norwich C | 61 | Coventry C* | 54 | Reading* | 54 |
| 1934–35a | Charlton Ath | 61 | Reading | 53 | Coventry C | 51 |
| 1935–36a | Coventry C | 57 | Luton T | 56 | Reading | 54 |
| 1936–37a | Luton T | 58 | Notts Co | 56 | Brighton & HA | 53 |
| 1937–38a | Millwall | 56 | Bristol C | 55 | QPR* | 53 |
| 1938–39a | Newport Co | 55 | Crystal Palace | 52 | Brighton & HA | 49 |

* *Won or placed on goal average/goal difference.*

| | First | Pts | Second | Pts | Third | Pts |
|---|---|---|---|---|---|---|
| 1939–46 | Competition cancelled owing to war. | | | | | |
| 1946–47a | Cardiff C | 66 | QPR | 57 | Bristol C | 51 |
| 1947–48a | QPR | 61 | Bournemouth | 57 | Walsall | 51 |
| 1948–49a | Swansea T | 62 | Reading | 55 | Bournemouth | 52 |
| 1949–50a | Notts Co | 58 | Northampton T* | 51 | Southend U | 51 |
| 1950–51b | Nottingham F | 70 | Norwich C | 64 | Reading* | 57 |
| 1951–52b | Plymouth Arg | 66 | Reading* | 61 | Norwich C | 61 |
| 1952–53b | Bristol R | 64 | Millwall* | 62 | Northampton T | 62 |
| 1953–54b | Ipswich T | 64 | Brighton & HA | 61 | Bristol C | 56 |
| 1954–55b | Bristol C | 70 | Leyton Orient | 61 | Southampton | 59 |
| 1955–56b | Leyton Orient | 66 | Brighton & HA | 65 | Ipswich T | 64 |
| 1956–57b | Ipswich T* | 59 | Torquay U | 59 | Colchester U | 58 |
| 1957–58b | Brighton & HA | 60 | Brentford* | 58 | Plymouth Arg | 58 |

### THIRD DIVISION—NORTH (1921–1958)
*Maximum points: a 76; b 84; c 80; d 92.*

| | First | Pts | Second | Pts | Third | Pts |
|---|---|---|---|---|---|---|
| 1921–22a | Stockport Co | 56 | Darlington* | 50 | Grimsby T | 50 |
| 1922–23a | Nelson | 51 | Bradford PA | 47 | Walsall | 46 |
| 1923–24b | Wolverhampton W | 63 | Rochdale | 62 | Chesterfield | 54 |
| 1924–25b | Darlington | 58 | Nelson* | 53 | New Brighton | 53 |
| 1925–26b | Grimsby T | 61 | Bradford PA | 60 | Rochdale | 59 |
| 1926–27b | Stoke C | 63 | Rochdale | 58 | Bradford PA | 55 |
| 1927–28b | Bradford PA | 63 | Lincoln C | 55 | Stockport Co | 54 |
| 1928–29g | Bradford C | 63 | Stockport Co | 62 | Wrexham | 52 |
| 1929–30b | Port Vale | 67 | Stockport Co | 63 | Darlington* | 50 |
| 1930–31b | Chesterfield | 58 | Lincoln C | 57 | Wrexham* | 54 |
| 1931–32c | Lincoln C* | 57 | Gateshead | 57 | Chester | 50 |
| 1932–33b | Hull C | 59 | Wrexham | 57 | Stockport Co | 54 |
| 1933–34b | Barnsley | 62 | Chesterfield | 61 | Stockport Co | 59 |
| 1934–35b | Doncaster R | 57 | Halifax T | 55 | Chester | 54 |
| 1935–36b | Chesterfield | 60 | Chester* | 55 | Tranmere R | 55 |
| 1936–37b | Stockport Co | 60 | Lincoln C | 57 | Chester | 53 |
| 1937–38b | Tranmere R | 56 | Doncaster R | 54 | Hull C | 53 |
| 1938–39b | Barnsley | 67 | Doncaster R | 56 | Bradford C | 52 |
| 1939–46 | Competition cancelled owing to war. | | | | | |
| 1946–47b | Doncaster R | 72 | Rotherham U | 60 | Chester | 56 |
| 1947–48b | Lincoln C | 60 | Rotherham U | 59 | Wrexham | 50 |
| 1948–49b | Hull C | 65 | Rotherham U | 62 | Doncaster R | 50 |
| 1949–50b | Doncaster R | 55 | Gateshead | 53 | Rochdale* | 51 |
| 1950–51d | Rotherham U | 71 | Mansfield T | 64 | Carlisle U | 62 |
| 1951–52d | Lincoln C | 69 | Grimsby T | 66 | Stockport Co | 59 |
| 1952–53d | Oldham Ath | 59 | Port Vale | 58 | Wrexham | 56 |
| 1953–54d | Port Vale | 69 | Barnsley | 58 | Scunthorpe U | 57 |
| 1954–55d | Barnsley | 65 | Accrington S | 61 | Scunthorpe U* | 58 |
| 1955–56d | Grimsby T | 68 | Derby Co | 63 | Accrington S | 59 |
| 1956–57d | Derby Co | 63 | Hartlepools U | 59 | Accrington S* | 58 |
| 1957–58d | Scunthorpe U | 66 | Accrington S | 59 | Bradford C | 57 |

\* Won or placed on goal average.

### PROMOTED AFTER PLAY-OFFS
(Not accounted for in previous section)

| | |
|---|---|
| 1986–87 | Aldershot to Division 3. |
| 1987–88 | Swansea C to Division 3. |
| 1988–89 | Leyton Orient to Division 3. |
| 1989–90 | Cambridge U to Division 3; Notts Co to Division 2; Sunderland to Division 1. |
| 1990–91 | Notts Co to Division 1; Tranmere R to Division 2; Torquay U to Division 3. |
| 1991–92 | Blackburn R to Premier League; Peterborough U to Division 1. |
| 1992–93 | Swindon T to Premier League; WBA to Division 1; York C to Division 2. |
| 1993–94 | Leicester C to Premier League; Burnley to Division 1; Wycombe W to Division 2. |
| 1994–95 | Huddersfield T to Division 1. |
| 1995–96 | Leicester C to Premier League; Bradford C to Division 1; Plymouth Arg to Division 2. |
| 1996–97 | Crystal Palace to Premier League; Crewe Alex to Division 1; Northampton T to Division 2. |
| 1997–98 | Charlton Ath to Premier League; Grimsby T to Division 1; Colchester U to Division 2. |

### LEAGUE TITLE WINS

FA PREMIER LEAGUE – Manchester U 4, Arsenal 1, Blackburn R 1.

LEAGUE DIVISION 1 – Liverpool 18, Arsenal 10, Everton 9, Manchester U 7, Aston Villa 7, Sunderland 7, Newcastle U 5, Sheffield W 4, Huddersfield T 3, Leeds U 3, Wolverhampton W 3, Blackburn R 2, Portsmouth 2, Preston NE 2, Burnley 2, Manchester C 2, Nottingham F 2, Tottenham H 2, Derby Co 2, Bolton W, Chelsea, Crystal Palace, Sheffield U, WBA, Ipswich T, Middlesbrough 1 each.

LEAGUE DIVISION 2 – Leicester C 6, Manchester C 6, Sheffield W 5, Birmingham C (one as Small Heath) 5, Derby Co 4, Liverpool 4, Ipswich T 3, Leeds U 3, Notts Co 3, Preston NE 3, Middlesbrough 3, Stoke C 3, Bury 2, Grimsby T 2, Norwich C 2, Nottingham F 2, Tottenham H 2, WBA 2, Aston Villa 2, Burnley 2, Chelsea 2, Manchester U 2, West Ham U 2, Wolverhampton W 2, Bolton W 2, Swindon T, Huddersfield T, Bristol C, Brentford, Bradford C, Everton, Fulham, Sheffield U, Newcastle U, Coventry C, Blackpool, Blackburn R, Sunderland, Crystal Palace, Luton T, QPR, Oxford U, Millwall, Oldham Ath, Reading 1, Watford 1 each.

LEAGUE DIVISION 3 – Portsmouth 2, Oxford U 2, Shrewsbury T 2, Carlisle U 2, Preston NE 2, Plymouth Arg, Southampton, Bury, Northampton T, Coventry C, Hull C, QPR, Watford, Leyton Orient, Aston Villa, Bolton W, Oldham Ath, Blackburn R, Hereford U, Mansfield T, Wrexham, Grimsby T, Rotherham U, Burnley, Bradford C, Bournemouth, Reading, Sunderland, Wolverhampton W, Bristol R, Cambridge U, Cardiff C, Wigan Ath 1, Notts Co 1 each.

LEAGUE DIVISION 4 – Chesterfield 2, Doncaster R 2, Peterborough U 2, Port Vale, Walsall, Millwall, Brentford, Gillingham, Brighton & HA, Stockport Co, Luton T, Notts Co, Grimsby T, Southport, Mansfield T, Lincoln C, Cambridge U, Watford, Reading, Huddersfield T, Southend U, Sheffield U, Wimbledon, York C, Swindon T, Northampton T, Wolverhampton W, Rotherham U, Exeter C, Darlington, Burnley 1 each.

**To 1957–58**

DIVISION 3 (South) – Bristol C 3; Charlton Ath, Ipswich T, Millwall, Notts Co, Plymouth Arg, Swansea T 2 each; Brentford, Bristol R, Cardiff C, Crystal Palace, Coventry C, Fulham, Leyton Orient, Luton T, Newport Co, Nottingham F, Norwich C, Portsmouth, QPR, Reading, Southampton, Brighton & HA 1 each.

DIVISION 3 (North) – Barnsley, Doncaster R, Lincoln C 3 each; Chesterfield, Grimsby T, Hull C, Port Vale, Stockport Co 2 each; Bradford PA, Bradford C, Darlington, Derby Co, Nelson, Oldham Ath, Rotherham U, Stoke C, Tranmere R, Wolverhampton W, Scunthorpe U 1 each.

### RELEGATED CLUBS

1891–92 League extended. Newton Heath, Sheffield W and Nottingham F admitted. *Second Division formed* including Darwen.
1892–93 In Test matches, Sheffield U and Darwen won promotion in place of Notts Co and Accrington S.
1893–94 In Tests, Liverpool and Small Heath won promotion. Newton Heath and Darwen relegated.
1894–95 After Tests, Bury promoted, Liverpool relegated.
1895–96 After Tests, Liverpool promoted, Small Heath relegated.
1896–97 After Tests, Notts Co promoted, Burnley relegated.
1897–98 Test system abolished after success of Stoke C and Burnley. League extended. Blackburn R and Newcastle U elected to First Division. *Automatic promotion and relegation introduced.*

### FA PREMIER LEAGUE TO DIVISION 1

| | |
|---|---|
| 1992–93 Crystal Palace, Middlesbrough, Nottingham F | 1995–96 Manchester C, QPR, Bolton W |
| 1993–94 Sheffield U, Oldham Ath, Swindon T | 1996–97 Sunderland, Middlesbrough, Nottingham F |
| 1994–95 Crystal Palace, Norwich C, Leicester C, Ipswich T | 1997–98 Bolton W, Barnsley, Crystal Palace |

### DIVISION 1 TO DIVISION 2

| | |
|---|---|
| 1898–99 Bolton W and Sheffield W | 1955–56 Huddersfield T and Sheffield U |
| 1899–1900 Burnley and Glossop | 1956–57 Charlton Ath and Cardiff C |
| 1900–01 Preston NE and WBA | 1957–58 Sheffield W and Sunderland |
| 1901–02 Small Heath and Manchester C | 1958–59 Portsmouth and Aston Villa |
| 1902–03 Grimsby T and Bolton W | 1959–60 Luton T and Leeds U |
| 1903–04 Liverpool and WBA | 1960–61 Preston NE and Newcastle U |
| 1904–05 League extended. Bury and Notts Co, two bottom clubs in First Division, re-elected. | 1961–62 Chelsea and Cardiff C |
| | 1962–63 Manchester C and Leyton Orient |
| 1905–06 Nottingham F and Wolverhampton W | 1963–64 Bolton W and Ipswich T |
| 1906–07 Derby Co and Stoke C | 1964–65 Wolverhampton W and Birmingham C |
| 1907–08 Bolton W and Birmingham C | 1965–66 Northampton T and Blackburn R |
| 1908–09 Manchester C and Leicester Fosse | 1966–67 Aston Villa and Blackpool |
| 1909–10 Bolton W and Chelsea | 1967–68 Fulham and Sheffield U |
| 1910–11 Bristol C and Nottingham F | 1968–69 Leicester C and QPR |
| 1911–12 Preston NE and Bury | 1969–70 Sunderland and Sheffield W |
| 1912–13 Notts Co and Woolwich Arsenal | 1970–71 Burnley and Blackpool |
| 1913–14 Preston NE and Derby Co | 1971–72 Huddersfield T and Nottingham F |
| 1914–15 Tottenham H and Chelsea* | 1972–73 Crystal Palace and WBA |
| 1919–20 Notts Co and Sheffield W | 1973–74 Southampton, Manchester U, Norwich C |
| 1920–21 Derby Co and Bradford PA | 1974–75 Luton T, Chelsea, Carlisle U |
| 1921–22 Bradford C and Manchester U | 1975–76 Wolverhampton W, Burnley, Sheffield U |
| 1922–23 Stoke C and Oldham Ath | 1976–77 Sunderland, Stoke C, Tottenham H |
| 1923–24 Chelsea and Middlesbrough | 1977–78 West Ham U, Newcastle U, Leicester C |
| 1924–25 Preston NE and Nottingham F | 1978–79 QPR, Birmingham C, Chelsea |
| 1925–26 Manchester C and Notts Co | 1979–80 Bristol C, Derby Co, Bolton W |
| 1926–27 Leeds U and WBA | 1980–81 Norwich C, Leicester C, Crystal Palace |
| 1927–28 Tottenham H and Middlesbrough | 1981–82 Leeds U, Wolverhampton W, Middlesbrough |
| 1928–29 Bury and Cardiff C | 1982–83 Manchester C, Swansea C, Brighton & HA |
| 1929–30 Burnley and Everton | 1983–84 Birmingham C, Notts Co, Wolverhampton W |
| 1930–31 Leeds U and Manchester U | 1984–85 Norwich C, Sunderland, Stoke C |
| 1931–32 Grimsby T and West Ham U | 1985–86 Ipswich T, Birmingham C, WBA |
| 1932–33 Bolton W and Blackpool | 1986–87 Leicester C, Manchester C, Aston Villa |
| 1933–34 Newcastle U and Sheffield U | 1987–88 Chelsea**, Portsmouth, Watford, Oxford U |
| 1934–35 Leicester C and Tottenham H | 1988–89 Middlesbrough, West Ham U, Newcastle U |
| 1935–36 Aston Villa and Blackburn R | 1989–90 Sheffield W, Charlton Ath, Millwall |
| 1936–37 Manchester U and Sheffield W | 1990–91 Sunderland and Derby Co |
| 1937–38 Manchester C and WBA | 1991–92 Luton T, Notts Co, West Ham U |
| 1938–39 Birmingham C and Leicester C | 1992–93 Brentford, Cambridge U, Bristol R |
| 1946–47 Brentford and Leeds U | 1993–94 Birmingham C, Oxford U, Peterborough U |
| 1947–48 Blackburn R and Grimsby T | 1994–95 Swindon T, Burnley, Bristol C, Notts Co |
| 1948–49 Preston NE and Sheffield U | 1995–96 Millwall, Watford, Luton T |
| 1949–50 Manchester C and Birmingham C | 1996–97 Grimsby T, Oldham Ath, Southend U |
| 1950–51 Sheffield W and Everton | 1997–98 Manchester C, Stoke C, Reading |
| 1951–52 Huddersfield T and Fulham | ***Relegated after play-offs.* |
| 1952–53 Stoke C and Derby Co | **Subsequently re-elected to Division 1 when League was* |
| 1953–54 Middlesbrough and Liverpool | *extended after the War.* |
| 1954–55 Leicester C and Sheffield W | |

### DIVISION 2 TO DIVISION 3

| | |
|---|---|
| 1920–21 Stockport Co | 1933–34 Millwall and Lincoln C |
| 1921–22 Bradford PA and Bristol C | 1934–35 Oldham Ath and Notts Co |
| 1922–23 Rotherham Co and Wolverhampton W | 1935–36 Port Vale and Hull C |
| 1923–24 Nelson and Bristol C | 1936–37 Doncaster R and Bradford C |
| 1924–25 Crystal Palace and Coventry C | 1937–38 Barnsley and Stockport Co |
| 1925–26 Stoke C and Stockport Co | 1938–39 Norwich C and Tranmere R |
| 1926–27 Darlington and Bradford C | 1946–47 Swansea T and Newport Co |
| 1927–28 Fulham and South Shields | 1947–48 Doncaster R and Millwall |
| 1928–29 Port Vale and Clapton Orient | 1948–49 Nottingham F and Lincoln C |
| 1929–30 Hull C and Notts Co | 1949–50 Plymouth Arg and Bradford PA |
| 1930–31 Reading and Cardiff C | 1950–51 Grimsby T and Chesterfield |
| 1931–32 Barnsley and Bristol C | 1951–52 Coventry C and QPR |
| 1932–33 Chesterfield and Charlton Ath | 1952–53 Southampton and Barnsley |

1953–54 Brentford and Oldham Ath
1954–55 Ipswich T and Derby Co
1955–56 Plymouth Arg and Hull C
1956–57 Port Vale and Bury
1957–58 Doncaster R and Notts Co
1958–59 Barnsley and Grimsby T
1959–60 Bristol C and Hull C
1960–61 Lincoln C and Portsmouth
1961–62 Brighton & HA and Bristol R
1962–63 Walsall and Luton T
1963–64 Grimsby T and Scunthorpe U
1964–65 Swindon T and Swansea T
1965–66 Middlesbrough and Leyton Orient
1966–67 Northampton T and Bury
1967–68 Plymouth Arg and Rotherham U
1968–69 Fulham and Bury
1969–70 Preston NE and Aston Villa
1970–71 Blackburn R and Bolton W
1971–72 Charlton Ath and Watford
1972–73 Huddersfield T and Brighton & HA
1973–74 Crystal Palace, Preston NE, Swindon T
1974–75 Millwall, Cardiff C, Sheffield W
1975–76 Oxford U, York C, Portsmouth
1976–77 Carlisle U, Plymouth Arg, Hereford U

1977–78 Blackpool, Mansfield T, Hull C
1978–79 Sheffield U, Millwall, Blackburn R
1979–80 Fulham, Burnley, Charlton Ath
1980–81 Preston NE, Bristol C, Bristol R
1981–82 Cardiff C, Wrexham, Orient
1982–83 Rotherham U, Burnley, Bolton W
1983–84 Derby Co, Swansea C, Cambridge U
1984–85 Notts Co, Cardiff C, Wolverhampton W
1985–86 Carlisle U, Middlesbrough, Fulham
1986–87 Sunderland**, Grimsby T, Brighton & HA
1987–88 Huddersfield T, Reading, Sheffield U**
1988–89 Shrewsbury T, Birmingham C, Walsall
1989–90 Bournemouth, Bradford C, Stoke C
1990–91 WBA and Hull C
1991–92 Plymouth Arg, Brighton & HA, Port Vale
1992–93 Preston NE, Mansfield T, Wigan Ath, Chester C
1993–94 Fulham, Exeter C, Hartlepool U, Barnet
1994–95 Cambridge U, Plymouth Arg, Cardiff C, Chester C, Leyton Orient
1995–96 Carlisle U, Swansea C, Brighton & HA, Hull C
1996–97 Peterborough U, Shrewsbury T, Rotherham U, Notts Co
1997–98 Brentford, Plymouth Arg, Carlisle U, Southend U

## DIVISION 3 TO DIVISION 4

1958–59 Rochdale, Notts Co, Doncaster R, Stockport Co
1959–60 Accrington S, Wrexham, Mansfield T, York C
1960–61 Chesterfield, Colchester U, Bradford C, Tranmere R
1961–62 Newport Co, Brentford, Lincoln C, Torquay U
1962–63 Bradford PA, Brighton & HA, Carlisle U, Halifax T
1963–64 Millwall, Crewe Alex, Wrexham, Notts Co
1964–65 Luton T, Port Vale, Colchester U, Barnsley
1965–66 Southend U, Exeter C, Brentford, York C
1966–67 Doncaster R, Workington, Darlington, Swansea T
1967–68 Scunthorpe U, Colchester U, Grimsby T, Peterborough U (demoted)
1968–69 Oldham Ath, Crewe Alex, Hartlepool, Northampton T
1969–70 Bournemouth, Southport, Barrow, Stockport Co
1970–71 Reading, Bury, Doncaster R, Gillingham
1971–72 Mansfield T, Barnsley, Torquay U, Bradford C
1972–73 Rotherham U, Brentford, Swansea C, Scunthorpe U
1973–74 Cambridge U, Shrewsbury T, Southport, Rochdale

1974–75 Bournemouth, Tranmere R, Watford, Huddersfield T
1975–76 Aldershot, Colchester U, Southend U, Halifax T
1976–77 Reading, Northampton T, Grimsby T, York C
1977–78 Port Vale, Bradford C, Hereford U, Portsmouth
1978–79 Peterborough U, Walsall, Tranmere R, Lincoln C
1979–80 Bury, Southend U, Mansfield T, Wimbledon
1980–81 Sheffield U, Colchester U, Blackpool, Hull C
1981–82 Wimbledon, Swindon T, Bristol C, Chester
1982–83 Reading, Wrexham, Doncaster R, Chesterfield
1983–84 Scunthorpe U, Southend U, Port Vale, Exeter C
1984–85 Burnley, Orient, Preston NE, Cambridge U
1985–86 Lincoln C, Cardiff C, Wolverhampton W, Swansea C
1986–87 Bolton W**, Carlisle U, Darlington, Newport Co
1987–88 Doncaster R, York C, Grimsby T, Rotherham U**
1988–89 Southend U, Chesterfield, Gillingham, Aldershot
1989–90 Cardiff C, Northampton T, Blackpool, Walsall
1990–91 Crewe Alex, Rotherham U, Mansfield T
1991–92 Bury, Shrewsbury T, Torquay U, Darlington
** *Relegated after play-offs.*

## APPLICATIONS FOR RE-ELECTION
### FOURTH DIVISION

**Eleven:** Hartlepool U.
**Seven:** Crewe Alex.
**Six:** Barrow (lost League place to Hereford U 1972), Halifax T, Rochdale, Southport (lost League place to Wigan Ath 1978), York C.
**Five:** Chester C, Darlington, Lincoln C, Stockport Co, Workington (lost League place to Wimbledon 1977).
**Four:** Bradford PA (lost League place to Cambridge U 1970), Newport Co, Northampton T.
**Three:** Doncaster R, Hereford U.
**Two:** Bradford C, Exeter C, Oldham Ath, Scunthorpe U, Torquay U.
**One:** Aldershot, Colchester U, Gateshead (lost League place to Peterborough U 1960), Grimsby T, Swansea C, Tranmere R, Wrexham, Blackpool, Cambridge U, Preston NE.
Accrington S resigned and Oxford U were elected 1962.
Port Vale were forced to re-apply following expulsion in 1968.
Aldershot expelled March 1992. Maidstone U resigned August 1992.

### THIRD DIVISIONS NORTH & SOUTH

**Seven:** Walsall.
**Six:** Exeter C, Halifax T, Newport Co.
**Five:** Accrington S, Barrow, Gillingham, New Brighton, Southport.
**Four:** Rochdale, Norwich C.
**Three:** Crystal Palace, Crewe Alex, Darlington, Hartlepool U, Merthyr T, Swindon T.
**Two:** Aberdare Ath, Aldershot, Ashington, Bournemouth, Brentford, Chester, Colchester U, Durham C, Millwall, Nelson, QPR, Rotherham U, Southend U, Tranmere R, Watford, Workington.
**One:** Bradford C, Bradford PA, Brighton & HA, Bristol R, Cardiff C, Carlisle U, Charlton Ath, Gateshead, Grimsby T, Mansfield T, Shrewsbury T, Torquay U, York C.

## LEAGUE STATUS FROM 1986–87

| **RELEGATED FROM LEAGUE** | | **PROMOTED TO LEAGUE** |
|---|---|---|
| 1986–87 | Lincoln C | Scarborough |
| 1987–88 | Newport Co | Lincoln C |
| 1988–89 | Darlington | Maidstone U |
| 1989–90 | Colchester U | Darlington |
| 1990–91 | — | Barnet |
| 1991–92 | — | Colchester U |
| 1992–93 | Halifax T | Wycombe W |
| 1993–94 | — | — |
| 1994–95 | — | — |
| 1995–96 | — | — |
| 1996–97 | Hereford U | Macclesfield T |
| 1997–98 | Doncaster R | Halifax T |

# LEAGUE ATTENDANCES SINCE 1946–47

| Season | Matches | Total | Div. 1 | Div. 2 | Div. 3 (S) | Div. 3 (N) |
|--------|---------|-------|--------|--------|------------|------------|
| 1946–47 | 1848 | 35,604,606 | 15,005,316 | 11,071,572 | 5,664,004 | 3,863,714 |
| 1947–48 | 1848 | 40,259,130 | 16,732,341 | 12,286,350 | 6,653,610 | 4,586,829 |
| 1948–49 | 1848 | 41,271,414 | 17,914,667 | 11,353,237 | 6,998,429 | 5,005,081 |
| 1949–50 | 1848 | 40,517,865 | 17,278,625 | 11,694,158 | 7,104,155 | 4,440,927 |
| 1950–51 | 2028 | 39,584,967 | 16,679,454 | 10,780,580 | 7,367,884 | 4,757,109 |
| 1951–52 | 2028 | 39,015,866 | 16,110,322 | 11,066,189 | 6,958,927 | 4,880,428 |
| 1952–53 | 2028 | 37,149,966 | 16,050,278 | 9,686,654 | 6,704,299 | 4,708,735 |
| 1953–54 | 2028 | 36,174,590 | 16,154,915 | 9,510,053 | 6,311,508 | 4,198,114 |
| 1954–55 | 2028 | 34,133,103 | 15,087,221 | 8,988,794 | 5,996,017 | 4,051,071 |
| 1955–56 | 2028 | 33,150,809 | 14,108,961 | 9,080,002 | 5,692,479 | 4,269,367 |
| 1956–57 | 2028 | 32,744,405 | 13,803,037 | 8,718,162 | 5,622,189 | 4,601,017 |
| 1957–58 | 2028 | 33,562,208 | 14,468,652 | 8,663,712 | 6,097,183 | 4,332,661 |

| | | | | | Div. 3 | Div. 4 |
|--------|---------|-------|--------|--------|--------|--------|
| 1958–59 | 2028 | 33,610,985 | 14,727,691 | 8,641,997 | 5,946,600 | 4,276,697 |
| 1959–60 | 2028 | 32,538,611 | 14,391,227 | 8,399,627 | 5,739,707 | 4,008,050 |
| 1960–61 | 2028 | 28,619,754 | 12,926,948 | 7,033,936 | 4,784,256 | 3,874,614 |
| 1961–62 | 2015 | 27,979,902 | 12,061,194 | 7,453,089 | 5,199,106 | 3,266,513 |
| 1962–63 | 2028 | 28,885,852 | 12,490,239 | 7,792,770 | 5,341,362 | 3,261,481 |
| 1963–64 | 2028 | 28,535,022 | 12,486,626 | 7,594,158 | 5,419,157 | 3,035,081 |
| 1964–65 | 2028 | 27,641,168 | 12,708,752 | 6,984,104 | 4,436,245 | 3,512,067 |
| 1965–66 | 2028 | 27,206,980 | 12,480,644 | 6,914,757 | 4,779,150 | 3,032,429 |
| 1966–67 | 2028 | 28,902,596 | 14,242,957 | 7,253,819 | 4,421,172 | 2,984,648 |
| 1967–68 | 2028 | 30,107,298 | 15,289,410 | 7,450,410 | 4,013,087 | 3,354,391 |
| 1968–69 | 2028 | 29,382,172 | 14,584,851 | 7,382,390 | 4,339,656 | 3,075,275 |
| 1969–70 | 2028 | 29,600,972 | 14,868,754 | 7,581,728 | 4,223,761 | 2,926,729 |
| 1970–71 | 2028 | 28,194,146 | 13,954,337 | 7,098,265 | 4,377,213 | 2,764,331 |
| 1971–72 | 2028 | 28,700,729 | 14,484,603 | 6,769,308 | 4,697,392 | 2,749,426 |
| 1972–73 | 2028 | 25,448,642 | 13,998,154 | 5,631,730 | 3,737,252 | 2,081,506 |
| 1973–74 | 2027 | 24,982,203 | 13,070,991 | 6,326,108 | 3,421,624 | 2,163,480 |
| 1974–75 | 2028 | 25,577,977 | 12,613,178 | 6,955,970 | 4,086,145 | 1,992,684 |
| 1975–76 | 2028 | 24,896,053 | 13,089,861 | 5,798,405 | 3,948,449 | 2,059,338 |
| 1976–77 | 2028 | 26,182,800 | 13,647,585 | 6,250,597 | 4,152,218 | 2,132,400 |
| 1977–78 | 2028 | 25,392,872 | 13,255,677 | 6,474,763 | 3,332,042 | 2,330,390 |
| 1978–79 | 2028 | 24,540,627 | 12,704,549 | 6,153,223 | 3,374,558 | 2,308,297 |
| 1979–80 | 2028 | 24,623,975 | 12,163,002 | 6,112,025 | 3,999,328 | 2,349,620 |
| 1980–81 | 2028 | 21,907,569 | 11,392,894 | 5,175,442 | 3,637,854 | 1,701,379 |
| 1981–82 | 2028 | 20,006,961 | 10,420,793 | 4,750,463 | 2,836,915 | 1,998,790 |
| 1982–83 | 2028 | 18,766,158 | 9,295,613 | 4,974,937 | 2,943,568 | 1,552,040 |
| 1983–84 | 2028 | 18,358,631 | 8,711,448 | 5,359,757 | 2,729,942 | 1,557,484 |
| 1984–85 | 2028 | 17,849,835 | 9,761,404 | 4,030,823 | 2,667,008 | 1,390,600 |
| 1985–86 | 2028 | 16,488,577 | 9,037,854 | 3,551,968 | 2,490,481 | 1,408,274 |
| 1986–87 | 2028 | 17,379,218 | 9,144,676 | 4,168,131 | 2,350,970 | 1,715,441 |
| 1987–88 | 2030 | 17,959,732 | 8,094,571 | 5,341,599 | 2,751,275 | 1,772,287 |
| 1988–89 | 2036 | 18,464,192 | 7,809,993 | 5,887,805 | 3,035,327 | 1,791,067 |
| 1989–90 | 2036 | 19,445,442 | 7,883,039 | 6,867,674 | 2,803,551 | 1,891,178 |
| 1990–91 | 2036 | 19,508,202 | 8,618,709 | 6,285,068 | 2,835,759 | 1,768,666 |
| 1991–92 | 2064* | 20,487,273 | 9,989,160 | 5,809,787 | 2,993,352 | 1,694,974 |

| | | Total | FA Premier | Div. 1 | Div. 2 | Div. 3 |
|--------|---------|-------|------------|--------|--------|--------|
| 1992–93 | 2028 | 20,657,327 | 9,759,809 | 5,874,017 | 3,483,073 | 1,540,428 |
| 1993–94 | 2028 | 21,683,381 | 10,644,551 | 6,487,104 | 2,972,702 | 1,579,024 |
| 1994–95 | 2028 | 21,856,020 | 11,213,168 | 6,044,293 | 3,037,752 | 1,560,807 |
| 1995–96 | 2036 | 21,844,416 | 10,469,107 | 6,566,349 | 2,843,652 | 1,965,308 |
| 1996–97 | 2036 | 22,783,163 | 10,804,762 | 6,931,539 | 3,195,223 | 1,851,639 |
| 1997–98 | 2036 | 24,692,608 | 11,092,106 | 8,330,018 | 3,503,264 | 1,767,220 |

*Figures include matches played by Aldershot.

# ENGLISH LEAGUE ATTENDANCES 1997–98

## FA CARLING PREMIERSHIP ATTENDANCES

| | Average Gate | | | Season 1997/98 | |
|---|---|---|---|---|---|
| | 1996/97 | 1997/98 | +/−% | Highest | Lowest |
| Arsenal | 37,821 | 38,053 | +0.61 | 38,269 | 37,324 |
| Aston Villa | 36,027 | 36,137 | +0.30 | 39,372 | 29,343 |
| Barnsley | 11,356 | 18,449 | +62.46 | 18,694 | 17,172 |
| Blackburn Rovers | 24,947 | 25,253 | +1.23 | 30,547 | 19,086 |
| Bolton Wanderers | 15,826 | 24,352 | +53.88 | 25,000 | 22,703 |
| Chelsea | 27,001 | 32,901 | +21.85 | 34,845 | 28,832 |
| Coventry City | 19,625 | 19,718 | +0.47 | 23,055 | 15,910 |
| Crystal Palace | 16,085 | 21,983 | +36.67 | 26,186 | 14,410 |
| Derby County | 17.889 | 29,105 | +62.70 | 30,492 | 25,625 |
| Everton | 36,186 | 35,376 | −2.24 | 40,479 | 28,533 |
| Leeds United | 32,109 | 34,725 | +8.15 | 39,943 | 28,926 |
| Leicester City | 20,184 | 20,615 | +2.14 | 21,699 | 18,553 |
| Liverpool | 39,777 | 40,628 | +2.14 | 44,532 | 34,705 |
| Manchester United | 55,081 | 55,168 | +0.16 | 55,306 | 55,008 |
| Newcastle United | 36,466 | 36,680 | +0.59 | 36,783 | 36,289 |
| Sheffield Wednesday | 25,693 | 28,709 | +11.74 | 39,427 | 21,087 |
| Southampton | 15,099 | 15,159 | +0.40 | 15,255 | 14,815 |
| Tottenham Hotspur | 31,067 | 29,143 | −6.19 | 35,995 | 25,097 |
| West Ham United | 23,242 | 24,967 | +7.42 | 25,908 | 22,477 |
| Wimbledon | 15,156 | 16,675 | +10.02 | 26,309 | 7,688 |

TOTAL ATTENDANCES: 11,092,106 (380 games)
Average 29,190 (+2.66%)
HIGHEST: 55,306 Manchester United v Wimbledon
LOWEST: 7,688 Wimbledon v Barnsley
HIGHEST AVERAGE: 55,168 Manchester United
LOWEST AVERAGE: 15,159 Southampton

## NATIONWIDE FOOTBALL LEAGUE: DIVISION ONE ATTENDANCES

| | Average Gate | | | Season 1997/98 | |
|---|---|---|---|---|---|
| | 1996/97 | 1997/98 | +/−% | Highest | Lowest |
| Birmingham City | 17,751 | 18,708 | +5.4 | 25,877 | 14,554 |
| Bradford City | 12,925 | 15,564 | +20.4 | 17,842 | 13,021 |
| Bury | 4,502 | 6,177 | +37.2 | 11,216 | 4,602 |
| Charlton Athletic | 11,081 | 13,275 | +19.8 | 15,815 | 9,850 |
| Crewe Alexandra | 3,978 | 5,243 | +31.8 | 5,759 | 4,176 |
| Huddersfield Town | 12,175 | 12,145 | −0.2 | 18,820 | 8,985 |
| Ipswich Town | 11,953 | 14,973 | +25.3 | 21,858 | 8,828 |
| Manchester City | 26,753 | 28,196 | +5.4 | 32,040 | 24,058 |
| Middlesbrough | 29,848 | 29,994 | +0.5 | 30,228 | 29,414 |
| Norwich City | 14,719 | 14,444 | −1.9 | 19,069 | 9,815 |
| Nottingham Forest | 24,587 | 20,584 | −16.3 | 29,302 | 16,701 |
| Oxford United | 7,608 | 7,512 | −1.3 | 9,484 | 5,726 |
| Port Vale | 7,385 | 8,432 | +14.2 | 13,853 | 5,244 |
| Portsmouth | 8,857 | 11,149 | +1.3 | 17,003 | 6,827 |
| Queens Park Rangers | 12,554 | 13,083 | +4.2 | 17,614 | 8,853 |
| Reading | 9,160 | 9,676 | +5.6 | 14,817 | 6,685 |
| Sheffield United | 16,638 | 17,942 | +7.8 | 24,536 | 14,120 |
| Stockport County | 6,424 | 8,322 | +29.5 | 11,351 | 6,148 |
| Stoke City | 12,698 | 15,025 | +18.3 | 26,664 | 8,423 |
| Sunderland | 20,865 | 33,492 | +60.5 | 40,712 | 24,642 |
| Swindon Town | 9,917 | 10,298 | +3.8 | 15,724 | 7,588 |
| Tranmere Rovers | 8,127 | 7,999 | −1.6 | 14,116 | 5,127 |
| West Bromwich Albion | 15,064 | 16,662 | +10.6 | 23,012 | 12,402 |
| Wolverhampton Wanderers | 24,763 | 23,281 | −6.0 | 28,244 | 19,785 |

TOTAL ATTENDANCES: 8,330,018 (552 games)
Average 15,091 (+20.2%)
HIGHEST: 40,712 Sunderland v Stoke City
LOWEST: 4,176 Crewe Alexandra v Swindon Town
HIGHEST AVERAGE: 33,492 Sunderland
LOWEST AVERAGE: 5,243 Crewe Alexandra

## NATIONWIDE FOOTBALL LEAGUE: DIVISION TWO ATTENDANCES

| | Average Gate | | | Season 1997/98 | |
|---|---|---|---|---|---|
| | 1996/97 | 1997/98 | +/−% | Highest | Lowest |
| AFC Bournemouth | 4,581 | 4,732 | +3.3 | 7,484 | 3,019 |
| Blackpool | 4,987 | 5,220 | +4.7 | 8,342 | 3,281 |
| Brentford | 5,832 | 5,029 | −13.8 | 10,510 | 3,424 |
| Bristol City | 10,802 | 11,846 | +9.7 | 19,141 | 8,330 |
| Bristol Rovers | 5,630 | 6,413 | +13.9 | 9,043 | 4,289 |
| Burnley | 10,053 | 10,481 | +4.3 | 18,811 | 8,256 |
| Carlisle United | 5,440 | 5,381 | −1.1 | 8,010 | 3,591 |
| Chesterfield | 4,639 | 4,756 | +2.5 | 7,406 | 3,420 |
| Fulham | 6,644 | 9,018 | +35.7 | 16,979 | 5,096 |
| Gillingham | 6,021 | 6,450 | +7.2 | 10,507 | 4,774 |
| Grimsby Town | 5,859 | 5,601 | −4.4 | 8,327 | 4,508 |
| Luton Town | 6,781 | 6,501 | −4.1 | 9,041 | 5,144 |
| Millwall | 7,743 | 7,023 | −9.3 | 10,291 | 4,647 |
| Northampton Town | 4,823 | 6,389 | +32.5 | 7,443 | 4,828 |
| Oldham Athletic | 7,045 | 5,586 | −20.7 | 9,781 | 4,244 |
| Plymouth Argyle | 6,495 | 5,323 | −18.0 | 9,390 | 2,994 |
| Preston North End | 9,411 | 9,460 | +0.5 | 13,500 | 6,992 |
| Southend United | 5,072 | 4,148 | −18.2 | 6.151 | 2,315 |
| Walsall | 3,892 | 4,062 | +4.4 | 6,634 | 2,598 |
| Watford | 8,894 | 11,532 | +29.7 | 16,072 | 7,274 |
| Wigan Athletic | 3,899 | 3,968 | +1.8 | 5,649 | 2,616 |
| Wrexham | 4,112 | 4,090 | −0.5 | 7,302 | 2,088 |
| Wycombe Wanderers | 5,232 | 5,415 | +3.5 | 8,090 | 3,635 |
| York City | 3,359 | 3,853 | +14.7 | 7,093 | 2,831 |

TOTAL ATTENDANCES: 3,503,264 (552 games)
Average 6,364 (+9.6%)
HIGHEST: 19,141 Bristol City v Watford
LOWEST: 2,088 Wrexham v Southend United
HIGHEST AVERAGE: 11,846 Bristol City
LOWEST AVERAGE: 3,853 York City

## NATIONWIDE FOOTBALL LEAGUE: DIVISION THREE ATTENDANCES

| | Average Gate | | | Season 1997/98 | |
|---|---|---|---|---|---|
| | 1996/97 | 1997/98 | +/−% | Highest | Lowest |
| Barnet | 2,141 | 2,254 | +5.3 | 3,449 | 1,246 |
| Brighton & Hove Albion | 5,844 | 2,329 | −60.1 | 6,339 | 1,025 |
| Cambridge United | 3,363 | 2,898 | −13.9 | 5,445 | 2,012 |
| Cardiff City | 3,594 | 3,610 | +0.4 | 6,862 | 2,340 |
| Chester City | 2,263 | 2,255 | −0.4 | 3,245 | 1,510 |
| Colchester United | 3,245 | 3,137 | −3.3 | 5,793 | 1,858 |
| Darlington | 2,796 | 2,314 | −17.2 | 3,169 | 1,399 |
| Doncaster Rovers | 2,091 | 1,715 | −18.0 | 3,562 | 729 |
| Exeter City | 3,014 | 3,988 | +32.3 | 8,315 | 2,754 |
| Hartlepool United | 2,107 | 2,258 | +7.2 | 3,905 | 1,588 |
| Hull City | 3,413 | 4,684 | +37.2 | 7,412 | 3,313 |
| Leyton Orient | 4,336 | 4,374 | +0.9 | 6,599 | 2,483 |
| Lincoln City | 3,163 | 3,968 | +25.5 | 9,890 | 2,276 |
| Macclesfield Town | 1,407 | 2,913 | +107.0 | 5,982 | 1,450 |
| Mansfield Town | 2,282 | 2,720 | +19.2 | 6,786 | 2,033 |
| Notts County | 4,239 | 5,711 | +34.7 | 12,431 | 3,104 |
| Peterborough United | 5,295 | 6,192 | +16.9 | 10,904 | 4,208 |
| Rochdale | 1,829 | 1,847 | +1.0 | 2,387 | 1,192 |
| Rotherham United | 2,844 | 3,648 | +28.3 | 5,995 | 2,914 |
| Scarborough | 2,455 | 2,489 | +1.4 | 3,831 | 1,408 |
| Scunthorpe United | 2,606 | 3,006 | +15.3 | 4,905 | 2,024 |
| Shrewsbury Town | 3,177 | 2,403 | −24.4 | 3,238 | 1,523 |
| Swansea City | 3,850 | 3,443 | −10.6 | 6.640 | 2,128 |
| Torquay United | 2,380 | 2,679 | +12.6 | 4,472 | 1,411 |

TOTAL ATTENDANCES: 1,767,220 (552 games)
Average 3,201 (−4.6%)
HIGHEST: 12,431 Notts County v Rotherham United
LOWEST: 729 Doncaster Rovers v Barnet
HIGHEST AVERAGE: 6,192 Peterborough United
LOWEST AVERAGE: 1,715 Doncaster Rovers

# LEAGUE CUP FINALISTS 1961–98

*Played as a two-leg final until 1966. All subsequent finals at Wembley.*

| Year | Winners | Runners-up | Score |
|------|---------|------------|-------|
| 1961 | Aston Villa | Rotherham U | 0-2, 3-0 (aet) |
| 1962 | Norwich C | Rochdale | 3-0, 1-0 |
| 1963 | Birmingham C | Aston Villa | 3-1, 0-0 |
| 1964 | Leicester C | Stoke C | 1-1, 3-2 |
| 1965 | Chelsea | Leicester C | 3-2, 0-0 |
| 1966 | WBA | West Ham U | 1-2, 4-1 |
| 1967 | QPR | WBA | 3-2 |
| 1968 | Leeds U | Arsenal | 1-0 |
| 1969 | Swindon T | Arsenal | 3-1 (aet) |
| 1970 | Manchester C | WBA | 2-1 (aet) |
| 1971 | Tottenham H | Aston Villa | 2-0 |
| 1972 | Stoke C | Chelsea | 2-1 |
| 1973 | Tottenham H | Norwich C | 1-0 |
| 1974 | Wolverhampton W | Manchester C | 2-1 |
| 1975 | Aston Villa | Norwich C | 1-0 |
| 1976 | Manchester C | Newcastle U | 2-1 |
| 1977 | Aston Villa | Everton | 0-0, 1-1 (aet), 3-2 (aet) |
| 1978 | Nottingham F | Liverpool | 0-0 (aet), 1-0 |
| 1979 | Nottingham F | Southampton | 3-2 |
| 1980 | Wolverhampton W | Nottingham F | 1-0 |
| 1981 | Liverpool | West Ham U | 1-1 (aet), 2-1 |

**MILK CUP**

| | | | |
|------|---------|------------|-------|
| 1982 | Liverpool | Tottenham H | 3-1 (aet) |
| 1983 | Liverpool | Manchester U | 2-1 (aet) |
| 1984 | Liverpool | Everton | 0-0 (aet), 1-0 |
| 1985 | Norwich C | Sunderland | 1-0 |
| 1986 | Oxford U | QPR | 3-0 |

**LITTLEWOODS CUP**

| | | | |
|------|---------|------------|-------|
| 1987 | Arsenal | Liverpool | 2-1 |
| 1988 | Luton T | Arsenal | 3-2 |
| 1989 | Nottingham F | Luton T | 3-1 |
| 1990 | Nottingham F | Oldham Ath | 1-0 |

**RUMBELOWS LEAGUE CUP**

| | | | |
|------|---------|------------|-------|
| 1991 | Sheffield W | Manchester U | 1-0 |
| 1992 | Manchester U | Nottingham F | 1-0 |

**COCA-COLA CUP**

| | | | |
|------|---------|------------|-------|
| 1993 | Arsenal | Sheffield W | 2-1 |
| 1994 | Aston Villa | Manchester U | 3-1 |
| 1995 | Liverpool | Bolton W | 2-1 |
| 1996 | Aston Villa | Leeds U | 3-0 |
| 1997 | Leicester C | Middlesbrough | 1-1 (aet), 1-0 (aet) |
| 1998 | Chelsea | Middlesbrough | 2-0 (aet) |

**LEAGUE CUP WINS**
Aston Villa 5, Liverpool 5, Nottingham F 4, Arsenal 2, Chelsea 2, Leicester C 2, Manchester C 2, Norwich C 2, Tottenham H 2, Wolverhampton W 2, Birmingham C 1, Leeds U 1, Luton T 1, Manchester U 1, Oxford U 1, QPR 1, Sheffield W 1, Stoke C 1, Swindon T 1, WBA 1.

**APPEARANCES IN FINALS**
Aston Villa 7, Liverpool 7, Nottingham F 6, Arsenal 5, Manchester U 4, Norwich C 4, Chelsea 3, Leicester C 3, Manchester C 3, Tottenham H 3, WBA 3, Everton 2, Leeds U 2, Luton T 2, Middlesbrough 2, QPR 2, Sheffield W 2, Stoke C 2, West Ham U 2, Wolverhampton W 2, Birmingham C 1, Bolton W 1, Newcastle U 1, Oldham Ath 1, Oxford U 1, Rochdale 1, Rotherham U 1, Southampton 1, Sunderland 1, Swindon T 1.

**APPEARANCES IN SEMI-FINALS**
Aston Villa 10, Liverpool 10, Arsenal 9, Tottenham H 8, Manchester U 7, West Ham U 7, Chelsea 6, Nottingham F 6, Leeds U 5, Manchester C 5, Norwich C 5, Middlesbrough 4, WBA 4, Birmingham C 3, Burnley 3, Everton 3, Leicester C 3, QPR 3, Sheffield W 3, Swindon T 3, Wolverhampton W 3, Blackburn R 2, Bolton W 2, Bristol C 2, Coventry C 2, Crystal Palace 2, Ipswich T 2, Luton T 2, Oxford U 2, Plymouth Arg 2, Southampton 2, Stoke C 2, Sunderland 2, Blackpool 1, Bury 1, Cardiff C 1, Carlisle U 1, Chester C 1, Derby Co 1, Huddersfield T 1, Newcastle U 1, Oldham Ath 1, Peterborough U 1, Rochdale 1, Rotherham U 1, Shrewsbury T 1, Stockport Co 1, Tranmere R 1, Walsall 1, Watford 1, Wimbledon 1.

# COCA-COLA CUP 1997–98

**FIRST ROUND, FIRST LEG**

**11 AUG**

**Doncaster R (0) 0**
**Nottingham F (3) 8** *(Thomas 11, Saunders 15, 78, Hjelde 30, 55, Van Hooijdonk 47, 83, Allen 86)* 4547
*Doncaster R:* Ingham; Darren Esdaille, Sanders, Warren, Gore, Brookes, David Esdaille (Cunningham), McDonald, Mike, Moncrieffe, Ireland.
*Nottingham F:* Pascolo; Lyttle, Rogers (Armstrong), Hjelde, Chettle, Thomas (Phillips), Bonalair (Moore), Gemmill, Van Hooijdonk, Saunders, Allen.

**12 AUG**

**Peterborough U (1) 2** *(Awford 8 (og), Carruthers 81)*
**Portsmouth (2) 2** *(Thorp 8, Hillier 24)* 3613
*Peterborough U:* Tiler; Linton, Lewis, Payne (Bullimore), Bodley (Cleaver), Edwards, Farrell, Castle, De Souza (Carruthers), Quinn, Houghton.
*Portsmouth:* Flahavan; Waterman, Thomson, McLoughlin, Whitbread, Hillier, Gurney, Awford (Pethick), Aloisi, Thorp, Igoe.

**Blackpool (0) 1** *(Preece 73)*
**Manchester C (0) 0** 8084
*Blackpool:* Banks; Bryan, Bradshaw, Butler, Lydiate, Brabin, Bonner, Clarkson, Quinn, Philpott (Malkin), Preece.
*Manchester C:* Margetson; Brightwell, Vaughan, Wiekens, Kernaghan, Summerbee, Brannan, Horlock, Bradbury, Kinkladze, Rosler.

**Bournemouth (0) 0**
**Torquay U (1) 1** *(Gibbs 43 (pen))* 3215
*Bournemouth:* Glass; Young, Vincent, Rolling (Murray), Cox, Bailey, Howe, Robinson (Brissett), O'Neill (Town), Fletcher, Rawlinson.
*Torquay U:* Gregg; Gurney, Gibbs, Robinson, Gittens, Watson, Oatway, Mitchell, Jack, Bedeau, Hill (Hapgood).

**Brentford (0) 1** *(Denys 65)*
**Shrewsbury T (0) 1** *(Currie 78)* 2040
*Brentford:* Dearden; Hurdle, Anderson, Hutchings, Bates, McGhee (Canham), Denys (Rapley), Wormull, Spencer, Barrowcliff, Taylor.
*Shrewsbury T:* Edwards; Blamey, Dempsey, Wilding, Walton, Herbert, Currie, Brown, Steele (Seabury), Evans, Taylor M (Jagielka).

**Bristol C (0) 0**
**Bristol R (0) 0** 9341
*Bristol C:* Welch; Locke, Bell, Paterson, Taylor, Edwards, Hewlett (Tisdale), Owers, Goater, Cramb (Bent), Tinnion.
*Bristol R:* Collett; Perry, Foster, Beadle (Bennett), Gayle, Tillson, Holloway, Penrice, Alsop, Cureton, Hayles.

**Cambridge U (0) 1** *(Kyd 57)*
**WBA (1) 1** *(Peschisolido 5)* 3520
*Cambridge U:* Barrett; Chenery, Wilson, Marc Joseph, Foster, Campbell, Wanless, Rees, Kyd (Benjamin), Butler, Williamson (Taylor).
*WBA:* Miller; McDermott, Nicholson, Sneekes, Mardon, Murphy, Flynn, Butler (Hamilton), Peschisolido, Hunt, Kilbane.

**Cardiff C (0) 1** *(Rollo 88)*
**Southend U (1) 1** *(Byrne 40)* 2804
*Cardiff C:* Hallworth; Young, Beech, Jarman, Harris, Fowler, Partridge, Middleton (Rollo) (Lloyd), White, Nugent, Carss (Stoker).
*Southend U:* Royce; Harris, Jones, Marsh, Roget, Dublin, Byrne, Beeston, Boere, Thomson (Rammell), Clarke.

**Chester C (0) 1** *(Woods 73)*
**Carlisle U (1) 2** *(Smart 33, Jansen 53)* 2367
*Chester C:* Sinclair; Davidson, Jenkins, Fisher, Whelan, Alsford, Bennett, Richardson, Rimmer, Flitcroft (Milner), Thomas (Woods).
*Carlisle U:* Caig; Delap, Archdeacon, Walling, Varty, Thorpe, Barr, Prokas, Smart (Dobie), Aspinall, Jansen.

**Colchester U (0) 0**
**Luton T (0) 1** *(Thorpe 87)* 2840
*Colchester U:* Emberson; Gregory, Stamps, Skelton (Forbes), Greene, Cawley, Wilkins, Buckle, Sale (Lock), Abrahams (Adcock), Hathaway.
*Luton T:* Feuer; Douglas, Thomas, Waddock, Davis S, Johnson, McLaren, Alexander, Oldfield (Harvey), Thorpe, Davies.

**Crewe Alex (2) 2** *(Lunt 7, Smith S 41)*
**Bury (2) 3** *(Armstrong 30, Jepson 34 (pen), Johnson 49)* 2618
*Crewe Alex:* Kearton; Unsworth, Smith S, Westwood, Pemberton (Lightfoot), Charnock, Rivers, Lunt, Adebola, Johnson, Little (Garvey).
*Bury:* Kiely; West, Armstrong, Daws, Lucketti, Butler, Gray (Hughes), Johnson (Randall), Jepson (Swan), Johnrose, Battersby.

**Darlington (1) 1** *(Roberts 14)*
**Notts Co (1) 1** *(White 3)* 2189
*Darlington:* Preece; Gray, Barnard, Brydon, Crosby, Hope, Oliver, Lowe, Roberts, Shutt, Naylor.
*Notts Co:* Ward; Hendon, Pearce, Redmile, Strodder, Derry, Finnan, Robinson, White (Baraclough), Jones, Robson.

**Gillingham (0) 0**
**Birmingham C (0) 1** *(Francis 85)* 5246
*Gillingham:* Moss; Ratcliffe, Butters, Smith, Green, Bryant, Hessenthaler, Galloway, Butler, Akinbiyi, O'Connor (Fortune-West).
*Birmingham C:* Bennett; Bass, Johnson, Wassall, Ablett, O'Connor, Devlin (Francis), Robinson (Grainger), Furlong, Hughes, Ndlovu.

**Huddersfield T (2) 2** *(Payton 6, Dreyer 45 (og))*
**Bradford C (1) 1** *(Steiner 17)* 8720
*Huddersfield T:* Francis (O'Connor); Jenkins, Ryan, Dyson, Morrison, Edwards, Beresford (Heary), Makel, Stewart, Payton, Burnett.
*Bradford C:* Prudhoe; Wilder, Jacobs, Beagrie, Youds, Dreyer, Lawrence, Pepper, Steiner (Blake), Edinho, Murray.

**Lincoln C (1) 1** *(Stant 39)*
**Burnley (0) 1** *(Howey 77)* 3010
*Lincoln C:* Vaughan; Barnett, Whitney, Hone, Holmes, Austin, Ainsworth, Miller, Stant, Thorpe, Fleming.
*Burnley:* Beresford; Huxford, Vinnicombe, Williams, Blatherwick, Brass, Winstanley, Ford, Howey, Barnes, Eyres (Matthew).

**Macclesfield T (0) 0**
**Hull C (0) 0** 2249
*Macclesfield T:* Price; Tinson, Rose, Payne, Howarth, Sodje, Askey (Mitchell), Wood, Landon, Mason (Power), Sorvel.
*Hull C:* Thomson; Trevitt, Mann, Wright, Brien, Dewhurst, Joyce, Rioch, Darby, Quigley (Hateley), Peacock.

**Mansfield T (2) 4** *(Gannon 32 (og), Christie 44, 46, 48)*
**Stockport Co (1) 2** *(Angell 36, Woodthorpe 75)* 2170
*Mansfield T:* Bowling; Ford, Harper, Watkiss, Eustace, Jones, Schofield, Sedgemore, Christie, Whitehall, Doolan.
*Stockport Co:* Gray; Connelly, Woodthorpe, Bennett, Flynn, Gannon, Durkan (Dinning), Marsden, Angell, Armstrong, Cooper.

**Northampton T (0) 2** *(Gayle 60, Seal 65)*
**Millwall (1) 1** *(Grant 33)*                        3773
*Northampton T:* Woodman; Clarkson, Frain, Sampson, Warburton, Brightwell, Parrish, Heggs (Gibb), Seal (Van Dullemen), Lee (Gayle), Hunter.
*Millwall:* Carter; Brown, Sturgess, Witter, Law, Fitzgerald, Allen, Savage, Sadlier, Grant, Newman.

**Norwich C (2) 2** *(Roberts 13, Adams 37)*
**Barnet (1) 1** *(Polston 35 (og))*                   5429
*Norwich C:* Marshall A; Fleming (Newman), Scott, Sutch, Segura, Polston, Adams, Fleck, Roberts, Bellamy, Bradshaw.
*Barnet:* Harrison; Stockley (McDonald), Harle, Heald, Howarth, Ford, Manuel (Wilson), Goodhind, Charley, Devine (Samuels), Mills.

**Oldham Ath (0) 1** *(Ritchie 77)*
**Grimsby T (0) 0**                                    5656
*Oldham Ath:* Kelly; Redmond, Serrant, Rickers (McNiven S), Sinnott, Garnett (Hodgson), Orlygsson, Duxbury, Ritchie, Barlow, Reid.
*Grimsby T:* Davison; McDermott, Gallimore, Handyside, Lever, Widdrington (Jobling), Donovan, Black (Rodger), Livingstone (Woods), Nogan, Groves.

**Oxford U (1) 2** *(Purse 24, Logan 78 (og))*
**Plymouth Arg (0) 0**                                 5083
*Oxford U:* Whitehead; Remy, Ford M, Robinson, Purse, Gilchrist, Ford R, Smith, Banger (Aldridge), Jemson, Beauchamp.
*Plymouth Arg:* Sheffield; Collins (Wilson), Williams, Mauge, Heathcote, Wotton, Rowbotham, Logan, Littlejohn, Corazzin, Anthony.

**Port Vale (1) 1** *(Mills 24)*
**York C (1) 2** *(Bull 32, Bushell 90)*               2749
*Port Vale:* Musselwhite; Hill, Tankard, Talbot (Porter), Aspin, Glover, McCarthy, Corden, Mills, Naylor (Foyle), Jansson.
*York C:* Samways; McMillan, Hall, Bushell, Tutill, Barras, Campbell (Stephenson), Tinkler, Rowe (Tolson), Bull, Pouton.

**QPR (0) 0**
**Wolverhampton W (1) 2** *(Froggatt 13, Paatelainen 36)*
                                                       8355
*QPR:* Harper; Perry (Graham), Brevett (Brazier), Barker, Rose, Morrow, Spencer, Peacock, Murray, Gallen (Slade), Sinclair.
*Wolverhampton W:* Stowell; Smith, Kubicki, Atkins, Sedgley, Curle, Keane (Paatelainen), Ferguson, Bull, Goodman, Froggatt.

**Reading (0) 2** *(Lambert 58, Roach 75)*
**Swansea C (0) 0**                                    4829
*Reading:* Mautone; Booty, Swales, Wdowczyk, McPherson, Primus, Bernal, Houghton (Holsgrove), Asaba, Hodges (Roach), Lambert.
*Swansea C:* Freestone; Price, Moreira, Walker, Edwards, Coates, Lacey, O'Gorman (Appleby), Bird, Ampadu, Puttnam (Jones G).

**Rochdale (0) 1** *(Painter 32)*
**Stoke C (1) 3** *(Kavanagh 26, Thorne 67, Forsyth 70)* 2509
*Rochdale:* Key; Fensome, Barlow, Hill, Farrell, Gouck, Bailey, Painter, Leonard, Carter, Stuart.
*Stoke C:* Muggleton; Pickering, Nyamah, Sigurdsson, Tweed, Keen, Forsyth, Wallace, Thorne, Stewart (Sturridge) (McMahon), Kavanagh.

**Rotherham U (0) 1** *(Richardson 77)*
**Preston NE (0) 3** *(Makin 54, Reeves 59, 61)*       2901
*Rotherham U:* Pettinger; Clark, Hurst, Thompson, Knill, Richardson, Berry, Goodwin, Druce (Bos), Glover, Roscoe.
*Preston NE:* Moilanen; Parkinson, Kidd, Murdock (Barrick), Jackson, Gregan, Cartwright (Appleton), Ashcroft, Reeves, Makin (Nogan), Rankine.

**Scarborough (0) 0**
**Scunthorpe U (1) 2** *(Calvo-Garcia 20, 73)*         1907
*Scarborough:* Martin; Kay, Sutherland, Bennett G (Mitchell), McIlhatton, Atkin, Van der Velden (Bennett T), Snodin, Worrall (Robinson), Brodie.
*Scunthorpe U:* Clarke; Walsh, Neil, Sertori, Wilcox, Hope, Walker, D'Auria (Stamp), Housham, Forrester, Calvo-Garcia.

**Tranmere R (0) 3** *(Jones L 57, Morrissey 70, Kelly 89)*
**Hartlepool U (1) 1** *(Howard 15)*                   3878
*Tranmere R:* Coyne; Stevens, Thompson, McGreal, Thorn, O'Brien (Irons), Morrissey, Cook (Morgan), Kelly, Jones G, Jones L.
*Hartlepool U:* Davis K; Knowles, Lucas, Ingram, Davies, Bradley, Allon (Halliday), Cullen, Baker, Beech, Howard.

**Walsall (0) 2** *(Platt 58, Boli 71)*
**Exeter C (0) 0**                                     2321
*Walsall:* Walker; Evans, Keates, Viveash, Mountfield, Donowa, Boli, Keister, Platt, Porter, Hodge.
*Exeter C:* Bayes; Gale, Cyrus, Curran, Blake, Richardson, Rowbotham, Minett, Flack, Gardner, McConnell (Fry).

**Wigan Ath (0) 1** *(Lee 50)*
**Chesterfield (0) 2** *(Willis 67, 82)*               3413
*Wigan Ath:* Butler L; Green, Johnson (Black), Greenall, McGibbon, Sharp, Lee, Lowe (Lancashire), O'Connell, Rogers, Kilford.
*Chesterfield:* Mercer; Hewitt, Holland, Curtis, Williams, Breckin, Willis, Beaumont, Lormor, Ebdon, Perkins.

**Wrexham (0) 1** *(Connolly 67 (pen))*
**Sheffield U (0) 1** *(Borbokis 63)*                  3644
*Wrexham:* Marriott; McGregor, Brace, Phillips, Jones B, Carey, Skinner, Russell, Connolly, Spink (Watkin), Ward.
*Sheffield U:* Tracey; Borbokis, Quinn (Nilsen), McGrath, Tiler, Holdsworth, Patterson, Parker, Fjortoft (Taylor), Deane, Whitehouse.

**Wycombe W (1) 1** *(Read 41)*
**Fulham (1) 2** *(Newhouse 28, Conroy 72)*            4360
*Wycombe W:* Taylor; Cornforth, Brown, Kavanagh, McCarthy, Forsyth, Carroll, Read, Stallard, McGavin (Parkin), Simpson.
*Fulham:* Walton; Lawrence, Herrera, Cullip, Smith, Cockerill, Newhouse (Scott), Hayward, Conroy (Moody), Morgan, Carpenter (McAree).

**13 AUG**

**Brighton & HA (0) 1** *(Minton 77 (pen))*
**Leyton Orient (1) 1** *(Griffiths 39)*               1073
*Brighton & HA:* Ormerod; Humphrey, Hobson, Minton, Morris, Johnson, Storer, Mayo, Reinelt, Maskell, McDonald (Westcott).
*Leyton Orient:* Hyde; Channing, Naylor, Smith, Hicks, Joseph, Ling, Warren, McGleish, West, Griffiths (Richards).
*at Gillingham.*

**Charlton Ath (0) 0**
**Ipswich T (1) 1** *(Venus 15)*                       6598
*Charlton Ath:* Petterson; Brown (Nicholls), Barness, Jones K, Rufus, Balmer, Newton, Kinsella, Robinson (Bright), Mendonca, Jones S.
*Ipswich T:* Wright; Stockwell, Taricco, Williams, Venus, Cundy, Dyer, Holland, Petta (Gregory), Scowcroft, Mason.

**Swindon T (0) 0**
**Watford (1) 2** *(Noel-Williams 12, Rosenthal 63)*   6271
*Swindon T:* Digby; Darras, Drysdale, Leitch, Seagraves (Walters), McDonald, Robinson, Cuervo, Finney (Cowe), Allison, Gooden.
*Watford:* Chamberlain; Gibbs, Kennedy, Page, Millen, Mooney, Noel-Williams, Hyde, Lee, Johnson R, Slater (Rosenthal).

**FIRST ROUND, SECOND LEG**

**26 AUG**

**Barnet (0) 3** *(Heald 68, Devine 69, 80)*
**Norwich C (0) 1** *(Roberts 46)* 2846
*Barnet:* Harrison; Stockley (Goodhind), Harle, Heald, Howarth, Ford (Mustafa), Manuel (Onwere), Simpson, Charley, Devine, Wilson.
*Norwich C:* Marshall; Segura, Newman, Grant, Sutch, Polston, Adams, Fleck (O'Neill), Roberts, Milligan, Eadie.
*Barnet won 4-3 on aggregate.*

**Birmingham C (0) 3** *(Furlong 68, Devlin 75, Ndlovu 78)*
**Gillingham (0) 0** 7921
*Birmingham C:* Bennett; Wassall, Grainger, Bruce (Johnson), Ablett, Holland, Devlin, Hey, Furlong, Hughes, Ndlovu (Francis).
*Gillingham:* Moss; Ratcliffe, Butters, Smith, Ashby, Bryant (Green), Hessenthaler, Galloway, Butler (Piper), Akinbiyi, Chapman (Corbett).
*Birmingham C won 4-0 on aggregate.*

**Bradford C (1) 1** *(Edinho 6)*
**Huddersfield T (0) 1** *(Burnett 77)* 8065
*Bradford C:* Zabica; Wilder, Jacobs, Beagrie, Youds, Dreyer, Lawrence (Sundgot), Pepper (Ramage), Steiner (Blake), Edinho, Murray.
*Huddersfield T:* Francis; Jenkins, Ryan, Dyson, Morrison, Browning, Baldry, Makel, Stewart, Dyer, Burnett.
*Huddersfield T won 3-2 on aggregate.*

**Bristol R (0) 1** *(Alsop 48)*
**Bristol C (0) 2** *(Taylor 59, Bent 118)* 5872
*Bristol R:* Collett; Perry, Pritchard, Bennett, Gayle, Tillson, Holloway, Penrice, Alsop (Beadle), Cureton (Lockwood), Hayles.
*Bristol C:* Welch; Locke, Bell, Paterson (Carey), Taylor, Edwards, Hewlett, Owers, Goater, Cramb (Bent), Tinnion.
*aet; Bristol C won 2-1 on aggregate.*

**Burnley (2) 2** *(Cooke 1, Eyres 16 (pen))*
**Lincoln C (1) 1** *(Ainsworth 25)* 4644
*Burnley:* Beresford; Huxford, Winstanley, Waddle, Blatherwick, Howey, Weller, Matthew, Cooke, Barnes, Eyres.
*Lincoln C:* Vaughan; Barnett, Whitney, Hone, Holmes, Chandler, Ainsworth, Miller, Stant (Fleming), Thorpe, Alcide.
*Burnley won 3-2 on aggregate.*

**Bury (2) 3** *(Gray 33, Johnson 35, Battersby 114 (pen))*
**Crewe Alex (2) 3** *(Rivers 22, Smith 36, Butler 90 (og))* 3296
*Bury:* Kiely; West, Armstrong (Hughes), Daws, Lucketti, Butler, Gray, Johnson (Randall), Jepson (Battersby), Johnrose, Swan.
*Crewe Alex:* Bankole; Rivers, Smith, Westwood, Lightfoot, Charnock, Whalley (Collins), Lunt (Adebola), Anthrobus, Johnson, Moralee (Garvey).
*aet; Bury won 6-5 on aggregate.*

**Carlisle U (2) 3** *(Walling 21, Jansen 38, 70)*
**Chester C (0) 0** 4208
*Carlisle U:* Caig; Couzens, Archdeacon, Walling, Varty, Pounewatchy, Barr (Milligan), Prokas, McAlindon, Aspinall (Dobie), Jansen (Boertien).
*Chester C:* Sinclair; Davidson, Jenkins, Fisher, Whelan, Alsford, Bennett (Milner), Richardson (Woods), McDonald, Flitcroft, Thomas (Murphy).
*Carlisle won 5-1 on aggregate.*

**Chesterfield (0) 1** *(Lormor 78)*
**Wigan Ath (0) 0** 4076
*Chesterfield:* Mercer; Hewitt, Jules (Beaumont), Curtis, Williams, Carr, Willis, Holland, Lormor, Ebdon, Perkins.
*Wigan Ath:* Carroll; Green, Johnson, Greenall, McGibbon, Martinez (Sharp), Lee, Jones (Saville), O'Connell, Rogers (Kilford), Lowe.
*Chesterfield won 3-1 on aggregate.*

**Exeter C (0) 0**
**Walsall (0) 1** *(Boli 50)* 2467
*Exeter C:* Bayes; Gale (Fry), Cyrus, Blake, Curran, Richardson, Rowbotham, Birch (Minett), Flack, Gardner, Braithwaite (Hare).
*Walsall:* Walker; Evans, Ryder, Viveash, Mountfield (Keates), Peron, Boli, Keister, Watson, Porter, Blake.
*Walsall won 3-0 on aggregate.*

**Fulham (3) 4** *(Newhouse 5, 41, Carpenter 24, Conroy 65)*
**Wycombe W (1) 4** *(Ryan 29, Scott 49, 81, Harkin 61)* 5055
*Fulham:* Walton; Lawrence, Herrera, Cullip, Smith, Brooker (McAree), Newhouse (Scott), Hayward, Conroy, Morgan, Carpenter (Cockerill).
*Wycombe W:* Taylor; Carroll (McGavin), Ryan (Brown), Kavanagh, McCarthy, Forsyth, Cornforth (Stallard), Scott, Read, Harkin, Simpson.
*Fulham won 6-5 on aggregate.*

**Grimsby T (3) 5** *(Lester 3, 6, 11, Livingstone 56, Donovan 79)*
**Oldham Ath (0) 0** 5078
*Grimsby T:* Davison; McDermott, Jobling, Handyside, Lever, Southall (Widdrington), Donovan, Gilbert, Nogan (Livingstone), Lester (Woods), Groves.
*Oldham Ath:* Ironside; Redmond, Serrant, Hughes (Hodgson), Graham, Garnett, McNiven S, Duxbury (Allott), McCarthy, Barlow, Reid.
*Grimsby won 5-1 on aggregate.*

**Hartlepool U (1) 2** *(Baker 24, Lee 75)*
**Tranmere R (1) 1** *(O'Brien 45)* 1626
*Hartlepool U:* Dobson; Knowles, Lucas, Ingram, Lee, Bradley, Barron, Cullen, Baker, Halliday, Howard.
*Tranmere R:* Coyne; Stevens, Thompson, McGreal, Thorn, O'Brien, Morrissey (Branch), Cook (Irons), Kelly, Jones G, Jones L.
*Tranmere R won 4-3 on aggregate.*

**Hull C (1) 2** *(Peacock 14, Joyce 117)*
**Macclesfield T (1) 1** *(Mason 42)* 3300
*Hull C:* Thomson; Dickinson (Mann), Doncel (Joyce), Brien, Wright, Dewhurst, Peacock, Rioch, Darby, Hateley, Hodges (Brown).
*Macclesfield T:* Price; Tinson, Rose, Payne, Howarth, Sodje, Askey, Wood (Mitchell), Landon (Power), Mason, Sorvel.
*aet; Hull C won 2-1 on aggregate.*

**Ipswich T (2) 3** *(Stein 31, Brown 45 (og), Scowcroft 61)*
**Charlton Ath (0) 1** *(Mendonca 88)* 10,989
*Ipswich T:* Wright; Stockwell, Taricco, Williams, Venus, Cundy, Dyer, Holland, Stein (Sonner), Scowcroft, Milton (Kerslake).
*Charlton Ath:* Petterson; Brown, Konchesky (Lisbie), Nicholls (Stuart), Chapple, Balmer, Newton, Kinsella, Robinson, Mendonca, Jones S (Bright).
*Ipswich T won 4-1 on aggregate.*

**Leyton Orient (1) 3** *(Griffiths 9, McGleish 73, Baker 89)*
**Brighton & HA (1) 1** *(Maskell 23)* 3690
*Leyton Orient:* Hyde; Joseph, Naylor, Smith, Hicks, Clark, Ling, Warren, Griffiths (Baker), McGleish, Richards.
*Brighton & HA:* Ormerod; Humphrey (Smith), Hobson, Minton (Westcott), Morris, Johnson, Storer, Mayo, Reinelt, Maskell, McDonald.
*Leyton Orient won 4-2 on aggregate.*

**Luton T (1) 1** *(Thorpe 34)*
**Colchester U (0) 1** *(Hathaway 52)* 2816
*Luton T:* Abbey; James, Thomas, Waddock, Davis S, Johnson, Davies (Douglas), McLaren, Oldfield, Thorpe, Marshall.
*Colchester U:* Emberson; Gregory, Stamps, Forbes, Greene, Cawley, Wilkins, Buckle, Sale, Abrahams (Adcock), Hathaway (Lock).
*Luton T won 2-1 on aggregate.*

**Manchester C (0) 1** *(Horlock 88)*
**Blackpool (0) 0**                                    12,563
*Manchester C:* Margetson; Brightwell, Vaughan, Wiekens, Symons, Summerbee, Brannan (McGoldrick), Horlock, Bradbury, Kinkladze (Dickov), Rosler (Van Blerk).
*Blackpool:* Banks; Bryan, Rogan, Butler, Linighan (Lydiate), Brabin, Bonner, Clarkson, Quinn (Malkin), Mellon, Preece (Ellis).
*aet; Blackpool won 4-2 on penalties.*

**Notts Co (1) 2** *(Baraclough 25 (pen), Hendon 103)*
**Darlington (0) 1** *(Naylor 90)*                    1925
*Notts Co:* Ward; Hendon, Pearce, Redmile, Strodder, Hogg, Finnan (Diuk), Richardson, White (Martindale), Jones, Baraclough.
*Darlington:* Preece; Gray, Barnard, Devos, Crosby, Hope (Turnbull), Oliver, Atkinson, Roberts, Shutt (Robinson), Lowe (Naylor).
*aet; Notts Co won 3-2 on aggregate.*

**Plymouth Arg (2) 3** *(Wilson 12, Logan 29, Smith 46 (og))*
**Oxford U (0) 5** *(Beauchamp 47, 88, Jemson 48, Purse 64, Murphy 74)*                               3037
*Plymouth Arg:* Sheffield; Billy, Williams, Wilson, Heathcote, Wotton, Rowbotham (Illman), Logan (Ashton), Littlejohn, Jean, Anthony.
*Oxford U:* Jackson; Remy, Marsh (Angel), Robinson, Purse, Wilsterman, Ford R, Smith, Aldridge (Murphy), Jemson, Beauchamp.
*Oxford U won 7-3 on aggregate.*

**Portsmouth (1) 1** *(Svensson 36)*
**Peterborough U (1) 2** *(Farrell 44, Quinn 56)*     6395
*Portsmouth:* Flahavan; Pethick, Thomson (Russell), McLoughlin, Whitbread, Perrett, Hall, Simpson, Aloisi (Turner), Svensson (Thorp), Hillier.
*Peterborough U:* Tyler; Linton, Lewis, Drury, Bodley, Edwards, Payne, Castle, Carruthers, Quinn, Farrell.
*Peterborough U won 4-3 on aggregate.*

**Preston NE (0) 2** *(Reeves 52, Makin 70)*
**Rotherham U (0) 0**                                 9441
*Preston NE:* Moilanen; Parkinson, Barrick, Appleton, Jackson, Kidd, Cartwright (Darby), Ashcroft, Reeves, Nogan (Makin), Rankine.
*Rotherham U:* Pettinger; Clark, Hurst, Bass, Knill (Goodwin), Richardson, Berry, Garner, Druce, Bos (Sedgwick), Roscoe.
*Preston NE won 5-1 on aggregate.*

**Scunthorpe U (1) 2** *(Calvo-Garcia 24, 61)*
**Scarborough (1) 1** *(Bennett G 6)*                 2149
*Scunthorpe U:* Clarke; Walsh, McAuley, Sertori, Wilcox, Hope, Walker, D'Auria, Eyre, Forrester, Calvo-Garcia (Shakespeare).
*Scarborough:* Martin; Kay, Sutherland (Atkin), Bennett G, McIlhatton, Rockett, Van der Velden, Bennett T, Robinson (Worrall), Brodie (Mitchell), Williams.
*Scunthorpe U won 4-1 on aggregate.*

**Sheffield U (1) 3** *(Deane 28, Whitehouse 74, Fjortoft 82)*
**Wrexham (1) 1** *(Spink 21)*                        7181
*Sheffield U:* Tracey; Borbokis, Quinn, White (Katchuro), Tiler, Holdsworth, Patterson, Marker, Fjortoft, Deane (Taylor), Whitehouse.
*Wrexham:* Marriott; McGregor, Brace, Phillips (Chalk), Jones B, Carey, Skinner, Brammer, Connolly, Spink, Ward.
*Sheffield U won 4-2 on aggregate.*

**Shrewsbury T (0) 3** *(Steele 55, 68, 82 (pen))*
**Brentford (3) 5** *(Rapley 15, 80, Taylor 30, 75, Bent 38)*
                                                      2136
*Shrewsbury T:* Edwards; Naylor, Hanmer, Wilding (Brown), Seabury (Berkley), Herbert, Taylor M (Nwadike), Jagielka, Steele, Evans, Scott.
*Brentford:* Dearden; Hurdle, Anderson, Hutchings (Goddard-Crawley), Bates, Barrowcliff, Denys, Canham, Bent (Wormull), Rapley, Taylor.
*Brentford won 6-4 on aggregate.*

**Southend U (2) 3** *(Williams 16, 18, Marsh 79)*
**Cardiff C (0) 1** *(Fowler 61)*                     3002
*Southend U:* Royce; Jones, Harris, Marsh, Roget, Dublin, Byrne, Beeston, Boere (Rammell), Williams (Hails), Clarke.
*Cardiff C:* Hallworth; Middleton (O'Sullivan), Beech, Young (Jarman), Harris (Lloyd), Fowler, Partridge, Stoker, Penney, White, Carss.
*Southend U won 4-2 on aggregate.*

**Stockport Co (2) 6** *(Dinning 28 (pen), Angell 45, Flynn 66, Armstrong 70, Mutch 88, Cooper 90)*
**Mansfield T (1) 3** *(Christie 14, Doolan 67, Ford 83)*  2840
*Stockport Co:* Gray; Connelly, Woodthorpe, Bennett (Cooper), Flynn, Gannon, Dinning, Marsden, Angell, Armstrong, Kalogeracus (Mutch).
*Mansfield T:* Bowling; Ford, Harper, Watkiss, Eustace, Jones, Schofield, Clarke, Christie, Whitehall, Doolan.
*Stockport Co won 8-7 on aggregate.*

**Swansea C (0) 1** *(Coates 49)*
**Reading (0) 1** *(Asaba 54)*                        3333
*Swansea C:* Freestone; Price, Moreira (Harris), Walker, Edwards, Coates, Appleby, O'Gorman, Bird, Ampadu, Puttnam.
*Reading:* Mautone; Booty, Bodin, Meaker (Roach), McPherson, Primus, Bernal, Houghton, Asaba, Hodges (Williams), Lambert.
*Reading won 3-1 on aggregate.*

**Torquay U (0) 1** *(Jack 116)*
**Bournemouth (1) 1** *(Rolling 25)*                  2278
*Torquay U:* Gregg; Gurney, Gibbs, Robinson, Gittens, Watson, Clayton, Mitchell, Jack, McFarlane, Hill (McCall).
*Bournemouth:* Glass; Young, Vincent, Rolling, Cox, Bailey, Beardsmore, Robinson, O'Neill (Harrington), Fletcher (Brissett), Rawlinson (Howe).
*aet; Torquay U won 2-1 on aggregate.*

**Watford (1) 1** *(Hyde 16)*
**Swindon T (0) 1** *(Leitch 58)*                     7712
*Watford:* Chamberlain; Melvang, Kennedy, Page, Millen (Palmer), Mooney, Noel-Williams, Hyde, Rosenthal (Andrews), Johnson R, Slater.
*Swindon T:* Talia; Darras, Drysdale, Leitch, Seagraves, McDonald, Walters, Cuervo, Hay, Allison, Gooden.
*Watford won 3-1 on aggregate.*

**York C (1) 1** *(Barras 37)*
**Port Vale (0) 1** *(Mills 89)*                      3195
*York C:* Samways; McMillan, Hall, Bushell, Reed, Barras, Stephenson, Tinkler, Rowe (Cresswell), Bull, Pouton (Greening).
*Port Vale:* Musselwhite; Hill, Tankard, Talbot, Aspin, Stokes, McCarthy, Bogie (Jansson), Mills, Naylor, Corden (Foyle).
*York C won 3-2 on aggregate.*

## 27 AUG

**Millwall (0) 2** *(Hockton 51, 61)*
**Northampton T (0) 1** *(Gayle 90)*                  4364
*Millwall:* Carter; Brown, Sturgess, Bowry, Law, McLeary, Allen, Newman, Hockton (Webber), Grant, Savage.
*Northampton T:* Woodman; Clarkson, Frain, Sampson, Warburton (Gibb), Brightwell, Parrish, Conway (Heggs), Seal, Gayle, Hunter.
*aet; Millwall won 2-0 on penalties.*

**Nottingham F (1) 2** *(Guinan 5, Van Hooijdonk 57)*
**Doncaster R (0) 1** *(Armstrong 72 (og))*           9908
*Nottingham F:* Fettis; Lyttle, Rogers, Armstrong, Thom, Bart-Williams (Woan), Howe, Johnson (Warner), Van Hooijdonk (Moore), Guinan, Allen.
*Doncaster R:* Ingham; Finley, Sanders, David Esdaille (Ramsay), Gore, Brookes, Cunningham, McDonald, Mike, Moncrieffe (Pemberton), Smith (Ireland).
*Nottingham F won 10-1 on aggregate.*

**Stoke C (0) 1** *(Kavanagh 85)*
**Rochdale (0) 1** *(Russell 90)*    12,768
*Stoke C:* Muggleton; Pickering, Griffin, Sigurdsson, Tweed (Whittle), Keen, Forsyth, Wallace (Schreuder), Thorne, Stewart, Kavanagh.
*Rochdale:* Key; Fensome, Bayliss, Hill, Farrell, Gouck, Russell, Painter, Leonard (Carter), Bailey (Smith), Stuart.
*Stoke C won 4-2 on aggregate.*

**WBA (0) 2** *(Hunt 86, Sneekes 103 (pen))*
**Cambridge U (1) 1** *(Butler 13)*    10,264
*WBA:* Spink; Holmes (Hughes) (Dobson), Nicholson, Sneekes, Mardon, Raven, Flynn (Hamilton), Butler, Peschisolido, Hunt, Kilbane.
*Cambridge U:* Barrett; Chenery, Wilson (Benjamin), Marc Joseph, Foster, Campbell, Wanless, Rees, Kyd (Matt Joseph), Butler, Williamson (Taylor).
*aet; WBA won 3-2 on aggregate.*

**Wolverhampton W (0) 1** *(Ferguson 62 (pen))*
**QPR (1) 2** *(Peacock 36, Murray 66)*    18,398
*Wolverhampton W:* Stowell; Smith, Kubicki, Atkins, Sedgley, Robinson, Paatelainen, Ferguson, Bull, Goodman, Froggatt.
*QPR:* Harper; Rose, Brevett, Barker, Maddix, Morrow, Perry, Peacock, Murray, Slade (Gallen), Sinclair.
*Wolverhampton W won 3-2 on aggregate.*

## SECOND ROUND, FIRST LEG

### 16 SEPT

**Blackpool (0) 1** *(Linighan 76)*
**Coventry C (0) 0**    5884
*Blackpool:* Banks; Bryan, Bradshaw, Lydiate, Linighan, Philpott, Bonner, Mellon, Quinn, Ellis, Preece (Malkin).
*Coventry C:* Ogrizovic; Nilsson, Burrows, Williams, Shaw, Soltvedt (Hall), Telfer (Breen), Johansen, Lightbourne, McAllister, Salako.

**Burnley (0) 0**
**Stoke C (1) 4** *(Thorne 37, 62, Kavanagh 68, 80)*    4175
*Burnley:* Beresford; Weller, Brass, Williams, Blatherwick, Moore, Matthew (Waddle), Ford, Howey (Little), Barnes, Eyres.
*Stoke C:* Muggleton; Pickering, Griffin, Sigurdsson, Tweed, Keen, Forsyth, Wallace (MacKenzie), Thorne, Andrade (Whittle), Kavanagh.

**Chesterfield (0) 1** *(Lormor 58 (pen))*
**Barnsley (0) 2** *(Redfearn 87 (pen), Ward 90)*    6318
*Chesterfield:* Mercer; Hewitt, Jules, Curtis, Williams, Breckin, Willis, Holland, Lormor, Howard, Beaumont.
*Barnsley:* Leese; Eaden (Appleby), Barnard, Shirtliff, Moses, Sheridan, Tinkler, Redfearn, Hristov (Ten-Heuvel), Ward, Krizan.

**Fulham (0) 0**
**Wolverhampton W (1) 1** *(Garcia Sanjuan 34)*    5933
*Fulham:* Arendse; Lawrence, Herrera, Cullip, Smith (Brooker), Cusack, Newhouse (Scott), Hayward, Moody, Morgan, Carpenter.
*Wolverhampton W:* Stowell; Smith, Kubicki, Atkins, Westwood, Robinson, Keane, Ferguson, Bull (Foley), Paatelainen, Froggatt (Garcia Sanjuan).

**Huddersfield T (0) 1** *(Dyer 75)*
**West Ham U (0) 0**    8525
*Huddersfield T:* Francis; Jenkins, Martin (Baldry), Dyson, Gray, Edmondson, Dalton (Hurst), Makel, Stewart, Dyer, Burnett.
*West Ham U:* Miklosko; Breacker, Hughes, Unsworth, Ferdinand, Potts, Lampard, Berkovic, Kitson (Dowie), Hartson, Lomas.

**Hull C (1) 1** *(Darby 22)*
**Crystal Palace (0) 0**    9323
*Hull C:* Thomson; Wright, Dewhurst, Bryan, Doncel, Lowthorpe, Peacock, Joyce, Darby (Quigley), Hateley (Fewings), Mann.
*Crystal Palace:* Miller; Hreidarsson, Gordon, Roberts, Tuttle, Linighan (Dyer), Muscat, Zohar, Shipperley, Freedman, Fullarton (Veart).

**Ipswich T (0) 1** *(Stockwell 89)*
**Torquay U (1) 1** *(McFarlane 1)*    8031
*Ipswich T:* Wright; Stockwell, Taricco, Williams, Venus, Swailes (Petta), Dyer, Holland, Stein, Scowcroft, Sonner (Mathie).
*Torquay U:* Gregg; Gurney, Gibbs, Robinson, Gittens, Watson (Thomas), Clayton, Hill, Jack, McFarlane, McCall (Barrow).

**Leyton Orient (1) 1** *(Inglethorpe 42)*
**Bolton W (2) 3** *(Todd 13, Frandsen 20, McGinlay 79)*    4128
*Leyton Orient:* Hyde; Channing, Naylor, Smith, Hicks (Richards), Clark, Ling, Warren, Griffiths, McLeish, Inglethorpe.
*Bolton W:* Branagan; McAnespie, Todd, Frandsen, Bergsson (Phillips), Strong, Pollock, Sellars (Johansen), Blake, McGinlay, Thompson.

**Luton T (1) 1** *(Douglas 25)*
**WBA (1) 1** *(Taylor 35)*    3437
*Luton T:* Dibble; Alexander, Harvey, Waddock, Davis S, Johnson (Davies), Evers (George), McLaren, Oldfield, Douglas, Marshall.
*WBA:* Miller; Holmes, Smith, Sneekes, Burgess, Raven, Coldicott, Hamilton, Taylor, Hunt, Kilbane.

**Middlesbrough (0) 1** *(Freestone 56)*
**Barnet (0) 0**    9611
*Middlesbrough:* Roberts; Fleming, Kinder (Liddle), Vickers, Festa, Emerson, Ormerod, Mustoe, Beck, Freestone, Campbell (Moore).
*Barnet:* Harrison; Stockley, Harle, Heald, Howarth, Ford, Goodhind, Simpson, Charlery, Devine (Samuels), Onwere.

**Notts Co (0) 0**
**Tranmere R (1) 2** *(Jones G 31, Kelly 60)*    1779
*Notts Co:* Ward; Hendon, Pearce (Cunnington), Redmile, Strodder, Baraclough, Finnan (Derry), Robinson, White (Dudley), Martindale, Otto.
*Tranmere R:* Coyne; Stevens, Thompson, McGreal, Thorne, O'Brien (Mahon), Morrissey (Branch), Cook, Kelly, Jones G (Irons), Jones L.

**Oxford U (0) 4** *(Robinson 53, Aldridge 62, Beauchamp 77, 81)*
**York C (1) 1** *(Rowe 43)*    2923
*Oxford U:* Jackson; Remy, Angel, Robinson, Purse, Gilchrist, Ford R, Smith, Aldridge (Banger), Jemson, Beauchamp.
*York C:* Samways; McMillan, Hall, Bushell, Tinkler, Barras, Murty, Pouton, Rowe (Bull), Tolson, Stephenson.

**Reading (0) 0**
**Peterborough U (0) 0**    5138
*Reading:* Mautone; Bernal (Booty), Swales, Roach (Houghton), McPherson, Primus, Parkinson, Hodges, Asaba, Meaker (Williams), Lambert.
*Peterborough U:* Tyler; McMenamin, Lewis, Payne, Bodley, Edwards, Farrell, Castle, Carruthers, Quinn, Houghton (Bullimore).

**Scunthorpe U (0) 0**
**Everton (1) 1** *(Farrelly 36)*    7145
*Scunthorpe U:* Clarke; Housham, McAuley, Sertori, Eyre, Hope, Walker, D'Auria, Laws, Forrester, Calvo-Garcia.
*Everton:* Gerrard; Short, Hinchcliffe, Williams, Watson, Bilic, Stuart, Farrelly, Ferguson, Oster (Cadamarteri), Speed.

**Southend U (0) 0**

**Derby Co (1) 1** *(Wanchope 43)* 4011

*Southend U:* Royce; Harris, Jones, Marsh, Roget (Rammell), Hails, Byrne (Lewis), Gridelet, Boere, Beeston (Williams), Clarke.
*Derby Co:* Poom; Elliott, Powell C, Powell D (Trollope), Dailly, Rowett, Wanchope, Van der Laan, Sturridge, Kozluk, Hunt (Simpson).

**Sunderland (1) 2** *(Williams 44, Bridges 56)*

**Bury (1) 1** *(Daws 43)* 18,775

*Sunderland:* Perez; Makin, Scott, Bracewell, Ball, Craddock, Johnston, Williams, Bridges (Rae), Russell, Gray.
*Bury:* Kiely; Hughes (Woodward), Armstrong, Daws, Lucketti, Butler, Randall (Linighan), Johnson, Jepson, Johnrose, Battersby.

**Watford (0) 1** *(Kennedy 89)*

**Sheffield U (1) 1** *(Scott 19)* 7154

*Watford:* Chamberlain; Gibbs, Kennedy, Page, Palmer, Mooney, Noel-Williams (Andrews), Hyde, Lee, Johnson R, Rosenthal.
*Sheffield U:* Kelly; Borbokis, Quinn, Nilsen, Tiler, Holdsworth, Patterson, Scott (Hutchison), Taylor, Katchuro (Beard), Whitehouse.

**Wimbledon (2) 5** *(Cort 23 (pen), 79, Clarke 44, Euell 56, Castledine 86)*

**Millwall (1) 1** *(Savage 16)* 6949

*Wimbledon:* Heald; Cunningham, Thatcher, Hughes C, McAllister, Perry, Jupp (Jones), Castledine, Clarke (Gayle), Cort, Euell (Holdsworth).
*Millwall:* Carter; Brown, Sturgess, Bowry, Law, McLeary, Allen, Newman, Hockton, Shaw, Savage.

**17 SEPT**

**Birmingham C (1) 4** *(Hughes 41, Robinson 51, Devlin 77 (pen), 87)*

**Stockport Co (0) 1** *(Angell 90)* 4900

*Birmingham C:* Bennett; Bass, Grainger, Wassall, Ablett, Holland, Devlin, Robinson, Furlong (Francis), Hughes, Ndlovu (Johnson).
*Stockport Co:* Nixon; Connelly, Woodthorpe, Bennett, McIntosh, Dinning, Gannon (Durkan), Marsden, Angell, Mutch (Travis), Cooper.

**Blackburn R (2) 6** *(Dahlin 26, 54, Sutton 29, Gallacher 78, Andersson 84, Bohinen 89)*

**Preston NE (0) 0** 22,564

*Blackburn R:* Flowers; Pedersen T, Kenna, Sherwood, Broomes, Croft, Duff (Gallacher), Dahlin, Sutton (Pedersen P), Andersson (Flitcroft), Bohinen.
*Preston NE:* Moilanen; Parkinson, Barrick, Kidd, Jackson, Gregan, Cartwright, Ashcroft, Reeves, Darby, Rankine (Macken).

**Grimsby T (1) 2** *(Groves 17, Livingstone 52)*

**Sheffield W (0) 0** 6429

*Grimsby T:* Pearcey; McDermott, Gallimore, Handyside, Lever, Widdrington, Donovan, Black, Nogan (Lester), Livingstone, Groves.
*Sheffield W:* Pressman; Atherton, Nolan, Pembridge, Newsome, Walker, Whittingham, Magilton, Clough, Collins (Briscoe), Di Canio.

**Leeds U (1) 3** *(Wetherall 20, Hasselbaink 70 (pen), Riberio 90)*

**Bristol C (0) 1** *(Goater 77)* 8806

*Leeds U:* Martyn; Halle, Robertson, Kelly, Radebe, Wetherall, Hopkin, Wallace, Hasselbaink (Riberio), Kewell, Molenaar.
*Bristol C:* Welch; Carey, Bell, Paterson, Taylor, Tisdale, Hewlett, Owers, Goater (Goodridge), Torpey, Tinnion.

**Nottingham F (0) 0**

**Walsall (0) 1** *(Skinner 53)* 7841

*Nottingham F:* Beasant; Lyttle, Rogers, Hjelde, Chettle, Phillips (Saunders), Johnson, Gemmill (Armstrong), Van Hooijdonk, Campbell, Bart-Williams.
*Walsall:* Walker; Evans, Rogers, Viveash, Mountfield (Roper), Peron, Boli, Skinner, Keates (Thomas), Watson, Hodge.

**Southampton (1) 3** *(Monkou 37, Davies 60, Evans 69)*

**Brentford (0) 1** *(Taylor 65)* 8004

*Southampton:* Jones; Dodd, Benali, Richardson, Lundekvam, Monkou, Oakley, Johansen (Davies), Evans, Neilson, Williams.
*Brentford:* Dearden; Hurdle, Anderson, Hutchings, Bates, Barrowcliff (Goddard-Crawley), Denys, Canham, Bent, Rapley, Taylor.

**Tottenham (1) 3** *(Fenn 1, Fox 73, Mahorn 78)*

**Carlisle U (2) 2** *(Couzens 40, Aspinall 45)* 19,255

*Tottenham:* Walker; Clemence, Edinburgh, Scales, Campbell, Mabbutt, Ginola, Nielsen, Fenn (Mahorn), Fox, Dominguez.
*Carlisle U:* Caig; Harrison (Dobie), Archdeacon, Prokas, Varty, Pounewatchy, Barr, Couzens, McAlindon, Jansen, Aspinall.

## SECOND ROUND, SECOND LEG

**23 SEPT**

**Barnet (0) 0**

**Middlesbrough (1) 2** *(Beck 45, Merson 67 (pen))* 3968

*Barnet:* Harrison; Stockley, Harle, Heald, Howarth, Ford, Goodhind (Samuels), Onwere (Manuel), Simpson, Charlery, Devine.
*Middlesbrough:* Schwarzer; Liddle, Harrison, Baker, Festa, Emerson, Ormerod (Campbell), Mustoe, Beck, Merson, Townsend.
*Middlesbrough won 3-0 on aggregate.*

**Bury (0) 1** *(Johnson 65)*

**Sunderland (2) 2** *(Smith 12, Rae 33)* 3928

*Bury:* Kiely; Hughes, Woodward, Daws, Lucketti (Barrass), Butler (Linighan), Gray, Johnson, Jepson (Randall), Johnrose, Battersby.
*Sunderland:* Zoetebier; Makin, Scott, Bracewell, Byrne, Craddock, Agnew (Russell), Williams (Ball), Smith, Rae, Gray.
*Sunderland won 4-2 on aggregate.*

**Peterborough U (0) 0**

**Reading (0) 2** *(Asaba 51, Williams 70)* 6067

*Peterborough U:* Tyler; McMenamin, Lewis, Payne, Bodley, Edwards, Farrell, Castle (Cleaver), Carruthers, Quinn (De Souza), Houghton (Bullimore).
*Reading:* Mautone; Booty, Swales, Williams, McPherson, Primus, Parkinson, Hodges, Asaba (Roach), Houghton, Lambert.
*Reading won 2-0 on aggregate.*

**Sheffield U (1) 4** *(Day 18 (og), Whitehouse 49, 80, Deane 56)*

**Watford (0) 0** 7511

*Sheffield U:* Tracey; Borbokis (Short), Quinn, Scott, Tiler, Holdsworth, Patterson, Marker, Katchuro, Deane, Whitehouse.
*Watford:* Day; Gibbs, Kennedy, Page, Palmer, Mooney, Slater, Hyde, Lee, Johnson R, Rosenthal (Easton).
*Sheffield U won 5-1 on aggregate.*

**Stockport Co (1) 2** *(Armstrong 37, Mutch 87)*

**Birmingham C (0) 1** *(Furlong 70 (pen))* 2074

*Stockport Co:* Nixon; Connelly, Woodthorpe, Bennett, McIntosh, Dinning, Gannon, Marsden, Angell, Armstrong, Cooper (Mutch).
*Birmingham C:* Bennett; Bass, Grainger, Wassall, Ablett, O'Connor, Devlin (Francis), Robinson, Furlong, Hughes, Ndlovu (Johnson).
*Birmingham C won 5-3 on aggregate.*

**Torquay U (0) 0**
**Ipswich T (1) 3** *(Holland 22, 61, Dyer 90)* 3598
*Torquay U:* Gregg; Gurney, Gibbs, Robinson, Gittens, Watson, Clayton, Hill, Jack, McFarlane, Hapgood (Bedeau).
*Ipswich T:* Wright; Kerslake, Venus, Williams, Mowbray, Cundy, Dyer, Holland, Stein (Mathie), Scowcroft, Petta.
*Ipswich T won 4-1 on aggregate.*

**Tranmere R (0) 0**
**Notts Co (1) 1** *(Dudley 43)* 3287
*Tranmere R:* Coyne; Stevens, Thompson, McGreal, Challinor, O'Brien (Morgan), Morrissey (Mahon), Cook, Kelly, Jones G, Jones L (Branch).
*Notts Co:* Ward; Hendon, Baraclough, Redmile, Richardson, Cunnington (Hogg), Finnan, Derry, Farrell (Jones), Dudley (Stevens), Otto.
*Tranmere R won 2-1 on aggregate.*

**WBA (1) 4** *(Raven 40, McDermott 52, Peschisolido 67, 88)*
**Luton T (1) 2** *(Davis S 37, Thorpe 74)* 7227
*WBA:* Miller; McDermott, Smith, Sneekes, Burgess, Raven, Flynn, Hamilton, Taylor (Peschisolido), Hunt, Kilbane.
*Luton T:* Dibble; Evers, Harvey, Waddock, Davis S, White, Gray, McLaren, Oldfield, Douglas (Thorpe), Davies (George).
*WBA won 5-3 on aggregate.*

**York C (0) 1** *(Murty 62)*
**Oxford U (0) 2** *(Aldridge 89, Banger 90)* 1555
*York C:* Samways; McMillan, Hall, Bushell, Reed, Barras, Murty, Tinkler, Tolson, Bull, Stephenson (Pouton).
*Oxford U:* Jackson; Whelan, Marsh (Angel), Robinson, Purse, Gilchrist, Ford R, Smith (Massey) (Aldridge), Banger, Jemson, Beauchamp.
*Oxford U won 6-2 on aggregate.*

**24 SEPT**
**Stoke C (1) 2** *(Keen 36, Thorne 71)*
**Burnley (0) 0** 6041
*Stoke C:* Muggleton; Pickering, Griffin, Sigurdsson, Tweed (Whittle), Keen (Kavanagh), McMahon, Wallace (Schreuder), Thorne, Crowe, MacKenzie.
*Burnley:* Beresford; Brass, Vinnicombe, Matthew (Huxford), Gentile, Moore, Waddle (Weller), Creaney, Cooke (Little), Cowans, Eyres.
*Stoke C won 6-0 on aggregate.*

**Walsall (0) 2** *(Watson 113, 117)*
**Nottingham F (0) 2** *(Van Hooijdonk 48, Armstrong 91)* 6037
*Walsall:* Walker; Evans, Rogers (Platt), Viveash, Mountfield (Roper), Peron, Boli, Skinner (Porter), Keates, Watson, Hodge.
*Nottingham F:* Beasant; Lyttle, Rogers, Cooper, Chettle (Johnson), Armstrong, Saunders, Gemmill, Van Hooijdonk, Campbell, Bart-Williams.
*aet; Walsall won 3-2 on aggregate.*

**Wolverhampton W (0) 1** *(Goodman 89)*
**Fulham (0) 0** 17,862
*Wolverhampton W:* Stowell; Smith, Kubicki, Atkins (Westwood), Williams, Robinson, Keane, Ferguson, Bull (Goodman), Paatelainen, Garcia Sanjuan.
*Fulham:* Arendse; Carpenter (Scott), Herrera, McAree, Cullip, Lawrence, Cockerill (Newhouse), Hayward, Conroy, Morgan, Moody (Cusack).
*Wolverhampton W won 2-0 on aggregate.*

**29 SEPT**
**West Ham U (2) 3** *(Hartson 31, 45, 77)*
**Huddersfield T (0) 0** 16,137
*West Ham U:* Miklosko; Breacker, Impey (Potts), Unsworth, Ferdinand, Pearce, Lampard, Dowie, Hartson, Berkovic, Lomas.
*Huddersfield T:* Francis; Jenkins, Edmondson, Collins, Morrison, Gray, Edwards (Lawson), Makel (Burnett), Stewart, Payton, Dyer.
*West Ham U won 3-1 on aggregate.*

**30 SEPT**
**Barnsley (2) 4** *(Liddell 37, Redfearn 44, Sheridan 55, Hristov 84)*
**Chesterfield (0) 1** *(Lormor 59 (pen))* 8417
*Barnsley:* Leese; Appleby (Bullock), Barnard, Krizan, Moses, De Zeeuw, Tinkler, Redfearn (Marcelle), Ward, Liddell (Hristov), Sheridan.
*Chesterfield:* Mercer; Hewitt (Gaughan), Jules, Curtis, Williams, Breckin, Beaumont, Wilkinson (Jackson), Lormor, Howard, Perkins.
*Barnsley won 6-2 on aggregate.*

**Bolton W (2) 4** *(Blake 8, 35, McGinlay 65 (pen), Gunnlaugsson 66)*
**Leyton Orient (2) 4** *(Inglethorpe 7, Griffiths 17, Baker 55, Warren 90)* 6444
*Bolton W:* Ward; Phillips, Whitlow, Frandsen, McAnespie, Todd, Johansen (Gunnlaugsson) (Strong), Beardsley, Blake (McGinlay), Pollock, Thompson.
*Leyton Orient:* Hyde; Warren, Naylor, Smith, Hicks, Clark, Ling, Baker (Channing), Griffiths, Harris (Joseph), Inglethorpe (Colkin).
*Bolton W won 7-5 on aggregate.*

**Brentford (0) 0**
**Southampton (2) 2** *(Le Tissier 31, 44)* 3957
*Brentford:* Dearden; Hurdle, Anderson, Hutchings, Bates, Townley, Denys (Canham), McGhee, Bent, Rapley (Reina), Taylor.
*Southampton:* Jones; Oakley, Todd, Richardson, Lundekvam, Dryden, Le Tissier (Williams), Palmer, Davies, Evans, Neilson (Charlton).
*Southampton won 5-1 on aggregate.*

**Bristol C (1) 2** *(Goodridge 41, Taylor 61)*
**Leeds U (1) 1** *(Hasselbaink 8)* 10,857
*Bristol C:* Welch; Locke, Bell, Dyche, Taylor, Edwards, Goodridge, Owers, Torpey, Doherty (Barclay), Tinnion.
*Leeds U:* Martyn; Molenaar (Halle), Robertson, Kelly, Radebe, Wetherall, Hopkin, Wallace, Hasselbaink, Haaland (Lilley), Bowyer.
*Leeds U won 4-3 on aggregate.*

**Carlisle U (0) 0**
**Tottenham H (1) 2** *(Ginola 43 (pen), Armstrong 51)* 13,571
*Carlisle U:* Caig; Barr, Archdeacon, Prokas, Varty, Pounewatchy, Harrison, Couzens (Boertien), McAlindon (Dobie), Jansen, Aspinall.
*Tottenham H:* Walker; Carr, Campbell, Scales, Calderwood, Vega, Fox, Clemence, Armstrong, Ferdinand, Ginola (Dominguez).
*Tottenham H won 5-2 on aggregate.*

**Crystal Palace (0) 2** *(Veart 56, Ndah 77)*
**Hull C (1) 1** *(Wright 30)* 6407
*Crystal Palace:* Miller; Edworthy, Gordon, Hreidarsson, Linighan, Boxall (Ndah), Fullarton, Warhurst, Shipperley, Zohar (Freedman), Veart (Rodger).
*Hull C:* Wilson; Greaves (Fewings), Rioch, Hocking, Wright, Brien, Peacock, Joyce, Doncel (Quigley), Hateley, Bettney (Gordon).
*aet; Hull C won on away goals.*

**Preston NE (1) 1** *(Barrick 15)*
**Blackburn R (0) 0** 11,472
*Preston NE:* Moilanen; Parkinson, Kidd, Murdock, Jackson, Gregan (Cartwright), Appleton, Ashcroft (Reeves), Macken (Holt), Rankine, Barrick.
*Blackburn R:* Flowers; Valery, Croft, Beattie, Pedersen T, Coleman, McKinlay, Johnson (Duff), Pedersen P, Andersson, Wilcox.
*Blackburn R won 6-1 on aggregate.*

**1 OCT**
**Coventry C (0) 3** *(McAllister 61 (pen), 89 (pen), Dublin 70)*
**Blackpool (1) 1** *(Linighan 36)* 9565
*Coventry C:* Ogrizovic; Hall, Burrows, Williams (Soltvedt), Shaw, Breen, O'Neill, Lightbourne (Ducros), Dublin, McAllister, Boland.
*Blackpool:* Banks; Bryan, Bradshaw, Lydiate, Linighan, Clarkson, Bonner, Mellon, Preece, Ellis, Philpott.
*Coventry C won 3-2 on aggregate.*

**Derby Co (1) 5** *(Rowett 43, 57, Wanchope 60, Sturridge 64, Trollope 83)*
**Southend U (0) 0** 18,490
*Derby Co:* Hoult; Rowett (Hunt), Powell C, Laursen (Van der Laan), Elliott, Dailly, Wanchope (Simpson), Solis, Sturridge, Trollope, Asanovic.
*Southend U:* Royce; Hails, Jones, Dublin, Lewis, Marsh, Allen, Gridelet, Rammell, Thomson, Clarke.
*Derby Co won 6-0 on aggregate.*

**Everton (2) 5** *(Stuart 11, Oster 23, 67, Barmby 66, Cadamateri 69)*
**Scunthorpe U (0) 0** 11,562
*Everton:* Southall; Thomas, Hinchcliffe, Ball, Watson (Phelan), Bilic, Stuart, Grant (Barmby), Cadamateri, Oster, Speed.
*Scunthorpe U:* Evans; Housham, McAuley, Sertori, D'Auria (Laws), Hope, Walker, Shakespeare, Eyre (Marshall), Forrester, Calvo-Garcia (Wilcox).
*Everton won 6-0 on aggregate.*

**Millwall (0) 1** *(Shaw 90 (pen))*
**Wimbledon (2) 4** *(Euell 22, 43, Castledine 47, Gayle 50)* 3591
*Millwall:* Nurse; Brown, Sturgess (Hockton), Newman, Webber, Witter, Doyle, Roche, Wilkinson, Shaw, Grant.
*Wimbledon:* Heald; Cunningham, Thatcher, Fear, McAllister, Perry (Reeves), Hughes C, Castledine, Gayle (Ekoku), Euell, Clarke.
*Wimbledon won 9-2 on aggregate.*

**Sheffield W (1) 3** *(Davison 16 (og), Di Canio 64, 88)*
**Grimsby T (0) 2** *(Nogan 46, Groves 48)* 11,120
*Sheffield W:* Pressman; Nolan, Briscoe (Poric), Pembridge, Stefanovic, Walker, Whittingham, Magilton, Di Canio, Carbone, Collins (Humphreys).
*Grimsby T:* Davison; McDermott, Gallimore, Handyside, Lever, Widdrington, Donovan, Black, Nogan, Livingstone (Lester), Groves.
*Grimsby T won 4-3 on aggregate.*

**THIRD ROUND**

**14 OCT**

**Arsenal (0) 4** *(Boa Morte 62, 108, Platt 99 (pen), Mendez 113)*
**Birmingham C (1) 1** *(Hey 20)* 27,097
*Arsenal:* Manninger; Dixon (Crowe), Upson, Grimandi, Marshall, Vernazza, Platt, Boa Morte (Muntasser), Wreh, Hughes, Mendez.
*Birmingham C:* Bennett; Wassall, Grainger, Bruce (Johnson), Ablett, O'Connor, Devlin (Bass), Hey, Holland (Francis), Robinson, Ndlovu.

**Barnsley (1) 1** *(Liddell 26)*
**Southampton (1) 2** *(Le Tissier 15, Davies 88)* 9019
*Barnsley:* Watson; Eaden, Barnard, Sheridan, De Zeeuw, Krizan, Bullock, Redfearn (Hristov), Ward, Liddell (Marcelle), Thompson.
*Southampton:* Jones; Dodd, Charlton (Benali), Richardson, Monkou, Lundekvam, Le Tissier, Palmer, Ostenstad (Evans), Davies, Oakley (Slater).

**Bolton W (0) 2** *(Pollock 91, McAllister 94 (og))*
**Wimbledon (0) 0** 9875
*Bolton W:* Branagan; Bergsson, Whitlow, Frandsen, Taggart, Todd, Pollock, Beardsley, McGinlay (Gunlaugsson), Sellars, Thompson.

**Wimbledon:** Sullivan; Cunningham, Thatcher, Jones, McAllister, Perry, Euell (Kimble), Earle, Ekoku (Cort), Castledine, Gayle (Clarke).

**Grimsby T (0) 3** *(Jobling 68, Livingstone 72, 78)*
**Leicester C (1) 1** *(Marshall 17)* 7738
*Grimsby T:* Davison; Butterfield (Jobling), Gallimore, Handyside, Rodger, Widdrington, Donovan, Black (Livingstone), Nogan, Lester, Groves.
*Leicester C:* Keller; Savage, Guppy, Elliott, Walsh (McMahon), Watts (Wilson), Lennon, Campbell, Cottee, Marshall, Fenton.

**Ipswich T (2) 2** *(Mathie 13, Tarrico 45)*
**Manchester U (0) 0** 22,173
*Ipswich T:* Wright; Stockwell, Tarrico, Williams (Stein), Mowbray, Cundy, Dyer, Holland, Mathie, Dozzell, Petta (Milton).
*Manchester U:* Van der Gouw; Curtis, Neville P, May, Johnsen (Irwin), Mulryne (Nevland), McClair, Cruyff, Cole, Poborsky, Thornley (Scholes).

**Oxford U (0) 1** *(Beauchamp 76)*
**Tranmere R (1) 1** *(Kelly 34)* 3878
*Oxford U:* Van Heusden; Remy, Angel, Robinson, Purse, Gilchrist (Murphy), Ford R, Smith, Banger, Aldridge, Beauchamp.
*Tranmere R:* Coyne; Stevens, Thompson, McGreal (O'Brien), Challinor, Irons, Morrissey, Branch, Kelly, Jones G, Jones L (Mahon).
*aet; Oxford U won 6-5 on penalties.*

**Reading (2) 4** *(Williams 33 (og), Parkinson 34, Meaker 46, McPherson 54)*
**Wolverhampton W (1) 2** *(Bull 44, 57)* 11,080
*Reading:* Mautone; Bernal, Swales, Williams, McPherson, Primus, Parkinson, Lambert (Caskey), Asaba (Roach), Houghton (Wdowczyk), Meaker.
*Wolverhampton W:* Stowell; Smith, Naylor, Atkins, Williams, Curle, Robinson, Ferguson (Keane), Bull, Paatelainen, Garcia Sanjuan (Foley).

**Walsall (0) 2** *(Watson 56, Tiler 87 (og))*
**Sheffield U (0) 1** *(Borbokis 49)* 8239
*Walsall:* Walker; Evans, Marsh, Viveash, Mountfield, Peron, Boli, Skinner, Keates, Watson, Hodge.
*Sheffield U:* Tracey; Borbokis, Quinn, McGrath, Tiler, Holdsworth, Patterson, Marker, Katchuro (Fjortoft), Deane, Whitehouse.

**15 OCT**
**Chelsea (0) 1** *(Di Matteo 61)*
**Blackburn R (0) 1** *(McKinlay 47)* 18,671
*Chelsea:* Hitchcock; Clarke, Granville, Gullit (Lee), Leboeuf, Nicholls, Babayaro, Di Matteo, Vialli, Hughes M (Hampshire), Newton (Sinclair).
*Blackburn R:* Flowers; Valery, Croft, McKinlay (Sherwood), Hendry (Henchoz), Pedersen T, Dahlin, Andersson, Sutton, Flitcroft, Duff (Bohinen).
*aet; Chelsea won 4-1 on penalties.*

**Coventry C (2) 4** *(Hall 6, Salako 33, 59, Haworth 62)*
**Everton (1) 1** *(Barmby 16)* 10,087
*Coventry C:* Ogrizovic; Nilsson, Burrows, Williams, Shaw, Breen, Hall, Haworth, Lightbourne, McAllister, Salako (Boland).
*Everton:* Gerrard; Short, Hinchcliffe, Williamson, Watson (Ball), Bilic, Stuart, Barmby, Ferguson (Cadamarteri), Oster, Speed.

**Middlesbrough (0) 2** *(Campbell 58, Hignett 90)*
**Sunderland (0) 0** 26,451
*Middlesbrough:* Schwarzer; Fleming, Harrison, Festa, Whyte, Emerson, Stamp (Hignett), Mustoe, Campbell (Freestone), Merson, Townsend.
*Sunderland:* Zoetebier; Makin, Scott, Clark, Ball, Craddock, Johnston, Williams, Russell (Smith), Bridges (Byrne), Gray.

**Newcastle U (0) 2** *(Hamilton 47, Rush 83)*
**Hull C (0) 0** 35,856
*Newcastle U:* Hislop; Barton, Beresford (Watson), Albert, Peacock, Howey, Hamilton (Brayson), Ketsbaia, Rush, Barnes, Tomasson.
*Hull C:* Wilson; Hocking, Rioch, Greaves (Quigley), Wright, Brien, Joyce (Peacock), Rocastle, Bettney, Hateley, Fewings (Ellington).

**Stoke C (0) 1** *(Kavanagh 66 (pen))*
**Leeds U (0) 3** *(Kewell 69, Wallace 93, 105)* 16,203
*Stoke C:* Muggleton; Pickering, Griffin, Sigurdsson, Tweed, Keen, Forsyth, Wallace, McMahon (Crowe), Andrade (Nyamah), Kavanagh (Whittle).
*Leeds U:* Martyn; Halle, Robertson, Kelly, Radebe, Wetherall, Hopkin (Bowyer), Wallace, Kewell, Riberio (Lilley), Haaland.

**Tottenham H (1) 1** *(Ginola 22)*
**Derby Co (1) 2** *(Wanchope 27, 71)* 20,390
*Tottenham H:* Walker; Carr, Edinburgh, Vega (Calderwood), Campbell, Howells, Ginola, Fox, Armstrong, Sinton, Dominguez.
*Derby Co:* Poom; Kozluk, Powell C, Carsley, Dailly, Rowett, Wanchope (Hunt), Van der Laan, Sturridge (Solis), Burton, Trollope.

**WBA (0) 0**
**Liverpool (0) 2** *(Berger 52, Fowler 89)* 21,986
*WBA:* Miller; Holmes, Smith, Sneekes, Burgess, Raven (Dobson), Flynn (Butler), Hamilton, Taylor (Hughes), Peschisolido, Kilbane.
*Liverpool:* James; McAteer, Bjornebye, Kvarme, Carragher (Leonhardsen), Ruddock, McManaman, Riedle, Fowler, Thomas, Berger (Harkness).

**West Ham U (2) 3** *(Hartson 9, 81, Lampard 17)*
**Aston Villa (0) 0** 20,360
*West Ham U:* Forrest; Breacker (Rowland), Impey, Potts, Ferdinand, Unsworth, Lampard, Dowie (Bishop), Hartson, Berkovic, Lomas.
*Aston Villa:* Bosnich; Nelson (Charles), Wright, Southgate (Grayson), Ehiogu, Scimeca, Taylor, Draper, Milosevic (Curcic), Collymore, Yorke.

**FOURTH ROUND**

**18 NOV**
**Arsenal (0) 1** *(Bergkamp 99)*
**Coventry C (0) 0** 30,199
*Arsenal:* Manninger; Dixon, Upson, Platt, Bould, Keown, Parlour, Mendez (Marshall), Anelka (Wreh), Bergkamp, Hughes.
*Coventry C:* Ogrizovic; Nilsson, Burrows, Williams, Shaw, Breen, Telfer, Hall, Dublin, McAllister, Haworth (Huckerby).

**Derby Co (0) 0**
**Newcastle U (0) 1** *(Tomasson 72)* 27,364
*Derby Co:* Poom; Eranio, Powell C, Laursen, Dailly, Rowett, Wanchope, Sturridge, Baiano, Hunt (Solis), Carsley.
*Newcastle U:* Hislop; Barton (Peacock), Beresford (Hamilton), Watson, Pistone, Albert, Lee, Batty, Tomasson, Barnes, Gillespie.

**Leeds U (1) 2** *(Wetherall 16, Bowyer 54)*
**Reading (1) 3** *(Asaba 9, Williams 66, Morley 85)* 15,069
*Leeds U:* Martyn; Maybury, Robertson, Haaland (Molenaar), Radebe, Wetherall, Hopkin, Wallace, Hasselbaink (Lilley), Riberio, Bowyer.
*Reading:* Hammond; Bernal, Swales, Caskey (Hodges), McPherson, Primus, Parkinson, Asaba, Morley, Houghton, Williams.

**Liverpool (2) 3** *(Owen 28, 45 (pen), 57)*
**Grimsby T (0) 0** 28,515
*Liverpool:* James; Jones, Bjornebye, Kvarme, Matteo, Leonhardsen, McManaman, Ince, Owen, Riedle, Redknapp (Berger).
*Grimsby T:* Davison; McDermott, Gallimore, Handyside, Lever, Widdrington, Donovan, Black (Livingstone), Nogan, Lester (Southall), Groves (Jobling).

**Middlesbrough (1) 2** *(Summerbell 39, Hignett 115)*
**Bolton W (1) 1** *(Thompson 33)* 22,801
*Middlesbrough:* Schwarzer; Maddison (Ormerod), Harrison, Vickers, Festa, Emerson, Hignett, Summerbell, Beck, Merson, Campbell (Baker).
*Bolton W:* Branagan; Bergsson, Whitlow, Fish, Todd, Pollock (Johansen), Frandsen, Sellars (Gunnlaugsson), Blake, Beardsley, Thompson.

**Oxford U (0) 1** *(Beauchamp 66)*
**Ipswich T (0) 2** *(Dozzell 63, Mowbray 93)* 5723
*Oxford U:* Van Heusden; Gray, Ford M (Powell), Robinson, Purse, Gilchrist, Ford R, Smith, Banger (Murphy), Jemson, Beauchamp.
*Ipswich T:* Wright; Stockwell, Taricco, Williams, Mowbray, Cundy, Dyer, Holland, Mathie (Gregory), Dozzell, Legg.

**19 NOV**
**Chelsea (0) 2** *(Flo 61, Morris 118)*
**Southampton (0) 1** *(Davies 52)* 20,968
*Chelsea:* Hitchcock; Lambourde, Granville, Gullit (Lee), Clarke, Sinclair, Nicholls, Morris, Flo, Crittenden, Wise (Hughes M).
*Southampton:* Jones; Dodd, Benali, Richardson (Johansen), Lundekvam (Spedding), Monkou, Le Tissier, Palmer, Hirst (Williams), Davies, Oakley.

**West Ham U (2) 4** *(Lampard 15, 73, 74, Hartson 16)*
**Walsall (1) 1** *(Watson 45)* 17,463
*West Ham U:* Forrest; Breacker, Lomas, Unsworth, Ferdinand, Pearce, Moncur, Lampard, Hartson, Berkovic, Abou.
*Walsall:* Walker; Evans, Marsh (Ricketts), Viveash, Mountfield, Peron, Boli, Keister (Porter), Keates, Watson, Hodge.

**FIFTH ROUND**

**6 JAN**
**Reading (0) 0**
**Middlesbrough (0) 1** *(Hignett 90)* 13,072
*Reading:* Hammond; Booty, Swales, Lambert, Bernal, Davies, Parkinson, Hodges, Asaba, Morley, Williams (Bowen).
*Middlesbrough:* Schwarzer; Vickers, Kinder, Festa, Pearson, Mustoe, Hignett, Swalwell, Beck, Merson, Maddison.

**West Ham U (0) 1** *(Abou 75)*
**Arsenal (1) 2** *(Wright 25, Overmars 52)* 24,770
*West Ham U:* Forrest; Potts, Lazaridis, Unsworth, Ferdinand, Pearce (Rowland), Impey, Berkovic, Kitson (Abou), Hartson, Lampard.
*Arsenal:* Seaman; Grimandi, Winterburn, Vieira, Bould, Keown, Parlour, Wright (Wreh), Petit, Bergkamp, Overmars (Hughes).

**7 JAN**
**Ipswich T (1) 2** *(Taricco 45, Mathie 62)*
**Chelsea (2) 2** *(Flo 32, Le Saux 45)* 22,088
*Ipswich T:* Wright; Stockwell, Taricco, Williams, Mowbray, Venus (Tanner), Dyer, Holland, Mathie (Petta), Scowcroft, Cundy.
*Chelsea:* De Goey; Lambourde, Granville, Sinclair (Clarke), Leboeuf, Myers (Gullit), Wise, Matteo, Flo (Hughes M), Zola, Le Saux.
*aet; Chelsea won 4-1 on penalties.*

**Newcastle U (0) 0**
**Liverpool (0) 2** *(Owen 95, Fowler 103)*        33,207
*Newcastle U:* Hislop; Watson, Beresford, Albert (Tomasson), Peacock, Batty, Lee, Gillespie (Ketsbaia), Rush, Barnes, Hughes.
*Liverpool:* James; McAteer, Harkness, Babb, Matteo, Leonhardsen, McManaman, Ince, Fowler, Owen (Riedle), Redknapp.

### SEMI-FINAL FIRST LEG

**27 JAN**
**Liverpool (1) 2** *(Redknapp 31, Fowler 82)*
**Middlesbrough (1) 1** *(Merson 29)*        33,438
*Liverpool:* James; McAteer, Harkness (Riedle), Babb, Matteo, Leonhardsen, McManaman, Ince, Fowler, Owen, Redknapp.
*Middlesbrough:* Schwarzer; Maddison, Kinder, Vickers, Pearson, Mustoe, Hignett (Harrison), Townsend, Beck, Merson, Baker.

**28 JAN**
**Arsenal (1) 2** *(Overmars 23, Hughes 47)*
**Chelsea (0) 1** *(Hughes M 68)*        38,114
*Arsenal:* Manninger; Grimandi (Platt), Winterburn, Hughes, Bould, Adams, Parlour, Anelka, Petit, Bergkamp, Overmars.
*Chelsea:* De Goey; Petrescu (Charvet), Le Saux, Sinclair (Vialli), Clarke, Duberry, Gullit, Newton, Flo (Hughes M), Zola, Lambourde.

### SEMI-FINAL SECOND LEG

**18 FEB**
**Chelsea (1) 3** *(Hughes M 10, Di Matteo 51, Petrescu 53)*
**Arsenal (0) 1** *(Bergkamp 82 (pen))*        34,330
*Chelsea:* De Goey; Petrescu, Le Saux, Duberry, Clarke, Zola, Di Matteo, Vialli (Newton), Hughes M, Wise.
*Arsenal:* Manninger; Dixon, Winterburn (Hughes), Vieira, Grimandi, Adams, Parlour (Platt), Anelka, Petit, Bergkamp, Overmars.

**Middlesbrough (2) 2** *(Merson 2 (pen), Branca 4)*
**Liverpool (0) 0**        29,828
*Middlesbrough:* Schwarzer; Kinder, Festa, Vickers, Pearson, Mustoe, Hignett (Baker), Branca, Beck, Merson, Townsend.
*Liverpool:* James; Jones, Bjornebye, Harkness, Matteo (Leonhardsen), Carragher, McManaman, Ince, Fowler, Owen, Berger (Riedle).

### FINAL

**29 MAR**
**Chelsea (0) 2** *(Sinclair 95, Di Matteo 107)*
**Middlesbrough (0) 0**        77,698
*Chelsea:* De Goey; Petrescu (Clarke), Le Saux, Sinclair, Leboeuf, Duberry, Newton, Di Matteo, Zola, Hughes M (Flo), Wise.
*Middlesbrough:* Schwarzer; Festa, Kinder, Vickers, Pearson, Mustoe, Ricard (Gascoigne), Townsend, Branca, Merson, Maddison (Beck).
*Referee:* P. Jones (Loughborough)

# FOOTBALL LEAGUE COMPETITION ATTENDANCES

## LEAGUE CUP ATTENDANCES

| Season | Attendances | Games | Average |
|---|---|---|---|
| 1960/61 | 1,204,580 | 112 | 10,755 |
| 1961/62 | 1,030,534 | 104 | 9,909 |
| 1962/63 | 1,029,893 | 102 | 10,097 |
| 1963/64 | 945,265 | 104 | 9,089 |
| 1964/65 | 962,802 | 98 | 9,825 |
| 1965/66 | 1,205,876 | 106 | 11,376 |
| 1966/67 | 1,394,553 | 118 | 11,818 |
| 1967/68 | 1,671,326 | 110 | 15,194 |
| 1968/69 | 2,064,647 | 118 | 17,497 |
| 1969/70 | 2,299,819 | 122 | 18,851 |
| 1970/71 | 2,035,315 | 116 | 17,546 |
| 1971/72 | 2,397,154 | 123 | 19,489 |
| 1972/73 | 1,935,474 | 120 | 16,129 |
| 1973/74 | 1,722,629 | 132 | 13,050 |
| 1974/75 | 1,901,094 | 127 | 14,969 |
| 1975/76 | 1,841,735 | 140 | 13,155 |
| 1976/77 | 2,236,636 | 147 | 15,215 |
| 1977/78 | 2,038,295 | 148 | 13,772 |
| 1978/79 | 1,825,643 | 139 | 13,134 |
| 1979/80 | 2,322,866 | 169 | 13,745 |
| 1980/81 | 2,051,576 | 161 | 12,743 |
| 1981/82 | 1,880,682 | 161 | 11,681 |
| 1982/83 | 1,679,756 | 160 | 10,498 |
| 1983/84 | 1,900,491 | 168 | 11,312 |
| 1984/85 | 1,876,429 | 167 | 11,236 |
| 1985/86 | 1,579,916 | 163 | 9,693 |
| 1986/87 | 1,531,498 | 157 | 9,755 |
| 1987/88 | 1,539,253 | 158 | 9,742 |
| 1988/89 | 1,552,780 | 162 | 9,585 |
| 1989/90 | 1,836,916 | 168 | 10,934 |
| 1990/91 | 1,675,496 | 159 | 10,538 |
| 1991/92 | 1,622,337 | 164 | 9,892 |
| 1992/93 | 1,558,031 | 161 | 9,677 |
| 1993/94 | 1,744,120 | 163 | 10,700 |
| 1994/95 | 1,530,478 | 157 | 9,748 |
| 1995/96 | 1,776,060 | 162 | 10,963 |
| 1996/97 | 1,529,321 | 163 | 9,382 |

## COCA-COLA CUP 1997–98

| Round | Aggregate | Games | Average |
|---|---|---|---|
| One | 345,284 | 70 | 4,933 |
| Two | 396,247 | 50 | 7,925 |
| Three | 267,116 | 16 | 16,695 |
| Four | 168,821 | 8 | 21,103 |
| Five | 93,781 | 4 | 23,445 |
| Semi-finals | 135,350 | 4 | 33,838 |
| Final | 77,698 | 1 | 77,698 |
| Total | 1,484,297 | 153 | 9,701 |

## AUTO WINDSCREENS SHIELD 1997–98

| Round | Aggregate | Games | Average |
|---|---|---|---|
| One | 24,790 | 16 | 1,549 |
| Two | 36,649 | 16 | 2,291 |
| Area Quarter-finals | 31,377 | 8 | 3,922 |
| Area Semi-finals | 27,684 | 4 | 6,921 |
| Area finals | 31,280 | 4 | 7,820 |
| Final | 62,432 | 1 | 62,432 |
| Total | 214,212 | 49 | 4,372 |

# AUTO WINDSCREENS SHIELD 1997–98

## FIRST ROUND

### 6 DEC

**Shrewsbury T (0) 1** *(Wilding 76)*

**Hartlepool U (0) 2** *(Lee 70, Pederson 85)*     1130

*Shrewsbury T:* Edwards; Taylor M, Hanmer, Wilding, Scott, Herbert, Berkley, White, Steele, Evans, Brown.

*Hartlepool U:* Hollund; Knowles, Lucas, Barron, Lee, Bradley, Beech, Cullen, Pederson, Halliday, Howard.

### 8 DEC

**Bristol R (0) 1** *(Cureton 46)*

**Cambridge U (0) 0**     2386

*Bristol R:* Higgs; Pritchard, Basford, Holloway, Perry, Smith (Tillson), Low, Parmenter (Lockwood), Beadle, Alsop (Hayles), Cureton.

*Cambridge U:* Barrett; Williamson, Hayes, Ashbee, Matt Joseph, Campbell, Rees, Youngs (Barnwell-Edinboro), McCammon (Kyd), Butler, Rodosthenous (Preece).

### 9 DEC

**Barnet (0) 1** *(Wilson 89)*

**Walsall (1) 2** *(Blake 38, Boli 57)*     754

*Barnet:* Harrison; Stockley, Sawyers, Goodhind, Howarth, Basham, Searle, Simpson (Wilson), Devine, Charlery (McGleish), Onwere (Manuel).

*Walsall:* Walker; Evans (Platt), Marsh, Viveash, Ryder, Peron, Boli, Porter (Blake), Keates, Ricketts, Hodge.

**Cardiff C (0) 0**

**Millwall (1) 2** *(Shaw 37, Grant 65)*     1219

*Cardiff C:* Elliott; Harriott (Phillips), Rollo, Young, Jarman, Partridge (Earnshaw), O'Sullivan, Stoker, Crowe, White, Carss.

*Millwall:* Spink; Brown, Bircham, Fitzgerald, Law, Doyle, Black (Hockton), Grant, Savage, Shaw (Stevens), Neill (Allen).

**Carlisle U (0) 1** *(McAlindon 99)*

**Oldham Ath (0) 0**     1518

*Carlisle U:* Caig; Hopper, Boertien, Barr, Varty, Milligan (Couzens), Anthony, Prokas, Stevens (Dobie), Jansen (McAlindon), Wright.

*Oldham Ath:* Kelly; McNiven S, Innes, Graham, Boxall, Garnett, Hughes (Rush) (Tipton), Duxbury (Richardson), McCarthy, Allott, Salt.

*aet; Carlisle U won on sudden death.*

**Chesterfield (0) 0**

**Grimsby T (0) 1** *(Nogan 71)*     1128

*Chesterfield:* Mercer; Perkins, Jules, Lomas, Williams (Pearce), Carr, Willis (Lenagh), Wilkinson, Jackson, Ebdon (Curtis), Dunn.

*Grimsby T:* Davison; McDermott, Gallimore, Handyside, Rodger, Jobling (Butterfield), Donovan, Widdrington, Nogan (Lester), Livingstone (Clare), Groves.

**Doncaster R (0) 0**

**Rochdale (1) 1** *(Reed 39)*     580

*Doncaster R:* Davis; Sanders, Smith M, Warren, Gore, Mike, Ireland, Dobbin, Helliwell, Moncrieffe (Brookes), Cunningham.

*Rochdale:* Edwards; Fensome, Barlow, Reed, Pender, Gouck, Bailey, Painter, Leonard, Farrell, Bryson (Stuart).

**Fulham (1) 1** *(Moody 18)*

**Watford (0) 0**     3364

*Fulham:* Taylor; Lawrence, Watson, Carpenter, Coleman (McAnespie), Neilson, Smith (Thomas), Hayward, Scott, Moody, Trollope.

*Watford:* Day; Ljung, Robinson, Rooney, Palmer, Pluck, Lowndes, Talboys (Ward), Lee, Grieves, Easton.

**Gillingham (0) 0**

**Peterborough U (0) 1** *(Farrell 55)*     905

*Gillingham:* Stannard; Statham, Masters (Corbett), Smith (Akinbiyi), Ashby, Bryant, Hessenthaler (Green), Ratcliffe, Onuora, Butler, Southall.

*Peterborough U:* Tyler; Linton, Drury, Castle (Rowe), Foran, Edwards, Rennie, Payne, Carruthers (Quinn), Gregory, Farrell.

**Hull C (1) 2** *(Darby 29, Atkin 49 (og))*

**Scarborough (0) 1** *(Campbell 71)*     1518

*Hull C:* Wilson; Gage (Lowthorpe), Rioch, Dewhurst, Hocking, Joyce, Morley (Fewings), McGinty, Darby, Hodges (Ellington), Mann.

*Scarborough:* Rhodes; Kay, Heckingbottom, Bennett G, Atkin, Rockett, Williams, McElhatton (Mitchell), Robinson (Tate), Bennett T (Brodie), Campbell.

**Leyton Orient (0) 1** *(Inglethorpe 51)*

**Colchester U (0) 0**     933

*Leyton Orient:* Mackenzie; Channing, Naylor, Smith, Inglethorpe, Clark, Ling, Warren, Griffiths (Simpson), Harris (Hanson), Baker.

*Colchester U:* Emberson; Dunne, Stamps, Skelton, Haydon, Cawley, Buckle (Forbes), Gregory D, Sale, Adcock (Lock), Rankin (Duguid).

**Northampton T (0) 1** *(Heggs 82)*

**Plymouth Arg (0) 1** *(O'Hagan 69)*     2631

*Northampton T:* Turley; Potter, Frain, Hill (Colkin), Warburton (Heggs), Brightwell, Gibb, Hunt, Seal, Gayle (Freestone), Hunter.

*Plymouth Arg:* Sheffield; Rowbotham, Williams, Hodges, Saunders, Collins, Barlow, Logan, O'Hagan (Wotton), Corazzin (Jean), Billy.

*aet; Northampton T won 5-3 on penalties.*

**Preston NE (1) 3** *(Appleton 28, Eyres 61, 110)*
**Darlington (0) 2** *(Atkinson 74 (pen), Midgley 85)*
                                                      2703
*Preston NE:* Lucas; Parkinson, Barrick, Kidd, Jackson, Gregan, Appleton, Ashcroft, Lormor (Macken), Murdock (Darby), Eyres.
*Darlington:* Preece; Shaw, Barnard, Devos (Hope), Crosby, Atkinson, Oliver (Midgley), Gaughan, Roberts (Robinson), Davies, Naylor.
*aet; Preston NE won on sudden death.*

**Scunthorpe U (0) 2** *(Eyre 67 (pen), 84 (pen))*
**Chester C (0) 1** *(Flitcroft 75 (pen))*          813
*Scunthorpe U:* Clarke; Walsh, McAuley, Sertori, Wilcox, Hope, Walker, D'Auria, Eyre (Ormondroyd), Forrester, Shakespeare.
*Chester C:* Brown; Davidson, Jenkins, Richardson (Wright), Whelan, Alsford, Jones, Priest, Rimmer, Flitcroft, Fisher.

**Southend U (0) 0**
**Wycombe W (1) 1** *(Stallard 43)*                1577
*Southend U:* Royce; Coulbault, Stimson (Jones), Perkins, Lewis, Beard, N'Diaye, Nielsen, Boere, Rammell (Thomson), Clarke.
*Wycombe W:* Taylor; Cousins (Wraight), Kavanagh, Ryan, McCarthy, Forsyth, Carroll, Harkin, Stallard, McGavin (Scott), Brown.

**Wigan Ath (0) 2** *(Jones 73, 89 (pen))*
**Lincoln C (0) 0**                                1467
*Wigan Ath:* Carroll; Green (Kilford), Bishop, Greenall (Martinez), McGibbon, Morgan, Lee, Rogers, Jones, Smeets, Lowe (Warne).
*Lincoln C:* Vaughan; Barnett, Whitney, Hone, Holmes (Brown S), Austin, Robertson, Stones (Bimson), Gordon (Alcide), Thorpe, Smith.


**SECOND ROUND**

**6 JAN**

**Blackpool (0) 1** *(Clarkson 87)*
**York C (1) 1** *(Rowe 23)*                       1105
*Blackpool:* Banks; Bryan, Dixon, Butler, Linighan, Hughes, Bent, Clarkson, Ormerod, Reed (Philpott), Preece.
*York C:* Warrington; Murty (Atkinson), Hall, Bushell, Reed, Tinkler, Pouton, Jordan, Cresswell, Rowe (Alderson), Greening.
*aet; Blackpool won 10-9 on penalties.*

**Bournemouth (0) 2** *(Jones 47, Robinson 87 (pen))*
**Leyton Orient (0) 0**                            1732
*Bournemouth:* Glass; Young, Vincent, Howe, Cox, Dean (O'Neill), Teather, Robinson, Jones (Brissett), Fletcher, Warren.
*Leyton Orient:* Hyde; Channing, Naylor, Smith, Cooper, Bennett (Hanson), Pitcher, Joseph, Griffiths, Richards (Baker), Simpson (Harris).

**Bristol C (1) 1** *(Locke 15)*
**Millwall (0) 0**                                 2557
*Bristol C:* Welch; Locke, Bell, Owers, Taylor, Carey, Murray, Edwards (Hewlett), Goater (Cramb), Torpey, Tinnion.
*Millwall:* Spink; Brown (Sturgess), Bircham, Newman, Law, Fitzgerald, Veart (Hockton), Grant (Doyle), Wilkinson, Shaw, Allen.

**Carlisle U (3) 6** *(Anthony 23, Pounewatchy 38, Stevens 42, 51, Wright 73, 78)*
**Rochdale (0) 1** *(Stuart (55))*                 2350
*Carlisle U:* Caig; Delap (Hopper), Thorpe, Barr, Varty, Wallwork, Anthony (Couzens), Pounewatchy, Stevens, Jansen (McAlindon), Wright.
*Rochdale:* Bywater; Fensome, Bayliss, Reed, Pender, Farrell, Bailey, Painter, Lancashire (Russell), Bryson (Gouck), Stuart.

**Exeter C (0) 1** *(Illman 56)*
**Bristol R (2) 2** *(Bennett 19, Tillson 45)*     1851
*Exeter C:* Bayes; Gale, Medlin (Flack), Blake (Baddeley), Clark, Richardson, Illman, Devlin, Ghazghazi, Fry, Gardner (McConnell).
*Bristol R:* Collett; Smith, Basford, Zabek, Tillson, Foster, Hayfield, Lockwood, Bennett, Alsop (Beadle), Low (Hayles).

**Grimsby T (1) 1** *(Butterfield 16)*
**Hull C (0) 0**                                   4778
*Grimsby T:* Davison; McDermott (Bloomer), Gallimore, Handyside, Lever, Jobling, Butterfield (Chapman), Black, Woods (Wrack), Clare, Groves.
*Hull C:* Wilson; Hocking, Edwards, Dewhurst, Wright, Joyce, Bettney, Quigley (McGinty), Darby, Hodges (Lowthorpe), Mann.

**Hartlepool U (0) 1** *(Lee 70)*
**Scunthorpe U (1) 2** *(Calvo-Garcia 44, Housham 88)*
                                                   1491
*Hartlepool U:* Hollund; Knowles, Clark, Barron, Lee, Bradley, Beech, Cullen, Pederson, Halliday (Larsen), Howard.
*Scunthorpe U:* Clarke; Walsh, Housham, Sertori, Wilcox, Hope, Murphy, D'Auria, Eyre, Forrester (Ormondroyd), Calvo-Garcia.

**Swansea C (1) 1** *(Bound 40)*
**Peterborough U (0) 2** *(Houghton 77, Quinn 89)* 1179
*Swansea C:* Freestone; Lacey, Hartfield, O'Leary, Casey, Bound, Cusack, Jenkins, Bird, O'Gorman (Coates), Clode.
*Peterborough U:* Tyler; Linton, Drury, McMenamin (Castle), Rennie, Edwards, Houghton, Payne, Carruthers (Cleaver), Quinn, Farrell.

**Walsall (2) 5** *(Watson 18, Boli 38, 83, Keates 52, Allan 80 (og))*
**Brighton & HA (0) 0**                            2562
*Walsall:* Walker; Evans, Marsh, Viveash, Mountfield (Roper), Peron, Boli, Porter, Keates (Blake), Watson (Platt), Hodge.
*Brighton & HA:* Ormerod; Saul, Tuck (Mayo), Armstrong, Smith, Allan, Storer, Reinelt, Barker, Ansah (Westcott), Linger (McNally).

**7 JAN**

**Mansfield T (0) 1** *(Whitehall 78 (pen))*

**Wrexham (0) 0** 1325

*Mansfield T:* Bowling; Williams, Harper, Thom, Sedgemore, Ford (Walker), Schofield, Kerr (Christie), Peacock, Whitehall, Tallon.

*Wrexham:* Marriott; McGregor, Hardy, Brammer (Skinner), Ridler, Carey, Wainwright, Owen, Connolly (Roberts), Spink, Ward (Phillips).

**13 JAN**

**Fulham (1) 3** *(Thomas 2, 87, Freeman 88)*

**Wycombe W (1) 1** *(Harkin 38)* 4319

*Fulham:* Walton; McAnespie, Herrera, Maher (Arnott), Blake, Lawrence, Thomas, Brooker, Scott (McAree), Freeman, Hayward.

*Wycombe W:* Taylor; Kerslake (Wraight), Kavanagh, Ryan, Mohan, Simpson, Carroll (Cornforth), Harkin, Stallard, McGavin, Brown.

**Luton T (0) 2** *(Thorpe 52, Oldfield 81)*

**Brentford (0) 1** *(Townley 90)* 3106

*Luton T:* Feuer; Patterson, Thomas, Evers, Davis S, White, Allen C, Davies, Oldfield, Thorpe (George), Alexander (Waddock).

*Brentford:* Dearden; Gleghorn (Adams), Wormull, Canham, Bates, Denys, Townley, Rapley (Dennis), Scott, Aspinall (Clark), Taylor.

**Macclesfield T (0) 0**

**Preston NE (0) 1** *(Cartwright 48)* 1618

*Macclesfield T:* Price; Howarth, Edey, Payne, McDonald, Sodje, Askey (Sorvel), Wood, Chambers, Power (Landon), Whittaker.

*Preston NE:* Lucas; Parkinson, Barrick, Davey, Jackson, Kidd, Cartwright, Rankine, Lormor, Nogan (Holt), Eyres.

**Northampton T (1) 5** *(Freestone 28, 64, Frain 51, Heggs 67, 80)*

**Torquay U (0) 1** *(Gittens 73)* 2845

*Northampton T:* Turley; Clarkson, Frain, Hill, Gibb (Warner), Colkin, Hunt, Dozzell, Freestone, Heggs, Hunter.

*Torquay U:* Veysey; Mitchell (Gomm), Hill, Thomas, Gittens, Watson, Clayton (Hapgood), Leadbitter, Jack (Bedeau), Roberts, Tully.

**20 JAN**

**Wigan Ath (1) 3** *(Jones 19, 58, Lowe 90)*

**Rotherham U (0) 0** 1495

*Wigan Ath:* Butler; Sharp, Morgan, Greenall, Fitzhenry, Martinez, Lee, Rogers, Jones, Smeets (Mustoe), Lowe.

*Rotherham U:* Pettinger; Scott, Roscoe, Richardson (Hayward), Monington, Knill, Goodwin, Thompson, White (Druce), Taylor, Shuttleworth (Hudson).

**27 JAN**

**Burnley (1) 2** *(Little 22, Cooke 61)*

**Notts Co (0) 0** 2442

*Burnley:* Beresford; Weller, Winstanley, Hoyland, Blatherwick, Little, Robertson, Ford (Vinnicombe), Cooke, Payton, Smith.

*Notts Co:* Ward; Mitchell (Henshaw), Pearce, Redmile (Randall), Robinson, Baraclough (Diuk), Robson, Cunnington, Martindale, Jackson, Kiwomya.

**QUARTER-FINALS**

**27 JAN**

**Blackpool (1) 1** *(Preece 15)*

**Wigan Ath (0) 0** 1687

*Blackpool:* Banks; Bryan, Hills, Carlisle, Strong, Lydiate, Hughes, Clarkson, Ormerod (Malkin), Bent (Brabin), Preece.

*Wigan Ath:* Carroll; Green, Sharp, Greenall, Kilford, Martinez, Lee (Warne), Morgan, Jones, Smeets, Lowe.

**Bournemouth (0) 1** *(Vincent 80)*

**Bristol C (0) 0** 2124

*Bournemouth:* Glass; Young, Vincent, Howe, Cox, Bailey, O'Neill, Robinson, Warren (Teather), Fletcher, Brissett (Hayter).

*Bristol C:* Welch; Locke (Goodridge), Bell, Murray, Taylor, Carey, Hewlett, Owers (Goater), Torpey, Cramb, Tinnion.

**Fulham (0) 1** *(Lightbourne 62)*

**Luton T (1) 2** *(Marshall 21, Thorpe 90)* 5103

*Fulham:* Walton; McAnespie, Maher (Arnott), Carpenter, Blake, Lawrence, Freeman (Scott), Collins, Brooker, Thomas, Lightbourne.

*Luton T:* Davis K; Patterson, Harvey, Evers, Davis S, White, Allen, McLaren (Waddock), Oldfield, Davies, Marshall (Thorpe).

**Peterborough U (1) 2** *(Castle 7, Edwards 60)*

**Northampton T (1) 1** *(Sampson 24)* 5516

*Peterborough U:* Tyler; McMenamin, Drury, Rennie, Bodley, Edwards, Farrell, Castle, Carruthers, Quinn, Payne.

*Northampton T:* Turley; Hill (Warner), Frain, Sampson, Warburton, Brightwell, Hunt, Dozzell (Gayle), Freestone, Lee (Seal), Hunter.

**Preston NE (1) 1** *(Nogan 39)*

**Mansfield T (0) 0** 3609

*Preston NE:* Lucas; Parkinson, Kidd, Davey, Jackson, Gregan, Cartwright, Rankine, Lormor (Macken), Nogan, Eyres.

*Mansfield T:* Bowling; Williams (Clarke), Harper, Thom, Kerr, Ford (Eustace), Schofield, Sedgemore, Peacock, Whitehall, Tallon.

**Scunthorpe U (0) 0**

**Grimsby T (0) 2** *(Groves 85, Burnett 90)* 4596

*Scunthorpe U:* Clarke; Walsh, Marshall, Sertori, Wilcox, Hope, Walker, D'Auria, Phillips (Eyre), Forrester (Ormondroyd), Calvo-Garcia.

*Grimsby T:* Davison; McDermott, Gallimore, Handyside, Lever, Burnett, Donovan, Black (Jobling), Livingstone, Clare (Lester), Groves.

**28 JAN**

**Bristol R (0) 0**

**Walsall (0) 1** *(Boli 91)*                    4165

*Bristol R:* Higgs; Perry, Lockwood, Penrice, White T,
Foster, Holloway, Basford, Beadle (White D),
Cureton, Hayles.
*Walsall:* Walker; Evans, Marsh, Ryder, Roper,
Peron, Boli, Porter, Keates, Watson, Hodge.
*aet; Walsall won on sudden death.*

**3 FEB**

**Burnley (1) 4** *(Payton 18, Vinnicombe 61, Cooke 73,*
*Henderson 89)*

**Carlisle U (0) 1** *(Prokas 55)*                4573

*Burnley:* Beresford; Williams (Brass), Vinnicombe,
Harrison, Moore, Blatherwick, Hoyland, Ford,
Cooke, Payton (Henderson), Smith.
*Carlisle U:* Caig; Delap, Bowman (Couzens), Prokas,
Varty, Wallwork, Anthony, Pounewatchy, Stevens,
Dobie, McAlindon.

**NORTHERN SEMI-FINALS**

**17 FEB**

**Burnley (1) 1** *(Payton 39)*

**Preston NE (0) 0**                            10,079

*Burnley:* Beresford; Brass, Winstanley, Harrison
(Hoyland), Moore, Little, Blatherwick, Robertson,
Cooke, Payton (Henderson), Matthew (Ford).
*Preston NE:* Moilanen; Parkinson, Barrick,
Murdock, Jackson, Gregan, Cartwright, Ashcroft,
Mullin, Nogan (Macken), Appleton.

**Grimsby T (0) 1** *(Burnett 77)*

**Blackpool (0) 0**                             8027

*Grimsby T:* Davison; McDermott, Gallimore,
Handyside, Lever (Lester), Burnett, Donovan,
Smith, Nogan, Livingstone, Groves.
*Blackpool:* Banks; Bryan, Hills, Butler, Hughes,
Linighan (Brabin), Bonner, Clarkson, Ormerod
(Quinn), Bent, Preece.

**SOUTHERN SEMI-FINALS**

**17 FEB**

**Bournemouth (0) 1** *(Rolling 86)*

**Luton T (0) 0**                              5367

*Bournemouth:* Glass; Young, Rawlinson, Rolling,
Cox, Bailey, O'Neill, Robinson, Warren, Fletcher S,
Brissett.
*Luton T:* Feuer; Alexander, Thomas, Evers, White,
Patterson, Allen, McLaren, Oldfield, Marshall,
Davies (Gray).

**Peterborough U (0) 1** *(De Souza 57)*

**Walsall (0) 2** *(Boli 80, Ricketts 81)*         4199

*Peterborough U:* Tiler; McMenamin (Cleaver),
Drury, Rennie, Bodley, Edwards, Davies (Lewis),
Bullimore (Rowe), De Souza, Quinn, Farrell.
*Walsall:* Walker; Evans, Marsh, Viveash, Roper,
Peron, Boli, Blake, Keates, Watson, Hodge
(Ricketts).

**NORTHERN FINAL FIRST LEG**

**10 MAR**

**Grimsby T (0) 1** *(Groves 78)*

**Burnley (1) 1** *(Payton 23)*                  6064

*Grimsby T:* Davison; McDermott, Gallimore
(Handyside), Livingstone, Lever (Black), Burnett,
Donovan, Smith, Nogan (Lester), Clare, Groves.
*Burnley:* Woods; Brass, Winstanley, Harrison,
Moore, Little, Vinnicombe, Ford, Cooke, Payton
(Howey), Matthew (Robertson).

**SOUTHERN FINAL FIRST LEG**

**10 MAR**

**Walsall (0) 0**

**Bournemouth (2) 2** *(Rolling 13, Beardsmore 30)*  6017

*Walsall:* Walker; Evans, Marsh (Platt), Ryder,
Roper, Eydelie, Boli, Porter, Ricketts, Tholot,
Hodge.
*Bournemouth:* Glass; Young, Vincent, Rolling, Cox,
Bailey, O'Neill (Howe), Robinson, Stein, Fletcher S,
Beardsmore.

**NORTHERN FINAL SECOND LEG**

**17 MAR**

**Burnley (0) 0**

**Grimsby T (1) 2** *(Nogan 10, Donovan 57)*      10,257

*Burnley:* Woods; Brass, Winstanley, Robertson
(Henderson), Moore, Vinnicombe, Weller, Ford,
Cook, Payton, Smith.
*Grimsby T:* Davison; McDermott, Gallimore,
Handyside, Lever, Burnett, Donovan, Smith, Nogan,
Lester, Groves.

**SOUTHERN FINAL SECOND LEG**

**17 MAR**

**Bournemouth (0) 2** *(Evans 55 (og), Rolling 82)*

**Walsall (0) 3** *(Thomas 47, Boli 53, Tholot 80)*   8972

*Bournemouth:* Glass; Young, Vincent, Rolling, Cox,
Bailey, O'Neill (Howe), Robinson, Stein, Fletcher S,
Beardsmore.
*Walsall:* Walker; Evans, Keates, Viveash, Roper,
Peron (Hodge), Boli, Porter, Platt, Ricketts
(Tholot), Thomas.

**FINAL (at Wembley)**

**19 APR**

**Bournemouth (1) 1** *(Bailey 31)*

**Grimsby T (0) 2** *(Glass 75 (og), Burnett 112)*  62,432

*Bournemouth:* Glass; Young, Vincent, Howe, Cox,
Bailey, Beardsmore (O'Neill), Robinson, Stein,
Fletcher S, Warren (Brissett).
*Grimsby T:* Davison; McDermott, Gallimore
(Black), Handyside, Lever, Burnett, Donovan,
Smith, Nogan (Jobling), Clare (Livingstone),
Groves.
*Referee:* M. Pierce (Portsmouth)
*aet; Grimsby T won on sudden death.*

# FA CUP FINALS 1872–1998

| | | | |
|---|---|---|---|
| 1872 and 1874–92 | Kennington Oval | 1911 | Replay at Old Trafford |
| 1873 | Lillie Bridge | 1912 | Replay at Bramall Lane |
| 1886 | Replay at Derby (Racecourse Ground) | | |
| 1893 | Fallowfield, Manchester | 1915 | Old Trafford, Manchester |
| 1894 | Everton | 1920–22 | Stamford Bridge |
| 1895–1914 | Crystal Palace | 1923 to date | Wembley |
| 1901 | Replay at Bolton | 1970 | Replay at Old Trafford |
| 1910 | Replay at Everton | | |

| Year | Winners | Runners-up | Score |
|---|---|---|---|
| 1872 | Wanderers | Royal Engineers | 1-0 |
| 1873 | Wanderers | Oxford University | 2-0 |
| 1874 | Oxford University | Royal Engineers | 2-0 |
| 1875 | Royal Engineers | Old Etonians | 2-0 (after 1-1 draw aet) |
| 1876 | Wanderers | Old Etonians | 3-0 (after 1-1 draw aet) |
| 1877 | Wanderers | Oxford University | 2-1 (aet) |
| 1878 | Wanderers* | Royal Engineers | 3-1 |
| 1879 | Old Etonians | Clapham R | 1-0 |
| 1880 | Clapham R | Oxford University | 1-0 |
| 1881 | Old Carthusians | Old Etonians | 3-0 |
| 1882 | Old Etonians | Blackburn R | 1-0 |
| 1883 | Blackburn Olympic | Old Etonians | 2-1 (aet) |
| 1884 | Blackburn R | Queen's Park, Glasgow | 2-1 |
| 1885 | Blackburn R | Queen's Park, Glasgow | 2-0 |
| 1886 | Blackburn R† | WBA | 2-0 (after 0-0 draw) |
| 1887 | Aston Villa | WBA | 2-0 |
| 1888 | WBA | Preston NE | 2-1 |
| 1889 | Preston NE | Wolverhampton W | 3-0 |
| 1890 | Blackburn R | Sheffield W | 6-1 |
| 1891 | Blackburn R | Notts Co | 3-1 |
| 1892 | WBA | Aston Villa | 3-0 |
| 1893 | Wolverhampton W | Everton | 1-0 |
| 1894 | Notts Co | Bolton W | 4-1 |
| 1895 | Aston Villa | WBA | 1-0 |
| 1896 | Sheffield W | Wolverhampton W | 2-1 |
| 1897 | Aston Villa | Everton | 3-2 |
| 1898 | Nottingham F | Derby Co | 3-1 |
| 1899 | Sheffield U | Derby Co | 4-1 |
| 1900 | Bury | Southampton | 4-0 |
| 1901 | Tottenham H | Sheffield U | 3-1 (after 2-2 draw) |
| 1902 | Sheffield U | Southampton | 2-1 (after 1-1 draw) |
| 1903 | Bury | Derby Co | 6-0 |
| 1904 | Manchester C | Bolton W | 1-0 |
| 1905 | Aston Villa | Newcastle U | 2-0 |
| 1906 | Everton | Newcastle U | 1-0 |
| 1907 | Sheffield W | Everton | 2-1 |
| 1908 | Wolverhampton W | Newcastle U | 3-1 |
| 1909 | Manchester U | Bristol C | 1-0 |
| 1910 | Newcastle U | Barnsley | 2-0 (after 1-1 draw) |
| 1911 | Bradford C | Newcastle U | 1-0 (after 0-0 draw) |
| 1912 | Barnsley | WBA | 1-0 (aet, after 0-0 draw) |
| 1913 | Aston Villa | Sunderland | 1-0 |
| 1914 | Burnley | Liverpool | 1-0 |
| 1915 | Sheffield U | Chelsea | 3-0 |
| 1920 | Aston Villa | Huddersfield T | 1-0 (aet) |
| 1921 | Tottenham H | Wolverhampton W | 1-0 |
| 1922 | Huddersfield T | Preston NE | 1-0 |
| 1923 | Bolton W | West Ham U | 2-0 |
| 1924 | Newcastle U | Aston Villa | 2-0 |
| 1925 | Sheffield U | Cardiff C | 1-0 |
| 1926 | Bolton W | Manchester C | 1-0 |
| 1927 | Cardiff C | Arsenal | 1-0 |
| 1928 | Blackburn R | Huddersfield T | 3-1 |
| 1929 | Bolton W | Portsmouth | 2-0 |
| 1930 | Arsenal | Huddersfield T | 2-0 |
| 1931 | WBA | Birmingham | 2-1 |
| 1932 | Newcastle U | Arsenal | 2-1 |
| 1933 | Everton | Manchester C | 3-0 |
| 1934 | Manchester C | Portsmouth | 2-1 |
| 1935 | Sheffield W | WBA | 4-2 |
| 1936 | Arsenal | Sheffield U | 1-0 |
| 1937 | Sunderland | Preston NE | 3-1 |
| 1938 | Preston NE | Huddersfield T | 1-0 (aet) |
| 1939 | Portsmouth | Wolverhampton W | 4-1 |
| 1946 | Derby Co | Charlton Ath | 4-1 (aet) |
| 1947 | Charlton Ath | Burnley | 1-0 (aet) |
| 1948 | Manchester U | Blackpool | 4-2 |
| 1949 | Wolverhampton W | Leicester C | 3-1 |
| 1950 | Arsenal | Liverpool | 2-0 |
| 1951 | Newcastle U | Blackpool | 2-0 |
| 1952 | Newcastle U | Arsenal | 1-0 |

| Year | Winners | Runners-up | Score |
|------|---------|-----------|-------|
| 1953 | Blackpool | Bolton W | 4-3 |
| 1954 | WBA | Preston NE | 3-2 |
| 1955 | Newcastle U | Manchester C | 3-1 |
| 1956 | Manchester C | Birmingham C | 3-1 |
| 1957 | Aston Villa | Manchester U | 2-1 |
| 1958 | Bolton W | Manchester U | 2-0 |
| 1959 | Nottingham F | Luton T | 2-1 |
| 1960 | Wolverhampton W | Blackburn R | 3-0 |
| 1961 | Tottenham H | Leicester C | 2-0 |
| 1962 | Tottenham H | Burnley | 3-1 |
| 1963 | Manchester U | Leicester C | 3-1 |
| 1964 | West Ham U | Preston NE | 3-2 |
| 1965 | Liverpool | Leeds U | 2-1 (aet) |
| 1966 | Everton | Sheffield W | 3-2 |
| 1967 | Tottenham H | Chelsea | 2-1 |
| 1968 | WBA | Everton | 1-0 (aet) |
| 1969 | Manchester U | Leicester C | 1-0 |
| 1970 | Chelsea | Leeds U | 2-1 (aet) |
| | *(after 2-2 draw, after extra time, at Wembley)* | | |
| 1971 | Arsenal | Liverpool | 2-1 (aet) |
| 1972 | Leeds U | Arsenal | 1-0 |
| 1973 | Sunderland | Leeds U | 1-0 |
| 1974 | Liverpool | Newcastle U | 3-0 |
| 1975 | West Ham U | Fulham | 2-0 |
| 1976 | Southampton | Manchester U | 1-0 |
| 1977 | Manchester U | Liverpool | 2-1 |
| 1978 | Ipswich T | Arsenal | 1-0 |
| 1979 | Arsenal | Manchester U | 3-2 |
| 1980 | West Ham U | Arsenal | 1-0 |
| 1981 | Tottenham H | Manchester C | 3-2 |
| | *(after 1-1 draw, after extra time, at Wembley)* | | |
| 1982 | Tottenham H | QPR | 1-0 |
| | *(after 1-1 draw, after extra time, at Wembley)* | | |
| 1983 | Manchester U | Brighton & HA | 4-0 |
| | *(after 2-2 draw, after extra time, at Wembley)* | | |
| 1984 | Everton | Watford | 2-0 |
| 1985 | Manchester U | Everton | 1-0 (aet) |
| 1986 | Liverpool | Everton | 3-1 |
| 1987 | Coventry C | Tottenham H | 3-2 (aet) |
| 1988 | Wimbledon | Liverpool | 1-0 |
| 1989 | Liverpool | Everton | 3-2 (aet) |
| 1990 | Manchester U | Crystal Palace | 1-0 |
| | *(after 3-3 draw, after extra time, at Wembley)* | | |
| 1991 | Tottenham H | Nottingham F | 2-1 (aet) |
| 1992 | Liverpool | Sunderland | 2-0 |
| 1993 | Arsenal | Sheffield W | 2-1 (aet) |
| | *(after 1-1 draw, after extra time, at Wembley)* | | |
| 1994 | Manchester U | Chelsea | 4-0 |
| 1995 | Everton | Manchester U | 1-0 |
| 1996 | Manchester U | Liverpool | 1-0 |
| 1997 | Chelsea | Middlesbrough | 2-0 |
| 1998 | Arsenal | Newcastle U | 2-0 |

\* *Won outright, but restored to the Football Association.*
† *A special trophy was awarded for third consecutive win.*

## FA CUP WINS

Manchester U 9, Tottenham H 8, Arsenal 7, Aston Villa 7, Blackburn R 6, Newcastle U 6, Everton 5, Liverpool 5, The Wanderers 5, WBA 5, Bolton W 4, Manchester C 4, Sheffield U 4, Wolverhampton W 4, Sheffield W 3, West Ham U 3, Bury 2, Chelsea 2, Nottingham F 2, Old Etonians 2, Preston NE 2, Sunderland 2, Barnsley 1, Blackburn Olympic 1, Blackpool 1, Bradford C 1, Burnley 1, Cardiff C 1, Charlton Ath 1, Clapham R 1, Coventry C 1, Derby Co 1, Huddersfield T 1, Ipswich T 1, Leeds U 1, Notts Co 1, Old Carthusians 1, Oxford University 1, Portsmouth 1, Royal Engineers 1, Southampton 1, Wimbledon 1.

## APPEARANCES IN FINALS

Manchester U 14, Arsenal 13, Everton 12, Newcastle U 12, Liverpool 11, Newcastle U 12, WBA 10, Aston Villa 9, Tottenham H 9, Blackburn R 8, Manchester C 8, Wolverhampton W 8, Bolton W 7, Preston NE 7, Old Etonians 6, Sheffield U 6, Sheffield W 6, Chelsea 5, Huddersfield T 5, *The Wanderers 5, Derby Co 4, Leeds U 4, Leicester C 4, Oxford University 4, Royal Engineers 4, Sunderland 4, West Ham U 4, Blackpool 3, Burnley 3, Nottingham F 3, Portsmouth 3, Southampton 3, Barnsley 2, Birmingham C 2, *Bury 2, Cardiff C 2, Charlton Ath 2, Clapham R 2, Notts Co 2, Queen's Park (Glasgow) 2, *Blackburn Olympic 1, *Bradford C 1, Brighton & HA 1, Bristol C 1, *Coventry C 1, Crystal Palace 1, Fulham 1, *Ipswich T 1, Luton T 4, Middlesbrough 1, *Old Carthusians 1, QPR 1, Watford 1, *Wimbledon 1.
  \* *Denotes undefeated.*

## APPEARANCES IN SEMI-FINALS

Everton 23, Manchester U 21, Liverpool 20, Arsenal 19, WBA 19, Aston Villa 18, Blackburn R 16, Sheffield W 16, Tottenham H 15, Newcastle U 14, Wolverhampton W 14, Chelsea 13, Derby Co 13, Bolton W 12, Nottingham F 12, Sheffield U 12, Sunderland 11, Manchester C 10, Preston NE 10, Southampton 10, Birmingham C 9, Burnley 8, Leeds U 8, Leicester C 8, Huddersfield T 7, Old Etonians 6, Oxford University 6, West Ham U 6, Fulham 5, Notts Co 5, Portsmouth 5, The Wanderers 5, Luton T 4, Queen's Park (Glasgow) 4, Royal Engineers 4, Blackpool 3, Cardiff C 3, Clapham R 3, Crystal Palace (professional club) 3, Ipswich T 3, Millwall 3, Norwich C 3, Old Carthusians 3, Oldham Ath 3, Stoke C 3, The Swifts 3, Watford 3, Barnsley 2, Blackburn Olympic 2, Bristol C 2, Bury 2, Charlton Ath 2, Grimsby T 2, Swansea T 2, Swindon T 2, Wimbledon 2, Bradford C 1, Brighton & HA 1, Cambridge University 1, Chesterfield 1, Coventry C 1, Crewe Alex 1, Crystal Palace (amateur club) 1, Darwen 1, Derby Junction 1, Glasgow R 1, Hull C 1, Marlow 1, Old Harrovians 1, Middlesbrough 1, Orient 1, Plymouth Arg 1, Port Vale 1, QPR 1, Reading 1, Shropshire W 1, York C 1.

# FA CUP 1997–98

## SPONSORED BY LITTLEWOODS POOLS

## PRELIMINARY AND QUALIFYING ROUNDS

**PRELIMINARY ROUND**

| | |
|---|---|
| Atherton Collieries v Maine Road | 1-2 |
| Billingham Synthonia v Brandon United | 1-1, 5-2 |
| Skelmersdale United v Pickering Town | 3-2 |
| Harrogate Railway v South Shields | 2-3 |
| Matlock Town v Curzon Ashton | 3-1 |
| Bedlington Terriers v Glapwell | 6-1 |
| Blackpool (Wren) Rovers v Burscough | 1-4 |
| Seaham Red Star v Ossett Town | 1-1, 0-1 |
| Denaby United v West Auckland Town | 3-1 |
| Droylsden v Cheadle Town | 4-1 |
| Blidworth MW v Rossendale United | 3-5 |
| Buxton v Ilkeston Town | 0-1 |
| Tow Law Town v RTM Newcastle | 1-2 |
| Peterlee Newtown v Warrington Town | 1-2 |
| Pontefract Collieries v Ossett Albion | 2-2, 3-0 |
| Arnold Town v Shildon | 3-1 |
| Billingham Town v Brodsworth | 3-0 |
| Maltby Main v Shotton Comrades | 0-1 |
| Kidsgrove Athletic v Whitley Bay | 1-1, 3-3 |
| *Whitley Bay won 5-3 on penalties* | |
| Netherfield v Chadderton | 1-1, 2-1 |
| Chester-le-Street Town v Ryhope CA | 0-2 |
| Congleton Town v Darwen | 1-1, 3-4 |
| St Helens Town v Sheffield | 3-1 |
| Great Harwood Town v Stockton | 2-1 |
| Louth United v Glasshoughton Welfare | 1-0 |
| Belper Town v Glossop North End | 2-2, 2-1 |
| Bootle v Bradford Park Avenue | 3-1 |
| Parkgate v Nantwich Town | 2-0 |
| Eccleshill United v Thackley | 1-1, 2-0 |
| Evenwood Town v Durham City | 0-3 |
| Crook Town v Mossley | 0-2 |
| Gretna v Haslingden | 4-2 |
| Tadcaster Albion v Stocksbridge Park Steels | 0-3 |
| Liversedge v Willington | 3-0 |
| Morpeth Town v Horden CW | 5-0 |
| Atherton LR v Hucknall Town | 0-1 |
| Brigg Town v Eastwood Town | 1-0 |
| Oldham Town v Northallerton | 4-2 |
| Guisborough Town v Worksop Town | 2-3 |
| Hebburn v Garforth Town | 0-5 |
| Borrowash Victoria v Jarrow Roofing Boldon CA | 1-2 |
| Castleton Gabriels v Clitheroe | 0-1 |
| Selby Town v Lincoln United | 1-3 |
| Flixton v Staveley MW | 2-3 |
| Hatfield Main v Dunston FB | 2-3 |
| Penrith v Trafford | 3-0 |
| Heanor Town v Salford City | 1-2 |
| *abandoned after 57 minutes; waterlogged pitch,* 1-0 | |
| Yorkshire Amateur v Easington Colliery | 1-4 |
| Harrogate Town v Armthorpe Welfare | 1-1, 3-1 |
| Fakenham Town v Stourbridge | 0-1 |
| Eynesbury Rovers v Pershore Town | 1-2 |
| Stratford Town v Desborough Town | 1-3 |
| Dudley Town withdrew v Bridgnorth Town w.o. | |
| Banbury United v Rushall Olympic | 3-2 |
| Blakenall v Great Yarmouth Town | 1-3 |
| Stewarts & Lloyds v Soham Town Rangers | 1-1, 3-1 |
| *at Soham Town* | |
| Hinckley United v Wednesfield | 2-0 |
| Boston Town v Stapenhill | 0-2 |
| Brackley Town v Cogenhoe United | 1-0 |
| Sutton Coldfield Town v Stowmarket Town | 1-3 |
| Rocester v West Midlands Police | 1-1, 3-0 |
| Stafford Rangers v Ely City | 1-1, 3-1 |
| Sandwell Borough v Spalding United | 0-4 |
| Raunds Town v Shifnall Town | 6-0 |
| Watton United withdrew v Lowestoft Town w.o. | |
| Lye Town v Evesham United | 2-1 |
| Redditch United v Wellingborough Town | 4-0 |
| Racing Club Warwick v St Neots Town | 3-1 |
| Willenhall Town v Gorleston | 4-1 |
| Pelsall Villa v Barwell | 2-3 |

| | |
|---|---|
| Newmarket Town v Stamford | 4-4, 4-1 |
| Histon v Oldbury United | 2-0 |
| VS Rugby v Chasetown | 1-0 |
| Diss Town v Bloxwich Town | 1-0 |
| Stourport Swifts v Woodbridge Town | 1-5 |
| Northampton Spencer v Warboys Town | 0-0, 3-2 |
| Wroxham v Paget Rangers | 3-1 |
| Long Buckby v Boldmere St Michaels | 2-4 |
| Littlehampton Town v Southend Manor | 6-2 |
| Folkestone Invicta v Marlow | 3-4 |
| Welwyn Garden City v East Thurrock United | 2-3 |
| Flackwell Heath v Barkingside | 5-0 |
| Grays Athletic v Langford | 10-0 |
| Ford United v Great Wakering Rovers | 0-4 |
| Pagham v Camberley Town | 1-3 |
| Chatham Town v Banstead Athletic | 0-7 |
| *at Corinthian* | |
| Horsham v Northwood | 3-1 |
| Croydon v Mile Oak | 2-1 |
| Tunbridge Wells v Chichester City | 4-4, 1-4 |
| Corinthian Casuals v Aveley | 0-2 |
| Leatherhead v Wealdstone | 2-0 |
| Langney Sports v Southall | 2-1 |
| Whitstable Town v Dorking | 1-1, 3-3 |
| *Dorking won 3-1 on penalties* | |
| Egham Town v Burnham | 1-1, 1-1 |
| *Burnham won 5-4 on penalties* | |
| Redhill v Ware | 1-1, 1-4 |
| Godalming & Guildford v Tonbridge | 0-6 |
| Worthing v Eastbourne Town | 8-1 |
| Epsom & Ewell v Canterbury City | 0-1 |
| Ringmer v Wick | 0-1 |
| Lewes v Tilbury | 0-1 |
| Wingate & Finchley v Corinthian | 1-1, 2-0 |
| Leighton Town v Ashford Town | 2-1 |
| Hailsham Town v Metropolitan Police | 0-4 |
| Erith Town v Harlow Town | 0-3 |
| Wivenhoe Town v Chipstead | 4-0 |
| Croydon Athletic v Beaconsfield SYCOB | 5-2 |
| Sheppey United v Windsor & Eton | 2-3 |
| *at Sittingbourne United* | |
| Hillingdon Borough v Stotfold | 4-2 |
| Tiptree United v Clapton | 1-4 |
| Hassocks v Barton Rovers | 1-2 |
| Milton Keynes v Viking Sports | 1-1, 0-1 |
| Kingsbury Town v Portfield | 1-2 |
| Witham Town v Deal Town | 1-1, 0-3 |
| Halstead Town v Berkhamsted Town | 0-3 |
| Peacehaven & Telscombe v Potton United | 0-3 |
| Oakwood v Potters Bar Town | 2-1 |
| Romford v Hertford Town | 2-0 |
| Hythe United v Chalfont St Peter | 3-2 |
| Three Bridges v Whitehawk | 1-2 |
| Selsey v Wembley | 0-3 |
| Wootton Blue Cross v Hemel Hempstead | 3-2 |
| London Colney v Fisher Athletic | 0-2 |
| Royston Town v Shoreham | 0-0, 1-2 |
| Maldon Town v Ruislip Manor | 0-3 |
| Slade Green v Erith & Belvedere | 1-1, 3-5 |
| Hornchurch v Arundel | 2-2, 3-4 |
| Arlesey Town v March Town United | 2-1 |
| Barking v Basildon United | 3-1 |
| Thamesmead Town v Saltdean United | 3-3, 0-4 |
| Hanwell Town v Tring Town | 3-1 |
| Horsham YMCA v Dartford | 2-4 |
| Abingdon Town v Devizes Town | 1-1, 3-0 |
| Bridgwater Town v Brislington | 1-0 |
| Paulton Rovers v Fareham Town | 5-0 |
| Cirencester Town v Tuffley Rovers | 3-4 |
| Cove v Brockenhurst | 1-3 |
| Bashley v Torrington | 9-0 |
| Chippenham Town v Eastleigh | 0-0, 1-0 |
| Westfields v Westbury United | 2-1 |
| Frome Town v Wokingham Town | 0-5 |

| | |
|---|---|
| Lymington v Endsleigh | 6-0 |
| *at Brockenhurst* | |
| Tiverton Town v Weymouth | 2-0 |
| St Blazey v Trowbridge Town | 1-0 |
| Wimborne Town v Falmouth Town | 3-2 |
| Odd Down v Backwell United | 3-1 |
| Fleet Town v Thame United | 0-0, 3-1 |
| Elmore v Hungerford Town | 4-5 |
| Welton Rovers v Calne Town | 1-5 |
| Clevedon Town v Bemerton Heath Harlequins | 4-0 |
| Bournemouth v Gosport Borough | 2-4 |
| Bridport v Buckingham Town | 1-2 |
| Newport AFC v Maidenhead United | 2-1 |
| Didcot Town v Taunton Town | 1-5 |
| Glastonbury v Chard Town | 0-2 |
| Andover v Portsmouth Royal Navy | 3-4 |
| Barnstaple Town v Carterton Town | 1-4 |
| Waterlooville v Reading Town | 2-0 |
| Melksham Town v Yate Town | 2-1 |
| Minehead v Mangotsfield United | 0-1 |

**FIRST QUALIFYING ROUND**

| | |
|---|---|
| Gateshead v Matlock Town | 2-0 |
| Billingham Synthonia v Maine Road | 0-0, 2-2 |
| *Maine Road won 5-3 on penalties* | |
| South Shields v Skelmersdale United | 3-0 |
| Witton Albion v Gainsborough Trinity | 0-5 |
| Halifax Town v Droylsden | 4-1 |
| Burscough v Bedlington Terriers | 3-3, 2-1 |
| Denaby United v Ossett Town | 2-3 |
| Leigh RMI v Accrington Stanley | 1-0 |
| Chorley v Pontefract Collieries | 3-1 |
| Ilkeston Town v Rossendale United | 3-0 |
| Warrington Town v RTM Newcastle | 1-2 |
| Ratcliffe Borough v Bishop Auckland | 1-3 |
| Whitby Town v Netherfield | 6-2 |
| Billingham Town v Arnold Town | 0-1 |
| Whitley Bay v Shotton Comrades | 0-0, 0-1 |
| Winsford United v Leek Town | 1-0 |
| Hyde United v Louth United | 3-0 |
| Darwen v Ryehope CA | 1-2 |
| Great Harwood Town v St Helens Town | 1-1, 1-3 |
| Lancaster City v Consett | 2-2, 2-1 |
| Knowsley United withdrew v Durham City w.o. | |
| Bootle v Belper Town | 2-3 |
| Eccleshill United v Parkgate | 1-2 |
| Workington v Emley | 0-3 |
| Frickley Athletic v Morpeth Town | 3-3, 1-4 |
| Gretna v Mossley | 3-0 |
| Liversedge v Stocksbridge Park Steels | 3-3, 3-2 |
| North Ferriby United v Barrow | 2-1 |
| Newcastle Town v Garforth Town | 3-5 |
| Brigg Town v Hucknall Town | 3-0 |
| Worksop Town v Oldham Town | 4-2 |
| Spennymoor United v Blyth Spartans | 1-1, 0-1 |
| Bamber Bridge v Dunston FB | 1-1, 3-2 |
| Clitheroe v Jarrow Roofing Boldon CA | 4-3 |
| Staveley MW v Lincoln United | 1-5 |
| Marine v Ashton United | 1-0 |
| Guiseley v Alfreton Town | 3-0 |
| Heanor Town v Penrith | 1-2 |
| Harrogate Town v Easington Colliery | 2-2, 1-4 |
| Ashington v Farsley Celtic | 0-2 |
| Telford United v Bedworth United | 1-2 |
| Pershore Town v Stourbridge | 0-7 |
| Bridgnorth Town v Desborough Town | 1-1, 3-1 |
| Bury Town v Nuneaton Borough | 1-2 |
| Kettering Town v Mirrlees Blackstone | 1-0 |
| Great Yarmouth Town v Banbury United | 2-1 |
| Hinckley United v Stewarts & Lloyds | 5-0 |
| Shepshed Dynamo v Cambridge City | 0-3 |
| Sudbury Wanderers v Stafford Rangers | 3-0 |
| Brackley Town v Stapenhill | 4-0 |
| Rocester v Stowmarket Town | 3-2 |
| Tamworth v Bromsgrove Rovers | 1-2 |
| Knypersley Victoria v Atherstone United | 1-0 |
| Raunds Town v Spalding United | 2-4 |
| Lye Town v Lowestoft Town | 2-3 |
| Holbeach United v Gresley Rovers | 3-6 |
| Rothwell Town v Corby Town | 2-1 |
| Racing Club Warwick v Redditch United | 1-2 |
| Barwell v Willenhall Town | 1-2 |
| Felixstowe Port & Town v Halesowen Town | 2-5 |
| Moor Green v Bilston Town | 0-2 |

| | |
|---|---|
| Histon v Newmarket Town | 1-3 |
| Diss Town v VS Rugby | 0-1 |
| Bourne Town v Kings Lynn | 1-3 |
| Solihull Borough v Burton Albion | 2-0 |
| Northampton Spencer v Woodbridge Town | 1-1, 1-3 |
| Boldmere St Michaels v Wroxham | 1-0 |
| Halesowen Harriers v Grantham Town | 0-1 |
| Whyteleafe v Crawley Town | 3-2 |
| Marlow v Littlehampton Town | 2-2, 2-2 |
| *Marlow won 11-10 on penalties* | |
| Flackwell Heath v East Thurrock United | 1-0 |
| Chertsey Town v Heybridge Swifts | 1-1, 1-2 |
| St Leonards Stamcroft v Bishop's Stortford | 1-0 |
| Great Wakering Rovers v Grays Athletic | 1-2 |
| Banstead Athletic v Camberley Town | 2-2, 1-2 |
| Brimsdown Rovers v Canvey Island | 1-2 |
| Hitchin Town v Bognor Regis Town | 0-2 |
| Croydon v Horsham | 2-1 |
| Aveley v Chichester City | 2-1 |
| Burnham Ramblers v Hastings Town | 0-1 |
| Sittingbourne v Molesey | 5-0 |
| Langney Sports v Leatherhead | 2-1 |
| Burnham v Dorking | 1-3 |
| *at Egham Town* | |
| Concord Rangers v Purfleet | 0-1 |
| Welling United v Leyton Pennant | 3-0 |
| Tonbridge v Ware | 1-0 |
| Canterbury City v Worthing | 1-1, 1-4 |
| Cheshunt v Sutton United | 0-4 |
| Walton & Hersham v Hampton | 2-0 |
| Tilbury v Wick | 3-1 |
| Leighton Town v Wingate & Finchley | 1-2 |
| Baldock Town v Slough Town | 0-0, 0-5 |
| Uxbridge v Dover Athletic | 0-2 |
| Harlow Town v Metropolitan Police | 0-2 |
| Croydon Athletic v Wivenhoe Town | 0-4 |
| Bedford United v Kingstonian | 0-5 |
| Gravesend & Northfleet v Braintree Town | 3-3, 1-4 |
| Hillingdon Borough v Windsor & Eton | 0-2 |
| Barton Rovers v Clapton | 1-0 |
| Bedfont v Chesham United | 2-4 |
| Margate v Bracknell Town | 5-0 |
| Portfield v Viking Sports | 2-1 |
| Berkhamsted Town v Deal Town | 1-1, 1-2 |
| Burgess Hill Town v Harrow Borough | 1-3 |
| Yeading v Chelmsford City | 4-2 |
| Oakwood v Potton United | 0-1 |
| Hythe United v Romford | 4-7 |
| Clacton Town v Stansted | 2-7 |
| Edgware Town v Aylesbury United | 2-5 |
| Wembley v Whitehawk | 3-1 |
| Fisher Athletic v Wootton Blue Cross | 5-0 |
| Harwich & Parkeston v Carshalton Athletic | 1-1, 0-4 |
| Tooting & Mitcham United v Billericay Town | 1-2 |
| Ruislip Manor v Shoreham | 4-1 |
| Arundel v Erith & Belvedere | 1-4 |
| Bedford Town v Dulwich Hamlet | 1-1, 0-2 |
| Herne Bay v Dartford | 1-2 |
| Barking v Arlesey Town | 4-1 |
| Hanwell Town v Saltdean United | 3-2 |
| Staines Town v Bromley | 3-1 |
| Merthyr Tydfil v Brockenhurst | 7-2 |
| Bridgwater Town v Abingdon Town | 1-1, 2-1 |
| Tuffley Rovers v Paulton Rovers | 1-3 |
| Thatcham Town v Cheltenham Town | 0-1 |
| Worcester City v Lymington | 3-2 |
| Chippenham Town v Bashley | 3-2 |
| Wokingham Town v Westfields | 1-1, 3-1 |
| Yeovil Town v Witney Town | 1-1, 2-1 |
| Oxford City v Dorchester Town | 1-1, 0-1 |
| St Blazey v Tiverton Town | 0-2 |
| Odd Down v Wimborne Town | 1-4 |
| Downton v Forest Green Rovers | 0-4 |
| Havant Town v Basingstoke Town | 1-1, 0-2 |
| Hungerford Town v Fleet Town | 1-4 |
| Clevedon Town v Calne Town | 1-1, 1-2 |
| Bideford v Bath City | 0-2 |
| Salisbury City v Chard Town | 3-0 |
| Buckingham Town v Gosport Borough | 1-1, 2-1 |
| Taunton Town v Newport AFC | 3-2 |
| Weston-Super-Mare v Cinderford Town | 0-0, 1-0 |
| Gloucester City v Mangotsfield United | 3-0 |
| Carterton Town v Portsmouth Royal Navy | 0-1 |
| Melksham Town v Waterlooville | 1-2 |
| Newport (IOW) v Aldershot Town | 2-1 |

**SECOND QUALIFYING ROUND**

| | |
|---|---|
| Gateshead v Gainsborough Trinity | 1-4 |
| South Shields v Maine Road | 2-0 |
| Halifax Town v Leigh RMI | 4-0 |
| Burscough v Ossett Town | 1-4 |
| Chorley v Bishop Auckland | 2-2, 3-2 |
| Ilkeston Town v RTM Newcastle | 7-1 |
| Whitby Town v Winsford United | 1-4 |
| Arnold Town v Shotton Comrades | 2-0 |
| Hyde United v Lancaster City | 4-1 |
| Ryehope CA v St Helens Town | 2-1 |
| Durham City v Emley | 0-5 |
| Belper Town v Parkgate | 2-2, 2-0 |
| Morpeth Town v North Ferriby United | 0-0, 0-1 |
| Gretna v Liversedge | 3-1 |
| Garforth Town v Blyth Spartans | 0-1 |
| Brigg Town v Worksop Town | 1-1, 1-3 |
| Bamber Bridge v Marine | 1-3 |
| Clitheroe v Lincoln United | 1-3 |
| Guiseley v Farsley Celtic | 0-0, 4-1 |
| Penrith v Easington Colliery | 6-3 |
| Bedworth United v Nuneaton Borough | 1-1, 0-6 |
| Stourbridge v Bridgnorth Town | 2-1 |
| Kettering Town v Cambridge City | 1-1, 4-2 |
| Hinckley United v Great Yarmouth Town | 2-0 |
| Sudbury Wanderers v Bromsgrove Rovers | 1-1, 0-2 |
| Brackley Town v Rocester | 0-0, 1-2 |
| Knypersley Victoria v Gresley Rovers | 3-1 |
| Spalding United v Lowestoft Town | 2-1 |
| Rothwell Town v Halesowen Town | 1-1, 1-4 |
| Redditch United v Willenhall Town | 3-1 |
| Bilston Town v Kings Lynn | 1-2 |
| Newmarket Town v VS Rugby | 1-2 |
| Solihull Borough v Grantham Town | 2-1 |
| Woodbridge Town v Boldmere St Michaels | 4-2 |
| Whyteleafe v Heybridge Swifts | 0-2 |
| Marlow v Flackwell Heath | 2-3 |
| St Leonards Stamcroft v Canvey Island | 2-0 |
| Grays Athletic v Camberley Town | 1-2 |
| Bognor Regis Town v Hastings Town | 2-1 |
| Croydon v Aveley | 2-0 |
| Sittingbourne v Purfleet | 2-1 |
| Langney Sports v Dorking | 3-0 |
| Welling United v Sutton United | 2-2, 1-2 |
| Tonbridge v Worthing | 3-0 |
| Walton & Hersham v Slough Town | 0-0, 0-0 |
| *Slough Town won 3-2 on penalties* | |
| Tilbury v Wingate & Finchley | 3-0 |
| Dover Athletic v Kingstonian | 0-4 |
| Metropolitan Police v Wivenhoe Town | 2-2, 1-2 |
| Braintree Town v Chesham United | 3-0 |
| Windsor & Eton v Barton Rovers | 2-5 |
| Margate v Harrow Borough | 4-0 |
| Portfield v Deal Town | 1-1, 1-2 |
| Yeading v Stansted | 3-0 |
| Potton United v Romford | 1-6 |
| Aylesbury United v Carshalton Athletic | 0-3 |
| Wembley v Fisher Athletic | 1-3 |
| Billericay Town v Dulwich Hamlet | 2-1 |
| Ruislip Manor v Erith & Belvedere | 0-0, 0-3 |
| Dartford v Staines Town | 1-2 |
| Barking v Hanwell Town | 3-0 |
| Merthyr Tydfil v Cheltenham Town | 0-2 |
| Bridgwater Town v Paulton Rovers | 2-4 |
| Worcester City v Yeovil Town | 1-2 |
| Chippenham Town v Wokingham Town | 1-1, 1-0 |
| Dorchester Town v Forest Green Rovers | 1-0 |
| Tiverton Town v Wimborne Town | 11-1 |
| Basingstoke Town v Bath City | 1-1, 3-1 |
| Fleet Town v Calne Town | 2-3 |
| Salisbury City v Weston-Super-Mare | 2-2, 2-2 |
| *Salisbury City won 4-3 on penalties* | |
| Buckingham Town v Taunton Town | 0-2 |
| Gloucester City v Newport (IOW) | 2-1 |
| Portsmouth Royal Navy v Waterlooville | 1-1, 0-7 |

**THIRD QUALIFYING ROUND**

| | |
|---|---|
| Gainsborough Trinity v South Shields | 3-2 |
| Halifax Town v Ossett Town | 5-0 |
| Chorley v Ilkeston Town | 1-3 |
| Winsford United v Arnold Town | 1-1, 0-0 |
| *Winsford United won 6-5 on penalties* | |
| Hyde United v Ryhope CA | 8-0 |
| Emley v Belper Town | 2-1 |
| North Ferriby United v Gretna | 2-0 |
| Blyth Spartans v Worksop Town | 4-0 |
| Marine v Lincoln United | 1-1, 1-4 |
| Guiseley v Penrith | 1-2 |
| Nuneaton Borough v Stourbridge | 4-1 |
| Kettering Town v Hinckley United | 0-1 |
| Bromsgrove Rovers v Rocester | 2-1 |
| Knypersley Victoria v Spalding United | 3-1 |
| Halesowen Town v Redditch United | 2-2, 3-0 |
| Kings Lynn v VS Rugby | 4-3 |
| Solihull Borough v Woodbridge Town | 6-0 |
| Heybridge Swifts v Flackwell Heath | 4-0 |
| St Leonards Stamcroft v Camberley Town | 1-3 |
| Bognor Regis Town v Croydon | 1-1, 2-2 |
| *Bognor Regis Town won 3-1 on penalties* | |
| Sittingbourne v Langney Sports | 2-1 |
| Sutton United v Tonbridge | 5-1 |
| Slough Town v Tilbury | 6-1 |
| Kingstonian v Wivenhoe Town | 1-0 |
| Braintree Town v Barton Rovers | 4-1 |
| Margate v Deal Town | 2-1 |
| Yeading v Romford | 0-2 |
| Carshalton Athletic v Fisher Athletic | 1-0 |
| Billericay Town v Erith & Belvedere | 4-1 |
| Staines Town v Barking | 3-1 |
| Cheltenham Town v Paulton Rovers | 5-0 |
| Yeovil Town v Chippenham Town | 4-0 |
| Dorchester Town v Tiverton Town | 0-1 |
| Basingstoke Town v Calne Town | 0-0, 2-1 |
| Salisbury City v Taunton Town | 3-0 |
| Gloucester City v Waterlooville | 2-0 |

**FOURTH QUALIFYING ROUND**

| | |
|---|---|
| Gainsborough Trinity v Halifax Town | 2-1 |
| Runcorn v Lincoln United | 1-2 |
| Hinckley United v Colwyn Bay | 1-2 |
| Halesowen Town v Northwich Victoria | 0-2 |
| Ilkeston Town v Hyde United | 3-2 |
| Blyth Spartans v Kidderminster Harriers | 2-1 |
| Nuneaton Borough v Emley | 2-3 |
| Winsford United v Penrith | 2-0 |
| Southport v North Ferriby United | 2-0 |
| Stalybridge Celtic v Solihull Borough | 3-3, 3-4 |
| Knypersley Victoria v Boston United | 0-1 |
| Altrincham v Morecambe | 0-2 |
| Billericay Town v Camberley Town | 1-1, 1-0 |
| Tiverton Town v Sudbury Town | 5-0 |
| Staines Town v Margate | 0-3 |
| Basingstoke Town v Braintree Town | 5-1 |
| Bognor Regis Town v Farnborough Town | 0-0, 1-2 |
| Rushden & Diamonds v Boreham Wood | 1-1, 0-1 |
| Yeovil Town v Hayes | 1-1, 0-1 |
| St Albans City v Hendon | 1-2 |
| Heybridge Swifts v Ashford Town | 5-2 |
| Cheltenham Town v Sutton United | 1-0 |
| Bromsgrove Rovers v Romford | 2-0 |
| Kings Lynn v Salisbury City | 5-0 |
| Gloucester City v Wisbech Town | 1-1, 2-3 |
| Enfield v Carshalton Athletic | 1-2 |
| Slough Town v Kingstonian | 2-1 |
| Sittingbourne v Hereford United | 2-2, 0-3 |

# FA CUP 1997–98
## SPONSORED BY LITTLEWOODS POOLS

## COMPETITION PROPER

**FIRST ROUND**

**14 NOV**

**Bristol R (1) 2** *(Alsop 19, Holloway 87)*
**Gillingham (1) 2** *(Onuora 42, Akinbiyi 82)*     4825
*Bristol R:* Collett; Pritchard (Low), Foster, Penrice, White, Tillson, Holloway, Alsop (French), Hayfield, Lockwood, Hayles.
*Gillingham:* Stannard; Patterson, Statham, Smith, Ashby, Butters, Hessenthaler, Galloway, Onuora (Ratcliffe), Akinbiyi, Butler.

**Swansea C (0) 1** *(Appleby 69)*
**Peterborough U (2) 4** *(Quinn 27, Castle 34, 70, Carruthers 86)*     2821
*Swansea C:* Freestone; Price, Clode (Ampadu), Walker, Edwards, Cusack, Coates, Newhouse (Watkin), Bird (Mainwaring), Appleby, O'Leary.
*Peterborough U:* Tyler; McMenamin, Lewis (Linton), Castle (Bullimore), Bodley, Edwards, Farrell, Payne, Carruthers, Quinn, Houghton.

**15 NOV**

**Barnet (1) 1** *(Charlery 9)*
**Watford (0) 2** *(Rosenthal 61, 67)*     4040
*Barnet:* Harrison; Stockley, Harle, Heald, Howarth, Ford, Searle, Wilson (Samuels), Charlery, McGleish, Manuel (Onwere).
*Watford:* Chamberlain; Gibbs, Kennedy, Page, Palmer, Mooney, Noel-Williams, Hyde, Lee (Thomas), Johnson R, Rosenthal.

**Billericay T (0) 2** *(Battram 76, Moore 89)*
**Wisbech T (1) 3** *(Munns 19, Ward 56, McLoughlin 88)*     1947
*Billericay T:* Root; Goldstone, Davidson, Moore, Waters, Hooker, Ridout (Kelly), Barry, Battram (Barnett), Gutzmore, Payne.
*Wisbech T:* Bray; Marshall, Lindsay, Irvine, Moore, Ward, McLoughlin, Rolph, Munns, Gallagher, Newell.

**Blackpool (1) 4** *(Preece 4, Linighan 59, Clarkson 71, 89)*
**Blyth S (2) 3** *(Henderson 10, Di Lella 44, Atkinson 84)*     4814
*Blackpool:* Banks; Lydiate, Dixon, Butler, Linighan, Philpott, Bonner, Clarkson, Bent (Longworth), Ellis (Ormerod), Preece.
*Blyth S:* Burridge; Farrey, Pike, Todd, Gamble, McGarrigle K, Renforth, Hislop, Henderson (Moat), Fletcher (Atkinson), Di Lella (Ainsley).

**Bournemouth (1) 3** *(Beardsmore 3, Robinson 58, 66)*
**Heybridge S (0) 0**     3385
*Bournemouth:* Glass; Young (Rolling), Vincent, Howe, Cox, O'Neill, Beardsmore, Robinson, Warren, Fletcher, Rawlinson (Harrington).
*Heybridge S:* Cheeswright; Cranfield, Cutbush, Vickers, Keen, Pollard, Greene (Adcock), Springett (Rayner), Calden (Harding), Jones, Kane.

**Brentford (1) 2** *(Taylor 9, 55)*
**Colchester U (1) 2** *(Sale 37, Gregory D 87)*     2899
*Brentford:* Dearden; Hurdle, Barrowcliff, Hutchings, Bates, Oatway, McGhee, Cockerill, Bent (Canham), Reina (Rapley), Taylor.
*Colchester U:* Emberson; Gregory D, Stamps, Skelton (Abrahams), Greene, Cawley, Wilkins (Dunne), Forbes (Adcock), Sale, Whitton, Duguid.

**Bristol C (1) 1** *(Taylor 25)*
**Millwall (0) 0**     8413
*Bristol C:* Welch; Locke, Bell, Doherty, Taylor, Carey, Goodridge (Langdon), Hewlett, Torpey, Goater, Tinnion.
*Millwall:* Spink; Brown, Sturgess (Bircham), Bowry, Law, McLeary, Newman, Savage, Wilkinson, Allen (Hockton), Doyle (Grant).

**Carlisle U (0) 0**
**Wigan Ath (1) 1** *(Jones 40)*     5182
*Carlisle U:* Caig; Boertien, Archdeacon, Barr, Varty, Pounewatchy, McAlindon (Hopper), Prokas, Stevens (Dobie), Jansen, Aspinall.
*Wigan Ath:* Butler; Green, Sharp, Greenall, McGibbon, Bradshaw, Lee, Kilford, Jones, Johnson, Lowe.

**Carshalton Ath (0) 0**
**Stevenage B (0) 0**     1405
*Carshalton Ath:* Blake; Robson, Smith, Saunders, Coney, Alexander, Jeffrey, Bassey, Bartley, Thompson, Kingsford.
*Stevenage B:* Gallagher; Kirby, March, Holden, Trott, Beevor, Smith, Perkins, Crawshaw, Trebble, Love.

**Cheltenham T (1) 2** *(Eaton 2, Walker 88)*
**Tiverton T (1) 1** *(Saunders 41)*     2781
*Cheltenham T:* Book; Duff (Milton), Victory, Banks, Freeman, Smith (Walker), Wright, Knight (Crisp), Eaton, Watkins, Bloomer.
*Tiverton T:* Edwards; Hynds, Saunders, Tatterton, Smith, Conning, Mancekivell, Varley, Everett, Daly, Leonard.

**Chester C (0) 2** *(Richardson 53, Priest 75)*
**Winsford U (1) 1** *(Steele 11)*     3885
*Chester C:* Brown; Jenkins, Fisher, Richardson, Whelan, Alsford, Bennett (Murphy), Priest, McDonald (Rimmer), Flitcroft, Thomas.
*Winsford U:* Oakes; Clegg, German, Came (Russell), Talbot, Byrne, Doherty, Bermingham, Shaugnessey (Dulson), Steele, Wheeler (Aspinall).

**Chesterfield (1) 1** *(Reeves 6)*
**Northwich Vic (0) 0**     5327
*Chesterfield:* Leaning; Hewitt, Jules, Beaumont, Williams, Breckin, Wilkinson (Dunn) (Jackson), Holland, Reeves, Ebdon, Howard.
*Northwich Vic:* Greygoose; Crookes, Fairclough, Billing, Simpson, Bishop (Sandeman), Stannard, Walters, Tait (Williams), Cooke, Duffy.

**Darlington (1) 1** *(Naylor 1)*
**Solihull B (0) 1** *(Cross 60)*     2318
*Darlington:* Preece; Shaw, Barnard, Brydon, Crosby, Hope (Shutt), Oliver (Turnbull), Atkinson, Roberts, Dorner (Robinson), Naylor.
*Solihull B:* Phillips; Abell, Wolsey, Bradley (Rowe), Brown, Brogan, Mitchell, Myers, Cross, Dowling, Byrne.

**Exeter C (1) 1** *(Rowbotham 32)*
**Northampton T (1) 1** *(Hunter 37)*     4605
*Exeter C:* Bayes; Gale, Cyrus, Blake, Clark, Richardson, Rowbotham, Birch, Ghazghazi (Braithwaite), Medlin, McConnell.
*Northampton T:* Woodman; Clarkson, Frain, Sampson, Warburton, Brightwell, Peer, Rennie (Gibb), Heggs, Gayle (Lee), Hunter.

**Farnborough T (0) 0**
**Dagenham & R (0) 1** *(Stimson 86)* 1236
*Farnborough T:* MacKenzie; Stemp (Miller), Underwood, Rowlands M, Baker N, Robson, Baker S, Harlow, Laidlaw, Mehew, Wingfield.
*Dagenham & R:* Gothard; Culverhouse, Pratt, Howard, Conner, Creaser, Parratt, Cobb, Broom, Stimson, Naylor (Flanaghan).

**Hartlepool U (0) 2** *(Beech 53, Pedersen 63)*
**Macclesfield T (0) 4** *(Wood 49, 81, Whittaker 71, 88)* 3165
*Hartlepool U:* Dobson; Knowles, Lucas, Ingram, Lee, Barron, Davies (Elliott), Cullen (Clark), Howard (Halliday), Beech, Pedersen.
*Macclesfield T:* Price; Tinson, Gardiner, Payne, Rose (Mitchell), Sodje, Whittaker, Wood, Peel (Irving) (Landon), Power, Sorvel.

**Hayes (0) 0**
**Boreham Wood (1) 1** *(Marshall 31)* 1343
*Hayes:* Meara; Brady, Flynn, Bunce, Sparks, Goodliffe, Hall (Boothe), Roddis (Haynes), Randall, Hammatt (Francis), Wilkinson.
*Boreham Wood:* Taylor; Daly, McCarthy, Robbins, Nisbet, Hollingdale, Shaw J, Marshall (Shaw P), Heffer, Samuels T, Brown (Hatchett).

**Hendon (1) 2** *(Simpson 25, 55)*
**Leyton Orient (2) 2** *(Harris 5, Smith 33)* 2421
*Hendon:* McCann; White, Clarke, Kelly P, Nugent, Bateman, Heard, Hyatt, Simpson (Lynch), Kelly T (Howard), Lewis.
*Leyton Orient:* Hyde; Warren, Naylor, Smith (Joseph), Hicks, Clark, Ling, Harris (Baker), Griffiths, Hanson, Channing.

**Hereford U (0) 2** *(Grayson 62, 73 (pen))*
**Brighton & HA (0) 1** *(Storer 66)* 5787
*Hereford U:* Debont; Rodgerson (McCue) Fishlock, Pitman, Warner, Walker, Cook, McGorry, Grayson, Foster, Mahon.
*Brighton & HA:* Rust; Smith, Tuck, Minton, Hobson, Allan, Westcott, Mayo, Storer, Maskell (Ansah), McDonald.

**Hull C (0) 0**
**Hednesford T (1) 2** *(Norbury 38 (pen), O'Connor 90)*
6091
*Hull C:* Wilson; Gage, Rioch, Wright, Greaves, Hocking, Peacock, Joyce, Darby, Hodges (Fewings), Mann (Ellington).
*Hednesford T:* Cooksey; Carty, Collins, Blades, Comyn, Beeston, Fitzpatrick, Ware, Norbury, Dennison (Hemmings), O'Connor.

**Ilkeston T (1) 2** *(Carmichael 25, 84)*
**Boston U (0) 1** *(Cavell 61)* 2504
*Ilkeston T:* Rigby; Fearon, Ludlum, Middleton, Law, Knapper, Eshelby (Huckerby), Robinson, Carmichael, Moore (Shaw), Ball.
*Boston U:* Bastock; Gowshall, Withe, Fee (Watts), Hardy, Charles, Stanhope, Appleby, Cavell, Chambers L, Mason.

**Kings Lynn (1) 1** *(Hudson 26)*
**Bromsgrove R (0) 0** 2847
*Kings Lynn:* Hollman; Matthews, Skelly, Ellis, Wright, Spearing, Hopkins, Williams, Roberts, McNamara, Hudson.
*Bromsgrove R:* Anstiss; Davies, Darkes, Skelding, Grocutt, Payne (Simpson), Softley (Mainwaring), Elmes, Whitehouse, Smith C, Gardner.

**Lincoln C (1) 1** *(Walling 15)*
**Gainsborough T (0) 1** *(Morrow 54)* 6014
*Lincoln C:* Richardson; Barnett, Whitney, Fleming, Holmes, Austin, Walling, Thorpe, Stant (Stones), Gordon (Brown S), Hone.
*Gainsborough T:* Sherwood; Price, Limber, Ogley, Timons, Ellender, Morrow, Circuit, Riley (Maxwell), Brown, Dennis.

**Luton T (0) 0**
**Torquay U (0) 1** *(Gibbs 74 (pen))* 3446
*Luton T:* Fewer; James, Harvey (Doherty), Waddock (Patterson), White, Spring (Davies), Fotiadis, McLaren, Oldfield, Thorpe, Alexander.
*Torquay U:* Gregg; Gurney, Gibbs, Robinson, Gittens, Watson, Clayton, Hill, Jack, Bedeau, Hapgood.

**Morecambe (1) 1** *(Bignall 37)*
**Emley (0) 1** *(Banks 63 (pen))* 1496
*Morecambe:* Banks; Burns, Hughes D (Takano), Hughes T, Mayers, Drummond, Monk (Ceroalo), Healy, Bignall (Parkinson), Norman, Shirley.
*Emley:* Marples; Nicholson, Jones, Thompson, Lacy, David, Banks, Hurst, Tonks (Graham), Wilson (Wood), Reynolds.

**Oldham Ath (1) 1** *(McCarthy 15)*
**Mansfield T (0) 1** *(Whitehall 66)* 5253
*Oldham Ath:* Kelly; McNiven S (Rush), Serrant, Garnett, Hodgson, Rickers, Wright (Hughes), Duxbury, McCarthy, Barlow (Allott), Reid.
*Mansfield T:* Bowling; Williams, Harper, Peters, Eustace, Hackett, Schofield, Clarke (Sedgemore), Peacock (Christie), Whitehall, Doolan.

**Plymouth Arg (0) 0**
**Cambridge U (0) 0** 4793
*Plymouth Arg:* Sheffield; Wilson (Illman), Williams, Mauge, Saunders, Wotton, Barlow, Jean, Littlejohn, Corazzin, Billy.
*Cambridge U:* Barrett; Ashbee, Wilson, Chenery, Foster, Campbell, Wanless, Preece, Kyd (Taylor), Butler, Beall.

**Preston NE (0) 3** *(Gregan 56, 65, Eyres 63)*
**Doncaster R (1) 2** *(Mike 6, Hammond 86)* 7953
*Preston NE:* Moilanen; Parkinson, Barrick (Murdock), Kidd, Gregan, Appleton, Ashcroft, Lormor, Rankine (Darby), Eyres.
*Doncaster R:* Williams; Ireland, Hilton, Warren, Gore, Brookes (Hammond), McDonald, Dobbin, Mike, Moncrieffe, Smith M (Ramsay).

**Rochdale (0) 0**
**Wrexham (0) 2** *(Roberts N 56, Connolly 65)* 3956
*Rochdale:* Edwards; Fensome, Barlow, Hill, Farrell, Gouck, Bryson, Painter, Leonard, Russell (Pender), Stuart.
*Wrexham:* Marriott; Jones, Hardy, Phillips, Humes, Ridler, Skinner (Chalk), Owen, Connolly, Roberts N, Ward.

**Rotherham U (2) 3** *(Roscoe 17, 66, Knill 36)*
**Burnley (2) 3** *(Cooke 24, Moore 37, Weller 55)* 5709
*Rotherham U:* Mimms; Clark, Warner, Garner, Knill, Richardson, Hayward, Thompson (Hudson), Roscoe (Shuttleworth), Glover, Hurst.
*Burnley:* Beresford; Brass, Vinnicombe (Blatherwick), Cowans (Harrison), Howey, Moore, Waddle (Smith), Williams, Cooke, Barnes, Weller.

**Scunthorpe U (1) 2** *(Wilcox 41, Calvo-Garcia 71)*
**Scarborough (0) 1** *(Robinson 52)* 3039
*Scunthorpe U:* Clarke; Walsh, Housham, Sertori, Wilcox, Hope, Walker (Laws), D'Auria, Eyre (Ormondroyd), Forrester, Calvo-Garcia.
*Scarborough:* Martin (Buxton); Brodie, Sutherland, Snodin, Atkin, Rockett, Williams, McElhatton, Robinson (Campbell), Mitchell (Tate), Bennett G.

**Shrewsbury (0) 1** *(Herbert 67)*
**Grimsby T (1) 1** *(Southall 15)* 3193
*Shrewsbury T:* Gall; Seabury, Hanmer, Taylor L (Edwards), Wilding, Herbert, Preece, White, Steele, Evans, Scott.
*Grimsby T:* Davison; McDermott, Gallimore, Handyside, Rodger, Southall, Donovan, Black (Livingstone), Nogan, Lester, Groves.

**Slough T (0) 1** *(Bolt 68)*
**Cardiff C (1) 1** *(O'Sullivan 16)* 2262
*Slough T:* Wilkerson; Smart, Hardyman, McGinnis, Hercules, Angus, Bailey, Browne (Owusu), Brazil, Abbott, Bolt.
*Cardiff C:* Hallworth; Middleton, Beech, Young, Harris, Fowler, O'Sullivan, Penney, Saville, Dale, Stoker (Carss).

**Southport (0) 0**
**York C (1) 4** *(Rowe 18, 68, Bolland 69 (og), Pouton 75)*
3952
*Southport:* Stewart; Farley, Ryan, Deary, Bolland, Futcher, Butler, Thompson (Mitten), Whittaker (Jones), Kielty, Formby (Gamble).
*York C:* Samways; Murty, Hall (Atkinson), Bushell, Reed, Barras, Pouton, Tinkler, Bull, Rowe (Cresswell), Stephenson (Himsworth).

**Walsall (1) 2** *(Watson 35, Boli 90)*
**Lincoln U (0) 0** 3279
*Walsall:* Walker; Evans, Marsh, Viveash, Roper (Mountfield), Peron, Boli, Keister, Keates, Watson (Hodge), Ricketts.
*Lincoln U:* Heath M; Casey (Barker), Carter, McDaid, Trotter, Heath B, Gray, Wright, Ranshaw, Munton (Simmons), Gibson (Farley).

**Woking (0) 0**
**Southend U (0) 2** *(Jones 88, Gridelet 90)* 4059
*Woking:* Batty; Betsy, Taylor, Howard (Sutton), Brown, Danzey, Thompson, Jones (Ellis), West, Hay (Steele), Smith.
*Southend U:* Royce; Hails, Jones, Coulbault, Harris, Lewis, Dublin, Gridelet, Rammell (Boere), Thomson, Clarke.

**Wycombe W (1) 2** *(Cornforth 16, 61 (pen))*
**Basingstoke T (0) 2** *(Coombs 68, Wilkinson 75)* 3932
*Wycombe W:* Taylor; Cousins, Kavanagh, Ryan, Mohan, Cornforth, Carroll (Simpson), Scott, Read, McGavin (Beeton), Harkin.
*Basingstoke T:* Beale; Barker, Richardson, Huxford, Harris, Morley, Wilkinson, Emsden, Mancy, Coombs, Tydeman.

**16 NOV**

**Margate (1) 1** *(Munday 6 (pen))*
**Fulham (1) 2** *(Carpenter 23, Scott 77)* 5100
*Margate:* Turner; O'Connell, Martin, Edwards, Blondrage, Dixon, Spiller, Munday, Sykes, Buglione (Lamb), Pilkington (Cory).
*Fulham:* Arendse; Blake, Herrera, Carpenter, Morgan, Lawrence, Smith, Bracewell, Scott, Peschisolido, Watson.

**Notts Co (0) 2** *(Hogg 58, Richardson 67)*
**Colwyn Bay (0) 0** 3074
*Notts Co:* Ward; Hogg, Pearce, Redmile, Strodder, Richardson, Finnan, Robinson (Derry), Farrell (Jones), Dudley, Robson (Hendon).
*Colwyn Bay:* Roberts R; McGosh, Mann (Drury), Graham, Caton, Price, Limbert (Donnelly), Roberts G, Jones T (Woods), Congerton, Lawton.

**FIRST ROUND REPLAYS**

**24 NOV**

**Stevenage B (3) 5** *(Love 7, 47, Perkins 11, Smith 22, Trott 69)*
**Carshalton Ath (0) 0** 2377
*Stevenage B:* Gallagher; Kirby, March (Dillnutt), Holden, Trott, Soloman, Smith, Perkins (Johansen), Crawshaw, Beevor, Love.
*Carshalton Ath:* Blake; Robson, Smith (Allen), Coney, Ford, Beard, Jeffrey, Bassey, Bartley, Thompson (Fowler), Kingsford (Adam).

**25 NOV**

**Basingstoke T (1) 2** *(Coombs 40, 85 (pen))*
**Wycombe W (1) 2** *(McGavin 17, 74)* 5085
*Basingstoke T:* Beale; Barker, Richardson, Line, Harris, Morley, Wilkinson, Emsden, Mancy, Coombs, Tydeman (Carey).
*Wycombe W:* Taylor; Cousins (Simpson), Beeton (Read), Ryan, Mohan, Forsyth, McCarthy (Kavanagh), Scott, Cornforth, McGavin, Brown.
*aet; Basingstoke T won 5–4 on penalties.*

**Burnley (0) 0**
**Rotherham U (1) 3** *(White 10, Berry 68, Garner 88)* 3118
*Burnley:* Beresford; Brass, Blatherwick, Cowans (Harrison), Howey, Moore, Waddle, Williams (Ford), Cooke, Barnes, Weller.
*Rotherham U:* Mimms; Clark, Hurst, Garner, Knill, Richardson, Berry (Hayward), Thompson, White, Glover, Roscoe.

**Cambridge U (0) 3** *(Beall 74, Benjamin 77, Wilson 95 (pen))*
**Plymouth Arg (2) 2** *(Mauge 21, Jean 45)* 3139
*Cambridge U:* Barrett; Chenery, Wilson, Ashbee, Foster, Campbell, Wanless, Preece (Benjamin), Taylor, Kyd (Butler), Beall.
*Plymouth Arg:* Sheffield; Logan, Williams, Mauge (Wilson), Saunders (Rowbotham), Wotton, Barlow, Jean, Littlejohn, Corazzin, Billy.

**Cardiff C (1) 3** *(Dale 22, Saville 55, White 114)*
**Slough T (1) 2** *(Owusu 5, Angus 74)* 2343
*Cardiff C:* Elliott; Middleton, Beech, Young (Jarman), Harris, Partridge (Rollo), O'Sullivan, Penney, Saville, Dale (White), Carss.
*Slough T:* Wilkerson; Smart, Hardyman (Simpson), McGinnis (West), Hercules, Angus, Bailey, Owusu, Brazil, Abbott, Bolt.

**Colchester U (0) 0**
**Brentford (0) 0** 3613
*Colchester U:* Emberson; Dunne, Betts, Gregory, Greene, Cawley, Abrahams (Hathaway), Adcock (Lock), Sale, Whitton (Skelton), Duguid.
*Brentford:* Dearden; McPherson (Hurdle), Townley, Hutchings, Bates, Oatway, McGhee, Cockerill, Bent, Reina (Bryan), Barrowcliff.
*aet; Colchester U won 4–2 on penalties.*

**Emley (1) 3** *(Hurst 43, 109, Marshall 120)*
**Morecambe (1) 3** *(Mayers 24, Takano 116, Monk 119)* 2439
*Emley:* Marples; Nicholson, Jones (Wood), Thompson, Lacy, Tonks (Calcutt), Banks, Hurst, Graham, Wilson, Reynolds (Marshall).
*Morecambe:* McIlhargey (Banks); Lowe, Takano, McKearney, Hughes T, Drummond, Burns (Monk), Healy, Ceroala (Williams), Norman, Mayers.
*aet; Emley won 3–1 on penalties.*

**Gainsborough T (2) 2** *(Maxwell 29, Price 39)*
**Lincoln C (3) 3** *(Walling 15, 17, Whitney 18)* 5726
*Gainsborough T:* Sherwood; Hanby, Limber, Ogley, Timons, Ellender, Brown, Circuit, Maxwell, Riley, Price (Taylor).
*Lincoln C:* Richardson; Barnett, Whitney, Fleming, Holmes, Austin, Walling, Gordon, Stant, Thorpe, Hone.
*at Lincoln.*

**Gillingham (0) 0**
**Bristol R (2) 2** *(Hayles 14, Penrice 28)* 4459
*Gillingham:* Stannard; Statham, Bryant (Fortune-West), Smith, Ashby, Butters, Hessenthaler, Onuora (Galloway), Butler, Akinbiyi, Patterson (Ratcliffe).
*Bristol R:* Collett; Pritchard, Perry, Penrice, White, Tillson, Low (French), Hayfield, Beadle, Lockwood, Hayles.

**Grimsby T (2) 4** *(Nogan 29, Herbert 45 (og), Lester 73, Jobling 89)*
**Shrewsbury T (0) 0**          3242
*Grimsby T:* Davison; McDermott, Gallimore, Handyside, Rodger, Jobling, Donovan, Black, Nogan (Livingstone), Lester (Clare), Groves (Southall).
*Shrewsbury T:* Gall; Seabury, Hanmer, Herbert, Taylor L, Wilding, Preece, White, Currie, Evans, Scott (Ward).

**Leyton Orient (0) 0**
**Hendon (0) 1** *(Lewis 72)*          3355
*Leyton Orient:* Hyde; Warren, Naylor, Smith, Hicks, Clark, Ling, Inglethorpe (Linger), Griffiths, Harris (Baker), Channing (Hanson).
*Hendon:* McCann; White, Clarke, Kelly P, Howard, Bateman, Heard, Hyatt, Simpson (Banton), Kelly T (Warmington), Lewis.

**Mansfield T (0) 0**
**Oldham Ath (1) 1** *(Serrant 43)*          4097
*Mansfield T:* Bowling; Williams, Harper, Peters, Eustace, Hackett, Schofield, Sedgemore (Christie), Peacock, Whitehall, Doolan.
*Oldham Ath:* Kelly; McNiven S, Serrant, Garnett, Graham, Redmond, Rickers, Duxbury, McCarthy, Allott (Barlow), Reid.

**Northampton T (1) 2** *(Hunter 10, Heggs 86)*
**Exeter C (1) 1** *(Clark 43)*          5259
*Northampton T:* Woodman; Clarkson, Frain, Sampson, Warburton, Brightwell, Peer, Heggs, Seal (Gibb), Lee (Wilson), Hunter.
*Exeter C:* Bayes; Gale, Fry, Blake, Clark, Richardson (Cyrus), Rowbotham, Birch, Flack, Baddeley, Gardner (Ghazghazi).

### 26 NOV

**Solihull B (1) 3** *(Dowling 43, 90, Cross 54)*
**Darlington (1) 3** *(Atkinson 44 (pen), Robinson 71, Dorner 88)*          2000
*Solihull B:* Phillips; Abell, Wolsey, Bradley (Woodley), Penny, Brogan, Mitchell, Beagan (Rowe), Cross, Dowling, Byrne.
*Darlington:* Preece; Shaw, Barnard (Resch), Devos, Crosby, Atkinson (Brumwell), Oliver, Naylor, Dorner, Shutt (Turnbull), Robinson.
*aet; Darlington won 4–2 on penalties.*

### SECOND ROUND

### 5 DEC

**Chester C (0) 0**
**Wrexham (2) 2** *(Connolly 38, 45)*          5224
*Chester C:* Brown; Jenkins, Fisher (Davidson), Richardson, Whelan, Alsford, Bennett, Priest, Rimmer (Jones), Flitcroft, Thomas.
*Wrexham:* Marriott; McGregor, Hardy, Russell, Ridler, Carey (Jones), Chalk, Owen, Connolly (Roberts), Spink, Ward.

### 6 DEC

**Cambridge U (0) 0** *(Butler 83)*
**Stevenage B (1) 1** *(Crawshaw 17 (pen))*          4847
*Cambridge U:* Barrett; Chenery (McCammon), Wilson, Ashbee, Foster, Campbell, Wanless, Benjamin, Taylor, Kyd (Butler), Beall.
*Stevenage B:* Gallagher; Kirby, Rogers (March), Holden, Trott, Soloman (Cretton), Smith, Love, Crawshaw, Wordsworth (Beevor), Trebble.

**Cardiff C (3) 3** *(Dale 20, 45, Saville 41)*
**Hendon (0) 1** *(Bashir 86)*          2578
*Cardiff C:* Hallworth; Middleton, Beech (Jarman), Young, Harris (Rollo), Partridge, O'Sullivan, Penney (Stoker), Saville, Dale, Carss.
*Hendon:* McCann; White, Clarke, Kelly (Banton), Nugent, Bateman, Heard (Bashir), Hyatt, Simpson, Howard (Tello), Lewis.

**Cheltenham T (0) 1** *(Howells 75)*
**Boreham Wood (1) 1** *(Marshall 13)*          3525
*Cheltenham T:* Book; Duff, Victory, Banks, Freeman, Milton (Crisp), Howells, Knight (Teague), Eaton, Walker, Wright.
*Boreham Wood:* Taylor; Daly, McCarthy, Robbins, Nisbet, Hollingdale, Shaw J, Marshall (Dixon), Heffer, Samuels, Hatchett.

**Colchester U (1) 1** *(Gregory D 10)*
**Hereford U (0) 1** *(Grayson 61)*          3558
*Colchester U:* Emberson; Dunne, Betts, Gregory D, Greene (Haydon), Skelton, Duguid, Buckle, Sale, Adcock (Lock), Hathaway (Stamps).
*Hereford U:* Debont; Norton, Fishlock, Pitman, Brough, Walker, Hargreaves, McGorry, Grayson, Warner, Mahon.

**Fulham (0) 1** *(Blake 57 (pen))*
**Southend U (0) 0**          8537
*Fulham:* Taylor; McAnespie (Moody), Herrera, Cullip, Blake, Neilson, Bracewell, Smith, Scott (Hayward), Peschisolido, Trollope.
*Southend U:* Royce; Hails, Jones, Coulbault, Harris, Dublin, N'Diaye (Lewis), Gridelet, Boere (Rammell), Thomson, Clarke (Henriksen).

**Grimsby T (2) 2** *(Rodger 8, Nogan 31)*
**Chesterfield (0) 2** *(Willis 52, Breckin 72)*          4762
*Grimsby T:* Davison; McDermott, Gallimore, Handyside, Rodger, Jobling, Donovan, Widdrington (Clare), Nogan, Lester (Livingstone), Groves.
*Chesterfield:* Leaning; Hewitt, Jules (Willis), Beaumont, Williams, Breckin, Wilkinson (Carr), Holland, Howard, Ebdon, Perkins.

**Hednesford T (0) 0**
**Darlington (0) 1** *(Roberts 49 (pen))*          1900
*Hednesford T:* Cooksey; Carty, Collins (Hemmings), Blades, Comyn, Fitzpatrick, Ware, Beeston, Norbury (Francis), Dennison, O'Connor.
*Darlington:* Preece; Shaw, Resch (Barnard), Devos, Crosby, Atkinson, Oliver, Gaughan, Roberts, Naylor, Robinson (Brydon).

**Lincoln C (1) 2** *(Fleming 12, 90)*
**Emley (1) 2** *(Hurst 45, Graham 85)*          3729
*Lincoln C:* Richardson; Barnett, Whitney (Alcide), Fleming, Holmes, Austin, Walling, Thorpe, Gordon, Brown S (Stant), Stones (Bimson).
*Emley:* Marples; Nicholson, Jones, Thompson, Wood, David, Calcutt, Hurst (Tonks), Graham, Wilson, Reynolds.

**Macclesfield T (0) 0**
**Walsall (2) 7** *(Boli 21, 57 (pen), Hodge 34 (pen), 90, Viveash 47, Porter 73, 85)*          3566
*Macclesfield T:* Price; Tinson, Howarth, Payne, Rose, Sodje, Whittaker (Mason), Mitchell (Irving), Peel, Power (Landon), Sorvel.
*Walsall:* Walker; Evans, Marsh, Viveash, Ryder, Peron, Boli (Ricketts), Porter, Keates, Watson (Platt), Hodge.

**Northampton T (1) 1** *(Seal 39)*
**Basingstoke T (0) 1** *(Carey 75)*          5881
*Northampton T:* Woodman; Clarkson, Frain, Hill, Warburton, Brightwell, Gibb, Heggs, Seal, Gayle (Hunt), Hunter.
*Basingstoke T:* Beale; Barker, Richardson, Huxford (Carey), Harris, Morley, Wilkinson, Emsden, Mancy, Coombs, Tydeman.

**Oldham Ath (0) 2** *(Graham 58, Barlow 81)*
**Blackpool (0) 1** *(Ellis 83)*          6590
*Oldham Ath:* Kelly; Rickers, Serrant, Graham, Hodgson, Redmond, Allott (Rush), Duxbury, Barlow (McNiven S), Ritchie, Reid.
*Blackpool:* Banks; Bryan, Dixon, Butler, Lydiate, Brabin, Bonner, Clarkson, Bent (Malkin), Ellis, Philpott.

**Peterborough U (1) 3** *(Carruthers 21, Quinn 74, 82)*
**Dagenham & R (0) 2** *(Cobb 47, Shipp 71)*  5572
*Peterborough U:* Tyler; Linton (Castle), Drury, McMenamin (Neal), Foran, Edwards, Farrell, Payne, Carruthers, Quinn, Lewis (Rowe).
*Dagenham & R:* Gothard; Culverhouse, Pratt, Bird (Double), Conner, Creaser, Parrott, Cobb, Stimson (Shipp), Cole (Flanagan), Broom.

**Preston NE (1) 2** *(Parkinson 22, Ashcroft 71)*
**Notts Co (1) 2** *(Finnan 35, Derry 84)*  7583
*Preston NE:* Lucas; Parkinson, Barrick, Kidd, Jackson, Gregan, Appleton, Ashcroft, Lormor, Darby (Macken), Eyres.
*Notts Co:* Ward; Hendon, Baraclough, Redmile, Strodder, Robinson (Pearce), Finnan, Derry, Robson, Jones (Jackson), Martindale (Dudley).

**Rotherham U (0) 6** *(Glover 48, Richardson 53, Garner 54, Druce 70, Berry 81, Hudson 90)*
**Kings Lynn (0) 0**  5883
*Rotherham U:* Mimms; Clark, Hurst (Goodwin), Garner (Hudson), Warner (Bass), Richardson, Berry, Thompson, Druce, Glover, Roscoe.
*Kings Lynn:* Hollman; Matthews, Skelly, Hoyle, Ellis, Spearing (Delicata), Hopkins, Wright, Roberts (Stock), McNamara, Hudson.

**Scunthorpe U (0) 1** *(Forrester 76)*
**Ilkeston T (0) 1** *(Robinson 52)*  4187
*Scunthorpe U:* Clarke; Walsh, McAuley (Ormondroyd), Sertori, Wilcox, Hope, Marshall (Shakespeare), D'Auria, Eyre, Forrester, Calvo-Garcia.
*Ilkeston T:* Rigby; Fearon, Ludlum, Wright, Law, Knapper, Shaw, Robinson, Carmichael, Moore (Eshelby), Ball.

**Torquay U (1) 1** *(Gurney 37)*
**Watford (1) 1** *(Noel-Williams 20)*  3416
*Torquay U:* Veysey; Gurney, Gibbs, Robinson, Gittens, Watson, Clayton, Hill (Leadbitter), Jack, Thomas, Hapgood.
*Watford:* Chamberlain; Gibbs, Kennedy, Page, Millen, Mooney, Noel-Williams (Palmer), Hyde, Thomas (Lowndes), Johnson R, Rosenthal.

**Wigan Ath (0) 2** *(Martinez 69, Lee 88)*
**York C (0) 1** *(Rowe 82)*  4021
*Wigan Ath:* Carroll; Green, Johnson (Sharp), Greenall, McGibbon, Martinez, Lee, O'Connell, Jones, Kilford, Lowe.
*York C:* Warrington; Murty, Himsworth, Bushell, Reed, Barras, Pouton (Jordan), Tinkler, Cresswell (Bull), Rowe, Stephenson.

**Wisbech T (0) 0**
**Bristol R (0) 2** *(Beadle 52, Hayles 79)*  3593
*Wisbech T:* Bray; Marshall (Newell), Lindsay, Irvine (McLaughlin), Moore, Ward, Parrott (Topliss), Childs, Munns, Gallagher, Williams.
*Bristol R:* Collett; Pritchard, Perry, Penrice, White, Tillson, Low, Hayfield, Beadle, Lockwood, Hayles.

**7 DEC**

**Bournemouth (1) 3** *(Carey 13 (og), O'Neill 79, Fletcher 90)*
**Bristol C (0) 1** *(Cramb 82)*  5687
*Bournemouth:* Glass; Young, Vincent, Howe, Cox, Bailey, Beardsmore (Rawlinson), Robinson, Warren, Fletcher, O'Neill.
*Bristol C:* Welch; Locke, Bell, Goodridge, Taylor, Carey, Edwards, Tisdale (Barclay), Goater, Cramb, Brennan (Tinnion).

**SECOND ROUND REPLAYS**

**15 DEC**

**Stevenage B (1) 2** *(Campbell 41 (og), Beevor 74)*
**Cambridge U (1) 1** *(Butler 17)*  4886
*Stevenage B:* Gallagher; Kirby, March, Smith, Trott, Beevor, Perkins, Trebble, Crawshaw, Wordsworth, Love.
*Cambridge U:* Barrett; Chenery, Wilson (Barnwell-Edinboro), Ashbee, Foster (Marc Joseph), Campbell, Wanless, Benjamin, Taylor (Kyd), Butler, Beall.

**16 DEC**

**Basingstoke T (0) 0**
**Northampton T (0) 0**  4943
*Basingstoke T:* Beale; Barker, Richardson, Carey (Huxford), Harris, Morley (Line), Wilkinson, Emsden, Mancy, Coombs, Tydeman (Ferrett).
*Northampton T:* Woodman; Clarkson, Frain, Hill, Peer, Brightwell, Hunt (Seal), Heggs, Gibb (Warner), Gayle, Hunter.
*aet; Northampton T won 4-3 on penalties.*

**Boreham Wood (0) 0**
**Cheltenham T (1) 2** *(Bloomer 42, Smith 68)*  1615
*Boreham Wood:* Taylor; Daly, McCarthy, Robbins, Nisbet, Hollingdale, Shaw J, Marshall, Heffer, Samuels, Brown (Dixon).
*Cheltenham T:* Book; Duff, Victory, Banks, Freeman, Milton (Crisp), Howells, Walker (Benton), Eaton (Smith), Watkins, Bloomer.

**Chesterfield (0) 0**
**Grimsby T (1) 2** *(Lester 22, Groves 79)*  4553
*Chesterfield:* Mercer; Hewitt, Jules, Beaumont (Reeves), Williams, Breckin, Willis, Holland, Wilkinson, Ebdon, Perkins.
*Grimsby T:* Davison; McDermott, Gallimore, Handyside, Rodger, Jobling, Donovan, Widdrington, Livingstone, Lester (Clare), Groves.

**Hereford U (0) 1** *(Grayson 48)*
**Colchester U (0) 1** *(Forbes 47)*  3725
*Hereford U:* Debont; Warner, Fishlock, Cook (Pitman), Brough, Walker, Hargreaves, McGorry, Grayson, McCue (Williams), Mahon. ·
*Colchester U:* Emberson; Dunne, Gregory, Skelton, Greene, Cawley, Wilkins (Lock), Haydon (Duguid), Forbes, Adcock, Stamps (Betts).
*aet; Hereford U won 5-4 on penalties.*

**Notts Co (0) 1** *(Farrell 51)*
**Preston NE (0) 2** *(Moyes 90, Eyres 96)*  3052
*Notts Co:* Ward; Hendon, Pearce, Redmile, Strodder (Martindale), Baraclough, Finnan, Derry, Farrell, Jones (Dudley), Robson (Robinson).
*Preston NE:* Moilanen; Parkinson, Barrick, Kidd (Holt), Jackson, Gregan, Appleton, Darby, Lormor (Moyes), Macken (Nogan), Eyres.

**Watford (0) 2** *(Noel-Williams 91, 108)*
**Torquay U (0) 1** *(Clayton 103)*  5848
*Watford:* Chamberlain; Gibbs, Kennedy, Page (Smith) (Robinson), Millen, Mooney, Noel-Williams, Hyde, Lee, Johnson, Palmer.
*Torquay U:* Veysey; Gurney, Gibbs, Robinson, Gittens, Watson, Clayton, Hill (Bedeau), Jack (Leadbitter), Thomas, Hapgood (Tully).

**17 DEC**

**Emley (0) 3** *(Graham 75, Nicholson 87, 111 (pen))*
**Lincoln C (0) 3** *(Whitney 65, Alcide 69, Hone 116)*  4891
*Emley:* Marples; Nicholson, Jones, Thompson, Lacy, David, Calcutt, Hurst, Graham (Viner), Wood (Tonks), Reynolds.
*Lincoln C:* Richardson; Barnett, Whitney, Fleming, Holmes, Austin, Walling, Hone, Gordon (Alcide), Thorpe, Brown S (Stant).
*aet; Emley won 4-3 on penalties.*

**Ilkeston T (0) 1** *(Moore 72)*
**Scunthorpe U (2) 2** *(Forrester 10, Wilcox 30)*  2109
*Ilkeston T:* Rigby; Fearon, Ludlam, Middleton, Law, Knapper (Simpson), Shaw (Eshelby), Robinson, Carmichael, Moore (Huckerby), Ball.
*Scunthorpe U:* Clarke; Walsh, McAuley, Sertori, Wilcox, Hope, Walker, D'Auria, Eyre, Forrester, Calvo-Garcia (Housham).

**THIRD ROUND**

**3 JAN**

**Arsenal (0) 0**

**Port Vale (0) 0**      37,471

*Arsenal:* Seaman; Grimandi, Winterburn, Vieira, Bould, Keown, Parlour (Wreh), Anelka (Boa Morte), Petit (Hughes), Bergkamp, Overmars.
*Port Vale:* Musselwhite; Hill, Tankard, Bogie, Aspin, Snijders, Ainsworth, Porter, Talbot (Glover), Naylor (Foyle), Corden.

**Barnsley (1) 1** *(Barnard 26)*

**Bolton W (0) 0**      15,042

*Barnsley:* Watson; Eaden, Barnard, Sheridan, Moses, De Zeeuw, Marcelle (Bullock), Redfearn, Hristov (Liddell), Ward, Tinkler.
*Bolton W:* Ward; Bergsson, Whitlow (Cox), Frandsen, Fish, Todd, Pollock (Beardsley), Sellars, Blake, Gunnlaugsson, Thompson.

**Blackburn R (2) 4** *(McGibbon 20 (og), Gallacher 37, 60, Sherwood 48)*

**Wigan Ath (0) 2** *(Lee 62, Lowe 68)*      22,402

*Blackburn R:* Flowers; Kenna, Valery, Henchoz, Hendry, Sherwood, Ripley (Bohinen) (Beattie), Gallacher (Wilcox), Sutton, Flitcroft, Duff.
*Wigan Ath:* Carroll; Green, Morgan, Greenall, McGibbon, Martinez, Lee, Rogers, Jones, Smeets, Kilford (Lowe).

**Bristol R (1) 1** *(Beadle 36)*

**Ipswich T (0) 1** *(Stockwell 71)*      8610

*Bristol R:* Collett; Pritchard, Lockwood, Penrice, White, Foster, Holloway, Ramasut (Bennett), Beadle, Cureton, Hayles.
*Ipswich T:* Wright; Stockwell, Taricco, Williams, Mowbray, Venus, Holland, Dyer, Johnson (Mathie), Scowcroft, Petta (Tanner).

**Cardiff C (1) 1** *(Fowler 18)*

**Oldham Ath (0) 0**      6635

*Cardiff C:* Hallworth; Middleton, Beech, Young, Harris, Fowler (Stoker), O'Sullivan (Eckhardt), Penney, Saville, Dale, Carss.
*Oldham Ath:* Kelly; McNiven S, Holt, Graham, Hodgson, Redmond, Rickers (Allott), Duxbury (Ritchie), McCarthy, Barlow (Rush), Reid.

**Charlton Ath (2) 4** *(Robinson 38, Brown 42, Leaburn 64, Mendonca 75)*

**Nottingham F (0) 1** *(Van Hooijdonk 56)*      13,827

*Charlton Ath:* Salmon; Brown, Bowen, Jones K (Parker), Rufus, Chapple, Newton, Kinsella, Robinson, Mendonca (Bright), Leaburn.
*Nottingham F:* Beasant; Little, Rogers, Cooper, Chettle, Hjelde, Bonalair, Gemmill, Moore, Campbell, Armstrong (Van Hooijdonk).

**Crewe Alex (1) 1** *(Rivers 31)*

**Birmingham C (1) 2** *(Furlong 22 (pen), 55)*      4607

*Crewe Alex:* Kearton; Bignot, Smith S, Unsworth, Walton, Charnock, Rivers, Holsgrove, Adebola, Johnson, Little.
*Birmingham C:* Bennett; Bass, Grainger, Bruce, Ablett, Marsden, McCarthy, O'Connor, Furlong, Hughes (Johnson), Forster (Francis).

**Crystal Palace (1) 2** *(Emblen 45, 87)*

**Scunthorpe U (0) 0**      11,624

*Crystal Palace:* Miller; Smith (Burton), Gordon, Roberts, Hreidarsson, Linighan, Edworthy, Warhurst (Ginty), Dyer, Rodger, Emblen.
*Scunthorpe U:* Clarke; Walsh (Laws), Housham, Sertori, Wilcox (Ormondroyd), Hope, Walker, D'Auria, Eyre, Forrester, Calvo-Garcia.

**Derby Co (0) 2** *(Baiano 68 (pen), Powell C 73)*

**Southampton (0) 0**      27,992

*Derby Co:* Poom; Kozluk, Powell C, Yates, Stimac, Rowett (Elliott), Powell D, Burton, Baiano (Willems), Wanchope, Carsley.
*Southampton:* Jones; Dodd, Benali, Richardson, Palmer, Monkou, Le Tissier, Hughes (Williams), Hirst (Ostenstad), Davies, Oakley.

**Grimsby T (1) 3** *(McDermott 25, Woods 48, Donovan 76)*

**Norwich C (0) 0**      8161

*Grimsby T:* Davison; McDermott, Gallimore, Handyside, Rodger, Jobling, Donovan (Butterfield), Black, Nogan (Woods), Clare (Lever), Groves.
*Norwich C:* Marshall A; Segura (Sutch), Mills, Grant, Scott, Fleming, Bellamy, Fleck (Llewellyn), Fuglestad, Milligan, O'Neill.

**Leeds U (2) 4** *(Radebe 17, Hasselbaink 45 (pen), Kewell 71, 72)*

**Oxford U (0) 0**      20,568

*Leeds U:* Martyn; Maybury, Halle, Kelly, Molenaar, Wetherall, Bowyer (Beeney), Wallace (Lilley), Hasselbaink (Harte), Kewell, Radebe.
*Oxford U:* Whitehead; Robinson, Ford (Remy), Robinson, Purse, Gilchrist, Massey (Angel), Smith, Powell, Jemson (Cook), Beauchamp.

**Leicester C (2) 4** *(Marshall 17, Parker 26 (pen), Savage 53, Cottee 58)*

**Northampton T (0) 0**      20,608

*Leicester C:* Keller; Savage, Guppy (Wilson), Elliott, Kamark, Prior, Lennon, Izzet (Fenton), Marshall (Cottee), Parker, Heskey.
*Northampton T:* Woodman; Clarkson, Frain, Bishop (Hunt), Hill (Gibb), Brightwell, Peer, Dozzell, Freestone, Gayle (Heggs), Hunter.

**Liverpool (1) 1** *(Redknapp 7)*

**Coventry C (1) 3** *(Huckerby 45, Dublin 62, Telfer 87)*      33,888

*Liverpool:* James; McAteer, Harkness, Kvarme (Murphy), Matteo, Leonhardsen (Berger), McManaman, Ince, Fowler, Riedle, Redknapp.
*Coventry C:* Hedman; Telfer, Burrows, Williams, Shaw, Breen, Boateng, Whelan, Dublin, Hall, Huckerby.

**Manchester C (2) 2** *(Rosler 35, Brown 42)*

**Bradford C (0) 0**      23,686

*Manchester C:* Wright; Brightwell, Shelia, Brown, Jeff Whitley, Wiekens (Jim Whitley), Brannan, Russell (Greenacre), Dickov (Van Blerk), Rosler.
*Bradford C:* Walsh; Wilder (McGinlay), Jacobs, Murray, Youds, O'Brien, Lawrence (Midgley), Pepper, Steiner, Blake, Beagrie.

**Portsmouth (2) 2** *(Foster 6, 40)*

**Aston Villa (1) 2** *(Staunton 41, Grayson 88)*      16,013

*Portsmouth:* Knight; Pethick, Thomson, McLoughlin, Waterman, Awford, Hall, Foster, Aloisi (Durnin), Svensson, Turner (Igoe).
*Aston Villa:* Bosnich; Nelson, Wright, Southgate (Scimeca), Ehiogu, Staunton, Taylor (Hendrie), Draper, Milosevic, Collymore (Joachim), Grayson.

**Preston NE (0) 1** *(Ashcroft 71 (pen))*

**Stockport Co (1) 2** *(Angell 30, 48)*      12,180

*Preston NE:* Moilanen; Parkinson (Cartwright), Kidd, Murdock, Jackson, Gregan, Appleton, Ashcroft (Holt), Macken, Rankine, Eyres.
*Stockport Co:* Nixon; Connelly, Searle, Bennett, Dinning, McIntosh, Gannon, Byrne, Angell, Armstrong, Cooper.

**QPR (1) 2** *(Spencer 6, Gallen 75)*

**Middlesbrough (1) 2** *(Hignett 33, Mustoe 63)*      13,379

*QPR:* Roberts; Yates, Brevett, Quashie, Maddix, Ready, Spencer (Gallen), Peacock, Murray, Sheron (Slade), Sinclair.
*Middlesbrough:* Schwarzer; Maddison, Kinder, Vickers, Pearson, Mustoe, Hignett, Townsend, Moreno, Merson, Stamp (Beck).

**Rotherham U (0) 1** *(Garner 68)*
**Sunderland (1) 5** *(Phillips 15 (pen), 55, 72, 76, Quinn 85)*
11,500
*Rotherham U:* Mimms; Richardson (Goodwin), Roscoe, Garner, Knill, Warner, Berry, Scott, White, Glover, Hurst.
*Sunderland:* Perez; Holloway, Gray, Clark, Craddock, Williams, Summerbee, Rae, Quinn, Phillips, Johnston.

**Sheffield U (0) 1** *(Fjortoft 65)*
**Bury (1) 1** *(Andy Gray 7)*
14,009
*Sheffield U:* Kelly; Borbokis, Woodhouse (Katchuro), Holdsworth, Ford, Nilsen, Saunders, Marker, Taylor (Fjortoft), Deane, Hutchison.
*Bury:* Kiely; Woodward, Armstrong, Daws, Lucketti, Swailes, Andy Gray, Dalglish (Jepson), Battersby, Johnrose, Patterson.

**Swindon T (1) 1** *(Walters 6)*
**Stevenage B (1) 2** *(Soloman 23, Grazioli 65)*
9422
*Swindon T:* Digby; Culverhouse, Robinson, Collins, Taylor, McDonald, Watson (Finney), Walters (Drysdale), Hay, Ndah, Gooden.
*Stevenage B:* Gallagher; Kirby, Love, Smith, Trott, Soloman, Perkins, Grazioli, Crawshaw, Wordsworth (Holden), Stapleton.

**Watford (0) 1** *(Kennedy 65)*
**Sheffield W (0) 1** *(Alexandersson 64)*
18,306
*Watford:* Chamberlain; Gibbs, Kennedy, Page, Millen, Mooney, Lowndes (Thomas), Hyde, Lee, Johnson R, Easton.
*Sheffield W:* Pressman; Atherton, Nolan, Pembridge, Newsome, Walker, Alexandersson, Rudi, Booth (Humphreys), Carbone, Di Canio.

**West Ham U (1) 2** *(Lampard 4, Hartson 82)*
**Emley (0) 1** *(David 56)*
18,629
*West Ham U:* Forrest; Breacker (Abou), Lazaridis, Potts, Pearce, Unsworth, Lampard, Berkovic, Kitson, Hartson, Ferdinand.
*Emley:* Marples; David, Lacey (Wilson) (Wood), Thompson, Jones, Calcutt (Tonks), Nicholson, Banks, Hurst, Graham, Reynolds.

**4 JAN**
**Chelsea (0) 3** *(Le Saux 78, Vialli 83, 88)*
**Manchester U (3) 5** *(Beckham 23, 28, Cole 45, 65, Sheringham 74)*
34,792
*Chelsea:* De Goey; Petrescu, Le Saux, Duberry, Leboeuf, Clarke, Nicholls (Myers), Di Matteo, Flo (Vialli), Hughes M, Zola.
*Manchester U:* Schmeichel; Neville G, Irwin, Johnsen, Scholes (Solskjaer), Pallister, Beckham, Butt, Cole, Sheringham, Giggs.

**Everton (0) 0**
**Newcastle U (0) 1** *(Rush 67)*
20,885
*Everton:* Myhre; Thomas, Ball, Thomsen (Oster), Dunne, Tyler, Farrelly, Barmby, Ferguson, Grant, Cadamarteri.
*Newcastle U:* Hislop; Watson, Beresford, Pistone, Peacock, Pearce, Lee, Hamilton, Asprilla (Rush), Barnes (Hughes), Gillespie.

**Wimbledon (0) 0**
**Wrexham (0) 0**
6349
*Wimbledon:* Sullivan; Cunningham, Kimble, Solbakken (Jones), Thatcher (Clarke), Perry, Ardley, Earle, Cort (Gayle), Hughes C, Hughes M.
*Wrexham:* Marriott; McGregor, Hardy, Russell, Ridler, Carey, Skinner, Owen, Connolly, Roberts (Spink), Ward.

**5 JAN**
**Tottenham H (2) 3** *(Clemence 20, Calderwood 28, Taylor 61 (og))*
**Fulham (0) 1** *(Smith 54)*
27,909
*Tottenham H:* Walker (Baardsen); Carr, Wilson, Vega, Calderwood, Campbell, Ginola (Mahorn), Clemence, Klinsmann, Brady, Dominguez.
*Fulham:* Taylor; Lawrence, Herrera, Trollope, Coleman, Neilson, Smith, Bracewell, Moody, Peschisolido, Hayward.

**13 JAN**
**Bournemouth (0) 0**
**Huddersfield T (1) 1** *(Stewart 15)*
7385
*Bournemouth:* Glass; Young, Vincent (Murray), Howe, Cox, Harrington (Rolling), O'Neill (Bailey), Robinson, Brissett, Fletcher, Warren.
*Huddersfield T:* Harper; Jenkins, Phillips, Dyson, Morrison, Gray, Dalton (Richardson), Horne, Stewart, Allison, Johnson (Makel).

**Cheltenham T (1) 1** *(Watkins 22 (pen))*
**Reading (0) 1** *(Morley 71)*
6000
*Cheltenham T:* Book; Duff, Victory, Banks, Freeman, Knight, Howells, Walker (Eaton), Smith (Benton), Watkins, Bloomer.
*Reading:* Hammond; Booty, Swales, Bernal, Davies, Parkinson, Bowen, Hodges (Caskey), Morley, Lovell (Meaker), Lambert.

**Hereford U (0) 0**
**Tranmere R (1) 3** *(Jones G 14, 53, Hill 59)*
7473
*Hereford U:* Debont; Rodgerson, Fishlock, Pitman, Brough, Walker, Hargreaves, McGorry, Grayson, Agana, Mahon.
*Tranmere R:* Simonsen; Challinor, Thompson, McGreal, Thorn (Hill), Irons, Jones G, Parkinson (Morrissey), Kelly, O'Brien, Mellon (Mahon).

**Peterborough U (0) 0**
**Walsall (1) 2** *(Watson 44, 73)*
12,809
*Peterborough U:* Tyler; Linton, Lewis, Castle, Bodley, Edwards, Houghton, Payne, Carruthers, Quinn, Farrell.
*Walsall:* Walker; Evans, Marsh, Viveash, Mountfield, Peron (Blake), Boli, Porter, Keates, Watson, Hodge.

**WBA (2) 3** *(Sneekes 28, 32, Kilbane 78)*
**Stoke C (0) 1** *(Gabbiadini 61)*
17,598
*WBA:* Miller; Holmes, Nicholson, Sneekes, Murphy, Dobson, Evans (Butler), Hamilton, Hughes, Hunt, Kilbane.
*Stoke C:* Muggleton; Pickering, Griffin, Sigurdsson, Tweed (Thorne), Keen, Forsyth, Wallace, Gabbiadini, Stewart, Whittle.

**THIRD ROUND REPLAYS**

**13 JAN**
**Bury (0) 1** *(Andy Gray 84)*
**Sheffield U (0) 2** *(Saunders 48, Fjortoft 70)*
4920
*Bury:* Kiely; Andy Gray, Armstrong, Daws, Lucketti, Butler, Swailes (Rigby), Battersby, Swan, Johnrose, Woodward (Jepson).
*Sheffield U:* Tracey; Borbokis (Beard), Nilsen, Ford, Hutchison, Holdsworth, Saunders, Marker, Fjortoft, Taylor (Katchuro), Stuart.

**Ipswich T (1) 1** *(Johnson 43)*
**Bristol R (0) 0**
11,362
*Ipswich T:* Wright; Stockwell, Taricco, Williams, Mowbray, Cundy, Tanner, Holland, Johnson, Scowcroft, Petta.
*Bristol R:* Collett; Pritchard (Perry), Lockwood, Penrice, White, Foster, Holloway, Ramasut (Hayfield), Beadle, Cureton (Bennett), Hayles.

**Middlesbrough (0) 2** *(Campbell 54, Mustoe 59)*
**QPR (0) 0**
21,817
*Middlesbrough:* Schwarzer; Stockdale, Harrison, Vickers, Festa, Maddison, Mustoe, Townsend, Campbell, Merson, Ormerod.
*QPR:* Harper; Yates, Brevett (Bruce), Quashie, Ready, Morrow, Spencer (Gallen), Peacock, Murray, Sheron (Slade), Sinclair.

**Wrexham (1) 2** *(Connolly 7, 46)*

**Wimbledon (3) 3** *(Hughes M 17, 26, Gayle 35)* 9539

*Wrexham:* Marriott; McGregor, Hardy, Phillips, Ridler, Carey, Wainwright, Owen, Connolly, Roberts, Ward (Chalk).
*Wimbledon:* Sullivan; Cunningham, Kimble, Jones, Blackwell, Perry, Ardley, Earle, Gayle, Cort (Ekoku), Hughes M.

## THIRD ROUND

### 14 JAN

**Darlington (0) 0**

**Wolverhampton W (1) 4** *(Freedman 18, Paatelainen 66, 90, Ferguson 90)* 5018

*Darlington:* Preece; Shaw, Barnard (Resch), Devos, Crosby (Brumwell), Atkinson, Oliver, Gaughan, Roberts, Dorner, Naylor (Robinson).
*Wolverhampton W:* Stowell; Muscat, Froggatt, Atkins, Richards, Curle, Goodman (Paatelainen), Ferguson, Robinson (Daley), Freedman, Sedgley.

## THIRD ROUND REPLAYS

### 14 JAN

**Aston Villa (1) 1** *(Milosevic 21)*

**Portsmouth (0) 0** 23,355

*Aston Villa:* Bosnich; Grayson, Wright, Scimeca, Ehiogu, Staunton, Taylor, Draper (Hendrie), Milosevic, Collymore, Yorke.
*Portsmouth:* Knight; Pethick, Thomson, McLoughlin, Whitbread, Awford, Hall, Simpson (Carter), Durnin, Foster (Svensson), Russell.

**Port Vale (0) 1** *(Corden 112)*

**Arsenal (0) 1** *(Bergkamp 100)* 14,964

*Port Vale:* Musselwhite; Hill, Tankard, Bogie, Aspin, Snijders, Ainsworth, Porter, Talbot (Foyle), Naylor (Mills), Corden.
*Arsenal:* Seaman; Dixon, Winterburn, Vieira (Grimandi), Bould, Keown, Parlour, Wright (Anelka), Hughes, Bergkamp, Overmars (Boa Morte).
*aet; Arsenal won 4-3 on penalties.*

**Sheffield W (0) 0**

**Watford (0) 0** 18,707

*Sheffield W:* Pressman; Nolan, Pembridge, Atherton, Newsome, Walker (Humphreys), Alexandersson (Oakes), Hyde, Booth, Rudi, Di Canio.
*Watford:* Chamberlain; Gibbs, Kennedy, Palmer, Millen, Mooney, Noel-Williams (Thomas), Hyde, Lee, Johnson R, Robinson.
*aet; Sheffield W won 5-3 on penalties.*

### 20 JAN

**Reading (1) 2** *(Morley 38, Booty 72)*

**Cheltenham T (0) 1** *(Walker 51)* 9686

*Reading:* Hammond; Booty, Swales, Bernal, Davies (Thorp), Parkinson, Bowen, Hodges (Houghton), Morley, Lovell, Lambert.
*Cheltenham T:* Book; Duff, Victory, Banks, Freeman, Benton (Wright), Crisp (Milton), Walker (Knight), Eaton, Watkins, Bloomer.

## FOURTH ROUND

### 24 JAN

**Aston Villa (1) 4** *(Grayson 4, Yorke 62, 64, Collymore 72)*

**WBA (0) 0** 39,372

*Aston Villa:* Bosnich; Grayson, Wright, Southgate, Ehiogu, Staunton (Charles), Taylor, Draper, Yorke, Collymore, Hendrie.
*WBA:* Miller; Holmes, Nicholson, Sneekes, Murphy, Dobson, Butler (Evans), Hamilton (Coldicott), Hughes (Flynn), Hunt, Kilbane.

**Birmingham C (1) 2** *(Hughes 32, 84)*

**Stockport Co (0) 1** *(Armstrong 66)* 15,882

*Birmingham C:* Bennett; Bass (Francis), Grainger (Robinson), Bruce, Ablett, Marsden, McCarthy, O'Connor, Furlong (Ndlovu), Hughes, Forster.
*Stockport Co:* Nixon; Connelly (Dinning), Searle (Byrne), Bennett, Flynn, McIntosh, Gannon, Cook (Travis), Angell, Armstrong, Cooper.

**Cardiff C (0) 1** *(Nugent 47)*

**Reading (0) 1** *(Asaba 56)* 10,174

*Cardiff C:* Hallworth; Middleton, Beech, Young, Harris, Fowler, Eckhardt, Penney, Nugent (Saville), Dale, Carss.
*Reading:* Hammond; Booty, Swales, Bernal, Bodin, Parkinson, Bowen (Meaker), Hodges (Houghton), Morley, Asaba (Lovell), Lambert.

**Charlton Ath (0) 1** *(Jones K 64)*

**Wolverhampton W (0) 1** *(Richards 47)* 15,540

*Charlton Ath:* Salmon; Brown, Bowen (Barness), Jones K (Allen), Rufus, Chapple, Newton, Kinsella, Robinson (Holmes), Bright, Mendonca.
*Wolverhampton W:* Stowell; Muscat, Froggatt, Atkins, Richards, Curle, Goodman, Robinson, Paatelainen, Freedman, Sedgley.

**Coventry C (2) 2** *(Dublin 38, 45)*

**Derby Co (0) 0** 22,824

*Coventry C:* Hedman; Nilsson, Burrows, Boateng (Gavin Strachan), Shaw, Breen, Telfer, Soltvedt, Dublin, Whelan (Hall), Huckerby (Moldovan).
*Derby Co:* Poom; Eranio, Powell C, Laursen, Stimac, Yates, Powell D, Burton (Rowett), Baiano (Willems), Wanchope, Carsley (Dailly).

**Crystal Palace (1) 3** *(Dyer 33, 62, 66)*

**Leicester C (0) 0** 15,489

*Crystal Palace:* Miller; Smith, Gordon, Roberts, Ismael, Linighan, Fullarton, Hreidarsson, Dyer, Edworthy, Brolin.
*Leicester C:* Keller; Savage, Guppy, Elliott, Walsh, Kamark (Cottee), Lennon, Izzet, Marshall (Wilson), Parker, Heskey.

**Huddersfield T (0) 0**

**Wimbledon (0) 1** *(Ardley 62)* 14,533

*Huddersfield T:* Harper; Jenkins, Phillips, Dyson, Morrison (Edmondson), Gray, Dalton (Edwards), Horne, Stewart, Allison, Johnson (Richardson).
*Wimbledon:* Sullivan; Cunningham, Kimble, Hughes C (Solbakken), Blackwell, Perry, Ardley, Earle (Castledine), Gayle (Clarke), Cort, Hughes M.

**Ipswich T (1) 1** *(Johnson 45)*

**Sheffield U (0) 1** *(Saunders 82)* 14,654

*Ipswich T:* Wright; Stockwell, Taricco, Williams, Tanner, Cundy, Uhlenbeek, Holland, Johnson, Scowcroft, Petta.
*Sheffield U:* Tracey; Short, Sandford, Ford (Morris), Beard, Holdsworth, Saunders, Marker, Stuart, Marcello, Katchuro.

**Leeds U (1) 2** *(Molenaar 45, Hasselbaink 79)*

**Grimsby T (0) 0** 29,598

*Leeds U:* Martyn; Kelly, Robertson, Hopkin, Molenaar, Wetherall, Bowyer, Wallace, Hasselbaink, Ribeiro, Kewell.
*Grimsby T:* Davison; McDermott, Gallimore, Handyside, Lever, Jobling (Clare), Donovan, Smith, Livingstone, Black, Groves.

**Manchester U (2) 5** *(Cole 10, 65, Solskjaer 39, 69, Johnsen 74)*

**Walsall (0) 1** *(Boli 72)* 54,669

*Manchester U:* Schmeichel; Irwin (Clegg), Neville P, Berg, Scholes (Mulryne), Johnsen, Beckham, McClair, Cole, Solskjaer, Thornley (Nevland).
*Walsall:* Walker; Evans, Marsh, Viveash, Mountfield, Peron (Blake), Boli, Porter, Keates, Watson, Hodge.

**Middlesbrough (0) 1** *(Merson 62)*
**Arsenal (2) 2** *(Overmars 2, Parlour 19)* 28,264
*Middlesbrough:* Schwarzer; Maddison, Harrison, Festa, Vickers, Mustoe, Ormerod (Hignett), Townsend, Moreno (Beck), Merson, Campbell (Baker).
*Arsenal:* Manninger; Dixon (Grimandi), Winterburn, Vieira, Bould, Adams, Parlour, Anelka, Petit, Bergkamp, Overmars.

**Tottenham H (1) 1** *(Campbell 30)*
**Barnsley (0) 1** *(Redfearn 59 (pen))* 28,722
*Tottenham H:* Baardsen; Carr, Wilson, Vega, Campbell, Berti, Ginola, Fox, Klinsmann, Ferdinand (Calderwood), Sinton.
*Barnsley:* Watson; Eaden, Barnard, Sheridan, Moses, De Zeeuw, Hendrie (Liddell), Redfearn, Ward, Marcelle, Tinkler (Bosancic).

**Tranmere R (0) 1** *(Parkinson 77)*
**Sunderland (0) 0** 14,055
*Tranmere R:* Simonsen; Morgan, Thompson, McGreal, Challinor, Hill, Jones G, Parkinson, Kelly, O'Brien, Mellon.
*Sunderland:* Perez; Holloway, Gray, Clark, Craddock, Makin, Summerbee, Rae, Quinn, Phillips, Johnston.

**25 JAN**

**Manchester C (0) 1** *(Kinkladze 59)*
**West Ham U (1) 2** *(Berkovic 28, Lomas 76)* 26,495
*Manchester C:* Wright; Brightwell, Shelia, Brown, Symons, Edghill, Jeff Whitley, Russell, Dickov, Kinkladze, Rosler.
*West Ham U:* Forrest; Potts, Lazaridis, Unsworth (Breacker), Ferdinand, Pearce, Lampard, Abou (Dowie), Hartson, Berkovic, Lomas.

**Stevenage B (1) 1** *(Grazioli 41)*
**Newcastle U (1) 1** *(Shearer 3)* 8040
*Stevenage B:* Gallagher; Dillnutt, Love (March), Smith, Trott, Soloman, Perkins, Grazioli (Wordsworth), Crawshaw, Trebble, Stapleton (Inman).
*Newcastle U:* Hislop; Watson, Pistone, Batty, Howey, Pearce, Lee, Gillespie, Shearer, Barnes (Ketsbaia), Beresford (Albert).

**26 JAN**

**Sheffield W (0) 0**
**Blackburn R (2) 3** *(Sutton 6, Sherwood 37, Duff 87)* 15,940
*Sheffield W:* Pressman; Nolan, Pembridge, Atherton, Newsome, Walker, Whittingham (Humphreys), Magilton (Oakes), Di Canio, Carbone, Rudi.
*Blackburn R:* Flowers; Kenna, McKinlay, Henchoz, Hendry, Sherwood, Ripley (Valery), Gallacher, Sutton, Duff (Andersson), Wilcox.

**FOURTH ROUND REPLAYS**

**3 FEB**

**Reading (0) 1** *(Morley 56)*
**Cardiff C (1) 1** *(Dale 40)* 11,808
*Reading:* Hammond; Booty, Swales, Bernal, Davies, Parkinson, Bowen, Houghton, Morley, Asaba, Williams (Hodges).
*Cardiff C:* Hallworth; Middleton, Beech, Young (Stoker), Harris, Eckhardt (Jarman), O'Sullivan (Fowler), Penney, Nugent, Dale, Carss.
*aet; Reading won 4-3 on penalties.*

**Sheffield U (1) 1** *(Hutchison 13 (pen))*
**Ipswich T (0) 0** 14,144
*Sheffield U:* Tracey; Short (Quinn), Sandford, Ford, Nilsen, Holdsworth, Saunders, Marker, Stuart, Marcello (Taylor), Hutchison.
*Ipswich T:* Wright; Stockwell, Taricco, Williams (Sonner), Tanner (Petta), Cundy, Uhlenbeek, Holland, Johnson (Mathie), Scowcroft, Dyer.

**Wolverhampton W (1) 3** *(Curle 29 (pen), Naylor 48, Paatelainen 65)*
**Charlton Ath (0) 0** 20,429
*Wolverhampton W:* Stowell; Muscat, Naylor, Sedgley, Richards (Atkins), Curle, Goodman (Simpson), Ferguson, Paatelainen, Freedman, Robinson.
*Charlton Ath:* Petterson; Brown, Bowen (Balmer), Holmes (Jones K), Rufus (Allen), Chapple, Newton, Kinsella, Robinson, Jones S, Bright.

**4 FEB**

**Barnsley (0) 3** *(Ward 50, Redfearn 58, Barnard 88)*
**Tottenham H (0) 1** *(Ginola 72)* 18,220
*Barnsley:* Watson; Eaden, Barnard, Morgan, Moses, De Zeeuw, Hendrie, Redfearn, Bullock, Ward, Bosancic.
*Tottenham H:* Baardsen; Carr, Wilson (Howells), Vega, Campbell, Clemence, Fox, Berti (Armstrong), Klinsmann (Brady), Ferdinand, Ginola.

**Newcastle U (1) 2** *(Shearer 16, 65)*
**Stevenage B (0) 1** *(Crawshaw 74)* 36,705
*Newcastle U:* Hislop; Watson (Barton), Pistone, Albert, Howey (Beresford), Pearce, Lee, Batty, Shearer, Tomasson (Ketsbaia), Gillespie.
*Stevenage B:* Gallagher; Dillnutt, March, Smith, Trott, Beevor, Perkins (Fenton), Wordsworth (Thompson), Crawshaw, Trebble, Stapleton (Inman).

**FIFTH ROUND**

**13 FEB**

**Sheffield U (0) 1** *(Sandford 87)*
**Reading (0) 0** 17,845
*Sheffield U:* Tracey; Borbokis, Quinn, Ford, Sandford, Holdsworth, Saunders (Katchuro), Marker, Taylor, Hutchison, Stuart (Marcello).
*Reading:* Bibbo; Booty, Swales, Bernal, Primus, Parkinson, Bowen, Houghton, Morley, Asaba (Williams), Hodges.

**14 FEB**

**Aston Villa (0) 0**
**Coventry C (0) 1** *(Moldovan 72)* 36,979
*Aston Villa:* Bosnich; Grayson, Wright, Southgate, Ehiogu, Scimeca, Joachim, Draper (Byfield), Hendrie, Collymore, Staunton.
*Coventry C:* Hedman; Nilsson, Burrows, Boateng, Shaw (Moldovan), Breen, Gavin Strachan (Boland), Soltvedt, Dublin, Hall, Huckerby.

**Leeds U (2) 3** *(Wallace 5, Hasselbaink 28, 87)*
**Birmingham C (0) 2** *(Ablett 63, Ndlovu 81)* 35,463
*Leeds U:* Martyn; Maybury (Harte), Halle, Kelly, Wetherall, Haaland, Bowyer, Wallace, Hasselbaink, Ribeiro, Kewell.
*Birmingham C:* Bennett; Bass, Grainger (Johnson), Bruce, Ablett, Charlton, McCarthy, O'Connor, Forster (Devlin), Hughes, Ndlovu.

**Newcastle U (1) 1** *(Shearer 22)*
**Tranmere R (0) 0** 36,675
*Newcastle U:* Given; Barton, Pistone, Batty, Howey, Pearce, Lee, Gillespie, Shearer, Tomasson (Ketsbaia), Speed (Barnes).
*Tranmere R:* Simonsen; Morgan, Thompson, McGreal, Challinor, Irons (Mellon), Morrissey, Hill, Kelly, O'Brien (Jones G), Branch (Parkinson).

**West Ham U (2) 2** *(Kitson 28, Berkovic 44)*
**Blackburn R (1) 2** *(Gallacher 3, Sutton 62)* 25,729
*West Ham U:* Forrest; Breacker (Potts), Lazaridis, Lomas, Ferdinand, Pearce, Lampard, Berkovic, Kitson (Hodges), Hartson, Impey.
*Blackburn R:* Flowers; Kenna, Croft (Duff), Henchoz, Hendry, McKinlay, Flitcroft, Gallacher, Sutton, Sherwood, Wilcox.

**Wimbledon (1) 1** *(Euell 14)*
**Wolverhampton W (0) 1** *(Paatelainen 67)* 15,322
*Wimbledon:* Sullivan; Jupp, Thatcher, Jones, Blackwell, Perry, Ardley, Fear, Euell, Cort (Clarke), Castledine.
*Wolverhampton W:* Stowell; Atkins, Naylor, Sedgley (Freedman), Richards, Curle, Goodman, Simpson, Paatelainen (Williams), Robinson, Osborn.

**15 FEB**
**Arsenal (0) 0**
**Crystal Palace (0) 0** 37,164
*Arsenal:* Manninger; Dixon, Winterburn, Hughes (Platt), Bould (Vieira), Grimandi, Parlour, Anelka (Wreh), Petit, Bergkamp, Overmars.
*Crystal Palace:* Miller; Smith, Gordon, Ismael, Hreidarsson, Edworthy, Fullarton, Roberts, Dyer, Rodger, Brolin.

**Manchester U (1) 1** *(Sheringham 42)*
**Barnsley (1) 1** *(Hendrie 39)* 54,700
*Manchester U:* Schmeichel; Clegg, Irwin, Berg, Neville P, Pallister, Nevland (Cruyff), Johnsen (Beckham), McClair (Neville G), Sheringham, Giggs.
*Barnsley:* Watson; Eaden, Krizan, Morgan, Moses, De Zeeuw (Appleby), Hendrie (Liddell), Redfearn, Ward, Bullock, Bosancic.

**FIFTH ROUND REPLAYS**

**25 FEB**
**Barnsley (2) 3** *(Hendrie 9, Jones 45, 65)*
**Manchester U (0) 2** *(Sheringham 56, Cole 81)* 18,655
*Barnsley:* Watson; Appleby (Sheridan), Barnard, Markstedt, Moses, Jones, Hendrie (Liddell), Redfearn, Ward, Bullock (Marcelle), Bosancic.
*Manchester U:* Schmeichel; Clegg (Twiss), Neville G, May, Neville P, Pallister, Beckham, McClair (Irwin), Cole, Nevland (Sheringham), Thornley.

**Blackburn R (0) 1** *(Ripley 114)*
**West Ham U (0) 1** *(Hartson 103)* 21,972
*Blackburn R:* Fettis; Kenna, Croft (Wilcox), Henchoz, Hendry, McKinlay (Flitcroft), Ripley (Dahlin), Gallacher, Sutton, Sherwood, Duff.
*West Ham U:* Forrest; Impey, Lazaridis, Unsworth, Ferdinand, Pearce, Moncur, Lampard, Hartson, Berkovic (Abou), Lomas.
*aet; West Ham U won 5-4 on penalties.*

**Crystal Palace (1) 1** *(Dyer 35)*
**Arsenal (2) 2** *(Anelka 2, Bergkamp 28)* 15,674
*Crystal Palace:* Miller; Smith (McKenzie), Gordon, Ismael, Hreidarsson, Edworthy, Fullarton, Roberts (Emblen), Dyer, Rodger, Brolin (Linighan).
*Arsenal:* Manninger; Dixon, Upson (Crowe), Vieira, Keown, Adams, Platt, Anelka, Hughes, Bergkamp (Overmars), Boa Morte.

**Wolverhampton W (0) 2** *(Robinson 63, Freedman 85)*
**Wimbledon (0) 1** *(Jones 48)* 25,112
*Wolverhampton W:* Stowell; Atkins, Naylor, Sedgley (Simpson), Richards, Curle, Paatelainen, Robinson, Keane (Williams), Freedman (Bull), Osborn.
*Wimbledon:* Sullivan; Jupp (Castledine), Thatcher, Jones, Blackwell, Perry, Ardley, Fear (Cort), Gayle, Euell (Clarke), Hughes M.

**SIXTH ROUND**

**7 MAR**
**Coventry C (1) 1** *(Dublin 32 (pen))*
**Sheffield U (1) 1** *(Marcello 45)* 23,084
*Coventry C:* Ogrizovic; Nilsson, Burrows, Boateng, Dublin, Breen, Telfer, Gavin Strachan (Soltvedt), Whelan, Moldovan (Hall), Huckerby.
*Sheffield U:* Kelly; Short (Beard), Quinn, Borbokis, Sandford, Holdsworth, Ford, Marker, Taylor, Marcello (Katchuro), Stuart.

**Leeds U (0) 0**
**Wolverhampton W (0) 1** *(Goodman 82)* 39,902
*Leeds U:* Martyn; Hiden, Harte, Halle, Radebe, Molenaar, Haaland, Wallace, Hasselbaink, Ribeiro (Kelly), Kewell.
*Wolverhampton W:* Segers; Muscat, Naylor, Williams, Richards, Curle, Goodman, Robinson, Bull (Keane), Freedman, Osborn.

**8 MAR**
**Arsenal (1) 1** *(Bergkamp 26 (pen))*
**West Ham U (1) 1** *(Pearce 12)* 38,077
*Arsenal:* Manninger; Dixon, Winterburn, Vieira, Keown, Adams, Parlour, Anelka (Wreh), Petit, Bergkamp, Overmars.
*West Ham U:* Lama; Impey, Lazaridis, Potts, Ferdinand, Pearce, Moncur, Lampard, Abou, Berkovic (Hodges), Lomas.

**Newcastle U (2) 3** *(Ketsbaia 16, Speed 27, Batty 90)*
**Barnsley (0) 1** *(Liddell 57)* 36,695
*Newcastle U:* Given; Barton, Pearce, Batty, Howey, Albert, Lee, Ketsbaia, Shearer, Andersson, Speed.
*Barnsley:* Watson; Eaden, Barnard, Morgan, Moses, De Zeeuw (Hristov), Marcelle (Bullock), Redfearn, Ward, Liddell, Sheridan.

**SIXTH ROUND REPLAYS**

**17 MAR**
**Sheffield U (0) 1** *(Holdsworth 89)*
**Coventry C (1) 1** *(Telfer 10)* 29,034
*Sheffield U:* Kelly; Short (Katchuro), Nilsen, Borbokis, Sandford, Holdsworth, Ford, Marker (Dellas), Taylor, Marcello (Morris), Quinn.
*Coventry C:* Ogrizovic; Nilsson, Burrows, Boateng, Dublin, Breen, Telfer, Soltvedt (Gavin Strachan), Whelan, Moldovan (Hayworth), Huckerby.
*aet; Sheffield U won 3-1 on penalties.*

**West Ham U (0) 1** *(Hartson 84)*
**Arsenal (1) 1** *(Anelka 45)* 25,859
*West Ham U:* Lama; Potts (Hodges), Lazaridis, Unsworth, Ferdinand, Pearce (Moncur), Lampard, Abou, Hartson, Berkovic, Lomas.
*Arsenal:* Manninger; Dixon, Winterburn, Vieira, Keown, Adams, Garde, Anelka (Wreh), Petit (Boa Morte), Bergkamp, Overmars (Hughes).
*aet; Arsenal won 4-3 on penalties.*

**SEMI-FINALS**

**5 APR**
**Sheffield U (0) 0**
**Newcastle U (0) 1** *(Shearer 60)* 53,452
*Sheffield U:* Kelly; Borbokis, Quinn, Nilsen, Sandford, Holdsworth, Ford, Marker (Dellas), Saunders (Katchuro), Marcello (Taylor), Stuart.
*Newcastle U:* Given; Barton, Pearce, Batty, Dabizas, Albert, Gillespie, Andersson (Ketsbaia), Shearer, Barnes, Speed.
*at Old Trafford.*

**Wolverhampton W (0) 0**
**Arsenal (1) 1** *(Wreh 12)* 39,372
*Wolverhampton W:* Segers; Muscat (Keane), Froggatt, Williams, Richards, Curle, Goodman (Bull), Sedgley, Claridge, Robinson (Slater), Simpson.
*Arsenal:* Seaman; Grimandi, Winterburn, Vieira, Keown (Bould), Adams, Parlour, Anelka (Platt), Petit, Wreh (Hughes), Overmars.
*at Villa Park.*

**FINAL (at Wembley)**

**16 MAY**
**Arsenal (1) 2** *(Overmars 23, Anelka 69)*
**Newcastle U (0) 0** 79,183
*Arsenal:* Seaman; Dixon, Winterburn, Vieira, Keown, Adams, Parlour, Anelka, Petit, Wreh (Platt), Overmars.
*Newcastle U:* Given; Pistone, Pearce (Andersson), Batty, Dabizas, Howey, Lee, Barton (Watson), Shearer, Ketsbaia (Barnes), Speed.
*Referee:* P. Durkin (Portland).

# FA CUP ATTENDANCES 1967–97

| | 1st Round | 2nd Round | 3rd Round | 4th Round | 5th Round | 6th Round | Semi-Finals & Final | Total | No. of matches | Average per match |
|---|---|---|---|---|---|---|---|---|---|---|
| 1996-97 | 209,521 | 122,324 | 651,139 | 402,293 | 199,873 | 67,035 | 191,813 | 1,843,998 | 151 | 12,211 |
| 1995-96 | 185,538 | 115,669 | 748,997 | 391,218 | 274,055 | 174,142 | 156,500 | 2,046,199 | 167 | 12,252 |
| 1994-95 | 219,511 | 125,629 | 640,017 | 438,596 | 257,650 | 159,787 | 174,059 | 2,015,249 | 161 | 12,517 |
| 1993-94 | 190,683 | 118,031 | 691,064 | 430,234 | 172,196 | 134,705 | 228,233 | 1,965,146 | 159 | 12,359 |
| 1992-93 | 241,968 | 174,702 | 612,494 | 377,211 | 198,379 | 149,675 | 293,241 | 2,047,670 | 161 | 12,718 |
| 1991-92 | 231,940 | 117,078 | 586,014 | 372,576 | 270,537 | 155,603 | 201,592 | 1,935,340 | 160 | 12,095 |
| 1990-91 | 194,195 | 121,450 | 594,592 | 530,279 | 276,112 | 124,826 | 196,434 | 2,038,518 | 162 | 12,583 |
| 1989-90 | 209,542 | 133,483 | 683,047 | 412,483 | 351,423 | 123,065 | 277,420 | 2,190,463 | 170 | 12,885 |
| 1988-89 | 212,775 | 121,326 | 690,199 | 421,255 | 206,781 | 176,629 | 167,353 | 1,966,318 | 164 | 12,173 |
| 1987-88 | 204,411 | 104,561 | 720,121 | 443,133 | 281,461 | 119,313 | 177,585 | 2,050,585 | 155 | 13,229 |
| 1986-87 | 209,290 | 146,761 | 593,520 | 349,342 | 263,550 | 119,396 | 195,533 | 1,877,400 | 165 | 11,378 |
| 1985-86 | 171,142 | 130,034 | 486,838 | 495,526 | 311,833 | 184,262 | 192,316 | 1,971,951 | 168 | 11,738 |
| 1984-85 | 174,604 | 137,078 | 616,229 | 320,772 | 269,232 | 148,690 | 242,754 | 1,909,359 | 157 | 12,162 |
| 1983-84 | 192,276 | 151,647 | 625,965 | 417,298 | 181,832 | 185,382 | 187,000 | 1,941,400 | 166 | 11,695 |
| 1982-83 | 191,312 | 150,046 | 670,503 | 452,688 | 260,069 | 193,845 | 291,162 | 2,209,625 | 154 | 14,348 |
| 1981-82 | 236,220 | 127,300 | 513,185 | 356,987 | 203,334 | 124,308 | 279,621 | 1,840,955 | 160 | 11,506 |
| 1980-81 | 246,824 | 194,502 | 832,578 | 534,402 | 320,530 | 288,714 | 339,250 | 2,756,800 | 169 | 16,312 |
| 1979-80 | 267,121 | 204,759 | 804,701 | 507,725 | 364,039 | 157,530 | 355,541 | 2,661,416 | 163 | 16,328 |
| 1978-79 | 243,773 | 185,343 | 880,345 | 537,748 | 243,683 | 263,213 | 249,897 | 2,604,002 | 166 | 15,687 |
| 1977-78 | 258,248 | 178,930 | 881,406 | 540,164 | 400,751 | 137,059 | 198,020 | 2,594,578 | 160 | 16,216 |
| 1976-77 | 379,230 | 192,159 | 942,523 | 631,265 | 373,330 | 205,379 | 258,216 | 2,982,102 | 174 | 17,139 |
| 1975-76 | 255,533 | 178,099 | 867,880 | 573,843 | 471,925 | 206,851 | 205,810 | 2,759,941 | 161 | 17,142 |
| 1974-75 | 283,956 | 170,466 | 914,994 | 646,434 | 393,323 | 268,361 | 291,369 | 2,968,903 | 172 | 17,261 |
| 1973-74 | 214,236 | 125,295 | 840,142 | 747,909 | 346,012 | 233,307 | 273,051 | 2,779,952 | 167 | 16,646 |
| 1972-73 | 259,432 | 169,114 | 938,741 | 735,825 | 357,386 | 241,934 | 226,543 | 2,928,975 | 160 | 18,306 |
| 1971-72 | 277,726 | 236,127 | 986,094 | 711,399 | 486,378 | 230,292 | 248,546 | 3,158,562 | 160 | 19,741 |
| 1970-71 | 329,687 | 230,942 | 956,683 | 757,852 | 360,687 | 304,937 | 279,644 | 3,220,432 | 162 | 19,879 |
| 1969-70 | 345,229 | 195,102 | 925,930 | 651,374 | 319,893 | 198,537 | 390,700 | 3,026,765 | 170 | 17,805 |
| 1968-69 | 331,858 | 252,710 | 1,094,043 | 883,675 | 464,915 | 188,121 | 216,232 | 3,431,554 | 157 | 21,857 |
| 1967-68 | 322,121 | 236,195 | 1,229,519 | 771,284 | 563,779 | 240,095 | 223,831 | 3,586,824 | 160 | 22,418 |

Marc Overmars opens the scoring for Arsenal in the 1998 FA Cup Final against Newcastle United at Wembley with a fine opportunist goal. (Colorsport)

# THE SCOTTISH SEASON 1997–98

What a last day to the League season! There was so much to be settled, so much elation – so much disappointment. For once the top place was still in doubt. From early on in the season, there were three teams challenging for the championship: Hearts led the field through November and most of December, but then Rangers drew ahead, and it looked like 'business as usual'. In the New Year's derby, Celtic beat Rangers – for the first time for a while in the league. This really opened up the race, but the Ibrox team lost itself for a while (there were all sorts of reasons and excuses, but the plain fact of some almost unreal results remained). So Celtic went ahead, and the gallant Hearts, for whom so many unattached observers hoped so much, gradually fell astern. Celtic went into an impregnable position, and then it at once became apparent that it was by no means so: Rangers failed to win here; Celtic threw points away there. So to the last day, where Celtic had to win to make sure: they did – to the delight of their fans, who almost immediately were shattered when it became known that their successful coach was leaving. There was much sadness, but it is silly to comment on a situation open to so many interpretations. So Celtic won the Premier Division, and thus robbed Rangers of their chance to record the tenth successive win.

That was at the top end of the table. In the middle Kilmarnock and St Johnstone vied for the prized fourth spot: two unlikely contenders for this honour, might have been the thought at the start of the season; however, two young and dedicated managers inspired their squads to great deeds, and in the end Kilmarnock just held on ahead.

For the rest it was a question of who was going to be at the foot of the table, and what was going to happen to the side in ninth place? Even towards the end of the season, this last question was not totally answered. Aberdeen and Dundee United, so often in the past in the top part of the table, were in dire straits, whilst Motherwell and Dunfermline, too, hovered in the nether regions. Hibs were a mile behind, but, with Alex McLeish in charge, were making up ground. On the penultimate weekend, Dundee United saved themselves from an awkward situation with a couple of late goals, and so consigned Hibs to the tenth place, and relegation. The rest could breathe a sigh of relief: no play-off, and all could look forward to a place in the new Scottish Premier League.

This new League had been hovering over the season. It appeared to stutter its way through (rather than over) the various hurdles, and is now ready to go. It is to be hoped that the bright future for it predicted by its protagonists is realised. It will be interesting to see how quickly it can settle down and get over the inevitable growing pains. Is it going to help Scottish football? See this column next year.

On now to the First Division, where Dundee – albeit with a change of managers midstream – forged ahead and won at a canter. Rarely did the chasing pack trouble them, but Falkirk took the runners-up position and the money, with Raith Rovers third. It was at the lower end that the drama unfolded: Stirling Albion finally fought a losing battle, but there was a scramble to avoid the second relegation place: on the final afternoon Ayr United beat Partick Thistle in a decider, and the Jags now head down into a region they have not seen before: may they soon regain former glory!

In the Second Division, Livingston and Clydebank made the running, and looked to be well set for promotion. An astonishing run by Stranraer: 9th in the table at the beginning of February, they won 12 out of their last 14 matches, and took top spot by a point, with Clydebank scoring their best win on the last afternoon and being the runners-up. The unfortunate Livingston, so near to success, could not contain the enigmatic Caley Thistle, and they missed promotion by the narrowest of margins. From December, Brechin were at the foot, and they went down, joined by Stenhousemuir, who just lost out to Clyde. Caley Thistle showed an aptitude for scoring goals, but they lost too many when it mattered: a mid-table position scarcely recognises their ability, though they did make a very poor start to the season. If the teams at the top of this division and the teams at the foot each had their own contests, yet the middle group had much influence on the table, and even till late in the season there were few games where the result was not crucial.

Fun, too, in the Third Division: here Alloa Athletic, Arbroath and Ross County held the high ground for most of the last months. Alloa took the lead in early February, and Arbroath were not too far behind; but Ross County, having their almost inexcusable lapses, nevertheless had a strong finish this time, and Arbroath needed to scramble a draw on the last day to finish in the second promotion spot. It was noted that the two teams promoted had much smaller selections of players during the season, and were thus able to field fairly constant teams.

In the Cups, the results overall were a good deal more predictable than usual: some teams had good runs: Falkirk won the League Challenge Cup, and then reached the semi-finals of the Scottish Cup, only the one stage short of the final which they contested last year; Caley Thistle only went out on penalties to Motherwell in the Coca-Cola, and then took Dundee United to a replay in the Scottish Cup, whilst Ross County also held Dundee at home, though they lost the replay at Dens; Queen of the South in the Challenge Cup eliminated three clubs in the upper division before losing by the odd goal to Falkirk in the final; both Edinburgh City and Annan Athletic saw that non-League clubs were represented in the Third Round of the Scottish Cup; whilst Ayr removed near rivals Kilmarnock, the Cup holders, in a local derby.

The Coca-Cola final was won by Celtic, with a comfortable victory over Dundee United: this was Celtic's first trophy for a while, and whetted the appetite of the fans for the further success at the end of the season. Hearts won the Scottish Cup after a gap of 42 years: this was a most popular win and Hearts certainly deserved something after their excellent season: Rangers were the disappointed losers in a close final, but it was good to see Jim Jefferies and his side generously applauded at the end of the game by many of the Rangers fans. Many would like to have seen Walter Smith taking a trophy in his last season as manager of Rangers: if in the end he was disappointed, nevertheless he has been a great ambassador for the game, and has achieved much with the club.

Scottish club sides again fared indifferently in Europe, and fans throughout the country always hope that next year may see a rise in the teams' successes abroad. If the club competitions have been below expectation, the international side has moved on steadily, and Craig Brown – surely one of the most talented national managers – led his side to the World Cup finals in France. After a courageous and rather unlucky defeat in the opening match against Brazil, the Scots fought a fine draw against the strong Norwegians before crashing to a disappointing defeat by Morocco. So the World Cup adventure was over, but the impact on the tournament of the colourful and noisy Tartan Army will long be remembered.

ALAN ELLIOTT

# ABERDEEN

## Premier League

*Year Formed:* 1903. *Ground & Address:* Pittodrie Stadium, Pittodrie St, Aberdeen AB24 5QH. *Telephone:* 01224 632328.
*Ground Capacity:* all seated: 21,634. All. *Size of Pitch:* 110yd × 72yd.
*Chairman:* Stewart Milne. *Secretary:* Richard A. M. Ramsay. *General Manager:* David Johnston.
*Manager:* Alex Miller. *Coach:* Tommy Craig. *Physios:* David Wylie, John Sharp.
*Managers since 1975:* Ally MacLeod; Billy McNeill; Alex Ferguson; Ian Porterfield; Alex Smith and Jocky Scott; Willie Miller, Roy Aitken. *Club Nicknames(s):* The Dons. *Previous Grounds:* None.
*Record Attendance:* 45,061 v Hearts, Scottish Cup 4th rd; 13 Mar, 1954.
*Record Transfer Fee received:* £1.75 million for Eoin Jess to Coventry City (February 1996).
*Record Transfer Fee paid:* £1m+ for Paul Bernard from Oldham Athletic (September 1995).
*Record Victory:* 13-0 v Peterhead, Scottish Cup; 9 Feb, 1923.
*Record Defeat:* 0-8 v Celtic, Division 1; 30 Jan, 1965.
*Most Capped Players:* Alex McLeish, 77, Scotland.
*Most League Appearances:* 556: Willie Miller, 1973-90.
*Most League Goals in Season (Individual):* 38: Benny Yorston, Division I; 1929-30.
*Most Goals Overall (Individual):* 199: Joe Harper.

## ABERDEEN 1997–98 LEAGUE RECORD

| Match No. | Date | Venue | Opponents | Result | H/T Score | Lg. Pos. | Goalscorers | Attendance |
|---|---|---|---|---|---|---|---|---|
| 1 | Aug 2 | H | Kilmarnock | D 0-0 | 0-0 | — | | 13,842 |
| 2 | 16 | A | Hearts | L 1-4 | 1-3 | 9 | Newell [12] | 12,367 |
| 3 | 23 | H | Motherwell | L 1-3 | 1-2 | 10 | Rowson [26] | 11,522 |
| 4 | 30 | H | Dundee U | D 1-1 | 1-1 | 9 | Dodds [44] | 12,060 |
| 5 | Sept 13 | A | Rangers | D 3-3 | 0-1 | 9 | Newell [58], Dodds [64], Inglis [78] | 50,030 |
| 6 | 20 | A | Celtic | L 0-2 | 0-2 | 10 | | 48,843 |
| 7 | 27 | H | Dunfermline Ath | L 1-2 | 1-1 | 10 | Dodds [40] | 10,702 |
| 8 | Oct 4 | A | St Johnstone | L 0-1 | 0-1 | 10 | | 6291 |
| 9 | 18 | H | Hibernian | W 2-0 | 2-0 | 10 | Glass [5], Dodds (pen) [37] | 11,708 |
| 10 | 25 | A | Motherwell | W 2-1 | 1-0 | 9 | Windass 2 [9, 89] | 6065 |
| 11 | Nov 1 | H | Hearts | L 1-4 | 1-0 | 9 | Windass [22] | 15,097 |
| 12 | 9 | A | Dundee U | L 0-5 | 0-3 | — | | 7893 |
| 13 | 15 | H | Rangers | D 1-1 | 1-0 | 10 | Jess [45] | 18,117 |
| 14 | 22 | A | Dunfermline Ath | D 1-1 | 0-0 | 10 | Dodds [66] | 6738 |
| 15 | Dec 6 | H | St Johnstone | D 1-1 | 0-0 | 10 | Rowson [49] | 10,974 |
| 16 | 9 | H | Celtic | L 0-2 | 0-1 | — | | 16,981 |
| 17 | 13 | A | Hibernian | D 2-2 | 1-1 | 10 | Dodds [43], Jess [68] | 10,008 |
| 18 | 20 | A | Kilmarnock | L 0-1 | 0-1 | 10 | | 8452 |
| 19 | 27 | A | Motherwell | W 3-0 | 0-0 | 9 | Windass [63], Jess 2 (1 pen) [83, 86 (p)] | 13,088 |
| 20 | Jan 3 | H | Dundee U | W 1-0 | 1-0 | 9 | Windass [26] | 17,025 |
| 21 | 10 | A | Rangers | L 0-2 | 0-2 | 9 | | 49,502 |
| 22 | 28 | H | Dunfermline Ath | W 2-0 | 1-0 | — | Jess [7], Smith [61] | 8661 |
| 23 | Feb 2 | A | Celtic | L 1-3 | 0-2 | — | Rowson [8] | 45,813 |
| 24 | 7 | H | Hibernian | W 3-0 | 1-0 | 7 | Newell [40], Jess [57], Miller [59] | 12,043 |
| 25 | 21 | A | St Johnstone | W 1-0 | 1-0 | 7 | Dodds [14] | 6570 |
| 26 | 25 | A | Hearts | L 1-3 | 0-1 | — | Jess [61] | 16,512 |
| 27 | 28 | H | Kilmarnock | D 0-0 | 0-0 | 7 | | 10,423 |
| 28 | Mar 14 | A | Dunfermline Ath | D 3-3 | 1-0 | 7 | Rowson 2 [19, 64], O'Neil [70] | 5931 |
| 29 | 21 | H | Celtic | L 0-1 | 0-1 | 7 | | 18,009 |
| 30 | 28 | A | Hibernian | D 1-1 | 0-0 | 8 | Jess [68] | 12,966 |
| 31 | Apr 4 | H | St Johnstone | L 0-1 | 0-1 | 8 | | 9002 |
| 32 | 11 | A | Dundee U | D 0-0 | 0-0 | 8 | | 9155 |
| 33 | 19 | H | Rangers | W 1-0 | 1-0 | — | Glass [28] | 17,981 |
| 34 | 25 | A | Kilmarnock | L 1-2 | 1-1 | 7 | Dodds [44] | 8212 |
| 35 | May 2 | H | Hearts | D 2-2 | 1-2 | 7 | Jess [26], Newell [46] | 12,899 |
| 36 | 9 | A | Motherwell | W 2-1 | 2-0 | 6 | Dodds 2 (1 pen) [2 (p), 22] | 5861 |

**Final League Position: 6**          1996–97 6

**Honours**
*League Champions:* Division I 1954-55. Premier Division 1979-80, 1983-84, 1984-85; *Runners-up:* Division I 1910-11, 1936-37, 1955-56, 1970-71, 1971-72. Premier Division 1977-78, 1980-81, 1981-82, 1988-89, 1989-90, 1990-91, 1992-93, 1993-94.
*Scottish Cup Winners:* 1947, 1970, 1982, 1983, 1984, 1986, 1990; *Runners-up:* 1937, 1953, 1954, 1959, 1967, 1978, 1993.
*League Cup Winners:* 1955-56, 1976-77, 1985-86, 1989-90, (Coca Cola cup) 1995-96; *Runners-up:* 1946-47, 1978-79, 1979-80, 1987-88, 1988-89, 1992-93.
*Drybrough Cup Winners:* 1971, 1980.

**European:** *European Cup:* 12 matches (1980-81, 1984-85, 1985-86); *Cup Winners' Cup:* 39 matches (1967-68, 1970-71, 1978-79, 1982-83 winners, 1983-84 semi-finals, 1986-87, 1990-91, 1993-94); *UEFA Cup:* 42 matches (*Fairs Cup:* 1968-69. *UEFA Cup:* 1971-72, 1972-73, 1973-74, 1977-78, 1979-80, 1981-82, 1987-88, 1988-89, 1989-90, 1991-92, 1994-95, 1996-97). *Club colours:* Shirt, Shorts, Stockings: Red with white trim.

**Goalscorers:** *League (39):* Dodds 10 (2 pens), Jess 9 (1 pen), Rowson 5, Windass 5, Newell 4, Glass 2, Inglis 1, Miller 1, O'Neil 1, Smith 1. *Scottish Cup (0): Coca Cola Cup (11):* Newell 4, Dodds 2, Miller 2, Glass 1, Jess 1, Windass 1.

| Stillie D 2 | Anderson R 20 + 6 | Tzvetanov T 10 + 1 | Bernard P 15 + 2 | Kombouare A 12 | O'Neil B 25 + 4 | Miller J 21 + 8 | Jess E 34 | Newell M 18 + 3 | Windass D 12 + 12 | Buchan J 9 + 1 | Dodds W 29 + 5 | Rowson D 24 + 6 | Leighton J 34 | Smith G 31 | Glass S 30 + 1 | Gillies R 5 + 16 | Inglis J 25 | Young D 2 + 3 | Kiriakov I 15 | Whyte D 19 | O'Neil M 4 + 2 | Match No. |
|---|---|---|---|---|---|---|---|---|---|---|---|---|---|---|---|---|---|---|---|---|---|---|
| 1 | 2 | 3 | 4 | 5 | 6 | 7² | 8 | 9¹ | 10 | 11 | 12 | 13 | | | | | | | | | | 1 |
| 1 | 2 | 3 | 4 | 5 | 6 | 7 | 8 | 9¹ | 10 | 11¹ | 13 | 12 | | | | | | | | | | 2 |
| | | 3 | 4 | | 6 | 7 | 8 | 9 | 12 | 2¹ | 10 | 11 | 1 | 5 | | | | | | | | 3 |
| | | 3 | 4 | | 6 | 7¹ | 8 | 9³ | 13 | | 10 | 2 | 1 | 5 | 11 | 12 | | | | | | 4 |
| | | | 4 | | 6 | 7 | 8¹ | 9³ | 13 | | 10 | 2 | 1 | 3 | 11 | 12 | 5 | | | | | 5 |
| | 14 | 3³ | | | 6 | 7¹ | 8 | 9 | 13 | | 10 | 2 | 1 | 4 | 11 | 12 | 5 | | | | | 6 |
| | 2 | 3 | 4 | | | 7 | 8¹ | 9 | 13 | | 10 | 6² | 1 | | 11 | 12 | 5 | | | | | 7 |
| | 2 | 3 | 4³ | | 6 | 7 | 8 | 9 | 13 | | 10 | 14 | 1 | | 11 | 12 | 5 | | | | | 8 |
| | 2 | 3 | 4¹ | 5 | | 7 | 13 | 9² | | | 10 | 8 | 1 | 6 | 11³ | 12 | | | 14 | | | 9 |
| | 2 | 3 | 4 | 5 | | 13 | 8 | 9¹ | | | 10 | 7 | 1 | 6 | 11² | 12 | | | | | | 10 |
| | 2 | | | 5 | 6 | 7 | 8 | 9 | | | 10 | 4 | 1 | 3 | 11 | 12 | | | | | | 11 |
| | 2 | 5 | 4 | 14 | | | 8³ | 9 | | | 10² | 7¹ | 1 | 6 | 11 | 13 | | 12 | 3 | | | 12 |
| | 2 | 12 | 4 | | | 7¹ | 8 | | | | 10 | 9 | 1 | 6 | 11 | 13 | | | 3² | | | 13 |
| | 2 | | 4 | 5 | | | 8 | | 13 | | 10² | 9 | 1 | 6 | 11 | 12 | | | 7¹ | 3 | | 14 |
| | 2 | 9 | | 5 | | 7¹ | 8 | | | | 10 | 3 | 1 | 6 | 11 | 4 | | 12 | | | | 15 |
| | 2 | 9 | | 5 | 12 | 14 | 8 | | | | 10 | 3¹ | 1 | 6 | 11³ | 13 | | 4 | 7² | | | 16 |
| | 2 | 12 | 3 | 5 | | | 8 | 9 | | | 10¹ | 7 | 1 | 6 | 11 | | | 4 | | | | 17 |
| | 2² | | 4 | | 7 | | 8 | 9¹ | 13 | | 10 | | 1 | 6 | 11 | 12 | 5 | | | 3 | | 18 |
| | 2 | | 4 | 12 | | 14 | 8 | 9² | | | 10³ | | 1 | 6 | 11³ | 13 | 5 | | 7 | 3 | | 19 |
| | 2 | | 4 | | 7 | | 8 | 9 | | | 10 | | 1 | 6 | 11 | | 5 | | | 3 | | 20 |
| | 13 | 2 | 4 | | | | 8 | | 12 | | 10² | | 1 | 6 | 11 | | 5 | | 7 | 3 | 9¹ | 21 |
| | 2 | | 4 | | | 7¹ | 8² | 9 | 12 | | 13 | | 1 | 6 | 11 | | 5 | | | 3 | 10 | 22 |
| | 13 | | 4 | | | | 8 | 9² | 12 | | 2 | | 1 | 6 | 11 | | 5 | | 7 | 3 | 10¹ | 23 |
| | | | 4³ | | | 7 | 8 | 9³ | 14 | | 13 | 12 | 1 | 6 | 11 | | 5 | 2 | | 3 | 10¹ | 24 |
| | 12 | | 4 | | | 7¹ | 8 | | | | 10² | 2 | 1 | 6 | 11 | | 5 | 9 | | 3 | 13 | 25 |
| | | | 4² | 12 | | | 8 | 9¹ | | | 10 | 7 | 1 | 6 | 11 | | 5 | 2 | | 3 | 13 | 26 |
| | | | 4 | | | 7 | 8 | 9 | | | 10 | | 1 | 6 | 11 | | 5 | 2 | | 3 | | 27 |
| | 2 | | 4 | 12 | | 7 | 8 | | | | 10 | 9 | 1 | 6 | 11¹ | | 5 | | | 3 | | 28 |
| | 2 | | 4 | | | 7¹ | 8 | | 13 | | 10² | 9 | 1 | 6 | 11 | 12 | 5 | | | 3 | | 29 |
| | 2¹ | | 4 | | | 7¹ | 8 | | 13 | 12 | 10 | 9 | 1 | 6 | 11² | 14 | 5 | | | 3 | | 30 |
| | | 11² | 4 | | | 7¹ | 8 | 9 | 12 | 2 | 10 | | 1 | 6 | 13 | | 5 | | | 3 | | 31 |
| | | | 4¹ | | | | 8 | 9 | 12 | 2 | 10 | | 1 | 6 | 11 | | 5 | | 7 | 3 | | 32 |
| | 12 | 13 | 4 | 14 | | | 8¹ | 9² | 2 | | 10³ | | 1 | 6 | 11 | | 5 | | 7 | 3 | | 33 |
| | 12 | | 4 | | | | 8 | 9 | 2¹ | | 10 | | 1 | 6 | 11 | | 5 | | 7 | 3 | | 34 |
| | 12 | 13 | 4¹ | | | | 8 | 9 | 2 | | 10 | | 1 | 6 | 11² | | 5 | | 7 | 3 | | 35 |
| | 2 | 13 | 4 | | | | 8 | 9 | 12 | | 10 | | 1 | 6 | 11¹ | | 5 | | 7² | 3 | | 36 |

# AIRDRIEONIANS
First Division

*Year Formed:* 1878. *Ground & Address:* Broadwood Stadium, Cumbernauld G68 9NE. Address for all correspondence: 32 Stirling Street, Airdrie, ML6 0AH *Telephone:* 01236 762067.
*Ground Capacity:* all seated: 6300. *Size of Pitch:* 112yd × 76yd.
*Chairman:* David W. Smith. *Secretary:* George W. Peat CA.
*Manager:* Alex MacDonald. *Physio:* Ian Constable. *Coach:* John Binnie.
*Managers since 1975:* I. McMillan; J. Stewart; R. Watson; W. Munro; A. MacLeod; D. Whiteford; G. McQueen; J. Bone.
*Club Nickname(s):* The Diamonds or The Waysiders. *Previous Grounds:* Mavisbank, Broomfield Park.
*Record Attendance:* 24,000 v Hearts, Scottish Cup; 8 Mar, 1952.
*Record Transfer Fee received:* £200,000 for Sandy Clark to West Ham U, May 1982.
*Record Transfer Fee paid:* £175,000 for Owen Coyle from Clydebank, February 1990.
*Record Victory:* 15-1 v Dundee Wanderers, Division II; 1 Dec, 1894.
*Record Defeat:* 1-11 v Hibernian, Division I; 24 Oct, 1959.
*Most Capped Player:* Jimmy Crapnell, 9, Scotland.
*Most League Appearances:* 523: Paul Jonquin, 1962-79.
*Most League Goals in Season (Individual):* 53, Hugh Baird, Division II, 1954-55. *Most Goals Overall (Individual):* —

## AIRDRIEONIANS 1997–98 LEAGUE RECORD

| Match No. | Date | Venue | Opponents | Result | H/T Score | Lg. Pos. | Goalscorers | Attendance |
|---|---|---|---|---|---|---|---|---|
| 1 | Aug 2 | H | St Mirren | L | 1-3 | 0-0 | — | Connolly P [62] | 2185 |
| 2 | 16 | A | Raith R | D | 1-1 | 1-0 | 8 | Cooper [37] | 3414 |
| 3 | 23 | H | Falkirk | D | 2-2 | 2-1 | 6 | Stewart [23], Cooper [38] | 2394 |
| 4 | 30 | H | Partick Th | D | 1-1 | 0-0 | 7 | Davies [56] | 2260 |
| 5 | Sept 13 | A | Greenock Morton | D | 1-1 | 0-0 | 9 | Cooper [60] | 2327 |
| 6 | 20 | A | Stirling A | D | 0-0 | 0-0 | 10 | | 1283 |
| 7 | 27 | H | Ayr U | W | 1-0 | 1-0 | 6 | Black (pen) [19] | 1392 |
| 8 | Oct 4 | A | Dundee | L | 0-1 | 0-0 | 7 | | 3086 |
| 9 | 18 | H | Hamilton A | D | 0-0 | 0-0 | 7 | | 1514 |
| 10 | 25 | A | St Mirren | W | 2-0 | 1-0 | 6 | Jack [42], Connolly P [74] | 2533 |
| 11 | Nov 1 | H | Raith R | W | 1-0 | 0-0 | 5 | Cooper [85] | 1945 |
| 12 | 8 | A | Partick Th | W | 2-1 | 0-1 | 5 | McPhee 2 (1 pen) [47, 57 (p)] | 2765 |
| 13 | 15 | H | Greenock Morton | D | 3-3 | 2-1 | 5 | Connolly P 2 [3, 77], Jack [28] | 1652 |
| 14 | 22 | A | Ayr U | L | 0-6 | 0-3 | 5 | | 1838 |
| 15 | 29 | H | Stirling A | W | 2-0 | 2-0 | 5 | Connolly P [10], Cooper [12] | 1320 |
| 16 | Dec 6 | H | Dundee | D | 0-0 | 0-0 | 5 | | 1996 |
| 17 | 20 | A | Falkirk | L | 1-2 | 1-1 | 5 | McPhee [9] | 2636 |
| 18 | 27 | H | St Mirren | W | 2-1 | 2-0 | 5 | Smith [2], Cooper [38] | 2312 |
| 19 | 30 | A | Hamilton A | D | 0-0 | 0-0 | — | | 1516 |
| 20 | Jan 6 | H | Partick Th | W | 2-1 | 1-1 | — | Connolly P [29], Johnston [89] | 1893 |
| 21 | 10 | A | Greenock Morton | W | 2-0 | 0-0 | 4 | McPhee 2 [48, 52] | 2038 |
| 22 | 31 | A | Stirling A | D | 2-2 | 1-0 | 4 | McPhee [5], Cooper [90] | 1292 |
| 23 | Feb 7 | H | Hamilton A | W | 3-2 | 1-1 | 4 | Cooper 3 [43, 72, 86] | 1316 |
| 24 | 10 | H | Ayr U | W | 2-0 | 1-0 | — | Connolly P 2 (1 pen) [45 (p), 89] | 1189 |
| 25 | 21 | A | Dundee | L | 0-1 | 0-0 | 4 | | 3239 |
| 26 | Mar 3 | H | Falkirk | L | 0-1 | 0-1 | — | | 1789 |
| 27 | 7 | A | Raith R | D | 1-1 | 0-1 | 4 | McEwan (og) [88] | 2635 |
| 28 | 14 | A | Ayr U | W | 2-0 | 1-0 | 4 | McPhee 2 [27, 64] | 1728 |
| 29 | 21 | H | Stirling A | W | 1-0 | 1-0 | 4 | McPhee [1] | 1284 |
| 30 | 28 | A | Hamilton A | W | 2-0 | 1-0 | 4 | Wilson [6], McPhee [73] | 1028 |
| 31 | Apr 4 | H | Dundee | L | 1-2 | 1-1 | 4 | Cooper [37] | 2058 |
| 32 | 11 | A | Partick Th | L | 0-2 | 0-2 | 4 | | 2102 |
| 33 | 18 | H | Greenock Morton | D | 1-1 | 1-0 | 4 | McPhee [5] | 1431 |
| 34 | 25 | A | St Mirren | W | 1-0 | 1-0 | 4 | Farrell [14] | 3329 |
| 35 | May 2 | H | Raith R | W | 1-0 | 1-0 | 4 | McPhee [11] | 1173 |
| 36 | 9 | A | Falkirk | W | 1-0 | 0-0 | 4 | Connolly G [47] | 3850 |

**Final League Position: 4**   1996–97 2

**Honours**
*League Champions:* Division II 1902-03, 1954-55, 1973-74; *Runners-up:* Division I 1922-23, 1923-24, 1924-25, 1925-26. First Division 1979-80, 1989-90, 1990-91, 1996-97. Division II 1900-01, 1946-47, 1949-50, 1965-66. *Scottish Cup Winners:* 1924; *Runners-up:* 1975, 1992, 1995. *Scottish Spring Cup Winners:* 1976. *League Cup semi-finalists:* 1991-92, 1994-95. *B&Q Cup Winners:* 1994-95.

**European:** *Cup Winners' Cup:* 2 matches (1992-93).
*Club colours:* Shirt: White with red diamond. Shorts: White. Stockings: Red.

**Goalscorers:** *League (42):* McPhee 12 (1 pen), Cooper 11, Connolly P 8 (1 pen), Jack 2, Black 1 (pen), Connolly G 1, Davies 1, Farrell 1, Johnston 1, Smith 1, Stewart 1, Wilson 1, own goal 1. *Scottish Cup (2):* Cooper 1, McPhee 1. *Coca Cola Cup (1):* Connolly P 1. *League Challenge Cup (3):* McPhee 2, Cooper 1.

| Rhodes A 4 | Stewart A 27+1 | McCann A 8+6 | McClelland J 1 | Sweeney M 29 | Wilson M 32+2 | Lawrence A 5+4 | Connolly P 22+1 | Cooper S 27+3 | McPhee B 15+14 | Smith A 30 | Rankin I —+1 | Johnston F 21+7 | Sandison J 31 | Davies J 11+8 | Mackay G 23+3 | Jack P 27+5 | Black K 24+3 | Connolly G 15+6 | Hogarth M 12 | Robertson A 3 | Martin J 20 | Farrell D 9+4 | Shaw G —+2 | Match No. |
|---|---|---|---|---|---|---|---|---|---|---|---|---|---|---|---|---|---|---|---|---|---|---|---|---|
| 1 | 2 | 3 | 4 | 5¹ | 6 | 7 | 8 | 9 | 10 | 11 | 12 | | | | | | | | | | | | | 1 |
| 1 | 2 | | | 5 | 8 | 14 | 10³ | 9¹ | 12 | 11 | | 3 | 4 | | 6 | 7² | 13 | | | | | | | 2 |
| 1 | 2 | | | 5¹ | 8 | | 10 | 9 | 13 | 11 | | 3 | 4 | | 6 | 7² | 12 | | | | | | | 3 |
| 1 | 2¹ | | | 5 | 8 | 13 | 10³ | 9² | | 11 | | 3 | 4 | | 7 | | 12 | 6 | 14 | | | | | 4 |
| | 2 | | | 5 | 8¹ | 7² | | 9 | | 11 | | 3 | 4 | 10 | | | 12 | 6 | 1 | | | | | 5 |
| | 2 | 11 | | 5 | 8 | | 7¹ | 9 | 12 | | | 3 | 4 | | 10¹ | | 6 | 13 | 1 | | | | | 6 |
| | 2 | | | 5 | 8² | 7¹ | | 9 | 12 | 11 | | 3 | 4 | 10 | | | 13 | 6 | 1 | | | | | 7 |
| | 2 | | | 5 | 8² | 12 | | 9 | | 11 | | 3 | 4 | 10 | 13 | | 6 | 7¹ | 1 | | | | | 8 |
| | 2 | 11 | | 5 | 8 | 10¹ | 13 | 9 | 12 | | | 4 | | 3 | 6 | 7² | | | 1 | | | | | 9 |
| | 2 | 14 | | 5 | 8 | | 9³ | | | 11 | | 4 | 13 | 12 | 3 | 6 | 7² | | 1 | | | 10¹ | | 10 |
| | 2 | | | 5 | 8 | 9 | 14 | 13 | | 11¹ | | 4 | 12 | 6 | 3 | 7² | | | 1 | | | 10² | | 11 |
| | 2 | | | 5 | 8 | 9³ | 14 | 13 | 11 | | | 4 | 12 | 6 | 3 | 7² | | | 1 | | | 10¹ | | 12 |
| | 2 | | | 5 | 8 | 10 | 9 | | 11 | | | 12 | 4 | 7² | 6 | 3¹ | 13 | | 1 | | | | | 13 |
| | 2 | 14 | | 5¹ | 8 | 10 | | 11 | 13 | | | 4 | 7 | 3¹ | 6² | 12 | | | 1 | | | | | 14 |
| | | | | 8 | 12 | 10 | 9 | 11 | 5 | | | 4 | 7¹ | 3 | 6 | | | | 1 | | | | | 15 |
| | | | | 8 | 10 | 9 | 11 | 5 | | | | 4 | 7 | 3 | 6 | | | | 1 | | | | | 16 |
| | 2 | | | 8 | 7² | 9 | 10 | 11 | | 5 | | 4¹ | 13 | 6² | 3 | 12 | | | | | 1 | 14 | | 17 |
| | 2 | | | 8 | 10¹ | 9 | 12 | 11 | | 4 | | 13 | 7 | 3 | 6² | | | | | | 1 | 5 | | 18 |
| | 2 | | | 8 | 10¹ | 9 | 12 | 11 | | 4 | | 13 | 7² | 3 | 6 | | | | | | 1 | 5 | | 19 |
| | 2 | | | 8 | 10 | 9 | 12 | 11¹ | | 13 | | 4 | 14 | 7 | 3 | 6² | | | | | 1 | 5¹ | | 20 |
| 12 | 14 | | | 8 | 10³ | 9 | 7² | 11 | | 4 | | 2 | 6 | 3¹ | 13 | | | | | | 1 | 5 | | 21 |
| | | | | 5 | 8 | 9¹ | 12 | 11 | | 2 | | 10 | 4 | 7¹ | 6 | 3 | | | | | 1 | | | 22 |
| | | 2 | | 5 | 8 | 10² | 9 | 13 | 11 | 12 | | 4 | 6 | 3 | 7¹ | | | | | | 1 | | | 23 |
| | | 2¹ | | 5 | 8 | 10² | 9 | 13 | 11 | 12 | | 4 | 6 | 3³ | 7 | | | | | | 1 | 14 | | 24 |
| | | | | 5 | 8 | 10 | 9 | 13 | 11² | 4 | | 7 | 6 | 3 | 12 | | | | | | 1 | 2¹ | | 25 |
| | 4 | | | 5 | 8 | 9¹ | 10³ | 11² | 2 | | | 7 | 3 | 6 | 12 | | | | | | 1 | 13 | 14 | 26 |
| | 2 | 13 | | 5 | | 10 | 9 | 11 | 4² | 12 | | 8 | 3 | 6 | 7¹ | | | | | | 1 | | | 27 |
| | 2 | 13 | | 5 | 12 | 9¹ | 10 | 11 | 4 | | | 8² | 3 | 6 | 7³ | | | | | | 1 | 14 | | 28 |
| | 2 | | | 5 | 12 | 9 | 10 | 11¹ | 4 | | | 8¹ | 3 | 6 | 7² | | | | | | 1 | | 13 | 29 |
| | 2 | | | 5 | 8 | 9 | 11 | 10¹ | 4 | | | 3 | 6 | 7 | | | | | | | 1 | | | 30 |
| | 2 | | | 5 | 8 | 9 | 10 | 11 | 4 | | | 7 | 3 | 6 | | | | | | | 1 | | | 31 |
| | 2 | 13 | | 5 | 8¹ | 9 | 10 | 11 | 4 | | | 7² | 3 | 6 | 12 | | | | | | 1 | | | 32 |
| | 2¹ | | | 5 | 8 | 9 | 11 | 12 | 4 | | | 3 | 6 | 7 | | | | | | | 1 | 10 | | 33 |
| | | | | 5 | 8 | 9 | 10 | 11 | 12 | 4 | | 3⁴ | 6 | 7 | | | | | | | 1 | 2 | | 34 |
| | | 3 | | 5 | 8 | 9¹ | 11 | 10 | 4 | 12 | | 6 | 7 | | | | | | | | 1 | 2 | | 35 |
| | | 3 | | 5 | 8 | 11 | 10 | 4 | 9 | | | 6 | 7 | | | | | | | | 1 | 2 | | 36 |

# ALBION ROVERS

## Third Division

*Year Formed:* 1882. *Ground & Address:* Cliftonhill Stadium, Main St, Coatbridge ML5 3RB. *Telephone:* 01236 606334.
*Ground capacity:* total: 2496, seated: 538. *Size of Pitch:* 110yd × 72yd.
*Chairman:* Andrew Dick, *Company Secretary:* David Shanks BSc. *General Manager:* John Reynolds.
*Commercial Manager:* Gordon Dishington.
*Manager:* Billy McLaren. *Assistant Manager:* Stuart Robertson. *Youth Development:* Jimmy Lindsay. *Physio:* Derek Kelly.
*Managers since 1975:* G. Caldwell; S. Goodwin; H. Hood; J. Baker; D. Whiteford; M. Ferguson; W. Wilson; B. Rooney;
A. Ritchie; T. Gemmell; D. Provan; M. Oliver; B. McLaren; T. Gemmell; T Spence; J. Crease; V. Moore.
*Club Nickname(s):* The Wee Rovers. *Previous Grounds:* Cowheath Park, Meadow Park, Whifflet.
*Record Attendance:* 27,381 v Rangers, Scottish Cup 2nd rd; 8 Feb, 1936.
*Record Transfer Fee received:* £40,000 from Motherwell for Bruce Cleland.
*Record Transfer Fee paid:* £7000 for Gerry McTeague to Stirling Albion, September 1989.
*Record Victory:* 12-0 v Airdriehill, Scottish Cup; 3 Sept, 1887.
*Record Defeat:* 1-11 v Partick T, League Cup, 11 August 1993.
*Most Capped Player:* Jock White, 1 (2), Scotland.
*Most League Appearances:* 399, Murdy Walls, 1921-36.
*Most League Goals in Season (Individual):* 41: Jim Renwick, Division II; 1932-33.
*Most Goals Overall (Individual):* 105: Bunty Weir, 1928-31.

## ALBION ROVERS 1997–98 LEAGUE RECORD

| Match No. | Date | | Venue | Opponents | Result | | H/T Score | Lg. Pos. | Goalscorers | Atten- dance |
|---|---|---|---|---|---|---|---|---|---|---|
| 1 | Aug | 5 | A | Montrose | W | 2-0 | 2-0 | — | Duncan [32], Bruce [33] | 471 |
| 2 | | 16 | H | Berwick R | W | 2-1 | 1-0 | 2 | Gardner 2 (1 pen) [30 (p), 70] | 374 |
| 3 | | 23 | A | Queen's Park | L | 1-5 | 0-0 | 5 | Gardner (pen) [70] | 567 |
| 4 | | 30 | A | Ross Co | L | 3-5 | 0-2 | 6 | Gardner (pen) [71], Dickson [87], Bruce [88] | 1285 |
| 5 | Sept | 13 | H | Dumbarton | W | 2-1 | 1-0 | 5 | Graham [45], Watters [78] | 495 |
| 6 | | 20 | H | Alloa Ath | W | 2-1 | 2-0 | 5 | Bruce [6], Gardner [33] | 405 |
| 7 | | 27 | A | Cowdenbeath | W | 4-1 | 1-0 | 3 | Watters 3 [11, 61, 63], Bruce [56] | 197 |
| 8 | Oct | 4 | A | Arbroath | L | 0-3 | 0-0 | 6 | | 535 |
| 9 | | 18 | H | East Stirling | W | 5-1 | 2-0 | 5 | Ross A [29], Dickson 2 (1 pen) [42 (p), 48], Bruce [51], Gardner [77] | 420 |
| 10 | | 25 | H | Queen's Park | D | 0-0 | 0-0 | 4 | | 508 |
| 11 | Nov | 1 | A | Berwick R | D | 1-1 | 1-1 | 4 | Duncan [11] | 401 |
| 12 | | 8 | H | Ross Co | W | 2-0 | 2-0 | 3 | Martin P [6], Mitchell [8] | 506 |
| 13 | | 15 | A | Dumbarton | D | 1-1 | 0-0 | 5 | Watters [66] | 425 |
| 14 | | 22 | H | Cowdenbeath | L | 0-1 | 0-0 | 5 | | 355 |
| 15 | | 29 | A | Alloa Ath | L | 0-4 | 0-1 | 5 | | 451 |
| 16 | Dec | 13 | A | East Stirling | L | 0-1 | 0-0 | 5 | | 335 |
| 17 | | 20 | H | Arbroath | L | 1-3 | 0-2 | 6 | Bruce [86] | 563 |
| 18 | | 27 | A | Queen's Park | W | 4-2 | 2-0 | 5 | Gardner 2 [21, 47], Watters [30], Dickson [63] | 643 |
| 19 | Jan | 10 | H | Montrose | W | 3-2 | 2-0 | 5 | Bruce [10], Harty [21], Shepherd [57] | 325 |
| 20 | | 31 | H | Alloa Ath | D | 3-3 | 0-2 | 5 | Gardner 2 [65, 83], Shepherd [68] | 435 |
| 21 | Feb | 7 | H | East Stirling | W | 3-2 | 2-1 | 5 | Watters [18], Sinclair 2 [41, 87] | 343 |
| 22 | | 10 | A | Cowdenbeath | L | 0-2 | 0-0 | — | | 231 |
| 23 | | 21 | A | Montrose | W | 3-1 | 1-0 | 5 | Ross A 2 (1 pen) [36, 48 (p)], Watters [50] | 292 |
| 24 | Mar | 7 | H | Dumbarton | D | 2-2 | 1-1 | 5 | Donaldson [19], Watters [46] | 417 |
| 25 | | 14 | H | Cowdenbeath | L | 0-1 | 0-1 | 5 | | 346 |
| 26 | | 17 | A | Ross Co | L | 2-6 | 0-5 | — | Ross A [70], Bruce [78] | 741 |
| 27 | | 21 | A | Alloa Ath | L | 1-3 | 1-1 | 5 | Ross A [17] | 478 |
| 28 | | 28 | A | East Stirling | L | 0-2 | 0-2 | 5 | | 291 |
| 29 | Apr | 4 | H | Arbroath | L | 0-1 | 0-0 | 5 | | 343 |
| 30 | | 11 | H | Ross Co | L | 1-3 | 0-1 | 5 | Dickson (pen) [82] | 504 |
| 31 | | 13 | A | Berwick R | W | 5-0 | 2-0 | — | Dickson [15], Watters 2 [35, 66], Ross A [55], Melvin [78] | 225 |
| 32 | | 18 | A | Dumbarton | L | 0-2 | 0-1 | 5 | | 398 |
| 33 | | 25 | H | Queen's Park | L | 1-2 | 0-1 | 5 | Docherty [81] | 403 |
| 34 | | 29 | A | Arbroath | L | 0-2 | 0-1 | — | | 409 |
| 35 | May | 2 | A | Berwick R | L | 2-5 | 1-2 | 6 | Watters [21], Dickson (pen) [53] | 519 |
| 36 | | 9 | H | Montrose | W | 4-2 | 3-0 | 5 | Watters [6], Harty [22], McIlhattan [34], Moore [68] | 239 |

**Final League Position: 5**      1996-97 5

**Honours**
*League Champions:* Division II 1933-34, Second Division 1988-89; *Runners-up:* Division II 1913-14, 1937-38, 1947-48.
*Scottish Cup Runners-up:* 1920. *League Cup:* —.
*Club Colours:* Shirt: Yellow with black trim. Shorts: Black. Stockings: Black.

**Goalscorers:** *League (60):* Watters 13, Gardner 10 (3 pens), Bruce 8, Dickson 7 (3 pens), Ross A 6 (1 pen), Duncan 2, Harty 2, Shepherd 2, Sinclair 2, Docherty 1, Donaldson 1, Graham 1, McIlhattan 1, Martin P 1, Melvin 1, Mitchell 1, Moore 1. *Scottish Cup (5):* Dickson 1, McKilligan 1, Ross A 1, Sinclair 1, Watters 1. *Coca Cola Cup (0). League Challenge Cup (1):* Bruce 1.

| Ross S 22 | Duncan G 9+3 | McGowan N 11+1 | Coyle R 16+3 | Martin P 18 | Cody S 7 | McInnes I 5+5 | Gardner L 32 | Watters W 28+7 | Moore V 17 | Bruce D 12+13 | McKilligan N 27+4 | Harty I 15+11 | Sinclair C 24+6 | Mitchell C 24+1 | Shepherd A 7+5 | Martin J 3 | Campbell D —+1 | Dickson J 19+7 | Graham A 2 | McKenzie D —+7 | Melvin M 24+1 | Kelly G —+1 | Ross A 19+4 | Alexander D —+2 | Duffy D 2 | Dinnie A 2 | Hamilton B —+1 | Greenock R 17 | Donaldson E 9 | Vincent R 2+2 | Docherty R 11 | Connolly J 8 | Baxter C 1 | Shaw M 1+4 | McLees J —+1 | Clark S —+1 | Mitchell A 1 | McIlhattan L 1 | Match No. |
|---|---|---|---|---|---|---|---|---|---|---|---|---|---|---|---|---|---|---|---|---|---|---|---|---|---|---|---|---|---|---|---|---|---|---|---|---|---|---|---|
| 1 | 2 | 3 | 4 | 5 | 6 | $7^1$ | 8 | 9 | $10^3$ | $11^2$ | 12 | 13 | 14 | | | | | | | | | | | | | | | | | | | | | | | | | | 1 |
| 1 | 6 | 3 | 4 | $5^1$ | 8 | $11^3$ | 7 | 13 | | $9^2$ | 12 | 10 | | 2 | 14 | | | | | | | | | | | | | | | | | | | | | | | | 2 |
| 1 | 6 | 3 | 4 | 5 | 8 | | 7 | $9^1$ | 10 | 12 | | 11 | | 2 | | | | | | | | | | | | | | | | | | | | | | | | | 3 |
| | | | 4 | | 8 | $10^3$ | 7 | $9^2$ | 5 | 13 | 3 | 11 | 6 | $2^1$ | | 1 | 12 | 14 | | | | | | | | | | | | | | | | | | | | | 4 |
| | 3 | 4 | 5 | $6^1$ | | 7 | 14 | $10^3$ | 13 | 12 | $11^2$ | | 2 | | 1 | 8 | 9 | | | | | | | | | | | | | | | | | | | | | | 5 |
| | 3 | 4 | 5 | | | 7 | 12 | 10 | $8^1$ | 6 | | 13 | 2 | | 1 | $11^2$ | 9 | | | | | | | | | | | | | | | | | | | | | | 6 |
| 1 | $6^2$ | | 4 | 5 | $8^3$ | | 7 | 9 | | $10^1$ | 14 | | 3 | 2 | | | | 11 | | 12 | 13 | | | | | | | | | | | | | | | | | | 7 |
| 1 | 8 | | 4 | 5 | $6^3$ | 12 | 7 | $9^2$ | | 10 | | | $3^1$ | 2 | | | | 11 | | 13 | | 14 | | | | | | | | | | | | | | | | | 8 |
| 1 | | | 4 | | | | 10 | 14 | $8^2$ | $11^1$ | 5 | 12 | 3 | 2 | 13 | | | 7 | | | 6 | | $9^3$ | | | | | | | | | | | | | | | | 9 |
| 1 | | | 4 | | | | 7 | 11 | 10 | $3^1$ | 5 | | 2 | | | | | 8 | | 12 | 6 | | 9 | | | | | | | | | | | | | | | | 10 |
| 1 | 8 | | 4 | | | | 10 | $11^2$ | | 5 | | | $3^3$ | 2 | 13 | | | 7 | | 12 | 6 | | $9^1$ | 14 | | | | | | | | | | | | | | | 11 |
| 1 | 13 | | $5^3$ | | | | 7 | 9 | 8 | | 4 | | 11 | $2^2$ | 6 | | | 14 | | 12 | 3 | | $10^1$ | | | | | | | | | | | | | | | | 12 |
| 1 | | | 5 | | | | 7 | 9 | 10 | 13 | 6 | | $3^1$ | 2 | 8 | | | 12 | | | 4 | | $11^2$ | | | | | | | | | | | | | | | | 13 |
| 1 | | | 5 | | | | 7 | $9^2$ | 10 | 13 | 2 | | $3^1$ | 12 | 6 | | | 8 | | $14$ | 4 | | $11^2$ | | | | | | | | | | | | | | | | 14 |
| | | | 5 | | | | $8^2$ | 12 | | 10 | 6 | 7 | 3 | 2 | 13 | | | 11 | | | | | $9^1$ | | 1 | 4 | | | | | | | | | | | | | 15 |
| | | 12 | 5 | | | | 7 | $9^2$ | | 13 | 3 | | 11 | 2 | 6 | | | $8^1$ | | | 4 | | 10 | | 1 | | | | | | | | | | | | | | 16 |
| 1 | $2^2$ | 13 | 5 | | | | | $9^4$ | | 12 | 3 | 10 | 11 | 6 | $8^1$ | | | 7 | | | 4 | | 14 | | | | | | | | | | | | | | | | 17 |
| 1 | | 4 | 5 | | | | $7^2$ | $9^1$ | | 10 | | 11 | 3 | 8 | | | | 12 | | | 6 | | 13 | | | | | 2 | | | | | | | | | | | 18 |
| 1 | | 4 | 5 | | | | 9 | | | 10 | | 11 | 3 | $7^2$ | 8 | | | 12 | | | 6 | | 14 | | | | | $13^3$ | | $6^1$ | 2 | | | | | | | | 19 |
| 1 | | 4 | 5 | | | | 7 | 9 | | $10^2$ | | $11^3$ | 3 | 8 | 12 | | | 13 | | | 6 | | 14 | | | | | | | | $2^1$ | | | | | | | | 20 |
| 1 | | | | | | | 8 | $9^1$ | | 13 | 5 | 12 | 11 | 6 | | | | 7 | | | 4 | | $10^2$ | | | | | | | | 2 | 3 | | | | | | | 21 |
| 1 | $4^2$ | | | | | | 7 | 9 | | 12 | 5 | 10 | 3 | 11 | $8^1$ | | | 13 | | | 6 | | | | | | | | | | 2 | | | | | | | | 22 |
| 1 | 12 | | | | | | 7 | $9^2$ | | 14 | 5 | 13 | $11^1$ | 6 | | | | | | | 4 | | $10^2$ | | | | | | | | 2 | 3 | | | | | | | 23 |
| 1 | 12 | | | | | | $7^2$ | 8 | 9 | | 13 | 4 | 14 | $11^1$ | $6^2$ | | | | | | 5 | | 10 | | | | | | | | 2 | 3 | | | | | | | 24 |
| 1 | | 5 | | | | | 7 | $9^1$ | | 13 | 4 | 12 | 11 | 8 | | | | | | | | | 10 | | | | | | | | 2 | 3 | $6^2$ | | | | | | 25 |
| 1 | | 4 | 5 | | | | $7^2$ | 14 | | 13 | 8 | | $11^3$ | | | | | | | | $6^1$ | | 9 | | | | | | | | 2 | 3 | 12 | 10 | | | | | 26 |
| | 14 | | | | | | | 13 | | $10^1$ | $6^3$ | 12 | 11 | 2 | | | | | | | 4 | | $9^2$ | | | | | 7 | 3 | | 8 | | 1 | 5 | | | | | 27 |
| | 4 | | | | | | 12 | $7^3$ | 11 | $8^2$ | | 2 | 14 | | | | | | | | 5 | | 9 | | | | | 3 | $6^1$ | | 10 | | 1 | | 13 | | | | 28 |
| | $4^2$ | | | | | | | 2 | | 8 | | 5 | $10^1$ | | | | | | 7 | | 6 | | 9 | | | | | 3 | 13 | 11 | | 1 | | 12 | | | | | 29 |
| 1 | 12 | | | | | | 14 | 6 | 9 | 8 | | 5 | $10^1$ | 13 | | | | 7 | | | 4 | | | $11^2$ | | | | $2^2$ | $3^1$ | | 11 | | | | | | | | 30 |
| 1 | 3 | | | | | | 6 | 9 | $10^1$ | | | 5 | 13 | 14 | | | | 7 | | | 4 | | $11^2$ | | | | | 2 | | | $8^1$ | 1 | | 12 | | | | | 31 |
| 1 | 3 | | | | | | 14 | 8 | 9 | | | $5^3$ | 12 | 13 | | | | 7 | | | 4 | | $10^1$ | | | | | 2 | | | 11 | 1 | | $6^2$ | | | | | 32 |
| 1 | 3 | | | | | | 6 | $9^2$ | 8 | | | 4 | 13 | 12 | | | | $7^1$ | | | 5 | | 10 | | | | | 2 | | | 11 | 1 | | | | | | | 33 |
| 1 | 3 | | | | | | 6 | 8 | | 5 | | 10 | 11 | 7 | | | | 4 | | | | | 2 | | | | | 6 | 1 | | | | | | | | | | 34 |
| 1 | 3 | | | | | | 12 | 8 | 9 | | | 5 | $10^2$ | 11 | | | | $7^1$ | | | $4^3$ | | | | | | | 2 | | | 6 | 1 | | | | 13 | 14 | | 35 |
| 1 | 3 | | | | | | $8^2$ | 9 | 4 | | | 5 | $10^3$ | $11^1$ | | | | | | | 13 | | $14$ | 2 | | | | | | | 7 | | | 12 | | | 1 | 6 | 36 |

# ALLOA ATHLETIC

## Second Division

*Year Formed:* 1883. *Ground & Address:* Recreation Park, Clackmannan Rd, Alloa FK10 1RR. *Telephone:* 01259 722695.
*Ground Capacity:* total: 931, seated: 414. *Size of Pitch:* 110yd × 75yd.
*Chairman:* Robert Hopkins. *Secretary:* E. G. Cameron. *Commercial Manager:* William McKie.
*Manager:* Tom Hendrie. *Assistant Manager:* John Coughlin. *Physio:* Alan Anderson.
*Managers since 1975:* H. Wilson; A. Totten; W. Garner; J. Thomson; D. Sullivan; G. Abel; B. Little; H. McCann; W. Lamont; Pat McAuley. *Club Nickname(s):* The Wasps. *Previous Grounds:* None.
*Record Attendance:* 13,000 v Dunfermline Athletic, Scottish Cup 3rd rd replay; 26 Feb, 1939.
*Record Transfer Fee received:* £60,000 for Paul Sheerin to Southampton (1992).
*Record Transfer Fee paid:* £10,000 for Douglas Lawrie from Stirling Albion.
*Record Victory:* 9-2 v Forfar Ath, Division II; 18 Mar, 1933.
*Record Defeat:* 0-10 v Dundee, Division II; 8 Mar, 1947: v Third Lanark, League Cup, 8 Aug, 1953.
*Most Capped Player:* Jock Hepburn, 1, Scotland.
*Most League Appearances:* —.
*Most League Goals in Season (Individual):* 49: William 'Wee' Crilley, Division II; 1921-22.
*Most Goals Overall (Individual):* —.

## ALLOA ATHLETIC 1997–98 LEAGUE RECORD

| Match No. | Date | Venue | Opponents | Result | H/T Score | Lg. Pos. | Goalscorers | Atten- dance |
|---|---|---|---|---|---|---|---|---|
| 1 | Aug 5 | A | Berwick R | W 2-0 | 1-0 | — | Irvine [29], Mathieson [54] | 549 |
| 2 | 16 | H | Cowdenbeath | W 1-0 | 1-0 | 1 | Irvine [44] | 462 |
| 3 | 23 | A | East Stirling | L 1-2 | 0-0 | 3 | Mathieson [90] | 502 |
| 4 | 30 | A | Dumbarton | W 1-0 | 0-0 | 3 | Wilson S [48] | 465 |
| 5 | Sept 13 | A | Montrose | W 5-1 | 2-0 | 1 | Mackay 2 [31, 36], Mathieson [58], Mailer (og) [62], Irvine [77] | 403 |
| 6 | 20 | A | Albion R | L 1-2 | 0-2 | 4 | Wilson S [83] | 405 |
| 7 | 27 | H | Arbroath | W 3-0 | 3-0 | 2 | Pew [10], Irvine [30], Simpson [45] | 555 |
| 8 | Oct 4 | A | Ross Co | W 4-2 | 0-2 | 1 | Haddow [48], McAneny [56], Irvine [75], Cameron [82] | 1823 |
| 9 | 18 | H | Queen's Park | L 3-4 | 0-3 | 3 | Pew 2 [47, 50], Mathieson [73] | 514 |
| 10 | 25 | H | East Stirling | L 0-2 | 0-0 | 5 | | 503 |
| 11 | Nov 1 | A | Cowdenbeath | W 3-0 | 2-0 | 3 | Ramsay [20], Pew [23], Simpson [82] | 214 |
| 12 | 8 | H | Dumbarton | L 1-2 | 1-1 | 4 | McAneny [30] | 424 |
| 13 | 15 | A | Montrose | W 2-0 | 1-0 | 3 | Irvine [26], Mackay [62] | 357 |
| 14 | 22 | A | Arbroath | W 3-2 | 2-0 | 2 | Pew [36], Irvine [45], Gilmour [87] | 751 |
| 15 | 29 | H | Albion R | W 4-0 | 1-0 | 2 | Simpson [38], Gilmour [73], Irvine 2 [74, 76] | 451 |
| 16 | Dec 13 | A | Queen's Park | L 0-3 | 0-2 | 4 | | 575 |
| 17 | 27 | A | East Stirling | W 3-0 | 1-0 | 4 | Simpson 2 [42, 73], Mackay [51] | 572 |
| 18 | 30 | H | Ross Co | W 1-0 | 1-0 | — | Shearer [11] | 778 |
| 19 | Jan 10 | H | Berwick R | L 1-3 | 0-0 | 2 | Pew [56] | 545 |
| 20 | 31 | A | Albion R | D 3-3 | 2-0 | 2 | Haddow 3 [22, 45, 65] | 435 |
| 21 | Feb 3 | H | Arbroath | W 3-1 | 2-0 | — | Irvine 2 [10, 38], Simpson [52] | 528 |
| 22 | 7 | A | Queen's Park | W 2-0 | 0-0 | 1 | Cameron [60], McKechnie [72] | 519 |
| 23 | 21 | A | Berwick R | D 1-1 | 1-1 | 1 | Simpson [38] | 435 |
| 24 | 24 | H | Cowdenbeath | W 2-0 | 0-0 | — | Irvine [52], Cameron [75] | 484 |
| 25 | 28 | A | Dumbarton | W 3-0 | 1-0 | 1 | McKechnie 2 [23, 64], Cameron [74] | 396 |
| 26 | Mar 7 | H | Montrose | W 3-2 | 1-0 | 1 | Irvine [29], Cameron 2 [60, 81] | 495 |
| 27 | 14 | A | Arbroath | L 0-3 | 0-2 | 1 | | 1012 |
| 28 | 21 | H | Albion R | W 3-1 | 1-1 | 1 | McKechnie [20], Ramsay [65], Irvine [86] | 478 |
| 29 | 24 | A | Ross Co | W 2-0 | 1-0 | — | Ramsay [10], Irvine [72] | 1327 |
| 30 | 24 | A | Queen's Park | D 1-1 | 0-1 | 1 | Cameron [55] | 549 |
| 31 | Apr 4 | A | Ross Co | D 1-1 | 0-0 | 1 | Irvine (pen) [70] | 624 |
| 32 | 11 | H | Dumbarton | W 3-0 | 0-0 | 1 | McKechnie [60], Irvine (pen) [63], Haddow [88] | 538 |
| 33 | 18 | A | Montrose | W 3-0 | 0-0 | 1 | Simpson 2 [47, 75], Irvine [74] | 463 |
| 34 | 25 | H | East Stirling | W 5-2 | 3-1 | 1 | Haddow 2 [2, 63], Mathieson 3 [35, 43, 71] | 788 |
| 35 | May 2 | A | Cowdenbeath | W 3-1 | 1-0 | 1 | Mathieson [32], McKechnie [63], Cameron [85] | 473 |
| 36 | 9 | H | Berwick R | W 1-0 | 1-0 | 1 | Haddow [18] | 894 |

**Final League Position: 1**      1996–97 4

**Honours**
*League Champions:* Division II 1921-22; Third Division 1997–98. *Runners-up:* Division II 1938-39. Second Division 1976-77, 1981-82, 1984-85, 1988-89.
*Scottish Cup:* —.
*League Cup:* —.
*Club colours:* Shirt: Gold with black trim. Shorts: Black. Stockings: Gold.

**Goalscorers:** *League (78):* Irvine 18 (2 pens), Simpson 9, Cameron 8, Haddow 8, Mathieson 8, McKechnie 6, Pew 6, Mackay 4, Ramsay 3, Gilmour 2, McAneny 2, Wilson S 2, Shearer 1, own goal 1. *Scottish Cup (2):* Irvine 1, Mackay 1. *Coca Cola Cup (3):* Irvine 2, Pew 1. *League Challenge Cup (1):* Irvine 1.

| Monaghan M 3 | Valentine C 36 | Haddow L 34 | McAneny P 20 + 3 | McCulloch K 2 | McCormack J 10 + 5 | Wilson M 15 + 2 | Wilson S 29 + 1 | Mathieson M 11 + 5 | Irvine W 33 | Pew D 22 + 11 | Ramsay S 24 + 6 | Simpson P 34 + 2 | Nelson M 20 + 6 | Little T — + 4 | Cairns M 29 | Mackay S 17 | Gilmour J 7 + 8 | Cowan M 30 | Cameron M 4 + 20 | Ellison S 4 | Smith B — + 1 | Shearer P 3 | McKechnie G 9 + 5 | Match No. |
|---|---|---|---|---|---|---|---|---|---|---|---|---|---|---|---|---|---|---|---|---|---|---|---|---|
| 1 | 2 | 3 | 4 | 5 | $6^1$ | 7 | 8 | $9^1$ | 10 | 11 | 12 | 13 | | | | | | | | | | | | 1 |
| 1 | 2 | 3 | 4 | 5 | | 7 | 8 | $9^1$ | 10 | 11 | 6 | 12 | | | | | | | | | | | | 2 |
| 1 | 2 | 3 | 4 | | $7^2$ | | 8 | 9 | 10 | $11^1$ | 6 | 5 | 12 | 13 | | | | | | | | | | 3 |
| | 2 | 3 | 4 | | | 7 | 8 | 9 | 10 | 11 | $6^1$ | 5 | 12 | | 1 | | | | | | | | | 4 |
| | 2 | $3^2$ | 4 | | | | 8 | 9 | 10 | 11 | $7^1$ | 5 | 12 | 13 | 1 | 6 | | | | | | | | 5 |
| | 2 | 3 | 4 | 12 | | 8 | | $9^1$ | 10 | 11 | $7^2$ | $5^1$ | 14 | | 1 | 6 | 13 | | | | | | | 6 |
| | 2 | $3^2$ | 4 | | | 8 | | 10 | 11 | 12 | 9 | 7 | | | 1 | $6^1$ | 13 | 5 | | | | | | 7 |
| | 2 | 3 | 4 | | | 8 | | 10 | $11^2$ | 12 | 9 | 7 | | | 1 | 6 | $5^1$ | 13 | | | | | | 8 |
| | 2 | $3^2$ | 4 | 13 | | 8 | 12 | 10 | 11 | 9 | $7^2$ | 14 | | | 1 | $6^1$ | 5 | | | | | | | 9 |
| | 2 | 3 | 4 | 7 | | $8^1$ | 9 | 11 | 10 | $12^3$ | | | | | 1 | $6^2$ | 13 | 5 | 14 | | | | | 10 |
| | 2 | 3 | 4 | | | $9^1$ | 11 | 7 | 10 | | | | | | 1 | 8 | 6 | 5 | 12 | | | | | 11 |
| | 2 | $10^2$ | 4 | | 14 | | 11 | $7^3$ | 9 | $3^1$ | 13 | | | | 1 | 8 | 6 | 5 | 12 | | | | | 12 |
| | 2 | 3 | 4 | | | | 10 | $11^1$ | 7 | 9 | | | | | 1 | 8 | 6 | 5 | 12 | | | | | 13 |
| | 2 | 3 | 4 | | | | 10 | 11 | 7 | 9 | | | | | 1 | 8 | 6 | 5 | | | | | | 14 |
| | 2 | 3 | 4 | 12 | | 13 | 10 | $11^3$ | $7^1$ | $9^2$ | | 8 | 6 | 5 | 14 | | | | | 1 | | | | 15 |
| | 2 | $4^1$ | 3 | | | 10 | 11 | 7 | 9 | 12 | | $8^2$ | 6 | 5 | $13^3$ | | | | | 1 | 14 | | | 16 |
| | 2 | | | 12 | 13 | 10 | 11 | $7^1$ | 9 | 4 | | $8^2$ | 6 | 5 | | | | | | 1 | | 3 | | 17 |
| | 2 | $3^1$ | | | | 7 | 10 | 11 | 12 | 9 | 4 | 8 | | 5 | | | | | | 1 | | 6 | | 18 |
| | 2 | $3^1$ | | | | 7 | 10 | $11^2$ | 14 | 9 | 4 | | 1 | $8^1$ | 12 | 5 | 13 | | | | | 6 | | 19 |
| | 2 | $3^1$ | 12 | | | $7^1$ | 8 | 10 | 11 | | 9 | 4 | | 1 | 6 | 5 | | | | | | | | 20 |
| | 2 | $3^1$ | 14 | | | $7^1$ | 8 | 10 | 12 | 9 | 4 | | 1 | $6^2$ | 13 | 5 | 11 | | | | | | | 21 |
| | 2 | 3 | | | | 7 | 8 | 10 | 13 | 6 | $9^1$ | 4 | | 1 | | 5 | | $11^2$ | | | | | 12 | 22 |
| | 2 | 3 | | | | 7 | 8 | 10 | 13 | 6 | $9^2$ | 4 | | 1 | | 5 | | $11^1$ | | | | | 12 | 23 |
| | 2 | 3 | | | 7 | | 8 | 10 | | 6 | $9^1$ | 4 | | 1 | | 5 | | 12 | | | | | 11 | 24 |
| | 2 | 3 | | | 7 | | 8 | $10^2$ | 13 | 6 | $9^1$ | 4 | | 1 | | 5 | | 12 | | | | | 11 | 25 |
| | 2 | $3^3$ | | | $7^1$ | 12 | 8 | 10 | 14 | 6 | $9^2$ | 4 | | 1 | | 5 | | 13 | | | | | 11 | 26 |
| | 2 | $3^4$ | 14 | | 7 | | 8 | 10 | 13 | $6^2$ | $9^1$ | 4 | | 1 | | 5 | | 12 | | | | | 11 | 27 |
| | 2 | 3 | | | | 7 | 8 | 10 | 13 | $6^3$ | $9^2$ | 4 | | 1 | | 14 | 5 | 12 | | | | | $11^1$ | 28 |
| | 2 | 3 | | | | 7 | $8^1$ | 10 | 13 | 6 | 9 | 4 | | 1 | | 5 | | 12 | | | | | $11^2$ | 29 |
| | 2 | $3^4$ | | | 7 | 6 | 8 | 10 | 13 | | $9^1$ | 4 | | 1 | | 14 | 5 | 12 | | | | | $11^2$ | 30 |
| | 2 | 3 | | | 7 | $8^2$ | 12 | 10 | 6 | | $9^1$ | 4 | | 1 | | 13 | 5 | 11 | | | | | | 31 |
| | 2 | 3 | 14 | | 7 | 6 | 12 | 10 | 8 | | $9^2$ | $4^3$ | | 1 | | 5 | 13 | | | | | | $11^1$ | 32 |
| | 2 | $3^1$ | 4 | | 7 | 8 | 13 | 10 | 12 | 6 | $9^1$ | | | 1 | | 5 | 14 | | | | | | $11^2$ | 33 |
| | 2 | 3 | 4 | | 7 | 8 | $11^2$ | 10 | | 6 | $9^1$ | | | 1 | | 5 | 13 | 12 | | | | | | 34 |
| | 2 | $3^1$ | 4 | | 7 | 8 | $11^2$ | 10 | 14 | 6 | $9^1$ | | | 1 | | 5 | 13 | 12 | | | | | | 35 |
| | 2 | 3 | 4 | | 7 | $8^3$ | $11^2$ | 10 | 14 | 6 | $9^1$ | | | 1 | | 5 | 13 | 12 | | | | | | 36 |

# ARBROATH

## Second Division

*Year Formed:* 1878. *Ground & Address:* Gayfield Park, Arbroath DD11 1QB. *Telephone and Fax:* 01241 872157.
*Ground Capacity:* 6488. seated: 715. *Size of Pitch:* 115yd × 71yd.
*President:* John D. Christison. *Secretary:* Charles Kinnear. *Commercial Manager:* Bill Thompson.
*Manager:* David Baikie. *Assistant Manager:* Graeme Irons. *Physio:* William Shearer. *Coaches:* John Martin, Ian Fairweather.
*Managers since 1975:* A. Henderson; I. J. Stewart; G. Fleming; J. Bone; J. Young; W. Borthwick; M. Lawson, D. McGrain MBE, J. Scott, J. Brogan, T. Campbell, G. Mackie, J. Brogan, T. Campbell, G. Mackie.
*Club Nickname(s):* The Red Lichties. *Previous Grounds:* None.
*Record Attendance:* 13,510 v Rangers, Scottish Cup 3rd rd; 23 Feb, 1952.
*Record Transfer Fee received:* £120,000 for Paul Tosh to Dundee (Aug 1993).
*Record Transfer Fee paid:* £20,000 for Douglas Robb from Montrose (1981).
*Record Victory:* 36-0 v Bon Accord, Scottish Cup 1st rd; 12 Sept, 1885.
*Record Defeat:* 1-9 v Celtic, League Cup 3rd rd; 25 Aug 1993.
*Most Capped Player:* Ned Doig, 2 (5), Scotland.
*Most League Appearances:* 445: Tom Cargill, 1966-81.
*Most League Goals in Season (Individual):* 45: Dave Easson, Division II; 1958-59.
*Most Goals Overall (Individual):* 120: Jimmy Jack; 1966-71.

## ARBROATH 1997–98 LEAGUE RECORD

| Match No. | Date | Venue | Opponents | Result | H/T Score | Lg. Pos. | Goalscorers | Atten- dance |
|---|---|---|---|---|---|---|---|---|
| 1 | Aug 16 | H | East Stirling | W 2-0 | 1-0 | — | Spence 2 [35, 65] | 387 |
| 2 | 23 | H | Montrose | W 3-0 | 1-0 | 2 | McWalter [10], Spence 2 [48, 78] | 921 |
| 3 | 30 | A | Berwick R | W 3-1 | 0-1 | 1 | Grant 3 [57, 60, 88] | 339 |
| 4 | Sept 9 | A | Queen's Park | L 2-3 | 1-1 | — | Burns [16], Scott [84] | 364 |
| 5 | 13 | H | Ross Co | D 2-2 | 0-0 | 2 | Crawford [85], Cooper (pen) [89] | 625 |
| 6 | 20 | H | Dumbarton | W 2-1 | 2-0 | 1 | Grant [25], Cooper (pen) [40] | 702 |
| 7 | 27 | A | Alloa Ath | L 0-3 | 0-3 | 5 | | 555 |
| 8 | Oct 4 | H | Albion R | W 3-0 | 0-0 | 2 | McWalter [50], Gallagher [65], Cooper (pen) [87] | 535 |
| 9 | 18 | A | Cowdenbeath | W 4-0 | 1-0 | 2 | McWalter [21], Cooper [53], Mitchell [66], Spence [87] | 252 |
| 10 | 25 | H | Montrose | L 1-2 | 1-1 | 2 | Cooper (pen) [21] | 1150 |
| 11 | Nov 1 | H | East Stirling | W 2-1 | 1-1 | 2 | Thomson N [15], Grant [50] | 413 |
| 12 | 8 | H | Berwick R | W 4-1 | 2-0 | 2 | Florence [35], Grant [41], Burns [64], Spence [84] | 500 |
| 13 | 15 | A | Ross Co | D 0-0 | 0-0 | 2 | | 1656 |
| 14 | 22 | A | Alloa Ath | L 2-3 | 0-2 | 4 | Thomson N [79], Spence [89] | 751 |
| 15 | 29 | A | Dumbarton | W 2-1 | 2-0 | 3 | Crawford [54], Spence [85] | 379 |
| 16 | Dec 6 | H | East Stirling | W 3-0 | 2-0 | 1 | McWalter [14], Crawford [29], Florence [63] | 646 |
| 17 | 13 | H | Cowdenbeath | W 3-2 | 2-2 | 1 | Burns [24], Spence [27], McWalter [75] | 630 |
| 18 | 20 | H | Albion R | W 3-1 | 2-0 | 1 | Cooper [37], Spence [44], Grant [89] | 563 |
| 19 | 27 | A | Montrose | L 0-1 | 0-0 | 1 | | 1496 |
| 20 | Jan 10 | H | Queen's Park | D 2-2 | 1-2 | 1 | Thomson R [4], Spence [67] | 741 |
| 21 | 31 | H | Dumbarton | D 2-2 | 2-2 | 1 | Tindal [17], Burns [20] | 666 |
| 22 | Feb 3 | A | Alloa Ath | L 1-3 | 0-2 | — | Thomson N [66] | 528 |
| 23 | 7 | A | Cowdenbeath | L 1-3 | 0-2 | 2 | Grant [87] | 248 |
| 24 | 21 | A | Queen's Park | W 2-0 | 0-0 | 2 | Grant [74], Gallagher (pen) [78] | 422 |
| 25 | 28 | A | Berwick R | D 0-0 | 0-0 | 2 | | 333 |
| 26 | Mar 7 | H | Ross Co | D 1-1 | 1-1 | 2 | Gallagher (pen) [12] | 784 |
| 27 | 14 | A | Alloa Ath | W 3-0 | 2-0 | 2 | Spence 2 [3, 85], Tindal [8] | 1012 |
| 28 | 21 | A | Dumbarton | W 2-1 | 0-0 | 2 | Spence 2 [65, 77] | 383 |
| 29 | 28 | H | Cowdenbeath | W 2-0 | 1-0 | 2 | Gallagher (pen) [23], McWalter [68] | 771 |
| 30 | Apr 4 | A | Albion R | W 1-0 | 0-0 | 2 | Grant [84] | 343 |
| 31 | 11 | H | Berwick R | W 1-0 | 0-0 | 2 | Tindal [54] | 823 |
| 32 | 18 | A | Ross Co | L 0-1 | 0-0 | 2 | | 1842 |
| 33 | 25 | H | Montrose | W 4-2 | 2-2 | 2 | Gallagher (pen) [30], Peters [42], Crawford [54], Tindal [74] | 1340 |
| 34 | 29 | A | Albion R | W 2-0 | 1-0 | — | Tindal [4], Spence [62] | 409 |
| 35 | May 2 | A | East Stirling | D 1-1 | 0-1 | 2 | Tindal [73] | 651 |
| 36 | 9 | H | Queen's Park | D 1-1 | 0-0 | 2 | Cooper (pen) [66] | 1950 |

**Final League Position: 2**   1996–97 10

**Honours**

*League Champions Runners-up:* Division II 1934-35, 1958-59, 1967-68, 1971-72; Third Division 1997–98.
*Scottish Cup: Quarter-finals:* 1993.
*League Cup:* —.
*Club colours:* Shirt: Maroon with white and sky blue trim. Shorts: White. Stockings: Maroon with white and sky blue hooped tops.

**Goalscorers:** *League (67):* Spence 16, Grant 10, Cooper 7 (5 pens), McWalter 6, Tindal 6, Gallagher 5 (4 pens), Burns 4, Crawford 4, Thomson N 3, Florence 2, Mitchell 1, Peters 1, Scott 1, Thomson R 1. *Scottish Cup (1):* Cooper 1. *Coca Cola Cup (0). League Challenge Cup (4):* Gallagher 1, Peters 1, Spence 1, Thomson N 1.

| Hinchcliffe C 25 | Mitchell B 34 + 1 | Gallagher J 35 + 1 | McAulay J 29 + 2 | Peters S 24 + 7 | Crawford J 33 | Cooper C 29 + 1 | Thomson N 30 + 4 | McWalter M 28 + 2 | Spence W 30 + 4 | Scott S 2 + 15 | Grant B 16 + 14 | Moonlight P —+ 5 | Burns K 17 + 12 | Florence S 24 + 1 | Butler D 1 + 4 | Thomson R 5 + 4 | Tindal K 11 + 1 | Scott D 12 | Sellars B —+ 2 | Wight C 11 | Match No. |
|---|---|---|---|---|---|---|---|---|---|---|---|---|---|---|---|---|---|---|---|---|---|
| 1 | 2 | 3 | 4 | 5 | 6 | $7^2$ | 8 | 9 | 10 | $11^1$ | 12 | 13 | | | | | | | | | 1 |
| 1 | 2 | 3 | 4 | 5 | 6 | 7 | 8 | | $10^2$ | 13 | $11^1$ | | 12 | | | | | | | | 2 |
| 1 | 2 | 3 | 4 | 5 | 6 | 7 | 8 | | $10^1$ | 12 | 9 | 13 | $11^2$ | | | | | | | | 3 |
| 1 | 2 | 3 | 4 | 5 | 6 | 7 | 8 | | 10 | 12 | 9 | | $11^1$ | | | | | | | | 4 |
| 1 | 2 | 3 | 4 | 5 | 6 | 7 | $8^2$ | $11^1$ | 10 | 12 | 9 | 13 | | | | | | | | | 5 |
| 1 | 2 | 3 | 4 | 5 | 6 | $7^1$ | 8 | 9 | 12 | 10 | 13 | | $11^2$ | 4 | | | | | | | 6 |
| 1 | 2 | 3 | 12 | 5 | 6 | 7 | 8 | 13 | $9^2$ | 10 | $11^1$ | | 4 | | | | | | | | 7 |
| 1 | 2 | 3 | 4 | $5^1$ | 6 | 7 | 8 | 10 | 9 | | 12 | 11 | | | | | | | | | 8 |
| 1 | 2 | 3 | 4 | 5 | 6 | 7 | $8^2$ | $10^1$ | $9^3$ | 12 | 14 | | 13 | 11 | | | | | | | 9 |
| 1 | 2 | 3 | 4 | 5 | 6 | 7 | 8 | $10^2$ | 9 | 13 | 12 | | $11^1$ | | | | | | | | 10 |
| 1 | 2 | 3 | 4 | 5 | 6 | | 8 | $9^1$ | | 10 | 11 | | 7 | 12 | | | | | | | 11 |
| 1 | 2 | 3 | 4 | $5^2$ | 6 | | 8 | $10^9$ | 12 | $9^1$ | 13 | | 11 | 7 | 14 | | | | | | 12 |
| 1 | 2 | 3 | 4 | 5 | 6 | 12 | 8 | $9^1$ | $10^2$ | | 11 | | 7 | 13 | | | | | | | 13 |
| 1 | 2 | 3 | 4 | 5 | 6 | 7 | 8 | 9 | 10 | | 11 | | | | | | | | | | 14 |
| 1 | 2 | 12 | 4 | 5 | 6 | $7^1$ | 8 | $10^2$ | 9 | 13 | 11 | | 3 | | | | | | | | 15 |
| 1 | 2 | 3 | 4 | | 6 | $7^1$ | 8 | $10^2$ | 9 | 12 | 13 | | 5 | 11 | | | | | | | 16 |
| 1 | 2 | 3 | 4 | | 6 | 7 | $8^2$ | 10 | $9^3$ | 14 | | | 5 | $11^1$ | 12 | | | | | | 17 |
| 1 | 2 | 3 | 4 | | 6 | $7^2$ | 8 | 10 | $9^3$ | 14 | | | 11 | $5^1$ | 12 | | | | | | 18 |
| 1 | 2 | 3 | 4 | $5^1$ | 6 | 7 | $8^2$ | 10 | 9 | 14 | | | 12 | $11^2$ | 13 | | | | | | 19 |
| 1 | 2 | 3 | 4 | | 6 | $7^1$ | 8 | $10^3$ | 9 | 14 | 12 | | 11 | | $5^2$ | 13 | | | | | 20 |
| 1 | 2 | 3 | $4^1$ | 13 | 6 | | 8 | 10 | 9 | 11 | | | 5 | 12 | | $7^2$ | | | | | 21 |
| 1 | 2 | 3 | 4 | $5^2$ | 6 | 7 | 8 | $10^3$ | 12 | | $9^1$ | | 11 | | 13 | 14 | | | | | 22 |
| 1 | 12 | $3^1$ | 4 | 2 | 6 | | 8 | 10 | 9 | | 13 | | 7 | $11^2$ | 5 | | | | | | 23 |
| 1 | 4 | 3 | | 11 | | | 8 | $10^1$ | $9^2$ | 13 | 12 | | $7^3$ | 2 | | 5 | | 6 | 14 | | 24 |
| 1 | 4 | 3 | | 7 | | | 8 | 12 | $9^1$ | | 10 | | 11 | 2 | | 5 | | 6 | | | 25 |
| | 4 | 11 | 12 | 2 | | 7 | $8^9$ | 10 | 13 | | $9^2$ | | 14 | 3 | | $5^1$ | 6 | | | 1 | 26 |
| | 5 | 3 | 4 | 12 | 6 | 7 | | $10^2$ | $9^2$ | | 13 | | 14 | 2 | | | $8^1$ | 11 | | 1 | 27 |
| | 5 | 3 | 4 | 12 | 6 | 7 | | $10^1$ | 9 | | | | 13 | 2 | | | $8^2$ | 11 | | 1 | 28 |
| | 5 | 3 | 4 | 14 | 6 | 7 | 12 | $10^2$ | 9 | | 13 | | | $2^9$ | | | $8^1$ | 11 | | 1 | 29 |
| | 3 | 4 | 5 | 6 | 7 | | 13 | $10^1$ | 9 | | 12 | | | 2 | | | $8^2$ | 11 | | 1 | 30 |
| | 5 | 3 | 4 | 14 | 6 | 7 | 13 | $10^9$ | 12 | | | | | 2 | | | $8^3$ | 11 | | 1 | 31 |
| | 5 | 3 | 4 | | 6 | 7 | 12 | | 9 | | $10^1$ | | | 2 | | | 8 | 11 | | 1 | 32 |
| | 5 | 3 | 4 | 12 | 6 | 7 | 11 | 10 | | 13 | $9^2$ | | 14 | $2^1$ | | | $8^3$ | | | 1 | 33 |
| | 5 | 3 | 4 | 12 | 6 | $7^2$ | 2 | 10 | 9 | | 13 | | | | | | $8^1$ | 11 | | 1 | 34 |
| | 5 | 3 | | 2 | 6 | $7^2$ | 4 | $10^3$ | $9^1$ | 14 | 12 | | 13 | | | | 8 | 11 | | 1 | 35 |
| | 5 | 3 | | 2 | 6 | 7 | 4 | $10^2$ | 12 | 13 | $9^1$ | | | | | | 8 | $11^3$ | 14 | 1 | 36 |

# AYR UNITED

## First Division

*Year Formed:* 1910. *Ground & Address:* Somerset Park, Tryfield Place, Ayr KA8 9NB. *Telephone:* 01292 263435.
*Ground Capacity:* 12,128. seated: 1450. *Size of Pitch:* 110yd × 72yd.
*Chairman:* W. J. Barr. *Administrator:* Brian Caldwell. *Secretary:* J. E. Eyley. *Lottery Manager:* Andrew Downie.
*Manager:* Gordon Dalziel. *Assistant Manager:* Alistair Dawson.
*Managers since 1975:* Alex Stuart; Ally MacLeod; Willie McLean; George Caldwell; Ally MacLeod; George Burley;
Simon Stainrod. *Club Nickname(s):* The Honest Men. *Previous Grounds:* None.
*Record Attendance:* 25,225 v Rangers, Division I; 13 Sept, 1969.
elticRecord *Transfer Fee received:* £300,000 for Steven Nicol to Liverpool (Oct 1981).
*Record Transfer Fee paid:* £50,000 for Peter Weir from St Mirren, June 1990.
*Record Victory:* 11-1 v Dumbarton, League Cup; 13 Aug, 1952.
*Record Defeat:* 0-9 in Division I v Rangers (1929); v Hearts (1931); B Division v Third Lanark (1954).
*Most Capped Player:* Jim Nisbet, 3, Scotland.
*Most League Appearances:* 459, John Murphy, 1963–78.
*Most League League and Cup Goals in Season (Individual):* 66, Jimmy Smith, 1927-28.
*Most  League and Cup Goals Overall (Individual):* 213, Peter Price, 1955–61.

## AYR UNITED 1997–98 LEAGUE RECORD

| Match No. | Date | | Venue | Opponents | Result | H/T Score | Lg. Pos. | Goalscorers | Attendance |
|---|---|---|---|---|---|---|---|---|---|
| 1 | Aug | 2 | H | Greenock Morton | L | 1-2 | 0-2 | — | Kerrigan [81] | 3481 |
| 2 | | 16 | A | Falkirk | L | 1-2 | 0-1 | 10 | Bell [67] | 2683 |
| 3 | | 23 | H | Partick Th | D | 2-2 | 2-1 | 10 | Ferguson [3], Hood [44] | 2398 |
| 4 | | 30 | A | Hamilton A | W | 2-0 | 2-0 | 6 | Kerrigan 2 [17, 24] | 915 |
| 5 | Sept | 13 | H | Dundee | L | 1-2 | 0-1 | 8 | Henderson [61] | 2180 |
| 6 | | 20 | H | Raith R | W | 1-0 | 1-0 | 4 | Ferguson [34] | 1987 |
| 7 | | 27 | A | Airdrieonians | L | 0-1 | 0-1 | 7 | | 1392 |
| 8 | Oct | 4 | H | Stirling A | W | 2-1 | 1-0 | 5 | Graham [11], D'Jaffo [50] | 1773 |
| 9 | | 18 | A | St Mirren | D | 1-1 | 0-1 | 5 | Millen [84] | 3021 |
| 10 | | 25 | A | Greenock Morton | D | 1-1 | 1-1 | 5 | D'Jaffo [5] | 2344 |
| 11 | Nov | 8 | H | Hamilton A | L | 1-2 | 0-2 | 6 | D'Jaffo [59] | 2093 |
| 12 | | 11 | H | Falkirk | L | 1-2 | 0-1 | — | D'Jaffo [87] | 2003 |
| 13 | | 15 | A | Dundee | L | 0-4 | 0-4 | 7 | | 2921 |
| 14 | | 22 | H | Airdrieonians | W | 6-0 | 3-0 | 6 | D'Jaffo 2 [20, 62], Ferguson [37], Dick [44], Traynor [46], Smith T [86] | 1838 |
| 15 | | 29 | A | Raith R | W | 1-0 | 0-0 | 6 | Dick [85] | 3015 |
| 16 | Dec | 6 | A | Stirling A | D | 1-1 | 0-0 | 6 | Graham [74] | 1023 |
| 17 | | 13 | H | St Mirren | L | 0-2 | 0-0 | 7 | | 2411 |
| 18 | | 20 | A | Partick Th | L | 0-3 | 0-1 | 7 | | 2967 |
| 19 | | 27 | H | Greenock Morton | W | 2-1 | 1-1 | 6 | Ferguson [21], Agnew [61] | 2581 |
| 20 | Jan | 10 | H | Dundee | L | 2-5 | 2-3 | 7 | D'Jaffo [12], Ferguson [14] | 2067 |
| 21 | | 31 | H | Raith R | D | 0-0 | 0-0 | 7 | | 1989 |
| 22 | Feb | 7 | A | St Mirren | L | 0-3 | 0-3 | 7 | | 2312 |
| 23 | | 10 | A | Airdrieonians | L | 0-2 | 0-1 | — | | 1189 |
| 24 | | 17 | A | Hamilton A | D | 1-1 | 0-1 | — | D'Jaffo [71] | 732 |
| 25 | | 21 | H | Stirling A | W | 1-0 | 0-0 | 8 | Burns [66] | 1637 |
| 26 | | 25 | A | Falkirk | L | 0-4 | 0-0 | — | | 2024 |
| 27 | | 28 | H | Partick Th | D | 2-2 | 0-0 | 8 | Duthie [48], Anderson [89] | 2539 |
| 28 | Mar | 14 | H | Airdrieonians | L | 0-2 | 0-1 | 9 | | 1728 |
| 29 | | 21 | A | Raith R | D | 0-0 | 0-0 | 8 | | 2800 |
| 30 | | 28 | H | St Mirren | D | 2-2 | 1-2 | 8 | D'Jaffo (pen) [26], Ferguson [84] | 2306 |
| 31 | Apr | 4 | A | Stirling A | L | 0-2 | 0-0 | 9 | | 1145 |
| 32 | | 11 | H | Hamilton A | W | 2-1 | 1-1 | 8 | Traynor [44], Millen [84] | 1680 |
| 33 | | 18 | A | Dundee | D | 1-1 | 1-1 | 8 | Shepherd [4] | 7564 |
| 34 | | 25 | A | Greenock Morton | W | 1-0 | 1-0 | 7 | Ferguson [34] | 2315 |
| 35 | May | 2 | H | Falkirk | L | 1-3 | 1-2 | 8 | Henderson [8] | 2809 |
| 36 | | 9 | A | Partick Th | W | 3-1 | 1-0 | 7 | Ferguson [22], D'Jaffo [56], McKeown [89] | 8653 |

**Final League Position: 7**          1996–97 DIV 2 1

**Honours**
*League Champions:* Division II 1911-12, 1912-13, 1927-28, 1936-37, 1958-59, 1965-66. Second Division 1987-88, 1996–97; *Runners-up:* Division II 1910-11, 1955-56, 1968-69.
*Scottish Cup:* —. *League Cup:* —.
*B&Q Cup: Runners-up:*1990-91, 1991-92.
*Club colours:* Shirt: White with black trim. Shorts: Black. Stockings: Black and white.

**Goalscorers:** *League (40):* D'Jaffo 10 (1 pen), Ferguson 8, Kerrigan 3, Dick 2, Graham 2, Henderson 2, Millen 2, Traynor 2, Agnew 1, Anderson 1, Bell 1, Burns 1, Duthie 1, Findlay 1, Hood 1, Shepherd 1, Smith T 1. *Scottish Cup (6):* Ferguson 5, Dick 1. *Coca Cola Cup (1):* Wordsworth 1. *League Challenge Cup (3):* Kerrigan 2, Wordsworth 1.

| McKeown K 2 | Robertson J 27 + 4 | Bonar P 6 + 4 | Hood G 12 + 1 | Warholm R — + 1 | Jamieson W 6 | Love G 12 | Agnew P 14 | McDonald C 2 + 2 | Nourredine M — + 2 | Wordsworth D 1 + 1 | Kristensen B 4 + 1 | Morley D 4 | Mainge W 8 + 2 | Henderson D 13 + 8 | Traynor J 29 + 4 | Kerrigan S 4 + 2 | Castilla D 23 | Smith T 13 + 5 | Nolan J — + 1 | Bell R 1 + 1 | Peroni J — + 1 | Ferguson J 32 + 1 | Sylla S — + 3 | Miller C 8 | Burns G 9 + 2 | Graham A 5 + 7 | Millen A 26 | Sonor L 9 | D'Jaffo L 21 + 3 | Davies J 8 | English I — + 1 | Smith H 2 + 1 | Ciardi M 8 | Bowman G 15 | Dick J 13 + 2 | Watson R 6 | Power L — + 4 | Donowa L 7 + 2 | Hogg K 1 + 5 | Shepherd P 6 | Finnbogason K 9 | Anderson D 12 | Duthie M 11 + 1 | Bradford J — + 2 | Findlay W 6 | Scally N 1 | Match No. |
|---|---|---|---|---|---|---|---|---|---|---|---|---|---|---|---|---|---|---|---|---|---|---|---|---|---|---|---|---|---|---|---|---|---|---|---|---|---|---|---|---|---|---|---|---|---|---|---|
| 1 | 2 | 3 | 4 | | 5 | $6^1$ | $7^2$ | | | | | | 8 | $9^3$ | 10 | 11 | 12 | 13 | 14 | | | | | | | | | | | | | | | | | | | | | | | | | | | | 1 |
| | 2 | $3^2$ | 4 | | 6 | 7 | 14 | | | 11 | | | 8 | | 5 | | | $9^2$ | 1 | $10^1$ | 12 | 13 | | | | | | | | | | | | | | | | | | | | | | | | 2 |
| | 2 | 3 | 4 | | 5 | | 7 | 12 | | | | | $10^1$ | 11 | | | 6 | | 1 | 8 | | | | 9 | | | | | | | | | | | | | | | | | | | | | | | 3 |
| | 2 | | 4 | | 5 | 3 | 7 | | | | | | $11^1$ | 12 | | | | 8 | $10^2$ | 1 | 6 | | | 9 | | | | | | | | | | | | | | | | | | | | | | | 4 |
| | 2 | | 4 | | 5 | 3 | $7^2$ | 13 | | | | | 12 | | | | | $11^1$ | 8 | 10 | 1 | 6 | | 9 | | | | | | | | | | | | | | | | | | | | | | | 5 |
| | 2 | | 4 | | | 3 | | | | | | | | 6 | 11 | | 8 | $10^1$ | 1 | 7 | | | 9 | 12 | 5 | | | | | | | | | | | | | | | | | | | | | | 6 |
| | 2 | | $4^2$ | | | 3 | | | | | | | | 6 | 11 | | 8 | 13 | 1 | 7 | | | 9 | 12 | 5 | $10^1$ | | | | | | | | | | | | | | | | | | | | | 7 |
| | 2 | | | | | 3 | | | | | | | | 7 | 11 | 12 | | 8 | 1 | | | | | $5^1$ | 9 | 4 | 6 | $10^2$ | 13 | | | | | | | | | | | | | | | | | 8 |
| | 2 | 5 | | | | 3 | | | | | | | | $7^2$ | 11 | 14 | | 8 | $6^2$ | 1 | | | 9 | | 13 | 12 | 4 | $10^1$ | | | | | | | | | | | | | | | | | | | 9 |
| | 2 | | 5 | | 3 | | | | | | | | | 11 | 6 | | 1 | 7 | | | | $9^1$ | | 12 | 8 | 4 | 10 | | | | | | | | | | | | | | | | | | | 10 |
| | 2 | | 5 | | 3 | | | | | | | | 13 | 12 | 6 | | 7 | | | | | $9^1$ | | | $8^1$ | 4 | 10 | 1 | $11^2$ | | | | | | | | | | | | | | | | | 11 |
| | 2 | 5 | | | | 3 | | | | | | | | 11 | 6 | | $1^4$ | 7 | | | | $9^1$ | | | 12 | 4 | 10 | 15 | 8 | | | | | | | | | | | | | | | | | 12 |
| | 2 | $5^2$ | | | | | | | | | | | | $7^1$ | 13 | 8 | | 12 | | 14 | | $9^3$ | | | 4 | 10 | 1 | 11 | 3 | 6 | | | | | | | | | | | | | | | | 13 |
| | 2 | | | | | | | | | | | | | 14 | 11 | | | | | | 9 | | 12 | $6^2$ | $8^1$ | $10^3$ | 3 | 7 | 5 | | | | | | | | | | | | | | | | | 14 |
| | 2 | | | | | | | | | | | | | 12 | 11 | | 1 | 13 | | | 9 | | | 4 | $6^2$ | 10 | $8^1$ | 3 | 7 | 5 | | | | | | | | | | | | | | | | 15 |
| | 2 | | | | | | | | | | | | | 12 | $11^1$ | | 1 | | | | 9 | | | 13 | 6 | 8 | $10^1$ | 3 | 7 | 5 | | | | | | | | | | | | | | | | 16 |
| | 2 | | | | | | | | | | | | | | 13 | | 1 | 14 | | | 9 | | | 12 | 4 | $6^2$ | $8^1$ | 10 | 3 | $7^3$ | 5 | 11 | | | | | | | | | | | | | | | 17 |
| | $2^2$ | | | | | | | | | | | | | 10 | 8 | | 1 | 14 | | | $9^1$ | | | 13 | 4 | 6 | 12 | | 3 | $7^3$ | 5 | 11 | | | | | | | | | | | | | | | 18 |
| | 12 | | | | | | 10 | | | | | | | 2 | | | 1 | 6 | | | 9 | | | | 4 | $5^1$ | 8 | | 11 | 3 | 7 | | | | | | | | | | | | | | | | 19 |
| 1 | 12 | | | | | $5^1$ | 10 | | | | | | | 2 | | | 6 | | | | 9 | | | 14 | 4 | $8^3$ | | | | 3 | 7 | $11^2$ | 13 | | | | | | | | | | | | | | 20 |
| | 12 | | | | | | 10 | | | | | | | 2 | | | 9 | 5 | | | 4 | | 8 | | | | | | 3 | | $7^1$ | | | 1 | 6 | 11 | | | | | | | | | 21 |
| | 7 | 14 | | | | | 10 | | | | | | | 2 | | | 9 | $5^2$ | | | 4 | | $8^1$ | | | | | | 3 | | | | 13 | | $6^1$ | 11 | 12 | | | | | | | | | 22 |
| | 12 | $5^1$ | | | | | 10 | | | | | | | 2 | | | 9 | 11 | | | 4 | $7^2$ | 8 | | | | | | 3 | | | | 13 | | 6 | 3 | | | | | | | | | | 23 |
| | 2 | 14 | | | | | 10 | | | | | | | 8 | | | 9 | 5 | | | $4^1$ | 13 | | | | | | | $11^2$ | | | | 12 | 1 | 6 | 7 | | | | | | | | $3^3$ | | 24 |
| | 2 | $3^2$ | 12 | 13 | | | $8^1$ | | | | | | | 5 | 1 | | 9 | 7 | | | 4 | 10 | | | | | | | | | | | | | | | 6 | 11 | | | | | | | | | 25 |
| | $2^1$ | 12 | 4 | | | | 8 | | | 14 | | | | 3 | 1 | | $9^3$ | 7 | | | | $10^2$ | | | | | | 5 | | 13 | | 6 | 11 | | | | | | | | | | | | 26 |
| | 2 | $3^1$ | | | | | 8 | | | 12 | | | | 4 | | | 9 | | | | | 10 | | | | | | | 7 | | | 5 | 1 | 6 | 11 | | | | | | | | | | | 27 |
| | 2 | $11^1$ | | | | | 8 | | | | | 5 | | 6 | | | 13 | 9 | | | | 4 | | | | | | 3 | $7^2$ | | | 1 | | 10 | 12 | | | | | | | | | | | 28 |
| | 2 | | | | | | | | | 5 | | $11^1$ | | | | | 9 | 6 | | | | 4 | | | 10 | 8 | | 3 | 7 | | | | 1 | 12 | | | | | | | | | | | 29 |
| | 2 | | | | | | | | | 5 | | 12 | | | | | 9 | 6 | | | | 4 | | | 10 | 8 | | 3 | $7^2$ | 13 | | | 1 | $11^1$ | | | | | | | | | | | 30 |
| | 14 | | | | | | | | | 5 | | | | | | | $9^1$ | 3 | | | | 4 | | | 10 | 8 | | $11^2$ | 7 | 13 | 12 | 2 | 1 | | | | $6^1$ | | | | | | | | 31 |
| | | | | | | | | | | $11^1$ | 5 | | | | | | 9 | 3 | | | | 4 | | | 13 | 12 | | $7^2$ | 2 | 1 | 6 | | 10 | | | | | | | | | | | | 32 |
| | 7 | | | | | | | | | 13 | 5 | | | | | | 9 | 3 | | | | 4 | | | 8 | 12 | | | 2 | $1^1$ | 6 | | $11^2$ | 10 | | | | | | | | | | | 33 |
| | | | | | | | | | | 11 | 5 | 1 | | | | | 9 | 3 | | | | 4 | | | 8 | $7^1$ | | 12 | 2 | 1 | 6 | | 10 | | | | | | | | | | | | 34 |
| | | | | | | | | | | 11 | 5 | 1 | | | | | 9 | $3^1$ | | | | 4 | | | 8 | | 12 | | 2 | 1 | 6 | 7 | 10 | | | | | | | | | | | | 35 |
| | | | | | | | | | | 11 | 5 | 1 | | | | | 9 | 3 | | | | 4 | | 12 | 8 | | $7^1$ | 2 | 1 | 6 | | 10 | | | | | | | | | | | | | 36 |

# BERWICK RANGERS     Third Division

*Year Formed:* 1881. *Ground & Address:* Shielfield Park, Tweedmouth, Berwick-upon-Tweed TD15 2EF. *Telephone:* 01289 307424. *Fax (to Secretary):* 01289 307424. Club 24 hour hotline 01891 800697. *Ground Capacity:* 4131. seated: 1366. *Size of Pitch:* 110yd × 70yd.
*Chairman:* Tom Davidson. *Vice-chairman:* Moray McLaren. *Club Secretary:* Dennis McCleary.
*Manager:* Paul Smith. *Assistant Manager:* John Clark. *Physio:* Ian Oliver. *Coaches:* Ian Oliver, Ian Smith
*Managers since 1975:* H. Melrose; G. Haig; W. Galbraith; D. Smith; F. Connor; J. McSherry; E. Tait; J. Thomson; J. Jefferies; J. Anderson, J. Crease, T. Hendrie, I. Ross, J. Thomson.
*Club Nickname(s):* The Borderers. *Previous Grounds:* Bull Stob Close, Pier Field, Meadow Field, Union Park, Old Shielfield.
*Record Attendance:* 13,365 v Rangers, Scottish Cup 1st rd; 28 Jan, 1967.
*Record Victory:* 8-1 v Forfar Ath. Division II; 25 Dec, 1965; v Vale of Leithen, Scottish Cup; Dec, 1966.
*Record Defeat:* 1-9 v Hamilton A, First Division; 9 Aug, 1980.
*Most Capped Player:* —.
*Most League Appearances:* 435;: Eric Tait, 1970-87.
*Most League Goals in Season (Individual):* 38: Ken Bowron, Division II; 1963-64.
*Most Goals Overall (Individual):* 115: Eric Tait, 1970-87.

## BERWICK RANGERS 1997–98 LEAGUE RECORD

| Match No. | Date | Venue | Opponents | Result | H/T Score | Lg. Pos. | Goalscorers | Attendance |
|---|---|---|---|---|---|---|---|---|
| 1 | Aug 5 | H | Alloa Ath | L 0-2 | 0-1 | — | | 549 |
| 2 | 16 | A | Albion R | L 1-2 | 0-1 | 8 | Laidler [87] | 374 |
| 3 | 23 | H | Dumbarton | W 5-3 | 3-2 | 7 | Forrester 4 [11, 13, 32, 50], Walton [55] | 304 |
| 4 | 30 | H | Arbroath | L 1-3 | 1-0 | 9 | Walton [6] | 339 |
| 5 | Sept 13 | A | Queen's Park | D 0-0 | 0-0 | 8 | | 488 |
| 6 | 20 | A | Ross Co | L 0-2 | 0-1 | 8 | | 1542 |
| 7 | 27 | H | East Stirling | L 2-3 | 0-1 | 8 | Fraser [65], Walton [89] | 328 |
| 8 | Oct 4 | H | Cowdenbeath | W 2-1 | 0-1 | 7 | Rafferty [77], Cunningham [87] | 319 |
| 9 | 18 | A | Montrose | W 2-1 | 1-1 | 7 | Walton [3], Rafferty [70] | 357 |
| 10 | 25 | A | Dumbarton | W 4-1 | 2-1 | 7 | Fraser [25], Walton 2 (1 pen) [41, 79 (p)], Forrester [61] | 413 |
| 11 | Nov 1 | H | Albion R | D 1-1 | 1-1 | 7 | Forrester [34] | 401 |
| 12 | 8 | A | Arbroath | L 1-4 | 0-2 | 7 | Escalaon [48] | 500 |
| 13 | 15 | A | Queen's Park | W 2-1 | 0-1 | 7 | Clark [47], Smith S [88] | 390 |
| 14 | 22 | A | East Stirling | L 0-4 | 0-1 | 7 | | 323 |
| 15 | 29 | H | Ross Co | D 0-0 | 0-0 | 7 | | 484 |
| 16 | Dec 13 | H | Montrose | L 1-2 | 1-0 | 7 | Forrester [1] | 322 |
| 17 | 20 | A | Cowdenbeath | W 2-0 | 1-0 | 7 | Escalaon [8], Finlayson [66] | 161 |
| 18 | 27 | H | Dumbarton | D 1-1 | 1-0 | 7 | Walton [37] | 449 |
| 19 | Jan 10 | A | Alloa Ath | W 3-1 | 0-0 | 7 | Martin [52], Walton (pen) [60], Neil [84] | 545 |
| 20 | 17 | H | East Stirling | W 3-1 | 1-0 | 7 | Martin [44], Clark [79], Forrester [88] | 366 |
| 21 | 31 | A | Ross Co | D 0-0 | 0-0 | 6 | | 1342 |
| 22 | Feb 7 | A | Montrose | D 2-2 | 1-2 | 6 | Craib (og) [6], McNicoll [61] | 300 |
| 23 | 14 | H | Cowdenbeath | L 0-2 | 0-0 | 6 | | 402 |
| 24 | 21 | H | Alloa Ath | D 1-1 | 1-1 | 6 | Martin [23] | 435 |
| 25 | 28 | H | Arbroath | D 0-0 | 0-0 | 6 | | 333 |
| 26 | Mar 7 | A | Queen's Park | L 1-2 | 1-0 | 6 | Forrester [32] | 430 |
| 27 | 14 | A | East Stirling | D 1-1 | 1-1 | 6 | Fraser [6] | 241 |
| 28 | 21 | H | Ross Co | D 1-1 | 0-1 | 7 | Forrester [52] | 428 |
| 29 | 28 | H | Montrose | D 1-1 | 0-0 | 7 | Beaton [47] | 318 |
| 30 | Apr 7 | A | Cowdenbeath | L 0-1 | 0-0 | — | | 164 |
| 31 | 11 | A | Arbroath | L 0-1 | 0-0 | 7 | | 823 |
| 32 | 13 | A | Albion R | L 0-5 | 0-2 | — | | 225 |
| 33 | 18 | A | Queen's Park | D 2-2 | 1-0 | 7 | Irvine [20], Rafferty [59] | 317 |
| 34 | 25 | A | Dumbarton | W 2-0 | 0-0 | 7 | Walton [60], Neil [82] | 310 |
| 35 | May 2 | H | Albion R | W 5-2 | 2-1 | 5 | Beaton 2 [30, 44], Neil [49], Fraser [63], Melvin (og) [87] | 519 |
| 36 | 9 | A | Alloa Ath | L 0-1 | 0-1 | 6 | | 894 |

**Final League Position: 6**     1996–97 DIV 2 10

**Honours**
*League Champions:* Second Division 1978-79. *Runners-up* Second Division 1993-94.
*Scottish Cup:* —.
*League Cup:* Semi-final 1963-64.
*Club colours:* Shirt: Black with 2 inch gold stripes. Shorts: Black, gold trim. Stockings: Black with gold trim.

**Goalscorers:** *League (47):* Forrester 10, Walton 9 (2 pens), Fraser 4, Beaton 3, Martin 3, Neil 3, Rafferty 3, Clark 2, Escalon 2, Cunningham 1, Finlayson 1, Irvine 1, Laidler 1, McNicoll 1, Smith S 1, own goals 2. *Scottish Cup (1):* Irvine 1. *Coca Cola Cup (2):* Forrester 1, Walton 1. *League Challenge Cup (2):* Walton 2.

| Collier D 1 | Irvine N 22 + 4 | Finlayson D 16 + 4 | Fraser G 29 + 1 | Clark J 24 | McNicoll G 19 + 2 | Rafferty K 29 + 7 | Smith P 2 + 1 | Forrester P 24 + 6 | Walton K 34 + 2 | Sloan S 1 | Clegg N — + 1 | Burgess M 8 | Cunningham T 26 + 2 | Ward B 2 + 3 | Graham T 3 + 4 | Laidler M 2 + 1 | Smith S 9 + 13 | O'Connor G 27 | Smith M 7 | Neil M 28 | Beaton D 28 | Laidlaw S 13 + 4 | Escalaon F 7 | Little B 1 + 7 | Martin J 13 + 5 | Robard U 2 + 1 | Harrison T 12 + 2 | Findlay M 3 | McLeod J 4 | Match No. |
|---|---|---|---|---|---|---|---|---|---|---|---|---|---|---|---|---|---|---|---|---|---|---|---|---|---|---|---|---|---|---|
| 1 | 2 | 3 | 4 | 5 | 6 | 7[1] | 8 | 9 | 10 | 11 | 12 | | | | | | | | | | | | | | | | | | | 1 |
| | 10 | 5 | 4 | 6 | 12 | 8[1] | 9 | 3 | | | | | 1 | 2 | 7 | 11[2] | 13 | | | | | | | | | | | | | 2 |
| | 8 | 5 | 12 | 4 | 6[1] | 7[2] | 9 | 10 | | | | | 1 | 2[3] | 14 | 13 | 3 | 11 | | | | | | | | | | | | 3 |
| | 8 | 3[2] | 6 | 4 | 5 | 7[1] | 12 | 9 | 10 | | | | 1 | 2 | | 13 | 11 | | | | | | | | | | | | | 4 |
| | 10 | | 5 | 8 | | 4 | | 9[1] | 6 | | | | 2 | 12 | | | | 11 | 1 | 3 | 7 | | | | | | | | | 5 |
| | 8[2] | | 5 | 6 | 4 | 13 | | 9 | 11 | | | | 2 | | 12 | | | 10[1] | 1 | 3 | 7 | | | | | | | | | 6 |
| | 10[1] | | 5 | 4 | 12 | 7 | | 9[2] | 6 | | | | 2 | 13 | 3 | | 11 | 1 | | 8 | | | | | | | | | | 7 |
| | 6 | 13 | 5 | | 4 | 12 | | 8 | 10 | | | | 2 | 9[1] | 11 | | | 1 | 3[2] | 7 | | | | | | | | | | 8 |
| | 6[2] | | 4 | 8 | 12 | 13 | | 10[3] | 11 | | | | 2[1] | | | | 14 | 1 | 3 | 7 | 5 | 9 | | | | | | | | 9 |
| | 14 | | 4 | 8 | | 6 | | 10[1] | 11 | | | | 2 | | 13 | | 12 | 1 | 3 | 7[3] | 5 | 9[2] | | | | | | | | 10 |
| | | | 4 | 8 | | 6[1] | | 9 | 11 | | | | 2 | | | | 12 | 1 | 3 | 7 | 5 | 10 | | | | | | | | 11 |
| | | | 4 | 8 | | 6 | | 9[2] | 11 | | | | 2[1] | | | | 12 | 1 | 3 | 7 | 5 | 10 | 13 | | | | | | | 12 |
| | 3 | | 4 | 8 | | 6 | | 9[1] | 11 | | | | 2 | | | | 12 | 1 | | 7 | 5 | 10 | | | | | | | | 13 |
| | 13 | 3 | 4 | 8 | | 6 | | | 11 | | 1 | | 2 | | | | 9[1] | | 7 | 5 | 10[2] | 12 | | | | | | | | 14 |
| | 3 | 4 | | 2 | 6 | | | 9 | 11 | | | | 8 | | | | 1 | | 7 | 5 | 10 | | | | | | | | | 15 |
| | 3 | 4 | | 2[2] | 6 | | | 9 | 11 | | | 13 | | | | | 8[1] | 1 | | 7 | 5 | 10 | 12 | | | | | | | 16 |
| | 3 | 4 | | | 6 | | | 9 | 11 | | | | 2 | | | | 12 | 1 | | 7 | 5 | 10 | | 8[1] | | | | | | 17 |
| | 12 | 3 | 4 | 10[1] | | 6 | | 9[2] | 11 | | | | 2 | | | | 13 | 1 | | 7 | 5 | | | 8 | | | | | | 18 |
| | 6[3] | 14 | 4 | 5 | 2 | 12 | | 13 | 11 | | | | | | | | 8[1] | 1 | | 7 | 3 | | | 9 | 10[3] | | | | | 19 |
| | 8 | 14 | 4 | 5 | 2 | 6 | | 13 | 11 | | | | | | | | | 1 | | 7 | 3[3] | 12 | | 9[2] | 10[1] | | | | | 20 |
| | 8 | 3 | | 4 | 2 | 6 | | 12 | 11 | | | | | | | | | 1 | | 7 | 5 | 10[1] | | 9[2] | 13 | | | | | 21 |
| | 8 | 3 | | 4 | 2 | 6 | | | 11 | | | | | | | | | 1 | | 7 | 5 | 10 | | 9 | | | | | | 22 |
| | | 5 | | 4 | 2[1] | 6[2] | | 13 | 11 | | | | 12 | | | | | 1 | | 7 | 3 | 9 | | 10 | | 8 | | | | 23 |
| | 5 | 8 | | 4 | 6 | | | 12 | 11 | | | | 2 | | | | 13 | 1 | | 3 | 9[1] | | | 10[2] | | 7 | | | | 24 |
| | 5 | 8 | | 4 | 6 | | | 9 | 11[1] | | | | 2 | | | | 13 | 1 | | 3 | 10[2] | 12 | | | 7 | | | | | 25 |
| | 13 | 3 | 8 | | 5 | 6 | | 7[2] | 11[1] | | | | 2 | | | | 12 | 1 | | 4 | 9 | | | 10 | | | | | | 26 |
| | 8 | | 5 | 4 | 2 | 6 | | 10 | 11 | | | | | | | | 1 | | | 3 | 12 | | | 9[1] | 7 | | | | | 27 |
| | 6 | | 5 | 4 | 8[1] | | | 10 | 12 | | | | 2 | | | | | 1 | | 7 | 3 | 13 | | 9[2] | 11 | | | | | 28 |
| | 6 | | | 5 | 12 | | | 9 | 11 | | | | 2 | | | | | 1 | | 7 | 3 | 13 | | 10[2] | | 8[1] | 4 | | | 29 |
| | 12 | | 4 | | 8 | | | 10 | 11 | | | | 2 | | | | | 1 | | 7 | 3 | 9 | | 13 | | 6[1] | 5[2] | | | 30 |
| | 8 | | 4 | 5 | 6[3] | | | 13 | 12 | | | | 2 | | | | 10 | 1 | | 7 | 3 | | | 11[1] | 9[2] | 14 | | | | 31 |
| | 8 | | 4 | 5 | 12 | | | 9[1] | 11 | | | | 2 | | | | | 1 | | 7 | 3 | 10 | | 14 | 13 | 6[2] | 2[1] | | | 32 |
| | 6 | | 4 | 5 | 8 | | | | 11 | | 1 | | 2 | | | | | | | 7 | 3 | | | 9 | 12 | 10[1] | | | | 33 |
| | 8 | | 4 | | | 6 | | | 3 | | 1 | | 2 | | | | 12 | | | 7 | 5 | 10[1] | | 13 | | 11 | | 9[2] | | 34 |
| | 8 | | 4 | | | 2 | | | 11 | | 1 | | 3 | | | | | | | 13 | | 7 | 5 | 10[2] | 14 | 12 | | 6[3] | 9[1] | | 35 |
| | 9 | | 4 | | | 6 | | | 3[3] | | 1 | | 2 | | | | | | | 13 | | 7 | 5 | 10[1] | 14 | 12 | | 8[2] | 11 | | 36 |

# BRECHIN CITY　　　　　　　　Third Division

*Year Formed:* 1906. *Ground & Address:* Glebe Park, Trinity Rd, Brechin, Angus DD9 6BJ. *Telephone:* 01356 622856.
*Fax (to Secretary):* 01356 625524.
*Ground Capacity:* total: 3980. seated: 1518. *Size of Pitch:* 110yd × 67yd.
*Chairman:* David Birse. *Vice-Chairman:* Hugh Campbell Adamson. *Secretary:* Ken Ferguson.
*Manager:* John Young. *Assistant Manager:* Jake Ferrier. *Youth Coach:* John Rankin. *Physio:* Tom Gilmartin.
*Managers since 1975:* Charlie Dunn; Ian Stewart; Doug Houston; Ian Fleming; John Ritchie, Ian Redford. *Club
Nickname(s):* The City. *Previous Grounds:* Nursery Park.
*Record Attendance:* 8122 v Aberdeen, Scottish Cup 3rd rd; 3 Feb, 1973.
*Record Transfer Fee received:* £100,000 for Scott Thomson to Aberdeen (1991).
*Record Transfer Fee paid:* £16,000 for Sandy Ross from Berwick Rangers (1991).
*Record Victory:* 12-1 v Thornhill, Scottish Cup 1st rd; 28 Jan, 1926.
*Record Defeat:* 0-10 v Airdrieonians, Albion R and Cowdenbeath, all in Division II; 1937-38.
*Most Capped Player:* —.
*Most League Appearances:* 459: David Watt, 1975-89.
*Most League Goals in Season (Individual):* 26: W. McIntosh, Division II; 1959-60.
*Most Goals Overall (Individual):* 131: Ian Campbell.

## BRECHIN CITY 1997–98 LEAGUE RECORD

| Match No. | Date | Venue | Opponents | Result | | H/T Score | Lg. Pos. | Goalscorers | Attendance |
|---|---|---|---|---|---|---|---|---|---|
| 1 | Aug 5 | A | Clydebank | L | 0-3 | 0-2 | — | | 316 |
| 2 | 16 | H | Inverness CT | D | 2-2 | 1-0 | 9 | Brown [26], Heddle [53] | 459 |
| 3 | 23 | A | Forfar Ath | W | 5-2 | 1-2 | 4 | McKellar 2 [14, 55], Brand [50], Campbell [77], Sorbie [83] | 607 |
| 4 | 30 | A | Stranraer | L | 0-4 | 0-1 | 6 | | 463 |
| 5 | Sept 13 | H | Livingston | L | 0-2 | 0-2 | 8 | | 402 |
| 6 | 20 | A | Clyde | D | 1-1 | 0-0 | 8 | Feroz [83] | 611 |
| 7 | 27 | H | Queen of the S | L | 0-3 | 0-0 | 9 | | 333 |
| 8 | Oct 4 | A | Stenhousemuir | L | 2-3 | 0-3 | 9 | Brand 2 [76, 83] | 329 |
| 9 | 18 | H | East Fife | D | 0-0 | 0-0 | 9 | | 406 |
| 10 | 25 | H | Forfar Ath | W | 2-0 | 0-0 | 9 | Brand [52], Campbell [74] | 620 |
| 11 | Nov 1 | H | Inverness CT | D | 0-0 | 0-0 | 9 | | 1905 |
| 12 | 8 | H | Stranraer | D | 2-2 | 0-0 | 10 | Feroz [53], McKellar [58] | 307 |
| 13 | 15 | A | Livingston | L | 2-5 | 0-2 | 10 | Christie [69], McNeill [74] | 1605 |
| 14 | 22 | A | Queen of the S | D | 0-0 | 0-0 | 9 | | 1356 |
| 15 | 29 | H | Clyde | W | 2-1 | 0-1 | 9 | Farnan [51], Sorbie [90] | 404 |
| 16 | Dec 13 | A | East Fife | L | 1-3 | 0-2 | 10 | McNeill [61] | 424 |
| 17 | 20 | H | Stenhousemuir | D | 1-1 | 0-1 | 10 | Hutcheon [75] | 256 |
| 18 | 27 | A | Forfar Ath | L | 0-5 | 0-1 | 10 | | 810 |
| 19 | Jan 10 | H | Clydebank | L | 0-1 | 0-1 | 10 | | 403 |
| 20 | 31 | A | Clyde | D | 2-2 | 0-1 | 10 | Farnan [52], Feroz [76] | 721 |
| 21 | Feb 3 | H | Queen of the S | D | 1-1 | 1-0 | — | Black [43] | 307 |
| 22 | 7 | H | East Fife | W | 2-1 | 2-0 | 10 | Feroz [7], McKellar [40] | 404 |
| 23 | 17 | A | Stenhousemuir | L | 1-3 | 0-2 | — | Sorbie [77] | 318 |
| 24 | 21 | A | Clydebank | L | 1-2 | 0-0 | 10 | Farnan [75] | 252 |
| 25 | 25 | H | Inverness CT | W | 3-1 | 1-1 | — | Feroz 2 [23, 89], Black [62] | 388 |
| 26 | Mar 4 | A | Stranraer | W | 2-0 | 2-0 | — | Brown [27], Farnan [43] | 398 |
| 27 | 14 | A | Queen of the S | D | 1-1 | 0-1 | 10 | Kerrigan [79] | 1216 |
| 28 | 17 | A | Livingston | L | 0-2 | 0-2 | — | | 345 |
| 29 | 21 | H | Clyde | L | 0-2 | 0-0 | 10 | | 329 |
| 30 | 28 | A | East Fife | L | 1-4 | 0-3 | 10 | Sorbie [51] | 623 |
| 31 | Apr 7 | H | Stenhousemuir | W | 4-3 | 1-2 | — | Brand [16], Sorbie [56], Feroz [68], Campbell [74] | 300 |
| 32 | 11 | H | Stranraer | L | 1-3 | 1-2 | 10 | Brand [45] | 324 |
| 33 | 18 | A | Livingston | L | 0-1 | 0-1 | 10 | | 1261 |
| 34 | 25 | H | Forfar Ath | D | 1-1 | 0-1 | 10 | Hutcheon [76] | 521 |
| 35 | May 2 | A | Inverness CT | L | 1-2 | 0-2 | 10 | Black [59] | 1955 |
| 36 | 9 | H | Clydebank | L | 1-6 | 1-5 | 10 | Kerrigan [14] | 408 |

**Final League Position: 10**　　　　1996–97 7

**Honours**
*League Champions:* Second Division 1982-83. C Division 1953-54. Second Division 1989-90. *Runners-up:* 1992-93. Third Division Runners-up 1995-96
*Scottish Cup:* —.
*League Cup:* —.
*Club colours:* Shirt, Shorts, Stockings: Red with white trimmings.

**Goalscorers:** *League (42):*Feroz 7, Brand 6, Sorbie 5, Farnan 4, McKellar 4, Black 3, Campbell 3, Brown 2, Hutcheon 2, Kerrigan 2, McNeill 2, Christie 1, Heddle 1. *Scottish Cup (1):* Sorbie 1. *Coca Cola Cup (0). League Challenge Cup (2):* Brand 1, Feroz 1.

| Garden S 33 | Farnan C 30 + 2 | Brown R 29 | Cairney H 22 | Dailly M 1 + 2 | Heddle 18 + 1 | Brand R 14 + 11 | Buick G 23 + 4 | Sorbie S 30 + 1 | Kerrigan S 6 + 14 | Campbell S 29 | Baillie R 21 + 1 | Smith G 23 + 1 | McKellar J 26 + 5 | Feroz C 30 + 4 | McNeill W 7 + 5 | Christie G 22 + 1 | Smart C 11 + 7 | Black R 18 + 1 | Hutcheon A 5 + 11 | Butter J 3 | Robertson H 5 + 2 | Match No. |
|---|---|---|---|---|---|---|---|---|---|---|---|---|---|---|---|---|---|---|---|---|---|---|
| 1 | 2 | 3 | 4 | 5 | 6 | 7 | 8 | 9 | $10^1$ | 11 | 12 | | | | | | | | | | | 1 |
| 1 | 2 | 3 | 4 | 13 | 6 | $10^1$ | 8 | 9 | | 11 | | | $5^2$ | 7 | 12 | | | | | | | 2 |
| 1 | 2 | 3 | 4 | 12 | 6 | $10^1$ | 8 | $9^3$ | | 11 | | | 5 | $7^2$ | 13 | 14 | | | | | | 3 |
| 1 | 2 | 3 | | | 6 | 9 | 8 | | 13 | 11 | 4 | | 12 | 7 | $10^2$ | $5^1$ | | | | | | 4 |
| 1 | | 3 | 4 | | $6^1$ | $9^2$ | 8 | | 13 | 11 | 2 | | 5 | 7 | $10^3$ | 12 | 14 | | | | | 5 |
| 1 | 5 | $3^2$ | 4 | | 6 | 12 | 8 | 9 | | 11 | 2 | | | $7^1$ | 10 | | 13 | | | | | 6 |
| 1 | 5 | 3 | 4 | | 6 | 13 | 8 | 12 | $9^1$ | 11 | 2 | | | $7^2$ | 10 | | | | | | | 7 |
| 1 | 8 | 3 | 4 | | $6^2$ | 12 | 13 | 9 | | 11 | 2 | | | $7^1$ | 10 | 5 | | | | | | 8 |
| 1 | 6 | 3 | | | | $10^1$ | 8 | 9 | | 11 | $2^2$ | 4 | 12 | 7 | | 5 | 13 | | | | | 9 |
| 1 | 6 | 3 | | | 14 | $10^2$ | 12 | 9 | | 11 | $2^1$ | 4 | 13 | 7 | | 5 | $8^3$ | | | | | 10 |
| 1 | 6 | 3 | | | | 10 | | | | 11 | 2 | 4 | 9 | $7^1$ | 12 | 5 | 8 | | | | | 11 |
| 1 | 6 | 3 | | | | | 8 | 9 | 12 | 11 | | 4 | | 10 | $7^1$ | 5 | 2 | | | | | 12 |
| 1 | 6 | $3^1$ | | | | $8^2$ | | $9^3$ | | 11 | 2 | 4 | 10 | 7 | 14 | 5 | 13 | 12 | | | | 13 |
| 1 | 6 | 3 | | | | | | $9^1$ | 12 | 11 | 2 | 4 | | 7 | 10 | 5 | 8 | | | | | 14 |
| 1 | 6 | 3 | | | | | | 9 | | 11 | 2 | 4 | | 7 | 10 | 5 | 8 | | | | | 15 |
| 1 | 6 | 3 | | | | | | 9 | 12 | 11 | 2 | 4 | | 7 | $10^1$ | 5 | 8 | | | | | 16 |
| 1 | 6 | | 4 | | | | | $9^1$ | | 13 | 11 | 2 | 3 | 7 | $10^2$ | 5 | 8 | | 12 | | | 17 |
| 1 | 6 | | 4 | | | | 12 | 14 | $9^1$ | | 11 | $2^3$ | 3 | $10^2$ | 7 | 5 | 8 | | 13 | | | 18 |
| 1 | 2 | 3 | 4 | | | | 13 | | 9 | | | 12 | 14 | 7 | $6^1$ | 5 | $8^2$ | 11 | $10^3$ | | | 19 |
| 1 | 2 | 3 | 4 | | | | 12 | 7 | 8 | 13 | | 5 | 14 | $9^1$ | $6^2$ | | | 11 | $10^1$ | | | 20 |
| 1 | | 3 | 4 | | | | 12 | 2 | 8 | | | 5 | 7 | 9 | | 11 | | 6 | $10^1$ | | | 21 |
| 1 | 2 | 3 | 4 | | | | | 8 | 10 | 11 | | 5 | 7 | $9^1$ | | | | 6 | 12 | | | 22 |
| 1 | 2 | 3 | 4 | | | | | 8 | 9 | 11 | | 5 | 7 | $10^1$ | | | | 6 | 12 | | | 23 |
| 1 | 12 | $3^1$ | 4 | | | | $8^2$ | 10 | | 11 | 2 | 5 | 7 | 9 | | | | 6 | 13 | | | 24 |
| 1 | 12 | 5 | 4 | | | | | 8 | | 11 | 3 | 2 | 7 | 9 | | | | 6 | $10^1$ | | | 25 |
| 1 | 8 | 5 | 4 | | | | | 10 | | 11 | 3 | | 7 | 9 | | 2 | | 6 | | | | 26 |
| | 5 | | | | | | $9^2$ | 8 | 10 | 14 | $11^3$ | 3 | 4 | 7 | | | $2^1$ | 12 | 6 | 13 | 1 | 27 |
| | | | | | | | $9^3$ | 8 | 10 | 13 | 11 | 3 | $4^1$ | 7 | 12 | | 5 | $2^1$ | 6 | 14 | 1 | 28 |
| | 4 | | | | | 13 | 14 | 8 | 9 | | $3^2$ | 2 | | $7^1$ | 10 | 5 | | $6^2$ | 12 | 1 | 11 | 29 |
| 1 | $8^1$ | 5 | 4 | | | | | 9 | | 13 | $2^3$ | 12 | 3 | 7 | $10^2$ | 14 | | | 6 | | 11 | 30 |
| 1 | 2 | $5^1$ | 4 | | | | | $9^3$ | 8 | 14 | | 3 | | 7 | 13 | 12 | | 6 | $10^2$ | | 11 | 31 |
| 1 | 2 | 5 | 4 | | | | | 9 | 8 | 13 | | 3 | | 7 | $10^2$ | 12 | | | 6 | | $11^1$ | 32 |
| 1 | 5 | | 4 | | | | | $9^2$ | 8 | 10 | $11^3$ | 13 | 3 | 7 | | $2^1$ | | 14 | 6 | | 12 | 33 |
| 1 | 5 | | 4 | | 6 | | | $9^1$ | 8 | 12 | 2 | 3 | | 7 | $10^2$ | | | | 11 | | 13 | 34 |
| 1 | 5 | | | | | | | 8 | $9^2$ | 13 | 2 | 4 | | 7 | $10^1$ | 3 | | 6 | 12 | | 11 | 35 |
| 1 | | 4 | 5 | | 6 | | | $8^2$ | $9^3$ | 12 | 2 | 14 | 3 | $7^1$ | 10 | | | | 11 | | 13 | 36 |

# CELTIC

# Premier League

*Year Formed:* 1888. *Ground & Address:* Celtic Park, Glasgow G40 3RE. *Telephone:* 0141 556 2611.
*Ground Capacity:* all seated: 60,294. *Size of Pitch:* 105yd × 68yd.
*Managing Director* Fergus McCann. *Secretary:* Kevin Sweeney.
*General Manager, Football:* Jock Brown. *Development Manager:* Eric Black. *Head Coach:* Dr Jozef Venglos.
*Reserve Coach:* Murdo MacLeod. *Head Youth Coach:* Willie McStay. *Kit Manager:* John Clark. *Physio:* Brian Scott.
*Assistant Physio:* Neil McLeod.
*Managers since 1975:* Jock Stein, Billy McNeill, David Hay, Billy McNeill, Liam Brady, Lou Macari, Tommy Burns,
Wim Jansen. *Club Nickname(s):* The Bhoys. *Previous Grounds:* None.
*Record Attendance:* 92,000 v Rangers, Division I; 1 Jan, 1938.
*Record Transfer Fee received:* £4,700,000 for Paolo Di Canio to Sheffield W, August 1997.
*Record Transfer Fee paid:* £4,500,000 for Alan Stubbs from Bolton W, July 1996.
*Record Victory:* 11-0 Dundee, Division I; 26 Oct, 1895.
*Record Defeat:* 0-8 v Motherwell, Division I; 30 Apr, 1937.
*Most Capped Player:* Paddy Bonner, 80, Republic of Ireland.
*Most League Appearances:* 486: Billy McNeill 1957-75.
*Most League Goals in Season (Individual):* 50: James McGrory, Division I; 1935-36.
*Most Goals Overall (Individual):* 397: James McGrory; 1922-39.

## CELTIC 1997–98 LEAGUE RECORD

| Match No. | Date | | Venue | Opponents | Result | H/T Score | Lg. Pos. | Goalscorers | Atten- dance |
|---|---|---|---|---|---|---|---|---|---|
| 1 | Aug | 3 | A | Hibernian | L | 1-2 | 1-1 | — | Mackay [29] | 13,216 |
| 2 | | 16 | H | Dunfermline Ath | L | 1-2 | 1-0 | 10 | Thom (pen) [40] | 45,120 |
| 3 | | 23 | A | St Johnstone | W | 2-0 | 1-0 | 7 | Larsson [45], Jackson [64] | 10,266 |
| 4 | Sept | 13 | A | Motherwell | W | 3-2 | 0-1 | 6 | Burley 2 [57, 75], Donnelly [81] | 11,550 |
| 5 | | 20 | H | Aberdeen | W | 2-0 | 2-0 | 4 | Larsson 2 [26, 38] | 48,843 |
| 6 | | 27 | A | Dundee U | W | 2-1 | 2-0 | 4 | Donnelly [29], O'Donnell [42] | 11,668 |
| 7 | Oct | 4 | A | Kilmarnock | W | 4-0 | 4-0 | 3 | Larsson 2 [18, 38], Donnelly [33], Wieghorst [35] | 47,955 |
| 8 | | 18 | A | Hearts | W | 2-1 | 2-0 | 2 | Rieper [16], Larsson [22] | 16,977 |
| 9 | | 25 | H | St Johnstone | W | 2-0 | 2-0 | 1 | Larsson [31], Donnelly (pen) [34] | 48,687 |
| 10 | Nov | 1 | A | Dunfermline Ath | W | 2-0 | 0-0 | 2 | Blinker [67], Larsson [86] | 12,659 |
| 11 | | 8 | A | Rangers | L | 0-1 | 0-1 | 3 | | 50,082 |
| 12 | | 15 | A | Motherwell | L | 0-2 | 0-1 | 3 | | 47,464 |
| 13 | | 19 | H | Rangers | D | 1-1 | 0-0 | — | Stubbs [90] | 49,427 |
| 14 | | 22 | H | Dundee U | W | 4-0 | 1-0 | 3 | Thom 2 (1 pen) [35 (p), 69], Larsson 2 [63, 77] | 48,200 |
| 15 | Dec | 6 | A | Kilmarnock | D | 0-0 | 0-0 | 3 | | 15,676 |
| 16 | | 9 | A | Aberdeen | W | 2-0 | 1-0 | — | Larsson [41], Jackson [73] | 16,981 |
| 17 | | 13 | H | Hearts | W | 1-0 | 0-0 | 3 | Burley [79] | 49,806 |
| 18 | | 20 | H | Hibernian | W | 5-0 | 2-0 | 2 | Burley 2 [23, 90], Wieghorst [38], McNamara [48], Larsson [64] | 48,605 |
| 19 | | 27 | A | St Johnstone | L | 0-1 | 0-0 | 3 | | 10,485 |
| 20 | Jan | 2 | H | Rangers | W | 2-0 | 0-0 | — | Burley [66], Lambert [85] | 49,396 |
| 21 | | 10 | A | Motherwell | D | 1-1 | 0-0 | 2 | Lambert [61] | 12,350 |
| 22 | | 27 | A | Dundee U | W | 2-1 | 0-1 | — | Donnelly [77], Burley [87] | 14,004 |
| 23 | Feb | 2 | H | Aberdeen | W | 3-1 | 2-0 | — | Wieghorst [21], Larsson [35], Jackson [83] | 45,813 |
| 24 | | 8 | A | Hearts | D | 1-1 | 1-0 | — | McNamara [40] | 17,657 |
| 25 | | 21 | H | Kilmarnock | W | 4-0 | 2-0 | 2 | Brattbakk 4 [11, 36, 70, 87] | 48,477 |
| 26 | | 25 | H | Dunfermline Ath | W | 5-1 | 3-0 | — | Larsson [3], Brattbakk 2 [27, 40], O'Donnell [61], Wieghorst [68] | 48,576 |
| 27 | | 28 | A | Hibernian | W | 1-0 | 1-0 | 1 | Rieper [25] | 15,137 |
| 28 | Mar | 15 | H | Dundee U | D | 1-1 | 1-0 | 1 | Donnelly [27] | 48,564 |
| 29 | | 21 | A | Aberdeen | W | 1-0 | 1-0 | 1 | Burley (pen) [45] | 18,009 |
| 30 | | 28 | H | Hearts | D | 0-0 | 0-0 | 1 | | 49,978 |
| 31 | Apr | 8 | A | Kilmarnock | W | 2-1 | 1-1 | — | Larsson [19], Donnelly [55] | 18,076 |
| 32 | | 12 | A | Rangers | L | 0-2 | 0-1 | — | | 50,042 |
| 33 | | 18 | H | Motherwell | W | 4-1 | 2-1 | — | Burley 2 [25, 43], Donnelly 2 [49, 62] | 49,351 |
| 34 | | 25 | H | Hibernian | D | 0-0 | 0-0 | 1 | | 49,619 |
| 35 | May | 3 | A | Dunfermline Ath | D | 1-1 | 1-0 | — | Donnelly [35] | 12,719 |
| 36 | | 9 | H | St Johnstone | W | 2-0 | 1-0 | 1 | Larsson [3], Brattbakk [72] | 49,701 |

**Final League Position: 1** 1996–97 2

**Honours**

*League Champions:* (36 times) Division I 1892-93, 1893-94, 1895-96, 1897-98, 1904-05, 1905-06, 1906-07, 1907-08, 1908-09, 1909-10, 1913-14, 1914-15, 1915-16, 1916-17, 1918-19, 1921-22, 1925-26, 1935-36, 1937-38, 1953-54, 1965-66, 1966-67, 1967-68, 1968-69, 1969-70, 1970-71, 1971-72, 1972-73, 1973-74. Premier Division 1976-77, 1978-79, 1980-81, 1981-82, 1985-86, 1987-88, 1997-98. *Runners-up:* 24 times.
*Scottish Cup Winners:* (30 times) 1892, 1899, 1900, 1904, 1907, 1908, 1911, 1912, 1914, 1923, 1925, 1927, 1931, 1933, 1937, 1951, 1954, 1965, 1967, 1969, 1971, 1972, 1974, 1975, 1977, 1980, 1985, 1988, 1989, 1995; *Runners-up:* 16 times.
*League Cup Winners:* (10 times) 1956-57, 1957-58, 1965-66, 1966-67, 1967-68, 1968-69, 1969-70, 1974-75, 1982-83, 1997-98; *Runners-up:* 10 times.

**European:** *European Cup:* 78 matches (1966-67 winners, 1967-68, 1968-69, 1969-70 runners-up, 1970-71, 1971-72 semi-finals, 1972-73, 1973-74 semi-finals, 1974-75, 1977-78, 1979-80, 1981-82, 1982-83, 1986-87, 1988-89). *Cup Winners' Cup:* 39 matches (1963-64 semi-finals, 1965-66 semi-finals, 1975-76, 1980-81, 1984-85, 1985-86, 1989-90, 1995-96). *UEFA Cup:* 38 matches (*Fairs Cup:* 1962-63, 1964-65. *UEFA Cup:* 1976-77, 1983-84, 1987-88, 1991-92, 1992-93, 1993-94, 1996-97, 1997-98).
*Club colours:* Shirt: Green and white hoops. Shorts: White. Stockings: White.

**Goalscorers:** *League (64):* Larsson 16, Burley 10 (1 pen), Donnelly 10 (1 pen), Brattbakk 7, Wieghorst 4, Jackson 3, Thom 3 (2 pens), Lambert 2, McNamara 2, O'Donnell 2, Rieper 2, Blinker 1, Mackay 1, Stubbs 1. *Scottish Cup (8):* Brattbakk 3, Burley 1, Jackson 1, Mahe 1, Wieghorst 1, own goal 1. *Coca Cola Cup (13):* Donnelly 3 (1 pen), Larsson 3, Burley 2, Blinker 1, Jackson 1, Rieper 1, Thom 1, Wieghorst 1.

| Marshall G 1 | Boyd T 33 | McKinlay T 2+3 | McNamara J 28+3 | Mackay M 3+1 | Stubbs A 29 | Donnelly S 21+9 | Burley C 35 | Johnson T 1+1 | Jackson D 9+14 | Thom A 8+7 | Larsson H 34+1 | Wieghorst M 26+5 | Gould J 35 | Hannah D 9+6 | Blinker R 13+3 | O'Donnell P 6+8 | Mahe S 23 | Rieper M 30 | Annoni E 14+6 | Lambert P 25+1 | Brattbakk H 11+7 | Match No |
|---|---|---|---|---|---|---|---|---|---|---|---|---|---|---|---|---|---|---|---|---|---|---|
| 1 | 2 | $3^2$ | 4 | 5 | 6 | 7 | 8 | 9 | 10 | $11^1$ | 12 | 13 | | | | | | | | | | 1 |
| | 2 | $3^2$ | 4 | 5 | | 12 | 8 | | 9 | $10^1$ | 7 | | 1 | | 6 | 11 | 13 | | | | | 2 |
| | 2 | | | 5 | | 9 | 8 | | 10 | 7 | 6 | | 1 | 4 | $11^1$ | 12 | 3 | | | | | 3 |
| | 2 | 12 | | | 6 | 9 | 8 | | $10^1$ | 7 | 4 | | 1 | | 11 | | 3 | 5 | | | | 4 |
| | 2 | $4^1$ | | | $6^2$ | 9 | 8 | | 10 | 7 | 11 | | 1 | 13 | | 12 | 3 | 5 | | | | 5 |
| | 2 | 13 | 4 | | 6 | 9 | 8 | | $10^1$ | 7 | $11^2$ | | 1 | 3 | | 12 | | 5 | | | | 6 |
| | 2 | 12 | 4 | | $6^3$ | 9 | 8 | | $10^1$ | 7 | $11^2$ | | 1 | 13 | | | 5 | 14 | | | | 7 |
| | 2 | | 4 | | 6 | $9^2$ | 8 | | 12 | 7 | 10 | | 1 | 13 | $11^1$ | | 3 | 5 | | | | 8 |
| | 2 | | 4 | | 6 | 9 | 8 | | | $7^2$ | 10 | | 1 | 13 | $11^1$ | 12 | 3 | 5 | | | | 9 |
| | 2 | | 4 | | 6 | 9 | 8 | | 12 | $7^1$ | 10 | | 1 | | 11 | | 3 | 5 | | | | 10 |
| | $2^3$ | | 4 | | $6^1$ | 9 | 8 | | 13 | 7 | 10 | | 1 | | $11^2$ | | 3 | 5 | 12 | 14 | | 11 |
| | 2 | | 4 | | 6 | $9^2$ | 8 | | 13 | 7 | 12 | | 1 | $3^1$ | 11 | | | 5 | 14 | $10^3$ | | 12 |
| | $2^2$ | | 4 | | 6 | $9^1$ | 8 | 12 | 13 | 7 | 11 | | 1 | | | | 3 | 5 | | 10 | | 13 |
| | 2 | 14 | 4 | | 12 | | | 13 | $9^1$ | 7 | 8 | | 1 | 6 | $11^2$ | | 3 | 5 | | $10^1$ | | 14 |
| | 2 | | 4 | | 6 | 9 | 8 | 12 | $11^1$ | 7 | | | 1 | | | | 3 | 5 | | 10 | | 15 |
| | 2 | | 4 | | 6 | 12 | 8 | $9^1$ | | 7 | | | 1 | | 11 | | 3 | 5 | | 10 | | 16 |
| | 2 | | 4 | | 6 | | 8 | 14 | | $7^3$ | 9 | | 1 | | $11^2$ | | 3 | $5^1$ | 12 | 10 | 13 | 17 |
| | 2 | | 4 | | 6 | | 8 | 13 | 14 | $7^2$ | $9^1$ | | 1 | 3 | $11^3$ | | | 5 | | 10 | 12 | 18 |
| | 2 | | 4 | | $6^2$ | | 8 | | $7^1$ | 13 | 9 | | 1 | 3 | 11 | | | 5 | | 10 | 12 | 19 |
| | 2 | | 4 | | 6 | | 8 | 12 | | 7 | 11 | | 1 | | | | 3 | 5 | | 10 | $9^1$ | 20 |
| | 2 | | 4 | | 6 | | 8 | 12 | | 7 | $11^2$ | | 1 | 13 | | | 3 | 5 | | 10 | $9^1$ | 21 |
| | | $4^1$ | | | 12 | 8 | 13 | | 7 | 11 | | 6 | 1 | | | | 3 | 5 | 2 | 10 | $9^2$ | 22 |
| | | 4 | | 6 | 13 | 8 | 12 | | $7^2$ | 11 | | | 1 | | | | 3 | 5 | 2 | 10 | $9^1$ | 23 |
| | | 4 | | 6 | | 8 | 12 | | 7 | 11 | | | 1 | | | | 3 | 5 | 2 | 10 | $9^1$ | 24 |
| | 2 | | $4^1$ | | 6 | 12 | 8 | 14 | | $7^3$ | 11 | | 1 | | | | 3 | $5^2$ | 13 | 10 | 9 | 25 |
| | 2 | 14 | | | 4 | $8^1$ | $13^3$ | | $7^2$ | 11 | | 6 | 1 | 12 | | | 3 | 5 | | 10 | 9 | 26 |
| | 2 | $4^2$ | | | 6 | 12 | 8 | | 7 | 11 | | | 1 | 13 | | | 3 | 5 | | 10 | $9^1$ | 27 |
| | 2 | | | $4^2$ | 6 | 8 | | 12 | 7 | $11^3$ | | | 1 | 14 | | | 3 | 5 | 13 | 10 | $9^1$ | 28 |
| | 2 | $4^2$ | | | 13 | 8 | 12 | | 7 | 11 | | 14 | 1 | | | | 3 | 5 | 6 | $10^3$ | $9^1$ | 29 |
| | 2 | $4^1$ | | 6 | 12 | 8 | 13 | | 7 | 11 | | 14 | 1 | | | | $3^1$ | 5 | | 10 | $9^2$ | 30 |
| | 2 | | | 4 | 8 | $9^1$ | | 7 | 11 | | | 6 | 1 | | | | 5 | 3 | | 10 | 12 | 31 |
| | 2 | | 6 | 4 | 8 | $9^1$ | | 7 | | | | 11 | 1 | | | | 5 | 3 | | 10 | 12 | 32 |
| | 2 | 12 | 6 | 4 | 8 | $9^1$ | | 7 | | | | 11 | 1 | | | | 5 | 3 | | 10 | | 33 |
| | 2 | 12 | 6 | $4^2$ | $8^3$ | $9^1$ | | 7 | 14 | | | 13 | 1 | 11 | | | 5 | 3 | | 10 | | 34 |
| | 2 | $4^1$ | 6 | 9 | 8 | | 7 | 13 | | | 1 | $11^2$ | | | 5 | | 3 | 10 | | | 12 | 35 |
| | 2 | 4 | 6 | $9^1$ | 8 | | $7^3$ | 13 | | | 1 | 14 | 11 | | | 5 | | 3 | $10^2$ | | 12 | 36 |

# CLYDE

Second Division

*Year Formed:* 1878. *Ground & Address:* Broadwood Stadium, Cumbernauld, G68 9NE. *Telephone:* 01236 451511.
*Ground Capacity:* total: 8200 all seated. *Size of Pitch:* 112yd × 76yd.
*Chairman:* W. B. Carmichael. *Secretary:* John D. Taylor. *Commercial Manager:* John Donnelly.
*Manager:* Gardner Speirs. *Physio:* J. Watson: *Coaches:* Gordon Wylde, Steven Clarke.
*Managers since 1975:* S. Anderson; C. Brown; J. Clark, A. Smith. *Club Nickname(s):* The Bully Wee. *Previous Grounds:*
Barrowfield & Shawfield Stadium.
*Record Attendance:* 52,000 v Rangers, Division I; 21 Nov, 1908.
*Record Transfer Fee received:* £95,000 for Pat Nevin to Chelsea (July 1983).
*Record Transfer Fee paid:* £14,000 for Harry Hood from Sunderland (1966).
*Record Victory:* 11-1 v Cowdenbeath, Division II; 6 Oct, 1951.
*Record Defeat:* 0-11 v Dumbarton, Scottish Cup 4th rd, 22 Nov, 1879; v Rangers, Scottish Cup 4th rd, 13 Nov, 1880.
*Most Capped Player:* Tommy Ring, 12, Scotland.
*Most League Appearances:* 428: Brian Ahern.
*Most League Goals in Season (Individual):* 32: Bill Boyd, 1932-33.
*Most Goals Overall (Individual):* —.

## CLYDE 1997–98 LEAGUE RECORD

| Match No. | Date | Venue | Opponents | Result | H/T Score | Lg. Pos. | Goalscorers | Atten- dance |
|---|---|---|---|---|---|---|---|---|
| 1 | Aug 6 | A | Stranraer | D | 0-0 | 0-0 | — | 509 |
| 2 | 16 | H | Forfar Ath | L | 1-2 | 1-1 | 7 | Gauley [19] | 732 |
| 3 | 23 | A | Clydebank | D | 2-2 | 2-1 | 8 | King [20], Carrigan [42] | 571 |
| 4 | 30 | A | East Fife | L | 0-3 | 0-1 | 9 | | 720 |
| 5 | Sept 13 | H | Stenhousemuir | W | 2-0 | 1-0 | 7 | McStay [17], Brownlie [83] | 706 |
| 6 | 20 | H | Brechin C | D | 1-1 | 0-0 | 7 | Brownlie [56] | 611 |
| 7 | 27 | A | Inverness CT | W | 2-1 | 1-1 | 7 | Brownlie [41], King [63] | 1751 |
| 8 | Oct 4 | H | Livingston | W | 1-0 | 1-0 | 7 | Rice (pen) [21] | 822 |
| 9 | 18 | A | Queen of the S | L | 3-4 | 2-1 | 7 | Brownlie [24], Gibson [29], O'Neill [73] | 1232 |
| 10 | 25 | H | Clydebank | L | 0-1 | 0-1 | 8 | | 1007 |
| 11 | Nov 1 | A | Forfar Ath | D | 2-2 | 2-0 | 8 | McStay [3], Brownlie [23] | 527 |
| 12 | 8 | H | East Fife | W | 3-0 | 2-0 | 6 | Carrigan [4], McStay [18], Rice (pen) [73] | 598 |
| 13 | 15 | A | Stenhousemuir | D | 0-0 | 0-0 | 5 | | 581 |
| 14 | 22 | H | Inverness CT | W | 4-3 | 3-1 | 4 | Brownlie 2 [5, 21], Scott 2 [41, 57] | 953 |
| 15 | 29 | A | Brechin C | L | 1-2 | 1-0 | 4 | McStay [25] | 404 |
| 16 | Dec 16 | A | Queen of the S | D | 0-0 | 0-0 | — | | 510 |
| 17 | 20 | H | Livingston | W | 2-0 | 2-0 | 3 | Carrigan [7], Gibson [32] | 1333 |
| 18 | 27 | A | Clydebank | L | 1-2 | 1-1 | 5 | Gibson [24] | 710 |
| 19 | Jan 13 | H | Stranraer | L | 0-1 | 0-1 | — | | 515 |
| 20 | 17 | A | Inverness CT | L | 1-5 | 0-2 | 7 | O'Neill [75] | 1505 |
| 21 | 31 | H | Brechin C | D | 2-2 | 1-0 | 7 | Gibson [5], Graham [87] | 721 |
| 22 | Feb 7 | A | Queen of the S | D | 0-0 | 0-0 | 7 | | 1230 |
| 23 | 17 | H | Livingston | L | 0-3 | 0-1 | — | | 528 |
| 24 | 21 | A | Stranraer | L | 0-3 | 0-2 | 9 | | 484 |
| 25 | 25 | H | Forfar Ath | L | 1-2 | 0-1 | — | Cameron [67] | 401 |
| 26 | 28 | A | East Fife | D | 1-1 | 1-1 | 9 | King [31] | 670 |
| 27 | Mar 7 | H | Stenhousemuir | D | 0-0 | 0-0 | 9 | | 619 |
| 28 | 14 | H | Inverness CT | L | 1-6 | 0-3 | 9 | McStay (pen) [69] | 766 |
| 29 | 21 | A | Brechin C | W | 2-0 | 0-0 | 9 | McGraw 2 [57, 83] | 329 |
| 30 | 28 | H | Queen of the S | W | 3-1 | 2-1 | 9 | McGraw 2 [18, 31], Brownlie [47] | 726 |
| 31 | Apr 7 | A | Livingston | L | 0-4 | 0-0 | — | | 1192 |
| 32 | 11 | H | East Fife | D | 0-0 | 0-0 | 9 | | 629 |
| 33 | 18 | A | Stenhousemuir | D | 1-1 | 1-0 | 9 | Graham [62] | 682 |
| 34 | 25 | H | Clydebank | W | 2-0 | 1-0 | 9 | Graham [44], King [66] | 649 |
| 35 | May 2 | A | Forfar Ath | W | 1-0 | 0-0 | 8 | Graham [76] | 583 |
| 36 | 9 | H | Stranraer | L | 0-1 | 0-0 | 8 | | 1649 |

**Final League Position: 8**   1996–97 4

**Honours**
*League Champions:* Division II 1904-05, 1951-52, 1956-57, 1961-62, 1972-73. Second Division 1977-78, 1981-82, 1992-93.
*Runners-up:* Division II 1903-04, 1905-06, 1925-26, 1963-64.
*Scottish Cup Winners:* 1939, 1955, 1958; *Runners-up:* 1910, 1912, 1949.
*League Cup: —*
*Club colours:* Shirt: White with red and black trim. Shorts: Black. Stockings: Black with red and white tops.

**Goalscorers:** *League (40):*Brownlie 8, McStay 5 (1 pen), Gibson 4, Graham 4, King 4, McGraw 4, Carrigan 3, O'Neill 2, Rice 2 (pens), Scott 2, Cameron 1, Gauley 1. *Scottish Cup (0): Coca Cola Cup (0).·League Challenge Cup (2):* Gauley 1, Gibson 1.

| McLean M 25 | McStay J 35 | Donaldson E 10+7 | Brown J 2 | Baptie C 30 | Rice B 31 | Gibson A 33 | King T 31 | Scott R 12+3 | McInulty S 13 | Brownlie P 26+6 | Carrigan B 25+9 | Gauley S 3+16 | Prunty J 19+3 | McPhee G 15+3 | Campbell P 9+3 | Tortolano J 16+5 | Stewart P —+1 | O'Neill M 9+10 | Balfour R 11 | Cameron I 12 | Graham A 12+3 | McMillan A 8 | McGraw M 9 | Match No. |
|---|---|---|---|---|---|---|---|---|---|---|---|---|---|---|---|---|---|---|---|---|---|---|---|---|
| 1 | 2 | 3 | 4 | 5 | 6 | 7 | 8 | $9^2$ | $10^1$ | 11 | 12 | 13 | | | | | | | | | | | | 1 |
| 1 | 4 | 3 | | 5 | 10 | 6 | 8 | | | 12 | 9 | $11^1$ | 2 | $7^2$ | 13 | | | | | | | | | 2 |
| 1 | 4 | 3 | | 5 | 10 | 6 | 8 | 12 | | | 9 | $11^1$ | 2 | 7 | | | | | | | | | | 3 |
| 1 | 4 | $11^1$ | | 5 | 6 | 10 | 8 | 9 | 3 | 7 | | 12 | 2 | | | | | | | | | | | 4 |
| 1 | 2 | 3 | | 5 | 10 | $7^2$ | 8 | | | $6^2$ | 9 | $11^1$ | 4 | | | 13 | 14 | | | | | | | 5 |
| 1 | 2 | 3 | | 5 | 10 | 7 | 8 | 13 | | $6^1$ | $11^2$ | 9 | 4 | | 12 | | | | | | | | | 6 |
| 1 | 2 | 3 | | 5 | 10 | 7 | 8 | $9^1$ | | 6 | $11^2$ | 13 | 4 | | 12 | | | | | | | | | 7 |
| 1 | 2 | 3 | | 5 | $10^1$ | 7 | 8 | $9^2$ | | 6 | $11^3$ | 14 | 4 | | 12 | 13 | | | | | | | | 8 |
| 1 | 2 | 3 | | 5 | 10 | 7 | 8 | $9^2$ | | $6^1$ | $11^3$ | 14 | 4 | | 12 | 13 | | | | | | | | 9 |
| 1 | 2 | 14 | | 5 | 6 | 10 | $8^2$ | | | 11 | 7 | 12 | $4^3$ | | 13 | 3 | | $9^1$ | | | | | | 10 |
| 1 | 2 | 12 | | 5 | 6 | 10 | 8 | 9 | | 11 | $7^1$ | | | | 4 | 3 | | | | | | | | 11 |
| 1 | 2 | | | 5 | 6 | 10 | 4 | 9 | | | 7 | 11 | | | 8 | 3 | | | | | | | | 12 |
| 1 | 2 | 12 | | 5 | 6 | 10 | 4 | 9 | | | $7^1$ | 11 | | | 8 | 3 | | | | | | | | 13 |
| 1 | 2 | | | 5 | 6 | 10 | 4 | $9^1$ | | | 7 | 11 | | | 8 | 3 | | 12 | | | | | | 14 |
| 1 | 2 | 12 | | 5 | 6 | 10 | 4 | 9 | | | $7^1$ | 11 | | | 8 | 3 | | | | | | | | 15 |
| 1 | 2 | 13 | | 5 | 6 | 10 | 4 | $9^1$ | | | 12 | 11 | | 7 | $8^2$ | 3 | | | | | | | | 16 |
| 1 | 2 | 12 | | 5 | 6 | 10 | 4 | $9^1$ | | | | 11 | 7 | | 8 | 3 | | | | | | | | 17 |
| 1 | 2 | 11 | | 5 | 6 | 10 | 4 | | | | 7 | 9$^1$ | | 8 | | 3 | | 12 | | | | | | 18 |
| 1 | $2^3$ | 13 | | 5 | 6 | 10 | 4 | | $8^1$ | 7 | 11 | | 14 | 12 | | 3 | | $9^2$ | | | | | | 19 |
| | | | | 5 | 6 | $10^1$ | | | | $11^2$ | 7 | 2 | 13 | | | 3 | | 12 | 1 | | | 8 | 9 | 20 |
| | 2 | | | 5 | 6 | 10 | 4 | 12 | | 13 | 11 | 7$^2$ | | | | 3 | | | 1 | | $8^1$ | | 9 | 21 |
| | 4 | | | 5 | 6 | 10 | | 3 | | 12 | 11 | 2 | $7^1$ | | | | | | 1 | | 8 | | 9 | 22 |
| | 5 | | | 6 | $10^1$ | 4 | | 3 | | 11 | 12 | 2 | 7 | | | | | | 1 | | 8 | | 9 | 23 |
| 1 | 4 | | | 5 | $6^1$ | 10 | | 3$^2$ | | 7$^3$ | 14 | 2 | 12 | | 13 | | | | | | 8 | | 9 | 24 |
| 1 | 5 | | | $6^1$ | 10 | 4 | | | | 11 | 13 | 14 | 2 | 7$^2$ | 12 | 3 | | | | | $8^3$ | | 9 | 25 |
| 1 | 5 | | | | 7 | 4 | | 6 | | 8 | 12 | | | | 10 | 3 | | $11^1$ | | | 9 | 2 | | 26 |
| 1 | 5 | | | | | | | | | 12 | 8 | 13 | 2 | 7 | 4 | 3 | | 11 | | $10^1$ | $9^2$ | 6 | | 27 |
| 1 | 5 | | | | | | | | | $8^1$ | 12 | 2 | 7 | 4 | 3 | 13 | | 10 | | $9^2$ | 6 | 11 | | 28 |
| 1 | 2 | | | 5 | 6 | | | 3 | | 7 | 11 | 12 | | 4 | | | | $9^1$ | | 10 | | | 8 | 29 |
| | 2 | | | 5 | 6 | 4 | 3 | | | $7^3$ | $11^1$ | 13 | 12 | | | | | $9^2$ | 1 | 10 | 14 | | 8 | 30 |
| | 2 | | | 5 | 6 | $4^3$ | 3 | | | 11 | $7^1$ | 12 | 14 | | | | | $9^2$ | 1 | 10 | 13 | | 8 | 31 |
| | 4 | | | 5 | 3 | 7 | 6 | | | $11^2$ | 13 | | | 10 | | | | $9^1$ | 1 | 10 | 12 | 2 | 8 | 32 |
| | 4 | | | 5 | 3 | $7^1$ | 6 | | | 11 | 13 | | | 10 | | | | 12 | 1 | | 9 | 2 | $8^2$ | 33 |
| | 4 | | | 5 | 3 | 7 | 6 | | | $11^2$ | 13 | 14 | | 10 | | | | 12 | 1 | | $9^3$ | 2 | $8^1$ | 34 |
| | 4 | | | 5 | | 7 | 6 | | | $11^3$ | 13 | 14 | | $10^2$ | | 3 | | 12 | 1 | | 9 | 2 | $8^1$ | 35 |
| | 4 | | | 5 | | 7 | 6 | | | 11 | 12 | 13 | | 10 | | 3 | | $9^1$ | 1 | | | 2 | $8^2$ | 36 |

# CLYDEBANK

## First Division

*Year Formed:* 1965. *Ground:* Boghead Park, Miller St, Dumbarton G82 2JA. *Telephone:* 0141 955 9048. *Fax:* 0141 955 9049
*Ground Capacity:* 5503. *Size of Pitch:* 110yd × 68yd.
*Chairman:* Dr John Hall. *Commercial Manager:* David Curwood.
*Team Manager:* Ian McCall. *Assistant Manager:* Gordon Chisholm. *First Team Coach:* Stephen Morrison. *Secretary:*
Alex D. Moffat. *Physio:* Peter Salila.
*Club Nickname(s):* The Bankies. *Previous Grounds:* None.
*Record Attendance:* 14,900 v Hibernian, Scottish Cup 1st rd; 10 Feb, 1965.
*Record Transfer Fee received:* £175,000 for Owen Coyle from Airdrieonians, (Feb 1990).
*Record Transfer Fee paid:* £50,000 for Gerry McCabe from Clyde.
*Record Victory:* 8-1 Arbroath, First Division; 3 Jan 1977.
*Record Defeat:* 1-9 v Gala Fairydean, Scottish Cup qual rd; 15 Sept, 1965.
*Most Capped Player:* —.
*Most League Appearances:* 620: Jim Fallon; 1968-86.
*Most League Goals in Season (Individual):* 29: Ken Eadie, First Division, 1990-91.
*Most League Goals Overall (Individual):* 138, Ken Eadie 1988-95.

## CLYDEBANK 1997–98 LEAGUE RECORD

| Match No. | Date | Venue | Opponents | Result | H/T Score | Lg. Pos. | Goalscorers | Atten-dance |
|---|---|---|---|---|---|---|---|---|
| 1 | Aug 5 | H | Brechin C | W 3-0 | 2-0 | — | Lovering [20], Teale [35], Wishart [85] | 316 |
| 2 | 16 | A | Queen of the S | D 2-2 | 2-0 | 2 | Docherty [5], Teale [15] | 1284 |
| 3 | 23 | H | Clyde | D 2-2 | 1-2 | 2 | Cadette [44], Nicholls [89] | 571 |
| 4 | 30 | A | Forfar Ath | W 2-0 | 2-0 | 2 | Docherty [2], Lovering [30] | 449 |
| 5 | Sept 13 | H | East Fife | L 1-2 | 1-1 | 4 | Murdoch (pen) [40] | 358 |
| 6 | 20 | H | Stenhousemuir | W 1-0 | 0-0 | 3 | McCall [72] | 336 |
| 7 | 27 | A | Livingston | D 0-0 | 0-0 | 2 | | 1707 |
| 8 | Oct 4 | H | Stranraer | D 0-0 | 0-0 | 4 | | 298 |
| 9 | 18 | A | Inverness CT | D 0-0 | 0-0 | 5 | | 1542 |
| 10 | 25 | A | Clyde | W 1-0 | 1-0 | 2 | McWilliams [25] | 1007 |
| 11 | Nov 5 | H | Queen of the S | W 4-0 | 1-0 | — | Brown A [3], Murdoch [46], Miller [65], Kaljob [82] | 297 |
| 12 | 8 | A | Forfar Ath | D 1-1 | 0-0 | 2 | McWilliams [85] | 325 |
| 13 | 15 | A | East Fife | W 3-2 | 1-1 | 2 | Brown A [6], McDonald 2 [46, 58] | 600 |
| 14 | 22 | H | Livingston | D 1-1 | 1-0 | 2 | Lovering [34] | 490 |
| 15 | 29 | A | Stenhousemuir | W 3-2 | 2-2 | 1 | McDonald 2 [8, 24], Lovering [66] | 483 |
| 16 | Dec 13 | A | Inverness CT | D 1-1 | 1-0 | 2 | McDonald [16] | 326 |
| 17 | 20 | A | Stranraer | W 1-0 | 0-0 | 1 | Adams [63] | 563 |
| 18 | 27 | H | Clyde | W 2-1 | 1-1 | 1 | McDonald [28], McWilliams [77] | 710 |
| 19 | Jan 10 | A | Brechin C | W 1-0 | 1-0 | 1 | Ward K [30] | 403 |
| 20 | 31 | H | Stenhousemuir | W 1-0 | 0-0 | 1 | McWilliams [63] | 309 |
| 21 | Feb 7 | A | Inverness CT | L 2-3 | 1-1 | 1 | McDonald [25], Teale [78] | 1863 |
| 22 | 10 | A | Livingston | W 3-0 | 1-0 | — | Teale 2 [36, 56], McLaughlin [47] | 1466 |
| 23 | 14 | H | Stranraer | L 0-1 | 0-0 | 1 | | 325 |
| 24 | 21 | H | Brechin C | W 2-1 | 0-0 | 1 | McDonald 2 [70, 71] | 252 |
| 25 | 24 | A | Queen of the S | D 0-0 | 0-0 | — | | 1148 |
| 26 | 28 | A | Forfar Ath | D 0-0 | 0-0 | 1 | | 497 |
| 27 | Mar 14 | H | Livingston | L 0-2 | 0-2 | 1 | | 407 |
| 28 | 17 | H | East Fife | L 0-3 | 0-1 | — | | 182 |
| 29 | 21 | A | Stenhousemuir | D 0-0 | 0-0 | 1 | | 487 |
| 30 | 28 | H | Inverness CT | W 1-0 | 0-0 | 1 | McWilliams [70] | 344 |
| 31 | Apr 4 | A | Stranraer | L 1-2 | 1-2 | 1 | McDonald [42] | 598 |
| 32 | 11 | H | Forfar Ath | L 0-1 | 0-0 | 2 | | 276 |
| 33 | 18 | A | East Fife | W 2-0 | 0-0 | 2 | McDonald [55], Teale [85] | 710 |
| 34 | 25 | A | Clyde | L 0-2 | 0-1 | 2 | | 649 |
| 35 | May 2 | H | Queen of the S | D 1-1 | 1-0 | 3 | McWilliams [17] | 533 |
| 36 | 9 | A | Brechin C | W 6-1 | 5-1 | 2 | McLaughlin [12], McDonald 2 [21, 25], Ward K 2 [26, 75], McWilliams [41] | 408 |

**Final League Position: 2**        1996–97 DIV 1 9

**Honours**
*League Champions:* Second Division 1975-76; *Runners-up:* 1997-98; *Runners-up:* First Division 1976-77, 1984-85.
*Scottish Cup:* Semi-finalists 1990. *League Cup:* —.
*Club colours:* Shirt: Vertical red and white stripes. Shorts: Black. Stockings: Black.

**Goalscorers:** *League (48):* McDonald 13, McWilliams 7 (1 pen), Teale 6, Lovering 4, Ward K 3, Brown A 2, Docherty 2, McLaughlin 2, Murdoch 2 (1 pen), Adams 1, Cadette 1, Kaljob 1, McCall 1, Miller 1, Nichols 1, Wishart 1. *Scottish Cup (6):* Brown A 1, Lovering 1, McWilliams 1, Murdoch 1, Nichols 1, Ward K 1. *Coca Cola Cup (0). League Challenge Cup (2):* Lovering 1, McCall 1.

| Hillcoat J 7 | Wishart F 30 | Lovering P 32 | Murdoch S 28 | McLaughlin J 32 | Brannigan K 26 | Connell G 17 + 10 | Nichols D 32 | Teale G 13 + 14 | McCall I 2 + 19 | Docherty S 30 | Melvin W 2 + 12 | Lorimer D 1 + 2 | Cadette R 4 | Miller S 16 + 5 | Brown A 14 + 6 | MacFarlane J 24 | Brown J — + 1 | Kaljob S 3 + 2 | McWilliams D 26 | Ward K 16 + 8 | McDonald C 23 | Adams C 6 + 5 | Inglis N 5 | Charnley J 1 | McKinstrey J 2 | Arnason H 1 | Shaw G 3 + 3 | Ward H — + 2 | Match No. |
|---|---|---|---|---|---|---|---|---|---|---|---|---|---|---|---|---|---|---|---|---|---|---|---|---|---|---|---|---|---|
| 1 | 2 | 3 | 4 | 5 | 6 | 7 | 8 | 9¹ | 10 | 11 | 12 | | | | | | | | | | | | | | | | | | 1 |
| 1 | 2 | 3 | 4 | 5 | 6 | 9 | 8 | 7² | 10 | 11¹ | 12 | 13 | | | | | | | | | | | | | | | | | 2 |
| 1 | 2 | 3 | 4 | 5 | 6 | 11 | 8 | 7 | 12 | | 10¹ | | | 9 | | | | | | | | | | | | | | | 3 |
| 1 | 2 | 3 | 4 | 5 | 6 | 11 | 8² | 7 | | | 10¹ | | 12 | 9 | 13 | | | | | | | | | | | | | | 4 |
| 1 | 2 | 3 | 4 | 5 | 6 | 11³ | 8 | 12 | 13 | 10 | 14 | | | 7² | 9¹ | | | | | | | | | | | | | | 5 |
| 1 | 2 | 3 | 4 | 5 | 6 | | 8 | 7¹ | 12 | 10 | | | | 9 | 11 | | | | | | | | | | | | | | 6 |
| 1 | 2 | 3 | 4 | 5 | 6 | 11 | 8² | 7¹ | 13 | 10 | 14 | | | 12 | 9³ | | | | | | | | | | | | | | 7 |
| | 3 | 5 | 4 | | 6 | 2 | 8 | 7² | 12 | 10¹ | 14 | | | 11³ | 9 | 1 | 13 | | | | | | | | | | | | 8 |
| | 2 | 3 | 4 | 5 | 6 | | 8² | | 12 | 13 | 10 | | 14 | | 9¹ | 1 | | 7² | 11 | | | | | | | | | | 9 |
| | | 3 | 4 | 5 | 6 | | 8¹ | | | 13 | 10 | | 12 | 2 | 9 | 1 | | | 11² | 7 | | | | | | | | | 10 |
| | | 3 | 4 | 5 | 6 | | 8 | | | 13 | 10¹ | | 14 | 2 | 9 | 1 | | 12 | 11² | 7² | | | | | | | | | 11 |
| | | 3 | 4 | 5 | 6 | 12 | | | | 13 | 10¹ | | | 2 | 9 | 1 | | 8¹ | 11 | 7² | | | | | | | | | 12 |
| | | 3 | | 5 | 6 | 12 | | | 4 | 13 | 10 | | | 2 | 9 | 1 | | 14 | 11¹ | 7² | 8³ | | | | | | | | 13 |
| | | 3 | 4 | 5 | 6 | 12 | | | | 13 | 10 | | | 2 | 9 | 1 | | | 11 | 7¹ | 8² | | | | | | | | 14 |
| | | 3 | 4 | 5 | 6 | 12 | | | | 13 | 10¹ | | | 2 | 9 | 1 | | | 11 | 7 | 8² | | | | | | | | 15 |
| | | 3 | 4 | 5 | 6 | 2 | | | 13 | 10 | 12 | | 14 | 2 | 9 | 1 | | | 11² | 7¹ | 8³ | | | | | | | | 16 |
| | | 3 | 4 | 5 | 6¹ | 12 | | 7 | 10³ | | | | | 2 | 9² | 1 | | 14 | 11 | | 8 | 13 | | | | | | | 17 |
| | 2 | 3 | 4 | 5 | 6 | | | | | 13 | 10 | | | 12 | 14 | 1 | | | 11 | 7¹ | 8³ | 9² | | | | | | | 18 |
| | 2 | 3 | 4 | 5 | | | | | | 13 | 6 | | 14 | | 9³ | 1 | | | 11 | 7² | 8¹ | 12 | | | | | | | 19 |
| | 2 | 3 | 4 | 5 | 6¹ | | | 7 | | 10 | | | 14 | 12 | | 1 | | | 11 | 13 | 8³ | 9² | | | | | | | 20 |
| | 2 | 3 | 4 | 5 | 6¹ | | | 7 | 13 | 10 | | | 14 | | | 1 | | | 11 | 12 | 8³ | 9² | | | | | | | 21 |
| | 2¹ | 3 | 4 | 5 | | 12 | | 7 | 9 | 10 | | | 14 | | | 1 | | | 11 | 6² | 8³ | 13 | | | | | | | 22 |
| | | 3 | 4 | 5 | | | | 7 | 10 | | 9² | 13 | 14 | 12 | | 1 | | | 11 | 6¹ | 8 | 2⁴ | | | | | | | 23 |
| | 2 | 3 | 4 | 5 | | | | 7 | 10² | 12 | 13 | | | | 9¹ | 1 | | | 11 | 6 | 8 | | | | | | | | 24 |
| | 2 | 3 | 4 | 5 | | | | 7 | 10 | | 9² | | | | | 1 | | | 11¹ | 13 | 8 | 12 | 6 | | | | | | 25 |
| | 2 | 3 | 4¹ | 5 | | | | 7 | 10 | 13 | 14 | | | 12 | | 1 | | | 11 | 6² | 8 | 9² | | 11 | | | | | 26 |
| | 2 | | 4² | 5 | 6 | 14 | | 7 | 10 | 12 | | | 13 | 3 | | 1 | | | 11 | | 8³ | 9¹ | | | | | | | 27 |
| | | | 4 | 5 | 6 | 2¹ | | 7 | 10 | | 12 | | 14 | 3² | | 1 | | | 11 | 13 | 8 | | | | | | | | 28 |
| | 2 | | 4 | 5 | 6 | | | 7 | 10 | | 12 | | | 3 | | 1 | | | 11 | 13 | 8¹ | 9² | | | | | | | 29 |
| | 2 | | | 5 | 6 | | | 7 | 10² | | 12 | | | 3 | | 1 | | | 11 | 13 | 8¹ | | | | | | 4 | 9 | 30 |
| | 2³ | 3 | 4² | 5 | 6 | 12 | | 7 | 10 | 13 | | | | | | 1 | | | 11 | | 8¹ | | | | | | 9 | 14 | 31 |
| | | 3 | 4 | 5 | 6 | | | 7 | 10 | 13 | | | | | | 1 | | | 11 | 8¹ | | | | | 2 | | 9² | 12 | 32 |
| | 2 | 3 | 4 | 5 | 6 | | | 7 | 10 | | 12 | | | 9² | | 1 | | | 11 | | 8¹ | | | | | | 13 | | 33 |
| | 2¹ | 3 | 4³ | 5 | 6 | 14 | | 7 | 10 | | 12 | | | 9 | | 1 | | | 11² | | 8 | | | | | | 13 | | 34 |
| | 2 | 3 | 4¹ | 5 | 6 | | | 7 | 10 | | | | | 9² | | 1 | | | 11 | 12 | 8 | | | | | | 13 | | 35 |
| | 2 | 3 | 4 | 5 | 6 | | | 7 | 13 | | 10¹ | | | | | 1 | | | 11 | 9 | 8² | | | | | | 12 | | 36 |

# COWDENBEATH

## Third Division

*Year Formed:* 1881. *Ground & Address:* Central Park, Cowdenbeath KY4 9EY. *Telephone:* 01383 610166. *Fax:* 01383 512132.
*Ground Capacity:* total: 5268. seated: 1622. *Size of Pitch:* 107yd × 66yd.
*Chairman:* Gordon McDougall. *Secretary:* Tom Ogilvie. *Commercial Manager:* Joe McNamara.
*Manager:* Craig Levein. *Coach:* Bert Oliver. *Physio:* Brian McNeill
*Managers since 1975:* D. McLindon; F. Connor; P. Wilson; A. Rolland; H. Wilson; W. McCulloch; J. Clark; J. Craig; R.
Campbell; J. Blackley; J. Brownlie, A. Harrow, J. Reilly, P Dolan, T. Steven, S. Conn. *Previous Grounds:* North End
Park, Cowdenbeath.
*Record Attendance:* 25,586 v Rangers, League Cup quarter-final; 21 Sept, 1949.
*Record Transfer Fee received:* £30,000 for Nicky Henderson to Falkirk, (March 1994).
*Record Transfer Fee paid:* —
*Record Victory:* 12-0 v Johnstone, Scottish Cup 1st rd; 21 Jan, 1928.
*Record Defeat:* 1-11 v Clyde, Division II; 6 Oct, 1951.
*Most Capped Player:* Jim Paterson, 3, Scotland.
*Most League and Cup Appearances:* 491 Ray Allan 1972-75, 1979-89.
*Most League Goals in Season (Individual):* 54, Rab Walls, Division II, 1938-39.
*Most Goals Overall (Individual):* 127, Willie Devlin, 1922-26, 1929-30.

## COWDENBEATH 1997–98 LEAGUE RECORD

| Match No. | Date | Venue | Opponents | Result | H/T Score | Lg. Pos. | Goalscorers | Attendance |
|---|---|---|---|---|---|---|---|---|
| 1 | Aug 5 | H | Dumbarton | L 0-2 | 0-1 | — | | 232 |
| 2 | 16 | A | Alloa Ath | L 0-1 | 0-1 | 9 | | 462 |
| 3 | 23 | H | Ross Co | L 0-1 | 0-0 | 10 | | 261 |
| 4 | 30 | A | Montrose | L 0-2 | 0-1 | 10 | | 287 |
| 5 | Sept 13 | H | East Stirling | W 1-0 | 1-0 | 10 | Stewart 44 | 176 |
| 6 | 20 | A | Queen's Park | L 0-1 | 0-0 | 10 | | 476 |
| 7 | 27 | H | Albion R | L 1-4 | 0-1 | 10 | Brown 73 | 197 |
| 8 | Oct 4 | A | Berwick R | L 1-2 | 1-0 | 10 | Brown 40 | 319 |
| 9 | 18 | H | Arbroath | L 0-4 | 0-1 | 10 | | 252 |
| 10 | 25 | A | Ross Co | L 0-5 | 0-3 | 10 | | 1233 |
| 11 | Nov 1 | H | Alloa Ath | L 0-3 | 0-2 | 10 | | 214 |
| 12 | 8 | H | Montrose | W 3-1 | 1-1 | 10 | Hunter 1, McMahon 58, Winter (pen) 61 | 132 |
| 13 | 15 | A | East Stirling | L 0-4 | 0-2 | 10 | | 287 |
| 14 | 22 | A | Albion R | W 1-0 | 0-0 | 10 | Brown 78 | 355 |
| 15 | 29 | H | Queen's Park | D 0-0 | 0-0 | 10 | | 220 |
| 16 | Dec 13 | A | Arbroath | L 2-3 | 2-2 | 10 | Winter 12, Millar 25 | 630 |
| 17 | 20 | H | Berwick R | L 0-2 | 0-1 | 10 | | 161 |
| 18 | 27 | H | Ross Co | L 0-2 | 0-0 | 10 | | 273 |
| 19 | Jan 10 | A | Dumbarton | W 2-1 | 1-0 | 10 | Mitchell 23, Holmes (pen) 77 | 338 |
| 20 | 31 | A | Queen's Park | W 4-0 | 2-0 | 10 | Sinclair 4, Stewart 17, Holmes 55, Urquhart 70 | 554 |
| 21 | Feb 7 | H | Arbroath | W 3-1 | 2-0 | 10 | Hamilton 22, Holmes 32, Crawford (og) 71 | 248 |
| 22 | 10 | H | Albion R | W 2-0 | 0-0 | — | Holmes 2 50, 58 | 231 |
| 23 | 14 | A | Berwick R | W 2-0 | 0-0 | 8 | Stewart 50, Hamilton 73 | 402 |
| 24 | 21 | A | Dumbarton | W 2-0 | 2-0 | 8 | Winter 32, Stewart 36 | 255 |
| 25 | 24 | A | Alloa Ath | L 0-2 | 0-0 | — | | 484 |
| 26 | 28 | A | Montrose | L 1-3 | 0-0 | 9 | Welsh 77 | 289 |
| 27 | Mar 9 | H | East Stirling | L 0-1 | 0-0 | — | | 174 |
| 28 | 14 | A | Albion R | W 1-0 | 1-0 | 8 | Burns J 37 | 346 |
| 29 | 21 | H | Queen's Park | L 1-2 | 0-1 | 8 | Stewart 69 | 235 |
| 30 | 28 | A | Arbroath | L 0-2 | 0-1 | 9 | | 771 |
| 31 | Apr 7 | H | Berwick R | W 1-0 | 0-0 | — | Stewart 80 | 164 |
| 32 | 11 | H | Montrose | D 0-0 | 0-0 | 9 | | 194 |
| 33 | 18 | A | East Stirling | L 1-2 | 1-0 | 8 | Burns J 30 | 284 |
| 34 | 25 | A | Ross Co | L 0-1 | 0-0 | 8 | | 1201 |
| 35 | May 2 | H | Alloa Ath | L 1-3 | 0-1 | 9 | Burns J 76 | 473 |
| 36 | 9 | A | Dumbarton | W 3-2 | 0-1 | 8 | Murray 51, Welsh (pen) 66, Ritchie 78 | 413 |

**Final League Position: 8**          1997-98 8

**Honours**
*League Champions:* Division II 1913-14, 1914-15, 1938-39; *Runners-up:* Division II 1921-22, 1923-24, 1969-70. Second Division 1991-92.
*Scottish Cup: Quarter-finals:* 1931.
*League Cup: Semi-finals:* 1959-60, 1970-71.
*Club colours:* Shirt: Royal blue 1" vertical stripe with red piping on sleeve seam. Shorts: White with blue side stripe. Stockings: Royal blue.

**Goalscorers:** *League (33):* Stewart 6, Holmes 5 (1 pen), Brown 3, Burns JP 3, Winter 3 (1 pen), Hamilton 2, Welsh 2 (1 pen), Hunter 1, McMahon 1, Millar 1, Mitchell 1, Murray 1, Ritchie 1, Sinclair 1, Urquhart 1, own goal 1. *Scottish Cup (1):* Winter 1. *Coca Cola Cup (0). League Challenge Cup (0).*

| Russell N 3 | Munro K 4 | Ritchie A 23 + 5 | Meldrum G 24 | Humphreys M 26 + 1 | Bailie R 10 + 5 | Sinclair C 25 + 2 | Jack S 1 | Robertson M 3 + 2 | Hunter R 5 + 2 | Nolan T 10 | Bowsher C 7 | Bowmaker K 2 | Stewart W 30 + 4 | Dinse R — + 1 | Scott M — + 1 | McMahon B 12 + 2 | Winter C 27 | Coulston D 5 + 1 | Hamilton A 26 + 5 | Brown G 9 + 21 | Millar P 10 + 10 | Godfrey R 5 | Burns W 4 | Manson S 3 + 2 | Foster B 2 + 1 | Shields P — + 1 | Melvin A — + 1 | Maskrey S 5 | Moffat J 2 | Wright G 2 | Urquhart M 17 + 1 | Duncan B 2 + 2 | Hutchison S 26 | Cook P 4 + 1 | Welsh B 8 + 6 | Holmes D 13 | Murray D 7 | Mitchell G 11 | Prytz R 1 | Gaughan M 1 | Carson A — + 2 | Snedden S 11 | Burns J 10 | Match No. |
|---|---|---|---|---|---|---|---|---|---|---|---|---|---|---|---|---|---|---|---|---|---|---|---|---|---|---|---|---|---|---|---|---|---|---|---|---|---|---|---|---|---|---|---|---|
| 1 | 2 | 3 | 4 | 5 | 6³ | 7¹ | 8 | | 9² | 10 | | 11 | 12 | | | 13 | 14 | | | | | | | | | | | | | | | | | | | | | | | | | | | 1 |
| 1 | 2 | 3 | 4 | 5 | 14 | 11 | | | 13 | 10 | | | 6² | | | 9¹ | 8² | 7 | 12 | | | | | | | | | | | | | | | | | | | | | | | | | 2 |
| 1 | 2 | 3 | 4 | 5 | 13 | 11 | | | | 10 | | | 9¹ | | | 8 | 6³ | 7² | 12 | 14 | | | | | | | | | | | | | | | | | | | | | | | | 3 |
| | 2 | 3⁴ | 4 | 5 | 6 | | 8 | | 13 | 10 | | | 9² | | | | 7 | | 11¹ | 12 | 14 | 1 | | | | | | | | | | | | | | | | | | | | | | 4 |
| | | | 4 | 5 | 3 | | 8 | | | 10 | | | 9¹ | | | 11 | 6 | 7 | | 2 | 12 | 1 | | | | | | | | | | | | | | | | | | | | | | 5 |
| 13 | | | 4 | 5 | 3 | | 8 | | | 10 | | | 9¹ | | | 11 | 6² | 7³ | 2 | 12 | 14 | 1 | | | | | | | | | | | | | | | | | | | | | | 6 |
| | | | 4 | 7 | 6 | 8 | | | | 10 | | | 2 | | | | 11¹ | 3 | 9³ | | 1 | | 5² | | | | | 12 | 13 | 14 | | | | | | | | | | | | | | 7 |
| | | 3 | 5 | | 6 | | | | | 10 | | | 11 | | | | 2 | 9¹ | | | | 4 | 12 | 8 | | 1 | 7 | | | | | | | | | | | | | | | | | 8 |
| | | 3 | 2 | 6¹ | 8 | | | | | 10 | | | 11² | | | | 7 | | 13 | 9 | | 1 | 4 | | 5 | | | | 12 | | | | | | | | | | | | | | | 9 |
| | | 3¹ | 4 | 6³ | 8 | | | | | 10² | | | 9 | | | 5 | 11 | | 7 | 13 | 12 | 1 | 2 | 14 | | | | | | | | | | | | | | | | | | | | 10 |
| | | | 4 | 6¹ | 3 | 8² | | | | 13 | | | 10 | | | | 12 | 9 | 14 | 7² | 11 | | 2 | | | | | 1 | 5 | | | | | | | | | | | | | | | 11 |
| 13 | | 4 | 2 | 3 | | | | | | 11³ | | | 12 | | | | 6 | 9¹ | 14 | | | | 7² | 8 | | 1 | 5 | | 10 | | | | | | | | | | | | | | | 12 |
| | | 4 | 2 | 3 | 12 | | | | | 11³ | | | 13 | | | | 6 | 9 | 14 | | | | 7² | 8¹ | | 1 | 5 | | 10 | | | | | | | | | | | | | | | 13 |
| 11¹ | | 3 | 4 | 13 | 8 | | | | | 9 | | | 5 | | | 7 | | | 2² | 12 | | | | | | 1 | | | 6 | 10 | | | | | | | | | | | | | | 14 |
| 11² | | 3 | 4 | 13 | 6 | | | | | 9 | | | 5¹ | | | 7 | | | 2 | 14 | | | | | | 1 | 12 | | 8² | 10 | | | | | | | | | | | | | | 15 |
| 3² | | 4 | 13 | 6 | | | | | | 9¹ | | | 11 | | | | 2 | 12 | 8¹ | | 7 | | | | | 1 | 5 | | 14 | 10 | | | | | | | | | | | | | | 16 |
| 14 | | 2 | 6 | | | | | | | 5 | | | 11 | | | 13 | 9³ | 12 | | 7² | | | | | 1 | | | 10 | 3 | 4 | 8¹ | | | | | | | | | | | | | 17 |
| | | 3 | 12 | | | | | | | 7 | | | 5¹ | | | 8 | | | 9² | 6 | | | 1 | | | | | 10 | 11 | 4 | | 2 | 13 | | | | | | | | | | | 18 |
| | | 3 | 4 | 6 | | | | | | 9 | | | 11 | | | 7 | | | 8¹ | | | | 2 | | | | | 1 | 12 | 10 | 5 | | | | | | | | | | | | | 19 |
| | | 3 | 5 | 6 | | | | | | 9¹ | | | 7 | | | | 8 | 12 | | | | | 2² | | | | | 1 | 13 | 10 | 11 | 4 | | | | | | | | | | | | 20 |
| | | 3 | 5 | 6 | | | | | | 9 | | | 7 | | | | 8 | | | | | | 2 | | | | | 1 | | 10 | 11 | 4 | | | | | | | | | | | | 21 |
| | | 3 | 5 | 6 | | | | | | 9¹ | | | 7 | | | | 8 | 12 | | | | | 2 | | | | | 1 | | 10 | 11 | 4 | | | | | | | | | | | | 22 |
| | | 3 | 5 | 6 | | | | | | 9³ | | | 7 | | | | 8² | 14 | 12 | | | | 2 | | | | | 1 | 13 | 10 | 11¹ | 4 | | | | | | | | | | | | 23 |
| 11 | | 3 | 5 | 6¹ | | | | | | 9² | | | 7 | | | | 8 | 12 | 13 | | | | 2 | | | | | 1 | | 10 | 4 | | | | | | | | | | | | | 24 |
| 11² | | 3 | 5¹ | 6 | | | | | | 9 | | | 7 | | | | 8 | 13 | 12 | | | | 2³ | | | | | 1 | 14 | 10 | 4 | | | | | | | | | | | | 25 |
| 11 | | 3 | | 12 | | | | | | 9 | | | 7 | | | | 6 | 8 | 2² | | | | 1 | 13 | 10¹ | 4 | | | | 5 | | | | | | | | | | | | | | 26 |
| 11¹ | | 3 | | 6 | | | | | | 10 | 4 | | 7 | | | | 8 | 12 | | | | | 2 | | | | | 1 | | 5 | 9 | | | | | | | | | | | | | 27 |
| 11 | | 3 | | 6 | | 8¹ | | | | 7² | 13 | | 10 | | | | 2 | | | | | | 1 | | 4 | | | 5 | 9 | | | | | | | | | | | | | | 28 |
| 11 | | 3² | 4 | | 8 | 6 | | | | 2 | 10 | 12 | 7 | 13 | | | | | | | | | 1 | | 5 | 9 | | | | | | | | | | | | | | | | | | 29 |
| 13 | | 3 | | 6¹ | | 5 | 9 | | | 2 | 10¹ | 8 | 12 | | | | 1 | | 7² | | | | 14 | 4 | 11 | | | | | | | | | | | | | | | | | | | 30 |
| | | 3 | 2¹ | | 12 | 4 | 7 | | | | 8 | 6 | | | | | 9 | 10 | | | | 1 | | | 5 | 11 | | | | | | | | | | | | | | | | | | 31 |
| | | 3 | | 4 | 9 | | 7 | 8 | 12 | 6 | | | 10¹ | | | | 2 | | | | 1 | | | 5 | 11 | | | | | | | | | | | | | | | | | | | 32 |
| | | 3 | 4 | | 10² | | 7 | 12 | 13 | 6¹ | | | 9 | 8 | 2 | | 1 | | | | 5 | 11 | | | | | | | | | | | | | | | | | | | | | | 33 |
| | | | 4 | 10 | | 8² | 7 | 12 | 13 | | | | 9 | | | | 2¹ | 1 | | | 6 | | | 5 | 11 | | | | | | | | | | | | | | | | | | | 34 |
| | | 3 | | 5 | 10 | | 7 | 2 | 13 | 8 | | | 9² | | | | 12 | 1 | 6 | | | | 4 | 11 | | | | | | | | | | | | | | | | | | | | 35 |
| | | 13 | | | 12 | | 4 | 10 | | | | | 6² | 2 | 9 | 8¹ | | 1 | | | 7 | 3 | | | 5 | 11 | | | | | | | | | | | | | | | | | | 36 |

# DUMBARTON

## Third Division

*Year Formed:* 1872. *Ground & Address:* Boghead Park, Miller St, Dumbarton G82 2JA. *Telephone:* 01389 762569/767864. *Fax:* 01389 762629
*Ground Capacity:* total: 5503. seated: 303. *Size of Pitch:* 110yd × 68yd.
*Chairman:* D. Dalglish. *Company Secretary:* Colin J. Hosie.
*Manager:* Ian Wallace. *Assistant Manager:* Jimmy Brown. *Coach:* Ringo Watts. *Physio:* David Stobie.
*Managers since 1975:* A. Wright; D. Wilson; S. Fallon; W. Lamont; D. Wilson; D. Whiteford; A. Totten; M. Clougherty; R. Auld; J. George; W. Lamont; M. MacLeod, J. Fallon. *Club Nickname(s):* The Sons. *Previous Grounds:* Broadmeadow, Ropework Lane, Townend Ground.
*Record Attendance:* 18,000 v Raith Rovers, Scottish Cup; 2 Mar, 1957.
*Record Transfer Fee received:* £125,000 for Graeme Sharp to Everton (March 1982).
*Record Transfer Fee paid:* £50,000 for Charlie Gibson from Stirling Albion (1989).
*Record Victory:* 13-1 v Kirkintilloch Central. 1st Rd; 1 Sept, 1888.
*Record Defeat:* 1-11 v Albion Rovers, Division II; 30 Jan, 1926: v Ayr United, League Cup; 13 Aug, 1952.
*Most Capped Player:* James McAulay, 9, Scotland.
*Most League Appearances:* 297: Andy Jardine, 1957-67.
*Most Goals in Season (Individual):* 38: Kenny Wilson, Division II; 1971-72. *(League and Cup):* 46 Hughie Gallacher, 1955-56.

## DUMBARTON 1997–98 LEAGUE RECORD

| Match No. | Date | | Venue | Opponents | Result | H/T Score | Lg. Pos. | Goalscorers | Attendance |
|---|---|---|---|---|---|---|---|---|---|
| 1 | Aug | 5 | A | Cowdenbeath | W 2-0 | 1-0 | — | McKinnon [7], Reilly [50] | 232 |
| 2 | | 16 | H | Montrose | D 2-2 | 2-0 | 3 | McKinnon [17], Ward [33] | 395 |
| 3 | | 23 | A | Berwick R | L 3-5 | 2-3 | 6 | McKinnon 2 [9, 58], Mellis [40] | 304 |
| 4 | | 30 | H | Alloa Ath | L 0-1 | 0-0 | 7 | | 465 |
| 5 | Sept | 13 | A | Albion R | L 1-2 | 0-1 | 7 | Brittain [84] | 495 |
| 6 | | 20 | A | Arbroath | L 1-2 | 0-2 | 7 | Gow [61] | 702 |
| 7 | | 27 | H | Queen's Park | D 0-0 | 0-0 | 7 | | 436 |
| 8 | Oct | 4 | A | East Stirling | L 1-3 | 1-0 | 8 | McKinnon [1] | 321 |
| 9 | | 18 | H | Ross Co | D 2-2 | 0-1 | 8 | Ward 2 [70, 71] | 452 |
| 10 | | 25 | H | Berwick R | L 1-4 | 1-2 | 9 | Glancy [36] | 413 |
| 11 | Nov | 1 | A | Montrose | D 2-2 | 0-1 | 9 | Brittain [54], Sharp [73] | 347 |
| 12 | | 8 | A | Alloa Ath | W 2-1 | 1-1 | 8 | Grace [43], Sharp [55] | 424 |
| 13 | | 15 | H | Albion R | D 1-1 | 0-0 | 8 | McKinnon [90] | 425 |
| 14 | | 22 | A | Queen's Park | W 3-2 | 0-2 | 8 | McKinnon [50], Sharp 2 [72, 85] | 548 |
| 15 | | 29 | H | Arbroath | L 1-2 | 0-0 | 8 | Meechan J [60] | 379 |
| 16 | Dec | 13 | A | Ross Co | W 3-2 | 2-2 | 8 | Meechan J 2 [18, 42], Glancy [75] | 1226 |
| 17 | | 20 | H | East Stirling | L 0-1 | 0-1 | 8 | | 323 |
| 18 | | 27 | A | Berwick R | D 1-1 | 0-1 | 8 | McKinnon [60] | 449 |
| 19 | Jan | 10 | H | Cowdenbeath | L 1-2 | 0-1 | 8 | Mooney [73] | 338 |
| 20 | | 17 | A | Queen's Park | D 0-0 | 0-0 | 8 | | 408 |
| 21 | | 31 | A | Arbroath | D 2-2 | 2-2 | 8 | Grace [18], Meechan J [45] | 666 |
| 22 | Feb | 7 | H | Ross Co | L 0-1 | 0-0 | 8 | | 447 |
| 23 | | 17 | A | East Stirling | L 0-1 | 0-0 | — | | 181 |
| 24 | | 21 | A | Cowdenbeath | L 0-2 | 0-2 | 10 | | 255 |
| 25 | | 25 | H | Montrose | L 2-3 | 1-3 | — | McKinnon [22], Mooney [58] | 315 |
| 26 | | 28 | H | Alloa Ath | L 0-3 | 0-1 | 10 | | 396 |
| 27 | Mar | 7 | A | Albion R | D 2-2 | 1-1 | 10 | Grace [41], Sharp (pen) [55] | 417 |
| 28 | | 14 | H | Queen's Park | W 2-0 | 2-0 | 10 | Grace [21], Sharp (pen) [24] | 528 |
| 29 | | 21 | A | Arbroath | L 1-2 | 0-0 | 10 | Sharp [67] | 383 |
| 30 | | 28 | A | Ross Co | D 0-0 | 0-0 | 10 | | 1475 |
| 31 | Apr | 4 | H | East Stirling | W 1-0 | 1-0 | 10 | Wilson [30] | 338 |
| 32 | | 11 | A | Alloa Ath | L 0-3 | 0-0 | 10 | | 538 |
| 33 | | 18 | H | Albion R | W 2-0 | 1-0 | 10 | Meechan J [41], Mooney [77] | 398 |
| 34 | | 25 | H | Berwick R | L 0-2 | 0-0 | 10 | | 310 |
| 35 | May | 2 | A | Montrose | L 1-2 | 0-2 | 10 | Mooney [64] | 305 |
| 36 | | 9 | H | Cowdenbeath | L 2-3 | 1-0 | 10 | Mooney [20], McKinnon [52] | 413 |

**Final League Position: 10**          1996–97 DIV 2 9

*Most Goals Overall (Individual):* 169: Hughie Gallacher, 1954-62 (including C Division 1954-55). *(League and Cup):* 202 Hughie Gallacher, 1954-62

**Honours**
*League Champions:* Division I 1890-91 (shared with Rangers), 1891-92. Division II 1910-11, 1971-72. Second Division 1991-92; *Runners-up:* First Division 1983-84. Division II 1907-08.
*Scottish Cup Winners:* 1883; *Runners-up:* 1881, 1882, 1887, 1891, 1897. *League Cup:* —.
*Club colours:* Shirt: White with yellow horizontal band between two black bands. Shorts: White. Stockings: White with black and gold hooped tops.

**Goalscorers:** *League (42):* McKinnon 10, Sharp 7 (2 pens), Meechan J 5, Mooney 5, Grace 4, Ward 3, Brittain 2, Glancy 2, Gow 1, Mellis 1, Reilly 1, Wilson 1. *Scottish Cup (2):* McCuaig 1, Sharp 1 (pen). *Coca Cola Cup (2):* Bruce 1, McKinnon 1. *League Challenge Cup (0).*

| Meechan K 30 | Wilson W 30+2 | Brittain C 23 | Bruce J 21+1 | Gow S 21 | Mooney M 26+4 | McKinnon C 32+1 | Meechan J 36 | Reilly R 4+2 | Sharp L 34 | Glancy M 11+10 | Mellis A 5+11 | Reid D 15+1 | Melvin M 1 | Ward H 9+11 | Grace A 23+5 | Prytz R 3 | Falconer M 6+2 | Davidson W 4+2 | Currie T 15 | Ewing C 1+1 | McCuaig R 12+4 | Hingsson H 2 | Flannery P 5+6 | Jack S 11+1 | Barnes D 6 | Dalrymple C 3 | Orismaa T —+1 | Melvin W 7 | Match No. |
|---|---|---|---|---|---|---|---|---|---|---|---|---|---|---|---|---|---|---|---|---|---|---|---|---|---|---|---|---|---|
| 1 | 2 | 3 | 4 | 5 | 6 | 7 | 8 | 9¹ | 10 | 11 | 12 | | | | | | | | | | | | | | | | | | 1 |
| 1 | 8 | 3 | | 10¹ | 7 | 5 | | 6 | | 9 | | | | 2 | 4 | 11 | 12 | | | | | | | | | | | | 2 |
| 1 | 7² | 3 | 4 | 8 | 9 | 5 | 12 | 6 | 10¹ | 11 | 2 | | | 13 | | | | | | | | | | | | | | | 3 |
| 1 | 2 | 3 | | 5 | 10 | 9 | 4 | 11¹ | 6² | 7² | 13 | | | 14 | | 8 | 12 | | | | | | | | | | | | 4 |
| 1 | 2 | 3 | 5 | | 8 | 9 | 4 | 12 | 11¹ | 13 | | | | 7² | 6 | 10 | | | | | | | | | | | | | 5 |
| 1 | 2² | 3 | 5 | 4 | 7 | | 8 | 9 | 6 | 11 | | | | 12 | | 10¹ | 13 | | | | | | | | | | | | 6 |
| 1 | | 3 | 5 | | 13 | | 6 | | 4 | 12 | | 2 | | 11 | 10 | 7 | 9¹ | 8² | | | | | | | | | | | | 7 |
| 1 | 12 | 3 | 5 | | 9 | 8 | 10 | 4 | | | 2¹ | | | 13 | 6 | 7² | 11 | | | | | | | | | | | | 8 |
| 1 | 7² | 11 | 4 | | 5 | 9 | 6 | | | 12 | | 2 | | 13 | 8 | | | | 3 | 10¹ | | | | | | | | | 9 |
| 1 | | 6 | 5 | | 8 | 9 | 4 | | | 10 | | 2 | | 11 | 7¹ | 12 | | 3 | | | | | | | | | | | 10 |
| 1 | | 6 | 4 | | 11 | 8 | | 3 | | 12 | 2 | | | 7 | | | 5 | | 9¹ | 10 | | | | | | | | | 11 |
| 1 | 13 | 11 | 5 | | | 8 | 6 | | 3 | 12 | 2 | | | 7² | | | 4 | | 10¹ | 9 | | | | | | | | | 12 |
| 1 | 11 | 5 | | | 8 | 6 | | 3 | 13 | 7 | 2 | | | 12 | | 9¹ | 4 | | 10² | | | | | | | | | | 13 |
| 1 | 2 | 11 | 5 | 12 | 8 | 6 | | 3 | | 7 | | | | 13 | | 9¹ | 4 | | 10² | | | | | | | | | | 14 |
| 1 | 2 | 11 | 5 | 10 | 8 | 6 | | 3 | 12 | 7¹ | | | | 9 | | | 4 | | | | | | | | | | | | 15 |
| 1 | 2 | 11 | 5 | 10 | 8 | 6 | | 3 | 12 | | | | | 9¹ | | 7 | 4 | | | | | | | | | | | | 16 |
| 1 | 2 | 11¹ | 5 | 10 | 8 | 6 | | 3 | 9 | 13 | | | | 12 | | 7² | 4 | | | | | | | | | | | | 17 |
| 1 | 2 | 11 | 5 | 10¹ | 8 | 6 | | 3 | 13 | | | | | 7³ | | 14 | 4 | | 12 | 9² | | | | | | | | | 18 |
| 1 | 2 | 11 | 5¹ | 14 | 9 | 6 | | 3 | | 7² | | | | 13 | 12 | | 4 | | 10³ | 8 | | | | | | | | | 19 |
| 1 | 2 | 3⁴ | | 5 | 10 | 11 | | 8 | 6 | 12 | | | | 13 | 14 | | 4 | | 7² | 9¹ | | | | | | | | | 20 |
| 1 | 2 | 3¹ | 4 | 5 | 6 | | 9 | 8 | 11 | | | | | 12 | 7 | | | | 13 | 10² | | | | | | | | | 21 |
| 1 | 2 | | 4 | 5 | | 9 | 8 | | 3 | 13 | | | | 11² | 7 | | | 12 | | 10¹ | 6 | | | | | | | | 22 |
| 1 | 2 | | 4 | 5 | | 9 | 8 | | 11 | | | | | | 7 | | | 3 | 10 | | 6 | | | | | | | | 23 |
| 1 | 2 | | 4 | 5 | 13 | 9 | 8 | | 11 | | | | | 12 | 7² | | | 3 | 10³ | 14 | 6¹ | | | | | | | | 24 |
| 1 | 2 | | 4 | 6 | 9 | 8 | | 3 | | | | | | 11 | 7 | | | 5 | 10¹ | 12 | | | | | | | | | 25 |
| 1 | 2 | | 5 | 4 | 6² | 9 | 8 | | 3 | | | | | 11 | 7 | | | | 10¹ | 12 | 13 | | | | | | | | 26 |
| | | | | | 10 | | 4 | 8 | 5 | | 11 | | | 2 | 7 | | 12 | | 9¹ | | | | 6 | 1 | 3 | | | | 27 |
| | | | | | 10 | | 4 | 8 | 12 | 5 | 11 | | | 13 | 7 | | | | 9² | | | | 6 | 1 | 3¹ | | | | 28 |
| | | | | | 10 | | 4 | 8 | 9² | 5 | 11 | | | 13 | 7 | | | | | | | | 6 | 1 | 3¹ | 12 | | | 29 |
| | | | | | 10¹ | | 4 | 8 | 9 | 5 | 3 | | | 12 | 7 | | | | | | | | 6 | 1 | | | | 11 | 30 |
| | | | | | 10 | | 4 | 8¹ | 9 | 5 | 3 | 12 | | 13 | 7 | | | | 2² | | | | 6 | 1 | | | | 11 | 31 |
| | | | | | 10 | | 4 | 8 | 9 | 5 | 3 | | | 12 | 7 | | | | 2¹ | | | | 6 | 1 | | | | 11 | 32 |
| 1 | 10 | | 4 | | 8 | 9 | 5 | | 3 | | | | | 2¹ | 12 | | | | 7² | | 13 | 6 | | | | | | 11 | 33 |
| 1 | 10 | | 4 | | 8 | 9 | 5 | | 3 | | | | | 2 | 7 | | | | | | 12 | 6¹ | | | | | | 11 | 34 |
| 1 | 2 | 3 | 12 | 5 | 8 | 9 | 6 | | 4 | 11² | | | | 10 | | | | | 13 | | | | | | | | | 7¹ | 35 |
| 1 | 10 | 6 | | 4 | 8 | 9 | 5 | | 3 | 2² | | | | 14 | 7¹ | | | | 12 | | 13 | | | | | | | 11³ | 36 |

# DUNDEE                                    Premier League

*Year Formed:* 1893. *Ground & Address:* Dens Park Stadium, Sandeman St, Dundee DD3 7JY. *Telephone:* 01382 826104.
*Fax:* 01382 832284.
*Ground Capacity:* 14,177. seated: 10,877. *Size of Pitch:* 110yd × 72yd.
*Chairman:* Jim Marr. *Chief Executive:* Peter Marr.
*Manager:* John Scott. *Assistant Manager:* Jimmy Bone. *Youth Coach:* Ray Farningham. *Physio:* Jim Crosby. *Youth Development:* Kenny Cameron.
*Managers since 1975:* David White; Tommy Gemmell; Donald Mackay; Archie Knox; Jocky Scott; Dave Smith; Gordon Wallace; Iain Munro; Simon Stainrod; Jim Duffy, John McCormack. *Club Nickname(s):* The Dark Blues or The Dee.
*Previous Grounds:* Carolina Port 1893-98.
*Record Attendance:* 43,024 v Rangers, Scottish Cup; 1953.
*Record Transfer Fee received:* £500,000 for Tommy Coyne to Celtic (March 1989).
*Record Transfer Fee paid:* £200,000 for Jim Leighton (Feb 1992).
*Record Victory:* 10-0 Division II v Alloa; 9 Mar, 1947 and v Dunfermline Ath; 22 Mar, 1947.
*Record Defeat:* 0-11 v Celtic, Division I; 26 Oct, 1895.
*Most Capped Player:* Alex Hamilton, 24, Scotland.
*Most League Appearances:* 341: Doug Cowie 1945-61.
*Most League Goals in Season (Individual):* 52: Alan Gilzean, 1963-64.
*Most Goals Overall (Individual):* 113: Alan Gilzean.

## DUNDEE 1997–98 LEAGUE RECORD

| Match No. | Date | Venue | Opponents | Result | H/T Score | Lg. Pos. | Goalscorers | Attendance |
|---|---|---|---|---|---|---|---|---|
| 1 | Aug 2 | H | Falkirk | W 3-0 | 1-0 | — | O'Driscoll [25], Annand [60], Elliott (pen) [89] | 4427 |
| 2 | 16 | A | Partick Th | W 3-0 | 1-0 | 1 | Annand (pen) [30], Grady [65], Maddison [75] | 2450 |
| 3 | 23 | H | St Mirren | W 1-0 | 1-0 | 1 | Annand [18] | 3571 |
| 4 | 30 | H | Raith R | D 2-2 | 2-0 | 1 | Grady [20], Annand [30] | 4461 |
| 5 | Sept13 | A | Ayr U | W 2-1 | 1-0 | 1 | Annand [30], Anderson (pen) [77] | 2180 |
| 6 | 20 | H | Hamilton A | L 0-2 | 0-2 | 2 | | 3611 |
| 7 | 27 | A | Greenock Morton | W 2-0 | 0-0 | 2 | Kelly [62], Anderson [80] | 2342 |
| 8 | Oct 4 | H | Airdrieonians | W 1-0 | 0-0 | 2 | Rogers [83] | 3086 |
| 9 | 18 | A | Stirling A | W 2-1 | 0-1 | 1 | Anderson [67], Smith [86] | 1538 |
| 10 | 25 | H | Falkirk | D 1-1 | 0-1 | 1 | Elliott [64] | 4076 |
| 11 | Nov 1 | H | Partick Th | D 0-0 | 0-0 | 2 | | 3560 |
| 12 | 8 | A | Raith R | W 1-0 | 0-0 | 2 | McInally [70] | 4763 |
| 13 | 15 | H | Ayr U | W 4-0 | 4-0 | 1 | Grady 2 [2, 18], Annand [25], Kelly [38] | 2921 |
| 14 | 22 | A | Greenock Morton | L 0-1 | 0-0 | 1 | | 3489 |
| 15 | 29 | A | Hamilton A | W 4-0 | 1-0 | 1 | Grady 3 (1 pen) [38, 57, 83 (pl)], McCulloch (og) [64] | 1967 |
| 16 | Dec 6 | A | Airdrieonians | D 0-0 | 0-0 | 1 | | 1996 |
| 17 | 13 | H | Stirling A | D 0-0 | 0-0 | 1 | | 2751 |
| 18 | 20 | A | St Mirren | W 2-0 | 0-0 | 1 | Anderson [80], Grady [89] | 3165 |
| 19 | 27 | H | Falkirk | L 0-1 | 0-1 | 1 | | 5074 |
| 20 | Jan 3 | A | Raith R | D 1-1 | 0-1 | 1 | Anderson [48] | 5304 |
| 21 | 10 | A | Ayr U | W 5-2 | 3-2 | 1 | Irvine [18], Grady 3 [25, 55, 65], McCormick [30] | 2067 |
| 22 | 17 | A | Greenock Morton | D 0-0 | 0-0 | 1 | | 2200 |
| 23 | 31 | H | Hamilton A | D 1-1 | 1-0 | 1 | McCormick [44] | 3028 |
| 24 | Feb 7 | A | Stirling A | W 3-1 | 2-0 | 1 | McGlashan [35], McCormick [40], Grady [70] | 1632 |
| 25 | 21 | A | Airdrieonians | W 1-0 | 0-0 | 1 | McCormick [70] | 3239 |
| 26 | 25 | A | Partick Th | W 2-1 | 1-1 | — | Annand 2 [1, 76] | 2244 |
| 27 | 28 | H | St Mirren | W 1-0 | 1-0 | 1 | Grady [2] | 3365 |
| 28 | Mar 14 | H | Greenock Morton | W 2-0 | 2-0 | 1 | Anderson [12], Adamczuk [41] | 3432 |
| 29 | 21 | A | Hamilton A | W 2-1 | 2-1 | 1 | Grady [12], Robertson [40] | 1180 |
| 30 | 28 | A | Stirling A | W 2-0 | 2-0 | 1 | Annand 2 [10, 30] | 3142 |
| 31 | Apr 4 | H | Airdrieonians | W 2-1 | 1-1 | 1 | Annand [17], McCormick [84] | 2058 |
| 32 | 11 | A | Raith R | D 1-1 | 0-0 | 1 | Annand [60] | 6985 |
| 33 | 18 | H | Ayr U | D 1-1 | 1-1 | 1 | Grady (pen) [34] | 7564 |
| 34 | 25 | A | Falkirk | L 0-1 | 0-0 | 1 | | 4169 |
| 35 | May 2 | H | Partick Th | L 0-3 | 0-3 | 1 | | 3609 |
| 36 | 9 | A | St Mirren | L 0-1 | 0-1 | 1 | | 2460 |

**Final League Position: 1**          1996–97 3

**Honours**

*League Champions:* Division I 1961-62. First Division 1978-79, 1991-92, 1997-98. Division II 1946-47; *Runners-up:* Division I 1902-03, 1906-07, 1908-09, 1948-49, 1980-81.
*Scottish Cup Winners:* 1910; *Runners-up:* 1925, 1952, 1964.
*League Cup Winners:* 1951-52, 1952-53, 1973-74; *Runners-up:* 1967-68, 1980-81. *(Coca-Cola Cup):* 1995–96.
*B&Q (Centenary) Cup: Winners:* 1990-91 *Runners-up:* 1994-95.

**European:** *European Cup:* 8 matches (1962-63 semi-finals). *Cup Winners' Cup:* 2 matches: (1964-65).
*UEFA Cup:* 18 matches: (*Fairs Cup:* 1967-68 semi-finals. *UEFA Cup:* 1971-72, 1973-74, 1974-75).
*Club colours:* Shirt: Dark blue with red and white trim. Shorts: White. Stockings: Blue and white.

**Goalscorers:** *League (52):* Grady 15 (2 pens), Annand 12 (1 pen), Anderson 6 (1 pen), McCormick 5, Elliott 2 (1 pen), Kelly 2, Adamczuk 1, Irvine 1, McGlashan 1, McInally 1, Maddison 1, O'Driscoll 1, Robertson 1, Rogers 1 (pen), Smith 1, own goal 1. *Scottish Cup (9):* Grady 3, Annand 2, McCormick 1, McGlashan 1, Maddison 1, Raeside 1. *Coca Cola Cup (1):* O'Driscoll 1. *League Challenge Cup (0).*

| Douglas R 36 | Smith B 34 | Maddison L 19 + 5 | Adamczuk D 34 | Irvine B 36 | Rogers D 31 + 1 | Magee D 11 + 6 | Grady J 38 | Annand E 27 + 7 | O'Driscoll J 1 + 12 | McInally J 32 | Anderson I 32 + 4 | Elliott J 1 + 16 | McGlashan J 5 + 3 | Tully C 4 + 10 | Kelly R 16 + 3 | Fleming D 15 + 2 | Rae G 1 + 5 | Bayne G — + 2 | Milne K 1 + 1 | McCormick S 6 + 8 | Raeside R 9 + 2 | Robertson J 4 | Grant B 5 + 3 | Farningham R — + 1 | Match No. |
|---|---|---|---|---|---|---|---|---|---|---|---|---|---|---|---|---|---|---|---|---|---|---|---|---|---|
| 1 | 2 | 3 | 4 | 5 | 6 | 7 | 8 | 9¹ | 10² | 11 | 12 | 13 | | | | | | | | | | | | | 1 |
| 1 | 2 | 3 | 4 | 5 | 6 | 10¹ | 8 | 9³ | 12 | 11² | 7 | | 13 | 14 | | | | | | | | | | | 2 |
| 1 | 2 | 3 | 4 | 5 | 6 | 10 | 8 | 9¹ | 12 | 11 | 7² | | 13 | | | | | | | | | | | | 3 |
| 1 | 2 | 3 | 4² | 5 | 6 | 10¹ | 8 | 9 | | 11 | 7 | 12 | 13 | | | | | | | | | | | | 4 |
| 1 | 2 | 3¹ | 4 | 5 | 6 | 10 | 8 | 9 | 13 | 11 | 7 | | 12² | | | | | | | | | | | | 5 |
| 1 | 2 | | 4 | 5² | 6 | 10 | 8² | 9¹ | 12 | 11 | 7 | 14 | | | | 3 | 13 | | | | | | | | 6 |
| 1 | 2 | | 4 | 5 | 6 | 10 | 8 | 9 | | 11 | 7 | | | | 8¹ | 3 | 12 | | | | | | | | 7 |
| 1 | 2 | | 4 | 5 | 6² | 10 | 13 | 9¹ | 12 | 11 | 7 | 14 | | | 8² | 3 | | | | | | | | | 8 |
| 1 | 2 | | 4¹ | 5 | 6 | 10 | | 9 | | 11 | 7³ | 14 | 13 | 12 | 8² | 3 | | | | | | | | | 9 |
| 1 | 2 | 13 | 4 | 5 | 6 | 10 | | 9 | | 11 | 7¹ | | | 12 | 8² | 3 | | | | | | | | | 10 |
| 1 | 2 | | 4 | 5 | 6 | 10 | | 9² | 13 | 11 | 7³ | 14 | | | 8¹ | 12 | 3 | | | | | | | | 11 |
| 1 | 2 | 8 | 4 | 5 | 6 | 10¹ | 7² | 9¹ | | 11 | 13 | 14 | 12 | | | 3 | | | | | | | | | 12 |
| 1 | 2 | 3 | 4 | 5 | 6 | 10² | 14 | 9¹ | 13 | 11 | 7 | 12 | | | 8³ | | | | | | | | | | 13 |
| 1 | 2 | 3¹ | 4 | 5 | 6 | 10 | | 9¹ | 12 | 11 | 7 | | | | 8² | 13 | 14 | | | | | | | | 14 |
| 1 | 2 | 12 | 4¹ | 5 | 6 | 10² | 14 | 9 | | 11 | 7 | 13 | | | 8³ | 3 | | | | | | | | | 15 |
| 1 | 2 | 14 | 4 | 5 | 6 | 10² | | 9¹ | 12 | 11 | 7 | 13 | | | 8 | 3³ | | | | | | | | | 16 |
| 1 | 2 | | 4 | 5 | 6 | 10 | | 9¹ | | 11 | 7 | 12 | | | 8² | 3 | 13 | | | | | | | | 17 |
| 1 | 2 | 13 | | 5 | 6 | 10 | 14 | | | 11¹ | 7 | | | 4² | 8 | 3 | 12 | | | 9³ | | | | | 18 |
| 1 | 2 | 13 | 4² | 5³ | 6 | 10 | | 9¹ | 12 | 11 | 7 | | | | 8 | 3 | | | 14 | | | | | | 19 |
| 1 | 2 | | 4 | 5 | 6 | 10 | | | | 11 | | 12 | | | 8 | 3 | | 4² | | 9¹ | | | | | 20 |
| 1 | 2 | 3 | 4 | 5 | 6 | 10¹ | | | 12 | 11² | 7 | 14 | 13 | | 8 | | | | | 9¹ | | | | | 21 |
| 1 | 2 | 3 | 4 | 5 | 6 | 10 | | | 13 | 11¹ | 7 | 14 | 12 | | 8³ | | | | | 9² | | | | | 22 |
| 1 | 2 | 3 | 4 | 5 | 6 | 10 | | | 12 | 11 | 7 | 13 | | | 8¹ | | | | | 9² | | | | | 23 |
| 1 | 2 | 3¹ | 4 | 5 | 6 | 10 | | 14 | 12 | 11 | 7¹ | 13 | | | 8 | | | | | 9² | | | | | 24 |
| 1 | 2 | 8 | 4 | 5 | 6² | 10 | | 9 | | 11¹ | 7³ | 13 | 14 | 12 | | 3 | | | | | | | | | 25 |
| 1 | 2 | 3 | 4 | 5 | 6 | 10 | | 9 | | 11 | 7² | 12 | 13 | | | | | | | | 8¹ | | | | 26 |
| 1 | 2 | 7² | 4 | 5 | 6 | 10 | | 9¹ | | 11 | | 12 | 13 | 14 | | | | | | | 3³ | 8 | | | 27 |
| 1 | 2 | 3 | 4² | 5 | 6¹ | 10 | 8 | | | 11 | 7 | 14 | | | | | | | | 12 | 9³ | | 13 | | 28 |
| 1 | 2 | 3¹ | 4 | 5 | 12 | 10 | | | 13 | 11 | 7³ | 14 | | | | | | | | 9 | 8² | | 6 | | 29 |
| 1 | 2 | 3 | 4 | 5 | | 10 | 8 | 9 | | 11 | 7¹ | | | | | | | | | 12 | 6 | | | | 30 |
| 1 | 2 | 3 | 4 | 5 | | 10 | 8 | 9² | | 11 | | 12 | 13 | | | | | | | | 6 | 7¹ | | | 31 |
| 1 | 2 | 3 | 4 | 5¹ | | 10 | 8 | 9² | | 11 | 7³ | | 13 | 14 | | | | | | | 6 | | 12 | | 32 |
| 1 | 2 | | 4 | 5 | | 10 | | 9 | 13 | 11 | 7² | | 3³ | 14 | | | | | | | 6¹ | | 12 | | 33 |
| 1 | 2¹ | | 4 | 5 | | 10 | | 9² | | 11 | 7 | 8 | | | | 3 | | | | 12 | 6 | | 13 | | 34 |
| 1 | | 3³ | 4 | 5 | | 10 | | 9 | 13 | 11 | 7 | | | 14 | 8² | | | | | | 6¹ | 2 | 12 | | 35 |
| 1 | | 3 | | 5 | | 10 | | | | 11 | 7 | 12 | | | 8 | | | | | 9¹ | 6 | 2 | 4² | 13 | 36 |

# DUNDEE UNITED

## Premier League

*Year Formed:* 1909 (1923). *Ground & Address:* Tannadice Park, Tannadice St, Dundee DD3 7JW. *Telephone:* 01382 833166. *Fax:* 01382 889398. *Ground Capacity:* total: 14,209 all seated: stands: east 2868, west 2096, south 2201, Fair Play 1601, George Fox 5151, executive boxes 292.
*Size of Pitch:* 110yd × 74yd.
*Chairman:* James Y. McLean. *Company Secretary:* Miss Priti Trivedi. *Commercial Manager:* Bill Campbell.
*Manager:* Thomas McLean. *Coaches:* Maurice Malpas, Gordon Wallace. *Physio:* David Rankine.
*Managers since 1975:* J. McLean, I.Golac, W. Kirkwood. *Club Nickname(s):* The Terrors. *Previous Grounds:* None.
*Record Attendance:* 28,000 v Barcelona, Fairs Cup; 16 Nov, 1966.
*Record Transfer Fee received:* £4,000,000 for Duncan Ferguson from Rangers (July 1993).
*Record Transfer Fee paid:* £750,000 for Steven Pressley from Coventry C (July 1995).
*Record Victory:* 14-0 v Nithsdale Wanderers, Scottish Cup 1st rd; 17 Jan, 1931.
*Record Defeat:* 1-12 v Motherwell, Division II; 23 Jan, 1954.
*Most Capped Player:* Maurice Malpas, 55, Scotland.
*Most League Appearances:* 612, Dave Narey; 1973-94.
*Most Appearances in European Matches:* 76, Dave Narey (record for Scottish player).
*Most League Goals in Season (Individual):* 41: John Coyle, Division II; 1955-56.
*Most Goals Overall (Individual):* 158: Peter McKay.

## DUNDEE UNITED 1997–98 LEAGUE RECORD

| Match No. | Date | Venue | Opponents | Result | H/T Score | Lg. Pos. | Goalscorers | Attendance |
|---|---|---|---|---|---|---|---|---|
| 1 | Aug 2 | A | St Johnstone | D | 1-1 | 1-0 | — | Olofsson [12] | 6492 |
| 2 | 17 | H | Hibernian | D | 1-1 | 1-0 | 7 | Winters [22] | 7344 |
| 3 | 23 | A | Rangers | L | 1-5 | 0-3 | 8 | Pressley (pen) [68] | 48,599 |
| 4 | 30 | A | Aberdeen | D | 1-1 | 1-1 | 8 | Winters [32] | 12,060 |
| 5 | Sept13 | H | Kilmarnock | L | 1-2 | 0-1 | 10 | Olofsson [63] | 6883 |
| 6 | 20 | A | Hearts | L | 1-2 | 1-1 | 9 | Olofsson [45] | 13,515 |
| 7 | 27 | H | Celtic | L | 1-2 | 0-2 | 9 | Olofsson [60] | 11,668 |
| 8 | Oct 4 | A | Dunfermline Ath | D | 3-3 | 3-0 | 9 | Winters 2 [7, 42], McLaren [45] | 5829 |
| 9 | 18 | H | Motherwell | W | 4-0 | 2-0 | 9 | Olofsson [2], Winters [12], McSwegan [80], McLaren [88] | 7337 |
| 10 | 25 | H | Rangers | W | 2-1 | 1-0 | 8 | Winters [16], Pressley (pen) [72] | 12,600 |
| 11 | Nov 1 | A | Hibernian | W | 3-1 | 1-0 | 5 | Olofsson 2 [26, 87], McSwegan [89] | 10,110 |
| 12 | 9 | H | Aberdeen | W | 5-0 | 3-0 | — | Olofsson 2 [17, 83], Zetterlund [18], McLaren [21], Easton [87] | 7893 |
| 13 | 15 | A | Kilmarnock | W | 3-1 | 0-1 | 4 | Perry [65], McSwegan [77], Olofsson [84] | 7402 |
| 14 | 22 | A | Celtic | L | 0-4 | 0-1 | 4 | | 48,200 |
| 15 | Dec 6 | H | Dunfermline Ath | D | 0-0 | 0-0 | 4 | | 6685 |
| 16 | 9 | H | Hearts | D | 0-0 | 0-0 | — | | 10,402 |
| 17 | 13 | A | Motherwell | L | 0-1 | 0-0 | 4 | | 4555 |
| 18 | 20 | H | St Johnstone | W | 2-1 | 2-0 | 4 | McLaren [10], Olofsson [27] | 7342 |
| 19 | 27 | A | Rangers | L | 1-4 | 1-2 | 5 | Olofsson [28] | 50,017 |
| 20 | Jan 3 | A | Aberdeen | L | 0-1 | 0-1 | 6 | | 17,025 |
| 21 | 10 | H | Kilmarnock | D | 1-1 | 1-0 | 6 | Winters [15] | 7541 |
| 22 | 27 | H | Celtic | L | 1-2 | 1-0 | — | Olofsson [23] | 14,004 |
| 23 | 31 | A | Hearts | L | 0-2 | 0-1 | 6 | | 14,414 |
| 24 | Feb 7 | H | Motherwell | W | 1-0 | 0-0 | 6 | Olofsson [68] | 6532 |
| 25 | 21 | A | Dunfermline Ath | D | 2-2 | 1-0 | 6 | McSwegan 2 [40, 90] | 5250 |
| 26 | 24 | H | Hibernian | D | 1-1 | 0-0 | — | Dow (og) [73] | 7989 |
| 27 | 28 | A | St Johnstone | D | 1-1 | 1-0 | 6 | Winters [23] | 5637 |
| 28 | Mar 15 | A | Celtic | D | 1-1 | 0-1 | — | Olofsson [75] | 48,564 |
| 29 | 21 | H | Hearts | L | 0-1 | 0-1 | 6 | | 10,400 |
| 30 | 28 | A | Motherwell | D | 0-0 | 0-0 | 6 | | 5012 |
| 31 | Apr 7 | A | Dunfermline Ath | D | 2-2 | 0-2 | — | Olofsson [48], Malpas [70] | 7769 |
| 32 | 11 | H | Aberdeen | D | 0-0 | 0-0 | 6 | | 9155 |
| 33 | 18 | A | Kilmarnock | L | 0-1 | 0-1 | 6 | | 7468 |
| 34 | 25 | H | St Johnstone | L | 0-2 | 0-0 | 8 | | 8045 |
| 35 | May 2 | A | Hibernian | W | 2-1 | 0-1 | 6 | Olofsson 2 [72, 78] | 13,413 |
| 36 | 9 | H | Rangers | L | 1-2 | 0-1 | 7 | Zetterlund [65] | 14,200 |

**Final League Position: 7**        1996–97 3

**Honours**

*League Champions:* Premier Division 1982-83. Division II 1924-25, 1928-29; *Runners-up:* Division II 1930-31, 1959-60. First Division Runners-up 1995-96.

*Scottish Cup Winners:* 1994; *Runners-up:* 1974, 1981, 1985, 1987, 1988, 1991.

*League Cup Winners:* 1979-80, 1980-81;*Runners-up:* 1981-82, 1984-85, 1997-98.

*Summer Cup Runners-up:* 1964-65. *Scottish War Cup Runners-up:* 1939-40.

**European:** *European Cup:* 8 matches (1983-84, semi-finals). *Cup Winners' Cup:* 10 matches (1974-75, 1988-89, 1994-95). *UEFA Cup:* 84 matches (*Fairs Cup:* 1966-67, 1969-70, 1970-71. *UEFA Cup:* 1975-76, 1977-78, 1978-79, 1979-80, 1980-81, 1981-82, 1982-83, 1984-85, 1985-86, 1986-87 runners-up, 1987-88, 1989-90, 1990-91, 1993-94, 1997-98).

*Club colours:* Tangerine and black shirt, black shorts, tangerine and black hoops.

**Goalscorers:** *League (43):* Olofsson 18, Winters 8, McSwegan 5, McLaren 4, Pressley 2 (pens), Zetterlund 2, Easton 1, Malpas 1, Perry 1, own goal 1. *Scottish Cup (7):* Olofsson 4, McSwegan 1, Winters 1, Zetterlund 1. *Coca Cola Cup (10):* McSwegan 5, Winters 2, Easton 1, Thompson 1, Zetterlund 1.

| Dijkstra S 36 | McKimmie S 3 + 1 | Malpas M 31 | Pressley S 29 | Perry M 32 | Pedersen E 32 | Olofsson K 31 + 1 | Zetterlund L 32 + 1 | Winters R 23 + 7 | Bowman D 15 + 4 | McSwegan G 17 + 14 | McLaren A 15 + 12 | Dolan J 21 + 5 | Thompson S 3 + 5 | Duffy C 1 + 6 | Easton C 20 + 9 | McKinnon R 7 + 2 | Walker P 1 | Marklund G 1 + 2 | Skoldmark M 15 + 4 | Sinclair D — + 4 | Andersson M 1 + 2 | Jonsson S 14 + 1 | Misse-Misse J 4 | Omoyinmi E 1 + 3 | Crawford J — + 2 | Jenkins I 7 | Alsford J 3 | Vaile O 1 | Gill W — + 2 | Match No. |
|---|---|---|---|---|---|---|---|---|---|---|---|---|---|---|---|---|---|---|---|---|---|---|---|---|---|---|---|---|---|---|
| 1 | 2² | 3 | 4 | 5 | 6 | 7 | 8 | 9¹ | 10 | 11 | 12 | 13 | | | | | | | | | | | | | | | | | | 1 |
| 1 | | 3 | 4 | 5 | 6 | 14 | 8 | 7³ | 2 | 9¹ | 12 | 10 | 11¹² | 13 | | | | | | | | | | | | | | | | 2 |
| 1 | 3 | 4 | 5 | 6 | 7 | 8 | 9² | 2 | 13 | | | 12 | | | 11¹ | 10 | | | | | | | | | | | | | | 3 |
| 1 | 3 | 4 | 5 | 6 | | 8 | 9² | 2 | 13 | 11 | 12 | | | | 7¹ | 10 | | | | | | | | | | | | | | 4 |
| 1 | 3 | 4 | 5 | 6 | 7 | 8 | | 9 | 13 | 10¹ | | | | | 14 | 2³ | | 11² | 12 | | | | | | | | | | | 5 |
| 1 | | 4 | 5 | 6 | 7 | 8 | | 2 | | 11² | 10¹ | | | | 13 | | | 9 | 12 | | 3 | | | | | | | | | 6 |
| 1 | 3 | 4 | 5 | 6 | 7 | 8 | | 9 | 13 | 14 | 12 | | | | 4¹ | | | 10² | 2³ | | | | | | | | | | | 7 |
| 1 | 3 | 4 | 5 | 6 | 7 | 8 | 9² | 10 | 13 | 11¹ | 12 | | | | 2 | | | | | | | | | | | | | | | 8 |
| 1 | 3 | 4 | 5 | 6 | 7³ | 8 | 9¹ | 12 | 11 | 2 | 13 | | | | 10 | | | | | | | | | | | | | | | 9 |
| 1 | 3 | 4 | 5 | 6 | 7 | 8 | 9² | | 13 | 11 | 2¹ | | | | 10 | | | 12 | | | | | | | | | | | | 10 |
| 1 | 3 | 4 | 5 | 6 | 7 | 8 | 9¹ | 12 | 11² | | | | | | 10 | | | 2 | 13 | | | | | | | | | | | 11 |
| 1 | 3 | 4 | 5 | 6 | 7 | 8 | 9³ | 14 | 11² | 12 | | | | | 10 | | | 2¹ | 13 | | | | | | | | | | | 12 |
| 1 | 14 | 3 | 4 | 5 | 6 | 7 | 8 | 9 | 13 | 12 | 2¹ | | | | 10 | | | | 11² | | | | | | | | | | | 13 |
| 1 | 2³ | 3 | 4 | 5 | 6 | 7 | 8 | 12 | | 9¹ | | 11² | | | 10 | | | | 13 | 14 | | | | | | | | | | 14 |
| 1 | 3¹ | 4 | 5 | 6 | 7 | 8 | 9 | 14 | 11³ | | | | | | 10 | 13 | | 12 | | | 2² | | | | | | | | | 15 |
| 1 | 3 | 4 | 5 | 6 | 7³ | 8 | 9 | 2¹ | 13 | 11 | | | | | 10 | | | 12 | | | | | | | | | | | | 16 |
| 1 | 3 | 4 | 5 | 6 | 7 | 8 | 9 | 12 | 13 | 11 | | | | | 10² | | | 2¹ | | | | | | | | | | | | 17 |
| 1 | 3 | 4 | 5 | 6 | 7 | 8 | 13 | 9² | 11 | 2 | | 12 | | | 10¹ | | | 12 | | | | | | | | | | | | 18 |
| 1 | 3 | 4 | 5 | 6³ | 7 | 8 | 13 | 9 | 11² | | | 10¹ | 14 | | 12 | | | | 2 | | | | | | | | | | | 19 |
| 1 | 3 | 4 | 5 | | 7 | 8² | 9 | 10² | 13 | 12 | | 14 | | 11¹ | 6 | | | 2 | | | | | | | | | | | | 20 |
| 1 | | 4 | 5 | 6 | 7 | 8² | 9 | 13 | | 12 | | | | | 10 | | | 3 | | | 2 | 11¹ | | | | | | | | 21 |
| 1 | | 4 | 5 | 6 | 7¹ | 8 | 12 | 3 | 9 | 11 | | | | | | 13 | | | 2 | | | 10 | | | | | | | | 22 |
| 1 | 3 | 4 | 5 | 6 | 7 | 8 | 12 | 2² | 9¹ | 11 | | | | | 13 | | | | | | | 10 | | | | | | | | 23 |
| 1 | 3 | 4 | 5 | 6 | | 8 | 7 | 9¹ | | 12 | 10 | | | | | | | 2 | | | | 11 | | | | | | | | 24 |
| 1 | 3 | 4 | 5 | 6 | | 8 | 7 | | 9² | 10 | | | | | 13 | | | 2 | | | | 11¹ | 12 | | | | | | | 25 |
| 1 | 3 | 4 | 5 | 6 | | 8 | 7 | 2³ | 9² | | 10 | | | | 12 | | | | | | | 11¹ | 13 | 14 | | | | | | 26 |
| 1 | 3 | 4 | 5 | 6 | | 8 | | 9³ | | 11² | 13 | 14 | 12 | 10 | | | | | 2¹ | | 7 | | | | | | | | | 27 |
| 1 | 3 | 4 | 5 | 6 | 7 | | 8¹ | 9² | 2 | | 12 | 10 | | 11 | | | 4 | | | | | 2 | | | | 13 | | | | 28 |
| 1 | 3 | | 5 | 6 | 7 | | 2 | 13 | | 10¹ | 9³ | 14 | 8 | 11² | 4 | | | | | | | 12 | | | | | | | | 29 |
| 1 | | 5 | 6 | 7 | 11¹ | 13 | 9 | | 10 | | 12 | 8 | | | | | | 2 | | | | | | 3 | 4² | | | | | 30 |
| 1 | 3 | | 6² | 7 | | 11³ | 12 | 9 | | 10 | 14 | 13 | | | | | | 4¹ | | | 8 | | | 2 | 5 | | | | | 31 |
| 1 | 3 | | 6 | 7 | | | 12 | 9² | 11 | 10 | 13 | 8 | | | | | | | | | 4 | | | 2 | 5¹ | | | | | 32 |
| 1 | 3 | 4¹ | 5 | | 7 | 12 | 13 | 14 | 9¹ | 10 | | | | 8 | | | | | | | 6 | | | 2 | | | 11² | | | 33 |
| 1 | 3 | | 5 | 6 | 7 | 8³ | 11 | 9 | 12 | 10² | | 8 | | 14 | | | | 4 | | | | | | 2 | | | | 13 | | 34 |
| 1 | 3 | 4 | | 7 | 8³ | 6 | 9 | 12 | 10² | | 13 | 11¹ | | 14 | | | 5 | | | | | | | 2 | | | | | | 35 |
| 1 | 3 | | 7 | 8³ | 6 | 9 | 11² | | 13 | 10 | | | | 4 | 12 | | | 5¹ | | | | | | 2 | | | | 14 | | 36 |

# DUNFERMLINE ATHLETIC  Premier League

*Year Formed:* 1885. *Ground & Address:* East End Park, Halbeath Rd, Dunfermline KY12 7RB. *Telephone:* 01383 724295. *Fax:* 01383 723468.
*Ground Capacity:* 12,500 (all seated). *Size of Pitch:* 115yd × 71yd.
*Chairman:* C. R. Woodrow. *Secretary:* P. A. M. D'Mello. *Commercial Manager:* Miss Audrey Bastianelli.
*Manager:* Bert Paton. *Assistant Manager:* Dick Campbell.
*Physio:* Philip Yeates, MCSP. *Youth Development Manager:* David McParland.
*Managers since 1975:* G. Miller; H. Melrose; P. Stanton; T. Forsyth; J. Leishman; I. Munro; J. Scott. *Club Nickname(s):* The Pars. *Previous Grounds:* None.
*Record Attendance:* 27,816 v Celtic, Division I, 30 April, 1968.
*Record Transfer Fee received:* £650,000 for Jackie McNamara to Celtic (Oct 1995).
*Record Transfer Fee paid:* £540,000 for Istvan Kozma from Bordeaux (Sept 1989).
*Record Victory:* 11-2 v Stenhousemuir, Division II, 27 Sept, 1930.
*Record Defeat:* 1-11 v Hibernian, Scottish Cup, 3rd rd replay, 26 Oct, 1889.
*Most Capped Player:* Colin Miller 15(59), Canada.
*Most League Appearances:* 497: Norrie McCathie; 1981-96.
*Most League Goals in Season (Individual):* 53: Bobby Skinner, Division II, 1925-26.
*Most Goals Overall (Individual):* 154: Charles Dickson.

## DUNFERMLINE ATHLETIC 1997–98 LEAGUE RECORD

| Match No. | Date | Venue | Opponents | Result | | H/T Score | Lg. Pos. | Goalscorers | Atten- dance |
|---|---|---|---|---|---|---|---|---|---|
| 1 | Aug 2 | H | Motherwell | L | 0-2 | 0-0 | — | | 5624 |
| 2 | 16 | A | Celtic | W | 2-1 | 0-1 | 6 | Bingham [46], French (pen) [76] | 45,120 |
| 3 | 23 | H | Hearts | W | 2-1 | 0-0 | 4 | Smith [58], Tod [68] | 8823 |
| 4 | 30 | H | St Johnstone | D | 2-2 | 1-0 | 2 | Tod 2 [16, 73] | 6354 |
| 5 | Sept 13 | A | Hibernian | L | 2-5 | 1-3 | 4 | Millar M (pen) [17], Petrie [80] | 10,002 |
| 6 | 21 | H | Kilmarnock | D | 1-1 | 0-0 | — | Smith [65] | 5374 |
| 7 | 27 | A | Aberdeen | W | 2-1 | 1-1 | 5 | Bingham [13], Britton [84] | 10,702 |
| 8 | Oct 4 | H | Dundee U | D | 3-3 | 0-3 | 5 | Smith [65], French [69], Bingham [80] | 5829 |
| 9 | 18 | A | Rangers | L | 0-7 | 0-3 | 6 | | 49,696 |
| 10 | 29 | A | Hearts | L | 1-3 | 0-1 | — | Smith [70] | 14,493 |
| 11 | Nov 1 | H | Celtic | L | 0-2 | 0-0 | 7 | | 12,659 |
| 12 | 8 | A | St Johnstone | W | 2-0 | 1-0 | 5 | Smith [8], Bingham [82] | 5239 |
| 13 | 15 | A | Hibernian | W | 2-1 | 1-0 | 5 | Smith 2 [27, 81] | 6952 |
| 14 | 22 | H | Aberdeen | D | 1-1 | 0-0 | 5 | Petrie [81] | 6738 |
| 15 | 29 | A | Kilmarnock | L | 1-2 | 1-2 | 5 | Smith [39] | 6667 |
| 16 | Dec 6 | A | Dundee U | D | 0-0 | 0-0 | 5 | | 6685 |
| 17 | 13 | H | Rangers | D | 0-0 | 0-0 | 5 | | 12,443 |
| 18 | 20 | H | Motherwell | L | 0-2 | 0-0 | 6 | | 4607 |
| 19 | 27 | H | Hearts | L | 1-3 | 1-3 | 7 | Bingham (pen) [17] | 11,722 |
| 20 | Jan 3 | H | St Johnstone | L | 0-1 | 0-1 | 7 | | 6591 |
| 21 | 10 | A | Hibernian | L | 0-1 | 0-1 | 7 | | 10,616 |
| 22 | 28 | A | Aberdeen | L | 0-2 | 0-1 | — | | 8661 |
| 23 | 31 | H | Kilmarnock | W | 3-2 | 1-1 | 7 | Barnett [41], Smith [67], Shaw [76] | 4903 |
| 24 | Feb 7 | A | Rangers | D | 1-1 | 0-0 | 8 | Curran [90] | 49,019 |
| 25 | 21 | H | Dundee U | D | 2-2 | 0-1 | 8 | Smith 2 [51, 90] | 5250 |
| 26 | 25 | A | Celtic | L | 1-5 | 0-3 | — | Tod [75] | 48,576 |
| 27 | Mar 7 | H | Motherwell | W | 2-1 | 1-1 | 8 | Smith 2 [23, 67] | 4811 |
| 28 | 14 | A | Aberdeen | D | 3-3 | 0-1 | 8 | Tod 2 [46, 53], Shaw [80] | 5931 |
| 29 | 21 | A | Kilmarnock | L | 0-3 | 0-0 | 8 | | 8230 |
| 30 | 28 | H | Rangers | L | 2-3 | 1-1 | 9 | Smith 2 [35, 63] | 11,531 |
| 31 | Apr 7 | A | Dundee U | D | 2-2 | 2-0 | — | Millar M [19], Britton [25] | 7769 |
| 32 | 11 | A | St Johnstone | D | 0-0 | 0-0 | 9 | | 5311 |
| 33 | 18 | H | Hibernian | D | 1-1 | 0-0 | 8 | Brebner (og) [48] | 12,749 |
| 34 | 25 | A | Motherwell | W | 3-1 | 2-1 | 6 | Smith [18], Ireland [32], Britton [54] | 5745 |
| 35 | May 3 | H | Celtic | D | 1-1 | 0-1 | — | Faulconbridge [83] | 12,719 |
| 36 | 9 | A | Hearts | L | 0-2 | 0-1 | 8 | | 13,888 |

**Final League Position: 8**          1996–97 5

## Honours
*League Champions:* First Division 1988-89, 1995-96. Division II 1925-26. Second Division 1985-86; *Runners-up:* First Division 1986-87, 1993-94, 1994-95. Division II 1912-13, 1933-34, 1954-55, 1957-58, 1972-73. Second Division 1978-79.
*Scottish Cup Winners:* 1961, 1968; *Runners-up:* 1965.
*League Cup Runners-up:* 1949-50, 1991-92.

**European**: *Cup Winners' Cup:* 14 matches (1961-62, 1968-69 semi-finals). *UEFA Cup:* 28 matches (*Fairs Cup:* 1962-63, 1964-65, 1965-66, 1966-67, 1969-70).
*Club colours:* Shirt: Black and white vertical stripes, stippled with red dots. Shorts: Black with white side panel. Stockings: White with red chevrons.

**Goalscorers:** *League (43):* Smith 16, Tod 6, Bingham 5 (1 pen), Britton 3, French 2 (1 pen), Millar M 2 (1 pen), Petrie 2, Shaw 2, Barnett 1, Curran 1, Faulconbridge 1, Ireland 1, own goal 1. *Scottish Cup (8):* Smith 5 (1 pen), Bingham 1, Miller C 1, Robertson 1. *Coca Cola Cup (8):* Smith 5, French 2 (1 pen), Moore 1.

| Westwater I 36 | Shields G 36 | Sharp R 1 + 2 | Tod A 35 | Barnett D 21 | Ireland C 12 | Curran H 15 + 2 | Miller C 13 + 2 | Smith A 33 | French J 33 + 1 | Fraser J 3 + 4 | Moore A 11 + 11 | Petrie S 19 + 8 | Bingham D 18 + 12 | Den Bieman I 11 + 14 | Fleming D 1 + 1 | Millar M 10 + 2 | Welsh S 4 + 2 | Shaw G 12 + 11 | Robertson C 21 | Britton G 12 + 4 | Duarte S 9 + 7 | McCulloch S 18 | McDonald P 1 + 2 | Huxford R 9 + 1 | Faulconbridge C — + 7 | Squires J 2 + 3 | Match No. |
|---|---|---|---|---|---|---|---|---|---|---|---|---|---|---|---|---|---|---|---|---|---|---|---|---|---|---|---|
| 1 | 2 | $3^{2}$ | 4 | 5 | 6 | 7 | 8 | 9 | 10 | $11^{1}$ | 12 | 13 | | | | | | | | | | | | | | | 1 |
| 1 | 2 | | 4 | 5 | 6 | 3 | | $9^{1}$ | 10 | 14 | 7 | $11^{2}$ | $8^{1}$ | 12 | 13 | | | | | | | | | | | | 2 |
| 1 | 2 | | 4 | 5 | 6 | 3 | | 9 | 10 | 13 | $7^{1}$ | 11 | $8^{2}$ | 12 | | | | | | | | | | | | | 3 |
| 1 | 2 | | 4 | 5 | 6 | 3 | | 9 | 10 | | 7 | 11 | $8^{1}$ | 12 | | | | | | | | | | | | | 4 |
| 1 | 2 | | 4 | $5^{1}$ | 6 | 3 | | 9 | 10 | | $7^{2}$ | 13 | 14 | 12 | | $11^{3}$ | 8 | | | | | | | | | | 5 |
| 1 | 2 | | 4 | | | 3 | 6 | $9^{2}$ | | | 7 | 10 | 11 | 13 | | $8^{1}$ | 5 | 12 | | | | | | | | | 6 |
| 1 | 2 | | 4 | | | $3^{1}$ | | $9$ | 10 | | 11 | $7^{2}$ | 12 | | | 6 | 5 | 13 | 8 | 14 | | | | | | | 7 |
| 1 | 2 | | 4 | | | | | 9 | 10 | | 7 | $11^{2}$ | 8 | 12 | | 3 | | $5^{1}$ | 13 | 6 | | | | | | | 8 |
| 1 | 2 | | 4 | 5 | 13 | 3 | 9 | 8 | | | $7^{3}$ | | 12 | | | $11^{2}$ | 14 | $10^{1}$ | 6 | | | | | | | | 9 |
| 1 | 2 | | 4 | 5 | | 3 | | 9 | 10 | | 12 | | | | | 6 | 7 | $11^{1}$ | 8 | | | | | | | | 10 |
| 1 | 2 | | 4 | 5 | $6^{1}$ | 3 | | 9 | 10 | | 13 | 12 | | | | 14 | $7^{2}$ | $11^{3}$ | 8 | | | | | | | | 11 |
| 1 | 2 | | 4 | 5 | 6 | | | 9 | 10 | | 13 | 14 | 12 | 3 | | $7^{3}$ | 11 | $8^{1}$ | | | | | | | | | 12 |
| 1 | 2 | | 4 | 5 | 6 | | | $9^{1}$ | 10 | | 14 | 12 | 13 | 3 | | $7^{1}$ | $11^{2}$ | 8 | | | | | | | | | 13 |
| 1 | 2 | | 4 | 5 | $6^{2}$ | | | 9 | 10 | | 12 | 13 | $11^{3}$ | 3 | | $7^{1}$ | 14 | 8 | | | | | | | | | 14 |
| 1 | 2 | | 4 | 5 | 6 | | | 9 | 10 | | $7^{2}$ | $11^{1}$ | 13 | 3 | | 12 | 14 | $8^{3}$ | | | | | | | | | 15 |
| 1 | 2 | | 4 | 5 | 6 | | | 9 | 10 | | $11^{2}$ | $7^{3}$ | 5 | | | 12 | 13 | 8 | 14 | $3^{1}$ | | | | | | | 16 |
| 1 | 2 | | 4 | 5 | 6 | | | 12 | 9 | | $11^{2}$ | 7 | | | | $10^{1}$ | 8 | 13 | 3 | | | | | | | | 17 |
| 1 | 2 | | 4 | 5 | 6 | | | 10 | 12 | | $9^{1}$ | 11 | $7^{3}$ | | | 14 | 8 | 13 | $3^{2}$ | | | | | | | | 18 |
| 1 | 2 | | 4 | 5 | $6^{2}$ | | | 9 | 10 | | 12 | 11 | 3 | | | $7^{1}$ | 8 | 13 | | | | | | | | | 19 |
| 1 | 2 | | 4 | 5 | | | | 10 | 13 | | $7^{2}$ | 9 | $11^{1}$ | 12 | | | 8 | 6 | 3 | | | | | | | | 20 |
| 1 | 2 | | 4 | 5 | | | 13 | 9 | 10 | | $7^{3}$ | | $6^{1}$ | 12 | | | 8 | 14 | $3^{2}$ | 11 | | | | | | | 21 |
| 1 | 2 | 14 | 4 | | | $6^{2}$ | $3^{3}$ | 9 | 10 | | $7^{1}$ | 11 | | 5 | | | 12 | 8 | 13 | | | | | | | | 22 |
| 1 | $2^{1}$ | 13 | 4 | 5 | | $3^{1}$ | | 9 | 10 | 6 | | $11^{3}$ | 14 | 12 | | | 7 | 8 | | | | | | | | | 23 |
| 1 | 2 | | 4 | 5 | | 12 | 14 | 9 | | $6^{1}$ | | 11 | 13 | $10^{3}$ | | $7^{2}$ | 8 | | 3 | | | | | | | | 24 |
| 1 | 2 | | 4 | $5^{1}$ | | | | 9 | 10 | 12 | 13 | 11 | $6^{3}$ | | | $7^{2}$ | 8 | | 3 | 14 | | | | | | | 25 |
| 1 | 2 | | 4 | | 5 | | $6^{3}$ | 9 | 10 | | 12 | $11^{1}$ | 13 | | | 14 | 8 | | $3^{2}$ | 7 | | | | | | | 26 |
| 1 | 2 | | 4 | 5 | 6 | | | 9 | $10^{1}$ | | | $11^{2}$ | 7 | | | 12 | 8 | | 3 | 13 | | | | | | | 27 |
| 1 | 2 | | 4 | 5 | | | | 9 | $10^{2}$ | | | $11^{3}$ | $7^{1}$ | 12 | | 14 | 13 | 8 | | 3 | 6 | | | | | | 28 |
| 1 | 2 | | 4 | 5 | | | | 9 | 10 | | | $11^{2}$ | $6^{1}$ | 12 | | 13 | $7^{3}$ | 8 | | 3 | 14 | | | | | | 29 |
| 1 | 2 | | 5 | | | | | 9 | 10 | 4 | | $11^{1}$ | | 14 | | 8 | $7^{2}$ | 12 | $3^{3}$ | 6 | 13 | | | | | | 30 |
| 1 | 2 | | 4 | 5 | | | | 9 | 10 | | 14 | | 13 | $11^{2}$ | | 8 | $7^{1}$ | 3 | 6 | $12^{2}$ | | | | | | | 31 |
| 1 | 2 | | 4 | 5 | | | | 9 | 10 | | 13 | | $11^{1}$ | 8 | | $7^{2}$ | 3 | $6^{3}$ | 12 | 14 | | | | | | | 32 |
| 1 | $2^{2}$ | | 4 | 5 | | | | 9 | 10 | | 14 | | $11^{3}$ | 8 | | $7^{1}$ | 3 | 6 | 12 | 13 | | | | | | | 33 |
| 1 | 2 | | 4 | 5 | | | | $9^{2}$ | 10 | | 14 | | 11 | $8^{1}$ | | $7^{3}$ | 3 | 6 | 13 | 12 | | | | | | | 34 |
| 1 | 2 | | 4 | 5 | | | | 9 | $10^{1}$ | | 12 | 13 | $11^{2}$ | | | $7^{3}$ | 3 | 6 | 14 | 8 | | | | | | | 35 |
| 1 | 2 | $4^{3}$ | 5 | | | | | 9 | 13 | | 12 | $10^{1}$ | $11^{2}$ | | | 7 | 3 | 6 | 14 | 8 | | | | | | | 36 |

# EAST FIFE                                    Second Division

*Year Formed:* 1903. *Ground & Address:* Stadium, South St, Methil, Fife (from September). *Telephone:* 01333 426323.
*Fax:* 01333 426376. *Old Address:* Bayview Park, Methil, KY8 3AG (until September).
*Ground Capacity:* total: 2000 (all seated). *Size of Pitch:* 110yd × 71yd.
*Chairman:* Julian Danskin. *Secretary:* J. Derrick Brown. *Commercial Manager:* Patrick McAuley.
*Manager:* Steve Kirk. *Assistant Manager:* Andy Harrow. *General Manager:* Pat McAuley. *Youth Manager:* Don Mackay.
*Physio:* John Cooper. *Coach:* Gordon Rae.
*Managers since 1975:* Frank Christie; Roy Barry; David Clarke; Gavin Murray, Alex Totten, Steve Archibald, James
Bone. *Club Nickname(s):* The Fifers. *Previous Grounds:* None.
*Record Attendance:* 22,515 v Raith Rovers, Division I; 2 Jan, 1950.
*Record Transfer Fee received:* £150,000 for Paul Hunter from Hull C (March 1990).
*Record Transfer Fee paid:* £70,000 for John Sludden from Kilmarnock (July 1991).
*Record Victory:* 13-2 v Edinburgh City, Division II; 11 Dec, 1937.
*Record Defeat:* 0-9 v Hearts, Division I; 5 Oct, 1957.
*Most Capped Player:* George Aitken, 5 (8), Scotland.
*Most League Appearances:* 517: David Clarke, 1968-86.
*Most League Goals in Season (Individual):* 41: Jock Wood, Division II; 1926-27 and Henry Morris, Division II; 1947-48.
*Most Goals Overall (Individual):* 225: Phil Weir (215 in League).

## EAST FIFE 1997–98 LEAGUE RECORD

| Match No. | Date | Venue | Opponents | Result | H/T Score | Lg. Pos. | Goalscorers | Attendance |
|---|---|---|---|---|---|---|---|---|
| 1 | Aug 16 | H | Stenhousemuir | L | 0-3 | 0-1 | — | 643 |
| 2 | 23 | A | Inverness CT | W | 1-0 | 0-0 | 7 | Cherry (og) [56] | 1746 |
| 3 | 30 | H | Clyde | W | 3-0 | 1-0 | 5 | Donaghy [44], Allan [62], Ritchie [65] | 720 |
| 4 | Sept 7 | A | Forfar Ath | W | 2-1 | 2-1 | — | Dyer [12], Johnston [34] | 587 |
| 5 | 13 | A | Clydebank | W | 2-1 | 1-1 | 1 | Cusick [16], Ritchie [61] | 358 |
| 6 | 20 | H | Livingston | L | 2-3 | 1-1 | 2 | Moffat 2 [42, 63] | 986 |
| 7 | 27 | A | Stranraer | L | 2-3 | 0-2 | 4 | Ronald (pen) [56], Moffat [72] | 474 |
| 8 | Oct 4 | H | Queen of the S | W | 3-2 | 1-1 | 2 | Abercromby [36], Allan [60], Johnston [69] | 656 |
| 9 | 18 | A | Brechin C | D | 0-0 | 0-0 | 2 | | 406 |
| 10 | 25 | H | Inverness CT | L | 1-5 | 1-3 | 3 | Gibb [41] | 772 |
| 11 | Nov 1 | A | Stenhousemuir | D | 0-0 | 0-0 | 3 | | 439 |
| 12 | 8 | A | Clyde | L | 0-3 | 0-2 | 5 | | 598 |
| 13 | 15 | H | Clydebank | L | 2-3 | 1-1 | 7 | Allan (pen) [10], Dyer [47] | 600 |
| 14 | 22 | H | Stranraer | D | 2-2 | 1-1 | 7 | Donaghy [1], Dyer [87] | 563 |
| 15 | Dec 3 | A | Livingston | L | 0-1 | 0-1 | — | | 876 |
| 16 | 13 | H | Brechin C | W | 3-1 | 2-0 | 4 | Ronald 2 [19, 83], Moffat [28] | 424 |
| 17 | 20 | A | Queen of the S | L | 1-2 | 0-1 | 7 | Moffat (pen) [67] | 1013 |
| 18 | 27 | A | Inverness CT | L | 0-4 | 0-2 | 7 | | 2134 |
| 19 | Jan 11 | H | Forfar Ath | W | 1-0 | 1-0 | — | Prytz [34] | 902 |
| 20 | 17 | A | Stranraer | W | 3-2 | 1-1 | 4 | Dyer [33], Ronald [50], Kirk [89] | 524 |
| 21 | 31 | H | Livingston | W | 2-0 | 0-0 | 4 | Ronald [62], Allan [73] | 899 |
| 22 | Feb 7 | A | Brechin C | L | 1-2 | 0-2 | 4 | Kirk [64] | 404 |
| 23 | 15 | A | Queen of the S | L | 1-5 | 1-1 | — | Moffat [21] | 887 |
| 24 | 21 | A | Forfar Ath | L | 0-1 | 0-0 | 7 | | 460 |
| 25 | 25 | H | Stenhousemuir | W | 2-1 | 2-0 | — | Allan 2 [21, 32] | 511 |
| 26 | 28 | H | Clyde | D | 1-1 | 1-1 | 6 | Allan (pen) [17] | 670 |
| 27 | Mar 14 | A | Stranraer | L | 0-3 | 0-2 | 8 | | 571 |
| 28 | 17 | A | Clydebank | W | 3-0 | 1-0 | — | Fisher [35], Ronald [66], Dyer [71] | 182 |
| 29 | 21 | A | Livingston | D | 2-2 | 1-1 | 6 | Allan [44], Dyer [56] | 1309 |
| 30 | 28 | H | Brechin C | W | 4-1 | 3-0 | 5 | Dyer 2 [1, 43], Kirk [1], Cusick [83] | 623 |
| 31 | Apr 5 | A | Queen of the S | W | 4-1 | 3-0 | — | Johnston [7], Dyer [12], Prytz [14], Munro [51] | 1276 |
| 32 | 11 | A | Clyde | D | 0-0 | 0-0 | 4 | | 629 |
| 33 | 18 | H | Clydebank | L | 0-2 | 0-0 | 5 | | 710 |
| 34 | 25 | H | Inverness CT | L | 0-1 | 0-1 | 5 | | 650 |
| 35 | May 2 | A | Stenhousemuir | W | 3-2 | 2-0 | 5 | Dyer 2 [14, 41], Prytz (pen) [77] | 554 |
| 36 | 9 | H | Forfar Ath | L | 0-1 | 0-0 | 6 | | 816 |

**Final League Position: 6**          1996–97 DIV 1 10

**Honours**
*League Champions:* Division II 1947-48; *Runners-up:* Division II 1929-30, 1970-71. Second Division 1983-84., 1995-96
*Scottish Cup Winners:* 1938; *Runners-up:* 1927, 1950.
*League Cup Winners:* 1947-48, 1949-50, 1953-54.
*Club colours:* Shirt: Amber and black diamonds. Shorts: Black with two amber stripes. Stockings: Amber with 3 black stripes on top.

**Goalscorers:** *League (51):* Dyer 11, Allan 8 (2 pens), Moffat 6 (1 pen), Ronald 6 (1 pen), Johnston 3, Kirk 3, Prytz 3 (1 pen), Cusick 2, Donaghy 2, Ritchie 2, Abercromby 1, Fisher 1, Gibb 1, Munro 1, own goal 1. *Scottish Cup (2):* Johnston 1, Moffat 1. *Coca Cola Cup (0). League Challenge Cup (2):* Dyer 1, Moffat 1.

| McCulloch W 17 | Dixon A 15 + 4 | Gibb R 27 + 1 | Ritchie I 30 | Johnston G 33 | Ryan R 15 | Allan G 33 + 1 | Donaghy M 13 + 3 | Dyer M 21 + 6 | Ronald P 32 + 2 | Moffat B 15 + 9 | Cusick J 14 + 6 | Nicoll G — + 4 | Gillies K 20 + 1 | MacFarlane C 3 + 2 | Fisher D 7 + 12 | Gartshore P 5 + 11 | Munro K 15 + 5 | Abercromby M 13 + 3 | McPherson G — + 1 | Masson G 1 | Reid A — + 1 | Strathdee J 14 + 1 | Thomson B 1 | Stewart A 18 | Prytz R 18 | Kirk S 11 + 6 | Essandoh R 5 | Roberts P — + 8 | Match No. |
|---|---|---|---|---|---|---|---|---|---|---|---|---|---|---|---|---|---|---|---|---|---|---|---|---|---|---|---|---|---|
| 1 | 2 | 3 | 4 | 5 | $6^1$ | 7 | $8^2$ | 9 | 10 | 11 | 12 | 13 | | | | | | | | | | | | | | | | | 1 |
| 1 | 13 | 3 | 4 | 5 | 11 | $7^1$ | 8 | 12 | 10 | $9^2$ | 2 | | | $6^3$ | 14 | | | | | | | | | | | | | | 2 |
| 1 | 13 | $3^2$ | 4 | 5 | 11 | 7 | 8 | 12 | 10 | $9^1$ | 2 | | 6 | | | | | | | | | | | | | | | | 3 |
| 1 | 8 | $11^1$ | 4 | 5 | 3 | 7 | | 9 | 10 | $12^3$ | $2^2$ | 14 | 6 | | 13 | | | | | | | | | | | | | | 4 |
| 1 | $8^2$ | 11 | 4 | | 3 | 7 | | $9^1$ | 10 | | $2^3$ | 14 | 6 | 5 | 12 | 13 | | | | | | | | | | | | | 5 |
| 1 | 8 | | 4 | | 3 | $7^3$ | | 9 | 10 | | 2 | 14 | 6 | $5^1$ | | | $11^2$ | 12 | 13 | | | | | | | | | | 6 |
| 1 | | | 4 | 5 | | 7 | 10 | 9 | | | | | 6 | 3 | | | 11 | $2^1$ | | | | 8 | | | | | | 12 | 7 |
| 1 | | | 4 | 5 | 3 | | 12 | 10 | $9^1$ | $11^2$ | 14 | | 6 | | | | 13 | 2 | | | | 8 | | $7^3$ | | | | | 8 |
| 1 | 12 | 11 | 4 | 5 | 3 | $7^1$ | | $9^2$ | $10^2$ | | | 13 | 6 | | | | 14 | 2 | | | | 8 | | | | | | | 9 |
| 1 | $8^2$ | $11^1$ | | 5 | 3 | 7 | | 9 | 10 | 12 | | | 6 | | | | 13 | 2 | 4 | | | | | | | | | | 10 |
| 1 | 6 | $11^2$ | | 5 | 3 | 7 | | 9 | 10 | | | 13 | | | | $8^1$ | 4 | 2 | | 12 | | | | | | | | | 11 |
| 1 | 6 | 13 | 4 | 5 | 3 | 7 | | 9 | 10 | | | | | | | $8^1$ | $11^2$ | 2 | | | 12 | | | | | | | | 12 |
| | | $6^2$ | 4 | 5 | 3 | 7 | | $9^1$ | 10 | | | 14 | | | | 12 | 13 | $2^1$ | | | | | 1 | | | | | | 13 |
| 1 | 14 | $11^1$ | 4 | 5 | 3 | 7 | 8 | 9 | 10 | | | 12 | | | | 13 | $6^2$ | | | | | $2^3$ | | | | | | | 14 |
| 1 | | | 4 | 5 | 3 | 7 | 8 | $9^2$ | 10 | | | 13 | | | | 12 | $6^1$ | $14^{}$ | $11^3$ | | | 2 | | | | | | | 15 |
| 1 | | 3 | 4 | 5 | | 7 | 6 | | 10 | 9 | | | | | | 11 | | | | | | 8 | | 2 | | | | | 16 |
| 1 | | 3 | 4 | 5 | | $7^1$ | 6 | 12 | 10 | 9 | | | | | | 11 | | | | | | 8 | | 2 | | | | | 17 |
| 1 | 2 | | 4 | 5 | 3 | $7^2$ | 8 | 12 | $10^1$ | 9 | | | | | | 6 | 13 | | | | | 11 | | | | | | | 18 |
| | 2 | 3 | | 5 | | 7 | 12 | 14 | $10^3$ | 9 | | | | | | $8^2$ | 11 | $6^1$ | | | | 13 | | 1 | 4 | | | | 19 |
| | $2^1$ | 3 | | 5 | | $7^3$ | 12 | $9^2$ | 10 | | | | | | | 8 | 11 | 6 | | | | 14 | | 1 | 4 | | | 13 | 20 |
| | | 3 | | 5 | | $7^1$ | 2 | | 10 | | | | | | | 8 | 11 | 6 | | | | 13 | | 1 | 4 | $9^2$ | | 12 | 21 |
| | | 3 | | 5 | | 7 | $2^2$ | 12 | $10^1$ | | | | | | | 8 | 11 | 6 | | | | 13 | | 1 | 4 | 9 | | | 22 |
| | | $3^2$ | 2 | 5 | | 7 | 14 | | 10 | | | | | | | $8^3$ | 12 | 6 | | | | 13 | | 1 | 4 | 9 | | $11^1$ | 23 |
| | $2^2$ | | | 5 | 6 | 7 | 3 | | 10 | | | | | | | $8^1$ | 11 | | | | | 12 | | 1 | 4 | 9 | | 13 | 24 |
| | 2 | 3 | | 5 | 6 | 7 | | 12 | $10^3$ | 14 | | | | | | $8^2$ | 11 | | | | | 13 | | 1 | 4 | $9^1$ | | | 25 |
| | 2 | 3 | | 5 | 6 | 7 | | 12 | 10 | | | | | | | 8 | 11 | | | | | | | 1 | 4 | $9^1$ | | | 26 |
| | $2^2$ | $3^3$ | | 5 | | | | 12 | 10 | 9 | | 14 | | | | $8^1$ | 11 | 6 | | | | | | 1 | 4 | | 7 | 13 | 27 |
| | | 3 | | 5 | 6 | $7^1$ | | 12 | $10^2$ | | | 14 | | | | $8^3$ | 11 | | | | | 2 | | 1 | 4 | 9 | | 13 | 28 |
| | | 3 | | 5 | 6 | $7^1$ | | | 10 | | | | | | | $8^2$ | 11 | | | | | 2 | | 1 | 4 | 9 | | 12 | 29 |
| | | 3 | | 5 | 6 | $7^1$ | | 12 | 10 | | | 14 | | | | $8^2$ | 11 | | | | | 2 | | 1 | $4^3$ | 9 | | 13 | 30 |
| | | 3 | | 5 | 6 | $7^2$ | | 8 | $10^3$ | 13 | | | | | | | 12 | 11 | | | | 2 | | 1 | 4 | $9^1$ | | 14 | 31 |
| | | 3 | | 5 | 6 | | | 12 | 7 | 10 | | 8 | | | | | | 11 | | | | 2 | | 1 | $4^1$ | 9 | | | 32 |
| | | 3 | | 5 | 6 | | | 8 | $7^2$ | $10^1$ | | | | | | | 14 | 13 | | | | $2^3$ | | 1 | $4^2$ | 9 | | 12 | 33 |
| | | $3^3$ | | 5 | 6 | | | 8 | $7^2$ | $10^1$ | | | | | | | 14 | $9^2$ | | | | 2 | | 1 | 4 | 13 | | 14 | 34 |
| | | $3^3$ | | 5 | 6 | | | 12 | 7 | 10 | | | | | | | $9^1$ | 13 | | | | 2 | | 1 | $4^2$ | 8 | | 14 | 35 |
| | | 3 | | 5 | 6 | | | $8^2$ | $7^3$ | $10^1$ | | | | | | | 13 | 9 | | | | 2 | | 1 | 4 | 14 | | 12 | 36 |

# EAST STIRLINGSHIRE   Third Division

*Year Formed:* 1880. *Ground & Address:* Firs Park, Firs St, Falkirk FK2 7AY. *Telephone:* 01324 623583. *Fax:* 01324 637 862
*Ground Capacity:* total: 1880. seated: 200. *Size of Pitch:* 112yd × 72yd.
*Chairman:* Leslie G. Thomson. *Vice Chairman:* Tom Kirk. *Secretary:* Margaret Thomson.
*Manager:* Hugh McCann. *Physio:* Paul Green.
*Managers since 1975:* I. Ure; D. McLinden; W. P. Lamont; A. Ferguson; W. Little; D. Whiteford; D. Lawson; J. D.
Connell; A. Mackin; Dom Sullivan; Bobby McCulley; Billy Little, John Brownlie. *Club Nickname(s):* The Shire.
*Previous Grounds:* Burnhouse, Randyford Park, Merchiston Park, New Kilbowie Park.
*Record Attendance:* 12,000 v Partick T, Scottish Cup 3rd rd; 19 Feb 1921.
*Record Transfer Fee received:* £35,000 for Jim Docherty to Chelsea (1978).
*Record Transfer Fee paid:* £6,000 for Colin McKinnon from Falkirk (March 1991).
*Record Victory:* 11-2 v Vale of Bannock, Scottish Cup 2nd rd; 22 Sept, 1888.
*Record Defeat:* 1-12 v Dundee United, Division II; 13 Apr, 1936.
*Most Capped Player:* Humphrey Jones, 5 (14), Wales.
*Most League Appearances:* 379: Gordon Simpson, 1968-80.
*Most League Goals in Season (Individual):* 36: Malcolm Morrison, Division II; 1938-39.
*Most Goals Overall (Individual):* —.

## EAST STIRLINGSHIRE 1997–98 LEAGUE RECORD

| Match No. | Date | Venue | Opponents | Result | H/T Score | Lg. Pos. | Goalscorers | Atten- dance |
|---|---|---|---|---|---|---|---|---|
| 1 | Aug 5 | H | Ross Co | L 1-3 | 0-3 | — | Watt 73 | 474 |
| 2 | 16 | A | Arbroath | L 0-2 | 0-1 | 10 | | 387 |
| 3 | 23 | H | Alloa Ath | W 2-1 | 0-0 | 8 | Muirhead 56, Barr 89 | 502 |
| 4 | 30 | H | Queen's Park | W 1-0 | 0-0 | 5 | Watt 49 | 457 |
| 5 | Sept13 | A | Cowdenbeath | L 0-1 | 0-1 | 6 | | 176 |
| 6 | 20 | H | Montrose | W 4-1 | 3-1 | 6 | Watt 3 18, 19, 51, Hunter 31 | 279 |
| 7 | 27 | A | Berwick R | W 3-2 | 1-0 | 6 | Hunter 11, Muirhead 66, Patterson 70 | 328 |
| 8 | Oct 4 | H | Dumbarton | W 3-1 | 0-1 | 5 | Neill 2 (1 pen) 75, 85 (p), Hunter 81 | 321 |
| 9 | 18 | A | Albion R | L 1-5 | 0-2 | 6 | Neill 69 | 420 |
| 10 | 25 | A | Alloa Ath | W 2-0 | 0-0 | 6 | Watt 46, Kennedy 61 | 503 |
| 11 | Nov 1 | H | Arbroath | L 1-2 | 1-1 | 6 | Patterson 24 | 413 |
| 12 | 8 | A | Queen's Park | W 1-0 | 1-0 | 5 | Barr 8 | 432 |
| 13 | 15 | H | Cowdenbeath | W 4-0 | 2-0 | 4 | Barr 19, Watt 25, McPherson 60, McBride 88 | 287 |
| 14 | 22 | H | Berwick R | W 4-0 | 1-0 | 3 | Parks 41, McPherson 2 60, 85, Watt 86 | 323 |
| 15 | 29 | A | Montrose | D 1-1 | 1-0 | 4 | McPherson 23 | 268 |
| 16 | Dec 6 | A | Arbroath | L 0-3 | 0-2 | 4 | | 646 |
| 17 | 13 | H | Albion R | W 1-0 | 0-0 | 3 | Watt 65 | 335 |
| 18 | 20 | H | Dumbarton | W 1-0 | 1-0 | 2 | Watt 21 | 323 |
| 19 | 27 | H | Alloa Ath | L 0-3 | 0-1 | 3 | | 572 |
| 20 | Jan 17 | A | Berwick R | L 1-3 | 0-1 | 4 | Barr 55 | 366 |
| 21 | 31 | H | Montrose | L 1-2 | 0-0 | 4 | Barr 75 | 177 |
| 22 | Feb 7 | A | Albion R | L 2-3 | 1-2 | 4 | Hunter 26, Barr 80 | 343 |
| 23 | 10 | A | Ross Co | D 0-0 | 0-0 | — | | 910 |
| 24 | 17 | H | Dumbarton | W 1-0 | 0-0 | — | Hunter 67 | 181 |
| 25 | 21 | H | Ross Co | W 1-0 | 0-0 | 3 | Campbell 60 | 340 |
| 26 | Mar 4 | A | Queen's Park | D 0-0 | 0-0 | — | | 196 |
| 27 | 9 | A | Cowdenbeath | W 1-0 | 0-0 | 4 | Patterson 81 | 174 |
| 28 | 14 | H | Berwick R | D 1-1 | 1-1 | 4 | Hunter 8 | 241 |
| 29 | 21 | A | Montrose | D 1-1 | 0-1 | 4 | Patterson 78 | 224 |
| 30 | 28 | H | Albion R | W 2-0 | 2-0 | 4 | Neill 26, Watt 33 | 291 |
| 31 | Apr 4 | A | Dumbarton | L 0-1 | 0-1 | 4 | | 338 |
| 32 | 11 | A | Queen's Park | W 2-0 | 1-0 | 4 | Barr 3, Muirhead 60 | 412 |
| 33 | 18 | H | Cowdenbeath | W 2-1 | 0-1 | 4 | Watt 52, Patterson 86 | 284 |
| 34 | 25 | A | Alloa Ath | L 2-5 | 1-3 | 4 | Watt 7, Hunter 89 | 788 |
| 35 | May 2 | H | Arbroath | D 1-1 | 1-0 | 4 | Kennedy 22 | 651 |
| 36 | 9 | A | Ross Co | L 2-5 | 1-3 | 4 | Patterson 10, Barr 69 | 1605 |

**Final League Position: 4**      1996–97 9

**Honours**
*League Champions:* Division II 1931-32; C Division 1947-48. *Runners-up:* Division II 1962-63. Second Division 1979-80. Division Three 1923-24.
*Scottish Cup:* —.
*League Cup:* —.
*Club colours:* Shirt: Black and white stripes. Shorts: Black and white. Stockings: Black with 3 tangerine bands on top.

**Goalscorers:** *League (50):* Watt 13, Barr 8, Hunter 7, Patterson 6, McPherson 4, Neill 4 (1 pen), Muirhead 3, Kennedy 2, Campbell 1, McBride 1, Parks 1. *Scottish Cup (1):* Watt 1. *Coca Cola Cup (3):* Abercromby 1, Campbell 1, Patterson 1. *League Challenge Cup (1):* Parks 1.

| McDougall G 34 | Russell G 12 | Neill A 33 | Campbell C 34 | Gardiner D 10 + 7 | Snedden S 1 | McBride M 20 + 16 | Watt D 35 + 1 | Abercromby M 5 | Muirhead D 32 + 2 | Patterson P 29 + 6 | Rae D 6 + 1 | Hunter M 20 + 2 | Parks G 7 + 14 | Barr A 24 + 8 | Kennedy K 7 + 3 | Welsh B — + 1 | Ross B 19 + 3 | Bowsher C 12 | McPherson D 9 + 4 | Cochrane M 4 + 7 | McConnell I 8 | Starrar A 11 + 4 | Balfour R 2 | Walker S 17 | Hamilton G 3 + 1 | McBeth P 1 + 1 | Little T 1 + 1 | McPeake S — + 3 | Match No. |
|---|---|---|---|---|---|---|---|---|---|---|---|---|---|---|---|---|---|---|---|---|---|---|---|---|---|---|---|---|---|
| 1 | 2 | 3 | 4 | 5 | $6^1$ | $7^3$ | 8 | 9 | $10^2$ | 11 | 12 | 13 | 14 | | | | | | | | | | | | | | | | 1 |
| 1 | $2^1$ | 3 | 4 | 5 | | $7^3$ | 13 | 9 | 8 | 11 | | | 14 | 12 | 6 | | $10^2$ | | | | | | | | | | | | 2 |
| 1 | $2^1$ | 3 | 4 | | | 7 | 8 | 9 | 5 | 13 | | $11^3$ | $10^2$ | 12 | 6 | | 14 | | | | | | | | | | | | 3 |
| 1 | 2 | 3 | 4 | 12 | | 7 | 8 | $9^2$ | $5^1$ | 11 | | 10 | 13 | | 6 | | | | | | | | | | | | | | 4 |
| 1 | | 3 | 4 | 13 | | 7 | 8 | 9 | 12 | $10^2$ | | | | | $6^1$ | | 2 | 5 | 11 | | | | | | | | | | 5 |
| 1 | | 3 | 4 | 6 | | 7 | $2^3$ | 8 | 13 | $11^1$ | | $10^2$ | 9 | 12 | | | | 5 | | 14 | | | | | | | | | 6 |
| 1 | | 3 | $4^3$ | 6 | | $7^2$ | 2 | 8 | 12 | $11^2$ | 10 | $9^1$ | 13 | | | | | 5 | | 14 | | | | | | | | | 7 |
| 1 | | 3 | $4^3$ | 6 | | $7^2$ | 2 | $8^1$ | 9 | 11 | 10 | 13 | 14 | | | | | 5 | 12 | | | | | | | | | | 8 |
| 1 | | 3 | 4 | | | $7^3$ | 2 | 14 | 9 | $11^1$ | $10^2$ | 13 | 8 | | | | | 5 | 12 | 6 | | | | | | | | | 9 |
| 1 | 2 | 3 | 4 | | | 13 | 8 | | 14 | $10^1$ | | 12 | $7^3$ | $9^2$ | | | | 5 | 11 | 6 | | | | | | | | | 10 |
| 1 | 2 | 3 | $4^2$ | 13 | | 12 | 8 | | 11 | 10 | | | 7 | $9^1$ | | | | 5 | | 6 | | | | | | | | | 11 |
| 1 | 2 | 3 | 4 | | | $7^1$ | 8 | | $11^2$ | 9 | | 12 | 10 | | | | | 5 | 13 | 6 | | | | | | | | | 12 |
| 1 | 2 | 3 | 4 | 13 | | 14 | 8 | | 11 | 9 | | $7^3$ | $10^1$ | | | | | 5 | 12 | $6^2$ | | | | | | | | | 13 |
| 1 | $2^3$ | 3 | $4^2$ | 13 | | 12 | 8 | | 11 | $9^1$ | | 7 | | 14 | | | 5 | 10 | | 6 | | | | | | | | | 14 |
| 1 | 2 | 3 | 4 | | | 13 | 8 | | $11^1$ | 9 | | $7^2$ | 12 | | | | | 5 | 10 | 6 | | | | | | | | | 15 |
| 1 | 2 | 3 | 4 | | | 13 | 8 | | 11 | $9^2$ | | 7 | 12 | 14 | | | $5^1$ | 10 | | $6^1$ | | | | | | | | | 16 |
| 1 | | 3 | 4 | | | 7 | 8 | | 11 | $9^2$ | | 13 | 6 | | 5 | | $10^1$ | | | | | 12 | | | | | | | 17 |
| | 3 | | 5 | | | $7^2$ | $8^3$ | | 11 | 9 | | 13 | 6 | | 2 | | | | | | | 12 | 1 | 4 | 14 | | | | 18 |
| | 3 | | | | | $7^1$ | 8 | | 11 | $9^3$ | | | $6^2$ | 12 | 2 | | 10 | 14 | | | 13 | 1 | 4 | 5 | | | | | 19 |
| 1 | | 3 | 4 | 5 | | $7^3$ | 8 | | 11 | 13 | | | 14 | 12 | 6 | | 10 | | $9^2$ | $2^1$ | | | | | | | | | 20 |
| 1 | | 3 | 5 | | | 14 | 7 | | 8 | $10^3$ | | $9^1$ | 12 | 4 | | | | $11^2$ | | | | 6 | 2 | 13 | | | | | 21 |
| 1 | | 3 | 5 | 6 | | 13 | 7 | | 8 | 12 | | $9^1$ | 11 | 14 | | | | | | 13 | | 4 | $2^1$ | $10^2$ | | | | | 22 |
| 1 | | 3 | 5 | | | 12 | 11 | | 8 | 10 | | 9 | $7^1$ | 4 | | | | | 13 | $2^2$ | | 6 | | | | | | | 23 |
| 1 | | 3 | 5 | 12 | | $2^1$ | 7 | | | 10 | | 9 | 11 | 4 | | | | | $8^1$ | | | 6 | | 13 | | | | | 24 |
| 1 | | 3 | 5 | | | 12 | 7 | | 8 | $10^1$ | | 9 | 11 | 4 | | | | | 12 | 2 | | 6 | | | | | | | 25 |
| 1 | | 3 | 5 | | | 13 | 7 | | $8^1$ | 10 | | $9^2$ | 11 | 4 | | | | | 12 | 2 | | 6 | | | | | | | 26 |
| 1 | | 3 | 5 | | | 12 | 8 | | 10 | $7^2$ | | 9 | 2 | 4 | | | | | 13 | | | 6 | | | | $11^1$ | | | 27 |
| 1 | | 3 | 5 | | | 12 | 7 | | 8 | 10 | | $9^2$ | $11^1$ | 13 | 4 | | | | | 2 | | 6 | | | | | | | 28 |
| 1 | | 3 | 5 | | | 7 | 11 | | 8 | 10 | | 12 | | $9^1$ | 4 | | | | | 2 | | 6 | | | | | | | 29 |
| 1 | | 3 | 5 | | | $7^1$ | 11 | | 8 | 10 | | 13 | 12 | $9^2$ | 4 | | | | | 2 | | 6 | | | | | | | 30 |
| 1 | | 3 | 4 | 6 | | 7 | 2 | | 8 | 10 | | 9 | | | | | | | $11^1$ | 5 | | | | | | | | 12 | 31 |
| 1 | | 3 | 5 | | | 12 | 7 | | 8 | $10^2$ | | 9 | $11^1$ | 4 | | | | | | 2 | | 6 | | | | | 13 | | 32 |
| 1 | $3^1$ | 5 | 13 | | | 12 | 7 | | 8 | 10 | | 9 | $11^1$ | 4 | | | | | | 2 | | 6 | | | | | | | 33 |
| 1 | | 5 | $3^1$ | | | 13 | 7 | | 11 | 10 | | 9 | | $2^2$ | 12 | | | | | 8 | | 6 | | | | | | | 34 |
| 1 | | 5 | | | | 7 | 3 | | 8 | 10 | | 9 | | 11 | $2^1$ | | 4 | | | | | 12 | | | | | 6 | | 35 |
| 1 | | 5 | | | | $7^3$ | 3 | | 8 | 10 | | 9 | 13 | 11 | $2^2$ | | 4 | | | | | 12 | | $6^1$ | | | | 14 | 36 |

# FALKIRK
First Division

*Year Formed:* 1876. *Ground & Address:* Brockville Park, Hope St, Falkirk FK1 5AX. *Telephone:* 01324 624121.
*Fax:* 01324 612418.
*Ground Capacity:* total: 9706. seated: 2661. *Size of Pitch:* 110yd × 72yd.
*Chairman:* Douglas McIntyre. *Secretary:* Alex Blackwood. *General Manager:* Jim Hendry.
*Manager:* Alex Totten. *Assistant Manager:* Walter Kidd. *Physio:* A. McQueen. *Coach:* Willie Wilson.
*Managers since 1975:* J. Prentice; G. Miller; W. Little; J. Hagart; A. Totten; G. Abel; W. Lamont; D. Clarke; J. Duffy;
W. Lamont; J. Jefferies; J. Lambie E. Bannon; A. Totten. *Club Nickname(s):* The Bairns. *Previous Grounds:* Randyford
1876–81; Blinkbonny Grounds 1881–83; Brockville Park 1883 to present.
*Record Attendance:* 23,100 v Celtic, Scottish Cup 3rd rd; 21 Feb, 1953.
*Record Transfer Fee received:* £380,000 for John Hughes to Celtic (Aug 1995).
*Record Transfer Fee paid:* £225,000 to Chelsea for Kevin McAllister (Aug 1991).
*Record Victory:* 12-1 v Laurieston, Scottish Cup 2nd rd; 23 Sept, 1893.
*Record Defeat:* 1-11 v Airdrieonians, Division I; 28 Apr, 1951.
*Most Capped Player:* Alex Parker, 14 (15), Scotland.
*Most League Appearances:* (post-war): 353, George Watson, 1975–87.
*Most League Goals in Season (Individual):* 43: Evelyn Morrison, Division I; 1928-29.
*Most Goals Overall (Individual):* Dougie Moran, 86, 1957–61 and 1964–67.

## FALKIRK 1997–98 LEAGUE RECORD

| Match No. | Date | Venue | Opponents | Result | H/T Score | Lg. Pos. | Goalscorers | Attendance |
|---|---|---|---|---|---|---|---|---|
| 1 | Aug 2 | A | Dundee | L 0-3 | 0-1 | — | | 4427 |
| 2 | 16 | H | Ayr U | W 2-1 | 1-0 | 5 | Moss [27], McGrillen [66] | 2683 |
| 3 | 23 | A | Airdrieonians | D 2-2 | 1-2 | 5 | Crabbe (pen) [16], Moss [75] | 2394 |
| 4 | 30 | A | Stirling A | W 3-2 | 1-1 | 4 | McKenzie [9], Crabbe [52], McGrillen [75] | 2485 |
| 5 | Sept 13 | H | Hamilton A | L 1-4 | 1-3 | 5 | McGrillen (pen) [24] | 2539 |
| 6 | 20 | H | St Mirren | W 3-1 | 0-1 | 3 | McCart [55], McGrillen [71], McGowan [77] | 3039 |
| 7 | 27 | A | Raith R | L 0-2 | 0-2 | 4 | | 3564 |
| 8 | Oct 4 | A | Partick Th | W 4-3 | 2-0 | 3 | McGrillen [25], Keith 2 [45, 57], McKenzie [54] | 2439 |
| 9 | 18 | H | Greenock Morton | W 1-0 | 0-0 | 3 | Lawrie [87] | 2642 |
| 10 | 25 | H | Dundee | D 1-1 | 1-0 | 4 | Moss [12] | 4076 |
| 11 | Nov 8 | H | Stirling A | W 3-2 | 1-0 | 3 | Craig 2 [12, 87], James [68] | 2467 |
| 12 | 11 | A | Ayr U | W 2-1 | 1-0 | — | McAllister [48], James [77] | 2003 |
| 13 | 15 | A | Hamilton A | D 1-1 | 1-0 | 3 | Hagen [26] | 1777 |
| 14 | 22 | H | Raith R | L 0-1 | 0-1 | 4 | | 3248 |
| 15 | 29 | A | St Mirren | L 0-2 | 0-1 | 4 | | 2658 |
| 16 | Dec 6 | H | Partick Th | L 0-1 | 0-0 | 4 | | 2667 |
| 17 | 13 | A | Greenock Morton | W 2-0 | 1-0 | 4 | Hagen [38], James [81] | 2462 |
| 18 | 20 | H | Airdrieonians | W 2-1 | 1-1 | 3 | Craig [43], James [51] | 2636 |
| 19 | 27 | A | Dundee | W 1-0 | 1-0 | 2 | Moss [38] | 5074 |
| 20 | Jan 3 | A | Stirling A | W 6-0 | 4-0 | 2 | Crabbe [12], Keith [26], McAllister [38], Craig (pen) [45], Moss [59], Hagen [70] | 2954 |
| 21 | 10 | H | Hamilton A | W 3-1 | 1-1 | 2 | Keith [14], Craig [46], Crabbe [50] | 3115 |
| 22 | 31 | H | St Mirren | D 2-2 | 1-0 | 2 | Keith [41], Moss [72] | 3296 |
| 23 | Feb 3 | A | Raith R | L 0-2 | 0-1 | — | | 4666 |
| 24 | 7 | H | Greenock Morton | D 1-1 | 1-0 | 3 | Moss [2] | 2800 |
| 25 | 21 | A | Partick Th | D 0-0 | 0-0 | 3 | | 2972 |
| 26 | 25 | H | Ayr U | W 4-0 | 0-0 | — | Moss 2 [48, 75], Keith 2 [56, 72] | 2024 |
| 27 | Mar 3 | A | Airdrieonians | W 1-0 | 1-0 | — | McKenzie [21] | 1789 |
| 28 | 14 | H | Raith R | L 0-1 | 0-1 | 2 | | 3512 |
| 29 | 21 | A | St Mirren | W 2-1 | 2-0 | 2 | Crabbe [2], Keith [29] | 2694 |
| 30 | 24 | H | Partick Th | D 1-1 | 0-0 | — | Keith [45] | 4815 |
| 31 | 28 | A | Greenock Morton | D 1-1 | 0-0 | 3 | Moss [46] | 2672 |
| 32 | Apr 11 | H | Stirling A | W 1-0 | 0-0 | 2 | Moss [73] | 3521 |
| 33 | 18 | A | Hamilton A | W 2-1 | 1-0 | 2 | Hagen [7], McGrillen [80] | 1159 |
| 34 | 25 | H | Dundee | W 1-0 | 0-0 | 2 | McGrillen [64] | 4169 |
| 35 | May 2 | A | Ayr U | W 3-1 | 2-1 | 2 | McGowan [19], Moss [33], Keith [90] | 2809 |
| 36 | 9 | H | Airdrieonians | L 0-1 | 0-0 | 2 | | 3850 |

**Final League Position: 2**  1996–97 5

**Honours**
*League Champions:* Division II 1935-36, 1969-70, 1974-75. First Division 1990-91, 1993-94. Second Division 1979-80;
*Runners-up:* Division I 1907-08, 1909-10. First Division 1985-86, 1988-89. Division II 1904-05, 1951-52, 1960-61.
*Scottish Cup Winners:* 1913, 1957; *Runners-up:* 1997. *League Cup Runners-up:* 1947-48. *B&Q Cup Winners:* 1993-94.
*League Challenge Cup Winners:* 1997-98.
*Club colours:* Shirt: Navy blue. Shorts: White. Stockings: Navy blue.

**Goalscorers:** *League (56):* Moss 12, Keith 10, McGrillen 7 (1 pen), Crabbe 5 (1 pen), Craig 5 (1 pen), Hagen 4, James 4, McKenzie 3, McAllister 2, McGowan 2, Lawrie 1, McCart 1. *Scottish Cup (10):* Moss 3, Crabbe 2, McAllister 2, Hagen 1, Keith 1, Seaton 1. *Coca Cola Cup (4):* Moss 2, Crabbe 1, James 1. *League Challenge Cup (11):* Craig 4 (1 pen), Hagen 2, Corrigan 1, McAllister 1, McGowan 1, McGraw 1, McGrillen 1

| Nelson C 7 | McGowan J 33 | Seaton A 24+6 | Oliver N 23+1 | James K 17 | McCart C 14+2 | Hagen D 25+8 | Craig A 16+10 | Crabbe S 27+4 | McKenzie S 29 | McGrillen P 19+11 | Hamilton B 3+10 | McGraw M —+2 | Corrigan M 24+4 | Mathers P 29 | McAllister K 35 | Moss D 30 | Cunning J —+2 | Keith M 26+6 | Lawrie A 5+1 | Ward K —+2 | Berry N 10 | Ferguson D —+4 | Match No. |
|---|---|---|---|---|---|---|---|---|---|---|---|---|---|---|---|---|---|---|---|---|---|---|---|
| 1 | 2 | 3 | 4 | 5 | 6 | 7 | 8¹ | 9² | 10 | 11³ | 12 | 13 | 14 |  |  |  |  |  |  |  |  |  | 1 |
|  | 2 | 3 | 4 | 5 |  | 11 |  | 8 | 6¹ | 9³ | 12 | 13 | 14 | 1 | 7² | 10 |  |  |  |  |  |  | 2 |
|  | 2 | 3 | 4 | 5 |  | 11 |  | 8 | 6¹ | 9 | 12 |  |  | 1 | 7 | 10 |  |  |  |  |  |  | 3 |
| 1 | 3 |  | 2 | 5 | 4 | 11³ | 12 | 8¹ | 6 | 9¹ |  |  | 14 |  | 7 | 10 | 13 |  |  |  |  |  | 4 |
| 1 | 3 |  | 2 | 5² | 4 | 11 | 14 | 8 | 6³ | 9¹ |  |  | 13 |  | 7 | 10 |  | 12 |  |  |  |  | 5 |
|  | 5 | 3¹ | 4 |  | 6 | 12 | 14 | 13 | 8³ | 9 |  |  | 2 | 1 | 7 | 10² |  | 11 |  |  |  |  | 6 |
|  | 5 | 3¹ | 4 |  | 6 | 12 | 13 | 10 | 8² | 9 |  |  | 2 | 1 | 7 |  |  | 11 |  |  |  |  | 7 |
|  | 5 | 3 |  |  | 6 | 11 |  | 8¹ | 4 | 9² |  |  | 2 | 1 | 7 | 10 |  | 12 | 13 |  |  |  | 8 |
|  | 3 |  |  |  |  | 11 | 12 | 4¹ |  | 9 |  |  | 2 | 1 | 7 | 10 |  | 8 | 6 |  | 5 |  | 9 |
|  | 3 |  |  |  |  | 11² | 12 | 4 |  | 9 |  |  | 2 | 1 | 7 | 10¹ |  | 8 | 6 | 13 | 5 |  | 10 |
|  | 3 | 13 |  | 5 |  | 11 | 8 | 4¹ |  | 9 |  |  | 2² | 1 | 7 | 10 |  | 12 |  |  | 6 |  | 11 |
|  | 3 | 13 | 12 | 5 |  | 11 |  | 4² |  | 9 |  |  | 2 | 1 | 7 | 10 |  | 8 |  |  | 6¹ |  | 12 |
|  | 3 | 13 | 4 | 5 |  | 11 | 12 |  |  | 9 |  |  | 2 | 1 | 7 | 10² |  | 8¹ |  |  | 6 |  | 13 |
|  | 3 | 4¹ | 5 |  |  | 11 | 8 | 12 |  | 9 |  |  | 2 | 1 | 7 | 10² |  | 13 |  |  | 6 |  | 14 |
|  | 3 | 13 | 4 | 5 |  | 11 | 8 |  |  | 9 |  |  | 2 | 1 | 7 | 10¹ |  | 12 |  |  | 6² |  | 15 |
| 1 | 3 |  | 4 | 5 |  | 13 | 12 | 8¹ | 6² | 11 |  |  | 2 |  | 7 | 10 |  | 9 |  |  |  |  | 16 |
| 1 | 3 |  | 2 | 5 | 6 | 11 |  | 8¹ | 4 | 12 |  |  |  |  | 7 | 10 |  | 9 |  |  |  |  | 17 |
| 1 | 3 | 13 | 2 | 5 | 6 |  | 8² | 9 | 4 | 12 |  |  |  |  | 7 | 10 |  | 11 |  |  |  |  | 18 |
| 1 | 6 | 3 | 2 | 5 | 12 | 8 | 9¹ | 4 | 13 |  |  |  |  |  | 7 | 10 |  | 11¹ |  |  |  |  | 19 |
|  | 6 | 3 | 2 | 5 | 12 | 8¹ | 9 | 4 | 13 |  |  |  |  | 1 | 7 | 10 |  | 11 |  |  |  |  | 20 |
|  | 6 | 3 | 2 | 5 | 12 | 8² | 9 | 4¹ | 14 | 13 |  |  |  | 1 | 7 | 10 |  | 11³ |  |  |  |  | 21 |
|  | 4 | 3 | 2 |  | 6 | 8 | 9 | 12 |  |  |  |  |  | 1 | 7 | 10 |  | 11¹ | 5 |  |  |  | 22 |
|  | 4 | 3 | 2 | 5 | 6 | 8 | 9 |  |  |  |  |  |  | 1 | 7 | 10 |  | 11 |  |  |  |  | 23 |
|  | 4 | 3 |  | 5 | 6¹ | 8 | 9 | 12 |  |  |  |  | 2 | 1 | 7 | 10 |  | 11 |  |  |  |  | 24 |
|  | 4 | 3 |  | 5 | 12 | 8¹ | 9² | 6 | 13 |  |  |  | 2 | 1 | 7 | 10 |  | 11 |  |  |  |  | 25 |
|  | 4 | 3 |  | 5 | 12 | 8 | 9¹ | 6 | 13 |  |  |  | 2 | 1 | 7 | 10² |  | 11 |  |  |  |  | 26 |
|  | 4 | 3 |  | 5 |  | 9 | 8² | 12 | 6 | 13 |  |  | 2 | 1 | 7 | 10 |  | 11¹ |  |  |  |  | 27 |
|  | 4 | 3 | 5¹ | 12 | 10 | 9¹ | 6 | 14 | 8² |  |  |  | 2 | 1 | 7 |  |  | 11 |  |  | 13 |  | 28 |
|  | 4 | 3 |  | 5 | 10 | 9 | 6 | 12 | 8 |  |  |  | 2 | 1 | 7 |  |  | 11¹ |  |  |  |  | 29 |
|  | 4 | 3 |  | 5 | 10² | 14 | 9 | 6³ | 13 | 8¹ |  |  | 2 | 1 | 7 |  |  | 11 |  |  | 12 |  | 30 |
|  | 4 | 3 |  |  | 8 | 9¹ | 6 | 12 |  |  |  |  | 2 | 1 | 7 | 10 |  | 11 | 5 |  |  |  | 31 |
|  | 4 | 3 |  | 12 | 8² | 9 | 6 | 13 |  |  |  |  | 2 | 1 | 7 | 10³ |  | 11 | 5¹ | 14 |  |  | 32 |
|  | 4 | 3² | 5 | 8 | 12 | 9 | 6 | 13 |  |  |  |  | 2 | 1 | 7 | 10¹ |  | 11² |  |  |  | 14 | 33 |
|  | 3 |  | 5 | 11 | 12 | 9² | 6¹ | 8 |  |  |  |  | 2 | 1 | 7 | 10 | 13 |  |  |  | 4 |  | 34 |
|  | 3¹ | 12 | 5 | 11 |  | 9 | 6 | 8² |  |  |  |  | 2 | 1 | 7 | 10 | 13 |  |  |  | 4 |  | 35 |
|  | 3 |  | 5 | 6¹ |  | 9 |  | 8 | 13 |  |  |  | 2 | 1 | 7 | 10 | 12 | 11² |  |  | 4 |  | 36 |

# FORFAR ATHLETIC

## Second Division

*Year Formed:* 1885. *Ground & Address:* Station Park, Carseview Road, Forfar. *Telephone:* 01307 463576/462259. *Fax:* 01307 466956.
*Ground Capacity:* total: 8732. seated: 739. *Size of Pitch:* 115yd × 69yd.
*Chairman and Secretary:* David McGregor.
*Manager:* Ian McPhee. *Assistant Manager:* Billy Bennett. *Physio:* Jim Peacock. *Coaches:* Raymond Lorimer, Malcolm Lowe.
*Managers since 1975:* Jerry Kerr; Archie Knox; Alex Rae; Doug Houston; Henry Hall; Bobby Glennie; Paul Hegarty; Tommy Campbell. *Club Nickname(s):* Loons. *Previous Grounds:* None.
*Record Attendance:* 10,780 v Rangers, Scottish Cup 2nd rd; 2 Feb, 1970.
*Record Transfer Fee received:* £65,000 for David Bingham to Dunfermline Ath (September 1995).
*Record Transfer Fee paid:* £50,000 for Ian McPhee from Airdrieonians (1991).
*Record Victory:* 14-1 v Lindertis, Scottish Cup 1st rd; 1 Sept 1988.
*Record Defeat:* 2-12 v King's Park, Division II; 2 Jan, 1930.
*Most Capped Player:* —.
*Most League Appearances:* 484: Ian McPhee, 1978–88 and 1991–98.

## FORFAR ATHLETIC 1997–98 LEAGUE RECORD

| Match No. | Date | Venue | Opponents | Result | H/T Score | Lg. Pos. | Goalscorers | Atten- dance |
|---|---|---|---|---|---|---|---|---|
| 1 | Aug 16 | A | Clyde | W 2-1 | 1-1 | — | Cargill [43], Honeyman [57] | 732 |
| 2 | 23 | H | Brechin C | L 2-5 | 2-1 | 6 | Morgan [15], Cargill [18] | 607 |
| 3 | 30 | H | Clydebank | L 0-2 | 0-2 | 7 | | 449 |
| 4 | Sept 7 | H | East Fife | L 1-2 | 1-2 | — | Mann [26] | 587 |
| 5 | 13 | A | Queen of the S | W 1-0 | 0-0 | 6 | McLauchlan [88] | 1011 |
| 6 | 20 | H | Stranraer | W 3-1 | 2-0 | 5 | Honeyman 2 [4, 70], McPhee [43] | 420 |
| 7 | 27 | A | Stenhousemuir | W 4-1 | 2-0 | 3 | Craig [13], Loney [15], Honeyman [70], McLauchlan [88] | 431 |
| 8 | Oct 4 | H | Inverness CT | W 2-1 | 0-1 | 3 | McLauchlan [83], Craig [88] | 531 |
| 9 | 18 | A | Livingston | L 3-4 | 1-1 | 4 | Honeyman 2 [19, 89], McLauchlan [67] | 1467 |
| 10 | 25 | A | Brechin C | L 0-2 | 0-0 | 5 | | 620 |
| 11 | Nov 1 | H | Clyde | D 2-2 | 0-2 | 5 | Loney [87], Honeyman [88] | 527 |
| 12 | 8 | A | Clydebank | D 1-1 | 0-0 | 4 | Gray [66] | 325 |
| 13 | 15 | H | Queen of the S | L 2-4 | 1-1 | 6 | Cargill [29], Honeyman (pen) [89] | 497 |
| 14 | 22 | H | Stenhousemuir | D 1-1 | 1-0 | 6 | Honeyman [24] | 385 |
| 15 | 29 | A | Stranraer | D 2-2 | 2-0 | 6 | Loney [15], Cargill [40] | 486 |
| 16 | Dec 13 | H | Livingston | D 2-2 | 2-1 | 7 | Watson (og) [20], McLauchlan [37] | 410 |
| 17 | 20 | A | Inverness CT | D 2-2 | 2-1 | 6 | Mann [24], Cargill [38] | 1521 |
| 18 | 27 | A | Brechin C | W 5-0 | 1-0 | 4 | Mann 2 (1 pen) [37, 60 ip], McLauchlan [64], Farningham [72], Nairn [75] | 810 |
| 19 | Jan 11 | A | East Fife | L 0-1 | 0-1 | — | | 902 |
| 20 | 31 | H | Stranraer | W 2-1 | 2-0 | 5 | McLauchlan [2], Cargill [14] | 410 |
| 21 | Feb 3 | A | Stenhousemuir | D 2-2 | 0-1 | — | Nairn [50], McLauchlan [80] | 298 |
| 22 | 7 | A | Livingston | L 0-4 | 0-3 | 5 | | 990 |
| 23 | 21 | H | East Fife | W 1-0 | 0-0 | 6 | Honeyman (pen) [61] | 460 |
| 24 | 25 | A | Clyde | W 2-1 | 1-0 | — | Honeyman [4], Mann [61] | 401 |
| 25 | 28 | H | Clydebank | D 0-0 | 0-0 | 4 | | 497 |
| 26 | Mar 7 | A | Queen of the S | L 1-5 | 1-2 | 5 | McLauchlan [33] | 1209 |
| 27 | 10 | H | Inverness CT | L 1-2 | 0-2 | — | Honeyman [76] | 432 |
| 28 | 14 | H | Stenhousemuir | L 0-1 | 0-1 | 7 | | 404 |
| 29 | 21 | A | Stranraer | L 0-4 | 0-1 | 8 | | 472 |
| 30 | 28 | H | Livingston | W 2-1 | 1-0 | 7 | McLauchlan [6], Allison [84] | 522 |
| 31 | Apr 4 | A | Inverness CT | D 0-0 | 0-0 | 6 | | 1315 |
| 32 | 11 | A | Clydebank | W 1-0 | 0-0 | 6 | Gray [65] | 276 |
| 33 | 18 | H | Queen of the S | L 2-4 | 1-1 | 6 | McLauchlan 2 [30, 89] | 490 |
| 34 | 25 | A | Brechin C | D 1-1 | 1-0 | 7 | McLauchlan [29] | 521 |
| 35 | May 2 | H | Clyde | L 0-1 | 0-0 | 7 | | 583 |
| 36 | 9 | A | East Fife | W 1-0 | 0-0 | 7 | McLauchlan [81] | 816 |

**Final League Position: 7**       1996–97 DIV 3 2

*Most League Goals in Season (Individual):* 45: Dave Kilgour, Division II; 1929–30.
*Most Goals Overall (Individual):* 124, John Clark.

**Honours**
*League Champions:* Second Division 1983–84. Third Division 1994–95; *Runners-up:* 1996–97. C Division 1948–49.
*Scottish Cup:* Semi-finals 1982.
*League Cup:* Semi-finals 1982.
*Scottish Cup:* Semi-finals 1977–78.
*Club colours:* Shirt: Sky blue with navy piping. Shorts: Navy. Stockings: Navy.

**Goalscorers:** *League (51):* McLauchlan 14, Honeyman 12 (2 pens), Cargill 6, Mann 5 (1 pen), Loney 3, Craig 2, Gray 2, Nairn 2, Allison 1, Farningham 1, McPhee 1, Morgan 1, own goal 1. *Scottish Cup (1):* Honeyman 1. *Coca Cola Cup (1):* Honeyman 1. *League Challenge Cup (3):* Glennie 1, Mann 1, Morgan 1 (pen).

| Robertson D 29 | McCheyne G 24+2 | Craig D 29+2 | Hamilton J 36 | Mann R 24 | Glennie S 4+2 | Cargill A 34 | Allison J 28+4 | Morgan A 3 | Honeyman B 29+5 | Lee I 20+1 | Nairn J 21+4 | Loney J 16+8 | Hannigan P 4+14 | Ferguson G 27+1 | McLauchlan M 25+3 | Roberts P 2+6 | McPhee I 4 | Farningham R 9 | Gray A 14+5 | Donegan J 7+1 | Scott R 7 | McLean B —+1 | Match No. |
|---|---|---|---|---|---|---|---|---|---|---|---|---|---|---|---|---|---|---|---|---|---|---|---|
| 1 | 2 | 3 | 4 | 5 | 6 | 7 | 8 | 9[1] | 10 | 11 | 12 | | | | | | | | | | | | 1 |
| 1 | 2 | 3 | 4 | 5 | | 7 | | | 9 | 10 | 11 | 6[1] | 8 | 12 | | | | | | | | | 2 |
| 1 | 2 | 3[1] | 4 | | 6 | 7 | 12 | 9 | 10 | 11[3] | | | 8[2] | 5 | 13 | 14 | | | | | | | 3 |
| 1 | 2[1] | 3[2] | 4 | 5[2] | 6 | 7 | 8 | | 10 | 11 | 13 | 12 | 14 | 9 | | | | | | | | | 4 |
| 1 | | 3 | 4 | | | 8 | 2 | | 10 | | 11 | | | 5 | 7 | 9 | 6 | | | | | | 5 |
| 1 | | 3 | 4 | | 14 | 8 | 2 | | 9 | 11[3] | 10 | 12 | | 5 | 7[2] | 13 | 6[1] | | | | | | 6 |
| 1 | 13 | 3 | 4 | | 12 | 8[3] | 2 | | 9[2] | 11 | 14 | 10 | | 5 | 7 | | 6[1] | | | | | | 7 |
| 1 | 2 | 3 | 4 | | | 8 | 6 | | 9 | 11 | 10 | | | 5 | 7 | | | | | | | | 8 |
| 1 | 2 | 3 | 4 | | | 8 | 6 | | 9 | 11 | 10 | | | 5 | 7 | | | | | | | | 9 |
| 1 | 2 | 3 | 4[2] | | | 6 | | | 9 | 11 | 13 | 10[1] | 12 | 5 | 7 | | | 8 | | | | | 10 |
| 1 | 2 | 3[1] | 4 | | | 8 | 6[2] | | 9 | 11 | 13 | 10 | 12 | 5 | 7[1] | 14 | | | | | | | 11 |
| 1 | 2 | 12 | 4 | 3 | | 6 | | | 11 | | 10 | | | 7 | 5 | | | 8 | 9[1] | | | | 12 |
| 1 | 2 | | 4 | 3 | | 6 | | | 7 | | 11 | 10 | 12 | 5[1] | | | | 8 | 9 | | | | 13 |
| 1 | 2[2] | 6 | 4 | 5 | | 7 | 13 | | 9 | | 10 | 11[1] | 12 | | | | | 8 | 3 | | | | 14 |
| 1 | 2 | 6 | 4 | 5 | | 8[1] | | | 9 | 11 | 10 | 12 | | | | | | 7 | 3 | | | | 15 |
| | 2 | 3 | 4 | 5 | | 12 | | | 10 | | | | 8 | 11[1] | 9 | 7 | 6 | 1 | | | | | 16 |
| | 2[1] | 3 | 4 | 5 | | 11 | 12 | | 10 | | | 8 | 13 | 6[1] | 9[2] | 7 | 14 | 1 | | | | | 17 |
| | | 3 | 4 | 5 | | 11[3] | 2 | | 10[1] | 8 | | 12 | 13 | 6 | 9[2] | 7 | 14 | 1 | | | | | 18 |
| | | 3 | 4[1] | 5 | | 8 | 2 | | 9 | 10 | 11 | 12 | | 6 | 7 | | | 1 | | | | | 19 |
| | 2 | 3 | 4 | | | 7 | 6[1] | | 10 | 8 | | 12 | 11 | 5 | 9 | | | 1 | | | | | 20 |
| | 2[2] | 3 | 4 | | | 7 | 6 | | 10 | 8 | | 12 | 11[1] | 5 | 9 | 13 | | 1 | | | | | 21 |
| | 2[1] | 3 | 4 | 11 | | 7 | 6[2] | | 10 | 8 | | 13 | 12 | 5 | 9 | | | 1 | | | | | 22 |
| 1 | | 3 | 4 | | | 9 | 2 | | 10 | 11 | | 8 | | 5 | 7 | | | | 6 | | | | 23 |
| 1 | | 3 | 4 | | 6 | 9 | 2 | | 10[1] | 11 | | 8 | 12 | 5 | 7 | | | | | | | | 24 |
| 1 | | 3 | 4 | | 6 | 9 | 2 | | 10[1] | 11 | | 8 | | 5 | 7 | 12 | | | | | | | 25 |
| 1 | | 3 | 4 | | 6 | 9 | 2 | | 10[2] | 11 | | | 14 | 5 | 7[3] | 13 | | 8[1] | 12 | | | | 26 |
| 1 | | 3[1] | 4 | | 6 | 9 | 2 | | 10 | 8[2] | | 11 | | 5 | 7 | 13 | | 12 | | | | | 27 |
| 1 | | | 4 | 5 | | 11 | 2 | | 10 | 13 | | 8 | 12 | 6 | 7[1] | | | | 3[2] | | 9 | | 28 |
| 1 | 12 | | 4 | 5 | | 7 | 2 | | 10[3] | 11[1] | | 8 | 14 | 6 | 13 | | | | 3 | | 9[2] | | 29 |
| 1 | 2 | | 4 | | 6 | 10 | 7 | | 12 | | | 8 | | 5 | 11 | | | | 3 | | 9[1] | | 30 |
| 1 | 2 | | 4 | | 6 | 10 | 7 | | 12 | | | 8 | | 5 | 11 | | | | 3 | | 9[1] | | 31 |
| 1 | 2 | 12 | 4 | | 6 | 10[2] | 7 | | 13 | | | 8 | 14 | 5 | 11[2] | | | | 3 | | 9[1] | | 32 |
| 1 | 2 | 5 | 4[1] | | 6 | 10 | 7 | | 12 | | | 8 | | | 11 | | | | 3 | | 9 | | 33 |
| 1 | 2 | 5 | 4 | | 6 | 10 | 7 | | 12 | | | 8 | | | 11 | | | | 3 | | 9[1] | | 34 |
| 1[6] | 2 | 5 | 4 | | 6 | 10 | 7 | | 11 | | | 8[1] | | 9 | | | | | 3 | 15 | | 12 | 35 |
| 1 | 2 | 3 | 4 | | 6 | 10 | 7 | | 11[1] | | | 8 | 12 | 5 | | | | | | | 9 | | 36 |

# GREENOCK MORTON

## First Division

*Year Formed:* 1874. *Ground & Address:* Cappielow Park, Sinclair St, Greenock. *Telephone:* 01475 723571.
*Ground Capacity:* total: 14,267. seated: 5257. *Size of Pitch:* 110yd × 71yd.
*Chairman:* Hugh Scott. *Secretary:* Mrs Jane Rankin.
*Manager:* Billy Stark. *Assistant Manager:* Peter Cormack, Sr. *Physio:* John Tierney. *Coach:* John McMaster.
*Managers since 1975:* Joe Gilroy; Benny Rooney; Alex Miller; Tommy McLean; Willie McLean, Allan McGraw. *Club
Nickname(s):* The Ton. *Previous Grounds:* Grant Street 1874, Garvel Park 1875, Cappielow Park 1879, Ladyburn Park
1882, (Cappielow Park 1883).
*Record Attendance:* 23,500 v Celtic; 1922.
*Record Transfer Fee received:* £350,000 for Neil Orr to West Ham U.
*Record Transfer Fee paid:* £150,000 for Allan Mahood from Nottingham Forest.
*Record Victory:* 11-0 v Carfin Shamrock, Scottish Cup 1st rd; 13 Nov, 1886.
*Record Defeat:* 1-10 v Port Glasgow Ath, Division II; 5 May, 1894 and v St Bernards, Division II; 14 Oct, 1933.
*Most Capped Player:* Jimmy Cowan, 25, Scotland.
*Most League Appearances:* 358: David Hayes, 1969-84.
*Most League Goals in Season (Individual):* 58: Allan McGraw, Division II; 1963-64.

## GREENOCK MORTON 1997–98 LEAGUE RECORD

| Match No. | Date | | Venue | Opponents | Result | | H/T Score | Lg. Pos. | Goalscorers | Attendance |
|---|---|---|---|---|---|---|---|---|---|---|
| 1 | Aug | 2 | A | Ayr U | W | 2-1 | 2-0 | — | Flannery (pen) 4, Mahood 41 | 3481 |
| 2 | | 16 | H | Hamilton A | L | 0-2 | 0-0 | 4 | | 2524 |
| 3 | | 23 | A | Stirling A | W | 3-1 | 3-0 | 3 | Hawke 2 6, 25, Blair 41 | 1337 |
| 4 | | 30 | A | St Mirren | L | 1-2 | 1-0 | 5 | Blair 4 | 5654 |
| 5 | Sept | 13 | H | Airdrieonians | D | 1-1 | 0-0 | 4 | Collins 85 | 2327 |
| 6 | | 20 | A | Partick Th | L | 1-2 | 1-1 | 6 | Anderson 31 | 2136 |
| 7 | | 27 | H | Dundee | L | 0-2 | 0-0 | 8 | | 2342 |
| 8 | Oct | 4 | H | Raith R | L | 1-3 | 0-2 | 8 | Blaikie 82 | 2309 |
| 9 | | 18 | A | Falkirk | L | 0-1 | 0-0 | 8 | | 2642 |
| 10 | | 25 | H | Ayr U | D | 1-1 | 1-1 | 8 | Anderson 26 | 2344 |
| 11 | Nov | 1 | A | Hamilton A | L | 0-1 | 0-0 | 9 | | 1272 |
| 12 | | 8 | H | St Mirren | W | 3-0 | 2-0 | 8 | Duffield 2 3, 47, Hawke 9 | 4013 |
| 13 | | 15 | A | Airdrieonians | D | 3-3 | 1-2 | 6 | Collins 11, Hawke 2 80, 84 | 1652 |
| 14 | | 22 | A | Dundee | W | 1-0 | 0-0 | 7 | Hawke 73 | 3489 |
| 15 | | 29 | H | Partick Th | W | 3-2 | 1-1 | 7 | Reid 27, Archdeacon 62, Gray 68 | 3384 |
| 16 | Dec | 6 | A | Raith R | D | 0-0 | 0-0 | 7 | | 2792 |
| 17 | | 13 | H | Falkirk | L | 0-2 | 0-1 | 8 | | 2462 |
| 18 | | 20 | H | Stirling A | L | 1-3 | 1-2 | 8 | Duffield 9 | 1903 |
| 19 | | 27 | A | Ayr U | L | 1-2 | 1-1 | 10 | Hawke 19 | 2581 |
| 20 | Jan | 7 | A | St Mirren | L | 2-3 | 0-2 | — | Blair 49, Mahood 62 | 4554 |
| 21 | | 10 | A | Airdrieonians | L | 0-2 | 0-0 | 10 | | 2038 |
| 22 | | 17 | H | Dundee | D | 0-0 | 0-0 | 10 | | 2200 |
| 23 | | 31 | A | Partick Th | D | 3-3 | 2-1 | 10 | Twaddle 33, Reid 36, Duffield 56 | 3156 |
| 24 | Feb | 7 | A | Falkirk | D | 1-1 | 0-1 | 10 | Twaddle 55 | 2800 |
| 25 | | 14 | A | Hamilton A | W | 3-1 | 2-1 | 7 | Anderson 2 13, 63, Mahood 41 | 1717 |
| 26 | | 21 | H | Raith R | W | 3-1 | 2-0 | 7 | Collins 6, Mahood 10, Duffield 86 | 2289 |
| 27 | | 28 | A | Stirling A | D | 2-2 | 2-0 | 7 | Duffield 25, Mahood 33 | 1507 |
| 28 | Mar | 14 | A | Dundee | L | 0-2 | 0-2 | 7 | | 3432 |
| 29 | | 21 | H | Partick Th | W | 1-0 | 0-0 | 7 | Mahood 60 | 2989 |
| 30 | | 28 | H | Falkirk | D | 1-1 | 0-0 | 7 | Duffield 90 | 2672 |
| 31 | Apr | 4 | A | Raith R | W | 2-1 | 1-0 | 6 | Duffield 9, McPherson 86 | 2400 |
| 32 | | 11 | H | St Mirren | W | 2-0 | 1-0 | 5 | Morrow 3, Curran 56 | 4728 |
| 33 | | 18 | H | Airdrieonians | D | 1-1 | 0-1 | 5 | Hawke 86 | 1431 |
| 34 | | 25 | H | Ayr U | L | 0-1 | 0-1 | 5 | | 2315 |
| 35 | May | 2 | A | Hamilton A | W | 3-0 | 2-0 | 5 | Hawke 9, Craig (og) 43, Duffield 69 | 1089 |
| 36 | | 9 | H | Stirling A | W | 1-0 | 0-0 | 5 | Hawke 72 | 1819 |

**Final League Position: 5**          1996–97 8

**Honours**
*League Champions:* First Division 1977-78, 1983-84, 1986-87. Division II 1949-50, 1963-64, 1966-67. Second Division 1994-95. *Runners-up:* Division 1 1916-17, Division II 1899-1900, 1928-29, 1936-37.
*Scottish Cup Winners:* 1922; *Runners-up:* 1948. *League Cup Runners-up:* 1963-64.
*B&Q Cup: Runners-up:* 1992-93.

**European:** *UEFA Cup:* 2 matches (*Fairs Cup:* 1968-69).
*Club colours:* Shirt: Royal blue and white 4" Hoops. Shorts: White with royal blue panel down side. Stockings: Royal blue and white hoops.

**Goalscorers:** *League (47):* Hawke 10, Duffield 9, Mahood 6, Anderson 4, Blair 3, Collins 3, Reid 2, Twaddle 2, Archdeacon 1, Blaikie 1, Curran 1, Flannery 1, Gray 1, McPherson 1, Morrow 1, own goal 1. *Scottish Cup (0): Coca Cola Cup (4):* Hawke 3, Aitken 1 (pen). *League Challenge Cup (6):* Blaikie 2, Flannery 2, Anderson 1, McArthur 1.

| Wylie D 27 | Collins D 34 | Sukatia M 3 | Anderson J 33 | McCahill S 11 | Reid B 33 | Flannery P 2+3 | Mahood A 24 | Hawke W 32 | Cormack P 7+4 | McPherson C 26+7 | McArthur S 10+3 | Blair P 11+15 | Blaikie A 13+9 | Mason B —+1 | Juttla J 6+4 | McGraw M 7+6 | Aitken S 10+3 | Matheson R 7+2 | Gray S 14 | Seatelli V 1 | Gavin M 1 | Duffield P 25 | Archdeacon O 23 | Morrow J 4+5 | Hillcoat J 9 | Twaddle K 14 | Curran H 9 | George M —+2 | Match No. |
|---|---|---|---|---|---|---|---|---|---|---|---|---|---|---|---|---|---|---|---|---|---|---|---|---|---|---|---|---|---|
| 1 | 2 | 3 | 4 | 5 | 6 | 7² | 8¹ | 9 | 10 | 11 | 12 | 13 | | | | | | | | | | | | | | | | | 1 |
| 1 | 2 | | 4 | 5 | 6 | 7 | 8 | 9 | 10 | 11 | 3¹ | 12 | | | | | | | | | | | | | | | | | 2 |
| 1 | 2 | 3 | | 5 | 6 | 12 | 8 | 9 | | 4 | 10 | 7 | 11¹ | | | | | | | | | | | | | | | | 3 |
| 1 | 2 | 3 | 4 | 5 | 6 | 13 | | 9 | | 11² | 10 | 7 | 8¹ | 12 | | | | | | | | | | | | | | | 4 |
| 1 | 2 | | 4 | 5 | 6 | | 9 | 13 | 10 | 3² | 7 | 11¹ | | | 8 | 12 | | | | | | | | | | | | | 5 |
| 1 | 2 | | 4 | 5 | 6 | | 9 | | | 3 | 11² | | 13 | | 8 | 10 | 7¹ | 12 | | | | | | | | | | | 6 |
| 1 | 2 | | 4 | 5 | 6 | | 9 | | | 3 | 11¹ | | 12 | | 8 | 10 | | 7 | | | | | | | | | | | 7 |
| 1 | 2 | | | 5 | 6 | | 9 | | | 3¹ | | 8 | 11 | | 7 | 12 | | 4 | 10 | | | | | | | | | | 8 |
| 1 | 2 | | | 5 | 6 | 13 | 9 | | 11 | 3 | 7¹ | 8 | | | 12 | 10² | | | 4 | | | | | | | | | | 9 |
| 1 | 2 | | 4 | 5 | 6 | | 9 | 13 | 11 | 3 | 12 | 7 | | | | 10¹ | 8² | | | | | | | | | | | | 10 |
| 1 | 2 | | 5 | | 6 | | 9 | | 11 | 3 | | 8 | | | 7 | 12 | 10¹ | | 4 | | | | | | | | | | 11 |
| 1 | 2 | | 5 | | 6 | | 10 | 13 | 11 | 3 | | 8² | | | | 12 | 7¹ | | 4 | | | 9 | | | | | | | 12 |
| 1 | 2 | | 5 | | 6 | | 10 | | 11 | 3¹ | | 8 | | | 7 | 12 | | | 4 | | | 9 | | | | | | | 13 |
| 1 | 2 | | 5 | | 6 | | 10 | | 11³ | | | 8² | | 14 | 7¹ | 12 | | 13 | 4 | | | 9 | 3 | | | | | | 14 |
| 1 | 2 | | 5 | | 6 | | 10 | | 11² | | | 8 | 13 | | 7¹ | | | | 4 | | | 9 | 3 | 12 | | | | | 15 |
| 1 | 2 | | 5 | | 6 | | 10³ | | 11² | | | 8 | 13 | 14 | | 12 | | | 4 | | | 9 | 3 | 7¹ | | | | | 16 |
| 1 | 2¹ | | 5 | | 6 | | 10 | | 11 | | | 8² | | | 7 | 12 | | | 4 | | | 9 | 3 | 13 | | | | | 17 |
| 1 | 2 | | 5 | 6² | | | 10 | | 11 | | | 8 | 13 | | 7¹ | 12 | | | 4 | | | 9 | 3 | | | | | | 18 |
| 1 | 2¹ | | 5 | | 6 | | 10 | | 11² | | | 8 | 13 | | 7 | 12 | | | 4 | | | 9 | 3 | | | | | | 19 |
| | | | 5 | | 6 | | 10 | | 11² | | | 8 | 13 | | 7 | 12 | | 13 | 4¹ | | 2 | 9 | 3 | | 1 | | | | 20 |
| | | | 5 | | 6 | | 10 | | 11 | | | 8 | | | 7¹ | 12 | | | 4 | | 2 | 9 | 3 | | 1 | | | | 21 |
| | 2 | | 5 | | 6 | | 10 | | 11 | | | 8 | | | | 12 | | | 4 | | | 9 | 3 | | 1 | 7¹ | | | 22 |
| | 2 | | 5 | | 6 | | 9 | | 11 | | | 8¹ | | | | 12 | | | 4 | | | 10 | 3 | | 1 | 7 | | | 23 |
| | 2 | | 5 | | 6 | | | 9¹ | 11 | | | 8 | 13 | | | 12 | | | 4 | | | 10 | 3 | | 1 | 7² | | | 24 |
| | 2 | | 5 | | 6 | | | 13 | 11¹ | | | 8 | | | | 12 | | 9 | 4 | | | 10 | 3 | | 1 | 7² | | | 25 |
| | 2 | | 5 | | 6 | | | 13 | 11¹ | | | 8 | | 14 | | 12 | 9 | | 4 | | | 10³ | 3 | | 1 | 7² | | | 26 |
| | 2 | | 5 | | 6 | | 9 | | 11 | | | 8 | | | | 12 | | | 4 | | | 10³ | 3 | | | 7¹ | 4 | | 27 |
| | 2 | | 5 | | 6 | | 9 | | 11¹ | | | 8 | | | | 12 | | | | | | 10 | 3 | | 1 | 7 | 4 | | 28 |
| 1 | 2 | | 5 | | 6 | | 9 | | 11 | | | 8² | | | | 12 | | 13 | | | | 10¹ | 3 | | | 7 | 4 | | 29 |
| 1 | 2 | | 5 | | 6 | | 9 | | 11¹ | | | 8 | | | | | | | | | | 10 | 3 | 12 | | 7 | 4 | | 30 |
| 1 | 2 | | 5 | | 6 | | | | 11¹ | | | 8² | | 14 | | 12 | | 13 | | | | 10² | 3 | 9 | | 7 | 4 | | 31 |
| 1 | 2 | | 5 | | 6 | | 9 | | 11 | | | 8 | | | | 12 | | 13 | | | | 10¹ | 3 | 7² | | | 4 | | 32 |
| 1 | 2 | | 5 | | | | 9 | 6 | | | | 8 | | | | 12 | | | | | | 10 | 3 | 7¹ | | 11 | 4 | | 33 |
| 1 | 2 | | 5 | | 6 | | 9 | | 11² | | | 8 | 13 | | | | | | | | | 10 | 3 | 12 | | 7¹ | 4 | | 34 |
| 1 | 2 | | 5 | | 6 | | 9 | | 11² | | | 8 | | | | | | | | | | 10 | 3 | 12 | | 7¹ | 4 | 13 | 35 |
| 1 | 2 | | 5 | | 6 | | 9 | | 11¹ | | | 8 | 14 | | | | | 13 | | | | 10 | 3 | | | 7³ | 4² | 12 | 36 |

# HAMILTON ACADEMICAL   First Division

*Year Formed:* 1874. *Ground:* Firhill Park, Glasgow G20 7BA. *Telephone (match days only):* 0141 945 4811. *(Weekdays):* 01698 286103. *Club Address:* Enable Building, Prospect House, New Park St, Hamilton ML3 0BN. *Telephone:* 01698 286103. *Ground Capacity:* 20,876. *Size of Pitch:* 110yd × 74yd.
*Secretary:* Scott A. Struthers BA. *Commercial Manager:* Gary Clark
*Manager:* Sandy Clark. *Physio:* Jim Fallon.
*Managers since 1975:* J. Eric Smith; Dave McParland; John Blackley; Bertie Auld; John Lambie; Jim Dempsey; John Lambie; Billy McLaren; Iain Munro. *Club Nickname(s):* The Accies. *Previous Grounds:* Bent Farm, South Avenue, South Haugh.
*Record Attendance:* 28,690 v Hearts, Scottish Cup 3rd rd; 3 Mar, 1937.
*Record Transfer Fee received:* £380,000 for Paul Hartley to Millwall (July 1996).
*Record Transfer Fee paid:* £60,000 for Paul Martin from Kilmarnock (Oct 1988) and for John McQuade from Dumbarton (Aug 1993).
*Record Victory:* 11-1 v Chryston, Lanarkshire Cup; 28 Nov, 1885.
*Record Defeat:* 1-11 v Hibernian, Division I; 6 Nov, 1965.
*Most Capped Player:* Colin Miller, 29, Canada, 1988-94.
*Most League Appearances:* 452: Rikki Ferguson, 1974-88.
*Most League Goals in Season (Individual):* 34: David Wilson, Division I; 1936-37.
*Most Goals Overall (Individual):* 246: David Wilson, 1928-39.

## HAMILTON ACADEMICAL 1997–98 LEAGUE RECORD

| Match No. | Date | Venue | Opponents | Result | H/T Score | Lg. Pos. | Goalscorers | Attendance |
|---|---|---|---|---|---|---|---|---|
| 1 | Aug 2 | H | Partick Th | D | 1-1 | 1-0 | — | McCormick [3] | 1221 |
| 2 | 16 | A | Greenock Morton | W | 2-0 | 0-0 | 3 | Clark [59], Cunnington [73] | 2524 |
| 3 | 23 | H | Raith R | W | 2-0 | 0-0 | 2 | Sherry [52], Ritchie [66] | 1140 |
| 4 | 30 | H | Ayr U | L | 0-2 | 0-2 | 3 | | 915 |
| 5 | Sept 13 | A | Falkirk | W | 4-1 | 3-1 | 2 | Sherry [15], Quitongo [31], McFarlane 2 [40, 78] | 2539 |
| 6 | 20 | A | Dundee | W | 2-0 | 2-0 | 1 | Cunnington [27], McFarlane [36] | 3611 |
| 7 | 27 | H | Stirling A | W | 3-2 | 2-2 | 1 | Quitongo [25], Clark [27], McFarlane [52] | 910 |
| 8 | Oct 4 | H | St Mirren | W | 2-0 | 1-0 | 1 | Clark [35], McCormick [54] | 1758 |
| 9 | 18 | A | Airdrieonians | D | 0-0 | 0-0 | 2 | | 1514 |
| 10 | 25 | H | Partick Th | D | 3-3 | 1-2 | 2 | Clark [1], Renicks [62], McCulloch [90] | 2316 |
| 11 | Nov 1 | H | Greenock Morton | W | 1-0 | 0-0 | 1 | McEntegart [83] | 1272 |
| 12 | 8 | A | Ayr U | W | 2-1 | 2-0 | 1 | Sherry [12], Ritchie [19] | 2093 |
| 13 | 15 | H | Falkirk | D | 1-1 | 0-1 | 2 | Berry (og) [48] | 1777 |
| 14 | 22 | A | Stirling A | L | 1-2 | 0-0 | 2 | McEntegart [84] | 921 |
| 15 | 29 | H | Dundee | L | 0-4 | 0-1 | 2 | | 1967 |
| 16 | Dec 6 | A | St Mirren | L | 1-2 | 1-1 | 2 | Geraghty [38] | 2992 |
| 17 | 20 | A | Raith R | L | 1-3 | 1-0 | 4 | Clark [21] | 2789 |
| 18 | 27 | H | Partick Th | L | 0-1 | 0-1 | 4 | | 2049 |
| 19 | 30 | H | Airdrieonians | D | 0-0 | 0-0 | — | | 1516 |
| 20 | Jan 10 | A | Falkirk | L | 1-3 | 1-1 | 5 | Hillcoat C [11] | 3115 |
| 21 | 31 | A | Dundee | D | 1-1 | 0-1 | 5 | Thomson [84] | 3028 |
| 22 | Feb 7 | A | Airdrieonians | L | 2-3 | 1-1 | 5 | Ritchie [15], Thomson [73] | 1316 |
| 23 | 14 | A | Greenock Morton | L | 1-3 | 1-2 | 5 | Craig [18] | 1717 |
| 24 | 17 | H | Ayr U | D | 1-1 | 1-0 | — | Ritchie (pen) [25] | 732 |
| 25 | 23 | H | St Mirren | D | 1-1 | 0-1 | — | McQuade [70] | 1459 |
| 26 | Mar 3 | H | Stirling A | D | 2-2 | 2-1 | — | McQuade [3], Ritchie [12] | 802 |
| 27 | 14 | A | Stirling A | W | 1-0 | 0-0 | 5 | Craig [81] | 1104 |
| 28 | 17 | H | Raith R | L | 1-4 | 1-1 | — | Clark [12] | 711 |
| 29 | 21 | H | Dundee | L | 1-2 | 1-2 | 5 | Thomson [9] | 1180 |
| 30 | 28 | A | Airdrieonians | L | 0-2 | 0-1 | 5 | | 1028 |
| 31 | Apr 4 | A | St Mirren | D | 2-2 | 2-1 | 5 | Ritchie 2 [23, 33] | 1885 |
| 32 | 11 | A | Ayr U | L | 1-2 | 1-1 | 6 | McQuade [40] | 1680 |
| 33 | 18 | H | Falkirk | L | 1-2 | 0-1 | 6 | McCormick [56] | 1159 |
| 34 | 25 | A | Partick Th | D | 0-0 | 0-0 | 6 | | 2993 |
| 35 | May 2 | H | Greenock Morton | L | 0-3 | 0-2 | 6 | | 1089 |
| 36 | 9 | A | Raith R | L | 1-2 | 1-0 | 8 | Fotheringham (og) [14] | 2036 |

**Final League Position: 8**        1996–97 DIV 2 2

**Honours**
*League Champions:* First Division 1985-86, 1987-88; *Runners-up:* Second Division 1996–97. Division II 1903-04; *Runners-up:* Division II 1952-53, 1964-65.
*Scottish Cup Runners-up:* 1911, 1935. *League Cup:* Semi-finalists three times.
*B&Q Cup Winners:* 1991-92 and 1992-93.
*Club colours:* Shirt: Red and white hoops. Shorts: White. Stockings: White.

**Goalscorers:** *League (43):* Ritchie 7 (1 pen), Clark 6, McFarlane 4, McCormick 3, McQuade 3, Sherry 3, Thomson 3, Craig 2, Cunnington 2, McEntegart 2, Quitongo 2, Geraghty 1, Hillcoat C 1, McCulloch 1, Renicks 1, own goals 2. *Scottish Cup (1):* McCormick 1. *Coca Cola Cup (0). League Challenge Cup (9):* Cunnington 2, Geraghty 2, Ritchie 2, Clark 1, Davidson 1, McFarlane 1.

| Ferguson A 25 | Hillcoat C 18 + 2 | Renicks S 34 | Thomson S 35 | McCulloch S 15 | McIntosh M 1 | Quitongo J 6 | Sherry J 26 | Ritchie P 23 + 6 | McCormick S 23 + 7 | Cunnington E 25 + 3 | Geraghty M 4 + 4 | McFarlane D 23 + 8 | Clark G 23 + 3 | McQuade J 15 + 11 | McKenzie P 17 + 10 | Bonnar M 1 + 4 | Davidson W — + 3 | McEntegart S 29 + 1 | Craig D 32 | McCondichie A 5 | Hillcoat J 1 | Wales G — + 3 | Hogarth M 5 | Krivokapic M 2 | McArthur S 8 | McLaren R — + 1 | Match No. |
|---|---|---|---|---|---|---|---|---|---|---|---|---|---|---|---|---|---|---|---|---|---|---|---|---|---|---|---|
| 1 | 2 | 3 | 4 | 5 | 6 | 7 | 8 | 9¹ | 10² | 11 | 12 | 13 |  |  |  |  |  |  |  |  |  |  |  |  |  |  | 1 |
| 1 | 2 | 3 | 4 | 5 |  | 7 | 8 | 9² | 10¹ | 6 | 12 | 13 | 11 |  |  |  |  |  |  |  |  |  |  |  |  |  | 2 |
| 1 | 2 | 3 | 4 | 5 |  | 7² | 8 | 9¹ | 6 |  |  | 10² | 11 | 12 | 13 | 14 |  |  |  |  |  |  |  |  |  |  | 3 |
| 1 | 2 | 3 | 4² | 5 |  | 7 | 8 |  | 6 |  |  | 9¹ | 10 | 11 | 12 | 13 |  |  |  |  |  |  |  |  |  |  | 4 |
| 1 |  | 3 | 2 | 5¹ |  | 7 | 8² |  |  | 12 | 11 | 14 | 9 | 10³ |  | 13 |  | 4 | 6 |  |  |  |  |  |  |  | 5 |
|  |  | 3 | 2 | 5¹ |  | 7 | 8 |  |  | 13 | 11 | 12 | 9² | 10 | 7 |  |  | 4 | 6 | 1 |  |  |  |  |  |  | 6 |
| 1 |  | 3 | 2 | 5 |  | 7 |  |  |  | 12 | 11 |  | 9 | 10 | 8¹ |  |  | 4 | 6 |  |  |  |  |  |  |  | 7 |
| 1 |  | 3 | 2 | 5 |  |  |  |  |  | 7 | 11 |  | 9¹ | 10 | 12 | 8 |  | 4 | 6 |  |  |  |  |  |  |  | 8 |
| 1 |  | 3 | 2 | 5 |  |  | 8 |  |  | 13 | 11 |  | 9² | 10¹ | 12 | 7 |  | 4 | 6 |  |  |  |  |  |  |  | 9 |
| 1 |  | 3 | 2 | 5 |  |  | 8 |  |  | 13 | 11 |  | 9 | 10¹ | 7² | 12 |  | 4 | 6 |  |  |  |  |  |  |  | 10 |
| 1 |  | 3 | 2 | 5 |  |  | 8 |  |  | 9¹ | 10 | 11 | 7² | 12 | 13 |  |  | 4 | 6 |  |  |  |  |  |  |  | 11 |
| 1 |  | 3 | 2 | 5 |  |  | 8 |  |  | 9 | 10² | 11 | 7¹ | 12 | 13 |  |  | 4 | 6 |  |  |  |  |  |  |  | 12 |
| 1 | 12 | 3 | 2 | 5 |  |  | 8 |  |  | 9 | 10 | 11 | 7¹ |  |  |  |  | 4 | 6 |  |  |  |  |  |  |  | 13 |
|  | 2 | 3 |  | 5¹ |  |  | 8 |  |  |  |  | 14 | 9² | 10 | 7¹ | 11 | 12 | 4 | 6 |  | 1 | 13 |  |  |  |  | 14 |
| 1 | 2 | 3 | 10 | 5 |  |  | 8³ |  |  |  |  | 14 | 9¹ | 12 | 11² | 7 | 13 | 4 | 6 |  |  |  |  |  |  |  | 15 |
| 1 | 2 |  |  | 5 |  |  | 8 |  |  | 12 | 7² | 3 | 9 | 10¹ | 11 | 13 |  | 4 | 6 |  |  |  |  |  |  |  | 16 |
|  | 2 | 3 |  | 5 |  |  | 8 |  |  | 9 | 13 |  | 10¹ | 11 | 7² | 12 |  | 4 | 6 |  |  |  | 1 |  |  |  | 17 |
|  | 2 | 3 |  | 5 |  |  | 8 |  |  | 9² | 10 |  | 11¹ | 12 | 7 | 13 |  | 4 | 6 |  |  |  | 1 |  |  |  | 18 |
|  | 2 | 3 | 4 |  |  |  | 8 |  |  |  |  | 10 | 9 | 11 |  |  |  | 7 | 6 |  |  |  | 1 |  | 5 |  | 19 |
|  | 2 | 3 | 4 |  |  |  | 8 |  |  | 14 | 10 | 12 | 9³ | 13 | 11² |  |  | 7 | 6 |  |  |  | 1 |  | 5¹ |  | 20 |
|  |  | 3 | 2 |  |  |  |  |  |  | 9 | 7² | 5 | 13 | 10 | 12 | 11¹ |  | 4 | 6 | 1 |  | 8 |  |  |  |  | 21 |
|  |  | 3 | 2 |  |  |  |  |  |  | 9 |  | 11 | 7¹ | 10 | 12 | 5 |  | 4 | 6 | 1 |  | 8 |  |  |  |  | 22 |
|  |  | 3 | 2 |  |  |  | 8² |  |  | 9 |  | 11 | 7 | 10¹ | 12 | 5 | 13 | 4 | 6 | 1 |  |  |  |  |  |  | 23 |
|  |  | 3 | 2 |  |  |  | 8 |  |  | 9 |  | 12 | 5 | 7¹ | 10 | 11 |  | 4 | 6 | 1 |  |  |  |  |  |  | 24 |
| 1 |  | 3 | 2 |  |  |  | 8 |  |  | 9 |  | 5 | 7 | 10 | 11 |  |  | 4 | 6 |  |  |  |  |  |  |  | 25 |
| 1 |  | 3 | 2 |  |  |  | 8 |  |  | 9 |  | 5 | 7¹ | 12 | 10 | 11 |  | 4 | 6 |  |  |  |  |  |  |  | 26 |
| 1 |  | 3 | 2 |  |  |  |  |  |  | 9² | 7¹ |  | 12 | 11 | 10 | 8 | 13 | 4 | 6 |  |  |  |  |  | 5 |  | 27 |
| 1 | 12 | 3 | 2 |  |  |  |  |  |  | 9 | 7³ | 13 | 11 | 10² | 8 | 14 |  | 4¹ | 6 |  |  |  |  |  | 5 |  | 28 |
|  |  | 3 | 2 |  |  |  |  |  |  | 9 | 7 | 12 | 11 | 10 | 8¹ |  |  | 4 | 6 |  |  |  | 1 |  | 5 |  | 29 |
| 1 | 2 | 3 |  |  |  |  |  |  |  | 9 | 7 | 12 | 11 | 10 | 8¹ |  |  | 4 | 6 |  |  |  |  |  | 5 |  | 30 |
| 1 | 2 | 3 |  |  |  |  | 8 |  |  | 9 | 7² | 5 | 13 | 11¹ | 10 | 12 |  | 4 | 6 |  |  |  |  |  |  |  | 31 |
| 1 | 2 | 3 | 4 |  |  |  | 8 |  |  | 9 | 7 |  | 11¹ | 12 | 10 |  |  |  | 6 |  |  |  |  |  | 5 |  | 32 |
| 1 | 2 | 3 | 4 |  |  |  | 8 |  |  | 9 | 7 | 13 | 11² | 10¹ | 12 |  |  |  | 6 |  |  |  |  |  | 5¹ |  | 33 |
| 1 | 2 | 3 | 4 |  |  |  | 8 |  |  | 12 | 7² | 5 | 9 | 11 | 10¹ | 13 |  |  | 6 |  |  |  |  |  |  |  | 34 |
| 1 | 2 | 3 | 4 |  |  |  | 8 |  |  | 13 | 7¹ | 5 | 9² | 10 |  | 11 |  |  | 6 |  |  |  |  | 12 |  |  | 35 |
| 1 | 2 | 3 | 4 |  |  |  |  |  |  | 12 | 7² | 11³ | 9¹ | 10 |  | 8 |  | 5 | 6 |  |  |  |  | 13 |  | 14 | 36 |

# HEART OF MIDLOTHIAN   Premier League

*Year Formed:* 1874. *Ground & Address:* Tynecastle Park, Gorgie Rd, Edinburgh EH11 2NL. *Telephone:* 0131 337 6132.
*Fax:* 0131 346 0699. *Website:* www.heartsfc.co.uk.
*Ground Capacity:* 18,300. *Size of Pitch:* 108yd × 73yd.
*Chairman:* Leslie Deans. *Chief Executive:* Christopher Robinson. *Sales and Marketing Manager:* Susan Bonnar.
*Commercial Manager:* Tommy Dickson.
*Manager:* Jim Jefferies. *Assistant Manager:* Billy Brown.
*Physio:* Alan Rae. *Coach:* Peter Houston.
*Managers since 1975:* J. Hagart; W. Ormond; R. Moncur; T. Ford; A. MacDonald; A. MacDonald & W. Jardine; A. MacDonald; J. Jordan, S. Clark, T. McLean.
*Club Nickname(s):* Hearts. *Previous Grounds:* The Meadows 1874, Powderhall 1878, Old Tynecastle 1881, (Tynecastle Park, 1886).
*Record Attendance:* 53,396 v Rangers, Scottish Cup 3rd rd; 13 Feb, 1932.
*Record Transfer Fee received:* £2,100,000 for Alan McLaren from Rangers (October 1994).
*Record of Transfer paid:* £750,000 for Derek Ferguson to Rangers (July 1990).
*Record Victory:* 21-0 v Anchor, EFA Cup 30th October 1880.
*Record Defeat:* 1-8 v Vale of Leven, Scottish Cup, 1888.
*Most Capped Player:* Bobby Walker, 29, Scotland.
*Most League Appearances:* 515: Gary Mackay, 1980-97.
*Most League Goals in Season (Individual):* 44: Barney Battles.
*Most Goals Overall (Individual):* 214: John Robertson, 1983-98.

## HEART OF MIDLOTHIAN 1997–98 LEAGUE RECORD

| Match No. | Date | Venue | Opponents | Result | H/T Score | Lg. Pos. | Goalscorers | Attendance |
|---|---|---|---|---|---|---|---|---|
| 1 | Aug 4 | A | Rangers | L | 1-3 | 0-2 | — | Cameron [86] | 48,257 |
| 2 | 16 | H | Aberdeen | W | 4-1 | 3-1 | 3 | Robertson (pen) [35], Fulton [37], Cameron [41], Flögel [89] | 12,367 |
| 3 | 23 | A | Dunfermline Ath | L | 1-2 | 0-0 | 6 | Hamilton [89] | 8823 |
| 4 | 30 | A | Hibernian | W | 1-0 | 1-0 | 5 | McCann [7] | 15,565 |
| 5 | Sept 13 | A | St Johnstone | W | 2-1 | 1-0 | 2 | Hamilton 2 [19, 65] | 5836 |
| 6 | 20 | H | Dundee U | W | 2-1 | 1-1 | — | Pressley (og) [44], Robertson [60] | 13,515 |
| 7 | 27 | A | Kilmarnock | W | 3-0 | 3-0 | 1 | Weir [6], Hamilton [14], Adam [43] | 7875 |
| 8 | Oct 4 | A | Motherwell | W | 4-1 | 3-1 | 1 | Cameron [6], Adam [14], McCann [20], Hamilton [73] | 8886 |
| 9 | 18 | H | Celtic | L | 1-2 | 0-2 | 3 | Cameron [65] | 16,977 |
| 10 | 29 | H | Dunfermline Ath | W | 3-1 | 1-0 | — | McCann [12], Adam [70], Fulton [89] | 14,493 |
| 11 | Nov 1 | A | Aberdeen | W | 4-1 | 0-1 | 1 | McCann [54], Flögel 2 [65, 82], Robertson [77] | 15,097 |
| 12 | 8 | H | Hibernian | W | 2-0 | 1-0 | 1 | Robertson [17], Quitongo [86] | 16,739 |
| 13 | 15 | H | St Johnstone | W | 2-1 | 0-0 | 1 | Flögel [48], Cameron (pen) [90] | 13,611 |
| 14 | 23 | H | Kilmarnock | W | 5-3 | 2-1 | 1 | Adam 3 [10, 61, 70], McCann [28], Quitongo [88] | 16,015 |
| 15 | Dec 6 | H | Motherwell | W | 2-0 | 1-0 | 1 | Cameron (pen) [45], Flögel [68] | 12,706 |
| 16 | 9 | A | Dundee U | D | 0-0 | 0-0 | — | | 10,402 |
| 17 | 13 | A | Celtic | L | 0-1 | 0-0 | 1 | | 49,806 |
| 18 | 20 | H | Rangers | L | 2-5 | 1-2 | 3 | Robertson [18], Hamilton [85] | 17,092 |
| 19 | 27 | A | Dunfermline Ath | W | 3-1 | 3-1 | 2 | Hamilton [7], Westwater (og) [17], Salvatori [28] | 11,722 |
| 20 | Jan 1 | H | Hibernian | D | 2-2 | 2-0 | — | Fulton 2 [6, 10] | 17,564 |
| 21 | 12 | A | St Johnstone | W | 3-2 | 2-0 | — | Hamilton 2 [29, 70], Naysmith [36] | 5408 |
| 22 | 17 | A | Kilmarnock | D | 2-2 | 2-1 | 2 | McCann [6], MacPherson (og) [45] | 11,079 |
| 23 | 31 | A | Dundee U | W | 2-0 | 1-0 | 2 | Cameron 2 [30, 79] | 14,414 |
| 24 | Feb 8 | H | Celtic | D | 1-1 | 0-1 | — | Quitongo [90] | 17,657 |
| 25 | 21 | A | Motherwell | W | 4-2 | 1-2 | 3 | Hamilton 2 [38, 58], Fulton [64], Adam [87] | 8375 |
| 26 | 25 | H | Aberdeen | W | 3-1 | 1-0 | — | Hamilton 2 [2], Naysmith [63], McCann [77] | 16,512 |
| 27 | 28 | A | Rangers | D | 2-2 | 1-1 | 2 | McCann [31], Hamilton [76] | 50,046 |
| 28 | Mar 14 | H | Kilmarnock | D | 1-1 | 1-1 | 2 | McPherson [23] | 15,338 |
| 29 | 21 | A | Dundee U | W | 1-0 | 1-0 | 2 | Hamilton [8] | 10,400 |
| 30 | 28 | A | Celtic | D | 0-0 | 0-0 | 2 | | 49,978 |
| 31 | Apr 8 | H | Motherwell | D | 1-1 | 0-0 | — | McCann [61] | 14,737 |
| 32 | 11 | A | Hibernian | L | 1-2 | 0-0 | 3 | Robertson [68] | 15,530 |
| 33 | 18 | H | St Johnstone | D | 1-1 | 0-0 | 3 | McPherson [75] | 15,034 |
| 34 | 25 | A | Rangers | L | 0-3 | 0-0 | 3 | | 17,415 |
| 35 | May 2 | A | Aberdeen | D | 2-2 | 2-1 | 3 | McCann [10], McPherson [29] | 12,899 |
| 36 | 9 | H | Dunfermline Ath | W | 2-0 | 1-0 | 3 | Adam [22], Holmes [83] | 13,888 |

**Final League Position: 3**          1996–97 4

**Honours**

*League Champions:* Division I 1894-95, 1896-97, 1957-58, 1959-60. First Division 1979-80; *Runners-up:* Division I 1893-94, 1898-99, 1903-04, 1905-06, 1914-15, 1937-38, 1953-54, 1956-57, 1958-59, 1964-65. Premier Division 1985-86, 1987-88, 1991-92. First Division 1977-78, 1982-83.
*Scottish Cup Winners:* 1891, 1896, 1901, 1906, 1956, 1998 *Runners-up:* 1903, 1907, 1968, 1976, 1986, 1996.
*League Cup Winners:* 1954-55, 1958-59, 1959-60, 1962-63; *Runners-up:* 1961-62, 1996–97.

**European:** *European Cup:* 4 matches (1958-59, 1960-61). *Cup Winners' Cup:* 6 matches (1976-77, 1996-97). *UEFA Cup:* 33 matches (*Fairs Cup:* 1961-62, 1963-64, 1965-66. *UEFA Cup:* 1984-85, 1986-87, 1988-89, 1990-91, 1992-93, 1993-94).
*Club colours:* Shirt: Maroon. Shorts: White. Stockings: Maroon with white tops.

**Goalscorers:** *League (70):* Hamilton 14, McCann 10, Adam 8, Cameron 8 (2 pens), Robertson 6 (1 pen), Flögel 5, Fulton 5, McPherson 3, Quitongo 3, Naysmith 2, Holmes 1, Salvatori 1, Weir 1, own goals 3. *Scottish Cup (14):* Adam 3, Cameron 2 (pens), Flögel 2, Quitongo 2, Fulton 1, Hamilton 1, McCann 1, Ritchie 1, Weir 1. *Coca Cola Cup (4):* McCann 2, Adam 1, Weir 1.

| Rousset G 32 | Frail S 6+5 | Pointon N 19+1 | Weir D 35 | Murray G 8+2 | Ritchie P 34 | Salvatori S 29+3 | Flögel T 13+16 | Hamilton J 20+12 | Fulton S 36 | McCann N 35 | Cameron C 30+1 | Adam S 28+2 | Robertson J 10+11 | McManus A 8+4 | Thomas K —+1 | Locke G 16+5 | McKenzie R 4 | Quitongo J 3+14 | Naysmith G 16 | McPherson D 10+3 | Murie D —+1 | Makel L 3+2 | Callaghan S 1 | Bradley M —+1 | Holmes D —+1 | Match No. |
|---|---|---|---|---|---|---|---|---|---|---|---|---|---|---|---|---|---|---|---|---|---|---|---|---|---|---|
| 1 | 2 | 3 | 4 | 5 | 6 | 7 | 8[1] | 9[2] | 10 | 11 | 12 | 13 | | | | | | | | | | | | | | 1 |
| 1 | 2[1] | 3 | 4 | 13 | 6 | 5 | 12 | | 8 | 7 | 10 | 11 | 9[1] | | | | | | | | | | | | | 2 |
| 1 | 2 | 3 | 4 | | 6 | 5[1] | 13 | 11 | 8 | 7 | 10[2] | | | 9[3] | 12 | 14 | | | | | | | | | | 3 |
| 1 | 2[1] | 3[2] | 4 | | 6 | 12 | 13 | 14 | 8 | 7 | 10 | 11 | 9[3] | 5 | | | | | | | | | | | | 4 |
| 1 | | 3 | 4 | | 6 | 5 | | 9[2] | 8 | 7 | 10[1] | 11 | 13 | 2 | | 12 | | | | | | | | | | 5 |
| 1 | | 3 | 4 | | 6 | 5 | | 9 | 8 | 7 | 10 | 11 | 12 | 2 | | | 1 | | | | | | | | | 6 |
| 1 | 12 | 3 | 4 | | 6 | 5[1] | 14 | 9 | 8 | 7 | 10[2] | 11[3] | | 2 | | 13 | | | | | | | | | | 7 |
| 1 | 13 | 3[1] | 4 | | 6 | 5[2] | | 9 | 8 | 7 | 10 | 11[3] | 14 | 2 | | 12 | | | | | | | | | | 8 |
| 1 | | 3 | 4 | | 6 | 5 | 14 | 9[2] | 8 | 7[3] | 10 | 11 | 13 | 2[1] | | 12 | | | | | | | | | | 9 |
| 1 | | 3[1] | 4 | | 6 | 5 | | 9 | 8 | 7 | 10 | 11 | | 12 | | | | | | | | | | | | 10 |
| 1 | | 3 | 4 | | 6 | 5 | 11 | 14 | 8[2] | 7 | 10[1] | | 9[3] | 13 | | 2 | | 12 | | | | | | | | 11 |
| 1 | | 3 | 4 | | 6 | 5 | 11[2] | 13 | 8 | 7 | 10 | | 9[1] | | | 2 | | 12 | | | | | | | | 12 |
| 1 | | | 4 | | 6 | 5 | 11[1] | 14 | 8 | 7 | 10 | 13 | 9[2] | | | 2 | | 12 | 3[3] | | | | | | | 13 |
| 1 | 3[1] | | 4 | | 6 | 5 | 11[2] | 12 | 8 | 7[3] | 10 | | 9 | 13 | | 2 | | 14 | | | | | | | | 14 |
| 1 | | 3 | 4 | | 6 | 5 | 11[2] | 12 | 8[1] | 7 | 10 | | 9[3] | 13 | | 2 | | 14 | | | | | | | | 15 |
| 1 | 3[2] | | 4 | | 6 | 5 | 11 | 13 | 8 | 7 | 10 | | 9 | | 12 | 2[1] | | | | | | | | | | 16 |
| 1 | 12 | 3[1] | 4 | | 6 | 5 | 11[2] | 14 | 8 | 7 | 10 | | 9[1] | 2 | | 13 | | | | | | | | | | 17 |
| 1 | | 3[1] | 4 | | 6 | 5 | 14 | 13 | 8 | 7 | 10[3] | 11[2] | 9 | 2 | | 12 | | | | | | | | | | 18 |
| 1 | 12 | 3 | 4 | | 6 | 5 | 13 | 11 | 8 | | 10[2] | | 9 | 2 | | 7[1] | | | | | | | | | | 19 |
| 1 | | 3[1] | 4 | | 6 | 5 | 12 | 13 | 8 | 7[2] | 10 | 11 | 9 | 2 | | | | | | | | | | | | 20 |
| 1 | 2[1] | | 4 | | 6 | | 12 | 11 | 8 | 7 | 10 | | 9[2] | | | | | 13 | 3 | 5 | | | | | | 21 |
| 1 | 12 | | 4 | | 6 | 5 | 11[2] | 13 | 8 | 7 | 10[1] | | 9[3] | | | | | 14 | 3 | 2 | | | | | | 22 |
| | | | | 12 | 6 | 5 | 11[1] | 13 | 8 | 7 | 10 | | 9 | 2 | | | 1 | | 3 | 4 | | | | | | 23 |
| | | | 4 | | 6 | | 11[1] | 14 | 8 | 7 | 10[3] | 13 | 9[2] | 2 | | | 1 | 12 | 3 | 5 | | | | | | 24 |
| 1 | | | 4 | | 6 | 2[1] | 13 | 11 | 8[2] | 7 | 10 | | 9 | | | | | 12 | 3 | 5 | | | | | | 25 |
| 1 | | | 4 | 5 | 6 | 13 | 12 | | 8 | 7 | 10[3] | | 9[2] | 2[1] | | | | 14 | 3 | | | | | | | 26 |
| 1 | | | 4 | 5 | 6 | 13 | 12 | 11[2] | 8 | 7 | 10 | | 9[1] | 2 | | | | | 3 | | | | | | | 27 |
| 1 | | | 4 | | 6 | 10 | 9[2] | 11 | 8 | 7 | | | | 2[1] | | 13 | | | 3 | 5 | | 12 | | | | 28 |
| 1 | | | 4 | 2[1] | 6 | 5 | 12 | 11 | 8 | 7 | 10 | | 9[1] | | | | | 13 | 3 | | | | | | | 29 |
| 1 | | | 4 | 2 | 6 | 5 | 12 | 11 | 8 | 7 | 10 | | 9[1] | | | | | | 3 | | | | | | | 30 |
| 1 | | | 4 | 2 | | 5 | | 11 | 8[2] | 7 | | 13 | 9 | | | | | 12 | 3 | 6 | | | 10[1] | | | 31 |
| 1 | | | 4 | 2[1] | 6 | 5[2] | 11 | | 8 | 7 | 10 | 13 | 9[3] | | | | | 14 | 3 | 12 | | | | | | 32 |
| | 3[1] | | 4 | 2[1] | 6 | 5 | | 11 | 8 | 7 | | 13 | 9[3] | | | | 1 | 14 | | 12 | | | 10 | | | 33 |
| 1 | | | 4 | | 6 | | 9 | | 8 | 7 | 12 | | | 5 | | | | | 3 | 2 | | | 10 | 11[1] | | 34 |
| 1 | | | 4 | | 6 | 5 | 12 | 11 | 8 | 7 | 10[2] | | 9[1] | | | | | | 3 | 2 | | | | 13 | | 35 |
| 1 | 13 | | 4 | | 6 | 5 | | 11 | 8 | 7[1] | 10[3] | | 9[2] | | | | | | 3 | 2 | | | 12 | | 14 | 36 |

# HIBERNIAN

## First Division

*Year Formed:* 1875. *Ground & Address:* Easter Road Stadium, Albion Rd, Edinburgh EH7 5QG. *Telephone:* 0131 661 2159. *Fax:* 0131 659 6488.
*Ground Capacity:* total: 16,218. *Size of Pitch:* 112yd × 74yd.
*Chairman:* Tom O'Malley. *Secretary:* Mary Anne McAdam. *Commercial Manager:* Ian Erskine.
*Manager:* Alex McLeish. *Assistant Manager:* Andrew Watson.
*Physio:* Malcolm Colquhoun. *Coach:* D. Park.
*Managers since 1975:* Eddie Turnbull; Willie Ormond; Bertie Auld; Pat Stanton; John Blackley, Alex Miller, Jim Duffy.
*Club Nickname(s):* Hibees. *Previous Grounds:* Meadows 1875-78, Powderhall 1878-79, Mayfield 1879-80, First Easter Road 1880-92, Second Easter Road 1892-.
*Record Attendance:* 65,860 v Hearts, Division I; 2 Jan, 1950.
*Record Transfer Fee received:* £1,000,000 for Andy Goram to Rangers (June 1991).
*Record Transfer Fee paid:* £420,000 for Keith Wright from Dundee.
*Record Victory:* 22-1 v 42nd Highlanders; 3 Sept, 1881.
*Record Defeat:* 0-10 v Rangers; 24 Dec, 1898.
*Most Capped Player:* Lawrie Reilly, 38, Scotland.
*Most League Appearances:* 446: Arthur Duncan.
*Most League Goals in Season (Individual):* 42: Joe Baker.
*Most Goals Overall (Individual):* 364: Gordon Smith.

## HIBERNIAN 1997–98 LEAGUE RECORD

| Match No. | Date | | Venue | Opponents | Result | H/T Score | Lg. Pos. | Goalscorers | Atten- dance |
|---|---|---|---|---|---|---|---|---|---|
| 1 | Aug | 3 | H | Celtic | W 2-1 | 1-1 | — | Power [24], Charnley [75] | 13,216 |
| 2 | | 17 | A | Dundee U | D 1-1 | 0-1 | 4 | Tosh [75] | 7344 |
| 3 | | 23 | H | Kilmarnock | W 4-0 | 2-0 | 1 | Crawford [6], Lavety [24], Miller W [64], McGinlay [89] | 9559 |
| 4 | | 30 | H | Hearts | L 0-1 | 0-1 | 1 | | 15,565 |
| 5 | Sept | 13 | A | Dunfermline Ath | W 5-2 | 3-1 | 1 | Charnley 2 [25, 79], Lavety [31], Crawford [38], McGinlay [55] | 10,002 |
| 6 | | 20 | A | Motherwell | D 1-1 | 0-0 | 2 | Rougier [48] | 7420 |
| 7 | | 27 | H | St Johnstone | D 1-1 | 1-1 | 3 | Crawford [2] | 11,104 |
| 8 | Oct | 4 | H | Rangers | L 3-4 | 2-1 | 4 | Lavety [19], McGinlay [28], Crawford [46] | 15,169 |
| 9 | | 18 | A | Aberdeen | L 0-2 | 0-2 | 4 | | 11,708 |
| 10 | | 25 | A | Kilmarnock | L 1-2 | 0-0 | 4 | Larasson [79] | 7541 |
| 11 | Nov | 1 | H | Dundee U | L 1-3 | 0-1 | 6 | Crawford [85] | 10,110 |
| 12 | | 8 | A | Hearts | L 0-2 | 0-1 | 8 | | 16,739 |
| 13 | | 15 | A | Dunfermline Ath | L 1-2 | 0-1 | 8 | Crawford [89] | 6952 |
| 14 | | 22 | A | St Johnstone | L 0-1 | 0-1 | 8 | | 5411 |
| 15 | | 29 | H | Motherwell | D 1-1 | 0-0 | 8 | Dods [74] | 9999 |
| 16 | Dec | 7 | A | Rangers | L 0-1 | 0-0 | — | | 48,070 |
| 17 | | 13 | H | Aberdeen | D 2-2 | 1-1 | 9 | Walker 2 [2, 84] | 10,008 |
| 18 | | 20 | A | Celtic | L 0-5 | 0-2 | 9 | | 48,605 |
| 19 | | 27 | H | Kilmarnock | L 0-1 | 0-1 | 10 | | 10,475 |
| 20 | Jan | 1 | H | Hearts | D 2-2 | 0-2 | — | Walker [51], McGinlay [67] | 17,564 |
| 21 | | 10 | H | Dunfermline Ath | W 1-0 | 1-0 | 10 | Crawford [36] | 10,616 |
| 22 | | 17 | H | St Johnstone | L 0-1 | 0-0 | 10 | | 9107 |
| 23 | | 31 | A | Motherwell | L 2-6 | 2-3 | 10 | Crawford [2], Lavety [10] | 6169 |
| 24 | Feb | 7 | A | Aberdeen | L 0-3 | 0-1 | 10 | | 12,043 |
| 25 | | 21 | H | Rangers | L 1-2 | 1-1 | 10 | Lavety [18] | 13,968 |
| 26 | | 24 | A | Dundee U | D 1-1 | 0-0 | — | Hughes [74] | 7989 |
| 27 | | 28 | H | Celtic | L 0-1 | 0-1 | 10 | | 15,137 |
| 28 | Mar | 14 | A | St Johnstone | D 1-1 | 0-0 | 10 | Rougier (pen) [86] | 6472 |
| 29 | | 21 | A | Motherwell | W 1-0 | 1-0 | 10 | Lavety [35] | 10,582 |
| 30 | | 28 | H | Aberdeen | D 1-1 | 0-0 | 10 | Rougier (pen) [90] | 12,966 |
| 31 | Apr | 1 | A | Rangers | L 0-3 | 0-0 | — | | 48,488 |
| 32 | | 11 | H | Hearts | W 2-1 | 0-0 | 10 | Lavety [56], Harper [81] | 15,530 |
| 33 | | 18 | A | Dunfermline Ath | D 1-1 | 0-0 | 10 | Welsh [90] | 12,749 |
| 34 | | 25 | A | Celtic | D 0-0 | 0-0 | 10 | | 49,619 |
| 35 | May | 2 | H | Dundee U | L 1-2 | 1-0 | 10 | Brebner [28] | 13,413 |
| 36 | | 9 | A | Kilmarnock | D 1-1 | 0-1 | 10 | Crawford [90] | 12,493 |

**Final League Position: 10**        1996–97 9

**Honours**
*League Champions:* Division I 1902-03, 1947-48, 1950-51, 1951-52. First Division 1980-81. Division II 1893-94, 1894-95, 1932-33; *Runners-up:* Division I 1896-97, 1946-47, 1949-50, 1952-53, 1973-74, 1974-75.
*Scottish Cup Winners:* 1887, 1902; *Runners-up:* 1896, 1914, 1923, 1924, 1947, 1958, 1972, 1979.
*League Cup Winners:* 1972-73, 1991-92; *Runners-up:* 1950-51, 1968-69, 1974-75, 1993-94.

**European:** *European Cup:* 6 matches (1955-56 semi-finals). *Cup Winners' Cup:* 6 matches (1972-73). *UEFA Cup:* 59 matches (*Fairs Cup:* 1960-61 semi-finals, 1961-62, 1962-63, 1965-66, 1967-68, 1968-69, 1970-71. *UEFA Cup:* 1973-74, 1974-75, 1975-76, 1976-77, 1978-79, 1989-90, 1992-93).
*Club colours:* Shirt: Green with white sleeves. Shorts: White. Stockings: Green with white trim.

**Goalscorers:** *League (38):* Crawford 9, Lavety 7, McGinlay 4, Charnley 3, Rougier 3 (2 pens), Walker 3, Brebner 1, Dods 1, Harper 1, Hughes 1, Larsson 1, Miller W 1, Power 1, Tosh 1, Welsh 1. *Scottish Cup (1):* McGinlay 1. *Coca Cola Cup (4):* Lavety 2, Charnley 1, McGinlay 1.

| Gottskalksson O 16 | Miller W 31 | Boco J 30 | Charnley J 17+3 | Hughes J 24+1 | Welsh B 15+2 | Dow A 23+9 | Power L 3+2 | Crawford S 35 | Rougier A 24+6 | McGinlay P 33 | Miller G —+3 | Tosh P 4+11 | Lavety B 22+4 | Harper K 20+7 | Grant B 1+4 | Dods D 28 | Jackson C 11+4 | McCaffrey S —+2 | Larsson S 3+4 | Renwick M 3+3 | Miller K 1+6 | Reid C 8 | Walker A 7+1 | McQuilken J 1 | Dennis S 5 | Donald G 1+3 | Gunn B 12 | Brebner G 9 | Elliot D 4 | Skinner W 5+1 | Bannerman S —+1 | Match No. |
|---|---|---|---|---|---|---|---|---|---|---|---|---|---|---|---|---|---|---|---|---|---|---|---|---|---|---|---|---|---|---|---|---|
| 1 | 2 | 3 | 4 | 5 | 6 | 7 | 8¹ | 9² | 10 | 11 | 12 | 13 | | | | | | | | | | | | | | | | | | | | 1 |
| 1 | 2 | 3 | 4 | 5 | 6¹ | 7 | 8² | 9³ | 10 | 11 | 12 | 13 | 14 | | | | | | | | | | | | | | | | | | | 2 |
| 1 | 2 | 3 | 6 | 5 | | 7 | | 9 | 10³ | 11 | | 13 | 14 | 8² | | 4 | 12 | | | | | | | | | | | | | | | 3 |
| 1 | 2 | 3 | 6² | 5 | | 7 | | 9 | 10 | 11 | | 13 | | 8¹ | 4 | 12 | | | | | | | | | | | | | | | | 4 |
| 1 | 2³ | 3 | 4² | 5 | 6 | 7 | | 9 | 10¹ | 11 | | 13 | 14 | 8 | | | 12 | | | | | | | | | | | | | | | 5 |
| 1 | 2 | 3 | 4 | 5 | 6 | 7¹ | | 9 | 10² | 11 | | 13 | | 8 | | | 12 | | | | | | | | | | | | | | | 6 |
| 1 | 2 | 3 | | 5 | 6¹ | 7² | | 9 | 10 | 11 | | 13 | | 8 | | 4 | 12 | | | | | | | | | | | | | | | 7 |
| 1 | 2 | 3 | 6 | 5 | | 7² | | 9 | 10¹ | 11 | | 13 | | 8 | | 4 | 12 | | | | | | | | | | | | | | | 8 |
| 1 | 2 | 3² | 6 | 5 | | 7 | | 9 | 10¹ | 11 | | 13 | | 8 | | 4 | 12 | | | | | | | | | | | | | | | 9 |
| 1 | 2 | 3 | 6¹ | 5 | | 7² | | 9 | 10 | 11 | | 13 | 14 | 8 | | 4³ | 12 | | | | | | | | | | | | | | | 10 |
| 1 | 2 | 3 | 6² | 5 | | 7¹ | | 9 | 10³ | 11 | | 13 | 14 | 8 | | 4 | 12 | | | | | | | | | | | | | | | 11 |
| 1 | 2 | 3 | 6² | 5 | | 7 | | 9 | 10¹ | 11 | | 13 | 14 | 8³ | | 4 | 12 | | | | | | | | | | | | | | | 12 |
| 1 | 2 | 3 | 6 | 5 | | 7² | | 9 | 10¹ | 11 | | 13 | | 8 | | 4 | 12 | | | | | | | | | | | | | | | 13 |
| 1 | 2³ | 3 | 6 | 5 | | 7 | | 9 | 10¹ | 11 | | 13 | 14 | 8² | | 4 | 12 | | | | | | | | | | | | | | | 14 |
| 1 | 2 | 3 | 6¹ | 5 | | 7 | | 9 | 10 | 11 | | 13 | | 8² | | 4 | 12 | | | | | | | | | | | | | | | 15 |
| | 2² | 3 | 6 | 5 | | 7 | | 9 | 10¹ | 11 | | 13 | | 8 | | 4 | 12 | | | | | 1 | | | | | | | | | | 16 |
| | 2 | 3 | 6¹ | 5 | | 7 | | 9 | 10² | 11 | | 13 | | 8 | | 4 | 12 | | | | | 1 | | | | | | | | | | 17 |
| | 2 | 3 | 6 | 5 | | 7¹ | | 9³ | 10² | 11 | | 13 | 14 | 8 | | 4 | 12 | | | | | 1 | | | | | | | | | | 18 |
| | 2 | 3 | 6² | 5¹ | | 7 | | 9 | 10 | 11 | | 13 | | 8 | | 4 | 12 | | | | | 1 | | | | | | | | | | 19 |
| | 2 | 3² | 6 | 5 | | 7 | | 9 | 10¹ | 11 | | 13 | | 8 | | 4 | 12 | | | | | 1 | | | | | | | | | | 20 |
| | 2 | 3 | 6 | 5 | | 7 | | 9 | 10¹ | 11 | | | | 8 | | 4 | 12 | | | | | 1 | | | | | | | | | | 21 |
| | 2 | 3 | 6 | 5 | | 7 | | 9 | 10 | 11 | | | | 8¹ | | 4 | 12 | | | | | 1 | | | | | | | | | | 22 |
| | 2 | 3 | 6 | 5 | | 7 | | 9 | 10 | 11 | | 13 | | 8² | | 4¹ | 12 | | | | | 1 | | | | | | | | | | 23 |
| 1 | 2 | 3 | 6 | 5 | | 7 | | 9 | 10 | 11 | | | | 8¹ | | 4 | 12 | | | | | | | | | | | | | | | 24 |
| | 2 | 3 | 6 | 5 | | 7 | | 9 | 10² | 11 | | 13 | | 8 | | 4¹ | 12 | | | | | | 13 | | | | 1 | | | | | 25 |
| | 2 | 3 | 6 | 5 | | 7 | | 9 | 10¹ | 11 | | | | 8 | | 4² | 12 | | | | | | 13 | | | | 1 | | | | | 26 |
| | 2 | 3 | 6 | 5 | | 7¹ | | 9 | 10 | 11 | | | | 8 | | 4 | 12 | | | | | | | | | | 1 | | | | | 27 |
| | 2 | 3¹ | 6 | 5 | | 7 | | 9³ | 10 | 11 | | 13 | 14 | 8² | | | 12 | | | | | | | | | | 1 | 4 | | | | 28 |
| | 2 | | 6 | 5 | | 7³ | | 9 | 10² | 11 | | 13 | 14 | 8¹ | | | 12 | | | | | | | | | | 1 | 4 | 3 | | | 29 |
| | 2 | 3² | 6 | 5 | | 7 | | 9 | 10¹ | 11 | | 13 | | 8 | | | 12 | | | | | | | | | | 1 | 4 | | | | 30 |
| | 2 | 3 | 6 | 5 | | 7¹ | | 9 | 10² | 11 | | 13 | | 8 | | | 12 | | | | | | | | | | 1 | 4 | | | | 31 |
| | 2 | 3 | 6 | 5 | | 7 | | 9 | 10¹ | 11 | | | | 8 | | | 12 | | | | | | | | | | 1 | 4 | | | | 32 |
| | 2 | 3 | 6 | 5 | | 7 | | 9¹ | 10 | 11 | | 13 | | 8 | | | 12 | | | | | | | | | | 1 | 4 | 13 | | | 33 |
| | 2 | 3 | 6 | 5 | | 7 | | 9² | 10 | 11 | | 13 | | 8¹ | | | 12 | | | | | | | | | | 1 | 4 | | 3 | | 34 |
| | 2 | | 6 | 5 | | 7¹ | | 9 | 10 | 11 | | 13 | | 8² | | | 12 | | | | | | | | | | 1 | 4 | | 3 | | 35 |
| | 2 | | 6 | 5 | | 7¹ | | 9 | 10 | 11 | | | | 8² | | | 12 | | | | | | | | | | 1 | 4 | | 3 | 13 | 36 |

# INVERNESS CALEDONIAN THISTLE
## Second Division

*Year Formed:* 1994. *Ground & Address:* Caledonian Stadium, East Longman, Inverness IV1 1FF. *Telephone:* 01463 222880.
*Ground Capacity:* 5600, seated 2200. *Size of Pitch:* 114yd × 74yd.
*President:* Dugald McGilvray. *Hon. Life President:* John S.McDonald. *Secretary:* Jim Falconer.
*Manager:* Steven W. Paterson. *Assistant Manager:* Alex Caldwell. *Physio:* Ian Manning. *Coach:* Alex Young. *Youth Development Officer:* Duncan Shearer.
*Record Attendance:* 5821 v Dundee United, Scottish Cup 4th rd replay, 18 February 1998.
*Record Victory:* 8-1, v Annan Ath, Scottish Cup 3rd rd, 24 January 1998.
*Record Defeat:* 0-4, v Queen's Park, Third Division, 20 August 1994 and v Montrose, Third Division, 14 February 1995.
*Most League Appearances:* 108, R. Hastings, 1995-98.
*Most League Goals in Season:* 27, Ian Stewart, 1996-97.
*Most Goals Overall (Individual):* 66, Ian Stewart, 1995-98.

### INVERNESS CALEDONIAN TH 1997–98 LEAGUE RECORD

| Match No. | Date | | Venue | Opponents | Result | H/T Score | Lg. Pos. | Goalscorers | Atten- dance |
|---|---|---|---|---|---|---|---|---|---|
| 1 | Aug | 6 | H | Livingston | D 1-1 | 0-0 | — | Thomson [88] | 2232 |
| 2 | | 16 | A | Brechin C | D 2-2 | 0-1 | 5 | Thomson [52], Stewart [77] | 459 |
| 3 | | 23 | H | East Fife | L 0-1 | 0-0 | 9 | | 1746 |
| 4 | | 30 | A | Stenhousemuir | L 2-3 | 0-2 | 8 | Thomson (pen) [47], Addicoat [85] | 442 |
| 5 | Sept | 13 | H | Stranraer | D 2-2 | 1-0 | 9 | Shearer [7], Stewart [82] | 1571 |
| 6 | | 20 | A | Queen of the S | L 1-2 | 0-0 | 10 | Wilson [63] | 1145 |
| 7 | | 27 | H | Clyde | L 1-2 | 1-1 | 10 | McCulloch [44] | 1751 |
| 8 | Oct | 4 | A | Forfar Ath | L 1-2 | 1-0 | 10 | Stewart [22] | 531 |
| 9 | | 18 | H | Clydebank | D 0-0 | 0-0 | 10 | | 1542 |
| 10 | | 25 | A | East Fife | W 5-1 | 3-1 | 10 | Shearer [5], Stewart 3 [7, 80, 82], Cherry [31] | 772 |
| 11 | Nov | 1 | H | Brechin C | D 0-0 | 0-0 | 10 | | 1905 |
| 12 | | 8 | H | Stenhousemuir | W 4-1 | 2-0 | 9 | Thomson [37], Wilson [44], Addicoat [71], Stewart [82] | 1669 |
| 13 | | 15 | A | Stranraer | L 1-2 | 1-0 | 9 | Thomson (pen) [19] | 644 |
| 14 | | 22 | A | Clyde | L 3-4 | 1-3 | 10 | Thomson [10], Cherry [46], Stewart [71] | 953 |
| 15 | | 29 | H | Queen of the S | W 2-1 | 1-0 | 10 | Stewart 2 (1 pen) [18, 70 (p)] | 1820 |
| 16 | Dec | 13 | A | Clydebank | D 1-1 | 0-0 | 9 | Ross [88] | 326 |
| 17 | | 20 | H | Forfar Ath | D 2-2 | 1-2 | 9 | Cherry 2 [11, 77] | 1521 |
| 18 | | 27 | A | East Fife | W 4-0 | 2-0 | 9 | Cherry [22], Robson [41], Teasdale [65], Wilson [85] | 2134 |
| 19 | Jan | 17 | H | Clyde | W 5-1 | 2-0 | 8 | Thomson [2], Wilson [20], Stewart 2 [69, 85], Robertson [80] | 1505 |
| 20 | | 31 | A | Queen of the S | L 0-1 | 0-1 | 9 | | 1322 |
| 21 | Feb | 7 | A | Clydebank | W 3-2 | 1-1 | 8 | Thomson (pen) [35], Shearer 2 [53, 59] | 1863 |
| 22 | | 21 | H | Livingston | D 2-2 | 2-2 | 8 | Shearer [37], McCulloch [44] | 2197 |
| 23 | | 25 | A | Brechin C | L 1-3 | 1-1 | — | Cherry [22] | 388 |
| 24 | | 28 | A | Stenhousemuir | W 3-0 | 1-0 | 8 | Robson [45], Thomson [55], Cherry [77] | 643 |
| 25 | Mar | 3 | A | Livingston | D 2-2 | 1-2 | — | Robson [19], Wilson [81] | 751 |
| 26 | | 7 | A | Stranraer | L 1-2 | 0-1 | 8 | Cherry [80] | 1582 |
| 27 | | 10 | A | Forfar Ath | W 2-1 | 2-0 | — | Sheerin 2 [19, 23] | 432 |
| 28 | | 14 | A | Clyde | W 6-1 | 3-0 | 6 | Thomson 2 [22, 83], Wilson [27], Sheerin [45], McLean [66], Stewart [85] | 766 |
| 29 | | 21 | H | Queen of the S | L 0-2 | 0-1 | 7 | | 1989 |
| 30 | | 28 | A | Clydebank | L 0-1 | 0-0 | 8 | | 344 |
| 31 | Apr | 4 | H | Forfar Ath | D 0-0 | 0-0 | 8 | | 1315 |
| 32 | | 11 | H | Stenhousemuir | W 2-1 | 1-1 | 7 | Teasdale 2 [31, 61] | 1414 |
| 33 | | 18 | A | Stranraer | L 1-3 | 1-0 | 7 | Stewart [14] | 667 |
| 34 | | 25 | A | East Fife | W 1-0 | 1-0 | 6 | Thomson [9] | 650 |
| 35 | May | 2 | H | Brechin C | W 2-1 | 2-0 | 6 | Thomson [38], Stewart [39] | 1955 |
| 36 | | 9 | A | Livingston | W 2-1 | 1-0 | 5 | Stewart [34], Sheerin [74] | 2812 |

**Final League Position: 5**          1996–97 DIV 3 1

**Honours**
*Scottish Cup:* Quarter-finals 1996.
*League Champions:* Third Division 1996–97.
*Club Colours:* Shirts: Blue with white stripes and thin red stripe. Shorts: Blue. Stockings: Blue with red tops.

**Goalscorers:** *League (65):* Stewart 16 (1 pen), Thomson 13 (3 pens), Cherry 8, Wilson 6, Shearer 5, Sheerin 4, Robson 3, Teasdale 3, Addicoat 2, McCulloch 2, McLean 1, Robertson 1, Ross 1. *Scottish Cup (16):* Stewart 4, Thomson 3, Wilson 3, Robson 2, McCulloch 1, Shearer 1, Sheerin 1, own goal 1. *Coca Cola Cup (7):* Thomson 4 (2 pens), Addicoat 1, Christie 1, Wilson 1. *League Challenge Cup (0).*

| Fridge L 15 | Teasdale M 18 + 4 | Hastings R 35 | MacArthur I 20 + 1 | Andersen V 30 + 2 | Cherry P 30 + 1 | Wilson B 24 + 9 | Thomson B 29 + 5 | Stewart J 25 + 5 | Christie C 13 + 1 | Ross D 12 + 13 | De-Barros M — + 1 | Addicoat W 3 + 20 | Noble M 2 + 2 | McCulloch M 32 | Shearer D 17 + 7 | Tokely R 13 + 5 | Robson B 15 + 8 | Calder J 21 | Robertson A 16 | Sheerin P 18 | McLean S 5 + 1 | Hood G 3 | Match No. |
|---|---|---|---|---|---|---|---|---|---|---|---|---|---|---|---|---|---|---|---|---|---|---|---|
| 1 | 2 | 3 | 4 | 5[2] | 6 | 7 | 8 | 9[2] | 10 | 11[1] | 12 | 13 | 14 | | | | | | | | | | 1 |
| 1 | 3 | 2 | 5 | 6 | 7[1] | 8 | 9 | 10 | 11 | | | 12 | 4 | | | | | | | | | | 2 |
| 1 | 2 | 3 | 4 | 5 | 6[1] | 7 | 8 | 9 | 10 | 13 | | 12 | | 11 | | | | | | | | | 3 |
| 1 | 2 | 3 | 4 | 5 | 6[1] | 7 | 8 | 9[2] | 10 | 12 | | 13 | | 11 | | | | | | | | | 4 |
| 1 | | 3 | 4 | 6 | 13 | 7 | | 9[1] | 12 | 10 | 2[3] | | 14 | 5[2] | 11 | | 8 | | | | | | 5 |
| 1 | 3 | 4 | 5 | 2[2] | 7 | 12 | | 9 | 10 | 11[3] | | | 14 | 13 | 6 | | 8[1] | | | | | | 6 |
| 1 | 12 | 3 | 4 | 5 | 2 | 7 | 10 | 9 | | 13 | | | 11[1] | 6 | | | 8 | | | | | | 7 |
| 1 | 5 | 4 | 3 | 2 | 12 | | | 9 | 10 | 13 | | | | 6 | 8 | 7[2] | 11[1] | | | | | | 8 |
| 1 | 5 | 2 | 3 | 6 | 7 | 10[2] | | 9 | 13 | | | | | 4 | 8 | 12 | 11 | | | | | | 9 |
| 1 | 5 | 3 | | | 6 | 7 | 10 | 9 | 12 | | | | | 4 | 8 | 2 | 11[1] | | | | | | 10 |
| 1 | 5 | 13 | 3 | | 6 | 7 | 10[1] | 9 | 12 | | | | 14 | 4 | 8[3] | 2 | 11[2] | | | | | | 11 |
| 1 | 5 | 2 | 3 | | 6 | 7 | 11 | 9 | 12 | | | | | 4 | 8[1] | | 10 | | | | | | 12 |
| 1 | 13 | 5 | 3 | 2 | 6 | 7[1] | 11 | 9[2] | 12 | | | | 14 | 4 | 8[3] | | 10 | | | | | | 13 |
| 1 | 5 | 2 | 3 | | 6 | | 10 | 9 | | 13 | | | 11[2] | 4 | 8 | 7[1] | 12 | | | | | | 14 |
| | 5 | 2[1] | 3 | | 6 | 7 | 13 | 8 | | | | | 14 | 4 | 9[3] | 12 | 11[2] | 1 | 10 | | | | 15 |
| | 2 | 5[1] | 3 | | 6 | 7 | 13 | 8[2] | | 11 | | | 14 | 4 | 9[3] | 12 | | 1 | 10 | | | | 16 |
| | 2 | 5 | 3 | | 6 | 7 | 8 | 9[1] | | | | | 14 | 4 | 11[3] | 13 | 12 | 1 | 10 | | | | 17 |
| | 2 | 5 | 3 | | 6 | 7 | 8[2] | 9[3] | 12 | | | | 14 | 4 | | 13 | 11[1] | 1 | 10 | | | | 18 |
| | 2 | 5 | 3 | | 6 | 7[1] | 8 | 9 | 12 | | | | | 4 | | 13 | 11[2] | 1 | 10 | | | | 19 |
| | 2 | 5 | 3 | | 6[1] | 7[4] | 8[2] | 9 | | | | | 14 | 4 | | 13 | 12 | 1 | 10 | 11 | | | 20 |
| | 2 | 5 | | | 6 | 7[4] | 8 | 9[1] | 12 | | | | 13 | 4 | | | 11 | 1 | 10 | | | 3 | 21 |
| | 2 | 5 | | | 6 | 7 | 8 | 9[2] | | | | | 11[1] | 4 | | 13 | 12 | 1 | 10 | | | 3 | 22 |
| | 2[1] | 5 | 12 | | 6 | 7[4] | 8 | 9[3] | | 11 | | | 14 | 4 | | 13 | | 1 | 10 | | | 3 | 23 |
| | 14 | 5 | 3 | 2 | 6 | 7 | 8[2] | 9[1] | 12 | | | | | 4 | | 13 | 11[3] | 1 | 10 | | | | 24 |
| | 5 | | 3[1] | 2 | 6 | 7[3] | 8 | 9[2] | 12 | | | | 14 | 4 | | 13 | 11 | 1 | 10 | | | | 25 |
| 1 | 5 | | 3 | 2 | 6 | 7 | 8[2] | 9 | 12 | | | | | 4 | | | | | 10 | 11[1] | 13 | | 26 |
| | 5 | | 3 | 2 | 6 | 7[3] | 8 | 9[1] | 12 | | | | 14 | 4 | | 13 | | 1 | 10[2] | 11 | | | 27 |
| | 5 | | 3 | 2 | 11[1] | 7 | 8 | 9[2] | 12 | | | | | 4 | | 13 | | 1 | 10 | 6 | | | 28 |
| | 13 | | 3 | 2[1] | 11 | 7 | 8 | 9[2] | 12 | | | | 14 | 4 | | | | 1 | 10[3] | 6 | | | 29 |
| | 5 | 2 | 3 | | | 7[2] | 8 | 9[1] | | | | | 14 | | | 13 | 11[3] | 1 | 10 | 6 | | 4 | 30 |
| | 5 | 2 | 3 | | | 7[1] | 8[2] | | | | | | 14 | | | 13 | 11 | 1 | | 6 | 9[3] | 4 | 31 |
| | 7 | | 3 | 2[2] | | | 8 | 9[1] | 12 | 11 | | | 14 | 4 | | 13 | 10 | 1 | | 6 | 5[1] | | 32 |
| | 7 | 5 | 2 | 3 | 6 | | 10 | 8[1] | 12 | | | | | 4 | 9 | 13 | | 1 | | 11[2] | | | 33 |
| | 7 | 5 | 2[1] | 3 | 6 | | 8 | | 12 | | | | | 4 | 9 | | 10 | 1 | | 11 | | | 34 |
| | 7 | 5[1] | 2 | 3[2] | 6 | | 8 | | 12 | | | | | 4 | 9 | 13 | 10 | 1 | | 11 | | | 35 |
| | 5[1] | 2 | 3 | | 6 | | | | 12 | | | | | 4 | 9 | 7 | 8 | 1 | 10 | 11 | | | 36 |

# KILMARNOCK                    Premier League

*Year Formed:* 1869. *Ground & Address:* Rugby Park, Kilmarnock KA1 2DP. *Telephone:* 01563 525184. *Fax:* 01563 522181. *Website:* www.kilmarnockfc.co.uk.
*Ground Capacity:* total: 18,128 seated. *Size of Pitch:* 114yd × 72yd.
*Chairman:* W. Costley. *Chief Executive:* I. Walsh. *Secretary:* Kevin Collins. *Commercial Manager:* J. McSherry. *Stadium Manager:* M. Gallagher.
*Manager:* Bobby Williamson. *Assistant Managers:* Jim Clark, Gerry McCabe. *Physio:* A. MacFie.
*Managers since 1975:* W. Fernie; D. Sneddon; J. Clunie; E. Morrison; J. Fleeting; T. Burns; A. Totten. *Club Nickname(s):* Killie. *Previous Grounds:* Rugby Park (Dundonald Road); The Grange; Holm Quarry; Present ground since 1899.
*Record Attendance:* 35,995 v Rangers, Scottish Cup; 10 March, 1962.
*Record Transfer Fee received:* £300,000 for Shaun McSkimming to Motherwell,1995.
*Record Transfer Fee paid:* £300,000 for Paul Wright from St Johnstone, 1995.
*Record Victory:* 11-1 v Paisley Academical, Scottish Cup; 18 Jan, 1930 (15-0 v Lanemark, Ayrshire Cup; 15 Nov, 1890).
*Record Defeat:* 1-9 v Celtic, Division I; 13 Aug, 1938.
*Most Capped Player:* Joe Nibloe, 11, Scotland.
*Most League Appearances:* 481: Alan Robertson, 1972-88.
*Most League Goals in Season (Individual):* 34: Harry 'Peerie' Cunningham 1927-28 and Andy Kerr 1960-61.
*Most Goals Overall (Individual):* 148: W. Culley; 1912-23.

## KILMARNOCK 1997–98 LEAGUE RECORD

| Match No. | Date | | Venue | Opponents | Result | H/T Score | Lg. Pos. | Goalscorers | Attendance |
|---|---|---|---|---|---|---|---|---|---|
| 1 | Aug | 2 | A | Aberdeen | D 0-0 | 0-0 | — | | 13,842 |
| 2 | | 23 | A | Hibernian | L 0-4 | 0-2 | 9 | | 9559 |
| 3 | Sept | 13 | A | Dundee U | W 2-1 | 1-0 | 8 | Wright 2 (1 pen) [15, 53 (p)] | 6883 |
| 4 | | 21 | A | Dunfermline Ath | D 1-1 | 0-0 | — | Wright (pen) [87] | 5374 |
| 5 | | 24 | H | Rangers | L 0-3 | 0-0 | — | | 15,367 |
| 6 | | 27 | H | Hearts | L 0-3 | 0-3 | 8 | | 7875 |
| 7 | Oct | 4 | A | Celtic | L 0-4 | 0-4 | 8 | | 47,955 |
| 8 | | 8 | H | Motherwell | W 2-1 | 2-1 | — | Vareille [30], Burke [37] | 6588 |
| 9 | | 18 | H | St Johnstone | L 0-1 | 0-1 | 8 | | 6572 |
| 10 | | 25 | H | Hibernian | W 2-1 | 0-0 | 7 | Roberts [54], Nevin [57] | 7541 |
| 11 | Nov | 1 | A | Rangers | L 1-4 | 1-1 | 8 | Mitchell [43] | 49,413 |
| 12 | | 8 | A | Motherwell | W 1-0 | 0-0 | 6 | Roberts (pen) [70] | 5346 |
| 13 | | 15 | A | Dundee U | L 1-3 | 1-0 | 7 | Roberts (pen) [10] | 7402 |
| 14 | | 23 | A | Hearts | L 3-5 | 1-2 | — | Nevin [6], Holt [60], Roberts [75] | 16,015 |
| 15 | | 29 | H | Dunfermline Ath | W 2-1 | 2-1 | 7 | Nevin 2 [28, 35] | 6667 |
| 16 | Dec | 6 | H | Celtic | D 0-0 | 0-0 | 7 | | 15,676 |
| 17 | | 13 | A | St Johnstone | D 1-1 | 0-0 | 7 | Mitchell [71] | 4385 |
| 18 | | 20 | H | Aberdeen | W 1-0 | 1-0 | 5 | Wright [27] | 8452 |
| 19 | | 27 | H | Hibernian | W 1-0 | 1-0 | 4 | Wright [42] | 10,475 |
| 20 | Jan | 3 | A | Motherwell | W 4-1 | 3-1 | 4 | Wright 2 [8, 33], Mitchell [44], Roberts [88] | 8724 |
| 21 | | 10 | A | Dundee U | D 1-1 | 0-1 | 4 | Reilly [79] | 7541 |
| 22 | | 17 | H | Hearts | D 2-2 | 1-2 | 4 | Wright [40], Reilly [76] | 11,079 |
| 23 | | 31 | A | Dunfermline Ath | L 2-3 | 1-1 | 5 | Vareille [2], Roberts [85] | 4903 |
| 24 | Feb | 7 | H | St Johnstone | W 1-0 | 0-0 | 4 | Reilly [90] | 7408 |
| 25 | | 21 | A | Celtic | L 0-4 | 0-2 | 4 | | 48,477 |
| 26 | | 24 | H | Rangers | D 1-1 | 1-1 | — | Wright [15] | 15,931 |
| 27 | | 28 | A | Aberdeen | D 0-0 | 0-0 | 4 | · | 10,423 |
| 28 | Mar | 14 | A | Hearts | D 1-1 | 1-1 | 4 | Henry [35] | 15,338 |
| 29 | | 21 | H | Dunfermline Ath | W 3-0 | 0-0 | 4 | Wright (pen) [62], Nevin [65], McIntyre [69] | 8230 |
| 30 | | 28 | A | St Johnstone | L 0-1 | 0-1 | 4 | | 4982 |
| 31 | Apr | 8 | H | Celtic | L 1-2 | 1-1 | — | Burke [40] | 18,076 |
| 32 | | 11 | A | Motherwell | D 1-1 | 1-0 | 5 | Holt [28] | 6209 |
| 33 | | 18 | H | Dundee U | W 1-0 | 1-0 | 4 | Burke [2] | 7468 |
| 34 | | 25 | H | Aberdeen | W 2-1 | 1-1 | 4 | Vareille 2 [33, 85] | 8212 |
| 35 | May | 2 | A | Rangers | W 1-0 | 0-0 | 4 | Mitchell [90] | 50,116 |
| 36 | | 9 | H | Hibernian | D 1-1 | 1-0 | 4 | Roberts [15] | 12,493 |

**Final League Position: 4**                    1996–97 7

**Honours**
League Champions: Division I 1964-65. Division II 1897-98, 1898-99; *Runners-up:* Division I 1959-60, 1960-61, 1962-63, 1963-64. First Division 1975-76, 1978-79, 1981-82, 1992-93. Division II 1953-54, 1973-74. Second Division 1989-90.
*Scottish Cup Winners:* 1920, 1929, 1997; *Runners-up:* 1898, 1932, 1938, 1957, 1960.
*League Cup Runners-up:* 1952-53, 1960-61, 1962-63.

**European:** *European Cup:* 4 matches (1965-66). *Cup Winners' Cup:* 4 matches (1997-98). *UEFA Cup:* 12 matches (*Fairs Cup:* 1964-65, 1966-67, 1969-70, 1970-71).
*Club colours:* Shirt: Blue and white vertical stripes. Shorts: Blue. Stockings: Blue.

**Goalscorers:** *League (40):* Wright 10 (2 pens), Roberts 7 (1 pen), Nevin 5, Mitchell 4, Vareille 4, Burke 3, Reilly 3, Holt 2, Henry 1, McIntyre 1. *Scottish Cup (2):* Roberts 1, Vareille 1. *Coca Cola Cup (4):* Vareille 2, Findlay 1, Wright 1.

| Lekovic D 13 | MacPherson A 25 | Baker M 18 + 1 | Montgomerie R 27 | McGowne K 21 + 5 | Reilly M 36 | Mitchell A 22 + 11 | Findlay W 2 + 3 | Wright P 26 + 2 | McIntyre J 6 + 2 | Bagan D 4 + 3 | Vareille J 24 + 10 | Nevin P 26 + 5 | Hamilton S 5 + 1 | Meldrum C 11 | Whitworth N 10 + 1 | Vincent R — + 2 | Roberts M 17 + 14 | Burke A 16 + 3 | Henry J 13 + 13 | Kerr D 14 | McCutcheon G — + 1 | Holt G 25 + 2 | Anderson D — + 1 | Lauchlan J 22 | Doig K 1 | Marshall G 12 | O'Neill M — + 2 | Match No. |
|---|---|---|---|---|---|---|---|---|---|---|---|---|---|---|---|---|---|---|---|---|---|---|---|---|---|---|---|---|
| 1 | 2 | 3 | 4 | 5 | 6 | 7 | 8 | 9 | 10¹ | 11² | 12 | 13 | | | | | | | | | | | | | | | | 1 |
| 1 | 2 | 3 | 4 | 5 | 6 | 8 | 14 | 9³ | 13 | 7 | 10² | 11¹ | 12 | | | | | | | | | | | | | | | 2 |
| | 3 | 2 | | 5 | 6 | 10 | 8 | 9² | 12 | 11³ | 7¹ | | | 1 | 4 | | 13 | 14 | | | | | | | | | | 3 |
| | 2 | 3 | | 5 | 6² | 8 | 7 | 9 | | 11¹ | 10 | | | 1 | 4 | | 13 | 12 | | | | | | | | | | 4 |
| | 2 | | 3² | 5 | 6 | 8 | | 9³ | | 12 | 7¹ | 10 | | 1 | 4 | | 13 | 14 | 11 | | | | | | | | | 5 |
| | 2 | 5¹ | 4 | | 6 | 7 | 8 | 9³ | | 13 | 10 | 11² | | 1 | 4 | | 14 | 12 | | | | | | | | | | 6 |
| 1 | | 3 | 4 | | 6 | 8¹ | 12 | 9² | | | 7 | | 2 | 5 | 10 | | 13 | 11 | | | | | | | | | | 7 |
| 1 | | | 4 | 5 | 6 | 12 | | 9 | | | 10² | 7¹ | 2 | | 14 | | 13 | 11 | 8³ | 3 | | | | | | | | 8 |
| 1 | | | 4 | 5 | 6 | 12 | | 9 | | | 7¹ | | 2² | | 10 | | 11³ | 8 | 3 | 13 | 14 | | | | | | | 9 |
| | | | 4 | 5 | 6 | 13 | 12 | 9² | | | 10 | 7³ | 2 | 1 | 11 | | 8¹ | 3 | | 14 | | | | | | | | 10 |
| | 2 | | 4 | 3 | 10 | 12 | | 9¹ | | | 7² | | | 1 | 5 | | 11 | 8 | 6 | 13 | | | | | | | | 11 |
| | | | 4 | | 6 | 8 | | 9¹ | | | 7 | | | 1 | 5 | | 11 | 12 | | 3 | | 2 | | | | | | 12 |
| | | | 4 | 12 | 6 | 8 | 13 | 9² | | | 7² | | | 1 | 5 | | 11¹ | 14 | | 3 | | 2 | | | | | | 13 |
| 1 | 2 | 3 | | 5 | 6 | 11 | | 10 | | | 7 | | | | 9 | | | | | | | 8 | 4 | | | | | 14 |
| 1 | 2 | | | 5 | 8¹ | 11 | 13 | 10 | | | 7 | | | | 9² | | 12 | | | 3 | | 6 | 4 | | | | | 15 |
| 1 | 2 | | | 5 | 8 | | 9 | 10 | | | 7 | | | | 11¹ | | 12 | | | 3 | | 6 | 4 | | | | | 16 |
| 1 | 2 | | 5 | | 6 | 11 | 9² | 10¹ | | | 7 | | | | 12 | | | 13 | | 3 | | 8 | 4 | | | | | 17 |
| 1 | 2 | | 5 | | 6 | 8 | 9 | 10 | | | 7 | | | | 11 | | | | | 3 | | 8 | 4 | | | | | 18 |
| 1 | 2 | 14 | 5 | | 6 | 11 | 9² | 10¹ | | | | 12 | | | 7² | | 13 | | | 3 | | 8 | 4 | | | | | 19 |
| 1 | 2 | | 5 | | 6 | 7 | 9² | 10¹ | 13 | | | | | | 14 | 11¹ | 12 | | | 3 | | 8 | 4 | | | | | 20 |
| 1 | | | 5 | 6 | 7² | 9 | | 11¹ | 12 | | | | | | 10 | | 13 | | | 3 | | 8 | 4 | 2 | | | | 21 |
| | 2 | | 5 | 6 | 7¹ | 9 | 13 | 11 | | | | 1 | | | 10² | | 12 | | | 3 | | 8 | 4 | | | | | 22 |
| | 2 | 3 | 5 | 6¹ | 7 | 9² | 13 | 11 | | | | 1 | | | 10 | | 12 | | | | | 8 | 4 | | | | | 23 |
| | 2 | 3 | 5 | 6 | 7 | 9 | 12 | 11 | | | | 1 | | | 10¹ | | | | | | | 8 | 4 | | | | | 24 |
| | 2 | 3 | 5 | 6 | 7³ | 9¹ | 10² | 12 | | | | | | | 13 | | 11 | | | | | 8 | 4 | | 1 | 14 | | 25 |
| | 2 | 3 | 4 | 5 | 6 | 14 | 9² | 10¹ | 12 | | 7 | | | | 13 | | 11³ | | | | | 8 | | | 1 | | | 26 |
| | 2 | 3 | 4 | 5 | 6 | 12 | 9 | 10 | | | 7¹ | | | | | | 11 | | | | | 8 | | | 1 | | | 27 |
| | 2 | 3 | 4 | 5 | 6 | | 9¹ | 11² | 13 | | 7 | | | | 12 | | 10 | | | | | 8 | | | 1 | | | 28 |
| | | 3 | 4 | | 6³ | | 9¹ | 11² | 13 | | 7 | 2 | | | 12 | | 10 | | | | | 8 | 5 | | 1 | 14 | | 29 |
| | | 3 | 5 | | 6 | 12 | 9² | | | | 11 | 7 | 2 | | 13 | | 10¹ | | | | | 8 | 4 | | 1 | | | 30 |
| | 2 | 3 | 5 | | 6 | 14 | 9¹ | | | | 13 | 7 | | | 12 | | 11³ | 10² | | | | 8 | 4 | | 1 | | | 31 |
| | 2 | 3 | 5 | 12 | 6 | 7 | 9 | | | | 14 | 13 | | | | | 11³ | 10² | | | | 8 | 4¹ | | 1 | | | 32 |
| | 2 | 3 | 5 | | 6¹ | 12 | 9 | | | | 13 | 7 | | | 10 | | 11² | | | | | 8 | 4 | | 1 | | | 33 |
| | 2 | | 5 | 14 | 6 | 12 | | 10 | | | 7¹ | | | | 9² | | 11 | 13 | 3³ | | | 8 | 4 | | 1 | | | 34 |
| | 2 | | 5 | 14 | 6 | 12 | | | | | 10² | 7 | | | 9² | | 11¹ | 13 | 3 | | | 8 | 4 | | 1 | | | 35 |
| | 2 | | 5 | 14 | 6¹ | 12 | | | | | 10 | 7 | | | 9³ | | 11² | 13 | 3 | | | 8 | 4 | | 1 | | | 36 |

# LIVINGSTON

## Second Division

*Year Formed:* 1974. *Ground:* Almondvale Stadium, Almondvale Stadium Road, Livingston EH54 7DN. *Telephone:* 01506 417000. *Fax:* 01506 418888.
*Ground Capacity:* total: 6100. Main stand only used 7500. *Size of Pitch:* 105yd × 72yd.
*Chairman:* Dominic Keane. *Secretary:* J.R.S.Renton.
*Manager:* Jim Leishman. *Club Doctor:* Dr Box. *Physio:* Arthur Duncan. *Coach:* George McNeil.
*Managers since 1975:* John Bain; Alec Ness; Willie MacFarlane; Terry Christie; Michael Lawson. *Club Nickname:* Livvy Lions. *Previous Grounds:* None.
*Record Attendance:* 4000 v Albion Rovers, League Cup 1st rd; 9 Sept, 1974.
*Record Transfer Fee received:* £115,000 for John Inglis to St Johnstone (1990).
*Record Transfer Fee paid:* £28,000 for Victor Kasule from Albion Rovers (1987).
*Record Victory:* 6-0 v Raith R, Second Division, 1985.
*Record Defeat:* 0-8 v Hamilton A. Division II; 14 Dec, 1974.
*Most Capped Player (under 18):* I. Little.
*Most League Appearances:* 446: Walter Boyd, 1979-89.
*Most League Goals in Season (Individual):* 21: John McGachie, 1986-87. *(Team):* 69; Second Division, 1986-87.
*Most Goals Overall (Individual):* 64: David Roseburgh, 1986-93.

## LIVINGSTON 1997–98 LEAGUE RECORD

| Match No. | Date | Venue | Opponents | Result | H/T Score | Lg. Pos. | Goalscorers | Attendance |
|---|---|---|---|---|---|---|---|---|
| 1 | Aug 6 | A | Inverness CT | D 1-1 | 0-0 | — | Graham [47] | 2232 |
| 2 | 16 | H | Stranraer | W 1-0 | 0-0 | 3 | Harvey [84] | 1058 |
| 3 | 23 | A | Stenhousemuir | D 1-1 | 0-0 | 3 | Raynes [80] | 514 |
| 4 | 30 | H | Queen of the S | W 3-1 | 2-0 | 3 | Harvey 3 (2 pens) [3, 24 (p), 49 (p)] | 1285 |
| 5 | Sept 13 | A | Brechin C | W 2-0 | 2-0 | 2 | Forrest [20], Young [32] | 402 |
| 6 | 20 | A | East Fife | W 3-2 | 1-1 | 2 | Duthie (pen) [39], Magee [67], Foster [75] | 986 |
| 7 | 27 | H | Clydebank | D 0-0 | 0-0 | 1 | | 1707 |
| 8 | Oct 4 | A | Clyde | L 0-1 | 0-1 | 1 | | 822 |
| 9 | 18 | H | Forfar Ath | W 4-3 | 1-1 | 1 | Foster [1], McLeod [50], Magee [55], Bailey [80] | 1467 |
| 10 | 25 | H | Stenhousemuir | W 2-1 | 1-0 | 1 | McLeod [28], Young [49] | 1691 |
| 11 | Nov 1 | A | Stranraer | D 1-1 | 0-0 | 1 | Forrest [74] | 609 |
| 12 | 8 | A | Queen of the S | L 0-1 | 0-1 | 1 | | 1210 |
| 13 | 15 | H | Brechin C | W 5-2 | 2-0 | 1 | Harvey [5], Bailey [32], Raynes [55], Maskrey [61], Christie (og) [75] | 1605 |
| 14 | 22 | A | Clydebank | D 1-1 | 0-1 | 1 | Foster [85] | 490 |
| 15 | Dec 3 | H | East Fife | W 1-0 | 1-0 | — | Bailey [11] | 876 |
| 16 | 13 | A | Forfar Ath | D 2-2 | 1-2 | 1 | Conway [5], Young [65] | 410 |
| 17 | 20 | H | Clyde | L 0-2 | 0-2 | 2 | | 1333 |
| 18 | 27 | A | Stenhousemuir | W 2-1 | 1-1 | 2 | Bailey [41], Harvey [73] | 587 |
| 19 | Jan 31 | A | East Fife | L 0-2 | 0-0 | 2 | | 899 |
| 20 | Feb 7 | H | Forfar Ath | W 4-0 | 3-0 | 2 | Young [4], Forrest 2 [8, 46], Harvey [42] | 990 |
| 21 | 10 | H | Clydebank | L 0-3 | 0-1 | — | | 1466 |
| 22 | 17 | A | Clyde | W 3-0 | 1-0 | 2 | McLeod [30], Graham [70], Harvey [75] | 528 |
| 23 | 21 | A | Inverness CT | D 2-2 | 2-2 | 2 | Harvey 2 [15, 20] | 2197 |
| 24 | 25 | H | Stranraer | L 0-1 | 0-0 | — | | 689 |
| 25 | Mar 3 | H | Inverness CT | D 2-2 | 2-1 | — | Harvey 2 [29, 38] | 751 |
| 26 | 14 | A | Clydebank | W 2-0 | 2-0 | 2 | McLeod (pen) [10], Callaghan [23] | 407 |
| 27 | 17 | A | Brechin C | W 2-0 | 2-0 | — | Callaghan [31], Moore [44] | 345 |
| 28 | 21 | H | East Fife | D 2-2 | 1-1 | 2 | Callaghan [40], Fleming [82] | 1309 |
| 29 | 25 | H | Queen of the S | D 1-1 | 0-0 | — | Callaghan [51] | 1269 |
| 30 | 28 | A | Forfar Ath | L 1-2 | 0-1 | 2 | Harvey (pen) [88] | 522 |
| 31 | Apr 7 | H | Clyde | W 4-0 | 0-0 | — | Harvey 2 [60, 70], Callaghan 2 [76, 82] | 1192 |
| 32 | 11 | A | Queen of the S | W 1-0 | 1-0 | 1 | Conway [5] | 1210 |
| 33 | 18 | H | Brechin C | W 1-0 | 1-0 | 1 | Fleming [10] | 1261 |
| 34 | 25 | H | Stenhousemuir | D 1-1 | 0-0 | 1 | Wright T [47] | 1282 |
| 35 | May 2 | A | Stranraer | L 0-2 | 0-0 | 1 | | 1061 |
| 36 | 9 | H | Inverness CT | L 1-2 | 0-1 | 3 | Graham [48] | 2812 |

**Final League Position: 3**       1996–97 3

**Honours**

*League Champions:* Second Division 1986-87. Third Division 1995-96; *Runners-up:* Second Division 1982-83. First Division 1987-88.
*Scottish Cup:* —. *League Cup:* Semi-finals 1984-85. *B&Q Cup:* Semi-finals 1992-93, 1993-94.
*Club colours:* Shirt: Black with yellow trim. Shorts: Black. Stockings: Black.

**Goalscorers:** *League (56):* Harvey 15 (3 pens), Callaghan 6, Bailey 4, Forrest 4, McLeod 4 (1 pen), Young 4, Foster 3, Graham 3, Conway 2, Fleming 2, Magee 2, Raynes 2, Duthie 1 (pen), Maskrey 1, Moore 1, Wright 1, own goal 1. *Scottish Cup (5):* Harvey 2, Duthie 1 (pen), Forrest 1, McMartin 1. *Coca Cola Cup (0). League Challenge Cup (2):* Magee 1, Raynes 1.

| McCaldon I 36 | Davidson G 10 | Duthie M 17 | Graham T 18 | Conway F 32 | McLeod G 9+1 | McMartin G 35+1 | Wright G 1 | Harvey G 25+5 | Maskrey S 4+10 | Magee K 18+13 | Watson G 28+6 | Young J 15+10 | Williamson S 23+2 | Raynes S 31+1 | Etot C 1 | Callaghan W 16+2 | Forrest G 26+1 | Bailey L 9+10 | Laidlaw S —+3 | Foster W 5+9 | Hegarty R —+3 | Sinclair D 5 | Moore A 6+1 | Wright T 8+1 | Alleyne D 2 | Fleming D 9 | Robertson A 6 | Miller G 1+4 | Match No. |
|---|---|---|---|---|---|---|---|---|---|---|---|---|---|---|---|---|---|---|---|---|---|---|---|---|---|---|---|---|---|
| 1 | 2 | 3 | 4 | 5 | $6^1$ | 7 | 8 | $9^2$ | 10 | 11 | 12 | 13 | | | | | | | | | | | | | | | | | 1 |
| 1 | 3 | $5^1$ | 4 | | | 7 | | $9^1$ | $8^2$ | 11 | 12 | 13 | 2 | 6 | 10 | 14 | | | | | | | | | | | | | 2 |
| 1 | $3^1$ | | 6 | | | 7 | | 9 | 8 | 11 | 12 | 10 | 2 | | | 5 | 4 | | | | | | | | | | | | 3 |
| 1 | | | | 5 | | 7 | | $10^1$ | | 6 | 2 | $11^2$ | 4 | 3 | | 9 | 8 | 12 | 13 | | | | | | | | | | 4 |
| 1 | 6 | | 4 | | | 7 | | $10^1$ | 13 | 11 | 2 | $9^2$ | 5 | 3 | | 8 | 12 | | | | | | | | | | | | 5 |
| 1 | 3 | | | 5 | | 7 | | $9^1$ | 13 | 6 | 2 | $11^2$ | 4 | 10 | | 8 | 12 | | | | | | | | | | | | 6 |
| 1 | 3 | | | 5 | | 7 | | 9 | 12 | $11^2$ | 2 | $10^1$ | 6 | 4 | | 8 | 13 | | | | | | | | | | | | 7 |
| 1 | 3 | | | 5 | | 7 | | $9^2$ | $10^1$ | 11 | 2 | | 6 | 4 | | 8 | 13 | 12 | | | | | | | | | | | 8 |
| 1 | 4 | 3 | | 5 | 6 | 7 | | | 12 | 11 | 2 | | $8^2$ | 10 | | 13 | | $9^1$ | | | | | | | | | | | 9 |
| 1 | 3 | 5 | 4 | | 8 | 6 | | 9 | 12 | 11 | $2^1$ | | | 7 | | 10 | | | | | | | | | | | | | 10 |
| 1 | $4^3$ | 3 | | $5^1$ | 6 | 7 | | $9^1$ | 12 | 11 | 2 | 13 | 14 | | | 8 | 10 | | | | | | | | | | | | 11 |
| 1 | 3 | | | 5 | | 7 | | 10 | 14 | 11 | 2 | $9^1$ | 4 | $6^2$ | | 8 | 12 | $13^3$ | | | | | | | | | | | 12 |
| 1 | 3 | | | 5 | | $7^1$ | | 9 | 12 | 11 | 2 | 13 | 4 | 6 | | 8 | $10^2$ | | | | | | | | | | | | 13 |
| 1 | 3 | | | 5 | | 7 | | $9^1$ | 14 | 11 | 2 | 13 | $4^3$ | 6 | | 8 | $10^1$ | 12 | | | | | | | | | | | 14 |
| 1 | 3 | | | 5 | | 7 | | $9^2$ | 13 | 11 | 2 | 12 | 4 | 6 | | 8 | $10^1$ | | | | | | | | | | | | 15 |
| 1 | 3 | | | 5 | | 7 | | | 13 | 11 | 2 | 12 | 4 | 6 | | 8 | $10^1$ | $9^2$ | | | | | | | | | | | 16 |
| 1 | 3 | | | 5 | | 7 | | $9^2$ | 14 | $11^1$ | 2 | 13 | 4 | 6 | | 8 | $10^2$ | 12 | | | | | | | | | | | 17 |
| 1 | 3 | | | 5 | | $7^1$ | | 9 | | $11^3$ | 14 | 2 | 13 | 4 | 6 | 8 | $10^2$ | 12 | | | | | | | | | | | 18 |
| 1 | 4 | | | | 6 | 13 | | 7 | 9 | 11 | $2^2$ | 12 | 5 | 3 | | 8 | $10^1$ | | | | | | | | | | | | 19 |
| 1 | 4 | | | 6 | | $11^3$ | | 7 | $9^1$ | 12 | 14 | 2 | $10^2$ | 5 | 3 | 8 | 13 | | | | | | | | | | | | 20 |
| 1 | 3 | | $4^1$ | | 6 | 7 | | 9 | 13 | | $2^2$ | 10 | $5^3$ | 11 | | 8 | 12 | 14 | | | | | | | | | | | 21 |
| 1 | 2 | | $4^3$ | 5 | 11 | 7 | | $9^2$ | 14 | | $10^1$ | | 3 | | | 8 | 13 | 12 | 6 | | | | | | | | | | 22 |
| 1 | 2 | | | 5 | 6 | 11 | 7 | 9 | | | $10^1$ | | 3 | | | 8 | 12 | | 4 | | | | | | | | | | 23 |
| 1 | $2^1$ | | 4 | 10 | 7 | | | 9 | 12 | $11^1$ | 5 | | $3^3$ | | | 8 | 14 | 13 | 6 | | | | | | | | | | 24 |
| 1 | | | | 5 | 6 | $10^2$ | 7 | 9 | | | 2 | | 3 | 13 | | 8 | 12 | $11^1$ | 4 | | | | | | | | | | 25 |
| 1 | | | | 5 | $6^1$ | 8 | | | | 2 | 4 | 3 | 11 | | | 12 | | 10 | 7 | 9 | | | | | | | | | 26 |
| 1 | | | | 5 | | 7 | | | 13 | 2 | 12 | 4 | 3 | 10 | | $8^1$ | | | | $9^2$ | 11 | 6 | | | | | | | 27 |
| 1 | | $4^1$ | 5 | | | 7 | | 13 | 14 | 2 | 12 | 6 | 9 | | | 8 | $10^2$ | | | | $11^3$ | | 3 | | | | | | 28 |
| 1 | | 5 | 6 | | | 7 | | $10^2$ | 13 | 2 | 4 | 8 | 11 | | | | | | | $9^1$ | 12 | | 3 | | | | | | 29 |
| 1 | | 4 | | | | 7 | | 13 | 12 | 2 | $9^2$ | 5 | 6 | $10^3$ | | $8^1$ | 14 | | | 11 | | | 3 | | | | | | 30 |
| 1 | | 4 | 5 | | 12 | | | 13 | | $14^2$ | 2 | 6 | 9 | | | | | | | $7^1$ | $11^3$ | | 3 | 8 | $10^2$ | | | | 31 |
| 1 | | 5 | 4 | | | 7 | | 10 | | 12 | 2 | 6 | $9^2$ | | | | | | | $11^1$ | | | 3 | 8 | 13 | | | | 32 |
| 1 | | $5^1$ | 4 | | | 7 | | $10^2$ | | 12 | 2 | | 9 | | | 11 | 6 | | | 11 | | | 3 | 8 | 13 | | | | 33 |
| 1 | | | 5 | | 9 | | | 12 | | | 2 | 4 | 6 | 10 | | | | | | $7^2$ | $11^1$ | | 3 | 8 | 13 | | | | 34 |
| 1 | | $5^1$ | 6 | | | $2^1$ | | | 11 | | 4 | 10 | 9 | 12 | | | 14 | | | $7^3$ | | | 3 | 8 | 13 | | | | 35 |
| 1 | | 5 | 4 | | | 7 | | $9^3$ | 13 | | $2^2$ | | 14 | 6 | | 11 | $8^1$ | | | 12 | | | 3 | 10 | | | | | 36 |

# MONTROSE

## Third Division

*Year Formed:* 1879. *Ground & Address:* Links Park, Wellington St, Montrose DD10 8QD. *Telephone:* 01674 673200.
*Ground Capacity:* total: 4338. seated: 1338. *Size of Pitch:* 113yd × 70yd.
*Chairman:* Michael Craig. *Secretary:* Malcolm J. Watters.
*Manager:* Tommy Campbell. *Assistant Manager:* Brian McLaughlin. *Physio:* Allan Borthwick.
*Managers since 1975:* A. Stuart; K. Cameron; R. Livingstone; S. Murray; D. D'Arcy; I. Stewart; C. McLelland; D. Rougvie; J. Leishman, J Holt, A. Dornan, D. Smith.
*Club Nickname(s):* The Gable Endies. *Previous Grounds:* None.
*Record Attendance:* 8983 v Dundee, Scottish Cup 3rd rd; 17 Mar, 1973.
*Record Transfer Fee received:* £50,000 for Gary Murray to Hibernian (Dec 1980).
*Record Transfer Fee paid:* £17,500 for Jim Smith from Airdrieonians (Feb 1992).
*Record Victory:* 12-0 v Vale of Leithen, Scottish Cup 2nd rd; 4 Jan, 1975.
*Record Defeat:* 0-13 v Aberdeen; 17 Mar, 1951.
*Most Capped Player:* Alexander Keillor, 2 (6), Scotland.
*Most League Appearances:* 426: David Larter, 1987-98.
*Most League Goals in Season (Individual):* 28: Brian Third, Division II; 1972-73.

## MONTROSE 1997–98 LEAGUE RECORD

| Match No. | Date | Venue | Opponents | Result | H/T Score | Lg. Pos. | Goalscorers | Atten- dance |
|---|---|---|---|---|---|---|---|---|
| 1 | Aug 5 | H | Albion R | L | 1-2 | 0-2 | — | Smith [76] | 471 |
| 2 | 16 | A | Dumbarton | D | 2-2 | 0-2 | 7 | Taylor [50], Winiarski [85] | 395 |
| 3 | 23 | H | Arbroath | L | 0-3 | 0-1 | 9 | | 921 |
| 4 | 30 | H | Cowdenbeath | W | 2-0 | 1-0 | 8 | McGlashan [43], Fisher [89] | 287 |
| 5 | Sept 13 | A | Alloa Ath | L | 1-5 | 0-2 | 9 | McGlashan [85] | 403 |
| 6 | 20 | A | East Stirling | L | 1-4 | 1-3 | 9 | McGlashan (pen) [69] | 279 |
| 7 | 27 | H | Ross Co | L | 3-4 | 1-2 | 9 | Andrew [31], Tindal [60], McGlashan [72] | 453 |
| 8 | Oct 4 | A | Queen's Park | D | 1-1 | 0-0 | 9 | McGlashan [49] | 479 |
| 9 | 18 | H | Berwick R | L | 1-2 | 1-1 | 9 | Cunningham (og) [19] | 357 |
| 10 | 25 | A | Arbroath | W | 2-1 | 1-1 | 8 | Higgins [39], Tindal [49] | 1150 |
| 11 | Nov 1 | H | Dumbarton | D | 2-2 | 1-0 | 8 | McGlashan (pen) [7], Higgins [80] | 347 |
| 12 | 8 | A | Cowdenbeath | L | 1-3 | 1-1 | 9 | Higgins [22] | 132 |
| 13 | 15 | H | Alloa Ath | L | 0-2 | 0-1 | 9 | | 357 |
| 14 | 22 | A | Ross Co | L | 1-8 | 1-4 | 9 | Higgins [21] | 1328 |
| 15 | 29 | H | East Stirling | D | 1-1 | 0-1 | 9 | Watt [48] | 268 |
| 16 | Dec 13 | A | Berwick R | W | 2-1 | 0-1 | 9 | McGlashan 2 (1 pen) [48 (p), 85] | 322 |
| 17 | 20 | H | Queen's Park | L | 1-3 | 0-1 | 9 | McGlashan [59] | 290 |
| 18 | 27 | A | Arbroath | W | 1-0 | 0-0 | 9 | Taylor [62] | 1496 |
| 19 | Jan 10 | A | Albion R | L | 2-3 | 0-2 | 9 | McGlashan 2 [69, 71] | 325 |
| 20 | 31 | A | East Stirling | W | 2-1 | 0-0 | 9 | Watt [61], McGlashan [82] | 177 |
| 21 | Feb 7 | H | Berwick R | D | 2-2 | 2-1 | 9 | Coulston [14], Higgins [27] | 300 |
| 22 | 14 | A | Queen's Park | W | 2-0 | 1-0 | 9 | Higgins [23], Taylor [90] | 501 |
| 23 | 21 | H | Albion R | L | 1-3 | 0-1 | 9 | Taylor [60] | 292 |
| 24 | 25 | A | Dumbarton | W | 3-2 | 3-1 | — | Taylor 2 [20, 30], McGlashan [25] | 315 |
| 25 | 28 | H | Cowdenbeath | W | 3-1 | 0-0 | 7 | Higgins 2 [47, 74], Taylor [72] | 289 |
| 26 | Mar 7 | A | Alloa Ath | L | 2-3 | 0-1 | 8 | McGlashan (pen) [72], Wylie [80] | 495 |
| 27 | 10 | H | Ross Co | L | 0-2 | 0-0 | — | | 321 |
| 28 | 14 | A | Ross Co | L | 1-2 | 0-1 | 9 | MacDonald [51] | 1209 |
| 29 | 21 | H | East Stirling | D | 1-1 | 1-0 | 9 | Andrew [14] | 224 |
| 30 | 28 | A | Berwick R | D | 1-1 | 0-0 | 8 | Winiarski [62] | 318 |
| 31 | Apr 4 | H | Queen's Park | W | 4-3 | 1-1 | 8 | McGlashan 2 (1 pen) [36 (p), 89], Taylor 2 [76, 80] | 244 |
| 32 | 11 | A | Cowdenbeath | D | 0-0 | 0-0 | 8 | | 194 |
| 33 | 18 | H | Alloa Ath | L | 0-3 | 0-0 | 9 | | 463 |
| 34 | 25 | A | Arbroath | L | 2-4 | 2-2 | 9 | McGlashan 2 [12, 18] | 1340 |
| 35 | May 2 | H | Dumbarton | W | 2-1 | 2-0 | 8 | Higgins [10], Henry [38] | 305 |
| 36 | 9 | A | Albion R | L | 2-4 | 0-3 | 9 | McGlashan 2 [53, 86] | 239 |

**Final League Position: 9**          1996–97 6

## Honours

*League Champions:* Second Division 1984-85, *Runners-up:* 1990-91. Third Division, *Runners-up:* 1994-95.
*Scottish Cup:* Quarter-finals 1973, 1976.
*League Cup:* Semi-finals 1975-76.
*B&Q Cup:* Semi-finals: 1992-93.
*League Challenge Cup:* semi-finals: 1996–97.
*Club colours:* Shirt: Royal blue with white sleeves. Shorts: White. Stockings: Royal blue.

**Goalscorers:** *League (53):* McGlashan 20 (5 pens), Higgins 9, Taylor 9, Andrew 2, Tindal 2, Watt 2, Winiarski 2, Coulston 1, Fisher 1, Henry 1, MacDonald 1, Smith M 1, Wylie 1, own goal 1. *Scottish Cup (2):* McGlashan 1, Taylor 1. *Coca Cola Cup (1):* Taylor 1. *League Challenge Cup (0).*

| Larter D 18 | Winiarski S 22+10 | Glass S 4+1 | Mailer C 35 | Wylie R 18 | Craib M 36 | Taylor S 25+9 | Fisher D 1+1 | McGlashan C 36 | MacDonald I 16+5 | Smith M 2+2 | Ferrie A 2+1 | Dorward R 1+5 | Hildersley R 4+1 | Andrew B 25+3 | Reynolds C 1+4 | Masson P 2+2 | Tindal K 10 | Masson C 6+4 | Watt J 29 | Henry J 20+7 | Higgins G 23+1 | Coulston D 23+4 | Russell N 1 | Arthur G —+1 | Hutton D 16+2 | Murray M 17 | Thompson B —+1 | Niddrie K 3 | Stevenson C —+2 | Match No. |
|---|---|---|---|---|---|---|---|---|---|---|---|---|---|---|---|---|---|---|---|---|---|---|---|---|---|---|---|---|---|---|
| 1 | 2 | 3 | 4 | 5 | 6 | 7 | $8^1$ | 9 | 10 | 11 | 12 | | | | | | | | | | | | | | | | | | | 1 |
| 1 | 12 | 13 | 5 | 4 | 2 | 10 | | 9 | 8 | $11^1$ | | | $3^4$ | 6 | | $7^3$ | 14 | | | | | | | | | | | | | 2 |
| 1 | 6 | $3^1$ | 5 | 4 | $2^3$ | 10 | | 9 | $11^2$ | 13 | | 12 | 8 | 7 | | | 14 | | | | | | | | | | | | | 3 |
| 1 | 2 | | 6 | 5 | 3 | 8 | 13 | $9^1$ | $12^2$ | 11 | | | 4 | 7 | | 10 | | | | | | | | | | | | | | 4 |
| 1 | 13 | 3 | 6 | 5 | 2 | 12 | | 9 | $11^1$ | | | | $4^2$ | 7 | 10 | | 8 | | | | | | | | | | | | | 5 |
| 1 | 2 | $3^1$ | 10 | $6^2$ | 4 | 12 | | 9 | $11^3$ | | | 13 | 7 | 14 | | 8 | 5 | | | | | | | | | | | | | 6 |
| 1 | 12 | | 2 | 5 | 4 | 10 | | 9 | 11 | | | | 7 | | | | 6 | | 3 | $8^1$ | | | | | | | | | | 7 |
| 1 | 12 | | 2 | $5^1$ | 4 | 10 | | 9 | $11^1$ | | | | 7 | 13 | | | 6 | 14 | $3^2$ | 8 | | | | | | | | | | 8 |
| 1 | 2 | | | 5 | $4^1$ | 13 | | 9 | | | | | 7 | | | | 6 | 12 | $3^3$ | 8 | 10 | 11 | | | | | | | | 9 |
| 1 | 12 | | 5 | | 4 | 13 | | 9 | | | | | $7^2$ | | $2^1$ | 6 | | 3 | 8 | 10 | 11 | | | | | | | | | 10 |
| 1 | 7 | | 5 | 2 | 4 | 12 | | 9 | | | | 13 | | | | | $6^2$ | $3^1$ | 8 | 10 | 11 | | | | | | | | | 11 |
| 1 | 2 | | 5 | | 4 | 7 | | 9 | | | | 12 | | | | | 6 | 3 | 8 | 10 | $11^1$ | | | | | | | | | 12 |
| $7^1$ | 4 | 5 | 6 | 13 | | 9 | 12 | | | | | | | | | $2^2$ | 3 | 8 | 10 | 11 | $1^6$ | 15 | | | | | | | 13 |
| 1 | 12 | $6^1$ | 5 | 2 | 13 | | 9 | 11 | | | | $7^2$ | | | | 3 | 4 | 10 | 8 | | | | | | | | | 14 |
| 1 | 6 | 5 | | 4 | 13 | | 9 | $11^2$ | | | | $7^1$ | | 2 | 14 | 3 | 12 | $10^3$ | 8 | | | | | | | | | 15 |
| 1 | 12 | | 2 | 6 | 10 | | 9 | $11^2$ | | | | $8^1$ | | | | 5 | 3 | 7 | | 4 | | | 13 | | | | | | 16 |
| 1 | $4^1$ | | 2 | 6 | 10 | | 9 | 11 | | | | 8 | | | | 5 | 3 | 7 | 12 | | | | | | | | | | 17 |
| 1 | 8 | | 2 | 5 | 4 | 11 | | $9^1$ | 12 | | | | $7^1$ | | | 3 | 6 | 10 | 13 | | | | | | | | | | 18 |
| 1 | 8 | | 2 | | 4 | 11 | | 9 | 13 | | | | 7 | | | $3^2$ | $6^1$ | 10 | 12 | | 5 | | | | | | | | 19 |
| | 12 | 2 | 5 | 4 | 11 | | 9 | 8 | | | | | 13 | | | $6^1$ | 10 | $7^2$ | | | 3 | 1 | | | | | | 20 |
| | 12 | 2 | 5 | 4 | 11 | | 9 | $8^2$ | | | | | 13 | | | $6^1$ | 10 | 7 | | | 3 | 1 | | | | | | 21 |
| | 12 | 2 | 5 | 4 | 11 | | 9 | 8 | | | | | 13 | | | $6^1$ | $10^2$ | 7 | | | 3 | 1 | | | | | | 22 |
| | 2 | 5 | 4 | 11 | | 9 | | 8 | | | | | 13 | | | $6^2$ | 12 | 10 | $7^1$ | | 3 | 1 | | | | | | 23 |
| | 2 | 5 | 4 | 11 | | 9 | | 7 | | | | | | | | 6 | 12 | 10 | $8^1$ | | 3 | 1 | | | | | | 24 |
| | $2^1$ | 5 | 4 | 11 | | 9 | | 7 | | | | | | | | 6 | 12 | 10 | 8 | | 3 | 1 | | | | | | 25 |
| | 5 | 2 | 4 | 11 | | 9 | 12 | | | | | | | | | 6 | $10^1$ | 8 | | | 3 | 1 | | | | | | 26 |
| $10^2$ | 2 | 5 | 4 | 11 | | 9 | 12 | | | | | | 7 | | | 6 | 13 | | $8^1$ | | 3 | 1 | | | | | | 27 |
| 11 | 2 | | 4 | 12 | | 9 | 10 | | | | | 7 | | | | 5 | $6^1$ | 8 | | | 3 | 1 | | | | | | 28 |
| 6 | 2 | | 4 | | 9 | 11 | | | | | | 7 | | | | 5 | 12 | 10 | $8^1$ | | 3 | 1 | | | | | | 29 |
| 8 | 2 | | 4 | | 9 | 11 | | | | | | | | | 5 | 6 | 12 | 10 | 7 | | $3^1$ | $1^6$ | 15 | | | | | 30 |
| 8 | 2 | | 4 | 11 | | 9 | | | | | | 1 | | | | 5 | 3 | 6 | 10 | 7 | | | 1 | | 5 | | | 31 |
| $8^1$ | 2 | | 4 | 11 | | 9 | | | | | | | | | | 5 | 3 | 6 | 10 | 7 | | 12 | 1 | | | | | 32 |
| | 2 | | 4 | 11 | | 9 | | | 14 | | | | | | 12 | | 5 | $3^3$ | 6 | 10 | $7^2$ | | $8^1$ | 1 | | 13 | | 33 |
| 2 | | 5 | 4 | 11 | | 9 | | | | | | | $7^1$ | | | | 6 | 8 | 10 | 12 | | | 3 | 1 | | | | 34 |
| | 5 | 2 | 4 | 11 | | 9 | | | | | | | 7 | | | | 6 | 8 | 10 | 12 | | | 3 | 1 | | $2^1$ | | 35 |
| | 2 | | $4^1$ | 11 | | 9 | | | 13 | | | | 7 | | 12 | | | 8 | $10^2$ | 6 | | | $3^3$ | 1 | | 5 | 14 | 36 |

# MOTHERWELL

## Premier League

*Year Formed:* 1886. *Ground & Address:* Fir Park, Motherwell ML1 2QN. *Telephone:* 01698 333333. *Fax:* 01698 276333.
*Ground Capacity:* total: 13,742 all seated. *Size of Pitch:* 110yd × 75yd.
*Chairman:* John C. Chapman. *Secretary:* Alan C. Dick. *Commercial Manager:* John Swinburne.
*Manager:* Harri Kampman. *Assistant Manager:* Jim Griffin. *Physio:* John Porteous. *Coach:* Willie McLean.
*Managers since 1975:* Ian St. John; Willie McLean; Rodger Hynd; Ally MacLeod; David Hay; Jock Wallace; Bobby
Watson, Tommy McLean, Alex McLeish.
*Club Nickname(s):* The Well. *Previous Grounds:* Roman Road, Dalziel Park.
*Record Attendance:* 35,632 v Rangers, Scottish Cup 4th rd replay; 12 Mar, 1952.
*Record Transfer Fee received:* £1,750,000 for Phil O'Donnell to Celtic, September 1994.
*Record Transfer Fee paid:* £400,000 for Mitchell Van Der Gaag from PSV Eindhoven, March 1995.
*Record Victory:* 12-1 v Dundee U, Division II; 23 Jan, 1954.
*Record Defeat:* 0-8 v Aberdeen, Premier Division; 26 Mar, 1979.
*Most Capped Player:* Tommy Coyne, 13, Republic of Ireland.
*Most League Appearances:* 626: Bobby Ferrier, 1918-37.
*Most League Goals in Season (Individual):* 52: Willie McFadyen, Division I; 1931-32.
*Most Goals Overall (Individual):* 283: Hugh Ferguson, 1916-25.

## MOTHERWELL 1997–98 LEAGUE RECORD

| Match No. | Date | | Venue | Opponents | Result | H/T Score | Lg. Pos. | Goalscorers | Attendance |
|---|---|---|---|---|---|---|---|---|---|
| 1 | Aug | 2 | A | Dunfermline Ath | W 2-0 | 0-0 | — | Coyne T 2 (1 pen) [64 (p), 85] | 5624 |
| 2 | | 16 | H | St Johnstone | L 0-1 | 0-0 | 5 | | 5036 |
| 3 | | 23 | A | Aberdeen | W 3-1 | 2-1 | 3 | Weir 2 [9, 55], Coyne T [29] | 11,522 |
| 4 | Sept | 13 | H | Celtic | L 2-3 | 1-0 | 5 | Coyne T 2 [4, 59] | 11,550 |
| 5 | | 20 | H | Hibernian | D 1-1 | 0-0 | 5 | Coyne T [77] | 7420 |
| 6 | | 27 | A | Rangers | D 2-2 | 2-1 | 6 | Coyne T [7], Shivute [44] | 48,672 |
| 7 | Oct | 4 | H | Hearts | L 1-4 | 1-3 | 7 | Coyne T (pen) [44] | 8886 |
| 8 | | 8 | A | Kilmarnock | L 1-2 | 1-2 | — | Shivute [17] | 6588 |
| 9 | | 18 | A | Dundee U | L 0-4 | 0-2 | 7 | | 7337 |
| 10 | | 25 | H | Aberdeen | L 1-2 | 0-1 | 10 | Davies [67] | 6065 |
| 11 | Nov | 1 | A | St Johnstone | L 3-4 | 0-2 | 10 | Hendry (pen) [61], Davies [65], Coyle O [76] | 4566 |
| 12 | | 8 | H | Kilmarnock | L 0-1 | 0-0 | 10 | | 5346 |
| 13 | | 15 | A | Celtic | W 2-0 | 1-0 | 9 | Coyle O [28], Weir [89] | 47,464 |
| 14 | | 22 | A | Rangers | D 1-1 | 0-0 | 9 | Coyne T [79] | 12,018 |
| 15 | | 29 | A | Hibernian | D 1-1 | 0-0 | 9 | Coyle O [89] | 9999 |
| 16 | Dec | 6 | A | Hearts | L 0-2 | 0-1 | 9 | | 12,706 |
| 17 | | 13 | H | Dundee U | W 1-0 | 0-0 | 8 | Coyle O [52] | 4555 |
| 18 | | 20 | A | Dunfermline Ath | W 2-0 | 0-0 | 8 | Coyle O 2 [62, 71] | 4607 |
| 19 | | 27 | A | Aberdeen | L 0-3 | 0-0 | 8 | | 13,088 |
| 20 | Jan | 3 | A | Kilmarnock | L 1-4 | 1-3 | 8 | Coyle O [14] | 8724 |
| 21 | | 10 | H | Celtic | D 1-1 | 0-0 | 8 | Falconer [57] | 12,350 |
| 22 | | 17 | A | Rangers | L 0-1 | 0-1 | 8 | | 49,443 |
| 23 | | 31 | H | Hibernian | W 6-2 | 3-2 | 8 | Arnott [10], Weir [24], Garcin [43], McCulloch 2 [81, 89], Coyne T [88] | 6169 |
| 24 | Feb | 7 | A | Dundee U | L 0-1 | 0-0 | 9 | | 6532 |
| 25 | | 21 | H | Hearts | L 2-4 | 2-1 | 9 | Coyle O [6], Falconer [37] | 8375 |
| 26 | | 25 | H | St Johnstone | W 2-1 | 2-0 | — | Coyne T 2 [11, 20] | 4517 |
| 27 | Mar | 7 | A | Dunfermline Ath | L 1-2 | 1-1 | 9 | Coyne T [12] | 4811 |
| 28 | | 14 | H | Rangers | W 2-1 | 1-1 | 9 | Coyle O [44], Falconer [87] | 11,779 |
| 29 | | 21 | A | Hibernian | L 0-1 | 0-1 | 9 | | 10,582 |
| 30 | | 28 | H | Dundee U | W 1-0 | 0-0 | 7 | Coyle O [54] | 5012 |
| 31 | Apr | 8 | A | Hearts | D 1-1 | 0-0 | — | Coyne T [77] | 14,737 |
| 32 | | 11 | H | Kilmarnock | D 1-1 | 0-1 | 7 | Lindquist [80] | 6209 |
| 33 | | 18 | A | Celtic | L 1-4 | 1-2 | 7 | McMillan [12] | 49,351 |
| 34 | | 25 | H | Dunfermline Ath | L 1-3 | 1-2 | 9 | Shivute [28] | 5745 |
| 35 | May | 2 | A | St Johnstone | L 2-3 | 1-1 | 9 | Martin [3], Coyne T (pen) [56] | 6760 |
| 36 | | 9 | H | Aberdeen | L 1-2 | 0-2 | 9 | Ross [66] | 5861 |

**Final League Position: 9**     1996–97 8

**Honours**
*League Champions:* Division I 1931-32. First Division 1981-82, 1984-85. Division II 1953-54, 1968-69; *Runners-up:* Premier Division 1994-95. Division I 1926-27, 1929-30, 1932-33, 1933-34. Division II 1894-95, 1902-03. *Scottish Cup:* 1952, 1991; *Runners-up:* 1931, 1933, 1939, 1951.
*League Cup:* 1950-51. *Runners-up:* 1954-55 *Scottish Summer Cup:* 1944, 1965.
*Club colours:* Shirt: Amber with claret hoop and trimmings. Shorts: White. Stockings: Claret.

**European:** *Cup Winners' Cup:* 2 matches (1991-92). *UEFA Cup:* 6 matches (1994-95, 1995-96).

**Goalscorers:** *League (46):* Coyne T 15 (3 pens), Coyle O 10, Weir 4, Falconer 3, Shivute 3, Davies 2, McCulloch 2, Arnott 1, Garcin 1, Hendry 1 (pen), Lindqvist 1, McMillan 1, Martin 1, Ross 1. *Scottish Cup (4):* Coyle O 1, Coyne T 1, McSkimming 1, own goal 1. *Coca Cola Cup (5):* Coyle O 4, Falconer 1.

| Woods S 35 | May E 20+5 | Resch F 3 | Valakari S 24+4 | Martin B 26 | Denham G 18 | Weir M 13+5 | McMillan S 33+1 | Coyne T 33+1 | Falconer W 21+1 | Coyle O 34+2 | Craigan S 9+5 | Philliben J 10+3 | Dorner M 1+1 | Davies W 12+5 | Ross I 16+6 | Christie K 20+1 | McCulloch L 6+19 | Shivute E 12+11 | Hendry J 10+3 | Jonsson G 2 | Garcin E 7+4 | McSkimming S 11+1 | Arnott D 3+4 | Newman R 11 | Lindquist S 5+1 | Thomson S 1 | Match No. |
|---|---|---|---|---|---|---|---|---|---|---|---|---|---|---|---|---|---|---|---|---|---|---|---|---|---|---|---|
| 1 | 2 | 3 | 4 | 5 | 6 | 7 | 8 | 9 | 10 | 11 | | | | | | | | | | | | | | | | | 1 |
| 1 | 2 | $3^9$ | 8 | | | 7 | $6^2$ | 12 | 10 | 11 | 4 | 5 | | $9^1$ | 13 | 14 | | | | | | | | | | | 2 |
| 1 | 2 | $3^1$ | 13 | 5 | 6 | 7 | 8 | $9^{10}$ | 10 | 11 | | | | | 14 | | 12 | $4^2$ | | | | | | | | | 3 |
| 1 | 2 | $8^1$ | | 5 | 6 | 7 | 3 | 9 | 10 | 11 | | | | | $4^2$ | | 12 | 13 | | | | | | | | | 4 |
| 1 | 2 | | 4 | 5 | | $7^1$ | 3 | 9 | 10 | 11 | 6 | | | | | | 12 | 8 | | | | | | | | | 5 |
| 1 | | | 4 | $5^2$ | 6 | 7 | 3 | 9 | 10 | 11 | 13 | | | | 2 | | 12 | $8^1$ | | | | | | | | | 6 |
| 1 | 2 | | 4 | $5^1$ | 6 | 7 | 3 | 9 | 10 | 11 | 12 | | | | | | | 8 | | | | | | | | | 7 |
| 1 | 2 | | | $6^3$ | | 7 | $3^1$ | 9 | 10 | $11^2$ | 14 | | | | 12 | 5 | 4 | 8 | 13 | | | | | | | | 8 |
| 1 | | | 4 | $5^3$ | | $7^1$ | 3 | 9 | $10^2$ | 12 | 6 | 14 | | | 11 | 2 | | 8 | 13 | | | | | | | | 9 |
| 1 | 8 | | | 6 | | $7^1$ | 3 | | 11 | 14 | 5 | | | | 13 | $2^3$ | 9 | 12 | $10^3$ | 4 | | | | | | | 10 |
| 1 | 14 | | | 6 | | | 3 | 9 | 13 | | | | | | 8 | $11^2$ | 2 | 12 | 7 | 10 | $5^1$ | $4^3$ | | | | | 11 |
| 1 | 2 | | | 6 | | 6 | | 9 | 11 | 5 | | | | | $8^1$ | | 7 | 12 | 13 | | $4^2$ | 10 | | | | | 12 |
| 1 | 8 | | | | 13 | | 3 | | 11 | 5 | 4 | | | | 6 | 2 | $9^1$ | | $7^2$ | | 10 | 12 | | | | | 13 |
| 1 | $2^1$ | | 8 | | | | 3 | $9^2$ | 11 | 5 | 6 | | | | 4 | | 13 | | 7 | | 10 | 12 | | | | | 14 |
| 1 | 2 | | $8^3$ | | | | 3 | $9^1$ | 11 | $5^2$ | 6 | | | | 13 | 4 | 14 | | 7 | | 10 | 12 | | | | | 15 |
| 1 | 2 | | | | | | 3 | $9^1$ | 11 | 5 | 6 | | | | 8 | 4 | | 12 | $7^2$ | | 10 | 13 | | | | | 16 |
| 1 | $2^2$ | | 5 | 12 | | | 3 | 9 | $11^1$ | | 6 | | | | 13 | | 8 | | 7 | | 10 | | 4 | | | | 17 |
| 1 | 2 | | 5 | 13 | | | $3^1$ | 9 | 11 | | 6 | | | | 12 | | 8 | | $7^2$ | | 10 | | 4 | | | | 18 |
| 1 | 2 | | 5 | 13 | | | 3 | 9 | 11 | | 6 | | | | 12 | | 8 | | $7^2$ | | $10^1$ | | 4 | | | | 19 |
| 1 | 2 | | 5 | 12 | | | 3 | 9 | 11 | | $6^1$ | | | | 8 | | 13 | | 7 | | $10^2$ | | 4 | | | | 20 |
| 1 | 2 | | 12 | 5 | | | 3 | $9^2$ | 6 | 11 | | | | | | | 7 | 13 | | | $8^1$ | 10 | 4 | | | | 21 |
| 1 | $2^1$ | | 12 | 5 | | $7^2$ | 9 | | 6 | 11 | 3 | | | | | | 14 | 13 | | | $8^3$ | 10 | 4 | | | | 22 |
| 1 | | | $5^1$ | | | 7 | 9 | | 6 | 11 | 12 | 3 | | | 2 | | 14 | | | | $8^2$ | 13 | $10^3$ | 4 | | | 23 |
| 1 | 2 | | | | | $7^1$ | 13 | 9 | 6 | 11 | 3 | | | | 5 | | 12 | | | | 8 | | $10^2$ | 4 | | | 24 |
| 1 | $2^3$ | | 7 | 5 | | | 3 | 9 | 6 | 11 | | | | | $10^2$ | $8^1$ | 13 | 12 | | | 14 | | | 4 | | | 25 |
| 1 | 12 | | $7^3$ | 5 | | | 3 | 9 | 6 | 11 | | | | | 10 | $8^2$ | $2^1$ | 14 | | | 13 | | | 4 | | | 26 |
| 1 | 12 | | $7^3$ | 5 | | | 3 | 9 | 6 | 11 | | | | | 10 | $8^2$ | $2^1$ | 14 | | | 13 | | | 4 | | | 27 |
| 1 | 13 | | 7 | 5 | 4 | | 3 | 9 | 6 | 11 | | | | | $10^2$ | $8^1$ | 2 | 12 | | | | | | | | | 28 |
| 1 | 12 | | $7^3$ | 5 | 4 | | 3 | 9 | 6 | 11 | | | | | 10 | 13 | $2^1$ | $8^2$ | | | 14 | | | | | | 29 |
| 1 | | | 7 | 5 | 4 | | 3 | 9 | 6 | 11 | | | | | $10^1$ | | 2 | 12 | 13 | | | | | | 8 | | 30 |
| 1 | | | 7 | 5 | 4 | | 3 | 9 | | 11 | | | | | $10^1$ | $6^2$ | 2 | 13 | 12 | | | | | | 8 | | 31 |
| 1 | | | 7 | 5 | 4 | | 3 | 9 | | 11 | | | | | $6^1$ | 2 | 12 | 13 | | | $10^2$ | | | | 8 | | 32 |
| 1 | 13 | | 7 | 5 | 4 | | 3 | $9^2$ | 6 | $11^1$ | | | | | | 2 | 12 | 10 | | | | | | | 8 | | 33 |
| 1 | | | 7 | 5 | 4 | | 3 | 9 | 6 | 11 | 2 | | | | 12 | | 13 | $10^2$ | | | | | | | 8 | | 34 |
| 1 | 2 | | 7 | 5 | 6 | | 3 | $9^2$ | 12 | $11^3$ | | | | | 10 | 4 | | 13 | | | | $8^1$ | | 14 | | | 35 |
| | $2^2$ | | 7 | $5^3$ | 4 | | 3 | 9 | | 11 | 13 | 14 | | | $10^1$ | 6 | | 12 | 8 | | | | | | | 1 | 36 |

# PARTICK THISTLE  Second Division

*Year Formed:* 1876. *Ground & Address:* Firhill Park, 80 Firhill Rd, Glasgow G20 7BA. *Telephone:* 0141 945 4811. *Fax:* 0141 945 1525
*Ground Capacity:* total: 20,876. seated: 9076. *Size of Pitch:* 110yd × 74yd.
*Chairman:* T. Brown McMaster. *Secretary:* Robert W. Reid. *Commercial Manager:* Peter Queen.
*Head Coach:* Tommy Bryce. *Assistant Head Coach:* Samuel Johnston. *Physio:* Walter Cannon.
*Managers since 1975:* R. Auld; P. Cormack; B. Rooney; R. Auld; D. Johnstone; W. Lamont; S. Clark; J. Lambie, M. MacLeod, John McVeigh. *Club Nickname(s):* The Jags. *Previous Grounds:* Jordanvale Park; Muirpark; Inchview; Meadowside Park.
*Record Attendance:* 49,838 v Rangers, Division I; 18 Feb, 1922.
*Record Transfer Fee received:* £200,000 for Mo Johnston to Watford.
*Record Transfer Fee paid:* £85,000 for Andy Murdoch from Celtic (Feb 1991).
*Record Victory:* 16-0 v Royal Albert, Scottish Cup 1st rd; 17 Jan, 1931.
*Record Defeat:* 0-10 v Queen's Park, Scottish Cup; 3 Dec, 1881.
*Most Capped Player:* Alan Rough, 51 (53), Scotland.
*Most League Appearances:* 410: Alan Rough, 1969-82.
*Most League Goals in Season (Individual):* 41: Alec Hair, Division I; 1926-27.

## PARTICK THISTLE 1997–98 LEAGUE RECORD

| Match No. | Date | Venue | Opponents | Result | H/T Score | Lg. Pos. | Goalscorers | Attendance |
|---|---|---|---|---|---|---|---|---|
| 1 | Aug 2 | A | Hamilton A | D 1-1 | 0-1 | — | Martin [85] | 1221 |
| 2 | 16 | H | Dundee | L 0-3 | 0-1 | 9 | | 2450 |
| 3 | 23 | A | Ayr U | D 2-2 | 1-2 | 9 | Hetherston [4], Adams [86] | 2398 |
| 4 | 30 | A | Airdrieonians | D 1-1 | 0-0 | 9 | Gaughan [87] | 2260 |
| 5 | Sept 13 | H | Stirling A | L 1-2 | 1-2 | 10 | Adams [36] | 1883 |
| 6 | 20 | H | Greenock Morton | W 2-1 | 1-1 | 9 | Morgan [30], Henderson [56] | 2136 |
| 7 | 27 | A | St Mirren | L 0-1 | 0-0 | 10 | | 3348 |
| 8 | Oct 4 | H | Falkirk | L 3-4 | 0-2 | 10 | Stirling (pen) [55], Adams [65], Morgan [70] | 2439 |
| 9 | 18 | A | Raith R | L 0-2 | 0-1 | 10 | | 3417 |
| 10 | 25 | H | Hamilton A | D 3-3 | 2-1 | 9 | Stirling 2 (2 pens) [20, 33], Adams [71] | 2316 |
| 11 | Nov 1 | A | Dundee | D 0-0 | 0-0 | 8 | | 3560 |
| 12 | 8 | H | Airdrieonians | L 1-2 | 1-0 | 9 | Nicholson [33] | 2765 |
| 13 | 15 | A | Stirling A | D 2-2 | 0-2 | 9 | Stirling [78], Boyle (pen) [89] | 1656 |
| 14 | 22 | H | St Mirren | D 2-2 | 1-2 | 10 | Archibald [16], Boyle (pen) [90] | 4661 |
| 15 | 29 | A | Greenock Morton | L 2-3 | 1-1 | 10 | Watson [32], Morgan [51] | 3384 |
| 16 | Dec 6 | A | Falkirk | W 1-0 | 0-0 | 9 | Lyons [68] | 2667 |
| 17 | 13 | H | Raith R | L 1-3 | 0-1 | 10 | Morgan (pen) [81] | 3108 |
| 18 | 20 | H | Ayr U | W 3-0 | 1-0 | 9 | Lyons 2 [14, 51], Morgan [86] | 2967 |
| 19 | 27 | A | Hamilton A | W 1-0 | 1-0 | 8 | Lawrence [21] | 2049 |
| 20 | Jan 6 | A | Airdrieonians | L 1-2 | 1-1 | — | Lawrence [6] | 1893 |
| 21 | 10 | H | Stirling A | L 1-3 | 0-1 | 9 | Henderson [59] | 2880 |
| 22 | 17 | A | St Mirren | W 1-0 | 0-0 | 8 | Lawrence [59] | 3052 |
| 23 | 31 | H | Greenock Morton | D 3-3 | 1-2 | 8 | Gaughan [31], Lyons [72], Henderson [80] | 3156 |
| 24 | Feb 7 | A | Raith R | L 0-2 | 0-0 | 8 | | 3675 |
| 25 | 21 | H | Falkirk | D 0-0 | 0-0 | 9 | | 2972 |
| 26 | 25 | H | Dundee | L 1-2 | 1-1 | — | McKenzie [7] | 2244 |
| 27 | 28 | A | Ayr U | D 2-2 | 0-0 | 9 | Milne [58], Nicholson [77] | 2539 |
| 28 | Mar 14 | H | St Mirren | L 1-2 | 0-2 | 10 | Lyons [86] | 3545 |
| 29 | 21 | A | Greenock Morton | L 0-1 | 0-0 | 10 | | 2989 |
| 30 | 24 | A | Falkirk | D 1-1 | 0-0 | — | McGowan (og) [57] | 4815 |
| 31 | 28 | H | Raith R | L 1-2 | 0-1 | 10 | Stirling (pen) [50] | 2308 |
| 32 | Apr 11 | H | Airdrieonians | W 2-0 | 2-0 | 10 | Evans [23], Henderson [44] | 2102 |
| 33 | 18 | A | Stirling A | W 1-0 | 1-0 | 9 | Evans [2] | 2219 |
| 34 | 25 | H | Hamilton A | D 0-0 | 0-0 | 10 | | 2993 |
| 35 | May 2 | A | Dundee | W 3-0 | 3-0 | 9 | Evans 2 [12, 32], Stirling (pen) [19] | 3609 |
| 36 | 9 | H | Ayr U | L 1-3 | 0-1 | 9 | Evans [44] | 8653 |

**Final League Position: 9**       1996–97 6

**Honours**

*League Champions:* First Division 1975-76. Division II 1896-97, 1899-1900, 1970-71; *Runners-up:* First Division 1991-92. Division II 1901-02.

*Scottish Cup Winners:* 1921; *Runners-up:* 1930.

*League Cup Winners:* 1971-72; *Runners-up:* 1953-54, 1956-57, 1958-59.

**European:** *Fairs Cup:* 4 matches (1963-64). *UEFA Cup:* 2 matches (1972-73).

*Club colours:* Shirt: Red and yellow hoops. Shorts: Black. Stockings: Red with two yellow leg bands, tops red with one broad yellow band.

**Goalscorers:** *League (45):* Stirling 6 (5 pens), Evans 5, Lyons 5, Morgan 5 (1 pen), Adams 4, Henderson 4, Lawrence 3, Boyle 2 (pens), Gaughan 2, Nicholson 2, Archibald 1, Hetherston 1, McKenzie 1, Martin 1, Milne 1, Watson 1, own goal 1. *Scottish Cup (0). Coca Cola Cup (2):* Farrell 1, Lyons 1. *League Challenge Cup (1):* Hetherston 1.

| O'Connor G 3 | Boyle J 36 | Lyons A 26 + 1 | Milne C 23 + 1 | Farrell D 11 | Watson G 31 + 2 | Hetherston P 5 | Macdonald W 21 + 5 | Adams C 8 + 7 | Connor R 2 | Dunn R 3 + 9 | Graham A 2 + 2 | Martin A 3 + 15 | Evans G 17 + 3 | McKenzie J 8 + 8 | Caesar G 1 | Stewart A 9 | Gaughan K 14 + 1 | Henderson N 28 + 5 | Nicholson I 25 + 7 | Morgan A 18 | Honor C 2 | Archibald A 26 + 3 | Stirling J 22 | Arthur K 19 | Lawrence A 17 | Lauchlan M 5 + 5 | Charnley J 5 | McKee C 1 | Hamilton L 5 | Match No. |
|---|---|---|---|---|---|---|---|---|---|---|---|---|---|---|---|---|---|---|---|---|---|---|---|---|---|---|---|---|---|---|
| 1 | 2 | 3 | 4 | 5 | 6 | 7 | 8 | 9² | 10 | 11¹ | 12 | 13 | | | | | | | | | | | | | | | | | | 1 |
| 1 | 2 | 3 | 4 | 5 | 6 | 10² | 11 | 12 | | | | 13 | 9 | 7¹ | 8 | | | | | | | | | | | | | | | 2 |
| 1 | 2 | 3 | 4 | 8 | 6 | 10 | 12 | 7 | 11 | | | 9² | 13 | | 5¹ | | | | | | | | | | | | | | | 3 |
| | 2 | 3 | 4 | 8 | 6 | 10¹ | 11² | 7³ | | | | 9 | 14 | 12 | | 1 | 5 | 13 | | | | | | | | | | | | 4 |
| | 2 | | 4 | 8 | 6 | 10¹ | 11 | | | | | 9 | | | | 1 | 5 | 12 | 3 | 7 | | | | | | | | | | 5 |
| 7 | | 3 | 4 | | 6 | | 12 | | | | | 9 | | | | 1 | 5 | 10 | 8 | 11¹ | 2² | 13 | | | | | | | | 6 |
| 7² | | 5 | 4 | | 6 | | 12 | | | | | 13 | 9 | | | 1 | | 10 | 8 | 11¹ | 2 | 3 | | | | | | | | 7 |
| 7¹ | 2 | | 4 | 5 | | 8² | 12 | 13 | | | | | 9 | | | 1 | | 10 | 6 | 11 | | 3 | | | | | | | | 8 |
| 7 | 11³ | 2 | 4 | 6 | | 8² | | 10 | | | | 12 | | | | 1 | 13 | 5 | 9 | 14 | | 3¹ | | | | | | | | 9 |
| | 2² | 11 | 4 | | 8 | 9 | | | | | | 14 | 7¹ | 13 | | 1 | 12 | 6 | 10³ | | | 5 | 3 | | | | | | | 10 |
| | 2² | 11 | 4 | 13 | 8 | 9 | | | | | | 14 | 12 | | | 1 | 7³ | 6 | 10¹ | | | 5 | 3 | | | | | | | 11 |
| | 2¹ | 11 | 4 | 12 | 8² | 9 | | | | | | 14 | 10 | 13 | | 1 | 7³ | 6 | | | | 5 | 3 | | | | | | | 12 |
| | 2 | | 4 | 11 | 8 | 13 | | | | | | 9 | 14 | | | | 12 | 7 | 6¹ | 10⁴ | | 5 | 3³ | 1 | | | | | | 13 |
| | 2 | 11 | | 6 | 12 | | | | | | | 9 | | | | | 4 | 8 | 7 | 10 | | 5 | 3¹ | 1 | | | | | | 14 |
| | 2 | 11 | | 6 | 12 | | | | | | | 9 | | | | | 5 | 8 | 7 | 10 | | 4 | 3¹ | 1 | | | | | | 15 |
| | 7 | 11 | 4 | 2 | | | | | | | | 13 | 9 | 6¹ | | | 5 | 8 | 12 | 10² | | 3 | | 1 | | | | | | 16 |
| | 7² | 3 | 6 | 2 | | | | | | | | 12 | 9¹ | 8 | | | 5 | 10 | 13 | 11 | | 4 | | 1 | | | | | | 17 |
| | 7 | 11 | 2 | 4¹ | 13 | | | | | | | | | | | | 5 | 8 | 12 | 10 | | 3 | 6 | 1 | 9² | | | | | 18 |
| | 7 | 11 | 2 | | 12 | | | | | | | | | | | | 5 | 8 | 4 | 10 | | 3 | 6 | 1 | 9¹ | | | | | 19 |
| | 7 | 11 | 12 | 2 | 13 | | | | | | | 14 | | | | | 5 | 8² | 4 | 10¹ | | 3 | 6 | 1 | 9³ | | | | | 20 |
| | 7 | 4² | 2 | | 12 | | | | | | | | | 13 | | | 5 | 11 | 8 | 10 | | 3 | 6¹ | 1 | 9 | | | | | 21 |
| | 7 | 3 | 2 | 8 | 13⁴ | | | | | | | | | 4 | | | 5 | 11 | 14 | 10² | 12 | | 6¹ | 1 | 9 | | | | | 22 |
| | 7 | 11 | 2 | 4¹ | | | | | | | | 14 | 10³ | 6² | | | 5 | 8 | 12 | | | 3 | | 1 | 9 | 13 | | | | 23 |
| | 7 | 11 | 4 | | 6 | | | | | | | | | | | | 5 | 8 | 2 | 10¹ | | 3 | | 1 | 9 | 12 | | | | 24 |
| | 2 | 11 | 4 | 5 | 8 | | | | | | | 12 | 7 | | | | 9 | 10 | | | | 3 | 6¹ | 1 | | | | | | 25 |
| | 2 | 11 | 4 | 5 | 8 | | | | | | | 9 | 7¹ | | | | 10 | 6 | | | | 3 | | 1 | | 12 | | | | 26 |
| | 7 | 11 | 4 | 5 | 6¹ | | | | | | | 12 | | | | | 8 | 2 | | | | 3 | | 1 | 9 | | 10 | | | 27 |
| | 7² | 11 | 4 | 5 | 13 | | | | | | | 14 | | 2 | | | 12 | 8 | | | | 3 | 6¹ | 1 | 9³ | | 10 | | | 28 |
| | 2 | 11 | 4 | 5 | | | | | | | | 8 | | | | | 7 | 6 | | | | 3 | | 1 | 9 | | 10 | | | 29 |
| | 2 | 11 | 4 | 5 | 12 | | | | | | | 8¹ | | | | | 7 | 6 | | | | 3 | | 1 | 9 | 13 | 10² | | | 30 |
| | 2 | 11 | | 5 | 12 | | | | | | | | | | | | 7 | 6¹ | | | | 3 | 4 | 1 | 9 | 13 | 10 | 8² | | 31 |
| | 2 | | 4 | 5 | 13 | | | | | | | 7¹ | 12 | | | | 10 | 8 | | | | 3 | 6 | | 9² | 11 | | | 1 | 32 |
| | 2 | | 4 | 5 | 14 | | | | | | | 13 | 7¹ | 12 | | | 10 | 8 | | | | 3 | 6 | | 9³ | 11² | | | 1 | 33 |
| | 2 | 12 | 4 | 5 | | | | | | | | 13 | 7 | | | | 10 | 8¹ | | | | 3 | 6 | | 9 | 11² | | | 1 | 34 |
| | 2 | 11 | 4 | 5² | | | | | | | | 13 | 10 | 12 | | | 8 | 14 | | | | 3 | 6 | | 9² | 7¹ | | | 1 | 35 |
| | 2 | 11 | 4 | 5 | | | | | | | | 13 | 10 | | | | 8 | 12 | | | | 3 | 6² | | 9 | 7¹ | | | 1 | 36 |

# QUEEN OF THE SOUTH  Second Division

*Year Formed:* 1919. *Ground & Address:* Palmerston Park, Dumfries DG2 9BA. *Telephone and Fax:* 01387 254853.
*Ground Capacity:* total: 8352. seated: 3549. *Size of Pitch:* 112yd × 73yd.
*Chairman:* Norman Blount. *Secretary:* Richard Shaw MBE. *Commercial Manager:* Rowan Alexander.
*Manager:* Rowan Alexander.
*Managers since 1975:* M. Jackson; W. Hunter; B. Little; G. Herd; H. Hood; A. Busby; R. Clark; M. Jackson; D. Wilson; W. McLaren; F. McGarvey; A. MacLeod; D. Frye; W. McLaren; M. Shanks. *Club Nickname(s):* The Doonhamers.
*Previous Grounds:* None.
*Record Attendance:* 24,500 v Hearts, Scottish Cup 3rd rd; 23 Feb, 1952.
*Record Transfer Fee received:* £250,000 for Andy Thomson to Southend U (1994).
*Record Transfer Fee paid:* £30,000 for Jim Butter from Alloa Athletic (1995).
*Record Victory:* 11-1 v Stranraer, Scottish Cup 1st rd; 16 Jan, 1932.
*Record Defeat:* 2-10 v Dundee, Division I; 1 Dec, 1962.
*Most Capped Player:* Billy Houliston, 3, Scotland.
*Most League Appearances:* 731: Allan Ball, 1963–82.
*Most League Goals in Season (Individual):* 37: Jimmy Gray, Division II; 1927-28.
*Most Goals in Season:* 41: Jimmy Rutherford, 1931–32.
*Most Goals Overall (Individual):* 250: Jim Patterson, 1949–63.

## QUEEN OF THE SOUTH 1997–98 LEAGUE RECORD

| Match No. | Date | | Venue | Opponents | Result | H/T Score | Lg. Pos. | Goalscorers | Atten-dance |
|---|---|---|---|---|---|---|---|---|---|
| 1 | Aug | 5 | A | Stenhousemuir | L 1-2 | 0-1 | — | Eadie [60] | 456 |
| 2 | | 16 | H | Clydebank | D 2-2 | 0-2 | 6 | Bryce (pen) [48], Townsley [83] | 1284 |
| 3 | | 23 | A | Stranraer | L 1-2 | 0-0 | 10 | Thomson [86] | 643 |
| 4 | | 30 | A | Livingston | L 1-3 | 0-2 | 10 | Flannigan [74] | 1285 |
| 5 | Sept | 13 | H | Forfar Ath | L 0-1 | 0-0 | 10 | | 1011 |
| 6 | | 20 | H | Inverness CT | W 2-1 | 0-0 | 9 | Flannigan [51], Bryce [64] | 1145 |
| 7 | | 27 | A | Brechin C | W 3-0 | 0-0 | 8 | Thomson [58], Cairney (og) [60], Eadie [64] | 333 |
| 8 | Oct | 4 | A | East Fife | L 2-3 | 1-1 | 8 | Townsley [20], Aitken [87] | 656 |
| 9 | | 18 | H | Clyde | W 4-3 | 1-2 | 8 | Cleeland [15], Mallan 2 [58, 80], Eadie [84] | 1232 |
| 10 | | 25 | H | Stranraer | W 2-1 | 1-0 | 6 | Bryce [9], Townsley [54] | 1607 |
| 11 | Nov | 5 | A | Clydebank | L 0-4 | 0-1 | — | | 297 |
| 12 | | 8 | H | Livingston | W 1-0 | 1-0 | 7 | Bryce [44] | 1210 |
| 13 | | 15 | A | Forfar Ath | W 4-2 | 1-1 | 4 | Flannigan 2 [26, 54], Mallan 2 [80, 87] | 497 |
| 14 | | 22 | H | Brechin C | D 0-0 | 0-0 | 5 | | 1356 |
| 15 | | 29 | A | Inverness CT | L 1-2 | 0-0 | 5 | McKeown [75] | 1820 |
| 16 | Dec | 16 | A | Clyde | D 0-0 | 0-0 | — | | 510 |
| 17 | | 20 | H | East Fife | W 2-1 | 1-0 | 4 | Eadie [20], Mallan [85] | 1013 |
| 18 | | 27 | A | Stranraer | W 4-3 | 2-1 | 3 | Bryce (pen) [40], Eadie [45], Mallan 2 [73, 81] | 1045 |
| 19 | Jan | 20 | H | Stenhousemuir | L 0-1 | 0-1 | — | | 1405 |
| 20 | | 31 | H | Inverness CT | W 1-0 | 1-0 | 3 | Weir [11] | 1322 |
| 21 | Feb | 3 | A | Brechin C | D 1-1 | 0-1 | — | Townsley [87] | 307 |
| 22 | | 7 | H | Clyde | D 0-0 | 0-0 | 3 | | 1230 |
| 23 | | 15 | A | East Fife | W 5-1 | 1-1 | — | Eadie [38], McKeown [47], Townsley [55], Pettit [78], Aitken [86] | 887 |
| 24 | | 21 | A | Stenhousemuir | L 0-2 | 0-2 | 3 | | 522 |
| 25 | | 28 | H | Clydebank | D 0-0 | 0-0 | — | | 1148 |
| 26 | Mar | 7 | A | Forfar Ath | W 5-1 | 2-1 | 3 | Eadie 2 [23, 56], Townsley (pen) [36], Cleeland [62], Mallan [84] | 1209 |
| 27 | | 14 | H | Brechin C | D 1-1 | 1-0 | 4 | Mallan [1] | 1216 |
| 28 | | 21 | A | Inverness CT | W 2-0 | 1-0 | 4 | Bryce 2 [13, 77] | 1989 |
| 29 | | 25 | A | Livingston | D 1-1 | 0-0 | 4 | Watson (og) [55] | 1269 |
| 30 | | 28 | A | Clyde | L 1-3 | 1-2 | 4 | Mallan [17] | 726 |
| 31 | Apr | 5 | H | East Fife | L 1-4 | 0-3 | — | McKeown [63] | 1276 |
| 32 | | 11 | H | Livingston | L 0-1 | 0-1 | 5 | | 1210 |
| 33 | | 18 | A | Forfar Ath | W 4-2 | 1-1 | 4 | McKeown [15], Leslie [51], Connor [58], Bryce [76] | 490 |
| 34 | | 25 | H | Stranraer | W 3-2 | 0-1 | 4 | Bryce 2 (1 pen) [58 (p), 87], Payne [65] | 1615 |
| 35 | May | 2 | A | Clydebank | D 1-1 | 0-1 | 4 | McKeown [78] | 533 |
| 36 | | 9 | H | Stenhousemuir | W 1-0 | 1-0 | 4 | Bryce [7] | 1260 |

**Final League Position: 4**        1996–97 5

## Honours
*League Champions:* Division II 1950-51; *Runners-up:* Division II 1932-33, 1961-62, 1974-75. Second Division 1980-81, 1985-86.
*Scottish Cup:* semi-finalists 1949–50.
*League Cup:* semi-finalists 1950–51, 1960–61.
*B&Q Cup:* semi-finalists 1991–92. *League Challenge Cup:* runners-up 1997–98.
*Club colours:* Shirt: Royal blue. Shorts: White. Stockings: Royal blue with white tops.

**Goalscorers:** *League (57):* Bryce 11 (3 pens), Mallan 10, Eadie 8, Townsley 6 (1 pen), McKeown 5, Flannigan 4, Aitken 2, Cleeland 2, Thomson 2, Connor 1, Leslie 1, Payne 1, Pettit 1, Weir 1, own goals 2. *Scottish Cup (6):* Bryce 1, Eadie 1, McAllister 1, Mallan 1, Townsley 1, Weir 1. *Coca Cola Cup (6):* Mallan 2, Bryce 1 (pen), Eadie 1, Flannigan 1, Townsley 1. *League Challenge Cup (9):* Mallan 5, Flannigan 3, Rowe 1.

| Mathieson D 36 | MacLeod J 11 | McKeown D 30+1 | Aitken A 32+1 | Rowe G 29+2 | Townsley D 27+2 | McCluskey J 2 | Bryce T 35 | Eadie K 19+4 | Flannigan C 11+1 | Cleeland M 18+4 | Mallan S 25+6 | Weir M 6+7 | Thomson J 31 | Irving C 4+3 | Alexander R 1+5 | Kennedy D 14+4 | McAllister J 3+12 | Lilley D 2 | Connor R 24 | Ferguson D 1+1 | Boyle D 2+4 | Leslie S 9+5 | Pettit S —+5 | Payne D 12 | Love G 12 | Minchella M —+1 | Moffat A —+2 | Match No. |
|---|---|---|---|---|---|---|---|---|---|---|---|---|---|---|---|---|---|---|---|---|---|---|---|---|---|---|---|---|
| 1 | 2 | 3 | 4 | 5 | 6² | 7 | 8 | 9 | 10¹ | 11 | 12 | 13 |  |  |  |  |  |  |  |  |  |  |  |  |  |  |  | 1 |
| 1 | 2 | 3 | 4 |  | 6 |  | 8 | 10 | 11 | 9 | 12 |  | 5 |  | 7¹ |  |  |  |  |  |  |  |  |  |  |  |  | 2 |
| 1 | 2 | 3 | 4 |  | 6¹ | 7 | 8 | 10 | 9 | 11 |  |  | 5 |  | 12 |  |  |  |  |  |  |  |  |  |  |  |  | 3 |
| 1 | 2 | 3 | 4 |  | 6 |  | 8 | 10 | 11³ | 9 | 7² |  | 5 |  | 12 | 14 | 13 |  |  |  |  |  |  |  |  |  |  | 4 |
| 1 | 2¹ | 3 | 4 |  | 6 |  | 8 | 13 | 10² | 11 | 9³ | 7 | 5 |  | 12 | 14 |  |  |  |  |  |  |  |  |  |  |  | 5 |
| 1 | 2 | 3 | 4 |  | 6 |  | 8 | 10 | 11 | 9 |  |  | 5 | 7¹ | 12 |  |  |  |  |  |  |  |  |  |  |  |  | 6 |
| 1 | 2 | 3 | 4 |  | 6² |  | 8 | 9 | 10¹ | 11 | 12 | 7 | 5 |  |  |  | 13 |  |  |  |  |  |  |  |  |  |  | 7 |
| 1 | 2 | 3 | 4 |  | 6 |  | 8 | 10 | 11 | 9 |  | 7¹ | 5 |  | 12 |  |  |  |  |  |  |  |  |  |  |  |  | 8 |
| 1 | 2¹ | 3 | 4 |  | 6 |  | 8 | 10 | 11³ | 9 |  | 7 | 5 |  | 12 |  | 13 |  |  |  |  |  |  |  |  |  |  | 9 |
| 1 | 2 | 3 | 4 |  | 6 |  | 8 | 10¹ | 11 | 9 | 12 | 7 | 5 |  |  |  |  |  |  |  |  |  |  |  |  |  |  | 10 |
| 1 | 2 | 3 | 4 |  | 6 |  | 8 | 10 | 11¹ | 9 |  | 7 | 5 |  | 12 |  |  |  |  |  |  |  |  |  |  |  |  | 11 |
| 1 | 2 | 3 | 4 |  |  |  | 8 | 10 | 11² |  | 12 | 7¹ | 5 |  |  | 14 | 13 |  | 6 | 9³ |  |  |  |  |  |  |  | 12 |
| 1 | 2 | 3 | 4 |  | 6¹ |  | 8 | 10 | 11 | 9 |  |  | 5 |  | 12 |  |  |  | 7 |  |  |  |  |  |  |  |  | 13 |
| 1 | 2 | 3 | 4 |  |  |  | 8 | 9² | 10 | 11 | 12 |  | 5 | 7¹ |  |  | 13 |  | 6 |  |  |  |  |  |  |  |  | 14 |
| 1 | 2 | 3 | 4 |  |  |  | 8 | 9 | 11 | 10¹ |  |  | 5 | 7² |  |  | 13 |  | 6 |  | 12 |  |  |  |  |  |  | 15 |
| 1 | 2 | 3 | 4 |  |  |  | 8 | 9 | 10 | 11 |  |  | 5 | 7¹ |  |  |  |  | 6 |  | 12 |  |  |  |  |  |  | 16 |
| 1 | 2 | 3 | 4 |  | 6¹ |  | 8² | 9 | 10 | 11 |  |  | 5 |  |  |  | 13 |  | 7 |  | 12 |  |  |  |  |  |  | 17 |
| 1 | 2 | 3 | 4 | 5 | 6¹ |  | 8³ | 9 | 10 | 11² |  |  |  |  |  | 14 | 13 |  | 7 |  | 12 |  |  |  |  |  |  | 18 |
| 1 | 2 | 3 | 4 |  | 6 |  | 8 | 9 | 10 | 11 |  |  | 5 |  |  |  |  |  | 7 |  |  |  |  |  |  |  |  | 19 |
| 1 | 2 | 3 | 4 |  | 6¹ |  | 8 | 9 | 10² | 11 |  |  | 5 |  |  |  | 13 |  | 7 |  | 12 |  |  |  |  |  |  | 20 |
| 1 | 2¹ | 3 | 4 |  | 6⁴ |  | 8 | 9 | 10 | 11³ |  |  | 5 |  |  | 14 | 13 |  | 7 |  | 12 |  |  |  |  |  |  | 21 |
| 1 | 2 | 3 | 4 |  | 6 |  | 8 | 9 | 10² | 11¹ |  |  | 5 |  |  |  |  |  | 7 |  | 12 | 13 |  |  |  |  |  | 22 |
| 1 |  | 3 | 4 |  |  | 7 | 8 | 9 | 10¹ | 11 |  |  | 5 |  |  |  |  |  | 6 |  |  | 12 |  | 2 |  |  |  | 23 |
| 1 |  | 3 | 4 |  |  | 7 | 8 | 9 | 10 | 11 |  |  | 5 |  |  |  |  |  | 6 |  |  | 12 |  | 2¹ |  |  |  | 24 |
| 1 |  | 3 | 4 |  | 6 |  | 8² | 9¹ | 10 | 11 |  |  | 5 |  |  | 14 | 13 |  | 7 |  |  | 12 |  | 2³ | 5 |  |  | 25 |
| 1 |  | 3 | 4 |  | 6 |  | 8 | 9² | 10 | 11 |  |  | 5 |  |  |  | 13 |  | 7 |  |  | 12 |  | 2³ | 3 |  |  | 26 |
| 1 |  | 3 | 4 |  | 6 |  | 8 | 9 | 10 | 11 | 12 |  | 5 |  |  |  |  |  | 7 |  |  |  |  | 2³ | 3 |  |  | 27 |
| 1 | 2 | 3 | 4 |  | 6 |  | 8 | 9² | 10 | 11 |  |  | 5 | 7¹ |  |  | 13 |  |  |  | 12 |  |  |  |  |  |  | 28 |
| 1 | 2 | 3 | 4 |  | 6 |  | 8 | 9 | 10 | 11 | 12 |  | 5 | 7¹ |  |  |  |  |  |  |  |  |  |  |  |  |  | 29 |
| 1 | 2 | 3² | 4 |  | 6 |  | 8 | 9 | 10 | 11¹ | 12 |  | 5 |  |  |  | 13 |  | 7 |  |  |  |  |  |  |  |  | 30 |
| 1 |  | 3² | 4 |  | 6 |  | 8 | 9 | 10 | 11 | 12 |  | 5 |  |  | 14 | 13 |  | 7 |  |  |  |  | 2¹ |  |  |  | 31 |
| 1 | 2 | 3 | 4 |  |  |  | 8 | 9 | 10 | 11³ | 12 |  | 5 | 7² |  | 14 | 13 |  | 6³ |  |  |  |  |  |  |  |  | 32 |
| 1 |  | 3 | 4 |  |  |  | 8 | 9 | 10 | 11 | 12 |  | 5 | 7¹ |  |  | 13 |  | 6³ |  |  |  |  | 2² |  |  | 14 | 33 |
| 1 |  | 3 | 4 |  | 6 |  | 8 | 9 | 10 | 11³ |  |  | 5¹ |  |  | 14 | 13 |  | 7 |  | 12² |  |  | 2² |  |  |  | 34 |
| 1 |  | 3 | 4¹ |  | 6 |  | 8 | 9 | 10 | 11 | 12 |  | 5 | 7² | 12² | 14 | 13 |  |  |  |  |  |  | 2³ |  |  |  | 35 |
| 1 |  | 3 | 4 |  | 6 |  | 8 | 9 | 10² | 11 | 12 |  | 5¹ |  |  |  | 13 |  | 7 |  |  |  |  | 2³ |  |  | 14 | 36 |

# QUEEN'S PARK                    Third Division

*Year Formed:* 1867. *Ground & Address:* Hampden Park, Mount Florida, Glasgow G42 9BA. *Telephone:* 0141 632 1275.
*Fax:* 0141 636 1612.
*Ground Capacity:* total: 9222 during reconstruction. *Size of Pitch:* 115yd × 75yd.
*President:* H. Gordon Wilson. *Secretary:* Alistair Mackay. *Physio:* R.C.Findlay. *Player/Coach:* John McCormack.
*Commercial Manager:* Miss Carol J. Cairns.
*Coaches since 1975:* D.McParland, J.Gilroy, E Hunter, H. McCann. *Club Nickname(s):* The Spiders. *Previous Grounds:*
1st Hampden (Recreation Ground); (Titwood Park was used as an interim measure between 1st & 2nd Hampdens); 2nd
Hampden (Cathkin); 3rd Hampden.
*Record Attendance:* 95,772 v Rangers, Scottish Cup, 18 Jan, 1930.
*Record for Ground:* 149,547 Scotland v England, 1937.
*Record Transfer Fee received:* Not applicable due to amateur status.
*Record Transfer Fee paid:* Not applicable due to amateur status.
*Record Victory:* 16-0 v St. Peters, Scottish Cup 1st rd; 29 Aug, 1885.
*Record Defeat:* 0-9 v Motherwell, Division I; 26 Apr, 1930.
*Most Capped Player:* Walter Arnott, 14, Scotland.
*Most League Appearances:* 473: J. B. McAlpine.

## QUEEN'S PARK 1997–98 LEAGUE RECORD

| Match No. | Date | | Venue | Opponents | Result | | H/T Score | Lg. Pos. | Goalscorers | Atten- dance |
|---|---|---|---|---|---|---|---|---|---|---|
| 1 | Aug | 16 | A | Ross Co | W | 1-0 | 0-0 | — | Edgar [82] | 1152 |
| 2 | | 23 | H | Albion R | W | 5-1 | 0-0 | 1 | Arbuckle 3 [73, 82, 89], Mitchell (og) [74], Edgar [76] | 567 |
| 3 | | 30 | A | East Stirling | L | 0-1 | 0-0 | 4 | | 457 |
| 4 | Sept | 9 | H | Arbroath | W | 3-2 | 1-1 | — | Miller [11], O'Brien [68], Mercer [90] | 364 |
| 5 | | 13 | H | Berwick R | D | 0-0 | 0-0 | 3 | | 488 |
| 6 | | 20 | H | Cowdenbeath | W | 1-0 | 0-0 | 3 | Hardie [68] | 476 |
| 7 | | 27 | A | Dumbarton | D | 0-0 | 0-0 | 4 | | 436 |
| 8 | Oct | 4 | H | Montrose | D | 1-1 | 0-0 | 4 | Caven [85] | 479 |
| 9 | | 11 | A | Ross Co | L | 1-2 | 1-0 | 4 | Mercer [10] | 1039 |
| 10 | | 18 | A | Alloa Ath | W | 4-3 | 3-0 | 4 | Edgar [7], O'Brien 2 [14, 58], Maxwell [31] | 514 |
| 11 | | 25 | A | Albion R | D | 0-0 | 0-0 | 3 | | 508 |
| 12 | Nov | 1 | H | Ross Co | L | 0-3 | 0-1 | 5 | | 838 |
| 13 | | 8 | H | East Stirling | L | 0-1 | 0-1 | 6 | | 432 |
| 14 | | 15 | A | Berwick R | L | 1-2 | 1-0 | 6 | Hardie [41] | 390 |
| 15 | | 22 | H | Dumbarton | L | 2-3 | 2-0 | 6 | Conroy [5], Edgar [31] | 548 |
| 16 | | 29 | A | Cowdenbeath | D | 0-0 | 0-0 | 6 | | 220 |
| 17 | Dec | 13 | H | Alloa Ath | W | 3-0 | 2-0 | 6 | Arbuckle [19], Mercer [25], Edgar [46] | 575 |
| 18 | | 20 | A | Montrose | W | 3-1 | 1-0 | 5 | Mercer 2 [29, 62], Edgar [82] | 290 |
| 19 | | 27 | H | Albion R | L | 2-4 | 0-2 | 6 | O'Brien [71], Edgar [75] | 643 |
| 20 | Jan | 10 | A | Arbroath | D | 2-2 | 2-1 | 6 | Arbuckle [37], Ferry [38] | 741 |
| 21 | | 17 | A | Dumbarton | D | 0-0 | 0-0 | 6 | | 408 |
| 22 | | 31 | H | Cowdenbeath | L | 0-4 | 0-2 | 7 | | 554 |
| 23 | Feb | 7 | A | Alloa Ath | L | 0-2 | 0-0 | 7 | | 519 |
| 24 | | 14 | H | Montrose | L | 0-2 | 0-1 | 7 | | 501 |
| 25 | | 21 | H | Arbroath | L | 0-2 | 0-0 | 7 | | 422 |
| 26 | Mar | 4 | A | East Stirling | D | 0-0 | 0-0 | — | | 196 |
| 27 | | 7 | H | Berwick R | W | 2-1 | 0-1 | 7 | Finlayson [70], Mercer [78] | 430 |
| 28 | | 14 | H | Dumbarton | L | 0-2 | 0-2 | 7 | | 528 |
| 29 | | 21 | A | Cowdenbeath | W | 2-1 | 1-0 | 6 | Hardie [33], Caven [70] | 235 |
| 30 | | 28 | H | Alloa Ath | D | 1-1 | 1-0 | 6 | Mercer [42] | 549 |
| 31 | Apr | 4 | A | Montrose | L | 3-4 | 1-1 | 6 | Hardie [17], Arbuckle [61], O'Donnell [85] | 244 |
| 32 | | 11 | H | East Stirling | L | 0-2 | 0-1 | 6 | | 412 |
| 33 | | 18 | A | Berwick R | D | 2-2 | 0-1 | 6 | Maxwell [54], Mercer [73] | 317 |
| 34 | | 25 | A | Albion R | W | 2-1 | 1-0 | 6 | Edgar [41], Hardie [63] | 403 |
| 35 | May | 2 | H | Ross Co | L | 0-4 | 0-1 | 7 | | 605 |
| 36 | | 9 | A | Arbroath | D | 1-1 | 0-0 | 7 | Maxwell (pen) [80] | 1950 |

**Final League Position: 7**          1996–97 8

*Most League Goals in Season (Individual):* 30: William Martin, Division I; 1937-38.
*Most Goals Overall (Individual):* 163: J. B. McAlpine.

**Honours**
*League Champions:* Division II 1922-23. B Division 1955-56. Second Division 1980-81.
*Scottish Cup Winners:* 1874, 1875, 1876, 1880, 1881, 1882, 1884, 1886, 1890, 1893; *Runners-up:* 1892, 1900.
*League Cup:* —.
*FA Cup runners-up:* 1884, 1885.
*Club colours:* Shirt: White and black hoops. Shorts: White. Stockings: White with black hoops.

**Goalscorers:** *League (42):* Edgar 8, Mercer 8, Arbuckle 6, Hardie 5, O'Brien 4, Maxwell 3 (1 pen), Caven 2, Conroy 1, Ferry 1, Finlayson 1, Miller 1, O'Donnell 1, own goal 1. *Scottish Cup (0). Coca Cola Cup (1):* Edgar 1. *League Challenge Cup (0).*

| Hamilton L 24 | Rossiter B 26 + 1 | Cullie S 2 + 2 | Elder G 32 | McNamee P 21 + 1 | Maxwell J 34 | O'Brien P 26 + 4 | Caven R 16 + 2 | Edgar S 31 + 1 | Mercer J 30 + 2 | Hardie M 16 + 7 | Arbuckle D 33 + 2 | Wilson D 4 + 3 | Ferry D 7 + 19 | McGoldrick K 7 + 1 | Miller G 10 + 6 | Smith M 4 + 1 | Bruce G 12 | Fitzpatrick I 1 + 3 | Orr G 14 + 2 | Ramsay S — + 1 | Conroy J 13 + 6 | Graham D 15 + 1 | Finlayson K 8 + 6 | King D 1 + 1 | Connaghan D 4 + 2 | Agostini D 3 + 1 | Ritchie J — + 1 | O'Donnell B 2 + 2 | | Match No. |
|---|---|---|---|---|---|---|---|---|---|---|---|---|---|---|---|---|---|---|---|---|---|---|---|---|---|---|---|---|---|---|
| 1 | 2² | 3 | 4 | 5 | 6 | 7 | 8¹ | 9 | 10 | 11³ | 12 | 13 | 14 | | | | | | | | | | | | | | | | | 1 |
| 1 | 2 | 12 | 4 | 5¹ | 6 | 8 | | 9 | 10 | 11² | 7 | 14 | 13 | 3¹ | | | | | | | | | | | | | | | | 2 |
| 1 | | 3¹ | 4 | 5 | 6 | 8 | | 9 | 10 | 11² | 7 | 2¹ | 14 | | 12 | 13 | | | | | | | | | | | | | | 3 |
| | 13 | | 4 | 5 | 6 | 10 | | 9 | 11 | 12 | 7 | 2 | | 3² | 8¹ | 1 | | | | | | | | | | | | | | 4 |
| 1 | | | 4 | 5 | 6 | 11 | | 10 | 9 | | 8 | 2 | | 3 | 7 | | | | | | | | | | | | | | | 5 |
| 1 | | | 4 | 5 | 6 | 10 | | 9 | 11¹ | 12 | 7 | 2 | 13 | 3 | 8² | | | | | | | | | | | | | | | 6 |
| 1 | 2 | | 4 | 5 | 6 | 10 | | 9 | 11² | 12 | 7 | 14 | | 3³ | 8¹ | 13 | | | | | | | | | | | | | | 7 |
| 1 | 2 | | 4 | 5 | 6 | 8 | 12 | 9 | 11 | | 7 | | 13 | 3² | | | 10¹ | | | | | | | | | | | | | 8 |
| 1 | 2 | 4² | 5 | 6 | 8 | 11 | | 9 | 10¹ | 3 | 7 | | 12 | | | | | 13 | | | | | | | | | | | | 9 |
| 1 | 2 | | 4 | 5 | 6 | 8¹ | 11 | 9 | 10¹ | 3² | 7 | | 14 | | | | | 12 | 13 | | | | | | | | | | | 10 |
| 1 | 2 | | 4 | 5 | 6 | 8 | 11 | 9 | 10 | | 7 | | | 3 | | | | | | | | | | | | | | | | 11 |
| 1 | 2 | | 4 | 5 | 6 | 8² | 11¹ | 9 | 10³ | | 7 | | 13 | 3 | | | | 14 | | 12 | | | | | | | | | | 12 |
| 1 | 2 | | 4 | 5¹ | 6 | 8² | 7 | 9 | 10¹ | 11 | 14 | | 12 | 3 | | | | | | | 13 | | | | | | | | | 13 |
| 1 | 2 | | 4 | 5¹ | 6 | 12 | | 9 | 14 | 7 | 8 | | 13 | | | | | | 11² | | 10 | 3¹ | | | | | | | | 14 |
| 1 | 2 | | 4 | | 6 | 8¹ | 7² | 9 | | 13 | 5 | | 12 | 3 | | | | | | | 10 | 11 | | | | | | | | 15 |
| 1 | 2 | | 4 | | 6 | 8 | 7 | 9 | | | 5 | | 12 | 3 | | | | | | | 10¹ | 11 | | | | | | | | 16 |
| 1 | 2 | | 4 | 5 | 6 | 8 | | 9 | 10 | 12 | 7 | | | | | | | | 3¹ | | | 11 | | | | | | | | 17 |
| 1 | 2 | | 4 | 5 | 6 | 8 | | 9 | 10¹ | | 7 | | | | | | | | 3 | | 12 | 11 | | | | | | | | 18 |
| 1 | 2 | | 4 | 5 | 6 | 8 | | 9 | 10¹ | 11 | 7 | | 12 | | | | | | | | 3² | | 13 | | | | | | | 19 |
| 1 | 2 | | 4 | 5 | 6 | 8 | | 9¹ | 10 | | 7 | | 12 | | | | | | 3 | | | 11 | | | | | | | | 20 |
| 1 | 2 | | 4 | 5 | 6 | 6¹ | 8 | | 9¹ | 10 | 7 | | | 13 | | | | | 3² | | 14 | 11 | | 12 | | | | | | 21 |
| 1 | 2 | | | 5² | 6 | 8 | | 9¹ | 10 | | 7 | | 14 | 13 | | | | | 3¹ | | 12 | 11 | | 4 | | | | | | 22 |
| 1 | 2 | | | 5 | 7 | | 9 | 8 | 6 | 4 | | 13 | | | | | | | 3¹ | | 11² | 10 | 12 | | | | | | | 23 |
| 1 | 2 | | | 5 | 6 | 8 | 9² | 10 | 14 | 4 | | 13 | | 3 | | | | | | | 12 | 11² | 7¹ | | | | | | | 24 |
| 1 | 2 | | | 5 | 6 | 8 | 9 | 10 | | 4 | | 12 | | | | | | | | | | 11 | 7¹ | | 3 | | | | | 25 |
| | 2 | 4² | | 5 | 13 | 8 | 9 | 10 | 12 | 7 | | 11 | | 6¹ | | 1 | | | | | | | 3 | | | | | | 26 |
| | 2³ | | 4 | | 5 | 12 | 7 | 9³ | 11 | 6 | 8 | | 10 | 14 | | 1 | | | | | | 13 | | 3¹ | | | | | 27 |
| | 2 | 4¹ | | 5 | 8 | | | 9³ | | 11 | 10 | | 3 | 1 | | | | | 12 | | 7 | | 6² | 13 | 14 | | | | 28 |
| | | 4 | | 5 | | 8 | | 9 | 2 | 11 | 10 | | 13 | 1 | | | 3 | | 6² | | 12 | | | | | | 7¹ | | 29 |
| 2 | | 4 | | 5 | 13 | 7 | | 9 | 3 | 8 | 10³ | | 14 | | | 1 | | | 11² | | 12 | | | | | | 6¹ | | 30 |
| | 2² | 4 | | | 11 | | | 9 | 5 | 8 | 10 | | | 1 | | 3 | | 6 | | | 7¹ | | 13 | | | | 12 | | 31 |
| | 14 | 4 | | | | 8 | 9 | | 5 | 10 | 11¹ | | | 1 | | 2³ | | 6 | 3² | 7 | | 12 | | 13 | | | | | 32 |
| | | 4 | 5 | | 10 | 9² | 11 | | 8 | 13 | 12 | | | 1 | | 2³ | | 6¹ | 14 | 7 | | | 3 | | | | | | 33 |
| | | 4 | 6 | | 9 | | 8 | 7 | | 3 | | | 1 | | 2 | | 10¹ | 11 | 12 | | 5 | | | | | | | | 34 |
| | | 4 | 12 | 6 | | 9 | 13 | 8 | | | 3 | | | 1 | | 2 | | 11 | 10 | 7² | | 5¹ | | | | | | | 35 |
| | | 4 | 5 | 6 | | 13 | 12 | 9 | | 8 | | | 3 | | 1 | | 2 | | 11¹ | 10 | 7² | | | | | | | | 36 |

# RAITH ROVERS

First Division

*Year Formed:* 1883. *Ground & Address:* Stark's Park, Pratt St, Kirkcaldy KY1 1SA. *Telephone:* 01592 263514. *Fax:* 01592 642833.
*Ground Capacity:* 10,271 (all seated). *Size of Pitch:* 113yd × 70yd.
*Chairman:* Alan Kelly. *Office Manager:* Keri Gooding.
*Manager:* Jimmy Nicholl. *Assistant Manager:* Alex Smith. *Physio:* John McCreadie. *Coach:* Terry Butcher. *Youth Development Coach:* John Brownlie.
*Managers since 1975:* R. Paton; A. Matthew; W. McLean; G. Wallace; R. Wilson; F. Connor; J. Nicholl; J. Thomson; T. McLean; I. Munro. *Club Nickname:* Rovers. *Previous Grounds:* Robbie's Park.
*Record Attendance:* 31,306 v Hearts, Scottish Cup 2nd rd; 7 Feb, 1953.
*Record Transfer Fee received:* £900,000 for S. McAnespie to Bolton Wanderers (Sept 1995).
*Record Transfer Fee paid:* £225,000 for Paul Harvey from Airdrieonians (1996).
*Record Victory:* 10-1 v Coldstream, Scottish Cup 2nd rd; 13 Feb, 1954.
*Record Defeat:* 2-11 v Morton, Division II; 18 Mar, 1936.
*Most Capped Player:* David Morris, 6, Scotland.
*Most League Appearances:* 430: Willie McNaught.
*Most League Goals in Season (Individual):* 38: Norman Haywood, Division II; 1937-38.
*Most Goals Overall (Individual):* 154: Gordon Dalziel (League), 1987-94.

## RAITH ROVERS 1997–98 LEAGUE RECORD

| Match No. | Date | Venue | Opponents | Result | H/T Score | Lg. Pos. | Goalscorers | Attendance |
|---|---|---|---|---|---|---|---|---|
| 1 | Aug 2 | A | Stirling A | D 1-1 | 1-1 | — | Duffield [25] | 2159 |
| 2 | 16 | H | Airdrieonians | D 1-1 | 0-1 | 7 | Wright [78] | 3414 |
| 3 | 23 | A | Hamilton A | L 0-2 | 0-0 | 8 | | 1140 |
| 4 | 30 | A | Dundee | D 2-2 | 0-2 | 8 | McGill [78], Lennon [83] | 4461 |
| 5 | Sept 13 | H | St Mirren | W 2-1 | 0-0 | 6 | Dair L [62], Wright [75] | 3311 |
| 6 | 20 | A | Ayr U | L 0-1 | 0-1 | 8 | | 1987 |
| 7 | 27 | H | Falkirk | W 2-0 | 2-0 | 5 | Dair L [20], McEwan [23] | 3564 |
| 8 | Oct 4 | A | Greenock Morton | W 3-1 | 2-0 | 4 | Dair L [11], Dargo [29], McGill [60] | 2309 |
| 9 | 18 | H | Partick Th | W 2-0 | 1-0 | 4 | Hartley [13], Lennon [90] | 3417 |
| 10 | 25 | H | Stirling A | W 2-0 | 1-0 | 3 | Hartley [38], Wright [84] | 3280 |
| 11 | Nov 1 | A | Airdrieonians | L 0-1 | 0-0 | 3 | | 1945 |
| 12 | 8 | H | Dundee | L 0-1 | 0-0 | 4 | | 4763 |
| 13 | 15 | A | St Mirren | W 3-2 | 1-2 | 4 | Dair L [43], Hartley [75], Lennon [79] | 2441 |
| 14 | 22 | A | Falkirk | W 1-0 | 1-0 | 3 | Hartley [11] | 3248 |
| 15 | 29 | H | Ayr U | L 0-1 | 0-0 | 3 | | 3015 |
| 16 | Dec 6 | H | Greenock Morton | D 0-0 | 0-0 | 3 | | 2792 |
| 17 | 13 | A | Partick Th | W 3-1 | 1-0 | 2 | Browne [38], Wright 2 [71, 72] | 3108 |
| 18 | 20 | H | Hamilton A | W 3-1 | 0-1 | 2 | Browne [76], Wright 2 [85, 90] | 2789 |
| 19 | 27 | A | Stirling A | L 2-3 | 2-1 | 2 | Wright 2 [8, 24] | 2087 |
| 20 | Jan 3 | A | Dundee | D 1-1 | 1-0 | 3 | Kelly (og) [45] | 5304 |
| 21 | 10 | H | St Mirren | W 4-1 | 2-1 | 3 | Dargo 3 [33, 47, 74], Hartley [42] | 3431 |
| 22 | 31 | A | Ayr U | D 0-0 | 0-0 | 3 | | 1989 |
| 23 | Feb 3 | H | Falkirk | W 2-0 | 1-0 | — | Lennon [29], Dargo [70] | 4666 |
| 24 | 7 | A | Partick Th | W 2-0 | 0-0 | 2 | Dargo [59], Millar [68] | 3675 |
| 25 | 21 | A | Greenock Morton | L 1-3 | 0-2 | 2 | Thomson [64] | 2289 |
| 26 | Mar 7 | H | Airdrieonians | D 1-1 | 1-0 | 3 | Fotheringham [35] | 2635 |
| 27 | 14 | A | Falkirk | W 1-0 | 1-0 | 3 | Walker (pen) [7] | 3512 |
| 28 | 17 | A | Hamilton A | W 4-1 | 1-1 | — | Hartley [16], Walker [59], McGill 2 [79, 86] | 711 |
| 29 | 21 | H | Ayr U | D 0-0 | 0-0 | 3 | | 2800 |
| 30 | 28 | A | Partick Th | W 2-1 | 1-0 | 2 | Hartley 2 [28, 63] | 2308 |
| 31 | Apr 4 | H | Greenock Morton | L 1-2 | 0-1 | 2 | Browne [84] | 2400 |
| 32 | 11 | H | Dundee | D 1-1 | 0-0 | 3 | Hartley [52] | 6985 |
| 33 | 18 | A | St Mirren | W 2-0 | 1-0 | 3 | Wright [30], Dargo [90] | 2285 |
| 34 | 25 | H | Stirling A | L 0-1 | 0-0 | 3 | | 2326 |
| 35 | May 2 | A | Airdrieonians | L 0-1 | 0-1 | 3 | | 1173 |
| 36 | 9 | H | Hamilton A | W 2-1 | 0-1 | 3 | Dargo [70], Hartley [88] | 2036 |

**Final League Position: 3**      1996–97 PREM 10

**Honours**

*League Champions:* First Division: 1992-93, 1994-95. Division II 1907-08, 1909-10 (shared), 1937-38, 1948-49; *Runners-up:* Division II 1908-09, 1926-27, 1966-67. Second Division 1975-76, 1977-78, 1986-87.
*Scottish Cup Runners-up:* 1913. *League Cup Winners: (Coca-Cola Cup):* 1994-95. *Runners-up:* 1948-49.
*Club colours:* Shirt: Navy blue, white trim. Shorts: White. Stockings: White.

**European:** *UEFA Cup:* 6 matches (1995-96).

**Goalscorers:** *League (51):* Hartley 10, Wright 10, Dargo 8, Dair L 4, Lennon 4, McGill 4, Browne 3, Walker 2 (1 pen), Duffield 1, Fotheringham 1, McEwan 1, Millar J 1, Thomson 1, own goal 1. *Scottish Cup (3):* Millar J 2, Thomson 1. *Coca Cola Cup (6):* Duffield 3, Cameron 1, Millen 1, Wright 1. *League Challenge Cup (4):* Cameron 1, Dair L 1, Lennon 1, Wright 1.

| Van De Kamp G 36 | McEwan C 33 | Thomson S 30 + 1 | Kirkwood D 15 + 1 | Craig D 3 | Millen A 6 | Lennon D 32 | Harvey P 1 | Duffield P 5 + 4 | Wright K 17 + 7 | Cameron 17 + 1 | Kirk S — + 3 | Twaddle K 4 + 6 | Fotheringham K 32 | Dair L 14 + 9 | Mitchell G 2 + 1 | Millar J 19 + 5 | Hartley P 28 + 2 | McGill D 11 + 5 | Dair J 15 + 10 | Browne P 30 + 1 | Dargo C 21 + 6 | Stein J 7 + 12 | McCulloch G 7 + 4 | Galloway A 1 + 3 | Andrews M 6 | Walker A 5 + 2 | Tosh S 6 | Blunt J — + 1 | McPherson D 2 | Venables R 1 + 1 | Byers K — + 1 | Smart C — + 1 | Match No. |
|---|---|---|---|---|---|---|---|---|---|---|---|---|---|---|---|---|---|---|---|---|---|---|---|---|---|---|---|---|---|---|---|---|---|
| 1 | 2 | 3 | 4 | 5 | 6 | 7 | $8^2$ | 9 | $10^1$ | 11 | 12 | 13 | | | | | | | | | | | | | | | | | | | | | 1 |
| 1 | 2 | | $4^1$ | 5 | 6 | 7 | | 9 | 10 | 11 | 14 | | $3^3$ | $8^2$ | 12 | 13 | | | | | | | | | | | | | | | | | 2 |
| 1 | | | 4 | 5 | 6 | | | $9^2$ | 10 | 11 | 12 | 7 | 3 | 13 | $2^1$ | 8 | | | | | | | | | | | | | | | | | 3 |
| 1 | 2 | 11 | 4 | | 6 | 8 | | 13 | 9 | $10^2$ | | | $3^3$ | 12 | $5^1$ | 7 | 14 | | | | | | | | | | | | | | | | 4 |
| 1 | 2 | 3 | 4 | | 6 | 8 | | $9^2$ | 12 | 10 | | | 5 | 7 | | | 13 | $11^1$ | | | | | | | | | | | | | | | 5 |
| 1 | 2 | 3 | 4 | | $6^3$ | 8 | | $9^1$ | 10 | 14 | | | 5 | 7 | | | 13 | $11^{12}$ | 12 | | | | | | | | | | | | | | 6 |
| 1 | 2 | 3 | 13 | | | | | 8 | 12 | | | | 6 | 11 | | 4 | $7^3$ | $9^1$ | 14 | 5 | $10^2$ | | | | | | | | | | | | 7 |
| 1 | 2 | 3 | | | | | | 8 | 12 | 13 | | | 6 | $11^3$ | | 4 | 7 | $9^1$ | 14 | 5 | $10^2$ | | | | | | | | | | | | 8 |
| 1 | 2 | 3 | | | | | | 8 | 12 | | | | 6 | $11^2$ | | 4 | 7 | 10 | 13 | 5 | $9^1$ | | | | | | | | | | | | 9 |
| 1 | 2 | 12 | 3 | | | | | 8 | 13 | | | | 6 | $11^2$ | | 4 | 7 | 10 | | 5 | $9^1$ | | | | | | | | | | | | 10 |
| 1 | 2 | 3 | 4 | | | | | 8 | 14 | $10^2$ | | | 6 | 12 | | $11^1$ | 7 | $9^3$ | 13 | 5 | | | | | | | | | | | | | 11 |
| 1 | 2 | 3 | 4 | | | | | 8 | 12 | | | | 6 | $11^3$ | | 13 | 7 | $10^2$ | 14 | 5 | $9^1$ | | | | | | | | | | | | 12 |
| 1 | 2 | $3^1$ | 4 | | | | | 8 | | | | 12 | 6 | 10 | | 14 | 7 | $9^2$ | $11^3$ | 5 | 13 | | | | | | | | | | | | 13 |
| 1 | 2 | 3 | | | | | | 8 | | | | 4 | 12 | 6 | $10^2$ | 13 | $7^1$ | 14 | 11 | 5 | $9^2$ | | | | | | | | | | | | 14 |
| 1 | 2 | 3 | | | | | | 8 | | | | $4^1$ | 12 | 6 | $10^2$ | | 7 | 13 | 11 | 5 | 9 | | | | | | | | | | | | 15 |
| 1 | 2 | 3 | | | | | | 8 | | | | | 6 | 11 | | 13 | 7 | $10^2$ | $4^1$ | 5 | 9 | 12 | | | | | | | | | | | 16 |
| 1 | 2 | 3 | | | | | | 8 | 10 | | | | $11^2$ | 6 | 12 | 4 | 7 | | 5 | $9^1$ | 13 | | | | | | | | | | | | 17 |
| 1 | $2^3$ | 3 | | | | | | 8 | 10 | | | | $11^1$ | 6 | $7^3$ | 4 | | 13 | 5 | 9 | 12 | 14 | | | | | | | | | | | 18 |
| 1 | 2 | 3 | | | | | | 8 | 10 | | | | 13 | 6 | 12 | 4 | | 7 | 5 | $9^1$ | $11^2$ | | | | | | | | | | | | 19 |
| 1 | 2 | 3 | 4 | | | | | 8 | 10 | | | | 12 | 6 | | 8 | 7 | 5 | 9 | $11^1$ | | | | | | | | | | | | | 20 |
| 1 | 2 | 3 | 4 | | | | | $8^1$ | 10 | | | | $6^3$ | | | 11 | 7 | 13 | 5 | $9^1$ | 12 | | 14 | | | | | | | | | | 21 |
| 1 | 2 | 3 | $4^1$ | | | | | 8 | $10^2$ | | | | 6 | | | 11 | 7 | 13 | 5 | 9 | 12 | | | | | | | | | | | | 22 |
| 1 | 2 | 3 | | | | | | 8 | $10^2$ | | | | 6 | 14 | | 4 | $7^3$ | $11^1$ | 5 | 9 | 13 | | 12 | | | | | | | | | | 23 |
| 1 | 2 | 3 | | | | | | 8 | $10^1$ | | | | 6 | | | 4 | 7 | 11 | 5 | 9 | 12 | | | | | | | | | | | | 24 |
| 1 | 2 | 3 | | | | | | 8 | 12 | | | | | $11^3$ | | 4 | 7 | $10^1$ | 5 | 9 | 13 | 14 | $6^2$ | | | | | | | | | | 25 |
| 1 | 2 | 3 | | | | | | 8 | | | | | | 10 | 12 | 4 | 7 | 13 | 6 | $9^2$ | $11^1$ | | | | | 5 | | | | | | | 26 |
| 1 | 2 | 3 | | | | | | 8 | | | | | | 11 | | 4 | 7 | $9^2$ | 13 | 6 | 12 | | | | | 5 | $10^1$ | | | | | | 27 |
| 1 | 2 | 3 | | | | | | 8 | | | | | | 11 | | 4 | 7 | 9 | 12 | $6^2$ | | | 13 | | | 5 | $10^1$ | | | | | | 28 |
| 1 | 2 | 3 | | | | | | 8 | | | | | | 11 | | | 7 | $9^1$ | 4 | 6 | 12 | 13 | | | | 5 | $10^1$ | | | | | | 29 |
| 1 | $2^1$ | 3 | | | | | | 8 | | | | | | 11 | | $10^3$ | 6 | 13 | 12 | 4 | 14 | 5 | | | | $9^2$ | | | | | | | 30 |
| 1 | | 3 | | | | | | 8 | | | | | 6 | | | | 7 | $10^2$ | 5 | 12 | 11 | 2 | | | | | | | $9^1$ | 4 | 13 | | 31 |
| 1 | 2 | 3 | | | | | | 8 | 12 | | | | 6 | | | | 7 | 5 | $9^1$ | $11^2$ | 4 | | | | | | | | 13 | 10 | | | 32 |
| 1 | 2 | 10 | | | | | | 8 | $9^2$ | | | | 6 | 13 | | 7 | | 5 | 12 | $11^1$ | 3 | | | | | 4 | | | | | | | 33 |
| 1 | $2^3$ | 11 | | | | | | $8^2$ | 9 | | | | 6 | 7 | | 14 | | 5 | $10^1$ | 13 | 3 | | | | | 12 | 4 | | | | | | 34 |
| 1 | 2 | $8^3$ | | | | | | | 9 | | | | 13 | | | 7 | | 6 | 12 | $11^2$ | 3 | | 5 | | | 4 | | | $10^1$ | 14 | | | 35 |
| 1 | | | | | | | | | | | | | 6 | $9^2$ | | | 7 | 11 | 5 | 10 | 14 | 2 | | | | 4 | | | $3^3$ | $8^1$ | 12 | 13 | 36 |

# RANGERS
## Premier League

*Year Formed:* 1873. *Ground & Address:* Ibrox Stadium, Edminston Drive, Glasgow G51 2XD. *Telephone:* 0141 427 8500. *Fax:* 0141 427 2676.
*Ground Capacity:* total: 50,500. *Size of Pitch:* 115yd × 78yd.
*Chairman:* David Murray. *Secretary:* R. C. Ogilvie. *Commercial & Marketing Manager:* Martin Bain.
*Manager:* Dick Advocaat. *Assistant Manager:* Bert Van Lingen. *Physio:* Grant Downie. *Coach:* Tommy Moller Nielsen.
*Reserve team coaches:* John McGregor, John Brown.
*Managers since 1975:* Jock Wallace; John Greig; Jock Wallace; Graeme Souness. *Club Nickname(s):* The Gers. *Previous Grounds:* Burnbank, Kinning Park.
*Record Attendance:* 118,567 v Celtic, Division I; 2 Jan, 1939.
*Record Transfer Fee received:* £5,580,000 for Trevor Steven to Marseille (Aug 1991).
*Record Transfer Fee paid:* £5.5 million for Andrei Kanchelskis from Fiorentina (July 1998).
*Record Victory:* 14-2 v Blairgowrie, Scottish Cup 1st rd; 20 Jan, 1934.
*Record Defeat:* 2-10 v Airdrieonians; 1886.
*Most Capped Player:* Ally McCoist, 59, Scotland.
*Most League Appearances:* 496: John Greig, 1962-78.
*Most League Goals in Season (Individual):* 44: Sam English, Division I; 1931–32.
*Most Goals Overall (Individual):* 250: Ally McCoist; 1985–98.

## RANGERS 1997–98 LEAGUE RECORD

| Match No. | Date | Venue | Opponents | Result | H/T Score | Lg. Pos. | Goalscorers | Attendance |
|---|---|---|---|---|---|---|---|---|
| 1 | Aug 4 | H | Hearts | W 3-1 | 2-0 | — | Negri 2 [39, 40], Cleland [85] | 48,257 |
| 2 | 23 | H | Dundee U | W 5-1 | 3-0 | 2 | Negri 5 [34, 42, 43, 65, 85] | 48,599 |
| 3 | Sept13 | H | Aberdeen | D 3-3 | 1-0 | 3 | Negri (pen) [43], Albertz [54], Laudrup [76] | 50,030 |
| 4 | 20 | A | St Johnstone | W 2-0 | 1-0 | 3 | Negri 2 [7, 46] | 10,093 |
| 5 | 24 | A | Kilmarnock | W 3-0 | 0-0 | — | Negri 2 [49, 62], Stensaas [90] | 15,367 |
| 6 | 27 | H | Motherwell | D 2-2 | 1-2 | 2 | Negri [16], Porrini [63] | 48,672 |
| 7 | Oct 4 | A | Hibernian | W 4-3 | 1-2 | 2 | Negri 2 (1 pen) [25 (p), 59], Gascoigne [50], Albertz [53] | 15,169 |
| 8 | 18 | H | Dunfermline Ath | W 7-0 | 3-0 | 1 | Laudrup [16], Negri 4 [19, 35, 79, 88], Gascoigne 2 [54, 82] | 49,696 |
| 9 | 25 | A | Dundee U | L 1-2 | 0-1 | 2 | Negri [57] | 12,600 |
| 10 | Nov 1 | H | Kilmarnock | W 4-1 | 1-1 | 3 | Negri 3 (1 pen) [4, 87 (p), 90], Porrini [85] | 49,413 |
| 11 | 8 | H | Celtic | W 1-0 | 1-0 | 2 | Gough [29] | 50,082 |
| 12 | 15 | A | Aberdeen | D 1-1 | 0-1 | 2 | Albertz [49] | 18,117 |
| 13 | 19 | A | Celtic | D 1-1 | 0-0 | — | Negri [71] | 49,427 |
| 14 | 22 | A | Motherwell | D 1-1 | 1-0 | 2 | McCoist [21] | 12,018 |
| 15 | 29 | H | St Johnstone | W 3-2 | 2-1 | 2 | Gattuso [6], Negri 2 [42, 56] | 49,142 |
| 16 | Dec 7 | H | Hibernian | W 1-0 | 0-0 | — | Negri [50] | 48,070 |
| 17 | 13 | A | Dunfermline Ath | D 0-0 | 0-0 | 2 | | 12,443 |
| 18 | 20 | A | Hearts | W 5-2 | 2-1 | 1 | Durie 3 [7, 35, 84], Negri (pen) [68], Albertz [78] | 17,092 |
| 19 | 27 | H | Dundee U | W 4-1 | 2-1 | 1 | Laudrup [42], Cleland [43], Negri 2 (1 pen) [81, 99 (p)] | 50,017 |
| 20 | Jan 2 | A | Celtic | L 0-2 | 0-0 | — | | 49,396 |
| 21 | 10 | H | Aberdeen | W 2-0 | 2-0 | 1 | Porrini [9], Laudrup [12] | 49,502 |
| 22 | 17 | A | Motherwell | W 1-0 | 1-0 | 1 | Cleland [22] | 49,443 |
| 23 | 31 | A | St Johnstone | L 0-2 | 0-1 | 1 | | 10,441 |
| 24 | Feb 7 | H | Dunfermline Ath | D 1-1 | 0-0 | 1 | Porrini [72] | 49,019 |
| 25 | 21 | A | Hibernian | W 2-1 | 1-1 | 1 | Negri [35], Albertz [87] | 13,968 |
| 26 | 24 | A | Kilmarnock | D 1-1 | 1-1 | 1 | Thern [35] | 15,931 |
| 27 | 28 | H | Hearts | D 2-2 | 1-1 | 3 | Albertz 2 [40, 90] | 50,046 |
| 28 | Mar 14 | A | Motherwell | L 1-2 | 1-1 | 3 | McCoist [11] | 11,779 |
| 29 | 21 | H | St Johnstone | W 2-1 | 1-1 | 3 | Negri [26], Thern [56] | 49,788 |
| 30 | 28 | A | Dunfermline Ath | W 3-2 | 1-1 | 3 | McCoist 2 [26, 48], Thern [68] | 11,531 |
| 31 | Apr 1 | H | Hibernian | W 3-0 | 0-0 | — | McCoist [56], Thern [58], Durie [75] | 48,488 |
| 32 | 12 | H | Celtic | W 2-0 | 1-0 | — | Thern [25], Albertz [66] | 50,042 |
| 33 | 19 | A | Aberdeen | L 0-1 | 0-1 | — | | 17,981 |
| 34 | 26 | A | Hearts | W 3-0 | 0-0 | 2 | Gattuso 2 [49, 78], Albertz [65] | 17,415 |
| 35 | May 2 | H | Kilmarnock | L 0-1 | 0-0 | 2 | | 50,116 |
| 36 | 9 | A | Dundee U | W 2-1 | 1-0 | 2 | Laudrup [30], Albertz (pen) [52] | 14,200 |

**Final League Position: 2**    1996–97 1

**Honours**

*League Champions:* (47 times) Division I 1890-91 (shared), 1898-99, 1899-1900, 1900-01, 1901-02, 1910-11, 1911-12, 1912-13, 1917-18, 1919-20, 1920-21, 1922-23, 1923-24, 1924-25, 1926-27, 1927-28, 1928-29, 1929-30, 1930-31, 1932-33, 1933-34, 1934-35, 1936-37, 1938-39, 1946-47, 1948-49, 1949-50, 1952-53, 1955-56, 1956-57, 1958-59, 1960-61, 1962-63, 1963-64, 1974-75. Premier Division: 1975-76, 1977-78, 1986-87, 1988-89, 1989-90, 1990-91, 1991-92, 1992-93, 1993-94, 1994-95, 1995-96, 1996–97; *Runners-up:* 24 times.
*Scottish Cup Winners:* (27 times) 1894, 1897, 1898, 1903, 1928, 1930, 1932, 1934, 1935, 1936, 1948, 1949, 1950, 1953, 1960, 1962, 1963, 1964, 1966, 1973, 1976, 1978, 1979, 1981, 1992, 1993, 1996; *Runners-up:* 17 times.
*League Cup Winners:* (20 times) 1946-47, 1948-49, 1960-61, 1961-62, 1963-64, 1964-65, 1970-71, 1975-76, 1977-78, 1978-79, 1981-82, 1983-84, 1984-85, 1986-87, 1987-88, 1988-89, 1990-91, 1992-93, 1993-94, 1996–97; *Runners-up:* 7 times.

**European:** *European Cup:* 91 matches (1956-57, 1957-58, 1959-60 semi-finals, 1961-62, 1963-64, 1964-65, 1975-76, 1976-77, 1978-79, 1987-88, 1989-90, 1990-91, 1991-92, 1992-93 final pool, 1993-94, 1994-95, 1995-96; 1996-97, 1997-98).
*Cup Winners' Cup:* 54 matches (1960-61 runners-up, 1962-63, 1966-67 runners-up, 1969-70, 1971-72 winners, 1973-74, 1977-78, 1979-80, 1981-82, 1983-84). *UEFA Cup:* 40 matches (*Fairs Cup:* 1967-68, 1968-69 semi-finals, 1970-71. *UEFA Cup:* 1982-83, 1984-85, 1985-86, 1986-87, 1988-89, 1997-98).
*Club colours:* Shirt: Royal blue with red and blue panels. Shorts: White with red and blue panels. Stockings: Red with black tops.

**Goalscorers:** *League (76):* Negri 32 (5 pens), Albertz 10 (1 pen), Laudrup 5, McCoist 5, Thern 5, Durie 4, Porrini 4, Cleland 3, Gascoigne 3, Gattuso 3, Gough 1, Stensaas 1. *Scottish Cup (12):* McCoist 4, Albertz 3, Durie 3, Gough 1, Negri 1. *Coca Cola Cup (5):* McCoist 4 (1 pen), Stensaas 1.

| Goram A 24 | Cleland A 27+2 | Stensaas S 17+3 | Porrini S 26 | Moore C 8+2 | Bjorklund J 31 | Thern J 22 | Ferguson I 9+2 | Negri M 28+1 | Albertz J 27+4 | Laudrup B 26+2 | Gattuso G 22+7 | Durie G 14+12 | Gascoigne P 14+6 | Miller C 5+2 | Snelders T 7 | Vidmar A 8+4 | McCoist A 7+8 | McCall S 26+4 | Petric G 6 | Gough R 24 | Durrant I 1+7 | Johansson J 1+5 | Ferguson B 6+1 | Bollan G —+1 | Niemi A 5 | Rozental S 1+1 | Van Vossen P —+1 | Amoruso L 4 | Match No. |
|---|---|---|---|---|---|---|---|---|---|---|---|---|---|---|---|---|---|---|---|---|---|---|---|---|---|---|---|---|---|
| 1 | 2 | 3 | 4 | 5[1] | 6 | 7 | 8 | 9 | 10 | 11 | 12 | | | | | | | | | | | | | | | | | | 1 |
| 1 | 13 | 3 | 4 | 2 | 6 | 11 | 5 | 9 | | | | 12 | 7 | | | | 8[1] | 10[2] | | | | | | | | | | | 2 |
| | 2[1] | 3 | 4 | 5 | | | 10[3] | 9 | 12 | 11 | 7 | 8[2] | 13 | 1 | 6 | 14 | | | | | | | | | | | | | 3 |
| 1 | | 3[1] | 4 | | 6 | | | 9 | 10[1] | 11 | 7 | 13 | 12 | | | 1 | 5 | 8 | | | | | | | | | | | 4 |
| 1 | | 3 | 4 | | 6 | | | 9 | 10 | 11 | 7 | | 12 | | | 1 | 5 | 8[1] | | | | | | | | | | | 5 |
| 1 | 2 | 3 | 4 | | 6[2] | | | 9 | 13 | 11[1] | 7 | 12 | 8 | 10[2] | | | 5 | 14 | | | | | | | | | | | 6 |
| | 2 | 3 | 4[1] | | | | | 9 | 10 | 11 | 13 | 8 | 7[1] | 1 | 6 | | 12 | 5 | | | | | | | | | | | 7 |
| 1 | | 3 | 5 | 6 | | | | 9 | | 11 | 7 | | 8 | 2 | | | 10 | | | 4 | | | | | | | | | 8 |
| 1 | | 3 | | 6[2] | | | | 9 | | 11 | 7 | 12 | 8 | 2[1] | | 13 | | 10 | 5 | 4 | | | | | | | | | 9 |
| 1 | | 3 | 5 | 6 | 7[2] | | | 9 | 14 | 11 | 10[3] | 12 | 8 | 13 | | 2[1] | | | | 4 | | | | | | | | | 10 |
| 1 | 3 | | 5 | 6 | 7 | | | 9 | 13 | 11[1] | 10 | 12 | 8[2] | | | 2 | | | | 4 | | | | | | | | | 11 |
| 1 | 2 | 3 | | 6 | 7 | | | 9 | 5 | 11[1] | 10[2] | 12 | | | | 13 | 8 | | | 4 | | | | | | | | | 12 |
| 1 | 3 | 12 | | 6 | 5 | | | 9[2] | 10 | 11[1] | 7 | 8 | | | | 13 | 2 | | | 4 | | | | | | | | | 13 |
| 1 | 3 | 13 | | 5 | 6 | 7 | 8[2] | 9 | 11[3] | | | | | | | 10[1] | 2 | | | 4 | 12 | 14 | | | | | | | 14 |
| 1 | 14 | 13 | 5[2] | 6 | 7 | | | 9 | 3[3] | 11[3] | 10 | 12 | 8 | | | 2 | | | | 4 | | | | | | | | | 15 |
| 1 | 2 | 3 | | 6 | 7 | | | 9[2] | 8 | 10[1] | 11 | | | | | 5 | | | | 4 | 13 | | 12 | | | | | | 16 |
| | 2 | 3[2] | 5 | 6 | 7 | | | 9 | 10 | 11 | | | | 1 | | | | | | 4[1] | 13 | | 12 | | | | | | 17 |
| | 2 | 3 | 5 | 6 | | 8 | 9[1] | 11 | 12 | 10 | 7 | | | 1 | | | | | | 4 | | | | | | | | | 18 |
| | 2 | 3[1] | 5 | 6 | | 8[3] | 9 | 10 | 11[2] | | | | | 1 | 12 | 14 | 4 | | | 13 | | | 7 | | | | | | 19 |
| 1 | 3 | | 5 | | 7 | 8 | 9 | 6[2] | 11 | 10[1] | 12 | 13 | | | | 2 | | | | 4 | | | | | | | | | 20 |
| 1 | 2 | | 5 | 6 | 7 | | 3 | 11 | | 9 | | | | | | 10 | 4 | | | 8 | | | | | | | | | 21 |
| 1 | 2 | | 5 | 6 | 7 | | 3 | | 9 | 8[2] | | 12 | 10[1] | 4 | | | 13 | 11 | | | | | | | | | | | 22 |
| 1 | | 5 | 14 | 6 | | | | 10[2] | 11 | 7[3] | 9 | 12 | | 3 | 2 | 4 | | 13 | 8[1] | | | | | | | | | | 23 |
| | | 5 | | 6 | | | 9 | 3 | 11 | 7 | 12 | 8 | | 2[1] | 10 | 4 | | | | 1 | | | | | | | | | 24 |
| 1 | 2 | | 5 | 6 | | 8[1] | 9 | 3 | 11 | 10 | 12 | | | 13 | | 4 | | | | 7[2] | | | | | | | | | 25 |
| 1 | | 5 | 2 | 6[2] | 7 | | 9 | | 11 | 12[3] | 8[1] | | | 13 | | | 4 | 14 | 3 | | | 10 | | | | | | | 26 |
| 1 | 2 | | 5 | 6 | 7 | | 9 | 3 | 11[2] | 8[1] | | | | | | 10 | 4 | | | 12 | | | 13 | | | | | | 27 |
| 1 | 3 | | | 4 | 6 | 7 | | 9 | 10[1] | 2 | | | | 8 | | | 5 | 13 | 11[2] | | | 12 | | | | | | | 28 |
| 1 | 2 | | 4[1] | 6 | 7 | | 9 | 3 | 12 | 13 | 14 | | | 8[2] | | 10 | 5 | | | 11[3] | | | | | | | | | 29 |
| 1 | 2 | | 5 | | 7 | | 9 | 3 | 11[1] | 12 | | | | 8 | 10 | 6 | 4 | | | | | | | | | | | | 30 |
| | 2 | | 6 | | 7 | | 9 | 3[1] | 11[3] | 12 | 13 | | | 8[2] | 10 | 5 | 4 | 14 | | | 1 | | | | | | | | 31 |
| 1 | 2 | | | 6 | 7 | | 3 | 11 | 12 | 9[1] | | | | 8 | 10 | 4 | | | | | | | | | | 5 | | | 32 |
| 1 | 2[3] | | 14 | 6 | 7 | 13 | 3 | 11 | 12 | 9 | | | | 8[2] | 10[1] | 4 | | | | | | | | | | 5 | | | 33 |
| | 2 | 3 | 5 | 6 | 7[1] | 12 | | 10 | 11[3] | 8 | 9 | | | 14 | 13 | 4 | | | | | | 1 | | | | | | | 34 |
| | 2 | 3[2] | | 6[1] | 13 | | | 10 | 11 | 8 | 9 | | | 12 | 7[3] | 4 | 14 | | | | | 1 | | | | | | 5 | 35 |
| | | 3 | 2 | 6[1] | | 8 | | 10 | 11[2] | 7 | 9 | | | 13 | 12 | 4 | | | | | | 1 | | | | | | 5 | 36 |

# ROSS COUNTY

## Third Division

*Year Formed:* 1929. *Ground & Address:* Victoria Park, Dingwall IV15 9QW. *Telephone:* 01349 862253. *Fax:* 01349 866277.
*Ground Capacity:* total 5400, seated 1520. *Size of Ground:* 110×75yd.
*Chairman:* Roy McGregor. *Chief Executive:* Donald MacLean. *Secretary:* Donnie MacBean. *Facilities Manager:* Brian Campbell.
*Manager:* Neale Cooper. *Assistant Manager:* Jim Kelly. *Physio:* Douglas Sim. *Record Attendance:* 8000, v Rangers, Scottish Cup, 28 February 1966.
*Record Transfer Fee Received:* £40,000 for Barry Wilson to Raith R, Sept.1994.
*Record Transfer Fee Paid:* £25,000 for Barry Wilson from Southampton, Oct.1992.
*Record Victory:* 11-0 v St Cuthbert Wanderers, Scottish Cup, Dec.1993.
*Record Defeat:* 1-10 v Inverness Thistle, Highland League.
*Most League Appearances:* 124: W. Herd, 1995–98.
*Most League Goals in Season:* 22: D. Adams, 1996–97.
*Most League Goals (Overall):* 38: D. Adams, 1996–98.
*Club Colours:* Shirt: Dark Blue with White trim. Shorts: White. Stockings: Red.

## ROSS COUNTY 1997–98 LEAGUE RECORD

| Match No. | Date | Venue | Opponents | Result | H/T Score | Lg. Pos. | Goalscorers | Attendance |
|---|---|---|---|---|---|---|---|---|
| 1 | Aug 5 | A | East Stirling | W 3-1 | 3-0 | — | Haro 2 [4, 42], Sneddon (og) [45] | 474 |
| 2 | 16 | H | Queen's Park | L 0-1 | 0-0 | 5 | | 1152 |
| 3 | 23 | A | Cowdenbeath | W 1-0 | 0-0 | 4 | Wood [78] | 261 |
| 4 | 30 | H | Albion R | W 5-3 | 2-0 | 2 | Adams 3 (1 pen) [30 (p), 51, 90], Wood [33], Ross A [81] | 1285 |
| 5 | Sept13 | A | Arbroath | D 2-2 | 0-0 | 4 | Wood [49], Bradshaw [71] | 625 |
| 6 | 20 | H | Berwick R | W 2-0 | 1-0 | 2 | Ferguson [29], Callaghan [83] | 1542 |
| 7 | 27 | A | Montrose | W 4-3 | 2-1 | 1 | Adams 3 (2 pens) [6 (p), 28 (p), 49], McBain [84] | 453 |
| 8 | Oct 4 | H | Alloa Ath | L 2-4 | 2-0 | 3 | Ferguson [6], Adams [30] | 1823 |
| 9 | 11 | H | Queen's Park | W 2-1 | 0-1 | 1 | Herd [46], Adams (pen) [76] | 1039 |
| 10 | 18 | A | Dumbarton | D 2-2 | 1-0 | 1 | Golabek [29], Adams [56] | 452 |
| 11 | 25 | H | Cowdenbeath | W 5-0 | 3-0 | 1 | Adams [2], Herd [40], Ferguson [45], Humphreys (og) [64], Haro [70] | 1233 |
| 12 | Nov 1 | A | Queen's Park | W 3-0 | 1-0 | 1 | Farrell [39], Maxwell (og) [47], Campbell [87] | 838 |
| 13 | 8 | A | Albion R | L 0-2 | 0-2 | 1 | | 506 |
| 14 | 15 | H | Arbroath | D 0-0 | 0-0 | 1 | | 1656 |
| 15 | 22 | H | Montrose | W 8-1 | 4-1 | 1 | Ferguson [6], Furphy [17], Adams 3 [36, 45, 69], Wood [49], McBain [57], Farrell [68] | 1328 |
| 16 | 29 | A | Berwick R | D 0-0 | 0-0 | 1 | | 484 |
| 17 | Dec 13 | H | Dumbarton | L 2-3 | 2-2 | 2 | Wood 2 [12, 32] | 1226 |
| 18 | 27 | A | Cowdenbeath | W 2-0 | 0-0 | 2 | Wood [62], Mitchell (og) [89] | 273 |
| 19 | 30 | A | Alloa Ath | L 0-1 | 0-1 | — | | 778 |
| 20 | Jan 31 | H | Berwick R | D 0-0 | 0-0 | 3 | | 1342 |
| 21 | Feb 7 | A | Dumbarton | W 1-0 | 0-0 | 3 | Adams (pen) [73] | 447 |
| 22 | 10 | A | East Stirling | D 0-0 | 0-0 | — | | 910 |
| 23 | 21 | A | East Stirling | L 0-1 | 0-0 | 4 | | 340 |
| 24 | Mar 7 | A | Arbroath | D 1-1 | 1-1 | 4 | King [32] | 784 |
| 25 | 10 | A | Montrose | W 2-0 | 0-0 | 4 | McBain [73], Gilbert [89] | 321 |
| 26 | 14 | H | Montrose | W 2-1 | 1-0 | 3 | Campbell [14], Ferguson [56] | 1209 |
| 27 | 17 | H | Albion R | W 6-2 | 5-0 | — | Farrell [13], Campbell [21], McBain [24], Coyle (og) [25], Adams [45], Haro [89] | 741 |
| 28 | 21 | A | Berwick R | D 1-1 | 1-0 | 3 | Ferguson (pen) [28] | 428 |
| 29 | 24 | H | Alloa Ath | L 0-2 | 0-1 | — | | 1327 |
| 30 | 28 | H | Dumbarton | D 0-0 | 0-0 | 3 | | 1475 |
| 31 | Apr 4 | A | Alloa Ath | D 1-1 | 0-0 | 3 | Tarrant [63] | 624 |
| 32 | 11 | A | Albion R | W 3-1 | 1-0 | 3 | Ferguson [30], Taylor [47], Adams [80] | 504 |
| 33 | 18 | A | Arbroath | W 1-0 | 0-0 | 3 | Taylor [89] | 1842 |
| 34 | 25 | H | Cowdenbeath | W 1-0 | 0-0 | 3 | Tarrant [60] | 1201 |
| 35 | May 2 | A | Queen's Park | W 4-0 | 1-0 | 3 | Ferguson 2 (1 pen) [30 (p), 90], Ross D [56], Hardie (og) [81] | 605 |
| 36 | 9 | H | East Stirling | W 5-2 | 3-1 | 3 | Ross D [25], Herd [44], Taylor 2 [45, 76], Tarrant [67] | 1605 |

**Final League Position: 3**     1996–97 3

**Goalscorers:** *League (71):* Adams 16 (5 pens), Ferguson 9 (2 pens), Wood 7, Haro 4, McBain 4, Taylor 4, Campbell 3, Farrell 3, Herd 3, Ross 3, Tarrant 3, Bradshaw 1, Callaghan 1, Furphy 1, Gilbert 1, Golabek 1, King 1, own goals 6. *Scottish Cup (7):* Adams 5 (1 pen), Ferguson 1, Haro 1. *Coca Cola Cup (2):* Wood 2. *League Challenge Cup (1):* Wood 1.

| Morgan K 9 | Farrell G 25+2 | Matheson D 4 | Haro M 31+1 | Furphy W 16+1 | Gilbert K 30+2 | Ferguson S 31 | Taylor A 19+8 | Wood G 18+1 | MacPherson J 2+8 | McBain R 27+6 | Ross A 2+5 | Williamson R 1+2 | Golabek S 18+6 | MacLeod A 1 | Adams D 31+3 | Bradshaw P 3+2 | Mackay D 32 | Callaghan T 2+6 | Herd W 27+1 | Campbell C 13+8 | Hart R 3+7 | Hutchison S 1 | Walker N 26 | Tarrant N 7+4 | Cooper N —+1 | Escalon F 7+6 | King C 4+2 | Ferries K —+1 | Addicoat W 1 | Ross D 5 | Match No. |
|---|---|---|---|---|---|---|---|---|---|---|---|---|---|---|---|---|---|---|---|---|---|---|---|---|---|---|---|---|---|---|---|
| 1 | 2 | 3 | 4 | 5 | 6 | 7 | $8^2$ | 9 | $10^1$ | 11 | 12 | 13 | | | | | | | | | | | | | | | | | | | 1 |
| 1 | 2 | | 4 | 5 | 6 | 7 | 8 | $9^2$ | | 11 | | 13 | 3 | | $10^1$ | 12 | | | | | | | | | | | | | | | 2 |
| 1 | 2 | | 4 | 5 | 6 | 7 | 13 | 9 | | $11^{11}$ | 12 | 10 | 3 | | $8^2$ | | | | | | | | | | | | | | | | 3 |
| 1 | 2 | $5^1$ | 4 | | 6 | 7 | $10^3$ | 9 | 14 | 13 | $12^2$ | | 3 | | 8 | 11 | | | | | | | | | | | | | | | 4 |
| | | | 4 | 5 | 6 | $7^1$ | $10^2$ | 9 | | | | 12 | 3 | | 8 | 11 | 2 | 13 | | | | | | | | | | | | | 5 |
| 1 | 5 | | | | $6^2$ | $7^3$ | 10 | 12 | 9 | | | | 3 | | 8 | $11^1$ | 2 | 13 | 4 | 14 | | | | | | | | | | | 6 |
| 1 | 5 | | | | 6 | $7^2$ | 8 | 11 | $9^1$ | | | | 3 | | 10 | | 2 | 13 | 4 | 12 | | | | | | | | | | | 7 |
| 1 | $5^3$ | | | | 6 | 7 | $10^2$ | $9^1$ | | 11 | 12 | | 3 | | 8 | | 2 | 13 | 4 | 14 | | | | | | | | | | | 8 |
| 2 | 5 | | | | 6 | 7 | 12 | | | 11 | | | 3 | | 8 | | $10^1$ | 4 | 9 | | | | 1 | | | | | | | | 9 |
| 2 | 5 | | | | 6 | 7 | 13 | $9^1$ | | 11 | | | 3 | | 8 | | $10^2$ | 4 | 12 | | | | 1 | | | | | | | | 10 |
| 2 | 5 | | | | 6 | $7^3$ | 9 | | | 12 | | 3 | | | $8^1$ | | 10 | 14 | 4 | $11^2$ | 13 | | 1 | | | | | | | | 11 |
| 2 | 5 | 12 | | | 6 | 7 | 9 | | | 11 | | | 3 | | 8 | | $4^1$ | 10 | | | | | 1 | | | | | | | | 12 |
| 2 | 5 | | | | 6 | $7^2$ | 12 | 9 | | 11 | | | 3 | | 8 | | 13 | 4 | $10^1$ | | | | 1 | | | | | | | | 13 |
| 2 | $5^1$ | | | | 6 | 7 | 10 | | | 11 | | 3 | | | 13 | 8 | 4 | 9 | 12 | | | | 1 | | | | | | | | 14 |
| 2 | | 6 | | | | $10^2$ | $7^3$ | $9^1$ | 3 | | | | | | 8 | 5 | 14 | 4 | 13 | 11 | 1 | 12 | | | | | | | | | | 15 |
| 2 | 5 | | | | 6 | 7 | 10 | 9 | | | | | | | 8 | 6 | 4 | | 11 | | | 1 | | | | | | | | | 16 |
| 2 | 6 | 13 | | | | $7^2$ | $10^2$ | 9 | | | | | 3 | | 8 | 5 | 4 | | 12 | | 1 | | | $11^1$ | 14 | | | | | | | 17 |
| 2 | 6 | 12 | | | | $7^2$ | $11^1$ | 9 | | | | | 14 | | 8 | 5 | 4 | | | | 1 | | 13 | | $10^3$ | | | | | | 18 |
| 12 | 5 | 2 | | | | 7 | 9 | | | 11 | | | $3^2$ | | 8 | 6 | 4 | | | | 1 | | 13 | | $10^5$ | | | | | | 19 |
| 13 | 5 | | | | 6 | 7 | 10 | $9^2$ | | | | | | | 8 | 2 | 4 | 12 | | | 1 | | $3^1$ | | 11 | | | | | | 20 |
| 2 | 5 | | | | 6 | | $11^1$ | $9^2$ | 14 | 3 | | | 12 | | 8 | 10 | 4 | | | | 1 | | | | $7^2$ | 13 | | | | | 21 |
| 7 | 5 | | | | 6 | | $9^2$ | 12 | $10^1$ | 3 | | | 8 | | 2 | 4 | | | | | 1 | | | | 13 | 11 | | | | | 22 |
| 1 | 7 | 5 | | | 6 | | 12 | $9^1$ | 13 | 3 | | | 8 | | 2 | 4 | | | | | | | | | $10^2$ | 11 | | | | | 23 |
| 7 | $5^2$ | 8 | | | 6 | | 12 | 13 | | 3 | | 14 | | | 2 | 4 | 9 | | | | 1 | | | | $10^1$ | $11^3$ | | | | | 24 |
| 10 | 5 | | | | 6 | 7 | 12 | 3 | | 11 | | | $8^1$ | | 2 | 4 | $9^2$ | | | | 1 | | | | 13 | | | | | | 25 |
| 10 | 5 | | | | 6 | 7 | 12 | 13 | | $3^1$ | | 11 | | | 8 | 2 | 4 | $9^2$ | | | | 1 | | | | | | | | | 26 |
| 10 | 5 | $4^1$ | | | 6 | $7^4$ | | 3 | | 11 | | | 8 | | 2 | 12 | 9 | | | | 1 | | | | 13 | | | | | | 27 |
| 10 | 5 | 4 | | | 6 | $7^1$ | | 3 | | 11 | | | 8 | | 2 | 9 | | | | | 1 | | | | 12 | | | | | | 28 |
| 2 | 5 | 4 | | | | 7 | 14 | $12^2$ | 13 | 3 | | | $11^3$ | | 8 | 6 | 9 | | | | 1 | | | | $10^1$ | | | | | | 29 |
| 10 | 5 | 4 | | | 6 | $7^1$ | 11 | $3^2$ | | 8 | | 2 | 9 | 13 | 1 | | | | | | | | | | | | 12 | | | | 30 |
| 3 | 2 | 5 | | | 6 | $7^3$ | | 14 | | 13 | | 8 | 4 | $10^1$ | 1 | 12 | | | | | | | | | | $9^2$ | 11 | | | | 31 |
| 3 | $5^2$ | 6 | | | | 7 | 10 | 14 | 12 | | | 8 | 4 | 13 | 1 | $9^3$ | | | | | | | | | | | $11^1$ | | | | 32 |
| $2^2$ | 12 | $10^1$ | 6 | 7 | | 11 | | $3^3$ | | 8 | 5 | 4 | 13 | 1 | 9 | 14 | | | | | | | | | | | | | | | 33 |
| | 5 | | | | 6 | $7^2$ | 10 | 12 | | 13 | | 8 | 2 | 4 | $11^2$ | 1 | 9 | 14 | | | | | | | | $3^1$ | | | | | 34 |
| | 5 | | | | 6 | 7 | 10 | 3 | | 14 | | $8^3$ | 2 | 4 | 12 | 1 | $9^1$ | 13 | | | | | | | | $11^2$ | | | | | 35 |
| | 5 | | | | 6 | | 10 | 3 | | 12 | | $8^2$ | 2 | 4 | 14 | 13 | 1 | $9^3$ | | | | | | | $7^1$ | 11 | | | | | 36 |

682

# ST JOHNSTONE Premier League

*Year Formed:* 1884. *Ground & Address:* McDiarmid Park, Crieff Road, Perth PH1 2SJ. *Telephone:* 01738 626961. *Fax:* 01738 625 771. *Clubcall:* 0898 121559.
*Ground Capacity:* total: 10,673 (all seated). *Size of Pitch:* 115yd × 75yd.
*Chairman:* G.S.Brown. *Secretary and Managing Director:* Stewart Duff.
*Manager:* Paul Sturrock. *Sales Executive:* Helen Harcus. *Physio:* David Henderson. *Coach:* John Blackley. *Youth Development Coach:* Alistair Stevenson.
*Managers since 1975:* J. Stewart; J. Storrie; A. Stuart; A. Rennie; I. Gibson; A. Totten, J. McClelland. *Club Nickname(s):* Saints. *Previous Grounds:* Recreation Grounds, Muirton Park.
*Record Attendance:* (McDiarmid Park): 10,504 v Rangers, Premier Division; 20 Oct, 1990.
*Record Transfer Fee received:* £1,750,000 for Calum Davidson to Blackburn R, March 1998.
*Record Transfer Fee paid:* £300,000 for Billy Dodds from Dundee, 1994.
*Record Victory:* 9-0 v Albion R, League Cup; 9 March, 1946.
*Record Defeat:* 1-10 v Third Lanark, Scottish Cup; 24 January, 1903.
*Most Capped Player:* George O'Boyle, 10, Northern Ireland.
*Most League Appearances:* 298: Drew Rutherford.
*Most League Goals in Season (Individual):* 36: Jimmy Benson, Division II; 1931-32.
*Most Goals Overall (Individual):* 140: John Brogan, 1977-83.

## ST JOHNSTONE 1997–98 LEAGUE RECORD

| Match No. | Date | | Venue | Opponents | Result | | H/T Score | Lg. Pos. | Goalscorers | Atten- dance |
|---|---|---|---|---|---|---|---|---|---|---|
| 1 | Aug | 2 | H | Dundee U | D | 1-1 | 0-1 | — | McKimmie (og) [61] | 6492 |
| 2 | | 16 | A | Motherwell | W | 1-0 | 0-0 | 1 | Grant [65] | 5036 |
| 3 | | 23 | H | Celtic | L | 0-2 | 0-1 | 5 | | 10,266 |
| 4 | | 30 | A | Dunfermline Ath | D | 2-2 | 0-1 | 6 | Sekerlioglu [67], O'Boyle [80] | 6354 |
| 5 | Sept | 13 | H | Hearts | L | 1-2 | 0-1 | 7 | Tosh [70] | 5836 |
| 6 | | 20 | H | Rangers | L | 0-2 | 0-1 | 7 | | 10,093 |
| 7 | | 27 | A | Hibernian | D | 1-1 | 1-1 | 7 | Farquhar [16] | 11,104 |
| 8 | Oct | 4 | H | Aberdeen | W | 1-0 | 1-0 | 6 | O'Neil [11] | 6291 |
| 9 | | 18 | A | Kilmarnock | W | 1-0 | 1-0 | 5 | O'Halloran [13] | 6572 |
| 10 | | 25 | A | Celtic | L | 0-2 | 0-2 | 5 | | 48,687 |
| 11 | Nov | 1 | H | Motherwell | W | 4-3 | 2-0 | 4 | Kernaghan [18], O'Neil 2 [33, 60], Grant (pen) [49] | 4566 |
| 12 | | 8 | H | Dunfermline Ath | L | 0-2 | 0-1 | 4 | | 5239 |
| 13 | | 15 | A | Hearts | L | 1-2 | 0-0 | 6 | O'Boyle [77] | 13,611 |
| 14 | | 22 | H | Hibernian | W | 1-0 | 1-0 | 6 | Scott [3] | 5411 |
| 15 | | 29 | A | Rangers | L | 2-3 | 1-2 | 6 | Preston [43], O'Boyle [74] | 49,142 |
| 16 | Dec | 6 | A | Aberdeen | D | 1-1 | 0-0 | 6 | Grant [80] | 10,974 |
| 17 | | 13 | H | Kilmarnock | D | 1-1 | 0-0 | 6 | O'Boyle (pen) [79] | 4385 |
| 18 | | 20 | A | Dundee U | L | 1-2 | 0-2 | 7 | Kane [85] | 7342 |
| 19 | | 27 | H | Celtic | W | 1-0 | 0-0 | 6 | O'Boyle [72] | 10,485 |
| 20 | Jan | 3 | A | Dunfermline Ath | W | 1-0 | 1-0 | 5 | Barnett (og) [7] | 6591 |
| 21 | | 12 | H | Hearts | L | 2-3 | 0-2 | — | Davidson [48], O'Boyle [63] | 5408 |
| 22 | | 17 | A | Hibernian | W | 1-0 | 0-0 | 5 | Grant [83] | 9107 |
| 23 | | 31 | H | Rangers | W | 2-0 | 1-0 | 4 | O'Neil [36], O'Boyle [69] | 10,441 |
| 24 | Feb | 7 | A | Kilmarnock | L | 0-1 | 0-0 | 5 | | 7408 |
| 25 | | 21 | H | Aberdeen | L | 0-1 | 0-1 | 5 | | 6570 |
| 26 | | 25 | A | Motherwell | L | 1-2 | 0-2 | — | O'Boyle (pen) [61] | 4517 |
| 27 | | 28 | H | Dundee U | D | 1-1 | 0-1 | 5 | Grant [75] | 5637 |
| 28 | Mar | 14 | H | Hibernian | D | 1-1 | 0-0 | 5 | McQuillan [61] | 6472 |
| 29 | | 21 | A | Rangers | L | 1-2 | 1-1 | 5 | Kernaghan [15] | 49,788 |
| 30 | | 28 | H | Kilmarnock | W | 1-0 | 1-0 | 5 | O'Neil [1] | 4982 |
| 31 | Apr | 4 | A | Aberdeen | W | 1-0 | 1-0 | 4 | O'Boyle [19] | 9002 |
| 32 | | 11 | H | Dunfermline Ath | D | 0-0 | 0-0 | 4 | | 5311 |
| 33 | | 18 | A | Hearts | D | 1-1 | 0-0 | 5 | Grant [78] | 15,034 |
| 34 | | 25 | A | Dundee U | W | 2-0 | 0-0 | 5 | Jenkinson [66], O'Boyle [89] | 8045 |
| 35 | May | 2 | H | Motherwell | W | 3-2 | 1-1 | 5 | Jenkinson 2 [15, 88], McCluskey [70] | 6760 |
| 36 | | 9 | A | Celtic | L | 0-2 | 0-1 | 5 | | 49,701 |

**Final League Position: 5**     1996–97 DIV 1 1

**Honours**

*League Champions:* First Division 1982–83, 1989–90, 1996–97. Division II 1923–24, 1959–60, 1962–63; *Runners-up:* Division II 1931–32. Second Division 1987–88.
*Scottish Cup:* Semi-finals 1934, 1968, 1989, 1991.
*League Cup: Runners-up:* 1969.
*League Challenge Cup: Runners-up:* 1996–97.

**European:** *UEFA Cup:* 6 matches (1971–72).
*Club colours:* Shirt: Royal blue with white trim. Shorts: White. Stockings: Royal blue with white hoops.

**Goalscorers:** *League (38):* O'Boyle 10 (2 pens), Grant 6 (1 pen), O'Neil 5, Jenkinson 3, Kernaghan 2, Davidson 1, Farquhar 1, Kane 1, McCluskey 1, McQuillan 1, O'Halloran 1, Preston 1, Scott 1, Sekerlioglu 1, Tosh 1, own goals 2. *Scottish Cup (4):* Dasovic 1, Kernaghan 1, O'Boyle 1 (pen), own goal 1. *Coca Cola Cup (3):* O'Boyle 2, Griffin 1.

| Main A 34 | McQuillan J 34 | Davidson C 15 | Sekerlioglu A 16 + 1 | Weir J 25 | Griffin D 10 + 3 | Scott P 19 + 3 | Tosh S 4 + 4 | Ferguson I 1 + 1 | O'Boyle G 29 + 4 | Jenkinson L 16 + 8 | Grant R 19 + 15 | O'Halloran J 11 + 11 | McCluskey S 12 + 6 | Preston A 32 + 3 | Kane P 24 + 3 | McAnespie K 1 + 2 | O'Neil J 26 + 4 | Farquhar G 3 + 1 | Kernaghan A 28 | Bowman G 1 | Dasovic N 18 + 1 | Wright T 3 + 2 | Anderson T — + 3 | Robertson S 2 | Xausa D 1 | McMahon G 9 + 1 | Connolly P 2 + 2 | Whiteford A 1 | Match No. |
|---|---|---|---|---|---|---|---|---|---|---|---|---|---|---|---|---|---|---|---|---|---|---|---|---|---|---|---|---|---|
| 1 | 2 | 3 | 4 | 5 | 6 | 7 | 8 | 9¹ | 10² | 11 | 12 | 13 | | | | | | | | | | | | | | | | | 1 |
| 1 | 2 | 3 | 4 | 5 | | 7 | | 14 | 10 | 11 | 9³ | 8² | 6 | 12 | 13 | | | | | | | | | | | | | | 2 |
| 1 | 2 | 3 | 4¹ | 5 | 13 | 7 | | | 10 | | 9 | 12 | 6² | 11³ | 8 | 14 | | | | | | | | | | | | | 3 |
| 1 | 2 | 3 | 4 | | 6 | 7 | 12 | | 10 | | 13 | | 5 | 11 | 9² | | 8¹ | | | | | | | | | | | | 4 |
| 1 | 2 | 3 | 4² | | 6¹ | 7 | 12 | | 10 | | 9 | 14 | 5 | 11 | 8³ | | 13 | | | | | | | | | | | | 5 |
| 1 | 2 | 3 | 4 | | 6 | 7² | 12 | | 10 | | 13 | | 5¹ | 3 | 9 | | 8 | 11 | | | | | | | | | | | 6 |
| 1 | 2 | 3 | 4 | | 6 | | | | | 11 | 9 | 7 | 12 | | 8 | | 10¹ | 5 | | | | | | | | | | | 7 |
| 1 | 2 | 3 | 4¹ | | 6 | | | | 10 | 11² | 9 | 13 | 7 | 12 | 8 | | | 5 | | | | | | | | | | | 8 |
| 1 | 2 | | 4 | | 14 | | | | 13 | 11² | 9 | 7 | 6 | 3 | 8 | | 10¹ | 5³ | 12 | | | | | | | | | | 9 |
| 1 | 2 | | 4² | 5 | 12 | | | | 13 | 11 | 9 | 7¹ | 6 | 3 | | | 14 | 8 | 10³ | | | | | | | | | | 10 |
| 1 | 2 | | | | 6 | 7 | 11² | | 10¹ | | 9 | 13 | | 3 | 12 | | 8 | | | | 5 | 4 | | | | | | | 11 |
| 1 | 2 | | | | 6 | 7 | 11¹ | | 10 | 12 | 9 | 13 | | 3 | 4 | | 8² | | | | 5 | | | | | | | | 12 |
| 1 | 2 | | 6 | | | 7 | 13 | | 10 | 11² | 12 | 8¹ | | 3 | 9 | | | | | | 5 | 4 | | | | | | | 13 |
| 1 | 2 | | 6 | | | 7² | | | 10 | 11¹ | 8 | 13 | | 3 | 9 | | 12 | | | | 5 | 4 | | | | | | | 14 |
| 1 | 2 | 3 | 6 | | | 7 | | | 10 | 12 | 13 | 11¹ | | | 9 | | 8² | | | | 5 | 4 | | | | | | | 15 |
| 1 | 2 | 3 | 6 | 14 | 7³ | | | | 10 | 12 | 13 | 11² | | | 9¹ | | 8 | | | | 5 | 4 | | | | | | | 16 |
| 1 | 2 | 3¹ | 6 | | 7 | | | | 10 | 14 | 13 | 11 | | 9 | | | 8² | | | | 5 | 4³ | 12 | | | | | | 17 |
| 1 | | 5 | 2³ | | | | | | 10 | 11 | 12 | 13 | 14 | 3 | 9 | | 8 | | 6 | | | 4² | 7¹ | | | | | | 18 |
| 1 | 3 | | 5 | | 7 | | | | 10¹ | | 12 | | 2 | 11 | 9 | | 8 | | 6 | | | 4 | | | | | | | 19 |
| 1 | 2 | 3 | 5 | | 7 | | | | | 10¹ | | | | 11 | 9 | | | | 6 | | | 4 | 8 | 12 | | | | | 20 |
| 1 | 2 | 3 | 5 | | 7 | | | | 10 | | 13 | | | 11³ | 9 | | 12 | | 6 | | | 4² | 8¹ | 14 | | | | | 21 |
| 1 | 2 | 3¹ | 5 | | 7 | | | | 10 | | 12 | | | 11 | 9 | | 8 | | 6 | | | 4 | | | | | | | 22 |
| 1 | 2 | 3¹ | 5 | | 7 | | | | 10² | 12 | 13 | | | 11 | 9 | | 8 | | 6 | | | 4 | | | | | | | 23 |
| 1 | 2 | | 5 | | 7 | | | | 10 | 11 | | | | 3 | 9 | | 8 | | 6 | | | 4 | | | | | | | 24 |
| | 2 | | 5 | | 7¹ | | | | 10 | 11 | 13 | | | 3 | 9 | | 8² | | 6 | | | 4 | 12 | 1 | | | | | 25 |
| 1 | 2 | 13 | 5 | | | | | | 10 | 11 | 12 | | | 3 | 9 | | 8 | | 6 | | | 4² | | | | 7¹ | | | 26 |
| 1 | 2 | 8¹ | 5 | 13 | | | | | 10 | 11 | 12 | | 6 | 3 | 9² | 14 | | | | | | 4 | | | | 7³ | | | 27 |
| 1 | 2 | 4 | 5 | | | | | | | 9 | 13 | 12 | 3¹ | 8 | 11 | | 6 | | | | | | 14 | | | 7² | 10³ | | 28 |
| | 2 | 4 | 5 | | | | | | | 14 | 13 | 9 | 3 | 11² | 8 | | 12 | | 6 | | | | | 1 | | 7¹ | 10³ | | 29 |
| 1 | 2 | 4 | 5 | | | | | | 10³ | 14 | 9 | 12 | 13 | 3 | 8 | | 11 | | 6² | | | | | | | 7¹ | | | 30 |
| 1 | 2 | 4 | | | | | | | 10 | 12 | 9¹ | | 5 | 3 | 8 | | 11 | | 6 | | | | | | | 7 | | | 31 |
| 1 | 2 | | 5 | | | | | | 10² | 12 | 9 | 4 | | 3 | 8 | | 11 | | 6 | | | | | | | 7¹ | 13 | | 32 |
| 1 | 2 | | 5 | | | | | | 10 | 13 | 9 | 12 | | 3 | 8 | | 11 | | 6 | | | 4¹ | | | | 7² | | | 33 |
| 1 | 2¹ | | 5 | | | | | | 10 | 11 | 9 | 8 | 12 | 3 | 4 | | | | 6 | | | | | | | 7 | | | 34 |
| 1 | 2 | | 5¹ | | | | | | 10 | 11 | 9 | 8 | 12 | 3 | 13 | | 4 | | 6 | | | | | | | 7² | | | 35 |
| 1 | 2 | | 4² | 13 | | | | | 10 | 11 | 9² | 7¹ | 5 | 3 | 8 | | | | | | | | | | | 12 | 14 | 6 | 36 |

# ST MIRREN

## First Division

*Year Formed:* 1877. *Ground & Address:* St Mirren Park, Love St, Paisley PA3 2EJ. *Telephone:* 0141 889 2558/0141 840 1337. *Fax:* 0141 848 6444.
*Ground Capacity:* total: 15,410. seated 9395. *Size of Pitch:* 112yd × 73yd.
*Chairman:* Stewart Gilmour. *Vice-Chairman:* George Campbell. *Secretary:* Allan Marshall.
*Manager:* Tony Fitzpatrick. *Physio:* Andrew Binning. *Youth Development Officer:* Joe Hughes.
*Managers since 1975:* Alex Ferguson; Jim Clunie; Rikki MacFarlane; Alex Miller; Alex Smith; Tony Fitzpatrick; David Hay; Jimmy Bone. *Club Nickname(s):* The Buddies. *Previous Grounds:* Short Roods 1877-79, Thistle Park Greenhill 1879-83, Westmarch 1883-94.
*Record Attendance:* 47,438 v Celtic, League Cup, 20 Aug, 1949.
*Record Transfer Fee received:* £850,000 for Ian Ferguson to Rangers (1988).
*Record Transfer Fee paid:* £400,000 for Thomas Stickroth from Bayer Uerdingen (1990).
*Record Victory:* 15-0 v Glasgow University, Scottish Cup 1st rd; 30 Jan, 1960.
*Record Defeat:* 0-9 v Rangers, Division I; 4 Dec, 1897.
*Most Capped Player:* Godmundor Torfason, 29, Iceland.
*Most League Appearances:* 351: Tony Fitzpatrick, 1973-88.
*Most League Goals in Season (Individual):* 45: Dunky Walker, Division I; 1921-22.
*Most Goals Overall (Individual):* 221: David McCrae, 1923-24.

## ST MIRREN 1997–98 LEAGUE RECORD

| Match No. | Date | Venue | Opponents | Result | H/T Score | Lg. Pos. | Goalscorers | Atten- dance |
|---|---|---|---|---|---|---|---|---|
| 1 | Aug 2 | A | Airdrieonians | W 3-1 | 0-0 | — | Mendes 3 [69, 80, 89] | 2185 |
| 2 | 16 | H | Stirling A | D 2-2 | 2-1 | 2 | Mendes [40], Brown [45] | 2705 |
| 3 | 23 | A | Dundee | L 0-1 | 0-1 | 4 | | 3571 |
| 4 | 30 | H | Greenock Morton | W 2-1 | 0-1 | 2 | Watson [61], Hetherston [71] | 5654 |
| 5 | Sept 13 | H | Raith R | L 1-2 | 0-0 | 3 | Mendes [90] | 3311 |
| 6 | 20 | A | Falkirk | L 1-3 | 1-0 | 5 | Watson [2] | 3039 |
| 7 | 27 | H | Partick Th | W 1-0 | 0-0 | 3 | Mendes [50] | 3348 |
| 8 | Oct 4 | A | Hamilton A | L 0-2 | 0-1 | 6 | | 1758 |
| 9 | 18 | H | Ayr U | D 1-1 | 1-0 | 6 | Mendes [45] | 3021 |
| 10 | 25 | H | Airdrieonians | L 0-2 | 0-1 | 7 | | 2533 |
| 11 | Nov 1 | A | Stirling A | D 0-0 | 0-0 | 7 | | 1533 |
| 12 | 8 | A | Greenock Morton | L 0-3 | 0-2 | 7 | | 4013 |
| 13 | 15 | H | Raith R | L 2-3 | 2-1 | 8 | Watson [3], Yardley [10] | 2441 |
| 14 | 22 | A | Partick Th | D 2-2 | 2-1 | 8 | Roddie [6], Taylor [14] | 4661 |
| 15 | 29 | H | Falkirk | W 2-0 | 1-0 | 8 | Turner [16], Taylor [73] | 2658 |
| 16 | Dec 6 | H | Hamilton A | W 2-1 | 1-1 | 8 | Watson [45], Hillcoat (og) [83] | 2992 |
| 17 | 13 | A | Ayr U | W 2-0 | 0-0 | 6 | Turner [56], Yardley [87] | 2411 |
| 18 | 20 | H | Dundee | L 0-2 | 0-0 | 6 | | 3165 |
| 19 | 27 | A | Airdrieonians | L 1-2 | 0-2 | 7 | Turner (pen) [76] | 2312 |
| 20 | Jan 7 | H | Greenock Morton | W 3-2 | 2-0 | — | Mendes 2 [9, 14], Yardley [50] | 4554 |
| 21 | 10 | H | Raith R | L 1-4 | 1-2 | 6 | Turner [36] | 3431 |
| 22 | 17 | H | Partick Th | L 0-1 | 0-0 | 6 | | 3052 |
| 23 | 31 | A | Falkirk | D 2-2 | 0-1 | 6 | Watson [47], Fenwick [79] | 3296 |
| 24 | Feb 7 | H | Ayr U | W 3-0 | 3-0 | 6 | Murray [15], McGarry [30], McWhirter [45] | 2312 |
| 25 | 23 | A | Hamilton A | D 1-1 | 1-0 | — | Murray [32] | 1459 |
| 26 | 28 | A | Dundee | L 0-1 | 0-1 | 6 | | 3365 |
| 27 | Mar 7 | H | Stirling A | L 0-2 | 0-1 | 6 | | 2573 |
| 28 | 14 | A | Partick Th | W 2-1 | 2-0 | 6 | Yardley 2 [8, 36] | 3545 |
| 29 | 21 | H | Falkirk | L 1-2 | 0-2 | 6 | Yardley [70] | 2694 |
| 30 | 28 | A | Ayr U | D 2-2 | 2-1 | 6 | Brown [11], Yardley [43] | 2306 |
| 31 | Apr 4 | H | Hamilton A | D 2-2 | 1-2 | 7 | Brown [45], Turner [81] | 1885 |
| 32 | 11 | A | Greenock Morton | L 0-2 | 0-1 | 7 | | 4728 |
| 33 | 18 | H | Raith R | L 0-2 | 0-1 | 7 | | 2285 |
| 34 | 25 | H | Airdrieonians | L 0-1 | 0-1 | 8 | | 3329 |
| 35 | May 2 | A | Stirling A | W 1-0 | 0-0 | 7 | Murray [63] | 2605 |
| 36 | 9 | H | Dundee | W 1-0 | 1-0 | 6 | Murray [17] | 2460 |

**Final League Position: 6**        1996–97 4

**Honours**
*League Champions:* First Division 1976-77. Division II 1967-68; *Runners-up:* 1935-36.
*Scottish Cup Winners:* 1926, 1959, 1987. *Runners-up* 1908, 1934, 1962.
*League Cup:* Runners-up 1955-56.
*B&Q Cup:* Runners-up 1993-94. *Victory Cup:* 1919-20. *Summer Cup:* 1943-44. *Anglo-Scottish Cup:* 1979-80.

**European:** *Cup Winners' Cup:* 4 matches (1987-88). *UEFA Cup:* 10 matches (1980-81, 1983-84, 1985-86).
*Club colours:* Shirt: Black and white vertical stripes. Shorts: Black. Stockings: Black with white trim. Change colours: Predominantly red.

**Goalscorers:** *League (41):* Mendes 9, Yardley 7, Turner 5 (1 pen), Watson 5, Murray 4, Brown 3, Taylor 2, Fenwick 1, Hetherston 1, McGarry 1, McWhirter 1, Roddie 1, own goal 1. *Scottish Cup (2):* Iwelumo 1, Watson 1. *Coca Cola Cup (2):* Kelly 1, Milne 1. *League Challenge Cup (0).*

| Combe A 30 | Smith B 13 | Galloway G 17+1 | McWhirter N 32 | McLaughlin B 35 | Archdeacon P 5 | Murray H 27+1 | Dick J 4 | McGarry S 11+17 | Mendes J 25+4 | Kelly R 4 | Milne D 3+2 | Iwelumo C 5+7 | Turner T 24+1 | Brown T 20+5 | Winnie D 21+1 | Fenwick P 27+1 | Yardley M 19+10 | Watson S 23+4 | Hetherston B 8+4 | Taylor S 9+5 | Roddie A 19 | Marshall G 1 | Fallon W 1 | Drew C 5+2 | O'Brien B —+4 | Scrimgour D 5 | McNamee D 1 | Kerr C 1 | Prentice A 1 | Rudden P —+1 | Match No. |
|---|---|---|---|---|---|---|---|---|---|---|---|---|---|---|---|---|---|---|---|---|---|---|---|---|---|---|---|---|---|---|---|
| 1 | 2 | 3 | 4 | 5 | 6 | 7 | 8[1] | 9[2] | 10 | 11 | 12 | 13 | | | | | | | | | | | | | | | | | | | 1 |
| 1 | 2 | 3 | 4 | 5 | 6 | 7 | | 10[1] | 11 | | 12 | | 8 | 9 | | | | | | | | | | | | | | | | | 2 |
| 1 | | | 4 | 2 | 6[2] | 7[1] | | 10 | 11 | | | | 8 | 9 | 3 | 5 | 12 | 13 | | | | | | | | | | | | | 3 |
| 1 | | 3[1] | 4 | 2 | | | | 14 | 10 | 11[2] | | | 8 | 9 | 12 | 5 | 13 | 6 | 7[3] | | | | | | | | | | | | 4 |
| 1 | | | 4 | 2 | | | | 12 | 10 | | | | 8 | 9 | 3 | 5 | 11[1] | 6 | 7[2] | 13 | | | | | | | | | | | 5 |
| 1 | 11 | | 4 | 2 | | | | | 10 | | | | 8 | 9 | 3 | 5 | 12 | 6 | 7[1] | | | | | | | | | | | | 6 |
| 1 | 2 | | 4 | 5 | | 7 | | | 10 | 11 | 12 | | 8 | 9[1] | 3 | | | 6 | | | | | | | | | | | | | 7 |
| 1 | 2 | | 4 | 5 | | 7 | | 14 | 10[2] | 11[1] | 12 | 13 | 8 | 9 | 3 | | | 6[1] | | | | | | | | | | | | | 8 |
| 1 | | | 4 | 2 | | 7 | | | 10 | 11[2] | 12 | 13 | 8 | 9[1] | 3 | 5 | | 6 | | | | | | | | | | | | | 9 |
| 1 | | | 4 | 2 | | 7[3] | | | 10 | 11[2] | 12 | 13 | 8 | 9 | | 5 | | 6 | 14 | | 1 | | | | | | | | | | 10 |
| 1 | 2 | | 4 | 5 | | | | 9 | 10 | 11 | 12 | | 8 | | 3 | | | 6 | | 7[1] | | | | | | | | | | | 11 |
| 1 | 2 | | 4 | 5 | | 7[1] | | | 10 | 11 | 12 | 13 | 8 | 9[1] | 3 | | | 6 | | | | | | | | | | | | | 12 |
| 1 | | | 4 | 2 | | 7 | | | 10 | 11 | 12 | 13 | 8 | 9[2] | 3[1] | 5 | | 6 | 8 | | | | | | | | | | | | 13 |
| 1 | 3 | | 4 | 2 | | 7 | | | | 11[1] | 12 | | 8 | 9 | | 5 | | 6 | | | | | | | | | | | | | 14 |
| 1 | 3 | | 4 | 2 | | 7 | | | 10[1] | 11 | 12 | | 8 | 9 | | 5 | | 6 | | | | | | | | | | | | | 15 |
| 1 | 3 | | 4 | 2 | | | | | 10 | 11 | | | 8 | 9 | | 5 | | 6 | 7 | | | | | | | | | | | | 16 |
| 1 | 3 | | 4 | 2 | | | | | 10 | 11 | 12 | | 8 | 9[1] | | 5 | | 6 | 7 | | | | | | | | | | | | 17 |
| 1 | 3 | | 4 | 2 | | | | | 10[1] | 11 | 12 | | 8 | 9 | | 5 | | 6 | 7 | | | | | | | | | | | | 18 |
| 1 | 3[1] | | 4 | 2 | 6 | | | | 10 | 11 | 12 | | 8 | 9 | | 5 | | | 7 | | | | | | | | | | | | 19 |
| 1 | | | 4 | 2 | 6 | | | | 10 | 11 | 12 | 13 | 8 | 9[1] | 3 | 5 | | | 7[2] | | | | | | | | | | | | 20 |
| 1 | 2 | 14 | 4 | 5 | 6 | 7 | | | 10[1] | 11[2] | 12 | 13 | 8[3] | 9 | 3 | | | | | | | | | | | | | | | | 21 |
| 1 | 3 | | 4 | 2 | | 7[1] | | | 10 | 11 | 12 | 13 | 8 | 9[2] | | 5 | | 6 | | | | | | | | | | | | | 22 |
| 1 | 2 | 3 | 4 | | | 7 | | | 10 | 11[1] | | 13 | 8[2] | 9[1] | | 5 | | 6 | 14 | | | | | 12 | | | | | | | 23 |
| 1 | 2 | 3 | 4 | | | 7 | | | 10[1] | 11 | 12 | | 8 | 9[1] | | 5 | | 6[2] | 14 | | | | | 13 | | | | | | | 24 |
| 1 | | | 4 | 2 | | 7 | | | 10 | 11[2] | 12 | 13 | 8 | 9[1] | 3 | 5 | | 6 | | | | | | | | | | | | | 25 |
| 1 | | | 4 | 2 | | 7 | | | 10[1] | 11 | 12 | 13 | 8 | 9[1] | 3 | 5 | | 6[3] | 14 | | | | | | | | | | | | 26 |
| 1 | 3 | | 4 | 2 | | 7[1] | | | 10 | 11 | 12 | 13 | 8 | 9[2] | | 5 | | 6[3] | 14 | | | | | | | | | | | | 27 |
| 1 | 3 | | 4 | 2 | 6 | | | | | 11 | 12 | | 8 | 9 | | 5 | | | | 7 | 10[1] | | | | | | | | | | 28 |
| 1 | 3 | | 4 | 2 | 6[3] | 7 | | 14 | 10 | 11 | 12 | 13 | 8[1] | 9[1] | | 5 | | | | | | | | | | | | | | | 29 |
| | | 3 | 4 | 2 | | 7 | | | | 11 | 12 | | 8 | 9 | | 5 | | 6 | | 10[1] | 1 | | | | | | | | | | 30 |
| | | 3 | 4 | 2 | | 7 | | | | 11 | 12 | 13 | 8 | 9 | | 5 | | 6[1] | | 10[2] | 1 | | | | | | | | | | 31 |
| | | 3 | 4 | 2 | | 7 | | | | 11 | 12 | 13 | 8 | 9 | | 5 | | 6[2] | | 10[1] | 1 | | | | | | | | | | 32 |
| | 2 | 3 | 4 | | | 7[1] | | | 10[2] | 11[3] | 12 | 13 | 8 | 9 | 3 | 5 | | 6 | 14 | | 1 | | | | | | | | | | 33 |
| | 2 | 3 | 4 | | 6 | 7[3] | | 14 | 10[1] | 11[2] | 12 | 13 | 8 | 9 | | 5 | | | | | 1 | | | | | | | | | | 34 |
| 1 | 2 | 3 | 4 | | 6 | 7 | | | 10 | 11 | 12 | | 8[1] | 9 | | 5 | | | | | | | | | | | | | | | 35 |
| 1 | | | 4 | 5 | 6 | 7[2] | 8 | 14 | 10 | | 12 | 13 | | 9 | | | | | | | | | | | | | 2[3] | 3[1] | 11 | | 36 |

# STENHOUSEMUIR                Third Division

*Year Formed:* 1884. *Ground & Address:* Ochilview Park, Gladstone Rd, Stenhousemuir FK5 5QL. *Telephone:* 01324 562992.
*Ground Capacity:* total: 3520. seated: 310. *Size of Pitch:* 113yd × 74yd.
*Chairman:* A Terry Bulloch. *Secretary:* David O.Reid. *Commercial Manager:* John Sharp.
*Manager:* Terry Christie. *Assistant Manager:* Graeme Armstrong. *Physio:* Lee Campbell. *Coach:* Gordon Buchanan.
*Managers since 1975:* H. Glasgow; J. Black; A. Rose; W. Henderson; A. Rennie; J. Meakin; D. Lawson. *Club Nickname(s):* The Warriors. *Previous Grounds:* Tryst Ground 1884-86, Goschen Park 1886-90.
*Record Attendance:* 12,500 v East Fife, Scottish Cup 4th rd; 11 Mar, 1950.
*Record Transfer Fee received:* £30,000 for David Beaton to Falkirk (June 1989).
*Record Transfer Fee paid:* £7000 to Meadowbank T for Lee Bullen (Nov 1990).
*Record Victory:* 9-2 v Dundee U, Division II; 19 Apr, 1937.
*Record Defeat:* 2-11 v Dunfermline Ath. Division II; 27 Sept, 1930.
*Most Capped Player:* —.
*Most League Appearances:* 360: Archie Rose.
*Most League Goals in Season (Individual):* 32: Robert Taylor, Division II; 1925-26.
*Most Goals Overall (Individual):* —.

## STENHOUSEMUIR 1997–98 LEAGUE RECORD

| Match No. | Date | | Venue | Opponents | Result | H/T Score | Lg. Pos. | Goalscorers | Atten- dance |
|---|---|---|---|---|---|---|---|---|---|
| 1 | Aug | 5 | H | Queen of the S | W 2-1 | 1-0 | — | Little [15], Henderson [62] | 456 |
| 2 | | 16 | A | East Fife | W 3-0 | 1-0 | 1 | Little [39], Henderson [70], Innes [86] | 643 |
| 3 | | 23 | H | Livingston | D 1-1 | 0-0 | 1 | Little [75] | 514 |
| 4 | | 30 | H | Inverness CT | W 3-2 | 2-0 | 1 | Farrell [22], Fisher [45], Roseburgh (pen) [50] | 442 |
| 5 | Sept | 13 | A | Clyde | L 0-2 | 0-1 | 3 | | 706 |
| 6 | | 20 | A | Clydebank | L 0-1 | 0-0 | 4 | | 336 |
| 7 | | 27 | H | Forfar Ath | L 1-4 | 0-2 | 6 | Roseburgh [85] | 431 |
| 8 | Oct | 4 | H | Brechin C | W 3-2 | 3-0 | 5 | Sprott [32], Roseburgh [36], Hunter [40] | 329 |
| 9 | | 18 | A | Stranraer | L 1-4 | 1-2 | 6 | Henderson [12] | 494 |
| 10 | | 25 | A | Livingston | L 1-2 | 0-1 | 7 | Hunter [70] | 1691 |
| 11 | Nov | 1 | H | East Fife | D 0-0 | 0-0 | 6 | | 439 |
| 12 | | 8 | A | Inverness CT | L 1-4 | 0-2 | 8 | Little [48] | 1669 |
| 13 | | 15 | H | Clyde | D 0-0 | 0-0 | 8 | | 581 |
| 14 | | 22 | H | Forfar Ath | D 1-1 | 0-1 | 8 | Hutchison [63] | 385 |
| 15 | | 29 | A | Clydebank | L 2-3 | 2-2 | 8 | Sprott [5], Innes [15] | 483 |
| 16 | Dec | 13 | H | Stranraer | W 3-0 | 1-0 | 8 | McCutcheon 2 [42, 65], Little [73] | 376 |
| 17 | | 20 | A | Brechin C | D 1-1 | 1-0 | 8 | Little [30] | 256 |
| 18 | | 27 | H | Livingston | L 1-2 | 1-1 | 8 | Little [30] | 587 |
| 19 | Jan | 20 | A | Queen of the S | W 1-0 | 1-0 | — | Hutchison [28] | 1405 |
| 20 | | 31 | A | Clydebank | L 0-1 | 0-0 | 8 | | 309 |
| 21 | Feb | 3 | H | Forfar Ath | D 2-2 | 1-0 | — | Armstrong [44], Christie [70] | 298 |
| 22 | | 7 | A | Stranraer | W 2-1 | 1-0 | 6 | Banks [20], Paton [70] | 449 |
| 23 | | 17 | H | Brechin C | W 3-1 | 2-0 | — | Little [4], McCutcheon 2 [30, 52] | 318 |
| 24 | | 21 | H | Queen of the S | W 2-0 | 2-0 | 4 | McCutcheon 2 [17, 25] | 522 |
| 25 | | 25 | A | East Fife | L 1-2 | 0-2 | — | Little [67] | 511 |
| 26 | | 28 | A | Inverness CT | L 0-3 | 0-1 | 7 | | 643 |
| 27 | Mar | 7 | A | Clyde | D 0-0 | 0-0 | 6 | | 619 |
| 28 | | 14 | A | Forfar Ath | W 1-0 | 1-0 | 5 | Hutchison [45] | 404 |
| 29 | | 21 | H | Clydebank | D 0-0 | 0-0 | 5 | | 487 |
| 30 | | 28 | H | Stranraer | L 0-1 | 0-1 | 6 | | 428 |
| 31 | Apr | 7 | A | Brechin C | L 3-4 | 2-1 | — | Law [26], Little 2 [41, 49] | 300 |
| 32 | | 11 | A | Inverness CT | L 1-2 | 1-1 | 8 | Little [22] | 1414 |
| 33 | | 18 | H | Clyde | D 1-1 | 1-0 | 8 | McCutcheon [65] | 682 |
| 34 | | 25 | A | Livingston | D 1-1 | 0-0 | 8 | Little [85] | 1282 |
| 35 | May | 2 | H | East Fife | L 2-3 | 0-2 | 9 | Little 2 [56, 62] | 554 |
| 36 | | 9 | A | Queen of the S | L 0-1 | 0-1 | 9 | | 1260 |

**Final League Position: 9**          1996–97 6

**Honours**
*League Champions:* —. *Scottish Cup:* Semi-finals 1902-03. Quarter-finals 1994-95 *League Cup:* Quarter-finals 1947-48, 1960-61, 1975-76. *League Challenge Cup:* Winners 1995-96.
*Club colours:* Shirt: Maroon with silver stripe. Shorts: White with maroon insert. Stockings: White.

**Goalscorers:** *League (44):* Little 15, McCutcheon 7, Henderson 3, Hutchison 3, Roseburgh 3 (1 pen), Hunter 2, Innes 2, Sprott 2, Armstrong 1, Banks 1, Christie 1, Farrell 1, Fisher 1, Law 1, Paton 1. *Scottish Cup (5):* McCutcheon 2, Hutchison 1, Law 1, Little 1. *Coca Cola Cup (1):* Henderson 1. *League Challenge Cup (1):* Henderson 1.

| Alexander N 36 | Sprott A 29+1 | Banks A 22+4 | Armstrong G 36 | Innes C 30 | Christie M 19+1 | Farrell S 28+3 | Fisher J 20 | Little I 33 | Hutchison G 28+6 | Henderson J 15+5 | Brown S 5 | Law R 21+4 | Roseburgh D 12+12 | Campbell M 1+4 | Stewart I 1+6 | Hunter P 9 | McCutcheon G 20 | Kane K 6+3 | Paton E 16 | Tierney G 1 | McDonald I 3 | Hall M 5 | Match No. |
|---|---|---|---|---|---|---|---|---|---|---|---|---|---|---|---|---|---|---|---|---|---|---|---|
| 1 | 2 | 3 | 4 | 5 | 6 | 7 | 8 | 9 | 10 | 11 | | | | | | | | | | | | | 1 |
| 1 | 2 | 3 | 4 | 5 | | 7 | 8 | 9 | 10 | 11 | 6 | | | | | | | | | | | | 2 |
| 1 | 2 | 3 | $4^1$ | 5 | | 7 | 8 | 9 | 10 | $11^2$ | | 6 | 12 | 13 | | | | | | | | | 3 |
| 1 | 2 | | 4 | 5 | | 7 | 8 | 9 | | 11 | 10 | 6 | $3^1$ | 12 | | | | | | | | | 4 |
| 1 | 2 | | 4 | 5 | | 7 | $8^1$ | 9 | 12 | $11^2$ | 10 | 6 | 3 | | 13 | | | | | | | | 5 |
| 1 | 2 | 3 | 4 | 5 | | 7 | 8 | 9 | $10^1$ | 11 | | 6 | | | 12 | | | | | | | | 6 |
| 1 | 2 | $3^1$ | 4 | 5 | | 7 | 8 | 11 | 12 | | $10^3$ | $6^1$ | 14 | | 13 | 9 | | | | | | | 7 |
| 1 | 2 | | 4 | 5 | | 7 | 8 | | 10 | 6 | | | 3 | | 11 | 9 | | | | | | | 8 |
| 1 | 2 | 14 | 4 | 5 | $6^2$ | $7^1$ | 8 | $11^3$ | 12 | 10 | | | 3 | | 13 | 9 | | | | | | | 9 |
| 1 | 2 | | 4 | | | 7 | 8 | 11 | 10 | 5 | | 6 | 3 | | | 9 | | | | | | | 10 |
| 1 | 2 | | 4 | | | 7 | 8 | $10^2$ | | 5 | $11^1$ | 6 | 3 | 13 | 12 | 9 | | | | | | | 11 |
| 1 | 2 | 10 | 4 | 5 | | 7 | 8 | 11 | | 13 | | 6 | $3^1$ | 12 | | $9^2$ | | | | | | | 12 |
| 1 | 2 | 3 | 4 | 5 | | 7 | 8 | 11 | 10 | | | 6 | | | | 9 | | | | | | | 13 |
| 1 | 2 | 3 | 4 | 5 | 12 | $7^1$ | 8 | 11 | 10 | | | 6 | | 13 | | $9^2$ | | | | | | | 14 |
| 1 | 2 | 3 | 4 | 5 | | | 8 | 11 | 10 | 6 | | 7 | | 12 | | $9^1$ | | | | | | | 15 |
| 1 | 2 | 3 | 4 | 5 | | 7 | $8^2$ | 11 | 12 | $6^1$ | $10^3$ | | 14 | | | | 9 | 13 | | | | | 16 |
| 1 | 2 | 3 | 4 | 5 | | 7 | | 11 | | 6 | 10 | | | 12 | | | $9^1$ | | 8 | | | | 17 |
| 1 | 2 | 3 | 4 | 5 | | 7 | 8 | 11 | | 6 | 10 | | | | | | 9 | | | | | | 18 |
| 1 | 2 | 3 | 4 | 5 | | 7 | | 11 | | 6 | 10 | | 15 | | | | 9 | | 8 | | | | 19 |
| 1 | $2^1$ | 3 | 4 | 5 | | 7 | | 11 | | 6 | $10^2$ | | 13 | 12 | | | 9 | | 8 | | | | 20 |
| 1 | 2 | 3 | 4 | 5 | | 7 | | 11 | | 6 | 10 | | | | | | 9 | | 8 | | | | 21 |
| 1 | 2 | 3 | 4 | 5 | | 7 | | 11 | | 6 | 10 | | | | | | 9 | | 8 | | | | 22 |
| 1 | 2 | 3 | 4 | 5 | | $7^1$ | | 11 | | $6^2$ | 10 | | 13 | 12 | | | 9 | | 8 | | | | 23 |
| 1 | 2 | 3 | 4 | 5 | | 7 | | 11 | | 6 | 10 | | | | | | 9 | | 8 | | | | 24 |
| 1 | 2 | 3 | 4 | $5^1$ | | 7 | | 11 | | $6^2$ | 10 | | 13 | 12 | | | 9 | | 8 | | | | 25 |
| 1 | 2 | $3^1$ | 4 | 5 | | 7 | | 11 | | 6 | 10 | | | 12 | | | 9 | | 8 | | | | 26 |
| 1 | 2 | 3 | 4 | 5 | | 7 | | 11 | | 6 | $10^1$ | | | 12 | | | 9 | | 8 | | | | 27 |
| 1 | 2 | 3 | 4 | 5 | | 7 | | 11 | | 6 | 10 | | 3 | | | | 9 | | 8 | | | | 28 |
| 1 | 2 | 3 | 4 | 5 | | 7 | | 11 | | 6 | 10 | | $3^1$ | 12 | | | 9 | | 8 | | | | 29 |
| 1 | 2 | $3^1$ | 4 | 5 | | 7 | | 11 | | 6 | 10 | | | 12 | | | 9 | | 8 | | | | 30 |
| 1 | 2 | | 4 | $5^3$ | | 7 | 8 | $11^1$ | 12 | $6^2$ | 10 | | 3 | 13 | | | 9 | 14 | | | | | 31 |
| 1 | 2 | 14 | 4 | 5 | | 7 | $8^3$ | 11 | 12 | 6 | $10^2$ | | 3 | 13 | | | 9 | | | | | 3 | 32 |
| 1 | 2 | | 4 | 5 | | $7^2$ | 8 | 11 | 12 | $6^1$ | 10 | | | 13 | | | 9 | | | | | 3 | 33 |
| 1 | 2 | | 4 | 5 | | $7^2$ | 8 | 11 | 12 | 6 | 10 | | | 13 | | | 9 | | | | | $3^1$ | 34 |
| 1 | 2 | 12 | 4 | 5 | | 7 | $8^1$ | 11 | | 6 | 10 | | $3^2$ | | | | 9 | 13 | | | | | 35 |
| 1 | 2 | 3 | 4 | 5 | | $7^1$ | $8^3$ | 11 | 12 | 6 | $10^2$ | | | 13 | | | 9 | 14 | | | | | 36 |

# STIRLING ALBION

## Second Division

*Year Formed:* 1945. *Ground & Address:* Forthbank Stadium, Springkerse Industrial Estate, Stirling FK7 7UJ.
*Telephone:* 01786 450399. *Fax:* 01786 448592.
*Ground Capacity:* 3808. seated: 2508. *Size of Pitch:* 110yd × 74yd.
*Chairman:* Peter McKenzie. *Secretary:* Mrs Marlyn Hallam.
*Manager:* Kevin Drinkell. *Assistant Manager:* Ray Stewart. *Physio:* George Cameron.
*Managers since 1975:* A.Smith; G.Peebles; J.Fleeting, J.Brogan. *Club Nickname(s):* The Binos. *Previous Grounds:*
Annfield 1945–92.
*Record Attendance:* 26,400 (at Annfield) v Celtic, Scottish Cup 4th rd; 14 Mar, 1959. 3808 v Aberdeen, Scottish Cup
4th rd, 15 February 1996 (Forthbank).
*Record Transfer Fee received:* £70,000 for John Philliben to Doncaster R (Mar 1984).
*Record Transfer Fee paid:* £25,000 for Craig Taggart from Falkirk (Aug 1994).
*Record Victory:* 20-0 v Selkirk, Scottish Cup 1st rd; 8 Dec, 1984.
*Record Defeat:* 0-9 v Dundee U, Division I; 30 Dec, 1967.
*Most Capped Player:* —.
*Most League Appearances:* 504: Matt McPhee, 1967-81.

## STIRLING ALBION 1997–98 LEAGUE RECORD

| Match No. | Date | | Venue | Opponents | Result | H/T Score | Lg. Pos. | Goalscorers | Atten- dance |
|---|---|---|---|---|---|---|---|---|---|
| 1 | Aug | 2 | H | Raith R | D | 1-1 | 1-1 | — | Tait [40] | 2159 |
| 2 | | 16 | A | St Mirren | D | 2-2 | 1-2 | 6 | Taggart [20], Bone (pen) [70] | 2705 |
| 3 | | 23 | H | Greenock Morton | L | 1-3 | 0-3 | 7 | Bone [70] | 1337 |
| 4 | | 30 | H | Falkirk | L | 2-3 | 1-1 | 10 | Bone 2 (1 pen) [15 (p), 87] | 2485 |
| 5 | Sept | 13 | A | Partick Th | W | 2-1 | 2-1 | 7 | Bone [20], McLaren [42] | 1883 |
| 6 | | 20 | H | Airdrieonians | D | 0-0 | 0-0 | 7 | | 1283 |
| 7 | | 27 | A | Hamilton A | L | 2-3 | 2-2 | 9 | Bone [2], McQuilter [4] | 910 |
| 8 | Oct | 4 | A | Ayr U | L | 1-2 | 0-1 | 9 | Taggart [66] | 1773 |
| 9 | | 18 | H | Dundee | L | 1-2 | 1-0 | 9 | Carberry [37] | 1538 |
| 10 | | 25 | L | Raith R | L | 0-2 | 0-1 | 10 | | 3280 |
| 11 | Nov | 1 | H | St Mirren | D | 0-0 | 0-0 | 10 | | 1533 |
| 12 | | 8 | A | Falkirk | L | 2-3 | 0-1 | 10 | Zahani-Oni 2 [38, 65] | 2467 |
| 13 | | 15 | H | Partick Th | D | 2-2 | 2-0 | 10 | Tait [1], Price [21] | 1656 |
| 14 | | 22 | H | Hamilton A | W | 2-1 | 0-0 | 9 | Bone 2 [47, 68] | 921 |
| 15 | | 29 | A | Airdrieonians | L | 0-2 | 0-2 | 9 | | 1320 |
| 16 | Dec | 6 | H | Ayr U | D | 1-1 | 0-0 | 10 | Bone (pen) [64] | 1023 |
| 17 | | 13 | A | Dundee | D | 0-0 | 0-0 | 9 | | 2751 |
| 18 | | 20 | A | Greenock Morton | W | 3-1 | 2-1 | 10 | Bone [40], Bennett [42], Zahana-Oni [58] | 1903 |
| 19 | | 27 | H | Raith R | W | 3-2 | 1-2 | 9 | Bennett [44], Price [60], Paterson A [80] | 2087 |
| 20 | Jan | 3 | H | Falkirk | L | 0-6 | 0-4 | 10 | | 2954 |
| 21 | | 10 | A | Partick Th | W | 3-1 | 1-0 | 8 | Paterson A [32], Bone 2 (1 pen) [62 (p), 73] | 2880 |
| 22 | | 31 | H | Airdrieonians | D | 2-2 | 0-1 | 9 | Lumsden [71], Bone (pen) [90] | 1292 |
| 23 | Feb | 7 | A | Dundee | L | 1-3 | 0-2 | 9 | Price [75] | 1632 |
| 24 | | 21 | A | Ayr U | L | 0-1 | 0-0 | 10 | | 1637 |
| 25 | | 28 | H | Greenock Morton | D | 2-2 | 0-2 | 10 | Zahana-Oni [68], McLaren [90] | 1507 |
| 26 | Mar | 3 | A | Hamilton A | D | 2-2 | 1-2 | — | Paterson A [33], Price [86] | 802 |
| 27 | | 7 | A | St Mirren | W | 2-0 | 1-0 | 8 | Nilsen [30], Gibson [70] | 2573 |
| 28 | | 14 | H | Hamilton A | L | 0-1 | 0-0 | 8 | | 1104 |
| 29 | | 21 | A | Airdrieonians | L | 0-1 | 0-1 | 9 | | 1284 |
| 30 | | 28 | A | Dundee | L | 0-2 | 0-2 | 9 | | 3142 |
| 31 | Apr | 4 | A | Ayr U | W | 2-0 | 0-0 | 8 | Zahana-Oni [58], Price [74] | 1145 |
| 32 | | 11 | H | Falkirk | L | 0-1 | 0-0 | 9 | | 3521 |
| 33 | | 18 | H | Partick Th | L | 0-1 | 0-1 | 10 | | 2219 |
| 34 | | 25 | A | Raith R | W | 1-0 | 0-0 | 9 | Lorimer [89] | 2326 |
| 35 | May | 2 | H | St Mirren | L | 0-1 | 0-0 | 10 | | 2605 |
| 36 | | 9 | A | Greenock Morton | L | 0-1 | 0-0 | 10 | | 1819 |

**Final League Position: 10**        1996–97 7

*Most League Goals in Season (Individual):* 27: Joe Hughes, Division II; 1969-70.
*Most Goals Overall (Individual):* 129: Billy Steele, 1971-83.

**Honours**
*League Champions:* Division II 1952-53, 1957-58, 1960-61, 1964-65. Second Division 1976-77, 1990-91, 1995-96; *Runners-up:* Division II 1948-49, 1950-51.
*Scottish Cup:* —. *League Cup:* —.
*Club colours:* Shirt: Red and white halves. Shorts: Red and white halves. Stockings: Red.

**Goalscorers:** *League (40):* Bone 13 (5 pens), Price 5, Zahana-Oni 5, Paterson A 3, Bennett 2, McLaren 2, Taggart 2, Tait 2, Carberry 1, Gibson 1, Lorimer 1, Lumsden 1, McQuilter 1, Nilsen 1. *Scottish Cup (4):* Bone 2, Tait 2. *Coca Cola Cup (9):* McCormick 2, McLaren 2, Taggart 2, Gibson 1, Paterson A 1, Tait 1. *League Challenge Cup (2):* McKechnie 1, Paterson G 1.

| McGeown M 36 | Paterson A 36 | Deas P 33 | Carberry G 26 + 1 | McQuilter R 7 | Paterson G 30 | Bone A 24 | Tait T 34 + 2 | McLaren S 6 + 12 | Taggart C 4 + 2 | Bennett N 30 | McKechnie G — + 5 | Bain K 11 + 5 | Gibson J 19 + 6 | Chalmers J — + 1 | McCormick S 5 + 3 | Nicholas S — + 7 | Zahana-Oni L 24 + 4 | Lumsden T 17 + 2 | Nilsen A 20 + 1 | Price G 24 | Hjartarsson G 3 + 9 | Forrest E 1 + 1 | Thomas K 6 | Lorimer D — + 5 | Mortimer P — + 1 | Match No. |
|---|---|---|---|---|---|---|---|---|---|---|---|---|---|---|---|---|---|---|---|---|---|---|---|---|---|---|
| 1 | 2 | 3 | 4 | 5 | 6 | 7 | 8 | 9[1] | 10 | 11 |  | 12 |  |  |  |  |  |  |  |  |  |  |  |  |  | 1 |
| 1 | 2[2] | 3[1] | 4 | 5 | 6 | 7 | 8 | 9 | 10[3] | 13 |  | 11 | 12 | 14 |  |  |  |  |  |  |  |  |  |  |  | 2 |
| 1 | 2 | 3 | 4[2] |  | 6 | 7 | 8 | 12 | 10 | 13 |  | 5[1] | 11 |  | 9 |  |  |  |  |  |  |  |  |  |  | 3 |
| 1 | 2 | 3 | 4[2] |  | 6 | 7 | 8[1] | 14 | 10[3] | 11 |  | 13 | 12 |  | 9 |  |  |  |  |  |  |  |  |  |  | 4 |
| 1 | 2 | 3 | 4[1] | 5 | 6 | 7 | 8 | 9 |  | 11 |  | 12 | 10 |  |  |  |  |  |  |  |  |  |  |  |  | 5 |
| 1 | 2 | 3 | 4 | 5 | 6 | 7 | 8 | 9[1] |  | 11 |  |  | 10[2] |  | 12 | 13 |  |  |  |  |  |  |  |  |  | 6 |
| 1 | 2 |  | 4 | 5 | 6 | 7 | 8 | 9 | 14 | 11 | 12 | 13 | 3[2] |  | 10 |  |  |  |  |  |  |  |  |  |  | 7 |
| 1 | 2 |  | 4[1] | 5 | 6 | 7 | 8 | 9[2] | 12 | 11 |  | 3 | 13 |  | 10 |  |  |  |  |  |  |  |  |  |  | 8 |
| 1 | 2 | 3 | 4[2] |  |  | 7 | 13 | 12 |  | 11 |  |  | 6 |  | 9[1] |  | 10 | 5 | 8 |  |  |  |  |  |  | 9 |
| 1 | 2 | 3 | 4 |  | 6 | 7[2] | 13 | 12 |  | 11 |  |  | 5 |  | 9[1] |  | 10 |  | 8 |  |  |  |  |  |  | 10 |
| 1 | 2 | 3 |  |  | 6 | 7[1] | 4 |  |  | 11 |  | 13 | 5 |  | 12 |  | 10[1] |  | 8 | 9 |  |  |  |  |  | 11 |
| 1 | 2 | 3 |  |  | 6 | 7[1] | 4 |  |  | 11 |  |  | 5 |  |  |  | 10 |  | 8 | 9 | 12 |  |  |  |  | 12 |
| 1 | 2 | 3 |  |  | 6 | 7 | 4 |  |  | 11 |  |  | 5 |  | 12 |  | 10[2] |  | 8[1] | 9 | 13 |  |  |  |  | 13 |
| 1 | 2 | 3 |  |  | 6 | 7 | 4 |  |  | 11 |  |  |  |  | 12 |  | 10 | 5 | 8 | 9[1] |  |  |  |  |  | 14 |
| 1 | 2 | 3 |  |  | 6 | 7 | 4 |  |  | 11 |  |  |  |  | 12 |  | 10[1] | 5 | 8[2] | 9 | 13 |  |  |  |  | 15 |
| 1 | 2 | 3 | 10 |  | 6 | 7 | 4 |  |  | 11 |  |  |  |  |  |  |  | 5 | 8[1] | 9 | 12 |  |  |  |  | 16 |
| 1 | 2 | 3 | 10 |  | 6 | 7 | 4 |  |  | 11 |  |  |  |  | 12 |  |  | 8 | 5[1] | 9 |  |  |  |  |  | 17 |
| 1 | 2 | 3 | 10 |  | 6 | 7 | 4 |  |  | 11 |  |  |  |  | 12 |  |  | 8 | 5[1] | 9 |  |  |  |  |  | 18 |
| 1 | 2 | 3 | 8 |  | 6 | 7 | 4 |  |  | 11 |  |  |  |  | 5 |  |  | 10 |  | 9 |  |  |  |  |  | 19 |
| 1 | 2 | 3 | 8[1] |  | 6 | 7 | 4[2] | 13 |  | 11 |  |  |  |  | 5[3] |  |  | 10 | 14 | 9 | 12 |  |  |  |  | 20 |
| 1 | 2 | 3 | 8 |  | 6 | 7 | 4 |  |  | 11 |  |  |  |  | 8[1] |  |  | 10 | 5 | 9 |  |  |  |  |  | 21 |
| 1 | 2 | 3 |  |  | 6 | 7 | 4 |  |  | 11 |  |  |  |  | 8[1] |  |  | 10 | 5 | 9 | 12 |  |  |  |  | 22 |
| 1 | 2 | 3 |  |  | 6 |  | 4 | 12 |  | 11 |  |  |  |  | 5 |  | 8 | 10 |  | 9 | 7[1] |  |  |  |  | 23 |
| 1 | 2 | 3 |  |  | 6 |  | 4 | 11 |  | 12 |  |  |  |  | 8[2] | 13 | 10 | 5 |  | 7[1] | 9[3] | 14 |  |  |  | 24 |
| 1 | 2 | 3 |  |  | 6 | 7[1] | 4 | 13 |  | 11 |  |  |  |  | 10[2] | 12 |  | 5 | 8 | 9 |  |  |  |  |  | 25 |
| 1 | 2[2] | 3 |  |  | 6 |  | 4 | 12 |  | 11[3] |  |  |  |  | 13 | 14 | 10[1] | 7 | 5 | 8 | 9 |  |  |  |  | 26 |
| 1 | 2 | 3 |  |  | 6 |  | 4 |  |  | 11 |  |  |  |  | 10 | 12 | 7[1] | 5 | 8 | 9 |  |  |  |  |  | 27 |
| 1 | 2 | 3 | 13 |  | 6 |  | 4 |  |  | 11 |  |  |  |  | 10[1] | 12 | 7 | 5 | 8[2] | 9 |  |  |  |  |  | 28 |
| 1 | 2 | 3 | 10 |  | 6 | 7 | 4 | 13 |  | 11 |  |  |  |  | 12 |  |  | 5[1] |  | 9[2] |  |  |  |  |  | 29 |
| 1 | 2 | 3 | 10 |  | 6 |  | 4 | 13 |  | 11 |  |  |  |  | 5 |  | 7 |  | 8[1] | 9[2] | 12 |  |  |  |  | 30 |
| 1 | 2 | 3 | 5 |  | 6 |  | 4 |  |  | 11 |  |  |  |  |  |  | 10 |  | 8[1] | 9 |  |  | 7 | 12 |  | 31 |
| 1 | 2 | 3 | 5 |  | 6 |  | 4 | 14 |  | 11[1] |  |  |  |  |  |  | 10 | 12 | 8[2] | 9[3] |  |  | 7 | 13 |  | 32 |
| 1 | 2 | 3 | 5[1] |  | 6 |  | 4 | 13 |  | 11 |  |  |  |  |  |  | 10 |  | 8 | 9[2] |  |  | 7 | 12 |  | 33 |
| 1 | 2 | 3 | 5 |  |  |  | 4 |  |  | 11 |  |  |  |  | 14 |  | 10 | 6 | 8[2] | 9[1] | 12 |  | 7[3] | 13 |  | 34 |
| 1 | 2 |  | 5[2] |  |  |  | 4 |  |  | 11 |  |  |  |  | 13 |  | 10 | 6 | 8 | 9[1] | 12 | 3 | 7[1] | 14 |  | 35 |
| 1 | 2 | 5 | 10 |  | 8 | 6 | 3[2] | 12 | 9[1] | 4 |  | 13 | 11[3] |  |  |  |  |  |  |  |  |  | 7 | 14 |  | 36 |

# STRANRAER
## First Division

*Year Formed:* 1870. *Ground & Address:* Stair Park, London Rd, Stranraer DG9 8BS. *Telephone:* 01776 703271.
*Ground Capacity:* total: 6100. seated: 1800. *Size of Pitch:* 110yd × 70yd.
*Chairman/Secretary:* Graham Rodgers. *Commercial Manager:* T. L. Sutherland.
*Manager:* Campbell Money. *Assistant Manager/Coach:* Jim Denny.
*Managers since 1975:* J. Hughes; N. Hood; G. Hamilton; D. Sneddon; J. Clark; R. Clark; A. McAnespie. *Club Nickname(s):* The Blues. *Previous Grounds:* None.
*Record Attendance:* 6500 v Rangers, Scottish Cup 1st rd; 24 Jan, 1948.
*Record Transfer Fee received:* £30,000 for Duncan George to Ayr Utd.
*Record Transfer Fee paid:* £15,000 for Colin Harkness from Kilmarnock (Aug 1989).
*Record Victory:* 7-0 v Brechin C, Division II; 6 Feb, 1965.
*Record Defeat:* 1-11 v Queen of the South, Scottish Cup 1st rd; 16 Jan, 1932.
*Most Capped Player:* —.
*Most League Appearances:* 256: Danny McDonald.
*Most League Goals in Season (Individual):* 27: Derek Frye, Second Division; 1977-78.
*Most Goals Overall (Individual):* —.

## STRANRAER 1997–98 LEAGUE RECORD

| Match No. | Date | Venue | Opponents | Result | H/T Score | Lg. Pos. | Goalscorers | Atten- dance |
|---|---|---|---|---|---|---|---|---|
| 1 | Aug 6 | H | Clyde | D 0-0 | 0-0 | — | | 509 |
| 2 | 16 | A | Livingston | L 0-1 | 0-0 | 8 | | 1058 |
| 3 | 23 | A | Queen of the S | W 2-1 | 0-0 | 5 | Black [56], McIntyre [87] | 643 |
| 4 | 30 | H | Brechin C | W 4-0 | 1-0 | 4 | Campbell [5], Young 2 [59, 85], Kinnaird [66] | 463 |
| 5 | Sept 13 | A | Inverness CT | D 2-2 | 0-1 | 5 | Campbell [59], Docherty [65] | 1571 |
| 6 | 20 | A | Forfar Ath | L 1-3 | 0-2 | 6 | Black (pen) [83] | 420 |
| 7 | 27 | H | East Fife | W 3-2 | 2-0 | 5 | Knox [17], Docherty [44], McAulay [62] | 474 |
| 8 | Oct 4 | A | Clydebank | D 0-0 | 0-0 | 6 | | 298 |
| 9 | 18 | H | Stenhousemuir | W 4-1 | 2-1 | 3 | Black [21], Kinnaird [32], Young [57], McIntyre [76] | 494 |
| 10 | 25 | A | Queen of the S | L 1-2 | 0-1 | 4 | McIntyre [59] | 1607 |
| 11 | Nov 1 | H | Livingston | D 1-1 | 0-0 | 4 | Knox [59] | 609 |
| 12 | 8 | A | Brechin C | D 2-2 | 0-0 | 3 | Campbell [71], Ramsay [90] | 307 |
| 13 | 15 | H | Inverness CT | W 2-1 | 0-1 | 3 | McIntyre [61], Young [80] | 644 |
| 14 | 22 | A | East Fife | D 2-2 | 1-1 | 3 | Kinnaird [16], Campbell [78] | 563 |
| 15 | 29 | H | Forfar Ath | D 2-2 | 0-2 | 3 | Campbell [71], Docherty [75] | 486 |
| 16 | Dec 13 | A | Stenhousemuir | L 0-3 | 0-1 | 3 | | 376 |
| 17 | 20 | H | Clydebank | L 0-1 | 0-0 | 5 | | 563 |
| 18 | 27 | H | Queen of the S | L 3-4 | 1-2 | 6 | Black [19], McCaffrey [53], Knox [87] | 1045 |
| 19 | Jan 13 | A | Clyde | W 1-0 | 1-0 | — | English [20] | 515 |
| 20 | 17 | A | East Fife | L 2-3 | 1-1 | 5 | Young [28], Lansdowne [62] | 524 |
| 21 | 31 | A | Forfar Ath | L 1-2 | 0-2 | 6 | Kinnaird [73] | 410 |
| 22 | Feb 7 | H | Stenhousemuir | L 1-2 | 0-1 | 9 | Young [75] | 449 |
| 23 | 14 | A | Clydebank | W 1-0 | 0-0 | 5 | McAulay (pen) [78] | 325 |
| 24 | 21 | H | Clyde | W 3-0 | 2-0 | 5 | Geraghty [36], McAulay (pen) [45], Young [58] | 484 |
| 25 | 25 | A | Livingston | W 1-0 | 0-0 | — | Young [60] | 689 |
| 26 | Mar 4 | H | Brechin C | L 0-2 | 0-2 | — | | 398 |
| 27 | 7 | A | Inverness CT | W 2-1 | 1-0 | 4 | Campbell [37], Young [60] | 1582 |
| 28 | 14 | A | East Fife | W 3-0 | 2-0 | 3 | McIntyre [34], Young [41], Geraghty [90] | 571 |
| 29 | 21 | H | Forfar Ath | W 4-0 | 1-0 | 3 | Black [36], McIntyre 2 [57, 85], Ferguson (og) [71] | 472 |
| 30 | 28 | A | Stenhousemuir | W 1-0 | 1-0 | 3 | Johnstone [22] | 428 |
| 31 | Apr 4 | H | Clydebank | W 2-1 | 2-1 | 3 | Knox [13], Geraghty [43] | 598 |
| 32 | 11 | A | Brechin C | W 3-1 | 2-1 | 3 | Campbell [24], Geraghty [33], McAulay [47] | 324 |
| 33 | 18 | H | Inverness CT | W 3-1 | 0-1 | 3 | George [61], Young [64], Campbell [71] | 667 |
| 34 | 25 | A | Queen of the S | L 2-3 | 1-0 | 3 | Geraghty [35], McAulay (pen) [63] | 1615 |
| 35 | May 2 | H | Livingston | W 2-0 | 0-0 | 2 | George [57], English [73] | 1061 |
| 36 | 9 | A | Clyde | W 1-0 | 0-0 | 1 | Lansdowne [80] | 1649 |

**Final League Position: 1**   1996–97 8

## Honours

*League Champions:* Second Division 1993–94, 1997–98.
*Scottish Cup:* —.
*League Cup:* —.
*Qualifying Cup Winners:* 1937.
*League Challenge Cup Winners:* 1996–97.
*Club colours:* Shirt: Blue. Shorts: White. Stockings: Blue with red tops.

**Goalscorers:** *League (62):* Young 11, Campbell 8, McIntyre 7, Black 5 (1 pen), Geraghty 5, McAulay 5 (3 pens), Kinnaird 4, Knox 4, Docherty 3, English 2, George 2, Lansdowne 2, Johnstone 1, McCaffrey 1, Ramsay 1, own goal 1. *Scottish Cup (5):* Kinnaird 3, George 1, Knox 1. *Coca Cola Cup (1):* Docherty 1. *League Challenge Cup (5):* Young 2, Crawford 1, Docherty 1, Friels 1.

| Matthews G 35 | Knox K 34+1 | Black T 36 | McIntyre P 23+4 | Campbell M 36 | Hay G 1 | Ewing C 1 | George C 31 | Young G 30+4 | Docherty R 20+6 | Kinnaird P 25+7 | Crawford D 2+4 | McAulay I 29+1 | McCrindle S —+3 | Duffy B 1 | McCaffrey J 14 | Friels G 1+11 | Lansdowne A 16+11 | McMillan J —+3 | McInnes I —+5 | Ramsay S 1+5 | Watson P 21+2 | Jenkins A 1 | English I 9+11 | Geraghty M 14 | Johnstone D 15 | Match No. |
|---|---|---|---|---|---|---|---|---|---|---|---|---|---|---|---|---|---|---|---|---|---|---|---|---|---|---|
| 1 | 2 | 3 | 4 | 5 | 6 | $7^1$ | 8 | $9^3$ | 10 | $11^2$ | 12 | 13 | 14 | | | | | | | | | | | | | 1 |
| | 2 | 3 | $9^2$ | 5 | | | 4 | 12 | 8 | $11^1$ | 10 | 7 | | 1 | 6 | 13 | | | | | | | | | | 2 |
| 1 | 2 | 3 | 8 | 5 | | | 4 | 9 | 10 | $11^1$ | 12 | 7 | | | 6 | | | | | | | | | | | 3 |
| 1 | $2^3$ | 3 | 8 | 5 | | | $4^2$ | 9 | 10 | $11^1$ | 6 | 7 | 14 | | | | 12 | 13 | | | | | | | | 4 |
| 1 | | 3 | 8 | 5 | | | 4 | 9 | $10^2$ | $11^3$ | 13 | $7^1$ | 12 | | 6 | 14 | 2 | | | | | | | | | 5 |
| 1 | 13 | 3 | 8 | 5 | | | $4^3$ | 9 | 10 | $11^1$ | | $7^4$ | | | 6 | 12 | 2 | 14 | | | | | | | | 6 |
| 1 | 2 | 3 | 7 | 5 | | | 4 | 9 | 10 | 11 | | $8^1$ | | | 6 | 12 | | | | | | | | | | 7 |
| 1 | 2 | 3 | 7 | 5 | | | 4 | $9^2$ | 10 | $11^1$ | | 8 | | | 6 | 13 | 12 | | | | | | | | | 8 |
| 1 | 2 | 3 | 8 | 5 | | | $4^1$ | 9 | 10 | $11^3$ | | $7^2$ | | | 6 | 14 | 12 | 13 | | | | | | | | 9 |
| 1 | 2 | 3 | 8 | 5 | | | 4 | 9 | $10^2$ | 11 | | $7^1$ | | | 6 | 13 | 12 | | | | | | | | | 10 |
| 1 | 2 | 3 | 8 | 5 | | | 4 | 9 | 10 | $11^1$ | | $7^2$ | | | 6 | 12 | 13 | | | | | | | | | 11 |
| 1 | 2 | 3 | $8^1$ | 5 | | | 4 | 9 | 10 | 11 | | $7^2$ | | | 6 | 13 | 12 | | | | | | | | | 12 |
| 1 | 2 | 3 | 8 | 5 | | | 4 | 9 | 10 | $11^2$ | | $7^1$ | | | 6 | 13 | 12 | | | | | | | | | 13 |
| 1 | 2 | 3 | | 5 | | | 4 | 9 | 10 | 11 | | 8 | | | 6 | | | | | | 7 | | | | | 14 |
| 1 | 2 | 3 | | 5 | | | | 9 | 10 | 11 | | | | | $6^1$ | | 4 | | 12 | 13 | 7 | | $8^1$ | | | 15 |
| 1 | 2 | 3 | | 5 | | | 12 | | 10 | 11 | | 8 | | | 13 | | 4 | | | | $7^1$ | | 6 | $9^2$ | | 16 |
| 1 | 2 | 3 | 7 | 5 | | | | | 10 | 11 | | $8^1$ | | | | | 4 | | 12 | | | | 6 | $9^1$ | | 17 |
| 1 | 2 | 3 | | 5 | | | | | 10 | 11 | | 8 | | | 6 | | 4 | | 12 | | 7 | | | $9^1$ | | 18 |
| 1 | 2 | 3 | 12 | 5 | | | 4 | 9 | $10^1$ | $11^3$ | | 8 | 14 | | 6 | | 13 | | | | $7^2$ | | | | | 19 |
| 1 | 2 | 3 | 12 | 5 | | | 4 | 9 | $10^1$ | $11^2$ | | 8 | | | 6 | | 13 | | | | 7 | | | | | 20 |
| 1 | 2 | 3 | 7 | 5 | | | $4^3$ | 13 | 12 | 11 | | 8 | | | | | 6 | | | | | | $10^2$ | 9 | | 21 |
| 1 | 2 | 3 | $7^1$ | 5 | | | $4^3$ | 13 | 12 | 11 | | 8 | | | | | 14 | | | | | | $10^2$ | 9 | 6 | 22 |
| 1 | 2 | 3 | | 5 | | | 4 | $9^1$ | | 11 | | 8 | | | | | | | | | 7 | | 12 | 10 | 6 | 23 |
| 1 | 2 | 3 | 13 | 5 | | | $4^2$ | $9^1$ | 14 | $11^3$ | | 8 | | | | | | | | | 7 | | 12 | 10 | 6 | 24 |
| 1 | 2 | 3 | | 5 | | | 4 | $9^1$ | | 11 | | 8 | | | | | | | | | 7 | | 12 | 10 | 6 | 25 |
| 1 | $2^2$ | 3 | 13 | 5 | | | 4 | $9^2$ | 12 | 11 | | $8^1$ | | | | | | | | | 7 | | 14 | 10 | $6^2$ | 26 |
| 1 | 2 | 3 | 8 | 5 | | | 4 | $9^3$ | 13 | 12 | | | | | | | 11 | | | | 7 | | 14 | $10^1$ | $6^2$ | 27 |
| 1 | 2 | 3 | 8 | 5 | | | 4 | 9 | 12 | 13 | | $11^1$ | | | | | | | | | 7 | | $10^2$ | | 6 | 28 |
| 1 | 2 | 3 | 8 | 5 | | | $4^1$ | $9^2$ | 7 | $11^3$ | | | | | | | 12 | | 14 | | | | 13 | 10 | 6 | 29 |
| 1 | 2 | 3 | 8 | 5 | | | 4 | $9^3$ | 14 | $11^2$ | | | | | | | 13 | | | | 7 | | 12 | $10^1$ | 6 | 30 |
| 1 | $2^1$ | 3 | 8 | 5 | | | 4 | $9^3$ | 13 | 11 | | | | | | | 12 | | | | 7 | | 14 | $10^2$ | 6 | 31 |
| 1 | 2 | 3 | 8 | 5 | | | $4^1$ | $9^2$ | 14 | 11 | | | | | | | 12 | | | | 7 | | 13 | $10^3$ | 6 | 32 |
| 1 | 2 | 3 | 8 | 5 | | | 4 | $9^3$ | 12 | $11^2$ | | | | | | | 13 | | | | 7 | | 14 | $10^1$ | 6 | 33 |
| 1 | 2 | 3 | | 5 | | | 4 | $9^3$ | 13 | 11 | | 8 | | | | | | | | | 7 | | 12 | $10^2$ | 6 | 34 |
| 1 | 2 | 3 | | 5 | | | 4 | $9^1$ | | 11 | | 8 | | | | | 12 | | | | 7 | | 10 | | 6 | 35 |
| 1 | 2 | 3 | | 5 | | | | $9^2$ | 11 | 13 | | 8 | | | | | 12 | | 4 | | 7 | | $10^1$ | | 6 | 36 |

# SCOTTISH LEAGUE TABLES 1997–98

### Premier Division

| | | Home | | | Goals | | Away | | | Goals | | | |
|---|---|---|---|---|---|---|---|---|---|---|---|---|---|
| | P | W | D | L | F | A | W | D | L | F | A | Pt | GD |
| Celtic | 36 | 12 | 4 | 2 | 41 | 9 | 10 | 4 | 4 | 23 | 15 | 74 | +40 |
| Rangers | 36 | 13 | 4 | 1 | 46 | 16 | 8 | 5 | 5 | 30 | 22 | 72 | +38 |
| Hearts | 36 | 10 | 5 | 3 | 36 | 24 | 9 | 5 | 4 | 34 | 22 | 67 | +24 |
| Kilmarnock | 36 | 9 | 4 | 5 | 24 | 21 | 4 | 7 | 7 | 16 | 31 | 50 | –12 |
| St Johnstone | 36 | 7 | 5 | 6 | 20 | 21 | 6 | 4 | 8 | 18 | 21 | 48 | –4 |
| Aberdeen | 36 | 6 | 6 | 6 | 20 | 18 | 3 | 6 | 9 | 19 | 35 | 39 | –14 |
| Dundee U | 36 | 5 | 7 | 6 | 23 | 18 | 3 | 6 | 9 | 20 | 33 | 37 | –8 |
| Dunfermline Ath | 36 | 4 | 9 | 5 | 26 | 30 | 4 | 4 | 10 | 17 | 38 | 37 | –25 |
| Motherwell | 36 | 6 | 4 | 8 | 26 | 28 | 3 | 3 | 12 | 20 | 36 | 34 | –18 |
| Hibernian | 36 | 6 | 4 | 8 | 26 | 24 | 0 | 8 | 10 | 12 | 35 | 30 | –21 |

### First Division

| | | Home | | | Goals | | Away | | | Goals | | | |
|---|---|---|---|---|---|---|---|---|---|---|---|---|---|
| | P | W | D | L | F | A | W | D | L | F | A | Pts | GD |
| Dundee | 36 | 8 | 6 | 4 | 20 | 12 | 12 | 4 | 2 | 32 | 12 | 70 | +28 |
| Falkirk | 36 | 9 | 4 | 5 | 26 | 19 | 10 | 4 | 4 | 30 | 22 | 65 | +15 |
| Raith R | 36 | 9 | 5 | 4 | 25 | 12 | 8 | 4 | 6 | 26 | 21 | 60 | +18 |
| Airdrieonians | 36 | 9 | 6 | 3 | 24 | 17 | 7 | 6 | 5 | 18 | 18 | 60 | +7 |
| Greenock Morton | 36 | 7 | 4 | 7 | 21 | 22 | 5 | 6 | 7 | 26 | 26 | 46 | –1 |
| St Mirren | 36 | 7 | 3 | 8 | 22 | 24 | 4 | 5 | 9 | 19 | 29 | 41 | –12 |
| Ayr U | 36 | 6 | 4 | 8 | 27 | 29 | 4 | 6 | 8 | 13 | 27 | 40 | –16 |
| Hamilton A | 36 | 4 | 6 | 8 | 17 | 28 | 5 | 5 | 8 | 26 | 28 | 38 | –13 |
| Partick T | 36 | 3 | 5 | 10 | 26 | 35 | 5 | 7 | 6 | 19 | 20 | 36 | –10 |
| Stirling Albion | 36 | 3 | 7 | 8 | 20 | 31 | 5 | 3 | 10 | 20 | 25 | 34 | –16 |

### Second Division

| | | Home | | | Goals | | Away | | | Goals | | | |
|---|---|---|---|---|---|---|---|---|---|---|---|---|---|
| | P | W | D | L | F | A | W | D | L | F | A | Pts | GD |
| Stranraer | 36 | 10 | 3 | 5 | 38 | 22 | 8 | 4 | 6 | 24 | 22 | 61 | +18 |
| Clydebank | 36 | 7 | 6 | 5 | 21 | 17 | 9 | 6 | 3 | 27 | 14 | 60 | +17 |
| Livingston | 36 | 9 | 5 | 4 | 32 | 21 | 7 | 6 | 5 | 24 | 19 | 59 | +16 |
| Queen of the S | 36 | 9 | 5 | 4 | 25 | 19 | 6 | 4 | 8 | 32 | 32 | 54 | +6 |
| Inverness CT | 36 | 7 | 7 | 4 | 31 | 21 | 6 | 3 | 9 | 34 | 30 | 49 | +14 |
| East Fife | 36 | 7 | 2 | 9 | 27 | 34 | 7 | 4 | 7 | 24 | 25 | 48 | –8 |
| Forfar Ath | 36 | 6 | 4 | 8 | 28 | 30 | 6 | 6 | 6 | 23 | 31 | 46 | –10 |
| Clyde | 36 | 6 | 5 | 7 | 21 | 23 | 4 | 7 | 7 | 19 | 30 | 42 | –13 |
| Stenhousemuir | 36 | 6 | 6 | 6 | 26 | 26 | 4 | 4 | 10 | 18 | 27 | 40 | –9 |
| Brechin C | 36 | 5 | 6 | 7 | 22 | 32 | 2 | 5 | 11 | 20 | 41 | 32 | –31 |

### Third Division

| | | Home | | | Goals | | Away | | | Goals | | | |
|---|---|---|---|---|---|---|---|---|---|---|---|---|---|
| | P | W | D | L | F | A | W | D | L | F | A | Pts | GD |
| Alloa Ath | 36 | 13 | 1 | 4 | 42 | 19 | 11 | 3 | 4 | 36 | 20 | 76 | +39 |
| Arbroath | 36 | 11 | 5 | 2 | 41 | 16 | 9 | 3 | 6 | 26 | 19 | 68 | +28 |
| Ross Co | 36 | 10 | 4 | 4 | 41 | 20 | 9 | 6 | 3 | 30 | 16 | 67 | +35 |
| East Stirlingshire | 36 | 11 | 3 | 4 | 30 | 16 | 6 | 3 | 9 | 20 | 32 | 57 | +2 |
| Albion R | 36 | 9 | 3 | 6 | 35 | 25 | 4 | 2 | 12 | 25 | 48 | 44 | –13 |
| Berwick R | 36 | 5 | 8 | 5 | 28 | 27 | 5 | 4 | 9 | 19 | 28 | 42 | –8 |
| Queen's Park | 36 | 5 | 3 | 10 | 20 | 33 | 5 | 8 | 5 | 22 | 22 | 41 | –13 |
| Cowdenbeath | 36 | 6 | 2 | 10 | 15 | 26 | 6 | 0 | 12 | 18 | 31 | 38 | –24 |
| Montrose | 36 | 5 | 4 | 9 | 25 | 35 | 5 | 4 | 9 | 28 | 45 | 38 | –27 |
| Dumbarton | 36 | 2 | 5 | 11 | 16 | 29 | 5 | 5 | 8 | 26 | 32 | 31 | –19 |

# SCOTTISH LEAGUE HONOURS 1890–91 to 1997–98

*On goal average/difference.   †Held jointly after indecisive play-off.   ‡Won on deciding match.
††Held jointly.   ¶Two points deducted for fielding ineligible player.
Competition suspended 1940–45 during war; Regional Leagues operating.   ‡‡Two points deducted for registration
irregularities.

## PREMIER DIVISION

*Maximum points: 72*

|         | First | Pts | Second | Pts | Third | Pts |
|---------|-------|-----|--------|-----|-------|-----|
| 1975–76 | Rangers | 54 | Celtic | 48 | Hibernian | 43 |
| 1976–77 | Celtic | 55 | Rangers | 46 | Aberdeen | 43 |
| 1977–78 | Rangers | 55 | Aberdeen | 53 | Dundee U | 40 |
| 1978–79 | Celtic | 48 | Rangers | 45 | Dundee U | 44 |
| 1979–80 | Aberdeen | 48 | Celtic | 47 | St Mirren | 42 |
| 1980–81 | Celtic | 56 | Aberdeen | 49 | Rangers* | 44 |
| 1981–82 | Celtic | 55 | Aberdeen | 53 | Rangers | 43 |
| 1982–83 | Dundee U | 56 | Celtic* | 55 | Aberdeen | 55 |
| 1983–84 | Aberdeen | 57 | Celtic | 50 | Dundee U | 47 |
| 1984–85 | Aberdeen | 59 | Celtic | 52 | Dundee U | 47 |
| 1985–86 | Celtic* | 50 | Hearts | 50 | Dundee U | 47 |

*Maximum points: 88*

| 1986–87 | Rangers | 69 | Celtic | 63 | Dundee U | 60 |
| 1987–88 | Celtic | 72 | Hearts | 62 | Rangers | 60 |

*Maximum points: 72*

| 1988–89 | Rangers | 56 | Aberdeen | 50 | Celtic | 46 |
| 1989–90 | Rangers | 51 | Aberdeen* | 44 | Hearts | 44 |
| 1990–91 | Rangers | 55 | Aberdeen | 53 | Celtic* | 41 |

*Maximum points: 88*

| 1991–92 | Rangers | 72 | Hearts | 63 | Celtic | 62 |
| 1992–93 | Rangers | 73 | Aberdeen | 64 | Celtic | 60 |
| 1993–94 | Rangers | 58 | Aberdeen | 55 | Motherwell | 54 |

*Maximum points: 108*

| 1994–95 | Rangers | 69 | Motherwell | 54 | Hibernian | 53 |
| 1995–96 | Rangers | 87 | Celtic | 83 | Aberdeen* | 55 |
| 1996–97 | Rangers | 80 | Celtic | 75 | Dundee U | 60 |
| 1997–98 | Celtic | 74 | Rangers | 72 | Hearts | 67 |

## FIRST DIVISION

*Maximum points: 52*

| 1975–76 | Partick T | 41 | Kilmarnock | 35 | Montrose | 30 |

*Maximum points: 78*

| 1976–77 | St Mirren | 62 | Clydebank | 58 | Dundee | 51 |
| 1977–78 | Morton* | 58 | Hearts | 58 | Dundee | 57 |
| 1978–79 | Dundee | 55 | Kilmarnock* | 54 | Clydebank | 54 |
| 1979–80 | Hearts | 53 | Airdrieonians | 51 | Ayr U* | 44 |
| 1980–81 | Hibernian | 57 | Dundee | 52 | St Johnstone | 51 |
| 1981–82 | Motherwell | 61 | Kilmarnock | 51 | Hearts | 50 |
| 1982–83 | St Johnstone | 55 | Hearts | 54 | Clydebank | 50 |
| 1983–84 | Morton | 54 | Dumbarton | 51 | Partick T | 46 |
| 1984–85 | Motherwell | 50 | Clydebank | 48 | Falkirk | 45 |
| 1985–86 | Hamilton A | 56 | Falkirk | 45 | Kilmarnock | 44 |

*Maximum points: 88*

| 1986–87 | Morton | 57 | Dunfermline Ath | 56 | Dumbarton | 53 |
| 1987–88 | Hamilton A | 56 | Meadowbank T | 52 | Clydebank | 49 |

*Maximum points: 78*

| 1988–89 | Dunfermline Ath | 54 | Falkirk | 52 | Clydebank | 48 |
| 1989–90 | St Johnstone | 58 | Airdrieonians | 54 | Clydebank | 44 |
| 1990–91 | Falkirk | 54 | Airdrieonians | 53 | Dundee | 52 |

*Maximum points: 88*

| 1991–92 | Dundee | 58 | Partick T* | 57 | Hamilton A | 57 |
| 1992–93 | Raith R | 65 | Kilmarnock | 54 | Dunfermline Ath | 52 |
| 1993–94 | Falkirk | 66 | Dunfermline Ath | 65 | Airdrieonians | 54 |

*Maximum points: 108*

| 1994–95 | Raith R | 69 | Dunfermline Ath* | 68 | Dundee | 68 |
| 1995–96 | Dunfermline Ath | 71 | Dundee U* | 67 | Morton | 67 |
| 1996–97 | St Johnstone | 80 | Airdrieonians | 60 | Dundee* | 58 |
| 1997–98 | Dundee | 70 | Falkirk | 65 | Raith R* | 60 |

## SECOND DIVISION

*Maximum points: 52*

| 1975–76 | Clydebank* | 40 | Raith R | 40 | Alloa | 35 |

*Maximum points: 78*

| | | | | | | |
|---|---|---|---|---|---|---|
| 1976–77 | Stirling A | 55 | Alloa | 51 | Dunfermline Ath | 50 |
| 1977–78 | Clyde* | 53 | Raith R | 53 | Dunfermline Ath | 48 |
| 1978–79 | Berwick R | 54 | Dunfermline Ath | 52 | Falkirk | 50 |
| 1979–80 | Falkirk | 50 | East Stirling | 49 | Forfar Ath | 46 |
| 1980–81 | Queen's Park | 50 | Queen of the S | 46 | Cowdenbeath | 45 |
| 1981–82 | Clyde | 59 | Alloa* | 50 | Arbroath | 50 |
| 1982–83 | Brechin C | 55 | Meadowbank T | 54 | Arbroath | 49 |
| 1983–84 | Forfar Ath | 63 | East Fife | 47 | Berwick R | 43 |
| 1984–85 | Montrose | 53 | Alloa | 50 | Dunfermline Ath | 49 |
| 1985–86 | Dunfermline Ath | 57 | Queen of the S | 55 | Meadowbank T | 49 |
| 1986–87 | Meadowbank T | 55 | Raith R* | 52 | Stirling A* | 52 |
| 1987–88 | Ayr U | 61 | St Johnstone | 59 | Queen's Park | 51 |
| 1988–89 | Albion R | 50 | Alloa | 45 | Brechin C | 43 |
| 1989–90 | Brechin C | 49 | Kilmarnock | 48 | Stirling A | 47 |
| 1990–91 | Stirling A | 54 | Montrose | 46 | Cowdenbeath | 45 |
| 1991–92 | Dumbarton | 52 | Cowdenbeath | 51 | Alloa | 50 |
| 1992–93 | Clyde | 54 | Brechin C* | 53 | Stranraer | 53 |
| 1993–94 | Stranraer | 56 | Berwick R | 48 | Stenhousemuir* | 47 |

*Maximum points: 108*

| | | | | | | |
|---|---|---|---|---|---|---|
| 1994–95 | Morton | 64 | Dumbarton | 60 | Stirling A | 58 |
| 1995–96 | Stirling A | 81 | East Fife | 67 | Berwick R | 60 |
| 1996–97 | Ayr U | 77 | Hamilton A | 74 | Livingston | 64 |
| 1997–98 | Stranraer | 61 | Clydebank | 60 | Livingston | 59 |

### THIRD DIVISION

*Maximum points: 108*

| | | | | | | |
|---|---|---|---|---|---|---|
| 1994–95 | Forfar Ath | 80 | Montrose | 67 | Ross Co | 60 |
| 1995–96 | Livingston | 72 | Brechin C | 63 | Caledonian T | 57 |
| 1996–97 | Inverness CT | 76 | Forfar Ath* | 67 | Ross Co | 67 |
| 1997–98 | Alloa Ath | 76 | Arbroath | 68 | Ross Co | 67 |

### FIRST DIVISION to 1974–75

*Maximum points: a 36; b 44; c 40; d 52; e 60; f 68; g 76; h 84.*

| | First | Pts | Second | Pts | Third | Pts |
|---|---|---|---|---|---|---|
| 1890–91a | Dumbarton†† | 29 | Rangers†† | 29 | Celtic | 21 |
| 1891–92b | Dumbarton | 37 | Celtic | 35 | Hearts | 34 |
| 1892–93a | Celtic | 29 | Rangers | 28 | St Mirren | 20 |
| 1893–94a | Celtic | 29 | Hearts | 26 | St Bernard's | 23 |
| 1894–95a | Hearts | 31 | Celtic | 26 | Rangers | 22 |
| 1895–96a | Celtic | 30 | Rangers | 26 | Hibernian | 24 |
| 1896–97a | Hearts | 28 | Hibernian | 26 | Rangers | 25 |
| 1897–98a | Celtic | 33 | Rangers | 29 | Hibernian | 22 |
| 1898–99a | Rangers | 36 | Hearts | 26 | Celtic | 24 |
| 1899–1900a | Rangers | 32 | Celtic | 25 | Hibernian | 24 |
| 1900–01c | Rangers | 35 | Celtic | 29 | Hibernian | 25 |
| 1901–02a | Rangers | 28 | Celtic | 26 | Hearts | 22 |
| 1902–03b | Hibernian | 37 | Dundee | 31 | Rangers | 29 |
| 1903–04d | Third Lanark | 43 | Hearts | 39 | Celtic* | 38 |
| 1904–05d | Celtic‡ | 41 | Rangers | 41 | Third Lanark | 35 |
| 1905–06e | Celtic | 49 | Hearts | 43 | Airdrieonians | 38 |
| 1906–07f | Celtic | 55 | Dundee | 48 | Rangers | 45 |
| 1907–08f | Celtic | 55 | Falkirk | 51 | Rangers | 50 |
| 1908–09f | Celtic | 51 | Dundee | 50 | Clyde | 48 |
| 1909–10f | Celtic | 54 | Falkirk | 52 | Rangers | 46 |
| 1910–11f | Rangers | 52 | Aberdeen | 48 | Falkirk | 44 |
| 1911–12f | Rangers | 51 | Celtic | 45 | Clyde | 42 |
| 1912–13f | Rangers | 53 | Celtic | 49 | Hearts* | 41 |
| 1913–14g | Celtic | 65 | Rangers | 59 | Hearts* | 54 |
| 1914–15g | Celtic | 65 | Hearts | 61 | Rangers | 50 |
| 1915–16g | Celtic | 67 | Rangers | 56 | Morton | 51 |
| 1916–17g | Celtic | 64 | Morton | 54 | Rangers | 53 |
| 1917–18f | Rangers | 56 | Celtic | 55 | Kilmarnock* | 43 |
| 1918–19f | Celtic | 58 | Rangers | 57 | Morton | 47 |
| 1919–20h | Rangers | 71 | Celtic | 68 | Motherwell | 57 |
| 1920–21h | Rangers | 76 | Celtic | 66 | Hearts | 50 |
| 1921–22h | Celtic | 67 | Rangers | 66 | Raith R | 51 |
| 1922–23g | Rangers | 55 | Airdrieonians | 50 | Celtic | 46 |
| 1923–24g | Rangers | 59 | Airdrieonians | 50 | Celtic | 46 |
| 1924–25g | Rangers | 60 | Airdrieonians | 57 | Hibernian | 52 |
| 1925–26g | Celtic | 58 | Airdrieonians* | 50 | Hearts | 50 |
| 1926–27g | Rangers | 56 | Motherwell | 51 | Celtic | 49 |
| 1927–28g | Rangers | 60 | Celtic* | 55 | Motherwell | 55 |
| 1928–29g | Rangers | 67 | Celtic | 51 | Motherwell | 50 |

| | | | | | | |
|---|---|---|---|---|---|---|
| 1929–30g | Rangers | 60 | Motherwell | 55 | Aberdeen | 53 |
| 1930–31g | Rangers | 60 | Celtic | 58 | Motherwell | 56 |
| 1931–32g | Motherwell | 66 | Rangers | 61 | Celtic | 48 |
| 1932–33g | Rangers | 62 | Motherwell | 59 | Hearts | 50 |
| 1933–34g | Rangers | 66 | Motherwell | 62 | Celtic | 47 |
| 1934–35g | Rangers | 55 | Celtic | 52 | Hearts | 50 |
| 1935–36g | Celtic | 66 | Rangers* | 61 | Aberdeen | 61 |
| 1936–37g | Rangers | 61 | Aberdeen | 54 | Celtic | 52 |
| 1937–38g | Celtic | 61 | Hearts | 58 | Rangers | 49 |
| 1938–39g | Rangers | 59 | Celtic | 48 | Aberdeen | 46 |
| 1946–47e | Rangers | 46 | Hibernian | 44 | Aberdeen | 46 |
| 1947–48e | Hibernian | 48 | Rangers | 46 | Partick T | 36 |
| 1948–49e | Rangers | 46 | Dundee | 45 | Hibernian | 39 |
| 1949–50e | Rangers | 50 | Hibernian | 49 | Hearts | 43 |
| 1950–51e | Hibernian | 48 | Rangers* | 38 | Dundee | 38 |
| 1951–52e | Hibernian | 45 | Rangers | 41 | East Fife | 37 |
| 1952–53e | Rangers* | 43 | Hibernian | 43 | East Fife | 39 |
| 1953–54e | Celtic | 43 | Hearts | 38 | Partick T | 35 |
| 1954–55e | Aberdeen | 49 | Celtic | 46 | Rangers | 41 |
| 1955–56f | Rangers | 52 | Aberdeen | 46 | Hearts* | 45 |
| 1956–57f | Rangers | 55 | Hearts | 53 | Kilmarnock | 42 |
| 1957–58f | Hearts | 62 | Rangers | 49 | Celtic | 46 |
| 1958–59f | Rangers | 50 | Hearts | 48 | Motherwell | 44 |
| 1959–60f | Hearts | 54 | Kilmarnock | 50 | Rangers* | 42 |
| 1960–61f | Rangers | 51 | Kilmarnock | 50 | Third Lanark | 42 |
| 1961–62f | Dundee | 54 | Rangers | 51 | Celtic | 46 |
| 1962–63f | Rangers | 57 | Kilmarnock | 48 | Partick T | 46 |
| 1963–64f | Rangers | 55 | Kilmarnock | 49 | Celtic* | 47 |
| 1964–65f | Kilmarnock* | 50 | Hearts | 50 | Dunfermline Ath | 49 |
| 1965–66f | Celtic | 57 | Rangers | 55 | Kilmarnock | 45 |
| 1966–67f | Celtic | 58 | Rangers | 55 | Clyde | 46 |
| 1967–68f | Celtic | 63 | Rangers | 61 | Hibernian | 45 |
| 1968–69f | Celtic | 54 | Rangers | 49 | Dunfermline Ath | 45 |
| 1969–70f | Celtic | 57 | Rangers | 45 | Hibernian | 44 |
| 1970–71f | Celtic | 56 | Aberdeen | 54 | St Johnstone | 44 |
| 1971–72f | Celtic | 60 | Aberdeen | 50 | Rangers | 44 |
| 1972–73f | Celtic | 57 | Rangers | 56 | Hibernian | 45 |
| 1973–74f | Celtic | 53 | Hibernian | 49 | Rangers | 48 |
| 1974–75f | Rangers | 56 | Hibernian | 49 | Celtic | 45 |

### SECOND DIVISION to 1974–75

*Maximum points: a 76; b 72; c 68; d 52; e 60; f 36; g 44.*

| | | | | | | |
|---|---|---|---|---|---|---|
| 1893–94f | Hibernian | 29 | Cowlairs | 27 | Clyde | 24 |
| 1894–95f | Hibernian | 30 | Motherwell | 22 | Port Glasgow | 20 |
| 1895–96f | Abercorn | 27 | Leith Ath | 23 | Renton | 21 |
| 1896–97f | Partick T | 31 | Leith Ath | 27 | Kilmarnock* | 21 |
| 1897–98f | Kilmarnock | 29 | Port Glasgow | 25 | Morton | 22 |
| 1898–99f | Kilmarnock | 32 | Leith Ath | 27 | Port Glasgow | 25 |
| 1899–1900f | Partick T | 29 | Morton | 28 | Port Glasgow | 20 |
| 1900–01f | St Bernard's | 25 | Airdrieonians | 23 | Abercorn | 21 |
| 1901–02g | Port Glasgow | 32 | Partick T | 31 | Motherwell | 26 |
| 1902–03g | Airdrieonians | 35 | Motherwell | 28 | Ayr U* | 27 |
| 1903–04g | Hamilton A | 37 | Clyde | 29 | Ayr U | 28 |
| 1904–05g | Clyde | 32 | Falkirk | 28 | Hamilton A | 27 |
| 1905–06g | Leith Ath | 34 | Clyde | 31 | Albion R | 27 |
| 1906–07g | St Bernard's | 32 | Vale of Leven* | 27 | Arthurlie | 27 |
| 1907–08g | Raith R | 30 | Dumbarton*‡‡ | 27 | Ayr U | 27 |
| 1908–09g | Abercorn | 31 | Raith R* | 28 | Vale of Leven | 28 |
| 1909–10g | Leith Ath‡ | 33 | Raith R | 33 | St Bernard's | 27 |
| 1910–11g | Dumbarton | 31 | Ayr U | 27 | Albion R | 25 |
| 1911–12g | Ayr U | 35 | Abercorn | 30 | Dumbarton | 27 |
| 1912–13d | Ayr U | 34 | Dunfermline Ath | 33 | East Stirling | 32 |
| 1913–14g | Cowdenbeath | 31 | Albion R | 27 | Dunfermline Ath* | 26 |
| 1914–15d | Cowdenbeath* | 37 | St Bernard's* | 37 | Leith Ath | 37 |
| 1921–22a | Alloa | 60 | Cowdenbeath | 47 | Armadale | 45 |
| 1922–23a | Queen's Park | 57 | Clydebank¶ | 50 | St Johnstone¶ | 45 |
| 1923–24a | St Johnstone | 56 | Cowdenbeath | 55 | Bathgate | 44 |
| 1924–25a | Dundee U | 50 | Clydebank | 48 | Clyde | 47 |
| 1925–26a | Dunfermline Ath | 59 | Clyde | 53 | Ayr U | 52 |
| 1926–27a | Bo'ness | 56 | Raith R | 49 | Clydebank | 45 |
| 1927–28a | Ayr U | 54 | Third Lanark | 45 | King's Park | 44 |
| 1928–29b | Dundee U | 51 | Morton | 50 | Arbroath | 47 |
| 1929–30a | Leith Ath* | 57 | East Fife | 57 | Albion R | 54 |
| 1930–31a | Third Lanark | 61 | Dundee U | 50 | Dunfermline Ath | 47 |

| 1931–32a | East Stirling* | 55 | St Johnstone | 55 | Raith R* | 46 |
|---|---|---|---|---|---|---|
| 1932–33c | Hibernian | 54 | Queen of the S | 49 | Dunfermline Ath | 47 |
| 1933–34c | Albion R | 45 | Dunfermline Ath* | 44 | Arbroath | 44 |
| 1934–35c | Third Lanark | 52 | Arbroath | 50 | St Bernard's | 47 |
| 1935–36c | Falkirk | 59 | St Mirren | 52 | Morton | 48 |
| 1936–37c | Ayr U | 54 | Morton | 51 | St Bernard's | 48 |
| 1937–38c | Raith R | 59 | Albion R | 48 | Airdrieonians | 47 |
| 1938–39c | Cowdenbeath | 60 | Alloa* | 48 | East Fife | 48 |
| 1946–47d | Dundee | 45 | Airdrieonians | 42 | East Fife | 31 |
| 1947–48e | East Fife | 53 | Albion R | 42 | Hamilton A | 40 |
| 1948–49e | Raith R* | 42 | Stirling A | 42 | Airdrieonians* | 41 |
| 1949–50e | Morton | 47 | Airdrieonians | 44 | Dunfermline Ath* | 36 |
| 1950–51e | Queen of the S* | 45 | Stirling A | 45 | Ayr U* | 36 |
| 1951–52e | Clyde | 44 | Falkirk | 43 | Ayr U | 39 |
| 1952–53e | Stirling A | 44 | Hamilton A | 43 | Queen's Park | 37 |
| 1953–54e | Motherwell | 45 | Kilmarnock | 42 | Third Lanark* | 36 |
| 1954–55e | Airdrieonians | 46 | Dunfermline Ath | 42 | Hamilton A | 39 |
| 1955–56b | Queen's Park | 54 | Ayr U | 51 | St Johnstone | 49 |
| 1956–57b | Clyde | 64 | Third Lanark | 51 | Cowdenbeath | 45 |
| 1957–58b | Stirling A | 55 | Dunfermline Ath | 53 | Arbroath | 47 |
| 1958–59b | Ayr U | 60 | Arbroath | 51 | Stenhousemuir | 46 |
| 1959–60b | St Johnstone | 53 | Dundee U | 50 | Queen of the S | 49 |
| 1960–61b | Stirling A | 55 | Falkirk | 54 | Stenhousemuir | 50 |
| 1961–62b | Clyde | 54 | Queen of the S | 53 | Morton | 44 |
| 1962–63b | St Johnstone | 55 | East Stirling | 49 | Morton | 48 |
| 1963–64b | Morton | 67 | Clyde | 53 | Arbroath | 46 |
| 1964–65b | Stirling A | 59 | Hamilton A | 50 | Queen of the S | 45 |
| 1965–66b | Ayr U | 53 | Airdrieonians | 50 | Queen of the S | 47 |
| 1966–67a | Morton | 69 | Raith R | 58 | Arbroath | 57 |
| 1967–68b | St Mirren | 62 | Arbroath | 53 | East Fife | 49 |
| 1968–69b | Motherwell | 64 | Ayr U | 53 | East Fife* | 48 |
| 1969–70b | Falkirk | 56 | Cowdenbeath | 55 | Queen of the S | 50 |
| 1970–71b | Partick T | 56 | East Fife | 51 | Arbroath | 46 |
| 1971–72b | Dumbarton* | 52 | Arbroath | 52 | Stirling A | 50 |
| 1972–73b | Clyde | 56 | Dumfermline Ath | 52 | Raith R* | 47 |
| 1973–74b | Airdrieonians | 60 | Kilmarnock | 58 | Hamilton A | 55 |
| 1974–75a | Falkirk | 54 | Queen of the S* | 53 | Montrose | 53 |

Elected to First Division: 1894 Clyde; 1895 Hibernian; 1896 Abercorn; 1897 Partick T; 1899 Kilmarnock; 1900 Morton and Partick T; 1902 Port Glasgow and Partick T; 1903 Airdrieonians and Motherwell; 1905 Falkirk and Aberdeen; 1906 Clyde and Hamilton A; 1910 Raith R; 1913 Ayr U and Dumbarton.

## RELEGATED FROM PREMIER DIVISION

1974–75 *No relegation due to League reorganization*
1975–76 Dundee, St Johnstone
1976–77 Hearts, Kilmarnock
1977–78 Ayr U, Clydebank
1978–79 Hearts, Motherwell
1979–80 Dundee, Hibernian
1980–81 Kilmarnock, Hearts
1981–82 Partick T, Airdrieonians
1982–83 Morton, Kilmarnock
1983–84 St Johnstone, Motherwell
1984–85 Dumbarton, Morton
1985–86 *No relegation due to League reorganization*
1986–87 Clydebank, Hamilton A
1987–88 Falkirk, Dunfermline Ath, Morton
1988–89 Hamilton A
1989–90 Dundee
1990–91 None
1991–92 St Mirren, Dunfermline Ath
1992–93 Falkirk, Airdrieonians
1993–94 *See footnote*
1994–95 Dundee U
1995–96 Partick T, Falkirk
1996–97 Raith R
1997–98 Hibernian

## RELEGATED FROM DIVISION 1

1974–75 *No relegation due to League reorganization*
1975–76 Dunfermline Ath, Clyde
1976–77 Raith R, Falkirk
1977–78 Alloa Ath, East Fife
1978–79 Montrose, Queen of the S
1979–80 Arbroath, Clyde
1980–81 Stirling A, Berwick R
1981–82 East Stirling, Queen of the S
1982–83 Dunfermline Ath, Queen's Park
1983–84 Raith R, Alloa
1984–85 Meadowbank T, St Johnstone
1985–86 Ayr U, Alloa
1986–87 Brechin C, Montrose
1987–88 East Fife, Dumbarton
1988–89 Kilmarnock, Queen of the S
1989–90 Albion R, Alloa
1990–91 Clyde, Brechin C
1991–92 Montrose, Forfar Ath
1992–93 Meadowbank T, Cowdenbeath
1993–94 *See footnote*
1994–95 Ayr U, Stranraer
1995–96 Hamilton A, Dumbarton
1996–97 Clydebank, East Fife
1997–98 Partick T, Stirling A

## RELEGATED FROM DIVISION 2

1994–95 Meadowbank T, Brechin C
1995–96 Forfar Ath, Montrose

1996–97 Dumbarton, Berwick R
1997–98 Stenhousemuir, Brechin C

## RELEGATED FROM DIVISION 1 (TO 1973–74)

| | |
|---|---|
| 1921–22  *Queen's Park, Dumbarton, Clydebank | 1951–52  Morton, Stirling A |
| 1922–23  Albion R, Alloa Ath | 1952–53  Motherwell, Third Lanark |
| 1923–24  Clyde, Clydebank | 1953–54  Airdrieonians, Hamilton A |
| 1924–25  Third Lanark, Ayr U | 1954–55  *No clubs relegated* |
| 1925–26  Raith R, Clydebank | 1955–56  Stirling A, Clyde |
| 1926–27  Morton, Dundee U | 1956–57  Dunfermline Ath, Ayr U |
| 1927–28  Dunfermline Ath, Bo'ness | 1957–58  East Fife, Queen's Park |
| 1928–29  Third Lanark, Raith R | 1958–59  Queen of the S, Falkirk |
| 1929–30  St Johnstone, Dundee U | 1959–60  Arbroath, Stirling A |
| 1930–31  Hibernian, East Fife | 1960–61  Ayr U, Clyde |
| 1931–32  Dundee U, Leith Ath | 1961–62  St Johnstone, Stirling A |
| 1932–33  Morton, East Stirling | 1962–63  Clyde, Raith R |
| 1933–34  Third Lanark, Cowdenbeath | 1963–64  Queen of the S, East Stirling |
| 1934–35  St Mirren, Falkirk | 1964–65  Airdrieonians, Third Lanark |
| 1935–36  Airdrieonians, Ayr U | 1965–66  Morton, Hamilton A |
| 1936–37  Dunfermline Ath, Albion R | 1966–67  St Mirren, Ayr U |
| 1937–38  Dundee, Morton | 1967–68  Motherwell, Stirling A |
| 1938–39  Queen's Park, Raith R | 1968–69  Falkirk, Arbroath |
| 1946–47  Kilmarnock, Hamilton A | 1969–70  Raith R, Partick T |
| 1947–48  Airdrieonians, Queen's Park | 1970–71  St Mirren, Cowdenbeath |
| 1948–49  Morton, Albion R | 1971–72  Clyde, Dunfermline Ath |
| 1949–50  Queen of the S, Stirling A | 1972–73  Kilmarnock, Airdrieonians |
| 1950–51  Clyde, Falkirk | 1973–74  East Fife, Falkirk |

*Season 1921–22 – only 1 club promoted, 3 clubs relegated.

**Scottish League championship wins:** Rangers 47, Celtic 36, Aberdeen 4, Hearts 4, Hibernian 4, Dumbarton 2, Dundee 1, Dundee U 1, Kilmarnock 1, Motherwell 1, Third Lanark 1.

*At the end of the 1993–94 season four divisions were created assisted by the admission of two new clubs Ross County and Caledonian Thistle. Only one club was promoted from Division 1 and Division 2. The three relegated from the Premier joined with teams finishing second to seventh in Division 1 to form the new Division 1. Five relegated from Division 1 combined with those who finished second to sixth to form a new Division 2 and the bottom eight in Division 2 linked with the two newcomers to form a new Division 3. At the end of the 1997–98 season the nine clubs remaining in the Premier Division plus the promoted team from Division 1 formed a breakaway Premier League.*

Henrik Larsson celebrates after scoring Celtic's first goal against St Johnstone in a Scottish Premier Division encounter. (Colorsport)

# SCOTTISH LEAGUE CUP FINALS 1946–98

| Season | Winners | Runners-up | Score |
|--------|---------|------------|-------|
| 1946–47 | Rangers | Aberdeen | 4-0 |
| 1947–48 | East Fife | Falkirk | 4-1 after 0-0 draw |
| 1948–49 | Rangers | Raith R | 2-0 |
| 1949–50 | East Fife | Dunfermline Ath | 3-0 |
| 1950–51 | Motherwell | Hibernian | 3-0 |
| 1951–52 | Dundee | Rangers | 3-2 |
| 1952–53 | Dundee | Kilmarnock | 2-0 |
| 1953–54 | East Fife | Partick T | 3-2 |
| 1954–55 | Hearts | Motherwell | 4-2 |
| 1955–56 | Aberdeen | St Mirren | 2-1 |
| 1956–57 | Celtic | Partick T | 3-0 after 0-0 draw |
| 1957–58 | Celtic | Rangers | 7-1 |
| 1958–59 | Hearts | Partick T | 5-1 |
| 1959–60 | Hearts | Third Lanark | 2-1 |
| 1960–61 | Rangers | Kilmarnock | 2-0 |
| 1961–62 | Rangers | Hearts | 3-1 after 1-1 draw |
| 1962–63 | Hearts | Kilmarnock | 1-0 |
| 1963–64 | Rangers | Morton | 5-0 |
| 1964–65 | Rangers | Celtic | 2-1 |
| 1965–66 | Celtic | Rangers | 2-1 |
| 1966–67 | Celtic | Rangers | 1-0 |
| 1967–68 | Celtic | Dundee | 5-3 |
| 1968–69 | Celtic | Hibernian | 6-2 |
| 1969–70 | Celtic | St Johnstone | 1-0 |
| 1970–71 | Rangers | Celtic | 1-0 |
| 1971–72 | Partick T | Celtic | 4-1 |
| 1972–73 | Hibernian | Celtic | 2-1 |
| 1973–74 | Dundee | Celtic | 1-0 |
| 1974–75 | Celtic | Hibernian | 6-3 |
| 1975–76 | Rangers | Celtic | 1-0 |
| 1976–77 | Aberdeen | Celtic | 2-1 |
| 1977–78 | Rangers | Celtic | 2-1 |
| 1978–79 | Rangers | Aberdeen | 2-1 |
| 1979–80 | Dundee U | Aberdeen | 3-0 after 0-0 draw |
| 1980–81 | Dundee U | Dundee | 3-0 |
| 1981–82 | Rangers | Dundee U | 2-1 |
| 1982–83 | Celtic | Rangers | 2-1 |
| 1983–84 | Rangers | Celtic | 3-2 |
| 1984–85 | Rangers | Dundee U | 1-0 |
| 1985–86 | Aberdeen | Hibernian | 3-0 |
| 1986–87 | Rangers | Celtic | 2-1 |
| 1987–88 | Rangers | Aberdeen | 3-3 |
| | | *(Rangers won 5-3 on penalties)* | |
| 1988–89 | Rangers | Aberdeen | 3-2 |
| 1989–90 | Aberdeen | Rangers | 2-1 |
| 1990–91 | Rangers | Celtic | 2-1 |
| 1991–92 | Hibernian | Dunfermline Ath | 2-0 |
| 1992–93 | Rangers | Aberdeen | 2-1 |
| 1993–94 | Rangers | Hibernian | 2-1 |
| 1994–95 | Raith R | Celtic | 2-2 |
| | | *(Raith R won 6-5 on penalties)* | |
| 1995–96 | Aberdeen | Dundee | 2-0 |
| 1996–97 | Rangers | Hearts | 4-3 |
| 1997–98 | Celtic | Dundee U | 3-0 |

## SCOTTISH LEAGUE CUP WINS

Rangers 20, Celtic 10, Hearts 4, Aberdeen 5, Dundee 3, East Fife 3, Dundee U 2, Hibernian 2, Motherwell 1, Partick T 1, Raith R 1.

## APPEARANCES IN FINALS

Rangers 26, Celtic 22, Aberdeen 11, Hibernian 7, Dundee 6, Hearts 6, Dundee U 5, Partick T 4, East Fife 3, Kilmarnock 3, Dunfermline Ath 2, Motherwell 2, Raith R 2, Falkirk 1, Morton 1, St Johnstone 1, St Mirren 1, Third Lanark 1.

# SCOTTISH COCA-COLA CUP 1997–98

**FIRST ROUND**

**2 AUG**

**Arbroath (0) 0**

**Queen of the S (1) 4** *(Townsley 45, Flannigan 51, Bryce 53 (pen), Eadie 63)*          466

*Arbroath:* Dunn; Mitchell, Gallagher, Crawford, Wylie, Peters, Grant, McAulay, McWalter, Spence (Scott), Burns K.
*Queen of the S:* Mathieson; MacLeod, McKeown, Rowe, Thomson (McAllister), Townsley, McLuskey (Irving), Bryce, Eadie, Flannigan (Mallan), Cleeland.

**Berwick R (1) 2** *(Forrester 13, Walton 86)*

**Brechin C (0) 0**

*Berwick R:* Collier; Cunningham, Finlayson, Fraser, Clark, McNicoll, Rafferty, Smith P, Forrester, Walton, Sloan.
*Brechin C:* Garden; Baillie (Heddle), Brown, Cairney, Farnan, Dailly, McNeill (Kerrigan), Buick, Sorbie, Brand, Campbell.

**Cowdenbeath (0) 0**

**Alloa Ath (1) 2** *(Irvine 44, Pew 74)*          270

*Cowdenbeath:* Godfrey; Hamilton, Ritchie, Meldrum (Scott), Humphreys, McMahon (Stewart), Munro, Jack, Hunter, Nolan, Bowmaker (Baillie).
*Alloa Ath:* Monaghan; Valentine, Haddow, McAneny, McCulloch, McCormack, Nelson (Wilson M), Wilson S, Mathieson, Irvine, Pew.

**Dumbarton (0) 1** *(Bruce 87)*

**Queen's Park (1) 1** *(Edgar 29)*          544

*Dumbarton:* Meechan K; Wilson, Brittain, Bruce, Gow, Mooney, McKinnon (Reilly), Meechan J, Mellis (Ward), Glancy, Sharp.
*Queen's Park:* Hamilton; Rossiter, Hardie, McNamee, Smith J, Maxwell, Caven, O'Brien (Cullie), Edgar, Conroy (Finlayson), McGoldrick.
*aet.(Dumbarton won 6-5 on penalties).*

**East Stirling (2) 3** *(Patterson 12, Campbell 29, Abercromby 90)*

**Stranraer (1) 1** *(Docherty 27)*          361

*East Stirling:* McDougall; Russell, Neill, Ross (Snedden), Gardiner, Campbell, McBride (Parks), Watt, Abercromby, Barr (Muirhead), Patterson.
*Stranraer:* Duffy; Lansdowne (McCrindle), Black, George, Campbell, McCaffrey, Ewing (McMillan), Docherty, Young, Crawford, Kinnaird.

**Forfar Ath (0) 1** *(Honeyman 73)*

**Albion R (0) 0**          401

*Forfar Ath:* Robertson; McCheyne, Craig, Hamilton, Mann, Cargill (Glennie), McLauchlan, Allison (Nairn), Hannigan (Loney), Lee, Honeyman.
*Albion R:* Ross; McKilligan, McGowan, Coyle (McInnes), Martin, Duncan, Gardner, Cody, Watters, Bruce, Harty (McKenzie).

**Inverness CT (1) 5** *(Christie 32, Thomson 68 (pen), 87, 88, Wilson 80)*

**Stenhousemuir (1) 1** *(Henderson 12)*          1715

*Inverness CT:* Fridge; Teasdale, Hastings, MacArthur, Andersen, Cherry, Wilson, Thomson, Stewart, Christie, Ross (Tokely)(De-Barros).
*Stenhousemuir:* Alexander; Law (Brown), Banks, Armstrong, Innes, Christie (Stewart), Farrell, Fisher, Little, Hutchison, Henderson.

**Ross Co (0) 2** *(Wood 57, 64)*

**Montrose (0) 1** *(Taylor 75)*          1051

*Ross Co:* Morgan; Ferguson, Matheson, Haro, Furphy, Gilbert, Hart (Adams), Taylor (Williamson), Wood (Ross), MacPherson, McBain.
*Montrose:* Larter (Butter); Winiarski (Masson C), Glass, MacDonald, Craib, Mailer, Fisher, Taylor, McGlashan, Smith S, Dorward (Ferrie).

**SECOND ROUND**

**7 AUG**

(at Fir Park)

**Hamilton A (0) 0**

**Rangers (0) 1** *(McCoist 62)*          8866

*Hamilton A:* Ferguson; Hillcoat, Renicks, Thomson, McCulloch, McIntosh, Quitongo, Sherry, McCormick (McFarlane), Clark, Cunnington.
*Rangers:* Snelders; Cleland, Stensaas (McCoist), McInnes, Petric, Bollan, Durie, Miller, Anderson, Durrant, Gattuso.

**9 AUG**

(at Tynecastle Stadium)

**Berwick R (0) 0**

**Celtic (5) 7** *(Jackson 16, Larsson 21, Blinker 28, Wieghorst 38, Thom 41, Donnelly 70, 84)*          6267

*Berwick R:* Collier (Burgess); Cunningham, Finlayson, Fraser, Clark, McNicoll, Irvine, Smith (Laidler), Forrester, Walton (Rafferty), Sloan.
*Celtic:* Gould; Boyd, Mahe (McNamara), Wieghorst, Mackay, Stubbs, Larsson (O'Donnell), Burley, Jackson, Thom (Donnelly), Blinker.

**Dumbarton (1) 1** *(McKinnon 16)*

**Aberdeen (3) 5** *(Miller 32, Newell 43, 55, 81, Jess 44)*          1739

*Dumbarton:* Meechan K; Wilson, Brittain, Bruce (Melvin), Gow (Grace), Mooney, McKinnon, Meechan J, Reilly, Sharp, Glancy (Ward).
*Aberdeen:* Stillie; Anderson, Tzvetanov, Bernard, Kombouare, O'Neil, Miller (Rowson), Jess, Newell, Windass (Dodds), Buchan (Craig).

**Dundee (0) 1** *(O'Driscoll 67)*

**East Stirling (0) 0**          2515

*Dundee:* Douglas; Smith, Maddison, Adamczuk, Irvine, Rogers, Grady, Magee (Farningham), Annand (Anderson), O'Driscoll (Elliott), McInally.
*East Stirling:* McDougall; Russell, Neill, Campbell, Gardiner, Barr (Hunter), McBride, Watt (Muirhead), Abercromby, Kennedy, Patterson (Parks).

**Dunfermline Ath (4) 5** *(Smith 6, 21, 39, 72, French 43 (pen))*

**Ayr U (1) 1** *(Wordsworth 28)*          3283

*Dunfermline Ath:* Westwater; Shields, Miller (Sharp), Tod, Barnett, Curran (Fraser), Moore, Bingham, Smith, French (Fleming), Petrie.
*Ayr U:* McKeown; Robertson, Bonar, Hood, Jamieson (Love), Mainge, Agnew, Bell, Wordsworth, McDonald (Kerrigan), Kristensen.

**East Fife (0) 0**

**Kilmarnock (1) 2** *(Findlay 45, Vareille 82)*          1169

*East Fife:* McCulloch; Cusick, Gibb, Ritchie, Johnston, Gillies, Allan, Donaghy, Dyer, Ronald (Moffat), Dixon (Ryan).
*Kilmarnock:* Lekovic; MacPherson, Baker, Montgomerie, McGowne, Reilly, Bagan (Burke), Findlay, Wright, McIntyre (Vareille), Mitchell (Nevin).

**Greenock Morton (0) 4** *(Hawke 69, 92, 114, Aitken 118 (pen))*
**Airdrieonians (1) 1** *(Connolly P 8) aet*                    2854
*Greenock Morton:* Wylie; Collins, Sukalia (Morrow), Anderson, McCahill (Blair), Reid, Flannery (Aitken), Mahood, Hawke, McArthur, McPherson.
*Airdrieonians:* Rhodes; Stewart, McCann, Johnston (McClelland), Sweeney, Wilson, Lawrence (McPhee), Davies, Cooper, Connolly P, Smith.

**Hibernian (2) 3** *(Lavety 9, Charnley 29, McGinlay 49)*
**Alloa Ath (0) 1** *(Irvine 50)*                              7407
*Hibernian:* Gottskalksson; Miller W, Boco, Dods, Hughes, Charnley (Grant), Dow, Lavety (Miller G), Crawford, Rougier (Paton), McGinlay.
*Alloa Ath:* Monaghan; Valentine, Haddow, McAneny, McCulloch, Ramsay, Wilson M (Nelson), Wilson S, Mathieson (Simpson), Irvine, Pew.

**Livingston (0) 0**
**Hearts (2) 2** *(McCann 25, 26)*                             4869
*Livingston:* McCaldon; Davidson, Duthie, Wright, Graham, Conway, McMartin, Alleyne (Watson), Maskrey (Young), Raynes, Magee (Callaghan).
*Hearts:* Rousset; Frail, Pointon, Weir, Murray, Ritchie, McCann, Fulton, Adam, Cameron (Salvatori), Hamilton (Thomas).

**Motherwell (2) 2** *(Falconer 16, Coyle 22)*
**Inverness CT (0) 2** *(Thomson 55 (pen), Addicoat 87)* 4247
*Motherwell:* Woods; May (Valakari), Resch (Dorner), Davies, Martin, Denham (Ross), Weir, McMillan, Coyne, Falconer, Coyle.
*Inverness CT:* Fridge; Teasdale, Hastings, MacArthur, Andersen, Cherry, Wilson (Addicoat), Thomson, Stewart, Christie, Ross (De-Barros)(Noble).
*aet (Motherwell won 4-1 on penalties).*

**Partick T (1) 2** *(Farrell 40, Lyons 64)*
**Stirling Albion (2) 3** *(McLaren 16, 33, Taggart 58)*   2109
*Partick T:* O'Connor; Boyle (Tait), Lyons, Milne, Farrell, Watson, Hetherston, Macdonald (Adams), Graham (Evans), Connor, Martin.
*Stirling Albion:* McGeown; Paterson A, Deas, Carberry, McQuilter, Paterson G, Bone, Tait, McLaren, Taggart, Bennett (Bain).

**Queen of the S (0) 2** *(Mallan 80, 88)*
**Dundee U (2) 4** *(McSwegan 21, 31, 78, Thompson 85)* 2438
*Queen of the S:* Mathieson; MacLeod, Aitken, Rowe, Thomson, Townsley (Lilley), Cleeland (Weir), Bryce, Eadie (Mallan), Flannigan, McKeown.
*Dundee U:* Dijkstra; Bowman (Thompson), Malpas, Pressley, Perry, Pedersen, Olafsson, Zetterlund, McSwegan, Dolan, McLaren (Winters).

**Raith R (3) 5** *(Duffield 23, 27, 43, Millen 48, Cameron 56)*
**Forfar Ath (0) 0**                                           2942
*Raith R:* Van De Kamp; McEwan, Fotheringham (Mitchell), Kirkwood (Dair L), Craig, Millen, Lennon, Twaddle, Duffield (Kirk), Wright, Cameron.
*Forfar Ath:* Robertson; McCheyne, Craig, Hamilton, Mann, Cargill, McLauchlan (Loney), Allison (Glennie), Morgan (Hannigan), Lee, Honeyman.

**Ross Co (0) 0**
**Falkirk (2) 3** *(Moss 2, 30, Crabbe 60)*                  1823
*Ross Co:* Morgan; Farrell, Golabek, Haro, Furphy, Gilbert, Ferguson, Taylor, Wood, MacPherson (Williamson), McBain (Ross).
*Falkirk:* Nelson; McGowan, Seaton, Oliver, James, McKenzie (Craig), McAllister, Crabbe, McGrillen (McGraw), Moss, Hagen (Corrigan).

**St Johnstone (1) 3** *(O'Boyle 43, 87, Griffin 54)*
**Clyde (0) 0**                                                2945
*St Johnstone:* Main; McQuillan, Davidson (Preston), Kane, Weir, Griffin, Scott, Tosh (O'Halloran), Grant, O'Boyle, Jenkinson.
*Clyde:* McLean; McStay, McInulty, Baptie, Brown, Donaldson, Gibson (Carrigan), King, Scott (Gauley), Rice, Brownlie.

**St Mirren (1) 2** *(Kelly 31, Milne 63)*
**Clydebank (0) 0**                                            2599
*St Mirren:* Combe; Smith, Galloway, McWhirter, McLaughlin, Archdeacon, Murray, Milne, McGarry (Iwelumo), Mendes, Kelly.
*Clydebank:* Hillcoat; Wishart, Lovering, Murdoch, McLaughlin, Brannigan, Teale (Lorimer), Nicholls, Connell (Melvin), McCall, Docherty.

### THIRD ROUND

**19 AUG**
**Dundee (0) 0**
**Aberdeen (1) 3** *(Dodds 17, 60, Newell 80)*               7457
*Dundee:* Douglas; Smith, Maddison (Elliott), Adamczuk, Irvine, Rogers, Anderson, Magee, Annand (O'Driscoll), Grady, McInally (McGlashan).
*Aberdeen:* Stillie; Anderson (Young), Tzvetanov, Bernard, Smith, O'Neil, Miller, Jess, Newell (Windass), Dodds, Rowson.

**Raith R (0) 1** *(Wright 60)*
**Hearts (0) 2** *(Weir 61, Adam 65)*                         7146
*Raith R:* Van De Kamp; McEwan (Twaddle), Fotheringham, Kirkwood, Craig, Millen, Lennon, Millar, Duffield, Wright, Cameron.
*Hearts:* Rousset; Frail (Murray), Pointon, Weir, Salvatori, Ritchie, McCann, Fulton, Robertson (Hamilton), Cameron (Flögel), Adam.

**Rangers (1) 4** *(McCoist 43, 82, 89 (pen), Stensaas 71)*
**Falkirk (1) 1** *(James 36)*                               43,606
*Rangers:* Goram; Cleland (Van Vossen), Stensaas, Porrini, Moore, Vidmar, Durie, Ferguson I, McCoist, Negri, Miller (Gattuso).
*Falkirk:* Mathers; McGowan, Seaton, Oliver, James, McKenzie, McAllister, Crabbe (Hamilton), McGrillen (McGraw), Moss, Hagen.

**St Johnstone (0) 0**
**Celtic (0) 1** *(Donnelly 103 (pen)) aet*                   7488
*St Johnstone:* Main; McQuillan, Davidson, Sekerlioglu, Weir, McCluskey, Scott (Farquhar), O'Halloran (O'Neil), Kane, O'Boyle, Preston (Grant).
*Celtic:* Gould; Boyd, Mahe, Hannah, Mackay, Wieghorst (Grant), Larsson, Burley, Donnelly, Jackson (Thom), O'Donnell.

**20 AUG**
**Dundee U (1) 2** *(Zetterlund 90, McSwegan 92)*
**Hibernian (1) 1** *(Lavety 3) aet*                          7692
*Dundee U:* Dijkstra; Bowman, Malpas, Pressley, Perry, Pedersen, Olofsson, Zetterlund, Winters (McSwegan), Duffy (Thompson), McLaren (Easton).
*Hibernian:* Reid; Miller W, Boco (Grant), Dods, Hughes, Charnley, Dow, Power (Crawford), Lavety, Harper (Tosh), McGinlay.

**Dunfermline Ath (1) 2** *(French 2, Smith 47)*
**St Mirren (0) 0**                                           4576
*Dunfermline Ath:* Westwater; Shields, Miller C, Tod, Den Bieman, Curran, Moore, Bingham, Smith, French, Petrie.
*St Mirren:* Combe; Smith, Galloway (Winnie), McWhirter, McLaughlin, Archdeacon, Murray (Milne), Turner, Brown, Mendes, Kelly (Yardley).

**Motherwell (2) 3** *(Coyle O 9, 39, 62)*
**Greenock Morton (0) 0** 4576
*Motherwell:* Woods; May, Resch, Christie, Martin, Denham, Weir (Ross), McMillan, Coyne T, Falconer (Dorner), Coyle O (McCulloch).
*Greenock Morton:* Wylie; Collins, Sukalia, Anderson, McCahill, Reid, Flannery, Mahood, Hawke, McArthur, McPherson (Blair).

**Stirling Albion (2) 6** *(Paterson A 37, Gibson 40, Tait 55, McCormick 70, 73, Taggart 89)*
**Kilmarnock (0) 2** *(Vareille 58, Wright 74)* 2154
*Stirling Albion:* McGeown; Paterson A, Deas, Carberry, McQuilter, Paterson G, Bone, Tait, McLaren (McCormick), Taggart, Gibson.
*Kilmarnock:* Meldrum; MacPherson, Baker, Anderson, McGowne, Reilly, Nevin, Findlay (Mitchell), Wright, Vareille, Burke (McIntyre).


## QUARTER-FINALS

### 9 SEPT

**Dunfermline Ath (0) 1** *(Moore 114)*
**Hearts (0) 0** *aet* 11,106
*Dunfermline Ath:* Westwater; Shields, Fleming, Tod, Barnett, Curran (Miller C), Moore, Bingham (Den Bieman), Smith, French, Petrie (Millar M).
*Hearts:* Rousset; McManus (Locke), Pointon, Weir, Salvatori (Robertson), Ritchie, McCann, Fulton (Flögel), Hamilton, Cameron, Adam.


**Rangers (0) 0**
**Dundee U (0) 1** *(McSwegan 98)* 44,440
*Rangers:* Goram; Cleland, Stensaas, Porrini (Van Vossen), Moore, Vidmar, Miller (McCoist), Ferguson, Negri, Albertz (McCall), Gattuso.
*Dundee U:* Dijkstra; McKinnon, Malpas, Pressley, Perry, Pedersen, Olofsson (McSwegan), Zetterlund, Winters (Easton), Dolan, McLaren.
*aet*


### 10 SEPT

**Celtic (1) 1** *(Larsson 29)*
**Motherwell (0) 0** 35,582
*Celtic:* Gould; Boyd, Mahe, Hannah, Mackay, O'Donnell, Larsson, Burley, Donnelly, Thom (McKinlay), Blinker (McNamara).

*Motherwell:* Woods; May, McMillan (Ross), Christie (Shivute), Martin, Denham, Weir, Valakari (McCulloch), Coyne T, Falconer, Coyle O.

**Stirling Albion (0) 0**
**Aberdeen (2) 2** *(Miller 8, Glass 17)* 3370
*Stirling Albion:* McGeown; Paterson A, Deas, Carberry (Bain), McQuilter, Paterson G, Bone, Tait, McCormick, Gibson (McLaren), Bennett.
*Aberdeen:* Leighton; Rowson, Tzvetanov (Kombouare), Bernard, Inglis, O'Neil, Miller, Jess, Newell, Dodds (Windass), Glass (Gillies).


## SEMI-FINALS

### 14 OCT

(at Ibrox Stadium)
**Dunfermline Ath (0) 0**
**Celtic (0) 1** *(Burley 69)* 27,796
*Dunfermline Ath:* Westwater; Shields, Millar M (Miller C), Tod, Barnett, Duarte (Den Bieman), Moore, Curran, Smith, French, Bingham (Britton).
*Celtic:* Gould; Boyd, Mahe, McNamara, Rieper, Stubbs, Larsson, Burley, Donnelly, O'Donnell, Blinker (Thom).

### 15 OCT

(at Tynecastle Stadium)
**Aberdeen (0) 1** *(Windass 47)*
**Dundee U (1) 3** *(Winters 34, 70, Easton 54)* 10,459
*Aberdeen:* Leighton; Smith (Gillies), Tzvetanov, Bernard, Inglis (Kombouare), O'Neil, Miller, Rowson, Newell, Windass, Glass.
*Dundee U:* Dijkstra; Bowman, Malpas, Pressley, Perry (Skoldmark), Pedersen, Olofsson, Zetterlund, Winters, Dolan (McLaren), Easton.


## FINAL AT IBROX STADIUM

### 30 NOV

**Celtic (2) 3** *(Rieper 20, Larsson 23, Burley 58)*
**Dundee U (0) 0** 49,305
*Celtic:* Gould; Boyd, Mahe, McNamara (Annoni), Rieper, Stubbs, Larsson, Burley, Thom (Donnelly), Wieghorst, Blinker (Lambert).
*Dundee U:* Dijkstra; Skoldmark (McSwegan), Malpas, Pressley, Perry, Pedersen, Olofsson, Zetterlund, Winters, Easton, Bowman.
*Referee:* J. McCluskey (Stewarton)

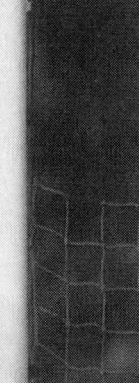

A jubilant Craig Burley acknowledges his third goal for Celtic against Dundee United in the Scottish Coca-Cola Cup Final. (Action Images)

# SCOTTISH CUP FINALS 1874–1998

| Year | Winners | Runners-up | Score |
|------|---------|------------|-------|
| 1874 | Queen's Park | Clydesdale | 2-0 |
| 1875 | Queen's Park | Renton | 3-0 |
| 1876 | Queen's Park | Third Lanark | 2-0 after 1-1 draw |
| 1877 | Vale of Leven | Rangers | 3-2 after 0-0 and 1-1 draws |
| 1878 | Vale of Leven | Third Lanark | 1-0 |
| 1879 | Vale of Leven* | Rangers | |
| 1880 | Queen's Park | Thornlibank | 3-0 |
| 1881 | Queen's Park† | Dumbarton | 3-1 |
| 1882 | Queen's Park | Dumbarton | 4-1 after 2-2 draw |
| 1883 | Dumbarton | Vale of Leven | 2-1 after 2-2 draw |
| 1884 | Queen's Park‡ | Vale of Leven | |
| 1885 | Renton | Vale of Leven | 3-1 after 0-0 draw |
| 1886 | Queen's Park | Renton | 3-1 |
| 1887 | Hibernian | Dumbarton | 2-1 |
| 1888 | Renton | Cambuslang | 6-1 |
| 1889 | Third Lanark§ | Celtic | 2-1 |
| 1890 | Queen's Park | Vale of Leven | 2-1 after 1-1 draw |
| 1891 | Hearts | Dumbarton | 1-0 |
| 1892 | Celtic¶ | Queen's Park | 5-1 |
| 1893 | Queen's Park | Celtic | 2-1 |
| 1894 | Rangers | Celtic | 3-1 |
| 1895 | St Bernard's | Renton | 2-1 |
| 1896 | Hearts | Hibernian | 3-1 |
| 1897 | Rangers | Dumbarton | 5-1 |
| 1898 | Rangers | Kilmarnock | 2-0 |
| 1899 | Celtic | Rangers | 2-0 |
| 1900 | Celtic | Queen's Park | 4-3 |
| 1901 | Hearts | Celtic | 4-3 |
| 1902 | Hibernian | Celtic | 1-0 |
| 1903 | Rangers | Hearts | 2-0 after 1-1 and 0-0 draws |
| 1904 | Celtic | Rangers | 3-2 |
| 1905 | Third Lanark | Rangers | 3-1 after 0-0 draw |
| 1906 | Hearts | Third Lanark | 1-0 |
| 1907 | Celtic | Hearts | 3-0 |
| 1908 | Celtic | St Mirren | 5-1 |
| 1909 | •• | | |
| 1910 | Dundee | Clyde | 2-1 after 2-2 and 0-0 draws |
| 1911 | Celtic | Hamilton A | 2-0 after 0-0 draw |
| 1912 | Celtic | Clyde | 2-0 |
| 1913 | Falkirk | Raith R | 2-0 |
| 1914 | Celtic | Hibernian | 4-1 after 0-0 draw |
| 1920 | Kilmarnock | Albion R | 3-2 |
| 1921 | Partick T | Rangers | 1-0 |
| 1922 | Morton | Rangers | 1-0 |
| 1923 | Celtic | Hibernian | 1-0 |
| 1924 | Airdrieonians | Hibernian | 2-0 |
| 1925 | Celtic | Dundee | 2-1 |
| 1926 | St Mirren | Celtic | 2-0 |
| 1927 | Celtic | East Fife | 3-1 |
| 1928 | Rangers | Celtic | 4-0 |
| 1929 | Kilmarnock | Rangers | 2-0 |
| 1930 | Rangers | Partick T | 2-1 after 0-0 draw |
| 1931 | Celtic | Motherwell | 4-2 after 2-2 draw |
| 1932 | Rangers | Kilmarnock | 3-0 after 1-1 draw |
| 1933 | Celtic | Motherwell | 1-0 |
| 1934 | Rangers | St Mirren | 5-0 |
| 1935 | Rangers | Hamilton A | 2-1 |
| 1936 | Rangers | Third Lanark | 1-0 |
| 1937 | Celtic | Aberdeen | 2-1 |
| 1938 | East Fife | Kilmarnock | 4-2 after 1-1 draw |
| 1939 | Clyde | Motherwell | 4-0 |
| 1947 | Aberdeen | Hibernian | 2-1 |
| 1948 | Rangers | Morton | 1-0 after 1-1 draw |
| 1949 | Rangers | Clyde | 4-1 |
| 1950 | Rangers | East Fife | 3-0 |
| 1951 | Celtic | Motherwell | 1-0 |
| 1952 | Motherwell | Dundee | 4-0 |
| 1953 | Rangers | Aberdeen | 1-0 after 1-1 draw |
| 1954 | Celtic | Aberdeen | 2-1 |
| 1955 | Clyde | Celtic | 1-0 after 1-1 draw |
| 1956 | Hearts | Celtic | 3-1 |
| 1957 | Falkirk | Kilmarnock | 2-1 after 1-1 draw |
| 1958 | Clyde | Hibernian | 1-0 |
| 1959 | St Mirren | Aberdeen | 3-1 |
| 1960 | Rangers | Kilmarnock | 2-0 |
| 1961 | Dunfermline Ath | Celtic | 2-0 after 0-0 draw |
| 1962 | Rangers | St Mirren | 2-0 |
| 1963 | Rangers | Celtic | 3-0 after 1-1 draw |
| 1964 | Rangers | Dundee | 3-1 |

| Year | Winners | Runners-up | Score |
|------|---------|------------|-------|
| 1965 | Celtic | Dunfermline Ath | 3-2 |
| 1966 | Rangers | Celtic | 1-0 after 0-0 draw |
| 1967 | Celtic | Aberdeen | 2-0 |
| 1968 | Dunfermline Ath | Hearts | 3-1 |
| 1969 | Celtic | Rangers | 4-0 |
| 1970 | Aberdeen | Celtic | 3-1 |
| 1971 | Celtic | Rangers | 2-1 after 1-1 draw |
| 1972 | Celtic | Hibernian | 6-1 |
| 1973 | Rangers | Celtic | 3-2 |
| 1974 | Celtic | Dundee U | 3-0 |
| 1975 | Celtic | Airdrieonians | 3-1 |
| 1976 | Rangers | Hearts | 3-1 |
| 1977 | Celtic | Rangers | 1-0 |
| 1978 | Rangers | Aberdeen | 2-1 |
| 1979 | Rangers | Hibernian | 3-2 after 0-0 and 0-0 draws |
| 1980 | Celtic | Rangers | 1-0 |
| 1981 | Rangers | Dundee U | 4-1 after 0-0 draw |
| 1982 | Aberdeen | Rangers | 4-1 (aet) |
| 1983 | Aberdeen | Rangers | 1-0 (aet) |
| 1984 | Aberdeen | Celtic | 2-1 (aet) |
| 1985 | Celtic | Dundee U | 2-1 |
| 1986 | Aberdeen | Hearts | 3-0 |
| 1987 | St Mirren | Dundee U | 1-0 (aet) |
| 1988 | Celtic | Dundee U | 2-1 |
| 1989 | Celtic | Rangers | 1-0 |
| 1990 | Aberdeen | Celtic | 0-0 (aet) |
|      |         | *(Aberdeen won 9-8 on penalties)* |  |
| 1991 | Motherwell | Dundee U | 4-3 (aet) |
| 1992 | Rangers | Airdrieonians | 2-1 |
| 1993 | Rangers | Aberdeen | 2-1 |
| 1994 | Dundee U | Rangers | 1-0 |
| 1995 | Celtic | Airdrieonians | 1-0 |
| 1996 | Rangers | Hearts | 5-1 |
| 1997 | Kilmarnock | Falkirk | 1-0 |
| 1998 | Hearts | Rangers | 2-1 |

*Vale of Leven awarded cup, Rangers failing to appear for replay after 1-1 draw.
†After Dumbarton protested the first game, which Queen's Park won 2-1.
‡Queen's Park awarded cup, Vale of Leven failing to appear.
§Replay by order of Scottish FA because of playing conditions in first match, won 3-0 by Third Lanark.
¶After mutually protested game which Celtic won 1-0.
••Owing to riot, the cup was withheld after two drawn games – between Celtic and Rangers 2-2 and 1-1.

## SCOTTISH CUP WINS

Celtic 30, Rangers 27, Queen's Park 10, Aberdeen 7, Hearts 6, Clyde 3, Kilmarnock 3, St Mirren 3, Vale of Leven 3, Dunfermline Ath 2, Falkirk 2, Hibernian 2, Motherwell 2, Renton 2, Third Lanark 2, Airdrieonians 1, Dumbarton 1, Dundee 1, Dundee U 1, East Fife 1, Morton 1, Partick T 1, St Bernard's 1.

## APPEARANCES IN FINAL

Celtic 47, Rangers 44, Aberdeen 14, Queen's Park 12, Hearts 12, Hibernian 10, Kilmarnock 8, Vale of Leven 7, Clyde 6, Dumbarton 6, St Mirren 6, Third Lanark 6, Dundee U 7, Motherwell 6, Renton 5, Airdrieonians 4, Dundee 4, Dunfermline Ath 3, East Fife 3, Falkirk 3, Hamilton A 2, Morton 2, Partick T 2, Albion R 1, Cambuslang 1, Clydesdale 1, Raith R 1, St Bernard's 1, Thornlibank 1.

Hearts take the lead against Rangers in the Scottish Cup Final with a Colin Cameron penalty. (Action Images)

# TENNENTS SCOTTISH CUP 1997–98

**FIRST ROUND**

**6 DEC**

**Cowdenbeath (0) 0**

**Montrose (0) 0**      300

*Cowdenbeath:* Hutchison; Hamilton, Meldrum, Humphreys, Cook, Welsh (Brown), Winter, Sinclair, Stewart, Hunter (Millar), Ritchie (Baillie).
*Montrose:* Larter; Tindal, Watt, Coulston (Henry), Wylie, Craib, Andrew (Winiarski), Masson P, McGlashan, Taylor, MacDonald.

**East Fife (1) 2** *(Johnston 40, Moffat 85)*

**Stranraer (1) 3** *(Kinnaird 42, Knox 68, George 86)*    497

*East Fife:* McCulloch; Strathdee, Ryan, Ritchie, Johnston, Gillies (Moffat), Allan, Donaghy, Dyer, Ronald, Abercromby.
*Stranraer:* Matthews; Knox, Black, George, Campbell, Watson, Lansdowne, McAulay, Frew, Docherty, Kinnaird.

**Inverness CT (2) 3** *(Stewart 4 (pen), 19, Wilson 79)*

**Whitehill Welfare (0) 1** *(Martin 66)*      1173

*Inverness CT:* Calder; Teasdale, Andersen, McCulloch, Hastings, Cherry, Wilson, Stewart, Shearer (Ross), Thomson (Tokely), Robson (Addicoat).
*Whitehill Welfare:* Cantley; Jardine (Wood), Gowrie, Purves, Sneddon H, Millar, Thorburn, Bennett, McGovern (Sneddon M), Martin, Tulloch.

**FIRST ROUND REPLAY**

**9 DEC**

**Montrose (1) 2** *(McGlashan 45, Taylor 50)*

**Cowdenbeath (0) 1** *(Winter 63)*      349

*Montrose:* Larter; Tindal, Watt, Coulston, Wylie, Craib, Henry (Winiarski), Masson P (Mailer), McGlashan, Taylor, MacDonald (Andrew).
*Cowdenbeath:* Hutchison; Hamilton, Meldrum, Cook, Humphreys, Welsh (Millar), Winter, Sinclair, Stewart, Hunter (Manson), Ritchie (Brown).

**FIRST ROUND**

**13 DEC**

**Fraserburgh (1) 1** *(Keith 9)*

**Clyde (0) 0**      270

*Fraserburgh:* Gordon; Milne, Scott R (Michie), Young, Stephen, Murray, Scott J, McBride, Keith, Hunter, Stephen.
*Clyde:* McLean; McStay, Tortolano, King, Baptie, Rice, McPhee (McInulty), Campbell (Carrigan), Scott (Donaldson), Gibson, Brownlie.

**SECOND ROUND**

**3 JAN**

**Annan Ath (0) 3** *(Montgomery 60, 79, Gillie 76 (og))*

**Vale of Leithen (1) 1** *(Hood 7)*      1029

*Annan Ath:* McColm; Middlemiss, Proudfoot, Elliot, Sutherland, Brown, Hewitt, Cochrane, Brydson, Montgomery, Nicoll (Smith).
*Vale of Leithen:* Reid; Hood (Biggs), Wallace, Fairgrieve, Curran, Gillie, Notman, Whiteford, Rathie (Diamond), Moffat (Darling), Selkirk.

**Forfar Ath (0) 1** *(Honeyman 55)*

**Albion R (0) 2** *(McKilligan 61, Dickson 86)*    660

*Forfar Ath:* Donegan; Allison, Craig, Hamilton, Mann, Ferguson, McLauchlan, Nairn, Honeyman, Cargill, Gray.
*Albion R:* Ross S; McKilligan, Sinclair, Coyle, Martin, Melvin, Gardner (Dickson), Shepherd, Watters (Ross A), Bruce, Harty.

**Inverness CT (0) 2** *(Robson 52, Stewart 59)*

**Queen's Park (0) 0**      1281

*Inverness CT:* Calder; Teasdale, Andersen, McCulloch, Hastings, Cherry, Ross (Shearer), Thomson, Stewart, Robertson, Robson (Addicoat).
*Queen's Park:* Hamilton; Orr (Ferry), Miller, King, McNamee, Maxwell, Arbuckle, O'Brien, Edgar, Mercer, Caven.

**Lossiemouth (0) 0**

**Dumbarton (0) 1** *(McCuaig 58)*      509

*Lossiemouth:* McRitchie M; Fiske, Mair, Masson, Gerrard, Smith (McLean), Rattary, Cormack, McKenzie (Richmond), Caldwell, Clinton.
*Dumbarton:* Meechan K; Wilson, Sharp, Currie, Bruce, Meechan J, Ward (Mellis), Mooney, McKinnon, McCuaig (Reilly), Brittain.

**Peterhead (0) 0**

**Alloa Ath (1) 2** *(Mackay 33, Irvine 84)*    1150

*Peterhead:* Pirie; Clark S, Cheyne, King, Simpson, Yule, Smith, Baxter, Milne (Clark G), Brown, Livingstone (McKenzie).
*Alloa Ath:* Cairns; Valentine, Haddow, Nelson (McAneny), Cowan, Gilmour (Ramsay), Wilson, Mackay, Simpson, Irvine, Pew (Cameron).

**Ross Co (1) 3** *(Adams 37, 49, 82)*

**Brechin C (0) 1** *(Sorbie 69)*      1296

*Ross Co:* Walker; Farrell, McBain, Herd, Haro, Mackay, Ferguson, Adams, Wood (Campbell), Gilbert (Tarrant), Taylor.
*Brechin C:* Garden; Baillie, Campbell, Cairney, Christie, Farnan (McKellar), Feroz (Hutcheon), Smart, Sorbie, McNeill, Black.

**6 JAN**

**Arbroath (1) 1** *(Cooper 38)*

**Queen of the S (0) 1** *(McAllister 58)*    767

*Arbroath:* Wight; Mitchell, Gallagher, McAulay, Thomson, Crawford, Cooper, Thomson, Spence (Grant), McWalter, Burns.
*Queen of the S:* Mathieson; Kennedy, Aitken (Weir), Rowe, Thomson, Townsley, Connor, Bryce (Leslie), Mallan, Eadie, McAllister.

**7 JAN**

**Livingston (0) 2** *(Harvey 61, McMartin 68)*

**Berwick R (0) 1** *(Irvine 67)*      509

*Livingstone:* McCaldon; Watson, Duthie, Williamson, Conway, Raynes, McMartin, Forrest, Harvey (Young), Bailey (Magee), Maskrey (Foster).
*Berwick R:* O'Connor; McNicoll, Finlayson, Fraser, Beaton, Rafferty (Forrester), Neil, Irvine, Martin, Clark (Smith), Walton.

**10 JAN**

**East Stirling (0) 1** *(Watt 61)*

**Edinburgh City (0) 1** *(Wallace 72)*    448

*East Stirling:* Balfour; Hamilton, Neill, Campbell, Gardiner, Ross, Parks (Patterson), Watt, Kennedy, McPherson, Muirhead.
*Edinburgh City:* MacIntosh; Catterson, Wallace (Devine), Summerville, Erskine, Nolan P, Scott (Henderson), Irving, Foggo, Nolan T, Vaughan (Doig).

**Stenhousemuir (1) 4** *(McCutcheon 23, 87, Law 53, Hutchison 60)*

**Deveronvale (0) 0**      689

*Stenhousemuir:* Alexander; Farrell, Banks, Armstrong, Innes, Hutchison (Sprott), Law, Fisher (Kane), McCutcheon, Christie (Roseburgh), Little.
*Deveronvale:* Grant; Watt, Simmers (Milne), Montgomery, Henderson, Anderson, Christie (Binnie), Douglas, Rowley, Stewart (Ellis), Dolan.

**Stranraer (2) 2** *(Kinnaird 2, 26)*
**Fraserburgh (0) 1** *(Hunter 85)* 612
*Stranraer:* Matthews; Knox, Black, George, Campbell, Watson, McAulay, Lansdowne, Young (English), Docherty, Kinnaird.
*Fraserburgh:* Gordon; Milne, Michie, Scott (Thomson), Stephen, Young (Killoh), Norris, McBride (McCafferty), Keith, Hunter, Stephen.

**12 JAN**

**Clydebank (3) 6** *(Brown 4, Murdoch 24, McWilliams 38, Ward 58, Nichols 70, Lovering 74)*
**Montrose (0) 0** 263
*Clydebank:* McFarlane; Wishart, Lovering, Murdoch (Miller), McLaughlin, Brannigan, Nichols, McDonald (Adams), Brown, Docherty, McWilliams (Ward).
*Montrose:* Larter (Watt); Mailer, Winiarski, Craib, Wylie, Coulston, Andrew (Hutton), MacDonald (Henry), McGlashan, Higgins, Taylor.

**SECOND ROUND REPLAYS**

**12 JAN**

**Edinburgh City (0) 0**
**East Stirling (0) 0** 460
*Edinburgh City:* MacIntosh; Catterson, Hume, Devine, Erskine, Summerville, Scott (Doig), Irving, Foggo, Nolan T, Vaughan (Henderson).
*East Stirling:* McDougall; Hamilton (Cochrane), Neill, Barr, Gardiner, Ross, Patterson, Watt, Kennedy (Parks), McPherson, Muirhead.
*aet (Edinburgh City won 4-3 on penalties)*

**Queen of the S (3) 4** *(Eadie 8, Bryce 22, Mallan 38, Townsley 73)*
**Arbroath (0) 0** 2167
*Queen of the S:* Mathieson; Kennedy, Aitken (Weir), Rowe, Thomson, Townsley (Cleeland), Connor, Bryce (Leslie), Mallan, Eadie, McAllister.
*Arbroath:* Hinchcliffe; Mitchell, Gallagher, McAulay, Thomson (Peters), Crawford, Florence, Thomson, Spence (Scott), Grant, Burns.

**THIRD ROUND**

**24 JAN**

**Airdrieonians (2) 2** *(McPhee 17, Cooper 21)*
**Ross Co (1) 2** *(Haro 42, Ferguson 79)* 1834
*Airdrieonians:* Martin; Jack, Smith, Sandison, Sweeney, Mackay (Connelly G), Davies, Wilson, Cooper, Connolly P (Johnston), McPhee.
*Ross Co:* Walker; Farrell, Mackay, Herd, Haro (MacPherson), Gilbert, Ferguson, Adams, Wood (Tarrant), Taylor, McBain.

**Alloa Ath (0) 0**
**Ayr U (1) 3** *(Ferguson 19, 64, 90)* 941
*Alloa Ath:* Cairns; Valentine, Haddow (McCormack), Nelson, Cowan, Gilmour (Ramsay), Wilson, Mackay, Simpson, Irvine, Pew (McAneny).
*Ayr U:* Castilla; Robertson, Bowman, Millen, Burns, Traynor, Donowa, D'Jaffo (Hogg), Ferguson, Henderson, Bonar (Agnew).

**Celtic (1) 2** *(Brattbakk 7, Jackson 84)*
**Greenock Morton (0) 0** 39,933
*Celtic:* Gould; Boyd, Mahe (Annoni), McNamara, Rieper, Stubbs, Larsson, Burley, Brattbakk (Jackson), Lambert, Blinker (Wieghorst).
*Greenock Morton:* Hillcoat; Collins, Archdeacon, Aitken (Juttla), Anderson, Reid, Blair, Mahood (McGraw), Duffield, Hawke, Blaikie (McPherson).

**Dumbarton (0) 1** *(Sharp 75 (pen))*
**Motherwell (0) 1** *(McSkimming 48)* 2412
*Dumbarton:* Meechan K; Wilson, Brittain (Grace), Bruce, Gow, Sharp, McCuaig (Ward), Meechan J, Flannery (Glancy), Mooney, McKinnon.
*Motherwell:* Woods; May (Philliben), McMillan, Newman, Martin, Falconer, Weir, McCulloch, Coyne T, McSkimming, Coyle O (Arnott).

**Dundee U (1) 1** *(Winters 13)*
**Aberdeen (0) 0** 11,669
*Dundee U:* Dijkstra; Skoldmark, Malpas, Pressley, Perry, Pedersen, Olofsson, Zetterlund, Winters (McSwegan), Jonsson, McLaren.
*Aberdeen:* Leighton; Bernard, Whyte, O'Neil B (O'Neill M), Inglis, Smith, Kiriakov, Jess, Windass, Dodds (Newell), Glass.

**Dunfermline Ath (3) 7** *(Miller 3, Robertson 6, Smith 32, 60, 69, 73 (pen), 77)*
**Edinburgh City (1) 2** *(Foggo 16, Nolan T 88)* 4191
*Dunfermline Ath:* Westwater; Shields, Miller, Tod, Barnett, Curran, Moore, Robertson (Den Bieman), Smith (McDonald), French (Shaw), Petrie.
*Edinburgh City:* MacIntosh; Catterson, Devine, Summerville, Erskine, Nolan P (Hume), Scott (Doig), Irving (Henderson), Foggo, Nolan T, Vaughan.

**Hamilton A (1) 1** *(McCormick 31)*
**Rangers (1) 2** *(Durie 42, Gough 90)* 11,915
*Hamilton A:* McCondichie; Thomson, Renicks, McEntegart, Cunnington, Craig, McCormick, Sherry (McQuade), Ritchie, Clark, McKenzie.
*Rangers:* Goram; Cleland, Stensaas (Albertz), Gough, Porrini, Bjorklund, Thern, Gascoigne (Johansson), Durie, Ferguson B (McCall), Laudrup.

**Hearts (1) 2** *(Flögel 31, Weir 61)*
**Clydebank (0) 0** 12,699
*Hearts:* McKenzie; Locke, Naysmith, Weir, Salvatori, Ritchie, McCann (Cameron), Fulton, Adam, Flögel (Quitongo), Hamilton (Robertson).
*Clydebank:* MacFarlane; Wishart, Lovering, Murdoch, McLaughlin, Brannigan, Nicholls, McDonald (Brown), Adams, Docherty (Ward), McWilliams (Miller).

**Hibernian (1) 1** *(McGinlay 22)*
**Raith R (2) 2** *(Millar 10,21)* 11,411
*Hibernian:* Reid; Miller W, Boco, Dods, Dennis, Dow (Charnley), Harper, Jackson (Lavety), Crawford, Walker, McGinlay.
*Raith R:* Van De Kamp; McEwan, Thomson, Kirkwood (Galloway), Browne, Fotheringham, Hartley (Stein), Lennon, Dargo (Dair J), Wright, Millar.

**Inverness CT (4) 8** *(Wilson 14, 84, Stewart 17, Thomson 20, 55, Robson 38, Leslie 74 (og), Shearer 86)*
**Annan Ath (1) 1** *(Montgomery 8)* 1836
*Inverness CT:* Calder; Teasdale, Andersen, McCulloch, Hastings, Cherry (Tokely), Wilson, Thomson, Stewart, Robertson, Robson (Shearer).
*Annan Ath:* McColm; Smith, Leslie, Elliot, Sutherland, Brown, Middlemiss, Cochrane, Brydson, Montgomery (Hewitt), Proudfoot (Pratt).

**Livingston (2) 3** *(Forrest 8, Duthie 22 (pen), Harvey 56)*
**Albion R (2) 3** *(Watters 30, Sinclair 43, Ross A 89)* 1187
*Livingston:* McCaldon; Watson, Duthie, Davidson, Williamson, Conway, McMartin, Forrest, Harvey (Young), Bailey (Foster), Raynes.
*Albion R:* Ross S; McKilligan, Sinclair, Coyle, Martin, Melvin, Gardner, Mitchell, Watters, Bruce (Dickson), Harty (Ross A).

**Queen of the S (1) 1** *(Weir 38)*
**Stirling Albion (1) 3** *(Bone 41, 80, Tait 65)* 2551
*Queen of the S:* Mathieson; Leslie, Aitken, Rowe, Thomson, Townsley, Connor, Bryce (Cleeland), Mallan, Eadie, Weir.
*Stirling Albion:* McGeown; Paterson A, Deas, Tait, Lumsden, Paterson G, Bone, Gibson, Price, Zahana-Oni, Bennett.

**St Johnstone (1) 1** *(Kernaghan 3)*

**Partick T (0) 0**                    4760

*St Johnstone:* Main; McQuillan, Preston, Kane, Weir, Kernaghan, Scott (Tosh), O'Neil, Grant, O'Boyle, Jenkinson.
*Partick T:* Arthur; Watson, Archibald, Milne, Gaughan, Macdonald (Nicolson), Boyle, Henderson, Lawrence, Dunn (Martin), Lyons.

**Stenhousemuir (0) 1** *(Little 64)*

**Falkirk (2) 3** *(Hagen 5, Moss 33, Crabbe 85)*    2654

*Stenhousemuir:* Ellison; Sprott, Banks, Armstrong, Innes, Hutchison, Law, Farnell (Kane), McCutcheon, Christie, Little.
*Falkirk:* Mathers; Oliver, Seaton, McGowan, James, Hagen, McAllister, Craig, Crabbe, Moss (Hamilton), Keith.

**Stranraer (0) 0**

**Kilmarnock (1) 2** *(Vareille 35, Roberts 49)*    4304

*Stranraer:* Matthews; Knox, Black, McIntyre, Campbell, Watson, McAulay, Lansdowne, Young (Ramsay), English, Kinnaird.
*Kilmarnock:* Marshall; MacPherson, Kerr, Lauchlan, McGowne, Reilly, Mitchell, Holt, Wright, Roberts, Vareille.

**25 JAN**

**Dundee (3) 4** *(McCormick 14, Grady 21, 56, Maddison 44)*

**St Mirren (0) 2** *(Watson 61, Iwelumo 89)*    4877

*Dundee:* Douglas; Smith, Maddison, Adamczuk, Irvine (Elliott), Rogers, Anderson, Kelly, McCormick (Annand), Grady, McInally (Fleming).
*St Mirren:* Combe; Smith, McLaughlin, McWhirter, Fenwick, Watson, Murray (Taylor), Turner (Hetherston), Iwelumo, McGarry (Yardley), Roddie.

**THIRD ROUND REPLAYS**

**27 JAN**

**Motherwell (0) 1** *(Coyle 75)*

**Dumbarton (0) 0**                    4202

*Motherwell:* Woods; May (Arnott), McMillan, Newman, Martin, Falconer, Weir (Philliben), McCulloch, Coyne, McSkimming (Davies), Coyle.
*Dumbarton:* Meechan K; Wilson, Brittain, Bruce, Gow, Mooney, Grace (Ward), Meechan J, McKinnon, Flannery (Glancy), Sharp.

**2 FEB**

**Albion R (0) 0**

**Livingston (0) 0**                    617

*Albion R:* Ross S; McKilligan, Sinclair (Dickson), Coyle, Martin, Melvin, Mitchell, Shepherd (Harty), Watters, Gardner, Ross A (Bruce).
*Livingston:* McCaldon; Watson, Raynes, Graham, Williamson, McLeod (Alleyne), McMartin, Forrest, Harvey, Young, Magee.
*aet (Albion R won 6-5 on penalties)*

**3 FEB**

**Ross Co (0) 1** *(Adams 89 (pen))*

**Airdrieonians (0) 0**                    2314

*Ross Co:* Walker; Mackay, McBain, Herd, Haro, Gilbert, Ferguson, Wood, MacPherson (Adams), Farrell, Taylor.
*Airdrieonians:* Martin; Johnston, Jack (McCann), Sandison, Sweeney, Black, Mackay, Davies (Connolly P), Cooper, McPhee, Smith.

**FOURTH ROUND**

**14 FEB**

**Ayr U (0) 2** *(Dick 83, Ferguson 85)*

**Kilmarnock (0) 0**                    9286

*Ayr U:* Finnbogason; Robertson, Hogg (D'Jaffo), Millen, Burns, Anderson, Dick, Traynor, Ferguson, Agnew, Bowman.
*Kilmarnock:* Marshall; MacPherson, Baker, Lauchlan, McGowne, Reilly, Mitchell (Bagan), Holt, Wright, Roberts (Henry), Vareille (McIntyre).

**Dundee U (0) 1** *(Olofsson 81)*

**Inverness CT (1) 1** *(Sheerin 27)*    8770

*Dundee U:* Dijkstra; Jonsson, Malpas, Pressley, Perry, Pedersen, Olofsson, McKinnon (McLaren), McSwegan, Dolan (Marklund), Misse-Misse (Skoldmark)).
*Inverness CT:* Calder; Teasdale, Andersen, McCulloch, Hastings, Cherry, Wilson (Ross), Thomson, Stewart (Shearer), Robertson, Sheerin.

**Hearts (0) 3** *(Quitongo 61, 88, Cameron 66 (pen))*

**Albion R (0) 0**                    12,634

*Hearts:* Rousset; Murie, Naysmith, Weir, Fulton, Ritchie, McCann, Flögel (Robertson), Quitongo, Cameron, Hamilton (Adam).
*Albion R:* Ross S; Greenock, McKilligan, Coyle, Melvin, Shepherd (Dickson), Gardner, Mitchell (Ross A), Watters, Harty (Bruce), Sinclair.

**Motherwell (1) 2** *(Coyne 19, Gough 77 (og))*

**Rangers (1) 2** *(Negri 26, Durie 83)*    12,602

*Motherwell:* Woods; May, McMillan, Newman, Martin, Falconer, Christie, Garcin (Valakari), Coyne, Arnott (McCulloch), Coyle.
*Rangers:* Goram; Cleland, Albertz, Gough, Porrini, Bjorklund, Durie, Gascoigne (Johansson), Negri, McCall, Gattuso (Ferguson B).

**Raith R (0) 1** *(Thomson 84)*

**Falkirk (2) 3** *(Keith 21, Crabbe 38, McAllister 64)*    6259

*Raith R:* Van De Kamp; McCulloch (Galloway), Thomson, Millar, Browne, Fotheringham, Hartley, Lennon, Dargo (Stein), Wright, Dair J (Dair L).
*Falkirk:* Mathers; Corrigan, Seaton, McGowan, Oliver (Lawrie), McKenzie, McAllister, Craig, Crabbe (Hagen), Moss (Hamilton), Keith.

**Ross Co (0) 1** *(Adams 54)*

**Dundee (0) 1** *(McGlashan 62)*    4500

*Ross Co:* Walker; Mackay, McBain (Golabek), Herd, Haro, Gilbert, Farrell, Adams, MacPherson (Wood), Escalon (Hart), King.
*Dundee:* Douglas; Smith, Fleming, Tully (Adamczuk), Irvine, Rogers, Anderson, McGlashan, McCormick (Annand), Grady, McInally.

**St Johnstone (1) 3** *(Dasovic 45, O'Boyle 78 (pen), Lumsden 90 (og))*

**Stirling Albion (0) 1** *(Tait 87)*    3063

*St Johnstone:* Main; McQuillan, Preston, Dasovic, Weir, Kernaghan, Tosh (O'Neil), Wright (O'Halloran), Kane, O'Boyle, Jenkinson.
*Stirling Albion:* McGeown; Paterson A, Deas, Tait, Lumsden, Paterson G, Bone (Hjartarson), Gibson (Nilsen), Price, Zahana-Oni, Bennett.

**16 FEB**

**Dunfermline Ath (0) 1** *(Bingham 81)*

**Celtic (0) 2** *(Mahe 50, Brattbakk 67)*    12,322

*Dunfermline Ath:* Westwater; Shields, McCulloch, Tod, Barnett, Fraser (French), Shaw (Bingham), Robertson, Smith, Den Bieman (Curran), Petrie.
*Celtic:* Gould; Boyd, Mahe, McNamara (Donnelly), Rieper, Stubbs, Larsson, Burley, Brattbakk (Jackson), Lambert, Wieghorst.

## FOURTH ROUND REPLAYS

**17 FEB**

**Dundee (0) 3** *(Annand 49, 75, Raeside 52)*
**Ross Co (0) 0** 4307
*Dundee:* Douglas; Smith, Raeside (Tully), Adamczuk, Irvine, Rogers, Anderson, McGlashan (Fleming), Annand, Grady (McCormick), McInally.
*Ross Co:* Walker; Farrell, McBain, Herd, Haro, Gilbert, Ferguson (Taylor), Adams, Wood, Escalon (MacPherson), King.

**Rangers (2) 3** *(Albertz 37, 86, Durie 39)*
**Motherwell (0) 0** 42,011
*Rangers:* Goram; Cleland, Albertz, Gough, Moore, Bjorklund, Ferguson B (McCall), Ferguson I (Gascoigne), Negri, Durie, Laudrup (Rozental).
*Motherwell:* Woods; May, McMillan, Newman, Martin, Falconer, Christie (Valakari), Garcin, Coyne, McSkimming (McCulloch), Coyle.

**18 FEB**

**Inverness CT (0) 2** *(Thomson 86, McCulloch 90)*
**Dundee U (1) 3** *(Olofsson 8, McSwegan 85, Zetterlund 108) aet* 5821
*Inverness CT:* Calder; Teasdale, Andersen (Robson), McCulloch, Hastings, Cherry, Wilson, Thomson, Shearer (Addicoat), Robertson, Sheerin.
*Dundee U:* Dijkstra; Dolan, Malpas, Pressley, Perry, Pedersen, Olofsson, Zetterlund, Winters (Misse-Misse), McKinnon (Skoldmark), McLaren (McSwegan).

## QUARTER-FINALS

**7 MAR**

**Falkirk (2) 3** *(Seaton 19, Moss 34, 48)*
**St Johnstone (0) 0** 6070
*Falkirk:* Mathers; Corrigan, Seaton (McCart), McGowan, Oliver, McKenzie, McAllister (Hamilton), Hagen, Crabbe (McGrillen), Moss, Keith.
*St Johnstone:* Main; McQuillan, Preston, Dasovic (Sekerlioglu), Weir, Kernaghan, Scott (O'Halloran), O'Neil (Grant), Kane, O'Boyle, Jenkinson.

**Hearts (2) 4** *(Ritchie 9, Flögel 17, Fulton 66, Hamilton 83)*
**Ayr U (1) 1** *(Ferguson 19)* 15,761
*Hearts:* Rousset; Locke, Naysmith, Weir, Salvatori (Quitongo), Ritchie, McCann (Callaghan), Fulton, Flögel, Cameron (Murray), Hamilton.
*Ayr U:* Finnbogason; Robertson, Bowman, Millen, Traynor, Anderson, Dick, Agnew, Ferguson, D'Jaffo (Bonar), Burns (Hogg).

**8 MAR**

**Dundee U (1) 2** *(Olofsson 19,52)*
**Celtic (1) 3** *(Brattbakk 11, Wieghorst 56, Pedersen 89 (og))* 12,640
*Dundee U:* Dijkstra; Bowman, Malpas, Pressley (Skoldmark), Perry, Pedersen, Olofsson, Zetterlund, Winters, Dolan (Easton), McLaren (Omoyimni).
*Celtic:* Gould; Boyd, Mahe, Donnelly, Rieper, Stubbs, Larsson, Burley, Brattbakk, Lambert, Wieghorst.

**9 MAR**

**Rangers (0) 0**
**Dundee (0) 0** 40,309
*Rangers:* Goram; Cleland, Albertz, Petric, Porrini (Moore), Bjorklund, Thern (Rozental), McCall, Negri, Ferguson B, Johansson (McCoist).
*Dundee:* Douglas; Smith, Raeside, Adamczuk, Irvine, Rogers, Maddison, Magee (Anderson), Annand (McCormick), Grady, McInally.

## QUARTER-FINAL REPLAY

**18 MAR**

**Dundee (1) 1** *(Grady 11)*
**Rangers (1) 2** *(McCoist 18, 55)* 12,418
*Dundee:* Douglas; Smith, Maddison (Tully), Adamczuk, Irvine, Raeside, Anderson (Rogers), Magee, McCormick, Grady (Annand), McInally.
*Rangers:* Goram; Cleland, Vidmar, Gough, Petric, Moore, McCall, McCoist, Negri, Durrant, Gattuso.

## SEMI-FINALS

**4 APR**

(at Ibrox Stadium)
**Falkirk (0) 1** *(McAllister 85)*
**Hearts (1) 3** *(Adam 5, 89, McCann 90)* 31,587
*Falkirk:* Mathers; Corrigan, Seaton, McGowan, Berry, McKenzie, McAllister, Craig (Hagen), Crabbe, Moss, Keith (McGrillen).
*Hearts:* Rousset; Murray, Naysmith, Weir, Salvatori, Ritchie, McCann, Flögel (Makel) Adam, Cameron (Quitongo), Hamilton.

**5 APR**

(at Celtic Park)
**Celtic (0) 1** *(Burley 90)*
**Rangers (0) 2** *(McCoist 75, Albertz 88)* 48,000
*Celtic:* Gould; Boyd, Annoni, Donnelly, Rieper, Stubbs (Hannah), Larsson, Burley, Brattbakk (Jackson), Lambert, O'Donnell.
*Rangers:* Goram; Cleland, Albertz, Gough, Petric (Amoruso), Bjorklund, Thern, McCoist (Durie), Gattuso, McCall, Laudrup.

## FINAL AT CELTIC PARK

**16 MAY**

**Hearts (1) 2** *(Cameron 1 (pen), Adam 52)*
**Rangers (0) 1** *(McCoist 80)* 48,946
*Hearts:* Rousset; McPherson, Naysmith, Weir, Salvatori, Ritchie, McCann, Fulton, Adam (Hamilton), Cameron, Flögel.
*Rangers:* Goram; Porrini, Stensaas (McCoist), Gough, Amoruso, Bjorklund, Gattuso, Ferguson I, Durie, McCall (Durrant), Laudrup.
*Referee:* W. Young (Clarkston)

# SCOTTISH LEAGUE CHALLENGE CUP 1997-98

**FIRST ROUND**

**9 AUG**

**Stranraer (2) 4** *(Young 15, Docherty 25, Friels 70, Crawford 119)*
**Arbroath (1) 4** *(Thomson 3, Peters 86, Gallagher 90, Spence 116)* 357
*Stranraer:* Matthews; Knox, Black, George, Campbell, Hay (McCrindle), Friels, McIntyre, Young (McAulay), Docherty, Kinnaird (Crawford).
*Arbroath:* Hinchcliffe; Mitchell, Gallagher, McAulay, Crawford, Peters, Cooper, Thomson, McWalter, Spence, Scott.
*aet (Stranraer won 4-2 on penalties)*

**12 AUG**

**Ayr U (1) 3** *(Kerrigan 10, 59, Wordsworth 73)*
**Queen's Park (0) 0** 1255
*Ayr U:* Castilla; Robertson (Jamieson), Bonar P, Hood, Traynor, Love, Bell, Mainge, Kerrigan (English), Wordsworth (McDonald), Kristensen.
*Queen's Park:* Bruce; Rossiter (Wilson D), Cullie, McNamee, Smith J, Maxwell, Hardie, Caven, Edgar, McGoldrick (Mercer), O'Brien.

**Berwick R (1) 1** *(Walton 63)*
**Montrose (0) 0** 321
*Berwick R:* Burgess; Cunningham, Walton, Clark, Finlayson, McNicoll, Ward (Rafferty), Smith P, Forrester, Irvine, Graham.
*Montrose:* Larter; Winiarski, Glass, Mailer, Wylie, Craib, MacDonald, Ferrie (Smith S), McGlashan, Taylor, Smith M.

**Clyde (1) 2** *(Gauley 37, Gibson 60)*
**Raith R (2) 4** *(Wright 12, Cameron 18, Lennon 63, Dair L 72)* 942
*Clyde:* McLean; McStay, Donaldson, Brown (Prunty), Baptie, McInulty, Gibson (McPhee), King, Carrigan, Rice, Gauley (Brownlie).
*Raith R:* Van De Kamp; McEwan, Fotheringham (Mitchell), Kirkwood, Craig, Millen, Lennon, Twaddle (Dair L), Duffield, Wright, Cameron.

**Cowdenbeath (0) 0**
**Clydebank (1) 1** *(Lovering 4)* 173
*Cowdenbeath:* Russell; Munro, Ritchie (Hunter), Humphreys, Jack, Winter, McMahon, Sinclair, Nolan, Stewart (Scott), Bowmaker.
*Clydebank:* MacFarlane; McKinstrey, Lovering, Murdoch, McLaughlin, Brannigan, Teale, Nicholls, Connell, McCall, Docherty.

**Dumbarton (0) 0**
**Falkirk (2) 2** *(Corrigan 12, McGraw 35)* 447
*Dumbarton:* Meechan K; Wilson, Brittain, Melvin, Sharp, Mooney (Reid), Mellis, McKinnon, Reilly, Ward (Hamill), Glancy (Grace).
*Falkirk:* Mathers; Corrigan, Seaton, Oliver, Berry, Hamilton, McAllister, Craig, McGraw, Moss, Hagen (Cunning).

**East Fife (0) 1** *(Dyer 114)*
**St Mirren (0) 0** *aet* 726
*East Fife:* McCulloch; Dixon (MacFarlane), Gibb, Ritchie, Johnston, Gillies, Allan, Ryan (Cusick), Dyer, Ronald, Moffat (McPherson).
*St Mirren:* Combe; Smith, Galloway, Fenwick, Winnie, Watson, Taylor, Dick, Brown, Hetherston (Mendes), Yardley (Iwelumo).

**Forfar Ath (1) 2** *(Mann 3, Glennie 83)*
**East Stirling (0) 1** *(Parks 72)* 298
*Forfar Ath:* Robertson (Nairn); McCheyne, Craig, Hamilton, Mann, Glennie, Allison, Cargill, Loney (McLauchlan), Honeyman, Lee.

*East Stirling:* McDougall; Russell, Neill, Campbell, Gardiner, Barr (Muirhead), Abercromby (Hunter), Watt, Parks, Kennedy (McBride), Patterson.

**Greenock Morton (2) 3** *(Flannery 5, 34, Anderson 76)*
**Albion R (0) 1** *(Bruce 76)* 1502
*Greenock Morton:* Wylie; Collins, Sukalia, Anderson, McCahill, Reid, Flannery, Mahood, Hawke, Morrow (Blair), McArthur (Aitken).
*Albion R:* Ross; McKilligan, McGowan, Coyle, Martin, Duncan, Gardner, Cody (Shepherd), Watters (Harty), Bruce, McInnes (Sinclair).

**Hamilton A (0) 2** *(Ritchie 72, 87)*
**Partick T (1) 1** *(Hetherston 23)* 863
*Hamilton A:* Ferguson; Hillcoat, Renicks, Thomson, McCulloch, Cunnington, Quitongo, Sherry, Ritchie, McCormick, Clark (McEntegart).
*Partick T:* O'Connor; McKenzie, Lyons, Boyle, Tait, Watson (Martin), Evans, Macdonald (Archibald), Farrell, Graham (Adams), Hetherston.

**Stenhousemuir (0) 1** *(Henderson 99)*
**Livingston (0) 1** *(Magee 116)* 460
*Stenhousemuir:* Alexander; Sprott, Banks, Armstrong, Innes, Christie (Brown), Farrell, Fisher, Little (Stewart), Hutchison, Henderson.
*Livingston:* McCaldon; Watson, Duthie, Wright (McMartin), Williamson, Callaghan, Raynes, Alleyne (Davidson)(Laidlaw), Bailey, Young, Magee.
*aet (Livingston won 5-4 on penalties)*

**13 AUG**

**Airdrieonians (0) 1** *(Cooper 88)*
**Dundee (0) 0** 929
*Airdrieonians:* Rhodes; Stewart, McCann, Johnston, Smith, Davies, Lawrence (Connelly G), Wilson, Cooper (McPhee), Mackay (McClelland), Connolly P.
*Dundee:* Douglas; Smith B, Tully, Adamczuk, Irvine (Fotheringham), Rogers, Anderson (Elliott), Magee, O'Driscoll (Annand), Grady, McInally.

**Inverness CT (0) 0**
**Queen of the S (0) 2** *(Flannigan 57, Rowe 67)* 944
*Inverness CT:* Fridge; Teasdale, Hastings, MacArthur, Noble (Christie), Cherry, Wilson, Thomson (Addicoat), Stewart, Andersen, Ross.
*Queen of the S:* Mathieson; MacLeod, McKeown (Aitken), Rowe, Thomson, Townsley (Weir), Irving, Bryce, Mallan, Flannigan (Alexander), Cleeland.

**Stirling Albion (1) 2** *(Paterson G 19, McKechnie 70)*
**Alloa Ath (0) 1** *(Irvine 51)* 532
*Stirling Albion:* Chalmers; Forrest (Paterson A), Deas, Storrar, McQuilter, Paterson G (Mortimer), Gibson (McLaren), Tait, McKechnie, Taggart, Bain.
*Alloa Ath:* Cairns; Valentine, Little, McAneny, McCulloch, Ramsay (Pew), Nelson, Wilson S (Irvine), Simpson, Gilmour, Haddow (McCormack).

**SECOND ROUND**

**26 AUG**

**Ayr U (0) 0**
**Clydebank (0) 1** *(McCall 110) aet* 1281
*Ayr U:* Castilla; Robertson, Bonar P (McDonald), Traynor, Jamieson, Love, Agnew (Hood), Mainge, Ferguson (Kerrigan), Kristensen, Smith T.
*Clydebank:* Hillcoat; Wishart, Lovering, Murdoch, McLaughlin, Brannigan, Teale (Connachan), Nicholls, Cadette (McCall), Melvin (Lorimer), Connell.

**Berwick R (0) 1** *(Walton 47)*
**Airdrieonians (3) 4** *(Lawrence 10, Connelly G 27, Black 43, Cooper 49)* 469
*Berwick R:* Burgess; Cunningham, Laidler (Irvine), Clark, Finlayson, McNicoll, Rafferty, Fraser, Ward, Walton, Graham.
*Airdrieonians:* Rhodes; Stewart, Jack, Sandison, Sweeney, Black, Lawrence, Wilson, Cooper (McPhee), Connelly G, McCann.

**Brechin C (2) 2** *(Brand 4, Feroz 28)*
**Livingston (0) 1** *(Raynes 75)* 321
*Brechin C:* Garden; Baillie, Brown, Cairney, Smith, Heddle, Feroz, Dailly (Buick), Sorbie (Kerrigan), Brand (McNeill), Campbell.
*Livingston:* McCaldon; Watson, Raynes, Conway, Graham, Alleyne, Maskrey (McMartin), Forrest (Young), Laidlaw, Bailey (Callaghan), Magee.

**Falkirk (2) 3** *(Craig 19 (pen),46, 76)*
**Forfar Ath (1) 1** *(Morgan 36 (pen))* 1436
*Falkirk:* Nelson; Oliver, Seaton, McCart, James, Hamilton (Crabbe), Corrigan (Ward), Craig, McGrillen, Hagen, Cunning.
*Forfar Ath:* Robertson; McCheyne, Craig, Hamilton, Mann, Glennie, Cargill, Loney (Roberts), Morgan, Honeyman, Lee.

**Hamilton A (1) 2** *(Cunnington 44, Davidson 81)*
**East Fife (1) 1** *(Moffat 27)* 599
*Hamilton A:* Ferguson; Hillcoat, Renicks, Thomson, McCulloch, Cunnington, Quitongo, Sherry, McQuade (Davidson), McFarlane, Clark.
*East Fife:* McCulloch; Cusick, Gibb, Ritchie, Johnston, Gillies, Allan, Donaghy (Dixon), Moffat (Dyer), Ronald, Ryan.

**Queen of the S (0) 2** *(Mallan 54, 55)*
**Stirling Albion (0) 0** 1016
*Queen of the S:* Mathieson; MacLeod, Aitken, Rowe, Thomson, Townsley, McKeown, Boyce, Mallan, Flannigan, Cleeland (Kennedy).
*Stirling Albion:* McGeown; Paterson A, Deas, Carberry, McQuilter, Paterson G, Bone, Tait, McCormick, McLaren (Bennett), Gibson (Taggart).

**Raith R (0) 0**
**Stranraer (0) 1** *(Young 69)* 1970
*Raith R:* Van De Kamp; McEwan, Thomson, Kirkwood, Craig, Millen, Lennon, Twaddle (Duffield), Hartley (Browne), Kirk, Cameron (Dair L).
*Stranraer:* Matthews; Knox, Black, George, Campbell, McCaffrey, McAulay, McIntyre, Young, Docherty, Kinnaird.

**Ross Co (0) 1** *(Wood 89)*
**Greenock Morton (1) 2** *(Blaikie 7, 74)* 4338
*Ross Co:* Hutchison; Mackay, Golabek, Furphy, Haro, Gilbert, Taylor (Ferguson), Williamson, Wood, Ross (Adams), Callaghan (Bradshaw).
*Greenock Morton:* Inglis; Collins, Sukalia, McPherson, McCahill, Reid, Blair (Aitken), Mahood (Anderson), Hawke (Flannery), McArthur, Blaikie.

## QUARTER-FINALS

### 2 SEPT

**Queen of the S (2) 3** *(Mallan 26, 42, Flannigan 66)*
**Airdrieonians (1) 2** *(McPhee 45, 80)* 1230
*Queen of the S:* Mathieson; MacLeod, Aitken, Rowe, Thomson, Townsley (Irving), Cleeland, Bryce, Mallan, Flannigan, McKeown.

*Airdrieonians:* Rhodes; Johnston, McCann (Davies), Sandison, Sweeney, Black (Lawrence), Connelly G, Wilson, McPhee, Mackay, Smith.

### 3 SEPT

**Falkirk (0) 3** *(Craig 72, McGrillen 77, Hagen 90)*
**Stranraer (0) 0** 1465
*Falkirk:* Nelson; Oliver, McGowan (Seaton), McCart, James, McKenzie (Corrigan), McAllister, Crabbe (Craig), McGrillen, Cunning, Hagen.
*Stranraer:* Matthews; Lansdowne, Black, George, Campbell, McCaffrey, McAulay (McCrindle), McIntyre, Young, Docherty, Crawford (Friels).

**Greenock Morton (0) 1** *(McArthur 86)*
**Clydebank (0) 0** 1495
*Greenock Morton:* Wylie; Collins, McArthur, Anderson, McCahill, Reid, Blair (Mason), Aitken (Juttla), Hawke, McPherson, Blaikie (Flannery).
*Clydebank:* Hillcoat; Wishart, Lovering, Murdoch, McLaughlin, Brannigan, Teale (Miller), Nicholls, Cadette (McCall), Docherty, Connell.

### 5 SEPT

**Hamilton A (0) 4** *(McFarlane 48, Cunnington 52, Geraghty 62, 85)*
**Brechin C (0) 0** 543
*Hamilton A:* Ferguson; Thomson, Renicks, McEntegart, McCulloch, Cunnington, Quitongo, Sherry (McKenzie), Geraghty, McFarlane (Clark), Davidson
*Brechin C:* Garden; Baillie, Campbell, Cairney, Brown, Heddle, McKellar, Buick, Brand (Kerrigan), McNeill, Feroz.

## SEMI-FINALS

### 15 SEPT

**Hamilton A (0) 1** *(Clark 90)*
**Falkirk (1) 2** *(McAllister 22, McGowan 56)* 1284
*Hamilton A:* Ferguson; Thomson, Renicks, McEntegart, McKenzie, Cunnington, Quitongo, Sherry, McFarlane (Geraghty), McCormick (McQuade), Clark.
*Falkirk:* Mathers; Corrigan, Seaton, Oliver, McGowan, McCart, McAllister (Hagen), McKenzie, McGrillen, Moss (Craig), Keith.

### 17 SEPT

**Greenock Morton (0) 0**
**Queen of the S (1) 2** *(Flannigan 2, Mallan 54)* 1752
*Greenock Morton:* Wylie; Collins, McArthur, Anderson, McCahill, Cormack, Blair, Juttla, Matheson, McPherson, Blaikie (Flannery).
*Queen of the S:* Mathieson; MacLeod, Aitken, Rowe, Thomson, Townsley, Kennedy, Bryce, Mallan, Flannigan, McKeown.

## FINAL AT FIR PARK

### 2 NOV

**Falkirk (0) 1** *(Hagen 65)*
**Queen of the S (0) 0** 9735
*Falkirk:* Mathers; Corrigan, McGowan, McKenzie, James, Berry, McAllister, Craig, McGrillen (Keith), Moss, Hagen.
*Queen of the S:* Mathieson; Kennedy, Aitken, Rowe, Thomson, Townsley, Cleeland (Irving), Bryce, Mallan, Eadie (Flannigan), McKeown (McAllister).
*Referee:* B. Tait (East Kilbride)

# WELSH FOOTBALL 1997–98

Forty years ago, Wales made their one and only appearance in the World Cup finals. After sneaking in through the back door when Middle East tensions enabled them to beat Israel in a play-off, they reached the quarter-finals of the 1958 tournament in Sweden before succumbing to a deflected goal from a young Brazilian called Pele. It was a defeat which set a frustrating trend for Welsh football almost until the end of the Millennium—spirited performances ending in glorious failure and non-qualification for major international competitions.

In fact, the nearest Wales got to France 98 was an end-of-season mini-tour to Malta and North Africa in the week before the tournament began. After an encouraging 3-0 win over Malta, they came back down to earth with a bump as Tunisia—one of England's group opponents—crushed them 4-0 in their final warm-up match.

It came as no surprise when the latest Welsh attempt to scramble onto the world stage ended with a bang and then a whimper. Eleven goals were conceded in three defeats—two by Belgium and one in Turkey—as Wales finished above only San Marino in their World Cup qualifying group. These results inevitably increased the pressure on manager Bobby Gould but, armed with a new two-year contract and a part-time assistant, former Welsh international full back Graham Williams, he immediately charted a course for the 2000 European Championships by boldly continuing the policy of putting his faith in youth.

A 3-0 defeat in Brazil was followed by a 0-0 draw in Cardiff against France-bound Jamaica before the two friendlies in Malta and Tunisia. With Mark Hughes unavailable, only Dean Saunders remained from the old guard as Gould rang the changes. Seventeen-year-old Ryan Green, a First Division YTS player, became the youngest ever full Welsh international when he played against Malta. The Cardiff-born defender had yet to make his league debut for Wolves when he beat by 106 days the record set by Ryan Giggs against Germany in 1991. Green acquitted himself well—as did Southampton's Andy Williams and Craig Bellamy of Norwich who were both making their full appearances.

Midfielder Bellamy, having scored the opening goal and made the second, seems to be one not so much for the future but for the immediate present. But he was powerless to stop the Welsh being swept aside in Tunis in a lacklustre display. Bobby Gould might consider FIFA's world rankings to be meaningless—Wales were 101st and Tunisia 26th—but the scoreline reflected the huge gulf between the two sides—even allowing for the heat and the weary legs of the inexperienced Welsh side. The result showed why Tunisia and not Wales were on their way to France but the jury must still be out on Gould as he guides his adopted country through a crucial transitional period.

On the club scene, it was another anti-climactic season. After two near-misses, Wrexham looked likely to make it third time lucky by reaching the Nationwide Second Division play-offs. Third with eight games to go, they fell away badly and, despite rediscovering the winning habit at Southend in their very last match, they failed to finish in the top six by scoring one goal less than Fulham.

After nearly nine years as manager, Brian Flynn then reaffirmed his commitment to Wrexham following approaches about vacancies at Burnley and Norwich. In contrast to the season at the Racecourse, both Swansea and Cardiff suffered promotion play-off hangovers which were to cost Jan Molby and Russell Osman their jobs. Swansea's poor start led to the former Liverpool star being sacked as manager in October while Cardiff's dismal form—they jointly set the record for the number of draws in a Division Three season—saw Osman replaced by former Cardiff manager Frank Burrows with Kenny Hibbitt being freed to concentrate on his job as director of football.

Fresh from his sacking as Fulham manager, Micky Adams succeeded Molby and lasted a mere 13 days before walking out after a disagreement over money for new players. His assistant Alan Cork, a former member of the Wimbledon Crazy Gang, took over but, with Doncaster destined for the drop to the Vauxhall Conference, neither Swansea nor Cardiff were ever in danger of losing their league status.

Further down the English pyramid, Colwyn Bay completed a mediocre season in the Unibond League but enjoyed another good FA Cup run before losing to runaway winners of Division Three, Notts County while Merthyr went close to reclaiming their place in the GM Vauxhall Conference. After leading the Dr Martens League Premier Division for much of the season, it all came down to their penultimate game at close rivals Forest Green Rovers. A second-half sending-off proved the catalyst for a 3-1 defeat and the Gloucestershire side finished well clear at the top. They deserved their second successive promotion but an untimely row over Merthyr's financial suitability for the Conference can hardly have helped during the run-in.

The League of Wales champions Barry Town looked set to complete a treble for the second year on the trot as the season drew to a close. In the end, they retained their title by another huge margin—26 points—and the Gilbert League Cup after beating Bangor City on penalties for the second successive season. The North Wales club, after overcoming Newtown in their semi-final, had expected to meet the league champions in the Welsh Cup Final. They—and Barry—had reckoned without the fighting qualities of Connah's Quay Nomads who pulled off the shock of the season with a 2-1 win over the holders. Sadly, the Nomads narrowly failed to qualify for Europe for the first time when, with the teams tied at 1-1 after extra time, they lost on penalties to Bangor in the final at Wrexham. Bangor soon parted company with manager Graeme Sharpe and his assistant John Hulse in a row over money and later appointed John King from Altrincham in their place.

The Racecourse in Wrexham was also the venue for the final of the FAW Invitation Cup—a competition created and lavishly sponsored by BBC Wales. After a slow start, the cup scuppered the sceptics—including this one—and made a creditable stab at reuniting Welsh football in the aftermath of the creation of the League of Wales. The group games attracted very small crowds but incredible viewing figures—more than justifying the BBC's decision to join forces with the FAW.

Keenly-contested quarter and semi-final ties—especially Merthyr's defeat of Barry in the Battle of the Non-Nationwide teams—led to Wrexham beating Cardiff 2-1 after extra time to collect the £100,000 first prize and confirm their position as the best team in Wales. Next season, the competition will have a new format as well as a new name. The FAW Premier Cup will be contested by 12 rather than 8 teams in three instead of two groups.

It is perhaps a sad reflection on the state of Welsh football that the supposedly premier competition, the League of Wales, as well as having to settle a row over relegation with the four affected clubs, is still struggling to find a sponsor. European football may well provide the qualifying teams with their fifteen minutes of fame—both Barry and Inter Cable-Tel had plum ties against Dinamo Kiev and Celtic last season—but, when it comes to making serious money, then charity, in the shape of the FAW Premier Cup, does indeed begin at home.

GRAHAME LLOYD

## LEAGUE OF WALES

| | Aberystwyth T | Bangor City | Barry Town | Caernarfon Town | Caersws | Carmarthen Town | Cemaes Ynys Mon | Connah's Quay Nomads | Conwy United | Cwmbran Town | Ebbw Vale | Flint Town United | Haverfordwest County | Inter Cable-Tel | Newtown | Porthmadog | Rhayader Town | Rhyl | Total Network Solutions | Welshpool Town |
|---|---|---|---|---|---|---|---|---|---|---|---|---|---|---|---|---|---|---|---|---|
| Aberystwyth Town | — | 3-1 | 0-2 | 3-0 | 1-0 | 3-1 | 2-5 | 0-1 | 3-0 | 2-4 | 1-1 | 2-1 | 4-0 | 1-0 | 0-1 | 2-2 | 3-2 | 1-1 | 2-2 | 5-0 |
| Bangor City | 1-0 | — | 1-4 | 1-0 | 3-2 | 2-2 | 6-0 | 0-2 | 1-1 | 2-2 | 1-0 | 2-1 | 1-2 | 2-1 | 0-3 | 3-3 | 3-1 | 2-0 | 2-0 | 5-1 |
| Barry Town | 6-1 | 5-0 | — | 4-0 | 6-1 | 6-3 | 12-0 | 2-1 | 3-1 | 2-1 | 1-1 | 2-0 | 3-2 | 2-1 | 5-5 | 3-0 | 2-0 | 3-2 | 10-0 | 8-0 |
| Caernarfon Town | 1-1 | 1-1 | 2-5 | — | 0-1 | 5-0 | 4-0 | 0-1 | 1-1 | 1-4 | 2-3 | 0-0 | 3-1 | 1-3 | 1-5 | 2-2 | 4-1 | 1-1 | 3-1 | 3-0 |
| Caersws | 5-3 | 1-3 | 0-2 | 4-2 | — | 6-1 | 3-0 | 0-2 | 1-4 | 2-1 | 1-2 | 2-3 | 3-1 | 2-0 | 1-2 | 4-1 | 0-1 | 1-2 | 2-0 | 0-4 |
| Carmarthen Town | 1-1 | 0-3 | 3-5 | 0-2 | 0-0 | — | 4-0 | 2-2 | 0-1 | 1-2 | 2-2 | 3-0 | 0-1 | 2-0 | 2-2 | 3-1 | 1-0 | 2-2 | 1-3 | 1-1 |
| Cemaes Ynys Mon | 2-2 | 0-2 | 0-3 | 0-5 | 0-2 | 3-3 | — | 1-4 | 1-2 | 2-5 | 0-2 | 1-2 | 4-0 | 0-3 | 0-1 | 1-2 | 1-3 | 0-2 | 1-5 | 2-3 |
| Connah's Quay Nomads | 1-0 | 2-2 | 1-4 | 2-0 | 3-1 | 0-2 | 1-4 | — | 2-2 | 1-5 | 2-3 | 3-2 | 5-2 | 0-0 | 1-1 | 2-2 | 2-1 | 1-1 | 2-2 | 2-1 |
| Conwy United | 1-3 | 0-2 | 1-3 | 0-2 | 3-0 | 0-2 | 10-0 | 2-2 | — | 1-2 | 2-3 | 2-0 | 2-0 | 1-2 | 3-1 | 1-0 | 4-1 | 2-1 | 2-2 | 0-0 |
| Cwmbran Town | 1-1 | 0-1 | 0-3 | 1-2 | 3-1 | 1-1 | 4-0 | 2-2 | 2-1 | — | 1-2 | 4-3 | 6-0 | 0-0 | 3-1 | 3-1 | 3-0 | 2-0 | 2-1 | 3-2 |
| Ebbw Vale | 1-1 | 2-3 | 1-1 | 1-1 | 3-3 | 3-1 | 2-0 | 2-0 | 4-3 | 1-2 | — | 5-0 | 6-1 | 4-0 | 0-4 | 3-1 | 1-1 | 3-3 | 1-1 | 1-1 |
| Flint Town United | 1-1 | 1-4 | 1-2 | 0-2 | 2-0 | 1-2 | 10-1 | 1-2 | 1-6 | 1-1 | 0-4 | — | 1-1 | 1-2 | 2-3 | 3-1 | 0-2 | 3-3 | 2-2 | 1-1 |
| Haverfordwest County | 1-1 | 2-2 | 0-1 | 3-0 | 1-0 | 1-1 | 3-0 | 1-1 | 3-0 | 1-1 | 1-4 | 1-3 | — | 0-2 | 1-6 | 2-1 | 2-4 | 0-1 | 2-1 | 3-0 |
| Inter Cable-Tel | 3-0 | 2-0 | 0-0 | 3-1 | 1-1 | 3-0 | 5-0 | 0-2 | 3-0 | 2-0 | 2-0 | 1-3 | 3-0 | — | 0-1 | 1-0 | 1-0 | 2-0 | 1-1 | 3-1 |
| Newtown | 4-0 | 4-2 | 0-2 | 2-1 | 1-1 | 2-0 | 3-0 | 4-1 | 3-0 | 0-1 | 1-2 | 3-2 | 5-2 | 0-1 | — | 4-0 | 3-1 | 1-1 | 1-1 | 3-0 |
| Porthmadog | 5-3 | 0-1 | 0-3 | 2-0 | 3-2 | 0-1 | 11-1 | 4-0 | 1-3 | 1-2 | 0-2 | 0-1 | 2-3 | 4-0 | 1-4 | — | 1-2 | 0-2 | 3-1 | 3-1 |
| Rhayader Town | 1-3 | 2-1 | 2-2 | 1-2 | 2-4 | 2-1 | 7-0 | 3-1 | 1-3 | 1-2 | 2-2 | 1-3 | 3-1 | 1-0 | 0-4 | 1-3 | — | 0-3 | 1-1 | 3-2 |
| Rhyl | 2-2 | 2-1 | 0-1 | 2-1 | 2-0 | 3-0 | 5-0 | 0-1 | 0-3 | 1-0 | 5-2 | 2-0 | 0-2 | 0-1 | 3-2 | 1-1 | 2-0 | — | 2-1 | 3-2 |
| Total Network Solutions | 1-0 | 1-1 | 0-1 | 2-0 | 1-1 | 2-3 | 1-1 | 0-0 | 2-1 | 3-3 | 2-3 | 1-0 | 2-2 | 1-1 | 2-4 | 2-1 | 2-2 | 1-0 | — | 3-1 |
| Welshpool Town | 1-3 | 1-3 | 0-5 | 4-1 | 0-3 | 1-5 | 8-0 | 2-4 | 1-2 | 0-1 | 2-3 | 4-2 | 2-2 | 0-2 | 0-1 | 1-2 | 3-3 | 3-3 | 1-0 | — |

## LEAGUE OF WALES

| | | Home | | | Goals | | Away | | | Goals | | | |
|---|---|---|---|---|---|---|---|---|---|---|---|---|---|
| | P | W | D | L | F | A | W | D | L | F | A | GD | Pts |
| Barry Town | 38 | 17 | 2 | 0 | 85 | 19 | 16 | 3 | 0 | 49 | 12 | +103 | 104 |
| Newtown | 38 | 10 | 6 | 3 | 50 | 22 | 13 | 3 | 3 | 51 | 25 | +54 | 78 |
| Ebbw Vale | 38 | 10 | 7 | 2 | 53 | 27 | 12 | 4 | 3 | 41 | 28 | +39 | 77 |
| Inter Cable-Tel | 38 | 15 | 1 | 3 | 36 | 10 | 8 | 4 | 7 | 22 | 18 | +30 | 74 |
| Cwmbran Town | 38 | 11 | 4 | 4 | 39 | 22 | 11 | 3 | 5 | 39 | 25 | +31 | 73 |
| Bangor City | 38 | 11 | 4 | 4 | 38 | 25 | 9 | 4 | 6 | 33 | 29 | +17 | 68 |
| Connah's Quay Nomads | 38 | 8 | 7 | 4 | 42 | 31 | 10 | 5 | 4 | 33 | 23 | +21 | 66 |
| Rhyl | 38 | 12 | 2 | 5 | 33 | 21 | 5 | 8 | 6 | 28 | 28 | +12 | 61 |
| Conwy United | 38 | 8 | 3 | 8 | 31 | 26 | 7 | 5 | 7 | 35 | 33 | +7 | 53 |
| Aberystwyth Town | 38 | 10 | 4 | 5 | 38 | 24 | 3 | 8 | 8 | 26 | 39 | +1 | 51 |
| Caersws | 38 | 9 | 0 | 10 | 38 | 34 | 5 | 4 | 10 | 26 | 37 | −7 | 46 |
| Carmarthen Town | 38 | 5 | 7 | 7 | 28 | 28 | 6 | 4 | 9 | 29 | 44 | −15 | 44 |
| Caernarfon Town | 38 | 6 | 6 | 7 | 35 | 31 | 6 | 1 | 12 | 22 | 35 | −9 | 43 |
| Total Network Solutions | 38 | 7 | 8 | 4 | 29 | 24 | 2 | 7 | 10 | 25 | 42 | −12 | 42 |
| Rhayader Town | 38 | 6 | 3 | 10 | 30 | 39 | 5 | 3 | 11 | 25 | 38 | −22 | 39 |
| Haverfordwest County | 38 | 6 | 5 | 8 | 31 | 32 | 4 | 3 | 12 | 23 | 55 | −33 | 38 |
| Porthmadog | 38 | 7 | 0 | 12 | 31 | 34 | 3 | 5 | 11 | 23 | 43 | −23 | 35 |
| Flint Town United | 38 | 3 | 6 | 10 | 24 | 38 | 6 | 1 | 12 | 26 | 39 | −27 | 34 |
| Welshpool Town | 38 | 4 | 3 | 12 | 34 | 45 | 2 | 4 | 13 | 21 | 52 | −42 | 25 |
| Cemaes Bay | 38 | 1 | 2 | 16 | 21 | 54 | 1 | 1 | 17 | 9 | 101 | −125 | 9 |

## WELSH CUP 1997–98

**Preliminary Round**

| | |
|---|---|
| Abercynon Athletic v Ferndale Athletic | 0-2 |
| British Aerospace v Penley | 4-1 |
| Halkyn United v Colwyn Bay YMCA | 1-4 |
| Montgomery Town v Berriew | 3-1 |
| Morriston Town v Ely Rangers | 0-2 |
| Panteg v Skewen Athletic | 2-3 |
| Pontlottyn Blast Furnace v Newport YMCA | 2-5 |
| South Wales Police v Tonyrefail Welfare | 5-3 |

**First Round**

| | |
|---|---|
| Aberaman Athletic v Porth Tywyn Suburbs | 2-2 |
| Abergavenny Thursdays v Treharris Athletic | 0-7 |
| AFC Rhondda v Briton Ferry Athletic | 5-5 |
| Ammanford Town v Risca United | 1-0 |
| Blaenrhondda v Pontypridd Town | 2-2 |
| Brecon Corinthians v Afan Lido | 0-5 |
| Bridgend Town v Port Talbot Athletic | 4-2 |
| Brymbo Broughton v Colwyn Bay YMCA | 1-0 |
| Caerleon v Goytre United | 2-7 |
| Cardiff Civil Service v Ferndale Athletic | 2-4 |
| Castell Alun Colts v Buckley Town | 1-7 |
| Cefn Druids v Prestatyn Town | 4-1 |
| Chepstow Town v Penrhiwceiber Rangers | 2-2 |
| Chirk AAA v Glantraeth | 3-2 |
| Corwen Amateurs v Lex XI | 3-6 |
| Denbigh Town v Presteigne St Andrews | 2-4 |
| Ely Rangers v Newport YMCA | 5-4 |
| Fields Park Pontllanfraith v Albion Rovers | 5-1 |
| Garw v UWIC | 1-1 |
| Grange Harlequins v Caerau United | 4-3 |
| Holyhead Hotspurs v Rhydymwyn | 2-1 |
| Hoover Sports v Taffs Well | 2-0 |
| Llandyrnog United v Mold Alexandra | 2-2 |
| Llangefni Town v British Aerospace | 3-2 |
| Llanidloes Town v Knighton Town | 3-6 |
| Llanwern v Llanelli | 3-1 |
| Maesteg Park Athletic v Porthcawl Town | 0-2 |
| Mostyn v Llandrindod Wells | 0-4 |
| Nantlle Vale v Llandudno | 3-0 |
| Oswestry Town v Montgomery Town | 5-1 |
| Penrhyncoch v Holywell Town | 0-1 |
| Penycae v Guilsfield | 0-1 |
| Pontardawe Athletic v Caldicot Town | 4-1 |
| Pontyclun v BP Llandarcy | 1-2 |
| Ruthin Town v Rhos Aelwyd | 3-1 |
| Skewen Athletic v Gwynfi United | 2-1 |
| Ton Pentre v South Wales Police | 5-0 |
| Treowen Stars v Cardiff Corinthians | 2-0 |

**Replays**

| | |
|---|---|
| Briton Ferry Athletic v AFC Rhondda | 3-1 |
| Mold Alexandra v Llandyrnog United | 3-1 |
| Penrhiwceiber v Chepstow Town | 0-5 |
| Pontypridd Town v Blaenrhondda | 1-4 |
| Porth Tywyn Suburbs v Aberaman Athletic | 5-0 |
| UWIC v Garw | 3-2 |

**Second Round**

| | |
|---|---|
| Afan Lido v Ton Pentre | 0-0 |
| BP Llandarcy v Haverfordwest County | 1-1 |
| Brymbo Broughton v Flint Town United | 1-3 |
| Buckley Town v Lex XI | 2-5 |
| Caernarfon Town v Chirk AAA | 6-1 |
| Carmarthen Town v Porth Tywyn Suburbs | 1-0 |
| Cefn Druids v Nantlle Vale | 4-1 |
| Connah's Quay Nomads v Porthmadog | 4-1 |
| Ely Rangers v Blaenrhondda | 5-1 |
| Fields Park Pontllanfraith v Briton Ferry Athletic | 0-1 |
| Goytre United v Chepstow Town | 6-1 |
| Guilsfield v Holywell Town | 0-4 |
| Knighton Town v Oswestry Town | 3-0 |
| Llandrindod Wells v Holyhead Hotspurs | 0-2 |
| Llanwern v Skewen Athletic | 2-0 |
| Mold Alexandra v Llangefni Town | 1-0 |
| Newtown v Rhyl | 2-0 |
| Pontardawe Athletic v Hoover Sports | 4-6 |
| Porthcawl Town v Bridgend Town | 1-1 |
| Presteigne St Andrews v Caersws | 1-8 |
| Rhayader Town v Total Network Solutions | 2-2 |
| Ruthin Town v Cemaes Ynys Mon | 3-1 |
| Treharris Athletic v Ferndale Athletic | 4-0 |
| Treowen Stars v Ammanford Town | 4-1 |
| UWIC v Grange Harlequins | 5-1 |
| Welshpool Town v Bangor City | 0-7 |

**Replays**

| | |
|---|---|
| Bridgend Town v Porthcawl Town | 0-2 |
| Haverfordwest County v BP Llandarcy | 2-1 |
| *(aet)* | |
| Ton Pentre v Afan Lido | 3-0 |
| Total Network Solutions v Rhayader Town | 3-3 |
| *(aet) (Total Network Solutions won 8-7 on penalties)* | |

**Third Round**

| | |
|---|---|
| Hoover Sports v Holywell Town | 2-2 |
| Briton Ferry Athletic v Inter Cable-Tel | 1-7 |
| Caernarfon Town v Cefn Druids | 0-0 |
| Carmarthen Town v Ely Rangers | 2-0 |
| Connah's Quay Nomads v Goytre United | 1-1 |
| Flint Town United v Bangor City | 0-3 |
| Haverfordwest County v Ebbw Vale | 2-3 |
| Holyhead Hotspurs v Cwmbran Town | 2-5 |
| Knighton Town v Conwy United | 4-1 |
| Lex XI v Barry Town | 0-3 |
| Llanwern v Treharris Athletic | 1-0 |
| Newtown v Treowen Stars | 2-0 |
| Porthcawl Town v Aberystwyth Town | 3-4 |
| Ton Pentre v Mold Alexandra | 5-0 |
| Total Network Solutions v Ruthin Town | 4-1 |
| UWIC v Caersws | 0-4 |

**Replays**

| | |
|---|---|
| Cefn Druids v Caernarfon Town | 0-2 |
| Goytre United v Connah's Quay Nomads | 1-4 |

Holywell Town v Hoover Sports — 0-1

**Fourth Round**
Aberystwyth Town v Bangor City — 1-3
Caernarfon Town v Carmarthen Town — 2-1
Connah's Quay Nomads v Llanwern — 4-0
Cwmbran Town v Hoovers Sports — 6-1
Ebbw Vale v Newtown — 0-4
Inter Cable-Tel v Caersws — 2-3
Knighton Town v Barry Town — 0-8
Ton Pentre v Total Network Solutions — 1-2

**Fifth Round**
Bangor City v Caernarfon Town — 2-0
Barry Town v Total Network Solutions — 3-1
Caersws v Newtown — 1-1
Connah's Quay Nomads v Cwmbran Town — 3-2

**Replay**
Newtown v Caersws — 4-2

**Semi-final**
Bangor City v Newtown — 2-1
Barry Town v Connah's Quay Nomads — 1-2

**Final**

**Bangor City (0) 1 Connah's Quay Nomads (0) 1**

*(at The Racecourse, Wrexham 10 May 1998)*

*(aet, Bangor City won 4-2 on penalties)*

*Bangor City:* Williams; Humphries (McGoona 45), Edwards, Allan, Whelan, Ashton, Waring, Lloyd-Williams, Brookman, McKenna, Noble.
*Scorer:* McKenna 89.
*Connah's Quay Nomads:* Collister; Thomas (Cody 93), Carroll, Hutchinson, Jardine, Smyth, Futcher, Davies C (Davies N 61), Hughes, Keep (Allen 67), Wynne.
*Scorer:* Futcher 73.
*Referee:* D.C. Richards (Llanelli).
*Attendance:* 2023.

## FAW INVITATION CUP

| Group A | P | W | D | L | F | A | Pts |
|---|---|---|---|---|---|---|---|
| Barry Town | 6 | 5 | 0 | 1 | 24 | 5 | 15 |
| Bangor City | 6 | 3 | 1 | 2 | 8 | 6 | 10 |
| Swansea City | 6 | 2 | 2 | 2 | 7 | 6 | 8 |
| Conwy United | 6 | 0 | 1 | 5 | 0 | 22 | 1 |

| Group B | P | W | D | L | F | A | Pts |
|---|---|---|---|---|---|---|---|
| Cardiff City | 6 | 3 | 3 | 0 | 7 | 4 | 12 |
| Wrexham | 6 | 3 | 2 | 1 | 11 | 5 | 11 |
| Newtown | 6 | 1 | 3 | 2 | 9 | 10 | 6 |
| Merthyr Tydfil | 6 | 0 | 2 | 4 | 4 | 12 | 2 |

**Quarter-finals**
Barry Town v Merthyr Tydfil — 0-1
*(aet)*
Cardiff City v Conwy United — 4-0
Wrexham v Swansea City — 2-2
*(aet) (1-1 after 90 mins; Wrexham won 5-4 on penalties)*
Bangor City v Newtown — 3-5

**Semi-finals (two-legs)**
Merthyr Tydfil v Cardiff City — 0-4
Cardiff City v Merthyr Tydfil — 3-1
Wrexham v Newtown — 2-0
Newtown v Wrexham — 0-2

**Final**
Wrexham v Cardiff City — 2-1
*(aet) (1-1 after 90 mins)*

## CC SPORTS WELSH LEAGUE

**Division One**

| | P | W | D | L | F | A | Pts |
|---|---|---|---|---|---|---|---|
| Ton Pentre | 36 | 28 | 4 | 4 | 122 | 39 | 88 |
| Afan Lido | 36 | 27 | 4 | 5 | 86 | 26 | 85 |
| Llanelli | 36 | 26 | 4 | 6 | 88 | 30 | 82 |
| Treowen | 36 | 24 | 2 | 10 | 76 | 43 | 74 |
| Port Talbot | 36 | 22 | 5 | 9 | 70 | 51 | 71 |
| Goytre United | 36 | 20 | 3 | 13 | 89 | 42 | 63 |
| UWIC | 36 | 18 | 7 | 11 | 59 | 35 | 61 |
| AFC Rhondda | 36 | 15 | 13 | 8 | 73 | 51 | 58 |
| Bridgend Town* | 36 | 14 | 7 | 15 | 80 | 65 | 48 |
| Maesteg Park | 36 | 13 | 8 | 15 | 82 | 73 | 47 |
| Grange Harlequins | 36 | 13 | 6 | 17 | 54 | 66 | 45 |
| Porthcawl | 36 | 13 | 3 | 20 | 63 | 78 | 42 |
| Cardiff Corries | 36 | 9 | 12 | 15 | 63 | 66 | 39 |
| Briton Ferry Athletic | 36 | 12 | 3 | 21 | 63 | 94 | 39 |
| Cardiff Civil Service | 36 | 11 | 5 | 20 | 50 | 83 | 38 |
| Aberaman | 36 | 9 | 4 | 23 | 43 | 77 | 31 |
| Taffs Well | 36 | 6 | 9 | 21 | 46 | 83 | 27 |
| Llanwern** | 36 | 6 | 10 | 20 | 53 | 79 | 25 |
| Abergavenny Thursdays | 36 | 0 | 3 | 33 | 31 | 210 | 3 |

*1 point deducted – breach of rule.
**3 points deducted – breach of rule.

## ERIC EVANS CARS CYMRU ALLIANCE

| | P | W | D | L | F | A | Pts |
|---|---|---|---|---|---|---|---|
| Rhydymwyn | 36 | 25 | 6 | 5 | 86 | 34 | 81 |
| Holywell Town* | 36 | 24 | 5 | 7 | 72 | 29 | 77 |
| Cefn Druids | 36 | 21 | 12 | 3 | 100 | 30 | 75 |
| Knighton Town | 36 | 21 | 8 | 7 | 74 | 41 | 71 |
| Glantraeth | 36 | 18 | 6 | 12 | 88 | 63 | 60 |
| Penrhyncoch | 36 | 16 | 8 | 12 | 72 | 67 | 56 |
| Denbigh Town | 36 | 15 | 8 | 13 | 83 | 78 | 53 |
| Oswestry Town** | 36 | 17 | 11 | 8 | 72 | 49 | 50 |
| Llandudno | 36 | 14 | 7 | 15 | 60 | 66 | 49 |
| Lex XI | 36 | 12 | 11 | 13 | 64 | 66 | 47 |
| Llandrindod Wells | 36 | 12 | 11 | 13 | 53 | 56 | 47 |
| Ruthin Town | 36 | 12 | 9 | 15 | 57 | 53 | 45 |
| Brymbo Broughton | 36 | 12 | 9 | 15 | 39 | 41 | 45 |
| Mostyn | 36 | 11 | 8 | 17 | 42 | 65 | 41 |
| Buckley Town | 36 | 11 | 8 | 17 | 62 | 88 | 41 |
| Penycae | 36 | 10 | 6 | 20 | 52 | 95 | 36 |
| Chirk AAA | 36 | 10 | 4 | 22 | 46 | 74 | 34 |
| Llanidloes Town | 36 | 4 | 7 | 25 | 54 | 110 | 19 |
| Mold Alexandra | 36 | 2 | 6 | 28 | 32 | 102 | 12 |

*Holywell Town promoted because Rhydymwyn's facilities not up to required standard.
**12 points deducted for twice fielding ineligible players.

# NORTHERN IRISH FOOTBALL 1997–98

Northern Ireland experienced a traumatic season particularly at international level after a disappointing World Cup series with only seven points out of a possible 30, slumping to 92nd in the FIFA world rankings.

This crisis situation led to the early termination of manager Bryan Hamilton's and his assistant Gerry Armstrong's contracts by the Irish FA International Committee who were, however, "conscious of the valuable public relations work carried out by the manager as an adjunct to his main duties and responsibilities".

Jim Boyce, Irish FA President and David Bowen, General Secretary, spent three months seeking replacements "from suitable candidates of the requisite quality and experience". This exercise resulted in the appointment of Lawrie McMenemy, former assistant to England manager Graham Taylor, Joe Jordan, ex-Manchester United and AC Milan striker, and the legendary Pat Jennings as the goalkeeping coach. Later Chris Nicholl, former Southampton centre-back and Grimsby manager, was invited to take charge of the Under-21 team which will compete in the European Championship for the first time. Roy Millar, Director of Coaching, remains in charge of all youth squads.

What was labelled as "The Dream Management Team" had an excellent start with victories over Slovakia and Switzerland as they laid the basis for the European championship. "Our target is qualification" said McMenemy, first Englishman to be appointed manager.

Progress has been made at youth and B international level while the under-21 side defeated Switzerland 1-0 and then went on to win a triangular tournament in the West of Ireland involving Scotland and the Republic. There is a nucleus of a reasonably talented senior squad but a need for more players to be featuring regularly in the Premiership. Too many either languish on the bench or in the reserves.

It was also an Irish managerial merry-go-round with changes at many clubs some of whom faced possible bankruptcy with increased expenditure and reduced income and attendances. Promotion and relegation introduced three seasons ago has meant managements paying out huge sums which they simply cannot afford to ensure either gaining promotion or avoiding relegation. Consequently, massive cost cutting exercises have been undertaken—even at Linfield, Ireland's wealthiest and best supported club.

Cliftonville won the Smirnoff Irish League championship for the first time in 88 years which brought them a European Champions Cup place. Marty Quinn, who built the side on a shoestring budget, justifiably earned the Manager of the Year Award and his veteran centre-back Marty Tabb the Player of the Year while the Young Player trophy went to Linfield's Lee Feeney.

Glentoran, under Roy Coyle, who succeeded Tommy Cassidy, now with Ards, showed remarkable improvement from January and climaxed the transformation with a 1-0 victory over Glenavon in the Irish Cup Final, a competition sponsored for 20 years by Bass who have signed a three year deal taking them into the new millennium.

Domestically, Northern Ireland football faces quite a few problems but they are not insurmountable provided there is proper business acumen, continued sponsorship and a cutback in the number of competitions which would avoid supporters being satiated with a surfeit of matches and, more important, avoiding clashes with the live televising of European and English midweek tournaments. Local football just cannot compete.

Internationally, a vibrancy exists in the squad but formidable hurdles loom in the European Championship with matches against holders Germany, Moldova, Turkey and Finland. Qualification for the finals will be difficult—very difficult.

MALCOLM BRODIE

## WILKINSON SWORD LEAGUE CUP

### Semi-finals

| | |
|---|---|
| Linfield v Portadown (at the Oval) | 2-1 |
| Glentoran v Glenavon (at Windsor Park) | 1-0 |

### Final

**Linfield 1 Glentoran 0** (at Windsor Park)
*Linfield:* Geddes; McDonald (Easton), Spiers, Campbell, McLean, Beatty, Barker, McNamara, Millar, McBride (Gorman), Bailie.
*Scorer:* Spiers.
*Glentoran:* Russell; Nixon, Smyth, Walker, Devine, Parker, Mathieson, Mitchell (Elliott), Hamill (Kirk), Livingstone, McBride J.
*Referee:* L. Irvine (Limavady).
*Attendance:* 6431.

## COCA-COLA FLOODLIT CUP

### Semi-finals

| | |
|---|---|
| Linfield v Glenavon (at Seaview) | 1-0 |
| Ballymena United v Cliftonville (at Windsor Park) | 1-2 |

### Final

**Linfield 2 Cliftonville 0** (at Windsor Park)
*Linfield:* Geddes; McDonald, McShane, Byrne (Marks), Murphy, Beatty (McNamara), Larmour, Gorman, Ferguson, Feeney, Bailie.
*Scorers:* Larmour, Feeney.
*Cliftonville:* Reece; Small (Collins), Flynn, Tabb, Davey, Sliney, McCann T, O'Connor, Tolan, McCann M (McCourt), Donnelly.
*Referee:* M. Ross (Carrickfergus).
*Attendance:* 5168 (police restricted allocation of tickets to 6000).

## SMIRNOFF IRISH LEAGUE

### Premier Division

| | P | W | D | L | F | A | GD | Pts |
|---|---|---|---|---|---|---|---|---|
| Cliftonville | 36 | 20 | 8 | 8 | 49 | 37 | +12 | 68 |
| Linfield | 36 | 17 | 13 | 6 | 50 | 19 | +31 | 64 |
| Portadown | 36 | 17 | 9 | 10 | 50 | 38 | +12 | 60 |
| Glentoran | 36 | 17 | 8 | 11 | 52 | 34 | +18 | 59 |
| Crusaders | 36 | 13 | 12 | 11 | 51 | 51 | 0 | 51 |
| Ballymena United | 36 | 14 | 9 | 13 | 54 | 55 | –1 | 51 |
| Coleraine | 36 | 11 | 10 | 15 | 41 | 46 | –5 | 43 |
| Glenavon | 36 | 9 | 12 | 15 | 46 | 56 | –10 | 39 |
| Omagh Town | 36 | 7 | 10 | 19 | 43 | 68 | –25 | 31 |
| Ards | 36 | 4 | 11 | 21 | 31 | 63 | –32 | 23 |

### First Division

| | P | W | D | L | F | A | GD | Pts |
|---|---|---|---|---|---|---|---|---|
| Newry Town | 28 | 20 | 5 | 3 | 61 | 18 | +43 | 65 |
| Bangor | 28 | 18 | 4 | 6 | 51 | 26 | +25 | 58 |
| Distillery | 28 | 15 | 6 | 7 | 48 | 34 | +14 | 51 |
| Dungannon Sw | 28 | 14 | 6 | 8 | 63 | 49 | +14 | 48 |
| Ballyclare Com | 28 | 13 | 3 | 12 | 47 | 45 | +2 | 42 |
| Larne | 28 | 8 | 2 | 18 | 30 | 58 | –28 | 26 |
| Limavady United | 28 | 6 | 2 | 20 | 29 | 60 | –31 | 20 |
| Carrick Rangers | 28 | 3 | 2 | 23 | 20 | 59 | –39 | 11 |

**Irish League leading scorers:** 34—Vinny Arkins (Portadown); 34—Crawford McCrae (Ballyclare); 27—Tony Grant (Glenavon); 25—Glenn Ferguson (Linfield); 24—David Larmour (Linfield),, Darren Armour (Distillery); 23—Barry Patton (Ballymena); 22—Michael McHugh (Omagh Town), Andy Kirk (Glentoran); 21—Justin McBride (Glentoran); 21—Philip Dykes (Distillery); 20—Gavin Arthur (Crusaders), Glenn Hunter (Ballymena), Dessie Gorman (Newry Town).

## IRISH LEAGUE CHAMPIONSHIP WINNERS

| | | | | | | | | | |
|---|---|---|---|---|---|---|---|---|---|
| 1891 | Linfield | 1910 | Cliftonville | 1934 | Linfield | 1961 | Linfield | 1981 | Glentoran |
| 1892 | Linfield | 1911 | Linfield | 1935 | Linfield | 1962 | Linfield | 1982 | Linfield |
| 1893 | Linfield | 1912 | Glentoran | 1936 | Belfast Celtic | 1963 | Distillery | 1983 | Linfield |
| 1894 | Glentoran | 1913 | Glentoran | 1937 | Belfast Celtic | 1964 | Glentoran | 1984 | Linfield |
| 1895 | Linfield | 1914 | Linfield | 1938 | Belfast Celtic | 1965 | Derry City | 1985 | Linfield |
| 1896 | Distillery | 1915 | Belfast Celtic | 1939 | Belfast Celtic | 1966 | Linfield | 1986 | Linfield |
| 1897 | Glentoran | 1920 | Belfast Celtic | 1940 | Belfast Celtic | 1967 | Glentoran | 1987 | Linfield |
| 1898 | Linfield | 1921 | Glentoran | 1948 | Belfast Celtic | 1968 | Glentoran | 1988 | Glentoran |
| 1899 | Distillery | 1922 | Linfield | 1949 | Linfield | 1969 | Linfield | 1989 | Linfield |
| 1900 | Belfast Celtic | 1923 | Linfield | 1950 | Linfield | 1970 | Glentoran | 1990 | Portadown |
| 1901 | Distillery | 1924 | Queen's Island | 1951 | Glentoran | 1971 | Linfield | 1991 | Portadown |
| 1902 | Linfield | 1925 | Glentoran | 1952 | Glenavon | 1972 | Glentoran | 1992 | Glentoran |
| 1903 | Distillery | 1926 | Belfast Celtic | 1953 | Glentoran | 1973 | Crusaders | 1993 | Linfield |
| 1904 | Linfield | 1927 | Belfast Celtic | 1954 | Linfield | 1974 | Coleraine | 1994 | Linfield |
| 1905 | Glentoran | 1928 | Belfast Celtic | 1955 | Linfield | 1975 | Linfield | 1995 | Crusaders |
| 1906 | Cliftonville | 1929 | Belfast Celtic | 1956 | Linfield | 1976 | Crusaders | 1996 | Portadown |
| | Distillery | 1930 | Linfield | 1957 | Glentoran | 1977 | Glentoran | 1997 | Crusaders |
| 1907 | Linfield | 1931 | Glentoran | 1958 | Ards | 1978 | Linfield | 1998 | Cliftonville |
| 1908 | Linfield | 1932 | Linfield | 1959 | Linfield | 1979 | Linfield | | |
| 1909 | Linfield | 1933 | Belfast Celtic | 1960 | Glenavon | 1980 | Linfield | | |

## FIRST DIVISION

| | |
|---|---|
| 1996 | Coleraine |
| 1997 | Ballymena United |
| 1998 | Newry Town |

### ULSTER CUP FINAL TABLE

| | P | W | D | L | F | A | Pts |
|---|---|---|---|---|---|---|---|
| Ballyclare Comrades | 7 | 6 | 1 | 0 | 16 | 4 | 19 |
| Distillery | 7 | 4 | 1 | 2 | 13 | 8 | 13 |
| Bangor | 7 | 3 | 2 | 2 | 11 | 8 | 11 |
| Newry Town | 7 | 3 | 2 | 2 | 10 | 8 | 11 |
| Carrick Rangers | 7 | 2 | 3 | 2 | 8 | 9 | 9 |
| Larne | 7 | 1 | 3 | 3 | 7 | 16 | 6 |
| Limavady United | 7 | 1 | 2 | 4 | 6 | 13 | 5 |
| Dungannon Swifts | 7 | 1 | 0 | 6 | 10 | 15 | 3 |

*Note: This competition was run on the League principle and confined to First Division clubs.*

### COCA-COLA YOUTH LEAGUE

| | P | W | D | L | F | A | GD | Pts |
|---|---|---|---|---|---|---|---|---|
| Crusaders Colts | 24 | 19 | 2 | 3 | 68 | 30 | +38 | 59 |
| Glentoran Colts | 24 | 19 | 1 | 4 | 72 | 25 | +47 | 58 |
| Linfield Rangers | 24 | 15 | 4 | 5 | 66 | 33 | +33 | 49 |
| Bangor Colts | 24 | 13 | 5 | 6 | 49 | 33 | +16 | 44 |
| Coleraine Colts | 24 | 13 | 3 | 8 | 71 | 53 | +18 | 42 |
| Glenavon III | 24 | 11 | 4 | 9 | 74 | 55 | +19 | 37 |
| Cliftonville Strollers | 24 | 8 | 6 | 10 | 57 | 53 | +4 | 30 |
| Ballymena Utd III | 24 | 9 | 2 | 13 | 46 | 74 | –28 | 29 |
| Ards Colts | 24 | 7 | 5 | 12 | 45 | 65 | –20 | 26 |
| Portadown III | 24 | 6 | 6 | 12 | 44 | 52 | –8 | 24 |
| Carrick Rngrs Colts | 24 | 7 | 2 | 15 | 47 | 58 | –11 | 23 |
| Newry Town Wdrs | 24 | 2 | 6 | 16 | 21 | 64 | –43 | 12 |
| Chimney Crnr Colts | 24 | 3 | 2 | 19 | 28 | 93 | –65 | 11 |

## ULSTER CUP WINNERS

| | | | | | | | | | |
|---|---|---|---|---|---|---|---|---|---|
| 1949 | Linfield | 1959 | Glenavon | 1969 | Coleraine | 1979 | Linfield | 1989 | Glentoran |
| 1950 | Larne | 1960 | Linfield | 1970 | Linfield | 1980 | Ballymena U | 1990 | Portadown |
| 1951 | Glentoran | 1961 | Ballymena U | 1971 | Linfield | 1981 | Glentoran | 1991 | Bangor |
| 1952 | | 1962 | Linfield | 1972 | Coleraine | 1982 | Glentoran | 1992 | Linfield |
| 1953 | Glentoran | 1963 | Crusaders | 1973 | Ards | 1983 | Glentoran | 1993 | Crusaders |
| 1954 | Crusaders | 1964 | Linfield | 1974 | Linfield | 1984 | Linfield | 1994 | Bangor |
| 1955 | Glenavon | 1965 | Coleraine | 1975 | Coleraine | 1985 | Coleraine | 1995 | Portadown |
| 1956 | Linfield | 1966 | Glentoran | 1976 | Glentoran | 1986 | Coleraine | 1996 | Portadown |
| 1957 | Linfield | 1967 | Linfield | 1977 | Linfield | 1987 | Larne | 1997 | Coleraine |
| 1958 | Distillery | 1968 | Coleraine | 1978 | Linfield | 1988 | Glentoran | 1998 | Ballyclare Comrades |

### IRISH LEAGUE 'B' DIVISION—SECTION 1

| | P | W | D | L | F | A | GD | Pts |
|---|---|---|---|---|---|---|---|---|
| Loughgall | 26 | 21 | 1 | 4 | 76 | 21 | +55 | 64 |
| Chimney Corner | 26 | 19 | 5 | 2 | 60 | 23 | +37 | 62 |
| Dundela | 26 | 15 | 7 | 4 | 55 | 22 | +33 | 52 |
| Armagh City | 26 | 15 | 2 | 9 | 61 | 49 | +12 | 47 |
| RUC | 26 | 14 | 4 | 8 | 43 | 33 | +10 | 46 |
| Institute | 26 | 12 | 5 | 9 | 40 | 32 | +8 | 41 |
| H&W Welders | 26 | 9 | 9 | 8 | 41 | 35 | +6 | 36 |
| Ballymoney Utd | 26 | 11 | 2 | 13 | 50 | 55 | –5 | 35 |
| Tobermore Utd | 26 | 6 | 8 | 12 | 36 | 46 | –10 | 26 |
| Ballinamallard Utd | 26 | 5 | 10 | 11 | 31 | 45 | –14 | 25 |
| Moyola Park | 26 | 7 | 3 | 16 | 38 | 69 | –31 | 24 |
| Banbridge Town | 26 | 3 | 12 | 11 | 28 | 49 | –21 | 21 |
| Brantwood | 26 | 3 | 6 | 17 | 32 | 73 | –41 | 15 |
| Cookstown Utd | 26 | 2 | 6 | 18 | 17 | 56 | –39 | 12 |

### IRISH LEAGUE 'B' DIVISION—SECTION 2

| | P | W | D | L | F | A | GD | Pts |
|---|---|---|---|---|---|---|---|---|
| Glentoran II | 32 | 24 | 6 | 2 | 92 | 26 | +66 | 78 |
| Linfield Swifts | 32 | 24 | 4 | 4 | 104 | 19 | +85 | 76 |
| Portadown Res | 32 | 16 | 7 | 9 | 70 | 56 | +14 | 55 |
| Crusaders Res | 32 | 17 | 3 | 12 | 74 | 36 | +38 | 54 |
| Glenavon Res | 32 | 15 | 7 | 10 | 67 | 50 | +17 | 52 |
| Ballymena Utd Res | 32 | 14 | 9 | 9 | 58 | 61 | –3 | 51 |
| Carrick Rngrs Res | 32 | 14 | 8 | 10 | 53 | 55 | –2 | 50 |
| Bangor Res | 32 | 14 | 6 | 12 | 41 | 41 | 0 | 48 |
| Limavady Utd Res | 32 | 13 | 5 | 14 | 46 | 63 | –17 | 44 |
| Cliftonville Olympic | 32 | 12 | 5 | 15 | 63 | 67 | –4 | 41 |
| Dungannon Sw Res | 32 | 12 | 5 | 15 | 59 | 82 | –23 | 41 |
| Larne Olympic | 32 | 11 | 4 | 17 | 51 | 73 | –22 | 37 |
| Ards II | 32 | 9 | 7 | 16 | 40 | 61 | –21 | 34 |
| Coleraine Res | 32 | 8 | 8 | 16 | 51 | 74 | –23 | 32 |
| Newry Town Res | 32 | 8 | 3 | 21 | 50 | 82 | –32 | 27 |
| Ballyclare Com Res | 32 | 5 | 9 | 18 | 33 | 69 | –36 | 24 |
| Distillery II | 32 | 5 | 6 | 21 | 39 | 76 | –37 | 21 |

## BASS IRISH CUP 1997–98

**Fifth Round**

| | |
|---|---|
| Coleraine v Chimney Corner | 3-1 |
| Loughgall v Crumlin United | 4-0 |
| Linfield v Tobermore United | 1-0 |
| Cliftonville v Glenavon | 0-2 |
| Dungannon Swifts v Ballinamallard United | 6-2 |
| Ards v Institute | 0-2 |
| Drumaness Mills v Killyleagh | 0-0, 0-2 |
| Ballyclare Comrades v Ballymoney United | 5-1 |
| Larne v Portadown | 1-2 |
| Distillery v RUC | 2-0 |
| Ballymena United v Glentoran | 1-1, 1-2 |
| Omagh Town v Limavady United | 3-0 |
| Newry Town v Dundela | 1-0 |
| Crusaders v Bangor | 1-0 |
| Carrick Rangers v Armagh City | 2-3 |
| Dunmurry Rec v Ards Rangers | 0-4 |

**Sixth Round**

| | |
|---|---|
| Glenavon v Ballyclare Comrades | 0-0, 4-0 |
| Armagh City v Ards Rangers | 0-0, 3-1 |
| Portadown v Omagh Town | 2-0 |
| Glentoran v Coleraine | 3-2 |
| Loughgall v Distillery | 1-2 |

| | |
|---|---|
| Dungannon Swifts v Institute | 0-1 |
| Linfield v Newry Town | 2-1 |
| Crusaders v Killyleagh | 2-1 |

**Quarter-finals**

| | |
|---|---|
| Armagh City v Glentoran | 1-3 |
| Crusaders v Institute | 4-0 |
| Distillery v Glenavon | 0-2 |
| Linfield v Portadown | 3-0 |

**Semi-finals**

| | |
|---|---|
| Glenavon v Crusaders *(at The Oval)* | 3-1 |
| Linfield v Glentoran *(at Windsor Park)* | 1-2 |

**Final**

**Glentoran 1 Glenavon 0** *(aet)*

*Glentoran:* Russell; Nixon, Kennedy, Walker, Devine, Leeman (Livingstone), Mitchell, Finlay, Kirk, Batey, Hamill.

*Scorer:* Kennedy.

*Glenavon:* O'Neill (Welch); Wright (O'Flaherty), Glendinning, Quigley, Cash (Murphy), Smyth G, McCoy, Byrne, Shepherd, Grant, Caffrey.

*Referee:* L. Irvine (Limavady).

*Attendance:* 8250 (All ticket limit by police).

## IRISH CUP FINALS (from 1946–47)

| | | | |
|---|---|---|---|
| 1946–47 | Belfast Celtic 1, Glentoran 0 | 1972–73 | Glentoran 3, Linfield 2 |
| 1947–48 | Linfield 3, Coleraine 0 | 1973–74 | Ards 2, Ballymena U 1 |
| 1948–49 | Derry City 3, Glentoran 1 | 1974–75 | Coleraine 1:0:1, Linfield 1:0:0 |
| 1949–50 | Linfield 2, Distillery 1 | 1975–76 | Carrick Rangers 2, Linfield 1 |
| 1950–51 | Glentoran 3, Ballymena U 1 | 1976–77 | Coleraine 4, Linfield 1 |
| 1951–52 | Ards 1, Glentoran 0 | 1977–78 | Linfield 3, Ballymena U 1 |
| 1952–53 | Linfield 5, Coleraine 0 | 1978–79 | Cliftonville 3, Portadown 2 |
| 1953–54 | Derry City 1, Glentoran 0 | 1979–80 | Linfield 2, Crusaders 0 |
| 1954–55 | Dundela 3, Glenavon 0 | 1980–81 | Ballymena U 1, Glenavon 0 |
| 1955–56 | Distillery 1, Glentoran 0 | 1981–82 | Linfield 2, Coleraine 1 |
| 1956–57 | Glenavon 2, Derry City 0 | 1982–83 | Glentoran 1:2, Linfield 1:1 |
| 1957–58 | Ballymena U 2, Linfield 0 | 1983–84 | Ballymena U 4, Carrick Rangers 1 |
| 1958–59 | Glenavon 2, Ballymena U 0 | 1984–85 | Glentoran 1:1, Linfield 1:0 |
| 1959–60 | Linfield 5, Ards 1 | 1985–86 | Glentoran 2, Coleraine 1 |
| 1960–61 | Glenavon 5, Linfield 1 | 1986–87 | Glentoran 1, Larne 0 |
| 1961–62 | Linfield 4, Portadown 0 | 1987–88 | Glentoran 1, Glenavon 0 |
| 1962–63 | Linfield 2, Distillery 1 | 1988–89 | Ballymena U 1, Larne 0 |
| 1963–64 | Derry City 2, Glentoran 0 | 1989–90 | Glentoran 3, Portadown 0 |
| 1964–65 | Coleraine 2, Glenavon 1 | 1990–91 | Portadown 2, Glenavon 1 |
| 1965–66 | Glentoran 2, Linfield 0 | 1991–92 | Glenavon 2, Linfield 1 |
| 1966–67 | Crusaders 3, Glentoran 1 | 1992–93 | Bangor 1:1:1, Ards 1:1:0 |
| 1967–68 | Crusaders 2, Linfield 0 | 1993–94 | Linfield 2, Bangor 0 |
| 1968–69 | Ards 4, Distillery 2 | 1994–95 | Linfield 3, Carrick Rangers 1 |
| 1969–70 | Linfield 2, Ballymena U 1 | 1995–96 | Glentoran 1, Glenavon 0 |
| 1970–71 | Distillery 3, Derry City 0 | 1996–97 | Glenavon 1, Cliftonville 0 |
| 1971–72 | Coleraine 2, Portadown 1 | 1997–98 | Glentoran 1, Glenavon 0 |

## NATIONWIDE GOLD CUP

| Section A | P | W | D | L | F | A | GD | Pts |
|---|---|---|---|---|---|---|---|---|
| Crusaders | 5 | 4 | 1 | 0 | 12 | 6 | +6 | 13 |
| Glenavon | 5 | 3 | 2 | 0 | 12 | 5 | +7 | 11 |
| Dungannon Swifts | 5 | 2 | 0 | 3 | 10 | 13 | –3 | 6 |
| Larne | 5 | 2 | 0 | 3 | 6 | 10 | –4 | 6 |
| Ballymena United | 5 | 1 | 1 | 3 | 8 | 9 | –1 | 4 |
| Ballyclare Comrades | 5 | 1 | 0 | 4 | 7 | 12 | –5 | 3 |

| Section B | P | W | D | L | F | A | GD | Pts |
|---|---|---|---|---|---|---|---|---|
| Distillery | 5 | 3 | 1 | 1 | 10 | 6 | +4 | 10 |
| Linfield | 5 | 3 | 0 | 2 | 15 | 5 | +10 | 9 |
| Coleraine | 5 | 3 | 0 | 2 | 13 | 10 | +3 | 9 |
| Bangor | 5 | 2 | 1 | 2 | 7 | 6 | +1 | 7 |
| Ards | 5 | 2 | 1 | 2 | 9 | 13 | –4 | 7 |
| Limavady United | 5 | 0 | 1 | 4 | 4 | 18 | –14 | 1 |

| Section C | P | W | D | L | F | A | GD | Pts |
|---|---|---|---|---|---|---|---|---|
| Omagh Town | 5 | 3 | 2 | 0 | 9 | 3 | +6 | 11 |
| Cliftonville | 5 | 2 | 3 | 0 | 6 | 1 | +5 | 9 |
| Newry Town | 5 | 3 | 0 | 2 | 5 | 4 | +1 | 9 |
| Portadown | 5 | 2 | 1 | 2 | 14 | 8 | +6 | 7 |
| Glentoran | 5 | 1 | 1 | 3 | 6 | 13 | –7 | 4 |
| Carrick Rangers | 5 | 0 | 1 | 4 | 2 | 13 | –11 | 1 |

### Quarter-finals

| | |
|---|---|
| Newry Town v Crusaders | 0-1 |
| Cliftonville v Coleraine | 0-1 |
| *(aet)* | |
| Linfield v Glenavon | 0-1 |
| Omagh Town v Distillery | 3-1 |

### Semi-finals

| | |
|---|---|
| Glenavon v Crusaders | 3-1 |
| Omagh Town v Coleraine | 1-2 |

### Final

**Glenavon 4 Coleraine 2** *(at Windsor Park)*

*Glenavon:* O'Neill; Wright, Quigley, Smyth, Murphy, Byrne, Doherty (Gregg), Caffrey, Tumilty, Grant (Patton), Ferguson.

*Scorers:* Grant, Tumilty, Ferguson 2.

*Coleraine:* Lamont; McAuley, Gaston, Jamieson, McKeever, Young, Clanachan (Aspinall), McCallion, McIvor, Shiels, Kerrigan.

*Scorers:* McCallion, Gaston.

*Referee:* T. Ferry (Londonderry).

*Attendance:* 2036.

## WHERE THE TROPHIES WENT

| | Winners | Runners-up |
|---|---|---|
| **Smirnoff Irish League** | | |
| Premier Division | Cliftonville | Linfield |
| First Division | Newry Town | Bangor |
| Bass Irish Cup | Glentoran | Glenavon |
| Nationwide Gold Cup | Glenavon | Coleraine |
| Wilkinson Sword League Cup | Linfield | Glentoran |
| Ulster Cup | Ballyclare Comrades | Distillery |
| Calor County Antrim Shield | Linfield | Crusaders |
| Calor County Antrim Junior Shield | Grange Rangers | Tollymore United |
| Coca-Cola League Cup | Linfield | Cliftonville |
| Belfast Telegraph Intermediate Cup | Loughgall | H & W Welders |
| Silverwood Mid Ulster Cup | Dungannon Swifts | Portadown |
| Mid Ulster Shield | Hill Street | Parkview |
| North West Senior Cup | Institute | Limavady United |
| Bob Radcliffe Mem Cup | Lurgan Celtic Bhoys | Glenavon Res |
| Smirnoff Knockout Cup | H & W Welders | Chimney Corner |
| Irish News Cup | Ballymena United | Omagh Town |
| Calor Steel and Sons Cup | Linfield Swifts | Dundela |
| Harry Cavan Coca-Cola Youth Cup | Crusaders Colts | Portadown Boys |
| Irish Youth League Cup | Crusaders Colts | Glenavon III |
| George Wilson Cup | Bangor Res | Linfield Swifts |
| **Irish League B Division** | | |
| Section One | Loughgall | Chimney Corner |
| Section Two | Glentoran II | Linfield Swifts |
| Irish Junior Cup Final | Oxford United | Coagh United II |

# EUROPEAN CUP

## EUROPEAN CUP FINALS 1956–98

| Year | Winners | Runners-up | Venue | Attendance | Referee |
|------|---------|------------|-------|-----------|---------|
| 1956 | Real Madrid 4 | Reims 3 | Paris | 38,000 | Ellis (E) |
| 1957 | Real Madrid 2 | Fiorentina 0 | Madrid | 124,000 | Horn (Ho) |
| 1958 | Real Madrid 3 | AC Milan 2 *(aet)* | Brussels | 67,000 | Alsteen (Bel) |
| 1959 | Real Madrid 2 | Reims 0 | Stuttgart | 80,000 | Dutsch (WG) |
| 1960 | Real Madrid 7 | Eintracht Frankfurt 3 | Glasgow | 135,000 | Mowat (S) |
| 1961 | Benfica 3 | Barcelona 2 | Berne | 28,000 | Dienst (Sw) |
| 1962 | Benfica 5 | Real Madrid 3 | Amsterdam | 65,000 | Horn (Ho) |
| 1963 | AC Milan 2 | Benfica 1 | Wembley | 45,000 | Holland (E) |
| 1964 | Internazionale 3 | Real Madrid 1 | Vienna | 74,000 | Stoll (A) |
| 1965 | Internazionale 1 | Benfica 0 | Milan | 80,000 | Dienst (Sw) |
| 1966 | Real Madrid 2 | Partizan Belgrade 1 | Brussels | 55,000 | Kreitlein (WG) |
| 1967 | Celtic 2 | Internazionale 1 | Lisbon | 56,000 | Tschenscher (WG) |
| 1968 | Manchester U 4 | Benfica 1 *(aet)* | Wembley | 100,000 | Lo Bello (I) |
| 1969 | AC Milan 4 | Ajax 1 | Madrid | 50,000 | Ortiz (Sp) |
| 1970 | Feyenoord 2 | Celtic 1 *(aet)* | Milan | 50,000 | Lo Bello (I) |
| 1971 | Ajax 2 | Panathinaikos 0 | Wembley | 90,000 | Taylor (E) |
| 1972 | Ajax 2 | Internazionale 0 | Rotterdam | 67,000 | Helies (F) |
| 1973 | Ajax 1 | Juventus 0 | Belgrade | 93,500 | Guglovic (Y) |
| 1974 | Bayern Munich 1 | Atletico Madrid 1 | Brussels | 65,000 | Loraux (Bel) |
| *Replay* | Bayern Munich 4 | Atletico Madrid 0 | Brussels | 65,000 | Delcourt (Bel) |
| 1975 | Bayern Munich 2 | Leeds U 0 | Paris | 50,000 | Kitabdjian (F) |
| 1976 | Bayern Munich 1 | St Etienne 0 | Glasgow | 54,864 | Palotai (H) |
| 1977 | Liverpool 3 | Moenchengladbach 1 | Rome | 57,000 | Wurtz (F) |
| 1978 | Liverpool 1 | FC Brugge 0 | Wembley | 92,000 | Corver (Ho) |
| 1979 | Nottingham F 1 | Malmo 0 | Munich | 57,500 | Linemayr (A) |
| 1980 | Nottingham F 1 | Hamburg 0 | Madrid | 50,000 | Garrido (P) |
| 1981 | Liverpool 1 | Real Madrid 0 | Paris | 48,360 | Palotai (H) |
| 1982 | Aston Villa 1 | Bayern Munich 0 | Rotterdam | 46,000 | Konrath (F) |
| 1983 | Hamburg 1 | Juventus 0 | Athens | 75,000 | Rainea (R) |
| 1984 | Liverpool 1 | Roma 1 | Rome | 69,693 | Fredriksson (Se) |
| | *(aet; Liverpool won 4–2 on penalties)* | | | | |
| 1985 | Juventus 1 | Liverpool 0 | Brussels | 58,000 | Daina (Sw) |
| 1986 | Steaua Bucharest 0 | Barcelona 0 | Seville | 70,000 | Vautrot (F) |
| | *(aet; Steaua won 2–0 on penalties)* | | | | |
| 1987 | Porto 2 | Bayern Munich 1 | Vienna | 59,000 | Ponnet (Bel) |
| 1988 | PSV Eindhoven 0 | Benfica 0 | Stuttgart | 70,000 | Agnolin (I) |
| | *(aet; PSV won 6–5 on penalties)* | | | | |
| 1989 | AC Milan 4 | Steaua Bucharest 0 | Barcelona | 97,000 | Tritschler (WG) |
| 1990 | AC Milan 1 | Benfica 0 | Vienna | 57,500 | Kohl (A) |
| 1991 | Red Star Belgrade 0 | Marseille 0 | Bari | 56,000 | Lanese (I) |
| | *(aet; Red Star won 5–3 on penalties)* | | | | |
| 1992 | Barcelona 1 | Sampdoria 0 *(aet)* | Wembley | 70,827 | Schmidhuber (G) |
| 1993 | Marseille* 1 | AC Milan 0 | Munich | 64,400 | Rothlisberger (Sw) |
| 1994 | AC Milan 4 | Barcelona 0 | Athens | 70,000 | Don (E) |
| 1995 | Ajax 1 | AC Milan 0 | Vienna | 49,730 | Craciunescu (Ro) |
| 1996 | Juventus 1 | Ajax 1 | Rome | 67,000 | Vega (Sp) |
| | *(aet; Juventus won 4–2 on penalties)* | | | | |
| 1997 | Borussia Dortmund 3 | Juventus 1 | Munich | 59,000 | Puhl (H) |
| 1998 | Juventus 0 | Real Madrid 1 | Amsterdam | 47,500 | Krug (G) |

*Subsequently stripped of title.

# EUROPEAN CUP 1997–98

## QUALIFYING ROUND, FIRST LEG

Anorthosis (1) 3 *(Chrismarevic 20, Okkas 47, 81)*,
Kareda (0) 0     7000
Constructorul (1) 1 *(Apachieti 18)*, MPKC (1) 1
*(Berishvili 23)*     3000
Crusaders (0) 1 *(Baxter 71)*, Dynamo Tbilisi (1) 3
*(Kiknadze 31, Gogichaishvili 50, Mujiri 65)*     1000
Derry City (0) 0, Branik Maribor (0) 2 *(Zidan 59, Gajser
77)*     3120
Dynamo Kiev (1) 2 *(Rebrov 20, Maximov 83)*, Barry
Town (0) 0     12,000
GI Gotu (0) 0, Rangers (2) 5 *(Negri 19, Durie 25, 80,
McCoist 66, 90)*     3000
Kosice (1) 3 *(Semenik 30, Toth 48, Sovic 73)*,
IA Akranes (0) 0     10,000
Lantana (0) 0, Jazz Pori (1) 2 *(Nieminen 4, 76)*     1000
Neftchi Baku (0) 0, Widzew Lodz (2) 2 *(Szarpak 23,
Dembinski 43)*     12,000
Partizan Belgrade (0) 1 *(Isailovic 84)*, Croatia
Zagreb (0) 0     35,000
Pyunik (0) 0, MTK (0) 2 *(Illes 83, Preisinger 89)*     5000
Sileks (0) 1 *(Karanfilovski 54 (pen))*, Beitar
Jerusalem (0) 0     3000
Sion (3) 4 *(Lipawsky 5, 45, Seone 15, Derivaz 61)*,
Jeunesse Esch (0) 0     7000
Steaua (1) 3 *(Rotariu 8, Lacatus 71, Munteanu 83)*, CSKA
Sofia (0) 3 *(Andonov 47, Nankov 49, 67)*     12,000
Valletta (1) 1 *(Galea 15)*, Skonto Riga (0) 0     2000

## QUALIFYING ROUND, SECOND LEG

Barry Town (0) 0, Dynamo Kiev (0) 4 *(Belkevich 52,
Maximov 67, 78, Vashchuk 80)*     2300
Beitar Jerusalem (2) 3 *(Salloi 15, Ohana 40, Hamar 55)*,
Sileks (0) 0     8000
Branik Maribor (0) 1 *(Drobne 48)*, Derry City (0) 0     7000
Croatia Zagreb (4) 5 *(Maric 13, 42, Cvitanovic 15, 69,
Viduka 24)*, Partizan Belgrade (0) 0     30,000
CSKA Sofia (0) 0, Steaua (1) 2 *(Serban 35, Reghecampf
49)*     25,000
Dynamo Tbilisi (3) 5 *(Iashvili 21, 36, Mujiri 44, 63,
Khomeriki 83)*, Crusaders (0) 1 *(Hunter 61)*     10,000
IA Akranes (0) 0, Kosice (0) 1 *(Faktor 66)*     1200
Jazz Pori (0) 1 *(Marco 65)*, Lantana (0) 0     3760
Jeunesse Esch (0) 0, Sion (0) 1 *(Zambaz 88)*     1600
Kareda (1) 1 *(Mikalajunas 24)*, Anorthosis (1) 1
*(Mihajlovic 10)*     5000
MPKC (1) 3 *(Denisyuk 7, Lovchev 49, Kouchnir 70)*,
Constructorul (1) 2 *(Oleksa 31, Comleonoc 68)*     500
MTK (2) 4 *(Illes 18, Halmai 41, Preisinger 47, Kuttor 75)*,
Pyunik (0) 3 *(Sanamyan 81, 86, Chageldian 85)*     3500
Rangers (2) 6 *(Durie 22, Negri 42, 90, McCoist 48, Albertz
58, Ferguson 84)*, GI Gotu (0) 0     44,433
Skonto Riga (2) 2 *(Astafyev 14, Mikholap 26)*, Valletta
(0) 0     5500
Widzew Lodz (5) 8 *(Szarpak 3, 70 (pen), 76, Kobylanski
8, Zajac 14, Dembinski 25, 30, Curtianu 68)*, Neftchi
Baku (0) 0     7000

## SECOND QUALIFYING ROUND, FIRST LEG

Anorthosis (1) 2 *(Okkas 42, Mihajlovic 90)*, Lierse (0) 0     12,000
Barcelona (1) 3 *(Giovanni 26, 70, Stoichkov 90 (pen))*,
Skonto Riga (1) 2 *(Babichev 25, Abelardo 46 (og))*     50,000
Beitar Jerusalem (0) 0, Sporting Lisbon (0) 0     12,000
Besiktas (0) 0, Branik Maribor (0) 0     15,000
Brondby (1) 2 *(Bagger 22, Daugaard 87)*, Dynamo Kiev
(2) 4 *(Gusin 8, Shevchenko 35, Rebrov 74, Golovko 81)*     10,318
Feyenoord (3) 6 *(Van Gastel 14 (pen), 65 (pen), Vosz 22,
39, Sanchez 58, Van Bronckhorst 85)*, Jazz Pori (1) 2
*(Marco 28, 70)*     28,000
IFK Gothenburg (0) 3 *(Pettersson 56, Karlsson 58,
Eriksson 88)*, Rangers (0) 0     9270
Kosice (2) 2 *(Kozlej 16, Kozak 43)*, Spartak Moscow (1)
1 *(Dimitriev 38)*     9270
Leverkusen (2) 6 *(Lehnhoff 5, Ramelow 43, Meijer 47, 62,
Kirsten 56, Rink 86)*, Dynamo Tbilisi (0) 1 *(Iashvili 59)*     20,500
MTK (0) 0, Rosenborg (0) 1 *(Rushfeldt 88)*     5000

Newcastle U (1) 2 *(Beresford 22, 76)*, Croatia Zagreb (0)
1 *(Cvitanovic 52)*     34,465
Olympiakos (0) 5 *(Niniadis 59, Gogic 63, 67, Georgatos
75, Alexandris 83)*, MPKC (0) 0     42,000
Salzburg (0) 0, Sparta Prague (0) 0     7000
Sion (1) 1 *(Lonfat 32)*, Galatasaray (2) 4 *(Milton 4 (og),
Arif 9, Ilie 61, Suat 86)*     12,500
Steaua (0) 3 *(Rotariu 54 (pen), Serban 71, Lacatus 79)*,
Paris St Germain (1) 2 *(Guerin 49, Maurice 64)*     16,000
Widzew Lodz (0) 1 *(Mikhalchuk 53)*, Parma (1) 3 *(Chiesa
28, 47, 49)*     15,000

## SECOND QUALIFYING ROUND, SECOND LEG

Branik Maribor (0) 1 *(Zidan 86)*, Besiktas (1) 3 *(Mehmet
45, Amokachi 61, Tayfur 62)*     7000
Croatia Zagreb (0) 2 *(Simic D 59, Cvitanovic 90)*,
Newcastle U (1) 2 *(Asprilla 44 (pen), Ketsbaia 120)*     34,000
Dynamo Kiev (0) 0, Brondby (1) 1 *(Colding 19)*     20,000
Dynamo Tbilisi (1) 1 *(Mujiri 11)*, Leverkusen (0) 0 30,000
Galatasaray (1) 4 *(Ilie 40, 52, 56, Fatih 61)*, Sion (0) 1
*(Ouattara 70)*     30,000
Jazz Pori (1) 1 *(Laaksonen 37)*, Feyenoord (1) 2 *(Boateng
21, Van Gastel 89)*     2720
Lierse (1) 3 *(Van Meir 22 (pen), Hasenhuttl 47, Tomic 84
(og))*, Anorthosis (0) 0     6,500
MPKC (2) 2 *(Berisvili 5, Kusjnir 19)*, Olympiakos (1) 2
*(Anatolakis 9, Niniadis 54)*     4000
Paris St Germain (4) 5 *(Rai 3 (pen), 22, 55, Simone 32,
Maurice 41)*, Steaua (0) 0     46,286
Parma (2) 4 *(Pedros 37, Sensini 41, 52, Adailton 79)*,
Widzew Lodz (0) 0     25,000
Rangers (1) 1 *(Miller 24)*, IFK Gothenburg (0) 1
*(Andersson R 49)*     45,585
Rosenborg (2) 3 *(Jakobsen 14, 16, Brattbakk 84)*, MTK
(0) 1 *(Kuttor 77)*     15,014
Skonto Riga (0) 0, Barcelona (0) 1 *(Anderson 50)*     12,000
Spartak Moscow (0) 0, Kosice (0) 0     20,000
Sparta Prague (2) 3 *(Baranek 28, Lokvenc 43, Svoboda
66)*, Salzburg (0) 0     15,628
Sporting Lisbon (1) 3 *(Yordanov 5, Leandro 55, 63)*,
Beitar Jerusalem (0) 0     50,000

## CHAMPIONS LEAGUE

### GROUP A

Galatasaray (0) 0, Borussia Dortmund (0) 1 *(Chapuisat
74)*     22,000
Sparta Prague (0) 0, Parma (0) 0     17,846
Borussia Dortmund (1) 4 *(Herrlich 20, Chapuisat 59, 75,
Heinrich 69)*, Sparta Prague (0) 1 *(Siegl 76)*     46,500
Parma (2) 2 *(Sensini 23, Crespo 38)*, Galatasaray (0) 0     15,922
Parma (0) 1 *(Crespo 63)*, Borussia Dortmund (0) 0 13,449
Sparta Prague (1) 3 *(Siegl 34, Gabrel 66, Obajdin 87)*,
Galatasaray (0) 0     11,108
Borussia Dortmund (0) 2 *(Moller 50, 74 (pen))*, Parma
(0) 0     40,000
Galatasaray (0) 2 *(Tugay 55, 88)*, Sparta Prague (0) 0     25,000
Borussia Dortmund (2) 4 *(But 22, Herrlich 34, Zorc 47,
86 (pen))*, Galatasary (0) 1 *(Ergun 47)*     45,000
Parma (1) 2 *(Chiesa 21, 90 (pen))*, Sparta Prague (0) 2
*(Novotny 90, Obajdin 90)*     16,200
Galatasaray (0) 1 *(Ilie 52)*, Parma (0) 1 *(Chiesa 50)* 30,000
Sparta Prague (0) 0, Borussia Dortmund (1) 3 *(Moller 30,
Kirovski 47, Booth 71)*     10,925

### FINAL TABLE

| | P | W | D | L | F | A | Pts |
|---|---|---|---|---|---|---|---|
| Borussia Dortmund | 6 | 5 | 0 | 1 | 14 | 3 | 15 |
| Parma | 6 | 2 | 3 | 1 | 6 | 5 | 9 |
| Sparta Prague | 6 | 1 | 2 | 3 | 6 | 11 | 5 |
| Galatasaray | 6 | 1 | 1 | 4 | 4 | 11 | 4 |

### GROUP B

Kosice (0) 0, Manchester U (1) 3 *(Irwin 29, Berg 60, Cole
88)*     10,000

Juventus (3) 5 *(Del Piero 3, 10 (pen), Inzaghi 34, Zidane 76, Birindelli 81)*, Feyenoord (0) 1 *(Van Gastel 75)*
12,622
Feyenoord (2) 2 *(Van Gastel 26 (pen), Cruz 34)*, Kosice (0) 0
35,408
Manchester U (1) 3 *(Sheringham 37, Scholes 69, Giggs 89)*, Juventus (1) 2 *(Del Piero 1, Zidane 90)*
53,428
Kosice (0) 0, Juventus (1) 1 *(Del Piero 33)*
10,000
Manchester U (1) 2 *(Scholes 32, Irwin 72 (pen))*, Feyenoord (0) 1 *(Vosz 83)*
53,188
Feyenoord (0) 1 *(Korneev 87)*, Manchester U (2) 3 *(Cole 31, 44, 75)*
45,000
Juventus (1) 3 *(Del Piero 44, Amoruso 58, Fonseca 61)*, Kosice (0) 2 *(Ljubarski 66, Kozak 70)*
17,000
Feyenoord (0) 2 *(Cruz 66, 88)*, Juventus (0) 0
45,000
Manchester U (1) 3 *(Cole 40, Faktor 85 (og), Sheringham 90)*, Kosice (0) 0
53,535
Kosice (0) 0, Feyenoord (0) 1 *(Van Bronckhorst 82)*
2500
Juventus (0) 1 *(Inzaghi 83)*, Manchester U (0) 0
47,786

**FINAL TABLE**

|              | P | W | D | L | F  | A  | Pts |
|--------------|---|---|---|---|----|----|-----|
| Manchester U | 6 | 5 | 0 | 1 | 14 | 5  | 15  |
| Juventus     | 6 | 4 | 0 | 2 | 12 | 8  | 12  |
| Feyenoord    | 6 | 3 | 0 | 3 | 8  | 10 | 9   |
| Kosice       | 6 | 0 | 0 | 6 | 2  | 13 | 0   |

## GROUP C

Newcastle U (2) 3 *(Asprilla 22 (pen), 30, 48)*, Barcelona (0) 2 *(Luis Enrique 72, Figo 88)*
35,274
PSV Eindhoven (1) 1 *(Jonk 40)*, Dynamo Kiev (1) 3 *(Maximov 33, Rebrov 47, Shevchenko 90)*
25,000
Barcelona (0) 2 *(Luis Enrique 64, 75)*, PSV Eindhoven (0) 2 *(De Bilde 70, Moller 86)*
80,000
Dynamo Kiev (2) 2 *(Rebrov 3, Shevchenko 28)*, Newcastle U (0) 2 *(Beresford 78, 85)*
100,000
Dynamo Kiev (2) 3 *(Rebrov 5, Maximov 32, Kalitvintsev 65)*, Barcelona (0) 0
100,000
PSV Eindhoven (1) 1 *(Jonk 38)*, Newcastle U (0) 0 29,200
Barcelona (0) 0, Dynamo Kiev (3) 4 *(Shevchenko 10, 33, 44 (pen), Rebrov 77)*
60,000
Newcastle U (0) 0, PSV Eindhoven (1) 2 *(Nilis 32, De Bilde 90)*
35,214
Barcelona (1) 1 *(Giovanni 17)*, Newcastle U (0) 0 25,000
Dynamo Kiev (1) 1 *(Rebrov 19)*, PSV Eindhoven (0) 1 *(De Bilde 65)*
80,000
Newcastle U (2) 2 *(Barnes 10, Pearce 21)*, Dynamo Kiev (0) 0
33,694
PSV Eindhoven (0) 2 *(Jonk 54, De Bilde 56)*, Barcelona (1) 2 *(Abelardo 30, Giovanni 67)*
30,000

**FINAL TABLE**

|               | P | W | D | L | F  | A  | Pts |
|---------------|---|---|---|---|----|----|-----|
| Dynamo Kiev   | 6 | 3 | 2 | 1 | 13 | 6  | 11  |
| PSV Eindhoven | 6 | 2 | 3 | 1 | 9  | 8  | 9   |
| Newcastle U   | 6 | 2 | 1 | 3 | 7  | 8  | 7   |
| Barcelona     | 6 | 1 | 2 | 3 | 7  | 14 | 5   |

## GROUP D

Olympiakos (1) 1 *(Giannakopoulos 6)*, Porto (0) 0 75,000
Real Madrid (3) 4 *(Panucci 4, Ze Roberto 38, Raul 43, Morientes 83)*, Rosenborg (1) 1 *(Jakobsen 14)*  53,000
Porto (0) 0, Real Madrid (1) 2 *(Hierro 14, Raul 79)* 40,000
Rosenborg (3) 5 *(Brattbakk 14, 80, Strand 33, 43, Rushfeldt 56)*, Olympiakos (0) 1 *(Ofori-Quaye 69)*
16,038
Real Madrid (2) 5 *(Suker 33 (pen), 67 (pen), Morientes 44, Victor 85, Roberto Carlos 90)*, Olympiakos (1) 1 *(Dabizas 18)*
50,000
Rosenborg (2) 2 *(Rushfeldt 7, Brattbakk 37)*, Porto (0) 0
17,214
Porto (1) 1 *(Jardel 7)*, Rosenborg (0) 1 *(Strand 87)* 25,000
Olympiakos (0) 0, Real Madrid (0) 0
50,000
Porto (1) 2 *(Jardel 27, 53)*, Olympiakos (1) 1 *(Georgatos 21)*
8000
Rosenborg (1) 2 *(Strand 42, Brattbakk 53)*, Real Madrid (0) 0
19,147
Olympiakos (1) 2 *(Mavrogenidis 27, Djordjevic 89)*, Rosenborg (1) 2 *(Rushfeldt 28, 70)*
25,000
Real Madrid (2) 4 *(Hierro 5, Suker 30, 72 (pen), Roberto Carlos 49)*, Porto (0) 0
70,000

**FINAL TABLE**

|             | P | W | D | L | F  | A  | Pts |
|-------------|---|---|---|---|----|----|-----|
| Real Madrid | 6 | 4 | 1 | 1 | 15 | 4  | 13  |
| Rosenborg   | 6 | 3 | 2 | 1 | 13 | 8  | 11  |
| Olympiakos  | 6 | 1 | 2 | 3 | 6  | 14 | 5   |
| Porto       | 6 | 1 | 1 | 4 | 3  | 11 | 4   |

## GROUP E

Bayern Munich (1) 2 *(Helmer 3, Basler 70)*, Besiktas (0) 0
38,000
Paris St Germain (1) 3 *(N'Gotty 27, Lucic 51 (og), Rai 81 (pen))*, IFK Gothenburg (0) 0
26,189
Besiktas (2) 3 *(Oktay 4, 41, Ertugrul 84)*, Paris St Germain (0) 1 *(Simone 66)*
30,000
IFK Gothenburg (0) 1 *(Lucic 86)*, Bayern Munich (2) 3 *(Jancker 2, Hamann 35, Elber 90)*
26,503
Bayern Munich (2) 5 *(Elber 3, 72, Jancker 21, 47, Helmer 51)*, Paris St Germain (0) 1 *(Simone 48)*
45,000
Besiktas (1) 1 *(Oktay 6)*, IFK Gothenburg (0) 0  30,000
IFK Gothenburg (2) 2 *(Pettersson 17 (pen), Andersson R 22)*, Besiktas (1) 1 *(Oktay 44)*
12,000
Paris St Germain (1) 3 *(Gava 18, Maurice 73, Leroy 75)*, Bayern Munich (1) 1 *(Babbel 29)*
32,274
Besiktas (0) 0, Bayern Munich (2) 2 *(Jancker 5, Helmer 32)*
30,000
IFK Gothenburg (0) 0, Paris St Germain (0) 1 *(Rabesandratana 90)*
19,323
Bayern Munich (0) 0, IFK Gothenburg (0) 1 *(Babbel 51 (og)*
27,000
Paris St Germain (1) 2 *(Gava 24, Simone 60)*, Besiktas (1) 1 *(Ozdilek 40)*
34,038

**FINAL TABLE**

|                  | P | W | D | L | F  | A  | Pts |
|------------------|---|---|---|---|----|----|-----|
| Bayern Munich    | 6 | 4 | 0 | 2 | 13 | 6  | 12  |
| Paris St Germain | 6 | 4 | 0 | 2 | 11 | 10 | 12  |
| Besiktas         | 6 | 2 | 0 | 4 | 6  | 9  | 6   |
| IFK Gothenburg   | 6 | 2 | 0 | 4 | 4  | 9  | 6   |

## GROUP F

Leverkusen (1) 1 *(Beinlich 40)*, Lierse (0) 0     22,500
Sporting Lisbon (2) 3 *(Oceano 3, Hadji 8, Leandro 75)*, Monaco (0) 0
32,000
Lierse (0) 1 *(Huistra 88)*, Sporting Lisbon (0) 1 *(Leandro 86)*
10,000
Monaco (1) 4 *(Henry 30, 84, Ikpeba 74, 90)*, Leverkusen (0) 0
6000
Monaco (1) 5 *(Henry 33, Collins 51, Ikpeba 66, Trezeguet 83, 87)*, Lierse (0) 1 *(Van Meir 60)*
7000
Sporting Lisbon (0) 0, Leverkusen (0) 2 *(Beinlich 71, Emerson 82)*
35,000
Leverkusen (1) 4 *(Emerson 15, 73, Rink 84, Frydek 90)*, Sporting Lisbon (1) 1 *(Hadji 44)*
22,500
Lierse (0) 0, Monaco (0) 1 *(Ikpeba 74)*
7500
Lierse (0) 0, Leverkusen (0) 2 *(Emerson 55, Kirsten 66)*
8000
Monaco (0) 3 *(Trezeguet 66, Henry 75, 90)*, Sporting Lisbon (2) 2 *(Miguel 30, Oceano 38 (pen))*  11,000
Leverkusen (1) 2 *(Beinlich 29, Meijer 57)*, Monaco (0) 2 *(Pignol 63, Henry 81)*
22,500
Sporting Lisbon (0) 2 *(Ramirez 47, Gimenez 65)*, Lierse (1) 1 *(Haagdoren 17)*
13,000

**FINAL TABLE**

|                 | P | W | D | L | F  | A  | Pts |
|-----------------|---|---|---|---|----|----|-----|
| Monaco          | 6 | 4 | 1 | 1 | 15 | 8  | 13  |
| Leverkusen      | 6 | 4 | 1 | 1 | 11 | 7  | 13  |
| Sporting Lisbon | 6 | 2 | 1 | 3 | 9  | 11 | 7   |
| Lierse          | 6 | 0 | 1 | 5 | 3  | 12 | 1   |

## QUARTER-FINALS, FIRST LEG

Monaco (0) 0, Manchester U (0) 0
15,000
Leverkusen (1) 1 *(Beinlich 17)*, Real Madrid (0) 1 *(Karembeu 73)*
22,500
Bayern Munich (0) 0, Borussia Dortmund (0) 0  60,000
Juventus (0) 1 *(Inzaghi 70)*, Dynamo Kiev (0) 1 *(Gusin 56)*
40,723

## QUARTER-FINALS, SECOND LEG

Borussia Dortmund (0) 1 *(Chapuisat 109 (pen))*, Bayern Munich (0) 0
48,500
Dynamo Kiev (0) 1 *(Rebrov 55)*, Juventus (1) 4 *(Inzaghi 29, 66, 72, Del Piero 88)*
100,000
Manchester U (1) 1 *(Solskjaer 53)*, Monaco (1) 1 *(Trezeguet 6)*
53,683
Real Madrid (0) 3 *(Karembeu 50, Morientes 58, Hierro 90 (pen))*, Leverkusen (0) 0
90,000

**SEMI-FINALS, FIRST LEG**
Juventus (2) 4 *(Del Piero 35, 45 (pen), 62 (pen), Zidane 88)*, Monaco (1) 1 *(Da Costa 44)* 56,550
Real Madrid (1) 2 *(Morientes 26, Karembeu 67)*, Borussia Dortmund (0) 0 85,000

**SEMI-FINALS, SECOND LEG**
Borussia Dortmund (0) 0, Real Madrid (0) 0 48,500
Monaco (1) 3 *(Leonard 39, Henry 50, Spehar 83)*, Juventus (1) 2 *(Amoruso 15, Del Piero 74)* 12,000

**FINAL**

**Juventus (0) 0, Real Madrid (0) 1**

(in Amsterdam, 20 May 1998, 47,500)

*Juventus:* Peruzzi; Torricelli, Montero, Juliano, Di Livio (Tacchinardi 46), Deschamps (Conte 77), Davids, Pessotto (Fonseca 70), Inzaghi, Del Piero, Zidane.
*Real Madrid:* Illgner; Panucci, Roberto Carlos, Seedorf, Sanchis, Hierro, Redondo, Karembeu, Raul (Amavisca 90), Mijatovic (Suker 88), Morientes (Jaime 81).
*Scorer:* Mijatovic 67.
*Referee:* H. Krug (Germany).

Real Madrid players celebrate with the European Cup following their final success against Juventus. (Colorsport)

# EUROPEAN CUP 1997–98 – BRITISH AND IRISH CLUBS

**FIRST QUALIFYING ROUND, FIRST LEG**
**23 JULY**

**Crusaders (0) 1** *(Baxter 71)*
**Dynamo Tbilisi (1) 3** *(Kiknadze 31, Gogichaishvili 50, Mujiri 65)* 1000
*Crusaders:* Grant; Dornan (Deegan 65), McCartney (Morgan 65), Dunlop, O'Brien, Lawlor, Mellon, Dwyer (McMullan 55), Arthur, Baxter, Hunter G.
*Dynamo Tbilisi:* Zoidze; Kaladze, Didava, Machavariani, Chikhaidze, Kiknadze, Tskitishvili, Mujiri (Khomeriki 89), Iashvili (Kizilashvili 79), Anchabadze, Gogichaishvili (Aleksidze 90).

**Derry City (0) 0**
**Branik Maribor (1) 2** *(Zidan 59, Gajser 77)* 3120
*Derry City:* Devine; Doherty, Curran, Dykes, Brady (Coyle R 62), Mahon, Hegarty, Hutton, Hargan, Coyle L, Beckett.
*Branik Maribor:* Simeunovic; Kek, Fridl, Sharkevi, Bulajic, Sterbal, Fricelj (Ceh 84), Gajser (Vuksanovic 84), Zidan, Paco, Drobne (Munishi 66).

**Dynamo Kiev (1) 2** *(Rebrov 20, Maximov 83)*
**Barry Town (0) 0** 12,000
*Dynamo Kiev:* Shovkovsky; Golovko, Vashchuk, Dmitrulin, Kalitvintsev, Rebrov, Gusin, Khatskevich (Mikhailenko 65), Shkapenko (Maximov 65), Radchenko, Belkevich.
*Barry Town:* Ovendale; Evans T, Knott, Lloyd, York, Loss, Bird, Ryan, Johnson, Huggins, Evans C (O'Gorman 73).

**GI Gotu (0) 0**
**Rangers (2) 5** *(Negri 19, Durie 25, 80, McCoist 66, 90)* 3000
*GI Gotu:* Knudsen; Rasmussen, Hojgaard, Justinussen S, Justinussen R, Jarnskor H, Jarnskor M, Jarnskor P (Tvorfoss 71), Joensen S, Hansen, Magnussen (Jacobsen 60).
*Rangers:* Niemi; Cleland, Bjorklund, Moore (Wright 78), Vidmar, Thern, Albertz, Ferguson I, Laudrup (McCoist 37), Durie, Negri.

**FIRST QUALIFYING ROUND, SECOND LEG**
**30 JULY**

**Barry Town (0) 0**
**Dynamo Kiev (0) 4** *(Belkevich 53, Maximov 67, 78, Vashchuk 80)* 2300
*Barry Town:* Ovendale; Evans T, York, Lloyd, Huggins, Jones, Barnett (Evans C 57), Ryan, O'Gorman, Bird, Pike (Loss 46).
*Dynamo Kiev:* Shovkovsky; Luzhny, Golovko, Vashchuk, Dmitrulin, Kalitvintsev, Rebrov, Gusin, Khatskevich (Radchenko 65), Shkapenko (Shmatovalenko 26), Belkevich (Maximov 64).

**Branik Maribor (0) 1** *(Drobne 48)*
**Derry City (0) 0** 7000
*Branik Maribor:* Simeunovic; Sterbal, Fridl, Bulajic, Kek, Sharkevi, Fricelj, Zidan (Vuksanovic 79), Paco, Gajser (Ceh 79), Drobne.
*Derry City:* O'Dowd; Doherty, Brady (Gallagher 66), Hutton, Curran, Dykes, Mohan, Hegarty, Coyle L (Sempe 67), Coyle R, Hargan.

**Dynamo Tbilisi (3) 5** *(Iashvili 21, 36, Mujiri 44, 63, Khomeriki 83)*
**Crusaders (0) 1** *(Hunter G 61)* 10,000
*Dynamo Tbilisi:* Zoidze; Kaladze, Didava, Machavariani (Rati 71), Gogichaishvili (Khomeriki 78), Kiknadze, Anchabadze, Iashvili, Tskitishvili, Chikhaidze, Mujiri.
*Crusaders:* Grant; Dunlop, Callaghan, Lawlor (Dwyer 45), Walker, McMullan, O'Brien (Hunter K 72), Deegan, Baxter, Hunter G, Arthur (Morgan).

**Rangers (2) 6** *(Durie 22, Negri 42, 90, McCoist 48, Albertz 58, Ferguson I 84)*
**GI Gotu (0) 0** 44,433
*Rangers:* Niemi; Moore, Bjorklund, Porrini (Cleland 83), Vidmar, Thern, Durie (Durrant 77), Gascoigne (Albertz 46), Negri, McCoist, Ferguson I.
*GI Gotu:* Knudsen; Rasmussen, Jarnskor H, Joensen, Hansen, Hojgaard, Jarnskor M, Justinussen S, Justinussen R, Olsen, Tvorfoss (Jarnskor P 72).

**SECOND QUALIFYING ROUND, FIRST LEG**
**13 AUG**

**IFK Gothenburg (0) 3** *(Pettersson 56, Karlsson 58, Eriksson 88)*
**Rangers (0) 0** 20,000
*IFK Gothenburg:* Ravelli; Johansson, Erlingmark, Lucic, Magnusson, Alexandersson, Pettersson, Lindqvist, Karlsson (Eriksson 71), Andersson A (Ekstrom 87), Andersson R.
*Rangers:* Goram; Cleland, Stensaas, Bjorklund, Porrini, Vidmar, Thern, Gascoigne, Negri (McCoist 69), Durie, Albertz (Ferguson I 69).

**Newcastle U (1) 2** *(Beresford 22, 76)*
**Croatia Zagreb (0) 1** *(Cvitanovic 52)* 34,465
*Newcastle U:* Given; Watson, Beresford, Albert (Howey 68), Pistone, Pearce, Lee, Batty, Asprilla, Tomasson (Gillespie 57), Ketsbaia.
*Croatia Zagreb:* Ladic; Mladinic, Juric, Simic D, Saric (Tomas 85), Maric (Mujcin 88), Jurcic, Krznar, Prosinecki, Viduka, Cvitanovic.

**SECOND QUALIFYING ROUND, SECOND LEG**
**27 AUG**

**Croatia Zagreb (0) 2** *(Simic D 59, Cvitanovic 90)*
**Newcastle U (1) 2** *(Asprilla 44 (pen), Ketsbaia 120)* 34,000
*Croatia Zagreb:* Ladic; Saric (Simic J 78) (Tomas 97), Juric, Simic D, Mladinic, Maric, Jurcic, Prosinecki, Mujcin, Viduka (Petrovic 73), Cvitanovic.
*Newcastle U:* Given; Watson, Beresford (Gillespie 82), Albert, Pistone, Pearce (Howey 30), Lee, Batty, Asprilla, Tomasson (Ketsbaia 102), Barton.

**Rangers (1) 1** *(Miller 24)*
**IFK Gothenburg (0) 1** *(Andersson R 49)* 45,585
*Rangers:* Goram; Moore, Stensaas, Bjorklund, Porrini, Miller (Albertz 79), Thern, Gascoigne, Negri, McCoist (Durie 64), Ferguson I (Laudrup 54).
*IFK Gothenburg:* Ravelli; Magnusson, Lucic, Erlingmark, Neilson, Alexandersson, Pettersson (Johansson 46), Lindqvist, Eriksson, Andersson R (Tetteh 73), Andersson A (Ekstrom 84).

**GROUP B**
**17 SEPT**

**Kosice (0) 0** 10,000
**Manchester U (1) 3** *(Irwin 29, Berg 60, Cole 88)*
*Kosice:* Molnar; Spilar, Telek, Kozak, Janocko, Lubarsky (Rusnak 7), Kozlej (Faktor 76), Semenik, Zvara, Sovic, Kral.
*Manchester U:* Schmeichel; Neville G, Irwin, Berg, Keane, Pallister, Beckham (McClair 75), Butt, Cole, Scholes, Poborsky.

**1 OCT**

**Manchester U (1) 3** *(Sheringham 37, Scholes 69, Giggs 89)*
**Juventus (1) 2** *(Del Piero 1, Zidane 90)* 53,428
*Manchester U:* Schmeichel; Neville G, Irwin, Berg, Johnsen, Pallister, Beckham, Butt (Scholes 37), Solskjaer (Neville P 49), Sheringham, Giggs.
*Juventus:* Peruzzi; Ferrara, Montero, Pecchia (Juliano 70), Dimas, Inzaghi, Del Piero (Amoruso 77), Deschamps, Birindelli, Tacchinardi (Pessotto 18), Zidane.

**22 OCT**

**Manchester U (1) 2** *(Scholes 32, Irwin 72 (pen))*
**Feyenoord (0) 1** *(Vosz 83)* 53,188
*Manchester U:* Schmeichel; Irwin, Neville P, Neville G, Scholes, Pallister, Beckham, Butt, Cole (Solskjaer 81), Sheringham, Giggs.
*Feyenoord:* Dudek; Van Gobbel, Van Wonderen, Picun, Schuiteman, Graff, Bosvelt, Van Gastel, Van Bronckhorst (Korneev 37), Sanchez (Boateng 75), Connolly (Vosz 72).

**5 NOV**

**Feyenoord (0) 1** *(Korneev 87)*
**Manchester U (2) 3** *(Cole 31, 44, 75)* 45,000
*Feyenoord:* Dudek; Van Gobbel, Schuiteman, Van Gastel, Van Wonderen, Graff (Claeys 32), Bosvelt (Zwijnenberg 83), Boateng, Van Bronckhorst, Korneev, Cruz (Vosz 77).
*Manchester U:* Schmeichel; Neville G, Irwin (Neville P 84), Berg, Scholes (Poborsky 78), Pallister, Beckham, Butt, Cole (Solskjaer 78), Sheringham, Giggs.

**27 NOV**

**Manchester U (1) 3** *(Cole 40, Faktor 85 (og), Sheringham 90)*
**Kosice (0) 0** 53,535
*Manchester U:* Schmeichel; Neville G, Neville P (Berg 75), Johnsen, Scholes, Pallister, Beckham, Butt (Solskjaer 55), Cole, Sheringham, Giggs (Poborsky 75).
*Kosice:* Molnar; Kozak, Semenik, Spilar, Toth, Sovic, Dzurik, Zvara (Faktor 82), Janocko (Rusnak 31), Kozlej, Lubarsky.

**10 DEC**

**Juventus (0) 1** *(Inzaghi 83)*
**Manchester U (0) 0** 47,786
*Juventus:* Peruzzi; Birindelli (Dimas 75), Ferrara, Juliano, Torricelli, Di Livio, Conte (Montero 65), Tacchinardi (Pecchia 46), Zidane, Fonseca, Inzaghi.
*Manchester U:* Schmeichel; Neville P, Neville G, Berg, Johnsen, Pallister, Beckham, Poborsky (McClair 80), Solskjaer (Cole 73), Sheringham, Giggs.

**GROUP C**

**17 SEPT**

**Newcastle U (2) 3** *(Asprilla 22 (pen), 30, 48)*
**Barcelona (0) 2** *(Luis Enrique 72, Figo 88)* 35,274
*Newcastle U:* Given; Watson, Beresford, Batty, Albert, Barton, Lee, Gillespie, Asprilla, Barnes (Ketsbaia 79), Tomasson (Peacock 76).
*Barcelona:* Hesp; Reiziger, Celades, Nadal, Sergi, De La Pena, Figo, Luis Enrique, Rivaldo, Amunike (Ciric 46), Anderson (Dugarry 54).

**1 OCT**

**Dynamo Kiev (2) 2** *(Rebrov 3, Shevchenko 28)*
**Newcastle U (0) 2** *(Beresford 78, 85)* 100,000
*Dynamo Kiev:* Shovkovsky; Luzhny (Bezhenar 41), Golovko, Vashchuk, Dmitrulin, Kossovsky, Gusin, Khatskevich (Radchenko 72), Belkevich (Mikhailenko 69), Rebrov, Shevchenko.
*Newcastle U:* Given; Watson, Beresford, Batty, Peacock, Albert, Lee (Ketsbaia 46), Barton, Asprilla (Tomasson 28), Barnes, Gillespie.

**22 OCT**

**PSV Eindhoven (1) 1** *(Jonk 38)*
**Newcastle U (0) 0** 29,200
*PSV Eindhoven:* Waterreus; Vampeta, Stam, Faber, Numan, Iwan (Stinga 63), Cocu, Jonk, Petrovic (Moller 80), Nilis (Bruggink 80), De Bilde.
*Newcastle U:* Given; Barton (Albert 80), Watson, Batty, Peacock, Howey, Lee, Gillespie, Rush, Tomasson, Beresford (Ketsbaia 67).

**5 NOV**

**Newcastle U (0) 0**
**PSV Eindhoven (1) 2** *(Nilis 32, De Bilde 90)* 35,214
*Newcastle U:* Given; Watson, Beresford, Barton, Pistone, Albert, Hamilton, Ketsbaia, Tomasson, Barnes, Gillespie.
*PSV Eindhoven:* Waterreus; Vampeta, Stam, Faber, Numan, Petrovic, Jonk, Cocu, Iwan, Nilis, De Bilde.

**26 NOV**

**Barcelona (1) 1** *(Giovanni 17)*
**Newcastle U (0) 0** 25,000
*Barcelona:* Hesp; Fernando Couto, Abelardo, Ferrer, Celades, Reiziger, Ciric, Guardiola (Amor 64), Rivaldo, Anderson (Pizzi 55), Giovanni (Nadal 80).
*Newcastle U:* Hislop; Watson, Beresford, Albert (Hughes 46), Peacock (Pearce 30), Pistone, Hamilton, Batty, Tomasson, Barnes, Ketsbaia.

**10 DEC**

**Newcastle U (2) 2** *(Barnes 10, Pearce 21)*
**Dynamo Kiev (0) 0** 33,694
*Newcastle U:* Hislop; Watson, Pearce, Albert, Peacock, Pistone (Hughes 46), Lee, Batty, Asprilla (Ketsbaia 57), Barnes, Gillespie.
*Dynamo Kiev:* Shovkovsky; Bezhenar, Luzhny, Volosyanko (Radchenko 80), Gusin, Mikhailenko (Venglinski 80), Dmitrulin, Kalitvintsev, Kossovsky, Rebrov, Shevchenko.

**QUARTER-FINALS, FIRST LEG**

**4 MAR**

**Monaco (0) 0**
**Manchester U (0) 0** 15,000
*Monaco:* Barthez; Sagnol, Dumas, Konjic, Leonard, Djetou, Collins, Legwinsky, Benarbia (Carnot 75), Henry, Ikpeba (Spehar 60).
*Manchester U:* Schmeichel; Neville G, Irwin (McClair 65), Berg, Neville P, Johnsen, Beckham, Butt, Cole, Sheringham, Scholes.

**QUARTER-FINALS, SECOND LEG**

**18 MAR**

**Manchester U (0) 1** *(Solskjaer 53)*
**Monaco (1) 1** *(Trezeguet 6)* 53,683
*Manchester U:* Van der Gouw; Neville P, Irwin, Neville G (Berg 32), Scholes (Clegg 46), Johnsen, Beckham, Butt, Cole, Sheringham, Solskjaer.
*Monaco:* Barthez; Sagnol, Djetou, Dumas, Konjic (Da Costa 74), Leonard, Diawara, Benarbia (Carnot 66), Collins, Ikpeba (Henry 60), Trezeguet.

# EUROPEAN CUP-WINNERS' CUP

## EUROPEAN CUP-WINNERS' CUP FINALS 1961–98

| Year | Winners | | Runners-up | | Venue | Attendance | Referee |
|---|---|---|---|---|---|---|---|
| 1961 | Fiorentina | 2 | Rangers | 0 *(1st Leg)* | Glasgow | 80,000 | Steiner (A) |
| | Fiorentina | 2 | Rangers | 1 *(2nd Leg)* | Florence | 50,000 | Hernadi (H) |
| 1962 | Atletico Madrid | 1 | Fiorentina | 1 | Glasgow | 27,389 | Wharton (S) |
| *Replay* | Atletico Madrid | 3 | Fiorentina | 0 | Stuttgart | 45,000 | Tschenscher (WG) |
| 1963 | Tottenham Hotspur | 5 | Atletico Madrid | 1 | Rotterdam | 25,000 | Van Leuwen (Ho) |
| 1964 | Sporting Lisbon | 3 | MTK Budapest | 3 *(aet)* | Brussels | 9000 | Van Nuffel (Bel) |
| *Replay* | Sporting Lisbon | 1 | MTK Budapest | 0 | Antwerp | 18,000 | Versyp (Bel) |
| 1965 | West Ham U | 2 | Munich 1860 | 0 | Wembley | 100,000 | Szolt (H) |
| 1966 | Borussia Dortmund | 2 | Liverpool | 1 *(aet)* | Glasgow | 41,657 | Schwinte (F) |
| 1967 | Bayern Munich | 1 | Rangers | 0 *(aet)* | Nuremberg | 69,480 | Lo Bello (I) |
| 1968 | AC Milan | 2 | Hamburg | 0 | Rotterdam | 60,000 | Ortiz (Sp) |
| 1969 | Slovan Bratislava | 3 | Barcelona | 2 | Basle | 40,000 | Van Ravens (Ho) |
| 1970 | Manchester C | 2 | Gornik Zabrze | 1 | Vienna | 10,000 | Schiller (A) |
| 1971 | Chelsea | 1 | Real Madrid | 1 *(aet)* | Athens | 42,000 | Scheurer (Sw) |
| *Replay* | Chelsea | 2 | Real Madrid | 1 *(aet)* | Athens | 24,000 | Bucheli (Sw) |
| 1972 | Rangers | 3 | Moscow Dynamo | 2 | Barcelona | 35,000 | Ortiz (Sp) |
| 1973 | AC Milan | 1 | Leeds U | 0 | Salonika | 45,000 | Mihas (Gr) |
| 1974 | Magdeburg | 2 | AC Milan | 0 | Rotterdam | 5000 | Van Gemert (Ho) |
| 1975 | Dynamo Kiev | 3 | Ferencvaros | 0 | Basle | 13,000 | Davidson (S) |
| 1976 | Anderlecht | 4 | West Ham U | 2 | Brussels | 58,000 | Wurtz (F) |
| 1977 | Hamburg | 2 | Anderlecht | 0 | Amsterdam | 65,000 | Partridge (E) |
| 1978 | Anderlecht | 4 | Austria/WAC | 0 | Paris | 48,679 | Adlinger (WG) |
| 1979 | Barcelona | 4 | Fortuna Dusseldorf | 3 *(aet)* | Basle | 58,000 | Palotai (H) |
| 1980 | Valencia | 0 | Arsenal | 0 | Brussels | 40,000 | Christov (Cz) |
| | *(aet; Valencia won 5-4 on penalties)* | | | | | | |
| 1981 | Dynamo Tbilisi | 2 | Carl Zeiss Jena | 1 | Dusseldorf | 9000 | Lattanzi (I) |
| 1982 | Barcelona | 2 | Standard Liege | 1 | Barcelona | 100,000 | Eschweiler (WG) |
| 1983 | Aberdeen | 2 | Real Madrid | 1 *(aet)* | Gothenburg | 17,804 | Menegali (I) |
| 1984 | Juventus | 2 | Porto | 1 | Basle | 60,000 | Prokop (EG) |
| 1985 | Everton | 3 | Rapid Vienna | 1 | Rotterdam | 30,000 | Casarin (I) |
| 1986 | Dynamo Kiev | 3 | Atletico Madrid | 0 | Lyon | 39,300 | Wohrer (A) |
| 1987 | Ajax | 1 | Lokomotiv Leipzig | 0 | Athens | 35,000 | Agnolin (I) |
| 1988 | Mechelen | 1 | Ajax | 0 | Strasbourg | 39,446 | Pauly (WG) |
| 1989 | Barcelona | 2 | Sampdoria | 0 | Berne | 45,000 | Courtney (E) |
| 1990 | Sampdoria | 2 | Anderlecht | 0 | Gothenburg | 20,103 | Galler (Sw) |
| 1991 | Manchester U | 2 | Barcelona | 1 | Rotterdam | 45,000 | Karlsson (Se) |
| 1992 | Werder Bremen | 2 | Monaco | 0 | Lisbon | 16,000 | D'Elia (I) |
| 1993 | Parma | 3 | Antwerp | 1 | Wembley | 37,393 | Assenmacher (G) |
| 1994 | Arsenal | 1 | Parma | 0 | Copenhagen | 33,765 | Krondl (Czr) |
| 1995 | Zaragoza | 2 | Arsenal | 1 | Paris | 42,424 | Ceccarini (I) |
| 1996 | Paris St Germain | 1 | Rapid Vienna | 0 | Brussels | 37,500 | Pairetto (I) |
| 1997 | Barcelona | 1 | Paris St Germain | 0 | Rotterdam | 40,000 | Merk (G) |
| 1998 | Chelsea | 1 | Stuttgart | 0 | Stockholm | 30,216 | Braschi (I) |

# EUROPEAN CUP-WINNERS' CUP 1997-98

## QUALIFYING ROUND, FIRST LEG

Balzers (1) 1 *(Wornhard 5)*, BVSC (0) 3 *(Telsor 57 (og),*
 *Fuezi 76, Csordas 84)* 660
Cwmbran Town (0) 2 *(Parfitt 76 (pen), Townsend 84)*,
 National (1) 5 *(Vasc 34, Niculescu 47, 62, Lita 77, 80)*
 1600
Dinaburg (1) 1 *(Tarasovs 35)*, Kapaz (0) 0 1000
Dynamo Batumi (2) 4 *(Chuchua 24, 32, Glonti 77,*
 *Shekiladze 88)*, Ararat Erevan (0) 2 *(Ter-Petrossian 59,*
 *Nazarjan 82)* 8000
*UEFA decision Ararat win 3–0*
Glenavon (0) 1 *(Grant 59)*, Legia Warsaw (1) 1
 *(Sokolowski 32)* 1115
HB Torshavn (1) 1 *(Arge 19)*, Apoel (1) 1 *(Alexis 40)* 100
Hibernians (0) 0, IBV (0) 1 *(Johanesson 70)* 800
HJK Helsinki (0) 1 *(Helin 59)*, Red Star Belgrade (0) 0
 5140
Kilmarnock (0) 2 *(Wright 65 (pen), 90)*, Shelbourne (1) 1
 *(Rutherford 12)* 9041
Levski (1) 1 *(Ivanov 18)*, Slovan Bratislava (0) 1 *(Novak*
 *65)* 25,000
Primorje (1) 2 *(Sabadin 37, Sculac 86 (pen))*, Union
 Luxembourg (0) 0 2000
Sadam (0) 1 *(Olumets 49)*, Belshina (1) 1 *(Hripuch 18)*
 500
Sloga (0) 1 *(Petkov 69)*, NK Zagreb (0) 2 *(Bule 77,*
 *Cizmek 90)* 4000
Zalgiris (0) 0, Hapoel Beer Sheba (0) 0 2000
Zimbru Chisinau (0) 1 *(Zgura 75)*, Donetsk (1) 1
 *(Atelkin 45)* 9000

## QUALIFYING ROUND, SECOND LEG

Apoel (2) 6 *(Hortnagel 14, 21, Sotiriou 52, Ioannu 77, 81,*
 *Fasouliotis 83)*, HB Torshavn (0) 0 7000
Ararat Erevan (0) 0, Dynamo Batumi (2) 2 *(Torgashvili*
 *2, Makharadze 38)* 5000
Belshina (1) 4 *(Smirnykh 3, Timofeyev 57, Khlebosolov*
 *73, Putrash 75)*, Sadam (0) 1 *(Ryzhkov 64 (pen))* 7000
BVSC (1) 2 *(Komlosi 12, Bukszegi 90)*, Balzers (0) 0 1500
Donetsk (2) 3 *(Orbu 25, Atelkin 43, Kriventsov 82)*,
 Zimbru Chisinau (0) 0 10,000
Hapoel Beer Sheba (0) 2 *(Radjos 96, Bochnik 116)*,
 Zalgiris (0) 1 *(Benayoun 105 (pen))* 9000
IBV (2) 3 *(Helgason 21, Gudmundsson T 33, 90)*,
 Hibernians (0) 0 1000
Kapaz (0) 0, Dinaburg (0) 1 *(Isayev 50)* 7000
Legia Warsaw (0) 4 *(Kacprzak 74, Sokolowski 76, 90*
 *(pen), Skrzypek 86)*, Glenavon (0) 0 3500
National (5) 7 *(Niculescu 15, Pigulea 20, 41, 75, Necula*
 *30, Albeanu 39, Savu 47)*, Cwmbran Town (0) 0 2500
NK Zagreb (2) 2 *(Sopic 2, Bule 8)*, Sloga (0) 0 2000
Red Star Belgrade (2) 3 *(Stankovic 6, 26, Njegus 89)*,
 HJK Helsinki (0) 0 36,000
Shelbourne (1) 1 *(Baker 39)*, Kilmarnock (1) 1 *(McIntyre*
 *21)* 8100
Slovan Bratislava (1) 2 *(Novak 15, Muzlay 52)*, Levski (1)
 1 *(Todorov 2)* 6850
Union Luxembourg (0) 0, Primorje (1) 1 *(Rudonja 18)*
 1000

## FIRST ROUND, FIRST LEG

AEK Athens (2) 5 *(Kopitsis 36 (pen), 45, Katsavos 64,*
 *Kalitzakis 67, Marcelo 77)*, Dinaburg (0) 0 14,000
AIK Stockholm (0) 0, Primorje (0) 1 *(Rudonja 85)* 4100
Apoel (0) 0, Sturm Graz (0) 1 *(Spiteri 81)* 5000
Belshina (1) 1 *(Khlebosolov 14 (pen))*, Lokomotiv
 Moscow (0) 2 *(Loskov 49, Borodjoek 71)* 7000
Betis (0) 2 *(Alfonso 58, 72)*, BVSC (0) 0 33,000
Boavista (0) 2 *(Rui Miguel 34, Magalhaes 44)*, Donetsk
 (1) 3 *(Zubov 24, Atelkin 62, 64)* 5000
Chelsea (2) 2 *(Di Matteo 6, Granville 80)*, Slovan
 Bratislava (0) 0 23,067
FC Copenhagen (1) 3 *(Jonsson 17, Hojer 53, Tur 87)*,
 Ararat Erevan (0) 0 7563
Ekeren (1) 3 *(Kovacs 16, Hofmans 58, Dauwe 69)*, Red
 Star Belgrade (2) 2 *(Ognjenovic 60, Stankovic 62)* 3700
Hapoel Beer Sheba (0) 1 *(Benhayoun 63)*, Roda (4) 4
 *(Van Houdt 15, 31, Torma 18, 35)* 6500
IBV (1) 1 *(Olafsson 40)*, Stuttgart (2) 3 *(Bobic 9, 12,*
 *Akpoborie 70)* 4000
Kocaeli (2) 2 *(Erhan 41, Moshoeu 45)*, National (0) 0
 20,000

Nice (1) 3 *(Kohn 13, 48, Rol 79)*, Kilmarnock (0) 1
 *(Wright 78 (pen))* 10,812
NK Zagreb (1) 3 *(Lalic 44, Sopic 50, Baturina 52)*,
 Tromso (0) 2 *(Johansen 55, Arst 80)* 5000
Slavia Prague (2) 4 *(Asanin 5, Vacha 14, Vagner 49,*
 *Labant 54)*, Lucerne (1) 2 *(Aleksandrov 7, Koilov 76)*
 5614
Vicenza (2) 2 *(Luiso 11, Ambrosetti 24)*, Legia Warsaw
 (0) 0 10,081

## FIRST ROUND, SECOND LEG

Ararat Erevan (0) 0, FC Copenhagen (0) 2 *(Nielsen M*
 *87, Sesta 89)* 700
BVSC (0) 0, Betis (1) 2 *(Alexis 8, Alfonso 48)* 1000
Dinaburg (1) 2 *(Fedotov 34, Isayev 62)*, AEK Athens (1)
 4 *(Nikolaidis 35, 78, Vlachos 50, Kostis 72)* 1500
Donetsk (0) 1 *(Patchvetia 78)*, Boavista (0) 1 *(Couto 87)*
 25,000
Kilmarnock (1) 1 *(Reilly 31)*, Nice (0) 1 *(Milinkovic 76)*
 8402
Legia Warsaw (0) 1 *(Kacprzak 56)*, Vicenza (0) 1 *(Zauli*
 *86)* 7000
Lokomotiv Moscow (2) 3 *(Maminov 23, Kharlachyev 41,*
 *Loskov 74)*, Belshina (0) 0 3000
Lucerne (0) 0, Slavia Prague (0) 2 *(Koilov 55 (og),*
 *Vagner 74)* 5000
National (0) 0, Kocaeli (0) 1 *(Nuri 79)* 8000
Primorje (0) 1 *(Rudonja 110)*, AIK Stockholm (0) 1
 *(Novakovic 77)* 3000
Red Star Belgrade (1) 1 *(Drulic 17)*, Ekeren (0) 1
 *(Radzinski 67)* 48,000
Roda (3) 10 *(Van Houdt 19, 32, 70, Lawal 41, 63, Ooijer*
 *49, 86 (pen), Vrede 54, Torma 72, 90)*, Hapoel Beer
 Sheba (0) 0 5000
Slovan Bratislava (0) 0, Chelsea (1) 2 *(Vialli 27, Di*
 *Matteo 60)* 15,000
Sturm Graz (3) 3 *(Reinmayr 3, Vastic 29, Haas 42)*, Apoel
 (0) 0 11,500
Stuttgart (0) 2 *(Akpoborie 73, 76)*, IBV (0) 1 *(Larusson*
 *80)* 10,000
Tromso (1) 4 *(Sabitovic 15 (og), Arst 75, Johansen S 90,*
 *Lange 115)*, NK Zagreb (0) 2 *(Vukic 55, Bule 59)* 3893

## SECOND ROUND, FIRST LEG

AEK Athens (0) 2 *(Batista 74, Marcelo 84)*, Sturm Graz
 (0) 0 15,000
Betis (2) 2 *(Oli 29, Canas 40)*, FC Copenhagen (0) 0
 17,000
Donetsk (0) 1 *(Zubov 62)*, Vicenza (1) 3 *(Luiso 1, 90,*
 *Beghetto 55)* 30,000
Ekeren (0) 0, Stuttgart (1) 4 *(Bobic 44, 63, Akpoborie 57,*
 *77)* 5000
Lokomotiv Moscow (1) 2 *(Kharlachyev 32, Dzjanasjia*
 *82)*, Kocaeli (0) 1 *(Uzun 73)* 3000
Nice (1) 2 *(Aulanier 5 (pen), 78)*, Slavia Prague (2) 2
 *(Vacha 14, 35)* 14,274
Primorje (0) 0, Roda (1) 2 *(Lawal 15, Van Houdt 68)*
 1250
Tromso (2) 3 *(Nilsen S 6, Fermann 19, Arst 86)*, Chelsea
 (0) 2 *(Vialli 85, 90)* 6438

## SECOND ROUND, SECOND LEG

Chelsea (3) 7 *(Petrescu 13, 86, Vialli 24, 61, 76, Zola 43,*
 *Leboeuf 55 (pen))*, Tromso (1) 1 *(Johansen B 39)* 29,363
FC Copenhagen (0) 1 *(Nielsen P 61 (pen))*, Betis (0) 1
 *(Urena 78)* 10,140
Kocaeli (0) 0, Lokomotiv Moscow (0) 0 12,000
Roda (1) 4 *(Van de Luer 45, Peeters 49, Zafarin 75,*
 *Valgaeren 85)*, Primorje (0) 0 5000
Slavia Prague (0) 1 *(Labant 80)*, Nice (0) 1 *(Vandecasteele*
 *75)* 7312
Sturm Graz (0) 1 *(Spiteri 82)*, AEK Athens (0) 0 15,400
Stuttgart (2) 2 *(Verlaat 13, Poschner 35)*, Ekeren (2) 4
 *(Van Ankeren 44, 83, Van Geneugden 45, Karagiannis*
 *73)* 11,000
Vicenza (1) 2 *(Luiso 24, Viviani 70)*, Donetsk (1) 1
 *(Atelkin 59)* 9500

## QUARTER-FINALS, FIRST LEG

AEK Athens (0) 0, Lokomotiv Moscow (0) 0 30,000
Betis (0) 1 *(Alfonso 46)*, Chelsea (2) 2 *(Flo 9, 12)* 31,000

Roda (0) 1 *(Peeters 73)*, Vicenza (3) 4 *(Luiso 17, 39,*
  *Belotti 29, Otero 68)* 20,000
Slavia Prague (1) 1 *(Vacha 40)*, Stuttgart (0) 1 *(Poschner*
  *51)* 8712

### QUARTER-FINALS, SECOND LEG

Chelsea (1) 3 *(Sinclair 30, Di Matteo 50, Zola 90)*, Betis
  (1) 1 *(Finidi George 21)* 32,300
Lokomotiv Moscow (0) 2 *(Kharlachyev 53, Chugainov*
  *90)*, AEK Athens (0) 1 *(Kopitsis 66 (pen))* 20,000
Stuttgart (1) 2 *(Balakov 10, 90)*, Slavia Prague (0) 0 18,000
Vicenza (4) 5 *(Luiso 5, Firmani 24, Mendez 38,*
  *Ambrosetti 43, Zauli 48)*, Roda (0) 0 15,000

### SEMI-FINALS, FIRST LEG

Stuttgart (1) 2 *(Akpoborie 43, Bobic 90)*, Lokomotiv
  Moscow (1) 1 *(Janashia 23)* 14,500
Vicenza (1) 1 *(Zauli 16)*, Chelsea (0) 0 20,900

### SEMI-FINALS, SECOND LEG

Chelsea (1) 3 *(Poyet 35, Zola 51, Hughes M 76)*, Vicenza
  (1) 1 *(Luiso 32)* 33,810
Lokomotiv Moscow (0) 0, Stuttgart (1) 1 *(Bobic 24)*
  18,000

### FINAL

**Chelsea (0) 1, Stuttgart (0) 0**

(in Stockholm, 13 May 1998, 30,216)

*Chelsea:* De Goey; Petrescu, Granville, Duberry,
  Leboeuf, Clarke, Poyet (Newton 81), Di Matteo, Vialli,
  Flo (Zola 70), Wise.
*Scorer:* Zola 71.
*Stuttgart:* Wohlfahrt; Schneider (Endress 55), Yakin,
  Berthold, Haber (Djordjevic 74), Soldo, Poschner,
  Hagner (Ristic 77), Balakov, Bobic, Akpoborie.
*Referee:* Braschi (Italy).

Gianfranco Zola of Chelsea scores the only goal of the Cup-Winners' Cup Final against Stuttgart. (Colorsport)

# EUROPEAN CUP-WINNERS' CUP 1997–98 – BRITISH AND IRISH CLUBS

**QUALIFYING ROUND, FIRST LEG**

**14 AUG**

**Cwmbran Town (0) 2** *(Parfitt 76 (pen), Townsend 84)*
**National (1) 5** *(Vasc 34, Niculescu 47, 62, Lita 77, 80)*1600
*Cwmbran Town:* O'Hagan (Speare 46); Carter (Powell 72), Jones, Gibbins, Blackie, Moore, Dyer (Johnson 72), Watkins, James, Parfitt, Townsend.
*National:* Stefanescu; Petre, Ciobotariu, Sburlea (Vochin 71), Necula, Marin, Carabas (Lita 61), Pigulea, Vasc, Niculescu (Albeanu 76), Duna.

**Glenavon (0) 1** *(Grant 59)*
**Legia Warsaw (1) 1** *(Sokolowski 32)*                                     1115
*Glenavon:* O'Neill; Greg, Byrne, Quigley, Murphy (McCartan 45), Glendinning, Doherty, Prizeman, Caffrey, Ferguson, Grant.
*Legia Warsaw:* Szamotulski; Skrmez, Bednarz, Zielinski, Kacprzak, Mieciel, Sokolowski, Wlodarczyk, Solnica (Koziok 74), Magiera.

**Kilmarnock (0) 2** *(Wright 65 (pen), 90)*
**Shelbourne (1) 1** *(Rutherford 12)*                                        9041
*Kilmarnock:* Lekovic; MacPherson, Montgomerie, McGowne, Baker, Findlay, Reilly, Burke, Mitchell (Nevin 57), Wright, McIntyre (Varielle 56).
*Shelbourne:* Gough; Veudequin (Costello 78), Geoghegan D, Neville (McCartney 66), Campbell, Scully, Baker (Geoghegan S 82), Sheridan, Rutherford, Fenton, Smith.

**QUALIFYING ROUND, SECOND LEG**

**28 AUG**

**Legia Warsaw (0) 4** *(Kacprzak 74, Sokolowski 76, 90 (pen), Skrzypek 86)*
**Glenavon (0) 0**                                                           3500
*Legia Warsaw:* Szamotulski; Magiera, Bednarz, Czereszewski, Zielinski, Kacprzak, Zeigbo, Sokolowski, Wlodarczyk (Solnica 68), Karwan, Skrzypek.
*Glenavon:* O'Neill; Caffrey, Glendinning, Doherty (Prizeman 38), Byrne, Smyth, McCartan (McCoy 65), Quigley (Russell 73), Ferguson, Grant, Grett.

**National (5) 7** *(Niculescu 15, Pigulea 20, 41, 75, Necula 30, Albeanu 39, Savu 47)*
**Cwmbran Town (0) 0**                                                       2500
*National:* Stefanescu; Petre (Lita 53), Ciobotariu, Sburlea (Vochin 46), Necula, Marin, Pigulea, Vasc, Carabas, Niculescu, Albeanu (Savu 46).
*Cwmbran Town:* Speare; Jones, Gibbins (James 46), Blackie, Moore, Powell, Dyer, Goodridge, Townsend (Watkins 66), Parfitt, Walker (Davies 66).

**Shelbourne (1) 1** *(Baker 39)*
**Kilmarnock (1) 1** *(McIntyre 21)*                                         8100
*Shelbourne:* Gough; Veudequin (Geoghegan S 65), Geoghegan D, Neville, Campbell, Scully, Baker, Sheridan, Rutherford, Fenton, Smith.
*Kilmarnock:* Lekovic; MacPherson, Montgomerie, McGowne, Baker, Mitchell, Findlay, Reilly, McIntyre, Nevin (Varielle 84).

**FIRST ROUND, FIRST LEG**

**18 SEPT**

**Chelsea (1) 2** *(Di Matteo 6, Granville 80)*
**Slovan Bratislava (0) 0**                                                  23,067
*Chelsea:* De Goey; Petrescu, Granville, Duberry, Leboeuf, Hughes P, Poyet, Di Matteo, Vialli, Zola, Wise.
*Slovan Bratislava:* Konig; Glonek, Antalovic, Pecko, Sobona, Gunda, Tomaschek, Hornyak, Kereszduri (Moder 81), Borisenko (Muzlay 62), Novak (Timko 50).

**Nice (1) 3** *(Kohn 13, 48, Rol 79)*
**Kilmarnock (0) 1** *(Wright 78 (pen))*                                     10,812
*Nice:* Huc; Stefano, Kartalija, Angan, Rol, Milinkovic, Savini (Aubame 76), Aulanier, Vandecasteele, Kohn, Angibeaud.
*Kilmarnock:* Meldrum; Montgomerie, Baker, MacPherson, McGowne, Reilly, Nevin (Bagen 65), Findlay (O'Neill 87), Wright, Mitchell, Varielle (Roberts 84).

**FIRST ROUND, SECOND LEG**

**2 OCT**

**Kilmarnock (1) 1** *(Reilly 31)*
**Nice (0) 1** *(Milinkovic 76)*                                            8402
*Kilmarnock:* Lekovic; MacPherson, Kerr, McGowne, Whitworth, Bagen (Henry 53), Mitchell (Nevin 80), Reilly, Burke, Varielle (Roberts 80), Wright.
*Nice:* Huc; Angan, Kartalija, Kohn (Pottier 9), Aulanier, Vandecasteele, Rol, Stefano (Aubame 69), Angibeaud, Savini, Milinkovic.

**Slovan Bratislava (0) 0**
**Chelsea (1) 2** *(Vialli 27, Di Matteo 60)*                               15,000
*Slovan Bratislava:* Konig; Gunda, Pecko, Tomaschek, Muzlay, Pukalovic (Puchner 72), Moder, Hornyak, Kereszduri, Borisenko (Nagy 62), Novak.
*Chelsea:* De Goey; Petrescu (Nicholls 72), Le Saux (Granville 65), Sinclair, Leboeuf, Lambourde, Poyet (Babayaro 46), Di Matteo, Vialli, Flo, Wise.

**SECOND ROUND, FIRST LEG**

**23 OCT**

**Tromso (0) 3** *(Nilsen S 6, Fermann 19, Arst 86)*
**Chelsea (0) 2** *(Vialli 85, 90)*                                         6438
*Tromso:* Grenersen; Johansen SM, Nilsen S, Johansen B (Hafstad 68), Kraemer, Berntsen, Christensen, Fermann (Bailing 72), Hanssen, Arst, Lange.
*Chelsea:* De Goey; Sinclair, Granville (Hughes M 46), Babayaro, Leboeuf (Myers 87), Clarke, Zola, Di Matteo, Vialli, Newton, Wise.

**SECOND ROUND, SECOND LEG**

**6 NOV**

**Chelsea (3) 7** *(Petrescu 13, 86, Vialli 24, 61, 76, Zola 43, Leboeuf 55 (pen))*
**Tromso (1) 1** *(Johansen B 39)*                                          29,363
*Chelsea:* De Goey; Petrescu, Babayaro, Sinclair, Leboeuf, Myers, Zola, Di Matteo (Lambourde 80), Vialli (Flo 87), Newton (Clarke 70), Wise.
*Tromso:* Grenersen; Johansen SM, Nilsen S, Hanssen, Kraemer, Berntsen (Hafstad 57), Johansen B, Christensen, Fermann, Arst (Johansen SB 70), Lange.

**QUARTER-FINALS, FIRST LEG**

**5 MAR**

**Betis (0) 1** *(Alfonso 46)*
**Chelsea (2) 2** *(Flo 9, 12)*                                             31,000
*Betis:* Prats; Solozabal, Vidakovic (Marquez 43), Olias, Merino, Canas (Oli 65), Alexis, Fernando, Finidi George, Alfonso, Jarni.
*Chelsea:* De Goey; Petrescu, Clarke, Sinclair, Leboeuf, Duberry, Newton, Di Matteo, Flo (Hughes M 84), Zola (Nicholls 79), Wise.

**QUARTER-FINALS, SECOND LEG**

**19 MAR**

**Chelsea (1) 3** *(Sinclair 30, Di Matteo 50, Zola 90)*
**Betis (1) 1** *(Finidi George 21)*                32,300
*Chelsea:* De Goey; Petrescu (Lambourde 87), Clarke, Sinclair, Leboeuf, Duberry, Zola, Di Matteo, Vialli, Newton, Wise.
*Betis:* Prats; Merino, Olias, Josete, Marquez, Canas (Oli 61), Alexis, Luis Fernandez (Cuellar 72), Finidi George, Alfonso, Jarni.

**SEMI-FINALS, FIRST LEG**

**2 APR**

**Vicenza (1) 1** *(Zauli 16)*
**Chelsea (0) 0**                                    20,900
*Vicenza:* Brivio; Mendez, Belotti, Dicara, Viviani, Schenardi (Stovini 67), Di Carlo, Ambrosini, Ambrosetti (Beghetto 67), Zauli, Luiso.
*Chelsea:* De Goey; Petrescu (Flo 59), Le Saux, Duberry, Leboeuf, Clarke, Zola (Morris 89), Di Matteo, Vialli, Newton, Wise.

**SEMI-FINALS, SECOND LEG**

**16 APR**

**Chelsea (1) 3** *(Poyet 35, Zola 51, Hughes M 76)*
**Vicenza (1) 1** *(Luiso 32)*                      33,810
Chelsea: De Goey; Clarke, Le Saux, Morris (Hughes M 70), Leboeuf, Duberry, Poyet, Newton (Charvet 70), Vialli, Zola (Myers 82), Wise.
*Vicenza:* Brivio; Mendez, Belotti, Dicara, Viviani (Stovini 60), Schenardi, Di Carlo (Otero 82), Ambrosini, Ambrosetti, Zauli, Luiso (Di Napoli 82).

**FINAL**

**Chelsea (0) 1, Stuttgart (0) 0**

(in Stockholm, 13 May 1998, 30,216)

*Chelsea:* De Goey; Petrescu, Granville, Duberry, Leboeuf, Clarke, Poyet (Newton 81), Di Matteo, Vialli, Flo (Zola 70), Wise.
*Scorer:* Zola 71.
*Stuttgart:* Wohlfahrt; Schneider (Endress 55), Yakin, Berthold, Haber (Djordjevic 74), Soldo, Poschner, Hagner (Ristic 77), Balakov, Bobic, Akpoborie.
*Referee:* Braschi (Italy).

# EUROPEAN CUP DRAWS 1998–99

## EUROPEAN CUP

**European Cup First Qualifying Round**
Celtic v St Patrick's Ath
Dynamo Kiev v Barry Town
Cliftonville v Kosice

**Second Qualifying Round**
Manchester U v LKS Lodz or Kapaz
Celtic or St Patrick's Ath v Croatia Zagreb
Dynamo Kiev or Barry Town v Sparta Prague
Kosice or Cliftonville v Brondby

### EUROPEAN CUP-WINNERS' CUP

Cork City v CSKA Kiev
Bangor v Haka
Lantana v Hearts
Glentoran v Maccabi Haifa

## UEFA CUP

Linfield v Omonia

**Group C**
Zeljeznicar v Kilmarnock

**Group D**
Shelbourne v Rangers

**Group E**
Newtown v Wisla

# INTER-CITIES FAIRS & UEFA CUP

## FAIRS CUP FINALS 1958–71
*(Winners in italics)*

| Year | First Leg | Attendance | Second Leg | Attendance |
|------|-----------|-----------|-----------|-----------|
| 1958 | London 2 Barcelona 2 | 45,466 | *Barcelona* 6 London 0 | 62,000 |
| 1960 | Birmingham C 0 Barcelona 0 | 40,500 | *Barcelona* 4 Birmingham C 1 | 70,000 |
| 1961 | Birmingham C 2 Roma 2 | 21,005 | *Roma* 2 Birmingham C 0 | 60,000 |
| 1962 | Valencia 6 Barcelona 2 | 65,000 | Barcelona 1 *Valencia* 1 | 60,000 |
| 1963 | Dynamo Zagreb 1 Valencia 2 | 40,000 | *Valencia* 2 Dynamo Zagreb 0 | 55,000 |
| 1964 | *Zaragoza* 2 Valencia 1 | 50,000 | (in Barcelona) | |
| 1965 | *Ferencvaros* 1 Juventus 0 | 25,000 | (in Turin) | |
| 1966 | Barcelona 0 Zaragoza 1 | 70,000 | Zaragoza 2 *Barcelona* 4 | 70,000 |
| 1967 | Dynamo Zagreb 2 Leeds U 0 | 40,000 | Leeds U 0 *Dynamo Zagreb* 0 | 35,604 |
| 1968 | Leeds U 1 Ferencvaros 0 | 25,368 | Ferencvaros 0 *Leeds U* 0 | 70,000 |
| 1969 | Newcastle U 3 Ujpest Dozsa 0 | 60,000 | Ujpest Dozsa 2 *Newcastle U* 3 | 37,000 |
| 1970 | Anderlecht 3 Arsenal 1 | 37,000 | *Arsenal* 3 Anderlecht 0 | 51,612 |
| 1971 | Juventus 0 Leeds U 0 *(abandoned 51 minutes)* | 42,000 | | |
| | Juventus 2 Leeds U 2 | 42,000 | *Leeds U* 1* Juventus 1 | 42,483 |

## UEFA CUP FINALS 1972–97
*(Winners in italics)*

| Year | First Leg | Attendance | Second Leg | Attendance |
|------|-----------|-----------|-----------|-----------|
| 1972 | Wolverhampton W 1 Tottenham H 2 | 45,000 | *Tottenham H* 1 Wolverhampton W 1 | 48,000 |
| 1973 | Liverpool 0 Moenchengladbach 0 | | | |
| | *(abandoned 27 minutes)* | 44,967 | | |
| | Liverpool 3 Moenchengladbach 0 | 41,169 | Moenchengladbach 2 *Liverpool* 0 | 35,000 |
| 1974 | Tottenham H 2 Feyenoord 2 | 46,281 | *Feyenoord* 2 Tottenham H 0 | 68,000 |
| 1975 | Moenchengladbach 0 Twente 0 | 45,000 | Twente 1 *Moenchengladbach* 5 | 24,500 |
| 1976 | Liverpool 3 FC Brugge 2 | 56,000 | FC Brugge 1 *Liverpool* 1 | 32,000 |
| 1977 | Juventus 1 Athletic Bilbao 0 | 75,000 | Athletic Bilbao 2 *Juventus* 1* | 43,000 |
| 1978 | Bastia 0 PSV Eindhoven 0 | 15,000 | *PSV Eindhoven* 3 Bastia 0 | 27,000 |
| 1979 | Red Star Belgrade 1 Moenchengladbach 1 | 87,500 | *Moenchengladbach* 1 Red Star Belgrade 0 | 45,000 |
| 1980 | Moenchengladbach 3 Eintracht Frankfurt 2 | 25,000 | *Eintracht Frankfurt* 1* Moenchengladbach 0 | 60,000 |
| 1981 | Ipswich T 3 AZ 67 Alkmaar 0 | 27,532 | AZ 67 Alkmaar 4 *Ipswich T* 2 | 28,500 |
| 1982 | Gothenburg 1 Hamburg 0 | 42,548 | Hamburg 0 *Gothenburg* 3 | 60,000 |
| 1983 | Anderlecht 1 Benfica 0 | 45,000 | Benfica 1 *Anderlecht* 1 | 80,000 |
| 1984 | Anderlecht 1 Tottenham H 1 | 40,000 | *Tottenham H* 1[1] Anderlecht 1 | 46,258 |
| 1985 | Videoton 0 Real Madrid 3 | 30,000 | *Real Madrid* 0 Videoton 1 | 98,300 |
| 1986 | Real Madrid 5 Cologne 1 | 80,000 | Cologne 2 *Real Madrid* 0 | 15,000 |
| 1987 | Gothenburg 1 Dundee U 0 | 50,023 | Dundee U 1 *Gothenburg* 1 | 20,911 |
| 1988 | Espanol 3 Bayer Leverkusen 0 | 42,000 | *Bayer Leverkusen* 3[2] Espanol 0 | 22,000 |
| 1989 | Napoli 2 Stuttgart 1 | 83,000 | Stuttgart 3 *Napoli* 3 | 67,000 |
| 1990 | Juventus 3 Fiorentina 1 | 45,000 | Fiorentina 0 *Juventus* 0 | 32,000 |
| 1991 | Internazionale 2 Roma 0 | 68,887 | Roma 1 *Internazionale* 0 | 70,901 |
| 1992 | Torino 2 Ajax 2 | 65,377 | Ajax 0* Torino 0 | 40,000 |
| 1993 | Borussia Dortmund 1 Juventus 3 | 37,000 | *Juventus* 3 Borussia Dortmund 0 | 62,781 |
| 1994 | Salzburg 0 Internazionale 1 | 47,500 | *Internazionale* 1 Salzburg 0 | 80,326 |
| 1995 | Parma 1 Juventus 0 | 23,000 | Juventus 1 *Parma* 1 | 80,750 |
| 1996 | Bayern Munich 2 Bordeaux 0 | 62,000 | Bordeaux 1 *Bayern Munich* 3 | 36,000 |
| 1997 | Schalke 1 Internazionale 0 | 56,824 | Internazionale 1 *Schalke* 0[3] | 81,670 |

*won on away goals    [1]*Tottenham H won 4-3 on penalties aet*    [2]*Bayer Leverkusen won 3-2 on penalties aet*
[3]*Schalke won 4-1 on penalties aet*

## UEFA CUP FINALS 1998 –

| Year | Winners | Runners-up | Venue | Attendance | Referee |
|------|---------|-----------|-------|-----------|---------|
| 1998 | Internazionale 3 | Lazio 0 | Paris | 42,938 | Nieto (Sp) |

# UEFA CUP 1997–98

**FIRST QUALIFYING ROUND, FIRST LEG**
Birkirkara (0) 0, Spartak Trnava (1) 1 *(Tittel 14)* 3000
Bohemians (0) 0, Ferencvaros (1) 1 *(Zavadszky 30)* 3000
Brann (2) 2 *(Mjelde 22, Lovvik 28)*, Neftokhimik (0) 1
*(Kishishev 81)* 6418
Daugava (0) 1 *(Vutsans 75)*, Vorskla (0) 3 *(Kobzar 51,
Chuychenko 57, Antyukhin 70)* 1800
Dnepr (1) 6 *(Getsko 31, Sharan 55, 62, 74, Palyanytsya
60, Moroz 72)*, Erevan (0) 1 *(Mallai 81)* 5500
Dynamo Minsk (0) 1 *(Chernyavsky 12)*, Kolkheti (0) 0
2000
Gorica (1) 2 *(Demirovic 30, Becaj 90)*, Otelul (0) 0 3000
Grasshoppers (2) 3 *(Yakin 32, Aspinall 34 (og), Subiat
79)*, Coleraine (0) 0 5100
Grevenmacher (0) 1 *(Thill S 69)*, Hajduk Split (3) 4
*(Erceg 9, Tudor 23, Vulic 29, 89)* 1200
Hapoel Petah Tikvah (0) 1 *(Marton 90)*, Flora Tallinn
(0) 0 2000
Inkaras (1) 3 *(Pribyl 14 (og), Slekys 65 (pen), Rudzionis
75)*, Boby Brno (1) 1 *(Golomek 5)* 5000
Inter Cable-Tel (0) 0, Celtic (2) 3 *(Thom 6 (pen),
Johnson 45, Wieghorst 81)* 6980
Jablonec (4) 5 *(Holub 7, 76, Neumann 11, 37, Hromadko
26)*, Karabach (0) 0 2830
KR (1) 2 *(Danielsson 26, Dadason 51 (pen))*, Dynamo
Bucharest (0) 0 4000
MyPa (1) 1 *(Enberg 36)*, Apollon (0) 1 *(Tsolakis 86)* 1000
Neuchatel Xamax (3) 7 *(Isabella 9, 16, Kunz 15, Sandjak
70, Perret 72, Rothenbuhler 76, Gigon 90)*, Tiligul (0) 0
3700
Odra (1) 3 *(Polak 33, Paluch 48, Nosal 68)*, Pobeda (0) 0
3000
Principat (0) 0, Dundee U (2) 8 *(Winters 14, 31, 75, 77,
McSwegan 46, 73, 76, Zetterlund 48)* 700
Ujpest (5) 6 *(Kovacs Z 6, 12, 86, Herczeg 9, 27, Jenei 38)*,
KI Klaksvik (0) 0 4000
Vojvodina (0) 0, Viking (0) 2 *(Skogheim 52, Andersen 67)*
6000

**FIRST QUALIFYING ROUND, SECOND LEG**
Apollon (0) 3 *(Mladenovic 50, Tsolakis 51, Pittas 83)*,
MyPa (0) 0 8000
Boby Brno (3) 6 *(Chaloupka 7, 50, Valnoha 15, 54,
Golomek P 25, Kolomaznik 63)*, Inkaras (1) 1
*(Rudjionas 15)* 16,800
Celtic (3) 5 *(Thom 19 (pen), Jackson 42, Johnson 45,
Hannah 63, Hay 85)*, Inter Cable-Tel (0) 0 41,557
Coleraine (1) 1 *(O'Dowd 22)*, Grasshoppers (3) 7
*(Magnin 15, Esposito 27, Ahinful 33, Shiels 51 (og),
Tikva 63, Yakin 64, Aspinall 83 (og))* 771
Dundee U (5) 9 *(McSwegan 8, 24, 65, Winters 23, 42,
McLaren 37, Olafsson 55, Zetterlund 59, Thompson
88)*, Principat (0) 0 6695
Dynamo Bucharest (1) 1 *(Chirita 41)*, KR (2) 2 *(Dadason
13, 33)* 7000
Erevan (0) 0, Dnepr (1) 2 *(Getsko 41, Belkin 89)* 500
Ferencvaros (1) 5 *(Albert 15, Jagodics 47, 74, Schultz 58,
Zavadszky 71)*, Bohemians (0) 0 10,000
Flora Tallinn (1) 1 *(Oper 16)*, Hapoel Petah Tikvah (0) 2
*(Offri 49, Kakun 62)* 2000
Hajduk Split (0) 2 *(Bulat 60, Erceg 90)*, Grevenmacher
(0) 0 9000
Karabach (0) 0, Jablonec (0) 3 *(Prochazka 73, Holub 80,
Vukol 87)* 10,000
KI Klaksvik (0) 2 *(Danielsen 14, Morkore K 73)*, Ujpest
(1) 3 *(Szanyo 39, Sebok 77, 89)* 205
Kolkheti (1) 2 *(Mikaberidze 40, Gaganidze 61)*, Dynamo
Minsk (1) 1 *(Makovski 18)* 5000
Neftokhimik (2) 3 *(Trendafilov 10, Parushev 28,
Kiselichkov 77)*, Brann (0) 2 *(Hasund 60, 82)* 17,000
Otelul (0) 4 *(Stefan 19, 23, State 63, Viorel I 76)*, Gorica
(0) 2 *(Protega 87, Demirovic 89)* 6000
Pobeda (0) 2 *(Oliveira 83, 87)*, Odra (1) 1 *(Zagorski 17)*
6000
Spartak Trnava (2) 3 *(Timko 30, Hadviger 45, Formanko
88)*, Birkirkara (0) 1 *(Galea 86)* 11,095
Tiligul (1) 1 *(Loukiantchikov 13)*, Neuchatel Xamax (2) 3
*(Sandjak 11, Martin 28, Jeanneret 78)* 1500
Viking (0) 0, Vojvodina (1) 2 *(Vulevic D 4, 88)* 2377

*Viking won 5-4 on penalties.*
Vorskla (1) 2 *(Chuychenko 30, Antyukhin 58)*, Daugava
(0) 1 *(Vutsans 49)* 15,000

**SECOND QUALIFYING ROUND, FIRST LEG**
Alania (1) 2 *(Jutautas 15, Ashvelia 58)*, Dnepr (1) 1
*(Palyanytsya 8)* 32,000
Anderlecht (1) 2 *(Petersen 19, Stoica 89)*, Vorskla (0) 0
18,167
Apollon (0) 0, Mouscron (0) 0 9000
Dynamo Minsk (0) 0, Lillestrom (1) 2 *(Mamadu 43,
75(pen))* 1200
Gorica (0) 3 *(Osterc 62, 64, 83)*, FC Brugge (5) 5
*(Claessens 10, 26, Staelens 14 (pen), 21, 42 (pen))* 2800
Grasshoppers (0) 3 *(Magnin 50, Turkyilmaz 65, Thuler
83)*, Brann (0) 0 5650
Hajduk Split (0) 3 *(Skoko 78, Sedloski 80, Sarr 90)*,
Malmo (1) 2 *(Wirmola 11, Gudmundsen 60)* 15,000
Helsingborg (0) 0, Ferencvaros (1) 1 *(Vincze 41)* 6523
Jablonec (1) 1 *(Hromadko 20)*, Orebro (0) 1 *(Sahlin 67)*
2792
KR (0) 0, Ofi Crete (0) 0 1900
Neuchatel Xamax (0) 3 *(Sandjak 53, 80, Fuglestad 59
(og))*, Viking (0) 0 4813
PAOK Salonika (3) 5 *(Zagorakis 31 (pen), Maragos 35,
45, Franzeskos 52, Olivares 80)*, Spartak Trnava (3) 3
*(Ulaki 22, 28, Luhovy L 24)* 40,000
Rapid Vienna (2) 6 *(Ipoua 36, 62, Stoger 45, Prosenik 78,
79, Stumpf 80)*, Boby Brno (0) 1 *(Dostalek 53)* 14,000
Tirol (2) 2 *(Mayrleb 22, 28)*, Celtic (0) 1 *(Stubbs 84)* 6700
Trabzonspor (0) 1 *(Hami 77 (pen))*, Dundee U (0) 0
25,000
Ujpest (0) 0, Aarhus (0) 0 5000
Vejle (0) 0, Hapoel Petah Tikva (0) 0 3070
Volgograd (0) 2 *(Niedergeus 75, Veretennikov 89)*, Odra
(0) 0 30,000

**SECOND QUALIFYING ROUND, SECOND LEG**
Aarhus (1) 3 *(Rieper 25, Hallum 67, Sorensen 70)*, Ujpest
(1) 2 *(Sebok 29, Kovacs 76)* 5900
Boby Brno (2) 2 *(Pacanda 4, Valnoha 45)*, Rapid Vienna
(0) 0 6500
Brann (2) 2 *(Paldan 41, 44)*, Grasshoppers (0) 0 2909
FC Brugge (1) 3 *(Jbari 5, De Brul 82, Van der Elst 86)*,
Gorica (0) 0 4000
Celtic (2) 6 *(Donnelly 34, 68 (pen), Thom 44, Burley 70,
90, Annoni 88)*, Tirol (2) 3 *(Mayrleb 39, Sebereyns 45,
Krinner 82)* 47,017
Dnepr (1) 1 *(Sharan 23)*, Alania (4) 4 *(Gakhokidze 2, 27,
Yanovski 33, Kobiashvili 44)* 15,000
Dundee U (0) 1 *(McLaren 56)*, Trabzonspor (0) 1 *(Hami
81)* 10,232
Ferencvaros (0) 0, Helsingborg (1) 1 *(Jacobsson 43)*
*Ferencvaros won 4–3 on penalties* 12,000
Hapoel Petah Tikva (1) 1 *(Scholz 32 (og))*, Vejle (0) 0
6000
Lillestrom (1) 1 *(Diallo 40)*, Dynamo Minsk (0) 0 1906
Malmo (0) 0, Hajduk Split (1) 2 *(Vucko 45, Erceg 90)*
6462
Mouscron (1) 3 *(Pierre 31, 65, Vidovic 53)*, Apollon (0) 0
11,000
Odra (3) 3 *(Staniek 34, Zagorski 44, Brzoza 45)*,
Volgograd (1) 4 *(Berketov 5, Abramov 50,
Veretennikov 69, 72)* 5000
Ofi Crete (1) 3 *(Anastasiou 10, Mitic 65, Papadopoulos
72)*, KR (1) 1 *(Bjornsson 40)* 12,000
Orebro (0) 0, Jablonec (0) 0 3096
Spartak Trnava (0) 0, PAOK Salonika (0) 1 *(Zagorakis
80)* 16,000
Viking (0) 2 *(Skogheim 54, Mansson 85)*, Neuchatel
Xamax (0) 1 *(Kunz 48)* 1877
Vorskla (0) 0, Anderlecht (2) 2 *(Zetterberg 31, Scifo 43)*
1300

**FIRST ROUND, FIRST LEG**
Aarhus (1) 2 *(Piechnik 18, Halum 77)*, Nantes (2) 2
  *(Gourvennec 12, N'Diaye 24)* 5425
Atletico Madrid (0) 2 *(Juninho 70, Vieri 72 (pen))*,
  Leicester C (1) 1 *(Marshall 11)* 35,000
Bastia (0) 1 *(Andre 80)*, Benfica (0) 0 10,080
Beitar Jerusalem (0) 2 *(Pisont 46, Salloi 50)*, FC Brugge
  (0) 1 *(Jbari 58)* 7500
Bordeaux (0) 0, Aston Villa (0) 0 16,800
Branik Maribor (0) 1 *(Ceh 47)*, Ajax (0) 1 *(Litmanen 67)*
   7000
Celtic (0) 2 *(McNamara 53, Donnelly 74 (pen))*,
  Liverpool (1) 2 *(Owen 6, McManaman 89)* 48,526
Croatia Zagreb (2) 4 *(Saric 23, Viduka 41, Prosinecki 58
  (pen), Cvitanovic 78)*, Grasshoppers (1) 4 *(Moldovan
  20, 79, Mladinic 62 (og), Turkyilmaz 65)* 18,000
Guimaraes (0) 0, Lazio (0) 4 *(Casiraghi 48, Fuser 62,
  Nedved 69, Nesta 79)* 15,000
Internazionale (0) 2 *(Ronaldo 58, Ze Elias 71)*, Neuchatel
  Xamax (0) 0 15,225
Jazz Pori (0) 0, Munich 1860 (0) 1 *(Pele 90)* 2000
Karlsruhe (1) 2 *(Regis 12, Schroth 88)*, Anorthosis (1) 1
  *(Charalambous 34)* 12,000
La Coruna (0) 1 *(Djalminha 87)*, Auxerre (0) 2 *(Diomede
  72, Guivarc'h 84)* 18,000
Lyon (1) 4 *(Kanoute 20, Linares 50, Carteron 58, Giuly
  76)*, Brondby (1) 1 *(Daugaard 34 (pen))* 12,000
Mouscron (0) 0, Metz (2) 2 *(Meyrieu 22, Rodriguez 26)*
   6700
MPKC (0) 1 *(Kushnir 50)*, Dynamo Tbilisi (1) 1 *(Mujiri
  42)* 5900
MTK (0) 3 *(Illes 55, Preisinger 71, Lorincz 88)*, Alania (0)
  0 3000
Ofi Crete (1) 3 *(Papadopoulos 20 (pen), Gounenakis 56,
  Nioplias 85)*, Ferencvaros (0) 0 8000
PAOK Salonika (0) 1 *(Franzeskos 61)*, Arsenal (0) 0
   42,000
Rapid Vienna (1) 1 *(Freund 37)*, Hapoel Petah Tikva
  (0) 0 10,000
Salzburg (1) 4 *(Klausz 33, 53, Glieder 50, 64 (pen))*,
  Anderlecht (1) 3 *(Iachtchouk 34, Goor 59, Stoica 80)*
   4000
Sampdoria (0) 1 *(Boghossian 74)*, Athletic Bilbao (1) 2
  *(Rios 19, Larrainzar 62)* 26,191
Schalke (2) 2 *(Goossens 7, 23)*, Hajduk Split (0) 0 53,250
Sion (0) 0, Spartak Moscow (0) 1 *(Kechinov 73)* 6000
Steaua (0) 0, Fenerbahce (0) 0 16,000
Strasbourg (1) 2 *(Baticle 44 (pen), 60 (pen))*, Rangers (0)
  1 *(Albertz 49 (pen))* 12,450
Trabzonspor (2) 2 *(Hami 23 (pen), Cetin 44)*, Bochum (1)
  1 *(Baluszynski 2 (pen))* 12,000
Twente (0) 0, Lillestrom (1) 1 *(Diallo 25 (pen))* 7948
Valladolid (1) 2 *(Juan Carlos 33 (pen), Edu 60)*, Skonto
  Riga (0) 0 8300
Vitesse (1) 2 *(Curovic 33, Karoglan 90 (pen))*, Braga (0)
  1 *(Trustfull 85 (pen))* 5900
Volgograd (1) 2 *(Burlachenko 42, Veretennikov 65)*,
  Orebro (1) 2 26,000
Widzew Lodz (0) 1 *(Bogusz 63)*, Udinese (0) 0 10,000

**FIRST ROUND, SECOND LEG**
Ajax (5) 9 *(Arveladze S 1, 25, 79, Litmanen 21, Witschge
  36, Babangida 40, Frank de Boer 63, Oliseh 85,
  McCarthy 87)*, Branik Maribor (0) 1 *(Ljubobratovic
  83)* 41,000
Alania (1) 1 *(Moroz 17)*, MTK (0) 1 *(Halmai 85)* 22,000
Anderlecht (0) 4 *(Peiremans 46, 67, Iachtchouk 57,
  Dheedene 66)*, Salzburg (2) 2 *(Glieder 5, Ivanauskas
  30)* 14,000
Anorthosis (1) 1 *(Mihajlovic 12)*, Karlsruhe (1) 1
  *(Schepens 42)* 7000
Arsenal (1) 1 *(Bergkamp 22)*, PAOK Salonika (0) 1
  *(Vrizas 86)* 37,982
Aston Villa (0) 1 *(Milosevic 111)*, Bordeaux (0) 0 33,072
Athletic Bilbao (1) 2 *(Larrazabal 39 (pen), Ziganda 47)*,
  Sampdoria (0) 0 42,000
Auxerre (0) 0, La Coruna (0) 0 12,000
Benfica (0) 0, Bastia (0) 0 35,000
Bochum (2) 5 *(Stickroth 22, Joeran 44, 52, Dickhaut 60,
  Peschel 68)*, Trabzonspor (1) 3 *(Misse-Misse 31, Ogun
  73, Osman 78)* 24,500
Braga (2) 2 *(Artur Jorge 15 (pen), 28 (pen))*, Vitesse (0) 0
  17,500
Brondby (2) 2 *(Sand 6, Daugaard 11 (pen)*, Lyon (1) 3
  *(Giuly 14 (pen), Job 81, Bardon 88)* 8138

FC Brugge (0) 3 *(Jbari 66, Fadiga 70, Verheyen 81)*,
  Beitar Jerusalem (0) 0 8000
Dynamo Tbilisi (0) 1 *(Aleksidze 73)*, MPKC (0) 0 17,000
Fenerbahce (0) 1 *(Bolic 63)*, Steaua (2) 2 *(Militaru 10,
  Ciocoiu 44)* 15,000
Ferencvaros (1) 2 *(Nichenko 70, Horvath 85 (pen))*, Ofi
  Crete (1) 1 *(Nioplias 14)* 12,000
Grasshoppers (0) 0, Croatia Zagreb (2) 5 *(Cvitanovic 25,
  32, 89, Prosinecki 86, 90 (pen))* 16,000
Hajduk Split (2) 3 *(Vulic 20, Racunica 35)*, Schalke (1) 3
  *(Wilmots 21, Eijkelkamp 68, 73)* 37,000
Hapoel Petah Tikva (1) 1 *(Kakun 30 (pen))*, Rapid
  Vienna (0) 1 *(Penksa 73)* 6000
Lazio (1) 2 *(Signori 41, Nedved 73)*, Guimaraes (1) 1
  *(Paas 1)* 5000
Leicester C (0) 0, Atletico Madrid (0) 2 *(Juninho 72,
  Kiko 88)* 20,776
Lillestrom (0) 1 *(Diallo 88 (pen))*, Twente (0) 2
  *(Vennegoor of Hesselink 55, Van Halst 90 (pen))* 3437
Liverpool (0) 0, Celtic (0) 0 38,205
Metz (3) 4 *(Rodriguez 4, 26, Kastendeuch 40, Gaillot 90)*,
  Mouscron (1) 1 *(Van Durme 9)* 7455
Munich 1860 (2) 6 *(Winkler 34, 71, Cerny 45, Bohme 50,
  Nowak 52, Hamann 68)*, Jazz Pori (0) 1 *(Mendez 83)*
   7500
Nantes (0) 0, Aarhus (1) 1 *(Piechnik 45)* 15,000
Neuchatel Xamax (0) 0, Internazionale (1) 2 *(Moriero 26,
  Ganz 69)* 15,000
Orebro (0) 1 *(Karlsson 84)*, Volgograd (2) 4 *(Nidergaus
  25, 67, Zernov 40, Veretennikov 72)* 3143
Rangers (1) 1 *(Gattuso 11)*, Strasbourg (1) 2 *(Baticle 35,
  Zitelli 49)* 40,145
Skonto Riga (1) 1 *(Mikholap 6)*, Valladolid (0) 0 2000
Spartak Moscow (1) 2 *(Shyrko 19, Alenichev 54)*,
  Sion (1) 2 *(Lota 4, 73)* 18,000
  *(Replay ordered; goalposts incorrect height)*
Spartak Moscow (3) 5 *(Busnukin 5, Titov 34, Kechinov
  41, Tikhonov 60, Romaschenko 83)*, Sion (0) 1
  *(Camadini 65)* 24,500
Udinese (2) 3 *(Bierhoff 2, Poggi 6, Locatelli 89)*, Widzew
  Lodz (0) 0 15,000

**SECOND ROUND, FIRST LEG**
Aarhus (1) 1 *(Molby 41 (pen)*, Twente (1) 1 *(Sumiala 16)*
   7353
Ajax (1) 1 *(Dani 28)*, Udinese (0) 0 46,000
Athletic Bilbao (0) 0, Aston Villa (0) 0 39,000
Atletico Madrid (3) 5 *(Vieri 9, 32, 53, Lardin 11, Kiko
  73)*, PAOK Salonika (1) 2 *(Franzeskos 20, Marangos
  64)* 50,000
Auxerre (1) 3 *(Sibierski 18, Guivarc'h 49, 90)*, Ofi Crete
  (1) 1 *(Nioplias 16)* 9000
Braga (1) 4 *(Rodrigao 22, Toni 55, Karoglan 66, Bruno
  77)*, Dynamo Tbilisi (0) 0 15,000
FC Brugge (0) 1 *(Jbari 79)*, Bochum (0) 0 12,500
Internazionale (0) 1 *(Ganz 71)*, Lyon (1) 2 *(Giuly 23,
  Coveglio 81 (pen))* 16,085
Metz (0) 0, Karlsruhe (2) 2 *(Hassler 13, 39)* 14,000
MTK (0) 1 *(Lorincz 82)*, Croatia Zagreb (0) 0 10,000
Rapid Vienna (1) 3 *(Stoger 45 (pen), Schottel 64, Penksa
  81)*, Munich 1860 (0) 0 26,500
Schalke (1) 1 *(Thon 18)*, Anderlecht (0) 0 56,824
Spartak Moscow (0) 2 *(Tikhonov 61, Titov 85)*,
  Valladolid (0) 0 17,000
Steaua (0) 1 *(Hrib 66)*, Bastia (0) 0 20,000
Strasbourg (1) 3 *(Zitelli 20, 63, Conteh 69)*, Liverpool
  (0) 0 18,813
Volgograd (0) 0, Lazio (0) 0 24,000

**SECOND ROUND, SECOND LEG**
Anderlecht (1) 1 *(De Boeck 16)*, Schalke (0) 2 *(Van
  Hoogdalem 57, Wilmots 65)* 20,000
Aston Villa (1) 2 *(Taylor 27, Yorke 50)*, Athletic Bilbao
  (0) 1 *(Javi Gonzalez 70)* 35,915
Bastia (0) 2 *(Prince 52, 68, Mendy 77)*, Steaua (2) 2
  *(Munteanu 14, 40)* 10,000
Bochum (1) 4 *(Donkov 13 (pen), 56, Joeran 83, Wosz 90)*,
  FC Brugge (1) 1 *(Jbari 37)* 24,500
Croatia Zagreb (1) 2 *(Prosinecki 12, 56)*, MTK (0) 0
   25,000
Dynamo Tbilisi (0) 0, Braga (0) 1 *(Toni 49)* 15,000
Karlsruhe (1) 1 *(Hassler 38)*, Metz (1) 1 *(Boffin 10)* 13,500
Lazio (2) 3 *(Casiraghi 5, Mancini 35, Signori 89)*,
  Volgograd (0) 0 28,462

Liverpool (0) 2 *(Fowler 63 (pen), Riedle 84)*, Strasbourg
(0) 0                                                    32,426
Lyon (0) 1 *(Bak 67)*, Internazionale (2) 3 *(Moriero 9, 69,
Cauet 48)*                                              30,000
Munich 1860 (2) 2 *(Borimirov 6, Winkler 23 (pen))*,
Rapid Vienna (0) 1 *(Zingler 70)*                       25,000
Ofi Crete (0) 3 *(Papadopoulos 57, 75, Anastasiou 90)*,
Auxerre (1) 2 *(Guivarc'h 37, Deniaud 60)*              9000
PAOK Salonika (1) 4 *(Franzeskos 17, Olivares 54,
Zagorakis 75, Zouboulis 82)*, Atletico Madrid (2) 4
*(Lardin 2, Bogdanovic 28, Santi 51, Kiko 90)*         25,000
Twente (0) 0, Aarhus (0) 0                              10,150
Udinese (2) 2 *(Poggi 26, Bierhoff 32)*, Ajax (0) 1
*(Arveladze S 80)*                                      41,500
Valladolid (0) 1 *(Juan Carlos 88)*, Spartak Moscow (0) 2
*(Shyrko 64, 90)*                                       20,000

**THIRD ROUND, FIRST LEG**
Ajax (4) 4 *(Laudrup 34, 35, Arveladze S 37, Frank de
Boer 45)*, Bochum (2) 2 *(Reis 19, Waldoch 23)*        50,000
Braga (0) 0, Schalke (0) 0                              15,000
Croatia Zagreb (1) 1 *(Mujcin 2)*, Atletico Madrid (0) 1
*(Caminero 61)*                                         35,000
Karlsruhe (0) 0, Spartak Moscow (0) 0                   12,500
Rapid Vienna (0) 0, Lazio (1) 2 *(Casiraghi 38, Mancini
62)*                                                    34,000
Steaua (2) 2 *(Oakes 29 (og), Ciocoiu 32)*, Aston Villa
(0) 1 *(Yorke 54)*                                      24,000
Strasbourg (2) 2 *(Baticle 11, Ismael 19)*, Internazionale
(0) 0                                                   25,101
Twente (0) 0, Auxerre (0) 1 *(Diomede 70)*             15,000

**THIRD ROUND, SECOND LEG**
Aston Villa (0) 2 *(Milosevic 71, Taylor 85)*, Steaua (0) 0
                                                        35,102
Atletico Madrid (1) 1 *(Caminero 45)*, Croatia Zagreb
(0) 0                                                   40,000
Auxerre (1) 2 *(Marlet 3, Guivarc'h 82)*, Twente (0) 0
                                                        20,000
Bochum (0) 2 *(Hofmann 59, Mamic 70)*, Ajax (0) 2
*(Arveladze S 51, Dani 73)*                             24,034
Internazionale (1) 3 *(Ronaldo 27, Zanetti 48, Simeone
73)*, Strasbourg (0) 0                                  45,000
Lazio (0) 1 *(Venturin 85)*, Rapid Vienna (0) 0        12,000
Schalke (0) 2 *(Max 46, Eijkelkamp 63)*, Braga (0) 0   56,824
Spartak Moscow (0) 1 *(Shyrko 109)*, Karlsruhe (0) 0
                                                        28,000

**QUARTER-FINALS, FIRST LEG**
Ajax (0) 1 *(Arveladze S 57)*, Spartak Moscow (1) 3
*(Shyrko 26, 52, Kechinov 84)*                          47,000
Atletico Madrid (1) 1 *(Vieri 41 (pen))*, Aston Villa (0) 0
                                                        51,000
Internazionale (1) 1 *(Ronaldo 16)*, Schalke (0) 0     44,900
Lazio (0) 1 *(Casiraghi 64)*, Auxerre (0) 0            30,000

**QUARTER-FINALS, SECOND LEG**
Aston Villa (0) 2 *(Taylor 72, Collymore 74)*, Atletico
Madrid (1) 1 *(Caminero 28)*                            39,163
Auxerre (1) 2 *(Guivarc'h 39, 80)*, Lazio (2) 2 *(Mancini 7
(pen), Gottardi 12)*                                    20,000
Schalke (0) 1 *(Goossens 90)*, Internazionale (0) 1 *(West
91)*                                                    56,824
Spartak Moscow (0) 1 *(Shyrko 85)*, Ajax (0) 0         32,000

**SEMI-FINALS, FIRST LEG**
Atletico Madrid (0) 0, Lazio (1) 1 *(Jugovic 33)*      54,000
Internazionale (1) 2 *(Zamorano 45, Ze Elias 90)*, Spartak
Moscow (0) 1 *(Alenichev 48)*                           57,803

**SEMI-FINALS, SECOND LEG**
Lazio(0) 0, Atletico Madrid (0) 0                       55,000
Spartak Moscow (1) 1 *(Tikhonov 13)*, Internazionale
(1) 2 *(Ronaldo 45, 79)*                                34,000


**FINAL**

**Lazio (0) 0, Internazionale (1) 3**

(in Paris, 6 May 1998, 42,938)

*Lazio:* Marchegiani; Grandoni (Gottardi 55), Nesta,
Negro, Favalli, Fuser, Venturin (Almeyda 48), Jugovic,
Nedved, Casiraghi, Mancini.
*Internazionale:* Pagliuca; Fresi, Colonnese, West, Winter
(Cauet 69), Ze Élias, Djorkaeff (Moriero 69), Simeone,
Zanetti, Ronaldo, Zamorano (Sartor 74).
*Scorers:* Zamorano 5, Zanetti 60, Ronaldo 70.
*Referee:* Nieto (Spain).

Ronaldo of Internazionale takes the ball round Lazio goalkeeper Luca Marchegiani in the UEFA Cup Final in Paris.
(Action Images)

# UEFA CUP 1997–98 – BRITISH AND IRISH CLUBS

**PRELIMINARY ROUND, FIRST LEG**

**23 JULY**

**Bohemians (0) 0**

**Ferencvaros (1) 1** *(Zavadsky 30)*                                3000

*Bohemians:* Dempsey; Broughan, Best, O'Driscoll, Mullen, Byrne (Parkes 79), O'Connor (Wade 80), Hanrahan Lawlor, McGrath, Swan.

*Ferencvaros:* Udvaracz; Limperger, Dragoner, Lipcsei, Paling, Albert, Jagodics (Milovanovics 90), Schultz (Szucs 63), Nagy, Zavadszky, Horvath (Sitku 19).

**Grasshoppers (2) 3** *(Yakin 32, Aspinall 34 (og), Subiat 79)*

**Coleraine (0) 0**                                                  5100

*Grasshoppers:* Walker; Thuler, Gren, Christ, Esposito (Mazzarelli 64), Moldovan (Subiat 75), Haas, Vogel (Tikva 46), Ahinful, Magnin, Yakin.

*Coleraine:* Lamont; McAuley, Brunton, Gaston, Aspinall, McCallion (Clanaghan 59), O'Dowd, McCallan (Shipp 64), McAllister, Young, McKeever (Shiels 80).

**Inter Cable-Tel (0) 0**

**Celtic (2) 3** *(Thom 6 (pen), Johnson 45, Wieghorst 81)*
                                                                     6980

*Inter Cable-Tel:* Ellacott; Philpott, Rickard, David, Hewitt, Williams, Wharton, Gibson (Murray 62), Davies, Burrows (Jenkins 69), Haig (Wyle 79).

*Celtic:* Marshall; McNamara, Stubbs, Boyd, Hannah, McKinlay, Wieghorst, Gray, Thom, Donnelly, Johnson (Jackson 69).

**Principat (0) 0**

**Dundee U (2) 8** *(Winters 14, 31, 75, 77, McSwegan 46, 73, 76, Zetterlund 48)*                                          700

*Principat:* Castro; Andres, Coto, Blanco (Vicenc 80), Felix (Pascual 46), Patri, Lorenzatti (Marin 60), Pablo, Bazan, Lucendo, Emiliano.

*Dundee U:* Dykstra; McKimmie (McSwegan 46), Malpas, Pressley, Perry, Pedersen (Bowman 59), Olafsson (Walker 73), Zetterlund, Winters, Dolan, McLaren.

**PRELIMINARY ROUND, SECOND LEG**

**29 JULY**

**Celtic (3) 5** *(Thom 19 (pen), Jackson 42, Johnson 45, Hannah 63, Hay 85)*

**Inter Cable-Tel (0) 0**                                           41,557

*Celtic:* Marshall; Boyd, McKinlay, McNamara, Stubbs, Hannah (McBride 81), Donnelly, Gray (Annoni 46), Jackson, Johnson (Hay 75), Thom.

*Inter Cable-Tel:* Ellacott; Hewitt, Rickard, David, Philpott, Davies, Wharton, Burrows (Jenkins 56), Haig, Gibson (Copeman 66), Williams (Richards 83).

**Ferencvaros (1) 5** *(Albert 15, Jagodics 47, 74, Schultz 58, Zavadsky 71)*

**Bohemians (0) 0**                                                 10,000

*Ferencvaros:* Udvaracz (Szeiler 66); Dragoner, Szucs, Lipcsei, Paling (Schultz 46), Nyilas, Albert (Sitku 46), Jagodics, Nagy, Zavadsky, Nichenko.

*Bohemians:* Dempsey; Broughan, Best, O'Driscoll, Mullen, Byrne, O'Connor (Maher 66), Doolin, Hanrahan (Lawlor 13), McGrath, Swan (Parkes 78).

**30 JULY**

**Coleraine (1) 1** *(O'Dowd 22)*

**Grasshoppers (3) 7** *(Magnin 15, Esposito 27, Ahinful 33, Shiels 51 (og), Tikva 63, Yakin 64, Aspinall 83 (og))*    771

*Coleraine:* Lamont; McAuley, Brunton, Gaston (Clanaghan 45), Aspinall, McCallion, O'Dowd, McCallan, McAllister (McKeever 18), Young, Shiels (Shipp 85).

*Grasshoppers:* Walker; Thuler, Christ, Esposito (Tikva 45), Moldovan (Yakin 59), Haas, Ahinful, Magnin (Gamperle 69), Mazzarelli, Subiat, Smiljanic.

**Dundee U (5) 9** *(McSwegan 8, 24, 65, Winters 23, 42, McLaren 37, Olafsson 55, Zetterlund 59, Thompson 88)*

**Principat (0) 0**                                                 6695

*Dundee U:* Dykstra; McKimmie, Malpas, Perry, Pedersen, Olafsson, Zetterlund (Easton 76), Winters (Walker 55), Bowman, McLaren (Thompson 68), McSwegan.

*Principat:* Espot; Andres, Coto (Carlos 46), Pablo (Manuel 54), Patri, Bazan (Mario 46), Lorenzatti, Cavito, Emiliano, Pascual, Sandro.

**SECOND QUALIFYING ROUND, FIRST LEG**

**12 AUG**

**Tirol (2) 2** *(Mayrleb 22, 28)*

**Celtic (0) 1** *(Stubbs 84)*                                      6700

*Tirol:* Cherchesov; Tangen, Kirchler, Vulic, Severeyns, Brzeczek, Prudlo, Knavs, Marasek, Mayrleb, El Dahab (Yilmaz 65).

*Celtic:* Gould; Boyd, McKinlay, MacKay, Stubbs, Larsson, Burley, Thom, Jackson (Donnelly 80), Mahe (McNamara 46), Wieghorst (Hannah 68).

**Trabzonspor (0) 1** *(Hami 77 (pen))*

**Dundee U (0) 0**                                                  16,000

*Trabzonspor:* Metin; Okan, Rada (Orhan 16), Iskender, Kazin, Unal, Ogun, Misse-Misse, Abdullah, Cetin, Hami.

*Dundee U:* Dykstra; McKimmie, Malpas, Pressley, Perry, Pedersen, Olafsson (Duffy 79), Zetterlund, Winters (McSwegan 85), Dolan (McLaren 72), Bowman.

**SECOND QUALIFYING ROUND, SECOND LEG**

**26 AUG**

**Celtic (2) 6** *(Donnelly 34, 68 (pen), Thom 44, Burley 70, 90, Annoni 88)*

**Tirol (2) 3** *(Mayrleb 39, Severeyns 45, Krinner 82)* 47,017

*Celtic:* Gould; Boyd, Mahe, Mackay, Hannah, Donnelly, Burley, Wieghorst, O'Donnell (McNamara 56), Larsson, Thom (Stubbs 90).

*Tirol:* Cherchesov (Weber 13); Tangen, Kirchler, Baur (Krinner 81), Severeyns, Brzeczek, Prudlo, Knavs (Jochum 78), Mayrleb, Marasek, El Dahab.

**Dundee U (0) 1** *(McLaren 56)*

**Trabzonspor (1) 1** *(Hami 81)*                                   10,232

*Dundee U:* Dykstra; Malpas, Pressley, Perry, Pedersen, Olafsson, Zetterlund, McSwegan (Winters 68), Dolan (Duffy 68), McLaren (Thompson 83), Bowman.

*Trabzonspor:* Metin; Kazin, Abdullah, Iskender, Okan, Vugrinec (Cetin 68), Unal, Ogun, Misse-Misse (Orhan 42), Hami (Osman 87), Tolunay.

**FIRST ROUND, FIRST LEG**

**16 SEPT**

**Atletico Madrid (0) 2** *(Juninho 70, Vieri 72 (pen))*

**Leicester C (1) 1** *(Marshall 11)*                               35,000

*Atletico Madrid:* Molina; Toni (Jose Mari 58), Lardin, Andrei, Vizcaino (Bejbl 63), Caminero (Pantic 77), Geli, Prodan, Vieri, Juninho, Kiko.

*Leicester C:* Keller; Kamark, Guppy, Elliott, Walsh, Prior, Lennon, Izzet, Marshall (Claridge 31), Parker (Fenton 71), Heskey.

**Bordeaux (0) 0**
**Aston Villa (0) 0**                                     16,800
*Bordeaux:* Rame; Saveljic, Gralak, Afanou, Wiltord, Luccin (Diabate 84), Pavon, Musampa, Grenet (Ferrier 73), Laslandes, Papin (Diawara 84).
*Aston Villa:* Bosnich; Nelson, Wright, Southgate, Ehiogu, Staunton, Taylor, Draper, Grayson (Curcic 53), Collymore, Yorke.

**Celtic (0) 2** *(McNamara 53, Donnelly 74 (pen))*
**Liverpool (1) 2** *(Owen 6, McManaman 89)*         48,526
*Celtic:* Gould; McNamara, Boyd, Hannah, Stubbs, Mahe, Wieghorst, Burley, Blinker (O'Donnell 46), Larsson, Donnelly.
*Liverpool:* James; Jones, Bjornebye, Kvarme, Wright, Matteo, McManaman, Ince, Owen, Riedle, Thomas.

**PAOK Salonika (0) 1** *(Franzeskos 61)*
**Arsenal (0) 0**                                        42,000
*PAOK Salonika:* Mihopoulos; Zagorakis, Tassiopoulos, Kolobourdas, Olivares, Toursounidis (Sidiropoulos 71), Nagbe (Velis 74), Franzeskos, Zafiriou, Vrizas (Kapetanopoulos 58), Zouboulis.
*Arsenal:* Seaman; Dixon, Winterburn, Vieira, Bould, Adams, Parlour (Platt 70), Wright, Petit, Anelka (Wreh 81), Overmars (Boa Morte 70).

**Strasbourg (1) 2** *(Baticle 44 (pen), 60 (pen))*
**Rangers (0) 1** *(Albertz 49 (pen))*               12,450
*Strasbourg:* Vencel; N'Ghoghi, Suchoparek, Okpara, Raschke, Collet (Kinet 35), Arpinon (Miceli 12), Dacourt, Baticle, Conteh (Rabbah 78), Nouma.
*Rangers:* Snelders; Porrini, Petric, Bjorklund, Vidmar (Andersen 70), Gatusso (Miller 46), McCall, Gascoigne, Albertz, Durie, Laudrup.

## FIRST ROUND, SECOND LEG
### 30 SEPT

**Arsenal (1) 1** *(Bergkamp 22)*
**PAOK Salonika (0) 1** *(Vrizas 86)*                37,982
*Arsenal:* Seaman; Dixon, Winterburn, Vieira, Bould, Adams, Parlour (Anelka 87), Wright, Petit, Bergkamp, Overmars (Platt 75).
*PAOK Salonika:* Mihopoulos; Zagorakis, Tassiopoulos, Kolobourdas (Kapetanopoulos 81), Olivares, Toursounidis, Nagbe, Zafiriou (Sidiropoulos 33), Velis, Franzeskos (Zouboulis 89), Vrizas.

**Aston Villa (0) 1** *(Milosevic 111)*
**Bordeaux (0) 0**                                       33,072
*Aston Villa:* Bosnich; Nelson (Charles 106), Wright, Southgate, Ehiogu, Staunton, Taylor, Grayson, Milosevic, Collymore, Yorke.
*Bordeaux:* Rame; Saveljic, Gralak, Afanou, Wiltord, Diabate, Pavon, Micoud (Luccin 106), Grenet, Papin (Musampa 62), Laslandes (Diawara 83).

**Leicester C (0) 0**
**Atletico Madrid (0) 2** *(Juninho 72, Kiko 88)*    20,776
*Leicester C:* Keller; Kamark, Guppy, Elliott, Watts (Savage 77), Prior (Cottee 65), Lennon, Izzet, Marshall (Fenton 90), Parker, Heskey.
*Atletico Madrid:* Molina; Lopez, Santi, Andrei, Geli (Prodan 85), Caminero (Vizcaino 72), Bejbl, Juninho, Lardin, Vieri (Jose Mari 64), Kiko.

**Liverpool (0) 0**
**Celtic (0) 0**                                         38,205
*Liverpool:* James; Jones, Bjornebye, Kvarme, Carragher, Babb, McManaman, Ince, Fowler (Riedle 85), Owen, Berger.
*Celtic:* Gould; Annoni, Mahe, Hannah, Stubbs, McNamara, Burley, Wieghorst, Larsson, Donnelly, McKinlay.

**Rangers (1) 1** *(Gattuso 11)*
**Strasbourg (1) 2** *(Baticle 35, Zitelli 49)*      40,145
*Rangers:* Goram; Cleland, Bjorklund (Miller 71), McCall, Porrini, Stensaas, Gattuso, Gascoigne, Durie (Johansson 78), Laudrup (Andersen 66), Negri.
*Strasbourg:* Vencel; Raschke, Suchoparek, Okpara, M'Ghoghi, Collet (Keller 90), Dacourt, Miceli (Zitelli 19), Baticle, Conteh (Rott 68), Kinet.

## SECOND ROUND, FIRST LEG
### 21 OCT

**Athletic Bilbao (0) 0**
**Aston Villa (0) 0**                                    39,000
*Athletic Bilbao:* Imanol Etxeberria; Rios, Carlos Garcia, Alkorta, Larrainzar, Urrutia, Alkiza, Lasa (Larrazabal 62), Joseba Etxeberria, Ziganda, Javi Gonzalez (Bernejo 76).
*Aston Villa:* Bosnich; Nelson, Wright, Southgate, Scimeca, Staunton, Taylor (Grayson), Draper, Milosevic, Collymore, Yorke.

**Strasbourg (1) 3** *(Zitelli 20, 63, Conteh 69)*
**Liverpool (0) 0**                                      18,813
*Strasbourg:* Vencel; Okpara, Suchoparek, Raschke, Collet, Arpinon, Dacourt, M'Ghoghi (Rott 77), Baticle, Conteh, Zitelli (Rabbah 88).
*Liverpool:* James; McAteer, Bjornebye, Kvarme, Harkness, Ruddock (Owen 75), McManaman, Ince, Fowler, Redknapp, Leonhardsen.

## SECOND ROUND, SECOND LEG
### 4 NOV

**Aston Villa (1) 2** *(Taylor 27, Yorke 50)*
**Athletic Bilbao (0) 1** *(Javi Gonzalez 70)*       35,915
*Aston Villa:* Bosnich; Charles, Wright, Southgate, Scimeca, Staunton, Nelson (Grayson 87), Draper, Milosevic, Taylor, Yorke.
*Athletic Bilbao:* Imanol Etxeberria; Rios, Alkorta, Ferreira (Lasa 50), Larrazabal, Larrainzar, Urrutia (Javi Gonzalez 69), Alkiza, Joseba Etxeberria, Urzaiz, Ziganda (Guerrero 53).

**Liverpool (0) 2** *(Fowler 63 (pen), Riedle 84)*
**Strasbourg (0) 0**                                     32,426
*Liverpool:* James; Jones (Riedle 55), Bjornebye (Berger 51), Kvarme, Matteo, Leonhardsen, McManaman, Ince, Fowler, Owen, Redknapp.
*Strasbourg:* Vencel; Ismael (Rott 53), Suchoparek, Okpara, Dacourt, M'Ghoghi, Collet, Kinet (Rabbah 57), Baticle, Zitelli (Miceli 88), Conteh.

## THIRD ROUND, FIRST LEG
### 25 NOV

**Steaua (2) 2** *(Oakes 29 (og), Ciocoiu 32)*
**Aston Villa (0) 1** *(Yorke 54)*                   24,000
*Steaua:* Ritli; Csik, Rachita, Miu, Reghecampf, Rotariu, Lincar (Hrib 69), Munteanu, Militaru, Lacatus (Raducan 88), Ciocoiu (Luca 75).
*Aston Villa:* Oakes; Nelson (Charles 69), Wright, Scimeca, Ehiogu, Staunton, Taylor, Draper, Milosevic, Collymore, Yorke.

## THIRD ROUND, SECOND LEG
### 9 DEC

**Aston Villa (0) 2** *(Milosevic 71, Taylor 85)*
**Steaua (0) 0**                                         35,102
*Aston Villa:* Bosnich; Charles, Wright, Southgate, Ehiogu, Staunton, Taylor, Draper (Nelson 82), Milosevic, Collymore, Grayson (Hendrie 62).
*Steaua:* Ritli; Matei, Rachita (Lincar 88), Csik, Reghecampf, Militaru, Rotariu, Munteanu, Miu, Lacatus (Luca 68), Ciocoiu (Hrib 77).

**QUARTER-FINALS, FIRST LEG**

**3 MAR**

**Atletico Madrid (1) 1** *(Vieri 41 (pen))*

**Aston Villa (0) 0**        51,000

*Atletico Madrid:* Molina; Aguilera, Santi, Andrei, Toni, Jose Mari (Paunovic 60), Pantic (Nimny 74), Vizcaino, Caminero, Vieri, Kiko.
*Aston Villa:* Bosnich; Grayson, Wright, Southgate, Ehiogu, Scimeca (Staunton 42), Taylor, Draper, Yorke, Collymore (Joachim 51), Hendrie.

**QUARTER-FINALS, SECOND LEG**

**17 MAR**

**Aston Villa (0) 2** *(Taylor 72, Collymore 74)*

**Atletico Madrid (1) 1** *(Caminero 28)*     39,163

*Aston Villa:* Bosnich; Joachim, Wright, Southgate, Ehiogu, Staunton, Taylor, Draper (Nelson 53) (Charles 87), Milosevic (Collymore 53), Hendrie, Yorke.
*Atletico Madrid:* Molina; Aguilera (Toni 82), Santi, Andrei (Prodan 60), Geli, Pantic (Lardin 58), Bejbl, Vizcaino, Caminero, Kiko, Vieri.

Savo Milosevic of Aston Villa makes progress against Athletic Bilbao's Rafael Alkorta. (Action Images)

# Summary of Appearances

## EUROPEAN CUP (1955–98)

**English clubs**
12 Liverpool
9 Manchester U
3 Nottingham F, Leeds U
2 Derby Co, Wolverhampton W, Everton, Aston Villa, Arsenal
1 Burnley, Tottenham H, Ipswich T, Manchester C, Blackburn R, Newcastle U

**Scottish clubs**
19 Rangers
15 Celtic
3 Aberdeen
2 Hearts
1 Dundee, Dundee U, Kilmarnock, Hibernian

**Welsh clubs**
1 Barry T, Cwmbran

**Northern Ireland clubs**
18 Linfield
8 Glentoran
3 Crusaders
2 Portadown
1 Glenavon, Ards, Distillery, Derry C, Coleraine

**Eire clubs**
7 Shamrock R, Dundalk
6 Waterford
3 Drumcondra
2 Bohemians, Limerick, Athlone T, Shelbourne, Derry C*
1 Cork Hibs, Cork Celtic, Cork City, Sligo R, St Patrick's Ath

**Winners: Celtic 1966–67; Manchester U 1967–68; Liverpool 1976–77, 1977–78, 1980–81, 1983–84; Nottingham F 1978–79, 1979–80; Aston Villa 1981–82**

**Finalists: Celtic 1969–70; Leeds U 1974–75; Liverpool 1984–85**

## EUROPEAN CUP-WINNERS' CUP (1960–98)

**English clubs**
6 Tottenham H
5 Manchester U, Liverpool
4 West Ham U, Chelsea
3 Arsenal, Everton
2 Manchester C
1 Wolverhampton W, Leicester C, WBA, Leeds U, Sunderland, Southampton, Ipswich T

**Scottish clubs**
10 Rangers
8 Aberdeen, Celtic
2 Dunfermline Ath, Hearts, Dundee U
1 Dundee, Hibernian, St Mirren, Motherwell, Airdrieonians, Kilmarnock

**Welsh clubs**
14 Cardiff C
8 Wrexham
7 Swansea C
2 Bangor C
1 Borough U, Newport Co, Merthyr Tydfil, Barry T, Llansantffraid, Cwmbran

**Northern Ireland clubs**
8 Glentoran
5 Glenavon
4 Ballymena U, Coleraine
3 Crusaders, Linfield
2 Ards, Bangor
1 Derry C, Distillery, Portadown, Carrick Rangers, Cliftonville

**Eire clubs**
6 Shamrock R
4 Shelbourne
3 Limerick, Waterford, Dundalk, Bohemians
2 Cork Hibs, Galway U, Sligo R, Derry C*
1 Cork Celtic, St Patrick's Ath, Finn Harps, Home Farm, University College Dublin, Cork City, Bray W

**Winners: Tottenham H 1962–63; West Ham U 1964–65; Manchester C 1969–70; Chelsea 1970–71, 1997–98; Rangers 1971–72; Aberdeen 1982–83; Everton 1984–85; Manchester U 1990-91; Arsenal 1993–94**

**Finalists: Rangers 1960–61, 1966–67; Liverpool 1965–66; Leeds U 1972–73; West Ham U 1975–76; Arsenal 1979–80, 1994–95**

## EUROPEAN FAIRS CUP & UEFA CUP (1955–98)

**English clubs**
9 Leeds U
8 Ipswich T, Liverpool, Aston Villa, Arsenal
7 Manchester U
6 Everton, Newcastle U
5 Southampton, Tottenham H, Nottingham F
4 Manchester C, Birmingham C, Wolverhampton W, WBA
3 Chelsea, Sheffield W
2 Stoke C, Derby Co, QPR
1 Burnley, Coventry C, Norwich C, London Rep XI, Watford, Blackburn R, Leicester C

**Scottish clubs**
18 Dundee U
14 Hibernian
13 Aberdeen
11 Celtic,
9 Hearts, Rangers
5 Dunfermline Ath
4 Dundee, Kilmarnock
3 St Mirren
2 Partick T, Motherwell
1 Morton, St Johnstone, Raith R

**Welsh Clubs**
2 Bangor C
1 Inter Cardiff, Afan Lido, Newtown, Barry T, Inter Cable-Tel

**Northern Ireland clubs**
11 Glentoran
7 Coleraine
5 Linfield
4 Glenavon, Portadown
3 Crusaders
1 Ards, Ballymena U, Bangor

**Eire clubs**
10 Bohemians
5 Dundalk
4 Shamrock R
3 Finn Harps, Shelbourne, St Patrick's Ath
2 Drumcondra, Derry C*, Cork City
1 Cork Hibs, Athlone T, Limerick, Drogheda U, Galway U

**Winners: Leeds U 1967–68, 1970–71; Newcastle U 1968–69; Arsenal 1969–70; Tottenham H 1971–72, 1983–84; Liverpool 1972–73, 1975–76; Ipswich T 1980–81**

**Finalists: London 1955–58, Birmingham C 1958–60, 1960–61; Leeds U 1966–67; Wolverhampton W 1971–72; Tottenham H 1973–74; Dundee U 1986–87**

*Now play in League of Ireland*

# INTER-TOTO CUP 1997

### Group 1
|  | P | W | D | L | F | A | Pts |
|---|---|---|---|---|---|---|---|
| Duisburg | 4 | 3 | 1 | 0 | 5 | 0 | 10 |
| Dynamo Minsk | 4 | 2 | 0 | 2 | 6 | 4 | 6 |
| Aalborg | 4 | 2 | 0 | 2 | 6 | 11 | 6 |
| Heerenveen | 4 | 1 | 1 | 2 | 8 | 5 | 4 |
| Polonia | 4 | 0 | 2 | 2 | 1 | 6 | 2 |

### Group 2
|  | P | W | D | L | F | A | Pts |
|---|---|---|---|---|---|---|---|
| Bastia | 4 | 3 | 0 | 1 | 5 | 3 | 9 |
| Graz | 4 | 2 | 1 | 1 | 5 | 4 | 7 |
| Silkeborg | 4 | 2 | 0 | 2 | 11 | 4 | 6 |
| Dragovoljac | 4 | 2 | 0 | 2 | 7 | 7 | 6 |
| Ebbw Vale | 4 | 0 | 1 | 3 | 2 | 12 | 1 |

### Group 3
|  | P | W | D | L | F | A | Pts |
|---|---|---|---|---|---|---|---|
| Auxerre | 4 | 3 | 1 | 0 | 19 | 2 | 10 |
| Lausanne | 4 | 2 | 2 | 0 | 13 | 4 | 8 |
| Antwerp | 4 | 2 | 1 | 1 | 7 | 7 | 7 |
| Salamina | 4 | 1 | 0 | 3 | 6 | 19 | 3 |
| Ards | 4 | 0 | 0 | 4 | 1 | 14 | 0 |

### Group 4
|  | P | W | D | L | F | A | Pts |
|---|---|---|---|---|---|---|---|
| Cologne | 4 | 3 | 1 | 0 | 9 | 2 | 10 |
| Maccabi Petah Tikva | 4 | 1 | 2 | 1 | 2 | 3 | 5 |
| Standard | 4 | 0 | 4 | 0 | 1 | 1 | 4 |
| Cork City | 4 | 0 | 3 | 1 | 0 | 2 | 3 |
| Aarau | 4 | 0 | 2 | 2 | 0 | 4 | 2 |

### Group 5
|  | P | W | D | L | F | A | Pts |
|---|---|---|---|---|---|---|---|
| Dynamo Moscow | 4 | 3 | 1 | 0 | 7 | 4 | 10 |
| Genk | 4 | 3 | 0 | 1 | 15 | 8 | 9 |
| Stabaek | 4 | 1 | 2 | 1 | 10 | 6 | 5 |
| Panachaiki | 4 | 1 | 1 | 2 | 8 | 9 | 4 |
| Boltfelagio | 4 | 0 | 0 | 4 | 2 | 15 | 0 |

### Group 6
|  | P | W | D | L | F | A | Pts |
|---|---|---|---|---|---|---|---|
| Hamburg | 4 | 4 | 0 | 0 | 9 | 4 | 12 |
| Samsun | 4 | 3 | 0 | 1 | 7 | 3 | 9 |
| FBK Kaunas | 4 | 1 | 1 | 2 | 6 | 7 | 4 |
| Leiftur | 4 | 1 | 0 | 3 | 7 | 11 | 3 |
| Odense | 4 | 0 | 1 | 3 | 6 | 10 | 1 |

### Group 7
|  | P | W | D | L | F | A | Pts |
|---|---|---|---|---|---|---|---|
| Istanbul | 4 | 3 | 1 | 0 | 10 | 3 | 10 |
| Vasas | 4 | 3 | 0 | 1 | 9 | 3 | 9 |
| Werder Bremen | 4 | 2 | 1 | 1 | 5 | 3 | 7 |
| Osters | 4 | 1 | 0 | 3 | 6 | 10 | 3 |
| Universitate | 4 | 0 | 0 | 4 | 2 | 13 | 0 |

### Group 8
|  | P | W | D | L | F | A | Pts |
|---|---|---|---|---|---|---|---|
| Halmstad | 4 | 3 | 1 | 0 | 10 | 3 | 10 |
| Lommel | 4 | 1 | 3 | 0 | 6 | 5 | 6 |
| Hajduk Kula | 4 | 2 | 0 | 2 | 6 | 5 | 6 |
| TPS Turku | 4 | 1 | 1 | 2 | 5 | 9 | 4 |
| Kongsvinger | 4 | 0 | 1 | 3 | 2 | 7 | 1 |

### Group 9
|  | P | W | D | L | F | A | Pts |
|---|---|---|---|---|---|---|---|
| Lyon | 4 | 4 | 0 | 0 | 14 | 3 | 12 |
| Rapid Bucharest | 4 | 2 | 1 | 1 | 8 | 5 | 7 |
| Odra | 4 | 1 | 1 | 2 | 9 | 10 | 4 |
| Zilina | 4 | 1 | 1 | 2 | 3 | 8 | 4 |
| FK Austria | 4 | 0 | 1 | 3 | 3 | 11 | 1 |

### Group 10
|  | P | W | D | L | F | A | Pts |
|---|---|---|---|---|---|---|---|
| Montpellier | 4 | 3 | 1 | 0 | 9 | 3 | 10 |
| Groningen | 4 | 3 | 0 | 1 | 7 | 4 | 9 |
| Cukaricki | 4 | 2 | 0 | 2 | 7 | 6 | 6 |
| Gloria | 4 | 1 | 0 | 3 | 6 | 10 | 3 |
| Spartak Varna | 4 | 0 | 1 | 3 | 2 | 8 | 1 |

### Group 11
|  | P | W | D | L | F | A | Pts |
|---|---|---|---|---|---|---|---|
| Novgorod | 4 | 4 | 0 | 0 | 8 | 1 | 12 |
| Publikum | 4 | 1 | 2 | 1 | 3 | 3 | 5 |
| Proleter | 4 | 1 | 1 | 2 | 4 | 2 | 4 |
| Antalya | 4 | 1 | 1 | 2 | 2 | 4 | 4 |
| Maccabi Haifa | 4 | 1 | 0 | 3 | 2 | 9 | 3 |

### Group 12
|  | P | W | D | L | F | A | Pts |
|---|---|---|---|---|---|---|---|
| Torpedo Moscow | 4 | 4 | 0 | 0 | 9 | 1 | 12 |
| Merani | 4 | 2 | 2 | 0 | 2 | 8 | 6 |
| Ried | 4 | 2 | 0 | 2 | 6 | 7 | 6 |
| Iraklis | 4 | 2 | 0 | 2 | 5 | 7 | 6 |
| Valletta | 4 | 0 | 0 | 4 | 1 | 9 | 0 |

**SEMI-FINALS**
Novgorod 0, 0, Halmstad 0, 1
Hamburg 0, 1, Bastia 1, 1
Istanbul 2, 0, Lyon 1, 2
Auxerre 3, 1, Torpedo Moscow 0, 4
Cologne 0, 2, Montpellier 1, 1
Dynamo Moscow 2, 1, Duisburg 2, 3

**FINALS, FIRST LEG**
Halmstad 0, Bastia 1
Montpellier 0, Lyon 1
Duisburg 0, Auxerre 0

**FINALS, SECOND LEG**
Bastia* 1, Halmstad 1
Lyon* 3, Montpellier 2
Auxerre* 2, Duisburg 0

*Three successful clubs gain access to the first round of the 1997–98 UEFA Cup.

# WORLD CLUB CHAMPIONSHIP

Played annually up to 1974 and intermittently since then between the winners of the European Cup and the winners of the South American Champions Cup — known as the Copa Libertadores. In 1980 the winners were decided by one match arranged in Tokyo in February 1981 and the venue has been the same since. AC Milan replaced Marseille who had been stripped of their European Cup title in 1993.

| | |
|---|---|
| 1960 | Real Madrid beat Penarol 0-0, 5-1 |
| 1961 | Penarol beat Benfica 0-1, 5-0, 2-1 |
| 1962 | Santos beat Benfica 3-2, 5-2 |
| 1963 | Santos beat AC Milan 2-4, 4-2, 1-0 |
| 1964 | Inter-Milan beat Independiente 0-1, 2-0, 1-0 |
| 1965 | Inter-Milan beat Independiente 3-0, 0-0 |
| 1966 | Penarol beat Real Madrid 2-0, 2-0 |
| 1967 | Racing Club beat Celtic 0-1, 2-1, 1-0 |
| 1968 | Estudiantes beat Manchester United 1-0, 1-1 |
| 1969 | AC Milan beat Estudiantes 3-0, 1-2 |
| 1970 | Feyenoord beat Estudiantes 2-2, 1-0 |
| 1971 | Nacional beat Panathinaikos* 1-1, 2-1 |
| 1972 | Ajax beat Independiente 1-1, 3-0 |
| 1973 | Independiente beat Juventus* 1-0 |
| 1974 | Atlético Madrid* beat Independiente 0-1, 2-0 |
| 1975 | Independiente and Bayern Munich could not agree dates; no matches. |
| 1976 | Bayern Munich beat Cruzeiro 2-0, 0-0 |
| 1977 | Boca Juniors beat Borussia Moenchengladbach* 2-2, 3-0 |
| 1978 | Not contested |
| 1979 | Olimpia beat Malmö* 1-0, 2-1 |

| | |
|---|---|
| 1980 | Nacional beat Nottingham Forest 1-0 |
| 1981 | Flamengo beat Liverpool 3-0 |
| 1982 | Penarol beat Aston Villa 2-0 |
| 1983 | Gremio Porto Alegre beat SV Hamburg 2-1 |
| 1984 | Independiente beat Liverpool 1-0 |
| 1985 | Juventus beat Argentinos Juniors 4-2 on penalties after a 2-2 draw |
| 1986 | River Plate beat Steaua Bucharest 1-0 |
| 1987 | FC Porto beat Penarol 2-1 after extra time |
| 1988 | Nacional (Uru) beat PSV Eindhoven 7-6 on penalties after 1-1 draw |
| 1989 | AC Milan beat Atletico Nacional (Col) 1-0 after extra time |
| 1990 | AC Milan beat Olimpia 3-0 |
| 1991 | Red Star Belgrade beat Colo Colo 3-0 |
| 1992 | Sao Paulo beat Barcelona 2-1 |
| 1993 | Sao Paulo beat AC Milan 3-2 |
| 1994 | Velez Sarsfield beat AC Milan 2-0 |
| 1995 | Ajax beat Gremio Porto Alegre 4-3 on penalties after 0-0 draw |
| 1996 | Juventus beat River Plate 1-0 |

*European Cup runners-up; winners declined to take part.

**1997**

**2 December in Tokyo**

**Borussia Dortmund (1) 2**

**Cruzeiro (0) 0**    46,953

*Borussia Dortmund:* Klos; Heinrich, Julio Cesar, Feiersinger, Freund, Zorc (Kirovski 80), Reuter, Moller, Paulo Sousa, Chapuisat (Decheiver 75), Herrlich.
*Scorers:* Zorc 34, Herrlich 85.
*Cruzeiro:* Dida; Victor, Joao Carlos, Goncalves, Fabinho, Cleison, Roberto Palacios (Marcelo 64), Ricardinho, Elivelton, Bebeto, Donizete.
*Referee:* Aranda (Spain).

# EUROPEAN SUPER CUP

Played annually between the winners of the European Champions' Cup and the European Cup-Winners' Cup. AC Milan replaced Marseille in 1993–94.

**Previous Matches**

| | |
|---|---|
| 1972 | Ajax beat Rangers 3-1, 3-2 |
| 1973 | Ajax beat AC Milan 0-1, 6-0 |
| 1974 | Not contested |
| 1975 | Dynamo Kiev beat Bayern Munich 1-0, 2-0 |
| 1976 | Anderlecht beat Bayern Munich 4-1, 1-2 |
| 1977 | Liverpool beat Hamburg 1-1, 6-0 |
| 1978 | Anderlecht beat Liverpool 3-1, 1-2 |
| 1979 | Nottingham F beat Barcelona 1-0, 1-1 |
| 1980 | Valencia beat Nottingham F 1-0, 1-2 |
| 1981 | Not contested |
| 1982 | Aston Villa beat Barcelona 0-1, 3-0 |
| 1983 | Aberdeen beat Hamburg 0-0, 2-0 |
| 1984 | Juventus beat Liverpool 2-0 |
| 1985 | Juventus v Everton not contested due to UEFA ban on English clubs |
| 1986 | Steaua Bucharest beat Dynamo Kiev 1-0 |
| 1987 | FC Porto beat Ajax 1-0, 1-0 |
| 1988 | KV Mechelen beat PSV Eindhoven 3-0, 0-1 |
| 1989 | AC Milan beat Barcelona 1-1, 1-0 |
| 1990 | AC Milan beat Sampdoria 1-1, 2-0 |
| 1991 | Manchester U beat Red Star Belgrade 1-0 |
| 1992 | Barcelona beat Werder Bremen 1-1, 2-1 |
| 1993 | Parma beat AC Milan 0-1, 2-0 |
| 1994 | AC Milan beat Arsenal 0-0, 2-0 |
| 1995 | Ajax beat Zaragoza 1-1, 4-0 |
| 1996 | Juventus beat Paris St. Germain 6-1, 3-1 |

**1997–98**

**First Leg, 8 January 1998, Barcelona**

**Barcelona (1) 2** *(Luis Enrique 8, Rivaldo 61 (pen))*

**Borussia Dortmund (0) 0**    50,000

*Barcelona:* Hesp; Bogarde, Albert Celades, Reiziger (Abelardo 70), Ferrer, Sergi, Ivan de la Pena, Rivaldo (Giovanni 86), Luis Enrique, Luis Figo (Stoichkov 86), Anderson.
*Borussia Dortmund:* Klos; Kree, Schneider (Reinhardt 46), Binz, Heinrich, But (Zorc 77), Ricken, Freund, Tanko (Chapuisat 58), Kirovski, Decheiver.
*Referee:* Elleray (England).

**Second Leg, 11 March 1998, Dortmund**

**Borussia Dortmund (0) 1** *(Heinrich 64)*

**Barcelona (1) 1** *(Giovanni 8)*    32,500

*Borussia Dortmund:* Klos; Schneider, Freund (Mehnert 20), Zorc, Kohler (Kirovski 73), Kree, Heinrich, Ricken, Binz, Decheiver, Chapuisat (Gambo 46).
*Barcelona:* Hesp; Ferrer, Bogarde, Nadal, Sergi, Luis Figo, Albert Celedes (Amor 79), Luis Enrique (Ciric 89), Anderson (Oscar Garcia 71), Giovanni, Rivaldo.
*Referee:* Ceccarini (Italy).

# INTERNATIONAL DIRECTORY

The latest available information has been given regarding numbers of clubs and players registered with FIFA, the world governing body. Where known, official colours are listed. With European countries, League tables show a number of signs. * indicates relegated teams, + play-offs, *+ relegated after play-offs, ++ promoted.

There are 197 member associations and one provisional member, Palestine. The four home countries, England, Scotland, Northern Ireland and Wales, are dealt with elsewhere in the Yearbook; but basic details appear in this directory.

## EUROPE

### ALBANIA

**Federation Albanaise De Football,** Rruga Dervish Hima Nr. 31, Tirana.
*Founded:* 1930; *Number of Clubs:* 49; *Number of Players:* 5,192; *National Colours:* All red.
*Telephone:* 00–355–42 27 877; *Cable:* ALBSPORT TIRANA; *Telex:* 2228 bfssh ab. *Fax:* 00 355–42 27 877 (27922).

**League Championship wins (1930-37; 1945–98)**
Dinamo Tirana 15; Partizani Tirana 15; SK Tirana 9; 17 Nentori 8; Vllaznia 8; Flamurtari 1; Labinoti 1; Skenderbeu 1, Teuta 1.

**Cup wins (1948–98)**
Partizani Tirana 14; Dinamo Tirana 12; 17 Nentori 6; Vllaznia 5; Flamurtari 2; SK Tirana 2; Labinoti 1; Elbasan 1; Teuta 1; Apolonia 1.

**Final League Table 1997–98**
|  | P | W | D | L | F | A | Pts |
|---|---|---|---|---|---|---|---|
| Vllaznia | 34 | 22 | 6 | 6 | 42 | 24 | 72 |
| SK Tirana | 34 | 19 | 8 | 7 | 54 | 19 | 65 |
| Partizani | 34 | 20 | 4 | 10 | 62 | 27 | 64 |
| Shkumbini | 34 | 17 | 3 | 14 | 56 | 49 | 54 |
| Teuta | 34 | 17 | 3 | 14 | 39 | 38 | 54 |
| Elbasan | 34 | 16 | 4 | 14 | 48 | 31 | 52 |
| Apolonia | 34 | 15 | 7 | 12 | 38 | 34 | 52 |
| Laci | 34 | 15 | 3 | 16 | 47 | 48 | 48 |
| Lushnja | 34 | 14 | 5 | 15 | 54 | 38 | 47 |
| Tomori | 34 | 15 | 2 | 17 | 36 | 45 | 47 |
| Skenderbeu | 34 | 13 | 7 | 14 | 40 | 50 | 46 |
| Dinamo | 34 | 12 | 9 | 13 | 42 | 36 | 45 |
| Bylis | 34 | 13 | 6 | 15 | 41 | 39 | 45 |
| Besa | 34 | 13 | 5 | 16 | 45 | 47 | 44 |
| Flamurtari | 34 | 12 | 7 | 15 | 37 | 41 | 43 |
| Shquiponia* | 34 | 12 | 4 | 18 | 34 | 55 | 40 |
| Sopoti* | 34 | 10 | 5 | 19 | 39 | 64 | 35 |
| Albpetrol* | 34 | 5 | 4 | 25 | 24 | 93 | 19 |

*Top scorer:* Bubeqi (Shkumbini) 26.
*Cup Final:* Apolonia 1, Lushnja 0.

### ANDORRA

**Federacio Andorrana de Futbol,** Camp d'Esports d'Aixovall, Carretera d'Os de Civis, s/n Saint Julia de Loria.
*Founded:* 1994; *Number of Clubs:* 12; *Number of Players:* 300; *National Colours:* Yellow shirts, red shorts, yellow stockings.
*Telephone:* 00376 842224; *Fax:* 00376 842225.

### ARMENIA

**Football Federation of Armenia,** 9, Abovian Str. 375001 Erevan, Armenia.
*Founded:* 1992; *Number of Clubs:* 32; *Number of Players:* 15,000; *National Colours:* Red shirts, blue shorts, orange stockings.
*Telephone:* 00374 2/589480; *Telex:* 243337 minor su; *Fax:* 00374 2/151573.

**League Championship wins (1992–98)**
Shirak Gyumri 2; Pyunik 2; Ararat Erevan 1; Homenmen 1; FC Erevan 1.

**Cup wins (1992–94)**
Ararat Erevan 2.

### Final League Table 1997–98
|  | P | W | D | L | F | A | Pts |
|---|---|---|---|---|---|---|---|
| FC Erevan | 18 | 13 | 4 | 1 | 41 | 10 | 43 |
| Shirak | 18 | 12 | 5 | 1 | 46 | 8 | 41 |
| Erebouni | 18 | 11 | 2 | 5 | 35 | 20 | 35 |
| Pyunik | 18 | 11 | 2 | 5 | 42 | 16 | 35 |
| Tsement | 18 | 8 | 3 | 7 | 28 | 27 | 27 |
| Ararat | 18 | 7 | 6 | 5 | 32 | 21 | 27 |
| Kotiak | 18 | 5 | 4 | 9 | 31 | 33 | 19 |
| Karabach | 18 | 5 | 3 | 10 | 13 | 28 | 18 |
| Dvinn | 18 | 1 | 4 | 13 | 16 | 52 | 7 |
| Lori* | 18 | 0 | 1 | 17 | 7 | 76 | 1 |

*Top scorer:* Petrossian (Shirak) 18.

### AUSTRIA

**Oesterreichischer Fussball-Bund,** Ernst-Happel Stadion, Postfach 340, Meierestrasse, A-1021 Wien.
*Founded:* 1904; *Number of Clubs:* 2,081; *Number of Players:* 253,576; *National Colours:* White shirts, black shorts, white stockings.
*Telephone:* 0043 1 727 180; *Cable:* FOOTBALL WIEN; *Telex:* 111919 oefb a; *Fax:* 0043 1 728 1632.

**League Championship wins (1912–98)**
Rapid Vienna 30; FK Austria 22; Admira-Energie-Wacker 9; First Vienna 6; Tirol-Svarowski-Innsbruck 7; Wiener Sportklub 3; Austria Salzburg 3; FAC 1; Hakoah 1; Linz ASK 1; WAF 1; Voest Linz 1; Sturm Graz 1.

**Cup wins (1919–98)**
FK Austria 25; Rapid Vienna 14; TS Innsbruck (prev. Wacker Innsbruck) 7; Admira-Energie-Wacker (prev. Sportklub Admira & Admira-Energie) 5; First Vienna 3; Sturm Graz 2; Linz ASK 1; Wacker Vienna 1; WAF 1; Wiener Sportklub 1; Graz 1; Stockerau 1; Ried 1.

**Final League Table 1997–98**
|  | P | W | D | L | F | A | Pts |
|---|---|---|---|---|---|---|---|
| Sturm Graz | 36 | 24 | 9 | 3 | 80 | 28 | 81 |
| Rapid | 36 | 18 | 8 | 10 | 42 | 36 | 62 |
| Graz | 36 | 18 | 7 | 11 | 53 | 33 | 61 |
| Austria Salzburg | 36 | 16 | 8 | 12 | 48 | 31 | 56 |
| Linz ASK | 36 | 17 | 4 | 15 | 67 | 57 | 55 |
| Innsbruck | 36 | 12 | 12 | 12 | 48 | 51 | 48 |
| FK Austria | 36 | 10 | 10 | 16 | 38 | 54 | 40 |
| Ried | 36 | 10 | 9 | 17 | 41 | 55 | 39 |
| Lustenau | 36 | 6 | 14 | 16 | 38 | 59 | 32 |
| Modling* | 36 | 5 | 7 | 24 | 34 | 85 | 22 |

*Top scorer:* Frigard (Linz ASK) 23.
*Cup Final:* Ried 3, Sturm Graz 1.

### AZERBAIJAN

Association of Football Federations of Azerbaijan, Husu Haciyev kuc., 42, 370009 Baku, Azerbaijan.
*Founded:* 1992; *Number of Clubs:* 1,500;. *Number of Players:* 95,000; *National Colours:* White shirts with blue stripes, blue shorts, white stockings.
*Telephone:* 00994 12 94 49 16; *Cable:* FOOTBALL ASSOCIATION, AZ; *Fax:* 00994 12 98 93 93.

**League Championship wins (1992–97)**
Neftchi 3; Karabach 1; Kopaz 1; Turan 1; Kepez 1.

**Cup wins (1992–98)**
Kopaz 3; Karabach 2; Neftchi 1; Inshatchi 1.
*Cup Final:* Kopaz 2, Agdam 0.

## BELARUS

Belarus Football Association, 8–2 Kyrov Str. 220600 Minsk, Belarus.
*Founded: 1989; Number of Clubs:* 455; *Number of Players:* 120,000; *National Colours:* All green.
*Telephone:* 007 0172 375 272325; *Telex:*252175 athlet su; *Fax:* 007 0172 27 29 20.

**League Championship wins (1992–97)**
Dynamo Minsk 6; MPKC Mozyr 1.

**Cup wins (1992–97)**
Dynamo Minsk 2; Neman 1; Dynamo 93 Minsk 1; MPKC Mozyr 1; Belshina 1; Lokomotiv 96 1.

**Final Table 1997**

|  | P | W | D | L | F | A | Pts |
|---|---|---|---|---|---|---|---|
| Dynamo Minsk | 30 | 21 | 7 | 2 | 74 | 24 | 70 |
| Belshina | 30 | 21 | 3 | 6 | 67 | 30 | 66 |
| Lokomotiv 96 | 30 | 18 | 5 | 7 | 46 | 30 | 59 |
| Dnepr Mogilev | 30 | 15 | 7 | 8 | 48 | 32 | 52 |
| Dynamo 93 Minsk | 30 | 14 | 7 | 9 | 53 | 30 | 49 |
| MPKC Mozyr | 30 | 12 | 7 | 11 | 39 | 30 | 43 |
| Dynamo Brest | 30 | 12 | 6 | 12 | 44 | 52 | 42 |
| Torpedo Minsk | 30 | 12 | 6 | 12 | 45 | 43 | 42 |
| Naftan | 30 | 10 | 9 | 11 | 40 | 33 | 39 |
| Neman | 30 | 10 | 8 | 12 | 32 | 41 | 38 |
| Kommunalnik | 30 | 9 | 3 | 18 | 32 | 61 | 30 |
| Ataka Aura | 30 | 8 | 6 | 16 | 29 | 44 | 30 |
| Molodechno | 30 | 7 | 9 | 14 | 28 | 44 | 30 |
| Transmash | 30 | 8 | 4 | 18 | 30 | 52 | 28 |
| Torpedo Mogilev* | 30 | 7 | 7 | 16 | 29 | 59 | 28 |
| Shakhter* | 30 | 6 | 6 | 18 | 22 | 53 | 24 |

*Top scorer:* Khlebosolov (Belshina) 19.
*Cup Final:* Dynamo Minsk 1, Lokomotiv 96, 2.

## BELGIUM

Union Royale Belge Des Societes De Football Association, 145 Avenue Houba de Strooper, B-1020 Bruxelles.
*Founded:* 1895; *Number of Clubs:* 2,120; *Number of Players:* 390,468; *National Colours:* All red.
*Telephone:* 0032 2 477 12 11; *Cable:* URBSFA BRUX-ELLES; *Telex:* 23257 bvbfbf b; *Fax:* 0032 2 478 23 91.

**League Championship wins (1896–1998)**
Anderlecht 24; Union St Gilloise 11; FC Brugge 11; Standard Liege 8; Beerschot 7; RC Brussels 6; FC Liege 5; Daring Brussels 5; Antwerp 4; Mechelen 4; Lierse SK 4; SV Brugge 3; Beveren 2; RWD Molenbeek 1.

**Cup wins (1954–98)**
Anderlecht 8; FC Brugge 7; Standard Liege 5; Beerschot 2; Waterschei 2; Beveren 2; Gent 2; Antwerp 2; Lierse SK 1; Racing Doornik 1; Waregem 1; SV Brugge 1; Mechelen 1; FC Liege 1; Ekeren 1; Genk 1.

**Final League Table 1997–98**

|  | P | W | D | L | F | A | Pts |
|---|---|---|---|---|---|---|---|
| FC Brugge | 34 | 26 | 6 | 2 | 78 | 29 | 84 |
| Genk | 34 | 20 | 6 | 8 | 65 | 40 | 66 |
| Ekeren | 34 | 17 | 7 | 10 | 60 | 48 | 58 |
| Anderlect | 34 | 16 | 9 | 9 | 53 | 37 | 57 |
| Harelbeke | 34 | 15 | 10 | 9 | 50 | 31 | 55 |
| Lokeren | 34 | 16 | 4 | 14 | 68 | 68 | 52 |
| Lierse | 34 | 14 | 8 | 12 | 54 | 45 | 50 |
| Gent | 34 | 11 | 14 | 9 | 50 | 44 | 47 |
| Standard Liege | 34 | 11 | 10 | 13 | 53 | 50 | 43 |
| Westerlo | 34 | 9 | 14 | 11 | 52 | 56 | 41 |
| Lommel | 34 | 10 | 11 | 13 | 46 | 50 | 41 |
| Mouscron | 34 | 11 | 8 | 15 | 39 | 45 | 41 |
| Charleroi | 34 | 9 | 12 | 13 | 46 | 57 | 39 |
| St Truiden | 34 | 8 | 13 | 13 | 32 | 45 | 37 |
| Aalst | 34 | 9 | 9 | 16 | 51 | 66 | 36 |
| Beveren | 34 | 7 | 11 | 16 | 30 | 48 | 32 |
| RWD Molenbeek* | 34 | 8 | 7 | 19 | 39 | 74 | 31 |
| Antwerp* | 34 | 6 | 7 | 21 | 38 | 71 | 25 |

*Top scorer:* Strupar (Genk) 22.
*Cup Final:* Genk 4, FC Brugge 0.

## BOSNIA HERZEGOVINA

Bosnia & Herzegovina Football Federation, Sime Milutinovico, 12/1 71000 Sarajevo.
*Founded:* 1992; *National Colours:* White shirts, blue shorts, white stockings.
*Telephone:* 00387 71/213881; *Fax:* 00387 71/444332.
*Cup Final:* Zeljeznicar 1, Sarajevo 0.**BULGARIA**
**Bulgarian Football Union,** Karnigradska 19, BG-1000 Sofia.
*Founded:* 1923; *Number of Clubs:* 376; *Number of Players:* 48,240; *National Colours:* White shirts, green shorts, white stockings.
*Telephone:* 00359 2 987 74 90; *Cable:* BULFUTBOL SOFIA; *Telex:* 23145 bfs bg; *Fax:* 00359 2 80 32 37.

**League Championship wins (1925–98)**
CSKA Sofia 28; Levski Sofia 19; Slavia Sofia 7; Vladislav Varna 3; Lokomotiv Sofia 3; Trakia Plovdiv 2; AC 23 Sofia 1; Botev Plovdiv 1; SC Sofia 1; Sokol Varna 1; Spartak Plovdiv 1; Tichka Varna 1; JSZ Sofia 1; Beroe Stara Zagora 1; Etur 1; Litets 1.
Cup wins (1946–98)
Levski Sofia 19; CSKA Sofia 15; Slavia Sofia 7; Lokomotiv Sofia 4; Botev Plovdiv 1; Spartak Plovdiv 1; Spartak Sofia 1; Marek Stanke 1; Trakia Plovdiv 1; Spartak Varna 1; Sliven 1.

**Final League Table 1997–98**

|  | P | W | D | L | F | A | Pts |
|---|---|---|---|---|---|---|---|
| Litets | 30 | 21 | 6 | 3 | 73 | 24 | 69 |
| Levski Sofia | 30 | 19 | 7 | 4 | 73 | 27 | 64 |
| CSKA Sofia | 30 | 18 | 7 | 5 | 70 | 29 | 61 |
| Neftochimik | 30 | 17 | 4 | 9 | 62 | 31 | 55 |
| Slavia Sofia | 30 | 14 | 9 | 7 | 47 | 34 | 51 |
| Levski Kustendil | 30 | 15 | 1 | 14 | 45 | 40 | 46 |
| Spartak Varna | 30 | 12 | 6 | 12 | 42 | 36 | 42 |
| Mineur | 30 | 12 | 5 | 13 | 32 | 35 | 41 |
| Lokomotiv Sofia | 30 | 11 | 6 | 13 | 42 | 40 | 39 |
| Metalurg | 30 | 11 | 4 | 15 | 28 | 36 | 37 |
| Botev Plovdiv | 30 | 11 | 3 | 16 | 35 | 48 | 36 |
| Dobrudja | 30 | 11 | 3 | 16 | 33 | 55 | 36 |
| Lokomotiv Plovdiv | 30 | 11 | 3 | 16 | 31 | 58 | 36 |
| Olimpik* | 30 | 11 | 2 | 17 | 26 | 50 | 35 |
| Spartak Pleven* | 30 | 7 | 0 | 23 | 32 | 75 | 21 |
| Etur* | 30 | 5 | 2 | 23 | 25 | 78 | 17 |

*Top scorers:* Spassov (Neftochimik) 17, Guentchev (CSKA Sofia) 17.
*Cup Final:* Levski Sofia 5, CSKA Sofia 0.

## CROATIA

Croatian Football Federation, Illica 31, CRO-10000 Zagreb, Croatia.
*Founded:* 1912; *Number of Clubs:* 1,221; *Number of Players:* 78,127; *National Colours:* Red/white shirts, white shorts, blue stockings.
*Telephone:* 00385 1/4554100. *Fax:* 00385 1 42 46 39.

**League Championship wins (1941-44; 1992–98)**
Croatia Zagreb 4; Hajduk Split 3; Gradanski 3; Concordia 1.

**Cup wins (1993–98)**
Croatia Zagreb 4, Hajduk Split 2.

**Final League Table 1997–98**

|  | P | W | D | L | F | A | Pts |
|---|---|---|---|---|---|---|---|
| Croatia Zagreb | 10 | 7 | 3 | 0 | 28 | 10 | 49 |
| Hajduk Split | 10 | 4 | 2 | 4 | 17 | 16 | 36 |
| Osijek | 10 | 5 | 1 | 4 | 13 | 12 | 32 |
| Dragovoljac | 10 | 4 | 2 | 4 | 7 | 12 | 32 |
| Zagreb | 10 | 2 | 3 | 5 | 16 | 16 | 30 |
| Zadarcommerce | 10 | 2 | 1 | 7 | 11 | 26 | 21 |

**Promotion/Relegation Table 1997–98**

|  | P | W | D | L | F | A | Pts |
|---|---|---|---|---|---|---|---|
| Rijeka | 10 | 4 | 3 | 3 | 16 | 13 | 28 |
| Sibenik | 10 | 5 | 3 | 2 | 16 | 8 | 27 |
| Slaven | 10 | 5 | 0 | 5 | 11 | 13 | 27 |
| Varteks | 10 | 4 | 2 | 4 | 11 | 13 | 26 |
| Mladost 127 | 10 | 4 | 1 | 5 | 10 | 12 | 25 |
| Samobor | 10 | 3 | 1 | 6 | 11 | 20 | 21 |

*Top scorer:* Baturina (Zagreb) 19.
*Cup Final:* Varteks 0, 1, Croatia Zagreb 1, 2.

## CYPRUS

Cyprus Football Association, 1 Stasinos Str., Engomi, P.O. Box 5071, CY-2404 Nicosia.
*Founded:* 1934; *Number of Clubs:* 85; *Number of Players:* 6,000; *National Colours:* Blue shirts, white shorts, blue stockings.
*Telephone:* 00357 2 /352341; *Cable:* FOOTBALL CYPRUS; *Telex:* 3880 football cy; *Fax:* 00357 2/590544.

**League Championship wins (1935–98)**
Omonia 17; Apoel 16; Anorthosis 9; AEL 5; EPA 3; Olympiakos 3; Apollon 2; Pezoporikos 2; Chetin Kayal 1; Trast 1.

**Cup wins (1935–98)**
Apoel 16; Omonia 10; AEL 6; EPA 5; Anorthosis 5; Apollon 4; Trast 3; Chetin Kayal 2; Olympiakos 1; Pezoporikos 1; Salamina 1.

**Final League Table 1997–98**

|            | P  | W  | D  | L  | F  | A  | Pts |
|------------|----|----|----|----|----|----|-----|
| Anorthosis | 26 | 21 | 3  | 2  | 87 | 18 | 66  |
| Omonia     | 26 | 19 | 5  | 2  | 90 | 20 | 62  |
| Apollon    | 26 | 16 | 7  | 3  | 50 | 25 | 55  |
| Ahna       | 26 | 13 | 8  | 5  | 35 | 28 | 47  |
| AEK        | 26 | 9  | 7  | 10 | 42 | 40 | 34  |
| Paralimni  | 26 | 10 | 3  | 13 | 45 | 49 | 33  |
| Apoel      | 26 | 8  | 7  | 11 | 48 | 51 | 31  |
| Salamina   | 26 | 10 | 1  | 15 | 43 | 59 | 31  |
| AEL        | 26 | 7  | 8  | 11 | 37 | 50 | 29  |
| Alki       | 26 | 9  | 2  | 15 | 46 | 65 | 29  |
| Evagoras   | 26 | 8  | 5  | 13 | 29 | 52 | 29  |
| Derynia*   | 26 | 7  | 6  | 13 | 37 | 65 | 27  |
| Apop*      | 26 | 7  | 5  | 14 | 40 | 59 | 26  |
| Assia*     | 26 | 3  | 3  | 20 | 28 | 76 | 12  |

*Top scorer:* Rauffman (Omonia) 42.
*Cup Final:* Anorthosis 3, Apollon 1.

## CZECH REPUBLIC

Football Association of Czech Republic, Diskarska 100, 169 00 Prague 6 - Strahov, Czech Republic.
*Founded:* 1901; *Number of Clubs:* 3,836; *Number of Players:* 319,500; *National Colours:* Red shirts, white shorts, blue stockings.
*Telephone:* 00422 20513575; *Cable:* SPORTSVAZ PRAHA; *Telex:* 122650 cstv c; *Fax:* 0042 2 35 27 84.

**League Championship wins (1926–93)**
Sparta Prague 20; Slavia Prague 12; Dukla Prague (prev. UDA) 11; Slovan Bratislava 7; Spartak Trnava 5; Banik Ostrava 3; Inter-Bratislava 1; Spartak Hradec Kralove 1; Viktoria Zizkov 1; Zbrojovka Brno 1; Bohemians 1; Vitkovice 1.

**Cup wins (1961–93)**
Dukla Prague 8; Sparta Prague 8; Slovan Bratislava 5; Spartak Trnava 4; Banik Ostrava 3; Lokomotiv Kosice 3; TJ Gottwaldov 1; Dunajska Streda 1.
*From 1993–94, there were two separate countries; the Czech Republic and Slovakia.*

**League Championship wins (1993–98)**
Sparta Prague 5; Slavia Prague 1.

**Cup wins (1994–98)**
Viktoria Zizkov 1; Spartak Hradec Kralove 1; Sparta Prague 1; Slavia Prague 1; Jablonec 1.

**Final League Table 1997–98**

|                | P  | W  | D  | L  | F  | A  | Pts |
|----------------|----|----|----|----|----|----|-----|
| Sparta Prague  | 30 | 22 | 5  | 3  | 53 | 19 | 71  |
| Slavia Prague  | 30 | 17 | 8  | 5  | 42 | 22 | 59  |
| Sigma Olomouc  | 30 | 16 | 7  | 7  | 38 | 21 | 55  |
| Banik Ostrava  | 30 | 13 | 11 | 6  | 51 | 35 | 50  |
| Slovan Liberec | 30 | 13 | 8  | 9  | 39 | 32 | 47  |
| Jablonec       | 30 | 12 | 10 | 8  | 47 | 33 | 46  |
| Teplice        | 30 | 10 | 10 | 10 | 36 | 30 | 40  |
| Viktoria Zizkov| 30 | 11 | 6  | 13 | 26 | 34 | 39  |
| Petra Drnovice | 30 | 10 | 8  | 12 | 35 | 43 | 38  |
| Boby Brno      | 30 | 10 | 7  | 13 | 42 | 42 | 37  |
| Kaucuk Opava   | 30 | 8  | 10 | 12 | 33 | 37 | 34  |
| Hradec Kralove | 30 | 8  | 10 | 12 | 25 | 36 | 34  |
| Viktoria Plzen | 30 | 9  | 6  | 15 | 37 | 47 | 33  |
| Dukla Prague   | 30 | 9  | 6  | 15 | 37 | 50 | 33  |
| Ceske Budejovice* | 30 | 8 | 7 | 15 | 26 | 43 | 31 |
| Lazne Bohdanec*| 30 | 2  | 5  | 23 | 18 | 61 | 11  |

*Top scorer:* Siegl (Sparta Prague) 13.
*Cup Final:* Jablonec 2, Petra Drnovice 1.

## DENMARK

Danish Football Association, Idraettens Hus, Brondby Stadion 20, DK-2605, Brondby.
*Founded:* 1889; *Number of Clubs:* 1,555; *Number of Players:* 268,517; *National Colours:* Red shirts, white shorts, red stockings.
*Telephone:* 0045 43/262222; *Cable:* DANSKBOLDSPIL COPENHAGEN; *Telex:* 15545 dbu dk; *Fax:* 0045 43/262245.

**League Championship wins (1913–98)**
KB Copenhagen 15; B 93 Copenhagen 10; AB (Akademisk) 9; Brondby 8; B 1903 Copenhagen 7; Frem 6; Esbjerg BK 5; Vejle BK 5; AGF Aarhus 5; Hvidovre 3; Odense BK 3; B 1909 Odense 2; Koge BK 2; Lyngby 2; FC Copenhagen 1; Silkeborg 1, AaB Aalborg 1.

**Cup wins (1955–98)**
Aarhus GF 9; Vejle BK 6; Randers Freja 3; Lyngby 3; OB Odense 3; Brondby 3; B1909 Odense 2; Aalborg BK 2; Esbjerg BK 2; Frem 2; B 1903 Copenhagen 2; FC Copenhagen 2; B 93 Copenhagen 1; KB Copenhagen 1; Vanlose 1; Hvidovre 1; B1913 Odense 1.

**Final League Table 1997–98**

|              | P  | W  | D  | L  | F  | A  | Pts |
|--------------|----|----|----|----|----|----|-----|
| Brondby      | 33 | 24 | 4  | 5  | 81 | 33 | 76  |
| Silkeborg    | 33 | 17 | 12 | 4  | 55 | 31 | 63  |
| FC Copenhagen| 33 | 18 | 7  | 8  | 66 | 48 | 61  |
| Vejle        | 33 | 16 | 4  | 13 | 53 | 51 | 52  |
| AB Copenhagen| 33 | 13 | 8  | 12 | 61 | 52 | 47  |
| Lyngby       | 33 | 13 | 6  | 14 | 53 | 62 | 45  |
| Aalborg      | 33 | 12 | 8  | 13 | 54 | 48 | 44  |
| Aarhus       | 33 | 11 | 10 | 12 | 53 | 52 | 43  |
| Herfolge     | 33 | 9  | 7  | 17 | 44 | 69 | 34  |
| Fremad       | 33 | 9  | 6  | 18 | 51 | 73 | 33  |
| Ikast*       | 33 | 8  | 5  | 20 | 51 | 86 | 29  |
| Odense*      | 33 | 6  | 7  | 20 | 40 | 57 | 25  |

*Top scorer:* Sand (Brondby) 28.
*Cup Final:* Brondby 4, FC Copenhagen 1.

## ENGLAND

The Football Association, 16 Lancaster Gate, London W2 3LW.
*Founded:* 1863; *Number of Clubs:* 42,000; *Number of Players:* 2,250,000; *National Colours:* White shirts with navy blue collar, navy blue shorts, white stockings with light blue top.
*Telephone:* 0171 262 4542, 0171 402 7151; *Cable:* FOOTBALL ASSOCIATION LONDON W2; *Telex:* 261110 faldn g; *Fax:* 0171 402 0486.

## ESTONIA

Estonian Football Association, Voidu 16, Tallinn EE 0012.
*Founded:* 1921; *Number of Clubs:* 40; *Number of Players:* 12,000; *National Colours:* Blue shirts, black shorts, white stockings.
*Telephone:* 00372 6/542715, 542716, 542717; *Fax:* 00372 6/542719.
**League Championship wins (1922-40; 1992–98)**
Sport 8; Estonia 5; Flora Tallinn 3; Norma Tallinn 2; Tallinn JK 2; Kalev 2; LFLS 1; Olimpia 1; Lantana 1.

**Cup wins (1992–98)**
Sadam 2; VMV Tallinn 1; Nikol Tallinn 1; Norma Tallinn 1, Lantana 1; Flora Tallinn 1.

**Final League Table 1997–98**

| | P | W | D | L | F | A | Pts |
|---|---|---|---|---|---|---|---|
| Flora | 10 | 7 | 2 | 1 | 34 | 10 | 42 |
| Sadam | 10 | 5 | 1 | 4 | 26 | 22 | 32 |
| Lantana | 10 | 4 | 3 | 3 | 17 | 17 | 25 |
| Trans | 10 | 5 | 1 | 4 | 14 | 19 | 24 |
| Tulevik | 10 | 2 | 3 | 5 | 11 | 15 | 19 |
| VMK | 10 | 2 | 0 | 8 | 4 | 23 | 13 |

*Half points added from qualifying table.*
*Top scorer:* Kolbassenko (Sadam) 18.
*Cup Final:* Flora 3, Lantana 2.

### FAEROE ISLANDS

Fotboltssamband Foroya, The Faeroes' Football Assn., Gundalur, P.O. Box 3028, FR-110, Torshavn.
*Founded:* 1979; *Number of Clubs:* 16; *Number of Players:* 1,014; *National Colours:* White shirts, blue shorts, white stockings.
*Telephone:* 00298 16 707; *Telex:* 81328 nspkkl fa; *Fax:* 00298 19 079.

**League Championship wins (1942–97)**
KI Klaksvik 15; HB Torshavn 14; TB Tvoroyri 7; GI Gotu 7; B36 Torshavn 6; B68 Toftir 3; SI Sorvag 1; IF Fuglafjordur 1; B71 Sandur 1.

**Cup wins (1955–97)**
HB Torshavn 24; TB Tvoroyri 4; KI Klaksvik 4; GI Gotu 4; B36 Torshavn 1; VB Vagur 1; NSI Runavik 1; B71 Sandur 1.

**Final League Table 1997**

| | P | W | D | L | F | A | Pts |
|---|---|---|---|---|---|---|---|
| B36 | 18 | 15 | 0 | 3 | 54 | 23 | 45 |
| FIB | 18 | 11 | 5 | 2 | 55 | 23 | 38 |
| VB | 18 | 12 | 1 | 5 | 34 | 18 | 37 |
| GI | 18 | 10 | 5 | 3 | 47 | 24 | 35 |
| KI | 18 | 10 | 2 | 6 | 52 | 25 | 32 |
| NSI | 18 | 5 | 4 | 9 | 24 | 36 | 19 |
| B68 | 18 | 4 | 4 | 10 | 23 | 39 | 16 |
| IF | 18 | 4 | 2 | 12 | 24 | 52 | 14 |
| B71* | 18 | 2 | 4 | 12 | 10 | 48 | 10 |
| FS* | 18 | 2 | 3 | 13 | 16 | 51 | 9 |

*Top scorer:* Arge (HB) 24.
*Cup Final:* GI 6, VB 0.

### FINLAND

Suomen Palloliitto Finlands Bollfoerbund, Lantinen Brahenkatu 2, P.O. Box 179, SF-00511 Helsinki.
*Founded:* 1907; *Number of Clubs:* 1,135; *Number of Players:* 66,100; *National Colours:* White shirts, blue shorts, white stockings.
*Telephone:* 00358 0 9701 01 01; *Cable:* SUOMIFOT-BOLL HELSINKI; *Telex:* 126033 spl sf; *Fax:* 00358 0 9701 01 099.

**League Championship wins (1949–97)**
Helsinki JK 10; Turun Palloseura 5; Kuopion Palloseura 5; Valkeakosken Haka 5; Kuusysi 4; Lahden Reipas 3; IF Kamraterna 3; Ilves-Kissat 2; Jazz Pori 2; Kotkan TP 2; OPS Oulu 1; Torun Pyrkiva 1; IF Kronohagens 1; Helsinki PS 1; Kokkolan PV 1; Vasa 1; TPV Tampere 1.

**Cup wins (1955–97)**
Valkeakosken Haka 10; Lahden Reipas 7; HJK Helsinki 5; Kotkan TP 4; Mikkeli 2; Kuusysi 2; Kuopion Palloseura 2; Ilves Tampere 2; TPS Turku 2; ; MyPa 2; IFK Abo 1; Drott 1; Helsinki PS 1; Pallo-Peikot 1; Rovaniemi PS 1.

**Final League Table 1997**

| | P | W | D | L | F | A | Pts |
|---|---|---|---|---|---|---|---|
| HJK Helsinki | 27 | 18 | 4 | 5 | 53 | 18 | 58 |
| VPS | 27 | 13 | 9 | 5 | 40 | 20 | 48 |
| FinnPa | 27 | 10 | 9 | 8 | 27 | 36 | 39 |
| TPS Turku | 27 | 10 | 8 | 9 | 43 | 41 | 38 |
| MyPa | 27 | 8 | 13 | 6 | 31 | 23 | 37 |
| RoPS Rovaniemi | 27 | 9 | 6 | 12 | 31 | 30 | 33 |
| Jazz Pori | 27 | 8 | 7 | 12 | 31 | 42 | 31 |
| Jaro | 27 | 8 | 4 | 15 | 34 | 48 | 28 |
| TP* | 27 | 5 | 12 | 10 | 20 | 36 | 27 |
| Inter* | 27 | 6 | 8 | 13 | 23 | 42 | 26 |

*Top scorer:* Rafael (HJK Helsinki) 11.
*Cup Final:* Haka 2, TPS Turku 1 aet.

### FRANCE

Federation Francaise De Football, 60 Bis Avenue D'Iena, F-75783 Paris, Cedex 16.
*Founded:* 1919; *Number of Clubs:* 21,629; *Number of Players:* 1,692,205; *National Colours:* Blue shirts, white shorts, red stockings.
*Telephone:* 0033 1 44 31 73 00; *Cable:* CEFI PARIS 034; *Telex:* 640000 fedfoot f; *Fax:* 0033 1 47 20 82 96.

**League Championship wins (1933–98)**
Saint Etienne 10; Olympique Marseille 8; Nantes 7; Stade de Reims 6; AS Monaco 6; OGC Nice 4; Girondins Bordeaux 4; Lille OSC 3; Paris St Germain 2; FC Sete 2; Sochaux 2; Racing Club Paris 1; Roubaix-Tourcoing 1; Strasbourg 1; Auxerre 1; Lens 1.

**Cup wins (1918–98)**
Olympique Marseille 10; Saint Etienne 6; Lille OSC 5; Racing Club Paris 5; Red Star 5; AS Monaco 5; Olympique Lyon 4; Paris St Germain 4; Girondins Bordeaux 3; OGC Nice 3; CAS Genereaux 2; Nancy 2; Racing Club Strasbourg 2; Sedan 2; FC Sete 2; Stade de Reims 2; SO Montpellier 2; Stade Rennes 2; Auxerre 2; AS Cannes 1; Club Français 1; Excelsior Roubaix 1; Le Havre 1; Olympique de Pantin 1; CA Paris 1; Sochaux 1; Toulouse 1; Bastia 1; Nantes 1; Metz 1.

**Final League Table 1997–98**

| | P | W | D | L | F | A | Pts |
|---|---|---|---|---|---|---|---|
| Lens | 34 | 21 | 5 | 8 | 55 | 30 | 68 |
| Metz | 34 | 20 | 8 | 6 | 48 | 28 | 68 |
| Monaco | 34 | 18 | 5 | 11 | 51 | 33 | 59 |
| Marseille | 34 | 16 | 9 | 9 | 47 | 27 | 57 |
| Bordeaux | 34 | 15 | 11 | 8 | 49 | 41 | 56 |
| Lyon | 34 | 16 | 5 | 13 | 39 | 37 | 53 |
| Auxerre | 34 | 14 | 9 | 11 | 55 | 45 | 51 |
| Paris St Germain | 34 | 14 | 8 | 12 | 43 | 35 | 50 |
| Bastia | 34 | 13 | 11 | 10 | 36 | 31 | 50 |
| Le Havre | 34 | 10 | 14 | 10 | 38 | 35 | 44 |
| Nantes | 34 | 11 | 8 | 15 | 35 | 41 | 41 |
| Montpellier | 34 | 10 | 11 | 13 | 32 | 42 | 41 |
| Strasbourg | 34 | 9 | 10 | 15 | 39 | 43 | 37 |
| Rennes | 34 | 9 | 9 | 16 | 36 | 48 | 36 |
| Toulouse | 34 | 9 | 9 | 16 | 26 | 46 | 36 |
| Guingamp* | 34 | 9 | 8 | 17 | 30 | 42 | 35 |
| Chateauroux* | 34 | 8 | 7 | 19 | 31 | 59 | 31 |
| Cannes* | 34 | 7 | 7 | 20 | 32 | 59 | 28 |

*Top scorer:* Guivarc'h (Auxerre) 21.
*Cup Final:* Paris St Germain 2, Lens 1.

### GEORGIA

Georgian Football Federation, 5 Shota Iamanidze Str, Tbilissi 380012, Georgia.
*Founded:* 1990; *Number of Clubs:* 4050. *Number of Players:* 115,000; *National Colours:* White shirts, black shorts, cherry stockings.
*Telephone:* 00995 32/960750; *Fax:* 00995 32/001128.

**League Championship wins (1990–97)**
Dynamo Tbilisi 8.

**Cup wins (1992–1998)**
Dynamo Tbilisi 7; Dynamo Batumi 1.

**Final League Table 1997–98**

|                | P  | W  | D | L  | F  | A  | Pts |
|----------------|----|----|---|----|----|----|-----|
| Dynamo Tbilisi | 30 | 23 | 5 | 2  | 84 | 18 | 69  |
| Dynamo Batumi  | 30 | 17 | 7 | 5  | 58 | 18 | 61  |
| Torpedo Kutaisi| 30 | 16 | 8 | 6  | 53 | 30 | 56  |
| Kolkheti       | 30 | 16 | 7 | 7  | 54 | 25 | 55  |
| Odishi         | 30 | 15 | 4 | 11 | 43 | 51 | 49  |
| Lokomotivi     | 30 | 12 | 8 | 10 | 34 | 37 | 44  |
| Merani 91      | 30 | 13 | 8 | 9  | 38 | 31 | 42  |
| TSU            | 30 | 11 | 6 | 13 | 35 | 33 | 39  |
| Georgia        | 30 | 10 | 8 | 12 | 29 | 37 | 38  |
| Dila Gori      | 30 | 11 | 4 | 15 | 31 | 36 | 37  |
| Samgurali      | 30 | 9  | 7 | 14 | 31 | 50 | 34  |
| Gorda          | 30 | 10 | 3 | 17 | 32 | 43 | 33  |
| Sioni          | 30 | 10 | 6 | 14 | 49 | 47 | 31  |
| Guria*         | 30 | 6  | 9 | 15 | 30 | 58 | 27  |
| Magharoeli*    | 30 | 7  | 5 | 18 | 25 | 59 | 26  |
| Margveti*      | 30 | 2  | 7 | 21 | 22 | 75 | 13  |

*Cup Final:* Dynamo Batumi 2, Dynamo Tbilisi 1.

## GERMANY

Deutsche Fussball-Bund, Postfach 710265, D-60492, Frankfurt Am Main.
*Founded:* 1900; *Number of Clubs:* 26,760; *Number of Players:* 5,260,320; *National Colours:* White shirts, black shorts, white stockings.
*Telephone:* 0049 69 678 80; *Telex:* 416815 dfb d; *Fax:* 0049 69 678 82 66.

**League Championship wins (1903–98)**
Bayern Munich 14; IFC Nuremberg 9; Schalke 04 7; SV Hamburg 6; Borussia Moenchengladbach 5; Borussia Dortmund 5; VfB Stuttgart 4; IFC Kaiserslautern 4; VfB Leipzig 3; Sp Vgg Furth 3; IFC Cologne 3; Werder Bremen 3; Viktoria Berlin 2; Hertha Berlin 2; Hanover 96 2; Dresden SC 2; Munich 1860 1; Union Berlin 1; FC Freiburg 1; Phoenix Karlsruhe 1; Karlsruher FV 1; Holsten Kiel 1; Fortuna Dusseldorf 1; Rapid Vienna 1; VfB Mannheim 1; Rot-Weiss Essen 1; Eintracht Frankfurt 1; Eintracht Brunswick 1.

**Cup wins (1935–98)**
Bayern Munich 9; IFC Cologne 4; Eintracht Frankfurt 4; IFC Nuremberg 3; SV Hamburg 3; Werder Bremen 3; Moenchengladbach 3; VfB Stuttgart 3; Dresden SC 2; Fortuna Dusseldorf 2; Karlsruhe SC 2; Munich 1860 2; Schalke 04 2; Borussia Dortmund 2; Kaiserslautern 2; First Vienna 1; VfB Leipzig 1; Kickers Offenbach 1; Rapid Vienna 1; Rot-Weiss Essen 1; SW Essen 1; Bayer Uerdingen 1; Hannover 96 1; Leverkusen 1.

**Final League Table 1997–98**

|                    | P  | W  | D  | L  | F  | A  | Pts |
|--------------------|----|----|----|----|----|----|-----|
| Kaiserslautern     | 34 | 19 | 11 | 4  | 63 | 39 | 68  |
| Bayern Munich      | 34 | 19 | 9  | 6  | 69 | 37 | 66  |
| Leverkusen         | 34 | 14 | 13 | 7  | 66 | 39 | 55  |
| Stuttgart          | 34 | 14 | 10 | 10 | 55 | 49 | 52  |
| Schalke            | 34 | 13 | 13 | 8  | 38 | 32 | 52  |
| Hansa Rostock      | 34 | 14 | 9  | 11 | 54 | 46 | 51  |
| Werder Bremen      | 34 | 14 | 8  | 12 | 43 | 47 | 50  |
| Duisburg           | 34 | 11 | 11 | 12 | 43 | 44 | 44  |
| Hamburg            | 34 | 11 | 11 | 12 | 38 | 46 | 44  |
| Borussia Dortmund  | 34 | 11 | 10 | 13 | 57 | 55 | 43  |
| Hertha             | 34 | 12 | 7  | 15 | 41 | 53 | 53  |
| Bochum             | 34 | 11 | 8  | 15 | 41 | 49 | 41  |
| Munich 1860        | 34 | 11 | 8  | 15 | 43 | 54 | 41  |
| Wolfsburg          | 34 | 11 | 6  | 17 | 38 | 54 | 39  |
| Moenchengladbach   | 34 | 9  | 11 | 14 | 54 | 59 | 38  |
| Karlsruhe*         | 34 | 9  | 11 | 14 | 48 | 60 | 38  |
| Cologne*           | 34 | 10 | 6  | 18 | 49 | 64 | 36  |
| Bielefeld*         | 34 | 8  | 8  | 18 | 43 | 56 | 32  |

*Top scorer:* Kirsten (Leverkusen) 22.
*Cup Final:* Bayern Munich 2, Duisburg 1.

## GREECE

Federation Hellenique De Football, Singrou Avenue 137, 17121 Athens.
*Founded:* 1926; *Number of Clubs:* 4,050; *Number of Players:* 180,000; *National Colours:* White shirts, blue shorts, white stockings.
*Telephone:* 0030 1 933 88 50; *Cable:* FOOTBALL ATHENS; *Telex:* 215328 epo gr; *Fax:* 0030 1 935 96 66.

**League Championship wins (1928–98)**
Olympiakos 27; Panathinaikos 18; AEK Athens 11; Aris Salonika 3; PAOK Salonika 2; Larissa 1.

**Cup wins (1932–98)**
Olympiakos 20; Panathinaikos 16; AEK Athens 11; PAOK Salonika 2; Panionios 2; Aris Salonika 1; Ethnikos 1; Iraklis 1; Kastoria 1; Larissa 1; Ofi Crete 1.

**Final League Table 1997–98**

|              | P  | W  | D | L  | F  | A  | Pts |
|--------------|----|----|---|----|----|----|-----|
| Olympiakos   | 34 | 29 | 1 | 4  | 88 | 27 | 88  |
| Panathinaikos| 34 | 28 | 1 | 5  | 90 | 24 | 85  |
| AEK Athens   | 34 | 22 | 8 | 4  | 61 | 30 | 74  |
| PAOK Salonika| 34 | 21 | 7 | 6  | 74 | 41 | 70  |
| Ionikos      | 34 | 18 | 8 | 8  | 46 | 31 | 62  |
| Iraklis      | 34 | 14 | 9 | 11 | 49 | 45 | 51  |
| Ofi Crete    | 34 | 15 | 4 | 15 | 45 | 53 | 49  |
| Xanthi       | 34 | 13 | 6 | 15 | 52 | 52 | 45  |
| Veria        | 34 | 12 | 6 | 16 | 38 | 48 | 42  |
| Paniliakos   | 34 | 9  | 9 | 16 | 41 | 54 | 36  |
| Panionios    | 34 | 10 | 6 | 18 | 41 | 54 | 36  |
| Apollon      | 34 | 10 | 6 | 18 | 37 | 51 | 36  |
| Kavala       | 34 | 10 | 5 | 19 | 40 | 58 | 35  |
| Proodeftiki  | 34 | 9  | 7 | 18 | 35 | 57 | 34  |
| Ethnikos     | 34 | 10 | 3 | 21 | 27 | 51 | 33  |
| Panachaiki*  | 34 | 9  | 5 | 20 | 29 | 62 | 32  |
| Kalamata*    | 34 | 7  | 8 | 19 | 27 | 50 | 29  |
| Athinaikos*  | 34 | 6  | 9 | 19 | 23 | 55 | 27  |

*Top scorer:* Vazecha (PAOK Salonika) 32.
*Cup Final:* Panionios 1, Panathinaikos 0.

## HOLLAND

Koninklijke Nederlandsche Voetbalbond, Woudenbergseweg 56-58, Postbus 515, NL-3700 AM, Zeist.
*Founded:* 1889; *Number of Clubs:* 3,097; *Number of Players:* 962,397; *National Colours:* Orange shirts, white shorts, orange stockings.
*Telephone:* 0031343 499211; *Cable:* VOETBAL ZEIST; *Telex:* 40497 knvb nl; *Fax:* 0031343 491487.

**League Championship wins (1898–1998)**
Ajax Amsterdam 27; Feyenoord 14; PSV Eindhoven 14; HVV The Hague 8; Sparta Rotterdam 6; Go Ahead Deventer 4; HBS The Hague 3; Willem II Tilburg 3; RCH Haarlem 2; RAP 2; Heracles 2; ADO The Hague 2; Quick The Hague 1; BVV Schiedam 1; NAC Breda 1; Eindhoven 1; Enschede 1; Volewijckers Amsterdam 1; Limburgia 1; Rapid JC Haarlem 1; DOS Utrecht 1; DWS Amsterdam 1; Haarlem 1; Be Quick Groningen 1; SVV Schiedam 1; AZ 67 Alkmaar 1.

**Cup wins (1899–1998)**
Ajax Amsterdam 13; Feyenoord 10; PSV Eindhoven 8; Quick The Hague 4; AZ 67 Alkmaar 3; Rotterdam 3; DFC 2; Fortuna Geleen 2; Haarlem 2; HBS The Hague 2; RCH 2; VOC 2; Wageningen 2; Willem II Tilburg 2; FC Den Haag 2; Concordia Rotterdam 1; CVV 1; Eindhoven 1; HVV The Hague 1; Longa 1; Quick Nijmegen 1; RAP 1; Roermond 1; Schoten 1; Velocitas Breda 1; Velocitas Groningen 1; VSV 1; VUC 1; VVV Groningen 1; ZFC 1; NAC Breda 1; Twente Enschede 1; Utrecht 1; Roda 1.

**Final League Table 1997–98**

| | P | W | D | L | F | A | Pts |
|---|---|---|---|---|---|---|---|
| Ajax | 34 | 29 | 2 | 3 | 112 | 22 | 89 |
| PSV Eindhoven | 34 | 21 | 9 | 4 | 95 | 44 | 72 |
| Vitesse | 34 | 21 | 7 | 6 | 85 | 48 | 70 |
| Feyenoord | 34 | 18 | 7 | 9 | 62 | 39 | 61 |
| Willem II | 34 | 17 | 4 | 13 | 66 | 58 | 55 |
| Heerenveen | 34 | 16 | 7 | 11 | 56 | 59 | 55 |
| Fortuna Sittard | 34 | 14 | 6 | 14 | 51 | 53 | 58 |
| NEC Nijmegen | 34 | 14 | 2 | 18 | 39 | 57 | 44 |
| Twente | 34 | 11 | 10 | 13 | 41 | 42 | 43 |
| Utrecht | 34 | 13 | 4 | 17 | 56 | 64 | 43 |
| De Graafschap | 34 | 11 | 9 | 14 | 45 | 49 | 42 |
| NAC Breda | 34 | 12 | 6 | 16 | 41 | 49 | 42 |
| Sparta | 34 | 10 | 11 | 13 | 50 | 59 | 41 |
| Roda JC | 34 | 10 | 8 | 16 | 44 | 45 | 38 |
| Maastricht | 34 | 9 | 5 | 20 | 35 | 75 | 32 |
| RKC Waalwijk+ | 34 | 8 | 7 | 19 | 48 | 71 | 31 |
| Groningen+ | 34 | 7 | 10 | 17 | 42 | 65 | 31 |
| Volendam* | 34 | 5 | 6 | 23 | 33 | 102 | 21 |

*Top scorer:* Machlas (Vitesse) 34.
*Cup Final:* Ajax 5, PSV Eindhoven 0.

**League Championship wins (1912–97)**
KR 20; Valur 19; Fram 18; IA Akranes 17; Vikingur 5; IBK Keflavik 3; IBV Vestmann 3; KA Akureyri 1.

**Cup wins (1960–97)**
KR 9; Valur 8; Fram 7; IA Akranes 6; IBV Vestmann 3; IBK Keflavik 2; IBA Akureyri 1; Vikingur 1.

**Final League Table 1997**

| | P | W | D | L | F | A | Pts |
|---|---|---|---|---|---|---|---|
| IBV | 18 | 12 | 4 | 2 | 44 | 17 | 40 |
| TA | 18 | 11 | 2 | 5 | 42 | 24 | 35 |
| Fram | 18 | 9 | 5 | 4 | 33 | 22 | 32 |
| Leiftur | 18 | 8 | 6 | 4 | 27 | 17 | 30 |
| IBK | 18 | 7 | 3 | 8 | 21 | 28 | 24 |
| KR | 18 | 6 | 6 | 6 | 38 | 23 | 23 |
| Valur | 18 | 6 | 3 | 9 | 20 | 36 | 21 |
| Grindavik | 18 | 5 | 4 | 9 | 20 | 30 | 19 |
| Skallagrimur* | 18 | 4 | 3 | 11 | 19 | 41 | 15 |
| Stjarnan* | 18 | 1 | 4 | 13 | 14 | 40 | 7 |

*Top scorer:* Gudmundsson (IBV) 19.
*Cup Final:* IBK 1, 0, IBV 1, 0.
*IBK won 5-4 on penalties in replay.*

## HUNGARY

Magyar Labdarugo Szovetseg, Hungarian Football Federation, Kiralyok utja 141-143, 1039 Budapest.
*Founded:* 1901; *Number of Clubs:* 1944; *Number of Players* 95,986; *National Colours:* Red shirts, white shorts, green stockings.
*Telephone:* 0036 1 4308351/52/54; *Telex:* 225782 misz h; *Fax:* 0036 1 4308353.

**League Championship wins (1901–98)**
Ferencvaros 26; MTK-VM Budapest 20; Ujpest Dozsa 20; Honved 13; Vasas Budapest 6; Csepel 4; Raba Gyor 3; BTC 2; Nagyvarad 1; Vac 1.

**Cup wins (1910–98)**
Ferencvaros 17; MTK-VM Budapest 11; Ujpest Dozsa 8; Raba Gyor 4; Kispest Honved 4; Vasas Budapest 3; Diósgyör 2; Bocskai 1; III Ker 1; Kispesti AC 1; Soroksar 1; Szolnoki MAV 1; Siofok Banyasz 1; Bekescsaba 1; Pecs 1.
*Cup not regularly held until 1964.*

**Final League Table 1997–98**

| | P | W | D | L | F | A | Pts |
|---|---|---|---|---|---|---|---|
| Ujpest | 34 | 21 | 10 | 3 | 62 | 25 | 73 |
| Ferencvaros | 34 | 20 | 7 | 7 | 62 | 42 | 67 |
| Vasas | 34 | 19 | 7 | 8 | 66 | 41 | 64 |
| Gyori | 34 | 18 | 9 | 7 | 47 | 31 | 63 |
| MTK | 34 | 17 | 7 | 10 | 60 | 35 | 58 |
| Vac | 34 | 15 | 6 | 13 | 45 | 47 | 51 |
| Zalaegerszeg | 34 | 15 | 5 | 14 | 58 | 42 | 50 |
| Gazszer | 34 | 12 | 13 | 9 | 55 | 45 | 49 |
| Debrecen | 34 | 13 | 9 | 12 | 46 | 48 | 48 |
| BVSC | 34 | 12 | 10 | 12 | 49 | 43 | 46 |
| Diosgyor | 34 | 12 | 8 | 14 | 46 | 41 | 44 |
| Siofok | 34 | 11 | 8 | 15 | 38 | 43 | 41 |
| Haladas | 34 | 9 | 9 | 16 | 38 | 47 | 36 |
| Kispest Honved | 34 | 10 | 6 | 18 | 41 | 58 | 36 |
| Tiszakecske | 34 | 8 | 8 | 18 | 36 | 75 | 32 |
| Videoton | 34 | 7 | 10 | 17 | 43 | 58 | 31 |
| Bekescsaba* | 34 | 7 | 10 | 17 | 28 | 61 | 31 |
| Stadler* | 34 | 4 | 10 | 20 | 29 | 67 | 22 |

*Top scorer:* Tiber (Gazszer) 19.
*Cup Final:* MTK 1, Ujpest 0.

## ICELAND

Knattspyrnusamband Island, Laugardal, 104 Reykjavik.
*Founded:* 1929; *Number of Clubs:* 73; *Number of Players:* 23,673; *National Colours;* All blue.
*Telephone:* 00354 5102900; *Cable* KSI REYKJAVIK; *Telex:* 2314 isi is; *Fax:* 00354 5689793.

## REPUBLIC OF IRELAND

The Football Association of Ireland, (Cumann Peile Na H-Eireann), 80 Merrion Square, South Dublin 2.
*Founded:* 1921; *Number of Clubs:* 3,190; *Number of Players:* 124,615; *National Colours:* Green shirts, white shorts, green and white stockings.
*Telephone:* 00353 1 676 68 64; *Telex:* 91397 fai ei; *Fax:* 00353 1 661 09 31.

**League Championship wins (1922–98)**
Shamrock Rovers 15; Dundalk 9; Shelbourne 8; Bohemians 7; St Patrick's Athletic 7; Waterford 6; Cork United 5; Drumcondra 5; St James's Gate 2; Cork Athletic 2; Sligo Rovers 2; Limerick 2; Athlone Town 2; Derry City 2; Dolphin 1; Cork Hibernians 1; Cork Celtic 1; Cork City 1.

**Cup wins (1922–98)**
Shamrock Rovers 24; Dundalk 8; Drumcondra 5; Bohemians 5; Shelbourne 5; Cork Athletic 2; Cork United 2; St James's Gate 2; St Patrick's Athletic 2; Cork Hibernians 2; Limerick 2; Waterford 2; Derry City 2; Athlone Town 2; Sligo 2; Alton United 1; Cork 1; Fordsons 1; Transport 1; Finn Harps 1; Home Farm 1; UCD 1; Bray Wanderers 1; Galway United 1; Cork City 1.

**Final League Table 1997–98**

| | P | W | D | L | F | A | Pts |
|---|---|---|---|---|---|---|---|
| St Patrick's Ath | 33 | 19 | 11 | 3 | 46 | 24 | 68 |
| Shelbourne | 33 | 20 | 7 | 6 | 58 | 32 | 67 |
| Cork City | 33 | 14 | 9 | 10 | 50 | 40 | 53 |
| Shamrock Rovers | 33 | 14 | 10 | 9 | 41 | 32 | 52 |
| Bohemians | 33 | 13 | 11 | 9 | 50 | 36 | 50 |
| Dundalk | 33 | 12 | 9 | 12 | 41 | 42 | 45 |
| Sligo Rovers | 33 | 10 | 14 | 9 | 46 | 49 | 44 |
| Finn Harps | 33 | 12 | 7 | 14 | 41 | 43 | 43 |
| Derry City | 33 | 10 | 10 | 13 | 30 | 31 | 40 |
| UCD | 33 | 9 | 12 | 12 | 36 | 38 | 39 |
| Kilkenny City* | 33 | 4 | 7 | 22 | 26 | 63 | 19 |
| Drogheda United* | 33 | 2 | 9 | 22 | 20 | 55 | 15 |

*Top scorer:* Geoghegan (Shelbourne) 17.
*Cup Final:* Cork City 1, Shelbourne 0.
*after 0-0 draw.*

## ISRAEL

Israel Football Association, Ramat-Gan Stadium, 299 Aba Hilell Street, Ramat-Gan 52594.
*Founded:* 1948; *Number of Clubs:* 544; *Number of Players:* 30,449; *National Colours:* Blue shirts, white shorts, blue stockings.
*Telephone:* 00972 3 570 59 99; *Cable:* CADUREGEL RAMAT-GAN; *Telex:* 361353 fa; *Fax:* 00972 3 570 20 44.

**League Championship wins (1932–98)**
Maccabi Tel Aviv 18; Hapoel Tel Aviv 12; Hapoel Petah
Tikva 6; Maccabi Haifa 5; Maccabi Netanya 5; Beitar
Jerusalem 4; Hakoah Ramat Gan 2; Hapoel Beersheba 2;
Bnei Yehouda 1; British Police 1; Hapoel Kfar Sava 1;
Hapoel Ramat Gan 1.

**Cup wins (1928–98)**
Maccabi Tel Aviv 19; Hapoel Tel Aviv 9; Beitar
Jerusalem 5; Maccabi Haifa 5; Hapoel Haifa 3; Hapoel
Kfar Sava 3; Beitar Tel Aviv 2; Bnei Yehouda 2; Hakoah
Ramat Gan 2; Hapoel Petah Tikva 2; Maccabi Petah
Tikva 2; British Police 1; Hapoel Jerusalem 1; Hapoel
Lod 1; Maccabi Netanya 1; Hapoel Beersheba 1.

**Final League Table 1997–98**

| | P | W | D | L | F | A | Pts |
|---|---|---|---|---|---|---|---|
| Beitar Jerusalem | 30 | 20 | 9 | 1 | 71 | 33 | 69 |
| Hapoel Tel Aviv | 30 | 21 | 5 | 4 | 44 | 16 | 68 |
| Hapoel Haifa | 30 | 17 | 9 | 4 | 59 | 27 | 60 |
| Maccabi Haifa | 30 | 15 | 7 | 8 | 49 | 34 | 52 |
| Hapoel Petah Tikva | 30 | 12 | 6 | 12 | 41 | 41 | 42 |
| Maccabi Tel Aviv | 30 | 10 | 9 | 11 | 42 | 35 | 39 |
| Hapoel Kfar Sabah | 30 | 10 | 8 | 12 | 39 | 39 | 38 |
| Maccabi Herzliya | 30 | 9 | 9 | 12 | 37 | 40 | 36 |
| Maccabi Petah Tikva | 30 | 8 | 12 | 10 | 27 | 31 | 36 |
| Hapoel Rishon | 30 | 10 | 6 | 14 | 42 | 52 | 36 |
| Hapoel Jerusalem | 30 | 8 | 10 | 12 | 35 | 45 | 34 |
| Maccabi Ironi | 30 | 8 | 9 | 13 | 39 | 57 | 33 |
| Hapoel Beit Shean | 30 | 8 | 7 | 15 | 35 | 51 | 31 |
| Bnei Yehuda | 30 | 8 | 7 | 15 | 26 | 42 | 31 |
| Hapoel Beersheba* | 30 | 7 | 9 | 14 | 38 | 57 | 30 |
| Hapoel Ashkelon | 30 | 5 | 6 | 19 | 26 | 50 | 21 |

*Top scorer:* Mizrahi (Maccabi Haifa) 18.
*Cup Final:* Maccabi Haifa 2, Hapoel Jerusalem 0.


## ITALY

Federazione Italiana Giuoco Calcio, Via Gregorio
Allegri 14, C.P. 2450, 1-00198, Roma.
*Founded:* 1898; *Number of Clubs:* 20,961; *Number of
Players:* 1,420,160; *National Colours:* Blue shirts, white
shorts, blue stockings with white trim.
*Telephone:* 0039 6 849 11; *Cable:* FEDERCALCIO
ROMA; *Telex:* 624132 calcio i; *Fax:* 0039 6 849 12 526.

**League Championship wins (1898–1998)**
Juventus 25; AC Milan 15; Inter-Milan 13; Genoa 9;
Torino 8; Pro Vercelli 7; Bologna 7; Fiorentina 2; Napoli
2; AS Roma 2; Casale 1; Novese 1; Cagliari 1; Lazio 1;
Verona 1; Sampdoria 1.

**Cup wins (1922–98)**
Juventus 9; AS Roma 8; Fiorentina 5; Torino 4; AC
Milan 4; Sampdoria 4; Inter-Milan 3; Napoli 3; Bologna 2;
Lazio 2; Atalanta 1; Genoa 1; Vado 1; Venezia 1; Parma
1; Vicenza 1.

**Final League Table 1997–98**

| | P | W | D | L | F | A | Pts |
|---|---|---|---|---|---|---|---|
| Juventus | 34 | 21 | 11 | 2 | 67 | 28 | 74 |
| Internazionale | 34 | 21 | 6 | 7 | 62 | 27 | 69 |
| Udinese | 34 | 19 | 7 | 8 | 62 | 40 | 64 |
| Roma | 34 | 16 | 11 | 7 | 67 | 42 | 59 |
| Fiorentina | 34 | 15 | 12 | 7 | 65 | 36 | 57 |
| Parma | 34 | 15 | 12 | 7 | 55 | 39 | 57 |
| Lazio | 34 | 16 | 8 | 10 | 53 | 30 | 56 |
| Bologna | 34 | 12 | 12 | 10 | 55 | 46 | 48 |
| Sampdoria | 34 | 13 | 9 | 12 | 52 | 55 | 48 |
| AC Milan | 34 | 11 | 11 | 12 | 37 | 43 | 44 |
| Bari | 34 | 10 | 8 | 16 | 30 | 45 | 38 |
| Empoli | 34 | 10 | 7 | 17 | 50 | 58 | 37 |
| Piacenza | 34 | 7 | 16 | 11 | 29 | 38 | 37 |
| Vicenza | 34 | 9 | 9 | 16 | 36 | 61 | 36 |
| Brescia* | 34 | 9 | 8 | 17 | 45 | 63 | 35 |
| Atalanta* | 34 | 7 | 11 | 16 | 25 | 48 | 32 |
| Lecce* | 34 | 6 | 8 | 20 | 32 | 72 | 26 |
| Napoli* | 34 | 2 | 8 | 24 | 25 | 76 | 14 |

*Top scorer:* Bierhoff (Udinese) 27.
*Cup Final:* AC Milan 1, 1, Lazio 0, 3.


## LATVIA

Latvian Football Federation, Augsiela, 1, LV-1009, Riga.
*Founded:* 1921; *Number of Clubs:* 50; *Number of
Players:* 12,000; *National Colours:* Carmine red shirts,
white shorts, carmine red stockings.
*Telephone:* 00371 2 29 29 88; *Fax:* 00371 7828331.

**League Championship wins (1922–97)**
ASK Riga 9; RFK Riga 8; Olympia Liepaya 7; Sarkanais
Metalurgs Liepaya 7; Skonto Riga 7; VEF Riga 6;
Energija Riga 4; Elektrons Riga 3; Torpedo Riga 3;
Daugava Liepaya 2; ODO Riga 2; Khimikis Daugavpils
2; RAF Yelgava 2; Keisermezhs Riga 2; Dinamo Riga 1;
Zhmilyeva Team 1; Darba Rezervi 1; REZ Riga 1; Start
Brotseni 1; Venta Ventspils 1; Yurnieks Riga 1; Alfa
Riga 1; Gauya Valmiera 1.

**Cup wins (1937–97)**
Elektrons Riga 7; Sarkanais Metalurgs Liepaya 5; ODO
Riga 3; VEF Riga 3; ASK Riga 3; Tseltnieks Riga 3; RAF
Yelgava 3; Skonto Riga 3; RFK Riga 2; Daugava Liepaya
2; Start Brotseni 2; Selmash Liepaya 2; Yurnieks Riga 2;
Khimikis Daugavpils 2; Rigas Vilki 1; Dinamo Liepaya 1;
Dinamo Riga 1; REZ Riga 1; Voulkan Kouldiga 1;
Baltija Liepaya 1; Venta Ventspils 1; Pilot Riga 1;
Lielupe Yurmala 1; Energija Riga 1; Torpedo Riga 1;
Daugava SKIF Riga 1; Tseltnieks Daugavpils 1; Olympia
Riga 1.

**Final League Table 1997**

| | P | W | D | L | F | A | Pts |
|---|---|---|---|---|---|---|---|
| Skonto Riga | 24 | 20 | 4 | 0 | 89 | 6 | 64 |
| Daugava Riga | 24 | 13 | 4 | 7 | 35 | 27 | 43 |
| Dinaburg Daugavpils | 24 | 12 | 6 | 6 | 37 | 19 | 42 |
| FK Ventspils | 24 | 12 | 6 | 6 | 32 | 21 | 42 |
| Metalurgs Liepaya | 24 | 9 | 4 | 11 | 27 | 32 | 31 |
| Universitate Riga | 24 | 8 | 5 | 11 | 25 | 42 | 29 |
| FK Valmiera | 24 | 8 | 4 | 12 | 29 | 43 | 28 |
| Lokomotive Daugavpils | 24 | 5 | 2 | 17 | 29 | 52 | 17 |
| FK Rezekne* | 24 | 1 | 5 | 18 | 10 | 69 | 8 |

*Top scorer:* Chaladze (Skonto Riga) 25.
*Cup Final:* Skonto Riga 2, Dinaburg Daugavpils 1.


## LIECHTENSTEIN

Liechtensteiner Fussball-Verband, Malbuner Huus
Altenbach 11, Postfach 165, 9490 Vaduz.
*Founded:* 1934; *Number of Clubs:* 7; *Number of Players:*
1,247; *National Colours:* Blue shirts, red shorts, blue
stockings.
*Telephone:* 004175 237 4747; *Cable:* FUSSBALLVER-
BAND VADUZ; *Fax:* 004175 237 4748.

Liechtenstein has no national league. Teams compete in
Swiss regional leagues.

**Cup wins (1946–97)**
Vaduz 27; Balzers 11; Triesen 8; Eschen/Mauren 4;
Schaan 2.
*Cup Final:* Vaduz 5, Eschen 1.


## LITHUANIA

Lithuanian Football Federation, Seimyniskiu str. 15, 2005
Vilnius.
*Founded:* 1922; *Number of Clubs:* 152; *Number of
Players:* 16,600; *National Colours:* Yellow shirts, green
shorts, yellow stockings.
*Telephone:* 00370 2/723654; *Fax:* 00370 2/723651.

**League Championship wins (1922–98)**
Kovas Kaunas 6; KSS Klaipeda 6; LFLS Kaunas 4;
Zalgiris Vilnius 3; LGSF Kaunas 2; Kareda 2; MSK
Kaunas 1; Ekranas Panevezys 1; Romar Mazeikiai 1;
Inkaras Grifas 1.

**Cup wins (1992–98)**
Zalgiris Vilnius 3; Inkaras 1; Kareda 1; Ekranas 1.

**Final League Table 1997–98**

| | P | W | D | L | F | A | Pts |
|---|---|---|---|---|---|---|---|
| Kareda | 30 | 25 | 4 | 1 | 106 | 14 | 79 |
| Zalgiris | 30 | 24 | 5 | 1 | 84 | 10 | 77 |
| Ekranas | 30 | 22 | 2 | 6 | 53 | 25 | 68 |
| Inkaras | 30 | 19 | 4 | 7 | 60 | 22 | 61 |
| FBK | 30 | 18 | 4 | 8 | 63 | 19 | 58 |
| Atlantas | 30 | 15 | 7 | 8 | 47 | 21 | 52 |
| Lokomotyvas | 30 | 14 | 4 | 12 | 35 | 29 | 46 |
| Ranga | 30 | 12 | 8 | 10 | 42 | 36 | 44 |
| Panerys | 30 | 10 | 9 | 11 | 36 | 39 | 39 |
| Nevezis | 30 | 9 | 4 | 17 | 25 | 52 | 31 |
| Mastis | 30 | 9 | 4 | 17 | 29 | 62 | 31 |
| Gelezinis | 30 | 7 | 6 | 17 | 31 | 44 | 27 |
| Banga | 30 | 7 | 3 | 20 | 34 | 57 | 24 |
| Interas* | 30 | 5 | 5 | 20 | 28 | 68 | 20 |
| Tauras* | 30 | 5 | 4 | 21 | 28 | 93 | 19 |
| Vienybe* | 30 | 2 | 1 | 27 | 15 | 125 | 7 |

*Top scorer:* Dancenka (Kareda) 26.
*Cup Final:* Ekranas 1, FBK 0.

**Cup wins (1993-98)**
Vardar 3; Sileks 1.

**Final Table 1997–98**

| | P | W | D | L | F | A | Pts |
|---|---|---|---|---|---|---|---|
| Sileks | 25 | 15 | 3 | 7 | 40 | 21 | 48 |
| Sloga | 25 | 12 | 7 | 6 | 25 | 16 | 43 |
| Makedonia | 25 | 12 | 6 | 7 | 34 | 21 | 42 |
| Vardar | 25 | 12 | 5 | 8 | 34 | 25 | 41 |
| Pobeda | 25 | 11 | 6 | 8 | 29 | 21 | 39 |
| Pelister | 25 | 10 | 7 | 8 | 31 | 24 | 37 |
| Borec | 25 | 9 | 6 | 10 | 27 | 30 | 33 |
| Balkan | 25 | 8 | 7 | 10 | 20 | 21 | 31 |
| Cement | 25 | 9 | 3 | 13 | 28 | 31 | 30 |
| Skopje | 25 | 9 | 3 | 13 | 31 | 45 | 30 |
| Tikves | 25 | 7 | 8 | 10 | 23 | 27 | 29 |
| Sasa | 25 | 8 | 5 | 12 | 21 | 32 | 29 |
| Belasica* | 25 | 8 | 4 | 13 | 25 | 35 | 28 |
| Bregalnica* | 13 | 4 | 0 | 9 | 13 | 32 | 12 |

*Top scorer:* Anatasov (Belasica) 12.
*Cup Final:* Vardar 2, Sloga 0.

## LUXEMBOURG

Federation Luxembourgeoise De Football, (F.L.F.), 50, Rue De Strasbourg, L-2560, Luxembourg.
*Founded:* 1908; *Number of Clubs:* 126; *Number of Players:* 21,684; *National Colours:* All red.
*Telephone:* 00352 48 86 65; *Cable:* FOOTBALL LUXEMBOURG; *Telex:* 2426 flf l; *Fax:* 00352 40 02 01.

**League Championship wins (1910–98)**
Jeunesse Esch 25; Spora Luxembourg 11; Stade Dudelange 10; Avenir Beggen 7; Red Boys Differdange 6; US Hollerich-Bonnevoie 5; Fola Esch 5; US Luxembourg 5; Aris Bonnevoie 3; Progres Niedercorn 3.

**Cup wins (1922–98)**
Red Boys Differdange 16; US Luxembourg 10; Jeunesse Esch 10; Spora Luxembourg 8; Avenir Beggen 6; Stade Dudelange 4; Progres Niedercorn 4; Fola Esch 3; Alliance Dudelange 2; US Rumelange 2; Grevenmacher 2; Aris Bonnevoie 1; US Dudelange 1; Jeunesse Hautcharage 1; National Schiffige 1; Racing Luxembourg 1; SC Tetange 1; Hesperange 1.

**Final Table 1996–98**

| | P | W | D | L | F | A | Pts |
|---|---|---|---|---|---|---|---|
| Jeunesse Esch | 22 | 17 | 3 | 2 | 69 | 19 | 54 |
| Union | 22 | 17 | 2 | 3 | 67 | 21 | 53 |
| Grevenmacher | 22 | 13 | 4 | 5 | 49 | 23 | 43 |
| F91 Dudelange | 22 | 10 | 6 | 6 | 44 | 32 | 36 |
| Avenir Beggen | 22 | 10 | 5 | 7 | 41 | 35 | 35 |
| Hobscheid | 22 | 8 | 7 | 7 | 38 | 35 | 31 |
| Sporting Mertzig | 22 | 8 | 6 | 8 | 44 | 41 | 30 |
| FC Wiltz 71 | 22 | 6 | 7 | 9 | 38 | 45 | 25 |
| Petange | 22 | 5 | 5 | 12 | 33 | 53 | 20 |
| Spora | 22 | 5 | 4 | 13 | 31 | 55 | 19 |
| Rumelange* | 22 | 4 | 4 | 14 | 25 | 74 | 16 |
| Red Boys* | 22 | 0 | 5 | 17 | 15 | 61 | 5 |

*Top scorer:* Zaritski (Sporting Mertzig) 29.
*Cup Final:* Grevenmacher 2, Avenir Beggen 0.

## MACEDONIA

Football Association of the Former Yugoslav Republic of Macedonia, VIII-ma Udarna Brigada 31A, PO Box 84, MAC-91000 Skopje.
*Founded:* 1948; *Number of Clubs:* 598; *Number of Players:* 15,165; *National Colours:* All red.
*Telephone:* 00389 1 22 90 42; *Fax:* 00389 1 23 54 48.

**League Championship wins (1993-98)**
Vardar 3; Sileks 3.

## MALTA

Malta Football Association, 280 St. Paul Street, Valletta VLT07.
*Founded:* 1900; *Number of Clubs:* 252; *Number of Players:* 5,544; *National Colours:* Red shirts, white shorts, red stockings.
*Telephone:* 00356 22 26 97; *Cable:* FOOTBALL MALTA VALLETTA; *Fax:* 00356 24 51 36.

**League Championship wins (1910–98)**
Floriana 25; Sliema Wanderers 23; Valletta 16; Hibernians 8; Hamrun Spartans 7; Rabat Ajax 2; St George's 1; KOMR 1.

**Cup wins (1935–98)**
Floriana 18; Sliema Wanderers 17; Valletta 8; Hamrun Spartans 6; Hibernians 6; Gzira United 1; Melita 1; Zurrieq 1; Rabat Ajax 1.

**Final League Table 1997–98**

| | P | W | D | L | F | A | Pts |
|---|---|---|---|---|---|---|---|
| Valletta | 27 | 20 | 5 | 2 | 66 | 19 | 65 |
| Birkirkara | 27 | 20 | 3 | 4 | 59 | 22 | 63 |
| Silema Wanderers | 27 | 18 | 2 | 7 | 64 | 26 | 56 |
| Hibernians | 27 | 15 | 4 | 8 | 50 | 33 | 46 |
| Floriana | 27 | 13 | 6 | 8 | 48 | 27 | 45 |
| Pieta Hotspurs | 27 | 10 | 2 | 15 | 40 | 44 | 32 |
| Naxxar Lions | 27 | 7 | 7 | 13 | 34 | 47 | 28 |
| Hamrun Spartans | 27 | 7 | 6 | 14 | 26 | 49 | 27 |
| Xghajra Tornados* | 27 | 2 | 6 | 19 | 18 | 71 | 12 |
| Tarxien Rainbows* | 27 | 1 | 3 | 23 | 14 | 81 | 6 |

*Top scorer:* Brincat (Birkirkara) 19.
*Cup Final:* Hibernians 2, Valletta 1.

## MOLDOVA

Moldavian Football Federation, 39 Tricolorului Str, 2012, Chisinau.
*Founded:* 1990; *Number of Clubs:* 143; *Number of Players:* 75,000; *National Colours:* Blue shirts, red shorts, yellow stockings.
*Telephone:* 00373 2 22 12 95. *Fax:* 00373 2 22 22 44.

**League Championship wins (1992–98)**
Zimbru Chisinau 6; Constructorul 1.

**Cup wins (1992–98)**
Tiligul 4; Zimbru Chisinau 2; Combat 1.

**Final League Table 1997–98**

| | P | W | D | L | F | A | Pts |
|---|---|---|---|---|---|---|---|
| Zimbru Chisinau | 26 | 22 | 3 | 1 | 75 | 8 | 69 |
| Tiligul | 26 | 19 | 2 | 5 | 45 | 20 | 59 |
| Constructorul | 26 | 17 | 3 | 6 | 54 | 32 | 54 |
| Otaci | 26 | 13 | 6 | 7 | 36 | 20 | 45 |
| Olimpia | 26 | 12 | 8 | 8 | 40 | 21 | 44 |
| Moldova-Gaz | 26 | 14 | 2 | 10 | 38 | 28 | 44 |
| Unisport | 26 | 11 | 5 | 10 | 23 | 32 | 38 |
| Roma | 26 | 10 | 7 | 9 | 40 | 32 | 37 |
| Agro | 26 | 10 | 3 | 13 | 27 | 35 | 33 |
| Locomotiva* | 26 | 6 | 7 | 13 | 21 | 43 | 25 |
| Victoria* | 26 | 6 | 6 | 14 | 20 | 42 | 24 |
| Bender* | 26 | 6 | 4 | 16 | 19 | 47 | 22 |
| Stimold* | 26 | 2 | 7 | 17 | 19 | 60 | 13 |
| Sperante* | 26 | 0 | 5 | 21 | 9 | 46 | 3 |

*Top scorer:* Clescenco (Zimbru Chisinau) 25.
*Cup Final:* Zimbru Chisinau 1, Constructorul 0.

## NORTHERN IRELAND

Irish Football Association Ltd, 20 Windsor Avenue, Belfast BT9 6EG.
*Founded:* 1880; *Number of Clubs:* 1,555; *Number of Players:* 24,558; *National Colours:* Green shirts, white shorts, green stockings.
*Telephone:* 01232 66 94 58; *Cable:* FOOTBALL BELFAST; *Telex:* 747317 ifa ni g; *Fax:* 01232 66 76 20.

## NORWAY

Norges Fotballforbund Ullevaal Stadion, Postboks 3823, Ulleval Hageby, 0805 Oslo 8.
*Founded:* 1902; *Number of Clubs:* 1,810; *Number of Players:* 300,000; *National Colours:* Red shirts, white shorts, blue stockings.
*Telephone:* 0047 22/024500 ; *Cable* FOTBALLFOR-BUND OSLO; *Telex:* 71722 nff n; *Fax:* 0047 22 95 10 10.

**League Championship wins (1938–97)**
Rosenborg Trondheim 11; Fredrikstad 9; Viking Stavanger 8; Lillestroem 6; Valerengen 4; Larvik Turn 3; Brann Bergen 2; Lyn Oslo 2; IK Start 2; Friedig 1; Fram 1; Skeid Oslo 1; Strömsgodset Drammen 1; Moss 1.

**Cup wins (1902–97)**
Odds Bk Skien 11; Fredrikstad 10; Lyn Oslo 8; Skeid Oslo 8; Sarpsborg FK 6; Rosenborg Trondheim 6; Brann Bergen 5; Orn F Horten 4; Lillestroem 4; Viking Stavanger 4; Strömsgodset Drammen 4; Frigg 3; Mjondalens F 3; Bodo-Glimt 2; Mercantile 2; Tromso 2; Valerengen 2; Grane Nordstrand 1; Kvik Halden 1; Sparta 1; Gjovik 1; Moss 1; Byrne 1, Molde 1.
*(Known as the Norwegian Championship for HM The King's Trophy).*

**Final League Table 1997**

| | P | W | D | L | F | A | Pts |
|---|---|---|---|---|---|---|---|
| Rosenborg | 26 | 18 | 7 | 1 | 87 | 20 | 61 |
| Brann | 26 | 15 | 5 | 6 | 59 | 37 | 50 |
| Stromsgodset | 26 | 14 | 4 | 8 | 58 | 44 | 46 |
| Molde | 26 | 13 | 6 | 7 | 47 | 36 | 45 |
| Stabaek | 26 | 13 | 4 | 9 | 33 | 35 | 43 |
| Kongsvinger | 26 | 11 | 5 | 10 | 43 | 48 | 38 |
| Bodo-Glimt | 26 | 10 | 7 | 9 | 39 | 34 | 37 |
| Viking | 26 | 8 | 10 | 8 | 42 | 34 | 34 |
| Haugesund | 26 | 9 | 5 | 12 | 31 | 38 | 32 |
| Lillestrom | 26 | 9 | 5 | 12 | 34 | 43 | 32 |
| Sogndal | 26 | 8 | 5 | 13 | 34 | 56 | 29 |
| Tromso | 26 | 6 | 10 | 10 | 37 | 44 | 28 |
| Lyn* | 26 | 4 | 5 | 17 | 28 | 58 | 17 |
| Skeid* | 26 | 3 | 4 | 19 | 27 | 72 | 13 |

*Top scorer:* Rushfeldt (Rosenborg) 25.
*Cup Final:* Valerengen 4, Stromsgodset 2.

## POLAND

Federation Polonaise De Foot-Ball, Al. Ujazdowskie 22, 00-478 Warszawa.
*Founded:* 1919; *Number of Clubs:* 5,881; *Number of Players:* 317,442; *National Colours:* White shirts, red shorts, white & red stockings.
*Telephone:* 0048 22 6223398; *Cable:* PEZETPEEN WARSZAWA; *Telex:* 825320 pzpn pl; *Fax:* 0048 22 629 24 89.

**League Championship wins (1921–98)**
Gornik Zabrze 14; Ruch Chorzow 13; Wisla Krakow 6; Legia Warsaw 6; Widzew Lodz 6; Lech Poznan 5; Pogon Lwow 4; Cracovia 3; Warta Poznan 2; Polonia Bytom 2; Stal Mielec 2; LKS Lodz 2; Garbarnia Krakow 1; Polonia Warsaw 1; Slask Wroclaw 1; Szombierki Bytom 1; Zaglebie Lubin 1.

**Cup wins (1951–98)**
Legia Warsaw 12; Gornik Zabrze 6; Zaglebie Sosnowiec 4; Lech Poznan 3; GKS Katowice 3; Ruch Chorzow 3; Slask Wroclaw 2; Gwardia Warsaw 1; LKS Lodz 1; Polonia Warsaw 1; Wisla Krakow 1; Stal Rzeszow 1; Arka Gdynia 1; Lechia Gdansk 1; Widzew Lodz 1; Miedz Legnica 1; Amica Wronki 1.

**Final League Table 1997–98**

| | P | W | D | L | F | A | Pts |
|---|---|---|---|---|---|---|---|
| LKS Lodz | 34 | 19 | 9 | 6 | 52 | 23 | 66 |
| Polonia | 34 | 18 | 9 | 7 | 46 | 30 | 63 |
| Wisla | 34 | 18 | 7 | 9 | 50 | 30 | 61 |
| Widzew | 34 | 18 | 7 | 9 | 53 | 34 | 61 |
| Legia | 34 | 16 | 11 | 7 | 50 | 32 | 59 |
| Ruch | 34 | 15 | 10 | 9 | 48 | 39 | 55 |
| Amica | 34 | 13 | 11 | 10 | 38 | 31 | 50 |
| Gornik Zabrze | 34 | 12 | 12 | 10 | 48 | 42 | 48 |
| Odra | 34 | 14 | 6 | 14 | 51 | 50 | 48 |
| Lech | 34 | 12 | 10 | 12 | 41 | 37 | 46 |
| Stomil | 34 | 12 | 9 | 13 | 38 | 45 | 45 |
| Katowice | 34 | 10 | 13 | 11 | 37 | 33 | 43 |
| Zaglebie Lubin | 34 | 12 | 7 | 15 | 39 | 40 | 43 |
| Pogon | 34 | 10 | 13 | 11 | 36 | 40 | 43 |
| Petrochemia* | 34 | 10 | 8 | 16 | 28 | 54 | 38 |
| Groclin* | 34 | 8 | 5 | 21 | 30 | 55 | 29 |
| Ostrowiec* | 34 | 6 | 6 | 22 | 24 | 47 | 24 |
| Rakow* | 34 | 4 | 5 | 25 | 21 | 68 | 17 |

*Top scorers:* Bak (Polonia) 14, Czereszewski (Legia) 14, Srutwa (Ruch) 14.
*Cup Final:* Amica 5, Aluminium 3.

## PORTUGAL

Federacao Portuguesa De Futebol, Praca De Alegria N.25, Apartado 21.100, P-1127, Lisboa Codex.
*Founded:* 1914; *Number of Clubs:* 204; *Number of Players:* 79,235; *National Colours:* Red shirts, green shorts, red stockings.
*Telephone:* 00351 1 342 8207/8/9/0; *Cable:* FUTEBOL LISBOA; *Telex:* 13489 fpf p; *Fax:* 00351 1 346 72 31.

**League Championship wins (1935–98)**
Benfica 30; FC Porto 17; Sporting Lisbon 16; Belenenses 1.

**Cup wins (1939–98)**
Benfica 23; Sporting Lisbon 12; FC Porto 9; Boavista 5; Belenenses 3; Vitoria Setubal 2; Academica Coimbra 1; Leixoes Porto 1; Sporting Braga 1; Amadora 1.

**Final League Table 1997–98**

|  | P | W | D | L | F | A | Pts |
|---|---|---|---|---|---|---|---|
| Porto | 34 | 24 | 5 | 5 | 75 | 38 | 77 |
| Benfica | 34 | 20 | 8 | 6 | 62 | 29 | 68 |
| Guimaraes | 34 | 17 | 8 | 9 | 42 | 25 | 59 |
| Sporting Lisbon | 34 | 15 | 11 | 8 | 45 | 33 | 56 |
| Maritimo | 34 | 16 | 8 | 10 | 44 | 35 | 56 |
| Boavista | 34 | 15 | 10 | 9 | 54 | 31 | 55 |
| Amadora | 34 | 14 | 8 | 12 | 42 | 41 | 50 |
| Salgueiros | 34 | 13 | 10 | 11 | 48 | 44 | 49 |
| Rio Ave | 34 | 12 | 10 | 12 | 43 | 43 | 46 |
| Braga | 34 | 11 | 12 | 11 | 48 | 49 | 45 |
| Campomaiorense | 34 | 11 | 7 | 16 | 53 | 58 | 40 |
| Leca | 34 | 10 | 8 | 16 | 29 | 52 | 38 |
| Setubal | 34 | 10 | 7 | 17 | 38 | 43 | 37 |
| Farense | 34 | 8 | 13 | 13 | 41 | 50 | 37 |
| Academica | 34 | 8 | 12 | 14 | 27 | 41 | 36 |
| Chaves* | 34 | 10 | 5 | 19 | 31 | 55 | 35 |
| Varzin* | 34 | 6 | 11 | 17 | 26 | 51 | 29 |
| Belenenses* | 34 | 5 | 9 | 20 | 22 | 52 | 24 |

*Top scorer:* Jardel (Porto) 26.
*Cup Final:* Porto 3, Braga 1.

## ROMANIA

Federatia Romana De Fotbal, Str. Poligrafiei 3, Sector 1, 71556 Bucharest.
*Founded:* 1909; *Number of Clubs:* 414; *Number of Players:* 22,920; *National Colours:* All yellow.
*Telephone:* 0040 1 2229993; *Cable:* SPORTROM BUCURESTI-FOTBAL; *Telex:* 10097 frf r; *Fax:* 0040 1 2226324

**League Championship wins (1910–98)**
Steaua Bucharest 20; Dinamo Bucharest 14; Venus Bucharest 8; Chinezul Timisoara 6; UT Arad 6; Ripensia Temesvar 4; Uni Craiova 4; Petrolul Ploesti 3; Olimpia Bucharest 2; Colentina Bucharest 2; Arges Pitesti 2; ICO Oradea 2; Soc RA Bucharest 1; Prahova Ploesti 1; Coltea Brasov 1; Juventus Bucharest 1; Metalochimia Resita 1; Ploesti United 1; Unirea Tricolor 1; Rapid Bucharest 1.

**Cup wins (1934–98)**
Steaua Bucharest 19; Rapid Bucharest 10; Dinamo Bucharest 7; Uni Craiova 6; UT Arad 2; Ripensia Temesvar 2; Politehnica Timisoara 2; Petrolul Ploesti 2; ICO Oradeo 1; Metalochimia Resita 1; Stinta Cluj 1; CFR Turnu Severin 1; Chimia Ramnicu Vilcea 1; Jiul Petroseni 1; Progresul Bucharest 1; Progresul Oradea 1; Gloria Bistrita 1.

**Final League Table 1997–98**

|  | P | W | D | L | F | A | Pts |
|---|---|---|---|---|---|---|---|
| Steaua | 34 | 25 | 5 | 4 | 83 | 36 | 80 |
| Rapid | 34 | 24 | 6 | 4 | 71 | 25 | 78 |
| Arges | 34 | 20 | 5 | 9 | 56 | 37 | 65 |
| Otelul | 34 | 20 | 4 | 10 | 54 | 28 | 64 |
| National | 34 | 18 | 6 | 10 | 56 | 39 | 60 |
| Dinamo | 34 | 17 | 3 | 14 | 65 | 49 | 54 |
| Resita | 34 | 15 | 6 | 13 | 55 | 49 | 51 |
| Uni Craiova | 34 | 15 | 4 | 15 | 46 | 49 | 49 |
| Ceahlaul | 34 | 14 | 7 | 13 | 46 | 49 | 49 |
| Bacau | 34 | 12 | 9 | 13 | 41 | 42 | 45 |
| Gloria | 34 | 13 | 5 | 16 | 56 | 63 | 44 |
| Constanta | 34 | 13 | 4 | 17 | 37 | 53 | 43 |
| Uni Cluj | 34 | 11 | 7 | 16 | 41 | 40 | 40 |
| Petrolul | 34 | 11 | 7 | 16 | 40 | 44 | 40 |
| Foresta | 34 | 10 | 9 | 15 | 32 | 41 | 39 |
| Tirgoviste* | 34 | 10 | 8 | 16 | 40 | 67 | 38 |
| Sportul* | 34 | 5 | 4 | 25 | 32 | 65 | 19 |
| Jiul* | 34 | 3 | 1 | 30 | 18 | 115 | 10 |

*Top scorer:* Dana (Gloria) 22.
*Cup Final:* Rapid 1, Uni Craiova 0.

## RUSSIA

Football Union of Russia; Luzhnetskaya Naberezyhnaja, 8. SU-119871 Moscow.
*Founded:* 1912; *Number of Clubs:* 43,700; *Number of Players:*785,000; *National Colours:* White shirts, blue shorts, red stockings.
*Telephone:* 0070 95 2011637; *Telex:* 411287 priz su; *Fax:* 0070 95 2011303;

**League Championship wins (1945–97)**
Spartak Moscow 16; Dynamo Kiev 13; Dynamo Moscow 11; CSKA Moscow 7; Torpedo Moscow 3; Dynamo Tbilisi 2; Dnepr Dnepropetrovsk 2; Saria Voroshilovgrad 1; Ararat Erevan 1; Dynamo Minsk 1; Zenit Leningrad 1; Spartak Vladikavkaz 1.

**Cup wins (1936–98)**
Spartak Moscow 12; Dynamo Kiev 10; Torpedo Moscow 7; Dynamo Moscow 7; CSKA Moscow 5; Donetsk Shaktyor 4; Lokomotiv Moscow 4; Dynamo Tbilisi 2; Ararat Erevan 2; Karpaty Lvov 1; SKA Rostov 1; Zenit Leningrad 1; Metallist Kharkov 1; Dnepr 1.

**Final League Table 1997**

|  | P | W | D | L | F | A | Pts |
|---|---|---|---|---|---|---|---|
| Spartak Moscow | 34 | 22 | 7 | 5 | 67 | 30 | 73 |
| Dynamo Moscow | 34 | 19 | 11 | 4 | 50 | 20 | 68 |
| Volgograd | 34 | 20 | 8 | 6 | 54 | 27 | 68 |
| Shinnik | 34 | 15 | 10 | 9 | 38 | 35 | 55 |
| Lokomotiv Moscow | 34 | 15 | 9 | 10 | 47 | 37 | 54 |
| Chernomorets | 34 | 13 | 14 | 7 | 40 | 26 | 53 |
| Baltika | 34 | 11 | 16 | 7 | 38 | 33 | 49 |
| Krylia Sovekov | 34 | 14 | 7 | 13 | 31 | 30 | 49 |
| Zenit | 34 | 13 | 10 | 11 | 28 | 29 | 49 |
| Vladikavkaz | 34 | 14 | 4 | 16 | 52 | 42 | 46 |
| Torpedo Moscow | 34 | 13 | 6 | 15 | 50 | 46 | 45 |
| CSKA Moscow | 34 | 11 | 9 | 14 | 31 | 42 | 42 |
| Rostov | 34 | 9 | 14 | 11 | 34 | 38 | 41 |
| Sotchi | 34 | 11 | 7 | 16 | 38 | 51 | 40 |
| Dynamo Gazovik | 34 | 9 | 7 | 18 | 28 | 46 | 34 |
| Fakel* | 34 | 7 | 5 | 22 | 25 | 49 | 26 |
| Novgorod* | 34 | 6 | 5 | 23 | 26 | 59 | 23 |
| Kamaz* | 34 | 8 | 3 | 23 | 38 | 75 | 21 |

*Top scorer:* Veretennikov (Volgograd) 22.
*Cup Final:* Spartak Moscow 1, Lokomotiv Moscow 0.

## SAN MARINO

Federazione Sammarinese Giuoco Calcio, Viale Campo dei Giudei, 14; 47031-Rep. San Marino.
*Founded:* 1931; *Number of Clubs:* 17; *Number of Players:* 1,033; *National Colours:* All light blue.
*Telephone:* 0039549 99 05 15; *Telex:* 0505284 cosmar so; *Fax:* 0039549 99 23 48.

**League Championship wins (1986–98)**
Tre Fiori 4; Fiorita 2; Faetano 2; Folgore 2; Domagnano 1; Montevito 1, Libertas 1.
*League Champions 1997-98:* Folgore.

**Cup wins (1986–97)**
Domagnano 4; Libertas 3; Faetano 1, Fiorita 1, Tre Fiori 1; Cosmos 1; Murata 1.
*Top scorer:* Vannucci (Virtus) 21.

## SCOTLAND

The Scottish Football Association Ltd, 6 Park Gardens, Glasgow G3 7YF.
*Founded:* 1873; *Number of Clubs:* 6,148; *Number of Players:* 135,474; *National Colours:* Dark blue shirts, white shorts, red stockings with dark blue tops.
*Telephone:* 0141 332 6372; *Cable:* EXECUTIVE GLASGOW; *Telex:* 778904 sfa g; *Fax:* 0141 332 7559.

## SLOVAKIA

Slovak Football Association, Junacka 6, 83280 Bratislava, Slovakia.
*Founded:* 1993; *Number of Clubs:* 2,140; *Number of Players:* 141,000; *National Colours:* All blue.
*Telephone:* 00421 75049151/5; *Fax:* 00421 75 049554.

**League Championship wins (1939-44; 1994-98)**
Slovan Bratislava 7; Kosice 2; Bystrica 1; OAP Bratislava 1.

**Cup wins (1994–98)**
Tatran Presov 1; Inter 1; Humenne 1; Slovan Bratislava 1; Spartak Trnava 1.

**Final League Table 1997–98**

| | P | W | D | L | F | A | Pts |
|---|---|---|---|---|---|---|---|
| Kosice | 30 | 21 | 5 | 4 | 71 | 24 | 68 |
| Spartak Trnava | 30 | 20 | 6 | 4 | 61 | 34 | 66 |
| Inter | 30 | 18 | 6 | 6 | 55 | 25 | 60 |
| Odu Trencin | 30 | 16 | 5 | 9 | 47 | 31 | 53 |
| Slovan Bratislava | 30 | 12 | 9 | 9 | 41 | 36 | 45 |
| Tauris | 30 | 12 | 8 | 10 | 39 | 34 | 44 |
| Zilina | 30 | 11 | 9 | 10 | 23 | 25 | 42 |
| Petrzalka | 30 | 11 | 6 | 13 | 27 | 28 | 39 |
| Humenne | 30 | 12 | 2 | 16 | 36 | 55 | 38 |
| Tatran Presov | 30 | 9 | 9 | 12 | 29 | 39 | 36 |
| Ruzomberok | 30 | 9 | 9 | 12 | 35 | 49 | 36 |
| Prievidza | 30 | 9 | 8 | 13 | 35 | 42 | 35 |
| Dukla Bystrica | 30 | 7 | 9 | 14 | 32 | 46 | 30 |
| Bardejov | 30 | 7 | 6 | 17 | 27 | 42 | 27 |
| Lokomotiv Kosice* | 30 | 7 | 5 | 18 | 31 | 54 | 26 |
| Dunajska Streda* | 30 | 5 | 6 | 19 | 26 | 51 | 21 |

*Top scorer:* Luhovy (Spartak Trnava) 17.
*Cup Final:* Spartak Trnava 2, Kosice 0.

## SLOVENIA

Football Association of Slovenia, P.P. 3986, 1001 Ljubljana, Slovenia.
*Founded:* 1920; *Number of Clubs:* 375; *Number of Players:* 20,117; *National Colours:* White shirts, green shorts, white stockings.
*Telephone:* 00386 61 1611500; *Fax:* 00386 61 612220.

**League Championship wins (1992–98)**
SCT Olimpija 4; Branik Maribor 2; Gorica 1.

**Cup wins (1992–98)**
Branik Maribor 3; SCT Olimpija 2; Mura 1; Rudar 1.

**Final League Table 1997–98**

| | P | W | D | L | F | A | Pts |
|---|---|---|---|---|---|---|---|
| Branik Maribor | 36 | 24 | 4 | 8 | 69 | 34 | 76 |
| Mura | 36 | 19 | 10 | 7 | 63 | 42 | 67 |
| Gorica | 36 | 20 | 5 | 11 | 64 | 36 | 65 |
| Primorje | 36 | 17 | 6 | 13 | 63 | 49 | 57 |
| Olimpija | 36 | 13 | 12 | 11 | 59 | 55 | 51 |
| Publikum | 36 | 14 | 7 | 15 | 57 | 57 | 49 |
| Rudar | 36 | 10 | 13 | 13 | 39 | 38 | 43 |
| Korotan | 36 | 10 | 9 | 17 | 31 | 59 | 39 |
| Beltinci+ | 36 | 9 | 7 | 20 | 44 | 73 | 34 |
| Set Vevce+ | 36 | 4 | 7 | 25 | 37 | 83 | 19 |

*Top scorer:* Ekmecic (Olimpija) 21.
*Cup Final:* Rudar 2, 3; Primorje 1, 0.

## SPAIN

Real Federacion Espanola De Futbol, Calle Alberto Bosch 13, Apartado Postal 347, E-28014 Madrid.
*Founded:* 1913; *Number of Clubs:* 10,240; *Number of Players:* 408,135; *National Colours:* Red shirts, blue shorts, blue stockings with red, blue & yellow border.
*Telephone:* 0034 1 420 13 62; *Cable:* FUTBOL MADRID; *Fax:* 0034 1 420 20 94.

**League Championship wins (1929-36; 1940–98)**
Real Madrid 27; Barcelona 15; Atletico Madrid 9; Athletic Bilbao 8; Valencia 4; Real Sociedad 2; Real Betis 1; Seville 1.

**Cup wins (1902–98)**
Barcelona 24; Athletic Bilbao 23; Real Madrid 17; Atletico Madrid 9; Valencia 5; Real Zaragoza 4; Real Union de Irun 3; Seville 3; Espanol 2; Arenas 1; Ciclista Sebastian 1; Racing de Irun 1; Vizcaya Bilbao 1; Real Betis 1; Real Sociedad 1, La Coruna 1.

**Final League Table 1997–98**

| | P | W | D | L | F | A | Pts |
|---|---|---|---|---|---|---|---|
| Barcelona | 38 | 23 | 5 | 10 | 78 | 56 | 74 |
| Athletic Bilbao | 38 | 17 | 14 | 7 | 52 | 42 | 65 |
| Real Sociedad | 38 | 16 | 15 | 7 | 60 | 37 | 63 |
| Real Madrid | 38 | 17 | 12 | 9 | 63 | 45 | 63 |
| Atletico Madrid | 38 | 16 | 12 | 10 | 79 | 56 | 60 |
| Mallorca | 38 | 16 | 12 | 10 | 55 | 39 | 60 |
| Celta | 38 | 17 | 9 | 12 | 54 | 47 | 60 |
| Betis | 38 | 17 | 8 | 13 | 49 | 50 | 59 |
| Valencia | 38 | 16 | 7 | 15 | 58 | 52 | 55 |
| Espanyol | 38 | 12 | 17 | 9 | 44 | 31 | 53 |
| Valladolid | 38 | 13 | 11 | 14 | 36 | 47 | 50 |
| La Coruna | 38 | 12 | 13 | 13 | 44 | 46 | 49 |
| Zaragoza | 38 | 12 | 12 | 14 | 45 | 53 | 48 |
| Salamanca | 38 | 12 | 9 | 17 | 46 | 46 | 45 |
| Santander | 38 | 12 | 9 | 17 | 46 | 55 | 45 |
| Tenerife | 38 | 11 | 12 | 15 | 44 | 57 | 45 |
| Compostela+ | 38 | 11 | 11 | 16 | 56 | 66 | 44 |
| Oviedo+ | 38 | 9 | 13 | 16 | 36 | 51 | 40 |
| Merida* | 38 | 9 | 12 | 17 | 33 | 53 | 39 |
| Sporting Gijon* | 38 | 2 | 7 | 29 | 31 | 80 | 13 |

*Top scorer:* Vieri (Atletico Madrid) 24.
*Cup Final:* Barcelona 1, Mallorca 1.
*Barcelona won 5-4 on penalties.*

## SWEDEN

Svenska Fotbollfoerbundet, Box 1216, S-17123 Solna.
*Founded:* 1904; *Number of Clubs:* 3,250; *Number of Players:* 485,000; *National Colours:* Yellow shirts, blue shorts, yellow stockings.
*Telephone:* 0046 8 735 09 00; *Cable:* FOOTBALL-S; *Fax:* 0046 8 27 51 47.

**League Championship wins (1896–1997)**
IFK Gothenburg 18; Oergryte IS Gothenburg 14; Malmo FF 14; IFK Norrköping 11; AIK Stockholm 9; Djurgaarden 8; GAIS Gothenburg 6; IF Helsingborg 5; Boras IF Elfsborg 4; Oster Vaxjo 4; Halmstad 3; Atvidaberg 2; IFK Ekilstune 1; IF Gavic Brynas 1; IF Gothenburg 1; Fassbergs 1; Norrköping IK Sleipner 1.

**Cup wins (1941–97)**
Malmo FF 13; IFK Norrköping 6; AIK Stockholm 6; IFK Gothenburg 4; Atvidaberg 2; Kalmar 2; Helsingborg 2; GAIS Gothenburg 1; IF Raa 1; Landskrona 1; Oster Vaxjo 1; Djurgaarden 1; Degerfors 1, Halmstad 1.

**Final League Table 1997**

| | P | W | D | L | F | A | Pts |
|---|---|---|---|---|---|---|---|
| Halmstad | 26 | 17 | 1 | 8 | 50 | 28 | 52 |
| IFK Gothenburg | 26 | 14 | 7 | 5 | 50 | 32 | 49 |
| Malmo | 26 | 12 | 10 | 4 | 48 | 28 | 46 |
| Orebro | 26 | 13 | 7 | 6 | 44 | 35 | 46 |
| Orgryte | 26 | 12 | 7 | 7 | 33 | 28 | 43 |
| Helsingborg | 26 | 10 | 11 | 5 | 40 | 28 | 41 |
| Elfsborg | 26 | 12 | 5 | 9 | 45 | 35 | 41 |
| AIK | 26 | 9 | 10 | 7 | 38 | 26 | 37 |
| Norrköping | 26 | 7 | 7 | 12 | 26 | 35 | 28 |
| Trelleborg | 26 | 8 | 4 | 14 | 32 | 48 | 28 |
| Osters | 26 | 4 | 11 | 11 | 28 | 44 | 23 |
| Vasteras | 26 | 6 | 5 | 15 | 26 | 49 | 23 |
| Degerfors* | 26 | 4 | 8 | 14 | 29 | 47 | 20 |
| Ljunskile* | 26 | 5 | 5 | 16 | 31 | 57 | 20 |

*Top scorers:* Mattiasson (Elfsborg) 14, Lilenberg (Halmstad) 14, Sahlin (Orebro) 14.
*Cup Final:* Helsingborg 1, 1, Orgryte 1, 1.
*Helsingborg won 3-0 on penalties.*

## SWITZERLAND

Schweizerisher Fussballverband, Postfach 3000 Berne 15.
*Founded:* 1895; *Number of Clubs:* 1,473; *Number of Players:* 185,286; *National Colours:* Red shirts, white shorts, red stockings.
*Telephone:* 0041 31 950 81 11; *Cable:* SWISSFOOT BERNE; *Fax:* 0041 31 950 81 81.

**League Championship wins (1898–1998)**
Grasshoppers 24; Servette 16; Young Boys Berne 11; FC Zurich 9; FC Basle 8; Lausanne 7; La Chaux-de-Fonds 3;

FC Lugano 3; Winterthur 3; FX Aarau 3; Neuchatel Xamax 3; Sion 2; FC Anglo-American 1; St Gallen 1; FC Brühl 1; Cantonal-Neuchatel 1; Biel 1; Bellinzona 1; FC Etoile Le Chaux-de-Fonds 1; Lucerne 1.

**Cup wins (1926–98)**

Grasshoppers 18; FC Sion 9; Lausanne 8; La Chaux-de-Fonds 6; Young Boys Berne 6; Servette 6; FC Basle 5; FC Zurich 5; Lucerne 2; FC Lugano 2; FC Granges 1; St Gallen 1; Urania Geneva 1; Young Fellows Zurich 1; Aarau 1.

**Qualifying Table 1997–98**

|  | P | W | D | L | F | A | Pts |
|---|---|---|---|---|---|---|---|
| Grasshoppers | 22 | 14 | 4 | 4 | 59 | 23 | 46 |
| Lausanne | 22 | 12 | 6 | 4 | 45 | 27 | 42 |
| Servette | 22 | 11 | 6 | 5 | 45 | 33 | 39 |
| Aarau | 22 | 10 | 5 | 7 | 38 | 31 | 35 |
| St Gallen | 22 | 7 | 9 | 6 | 38 | 34 | 30 |
| Zurich | 22 | 7 | 9 | 6 | 31 | 28 | 30 |
| Sion | 22 | 7 | 9 | 6 | 30 | 27 | 30 |
| Lucerne | 22 | 7 | 8 | 7 | 26 | 28 | 29 |
| Neuchatel Xamax | 22 | 7 | 5 | 10 | 37 | 39 | 26 |
| Kriens | 22 | 5 | 7 | 10 | 23 | 41 | 22 |
| Basle* | 22 | 5 | 4 | 13 | 28 | 46 | 19 |
| Etoile Carouge* | 22 | 1 | 6 | 15 | 20 | 63 | 9 |

*Top scorer:* Moldovan (Grasshoppers) 16.

**Final Table 1997–98**

|  | P | W | D | L | F | A | Pts |
|---|---|---|---|---|---|---|---|
| Grasshoppers | 14 | 11 | 1 | 2 | 39 | 16 | 57 |
| Servette | 14 | 5 | 6 | 3 | 18 | 15 | 41 |
| Lausanne | 14 | 5 | 4 | 5 | 17 | 17 | 40 |
| Zurich | 14 | 6 | 5 | 3 | 27 | 17 | 38 |
| Sion | 14 | 6 | 4 | 4 | 23 | 21 | 37 |
| St Gallen | 14 | 4 | 5 | 5 | 12 | 17 | 32 |
| Aarau | 14 | 1 | 4 | 9 | 13 | 27 | 25 |
| Lucerne | 14 | 1 | 5 | 8 | 10 | 29 | 23 |

*Teams take half points from qualifying table.*
*Top scorer:* Nonda (Zurich) 24.

**Promotion/Relegation Table 1997–98**

|  | P | W | D | L | F | A | Pts |
|---|---|---|---|---|---|---|---|
| Neuchatel Xamax | 14 | 7 | 5 | 2 | 35 | 22 | 26 |
| Lugano | 14 | 6 | 5 | 3 | 15 | 12 | 23 |
| Basle | 14 | 6 | 4 | 4 | 27 | 22 | 22 |
| Young Boys Berne | 14 | 6 | 4 | 4 | 20 | 23 | 22 |
| Soleure | 14 | 6 | 3 | 5 | 17 | 15 | 21 |
| Kriens* | 14 | 4 | 4 | 6 | 19 | 25 | 16 |
| Baden | 14 | 3 | 3 | 8 | 15 | 23 | 12 |
| Etoile Carouge* | 14 | 3 | 2 | 9 | 13 | 19 | 11 |

*Top scorer:* Maslov (Neuchatel Xamax) 11.
*Cup Final:* Lausanne 2, St Gallen 2.
*Lausanne won 4-3 on penalty kicks.*

## TURKEY

Turkiye Futbol Federasyonu, Konaklar Mah. Ihlamurlu Sok. 9, 80620 4 Levent, Istanbul.
*Founded:* 1923; *Number of Clubs:* 230; *Number of Players:* 64,521; *National Colours:* White shirts, white shorts, red and white stockings.
*Telephone:* 0090 212 282 70 10; *Cable:* ISTANBUL FUTBOL SPOR; *Telex:* 46308 btff tr; *Fax:* 0090 212 282 70 15.

**League Championship wins (1960–98)**

Fenerbahce 13; Galatasaray 12; Besiktas 10; Trabzonspor 6.

**Cup wins (1963–98)**

Galatasaray 11; Besiktas 6; Trabzonspor 5; Fenerbahce 4; Goztepe Izmir 2; Altay Izmir 2; Ankaragucu 2; Eskisehirspor 1; Bursapor 1; Genclerbirligi 1; Sakaryaspor 1; Kocaeli 1.

**Final League Table 1997–98**

|  | P | W | D | L | F | A | Pts |
|---|---|---|---|---|---|---|---|
| Galatasaray | 34 | 23 | 6 | 5 | 86 | 43 | 75 |
| Fenerbahce | 34 | 21 | 8 | 5 | 61 | 25 | 71 |
| Trabzonspor | 34 | 19 | 9 | 6 | 68 | 42 | 66 |
| Istanbul | 34 | 14 | 12 | 8 | 60 | 42 | 54 |
| Samsun | 34 | 14 | 7 | 13 | 42 | 42 | 49 |
| Besiktas | 34 | 13 | 9 | 12 | 56 | 41 | 48 |
| Altay | 34 | 12 | 11 | 11 | 45 | 52 | 47 |
| Bursa | 34 | 12 | 9 | 13 | 46 | 50 | 45 |
| Karabuk | 34 | 13 | 5 | 16 | 34 | 50 | 44 |
| Kocaeli | 34 | 12 | 7 | 15 | 46 | 46 | 43 |
| Dardanel | 34 | 10 | 11 | 13 | 37 | 40 | 41 |
| Antalya | 34 | 10 | 11 | 13 | 51 | 55 | 41 |
| Ankaragucu | 34 | 11 | 8 | 15 | 40 | 47 | 41 |
| Genclerbirligi | 34 | 9 | 11 | 14 | 42 | 46 | 38 |
| Gaziantep | 34 | 9 | 11 | 14 | 39 | 44 | 38 |
| Kayseri* | 34 | 11 | 5 | 18 | 42 | 60 | 38 |
| Seker* | 34 | 9 | 9 | 16 | 41 | 67 | 36 |
| Van* | 34 | 5 | 9 | 20 | 26 | 70 | 24 |

*Top scorer:* Hakan Sukur (Galatasaray) 32.
*Cup Final:* Besiktas 1, 1, Galatasaray 1, 1.
*Besiktas won 4-2 on penalties after the replay.*

## UKRAINE

Football Federation of Ukraine, Ulianovyh Street 1, P.O. Box 503, 252150 Kiev, Ukraine.
*Founded:* 1991; *Number of Clubs:* 1500; *Number of Players:*759,500; *National Colours:* Yellow and blue shirts, blue shorts, yellow stockings.
*Telephone:* 0070 44 264 72 98; *Fax:* 0070 44 264 75 64; *Telex:* 631461 uff ux.

**League Championship wins (1992–98)**

Dynamo Kiev 5; Tavria Simferopol 1.

**Cup wins (1992–98)**

Dynamo Kiev 3; Chernomorets 2; Shakhtjor Donetsk 2.

**Final League Table 1997–98**

|  | P | W | D | L | F | A | Pts |
|---|---|---|---|---|---|---|---|
| Dynamo Kiev | 30 | 23 | 3 | 4 | 70 | 15 | 72 |
| Karpaty | 30 | 16 | 9 | 5 | 36 | 20 | 57 |
| Dnepr | 30 | 17 | 4 | 9 | 47 | 27 | 55 |
| Vorskla | 30 | 15 | 4 | 11 | 41 | 46 | 49 |
| Ternopol | 30 | 12 | 4 | 14 | 37 | 39 | 40 |
| Metallurg Donetsk | 30 | 11 | 7 | 12 | 27 | 27 | 40 |
| Krivoj | 30 | 10 | 9 | 11 | 34 | 33 | 39 |
| Metallurg Zapor | 30 | 10 | 7 | 13 | 40 | 44 | 37 |
| CSKA | 30 | 9 | 6 | 15 | 30 | 35 | 33 |
| Simferopol | 30 | 8 | 9 | 13 | 35 | 41 | 33 |
| Prekarpate | 30 | 8 | 9 | 13 | 33 | 41 | 33 |
| Kirovograd | 30 | 9 | 6 | 15 | 27 | 48 | 33 |
| Mettallurg Mariupol | 30 | 8 | 9 | 13 | 27 | 48 | 33 |
| Chernomorets* | 30 | 8 | 8 | 14 | 31 | 40 | 32 |
| Torpedo* | 30 | 2 | 7 | 21 | 20 | 69 | 13 |

*Top scorer:* Rebrov (Dynamo Kiev) 22.
*Cup Final:* Dynamo Kiev 2, CSKA 1.

## WALES

The Football Association of Wales Limited, Plymouth Chambers, 3 Westgate Street, Cardiff, South Glamorgan CF1 1DD.
*Founded:* 1876; *Number of Clubs:* 2,326; *Number of Players:* 53,926; *National Colours:* All red.
*Telephone:* 01222 372325; *Telex:* 497 363 faw g; *Cable:* WELSOCCER CARDIFF; *Fax:* 01222 343961.

## YUGOSLAVIA

Yugoslav Football Association, P.O. Box 263, Terazije 35, 11000 Beograd.
*Founded:* 1919; *Number of Clubs:* 6,532; *Number of Players:* 229,024; *National Colours:* Blue shirts, white shorts, red stockings.
*Telephone:* 00381 11 323 3447; *Cable:* JUGOFUDBAL BEOGRAD; *Telex:* 11666 fsj yu; *Fax:* 00381 11 323 3433.

**League Championship wins (1923–98)**

Red Star Belgrade 20; Partizan Belgrade 15; Hajduk Split 9; Gradjanski Zagreb 5; BSK Belgrade 5; Dynamo Zagreb 4; Jugoslavija Belgrade 2; Concordia Zagreb 2;

FC Sarajevo 2; Vojvodina Novi Sad 2; HASK Zagreb 1; Zeljeznicar 1; Obilic 1.

**Cup wins (1947–98)**
Red Star Belgrade 16; Hajduk Split 9; Dynamo Zagreb 8; Partizan Belgrade 8; BSK Belgrade 2; OFK Belgrade 2; Rijeka 2; Velez Mostar 2; Vardar Skopje 1; Borac Banjaluka 1.

**Final League Table 1997–98**
Group A

|  | P | W | D | L | F | A | Pts |
|---|---|---|---|---|---|---|---|
| Obilic | 33 | 27 | 5 | 1 | 72 | 19 | 86 |
| Red Star Belgrade | 33 | 27 | 3 | 3 | 86 | 22 | 84 |
| Partizan Belgrade | 33 | 22 | 4 | 7 | 73 | 38 | 70 |
| Vojvodina | 33 | 14 | 7 | 12 | 57 | 63 | 49 |
| Rad | 33 | 12 | 6 | 15 | 35 | 39 | 42 |
| Zemun | 33 | 10 | 9 | 14 | 38 | 50 | 39 |
| Hajduk | 33 | 10 | 5 | 18 | 32 | 51 | 35 |
| Buducnost | 33 | 8 | 9 | 16 | 27 | 53 | 33 |
| Zeleznik | 33 | 9 | 5 | 19 | 43 | 62 | 32 |
| Proleter | 33 | 10 | 2 | 21 | 40 | 64 | 32 |
| Cukaricki+ | 33 | 9 | 4 | 20 | 32 | 45 | 31 |
| Mladost L* | 33 | 9 | 3 | 21 | 25 | 54 | 30 |

Group B

|  | P | W | D | L | F | A | Pts |
|---|---|---|---|---|---|---|---|
| OFK Belgrade | 33 | 19 | 8 | 6 | 61 | 34 | 65 |
| Sartid 1913 | 33 | 19 | 6 | 8 | 45 | 23 | 63 |
| Pristina | 33 | 17 | 9 | 7 | 57 | 28 | 60 |
| Spartak | 33 | 17 | 5 | 11 | 59 | 42 | 56 |
| Radnicki Nis | 33 | 14 | 12 | 7 | 46 | 33 | 54 |
| Radnicki Kragujevac+ | 33 | 16 | 5 | 12 | 52 | 46 | 53 |
| Buducnost V | 33 | 13 | 6 | 14 | 43 | 52 | 45 |
| Rudar | 33 | 13 | 4 | 16 | 42 | 51 | 43 |
| Sutjeska | 33 | 8 | 8 | 17 | 34 | 43 | 32 |
| Loznica | 33 | 7 | 7 | 19 | 24 | 46 | 28 |
| Borac | 33 | 7 | 7 | 19 | 32 | 65 | 28 |
| Becej | 33 | 8 | 3 | 22 | 22 | 54 | 27 |

*For 1998-99 the top ten in Group A and the top five in Group B will play in a Premier Division.*
*Top scorer: Markovic (Red Star Belgrade) 27.*
*Cup Final: Obilic 0, 0, Partizan Belgrade 0, 2*

# SOUTH AMERICA

## ARGENTINA

Asociacion Del Futbol Argentina, Viamonte 1366/76, 1053 Buenos Aires.
*Founded:* 1893; *Number of Clubs:* 3,035; *Number of Players:* 306,365; *National Colours:* Light blue & white striped shirts, black shorts, white stockings.
*Telephone:* 00541 371 4276; *Cable:* FUTBOL BUENOS AIRES; *Telex:* 17848 AFA AR; *Fax:* 00541 375 4410.

## BOLIVIA

Federacion Boliviana De Futbol, Av. Libertador Bolivar No. 1168, Casilla de Correo 484, Cochabamba, Bolivia.
*Founded:* 1925; *Number of Clubs:* 305; *Number of Players:* 15,290; *National Colours:* Green shirts with white borders, white shorts with green borders, green stockings.
*Telephone:* 0059142 44982; *Cable:* FEDFUTBOL COCHABAMBA; *Telex:* 6239 FEDBOL; *Fax:* 0059142 82132.

## BRAZIL

Confederacao Brasileira De Futebol, Rua Da Alfandega, 70, P.O. Box 1078, 20.070 Rio De Janeiro.
*Founded:* 1914; *Number of Clubs:* 12,987; *Number of Players:* 551,358; *National Colours:* Yellow shirts with green collar/cuffs, blue shorts, white stockings with green-yellow border.
*Telephone:* 005521 509 5937; *Cable:* DESPORTOS RIO DE JANEIRO; *Telex:* 21509 CBDS BR; *Fax:* 005521 252 9294.

## CHILE

Federacion De Futbol De Chile, Avda. Quillin No. 5635, Casilla postal 3733, Correo Central, Santiago de Chile.
*Founded:* 1895; *Number of Clubs:* 4,598; *Number of Players:* 609,724; *National Colours:* Red shirts with white collar & cuffs, blue shorts, white stockings.
*Telephone:* 00562 2849000; *Cable:* FEDFUTBOL SANTIAGO DE CHILE; *Fax:* 00562 2843510.

## COLOMBIA

Federacion Colombiana De Futbol, Avenida 32, No. 16-22 piso 40. Apartado Aereo 17602, Santafe de Bogota.
*Founded:* 1924; *Number of Clubs:* 3,685; *Number of Players:* 188,050; *National Colours:* White shirts with tricolour borders, blue shorts, Red stockings with tricolour borders.
*Telephone:* 00571 2853320; *Cable:* COLFUTBOL BOGOTA; *Fax:* 00571 2854340.

## ECUADOR

Federacion Ecuatoriana De Futbol, Calle Jose Mascote 1.103 (Piso 2), Luque, Casilla 7447, Guayaquil.
*Founded:* 1925; *Number of Clubs:* 170; *Number of Players:* 15,700; *National Colours:* Yellow shirts with blue and red fringes, blue shorts, red stockings.
*Telephone:* 005934 371674; *Cable:* ECUAFUTBOL GUAYAQUIL; *Fax:* 005934 515341.

## PARAGUAY

Liga Paraguaya De Futbol, Estadio De Sajonia, Calles Mayor Martinez Y Alejo Garcia, Asuncion.
*Founded:* 1906; *Number of Clubs:* 1,500; *Number of Players:* 140,000; *National Colours:* Red & white shirts, blue shorts, blue stockings.
*Telephone:* 0059521 480120; *Telex:* 38009 PY FUTBOL; *Fax:* 0059521 480124.

## PERU

Federacion Peruana De Futbol, Av. Aviacion Cdra. 20 s/n, San Luis, Lima.
*Founded:* 1922; *Number of Clubs:* 10,000; *Number of Players:* 325,650; *National Colours:* White shirts with red stripe, white shorts with red lines, white stockings with red line.
*Telephone:* 005114 2258236-9; *Cable* FEPEFUTBOL LIMA; *Fax:* 005114 2258240; *Telex:* 20066 FEPEFUT PE.

## URUGUAY

Asociacion Uruguaya De Futbol, Guayabo 1531, 11200 Montevideo.
*Founded:* 1900; *Number of Clubs:* 1,091; *Number of Players:* 134,310; *National Colours:* Sky blue shirts with white collar/cuffs, black shorts, black stockings with sky blue borders.
*Telephone:* 005982 4007101/06; *Cable:* FOOTBALL MONTEVIDEO; *Fax:* 005982 4007873; *Telex:* AUF UY 22607.

## VENEZUELA

Federacion Venezolana De Futbol, Avda S. Erminy, Torre Mega II Pent House B, e/Sabana Gr. y la Solano, Parroquia el Recreo, Caracas.
*Founded:* 1926; *Number of Clubs:* 1,753; *Number of Players:* 63,175; *National Colours:* Dark red shirts, white shorts, white stockings with black border.
*Telephone:* 00582 7620362; *Cable:* FEVEFUTBOL CARACAS; *Telex:* 26140 FVFCS VC; *Fax:* 00582 7620596.

# ASIA

## AFGHANISTAN

The Football Federation of National Olympic Committee, Kabul.
*Founded:* 1933; *Number of Clubs:* 30; *Number of Players:* 3,300; *National Colours:* All white with red lines.
*Telephone:* 0093 11420579; *Cable:* OLYMPIC KABUL.

## BAHRAIN

Bahrain Football Association, P.O. Box 5464, Manama.
*Founded:* 1957; *Number of Clubs:* 25; *Number of Players:* 2,030; *National Colours:* All red.
*Telephone:* 00973 252929; *Cable:* BAHKORA BAHRAIN; *Telex:* 9040 FAB BN; *Fax:* 00973 255560.

## BANGLADESH

Bangladesh Football Federation, National Stadium-1, Dhaka 1000.
*Founded:* 1972; *Number of Clubs:* 1,265; *Number of Players:* 30,385; *National Colours:* Orange shirts, white shorts, green stockings.
*Telephone:* 008802 9556072; *Cable:* FOOTBALFED DHAKA; *Fax:* 008802 9563419.

## BRUNEI

The Football Association of Brunei Darussalam, P.O. Box 2010, 1920 Bandar Seri Begawan.
*Founded:* 1959; *Number of Clubs:* 22; *Number of Players:* 830; *National Colours:* Yellow shirts, black shorts, yellow stockings.
*Telephone:* 006732 383883; *Cable:* BAFA BRUNEI; *Telex:* BU 2575 Attn: BAFA; *Fax:* 006732 382900.

## CAMBODIA

Cambodian Football Federation, PO Box 2327 PTT, Phnom-Penh 3.
*Founded:* 1933; *Number of Clubs:* 30; *Number of Players:* 650; *National Colours:* Blue, red and white shirts, white and blue shorts, red, white and blue stockings.
*Telephone:* 0085523 364889; *Cable:* CFF PHNOM PENH; *Fax:* 0088523 367191.

## CHINA PR

Football Association of The People's Republic of China, 9 Tiyuguan Road, Beijing 100763.
*Founded:* 1924; *Number of Clubs:* 1,045; *Number of Players:* 2,250,000; *National Colours:* All white.
*Telephone:* 008610 67117019; *Cable:* SPORTSCHINE BEIJING; *Telex:* 22034 ACSF CN; *Fax:* 008610 67142533.

## CHINA TAIPEI

Chinese Taipei Football Association, 100, Kuang-Fu South Road, Taipei, Taiwan.
*Founded:* 1936; *Number of Players:* 17,000; *National Colours:* Blue shirts, white shorts, red stockings.
*Telephone:* 008862 27117710; *Cable:* CTFA Taipei; *Fax:* 008862 27117713.

## GUAM

Guam Soccer Association, P.O.Box 5093, Agana, Guam 96932.
*Founded:* 1975; *National Colours:* Blue shirts, white shorts, blue stockings.
*Telephone:* 00671 4725523; *Fax:* 00671 4775424.

## HONG KONG

The Hong Kong Football Association Ltd, 55 Fat Kwong Street, Homantin, Kowloon, Hong Kong.
*Founded:* 1914; *Number of Clubs:* 69; *Number of Players:* 3,274; *National Colours:* All Red.
*Telephone:* 00852 27129122; *Cable:* FOOTBALL HONG KONG; *Telex:* 40518 FAHKG HX; *Fax:* 00852 27604303.

## INDIA

All India Football Federation , Mr KN Mour, Gen. Secretary, Youth Hostel Complex, Paltan Bazar, Guwahati - 781 008, Assam.
*Founded:* 1937; *Number of Clubs:* 2,000; *Number of Players:* 56,000; *National Colours:* Orange shirts, white shorts, green stockings.
*Telephone:* 0091361 525109; *Fax:* 0091 361525110.

## INDONESIA

All Indonesia Football Federation, Wisma Karsa Pemuda, Jl.Gerbang Pemuda No. 3, PO Box 2305, Jakarta 10023.
*Founded:* 1930; *Number of Clubs:* 2,880; *Number of Players:* 97,000; *National Colours:* Red shirts, white shorts, red and white stockings.
*Telephone:* 006221 5722948; *Cable:* PSSI JAKARTA; *Telex:* 65739 PSSI IA; *Fax:* 006221 5734386.

## IRAN

IR Iran Football Federation, Shahid Keshvari Sports Complex, Mirdamad Ave., Razan Jonoobi Str., PO Box 15875-6967 Tehran 15875.
*Founded:* 1920; *Number of Clubs:* 6,326; *Number of Players:* 306,000; *National Colours:* All white.
*Telephone:* 009821 2258116; *Cable:* FOOTBALL IRAN - TEHRAN; *Telex:* 212691 NOC IR; *Fax:* 009821 2258123.

## IRAQ

Iraqi Football Association, Olympic Committee Building, Palestine Street, PO Box 484, Baghdad.
*Founded:* 1948; *Number of Clubs:* 155; *Number of Players:* 4,400; *National Colours:* White shirts, green shorts, white stockings.
*Telephone:* 009641 7729990; *Cable:* BALL BAGHDAD; *Telex:* 213409 IRFA IK; *Fax:* 009641 7744475.

## JAPAN

Japan Football Association, 2nd Floor, Gotoh Ikueikai Bldg, 1-10-7 Dogenzaka, Shibuya-Ku, Tokyo 150, Japan.
*Founded:* 1921; *Number of Clubs:* 13,047; *Number of Players:* 358,989; *National Colours:* Blue shirts, white shorts, blue stockings.
*Telephone:* 00813 34762011; *Cable:* SOCCERJAPAN TOKYO; *Telex:* 2422975 FOTJPN J; *Fax:* 00813 34762291.

## JORDAN

Jordan Football Association, P.O. Box 1054, Amman.
*Founded:* 1949; *Number of Clubs:* 98; *Number of Players:* 4,305; *National Colours:* All white and red.
*Telephone:* 009626 825450; *Cable:* JORDAN FOOTBALL ASSN AMMAN; *Fax:* 009626 861530.

## KAZAKHSTAN

The Football Association of the Republic of Kazakhstan, 44 Abai Street, 480072 Almaty, Kazakhstan.
*Founded:* 1914; *Number of Clubs:* 5,793; *Number of Players:* 260,000.
*Telephone:* 0073272 671885; *Telex:* 251347 TREK SU; *Fax:* 0073272 671885.

## KOREA, NORTH

Football Association of The Democratic People's Rep. of Korea, Kumsong-dong 2, Mangyongdae Distr, Pyongyang.
*Founded:* 1945; *Number of Clubs:* 90; *Number of Players:* 3,420; *National Colours:* All white.
*Telephone:* 008502 814164; *Cable:* DPR KOREA FOOTBALL PYONGYANG; *Telex:* 5472 KP; *Fax:* 008502 814403.

## KOREA, SOUTH

Korea Football Association, 110-39, Kyeonji-Dong, Chongro-Ku, Seoul.
*Founded:* 1928; *Number of Clubs:* 476; *Number of Players:* 2,047; *National Colours:* Red shirts, black shorts, red stockings.
*Telephone:* 00822 7336764; *Cable:* FOOTBALLKOREA SEOUL; *Telex:* KFASEL K 25373; *Fax:* 00822 7352755.

## KUWAIT

Kuwait Football Association, P.O. Box 2029 Safat, 13021 Safat.
*Founded:* 1952; *Number of Clubs:* 14 (senior); *Number of Players:* 1,526; *National Colours:* Blue shirts, white shorts, blue stockings.
*Telephone:* 00965 2555851; *Cable:* FOOT KUWAIT; *Fax:* 00965 2549955.

## KYRGYZSTAN

Football Association of Kyrgyz Republic, Frunze Street, 503 Bishkek 720040, Kyrgyzstan.
*Founded:* 1992; *Number of Players:* 20,000; *National Colours:* Red shirts, white shorts, red stockings.
*Telephone:* 00331 2223507; *Fax:* 00331 2225492.

## LAOS

Federation Lao De Football, National Stadium, Vientiane.
*Founded:* 1951; *Number of Clubs:* 76; *Number of Players:* 2,060; *National Colours:* Red shirts, white shorts, blue stockings.
*Telephone:* 0085621 216008/9; *Cable:* FOOTBALL VIENTIANE; *Fax:* 0085621 216008.

## LEBANON

Federation Libanaise De Football-Association, P.O. Box 4732, Verdun Street, Radwan Centre Building, Beirut.
*Founded:* 1933; *Number of Clubs:* 105; *Number of Players:* 8,125; *National Colours:* Red shirts, white shorts, red stockings.
*Telephone:* 009611 347157; *Cable:* FOOTBALL BEIRUT; *Telex:* 21404 LIBALL; *Fax:* 009611 349529.

## MACAO

Associacao De Futebol De Macau (AFM), P.O. Box 920, Macau.
*Founded:* 1939; *Number of Clubs:* 52; *Number of Players:* 800; *National Colours:* Green shirts, black shorts, green stockings.
*Telephone:* 00853 71996; *Cable:* FOOTBALL MACAU; *Fax:* 00853 260148.

## MALAYSIA

Football Association of Malaysia, Wisma Fam, Tingkat 3, Jalan SS5A/9, Kelana Jaya, 47301 Petaling Jaya, Selangor.
*Founded:* 1933; *Number of Clubs:* 450; *Number of Players:* 11,250; *National Colours:* All yellow and black.
*Telephone:* 00603 7763766; *Cable:* FOOTB. PETALING JAYA SELANGO; *Telex:* FAM PJ MA 36701; *Fax:* 00603 7757984.

## MALDIVES REPUBLIC

Football Association of Maldives, National Stadium Ghalolhu, Male 20-04.
*Founded:* 1982; *Number of Clubs: Number of Players: National Colours:* Green shirts, white shorts, red stockings.
*Telephone:* 0096031 7006; *Fax:* 0096031 7005.

## MYANMAR

Myanmar Football Federation, Attn Maj. Naw Tawng, Gen. Secr. Youth Training Centre, Thuwunna, Yangon.
*Founded:* 1947; *Number of Clubs:* 600; *Number of Players:* 21,000; *National Colours:* Red shirts, white shorts, red stockings.
*Telephone:* 00951 577366; *Cable:* FOOTBALL YANGON; *Telex:* 21253 SPED BM; *Fax:* 00951 571253.

## NEPAL

All-Nepal Football Association, Dasharath Rangashala, Tripureshwor, PO Box 2090, Kathmandu.
*Founded:* 1951; *Number of Clubs:* 85; *Number of Players:* 2,550; *National Colours:* All red.
*Telephone:* 009771 241367; *Cable:* ANFA KATHMANDU; *Telex:* 2390 NSC NP; *Fax:* 009771 241365.

## OMAN

Oman Football Association, P.O. Box 3462, Ruwi Postal Code 112.
*Founded:* 1978; *Number of Clubs:* 47; *Number of Players:* 2,340; *National Colours:* Red shirts with white sleeves, red/white shorts and stockings.
*Telephone:* 00968 787638/9; *Cable:* FOOTBALL MUSCAT; *Telex:* FOOTBALL 3223 ON; *Fax:* 00968 787632/33.

## PAKISTAN

Pakistan Football Federation, 183, Abu Bakar Block, New Garden Town, Lahore, Pakistan.
*Founded:* 1948; *Number of Clubs:* 882; *Number of Players:* 21,000; *National Colours:* Green shirts, white shorts, green stockings.
*Telephone:* 009242 5832786; *Cable:* FOOTBALL LAHORE; *Telex:* 47643 PFF PK; *Fax:* 009242 7281541.

## PALESTINE

Palestinian Football Federation, Al-Yarmouk, Gaza.
*Telephone:* 009727 829433; *Fax:* 009727 825208.

## PHILIPPINES

Philippine Football Federation, Room 207 PSC, Administration Building, Rizal Memorial Sports Complex, P. Ocampo Street, Manila.
*Founded:* 1907; *Number of Clubs:* 650; *Number of Players:* 45,000; *National Colours:* Blue and red shirts, blue shorts, white stockings.
*Telephone:* 00632 5256502; *Cable:* FOOTBALL MANILA; *Telex:* 65014 POC PACA PN; *Fax:* 00632 5235909.

## QATAR

Qatar Football Association, P.O. Box 5333, Doha.
*Founded:* 1960; *Number of Clubs:* 8 (senior); *Number of Players:* 1,380; *National Colours:* All white.
*Telephone:* 00974 434455; *Cable:* FOOTQATAR DOHA; *Telex:* 4749 QATFOT DH; *Fax:* 00974 411660.

## SAUDI ARABIA

Saudi Arabian Football Federation, Al Mather Quarter (Olympic Complex), P.O. Box 5844, Riyadh 11432.
*Founded:* 1959; *Number of Clubs:* 120; *Number of*

*Players:* 9,600; *National Colours:* White shirts, green shorts, white stockings.
*Telephone:* 009661 4822240; *Cable:* KURA RIYADH; *Telex:* 404300 SAFOTB SJ; *Fax:* 009661 4821215.

### SINGAPORE

Football Association of Singapore, Jalan Besar Stadium, Tyrwhitt Road, Singapore 207542.
*Founded:* 1892; *Number of Clubs:* 250; *Number of Players:* 8,000; *National Colours:* All red.
*Telephone:* 0065 2931477; *Fax:* 0065 2933728.

### SRI LANKA

Football Federation of Sri Lanka, No. 2, Old Grand Stand, Race Course, Reid Avenue, Colombo 7.
*Founded:* 1939; *Number of Clubs:* 600; *Number of Players:* 18,825; *National Colours:* Maroon and gold shirts, white shorts and stockings.
*Telephone:* 00941 696179; *Cable:* SOCCER COLOMBO; *Telex:* 21537 METALIX CE; *Fax:* 00941 682471.

### SYRIA

Syrian Football Federation, Maysaloon St., PO Box 421, Damascus.
*Founded:* 1936; *Number of Clubs:* 102; *Number of Players:* 30,600; *National Colours:* All white.
*Telephone:* 0096311 3335866; *Cable:* FOOTBALL DAMASCUS; *Telex:* 411578 SPOFED SY; *Fax:* 0096311 3331511.

### TAJIKISTAN

Tajikistan National Football Federation, 44, Rudaki Ave., PO Box 26, 734025 Dushanbe, Tajikistan.
*Founded:* 1991; *Number of Clubs:* 1,804; *Number of Players:* 71,400; *National Colours:* Green shirts, white shorts, green stockings.
*Telephone:* 0073772 212363; *Telex:* 116286 SHAKH; *Fax:* 0073772 212447.

### THAILAND

The Football Association of Thailand, National Stadium, Rama I Road, Bangkok.
*Founded:* 1916; *Number of Clubs:* 168; *Number of Players:* 15,000; *National Colours:* All red.
*Telephone:* 00662 2141058; *Cable:* FOOTBALL BANGKOK; *Telex:* 20211 FAT TH; *Fax:* 00662 2154494.

### TURKMENISTAN

Turkmenistan Football Federation, 10 Turkmenbashi Avenue, 744005 Ashgabat, Turkmenistan.
*Founded:* 1992; *Number of Players:* 75,000; *National Colours:* Green shirts, white shorts, green stockings.
*Telephone:* 00363 2353739; *Fax:* 00363 2355327; *Telex:* 116175 TINTO SU.

### UNITED ARAB EMIRATES

United Arab Emirates Football Association, P.O. Box 916, Abu Dhabi.
*Founded:* 1971; *Number of Clubs:* 23 (senior); *Number of Players:* 1,787; *National Colours:* All white.
*Telephone:* 00971 2445600; *Cable:* FOOTBALL EMIRATES ABU DHABI; *Telex:* 22121 UAEFA EM; *Fax:* 00971 2448558.

### UZBEKISTAN

Uzbekistan Football Federation, Massiv Almazar Furkat Street 15/1, 700003 Tashkent, Uzbekistan.
*Founded:* 1946; *Number of Clubs:* 15,000; *Number of Players:* 217,000; *National Colours:* Blue shirts, white shorts, green stockings.
*Telephone:* 0073712 457106; *Telex:* 116108 PTB SU; *Fax:* 0073712 454948.

### VIETNAM

Vietnam Football Federation, 141 Nguyen Thai Hoc Str., Dis Dongda, Hanoi.
*Founded:* 1962; *Number of Clubs:* 55 (senior); *Number of Players:* 16,000; *National Colours:* All red.
*Telephone:* 008448 452480; *Cable:* AFBVN, 141 NGUYEN THAI HOC STR.; *Fax:* 008448 233119.

### YEMEN

Yemen Football Association, P.O. Box 908, Sana'a.
*Founded:* 1962; *Number of Clubs:* 26; *Number of Players:* 1750; *National Colours:* All green.
*Telephone:* 009671 264159. *Cable:* SANA'A FOOTBALL; *Telex:* 2710 YOUTH YE; *Fax:* 009671 263182.

## CONCACAF

### ANGUILLA

Anguilla Football Association, att. Lord Bletchley, General Secretary, 338 Bletchley Manor, The Valley, Anguilla.
*National Colours:* All blue.
*Telephone:* 001264 4975887; *Fax:* 001264 4975889.

### ANTIGUA & BARBUDA

The Antigua Football Association, P.O. Box 773, St. John's.
*Founded:* 1928; *Number of Clubs:* 60; *Number of Players:* 1,008; *National Colours:* Gold shirts, black shorts and stockings.
*Telephone:* 001809 4624863; *Cable:* AFA ANTIGUA; *Fax:* 001809 4624864.

### ARUBA

Arubaanse Voetbal Bond, PO Box 376, Oranjestad, Aruba.
*Founded:* 1932; *Number of Clubs:* 50; *Number of Players:* 1,000; *National Colours:* Yellow shirts, blue shorts, yellow and blue stockings.
*Telephone:* 00297 829550; *Cable:* AVB ARUBA; *Fax:* 00297 820624.

### BAHAMAS

Bahamas Football Association, P.O. Box N 8434, Nassau, N.P.
*Founded:* 1967; *Number of Clubs:* 14; *Number of Players:* 700; *National Colours:* Yellow shirts, black shorts, yellow stockings.
*Telephone:* 001809 3233426; *Cable:* BAHSOCA NASSAU; *Fax:* 001809 3288006.

### BARBADOS

Barbados Football Association, No. 7, 7th Avenue, Belleville, St. Michael, Barbados, W.I.
*Founded:* 1910; *Number of Clubs:* 92; *Number of Players:* 1,100; *National Colours:* Royal blue and gold shirts, gold shorts, white, gold and blue stockings.
*Tel:* 001246 2281707; *Cable:* FOOTBALL BRIDGETOWN; *Fax:* 001246 2286484.

### BELIZE

Belize National Football Association, P.O. Box 1742, Belize City.
*Founded:* 1980; *National Colours:* Red, white and blue shirts and shorts, red stockings.
*Telephone:* 005012 44794; *Fax:* 005012 35838.

## BERMUDA

The Bermuda Football Association, P.O. Box HM 745, Hamilton HM CX.
*Founded:* 1928; *Number of Clubs:* 30; *Number of Players:* 1,947; *National Colours:* Royal blue shirts, white shorts and stockings.
*Telephone:* 001809 2952199; *Cable:* FOOTBALL BERMUDA; *Telex:* 3441 BFA BA; *Fax:* 001809 2950773.

## BRITISH VIRGIN ISLANDS

British Virgin Islands Football Association, P.O. Box 34, Road Town, Tortola, BVI.
*Telephone:* 001809 4943783; *Fax:* 001809 4942220.

## CANADA

The Canadian Soccer Association, Place Soccer Canada, 237 Metcalfe Street, Ottawa, ONT K2P 1R2.
*Founded:* 1912; *Number of Clubs:* 1,600; *Number of Players:* 224,290; *National Colours:* All red.
*Telephone:* 001613 2377678; *Cable:* SOCCANADA OTTAWA; *Fax:* 001613 2371516.

## CAYMAN ISLANDS

Cayman Islands Football Association, PO Box 178 GT, George Town, Grand Cayman, Cayman Islands W1.
*Founded:* 1966; *Number of Clubs:* 25; *Number of Players:* 875; *National Colours:* Red shirts, blue shorts, white stockings.
*Telephone:* 001345 9497822328. *Fax:* 001345 9496064.

## COSTA RICA

Federacion Costarricense De Futbol, Apartado 670-1000, Calle 40, Avda CTL & I, San Jose.
*Founded:* 1921; *Number of Clubs:* 431; *Number of Players:* 12,429; *National Colours:* Red and white shirts, blue shorts, white stockings.
*Telephone:* 00506 2221544; *Cable:* FEDEFUTBOL SAN JOSE; *Telex:* 3394 DIDER CR; *Fax:* 00506 2552674.

## CUBA

Federacion Cubana De Futbol, c/o Comite Olimpico Cubano, Calle 13 No. 601, Esq. C. Vedado, La Habana, ZP 4.
*Founded:* 1924; *Number of Clubs:* 70; *Number of Players:* 12,900; *National Colours:* White shirts with red collar & cuffs, dark blue shorts, white and red stockings.
*Telephone:* 00537 403581; *Cable:* FOOTBALL HABANA; *Telex:* 511332 INDER CU; *Fax:* 00537 409037.

## DOMINICA

Dominica Football Association, P.O. Box 372, Roseau, Commonwealth of Dominica.
*Founded:* 1970; *Number of Clubs:* 30; *Number of Players:* 500; *National Colours:* Emerald green shirts, green shorts, yellow stockings.
*Telephone & fax:* 001767 4492173.

## DOMINICAN REPUBLIC

Federacion Dominicana De Futbol, Apartado De Correos No. 1953, Santo Domingo.
*Founded:* 1953; *Number of Clubs:* 128; *Number of Players:* 10,706; *National Colours:* Navy blue shirts, white shorts, red stockings.
*Telephone:* 001809542 6923. *Cable:* FEDOFUTBOL SANTO DOMINGO; *Telex:* 817240; *Fax:* 001809547 5363.

## EL SALVADOR

Federacion Salvadorena De Futbol, Av. J.M. Delgado, Col. Escalon, Frente Ctro Espanol, Apartado 1029, San Salvador.
*Founded:* 1935; *Number of Clubs:* 944; *Number of Players:* 21,294; *National Colours:* Blue shirts, white shorts, blue stockings.
*Telephone:* 00503 2637525/6; *Cable:* FESFUT SAN SALVADOR; *Fax:* 00503 2637583.

## GRENADA

Grenada Football Association, P.O. Box 326, St. Juilles Street, St George's, Grenada, West Indies.
*Founded:* 1924; *Number of Clubs:* 15; *Number of Players:* 200; *National Colours:* Green & yellow striped shirts, red shorts, yellow stockings.
*Telephone & fax:* 001809 4401986; *Cable:* GRENBALL GRENADA; *Telex:* 3431 CW BUR.

## GUATEMALA

Federacion Nacional De Futbol De Guatemala, Avenida Reforma 1-90 Zona 9, 11 Nivel, Edificio Masval, 01009 Ciudad Guatemala, C.A.
*Founded:* 1946; *Number of Clubs:* 1,611; *Number of Players:* 43,516; *National Colours:* Blue shirts, white shorts, blue stockings.
*Telephone:* 005023 314797; *Cable:* FEDFUTBOL GUATEMALA C.A.; *Fax:* 005023 600188.

## GUYANA

Guyana Football Association, Lot 65 King Street, P.O. Box 10727 Georgetown.
*Founded:* 1902; *Number of Clubs:* 103; *Number of Players:* 1,665; *National Colours:* Green shirts and shorts, yellow stockings.
*Telephone & fax:* 005922 62641; *Telex:* 2266 RICEBRD GY.

## HAITI

Federation Haitienne De Football, P.O. Box 2258, Port-Au-Prince.
*Founded:* 1904; *Number of Clubs:* 40; *Number of Players:* 4,000; *National Colours:* Blue and red shirts, blue shorts, blue and red stockings.
*Telephone:* 00509 464509; *Cable:* FEDHAFOOB PORT-AU-PRINCE; *Fax:* 00509 573001.

## HONDURAS

Federacion Nacional Autonoma De Futbol De Honduras, Apartado Postal 827, Costa Oeste Del Est. Nac, Tegucigalpa, D. C.
*Founded:* 1951; *Number of Clubs:* 1,050; *Number of Players:* 15,300; *National Colours:* Blue shirts, white shorts, blue stockings.
*Telephone:* 00504 311432/6; *Cable* FENAFUTH TEGU-CIGALPA; *Fax:* 00504 311428.

## JAMAICA

Jamaica Football Federation, General Secretariat, Room 8, Nat. Arena, Institue of Sports, Independence Park, Kingston 6.
*Founded:* 1910; *Number of Clubs:* 266; *Number of Players:* 45,200; *National Colours:* Gold shirts, black shorts, gold stockings.
*Telephone:* 001809 9290484; *Cable:* FOOTBALL JAMAICA KINGSTON; *Telex:* 2224 FEDLASCO JA; *Fax:* 001809 9290483.

## MEXICO

Federacion Mexicana De Futbol Asociacion, A.C., Abraham Gonzales 74, Col. Juarez, C.P. 06600, Mexico 6, D.F.

*Founded:* 1927; *Number of Clubs:* 77 (senior); *Number of Players:* 1,402,270; *National Colours:* Green shirts with white collar, white shorts, red stockings.
*Telephone:* 00525 5662155; *Cable:* MEXFUTBOL MEXICO; *Fax:* 00525 5667580.

## MONSERRAT

Monserrat Football Association, P.O. Box 46, Church Road, Plymouth, Monserrat.
*Telephone:* 001664 4912346; *Fax:* 001664 4912719.

## NETHERLANDS ANTILLES

Nederlands Antiliaanse Voetbal Unie, P.O. Box 341, Curacao, N.A.
*Founded:* 1921; *Number of Clubs:* 85; *Number of Players:* 4,500; *National Colours:* white shirts with red and blue strips, white shorts, red, white and blue stockings.
*Telephone:* 005999 688748; *Cable:* NAVU CURACAO; *Telex:* 1046 ENNIA NA; *Fax:* 005999 61.

## NICARAGUA

Federacion Nicaraguense De Futbol, Estadio Futbol Camilo Ortega (Cranshaw), Apdo Postal 976, Managua.
*Founded:* 1931; *Number of Clubs:* 31; *Number of Players:* 160 (senior); *National Colours:* Blue and white striped shirts, blue shorts, blue and white striped stockings.
*Telephone:* 005052 680006/7/8; *Cable:* FENIFUT MANAGUA; *Fax:* 005052 664134.

## PANAMA

Federacion Panamena De Futbol, Apartado Postal 8-391, Zona 8, Panama.
*Founded:* 1937; *Number of Clubs:* 65; *Number of Players:* 4,225; *National Colours:* Red shirts, blue shorts, white stockings.
*Telephone & fax:* 00507 2282238.

## PUERTO RICO

Federacion Puertorriquena De Futbol, Coliseo Roberto Clemente, P.O. Box 1944355, Hato Rey, P.R. 00919-4355.
*Founded:* 1940; *Number of Clubs:* 175; *Number of Players:* 4,200; *National Colours:* Blue shirts, blue and white shorts and stockings.
*Telephone & fax:* 001787 7642025.

## SAINT LUCIA

St Lucia National Football Association, PO Box 255, Castries, St Lucia.
*Founded:* 1979; *Number of Clubs:* 100; *Number of*

*Players:* 4,000; *National Colours:* Blue and white shirts, black shorts, blue stockings.
*Telephone:* 001453 0689; *Cable:* NFU ST. LUCIA; *Telex:* 6394 FOR AFF LC; *Fax:* 001452 2506.

## SAINT KITTS & NEVIS

St Kitts and Nevis Amateur Football Association, P.O. Box 465, Basseterre, St Kitts, W.I.
*Founded:* 1932; *Number of Clubs:* 36; *Number of Players:* 600; *National Colours:* Green and yellow shirts, red shorts, yellow stockings.
*Telephone:* 001809 4652521; *Cable:* HORSFORD ST. KITTS; *Telex:* 6822 HORSFDSKB KC; *Fax:* 001809 4651042.

## SAINT VINCENT & THE GRENADINES

St Vincent & The Grenadines Football Federation, PO Box 1278, Kingstown, St Vincent, W.I.
*Founded:* 1979; *Number of Clubs:* 500; *Number of Players:* 5,000; *National Colours:* Green shirts with yellow border, blue shorts, yellow stockings.
*Telephone:* 001809 4561659; *Fax:* 001809 4571659.

## SURINAM

Surinaamse Voetbal Bond, Letitia Vriesde Laan 7, P.O. Box 1223, Paramaribo.
*Founded:* 1920; *Number of Clubs:* 168; *Number of Players:* 4,430; *National Colours:* Red green and white shirts, white or green shorts and stockings.
*Telephone:* 00597 473112; *Cable:* SVB Paramaribo; *Fax:* 00597 479718.

## TRINIDAD AND TOBAGO

Trinidad & Tobago Football Association, Petrotrin Savannah Building, 9 Queen's Park West, P.O. Box 400, Port of Spain.
*Founded:* 1908; *Number of Clubs:* 124; *Number of Players:* 5,050; *National Colours:* Red shirts, black shorts, white stockings.
*Telephone:* 001809 6271011; *Fax:* 001809 6271007.

## USA

US Soccer, Soccer House, 1801-1811 S. Prairie Avenue, Chicago, Illinois 60616.
*Founded:* 1913; *Number of Clubs:* 7,000; *Number of Players:* 1,411,500; *National Colours:* All white.
*Telephone:* 001312 8081300; *Telex:* 450024 US SOCCER FED; *Fax:* 001312 8081301.

# OCEANIA

## AUSTRALIA

Soccer Australia, Sydney Football Stadium, Driver Avenue, P.O. Box 175, Paddington NSW 2021.
*Founded:* 1961; *Number of Clubs:* 6,816; *Number of Players:* 433,957; *National Colours:* Gold shirts with green trim, gold shorts, gold and green stockings.
*Telephone:* 0061 293806099; *Cable:* FOOTBALL SYDNEY; *Fax:* 0061 293806155.

## COOK ISLANDS

Cook Islands Football Federation, P.O. Box 29, Avarua, Rarotonga, Cook Islands.
*Founded:* 1971; *Number of Clubs:* 9; *National Colours:* Green shirts and shorts with golden stripes, gold and green stockings.
*Telephone:* 00682 21231; *Fax:* 00682 25912.

## FIJI

Fiji Football Association, Bob S. Kumar, Hon. Secretary, Government Bldgs, P.O.Box 2514, Suva.
*Founded:* 1938; *Number of Clubs:* 140: *Number of Players:* 21,300; *National Colours:* White shirts, blue shorts and stockings.
*Telephone:* 00679 300453; *Fax:* 00679 304642.

## NEW ZEALAND

Soccer New Zealand, P.O. Box 11-357, Ellerslie, Auckland.
*Founded:* 1891; *Number of Clubs:* 312; *Number of Players:* 52,969; *National Colours:* White shirts with black trim, white shorts and stockings.
*Telephone:* 00649 5256120; *Fax:* 00649 5256123.

### PAPUA NEW GUINEA

Papua New Guinea Football (Soccer) Association, c/o National Sports Institute, P.O. Box 337, Goroka, EHP 441.
*Founded:* 1962; *Number of Clubs:* 350; *Number of Players:* 8,250; *National Colours:* Red shirts, black shorts, red stockings.
*Telephone:* 00675 7321699; *Telex:* TOTOTRA NE 23436; *Fax:* 00675 7321941.

### SOLOMAN ISLANDS

Soloman Islands Football Federation, PO Box 854, Honiara, Soloman Islands.
*Founded:* 1978; *Number of Players:* 4,000; *National Colours:* Green, yellow and blue shirts and shorts, white stockings.
*Telephone & fax:* 00677 26200; *Telex:* HQ 66349.

### TAHITI

Federation Tahitienne de Football (F.T.F.), B.P.50 358, Pirae, Tahiti, French Polynesia.
*Founded:* 1989; *National Colours:* White shirts, red shorts, white stockings.
*Telephone:* 00689 540954; *Cable:* FOOTBALL TAHITI; *Fax:* 00689 419629.

### TONGA

Tonga Football Association, att. General Secretary, TASA Office, P.O. Box 1278, Nuku'alofa, Kingdom of Tonga.
*Founded:* 1965; *Number of Clubs:* 23; *Number of Players:* 350; *National Colours:* Red shirts, white shorts, red and white stockings.
*Telephone:* 00676 24127; *Cable:* SOCCER NUKU'ALO-FA; *Fax:* 00676 21041.

### VANUATU

Vanuatu Football Federation, P.O. Box 226, Port Vila, Vanuatu.
*Founded:* 1934; *National Colours:* Gold and black shirts, black shorts, gold and black stockings.
*Telephone:* 00678 26873; *Cable:* FUTBOL BLONG VANUATU; *Fax:* 00678 27400.

### WESTERN SAMOA

Samoa Football (Soccer) Association, P.O. Box 960, Apia.
*Founded:* 1968; *National Colours:* Royal blue shirts, white shorts, royal blue and white stockings.
*Telephone:* 00685 22822; *Telex:* 233 TREASURY SX; *Fax:* 00685 21312.

# AFRICA

### ALGERIA

Federation Algerienne De Foot-ball, Chemin Ahmed Ouaked, Boite Postale No. 39, Dely-Ibrahim-Alger.
*Founded:* 1962; *Number of Clubs:* 780; *Number of Players:* 58,567; *National Colours:* Green shirts, white shorts, green stockings.
*Telephone:* 002132 365938; *Cable:* FAFOOT ALGER; *Telex:* 61378. *Fax:* 002132 365949.

### ANGOLA

Federation Angolaise De Football, Compl. da Cidadela Desportiva, B.P. 3449, Luanda.
*Founded:* 1979; *Number of Clubs:* 276; *Number of Players:* 4,269; *National Colours:* Red shirts, black shorts, red stockings.
*Telephone:* 002442 364948; *Cable:* FUTANGOLA; *Telex:* 2580 PALANCA AN; *Fax:* 002442 333147.

### BENIN

Federation Beninoise De Football, B.P. 965, Cotonou.
*Founded:* 1962; *Number of Clubs:* 117; *Number of Players:* 6,700; *National Colours:* Yellow shirts, green shorts, red stockings.
*Telephone:* 00229 330537; *Cable:* FEBEFOOT COTO-NOU; *Telex:* 5245 SONACOP COTONOU; *Fax:* 00229 312485.

### BOTSWANA

Botswana Football Association, P.O. Box 1396, Gabarone.
*Founded:* 1970; *National Colours:* Blue and white shirts, blue, white and black shorts, blue, white and black striped stockings.
*Telephone:* 00267 300279; *Cable:* BOTSBALL GABARONE; *Telex:* 2977 BD; *Fax:* 00267 300280.

### BURKINA FASO

Federation Burkinabe De Foot-Ball, 01 B.P. 57, Ouagadougou 01.
*Founded:* 1960; *Number of Clubs:* 57; *Number of Players:* 4,672; *National Colours:* Red shirts, green shorts with yellow star, red stockings.
*Telephone:* 00226 318815; *Cable:* FEDEFOOT OUA-GADOUGOU; *Fax:* 00226 318843.

### BURUNDI

Federation De Football Du Burundi, B.P. 3426, Bujumbura.
*Founded:* 1948; *Number of Clubs:* 132; *Number of Players:* 3,930; *National Colours:* Red shirts, white shorts, green stockings.
*Telephone & fax:* 00257 212891; *Cable:* FFB BUJA.

### CAMEROON

Federation Camerounaise De Football, B.P. 1116, Yaounde.
*Founded:* 1959; *Number of Clubs:* 200; *Number of Players:* 9,328; *National Colours:* Green shirts, red shorts, yellow stockings.
*Telephone:* 00237 232369; *Cable:* FECAFOOT YAOUNDE; *Telex:* 8568 JEUNESPO KN; *Fax:* 00237 222430, 234396.

### CAPE VERDE ISLANDS

Federacao Cabo-Verdiana De Futebol, P.O. Box 234, Praia.
*Founded:* 1982; *National Colours:* All green.
*Telephone & fax:* 00238 611362; *Cable:* FUTEBOL PRAIA CV; *Telex:* 6005 ACAS CV.

### CENTRAL AFRICAN REPUBLIC

Federation Centrafricaine De Football Amateur, B.P. 344, Bangui.
*Founded:* 1937; *Number of Clubs:* 256; *Number of Players:* 7,200; *National Colours:* Grey & blue shirts with Nat. emblem and star, white shorts, red stockings with yellow trim.
*Telephone:* 00236 612433; *Cable:* FOOTBANGUI BAN-GUI; *Fax:* 00236 611637.

## CHAD

Federation Tchadienne de Football, B.P. 886, N'Djamena.
*Founded:* 1962; *National Colours:* Blue shirts, yellow shorts, red stockings.
*Telephone:* 00235/519204; *Telex:* 5248 kd; *Fax:* 00235/519204.

## CONGO

Federation Congolaise De Football, B.P. 4041, Brazzaville.
*Founded:* 1962; *Number of Clubs:* 250; *Number of Players:* 5,940; *National Colours:* All red.
*Telephone:* 00242 834885; *Cable:* FECOFOOT BRAZ-ZAVILLE; *Telex:* 5210 KG; *Fax:* 00242 820582.

## CONGO DR

Federation Congolaise De Football-Association (FECO-FA), P.O. Box 1284, Av. De L'Enseignem. 210, Z/Kasa-Vubu, Kinshasa 1.
*Founded:* 1919; *Number of Clubs:* 3,800; *Number of Players:* 64,627; *National Colours:* Green shirts, yellow shorts, red stockings.
*Telephone & fax:* 001212 3769411; *Cable:* FECOFA KINSHASA.

## DJIBOUTI

Federation Djiboutienne de Football, B.P. 2694, Djibouti.
*Founded:* 1977; *Number of Players:* 2,000; *National Colours:* Green shirts, white shorts, blue stockings.
*Telephone:* 00253 342049; *Fax:* 00253 356793.

## EGYPT

Egyptian Football Association, 5, Shareh Gabalaya, Guezira, Al Borg Post Office, Cairo.
*Founded:* 1921; *Number of Clubs:* 247; *Number of Players:* 19,735; *National Colours:* Red shirts, white shorts, black stockings.
*Telephone:* 00202 3401793; *Cable:* KORA CAIRO; *Telex:* 93506 KORA UN; *Fax:* 00202 3417817.

## ETHIOPIA

Ethiopia Football Federation, Addis Ababa Stadium, P.O. Box 1080, Addis Ababa.
*Founded:* 1943; *Number of Clubs:* 767; *Number of Players:* 20,594; *National Colours:* Green shirts, yellow shorts, red stockings.
*Telephone:* 002511 514453; *Telex:* 21377 NESCO ET; *Fax:* 002511 513345.

## GABON

Federation Gabonaise De Football, B.P. 181, Libreville.
*Founded:* 1962; *Number of Clubs:* 320; *Number of Players:* 10,000; *National Colours:* Green, yellow and blue shirts, blue and yellow shorts, white stockings with tri-colour trims.
*Telephone:* 00241 730460; *Cable:* FEGAFOOT LIBRE-VILLE; *Telex:* 5526 GO; *Fax:* 00241 746047.

## GAMBIA

Gambia Football Association, Independence Stadium, Bakau, P.O. Box 523, Banjul.
*Founded:* 1952; *Number of Clubs:* 30; *Number of Players:* 860; *National Colours:* White shirts with striped band, white shorts, white stockings with red tops.
*Telephone:* 00220 496980; *Cable:* SPORTS GAMBIA BANJUL; *Telex:* 2262 FISCO GV; *Fax:* 00220 394962.

## GHANA

Ghana Football Association, P.O. Box 1272, Accra.
*Founded:* 1957; *Number of Clubs:* 347; *Number of Players:* 11,275; *National Colours:* All yellow.
*Telephone:* 0023321 666697; *Cable:* GFA ACCRA; *Telex:* 2519 SPORTS GH; *Fax:* 0023321 668590.

## GUINEA

Federation Guineenne De Football, P.O. Box 3645, Conakry.
*Founded:* 1959; *Number of Clubs:* 351; *Number of Players:* 10,000; *National Colours:* Red shirts, yellow shorts, green stockings.
*Telephone:* 00224 461159; *Cable:* GUINEFOOT CONAKRY; *Telex:* 22302 MJ GE; Fax: 00224 411926.

## GUINEA-BISSAU

Federacao De Football Da Guinea-Bissau, Rua 4 No. 10-C, Apartado 375, 1035 Bissau- Codex.
*Founded:* 1974; *National Colours:* All red..
*Telephone & fax:* 00245 201918; *Cable:* FUTEBOL BISSAU.

## GUINEA, EQUATORIAL

Federacion Ecuatoguineana De Futbol, Malabo.
*Founded:* 1986; *National Colours:* All red.
*Telephone:* 002409 2392; *Cable:* FEGUIFUT MALABO; *Telex:* 9991111 EG; *Fax:* 002409 3353.

## IVORY COAST

Federation Ivoirienne De Football, Av. 1 Treichville, 01 B.P. 1202, Abidjan 01.
*Founded:* 1960; *Number of Clubs:* 84 (senior); *Number of Players:* 3,655; *National Colours:* Orange shirts, white shorts, green stockings.
*Telephone:* 00225 242301; *Cable:* FIF ABIDJAN; *Telex:* 42344 FIF CI; *Fax:* 00225 257111.

## KENYA

Kenya Football Federation, Nyayo National Stadium, P.O. Box 40234, Nairobi.
*Founded:* 1960; *Number of Clubs:* 351; *Number of Players:* 8,880; *National Colours:* Red, green and white shirts, red, green and black shorts and stockings.
*Telephone:* 002542 501825/35; *Cable:* KEFF NAIROBI; *Telex:* 24069 SPICERS KE; *Fax:* 002542 501120.

## LESOTHO

Lesotho Football Association, P.O. Box 1879, Maseru-100, Lesotho.
*Founded:* 1932; *Number of Clubs:* 88; *Number of Players:* 2,076; *National Colours:* Blue shirts, green shorts, white stockings.
*Telephone:* 00266 311291; *Cable:* LEFA MASERU; *Telex:* 4493, 4228; *Fax:* 00266 310194.

## LIBERIA

Liberia Football Association, 110 Camp Johnson Road, P.O. Box 10-1066, 1000 Monrovia 10.
*Founded:* 1936; *National Colours:* Red shirts, white shorts, blue stockings.
*Telephone:* 00231 226284; *Cable:* LIBFOTASS MONROVIA; *Telex:* 44220 EXM IBR. *Fax:* 00231 225217.

## LIBYA

Libyan Arab Football Federation, 7th October Stadium, P.O. Box 5137, Tripoli.
*Founded:* 1963; *Number of Clubs:* 89; *Number of Players:* 2,941; *National Colours:* Green shirts, white shorts, green stockings.
*Telephone:* 0021821 333 0078/9; *Telex:* 20896 LY. *Fax:* 0021821 4446610.

## MADAGASCAR

Federation Malagasy De Football, P. O. Box 4409, Antananarivo 101.
*Founded:* 1961; *Number of Clubs:* 775; *Number of Players:* 23,536; *National Colours:* Red shirts, white shorts, green stockings.
*Telephone:* 0026120 2228433; *Telex:* 22265 AROSUR MG; *Fax:* 0026120 2234464.

## MALAWI

Football Association of Malawi, P.O. Box 865, Blantyre.
*Founded:* 1966; *Number of Clubs:* 465; *Number of Players:* 12,500; *National Colours:* Red shirts, red and green shorts, green stockings.
*Telephone & fax:* 00265 674290; *Cable:* FOOTBALL BLANTYRE; *Telex:* 4526 SPORTS MI.

## MALI

Federation Malienne De Football, Stade Mamdou Konate, B.P. 1020, Bamako.
*Founded:* 1960; *Number of Clubs:* 128; *Number of Players:* 5,480; *National Colours:* Green shirts, yellow shorts, red stockings.
*Telephone:* 00223 224254; *Cable:* MALIFOOT BAMAKO; Telex: 0985 1200 MJ; *Fax:* 00356 245136.

## MAURITANIA

Federation De Foot-Ball De La Rep. Islamique. De Mauritanie, B.P. 566, Nouakchott.
*Founded:* 1961; *Number of Clubs:* 59; *Number of Players:* 1,930; *National Colours:* Green and yellow shirts, yellow shorts, green stockings.
*Telephone & fax:* 00222 259057; *Cable:* FOOTRIM NOUAKCHOTT; *Telex:* 577 MTN NKTT RIM.

## MAURITIUS

Mauritius Football Association, Chancery House, 2nd Floor Nos. 303-305, 14 Lislet Geoffroy Street, Port Louis.
*Founded:* 1952; *Number of Clubs:* 397; *Number of Players:* 29,375; *National Colours:* Red shirts, white shorts, red stockings with white tops.
*Telephone:* 00230 2121418; *Cable:* MFA PORT LOUIS; *Fax:* 00230 2084100.

## MOROCCO

Federation Royale Marocaine De Football, Av. Ibn Sina, C.N.S. Bellevue, B.P. 51, Rabat.
*Founded:* 1955; *Number of Clubs:* 350; *Number of Players:* 19,768; *National Colours:* All red.
*Telephone:* 002127 672706/08; *Cable:* FERMAFOOT RABAT; *Telex:* 32940 FERMFOOT M. *Fax:* 002127 671070.

## MOZAMBIQUE

Federacao Mocambicana De Futebol, Av. Samora Machel, 11-2, Caixa Postal 1467, Maputo.
*Founded:* 1978; *Number of Clubs:* 144; *National Colours:* Red shirts, black shorts, black and red stockings.
*Telephone:* 002581 300366; *Cable:* MOCAMBOLA MAPUTO; *Telex:* 6-747 MCID MO; *Fax:* 002581 300367.

## NAMIBIA

Namibia Football Federation, Abraham Mashego Street 8521, Katurua Council of Churches in Namibia, PO Box 1345, Windhoek, Namibia.
*Founded:* 1990*Number of Clubs:* 244; *Number of Players:* 7320; *National Colours:* All blue, red, green, yellow and white.
*Telephone:* 0026461 249441; *Fax:* 0026461 249442.

## NIGER

Federation Nigerienne De Football (Fenifoot), Stade du 29 Juillet, B.P. 10299, Niamey.
*Founded:* 1967; *Number of Clubs:* 64; *Number of Players:* 1,525; *National Colours:* Orange shirts, white shorts, green stockings.
*Telephone:* 00227 725127-6; *Cable:* FEDERFOOT NIGER NIAMEY; *Telex:* 5527; *Fax:* 00227 734694.

## NIGERIA

Nigeria Football Association, Plot 2033, Olusegun Obasanjo Way, Wuse Zone 7, Abuja, Nigeria.
*Founded:* 1945; *Number of Clubs:* 326; *Number of Players:* 80,190; *National Colours:* Green shirts, white shorts, green stockings.
*Telephone:* 002349 5237326; *Cable:* FOOTBALL ABUJA; *Telex:* 26570 NFA NG; *Fax:* 002349 5237327.

## RWANDA

Federation Rwandaise De Football Amateur, B.P. 2000, Kigali.
*Founded:* 1972; *Number of Clubs:* 167; *National Colours:* Red, green and yellow shirts, green shorts, red stockings.
*Telephone:* 00250 84999; *Cable:* FERWAFA KIGALI; *Telex:* 22504 PUBLIC RW; *Fax:* 00250 76574.

## SENEGAL

Federation Senegalaise De Football, Stade L.S. Senghor, Route De L'Aeroport De Yoff, B.P. 130 21, Dakar.
*Founded:* 1960; *Number of Clubs:* 75 (senior); *Number of Players:* 3,977; *National Colours:* Green shirts, yellow shorts, red stockings.
*Telephone & fax:* 00221 273524; *Cable:* SENEFOOT DAKAR ; *Telex:* 13048 PUBLIDK SG.

## SEYCHELLES

Seychelles Football Federation, P.O. Box 843, People's Stadium, Victoria-Mahe, Seychelles.
*Founded:* 1979; *National Colours:* Red and blue shirts, blue and red shorts, white stockings.
*Telephone:* 00248 323908 ext. 244; *Fax:* 00248 225468.

## ST. THOMAS AND PRINCIPE

Federation Santomense De Futebol, P.O. Box 42, Sao Tome.
*Founded:* 1975; *National Colours:* All green and yellow.
*Telephone:* 0023912 23431; *Telex:* 213 PUBLICO STP; *Fax:* 0023912 21365.

## SIERRA LEONE

Sierra Leone Football Association, att Mr. Alimu Bah, Gen. Secretary, c/o Fed. Guineenne de Football, B.P. 3645 Conakry, (Guinea).
*Founded:* 1967; *Number of Clubs:* 104; *Number of Players:* 8,120; *National Colours:* Green, white and blue shirts, white shorts, blue stockings with white tops.
*Telephone:* 00224 461159; *Fax:* 00224 411926.

## SOMALIA

Somali Football Federation, c/o Conf. Afric. de Football, 5 Gabalaya Street, 11567, El Borg, Cairo, Egypt.
*Founded:* 1951; *Number of Clubs:* 46 (senior); *Number of Players:* 1,150; *National Colours:* All sky blue and white.
*Telephone:* 0020 2/3412497; *Cable:* SOMALIA FOOTBALL CAIRO; *Telex:* 93162 CAF UN; *Fax:* 0020 2/3420114 (CAF).

## SOUTH AFRICA

South African Football Association, First National Bank Stadium, Nasrec/ PO Box 910, Johannesburg 2000; South Africa.
*Founded:* 1991; *Number of Teams:* 51,944; *Number of Players:* 1,039,880; *National Colours:* Gold and black shirts, green shorts, white stockings.
*Telephone:* 002711 4943522; Fax: 002711 4943013.

## SUDAN

Sudan Football Association, P.O. Box 437, Khartoum.
*Founded:* 1936; *Number of Clubs:* 750; *Number of Players:* 42,200; *National Colours:* Green shirts, white shorts, green stockings.
*Telephone & fax:* 0024911 776633; *Cable:* ALKOURA KHARTOUM; *Telex:* 23007 KORA SD.

## SWAZILAND

National Football Association of Swaziland, P.O. Box 641, Mbabane.
*Founded:* 1968; *Number of Clubs:* 136; *National Colours:* Blue shirts, gold shorts, white stockings.
*Telephone:* 00268 46852; *Telex:* 2245 EXP WD; *Fax:* 00268 46206.

## TANZANIA

Football Association of Tanzania, P.O. Box 1574, Dar Es Salaam.
*Founded:* 1930; *Number of Clubs:* 51; *National Colours:* Yellow shirts with black stripes, yellow shorts, yellow and black stockings with horiz. stripe.
*Telephone:* 0025551 117931; *Cable:* FAT DAR- ES-SALAAM; *Telex:* 41873 TZ; *Fax:* 0025551 117930.

## TOGO

Federation Togolaise De Football, C.P. 5, Lome.
*Founded:* 1960; *Number of Clubs:* 144; *Number of Players:* 4,346; *National Colours:* White shirts, green shorts, red and yellow stockings with green stripes.
*Telephone:* 00228 221412; *Cable:* TOGOFOOT LOME; *Telex:* 5015 CNOT TG. *Fax:* 00228 221413.

## TUNISIA

Federation Tunisienne De Football, 16 Rue de la Ligue Arabe, El-Menzah VI, Tunis 1004.
*Founded:* 1956; *Number of Clubs:* 215; *Number of Players:* 18,300; *National Colours:* Red shirts, white shorts, red stockings.
*Telephone:* 002161 233303; *Cable:* FOOTBALL TUNIS; *Telex:* 14783 FTFOOT TN; *Fax:* 002161 767929.

## UGANDA

Federation of Uganda Football Associations, P.O. Box 22518, Kampala, Uganda.
*Founded:* 1924; *Number of Clubs:* 400; *Number of Players:* 1,518; *National Colours:* Yellow shirts with black stripes, black shorts with yellow stripes, yellow and red stockings.
*Telephone:* 0025641 342731; *Cable:* FUFA LUGOGO STADIUM, KAMPALA; *Telex:* 61605; *Fax:* 0025641 257456.

## ZAMBIA

Football Association of Zambia, P.O. Box 34751, Lusaka.
*Founded:* 1929; *Number of Clubs:* 20 (senior); *Number of Players:* 4,100; *National Colours:* Copper shirts, black shorts, copper stockings.
*Telephone:* 002601 221145; *Cable:* FOOTBALL LUSAKA; *Fax:* 002601 225046.

## ZIMBABWE

Zimbabwe Football Association, P.O. Box CY 114, Causeway, Harare.
*Founded:* 1965; *National Colours:* Green shirts, gold shorts, green and gold stockings.
*Telephone:* 002634 731262; *Cable:* SOCCER HARARE; *Telex:* 22299 SOCCER ZW; *Fax:* 002634 731265.

# FIFA/CONFEDERATIONS CUP

### (In Saudi Arabia)

**GROUP A**
Saudi Arabia 0, Brazil 3
Mexico 1, Australia 3
Saudi Arabia 0, Mexico 5
Australia 0, Brazil 0
Saudi Arabia 1, Australia 0
Brazil 3, Mexico 2

**GROUP B**
UAE 0, Uruguay 2
South Africa 2, Czech Republic 2
UAE 1, South Africa 3
Czech Republic 1, Uruguay 2
UAE 1, Czech Republic 6
Uruguay 4, South Africa 3

**SEMI-FINALS**
Brazil 2, Czech Republic 0
Uruguay 0, Australia 1
aet; Australia won sudden death.

**3RD/4TH PLACE**
Czech Republic 1, Uruguay 0

**FINAL**
Brazil 6, Australia 0

# THE WORLD CUP 1930–98

| Year | Winners | | Runners-up | | Venue | Attendance | Referee |
|------|---------|--|------------|--|-------|-----------|---------|
| 1930 | Uruguay | 4 | Argentina | 2 | Montevideo | 90,000 | Langenus (B) |
| 1934 | Italy | 2 | Czechoslovakia | 1 | Rome | 50,000 | Eklind (Se) |
| | *(after extra time)* | | | | | | |
| 1938 | Italy | 4 | Hungary | 2 | Paris | 45,000 | Capdeville (F) |
| 1950 | Uruguay | 2 | Brazil | 1 | Rio de Janeiro | 199,854 | Reader (E) |
| 1954 | West Germany | 3 | Hungary | 2 | Berne | 60,000 | Ling (E) |
| 1958 | Brazil | 5 | Sweden | 2 | Stockholm | 49,737 | Guigue (F) |
| 1962 | Brazil | 3 | Czechoslovakia | 1 | Santiago | 68,679 | Latychev (USSR) |
| 1966 | England | 4 | West Germany | 2 | Wembley | 93,802 | Dienst (Sw) |
| | *(after extra time)* | | | | | | |
| 1970 | Brazil | 4 | Italy | 1 | Mexico City | 107,412 | Glockner (EG) |
| 1974 | West Germany | 2 | Holland | 1 | Munich | 77,833 | Taylor (E) |
| 1978 | Argentina | 3 | Holland | 1 | Buenos Aires | 77,000 | Gonella (I) |
| | *(after extra time)* | | | | | | |
| 1982 | Italy | 3 | West Germany | 1 | Madrid | 90,080 | Coelho (Br) |
| 1986 | Argentina | 3 | West Germany | 2 | Mexico City | 114,580 | Filho (Br) |
| 1990 | West Germany | 1 | Argentina | 0 | Rome | 73,603 | Codesal (Mex) |
| 1994 | Brazil | 0 | Italy | 0 | Los Angeles | 94,194 | Puhl (H) |
| | *(Brazil won 3-2 on penalties aet)* | | | | | | |
| 1998 | France | 3 | Brazil | 0 | St-Denis | 75,000 | Belqola (Mor) |

## GOALSCORING AND ATTENDANCES IN WORLD CUP FINAL ROUNDS

| Venue | Matches | Goals (av) | Attendance (av) |
|-------|---------|-----------|-----------------|
| 1930, Uruguay | 18 | 70 (3.9) | 434,500 (24,138) |
| 1934, Italy | 17 | 70 (4.1) | 395,000 (23,235) |
| 1938, France | 18 | 84 (4.6) | 483,000 (26,833) |
| 1950, Brazil | 22 | 88 (4.0) | 1,337,000 (60,772) |
| 1954, Switzerland | 26 | 140 (5.4) | 943,000 (36,270) |
| 1958, Sweden | 35 | 126 (3.6) | 868,000 (24,800) |
| 1962, Chile | 32 | 89 (2.8) | 776,000 (24,250) |
| 1966, England | 32 | 89 (2.8) | 1,614,677 (50,458) |
| 1970, Mexico | 32 | 95 (2.9) | 1,673,975 (52,311) |
| 1974, West Germany | 38 | 97 (2.5) | 1,774,022 (46,684) |
| 1978, Argentina | 38 | 102 (2.7) | 1,610,215 (42,374) |
| 1982, Spain | 52 | 146 (2.8) | 2,064,364 (38,816) |
| 1986, Mexico | 52 | 132 (2.5) | 2,441,731 (46,956) |
| 1990, Italy | 52 | 115 (2.2) | 2,515,168 (48,368) |
| 1994, USA | 52 | 141 (2.7) | 3,567,415 (68,604) |
| 1998, France | 64 | 171 (2.6) | 2,775,400 (43,366) |

## LEADING GOALSCORERS

| Year | Player | Goals |
|------|--------|-------|
| 1930 | Guillermo Stabile (Argentina) | 8 |
| 1934 | Angelo Schiavio (Italy) | |
| | Oldrich Nejedly (Czechoslovakia) | |
| | Edmund Conen (Germany) | 4 |
| 1938 | Leonidas da Silva (Brazil) | 8 |
| 1950 | Ademir (Brazil) | 9 |
| 1954 | Sandor Kocsis (Hungary) | 11 |
| 1958 | Just Fontaine (France) | 13 |
| 1962 | Valentin Ivanov (USSR), Leonel Sanchez (Chile), Garrincha, Vava (both Brazil), Florian Albert (Hungary), Drazen Jerkovic (Yugoslavia) | 4 |
| 1966 | Eusebio (Portugal) | 9 |
| 1970 | Gerd Muller (West Germany) | 10 |
| 1974 | Grzegorz Lato (Poland) | 7 |
| 1978 | Mario Kempes (Argentina) | 6 |
| 1982 | Paolo Rossi (Italy) | 6 |
| 1986 | Gary Lineker (England) | 6 |
| 1990 | Salvatore Schillaci (Italy) | 6 |
| 1994 | Oleg Salenko (Russia) | |
| | Hristo Stoichkov (Bulgaria) | 6 |
| 1998 | Davor Suker (Croatia) | 6 |

The victorious French players celebrate World Cup victory after beating Brazil 3–0 in the final. (Colorsport)

# 1998 FIFA WORLD CUP – QUALIFYING COMPETITION

**OCEANIA** (Members 10, Entries 10)
Either one or no team qualifies
**First Round** (League System + 1 play-off match)
*Melanesian Group:* Papua New Guinea 1, Soloman Islands 1; Soloman Islands 1, Vanuatu 1; Papua New Guinea 2, Vanuatu 1.
*Polynesian Group:* Tonga 2, Cook Islands 0; Western Samoa 2, Cook Islands 1; Tonga 1, Western Samoa 0.
*Play-off:* Tonga 0, Soloman Islands 4; Soloman Islands 9, Tonga 0.
**Second Round** (League System)
*Group 1:* Australia 13, Soloman Islands 0; Australia 5, Tahiti 0; Soloman Islands 4, Tahiti 1; Soloman Islands 2, Australia 6; Tahiti 0, Australia 2; Tahiti 1, Soloman Islands 1.
*Group 2:* Papua New Guinea 1, New Zealand 1; Fiji 0, New Zealand 1; New Zealand 7, Papua New Guinea 0; Fiji 3, Papua New Guinea 1; New Zealand 5, Fiji 0; Papua New Guinea 0, Fiji 1.
**Third Round** (Cup System)
Winner of group 1 v winner of group 2
Third Round Winner plays team finishing fourth in Asia.
New Zealand 0, Australia 3; Australia 2, New Zealand 0.
**Play-Off**
Iran 1, Australia 1; Australia 2, Iran 2.
**Iran qualify for finals (29.11.97).**

**ASIA** (Members 41 +1, Entries 36)
Three or four teams qualify
**First Round** (League System)
*Group 1:* Taiwan 0, Saudi Arabia 2; Malaysia 2, Bangladesh 0; Bangladesh 1, Taiwan 3; Malaysia 0, Saudi Arabia 0; Bangladesh 1, Saudi Arabia 4; Malaysia 2, Taiwan 0; Taiwan 1, Malaysia 0; Saudi Arabia 3, Bangladesh 0; Taiwan 1, Bangladesh 2; Saudi Arabia 3, Malaysia 0; Bangladesh 0, Malaysia 1; Saudi Arabia 6, Taiwan 0.
*Group 2:* Maldives 0, Iran 17; Syria 12, Maldives 0; Kyrgyzstan 0, Iran 7; Syria 0, Iran 1; Kyrgyzstan 3, Maldives 0; Iran 3, Kyrgyzstan 1; Maldives 0, Syria 12; Iran 9, Maldives 0; Kyrgyzstan 2, Syria 1; Iran 2, Syria 2; Maldives 0, Kyrgyzstan 6.
*Group 3:* Jordan 0, United Arab Emirates 0; Bahrain 1, United Arab Emirates 2; Bahrain 1, Jordan 0; Jordan 4, Bahrain 1; United Arab Emirates 3, Bahrain 0; United Arab Emirates 2, Jordan 0.
*Group 4:* Nepal 1, Macao 1; Oman 0, Japan 1; Macao 0, Japan 10; Oman 1, Nepal 0; Nepal 0, Japan 6; Oman 4, Macao 0; Japan 10, Macao 0; Nepal 0, Oman 6; Japan 3, Nepal 0; Macao 0, Oman 2; Japan 1, Oman 1; Macao 2, Nepal 1.
*Group 5:* Indonesia 8, Cambodia 0; Indonesia 0, Yemen 0; Cambodia 0, Yemen 1, Cambodia 1, Indonesia 1; Yemen 0, Uzbekistan 1; Yemen 7, Cambodia 0; Uzbekistan 6, Cambodia 0; Indonesia 1, Uzbekistan 1; Yemen 1, Indonesia 1; Uzbekistan 3, Indonesia 0; Cambodia 1, Uzbekistan 4.
*Group 6:* Hong Kong 0, Korea Republic 2; Thailand 1, Korea Republic 3; Thailand 2, Hong Kong 0; Hong Kong 3, Thailand 2; Korea Republic 4, Hong Kong 0; Korea Republic 0, Thailand 0.
*Group 7:* Lebanon 1, Singapore 1; Singapore 0, Kuwait 1; Kuwait 2, Lebanon 0; Singapore 1, Lebanon 2; Kuwait 4, Singapore 0; Lebanon 1, Kuwait 3.
*Group 8:* Tajikistan 4, Vietnam 0; Turkmenistan 1, China 4, Tajikistan 0; China 1; Turkmenistan 2, Vietnam 1; Vietman 1, China 3; Turkmenistan 1, Tajikistan 2; China 1, Turkmenistan 0; Vietnam 0, Tajikistan 4; China 0, Tajikistan 0; Vietnam 0, Turkmenistan 4; China 4, Vietnam 0; Tajikistan 5, Turkmenistan 0.
*Group 9:* Kazakhstan 2, Pakistan 0; Pakistan 2, Iraq 6; Iraq 1, Kazakhstan 2; Pakistan 0, Kazakhstan 7; Iraq 6, Pakistan 1; Kazakhstan 1, Iraq 1.
*Group 10:* Qatar 3, Sri Lanka 0; India 2, Philippines 0; Qatar 5, Philippines 0; Sri Lanka 1, India 1; Philippines 0, Sri Lanka 3; Qatar 6, India 0.
**Second Round** (League System)
*Group A:* China 2, Iran 4; Saudi Arabia 2, Kuwait 1; Iran 1, Saudi Arabia 1; Qatar 0, Kuwait 2; Kuwait 1, Iran 1;

Qatar 1, China 1; China 1, Saudi Arabia 0; Iran 3, Qatar 0; Kuwait 1, China 2; Saudi Arabia 1, Qatar 0; Iran 4, China 1; Kuwait 2, Saudi Arabia 1; Kuwait 0, Qatar 1; Saudi Arabia 1, Iran 0; China 2, Qatar 3; Iran 0, Kuwait 0; Saudi Arabia 1, China 1; Qatar 2, Iran 0; China 1, Kuwait 0; Qatar 0, Saudi Arabia 1.
**Saudi Arabia qualify for finals (12.11.97).**
*Group B:* Korea Republic 3, Kazakhstan 0; Japan 6, Uzbekistan 3; Korea Republic 2, Uzbekistan 1; Kazakhstan 0; UAE 0, Japan 0; Kazakhstan 1, Uzbekistan 1; Uzbekistan 3, UAE 3; Japan 1, Korea Republic 2; Korea Republic 3, UAE 0; Kazakhstan 1, Japan 1; Uzbekistan 1, Japan 1; Kazakhstan 1, Korea Republic 1; Uzbekistan 1, Korea Republic 5; Kazakhstan 3, UAE 0; Uzbekistan 4, Kazakhstan 0; Japan 1, UAE 1; Korea Republic 0, Japan 2; UAE 0, Uzbekistan 0; Japan 5, Kazakhstan 1; UAE 1, Korea Republic 3.
**Korea Republic qualify for finals (26.10.97).**

**Third Place Play-Off**
Japan 3, Iran 2.
(Japan won on sudden death).
**Japan qualify for finals (16.11.97).**
For Iran, see Oceania Group.

**CONCACAF** (Members 30, Entries 30, including 2 late entries Bermuda and Cuba)
Three teams qualify
**First Round** (Cup System - Caribbean zone)
Dominican Republic 3, Aruba 2; Aruba 1, Dominican Republic 3; Bahamas withdrew v St Kitts & Nevis w.o.; Guyana 1, Grenada 2; Grenada 6, Guyana 0; Dominica 3, Antigua 3; Antigua 1, Dominica 3.
**Second Round** (Cup System - Caribbean zone)
Bermuda withdrew v Trinidad & Tobago w.o.; Puerto Rico 1, St Vincent & the Grenadines 2; St Vincent & the Grenadines 7, Puerto Rico 0; Cuba 1, Cayman Islands 0; Cayman Islands 0, Cuba 5; St Kitts & Nevis 5, St Lucia 1; St Lucia 0, St Kitts & Nevis 1; Haiti 6, Grenada 1; Grenada 0, Haiti 1; Syrinam 0, Jamaica 1; Jamaica 1, Syrinam 0; Dominica 0, Barbados 1; Barbados 1, Dominica 0; Dominican Republic 2, Netherlands Antilles 1; Netherlands Antilles 0, Dominican Republic 0.
**Third Round** (Cup System - Caribbean zone)
Cuba 5, Haiti 1; Haiti 1, Cuba 0; Dominican Republic 1, Trinidad & Tobago 4; Trinidad & Tobago 8, Dominican Republic 0; Barbados 0, Jamaica 2; Jamaica 2, Barbados 0; St Kitts & Nevis 2, St Vincent 0; St Vincent 0, St Kitts & Nevis 0.
**First Round** (Cup System - Central American zone)
Nicaragua 0, Guatemala 1; Guatemala 2, Nicaragua 1; Belize 1, Panama 2; Panama 4, Belize 1.
**Semi-final Round** (League System)
*Group 1:* Trinidad & Tobago 0, Costa Rica 1; Trinidad & Tobago 1, Guatemala 1; USA 4, Guatemala 0; USA 2, Trinidad & Tobago 0; Costa Rica 3, Guatemala 0; Guatemala 1, Costa Rica 1; Trinidad & Tobago 0, USA 1; Costa Rica 2, USA 1; Guatemala 2, Trinidad & Tobago 1; USA 2, Costa Rica 1; Costa Rica 2, Trinidad & Tobago 1; Guatemala 2, USA 2.
*Group 2:* Canada 3, Cuba 0; Cuba 0, El Salvador 5; Cuba 1, Panama 0; Panama 1, El Salvador 1; Canada 2, Cuba 0; Cuba 0, Canada 0; Panama 0, Canada 0; Canada 1, El Salvador 0; El Salvador 3, Panama 2; El Salvador 3, Cuba 0; Panama 5, Cuba 1; El Salvador 0, Canada 2.
*Group 3:* Jamaica 3, Honduras 0; St Vincent & the Genadines 0, Mexico 3; Honduras 2, Mexico 1; St Vincent & the Grenadines 1, Jamaica 2; St Vincent & the Grenadines 1, Honduras 4; Mexico 2, Jamaica 1; Honduras 0, Jamaica 0; Mexico 5, St Vincent & the Grenadines 1; Mexico 3, Honduras 1; Jamaica 5, St Vincent & the Grenadines 0; Honduras 11, St Vincent & the Grenadines 3; Jamaica 1, Mexico 0.
**Final Round** (League System)
Jamaica 0, USA 0; Mexico 4, Canada 0; Costa Rica 0, Mexico 0; USA 3, Canada 0; Costa Rica 3, USA 2; Canada 0, El Salvador 0; Mexico 6, Jamaica 0; USA 2, Mexico 2; Canada 0, Jamaica 0; El Salvador 2, Costa Rica 1; Costa Rica 3, Jamaica 1; Jamaica 1, El Salvador 0;

Canada 1, Costa Rica 0; El Salvador 0, Mexico 1; El Salvador 1, USA 1; Costa Rica 0, El Salvador 0; USA 1, Costa Rica 0; Jamaica 1, Canada 0; Jamaica 1, Costa Rica 0; El Salvador 4, Canada 1; USA 1, Jamaica 1; Mexico 5, El Salvador 0; Canada 2, Mexico 2; Mexico 0, USA 0; Canada 0, USA 3; El Salvador 2, Jamaica 2; Mexico 3, Costa Rica 3; Jamaica 0, Mexico 0; Costa Rica 3, Canada 1; USA 4, El Salvador 2.

**Mexico qualify for finals (2.11.97); USA (9.11.97) and Jamaica (16.11.97).**

## AFRICA (Members 51, Entries 38, Withdrawals 2)

Five teams qualify

**First Round** (Cup System)
Sudan 2, Zambia 0; Namibia 2, Mozambique 0; Tanzania 0, Ghana 0; Swaziland 0, Gabon 1; Uganda 0, Angola 2; Mauritius 1, Zaire 5; Malawi 0, South Africa 1; Madagascar 1, Zimbabwe 2; Guinea-Bissau 3, Guinea 2; Rwanda 1,Tunisia 3; Congo 2, Ivory Coast 0; Kenya 3, Algeria 1; Burundi 1, Sierra Leone 0; Mauritania 0, Burkina Faso 0; Togo 2, Senegal 1; Gambia 2, Liberia 1; Algeria 1, Kenya 0; Senegal 1, Togo 1; South Africa 3, Malawi 0; Sierra Leone 0, Burundi 1; Angola 3, Uganda 1; Gabon 2, Swaziland 0; Guinea 3, Guinea-Bissau 1; Ivory Coast 1, Congo 1; Mozambique 1, Namibia 1; Tunisia 2, Rwanda 0; Burkina Faso 2, Mauritania 0; Zaire 2, Mauritius 0; Zambia 3, Sudan 0; Zimbabwe 2, Madagascar 2; Ghana 2, Tanzania 1; Liberia 4, Gambia 0.

**Second Round** (League System)
*Group 1:* Nigeria 2, Burkina Faso 0; Guinea 3, Kenya 1; Kenya 1, Nigeria 1; Burkina Faso 0, Guinea 2; Nigeria 2, Guinea 1; Kenya 4, Burkina Faso 3; Kenya 1, Guinea 0; Burkina Faso 1, Nigeria 2; Nigeria 3, Kenya 0; Guinea 3, Burkina Faso 1; Burkina Faso 2, Kenya 4; Guinea 1, Nigeria 0.
**Nigeria qualify for finals (7.6.97).**
*Group 2:* Egypt 7, Namibia 1; Liberia 0, Tunisia 1; Namibia 0, Liberia 0; Tunisia 1, Egypt 0; Liberia 1, Egypt 0; Namibia 1, Tunisia 2; Namibia 2, Egypt 3; Tunisia 2, Liberia 0; Egypt 0, Tunisia 0; Liberia 1, Namibia 2; Tunisia 4, Namibia 0; Egypt 5, Liberia 0.
**Tunisia qualify for finals (8.6.97).**
*Group 3:* South Africa 1, Zaire 0; Congo 1, Zambia 0; Zambia 0, South Africa 0; Zaire 1, Congo 1; Congo 2, South Africa 0; Zaire 2, Zambia 2; Zaire 1, South Africa 2; Zambia 3, Congo 0; Congo 1, Zaire 0; South Africa 3, Zambia 0; Zambia 2, Zaire 0; South Africa 1, Congo 0.
**South Africa qualify for finals (16.8.97).**
*Group 4:* Angola 2, Zimbabwe 1; Togo 2, Cameroon 4; Cameroon 0, Angola 0; Zimbabwe 3, Togo 0; Angola 3, Togo 1; Cameroon 1, Zimbabwe 0; Cameroon 2, Togo 0; Zimbabwe 0, Angola 0; Angola 1, Cameroon 1; Togo 2, Zimbabwe 1; Togo 1, Angola 1; Zimbabwe 1, Cameroon 2.
**Cameroon qualify for finals (17.8.97).**
*Group 5:* Morocco 4, Sierra Leone 0; Gabon 1, Ghana 1; Sierra Leone 1, Gabon 0; Ghana 2, Morocco 2; Sierra Leone 1, Ghana 1; Gabon 0, Morocco 4; Sierra Leone 0, Morocco 1; Ghana 3, Gabon 0; Morocco 1, Ghana 0; Morocco 2, Gabon 0; Ghana 0, Sierra Leone 2.
**Morocco qualify for finals (7.6.97).**

## EUROPE (Members 49 + 1, Entries)

Fifteen teams qualify including France as the host nation. The nine group winners and the best runner-up qualify. The eight other runners-up will be drawn in pairs, the four winners also qualifying for the final.

### GROUP 1
Athens, 24 April 1996, 9000

**Greece (0) 2** *(Batista 56, Nikolaidis 66)*
**Slovenia (0) 0**

*Greece:* Atmatsidis; Apostolakis, Kassapis, Ouzounidis, Kallitzakis, Kostantinidis (Alexandris 46), Zagorakis, Vrizas, Batista, Tsartas (Frantzeskos 82), Donis (Nikolaidis 61).
*Slovenia:* Boskovic; Galic, Englaro, Milanic, Jermanis, Ceh, Novak, Zidan (Gajser 36), Udovic (Gliha 70), Gregor, Florjancic.
*Referee:* Pedersen (Denmark).

---

Kalamata, 1 September 1996, 6000

**Greece (1) 3** *(Ouzounidis 41, Apostolakis 77, Nikolaidis 83)*
**Bosnia (0) 0**

*Greece:* Atmatsidis; Apostolakis, Kassapis, Ouzounidis, Kallitzakis, Dabizas, Zagorakis, Vrizas (Batista 34), Tsartas (Frantzeskos 75), Donis (Alexandris 46), Nikolaidis.
*Bosnia:* Omerovic; Sabic, Katana, Glavas, Konjic, Smajic (Sasivarevic 64), Bazdarevic, Baljic, Begic (Varesanovic 67), Kodro, Bolic (Music 60).
*Referee:* Benko (Austria).

---

Ljubljana, 1 September 1996, 5000

**Slovenia (0) 0**
**Denmark (0) 2** *(Nielsen A 78, Schjonberg 89)*

*Slovenia:* Boskovic; Galic, Krizan, Englaro, Binkovski, Ceh, Novak, Karic, Zahovic, Udovic (Kokol 72), Florjancic.
*Denmark:* Schmeichel; Helveg, Friis-Hansen, Hogh, Laursen, Bjur (Goldbaek 22), Nielsen A, Steen Nielsen (Schjonberg 61), Thomsen, Laudrup M (Andersen S 85), Laudrup B.
*Referee:* Meier (Switzerland).

---

Bologna, 8 October 1996, 1500

**Bosnia (1) 1** *(Salihamidzic 25)*
**Croatia (2) 4** *(Bilic 14, Vlaovic 33, Boksic 64, 83)*

*Bosnia:* Omerovic; Sabic (Begic 53), Geca, Konjic (Pintul 65), Katana, Besirevic, Teljigovic (Halilovic 60), Bazdarevic, Smajic, Salihamidzic, Bolic.
*Croatia:* Ladic; Soldo, Jerkan, Bilic (Mamic 80), Jurcevic (Simic 44), Boban, Vlaovic (Cvitanovic 85), Asanovic, Jarni, Boksic, Suker.
*Referee:* Ouzounov (Bulgaria).

---

Copenhagen, 9 October 1996, 40,226

**Denmark (1) 2** *(Zagorakis 25 (og), Laudrup B 52)*
**Greece (1) 1** *(Donis 35)*

*Denmark:* Schmeichel; Helveg, Rieper, Hogh, Laursen, Nielsen P (Goldbaek 53), Thomsen, Nielsen A, Laudrup M (Schjonberg 75), Moller (Andersen S 87), Laudrup B.
*Greece:* Atmatsidis; Efstratios, Ouzounidis, Kallitzakis, Kassapis, Zagorakis (Konstantinidis 64), Ntampizas, Nikolaidis, Tsartas (Niniadis 75), Lima (Alexandris 59), Donis.
*Referee:* Durkin (England).

---

Zagreb, 10 November 1996, 30,000

**Croatia (1) 1** *(Suker 45)*
**Greece (1) 1** *(Nikolaidis 9)*

*Croatia:* Ladic; Stimac (Soldo 52), Jerkan, Bilic, Stanic, Asanovic, Prosinecki (Vlaovic 75), Boban, Jarni, Suker, Boksic.
*Greece:* Atmatsidis; Apostolakis, Karataidis, Kallitzakis, Danbitzas, Kassapis, Zagorakis (Vlahos 46), Kostantinidis, Tsartas (Vrizas 83), Donis (Georgiadis 65), Nikolaidis.
*Referee:* Van der Ende (Holland).

---

Ljubljana, 10 November 1996, 4000

**Slovenia (1) 1** *(Zahovic 41)*
**Bosnia (2) 2** *(Bolic 6, Kodro 33)*

*Slovenia:* Boskovic; Englaro, Krizan, Milanic, Jermanis, Ceh, Novak, Karic (Binkovski 78), Zahovic, Simundza (Vulic 46), Udovic.
*Bosnia:* Dedic; Sabic (Kapetanovic 89), Besirevic, Konjic, Begic, Jasarevic, Glavas, Halilovic, Kodro, Salihamidzic (Baljic 75), Bolic (Brkic 85).
*Referee:* Agius (Malta).

### Split, 29 March 1997, 34,000

**Croatia (0) 1** *(Suker 50)*

**Denmark (0) 1** *(Laudrup B 82)*

*Croatia:* Ladic; Kovac, Jarni, Soldo, Jerkan, Bilic, Asanovic (Pralija 84), Prosinecki, Suker, Boban, Boksic (Vlaovic 75).
*Denmark:* Schmeichel; Laursen, Rieper, Hogh (Schjonbjerg 14), Heintze, Helveg, Frandsen (Tomasson 70), Thomsen, Nielsen A, Beck (Pedersen P 57), Laudrup B.
*Referee:* Ceccarini (Italy).

### Sarajevo, 2 April 1997, 40,000

**Bosnia (0) 0**

**Greece (0) 1** *(Franzeskos 74)*

*Bosnia:* Dedic; Sabic (Brkic 86), Besirevic (Music 79), Ramcic, Katana, Jasarevic, Glavas (Baljic 79), Halilovic, Kodro, Salihamidzic, Bolic.
*Greece:* Atmatsidis; Apostolakis, Karataidis, Ouzounidis, Kalitzakis, Kursaidis, Zagorakis, Nikolaidis, Kostis (Georgatos 46), Tsartas (Franzeskos 67), Donis (Georgiadis GH 87).
*Referee:* Sars (France).

### Split, 2 April 1997, 15,000

**Croatia (2) 3** *(Prosinecki 33, Boban 43, 60)*

**Slovenia (1) 3** *(Gliha 45, 65, 67)*

*Croatia:* Gabric (Mrmic 46); Simic, Jerkan, Bilic, Asanovic, Prosinecki, Vlaovic (Pralija 68), Boban, Boksic, Juric, Cvitanovic.
*Slovenia:* Boskovic; Englaro, Srebrnic, Krizan, Rudonja, Novak, Ceh (Seslar 68), Zahovic, Gajser (Karic 46), Udovic (Siljak 46), Gliha.
*Referee:* Durkin (England).

### Copenhagen, 30 April 1997, 41,278

**Denmark (2) 4** *(Nielsen A 4, 56, Pedersen P 27, Laudrup B 51)*

**Slovenia (0) 0**

*Denmark:* Schmeichel; Laursen (Bisgaard 58), Rieper, Hogh, Heintze, Helveg, Nielsen A, Thomsen (Frandsen 86), Tomasson, Pedersen P (Beck 70), Laudrup B.
*Slovenia:* Boskovic; Englaro, Krizan, Milanic, Rudonja (Karic 46), Jermanis, Novak, Gajser (Seslar 60), Ceh, Gliha, Siljak (Valentincic 80).
*Referee:* Krug (Germany).

### Salonika, 30 April 1997, 35,000

**Greece (0) 0**

**Croatia (0) 1** *(Suker 74)*

*Greece:* Atmatsidis; Apostolakis (Kostantinidis 46), Kassapis, Ouzounidis, Karataidis, Dabizas, Zagorakis, Nikolaidis (Mahlas 13), Poursanidis, Franzeskos, Donis.
*Croatia:* Ladic; Jarni, Bilic, Asanovic, Prosinecki (Vlaovic 72), Boban, Simic, Soldo (Maric 53), Juric, Suker, Boksic (Cvitanovic 67).
*Referee:* Nieto (Spain).

### Copenhagen, 8 June 1997, 41,592

**Denmark (0) 2** *(Rieper 67, Molnar 90)*

**Bosnia (0) 0**

*Denmark:* Schmeichel; Laursen, Rieper, Hogh, Heintze (Schjonberg 80), Helveg, Nielsen A, Thomsen, Tomasson (Frandsen 52), Pedersen P (Molnar 66), Laudrup B.
*Bosnia:* Dedic; Sabic (Music 71), Katana, Konjic (Ramcic 17), Besirevic, Hibic, Glavas, Halilovic, Baljic, Kodro (Majcin 37), Bolic.
*Referee:* Ihring (Slovakia).

### Sarajevo, 20 August 1997, 35,000

**Bosnia (3) 3** *(Mujcin 18, Bolic 26 (pen), 34 (pen))*

**Denmark (0) 0**

*Bosnia:* Dedic; Sabic (Repuh 54), Besirevic, Konjic, Ramcic, Hibic, Baljic E, Mujcin (Demirovic 84), Kodro, Salihamidzic, Bolic (Beganovic 86).
*Denmark:* Schmeichel; Laursen, Rieper, Hogh, Heintze, Helveg (Colding 76), Nielsen A, Thomsen (Molnar 54), Laudrup M (Schjonberg 54), Tomasson, Moller.
*Referee:* Pereira (Portugal).

### Zagreb, 6 September 1997, 25,000

**Croatia (2) 3** *(Bilic 27, Maric 40, Boban 80)*

**Bosnia (1) 2** *(Baljic 19, Salihamdzic 55)*

*Croatia:* Ladic; Simic, Jarni, Huric, Stimac, Bilic, Boban, Maric (Erceg 74), Cvitanovic (Jurcic 67), Suker, Boksic (Asanovic 46).
*Bosnia:* Dedic; Repuh (Dadic 52), Besirevic, Konjic, Varesanovic, Jasarevic, Mujcin (Bolic 46), Halilovic (Zeric 78), Demirovic, Salihamdzic, Baljic.
*Referee:* Dallas (Scotland).

### Ljubljana, 6 September 1997, 2500

**Slovenia (0) 0**

**Greece (0) 3** *(Alexandris 54, Constantinidis 89, Mahlas 90)*

*Slovenia:* Boskovic; Englaro, Milanic, Krizan, Novak, Karic (Gajser 63), Ceh, Istenic, Zahovic (Seslar 81), Gliha, Siljak (Osterc 68).
*Greece:* Atmatzidis; Apostolakis (Georgiadis 80), Kassapis, Ouzounidis, Kalitzakis, Karataidis, Zagorakis, Franzeskos (Constantinidis 59), Georgatos, Mahlas, Alexandris.
*Referee:* Ihring (Slovakia).

### Sarajevo, 10 September 1997, 22,000

**Bosnia (1) 1** *(Bolic 22)*

**Slovenia (0) 0**

*Bosnia:* Dedic; Sabic, Jasarevic, Konjic, Varesanovic, Mujcin (Besirevic 71), Bolic (Dadic 89), Halilovic, Salihamidzic, Baljic, Kodro (Demirovic 83).
*Slovenia:* Boskovic; Galic, Krizan, Milanic, Istenic, Ceh, Novak, Seslar (Osterc 46), Gajser, Gliha (Gasek 77), Rudonja.
*Referee:* Bezubiak (Russia).

### Copenhagen, 10 September 1997, 41,381

**Denmark (3) 3** *(Laudrup B 13, Laudrup M 32, Molnar 38)*

**Croatia (1) 1** *(Suker 40)*

*Denmark:* Schmeichel; Tobiasen, Hogh, Schjonberg, Helveg, Nielsen A, Frandsen, Heintze, Laudrup M, Laudrup B (Wieghorst 82), Molnar (Moller 72).
*Croatia:* Mrmic (Gabric 7); Bilic, Juric, Stimac, Maric (Erceg 69), Soldo, Asanovic, Boban, Jarni, Suker, Boksic.
*Referee:* Puhl (Hungary).

### Athens, 11 October 1997, 77,000

**Greece (0) 0**

**Denmark (0) 0**

*Greece:* Atmatzidis; Kalitzakis, Ouzounidis, Dabizas, Apostolakis, Karataidis, Zagorakis (Alexandris 78), Georgiadis G (Franzeskos 46), Georgatos (Kostandinidis 46), Mahlas, Nikolaidis.
*Denmark:* Schmeichel; Tobiasen, Rieper, Hogh, Schjonberg, Wieghorst (Colding 57), Nielsen A, Helveg, Heintze, Molnar (Moller 73), Laudrup B (Beck 86).
*Referee:* Veissiere (France).

### Ljubljana, 11 October 1997, 5000

**Slovenia (0) 1** *(Zahovic 72)*

**Croatia (2) 3** *(Suker 11, Soldo 39, Boksic 50)*

*Slovenia:* Boskovic; Englaro (Srebrnic 70), Krizan, Milanic (Galic 46), Rudonja, Gaiser (Karic 46), Novak, Zahovic, Istenic, Gliha, Siljak.
*Croatia:* Ladic; Juric, Bilic, Soldo (Jurcic 64), Saric, Simic, Cvitanovic, Prosinecki, Boban, Suker (Vlaovic 75), Boksic (Kovac 85).
*Referee:* Ancion (Belgium).

### Group 1

| | P | W | D | L | F | A | Pts |
|---|---|---|---|---|---|---|---|
| Denmark | 8 | 5 | 2 | 1 | 14 | 6 | 17 |
| Croatia | 8 | 4 | 3 | 1 | 17 | 12 | 15 |
| Greece | 8 | 4 | 2 | 2 | 11 | 4 | 14 |
| Bosnia | 8 | 3 | 0 | 5 | 9 | 14 | 9 |
| Slovenia | 8 | 0 | 1 | 7 | 5 | 20 | 1 |

**Denmark qualify for finals (11.10.97).**

## GROUP 2
### Chisinau, 1 September 1996, 15,000
**Moldova (0) 0**
**England (2) 3** *(Barmby 23, Gascoigne 24, Shearer 61)*
*Moldova:* Romanenco; Secu, Nani, Testimitanu, Gaidamasciuc, Belous (Siscin 58), Epureanu, Curtianu, Clescenco, Miterev (Rebeja 61), Popovici.
*England:* Seaman; Neville G, Pearce, Southgate, Pallister, Hinchcliffe, Barmby (Le Tissier 81), Ince, Shearer, Gascoigne (Batty 81), Beckham.
*Referee:* Koho (Finland).

### Chisinau, 5 October 1996, 11,000
**Moldova (1) 1** *(Curtianu 12)*
**Italy (1) 3** *(Ravanelli 9, 86 (pen), Casiraghi 69)*
*Moldova:* Romanenco; Secu, Tolokonnikov, Culibaba, Testimitanu, Gaidamasciuc, Curtianu (Miterev 52), Epureanu, Siscin, Rebeja (Rogaciov 78), Clescenco.
*Italy:* Toldo; Nesta, Ferrara, Costacurta, Maldini, Conte, Di Matteo, Carboni (Zola 70), Chiesa (Di Livio 46), Casiraghi, Ravanelli.
*Referee:* Grabher (Austria).

### Wembley, 9 October 1996, 74,663
**England (2) 2** *(Shearer 24, 38)*
**Poland (1) 1** *(Citko 7)*
*England:* Seaman; Neville G, Pearce, Southgate (Pallister 51), Ince, Hinchcliffe, McManaman, Gascoigne, Shearer, Ferdinand, Beckham.
*Poland:* Wozniak; Waldoch, Zielinski, Juskowiak, Hajto, Michalski, Baluszynski, Wojtala, Nowak, Citko, Warzycha (Sagamowski 75).
*Referee:* Krug (Germany).

### Perugia, 9 October 1996, 16,146
**Italy (1) 1** *(Ravanelli 43)*
**Georgia (0) 0**
*Italy:* Toldo; Pessotto, Nesta, Ferrara, Maldini, Di Livio (Panucci 82), Conte (Dino Baggio 60), Di Matteo, Carboni (Zola 17), Casiraghi, Ravanelli.
*Georgia:* Zoidze; Lobjanidze, Koudinov (Inalishvili 46), Tskhadadze, Shelia, Kobiashvili, Gogichaishvili, Nemsadze, Kinkladze, Ketsbaia, Gogrichiani (Aveladze R 30).
*Referee:* Blareau (Belgium).

### Tbilisi, 9 November 1996, 48,000
**Georgia (0) 0**
**England (2) 2** *(Sheringham 15, Ferdinand 37)*
*Georgia:* Zoidze; Lobjanidze, Tskhadadze, Shelia, Gogichaishvili (Gudushauri 60), Nemsadze, Kinkladze, Jamarauli, Kobiashvili, Ketsbaia, Aveladze S (Gogrichiani 52).
*England:* Seaman; Campbell, Hinchcliffe, Batty, Southgate, Adams, Beckham, Gascoigne, Ferdinand (Wright 81), Sheringham, Ince.
*Referee:* Monteiro (Portugal).

### Katowice, 10 November 1996, 10,000
**Poland (1) 2** *(Baluszynski 4, Warzycha 76 (pen))*
**Moldova (0) 1** *(Clescenco 83 (pen))*
*Poland:* Szamotulski; Zielinski, Wojtala, Michalski, Juskowiak, Czerwiec (Waldoch 46), Hajto, Baluszynski (Kucharski 72), Nowak, Warzycha (Staniek 87), Citko.
*Moldova:* Romanenco; Secu, Tolokonnikov, Testimitanu, Culibaba, Gaidamasciuc, Curtianu, Epureanu (Cebotari 28) (Miterev 59), Siscin, Popovici (Martin 67), Clescenco.
*Referee:* Vorgias (Greece).

### Wembley, 12 February 1997, 75,055
**England (0) 0**
**Italy (1) 1** *(Zola 18)*
*England:* Walker; Neville G, Pearce, Ince, Campbell, Batty (Wright 88), McManaman (Merson 76), Le Tissier (Ferdinand 60), Shearer, Beckham, Le Saux.
*Italy:* Peruzzi; Ferrara, Costacurta, Cannavaro, Di Livio, Dino Baggio, Albertini, Di Matteo, Maldini, Zola (Fuser 90), Casiraghi (Ravanelli 76).
*Referee:* Puhl (Hungary).

### Trieste, 29 March 1997, 20,767
**Italy (2) 3** *(Maldini 24, Zola 44, Vieri 49)*
**Moldova (0) 0**
*Italy:* Peruzzi; Ferrara, Maldini, Costacurta, Nesta (Cannavaro 31), Albertini, Di Matteo, Di Livio (Eranio 75), Dino Baggio, Zola, Vieri (Padovano 68).
*Moldova:* Romanenco; Fistican, Tolokonnikov, Culibaba, Testimitanu, Gaidamasciuc (Cebotar 61), Siscin, Epureanu, Curtianu, Spinu (Suharev 61), Clescenco.
*Referee:* Veissiere (France).

### Chorzow, 2 April 1997, 32,000
**Poland (0) 0**
**Italy (0) 0**
*Poland:* Wozniak; Skrzypek, Zielinski, Wojtala, Waldoch, Citko, Swierczewski P (Kowalczyk 46), Juskowiak, Nowak (Sokolowski 44), Baluszynski (Kaluzny 65), Ledwon.
*Italy:* Peruzzi; Ferrara, Maldini, Dino Baggio, Cannavaro, Costacurta, Di Livio, Fuser (Carboni 84), Vieri, Di Matteo, Zola.
*Referee:* Nielsen (Denmark).

### Wembley, 30 April 1997, 71,206
**England (1) 2** *(Sheringham 42, Shearer 90)*
**Georgia (0) 0**
*England:* Seaman; Neville G, Le Saux, Batty, Campbell, Adams (Southgate 87), Lee, Ince (Redknapp 77), Shearer, Sheringham, Beckham.
*Georgia:* Zoidze; Chikhradze, Sheqiladze, Tskhadadze, Shelia, Machavariani (Gogrichiani 30) (Arveladze A 76), Nemsadze, Jamarauli, Ketsbaia, Kinkladze (Gakhokidze 61), Arveladze S.
*Referee:* Harrel (France).

### Naples, 30 April 1997, 37,500
**Italy (2) 3** *(Di Matteo 23, Maldini 37, Roberto Baggio 66)*
**Poland (0) 0**
*Italy:* Peruzzi; Ferrara (Panucci 85), Di Livio, Costacurta, Cannavaro, Maldini, Di Matteo, Albertini, Dino Baggio (Fuser 85), Zola (Roberto Baggio 51), Ravanelli.
*Poland:* Wozniak; Skrzypek, Zielinski, Wojtala, Waldoch (Majak 46), Citko, Kaluzny, Baluszynski (Hajto 66), Kucharski (Warzycha K 46), Nowak, Ledwon.
*Referee:* Aranda (Spain).

### Katowice, 31 May 1997, 35,000
**Poland (0) 0**
**England (1) 2** *(Shearer 6, Sheringham 90)*
*Poland:* Wozniak; Jozwiak, Zielinski, Kaluzny, Ledwon, Bukalski (Swierczewski P 46), Nowak (Kucharski 57), Majak, Juskowiak (Adamczyk 51), Dembinski.
*England:* Seaman; Neville G, Le Saux, Southgate, Campbell, Ince, Lee, Gascoigne (Batty 16), Shearer, Sheringham, Beckham (Neville P 88).
*Referee:* Meier (Switzerland).

### Batumi, 7 June 1997, 17,000
**Georgia (1) 2** *(Arveladze S 27, Kinkladze 51 (pen))*
**Moldova (0) 0**
*Georgia:* Zoidze; Lobjanidze, Tskhadadze, Kobiashvili, Chikhradze, Gogichaishvili, Nemsadze, Jamarauli, Ketsbaia (Janashia 80), Kinkladze, Arveladze S.
*Moldova:* Romanenco; Fistican, Tolokonnikov, Testimitanu, Culibaba, Epureanu, Siscin (Spinu 29), Popovici, Suharev, Miterev (Rogaciov 29), Clescenco.
*Referee:* Agius (Malta).

**Katowice, 14 June 1997, 1500**

**Poland (2) 4** *(Ledwon 33, Trzeciak 35, Bukalski 75 (pen), Nowak 90)*

**Georgia (1) 1** *(Aveladze S 25)*

*Poland:* Szamotulski; Skrzypek, Kukielka, Michalski, Kaluzny, Sokolowski, Bukalski, Ledwon, Dembinski (Adamczyk 88), Nowak, Trzeciak (Kucharski 60).
*Georgia:* Zoidze; Lobjanidze, Tskhadadze, Kobiashvili (Kavelashvili 72), Kaladze, Gogichaishvili (Kiknadze 46), Nemsadze, Jamarauli (Aveladze A 46), Ketsbaia, Kinkladze, Aveladze S.
*Referee:* Benko (Austria).

**Wembley, 10 September 1997, 74,102**

**England (1) 4** *(Scholes 28, Wright 46, 90, Gascoigne 80)*

**Moldova (0) 0**

*England:* Seaman; Neville G, Neville P, Batty, Campbell, Southgate, Beckham (Ripley 68) (Butt 75), Gascoigne, Wright, Ferdinand (Collymore 83), Scholes.
*Moldova:* Romanenco; Fistican, Testimitanu, Stroenco, Culibaba (Suharev 53), Rebeja, Spanu, Sischin (Popovici 61), Curtianu, Miterev, Rogaciov (Cebotari 75).
*Referee:* Nilsson (Sweden).

**Tbilisi, 10 September 1997, 25,000**

**Georgia (0) 0**

**Italy (0) 0**

*Georgia:* Togonidze; Shekiladze, Shelia, Chikhradze, Tskhadadze (Kaladze 20), Kobiashvili, Arveladze A (Daraselia 77), Kavelashvili, Ketsbaia, Kinkladze (Gogichaishvili 65), Arveladze S.
*Italy:* Peruzzi; Lombardo (Roberto Baggio 73), Nesta, Cannavaro, Ferrara, Maldini, Dino Baggio, Di Livio, Di Matteo, Vieri (Casiraghi 65), Zola (Inzaghi 80).
*Referee:* Pedersen (Norway).

**Chisinau, 24 September 1997, 9000**

**Moldova (0) 0**

**Georgia (1) 1** *(Ketsbaia 9)*

*Moldova:* Romanenco; Fistican (Chirilov 65), Testimitanu, Culibaba, Gaidamasciuc (Rebeja 55), Stroenco, Curtianu, Popovici, Clescenco, Miterev (Cebotari 53), Rogaciov.
*Georgia:* Togonidze; Lobjanidze, Shekiladze, Kaladze, Chikhradze, Kahokidze (Jamarauli 89), Nemsadze, Kiknadze, Kavelashvili (Shelia 84), Ketsbaia, Arveladze A.
*Referee:* Koren (Israel).

**Chisinau, 8 October 1997, 3000**

**Moldova (0) 0**

**Poland (1) 3** *(Juskowiak 23, 55, 61)*

*Moldova:* Romanenco; Fistican, Stroenco, Culibaba (Cebotari 32), Testimitanu, Spanu (Gaidamasciuc 65), Sischin, Epureanu, Popovici (Rogaciov 65), Clescenco, Miterev.
*Poland:* Klak; Jozwiak, Lapinski, Kozminski, Swierczewski, Michalski (Waldoch 74), Brzeczek, Majak, Iwan, Juskowiak (Bukalski 78), Kowalczyk (Kucharski 62).
*Referee:* Tokat (Turkey).

**Tbilisi, 11 October 1997, 12,000**

**Georgia (0) 3** *(Arveladze A 55, Tskhadadze 70, Ketsbaia 75)*

**Poland (0) 0**

*Georgia:* Togonidze; Lobzhanidze, Tskhadadze, Shelia, Chikhradze, Kachokidze (Jamarauli 63), Nemsadze, Ketsbaia (Kiknadze 88), Arveladze A (Gogichaishvili 80), Kavelashvili, Arveladze S.
*Poland:* Klak; Jozwiak, Lapinski, Kozminski, Swierczewski (Ledwon 63), Waldoch, Brzeczek, Majak, Iwan, Juskowiak (Kucharski 84), Gilewicz (Bukalski 74).
*Referee:* Michel (Slovakia).

**Rome, 11 October 1997, 81,200**

**Italy (0) 0**

**England (0) 0**

*Italy:* Peruzzi; Nesta, Costacurta, Cannavaro, Di Livio, Albertini, Dino Baggio, Maldini (Benarrivo 31), Zola (Del Piero 63), Vieri, Inzaghi (Chiesa 46).
*England:* Seaman; Campbell, Le Saux, Southgate, Adams, Batty, Beckham, Gascoigne (Butt 87), Wright, Sheringham, Ince.
*Referee:* Van der Ende (Holland).

**Group 2**

|         | P | W | D | L | F  | A  | Pts |
|---------|---|---|---|---|----|----|-----|
| England | 8 | 6 | 1 | 1 | 15 | 2  | 19  |
| Italy   | 8 | 5 | 3 | 0 | 11 | 1  | 18  |
| Poland  | 8 | 3 | 1 | 4 | 10 | 12 | 10  |
| Georgia | 8 | 3 | 1 | 4 | 7  | 9  | 10  |
| Moldova | 8 | 0 | 0 | 8 | 2  | 21 | 0   |

**England qualify for finals (11.10.97).**

## GROUP 3

**Oslo, 2 June 1996, 14,012**

**Norway (2) 5** *(Solbakken 8, 46, Solskjaer 37, 90, Strandli 60)*

**Azerbaijan (0) 0**

*Norway:* Grodas; Haaland, Berg, Johnsen R, Bjornebye, Rudi, Solbakken (Larsen 79), Rekdal, Leonhardsen (Flo T 46), Solskjaer, Strandli.
*Azerbaijan:* Jidkov; Gasimov, Getman, Ahmedov, Agayev (Nosenko 40), Idigov, Abusev (Asadov 79), Rzayev (Kurbanov 46), Guseynov, Lichkin, Suleimanov.
*Referee:* Snoddy (N Ireland).

**Baku, 31 August 1996, 30,000**

**Azerbaijan (1) 1** *(Rzayev 28)*

**Switzerland (0) 0**

*Azerbaijan:* Jidkov; Gasimov, Asadov, Abusev, Agayev (Getman 86), Ahmedov, Rzayev (Kurbanov 69), Idigov, Lichkin (Alekperov 90), Suleimanov, Guseynov.
*Switzerland:* Pascolo; Hottiger, Vega, Henchoz, Quentin, Ohrel (Sesa 75), Yakin, Sforza, Comisetti (Bonvin 81), Knup (Chapuisat 67), Turkyilmaz.
*Referee:* Wojcik (Poland).

**Budapest, 1 September 1996, 12,500**

**Hungary (1) 1** *(Orosz 16)*

**Finland (0) 0**

*Hungary:* Safar; Mracsko, Telek, Nagy N, Sebok, Halmai, Dombi (Plokai 18), Urban, Orosz (Balog 62), Sandor (Egressy 87), Klausz.
*Finland:* Niemi; Rissanen, Hyypia, Nieminen (Huhtamaki 46), Koskinen, Lindberg, Sumiala, Mahlio (Suominen 81), Jarvinen, Nyyssonen (Kolkka 65), Vanhala.
*Referee:* Strampe (Germany).

**Helsinki, 6 October 1996, 7217**

**Finland (1) 2** *(Sumiala 41 (pen), Kolkka 75)*

**Switzerland (2) 3** *(Lombardo 14, Sforza 34, Yakin 54)*

*Finland:* Niemi; Huhtamaki, Rissanen, Hyrylainen, Myyry, Lindberg (Kolkka 37), Suominen, Gronlund, Koskinen, Sumiala (Hyypia 82), Vanhala.
*Switzerland:* Pascolo; Haas, Vega, Henchoz, Walker, Lombardo, Yakin, Sforza, Vogel (Wicky 90), Chapuisat (Bonvin 78), Kunz (Knup 78).
*Referee:* Orasson (Iceland).

**Oslo, 9 October 1996, 22,480**

**Norway (0) 3** *(Rekdal 83, 89, 90 (pen))*

**Hungary (0) 0**

*Norway:* Grodas; Haaland, Berg, Johnsen R, Bjornebye, Bohinen, Mykland, Rekdal, Leonhardsen, Solskjaer (Flo T 64), Strandli (Ostenstad 83).
*Hungary:* Safar; Banfi, Sebok, Mracsko, Nyilas (Illes 83), Urban, Halmai (Torma 87), Balog, Nagy N, Dombi, Klausz.
*Referee:* Dallas (Scotland).

Baku, 10 November 1996, 35,000

**Azerbaijan (0) 0**

**Hungary (1) 3** *(Nyilas 42, 70 (pen), Urban 83)*

*Azerbaijan:* Jidkov (Koudijev 89); Kasumov, Asadov, Abusev, Agayev (Getman 85), Ahmedov, Rzayev, Idigov, Lichkin (Hasanbekov 46), Suleimanov, Kurbanov.
*Hungary:* Safar; Banfi, Mracsko, Kuttor, Nyilas, Urban (Szlezak 89), Illes (Sandor 75), Halmai, Nagy N, Torma (Dombi 63), Klausz.
*Referee:* Poljak (Croatia).

Berne, 10 November 1996, 23,000

**Switzerland (0) 0**

**Norway (1) 1** *(Leonhardsen 32)*

*Switzerland:* Pascolo; Wicky, Vega, Henchoz, Walker, Lombardo (Subiat 67), Yakin (Piffaretti 88), Sforza, Vogel, Turkyilmaz, Chapuisat (Bonvin 85).
*Norway:* Grodas; Haaland, Berg, Johnsen R, Nilsen, Flo T (Solskjaer 75), Mykland (Solbakken 61), Rekdal, Leonhardsen, Strandli, Ostenstad (Flo H 87).
*Referee:* Vega (Spain).

Baku, 2 April 1997, 20,000

**Azerbaijan (0) 1** *(Suleimanov 80 (pen))*

**Finland (1) 2** *(Litmanen 25, Paatelainen 66)*

*Azerbaijan:* Jidkov; Agayev, Isayev (Kurbanov M 80), Ahmedov, Lichkin, Abusev, Guseynov, Guliyev, Kurbanov G, Suleimanov, Junuyov.
*Finland:* Niemi; Nuorela, Makela (Rissanen 73), Hyypia, Koskinen, Nurmela, Mahlio, Litmanen (Myyry 73), Wiss, Sumiala, Paatelainen.
*Referee:* Poll (England).

Oslo, 30 April 1997, 22,287

**Norway (0) 1** *(Solskjaer 83)*

**Finland (0) 1** *(Sumiala 60)*

*Norway:* Grodas; Eggen, Berg, Johnsen R (Halle 28), Bjornebye, Solskjaer, Mykland, Rekdal, Solbakken, Strandli (Flo J 62), Flo TA.
*Finland:* Niemi; Tuomela, Hyypia (Lehkusou 4), Nuorela, Koskinen, Mahlio, Rissanen, Nurmela (Makela 86), Sumiala, Litmanen, Johansson J (Kolkka 82).
*Referee:* Merk (Germany).

Zurich, 30 April 1997, 17,300

**Switzerland (0) 1** *(Turkyilmaz 83)*

**Hungary (0) 0**

*Switzerland:* Lehmann; Ohrel, Walker, Vega, Wicky (Lombardo 62), Yakin, Kunz (Chassot 56), Vogel, Turkyilmaz, Sforza, Chapuisat (Grassi 73).
*Hungary:* Safar; Kuttor, Banfi, Nagy N (Szlezak 56), Lorincz, Kereszturi, Mracsko (Nyilas 69), Urban, Orosz (Halmai 80), Illes, Klausz.
*Referee:* Sundell (Sweden).

Helsinki, 8 June 1997, 13,417

**Finland (0) 3** *(Vanhala 60, Litmanen 65, Sumiala 82)*

**Azerbaijan (0) 0**

*Finland:* Niemi; Nuorela, Rissanen, Hyypia, Koskinen, Nurmela (Valakari 46), Litmanen (Nyyssonen 84), Mahlio, Johansson (Kolkka 62), Sumiala, Vanhala.
*Azerbaijan:* Jidkov; Jabarov, Gaisumov, Ahmedov (Moussaev 65), Lichkin, Abusev, Guseynov, Agayev (Isaev 89), Guliyev, Kurbanov, Kasumov (Tagizadze 60).
*Referee:* Hamer (Luxembourg).

Budapest, 8 June 1997, 30,000

**Hungary (1) 1** *(Kovacs Z 21)*

**Norway (1) 1** *(Rudi 10)*

*Hungary:* Babos; Lorincz, Banfi, Kuttor, Dombi, Farkashazy, Sandor (Nyilas 79), Halmai, Nagy N (Szlezak 60), Orosz (Dragoner 86), Kovacs Z.
*Norway:* Grodas; Haaland, Berg, Johnsen R, Bjornebye, Rudi, Mykland (Flo J 66), Rekdal, Leonhardsen (Solbakken 76), Strandli, Flo T (Ostenstad 81).
*Referee:* Elleray (England).

Helsinki, 20 August 1997, 35,520

**Finland (0) 0**

**Norway (2) 4** *(Solbakken 9, Rudi 12, Flo J 48, Flo T A 84)*

*Finland:* Moilanen; Rissanen, Nuorela, Tuomela, Koskinen, Mahlio, Lehkosuo, Wiss (Johansson 46), Litmanen, Sumiala, Paatelainen.
*Norway:* Grodas; Halle, Berg, Eggen, Bjornebye, Rudi, Mykland (Strandli 71), Rekdal (Skammelsrud 63), Solbakken, Flo J (Haaland 86), Flo T A.
*Referee:* Jouk (Belarus).

Budapest, 20 August 1997, 30,000

**Hungary (0) 1** *(Klausz 53)*

**Switzerland (0) 1** *(Chapuisat 90)*

*Hungary:* Safar; Mracsko, Dragoner (Halmai 46), Kuttor, Kereszturi, Dombi, Urban, Lipcsei, Illes (Nyilas 46), Kovacs Z (Nagy N 75), Klausz.
*Switzerland:* Lehmann; Ohrel (Kunz 75), Wolf, Henchoz, Walker, Wicky, Yakin, Sforza, Cantaluppi (Zambaz 83), Sesa (De Napoli 66), Chapuisat.
*Referee:* Piraux (Belgium).

Baku, 6 September 1997, 18,000

**Azerbaijan (0) 0**

**Norway (1) 1** *(Flo T A 43)*

*Azerbaijan:* Jidkov; Agayev, Jabarov, Gaisumov, Abusev (Kerimov 68), Lichkin (Musaev 86), Guseynov (Rzayev 78), Kuliyev, Sirkaev, Suleimanov, Kurbanov G.
*Norway:* Grodas; Berg, Eggen, Bjornebye, Rekdal (Skammelsrud 74), Rudi, Solbakken, Strandli (Halle 46), Mykland, Flo J (Steiner 83), Flo T A.
*Referee:* Benko (Austria).

Lausanne, 6 September 1997, 13,000

**Switzerland (0) 1** *(Kunz 90)*

**Finland (1) 2** *(Litmanen 16, Sumiala 79)*

*Switzerland:* Lehmann; Ohrel, Wolf, Henchoz, Walker, Cantaluppi (Zambaz 70), Wicky, Fournier, Zuffi, Sesa (Kunz 68), Chapuisat.
*Finland:* Niemi; Tuomela, Reini, Rissanen, Koskinen, Vanhala (Lahkosuo 46), Mahlio, Valakara (Kuivasto 35), Paatelainen, Litmanen, Sumiala.
*Referee:* Braschi (Italy).

Budapest, 10 September 1997, 10,000

**Hungary (2) 3** *(Klausz 8, Halmai 44, Illes 89)*

**Azerbaijan (0) 1** *(Lichkin 71)*

*Hungary:* Safar; Urban, Mracsko, Kereszturi, Dombi (Illes 60), Lipcsei, Nyilas (Farkashazy 83), Halmai, Egressy, Kovacs Z (Orosz 59), Klausz.
*Azerbaijan:* Jidkov; Gaisumov, Jabarov, Abusev, Agayev (Kerimov 34), Rzayev (Guseynov 61), Kuliyev, Lichkin, Sirkaev, Kurbanov G, Suleimanov (Musaev 78).
*Referee:* Ouzoumov (Bulgaria).

Oslo, 10 September 1997, 22,603

**Norway (0) 5** *(Jakobsen 47, Solbakken 51, Eggen 66, Ostenstad 75, Flo T A 86)*

**Switzerland (0) 0**

*Norway:* Grodas; Halle (Haaland 83), Berg, Eggen, Bjornebye, Flo J (Ostenstad 46), Solbakken, Rekdal, Rudi, Jakobsen (Strandli 72), Flo T A.
*Switzerland:* Lehmann; Ohrel (Zambaz 54), Wolf, Henchoz, Walker, Wicky, Yakin, Sforza, Fournier, Kunz (Sesa 60), Chapuisat (Vogel 69).
*Referee:* Krug (Germany).

Helsinki, 11 October 1997, 31,617

**Finland (0) 1** *(Sumiala 62)*

**Hungary (0) 1** *(Sebok 90)*

*Finland:* Moilanen; Ylonen, Tuomela, Hyypia, Koskinen (Rissanen 82), Mahlio, Reini, Litmanen, Valakari, Sumiala (Johansson 89), Paatelainen.
*Hungary:* Safar; Mracsko, Halmai, Kereszturi, Lorincz, Lipcsei, Egressy (Dombi 81), Sebok, Orosz, Nyilas (Horvath 57), Kovacs (Illes 57).
*Referee:* Heynemann (Germany).

Zurich, 11 October 1997, 7600

**Switzerland (3) 5** *(Turkyilmaz 13, 23, 69 (pen), Yakin 43, Chapuisat 51)*

**Azerbaijan (0) 0**

*Switzerland:* Lehmann; Ohrel (Sesa 46), Henchoz, Vega, Walker, Cantaluppi (Zambaz 74), Yakin, Wicky, Zuffi, Turkyilmaz, Chapuisat (Kunz 63).
*Azerbaijan:* Jidkov; Vasenko (Kerimov 44), Abusev, Musaev, Lichkin, Guseynov, Kurbanov M, Kuliyev, Kurbanov G, Suleimanov (Tagizade 76), Sirkaev.
*Referee:* Rowbotham (Scotland).

**Group 3**

| | P | W | D | L | F | A | Pts |
|---|---|---|---|---|---|---|---|
| Norway | 8 | 6 | 2 | 0 | 21 | 2 | 20 |
| Hungary | 8 | 3 | 3 | 2 | 10 | 8 | 12 |
| Finland | 8 | 3 | 2 | 3 | 11 | 12 | 11 |
| Switzerland | 8 | 3 | 1 | 4 | 11 | 12 | 10 |
| Azerbaijan | 8 | 1 | 0 | 7 | 3 | 22 | 3 |

**Norway qualify for finals (6.9.97).**

GROUP 4
Stockholm, 1 June 1996, 30,014

**Sweden (2) 5** *(Andersson K 20 (pen), 62, Dahlin 30, Andersson P 77, Larsson 88)*

**Belarus (0) 1** *(Belkevich 75)*

*Sweden:* Andersson B; Nilsson R, Andersson P, Bjorklund, Sundgren, Ingesson (Mild 85), Thern, Zetterberg, Limpar, Dahlin (Larsson 77), Andersson K.
*Belarus:* Satsunkhevich; Gurenko, Khatskevich, Shtanyuk, Kashentsev (Kulchi 63), Vergeichik, Belkevich, Maleyev, Romashchenko (Katchuro 57), Makovski, Baranov.
*Referee:* Harrel (France).

Vienna, 31 August 1996, 29,500

**Austria (0) 0**

**Scotland (0) 0**

*Austria:* Konsel; Schopp, Schottel, Pfeffer, Feiersinger, Marasek, Ramusch (Ogris 76), Kuhbauer, Polster (Sabitzer 68), Herzog, Heraf.
*Scotland:* Goram; Burley, McKinlay T, Calderwood, Hendry, Boyd, McCall, Ferguson, McCoist (Durie 75), McAllister, Collins.
*Referee:* Piraux (Belgium).

Minsk, 31 August 1996, 7000

**Belarus (1) 1** *(Makovski 35)*

**Estonia (0) 0**

*Belarus:* Shantalosov; Gurenko, Orlovski, Shtanyuk, Yakhimovich, Oreshnikov, Kulchi, Baranov, Belkevich (Romashchenko 85), Makovski (Tchernyavski 70), Katchuro.
*Estonia:* Poom (Pareiko 7); Lemsalu, Rooba U, Hohlov-Simson, Lindmaa, Alonen (Kirs 57), Rooba M, Zelinski, Kristal, Reim, Oper (Arbeiter 64).
*Referee:* Khoussainov (Russia).

Riga, 1 September 1996, 2000

**Latvia (0) 1** *(Rimkus 55)*

**Sweden (2) 2** *(Dahlin 18, Andersson K 21)*

*Latvia:* Karavayev; Zakreshevsky (Troitsky 59), Stepanov, Shevlyakov, Bleidelis, Ivanov, Zemlinsky, Rimkus, Boulders (Babichev 74), Stradinsh (Pakhar 28), Shtolcers.
*Sweden:* Andersson B; Nilsson R, Andersson P, Bjorklund, Sundgren, Mild (Limpar 82), Zetterberg (Schwarz 85), Thern, Blomqvist, Dahlin (Andersson A 77), Andersson K.
*Referee:* Wagner (Hungary).

Tallinn, 5 October 1996, 2000

**Estonia (0) 1** *(Hohlov-Simson 52)*

**Belarus (0) 0**

*Estonia:* Poom; Lemsalu, Hohlov-Simson, Rooba U, Zelinski, Alonen, Rooba M (Kallaste T 59), Lindmaa, Kristal (Arbeiter 90), Reim, Oper (Kirs 26).
*Belarus:* Shantalosov; Gurenko, Ostrovski, Shtanyuk, Khasskevich, Vergeichik (Baranov 43) (Tchernyavski 77), Kulchi, Maleyev, Belkevich, Makovski, Kachuro.
*Referee:* O'Hanlon (Rep of Ireland).

Riga, 5 October 1996, 9500

**Latvia (0) 0**

**Scotland (1) 2** *(Collins 18, Jackson 78)*

*Latvia:* Karavayev; Troitsky, Astafyev, Zemlinsky, Shevlyakov, Stepanov, Ivanov, Bleidelis, Rimkus (Boulders 78), Babichev (Shtolcers 46), Pakhar.
*Scotland:* Goram; Burley, Boyd, McKinlay T (McNamara 65), Calderwood, Whyte, Spencer (Dodds 59), McCall (Lambert 46), Jackson, McAllister, Collins.
*Referee:* Ulrich (Czech Republic).

Minsk, 9 October 1996, 5000

**Belarus (0) 1** *(Makovski 78)*

**Latvia (1) 1** *(Zemlinksy 16)*

*Belarus:* Shantalosov; Gurenko, Shtanyuk, Bezmen, Ostrovski, Kulchi, Orlovski, Makovski, Tchernyavski (Vergeichik 90), Maleyev, Katchuro (Vyajevich 60).
*Latvia:* Karavayev; Troitsky, Zemlinsky, Shevlyakov (Zakreshevsky 64), Astafyev, Ivanov, Stepanov, Zeiberlinsh (Babichev 46), Bleidelis, Rimkus (Boulders 67), Pakhar.
*Referee:* Kvarastskhelia (Georgia).

Tallinn, 9 October 1996,

**Estonia (0) 0**

**Scotland (0) 0**

*Estonia:* .
*Scotland:* .
*Game abandoned.*

Stockholm, 9 October 1996, 36,859

**Sweden (0) 0**

**Austria (1) 1** *(Herzog 11)*

*Sweden:* Ravelli; Nilsson R, Bjorklund, Andersson P, Schwarz, Thern, Blomqvist, Zetterberg, Ingesson (Mild 67), Dahlin (Andersson A 83), Andersson K (Larsson H 42).
*Austria:* Konsel; Schopp (Hatz 77), Pfeffer, Schottel, Feiersinger, Hutter A, Heraf, Herzog, Stoger (Ramusch 71), Polster, Wetl.
*Referee:* Krondl (Czech Republic).

Vienna, 9 November 1996, 15,700

**Austria (1) 2** *(Polster 43, Herzog 73)*

**Latvia (1) 1** *(Rimkus 45)*

*Austria:* Konsel; Schottel, Kartalija, Pfeffer, Heraf, Schopp, Stoger (Kuhbauer 60), Hutter (Ramusch 60), Herzog, Wetl, Polster.
*Latvia:* Karavayev; Troitsky, Stepanov, Shevlyakov, Bleidelis, Zemlinsky, Shtolcers, Astafyev, Ivanov, Rimkus, Babichev (Pakhar 65).
*Referee:* Mitrovic (Slovenia).

Hampden Park, 10 November 1996, 50,000

**Scotland (1) 1** *(McGinlay 8)*

**Sweden (0) 0**

*Scotland:* Leighton; McNamara (Lambert 46), Boyd, Calderwood, Hendry, McKinlay T, Burley, McKinlay W, Jackson (Gallacher 78), McGinlay (McCoist 84), Collins.
*Sweden:* Ravelli; Nilsson R, Andersson P, Bjorklund, Sundgren, Alexandersson (Larsson 68), Thern, Zetterberg (Andersson A 76), Schwarz, Blomqvist, Dahlin (Andersson K 16).
*Referee:* Aranda (Spain).

## Monaco, 11 February 1997, 4000

**Estonia (0) 0**

**Scotland (0) 0**

*Estonia:* Poom; Kirs, Hohlov-Simson, Lemsalu, Rooba U, Reim, Leetma (Oper 75), Rooba M (Pari 67), Alonen, Kristal, Zelinski.
*Scotland:* Goram; McNamara (McKinlay T 75), Boyd, McStay (Ferguson I 63), Hendry, Calderwood, Gallacher, McAllister, Ferguson D, McGinlay (McCoist 72), Collins.
*Referee:* Radoman (Yugoslavia).

## Kilmarnock, 29 March 1997, 17,996

**Scotland (1) 2** *(Boyd 25, Meet 52 (og))*

**Estonia (0) 0**

*Scotland:* Leighton; Burley, McKinlay T, Calderwood, Hendry (McKinlay W 65), Boyd, Gemmill, Jackson (McGinlay 83), Gallacher, McAllister, McStay.
*Estonia:* Poom; Kirs, Hohlov-Simson, Lemsalu, Meet, Reim, Viikmae (Leetma 72), Zelinski (Arbeiter 81), Pari (Rooba M 54), Kristal, Oper.
*Referee:* Heynemann (Germany).

## Celtic Park, 2 April 1997, 43,295

**Scotland (1) 2** *(Gallacher 24, 77)*

**Austria (0) 0**

*Scotland:* Leighton; Burley, Boyd, Lambert, Hendry, Calderwood, McKinlay T, Gallacher (McCoist 85), Jackson (McGinlay 75), McAllister (McStay 89), Collins.
*Austria:* Konsel; Schottel (Kogler W 46), Feiersinger, Pfeffer, Schopp, Heraf, Aigner (Ogris 81), Wetl, Stoger (Vastic 67), Herzog, Polster.
*Referee:* Levnikov (Russia).

## Vienna, 30 April 1997, 27,500

**Austria (0) 2** *(Vastic 48, Stoger 87)*

**Estonia (0) 0**

*Austria:* Konsel; Feiersinger, Schottel (Kogler W 69), Pfeffer, Cerny, Heraf, Kuhbauer, Herzog, Wetl, Vastic (Stoger 51), Polster.
*Estonia:* Poom; Kirs, Hohlov-Simson, Lemsalu, Meet, Viikmae (Leetma 83), Pari, Reim, Alonen (Arbeiter 80), Kristal, Oper.
*Referee:* Ancion (Belgium).

## Riga, 30 April 1997, 3000

**Latvia (1) 2** *(Shevlyakov 38, 83)*

**Belarus (0) 0**

*Latvia:* Karavayev; Troitsky, Astafyev (Strandinsh 82), Zemlinsky, Shevlyakov, Blagonadezhdin, Ivanov, Pakhar (Zakreshevsky 66), Rimkus, Babichev (Bleidelis 46), Shtolcers.
*Belarus:* Shantolosov; Gurenko, Shtanuk, Yakhimovich, Hackevich (Gerasimenko 46), Ostrovsky, Belkevich, Melitski, Katchuro, Antonovich (Gerasimets 46), Orlovski (Makovetsky 66).
*Referee:* Koho (Finland).

## Gothenburg, 30 April 1997, 40,000

**Sweden (1) 2** *(Andersson K 44, 64)*

**Scotland (0) 1** *(Gallacher 84)*

*Sweden:* Ravelli; Sundgren, Andersson P, Bjorklund, Kamark, Thern, Zetterberg, Schwarz (Mild 12), Andersson A, Andersson K, Dahlin.
*Scotland:* Leighton; Burley, Boyd, Lambert, Hendry, Calderwood, McKinlay T (Gemmill 67), Gallacher, Jackson (Durie 66), McAllister, Collins.
*Referee:* Collina (Italy).

## Tallinn, 18 May 1997, 3000

**Estonia (1) 1** *(Zelinski 5)*

**Latvia (0) 3** *(Babichev 53, Yeliseyev 80, Lemsalu 87 (og))*

*Estonia:* Poom; Lemsalu, Kirs, Nommik, Meet, Alonen, Viikmae (Arbeiter 81), Zelinski, Kristal, Reim, Oper (Rooba M 84).
*Latvia:* Karavayev; Stepanov, Astafyev, Zemlinsky, Shevlyakov, Bleidelis, Ivanov, Pakhar, Babichev (Troitsky 90), Rimkus (Boulders 73), Shtolcers (Yeliseyev 46).
*Referee:* Cvitkovic (Croatia).

## Minsk, 8 June 1997, 12,000

**Belarus (0) 0**

**Scotland (0) 1** *(McAllister G 49 (pen))*

*Belarus:* Satsunkhevich; Lavrik, Ostrovski, Yakhimovich, Gurenko, Dovnar (Belkevich 53), Romashchenko, Shtanyuk, Orlovski (Balachov 66), Khlebossolov (Makovski 61), Gerasimets.
*Scotland:* Leighton; Burley, Boyd, Lambert, Dailly, Hopkin (Gemmill 68), McKinlay T (McAllister B 79), Gallacher, Jackson (Dodds 87), McAllister G, Durie.
*Referee:* Cakar (Turkey).

## Tallinn, 8 June 1997, 4000

**Estonia (0) 2** *(Kristal 75, 84)*

**Sweden (1) 3** *(Dahlin 13, Zetterberg 53 (pen), Andersson K 71)*

*Estonia:* Poom; Kirs, Lemsalu, Hohlov-Simson, Meet, Leetma (Viikmae 46), Rooba M (Pari 65), Oper, Kristal, Reim, Zelinski (Arbeiter 85).
*Sweden:* Hedman; Nilsson R, Andersson P, Bjorklund, Sundgren, Thern, Zetterberg, Mild (Alexandersson 76), Andersson A, Dahlin (Pettersson 72), Andersson K.
*Referee:* Wojcik (Poland).

## Riga, 8 June 1997, 5000

**Latvia (0) 1** *(Pakhar 39)*

**Austria (0) 3** *(Heraf 55, Polster 79, Stoger 80)*

*Latvia:* Karavayev; Troitsky, Astafyev, Zemlinsky, Shevlyakov, Stepanov, Ivanov, Pakhar, Babichev (Zakreshevsky 68), Rimkus (Yeliseyev 59), Bleidelis (Shtolcers 64).
*Austria:* Konsel; Schottel, Pfeffer, Feiersinger, Cerny (Ramusch 85), Heraf, Kuhbauer, Herzog (Stoger 78), Wetl (Pfeifenberger 46), Vastic, Polster.
*Referee:* Jol (Holland).

## Minsk, 20 August 1997, 10,000

**Belarus (0) 1** *(Guernko 39)*

**Sweden (1) 2** *(Andersson K 76, Zetterberg 85)*

*Belarus:* Shantalosov; Gerashchenko, Shtanyuk, Ostrovski, Lavrik (Yaskovich 22), Romashchenko, Orlovski (Balashov 58), Gurenko, Belkevich, Katchuro, Gerasimets (Khlebosolov 66).
*Sweden:* Ravelli; Sundgren, Andersson P, Bjorklund, Kamark, Alexandersson, Zetterberg, Andersson A (Blomqvist 55), Thern, Dahlin (Mild 89), Petersson (Andersson K 55).
*Referee:* Gallacher (England).

## Tallinn, 20 August 1997, 1500

**Estonia (0) 0**

**Austria (0) 3** *(Polster 47, 70, 90)*

*Estonia:* Poom; Lemsalu, Kirs (Leetma 79), Hohlov-Simson, Meet, Viikmae (Terehhov 70), Arbeiter (Rooba M 77), Oper, Kristal, Reim, Zelinski.
*Austria:* Konsel; Cherny (Schopp 86), Kogler W, Pfeffer, Pfeifenberger, Mahlich, Kuhbauer, Herzog (Stoger P 71), Prilasnig, Vastic, Polster.
*Referee:* Fassolis (Greece).

### Vienna, 6 September 1997, 48,000

**Austria (0) 1** *(Herzog 76)*
**Sweden (0) 0**

*Austria:* Konsel; Schottel, Feiersinger, Pfeffer, Cerny, Mahlich, Pfeifenberger, Herzog (Wohlfahrt 83), Prilasnig, Polster, Vastic (Stoger 66).
*Sweden:* Ravelli; Nilsson R, Andersson P, Bjorklund, Kamark, Alexandersson, Thern, Zetterberg, Mild (Blomqvist 55), Andersson K, Dahlin.
*Referee:* Nieto (Spain).

### Riga, 6 September 1997, 1500

**Latvia (0) 1** *(Zemlinsky 87 (pen))*
**Estonia (0) 0**

*Latvia:* Karavayev; Troitsky (Shtolcers 56), Zemlinsky, Stepanov, Astafyev (Balgonadezhdin 74), Shevlyakov, Ivanov, Bleidelis, Rimkus, Babichev, Yeliseyev (Zakreshevsky 69).
*Estonia:* Poom; Lemsalu, Hohlov-Simson, Meet, Kirs, Alonen, Arbeiter, Oper, Kristal, Reim, Viikmae (Zelinski 60).
*Referee:* Guntadze (Georgia).

### Aberdeen, 7 September 1997, 20,160

**Scotland (1) 4** *(Gallacher 6, 58, Hopkin 54, 88)*
**Belarus (0) 1** *(Katchuro 74 (pen))*

*Scotland:* Leighton; Burley, McKinlay T, Calderwood, Boyd, Dailly, Lambert, Gallacher (Dodds 85), Durie (McCoist 46), McAllister (Hopkin 50), Collins.
*Belarus:* Shantalosov; Lavrik, Ostrovski, Gerashchenko, Dovnar, Gerasimets (Balashov 78) Belkevich, Jouravel (Tchernyavski 65), Kulchi, Gurenko (Orlovski 52), Katchuro.
*Referee:* Van der Ende (Holland).

### Minsk, 10 September 1997, 5000

**Belarus (0) 0**
**Austria (0) 1** *(Pfeifenberger 50)*

*Belarus:* Satsunkhevich; Gerashchenko, Dovnar (Orlovski 76), Shtanyuk, Ostrovski, Tchernyavski (Gerasimets 55), Kulchi, Gurenko, Belkevich, Katchuro, Romashchenko.
*Austria:* Wohlfahrt; Cerny, Schottel, Kogler, Feiersinger, Mahlic, Vastic (Stoger 46), Prilassnig, Pfeifenberger, Polster, Herzog (Hutter 71).
*Referee:* Muhmenthaler (Switzerland).

### Solna, 10 September 1997, 20,251

**Sweden (0) 1** *(Jonsson 88)*
**Latvia (0) 0**

*Sweden:* Ravelli; Sundgren, Andersson P, Bjorklund, Kamark, Alexandersson, Zetterberg, Thern, Mild (Blomqvist 46), Dahlin (Andersson A 58), Andersson K (Jonsson 68).
*Latvia:* Karavayev; Lobanyov, Stepanov, Troitsky (Zakreshevsky 46), Bleidelis, Astafyev, Blagonadezhdin, Babichev (Shtolcers 52), Ivanov, Pakhar, Rimkus (Yeliseyev 61).
*Referee:* Merk (Germany).

### Vienna, 11 October 1997, 48,000

**Austria (4) 4** *(Polster 3, 16 (pen), Stoger 6, 42)*
**Belarus (0) 0**

*Austria:* Konsel; Kogler, Feiersinger, Pfeffer, Cerny (Ramusch 75), Pfeifenberger, Mahlich, Stoger, Prilasnig (Schopp 66), Polster, Herzog (Reinmayr 66).
*Belarus:* Satsunkhevich; Lavrik, Shtanyuk, Ostrovski, Orlovski, Gerasimets (Tchernyavski 78) Romashchenko, Kulchi, Belkevich (Balashov 54) (Razumov 83), Gurenko, Makovski.
*Referee:* Huzu (Romania).

### Parkhead, 11 October 1997, 47,613

**Scotland (1) 2** *(Gallacher 43, Durie 80)*
**Latvia (0) 0**

*Scotland:* Leighton; Burley (McKinlay W 85), Boyd (McKinlay T 81), Calderwood, Hendry, Dailly, Lambert, Gallacher, Durie (Donnelly 84), McAllister, Collins.
*Latvia:* Karavayev; Stepanov, Lobanyov, Zemlinsky, Shevlyakov, Blagonadezhdin (Shtolcers 61), Ivanov, Bleidelis, Pakhar, Babichev, Yeliseyev (Rimkus 68).
*Referee:* Pilier (Hungary).

### Stockholm, 11 October 1997, 18,702

**Sweden (1) 1** *(Zetterberg 25)*
**Estonia (0) 0**

*Sweden:* Ravelli; Nilsson, Andersson P, Matovac, Sundgren, Alexandersson, Mild, Zetterberg, Blomqvist (Andreas Andersson 66), Larsson (Jonsson 66), Dahlin (Anders Andersson 80).
*Estonia:* Poom; Kirs, Hohlov-Simson, Lemsalu, Meet, Viikmae, Arbeiter (Zelinski 70), Reim, Alonen, Kristal, Oper.
*Referee:* Ormandjev (Bulgaria).

### Group 4

| | P | W | D | L | F | A | Pts |
|---|---|---|---|---|---|---|---|
| Austria | 10 | 8 | 1 | 1 | 17 | 4 | 25 |
| Scotland | 10 | 7 | 2 | 1 | 15 | 3 | 23 |
| Sweden | 10 | 7 | 0 | 3 | 16 | 9 | 21 |
| Latvia | 10 | 3 | 1 | 6 | 10 | 14 | 10 |
| Estonia | 10 | 1 | 1 | 8 | 4 | 16 | 4 |
| Belarus | 10 | 1 | 1 | 8 | 5 | 21 | 4 |

**Austria and Scotland (as best runner-up) qualify for finals (11.10.97).**

### GROUP 5

### Tel Aviv, 1 September 1996, 25,000

**Israel (1) 2** *(Harazi R 34, Banin 62 (pen))*
**Bulgaria (1) 1** *(Balakov 2 (pen))*

*Israel:* Cohen; Halfon (Harazi A 90), Benado, Shelah, Amsalem, Banin, Hazan, Nimni, Revivo, Rosenthal (Berkovic 83), Harazi R (Klinger 77).
*Bulgaria:* Mikhailov; Kishishev, Hubchev, Ivanov T (Borimirov 75), Tsvetanov, Lechkov, Yankov, Balakov, Yordanov, Donkov (Iliev 62), Kostadinov.
*Referee:* Trentalange (Italy).

### Moscow, 1 September 1996, 15,000

**Russia (2) 4** *(Nikiforov 7, 50, Kolyvanov 34, Bestchastnykh 82)*
**Cyprus (0) 0**

*Russia:* Cherchesov; Radimov (Charlashev 68), Nikiforov, Mamedov, Ternavsky, Tetradze, Onopko, Kanchelskis, Bestchastnykh, Kolyvanov (Tikhonov 55), Radchenko (Kanischev 46).
*Cyprus:* Petrides; Larkou (Timotheou 61), Pittas, Ioannou D, Christodolou G, Andreou A, Christodolou M, Panayi, Gogic, Ioannou I (Theodotou 90), Alexandrou (Malekos 78).
*Referee:* Nilsson (Sweden).

### Luxembourg, 8 October 1996, 3775

**Luxembourg (1) 1** *(Langers 20)*
**Bulgaria (2) 2** *(Balakov 14 (pen), Kostadinov 37)*

*Luxembourg:* Koch; Deville, Vanek, Weis, Strasser, Posing (Ganser 46), Saibene, Birsens, Hellers, Cardoni (Theis 27), Langers.
*Bulgaria:* Mikhailov; Kishishev, Antonov (Vassiliev 46), Ivanov T (Borimirov 62), Tsvetanov, Lechkov, Ivanov G, Yankov, Balakov, Hristov (Vidolov 46), Kostadinov.
*Referee:* Kollari (Albania).

Tel Aviv, 9 October 1996, 34,000

**Israel (0) 1** *(Bromer G 62)*

**Russia (0) 1** *(Kolyvanov 80)*

*Israel:* Cohen; Halfon (Benado 81), Shelah, Bromer G, Amsalem, Hazan, Nimni, Berkovic (Zohar 89), Banin, Revivo, Harazi R (Rosenthal 78).
*Russia:* Cherchesov; Bushmanov (Radimov 67), Tetradze, Nikiforov, Minko, Kanchelskis, Onopko, Karpin, Kolyvanov, Radchenko (Tikhonov 46), Bestchastnykh.
*Referee:* Batta (France).

Limassol, 10 November 1996, 15,000

**Cyprus (2) 2** *(Gogic 8, 14)*

**Israel (0) 0**

*Cyprus:* Panayiotou; Aristocleous, Pittas, Ioannou D (Misos 71), Christodolou G, Stavrou, Ioannou G (Timotheou 58), Andreou, Gogic, Christodolou M, Alexandrou (Malekos 78).
*Israel:* Cohen; Halfon (Benado 36), Bromer G, Shelah, Amsalem (Harazi R 36), Hazan, Banin, Berkovic, Nimni, Revivo, Rosenthal (Drieks 72).
*Referee:* Constantin (Romania).

Luxembourg, 10 November 1996, 5650

**Luxembourg (0) 0**

**Russia (2) 4** *(Tikhonov 34, Kanchelskis 38, Bestchatnykh 56, Karpin 79)*

*Luxembourg:* Koch; Vanek, Deville, Birsens, Strasser, Saibene, Ganser (Holtz 46), Weis, Thill (Amodio 82), Groff, Langers.
*Russia:* Cherchesov (Ovchinnikov 75); Minko, Nikiforov, Tetradze, Karpin, Onopko, Mostovoi, Tikhonov, Kanchelskis, Bestchastnykh (Radimov 80), Kolyvanov.
*Referee:* Hirviniemi (Finland).

Limassol, 14 December 1996, 16,000

**Cyprus (1) 1** *(Pittas 29)*

**Bulgaria (2) 3** *(Balakov 23, 34, Iliev 70)*

*Cyprus:* Panayiotou; Aristocleous (Theodotou 61), Pittas, Ioannou D, Christodoulou G, Andreou S, Christodoulou M, Stravrou (Larkou 46), Gogic, Ioannou G (Xiouroupas 81), Malekos.
*Bulgaria:* Mikhailov (Zdravkov 46); Kishishev (Antonov G 78), Ivanov T, Tsvetanov, Guentchev, Yordanov, Kostadinov, Nankov, Donkov (Vidolov 61), Balakov, Iliev.
*Referee:* Rowbotham (Scotland).

Ramatgan, 15 December 1996, 28,000

**Israel (1) 1** *(Ohana 39)*

**Luxembourg (0) 0**

*Israel:* Korenfain; Amsalem, Shelah, Klinger, Hazan, Nimni, Banin, Berkovic, Abuksis, Revivo (Zohar 82), Ohana (Bromer A 90).
*Luxembourg:* Koch; Vanek, Weis, Strasser, Deville, Saibene, Hellers, Birsens (Holtz 28), Fanelli, Cardoni (Ganser 78), Langers.
*Referee:* Ashman (Wales).

Nicosia, 29 March 1997, 4000

**Cyprus (1) 1** *(Gogic 29)*

**Russia (1) 1** *(Simutenkov 31)*

*Cyprus:* Petrides; Theodotou, Pittas, Andreou A, Misos, Larkou, Papavassiliou, Malekos (Melanargitis 86), Ioannou G (Engomitis 77), Gogic (Okkas 84), Timotheou.
*Russia:* Cherchesov; Onopko, Tetradze, Popov, Chugainov, Kanchelskis, Karpin, Mostovoi, Tsymbalar (Gerasimenko 69), Kolyvanov, Simutenkov.
*Referee:* Roca (Spain).

Luxembourg, 31 March 1997, 6066

**Luxembourg (0) 0**

**Israel (1) 3** *(Zohar 11, 80, Banin 56)*

*Luxembourg:* Koch; Vanek, Deville (Amodio 65), Birsens, Strasser, Saibene, Holtz (Posing 75), Thill, Langers, Cardoni, Groff.
*Israel:* Cohen; Halfon, Amsalem, Shelah, Benado, Rosenthal (Klinger 83), Banin, Revivo, Berkovic (Ben-Shimon 46), Zohar, Ohana (Mizrahi 46).
*Referee:* Temmink (Holland).

Sofia, 2 April 1997, 33,000

**Bulgaria (2) 4** *(Borimirov 2, Kostadinov 36, 45, Yordanov 66)*

**Cyprus (0) 1** *(Okkas 61)*

*Bulgaria:* Zdravkov; Kishishev, Ivanov T, Genchev, Yordanov, Yankov (Mitov 80), Kostadinov, Borimirov (Nankov 58), Donkov (Vidolov 73), Balakov, Iliev.
*Cyprus:* Petrides; Pittas (Melanargitis 77), Theodotou, Yiannaki, Misos, Larkou, Papavassiliou, Engomitis (Hadjilucas 46), Charalambous, Alexandrou (Okkas 46), Timotheou.
*Referee:* Muhmenthaler (Switzerland).

Tel Aviv, 30 April 1997, 34,000

**Israel (1) 2** *(Ohana 3, 72)*

**Cyprus (0) 0**

*Israel:* Cohen; Harazi A, Glam, Hazan A, Shelah, Benado, Banin, Mizrahi (Jano 85), Berkovic, Zohar (Atar 88), Ohana.
*Cyprus:* Panayiotou; Theodotou, Pittas, Misos, Charalambous, Larkou (Okkas 46), Timotheou, Andreou, Gogic, Malekos (Ioannou G 46), Papavassiliou (Engomitis 88).
*Referee:* Melnitchuk (Ukraine).

Moscow, 30 April 1997, 10,000

**Russia (1) 3** *(Kechinov 20, Grishin 58, Simutenkov 60)*

**Luxembourg (0) 0**

*Russia:* Ovchinnikov; Kovtun, Tetradze (Popov 24), Chugainov, Onopko, Radimov (Zubkov 69), Kosolapov, Alenichev, Bestchastnykh (Grishin 46), Kechinov, Simutenkov.
*Luxembourg:* Koch; Vanek, Strasser, Weis, Saibene (Amodio 88), Deville, Posing, Birsens, Hellers, Cardoni (Lamborelle 75), Langers (Thill 71).
*Referee:* Rowbotham (Scotland).

Bourgas, 8 June 1997, 20,000

**Bulgaria (1) 4** *(Stoichkov 43 (pen), Kostadinov 47, Balakov 49 (pen), Lechkov 80)*

**Luxembourg (0) 0**

*Bulgaria:* Zdravkov; Nankov, Ivanov T, Yordanov, Petkov, Yankov (Lechkov 56), Balakov, Iliev (Trendafilov 84), Kostadinov, Penev (Borimirov 67), Stoichkov.
*Luxembourg:* Koch; Vanek, Weis, Deville, Holt (Thill 73), Birsens, Ganser (Amodio 81), Hellers, Theis, Cardoni, Langers (Posing 87).
*Referee:* Batista (Portugal).

Moscow, 8 June 1997, 30,000

**Russia (2) 2** *(Radimov 8, Kosolapov 38)*

**Israel (0) 0**

*Russia:* Ovchinnikov; Tsveiba, Nikiforov, Onopko, Yanovski, Grishin (Tessipov 90), Kosolapov, Alenichev, Radimov, Tcherychev (Kovtun 83), Bestchastnykh (Tikhonov 60).
*Israel:* Cohen; Halfon, Amsalem, Hazan, Shelah, Benado, Rosenthal (Harazi A 46), Revivo (Zohar 56), Berkovic, Nimni, Ohana (Mizrahi 72).
*Referee:* Grabher (Austria).

Sofia, 20 August 1997, 20,000

**Bulgaria (0) 1** *(Penev 71)*

**Israel (0) 0**

*Bulgaria:* Zdravkov; Nankov, Ivanov T, Petkov (Penev 46), Yordanov, Kichichev, Borimirov (Lechkov 60), Yankov, Balakov, Kostadinov (Guintchev 73), Stoichkov.
*Israel:* Cohen; Halfon (Harazi A 72), Benado, Shelach, Ben-Shimon, Amsalem, Hazan, Banin, Revivo, Nimni, Ohana (Mizrahi A 73).
*Referee:* Piller (Hungary).

Luxembourg, 7 September 1997, 3022

**Luxembourg (1) 1** *(Amodio 8)*

**Cyprus (1) 3** *(Papavassiliou 6, Ioannou 55, 80)*

*Luxembourg:* Koch; Weis, Lamborelle, Vanek, Saibene, Hellers, Thil, Amodio, Groff, Cardoni, Langers (Theis 67).
*Cyprus:* Panayiotou; Costa, Pittas, Christodolou, Charalambos, Pounnas, Melanarkitis (Engomitis 58), Ioannou, Papavassiliou (Kaiafas 81), Gogic (Okkas 84), Malekos.
*Referee:* Orrassen (Sweden).

Sofia, 10 September 1997, 45,000

**Bulgaria (0) 1** *(Ivanov 57)*

**Russia (0) 0**

*Bulgaria:* Zdravkov; Kishishev, Ivanov, Guentchev, Petkov M, Yankov, Lechkov, Balakov, Stoichkov (Petkov I 85), Kostadinov (Iliev 73), Penev.
*Russia:* Ovchinnikov; Kovtun, Nikiforov, Tsveiba, Yanovski, Kanchelskis, Onopko, Kosolapov (Hohlov 46), Alenichev, Kolyvanov, Simutenkov (Tcherychev 75).
*Referee:* Krondl (Czech Republic).

Limassol, 11 October 1997, 5000

**Cyprus (0) 2** *(Papavassiliou 80, Spoljaric 85)*

**Luxembourg (0) 0**

*Cyprus:* Panayiotou; Costa, Pittas, Christodolou, Ioannou D, Pounnas, Engomitis, Spoljaric, Ioannou I (Agathocleous 68), Papavassiliou, Malekos (Okkas 57).
*Luxembourg:* Koch; Funck, Thill, Birsens, Vanek, Saibene, Hellers, Theis, Langers (Amodio 43), Cardoni (Holtz 75), Groff (Posing 83).
*Referee:* Pregia (Albania).

Moscow, 11 October 1997, 20,000

**Russia (2) 4** *(Alenichev 13, 57, Kolyvanov 40 (pen), Yuran 52 (pen))*

**Bulgaria (0) 2** *(Grouev 68, Kostadinov 78)*

*Russia:* Ovchinnikov; Popov, Tchougainov, Tsveiba, Janovski, Tichonov, Onopko, Simutenkov (Radimov 46), Alenichev (Kossolapov 84), Yuran (Veretennikov 67), Kolyvanov.
*Bulgaria:* Zdravkov; Kishishev, Ivanov, Petkov, Ginchev, Jankov, Zafirov, Lechkov (Borimirov 55), Iliev (Grouev 67), Penev, Stoichkov (Kostadinov 55).
*Referee:* Pairetto (Italy).

**Group 5**

| | P | W | D | L | F | A | Pts |
|---|---|---|---|---|---|---|---|
| Bulgaria | 8 | 6 | 0 | 2 | 18 | 9 | 18 |
| Russia | 8 | 5 | 2 | 1 | 19 | 5 | 17 |
| Israel | 8 | 4 | 1 | 3 | 9 | 7 | 13 |
| Cyprus | 8 | 3 | 1 | 4 | 10 | 15 | 10 |
| Luxembourg | 8 | 0 | 0 | 8 | 2 | 22 | 0 |

**Bulgaria qualify for finals (10.9.97).**

## GROUP 6

Belgrade, 24 April 1996, 25,000

**Yugoslavia (3) 3** *(Savicevic 3, 30, Milosevic 38)*

**Faeroes (0) 1** *(Petersen 54)*

*Yugoslavia:* Kocic; Curcic (Mirkovic 75), Djorovic, Jokanovic, Brnovic, Mihajlovic (Pantic 40), Jugovic, Savicevic, Mijatovic, Stojkovic, Milosevic (Nadj 87).
*Faeroes:* Knudsen; Johannesen O, Hansen J, Hansen A, Johnsson J, Morkore A, Jarnskor H, Dam, Muller, Petersen, Rasmussen JE (Jarnskor M 75).
*Referee:* Bec (Liechtenstein).

Belgrade, 2 June 1996, 20,000

**Yugoslavia (3) 6** *(Milosevic 2, 68, Mijatovic 39, Stojkovic 45, Savicevic 71, 73)*

**Malta (0) 0**

*Yugoslavia:* Kocic; Mirkovic, Djorovic (Saveljic 85), Jokanovic, Djukic, Mihajlovic, Jugovic (Nadj 50), Savicevic, Mijatovic, Stojkovic, Milosevic (Kovacevic 79).
*Malta:* Cluett; Attard (Woods 46), Buhagiar, Vella S, Debono, Zammit (Camilleri 75), Busuttil, Turner, Brincat, Chetcuti, Agius.
*Referee:* Albrecht (Germany).

Toftir, 31 August 1996, 1445

**Faeroes (0) 1** *(Muller 60)*

**Slovakia (0) 2** *(Moravcik 58, Dubovsky 89)*

*Faeroes:* Knudsen; Morkore A, Johannesen O, Hansen J, Jarnskor H, Johnsson J, Dam, Hansen O, Petersen, Muller (Arge 75), Joensen.
*Slovakia:* Molnar; Kozak, Tittel, Zeman, Kinder, Juriga, Balis (Ujlaky 73), Simon (Jancula 69), Moravcik, Timko (Maixner 69), Dubovsky.
*Referee:* Hauge (Norway).

Toftir, 4 September 1996, 3500

**Faeroes (0) 2** *(Jonsson T 47, Arge 90)*

**Spain (1) 6** *(Luis Enrique 37, Alfonso 63, 83, 86, Johanessen O 70 (og), Hierro 85)*

*Faeroes:* Knudsen; Johannesen O, Morkore A, Joensen, Hansen J, Johnsson J, Hansen O, Petersen (Eliasen 90), Muller (Arge 74), Jarnskor H, Jonsson T.
*Spain:* Zubizarreta; Belsue, Alkorta (Abelardo 46), Nadal, Aranzabal (Guerrero 71), Sergi, Hierro, Guardiola, Pizzi (Alfonso 59), Kiko, Luis Enrique.
*Referee:* Leduc (France).

Teplice, 18 September 1996, 18,000

**Czech Republic (2) 6** *(Berger 11, 62 (pen), Nedved 24, Kubik 77, Smicer 83, Frydek 87)*

**Malta (0) 0**

*Czech Republic:* Srnicek; Kubik, Hornak (Smicer 63), Suchoparek, Latal, Bejbl, Nedved (Frydek 81), Nemec, Poborsky (Verbir 86), Berger, Kuka.
*Malta:* Cini; Saliba, Attard, Buhagiar, Vella S, Zammit (Agius 83), Sant Fournier, Chetcuti, Debono (Said 88), Zahra, Carabott (Suda 69).
*Referee:* Beusen (Croatia).

Bratislava, 22 September 1996, 2236

**Slovakia (3) 6** *(Tittel 13, 81, Simon 16, Zeman 36, Timko 56, Dubovsky 59)*

**Malta (0) 0**

*Slovakia:* Vencel; Zeman (Kozak 73), Karhan, Tomaschek, Kinder, Tittel, Slovak, Simon, Timko (Ujlaky 65), Dubovsky, Moravcik (Jancula 46).
*Malta:* Cini; Attard, Bonnici, Vella S, Chetcuti (Saliba 33), Zammit, Suda, Said, Carabott, Sant Fournier, Zahra (Agius 71).
*Referee:* Bikas (Greece).

Toftir, 6 October 1996, 1017

**Faeroes (1) 1** *(Muller 26)*

**Yugoslavia (5) 8** *(Milosevic 8, 38, 45, Jokanovic 12, 58, Mijatovic 30, Jugovic 70, Stojkovic 90 (pen))*

*Faeroes:* Knudsen; Johannesen, Hansen J (Hansen T 46), Hansen A, Joensen, Morkore A, Jonsson J, Dam, Jonson T, Muller (Arge 75), Petersen.
*Yugoslavia:* Kocic; Brnovic, Vidakovic (Djorovic 67), Djukic, Mihajlovic, Jugovic, Jokanovic, Stojkovic, Savicevic (Nadj 76), Mijatovic, Milosevic (Drobnjak 72).
*Referee:* Irvine (N Ireland).

Prague, 9 October 1996, 21,750

**Czech Republic (0) 0**

**Spain (0) 0**

*Czech Republic:* Srnicek; Hornak, Kadlec, Suchoparek, Latal, Bejbl, Nedved (Frydek 86), Poborsky (Smicer 58), Berger, Nemec, Kuka.
*Spain:* Zubizarreta; Alkorta, Nadal, Abelardo, Sergi, Luis Enrique, Hierro, Amor (Urzaiz 79), Guerrero (Guardiola 53), Raul, Alfonso (Rios 72).
*Referee:* Frisk (Sweden).

Bratislava, 23 October 1996, 5400

**Slovakia (1) 3** *(Dubovsky 20, Jancula 44, Simon 57 (pen))*

**Faeroes (0) 0**

*Slovakia:* Vencel; Zeman, Karhan (Kozak 84), Tomaschek, Kinder, Tittel, Balis (Kozlej 68), Simon, Jancula, Dubovsky, Timko (Ujlaky 68).
*Faeroes:* Knudsen; Johannesen O, Jarnskor H, Hansen A, Hansen O, Morkore A, Johnsson J, Dam (Ennigard 63), Muller, Jonsson T (Arge 46), Petersen (Eliasen 35).
*Referee:* Prolic (Bosnia).

Belgrade, 10 November 1996, 50,000

**Yugoslavia (1) 1** *(Mijatovic 18)*

**Czech Republic (0) 0**

*Yugoslavia:* Kocic; Jokanovic, Djukic, Djorovic, Vidakovic, Brnovic, Stojkovic, Jugovic, Mihajlovic, Mijatovic, Milosevic (Curcic 76).
*Czech Republic:* Srnicek; Hornak, Kadlec, Suchoparek, Latal (Poborsky 86), Nedved (Frydek 78), Berger, Bejbl, Nemec, Smicer, Kuka (Drulak 71).
*Referee:* Jol (Holland).

Tenerife, 13 November 1996, 15,000

**Spain (1) 4** *(Pizzi 30, Amor 46, Luis Enrique 57, Hierro 61)*

**Slovakia (1) 1** *(Tittel 39)*

*Spain:* Zubizarreta; Belsue, Alkorta, Nadal, Sergi, Luis Enrique, Hierro (Rios 80), Amor (Guardiola 59), Guerrero (Kiko 58), Raul, Pizzi.
*Slovakia:* Vencel; Zeman, Kozak, Tittel, Kinder, Tomaschek, Ujlaky (Kostka 65), Slovak, Simon, Jancula, Timko.
*Referee:* Merk (Germany).

Valencia, 14 December 1996, 40,000

**Spain (2) 2** *(Guardiola 19 (pen), Raul 37)*

**Yugoslavia (0) 0**

*Spain:* Zubizarreta; Abelardo, Alkorta, Nadal, Rios, Luis Enrique, Guardiola, Alfonso (Amor 62), Sergi, Kiko (Manjarin 75), Raul (Guerrero 88).
*Yugoslavia:* Kocic; Saveljic, Djukic, Vidakovic (Pantic 75) (Nadj 79), Djorovic, Jokanovic, Jugovic, Stojkovic D, Brnovic, Mijatovic, Savicevic.
*Referee:* Muhmenthaler (Switzerland).

Ta'Qali, 18 December 1996, 2000

**Malta (0) 0**

**Spain (3) 3** *(Guerrero 8, 25, 33)*

*Malta:* Cini; Chetcuti, Buhagiar, Vella, Debono, Zammit, Turner, Suda (Said 70), Brincat, Agius (Sultana 81), Zahra.
*Spain:* Zubizarreta; Belsue (Alvarez 70), Nadal, Abelardo, Aranzabal, Rios, Guardiola (Amor 61), Guerrero, Luis Enrique, Pizzi, Raul (Manjarin 61).
*Referee:* Levnikov (Russia).

Alicante, 12 February 1997, 32,000

**Spain (2) 4** *(Guardiola 25, Alfonso 40, 47, Pizzi 90)*

**Malta (0) 0**

*Spain:* Zubizarreta; Armando, Nadal, Abelardo, Aranzabal, Hierro (Rios 46), Guardiola, Manjarin, Raul (Pizzi 46), Alfonso, Luis Enrique.
*Malta:* Cini; Brincat (Galea 85), Buhagiar, Vella, Chetcuti, Agius (Debono 60), Zammit (Camilleri 80), Sultana, Turner, Zahra, Suda.
*Referee:* Lodge (England).

Valletta, 31 March 1997, 5000

**Malta (0) 0**

**Slovakia (1) 2** *(Jancula 38, Tittel 90)*

*Malta:* Muscat; Cauchi, Chetcuti, Attard, Debono, Saliba, Agius, Turner, Sultana (Suda 65), Brincat, Carabott.
*Slovakia:* Vencel; Kozak, Karhan, Zeman, Spilar, Tittel, Slovak (Zvara 57), Simon, Jancula (Majoros 50), Semenik, Moravcik.
*Referee:* Kowalczyk (Poland).

Prague, 2 April 1997, 19,137

**Czech Republic (0) 1** *(Bejbl 75)*

**Yugoslavia (1) 2** *(Mijatovic 28, Milosevic 90)*

*Czech Republic:* Miklosko; Latal (Berger 46), Repka, Nedved (Frydek 83), Kadlec, Hornak, Cizek, Poborsky, Kuka, Smicer (Siegl 67), Bejbl.
*Yugoslavia:* Kralj; Mirkovic, Govedarica, Jokanovic, Djukic, Mihajlovic (Brnovic 14), Jugovic, Savicevic (Milosevic 82), Mijatovic, Stojkovic (Drulovic 86), Nadj.
*Referee:* Batta (France).

Valletta, 30 April 1997, 5000

**Malta (1) 1** *(Sultana 8)*

**Faeroes (0) 2** *(Hansen O 60 (pen), Jonsson T 90)*

*Malta:* Muscat; Attard (Turner 50), Chetcuti, Vella S, Debono, Zammit, Agius, Saliba, Sultana, Brincat, Zahra.
*Faeroes:* Knudsen; Ennigard, Hansen K, Johannesen O, Jarnskor H, Johansen J, Thomasen, Petersen (Rasmussen JE 55), Hansen O, Morkore A, Jonsson T.
*Referee:* Koren (Israel).

Belgrade, 30 April 1997, 53,000

**Yugoslavia (0) 1** *(Mijatovic 87 (pen))*

**Spain (1) 1** *(Hierro 19 (pen))*

*Yugoslavia:* Kralj; Mirkovic, Djorovic, Vidakovic (Petrovic 46), Djukic, Mihajlovic (Ciric 79), Govedarica, Savicevic (Milosevic 36), Mijatovic, Stojkovic D, Drulovic.
*Spain:* Zubizarreta; Abelardo, Sergi, Alkorta, Nadal, Hierro, Kiko (Luis Enrique 55), Rios (Lopez 57), Guardiola, Raul, Alfonso (Amor 68).
*Referee:* Pedersen (Norway).

Toftir, 8 June 1997, 6400

**Faeroes (2) 2** *(Arge 6, Jonsson T 41)*

**Malta (0) 1** *(Agius 47 (pen))*

*Faeroes:* Knudsen; Johannesen O, Thorsteinsson, Hansen O, Hansen J, Morkore A, Jarnskor H, Dam, Johnsson J, Jonsson T, Arge.
*Malta:* Muscat; Chetcuti, Debono (Attard 33), Turner, Vella S, Zammit, Agius, Carabott, Brincat, Saliba, Sultana.
*Referee:* O'Hanlon (Republic of Ireland).

Valladolid, 8 June 1997, 30,000

**Spain (1) 1** *(Hierro 49 (pen))*

**Czech Republic (0) 0**

*Spain:* Zubizarreta; Ferrer, Alkorta, Abelardo, Guardiola, Hierro, Amavisca (Amor 74), Manjarin (Urzaiz 55), Alfonso, Kiko (Rios 85), Raul.
*Czech Republic:* Srnicek; Repka, Rada, Kadlec, Hornak, Latal (Poborsky 70), Nedved, Nemec, Cizek (Frydek 69), Smicer, Wagner (Siegl 73).
*Referee:* Dallas (Scotland).

Belgrade, 8 June 1997, 30,000

**Yugoslavia (1) 2** *(Savicevic 17, Mijatovic 78)*

**Slovakia (0) 0**

*Yugoslavia:* Kralj; Mirkovic, Djorovic, Djukic, Jokanovic, Mihajlovic, Jugovic, Stojkovic, Nadj (Drulovic 70), Savicevic (Govedarica 89), Mijatovic.
*Slovakia:* Molnar; Zeman, Tittel, Karhan, Kinder, Spilar, Tomaschek (Simon 46), Balis, Majoros (Nemeth 75), Moravcik, Jancula (Kozlej 83).
*Referee:* Mikkelsen (Denmark).

Teplici, 20 August 1997, 8332

**Czech Republic (2) 2** *(Kuka 14 (pen), Kozel 26)*

**Faeroes (0) 0**

*Czech Republic:* Srnicek; Hornak, Suchoparek, Kozel, Latal, Poborsky (Frydek 63), Nedved, Cizek (Bejbl 18), Nemec, Kuka, Smicer (Verbir 74).
*Faeroes:* Knudsen; Johannesen O, Thorsteinsson, Johnsson J, Hansen J, Morkore A, Jarnskor M, Jarnskor H, Arge (Rasmussen JE 73), Muller J, Petersen J (Joensen 61).
*Referee:* Dubinskas (Lithuania).

Bratislava, 24 August 1997, 27,000

**Slovakia (1) 2** *(Jancula 45, Majoros 55)*

**Czech Republic (1) 1** *(Smicer 14)*

*Slovakia:* Molnar; Kozak (Karhan 42), Kinder, Tittel, Spilar, Balis, Tomaschek, Simon (Zatek 84), Majoros, Jancula, Kozlej (Uljaky 84).
*Czech Republic:* Srnicek; Latal, Suchoparek, Hornak, Kozel, Poborsky (Sloncik 64), Nemec, Nedved (Vicek 56), Bejbl, Kuka, Smicer.
*Referee:* Ceccarini (Italy).

Toftir, 6 September 1997, 2700

**Faeroes (0) 0**

**Czech Republic (2) 2** *(Smicer 16, Kuka 32 (pen))*

*Faeroes:* Knudsen; Johannesen O, Hansen J, Thorsteinsson, Hansen O, Morkore A, Jarnskor M (Joensen 72), Dam, Jonsson T, Muller (Arge 72), Petersen.
*Czech Republic:* Srnicek; Latal, Suchoparek, Vicek, Repka, Nemec, Sloncik (Svoboda 85), Bejbl, Lasota (Hasek 73), Kuka (Vacha 55), Smicer.
*Referee:* Saules (France).

Bratislava, 10 September 1997, 22,510

**Slovakia (0) 1** *(Majoros 66)*

**Yugoslavia (0) 1** *(Mihajlovic 80)*

*Slovakia:* Molnar; Titel, Kozak, Spilar, Kinder, Balis (Ujlaky 71), Tomaschek, Zvara (Simon 85), Jancula, Kozlej (Luhovy 84), Majoros.
*Yugoslavia:* Lekovic (Kocic 64); Mirkovic, Djorovic, Djukic, Nadj (Drulovic 67), Jokanovic, Stojkovic, Jugovic, Mihajlovic, Mijatovic, Savicevic.
*Referee:* Frisk (Sweden).

Valletta, 24 September 1997, 3500

**Malta (0) 0**

**Czech Republic (1) 1** *(Bejbl 32)*

*Malta:* Muscat; Giglio, Chetcuti, Vella S, Camilleri, Debono, Zahra (Galea 67), Suda, Brincat, Agius (Sultana 80), Buhagiar (Turner 46).
*Czech Republic:* Srnicek; Novotny, Lasota, Vicek, Sloncik, Svoboda, Nemec (Kozel 46), Lokvenc (Ulich 54), Bejbl, Kuka, Smicer.
*Referee:* Ancion (Belgium).

Bratislava, 24 September 1997, 15,000

**Slovakia (0) 1** *(Majoros 74)*

**Spain (0) 2** *(Kiko 46, Amor 76)*

*Slovakia:* Molnar; Kozak, Tittel, Spilar, Balis, Simon (Zvara 64), Tomaschek, Majoros, Kinder, Jancula (Uljaky 85), Kozlej (Luhovy 53).
*Spain:* Zubizarreta; Ferrer (Aguilera 62), Nadal, Rios, Alkorta, Luis Enrique, Hierro, Raul, Sergi, Kiko (Oli 87), Alfonso (Amor 71).
*Referee:* Vagner (Hungary).

Prague, 11 October 1997, 5048

**Czech Republic (0) 3** *(Smicer 53, Siegl 70, Novotny 73)*

**Slovakia (0) 0**

*Czech Republic:* Srnicek; Suchoparek, Cizek (Lasota 57), Repka, Latal, Svoboda, Nemec, Novotny, Bejbl, Smicer, Siegl (Lokvenc 80).
*Slovakia:* Vencel; Kozak, Spilar, Tomaschek (Zatek 86), Kinder, Tittel, Balis, Zvara (Kozlej 75), Jancula (Simon 75), Majoros.
*Referee:* Meier (Switzerland).

Valletta, 11 October 1997, 300

**Malta (0) 0**

**Yugoslavia (3) 5** *(Milosevic 8, Mihajlovic 24, Savicevic 44, Mijatovic 55, Jugovic 76)*

*Malta:* Muscat; Said (Carabott 46), Chetcuti, Vella S (Busuttil 57), Debono, Camillieri, Agius, Zahra (Turner 50), Suda, Brincat, Buhagiar.
*Yugoslavia:* Kralj; Patrovic, Vidakovic, Jokanovic, Djukic, Milosevic (Govedarica 76), Jugovic, Savicevic (Brnovic 46), Mihajlovic, Stojkovic (Drulovic 65), Mijatovic.
*Referee:* Gallagher (England).

Gijon, 11 October 1997, 25,000

**Spain (2) 3** *(Luis Enrique 19, 84, Oli 25)*

**Faeroes (1) 1** *(Hansen J 44)*

*Spain:* Zubizarreta; Aguilera (Ferrer 75), Santi, Abelardo, Sergi, Luis Enrique, Hierro (Guardiola 59), Amor, Oli, Raul, Pizzi (Amavisca 70).
*Faeroes:* Knudsen; Johannsen O, Hansen J (Danielsen 80), Thorsteinsson, Hansen O, Dam, Jarnskor H, Jonsson T, Muller, Joensen (Rasmussen JE 88), Petersen (Rasmussen J 47).
*Referee:* Granat (Poland).

**Group 6**

|              | P  | W | D | L  | F  | A  | Pts |
|--------------|----|---|---|----|----|----|-----|
| Spain        | 10 | 8 | 2 | 0  | 26 | 6  | 26  |
| Yugoslavia   | 10 | 7 | 2 | 1  | 29 | 7  | 23  |
| Czech Republic | 10 | 5 | 1 | 4 | 16 | 6  | 16  |
| Slovakia     | 10 | 5 | 1 | 4  | 18 | 14 | 16  |
| Faeroes      | 10 | 2 | 0 | 8  | 10 | 31 | 6   |
| Malta        | 10 | 0 | 0 | 10 | 2  | 37 | 0   |

**Spain qualify for finals (24.9.97).**

## GROUP 7

Serravalle, 2 June 1996, 1613

**San Marino (0) 0**

**Wales (3) 5** *(Melville 20, Hughes M 32, 43, Giggs 50, Pembridge 85)*

*San Marino:* Muccioli S; Gasperoni L, Valentini M, Guerra, Gobbi, Manzaroli, Pasolini (Muccioli R 69), Mazza, Casadei (Peverani 74), Mularoni M (Valentini V 46), Montagna.
*Wales:* Southall; Bowen, Melville, Coleman, Pembridge, Browning (Gos 74), Horne (Savage 81), Robinson (Legg 80), Hughes M, Saunders, Giggs.
*Referee:* Lubos (Slovakia).

Brussels, 31 August 1996, 38,000

**Belgium (2) 2** *(Degryse 11, Oliveira 36)*

**Turkey (0) 1** *(Sergen 56)*

*Belgium:* De Wilde; Crasson, Medved, Renier, Claeys, Verheyen (Peiremans 59), Scifo, Degryse, Schepens (Van Kerckhoven 77), Oliveira (De Bilde 83), Nilis.
*Turkey:* Rustu; Recep, Ogun, Alpay, Hakan Unsal (Arif 58), Tolunay, Oguz (Sergen 53), Tayfun, Abdullah, Hakan Sukur, Saffet (Orhan 74).
*Referee:* Elleray (England).

Cardiff, 31 August 1996, 15,150

**Wales (4) 6** *(Saunders 2, 75, Hughes M 24, 54, Melville 34, Robinson 45)*

**San Marino (0) 0**

*Wales:* Southall (Roberts 72); Bowen, Melville, Coleman (Taylor 81), Pembridge, Robinson (Speed 78), Browning, Horne, Saunders, Hughes M, Giggs.
*San Marino:* Muccioli S; Gasperoni L (Matteoni 67), Guerra, Gobbi, Valentini V, Mazza (Pasolini 80), Gennari, Bacciocchi (Francini 44), Gasperoni B, Manzaroli, Montagna.
*Referee:* Hamer (Luxembourg).

Cardiff, 5 October 1996, 37,000

**Wales (1) 1** *(Saunders 17)*
**Holland (0) 3** *(Van Hooijdonk 72, 75, Ronald de Boer 80)*

*Wales:* Southall; Bowen, Pembridge (Legg 65), Browning (Jenkins 83), Symons, Melville, Robinson, Horne, Saunders, Hughes M, Speed.
*Holland:* Van der Sar; Vierklau (Van Hooijdonk 71), Frank de Boer, Valckx, Bogarde, Winter, Jonk, Seedorf, Cocu, Cruyff (Makaay 46), Ronald de Boer (Van Bronckhorst 90).
*Referee:* Nieto (Spain).

San Marino, 9 October 1996, 1353

**San Marino (0) 0**
**Belgium (2) 3** *(Verheyen 11, Nilis 20, 48)*

*San Marino:* Gasperoni F; Gobbi, Gennari, Bacciocchi, Gasperoni L, Guerra, Muccioli R (Bianchi 68), Mazza (Peverani 74), Montagna, Francini, Pasolini (Vannucci 52).
*Belgium:* De Wilde; Crasson, Medved, Renier, Leonard, Verheyen (Pierre 66), Staelens, Degryse, Schepens (Van Kerckhoven 63), Nilis, Oliveira (De Bilde 81).
*Referee:* Oganessian (Armenia).

Eindhoven, 9 November 1996, 25,000

**Holland (4) 7** *(Bergkamp 22, 72, 78, Jonk 34, Ronald de Boer 33, Frank de Boer 45, Cocu 61)*
**Wales (1) 1** *(Saunders 40)*

*Holland:* Van der Sar; Stam, Frank de Boer, Numan, Reiziger, Winter, Jonk (Van Bronckhorst 82), Cocu, Seedorf (Van Hooijdonk 69), Bergkamp, Ronald de Boer (Overmars 58).
*Wales:* Southall; Bowen M, Nielson, Symons, Melville, Jones, Bowen J (Robinson 58), Hartson (Taylor 67), Saunders, Pembridge, Speed.
*Referee:* Pereira (Portugal).

Istanbul, 10 November 1996, 35,000

**Turkey (2) 7** *(Oktay 24, 38, 50, 60, Hakan Sukur 55, 65, Urtugrul 80)*
**San Marino (0) 0**

*Turkey:* Rustu; Recep, Bulent K, Celil, Alpay, Oktay (Ertugrul 87), Ogun, Tugay, Abdullah, Hami (Arif 87), Hakan Sukur.
*San Marino:* Gasperoni F; Valentini M, Gennari, Gasperoni L, Guerra, Manzaroli, Francini, Matteoni, Bacciocchi (Ugolini 70), Pasolini (Gatti 80), Mularoni M (Mularoni L 90).
*Referee:* Antonov (Moldova).

Brussels, 14 December 1996, 38,000

**Belgium (0) 0**
**Holland (2) 3** *(Bergkamp 24, Seedorf 28, Jonk 89 (pen))*

*Belgium:* De Wilde; Deflandre (Jbari 77), Albert, Van Meir, Renier, Leonard (Van Kerckhoven 34), Staelens, Wilmots, Degryse (Pierre 59), Oliveira, Nilis.
*Holland:* Van der Sar; Reiziger, Stam, Frank de Boer, Numan, Winter, Seedorf, Jonk, Cocu, Ronald de Boer (Overmars 88), Bergkamp (Kluivert 64).
*Referee:* Parietto (Italy).

Cardiff, 14 December 1996, 14,200

**Wales (0) 0**
**Turkey (0) 0**

*Wales:* Southall; Page, Jenkins, Jones, Melville, Pembridge, Speed, Horne, Saunders (Hartson 81), Hughes M, Giggs.
*Turkey:* Engin; Recep, Alpay, Ogun, Bulent K, Ilker (Tolunay 88), Kemalettin (Saffet 88), Tugay, Abdullah, Arif (Oktay 70), Hakan Sukur.
*Referee:* Huzu (Romania).

Amsterdam, 29 March 1997, 47,000

**Holland (1) 4** *(Kluivert 44, Frank de Boer 59, 90, Van Hooijdonk 82)*
**San Marino (0) 0**

*Holland:* Van der Sar; Reiziger, Stam, Frank de Boer, Numan, Seedorf (Van Hooijdonk 74), Winter (Overmars 33), Jonk, Cocu, Bergkamp, Kluivert.
*San Marino:* Gasperoni F; Valentini M, Gobbi L (Valentini V 54), Matteoni, Guerra, Vanucci (Gennari 78), Mazza M, Gasperoni B, Muccioli R, Francini, Montagna (Bacciocchi 81).
*Referee:* Klein (Israel).

Cardiff, 29 March 1997, 15,000

**Wales (0) 1** *(Speed 67)*
**Belgium (2) 2** *(Crasson 24, Staelens 44)*

*Wales:* Southall; Blackmore, Page, Symons, Pembridge, Jones, Horne, Hughes M, Saunders (Hartson 64), Speed, Giggs.
*Belgium:* De Wilde; De Roover, Van Meir, Smidts, Crasson, Van der Elst F, Staelens, Lemoine, Van Kerckhoven, Mpenza L (Mpenza M 64), Oliveira (Scifo 79).
*Referee:* Fallstrom (Sweden).

Bursa, 2 April 1997, 30,000

**Turkey (0) 1** *(Hakan Sukur 53)*
**Holland (0) 0**

*Turkey:* Rustu; Ilker, Bulent K, Alpay, Ogun, Tafun, Tolunay, Tugay (Tayfur 80), Abdullah (Oguz 87), Hakan Sukur, Celil (Hakan Unsal 70).
*Holland:* Van der Sar; Reiziger (Overmars 80), Stam, Frank de Boer, Numan, Winter (Van Hooijdonk 76), Jonk, Seedorf, Cocu, Kluivert, Ronald de Boer.
*Referee:* Vega (Spain).

Serravalle, 30 April 1997, 2800

**San Marino (0) 0**
**Holland (1) 6** *(Bergkamp 40, 90, Winter 63, Van Hooijdonk 70, Frank de Boer 74, Bosman 85)*

*San Marino:* Gasperoni F; Valentini M, Vanucci, Gobbi L, Guerra, Matteoni, Gasperoni B (Gasperoni L 78), Mazza M, Montagna (Bianchi 50), Francini, Muccioli R.
*Holland:* Van der Sar; Winter (Reiziger 73), Stam, Frank de Boer, Numan, Jonk, Van Hooijdonk, Seedorf, Zenden, Ronald de Boer (Bosman 65), Bergkamp.
*Referee:* Georgiou (Cyprus).

Istanbul, 30 April 1997, 29,000

**Turkey (1) 1** *(Oktay 35)*
**Belgium (3) 3** *(Oliveira 12, 31, 45)*

*Turkey:* Rustu; Recep, Bulent K, Tolunay, Hakan Unsal (Celil 46), Arif (Tayfun 46), Tayfur, Ogun, Hakan Sukur, Tugay (Hami 75), Oktay.
*Belgium:* De Wilde; Crasson, De Roover, Van Meir, Smidts (Doll 58), Van der Elst F, Staelens, Oliveira, Mpenza E (Lemoine 69), Scifo, Van Kerckhoven.
*Referee:* Heynemann (Germany).

Brussels, 7 June 1997, 22,000

**Belgium (5) 6** *(Staelens 16, 85, Van Meir 26, Mpenza L 27, 45, Oliveira 33)*
**San Marino (0) 0**

*Belgium:* De Wilde; Crasson (Haagdoren 73), Van Meir, Vidovic, De Roover, Van der Elst F (Smidts 85), Staelens, Lemoine, Van Kerckhoven, Oliveira, Mpenza L (De Bilde 73).
*San Marino:* Gasperoni F; Valentini V, Valentini M, Gobbi L (Manzaroli 72), Vanucci, Guerra, Mazza M, Della Valle, Gasperoni B, Montagna (Gatti 55), Bacciocchi (Mularoni L 82).
*Referee:* Jirku (Czech Republic).

**Istanbul, 20 August 1997, 25,000**

**Turkey (3) 6** *(Hakan Sukur 5, 37, 77, 82, Oguz 8, Ogun 61)*
**Wales (3) 4** *(Blake 17, Savage 20, Saunders 32, Melville 52)*

*Turkey:* Rustu; Bulent K, Ogun (Fatih 63), Alpay, Ilker, Tolunay, Oguz, Abdullah (Ergun 85), Arif, Hakan Sukur, Saffet (Hami 59).
*Wales:* Southall (Jones P 46); Jenkins, Speed, Page, Melville, Savage, Hughes C (Edwards 68), Saunders (Jones L 68), Blake, Hughes M, Giggs.
*Referee:* Kowalczyk (Poland).

**Rotterdam, 6 September 1997, 52,000**

**Holland (1) 3** *(Stam 32, Kluivert 53, Bergkamp 84)*
**Belgium (0) 1** *(Staelens 67 (pen))*

*Holland:* Van der Sar; Reiziger, Stam, Frank de Boer, Numan (Bogarde 71), Seedorf (Van Bronchkorst 87), Ronald de Boer (Winter 71), Jonk, Cocu, Bergkamp, Kluivert.
*Belgium:* De Wilde; Crasson (Genaux 46), Van Meir, Vidovic, Albert, Staelens, Van der Elst F, Scifo (De Bilde 77), Van Kerckhoven, Mpenza E (Schepens 87), Oliveira.
*Referee:* Nielsen (Denmark).

**Serravalle, 10 September 1997, 500**

**San Marino (0) 0**
**Turkey (2) 5** *(Gobbi 26 (og), Arif 29, 80, Hakan Sukur 74, Hami 76)*

*San Marino:* Gasperoni F; Manzaroli, Vannucci, Gobbi, Valentini M, Matteoni, Bacciocchi, Muccioli R, Gualtieri, Francini, Gasperoni B.
*Turkey:* Rustu; Tayfun, Tayfur, Fatih, Alpay, Abdullah, Arif, Sergen (Mehmet 65), Hakan Sukur, Oguz, Saffet (Hami 46).
*Referee:* Tatulian (Armenia).

**Brussels, 11 October 1997, 33,000**

**Belgium (3) 3** *(Staelens 4 (pen), Claessens 63, Wilmots 38)*
**Wales (0) 2** *(Pembridge 52 (pen), Giggs 60)*

*Belgium:* De Wilde; Deflandre, De Roover (Verstraeten 65), Staelens, Smidts, Van Kerckhoven (Borkelmans 77), Van der Elst F, Wilmots, Boffin, Oliveira, Claessens (Nilis 68).
*Wales:* Marriott; Jenkins, Ready, Pembridge, Edwards, Savage, Robinson, Saunders, Hartson (Taylor 84), Hughes C (Page 46), Giggs.
*Referee:* Pereira (Portugal).

**Amsterdam, 11 October 1997, 50,000**

**Holland (0) 0**
**Turkey (0) 0**

*Holland:* Van der Sar; Reiziger (Van Hooijdonk 79), Stam, Frank de Boer, Numan, Winter, Cocu, Seedorf (Bogarde 70), Van Bronckhorst (Overmars 54), Bergkamp, Kluivert.
*Turkey:* Rustu; Ilker (Celil 79), Fatih, Selim, Alpay, Abdullah, Tayfun, Arif (Hami 89), Tayfur, Hakan Suker, Oguz (Mehmet 86).
*Referee:* Sundell (Sweden).

**Group 7**

|              | P | W | D | L | F  | A  | Pts |
|--------------|---|---|---|---|----|----|-----|
| Holland      | 8 | 6 | 1 | 1 | 26 | 4  | 19  |
| Belgium      | 8 | 6 | 0 | 2 | 20 | 11 | 18  |
| Turkey       | 8 | 4 | 2 | 2 | 21 | 9  | 14  |
| Wales        | 8 | 2 | 1 | 5 | 20 | 21 | 7   |
| San Marino   | 8 | 0 | 0 | 8 | 0  | 42 | 0   |

**Holland qualify for finals (11.10.97).**

**GROUP 8**

**Skopje, 24 April 1996, 12,000**

**Macedonia (1) 3** *(Milosevski 5, Babunski 49 (pen), Zaharievski 80)*
**Liechtenstein (0) 0**

*Macedonia:* Celeski; Babunski, Markovski (Nikolovski 60), Jovanovski, Stojkovski, Milosevski, Milosavov, Gosev (Zaharievski 75), Ciric, Boskovski, Hristov (Naumovski 71).
*Liechtenstein:* Heeb; Hanselmann, Hasler, Stocker (Quaderer 46), Zech J, Frick C, Frick D, Frick M, Hilti, Oehri, Telser D (Sele 51).
*Referee:* Loizou (Cyprus).

**Reykjavik, 1 June 1996, 5000**

**Iceland (0) 1** *(Gudjohnsen A 63)*
**Macedonia (0) 1** *(Memed 62)*

*Iceland:* Kristinsson B; Sigurdsson L, Gretarsson A, Jonsson S, Adolfsson, Kristinsson R, Bergsson, Gudjohnsson A, Thordarson O (Stefansson 68), Thordur Gudjonsson (Benediktsson 81), Gunnlaugsson B (Gylfason 29).
*Macedonia:* Celeski; Milosavov, Markovski, Nikolovski, Stojkovski, Sedloski, Memed, Gosev, Ciric (Saciri 36), Hristov (Borov 84), Milosevski.
*Referee:* Luinge (Holland).

**Eschen, 31 August 1996, 4000**

**Liechtenstein (0) 0**
**Republic of Ireland (4) 5** *(Townsend 5, O'Neill 9, Quinn 12, 61, Harte 20)*

*Liechtenstein:* Heeb; Hefti, Hasler, Stocklasa, Quaderer, Hilti, Hanselmann (Telser D 82), Zech H (Bicker 65), Schadler F (Klaunzer 78), Frick M, Schadler H.
*Republic of Ireland:* Given; Irwin, Kenna, McLoughlin, Breen, Staunton, Houghton, Townsend (Cascarino 83), Quinn, O'Neill (Moore 73), Harte.
*Referee:* Shmolik (Belarus).

**Bucharest, 31 August 1996, 9000**

**Romania (1) 3** *(Moldovan 20, Petrescu 65, Galca 77)*
**Lithuania (0) 0**

*Romania:* Prunea (Gherasim 83); Petrescu (Popescu 80), Papura, Prodan, Selymes, Lupescu (Stinga 81), Filipescu, Galca, Munteanu, Moldovan, Ilie A.
*Lithuania:* Stauce; Ziukas, Vainoras, Gvildys (Zutautas 84), Miknevicius (Razanauskas 64), Baltusnikas, Maciulevicius, Tereskinas, Jankauskas, Skarbalius, Zvingilas.
*Referee:* Melnitchouk (Ukraine).

**Vilnius, 5 October 1996, 8000**

**Lithuania (1) 2** *(Jankauskas 22 (pen), Slekys 71)*
**Iceland (0) 0**

*Lithuania:* Stauce; Tereskinas, Vainoras, Sukristovas, Miknevicius, Skarbalius, Zutautas, Maciulevicius (Baltusnikas 46), Slekys, Narbekovas (Zvingilas 90), Jankauskas.
*Iceland:* Kristinsson B; Sigurdsson L (Thordarson O 82), Thorsteinn Gudjonsson, Jonsson S, Adolfsson, Kristinsson R, Bergsson, Gudjonsson H (Gretarsson A 76), Dadason, Gudjohnsen A (Gunnlaugsson A 56), Sverrisson.
*Referee:* Marnix (Belgium).

**Reykjavik, 9 October 1996, 3500**

**Iceland (0) 0**
**Romania (1) 4** *(Munteanu 21, Hagi 60, Popescu 75, Petrescu 81)*

*Iceland:* Kristinsson B; Sigurdsson L (Thordarsson A 68), Thorsteinn Gudjonsson, Jonsson S, Adolfsson, Kristinsson R, Bergsson, Gudjonsson A, Dadason (Sigurdsson H 66), Gunnlaugsson B (Gunnlaugsson A 70), Sverisson.
*Romania:* Stelea; Petrescu, Prodan, Dobos, Selymes, Popescu, Galca, Munteanu, Hagi (Vladoiu 82), Moldovan (Dumitrescu 82), Ilie A (Filipescu 75).
*Referee:* Detruche (Switzerland).

Vilnius, 9 October 1996, 5000

**Lithuania (1) 2** *(Jankauskas 43, Narbekovas 55)*
**Liechtenstein (0) 1** *(Zech H 53)*

*Lithuania:* Stauce; Tereskinas, Vainoras, Sukristovas, Miknevicius, Slekys, Zutautas, Maciulevicius (Zvingilas 57) (Baltusnikas 82), Narbekovas, Skarbalius, Jankauskas.
*Liechtenstein:* Heeb; Ospelt, Hilti, Hanselmann, Telser D, Beck, Schadler S (Schadler A 75), Zech H, Hasler, Frick M, Hassler (Marxer 63).
*Referee:* Mamedov (Azerbaijan).

Dublin, 9 October 1996, 31,671

**Republic of Ireland (1) 3** *(McAteer 8, Cascarino 46, 70)*
**Macedonia (0) 0**

*Republic of Ireland:* Kelly A; Kenna, Irwin, McAteer, Breen, Staunton, Townsend, McLoughlin (O'Brien 85), Cascarino, Harte (Moore 83), O'Neill (Aldridge 81).
*Macedonia:* Celeski; Sedloski, Nikolovski, Jovanovski, Milosavov, Gosev, Beganovic (Saciri 73), Micevski T, Ciric, Milosevski (Zaharievski 57), Hristov.
*Referee:* Fisker (Denmark).

Eschen, 9 November 1996, 2600

**Liechtenstein (1) 1** *(Schadler F 34)*
**Macedonia (8) 11** *(Gavevski 8, 13, 60, Ciric 9, 43, Hristov 23, Stojkovski 38, 44, Micevski T 45, 49, Micevski V 90)*

*Liechtenstein:* Heeb; Ospelt, Telser D (Telser M 53), Hilti (Bicker 48), Hanselmann, Oehri, Quaderer (Marxer 73), Zech, Hasler, Hassler, Schadler F.
*Macedonia:* Celeski; Sedloski, Stojkovski (Milosevski 65), Markovski, Nikolovski, Zaharievski, Gosev, Micevski T (Naumoski 73), Hristov, Ciric, Gavevski (Micevski V 70).
*Referee:* Lipkowitz (Israel).

Dublin, 10 November 1996, 33,869

**Republic of Ireland (0) 0**
**Iceland (0) 0**

*Republic of Ireland:* Kelly A; Kenna (Cunningham 65), Irwin (Harte 65), Keane, Breen, Babb, McLoughlin, McAteer, Kelly D (Moore 80), Cascarino, Townsend.
*Iceland:* Kristinsson B; Adolfsson, Jonsson S, Sigurdsson L, Birgisson, Gudjonsson H (Thordarson O 86), Kristinsson R (Gretarsson A 71), Sverrisson, Gylfason, Thordur Gudjonsson, Sigurdsson H.
*Referee:* Ormandjiev (Bulgaria).

Skopje, 14 December 1996, 14,000

**Macedonia (0) 0**
**Romania (2) 3** *(Popescu 36, 45, 90 (pen))*

*Macedonia:* Celeski; Sedloski, Glavevski, Nikolovski, Markovski, Zaharievski, Micevski T (Stojkovski 83), Hristov, Ciric (Milosevski 64), Glosevski, Micevski H.
*Romania:* Stelea; Petrescu, Prodan, Dobos, Selymes, Filipescu, Galca, Popescu, Munteanu (Stinga 83), Craioveanu (Panduru 67), Vladoiu (Viorel 88).
*Referee:* Filippi (Luxembourg).

Bucharest, 29 March 1997, 5000

**Romania (3) 8** *(Moldovan 10, Popescu 29, 30, 67, 82, Hagi 46, Petrescu 47, Craioveanu 79)*
**Liechtenstein (0) 0**

*Romania:* Stingaciu (Prunea 62); Petrescu (Filipescu 68), Dobos, Prodan, Galca, Popescu, Selymes, Ilie A, Moldovan (Craioveanu 62), Hagi, Vladoiu.
*Liechtenstein:* Heeb; Stocklasa, Hefti, Zech J, Hanselmann, Hasler D, Telser D, Frick C (Ackermann 71), Schadler (Frick D 46), Klaunzer (Telser M 85), Ospelt.
*Referee:* Laskus (Lativa).

Vilnius, 2 April 1997, 10,000

**Lithuania (0) 0**
**Romania (0) 1** *(Moldovan 73)*

*Lithuania:* Stauce; Suliauskas (Baltunikas 75), Ziukas, Tereskinas, Vainoras, Slekys, Zutautas, Maciulevicius, Preiksaitis (Stumbrys 62), Ivanauskas, Jankauskas.
*Romania:* Stelea; Petrescu, Dobos, Prodan, Selymes, Galca, Popescu, Hagi, Munteanu, Vladoiu (Craioveanu 62), Moldovan (Ilie A 75).
*Referee:* Steinberg (Germany).

Skopje, 2 April 1997, 8000

**Macedonia (2) 3** *(Stojkovski 28 (pen), 44 (pen), Hristov 59)*
**Republic of Ireland (1) 2** *(McLoughlin 8, Kelly D 78)*

*Macedonia:* Celeski; Sedloski, Nikolovski, Markovski, Gosev, Milosavov, Sainovski (Georgioski 82), Stojkovski, Saciri, Hristov (Beganovic 78), Glavevski (Micevski V 87).
*Republic of Ireland:* Kelly A; McAteer, Irwin, McLoughlin, Breen, Staunton, Townsend, Keane, Cascarino (O'Neill 46) (Kelly D 76), Goodman, Phelan (Harte 57).
*Referee:* Trentalange (Italy).

Vaduz, 30 April 1997, 800

**Liechtenstein (0) 0**
**Lithuania (0) 2** *(Razanauskas 65, Skarbalius 90)*

*Liechtenstein:* Heeb; Stocklasa, Hefti, Ospelt (Bicker 72), Hanselmann, Frick C (Ackermann 64), Telser D, Hasler D, Klaunzer (Telser M 75), Schadler, Frick D.
*Lithuania:* Stauce; Ziukas, Tereskinas, Suika, Vainoras, Zutautas, Maciulevicius, Ivanauskas, Stumbrys (Razanauskas 46), Jankauskas, Skarbalius.
*Referee:* Pregia (Albania).

Bucharest, 30 April 1997, 21,500

**Romania (1) 1** *(Ilie A 32)*
**Republic of Ireland (0) 0**

*Romania:* Stelea; Petrescu, Dobos, Prodan, Hagi (Craioveanu 87), Filipescu, Georghe Popescu (Rotariu 72), Munteanu, Selymes, Moldovan, Ilie A (Gabriel Popescu 83).
*Republic of Ireland:* Kelly A; Kelly G, Irwin (Kenna 46), Cunningham, Staunton, Harte (Cascarino 75), Townsend, Keane, Connolly (Goodman 75), Houghton, Kennedy.
*Referee:* Van den Ende (Holland).

Dublin, 21 May 1997, 28,575

**Republic of Ireland (3) 5** *(Connolly 29, 34, 40, Cascarino 60, 77)*
**Liechtenstein (0) 0**

*Republic of Ireland:* Given; Kenna, Cunningham, Keane, Harte, Staunton, Houghton (Cascarino 53), Kelly G, Connolly (Goodman 77), Townsend, Kennedy (Fleming 63).
*Liechtenstein:* Heeb; Telser D (Verling 58), Stocklasa, Hefti, Hanselmann (Ackermann 80), Frick C, Hasler D, Schadler, Frick M (Ospelt 46), Klaunzer, Frick D.
*Referee:* Boutenko (Russia).

Skopje, 7 June 1997, 15,000

**Macedonia (0) 0**
**Iceland (0) 1** *(Hristov 53)*

*Macedonia:* Ilic; Sedloski, Markovski, Babunski, Nikolovski, Zaharievski, Gosev (Milosevic 83), Saciri (Trenevski 46), Glavevski (Sainovski 71), Hristov, Micevski T.
*Iceland:* Finnbogason; Sigurdsson L, Gretarsson A, Bergsson, Gislason (Dadason 85), Jonsson S, Gudjonsson B, Gudjonsson T, Gudjohnsen A (Sigurdsson H 78), Gunnlaugsson B, Sverrisson.
*Referee:* Tsjoek (Belarus).

Reykjavik, 11 June 1997, 4500

**Iceland (0) 0**
**Lithuania (0) 0**
*Iceland:* Finnbogason; Sigurdsson L, Jonsson S, Gudjonsson H (Dadason 82), Gislason (Gretarsson 79), Kristinsson R, Gudjohnsen A, Bergsson, Gunnlaugsson B, Gunnlaugsson A (Sigurdsson H 72), Sverrisson.
*Lithuania:* Stauce; Ziukas, Tereskinas, Vainoras, Zutautas G, Stumbrys, Zutautas R, Slekys, Skarbalius, Preitsaitis, Jankauskas.
*Referee:* Irvine (N Ireland).

Eschen, 20 August 1997, 550

**Liechtenstein (0) 0**
**Iceland (2) 4** *(Danielsson 28, Gunnarsson 41, Jonsson S 61, Gudmundsson 63)*
*Liechtenstein:* Heeb; Hefti, Telser D, Ospelt, Klaunzer (Telser M 74), Hanselmann, Hasler, Schadler F (Marxier 46), Stocklasa, Frick M, Frick D.
*Iceland:* Finnbogason; Sigurdsson L, Bergsson, Sverisson, Hreidarsson, Kristinsson R, Jonsson S (Gudjonsson 65), Gunnarsson, Danielsson (Gudmundsson 53), Gudjohnsen A (Gretarsson 73), Sigurdsson H.
*Referee:* Timofejev (Estonia).

Dublin, 20 August 1997, 32,600

**Republic of Ireland (0) 0**
**Lithuania (0) 0**
*Republic of Ireland:* Given; Kenna, Staunton, Cunningham, Harte, Keane, Townsend (Kelly D 83), Houghton, Quinn (Cascarino 59), Connolly, Kennedy (McLoughlin 73).
*Lithuania:* Stauce; Ziukas, Skerla, Vainoras, Kanchelskis, Tereskinas, Zutautas, Narbekovas, Mikalajunas, Preitsaitis (Suliauskas 46), Jankauskas (Buitkus 57) (Sulka 79).
*Referee:* Monteiro (Portugal).

Bucharest, 20 August 1997, 20,000

**Romania (2) 4** *(Moldovan 36 (pen), 63, Galca 40, Dumitrescu 66)*
**Macedonia (0) 2** *(Dzokic 52, 90)*
*Romania:* Stelea; Petrescu, Prodan (Cibatariu 74), Dobos, Selymes, Galca (Gabriel Popescu 84), Gica Popescu, Serban, Ilie A, Moldovan (Craioveanu 80), Dumitrescu.
*Macedonia:* Ilic; Milosavov, Sedloski, Nikolovski, Milosevic, Markovski, Zaharievski (Milosevski 68), Zainovski (Dzokic 46), Saciri, Hristov, Trenevski (Memed 68).
*Referee:* Tokat (Turkey).

Reykjavik, 6 September 1997, 5000

**Iceland (1) 2** *(Gunnarsson 45, Sigurdsson H 47)*
**Republic of Ireland (1) 4** *(Connolly 13, Keane 54, 64, Finnbogason 79 (og))*
*Iceland:* Finnbogason; Sigurdsson L, Bergsson, Sverisson, Hreidarsson, Kristinsson R, Gudjonsson T, Jonsson S, Gunnarsson (Gudjonsson B 88), Sigurdsson H (Dadason 67), Danielsson (Gudmundsson T 70).
*Republic of Ireland:* Given; Kenna (McAteer 64), Staunton, Cunningham, Harte, Kelly G, McLoughlin, Keane, Connolly, Townsend (Cascarino 88), Kilbane (Kennedy 46).
*Referee:* Kulusic (Croatia).

Eschen, 6 September 1997, 1800

**Liechtenstein (0) 1** *(Frick M 64)*
**Romania (6) 8** *(Moldovan 6, Craioveanu 10, 32, Dobos 36, Munteanu 44, 45, 69, Barbu 55)*
*Liechtenstein:* Heeb; Ospelt, Hefti, Stocklasa, Hanselmann, Frick M, Hasler, Frick C (Telser M 72), Klaunzer (Schadler F 56), Frick D, Telser D.
*Romania:* Stelea; Petrescu, Prodan, Dobos (Potcianu 46), Selymes (Stefan 59), Munteanu, Galca, Serban, Dumitrescu, Moldovan, Craioveanu (Barbu 46).
*Referee:* Michallef (Malta).

Vilnius, 6 September 1997, 7000

**Lithuania (1) 2** *(Ivanauskas 26, Preiksatis 88)*
**Macedonia (0) 0**
*Lithuania:* Stauce; Ziukas, Vainoras, Kanchelskis, Tereskinas, Slekys, Skerla, Narbekovas (Zvingilas 86), Mikalajunas (Baltusnikas 83), Ivanauskas, Jankauskas (Preiksatis 81).
*Macedonia:* Ilic; Milosavov (Trenevski 47), Sedloski, Stojkovski, Nikolovski, Markovski, Zaharievski (Sakiri 65), Dzokic (Memed 72), Micevski, Babunski, Hristov.
*Referee:* Lucilio (Portugal).

Vilnius, 10 September 1997, 7000

**Lithuania (0) 1** *(Ziukas 52)*
**Republic of Ireland (1) 2** *(Cascarino 17, 71)*
*Lithuania:* Stauce; Skerla, Vainoras, Kanchelskis, Tereskinas (Slekys 76), Ziukas, Zutautas R, Mikalajunas (Zvingilas 46), Preitsaitis (Jankauskas 46), Narbekovas, Ivanauskas.
*Republic of Ireland:* Given; Kelly G, Irwin, McAteer (Babb 83), Cunningham, Harte, McLoughlin, Keane, Connolly (Breen 90), Cascarino, Staunton.
*Referee:* Bikas (Greece).

Bucharest, 10 September 1997, 12,000

**Romania (2) 4** *(Hagi 9, 82 (pen), Petrescu 41, Galca 65)*
**Iceland (0) 0**
*Romania:* Stelea; Petrescu, Dobos, Prodan, Munteanu, Gica Popescu, Galca (Gabriel Popescu 75), Hagi, Dumitrescu, Illie A (Barbu 66), Craioveanu (Selymes 46).
*Iceland:* Gottskalksson; Jonsson G, Hreidarsson, Jonsson S, Gunnarsson, Kristinsson R, Adolfsson, Danielsson (Gudmundsson 82), Gretarsson (Thorvaldsson 81), Gudjonsson T, Sigurdsson H (Dadason 75).
*Referee:* Elleray (England).

Reykjavik, 11 October 1997, 1651

**Iceland (0) 4** *(Gudjohnsson T 55, Gudmundsson 59, Gudjohnsson A 68, Gudjohnsson B 73)*
**Liechtenstein (0) 0**
*Iceland:* Gottskalksson; Gudjohnsson B, Hreidarsson, Sigurdsson L, Gunnarsson, Kristinsson R, Gujonsson T, Sverisson S, Gudmundsson, Gudjohnsson A, Sverisson.
*Liechtenstein:* Oehry; Hefti, Stocklasa, Marxer, Hanselmann, Telser, Ospelt, Frick C, Klaunzer, Frick M, Schadler.
*Referee:* Howells (Wales).

Skopje, 11 October 1997, 4000

**Macedonia (1) 1** *(Saciri 45)*
**Lithuania (0) 2** *(Buitkus 69, 83)*
*Macedonia:* Celeski; Sedloski, Jovanovski, Markovski, Nikolovski, Zaharievski, Sainovski, Memed (Miserdovski 72), Hristov, Trenevski, Saciri.
*Lithuania:* Stauce; Zutautas, Ziukas, Tereskinas, Gleveckas, Skerla, Skinderis, Mikalajunas, Slekys (Buitkus 46), Jankauskas, Preitsaitis.
*Referee:* Liba (Czech Republic).

Dublin, 11 October 1997, 49,000

**Republic of Ireland (0) 1** *(Cascarino 84)*
**Romania (0) 1** *(Hagi 53)*
*Republic of Ireland:* Kelly A; Kenna, Phelan (Fleming 89), McAteer, Breen, Babb, McLoughlin (Kelly D 62), Houghton, Cascarino (Evans 85), Carsley, Kennedy.
*Romania:* Stelea; Petrescu, Dobos, Ciobotariu, Popescu, Galca C, Selymes, Hagi (Dumitrescu 84), Munteanu, Moldovan (Filipescu 62), Ilie A (Lacatus 76).
*Referee:* Levnikov (Russia).

**Group 8**

|  | P | W | D | L | F | A | Pts |
|---|---|---|---|---|---|---|---|
| Romania | 10 | 9 | 1 | 0 | 37 | 4 | 28 |
| Republic of Ireland | 10 | 5 | 3 | 2 | 22 | 8 | 18 |
| Lithuania | 10 | 5 | 2 | 3 | 11 | 8 | 17 |
| Macedonia | 10 | 4 | 1 | 5 | 22 | 18 | 13 |
| Iceland | 10 | 2 | 3 | 5 | 11 | 16 | 9 |
| Liechtenstein | 10 | 0 | 0 | 10 | 3 | 52 | 0 |

**Romania qualify for finals (20.8.97).**

## GROUP 9

### Erevan, 31 August 1996, 5000

**Armenia (0) 0**

**Portugal (0) 0**

*Armenia:* Berezovski; Soukiassian, Khachatrian V, Zakarian (Minassian 9), Hovsepian, Vardanian, Art Petrossian, Grigorian (Adamian 65), Mikhitarian H, Avetissian V, Avetissian A (Essayan 60).
*Portugal:* Vitor Baia; Secretario, Fernando Couto, Helder, Dimas, Oceano, Rui Barros, Rui Costa (Paulo Alves 80), Sa Pinto, Joao Pinto II, Folha (Cadete 46).
*Referee:* Ehring (Sweden).

### Belfast, 31 August 1996, 9358

**Northern Ireland (0) 0**

**Ukraine (0) 1** *(Rebrov 79)*

*Northern Ireland:* Fettis; Griffin (O'Neill 52), Rowland (Magilton 84), Lomas, Morrow, Hill, Gillespie, Lennon, Dowie, Gray, Hughes.
*Ukraine:* Shovkovskyi; Luzhnyi (Parfenov 70), Skrypnyk, Golovko, Bezhenar, Popov, Orbu, Kalitvintsev (Kriventsov 74), Luchkeyvich (Rebrov 46), Maximov, Leonenko.
*Referee:* Sars (France).

### Belfast, 5 October 1996, 8357

**Northern Ireland (1) 1** *(Lennon 29)*

**Armenia (1) 1** *(Assadourian 7)*

*Northern Ireland:* Fettis; Nolan, Rowland, Lomas, Hunter, Hill, Gillespie (O'Neill 80), Lennon (Magilton 60), Dowie, Gray P (McMahon 60), Hughes.
*Armenia:* Berezovski; Soukiassian, Kachatrian V, Hovsepian, Hovhaffifyaf, Vardanian, Art Petrossian (Avetissian A 82), Tonoyan (Minassian 56), Mikhitarian H, Assadourian, Mikayelian (Ter-Petrossian 70).
*Referee:* Danilovski (Macedonia).

### Kiev, 5 October 1996, 51,300

**Ukraine (1) 2** *(Popov 4, Maximov 88)*

**Portugal (0) 1** *(Joao Pinto II 83)*

*Ukraine:* Suslov; Dmitrulin, Golovko, Vachtsjaek, Popov, Skrypnyk, Zubov (Jesin 53), Maximov, Kriventsov (Luzhnyi 66), Kosovski, Rebrov (Guseinov 75).
*Portugal:* Vitor Baia; Secretario, Helder, Santos, Figo, Oceano (Bento 66), Paulo Sousa, Rui Costa, Joao Pinto II, Domingos (Folha 15), Sa Pinto (Paulo Alves 64).
*Referee:* Nielsen (Denmark).

### Tirana, 10 October 1996, 10,000

**Albania (0) 0**

**Portugal (1) 3** *(Figo 10, Helder 75, Rui Costa 86)*

*Albania:* Strakosha; Dema (Kushta 46), Abazi (Malko 81), Xhumba, Vata R, Lekbello, Kacaj, Kola, Xola, Bozgo, Rraklli.
*Portugal:* Vitor Baia; Secretario, Fernando Couto, Helder, Santos, Oceano (Taira 83), Figo (Capucho 86), Rui Costa, Joao Pinto, Sa Pinto, Folha (Bento 67).
*Referee:* Sarvan (Turkey).

### Erevan, 10 October 1996, 40,000

**Armenia (0) 1** *(Mikayelian 85)*

**Germany (3) 5** *(Hassler 20, 39, Klinsmann 26, Bobic 69, Kuntz 81)*

*Armenia:* Berezovski; Soukiassian, Kachatrian V, Hovsepian, Der Zakarian, Ovannessian (Ter-Petrossian 46), Vardanian, Tonoyan (Avetissian A 46), Mikhitarian H, Assadourian, Mikayelian.
*Germany:* Kopke; Passlack, Babbel, Kohler, Reuter, Bode (Kuntz 73), Eilts, Hassler (Tarnat 76), Scholl, Klinsmann, Bierhoff (Bobic 63).
*Referee:* Collina (Italy).

### Tirana, 9 November 1996, 5000

**Albania (0) 1** *(Fraholli 58)*

**Armenia (0) 1** *(Ter Petrossian 90)*

*Albania:* Nallbani; Vata R, Xhumba, Malko, Vila, Kola (Shulku 83), Haxhi, Paco (Alliu 46), Fraholli, Rraklli (Fortuzi 67), Vata F.
*Armenia:* Arm Petrossian; Soukiassian, Khachatrian V, Hovsepian, Avetissian A (Ter-Petrossian 46), Vardanian (Avetissian V 72), Art Petrossian, Tonoyan (Minassian 46), Mikhitarian H, Assadourian, Mikayelian.
*Referee:* Stuchlik (Austria).

### Nuremburg, 9 November 1996, 40,700

**Germany (1) 1** *(Moller 41)*

**Northern Ireland (1) 1** *(Taggart 39)*

*Germany:* Kopke; Strunz, Reuter, Kohler, Babbel, Tarnat, Hassler, Eilts (Passlack 62), Moller, Klinsmann, Bobic (Bierhoff 70).
*Northern Ireland:* Wright; Hill, Nolan, Hunter, Taggart, Horlock, Morrow, Lomas, Dowie (Gray 78), Lennon (Rogan 85), Hughes.
*Referee:* Cakar (Turkey).

### Porto, 9 November 1996, 40,000

**Portugal (0) 1** *(Fernando Couto 58)*

**Ukraine (0) 0**

*Portugal:* Vitor Baia; Joao Pinto I, Fernando Couto, Helder, Dimas, Figo, Oceano, Rui Costa (Conceicao 64), Joao Pinto II, Sa Pinto (Bento 75), Folha (Porfifio 46).
*Ukraine:* Suslov; Dmitrulin, Skrypnyk, Golovko, Bezhnar, Popov, Maximov, Kalitvitsev (Kriventsov 58), Orbu (Kosovski V 64), Yessine (Zubov 46), Rebrov.
*Referee:* Sundell (Sweden).

### Belfast, 14 December 1996, 7935

**Northern Ireland (2) 2** *(Dowie 12, 21)*

**Albania (0) 0**

*Northern Ireland:* Wright; Nolan, Horlock, Hunter, Hill, Taggart, Lomas, Lennon, Dowie (Quinn 89), Morrow (McMahon 72), Hughes.
*Albania:* Nallbani; Dede (Tole 35), Vata R, Malko, Shulku, Vata F, Fakaj, Kola, Haxhi (Fraholli 38), Rraklli, Paco.
*Referee:* Georgiou (Cyprus).

### Lisbon, 14 December 1996, 55,000

**Portugal (0) 0**

**Germany (0) 0**

*Portugal:* Vitor Baia; Secretario, Dimas, Fernando Couto, Helder, Oceano, Paulinho Santos, Rui Barros (Cadete 78), Figo, Joao Pinto II, Rui Costa.
*Germany:* Kopke; Reuter, Sammer, Kohler, Ziege, Eilts, Basler (Kirsten 70), Moller, Babbel (Tarnat 84), Klinsmann, Bobic.
*Referee:* Puhl (Hungary).

### Grenada, 29 March 1997, 500

**Albania (0) 0**

**Ukraine (1) 1** *(Rebrov 39)*

*Albania:* Strakosha; Dema (Haxhi 46), Daja, Abazi, Vata R, Kacaj, Bozgo (Bujhaj 72), Bellai (Jphaza 82), Kola, Rraklli, Vata F.
*Ukraine:* Suslov; Starostyak, Golovko, Bezhnar, Vashchuk, Mikhailenko (Kardash 72), Orbu (Skrypnyk 18), Kalitvintsev (Kriventsov 86), Kossovski V, Shevchenko, Rebrov.
*played in Spain due to civil unrest in Albania.*
*Referee:* McDermott (N Ireland).

Belfast, 29 March 1997, 9392

**Northern Ireland (0) 0**

**Portugal (0) 0**

*Northern Ireland:* Wright; Gillespie, Hill, Morrow, Taggart, Nolan, Lennon, Lomas, Quinn (McMahon 68), Dowie, Magilton.
*Portugal:* Vitor Baia; Paulinho Santos, Fernando Couto, Jorge Costa, Dimas (Cadete 63), Conceicao, Paulo Sousa, Rui Costa, Oceano (Martins 63), Figo, Joao Pinto II.
*Referee:* Cesari (Italy).


Grenada, 2 April 1997, 8000

**Albania (0) 2** *(Kola 61 (pen), 90 (pen))*

**Germany (0) 3** *(Kirsten 64, 80, 84)*

*Albania:* Strakosha; Shpuza (Bellai 61), Shulku, Vata R, Kacaj, Abazi, Haxhi, Kola, Bushi (Lance 90), Rraklli, Tare (Vata F 74).
*Germany:* Kopke; Reuter (Heinrich 62), Kohler, Sammer, Helmer, Ziege, Moller, Eilts (Kirsten 63), Wosz, Klinsmann, Beirhoff.
*played in Spain due to civil unrest in Albania.*
*Referee:* Piraux (Belgium).


Kiev, 2 April 1997, 70,000

**Ukraine (1) 2** *(Kossovski V 2, Shevchenko 70)*

**Northern Ireland (1) 1** *(Dowie 14 (pen))*

*Ukraine:* Kossovski O; Luzhni, Bezhenar, Golovko, Skrypnyk, Mikhailenko, Kardash, Kalitvintsev (Kriventsov 88), Kossovski V (Orbu 77), Shevchenko, Rebrov.
*Northern Ireland:* Wright; Gillespie (McMahon 82), Nolan, Hill, Taggart, Morrow, Lennon (Quinn 75), Lomas, Dowie, Horlock, Hughes.
*Referee:* Krondl (Czech Republic).


Erevan, 30 April 1997, 10,000

**Armenia (0) 0**

**Northern Ireland (0) 0**

*Armenia:* Berezovski; Soukiassian, Khachatrian V, Hovsepian, Ter-Zakarian, Art Petrossian (Khodgoyan 84), Mikhitarian H, Yepiskoposyan (Minassian 86), Avalian (Avetissian A 76), Mikaelian, Assadourian.
*Northern Ireland:* Fettis; Jenkins, Morrow, Hill, Taggart, Lomas, McCarthy (Mulryne 71), Lennon, Quinn (McMahon 59), Dowie, Horlock.
*Referee:* Nielsen (Sweden).


Bremen, 30 April 1997, 33,242

**Germany (0) 2** *(Bierhoff 63, Basler 72)*

**Ukraine (0) 0**

*Germany:* Kopke; Helmer, Kohler, Heinrich, Eilts, Ziege, Basler, Wosz (Tarnat 83), Bobic (Novotny 13), Klinsmann, Bierhoff.
*Ukraine:* Shovkovskyi; Golovko, Luzhni, Skrypnyk (Orbu 70), Nagornyak (Vashchuk 70), Bezhenar, Maximov, Rebrov, Kalitvintsev (Mikhailenko 79), Kossovski V, Shevchenko.
*Referee:* Frisk (Sweden).


Kiev, 7 May 1997, 60,000

**Ukraine (1) 1** *(Shevchenko 6)*

**Armenia (0) 1** *(Art Petrossian 75)*

*Ukraine:* Shovkovskyi; Luzhni, Golovko, Vashchuk, Dmitrulin, Nagornyak (Orbu 66), Mikhailenko, Kalitvintsev (Kriventsov 79), Kossovski V, Rebrov (Zubov 83), Shevchenko.
*Armenia:* Berezovski; Soukiassian, Ter-Zakarian, Kocharyan, Oganessian, Art Petrossian, Vardanian, Mikhitarian H (Avalian 60), Sarkissian, Assadourian (Yessayan 89), Mikaelian (Avetissian A 68).
*Referee:* Ozonov (Russia).


Porto, 7 June 1997, 15,000

**Portugal (1) 2** *(Joao Pinto 14, Figo 70)*

**Albania (0) 0**

*Portugal:* Vitor Baia; Nelson, Jorge Costa, Fernando Couto, Paulinho Santos, Conceicao, Paulo Sousa, Figo (Cadete 87), Joao Pinto (Nuno Gomes 87), Domingos (Barbosa 20), Dani.
*Albania:* Mallisami; Shpuza (Tole 76), Xhumba, Vata R, Shulku, Kacaj, Abazi, Bushi, Haxhi, Tare, Zela (Vila 46).
*Referee:* Hauge (Norway).


Kiev, 7 June 1997, 55,000

**Ukraine (0) 0**

**Germany (0) 0**

*Ukraine:* Shovkovskyi; Luzhnyi, Golovko, Vachtsjaek, Koval, Dmitrulin, Maximov (Zhabchenko 74), Guseinov, Nagornyak (Bezhenar 88), Rebrov (Mikhailenko 84), Shevchenko.
*Germany:* Kopke; Heinrich, Kohler, Sammer, Helmer, Ziege, Eilts, Wosz (Scholl 69), Basler, Klinsmann, Kirsten (Bierhoff 87).
*Referee:* Vagner (Hungary).


Belfast, 20 August 1997, 12,035

**Northern Ireland (0) 1** *(Hughes 59)*

**Germany (0) 3** *(Bierhoff 73, 77, 79)*

*Northern Ireland:* Davison; Nolan, Morrow, Hill, Taggart, Horlock, Gillespie (McMahon 80), Magilton, Quinn, Lennon (Griffin 83), Hughes.
*Germany:* Kopke; Basler (Babbel 83), Worns (Hassler 62), Kohler, Helmer, Heinrich, Moller, Nowotny, Ziege, Kirsten (Bierhoff 69), Klinsmann.
*Referee:* Aranda (Spain).


Kiev, 20 August 1997, 38,000

**Ukraine (0) 1** *(Rebrov 85)*

**Albania (0) 0**

*Ukraine:* Shovkovsky; Luzhny, Golovko, Vashchuk, Zubov (Kossovski V 46), Dmitrulin (Kriventsov 56), Maximov, Kalitvintsev (Getsko 83), Guseinov, Shevchenko, Rebrov.
*Albania:* Strakosha; Tole, Xhumba (Gallo 46), Vata R, Shulku, Daiu, Paco (Peko 29), Bushi, Haxhi, Tare, Rraklli.
*Referee:* Lyubash (Slovenia).


Setubal, 21 August 1997, 15,000

**Portugal (2) 3** *(Domingos 22, Figo 30, Barbosa 53)*

**Armenia (0) 1** *(Assadourian 46)*

*Portugal:* Rui Correia; Conseicao, Fernando Couto, Helder, Paulinho Santos (Dimas 82), Figo, Paulo Sousa, Rui Costa, Barbosa, Joao Pinto (Dani 66), Domingos (Pauleta 77).
*Armenia:* Abrahamian; Ter-Petrossian (Art Petrossian 46), Vardanian, Hovsepian, Sargasian (Gsepian 83), Yessayan, Nazaryan, Avalayan (Georgian 79), Gogojan, Assadourian, Mikaelian.
*Referee:* Lica (Romania).


Erevan, 6 September 1997, 5000

**Armenia (0) 3** *(Vardanian 60, Assadourian 82, Avalayan 88 (pen))*

**Albania (0) 0**

*Armenia:* Berezovski; Krbachian, Nazaryan, Hovsepian, Avalayan, Vardanian, Art Petrossian (Yessayan 38), Sargasian (Ter-Petrossian 61), Mikhitarian, Assadourian, Mikaelian (Avetissian V 84).
*Albania:* Strakosha; Tole, Shulku, Dalu, Xhumba, Vata R, Peko (Vata F 77), Haxhi, Kova, Rrakli, Tare (Fortizi 74).
*Referee:* Radoman (Yugoslavia).

Berlin, 6 September 1997, 75,841

**Germany (0) 1** *(Kirsten 81)*
**Portugal (0) 1** *(Barbosa 71)*

*Germany:* Kopke; Helmer, Kohler, Reuter (Babbel 46), Heinrich (Wosz 79), Nowotny, Ziege, Basler, Hassler, Klinsmann, Bierhoff (Kirsten 70).
*Portugal:* Silvino; Santos, Beto, Helder, Dimas, Paulo Sousa, Oceano (Pauleter 84), Figo, Rui Costa, Barbosa, Joao Pinto (Conceicao 78).
*Referee:* Batta (France).

Zurich, 10 September 1997, 2600

**Albania (0) 1** *(Haxhi 69)*
**Northern Ireland (0) 0**

*Albania:* Strakosha; Tole, Shulku, Xhumba, Vata R, Fakaj, Peco (Halili 65), Haxhi (Gallo 83), Kola, Bushaj, Tare.
*Northern Ireland:* Wright; Hill, Griffin, McGibbon, Rowland (Mulryne 46), Lomas, Gillespie, Lennon (Sonner 83), Quinn (McMahon 76), Dowie, Horlock.
*Referee:* Philippi (Luxembourg).

Dortmund, 10 September 1997, 43,000

**Germany (0) 4** *(Klinsmann 70, 84, Hassler 86, Kirsten 90)*
**Armenia (0) 0**

*Germany:* Kopke; Heinrich, Worns, Thon, Helmer, Tarnat (Bierhoff 67), Hassler, Kmetsch (Ricken 46), Wosz (Nowotny 81), Kirsten, Klinsmann.
*Armenia:* Berezovski; Krbachian (Ter-Petrossian 62), Nazaryan, Hovsepian, Vardanian, Avalayan (Sargasian 46), Art Petrossian (Avetissian A 79), Schahgeldian, Mikhitarian, Mikaelian, Assadourian.
*Referee:* Mikkelsen (Denmark).

Erevan, 11 October 1997, 8000

**Armenia (0) 0**
**Ukraine (1) 2** *(Shevchenko 33, Maximov 58)*

*Armenia:* Berezovski; Vardanian, Nazaryan, Hovsepian, Krbachian (Hodjojan 54), Minassian (Assadourian 46), Art Petrossian (Avetissian V 84), Mikhitarian, Sargasian, Avalayan, Mikaelian.
*Ukraine:* Shovkovsky; Dmitrulin, Golovko, Vashchuk, Skrypnyk (Starostyak 70), Gusin, Maximov, Kalitvintsev, Kossovski V (Nagornyak 58), Rebrov, Shevchenko (Atelkin 82).
*Referee:* Vega (Spain).

Hanover, 11 October 1997, 44,522

**Germany (0) 4** *(Helmer 64, Bierhoff 73, 90, Marschall 86)*
**Albania (0) 3** *(Kola 55 (og), Tare 80, Vata R 88)*

*Germany:* Kahn; Kohler, Thon, Helmer, Reuter, Hassler, Moller, Kuntz (Marschall 72), Heinrich, Bierhoff, Bobic (Tarnat 60).
*Albania:* Strakosha; Xhumba, Shulku, Fakaj, Tole (Gallo 79), Bushi (Prenga 90), Kola, Vata R, Halili (Peco 55), Haxhi, Tare.
*Referee:* Pedersen (Norway).

Lisbon, 11 October 1997, 31,847

**Portugal (1) 1** *(Conceicao 17)*
**Northern Ireland (0) 0**

*Portugal:* Silvino; Paulinho Santos, Fernando Couto, Helder, Dimas, Conceicao (Dani 78), Oceano, Paulo Sousa, Figo, Joao Pinto, Pauleta (Cadete 62).
*Northern Ireland:* Fettis; Nolan, Morrow, Hill (McMahon 77), Taggart, Lomas, Lennon (McCarthy 77), Magilton, Dowie, Horlock, Hughes.
*Referee:* Mikkelsen (Denmark).

**Group 9**

| | P | W | D | L | F | A | Pts |
|---|---|---|---|---|---|---|---|
| Germany | 10 | 6 | 4 | 0 | 23 | 9 | 22 |
| Ukraine | 10 | 6 | 2 | 2 | 10 | 6 | 20 |
| Portugal | 10 | 5 | 4 | 1 | 12 | 4 | 19 |
| Armenia | 10 | 1 | 5 | 4 | 8 | 17 | 8 |
| Northern Ireland | 10 | 1 | 4 | 5 | 6 | 10 | 7 |
| Albania | 10 | 1 | 1 | 8 | 7 | 20 | 4 |

**Germany qualify for finals (11.10.97).**

# PLAY-OFFS

Zagreb, 29 October 1997, 20,000

**Croatia (1) 2** *(Bilic 11, Vlaovic 49)*
**Ukraine (0) 0**

*Croatia:* Ladic; Simic, Bilic, Juric, Saric, Jarni, Stanic (Asanovic 59), Boban, Prosinecki, Vlaovic (Cvitanovic 82), Suker.
*Ukraine:* Shovkovsky; Dmitrulin, Golovko, Vashchuk, Atelkin (Mikhailenko 53), Skrypnyk, Guseinov, Nagornyak (Zubov 59), Rebrov, Maximov (Getsko 86), Kossovski V.
*Referee:* Sars (France).

Budapest, 29 October 1997, 13,175

**Hungary (0) 1** *(Illes 89)*
**Yugoslavia (5) 7** *(Brnovic 2, Djukic 6, Savicevic 10, Mijatovic 26, 41, 51, Milosevic 65)*

*Hungary:* Safar; Lorincz, Sebok, Banfi, Dombi (Mracsko 32), Nyilas (Urban 41), Lipcsei, Halmai, Kereszturi, Orosz, Klausz (Illes 62).
*Yugoslavia:* Kralj; Mirkovic, Djukic, Mihajlovic, Djorovic, Stojkovic, Jokanovic, Brnovic (Petrovic 60), Jugovic, Savicevic (Govedarica 72), Mijatovic (Milosevic 54).
*Referee:* Pereira (Portugal).

Dublin, 29 October 1997, 32,305

**Republic of Ireland (1) 1** *(Irwin 8)*
**Belgium (1) 1** *(Nilis 30)*

*Republic of Ireland:* Given; Kelly G, Irwin, Harte, Cunningham, Staunton, Kennedy (Kenna 33), Houghton, Connolly (Coyne 81), Cascarino, Townsend (Carsley 75).
*Belgium:* De Wilde; Verstraeten, Vidovic, Van Meir, Genaux, Van der Elst F, Van Kerckhoven, Boffin, Wilmots, Goosens (Verheyen 88), Nilis (De Bilde 88).
*Referee:* Vagner (Hungary).

Moscow, 29 October 1997, 20,000

**Russia (0) 1** *(Yuran 51)*
**Italy (0) 1** *(Vieri 49)*

*Russia:* Ovchinnikov; Radimov, Kovtun, Onopko (Tsveiba 42), Chugainov, Kanchelskis (Khokhlov 46), Popov (Tikhonov 81), Alenichev, Ianovski, Yuran, Kolyvanov.
*Italy:* Pagliuca (Buffon 34); Nesta, Costacurta, Cannavaro, Maldini, Pessotto (Benarrivo 52), Dino Baggio, Albertini, Di Matteo, Vieri, Ravanelli (Del Piero 61).
*Referee:* Mikkelsen (Denmark).

Brussels, 15 November 1997, 38,000

**Belgium (1) 2** *(Oliveira 25, Nilis 68)*
**Republic of Ireland (0) 1** *(Houghton 58)*

*Belgium:* De Wilde; Deflandre, Verstraeten, De Boeck, Vidovic (Borkelmans 64), Verheyen, Van der Elst F, Claessens (Leonard 76), Boffin, Oliveira, Nilis (Goossens 89).
*Republic of Ireland:* Given; Kenna, Staunton, Kelly G, Cunningham, Harte, Carsley, McLoughlin (Houghton 48), Cascarino, Townsend (Kelly D 85), Kennedy (Connolly 73).
*Belgium qualify for final (15.11.97).*
*Referee:* Benko (Austria).

Naples, 15 November 1997, 76,500

**Italy (0) 1** *(Casiraghi 53)*
**Russia (0) 0**

*Italy:* Peruzzi; Pessotto (Nesta 76), Cannavaro, Costacurta, Ferrara, Maldini, Dino Baggio, Albertini, Di Matteo, Casiraghi, Ravanelli (Del Piero 76).
*Russia:* Ovchinnikov; Kovtun, Khokhlov, Nikiforov, Onopko, Popov, Alenichev, Radimov (Semak 66), Yanovski (Simoutenkov 59), Yuran (Bestchastnykh 79), Kolyvanov.
*Italy qualify for final (15.11.97).*
*Referee:* Muhmenthaler (Switzerland).

Kiev, 15 November 1997, 70,000

**Ukraine (1) 1** *(Shevchenko 4)*
**Croatia (1) 1** *(Boksic 28)*

*Ukraine:* Shovkovsky; Luzhny, Bezhenar, Golovko, Popov, Dmitrulin (Mikhailenko 60), Guseinov (Kriventsov 86), Kalitvintsev, Kossovski V, Schevchenko, Rebrov.
*Croatia:* Mrmic; Simic, Juric, Soldo, Saric (Kovac 55), Asanovic (Tudor 88), Boban, Jurcic, Jarni, Boksic (Vlaovic 84), Suker.
*Croatia qualify for final (15.11.97).*
*Referee:* Pedersen (Norway).

Belgrade, 15 November 1997, 60,000

**Yugoslavia (3) 5** *(Milosevic 17, Mijatovic 44, 45 (pen), 71, 88)*
**Hungary (0) 0**

*Yugoslavia:* Kralj (Lekovic 46); Mirkovic, Djorovic, Djukic, Mihajlovic, Stojkovic, Jokanovic (Drulovic 46), Brnovic, Savicevic, Mijatovic, Milosevic (Petrovic 60).
*Hungary:* Babos; Mracsko, Urban, Sebok, Kuttor, Kereszturi, Halmai, Dombi, Kovacs Z (Hamori 62), Illes (Horvath 88), Szlezak (Lipcsei 31).
*Yugoslavia qualify for final (15.11.97).*
*Referee:* Tokar (Turkey).

## SOUTH AMERICA

**SOUTH AMERICA** (Members 10, Entries 10)
Five teams qualify including Brazil as champions.
The nine competing teams play each other twice, the first four qualifying for the finals.

Buenos Aires, 24 April 1996, 60,000

**Argentina (2) 3** *(Ortega 8, 18, Batistuta 49)*
**Bolivia (1) 1** *(Baldivieso 42)*

*Argentina:* Passet; Zanetti, Ayala, Sensini, Chamot, Simeone, Almeyda, Ortega, Morales, Caniggia (Balbo 72), Batistuta (Lopez C 87).
*Bolivia:* Barrero; Rimba, Pena, Paraba, Sanchez O, Ramos (Castillo I 80), Coimbra (Paniagua 75), Tufino, Baldivieso, Etcheverry (Suarez 78), Castillo R.
*Referee:* Sanchez (Chile).

Barranquilla, 24 April 1996, 60,000

**Colombia (0) 1** *(Asprilla F 55)*
**Paraguay (0) 0**

*Colombia:* Mondragon; Perez W (Estrada 69), Bermudez, Mendoza, Moreno, Alvarez, Serna, Valderrama, Rincon, Valenciano (Valencia 75), Asprilla F.
*Paraguay:* Chilavert; Arce, Gamarra, Ayala, Rivarola, Jara (Sarabia 80), Acuna, Sotelo, Struway, Ferreira (Benitez 64), Campos J (Rojas A 69).
*Referee:* Castrilli (Argentina).

Guayaquil, 24 April 1996, 65,000

**Ecuador (0) 4** *(Hurtado E 54, 90, Tenorio 65, Gavica 77)*
**Peru (0) 1** *(Palacios 62)*

*Ecuador:* Morales; Rivera, Montano, Hurtado I (Abregon 84), Capurro, De Souza, Tenorio, Carabali W (Carabali H 46), Aguinaga, Fernandez (Gavica 76), Hurtado E.
*Peru:* Miranda; Solano, Reynoso, Marengo, Ferrari (Magallanes 67), Carranza, Jayo, Del Solar, Palacios, Maestri, Guadalupe (Ramirez 68).
*Referee:* Matto (Uruguay).

Caracas, 24 April 1996, 12,000

**Venezuela (0) 0**
**Uruguay (0) 2** *(Otero 54, Poyet 71)*

*Venezuela:* Angelucci; Filosa, Gonzalez W, Tortolero, Gonzalez L, Vallenilla, Valiente (Mackintosh 74), Hernandez, Castellin, Diaz (Rivas 55), Guerra.
*Uruguay:* Arbiza; Olivera, Herrera, Moas, Montero, Saralegui, Gutierrez, Bengoechea (Abeijon 90), Poyet, Otero (Cedres 87), Fonseca.
*Referee:* Tejada (Peru).

Quito, 2 June 1996, 55,000

**Ecuador (0) 2** *(Montano 52, Hurtado E 89)*
**Argentina (0) 0**

*Ecuador:* Morales; Rivera, Hurtado I (Obregon 84), Tenorio, Capurro, Montano, Gavica (Fernandez 46), Aguinaga, Carabali H, De Souza, Hurtado E.
*Argentina:* Bossio; Zanetti, Caceres, Sensini, Chamot, Almeyda, Simeone, Morales (Lopez G 76), Ortega (Cardoso 71), Batistuta (Crespo 76), Caniggia.
*Referee:* Perez (Colombia).

Lima, 2 June 1996, 45,000

**Peru (0) 1** *(Reynoso 48)*
**Colombia (0) 1** *(Aristizabal 60)*

*Peru:* Balerio; Marengo, Reynoso, Olivares, Legario, Carranza (Guadalupe 75), Solano, Del Solar, Maestri, Palacios, Zegarra (Magallanes 79).
*Colombia:* Mondragon; Mendoza, Moreno, Herrera, Bermudez, Valencia (Aristizabal 46), Estrada, Valderrama (Bolano 90), Asprilla F, Rincon, Alvarez.
*Referee:* Rodas (Ecuador).

Montevideo, 2 June 1996, 60,000

**Uruguay (0) 0**
**Paraguay (1) 2** *(Arce 10, Rojas A 89)*

*Uruguay:* Arbiza; Mendez, Herrera, Moas, Montero, Saralegui (Romero 46), Gutierrez (Dorta 69), Poyet, Bengoechea, Otero, Martinez (Cedres 60).
*Paraguay:* Chilavert; Arce, Rivarola, Ayala, Gamarra, Struway, Enciso, Bourdier, Acuna (Suarez 90), Baez E (Gonzalez 60), Baez R (Rojas A 70).
*Referee:* Rezende (Brazil).

Barinas, 2 June 1996, 9850

**Venezuela (1) 1** *(Guerra 7)*
**Chile (0) 1** *(Margas 90)*

*Venezuela:* Dudamel; Mackintosh, Tortolero, Gonzalez L, Diaz (Hezzel 67) (Urdaneta 85), Hernandez S, Valiente, Hernandez F, Rivas, Guerra, Castellin (Savarese 67).
*Chile:* Tapia; Mendoza, Ramirez, Fuentes, Margas, Vilches (Nunez 73), Estay, Vega (Rozental 46), Valencia (Musrri 46), Zamorano, Salas.
*Referee:* Gonzales (Paraguay).

Santiago, 6 July 1996, 75,000

**Chile (1) 4** *(Zamorano 21, 85, Salas 75, Estay 83)*
**Ecuador (0) 1** *(Aguinaga 74)*

*Chile:* Tapia; Castaneda C, Gonzalez, Margas, Miranda, Musrri, Valencia (Sierra 76), Vega (Sierra 76), Castaneda V (Mora 68), Salas, Zamorano.
*Ecuador:* Morales; Tenorio M (Gonzalez 78), Rivera, Montano (Tenorio B 46), Capurro, Hurtado I, Obregon (Fernandez 46), Carabali, Aguinaga, De Souza, Hurtado E.
*Referee:* Duran (Bolivia).

La Paz, 7 July 1996, 40,000

**Bolivia (2) 6** *(Sandy 3, Etcheverry 27 (pen), Baldivieso 49, Coimbra 67, Suarez 77, Paniagua 80)*
**Venezuela (0) 1** *(Tortolero 65 (pen))*

*Bolivia:* Trucco; Sanchez O, Quinteros, Sandy, Rimba, Pena, Cristaldo, Castillo R (Suarez 75), Baldivieso, Etcheverry (Moreno 68), Coimbra (Paniagua 78).
*Venezuela:* Dudamel; Filosa, Mackintosh, Tortolero, Hernandez S (Diaz 46), Vera, Gonzalez, Hernandez F, Rivas S (Urdaneta 46), Savarese (Miranda 46), Guerra.
*Referee:* Da Rosa (Uruguay).

Barranquilla, 7 July 1996, 40,000

**Colombia (2) 3** *(Asprilla F 10, Valderrama 22, De Avila 77)*
**Uruguay (0) 1** *(Cedres 55)*

*Colombia:* Mondragon; Cabrera, Bermudez, Mendoza, Moreno, Alvarez, Serna, Rincon, Valderrama, Asprilla F, Aristizabal (De Avila 64).
*Uruguay:* Arbiza; Oliveira (Bengoechea 36), Moas, Aguirregaray, Lima (Silva T 54), Pereyra, Dorta (Sosa H 71), Poyet, Saralegui, Cedres, Romero.
*Referee:* Ruscio (Argentina).

Lima, 7 July 1996, 45,000

**Peru (0) 0**
**Argentina (0) 0**

*Peru:* Balerio; Solano, Reynoso, Soto, Olivares, Jayo, Zegarra (Magallanes 68), Carranza (Farfan 83), Palacios, Julinho, Maestri.
*Argentina:* Burgos; Zanetti, Ayala, Sensini, Chamot, Almeyda, Simeone, Morales (Bassedas 46), Ortega (Lopez G 89), Caniggia (Paz 72), Balbo.
*Referee:* Souza (Brazil).

Buenos Aires, 1 September 1996, 57,886

**Argentina (1) 1** *(Batistuta 26)*
**Paraguay (1) 1** *(Chilavert 42 (pen))*

*Argentina:* Burgos; Zanetti (Albornoz 88), Caceres, Ayala, Chamot, Almeyda, Bassedas (Veron 53), Morales, Ortega, Schelotto (Lopez C 53), Batistuta.
*Paraguay:* Chilavert; Gamarra, Ayala, Rivarola, Suarez, Enciso, Sanabria V (Esteche 75), Acuna (Alcaraz 87), Bourdier, Baez R, Rojas A.
*Referee:* Da Silva (Brazil).

La Paz, 1 September 1996, 45,000

**Bolivia (0) 0**
**Peru (0) 0**

*Bolivia:* Trucco; Rimba, Sanchez O, Pena, Sandy, Castillo I, Baldivieso, Etcheverry, Sanchez E (Paniagua 85), Castillo R, Coimbra (Moreno 65).
*Peru:* Balerio; Olivares, Marengo, Jose Soto, Reynoso, Serrano (Julinho 47), Jayo, Zegarra, Pereda, Palacios (Jorge Soto 81), Maestri (Carty 80).
*Referee:* Velasquez (Paraguay).

Barranquilla, 1 September 1996, 35,000

**Colombia (3) 4** *(Asprilla F 4, 31, 47, Bermudez 43)*
**Chile (0) 1** *(Zamorano 56 (pen))*

*Colombia:* Mondragon; Santa, Bermudez, Mendoza, Galeano, Lozano, Serna, Quinonez (Lopez 58), Valderrama, Aristizabal (De Avila 52), Asprilla F (Ramirez 85).
*Chile:* Tapia; Rojas (Sierra 46), Margas, Gonzalez, Mora, Estay (Castaneda V 85), Musrri, Romero, Vega (Rozental 71), Salas, Zamorano.
*Referee:* Marinho (Brazil).

Quito, 1 September 1996, 45,000

**Ecuador (1) 1** *(Aguinaga 4)*
**Venezuela (0) 0**

*Ecuador:* Morales; Rivera, Hurtado I, Tenorio, Capurro, Diaz (Abregon 79), Carabali, Aguinaga, Garcia (Fernandez 46), De Souza, Hurtado E.
*Venezuela:* Dudamel; Filosa, Gonzalez W, Tortolero, Mackintosh, Hernandez S, Valiente (Urdaneta 40), Vera, Miranda, Socorro (Hernandez L 79), Garcia.
*Referee:* Robles (Chile).

Montevideo, 8 October 1996, 65,000

**Uruguay (0) 1** *(Pena 64 (og))*
**Bolivia (0) 0**

*Uruguay:* Siboldi; Sanguinetti, Herrera, Montero, Mendez, Saralegui (Gutierrez 82), Cedres, Poyet (Romero 62), Francescoli, Otero (Bengoechea 81), Fonseca.
*Bolivia:* Trucco; Cristaldo, Pena, Sandy, Sanchez O, Castillo S, Soria (Tufino 34), Baldivieso (Coimbra 71), Castillo R, Melgar, Moreno.
*Referee:* Borgosano (Venezuela).

Quito, 9 October 1996, 45,000

**Ecuador (0) 0**
**Colombia (0) 1** *(Asprilla F 72)*

*Ecuador:* Morales; Rivera, Montano, Tenorio M, Capurro, Hurtado I (Obregon 62), Carabali, De Souza (Fernandez 74), Aguinaga, Hurtado E, Delgado.
*Colombia:* Mondragon; Cabrera, Bermudez, Lopez, Galeano, Serna, Alvarez, Rincon (Lozano 62), Valderrama, Aristizabal (De Avila 62), Asprilla F.
*Referee:* Elizondo (Argentina).

Asuncion, 9 October 1996, 45,000

**Paraguay (1) 2** *(Gamarra 24, Rivarola 63)*
**Chile (1) 1** *(Margas 22)*

*Paraguay:* Chilavert; Arce, Ayala, Rivarola, Gamarra, Acuna, Struway, Enciso (Baez R 62), Caballero (Rojas A 46), Benitez, Cardoso (Alcaraz 70).
*Chile:* Ramirez; Fuentes, Reyes, Margas (Estay 80), Castaneda, Miranda, Musrri, Cornejo, Contreras (Rozental 65), Zamorano, Vergara (Goldberg 75).
*Referee:* Ruiz (Colombia).

San Cristobal, 9 October 1996, 30,000

**Venezuela (1) 2** *(Savarese 6, Dudamel 87)*
**Argentina (1) 5** *(Ortega 35, Sorin 68, Simeone 78, Morales 86, Albornoz 90)*

*Venezuela:* Dudamel; Mackintosh, Gonzalez L, Gonzalez W, Hernandez S, Hernandez F (Urdaneta 42), Miranda (Garcia 70), Savarese, Vera, Moran, Guerra (Filosa 46).
*Argentina:* Cavallero; Diaz, Ayala, Berizzo, Sorin, Simeone (Molina 88), Almeyda, Morales, Albornoz, Batistuta, Ortega (Lopez C 88).
*Referee:* Diuzaniewsky (Uruguay).

La Paz, 10 November 1996, 45,000

**Bolivia (2) 2** *(Sandy 15, Moreno 44)*
**Colombia (1) 2** *(Serna 40 (pen), Rincon 54)*

*Bolivia:* Trucco; Ochoaizpur, Sanchez O, Pena, Sandy, Cristaldo, Castillo, Melgar (Soria 70), Etcheverry, Ramallo (Coimbra 75), Moreno.
*Colombia:* Mondragon; Cabrera, Mendoza, Bermudez, Galeano, Alvarez, Serna, Valderrama, Rincon (Estrada 75), Asprilla F (Quinonez 75), De Avila (Angel 87).
*Referee:* Serna (Peru).

Asuncion, 10 November 1996, 37,000

**Paraguay (1) 1** *(Benitez 24)*
**Ecuador (0) 0**

*Paraguay:* Chilavert; Ayala, Rivarola, Gamarra, Arce, Caniza (Enciso 46), Struway, Acuna, Benitez, Baez R (Cardoso 46), Rojas A (Gonzalez 70).
*Ecuador:* Morales; Hurtado I, Rivera, Tenorio, Montano, Quinonez, De Souza, Aguinaga, De la Cruz, Hurtado E, Smith.
*Referee:* Gimenez (Argentina).

Lima, 10 November 1996, 31,000

**Peru (2) 4** *(Reynoso 5, Julinho 22, Palacios 49, 82)*
**Venezuela (0) 1** *(Vera 77)*

*Peru:* Balero; Solano, Jose Soto, Reynoso, Olivares, Lejario, Serrano (Maldonado 64), Palacios, Zegarra, Maestri (Carty 64), Julinho (Saenz 76).
*Venezuela:* Dudamel; Gonzalez, Tortolero, Mackintosh, Echenausi, Filosa, Hernandez (Diaz 46), Miranda (Vera 62), Valiente, Savarese (Moran 46), Garcia.
*Referee:* Betancourt (Bolivia).

Santiago, 12 November 1996, 70,000

**Chile (0) 1** *(Salas 60)*
**Uruguay (0) 0**

*Chile:* Tapia; Fuentes, Castaneda C, Reyes, Margas, Perez (Basay 46), Cornejo, Chavarria, Castaneda V (Contreras 69), Salas, Rozental (Mora 77).
*Uruguay:* Siboldi; Sanguinetti, Montero, Herrera, Mendez, Saralegui (Bengoechea 57), Gutierrez, Cedres (Recoba 72), Poyet, Otero, Francescoli (Romero 46).
*Referee:* Guevara (Ecuador).

Buenos Aires, 15 December 1996, 60,000

**Argentina (0) 1** *(Bastistuta 70 (pen))*
**Chile (1) 1** *(Cornejo 51)*

*Argentina:* Cavallero; Vivas (Lopez G 46), Ayala, Berizzo, Sorin, Almeyda, Zanetti, Morales (Camps 66), Albornoz (Balbo 36), Ortega, Batistuta.
*Chile:* Tapia; Castaneda C, Fuentes, Margas, Reyes, Mora, Chavarria, Cornejo, Castaneda V (Contreras 65), Rozental (Miranda 46), Salas (Zamorano 75).
*Referee:* Aquino (Paraguay).

La Paz, 15 December 1996, 45,000

**Bolivia (0) 0**
**Paraguay (0) 0**

*Bolivia:* Trucco; Rimba, Sandy, Pena, Castillo I, Ochaizpur, Tufino (Soria 46), Castillo R, Etcheverry, Moreno (Suarez B 60), Ramallo (Suarez R 46).
*Paraguay:* Chilavert; Acuna (Mesa 85), Villamayor, Ayala, Alcaraz, Caniza, Struway, Enciso, Benitez (Bourdier 64), Baez R (Cohener 75), Rojas A.
*Referee:* Nieves (Uruguay).

Montevideo, 15 December 1996, 55,000

**Uruguay (2) 2** *(Montero 2, Bengoechea 38)*
**Peru (0) 0**

*Uruguay:* Siboldi; Tais, Herrera, Montero, Sanguinetti, Abeijon (Saralegui 85), Moas (De los Santos G 77), Bengoechea, Francescoli, Otero, Fonseca (O'Neill 59).
*Peru:* Balerio; Marengo (Dulanto 46), Reynoso, Jose Soto, Olivares, Serrano, Jayo, Palacios, Zegarra (Carty 80), Maestri, Julinho (Saenz 84).
*Referee:* Russi (Colombia).

San Cristobal, 15 December 1996, 25,000

**Venezuela (0) 0**
**Colombia (1) 2** *(Bermudez 7, Valenciano 50)*

*Venezuela:* Dudamel; Filosa, Tortolero, Gonzalez W, Martinez, Hernandez F (Urdaneta 78), Hernandez S, Ramos, Paez, Savarese (Diaz 74), Castellin (Sanabria 82).
*Colombia:* Mondragon; Cabrera, Bermudez, Lopez (Valencia 68), Moreno, Serna, Lozano, Valderrama, Rincon, Valenciano (Ricard 65), De Avila (Aristizabal 65).
*Referee:* Gamboa (Peru).

La Paz, 12 January 1997, 37,000

**Bolivia (2) 2** *(Moreno 7, Etcheverry 12)*
**Ecuador (0) 0**

*Bolivia:* Trucco; Ochaizpur, Pena, Sandy, Sanchez O, Cristaldo, Baldivieso (Melgar 70), Soria, Castillo R (Gutierrez 65), Etcheverry, Moreno (Ramallo 75).
*Ecuador:* Morales; Rivera, Montano, Tenorio, Quinones, Carabali, Hurtado I, Aguinaga, De la Cruz (Gilson 46), Chala (Delgado 70), Fernandez (Hurtado E 46).
*Referee:* Acosta (Colombia).

Lima, 12 January 1997, 45,000

**Peru (2) 2** *(Maestri 15, Palacios 35)*
**Chile (0) 1** *(Zamorano 89)*

*Peru:* Miranda; Solano, Reynoso, Jose Soto, Olivarez, Jayo, Serrano, Palacios, Maldonado (Pereda 46), Julinho (Carty 70), Maestri (Jorge Soto 82).
*Chile:* Tapia; Castaneda C, Reyes, Gonzalez J, Miranda, Mora, Cornejo, Musrri (Riveros 58), Rozental (Contreras 83), Vergara (Gonzalez P 63), Zamorano.
*Referee:* Varela (Uruguay).

Montevideo, 12 January 1997, 70,000

**Uruguay (0) 0**
**Argentina (0) 0**

*Uruguay:* Siboldi; Tais, Herrera, Montero, Mendez, Moas, Abeijon, Cedres, Bengoechea, Francescoli (Recoba 73), Fonseca (Abreu 63).
*Argentina:* Gonzalez; Vivas, Sensini, Paz, Chamot, Almeyda, Simeone, Bassedas, Gorosito (Crespo 60), Ortega, Batistuta.
*Referee:* Rezende (Brazil).

Merida, 12 January 1997, 16,000

**Venezuela (0) 0**
**Paraguay (1) 2** *(Benitez 5, Enciso 62)*

*Venezuela:* Dudamel; Mackintosh, Medina, Echenique, Vallenilla, Ramos, Castellano (Tizamo 46), Nabollin (Valiente 68), Urdaneta, Savarese, Paez.
*Paraguay:* Diaz; Arce, Sarabia, Gamarra, Alcaraz, Enciso, Benitez (Mesa 73), Struway, Acuna, Rojas A (Baez R 73), Cohener (Ferreira 78).
*Referee:* Sanchez (Argentina).

La Paz, 12 February 1997, 45,000

**Bolivia (1) 1** *(Soria 28)*
**Chile (1) 1** *(Gonzalez P 45)*

*Bolivia:* Trucco; Sanchez O, Pena, Ochaizpur (Gutierrez 46), Sandy, Tufino, Soria, Castillo R (Castillo S 46), Cristaldo, Moreno, Etcheverry.
*Chile:* Tapia; Castaneda C, Reyes, Fuentes, Miranda, Chavarria, Castaneda V (Flores 56), Riveros (Contreras 76), Gonzalez P, Salas, Zamorano (Lee Chong 89).
*Referee:* Tejada (Peru).

Barranquilla, 12 February 1997, 60,000

**Colombia (0) 0**
**Argentina (1) 1** *(Lopez C 9)*

*Colombia:* Mondragon; Cabrera, Bermudez, Mendoza, Galeano (De Avila 58), Alvarez (Pacheco 46), Serna, Valderrama, Rincon, Valenciano, Asprilla F.
*Argentina:* Gonzalez; Diaz, Sensini, Berizzo, Paz, Simeone, Zapata, Veron, Ortega, Crespo (Vivas 46), Lopez C (Sorin 83).
*Referee:* Pereira (Brazil).

Quito, 12 February 1997, 25,000

**Ecuador (1) 4** *(Aguinaga 6, Delgado 69, 77, Chala 88)*
**Uruguay (0) 0**

*Ecuador:* Ibarra; Rivera, Montano, Hurtado I, Capurro, Ruiz, Blandon, De la Cruz (Chala 81), Gilson (Fernandez 81), Aguinaga, Delgado.
*Uruguay:* Siboldi; Tais, Montero, Herrera, Mendez, Moas, Abeijon, O'Neill, Cedres (Silva D 54), Francescoli (Saralegui 64), Abreu (Fonseca 54).
*Referee:* Castrilli (Argentina).

Asuncion, 12 February 1997, 35,000

**Paraguay (2) 2** *(Rivarola 12, Rojas A 40)*
**Peru (1) 1** *(Pereda 33)*

*Paraguay:* Chilavert; Ayala, Rivarola, Gamarra, Arce, Struway, Acuna (Bourdier 72), Enciso, Benitez, Soto (Cardozo 81), Rojas A (Campos 71).
*Peru:* Balerio; Reynoso, Jose Soto (Carty 53), Solano, Olivares, Jayo, Serrano, Pereda, Palacios (Saenz 72), Zegarra (Magallanes 67), Maestri.
*Referee:* Sanchez (Chile).

La Paz, 2 April 1997, 45,000

**Bolivia (1) 2** *(Sandy 7, Ochaizpur 48)*
**Argentina (1) 1** *(Gorosito 43 (pen))*

*Bolivia:* Trucco; Castillo S, Rimba, Sandy, Sanchez O, Castillo I, Ochaizpur (Melgar 89), Soria, Castillo R, Gutierrez (Blanco 51), Moreno (Angola 70).
*Argentina:* Gonzalez; Sensini, Vivas, Paz, Sorin, Diaz, Zapata, Cagna (Ortega 50), Gorosito (Veron 46), Delgado (Calderon 52), Cruz.
*Referee:* Marinho (Brazil).

Bogota, 2 April 1997, 42,000

**Colombia (1) 1** *(Serna 37 (pen))*
**Paraguay (1) 2** *(Gamarra 37, Soto 85)*

*Colombia:* Mondragon; Santa, Mendoza, Lopez, Galeano, Serna, Lozano (Pacheco 59), Alvarez (De Avila 89), Valderrama, Asprilla F, Aristizabal (Hamilton 76).
*Paraguay:* Chilavert; Ayala, Rivarola, Gamarra, Arce, Bourdier, Acuna, Enciso (Ruiz Diaz 77), Soto, Rojas A, Yegros (Sarabia 66).
*Referee:* Souza (Brazil).

Lima, 2 April 1997, 47,000

**Peru (0) 1** *(Palacios 58)*
**Ecuador (0) 1** *(Aguinaga 78 (pen))*

*Peru:* Balerio; Solano, Reynoso, Jose Soto, Olivares, Carranza, Carazas, Zegarra (Carty 82), Palacios, Maestri, Julinho (Saenz 63).
*Ecuador:* Ibarra; Rivera, Montano, Hurtado I, Capurro, Ruiz (Chala 63), Carabali, Blandon, Aguinaga, Delgado, Graziani (Hurtado E 46).
*Referee:* Toro (Colombia).

Montevideo, 2 April 1997, 45,000

**Uruguay (1) 3** *(De los Santos G 30, Montero 47, Otero 60)*
**Venezuela (0) 1** *(Castellin 57)*

*Uruguay:* Siboldi; Tais, Moas, Montero, De los Santos J, Saralegui, De los Santos G, Bengoechea, Francescoli (Martinez 70), Otero (Hernandez 76), Abreu (Romero 42).
*Venezuela:* Dudamel; Gonzalez W, Tortolero, Echenique, Martinez, Rodriguez (Paez 73), Ramos, Hernandez F, Gerson, Guerra, Castellin.
*Referee:* Ortube (Bolivia).

Santiago, 29 April 1997, 42,000

**Chile (3) 6** *(Zamorano 19, 26, 31, 47, 85, Reyes 66)*
**Venezuela (0) 0**

*Chile:* Tapia; Mora, Reyes, Gonzalez J, Ponce, Musrri, Acuna, Vega (Villarroel 81), Sierra (Castaneda V 68), Nunez (Goldberg 68), Zamorano.
*Venezuela:* Dudamel; Gonzalez W, Echenique, Tortolero, Martinez, Ramos, Rodriguez (Paez 46), Hernandez F, Gerson, Savarese, Guerra (Castellin 55).
*Referee:* Carter (Mexico).

Buenos Aires, 30 April 1997, 65,000

**Argentina (2) 2** *(Noriega 17 (og), Crespo 32)*
**Ecuador (0) 1** *(Aguinaga 67)*

*Argentina:* Roa; Ayala, Paz, Chamot, Almeyda, Simeone, Veron, Berti (Morales 80), Ortega, Lopez C (Berizzo 76), Crespo.
*Ecuador:* Ibarra; Rivera (Urbano 79), Noriega, Montano, Mendez, Blandon, Carabali, Gilson, Chala (De la Cruz 64), Aguinaga, Hurtado E.
*Referee:* Benegas (Paraguay).

Barranquilla, 30 April 1997, 30,000

**Colombia (0) 0**
**Peru (0) 1** *(Pereda 61)*

*Colombia:* Mondragon; Cabrera, Bermudez, Lopez (Palacios 44), Galeano, Gaviria (Lozano 46), Alvarez, Rincon, Valderrama, Valencia, De Avila (Ricard 57).
*Peru:* Balerio; Solano, Jose Soto, Reynoso, Olivares, Serrano (Bazalar 80), Jayo, Pereda, Palacios, Carazas (Jorge Soto 63), Carty (Julinho 84).
*Referee:* Rezende (Brazil).

Asuncion, 30 April 1997, 45,000

**Paraguay (1) 3** *(Rojas A 37, Cardozo 73 (pen), Soto 83)*
**Uruguay (0) 1** *(Dario Silva 87)*

*Paraguay:* Ruiz Diaz; Gamarra, Rivarola, Ayala, Villamayor, Enciso (Soto 33), Acuna, Struway, Benitez (Ferreira 57), Rojas A (Brizuela 76), Cardozo.
*Uruguay:* Siboldi; Mendez, Herrera, Moas, Ramos, Gutierrez, De los Santos G, Poyet, Francescoli, Otero (Dario Silva 65), Martinez (Bengoechea 46).
*Referee:* Pereira (Brazil).

Buenos Aires, 8 June 1997, 77,000

**Argentina (1) 2** *(Crespo 45, Simeone 46)*
**Peru (0) 0**

*Argentina:* Roa; Ayala, Sensini, Chamot, Diaz, Almeyda, Simeone, Berti (Borelli 65), Ortega (Bassedas 53), Crespo (Calderon 86), Lopez C.
*Peru:* Balerio; Solano, Reynoso, Jose Soto, Olivares, Jorge Soto, Serrano (Carranza 76), Jayo, Palacios, Saenz (Julinho 46), Maestri (Carty 62).
*Referee:* Cerdeira (Brazil).

Quito, 8 June 1997, 42,000

**Ecuador (1) 1** *(Graziani 43)*
**Chile (0) 1** *(Salas 53)*

*Ecuador:* Ibarra; Hurtado I, De la Cruz U, Montano, Mendez, Constante, Blandon, De la Cruz O (Hurtado E 60), Delgado (Gilson 60), Aguinaga, Graziani (Fernandez 65).
*Chile:* Ramirez; Castaneda, Margas, Gonzalez C, Miranda, Musrri (Cornejo 57), Acuna, Reyes, Sierra (Rivero 71), Gonzalez P (Nunez 52), Salas.
*Referee:* Tellez (Mexico).

Montevideo, 8 June 1997, 50,000

**Uruguay (1) 1** *(Dario Silva 7)*
**Colombia (0) 1** *(Ricard 51)*

*Uruguay:* Alvez; Mendez, Moas, Montero, Ramos, Abeijon (Ruben da Silva 60), De los Santos, O'Neill (Romero 83), Bengoechea, Dario Silva, Recoba (Martinez 60).
*Colombia:* Mondragon; Santa (Estrada 86), Asprilla C, Bermudez, Moreno, Cabrera, Gaviria, Serna (Perez J 11), Valderrama, Escobar (Bonilla 46), Ricard.
*Referee:* Dacildo (Brazil).

Valera, 8 June 1997, 7000

**Venezuela (0) 1** *(Savarese 63)*
**Bolivia (0) 1** *(Castillo R 73)*

*Venezuela:* Dudamel; Mackintosh, Rey, Vallenilla, Echenique, Gonzalez L, Gerson, Castellin, Miranda (Paez 69), Savarese, Socorro (Urdaneta 75).
*Bolivia:* Trucco; Pena, Sanchez O, Soria, Sandy, Castillo S (Castillo I 61), Etcheverry, Cristaldo, Baldivieso (Gutierrez 47), Moreno (Coimbra 47), Castillo R.
*Referee:* Zuluaga (Colombia).

Santiago, 5 July 1997, 75,000

**Chile (3) 4** *(Salas 16, 27, 41, Zamorano 90 (pen))*
**Colombia (0) 1** *(Ricard 53)*

*Chile:* Tapia; Castaneda C, Margas, Fuentes, Ponce, Vega (Valencia 75), Acuna, Musrri, Castaneda V (Cornejo 86), Zamorano, Salas.
*Colombia:* Mondragon; Santa, Bermudez, Mendoza, Moreno (Galeano 73), Alvarez (Morantes 46), Cabrera, Lozano, Valderrama, Angel (Ricard 46), Asprilla F.
*Referee:* Borgosano (Venezuela).

Asuncion, 6 July 1997, 35,000

**Paraguay (0) 1** *(Acuna 60 (pen))*
**Argentina (2) 2** *(Gallardo 30, Veron 40)*

*Paraguay:* Ruiz Diaz; Gamarra, Ayala, Struway (Ferreira 52), Esteche (Soto 46), Cardozo, Acuna, Jara, Rojas A, Rojas R, Enciso.
*Argentina:* Roa; Ayala, Chamot, Diaz, Almeyda, Sensini, Lopez G, Simeone, Veron (Zanetti 50), Crespo (Berti 77), Gallardo (Paz 80).
*Referee:* Rezende (Brazil).

Lima, 6 July 1997, 35,000

**Peru (1) 2** *(Carty 9, Jorge Soto 51)*
**Bolivia (0) 1** *(Cristaldo 54)*

*Peru:* Balerio; Jorge Soto, Reynoso, Jose Soto, Olivares, Carazas (Serrano 62), Jayo, Carranzo (Bazalar 83), Zegarra, Maestri (Rivera 68), Carty.
*Bolivia:* Trucco; Castillo S, Sanchez O, Pena, Sandy, Cristaldo, Soria, Baldivieso, Sanchez E, Etcheverry, Moreno (Gutierrez L 79).
*Referee:* Mendonca (Brazil).

Maracaibo, 6 July 1997, 12,000

**Venezuela (0) 1** *(Miranda 77)*
**Ecuador (0) 1** *(Hurtado I 54)*

*Venezuela:* Dudamel; Echenique, Rey, McIntosh, Pacheco, Rodallega, Gonzales L, Urdaneta (Martinez 89), Diaz (Miranda 55), Moran (Castellin 55), Savarese.
*Ecuador:* Ibarra; Burbano, Montano, Hurtado I, Mendez, Carabali (Smith 73), Blandon, Gavica (Gilson 70), Aguniga, Hurtado E, Graziani.
*Referee:* Angeles (USA).

Buenos Aires, 20 July 1997, 47,000

**Argentina (1) 2** *(Crespo 30, Paz 56)*
**Venezuela (0) 0**

*Argentina:* Roa; Sensini, Ayala (Paz 50), Chamot, Zanetti, Astrada, Simeone, Veron, Gallardo (Ortega 57), Crespo, Lopez C (Berti 75).
*Venezuela:* Dudamel; McIntosh, Echenique, Rey, Martinez, Gonzales, Rodallega, Moran (Lucena 60), Gerson (Palencia 72), Miranda, Savarese.
*Referee:* De Souza (Brazil).

La Paz, 20 July 1997, 20,680

**Bolivia (0) 1** *(Etcheverry 75)*

**Uruguay (0) 0**

*Bolivia:* Trucco; Castillo S, Sandy, Sanchez O, Rimba, Castillo I, Tufino (Moreno 58), Cristaldo, Sanchez E, Etcheverry (Blanco M 87), Coimbra (Angola 46).
*Uruguay:* Siboldi; Aguirregaray, Ramos (Romero 82), Moas, Rodriguez, Gomez, De los Santos G, Saralegui, Bengoechea, Francescoli (Lujambio 55), Martinez (Ruben Da Silva 74).
*Referee:* Brizio (Mexico).

Santiago, 20 July 1997, 75,143

**Chile (1) 2** *(Zamorano 8 (pen), 47)*

**Paraguay (0) 1** *(Brizuela 62)*

*Chile:* Tapia; Castaneda C, Fuentes, Margas, Ponce, Musrri, Acuna (Cornejo 82), Castaneda V, Vega (Valencia 70), Zamorano, Salas (Nunez 87).
*Paraguay:* Aceval; Gamarra, Rivarola, Ayala, Bourdier, Arce, Struway (Soto 68), Acuna, Enciso, Rojas A (Cardozo 46), Baez R (Brizuela 60).
*Referee:* Torrealba (Venezuela).

Barranquilla, 20 July 1997, 30,000

**Colombia (0) 1** *(De Avila 87)*

**Ecuador (0) 0**

*Colombia:* Cordoba O; Cabrera, Bermudez, Cordoba I, Moreno, Lozano, Perez J, Rincon (Pacheco 64), Valderrama, Aristizabal (De Avila 60), Asprilla F (Estrada 89).
*Ecuador:* Ceballos; Rivera, Montano, Hurtado I, Capurro, Blandon, Carabali, Sanchez W (Maldonaldo 57), Aguinaga, Gavica, Hurtado E (Graziani 57).
*Referee:* Rezende (Brazil).

Barranquilla, 20 August 1997, 38,000

**Colombia (2) 3** *(De Avila 1, Valderrama 30 (pen), Asprilla F 75)*

**Bolivia (0) 0**

*Colombia:* Cordoba O; Cabrera, Bermudez, Cordoba I, Galeano, Serna, Perez J, Rincon (Pacheco 73), Valderrama, De Avila, Asprilla F (Bolano 85).
*Bolivia:* Trucco; Pena, Sandy, Sanchez O, Castillo S, Cristaldo, Ochoaizpur, Tufino, Etcheverry, Sanchez E, Moreno (Angola 67).
*Referee:* Cedeira (Brazil).

Quito, 20 August 1997, 30,000

**Ecuador (0) 2** *(Aguinaga 54, Graziani 77)*

**Paraguay (1) 1** *(Baez R 5)*

*Ecuador:* Ceballos; De la Cruz, Montano (Rivera 46), Hurtado I, Capurro, Blandon, Carabali, Sanchez W (Maldonaldo 74), Aguinaga, Graziani, Hurtado E (Gavica 46).
*Paraguay:* Aceval; Arce, Gamarra, Alcaraz, Sarabia, Bourdier, Enciso, Struway, Acuna (Rojas A 75), Baez R (Morales 60), Ramirez (Roman 59).
*Referee:* Badillo (Costa Rica).

Montevideo, 20 August 1997, 45,000

**Uruguay (1) 1** *(Otero 20)*

**Chile (0) 0**

*Uruguay:* Siboldi; Mendez, Rodriguez, Montero, Silva T, Gutierrez, Poyet, Bengoechea (Romero M 74), Francescoli (Aguirregaray 81), Lujambo (Fonseca 56), Otero.
*Chile:* Tapia; Castaneda C (Cornejo 86), Reyes, Fuentes, Margas, Ponce, Acuna, Musrri (Ruiz 81), Vega (Valencia 72), Nunez, Salas.
*Referee:* Pereira (Brazil).

Barinas, 20 August 1997, 8,500

**Venezuela (0) 0**

**Peru (1) 3** *(Marengo 14, Julinho 56, Maestri 83)*

*Venezuela:* Dudamel; McIntosh, Echenique, Rey, Vallenilla, Gonzalez, Rodallega (Lucena 46), Garcia (Giraldo 70), Urdaneta, Savarese, Palencia (Moran 57).
*Peru:* Balerio; Marengo, Jose Soto, Reynoso, Solano, Jayo, Jorge Soto, Palacios (Rivera 70), Zegarra, Carthy (Maestri 57), Julinho (Bazalar 84).
*Referee:* Prendergast (Jamaica).

Santiago, 10 September 1997, 73,000

**Chile (1) 1** *(Salas 34)*

**Argentina (1) 2** *(Gallardo 25, Lopez C 85)*

*Chile:* Tapia; Castaneda C, Reyes, Margas, Ponce, Musrri, Parraguez, Contreras, Sierra, Salas, Vega (Goldberg 75).
*Argentina:* Roa; Sensini, Ayala, Paz, Veron, Almeyda, Simeone, Gallardo (Zanetti 86), Ortega, Lopez C, Crespo (Berti 71).
*Referee:* Dacildo (Brazil).

Barranquilla, 10 September 1997, 35,000

**Colombia (0) 1** *(Cabrera 68)*

**Venezuela (0) 0**

*Colombia:* Calero; Cabrera, Bermudez, Cordoba, Galeano, Bolano, Serna (Pacheco 46), Rincon, Valderrama, De Avila, Asprilla F.
*Venezuela:* Dudamel; Garcia C, Echenique, Gonzalez W, Vallenilla, Urdaneta (Garcia A 89), Madriz, Ramos, Perez, Garcia J (Lucena 82), Moran.
*Referee:* Pimental (Brazil).

Asuncion, 10 September 1997, 35,000

**Paraguay (2) 2** *(Benitez 27, Gamarra 36)*

**Bolivia (0) 1** *(Suarez 56)*

*Paraguay:* Chilavert; Rivarola, Ayala, Gamarra, Suarez, Arce, Enciso, Acuna, Baez R (Rojas A 75), Benitez, Ovelar (Morales 60).
*Bolivia:* Trucco; Castillo S, Sanchez O, Pena, Sandy, Rimba, Soria, Blanco (Castillo R 46), Ortiz (Coimbra 65), Etcheverry, Angola (Suarez 46).
*Referee:* Archundia (Mexico).

Lima, 10 September 1997, 45,000

**Peru (0) 2** *(Palacios 56, Carty 59)*

**Uruguay (1) 1** *(Recoba 44)*

*Peru:* Balerio; Solano, Marengo, Jose Soto, Olivares, Pereda (Carranza 79), Jayo, Palacios, Zegarra (Jorge Soto 46), Maestri (Rivera 75), Carty.
*Uruguay:* Siboldi; Mendez, Aguirregaray (Saralegui 66), Rodriguez, Silva, De Los Santos, Romero, Lopez, Bengoechea (Lujambio 77), Recoba, Fonseca.
*Referee:* Sfandiar (USA).

Buenos Aires, 12 October 1997, 65,000

**Argentina (0) 0**

**Uruguay (0) 0**

*Argentina:* Roa; Ayala, Sensini, Paz, Zenetti (Berti 65), Almeyda, Veron, Simeone, Ortega, Crespo (Esnaider 69), Lopez C (Posse 74).
*Uruguay:* Nicola; Sanguinetti, Pena, Montero, Adinolfi, Vespa, De los Santos, Barilko, Bengoechea (Fleurquin 67), Recoba, Lujanbio (Pacheco 53).
*Referee:* Cerdeira (Brazil).

Santiago, 12 October 1997, 75,000

**Chile (1) 4** *(Salas 13, 83, 87, Reyes 69)*

**Peru (0) 0**

*Chile:* Tapia; Rojas, Fuentes, Reyes, Ponce (Parraguez 46), Cornejo, Acuna, Sierra, Castaneda V (Vega 50), Salas, Barrera (Carreno 70).
*Peru:* Balerio; Solano, Reynoso, Jose Soto, Olivares, Jayo, Jorge Soto, Pereda (Rivera 59), Palacios (Zegarra 77), Maestri, Carty (Julinho 59).
*Referee:* Rezende (Brazil).

Guayaquil, 12 October 1997, 40,000

**Ecuador (1) 1** *(Graziani 28)*

**Bolivia (0) 0**

*Ecuador:* Cevallos; De la Cruz, Montano, Hurtado I, Capurro, Carabali, Blandon, Gavica (Aguinaga 46), Sanchez W (Fernandez A 76), Hurtado E (Smith 76), Graziani.
*Bolivia:* Trucco; Castillo S, Rimba, Jiguchi, Tufino, Cristaldo, Castillo I, Ochoaizpur (Ortiz 85), Castillo R (Blanco 77), Etcheverry, Suarez (Gutierrez 55).
*Referee:* Brizio (Mexico).

Asuncion, 12 October 1997, 30,000

**Paraguay (0) 1** *(Torres 69)*

**Venezuela (0) 0**

*Paraguay:* Chilavert; Rivarola, Ayala, Gamarra, Esteche, Suarez (Ramirez 65), Acuna, Enciso, Ovelar (Rojas 50), Benitez, Baez R (Torres 60).
*Venezuela:* Dudamel; Gonzalez W, Echenique, Rey, Valenilla, Ramos (Valiente 53), Madriz, Garcia, Urdaneta (Martinez 63), Dolgueta, Perez.
*Referee:* Bahamarst (USA).

Buenos Aires, 16 November 1997, 42,000

**Argentina (0) 1** *(Caceres 69)*

**Colombia (1) 1** *(Valderrama 10)*

*Argentina:* Roa; Ayala, Sensini, Caceres, Simeone, Astrada (Zapata 82), Veron, Ortega, Gallardo (Riquelme 81), Batistuta, Lopez C (Crespo 55).
*Colombia:* Cordoba O; Cabrera, Bermudez, Cordoba I, Perez, Rincon, Gaviria, Serna, Valderrama, De Avila (Canton 80), Aristizabal (Pacheco 73).
*Referee:* Rezende (Brazil).

Santiago, 16 November 1997, 75,000

**Chile (2) 3** *(Barrera 24, Salas 41, Carreno 85)*

**Bolivia (0) 0**

*Chile:* Tapia; Castaneda C, Margas, Reyes, Rojas F, Acuna, Musrri, Sierra (Carreno 82), Vega (Valencia 46), Salas, Barrera (Nunez 74).
*Bolivia:* Trucco; Castillo S (Soria 46), Rimba, Sanchez O, Sandy, Cristaldo, Baldivieso, Ochoaizpur, Tufino, Etcheverry, Moreno (Castillo I 70).
*Referee:* Mendonca (Brazil).

Lima, 16 November 1997, 25,000

**Peru (1) 1** *(Jorge Soto 36)*

**Paraguay (0) 0**

*Peru:* Balerio; Jorge Soto, Reynoso, Jose Soto, Solano, Carranza, Palacios (Bazalar 65), Pereda (Rebosio 46), Zegarra, Andrade (Carty 56), Maestri.
*Paraguay:* Ruiz Diaz; Arce, Saravia, Gamarra, Ayala, Struway, Caniza (Brizuela 73), Benitez, Enciso, Rojas A, Suarez (Gonzalez G 52).
*Referee:* Dacildo (Brazil).

Maldonado, 16 November 1997, 12,000

**Uruguay (2) 5** *(Saralegui 3, 12, Abreu 48, 50, Aguilera 63)*

**Ecuador (1) 3** *(Graziani 2, 60, 65)*

*Uruguay:* Nicola; Sanguinetti, Alzueta, Rodriguez (Ruben Silva 85), Adinolfi (Gomez 71), Barilko, Tito, Saralegui, Lopez, Aguilera, Abreu (Canobbio 77).
*Ecuador:* Ceballos; Hurtado I (Coronel 63), Noriega, Montano, De La Cruz, Blandon, Caravali, Gavica, Aguinaga, Hurtado E (Fernandez A 63), Graziani.
*Referee:* Marrufo (Mexico).

**SOUTH AMERICA**

|           | P  | W | D | L  | F  | A  | Pts |
|-----------|----|---|---|----|----|----|-----|
| Argentina | 16 | 8 | 6 | 2  | 23 | 13 | 30  |
| Paraguay  | 16 | 9 | 2 | 5  | 21 | 14 | 29  |
| Colombia  | 16 | 8 | 4 | 4  | 23 | 15 | 28  |
| Chile     | 16 | 7 | 4 | 5  | 32 | 18 | 25  |
| Peru      | 16 | 7 | 4 | 5  | 19 | 20 | 25  |
| Ecuador   | 16 | 6 | 3 | 7  | 22 | 21 | 21  |
| Uruguay   | 16 | 6 | 3 | 7  | 18 | 21 | 21  |
| Bolivia   | 16 | 4 | 5 | 7  | 18 | 21 | 17  |
| Venezuela | 16 | 0 | 3 | 13 | 8  | 41 | 3   |

**Argentina qualify for finals (10.9.97); Paraguay (10.9.97); Colombia (10.9.97) and Chile (16.11.97).**

Michael Owen made a memorable impact on the 1998 World Cup, scoring this outstanding individual goal against Argentina. Here, on the ground, he scores against Romania after coming on as substitute.

# WORLD CUP FINAL REVIEW

With a sense of timing that given France's history in the competition, Emmanuel Petit scored the 1,000th goal for his country in the dying seconds of the World Cup. Jules Rimet had been the Frenchman who was responsible for launching the symbol of world professional football supremacy. Pity the 1998 version will be remembered for many of the worst aspects of the game.

To say that Brazil, the beaten finalists were represented by the poorest team ever to wear the famous yellow shirts, does scant justice to France, who had the best defence in the tournament, a workmanlike midfield and no striker worth the description. But they did possess Zinedine Zidane, Zizou to his friends, a gifted attacking midfield player.

The entire competition might have been written for him. Sent off for a first-class stamp on Fouad Amin in an earlier match, he was in disgrace. But the Mistral Boy from Marseille returned as the Prodigal Son and as the saviour of France in the final with a couple of headed goals.

Brazil, like so many other teams in the unwieldy 32-team tournament, were hugely disappointing. Perhaps it was because coach Mario Zagalo had changed his name, adding another 'l' which had hitherto been absent. Instead they had the 'l' kicked out of them, metaphorically speaking.

Long before the final farce with Ronaldo, a case of fits and starts it appears, there were severe questions over the calibre of the defending champions. Only the captain Dunga emerged as a consistent performer in a World Cup strewn with inconsistency.

England, one of three teams to be eliminated from penalties along with Holland and Italy, scored two of the best goals: David Beckham's free-kick against Colombia and Michael Owen's individual effort against Argentina. But the best of France 98 came from Holland's Dennis Bergkamp against the Argies. He controlled a lofted 60 yard pass from Frank de Boer with one touch, beat his marker with the second and finished clinically with the third.

Bergkamp was fortunate not to have been sent off himself against Yugoslavia following a similar incident to the one in which Zidane was involved. But clearly the referee regarded the Arsenal player's misdemeanour to have been more of a second-class delivery. Strange that Beckham's moment of glory ended in a second of stupidity against Argentina.

Having been awash with wallcharts, saturated with supplements and brimming over with brochures before the finals, we were drowned in facts and figures once the serious side of everything began. These infinite details included a breakdown of Colombia's midfield player Carlos Valderrama before the match with England. Apparently he completed 143 passes in a previous game. You knew how many in each half, but the fact that 90% of these were either square or backwards and of no more than three yards in length, was not in evidence. Also the same source stated that when Italy beat Austria 2-1, they had no shots on target!

The statistics of the entire proceedings concluded that a record 22 red and 257 yellow cards had been flashed, 1881 shots taken by the 32 teams in 64 matches and 891 of them had been on target. There had been 667 corners and 379 offside decisions as well as 2,135 offences of one kind or another.

After Argentina had been knocked out, France were said to be the dirtiest team left in the competition. They finished by sharing the Fair Play trophy with England, having had three players sent off to England's one.

For TV viewers, the return to something like a panel of experts was not too successful. The only thing missing was the desk. Perhaps in 2002 we can have the desk back on its own. ITV did score over the BBC in totty spotting, managing to identify Suzana Werner, Ronaldo's girl friend (at the time?), while the BBC were striving to put a name to her. Against France, Brazil might have done better to shove her up front instead of Ronaldo. She would have been more likely to score.

The surprise successes were Croatia, who deservedly finished in third place. They gave France their biggest shock and had they not fallen asleep soon after taking the lead, might have caused an even bigger upset. Davor Suker with six goals was the top scorer and one of the few impressive strikers.

Mexico did well and were unlucky against the disappointing Germans. Denmark, Paraguay, Morocco and even Iran did better than expected in varying degrees. Along with the Germans, Brazil as mentioned, Italy and eventually Argentina failed to show the required level of consistency needed to make an impact.

Referees, drawn as they were from every part of the earth, were no better, no worse than in previous finals. They had their work cut out dealing with too many cheating, diving, shirt-pulling and elbow nudging players, who gave a poor example to impressionable youngsters watching around the world.

# 1998 FIFA WORLD CUP FINALS

## GROUP A

Saint-Denis, 10 June 1998, 80,000

**Brazil (1) 2** *(Cesar Sampaio 4, Boyd 73 (og))*
**Scotland (1) 1** *(Collins 38 (pen))*
*Brazil:* Taffarel; Cafu, Junior Baiano, Aldair, Roberto Carlos, Cesar Sampaio, Giovanni (Leonardo 46), Dunga, Rivaldo, Ronaldo, Bebeto (Denilson 70).
*Scotland:* Leighton; Calderwood, Hendry, Boyd, Burley, Lambert, Collins, Dailly (McKinlay T 85), Jackson (McKinlay W 79), Gallacher, Durie.
*Referee:* Aranda (Spain).

Montpellier, 10 June 1998, 29,750

**Morocco (1) 2** *(Hadji 38, Hadda 59)*
**Norway (1) 2** *(Chippo 45 (og), Eggen 61)*
*Morocco:* Benzekri; Rossi, Naybet, El Hadrioui, Saber, Chiba, El Khalej (Azzouzi 89), Chippo (Amzine 78), Hadji, Hadda (El Khattabi 87), Bassir.
*Norway:* Grodas; Berg, Eggen, Johnsen, Bjornebye, Flo H (Solbakken 72), Leonhardsen, Rekdal, Mykland, Solskjaer (Riseth 46), Flo T.
*Referee:* Un-Prasert (Thailand).

Nantes, 16 June 1998, 32,226

**Brazil (2) 3** *(Ronaldo 9, Rivaldo 45, Bebeto 50)*
**Morocco (0) 0**
*Brazil:* Taffarel; Cafu, Junior Baiano, Aldair, Roberto Carlos, Cesar Sampaio (Doriva 67), Dunga, Leonardo, Rivaldo (Denilson 87), Bebeto (Edmundo 71), Ronaldo.
*Morocco:* Benzekri; Saber (Abrami 75), Rossi, Naybet, El Hadrioui, Chiba (Amzine 75), El Khalej, Chippo, El Hadji, Bassir, Hadda (El Khattabi 88).
*Referee:* Levnikov (Russia).

Bordeaux, 16 June 1998, 30,236

**Scotland (0) 1** *(Burley 66)*
**Norway (0) 1** *(Flo H 46)*
*Scotland:* Leighton; Calderwood (Weir 59), Hendry, Boyd, Burley, Lambert, Collins, Dailly, Jackson (McNamara 62), Gallacher, Durie.
*Norway:* Grodas; Bjornebye, Eggen, Johnsen, Berg (Halle 82), Strand, Rekdal, Solbakken, Flo H (Jakobsen 60), Riseth (Ostenstad 72), Flo T.
*Referee:* Vagner (Hungary).

Marseille, 23 June 1998, 55,000

**Brazil (0) 1** *(Bebeto 78)*
**Norway (0) 2** *(Flo T 83, Rekdal 89 (pen))*
*Brazil:* Taffarel; Cafu, Junior Baiano, Goncalves, Roberto Carlos, Rivaldo, Dunga, Leonardo, Denilson, Bebeto, Ronaldo.
*Norway:* Grodas; Berg, Eggen, Johnsen, Bjornebye, Flo H (Solskjaer 68), Strand (Mykland 46), Rekdal, Leonhardsen, Riseth (Flo J 79), Flo T.
*Referee:* Baharmast (USA).

St Etienne, 23 June 1998, 35,500

**Scotland (0) 0**
**Morocco (1) 3** *(Bassir 22, 85, Hadda 47)*
*Scotland:* Leighton; Weir, Hendry, Boyd, McNamara (McKinlay T 54), Burley, Lambert, Collins, Dailly, Gallacher, Durie (Booth 83).
*Morocco:* Benzekri; Saber (Rossi 72), Naybet, Triki, Abrami, Amzine (Azzouzi 77), El Khalej, Chippo (Sellami 87), Hadji, Bassir, Hadda.
*Referee:* Bussaim (UAE).

## GROUP B

Toulouse, 11 June 1998, 31,800

**Cameroon (0) 1** *(Njanka 77)*
**Austria (0) 1** *(Polster 90)*
*Cameroon:* Songo'o; Njanka, Kalla Nkongo, Song, Ndo, Simo (Olembe 65), Mboma, Angibeaud, Wome Nlend, Omam Biyik (Tchami 83), Ipoua (Job 65).
*Austria:* Konsel; Schottel, Feiersinger, Pfeffer, Cerny (Haas 82), Mahlich, Kuhbauer, Pfeifenberger (Stoger 82), Wetl, Herzog (Vastic 82), Polster.
*Referee:* Chavez (Paraguay).

Bordeaux, 11 June 1998, 36,500

**Italy (1) 2** *(Vieri 10, Roberto Baggio 85 (pen))*
**Chile (1) 2** *(Salas 45, 50)*
*Italy:* Pagliuca; Nesta, Costacurta, Cannavaro, Di Livio (Chiesa 62), Dino Baggio, Albertini, Di Matteo (Di Biagio 57), Maldini, Vieri (Inzaghi 71), Roberto Baggio.
*Chile:* Tapia; Fuentes, Margas (Miguel Ramirez 63), Reyes, Estay (Sierra 81), Villarroel, Acuna (Cornejo 82), Parraguez, Rojas, Salas, Zamorano.
*Referee:* Bouchardeau (Nigeria).

St Etienne, 17 June 1998, 30,392

**Chile (0) 1** *(Salas 70)*
**Austria (0) 1** *(Vastic 90)*
*Chile:* Tapia; Margas, Fuentes, Reyes, Rojas, Parraguez, Acuna, Villarroel (Castaneda 67), Estay (Sierra 57), Salas, Zamorano.
*Austria:* Konsel; Pfeffer, Schottel, Feiersinger, Cerny (Schoppe 46), Kuhbauer (Herzog 46), Mahlich, Pfeifenberger, Wetl, Haas (Vastic 74), Polster.
*Referee:* Ghandour (Egypt).

Montpellier, 17 June 1998, 35,000

**Italy (1) 3** *(Di Biagio 8, Vieri 75, 89)*
**Cameroon (0) 0**
*Italy:* Pagliuca; Cannavaro, Costacurta, Nesta, Maldini, Dino Baggio, Albertini (Di Matteo 63), Di Biagio, Moriero (Di Livio 75), Vieri, Roberto Baggio (Del Piero 65).
*Cameroon:* Songo'o; Njanka, Kalla Nkongo, Song, Wome Nlend, Ndo, Angibeaud, Mboma (Eto'o 66), Olembe, Ipoua (Job 46), Omam-Biyik (Tchami 66).
*Referee:* Lennie (Australia).

Nantes, 23 June 1998, 39,500

**Chile (1) 1** *(Sierra 21)*
**Cameroon (0) 1** *(Mboma 56)*
*Chile:* Tapia; Reyes, Fuentes, Margas, Villarroel (Cornejo 70), Acuna, Sierra (Estay 70), Parraguez, Rojas (Miguel Ramirez 76), Zamorano, Salas.
*Cameroon:* Songo'o; Pensee, Njanka, Song, Ndo (Etame 82), Mahouve, Olembe (Angibeaud 68), Wome Nlend, Omam Biyik, Mboma, Job (Tchami 70).
*Referee:* Vagner (Hungary).

Saint-Denis, 23 June 1998, 75,000

**Italy (0) 2** *(Vieri 48, Roberto Baggio 90)*
**Austria (0) 1** *(Herzog 90 (pen))*
*Italy:* Pagliuca; Nesta (Bergomi 4), Costacurta, Cannavaro, Moriero, Dino Baggio, Di Biagio, Maldini, Del Piero (Roberto Baggio 72), Vieri (Inzaghi 60).
*Austria:* Konsel; Pfeffer, Feiersinger, Schottel, Mahlich, Kuhbauer (Stoger 74), Pfeifenberger (Herzog 79), Reinmayr, Wetl, Vastic, Polster (Haas 62).
*Referee:* Durkin (England).

| GROUP A | P | W | D | L | F | A | Pts |
|---|---|---|---|---|---|---|---|
| Brazil | 3 | 2 | 0 | 1 | 6 | 2 | 6 |
| Norway | 3 | 1 | 2 | 0 | 5 | 4 | 5 |
| Morocco | 3 | 1 | 1 | 1 | 5 | 5 | 4 |
| Scotland | 3 | 0 | 1 | 2 | 2 | 6 | 1 |

| GROUP B | P | W | D | L | F | A | Pts |
|---|---|---|---|---|---|---|---|
| Italy | 3 | 2 | 1 | 0 | 7 | 3 | 7 |
| Chile | 3 | 0 | 3 | 0 | 4 | 4 | 3 |
| Austria | 3 | 0 | 2 | 1 | 3 | 4 | 2 |
| Cameroon | 3 | 0 | 2 | 1 | 2 | 5 | 2 |

## GROUP C

### Marseille, 12 June 1998, 60,000

**France (1) 3** *(Dugarry 35, Issa 78 (og), 90 (og))*
**South Africa (0) 0**

*France:* Barthez; Desailly, Blanc, Lizarazu, Thuram, Deschamps, Petit (Boghossian 73), Henry, Zidane, Djorkaeff (Trezeguet 82), Guivarc'h (Dugarry 26).
*South Africa:* Vonk; Issa, Fish, Radebe, Nyathi, Jackson, Moshoeu, Fortune, Augustine (Mkhalele 57), McCarthy (Bartlett 88), Masinga.
*Referee:* De Freitas (Brazil).

### Lens, 12 June 1998, 38,140

**Saudi Arabia (0) 0**
**Denmark (0) 1** *(Rieper 68)*

*Saudi Arabia:* Al Deayea; Al Jahani, Al Khilaiwi, Zubromawi, Sulimani, Amin (Saleh 79), Saeed Owairan (Al Dosari O 79), Al Muwalid, Khamis Owairan, Al Shahrani, Al Jaber (Al Thyniyan 84).
*Denmark:* Schmeichel; Rieper, Hogh, Colding, Schjonberg Helveg, Wieghorst (Nielsen 66), Jorgensen (Frandsen 73), Laudrup M, Laudrup B (Heintze 84), Sand.
*Referee:* Castrilli (Argentina).

### Saint-Denis, 18 June 1998, 75,000

**France (1) 4** *(Henry 36, 77, Trezeguet 68, Lizarazu 85)*
**Saudi Arabia (0) 0**

*France:* Barthez; Desailly, Blanc, Lizarazu, Thuram, Deschamps, Boghossian, Henry (Pires 78), Zidane, Diomede, Dugarry (Trezeguet 30).
*Saudi Arabia:* Al Deayea; Al Jahni (Al Dosari A 76), Zubromawi, Al Khilaiwi, Sulimani, Amin, Khamis Owairan, Saleh, Al Shahrani, Saeed Owairan (Al Harbi 33 (Al Muwalid 63)), Al Jaber.
*Referee:* Carter (Mexico).

### Toulouse, 18 June 1998, 36,500

**South Africa (0) 1** *(McCarthy 52)*
**Denmark (1) 1** *(Nielsen 13)*

*South Africa:* Vonk; Fish, Issa, Radebe, Mkhalele, Augustine (Phiri 46), Moshoeu, Fortune, Nyathi (Buckley 88), Bartlett (Masinga 77), McCarthy.
*Denmark:* Schmeichel; Colding, Rieper, Hogh, Schjonberg (Wieghorst 82), Jorgensen, Helveg, Nielsen, Laudrup M (Heintze 58), Sand (Molnar 58), Laudrup B.
*Referee:* Rendon (Colombia).

### Lyon, 24 June 1998, 43,500

**France (1) 2** *(Djorkaeff 13 (pen), Petit 56)*
**Denmark (1) 1** *(Laudrup M 42 (pen))*

*France:* Barthez; Karembeu, Leboeuf, Desailly, Candela, Vieira, Petit (Boghossian 64), Diomede, Pires (Henry 71), Trezeguet (Guivarc'h 85), Djorkaeff.
*Denmark:* Schmeichel; Laursen (Colding 46), Rieper, Hogh, Heintze, Jorgensen (Sand 54), Helveg, Nielsen, Laudrup M, Schjonberg, Laudrup B (Tofting 75).
*Referee:* Collina (Italy).

### Bordeaux, 24 June 1998, 34,500

**South Africa (1) 2** *(Bartlett 18, 90 (pen))*
**Saudi Arabia (1) 2** *(Al Jaber 45 (pen), Al Thynyan 73 (pen))*

*South Africa:* Vonk; Fish, Issa, Jackson (Buckley 46), Nyathi, Mkhalele, Radebe, Fortune (Khumalo 66), Moshoeu, McCarthy (Sikhosana 46), Bartlett.
*Saudi Arabia:* Al Deayea; Al Jahani, Amin, Zubromawi, Sulimani, Al Temyat, Khamis Owairan, Al Thynyan (Al Harbi 81), Saleh, Al Jaber, Al Mehalel (Al Shahrani 64).
*Referee:* Yanten (Chile).

## GROUP D

### Montpellier, 12 June 1998, 27,650

**Paraguay (0) 0**
**Bulgaria (0) 0**

*Paraguay:* Chilavert; Gamarra, Ayala, Sarabia, Benitez, Morales (Caniza 42) Acuna, Paredes, Enciso, Cardozo (Ramirez 69), Campos (Yegros 77).
*Bulgaria:* Zdravkov; Nankov, Iordanov, Ivanov, Petkov, Iliev (Borimirov 77), Balakov, Kischicev, Yankov, Penev (Kostadinov 69), Stoichkov.
*Referee:* Al Zeid (Saudi Arabia).

### Nantes, 13 June 1998, 33,257

**Spain (1) 2** *(Hierro 21, Raul 47)*
**Nigeria (1) 3** *(Adepoju 24, Zubizarreta 73 (og), Oliseh 78)*

*Spain:* Zubizarreta; Ferrer (Amor 46), Alkorta, Campo, Sergi, Hierro, Nadal (Celades 76), Luis Enrique, Kiko, Raul, Alfonso (Etxeberria 57).
*Nigeria:* Rufai; Oparaku (Yekini 69), Uche, West, Babayaro, Finidi George, Oliseh, Adepoju, Lawal (Okpara G 90), Okocha, Ikpeba (Babangida 81).
*Referee:* Baharmast (USA).

### Paris, 19 June 1998, 48,500

**Nigeria (1) 1** *(Ikpeba 27)*
**Bulgaria (0) 0**

*Nigeria:* Rufai; Adepoju, Uche, West, Finidi George (Babangida 85), Oliseh, Okocha, Lawal, Babayaro, Amokachi (Kanu 66), Ikpeba (Yekini 75).
*Bulgaria:* Zdravkov; Kichichev, Ivanov, Ginchev, Iliev (Penev 67), Yankov (Batchev 85), Balakov, Hristov (Borimirov 46), Petkov, Kostadinov, Stoichkov.
*Referee:* Yanten (Chile).

### St Etienne, 19 June 1998, 35,300

**Spain (0) 0**
**Paraguay (0) 0**

*Spain:* Zubizarreta; Aguilera, Alkorta, Abelardo (Celades 56), Sergi, Hierro, Amor, Etxeberria, Luis Enrique, Raul (Kiko 66), Pizzi (Morientes 54).
*Paraguay:* Chilavert; Sarabia, Gamarra, Ayala, Caniza, Benitez, Arce, Enciso, Acuna (Yegros 74), Campos (Parades 46), Rojas A (Ramirez 84).
*Referee:* McLeod (South Africa).

### Toulouse, 24 June 1998, 36,500

**Nigeria (1) 1** *(Oruma 11)*
**Paraguay (1) 3** *(Ayala 1, Benitez 59, Cardozo 86)*

*Nigeria:* Rufai; Eguavoen, Okafor, West, Iroha, Oliseh (Okpara 46), Babangida, Oruma (Finidi George 69), Lawal, Yekini, Kanu.
*Paraguay:* Chilavert; Sarabia, Ayala, Gamarra, Arce, Enciso, Paredes, Caniza (Yegros 55), Benitez (Acuna 68), Cardozo, Brizuela (Rojas 78).
*Referee:* Un-Prasert (Thailand).

### Lens, 24 June 1998, 40,500

**Spain (2) 6** *(Hierro 6 (pen), Luis Enrique 18, Morientes 53, 81, Kiko 88, 90)*
**Bulgaria (0) 1** *(Kostadinov 56)*

*Spain:* Zubizarreta; Aguilera, Nadal, Alkorta, Sergi, Amor, Hierro, Luis Enrique (Guerrero 71), Alfonso (Kiko 65), Etxeberria (Raul 65), Morientes.
*Bulgaria:* Zdravkov; Ivanov, Kichichev, Iordanov, Ginchev, Nankov (Penev 29), Borimirov, Batchev, Balakov (Hristov 59), Kostadinov, Stoichkov (Iliev 46).
*Referee:* Van der Ende (Holland).

| GROUP C | P | W | D | L | F | A | Pts |
|---|---|---|---|---|---|---|---|
| France | 3 | 3 | 0 | 0 | 6 | 3 | 9 |
| Denmark | 3 | 1 | 1 | 1 | 3 | 3 | 4 |
| South Africa | 3 | 0 | 2 | 1 | 3 | 4 | 2 |
| Saudi Arabia | 3 | 0 | 1 | 2 | 2 | 9 | 1 |

| GROUP D | P | W | D | L | F | A | Pts |
|---|---|---|---|---|---|---|---|
| Nigeria | 3 | 2 | 0 | 1 | 5 | 5 | 6 |
| Paraguay | 3 | 1 | 2 | 0 | 3 | 1 | 5 |
| Spain | 3 | 1 | 1 | 1 | 8 | 4 | 4 |
| Bulgaria | 3 | 0 | 1 | 2 | 1 | 7 | 1 |

## GROUP E

### Saint-Denis, 13 June 1998, 75,000

**Holland (0) 0**
**Belgium (0) 0**

*Holland:* Van der Sar; Winter, Stam, Frank de Boer, Numan, Seedorf (Zenden 65), Ronald de Boer (Jonk 79), Cocu, Overmars, Kluivert, Hasselbaink (Bergkamp 65).
*Belgium:* De Wilde; Verstraeten, Staelens, Clement, Crasson (Deflandre 20), Boffin, Van Der Elst, Wilmots, Borkelmans, Oliveira (Mpenza L 60), Nilis.
*Referee:* Collina (Italy).

### Lyon, 13 June 1998, 37,588

**South Korea (1) 1** *(Ha 27)*

**Mexico (0) 3** *(Pelaez 51, Hernandez 74, 82)*

*South Korea:* Kim J; Kim T, Hong, Yoo, Lee M, Noh (Jang 56), Ha, Kim D K (Choi S 61), Ko (Seo J 71), Kim D H, Lee S.
*Mexico:* Campos; Pardo, Suarez, Davino, Luna (Arellano 46), Ordiales (Pelaez 46), Lara, Ramirez, Garcia Aspe (Bernal 72), Hernandez, Blanco.
*Referee:* Benko (Austria).

### Bordeaux, 20 June 1998, 34,750

**Belgium (1) 2** *(Wilmots 43, 48)*

**Mexico (0) 2** *(Garcia Aspe 56 (pen), Blanco 63)*

*Belgium:* De Wilde; Deflandre, Staelens, Vidovic, Borkelmans, Van der Elst (De Boeck 67), Wilmots, Boffin (Verheyen 18), Scifo, Nilis (Mpenza L 77), Oliveira.
*Mexico:* Campos; Pardo, Sanchez J, Davino, Ramirez, Garcia Aspe (Lara 68), Suarez, Ordiales (Villa 58), Palencia (Arellano 46), Hernandez, Blanco.
*Referee:* Dallas (Scotland).

### Marseille, 20 June 1998, 60,000

**Holland (2) 5** *(Cocu 37, Overmars 41, Bergkamp 71, Van Hooijdonk 79, Ronald de Boer 83)*

**South Korea (0) 0**

*Holland:* Van der Sar; Stam, Numan (Bogarde 80),Frank de Boer, Jonk, Winter, Ronald de Boer (Zenden 84), Davids, Cocu, Overmars, Bergkamp (Van Hooijdonk 78).
*South Korea:* Kim J; Choi Y, Lee M, Hong, Choi S (Kim T 53), Yoo, Kim D K, Lee S, Kim D H (Ko 70), Choi Y S, Seo J (Lee D 77).
*Referee:* Wojcik (Poland).

### Paris, 25 June 1998, 48,500

**Belgium (1) 1** *(Nilis 7)*

**South Korea (0) 1** *(Yoo 70)*

*Belgium:* Van de Walle; Staelens, Borkelmans, Vidovic, Deflandre, Wilmots, Van Kerckhoven, Clement (Mpenza L 74), Scifo (Van der Elst 67), Oliveira (Mpenza M 46), Nilis.
*South Korea:* Kim J; Hong, Lee S (Jang 68), Kim T, Choi S (Lee L 46), Kim D K (Ko 46), Ha, Lee M, Yoo, Choi Y S, Seo.
*Referee:* Rezende (Brazil).

### St Etienne, 25 June 1998, 35,500

**Holland (2) 2** *(Cocu 4, Ronald de Boer 19)*

**Mexico (0) 2** *(Pelaez 75, Hernandez 90)*

*Holland:* Van der Sar; Reiziger, Stam, Frank de Boer, Numan (Bogarde 72), Ronald de Boer, Jonk (Winter 70), Davids, Overmars, Bergkamp (Hasselbaink 80), Cocu.
*Mexico:* Campos; Sanchez (Pelaez 56), Suarez, Davino, Carmona, Villa, Ramirez, Garcia Aspe, Luna (Arellano 46), Blanco, Hernandez.
*Referee:* Al Zeid (Saudi Arabia).

| GROUP E | P | W | D | L | F | A | Pts |
|---|---|---|---|---|---|---|---|
| Holland | 3 | 1 | 2 | 0 | 7 | 2 | 5 |
| Mexico | 3 | 1 | 2 | 0 | 7 | 5 | 5 |
| Belgium | 3 | 0 | 3 | 0 | 3 | 3 | 3 |
| South Korea | 3 | 0 | 1 | 2 | 2 | 9 | 1 |

## GROUP F

### St Etienne, 14 June 1998, 30,392

**Yugoslavia (0) 1** *(Mihajlovic 73)*

**Iran (0) 0**

*Yugoslavia:* Kralj; Mirkovic, Djorovic, Mihajlovic, Petrovic, Jokanovic, Stojkovic (Kovacevic 67), Brnovic (Stankovic 50), Jugovic, Milosevic (Ognjenovic 57), Mijatovic.
*Iran:* Nakisa; Zarincheh, Khakpour, Mohammadkhani, Pashazadeh, Mahdavikia, Bagheri, Estili (Mansourian 67), Minavand Chal, Azizi, Daei.
*Referee:* Noriega (Peru).

### Paris, 15 June 1998, 43,815

**Germany (1) 2** *(Moller 9, Klinsmann 65)*

**USA (0) 0**

*Germany:* Kopke; Worns, Thon, Kohler, Reuter (Ziege 69), Jeremies, Moller (Babbel 89), Hassler (Hamann 50), Heinrich, Klinsmann, Bierhoff.
*USA:* Keller; Pope, Dooley, Regis, Burns (Hejduk 46), Deering (Ramos 70), Maisonneuve, Reyna, Jones, Wynalda (Wegerle 72), Stewart.
*Referee:* Belqola (Morocco).

### Lens, 21 June 1998, 40,775

**Germany (0) 2** *(Mihajlovic 73 (og), Bierhoff 80)*

**Yugoslavia (1) 2** *(Mijatovic 13, Stojkovic 54)*

*Germany:* Kopke; Thom, Kohler, Worns, Heinrich, Moller (Kirsten 58), Jeremies, Hamann (Matthaus 46), Ziege (Tarnat 67), Klinsmann, Bierhoff.
*Yugoslavia:* Kralj; Djorovic, Mihajlovic, Komljenovic, Petrovic (Stevic 75), Jokanovic, Stojkovic, Stankovic (Govedarica 68), Jugovic, Mijatovic, Kovacevic (Ognjenovic 58).
*Referee:* Nielsen (Denmark).

### Lyon, 21 June 1998, 44,000

**USA (0) 1** *(McBride 87)*

**Iran (1) 2** *(Estili 40, Mahdavikia 84)*

*USA:* Keller; Pope, Dooley (Maisonneuve 82), Regis, Moore, Hejduk, Ramos (Stewart 57), Reyna, Jones, McBride, Wegerle (Radosavljevic 57).
*Iran:* Abedzadeh; Zarincheh (Saadavi 77), Khakpour, Mohammadkhani (Peyravani 75), Pashazadeh, Mahdavikia, Minavand Chal, Bagheri, Estili, Azizi (Mansourian 71), Daei.
*Referee:* Meier (Switerland).

### Montpellier, 25 June 1998, 35,000

**Germany (0) 2** *(Bierhoff 50, Klinsmann 58)*

**Iran (0) 0**

*Germany:* Kopke; Kohler, Thon (Hamann 46), Worns, Heinrich, Matthaus, Helmer, Tarnat (Ziege 78), Hassler (Kirsten 70), Bierhoff, Klinsmann.
*Iran:* Abedzadeh; Khakpour; Mohammadkhani, Pashazadeh, Zarincheh (Din Mohammadi 71), Mahdavikia, Estili, Minavand Chal, Bagheri, Azizi, Daei.
*Referee:* Chavez (Paraguay).

### Nantes, 25 June 1998, 39,000

**USA (0) 0**

**Yugoslavia (1) 1** *(Komljenovic 4)*

*USA:* Friedel; Burns, Dooley (Balboa 82), Regis, Hejduk (Wynalda 64), Reyna, Maisonneuve, Stewart, Moore (Radosavljevic 58), Jones, McBride.
*Yugoslavia:* Kralj; Djorovic, Mihajlovic, Petrovic, Komljenovic, Stankovic (Brnovic 54), Stojkovic (Savicevic 63), Jugovic, Jokanovic, Milosevic, Mijatovic (Ognjenovic 31).
*Referee:* Ghandour (Egypt).

| GROUP F | P | W | D | L | F | A | Pts |
|---|---|---|---|---|---|---|---|
| Germany | 3 | 2 | 1 | 0 | 6 | 2 | 7 |
| Yugoslavia | 3 | 2 | 1 | 0 | 4 | 2 | 7 |
| Iran | 3 | 1 | 0 | 2 | 2 | 5 | 3 |
| USA | 3 | 0 | 0 | 3 | 1 | 5 | 0 |

## GROUP G

### Marseille, 15 June 1998, 54,587

**England (1) 2** *(Shearer 42, Scholes 90)*

**Tunisia (0) 0**

*England:* Seaman; Southgate, Adams, Campbell, Anderton, Batty, Scholes, Ince, Le Saux, Sheringham (Owen 84), Shearer.
*Tunisia:* El Ouaer; Boukadida, Badra, Trabelsi S, Trabelsi H (Thabet 78), Ghodbane, Souayah (Baya 46), Chihi, Clayton, Sellimi, Ben Slimane (Ben Younes 65).
*Referee:* Okada (Japan).

### Lyon, 15 June 1998, 37,572

**Romania (1) 1** *(Ilie 45)*

**Colombia (0) 0**

*Romania:* Stelea; Petrescu, Cibotariu, Gheorge Popescu, Filipescu, Gabriel Popescu (Stanga 67), Galca, Hagi (Marinescu 75), Munteanu, Moldovan (Niculescu 84), Ilie.
*Colombia:* Mondragon; Cabrera, Bermudez, Palacios, Santa, Aristizabal (Valencia 46), Lozano, Serna, Rincon, Valderrama, Asprilla (Preciado 84).
*Referee:* Chong (Mauritius).

### Montpellier, 22 June 1998, 35,000

**Colombia (0) 1** *(Preciado 83)*

**Tunisia (0) 0**

*Colombia:* Mondragon; Cabrera, Bermudez, Palacios, Santa, Rincon (Aristizabal 57), Serna (Bolano 61), Lozano, Valderrama, Valencia (Preciado 57), De Avila.
*Tunisia:* El Ouaer; Thabet (Ghodbane 78), Trabelsi S, Chouchene, Chihi, Clayton, Beya (Ben Ahmed 74), Ben Slimane, Bouazizi, Souayah, Sellimi (Ben Younes 69).
*Referee:* Heynemann (Germany).

### Toulouse, 22 June 1998, 37,500

**Romania (0) 2** *(Moldovan 47, Petrescu 90)*

**England (0) 1** *(Owen 83)*

*Romania:* Stelea; Petrescu, Ciobotariu, Gheorghe Popescu, Filipescu, Munteanu, Hagi (Stanga 73) (Marinescu 84), Galca, Gabriel Popescu, Moldovan (Lacatus 86), Ilie.
*England:* Seaman; Neville, Adams, Campbell, Anderton, Ince (Beckham 33), Scholes, Batty, Le Saux, Sheringham (Owen 73), Shearer.
*Referee:* Batta (France).

### Lens, 26 June 1998, 41,275

**Colombia (0) 0**

**England (2) 2** *(Anderton 20, Beckham 30)*

*Colombia:* Mondragon; Cabrera, Bermudez, Palacios, Moreno, Rincon, Serna (Aristazabal 46), Lozano, Valderrama, Preciado (Valencia 46), De Avila (Ricard 46).
*England:* Seaman; Neville, Adams, Campbell, Anderton (Lee 79), Beckham, Ince (Batty 82), Le Saux, Scholes (McManaman 73), Owen, Shearer.
*Referee:* Carter (Mexico).

### Saint-Denis, 26 June 1998, 80,000

**Romania (0) 1** *(Moldovan 72)*

**Tunisia (1) 1** *(Souayah 10 (pen))*

*Romania:* Stelea; Petrescu, Dulca (Gheorge Popescu 31), Dobos, Ciobotariu, Galca, Munteanu, Hagi, Marinescu, Dumitrescu (Moldovan 67), Lacatus (Ilie 46).
*Tunisia:* El Ouaer; Trabelsi S, Boukadida, Chouchane, Baya, Ghodbane (Thabet 83), Bouazizi, Chihi, Souayah (Ben Younes 90), Sellimi, Ben Slimane (Jelassi 55).
*Referee:* Lennie (Australia).

| GROUP G | P | W | D | L | F | A | Pts |
|---|---|---|---|---|---|---|---|
| Romania | 3 | 2 | 1 | 0 | 4 | 2 | 7 |
| England | 3 | 2 | 0 | 1 | 5 | 2 | 6 |
| Colombia | 3 | 1 | 0 | 2 | 1 | 3 | 3 |
| Tunisia | 3 | 0 | 1 | 2 | 1 | 4 | 1 |

## GROUP H

### Toulouse, 14 June 1998, 33,400

**Argentina (1) 1** *(Batistuta 28)*

**Japan (0) 0**

*Argentina:* Roa; Zanetti, Vivas, Ayala, Sensini (Chamot 75), Ortega, Almeyda, Veron, Simeone, Batistuta, Lopez (Balbo 63).
*Japan:* Kawaguchi; Narahashi, Nakanishi, Akita, Ihara, Soma (Hirano 87), Yamaguchi, Nanami, Nakayama (Lopes 69), Nakata, Jo.
*Referee:* Van der Ende (Holland).

### Lens, 14 June 1998, 38,058

**Jamaica (1) 1** *(Earle 45)*

**Croatia (1) 3** *(Stanic 27, Prosinecki 53, Suker 69)*

*Jamaica:* Barrett; Sinclair, Goodison, Lowe, Gardener, Earle (Williams 72), Whitmore, Cargill (Powell 70), Simpson, Burton, Hall (Boyd 82).
*Croatia:* Ladic; Stimac, Soldo, Bilic, Simac, Boban, Asanovic, Prosinecki, Jarni, Stanic (Vlaovic 73), Suker.
*Referee:* Pereira (Portugal).

### Nantes, 20 June 1998, 39,000

**Japan (0) 0**

**Croatia (0) 1** *(Suker 77)*

*Japan:* Kawaguchi; Narahashi (Morishima 79), Akita, Ihara, Soma, Nakanishi, Nanami (Lopes 84), Nakata, Yamaguchi, Jo, Nakayama (Okano 61).
*Croatia:* Ladic; Soldo, Stimac (Vlaovic 46), Bilic, Jarni, Simic, Jurcic, Asanovic, Prosinecki (Maric 67), Stanic (Tudor 88), Suker.
*Referee:* Rhamdan (Trinidad & Tobago).

### Paris, 21 June 1998, 48,500

**Argentina (1) 5** *(Ortega 32, 55, Batistuta 73, 79, 83 (pen))*

**Jamaica (0) 0**

*Argentina:* Roa; Sensini (Vivas 25), Ayala, Chamot, Simeone (Pineda 80), Lopez (Gallardo 75), Almeyda, Veron, Zanetti, Ortega, Batistuta.
*Jamaica:* Barrett; Malcolm (Boyd 62), Goodison, Dawes, Sinclair, Gardener, Simpson, Powell, Whitmore (Earle 72), Burton (Cargill 46), Hall.
*Referee:* Pedersen (Norway).

### Bordeaux, 26 June 1998, 35,000

**Argentina (1) 1** *(Pineda 36)*

**Croatia (0) 0**

*Argentina:* Roa; Vivas, Ayala, Paz, Zanetti (Simeone 67), Almeyda, Veron, Pineda, Gallardo (Berti 80), Ortega (Lopez 52), Batistuta.
*Croatia:* Ladic; Bilic, Soldo, Simic, Maric (Vlaovic 46), Prosinecki (Stimac 67), Boban, Asanovic, Jarni, Stanic, Suker.
*Referee:* Belqola (Morocco).

### Lyon, 26 June 1998, 44,000

**Japan (0) 1** *(Nakayama 75)*

**Jamaica (1) 2** *(Whitmore 39, 54)*

*Japan:* Kawaguchi; Narahashi, Soma, Ihara, Jo (Lopes 59), Akita, Nanami (Ono 79), Nakayama, Nakata, Yamaguchi, Omura (Hirano 59).
*Jamaica:* Lawrence; Goodison, Gardener, Sinclair, Malcolm, Dawes, Whitmore, Simpson (Earle 90), Lowe, Hall (Boyd 71), Gayle (Burton 80).
*Referee:* Benkoe (Austria).

| GROUP H | P | W | D | L | F | A | Pts |
|---|---|---|---|---|---|---|---|
| Argentina | 3 | 3 | 0 | 0 | 7 | 0 | 9 |
| Croatia | 3 | 2 | 0 | 1 | 4 | 2 | 6 |
| Jamaica | 3 | 1 | 0 | 2 | 3 | 9 | 3 |
| Japan | 3 | 0 | 0 | 3 | 1 | 5 | 0 |

## SECOND ROUND

### Paris, 27 June 1998, 48,500

**Brazil (3) 4** *(Cesar Sampaio 11, 27, Ronaldo 45 (pen), 70)*
**Chile (0) 1** *(Salas 68)*

*Brazil:* Taffarel; Cafu, Junior Baiano, Roberto Carlos, Aldair (Goncalves 77), Cesar Sampaio, Dunga, Rivaldo, Leonardo, Ronaldo, Bebeto (Denilson 65).
*Chile:* Tapia; Fuentes, Margas, Reyes, Miguel Ramirez (Vega 46), Aros, Cornejo, Acuna (Musrri 80), Sierra (Estay 46), Zamorano, Salas.
*Referee:* Batta (France).

### Marseille, 27 June 1998, 60,000

**Italy (1) 1** *(Vieri 18)*
**Norway (0) 0**

*Italy:* Pagliuca; Costacurta, Bergomi, Cannavaro, Moriero (Di Livio 63), Albertini (Pessotto 72), Di Biagio, Maldini, Dino Baggio, Vieri, Del Piero (Chiesa 77).
*Norway:* Grodas; Bjornebye, Johnsen, Eggen, Berg, Riseth, Leonhardsen (Strand 13) (Solbakken 40), Rekdal, Mykland, Flo H (Solskjaer 73), Flo T.
*Referee:* Heynemann (Germany).

### Lens, 28 June 1998, 41,275

**France (0) 1** *(Blanc 114)*
**Paraguay (0) 0**

*France:* Barthez; Blanc, Desailly, Lizarazu, Thuram, Deschamps, Petit (Boghossian 69), Henry (Pires 64), Djorkaeff, Diomede (Guivarc'h 76), Trezeguet.
*Paraguay:* Chilavert; Arce, Gamarra, Ayala, Sarabia, Benitez, Acuna, Enciso, Paredes (Caniza 74), Campos (Yegros 55), Cardozo (Rojas 94).
*France won in extra time on sudden death.*
*Referee:* Ali Bujsaim (UAE).

### Saint-Denis, 28 June 1998, 79,500

**Nigeria (0) 1** *(Babangida 77)*
**Denmark (2) 4** *(Moller 3, Laudrup B 12, Sand 59, Helveg 76)*

*Nigeria:* Rufai; Adepojou, Uche, West, Babayaro, Oliseh, Lawal (Babangida 73), Finidi George, Okocha, Kanu (Yekini 65), Ikpeba.
*Denmark:* Schmeichel; Colding, Rieper, Hogh, Heintze, Jorgensen, Helveg, Nielsen, Moller (Sand 59), Laudrup B (Wieghorst 78), Laudrup M (Frandsen 86).
*Referee:* Meier (Switzerland).

### Montpellier, 29 June 1998, 35,000

**Germany (0) 2** *(Klinsmann 75, Bierhoff 86)*
**Mexico (0) 1** *(Hernandez 47)*

*Germany:* Kopke; Heinrich (Moller 58), Worns, Matthaus, Babbel, Helmer (Ziege 37), Hassler (Kirsten 74), Hamann, Tarnat, Bierhoff, Klinsmann.
*Mexico:* Campos; Pardo, Lara, Suarez, Davino, Villa, Palencia (Arellano 55), Bernal (Carmona 46), Garcia Aspe (Pelaez 86), Blanco, Hernandez.
*Referee:* Pereira (Portugal).

### Toulouse, 29 June 1998, 36,000

**Holland (1) 2** *(Bergkamp 38, Davids 90)*
**Yugoslavia (0) 1** *(Komljenovic 49)*

*Holland:* Van der Sar; Reiziger, Stam, Frank de Boer, Numan, Ronald de Boer, Seedorf, Davids, Overmars, Cocu, Bergkamp.
*Yugoslavia:* Kralj; Petrovic, Djorovic, Mihajlovic (Saveljic 79), Komljenovic, Mirkovic, Brnovic, Jokanovic, Jugovic, Stojkovic (Savicevic 57), Mijatovic.
*Referee:* Aranda (Spain).

### St Etienne, 30 June 1998, 30,600

**Argentina (2) 2** *(Batistuta 6 (pen), Zanetti 45)*
**England (2) 2** *(Shearer 10 (pen), Owen 16)*

*Argentina:* Roa; Vivas, Ayala, Chamot, Zanetti, Almeyda, Simeone (Berti 91), Ortega, Veron, Batistuta (Crespo 68), Lopez (Gallardo 68).
*England:* Seaman; Neville, Adams, Campbell, Anderton (Batty 96), Beckham, Ince, Le Saux (Southgate 70), Scholes (Merson 78), Owen, Shearer.
*aet; Argentina won 4-3 on penalties:- Berti score; Shearer score; Crespo miss; Ince save; Veron score; Merson score; Gallardo score; Owen score; Ayala score; Batty save.*
*Referee:* Nielsen (Denmark).

### Bordeaux, 30 June 1998, 34,700

**Romania (0) 0**
**Croatia (1) 1** *(Suker 45 (pen))*

*Romania:* Stelea; Filipescu, Gheorghe Popescu, Ciobotariu, Petrescu (Marinescu 75), Galca, Gabriel Popescu (Niculescu 60), Munteanu, Hagi (Craioveanu 56), Moldovan, Ilie.
*Croatia:* Ladic; Simic, Stimac, Bilic, Boban, Stanic (Tudor 82), Jurcic, Asanovic, Jarni, Vlaovic (Krpan 76), Suker.
*Referee:* Castrilli (Argentina).

## QUARTER-FINALS

### Nantes, 3 July 1998, 39,500

**Brazil (2) 3** *(Bebeto 11, Rivaldo 26, 60)*
**Denmark (1) 2** *(Jorgensen 2, Laudrup B 50)*

*Brazil:* Taffarel; Cafu, Junior Baiano, Aldair, Roberto Carlos, Dunga, Leonardo (Emerson 71), Cesar Sampaio, Rivaldo (Ze Roberto 87), Ronaldo, Bebeto (Denilson 63).
*Denmark:* Schmeichel; Colding, Rieper, Hogh, Heintze, Jorgensen, Helveg (Schjonberg 87), Nielsen (Tofting 46), Laudrup M, Laudrup B, Moller (Sand 66).
*Referee:* Ghandour (Egypt).

### Saint Denis, 3 July 1998, 77,000

**France (0) 0**
**Italy (0) 0**

*France:* Barthez; Thuram, Blanc, Desailly, Karembeu (Henry 65), Deschamps, Petit, Lizarazu, Zidane, Djorkaeff, Guivarc'h (Trezeguet 65).
*Italy:* Pagliuca; Cannavaro, Bergomi, Costacurta, Pessotto (Di Livio 93), Moriero, Dino Baggio (Albertini 52), Di Biagio, Maldini, Del Piero (Roberto Baggio 67), Vieri.
*aet; France won 4-3 on penalties:- Zidane score; Roberto Baggio score; Lizarazu save; Albertini save; Trezeguet score; Costacurta score; Henry score; Vieri score; Blanc score; Di Biagio miss.*
*Referee:* Dallas (Scotland).

### Lyon, 4 July 1998, 39,100

**Germany (0) 0**
**Croatia (1) 3** *(Jarni 45, Vlaovic 80, Suker 85)*

*Germany:* Kopke; Kohler, Matthaus, Worns, Heinrich, Jeremies, Hamann (Marschall 78), Tarnat, Hassler (Kirsten 69), Bierhoff, Klinsmann.
*Croatia:* Ladic; Stimac, Bilic, Simic, Stanic, Boban, Jarni, Soldo, Asanovic, Vlaovic (Maric 84), Suker.
*Referee:* Pedersen (Norway).

### Marseille, 4 July 1998, 55,000

**Holland (1) 2** *(Kluivert 12, Bergkamp 90)*
**Argentina (1) 1** *(Lopez 18)*

*Holland:* Van der Sar; Reiziger, Stam, Frank de Boer, Numan, Ronald de Boer (Overmars 64), Jonk, Davids, Cocu, Kluivert, Bergkamp.
*Argentina:* Roa; Sensini, Ayala, Chamot (Balbo 90), Zanetti, Simeone, Veron, Almeyda (Pineda 67), Ortega, Batistuta, Lopez.
*Referee:* Carter (Mexico).

### SEMI-FINAL

Marseille, 7 July 1998, 54,000

**Brazil (0) 1** *(Ronaldo 46)*
**Holland (0) 1** *(Kluivert 87)*

*Brazil:* Taffarel; Ze Carlos, Junior Baiano, Aldair, Roberto Carlos, Dunga, Leonardo (Emerson 84), Cesar Sampaio, Rivaldo, Ronaldo, Bebeto (Denilson 69).
*Holland:* Van der Sar; Reiziger (Winter 56), Stam, Frank de Boer, Cocu, Ronald de Boer, Jonk (Seedorf 110), Davids, Zenden (Van Hooijdonk 74), Kluivert, Bergkamp.
*aet; Brazil won 4-2 on penalties:- Ronaldo score, Frank de Boer score, Rivaldo score, Bergkamp score, Emerson score, Cocu save, Dunga score, Ronald de Boer save.*
*Referee:* Bujsaim (UAE).

### SEMI-FINAL

Saint-Denis, 8 July 1998, 76,000

**France (0) 2** *(Thuram 47, 70)*
**Croatia (0) 1** *(Suker 46)*

*France:* Barthez; Thuram, Blanc, Desailly, Lizarazu, Karembeu (Henry 61), Deschamps, Petit, Zidane, Djorkaeff (Leboeuf 75), Guivarc'h (Trezeguet 69).
*Croatia:* Ladic; Simic, Stimac, Bilic, Stanic (Prosinecki 90), Soldo, Asanovic, Jarni, Boban (Maric 65), Vlaovic, Suker.
*Referee:* Aranda (Spain).

### 3rd & 4th PLACE PLAY-OFF
### Paris, 11 July 1998, 45,500

**Holland (1) 1** *(Zenden 21)*
**Croatia (2) 2** *(Prosinecki 13, Suker 36)*

*Holland:* Van der Sar, Seedorf, Stam, Frank de Boer, Numan, Zenden, Jonk, Davids, Cocu (Overmars 46), Bergkamp (Van Hooijdonk 58), Kluivert.
*Croatia:* Ladic, Billic, Stimac, Soldo, Stanic, Prosinecki (Vlaovic 78), Jurcic, Asanovic, Jarni, Boban (Tudor 86), Suker.
*Referee:* Chavez (Paraguay)

### FINAL
### Saint-Denis, 12 July 1998, 75,000

**Brazil (0) 0**
**France (2) 3** *(Zidane 27, 45, Petit 90)*

*Brazil:* Taffarel, Cafu, Junior Baiano, Aldair, Roberto Carlos, Dunga, Leonardo (Denilson 46), Cesar Sampaio (Edmundo 74), Rivaldo, Bebeto, Ronaldo.
*France:* Barthez, Thuram, Leboeuf, Desailly, Lizarazu, Karembeu (Boghossian 56), Deschamps, Petit, Zidane, Djorkaeff (Vieira 75), Guivarc'h (Dugarry 66).
*Referee:* Belqola (Morocco).

**Red cards:** *France:* Zidane 70 mins v Saudi Arabia; Blanc 74 v Croatia; Desailly 68 v Brazil; *Holland:* Kluivert 80 v Belgium; Numan 76 v Argentina; *Argentina:* Ortega 88 v Holland; *Germany:* Worns 40 v Croatia; *Denmark:* Molnar 67, Wieghorst 85 v South Africa; *England:* Beckham 47 v Argentina; *Mexico:* Pardo 29 v Belgium; Ramirez 89 v Holland; *Belgium:* Verheyen 55 v Mexico; *Jamaica:* Powell 45 v Argentina; *South Africa:* Phiri 65 v Denmark; *Cameroon:* Kalla Nkongo 43 v Italy; Song 52, Etame 89 v Chile; *Scotland:* Burley 54 v Morocco; *Bulgaria:* Nankov 88 v Paraguay; *Saudi Arabia:* Al Khilaiwi 19 v France; *South Korea:* Ha 30 v Mexico.

Zinedine Zidane heads France into the lead against Brazil in the 1998 World Cup Final. (Colorsport)

# BRITISH AND IRISH INTERNATIONAL RESULTS 1872–1998

*Note:* In the results that follow, wc=World Cup, ec=European Championship, ui=Umbro International Trophy. tf = Tournoi de France. For Ireland, read Northern Ireland from 1921.

## ENGLAND v SCOTLAND

*Played:* 108; England won 44, Scotland won 40, Drawn 24. *Goals:* England 190, Scotland 168.

| | | | E | S | | | | E | S |
|---|---|---|---|---|---|---|---|---|---|
| 1872 | 30 Nov | Glasgow | 0 | 0 | 1931 | 28 Mar | Glasgow | 0 | 2 |
| 1873 | 8 Mar | Kennington Oval | 4 | 2 | 1932 | 9 Apr | Wembley | 3 | 0 |
| 1874 | 7 Mar | Glasgow | 1 | 2 | 1933 | 1 Apr | Glasgow | 1 | 2 |
| 1875 | 6 Mar | Kennington Oval | 2 | 2 | 1934 | 14 Apr | Wembley | 3 | 0 |
| 1876 | 4 Mar | Glasgow | 0 | 3 | 1935 | 6 Apr | Glasgow | 0 | 2 |
| 1877 | 3 Mar | Kennington Oval | 1 | 3 | 1936 | 4 Apr | Wembley | 1 | 1 |
| 1878 | 2 Mar | Glasgow | 2 | 7 | 1937 | 17 Apr | Glasgow | 1 | 3 |
| 1879 | 5 Apr | Kennington Oval | 5 | 4 | 1938 | 9 Apr | Wembley | 0 | 1 |
| 1880 | 13 Mar | Glasgow | 4 | 5 | 1939 | 15 Apr | Glasgow | 2 | 1 |
| 1881 | 12 Mar | Kennington Oval | 1 | 6 | 1947 | 12 Apr | Wembley | 1 | 1 |
| 1882 | 11 Mar | Glasgow | 1 | 5 | 1948 | 10 Apr | Glasgow | 2 | 0 |
| 1883 | 10 Mar | Sheffield | 2 | 3 | 1949 | 9 Apr | Wembley | 1 | 3 |
| 1884 | 15 Mar | Glasgow | 0 | 1 | wc1950 | 15 Apr | Glasgow | 1 | 0 |
| 1885 | 21 Mar | Kennington Oval | 1 | 1 | 1951 | 14 Apr | Wembley | 2 | 3 |
| 1886 | 31 Mar | Glasgow | 1 | 1 | 1952 | 5 Apr | Glasgow | 2 | 1 |
| 1887 | 19 Mar | Blackburn | 2 | 3 | 1953 | 18 Apr | Wembley | 2 | 2 |
| 1888 | 17 Mar | Glasgow | 5 | 0 | wc1954 | 3 Apr | Glasgow | 4 | 2 |
| 1889 | 13 Apr | Kennington Oval | 2 | 3 | 1955 | 2 Apr | Wembley | 7 | 2 |
| 1890 | 5 Apr | Glasgow | 1 | 1 | 1956 | 14 Apr | Glasgow | 1 | 1 |
| 1891 | 6 Apr | Blackburn | 2 | 1 | 1957 | 6 Apr | Wembley | 2 | 1 |
| 1892 | 2 Apr | Glasgow | 4 | 1 | 1958 | 19 Apr | Glasgow | 4 | 0 |
| 1893 | 1 Apr | Richmond | 5 | 2 | 1959 | 11 Apr | Wembley | 1 | 0 |
| 1894 | 7 Apr | Glasgow | 2 | 2 | 1960 | 9 Apr | Glasgow | 1 | 1 |
| 1895 | 6 Apr | Everton | 3 | 0 | 1961 | 15 Apr | Wembley | 9 | 3 |
| 1896 | 4 Apr | Glasgow | 1 | 2 | 1962 | 14 Apr | Glasgow | 0 | 2 |
| 1897 | 3 Apr | Crystal Palace | 1 | 2 | 1963 | 6 Apr | Wembley | 1 | 2 |
| 1898 | 2 Apr | Glasgow | 3 | 1 | 1964 | 11 Apr | Glasgow | 0 | 1 |
| 1899 | 8 Apr | Birmingham | 2 | 1 | 1965 | 10 Apr | Wembley | 2 | 2 |
| 1900 | 7 Apr | Glasgow | 1 | 4 | 1966 | 2 Apr | Glasgow | 4 | 3 |
| 1901 | 30 Mar | Crystal Palace | 2 | 2 | ec1967 | 15 Apr | Wembley | 2 | 3 |
| 1902 | 3 Mar | Birmingham | 2 | 2 | ec1968 | 24 Jan | Glasgow | 1 | 1 |
| 1903 | 4 Apr | Sheffield | 1 | 2 | 1969 | 10 May | Wembley | 4 | 1 |
| 1904 | 9 Apr | Glasgow | 1 | 0 | 1970 | 25 Apr | Glasgow | 0 | 0 |
| 1905 | 1 Apr | Crystal Palace | 1 | 0 | 1971 | 22 May | Wembley | 3 | 1 |
| 1906 | 7 Apr | Glasgow | 1 | 2 | 1972 | 27 May | Glasgow | 1 | 0 |
| 1907 | 6 Apr | Newcastle | 1 | 1 | 1973 | 14 Feb | Glasgow | 5 | 0 |
| 1908 | 4 Apr | Glasgow | 1 | 1 | 1973 | 19 May | Wembley | 1 | 0 |
| 1909 | 3 Apr | Crystal Palace | 2 | 0 | 1974 | 18 May | Glasgow | 0 | 2 |
| 1910 | 2 Apr | Glasgow | 0 | 2 | 1975 | 24 May | Wembley | 5 | 1 |
| 1911 | 1 Apr | Everton | 1 | 1 | 1976 | 15 May | Glasgow | 1 | 2 |
| 1912 | 23 Mar | Glasgow | 1 | 1 | 1977 | 4 June | Wembley | 1 | 2 |
| 1913 | 5 Apr | Chelsea | 1 | 0 | 1978 | 20 May | Glasgow | 1 | 0 |
| 1914 | 14 Apr | Glasgow | 1 | 3 | 1979 | 26 May | Wembley | 3 | 1 |
| 1920 | 10 Apr | Sheffield | 5 | 4 | 1980 | 24 May | Glasgow | 2 | 0 |
| 1921 | 9 Apr | Glasgow | 0 | 3 | 1981 | 23 May | Wembley | 0 | 1 |
| 1922 | 8 Apr | Aston Villa | 0 | 1 | 1982 | 29 May | Glasgow | 1 | 0 |
| 1923 | 14 Apr | Glasgow | 2 | 2 | 1983 | 1 June | Wembley | 2 | 0 |
| 1924 | 12 Apr | Wembley | 1 | 1 | 1984 | 26 May | Glasgow | 1 | 1 |
| 1925 | 4 Apr | Glasgow | 0 | 2 | 1985 | 25 May | Glasgow | 0 | 1 |
| 1926 | 17 Apr | Manchester | 0 | 1 | 1986 | 23 Apr | Wembley | 2 | 1 |
| 1927 | 2 Apr | Glasgow | 2 | 1 | 1987 | 23 May | Glasgow | 0 | 0 |
| 1928 | 31 Mar | Wembley | 1 | 5 | 1988 | 21 May | Wembley | 1 | 0 |
| 1929 | 13 Apr | Glasgow | 0 | 1 | 1989 | 27 May | Glasgow | 2 | 0 |
| 1930 | 5 Apr | Wembley | 5 | 2 | ec1996 | 15 June | Wembley | 2 | 0 |

## ENGLAND v WALES

*Played:* 97; England won 62, Wales won 14, Drawn 21. *Goals:* England 239, Wales 90.

| | | | E | W | | | | E | W |
|---|---|---|---|---|---|---|---|---|---|
| 1879 | 18 Jan | Kennington Oval | 2 | 1 | 1882 | 13 Mar | Wrexham | 3 | 5 |
| 1880 | 15 Mar | Wrexham | 3 | 2 | 1883 | 3 Feb | Kennington Oval | 5 | 0 |
| 1881 | 26 Feb | Blackburn | 0 | 1 | 1884 | 17 Mar | Wrexham | 4 | 0 |

| | | | E | W | | | | E | W |
|---|---|---|---|---|---|---|---|---|---|
| 1885 | 14 Mar | Blackburn | 1 | 1 | 1934 | 29 Sept | Cardiff | 4 | 0 |
| 1886 | 29 Mar | Wrexham | 3 | 1 | 1936 | 5 Feb | Wolverhampton | 1 | 2 |
| 1887 | 26 Feb | Kennington Oval | 4 | 0 | 1936 | 17 Oct | Cardiff | 1 | 2 |
| 1888 | 4 Feb | Crewe | 5 | 1 | 1937 | 17 Nov | Middlesbrough | 2 | 1 |
| 1889 | 23 Feb | Stoke | 4 | 1 | 1938 | 22 Oct | Cardiff | 2 | 4 |
| 1890 | 15 Mar | Wrexham | 3 | 1 | 1946 | 13 Nov | Manchester | 3 | 0 |
| 1891 | 7 May | Sunderland | 4 | 1 | 1947 | 18 Oct | Cardiff | 3 | 0 |
| 1892 | 5 Mar | Wrexham | 2 | 0 | 1948 | 10 Nov | Aston Villa | 1 | 0 |
| 1893 | 13 Mar | Stoke | 6 | 0 | wc1949 | 15 Oct | Cardiff | 4 | 1 |
| 1894 | 12 Mar | Wrexham | 5 | 1 | 1950 | 15 Nov | Sunderland | 4 | 2 |
| 1895 | 18 Mar | Queen's Club, Kensington | 1 | 1 | 1951 | 20 Oct | Cardiff | 1 | 1 |
| | | | | | 1952 | 12 Nov | Wembley | 5 | 2 |
| 1896 | 16 Mar | Cardiff | 9 | 1 | wc1953 | 10 Oct | Cardiff | 4 | 1 |
| 1897 | 29 Mar | Sheffield | 4 | 0 | 1954 | 10 Nov | Wembley | 3 | 2 |
| 1898 | 28 Mar | Wrexham | 3 | 0 | 1955 | 27 Oct | Cardiff | 1 | 2 |
| 1899 | 20 Mar | Bristol | 4 | 0 | 1956 | 14 Nov | Wembley | 3 | 1 |
| 1900 | 26 Mar | Cardiff | 1 | 1 | 1957 | 19 Oct | Cardiff | 4 | 0 |
| 1901 | 18 Mar | Newcastle | 6 | 0 | 1958 | 26 Nov | Aston Villa | 2 | 2 |
| 1902 | 3 Mar | Wrexham | 0 | 0 | 1959 | 17 Oct | Cardiff | 1 | 1 |
| 1903 | 2 Mar | Portsmouth | 2 | 1 | 1960 | 23 Nov | Wembley | 5 | 1 |
| 1904 | 29 Feb | Wrexham | 2 | 2 | 1961 | 14 Oct | Cardiff | 1 | 1 |
| 1905 | 27 Mar | Liverpool | 3 | 1 | 1962 | 21 Oct | Wembley | 4 | 0 |
| 1906 | 19 Mar | Cardiff | 1 | 0 | 1963 | 12 Oct | Cardiff | 4 | 0 |
| 1907 | 18 Mar | Fulham | 1 | 1 | 1964 | 18 Nov | Wembley | 2 | 1 |
| 1908 | 16 Mar | Wrexham | 7 | 1 | 1965 | 2 Oct | Cardiff | 0 | 0 |
| 1909 | 15 Mar | Nottingham | 2 | 0 | EC1966 | 16 Nov | Wembley | 5 | 1 |
| 1910 | 14 Mar | Cardiff | 1 | 0 | EC1967 | 21 Oct | Cardiff | 3 | 0 |
| 1911 | 13 Mar | Millwall | 3 | 0 | 1969 | 7 May | Wembley | 2 | 1 |
| 1912 | 11 Mar | Wrexham | 2 | 0 | 1970 | 18 Apr | Cardiff | 1 | 1 |
| 1913 | 17 Mar | Bristol | 4 | 3 | 1971 | 19 May | Wembley | 0 | 0 |
| 1914 | 16 Mar | Cardiff | 2 | 0 | 1972 | 20 May | Cardiff | 3 | 0 |
| 1920 | 15 Mar | Highbury | 1 | 2 | wc1972 | 15 Nov | Cardiff | 1 | 0 |
| 1921 | 14 Mar | Cardiff | 0 | 0 | wc1973 | 24 Jan | Wembley | 1 | 1 |
| 1922 | 13 Mar | Liverpool | 1 | 0 | 1973 | 15 May | Wembley | 3 | 0 |
| 1923 | 5 Mar | Cardiff | 2 | 2 | 1974 | 11 May | Cardiff | 2 | 0 |
| 1924 | 3 Mar | Blackburn | 1 | 2 | 1975 | 21 May | Wembley | 2 | 2 |
| 1925 | 28 Feb | Swansea | 2 | 1 | 1976 | 24 Mar | Wrexham | 2 | 1 |
| 1926 | 1 Mar | Crystal Palace | 1 | 3 | 1976 | 8 May | Cardiff | 1 | 0 |
| 1927 | 12 Feb | Wrexham | 3 | 3 | 1977 | 31 May | Wembley | 0 | 1 |
| 1927 | 28 Nov | Burnley | 1 | 2 | 1978 | 3 May | Cardiff | 3 | 1 |
| 1928 | 17 Nov | Swansea | 3 | 2 | 1979 | 23 May | Wembley | 0 | 0 |
| 1929 | 20 Nov | Chelsea | 6 | 0 | 1980 | 17 May | Wrexham | 1 | 4 |
| 1930 | 22 Nov | Wrexham | 4 | 0 | 1981 | 20 May | Wembley | 0 | 0 |
| 1931 | 18 Nov | Liverpool | 3 | 1 | 1982 | 27 Apr | Cardiff | 1 | 0 |
| 1932 | 16 Nov | Wrexham | 0 | 0 | 1983 | 23 Feb | Wembley | 2 | 1 |
| 1933 | 15 Nov | Newcastle | 1 | 2 | 1984 | 2 May | Wrexham | 0 | 1 |

## ENGLAND v IRELAND

*Played:* 96; England won 74, Ireland won 6, Drawn 16. *Goals:* England 319, Ireland 80.

| | | | E | I | | | | E | I |
|---|---|---|---|---|---|---|---|---|---|
| 1882 | 18 Feb | Belfast | 13 | 0 | 1903 | 14 Feb | Wolverhampton | 4 | 0 |
| 1883 | 24 Feb | Liverpool | 7 | 0 | 1904 | 12 Mar | Belfast | 3 | 1 |
| 1884 | 23 Feb | Belfast | 8 | 1 | 1905 | 25 Feb | Middlesbrough | 1 | 1 |
| 1885 | 28 Feb | Manchester | 4 | 0 | 1906 | 17 Feb | Belfast | 5 | 0 |
| 1886 | 13 Mar | Belfast | 6 | 1 | 1907 | 16 Feb | Everton | 1 | 0 |
| 1887 | 5 Feb | Sheffield | 7 | 0 | 1908 | 15 Feb | Belfast | 3 | 1 |
| 1888 | 31 Mar | Belfast | 5 | 1 | 1909 | 13 Feb | Bradford | 4 | 0 |
| 1889 | 2 Mar | Everton | 6 | 1 | 1910 | 12 Feb | Belfast | 1 | 1 |
| 1890 | 15 Mar | Belfast | 9 | 1 | 1911 | 11 Feb | Derby | 2 | 1 |
| 1891 | 7 Mar | Wolverhampton | 6 | 1 | 1912 | 10 Feb | Dublin | 6 | 1 |
| 1892 | 5 Mar | Belfast | 2 | 0 | 1913 | 15 Feb | Belfast | 1 | 2 |
| 1893 | 25 Feb | Birmingham | 6 | 1 | 1914 | 14 Feb | Middlesbrough | 0 | 3 |
| 1894 | 3 Mar | Belfast | 2 | 2 | 1919 | 25 Oct | Belfast | 1 | 1 |
| 1895 | 9 Mar | Derby | 9 | 0 | 1920 | 23 Oct | Sunderland | 2 | 0 |
| 1896 | 7 Mar | Belfast | 2 | 0 | 1921 | 22 Oct | Belfast | 1 | 1 |
| 1897 | 20 Feb | Nottingham | 6 | 0 | 1922 | 21 Oct | West Bromwich | 2 | 0 |
| 1898 | 5 Mar | Belfast | 3 | 2 | 1923 | 20 Oct | Belfast | 1 | 2 |
| 1899 | 18 Feb | Sunderland | 13 | 2 | 1924 | 22 Oct | Everton | 3 | 1 |
| 1900 | 17 Mar | Dublin | 2 | 0 | 1925 | 24 Oct | Belfast | 0 | 0 |
| 1901 | 9 Mar | Southampton | 3 | 0 | 1926 | 20 Oct | Liverpool | 3 | 3 |
| 1902 | 22 Mar | Belfast | 1 | 0 | 1927 | 22 Oct | Belfast | 0 | 2 |

| | | | E | I |
|---|---|---|---|---|
| 1928 | 22 Oct | Everton | 2 | 1 |
| 1929 | 19 Oct | Belfast | 3 | 0 |
| 1930 | 20 Oct | Sheffield | 5 | 1 |
| 1931 | 17 Oct | Belfast | 6 | 2 |
| 1932 | 17 Oct | Blackpool | 1 | 0 |
| 1933 | 14 Oct | Belfast | 3 | 0 |
| 1935 | 6 Feb | Everton | 2 | 1 |
| 1935 | 19 Oct | Belfast | 3 | 1 |
| 1936 | 18 Nov | Stoke | 3 | 1 |
| 1937 | 23 Oct | Belfast | 5 | 1 |
| 1938 | 16 Nov | Manchester | 7 | 0 |
| 1946 | 28 Sept | Belfast | 7 | 2 |
| 1947 | 5 Nov | Everton | 2 | 2 |
| 1948 | 9 Oct | Belfast | 6 | 2 |
| wc1949 | 16 Nov | Manchester | 9 | 2 |
| 1950 | 7 Oct | Belfast | 4 | 1 |
| 1951 | 14 Nov | Aston Villa | 2 | 0 |
| 1952 | 4 Oct | Belfast | 2 | 2 |
| wc1953 | 11 Nov | Everton | 3 | 1 |
| 1954 | 2 Oct | Belfast | 2 | 0 |
| 1955 | 2 Nov | Wembley | 3 | 0 |
| 1956 | 10 Oct | Belfast | 1 | 1 |
| 1957 | 6 Nov | Wembley | 2 | 3 |
| 1958 | 4 Oct | Belfast | 3 | 3 |
| 1959 | 18 Nov | Wembley | 2 | 1 |
| 1960 | 8 Oct | Belfast | 5 | 2 |
| 1961 | 22 Nov | Wembley | 1 | 1 |
| 1962 | 20 Oct | Belfast | 3 | 1 |
| 1963 | 20 Nov | Wembley | 8 | 3 |
| 1964 | 3 Oct | Belfast | 4 | 3 |
| 1965 | 10 Nov | Wembley | 2 | 1 |
| EC1966 | 20 Oct | Belfast | 2 | 0 |
| EC1967 | 22 Nov | Wembley | 2 | 0 |
| 1969 | 3 May | Belfast | 3 | 1 |
| 1970 | 21 Apr | Wembley | 3 | 1 |
| 1971 | 15 May | Belfast | 1 | 0 |
| 1972 | 23 May | Wembley | 0 | 1 |
| 1973 | 12 May | Everton | 2 | 1 |
| 1974 | 15 May | Wembley | 1 | 0 |
| 1975 | 17 May | Belfast | 0 | 0 |
| 1976 | 11 May | Wembley | 4 | 0 |
| 1977 | 28 May | Belfast | 2 | 1 |
| 1978 | 16 May | Wembley | 1 | 0 |
| EC1979 | 7 Feb | Wembley | 4 | 0 |
| 1979 | 19 May | Belfast | 2 | 0 |
| EC1979 | 17 Oct | Belfast | 5 | 1 |
| 1980 | 20 May | Wembley | 1 | 1 |
| 1982 | 23 Feb | Wembley | 4 | 0 |
| 1983 | 28 May | Belfast | 0 | 0 |
| 1984 | 24 Apr | Wembley | 1 | 0 |
| wc1985 | 27 Feb | Belfast | 1 | 0 |
| wc1985 | 13 Nov | Wembley | 0 | 0 |
| EC1986 | 15 Oct | Wembley | 3 | 0 |
| EC1987 | 1 Apr | Belfast | 2 | 0 |

## SCOTLAND v WALES

*Played:* 102; Scotland won 60, Wales won 19, Drawn 23. *Goals:* Scotland 238, Wales 112.

| | | | S | W |
|---|---|---|---|---|
| 1876 | 25 Mar | Glasgow | 4 | 0 |
| 1877 | 5 Mar | Wrexham | 2 | 0 |
| 1878 | 23 Mar | Glasgow | 9 | 0 |
| 1879 | 7 Apr | Wrexham | 3 | 0 |
| 1880 | 3 Apr | Glasgow | 5 | 1 |
| 1881 | 14 Mar | Wrexham | 5 | 1 |
| 1882 | 25 Mar | Glasgow | 5 | 0 |
| 1883 | 12 Mar | Wrexham | 4 | 1 |
| 1884 | 29 Mar | Glasgow | 4 | 1 |
| 1885 | 23 Mar | Wrexham | 8 | 1 |
| 1886 | 10 Apr | Glasgow | 4 | 1 |
| 1887 | 21 Mar | Wrexham | 2 | 0 |
| 1888 | 10 Mar | Edinburgh | 5 | 1 |
| 1889 | 15 Apr | Wrexham | 0 | 0 |
| 1890 | 22 Mar | Paisley | 5 | 0 |
| 1891 | 21 Mar | Wrexham | 4 | 3 |
| 1892 | 26 Mar | Edinburgh | 6 | 1 |
| 1893 | 18 Mar | Wrexham | 8 | 0 |
| 1894 | 24 Mar | Kilmarnock | 5 | 2 |
| 1895 | 23 Mar | Wrexham | 2 | 2 |
| 1896 | 21 Mar | Dundee | 4 | 0 |
| 1897 | 20 Mar | Wrexham | 2 | 2 |
| 1898 | 19 Mar | Motherwell | 5 | 2 |
| 1899 | 18 Mar | Wrexham | 6 | 0 |
| 1900 | 3 Feb | Aberdeen | 5 | 2 |
| 1901 | 2 Mar | Wrexham | 1 | 1 |
| 1902 | 15 Mar | Greenock | 5 | 1 |
| 1903 | 9 Mar | Cardiff | 1 | 0 |
| 1904 | 12 Mar | Dundee | 1 | 1 |
| 1905 | 6 Mar | Wrexham | 1 | 3 |
| 1906 | 3 Mar | Edinburgh | 0 | 2 |
| 1907 | 4 Mar | Wrexham | 0 | 1 |
| 1908 | 7 Mar | Dundee | 2 | 1 |
| 1909 | 1 Mar | Wrexham | 2 | 3 |
| 1910 | 5 Mar | Kilmarnock | 1 | 0 |
| 1911 | 6 Mar | Cardiff | 2 | 2 |
| 1912 | 2 Mar | Tynecastle | 1 | 0 |
| 1913 | 3 Mar | Wrexham | 0 | 0 |
| 1914 | 28 Feb | Glasgow | 0 | 0 |
| 1920 | 26 Feb | Cardiff | 1 | 1 |
| 1921 | 12 Feb | Aberdeen | 2 | 1 |
| 1922 | 4 Feb | Wrexham | 1 | 2 |
| 1923 | 17 Mar | Paisley | 2 | 0 |
| 1924 | 16 Feb | Cardiff | 0 | 2 |
| 1925 | 14 Feb | Tynecastle | 3 | 1 |
| 1925 | 31 Oct | Cardiff | 3 | 0 |
| 1926 | 30 Oct | Glasgow | 3 | 0 |
| 1927 | 29 Oct | Wrexham | 2 | 2 |
| 1928 | 27 Oct | Glasgow | 4 | 2 |
| 1929 | 26 Oct | Cardiff | 4 | 2 |
| 1930 | 25 Oct | Glasgow | 1 | 1 |
| 1931 | 31 Oct | Wrexham | 3 | 2 |
| 1932 | 26 Oct | Edinburgh | 2 | 5 |
| 1933 | 4 Oct | Cardiff | 2 | 3 |
| 1934 | 21 Nov | Aberdeen | 3 | 2 |
| 1935 | 5 Oct | Cardiff | 1 | 1 |
| 1936 | 2 Dec | Dundee | 1 | 2 |
| 1937 | 30 Oct | Cardiff | 1 | 2 |
| 1938 | 9 Nov | Edinburgh | 3 | 2 |
| 1946 | 19 Oct | Wrexham | 1 | 3 |
| 1947 | 12 Nov | Glasgow | 1 | 2 |
| wc1948 | 23 Oct | Cardiff | 3 | 1 |
| 1949 | 9 Nov | Glasgow | 2 | 0 |
| 1950 | 21 Oct | Cardiff | 3 | 1 |
| 1951 | 14 Nov | Glasgow | 0 | 1 |
| wc1952 | 18 Oct | Cardiff | 2 | 1 |
| 1953 | 4 Nov | Glasgow | 3 | 3 |
| 1954 | 16 Oct | Cardiff | 1 | 0 |
| 1955 | 9 Nov | Glasgow | 2 | 0 |
| 1956 | 20 Oct | Cardiff | 2 | 2 |
| 1957 | 13 Nov | Glasgow | 1 | 1 |
| 1958 | 18 Oct | Cardiff | 3 | 0 |
| 1959 | 4 Nov | Glasgow | 1 | 1 |
| 1960 | 20 Oct | Cardiff | 0 | 2 |
| 1961 | 8 Nov | Glasgow | 2 | 0 |
| 1962 | 20 Oct | Cardiff | 3 | 2 |
| 1963 | 20 Nov | Glasgow | 2 | 1 |
| 1964 | 3 Oct | Cardiff | 2 | 3 |
| EC1965 | 24 Nov | Glasgow | 4 | 1 |
| EC1966 | 22 Oct | Cardiff | 1 | 1 |

| | | | S | W | | | | S | W |
|---|---|---|---|---|---|---|---|---|---|
| 1967 | 22 Nov | Glasgow | 3 | 2 | wc1977 | 12 Oct | Liverpool | 2 | 0 |
| 1969 | 3 May | Wrexham | 5 | 3 | 1978 | 17 May | Glasgow | 1 | 1 |
| 1970 | 22 Apr | Glasgow | 0 | 0 | 1979 | 19 May | Cardiff | 0 | 3 |
| 1971 | 15 May | Cardiff | 0 | 0 | 1980 | 21 May | Glasgow | 1 | 0 |
| 1972 | 24 May | Glasgow | 1 | 0 | 1981 | 16 May | Swansea | 0 | 2 |
| 1973 | 12 May | Wrexham | 2 | 0 | 1982 | 24 May | Glasgow | 1 | 0 |
| 1974 | 14 May | Glasgow | 2 | 0 | 1983 | 28 May | Cardiff | 2 | 0 |
| 1975 | 17 May | Cardiff | 2 | 2 | 1984 | 28 Feb | Glasgow | 2 | 1 |
| 1976 | 6 May | Glasgow | 3 | 1 | wc1985 | 27 Mar | Glasgow | 0 | 1 |
| wc1976 | 17 Nov | Glasgow | 1 | 0 | wc1985 | 10 Sept | Cardiff | 1 | 1 |
| 1977 | 28 May | Wrexham | 0 | 0 | 1997 | 27 May | Kilmarnock | 0 | 1 |

## SCOTLAND v IRELAND

*Played:* 92; Scotland won 61, Ireland won 15, Drawn 16. *Goals:* Scotland 254, Ireland 81.

| | | | S | I | | | | S | I |
|---|---|---|---|---|---|---|---|---|---|
| 1884 | 26 Jan | Belfast | 5 | 0 | 1934 | 20 Oct | Belfast | 1 | 2 |
| 1885 | 14 Mar | Glasgow | 8 | 2 | 1935 | 13 Nov | Edinburgh | 2 | 1 |
| 1886 | 20 Mar | Belfast | 7 | 2 | 1936 | 31 Oct | Belfast | 3 | 1 |
| 1887 | 19 Feb | Glasgow | 4 | 1 | 1937 | 10 Nov | Aberdeen | 1 | 1 |
| 1888 | 24 Mar | Belfast | 10 | 2 | 1938 | 8 Oct | Belfast | 2 | 0 |
| 1889 | 9 Mar | Glasgow | 7 | 0 | 1946 | 27 Nov | Glasgow | 0 | 0 |
| 1890 | 29 Mar | Belfast | 4 | 1 | 1947 | 4 Oct | Belfast | 0 | 2 |
| 1891 | 28 Mar | Glasgow | 2 | 1 | 1948 | 17 Nov | Glasgow | 3 | 2 |
| 1892 | 19 Mar | Belfast | 3 | 2 | 1949 | 1 Oct | Belfast | 8 | 2 |
| 1893 | 25 Mar | Glasgow | 6 | 1 | 1950 | 1 Nov | Glasgow | 6 | 1 |
| 1894 | 31 Mar | Belfast | 2 | 1 | 1951 | 6 Oct | Belfast | 3 | 0 |
| 1895 | 30 Mar | Glasgow | 3 | 1 | 1952 | 5 Nov | Glasgow | 1 | 1 |
| 1896 | 28 Mar | Belfast | 3 | 3 | 1953 | 3 Oct | Belfast | 3 | 1 |
| 1897 | 27 Mar | Glasgow | 5 | 1 | 1954 | 3 Nov | Glasgow | 2 | 2 |
| 1898 | 26 Mar | Belfast | 3 | 0 | 1955 | 8 Oct | Belfast | 1 | 2 |
| 1899 | 25 Mar | Glasgow | 9 | 1 | 1956 | 7 Nov | Glasgow | 1 | 0 |
| 1900 | 3 Mar | Belfast | 3 | 0 | 1957 | 5 Oct | Belfast | 1 | 1 |
| 1901 | 23 Feb | Glasgow | 11 | 0 | 1958 | 5 Nov | Glasgow | 2 | 2 |
| 1902 | 1 Mar | Belfast | 5 | 1 | 1959 | 3 Oct | Belfast | 4 | 0 |
| 1903 | 21 Mar | Glasgow | 0 | 2 | 1960 | 9 Nov | Glasgow | 5 | 2 |
| 1904 | 26 Mar | Dublin | 1 | 1 | 1961 | 7 Oct | Belfast | 6 | 1 |
| 1905 | 18 Mar | Glasgow | 4 | 0 | 1962 | 7 Nov | Glasgow | 5 | 1 |
| 1906 | 17 Mar | Dublin | 1 | 0 | 1963 | 12 Oct | Belfast | 1 | 2 |
| 1907 | 16 Mar | Glasgow | 3 | 0 | 1964 | 25 Nov | Glasgow | 3 | 2 |
| 1908 | 14 Mar | Dublin | 5 | 0 | 1965 | 2 Oct | Belfast | 2 | 3 |
| 1909 | 15 Mar | Glasgow | 5 | 0 | 1966 | 16 Nov | Glasgow | 2 | 1 |
| 1910 | 19 Mar | Belfast | 0 | 1 | 1967 | 21 Oct | Belfast | 0 | 1 |
| 1911 | 18 Mar | Glasgow | 2 | 0 | 1969 | 6 May | Glasgow | 1 | 1 |
| 1912 | 16 Mar | Belfast | 4 | 1 | 1970 | 18 Apr | Belfast | 1 | 0 |
| 1913 | 15 Mar | Dublin | 2 | 1 | 1971 | 18 May | Glasgow | 0 | 1 |
| 1914 | 14 Mar | Belfast | 1 | 1 | 1972 | 20 May | Glasgow | 2 | 0 |
| 1920 | 13 Mar | Glasgow | 3 | 0 | 1973 | 16 May | Glasgow | 1 | 2 |
| 1921 | 26 Feb | Belfast | 2 | 0 | 1974 | 11 May | Glasgow | 0 | 1 |
| 1922 | 4 Mar | Glasgow | 2 | 1 | 1975 | 20 May | Glasgow | 3 | 0 |
| 1923 | 3 Mar | Belfast | 1 | 0 | 1976 | 8 May | Glasgow | 3 | 0 |
| 1924 | 1 Mar | Glasgow | 2 | 0 | 1977 | 1 June | Glasgow | 3 | 0 |
| 1925 | 28 Feb | Belfast | 3 | 0 | 1978 | 13 May | Glasgow | 1 | 1 |
| 1926 | 27 Feb | Glasgow | 4 | 0 | 1979 | 22 May | Glasgow | 1 | 0 |
| 1927 | 26 Feb | Belfast | 2 | 0 | 1980 | 17 May | Belfast | 0 | 1 |
| 1928 | 25 Feb | Glasgow | 0 | 1 | wc1981 | 25 Mar | Glasgow | 1 | 1 |
| 1929 | 23 Feb | Belfast | 7 | 3 | 1981 | 19 May | Glasgow | 2 | 0 |
| 1930 | 22 Feb | Glasgow | 3 | 1 | wc1981 | 14 Oct | Belfast | 0 | 0 |
| 1931 | 21 Feb | Belfast | 0 | 0 | 1982 | 28 Apr | Belfast | 1 | 1 |
| 1931 | 19 Sept | Glasgow | 3 | 1 | 1983 | 24 May | Glasgow | 0 | 0 |
| 1932 | 12 Sept | Belfast | 4 | 0 | 1983 | 13 Dec | Belfast | 0 | 2 |
| 1933 | 16 Sept | Glasgow | 1 | 2 | 1992 | 19 Feb | Glasgow | 1 | 0 |

## WALES v IRELAND

*Played:* 90; Wales won 42, Ireland won 27, Drawn 21. *Goals:* Wales 181, Ireland 126.

| | | | W | I | | | | W | I |
|---|---|---|---|---|---|---|---|---|---|
| 1882 | 25 Feb | Wrexham | 7 | 1 | 1886 | 27 Feb | Wrexham | 5 | 0 |
| 1883 | 17 Mar | Belfast | 1 | 1 | 1887 | 12 Mar | Belfast | 1 | 4 |
| 1884 | 9 Feb | Wrexham | 6 | 0 | 1888 | 3 Mar | Wrexham | 11 | 0 |
| 1885 | 11 Apr | Belfast | 8 | 2 | 1889 | 27 Apr | Belfast | 3 | 1 |

| | | | W | I |
|---|---|---|---|---|
| 1890 | 8 Feb | Shrewsbury | 5 | 2 |
| 1891 | 7 Feb | Belfast | 2 | 7 |
| 1892 | 27 Feb | Bangor | 1 | 1 |
| 1893 | 8 Apr | Belfast | 3 | 4 |
| 1894 | 24 Feb | Swansea | 4 | 1 |
| 1895 | 16 Mar | Belfast | 2 | 2 |
| 1896 | 29 Feb | Wrexham | 6 | 1 |
| 1897 | 6 Mar | Belfast | 3 | 4 |
| 1898 | 19 Feb | Llandudno | 0 | 1 |
| 1899 | 4 Mar | Belfast | 0 | 1 |
| 1900 | 24 Feb | Llandudno | 2 | 0 |
| 1901 | 23 Mar | Belfast | 1 | 0 |
| 1902 | 22 Mar | Cardiff | 0 | 3 |
| 1903 | 28 Mar | Belfast | 0 | 2 |
| 1904 | 21 Mar | Bangor | 0 | 1 |
| 1905 | 18 Apr | Belfast | 2 | 2 |
| 1906 | 2 Apr | Wrexham | 4 | 4 |
| 1907 | 23 Feb | Belfast | 3 | 2 |
| 1908 | 11 Apr | Aberdare | 0 | 1 |
| 1909 | 20 Mar | Belfast | 3 | 2 |
| 1910 | 11 Apr | Wrexham | 4 | 1 |
| 1911 | 28 Jan | Belfast | 2 | 1 |
| 1912 | 13 Apr | Cardiff | 2 | 3 |
| 1913 | 18 Jan | Belfast | 1 | 0 |
| 1914 | 19 Jan | Wrexham | 1 | 2 |
| 1920 | 14 Feb | Belfast | 2 | 2 |
| 1921 | 9 Apr | Swansea | 2 | 1 |
| 1922 | 4 Apr | Belfast | 1 | 1 |
| 1923 | 14 Apr | Wrexham | 0 | 3 |
| 1924 | 15 Mar | Belfast | 1 | 0 |
| 1925 | 18 Apr | Wrexham | 0 | 0 |
| 1926 | 13 Feb | Belfast | 0 | 3 |
| 1927 | 9 Apr | Cardiff | 2 | 2 |
| 1928 | 4 Feb | Belfast | 2 | 1 |
| 1929 | 2 Feb | Wrexham | 2 | 2 |
| 1930 | 1 Feb | Belfast | 0 | 7 |
| 1931 | 22 Apr | Wrexham | 3 | 2 |
| 1931 | 5 Dec | Belfast | 0 | 4 |
| 1932 | 7 Dec | Wrexham | 4 | 1 |
| 1933 | 4 Nov | Belfast | 1 | 1 |
| 1935 | 27 Mar | Wrexham | 3 | 1 |

| | | | W | I |
|---|---|---|---|---|
| 1936 | 11 Mar | Belfast | 2 | 3 |
| 1937 | 17 Mar | Wrexham | 4 | 1 |
| 1938 | 16 Mar | Belfast | 0 | 1 |
| 1939 | 15 Mar | Wrexham | 3 | 1 |
| 1947 | 16 Apr | Belfast | 1 | 2 |
| 1948 | 10 Mar | Wrexham | 2 | 0 |
| 1949 | 9 Mar | Belfast | 2 | 0 |
| wc1950 | 8 Mar | Wrexham | 0 | 0 |
| 1951 | 7 Mar | Belfast | 2 | 1 |
| 1952 | 19 Mar | Swansea | 3 | 0 |
| 1953 | 15 Apr | Belfast | 3 | 2 |
| wc1954 | 31 Mar | Wrexham | 1 | 2 |
| 1955 | 20 Apr | Belfast | 3 | 2 |
| 1956 | 11 Apr | Cardiff | 1 | 1 |
| 1957 | 10 Apr | Belfast | 0 | 0 |
| 1958 | 16 Apr | Cardiff | 1 | 1 |
| 1959 | 22 Apr | Belfast | 1 | 4 |
| 1960 | 6 Apr | Wrexham | 3 | 2 |
| 1961 | 12 Apr | Belfast | 5 | 1 |
| 1962 | 11 Apr | Cardiff | 4 | 0 |
| 1963 | 3 Apr | Belfast | 4 | 1 |
| 1964 | 15 Apr | Cardiff | 2 | 3 |
| 1965 | 31 Mar | Belfast | 5 | 0 |
| 1966 | 30 Mar | Cardiff | 1 | 4 |
| EC1967 | 12 Apr | Belfast | 0 | 0 |
| EC1968 | 28 Feb | Wrexham | 2 | 0 |
| 1969 | 10 May | Belfast | 0 | 0 |
| 1970 | 25 Apr | Swansea | 1 | 0 |
| 1971 | 22 May | Belfast | 0 | 1 |
| 1972 | 27 May | Wrexham | 0 | 0 |
| 1973 | 19 May | Everton | 0 | 1 |
| 1974 | 18 May | Wrexham | 1 | 0 |
| 1975 | 23 May | Belfast | 0 | 1 |
| 1976 | 14 May | Swansea | 1 | 0 |
| 1977 | 3 June | Belfast | 1 | 1 |
| 1978 | 19 May | Wrexham | 1 | 0 |
| 1979 | 25 May | Belfast | 1 | 1 |
| 1980 | 23 May | Cardiff | 0 | 1 |
| 1982 | 27 May | Wrexham | 3 | 0 |
| 1983 | 31 May | Belfast | 1 | 0 |
| 1984 | 22 May | Swansea | 1 | 1 |

## OTHER BRITISH INTERNATIONAL RESULTS 1908–1998

### ENGLAND

| | | v ALBANIA | E | A |
|---|---|---|---|---|
| wc1989 | 8 Mar | Tirana | 2 | 0 |
| wc1989 | 26 Apr | Wembley | 5 | 0 |

| | | v ARGENTINA | E | A |
|---|---|---|---|---|
| 1951 | 9 May | Wembley | 2 | 1 |
| 1953 | 17 May | Buenos Aires | 0 | 0 |
| (*abandoned after 21 mins*) | | | | |
| wc1962 | 2 June | Rancagua | 3 | 1 |
| 1964 | 6 June | Rio de Janeiro | 0 | 1 |
| wc1966 | 23 July | Wembley | 1 | 0 |
| 1974 | 22 May | Wembley | 2 | 2 |
| 1977 | 12 June | Buenos Aires | 1 | 1 |
| 1980 | 13 May | Wembley | 3 | 1 |
| wc1986 | 22 June | Mexico City | 1 | 2 |
| 1991 | 25 May | Wembley | 2 | 2 |
| wc1998 | 30 June | St Etienne | 2 | 2 |

| | | v AUSTRALIA | E | A |
|---|---|---|---|---|
| 1980 | 31 May | Sydney | 2 | 1 |
| 1983 | 11 June | Sydney | 0 | 0 |
| 1983 | 15 June | Brisbane | 1 | 0 |
| 1983 | 18 June | Melbourne | 1 | 1 |
| 1991 | 1 June | Sydney | 1 | 0 |

| | | v AUSTRIA | E | A |
|---|---|---|---|---|
| 1908 | 6 June | Vienna | 6 | 1 |
| 1908 | 8 June | Vienna | 11 | 1 |
| 1909 | 1 June | Vienna | 8 | 1 |
| 1930 | 14 May | Vienna | 0 | 0 |
| 1932 | 7 Dec | Chelsea | 4 | 3 |
| 1936 | 6 May | Vienna | 1 | 2 |
| 1951 | 28 Nov | Wembley | 2 | 2 |
| 1952 | 25 May | Vienna | 3 | 2 |
| wc1958 | 15 June | Boras | 2 | 2 |
| 1961 | 27 May | Vienna | 1 | 3 |
| 1962 | 4 Apr | Wembley | 3 | 1 |
| 1965 | 20 Oct | Wembley | 2 | 3 |
| 1967 | 27 May | Vienna | 1 | 0 |
| 1973 | 26 Sept | Wembley | 7 | 0 |
| 1979 | 13 June | Vienna | 3 | 4 |

| | | v BELGIUM | E | B |
|---|---|---|---|---|
| 1921 | 21 May | Brussels | 2 | 0 |
| 1923 | 19 Mar | Highbury | 6 | 1 |
| 1923 | 1 Nov | Antwerp | 2 | 2 |
| 1924 | 8 Dec | West Bromwich | 4 | 0 |
| 1926 | 24 May | Antwerp | 5 | 3 |
| 1927 | 11 May | Brussels | 9 | 1 |
| 1928 | 19 May | Antwerp | 3 | 1 |
| 1929 | 11 May | Brussels | 5 | 1 |
| 1931 | 16 May | Brussels | 4 | 1 |
| 1936 | 9 May | Brussels | 2 | 3 |
| 1947 | 21 Sept | Brussels | 5 | 2 |

| | | | E | B |
|---|---|---|---|---|
| 1950 | 18 May | Brussels | 4 | 1 |
| 1952 | 26 Nov | Wembley | 5 | 0 |
| wc1954 | 17 June | Basle | 4 | 4* |
| 1964 | 21 Oct | Wembley | 2 | 2 |
| 1970 | 25 Feb | Brussels | 3 | 1 |
| EC1980 | 12 June | Turin | 1 | 1 |
| wc1990 | 27 June | Bologna | 1 | 0* |
| 1998 | 29 May | Casablanca | 0 | 0 |

*After extra time

| **v BOHEMIA** | | | E | B |
|---|---|---|---|---|
| 1908 | 13 June | Prague | 4 | 0 |

| **v BRAZIL** | | | E | B |
|---|---|---|---|---|
| 1956 | 9 May | Wembley | 4 | 2 |
| wc1958 | 11 June | Gothenburg | 0 | 0 |
| 1959 | 13 May | Rio de Janeiro | 0 | 2 |
| wc1962 | 10 June | Vina del Mar | 1 | 3 |
| 1963 | 8 May | Wembley | 1 | 1 |
| 1964 | 30 May | Rio de Janeiro | 1 | 5 |
| 1969 | 12 June | Rio de Janeiro | 1 | 2 |
| wc1970 | 7 June | Guadalajara | 0 | 1 |
| 1976 | 23 May | Los Angeles | 0 | 1 |
| 1977 | 8 June | Rio de Janeiro | 0 | 0 |
| 1978 | 19 Apr | Wembley | 1 | 1 |
| 1981 | 12 May | Wembley | 0 | 1 |
| 1984 | 10 June | Rio de Janeiro | 2 | 0 |
| 1987 | 19 May | Wembley | 1 | 1 |
| 1990 | 28 Mar | Wembley | 1 | 0 |
| 1992 | 17 May | Wembley | 1 | 1 |
| 1993 | 13 June | Washington | 1 | 1 |
| UI1995 | 11 June | Wembley | 1 | 3 |
| TF1997 | 10 June | Paris | 0 | 1 |

| **v BULGARIA** | | | E | B |
|---|---|---|---|---|
| wc1962 | 7 June | Rancagua | 0 | 0 |
| 1968 | 11 Dec | Wembley | 1 | 1 |
| 1974 | 1 June | Sofia | 1 | 0 |
| EC1979 | 6 June | Sofia | 3 | 0 |
| EC1979 | 22 Nov | Wembley | 2 | 0 |
| 1996 | 27 Mar | Wembley | 1 | 0 |

| **v CAMEROON** | | | E | C |
|---|---|---|---|---|
| wc1990 | 1 July | Naples | 3 | 2* |
| 1991 | 6 Feb | Wembley | 2 | 0 |
| 1997 | 15 Nov | Wembley | 2 | 0 |

*After extra time

| **v CANADA** | | | E | C |
|---|---|---|---|---|
| 1986 | 24 May | Burnaby | 1 | 0 |

| **v CHILE** | | | E | C |
|---|---|---|---|---|
| wc1950 | 25 June | Rio de Janeiro | 2 | 0 |
| 1953 | 24 May | Santiago | 2 | 1 |
| 1984 | 17 June | Santiago | 0 | 0 |
| 1989 | 23 May | Wembley | 0 | 0 |
| 1998 | 11 Feb | Wembley | 0 | 2 |

| **v CHINA** | | | E | C |
|---|---|---|---|---|
| 1996 | 23 May | Beijing | 3 | 0 |

| **v CIS** | | | E | C |
|---|---|---|---|---|
| 1992 | 29 Apr | Moscow | 2 | 2 |

| **v COLOMBIA** | | | E | C |
|---|---|---|---|---|
| 1970 | 20 May | Bogota | 4 | 0 |
| 1988 | 24 May | Wembley | 1 | 1 |
| 1995 | 6 Sept | Wembley | 0 | 0 |
| wc1998 | 26 June | Lens | 2 | 0 |

| **v CROATIA** | | | E | C |
|---|---|---|---|---|
| 1996 | 24 Apr | Wembley | 0 | 0 |

| **v CYPRUS** | | | E | C |
|---|---|---|---|---|
| EC1975 | 16 Apr | Wembley | 5 | 0 |
| EC1975 | 11 May | Limassol | 1 | 0 |

| **v CZECHOSLOVAKIA** | | | E | C |
|---|---|---|---|---|
| 1934 | 16 May | Prague | 1 | 2 |
| 1937 | 1 Dec | Tottenham | 5 | 4 |
| 1963 | 29 May | Bratislava | 4 | 2 |
| 1966 | 2 Nov | Wembley | 0 | 0 |
| wc1970 | 11 June | Guadalajara | 1 | 0 |
| 1973 | 27 May | Prague | 1 | 1 |
| EC1974 | 30 Oct | Wembley | 3 | 0 |
| EC1975 | 30 Oct | Bratislava | 1 | 2 |
| 1978 | 29 Nov | Wembley | 1 | 0 |
| wc1982 | 20 June | Bilbao | 2 | 0 |
| 1990 | 25 Apr | Wembley | 4 | 2 |
| 1992 | 25 Mar | Prague | 2 | 2 |

| **v DENMARK** | | | E | D |
|---|---|---|---|---|
| 1948 | 26 Sept | Copenhagen | 0 | 0 |
| 1955 | 2 Oct | Copenhagen | 5 | 1 |
| wc1956 | 5 Dec | Wolverhampton | 5 | 2 |
| wc1957 | 15 May | Copenhagen | 4 | 1 |
| 1966 | 3 July | Copenhagen | 2 | 0 |
| EC1978 | 20 Sept | Copenhagen | 4 | 3 |
| EC1979 | 12 Sept | Wembley | 1 | 0 |
| EC1982 | 22 Sept | Copenhagen | 2 | 2 |
| EC1983 | 21 Sept | Wembley | 0 | 1 |
| 1988 | 14 Sept | Wembley | 1 | 0 |
| 1989 | 7 June | Copenhagen | 1 | 1 |
| 1990 | 15 May | Wembley | 1 | 0 |
| EC1992 | 11 June | Malmo | 0 | 0 |
| 1994 | 9 Mar | Wembley | 1 | 0 |

| **v ECUADOR** | | | E | Ec |
|---|---|---|---|---|
| 1970 | 24 May | Quito | 2 | 0 |

| **v EGYPT** | | | E | Eg |
|---|---|---|---|---|
| 1986 | 29 Jan | Cairo | 4 | 0 |
| wc1990 | 21 June | Cagliari | 1 | 0 |

| **v FIFA** | | | E | FIFA |
|---|---|---|---|---|
| 1938 | 26 Oct | Highbury | 3 | 0 |
| 1953 | 21 Oct | Wembley | 4 | 4 |
| 1963 | 23 Oct | Wembley | 2 | 1 |

| **v FINLAND** | | | E | F |
|---|---|---|---|---|
| 1937 | 20 May | Helsinki | 8 | 0 |
| 1956 | 20 May | Helsinki | 5 | 1 |
| 1966 | 26 June | Helsinki | 3 | 0 |
| wc1976 | 13 June | Helsinki | 4 | 1 |
| wc1976 | 13 Oct | Wembley | 2 | 1 |
| 1982 | 3 June | Helsinki | 4 | 1 |
| wc1984 | 17 Oct | Wembley | 5 | 0 |
| wc1985 | 22 May | Helsinki | 1 | 1 |
| 1992 | 3 June | Helsinki | 2 | 1 |

| **v FRANCE** | | | E | F |
|---|---|---|---|---|
| 1923 | 10 May | Paris | 4 | 1 |
| 1924 | 17 May | Paris | 3 | 1 |
| 1925 | 21 May | Paris | 3 | 2 |
| 1927 | 26 May | Paris | 6 | 0 |
| 1928 | 17 May | Paris | 5 | 1 |
| 1929 | 9 May | Paris | 4 | 1 |
| 1931 | 14 May | Paris | 2 | 5 |
| 1933 | 6 Dec | Tottenham | 4 | 1 |
| 1938 | 26 May | Paris | 4 | 2 |
| 1947 | 3 May | Highbury | 3 | 0 |
| 1949 | 22 May | Paris | 3 | 1 |
| 1951 | 3 Oct | Highbury | 2 | 2 |
| 1955 | 15 May | Paris | 0 | 1 |
| 1957 | 27 Nov | Wembley | 4 | 0 |
| EC1962 | 3 Oct | Sheffield | 1 | 1 |
| EC1963 | 27 Feb | Paris | 2 | 5 |
| wc1966 | 20 July | Wembley | 2 | 0 |
| 1969 | 12 Mar | Wembley | 5 | 0 |
| wc1982 | 16 June | Bilbao | 3 | 1 |

| | | | E | F |
|---|---|---|---|---|
| 1984 | 29 Feb | Paris | 0 | 2 |
| 1992 | 19 Feb | Wembley | 2 | 0 |
| EC1992 | 14 June | Malmo | 0 | 0 |
| TF1997 | 7 June | Montpellier | 1 | 0 |

| **v GEORGIA** | | | E | G |
|---|---|---|---|---|
| wc1996 | 9 Nov | Tbilisi | 2 | 0 |
| wc1997 | 30 Apr | Wembley | 2 | 0 |

| **v GERMANY** | | | E | G |
|---|---|---|---|---|
| 1930 | 10 May | Berlin | 3 | 3 |
| 1935 | 4 Dec | Tottenham | 3 | 0 |
| 1938 | 14 May | Berlin | 6 | 3 |
| 1991 | 11 Sept | Wembley | 0 | 1 |
| 1993 | 19 June | Detroit | 1 | 2 |
| EC1996 | 26 June | Wembley | 1 | 1* |

| **v EAST GERMANY** | | | E | EG |
|---|---|---|---|---|
| 1963 | 2 June | Leipzig | 2 | 1 |
| 1970 | 25 Nov | Wembley | 3 | 1 |
| 1974 | 29 May | Leipzig | 1 | 1 |
| 1984 | 12 Sept | Wembley | 1 | 0 |

| **v WEST GERMANY** | | | E | WG |
|---|---|---|---|---|
| 1954 | 1 Dec | Wembley | 3 | 1 |
| 1956 | 26 May | Berlin | 3 | 1 |
| 1965 | 12 May | Nuremberg | 1 | 0 |
| 1966 | 23 Feb | Wembley | 1 | 0 |
| wc1966 | 30 July | Wembley | 4 | 2* |
| 1968 | 1 June | Hanover | 0 | 1 |
| wc1970 | 14 June | Leon | 2 | 3* |
| EC1972 | 29 Apr | Wembley | 1 | 3 |
| EC1972 | 13 May | Berlin | 0 | 0 |
| 1975 | 12 Mar | Wembley | 2 | 0 |
| 1978 | 22 Feb | Munich | 1 | 2 |
| wc1982 | 29 June | Madrid | 0 | 0 |
| 1982 | 13 Oct | Wembley | 1 | 2 |
| 1985 | 12 June | Mexico City | 3 | 0 |
| 1987 | 9 Sept | Dusseldorf | 1 | 3 |
| wc1990 | 4 July | Turin | 1 | 1* |

*After extra time

| **v GREECE** | | | E | G |
|---|---|---|---|---|
| EC1971 | 21 Apr | Wembley | 3 | 0 |
| EC1971 | 1 Dec | Athens | 2 | 0 |
| EC1982 | 17 Nov | Athens | 3 | 0 |
| EC1983 | 30 Mar | Wembley | 0 | 0 |
| 1989 | 8 Feb | Athens | 2 | 1 |
| 1994 | 17 May | Wembley | 5 | 0 |

| **v HOLLAND** | | | E | H |
|---|---|---|---|---|
| 1935 | 18 May | Amsterdam | 1 | 0 |
| 1946 | 27 Nov | Huddersfield | 8 | 2 |
| 1964 | 9 Dec | Amsterdam | 1 | 1 |
| 1969 | 5 Nov | Amsterdam | 1 | 0 |
| 1970 | 14 Jun | Wembley | 0 | 0 |
| 1977 | 9 Feb | Wembley | 0 | 2 |
| 1982 | 25 May | Wembley | 2 | 0 |
| 1988 | 23 Mar | Wembley | 2 | 2 |
| EC1988 | 15 June | Dusseldorf | 1 | 3 |
| wc1990 | 16 June | Cagliari | 0 | 0 |
| wc1993 | 28 Apr | Wembley | 2 | 2 |
| wc1993 | 13 Oct | Rotterdam | 0 | 2 |
| EC1996 | 18 June | Wembley | 4 | 1 |

| **v HUNGARY** | | | E | H |
|---|---|---|---|---|
| 1908 | 10 June | Budapest | 7 | 0 |
| 1909 | 29 May | Budapest | 4 | 2 |
| 1909 | 31 May | Budapest | 8 | 2 |
| 1934 | 10 May | Budapest | 1 | 2 |
| 1936 | 2 Dec | Highbury | 6 | 2 |
| 1953 | 25 Nov | Wembley | 3 | 6 |
| 1954 | 23 May | Budapest | 1 | 7 |
| 1960 | 22 May | Budapest | 0 | 2 |

| | | | E | H |
|---|---|---|---|---|
| wc1962 | 31 May | Rancagua | 1 | 2 |
| 1965 | 5 May | Wembley | 1 | 0 |
| 1978 | 24 May | Wembley | 4 | 1 |
| wc1981 | 6 June | Budapest | 3 | 1 |
| wc1982 | 18 Nov | Wembley | 1 | 0 |
| EC1983 | 27 Apr | Wembley | 2 | 0 |
| EC1983 | 12 Oct | Budapest | 3 | 0 |
| 1988 | 27 Apr | Budapest | 0 | 0 |
| 1990 | 12 Sept | Wembley | 1 | 0 |
| 1992 | 12 May | Budapest | 1 | 0 |
| 1996 | 18 May | Wembley | 3 | 0 |

| **v ICELAND** | | | E | I |
|---|---|---|---|---|
| 1982 | 2 June | Reykjavik | 1 | 1 |

| **v REPUBLIC OF IRELAND** | | | E | RI |
|---|---|---|---|---|
| 1946 | 30 Sept | Dublin | 1 | 0 |
| 1949 | 21 Sept | Everton | 0 | 2 |
| wc1957 | 8 May | Wembley | 5 | 1 |
| wc1957 | 19 May | Dublin | 1 | 1 |
| 1964 | 24 May | Dublin | 3 | 1 |
| 1976 | 8 Sept | Wembley | 1 | 1 |
| EC1978 | 25 Oct | Dublin | 1 | 1 |
| EC1980 | 6 Feb | Wembley | 2 | 0 |
| 1985 | 26 Mar | Wembley | 2 | 1 |
| EC1988 | 12 June | Stuttgart | 0 | 1 |
| wc1990 | 11 June | Cagliari | 1 | 1 |
| EC1990 | 14 Nov | Dublin | 1 | 1 |
| EC1991 | 27 Mar | Wembley | 1 | 1 |
| 1995 | 15 Feb | Dublin | 0 | 1 |

*(abandoned after 27 mins)*

| **v ISRAEL** | | | E | I |
|---|---|---|---|---|
| 1986 | 26 Feb | Ramat Gan | 2 | 1 |
| 1988 | 17 Feb | Tel Aviv | 0 | 0 |

| **v ITALY** | | | E | I |
|---|---|---|---|---|
| 1933 | 13 May | Rome | 1 | 1 |
| 1934 | 14 Nov | Highbury | 3 | 2 |
| 1939 | 13 May | Milan | 2 | 2 |
| 1948 | 16 May | Turin | 4 | 0 |
| 1949 | 30 Nov | Tottenham | 2 | 0 |
| 1952 | 18 May | Florence | 1 | 1 |
| 1959 | 6 May | Wembley | 2 | 2 |
| 1961 | 24 May | Rome | 3 | 2 |
| 1973 | 14 June | Turin | 0 | 2 |
| 1973 | 14 Nov | Wembley | 0 | 1 |
| 1976 | 28 May | New York | 3 | 2 |
| wc1976 | 17 Nov | Rome | 0 | 2 |
| wc1977 | 16 Nov | Wembley | 2 | 0 |
| EC1980 | 15 June | Turin | 0 | 1 |
| 1985 | 6 June | Mexico City | 1 | 2 |
| 1989 | 15 Nov | Wembley | 0 | 0 |
| wc1990 | 7 July | Bari | 1 | 2 |
| wc1997 | 12 Feb | Wembley | 0 | 1 |
| TF1997 | 4 June | Nantes | 2 | 0 |
| wc1997 | 11 Oct | Rome | 0 | 0 |

| **v JAPAN** | | | E | J |
|---|---|---|---|---|
| UI1995 | 3 June | Wembley | 2 | 1 |

| **v KUWAIT** | | | E | K |
|---|---|---|---|---|
| wc1982 | 25 June | Bilbao | 1 | 0 |

| **v LUXEMBOURG** | | | E | L |
|---|---|---|---|---|
| 1927 | 21 May | Luxembourg | 5 | 2 |
| wc1960 | 19 Oct | Luxembourg | 9 | 0 |
| wc1961 | 28 Sept | Highbury | 4 | 1 |
| wc1977 | 30 Mar | Wembley | 5 | 0 |
| wc1977 | 12 Oct | Luxembourg | 2 | 0 |
| EC1982 | 15 Dec | Wembley | 9 | 0 |
| EC1983 | 16 Nov | Luxembourg | 4 | 0 |

| **v MALAYSIA** | | | E | M |
|---|---|---|---|---|
| 1991 | 12 June | Kuala Lumpur | 4 | 2 |

| | | v MALTA | E | M |
|---|---|---|---|---|
| EC1971 | 3 Feb | Valletta | 1 | 0 |
| EC1971 | 12 May | Wembley | 5 | 0 |

| | | v MEXICO | E | M |
|---|---|---|---|---|
| 1959 | 24 May | Mexico City | 1 | 2 |
| 1961 | 10 May | Wembley | 8 | 0 |
| wc1966 | 16 July | Wembley | 2 | 0 |
| 1969 | 1 June | Mexico City | 0 | 0 |
| 1985 | 9 June | Mexico City | 0 | 1 |
| 1986 | 17 May | Los Angeles | 3 | 0 |
| 1997 | 29 Mar | Wembley | 2 | 0 |

| | | v MOLDOVA | E | M |
|---|---|---|---|---|
| wc1996 | 1 Sept | Chisinau | 3 | 0 |
| wc1997 | 10 Sept | Wembley | 4 | 0 |

| | | v MOROCCO | E | M |
|---|---|---|---|---|
| wc1986 | 6 June | Monterrey | 0 | 0 |
| 1998 | 27 May | Casablanca | 1 | 0 |

| | | v NEW ZEALAND | E | NZ |
|---|---|---|---|---|
| 1991 | 3 June | Auckland | 1 | 0 |
| 1991 | 8 June | Wellington | 2 | 0 |

| | | v NIGERIA | E | N |
|---|---|---|---|---|
| 1994 | 16 Nov | Wembley | 1 | 0 |

| | | v NORWAY | E | N |
|---|---|---|---|---|
| 1937 | 14 May | Oslo | 6 | 0 |
| 1938 | 9 Nov | Newcastle | 4 | 0 |
| 1949 | 18 May | Oslo | 4 | 1 |
| 1966 | 29 June | Oslo | 6 | 1 |
| wc1980 | 10 Sept | Wembley | 4 | 0 |
| wc1981 | 9 Sept | Oslo | 1 | 2 |
| wc1992 | 14 Oct | Wembley | 1 | 1 |
| wc1993 | 2 June | Oslo | 0 | 2 |
| 1994 | 22 May | Wembley | 0 | 0 |
| 1995 | 11 Oct | Oslo | 0 | 0 |

| | | v PARAGUAY | E | P |
|---|---|---|---|---|
| wc1986 | 18 June | Mexico City | 3 | 0 |

| | | v PERU | E | P |
|---|---|---|---|---|
| 1959 | 17 May | Lima | 1 | 4 |
| 1962 | 20 May | Lima | 4 | 0 |

| | | v POLAND | E | P |
|---|---|---|---|---|
| 1966 | 5 Jan | Everton | 1 | 1 |
| 1966 | 5 July | Chorzow | 1 | 0 |
| wc1973 | 6 June | Chorzow | 0 | 2 |
| wc1973 | 17 Oct | Wembley | 1 | 1 |
| wc1986 | 11 June | Monterrey | 3 | 0 |
| wc1989 | 3 June | Wembley | 3 | 0 |
| wc1989 | 11 Oct | Katowice | 0 | 0 |
| EC1990 | 17 Oct | Wembley | 2 | 0 |
| EC1991 | 13 Nov | Poznan | 1 | 1 |
| wc1993 | 29 May | Katowice | 1 | 1 |
| wc1993 | 8 Sept | Wembley | 3 | 0 |
| wc1996 | 9 Oct | Wembley | 2 | 0 |
| wc1997 | 31 May | Katowice | 2 | 0 |

| | | v PORTUGAL | E | P |
|---|---|---|---|---|
| 1947 | 25 May | Lisbon | 10 | 0 |
| 1950 | 14 May | Lisbon | 5 | 3 |
| 1951 | 19 May | Everton | 5 | 2 |
| 1955 | 22 May | Oporto | 1 | 3 |
| 1958 | 7 May | Wembley | 2 | 1 |
| wc1961 | 21 May | Lisbon | 1 | 1 |
| wc1961 | 25 Oct | Wembley | 2 | 0 |
| 1964 | 17 May | Lisbon | 4 | 3 |
| 1964 | 4 June | São Paulo | 1 | 1 |
| wc1966 | 26 July | Wembley | 2 | 1 |
| 1969 | 10 Dec | Wembley | 1 | 0 |
| 1974 | 3 Apr | Lisbon | 0 | 0 |
| EC1974 | 20 Nov | Wembley | 0 | 0 |
| EC1975 | 19 Nov | Lisbon | 1 | 1 |
| wc1986 | 3 June | Monterrey | 0 | 1 |
| 1995 | 12 Dec | Wembley | 1 | 1 |
| 1998 | 22 Apr | Wembley | 3 | 0 |

| | | v ROMANIA | E | R |
|---|---|---|---|---|
| 1939 | 24 May | Bucharest | 2 | 0 |
| 1968 | 6 Nov | Bucharest | 0 | 0 |
| 1969 | 15 Jan | Wembley | 1 | 1 |
| wc1970 | 2 June | Guadalajara | 1 | 0 |
| wc1980 | 15 Oct | Bucharest | 1 | 2 |
| wc1981 | 29 April | Wembley | 0 | 0 |
| wc1985 | 1 May | Bucharest | 0 | 0 |
| wc1985 | 11 Sept | Wembley | 1 | 1 |
| 1994 | 12 Oct | Wembley | 1 | 1 |
| wc1998 | 22 June | Toulouse | 1 | 2 |

| | | v SAN MARINO | E | SM |
|---|---|---|---|---|
| wc1992 | 17 Feb | Wembley | 6 | 0 |
| wc1993 | 17 Nov | Bologna | 7 | 1 |

| | | v SAUDI ARABIA | E | SA |
|---|---|---|---|---|
| 1988 | 16 Nov | Riyadh | 1 | 1 |
| 1998 | 23 May | Wembley | 0 | 0 |

| | | v SOUTH AFRICA | E | SA |
|---|---|---|---|---|
| 1997 | 24 May | Old Trafford | 2 | 1 |

| | | v SPAIN | E | S |
|---|---|---|---|---|
| 1929 | 15 May | Madrid | 3 | 4 |
| 1931 | 9 Dec | Highbury | 7 | 1 |
| wc1950 | 2 July | Rio de Janeiro | 0 | 1 |
| 1955 | 18 May | Madrid | 1 | 1 |
| 1955 | 30 Nov | Wembley | 4 | 1 |
| 1960 | 15 May | Madrid | 0 | 3 |
| 1960 | 26 Oct | Wembley | 4 | 2 |
| 1965 | 8 Dec | Madrid | 2 | 0 |
| 1967 | 24 May | Wembley | 2 | 0 |
| EC1968 | 3 Apr | Wembley | 1 | 0 |
| EC1968 | 8 May | Madrid | 2 | 1 |
| 1980 | 26 Mar | Barcelona | 2 | 0 |
| EC1980 | 18 June | Naples | 2 | 1 |
| 1981 | 25 Mar | Wembley | 1 | 2 |
| wc1982 | 5 July | Madrid | 0 | 0 |
| 1987 | 18 Feb | Madrid | 4 | 2 |
| 1992 | 9 Sept | Santander | 0 | 1 |
| EC 1996 | 22 June | Wembley | 0 | 0 |

| | | v SWEDEN | E | S |
|---|---|---|---|---|
| 1923 | 21 May | Stockholm | 4 | 2 |
| 1923 | 24 May | Stockholm | 3 | 1 |
| 1937 | 17 May | Stockholm | 4 | 0 |
| 1947 | 19 Nov | Highbury | 4 | 2 |
| 1949 | 13 May | Stockholm | 1 | 3 |
| 1956 | 16 May | Stockholm | 0 | 0 |
| 1959 | 28 Oct | Wembley | 2 | 3 |
| 1965 | 16 May | Gothenburg | 2 | 1 |
| 1968 | 22 May | Wembley | 3 | 1 |
| 1979 | 10 June | Stockholm | 0 | 0 |
| 1986 | 10 Sept | Stockholm | 0 | 1 |
| wc1988 | 19 Oct | Wembley | 0 | 0 |
| wc1989 | 6 Sept | Stockholm | 0 | 0 |
| EC1992 | 17 June | Stockholm | 1 | 2 |
| UI1995 | 8 June | Leeds | 3 | 3 |

| | | v SWITZERLAND | E | S |
|---|---|---|---|---|
| 1933 | 20 May | Berne | 4 | 0 |
| 1938 | 21 May | Zurich | 1 | 2 |
| 1947 | 18 May | Zurich | 0 | 1 |
| 1948 | 2 Dec | Highbury | 6 | 0 |
| 1952 | 28 May | Zurich | 3 | 0 |
| wc1954 | 20 June | Berne | 2 | 0 |
| 1962 | 9 May | Wembley | 3 | 1 |
| 1963 | 5 June | Basle | 8 | 1 |
| EC1971 | 13 Oct | Basle | 3 | 2 |
| EC1971 | 10 Nov | Wembley | 1 | 1 |
| 1975 | 3 Sept | Basle | 2 | 1 |
| 1977 | 7 Sept | Wembley | 0 | 0 |
| wc1980 | 19 Nov | Wembley | 2 | 1 |
| wc1981 | 30 May | Basle | 1 | 2 |
| 1988 | 28 May | Lausanne | 1 | 0 |
| 1995 | 15 Nov | Wembley | 3 | 1 |
| EC1996 | 8 June | Wembley | 1 | 1 |
| 1998 | 25 Mar | Berne | 1 | 1 |

| v TUNISIA | | | E | T |
|---|---|---|---|---|
| 1990 | 2 June | Tunis | 1 | 1 |
| wc1998 | 15 June | Marseilles | 2 | 0 |

| v TURKEY | | | E | T |
|---|---|---|---|---|
| wc1984 | 14 Nov | Istanbul | 8 | 0 |
| wc1985 | 16 Oct | Wembley | 5 | 0 |
| EC1987 | 29 Apr | Izmir | 0 | 0 |
| EC1987 | 14 Oct | Wembley | 8 | 0 |
| EC1991 | 1 May | Izmir | 1 | 0 |
| EC1991 | 16 Oct | Wembley | 1 | 0 |
| wc1992 | 18 Nov | Wembley | 4 | 0 |
| wc1993 | 31 Mar | Izmir | 2 | 0 |

| v URUGUAY | | | E | U |
|---|---|---|---|---|
| 1953 | 31 May | Montevideo | 1 | 2 |
| wc1954 | 26 June | Basle | 2 | 4 |
| 1964 | 6 May | Wembley | 2 | 1 |
| wc1966 | 11 July | Wembley | 0 | 0 |
| 1969 | 8 June | Montevideo | 2 | 1 |
| 1977 | 15 June | Montevideo | 0 | 0 |
| 1984 | 13 June | Montevideo | 0 | 2 |
| 1990 | 22 May | Wembley | 1 | 2 |
| 1995 | 29 Mar | Wembley | 0 | 0 |

| v USA | | | E | USA |
|---|---|---|---|---|
| wc1950 | 29 June | Belo Horizonte | 0 | 1 |
| 1953 | 8 June | New York | 6 | 3 |
| 1959 | 28 May | Los Angeles | 8 | 1 |
| 1964 | 27 May | New York | 10 | 0 |
| 1985 | 16 June | Los Angeles | 5 | 0 |
| 1993 | 9 June | Foxboro | 0 | 2 |

| | | | E | USA |
|---|---|---|---|---|
| 1994 | 7 Sept | Wembley | 2 | 0 |

| v USSR | | | E | USSR |
|---|---|---|---|---|
| 1958 | 18 May | Moscow | 1 | 1 |
| wc1958 | 8 June | Gothenburg | 2 | 2 |
| wc1958 | 17 June | Gothenburg | 0 | 1 |
| 1958 | 22 Oct | Wembley | 5 | 0 |
| 1967 | 6 Dec | Wembley | 2 | 2 |
| EC1968 | 8 June | Rome | 2 | 0 |
| 1973 | 10 June | Moscow | 2 | 1 |
| 1984 | 2 June | Wembley | 0 | 2 |
| 1986 | 26 Mar | Tbilisi | 1 | 0 |
| EC1988 | 18 June | Frankfurt | 1 | 3 |
| 1991 | 21 May | Wembley | 3 | 1 |

| v YUGOSLAVIA | | | E | Y |
|---|---|---|---|---|
| 1939 | 18 May | Belgrade | 1 | 2 |
| 1950 | 22 Nov | Highbury | 2 | 2 |
| 1954 | 16 May | Belgrade | 0 | 1 |
| 1956 | 28 Nov | Wembley | 3 | 0 |
| 1958 | 11 May | Belgrade | 0 | 5 |
| 1960 | 11 May | Wembley | 3 | 3 |
| 1965 | 9 May | Belgrade | 1 | 1 |
| 1966 | 4 May | Wembley | 2 | 0 |
| EC1968 | 5 June | Florence | 0 | 1 |
| 1972 | 11 Oct | Wembley | 1 | 1 |
| 1974 | 5 June | Belgrade | 2 | 2 |
| EC1986 | 12 Nov | Wembley | 2 | 0 |
| EC1987 | 11 Nov | Belgrade | 4 | 1 |
| 1989 | 13 Dec | Wembley | 2 | 1 |

# SCOTLAND

| v ARGENTINA | | | S | A |
|---|---|---|---|---|
| 1977 | 18 June | Buenos Aires | 1 | 1 |
| 1979 | 2 June | Glasgow | 1 | 3 |
| 1990 | 28 Mar | Glasgow | 1 | 0 |

| v AUSTRALIA | | | S | A |
|---|---|---|---|---|
| wc1985 | 20 Nov | Glasgow | 2 | 0 |
| wc1985 | 4 Dec | Melbourne | 0 | 0 |
| 1996 | 27 Mar | Glasgow | 1 | 0 |

| v AUSTRIA | | | S | A |
|---|---|---|---|---|
| 1931 | 16 May | Vienna | 0 | 5 |
| 1933 | 29 Nov | Glasgow | 2 | 2 |
| 1937 | 9 May | Vienna | 1 | 1 |
| 1950 | 13 Dec | Glasgow | 0 | 1 |
| 1951 | 27 May | Vienna | 0 | 4 |
| wc1954 | 16 June | Zurich | 0 | 1 |
| 1955 | 19 May | Vienna | 4 | 1 |
| 1956 | 2 May | Glasgow | 1 | 1 |
| 1960 | 29 May | Vienna | 1 | 4 |
| 1963 | 8 May | Glasgow | 4 | 1 |
| *(abandoned after 79 mins)* | | | | |
| wc1968 | 6 Nov | Glasgow | 2 | 1 |
| wc1969 | 5 Nov | Vienna | 0 | 2 |
| EC1978 | 20 Sept | Vienna | 2 | 3 |
| EC1979 | 17 Oct | Glasgow | 1 | 1 |
| 1994 | 20 Apr | Vienna | 2 | 1 |
| wc1996 | 31 Aug | Vienna | 0 | 0 |
| wc1997 | 2 Apr | Celtic Park | 2 | 0 |

| v BELARUS | | | S | B |
|---|---|---|---|---|
| wc1997 | 8 June | Minsk | 1 | 0 |
| wc1997 | 7 Sept | Aberdeen | 4 | 1 |

| v BELGIUM | | | S | B |
|---|---|---|---|---|
| 1947 | 18 May | Brussels | 1 | 2 |
| 1948 | 28 Apr | Glasgow | 2 | 0 |
| 1951 | 20 May | Brussels | 5 | 0 |
| EC1971 | 3 Feb | Liège | 0 | 3 |
| EC1971 | 10 Nov | Aberdeen | 1 | 0 |
| 1974 | 2 June | Brussels | 1 | 2 |
| EC1979 | 21 Nov | Brussels | 0 | 2 |
| EC1979 | 19 Dec | Glasgow | 1 | 3 |
| EC1982 | 15 Dec | Brussels | 2 | 3 |
| EC1983 | 12 Oct | Glasgow | 1 | 1 |

| | | | S | B |
|---|---|---|---|---|
| EC1987 | 1 Apr | Brussels | 1 | 4 |
| EC1987 | 14 Oct | Glasgow | 2 | 0 |

| v BRAZIL | | | S | B |
|---|---|---|---|---|
| 1966 | 25 June | Glasgow | 1 | 1 |
| 1972 | 5 July | Rio de Janeiro | 0 | 1 |
| 1973 | 30 June | Glasgow | 0 | 1 |
| wc1974 | 18 June | Frankfurt | 0 | 0 |
| 1977 | 23 June | Rio de Janeiro | 0 | 2 |
| wc1982 | 18 June | Seville | 1 | 4 |
| 1987 | 26 May | Glasgow | 0 | 2 |
| wc1990 | 20 June | Turin | 0 | 1 |
| wc1998 | 10 June | Sant-Denis | 1 | 2 |

| v BULGARIA | | | S | B |
|---|---|---|---|---|
| 1978 | 22 Feb | Glasgow | 2 | 1 |
| EC1986 | 10 Sept | Glasgow | 0 | 0 |
| EC1987 | 11 Nov | Sofia | 1 | 0 |
| EC1990 | 14 Nov | Sofia | 1 | 1 |
| EC1991 | 27 Mar | Glasgow | 1 | 1 |

| v CANADA | | | S | C |
|---|---|---|---|---|
| 1983 | 12 June | Vancouver | 2 | 0 |
| 1983 | 16 June | Edmonton | 3 | 0 |
| 1983 | 20 June | Toronto | 2 | 0 |
| 1992 | 21 May | Toronto | 3 | 1 |

| v CHILE | | | S | C |
|---|---|---|---|---|
| 1977 | 15 June | Santiago | 4 | 2 |
| 1989 | 30 May | Glasgow | 2 | 0 |

| v CIS | | | S | C |
|---|---|---|---|---|
| EC1992 | 18 June | Norrkoping | 3 | 0 |

| v COLOMBIA | | | S | C |
|---|---|---|---|---|
| 1988 | 17 May | Glasgow | 0 | 0 |
| 1996 | 30 May | Miami | 0 | 1 |
| 1998 | 23 May | New York | 2 | 2 |

| v COSTA RICA | | | S | CR |
|---|---|---|---|---|
| wc1990 | 11 June | Genoa | 0 | 1 |

| v CYPRUS | | | S | C |
|---|---|---|---|---|
| wc1968 | 17 Dec | Nicosia | 5 | 0 |
| wc1969 | 11 May | Glasgow | 8 | 0 |
| wc1989 | 8 Feb | Limassol | 3 | 2 |
| wc1989 | 26 Apr | Glasgow | 2 | 1 |

## v CZECHOSLOVAKIA

| | | | S | C |
|---|---|---|---|---|
| 1937 | 22 May | Prague | 3 | 1 |
| 1937 | 8 Dec | Glasgow | 5 | 0 |
| wc1961 | 14 May | Bratislava | 0 | 4 |
| wc1961 | 26 Sept | Glasgow | 3 | 2 |
| wc1961 | 29 Nov | Brussels | 2 | 4* |
| 1972 | 2 July | Porto Alegre | 0 | 0 |
| wc1973 | 26 Sept | Glasgow | 2 | 1 |
| wc1973 | 17 Oct | Prague | 0 | 1 |
| wc1976 | 13 Oct | Prague | 0 | 2 |
| wc1977 | 21 Sept | Glasgow | 3 | 1 |

*After extra time*

## v DENMARK

| | | | S | D |
|---|---|---|---|---|
| 1951 | 12 May | Glasgow | 3 | 1 |
| 1952 | 25 May | Copenhagen | 2 | 1 |
| 1968 | 16 Oct | Copenhagen | 1 | 0 |
| EC1970 | 11 Nov | Glasgow | 1 | 0 |
| EC1971 | 9 June | Copenhagen | 0 | 1 |
| wc1972 | 18 Oct | Copenhagen | 4 | 1 |
| wc1972 | 15 Nov | Glasgow | 2 | 0 |
| EC1975 | 3 Sept | Copenhagen | 1 | 0 |
| EC1975 | 29 Oct | Glasgow | 3 | 1 |
| wc1986 | 4 June | Nezahualcayotl | 0 | 1 |
| 1996 | 24 Apr | Copenhagen | 0 | 2 |
| 1998 | 25 Mar | Glasgow | 0 | 1 |

## v ECUADOR

| | | | S | E |
|---|---|---|---|---|
| 1995 | 24 May | Toyama | 2 | 1 |

## v EGYPT

| | | | S | E |
|---|---|---|---|---|
| 1990 | 16 May | Aberdeen | 1 | 3 |

## v ESTONIA

| | | | S | E |
|---|---|---|---|---|
| wc1993 | 19 May | Tallinn | 3 | 0 |
| wc1993 | 2 June | Aberdeen | 3 | 1 |
| wc1997 | 11 Feb | Monaco | 0 | 0 |
| wc1997 | 29 Mar | Kilmarnock | 2 | 0 |

## v FAEROES

| | | | S | F |
|---|---|---|---|---|
| EC1994 | 12 Oct | Glasgow | 5 | 1 |
| EC1995 | 7 June | Toftir | 2 | 0 |

## v FINLAND

| | | | S | F |
|---|---|---|---|---|
| 1954 | 25 May | Helsinki | 2 | 1 |
| wc1964 | 21 Oct | Glasgow | 3 | 1 |
| wc1965 | 27 May | Helsinki | 2 | 1 |
| 1976 | 8 Sept | Glasgow | 6 | 0 |
| 1992 | 25 Mar | Glasgow | 1 | 1 |
| EC1994 | 7 Sept | Helsinki | 2 | 0 |
| EC1995 | 6 Sept | Glasgow | 1 | 0 |
| 1998 | 22 Apr | Edinburgh | 1 | 1 |

## v FRANCE

| | | | S | F |
|---|---|---|---|---|
| 1930 | 18 May | Paris | 2 | 0 |
| 1932 | 8 May | Paris | 3 | 1 |
| 1948 | 23 May | Paris | 0 | 3 |
| 1949 | 27 Apr | Glasgow | 2 | 0 |
| 1950 | 27 May | Paris | 1 | 0 |
| 1951 | 16 May | Glasgow | 1 | 0 |
| wc1958 | 15 June | Orebro | 1 | 2 |
| 1984 | 1 June | Marseilles | 0 | 2 |
| wc1989 | 8 Mar | Glasgow | 2 | 0 |
| wc1989 | 11 Oct | Paris | 0 | 3 |
| 1997 | 12 Nov | St Etienne | 1 | 2 |

## v GERMANY

| | | | S | G |
|---|---|---|---|---|
| 1929 | 1 June | Berlin | 1 | 1 |
| 1936 | 14 Oct | Glasgow | 2 | 0 |
| EC1992 | 15 June | Norrkoping | 0 | 2 |
| 1993 | 24 Mar | Glasgow | 0 | 1 |

## v EAST GERMANY

| | | | S | EG |
|---|---|---|---|---|
| 1974 | 30 Oct | Glasgow | 3 | 0 |
| 1977 | 7 Sept | East Berlin | 0 | 1 |
| EC1982 | 13 Oct | Glasgow | 2 | 0 |
| EC1983 | 16 Nov | Halle | 1 | 2 |
| 1985 | 16 Oct | Glasgow | 0 | 0 |
| 1990 | 25 Apr | Glasgow | 0 | 1 |

## v WEST GERMANY

| | | | S | WG |
|---|---|---|---|---|
| 1957 | 22 May | Stuttgart | 3 | 1 |
| 1959 | 6 May | Glasgow | 3 | 2 |
| 1964 | 12 May | Hanover | 2 | 2 |
| wc1969 | 16 Apr | Glasgow | 1 | 1 |
| wc1969 | 22 Oct | Hamburg | 2 | 3 |
| 1973 | 14 Nov | Glasgow | 1 | 1 |
| 1974 | 27 Mar | Frankfurt | 1 | 2 |
| wc1986 | 8 June | Queretaro | 1 | 2 |

## v GREECE

| | | | S | G |
|---|---|---|---|---|
| EC1994 | 18 Dec | Athens | 0 | 1 |
| EC1995 | 16 Aug | Glasgow | 1 | 0 |

## v HOLLAND

| | | | S | H |
|---|---|---|---|---|
| 1929 | 4 June | Amsterdam | 2 | 0 |
| 1938 | 21 May | Amsterdam | 3 | 1 |
| 1959 | 27 May | Amsterdam | 2 | 1 |
| 1966 | 11 May | Glasgow | 0 | 3 |
| 1968 | 30 May | Amsterdam | 0 | 0 |
| 1971 | 1 Dec | Rotterdam | 1 | 2 |
| wc1978 | 11 June | Mendoza | 3 | 2 |
| 1982 | 23 Mar | Glasgow | 2 | 1 |
| 1986 | 29 Apr | Eindhoven | 0 | 0 |
| EC1992 | 12 June | Gothenburg | 0 | 1 |
| 1994 | 23 Mar | Glasgow | 0 | 1 |
| 1994 | 27 May | Utrecht | 1 | 3 |
| EC1996 | 10 June | Birmingham | 0 | 0 |

## v HUNGARY

| | | | S | H |
|---|---|---|---|---|
| 1938 | 7 Dec | Glasgow | 3 | 1 |
| 1954 | 8 Dec | Glasgow | 2 | 4 |
| 1955 | 29 May | Budapest | 1 | 3 |
| 1958 | 7 May | Glasgow | 1 | 1 |
| 1960 | 5 June | Budapest | 3 | 3 |
| 1980 | 31 May | Budapest | 1 | 3 |
| 1987 | 9 Sept | Glasgow | 2 | 0 |

## v ICELAND

| | | | S | I |
|---|---|---|---|---|
| wc1984 | 17 Oct | Glasgow | 3 | 0 |
| wc1985 | 28 May | Reykjavik | 1 | 0 |

## v IRAN

| | | | S | I |
|---|---|---|---|---|
| wc1978 | 7 June | Cordoba | 1 | 1 |

## v REPUBLIC OF IRELAND

| | | | S | RI |
|---|---|---|---|---|
| wc1961 | 3 May | Glasgow | 4 | 1 |
| wc1961 | 7 May | Dublin | 3 | 0 |
| 1963 | 9 June | Dublin | 0 | 1 |
| 1969 | 21 Sept | Dublin | 1 | 1 |
| EC1986 | 15 Oct | Dublin | 0 | 0 |
| EC1987 | 18 Feb | Glasgow | 0 | 1 |

## v ISRAEL

| | | | S | I |
|---|---|---|---|---|
| wc1981 | 25 Feb | Tel Aviv | 1 | 0 |
| wc1981 | 28 Apr | Glasgow | 3 | 1 |
| 1986 | 28 Jan | Tel Aviv | 1 | 0 |

## v ITALY

| | | | S | I |
|---|---|---|---|---|
| 1931 | 20 May | Rome | 0 | 3 |
| wc1965 | 9 Nov | Glasgow | 1 | 0 |
| wc1965 | 7 Dec | Naples | 0 | 3 |
| 1988 | 22 Dec | Perugia | 0 | 2 |
| wc1992 | 18 Nov | Glasgow | 0 | 0 |
| wc1993 | 13 Oct | Rome | 1 | 3 |

## v JAPAN

| | | | S | J |
|---|---|---|---|---|
| 1995 | 21 May | Hiroshima | 0 | 0 |

## v LATVIA

| | | | S | L |
|---|---|---|---|---|
| wc1996 | 5 Oct | Riga | 2 | 0 |
| wc1997 | 11 Oct | Glasgow | 2 | 0 |

## v LUXEMBOURG

| | | | S | L |
|---|---|---|---|---|
| 1947 | 24 May | Luxembourg | 6 | 0 |
| EC1986 | 12 Nov | Glasgow | 3 | 0 |
| EC1987 | 2 Dec | Esch | 0 | 0 |

| | | v **MALTA** | S | M |
|---|---|---|---|---|
| 1988 | 22 Mar | Valletta | 1 | 1 |
| 1990 | 28 May | Valletta | 2 | 1 |
| wc1993 | 17 Feb | Glasgow | 3 | 0 |
| wc1993 | 17 Nov | Valletta | 2 | 0 |
| 1997 | 1 June | Valletta | 3 | 2 |

| | | v **MOROCCO** | S | M |
|---|---|---|---|---|
| wc1998 | 23 June | St Etienne | 0 | 3 |

| | | v **NEW ZEALAND** | S | NZ |
|---|---|---|---|---|
| wc1982 | 15 June | Malaga | 5 | 2 |

| | | v **NORWAY** | S | N |
|---|---|---|---|---|
| 1929 | 28 May | Oslo | 7 | 3 |
| 1954 | 5 May | Glasgow | 1 | 0 |
| 1954 | 19 May | Oslo | 1 | 1 |
| 1963 | 4 June | Bergen | 3 | 4 |
| 1963 | 7 Nov | Glasgow | 6 | 1 |
| 1974 | 6 June | Oslo | 2 | 1 |
| EC1978 | 25 Oct | Glasgow | 3 | 2 |
| EC1979 | 7 June | Oslo | 4 | 0 |
| wc1988 | 14 Sept | Oslo | 2 | 1 |
| wc1989 | 15 Nov | Glasgow | 1 | 1 |
| 1992 | 3 June | Oslo | 0 | 0 |
| wc1998 | 16 June | Bordeaux | 1 | 1 |

| | | v **PARAGUAY** | S | P |
|---|---|---|---|---|
| wc1958 | 11 June | Norrkoping | 2 | 3 |

| | | v **PERU** | S | P |
|---|---|---|---|---|
| 1972 | 26 Apr | Glasgow | 2 | 0 |
| wc1978 | 3 June | Cordoba | 1 | 3 |
| 1979 | 12 Sept | Glasgow | 1 | 1 |

| | | v **POLAND** | S | P |
|---|---|---|---|---|
| 1958 | 1 June | Warsaw | 2 | 1 |
| 1960 | 4 June | Glasgow | 2 | 3 |
| wc1965 | 23 May | Chorzow | 1 | 1 |
| wc1965 | 13 Oct | Glasgow | 1 | 2 |
| 1980 | 28 May | Poznan | 0 | 1 |
| 1990 | 19 May | Glasgow | 1 | 1 |

| | | v **PORTUGAL** | S | P |
|---|---|---|---|---|
| 1950 | 21 May | Lisbon | 2 | 2 |
| 1955 | 4 May | Glasgow | 3 | 0 |
| 1959 | 3 June | Lisbon | 0 | 1 |
| 1966 | 18 June | Glasgow | 0 | 1 |
| EC1971 | 21 Apr | Lisbon | 0 | 2 |
| EC1971 | 13 Oct | Glasgow | 2 | 1 |
| 1975 | 13 May | Glasgow | 1 | 0 |
| EC1978 | 29 Nov | Lisbon | 0 | 1 |
| EC1980 | 26 Mar | Glasgow | 4 | 1 |
| wc1980 | 15 Oct | Glasgow | 0 | 0 |
| wc1981 | 18 Nov | Lisbon | 1 | 2 |
| wc1992 | 14 Oct | Glasgow | 0 | 0 |
| wc1993 | 28 Apr | Lisbon | 0 | 5 |

| | | v **ROMANIA** | S | R |
|---|---|---|---|---|
| EC1975 | 1 June | Bucharest | 1 | 1 |
| EC1975 | 17 Dec | Glasgow | 1 | 1 |
| 1986 | 26 Mar | Glasgow | 3 | 0 |
| EC1990 | 12 Sept | Glasgow | 2 | 1 |
| EC1991 | 16 Oct | Bucharest | 0 | 1 |

| | | v **RUSSIA** | S | R |
|---|---|---|---|---|
| EC1994 | 16 Nov | Glasgow | 1 | 1 |
| EC1995 | 29 Mar | Moscow | 0 | 0 |

| | | v **SAN MARINO** | S | SM |
|---|---|---|---|---|
| EC1991 | 1 May | Serravalle | 2 | 0 |
| EC1991 | 13 Nov | Glasgow | 4 | 0 |
| EC1995 | 26 Apr | Serravalle | 2 | 0 |
| EC1995 | 15 Nov | Glasgow | 5 | 0 |

| | | v **SAUDI ARABIA** | S | SA |
|---|---|---|---|---|
| 1988 | 17 Feb | Riyadh | 2 | 2 |

| | | v **SPAIN** | S | Sp |
|---|---|---|---|---|
| wc1957 | 8 May | Glasgow | 4 | 2 |
| wc1957 | 26 May | Madrid | 1 | 4 |
| 1963 | 13 June | Madrid | 6 | 2 |
| 1965 | 8 May | Glasgow | 0 | 0 |
| EC1974 | 20 Nov | Glasgow | 1 | 2 |
| EC1975 | 5 Feb | Valencia | 1 | 1 |
| 1982 | 24 Feb | Valencia | 0 | 3 |
| wc1984 | 14 Nov | Glasgow | 3 | 1 |
| wc1985 | 27 Feb | Seville | 0 | 1 |
| 1988 | 27 Apr | Madrid | 0 | 0 |

| | | v **SWEDEN** | S | Sw |
|---|---|---|---|---|
| 1952 | 30 May | Stockholm | 1 | 3 |
| 1953 | 6 May | Glasgow | 1 | 2 |
| 1975 | 16 Apr | Gothenburg | 1 | 1 |
| 1977 | 27 Apr | Glasgow | 3 | 1 |
| wc1980 | 10 Sept | Stockholm | 1 | 0 |
| wc1981 | 9 Sept | Glasgow | 2 | 0 |
| wc1990 | 16 June | Genoa | 2 | 1 |
| 1995 | 11 Oct | Stockholm | 0 | 2 |
| wc1996 | 10 Nov | Glasgow | 1 | 0 |
| wc1997 | 30 Apr | Gothenburg | 1 | 2 |

| | | v **SWITZERLAND** | S | Sw |
|---|---|---|---|---|
| 1931 | 24 May | Geneva | 3 | 2 |
| 1948 | 17 May | Berne | 1 | 2 |
| 1950 | 26 Apr | Glasgow | 3 | 1 |
| wc1957 | 19 May | Basle | 2 | 1 |
| wc1957 | 6 Nov | Glasgow | 3 | 2 |
| 1973 | 22 June | Berne | 0 | 1 |
| 1976 | 7 Apr | Glasgow | 1 | 0 |
| EC1982 | 17 Nov | Berne | 0 | 2 |
| EC1983 | 30 May | Glasgow | 2 | 2 |
| EC1990 | 17 Oct | Glasgow | 2 | 1 |
| EC1991 | 11 Sept | Berne | 2 | 2 |
| wc1992 | 9 Sept | Berne | 1 | 3 |
| wc1993 | 8 Sept | Aberdeen | 1 | 1 |
| EC1996 | 18 June | Birmingham | 1 | 0 |

| | | v **TURKEY** | S | T |
|---|---|---|---|---|
| 1960 | 8 June | Ankara | 2 | 4 |

| | | v **URUGUAY** | S | U |
|---|---|---|---|---|
| wc1954 | 19 June | Basle | 0 | 7 |
| 1962 | 2 May | Glasgow | 2 | 3 |
| 1983 | 21 Sept | Glasgow | 2 | 0 |
| wc1986 | 13 June | Nezahualcoyotl | 0 | 0 |

| | | v **USA** | S | USA |
|---|---|---|---|---|
| 1952 | 30 Apr | Glasgow | 6 | 0 |
| 1992 | 17 May | Denver | 1 | 0 |
| 1996 | 26 May | New Britain | 1 | 2 |
| 1998 | 30 May | Washington | 0 | 0 |

| | | v **USSR** | S | USSR |
|---|---|---|---|---|
| 1967 | 10 May | Glasgow | 0 | 2 |
| 1971 | 14 June | Moscow | 0 | 1 |
| wc1982 | 22 June | Malaga | 2 | 2 |
| 1991 | 6 Feb | Glasgow | 0 | 1 |

| | | v **YUGOSLAVIA** | S | Y |
|---|---|---|---|---|
| 1955 | 15 May | Belgrade | 2 | 2 |
| 1956 | 21 Nov | Glasgow | 2 | 0 |
| wc1958 | 8 June | Vasteras | 1 | 1 |
| 1972 | 29 June | Belo Horizonte | 2 | 2 |
| wc1974 | 22 June | Frankfurt | 1 | 1 |
| 1984 | 12 Sept | Glasgow | 6 | 1 |
| wc1988 | 19 Oct | Glasgow | 1 | 1 |
| wc1989 | 6 Sept | Zagreb | 1 | 3 |

| | | v **ZAIRE** | S | Z |
|---|---|---|---|---|
| wc1974 | 14 June | Dortmund | 2 | 0 |

# WALES

| v ALBANIA | | W | A |
|---|---|---|---|
| EC1994 | 7 Sept Cardiff | 2 | 0 |
| EC1995 | 15 Nov Tirana | 1 | 1 |

| v ARGENTINA | | W | A |
|---|---|---|---|
| 1992 | 3 June Tokyo | 0 | 1 |

| v AUSTRIA | | W | A |
|---|---|---|---|
| 1954 | 9 May Vienna | 0 | 2 |
| EC1955 | 23 Nov Wrexham | 1 | 2 |
| EC1974 | 4 Sept Vienna | 1 | 2 |
| 1975 | 19 Nov Wrexham | 1 | 0 |
| 1992 | 29 Apr Vienna | 1 | 1 |

| v BELGIUM | | W | B |
|---|---|---|---|
| 1949 | 22 May Liège | 1 | 3 |
| 1949 | 23 Nov Cardiff | 5 | 1 |
| EC1990 | 17 Oct Cardiff | 3 | 1 |
| EC1991 | 27 Mar Brussels | 1 | 1 |
| wc1992 | 18 Nov Brussels | 0 | 2 |
| wc1993 | 31 Mar Cardiff | 2 | 0 |
| wc1997 | 29 Mar Cardiff | 1 | 2 |
| wc1997 | 11 Oct Brussels | 2 | 3 |

| v BRAZIL | | W | B |
|---|---|---|---|
| wc1958 | 19 June Gothenburg | 0 | 1 |
| 1962 | 12 May Rio de Janeiro | 1 | 3 |
| 1962 | 16 May São Paulo | 1 | 3 |
| 1966 | 14 May Rio de Janeiro | 1 | 3 |
| 1966 | 18 May Belo Horizonte | 0 | 1 |
| 1983 | 12 June Cardiff | 1 | 1 |
| 1991 | 11 Sept Cardiff | 1 | 0 |
| 1997 | 12 Nov Brasilia | 0 | 3 |

| v BULGARIA | | W | B |
|---|---|---|---|
| EC1983 | 27 Apr Wrexham | 1 | 0 |
| EC1983 | 16 Nov Sofia | 0 | 1 |
| EC1994 | 14 Dec Cardiff | 0 | 3 |
| EC1995 | 29 Mar Sofia | 1 | 3 |

| v CANADA | | W | C |
|---|---|---|---|
| 1986 | 10 May Toronto | 0 | 2 |
| 1986 | 20 May Vancouver | 3 | 0 |

| v CHILE | | W | C |
|---|---|---|---|
| 1966 | 22 May Santiago | 0 | 2 |

| v COSTA RICA | | W | CR |
|---|---|---|---|
| 1990 | 20 May Cardiff | 1 | 0 |

| v CYPRUS | | W | C |
|---|---|---|---|
| wc1992 | 14 Oct Limassol | 1 | 0 |
| wc1993 | 13 Oct Cardiff | 2 | 0 |

| v CZECHOSLOVAKIA | | W | C |
|---|---|---|---|
| wc1957 | 1 May Cardiff | 1 | 0 |
| wc1957 | 26 May Prague | 0 | 2 |
| EC1971 | 21 Apr Swansea | 1 | 3 |
| EC1971 | 27 Oct Prague | 0 | 1 |
| wc1977 | 30 Mar Wrexham | 3 | 0 |
| wc1977 | 16 Nov Prague | 0 | 1 |
| wc1980 | 19 Nov Cardiff | 1 | 0 |
| wc1981 | 9 Sept Prague | 0 | 2 |
| EC1987 | 29 Apr Wrexham | 1 | 1 |
| EC1987 | 11 Nov Prague | 0 | 2 |
| wc1993 | 28 Apr Ostrava† | 1 | 1 |
| wc1993 | 8 Sept Cardiff† | 2 | 2 |

†Czechoslovakia played as RCS (Republic of Czechs and Slovaks).

| v DENMARK | | W | D |
|---|---|---|---|
| wc1964 | 21 Oct Copenhagen | 0 | 1 |
| wc1965 | 1 Dec Wrexham | 4 | 2 |
| EC1987 | 9 Sept Cardiff | 1 | 0 |
| EC1987 | 14 Oct Copenhagen | 0 | 1 |
| 1990 | 11 Sept Copenhagen | 0 | 1 |

| v ESTONIA | | W | E |
|---|---|---|---|
| 1994 | 23 May Tallinn | 2 | 1 |

| v FINLAND | | W | F |
|---|---|---|---|
| EC1971 | 26 May Helsinki | 1 | 0 |
| EC1971 | 13 Oct Swansea | 3 | 0 |
| EC1987 | 10 Sept Helsinki | 1 | 1 |
| EC1987 | 1 Apr Wrexham | 4 | 0 |
| wc1988 | 19 Oct Swansea | 2 | 2 |
| wc1989 | 6 Sept Helsinki | 0 | 1 |

| v FAEROES | | W | F |
|---|---|---|---|
| wc1992 | 9 Sept Cardiff | 6 | 0 |
| wc1993 | 6 June Toftir | 3 | 0 |

| v FRANCE | | W | F |
|---|---|---|---|
| 1933 | 25 May Paris | 1 | 1 |
| 1939 | 20 May Paris | 1 | 2 |
| 1953 | 14 May Paris | 1 | 6 |
| 1982 | 2 June Toulouse | 1 | 0 |

| v GEORGIA | | W | G |
|---|---|---|---|
| EC1994 | 16 Nov Tbilisi | 0 | 5 |
| EC1995 | 7 June Cardiff | 0 | 1 |

| v GERMANY | | W | G |
|---|---|---|---|
| EC1995 | 26 Apr Dusseldorf | 1 | 1 |
| EC1995 | 11 Oct Cardiff | 1 | 2 |

| v EAST GERMANY | | W | EG |
|---|---|---|---|
| wc1957 | 19 May Leipzig | 1 | 2 |
| wc1957 | 25 Sept Cardiff | 4 | 1 |
| wc1969 | 16 Apr Dresden | 1 | 2 |
| wc1969 | 22 Oct Cardiff | 1 | 3 |

| v WEST GERMANY | | W | WG |
|---|---|---|---|
| 1968 | 8 May Cardiff | 1 | 1 |
| 1969 | 26 Mar Frankfurt | 1 | 1 |
| 1976 | 6 Oct Cardiff | 0 | 2 |
| 1977 | 14 Dec Dortmund | 1 | 1 |
| EC1979 | 2 May Wrexham | 0 | 2 |
| EC1979 | 17 Oct Cologne | 1 | 5 |
| wc1989 | 31 May Cardiff | 0 | 0 |
| wc1989 | 15 Nov Cologne | 1 | 2 |
| EC1991 | 5 June Cardiff | 1 | 0 |
| EC1991 | 16 Oct Nuremberg | 1 | 4 |

| v GREECE | | W | G |
|---|---|---|---|
| wc1964 | 9 Dec Athens | 0 | 2 |
| wc1965 | 17 Mar Cardiff | 4 | 1 |

| v HOLLAND | | W | H |
|---|---|---|---|
| wc1988 | 14 Sept Amsterdam | 0 | 1 |
| wc1989 | 11 Oct Wrexham | 1 | 2 |
| 1992 | 30 May Utrecht | 0 | 4 |
| wc1996 | 5 Oct Cardiff | 1 | 3 |
| wc1996 | 9 Nov Eindhoven | 1 | 7 |

| v HUNGARY | | W | H |
|---|---|---|---|
| wc1958 | 8 June Sanviken | 1 | 1 |
| wc1958 | 17 June Stockholm | 2 | 1 |
| 1961 | 28 May Budapest | 2 | 3 |
| EC1962 | 7 Nov Budapest | 1 | 3 |
| EC1963 | 20 Mar Cardiff | 1 | 1 |
| EC1974 | 30 Oct Cardiff | 2 | 0 |
| EC1975 | 16 Apr Budapest | 2 | 1 |
| 1985 | 16 Oct Cardiff | 0 | 3 |

| v ICELAND | | W | I |
|---|---|---|---|
| wc1980 | 2 June Reykjavik | 4 | 0 |
| wc1981 | 14 Oct Swansea | 2 | 2 |
| wc1984 | 12 Sept Reykjavik | 0 | 1 |
| wc1984 | 14 Nov Cardiff | 2 | 1 |
| 1991 | 1 May Cardiff | 1 | 0 |

| | | v IRAN | W | I |
|---|---|---|---|---|
| 1978 | 18 Apr | Teheran | 1 | 0 |

| | | v REPUBLIC OF IRELAND | W | RI |
|---|---|---|---|---|
| 1960 | 28 Sept | Dublin | 3 | 2 |
| 1979 | 11 Sept | Swansea | 2 | 1 |
| 1981 | 24 Feb | Dublin | 3 | 1 |
| 1986 | 26 Mar | Dublin | 1 | 0 |
| 1990 | 28 Mar | Dublin | 0 | 1 |
| 1991 | 6 Feb | Wrexham | 0 | 3 |
| 1992 | 19 Feb | Dublin | 1 | 0 |
| 1993 | 17 Feb | Dublin | 1 | 2 |
| 1997 | 11 Feb | Cardiff | 0 | 0 |

| | | v ISRAEL | W | I |
|---|---|---|---|---|
| wc1958 | 15 Jan | Tel Aviv | 2 | 0 |
| wc1958 | 5 Feb | Cardiff | 2 | 0 |
| 1984 | 10 June | Tel Aviv | 0 | 0 |
| 1989 | 8 Feb | Tel Aviv | 3 | 3 |

| | | v ITALY | W | I |
|---|---|---|---|---|
| 1965 | 1 May | Florence | 1 | 4 |
| wc1968 | 23 Oct | Cardiff | 0 | 1 |
| wc1969 | 4 Nov | Rome | 1 | 4 |
| 1988 | 4 June | Brescia | 1 | 0 |
| 1996 | 24 Jan | Terni | 0 | 3 |

| | | v JAMAICA | W | J |
|---|---|---|---|---|
| 1998 | 25 Mar | Cardiff | 0 | 0 |

| | | v JAPAN | W | J |
|---|---|---|---|---|
| 1992 | 7 June | Matsuyama | 1 | 0 |

| | | v KUWAIT | W | K |
|---|---|---|---|---|
| 1977 | 6 Sept | Wrexham | 0 | 0 |
| 1977 | 20 Sept | Kuwait | 0 | 0 |

| | | v LUXEMBOURG | W | L |
|---|---|---|---|---|
| EC1974 | 20 Nov | Swansea | 5 | 0 |
| EC1975 | 1 May | Luxembourg | 3 | 1 |
| EC1990 | 14 Nov | Luxembourg | 1 | 0 |
| EC1991 | 13 Nov | Cardiff | 1 | 0 |

| | | v MALTA | W | M |
|---|---|---|---|---|
| EC1978 | 25 Oct | Wrexham | 7 | 0 |
| EC1979 | 2 June | Valletta | 2 | 0 |
| 1988 | 1 June | Valletta | 3 | 2 |
| 1998 | 3 June | Valletta | 3 | 0 |

| | | v MEXICO | W | M |
|---|---|---|---|---|
| wc1958 | 11 June | Stockholm | 1 | 1 |
| 1962 | 22 May | Mexico City | 1 | 2 |

| | | v MOLDOVA | W | M |
|---|---|---|---|---|
| EC1994 | 12 Oct | Kishinev | 2 | 3 |
| EC1995 | 6 Sept | Cardiff | 1 | 0 |

| | | v NORWAY | W | N |
|---|---|---|---|---|
| EC1982 | 22 Sept | Swansea | 1 | 0 |
| EC1983 | 21 Sept | Oslo | 0 | 0 |
| 1984 | 6 June | Trondheim | 0 | 1 |
| 1985 | 26 Feb | Wrexham | 1 | 1 |
| 1985 | 5 June | Bergen | 2 | 4 |
| 1994 | 9 Mar | Cardiff | 1 | 3 |

| | | v POLAND | W | P |
|---|---|---|---|---|
| wc1973 | 28 Mar | Cardiff | 2 | 0 |
| wc1973 | 26 Sept | Katowice | 0 | 3 |
| 1991 | 29 May | Radom | 0 | 0 |

| | | v PORTUGAL | W | P |
|---|---|---|---|---|
| 1949 | 15 May | Lisbon | 2 | 3 |
| 1951 | 12 May | Cardiff | 2 | 1 |

| | | v ROMANIA | W | R |
|---|---|---|---|---|
| EC1970 | 11 Nov | Cardiff | 0 | 0 |
| EC1971 | 24 Nov | Bucharest | 0 | 2 |
| 1983 | 12 Oct | Wrexham | 5 | 0 |
| wc1992 | 20 May | Bucharest | 1 | 5 |
| wc1993 | 17 Nov | Cardiff | 1 | 2 |

| | | v SAN MARINO | W | SM |
|---|---|---|---|---|
| wc1996 | 2 June | Serravalle | 5 | 0 |
| wc1996 | 31 Aug | Cardiff | 6 | 0 |

| | | v SAUDI ARABIA | W | SA |
|---|---|---|---|---|
| 1986 | 25 Feb | Dahran | 2 | 1 |

| | | v SPAIN | W | S |
|---|---|---|---|---|
| wc1961 | 19 Apr | Cardiff | 1 | 2 |
| wc1961 | 18 May | Madrid | 1 | 1 |
| 1982 | 24 Mar | Valencia | 1 | 1 |
| wc1984 | 17 Oct | Seville | 0 | 3 |
| wc1985 | 30 Apr | Wrexham | 3 | 0 |

| | | v SWEDEN | W | S |
|---|---|---|---|---|
| wc1958 | 15 June | Stockholm | 0 | 0 |
| 1988 | 27 Apr | Stockholm | 1 | 4 |
| 1989 | 26 Apr | Wrexham | 0 | 2 |
| 1990 | 25 Apr | Stockholm | 2 | 4 |
| 1994 | 20 Apr | Wrexham | 0 | 2 |

| | | v SWITZERLAND | W | S |
|---|---|---|---|---|
| 1949 | 26 May | Berne | 0 | 4 |
| 1951 | 16 May | Wrexham | 3 | 2 |
| 1996 | 24 Apr | Lugano | 0 | 2 |

| | | v TUNISIA | W | T |
|---|---|---|---|---|
| 1998 | 6 June | Tunis | 0 | 4 |

| | | v TURKEY | W | T |
|---|---|---|---|---|
| EC1978 | 29 Nov | Wrexham | 1 | 0 |
| EC1979 | 21 Nov | Izmir | 0 | 1 |
| wc1980 | 15 Oct | Cardiff | 4 | 0 |
| wc1981 | 25 Mar | Ankara | 1 | 0 |
| wc1996 | 14 Dec | Cardiff | 0 | 0 |
| wc1997 | 20 Aug | Istanbul | 4 | 6 |

| | | v REST OF UNITED KINGDOM | | |
|---|---|---|---|---|
| | | | W | UK |
| 1951 | 5 Dec | Cardiff | 3 | 2 |
| 1969 | 28 July | Cardiff | 0 | 1 |

| | | v URUGUAY | W | U |
|---|---|---|---|---|
| 1986 | 21 Apr | Wrexham | 0 | 0 |

| | | v USSR | W | USSR |
|---|---|---|---|---|
| wc1965 | 30 May | Moscow | 1 | 2 |
| wc1965 | 27 Oct | Cardiff | 2 | 1 |
| wc1981 | 30 May | Wrexham | 0 | 0 |
| wc1981 | 18 Nov | Tbilisi | 0 | 3 |
| 1987 | 18 Feb | Swansea | 0 | 0 |

| | | v YUGOSLAVIA | W | Y |
|---|---|---|---|---|
| 1953 | 21 May | Belgrade | 2 | 5 |
| 1954 | 22 Nov | Cardiff | 1 | 3 |
| EC1976 | 24 Apr | Zagreb | 0 | 2 |
| EC1976 | 22 May | Cardiff | 1 | 1 |
| EC1982 | 15 Dec | Titograd | 4 | 4 |
| EC1983 | 14 Dec | Cardiff | 1 | 1 |
| 1988 | 23 Mar | Swansea | 1 | 2 |

# NORTHERN IRELAND

| v ALBANIA | | NI | A |
|---|---|---|---|
| wc1965 | 7 May | Belfast | 4 | 1 |
| wc1965 | 24 Nov | Tirana | 1 | 1 |
| EC1982 | 15 Dec | Tirana | 0 | 0 |
| EC1983 | 27 Apr | Belfast | 1 | 0 |
| wc1992 | 9 Sept | Belfast | 3 | 0 |
| wc1993 | 17 Feb | Tirana | 2 | 1 |
| wc1996 | 14 Dec | Belfast | 2 | 0 |
| wc1997 | 10 Sept | Zurich | 0 | 1 |

| v ALGERIA | | | NI | A |
|---|---|---|---|---|
| wc1986 | 3 June | Guadalajara | 1 | 1 |

| v ARGENTINA | | | NI | A |
|---|---|---|---|---|
| wc1958 | 11 June | Halmstad | 1 | 3 |

| v ARMENIA | | | NI | A |
|---|---|---|---|---|
| wc1996 | 5 Oct | Belfast | 1 | 1 |
| wc1996 | 30 Apr | Erevan | 0 | 0 |

| v AUSTRALIA | | | NI | A |
|---|---|---|---|---|
| 1980 | 11 June | Sydney | 2 | 1 |
| 1980 | 15 June | Melbourne | 1 | 1 |
| 1980 | 18 June | Adelaide | 2 | 1 |

| v AUSTRIA | | | NI | A |
|---|---|---|---|---|
| wc1982 | 1 July | Madrid | 2 | 2 |
| EC1982 | 13 Oct | Vienna | 0 | 2 |
| EC1983 | 21 Sept | Belfast | 3 | 1 |
| EC1990 | 14 Nov | Vienna | 0 | 0 |
| EC1991 | 16 Oct | Belfast | 2 | 1 |
| EC1994 | 12 Oct | Vienna | 2 | 1 |
| EC1995 | 15 Nov | Belfast | 5 | 3 |

| v BELGIUM | | | NI | B |
|---|---|---|---|---|
| wc1976 | 10 Nov | Liège | 0 | 2 |
| wc1977 | 16 Nov | Belfast | 3 | 0 |
| 1997 | 11 Feb | Belfast | 3 | 0 |

| v BRAZIL | | | NI | B |
|---|---|---|---|---|
| wc1986 | 12 June | Guadalajara | 0 | 3 |

| v BULGARIA | | | NI | B |
|---|---|---|---|---|
| wc1972 | 18 Oct | Sofia | 0 | 3 |
| wc1973 | 26 Sept | Sheffield | 0 | 0 |
| EC1978 | 29 Nov | Sofia | 2 | 0 |
| EC1979 | 2 May | Belfast | 2 | 0 |

| v CANADA | | | NI | C |
|---|---|---|---|---|
| 1995 | 22 May | Edmonton | 0 | 2 |

| v CHILE | | | NI | C |
|---|---|---|---|---|
| 1989 | 26 May | Belfast | 0 | 1 |
| 1995 | 25 May | Edmonton | 1 | 2 |

| v COLOMBIA | | | NI | C |
|---|---|---|---|---|
| 1994 | 4 June | Boston | 0 | 2 |

| v CYPRUS | | | NI | C |
|---|---|---|---|---|
| EC1971 | 3 Feb | Nicosia | 3 | 0 |
| EC1971 | 21 Apr | Belfast | 5 | 0 |
| wc1973 | 14 Feb | Nicosia | 0 | 1 |
| wc1973 | 8 May | London | 3 | 0 |

| v CZECHOSLOVAKIA | | | NI | C |
|---|---|---|---|---|
| wc1958 | 8 June | Halmstad | 1 | 0 |
| wc1958 | 17 June | Malmo | 2 | 1* |

*After extra time

| v DENMARK | | | NI | D |
|---|---|---|---|---|
| EC1978 | 25 Oct | Belfast | 2 | 1 |
| EC1979 | 6 June | Copenhagen | 0 | 4 |
| 1986 | 26 Mar | Belfast | 1 | 1 |
| EC1990 | 17 Oct | Belfast | 1 | 1 |
| EC1991 | 13 Nov | Odense | 1 | 2 |
| wc1992 | 18 Nov | Belfast | 0 | 1 |
| wc1993 | 13 Oct | Copenhagen | 0 | 1 |

| v FAEROES | | | NI | F |
|---|---|---|---|---|
| EC1991 | 1 May | Belfast | 1 | 1 |
| EC1991 | 11 Sept | Landskrona | 5 | 0 |

| v FINLAND | | | NI | F |
|---|---|---|---|---|
| wc1984 | 27 May | Pori | 0 | 1 |
| wc1984 | 14 Nov | Belfast | 2 | 1 |

| v FRANCE | | | NI | F |
|---|---|---|---|---|
| 1951 | 12 May | Belfast | 2 | 2 |
| 1952 | 11 Nov | Paris | 1 | 3 |
| wc1958 | 19 June | Norrkoping | 0 | 4 |
| 1982 | 24 Mar | Paris | 0 | 4 |
| wc1982 | 4 July | Madrid | 1 | 4 |
| 1986 | 26 Feb | Paris | 0 | 0 |
| 1988 | 27 Apr | Belfast | 0 | 0 |

| v GERMANY | | | NI | G |
|---|---|---|---|---|
| 1992 | 2 June | Bremen | 1 | 1 |
| 1996 | 29 May | Belfast | 1 | 1 |
| wc1996 | 9 Nov | Nuremberg | 1 | 1 |
| wc1997 | 20 Aug | Belfast | 1 | 3 |

| v WEST GERMANY | | | NI | WG |
|---|---|---|---|---|
| wc1958 | 15 June | Malmo | 2 | 2 |
| wc1960 | 26 Oct | Belfast | 3 | 4 |
| wc1961 | 10 May | Hamburg | 1 | 2 |
| 1966 | 7 May | Belfast | 0 | 2 |
| 1977 | 27 Apr | Cologne | 0 | 5 |
| EC1982 | 17 Nov | Belfast | 1 | 0 |
| EC1983 | 16 Nov | Hamburg | 1 | 0 |

| v GREECE | | | NI | G |
|---|---|---|---|---|
| wc1961 | 3 May | Athens | 1 | 2 |
| wc1961 | 17 Oct | Belfast | 2 | 0 |
| 1988 | 17 Feb | Athens | 2 | 3 |

| v HOLLAND | | | NI | H |
|---|---|---|---|---|
| 1962 | 9 May | Rotterdam | 0 | 4 |
| wc1965 | 17 Mar | Belfast | 2 | 1 |
| wc1965 | 7 Apr | Rotterdam | 0 | 0 |
| wc1976 | 13 Oct | Rotterdam | 2 | 2 |
| wc1977 | 12 Oct | Belfast | 0 | 1 |

| v HONDURAS | | | NI | H |
|---|---|---|---|---|
| wc1982 | 21 June | Zaragoza | 1 | 1 |

| v HUNGARY | | | NI | H |
|---|---|---|---|---|
| wc1988 | 19 Oct | Budapest | 0 | 1 |
| wc1989 | 6 Sept | Belfast | 1 | 2 |

| v ICELAND | | | NI | I |
|---|---|---|---|---|
| wc1977 | 11 June | Reykjavik | 0 | 1 |
| wc1977 | 21 Sept | Belfast | 2 | 0 |

| v REPUBLIC OF IRELAND | | | NI | RI |
|---|---|---|---|---|
| EC1978 | 20 Sept | Dublin | 0 | 0 |
| EC1979 | 21 Nov | Belfast | 1 | 0 |
| wc1988 | 14 Sept | Belfast | 0 | 0 |
| wc1989 | 11 Oct | Dublin | 0 | 3 |
| wc1993 | 31 Mar | Dublin | 0 | 3 |
| wc1993 | 17 Nov | Belfast | 1 | 1 |
| EC1994 | 16 Nov | Belfast | 0 | 4 |
| EC1995 | 29 Mar | Dublin | 1 | 1 |

| v ISRAEL | | | NI | I |
|---|---|---|---|---|
| 1968 | 10 Sept | Jaffa | 3 | 2 |
| 1976 | 3 Mar | Tel Aviv | 1 | 1 |
| wc1980 | 26 Mar | Tel Aviv | 0 | 0 |
| wc1981 | 18 Nov | Belfast | 1 | 0 |
| 1984 | 16 Oct | Belfast | 3 | 0 |
| 1987 | 18 Feb | Tel Aviv | 1 | 1 |

| | | v ITALY | NI | I |
|---|---|---|---|---|
| wc1957 | 25 Apr | Rome | 0 | 1 |
| 1957 | 4 Dec | Belfast | 2 | 2 |
| wc1958 | 15 Jan | Belfast | 2 | 1 |
| 1961 | 25 Apr | Bologna | 2 | 3 |
| 1997 | 22 Jan | Palermo | 0 | 2 |

| | | v LATVIA | NI | L |
|---|---|---|---|---|
| wc1993 | 2 June | Riga | 2 | 1 |
| wc1993 | 8 Sept | Belfast | 2 | 0 |
| EC1995 | 26 Apr | Riga | 1 | 0 |
| EC1995 | 7 June | Belfast | 1 | 2 |

| | | v LIECHTENSTEIN | NI | L |
|---|---|---|---|---|
| EC1994 | 20 Apr | Belfast | 4 | 1 |
| EC1995 | 11 Oct | Eschen | 4 | 0 |

| | | v LITHUANIA | NI | L |
|---|---|---|---|---|
| wc1992 | 28 Apr | Belfast | 2 | 2 |
| wc1993 | 25 May | Vilnius | 1 | 0 |

| | | v MALTA | NI | M |
|---|---|---|---|---|
| wc1988 | 21 May | Belfast | 3 | 0 |
| wc1989 | 26 Apr | Valletta | 2 | 0 |

| | | v MEXICO | NI | M |
|---|---|---|---|---|
| 1966 | 22 June | Belfast | 4 | 1 |
| 1994 | 11 June | Miami | 0 | 3 |

| | | v MOROCCO | NI | M |
|---|---|---|---|---|
| 1986 | 23 Apr | Belfast | 2 | 1 |

| | | v NORWAY | NI | N |
|---|---|---|---|---|
| EC1974 | 4 Sept | Oslo | 1 | 2 |
| EC1975 | 29 Oct | Belfast | 3 | 0 |
| 1990 | 27 Mar | Belfast | 2 | 3 |
| 1996 | 27 Mar | Belfast | 0 | 2 |

| | | v POLAND | NI | P |
|---|---|---|---|---|
| EC1962 | 10 Oct | Katowice | 2 | 0 |
| EC1962 | 28 Nov | Belfast | 2 | 0 |
| 1988 | 23 Mar | Belfast | 1 | 1 |
| 1991 | 5 Feb | Belfast | 3 | 1 |
| EC1995 | 3 Sept | Lisbon | 1 | 1 |
| wc1997 | 29 Mar | Belfast | 0 | 0 |

| | | v PORTUGAL | NI | P |
|---|---|---|---|---|
| wc1957 | 16 Jan | Lisbon | 1 | 1 |
| wc1957 | 1 May | Belfast | 3 | 0 |
| wc1973 | 28 Mar | Coventry | 1 | 1 |
| wc1973 | 14 Nov | Lisbon | 1 | 1 |
| wc1980 | 19 Nov | Lisbon | 0 | 1 |
| wc1981 | 29 Apr | Belfast | 1 | 0 |
| EC1994 | 7 Sept | Belfast | 1 | 2 |
| EC1995 | 3 Sept | Lisbon | 1 | 1 |
| wc1997 | 29 Mar | Belfast | 0 | 0 |
| wc1997 | 11 Oct | Lisbon | 0 | 1 |

| | | v ROMANIA | NI | R |
|---|---|---|---|---|
| wc1984 | 12 Sept | Belfast | 3 | 2 |
| wc1985 | 16 Oct | Bucharest | 1 | 0 |
| 1994 | 23 Mar | Belfast | 2 | 0 |

| | | v SLOVAKIA | NI | S |
|---|---|---|---|---|
| 1998 | 25 Mar | Belfast | 1 | 0 |

| | | v SPAIN | NI | S |
|---|---|---|---|---|
| 1958 | 15 Oct | Madrid | 2 | 6 |
| 1963 | 30 May | Bilbao | 1 | 1 |
| 1963 | 30 Oct | Belfast | 0 | 1 |
| EC1970 | 11 Nov | Seville | 0 | 3 |
| EC1972 | 16 Feb | Hull | 1 | 1 |
| wc1982 | 25 June | Valencia | 1 | 0 |
| 1985 | 27 Mar | Palma | 0 | 0 |
| wc1986 | 7 June | Guadalajara | 1 | 2 |
| wc1988 | 21 Dec | Seville | 0 | 4 |
| wc1989 | 8 Feb | Belfast | 0 | 2 |
| wc1992 | 14 Oct | Belfast | 0 | 0 |
| wc1993 | 28 Apr | Seville | 1 | 3 |
| 1998 | 2 June | Santander | 1 | 4 |

| | | v SWEDEN | NI | S |
|---|---|---|---|---|
| EC1974 | 30 Oct | Solna | 2 | 0 |
| EC1975 | 3 Sept | Belfast | 1 | 2 |
| wc1980 | 15 Oct | Belfast | 3 | 0 |
| wc1981 | 3 June | Solna | 0 | 1 |
| 1996 | 24 Apr | Belfast | 1 | 2 |

| | | v SWITZERLAND | NI | S |
|---|---|---|---|---|
| wc1964 | 14 Oct | Belfast | 1 | 0 |
| wc1964 | 14 Nov | Lausanne | 1 | 2 |
| 1998 | 22 Apr | Belfast | 1 | 0 |

| | | v THAILAND | NI | T |
|---|---|---|---|---|
| 1997 | 21 May | Bangkok | 0 | 0 |

| | | v TURKEY | NI | T |
|---|---|---|---|---|
| wc1968 | 23 Oct | Belfast | 4 | 1 |
| wc1968 | 11 Dec | Istanbul | 3 | 0 |
| EC1983 | 30 Mar | Belfast | 2 | 1 |
| EC1983 | 12 Oct | Ankara | 0 | 1 |
| wc1985 | 1 May | Belfast | 2 | 0 |
| wc1985 | 11 Sept | Izmir | 0 | 0 |
| EC1986 | 12 Nov | Izmir | 0 | 0 |
| EC1987 | 11 Nov | Belfast | 1 | 0 |

| | | v UKRAINE | NI | U |
|---|---|---|---|---|
| wc1996 | 31 Aug | Belfast | 0 | 1 |
| wc1997 | 2 Apr | Kiev | 1 | 2 |

| | | v URUGUAY | NI | U |
|---|---|---|---|---|
| 1964 | 29 Apr | Belfast | 3 | 0 |
| 1990 | 18 May | Belfast | 1 | 0 |

| | | v USSR | NI | USSR |
|---|---|---|---|---|
| wc1969 | 19 Sept | Belfast | 0 | 0 |
| wc1969 | 22 Oct | Moscow | 0 | 2 |
| EC1971 | 22 Sept | Moscow | 0 | 1 |
| EC1971 | 13 Oct | Belfast | 1 | 1 |

| | | v YUGOSLAVIA | NI | Y |
|---|---|---|---|---|
| EC1975 | 16 Mar | Belfast | 1 | 0 |
| EC1975 | 19 Nov | Belgrade | 0 | 1 |
| wc1982 | 17 June | Zaragoza | 0 | 0 |
| EC1987 | 29 Apr | Belfast | 1 | 2 |
| EC1987 | 14 Oct | Sarajevo | 0 | 3 |
| EC1990 | 12 Sept | Belfast | 0 | 2 |
| EC1991 | 27 Mar | Belgrade | 1 | 4 |

## REPUBLIC OF IRELAND

| | | v ALBANIA | RI | A |
|---|---|---|---|---|
| wc1992 | 26 May | Dublin | 2 | 0 |
| wc1993 | 26 May | Tirana | 2 | 1 |

| | | v ALGERIA | RI | A |
|---|---|---|---|---|
| 1982 | 28 Apr | Algiers | 0 | 2 |

| | | v ARGENTINA | RI | A |
|---|---|---|---|---|
| 1951 | 13 May | Dublin | 0 | 1 |
| 1979 | 29 May | Dublin | 0 | 0* |
| 1980 | 16 May | Dublin | 0 | 1 |
| 1998 | 22 Apr | Dublin | 0 | 2 |

\* Not considered a full international

| | | v AUSTRIA | RI | A |
|---|---|---|---|---|
| 1952 | 7 May | Vienna | 0 | 6 |
| 1953 | 25 Mar | Dublin | 4 | 0 |
| 1958 | 14 Mar | Vienna | 1 | 3 |
| 1962 | 8 Apr | Dublin | 2 | 3 |
| EC1963 | 25 Sept | Vienna | 0 | 0 |
| EC1963 | 13 Oct | Dublin | 3 | 2 |
| 1966 | 22 May | Vienna | 0 | 1 |
| 1968 | 10 Nov | Dublin | 2 | 2 |
| EC1971 | 30 May | Dublin | 1 | 4 |
| EC1971 | 10 Oct | Linz | 0 | 6 |
| EC1995 | 11 June | Dublin | 1 | 3 |
| EC1995 | 6 Sept | Vienna | 1 | 3 |

### v BELGIUM

| | | | RI | B |
|---|---|---|---|---|
| 1928 | 12 Feb | Liège | 4 | 2 |
| 1929 | 30 Apr | Dublin | 4 | 0 |
| 1930 | 11 May | Brussels | 3 | 1 |
| wc1934 | 25 Feb | Dublin | 4 | 4 |
| 1949 | 24 Apr | Dublin | 0 | 2 |
| 1950 | 10 May | Brussels | 1 | 5 |
| 1965 | 24 Mar | Dublin | 0 | 2 |
| 1966 | 25 May | Liège | 3 | 2 |
| wc1980 | 15 Oct | Dublin | 1 | 1 |
| wc1981 | 25 Mar | Brussels | 0 | 1 |
| EC1986 | 10 Sept | Brussels | 2 | 2 |
| EC1987 | 29 Apr | Dublin | 0 | 0 |
| wc1997 | 29 Oct | Dublin | 1 | 1 |
| wc1997 | 16 Nov | Brussels | 1 | 2 |

### v BOLIVIA

| | | | RI | B |
|---|---|---|---|---|
| 1994 | 24 May | Dublin | 1 | 0 |
| 1996 | 15 June | New Jersey | 3 | 0 |

### v BRAZIL

| | | | RI | B |
|---|---|---|---|---|
| 1974 | 5 May | Rio de Janeiro | 1 | 2 |
| 1982 | 27 May | Uberlandia | 0 | 7 |
| 1987 | 23 May | Dublin | 1 | 0 |

### v BULGARIA

| | | | RI | B |
|---|---|---|---|---|
| wc1977 | 1 June | Sofia | 1 | 2 |
| wc1977 | 12 Oct | Dublin | 0 | 0 |
| EC1979 | 19 May | Sofia | 0 | 1 |
| EC1979 | 17 Oct | Dublin | 3 | 0 |
| wc1987 | 1 Apr | Sofia | 1 | 2 |
| wc1987 | 14 Oct | Dublin | 2 | 0 |

### v CHILE

| | | | RI | C |
|---|---|---|---|---|
| 1960 | 30 Mar | Dublin | 2 | 0 |
| 1972 | 21 June | Recife | 1 | 2 |
| 1974 | 12 May | Santiago | 2 | 1 |
| 1982 | 22 May | Santiago | 0 | 1 |
| 1991 | 22 May | Dublin | 1 | 1 |

### v CHINA

| | | | RI | C |
|---|---|---|---|---|
| 1984 | 3 June | Sapporo | 1 | 0 |

### v CROATIA

| | | | RI | C |
|---|---|---|---|---|
| 1996 | 2 June | Dublin | 2 | 2 |

### v CYPRUS

| | | | RI | C |
|---|---|---|---|---|
| wc1980 | 26 Mar | Nicosia | 3 | 2 |
| wc1980 | 19 Nov | Dublin | 6 | 0 |

### v CZECHOSLOVAKIA

| | | | RI | C |
|---|---|---|---|---|
| 1938 | 18 May | Prague | 2 | 2 |
| EC1959 | 5 Apr | Dublin | 2 | 0 |
| EC1959 | 10 May | Bratislava | 0 | 4 |
| wc1961 | 8 Oct | Dublin | 1 | 3 |
| wc1961 | 29 Oct | Prague | 1 | 7 |
| EC1967 | 21 May | Dublin | 0 | 2 |
| EC1967 | 22 Nov | Prague | 2 | 1 |
| wc1969 | 4 May | Dublin | 1 | 2 |
| wc1969 | 7 Oct | Prague | 0 | 3 |
| 1979 | 26 Sept | Prague | 1 | 4 |
| 1981 | 29 Apr | Dublin | 3 | 1 |
| 1986 | 27 May | Reykjavik | 1 | 0 |

### v CZECH REPUBLIC

| | | | RI | C |
|---|---|---|---|---|
| 1994 | 5 June | Dublin | 1 | 3 |
| 1996 | 24 Apr | Prague | 0 | 2 |
| 1998 | 25 Mar | Olomouc | 1 | 2 |

### v DENMARK

| | | | RI | D |
|---|---|---|---|---|
| wc1956 | 3 Oct | Dublin | 2 | 1 |
| wc1957 | 2 Oct | Copenhagen | 2 | 0 |
| wc1968 | 4 Dec | Dublin | 1 | 1 |
| *(abandoned after 51 mins)* | | | | |
| wc1969 | 27 May | Copenhagen | 0 | 2 |

| | | | RI | D |
|---|---|---|---|---|
| wc1969 | 15 Oct | Dublin | 1 | 1 |
| EC1978 | 24 May | Copenhagen | 3 | 3 |
| EC1979 | 2 May | Dublin | 2 | 0 |
| wc1984 | 14 Nov | Copenhagen | 0 | 3 |
| wc1985 | 13 Nov | Dublin | 1 | 4 |
| wc1992 | 14 Oct | Copenhagen | 0 | 0 |
| wc1993 | 28 Apr | Dublin | 1 | 1 |

### v ECUADOR

| | | | RI | E |
|---|---|---|---|---|
| 1972 | 19 June | Natal | 3 | 2 |

### v EGYPT

| | | | RI | E |
|---|---|---|---|---|
| wc1990 | 17 June | Palermo | 0 | 0 |

### v ENGLAND

| | | | RI | E |
|---|---|---|---|---|
| 1946 | 30 Sept | Dublin | 0 | 1 |
| 1949 | 21 Sept | Everton | 2 | 0 |
| wc1957 | 8 May | Wembley | 1 | 5 |
| wc1957 | 19 May | Dublin | 1 | 1 |
| 1964 | 24 May | Dublin | 1 | 3 |
| 1976 | 8 Sept | Wembley | 1 | 1 |
| EC1978 | 25 Oct | Dublin | 1 | 1 |
| EC1980 | 6 Feb | Wembley | 0 | 2 |
| 1985 | 26 Mar | Wembley | 1 | 2 |
| EC1988 | 12 June | Stuttgart | 1 | 0 |
| wc1990 | 11 June | Cagliari | 1 | 1 |
| EC1990 | 14 Nov | Dublin | 1 | 1 |
| EC1991 | 27 Mar | Wembley | 1 | 1 |
| 1995 | 15 Feb | Dublin | 1 | 0 |
| *(abandoned after 27 mins)* | | | | |

### v FINLAND

| | | | RI | F |
|---|---|---|---|---|
| wc1949 | 8 Sept | Dublin | 3 | 0 |
| wc1949 | 9 Oct | Helsinki | 1 | 1 |
| 1990 | 16 May | Dublin | 1 | 1 |

### v FRANCE

| | | | RI | F |
|---|---|---|---|---|
| 1937 | 23 May | Paris | 2 | 0 |
| 1952 | 16 Nov | Dublin | 1 | 1 |
| wc1953 | 4 Oct | Dublin | 3 | 5 |
| wc1953 | 25 Nov | Paris | 0 | 1 |
| wc1972 | 15 Nov | Dublin | 2 | 1 |
| wc1973 | 19 May | Paris | 1 | 1 |
| wc1976 | 17 Nov | Paris | 0 | 2 |
| wc1977 | 30 Mar | Dublin | 1 | 0 |
| wc1980 | 28 Oct | Paris | 0 | 2 |
| wc1981 | 14 Oct | Dublin | 3 | 2 |
| 1989 | 7 Feb | Dublin | 0 | 0 |

### v GERMANY

| | | | RI | G |
|---|---|---|---|---|
| 1935 | 8 May | Dortmund | 1 | 3 |
| 1936 | 17 Oct | Dublin | 5 | 2 |
| 1939 | 23 May | Bremen | 1 | 1 |
| 1994 | 29 May | Hanover | 2 | 0 |

### v WEST GERMANY

| | | | RI | WG |
|---|---|---|---|---|
| 1951 | 17 Oct | Dublin | 3 | 2 |
| 1952 | 4 May | Cologne | 0 | 3 |
| 1955 | 28 May | Hamburg | 1 | 2 |
| 1956 | 25 Nov | Dublin | 3 | 0 |
| 1960 | 11 May | Dusseldorf | 1 | 0 |
| 1966 | 4 May | Dublin | 0 | 4 |
| 1970 | 9 May | Berlin | 1 | 2 |
| 1975 | 1 Mar | Dublin | 1 | 0† |
| 1979 | 22 May | Dublin | 1 | 3 |
| 1981 | 21 May | Bremen | 0 | 3† |
| 1989 | 6 Sept | Dublin | 1 | 1 |

†v West Germany 'B'

### v HOLLAND

| | | | RI | N |
|---|---|---|---|---|
| 1932 | 8 May | Amsterdam | 2 | 0 |
| 1934 | 8 Apr | Amsterdam | 2 | 5 |

| | | | RI | H |
|---|---|---|---|---|
| 1935 | 8 Dec | Dublin | 3 | 5 |
| 1955 | 1 May | Dublin | 1 | 0 |
| 1956 | 10 May | Rotterdam | 4 | 1 |
| wc1980 | 10 Sept | Dublin | 2 | 1 |
| wc1981 | 9 Sept | Rotterdam | 2 | 2 |
| EC1982 | 22 Sept | Rotterdam | 1 | 2 |
| EC1983 | 12 Oct | Dublin | 2 | 3 |
| EC1988 | 18 June | Gelsenkirchen | 0 | 1 |
| wc1990 | 21 June | Palermo | 1 | 1 |
| 1994 | 20 Apr | Tilburg | 1 | 0 |
| wc1994 | 4 July | Orlando | 0 | 2 |
| EC1995 | 13 Dec | Liverpool | 0 | 2 |
| 1996 | 4 June | Rotterdam | 1 | 3 |

| | | **v HUNGARY** | RI | H |
|---|---|---|---|---|
| 1934 | 15 Dec | Dublin | 2 | 4 |
| 1936 | 3 May | Budapest | 3 | 3 |
| 1936 | 6 Dec | Dublin | 2 | 3 |
| 1939 | 19 Mar | Cork | 2 | 2 |
| 1939 | 18 May | Budapest | 2 | 2 |
| wc1969 | 8 June | Dublin | 1 | 2 |
| wc1969 | 5 Nov | Budapest | 0 | 4 |
| wc1989 | 8 Mar | Budapest | 0 | 0 |
| wc1989 | 4 June | Dublin | 2 | 0 |
| 1991 | 11 Sept | Gyor | 2 | 1 |

| | | **v ICELAND** | RI | I |
|---|---|---|---|---|
| EC1962 | 12 Aug | Dublin | 4 | 2 |
| EC1962 | 2 Sept | Reykjavik | 1 | 1 |
| EC1982 | 13 Oct | Dublin | 2 | 0 |
| EC1983 | 21 Sept | Reykjavik | 3 | 0 |
| 1986 | 25 May | Reykjavik | 2 | 1 |
| wc1996 | 10 Nov | Dublin | 0 | 0 |
| wc1997 | 6 Sept | Reykjavik | 4 | 2 |

| | | **v IRAN** | RI | I |
|---|---|---|---|---|
| 1972 | 18 June | Recife | 2 | 1 |

| | | **v N. IRELAND** | RI | NI |
|---|---|---|---|---|
| EC1978 | 20 Sept | Dublin | 0 | 0 |
| EC1979 | 21 Nov | Belfast | 0 | 1 |
| wc1988 | 14 Sept | Belfast | 0 | 0 |
| wc1989 | 11 Oct | Dublin | 3 | 0 |
| wc1993 | 31 Mar | Dublin | 3 | 0 |
| wc1993 | 17 Nov | Belfast | 1 | 1 |
| EC1994 | 16 Nov | Belfast | 4 | 0 |
| EC1995 | 29 Mar | Dublin | 1 | 1 |

| | | **v ISRAEL** | RI | I |
|---|---|---|---|---|
| 1984 | 4 Apr | Tel Aviv | 0 | 3 |
| 1985 | 27 May | Tel Aviv | 0 | 0 |
| 1987 | 10 Nov | Dublin | 5 | 0 |

| | | **v ITALY** | RI | I |
|---|---|---|---|---|
| 1926 | 21 Mar | Turin | 0 | 3 |
| 1927 | 23 Apr | Dublin | 1 | 2 |
| EC1970 | 8 Dec | Rome | 0 | 3 |
| EC1971 | 10 May | Dublin | 1 | 2 |
| 1985 | 5 Feb | Dublin | 1 | 2 |
| wc1990 | 30 June | Rome | 0 | 1 |
| 1992 | 4 June | Foxboro | 0 | 2 |
| wc1994 | 18 June | New York | 1 | 0 |

| | | **v LATVIA** | RI | L |
|---|---|---|---|---|
| wc1992 | 9 Sept | Dublin | 4 | 0 |
| wc1993 | 2 June | Riga | 2 | 1 |
| EC1994 | 7 Sept | Riga | 3 | 0 |
| EC1995 | 11 Oct | Dublin | 2 | 1 |

| | | **v LIECHTENSTEIN** | RI | L |
|---|---|---|---|---|
| EC1994 | 12 Oct | Dublin | 4 | 0 |
| EC1995 | 3 June | Eschen | 0 | 0 |
| wc1996 | 31 Aug | Eschen | 5 | 0 |
| wc1997 | 21 May | Dublin | 5 | 0 |

| | | **v LITHUANIA** | RI | L |
|---|---|---|---|---|
| wc1993 | 16 June | Vilnius | 1 | 0 |
| wc1993 | 8 Sept | Dublin | 2 | 0 |
| wc1997 | 20 Aug | Dublin | 0 | 0 |
| wc1997 | 10 Sept | Vilnius | 2 | 1 |

| | | **v LUXEMBOURG** | RI | I |
|---|---|---|---|---|
| 1936 | 9 May | Luxembourg | 5 | 1 |
| wc1953 | 28 Oct | Dublin | 4 | 0 |
| wc1954 | 7 Mar | Luxembourg | 1 | 0 |
| EC1987 | 28 May | Luxembourg | 2 | 0 |
| EC1987 | 9 Sept | Dublin | 2 | 1 |

| | | **v MACEDONIA** | RI | M |
|---|---|---|---|---|
| wc1996 | 9 Oct | Dublin | 3 | 0 |
| wc1997 | 2 Apr | Skopje | 2 | 3 |

| | | **v MALTA** | RI | M |
|---|---|---|---|---|
| EC1983 | 30 Mar | Valletta | 1 | 0 |
| EC1983 | 16 Nov | Dublin | 8 | 0 |
| wc1989 | 28 May | Dublin | 2 | 0 |
| wc1989 | 15 Nov | Valletta | 2 | 0 |
| 1990 | 2 June | Valletta | 3 | 0 |

| | | **v MEXICO** | RI | M |
|---|---|---|---|---|
| 1984 | 8 Aug | Dublin | 0 | 0 |
| wc1994 | 24 June | Orlando | 1 | 2 |
| 1996 | 13 June | New Jersey | 2 | 2 |
| 1998 | 23 May | Dublin | 0 | 0 |

| | | **v MOROCCO** | RI | M |
|---|---|---|---|---|
| 1990 | 12 Sept | Dublin | 1 | 0 |

| | | **v NORWAY** | RI | N |
|---|---|---|---|---|
| wc1937 | 10 Oct | Oslo | 2 | 3 |
| wc1937 | 7 Nov | Dublin | 3 | 3 |
| 1950 | 26 Nov | Dublin | 2 | 2 |
| 1951 | 30 May | Oslo | 3 | 2 |
| 1954 | 8 Nov | Dublin | 2 | 1 |
| 1955 | 25 May | Oslo | 3 | 1 |
| 1960 | 6 Nov | Dublin | 3 | 1 |
| 1964 | 13 May | Oslo | 4 | 1 |
| 1973 | 6 June | Oslo | 1 | 1 |
| 1976 | 24 May | Dublin | 3 | 0 |
| 1978 | 21 May | Oslo | 0 | 0 |
| wc1984 | 17 Oct | Oslo | 0 | 1 |
| wc1985 | 1 May | Dublin | 0 | 0 |
| 1988 | 1 June | Oslo | 0 | 0 |
| wc1994 | 28 June | New York | 0 | 0 |

| | | **v POLAND** | RI | P |
|---|---|---|---|---|
| 1938 | 22 May | Warsaw | 0 | 6 |
| 1938 | 13 Nov | Dublin | 3 | 2 |
| 1958 | 11 May | Katowice | 2 | 2 |
| 1958 | 5 Oct | Dublin | 2 | 2 |
| 1964 | 10 May | Kracow | 1 | 3 |
| 1964 | 25 Oct | Dublin | 3 | 2 |
| 1968 | 15 May | Dublin | 2 | 2 |
| 1968 | 30 Oct | Katowice | 0 | 1 |
| 1970 | 6 May | Dublin | 1 | 2 |
| 1970 | 23 Sept | Dublin | 0 | 2 |
| 1973 | 16 May | Wroclaw | 0 | 2 |
| 1973 | 21 Oct | Dublin | 1 | 0 |
| 1976 | 26 May | Poznan | 2 | 0 |
| 1977 | 24 Apr | Dublin | 0 | 0 |
| 1978 | 12 Apr | Lodz | 0 | 3 |
| 1981 | 23 May | Bydgoszcz | 0 | 3 |
| 1984 | 23 May | Dublin | 0 | 0 |
| 1986 | 12 Nov | Warsaw | 0 | 1 |
| 1988 | 22 May | Dublin | 3 | 1 |
| EC1991 | 1 May | Dublin | 0 | 0 |
| EC1991 | 16 Oct | Poznan | 3 | 3 |

### v PORTUGAL

| | | | RI | P |
|---|---|---|---|---|
| 1946 | 16 June | Lisbon | 1 | 3 |
| 1947 | 4 May | Dublin | 0 | 2 |
| 1948 | 23 May | Lisbon | 0 | 2 |
| 1949 | 22 May | Dublin | 1 | 0 |
| 1972 | 25 June | Recife | 1 | 2 |
| 1992 | 7 June | Boston | 2 | 0 |
| EC1995 | 26 Apr | Dublin | 1 | 0 |
| EC1995 | 15 Nov | Lisbon | 0 | 3 |
| 1996 | 29 May | Dublin | 0 | 1 |

### v ROMANIA

| | | | RI | R |
|---|---|---|---|---|
| 1988 | 23 Mar | Dublin | 2 | 0 |
| WC1990 | 25 June | Genoa | 0 | 0* |
| WC1997 | 30 Apr | Bucharest | 0 | 1 |
| WC1997 | 11 Oct | Dublin | 1 | 1 |

*After extra time

### v RUSSIA

| | | | RI | R |
|---|---|---|---|---|
| 1994 | 23 Mar | Dublin | 0 | 0 |
| 1996 | 27 Mar | Dublin | 0 | 2 |

### v SCOTLAND

| | | | RI | S |
|---|---|---|---|---|
| WC1961 | 3 May | Glasgow | 1 | 4 |
| WC1961 | 7 May | Dublin | 0 | 3 |
| 1963 | 9 June | Dublin | 1 | 0 |
| 1969 | 21 Sept | Dublin | 1 | 1 |
| EC1986 | 15 Oct | Dublin | 0 | 0 |
| EC1987 | 18 Feb | Glasgow | 1 | 0 |

### v SPAIN

| | | | RI | S |
|---|---|---|---|---|
| 1931 | 26 Apr | Barcelona | 1 | 1 |
| 1931 | 13 Dec | Dublin | 0 | 5 |
| 1946 | 23 June | Madrid | 1 | 0 |
| 1947 | 2 Mar | Dublin | 3 | 2 |
| 1948 | 30 May | Barcelona | 1 | 2 |
| 1949 | 12 June | Dublin | 1 | 4 |
| 1952 | 1 June | Madrid | 0 | 6 |
| 1955 | 27 Nov | Dublin | 2 | 2 |
| EC1964 | 11 Mar | Seville | 1 | 5 |
| EC1964 | 8 Apr | Dublin | 0 | 2 |
| WC1965 | 5 May | Dublin | 1 | 0 |
| WC1965 | 27 Oct | Seville | 1 | 4 |
| WC1965 | 10 Nov | Paris | 0 | 1 |
| EC1966 | 23 Oct | Dublin | 0 | 0 |
| EC1966 | 7 Dec | Valencia | 0 | 2 |
| 1977 | 9 Feb | Dublin | 0 | 1 |
| EC1982 | 17 Nov | Dublin | 3 | 3 |
| EC1983 | 27 Apr | Zaragoza | 0 | 2 |
| 1985 | 26 May | Cork | 0 | 0 |
| WC1988 | 16 Nov | Seville | 0 | 2 |
| WC1989 | 26 Apr | Dublin | 1 | 0 |
| WC1992 | 18 Nov | Seville | 0 | 0 |
| WC1993 | 13 Oct | Dublin | 1 | 3 |

### v SWEDEN

| | | | RI | S |
|---|---|---|---|---|
| WC1949 | 2 June | Stockholm | 1 | 3 |
| WC1949 | 13 Nov | Dublin | 1 | 3 |
| 1959 | 1 Nov | Dublin | 3 | 2 |
| 1960 | 18 May | Malmo | 1 | 4 |
| EC1970 | 14 Oct | Dublin | 1 | 1 |
| EC1970 | 28 Oct | Malmo | 0 | 1 |

### v SWITZERLAND

| | | | RI | S |
|---|---|---|---|---|
| 1935 | 5 May | Basle | 0 | 1 |
| 1936 | 17 Mar | Dublin | 1 | 0 |
| 1937 | 17 May | Berne | 1 | 0 |
| 1938 | 18 Sept | Dublin | 4 | 0 |
| 1948 | 5 Dec | Dublin | 0 | 1 |
| EC1975 | 11 May | Dublin | 2 | 1 |
| EC1975 | 21 May | Berne | 0 | 1 |
| 1980 | 30 Apr | Dublin | 2 | 0 |
| WC1985 | 2 June | Dublin | 3 | 0 |
| WC1985 | 11 Sept | Berne | 0 | 0 |
| 1992 | 25 Mar | Dublin | 2 | 1 |

### v TRINIDAD & TOBAGO

| | | | RI | TT |
|---|---|---|---|---|
| 1982 | 30 May | Port of Spain | 1 | 2 |

### v TUNISIA

| | | | RI | T |
|---|---|---|---|---|
| 1988 | 19 Oct | Dublin | 4 | 0 |

### v TURKEY

| | | | RI | T |
|---|---|---|---|---|
| EC1966 | 16 Nov | Dublin | 2 | 1 |
| EC1967 | 22 Feb | Ankara | 1 | 2 |
| EC1974 | 20 Nov | Izmir | 1 | 1 |
| EC1975 | 29 Oct | Dublin | 4 | 0 |
| 1976 | 13 Oct | Ankara | 3 | 3 |
| 1978 | 5 Apr | Dublin | 4 | 2 |
| 1990 | 26 May | Izmir | 0 | 0 |
| EC1990 | 17 Oct | Dublin | 5 | 0 |
| EC1991 | 13 Nov | Istanbul | 3 | 1 |

### v URUGUAY

| | | | RI | U |
|---|---|---|---|---|
| 1974 | 8 May | Montevideo | 0 | 2 |
| 1986 | 23 Apr | Dublin | 1 | 1 |

### v USA

| | | | RI | USA |
|---|---|---|---|---|
| 1979 | 29 Oct | Dublin | 3 | 2 |
| 1991 | 1 June | Boston | 1 | 1 |
| 1992 | 29 Apr | Dublin | 4 | 1 |
| 1992 | 30 May | Washington | 1 | 3 |
| 1996 | 9 June | Boston | 1 | 2 |

### v USSR

| | | | RI | USSR |
|---|---|---|---|---|
| WC1972 | 18 Oct | Dublin | 1 | 2 |
| WC1973 | 13 May | Moscow | 0 | 1 |
| EC1974 | 30 Oct | Dublin | 3 | 0 |
| EC1975 | 18 May | Kiev | 1 | 2 |
| WC1984 | 12 Sept | Dublin | 1 | 0 |
| WC1985 | 16 Oct | Moscow | 0 | 2 |
| EC1988 | 15 June | Hanover | 1 | 1 |
| 1990 | 25 Apr | Dublin | 1 | 0 |

### v WALES

| | | | RI | W |
|---|---|---|---|---|
| 1960 | 28 Sept | Dublin | 2 | 3 |
| 1979 | 11 Sept | Swansea | 1 | 2 |
| 1981 | 24 Feb | Dublin | 1 | 3 |
| 1986 | 26 Mar | Dublin | 0 | 1 |
| 1990 | 28 Mar | Dublin | 1 | 0 |
| 1991 | 6 Feb | Wrexham | 3 | 0 |
| 1992 | 19 Feb | Dublin | 0 | 1 |
| 1993 | 17 Feb | Dublin | 2 | 1 |
| 1997 | 11 Feb | Cardiff | 0 | 0 |

### v YUGOSLAVIA

| | | | RI | Y |
|---|---|---|---|---|
| 1955 | 19 Sept | Dublin | 1 | 4 |
| 1988 | 27 Apr | Dublin | 2 | 0 |

# OTHER BRITISH AND IRISH INTERNATIONAL MATCHES 1997–98

## FRIENDLIES

**Wembley, 15 November 1997, 46,176**
**England (2) 2** *(Fowler 44, Scholes 45)*
**Cameroon (0) 0**
*England:* Martyn; Southgate (Ferdinand R 38), Hinchcliffe, Ince, Campbell, Neville P, Beckham, Gascoigne (Lee 72), Fowler, Scholes (Sutton 79), McManaman.
*Cameroon:* Ongandzi; Kalla, Song, Mimboe, Etchi, Ipoua, Foe, Etame (Olembe 72), Wome Nlend, Mboma (Njitap 76), Job.
*Referee:* Hauge (Norway).

**Wembley, 11 February 1998, 65,228**
**England (0) 0**
**Chile (1) 2** *(Salas 45, 79 (pen))*
*England:* Martyn; Neville G, Neville P (Le Saux 46), Batty (Ince 63), Adams, Campbell, Lee, Butt, Dublin, Sheringham (Shearer 63), Owen.
*Chile:* Tapia; Rojas, Villaroel, Fuentes, Margas, Reyes, Acuna, Parraguez, Salas, Barrera (Carreno 77), Sierra (Valenzuela 88).
*Referee:* Wojcik (Poland).

**Olomouc, 25 March 1998, 9405**
**Czech Republic (0) 2** *(Smicer 48, Lascta 75)*
**Republic of Ireland (1) 1** *(Breen 9)*
*Czech Republic:* Postulka; Latal, Kozei, Rada, Novotny, Cizek (Lascta 70), Nemec, Poborsky, Kuka (Lakvenc 59), Smicer (Fukal 88), Bejbl.
*Republic of Ireland:* Given; Maybury (Keane 46), Kenna, Carsley (Kavanagh 84) Cunningham, Breen, Kinsella, Farrelly (McLoughlin 60), Connolly (Kilbane 60), Kelly ?, Duff (Delap 72).
*Referee:* Juhos (Slovakia).

**Belfast, 25 March 1998, 7895**
**Northern Ireland (0) 1** *(Lomas 51)*
**Slovakia (0) 0**
*Northern Ireland:* Fettis; Jenkins, Hughes, Lomas, Morrow, Hill, Gillespie (McCarthy 90), Lennon, Quinn (O'Boyle 83), Dowie, Hughes.
*Slovakia:* Vencel; Zeman, Tittel, Timko (Zitak 80), Slovak (Balis 68), Dubovsky, Spilar, Moravcik (Sovic 68), Kinder, Pinte (Nemeth 46), Majoros.
*Referee:* Howells (Wales).

**Ibrox, 25 March 1998, 26,468**
**Scotland (0) 0**
**Denmark (1) 1** *(Laudrup B 37)*
*Scotland:* Leighton (Goram 46); McNamara (Weir 60), Boyd, Elliott, Hendry, Dailly, McKinlay W, Calderwood, Jackson (Donnelly 75), Booth (Jess 46), Gemmill (McCall 69).
*Denmark:* Krogh; Rieper, Laursen (Henriksen 46), Schjonberg, Helveg, Weghorst, Nielsen (Frandsen 62), Heintze, Laudrup M, Laudrup B (Goldbaek 80), Moller (Jorgensen 73).
*Referee:* Gallagher (England).

**Berne, 25 March 1998, 17,100**
**Switzerland (1) 1** *(Vega 37)*
**England (0) 1** *(Merson 70)*
*Switzerland:* Corminboeuf; Vega, Yakin, Henchoz, Vogel, Wicky (Lonfat 82), Sforza, Fournier, Sesa (Kunz 87), Grassi, Chapuisat.
*England:* Flowers; Lee, Hinchcliffe, Keown, Ferdinand R, Southgate, McManaman, Ince, Shearer, Merson (Batty 80), Owen (Sheringham 69).
*Referee:* Garibian (France).

**Ninian Park, 25 March 1998, 13,349**
**Wales (0) 0**
**Jamaica (0) 0**
*Wales:* Jones; Jenkins, Barnard, Adrian Williams, Coleman, Pembridge, Savage, Oster, Taylor (Bellamy 58), Hartson (Haworth 77), Speed (Trollope 46).
*Jamaica:* Lawrence (Barrett 46); Dixon, Dawes, Goodison, Cargill, Malcolm (Sewell 71), Earle (Williams 59), Simpson (Powell 67), Gardner, Hall (Lowe 76), Burton (Gayle 46).
*Referee:* Dougal (Scotland).

**Wembley, 22 April 1998, 63,463**
**England (1) 3** *(Shearer 5, 65, Sheringham 46)*
**Portugal (0) 0**
*England:* Seaman; Neville G (Neville P 81), Le Saux, Ince, Adams, Campbell, Beckham (Merson 46), Batty, Shearer, Sheringham (Owen 73), Scholes.
*Portugal:* Vitor Baia; Xavier, Fernando Couto, Beto, Calado, Paulo Sousa (Oceano 72), Paulinho Santos, Dimas (Barbosa 55), Cadete, Joao Pinto (Capucho 69), Figo.
*Referee:* Vega (Spain).

**Belfast, 22 April 1998, 8862**
**Northern Ireland (1) 1** *(Patterson 10)*
**Switzerland (0) 0**
*Northern Ireland:* Fettis; Jenkins, Hughes, Patterson, Morrow, Lomas, Gillespie, Lennon, Quinn (O'Boyle 67), Dowie, Hughes.
*Switzerland:* Corminboeuf (Zuberbuhler 46); Vega, Yakin, Henchoz, Vogel (Jeanneret 67) Wicky, Lonfat (Kunz 71), Fournier, Grassi, Chapuisat (Muller 60), Sesa.
*Referee:* Dallas (Scotland).

**Dublin, 22 April 1998, 38,500**
**Republic of Ireland (0) 0**
**Argentina (2) 2** *(Batistuta 27, Ortega 40)*
*Republic of Ireland:* Given (Kelly A 46); Kenna (Delap 76), Staunton, Kelly G, Breen, Harte (Babb 46), Carsley, Kinsella, Quinn, Keane R D, Kilbane (Irwin 46).
*Argentina:* Burgos; Vivas, Ayala, Sensini, Simeone, Almeyda, Veron, Berti (Pineda 62), Ortega, Lopez (Delgado 84), Batistuta.
*Referee:* Dougal (Scotland).

**Edinburgh, 22 April 1998, 14,315**
**Scotland (1) 1** *(Jackson 15)*
**Finland (1) 1** *(Johansson 10)*
*Scotland:* Leighton; Calderwood (Durie 70), Dailly (Boyd 85), Elliott (Weir 46), Hendry, Whyte, McKinlay W, Gemmill (Lambert 75), Jackson (Gallacher 46), Booth (Donnelly 75), Collins.
*Finland:* Niemi; Tuomela (Kinnunen 75), Ylonen, Hyypia, Reini (Turpeinen 46), Mahlio, Litmanen (Rihilahti 46), Valakari, Koskinen, Sumiala (Kolkkaa 38), Johansson (Paatelainen 58).
*Referee:* Van Dijk (Holland).

**New York, 23 May 1998, 56,404**
**Colombia (1) 2** *(Valderrama 22 (pen), Rincon 79)*
**Scotland (2) 2** *(Collins 25, Burley 33)*
*Colombia:* Calero; Cabrera, Bermudez, Cordoba, Santa, Lozano, Valderrama, Rincon, Serna, Asprilla, Valencia.
*Scotland:* Sullivan; McNamara (McKinlay W 71), Boyd, Calderwood, Hendry, Dailly, Burley, Lambert, Jackson (Booth 46), Durie (Donnelly 61), Collins.
*Referee:* Hall (USA).

**Wembley, 23 May 1998, 63,733**
**England (0) 0**
**Saudi Arabia (0) 0**
*England:* Seaman; Neville G, Hinchcliffe (Neville P 71), Batty, Adams, Southgate, Anderton, Beckham (Gascoigne 61), Shearer (Ferdinand L 74), Sheringham (Wright 61), Scholes.
*Saudi Arabia:* Al Daeya; Al Jahni, Al Khlaiwi, Zubromawi, Al Shahrani, Amin (Al Dosary 77), Al Muwalid, Al Owairan K, Solaimani, Al Owairan S (Al Temiyat 77), Al Jaber.
*Referee:* Jol (Holland).

**Dublin, 23 May 1998, 28,500**
**Republic of Ireland (0) 0**
**Mexico (0) 0**
*Republic of Ireland:* Given; Fleming, Harte, Babb, Breen, Kelly G, Carsley, Farrelly, Connolly (Delap 75), Keane R D, Duff (Kennedy 75).
*Mexico:* Campos; Pardo, Sanchez, Davino, Luna, Garcia Aspe, Ordiales (Palencia 46), Suarez, Ramirez (Pelaez 60), Hernandez (Chavez 85), Blanco.
*Referee:* Ashman (Wales).

**Casablanca, 27 May 1998, 80,000**
**England (0) 1** *(Owen 59)*
**Morocco (0) 0**
*England:* Flowers; McManaman, Le Saux, Keown, Southgate, Campbell, Anderton, Ince, Dublin (Ferdinand L 79), Wright (Owen 25), Gascoigne.
*Morocco:* Benzakri; Saber, Rossi, Neqrouz, El Haddrioui, Chiba (Amzine 62), Tahar, Chippo, Ouakili, Bassir, Rokki (El Khattabi 62).
*Referee:* Ghani (Tunisia).

**Casablanca, 29 May 1998, 25,000**
**England (0) 0**
**Belgium (0) 0**
*England:* Martyn; Neville G (Owen 46), Le Saux, Keown, Campbell (Dublin 75), Neville P (Ferdinand R 46), Lee, Gascoigne (Beckham 49), Ferdinand L, Merson, Butt.
*Belgium:* Van der Walle; Deflandre, Van Meir, Verstraeten, Verheyen, De Boeck, Scifo, Borkelmans, Goossens (Mpenza M 46), Mpenza E, Boffin.
*Belgium won 4-3 on penalties.*
*Referee:* Arjoune (Morocco).

**Washington, 30 May 1998, 46,737**
**USA (0) 0**
**Scotland (0) 0**
*USA:* Keller; Pope, Dooley, Regis, Burns, Moore, Stewart (Lalas 82), Deering, Ramos (Radosavljevic 56), Jones, Wegerle (Wynalda 62).
*Scotland:* Leighton; McKinlay T (McNamara 59), Boyd, Calderwood, Hendry, Dailly, McKinlay W (Burley 74), Lambert, Jackson, Gallacher (Donnelly 82), Collins.
*Referee:* Ramos (Mexico).

**Valletta, 3 June 1998, 3000**
**Malta (0) 0**
**Wales (1) 3** *(Bellamy 25, Hartson 65, Pembridge 77 (pen))*
*Malta:* Muscat; Turner (Buhagiar 61), Saliba, Magri (Aquilina 46), Debono (Giggio 77), Chetcuti (Grima 70), Zahra, Brincat, Camilleri, Busuttil (Theuma 71), Sultana (Nwoko 46).
*Wales:* Jones; Ready, Green, Coleman, Pembridge, Williams A (Llewellyn 76), Bellamy (Edwards 76), Trollope, Hartson (Haworth 73), Saunders, Speed.
*Referee:* Rodomonti (Italy).

**Santander, 3 June 1998, 18,120**
**Spain (2) 4** *(Pizzi 30, 37, Morientes 46, 56)*
**Northern Ireland (1) 1** *(Taggart 43)*
*Spain:* Canizares; Ferrer, Abelardo, Campo, Sergi (Aranzabal 46), Etxberria, Celades, Amor, Raul (Kiko 46), Guerrero (Morientes 46), Pizzi (Alfonso 46).
*Northern Ireland:* Fettis; Jenkins, Taggart, Morrow, Patterson (Hughes A 64), McCarthy, Magilton (Mulryne 75), Lennon (Jeff Whitley 84), Jim Whitley, Dowie, Hughes M.
*Referee:* Veissiere (France).

**Tunis, 6 June 1998, 30,000**
**Tunisia (2) 4** *(Ben Younes 18, Badra 28, 83 (pen), Jaballah 68)*
**Wales (0) 0**
*Tunisia:* El Ouaer; Chouchene (Jaballah 46), Badra, Trabelsi S, Trabelsi H (Thabet 46), Ghodhbane (Bouazizi 46), Souayah (Beya 46), Chihi, Clayton (Ben Ahmed 77), Sellimi (Melki 68), Ben Younes (Ben Slimane 46).
*Wales:* Marriott; Ready, Green, Coleman, Savage, Bellamy (Haworth 70), Pembridge, Trollope, Hartson (Edwards 60), Saunders (Llewellyn 79), Speed.
*Referee:* Mamad (Algeria).

# INTERNATIONAL APPEARANCES 1872–1998

This is a list of full international appearances by Englishmen, Irishmen, Scotsmen and Welshmen in matches against the Home Countries and against foreign nations. It does not include unofficial matches against Commonwealth and Empire countries. The year indicated refers to the season; ie 1998 is the 1997-98 season.

Explanatory code for matches played by all five countries: A represents Austria; Alb, Albania; Alg, Algeria; An, Angola; Arg, Argentina; Arm, Armenia; Aus, Australia; B, Bohemia; Bel, Belgium; Bl, Belarus; Bol, Bolivia; Br, Brazil; Bul, Bulgaria; C,CIS; Ca, Canada; Cam, Cameroon; Ch, Chile; Chn, China; Co, Colombia; Cr, Costa Rica; Cro, Croatia; Cy, Cyprus; Cz, Czechoslovakia; CzR, Czech Republic; D, Denmark; E, England; Ec, Ecuador; Ei, Republic of Ireland; EG, East Germany; Eg, Egypt; Es, Estonia; F, France; Fa, Faeroes; Fi, Finland; G, Germany; Ge, Georgia; Gr, Greece; H, Hungary; Ho, Holland; Hon, Honduras; I, Italy; Ic, Iceland; Ir, Iran; Is, Israel; J, Japan; Jam, Jamaica; K, Kuwait; L, Luxembourg; La, Latvia; Li, Lithuania; Lie, Liechtenstein; M, Mexico; Ma, Malta; Mac, Macedonia; Mal, Malaysia; Mol, Moldova; Mor, Morocco; N, Norway; Ni, Ng, Nigeria; Ni, Northern Ireland; Nz, New Zealand; P, Portugal; Para, Paraguay; Pe, Peru; Pol, Poland; R, Romania; RCS, Republic of Czechs and Slovaks; R of E, Rest of Europe; R of UK, Rest of United Kingdom; R of W, Rest of World; Ru, Russia; S.Af, South Africa; S.Ar, Saudi Arabia; S, Scotland; Se, Sweden; Slo, Slovakia; Sm, San Marino; Sp, Spain; Sw, Switzerland; T, Turkey; Th, Thailand; Tr, Trinidad & Tobago; Tun, Tunisia; U, Uruguay; Uk, Ukraine; US, United States of America; USSR, Soviet Union; W, Wales; WG, West Germany; Y, Yugoslavia; Z, Zaire.

*As at July 1998.*

## ENGLAND

Abbott, W. (Everton), 1902 v W (1)
A'Court, A. (Liverpool), 1958 v Ni, Br, A, USSR; 1959 v W (5)
Adams, T. A. (Arsenal), 1987 v Sp, T, Br; 1988 v WG, T, Y, Ho, H, S, Co, Sw, Ei, Ho, USSR; 1989 v D, Se, S.Ar.; 1991 v Ei (2); 1993 v N, T, Sm, T, Ho, Pol, N; 1994 v Pol, Ho, D, Gr, N; 1995 v US, R, Ei, U; 1996 v Co, N, Sw, P, Chn, Sw, S, Ho, Sp, G; 1997 v Ge (2); 1998 v I, Ch, P, S.Ar, Tun, R, Co, Arg (55)
Adcock, H. (Leicester C), 1929 v F, Bel, Sp; 1930 v Ni, W (5)
Alcock, C. W. (Wanderers), 1875 v S (1)
Alderson, J. T. (C Palace), 1923 v F (1)
Aldridge, A. (WBA), 1888 v Ni; (with Walsall Town Swifts), 1889 v Ni (2)
Allen, A. (Stoke C) 1960 v Se, W, Ni (3)
Allen, A. (Aston Villa), 1888 v Ni (1)
Allen, C. (QPR), 1984 v Br (sub), U, Ch; (with Tottenham H), 1987 v T; 1988 v Is (5)
Allen, H. (Wolverhampton W), 1888 v S, W, Ni; 1889 v S; 1890 v S (5)
Allen, J. P. (Portsmouth), 1934 v Ni, W (2)
Allen, R. (WBA), 1952 v Sw; 1954 v Y, S; 1955 v WG, W (5)
Alsford, W. J. (Tottenham H), 1935 v S (1)
Amos, A. (Old Carthusians), 1885 v S; 1886 v W (2)
Anderson, R. D. (Old Etonians), 1879 v W (1)
Anderson, S. (Sunderland), 1962 v A, S (2)
Anderson, V. (Nottingham F), 1979 v Cz; 1980 v Bul, Sp; 1981 v N, R, W, S; 1982 v Ni, Ic; 1984 v Ni; (with Arsenal), 1985 v T, Ni, Ei, R, Fi, S, M, USSR; 1986 v W; 1987 v Se, Ni (2); Y, Sp, T; (with Manchester U), 1988 v WG, H, Co (30)
Anderton, D. R. (Tottenham H), 1994 v D, Gr, N; 1995 v US, Ei, U, J, Se, Br; 1996 v H, Chn, Sw, S, Ho, Sp, G; 1998 v S.Ar, Mor, Tun, R, Co, Arg (22)
Angus, J. (Burnley), 1961 v A (1)
Armfield, J. C. (Blackpool), 1959 v Br, Pe, M, US; 1960 v Y, Sp, H, S; 1961 v L, P, Sp, M, I, A, W, Ni, S; 1962 v A, Sw, Pe, W, Ni, S, L, P, H, Arg, Bul, Br; 1963 v F (2), Br, EG, Sw, Ni, W, S; 1964 v R of W, W, Ni, S; 1966 v Y, Fi (43)
Armitage, G. H. (Charlton Ath), 1926 v Ni (1)
Armstrong, D. (Middlesbrough), 1980 v Aus; (with Southampton), 1983 v WG; 1984 v W (3)
Armstrong, K. (Chelsea), 1955 v S (1)
Arnold, J. (Fulham), 1933 v S (1)
Arthur, J. W. H. (Blackburn R), 1885 v S, W, Ni; 1886 v S, W; 1887 v W, Ni (7)
Ashcroft, J. (Woolwich Arsenal), 1906 v Ni, W, S (3)
Ashmore, G. S. (WBA), 1926 v Bel (1)
Ashton, C. T. (Corinthians), 1926 v Ni (1)
Ashurst, W. (Notts Co), 1923 v Se (2); 1925 v S, W, Bel (5)
Astall, G. (Birmingham C), 1956 v Fi, WG (2)
Astle, J. (WBA), 1969 v W; 1970 v S, P, Br (sub), Cz (5)
Aston, J. (Manchester U), 1949 v S, W, D, Sw, Se, N, F; 1950 v S, W, Ni, Ei, I, P, Bel, Ch, US; 1951 v W (17)
Athersmith, W. C. (Aston Villa), 1892 v Ni; 1897 v S, W, Ni; 1898 v S, Ni; 1899 v S, W, Ni; 1900 v S, W (12)
Atyeo, P. J. W. (Bristol C), 1956 v Br, Se, Sp; 1957 v D, Ei (2) (6)
Austin, S. W. (Manchester C), 1926 v Ni (1)

Bach, P. (Sunderland), 1899 v Ni (1)
Bache, J. W. (Aston Villa), 1903 v W; 1904 v W, Ni; 1905 v S; 1907 v Ni; 1910 v Ni; 1911 v S (7)
Baddeley, T. (Wolverhampton W), 1903 v S, Ni; 1904 v S, W, Ni (5)
Bagshaw, J. J. (Derby Co), 1920 v Ni (1)
Bailey, G. R. (Manchester U), 1985 v Ei, M (2)

Bailey, H. P. (Leicester Fosse), 1908 v W, A (2), H, B (5)
Bailey, M. A. (Charlton Ath), 1964 v US; 1965 v W (2)
Bailey, N. C. (Clapham Rovers), 1878 v S; 1879 v S, W; 1880 v S; 1881 v S; 1882 v S, W; 1883 v S, W; 1884 v S, W, Ni; 1885 v S, W, Ni; 1886 v S, W; 1887 v S, W (19)
Baily, E. F. (Tottenham H), 1950 v Sp; 1951 v Y, Ni, W; 1952 v A (2), Sw, W; 1953 v Ni (9)
Bain, J. (Oxford University), 1887 v S (1)
Baker, A. (Arsenal), 1928 v W (1)
Baker, B. H. (Everton), 1921 v Bel; (with Chelsea), 1926 v Ni (2)
Baker, J. H. (Hibernian), 1960 v Y, Sp, H, Ni, S; (with Arsenal) 1966 v Sp, Pol, Ni (8)
Ball, A. J. (Blackpool), 1965 v Y, WG, Se; 1966 v S, Sp, Fi, D, U, Arg, P, WG (2), Pol (2); (with Everton), 1967 v W, S, Ni, A, Cz, Sp; 1968 v W, S, USSR, Sp (2), Y, WG; 1969 v Ni, W, S, R (2), M, Br; U; 1970 v P, Co, Ec, R, Cz (sub), WG, W, S, Bel; 1971 v Ma, EG, Gr, Ma (sub), Ni, S; 1972 v Sw, Gr; (with Arsenal) WG (2), S; 1973 v W (3), Y, S (2), Cz, Ni, Pol; 1974 v P (sub); 1975 v WG, Cy (2), Ni, W, S (72)
Ball, J. (Bury), 1928 v Ni (1)
Balmer, W. (Everton), 1905 v Ni (1)
Bamber, J. (Liverpool), 1921 v W (1)
Bambridge, A. L. (Swifts), 1881 v W; 1883 v W; 1884 v Ni (3)
Bambridge, E. C. (Swifts), 1879 v S; 1880 v S; 1881 v S; 1882 v S, W, Ni; 1883 v W; 1884 v S, W, Ni; 1885 v S, W, Ni; 1886 v S, W; 1887 v S, W, Ni (18)
Bambridge, E. H. (Swifts), 1876 v S (1)
Banks, G. (Leicester C), 1963 v S, Br, Cz, EG; 1964 v W, Ni, S, R of W, U, P (2), US, Arg; 1965 v Ni, S, H, Y, WG, Se; 1966 v Ni, S, Sp, Pol (2), WG (2), Y, Fi, U, M, F, Arg, P; 1967 v Ni, W, S, Cz; (with Stoke C), 1968 v W, Ni, S, USSR (2), Sp, WG, Y; 1969 v Ni, S, R (2), F, U, Br; 1970 v W, Ni, S, Ho, Bel, Co, Ec, R, Br, Cz; 1971 v Gr, Ma (2), Ni, S; 1972 v Sw, Gr, WG (2), W, S (73)
Banks, H. E. (Millwall), 1901 v Ni (1)
Banks, T. (Bolton W), 1958 v USSR (3), Br, A; 1959 v Ni (6)
Bannister, W. (Burnley), 1901 v W; (with Bolton W), 1902 v Ni (2)
Barclay, R. (Sheffield U), 1932 v S; 1933 v Ni; 1936 v S (3)
Bardsley, D. J. (QPR), 1993 v Sp (sub), Pol (2)
Barham, M. (Norwich C), 1983 v Aus (2) (2)
Barkas, S. (Manchester C), 1936 v Bel; 1937 v S; 1938 v W, Ni, Cz (5)
Barker, J. (Derby Co), 1935 v I, Ho, S, W, Ni; 1936 v G, A, S, W, Ni; 1937 v W (11)
Barker, R. (Herts Rangers), 1872 v S (1)
Barker, R. R. (Casuals), 1895 v W (1)
Barlow, R. J. (WBA), 1955 v Ni (1)
Barmby, N.J. (Tottenham H), 1995 v U (sub), Se (sub); (with Middlesbrough), 1996 v Co, N, P, Chn, Sw (sub), Ho (sub), Sp (sub); 1997 v Mol (10)
Barnes, J. (Watford), 1983 v Ni (sub), Aus (sub), Aus (2); 1984 v U, S, Bel F (sub), S, USSR, Br, U, Ch; 1985 v EG, Fi, T, Ni, R, Fi, S, I (sub), M, WG (sub), US (sub); 1986 v R (sub), Is (sub), M (sub), Ca (sub), Arg (sub); 1987 v Se, T (sub), Br; (with Liverpool), 1988 v WG, T, Y, Is, Ho, S, Co, Sw, Ei, Ho, USSR; 1989 v Gr, Alb, Pol, D; 1990 v Se, I, Br, D, U, Tun, Ei, Ho, Eg, Bel, Cam; 1991 v H, Pol, Cam, Ei, T, USSR, Arg; 1992 v Cz, Fi; 1993 v Sm, T, Ho, Pol, US, G; 1995 v US, R, Ng, U, Se; 1996 v Co (sub) (79)
Barnes, P. S. (Manchester C), 1978 v I, WG, Br, W, S, H; 1979 v D, Ei, Cz, Ni (2), S, Bul, A; (with WBA), 1980 v D, W; 1981 v Sp (sub), Br, W, Sw (sub); (with Leeds U), 1982 v N (sub), Ho (sub) (22)

Barnet, H. H. (Royal Engineers), 1882 v Ni (1)
Barrass, M. W. (Bolton W), 1952 v W, Ni; 1953 v S (3)
Barrett, A. F. (Fulham), 1930 v Ni (1)
Barrett, E. D. (Oldham Ath), 1991 v Nz; 1993 v Br, G (3)
Barrett, J. W. (West Ham U), 1929 v Ni (1)
Barry, L. (Leicester C), 1928 v F, Bel; 1929 v F, Bel, Sp (5)
Barson, F. (Aston Villa), 1920 v W (1)
Barton, J. (Blackburn R), 1890 v Ni (1)
Barton, P. H. (Birmingham), 1921 v Bel; 1922 v Ni; 1923 v F; 1924 v Bel, S, W; 1925 v Ni (7)
Barton, W. D. (Wimbledon), 1995 v Ei; (with Newcastle U), Se, Br (sub) (3)
Bassett, W. I. (WBA), 1888 v Ni, 1889 v S, W; 1890 v S, W; 1891 v S, Ni; 1892 v S; 1893 v S, W; 1894 v S; 1895 v S, Ni; 1896 v S, W, Ni (16)
Bastard, S. R. (Upton Park), 1880 v S (1)
Bastin, C. S. (Arsenal), 1932 v W; 1933 v I, Sw; 1934 v S, Ni, W, H, Cz; 1935 v S, Ni, I; 1936 v S, W, G, A; 1937 v W, Ni; 1938 v S, G, Sw, F (21)
Batty, D. (Leeds U), 1991 v USSR (sub), Arg, Aus, Nz, Mal; 1992 v G, T, H (sub), F, Se; 1993 v N, Sm, US, Br; (with Blackburn R), 1994 v D (sub); 1995 v J, Br; (with Newcastle U), 1997 v Mol (sub), Ge, I, M, Ge, S.Af (sub), Pol (sub), F; 1998 v Mol, I, Ch, Sw (sub), P, S.Ar, Tun, R, Co (sub), Arg (sub) (35)
Baugh, R. (Stafford Road), 1886 v Ni; (with Wolverhampton W) 1890 v Ni (2)
Bayliss, A. E. J. M. (WBA), 1891 v Ni (1)
Baynham, R. L. (Luton T), 1956 v Ni, D, Sp (3)
Beardsley, P. A. (Newcastle U), 1986 v Eg (sub), Is, USSR, M, Ca (sub), P (sub), Pol, Para, Arg; 1987 v Ni (2), Y, Sp, Br, S; (with Liverpool), 1988 v WG, T, Y, Is, Ho, H, S, Co, Sw, Ei, Ho; 1989 v D, Se, S.Ar, Gr (sub), Alb (sub+1), Pol, D; 1990 v Se, Pol, I, Br, U (sub), Tun (sub), Ei, Eg (sub), Cam (sub), WG, I; 1991 v Pol (sub), Ei (2), USSR (sub); (with Newcastle U), 1994 v D, Gr, N; 1995 v Ng, Ei, U, J, Se; 1996 v P (sub), Chn (sub) (59)
Beasant, D. J. (Chelsea), 1990 v I (sub), Y (sub) (2)
Beasley, A. (Huddersfield T), 1939 v S (1)
Beats, W. E. (Wolverhampton W), 1901 v W; 1902 v S (2)
Beattie, T. K. (Ipswich T), 1975 v Cy (2), S; 1976 v Sw, P; 1977 v Fi, I (sub), Ho; 1978 v L (sub) (9)
Beckham, D. R. J. (Manchester U), 1997 v Mol, Pol, Ge, I, Ge, S.Af (sub), Pol, I, F; 1998 v Mol, I, Cam, P, S.Ar, Bel (sub), R (sub), Co, Arg (18)
Becton, F. (Preston NE), 1895 v Ni; (with Liverpool), 1897 v W (2)
Bedford, H. (Blackpool), 1923 v Se; 1925 v Ni (2)
Bell, C. (Manchester C), 1968 v Se, WG; 1969 v W, Bul, F, U, Br; 1970 v Ni (sub), Ho (2), P, Br (sub), Cz, WG (sub); 1972 v Gr, WG (2), W, Ni, S; 1973 v W (3), Y, S (2), Ni, Cz, Pol; 1974 v A, Pol, I, W, Ni, S, Arg, EG, Bul, Y; 1975 v Cz, P, WG, Cy (2), Ni, S; 1976 v Sw, Cz (48)
Bennett, W. (Sheffield U), 1901 v S, W (2)
Benson, R. W. (Sheffield U), 1913 v Ni (1)
Bentley, R. T. F. (Chelsea), 1949 v Se; 1950 v S, P, Bel, Ch, USA; 1953 v W, Bel; 1955 v W, WG, Sp, P (12)
Beresford, J. (Aston Villa), 1934 v Cz (1)
Berry, A. (Oxford University), 1909 v Ni (1)
Berry, J. J. (Manchester U), 1953 v Arg, Ch, U; 1956 v Se (4)
Bestall, J. G. (Grimsby T), 1935 v Ni (1)
Betmead, H. A. (Grimsby T), 1937 v Fi (1)
Betts, M. P. (Old Harrovians), 1877 v S (1)
Betts, W. (Sheffield W), 1889 v W (1)
Beverley, J. (Blackburn R), 1884 v S, W, Ni (3)
Birkett, R. H. (Clapham Rovers), 1879 v S (1)
Birkett, R. J. E. (Middlesbrough), 1936 v Ni (1)
Birley, F. H. (Oxford University), 1874 v S; (with Wanderers), 1875 v S (2)
Birtles, G. (Nottingham F), 1980 v Arg (sub), I; 1981 v R (3)
Bishop, S. M. (Leicester C), 1927 v S, Bel, L, F (4)
Blackburn, F. (Blackburn R), 1901 v S; 1902 v Ni; 1904 v S (3)
Blackburn, G. F. (Aston Villa), 1924 v F (1)
Blenkinsop, E. (Sheffield W), 1928 v F, Bel; 1929 v S, W, Ni, F, Bel, Sp; 1930 v S, W, Ni, G, A; 1931 v S, W, Ni, F, Bel; 1932 v S, W, Ni, Sp; 1933 v S, W, Ni, A (26)
Bliss, H. (Tottenham H), 1921 v S (1)
Blissett, L. (Watford), 1983 v WG (sub), L, W, Gr (sub), H, Ni, S (sub), Aus (1+1 sub); (with AC Milan), 1984 v D (sub), H, W (sub), S, USSR (14)
Blockley, J. P. (Arsenal), 1973 v Y (1)
Bloomer, S. (Derby Co), 1895 v S, Ni; 1896 v W, Ni; 1897 v S, W, Ni; 1898 v S; 1899 v S, W, Ni; 1900 v S; 1901 v S, W; 1902 v S, W, Ni; 1904 v S; 1905 v S, W, Ni; (with Middlesbrough), 1907 v S, W (23)
Blunstone, F. (Chelsea), 1955 v W, S, F, P; 1957 v Y (5)
Bond, R. (Preston NE), 1905 v Ni, W; 1906 v S, W, Ni; (with Bradford C), 1910 v S, W, Ni (8)

Bonetti, P. P. (Chelsea), 1966 v D; 1967 v Sp, A; 1968 v Sp; 1970 v Ho, P, WG (7)
Bonsor, A. G. (Wanderers), 1873 v S; 1875 v S (2)
Booth, F. (Manchester C), 1905 v Ni (1)
Booth, T. (Blackburn R), 1898 v W; (with Everton), 1903 v S (2)
Bould, S. A. (Arsenal), 1994 v Gr, N (2)
Bowden, E. R. (Arsenal), 1935 v W, I; 1936 v W, Ni, A; 1937 v H (6)
Bower, A. G. (Corinthians), 1924 v Ni, Bel; 1925 v W, Bel; 1927 v W (5)
Bowers, J. W. (Derby Co), 1934 v S, Ni, W (3)
Bowles, S. (QPR), 1974 v P, W, Ni; 1977 v I, Ho (5)
Bowser, S. (WBA), 1920 v Ni (1)
Boyer, P. J. (Norwich C), 1976 v W (1)
Boyes, W. (WBA), 1935 v Ho; (with Everton), 1939 v W, R of E (3)
Boyle, T. W. (Burnley), 1913 v Ni (1)
Brabrook, P. (Chelsea), 1958 v USSR; 1959 v Ni; 1960 v Sp (3)
Bracewell, P. W. (Everton), 1985 v WG (sub), US; 1986 v Ni (3)
Bradford, G. R. W. (Bristol R), 1956 v D (1)
Bradford, J. (Birmingham), 1924 v Ni; 1925 v Bel; 1928 v S; 1929 v Ni, W, F, Sp; 1930 v S, Ni, G, A; 1931 v W (12)
Bradley, W. (Manchester U), 1959 v I, US, M (sub) (3)
Bradshaw, F. (Sheffield W), 1908 v A (1)
Bradshaw, T. H. (Liverpool), 1897 v Ni (1)
Bradshaw, W. (Blackburn R), 1910 v W, Ni; 1912 v Ni; 1913 v W (4)
Brann, G. (Swifts), 1886 v S, W; 1891 v W (3)
Brawn, W. F. (Aston Villa), 1904 v W, Ni (2)
Bray, J. (Manchester C), 1935 v W; 1936 v S, W, Ni, G; 1937 v S (6)
Brayshaw, E. (Sheffield W), 1887 v Ni (1)
Bridges, B. J. (Chelsea), 1965 v S, H, Y; 1966 v A (4)
Bridgett, A. (Sunderland), 1905 v S; 1908 v S, A (2), H, B; 1909 v Ni, W, H (2), A (11)
Brindle, T. (Darwen), 1880 v S, W (2)
Brittleton, J. T. (Sheffield W), 1912 v S, W, Ni; 1913 v S; 1914 v W (5)
Britton, C. S. (Everton), 1935 v S, W, Ni, I; 1937 v S, Ni, H, N, Se (9)
Broadbent, P. F. (Wolverhampton W), 1958 v USSR; 1959 v S, W, Ni, I, Br; 1960 v S (7)
Broadis, I. A. (Manchester C), 1952 v S, A, I; 1953 v S, Arg, Ch, U, US; (with Newcastle U), 1954 v S, H, Y, Bel, Sw, U (14)
Brockbank, J. (Cambridge University), 1872 v S (1)
Brodie, J. B. (Wolverhampton W), 1889 v S, Ni; 1891 v Ni (3)
Bromilow, T. G. (Liverpool), 1921 v W; 1922 v S, W; 1923 v Bel; 1926 v Ni (5)
Bromley-Davenport, W. E. (Oxford University), 1884 v S, W (2)
Brook, E. F. (Manchester C), 1930 v Ni; 1933 v Sw: 1934 v S, W, Ni, F, H, Cz; 1935 v S, W, Ni, I; 1936 v S, W, Ni; 1937 v H; 1938 v W, Ni (18)
Brooking, T. D. (West Ham U), 1974 v P, Arg, EG, Bul, Y; 1975 v Cz (sub), P; 1976 v P, W, Br, I, Fi; 1977 v Ei, Fi, I, Ho, Ni; 1978 v I, WG, W, S (sub), H; 1979 v D, Ei, Ni, W (sub), S, Bul, Se (sub), A; 1980 v D, Ni, Arg (sub), W, Ni, S, Bel, Sp; 1981 v Sw, Sp, R, H; 1982 v H, S, Fi, Sp (sub) (47)
Brooks, J. (Tottenham H), 1957 v W, Y, D (3)
Broome, F. H. (Aston Villa), 1938 v G, Sw, F; 1939 v N, I, R, Y (7)
Brown, A. (Aston Villa), 1882 v S, W, Ni (3)
Brown, A. S. (Sheffield U), 1904 v W; 1906 v Ni (2)
Brown, A. (WBA), 1971 v W (1)
Brown, G. (Huddersfield T), 1927 v S, W, Ni, Bel, L, F; 1928 v W; 1929 v S; (with Aston Villa), 1933 v W (9)
Brown, J. (Blackburn R), 1881 v W; 1882 v Ni; 1885 v S, W, Ni (5)
Brown, J. H. (Sheffield W), 1927 v S, W, Bel, L, F; 1930 v Ni (6)
Brown, K. (West Ham U), 1960 v Ni (1)
Brown, W. (West Ham U), 1924 v Bel (1)
Bruton, J. (Burnley), 1928 v F, Bel; 1929 v S (3)
Bryant, W. I. (Clapton), 1925 v F (1)
Buchan, C. M. (Sunderland), 1913 v Ni; 1920 v W; 1921 v W, Bel; 1923 v F; 1924 v S (6)
Buchanan, W. S. (Clapham R), 1876 v S (1)
Buckley, F. C. (Derby Co), 1914 v Ni (1)
Bull, S. G. (Wolverhampton W), 1989 v S (sub), D (sub); 1990 v Y, Cz, D (sub), U (sub), Tun (sub), Ei (sub), Ho (sub), Eg, Bel (sub); 1991 v H, Pol (13)
Bullock, F. E. (Huddersfield T), 1921 v Ni (1)
Bullock, N. (Bury), 1923 v Bel; 1926 v W; 1927 v Ni (3)

Burgess, H. (Manchester C), 1904 v S, W, Ni; 1906 v S (4)

Burgess, H. (Sheffield W), 1931 v S, Ni, F, Bel (4)

Burnup, C. J. (Cambridge University), 1896 v S (1)

Burrows, H. (Sheffield W), 1934 v H, Cz; 1935 v Ho (3)

Burton, F. E. (Nottingham F), 1889 v Ni (1)

Bury, L. (Cambridge University), 1877 v S; (with Old Etonians), 1879 v W (2)

Butcher, T. (Ipswich T), 1980 v Aus; 1981 v Sp; 1982 v W, S, F, Cz, WG, Sp; 1983 v D, WG, L, W, Gr, H, Ni, S, Aus (3); 1984 v D, H, L, F, Ni; 1985 v EG, Fi, T, Ni, Ei, R, Fi, S, I, WG, US; 1986 v Is, USSR, S, M, Ca, P, Mor, Pol, Para, Arg; (with Rangers), 1987 v Se, Ni (2), Y, Sp, Br, S; 1988 v T, Y; 1989 v D, Se, Gr, Alb (2), Ch, S, Pol, D; 1990 v Se, Pol, I, Y, Br, Cz, D, U, Tun, Ei, Ho, Bel, Cam, WG (77)

Butler, J. D. (Arsenal), 1925 v Bel (1)

Butler, W. (Bolton W), 1924 v S (1)

Butt, N. (Manchester U), 1997 v M (sub), S.Af (sub); 1998 v Mol (sub), I (sub), Ch, Bel (6)

Byrne, G. (Liverpool), 1963 v S; 1966 v N (2)

Byrne, J. J. (C Palace), 1962 v Ni; (with West Ham U), 1963 v Sw; 1964 v S, U, P (2), Ei, Br, Arg; 1965 v W, S (11)

Byrne, R. W. (Manchester U), 1954 v S, H, Y, Bel, Sw, U; 1955 v S, W, Ni, WG, F, Sp, P; 1956 v S, W, Ni, Br, Se, Fi, WG, D, Sp; 1957 v S, W, Ni, Y, D (2), Ei (2); 1958 v W, Ni, F (33)

Callaghan, I. R. (Liverpool), 1966 v Fi, F; 1978 v Sw, L (4)

Calvey, J. (Nottingham F), 1902 v Ni (1)

Campbell, A. F. (Blackburn R), 1929 v W, Ni; (with Huddersfield T), 1931 v W, S, Ni; 1932 v W, Ni, Sp (8)

Campbell, S. (Tottenham H), 1996 v H (sub), S (sub); 1997 v Ge, I, S.Af (sub), Pol, F, Br; 1998 v Mol, I, Cam, Ch, P, Mor, Bel, Tun, R, Co, Arg (20)

Camsell, G. H. (Middlesbrough), 1929 v F, Bel; 1930 v Ni, W; 1934 v F; 1936 v S, G, A, Bel (9)

Capes, A. J. (Stoke C), 1903 v S (1)

Carr, J. (Middlesbrough), 1920 v Ni; 1923 v W (2)

Carr, J. (Newcastle U), 1905 v Ni; 1907 v Ni (2)

Carr, W. H. (Owlerton, Sheffield), 1875 v S (1)

Carter, H. S. (Sunderland), 1934 v S, H; 1936 v G; 1937 v S, Ni, H; (with Derby Co), 1947 v S, W, Ni, Ei, Ho, F, Sw (13)

Carter, J. H. (WBA), 1926 v Bel; 1929 v Bel, Sp (3)

Catlin, A. E. (Sheffield W), 1937 v W, Ni, H, N, Se (5)

Chadwick, A. (Southampton), 1900 v S, W (2)

Chadwick, E. (Everton), 1891 v S, W; 1892 v S; 1893 v S; 1894 v S; 1896 v Ni; 1897 v S (7)

Chamberlain, M (Stoke C), 1983 v L (sub); 1984 v D (sub), S, USSR, Br, U, Ch; 1985 v Fi (sub) (8)

Chambers, H. (Liverpool), 1921 v S, W, Bel; 1923 v S, W, Ni, Bel; 1924 v Ni (8)

Channon, M. R. (Southampton), 1973 v Y, S (2), Ni, W, Cz, USSR, I; 1974 v A, Pol, I, P, W, Ni, S, Arg, EG, Bul, Y; 1975 v Cz, P, WG, Cy (2), Ni (sub), W, S; 1976 v Sw, Cz, P, W, Ni, S, Br, I, Fi; 1977 v Fi, I, L, Ni, W, S, Br (sub), Arg, U; (with Manchester C), 1978 v Sw (46)

Charles, G. A. (Nottingham F), 1991 v Nz, Mal (2)

Charlton, J. (Leeds U), 1965 v S, H, Y, WG, Se; 1966 v W, Ni, S, A, Sp, Pol (2), WG (2), Y, Fi, D, U, M, F, Arg, P; 1967 v W, S, Ni, Cz; 1968 v W, Sp; 1969 v W, R, F; 1970 v Ho (2), P, Cz (35)

Charlton, R. (Manchester U), 1958 v S, P, Y; 1959 v S, W, Ni, USSR, I, Br, Pe, M, US; 1960 v W, S, Se, Y, Sp, H; 1961 v Ni, W, S, L, P, Sp, M, I, A; 1962 v W, Ni, S, A, Sw, Pe, L, P, H, Arg, Bul, Br; 1963 v S, F, Br, Cz, EG, Sw; 1964 v S, W, Ni, R of W, U, P, Ei, Br, Arg, US (sub); 1965 v Ni, S, Ho; 1966 v W, Ni, S, A, Sp, WG (2), Y, Fi, N, Pol, U, M, F, Arg, P; 1967 v Ni, W, S, Cz; 1968 v W, Ni, S, USSR (2), Sp (2), Se, Y; 1969 v S, W, Ni, R (2), Bul, M, Br; 1970 v W, Ni, Ho (2), P, Co, Ec, Cz, R, Br, WG (106)

Charnley, R. O. (Blackpool), 1963 v F (1)

Charsley, C. C. (Small Heath), 1893 v Ni (1)

Chedgzoy, S. (Everton), 1920 v W; 1921 v W, S, Ni; 1922 v Ni; 1923 v S; 1924 v W; 1925 v Ni (8)

Chenery, C. J. (C Palace), 1872 v S; 1873 v S; 1874 v S (3)

Cherry, T. J. (Leeds U), 1976 v W, S (sub), Br, Fi; 1977 v Ei, I, L, Ni, S (sub), Br, Arg, U; 1978 v Sw, L, I, Br, W; 1979 v Cz, W, Se; 1980 v Ei, Arg (sub), W, Ni, S, Aus, Sp (sub) (27)

Chilton, A. (Manchester U), 1951 v Ni; 1952 v F (2)

Chippendale, H. (Blackburn R), 1894 v Ni (1)

Chivers, M. (Tottenham H), 1971 v Ma (2), Gr, Ni, S; 1972 v Sw (1+1 sub), Gr, WG (2), Ni (sub), S; 1973 v W (3), S (2), Ni, Cz, Pol, USSR, I; 1974 v A, Pol (24)

Christian, E. (Old Etonians), 1879 v S (1)

Clamp, E. (Wolverhampton W), 1958 v USSR (2), Br, A (4)

Clapton, D. R. (Arsenal), 1959 v W (1)

Clare, T. (Stoke C), 1889 v Ni; 1892 v Ni; 1893 v W; 1894 v S (4)

Clarke, A. J. (Leeds U), 1970 v Cz; 1971 v EG, Ma, Ni, W (sub), S (sub); 1973 v S (2), W, Cz, Pol, USSR, I; 1974 v A, Pol, I; 1975 v P; 1976 v Cz, P (sub) (19)

Clarke, H. A. (Tottenham H), 1954 v S (1)

Clay, T. (Tottenham H), 1920 v W; 1922 v W, S, Ni (4)

Clayton, R. (Blackburn R), 1956 v Ni, Br, Se, Fi, WG, Sp; 1957 v S, W, Ni, Y, D (2), Ei (2); 1958 v S, W, Ni, F, P, Y, USSR; 1959 v S, W, Ni, USSR, I, Br, Pe, M, US; 1960 v W, Ni, S, Se, Y (35)

Clegg, J. C. (Sheffield W), 1872 v S (1)

Clegg, W. E. (Sheffield W), 1873 v S; (with Sheffield Albion), 1879 v W (2)

Clemence, R. N. (Liverpool), 1973 v W (2); 1974 v EG, Bul, Y; 1975 v Cz, P, WG, Cy, Ni, W, S; 1976 v Sw, Cz, P, W (2), Ni, S, Br, Fi; 1977 v Ei, Fi, I, Ho, L, S, Br, Arg, U; 1978 v Sw, L, I, WG, Ni, S; 1979 v D, Ei, Ni (2), S, Bul, A (sub); 1980 v D, Bul, Ei, Arg, W, S, Bel, Sp; 1981 v R, Sp, Br, Sw, H; (with Tottenham H), 1982 v N, Ni, Fi; 1983 v L; 1984 v L (61)

Clement, D. T. (QPR), 1976 v W (sub+1), I; 1977 v I, Ho (5)

Clough, B. H. (Middlesbrough), 1960 v W, Se (2)

Clough, N. H. (Nottingham F), 1989 v Ch; 1991 v Arg (sub), Aus, Mal; 1992 v F, Cz, C; 1993 v Sp, T (sub), Pol (sub), N (sub), US, Br, G (14)

Coates, R. (Burnley), 1970 v Ni; 1971 v Gr (sub); (with Tottenham H), Ma, W (4)

Cobbold, W. N. (Cambridge University), 1883 v S, Ni; 1885 v S, Ni; 1886 v S, W; (with Old Carthusians), 1887 v S, W, Ni (9)

Cock, J. G. (Huddersfield T), 1920 v Ni; (with Chelsea), v S (2)

Cockburn, H. (Manchester U), 1947 v W, Ni, Ei; 1948 v S, I; 1949 v S, Ni, D, Sw, Se; 1951 v Arg, P; 1952 v F (13)

Cohen, G. R. (Fulham), 1964 v U, P, Ei, US, Br; 1965 v W, S, Ni, Bel, H, Ho, Y, WG, Se; 1966 v W, S, Ni, A, Sp, Pol (2), WG (2), N, D, U, M, F, Arg, P; 1967 v W, S, Ni, Cz, Sp; 1968 v W, Ni (37)

Colclough, H. (C Palace), 1914 v W (1)

Cole, A. (Manchester U), 1995 v U (sub); 1997 v I (sub) (2)

Coleman, E. H. (Dulwich Hamlet), 1921 v W (1)

Coleman, J. (Woolwich Arsenal), 1907 v Ni (1)

Collymore, S. V. (Nottingham F), 1995 v J, Br (sub); (with Aston Villa), 1998 v Mol (sub) (3)

Common, A. (Sheffield U), 1904 v W, Ni; (with Middlesbrough), 1906 v W (3)

Compton, L. H. (Arsenal), 1951 v W, Y (2)

Conlin, J. (Bradford C), 1906 v S (1)

Connelly, J. M. (Burnley), 1960 v W, N, S, Se; 1962 v W, A, Sw, P; 1963 v W, F; (with Manchester U), 1965 v H, Y, Se; 1966 v W, Ni, S, A, N, D, U (20)

Cook, T. E. R. (Brighton), 1925 v W (1)

Cooper, C. T. (Nottingham F), 1995 v Se, Br (2)

Cooper, N. C. (Cambridge University), 1893 v Ni (1)

Cooper, T. (Derby Co), 1928 v Ni; 1929 v W, Ni, S, F, Bel, Sp; 1931 v F; 1932 v W, Sp; 1933 v S; 1934 v S, H, Cz; 1935 v W (15)

Cooper, T. (Leeds U), 1969 v W, S, F, M; 1970 v Ho, Bel, Co, Ec, R, Cz, Br, WG; 1971 v EG, Ma, Ni, W, S; 1972 v Sw (2); 1975 v P (20)

Coppell, S. J. (Manchester U), 1978 v I, WG, Br, W, Ni, S, H; 1979 v D, Ei, Cz, Ni (2), W (sub), S, Bul, A; 1980 v D, Ni, Ei (sub), Sp, Arg, W, S, Bel, I; 1981 v R (sub), Sw, R, Br, W, S, Sw, H; 1982 v H, S, Fi, F, Cz, K, WG; 1983 v L, Gr (42)

Copping, W. (Leeds U), 1933 v I, Sw; 1934 v S, Ni, W, F; (with Arsenal), 1935 v Ni, I; 1936 v A, Bel; 1937 v N, Se, Fi; 1938 v S, W, Ni, Cz; 1939 v W, R of E; (with Leeds U), R (20)

Corbett, B. O. (Corinthians), 1901 v W (1)

Corbett, R. (Old Malvernians), 1903 v W (1)

Corbett, W. S. (Birmingham), 1908 v A, H, B (3)

Corrigan, J. T. (Manchester C), 1978 v I (sub), Br; 1979 v W; 1980 v Ni, Aus; 1981 v W, S; 1982 v W, Ic (9)

Cottee, A. R. (West Ham U), 1987 v Se (sub), Ni (sub); 1988 v H (sub); (with Everton) 1989 v D (sub), Se (sub), Ch (sub), S (7)

Cotterill, G. H. (Cambridge University), 1891 v Ni; (with Old Brightonians), 1892 v W; 1893 v S, Ni (4)

Cottle, J. R. (Bristol C), 1909 v Ni (1)

Cowan, S. (Manchester C), 1926 v Bel; 1930 v A; 1931 v Bel (3)

Cowans, G. (Aston Villa), 1983 v W, H, Ni, S, Aus (3); (with Bari), 1986 v Eg, USSR; (with Aston Villa), 1991 v Ei (10)

Cowell, A. (Blackburn R), 1910 v Ni (1)

Cox, J. (Liverpool), 1901 v Ni; 1902 v S; 1903 v S (3)

Cox, J. D. (Derby Co), 1892 v Ni (1)

Crabtree, J. W. (Burnley), 1894 v Ni; 1895 v Ni, S; (with Aston Villa), 1896 v W, S, Ni; 1899 v S, W, Ni; 1900 v S, W, Ni; 1901 v W; 1902 v W (14)
Crawford, J. F. (Chelsea), 1931 v S (1)
Crawford, R. (Ipswich T), 1962 v Ni, A (2)
Crawshaw, T. H. (Sheffield W), 1895 v Ni; 1896 v S, W, Ni; 1897 v S, W, Ni; 1901 v Ni; 1904 v W, Ni (10)
Crayston, W. J. (Arsenal), 1936 v S, W, G, A, Bel; 1938 v W, Ni, Cz (8)
Creek, F. N. S. (Corinthians), 1923 v F (1)
Cresswell, W. (South Shields), 1921 v W; (with Sunderland), 1923 v F; 1924 v Bel; 1925 v Ni; 1926 v W; 1927 v Ni; (with Everton), 1930 v Ni (7)
Crompton, R. (Blackburn R), 1902 v S, W, Ni; 1903 v S, W; 1904 v S, W, Ni; 1906 v S, W, Ni; 1907 v S, W, Ni; 1908 v S, W, Ni, A (2), H, B; 1909 v S, W, Ni, H (2), A; 1910 v S, W; 1911 v S, W, Ni; 1912 v S, W, Ni; 1913 v S, W, Ni; 1914 v S, W, Ni (41)
Crooks, S. D. (Derby Co), 1930 v S, G, A; 1931 v S, W, Ni, F, Bel; 1932 v S, W, Ni, Sp; 1933 v Ni, W, A; 1934 v S, Ni, W, F, H, Cz; 1935 v Ni; 1936 v S, W; 1937 v W, H (26)
Crowe, C. (Wolverhampton W), 1963 v F (1)
Cuggy, F. (Sunderland), 1913 v Ni; 1914 v Ni (2)
Cullis, S. (Wolverhampton W), 1938 v S, W, Ni, F, Cz; 1939 v S, Ni, R of E, N, I, R, Y (12)
Cunliffe, A. (Blackburn R), 1933 v Ni, W (2)
Cunliffe, D. (Portsmouth), 1900 v Ni (1)
Cunliffe, J. N. (Everton), 1936 v Bel (1)
Cunningham, L. (WBA), 1979 v W, Se, A (sub); (with Real Madrid), 1980 v Ei, Sp (sub); 1981 v R (sub) (6)
Curle, K. (Manchester C), 1992 v C (sub), H, D (3)
Currey, E. S. (Oxford University), 1890 v S, W (2)
Currie, A. W. (Sheffield U), 1972 v Ni; 1973 v USSR, I; 1974 v A, Pol, I; 1976 v Sw; (with Leeds U), 1978 v Br, W (sub), Ni, S, H (sub); 1979 v Cz, Ni (2), W, Se (17)
Cursham, A. W. (Notts Co), 1876 v S; 1877 v S; 1878 v S; 1879 v W; 1883 v S, W (6)
Cursham, H. A. (Notts Co), 1880 v W; 1882 v S, W, Ni; 1883 v S, W, Ni; 1884 v Ni (8)

Daft, H. B. (Notts Co), 1889 v Ni; 1890 v S, W; 1891 v Ni; 1892 v Ni (5)
Daley, A. M. (Aston Villa), 1992 v Pol (sub), C, H, Br, Fi (sub), D (sub), Se (7)
Danks, T. (Nottingham F), 1885 v S (1)
Davenport, J. K. (Bolton W), 1885 v W; 1890 v Ni (2)
Davenport, P. (Nottingham F), 1985 v Ei (sub) (1)
Davis, G. (Derby Co), 1904 v W, Ni (2)
Davis, H. (Sheffield W), 1903 v S, W, Ni (3)
Davison, J. E. (Sheffield W), 1922 v W (1)
Dawson, J. (Burnley), 1922 v S, Ni (2)
Day, S. H. (Old Malvernians), 1906 v Ni, W, S (3)
Dean, W. R. (Everton), 1927 v S, W, F, Bel, L; 1928 v S, W, Ni, F, Bel; 1929 v S, W, Ni; 1931 v S; 1932 v Sp; 1933 v Ni (16)
Deane, B. C. (Sheffield U), 1991 v Nz (sub + 1); 1993 v Sp (sub) (3)
Deeley, N. V. (Wolverhampton W), 1959 v Br, Pe (2)
Devey, J. H. G. (Aston Villa), 1892 v Ni; 1894 v Ni (2)
Devonshire, A. (West Ham U), 1980 v Aus (sub), Ni; 1982 v Ho, Ic; 1983 v WG, W, Gr; 1984 v L (8)
Dewhurst, F. (Preston NE), 1886 v W, Ni; 1887 v S, W, Ni; 1888 v S, W, Ni; 1889 v W (9)
Dewhurst, G. P. (Liverpool Ramblers), 1895 v W (1)
Dickinson, J. W. (Portsmouth), 1949 v N, F; 1950 v S, W, Ei, P, Bel, Ch, US, Sp; 1951 v Ni, W, Y; 1952 v W, Ni, S, A (2), I, Sw; 1953 v W, Ni, S, Bel, Arg, Ch, U, US; 1954 v W, Ni, S, R of E, H (2), Y, Bel, Sw, U; 1955 v Sp, P; 1956 v W, Ni, S, D, Sp; 1957 v W, Y, D (48)
Dimmock, J. H. (Tottenham H), 1921 v S; 1926 v W, Bel (3)
Ditchburn, E. G. (Tottenham H), 1949 v Sw, Se; 1953 v US; 1957 v W, Y, D (6)
Dix, R. W. (Derby Co), 1939 v N (1)
Dixon, J. A. (Notts Co), 1885 v W (1)
Dixon, K. M. (Chelsea), 1985 v M (sub), WG, US; 1986 v Ni, Is, M (sub), Pol (sub); 1987 v Se (8)
Dixon, L. M. (Arsenal), 1990 v Cz; 1991 v H, Pol, Ei (2), Cam, T, Arg; 1992 v G, T, Pol, Cz (sub); 1993 v Sp, N, T, Sm, T, Ho, N, US; 1994 v Sm (21)
Dobson, A. T. C. (Notts Co), 1882 v Ni; 1884 v S, W, Ni (4)
Dobson, C. F. (Notts Co), 1886 v Ni (1)
Dobson, J. M. (Burnley), 1974 v P, EG, Bul, Y; (with Everton), 1975 v Cz (5)
Doggart, A. G. (Corinthians), 1924 v Bel (1)
Dorigo, A. R. (Chelsea), 1990 v Y (sub), Cz (sub), D (sub), I; 1991 v H (sub), USSR; (with Leeds U), 1992 v G, Cz (sub), H, Br; 1993 v Sm, Pol, US, Br; 1994 v H (15)
Dorrell, A. R. (Aston Villa), 1925 v W, Bel, F; 1926 v Ni (4)

Douglas, B. (Blackburn R), 1958 v S, W, Ni, F, P, Y, USSR (2), Br, A; 1959 v S, USSR; 1960 v Y, H; 1961 v Ni, W, S, L, P, Sp, M, I, A; 1962 v W, Ni, S, Pe, L, P, H, Arg, Bul, Br; 1963 v S, Br, Sw (36)
Downs, R. W. (Everton), 1921 v Ni (1)
Doyle, M. (Manchester C), 1976 v W, S (sub), Br, I; 1977 v Ho (5)
Drake, E. J. (Arsenal), 1935 v Ni, I; 1936 v W; 1937 v H; 1938 v F (5)
Dublin, D. (Coventry C), 1998 v Ch, Mor, Bel (sub) (3)
Ducat, A. (Woolwich Arsenal), 1910 v S, W, Ni; (with Aston Villa), 1920 v S, W; 1921 v Ni (6)
Dunn, A. T. B. (Cambridge University), 1883 v Ni; 1884 v Ni; (with Old Etonians), 1892 v S, W (4)
Duxbury, M. (Manchester U), 1984 v L, F, W, S, USSR, Br, U, Ch; 1985 v EG, Fi (10)

Earle, S. G. J. (Clapton), 1924 v F; (with West Ham U), 1928 v Ni (2)
Eastham, G. (Arsenal), 1963 v Br, Cz, EG; 1964 v W, Ni, S, R of W, U, P, Ei, US, Br, Arg; 1965 v H, WG, Se; 1966 v Sp, Pol, D (19)
Eastham, G. R. (Bolton W), 1935 v Ho (1)
Eckersley, W. (Blackburn R), 1950 v Sp; 1951 v S, Y, Arg, P; 1952 v A (2), Sw; 1953 v Ni, Arg, Ch, U, US; 1954 v W, Ni, R of E, H (17)
Edwards, D. (Manchester U), 1955 v S, F, Sp, P; 1956 v S, Br, Se, Fi, WG; 1957 v S, Ni, Ei (2), D (2); 1958 v W, Ni, F (18)
Edwards, J. H. (Shropshire Wanderers), 1874 v S (1)
Edwards, W. (Leeds U), 1926 v S, W; 1927 v W, Ni, S, F, Bel, L; 1928 v S, F, Bel; 1929 v S, W, Ni; 1930 v W, Ni (16)
Ehiogu, U. (Aston Villa), 1996 v Chn (sub) (1)
Ellerington, W. (Southampton), 1949 v N, F (2)
Elliott, G. W. (Middlesbrough), 1913 v Ni; 1914 v Ni; 1920 v W (3)
Elliott, W. H. (Burnley), 1952 v I, A; 1953 v Ni, W, Bel (5)
Evans, R. E. (Sheffield U), 1911 v S, W, Ni; 1912 v W (4)
Ewer, F. H. (Casuals), 1924 v F; 1925 v Bel (2)

Fairclough, P. (Old Foresters), 1878 v S (1)
Fairhurst, D. (Newcastle U), 1934 v F (1)
Fantham, J. (Sheffield W), 1962 v L (1)
Fashanu, J. (Wimbledon), 1989 v Ch, S (2)
Felton, W. (Sheffield W), 1925 v F (1)
Fenton, M. (Middlesbrough), 1938 v S (1)
Fenwick, T. (QPR), 1984 v W (sub), S, USSR, Br, U, Ch; 1985 v Fi, S, M, US; 1986 v R, T, Ni, Eg, M, P, Mor, Pol, Arg; (with Tottenham H), 1988 v Is (sub) (20)
Ferdinand, L. (QPR), 1993 v Sm, Ho, N, US; 1994 v Pol, Sm; 1995 v US (sub); (with Newcastle U), 1996 v P, Bul, H; 1997 v Pol, Ge, I (sub); (with Tottenham H), 1998 v Mol, S.Ar (sub), Mor (sub), Bel (17)
Ferdinand, R. G. (West Ham U), 1998 v Cam (sub), Sw, Bel (sub) (3)
Field, E. (Clapham Rovers), 1876 v S; 1881 v S (2)
Finney, T. (Preston NE), 1947 v W, Ni, Ei, Ho, F, P; 1948 v S, W, Ni, Bel, Se, I; 1949 v S, W, Ni, Se, N, F; 1950 v S, W, Ni, Ei, I, P, Bel, Ch, US, Sp; 1951 v S, Arg, P; 1952 v W, Ni, S, F, I, Sw, A; 1953 v W, Ni, S, Bel, Arg, Ch, U, US; 1954 v W, S, Bel, Sw, U, H, Y; 1955 v WG; 1956 v S, W, Ni, D, Sp; 1957 v S, W, Y, D (2), Ei (2); 1958 v W, S, F, P, Y, USSR (2); 1959 v Ni, USSR (76)
Fleming, H. J. (Swindon T), 1909 v S, H (2); 1910 v W, Ni; 1911 v W, Ni; 1912 v Ni; 1913 v S, W; 1914 v S (11)
Fletcher, A. (Wolverhampton W), 1889 v W; 1890 v W (2)
Flowers, R. (Wolverhampton W), 1955 v F; 1959 v S, W, I, Br, Pe, US, M (sub); 1960 v W, Ni, S, Se, Y, Sp, H; 1961 v Ni, W, S, L, P, Sp, M, I, A; 1962 v W, Ni, S, A, Se, Pe, L, P, H, Arg, Bul, Br; 1963 v Ni, W, S, F (2), Sw; 1964 v Ei, US, P; 1965 v W, Ho, WG; 1966 v N (49)
Flowers, T. D. (Southampton), 1993 v Br; (with Blackburn R), 1994 v Gr; 1995 v Ng, U, J, Se, Br; 1996 v Chn; 1997 v I; 1998 v Sw, Mor (13)
Forman, Frank (Nottingham F), 1898 v S, Ni; 1899 v S, W, Ni; 1901 v S; 1902 v S, Ni; 1903 v W (9)
Forman, F. R. (Nottingham F), 1899 v S, W, Ni (3)
Forrest, J. H. (Blackburn R), 1884 v W; 1885 v S, W, Ni; 1886 v S, W; 1887 v S, W, Ni; 1889 v S; 1890 v Ni (11)
Fort, J. (Millwall), 1921 v Bel (1)
Foster, R. E. (Oxford University), 1900 v W; (with Corinthians), 1901 v W, Ni, S; 1902 v W (5)
Foster, S. (Brighton & HA), 1982 v Ni, Ho, K (3)
Foulke, W. J. (Sheffield U), 1897 v W (1)
Foulkes, W. A. (Manchester U), 1955 v Ni (1)
Fowler, R. B. (Liverpool), 1996 v Bul (sub), Cro, Chn (sub), Ho (sub), Sp (sub); 1997 v M; 1998 v Cam (7)
Fox, F. S. (Millwall), 1925 v F (1)

Francis, G. C. J. (QPR), 1975 v Cz, P, W, S; 1976 v Sw, Cz, P, W, Ni, S, Br, Fi (12)
Francis, T. (Birmingham C), 1977 v Ho, L, S, Br; 1978 v Sw, L, I (sub), WG (sub), Br, W, S, H; (with Nottingham F), 1979 v Bul (sub), Se, A (sub); 1980 v Ni, Bul, Sp; 1981 v Sp, R, S (sub); Sw; (with Manchester C), 1982 v N, Ni, W, S (sub), Fi (sub), F, Cz, K, WG, Sp; (with Sampdoria), 1983 v D, Gr, H, Ni, S, Aus (3); 1984 v D, Ni, USSR; 1985 v EG (sub), T (sub), Ni (sub), R, Fi, S, I, M; 1986 v S (52)
Franklin, C. F. (Stoke C), 1947 v S, W, Ni, Ei, Ho, F, Sw, P; 1948 v S, W, Ni, Bel, Se, I; 1949 v S, W, Ni, D, Sw, N, F, Se; 1950 v W, S, Ni, Ei, I (27)
Freeman, B. C. (Everton), 1909 v S, W; (with Burnley), 1912 v S, W, Ni (5)
Froggatt, J. (Portsmouth), 1950 v Ni, I; 1951 v S; 1952 v S, A (2), I, Sw; 1953 v Ni, W, S, Bel, US (13)
Froggatt, R. (Sheffield W), 1953 v W, S, Bel, US (4)
Fry, C. B. (Corinthians), 1901 v Ni (1)
Furness, W. I. (Leeds U), 1933 v I (1)

Galley, T. (Wolverhampton W), 1937 v N, Se (2)
Gardner, T. (Aston Villa), 1934 v Cz; 1935 v Ho (2)
Garfield, B. (WBA), 1898 v Ni (1)
Garratty, W. (Aston Villa), 1903 v W (1)
Garrett, T. (Blackpool), 1952 v S, I; 1954 v W (3)
Gascoigne, P. J. (Tottenham H), 1989 v D (sub), S.Ar (sub), Alb (sub), Ch, S (sub); 1990 v Se (sub), Br (sub), Cz, D, U, Tun, Ei, Ho, Eg, Bel, Cam, WG; 1991 v H, Pol, Cam; (with Lazio), 1993 v N, T, Sm, T, Ho, Pol, N; 1994 v Pol, D; 1995 v J (sub), Se (sub), Br (sub); (with Rangers), 1996 v Co, Sw, P, Bul, Cro, Chn, Sw, S, Ho, Sp, G; 1997 v Mol, Pol, Ge, S.Af, Pol, I (sub), F, Br; 1998 v Mol, I, Cam; (with Middlesbrough), S.Ar (sub), Mor, Bel (57)
Gates, E. (Ipswich T), 1981 v N, R (2)
Gay, L. H. (Cambridge University), 1893 v S; (with Old Brightonians), 1894 v S, W (3)
Geary, F. (Everton), 1890 v Ni; 1891 v S (2)
Geaves, R. L. (Clapham Rovers), 1875 v S (1)
Gee, C. W. (Everton), 1932 v W, Sp; 1937 v Ni (3)
Geldard, A. (Everton), 1933 v I, Sw; 1935 v S; 1938 v Ni (4)
George, C. (Derby Co), 1977 v Ei (1)
George, W. (Aston Villa), 1902 v S, W, Ni (3)
Gibbins, W. V. T. (Clapton), 1924 v F; 1925 v F (2)
Gidman, J. (Aston Villa), 1977 v L (1)
Gillard, I. T. (QPR), 1975 v WG, W; 1976 v Cz (3)
Gilliat, W. E. (Old Carthusians), 1893 v Ni (1)
Goddard, P. (West Ham U), 1982 v Ic (sub) (1)
Goodall, F. R. (Huddersfield T), 1926 v S; 1927 v S, F, Bel, L; 1928 v S, W, F, Bel; 1930 v S, G, A; 1931 v S, W, Ni, Bel; 1932 v Ni; 1933 v W, Ni, A, I, Sw; 1934 v W, Ni, F (25)
Goodall, J. (Preston NE), 1888 v S, W; 1889 v S, W; (with Derby Co), 1891 v S, W; 1892 v S; 1893 v W; 1894 v S; 1895 v S, Ni; 1896 v S, W; 1898 v W (14)
Goodhart, H. C. (Old Etonians), 1883 v S, W, Ni (3)
Goodwyn, A. G. (Royal Engineers), 1873 v S (1)
Goodyer, A. C. (Nottingham F), 1879 v S (1)
Gosling, R. C. (Old Etonians), 1892 v W; 1893 v S; 1894 v W; 1895 v W, S (5)
Gosnell, A. A. (Newcastle U), 1906 v Ni (1)
Gough, H. C. (Sheffield U), 1921 v S (1)
Goulden, L. A. (West Ham U), 1937 v Se, N; 1938 v W, Ni, Cz, G, Sw, F; 1939 v S, W, R of E, I, R, Y (14)
Graham, L. (Millwall), 1925 v S, W (2)
Graham, T. (Nottingham F), 1931 v F; 1932 v Ni (2)
Grainger, C. (Sheffield U), 1956 v Br, Se, Fi, WG; 1957 v W, Ni; (with Sunderland), 1957 v S (7)
Gray, A. A. (C Palace), 1992 v Pol (1)
Greaves, J. (Chelsea), 1959 v Pe, M, US; 1960 v W, Se, Y, Sp; 1961 v Ni, W, S, L, Sp, I, A; (with Tottenham H), 1962 v S, Sw, Pe, H, Arg, Bul, Br; 1963 v Ni, W, S, F (2), Br, Cz, Sw; 1964 v W, Ni, R of W, P (2), Ei, Br, U, Arg; 1965 v Ni, S, Bel, Ho, H, Y; 1966 v W, A, Y, N, D, Pol, U, M, F; 1967 v S, Sp, A (57)
Green, F. T. (Wanderers), 1876 v S (1)
Green, G. H. (Sheffield U), 1925 v F; 1926 v S, Bel, W; 1927 v W, Ni; 1928 v F, Bel (8)
Greenhalgh, E. H. (Notts Co), 1872 v S; 1873 v S (2)
Greenhoff, B. (Manchester U), 1976 v W, Ni; 1977 v Ei, Fi, I, Ho, Ni, W, S, Br, Arg, U; 1978 v Br, W, Ni, S (sub), H (sub); (with Leeds U), 1980 v Aus (sub) (18)
Greenwood, D. H. (Blackburn R), 1882 v S, Ni (2)
Gregory, J. (QPR), 1983 v Aus (3); 1984 v D, H, W (6)
Grimsdell, A. (Tottenham H), 1920 v S, W; 1921 v S, Ni; 1923 v W, Ni (6)
Grosvenor, A. T. (Birmingham), 1934 v Ni, W, F (3)
Gunn, W. (Notts Co), 1884 v S, W (2)
Gurney, R. (Sunderland), 1935 v S (1)
Hacking, J. (Oldham Ath), 1929 v S, W, Ni (3)

Hadley, N. (WBA), 1903 v Ni (1)
Hagan, J. (Sheffield U), 1949 v D (1)
Haines, J. T. W. (WBA), 1949 v Sw (1)
Hall, A. E. (Aston Villa), 1910 v Ni (1)
Hall, G. W. (Tottenham H), 1934 v F; 1938 v S, W, Ni, Cz; 1939 v S, Ni, R of E, I, Y (10)
Hall, J. (Birmingham C), 1956 v S, W, Ni, Br, Se, Fi, WG, D, Sp; 1957 v S, W, Ni, Y, D (2), Ei (2) (17)
Halse, H. J. (Manchester U), 1909 v A (1)
Hammond, H. E. D. (Oxford University), 1889 v S (1)
Hampson, J. (Blackpool), 1931 v Ni, W; 1933 v A (3)
Hampton, H. (Aston Villa), 1913 v S, W; 1914 v S, W (4)
Hancocks, J. (Wolverhampton W), 1949 v Sw; 1950 v W; 1951 v Y (3)
Hapgood, E. (Arsenal), 1933 v I, Sw; 1934 v S, Ni, W, H, Cz; 1935 v S, Ni, W, I, Ho; 1936 v S, Ni, W, G, A, Bel; 1937 v Fi; 1938 v S, G, Sw, F; 1939 v S, Ni, R of E, N, I, Y (30)
Hardinge, H. T. W. (Sheffield U), 1910 v S (1)
Hardman, H. P. (Everton), 1905 v W; 1907 v S, Ni; 1908 v W (4)
Hardwick, G. F. M. (Middlesbrough), 1947 v S, W, Ni, Ei, Ho, F, Sw, P; 1948 v S, W, Ni, Bel, Se (13)
Hardy, H. (Stockport Co), 1925 v Bel (1)
Hardy, S. (Liverpool), 1907 v S, W, Ni; 1908 v S; 1909 v S, W, Ni, H (2), A; 1910 v S, W, Ni; 1912 v Ni; (with Aston Villa), 1913 v S; 1914 v Ni, W, S; 1920 v S, W, Ni (21)
Harford, M. G. (Luton T), 1988 v Is (sub); 1989 v D (2) (2)
Hargreaves, F. W. (Blackburn R), 1880 v W; 1881 v W; 1882 v Ni (3)
Hargreaves, J. (Blackburn R), 1881 v S, W (2)
Harper, E. C. (Blackburn R), 1926 v S (1)
Harris, G. (Burnley), 1966 v Pol (1)
Harris, P. P. (Portsmouth), 1950 v Ei; 1954 v H (2)
Harris, S. S. (Cambridge University), 1904 v S; (with Old Westminsters), 1905 v Ni, W; 1906 v S, W, Ni (6)
Harrison, A. H. (Old Westminsters), 1893 v S, Ni (2)
Harrison, G. (Everton), 1921 v Bel; 1922 v Ni (2)
Harrow, J. H. (Chelsea), 1923 v Ni, Se (2)
Hart, E. (Leeds U), 1929 v W; 1930 v W, Ni; 1933 v S, A; 1934 v S, H, Cz (8)
Hartley, F. (Oxford C), 1923 v F (1)
Harvey, A. (Wednesbury Strollers), 1881 v W (1)
Harvey, J. C. (Everton), 1971 v Ma (1)
Hassall, H. W. (Huddersfield T), 1951 v S, Arg, P; 1952 v F; (with Bolton W), 1954 v Ni (5)
Hateley, M. (Portsmouth), 1984 v USSR (sub), Br, U, Ch; (with AC Milan), 1985 v EG (sub), Fi, Ni, Ei, Fi, S, I, M; 1986 v R, T, Eg, S, M, Ca, P, Mor, Para (sub); 1987 v T (sub), Br (sub), S; (with Monaco), 1988 v WG (sub), Ho (sub), H (sub), Co (sub), Ei (sub), Ho (sub), USSR (sub); (with Rangers), 1992 v Cz (32)
Hawkes, R. M. (Luton T), 1907 v Ni; 1908 v A (2), H, B (5)
Haworth, G. (Accrington), 1887 v Ni, S, W; 1888 v S; 1890 v S (5)
Hawtrey, J. P. (Old Etonians), 1881 v S, W (2)
Haygarth, E. B. (Swifts), 1875 v S (1)
Haynes, J. N. (Fulham), 1955 v Ni; 1956 v S, Ni, Br, Se, Fi, WG, Sp; 1957 v W, Y, D, Ei (2); 1958 v W, Ni, S, F, P, Y, USSR (3), Br, A; 1959 v S, Ni, USSR, I, Br, Pe, M, US; 1960 v Ni, Y, Sp, H; 1961 v Ni, W, S, L, P, Sp, M, I, A; 1962 v W, Ni, S, A, Sw, Pe, P, H, Arg, Bul, Br (56)
Healless, H. (Blackburn R), 1925 v Ni; 1928 v S (2)
Hector, K. J. (Derby Co), 1974 v Pol (sub), I (sub) (2)
Hedley, G. A. (Sheffield U), 1901 v Ni (1)
Hegan, K. E. (Corinthians), 1923 v Bel, F; 1924 v Ni, Bel (4)
Hellawell, M. S. (Birmingham C), 1963 v Ni, F (2)
Henfrey, A. G. (Cambridge University), 1891 v Ni; (with Corinthians), 1892 v W; 1895 v W; 1896 v S, W (5)
Henry, R. P. (Tottenham H), 1963 v F (1)
Heron, F. (Wanderers), 1876 v S (1)
Heron, G. H. H. (Uxbridge), 1873 v S; 1874 v S; (with Wanderers), 1875 v S; 1876 v S; 1878 v S (5)
Hibbert, W. (Bury), 1910 v S (1)
Hibbs, H. E. (Birmingham), 1930 v S, W, A, G; 1931 v S, W, Ni; 1932 v W, Ni, Sp; 1933 v S, W, Ni, A, I, Sw; 1934 v Ni, W, F; 1935 v S, W, Ni, Ho; 1936 v G, W (25)
Hill, F. (Bolton W), 1963 v Ni, W (2)
Hill, G. A. (Manchester U), 1976 v I; 1977 v Ei (sub), Fi (sub), L; 1978 v Sw (sub), L (6)
Hill, J. H. (Burnley), 1925 v W; 1926 v S; 1927 v S, Ni, Bel, F; 1928 v Ni, W; (with Newcastle U), 1929 v F, Bel, Sp (11)
Hill, R. (Luton T), 1983 v D (sub), WG; 1986 v Eg (sub) (3)
Hill, R. H. (Millwall), 1926 v Bel (1)
Hillman, J. (Burnley), 1899 v Ni (1)
Hills, A. F. (Old Harrovians), 1879 v S (1)
Hilsdon, G. R. (Chelsea), 1907 v Ni; 1908 v S, W, Ni, A, H, B; 1909 v Ni (8)
Hinchcliffe, A. G. (Everton), 1997 v Mol, Pol, Ge; 1998 v Cam; (with Sheffield W), Sw, S.Ar (6)

Hine, E. W. (Leicester C), 1929 v W, Ni; 1930 v W, Ni; 1932 v W, Ni (6)

Hinton, A. T. (Wolverhampton W), 1963 v F; (with Nottingham F), 1965 v W, Bel (3)

Hirst, D. E. (Sheffield W), 1991 v Aus, Nz (sub); 1992 v F (3)

Hitchens, G. A. (Aston Villa), 1961 v M, I, A; (with Inter-Milan), 1962 v Sw, Pe, H, Br (7)

Hobbis, H. H. F. (Charlton Ath), 1936 v A, Bel (2)

Hoddle, G. (Tottenham H), 1980 v Bul, W, Aus, Sp; 1981 v Sp, W, S; 1982 v N, Ni, W, Ic, Cz (sub), K; 1983 v L (sub), Ni, S; 1984 v H, L, F; 1985 v Ei (sub), S, I (sub), M, WG, US; 1986 v R, T, Ni, Is, USSR, S, M, Ca, P, Mor, Pol, Para, Arg; 1987 v Se, Ni, Y, Sp, T, S; (with Monaco), 1988 v WG, T (sub), Y (sub), Ho (sub), H (sub), Co (sub), Ei (sub), Ho, USSR (53)

Hodge, S. B. (Aston Villa), 1986 v USSR (sub), S, Ca, P (sub), Mor (sub), Pol, Para, Arg; 1987 v Se, Ni, Y; (with Tottenham H), Sp, Ni, T, S; (with Nottingham F), 1989 v D; 1990 v I (sub), Y (sub), Cz, D, U, Tun; 1991 v Cam (sub), T (sub) (24)

Hodgetts, D. (Aston Villa), 1888 v S, W, Ni; 1892 v S, Ni; 1894 v Ni (6)

Hodgkinson, A. (Sheffield U), 1957 v S, Ei (2), D; 1961 v W (5)

Hodgson, G. (Liverpool), 1931 v S, Ni, W (3)

Hodkinson, J. (Blackburn R), 1913 v W, S; 1920 v Ni (3)

Hogg, W. (Sunderland), 1902 v S, W, Ni (3)

Holdcroft, G. H. (Preston NE), 1937 v W, Ni (2)

Holden, A. D. (Bolton W), 1959 v S, I, Br, Pe, M (5)

Holden, G. H. (Wednesbury OA), 1881 v S; 1884 v S, W, Ni (4)

Holden-White, C. (Corinthians), 1888 v W, S (2)

Holford, T. (Stoke), 1903 v Ni (1)

Holley, H. (Sunderland), 1909 v S, W, H (2), A; 1910 v W; 1912 v S, W, Ni; 1913 v S (10)

Holliday, E. (Middlesbrough), 1960 v W, Ni, Se (3)

Hollins, J. W. (Chelsea), 1967 v Sp (1)

Holmes, R. (Preston NE), 1888 v Ni; 1891 v S; 1892 v S; 1893 v S, W; 1894 v Ni; 1895 v Ni (7)

Holt, J. (Everton), 1890 v W; 1891 v S, W; 1892 v S, Ni; 1893 v S; 1894 v S, Ni; 1895 v S; (with Reading), 1900 v Ni (10)

Hopkinson, E. (Bolton W), 1958 v W, Ni, S, F, P, Y; 1959 v S, I, Br, Pe, M, US; 1960 v W, Se (14)

Hossack, A. H. (Corinthians), 1892 v W; 1894 v W (2)

Houghton, W. E. (Aston Villa), 1931 v Ni, W, F, Bel; 1932 v S, Ni; 1933 v A (7)

Houlker, A. E. (Blackburn R), 1902 v S; (with Portsmouth), 1903 v S, W; (with Southampton), 1906 v W, Ni (5)

Howarth, R. H. (Preston NE), 1887 v Ni; 1888 v S, W; 1891 v S; (with Everton), 1894 v Ni (5)

Howe, D. (WBA), 1958 v S, W, Ni, F, P, Y, USSR (3), Br, A; 1959 v S, W, Ni, USSR, I, Br, Pe, M, US; 1960 v W, Ni, Se (23)

Howe, J. R. (Derby Co), 1948 v I; 1949 v S, Ni (3)

Howell, L. S. (Wanderers), 1873 v S (1)

Howell, R. (Sheffield U), 1895 v Ni; (with Liverpool) 1899 v S (2)

Howey, S. N. (Newcastle U), 1995 v Ng; 1996 v Co, P, Bul (4)

Hudson, A. A. (Stoke C), 1975 v WG, Cy (2)

Hudson, J. (Sheffield), 1883 v Ni (1)

Hudspeth, F. C. (Newcastle U), 1926 v Ni (1)

Hufton, A. E. (West Ham U), 1924 v Bel; 1928 v S, Ni; 1929 v F, Bel, Sp (6)

Hughes, E. W. (Liverpool), 1970 v W, Ni, S, Ho, P, Bel; 1971 v EG, Ma (2), Gr, W; 1972 v Sw, Gr, WG (2), W, Ni, S; 1973 v W (3), S (2), Pol, USSR, I; 1974 v A, Pol, I, W, Ni, S, Arg, EG, Bul, Y; 1975 v Cz, P, Cy (sub), Ni; 1977 v I, L, W, S, Br, Arg, U; 1978 v Sw, L, I, WG, Ni, S, H; 1979 v D, Ei, Ni, W, Se; (with Wolverhampton W), 1980 v Sp (sub), Ni, S (sub) (62)

Hughes, L. (Liverpool), 1950 v Ch, US, Sp (3)

Hulme, J. H. A. (Arsenal), 1927 v S, Bel, F; 1928 v S, Ni, W; 1929 v Ni, W; 1933 v S (9)

Humphreys, P. (Notts Co), 1903 v S (1)

Hunt, G. S. (Tottenham H), 1933 v I, Sw, S (3)

Hunt, Rev K. R. G. (Leyton), 1911 v S, W (2)

Hunt, R. (Liverpool), 1962 v A; 1963 v EG; 1964 v S, US, P; 1965 v W; 1966 v S, Sp, Pol (2), WG (2), Fi, N, U, M, F, Arg, P; 1967 v Ni, W, Cz, Sp, A; 1968 v W, Ni, USSR (2), Sp (2), Se, Y; 1969 v R (2) (34)

Hunt, S. (WBA), 1984 v S (sub), USSR (sub) (2)

Hunter, J. (Sheffield Heeley), 1878 v S; 1880 v S, W; 1881 v S, W; 1882 v S, W (7)

Hunter, N. (Leeds U), 1966 v WG, Y, Fi, Sp (sub); 1967 v A; 1968 v Sp, Se, Y, WG, USSR; 1969 v R, W; 1970 v Ho, WG (sub); 1971 v Ma; 1972 v WG (2), W, Ni, S; 1973 v W (2) USSR (sub); 1974 v A, Pol, Ni (sub), S; 1975 v Cz (28)

Hurst, G. C. (West Ham U), 1966 v S, WG (2), Y, Fi, D, Arg, P; 1967 v Ni, W, S, Cz, Sp, A; 1968 v W, Ni, S, Se (sub), WG, USSR (2); 1969 v Ni, S, R (2), Bul, F, M, U, Br; 1970 v W, Ni, S, Ho (1+1 sub), Bel, Co, Ec, R, Br, WG; 1971 v EG, Gr, W, S; 1972 v Sw (2), Gr, WG (49)

Ince, P. E. C. (Manchester U), 1993 v Sp, N, T (2), Ho, Pol, US, Br, G; 1994 v Pol, Ho, Sm, D, N; 1995 v R, Ei; (with Internazionale), 1996 v Bul, Cro, H, Sw, S, Ho, G; 1997 v Mol, Pol, Ge, I, M, Ge, Pol, I, F (sub), Br; (with Liverpool), 1998 v I, Cam, Ch (sub), Sw, P, Mor, Tun, R, Co, Arg (43)

Iremonger, J. (Nottingham F), 1901 v S; 1902 v Ni (2)

Jack, D. N. B. (Bolton W), 1924 v S, W; 1928 v F, Bel; (with Arsenal), 1930 v S, G, A; 1933 v W, A (9)

Jackson, E. (Oxford University), 1891 v W (1)

James, D. B. (Liverpool), 1997 v M (1)

Jarrett, B. G. (Cambridge University), 1876 v S; 1877 v S; 1878 v S (3)

Jefferis, F. (Everton), 1912 v S, W (2)

Jezzard, B. A. G. (Fulham), 1954 v H; 1956 v Ni (2)

Johnson, D. E. (Ipswich T), 1975 v W, S; 1976 v Sw; (with Liverpool), 1980 v Ei, Arg, Ni, S, Bel (8)

Johnson, E. (Saltley College), 1880 v W; (with Stoke C), 1884 v Ni (2)

Johnson, J. A. (Stoke C), 1937 v N, Se, Fi, S, Ni (5)

Johnson, T. C. F. (Manchester C), 1926 v Bel; 1930 v W; (with Everton), 1932 v S, Sp; 1933 v Ni (5)

Johnson, W. H. (Sheffield U), 1900 v S, W, Ni; 1903 v S, W, Ni (6)

Johnston, H. (Blackpool), 1947 v S, Ho; 1951 v S; 1953 v Arg, Ch, U, US; 1954 v W, Ni, H (10)

Jones, A. (Walsall Swifts), 1882 v S, W; (with Great Lever), 1883 v S (3)

Jones, H. (Blackburn R), 1927 v S, Bel, L, F; 1928 v S, Ni (6)

Jones, H. (Nottingham F), 1923 v F (1)

Jones, M. D. (Sheffield U), 1965 v WG, Se; (with Leeds U), 1970 v Ho (3)

Jones, R. (Liverpool), 1992 v F; 1994 v Pol, Gr, N; 1995 v US, R, Ng, U (8)

Jones, W. (Bristol C), 1901 v Ni (1)

Jones, W. H. (Liverpool), 1950 v P, Bel (2)

Joy, B. (Casuals), 1936 v Bel (1)

Kail, E. I. L. (Dulwich Hamlet), 1929 v F, Bel, Sp (3)

Kay, A. H. (Everton), 1963 v Sw (1)

Kean, F. W. (Sheffield W), 1923 v S, Bel; 1924 v W; 1925 v Ni; 1926 v Ni, Bel; 1927 v L; (with Bolton W), 1929 v F, Sp (9)

Keegan, J. K. (Liverpool), 1973 v W (2); 1974 v W, Ni, Arg, EG, Bul, Y; 1975 v Cz, WG, Cy (2), Ni, S; 1976 v Sw, Cz, P, W (2), Ni, S, Br, Fi; 1977 v Ei, Fi, I, Ho, L; (with SV Hamburg), W, Br, Arg, U; 1978 v Sw, I, WG, Br, H; 1979 v D, Ei, Cz, Ni, W, S, Bul, Se, A; 1980 v D, Ni, Ei, Sp (2), Arg, Bel, I; (with Southampton), 1981 v Sp, Sw, H; 1982 v N, H, Ni, S, Fi, Sp (sub) (63)

Keen, E. R. L. (Derby Co), 1933 v A; 1937 v W, Ni, H (4)

Kelly, R. (Burnley), 1920 v S; 1921 v S, W, Ni; 1922 v S, W; 1923 v S; 1924 v Ni; 1925 v W, Ni, S; (with Sunderland), 1926 v W; (with Huddersfield T); 1927 v L; 1928 v S (14)

Kennedy, A. (Liverpool), 1984 v Ni, W (2)

Kennedy, R. (Liverpool), 1976 v W (2), Ni, S; 1977 v L, W, S, Br (sub), Arg (sub); 1978 v Sw, L; 1980 v Bul, Sp, Arg, W, Bel (sub), I (17)

Kenyon-Slaney, W. S. (Wanderers), 1873 v S (1)

Keown, M. R. (Everton), 1992 v F, Cz, C, H, Br, Fi, D, Fe, Se; (with Arsenal), 1993 v Ho, G (sub); 1997 v M, S.Af, I, Br; 1998 v Sw, Mor, Bel (18)

Kevan, D. T. (WBA), 1957 v S; 1958 v W, Ni, S, P, Y, USSR (3), Br, A; 1959 v M, US; 1961 v M (14)

Kidd, B. (Manchester U), 1970 v Ni, Ec (sub) (2)

King, R. S. (Oxford University), 1882 v Ni (1)

Kingsford, R. K. (Wanderers), 1874 v S (1)

Kingsley, M. (Newcastle U), 1901 v W (1)

Kinsey, G. (Wolverhampton C), 1892 v W; 1893 v S; (with Derby Co), 1896 v W, Ni (4)

Kirchen, A. J. (Arsenal), 1937 v N, Se, Fi (3)

Kirton, W. J. (Aston Villa), 1922 v Ni (1)

Knight, A. E. (Portsmouth), 1920 v Ni (1)

Knowles, C. (Tottenham H), 1968 v USSR, Sp, Se, WG (4)

Labone, B. L. (Everton), 1963 v Ni, W, F; 1967 v Sp, A; 1968 v S, Sp, Se, Y, USSR, WG; 1969 v Ni, S, R, Bul, M, U, Br; 1970 v S, W, Bel, Co, Ec, R, Br, WG (26)

Lampard, F. R. G. (West Ham U), 1973 v Y; 1980 v Aus (2)

Langley, E. J. (Fulham), 1958 v S, P, Y (3)

Mitchell, C. (Upton Park), 1880 v W; 1881 v S; 1883 v S, W; 1885 v W (5)
Mitchell, J. F. (Manchester C), 1925 v Ni (1)
Moffat, H. (Oldham Ath), 1913 v W (1)
Molyneux, G. (Southampton), 1902 v S; 1903 v S, W, Ni (4)
Moon, W. R. (Old Westminsters), 1888 v S, W; 1889 v S, W; 1890 v S, W; 1891 v S (7)
Moore, H. T. (Notts Co), 1883 v Ni; 1885 v W (2)
Moore, J. (Derby Co), 1923 v Se (1)
Moore, R. F. (West Ham U), 1962 v Pe, H, Arg, Bul, Br; 1963 v W, Ni, S, F (2), Br, Cz, EG, Sw; 1964 v W, Ni, S, R of W, U, P (2), Ei, Br, Arg; 1965 v Ni, S, Bel, H, Y, WG, Se; 1966 v W, Ni, S, A, Sp, Pol (2), WG (2), N, D, U, M, F, Arg, P; 1967 v W, Ni, S, Cz, Sp, A; 1968 v W, Ni, S, USSR (2), Sp (2), Se, Y, WG; 1969 v Ni, W, S, R, Bul, F, M, U, Br; 1970 v W, Ni, S, Ho, P, Bel, Co, Ec, R, Br, Cz, WG; 1971 v EG, Gr, Ma, Ni, S; 1972 v Sw (2), Gr, WG (2), W, S; 1973 v W (3), Y, S (2), Ni, Cz, Pol, USSR, I; 1974 v I (108)
Moore, W. G. B. (West Ham U), 1923 v Se (1)
Mordue, J. (Sunderland), 1912 v Ni; 1913 v Ni (2)
Morice, C. J. (Barnes), 1872 v S (1)
Morley, A. (Aston Villa), 1982 v H (sub), Ni, W, Ic; 1983 v D, Gr (6)
Morley, H. (Notts Co), 1910 v Ni (1)
Morren, T. (Sheffield U), 1898 v Ni (1)
Morris, F. (WBA), 1920 v S; 1921 v Ni (2)
Morris, J. (Derby Co), 1949 v N, F; 1950 v F (3)
Morris, W. W. (Wolverhampton W), 1939 v S, Ni, R (3)
Morse, H. (Notts Co), 1879 v S (1)
Mort, T. (Aston Villa), 1924 v W, F; 1926 v S (3)
Morten, A. (C Palace), 1873 v S (1)
Mortensen, S. H. (Blackpool), 1947 v P; 1948 v W, S, Ni, Bel, Se, I; 1949 v S, W, Ni, Se, N; 1950 v S, W, Ni, I, P, Bel, Ch, US, Sp; 1951 v S, Arg; 1954 v R of E, H (25)
Morton, J. R. (West Ham U), 1938 v Cz (1)
Mosforth, W. (Sheffield W), 1877 v S; (with Sheffield Albion), 1878 v S; 1879 v S, W; 1880 v S, W; (with Sheffield W), 1881 v W; 1882 v S, W (9)
Moss, F. (Arsenal), 1934 v S, H, Cz; 1935 v I (4)
Moss, F. (Aston Villa), 1922 v S, Ni; 1923 v Ni; 1924 v S, Bel (5)
Mosscrop, E. (Burnley), 1914 v S, W (2)
Mozley, B. (Derby Co), 1950 v W, Ni, Ei (3)
Mullen, J. (Wolverhampton W), 1947 v S; 1949 v N, F; 1950 v Bel (sub), Ch, US; 1954 v W, Ni, S, R of E, Y, Sw (12)
Mullery, A. P. (Tottenham H), 1965 v Ho; 1967 v Sp, A; 1968 v W, Ni, S, USSR, Sp (2), Se, Y; 1969 v Ni, S, R, Bul, F, M, U, Br; 1970 v W, Ni, S (sub), Ho (sub), Bel, P, Co, Ec, R, Cz, WG, Br; 1971 v Ma, EG, Gr; 1972 v Sw (35)

Neal, P. G. (Liverpool), 1976 v W, I; 1977 v W, S, Br, Arg, U; 1978 v Sw, I, WG, Ni, S, H; 1979 v D, Ei, Ni (2), S, Bul, A; 1980 v D, Ni, Sp, Arg, W, Bel, I; 1981 v R, Sw, Sp, Br, H; 1982 v N, H, W, Ho, Ic, F (sub), K; 1983 v D, Gr, L, W, Gr, H, Ni, S, Aus (2); 1984 v D (50)
Needham, E. (Sheffield U), 1894 v S; 1895 v S; 1897 v S, W, Ni; 1898 v S, W; 1899 v S, W, Ni; 1900 v S, Ni; 1901 v S, W, Ni; 1902 v W (16)
Neville, G. A. (Manchester U), 1995 v J, Br; 1996 v Co, N, Sw, P, Bul, Cro, H, Chn, Sw, S, Ho, Sp; 1997 v Mol, Pol, I, Ge, Pol, I (sub), F, Br (sub); 1998 v Mol, Ch, P, S.Ar, Bel, R, Co, Arg (30)
Neville, P. J. (Manchester U), 1996 v Chn; 1997 v S.Af, Pol (sub), I, F, Br; 1998 v Mol, Cam, Ch, P (sub), S.Ar (sub), Bel (12)
Newton, K. R. (Blackburn R), 1966 v S, WG; 1967 v Sp, A; 1968 v W, S, Sp, Se, Y, WG; 1969 v Ni, W, S, R, Bul, M, U, Br, F; (with Everton), 1970 v Ni, S, Ho, Co, Ec, R, Cz, WG (27)
Nicholls, J. (WBA), 1954 v S, Y (2)
Nicholson, W. E. (Tottenham H), 1951 v P (1)
Nish, D. J. (Derby Co), 1973 v Ni; 1974 v P, W, Ni, S (5)
Norman, M. (Tottenham H), 1962 v Pe, H, Arg, Bul, Br; 1963 v S, F, Br, Cz, EG; 1964 v W, U, P (2), US, Br, Arg; 1965 v Ni, Bel, Ho (23)
Nuttall, H. (Bolton W), 1928 v W, Ni; 1929 v S (3)

Oakley, W. J. (Oxford University), 1895 v W; 1896 v S, W, Ni; (with Corinthians), 1897 v S, W, Ni; 1898 v S, W, Ni; 1900 v S, W, Ni; 1901 v S, W, Ni (16)
O'Dowd, J. P. (Chelsea), 1932 v S; 1933 v Ni, Sw (3)
O'Grady, M. (Huddersfield T), 1963 v Ni; (with Leeds U), 1969 v F (2)
Ogilvie, R. A. M. M. (Clapham R), 1874 v S (1)
Oliver, L. F. (Fulham), 1929 v Bel (1)
Olney, B. A. (Aston Villa), 1928 v F, Bel (2)
Osborne, F. R. (Fulham), 1923 v Ni, F; (with Tottenham H), 1925 v Bel; 1926 v Bel (4)

Osborne, R. (Leicester C), 1928 v W (1)
Osgood, P. L. (Chelsea), 1970 v Bel, R (sub), Cz (sub); 1974 v I (4)
Osman, R. (Ipswich T), 1980 v Aus; 1981 v Sp, R, Sw; 1982 v N, Ic; 1983 v D, Aus (3); 1984 v D (11)
Ottaway, C. J. (Oxford University), 1872 v S; 1874 v S (2)
Owen, J. R. B. (Sheffield), 1874 v S (1)
Owen, M. J. (Liverpool), 1998 v Ch, Sw, P (sub), Mor (sub), Bel (sub), Tun (sub), R (sub), Co, Arg (9)
Owen, S. W. (Luton T), 1954 v H, Y, Bel (3)

Page, L. A. (Burnley), 1927 v S, W, Bel, L, F; 1928 v W, Ni (7)
Paine, T. L. (Southampton), 1963 v Cz, EG; 1964 v W, Ni, S, R of W, U, US, P; 1965 v Ni, H, Y, WG, Se; 1966 v W, A, Y, N, M (19)
Pallister, G. A. (Middlesbrough), 1988 v H; 1989 v S.Ar; (with Manchester U), 1991 v Cam (sub), T; 1992 v G; 1993 v N, US, Br, G; 1994 v Pol, Ho, Sm, D; 1995 v US, R, Ei, U, Se; 1996 v N, Sw; 1997 v Mol, Pol (sub) (22)
Palmer, C. L. (Sheffield W), 1992 v C, H, Br, Fi (sub), D, F, Se; 1993 v Sp (sub), N (sub), T, Sm, T, Ho, Pol, N, US, Br (sub); 1994 v Ho (18)
Pantling, H. H. (Sheffield U), 1924 v Ni (1)
Paravacini, P. J. de (Cambridge University), 1883 v S, W, Ni (3)
Parker, P. A. (QPR), 1989 v Alb (sub), Ch, D; 1990 v Y, U, Ho, Eg, Bel, Cam, WG, I; 1991 v H, Pol, USSR, Aus, Nz; (with Manchester U), 1992 v G; 1994 v Ho, D (19)
Parker, T. R. (Southampton), 1925 v F (1)
Parkes, P. B. (QPR), 1974 v P (1)
Parkinson, J. (Liverpool), 1910 v S, W (2)
Parr, P. C. (Oxford University), 1882 v W (1)
Parry, E. H. (Old Carthusians), 1879 v W; 1882 v W, S (3)
Parry, R. A. (Bolton W), 1960 v Ni, S (2)
Patchitt, B. C. A. (Corinthians), 1923 v Se (2) (2)
Pawson, F. W. (Cambridge University), 1883 v Ni; (with Swifts), 1885 v Ni (2)
Payne, J. (Luton T), 1937 v Fi (1)
Peacock, A. (Middlesbrough), 1962 v Arg, Bul; 1963 v Ni, W; (with Leeds U), 1966 v W, Ni (6)
Peacock, J. (Middlesbrough), 1929 v F, Bel, Sp (3)
Pearce, S. (Nottingham F), 1987 v Br, S; 1988 v WG (sub), Is, H; 1989 v D, Se, S.Ar, Gr, Alb (2), Ch, S, Pol, D; 1990 v Pol, I, Y, Br, Cz, D, U, Tun, Ei, Ho, Eg, Bel, Cam, WG; 1991 v H, Pol, Ei (2), Cam, T, Arg, Aus, Nz (2), Mal; 1992 v T, Pol, F, Cz, Br (sub), Fi, D, F, Se; 1993 v Sp, N, T; 1994 v Pol, Sm, Gr (sub); 1995 v R (sub), J, Br; 1996 v N, Sw, P, Bul, Cro, H, Sw, S, Ho, Sp, G; 1997 v Mol, Pol, I, M, S.Af, I (76)
Pearson, H. F. (WBA), 1932 v S (1)
Pearson, J. H. (Crewe Alex), 1892 v Ni (1)
Pearson, J. S. (Manchester U), 1976 v W, Ni, S, Br, Fi; 1977 v Ei, Ho (sub), W, S, Br, Arg, U; 1978 v I (sub), WG, Ni (15)
Pearson, S. C. (Manchester U), 1948 v S; 1949 v S, Ni; 1950 v Ni, I; 1951 v P; 1952 v S, I (8)
Pease, W. H. (Middlesbrough), 1927 v W (1)
Pegg, D. (Manchester U), 1957 v Ei (1)
Pejic, M. (Stoke C), 1974 v P, W, Ni, S (4)
Pelly, F. R. (Old Foresters), 1893 v Ni; 1894 v S, W (3)
Pennington, J. (WBA), 1907 v S, W; 1908 v S, W, Ni, A; 1909 v S, W, H (2), A; 1910 v S, W; 1911 v S, W, Ni; 1912 v S, W, Ni; 1913 v S, W; 1914 v S, Ni; 1920 v S, W (25)
Pentland, F. B. (Middlesbrough), 1909 v S, W, H (2), A (5)
Perry, C. (WBA), 1890 v Ni; 1891 v Ni; 1893 v W (3)
Perry, T. (WBA), 1898 v W (1)
Perry, W. (Blackpool), 1956 v Ni, S, Sp (3)
Perryman, S. (Tottenham H), 1982 v Ic (sub) (1)
Peters, M. (West Ham U), 1966 v Y, Fi, Pol, M, F, Arg, P, WG; 1967 v Ni, W, S, Cz; 1968 v W, Ni, S, USSR (2), Sp (2), Se, Y; 1969 v Ni, S, R, Bul, F, M, U, Br; 1970 v Ho (2), P (sub), Bel; (with Tottenham H), W, Ni, S, Co, Ec, R, Br, Cz, WG; 1971 v EG, Gr, Ma (2), Ni, W, S; 1972 v Sw, Gr, WG (1+1 sub), Ni (sub); 1973 v S (2), Ni, W, Cz, Pol, USSR, I; 1974 v A, Pol, I, P, S (67)
Phelan, M. C. (Manchester U), 1990 v I (sub) (1)
Phillips, L. H. (Portsmouth), 1952 v Ni; 1955 v W, WG (3)
Pickering, F. (Everton), 1964 v US; 1965 v Ni, Bel (3)
Pickering, J. (Sheffield U), 1933 v S (1)
Pickering, N. (Sunderland), 1983 v Aus (1)
Pike, T. M. (Cambridge University), 1886 v Ni (1)
Pilkington, B. (Burnley), 1955 v Ni (1)
Plant, J. (Bury), 1900 v S (1)
Platt, D. (Aston Villa), 1990 v I (sub), Y (sub), Br, D (sub), Tun (sub), Ho (sub), Eg (sub), Bel (sub), Cam, WG, I; 1991 v H, Pol, Ei (2), T, USSR, Arg, Aus, Nz (2), Mal; (with Bari), 1992 v G, T, Pol, Cz, C, Br, Fi, D, F, Se; (with Juventus), 1993 v Sp, N, T, Sm, T, Ho, Pol, N, Br (sub), G;

(with Sampdoria), 1994 v Pol, Ho, Sm, D, Gr, N; 1995 v US, Ng, Ei, U, J, Se, Br; (with Arsenal), 1996 v Bul (sub), Cro, H, Sw (sub), Ho (sub), Sp, G (62)

Plum, S. L. (Charlton Ath), 1923 v F (1)

Pointer, R. (Burnley), 1962 v W, L, P (3)

Porteous, T. S. (Sunderland), 1891 v W (1)

Priest, A. E. (Sheffield U), 1900 v Ni (1)

Prinsep, J. F. M. (Clapham Rovers), 1879 v S (1)

Puddefoot, S. C. (Blackburn R), 1926 v S, Ni (2)

Pye, J. (Wolverhampton W), 1950 v Ei (1)

Pym, R. H. (Bolton W), 1925 v S, W; 1926 v W (3)

Quantrill, A. (Derby Co), 1920 v S, W; 1921 v W, Ni (4)

Quixall, A. (Sheffield W), 1954 v W, Ni, R of E; 1955 v Sp, P (sub) (5)

Radford, J. (Arsenal), 1969 v R; 1972 v Sw (sub) (2)

Raikes, G. B. (Oxford University), 1895 v W; 1896 v W, Ni, S (4)

Ramsey, A. E. (Southampton), 1949 v Sw; (with Tottenham H), 1950 v S, I, P, Bel, Ch, US, Sp; 1951 v S, Ni, W, Y, Arg, P; 1952 v S, W, Ni, F, A (2), I, Sw; 1953 v Ni, W, S, Bel, Arg, Ch, U, US; 1954 v R of E, H (32)

Rawlings, A. (Preston NE), 1921 v Bel (1)

Rawlings, W. E. (Southampton), 1922 v S, W (2)

Rawlinson, J. F. P. (Cambridge University), 1882 v Ni (1)

Rawson, H. E. (Royal Engineers), 1875 v S (1)

Rawson, W. S. (Oxford University), 1875 v S; 1877 v S (2)

Read, A. (Tufnell Park), 1921 v Bel (1)

Reader, J. (WBA), 1894 v Ni (1)

Reaney, P. (Leeds U), 1969 v Bul (sub); 1970 v P; 1971 v Ma (3)

Redknapp, J. F. (Liverpool), 1996 v Co, N, Sw, Chn, S (sub); 1997 v M (sub), Ge (sub), S.Af (8)

Reeves, K. (Norwich C), 1980 v Bul; (with Manchester C), Ni (2)

Regis, C. (WBA), 1982 v Ni (sub), W (sub), Ic; 1983 v WG; (with Coventry C), 1988 v T (sub) (5)

Reid, P. (Everton), 1985 v M (sub), WG, US (sub); 1986 v R, S (sub), Ca (sub), Pol, Para, Arg; 1987 v Br; 1988 v WG, Y (sub), Sw (sub) (13)

Revie, D. G. (Manchester C), 1955 v Ni, S, F; 1956 v W, D; 1957 v Ni (6)

Reynolds, J. (WBA), 1892 v S; 1893 v S, W; (with Aston Villa), 1894 v S, Ni; 1895 v S; 1897 v S, W (8)

Richards, C. H. (Nottingham F), 1898 v Ni (1)

Richards, G. H. (Derby Co), 1909 v A (1)

Richards, J. P. (Wolverhampton W), 1973 v Ni (1)

Richardson, J. R. (Newcastle U), 1933 v I, Sw (2)

Richardson, K. (Aston Villa), 1994 v Gr (1)

Richardson, W. G. (WBA), 1935 v Ho (1)

Rickaby, S. (WBA), 1954 v Ni (1)

Rigby, A. (Blackburn R), 1927 v S, Bel, L, F; 1928 v W (5)

Rimmer, E. J. (Sheffield W), 1930 v S, G, A; 1932 v Sp (4)

Rimmer, J. J. (Arsenal), 1976 v I (1)

Ripley, S. E. (Blackburn R), 1994 v Sm; 1998 v Mol (sub) (2)

Rix, G. (Arsenal), 1981 v N, R, Sw (sub), Br, W, S; 1982 v Ho (sub), Fi (sub), F, Cz, K, WG, Sp; 1983 v D, WG (sub), Gr (sub); 1984 v Ni (17)

Robb, G. (Tottenham H), 1954 v H (1)

Roberts, C. (Manchester U), 1905 v Ni, W, S (3)

Roberts, F. (Manchester C), 1925 v S, W, Bel, F (4)

Roberts, G. (Tottenham H), 1983 v Ni, S; 1984 v F, Ni, S, USSR (6)

Roberts, H. (Arsenal), 1931 v S (1)

Roberts, H. (Millwall), 1931 v Bel (1)

Roberts, R. (WBA), 1887 v S; 1888 v Ni; 1890 v Ni (3)

Roberts, W. T. (Preston NE), 1924 v W, Bel (2)

Robinson, J. (Sheffield W), 1937 v Fi; 1938 v G, Sw; 1939 v W (4)

Robinson, J. W. (Derby Co), 1897 v S, Ni; (with New Brighton Tower), 1898 v S, W, Ni; (with Southampton), 1899 v W, S; 1900 v S, W, Ni; 1901 v Ni (11)

Robson, B. (WBA), 1980 v Ei, Aus; 1981 v N, R, Sw, Sp, R, Br, W, S, Sw, H; 1982 v N; (with Manchester U), H, Ni, W, Ho, S, Fi, F, Cz, WG, Sp; 1983 v D, Gr, L, S; 1984 v H, L, F, Ni, S, USSR, Br, U, Ch; 1985 v EG, Fi, T, Ei, R, Fi, S, M, I, WG, US; 1986 v R, T, Ni, Eg, Is, USSR, S, M, Ca, P, Mor, Pol, Sp, T, Br, S; 1988 v T, Y, Ho, H, S, Co, Sw, Ei, Ho, USSR; 1989 v S, Se, S.Ar, Gr, Alb (2), Ch, S, Pol, D; 1990 v Pol, I, Y, Cz, U, Tun, Ei, Ho; 1991 v Cam, Ei; 1992 v T (90)

Robson, R. (WBA), 1958 v F, USSR (2), Br, A; 1960 v Sp, H; 1961 v Ni, W, S, L, P, Sp, M, I; 1962 v W, Ni, Sw, L, P (20)

Rocastle, D. (Arsenal), 1989 v D, S.Ar, Gr, Alb (2), Pol (sub), D; 1990 v Se (sub), Pol, Y, D (sub); 1992 v Pol, Cz, Br (sub) (14)

Rose, W. C. (Wolverhampton W), 1884 v S, W, Ni; (with Preston NE), 1886 v Ni; (with Wolverhampton W), 1891 v Ni (5)

Rostron, T. (Darwen), 1881 v S, W (2)

Rowe, A. (Tottenham H), 1934 v F (1)

Rowley, J. F. (Manchester U), 1949 v Sw, Se, F; 1950 v Ni, I; 1952 v S (6)

Rowley, W. (Stoke C), 1889 v Ni; 1892 v Ni (2)

Royle, J. (Everton), 1971 v Ma; 1973 v Y; (with Manchester C), 1976 v Ni (sub), I; 1977 v Fi, L (6)

Ruddlesdin, H. (Sheffield W), 1904 v W, Ni; 1905 v S (3)

Ruddock, N. (Liverpool), 1995 v Ng (1)

Ruffell, J. W. (West Ham U), 1926 v S; 1927 v Ni; 1929 v S, W, Ni; 1930 v W (6)

Russell, B. B. (Royal Engineers), 1883 v W (1)

Rutherford, J. (Newcastle U), 1904 v S; 1907 v S, Ni, W; 1908 v S, Ni, W, A (2), H, B (11)

Sadler, D. (Manchester U), 1968 v Ni, USSR; 1970 v Ec (sub); 1971 v EG (4)

Sagar, C. (Bury), 1900 v Ni; 1902 v W (2)

Sagar, E. (Everton), 1936 v S, Ni, A, Bel (4)

Salako, J. A. (C Palace), 1991 v Aus (sub), Nz (sub + 1), Mal; 1992 v G (5)

Sandford, E. A. (WBA), 1933 v W (1)

Sandilands, R. R. (Old Westminsters), 1892 v W; 1893 v Ni; 1894 v W; 1895 v W; 1896 v W (5)

Sands, J. (Nottingham F), 1880 v W (1)

Sansom, K. (C Palace), 1979 v W; 1980 v Bul, Ei, Arg, W (sub), Ni, S, Bel, I; (with Arsenal), 1981 v N, R, Sw, Sp, R, Br, W, S, Sw; 1982 v Ni, W, Ho, S, Fi, F, Cz, WG, Sp; 1983 v D, WG, Gr, L, Gr, H, Ni, S; 1984 v D, H, L, F, S, USSR, Br, U, Ch; 1985 v EG, Fi, T, Ni, Ei, R, Fi, S, I, M, WG, US; 1986 v R, T, Ni, Eg, Is, USSR, S, M, Ca, P, Mor, Pol, Para, Arg; 1987 v Se, Ni (2), Y, Sp, T; 1988 v WG, T, Y, Ho, S, Co, Sw, Ei, Ho, USSR (86)

Saunders, F. E. (Swifts), 1888 v W (1)

Savage, A. H. (C Palace), 1876 v S (1)

Sayer, J. (Stoke C), 1887 v Ni (1)

Scales, J. R. (Liverpool), 1995 v J, Se (sub), Br (3)

Scattergood, E. (Derby Co), 1913 v W (1)

Schofield, J. (Stoke C), 1892 v W; 1893 v W; 1895 v Ni (3)

Scholes, P. (Manchester U), 1997 v S.Af (sub), I, Br; 1998 v Mol, Cam, P, S.Ar, Tun, R, Co, Arg (11)

Scott, L. (Arsenal), 1947 v S, W, Ni, Ei, Ho, F, Sw, P; 1948 v S, W, Ni, Bel, Se, I; 1949 v W, Ni, D (17)

Scott, W. R. (Brentford), 1937 v W (1)

Seaman, D. A. (QPR), 1989 v S.Ar, D (sub); 1990 v Cz (sub); (with Arsenal), 1991 v Cam, Ei, T, Arg; 1992 v Cz, H (sub); 1994 v Pol, Ho, Sm, D, N; 1995 v US, R, Ei; 1996 v Co, N, Sw, P, Bul, Cro, H, Sw, S, Ho, Sp, G; 1997 v Mol, Pol, Ge (2), Pol, F, Br; 1998 v Mol, I, P, S.Ar, Tun, R, Co, Arg (44)

Seddon, J. (Bolton W), 1923 v F, Se (2); 1924 v Bel; 1927 v W; 1929 v S (6)

Seed, J. M. (Tottenham H), 1921 v Bel; 1923 v W, Ni, Bel; 1925 v S (5)

Settle, J. (Bury), 1899 v S, W, Ni; (with Everton), 1902 v S, Ni; 1903 v Ni (6)

Sewell, J. (Sheffield W), 1952 v Ni, A, Sw; 1953 v Ni; 1954 v H (2) (6)

Sewell, W. R. (Blackburn R), 1924 v W (1)

Shackleton, L. F. (Sunderland), 1949 v W, D; 1950 v W; 1955 v W, WG (5)

Sharp, J. (Everton), 1903 v Ni; 1905 v S (2)

Sharpe, L. S. (Manchester U), 1991 v Ei (sub); 1993 v T (sub), N, US, Br, G; 1994 v Pol, Ho (8)

Shaw, G. E. (WBA), 1932 v S (1)

Shaw, G. L. (Sheffield U), 1959 v S, W, USSR, I; 1963 v W (5)

Shea, D. (Blackburn R), 1914 v W, Ni (2)

Shearer, A. (Southampton), 1992 v F, C, F; (with Blackburn R), 1993 v Sp, N, T; 1994 v Ho, D, Gr, N; 1995 v US, R, Ng, Ei, J, Se, Br; 1996 v Co, N, Sw, P, H (sub), Chn, Sw, S, Ho, Sp, G; (with Newcastle U), 1997 v Mol, Pol, I, Ge, Pol, F, Br; 1998 v Ch (sub), Sw, P, S.Ar, Tun, R, Co, Arg (43)

Shellito, K. J. (Chelsea), 1963 v Cz (1)

Shelton A. (Notts Co), 1889 v Ni; 1890 v S, W; 1891 v S, W; 1892 v S (6)

Shelton, C. (Notts Rangers), 1888 v Ni (1)

Shepherd, A. (Bolton W), 1906 v S; (with Newcastle U), 1911 v Ni (2)

Sheringham, E. P. (Tottenham H), 1993 v Pol, N; 1995 v US, R (sub), Ng (sub), U, J (sub), Se, Br; 1996 v Co (sub), N (sub), Sw, Bul, Cro, H, Sw, S, Ho, Sp, G; 1997 v Ge, M, Ge, S.Af, Pol, I, F (sub), Br; (with Manchester U), 1998 v I, Ch, Sw (sub), P, S.Ar, Tun, R (35)

Shilton, P. L. (Leicester C), 1971 v EG, W; 1972 v Sw, Ni; 1973 v Y, S (2), Ni, W, Cz, Pol, USSR, I; 1974 v A, Pol, I, W, Ni, S, Arg; (with Stoke C), 1975 v Cy; 1977 v Ni, W; (with Nottingham F), 1978 v W, H; 1979 v Cz, Se, A; 1980 v Ni, Sp, I; 1981 v N, Sw, R; 1982 v H, Ho, S, F, Cz, K, WG, Sp; (with Southampton), 1983 v D, WG, Gr, W, Gr, H, Ni, S, Aus (3); 1984 v D, H, F, Ni, W, S, USSR, Br, U, Ch; 1985 v EG, Fi, T, Ni, R, Fi, S, I, WG; 1986 v R, T, Ni, Eg, Is, USSR, S, M, Ca, P, Mor, Pol, Para, Arg; 1987 v Se, Ni (2), Sp, Br; (with Derby Co), 1988 v WG, T, Y, Ho, S, Co, Sw, Ei, Ho; 1989 v D, Se, Gr, Alb (2), Ch, S, Pol, D; 1990 v Se, Pol, I, Y, Br, Cz, D, U, Tun, Ei, Ho, Eg, Bel, Cam, WG, I (125)
Shimwell, E. (Blackpool), 1949 v Se (1)
Shutt, G. (Stoke C), 1886 v Ni (1)
Silcock, J. (Manchester U), 1921 v S, W; 1923 v Se (3)
Sillett, R. P. (Chelsea), 1955 v F, Sp, P (3)
Simms, E. (Luton T), 1922 v Ni (1)
Simpson, J. (Blackburn R), 1911 v S, W, Ni; 1912 v S, W, Ni; 1913 v S; 1914 v W (8)
Sinton, A. (QPR), 1992 v Pol, C, H (sub), Br, F, Se; 1993 v Sp, T, Br, G; (with Sheffield W), 1994 v Ho (sub), Sm (12)
Slater, W. J. (Wolverhampton W), 1955 v W, WG; 1958 v S, P, Y, USSR (3), Br, A; 1959 v USSR; 1960 v S (12)
Smalley, T. (Wolverhampton W), 1937 v W (1)
Smart, T. (Aston Villa), 1921 v S; 1924 v S, W; 1926 v Ni; 1930 v W (5)
Smith, A. (Nottingham F), 1891 v S, W; 1893 v Ni (3)
Smith, A. K. (Oxford University), 1872 v S (1)
Smith, A. M. (Arsenal), 1989 v S.Ar (sub), Gr, Alb (sub), Pol (sub); 1991 v T, USSR, Arg; 1992 v G, T, Pol (sub), H (sub), D, Se (sub) (13)
Smith, B. (Tottenham H), 1921 v S; 1922 v W (2)
Smith, C. E. (C Palace), 1876 v S (1)
Smith, G. O. (Oxford University), 1893 v Ni; 1894 v W, S; 1895 v W; 1896 v Ni, W, S; (with Old Carthusians), 1897 v Ni, W, S; 1898 v Ni, W, S; (with Corinthians), 1899 v Ni, W, S; 1899 v Ni, W, S; 1901 v S (20)
Smith, H. (Reading), 1905 v W, S; 1906 v W, Ni (4)
Smith, J. (WBA), 1920 v Ni; 1923 v Ni (2)
Smith, Joe (Bolton W), 1913 v Ni; 1914 v S, W; 1920 v W, Ni (5)
Smith, J. C. R. (Millwall), 1939 v Ni, N (2)
Smith, J. W. (Portsmouth), 1932 v Ni, W, Sp (3)
Smith, Leslie (Brentford), 1939 v R (1)
Smith, Lionel (Arsenal), 1951 v W; 1952 v W, Ni; 1953 v W, S, Bel (6)
Smith, R. A. (Tottenham H), 1961 v Ni, W, S, L, P, Sp; 1962 v S; 1963 v S, F, Br, Cz, EG; 1964 v W, Ni, R of W (15)
Smith, S. (Aston Villa), 1895 v S (1)
Smith, S. C. (Leicester C), 1936 v Ni (1)
Smith, T. (Birmingham C), 1960 v W, Se (2)
Smith, T. (Liverpool), 1971 v W (1)
Smith, W. H. (Huddersfield T), 1922 v W, S; 1928 v S (3)
Sorby, T. H. (Thursday Wanderers, Sheffield), 1879 v W (1)
Southgate, G. (Aston Villa), 1996 v P (sub), Bul, H (sub), Chn, Sw, S, Ho, Sp, G; 1997 v Mol, Pol, Ge, M, Ge (sub), S.Af, Pol, I, F, Br; 1998 v Mol, I, Cam, Sw, S.Ar, Mor, Tun, Arg (sub) (27)
Southworth, J. (Blackburn R), 1889 v W; 1891 v W; 1892 v S (3)
Sparks, F. J. (Herts Rangers), 1879 v S; (with Clapham Rovers), 1880 v S, W (3)
Spence, J. W. (Manchester U), 1926 v Bel; 1927 v Ni (2)
Spence, R. (Chelsea), 1936 v A, Bel (2)
Spencer, C. W. (Newcastle U), 1924 v S; 1925 v W (2)
Spencer, H. (Aston Villa), 1897 v S, W; 1900 v W; 1903 v Ni; 1905 v W, S (6)
Spiksley, F. (Sheffield W), 1893 v S, W; 1894 v S, Ni; 1896 v Ni; 1898 v S, W (7)
Spilsbury, B. W. (Cambridge University), 1885 v Ni; 1886 v Ni, S (3)
Spink, N. (Aston Villa), 1983 v Aus (sub) (1)
Spouncer, W. A. (Nottingham F), 1900 v W (1)
Springett, R. D. G. (Sheffield W), 1960 v Ni, S, Y, Sp, H; 1961 v Ni, S, L, P, Sp, M, I, A; 1962 v W, Ni, S, A, Sw, Pe, L, P, H, Arg, Bul, Br; 1963 v Ni, W, F (2), Sw; 1966 v W, A, N (33)
Sproston, B. (Leeds U), 1937 v W; 1938 v S, W, Ni, Cz, G, Sw, F; (with Tottenham H), 1939 v W, R of E; (with Manchester C), N (11)
Squire, R. T. (Cambridge University), 1886 v S, W, Ni (3)
Stanbrough, M. H. (Old Carthusians), 1895 v W (1)
Staniforth, R. (Huddersfield T), 1954 v S, H, Y, Bel, Sw, U; 1955 v W, WG (8)
Starling, R. W. (Sheffield W), 1933 v S; (with Aston Villa), 1937 v S (2)
Statham, D. (WBA), 1983 v W, Aus (2) (3)
Steele, F. C. (Stoke C), 1937 v S, W, Ni, N, Se, Fi (6)

Stein, B. (Luton T), 1984 v F (1)
Stephenson, C. (Huddersfield T), 1924 v W (1)
Stephenson, G. T. (Derby Co), 1928 v F, Bel; (with Sheffield W), 1931 v F (3)
Stephenson, J. E. (Leeds U), 1938 v S; 1939 v Ni (2)
Stepney, A. C. (Manchester U), 1968 v Se (1)
Sterland, M. (Sheffield W), 1989 v S.Ar (1)
Steven, T. M. (Everton), 1985 v Ni, Ei, R, Fi, I, US (sub); 1986 v T (sub), Eg, USSR (sub), M (sub), Pol, Para, Arg; 1987 v Se, Y (sub), Sp (sub); 1988 v T, Y, Ho, H, S, Sw, Ho, USSR; 1989 v S; (with Rangers), 1990 v Cz, Cam (sub), WG (sub), I; 1991 v Cam; (with Marseille), 1992 v G, C, Br, Fi, D, F (36)
Stevens, G. A. (Tottenham H), 1985 v Fi (sub), T (sub), Ni; 1986 v S (sub), M (sub), Mor (sub), Para (sub) (7)
Stevens, M. G. (Everton), 1985 v I, WG; 1986 v R, T, Ni, Eg, Is, S, Ca, P, Mor, Pol, Para, Arg; 1987 v Br, S; 1988 v T, Y, Is, Ho, H (sub), S, Sw, Ei, Ho, USSR; (with Rangers), 1989 v D, Se, Gr, Alb (2), S, Pol; 1990 v Se, Pol, I, Br, D, Tun, Ei, I; 1991 v USSR; 1992 v C, H, Br, Fi (46)
Stewart, J. (Sheffield W), 1907 v S, W; (with Newcastle U), 1911 v S (3)
Stewart, P. A. (Tottenham H), 1992 v G (sub), Cz (sub), C (sub) (3)
Stiles, N. P. (Manchester U), 1965 v S, H, Y, Se; 1966 v W, Ni, S, A, Sp, Pol (2), WG (2), N, D, U, M, F, Arg, P; 1967 v Ni, W, S, Cz; 1968 v USSR; 1969 v R; 1970 v Ni, S (28)
Stoker, J. (Birmingham), 1933 v W; 1934 v S, H (3)
Stone, S. B. (Nottingham F), 1996 v N (sub), Sw (sub), P, Bul, Cro, Chn (sub), Sw (sub), S (sub), Sp (sub) (9)
Storer, H. (Derby Co), 1924 v F; 1928 v Ni (2)
Storey, P. E. (Arsenal), 1971 v Gr, Ni, S; 1972 v Sw, WG, W, Ni, S; 1973 v W (3), Y, S (2), Ni, Cz, Pol, USSR, I (19)
Storey-Moore, I. (Nottingham F), 1970 v Ho (1)
Strange, A. H. (Sheffield W), 1930 v S, A, G; 1931 v S, W, Ni, F, Bel; 1932 v S, W, Ni, Sp; 1933 v S, Ni, A, I, Sw; 1934 v Ni, W, F (20)
Stratford, A. H. (Wanderers), 1874 v S (1)
Streten, B. (Luton T), 1950 v Ni (1)
Sturgess, A. (Sheffield U), 1911 v Ni; 1914 v S (2)
Summerbee, M. G. (Manchester C), 1968 v S, Sp, WG; 1972 v Sw, WG (sub), W, Ni; 1973 v USSR (sub) (8)
Sunderland, A. (Arsenal), 1980 v Aus (1)
Sutcliffe, J. W. (Bolton W), 1893 v W; 1895 v S, Ni; 1901 v S; (with Millwall), 1903 v W (5)
Sutton, C. R. (Blackburn R), 1998 v Cam (sub) (1)
Swan, P. (Sheffield W), 1960 v Y, Sp, H; 1961 v Ni, W, S, L, P, Sp, M, I, A; 1962 v W, Ni, S, A, Sw, L, P (19)
Swepstone, H. A. (Pilgrims), 1880 v S; 1882 v S, W; 1883 v S, W, Ni (6)
Swift, F. V. (Manchester C), 1947 v S, W, Ni, Ei, Ho, F, Sw, P; 1948 v S, W, Ni, Bel, Se, I; 1949 v S, W, Ni, D, N (19)

Tait, G. (Birmingham Excelsior), 1881 v W (1)
Talbot, B. (Ipswich T), 1977 v Ni (sub), S, Br, Arg, U; (with Arsenal), 1980 v Aus (6)
Tambling, R. V. (Chelsea), 1963 v W, F; 1966 v Y (3)
Tate, J. T. (Aston Villa), 1931 v F, Bel; 1933 v W (3)
Taylor, E. (Blackpool), 1954 v H (1)
Taylor, E. H. (Huddersfield T), 1923 v S, W, Ni, Bel; 1924 v S, Ni, F; 1926 v S (8)
Taylor, J. G. (Fulham), 1951 v Arg, P (2)
Taylor, P. H. (Liverpool), 1948 v W, Ni, Se (3)
Taylor, P. J. (C Palace), 1976 v W (sub+1), Ni, S (4)
Taylor, T. (Manchester U), 1953 v Arg, Ch, U; 1954 v Bel, Sw; 1956 v S, Br, Se, Fi, WG; 1957 v Ni, Y (sub), D (2), Ei (2); 1958 v W, Ni, F (19)
Temple, D. W. (Everton), 1965 v WG (1)
Thickett, H. (Sheffield U), 1899 v S, W (2)
Thomas, D. (Coventry C), 1983 v Aus (1+1 sub) (2)
Thomas, D. (QPR), 1975 v Cz (sub), P, Cy (sub+1), W, S (sub); 1976 v Cz (sub), P (sub) (8)
Thomas, G. R. (C Palace), 1991 v T, USSR, Arg, Aus, Nz (2), Mal; 1992 v Pol, F (9)
Thomas, M. L. (Arsenal), 1989 v S.Ar; 1990 v Y (2)
Thompson, P. (Liverpool), 1964 v P (2), Ei, US, Br, Arg; 1965 v N, W, S, Bel, Ho; 1966 v Ni; 1968 v Ni, WG; 1970 v S, Ho (sub) (16)
Thompson, P. B. (Liverpool), 1976 v W (2), Ni, S, Br, I, Fi; 1977 v Fi; 1979 v Ei (sub), Cz, Ni, S, Bul, Se (sub), A; 1980 v D, Ni, Bul, Ei, Sp (2), Arg, W, S, Bel, I; 1981 v N, R, H; 1982 v H, W, Ho, S, Fi, F, Cz, K, WG, Sp; 1983 v WG, Gr (42)
Thompson T. (Aston Villa), 1952 v W; (with Preston NE), 1957 v S (2)
Thomson, R. A. (Wolverhampton W), 1964 v Ni, US, P, Arg; 1965 v Bel, Ho, Ni, W (8)
Thornewell, G. (Derby Co), 1923 v Se (2); 1924 v F; 1925 v F (4)

Wilson, R. (Huddersfield T), 1960 v S, Y, Sp, H; 1962 v W, Ni, S, A, Sw, Pe, P, H, Arg, Bul, Br; 1963 v Ni, F, Br, Cz, EG, Sw; 1964 v W, S, R of W, U, P (2), Ei, Br, Arg; (with Everton), 1965 v S, H, Y, WG, Se; 1966 v WG (sub), W, Ni, A, Sp, Pol (2), Y, Fi, D, U, M, F, Arg, P, WG; 1967 v Ni, W, S, Cz, A; 1968 v Ni, S, USSR (2), Sp (2), Y (63)
Wilson, T. (Huddersfield T), 1928 v S (1)
Winckworth, W. N. (Old Westminsters), 1892 v W; 1893 v Ni (2)
Windridge, J. E. (Chelsea), 1908 v S, W, Ni, A (2), H, B; 1909 v Ni (8)
Wingfield-Stratford, C. V. (Royal Engineers), 1877 v S (1)
Winterburn, N. (Arsenal), 1990 v I (sub); 1993 v G (sub) (2)
Wise, D. F. (Chelsea), 1991 v T, USSR, Aus (sub), Nz (2); 1994 v N; 1995 v R (sub), Ng; 1996 v Co, N, P, H (sub) (12)
Withe, P. (Aston Villa), 1981 v Br, W, S; 1982 v N (sub), W, Ic; 1983 v H, Ni, S; 1984 v H (sub); 1985 v T (11)
Wollaston, C. H. R. (Wanderers), 1874 v S; 1875 v S; 1877 v S; 1880 v S (4)
Wolstenholme, S. (Everton), 1904 v S; (with Blackburn R), 1905 v W, Ni (3)
Wood, H. (Wolverhampton W), 1890 v S, W; 1896 v S (3)
Wood, R. E. (Manchester U), 1955 v Ni, W; 1956 v Fi (3)
Woodcock, A. S. (Nottingham F), 1978 v Ni; 1979 v Ei (sub), Cz, Bul (sub), Se; 1980 v Ni; (with Cologne), Bul, Ei, Sp (2), Arg, Bel, I; 1981 v N, R, Sw, R, W (sub), S; 1982 v Ni (sub), Ho, Fi (sub), WG (sub), Sp; (with Arsenal), 1983 v WG (sub), Gr, L, Gr; 1984 v L, F (sub), Ni, W, S, Br, U (sub); 1985 v EG, Fi, T, Ni; 1986 v R (sub), T (sub), Is (sub) (42)
Woodger, G. (Oldham Ath), 1911 v Ni (1)
Woodhall, G. (WBA), 1888 v S, W (2)
Woodley, V. R. (Chelsea), 1937 v S, N, Se, Fi; 1938 v S, W, Ni, Cz, G, Sw, F; 1939 v S, W, Ni, R of E, N, I, R, Y (19)
Woods, C. C. E. (Norwich C), 1985 v US; 1986 v Eg (sub), Is (sub), Ca (sub); (with Rangers), 1987 v Y, Sp (sub), Ni (sub), T, S; 1988 v Is, H, Sw (sub), USSR; 1989 v D (sub); 1990 v Br (sub), D (sub); 1991 v H, Pol, Ei, USSR, Aus, Nz (2), Mal; (with Sheffield W), 1992 v G, T, Pol, F, C, Br, Fi, D, F, Se; 1993 v Sp, N, T, Sm, T, Ho, Pol, N, US (43)
Woodward, V. J. (Tottenham H), 1903 v S, W, Ni; 1904 v S, Ni; 1905 v S, W, Ni; 1907 v S; 1908 v S, W, Ni, A (2), H, B;
1909 v W, Ni, H (2), A; (with Chelsea), 1910 v Ni; 1911 v W (23)
Woosnam, M. (Manchester C), 1922 v W (1)
Worrall, F. (Portsmouth), 1935 v Ho; 1937 v Ni (2)
Worthington, F. S. (Leicester C), 1974 v Ni (sub), S, Arg, EG, Bul, Y; 1975 v Cz, P (sub) (8)
Wreford-Brown, C. (Oxford University), 1889 v Ni; (with Old Carthusians), 1894 v W; 1895 v W; 1898 v S (4)
Wright, E, G. D. (Cambridge University), 1906 v W (1)
Wright, I. E. (C Palace), 1991 v Cam, Ei (sub), USSR, Nz; (with Arsenal), 1992 v H (sub); 1993 v N, T (2), Pol (sub), N (sub), US (sub), Br, G (sub); 1994 v Pol, Ho (sub), Sm, Gr (sub), N (sub); 1995 v US (sub), R; 1997 v Ge (sub), I (sub), M (sub), S.Af, I, F, Br (sub); 1998 v Mol, I, S.Ar (sub), Mor (31)
Wright, J. D. (Newcastle U), 1939 v N (1)
Wright, M. (Southampton), 1984 v W; 1985 v EG, Fi, T, Ei, R, I, WG; 1986 v R, T, Ni, Eg, USSR; 1987 v Y, Ni, S; (with Derby Co), 1988 v Is, Ho (sub), Co, Sw, Ei, Ho; 1990 v Cz (sub), Tun (sub), Ho, Eg, Bel, Cam, WG, I; 1991 v H, Pol, Ei (2), Cam, USSR, Arg, Aus, Nz, Mal; (with Liverpool), 1992 v F, Fi; 1993 v Sp; 1996 v Cro, H (45)
Wright, T. J. (Everton), 1968 v USSR; 1969 v R (2), M (sub), U, Br; 1970 v W, Ho, Bel, R (sub), Br (11)
Wright, W. A. (Wolverhampton W), 1947 v S, W, Ni, Ei, Ho, F, Sw, P; 1948 v S, W, Ni, Bel, Se, I; 1949 v S, W, Ni, D, Sw, Se, N, F; 1950 v S, W, Ni, Ei, I, P, Bel, Ch, US, Sp; 1951 v Ni, S, Arg; 1952 v W, Ni, S, F, A (2), I, Sw; 1953 v Ni, W, S, Bel, Arg, Ch, U, US; 1954 v W, Ni, S, R of E, H (2), Y, Bel, Sw, U; 1955 v W, Ni, S, WG, F, Sp, P; 1956 v Ni, W, S, Br, Se, Fi, WG, D, Sp; 1957 v S, W, Ni, Y, D (2), Ei (2); 1958 v W, Ni, S, P, Y, USSR (3), Br, A, F; 1959 v W, Ni, S, USSR, I, Br, Pe, M, US (105)
Wylie, J. G. (Wanderers), 1878 v S (1)

Yates, J. (Burnley), 1889 v Ni (1)
York, R. E. (Aston Villa), 1922 v S; 1926 v S (2)
Young, A. (Huddersfield T), 1933 v W; 1937 v S, H, N, Se; 1938 v G, Sw, F; 1939 v W (9)
Young, G. M. (Sheffield W), 1965 v W (1)
R. E. Evans also played for Wales against E, Ni, S; J. Reynolds also played for Ireland against E, W, S.

# NORTHERN IRELAND

Aherne, T. (Belfast C), 1947 v E; 1948 v S; 1949 v W; (with Luton T), 1950 v W (4)
Alexander, T. E. (Cliftonville), 1895 v S (1)
Allan, C. (Cliftonville), 1936 v E (1)
Allen, J. (Limavady), 1887 v E (1)
Anderson, T. (Manchester U), 1973 v Cy, E, S, W; 1974 v Bul, P; (with Swindon T), 1975 v S (sub); 1976 v Is; 1977 v Ho, Bel, WG, E, S, W, Ic; 1978 v Ic, Ho, Bel; (with Peterborough U), S, E, W; 1979 v D (sub) (22)
Anderson, W. (Linfield), 1898 v W, E, S; (with Cliftonville), 1899 v S (4)
Andrews, W. (Glentoran), 1908 v S; (with Grimsby T), 1913 v E, S (3)
Armstrong, G. J. (Tottenham H), 1977 v WG, E, W (sub), Ic (sub); 1978 v Bel, S, E, W; 1979 v Ei, D, Bul, E, Bul, E, S, W, D; 1980 v E, Ei, Is, S, E, W, Aus (3); 1981 v Se; (with Watford), P, S, P, S, Se; 1982 v S, Is, E, F, W, Y, Hon, Sp, A, F; 1983 v A, T, Alb, S, E, W; (with Real Mallorca), 1984 v A, WG, E, W, Fi; 1985 v R, Fi, E, Sp; (with WBA), 1986 v T, R (sub), E (sub), F (sub); (with Chesterfield), D (sub), Br (sub) (63)
Baird, G. (Distillery), 1896 v S, E, W (3)
Baird, H. C. (Huddersfield T), 1939 v E (1)
Balfe, J. (Shelbourne), 1909 v E; 1910 v W (2)
Bambrick, J. (Linfield), 1929 v W, S, E; 1930 v W, S, E; 1932 v W; (with Chelsea), 1935 v W; 1936 v E, S; 1938 v W (11)
Banks, S. J. (Cliftonville), 1937 v W (1)
Barr, H. H. (Linfield), 1962 v E; (with Coventry C), 1963 v E, Pol (3)
Barron, J. H. (Cliftonville), 1894 v E, W, S; 1895 v S; 1896 v S; 1897 v E, W (7)
Barry, J. (Cliftonville), 1888 v W, S; 1889 v E (3)
Barry, J. (Bohemians), 1900 v S (1)
Baxter, R. A. (Distillery), 1887 v S (1)
Baxter, S. N. (Cliftonville), 1887 v W (1)
Bennett, L. V. (Dublin University), 1889 v W (1)
Berry, J. (Cliftonville), 1888 v S, W; 1889 v E (3)
Best, G. (Manchester U), 1964 v W, U; 1965 v E, Ho (2), S, Sw (2), Alb; 1966 v S, E, Alb; 1967 v E; 1968 v S; 1969 v E, S, W, T; 1970 v S, E, W, USSR; 1971 v Cy (2), Sp, E, S, W;
1972 v USSR, Sp; 1973 v Bul; 1974 v P; (with Fulham), 1977 v Ho, Bel, WG; 1978 v Ic, Ho (37)
Bingham, W. L. (Sunderland), 1951 v F; 1952 v E, S, W; 1953 v E, S, F, W; 1954 v E, S, W; 1955 v E, S, W; 1956 v E, S, W; 1957 v E, S, W, P (2), I; 1958 v S, E, W, I (2), Arg, Cz (2), WG, F; (with Luton T), 1959 v E, S, W, Sp; 1960 v S, E, W; (with Everton), 1961 v E, S, WG (2), Gr, I; 1962 v E, Gr; 1963 v E, S, Pol (2), Sp; (with Port Vale), 1964 v S, E, Sp (56)
Black, K. T. (Luton T), 1988 v Fr (sub), Ma (sub); 1989 v Ei, H, Sp (2), Ch (sub); 1990 v H, N, U; 1991 v Y (2), D, A, Pol, Fa; (with Nottingham F), 1992 v Fa, A, D, S, Li, G; 1993 v Sp, D (sub), Alb, Ei (sub), Sp; 1994 v D (sub), Ei (sub), R (sub) (30)
Black, T. (Glentoran), 1901 v E (1)
Blair, H. (Portadown), 1931 v S; 1932 v S; (with Swansea), 1934 v S (3)
Blair, J. (Cliftonville), 1907 v W, E, S; 1908 v E, S (5)
Blair, R. V. (Oldham Ath), 1975 v Se (sub), S (sub), W; 1976 v Se, Is (5)
Blanchflower, R. D. (Barnsley), 1950 v S, W; 1951 v E, S; (with Aston Villa), 1952 v W; 1953 v E, S, W, F; 1954 v E, S, W; 1955 v E, S; (with Tottenham H), W; 1956 v E, S, W; 1957 v E, S, W, I, P (2); 1958 v E, S, W, I (2), Cz (2), Arg, F, WG; 1959 v E, S, W, Sp; 1960 v E, S, W; 1961 v E, S, W, WG (2); 1962 v E, S, W, Gr, Ho; 1963 v E, S, Pol (2) (56)
Blanchflower, J. (Manchester U), 1954 v W; 1955 v E, S; 1956 v S, W; 1957 v S, E, P; 1958 v S, E, I (2) (12)
Bookman, L. J. O. (Bradford C), 1914 v W; (with Luton T), 1921 v S, W; 1922 v E (4)
Bothwell, A. W. (Ards), 1926 v S, E, W; 1927 v E, W (5)
Bowler, G. C. (Hull C), 1950 v E, S, W (3)
Boyle, P. (Sheffield U), 1901 v E; 1902 v E; 1903 v S, W; 1904 v E (5)
Braithwaite, R. M. (Linfield), 1962 v W; 1963 v P, Sp; (with Middlesbrough), 1964 v W, U; 1965 v E, S, Sw (2), Ho (10)
Breen, T. (Belfast C), 1935 v E, W; 1937 v E, S; (with Manchester U), 1937 v W; 1938 v E, S; 1939 v W, S (9)
Brennan, B. (Bohemians), 1912 v W (1)

Brennan, R. A. (Luton T), 1949 v W; (with Birmingham C), 1950 v E, S, W; (with Fulham), 1951 v E (5)
Briggs, W. R. (Manchester U), 1962 v W; (with Swansea T), 1965 v Ho (2)
Brisby, D. (Distillery), 1891 v S (1)
Brolly, T. H. (Millwall), 1937 v W; 1938 v W; 1939 v E, W (4)
Brookes, E. A. (Shelbourne), 1920 v S (1)
Brotherston, N. (Blackburn R), 1980 v S, E, W, Aus (3); 1981 v Se, P; 1982 v S, Is, E, F, S, W, Hon (sub), A (sub); 1983 v A (sub), WG, Alb, T, Alb, S (sub), E (sub), W; 1984 v T; 1985 v Is (sub), T (27)
Brown, J. (Glenavon), 1921 v W; (with Tranmere R), 1924 v E, W (3)
Brown, J. (Wolverhampton W), 1935 v E, W; 1936 v E; (with Coventry C), 1937 v E, W; 1938 v S, W; (with Birmingham C), 1939 v E, S, W (10)
Brown, N. M. (Limavady), 1887 v E (1)
Brown, W. G. (Glenavon), 1926 v W (1)
Browne, F. (Cliftonville), 1887 v E, S, W; 1888 v E, S (5)
Browne, R. J. (Leeds U), 1936 v E, W; 1938 v E, W; 1939 v E, S (6)
Bruce, W. (Glentoran), 1961 v S; 1967 v W (2)
Buckle, H. R. (Sunderland), 1904 v E; (with Bristol R), 1908 v W (2)
Buckle, J. (Cliftonville), 1882 v E (1)
Burnett, J. (Distillery), 1894 v E, W, S; (with Glentoran), 1895 v E, W (5)
Burnison, J. (Distillery), 1901 v E, W (2)
Burnison, S. (Distillery), 1908 v E; 1910 v E, S; (with Bradford), 1911 v E, S, W; (with Distillery), 1912 v E; 1913 v W (8)
Burns, J. (Glenavon), 1923 v E (1)
Butler, M. P. (Blackpool), 1939 v W (1)

Campbell, A. C. (Crusaders), 1963 v W; 1965 v Sw (2)
Campbell, D. A. (Nottingham F), 1986 v Mor (sub), Br; 1987 v E (2), T, Y; (with Charlton Ath), 1988 v Y, T (sub), Gr (sub), Pol (sub) (10)
Campbell, James (Cliftonville), 1897 v E, S, W; 1898 v E, S, W; 1899 v E; 1900 v E, S; 1901 v S, W; 1902 v S; 1903 v E; 1904 v S (14)
Campbell, John (Cliftonville), 1896 v W (1)
Campbell, J. P. (Fulham), 1951 v E, S (2)
Campbell, R. M. (Bradford C), 1982 v S, W (sub) (2)
Campbell, W. G. (Dundee), 1968 v S, E; 1969 v T; 1970 v S, W, USSR (6)
Carey, J. J. (Manchester U), 1947 v E, S, W; 1948 v E; 1949 v E, S, W (7)
Carroll, E. (Glenavon), 1925 v S (1)
Carroll, R. E. (Wigan Ath), 1997 v Th (sub) (1)
Casey, T. (Newcastle U), 1955 v W; 1956 v W; 1957 v E, S, W, I, P (2); 1958 v WG, F; (with Portsmouth), 1959 v E, Sp (12)
Caskey, W. T.(Derby Co), 1979 v Bul, E, Bul, E, S (sub), D (sub); 1980 v E (sub); (with Tulsa R), 1982 v F (sub) (8)
Cassidy, T. (Newcastle U), 1971 v E (sub); 1972 v USSR (sub); 1974 v Bul (sub), S, E, W; 1975 v N; 1976 v S, E, W; 1977 v WG (sub); 1980 v E, Ei (sub), Is, S, E, W, Aus (3); (with Burnley), 1981 v Se, P; 1982 v Is, Sp (sub) (24)
Caughey, M. (Linfield), 1986 v F (sub), D (sub) (2)
Chambers, R. J. (Distillery), 1921 v W; (with Bury), 1928 v E, S, W; 1929 v E, S, W; 1930 v S, W; (with Nottingham F), 1932 v E, S, W (12)
Chatton, H. A. (Partick T), 1925 v E, S; 1926 v E (3)
Christian, J. (Linfield), 1889 v S (1)
Clarke, C. J. (Bournemouth), 1986 v F, D, Mor, Alg (sub), Sp, Br; (with Southampton), 1987 v E, T, Y; 1988 v Y, T, Gr, Pol, F, Ma; 1989 v Ei, H, Sp (1+1 sub); (with QPR), Ma, Ch; 1990 v H, Ei, N; (with Portsmouth), 1991 v Y (sub), D, A, Pol, Y (sub), Fa; 1992 v Fa, A, D, S, G; 1993 v Alb, Sp, D (38)
Clarke, R. (Belfast C), 1901 v E, S (2)
Cleary, J. (Glentoran), 1982 v S, W; 1983 v W (sub); 1984 v T (sub); 1985 v Is (5)
Clements, D. (Coventry C), 1965 v W, Ho; 1966 v M; 1967 v S, W; 1968 v S, E; 1969 v T (2), S, W; 1970 v S, E, W, USSR (2); 1971 v Sp, E, S, W, Cy; (with Sheffield W), 1972 v USSR (2), Sp, E, S, W; 1973 v Bul, Cy (2), P, E, S, W; (with Everton), 1974 v Bul, P, S, E, W; 1975 v N, Y, E, S, W; 1976 v Se, Y; (with New York Cosmos), E, W (48)
Clugston, J. (Cliftonville), 1888 v W; 1889 v W, S, E; 1890 v E, S; 1891 v E, W; 1892 v E, S, W; 1893 v E, S, W (14)
Cochrane, D. (Leeds U), 1939 v E, W; 1947 v E, S, W; 1948 v E, S, W; 1949 v S, W; 1950 v S, E (12)
Cochrane, G. T. (Coleraine), 1976 v N (sub); (with Burnley), 1978 v S (sub), E (sub), W (sub); 1979 v Ei (sub); (with Middlesbrough), D, Bul, E, Bul, E; 1980 v Is, E (sub), W (sub), Aus (1+2 sub); 1981 v Se (sub), P (sub), S, P, S, Se;

1982 v E (sub), F; (with Gillingham), 1984 v S, Fi (sub) (26)
Cochrane, M. (Distillery), 1898 v S, W, E; 1899 v E; 1900 v E, S, W; (with Leicester Fosse), 1901 v S (8)
Collins, F. (Celtic), 1922 v S (1)
Condy, J. (Distillery), 1882 v W; 1886 v E, S (3)
Connell, T. E. (Coleraine), 1978 v W (sub) (1)
Connor, J. (Glentoran), 1901 v S, E; (with Belfast C), 1905 v E, S, W; 1907 v E, S; 1908 v E, S; 1909 v W; 1911 v S, E, W (13)
Connor, M. J. (Brentford), 1903 v S, W; (with Fulham), 1904 v E (3)
Cook, W. (Celtic), 1933 v E, W, S; (with Everton), 1935 v E; 1936 v S, W; 1937 v E, S, W; 1938 v E, S, W; 1939 v E, S, W (15)
Cooke, S. (Belfast YMCA), 1889 v E; (with Cliftonville), 1890 v E, S (3)
Coulter, J. (Belfast C), 1934 v E, S, W; (with Everton), 1935 v E, S, W; 1937 v S, W; (with Grimsby T), 1938 v S, W; (with Chelmsford C), 1939 v S (11)
Cowan, J. (Newcastle U), 1970 v E (sub) (1)
Cowan, T. S. (Queen's Island), 1925 v W (1)
Coyle, F. (Coleraine), 1956 v E, S; 1957 v P; (with Nottingham F), 1958 v Arg (4)
Coyle, L. (Derry C), 1989 v Ch (sub) (1)
Coyle, R. I. (Sheffield W), 1973 v P, Cy (sub), W (sub); 1974 v Bul (sub), P (sub) (5)
Craig, A. B. (Rangers), 1908 v E, S, W; 1909 v S; (with Morton), 1912 v S; 1914 v E, S, W (9)
Craig, D. J. (Newcastle U), 1967 v W; 1968 v W; 1969 v T (2), E, S, W; 1970 v E, S, W, USSR; 1971 v Cy (2), Sp, S (sub); 1972 v USSR, S (sub); 1973 v Cy (2), E, S, W; 1974 v Bul, P; 1975 v N (25)
Crawford, A. (Distillery), 1889 v E, W; (with Cliftonville), 1891 v E, S, W; 1893 v E, W (7)
Croft, T. (Queen's Island), 1924 v E (1)
Crone, R. (Distillery), 1889 v S; 1890 v E, S, W (4)
Crone, W. (Distillery), 1882 v W; 1884 v E, S, W; 1886 v E, S, W; 1887 v E; 1888 v E, S, W; 1889 v S; 1890 v W (12)
Crooks, W. J. (Manchester U), 1922 v W (1)
Crossan, E. (Blackburn R), 1950 v S; 1951 v E; 1955 v W (3)
Crossan, J. A. (Sparta-Rotterdam), 1960 v E; (with Sunderland), 1963 v W, P, Sp; 1964 v E, S, W, S, U, Sp; 1965 v E, S, Sw (2); (with Manchester C), W, Ho (2), Alb; 1966 v S, E, Alb, WG; 1967 v E, S; (with Middlesbrough), 1968 v S (24)
Crothers, C. (Distillery), 1907 v W (1)
Cumming, L. (Huddersfield T), 1929 v W, S; (with Oldham Ath), 1930 v E (3)
Cunningham, W. (Ulster), 1892 v S, E, W; 1893 v E (4)
Cunningham, W. E. (St Mirren), 1951 v W; 1953 v E; 1954 v S; 1955 v S; (with Leicester C), 1956 v E, S, W; 1957 v E, S, W, I, P (2); 1958 v S, W, I, Cz (2), Arg, WG, F; 1959 v E, S, W; 1960 v E, S, W; (with Dunfermline Ath), 1961 v W; 1962 v W, Ho (30)
Curran, S. (Belfast C), 1926 v S, W; 1928 v S (3)
Curran, J. J. (Glenavon), 1922 v W; (with Pontypridd), 1923 v E, S; (with Glenavon), 1924 v E (4)
Cush, W. W. (Glenavon), 1951 v E, S; 1954 v S, E; 1957 v W, I, P (2); (with Leeds U), 1958 v I (2), W, Cz (2), Arg, WG, F; 1959 v E, S, W, Sp; 1960 v E, S, W; (with Portadown), 1961 v WG, Gr; 1962 v Gr (26)

Dalton, W. (YMCA), 1888 v S; (with Linfield), 1890 v S, W; 1891 v S, W; 1892 v E, S, W; 1894 v E, S, W (11)
D'Arcy, S. D. (Chelsea), 1952 v W; 1953 v E; (with Brentford), 1953 v S, W, F (5)
Darling, J. (Linfield), 1897 v E, S; 1900 v S; 1902 v E, S, W; 1903 v E, S, W; 1905 v E, S, W; 1906 v E, S, W; 1908 v W; 1909 v E; 1910 v E, S, W; 1912 v S (21)
Davey, H. H. (Reading), 1926 v E; 1927 v E, S; 1928 v E; (with Portsmouth), 1928 v W (5)
Davis, T. L. (Oldham Ath), 1937 v E (1)
Davison, A. J. (Bolton W), 1996 v Se; (with Bradford C), 1997 v Th; (with Grimsby T), 1998 v G (3)
Davison, J. R. (Cliftonville), 1882 v E, W; 1883 v E, W; 1884 v E, W, S; 1885 v E (8)
Dennison, R. (Wolverhampton W), 1988 v F, Ma; 1989 v H, Sp Ch (sub); 1990 v Ei, U; 1991 v Y (2), A, Pol, Fa (sub); 1992 v Fa, A, D (sub); 1993 v Sp (sub); 1994 v Co (sub); 1997 v I (sub) (18)
Devine, A. O. (Limavady), 1886 v E, W; 1887 v W; 1888 v W (4)
Devine, J. (Glentoran), 1990 v U (sub) (1)
Dickson, D. (Coleraine), 1970 v S (sub), W; 1973 v Cy, P (4)
Dickson, T. A. (Linfield), 1957 v S (1)
Dickson, W. (Chelsea), 1951 v W, F; 1952 v E, S, W; 1953 v E, S, W, F; (with Arsenal), 1954 v E, W; 1955 v E (12)
Diffin, W. J. (Belfast C), 1931 v W (1)

Dill, A. H. (Knock), 1882 v E, W; (with Down Ath), 1883 v W; (with Cliftonville), 1884 v E, S, W; 1885 v E, S, W (9)
Doherty, I. (Belfast C), 1901 v E (1)
Doherty, J. (Cliftonville), 1933 v E, W (2)
Doherty, L. (Linfield), 1985 v Is; 1988 v T (sub) (2)
Doherty, M. (Derry C), 1938 v S (1)
Doherty, P. D. (Blackpool), 1935 v E, W; 1936 v E, S; (with Manchester C), 1937 v E, W; 1938 v E, S; 1939 v E, W; (with Derby Co), 1947 v E; (with Huddersfield T), 1947 v W; 1948 v E, W; 1949 v S; (with Doncaster R), 1951 v S (16)
Donaghy, M. M. (Luton T), 1980 v S, E, W; 1981 v Se, P, S (sub); 1982 v S, Is, E, F, S, W, Y, Hon, Sp, F; 1983 v A, WG, Alb, T, Alb, S, E, W; 1984 v A, T, WG, S, E, W, Fi; 1985 v R, Fi, E, Sp, T; 1986 v T, R, E, F, D, Mor, Alg, Sp, Br; 1987 v E (2), T, Is, Y; 1988 v Y, T, Gr, Pol, F, Ma; 1989 v Ei, H; (with Manchester U), Sp (2), Ma, Ch; 1990 v Ei, N; 1991 v Y (2), D, A, Pol, Fa; 1992 v Fa, A, D, S, Li, G; (with Chelsea), 1993 v Alb, Sp, D, Alb, Ei, Sp, Li, La; 1994 v La, D, Ei, R, Lie, Co, M (91)
Donnelly, L. (Distillery), 1913 v W (1)
Doran, J. F. (Brighton), 1921 v E; 1922 v E, W (3)
Dougan, A. D. (Portsmouth), 1958 v Cz; (with Blackburn R), 1960 v S; 1961 v E, W, I, Gr; (with Aston Villa), 1963 v S, Pol (2); (with Leicester C), 1966 v S, E, W, M, Alb, WG; 1967 v E, S; (with Wolverhampton W), 1967 v W; 1968 v S, W,; 1969 v Is, T (2), E, S, W; 1970 v S, E, USSR (2); 1971 v Cy (2), Sp, E, S, W; 1972 v USSR (2), E, S, W; 1973 v Bul, Cy (43)
Douglas, J. P. (Belfast C), 1947 v E (1)
Dowd, H. O. (Glenavon), 1974 v W; (with Sheffield W), 1975 v N (sub), Se (3)
Dowie, I. (Luton T), 1990 v N (sub), U; 1991 v Y, D, A (sub), (with West Ham U), Y, Fa; (with Southampton) 1992 v Fa, A, D (sub), S (sub), Li; 1993 v Alb (2), Ei, Sp (sub), Li, La; 1994 v La, D, Ei (sub), R (sub), Lie, Co, M (sub); 1995 v A, Ei; (with C Palace) Ei, La, Ca, Ch, La; 1996 v P; (with West Ham U), A, N, G; 1997 v Uk, Arm, G, Alb, P, Uk, Arm, Th; 1998 v Alb, P; (with QPR), Slo, Sw, Sp (49)
Duggan, H. A. (Leeds U), 1930 v E; 1931 v E, W; 1933 v E; 1934 v E; 1935 v S, W; 1936 v S (8)
Dunlop, G. (Linfield), 1985 v Is; 1987 v E, Y; 1990 v Ei (4)
Dunne, J. (Sheffield U), 1928 v W; 1931 v W, E; 1932 v E, S; 1933 v E, W (7)

Eames, W. L. E. (Dublin U), 1885 v E, S, W (3)
Eglington, T. J. (Everton), 1947 v S, W; 1948 v E, S, W; 1949 v E (6)
Elder, A. R. (Burnley), 1960 v W; 1961 v S, E, W, WG (2), Gr; 1962 v E, S, Gr; 1963 v E, S, W, Pol (2); Sp; 1964 v W, U; 1965 v E, S, W, Sw (2), Ho (2), Alb; 1966 v E, S, W, M, Alb; 1967 v E, S, W; (with Stoke C), 1968 v E, W; 1969 v E (sub), S, W; 1970 v USSR (40)
Elleman, A. R. (Cliftonville), 1889 v W; 1890 v E (2)
Elwood, J. H. (Bradford), 1929 v W; 1930 v E (2)
Emerson, W. (Glentoran), 1920 v S, W; 1921 v E; 1922 v E, S; (with Burnley), 1922 v W; 1923 v E, S, W; 1924 v E (11)
English, S. (Rangers), 1933 v W, S (2)
Enright, J. (Leeds C), 1912 v S (1)

Falloon, E. (Aberdeen), 1931 v S; 1933 v S (2)
Farquharson, T. G. (Cardiff C), 1923 v S, W; 1924 v E, S, W; 1925 v E, S (7)
Farrell, P. (Distillery), 1901 v S, W (2)
Farrell, P. (Hibernian), 1938 v W (1)
Farrell, P. D. (Everton), 1947 v S, W; 1948 v E, S, W; 1949 v E, W (7)
Feeney, J. M. (Linfield), 1947 v S; (with Swansea T), 1950 v E (2)
Feeney, W. (Glentoran), 1976 v Is (1)
Ferguson, W. (Linfield), 1966 v M; 1967 v E (2)
Ferris, J. (Belfast C), 1920 v E, W; (with Chelsea), 1921 v S, E; (with Belfast C), 1928 v S (5)
Ferris, R. O. (Birmingham C), 1950 v S; 1951 v F; 1952 v S (3)
Fettis, A. W. (Hull C), 1992 v D, Li; 1993 v D; 1994 v M; 1995 v P, Ei, La, Ca, Ch, La; 1996 v P, Lie, A; (with Nottingham F), v N, G; 1997 v Uk, Arm (2); (with Blackburn R), 1998 v P, Slo, Sw, Sp (22)
Finney, T. (Sunderland), 1975 v N, E (sub), S, W; 1976 v N, Y, S; (with Cambridge U), 1980 v E, Is, S, E, W, Aus (2) (14)
Fitzpatrick, J. C. (Bohemians), 1896 v E, S (2)
Flack, H. (Burnley), 1929 v S (1)
Fleming, J. G. (Nottingham F), 1987 v E (2), Is, Y; 1988 v T, Gr, Pol; 1989 v Ma, Ch; (with Manchester C), 1990 v H, Ei; (with Barnsley), 1991 v Y; 1992 v Li (sub), G; 1993 v

Alb, Sp, D, Alb, Sp, Li, La; 1994 v La, D, Ei, R, Lie, Co, M; 1995 v P, A, Ei (31)
Forbes, G. (Limavady), 1888 v W; (with Distillery), 1891 v E, S (3)
Forde, J. T. (Ards), 1959 v Sp; 1961 v E, S, WG (4)
Foreman, T. A. (Cliftonville), 1899 v S (1)
Forsyth, J. (YMCA), 1888 v E, S (2)
Fox, W. T. (Ulster), 1887 v E, S (2)
Fulton, R. P. (Belfast C), 1930 v W; 1931 v E, S, W; 1932 v W, E; 1933 v E, S; 1934 v E, W, S; 1935 v E, W, S; 1936 v S, W; 1937 v E, S, W; 1938 v W (20)

Gaffikin, G. (Linfield Ath), 1890 v S, W; 1891 v S, W; 1892 v E, S, W; 1893 v E, S, W; 1894 v E, S, W; 1895 v E, W (15)
Galbraith, W. (Distillery), 1890 v W (1)
Gallagher, P. (Celtic), 1920 v E, S; 1922 v S; 1923 v S, W; 1924 v S, W; 1925 v S, W, E; (with Falkirk), 1927 v S (11)
Gallogly, C. (Huddersfield T), 1951 v E, S (2)
Gara, A. (Preston NE), 1902 v E, S, W (3)
Gardiner, A. (Cliftonville), 1930 v S, W; 1931 v S; 1932 v E, S (5)
Garrett, J. (Distillery), 1925 v W (1)
Gaston, R. (Oxford U), 1969 v Is (sub) (1)
Gaukrodger, G. (Linfield), 1895 v W (1)
Gaussen, A. D. (Moyola Park), 1884 v E, S; (with Magherafelt), 1888 v E, W; 1889 v E, W (6)
Geary, J. (Glentoran), 1931 v S; 1932 v S (2)
Gibb, J. T. (Wellington Park) 1884 v S, W; 1885 v S, E, W; 1886 v S; 1887 v S, E, W; (with Cliftonville), 1889 v S (10)
Gibb, T. J. (Cliftonville), 1936 v W (1)
Gibson W. K. (Cliftonville), 1894 v S, W, E; 1895 v S; 1897 v W; 1898 v S, W, E; 1901 v S, W, E; 1902 v S, W (13)
Gillespie, K.R. (Manchester U), 1995 v P, A, Ei; (with Newcastle U) Ei, La, Ca, Ch (sub), La (sub); 1996 v P, A, N, G; 1997 v Uk, Arm, Bel, P, Uk; 1998 v G, Alb, Slo, Sw (21)
Gillespie, S. (Hertford), 1886 v E, S, W; 1887 v E, S, W (6)
Gillespie, W. (Sheffield U), 1913 v E, S; 1914 v E, W; 1920 v S, W; 1921 v E; 1922 v E, S, W; 1923 v E, S, W; 1924 v E, S, W; 1925 v E, S; 1926 v S, W; 1927 v E, W; 1928 v E; 1929 v E; 1931 v E (25)
Gillespie, W. (West Down), 1889 v W (1)
Goodall, A. L. (Derby Co), 1899 v S, W; 1900 v E, W; 1901 v E; 1902 v S; 1903 v E, W; (with Glossop), 1904 v E, W (10)
Goodbody, M. F. (Dublin University), 1889 v E; 1891 v W (2)
Gordon, H. (Linfield), 1895 v E; 1896 v E, S (3)
Gordon R. W. (Linfield), 1891 v S; 1892 v W, E, S; 1893 v E, S, W (7)
Gordon, T. (Linfield), 1894 v W; 1895 v E (2)
Gorman, W. C. (Brentford), 1947 v E, S, W; 1948 v W (4)
Gowdy, J. (Glentoran), 1920 v E; (with Queen's Island), 1924 v W; (with Falkirk), 1926 v E, S; 1927 v E, S (6)
Gowdy, W. A. (Hull C), 1932 v S; (with Sheffield W), 1933 v S; (with Linfield), 1935 v E, S, W; (with Hibernian), 1936 v W (6)
Graham, W. G. L. (Doncaster R), 1951 v W, F; 1952 v E, S, W; 1953 v S, F; 1954 v E, W; 1955 v S, W; 1956 v E, S; 1959 v E (14)
Gray, P. (Luton T), 1993 v D (sub), Alb, Ei, Sp; (with Sunderland), 1994 v La, D, Ei, R, Lie (sub); 1995 v P, A, Ei, Ca, Ch (sub); 1996 v P (sub), Lie, A; (with Nancy), 1997 v Uk, Arm, G (sub) (20)
Greer, W. (QPR), 1909 v E, S, W (3)
Gregg, H. (Doncaster R), 1954 v W; 1957 v E, S, W, I, P (2); 1958 v E, I; (with Manchester U), 1958 v Cz, Arg, WG, F, W; 1959 v E, W; 1960 v S, E, W; 1961 v E, S; 1962 v S, Gr; 1964 v S, E (25)
Griffin, D. J. (St Johnstone), 1996 v G; 1997 v Uk, I, Bel (sub), Th; 1998 v G (sub), Alb (7)

Hall, G. (Distillery), 1897 v E (1)
Halligan, W. (Derby Co), 1911 v W; (with Wolverhampton W), 1912 v E (2)
Hamill, M. (Manchester U), 1912 v E; 1914 v E, S; (with Belfast C), 1920 v E, S, W; (with Manchester C), 1921 v S (7)
Hamilton, B. (Linfield), 1969 v T; 1971 v Cy (2), E, S, W; (with Ipswich T), 1972 v USSR (1+1 sub), Sp; 1973 v Bul, Cy (2), P, E, S, W; 1974 v Bul, S, E, W; 1975 v N, Se, Y, E; 1976 v Se, N, Y; (with Everton), Is, S, E, W; 1977 v Ho, Bel, WG, E, S, W, Ic; (with Millwall), 1978 v S, W; 1979 v Ei (sub); (with Swindon T), Bul (2), E, S, W, D; 1980 v Aus (2 sub) (50)
Hamilton, J. (Knock), 1882 v E, W (2)
Hamilton, R. (Rangers), 1928 v S; 1929 v E; 1930 v S, E; 1932 v S (5)
Hamilton, W. D. (Dublin Association), 1885 v W (1)
Hamilton, W. J. (Distillery), 1908 v W (1)

Hamilton, W. J. (Dublin Association), 1885 v W (1)
Hamilton, W. R. (QPR), 1978 v S (sub); (with Burnley), 1980 v S, E, W, Aus (2); 1981 v Se, P, S, P, S, Se; 1982 v S, Is, E, W, Y, Hon, Sp, A, F; 1983 v A, WG, Alb (2), S, E, W; 1984 v A, T, WG, S, E, W, Fi; (with Oxford U), 1985 v R, Sp; 1986 v Mor (sub), Alg, Sp (sub), Br (sub) (41)
Hampton, H. (Bradford C), 1911 v E, S, W; 1912 v E, W; 1913 v E, S, W; 1914 v E (9)
Hanna, J. (Nottingham F), 1912 v S, W (2)
Hanna, J. D. (Royal Artillery, Portsmouth), 1899 v W (1)
Hannon, D. J. (Bohemians), 1908 v E, S; 1911 v E, S; 1912 v W; 1913 v E (6)
Harkin, J. T. (Southport), 1968 v W; 1969 v T; (with Shrewsbury T), W (sub); 1970 v USSR; 1971 v Sp (5)
Harland, A. I. (Linfield), 1923 v E (1)
Harris, J. (Cliftonville), 1921 v W (1)
Harris, V. (Shelbourne), 1906 v E; 1907 v E, W; 1908 v E, W, S; (with Everton), 1909 v E, W, S; 1910 v E, S, W; 1911 v E, S, W; 1912 v E; 1913 v E, S; 1914 v S, W (20)
Harvey, M. (Sunderland), 1961 v I; 1962 v Ho; 1963 v W, Sp; 1964 v S, E, W, U, Sp; 1965 v E, S, W, Sw (2), Ho (2), Alb; 1966 v S, E, W, M, Alb, WG; 1967 v E, S; 1968 v E, W; 1969 v Is, T (2), E; 1970 v USSR; 1971 v Cy, W (sub) (34)
Hastings, J. (Knock), 1882 v E, W; (with Ulster), 1883 v W; 1884 v E, S; 1886 v E, S (7)
Hatton, S. (Linfield), 1963 v S, Pol (2)
Hayes, W. E. (Huddersfield T), 1938 v E, S; 1939 v E, S (4)
Healy, P, J. (Coleraine), 1982 v S, W, Hon (sub); (with Glentoran), 1983 v A (sub) (4)
Hegan, D. (WBA), 1970 v USSR; (with Wolverhampton W), 1972 v USSR, E, S, W; 1973 v Bul, Cy (7)
Henderson, J. (Ulster), 1885 v E, S, W (3)
Hewison, G. (Moyola Park), 1885 v S, E (2)
Hill, C. F. (Sheffield U), 1990 v N, U; 1991 v Pol, Y; 1992 v A, D; (with Leicester C) 1995 v Ei, La; 1996 v P, Lie, A, N, Se, G; 1997 v Uk, Arm, G, Alb, P, Uk, Arm, Th; (with Trelleborg), 1998 v Q, Alb, P; (with Northampton T), Slo (26)
Hill, M. J. (Norwich C), 1959 v W; 1960 v W; 1961 v WG; 1962 v S; (with Everton), 1964 v S, E, Sp (7)
Hinton, E. (Fulham), 1947 v S, W; 1948 v S, E, W; (with Millwall), 1951 v W, F (7)
Hopkins, J. (Brighton), 1926 v E (1)
Horlock, K. (Swindon U), 1995 v La, Ca; 1997 v G, Alb, I; (with Manchester C), v Bel, Uk, Arm, Th; 1998 v G, Alb, P (12)
Houston, J. (Linfield), 1912 v S, W; 1913 v W; (with Everton), 1913 v E, S; 1914 v S (6)
Houston, W. (Linfield), 1933 v W (1)
Houston, W. J. (Moyola Park), 1885 v E, S (2)
Hughes, A. W. (Newcastle U), 1998 v Slo, Sw, Sp (sub) (3)
Hughes, M. E. (Manchester C), 1992 v D, S, Li, G; (with Strasbourg), 1993 v Alb, Sp, D, Ei, Sp, Li, La; 1994 v La, D, Ei, R, Lie, Co, M; 1995 v P, A, Ei (2) La, Ca, Ch, La; 1996 v P, Lie, A, N, G; (with West Ham U), 1997 v Uk, Arm, G, Alb, I, Uk; 1998 v G; (with Wimbledon), P, Slo, Sw, Sp (42)
Hughes, P. A. (Bury), 1987 v E, T, Is (3)
Hughes, W. (Bolton W), 1951 v W (1)
Humphries, W. M. (Ards), 1962 v W; (with Coventry C), 1962 v Ho; 1963 v E, S, W, Pol, Sp; 1964 v S, E, Sp; 1965 v S, Ho; (with Swansea T), 1965 v W, Alb (14)
Hunter, A. (Distillery), 1905 v W; 1906 v W, E, S; (with Belfast C), 1908 v W; 1909 v W, E, S (8)
Hunter, A. (Blackburn R), 1970 v USSR; 1971 v Cy (2), E, S, W; (with Ipswich T), 1972 v USSR (2), Sp, E, S, W; 1973 v Bul, Cy (2), P, E, S, W; 1974 v Bul, S, E, W; 1975 v N, Se, Y, E, S, W; 1976 v Se, N, Y, Is, S, E, W; 1977 v Ho, Bel, WG, E, S, W, Ic; 1978 v Ic, Ho, Bel; 1979 v Ei, D, S, W, D; 1980 v E, Ei (53)
Hunter, B.V. (Wrexham), 1995 v La; 1996 v P, Lie, A, Se, G; (with Reading), 1997 v Arm, G, Alb, I, Bel (11)
Hunter, R. J. (Cliftonville), 1884 v E, S, W (3)
Hunter, V. (Coleraine), 1962 v E; 1964 v Sp (2)

Irvine, R. J. (Linfield), 1962 v Ho; 1963 v E, S, W, Pol (2), Sp; (with Stoke C), 1965 v W (8)
Irvine, R. W. (Everton), 1922 v S; 1923 v E, W; 1924 v E, S; 1925 v E; 1926 v E; 1927 v E, W; 1928 v E, S; (with Portsmouth), 1929 v E; 1930 v S; (with Connah's Quay), 1931 v E; (with Derry C), 1932 v W (15)
Irvine, W. J. (Burnley), 1963 v W, Sp; 1965 v S, W, Sw, Ho (2), Alb; 1966 v S, E, W, M, Alb; 1967 v E, S; 1968 v E, W; (with Preston NE), 1969 v Is, T, E; (with Brighton) 1972 v E, S, W (23)
Irving, S. J. (Dundee), 1923 v S, W; 1924 v S, E, W; 1925 v S, E, W; 1926 v S, W; (with Cardiff C), 1927 v S, E, W; 1928 v S, E, W; (with Chelsea), 1929 v E; 1931 v W (18)

Jackson, T. A. (Everton), 1969 v Is, E, S, W; 1970 v USSR (1+1 sub); (with Nottingham F), 1971 v Sp; 1972 v E, S, W; 1973 v Cy, E, S, W; 1974 v Bul, P, S (sub), E (sub), W (sub); 1975 v N (sub), Se, Y, E, S, W; (with Manchester U); 1976 v Se, N, Y; 1977 v Ho, Bel, WG, E, S, W, Ic (35)
Jamison, J. (Glentoran), 1976 v N (1)
Jenkins, I. (Chester C), 1997 v Arm, Th; 1998 v Slo; (with Dundee U), Sw, Sp (5)
Jennings, P. A. (Watford), 1964 v W, U; (with Tottenham H), 1965 v E, S, Sw (2), Ho, Alb; 1966 v S, E, W, Alb, WG; 1967 v E, S; 1968 v S, E, W; 1969 v Is, T (2), E, S, W; 1970 v S, E, USSR (2); 1971 v Cy (2), E, S, W; 1972 v USSR, Sp, S, E, W; 1973 v Bul, Cy, P, E, S, W; 1974 v P, S, E, W; 1975 v N, Se, Y, E, S, W; 1976 v N, Y, Is, S, E, W; 1977 v Ho, Bel, WG, E, S, W, Ic; (with Arsenal), 1978 v Ic, Ho, Bel; 1979 v Ei, D, Bul, E, Bul, E, S, W, D; 1980 v E, Ei, Is; 1981 v S, P, Se; 1982 v S, Is, E, W, Y, Hon, Sp, F; 1983 v Alb, S, E, W; 1984 v A, T, WG, S, W, Fi; 1985 v R, Fi, E, Sp, T; (with Tottenham H), 1986 v T, R, E, F, D, (with Everton), Mor; (with Tottenham H), Alg, Sp, Br (119)
Johnston, H. (Portadown), 1927 v W (1)
Johnston, R. S. (Distillery), 1882 v E, W; 1884 v E; 1886 v E, S (5)
Johnston, R. S. (Distillery), 1905 v W (1)
Johnston, S. (Linfield), 1890 v W; 1893 v S, W; 1894 v E (4)
Johnston, W. (Oldpark), 1885 v S, W (2)
Johnston, W. C. (Glenavon), 1962 v W; (with Oldham Ath), 1966 v M (sub) (2)
Jones, J. (Linfield), 1930 v S, W; 1931 v S, W, E; 1932 v S, E; 1933 v S, E, W; 1934 v S, E, W; 1935 v S, E, W; 1936 v E, S; (with Hibernian), 1936 v W; 1937 v E, W, S; (with Glenavon), 1938 v E (23)
Jones, J. (Glenavon), 1956 v W; 1957 v E, W (3)
Jones, S. (Distillery), 1934 v E; (with Blackpool), 1934 v W (2)
Jordan, T. (Linfield), 1895 v E, W (2)

Kavanagh, P. J. (Celtic), 1930 v E (1)
Keane, T. R. (Swansea T), 1949 v S (1)
Kearns, A. (Distillery), 1900 v E, S, W; 1902 v E, S, W (6)
Kee, P. V. (Oxford U), 1990 v N; 1991 v Y (2), D, A, Pol, Fa; (with Ards), 1995 v A, Ei (9)
Keith, R. M. (Newcastle U), 1958 v E, W, Cz (2), Arg, I, WG, F; 1959 v E, S, W, Sp; 1960 v S, E; 1961 v S, E, W, I, WG (2), Gr; 1962 v W, Ho (23)
Kelly, H. R. (Fulham), 1950 v E, W; (with Southampton), 1951 v E, S (4)
Kelly, J. (Glentoran), 1896 v E (1)
Kelly, J. (Derry C), 1932 v E, W; 1933 v E, W, S; 1934 v W; 1936 v E, S, W; 1937 v S, E (11)
Kelly, P. J. (Manchester C), 1921 v E (1)
Kelly, P. M. (Barnsley), 1950 v S (1)
Kennedy, A. L. (Arsenal), 1923 v W; 1925 v E (2)
Kernaghan, N. (Belfast C), 1936 v W; 1937 v S; 1938 v E (3)
Kirkwood, H. (Cliftonville), 1904 v W (1)
Kirwan, J. (Tottenham H), 1900 v W; 1902 v E, W; 1903 v E, S, W; 1904 v E, S, W; 1905 v E, S, W; (with Chelsea), 1906 v E, S, W; 1907 v W; (with Clyde), 1909 v S (17)

Lacey, W. (Everton), 1909 v E, S, W; 1910 v E, S, W; 1911 v E, S, W; 1912 v E; (with Liverpool), 1913 v W; 1914 v E, S, W; 1920 v E, S, W; 1921 v E, S, W; 1922 v E, S; (with New Brighton), 1925 v E (23)
Lawther, R. (Glentoran), 1888 v E, S (2)
Lawther, W. I. (Sunderland), 1960 v W; 1961 v I; (with Blackburn R), 1962 v S, Ho (4)
Leatham, J. (Belfast C), 1939 v W (1)
Ledwidge, J. J. (Shelbourne), 1906 v S, W (2)
Lemon, J. (Glentoran), 1886 v W; (with Belfast YMCA), 1888 v S; 1889 v W (3)
Lennon, N. F. (Crewe Alex), 1994 v M (sub); 1995 v Ch; 1996 v P, Lie, A; (with Leicester C), v N; 1997 v Uk, Arm, G, Alb, Bel, P, Uk, Arm, Th; 1998 v G, Alb, P, Slo, Sw, Sp (21)
Leslie, W. (YMCA), 1887 v E (1)
Lewis, J. (Glentoran), 1899 v S, E, W; (with Distillery), 1900 v S (4)
Lockhart, H. (Russell School), 1884 v W (1)
Lockhart, N. H. (Linfield), 1947 v E; (with Coventry C), 1950 v W; 1951 v W; 1952 v W; (with Aston Villa), 1954 v S, E; 1955 v W; 1956 v W (8)
Lomas, S. M. (Manchester C), 1994 v R, Lie, Co (sub), M; 1995 v P, A; 1996 v P, Lie, A, N, Se, G; 1997 v Uk, Arm, G, Alb, I, Bel; (with West Ham U), P, Uk, Arm, Th; 1998 v Alb, P, Slo, Sw (26)
Loyal, J. (Clarence), 1891 v S (1)
Lutton, R. J. (Wolverhampton W), 1970 v S, E; (with West Ham U), 1973 v Cy (sub), S (sub), W (sub); 1974 v P (6)

Lyner, D. R. (Glentoran), 1920 v E, W; 1922 v S, W; (with Manchester U), 1923 v E; (with Kilmarnock), 1923 v W (6)

Lytle, J. (Glentoran), 1898 W (1)

McAdams, W. J. (Manchester C), 1954 v W; 1955 v S; 1957 v E; 1958 v S, I; (with Bolton W), 1961 v E, S, W, I, WG (2), Gr; 1962 v E, Gr; (with Leeds U), Ho (15)

McAlery, J. M. (Cliftonville), 1882 v E, W (2)

McAlinden, J. (Belfast C), 1938 v S; 1939 v S; (with Portsmouth), 1947 v E; (with Southend U), 1949 v E (4)

McAllen, J. (Linfield), 1898 v E; 1899 v E, S, W; 1900 v E, S, W; 1901 v W; 1902 v S (9)

McAlpine, S. (Cliftonville), 1901 v S (1)

McArthur, A. (Distillery), 1886 v W (1)

McAuley, J. L. (Huddersfield T), 1911 v E, W; 1912 v E, S; 1913 v E, S (6)

McAuley, P. (Belfast C), 1900 v S (1)

McBride, S. D.(Glenavon), 1991 v D (sub), Pol (sub); 1992 v Fa (sub), D (4)

McCabe, J. J. (Leeds U), 1949 v S, W; 1950 v E; 1951 v W; 1953 v W; 1954 v S (6)

McCabe, W. (Ulster), 1891 v E (1)

McCambridge, J. (Ballymena), 1930 v S, W; (with Cardiff C), 1931 v W; 1932 v E (4)

McCandless, J. (Bradford), 1912 v W; 1913 v W; 1920 v W, S; 1921 v E (5)

McCandless, W. (Linfield), 1920 v E, W; 1921 v E; (with Rangers), 1921 v W; 1922 v S; 1924 v W, S; 1925 v S; 1929 v W (9)

McCann, P. (Belfast C), 1910 v E, S, W; 1911 v E; (with Glentoran), 1911 v S; 1912 v E; 1913 v W (7)

McCarthy, J. D. (Port Vale), 1996 v Se; 1997 v I, Arm, Th; (with Birmingham C), 1998 v P (sub), Slo (sub), Sp (7)

McCartney, A. (Ulster), 1903 v S, W; (with Linfield), 1904 v S, W; (with Everton), 1905 v E, S; (with Belfast C), 1907 v E, S, W; 1908 v E, S, W; (with Glentoran), 1909 v E, S, W (15)

McCashin, J. (Cliftonville), 1896 v W; 1898 v S, W; 1899 v S (4)

McCavana, W. T. (Coleraine), 1955 v S; 1956 v E, S (3)

McCaw, J. H. (Linfield), 1927 v W; 1930 v S; 1931 v E, S, W (5)

McClatchey, J. (Distillery), 1886 v E, S, W (3)

McClatchey, T. (Distillery), 1895 v S (1)

McCleary, J. W. (Cliftonville), 1955 v W (1)

McCleery, W. (Linfield), 1930 v E, W; 1931 v E, S, W; 1932 v S, W; 1933 v E, W (9)

McClelland, J. T. (Arsenal), 1961 v W, I, WG (2), Gr; (with Fulham), 1966 v M (6)

McClelland, J. (Mansfield T), 1980 v S (sub), Aus (3); 1981 v Se, S; (with Rangers), S, Se (sub); 1982 v S, W, Y, Hon, Sp, A, F; 1983 v A, WG, Alb, T, Alb, S, E, W; 1984 v A, T, WG, S, E, W, Fi; 1985 v R, Is; (with Watford), Fi, E, Sp, T; 1986 v T, F (sub); 1987 v E (2), T, Is, Y; 1988 v T, Gr, F, Ma; 1989 v Ei, H, Sp (2), Ma; (with Leeds U), 1990 v N (53)

McCluggage, A. (Bradford), 1924 v E; (with Burnley), 1927 v S, W; 1928 v S, E, W; 1929 v S, E, W; 1930 v W; 1931 v E, W (12)

McClure, G. (Cliftonville), 1907 v S, W; 1908 v E; (with Distillery), 1909 v E (4)

McConnell, E. (Cliftonville), 1904 v S, W; (with Glentoran), 1905 v S; (with Sunderland), 1906 v E; 1907 v E; 1908 v S, W; (with Sheffield W), 1909 v S, W; 1910 v S, W, E (12)

McConnell, P. (Doncaster R), 1928 v W; (with Southport), 1932 v E (2)

McConnell, W. G. (Bohemians), 1912 v W; 1913 v E, S; 1914 v E, S, W (6)

McConnell, W. H. (Reading), 1925 v W; 1926 v E, W; 1927 v E, S, W; 1928 v E, W (8)

McCourt, F. J. (Manchester C), 1952 v E, W; 1953 v E, S, W, F (6)

McCoy, R. K. (Coleraine), 1987 v Y (sub) (1)

McCoy, S. (Distillery), 1896 v W (1)

McCracken, R. (C Palace), 1921 v E; 1922 v E, S, W (4)

McCracken, R. W. (Distillery), 1902 v E, W; 1903 v E; 1904 v E, S, W; (with Newcastle U), 1905 v E, S, W; 1907 v E; 1920 v E; 1922 v E, S, W; (with Hull C), 1923 v S (15)

McCreery, D. (Manchester U), 1976 v S (sub), E, W; 1977 v Ho, Bel, WG, E, S, W, Ic; 1978 v Ic, Ho, Bel, S, E, W; 1979 v Ei, D, Bul, E, Bul, W, D; (with QPR), 1980 v E, Ei, S (sub), E (sub), W (sub), Aus (1+1 sub); 1981 v Se (sub); (with Tulsa R), S, P, Se; 1982 v S, Is, E (sub), F, Y, Hon, Sp, A, F; (with Newcastle U), 1983 v A; 1984 v T (sub); 1985 v R, Sp (sub); 1986 v T (sub), R, E, F, D, Alg, Sp, Br; 1987 v T, E, Y; 1988 v Y; 1989 v Sp, Ma, Ch; (with Hearts), 1990 v H, Ei, N, U (sub) (67)

McCrory, S. (Southend U), 1958 v E (1)

McCullough, K. (Belfast C), 1935 v W; 1936 v E; (with Manchester C), 1936 v S; 1937 v E, S (5)

McCullough, W. J. (Arsenal), 1961 v I; 1963 v Sp; 1964 v S, E, W, U, Sp; 1965 v E, Sw; (with Millwall), 1967 v E (10)

McCurdy, C. (Linfield), 1980 v Aus (sub) (1)

McDonald, A. (QPR), 1986 v R, E, F, D, Mor, Alg, Sp, Br; 1987 v E (2), T, Is, Y; 1988 v Y, T, Pol, F, Ma; 1989 v Ei, H, Sp, Ch; 1990 v H, Ei, U; 1991 v Y, D, A, Fa; 1992 v Fa, S, Li, G; 1993 v Alb, Sp, D, Alb, Ei, Sp, Li, La; 1994 v D, Ei; 1995 v P, A, Ei, La, Ca, Ch, La; 1996 v A (sub), N (52)

McDonald, R. (Rangers), 1930 v S; 1932 v E (2)

McDonnell, J. (Bohemians), 1911 v E, S; 1912 v W; 1913 v W (4)

McElhinney, G. M. A. (Bolton W), 1984 v WG, S, E, W, Fi; 1985 v R (6)

McFaul, W. S. (Linfield), 1967 v E (sub); (with Newcastle U), 1970 v W; 1971 v Sp; 1972 v USSR; 1973 v Cy; 1974 v Bul (6)

McGarry, J. K. (Cliftonville), 1951 v W, F, S (3)

McGaughey, M. (Linfield), 1985 v Is (sub) (1)

McGibbon, P. C. G. (Manchester U), 1995 v Ca (sub), Ch, La; 1996 v Lie (sub); 1997 v Th; (with Wigan Ath), 1998 v Alb (6)

McGrath, R. C. (Tottenham H), 1974 v S, E, W; 1975 v N; 1976 v Is (sub); 1977; (with Manchester U), Ho, Bel, WG, E, S, W, Ic; 1978 v Ic, Ho, Bel, S, E, W; 1979 v Bul (sub), E (2 sub) (21)

McGregor, S. (Glentoran), 1921 v S (1)

McGrillen, J. (Clyde), 1924 v S; (with Belfast C), 1927 v S (2)

McGuire, E. (Distillery), 1907 v S (1)

McIlroy, H. (Cliftonville), 1906 v E (1)

McIlroy, J. (Burnley), 1952 v E, S, W; 1953 v E, S, W; 1954 v E, S, W; 1955 v E, S, W; 1956 v E, S, W; 1957 v E, S, W, I, P (2); 1958 v E, S, W, I (2), Cz (2), Arg, WG, F; 1959 v E, S, W, Sp; 1960 v E, S, W; 1961 v E, W, WG (2), Gr; 1962 v E, S, Gr, Ho; 1963 v E, S, Pol (2); (with Stoke C), 1963 v W; 1966 v S, E, Alb (55)

McIlroy, S. B. (Manchester U), 1972 v Sp, S (sub); 1974 v S, E, W; 1975 v N, Se, Y, E, S, W; 1976 v Se, N, Y, S, E, W; 1977 v Ho, Bel, E, S, W, Ic; 1978 v Ic, Ho, Bel, S, E, W; 1979 v Ei, D, Bul, E, Bul, E, S, W, D; 1980 v E, Ei, Is, S, E, W; 1981 v Se, P, S, P, S, Se; 1982 v S, Is; (with Stoke C), E, F, S, W, Y, Hon, Sp, A, F; 1983 v A, WG, Alb, T, Alb, S, E, W; 1984 v A, T, S, E, W, Fi; 1985 v Fi, E, T; (with Manchester C), 1986 v T, R, E, F, D, Mor, Alg, Sp, Br; 1987 v E (sub) (88)

McIlvenny, P. (Distillery), 1924 v W (1)

McIlvenny, R. (Distillery), 1890 v E; (with Ulster), 1891 v E (2)

McKeag, W. (Glentoran), 1968 v S, W (2)

McKee, F. W. (Cliftonville), 1906 v S, W; (with Belfast C), 1914 v E, S, W (5)

McKelvey, H. (Glentoran), 1901 v W (1)

McKenna, J. (Huddersfield), 1950 v E, S, W; 1951 v E, S, F; 1952 v E (7)

McKenzie, H. (Distillery), 1923 v S (1)

McKenzie, R. (Airdrie), 1967 v W (1)

McKeown, N. (Linfield), 1892 v E, S, W; 1893 v S, W; 1894 v S, W (7)

McKie, H. (Cliftonville), 1895 v E, S, W (3)

McKinney, D. (Hull C), 1921 v S; (with Bradford C), 1924 v S (2)

McKinney, V. J. (Falkirk), 1966 v WG (1)

McKnight, A. D. (Celtic), 1988 v Y, T, Gr, Pol, F, Ma; (with West Ham U) 1989 v Ei, H, Sp (2) (10)

McKnight, J. (Preston NE), 1912 v S; (with Glentoran), 1913 v S (2)

McLaughlin, J. C. (Shrewsbury T), 1962 v E, S, W, Gr; 1963 v W; (with Swansea T), 1964 v W, U; 1965 v E, W, Sw (2); 1966 v W (12)

McLean, T. (Limavady), 1885 v S (1)

McMahon, G. J. (Tottenham H), 1995 v Ca (sub), Ch, La; 1996 v Lie, N (sub), Se, G; (with Stoke C), 1997 v Arm (sub), Alb (sub), Bel, P (sub), Uk (sub), Arm (sub), Th (sub); 1998 v G (sub), Alb (sub), P (sub) (17)

McMahon, J. (Bohemians), 1934 v S (1)

McMaster, G. (Glentoran), 1897 v E, S, W (3)

McMichael, A. (Newcastle U), 1950 v E, S; 1951 v E, S, F; 1952 v E, S, W; 1953 v E, S, W, F; 1954 v E, S, W; 1955 v E, W; 1956 v W; 1957 v E, S, W, I, P (2); 1958 v E, S, W, I (2), Cz (2), Arg, WG, F; 1959 v S, W, Sp; 1960 v E, S, W (40)

McMillan, G. (Distillery), 1903 v E; 1905 v W (2)

McMillan, S. T. (Manchester U), 1963 v E, S (2)

McMillen, W. S. (Manchester U), 1934 v E; 1935 v S; 1937 v S; (with Chesterfield), 1938 v S, W; 1939 v E, S (7)

McMordie, A. S. (Middlesbrough), 1969 v Is, T (2), E, S, W; 1970 v E, S, W, USSR; 1971 v Cy (2), E, S, W; 1972 v USSR, Sp, E, S, W; 1973 v Bul (21)

McMorran, E. J. (Belfast C), 1947 v E; (with Barnsley), 1951 v E, S, W; 1952 v E, S, W; 1953 v E, S, F; (with Doncaster R), 1953 v W; 1954 v E; 1956 v W; 1957 v I, P (15)

McMullan, D. (Liverpool), 1926 v E, W; 1927 v S (3)

McNally, B. A. (Shrewsbury T), 1986 v Mor; 1987 v T (sub); 1988 v Y, Gr, Ma (sub) (5)

McNinch, J. (Ballymena), 1931 v S; 1932 v S, W (3)

McParland, P. J. (Aston Villa), 1954 v W; 1955 v E, S; 1956 v E, S; 1957 v E, S, W, P; 1958 v E, S, W, I (2), Cz (2), Arg, WG, F; 1959 v E, S, W, Sp; 1960 v E, S, W; 1961 v E, S, W, I, WG (2), Gr; (with Wolverhampton W), 1962 v Ho (34)

McShane, J. (Cliftonville), 1899 v S; 1900 v E, S, W (4)

McVicker, J. (Linfield), 1888 v E; (with Glentoran), 1889 v S (2)

McWha, W. B. R. (Knock), 1882 v E, W; (with Cliftonville), 1883 v E, W; 1884 v E; 1885 v E, W (7)

Mackie, J. (Arsenal), 1923 v W; (with Portsmouth), 1935 v S, W (3)

Madden, O. (Norwich C), 1938 v E (1)

Magee, G. (Wellington Park), 1885 v E, S, W (3)

Magill, E. J. (Arsenal), 1962 v E, S, Gr; 1963 v E, S, W, Pol (2), Sp; 1964 v E, S, W, U, Sp; 1965 v E, S, Sw (2), Ho, Alb; 1966 v S, (with Brighton), E, Alb, W, WG, M (26)

Magilton, J. (Oxford U), 1991 v Pol, Y, Fa; 1992 v Fa, A, D, S, Li, G; 1993 v Alb, D, Alb, Ei, Li, La; 1994 v La, D, Ei; (with Southampton), R, Lie, Co, M; 1995 v P, A, Ei (2), Ca, Ch, La; 1996 v P, N, G; 1997 v Uk (sub), Arm (sub), Bel, P; 1998 v G; (with Sheffield W), P, Sp (39)

Maginnis, H. (Linfield), 1900 v E, S, W; 1903 v S, W; 1904 v E, S, W (8)

Mahood, J. (Belfast C), 1926 v S; 1928 v E, S, W; 1929 v E, S, W; 1930 v W; (with Ballymena), 1934 v S (9)

Manderson, R. (Rangers), 1920 v W, S; 1925 v S, E; 1926 v S (5)

Mansfield, J. (Dublin Freebooters), 1901 v E (1)

Martin, C. (Cliftonville), 1882 v E, W; 1883 v E (3)

Martin, C. (Bo'ness), 1925 v S (1)

Martin, C. J. (Glentoran), 1947 v S; (with Leeds U), 1948 v E, S, W; (with Aston Villa), 1949 v E; 1950 v W (6)

Martin, D. K. (Belfast C), 1934 v E, S, W; 1935 v S; (with Wolverhampton W), 1935 v E; 1936 v S, W; (with Nottingham F), 1937 v S; 1938 v E, S; 1939 v S (10)

Mathieson, A. (Luton T), 1921 v W; 1922 v E (2)

Maxwell, J. (Linfield), 1902 v W; 1903 v W, E; (with Glentoran), 1905 v W, S; (with Belfast C), 1906 v W; 1907 v S (7)

Meek, H. L. (Glentoran), 1925 v W (1)

Mehaffy, J. A. C. (Queen's Island), 1922 v W (1)

Meldon, P. A. (Dublin Freebooters), 1899 v S, W (2)

Mercer, H. V. A. (Linfield), 1908 v E (1)

Mercer, J. T. (Distillery), 1898 v E, S, W; 1899 v E; (with Linfield), 1902 v E, W; (with Distillery), 1903 v S, W; (with Derby Co), 1904 v E, W; 1905 v S (11)

Millar, W. (Barrow), 1932 v W; 1933 v S (2)

Miller, J. (Middlesbrough), 1929 v W, S; 1930 v E (3)

Milligan, D. (Chesterfield), 1939 v W (1)

Milne, R. G. (Linfield), 1894 v E, S, W; 1895 v E, W; 1896 v E, S, W; 1897 v E, S; 1898 v E, S, W; 1899 v E, W; 1901 v W; 1902 v E, S, W; 1903 v E, S; 1904 v E, S, W; 1906 v E, S, W (27)

Mitchell, E. J. (Cliftonville), 1933 v S; (with Glentoran), 1934 v W (2)

Mitchell, W. (Distillery), 1932 v E, W; 1933 v E, S, W; (with Chelsea), 1934 v W, S; 1935 v S, E; 1936 v S, E; 1937 v E, S, W; 1938 v E, S (15)

Molyneux, T. B. (Ligoniel), 1883 v E, W; (with Cliftonville), 1884 v E, W, S; 1885 v E, W; 1886 v E, W, S; 1888 v S (11)

Montgomery, F. J. (Coleraine), 1955 v E (1)

Moore, C. (Glentoran), 1949 v W (1)

Moore, P. (Aberdeen), 1933 v E (1)

Moore, R. (Linfield Ath), 1891 v E, S, W (3)

Moore, R. L. (Ulster), 1887 v S, W (2)

Moore, W. (Falkirk), 1923 v S (1)

Moorhead, F. W. (Dublin University), 1885 v E (1)

Moorhead, G. (Linfield), 1923 v S; 1928 v S; 1929 v S (3)

Moran, J. (Leeds C), 1912 v S (1)

Moreland, V. (Derby Co), 1979 v Bul (2 sub), E, S; 1980 v E, Ei (6)

Morgan, F. G. (Linfield), 1923 v E; (with Nottingham F), 1924 v S; 1927 v E; 1928 v E, S, W; 1929 v E (7)

Morgan, S. (Port Vale), 1972 v Sp; 1973 v Bul (sub), P, Cy, E, S, W; (with Aston Villa), 1974 v Bul, P, S, E; 1975 v Se; 1976 v Se (sub), N, Y; (with Brighton & HA), S, W (sub); (with Sparta Rotterdam), 1979 v D (18)

Morrison, R. (Linfield Ath), 1891 v E, W (2)

Morrison, T. (Glentoran), 1895 v E, S, W; (with Burnley), 1899 v W; 1900 v W; 1902 v E, S (7)

Morrogh, D. (Bohemians), 1896 v S (1)

Morrow, S. J. (Arsenal), 1990 v U (sub); 1991 v A (sub), Pol, Y; 1992 v Fa, S (sub), G (sub); 1993 v Sp (sub), Alb, Ei; 1994 v R, Co, M (sub); 1995 v P, Ei (2), La; 1996 v P, Se; 1997 v Uk, G, Alb, I, Bel; (with QPR), P, Uk, Arm; 1998 v G, P, Slo, Sw, Sp (32)

Morrow, W. J. (Moyola Park), 1883 v E, W; 1884 v S (3)

Muir, R. (Oldpark), 1885 v S, W (2)

Mullan, G. (Glentoran), 1983 v S, E, W, Alb (sub) (4)

Mulholland, S. (Celtic), 1906 v S, E (2)

Mulligan, J. (Manchester C), 1921 v S (1)

Mulryne, P. P. (Manchester U), 1997 v Bel (sub), Arm (sub), Th; 1998 v Alb (sub), Sp (sub) (5)

Murphy, J. (Bradford C), 1910 v E, S, W (3)

Murphy, N. (QPR), 1905 v E, S, W (3)

Murray, J. M. (Motherwell), 1910 v E, S; (with Sheffield W), 1910 v W (3)

Napier, R. J. (Bolton W), 1966 v WG (1)

Neill, W. J. T. (Arsenal), 1961 v I, Gr, WG; 1962 v E, S, W, Gr; 1963 v E, W, Pol, Sp; 1964 v S, E, W, U, Sp; 1965 v E, S, W, Sw, Ho (2), Alb; 1966 v S, E, W, Alb, WG, M; 1967 v S, W; 1968 v S, E; 1969 v E, S, W, Is, T (2); 1970 v S, E, W, USSR (2); (with Hull C), 1971 v Cy, Sp; 1972 v USSR (2), Sp, S, E, W; 1973 v Bul, Cy (2), P, E, S, W (59)

Nelis, P. (Nottingham F), 1923 v E (1)

Nelson, S. (Arsenal), 1970 v W, E (sub); 1971 v Cy, Sp, E, S, W; 1972 v USSR (2), Sp, E, S, W; 1973 v Bul, Cy, P; 1974 v S, E; 1975 v Se, Y; 1976 v Se, N, Is, E; 1977 v Bel (sub), WG, W, Ic; 1978 v Ic, Ho, Bel; 1979 v Ei, D, Bul, E, Bul, E, S, W, D; 1980 v E, Ei, Is; 1981 v S, P, S, Se; (with Brighton & HA), 1982 v E, S, Sp (sub), A (51)

Nicholl, C. J. (Aston Villa), 1975 v Se, Y, E, S, W; 1976 v Se, N, Y, S, E, W; 1977 v W; (with Southampton), 1978 v Bel (sub), S, E, W; 1979 v Ei, Bul, E, Bul, E, W; 1980 v Ei, Is, S, E, W, Aus (3); 1981 v Se, P, S, P, S, Se; 1982 v S, Is, E, F, W, Y, Hon, Sp, A, F; 1983 v S (sub), E, W; (with Grimsby T), 1984 v A, T (51)

Nicholl, H. (Belfast C), 1902 v E, W; 1905 v E (3)

Nicholl, J. M. (Manchester U), 1976 v Is, W (sub); 1977 v Ho, Bel, E, S, W, Ic; 1978 v Ic, Ho, Bel, S, E, W; 1979 v Ei, D, Bul, E, Bul, E, S, W, D; 1980 v E, Ei, Is, S, E, W, Aus (3); 1981 v Se, P, S, P, S, Se; 1982 v S, Is, E; (with Toronto B), F, W, Y, Hon, Sp, A, F; (with Sunderland), 1983 v A, WG, Alb, T, Alb; (with Toronto B), S, E, W; 1984 v T; (with Rangers), WG, S, E; (with Toronto B), Fi; 1985 v R; (with WBA), Fi, E, Sp, T; 1986 v T, R, E, F, Alg, Sp, Br (73)

Nicholson, J. J. (Manchester U), 1961 v S, W; 1962 v E, W, Gr, Ho; 1963 v E, S, Pol (2); (with Huddersfield T), 1965 v W, Ho (2), Alb; 1966 v S, E, W, Alb, M; 1967 v S, W; 1968 v S, E, W; 1969 v S, E, W, T (2); 1970 v S, E, W, USSR (2); 1971 v Cy (2), E, S, W; 1972 v USSR (2) (41)

Nixon, R. (Linfield), 1914 v S (1)

Nolan, I.R. (Sheffield W), 1997 v Arm, G, Alb, P, Uk; 1998 v G, P (7)

Nolan-Whelan, J. V. (Dublin Freebooters), 1901 v E, W; 1902 v S, W (4)

O'Boyle, G. (Dunfermline Ath), 1994 v Co (sub), M; (with St Johnstone), 1995 v P (sub), La (sub), Ca (sub), Ch (sub); 1996 v Se (sub), G (sub); 1997 v I (sub), Bel (sub); 1998 v Slo, Sw (sub) (12)

O'Brien, M. T. (QPR), 1921 v S; (with Leicester C), 1922 v S, W; 1924 v S, W; (with Hull C), 1925 v S, E; 1926 v W; (with Derby Co), 1927 v W (10)

O'Connell, P. (Sheffield W), 1912 v E, S; (with Hull C), 1914 v E, S, W (5)

O'Doherty, A. (Coleraine), 1970 v E, W (sub) (2)

O'Driscoll, J. F. (Swansea T), 1949 v E, S, W (3)

O'Hagan, C. (Tottenham H), 1905 v S, W; 1906 v S, W, E; (with Aberdeen), 1907 v E, S, W; 1908 v S, W; 1909 v E (11)

O'Hagan, W. (St Mirren), 1920 v E, W (2)

O'Hehir, J. C. (Bohemians), 1910 v W (1)

O'Kane, W. J. (Nottingham F), 1970 v E, W, S (sub); 1971 v Sp, E, S, W; 1972 v USSR (2); 1973 v P, Cy; 1974 v Bul, P, S, E, W; 1975 v N, Se, E, S (20)

O'Mahoney, M. T. (Bristol R), 1939 v S (1)

O'Neill, C. (Motherwell), 1989 v Ch (sub); 1990 v Ei (sub); 1991 v D (3)

O'Neill, J. P. (Leicester C), 1980 v Is, S, E, W, Aus (3); 1981 v P, S, P, S, Se; 1982 v S, Is, E, F, S, F (sub); 1983 v A, WG, Alb, T, Alb, S (sub); 1985 v Is, Fi, E, Sp, T; 1986 v T, R, E, F, D, Mor, Alg, Sp, Br (39)

O'Neill, J. (Sunderland), 1962 v W (1)

O'Neill, M. A. M. (Newcastle U), 1988 v Gr, Pol, F, Ma; 1989 v Ei, H, Sp (sub), Sp (sub), Ma (sub), Ch; (with Dundee U), 1990 v H (sub), Ei; 1991 v Pol; 1992 v Fa (sub), S (sub), G (sub); 1993 v Alb (sub + 1), Ei, Sp, Li, La; (with Hibernian), 1994 v Lie (sub); 1995 v A (sub), Ei; 1996 v Lie, A, N, Se; (with Coventry C), 1997 v Uk (sub), Arm (sub) (31)

O'Neill, M. H. M. (Distillery), 1972 v USSR (sub), (with Nottingham F), Sp (sub), W (sub); 1973 v P, Cy, E, S, W; 1974 v Bul, P, E (sub), W; 1975 v Se, Y, E, S; 1976 v Y (sub); 1977 v E (sub), S; 1978 v Ic, Ho, S, E, W; 1979 v Ei, D, Bul, E, Bul, D; 1980 v Ei, Is, Aus (3); 1981 v Se, P; (with Norwich C), P, S, Se; (with Manchester C), 1982 v S; (with Norwich C), E, F, S, Y, Hon, Sp, A, F; 1983 v A, WG, Alb, T, Alb, S, E; (with Notts Co), 1984 v A, T, WG, E, W, Fi; 1985 v R, Fi (64)

O'Reilly, H. (Dublin Freebooters), 1901 v S, W; 1904 v S (3)

Parke, J. (Linfield), 1964 v S; (with Hibernian), 1964 v E, Sp; (with Sunderland), 1965 v Sw, S, W, Ho (2), Alb; 1966 v WG; 1967 v E, S; 1968 v S, E (14)

Patterson, D. J. (C Palace), 1994 v Co (sub), M (sub); 1995 v Ei (sub+1), La, Ca, Ch (sub), La (sub); (with Luton T), 1996 v N (sub), Se; 1998 v Sw, Sp (12)

Peacock, R. (Celtic), 1952 v S; 1953 v F; 1954 v W; 1955 v E, S; 1956 v E, S; 1957 v W, I, P; 1958 v S, E, W, I (2), Arg, Cz (2), WG; 1959 v E, S, W; 1960 v S, E; 1961 v E, S, I, WG (2), Gr; (with Coleraine), 1962 v S (31)

Peden, J. (Distillery), 1887 v S, W; 1888 v W, E; 1889 v S, E; 1890 v W, S; 1891 v W, E; 1892 v W, E; 1893 v E, S, W; 1896 v W, E, S; 1897 v W, S; 1898 v W, E, S; 1899 v W (24)

Penney, S. (Brighton & HA), 1985 v Is; 1986 v T, R, E, F, D, Mor, Alg, Sp; 1987 v E, T, Is; 1988 v Pol, F, Ma; 1989 v Ei, Sp (17)

Percy, J. C. (Belfast YMCA), 1889 v W (1)

Platt, J. A. (Middlesbrough), 1976 v Is (sub); 1978 v S, E, W; 1980 v S, E, W, Aus (3); 1981 v Se, P; 1982 v F, S, W (sub), A; 1983 v A, WG, Alb, T; (with Ballymena U), 1984 v E, W (sub); (with Coleraine), 1986 v Mor (sub) (23)

Ponsonby, J. (Distillery), 1895 v S, W; 1896 v E, S, W; 1897 v E, S, W; 1899 v E (9)

Potts, R. M. C. (Cliftonville), 1883 v E, W (2)

Priestley, T. J. M. (Coleraine), 1933 v S; (with Chelsea), 1934 v E (2)

Pyper, Jas. (Cliftonville), 1897 v S, W; 1898 v S, E, W; 1899 v S; 1900 v E (7)

Pyper, John (Cliftonville), 1897 v E, S, W; 1899 v E, W; 1900 v E, W, S; 1902 v S (9)

Pyper, M. (Linfield), 1932 v W (1)

Quinn, J. M. (Blackburn R), 1985 v Is, Fi, E, Sp, T; 1986 v T, R, E, F, D (sub), Mor (sub); 1987 v E (sub), T; (with Swindon T), 1988 v Y (sub), T, Gr, Pol, F (sub), Ma; (with Leicester C), 1989 v Ei, H (sub), Sp (sub+1); (with Bradford C), Ma, Ch; 1990 v H, (with West Ham U), N; 1991 v Y (sub); (with Bournemouth), 1992 v Li; (with Reading), 1993 v Sp, D, Alb (sub), Ei (sub), La (sub); 1994 v La, D (sub), Ei, R, Lie, Co, M; 1995 v P, A (sub), La (sub); 1996 v Lie, A (sub) (46)

Quinn, S. J. (Blackpool), 1996 v Se (sub); 1997 v Alb (sub), I, Bel, P, Uk (sub), Arm, Th (sub); 1998 v G, Alb; (with WBA), Slo, Sw (12)

Rafferty, P. (Linfield), 1980 v E (sub) (1)

Ramsey, P. C. (Leicester C), 1984 v A, WG, S; 1985 v Is, E, Sp, T; 1986 v T, Mor; 1987 v Is, E, Y (sub); 1988 v Y; 1989 v Sp (14)

Rankine, J. (Alexander), 1883 v E, W (2)

Rattray, D. (Avoniel), 1882 v E; 1883 v E, W (3)

Rea, R. (Glentoran), 1901 v E (1)

Redmond, R. (Cliftonville), 1884 v W (1)

Reid, G. H. (Cardiff C), 1923 v S (1)

Reid, J. (Ulster), 1883 v E; 1884 v W; 1887 v S; 1889 v W; 1890 v S, W (6)

Reid, S. E. (Derby Co), 1934 v E, W; 1936 v E (3)

Reid, W. (Hearts), 1931 v E (1)

Reilly, M. M. (Portsmouth), 1900 v E; 1902 v E (2)

Renneville, W. T. J. (Leyton), 1910 v S, E, W; (with Aston Villa), 1911 v W (4)

Reynolds, J. (Distillery), 1890 v E, W; (with Ulster), 1891 v É, S, W (5)

Reynolds, R. (Bohemians), 1905 v W (1)

Rice, P. J. (Arsenal), 1969 v Is; 1970 v USSR; 1971 v E, S, W; 1972 v USSR, Sp, E, S, W; 1973 v Bul, Cy, E, S, W; 1974 v Bul, P, S, E, W; 1975 v N, Y, E, S, W; 1976 v Se, N, Y, Is, S, E, W; 1977 v Ho, Bel, WG, E, S, Ic; 1978 v Ic, Ho, Bel; 1979 v Ei, D, E (2), S, W, D; 1980 v E (49)

Roberts, F. C. (Glentoran) 1931 v S (1)

Robinson, P. (Distillery), 1920 v S; (with Blackburn R), 1921 v W (2)

Robinson, S. (Bournemouth), 1997 v Th (sub) (1)

Rogan, A. (Celtic), 1988 v Y (sub), Gr, Pol (sub); 1989 v Ei (sub), H, Sp (2), Ma (sub), Ch; 1990 v H, N (sub), U; 1991 v Y (2), D, A; (with Sunderland), 1992 v Li (sub); (with Millwall), 1997 v G (sub) (18)

Rollo, D. (Linfield), 1912 v W; 1913 v W; 1914 v W, E; (with Blackburn R), 1920 v S, W; 1921 v E, S, W; 1922 v E; 1923 v E; 1924 v S, W; 1925 v W; 1926 v E; 1927 v E (16)

Roper, E. O. (Dublin University), 1886 v W (1)

Rosbotham, A. (Cliftonville), 1887 v E, S, W; 1888 v E, S, W; 1889 v E (7)

Ross, W. E. (Newcastle U), 1969 v Is (1)

Rowland, K. (West Ham U), 1994 v La (sub); 1995 v Ca, Ch, La; 1996 v P (sub), Lie (sub), N (sub), Se, G (sub); 1997 v Uk, Arm, I (sub); 1998 v Alb (13)

Rowley, R. W. M. (Southampton), 1929 v S, W; 1930 v W, E; (with Tottenham H), 1931 v W; 1932 v S (6)

Russell, A. (Linfield), 1947 v E (1)

Russell, S. R. (Bradford C), 1930 v E, S; (with Derry C), 1932 v E (3)

Ryan, R. A. (WBA), 1950 v W (1)

Sanchez, L. P. (Wimbledon), 1987 v T (sub); 1989 v Sp, Ma (3)

Scott, E. (Liverpool), 1920 v S; 1921 v E, S, W; 1922 v E; 1925 v W; 1926 v E, S, W; 1927 v E, S, W; 1928 v E, S, W; 1929 v E, S, W; 1930 v E; 1931 v E; 1932 v W; 1933 v E, S, W; 1934 v E, S, W; (with Belfast C), 1935 v S; 1936 v E, S, W (31)

Scott, J. (Grimsby), 1958 v Cz, F (2)

Scott, J. E. (Cliftonville), 1901 v S (1)

Scott, L. J. (Dublin University), 1895 v S, W (2)

Scott, P. W. (Everton), 1975 v W; 1976 v Y; (with York C), Is, S, E (sub), W; 1978 v S, E, W; (with Aldershot), 1979 v S (sub) (10)

Scott, T. (Cliftonville), 1894 v E, S; 1895 v S, W; 1896 v S, E, W; 1897 v E, W; 1898 v E, S, W; 1900 v W (13)

Scott, W. (Linfield), 1903 v E, S, W; 1904 v E, S, W; (with Everton), 1905 v E, S; 1907 v E, S; 1908 v E, S, W; 1909 v E, S, W; 1910 v S, E; 1911 v E, S, W; 1912 v E; (with Leeds City), 1913 v E, S, W (25)

Scraggs, M. J. (Glentoran), 1921 v W; 1922 v E (2)

Seymour, H. C. (Bohemians), 1914 v W (1)

Seymour, J. (Cliftonville), 1907 v W; 1909 v W (2)

Shanks, T. (Woolwich Arsenal), 1903 v S; 1904 v W; (with Brentford), 1905 v E (3)

Sharkey, P. G. (Ipswich T), 1976 v S (1)

Sheehan, Dr G. (Bohemians), 1899 v S; 1900 v E, W (3)

Sheridan, J. (Everton), 1903 v W, E, S; 1904 v E, S; (with Stoke C), 1905 v E (6)

Sherrard, J. (Limavady), 1885 v S; 1887 v W; 1888 v W (3)

Sherrard, W. C. (Cliftonville), 1895 v E, W, S (3)

Sherry, J. J. (Bohemians), 1906 v E; 1907 v W (2)

Shields, R. J. (Southampton), 1957 v S (1)

Silo, M. (Belfast YMCA), 1888 v E (1)

Simpson, W. J. (Rangers), 1951 v W, F; 1954 v E, S; 1955 v E; 1957 v I, P; 1958 v S, E, W, I; 1959 v S (12)

Sinclair, J. (Knock), 1882 v V, W (2)

Slemin, J. C. (Bohemians), 1909 v W (1)

Sloan, A. S. (London Caledonians), 1925 v W (1)

Sloan, D. (Oxford U), 1969 v Is; 1971 v Sp (2)

Sloan, H. A. de B. (Bohemians), 1903 v E; 1904 v S; 1905 v E; 1906 v W; 1907 v E, W; 1908 v W; 1909 v S (8)

Sloan, J. W. (Arsenal), 1947 v W (1)

Sloan, T. (Cardiff C), 1926 v S, W, E; 1927 v W, S; 1928 v E, W; 1929 v E; (with Linfield), 1930 v W, S; 1931 v S (11)

Sloan, T. (Manchester U), 1979 v S, W (sub), D (sub) (3)

Small, J. M. (Clarence), 1887 v E; (with Cliftonville), 1893 v E, S, W (4)

Smith, E. E. (Cardiff C), 1921 v S; 1923 v W, E; 1924 v E (4)

Smith, J. E. (Distillery), 1901 v S, W (2)

Smyth, R. H. (Dublin University), 1886 v W (1)

Smyth, S. (Wolverhampton W), 1948 v E, S, W; 1949 v S, W; 1950 v E, S, W; (with Stoke C), 1952 v E (9)

Smyth, W. (Distillery), 1949 v E, S; 1954 v S, E (4)

Snape, A. (Airdrie), 1920 v E (1)

Sonner, D. J. (Ipswich T), 1998 v Alb (sub) (1)

Spence, D. W. (Bury), 1975 v Y, E, S, W; 1976 v Se, Is, E, W, S (sub); (with Blackpool), 1977 v Ho (sub), WG (sub), E (sub), S (sub), W (sub), Ic (sub); 1979 v Ei, D (sub), E (sub), Bul (sub), E (sub), S, W, D; 1980 v Ei; (with Southend U), Is (sub), Aus (sub); 1981 v S (sub), Se (sub); 1982 v F (sub) (29)

Spencer, S. (Distillery), 1890 v E, S; 1892 v E, S, W; 1893 v E (6)

Spiller, E. A. (Cliftonville), 1883 v E, W; 1884 v E, W, S (5)

Stanfield, O. M. (Distillery), 1887 v E, S, W; 1888 v E, S, W; 1889 v E, S, W; 1890 v E, S; 1891 v E, S, W; 1892 v E, S, W; 1893 v E, W; 1894 v E, S, W; 1895 v E, S; 1896 v E, S, W; 1897 v E, S, W (30)

Steele, A. (Charlton Ath), 1926 v W, S; (with Fulham), 1929 v W, S (4)

Stevenson, A. E. (Rangers), 1934 v E, S, W; (with Everton), 1935 v E, S; 1936 v S, W; 1937 v E, W; 1938 v E, W; 1939 v E, S, W; 1947 v S, W; 1948 v S (17)

Stewart, A. (Glentoran), 1967 v W; 1968 v S, E; (with Derby Co), 1968 v W; 1969 v Is, T (1+1 sub) (7)

Stewart, D. C. (Hull C), 1978 v Bel (1)

Stewart, I. (QPR), 1982 v F (sub); 1983 v A, WG, Alb, T, Alb, S, E, W; 1984 v A, T, WG, S, E, W, Fi; 1985 v R, Fi, Is, E, Sp, T; (with Newcastle U), 1986 v R, E, D, Mor, Alg (sub), Sp (sub), Br; 1987 v E, Is (sub) (31)

Stewart, R. K. (St Columb's Court), 1890 v E, S, W; (with Cliftonville), 1892 v E, S, W; 1893 v E, W; 1894 v E, S, W (11)

Stewart, T. C. (Linfield), 1961 v W (1)

Swan, S. (Linfield), 1899 v S (1)

Taggart, G. P. (Barnsley), 1990 v N, U; 1991 v Y, D, A, Pol, Fa; 1992 v Fa, A, D, S, Li, G; 1993 v Alb, Sp, D, Alb, Ei, Sp, Li, La; 1994 v La, D, Ei, R, Lie, Co, M; 1995 v P (sub), A, Ei (2), Ca, Ch, La; (with Bolton W), 1997 v G, Alb, I, Bel, P, Uk, Arm; 1998 v G, P, Sp (45)

Taggart, J. (Walsall), 1899 v W (1)

Thompson, F. W. (Cliftonville), 1910 v E, S, W; (with Linfield), 1911 v W; (with Bradford C), 1911 v E; 1912 v E, W; 1913 v E, S, W; (with Clyde), 1914 v E, S (12)

Thompson, J. (Belfast Ath), 1889 v S (1)

Thompson, J. (Distillery), 1897 v S (1)

Thunder, P. J. (Bohemians), 1911 v W (1)

Todd, S. J. (Burnley), 1966 v M (sub); 1967 v E; 1968 v W; 1969 v E, S, W; 1970 v S, USSR; (with Sheffield W), 1971 v Cy (2), Sp (sub) (11)

Toner, J. (Arsenal), 1922 v W; 1923 v W, E; 1924 v W, E; 1925 v E, S; (with St Johnstone), 1927 v E, S (8)

Torrans, R. (Linfield), 1893 v S (1)

Torrans, S. (Linfield), 1889 v S; 1890 v S, W; 1891 v S, W; 1892 v E, S, W; 1893 v E, S; 1894 v E, S, W; 1895 v E; 1896 v E, S, W; 1897 v E, S, W; 1898 v E, S; 1899 v E, W; 1901 v S, W (26)

Trainor, D. (Crusaders), 1967 v W (1)

Tully, C. P. (Celtic), 1949 v E; 1950 v E; 1952 v S; 1953 v E, S, W, F; 1954 v S; 1956 v E; 1959 v Sp (10)

Turner, E. (Cliftonville), 1896 v E, W (2)

Turner, W. (Cliftonville), 1886 v E, S; 1888 v S (3)

Twoomey, J. F. (Leeds U), 1938 v W; 1939 v E (2)

Uprichard, W. N. M. C. (Swindon T), 1952 v E, S, W; 1953 v E, S; (with Portsmouth), 1953 v W, F; 1955 v E, S, W; 1956 v E, S, W; 1958 v S, I, Cz; 1959 v S, Sp (18)

Vernon, J. (Belfast C), 1947 v E, S; (with WBA), 1947 v W; 1948 v E, S, W; 1949 v E, S, W; 1950 v E, S; 1951 v E, S, W, F; 1952 v S, E (17)

Waddell, T. M. R. (Cliftonville), 1906 v S (1)

Walker, J. (Doncaster R), 1955 v W (1)

Walker, T. (Bury), 1911 v S (1)

Walsh, D. J. (WBA), 1947 v S, W; 1948 v E, S, W; 1949 v E, S, W; 1950 v W (9)

Walsh, W. (Manchester C), 1948 v E, S, W; 1949 v E, S (5)

Waring, J. (Cliftonville), 1899 v E (1)

Warren, P. (Shelbourne), 1913 v E, S (2)

Watson, J. (Ulster), 1883 v E, W; 1886 v E, S, W; 1887 v S, W; 1889 v E, W (9)

Watson, P. (Distillery), 1971 v Cy (sub) (1)

Watson, T. (Cardiff C), 1926 v S (1)

Wattie, J. (Distillery), 1899 v E (1)

Webb, C. G. (Brighton), 1909 v S, W; 1911 v S (3)

Weir, E. (Clyde), 1939 v W (1)

Welsh, E. (Carlisle U), 1966 v W, WG, M; 1967 v W (4)

Whiteside, N. (Manchester U), 1982 v Y, Hon, Sp, A, F; 1983 v WG, Alb, T; 1984 v A, T, WG, S, E, W, Fi; 1985 v R, Fi, Is, E, Sp, T; 1986 v R, E, F, D, Mor, Alg, Sp, Br; 1987 v E (2), Is, Y; 1988 v T, Pol, F; (with Everton), 1990 v H, Ei (38)

Whiteside, T. (Distillery), 1891 v E (1)

Whitfield, E. R. (Dublin University), 1886 v W (1)

Whitley, Jeff (Manchester C), 1997 v Bel (sub), Th (sub); 1998 v Sp (sub) (3)

Whitley, Jim (Manchester C), 1998 v Sp (1)

Williams, J. R. (Ulster), 1886 v E, S (2)

Williams, P. A. (WBA), 1991 v Fa (sub) (1)

Williamson, J. (Cliftonville), 1890 v E; 1892 v S; 1893 v S (3)

Willighan, T. (Burnley), 1933 v W; 1934 v S (2)

Willis, G. (Linfield), 1906 v S, W; 1907 v S; 1912 v S (4)

Wilson, D. J. (Brighton & HA), 1987 v T, Is, E (sub); (with Luton T), 1988 v Y, T, Gr, Pol, F, Ma; 1989 v Ei, H, Sp, Ma, Ch; 1990 v H, Ei, N, U; (with Sheffield W), 1991 v Y, D, A, Fa; 1992 v A (sub), S (24)

Wilson, H. (Linfield), 1925 v W (1)

Wilson, K. J. (Ipswich T), 1987 v Is, E, Y; (with Chelsea), 1988 v Y, T, Gr (sub), Pol (sub), F (sub); 1989 v H (sub), Sp (2), Ma, Ch; 1990 v Ei (sub), N, U; 1991 v Y (2), A, Pol, Fa; 1992 v Fa, A, D, S; (with Notts Co), Li, G; 1993 v Alb, Sp, D, Sp, Li, La; 1994 v La, D, Ei, R, Lie, Co, M; (with Walsall), 1995 v Ei (sub), La (42)

Wilson, M. (Distillery), 1884 v E, S, W (3)

Wilson, R. (Cliftonville), 1888 v S (1)

Wilson, S. J. (Glenavon), 1962 v S; 1964 v S; (with Falkirk), 1964 v E, W, U, Sp; 1965 v E, Sw; (with Dundee), 1966 v W, WG; 1967 v S; 1968 v E (12)

Wilton, J. M. (St Columb's Court), 1888 v E, W; 1889 v S, E; (with Cliftonville), 1890 v E; (with St Columb's Court); 1893 v W, S (7)

Wood, T. J. (Walsall), 1996 v Lie (sub) (1)

Worthington, N. (Sheffield W), 1984 v W, Fi (sub); 1985 v Is, Sp (sub); 1986 v T, R (sub), E (sub), D, Alg, Sp; 1987 v E (2), T, Is, Y; 1988 v Y, T, Gr, Pol, F, Ma; 1989 v Ei, H, Sp, Ma; 1990 v H, Ei, U; 1991 v Y, D, A, Fa; 1992 v A, D, S, Li, G; 1993 v Alb, Sp, D, Ei, Sp, Li, La; 1994 v La, D, Ei, Lie, Co, M; (with Leeds U), 1995 v P, A, Ei (2), La, Ca (sub), Ch, La; 1996 v P, Lie, A, N, Se, G; (with Stoke C), 1997 v I, Bel (sub) (66)

Wright, J. (Cliftonville), 1906 v E, S, W; 1907 v E, S, W (6)

Wright, T. J. (Newcastle U), 1989 v Ma, Ch; 1990 v H, U; 1992 v Fa, A, S, G; 1993 v Alb, Sp, Alb, Ei, Sp, Li, La; 1994 v La; (with Nottingham F), D, Ei, R, Lie, Co, M (sub); 1997 v G, Alb, I, Bel; (with Manchester C), P, Uk; 1998 v Alb (29)

Young, S. (Linfield), 1907 v E, S; 1908 v E, S; (with Airdrie), 1909 v E; 1912 v S; (with Linfield), 1914 v E, S, W (9)

## SCOTLAND

Adams, J. (Hearts), 1889 v Ni; 1892 v W; 1893 v Ni (3)

Agnew, W. B. (Kilmarnock), 1907 v Ni; 1908 v W, Ni (3)

Aird, J. (Burnley), 1954 v N (2), A, U (4)

Aitken, A. (Newcastle U), 1901 v E; 1902 v E; 1903 v E, W; 1904 v E; 1905 v E, W; 1906 v E; (with Middlesbrough), 1907 v E, W; 1908 v E; (with Leicester Fosse), 1910 v E; 1911 v E, Ni (14)

Aitken, G. G. (East Fife), 1949 v E, F; 1950 v W, Ni, Sw; (with Sunderland), 1953 v W, Ni; 1954 v E (8)

Aitken, R. (Dumbarton), 1886 v E; 1888 v Ni (2)

Aitken, R. (Celtic), 1980 v Pe (sub), Bel, W (sub), E, Pol; 1983 v Bel, Ca (1+1 sub); 1984 v Bel (sub), Ni, W (sub); 1985 v E, Ic; 1986 v WG, EG, Aus (2), Is, R, E, D, WG, U; 1987 v Bul, Ei (2), L, Bel, E, Br; 1988 v H, Bel, Bul, L, S.Ar, Ma, Sp, Co, E; 1989 v N, Y, I, Cy, F, Cy, E, Ch; 1990 v Y, F, N; (with Newcastle U), Arg (sub), Pol, Ma, Cr, Se, Br; (with St Mirren), 1992 v R (sub) (57)

Aitkenhead, W. A. C. (Blackburn R), 1912 v Ni (1)

Albiston, A. (Manchester U), 1982 v Ni; 1984 v U, Bel, EG, W, E; 1985 v Y, Ic, Sp (2), W; 1986 v EG, Ho, U (14)

Alexander, D. (East Stirlingshire), 1894 v W, Ni (2)

Allan, D. S. (Queen's Park), 1885 v E, W; 1886 v W (3)

Allan, G. (Liverpool), 1897 v E (1)

Allan, H. (Hearts), 1902 v W (1)

Allan, J. (Queen's Park), 1887 v E, W (2)

Allan, T. (Dundee), 1974 v WG, N (2)

Ancell, R. F. D. (Newcastle U), 1937 v W, Ni (2)

Anderson, A. (Hearts), 1933 v E; 1934 v A, E, W, Ni; 1935 v E, W, Ni; 1936 v E, W, Ni; 1937 v G, E, W, Ni, A; 1938 v E, W, Ni, Cz, Ho; 1939 v W, H (23)

Anderson, F. (Clydesdale), 1874 v E (1)

Anderson, G. (Kilmarnock), 1901 v Ni (1)

Anderson, H. A. (Raith R), 1914 v W (1)

Anderson, J. (Leicester C), 1954 v Fi (1)

Anderson, K. (Queen's Park), 1896 v Ni; 1898 v E, Ni (3)

Anderson, W. (Queen's Park), 1882 v E; 1883 v E, W; 1884 v E; 1885 v E, W (6)

Andrews, P. (Eastern), 1875 v E (1)

Archibald, A. (Rangers), 1921 v W; 1922 v W, E; 1923 v Ni; 1924 v E, W; 1931 v E; 1932 v E (8)

Archibald, S. (Aberdeen), 1980 v P (sub); (with Tottenham H), Ni, Pol, H; 1981 v Se (sub), Is, Ni, Is, Ni, E; 1982 v Ni, P, Sp (sub), Ho, Nz (sub), Br, USSR; 1983 v EG, Sw (sub), Bel; 1984 v EG, E, F; (with Barcelona), 1985 v Sp, E, Ic (sub); 1986 v WG (27)

Armstrong, M. W. (Aberdeen), 1936 v W, Ni; 1937 v G (3)

Arnott, W. (Queen's Park), 1883 v W; 1884 v E, Ni; 1885 v E, W; 1886 v E; 1887 v E, W; 1888 v E; 1889 v E; 1890 v E; 1891 v E; 1892 v E; 1893 v E (14)

Auld, J. R. (Third Lanark), 1887 v E, W; 1889 v W (3)

Auld, R. (Celtic), 1959 v H, P; 1960 v W (3)

Baird, A. (Queen's Park), 1892 v Ni; 1894 v W (2)

Baird, D. (Hearts), 1890 v Ni; 1891 v E; 1892 v W (3)

Baird, H. (Airdrieonians), 1956 v A (1)

Baird, J. C. (Vale of Leven), 1876 v E; 1878 v W; 1880 v E (3)

Baird, S. (Rangers), 1957 v Y, Sp (2), Sw, WG; 1958 v F, Ni (7)

Baird, W. U. (St Bernard), 1897 v Ni (1)

Bannon, E. (Dundee U), 1980 v Bel; 1983 v Ni, W, E, Ca; 1984 v EG; 1986 v Is, R, E, D (sub), WG (11)

Barbour, A. (Renton), 1885 v Ni (1)

Barker, J. B. (Rangers), 1893 v W; 1894 v W (2)

Barrett, F. (Dundee), 1894 v Ni; 1895 v W (2)

Battles, B. (Celtic), 1901 v E, W, Ni (3)

Battles, B. jun. (Hearts), 1931 v W (1)

Bauld, W. (Hearts), 1950 v E, Sw, P (3)

Baxter, J. C. (Rangers), 1961 v Ni, Ei (2), Cz; 1962 v Ni, W, E, Cz, U; 1963 v W, Ni, E, A, N, Ei, Sp; 1964 v W, E, N, WG; 1965 v W, Ni, Fi; (with Sunderland), 1966 v P, Br, Ni, W, E; 1967 v W, E, USSR; 1968 v W (34)

Baxter, R. D. (Middlesbrough), 1939 v E, W, H (3)

Beattie, A. (Preston NE), 1937 v E, A, Cz; 1938 v E; 1939 v W, Ni, H (7)

Beattie, R. (Preston NE), 1939 v W (1)

Begbie, I. (Hearts), 1890 v Ni; 1891 v E; 1892 v W; 1894 v E (4)

Bell, A. (Manchester U), 1912 v Ni (1)

Bell, J. (Dumbarton), 1890 v Ni; 1892 v E; (with Everton), 1896 v E; 1897 v E; 1898 v E; (with Celtic), 1899 v E, W, Ni; 1900 v E, W (10)

Bell, M. (Hearts), 1901 v W (1)

Bell, W. J. (Leeds U), 1966 v P, Br (2)

Bennett, A. (Celtic), 1904 v W; 1907 v Ni; 1908 v W; (with Rangers), 1909 v W, Ni, E; 1910 v E, W; 1911 v E, W; 1913 v Ni (11)

Bennie, R. (Airdrieonians), 1925 v W, Ni; 1926 v Ni (3)

Bernard, P. R. J. (Oldham Ath), 1995 v J (sub), Ec (2)

Berry, D. (Queen's Park), 1894 v W; 1899 v W, Ni (3)

Berry, W. H. (Queen's Park), 1888 v E; 1889 v E; 1890 v E; 1891 v E (4)

Bett, J. (Rangers), 1982 v Ho; 1983 v Bel; (with Lokeren), 1984 v Bel, W, E, F; 1985 v Y, Ic, Sp (2), W, E, Ic; (with Aberdeen), 1986 v Is, Ho; 1987 v Bel; 1988 v H (sub); 1989 v Y; 1990 v F (sub), N, Arg, Eg, Ma, Cr (25)

Beveridge, W. W. (Glasgow University), 1879 v E, W; 1880 v W (3)

Black, A. (Hearts), 1938 v Cz, Ho; 1939 v H (3)

Black, D. (Hurlford), 1889 v Ni (1)

Black, E. (Metz), 1988 v H (sub), L (sub) (2)

Black, I. H. (Southampton), 1948 v E (1)

Blackburn, J. E. (Royal Engineers), 1873 v E (1)

Blacklaw, A. S. (Burnley), 1963 v N, Sp; 1966 v I (3)

Blackley, J. (Hibernian), 1974 v Cz, E, Bel, Z; 1976 v Sw; 1977 v W, Se (7)

Blair, D. (Clyde), 1929 v W, Ni; 1931 v E, A, I; 1932 v W, Ni; (with Aston Villa), 1933 v W (8)

Blair, J. (Sheffield W), 1920 v E, Ni; (with Cardiff C), 1921 v E; 1922 v E; 1923 v E, W, Ni; 1924 v W (8)

Blair, J. (Motherwell), 1934 v W (1)

Blair, J. A. (Blackpool), 1947 v W (1)

Blair, W. (Third Lanark), 1896 v W (1)

Blessington, J. (Celtic), 1894 v E, Ni; 1896 v E, Ni (4)

Blyth, J. A. (Coventry C), 1978 v Bul, W (2)

Bone, J. (Norwich C), 1972 v Y (sub); 1973 v D (2)

Booth, S. (Aberdeen), 1993 v G (sub), Es (2 subs); 1994 v Sw, Ma (sub); 1995 v Fa, Ru; 1996 v Fi, Sm, Aus (sub), US, Ho, Sw (sub); (with Borussia Dortmund), 1998 v D, Fi, Co (sub), Mor (sub) (17)

Bowie, J. (Rangers), 1920 v E, Ni (2)

Bowie, W. (Linthouse), 1891 v Ni (1)

Bowman, D. (Dundee U), 1992 v Fi, US (sub); 1993 v G, Es; 1994 v Sw, I (6)

Bowman, G. A. (Montrose), 1892 v Ni (1)

Boyd, J. M. (Newcastle U), 1934 v Ni (1)

Boyd, R. (Mossend Swifts), 1889 v Ni; 1891 v W (2)

Boyd, T. (Motherwell), 1991 v R (sub), Sw, Bul, USSR; (with Chelsea), 1992 v Sw, R; (with Celtic), Fi, Ca, N, C;

1993 v Sw, P, I, Ma, G, Es (2); 1994 v I, Ma (sub), Ho (sub), A; 1995 v Fi, Fa, Ru, Gr, Ru, Sm; 1996 v Gr, Fi, Se, Sm, Aus, D, US, Co, Ho, E, Sw; 1997 v A, La, Se, Es (2), A, Se, W, Ma, Bl; 1998 v Bl, La, F, D, Fi (sub), Co, US, Br, N, Mor (58)

Boyd, W. G. (Clyde), 1931 v I, Sw (2)

Breckenbridge, T. (Hearts), 1888 v Ni (1)

Bradshaw, T. (Bury), 1928 v E (1)

Brand, R. (Rangers), 1961 v Ni, Cz, Ei (2); 1962 v Ni, W, Cz, U (8)

Branden, T. (Blackburn R), 1896 v E (1)

Brazil, A. (Ipswich T), 1980 v Pol (sub), H; 1982 v Sp, Ho (sub), Ni, W, E, Nz, USSR (sub); 1983 v EG, Sw, (with Tottenham H), W, E (sub) (13)

Bremner, D. (Hibernian), 1976 v Sw (sub) (1)

Bremner, W. J. (Leeds U), 1965 v Sp; 1966 v E, Pol, P, Br, I (2); 1967 v W, Ni, E; 1968 v W, E; 1969 v W, E, Ni, D, A, WG, Cy (2); 1970 v Ei, WG, A; 1971 v E; 1972 v P, Bel, Ho, Ni, W, E, Y, Cz, Br; 1973 v D (2), E (2), Ni (sub), Sw, Br; 1974 v Cz, WG, Ni, W, E, Bel, N, Z, Br, Y; 1975 v Sp (2); 1976 v D (54)

Brennan, F. (Newcastle U), 1947 v W, Ni; 1953 v W, Ni, E; 1954 v Ni, E (7)

Breslin, B. (Hibernian), 1897 v W (1)

Brewster, G. (Everton), 1921 v E (1)

Brogan, J. (Celtic), 1971 v W, Ni, P, E (4)

Brown, A. (Middlesbrough), 1904 v E (1)

Brown, A. (St Mirren), 1890 v W; 1891 v W (2)

Brown, A. D. (East Fife), 1950 v Sw, P, F; (with Blackpool), 1952 v USA, D, Se; 1953 v W; 1954 v W, E, N (2), Fi, A, U (14)

Brown, G. C. P. (Rangers), 1931 v W; 1932 v E, W, Ni; 1933 v E; 1934 v A; 1935 v E, W; 1936 v E, W; 1937 v G, E, W, Ni, Cz; 1938 v E, W, Cz, Ho (19)

Brown, H. (Partick T), 1947 v W, Bel, L (3)

Brown, J. (Cambuslang), 1890 v W (1)

Brown, J. B. (Clyde), 1939 v W (1)

Brown, J. G. (Sheffield U), 1975 v R (1)

Brown, R. (Dumbarton), 1884 v W, Ni (2)

Brown, R. (Rangers), 1947 v Ni; 1949 v Ni; 1952 v E (3)

Brown, R. jun. (Dumbarton), 1885 v W (1)

Brown, W. D. F. (Dundee), 1958 v F; 1959 v E, W, Ni; (with Tottenham H), 1960 v W, Ni, Pol, A, H, T; 1962 v Ni, W, E, Cz; 1963 v W, Ni, E, A; 1964 v Ni, W, N; 1965 v E, Fi, Pol, Sp; 1966 v Ni, Pol, I (28)

Browning, J. (Celtic), 1914 v W (1)

Brownlie, J. (Hibernian), 1971 v USSR; 1972 v Pe, Ni, E; 1973 v D (2); 1976 v R (7)

Brownlie, J. (Third Lanark), 1909 v E, Ni; 1910 v E, W, Ni; 1911 v W, Ni; 1912 v W, Ni, E; 1913 v W, Ni, E; 1914 v W, Ni, E (16)

Bruce, D. (Vale of Leven), 1890 v W (1)

Bruce, R. F. (Middlesbrough), 1934 v A (1)

Buchan, M. M. (Aberdeen), 1972 v P (sub), Bel; (with Manchester U), W, Y, Cz, Br; 1973 v D (2), E; 1974 v WG, Ni, W, N, Br, Y; 1975 v EG, Sp, P; 1976 v D, R; 1977 v Fi, Cz, Ch, Arg, Br; 1978 v EG, W (sub), Ni, Pe, Ir, Ho; 1979 v A, N, P (34)

Buchanan, J. (Cambuslang), 1889 v Ni (1)

Buchanan, J. (Rangers), 1929 v E; 1930 v E (2)

Buchanan, P. S. (Chelsea), 1938 v Cz (1)

Buchanan, R. (Abercorn), 1891 v W (1)

Buckley, P. (Aberdeen), 1954 v N; 1955 v W, Ni (3)

Buick, A. (Hearts), 1902 v W, Ni (2)

Burley, C. W. (Chelsea), 1995 v J, Ec, Fa; 1996 v Gr, Se, Aus, D, US, Co (sub), Ho (sub), E (sub), Sw; 1997 v A, La, Se, Es, A, Se, Ma, Bl; (with Celtic), 1998 v Bl, La, F, Co, US (sub), Br, N, Mor (28)

Burley, G. (Ipswich T), 1979 v W, Ni, E, Arg, N; 1980 v P, Ni, E (sub), Pol; 1982 v W (sub), E (11)

Burns, F. (Manchester U), 1970 v A (1)

Burns, K. (Birmingham C), 1974 v WG; 1975 v EG (sub), Sp (2); 1977 v Cz (sub), W, Se, W (sub); (with Nottingham F), 1978 v Ni (sub), W, E, Pe, Ir; 1979 v N; 1980 v Pe, A, Bel; 1981 v Is, Ni, W (20)

Burns, T. (Celtic), 1981 v Ni; 1982 v Ho (sub), W; 1983 v Bel (sub), Ni, Ca (1 + 1 sub); 1988 v E (sub) (8)

Busby, M. W. (Manchester C), 1934 v W (1)

Cairns, T. (Rangers), 1920 v W; 1922 v E; 1923 v E, W; 1924 v Ni; 1925 v W, E, Ni (8)

Calderhead, D. (Queen of the South), 1889 v Ni (1)

Calderwood, C. (Tottenham H), 1995 v Ru, Sm, J, Ec, Fa; 1996 v Gr, Fi, Se, Sm, US, Co, Ho, E, Sw; 1997 v A, La, Se, Es (2), A, Se; 1998 v Bl, La, F, D, Fi, Co, US, Br, N (30)

Calderwood, R. (Cartvale), 1885 v Ni, E, W (3)

Caldow, E. (Rangers), 1957 v Sp (2), Sw, WG, E; 1958 v Ni, W, Sw, Par, H, Pol, Y, F; 1959 v E, W, Ni, WG, Ho, P;

1960 v E, W, Ni, A, H, T; 1961 v E, W, Ni, Ei (2), Cz; 1962 v Ni, W, E, Cz (2), U; 1963 v W, Ni, E (40)

Callaghan, P. (Hibernian), 1900 v Ni (1)

Callaghan, W. (Dunfermline Ath), 1970 v Ei (sub), W (2)

Cameron, J. (Rangers), 1886 v Ni (1)

Cameron, J. (Queen's Park), 1896 v Ni (1)

Cameron, J. (St Mirren), 1904 v Ni; (with Chelsea), 1909 v E (2)

Campbell, C. (Queen's Park), 1874 v E; 1876 v W; 1877 v E, W; 1878 v E; 1879 v E; 1880 v E; 1881 v E; 1882 v E, W; 1884 v E; 1885 v E; 1886 v E (13)

Campbell, H. (Renton), 1889 v W (1)

Campbell, Jas (Sheffield W), 1913 v W (1)

Campbell, J. (South Western), 1880 v W (1)

Campbell, J. (Kilmarnock), 1891 v Ni; 1892 v W (2)

Campbell, John (Celtic), 1893 v E, Ni; 1898 v E, Ni; 1900 v E, Ni; 1901 v E, W, Ni; 1902 v W, Ni; 1903 v W (12)

Campbell, John (Rangers), 1899 v E, W, Ni; 1901 v Ni (4)

Campbell, K. (Liverpool), 1920 v E, W, Ni; (with Partick T), 1921 v W, Ni; 1922 v W, Ni, E (8)

Campbell, P. (Rangers), 1878 v W; 1879 v W (2)

Campbell, P. (Morton), 1898 v W (1)

Campbell, R. (Falkirk), 1947 v Bel, L; (with Chelsea), 1950 v Sw, P, F (5)

Campbell, W. (Morton), 1947 v Ni; 1948 v E, Bel, Sw, F (5)

Carabine, J. (Third Lanark), 1938 v Ho; 1939 v E, Ni (3)

Carr, W. M. (Coventry C), 1970 v Ni, W, E; 1971 v D; 1972 v Pe; 1973 v D (sub) (6)

Cassidy, J. (Celtic), 1921 v W, Ni; 1923 v Ni; 1924 v W (4)

Chalmers, S. (Celtic), 1965 v W, Fi; 1966 v P (sub), Br; 1967 v Ni (5)

Chalmers, W. (Rangers), 1885 v Ni (1)

Chalmers, W. S. (Queen's Park), 1929 v Ni (1)

Chambers, T. (Hearts), 1894 v W (1)

Chaplin, G. D. (Dundee), 1908 v W (1)

Cheyne, A. G. (Aberdeen), 1929 v E, N, G, Ho; 1930 v F (5)

Christie, A. J. (Queen's Park), 1898 v W; 1899 v E, Ni (3)

Christie, R. M. (Queen's Park), 1884 v E (1)

Clark, J. (Celtic), 1966 v Br; 1967 v W, Ni, USSR (4)

Clark, R. B. (Aberdeen), 1968 v W, Ho; 1970 v Ni; 1971 v W, Ni, E, D, P, USSR; 1972 v Bel, Ni, W, E, Cz, Br; 1973 v D, E (17)

Clarke, S. (Chelsea), 1988 v H, Bel, Bul, S.Ar, Ma; 1994 v Ho (6)

Cleland, J. (Royal Albert), 1891 v Ni (1)

Clements, R. (Leith Ath), 1891 v Ni (1)

Clunas, W. L. (Sunderland), 1924 v E; 1926 v W (2)

Collier, W. (Raith R), 1922 v W (1)

Collins, J. (Hibernian), 1988 v S.Ar; 1990 v EG, Pol (sub), Ma (sub); (with Celtic), 1991 v Sw (sub), Bul (sub); 1992 v Ni (sub), Fi; 1993 v P, Ma, G, P, Es (2); 1994 v Sw, Ho (sub), A, Ho; 1995 v Fi, Fa, Ru, Gr, Ru, Sm, Fa; 1996 v Gr, Fi, Se, Sm, Aus, D, US (sub), Co, Ho, E, Sw; (with Monaco), 1997 v A, La, Se, Es, A, Se, Ma; 1998 v Bl, La, F, Fi, Co, US, Br, N, Mor (52)

Collins, R. Y. (Celtic), 1951 v W, Ni, A; 1955 v Y, A, H; 1956 v Ni, W; 1957 v E, W, Sp (2), Sw, WG; 1958 v Ni, W, Sw, H, Pol, Y, F, Par; (with Everton), 1959 v E, W, Ni, WG, Ho, P; (with Leeds U), 1965 v E, Pol, Sp (31)

Collins, T. (Hearts), 1909 v W (1)

Colman, D. (Aberdeen), 1911 v E, W, Ni; 1913 v Ni (4)

Colquhoun, E. P. (Sheffield U), 1972 v P, Ho, Pe, Y, Cz, Br; 1973 v D (2), E (9)

Colquhoun, J. (Hearts), 1988 v S.Ar (sub), Ma (sub) (2)

Combe, J. R. (Hibernian), 1948 v E, Bel, Sw (3)

Conn, A. (Hearts), 1956 v A (1)

Conn, A. (Tottenham H), 1975 v Ni (sub), E (2)

Connachan, E. D. (Dunfermline Ath), 1962 v Cz, U (2)

Connelly, G. (Celtic), 1974 v Cz, WG (2)

Connolly, J. (Everton), 1973 v Sw (1)

Connor, J. (Airdrieonians), 1886 v Ni (1)

Connor, J. (Sunderland), 1930 v F; 1932 v Ni; 1934 v E; 1935 v Ni (4)

Connor, R. (Dundee), 1986 v Ho; (with Aberdeen), 1988 v S.Ar (sub); 1989 v E; 1991 v R (4)

Cook, W. L. (Bolton W), 1934 v E; 1935 v W, Ni (3)

Cooke, C. (Dundee), 1966 v W, I; (with Chelsea), P, Br; 1968 v E, Ho; 1969 v W, Ni, A, WG (sub), Cy (2); 1970 v A; 1971 v Bel; 1975 v Sp, P (16)

Cooper, D. (Rangers), 1980 v Pe, A (sub); 1984 v W, E; 1985 v Y, Ic, Sp (2), W; 1986 v W (sub), EG, Aus (2), Ho, WG (sub), U (sub); 1987 v Bul, L, Ei, Br; (with Motherwell), 1990 v N, Eg (22)

Cormack, P. B. (Hibernian), 1966 v Br; 1969 v D (sub); 1970 v Ei, WG; (with Nottingham F), 1971 v D (sub), W, P, E; 1972 v Ho (sub) (9)

Cowan, J. (Aston Villa), 1896 v E; 1897 v E; 1898 v E (3)

Cowan, J. (Morton), 1948 v Bel, Sw; F; 1949 v E, W, F; 1950 v E, W, Ni, Sw, P, F; 1951 v E, W, Ni, A (2), D, F, Bel; 1952 v Ni, W, USA, D, Se (25)

Cowan, W. D. (Newcastle U), 1924 v E (1)

Cowie, D. (Dundee), 1953 v E, Se; 1954 v Ni, W, Fi, N, A, U; 1955 v W, Ni, A, H; 1956 v W, A; 1957 v Ni, W; 1958 v H, Pol, Y, Par (20)

Cox, C. J. (Hearts), 1948 v F (1)

Cox, S. (Rangers), 1949 v E, F; 1950 v E, F, W, Ni, Sw, P; 1951 v E, D, F, Bel, A; 1952 v Ni, W, USA, D, Se; 1953 v W, Ni, E; 1954 v W, Ni, E (24)

Craig, A. (Motherwell), 1929 v N, Ho; 1932 v E (3)

Craig, J. (Celtic), 1977 v Se (sub) (1)

Craig, J. P. (Celtic), 1968 v W (1)

Craig, T. (Rangers), 1927 v Ni; 1928 v Ni; 1929 v N, G, Ho; 1930 v Ni, E, W (8)

Craig, T. B. (Newcastle U), 1976 v Sw (1)

Crapnell, J. (Airdrieonians), 1929 v E, N, G; 1930 v F; 1931 v Ni, Sw; 1932 v E, F; 1933 v Ni (9)

Crawford, D. (St Mirren), 1894 v W, Ni; 1900 v W (3)

Crawford, J. (Queen's Park), 1932 v F, Ni; 1933 v E, W, Ni (5)

Crawford, S. (Raith R) 1995 v Ec (sub) (1)

Crerand, P. T. (Celtic), 1961 v Ei (2), Cz; 1962 v Ni, W, E, Cz (2), U; 1963 v W, Ni; (with Manchester U), 1964 v Ni; 1965 v E, Pol, Fi; 1966 v Pol (16)

Cringan, W. (Celtic), 1920 v W; 1922 v E, Ni; 1923 v W, E (5)

Crosbie, J. A. (Ayr U), 1920 v W; (with Birmingham), 1922 v E (2)

Croal, J. A. (Falkirk), 1913 v Ni; 1914 v E, W (3)

Cropley, A. J. (Hibernian), 1972 v P, Bel (2)

Cross, J. H. (Third Lanark), 1903 v Ni (1)

Cruickshank, J. (Hearts), 1964 v WG; 1970 v W, E; 1971 v D, Bel; 1976 v R (6)

Crum, J. (Celtic), 1936 v E; 1939 v Ni (2)

Cullen, M. J. (Luton T), 1956 v A (1)

Cumming, D. S. (Middlesbrough), 1938 v E (1)

Cumming, J. (Hearts), 1955 v E, H, P, Y; 1960 v E, Pol, A, H, T (9)

Cummings, G. (Partick T), 1935 v E; 1936 v W, Ni; (with Aston Villa), E; 1937 v G; 1938 v W, Ni, Cz; 1939 v E (9)

Cunningham, A. N. (Rangers), 1920 v Ni; 1921 v W, E; 1922 v Ni; 1923 v E, W; 1924 v E, Ni; 1926 v E, Ni; 1927 v E, W (12)

Cunningham, W. C. (Preston NE), 1954 v N (2), U, Fi, A; 1955 v W, E, H (8)

Curran, H. P. (Wolverhampton W), 1970 v A; 1971 v Ni, E, D, USSR (sub) (5)

Dailly, C. (Derby Co), 1997 v W, Ma, Bl; 1998 v Bl, La, F, D, Fi, Co, US, Br, N, Mor (13)

Dalglish, K. (Celtic), 1972 v Bel (sub), Ho; 1973 v D (1+1 sub), E (2), W, Ni, Sw, Br; 1974 v Cz (2), WG (2), Ni, W, E, Bel, N (sub), Z, Br, Y; 1975 v EG, Sp (sub+1), Se, P, W, Ni, E, R; 1976 v D (2), R, Sw, Ni, E; 1977 v Fi, Cz, W (2), Se, Ni, E, Ch, Arg, Br; (with Liverpool), 1978 v EG, Cz, W, Bul, Ni (sub), W, E, Pe, Ir, Ho; 1979 v A, N, P, W, Ni, E, Arg, N; 1980 v Pe, A, Bel (2), P, Ni, W, E, Pol, H; 1981 v Se, P, Is; 1982 v Se, H, P (sub), Sp, Ho, Ni, W, E, Nz, Br (sub); 1983 v Bel, Sw; 1984 v U, Bel, EG; 1985 v Y, Ic, Sp, W; 1986 v EG, Aus, R; 1987 v Bul (sub), L (102)

Davidson, D. (Queen's Park), 1878 v W; 1879 v W; 1880 v W; 1881 v E, W (5)

Davidson, J. A. (Partick T), 1954 v N (2), A, U; 1955 v W, Ni, E, H (8)

Davidson, S. (Middlesbrough), 1921 v E (1)

Dawson, A. (Rangers), 1980 v Pol (sub), H; 1983 v Ni, Ca (2) (5)

Dawson, J. (Rangers), 1935 v Ni; 1936 v E; 1937 v G, E, W, Ni, A, Cz; 1938 v W, Ho, Ni; 1939 v E, Ni, H (14)

Deans, J. (Celtic), 1975 v EG, Sp (2)

Delaney, J. (Celtic), 1936 v W, Ni; 1937 v G, E, A, Cz; 1938 v Ni; 1939 v W, Ni; (with Manchester U), 1947 v E; 1948 v E, W, Ni (13)

Divine, A. (Falkirk), 1910 v W (1)

Dewar, G. (Dumbarton), 1888 v Ni; 1889 v E (2)

Dewar, N. (Third Lanark), 1932 v E, F; 1933 v W (3)

Dick, J. (West Ham U), 1959 v E (1)

Dickie, M. (Rangers), 1897 v Ni; 1899 v Ni; 1900 v W (3)

Dickson, W. (Dumbarton), 1888 v Ni (1)

Dickson, W. (Kilmarnock), 1970 v Ni, W, E; 1971 v D, USSR (5)

Divers, J. (Celtic), 1895 v W (1)

Divers, J. (Celtic), 1939 v Ni (1)

Docherty, T. H. (Preston NE), 1952 v W; 1953 v E, Se; 1954 v N (2), A, U; 1955 v W, E, H (2), A; 1957 v E, Y, Sp (2), Sw, WG; 1958 v Ni, W, E, Sw; (with Arsenal), 1959 v W, E, Ni (25)

Dodds, D. (Dundee U), 1984 v U (sub), Ni (2)
Dodds, J. (Celtic), 1914 v E, W, Ni (3)
Dodds, W. (Aberdeen), 1997 v La (sub), W, Bl (sub); 1998 v Bl (sub) (4)
Doig, J. E. (Arbroath), 1887 v Ni; 1889 v Ni; (with Sunderland), 1896 v E; 1899 v E; 1903 v E (5)
Donachie, W. (Manchester C), 1972 v Pe, Ni, E, Y, Cz, Br; 1973 v D, E, W, Ni; 1974 v Ni; 1976 v R, Ni, W, E; 1977 v Fi, Cz, W (2), Se, Ni, E, Ch, Arg, Br; 1978 v EG, W, Bul, W, E, Ir, Ho; 1979 v A, N, P (sub) (35)
Donaldson, A. (Bolton W), 1914 v E, Ni, W; 1920 v E, Ni; 1922 v Ni (6)
Donnachie, J. (Oldham Ath), 1913 v E; 1914 v E, Ni (3)
Donnelly, S. (Celtic), 1997 v W (sub), Ma (sub); 1998 v La (sub), F (sub), D (sub), Fi (sub), Co (sub), US (sub) (8)
Dougall, C. (Birmingham C), 1947 v W (1)
Dougall, J. (Preston NE), 1939 v E (1)
Dougan, R. (Hearts), 1950 v Sw (1)
Douglas, A. (Chelsea), 1911 v W (1)
Douglas, J. (Renfrew), 1880 v W (1)
Dowds, P. (Celtic), 1892 v Ni (1)
Downie, R. (Third Lanark), 1892 v W (1)
Doyle, D. (Celtic), 1892 v E; 1893 v W; 1894 v E; 1895 v E, Ni; 1897 v E; 1898 v E, Ni (8)
Doyle, J. (Ayr U), 1976 v R (1)
Drummond, J. (Falkirk), 1892 v Ni; (with Rangers), 1894 v Ni; 1895 v Ni, E; 1896 v E, Ni; 1897 v Ni; 1898 v E; 1900 v E; 1901 v E; 1902 v E, W, Ni; 1903 v Ni (14)
Dunbar, M. (Cartvale), 1886 v Ni (1)
Duncan, A. (Hibernian), 1975 v P (sub), W, Ni, E, R; 1976 v D (sub) (6)
Duncan, D. (Derby Co), 1933 v E, W; 1934 v A, W; 1935 v E, W; 1936 v E, W, Ni; 1937 v G, E, W, Ni; 1938 v W (14)
Duncan, D. M. (East Fife), 1948 v Bel, Sw, F (3)
Duncan, J. (Alexandra Ath), 1878 v W; 1882 v W (2)
Duncan, J. (Leicester C), 1926 v W (1)
Duncanson, J. (Rangers), 1947 v Ni (1)
Dunlop, J. (St Mirren), 1890 v W (1)
Dunlop, W. (Liverpool), 1906 v E (1)
Dunn, J. (Hibernian), 1925 v W, Ni; 1927 v Ni; 1928 v Ni, E; (with Everton), 1929 v W (6)
Durie, G. S. (Chelsea), 1988 v Bul (sub); 1989 v I (sub), Cy; 1990 v Y, EG, Eg, Se; 1991 v Sw (sub), Bul (2), USSR (sub), Sm; (with Tottenham H), 1992 v Sw, R, Sm, Ni (sub), Fi, Ca, N (sub), Ho, G; 1993 v Sw, I; 1994 v Sw, I; (with Rangers), Ho (2); 1996 v US, Ho, E, Sw; 1997 v A (sub), Se (sub), Ma (sub), Bl; 1998 v Bl, La, F, Fi (sub), Co, Br, N, Mor (43)
Durrant, I. (Rangers), 1988 v H, Bel, Ma, Sp; 1989 v N (sub); 1993 v Sw (sub), P (sub), I, P (sub); 1994 v I (sub), Ma (11)

Dykes, J. (Hearts), 1938 v Ho; 1939 v Ni (2)

Easson, J. F. (Portsmouth), 1931 v A, Sw; 1934 v W (3)
Ellis, J. (Mossend Swifts), 1892 v Ni (1)
Elliott, M. S. (Leicester C), 1998 v F (sub), D, Fi (3)
Evans, A. (Aston Villa), 1982 v Ho, Ni, E, Nz (4)
Evans, R. (Celtic), 1949 v E, W, Ni, F; 1950 v W, Ni, Sw, P; 1951 v E, A; 1952 v Ni; 1953 v Se; 1954 v Ni, W, E, Ni, Fi; 1955 v Ni, P, Y, A, H; 1956 v Ni, W, A; 1957 v WG, Sp; 1958 v Ni, W, E, Sw, H, Pol, Y, Par, F; 1959 v E, WG, Ho, P; 1960 v E, Ni, W, Pol; (with Chelsea), 1960 v A, H, T (48)
Ewart, J. (Bradford C), 1921 v E (1)
Ewing, T. (Partick T), 1958 v W, E (2)

Farm, G. N. (Blackpool), 1953 v W, Ni, E, Se; 1954 v Ni, W, E; 1959 v WG, Ho, P (10)
Ferguson, D. (Rangers), 1988 v Ma, Co (sub) (2)
Ferguson, D. (Dundee U), 1992 v US (sub), Ca, Ho (sub); 1993 v G; (with Everton) 1995 v Gr; 1997 v A, Es (7)
Ferguson, I. (Rangers), 1989 v I, Cy (sub), F; 1993 v Ma (sub), Es; 1994 v Ma, A (sub), Ho (sub); 1997 v Es (sub) (9)
Ferguson, J. (Vale of Leven), 1874 v E; 1876 v E, W; 1877 v E, W; 1878 v W (6)
Ferguson, R. (Kilmarnock), 1966 v W, E, Ho, P, Br; 1967 v W, Ni (7)
Fernie, W. (Celtic), 1954 v Fi, A, U; 1955 v W, Ni; 1957 v E, Ni, W, Y; 1958 v W, Sw, Par (12)
Findlay, R. (Kilmarnock), 1898 v W (1)
Fitchie, T. T. (Woolwich Arsenal), 1905 v W; 1906 v W, Ni; (with Queen's Park), 1907 v W (4)
Flavell, R. (Airdrieonians), 1947 v Bel, L (2)
Fleck, R. (Norwich C), 1990 v Arg, Se, Br (sub); 1991 v USSR (4)
Fleming, C. (East Fife), 1954 v Ni (1)
Fleming, J. W. (Rangers), 1929 v G, Ho; 1930 v E (3)
Fleming, R. (Morton), 1886 v Ni (1)

Forbes, A. R. (Sheffield U), 1947 v Bel, L, E; 1948 v W, Ni; (with Arsenal), 1950 v E, P, F; 1951 v W, Ni, A; 1952 v W, D, Se (14)
Forbes, J. (Vale of Leven), 1884 v E, W, Ni; 1887 v W, E (5)
Ford, D. (Hearts), 1974 v Cz (sub), WG (sub), W (3)
Forrest, J. (Rangers), 1966 v W, I; (with Aberdeen), 1971 v Bel (sub), D, USSR (5)
Forrest, J. (Motherwell), 1958 v E (1)
Forsyth, A. (Partick T), 1972 v Y, Cz, Br; 1973 v D; (with Manchester U), E; 1975 v Sp, Ni (sub), R, EG; 1976 v D (10)
Forsyth, C. (Kilmarnock), 1964 v E; 1965 v W, Ni, Fi (4)
Forsyth, T. (Motherwell), 1971 v D; (with Rangers), 1974 v Cz; 1976 v Sw, Ni, W, E; 1977 v Fi, Se, W, Ni, E, Ch, Arg, Br; 1978 v Cz, W, Ni, W (sub), E, Pe, Ir (sub), Ho (22)
Foyers, R. (St Bernards), 1893 v W; 1894 v W (2)
Fraser, D. M. (WBA), 1968 v Ho; 1969 v Cy (2)
Fraser, J. (Moffat), 1891 v Ni (1)
Fraser, M. J. E. (Queen's Park), 1880 v W; 1882 v W, E; 1883 v W, E (5)
Fraser, J. (Dundee), 1907 v Ni (1)
Fraser, W. (Sunderland), 1955 v W, Ni (2)
Fulton, W. (Abercorn), 1884 v Ni (1)
Fyfe, J. H. (Third Lanark), 1895 v W (1)

Gabriel, J. (Everton), 1961 v W; 1964 v N (sub) (2)
Gallacher, H. K. (Airdrieonians), 1924 v Ni; 1925 v E, W, Ni; 1926 v W; (with Newcastle U), 1926 v E, Ni; 1927 v E, W, Ni; 1928 v E, W; 1929 v E, W, Ni; 1930 v W, Ni, F; (with Chelsea), 1934 v E; (with Derby Co), 1935 v E (20)
Gallacher, K. W. (Dundee U), 1988 v Co, E (sub); 1989 v N, I; (with Coventry C), 1991 v Sm; 1992 v R (sub), Sm (sub), Ni (sub), N (sub), Ho (sub), G (sub), C; 1993 v Sw (sub), P; (with Blackburn R), P, Es (2); 1994 v I, Ma; 1996 v Aus (sub), D, Co (sub), Ho; 1997 v Se (sub), Es (2), A, Se, W, Ma, Bl; 1998 v Bl, La, F, Fi (sub), US, Br, N, Mor (39)
Gallacher, P. (Sunderland), 1935 v Ni (1)
Galloway, M. (Celtic), 1992 v R (1)
Galt, J. H. (Rangers), 1908 v W, Ni (2)
Gardiner, I. (Motherwell), 1958 v W (1)
Gardner, D. R. (Third Lanark), 1897 v W (1)
Gardner, R. (Queen's Park), 1872 v E; 1873 v E; (with Clydesdale), 1874 v E; 1875 v E; 1878 v E (5)
Gemmell, T. (St Mirren), 1955 v P, Y (2)
Gemmell, T. (Celtic), 1966 v E; 1967 v W, Ni, E, USSR; 1968 v Ni, E; 1969 v W, Ni, E, D, A, WG, Cy; 1970 v E, Ei, WG; 1971 v Bel (18)
Gemmill, A. (Derby Co), 1971 v Bel; 1972 v P, Ho, Pe, Ni, W, E; 1976 v D, R, Ni, W, E; 1977 v Fi, Cz, W (2), Ni (sub), E (sub), Ch (sub), Arg, Br; 1978 v EG (sub); (with Nottingham F), Bul, Ni, W, E (sub), Pe (sub), Ir, Ho; 1979 v A, N, P, N; (with Birmingham C), 1980 v A, P, Ni, W, E, H; 1981 v Se, P, Is, Ni (43)
Gemmill, S. (Nottingham F), 1995 v J, Ec, Fa (sub); 1996 v Sm, D (sub), US; 1997 v Es, Se (sub), W, Ma (sub), Bl (sub); 1998 v D, Fi (13)
Gibb, W. (Clydesdale), 1873 v E (1)
Gibson, D. W. (Leicester C), 1963 v A, N, Ei, Sp; 1964 v Ni; 1965 v W, Fi (7)
Gibson, J. D. (Partick T), 1926 v E; 1927 v E, W, Ni; (with Aston Villa), 1928 v E, W; 1930 v W, Ni (8)
Gibson, N. (Rangers), 1895 v E, Ni; 1896 v E, Ni; 1897 v E, Ni; 1898 v E; 1899 v E, W, Ni; 1900 v E, Ni; 1901 v W; (with Partick T), 1905 v Ni (14)
Gilchrist, J. E. (Celtic), 1922 v E (1)
Gilhooley, M. (Hull C), 1922 v W (1)
Gillespie, G. (Rangers), 1880 v W; 1881 v E, W; 1882 v E; (with Queen's Park), 1886 v W; 1890 v W; 1891 v Ni (7)
Gillespie, G. T. (Liverpool), 1988 v Bel, Bul, Sp; 1989 v N, F, Ch; 1990 v Y, EG, Eg, Pol, Ma, Br (sub); 1991 v Bul (13)
Gillespie, Jas (Third Lanark), 1898 v W (1)
Gillespie, John (Queen's Park), 1896 v W (1)
Gillespie, R. (Queen's Park), 1927 v W; 1931 v W; 1932 v F; 1933 v E (4)
Gillick, T. (Everton), 1937 v A, Cz; 1939 v W, Ni, H (5)
Gilmour, J. (Dundee), 1931 v W (1)
Gilzean, A. J. (Dundee), 1964 v W, E, N, WG; 1965 v Ni, (with Tottenham H), Sp; 1966 v Ni, W, Pol, I; 1968 v W; 1969 v W, E, WG, Cy (2), A (sub); 1970 v Ni, E (sub), WG, A; 1971 v P (22)
Glavin, R. (Celtic), 1977 v Se (1)
Glen, A. (Aberdeen), 1956 v E, Ni (2)
Glen, R. (Renton), 1895 v W; 1896 v W; (with Hibernian), 1900 v Ni (3)
Goram, A. L. (Oldham Ath), 1986 v EG (sub), R, Ho; 1987 v Br; (with Hibernian) 1989 v Y, I; 1990 v EG, Pol, Ma; 1991 v R, Sw, Bul (2), USSR, Sm; (with Rangers), 1992 v Sw, R, Sm, Fi, N, Ho, G, C; 1993 v Sw, P, I, Ma, P; 1994 v

Ho; 1995 v Fi, Fa, Ru, Gr; 1996 v Se (sub), D (sub), Co, Ho, E, Sw; 1997 v A, La, Es; 1998 v D (43)

Gordon, J. E. (Rangers), 1912 v E, Ni; 1913 v E, Ni, W; 1914 v E, Ni; 1920 v W, E, Ni (10)

Gossland, J. (Rangers), 1884 v Ni (1)

Goudle, J. (Abercorn), 1884 v Ni (1)

Gough, C. R. (Dundee U), 1983 v Sw, Ni, W, E, Ca (3); 1984 v U, Bel, EG, Ni, W, E, F; 1985 v Sp, E, Ic; 1986 v W, EG, Aus, Is, R, E, D, WG, U; (with Tottenham H), 1987 v Bul, L, Ei (2), Bel, E, Br; 1988 v H; (with Rangers), S.Ar, Sp, Co, E; 1989 v Y, I, Cy, F, Cy; 1990 v F, Arg, EG, Eg, Pol, Ma, Cr; 1991 v USSR, Bul; 1992 v Sm, Ni, Ca, N, Ho, G, C; 1993 v Sw, P (61)

Gourlay, J. (Cambuslang), 1886 v Ni; 1888 v W (2)

Govan, J. (Hibernian), 1948 v E, W, Bel, Sw, F; 1949 v Ni (6)

Gow, D. R. (Rangers), 1888 v E (1)

Gow, J. J. (Queen's Park), 1885 v E (1)

Gow, J. R. (Rangers), 1888 v Ni (1)

Graham, A. (Leeds U), 1978 v EG (sub); 1979 v A (sub), N, W, Ni, E, Arg, N; 1980 v A; 1981 v W (10)

Graham, G. (Arsenal), 1972 v P, Ho, Ni, Y, Cz, Br; 1973 v D (2); (with Manchester U), E, W, Ni, Br (sub) (12)

Graham, J. (Annbank), 1884 v Ni (1)

Graham, J. A. (Arsenal), 1921 v Ni (1)

Grant, J. (Hibernian), 1959 v W, Ni (2)

Grant, P. (Celtic), 1989 v E (sub), Ch (2)

Gray, A. (Hibernian), 1903 v Ni (1)

Gray, A. M. (Aston Villa), 1976 v R, Sw; 1977 v Fi, Cz; 1979 v A, N; (with Wolverhampton W), 1980 v P, E (sub); 1981 v Se, P, Is (sub), Ni; 1982 v Se (sub), Ni (sub); 1983 v Ni, W, E, Ca (1+1 sub); (with Everton), 1985 v Ic (20)

Gray, D. (Rangers), 1929 v W, Ni, G, Ho; 1930 v W, E, Ni; 1931 v W; 1933 v W, Ni (10)

Gray, E. (Leeds U), 1969 v E, Cy; 1970 v WG, A; 1971 v W, Ni; 1972 v Bel, Ho; 1976 v W, E; 1977 v Fi, W (12)

Gray, F. T. (Leeds U), 1976 v Sw; 1979 v N, P, W, Ni, E, Arg (sub); (with Nottingham F), 1980 v Bel (sub); 1981 v Se, P, Is, Ni, Is, W; (with Leeds U), Ni, E; 1982 v Se, Ni, P, Sp, Ho, W, Nz, Br, USSR; 1983 v EG, Sw, Bel, Sw, W, E, Ca (32)

Gray, W. (Pollokshields Ath), 1886 v E (1)

Green, A. (Blackpool), 1971 v Bel (sub), P (sub), Ni, E; (with Newcastle U), 1972 v W, E (sub) (6)

Greig, J. (Rangers), 1964 v E, WG; 1965 v W, Ni, E, Fi (2), Sp, Pol; 1966 v Ni, W, E, Pol, I (2), Ho, Br; 1967 v W, Ni, E; 1968 v Ni, W, E, Ho; 1969 v W, Ni, E, D, A, WG, Cy (2); 1970 v W, E, Ei, WG, A; 1971 v D, Bel, W (sub), Ni, E; 1976 v D (44)

Groves, W. (Hibernian), 1888 v W; (with Celtic), 1889 v Ni; 1890 v E (3)

Guilliland, W. (Queen's Park), 1891 v W; 1892 v Ni; 1894 v E; 1895 v E (4)

Gunn, B. (Norwich C), 1990 v Eg; 1993 v Es (2); 1994 v Sw, I, Ho (sub) (6)

Haddock, H. (Clyde), 1955 v E, H (2), P, Y; 1958 v E (6)

Haddow, D. (Rangers), 1894 v E (1)

Haffey, F. (Celtic), 1960 v E; 1961 v E (2)

Hamilton, A. (Queen's Park), 1885 v E, W; 1886 v E; 1888 v E (4)

Hamilton, A. W. (Dundee), 1962 v Cz, U, W, E; 1963 v W, Ni, E, A, Ei; 1964 v Ni, W, E, N, WG; 1965 v Ni, W, E, Fi (2), Pol, Sp; 1966 v Pol, Ni (24)

Hamilton, G. (Aberdeen), 1947 v Ni; 1951 v Bel, A; 1954 v N (2) (5)

Hamilton, G. (Port Glasgow Ath), 1906 v Ni (1)

Hamilton, J. (Queen's Park), 1892 v W; 1893 v E, Ni (3)

Hamilton, J. (St Mirren), 1924 v Ni (1)

Hamilton, R. C. (Rangers), 1899 v E, W, Ni; 1900 v W; 1901 v E, Ni; 1902 v W, Ni; 1903 v E; 1904 v Ni; (with Dundee), 1911 v W (11)

Hamilton, T. (Hurlford), 1891 v Ni (1)

Hamilton, T. (Rangers), 1932 v E (1)

Hamilton, W. M. (Hibernian), 1965 v Fi (1)

Hannah, A. B. (Renton), 1888 v W (1)

Hannah, J. (Third Lanark), 1889 v W (1)

Hansen, A. D. (Liverpool), 1979 v W, Arg; 1980 v Bel, P; 1981 v P, Is; 1982 v Se, Ni, P, Sp, Ni (sub), W, E, Nz, Br, USSR; 1983 v EG, Sw, Bel, Sw; 1985 v W (sub); 1986 v R (sub); 1987 v Ei (2), L (26)

Hansen, J. (Partick T), 1972 v Bel (sub), Y (sub) (2)

Harkness, J. D. (Queen's Park), 1927 v E, Ni; 1928 v E; (with Hearts), 1929 v W, E, Ni; 1930 v E, W; 1932 v W, F; 1934 v Ni (11)

Harper, J. M. (Aberdeen), 1973 v D (1+1 sub); (with Hibernian), 1976 v D; (with Aberdeen), 1978 v Ir (sub) (4)

Harper, W. (Hibernian), 1923 v E, Ni, W; 1924 v E, Ni, W; 1925 v E, Ni, W; (with Arsenal), 1926 v E, Ni (11)

Harris, J. (Partick T), 1921 v W, Ni (2)

Harris, N. (Newcastle U), 1924 v E (1)

Harrower, W. (Queen's Park), 1882 v E; 1884 v Ni; 1886 v W (3)

Hartford, R. A. (WBA), 1972 v Pe, W (sub), E, Y, Cz, Br; (with Manchester C), 1976 v D, R, Ni (sub); 1977 v Cz (sub), W (sub), Se, W, Ni, E, Ch, Arg, Br; 1978 v EG, Cz, W, Bul, W, E, Pe, Ir, Ho; 1979 v N, P, W, Ni, E, Arg, N; (with Everton), 1980 v Pe, Bel; 1981 v Ni (sub), Is, W, Ni, E; 1982 v Se; (with Manchester C), Ni, P, Sp, Ni, W, E, Br (50)

Harvey, D. (Leeds U), 1973 v D; 1974 v Cz, WG, Ni, W, E, Bel, Z, Br, Y; 1975 v EG, Sp (2); 1976 v D (2); 1977 v Fi (sub) (16)

Hastings, A. C. (Sunderland), 1936 v Ni; 1938 v Ni (2)

Haughney, M. (Celtic), 1954 v E (1)

Hay, D. (Celtic), 1970 v Ni, W, E; 1971 v D, Bel, W, P, Ni; 1972 v P, Bel, Ho; 1973 v W, Ni, E, Sw, Br; 1974 v Cz (2), WG, Ni, W, E, Bel, N, Z, Br, Y (27)

Hay, J. (Celtic), 1905 v Ni; 1909 v Ni; 1910 v W, Ni, E; 1911 v Ni, E; (with Newcastle U), 1912 v E, W; 1914 v E, Ni (11)

Hegarty, P. (Dundee U), 1979 v W, Ni, E, Arg, N (sub); 1980 v W, E; 1983 v Ni (8)

Heggie, C. (Rangers), 1886 v Ni (1)

Henderson, G. H. (Rangers), 1904 v Ni (1)

Henderson, J. G. (Portsmouth), 1953 v Se; 1954 v Ni, E, N; 1956 v W; (with Arsenal), 1959 v W, Ni (7)

Henderson, W. (Rangers), 1963 v W, Ni, E, A, N, Ei, Sp; 1964 v Ni, E, N, WG; 1965 v Fi, Pol, E, Sp; 1966 v Ni, W, Pol, I, Ho; 1967 v W, Ni; 1968 v Ho; 1969 v Ni, E, Cy; 1970 v Ei; 1971 v P (29)

Hendry, E. C. J. (Blackburn R), 1993 v Es (2); 1994 v Ma, Ho, A, Ho; 1995 v Fi, Fa, Gr, Ru, Sm; 1996 v Fi, Se, Sm, Aus, D, US, Co, Ho, E, Sw; 1997 v A, Se, Es (2), A, Se; 1998 v La, D, Fi, Co, US, Br, N, Mor (35)

Hepburn, J. (Alloa Ath), 1891 v W (1)

Hepburn, R. (Ayr U), 1932 v Ni (1)

Herd, A. C. (Hearts), 1935 v Ni (1)

Herd, D. G. (Arsenal), 1959 v E, W, Ni; 1961 v Ei, Cz (5)

Herd, G. (Clyde), 1958 v E; 1960 v H, T; 1961 v W, Ni (5)

Herriot, J. (Birmingham C), 1969 v Ni, E, D, Cy (2), W (sub); 1970 v Ei (sub), WG (8)

Hewie, J. D. (Charlton Ath), 1956 v E, A; 1957 v E, Ni, W, Y, Sp (2), Sw, WG; 1958 v H, Pol, Y, F; 1959 v Ho, P; 1960 v Ni, W, Pol (19)

Higgins, A. (Kilmarnock), 1885 v Ni (1)

Higgins, A. (Newcastle U), 1910 v E, Ni; 1911 v E, Ni (4)

Highet, T. C. (Queen's Park), 1875 v E; 1876 v E, W; 1878 v E (4)

Hill, D. (Rangers), 1881 v E, W; 1882 v W (3)

Hill, D. A. (Third Lanark), 1906 v Ni (1)

Hill, F. R. (Aberdeen), 1930 v F; 1931 v W, Ni (3)

Hill, J. (Hearts), 1891 v E; 1892 v W (2)

Hogg, G (Hearts), 1896 v E, Ni (2)

Hogg, J. (Ayr U), 1922 v Ni (1)

Hogg, R. M. (Celtic), 1937 v Cz (1)

Holm, A. H. (Queen's Park), 1882 v W; 1883 v E, W (3)

Holt, D. D. (Hearts), 1963 v A, N, Ei, Sp; 1964 v WG (sub) (5)

Holton, J. A. (Manchester U), 1973 v W, Ni, E, Sw, Br; 1974 v Cz, WG, Ni, W, E, N, Z, Br, Y; 1975 v EG (15)

Hope, R. (WBA), 1968 v Ho; 1969 v D (2)

Hopkin, D. (Crystal Palace), 1997 v Ma, Bl; (with Leeds U), 1998 v Bl (sub), F (sub) (4)

Houliston, W. (Queen of the South), 1949 v E, Ni, F (3)

Houston, S. M. (Manchester U), 1976 v D (1)

Howden, W. (Partick T), 1905 v Ni (1)

Howe, R. (Hamilton A), 1929 v N, Ho (2)

Howie, J. (Newcastle U), 1905 v E; 1906 v E; 1908 v E (3)

Howie, H. (Hibernian), 1949 v W (1)

Howieson, J. (St Mirren), 1927 v Ni (1)

Hughes, J. (Celtic), 1965 v Pol, Sp; 1966 v Ni, I (2); 1968 v E; 1969 v A; 1970 v Ei (8)

Hughes, W. (Sunderland), 1975 v Se (sub) (1)

Humphries, W. (Motherwell), 1952 v Se (1)

Hunter, A. (Kilmarnock), 1972 v Pe, Y; (with Celtic), 1973 v E; 1974 v Cz (4)

Hunter, J. (Dundee), 1909 v W (1)

Hunter, J. (Third Lanark), 1874 v E; (with Eastern), 1875 v E; (with Third Lanark), 1876 v E; 1877 v W (4)

Hunter, R. (St Mirren), 1890 v Ni (1)

Hunter, W. (Motherwell), 1960 v H, T; 1961 v W (3)

Husband, J. (Partick T), 1947 v W (1)

Hutchison, T. (Coventry C), 1974 v Cz (2), WG (2), Ni, W, Bel (sub), N, Z (sub), Y (sub); 1975 v EG, Sp (2), P, E (sub), R (sub); 1976 v D (17)

Hutton, J. (Aberdeen), 1923 v E, W, Ni; 1924 v Ni; 1926 v W, E, Ni; (with Blackburn R), 1927 v Ni; 1928 v W, Ni (10)

Hutton, J. (St Bernards), 1887 v Ni (1)
Hyslop, T. (Stoke C), 1896 v E; (with Rangers), 1897 v E (2)

Imlach, J. J. S. (Nottingham F), 1958 v H, Pol, Y, F (4)
Imrie, W. N. (St Johnstone), 1929 v N, G (2)
Inglis, J. (Kilmarnock Ath), 1884 v Ni (1)
Inglis, J. (Rangers), 1883 v E, W (2)
Irons, J. H. (Queen's Park), 1900 v W (1)
Irvine, B. (Aberdeen), 1991 v R; 1993 v G, Es (2); 1994 v Sw, I, Ma, A, Ho (9)

Jackson, A. (Cambuslang), 1886 v W; 1888 v Ni (2)
Jackson, A. (Aberdeen), 1925 v E, W, Ni; (with Huddersfield T), 1926 v E, W, Ni; 1927 v W, Ni; 1928 v E, W; 1929 v E, W, Ni; 1930 v E, W, Ni, F (17)
Jackson, C. (Rangers), 1975 v Se, P (sub); W; 1976 v D, R, Ni, W, E (8)
Jackson, D. (Hibernian), 1995 v Ru, Sm, J, Ec, Fa; 1996 v Gr, Fi (sub), Se (sub), Sm (sub), Aus (sub), D (sub), US; 1997 v La, Se, Es, A, Se, W, Ma, Bl; (with Celtic), 1998 v D, Fi, Co, US, Br, N (26)
Jackson, J. (Partick T), 1931 v A, I, Sw; 1933 v E; (with Chelsea), 1934 v E; 1935 v E; 1936 v W, Ni (8)
Jackson, T. A. (St Mirren), 1904 v W, E, Ni; 1905 v W; 1907 v W, Ni (6)
James, A. W. (Preston NE), 1926 v W; 1928 v E; 1929 v E, Ni; (with Arsenal), 1930 v E, W, Ni; 1933 v W (8)
Jardine, A. (Rangers), 1971 v D (sub); 1972 v P, Bel, Ho; 1973 v E, Sw, Br; 1974 v Cz (2), WG (2), Ni, W, E, Bel, N, Z, Br, Y; 1975 v EG, Sp (2), Se, P, W, Ni, E; 1977 v Se (sub), Ch (sub), Br (sub); 1978 v Cz, W, Ni, Ir; 1980 v Pe, A, Bel (2) (38)
Jarvie, A. (Airdrieonians), 1971 v P (sub), Ni (sub), E (sub) (3)
Jenkinson, T. (Hearts), 1887 v Ni (1)
Jess, E. (Aberdeen), 1993 v I (sub), Ma; 1994 v Sw (sub), I, Ho (sub), A, Ho (sub); 1995 v Fi (sub); 1996 v Se (sub), Sm; (with Coventry C), US, Co (sub), E (sub); (with Aberdeen), 1998 v D (sub) (14)
Johnston, L. H. (Clyde), 1948 v Bel, Sw (2)
Johnston, M. (Watford), 1984 v W (sub), E (sub), F; 1985 v Y; (with Celtic), Ic, Sp (2), W; 1986 v EG; 1987 v Bul, Ei (2), L; (with Nantes), 1988 v H, Bel, I, S.Ar, Sp, Co, E; 1989 v N, Y, I, Cy, F, Cy, E, Ch (sub); (with Rangers), 1990 v F, N, EG, Pol, Ma, Cr, Se, Br; 1992 v Sw, Sm (sub) (38)
Johnston, R. (Sunderland), 1938 v Cz (1)
Johnston, W. (Rangers), 1966 v W, E, Pol, Ho; 1968 v W, E; 1969 v Ni (sub); 1970 v Ni; 1971 v D; (with WBA), 1977 v Se, W (sub), Ni, E, Ch, Arg, Br; 1978 v EG, Cz, W (2), E, Pe (22)
Johnstone, D. (Rangers), 1973 v W, Ni, E, Sw, Br; 1975 v EG (sub), Se (sub); 1976 v Sw, Ni (sub), E (sub); 1978 v Bul (sub), Ni, W; 1980 v Bel (14)
Johnstone, J. (Abercorn), 1888 v W (1)
Johnstone, J. (Celtic), 1965 v W, Fi; 1966 v E; 1967 v W, USSR; 1968 v W; 1969 v A, WG; 1970 v E, WG; 1971 v D, E; 1972 v P, Bel, Ho, Ni, E (sub); 1974 v W, E, Bel, N; 1975 v EG, Sp (23)
Johnstone, Jas (Kilmarnock), 1894 v W (1)
Johnstone, J. A. (Hearts), 1930 v W; 1933 v W, Ni (3)
Johnstone, R. (Hibernian), 1951 v E, D, F; 1952 v Ni, E; 1953 v E, Se; 1954 v W, E, N, Fi; 1955 v Ni, H; (with Manchester C), 1955 v E; 1956 v E, Ni, W (17)
Johnstone, W. (Third Lanark), 1887 v Ni; 1889 v W; 1890 v E (3)
Jordan, J. (Leeds U), 1973 v E (sub), Sw (sub), Br; 1974 v Cz (sub+1), WG (sub), Ni (sub), W, E, Bel, N, Z, Br, Y; 1975 v EG, Sp (2); 1976 v Ni, W, E; 1977 v Cz, W, Ni, E; 1978 v EG, Cz, W; (with Manchester U), Bul, Ni, E, Pe, Ir, Ho; 1979 v A, P, W (sub), Ni, E, N; 1980 v Bel, Ni (sub), W, E, Pol; 1981 v Is, W, E; (with AC Milan), 1982 v Se, Ho, W, E, USSR (52)

Kay, J. L. (Queen's Park), 1880 v E; 1882 v E, W; 1883 v E, W; 1884 v W (6)
Keillor, A. (Montrose), 1891 v W; 1892 v Ni; (with Dundee), 1894 v Ni; 1895 v W; 1896 v W; 1897 v W (6)
Keir, L. (Dumbarton), 1885 v W; 1886 v Ni; 1887 v E, W; 1888 v E (5)
Kelly, H. T. (Blackpool), 1952 v USA (1)
Kelly, J. (Renton), 1888 v E; (with Celtic), 1889 v E; 1890 v E; 1892 v E; 1893 v E, Ni; 1894 v W; 1896 v Ni (8)
Kelly, J. C. (Barnsley), 1949 v W, Ni (2)
Kelso, R. (Renton), 1885 v W, Ni; 1886 v W; 1887 v E, W; 1888 v E, Ni; (with Dundee), 1898 v Ni (8)
Kelso, T. (Dundee), 1914 v W (1)
Kennaway, J. (Celtic), 1934 v W, A (2)

Kennedy, A. (Eastern), 1875 v E; 1876 v E, W; (with Third Lanark), 1878 v E; 1882 v W; 1884 v W (6)
Kennedy, J. (Celtic), 1964 v W, E, WG; 1965 v W, Ni, Fi (6)
Kennedy, J. (Hibernian), 1897 v W (1)
Kennedy, S. (Aberdeen), 1978 v Bul, W, E, Pe, Ho; 1979 v A, P; 1982 v P (sub) (8)
Kennedy, S. (Partick T), 1905 v W (1)
Kennedy, S. (Rangers), 1975 v Se, P, W, Ni, E (5)
Ker, G. (Queen's Park), 1880 v E; 1881 v E, W; 1882 v W, E (5)
Ker, W. (Granville), 1872 v E; (with Queen's Park), 1873 v E (2)
Kerr, A. (Partick T), 1955 v A, H (2)
Kerr, P. (Hibernian), 1924 v Ni (1)
Key, G. (Hearts), 1902 v Ni (1)
Key, W. (Queen's Park), 1907 v Ni (1)
King, A. (Hearts), 1896 v E, W; (with Celtic), 1897 v Ni; 1898 v Ni; 1899 v Ni, W (6)
King, J. (Hamilton A), 1933 v Ni; 1934 v Ni (2)
King, W. S. (Queen's Park), 1929 v W (1)
Kinloch, J. D. (Partick T), 1922 v Ni (1)
Kinnaird, A. F. (Wanderers), 1873 v E (1)
Kinnear, D. (Rangers), 1938 v Cz (1)

Lambert, P. (Motherwell), 1995 v J, Ec (sub); (with Borussia Dortmund), 1997 v La (sub), Se (sub), A, Se, Bl; 1998 v Bl, La; (with Celtic), Fi (sub), Co, US, Br, N, Mor (15)
Lambie, J. A. (Queen's Park), 1886 v Ni; 1887 v Ni; 1888 v E (3)
Lambie, W. A. (Queen's Park), 1892 v Ni; 1893 v W; 1894 v E; 1895 v E, Ni; 1896 v E, Ni; 1897 v E, Ni (9)
Lamont, D. (Pilgrims), 1885 v Ni (1)
Lang, A. (Dumbarton), 1880 v W (1)
Lang, J. J. (Clydesdale), 1876 v W; (with Third Lanark), 1878 v W (2)
Latta, A. (Dumbarton), 1888 v W; 1889 v E (2)
Law, D. (Huddersfield T), 1959 v W, Ni, Ho, P; 1960 v Ni, W; (with Manchester C), 1960 v E, Pol, A; 1961 v E, Ni; (with Torino), 1962 v Cz (2), E; (with Manchester U), 1963 v W, Ni, E, A, N, Ei, Sp; 1964 v W, E, N; 1965 v W, Ni, E, Fi (2), Pol, Sp; 1966 v Ni, E, Pol; 1967 v W, E, USSR; 1968 v Ni; 1969 v Ni, A, WG; 1972 v Pe, Ni, W, E, Y, Cz, Br; (with Manchester C), 1974 v Cz (2), WG (2), Ni, Z (55)
Law, G. (Rangers), 1910 v E, Ni, W (3)
Law, T. (Chelsea), 1928 v E; 1930 v E (2)
Lawrence, J. (Newcastle U), 1911 v E (1)
Lawrence, T. (Liverpool), 1963 v Ei; 1969 v W, WG (3)
Lawson, D. (St Mirren), 1923 v E (1)
Leckie, R. (Queen's Park), 1872 v E (1)
Leggat, G. (Aberdeen), 1956 v E; 1957 v W; 1958 v Ni, H, Pol, Y, Par; (with Fulham), 1959 v E, W, Ni, WG, Ho; 1960 v E, Ni, W, Pol, A, H (18)
Leighton, J. (Aberdeen), 1983 v EG, Sw, Bel, Sw, W, E, Ca (2); 1984 v U, Bel, Ni, W, E, F; 1985 v Y, Ic, Sp (2), W, E, Ic; 1986 v W, EG, Aus (2), Is, D, WG, U; 1987 v Bul, Ei (2), L, Bel, E; 1988 v H, Bel, Bul, L, S.Ar, Ma, Sp; (with Manchester U), Co, E; 1989 v N, Cy, F, Cy, E, Ch; 1990 v Y, F, N, Arg, Ma (sub, Cr, Se, Br; (with Hibernian), 1994 v Ma, A, Ho; 1995 v Gr (sub), Ru, Sm, J, Ec, Fa; 1996 v Gr, Fi, Se, Sm, Aus, D, US; 1997 v Se, Es, A, Se, W (sub), Ma, Bl; (with Aberdeen), 1998 v Bl, La, D, Fi, US, Br, N, Mor (89)
Lennie, W. (Aberdeen), 1908 v W, Ni (2)
Lennox, R. (Celtic), 1967 v Ni, E, USSR; 1968 v W, L; 1969 v D, A, WG, Cy (sub); 1970 v W (sub) (10)
Leslie, L. G. (Airdrieonians), 1961 v W, Ni, Ei (2), Cz (5)
Levein, C. (Hearts), 1990 v Arg, EG, Eg (sub), Pol, Ma (sub), Se; 1992 v R, Sm; 1993 v P, G, P; 1994 v Sw, Ho; 1995 v Fi, Fa, Ru (16)
Liddell, W. (Liverpool), 1947 v W, Ni; 1948 v E, W, Ni; 1950 v E, W, P, F; 1951 v W, Ni, E, A; 1952 v W, Ni, E, USA, D, Se; 1953 v W, Ni, E; 1954 v W; 1955 v P, Y, A, H; 1956 v Ni (28)
Liddle, D. (East Fife), 1931 v A, I, Sw (3)
Lindsay, D. (St Mirren), 1903 v Ni (1)
Lindsay, J. (Dumbarton), 1880 v W; 1881 v W, E; 1884 v W, E; 1885 v W, E; 1886 v E (8)
Lindsay, J. (Renton), 1888 v E; 1893 v E, Ni (3)
Linwood, A. B. (Clyde), 1950 v W (1)
Little, R. J. (Rangers), 1953 v Se (1)
Livingstone, G. T. (Manchester C), 1906 v E; (with Rangers), 1907 v W (2)
Lochhead, A. (Third Lanark), 1889 v W (1)
Logan, J. (Ayr U), 1891 v W (1)
Logan, T. (Falkirk), 1913 v Ni (1)
Logie, J. T. (Arsenal), 1953 v Ni (1)
Loney, W. (Celtic), 1910 v W, Ni (2)
Long, H. (Clyde), 1947 v Ni (1)

Longair, W. (Dundee), 1894 v Ni (1)
Lorimer, P. (Leeds U), 1970 v A (sub); 1971 v W, Ni; 1972 v Ni (sub), W, E; 1973 v D (2), E (2); 1974 v WG (sub), E, Bel, N, Z, Br, Y; 1975 v Sp (sub); 1976 v D (2), R (sub) (21)
Love, A. (Aberdeen), 1931 v A, I, Sw (3)
Low, A. (Falkirk), 1934 v Ni (1)
Low, T. P. (Rangers), 1897 v Ni (1)
Low, W. L. (Newcastle U), 1911 v E, W; 1912 v Ni; 1920 v E, Ni (5)
Lowe, J. (Cambuslang), 1891 v Ni (1)
Lowe, J. (St Bernards), 1887 v Ni (1)
Lundie, J. (Hibernian), 1886 v W (1)
Lyall, J. (Sheffield W), 1905 v E (1)

McAdam, J. (Third Lanark), 1880 v W (1)
McAllister, B. (Wimbledon), 1997 v W, Ma, Bl (sub) (3)
McAllister, G. (Leicester C), 1990 v EG, Pol, Ma (sub); (with Leeds U), 1991 v R, Sw, Bul, USSR (sub), Sm; 1992 v Sw (sub), Sm, Ni, Fi (sub), US, Ca, N, Ho, G, C; 1993 v Sw, P, I, Ma; 1994 v Sw, I, Ma, Ho, A, Ho; 1995 v Fi, Ru, Gr, Ru, Sm; 1996 v Gr, Fi, Se, Sm, Aus, D, US (sub), Co, Ho, E, Sw; (with Coventry C), 1997 v A, La, Es (2), A, Se, W, Ma, Bl; 1998 v Bl, La, F (56)
McArthur, D. (Celtic), 1895 v E, Ni; 1899 v W (3)
McAtee, A. (Celtic), 1913 v W (1)
McAulay, J. (Dumbarton), 1882 v W; (with Arthurlie), 1884 v Ni (2)
McAulay, J. (Dumbarton), 1883 v E, W; 1884 v E; 1885 v E, W; 1886 v E; 1887 v E, W (8)
McAuley, R. (Rangers), 1932 v Ni, W (2)
McAvennie, F. (West Ham U), 1986 v Aus (2), D (sub), WG (sub); (with Celtic), 1988 v S.Ar (5)
McBain, E. (St Mirren), 1894 v W (1)
McBain, N. (Manchester U), 1922 v E; (with Everton), 1923 v Ni; 1924 v W (3)
McBride, J. (Celtic), 1967 v W, Ni (2)
McBride, P. (Preston NE), 1904 v E; 1906 v E; 1907 v E, W; 1908 v E; 1909 v W (6)
McCall, J. (Renton), 1886 v W; 1887 v E, W; 1888 v E; 1890 v E (5)
McCall, S. M. (Everton), 1990 v Arg, EG, Eg (sub); Pol, Ma, Cr, Se, Br; 1991 v Sw, USSR, Sm; (with Rangers), 1992 v Sw, R, Sm, US, Ca, N, Ho, G, C; 1993 v Sw, P (2); 1994 v I, Ho, A (sub), Ho; 1995 v Fi (sub), Ru, Gr; 1996 v Gr, D, US (sub), Co, Ho, E, Sw; 1997 v A, La; 1998 v D (sub) (40)
McCalliog, J. (Sheffield W), 1967 v E, USSR; 1968 v Ni; 1969 v D; (with Wolverhampton W), 1971 v P (5)
McCallum, N. (Renton), 1888 v Ni (1)
McCann, R. J. (Motherwell), 1959 v WG; 1960 v E, Ni, W; 1961 v E (5)
McCartney, W. (Hibernian), 1902 v Ni (1)
McClair, B. (Celtic), 1987 v L, Ei, E, Br (sub); (with Manchester U), 1988 v Bul, Ma (sub), Sp (sub); 1989 v N, Y, I (sub), Cy, F (sub); 1990 v N (sub), Arg (sub); 1991 v Bul (2), Sm; 1992 v Sw (sub), R, Ni, US, Ca (sub), N, Ho, G, C; 1993 v Sw, P (sub), Es (2) (30)
McClory, A. (Motherwell), 1927 v W; 1928 v Ni; 1935 v W (3)
McCloy, P. (Ayr U), 1924 v E; 1925 v E (2)
McCloy, P. (Rangers), 1973 v W, Ni, Sw, Br (4)
McCoist, A. (Rangers), 1986 v Ho; 1987 v L (sub), Ei (sub), Bel, E, Br; 1988 v H, Bel, Ma, Sp, Co, E; 1989 v Y (sub), F, Cy, E; 1990 v Y, F, N, EG (sub), Eg, Pol, Ma (sub), Cr (sub), Se (sub), Br; 1991 v R, Sw, Bul (2), USSR; 1992 v Sw, Sm, Ni, Fi (sub), US, Ca, N, Ho, G, C; 1993 v Sw, P, I, Ma, P; 1996 v Gr (sub), Fi (sub), Sm (sub), Aus, D (sub), Co, E (sub), Sw; 1997 v A, Se (sub), Es (sub), A (sub); 1998 v Bl (sub) (59)
McColl, A. (Renton), 1888 v Ni (1)
McColl, I. M. (Rangers), 1950 v E, F; 1951 v W, Ni, Bel; 1957 v E, Ni, W, Y, Sp, Sw, WG; 1958 v Ni, E (14)
McColl, R. S. (Queen's Park), 1896 v W, Ni; 1897 v Ni; 1898 v Ni; 1899 v W, Ni; 1900 v E, W; 1901 v E, W; (with Newcastle U), 1902 v E; (with Queen's Park), 1908 v Ni (13)
McColl, W. (Renton), 1895 v W (1)
McCombie, A. (Sunderland), 1903 v E, W; (with Newcastle U), 1905 v E, W (4)
McCorkindale, J. (Partick T), 1891 v W (1)
McCormick, R. (Abercorn), 1886 v W (1)
McCrae, D. (St Mirren), 1929 v N, G (2)
McCredie, A. (Rangers), 1893 v W; 1894 v E (2)
McCreadie, E. G. (Chelsea), 1965 v E, Sp, Fi, Pol; 1966 v P, Ni, W, Pol, I; 1967 v E, USSR; 1968 v Ni, W, E, Ho; 1969 v W, Ni, E, D, A, WG, Cy (2) (23)

McCulloch, D. (Hearts), 1935 v W; (with Brentford), 1936 v E; 1937 v W, Ni; 1938 v Cz; (with Derby Co), 1939 v H, W (7)
MacDonald, A. (Rangers), 1976 v Sw (1)
McDonald, J. (Edinburgh University), 1886 v E (1)
McDonald, J. (Sunderland), 1956 v W, Ni (2)
MacDougall, E. J. (Norwich C) 1975 v Se, P, W, Ni, E; 1976 v D, R (sub) (7)
McDougall, J. (Liverpool), 1931 v I, A (2)
McDougall, J. (Airdrieonians), 1926 v Ni (1)
McDougall, J. (Vale of Leven), 1877 v E, W; 1878 v E; 1879 v E, W (5)
McFadyen, W. (Motherwell), 1934 v A, W (2)
Macfarlane, A. (Dundee), 1904 v W; 1906 v W; 1908 v W; 1909 v Ni; 1911 v W (5)
McFarlane, R. (Greenock Morton), 1896 v W (1)
Macfarlane, W. (Hearts), 1947 v L (1)
McGarr, E. (Aberdeen), 1970 v Ei, A (2)
McGarvey, F. P. (Liverpool), 1979 v Ni (sub), Arg; (with Celtic), 1984 v U, Bel (sub), EG (sub), Ni, W (7)
McGeoch, A. (Dumbreck), 1876 v E, W; 1877 v E, W (4)
McGhee, J. (Hibernian), 1886 v W (1)
McGhee, M. (Aberdeen), 1983 v Ca (1+1 sub); 1984 v Ni (sub), E (4)
McGinlay, J. (Bolton W), 1994 v A, Ho; 1995 v Fa, Ru, Gr, Ru, Sm, Fa; 1996 v Se; 1997 v Se, Es (1 + sub), A (sub) (13)
McGonagle, W. (Celtic), 1933 v E; 1934 v A, E, Ni; 1935 v Ni, W (6)
McGrain, D. (Celtic), 1973 v W, Ni, E, Sw, Br; 1974 v Cz (2), WG, W (sub), E, Bel, N, Z, Br, Y; 1975 v Sp, Se, P, W, Ni, E, R; 1976 v D (2), Sw, Ni, W, E; 1977 v Fi, Cz, W (2), Se, Ni, E, Ch, Arg, Br; 1978 v EG, Cz; 1980 v Bel, P, Ni, W, E, Pol, H; 1981 v Se, P, Is, Ni, Is, W (sub), Ni, E; 1982 v Se, Sp, Ho, Ni, E, Nz, USSR (sub) (62)
McGregor, J. C. (Vale of Leven), 1877 v E, W; 1878 v E; 1880 v E (4)
McGrory, J. E. (Kilmarnock), 1965 v Ni, Fi; 1966 v P (3)
McGrory, J. (Celtic), 1928 v Ni; 1931 v E; 1932 v Ni, W; 1933 v E, Ni; 1934 v Ni (7)
McGuire, W. (Beith), 1881 v E, W (2)
McGurk, F. (Birmingham), 1934 v W (1)
McHardy, H. (Rangers), 1885 v Ni (1)
McInally, A. (Aston Villa), 1989 v Cy (sub), Ch; (with Bayern Munich), 1990 v Y (sub), F (sub), Arg, Pol (sub), Ma, Cr (8)
McInally, J. (Dundee U), 1987 v Bel, Br; 1988 v Ma (sub); 1991 v Bul (2); 1992 v US (sub), N (sub), C (sub); 1993 v G, P (10)
McInally, T. B. (Celtic), 1926 v Ni; 1927 v W (2)
McInnes, T. (Cowlairs), 1889 v Ni (1)
McIntosh, W. (Third Lanark), 1905 v Ni (1)
McIntyre, A. (Vale of Leven), 1878 v E; 1882 v E (2)
McIntyre, H. (Rangers), 1880 v W (1)
McIntyre, J. (Rangers), 1884 v W (1)
MacKay, D. (Celtic), 1959 v E, WG, Ho, P; 1960 v E, Pol, A, H, T; 1961 v W, Ni; 1962 v Ni, Cz, U (sub) (14)
Mackay, D. C. (Hearts), 1957 v Sp; 1958 v F; 1959 v W, Ni; (with Tottenham H), 1959 v WG, E; 1960 v W, Ni, A, Pol, H, T; 1961 v W, Ni, E; 1963 v E, A, N; 1964 v Ni, W, N; 1966 v Ni (22)
Mackay, G. (Hearts), 1988 v Bul (sub), L (sub), S.Ar (sub), Ma (4)
McKay, J. (Blackburn R), 1924 v W (1)
McKay, R. (Newcastle U), 1928 v W (1)
McKean, R. (Rangers), 1976 v Sw (sub) (1)
McKenzie, D. (Brentford), 1938 v Ni (1)
Mackenzie, J. A. (Partick T), 1954 v W, E, N, Fi, A, U; 1955 v E, H; 1956 v A (9)
McKeown, M. (Celtic), 1889 v Ni; 1890 v E (2)
McKie, J. (East Stirling), 1898 v W (1)
McKillop, T. R. (Rangers), 1938 v Ho (1)
McKimmie, S. (Aberdeen), 1989 v E, Ch; 1990 v Arg, Eg, Cr (sub); Br; 1991 v R, Sw, Bul, Sm; 1992 v Sw, R, Ni, Fi, US, Ca (sub), N (sub), Ho, G, C; 1993 v P, Es (sub); 1994 v Sw, I, Ho, A, Ho; 1995 v Fi, Fa, Ru, Gr, Ru, Fa; 1996 v Gr, Fi, Se, D, Co, Ho, E (40)
McKinlay, D. (Liverpool), 1922 v W, Ni (2)
McKinlay, T. (Celtic), 1996 v Gr, Fi, D, Co, E, Sw; 1997 v A, La, Se, Es (sub + 1), A, Se, W, Ma, Bl; 1998 v Bl, La (sub), F (sub), US, Br (sub), Mor (sub) (22)
McKinlay, W. (Dundee U), 1994 v Ma, Ho (sub), A, Ho; 1995 v Fa (sub), Ru, Gr, Ru (sub), Sm (sub), J, Ec, Fa; 1996 v Fi (sub), Se (sub); (with Blackburn R), Sm (sub), Aus, D (sub), Ho (sub); 1997 v Se, Es (sub); 1998 v La (sub), F, D, Fi, Co (sub), US, Br (sub) (27)
McKinnon, A. (Queen's Park), 1874 v E (1)

McKinnon, R. (Rangers), 1966 v W, E, I (2), Ho, Br; 1967 v W, Ni, E; 1968 v Ni, W, E, Ho; 1969 v D, A, WG, Cy; 1970 v Ni, W, E, Ei, WG, A; 1971 v D, Bel, P, USSR, D (28)

McKinnon, R. (Motherwell), 1994 v Ma; 1995 v J, Fa (3)

MacKinnon, W. (Dumbarton), 1883 v E, W; 1884 v E, W (4)

MacKinnon, W. W. (Queen's Park), 1872 v E; 1873 v E; 1874 v E; 1875 v E; 1876 v E, W; 1877 v E; 1878 v E; 1879 v E (9)

McLaren, A. (St Johnstone), 1929 v N, G, Ho; 1933 v W, Ni (5)

McLaren, A. (Preston NE), 1947 v E, Bel, L; 1948 v W (4)

McLaren, A. (Hearts), 1992 v US, Ca, N; 1993 v I, Ma, G, Es (sub + 1); 1994 v I, Ma, Ho, A; 1995 v Fi, Fa; (with Rangers), Ru, Gr, Ru, Sm, J, Ec, Fa; 1996 v Fi, Se, Sm (24)

McLaren, J. (Hibernian), 1888 v W; (with Celtic), 1889 v E; 1890 v E (3)

McLean, A. (Celtic), 1926 v W, Ni; 1927 v W, E (4)

McLean, D. (St Bernards), 1896 v W; 1897 v Ni (2)

McLean, D. (Sheffield W), 1912 v E (1)

McLean, G. (Dundee), 1968 v Ho (1)

McLean, T. (Kilmarnock), 1969 v D, Cy, W; 1970 v Ni, W; 1971 v D (6)

McLeish, A. (Aberdeen), 1980 v P, Ni, W, E, Pol, H; 1981 v Se, Is, Ni, Is, Ni, E; 1982 v Se, Sp, Ni, Br (sub); 1983 v Bel, Sw (sub), W, E, Ca (3); 1984 v U, Bel, EG, Ni, W, E, F; 1985 v Y, Ic, Sp (2), W, E, Ic; 1986 v W, EG, Aus (2), E, Ho, D; 1987 v Bel, E, Br; 1988 v Bel, Bul, L, S.Ar (sub), Ma, Sp, Co, E; 1989 v N, Y, I, Cy, F, Cy, E, Ch; 1990 v Y, F, N, Arg, EG, Eg, Cr, Se, Br; 1991 v R, Sw, USSR, Bul; 1993 v Ma (77)

McLeod, D. (Celtic), 1905 v Ni; 1906 v E, W, Ni (4)

McLeod, J. (Dumbarton), 1888 v Ni; 1889 v W; 1890 v Ni; 1892 v E; 1893 v W (5)

MacLeod, J. M. (Hibernian), 1961 v E, Ei (2), Cz (4)

MacLeod, M. (Celtic), 1985 v E (sub); 1987 v Ei, L, E, Br; (with Borussia Dortmund), 1988 v Co, E; 1989 v I, Ch; 1990 v Y, F, N (sub), Arg, EG, Pol, Se Br; (with Hibernian), 1991 v R, Sw, USSR (sub) (20)

McLeod, W. (Cowlairs), 1886 v Ni (1)

McLintock, A. (Vale of Leven), 1875 v E; 1876 v E; 1880 v E (3)

McLintock, F. (Leicester C), 1963 v N (sub), Ei, Sp; (with Arsenal), 1965 v Ni; 1967 v USSR; 1970 v Ni; 1971 v W, Ni, E (9)

McLuckie, J. S. (Manchester C), 1934 v W (1)

McMahon, A. (Celtic), 1892 v E; 1893 v E, Ni; 1894 v E; 1901 v Ni; 1902 v W (6)

McMenemy, J. (Celtic), 1905 v Ni; 1909 v Ni; 1910 v E, W; 1911 v Ni, W, E; 1912 v W; 1914 v W, Ni, E; 1920 v Ni (12)

McMenemy, J. (Motherwell), 1934 v W (1)

McMillan, J. (St Bernards), 1897 v W (1)

McMillan, I. L. (Airdrieonians), 1952 v E, USA, D; 1955 v E; 1956 v E; (with Rangers), 1961 v Cz (6)

McMillan, T. (Dumbarton), 1887 v Ni (1)

McMullan, J. (Partick T), 1920 v W; 1921 v W, Ni, E; 1924 v E, Ni; 1925 v E; 1926 v W; (with Manchester C), 1926 v E; 1927 v E, W; 1928 v E, W; 1929 v W, E, Ni (16)

McNab, A. (Morton), 1921 v E, Ni (2)

McNab, A. (Sunderland), 1937 v A; (with WBA), 1939 v E (2)

McNab, C. D. (Dundee), 1931 v E, W, A, I, Sw; 1932 v E (6)

McNab, J. S. (Liverpool), 1923 v W (1)

McNair, A. (Celtic), 1906 v W; 1907 v Ni; 1908 v E, W; 1909 v E; 1910 v W; 1912 v E, W, Ni; 1913 v E; 1914 v E, Ni; 1920 v E, W, Ni (15)

McNamara, J. (Celtic), 1997 v La (sub), Se, Es, W (sub); 1998 v D, Co, US (sub), N (sub), Mor (9)

McNaught, W. (Raith R), 1951 v A, W, Ni; 1952 v E; 1955 v Ni (5)

McNeill, W. (Celtic), 1961 v E, Ei (2), Cz; 1962 v Ni, E, Cz, U; 1963 v Ei, Sp; 1964 v W, E, WG; 1965 v E, Fi, Pol, Sp; 1966 v Ni, Pol; 1967 v USSR; 1968 v E; 1969 v Cy, W, E, Cy (sub); 1970 v WG; 1972 v Ni, W, E (29)

McNiel, H. (Queen's Park), 1874 v E; 1875 v E; 1876 v E, W; 1877 v W; 1878 v E; 1879 v E, W; 1881 v E, W (10)

McNiel, M. (Rangers), 1876 v W; 1880 v E (2)

McPhail, J. (Celtic), 1950 v W; 1951 v W, Ni, A; 1954 v Ni (5)

McPhail, R. (Airdrieonians), 1927 v E; (with Rangers), 1929 v W; 1931 v E, Ni; 1932 v W, Ni, F; 1933 v E, Ni; 1934 v A, Ni; 1935 v E; 1937 v G, E, Cz; 1938 v W, Ni (17)

McPherson, D. (Kilmarnock), 1892 v Ni (1)

McPherson, D. (Hearts), 1989 v Cy, E; 1990 v N, Ma, Cr, Se, Br; 1991 v Sw, Bul (2), USSR (sub), Sm; 1992 v Sw, R, Sm, Ni, Fi, US, Ca, N, Ho, G, C; (with Rangers), 1993 v Sw, I, Ma, P (27)

McPherson, J. (Clydesdale), 1875 v E (1)

McPherson, J. (Vale of Leven), 1879 v E, W; 1880 v E; 1881 v W; 1883 v E, W; 1884 v E; 1885 v Ni (8)

McPherson, J. (Kilmarnock), 1888 v W; (with Cowlairs), 1889 v E; 1890 v Ni, E; (with Rangers), 1892 v W; 1894 v E; 1895 v E, Ni; 1897 v Ni (9)

McPherson, J. (Hearts), 1891 v E (1)

McPherson, R. (Arthurlie), 1882 v E (1)

McQueen, G. (Leeds U), 1974 v Bel; 1975 v Sp (2), P, W, Ni, E, R; 1976 v D; 1977 v Cz, W (2), Ni, E; 1978 v EG, Cz, W; (with Manchester U), Bul, Ni, W; 1979 v A, N, P, Ni, E, N; 1980 v Pe, A, Bel; 1981 v W (30)

McQueen, M. (Leith Ath), 1890 v W; 1891 v W (2)

McRorie, D. M. (Morton), 1931 v W (1)

McSpadyen, A. (Partick T), 1939 v E, H (2)

McStay, P. (Celtic), 1984 v U, Bel, EG, Ni, W, E (sub); 1985 v Y, Ic, Sp (2), W; 1986 v EG (sub), Aus, Is, U; 1987 v Bul, Ei (1+1 sub), L (sub), Bel, E, Br; 1988 v H, Bel, Bul, L, S.Ar, Sp, Co, E; 1989 v N, Y, I, Cy, F, Cy, E, Ch; 1990 v Y, F, N, Arg, EG (sub), Eg, Pol (sub), Ma, Cr, Se (sub), Br; 1991 v R, USSR, Bul; 1992 v Sm, Fi, US, Ca, N, Ho, G, C; 1993 v Sw, P, I, Ma, P, Es (2); 1994 v I (sub), Ho; 1995 v Fi, Fa, Ru; 1996 v Aus; 1997 v Es (2), A (sub) (76)

McStay, W. (Celtic), 1921 v W, Ni; 1925 v E, Ni, W; 1926 v E, Ni, W; 1927 v E, Ni, W; 1928 v W, Ni (13)

McTavish, J. (Falkirk), 1910 v Ni (1)

McWattie, G. C. (Queen's Park), 1901 v W, Ni (2)

McWilliam, P. (Newcastle U), 1905 v E; 1906 v E; 1907 v E, W; 1909 v E, W; 1910 v E; 1911 v W (8)

Macari, L. (Celtic), 1972 v W (sub), E, Y, Cz, Br; 1973 v D; (with Manchester U), E (2), W (sub), Ni (sub); 1975 v Se, P (sub), W, E (sub), R; 1977 v Ni (sub), E (sub), Ch, Arg; 1978 v EG, W, Bul, Pe (sub), Ir (24)

Macauley, A. R. (Brentford), 1947 v E; (with Arsenal), 1948 v E, W, Ni, Bel, Sw, F (7)

Madden, J. (Celtic), 1893 v W; 1895 v W (2)

Main, F. R. (Rangers), 1938 v W (1)

Main, J. (Hibernian), 1909 v Ni (1)

Maley, W. (Celtic), 1893 v E, Ni (2)

Malpas, M. (Dundee U), 1984 v F; 1985 v E, Ic; 1986 v W, Aus (2), Is, R, E, Ho, D, WG; 1987 v Bul, Ei, Bel; 1988 v Bel, Bul, L, S.Ar, Ma; 1989 v N, Y, I, Cy, F, Cy, E, Ch; 1990 v Y, F, N, Eg, Pol, Ma, Cr, Se, Br; 1991 v R, Bul (2), USSR, Sm; 1992 v Sw, R, Sm, Ni, Fi, US, Ca (sub), N, Ho, G; 1993 v Sw, P, I (55)

Marshall, G. (Celtic), 1992 v US (1)

Marshall, H. (Celtic), 1899 v W; 1900 v Ni (2)

Marshall, J. (Middlesbrough), 1921 v E, W, Ni; 1922 v E, W, Ni; (with Llanelly), 1924 v W (7)

Marshall, J. (Third Lanark), 1885 v Ni; 1886 v W; 1887 v E, W (4)

Marshall, J. (Rangers), 1932 v E; 1933 v E; 1934 v E (3)

Marshall, R. W. (Rangers), 1892 v Ni; 1894 v Ni (2)

Martin, B. (Motherwell), 1995 v J, Ec (2)

Martin, F. (Aberdeen), 1954 v N (2), A, U; 1955 v E, H (6)

Martin, N. (Hibernian), 1965 v Fi, Pol; (with Sunderland), 1966 v I (3)

Martis, J. (Motherwell), 1961 v W (1)

Mason, J. (Third Lanark), 1949 v E, W, Ni; 1950 v Ni; 1951 v Ni, Bel, A (7)

Massie, A. (Hearts), 1932 v Ni, W, F; 1933 v Ni; 1934 v E, Ni; 1935 v E, Ni, W; 1936 v W, Ni; (with Aston Villa), 1936 v E; 1937 v G, E, W, Ni, A; 1938 v W (18)

Masson, D. S. (QPR), 1976 v Ni, W, E; 1977 v Fi, Cz, W, Ni, E, Ch, Arg, Br; 1978 v EG, Cz, W; (with Derby Co), Ni, E, Pe (17)

Mathers, D. (Partick T), 1954 v Fi (1)

Maxwell, W. S. (Stoke C), 1898 v E (1)

May, J. (Rangers), 1906 v W, Ni; 1908 v E, Ni; 1909 v W (5)

Meechan, P. (Celtic), 1896 v Ni (1)

Meiklejohn, D. D. (Rangers), 1922 v W; 1924 v W; 1925 v W, Ni, E; 1928 v W, Ni; 1929 v E, Ni; 1930 v E, Ni; 1931 v E; 1932 v W, Ni; 1934 v A (15)

Menzies, A. (Hearts), 1906 v E (1)

Mercer, R. (Hearts), 1912 v W; 1913 v Ni (2)

Middleton, R. (Cowdenbeath), 1930 v Ni (1)

Millar, A. (Hearts), 1939 v W (1)

Millar, J. (Rangers), 1897 v E; 1898 v E, W (3)

Millar, J. (Rangers), 1963 v A, Ei (2)

Miller, J. (St Mirren), 1931 v E, I, Sw; 1932 v F; 1934 v E (5)

Miller, P. (Dumbarton), 1882 v E; 1883 v E, W (3)

Miller, T. (Liverpool), 1920 v E; (with Manchester U), 1921 v E, Ni (3)

Miller, W. (Third Lanark), 1876 v E (1)

Miller, W. (Celtic), 1947 v E, W, Bel, L; 1948 v W, Ni (6)

Miller, W. (Aberdeen), 1975 v R; 1978 v Bul; 1980 v Bel, W, E, Pol, H; 1981 v Se, P, Is (sub), Ni, W, Ni, E; 1982 v Ni, P, Ho, Br, USSR; 1983 v EG, Sw (2), W, E, Ca (3); 1984 v U, Bel, EG, W, E, F; 1985 v Y, Ic, Sp (2), W, E, Ic; 1986 v W, EG, Aus (2), Is, R, E, Ho, D, WG, U; 1987 v Bul, E, Br;

Robertson, G. (Motherwell), 1910 v W; (with Sheffield W), 1912 v W; 1913 v E, Ni (4)

Robertson, G. (Kilmarnock), 1938 v Cz (1)

Robertson, H. (Dundee), 1962 v Cz (1)

Robertson, J. (Dundee), 1931 v A, I (2)

Robertson, J. (Hearts), 1991 v R, Sw, Bul (sub), Sm (sub); 1992 v Sm, Ni (sub), Fi; 1993 v I (sub), Ma (sub), G, Es; 1995 v J (sub), Ec, Fa (sub); 1996 v Gr (sub), Se (16)

Robertson, J. N. (Nottingham F), 1978 v Ni, W (sub), Ir; 1979 v P, N; 1980 v Pe, A, Bel (2), P; 1981 v Se, P, Is, Ni, Is, Ni, E; 1982 v Se, Ni (2), E (sub), Nz, Br, USSR; 1983 v EG, Sw; (with Derby Co), 1984 v U, Bel (28)

Robertson, J. G. (Tottenham H), 1965 v W (1)

Robertson, J. T. (Everton), 1898 v E; (with Southampton), 1899 v E; (with Rangers), 1900 v E, W; 1901 v W, Ni, E; 1902 v W, Ni, E; 1903 v E, W; 1904 v E, W, Ni; 1905 v W (16)

Robertson, P. (Dundee), 1903 v Ni (1)

Robertson, T. (Queen's Park), 1889 v Ni; 1890 v E; 1891 v W; 1892 v Ni (4)

Robertson, T. (Hearts), 1898 v Ni (1)

Robertson, W. (Dumbarton), 1887 v E, W (2)

Robinson, R. (Dundee), 1974 v WG (sub); 1975 v Se, Ni, R (sub) (4)

Rough, A. (Partick T), 1976 v Sw, Ni, W, E; 1977 v Fi, Cz, W (2), Se, Ni, E, Ch, Arg, Br; 1978 v Cz, W, Ni, E, Pe, Ir, Ho; 1979 v A, P, W, Arg, N; 1980 v Pe, A, Bel (2), P, W, E, Pol, H; 1981 v Se, P, Is, Ni, Is, W, E; 1982 v Se, Ni, Sp, Ho, W, E, Nz, Br, USSR; (with Hibernian), 1986 v W (sub), E (53)

Rougvie, D. (Aberdeen), 1984 v Ni (1)

Rowan, A. (Caledonian), 1880 v E; (with Queen's Park), 1882 v W (2)

Russell, D. (Hearts), 1895 v E, Ni; (with Celtic), 1897 v W; 1898 v Ni; 1901 v W, Ni (6)

Russell, J. (Cambuslang), 1890 v Ni (1)

Russell, W. F. (Airdrieonians), 1924 v W; 1925 v E (2)

Rutherford, E. (Rangers), 1948 v F (1)

St John, I. (Motherwell), 1959 v WG; 1960 v E, Ni, W, Pol, A; 1961 v E; (with Liverpool), 1962 v Ni, W, E, Cz (2), U; 1963 v W, Ni, E, N, Ei (sub); Sp; 1964 v Ni; 1965 v E (21)

Sawers, W. (Dundee), 1895 v W (1)

Scarff, J. (Celtic), 1931 v Ni (1)

Schaedler, E. (Hibernian), 1974 v WG (1)

Scott, A. S. (Rangers), 1957 v Ni, Y, WG; 1958 v W, Sw; 1959 v P; 1962 v Ni, W, E, Cz, U; (with Everton), 1964 v W, N; 1965 v Fi; 1966 v P, Br (16)

Scott, J. (Hibernian), 1966 v Ho (1)

Scott, J. (Dundee), 1971 v D (sub), USSR (2)

Scott, M. (Airdrieonians), 1898 v W (1)

Scott, R. (Airdrieonians), 1894 v Ni (1)

Scoular, J. (Portsmouth), 1951 v D, F, A; 1952 v E, USA, D, Se; 1953 v W, Ni (9)

Sellar, W. (Battlefield), 1885 v E; 1886 v E; 1887 v E, W; 1888 v E; (with Queen's Park), 1891 v E; 1892 v E; 1893 v E, Ni (9)

Semple, W. (Cambuslang), 1886 v W (1)

Shankly, W. (Preston NE), 1938 v E; 1939 v E, W, Ni, H (5)

Sharp, G. M. (Everton), 1985 v Ic; 1986 v W, Aus (2 sub), Is, R, U; 1987 v Ei; 1988 v Bel (sub), Bul, L, Ma (12)

Sharp, J. (Dundee), 1904 v W; (with Woolwich Arsenal), 1907 v W, E; 1908 v E; (with Fulham), 1909 v W (5)

Shaw, D. (Hibernian), 1947 v W, Ni; 1948 v E, Bel, Sw, F; 1949 v W, Ni (8)

Shaw, F. W. (Pollokshields Ath), 1884 v E, W (2)

Shaw, J. (Rangers), 1947 v E, Bel, L; 1948 v Ni (4)

Shearer, D. (Aberdeen), 1994 v A (sub), Ho (sub); 1995 v Fi, Ru (sub), Sm, Fa; 1996 v Gr (7)

Shearer, R. (Rangers), 1961 v E, Ei (2), Cz (4)

Sillars, D. C. (Queen's Park), 1891 v Ni; 1892 v E; 1893 v W; 1894 v E; 1895 v W (5)

Simpson, J. (Third Lanark), 1895 v E, W, Ni (3)

Simpson, J. (Rangers), 1935 v E, W, Ni; 1936 v E, W, Ni; 1937 v G, E, W, Ni, A, Cz; 1938 v W, Ni (14)

Simpson, N. (Aberdeen), 1983 v Ni; 1984 v U (sub), F (sub); 1987 v E; 1988 v E (5)

Simpson, R. C. (Celtic), 1967 v E, USSR; 1968 v Ni, E; 1969 v A (5)

Sinclair, G. L. (Hearts), 1910 v Ni; 1912 v W, Ni (3)

Sinclair, J. W. E. (Leicester C), 1966 v P (1)

Skene, L. H. (Queen's Park), 1904 v W (1)

Sloan, T. (Third Lanark), 1904 v W (1)

Smellie, R. (Queen's Park), 1887 v Ni; 1888 v W; 1889 v E; 1891 v E; 1893 v E, Ni (6)

Smith, A. (Rangers), 1898 v E; 1900 v E, Ni, W; 1901 v E, Ni, W; 1902 v E, Ni, W; 1903 v E, Ni, W; 1904 v Ni; 1905 v W; 1906 v Ni; 1907 v W; 1911 v E, Ni (20)

Smith, D. (Aberdeen), 1966 v Ho; (with Rangers), 1968 v Ho (2)

Smith, G. (Hibernian), 1947 v E, Ni; 1948 v W, Bel, Sw, F; 1952 v E, USA; 1955 v P, Y, A, H; 1956 v E, Ni, W; 1957 v Sp (2), Sw (18)

Smith, H. G. (Hearts), 1988 v S.Ar (sub); 1992 v Ni, Ca (3)

Smith, J. (Rangers), 1935 v Ni; 1938 v Ni (2)

Smith, J. (Ayr U), 1924 v E (1)

Smith, J. (Aberdeen), 1968 v Ho (sub); (with Newcastle U), 1974 v WG, Ni (sub), W (sub) (4)

Smith, J. E. (Celtic), 1959 v H, P (2)

Smith, Jas (Queen's Park), 1872 v E (1)

Smith, John (Mauchline), 1877 v E, W; 1879 v E, W; (with Edinburgh University), 1880 v E; (with Queen's Park), 1881 v W, E; 1883 v E, W; 1884 v E (10)

Smith, N. (Rangers), 1897 v E; 1898 v W; 1899 v E, W, Ni; 1900 v E, W, Ni; 1901 v Ni, W; 1902 v E, Ni (12)

Smith, R. (Queen's Park), 1872 v E; 1873 v E (2)

Smith, T. M. (Kilmarnock), 1934 v E; (with Preston NE), 1938 v E (2)

Somers, P. (Celtic), 1905 v E, Ni; 1907 v Ni; 1909 v W (4)

Somers, W. S. (Third Lanark), 1879 v E, W; (with Queen's Park), 1880 v W (3)

Somerville, G. (Queen's Park), 1886 v E (1)

Souness, G. J. (Middlesbrough), 1975 v EG, Sp, Se; (with Liverpool), 1978 v Bul, W, E (sub), Ho; 1979 v A, N, W, Ni, E; 1980 v Pe, A, Bel, P, Ni; 1981 v P, Is (2); 1982 v Ni, P, Sp, W, E, Nz, Br, USSR; 1983 v EG, Sw, Bel, Sw, W, E, Ca (2 + 1 sub); 1984 v U, Ni, W; (with Sampdoria), 1985 v Y, Ic, Sp (2), W, E, Ic; 1986 v EG, Aus (2), R, E, D, WG (54)

Speedie, D. R. (Chelsea), 1985 v E; 1986 v W, EG (sub), Aus, E; (with Coventry C), 1989 v Y (sub), I (sub), Cy (1+1 sub), Ch (10)

Speedie, F. (Rangers), 1903 v E, W, Ni (3)

Speirs, J. H. (Rangers), 1908 v W (1)

Spencer, J. (Chelsea), 1995 v Ru (sub), Gr (sub), Sm (sub), J; 1996 v Fi, Aus, D, US (sub), Co, Ho (sub), E, Sw (sub); 1997 v La; (with QPR), W (sub) (14)

Stanton, P. (Hibernian), 1966 v Ho; 1969 v Ni; 1970 v Ei, A; 1971 v D, Bel, P, USSR, D; 1972 v P, Bel, Ho, W; 1973 v W, Ni; 1974 v WG (16)

Stark, J. (Rangers), 1909 v E, Ni (2)

Steel, W. (Morton), 1947 v E, Bel, L; (with Derby Co), 1948 v F, E, W, Ni; 1949 v E, W, Ni, F; 1950 v E, W, Ni, Sw, P, F; (with Dundee), 1951 v W, Ni, E, A (2), D, F, Bel; 1952 v W; 1953 v W, E, Ni, Se (30)

Steele, D. M. (Huddersfield), 1923 v E, W, Ni (3)

Stein, C. (Rangers), 1969 v W, Ni, D, E, Cy (2); 1970 v A (sub), Ni (sub), W, E, Ei, WG; 1971 v D, USSR, Bel, D; 1972 v Cz (sub); (with Coventry C), 1973 v E (2 sub), W (sub), Ni (21)

Stephen, J. F. (Bradford), 1947 v W; 1948 v W (2)

Stevenson, G. (Motherwell), 1928 v W, Ni; 1930 v Ni, E, F; 1931 v E, W; 1932 v W, Ni; 1933 v Ni; 1934 v E; 1935 v Ni (12)

Stewart, A. (Queen's Park), 1888 v Ni; 1889 v W (2)

Stewart, A. (Third Lanark), 1894 v W (1)

Stewart, D. (Dumbarton), 1888 v Ni (1)

Stewart, D. (Queen's Park), 1893 v W; 1894 v Ni; 1897 v Ni (3)

Stewart, D. S. (Leeds U), 1978 v EG (1)

Stewart, G. (Hibernian), 1906 v W, E; (with Manchester C), 1907 v E, W (4)

Stewart, J. (Kilmarnock), 1977 v Ch (sub); (with Middlesbrough), 1979 v N (2)

Stewart, R. (West Ham U), 1981 v W, Ni, E; 1982 v Ni, P, W; 1984 v F; 1987 v Ei (2), L (10)

Stewart, W. E. (Queen's Park), 1898 v Ni; 1900 v Ni (2)

Storrier, D. (Celtic), 1899 v E, W, Ni (3)

Strachan, G. (Aberdeen), 1980 v Ni, W, E, Pol, H (sub); 1981 v Se, P; 1982 v Ni, P, Sp, Ho (sub), Nz, Br, USSR; 1983 v EG, Sw, Bel, Sw, Ni (sub), W, E, Ca (2 + 1 sub); 1984 v EG, Ni, E, F; (with Manchester U), 1985 v Sp (sub), E, Ic; 1986 v W, Aus, R, D, WG, U; 1987 v Bul, Ei (2); 1988 v H; 1989 v F (sub); (with Leeds U), 1990 v F; 1991 v USSR, Bul, Sm; 1992 v Sw, R, Ni, Fi (50)

Sturrock, P. (Dundee U), 1981 v W (sub), Ni, E (sub); 1982 v P, Ni (sub), W (sub), E (sub); 1983 v EG (sub), Sw, Bel (sub), Ca (3); 1984 v W; 1985 v Y (sub); 1986 v Is (sub), Ho, D, U; 1987 v Bel (20)

Sullivan, N. (Wimbledon), 1997 v W; 1998 v F, Co (3)

Summers, W. (St Mirren), 1926 v E (1)

Symon, J. S. (Rangers), 1939 v H (1)

Tait, T. S. (Sunderland), 1911 v W (1)

# WALES

Adams, H. (Berwyn R), 1882 v Ni, E; (with Druids), 1883 v Ni, E (4)

Aizlewood, M. (Charlton Ath), 1986 v S.Ar, Ca (2); 1987 v Fi; (with Leeds U), USSR, Fi (sub); 1988 v D (sub), Se, Ma, I; 1989 v Ho, Se (sub), WG; (with Bradford C), 1990 v Fi, WG, Ei, Cr; (with Bristol C), 1991 v D, Bel (2), L, Ei, Ic, Pol, WG; 1992 v Br, L, Ei, A, R, Ho, Arg, J; 1993 v Ei, Bel, Fa; 1994 v RCS, Cy; (with Cardiff C) 1995v Bul (39)

Allchurch, I. J. (Swansea T), 1951 v E, Ni, P, Sw; 1952 v E, S, Ni, R of UK; 1953 v S, E, Ni, F, Y; 1954 v S, E, Ni, A; 1955 v S, E, Ni, Y; 1956 v E, S, Ni, A; 1957 v E, S; 1958 v Ni, Is (2), H (2), M, Sw, Br; (with Newcastle U), 1959 v E, S, Ni; 1960 v E, S; 1961 v Ni, H, Sp (2); 1962 v E, S, Br (2), M; (with Cardiff C), 1963 v S, E, Ni, H (2); 1964 v E; 1965 v S, E, Ni, Gr, I, USSR; (with Swansea T), 1966 v USSR, E, S, D, Br (2), Ch (68)

Allchurch, L. (Swansea T), 1955 v Ni; 1956 v A; 1958 v S, Ni, EG, Is; 1959 v S; (with Sheffield U), 1962 v S, Ni, Br; 1964 v E (11)

Allen, B. W. (Coventry C), 1951 v S, E (2)

Allen, M. (Watford), 1986 v S.Ar (sub), Ca (1 + 1 sub); (with Norwich C), 1989 v Is (sub); 1990 v Ho, WG; (with Millwall), Ei, Se, Cr (sub); 1991 v L (sub), Ei (sub); 1992 v A; 1993 v Ei (sub); (with Newcastle U), 1994 v R (sub) (14)

Arridge, S. (Bootle), 1892 v S, Ni; (with Everton), 1894 v Ni; 1895 v Ni; 1896 v E; (with New Brighton Tower), 1898 v E, Ni; 1899 v E (8)

Astley, D. J. (Charlton Ath), 1931 v Ni; (with Aston Villa), 1932 v E; 1933 v E, S, Ni; 1934 v E, S; 1935 v S; 1936 v E, Ni; (with Derby Co), 1939 v E, S; (with Blackpool), F (13)

Atherton, R. W. (Hibernian), 1899 v E, Ni; 1903 v E, S, Ni; (with Middlesbrough), 1904 v E, S, Ni; 1905 v Ni (9)

Bailiff, W. E. (Llanelly), 1913 v E, S, Ni; 1920 v Ni (4)

Baker, C. W. (Cardiff C), 1958 v M; 1960 v S, Ni; 1961 v S, E, Ei; 1962 v S (7)

Baker, W. G. (Cardiff C), 1948 v Ni (1)

Bamford, T. (Wrexham), 1931 v E, S, Ni; 1932 v Ni; 1933 v F (5)

Barnard, D. S. (Barnsley), 1998 v Jam (1)

Barnes, W. (Arsenal), 1948 v E, S, Ni; 1949 v E, S, Ni; 1950 v E, S, Ni, Bel; 1951 v E, S, Ni, P; 1952 v E, S, Ni, R of UK; 1954 v E, S; 1955 v S, Y (22)

Bartley, T. (Glossop NE), 1898 v E (1)

Bastock, A. M. (Shrewsbury), 1892 v Ni (1)

Beadles, G. H. (Cardiff C), 1925 v E, S (2)

Bell, W. S. (Shrewsbury Engineers), 1881 v E, S; (with Crewe Alex), 1886 v E, S, Ni (5)

Bellamy, C. D. (Norwich C), 1998 v Jam (sub), Ma, Tun (3)

Bennion, S. R. (Manchester U), 1926 v S; 1927 v S; 1928 v S, E, Ni; 1929 v S, E, Ni; 1930 v S; 1932 v Ni (10)

Berry, G. F. (Wolverhampton W), 1979 v WG; 1980 v Ei, WG (sub), T; (with Stoke C), 1983 v E (sub) (5)

Blackmore, C. G. (Manchester U), 1985 v N (sub); 1986 v S (sub), H (sub), S.Ar, Ei, U; 1987 v Fi (2), USSR, Cz; 1988 v D (2), Cz, Y, Se, Ma, I; 1989 v Ho, Fi, Is, WG; 1990 v F; Ho, WG, Cr; 1991 v Bel, L; 1992 v Ei (sub), A, R (sub), Ho, Arg, J; 1993 v Fa, Cy, Bel, RCS; 1994 v Se (sub); (with Middlesbrough), 1997 v Bel (39)

Blake, N. A. (Sheffield U), 1994 v N, Se (sub); 1995 v Alb, Mol; 1996 v G (with Bolton W), I (sub); 1998 v T (17)

Blew, H. (Wrexham), 1899 v E, S, Ni; 1902 v S, Ni; 1903 v E, S; 1904 v E, S, Ni; 1905 v S, Ni; 1906 v E, S, Ni; 1907 v S; 1908 v E, S, Ni; 1909 v E, S; 1910 v E (22)

Boden, T. (Wrexham), 1880 v E (1)

Bodin, P. J. (Swindon T), 1990 v Cr; 1991 v D, Bel, L, Ei; (with C Palace), Bel, Ic, Pol, WG; 1992 v Br, G, L (sub); (with Swindon T), Ei (sub), Ho, Arg; 1993 v Ei, Bel, RCS, Fa; 1994 v R, Se, Es (sub); 1995 v Alb (23)

Boulter, L. M. (Brentford), 1939 v Ni (1)

Bowdler, H. E. (Shrewsbury), 1893 v S (1)

Bowdler, J. C. H. (Shrewsbury), 1890 v Ni; (with Wolverhampton W), 1891 v S; 1892 v Ni; (with Shrewsbury), 1894 v E (4)

Bowen, D. L. (Arsenal), 1955 v S, Y; 1957 v Ni, Cz, EG; 1958 v E, S, Ni, EG, Is (2), H (2), M, Se, Br; 1959 v E, S, Ni (19)

Bowen, E. (Druids), 1880 v S; 1883 v S (2)

Bowen, J. P. (Swansea C), 1994 v Es; (with Birmingham C), 1997 v Ho (2)

Bowen, M. R. (Tottenham H), 1986 v Ca (2 sub); (with Norwich C), 1988 v Y (sub); 1989 v Fi (sub), Is, Se, WG (sub); 1990 v Fi (sub), Ho, WG, Se; 1992 v Br (sub), G, L, Ei, A, R, Ho (sub), J; 1993 v Fa, Cy, Bel (1 + sub), RCS (sub); 1994 v RCS, Se; 1995 v Mol, Ge, Bul (2), G, Ge;

1996 v Mol, G, Alb, Sw, Sm; (with West Ham U), 1997 v Sm, Ho (2), Ei (sub) (41)

Bowsher, S. J. (Burnley), 1929 v Ni (1)

Boyle, T. (C Palace), 1981 v Ei, S (sub) (2)

Britten, T. J. (Parkgrove), 1878 v S; (with Presteigne), 1880 v S (2)

Brookes, S. J. (Llandudno), 1900 v E, Ni (2)

Brown, A. I. (Aberdare Ath), 1926 v Ni (1)

Browning, M. T. (Bristol R), 1996 v I (sub), Sm; 1997 v Sm, Ho (with Huddersfield T), S (sub) (5)

Bryan, T. (Oswestry), 1886 v E, Ni (2)

Buckland, T. (Bangor), 1899 v E (1)

Burgess, W. A. R. (Tottenham H), 1947 v E, S, Ni; 1948 v E, S; 1949 v E, S, Ni, P, Bel, Sw; 1950 v E, S, Ni, Bel; 1951 v S, Ni, P, Sw; 1952 v E, S, Ni, R of UK; 1953 v S, E, Ni, F, Y; 1954 v S, E, Ni, A (32)

Burke, T. (Wrexham), 1883 v E; 1884 v S; 1885 v E, S, Ni; (with Newton Heath), 1887 v E, S; 1888 v S (8)

Burnett, T. B. (Ruabon), 1877 v S (1)

Burton, A. D. (Norwich C), 1963 v Ni, H; (with Newcastle U), 1964 v E; 1969 v S, E, Ni, I, EG; 1972 v Cz (9)

Butler, J. (Chirk), 1893 v E, S, Ni (3)

Butler, W. T. (Druids), 1900 v S, Ni (2)

Cartwright, L. (Coventry C), 1974 v E (sub), S, Ni; 1976 v S (sub); 1977 v WG (sub); (with Wrexham), 1978 v Ir (sub); 1979 v Ma (7)

Carty, T. [s] See McCarthy [s] (Wrexham).

Challen, J. B. (Corinthians), 1887 v E, S; 1888 v E; (with Wellingborough GS), 1890 v E (4)

Chapman, T. (Newtown), 1894 v E, S, Ni; 1895 v S, Ni; (with Manchester C), 1896 v E; 1897 v E (7)

Charles, J. M. (Swansea C), 1981 v Cz, T (sub), S (sub), USSR (sub); 1982 v Ic; 1983 v N (sub), Y (sub), Bul (sub), S, Ni, Br; 1984 v Bul (sub); (with QPR), Y (sub), S; (with Oxford U), 1985 v Ic (sub), Sp, Ic; 1986 v Ei; 1987 v Fi (19)

Charles, M. (Swansea T), 1955 v Ni; 1956 v E, S, A; 1957 v E, Ni, Cz (2), EG; 1958 v E, S, EG, Is (2), H (2), M, Se, Br; 1959 v E, S; (with Arsenal), 1961 v Ni, H, Sp (2); 1962 v E, S; (with Cardiff C), 1962 v Br, Ni; 1963 v S, H (31)

Charles, W. J. (Leeds U), 1950 v Ni; 1951 v Sw; 1953 v Ni, F, Y; 1954 v E, S, Ni, A; 1955 v S, E, Ni, Y; 1956 v E, S, A, Ni; 1957 v E, S, Ni, Cz (2), EG; (with Juventus), 1958 v Is (2), H (2) M, Se; 1960 v S; 1962 v E, Br (2), M; (with Leeds U), 1963 v S; (with Cardiff C), 1964 v S; 1965 v S, USSR (38)

Clarke, R. J. (Manchester C), 1949 v E; 1950 v S, Ni, Bel; 1951 v E, S, Ni, P, Sw; 1952 v S, E, Ni, R of UK; 1953 v S, E; 1954 v E, S, Ni; 1955 v Y, S, E; 1956 v Ni (22)

Coleman, C. (C Palace), 1992 v A (sub); 1993 v Ei (sub); 1994 v N, Es; 1995 v Alb, Mol, Ge, Bul (2), G; 1996 v Mol; (with Blackburn R), I, Sw, Sm; 1997 v Sm; 1998 v Br; (with Fulham), Jam, Ma, Tun (19)

Collier, D. J. (Grimsby T), 1921 v S (1)

Collins, W. S. (Llanelly), 1931 v S (1)

Conde, C. (Chirk), 1884 v E, S, Ni (3)

Cook, F. C. (Newport Co), 1925 v E, S; (with Portsmouth), 1928 v E, S; 1930 v E, S, Ni; 1932 v E (8)

Cornforth, J.M. (Swansea C), 1995 v Bul (sub), Ge (2)

Coyne, D. (Tranmere R), 1996 v Sw (1)

Crompton, W. (Wrexham), 1931 v E, S, Ni (3)

Cross, E. A. (Wrexham), 1876 v S; 1877 v S (2)

Crosse, K. (Druids), 1879 v S; 1881 v E, S (3)

Crossley, M. G. (Nottingham F), 1997 v Ei (1)

Crowe, V. H. (Aston Villa), 1959 v E, Ni; 1960 v E, Ni; 1961 v S, E, Ni, Ei, H, Sp (2); 1962 v E, S, Br, M; 1963 v H (16)

Cumner, R. H. (Arsenal), 1939 v E, S, Ni (3)

Curtis, A. (Swansea C), 1976 v E, Y (sub), S, Ni, Y (sub), E; 1977 v WG, S (sub), Ni (sub); 1978 v WG, E, S; 1979 v WG, S; (with Leeds U), E, Ni, Ma; 1980 v Ei, WG, T; (with Swansea C), 1982 v Cz, Ic, USSR, Sp, E, S, Ni; 1983 v N; 1984 v R (sub); (with Southampton), S; 1985 v Sp, N (1 + 1 sub); 1986 v H; (with Cardiff C), 1987 v USSR (35)

Curtis, E. R. (Cardiff C), 1928 v S; (with Birmingham C), 1932 v S; 1934 v Ni (3)

Daniel, R. W. (Arsenal), 1951 v E, Ni, P; 1952 v E, S, Ni, R of UK; 1953 v S, E, Ni, F, Y; (with Sunderland), 1954 v E, S, Ni; 1955 v E, Ni; 1957 v S, E, Ni, Cz (21)

Darvell, S. (Oxford University), 1897 v S, Ni (2)

Davies, A. (Manchester U), 1983 v Ni, Br; 1984 v E, Ni; 1985 v Ic (2), N; (with Newcastle U), 1986 v H; (with Swansea C), 1988 v Ma, I; 1989 v Ho; (with Bradford C), 1990 v Fi, Ei (13)

Davies, A. (Wrexham), 1876 v S; 1877 v S (2)

Davies, A. (Druids), 1904 v S; (with Middlesbrough), 1905 v S (2)

Davies, A. O. (Barmouth), 1885 v Ni; 1886 v E, S; (with Swifts), 1887 v E, S; 1888 v E, Ni; (with Wrexham), 1889 v S; (with Crewe Alex), 1890 v E (9)

Davies, A. T. (Shrewsbury), 1891 v Ni (1)

Davies, C. (Charlton Ath), 1972 v R (sub) (1)

Davies, D. (Bolton W), 1904 v S, Ni; 1908 v E (sub) (3)

Davies, D. C. (Brecon), 1899 v Ni; (with Hereford); 1900 v Ni (2)

Davies, D. W. (Treharris), 1912 v Ni; (with Oldham Ath), 1913 v Ni (2)

Davies, E. Lloyd (Stoke C), 1904 v E; 1907 v E, S, Ni; (with Northampton T), 1908 v S; 1909 v Ni; 1910 v Ni; 1911 v E, S; 1912 v E, S; 1913 v E, S; 1914 v Ni, E, S (16)

Davies, E. R. (Newcastle U), 1953 v S, E; 1954 v E, S; 1958 v E, EG (6)

Davies, G. (Fulham), 1980 v T, Ic; 1982 v Sp (sub), F (sub); 1983 v E, Bul, S, Ni, Br; 1984 v R (sub), S (sub), E, Ni; 1985 v Ic; (with Manchester C), 1986 v S.Ar, Ei (16)

Davies, Rev. H. (Wrexham), 1928 v Ni (1)

Davies, Idwal (Liverpool Marine), 1923 v S (1)

Davies, J. E. (Oswestry), 1885 v E (1)

Davies, Jas (Wrexham), 1878 v S (1)

Davies, John (Wrexham), 1879 v S (1)

Davies, Jos (Newton Heath), 1888 v E, S, Ni; 1889 v S; 1890 v E; (with Wolverhampton W), 1892 v E; 1893 v E (7)

Davies, Jos (Everton), 1889 v S, Ni; (with Chirk), 1891 v Ni; (with Ardwick), v E, S; (with Sheffield U), 1895 v E, S, Ni; (with Manchester C), 1896 v E; (with Millwall), 1897 v E; (with Reading), 1900 v E (11)

Davies, J. P. (Druids), 1883 v E, Ni (2)

Davies, Ll. (Wrexham), 1907 v Ni; 1910 v Ni, S, E; (with Everton), 1911 v S, Ni; (with Wrexham), 1912 v Ni, S, E; 1913 v Ni, S, E; 1914 v Ni (13)

Davies, L. S. (Cardiff C), 1922 v E, S, Ni; 1923 v E, S, Ni; 1924 v E, S, Ni; 1925 v S, Ni; 1926 v E, Ni; 1927 v E, Ni; 1928 v S, Ni, E; 1929 v S, Ni, E; 1930 v E, S (23)

Davies, O. (Wrexham), 1890 v S (1)

Davies, R. (Wrexham), 1883 v Ni; 1884 v Ni; 1885 v Ni (3)

Davies, R. (Druids), 1885 v E (1)

Davies, R. O. (Wrexham), 1892 v Ni, E (2)

Davies, R. T. (Norwich C), 1964 v Ni; 1965 v E; 1966 v Br (2), Ch; (with Southampton), 1967 v S, E, Ni; 1968 v S, Ni, WG; 1969 v S, E, Ni, I, WG, R of UK; 1970 v E, S, Ni; 1971 v Cz, S, E, Ni; 1972 v R, E, S, N; (with Portsmouth), 1974 v E (29)

Davies, R. W. (Bolton W), 1964 v E; 1965 v E, S, Ni, D, Gr, USSR; 1966 v E, S, Ni, USSR, D, Br (2), Ch (sub); 1967 v S; (with Newcastle U), E; 1968 v S, Ni, WG; 1969 v S, E, Ni, I; 1970 v EG; 1971 v R, Cz; (with Manchester C), 1972 v E, S, Ni; (with Manchester U), 1973 v E, S (sub), Ni; (with Blackpool), 1974 v Pol (34)

Davies, S. I. (Manchester U), 1996 v Sw (sub) (1)

Davies, Stanley (Preston NE), 1920 v E, S, Ni; (with Everton), 1921 v E, S, Ni; (with WBA), 1922 v E, S, Ni; 1923 v S; 1925 v S, Ni; 1926 v S, E, Ni; 1927 v S; 1928 v S; (with Rotherham U), 1930 v Ni (18)

Davies, T. (Oswestry), 1886 v E (1)

Davies, T. (Druids), 1903 v E, Ni, S; 1904 v S (4)

Davies, W. (Wrexham), 1884 v Ni (1)

Davies, W. (Swansea T), 1924 v E, S, Ni; (with Cardiff C), 1925 v E, S, Ni; 1926 v E, S, Ni; 1927 v S; 1928 v Ni; (with Notts Co), 1929 v E, S, Ni; 1930 v E, S, Ni (17)

Davies, William (Wrexham), 1903 v Ni; 1905 v Ni; (with Blackburn R), 1908 v E, S; 1909 v E, S, Ni; 1911 v E, S, Ni; 1912 v Ni (11)

Davies, W. C. (C Palace), 1908 v S; (with WBA), 1909 v E; 1910 v S; (with C Palace), 1914 v E (4)

Davies, W. D. (Everton), 1975 v H, L, S, E, Ni; 1976 v Y (2), E, Ni; 1977 v WG, S (2), Cz, E, Ni; 1978 v K; (with Wrexham), S, Cz, WG, Ir, E, S, Ni; 1979 v Ma, T, WG, S, E, Ni, Ma; 1980 v Ei, WG, T, E, S, Ni, Ic; 1981 v T, Cz, Ei, T, S, E, USSR; (with Swansea C), 1982 v Cz, Ic, USSR, Sp, E, S, F; 1983 v Y (52)

Davies, W. H. (Oswestry), 1876 v S; 1877 v S; 1879 v E; 1880 v E (4)

Davies, W. O. (Millwall Ath), 1913 v E, S, Ni; 1914 v S, Ni (5)

Davis, G. (Wrexham), 1978 v Ir, E (sub), Ni (3)

Day, A. (Tottenham H), 1934 v Ni (1)

Deacy, N. (PSV Eindhoven), 1977 v Cz, S, E, Ni; 1978 v K (sub), S (sub), Cz (sub), WG, Ir, S (sub), Ni; (with Beringen), 1979 v T (12)

Dearson, D. J. (Birmingham), 1939 v S, Ni, F (3)

Derrett, S. C. (Cardiff C), 1969 v S, WG; 1970 v I; 1971 v Fi (4)

Dewey, F. T. (Cardiff Corinthians), 1931 v E, S (2)

Dibble, A. (Luton T), 1986 v Ca (1+1 sub); (with Manchester C), 1989 v Is (3)

Doughty, J. (Druids), 1886 v S; (with Newton Heath), 1887 v S, Ni; 1888 v E, S, Ni; 1889 v S; 1890 v E (8)

Doughty, R. (Newton Heath and Druids), 1888 v S, Ni (2)

Durban, A. (Derby Co), 1966 v Br (sub); 1967 v Ni; 1968 v E, S, Ni, WG; 1969 v EG, S, E, Ni, WG; 1970 v E, S, Ni, EG, I; 1971 v R, S, E, Ni, Cz, Fi; 1972 v Fi, Cz, E, S, Ni (27)

Dwyer, P. (Cardiff C), 1978 v Ir, E, S, Ni; 1979 v T, S, E, Ni, Ma (sub); 1980 v WG (10)

Edwards, C. (Wrexham), 1878 v S (1)

Edwards, C. N. H. (Swansea C), 1996 v Sw (sub) (1)

Edwards, G. (Birmingham C), 1947 v E, S, Ni; 1948 v E, S, Ni; (with Cardiff C), 1949 v Ni, P, Bel, Sw; 1950 v E, S (12)

Edwards, H. (Wrexham Civil Service), 1878 v S; 1880 v E, S; 1882 v E, S; 1883 v S; 1884 v Ni; 1887 v Ni (8)

Edwards, J. H. (Wanderers), 1876 v S (1)

Edwards, J. H. (Oswestry), 1895 v Ni; 1897 v E, Ni (3)

Edwards, J. H. (Aberystwyth), 1898 v Ni (1)

Edwards, L. T. (Charlton Ath), 1957 v Ni, EG (2)

Edwards, R. I. (Chester), 1978 v K (sub); 1979 v Ma, WG; (with Wrexham), 1980 v T (sub) (4)

Edwards, R. W. (Bristol C), 1998 v T (sub), Bel, Ma (sub), Tun (sub) (4)

Edwards, T. (Linfield), 1932 v S (1)

Egan, W. (Chirk), 1892 v S (1)

Ellis, B. (Motherwell), 1932 v E; 1933 v E, S; 1934 v S; 1936 v E; 1937 v S (6)

Ellis, E. (Nunhead), 1931 v S; (with Oswestry), E; 1932 v Ni (3)

Emanuel, W. J. (Bristol C), 1973 v E (sub), Ni (sub) (2)

England, H. M. (Blackburn R), 1962 v Ni, Br, M; 1963 v Ni, H; 1964 v S, Ni; 1965 v E, D, Gr (2), USSR, Ni, I; 1966 v E, S, Ni, USSR, D; (with Tottenham H), 1967 v S, E; 1968 v E, Ni, WG; 1969 v EG; 1970 v R of UK, EG, E, S, Ni, I; 1971 v R; 1972 v Fi, E, S, Ni; 1973 v E (3), S; 1974 v Pol; 1975 v H, L (44)

Evans, B. C. (Swansea C), 1972 v Fi, Cz; 1973 v E (2), Pol, S; (with Hereford U), 1974 v Pol (7)

Evans, D. G. (Reading), 1926 v Ni; 1927 v Ni, E; (with Huddersfield T), 1929 v S (4)

Evans, H. P. (Cardiff C), 1922 v E, S, Ni; 1924 v E, S, Ni (6)

Evans, I. (C Palace), 1976 v A, E, Y (2), E, Ni; 1977 v WG, S (2), Cz, E, Ni; 1978 v K (13)

Evans, J. (Oswestry), 1893 v Ni; 1894 v E, Ni (3)

Evans, J. (Cardiff C), 1912 v Ni; 1913 v Ni; 1914 v S; 1920 v S, Ni; 1922 v Ni; 1923 v E, Ni (8)

Evans, J. (Southend U), 1922 v E, S, Ni; 1923 v S (4)

Evans, Len (Aberdare Ath), 1927 v Ni; (with Cardiff C), 1931 v E, S; (with Birmingham), 1934 v Ni (4)

Evans, M. (Oswestry), 1884 v E (1)

Evans, R. (Clapton), 1902 v Ni (1)

Evans, R. E. (Wrexham), 1906 v E, S; (with Aston Villa), Ni; 1907 v E; 1908 v E, S; (with Sheffield U), 1909 v S; 1910 v E, S, Ni (10)

Evans, R. O. (Wrexham), 1902 v Ni; 1903 v E, S, Ni; (with Blackburn R), 1908 v Ni; (with Coventry C), 1911 v E, Ni; 1912 v E, S, Ni (10)

Evans, R. S. (Swansea T), 1964 v Ni (1)

Evans, T. J. (Clapton Orient), 1927 v S; 1928 v E, S; (with Newcastle U), Ni (4)

Evans, W. (Tottenham H), 1933 v Ni; 1934 v E, S; 1935 v S; 1936 v E, Ni (6)

Evans, W. A. W. (Oxford University), 1876 v S; 1877 v S (2)

Evans, W. G. (Bootle), 1890 v E; 1891 v E; (with Aston Villa), 1892 v E (3)

Evelyn, E. C. (Crusaders), 1887 v E (1)

Eyton-Jones, J. A. (Wrexham), 1883 v Ni; 1884 v Ni, E, S (4)

Farmer, G. (Oswestry), 1885 v E, S (2)

Felgate, D. (Lincoln C), 1984 v R (sub) (1)

Finnigan, R. J. (Wrexham), 1930 v Ni (1)

Flynn, B. (Burnley), 1975 v L (2 sub), H (sub), S, E, Ni; 1976 v A, E, Y (2), E, Ni; 1977 v WG (sub), S (2), Cz, E, Ni; 1978 v K (2), S; (with Leeds U), Cz, WG, Ir (sub), E, S, Ni; 1979 v Ma, T, S, E, Ni, Ma; 1980 v Ei, WG, E, S, Ni, Ic; 1981 v T, Cz, Ei, T, S, E, USSR; 1982 v Cz, USSR, E, S, Ni, F; 1983 v N; (with Burnley), Y, E, Bul, S, Ni, Br; 1984 v N, R, Bul, Y, S, N, Is (66)

Ford, T. (Swansea T), 1947 v S; (with Aston Villa), 1947 v Ni; 1948 v S, Ni; 1949 v E, S, Ni, P, Bel, Sw; 1950 v E, S, Ni, Bel; 1951 v S; (with Sunderland), 1951 v E, Ni, P, Sw; 1952 v E, S, Ni, R of UK; 1953 v S, E, Ni, F, Y; (with Cardiff C), 1954 v A; 1955 v S, E, Ni, Y; 1956 v S, Ni, E, A; 1957 v S (38)

Foulkes, H. E. (WBA), 1932 v Ni (1)

Foulkes, W. I. (Newcastle U), 1952 v E, S, Ni, R of UK; 1953 v E, S, F, Y; 1954 v E, S, Ni (11)
Foulkes, W. T. (Oswestry), 1884 v Ni; 1885 v S (2)
Fowler, J. (Swansea T), 1925 v E; 1926 v E, Ni; 1927 v S; 1928 v S; 1929 v E (6)

Garner, J. (Aberystwyth), 1896 v S (1)
Giggs, R. J. (Manchester U), 1992 v G (sub), L (sub), R (sub); 1993 v Fa (sub), Bel (sub + 1), RCS, Fa; 1994 v RCS, Cy, R; 1995 v Alb, Bul; 1996 v G, Alb, Sm; 1997 v Sm, T, Bel; 1998 v T, Bel (21)
Giles, D. (Swansea C), 1980 v E, S, Ni, Ic; 1981 v T, Cz, T (sub), E (sub), USSR (sub); (with C Palace), 1982 v Sp (sub); 1983 v Ni (sub), Br (12)
Gillam, S. G. (Wrexham), 1889 v S (sub), Ni; (with Shrewsbury), 1890 v E, Ni; (with Clapton), 1894 v S (5)
Glascodine, G. (Wrexham), 1879 v E (1)
Glover, E. M. (Grimsby T), 1932 v S; 1934 v Ni; 1936 v S; 1937 v E, S, Ni; 1939 v Ni (7)
Godding, G. (Wrexham), 1923 v S, Ni (2)
Godfrey, B. C. (Preston NE), 1964 v Ni; 1965 v D, I (3)
Goodwin, U. (Ruthin), 1881 v E (1)
Goss, J. (Norwich C), 1991 v Ic, Pol (sub); 1992 v A; 1994 v Cy (sub), R (sub), Se; 1995 v Alb; 1996 v Sw (sub), Sm (sub) (9)
Gough, R. T. (Oswestry White Star), 1883 v S (1)
Gray, A. (Oldham Ath), 1924 v E, S, Ni; 1925 v E, S, Ni; 1926 v E, S; 1927 v S; (with Manchester C), 1928 v E, S; 1929 v E, S, Ni; (with Manchester Central), 1930 v S; (with Tranmere R), 1932 v E, S, Ni; (with Chester), 1937 v E, S, Ni; 1938 v E, S, Ni (24)
Green, A. W. (Aston Villa), 1901 v Ni; (with Notts Co), 1903 v E; 1904 v S, Ni; 1906 v Ni, E; (with Nottingham F), 1907 v E; 1908 v S (8)
Green, C. R. (Birmingham C), 1965 v USSR, I; 1966 v E, S, USSR, Br (2); 1967 v E; 1968 v E, S, Ni, WG; 1969 v S, I, Ni (sub) (15)
Green, G. H. (Charlton Ath), 1938 v Ni; 1939 v E, Ni, F (4)
Green, R. M. (Wolverhampton W), 1998 v Ma, Tun (2)
Grey, Dr W. (Druids), 1876 v S; 1878 v S (2)
Griffiths, A. T. (Wrexham), 1971 v Cz (sub); 1975 v A, H (2), L (2), E, Ni; 1976 v A, E, S, E (sub), Ni, Y (2); 1977 v WG, S (17)
Griffiths, F. J. (Blackpool), 1900 v E, S (2)
Griffiths, G. (Chirk), 1887 v Ni (1)
Griffiths, J. H. (Swansea T), 1953 v Ni (1)
Griffiths, L. (Wrexham), 1902 v S (1)
Griffiths, M. W. (Leicester C), 1947 v Ni; 1949 v P, Bel; 1950 v E, S, Bel; 1951 v E, Ni, P, Sw; 1954 v A (11)
Griffiths, P. (Chirk), 1884 v Ni; 1888 v E; 1890 v S, Ni; 1891 v Ni (6)
Griffiths, P. H. (Everton), 1932 v S (1)
Griffiths, L. (Wrexham), 1902 v S (1)
Griffiths, T. P. (Everton), 1927 v E, Ni; 1929 v E; 1930 v E; 1931 v Ni; 1932 v Ni, S, E; (with Bolton W), 1933 v E, S, Ni; (with Middlesbrough), F; 1934 v E, S; 1935 v E, Ni; 1936 v S; (with Aston Villa), Ni; 1937 v E, S, Ni (21)

Hall, G. D. (Chelsea), 1988 v Y (sub), Ma, I; 1989 v Ho, Fi, Is; 1990 v Ei; 1991 v Ei; 1992 v A (sub) (9)
Hallam, J. (Oswestry), 1889 v E (1)
Hanford, H. (Swansea T), 1934 v Ni; 1935 v S; 1936 v E; (with Sheffield W), 1936 v Ni; 1938 v E, S; 1939 v F (7)
Harrington, A. C. (Cardiff C), 1956 v Ni; 1957 v E, S; 1958 v S, Ni, Is (2); 1961 v S, E; 1962 v E, S (11)
Harris, C. S. (Leeds U), 1976 v E, S; 1978 v WG, Ir, E, S, Ni; 1979 v Ma, T, WG, E (sub), Ma; 1980 v Ni (sub), Ic (sub); 1981 v T, Cz (sub), Ei, T, S, E, USSR; 1982 v Cz, Ic, E (sub) (24)
Harris, W. C. (Middlesbrough), 1954 v A; 1957 v EG, Cz; 1958 v E, S, EG (6)
Harrison, W. C. (Wrexham), 1899 v E; 1900 v E, S, Ni; 1901 v Ni (5)
Hartson, J. (Arsenal), 1995 v Bul, G (sub), Ge (sub); 1996 v Mol (sub), Sw; 1997 v Ho, T (sub), Ei; (with West Ham U), Bel (sub), S; 1998 v Bel, Jam, Ma, Tun (14)
Haworth, S. O. (Cardiff C), 1997 v S (sub); (with Coventry C), 1998 v Br, Jam (sub), Ma (sub), Tun (sub) (5)
Hayes, A. (Wrexham), 1890 v Ni; 1894 v Ni (2)
Hennessey, W. T. (Birmingham C), 1962 v Ni, Br (2); 1963 v S, E, H (2); 1964 v E, S; 1965 v S, E, D, Gr, USSR; 1966 v E, USSR; (with Nottingham F), 1966 v S, Ni, D, Br (2), Ch; 1967 v S, E; 1968 v E, S, Ni; 1969 v WG, EG, R of UK; 1970 v EG; (with Derby Co), E, S, Ni; 1972 v Fi, Cz, E, S; 1973 v E (39)
Hersee, A. M. (Bangor), 1886 v S, Ni (2)
Hersee, R. (Llandudno), 1886 v Ni (1)
Hewitt, R. (Cardiff C), 1958 v Ni, Is, Se, H, Br (5)

Hewitt, T. J. (Wrexham), 1911 v E, S, Ni; (with Chelsea), 1913 v E, S, Ni; (with South Liverpool), 1914 v E, S (8)
Heywood, D. (Druids), 1879 v E (1)
Hibbott, H. (Newtown Excelsior), 1880 v E, S; (with Newtown), 1885 v S (3)
Higham, G. O. (Oswestry), 1878 v S; 1879 v E (2)
Hill, M. R. (Ipswich T), 1972 v Cz, R (2)
Hockey, T. (Sheffield U), 1972 v Fi, R; 1973 v E (2); (with Norwich C), Pol, S, E, Ni; (with Aston Villa), 1974 v Pol (9)
Hoddinott, T. F. (Watford), 1921 v E, S (2)
Hodges, G. (Wimbledon), 1984 v N (sub), Is (sub); 1987 v USSR, Fi, Cz; (with Newcastle U), 1988 v D; (with Watford), D (sub), Cz (sub), Se, Ma (sub), I (sub); 1990 v Se, Cr; (with Sheffield U), 1992 v Br (sub), Ei (sub), A; 1996 v G (sub), I (18)
Hodgkinson, A. V. (Southampton), 1908 v Ni (1)
Holden, A. (Chester C), 1984 v Is (sub) (1)
Hole, B. G. (Cardiff C), 1963 v Ni; 1964 v Ni; 1965 v S, E, Ni, D, Gr (2), USSR, I; 1966 v E, S, Ni, USSR, D, Br (2), Ch; (with Blackburn R), 1967 v S, E, Ni; 1968 v E, S, Ni, WG; (with Aston Villa), 1969 v I, WG, EG; 1970 v I; (with Swansea C), 1971 v R (30)
Hole, W. J. (Swansea T), 1921 v Ni; 1922 v E; 1923 v E, Ni; 1928 v E, S, Ni; 1929 v E, S (9)
Hollins, D. M. (Newcastle U), 1962 v Br (sub), M; 1963 v Ni, H; 1964 v E; 1965 v Ni, Gr, I; 1966 v S, D, Br (11)
Hopkins, I. J. (Brentford), 1935 v S, Ni; 1936 v E, Ni; 1937 v E, S, Ni; 1938 v E, Ni; 1939 v E, S, Ni (12)
Hopkins, J. (Fulham), 1983 v Ni, Br; 1984 v N, R, Bul, Y, S, E, Ni, N, Is; 1985 v Ic (1 + 1 sub), N; (with C Palace), 1990 v Ho, Cr (16)
Hopkins, M. (Tottenham H), 1956 v Ni; 1957 v Ni, S, E, Cz (2), EG; 1958 v E, S, Ni, EG, Is (2), H (2), M, Se, Br; 1959 v E, S, Ni; 1960 v E, S; 1961 v Ni, H, Sp (2); 1962 v Ni, Br (2), M; 1963 v S, Ni, H (34)
Horne, B. (Portsmouth), 1988 v D (sub), Y, Se (sub), Ma, I; 1989 v Ho, Fi, Is; (with Southampton), Se, WG; 1990 v WG (sub), Ei, Se, Cr; 1991 v D, Bel (2), L, Ei, Ic, Pol, WG; 1992 v Br, G, L, Ei, A, R, Ho, Arg, J; (with Everton), 1993 v Fa, Cy, Bel, Ei, Bel, RCS, Fa; 1994 v RCS, Cy, R, N, Se, Es; 1995 v Mol, Ge, Bul, G, Ge; 1996 v Mol, G, I, Sw, Sm; (with Birmingham C), 1997 v Sm, Ho, T, Ei, Bel (59)
Howell, E. G. (Builth), 1888 v Ni; 1890 v E; 1891 v E (3)
Howells, R. G. (Cardiff C), 1954 v E, S (2)
Hugh, A. R. (Newport Co), 1930 v Ni (1)
Hughes, A. (Rhos), 1894 v E, S (2)
Hughes, A. (Chirk), 1907 v Ni (1)
Hughes, C. M. (Luton T), 1992 v Ho (sub); 1994 v N (sub), Se (sub), Es; 1996 v Alb; 1997 v Ei (sub); (with Wimbledon), 1998 v T, Bel (8)
Hughes, E. (Everton), 1899 v S, Ni; (with Tottenham H), 1901 v S; 1902 v Ni; 1904 v E, Ni, S; 1905 v E, Ni, S; 1906 v E, Ni; 1907 v E (14)
Hughes, E. (Wrexham), 1906 v S; (with Nottingham F), 1906 v Ni; 1908 v S, E; 1910 v Ni, E, S; 1911 v Ni, E, S; (with Wrexham), 1912 v Ni, E, S; (with Manchester C), 1913 v E, S; 1914 v Ni (16)
Hughes, F. W. (Northwich Victoria), 1882 v E, Ni; 1883 v E, Ni, S; 1884 v S (6)
Hughes, I. (Luton T), 1951 v E, Ni, P, Sw (4)
Hughes, J. (Cambridge University), 1877 v S; (with Aberystwyth), 1879 v S (2)
Hughes, J. (Liverpool), 1905 v E, S, Ni (3)
Hughes, J. I. (Blackburn R), 1935 v Ni (1)
Hughes, L. M. (Manchester U), 1984 v E, Ni; 1985 v Ic, Sp, Ic, N, S, Sp, N; 1986 v S, H, U; (with Barcelona), 1987 v USSR, Cz; 1988 v D (2), Cz, Se, Ma, I; (with Manchester U), 1989 v Ho, Fi, Is, Se, WG; 1990 v Fi, WG, Cr; 1991 v D, Bel (2), L, Ic, Pol, WG; 1992 v Br, G, L, Ei, R, Ho, Arg, J; 1993 v Fa, Cy, Bel, Ei, Bel, RCS, Fa; 1994 v RCS, Cy, N; 1995 v Ge, Bul, G, Ge; (with Chelsea), 1996 v Mol, I, Sm; 1997 v Sm, Ho, T, Ei, Bel; 1998 v T (66)
Hughes, P. W. (Bangor), 1887 v Ni; 1889 v Ni, E (3)
Hughes, W. (Bootle), 1891 v E; 1892 v S, Ni (3)
Hughes, W. A. (Blackburn R), 1949 v E, Ni, P, Bel, Sw (5)
Hughes, W. M. (Birmingham), 1938 v E, Ni, S; 1939 v E, Ni, S, F; 1947 v E, S, Ni (10)
Humphreys, J. V. (Everton), 1947 v Ni (1)
Humphreys, R. (Druids), 1888 v Ni (1)
Hunter, A. H. (FA of Wales Secretary), 1887 v Ni (1)

Jackett, K. (Watford), 1983 v N, Y, E, Bul, S; 1984 v N, R, Y, S, Ni, N, Is; 1985 v Ic, Sp, Ic, N, S, Sp, N; 1986 v S, H, S.Ar, Ei, Ca (2); 1987 v Fi (2); 1988 v D, Cz, Y, Se (31)
Jackson, W. (St Helens Rec), 1899 v Ni (1)
James, E. (Chirk), 1893 v E, Ni; 1894 v E, S, Ni; 1898 v S, E; 1899 v Ni (8)

James, E. G. (Blackpool), 1966 v Br (2), Ch; 1967 v Ni; 1968 v S; 1971 v Cz, S, E, Ni (9)

James, L. (Burnley), 1972 v Cz, R, S (sub); 1973 v E (3), Pol, S, Ni; 1974 v Pol, E, S, Ni; 1975 v A, H (2), L (2), S, E, Ni; 1976 v A; (with Derby Co), S, E, Y (2), Ni; 1977 v WG, S (2), Cz, E, Ni; 1978 v K (2); (with QPR), WG; (with Burnley), 1979 v T; (with Swansea C), 1980 v E, S, Ni, Ic; 1981 v T, Ei, T, S, E; 1982 v Cz, Ic, USSR, E (sub), S, Ni, F; (with Sunderland), 1983 v E (sub) (54)

James, R. M. (Swansea C), 1979 v Ma, WG (sub), S, E, Ni, Ma; 1980 v WG; 1982 v Cz (sub), Ic, Sp, E, S, Ni, F; 1983 v N, Y, E, Bul; (with Stoke C), 1984 v N, R, Bul, Y, S, E, Ni, N, Is; 1985 v Ic, Sp, Ic; (with QPR), N, S, Sp, N; 1986 v S, S.Ar, Ei, U, Ca (2); 1987 v Fi (2), USSR, Cz; (with Leicester C), 1988 v D (2); (with Swansea C), Y (47)

James, W. (West Ham U), 1931 v Ni; 1932 v Ni (2)

Jarrett, R. H. (Ruthin), 1889 v Ni; 1890 v S (2)

Jarvis, A. L. (Hull C), 1967 v S, E, Ni (3)

Jenkins, E. (Lovell's Ath), 1925 v E (1)

Jenkins, J. (Brighton), 1924 v Ni, E, S; 1925 v S, Ni; 1926 v E, S; 1927 v S (8)

Jenkins, R. W. (Rhyl), 1902 v Ni (1)

Jenkins, S. R. (Swansea C), 1996 v G; (with Huddersfield T), Alb, I; 1997 v Ho (sub), T, S; 1998 v T, Bel, Br, Jam (10)

Jenkyns, C. A. L. (Small Heath), 1892 v E, S, Ni; 1895 v E; (with Woolwich Arsenal), 1896 v S; (with Newton Heath), 1897 v Ni; (with Walsall), 1898 v S, E (8)

Jennings, W. (Bolton W), 1914 v E, S; 1920 v S; 1923 v Ni, E; 1924 v E, S, Ni; 1927 v S, Ni; 1929 v S (11)

John, R. F. (Arsenal), 1923 v S, Ni; 1925 v Ni; 1926 v E; 1927 v E; 1928 v E, Ni; 1930 v E, S; 1932 v E; 1933 v F, Ni; 1935 v Ni; 1936 v S; 1937 v E (15)

John, W. R. (Walsall), 1931 v Ni; (with Stoke C), 1933 v E, S, Ni, F; 1934 v E, S; (with Preston NE), 1935 v E, S; (with Sheffield U), 1936 v E, S, Ni; (with Swansea T), 1939 v E, S (14)

Johnson, M. G. (Swansea T), 1964 v Ni (1)

Jones, A. (Port Vale), 1987 v Fi, Cz (sub); 1988 v D, (with Charlton Ath), D (sub), Cz (sub); 1990 v Hol (sub) (6)

Jones, A. F. (Oxford University), 1877 v S (1)

Jones, A. T. (Nottingham F), 1905 v E; (with Notts Co), 1906 v E (2)

Jones, Bryn (Wolverhampton W), 1935 v Ni; 1936 v E, S, Ni; 1937 v E, S, Ni; 1938 v E, S, Ni; (with Arsenal), 1939 v E, S, Ni; 1947 v S, Ni; 1948 v E; 1949 v S (17)

Jones, B. S. (Swansea T), 1963 v S, E, Ni, H (2); 1964 v S, Ni; (with Plymouth Arg), 1965 v D; (with Cardiff C), 1969 v S, E, Ni, I (sub), WG, EG, R of UK (15)

Jones, Charlie (Nottingham F), 1926 v E; 1927 v S, Ni; 1928 v E; (with Arsenal), 1930 v E, S; 1932 v E; 1933 v F (8)

Jones, Cliff (Swansea T), 1954 v A; 1956 v E, Ni, S, A; 1957 v E, S, Ni, Cz (2), EG; 1958 v EG, E, S, Is (2); (with Tottenham H), 1958 v Ni, H (2), M, Se, Br; 1959 v Ni; 1960 v E, S, Ni; 1961 v S, E, Ni, Sp, H, Ei; 1962 v E, Ni, S, Br (2), M; 1963 v S, Ni, H; 1964 v E, S, Ni; 1965 v E, S, Ni, D, Gr (2), USSR, I; 1967 v S, E; 1968 v E, S, WG; (with Fulham), 1969 v I, R of UK (59)

Jones, C. W. (Birmingham), 1935 v Ni; 1939 v F (2)

Jones, D. (Chirk), 1888 v S, Ni; (with Bolton W), 1889 v E, S, Ni; 1890 v E; 1891 v S; 1892 v Ni; 1893 v E; 1894 v E; 1895 v E; 1898 v S; (with Manchester C), 1900 v E, Ni (14)

Jones, D. E. (Norwich C), 1976 v S, E (sub); 1978 v S, Cz, WG, Ir, E; 1980 v E (8)

Jones, D. O. (Leicester C), 1934 v E, Ni; 1935 v E, S; 1936 v E, Ni; 1937 v Ni (7)

Jones, Evan (Chelsea), 1910 v S, Ni; (with Oldham Ath), 1911 v E, S; 1912 v E, S; (with Bolton W), 1914 v Ni (7)

Jones, F. R. (Bangor), 1885 v E, Ni; 1886 v S (3)

Jones, F. W. (Small Heath), 1893 v S (1)

Jones, G. P. (Wrexham), 1907 v S, Ni (2)

Jones, H. (Aberaman), 1902 v Ni (1)

Jones, Humphrey (Bangor), 1885 v E, Ni, S; 1886 v E, Ni, S; (with Queen's Park), 1887 v E; (with East Stirlingshire), 1889 v E, Ni; 1890 v E, S, Ni; (with Queen's Park), 1891 v E, S (14)

Jones, Ivor (Swansea T), 1920 v S, Ni; 1921 v Ni, E; 1922 v S, Ni; (with WBA), 1923 v E, Ni; 1924 v S; 1926 v Ni (10)

Jones, Jeffrey (Llandrindod Wells), 1908 v Ni; 1909 v Ni; 1910 v S (3)

Jones, J. (Druids), 1876 v S (1)

Jones, J. (Berwyn Rangers), 1883 v S, Ni; 1884 v S (3)

Jones, J. (Wrexham), 1925 v Ni (1)

Jones, J. L. (Sheffield U), 1895 v E, S, Ni; 1896 v Ni, S, E; 1897 v Ni, S, E; (with Tottenham H), 1898 v Ni, E, S; 1899 v S, Ni; 1900 v S; 1902 v E, S, Ni; 1904 v E, S, Ni (21)

Jones, J. Love (Stoke C), 1906 v S; (with Middlesbrough), 1910 v Ni (2)

Jones, J. O. (Bangor), 1901 v S, Ni (2)

Jones, J. P. (Liverpool), 1976 v A, E, S; 1977 v WG, S (2), Cz, E, Ni; 1978 v K (2), S, Cz, WG, Ir, E, S, Ni; (with Wrexham), 1979 v Ma, T, WG, S, E, Ni, Ma; 1980 v Ei, WG, T, E, S, Ni, Ic; 1981 v T, Ei, T, S, E, USSR; 1982 v Cz, Ic, USSR, Sp, E, S, Ni, F; 1983 v N; (with Chelsea), Y, E, Bul, S, Ni, Br; 1984 v N, R, Bul, Y, S, E, Ni, N, Is; 1985 v Ic, N, S, N; (with Huddersfield T), 1986 v S, H, Ei, U, Ca (2) (72)

Jones, J. T. (Stoke C), 1912 v E, S, Ni; 1913 v E, Ni; 1914 v S, Ni; 1920 v E, S, Ni; (with C Palace), 1921 v E, S; 1922 v E, S, Ni (15)

Jones, K. (Aston Villa), 1950 v S (1)

Jones, Leslie J. (Cardiff C), 1933 v F; (with Coventry C), 1935 v Ni; 1936 v S; 1937 v E, S, Ni; (with Arsenal), 1938 v E, S, Ni; 1939 v E, S (11)

Jones, P. L. (Liverpool), 1997 v S (sub); (with Tranmere R), 1998 v T (sub) (2)

Jones, P. S. (Stockport Co), 1997 v S (sub); (with Southampton), 1998 v T (sub), Br, Jam, Ma (5)

Jones, P. W. (Bristol R), 1971 v Fi (1)

Jones, R. (Bangor), 1887 v S; 1889 v E; (with Crewe Alex), 1890 v E (3)

Jones, R. (Leicester Fosse), 1898 v S (1)

Jones, R. (Druids), 1899 v S (1)

Jones, R. (Bangor), 1900 v S, Ni (2)

Jones, R. (Millwall), 1906 v S, Ni (2)

Jones, R. A. (Druids), 1884 v E, Ni, S; 1885 v S (4)

Jones, R. A. (Sheffield W), 1994 v Es (1)

Jones, R. S. (Everton), 1894 v Ni (1)

Jones, S. (Wrexham), 1887 v Ni; (with Chester), 1890 v S (2)

Jones, S. (Wrexham), 1893 v S, Ni; (with Burton Swifts), 1895 v S; 1896 v E, Ni; (with Druids), 1899 v E (6)

Jones, T. (Manchester U), 1926 v Ni; 1927 v E, Ni; 1930 v Ni (4)

Jones, T. D. (Aberdare), 1908 v Ni (1)

Jones, T. G. (Everton), 1938 v Ni; 1939 v E, S, Ni; 1947 v E, S; 1948 v E, S, Ni; 1949 v E, Ni, P, Bel, Sw; 1950 v E, S, Bel (17)

Jones, T. J. (Sheffield W), 1932 v Ni; 1933 v F (2)

Jones, V. P. (Wimbledon), 1995 v Bul (2), G, Ge; 1996 v Sw; 1997 v Ho, T, Ei, Bel (9)

Jones, W. E. A. (Swansea T), 1947 v E, S; (with Tottenham H), 1949 v E, S (4)

Jones, W. J. (Aberdare), 1901 v E, S; (with West Ham U), 1902 v S, E (4)

Jones, W. Lot (Manchester C), 1905 v E, Ni; 1906 v E, S, Ni; 1907 v E, S, Ni; 1908 v S; 1909 v E, S, Ni; 1910 v E; 1911 v E; 1913 v E, S; 1914 v S, Ni; (with Southend U), 1920 v E, Ni (20)

Jones, W. P. (Druids), 1889 v E, Ni; (with Wynstay), 1890 v S, Ni (4)

Jones, W. R. (Aberystwyth), 1897 v S (1)

Keenor, F. C. (Cardiff C), 1920 v E, Ni; 1921 v E, Ni, S; 1922 v Ni; 1923 v E, Ni, S; 1924 v E, Ni, S; 1925 v E, Ni, S; 1926 v S; 1927 v E, Ni, S; 1928 v E, Ni, S; 1929 v E, Ni, S; 1930 v E, Ni, S; 1931 v E, Ni, S; (with Crewe Alex), 1933 v S (32)

Kelly, F. C. (Wrexham), 1899 v S, Ni; (with Druids), 1902 v Ni (3)

Kelsey, A. J. (Arsenal), 1954 v Ni, A; 1955 v S, Ni, Y; 1956 v E, Ni, S, A; 1957 v E, Ni, S, Cz (2), EG; 1958 v E, S, Ni, Is (2), H (2), M, Se, Br; 1959 v E, S; 1960 v E, Ni, S; 1961 v E, Ni, S, H, Sp (2); 1962 v E, S, Ni, Br (2) (41)

Kenrick, S. L. (Druids), 1876 v S; 1877 v S; (with Oswestry), 1879 v S, E; (with Shropshire Wanderers), 1881 v E (5)

Ketley, C. F. (Druids), 1882 v Ni (1)

King, J. (Swansea T), 1955 v E (1)

Kinsey, N. (Norwich C), 1951 v Ni, P, Sw; 1952 v E; (with Birmingham C), 1954 v Ni; 1956 v E, S (7)

Knill, A. R. (Swansea C), 1989 v Ho (1)

Krzywicki, R. L. (WBA), 1970 v EG, I; (with Huddersfield T), Ni, E, S; 1971 v R, Fi; 1972 v Cz (sub) (8)

Lambert, R. (Liverpool), 1947 v S; 1948 v E; 1949 v P, Bel, Sw (5)

Latham, G. (Liverpool), 1905 v E, S; 1906 v S; 1907 v E, S, Ni; 1908 v E; 1909 v Ni; (with Southport Central), 1910 v E; (with Cardiff C), 1913 v Ni (10)

Law, B. J. (QPR), 1990 v Se (1)

Lawrence, E. (Clapton Orient), 1930 v Ni; (with Notts Co), 1932 v S (2)

Lawrence, S. (Swansea T), 1932 v Ni; 1933 v F; 1934 v S, E, Ni; 1935 v E, S; 1936 v S (8)

Lea, A. (Wrexham), 1889 v E; 1891 v S, Ni; 1893 v Ni (4)

Lea, C. (Ipswich T), 1965 v Ni, I (2)

Leary, P. (Bangor), 1889 v Ni (1)

Leek, K. (Leicester C), 1961 v S, E, Ni, H, Sp (2); (with Newcastle U), 1962 v S; (with Birmingham C), v Br (sub),

M; 1963 v E; 1965 v S, Gr; (with Northampton T), 1965 v Gr (13)

Legg, A. (Birmingham C), 1996 v Sw, Sm (sub); 1997 v Ho (sub), Ei (4)

Lever, A. R. (Leicester C), 1953 v S (1)

Lewis, B. (Chester), 1891 v Ni; (with Wrexham), 1892 v S, E, Ni; (with Middlesbrough), 1893 v S, E; (with Wrexham), 1894 v S, E, Ni; 1895 v S (10)

Lewis, D. (Arsenal), 1927 v E; 1928 v Ni; 1930 v E (3)

Lewis, D. (Swansea C), 1983 v Br (sub) (1)

Lewis, D. J. (Swansea T), 1933 v E, S (2)

Lewis, D. M. (Bangor), 1890 v Ni, S (2)

Lewis, J. (Bristol R), 1906 v E (1)

Lewis, J. (Cardiff C), 1926 v S (1)

Lewis, T. (Wrexham), 1881 v E, S (2)

Lewis, W. (Bangor), 1885 v E; 1886 v E, S; 1887 v E, S; 1888 v E; 1889 v E, Ni, S; (with Crewe Alex), 1890 v E; 1891 v E, S; 1892 v E, S, Ni; 1894 v E, S, Ni; (with Chester), 1895 v S, Ni, E; 1896 v E, S, Ni; (with Manchester C), 1897 v E, S; (with Chester), 1898 v Ni (27)

Lewis, W. L. (Swansea T), 1927 v E, Ni; 1928 v E, Ni; 1929 v S; (with Huddersfield T), 1930 v E (6)

Llewellyn. C. M. (Norwich C), 1998 v Ma (sub), Tun (sub) (2)

Lloyd, B. W. (Wrexham), 1976 v A, E, S (3)

Lloyd, J. W. (Wrexham), 1879 v S; (with Newtown), 1885 v S (2)

Lloyd, R. A. (Ruthin), 1891 v Ni; 1895 v S (2)

Lockley, A. (Chirk), 1898 v Ni (1)

Lovell, S. (C Palace), 1982 v USSR (sub); (with Millwall), 1985 v N; 1986 v S (sub), H (sub), Ca (1+1 sub) (6)

Lowrie, G. (Coventry C), 1948 v E, S, Ni; (with Newcastle U), 1949 v P (4)

Lowndes, S. (Newport Co), 1983 v S (sub), Br (sub); (with Millwall), 1985 v N (sub); 1986 v S.Ar (sub), Ei, U, Ca (2); (with Barnsley), 1987 v Fi (sub); 1988 v Se (sub) (10)

Lucas, P. M. (Leyton Orient), 1962 v Ni, M; 1963 v S, E (4)

Lucas, W. H. (Swansea T), 1949 v S, Ni, P, Bel, Sw; 1950 v E; 1951 v E (7)

Lumberg, A. (Wrexham), 1929 v Ni; 1930 v E, S; (with Wolverhampton W), 1932 v S (4)

McCarthy, T. P. (Wrexham), 1899 v Ni (1)

McMillan, R. (Shrewsbury Engineers), 1881 v E, S (2)

Maguire, G. T. (Portsmouth), 1990 v Fi (sub), Ho, WG, Ei, Se; 1992 v Br (sub), G (7)

Mahoney, J. F. (Stoke C), 1968 v E; 1969 v EG; 1971 v Cz; 1973 v E (3), Pol, S, Ni; 1974 v Pol, E, S, Ni; 1975 v A, H (2), L (2), S, Ni; 1976 v A, Y (2), E, Ni; 1977 v WG, Cz, S, E, Ni; (with Middlesbrough), 1978 v K (2), S, Cz, Ir, E (sub), S, Ni; 1979 v WG, S, E, Ni, Ma; (with Swansea C), 1980 v Ei, WG, T (sub); 1982 v Ic, USSR; 1983 v Y, E (51)

Mardon, P. J. (WBA), 1996 v G (sub) (1)

Marriott, A. (Wrexham), 1996 v Sw (sub); 1997 v S; 1998 v Bel, Br (sub), Tun (5)

Martin, T. J. (Newport Co), 1930 v Ni (1)

Marustik, C. (Swansea C), 1982 v Sp, E, S, Ni, F; 1983 v N (4)

Mates, J. (Chirk), 1891 v Ni; 1897 v E, S (3)

Mathews, R. W. (Liverpool), 1921 v Ni; (with Bristol C), 1923 v E; (with Bradford), 1926 v Ni (3)

Matthews, W. (Chester), 1905 v Ni; 1908 v E (2)

Matthias, J. S. (Brymbo), 1896 v S, Ni; (with Shrewsbury), 1897 v E, S; (with Wolverhampton W), 1899 v S (5)

Matthias, T. J. (Wrexham), 1914 v S, E; 1920 v Ni, S, E; 1921 v S, E, Ni; 1922 v S, E, Ni; 1923 v S (12)

Mays, A. W. (Wrexham), 1929 v Ni (1)

Medwin, T. C. (Swansea T), 1953 v Ni, F, Y; (with Tottenham H), 1957 v E, S, Ni, Cz (2), EG; 1958 v E, S, Ni, Is (2), H (2), M, Br; 1959 v E, S, Ni; 1960 v E, S, Ni; 1961 v S, Ei, E, Sp; 1963 v E, H (30)

Melville, A. K. (Swansea C), 1990 v WG, Ei, Se, Cr (sub); (with Oxford U), 1991 v Ic, Pol, WG; 1992 v Br, G, L, R, Ho, J (sub); 1993 v RCS, Fa (sub); (with Sunderland), 1994 v RCS (sub), R, N, Se, Es; 1995 v Alb, Mol (sub), Ge, Bul; 1996 v G, Alb, Sm; 1997 v Sm, Ho (2), T; 1998 v T (32)

Meredith, S. (Chirk), 1900 v S; 1901 v S, E, Ni; (with Stoke C), 1902 v E; 1903 v Ni; 1904 v E; (with Leyton), 1907 v E (8)

Meredith, W. H. (Manchester C), 1895 v E, Ni; 1896 v E, Ni; 1897 v E, Ni, S; 1898 v E, Ni; 1899 v E; 1900 v E, Ni; 1901 v E, Ni; 1902 v E, S; 1903 v E, S, Ni; 1904 v E; 1905 v E, S; (with Manchester U), 1907 v E, S, Ni; 1908 v E, Ni; 1909 v E, S, Ni; 1910 v E, S, Ni; 1911 v E, S, Ni; 1912 v E, S, Ni; 1913 v E, S, Ni; 1914 v E, S, Ni; 1920 v E, S, Ni (48)

Mielczarek, R. (Rotherham U), 1971 v Fi (1)

Millership, H. (Rotherham Co), 1920 v E, S, Ni; 1921 v E, S, Ni (6)

Millington, A. H. (WBA), 1963 v S, E, H; (with C Palace), 1965 v E, USSR; (with Peterborough U), 1966 v Ch, Br; 1967 v E, Ni; 1968 v Ni, WG; 1969 v I, EG; (with Swansea T), 1970 v E, S, Ni; 1971 v Cz, Fi; 1972 v Fi (sub), Cz, R (21)

Mills, T. J. (Clapton Orient), 1934 v E, Ni; (with Leicester C), 1935 v E, S (4)

Mills-Roberts, R. H. (St Thomas' Hospital), 1885 v E, S, Ni; 1886 v E; 1887 v E; (with Preston NE), 1888 v E, Ni; (with Llanberis), 1892 v E (8)

Moore, G. (Cardiff C), 1960 v E, S, Ni; 1961 v Ei, Sp; (with Chelsea), 1962 v Br; 1963 v Ni, H; (with Manchester U), 1964 v S, Ni; (with Northampton T), 1966 v Ni, Ch; (with Charlton Ath), 1969 v S, E, Ni, R of UK; 1970 v E, S, Ni, I; 1971 v R (21)

Morgan, J. R. (Cambridge University), 1877 v S; (with Swansea T), 1879 v S; (with Derby School Staff), 1880 v E, S; 1881 v E, S; 1882 v E, S, Ni; (with Swansea T), 1883 v E (10)

Morgan, J. T. (Wrexham), 1905 v Ni (1)

Morgan-Owen, H. (Oxford University), 1902 v S; 1906 v E, Ni; (with Welshpool), 1907 v S (5)

Morgan-Owen, M. M. (Oxford University), 1897 v S, Ni; 1898 v E, S; 1899 v S; 1900 v E; (with Corinthians), 1901 v S, E; 1903 v S; 1906 v S, E, Ni; 1907 v E (13)

Morley, E. J. (Swansea T), 1925 v E; (with Clapton Orient), 1929 v E, S, Ni (4)

Morris, A. G. (Aberystwyth), 1896 v E, Ni, S; (with Swindon T), 1897 v E; 1898 v S; (with Nottingham F), 1899 v E, S; 1903 v E, S; 1905 v E, S; 1907 v E, S; 1908 v E; 1910 v E, S, Ni; 1911 v E, S, Ni; 1912 v E (21)

Morris, C. (Chirk), 1900 v E, S, Ni; (with Derby Co), 1901 v E, S, Ni; 1902 v E; 1903 v E, S, Ni; 1904 v Ni; 1905 v E, S, Ni; 1906 v S; 1907 v S; 1908 v E, S; 1909 v E, S, Ni; 1910 v E, S, Ni; (with Huddersfield T), 1911 v E, S, Ni (27)

Morris, E. (Chirk), 1893 v E, S, Ni (3)

Morris, H. (Sheffield U), 1894 v S; (with Manchester C), 1896 v E; (with Grimsby T), 1897 v E (3)

Morris, J. (Oswestry), 1887 v S (1)

Morris, J. (Chirk), 1898 v Ni (1)

Morris, R. (Chirk), 1900 v E, Ni; 1901 v Ni; 1902 v S; (with Shrewsbury T), 1903 v E, Ni (6)

Morris, R. (Druids), 1902 v E, S; (with Newtown), Ni; (with Liverpool), 1903 v S, Ni; 1904 v E, S, Ni; (with Leeds C), 1906 v S; (with Grimsby T), 1907 v Ni; (with Plymouth Arg), 1908 v Ni (11)

Morris, S. (Birmingham), 1937 v E, S; 1938 v E, S; 1939 v F (5)

Morris, W. (Burnley), 1947 v Ni; 1949 v E; 1952 v S, Ni, R of UK (5)

Moulsdale, J. R. B. (Corinthians), 1925 v Ni (1)

Murphy, J. P. (WBA), 1933 v F, E, Ni; 1934 v E, S; 1935 v E, S, Ni; 1936 v E, S, Ni; 1937 v S, Ni; 1938 v E, S (15)

Nardiello, D. (Coventry C), 1978 v Cz, WG (sub) (2)

Neal, J. E. (Colwyn Bay), 1931 v E, S (2)

Neilson, A. B. (Newcastle U), 1992 v Ei; 1994 v Se, Es; 1995 v Ge; (with Southampton), 1997 v Ho (5)

Newnes, J. (Nelson), 1926 v Ni (1)

Newton, L. F. (Cardiff Corinthians), 1912 v Ni (1)

Nicholas, D. S. (Stoke C), 1923 v S; (with Swansea T), 1927 v E, Ni (3)

Nicholas, P. (C Palace), 1979 v S (sub), Ni (sub), Ma; 1980 v Ei, WG, T, E, S, Ni, U; 1981 v T, Cz, E; (with Arsenal), T, S, E, USSR; 1982 v Cz, Ic, USSR, Sp, E, S, Ni, F; 1983 v Y, Bul, S, Ni; 1984 v N, Bul, N, Is; (with C Palace), 1985 v Sp; (with Luton T), N, S, Sp, N; 1986 v S, H, S.Ar, Ei, U, Ca (2); 1987 v Fi (2) USSR, Cz; (with Aberdeen), 1988 v D (2), Cz, Y, Se; (with Chelsea), 1989 v Ho, Fi, Is, Se, WG; 1990 v Fi, Ho, WG, Ei, Se, Cr; 1991 v D (sub), Bel, L, Ei; (with Watford), Bel, Pol, WG; 1992 v L (73)

Nicholls, J. (Newport Co), 1924 v E, Ni; (with Cardiff C), 1925 v S, E (4)

Niedzwiecki, E. A. (Chelsea), 1985 v N (sub); 1988 v D (2)

Nock, W. (Newtown), 1897 v Ni (1)

Nogan, L. M. (Watford), 1992 v A (sub); (with Reading), 1996 v Mol (2)

Norman, A. J. (Hull C), 1986 v Ei (sub), U, Ca; 1988 v Ma, I (5)

Nurse, M. T. G. (Swansea T), 1960 v E, Ni; 1961 v S, E, H, Ni, Ei, Sp (2); (with Middlesbrough), 1963 v E, H; 1964 v S (12)

O'Callaghan, E. (Tottenham H), 1929 v Ni; 1930 v S; 1932 v S, E; 1933 v Ni, S, E; 1934 v Ni, S, E; 1935 v E (11)

Oliver, A. (Blackburn R), 1905 v E; (with Bangor), S (2)

O'Sullivan, P. A. (Brighton), 1973 v S (sub); 1976 v S; 1979 v Ma (sub) (3)

Oster, J. M. (Everton), 1998 v Br, Jam (2)

Owen, D. (Oswestry), 1879 v E (1)
Owen, E. (Ruthin Grammar School), 1884 v E, Ni, S (3)
Owen, G. (Chirk), 1888 v S; (with Newton Heath), 1889 v S, Ni; 1893 v Ni (4)
Owen, J. (Newton Heath), 1892 v E (1)
Owen, Trevor (Crewe Alex), 1899 v E, S (2)
Owen, T. (Oswestry), 1879 v E (1)
Owen, W. (Chirk), 1884 v E; 1885 v Ni; 1887 v E; 1888 v E; 1889 v E, Ni, S; 1890 v S, Ni; 1891 v E, S, Ni; 1892 v E, S; 1893 v S, Ni (16)
Owen, W. P. (Ruthin), 1880 v E, S; 1881 v E, S; 1882 v E, S, Ni; 1883 v E, S; 1884 v E, S, Ni (12)
Owens, J. (Wrexham), 1902 v S (1)

Page, M. E. (Birmingham C), 1971 v Fi; 1972 v S, Ni; 1973 v E (1+1 sub), Ni; 1974 v S, Ni; 1975 v H, L, S, E, Ni; 1976 v E, Y (2), E, Ni; 1977 v WG, S; 1978 v K (sub+1), WG, Ir, E, S; 1979 v Ma, WG (28)
Page, R. J. (Watford), 1997 v T, Bel, S; 1998 v T, Bel (sub), Br (6)
Palmer, D. (Swansea T), 1957 v Cz; 1958 v E, EG (3)
Parris, J. E. (Bradford), 1932 v Ni (1)
Parry, B. J. (Swansea T), 1951 v S (1)
Parry, C. (Everton), 1891 v S; 1893 v E; 1894 v E; 1895 v E, S; (with Newtown), 1896 v E, S, Ni; 1897 v Ni; 1898 v E, S, Ni (13)
Parry, E. (Liverpool), 1922 v S; 1923 v E, Ni; 1925 v Ni; 1926 v Ni (5)
Parry, M. (Liverpool), 1901 v E, S, Ni; 1902 v E, S, Ni; 1903 v E, S; 1904 v E, Ni; 1906 v E; 1908 v E, S, Ni; 1909 v E, S (16)
Parry, T. D. (Oswestry), 1900 v E, S, Ni; 1901 v E, S, Ni; 1902 v E (7)
Parry, W. (Newtown), 1895 v Ni (1)
Pascoe, C. (Swansea C), 1984 v N, Is; (with Sunderland), 1989 v Fi, Is, WG (sub); 1990 v Ho (sub), WG (sub); 1991 v Ei, Ic (sub); 1992 v Br (10)
Paul, R. (Swansea T), 1949 v E, S, Ni, P, Sw; 1950 v E, S, Ni, Bel; (with Manchester C), 1951 v E, S, Ni, P, Sw; 1952 v E, S, Ni, R of UK; 1953 v S, E, Ni, F, Y; 1954 v E, S, Ni; 1955 v S, E, Y; 1956 v E, Ni, S, A (33)
Peake, E. (Aberystwyth), 1908 v Ni; (with Liverpool), 1909 v Ni, S, E; 1910 v S, Ni; 1911 v Ni; 1912 v E; 1913 v E, Ni; 1914 v Ni (11)
Peers, E. J. (Wolverhampton W), 1914 v Ni, S, E; 1920 v E, S; 1921 v S, Ni, E; (with Port Vale), 1922 v E, S, Ni; 1923 v E (12)
Pembridge, M. A. (Luton T), 1992 v Br, Ei, R (with Derby Co), Ho, J (sub); 1993 v Bel (sub), Ei; 1994 v N (sub); 1995 v Alb (sub), Mol, Ge (sub); (with Sheffield W), 1996 v Mol, G, Alb, Sw, Sm; 1997 v Sm, Ho (2), T, Ei, Bel, S; 1998 v Bel, Br, Jam, Ma, Tun (28)
Perry, E. (Doncaster R), 1938 v E, S, Ni (3)
Perry, J. (Cardiff C), 1994 v N (1)
Phennah, E. (Civil Service), 1878 v S (1)
Phillips, C. (Wolverhampton W), 1931 v Ni; 1932 v E; 1933 v S; 1934 v S, Ni; 1935 v S, Ni; 1936 v S; (with Aston Villa), 1936 v E, Ni; 1938 v S (13)
Phillips, D. (Plymouth Arg), 1984 v E, Ni, N; (with Manchester C), 1985 v Sp, Ic, S, Sp, N; 1986 v S, H, S.Ar, Ei, U; (with Coventry C), 1987 v Fi, Cz; 1988 v D (2), Cz, Y, Se; 1989 v Se, WG; (with Norwich C), 1990 v Fi, Ho, WG, Ei, Se; 1991 v D, Bel, Ic, Pol, WG; 1992 v L, Ei, A, R, Ho (sub), Arg, J; 1993 v Fa, Cy, Bel, Ei, Bel, RCS, Fa; (with Nottingham F), 1994 v RCS, Cy, R, N, Se, Es; 1995 v Alb, Mol, Ge, Bul (2), G, Ge; 1996 v Mol (sub), Alb, I (62)
Phillips, L. (Cardiff C), 1971 v Cz, S, E, Ni; 1972 v Cz, R, S, Ni; 1973 v E; 1974 v Pol (sub), Ni; 1975 v A; (with Aston Villa), H (2), L (2), S, E, Ni; 1976 v A, E, Y (2), E, Ni; 1977 v WG, S (2), Cz, E; 1978 v K (2), S, Cz, WG, E, S; 1979 v Ma; (with Swansea C), T, WG, S, E, Ni, Ma; 1980 v Ei, WG, T, S (sub), Ni, Ic; 1981 v T, Cz, T, S, E, USSR; (with Charlton Ath), 1982 v Cz, USSR (58)
Phillips, T. J. S. (Chelsea), 1973 v E; 1974 v E; 1975 v H (sub); 1978 v K (4)
Phoenix, H. (Wrexham), 1882 v S (1)
Poland, G. (Wrexham), 1939 v Ni, F (2)
Pontin, K. (Cardiff C), 1980 v E (sub), S (2)
Powell, A. (Leeds U), 1947 v E, S; 1948 v E, S, Ni; (with Everton), 1949 v E; 1950 v Bel; (with Birmingham C), 1951 v S (8)
Powell, D. (Wrexham), 1968 v WG; (with Sheffield U), 1969 v S, E, Ni, I, WG; 1970 v E, S, Ni, EG; 1971 v R (11)
Powell, I. V. (QPR), 1947 v E; 1948 v E, S, Ni; (with Aston Villa), 1949 v Bel; 1950 v S, Bel; 1951 v S (8)
Powell, J. (Druids), 1878 v S; 1880 v E, S; 1882 v E, S, Ni; 1883 v E, S, Ni; (with Bolton W), 1884 v E; (with Newton Heath), 1887 v E, S; 1888 v E, S, Ni (15)

Powell, Seth (WBA), 1885 v S; 1886 v E, Ni; 1891 v E, S; 1892 v E, S (7)
Price, H. (Aston Villa), 1907 v S; (with Burton U), 1908 v Ni; (with Wrexham), 1909 v S, E, Ni (5)
Price, J. (Wrexham), 1877 v S; 1878 v S; 1879 v E; 1880 v E, S; 1881 v E, S; (with Druids), 1882 v S, E, Ni; 1883 v S, Ni (12)
Price, P. (Luton T), 1980 v E, S, Ni, Ic; 1981 v T, Cz, Ei, T, S, E, USSR; (with Tottenham H), 1982 v USSR, Sp, F; 1983 v N, Y, E, Bul, S, Ni; 1984 v N, R, Bul, Y, S (sub) (25)
Pring, K. D. (Rotherham U), 1966 v Ch, D; 1967 v Ni (3)
Pritchard, H. K. (Bristol C), 1985 v N (sub) (1)
Pryce-Jones, A. W. (Newtown), 1895 v E (1)
Pryce-Jones, W. E. (Cambridge University), 1887 v S; 1888 v S, E, Ni; 1890 v Ni (5)
Pugh, A. (Rhostyllen), 1889 v S (sub) (1)
Pugh, D. H. (Wrexham), 1896 v S, Ni; 1897 v S, Ni; (with Lincoln C), 1900 v S, Ni; 1901 v S, E (7)
Pugsley, J. (Charlton Ath), 1930 v Ni (1)
Pullen, W. J. (Plymouth Arg), 1926 v E (1)

Rankmore, F. E. J. (Peterborough), 1966 v Ch (sub) (1)
Ratcliffe, K. (Everton), 1981 v Cz, Ei, T, S, E, USSR; 1982 v Cz, Ic, USSR, Sp, E; 1983 v Y, E, Bul, S, Ni, Br; 1984 v N, R, Bul, Y, S, E, Ni, N, Is; 1985 v Ic, Sp, Ic, N, S, Sp; 1986 v S, H, S.Ar, U; 1987 v Fi (2), USSR, Cz; 1988 v D (2), Cz; 1989 v Fi, Is, Se, WG; 1990 v Fi; 1991 v D, Bel (2), L, Ei, Ic, Pol, WG; 1992 v Br, G; (with Cardiff C), 1993 v Bel (59)
Rea, J. C. (Aberystwyth), 1894 v Ni, S, E; 1895 v S; 1896 v S, Ni; 1897 v S, Ni; 1898 v Ni (9)
Ready, K. (QPR), 1997 v Ei; 1998 v Bel, Br, Ma, Tun (5)
Reece, G. I. (Sheffield U), 1966 v E, S, Ni, USSR; 1967 v S; 1969 v R of UK (sub); 1970 v I (sub); 1971 v S, E, Ni, Fi; 1972 v Fi, R, E (sub), S, Ni; (with Cardiff C), 1973 v E (sub), Ni; 1974 v Pol (sub), E, S, Ni; 1975 v A, H (2), L (2), S, Ni (29)
Reed, W. G. (Ipswich T), 1955 v S, Y (2)
Rees, A. (Birmingham C), 1984 v N (sub) (1)
Rees, J. M. (Luton T), 1992 v A (sub) (1)
Rees, R. R. (Coventry C), 1965 v S, E, Ni, D, Gr (2), I, R; 1966 v S, Ni, R, D, Br (2), Ch; 1967 v E, Ni; 1968 v E, S, Ni; (with WBA), 1969 v I; (with Nottingham F), 1969 v WG, EG, S (sub), R of UK; 1970 v E, S, Ni, EG, I; 1971 v Cz, R, E (sub), Ni (sub), Fi; 1972 v Cz (sub), R (39)
Rees, W. (Cardiff C), 1949 v Ni, Bel, Sw; (with Tottenham H), 1950 v Ni (4)
Richards, A. (Barnsley), 1932 v S (1)
Richards, D. (Wolverhampton W), 1931 v Ni; 1933 v E, S, Ni; 1934 v E, S, Ni; 1935 v E, S, Ni; 1936 v S; (with Brentford), 1936 v E, Ni; 1937 v S, E; (with Birmingham), Ni; 1938 v E, S, Ni; 1939 v E, S (21)
Richards, G. (Druids), 1899 v E, S, Ni; (with Oswestry), 1903 v Ni; (with Shrewsbury), 1904 v S; 1905 v Ni (6)
Richards, R. W. (Wolverhampton W), 1920 v E, S; 1921 v Ni; 1922 v E, S; (with West Ham U), 1924 v E, S, Ni; (with Mold), 1926 v S (9)
Richards, S. V. (Cardiff C), 1947 v E (1)
Richards, W. E. (Fulham), 1933 v Ni (1)
Roach, J. (Oswestry), 1885 v Ni (1)
Robbins, W. W. (Cardiff C), 1931 v E, S; 1932 v Ni, E, S; (with WBA), 1933 v F, E, S, Ni; 1934 v S; 1936 v S (11)
Roberts, A. M. (QPR), 1993 v Ei (sub); 1997 v Sm (sub) (2)
Roberts, D. F. (Oxford U), 1973 v Pol, E (sub), Ni; 1974 v E, S; 1975 v A; (with Hull C), L, Ni; 1976 v S, Ni, Y; 1977 v E (sub), Ni; 1978 v K (1+1 sub), S, Ni (17)
Roberts, I. W. (Watford), 1990 v Ho; (with Huddersfield T), 1992 v A, Arg, J; (with Leicester C), 1994 v Se; 1995 v Alb (sub), Mol (7)
Roberts, Jas (Wrexham), 1913 v S, Ni (2)
Roberts, J. (Corwen), 1879 v S; 1880 v E, S; 1882 v E, S, Ni; (with Berwyn R), 1883 v E (7)
Roberts, J. (Ruthin), 1881 v S; 1882 v S (2)
Roberts, J. (Bradford), 1906 v Ni; 1907 v Ni (2)
Roberts, J. G. (Arsenal), 1971 v S, E, Ni, Fi; 1972 v Fi, E, Ni; (with Birmingham C), 1973 v E (2), Pol, S, Ni; 1974 v Pol, E, S, Ni; 1975 v A, H, S, E; 1976 v E, S (22)
Roberts, J. H. (Bolton), 1949 v Bel (1)
Roberts, P. S. (Portsmouth), 1974 v E; 1975 v A, H, L (4)
Roberts, R. (Druids), 1884 v S; (with Bolton W), 1887 v S; 1888 v S, E; 1889 v S, E; 1890 v S; 1892 v Ni; (with Preston NE), S (9)
Roberts, R. (Wrexham), 1886 v Ni; 1887 v Ni; 1891 v Ni (3)
Roberts, R. (Rhos), 1891 v Ni; (with Crewe Alex), 1893 v E (2)
Roberts, R. L. (Chester), 1890 v Ni (1)
Roberts, W. (Llangollen), 1879 v E, S; 1880 v E, S; (with Berwyn R), 1881 v S; 1883 v S (6)
Roberts, W. (Wrexham), 1886 v E, S, Ni; 1887 v Ni (4)

Roberts, W. H. (Ruthin), 1882 v E, S; 1883 v E, S, Ni; (with Rhyl), 1884 v S (6)

Robinson, J. R. C. (Charlton Ath), 1996 v Alb (sub), Sw, Sm; 1997 v Sm, Ho (1 + sub), Ei, S; 1998 v Bel, Br (10)

Rodrigues, P. J. (Cardiff C), 1965 v Ni, Gr (2); 1966 v USSR, E, S, D; (with Leicester C), Ni, Br (2), Ch; 1967 v S; 1968 v E, S, Ni; 1969 v E, Ni, EG, R of UK; 1970 v E, S, Ni, EG; (with Sheffield W), 1971 v R, E, S, Cz, Ni; 1972 v Fi, Cz, R, E, Ni (sub); 1973 v E (3), Pol, S, Ni; 1974 v Pol (40)

Rogers, J. P. (Wrexham), 1896 v E, S, Ni (3)

Rogers, W. (Wrexham), 1931 v E, S (2)

Roose, L. R. (Aberystwyth), 1900 v Ni; (with London Welsh), 1901 v E, S, Ni; (with Stoke C), 1902 v E, S; 1904 v E; (with Everton), 1905 v S, E; (with Stoke C), 1906 v E, S, Ni; 1907 v E, S, Ni; (with Sunderland), 1908 v E, S; 1909 v E, S, Ni; 1910 v E, S, Ni; 1911 v S (24)

Rouse, R. V. (C Palace), 1959 v Ni (1)

Rowlands, A. C. (Tranmere R), 1914 v E (1)

Rowley, T. (Tranmere R), 1959 v Ni (1)

Rush, I. (Liverpool), 1980 v S (sub), Ni; 1981 v E (sub); 1982 v Ic (sub), USSR, E, S, Ni, F; 1983 v N, Y, E, Bul; 1984 v N, R, Bul, Y, S, E, Ni; 1985 v Ic, N, S, Sp; 1986 v S, S.Ar, Ei, U; 1987 v Fi (2), USSR, Cz; (with Juventus), 1988 v D, Cz, Y, Se, Ma, I; (with Liverpool), 1989 v Ho, Fi, Se, WG; 1990 v Fi, Ei; 1991 v D, Bel (2), L, Ei, Pol, WG; 1992 v G, L, R; 1993 v Fa, Cy, Bel (2), RCS, Fa; 1994 v RCS, Cy, R, N, Se, Es; 1995 v Alb, Ge, Bul, G, Ge; 1996 v Mol, I (73)

Russell, M. R. (Merthyr T), 1912 v S, Ni; 1914 v E; (with Plymouth Arg), 1920 v E, S, Ni; 1921 v E, S, Ni; 1922 v E, Ni; 1923 v E, S, Ni; 1924 v E, S, Ni; 1925 v E; 1926 v E, S; 1928 v S; 1929 v E (23)

Sabine, H. W. (Oswestry), 1887 v Ni (1)

Saunders, D. (Brighton & HA), 1986 v Ei (sub), Ca (2); 1987 v Fi, USSR (sub); (with Oxford U), 1988 v Y, Se, Ma, I (sub); 1989 v Ho (sub), Fi; (with Derby Co), Is, Se, WG; 1990 v Fi, Ho, WG, Se, Cr; 1991 v D, Bel (2), L, Ei, Ic, Pol, WG; (with Liverpool), 1992 v Br, G, Ei, R, Ho, Arg, J; 1993 v Fa; (with Aston Villa), Cy, Bel (2), RCS, Fa; 1994 v RCS, Cy, R, N (sub); 1995 v Ge, Bul (2), G, Ge; (with Galatasaray), 1996 v G, Alb, Sm; (with Nottingham F), 1997 v Sm, Ho (2), T, Bel; S; 1998 v T, Bel, Br; (with Sheffield U), Ma, Tun (63)

Savage, R. W. (Crewe Alex), 1996 v Alb (sub), Sw (sub), Sm (sub); 1997 v Ei (sub), S; (with Leicester C), 1998 v T, Bel, Jam, Tun (9)

Savin, G. (Oswestry), 1878 v S (1)

Sayer, P. (Cardiff C), 1977 v Cz, S, E, Ni; 1978 v K (2), S (7)

Scrine, F. H. (Swansea T), 1950 v E, Ni (2)

Sear, C. R. (Manchester C), 1963 v E (1)

Shaw, E. G. (Oswestry), 1882 v Ni; 1884 v S, Ni (3)

Sherwood, A. T. (Cardiff C), 1947 v E, Ni; 1948 v S, Ni; 1949 v E, S, Ni, P, Sw; 1950 v E, S, Ni, Bel; 1951 v E, S, Ni, P, Sw; 1952 v E, S, Ni, R of UK; 1953 v S, E, Ni, F, Y; 1954 v S, Ni, A; 1955 v S, E, Y, Ni; 1956 v E, S, Ni, A; (with Newport Co), 1957 v E, S (41)

Shone, W. W. (Oswestry), 1879 v E (1)

Shortt, W. W. (Plymouth Arg), 1947 v Ni; 1950 v Ni, Bel; 1952 v E, S, Ni, R of UK; 1953 v S, E, Ni, F, Y (12)

Showers, D. (Cardiff C), 1975 v E (sub), Ni (2)

Sidlow, C. (Liverpool), 1947 v E, S; 1948 v E, S, Ni; 1949 v S; 1950 v E (7)

Sisson, H. (Wrexham Olympic), 1885 v Ni; 1886 v S, Ni (3)

Slatter, N. (Bristol R), 1983 v S; 1984 v Ni (sub), Is; 1985 v Ic, Sp, Ic, N, S, Sp, N; (with Oxford U), 1986 v H (sub), S.Ar, Ca (2); 1987 v Fi (sub), Cz; 1988 v D (2), Cz, Ma, I; 1989 v Is (sub) (22)

Smallman, D. P. (Wrexham), 1974 v E (sub), S (sub), Ni; (with Everton), 1975 v H (sub), E, Ni (sub); 1976 v A (7)

Southall, N. (Everton), 1982 v Ni; 1983 v N, E, Bul, S, Ni, Br; 1984 v N, R, Bul, Y, S, E, Ni, N, Is; 1985 v Ic, Sp, Ic, N, S, Sp, N; 1986 v S, H, S.Ar, Ei; 1987 v USSR, Fi, Cz; 1988 v D, Cz, Y, Se; 1989 v Ho, Fi, Se, WG; 1990 v Fi, Ho, WG, Ei, Se, Cr; 1991 v D, Bel (2), L, Ei, Ic, Pol, WG; 1992 v Br, G, L, Ei, A, R, Ho, Arg, J; 1993 v Fa, Cy, Bel, Ei, Bel, RCS, Fa; 1994 v RCS, Cy, R, N, Se, Es; 1995 v Alb, Mol, Ge, Bul (2), G, Ge; 1996 v Mol, G, Alb, I, Sm; 1997 v Sm, Ho (2), T, Bel; 1998 v T (92)

Speed, G. A. (Leeds U), 1990 v Cr (sub); 1991 v D, L (sub), Ei (sub), Ic, WG (sub); 1992 v R, G (sub), L, Ei, R, Ho,Arg,J; 1993 v Fa, Cy, Bel, Ei, Bel, Fa (sub); 1994 v RCS (sub), Cy, R, N, Se; 1995 v Alb, Mol, Ge, Bul (2), G; 1996 v Mol, G, I, Sw (sub); (with Everton), 1997 v Sm (sub), Ho (2), T, Ei, Bel, S; 1998 v T, Br; (with Newcastle U), Jam, Ma, Tun (47)

Sprake, G. (Leeds U), 1964 v S, Ni; 1965 v S, D, Gr; 1966 v E, Ni, USSR; 1967 v S; 1968 v E, S; 1969 v S, E, Ni, WG, R of UK; 1970 v EG, I; 1971 v R, S, E, Ni; 1972 v Fi, E, S,

Ni; 1973 v E (2), Pol, S, Ni; 1974 v Pol; (with Birmingham C), S, Ni; 1975 v A, H, L (37)

Stansfield, F. (Cardiff C), 1949 v S (1)

Stevenson, B. (Leeds U), 1978 v Ni; 1979 v Ma, T, S, E, Ni, Ma; 1980 v WG, T, Ic (sub); 1982 v Cz; (with Birmingham C), Sp, S, Ni, F (15)

Stevenson, N. (Swansea C), 1982 v E, S, Ni; 1983 v N (4)

Stitfall, R. F. (Cardiff C), 1953 v E; 1957 v Cz (2)

Sullivan, D. (Cardiff C), 1953 v Ni, F, Y; 1954 v Ni; 1955 v E, Ni; 1957 v E, S; 1958 v Ni, H (2), Se, Br; 1959 v S, Ni; 1960 v E, S (17)

Symons, C. J. (Portsmouth), 1992 v Ei, Ho, Arg, J; 1993 v Fa, Cy, Bel, Ei, RCS, Fa; 1994 v RCS, Cy, R; 1995 v Mol, Ge (sub), Bul, G, Ge; (with Manchester C), 1996 v Mol, G, I, Sw; 1997 v Ho (2), Ei, Bel, S (27)

Tapscott, D. R. (Arsenal), 1954 v A; 1955 v S, E, Ni, Y; 1956 v E, Ni, S, A; 1957 v Ni, Cz, EG; (with Cardiff C), 1959 v E, Ni (14)

Taylor, G. K. (C Palace), 1996 v Alb, I (sub); (with Sheffield U), Sw; 1997 v Sm (sub), Ho (sub), Ei (sub); 1998 v Bel (sub), Jam (8)

Taylor, J. (Wrexham), 1898 v E (1)

Taylor, O. D. S. (Newtown), 1893 v S, Ni; 1894 v S, Ni (4)

Thomas, C. (Druids), 1899 v Ni; 1900 v S (2)

Thomas, D. A. (Swansea T), 1957 v Cz; 1958 v EG (2)

Thomas, D. S. (Fulham), 1948 v E, S, Ni; 1949 v S (4)

Thomas, E. (Cardiff Corinthians), 1925 v E (1)

Thomas, G. (Wrexham), 1885 v E, S (2)

Thomas, H. (Manchester U), 1927 v E (1)

Thomas, M. (Wrexham), 1977 v WG, S (1+1 sub), Ni (sub); 1978 v K (sub), S, Cz, Ir, E, Ni (sub); 1979 v Ma; (with Manchester U), T, WG, Ma (sub); 1980 v Ei, WG (sub), T, E, S, Ni; 1981 v Cz, S, E, USSR; (with Everton), 1982 v Cz; (with Brighton & HA), USSR, Sp, E, S (sub), Ni (sub); 1983 (with Stoke C), v N, Y, E, Bul, S, Ni, Br; 1984 v R, Bul, Y; (with Chelsea), S, E; 1985 v Ic, Sp, Ic, S, Sp, N; 1986 v S; (with WBA), H, S.Ar (sub) (51)

Thomas, M. R. (Newcastle U), 1987 v Fi (1)

Thomas, R. J. (Swindon T), 1967 v Ni; 1968 v WG; 1969 v E, Ni, I, WG, R of UK; 1970 v E, S, Ni, EG, I; 1971 v S, E, Ni, R, Cz; 1972 v Fi, Cz, R, E, S, Ni; 1973 v E (3), Pol, S, Ni; 1974 v Pol; (with Derby Co), E, S, Ni; 1975 v H (2), L (2), S, E, Ni; 1976 v A, Y, E; 1977 v Cz, S, E, Ni; 1978 v K, S; (with Cardiff C), Cz (50)

Thomas, T. (Bangor), 1898 v S, Ni (2)

Thomas, W. R. (Newport Co), 1931 v E, S (2)

Thomson, D. (Druids), 1876 v S (1)

Thomson, G. F. (Druids), 1876 v S; 1877 v S (2)

Toshack, J. B. (Cardiff C), 1969 v S, E, Ni, WG, EG, R of UK; 1970 v EG, I; (with Liverpool), 1971 v S, E, Ni, Fi; 1972 v Fi, E; 1973 v E (3), Pol, S; 1975 v A, H (2), L (2), S, E; 1976 v Y (2), E; 1977 v S; 1978 v K (2), S, Cz; (with Swansea C), 1979 v WG (sub), S, E, Ni, Ma; 1980 v WG (40)

Townsend, W. (Newtown), 1887 v Ni; 1893 v Ni (2)

Trainer, H. (Wrexham), 1895 v E, S, Ni (3)

Trainer, J. (Bolton W), 1887 v S; (with Preston NE), 1888 v S; 1889 v E; 1890 v S; 1891 v S; 1892 v Ni, S; 1893 v E; 1894 v Ni, E; 1895 v Ni, E; 1896 v S; 1897 v Ni, S, E; 1898 v S, E; 1899 v Ni, S (20)

Trollope, P. J. (Derby Co), 1997 v S; 1998 v Br (sub); (with Fulham), Jam (sub), Ma, Tun (5)

Turner, H. G. (Charlton Ath), 1937 v E, S, Ni; 1938 v E, S, Ni; 1939 v Ni, F (8)

Turner, J. (Wrexham), 1892 v E (1)

Turner, R. E. (Wrexham), 1891 v E, Ni (2)

Turner, W. H. (Wrexham), 1887 v E, Ni; 1890 v S; 1891 v E, S (5)

Van Den Hauwe, P. W. R. (Everton), 1985 v Sp; 1986 v S, H; 1987 v USSR, Fi, Cz; 1988 v D (2), Cz, Y, I; 1989 v Fi, Se (13)

Vaughan, Jas (Druids), 1893 v Ni, S; 1899 v E (4)

Vaughan, John (Oswestry), 1879 v S; 1880 v S; 1881 v E, S; 1882 v S, Ni; 1883 v E, S, Ni; (with Bolton W), 1884 v E (11)

Vaughan, J. O. (Rhyl), 1885 v Ni; 1886 v Ni, S, E (4)

Vaughan, N. (Newport Co), 1983 v Y (sub), Br; 1984 v N; (with Cardiff C), R, Bul, Y, Ni (sub), N, Is; 1985 v Sp (sub) (10)

Vaughan, T. (Rhyl), 1885 v E (1)

Vearncombe, G. (Cardiff C), 1958 v EG; 1961 v Ei (2)

Vernon, T. R. (Blackburn R), 1957 v Ni, Cz (2), EG; 1958 v E, S, EG, Se; 1959 v S; (with Everton), 1960 v Ni; 1961 v S, E, Ei; 1962 v Ni, Br (2), M; 1963 v S, E, H; 1964 v E, S; (with Stoke C), 1965 v Ni, Gr, I; 1966 v E, S, Ni, USSR, D; 1967 v Ni; 1968 v E (32)

Villars, A. K. (Cardiff C), 1974 v E, S, Ni (sub) (3)

Vizard, E. T. (Bolton W), 1911 v E, S, Ni; 1912 v E, S; 1913 v S; 1914 v E, Ni; 1920 v E; 1921 v E, S, Ni; 1922 v E, S; 1923 v E, Ni; 1924 v E, S, Ni; 1926 v E, S; 1927 v S (22)

Walley, J. T. (Watford), 1971 v Cz (1)

Walsh, I. (C Palace), 1980 v Ei, T, E, S, Ic; 1981 v T, Cz, Ei, T, S, E, USSR; 1982 v Cz (sub), Ic; (with Swansea C), Sp, S (sub), Ni (sub), F (18)

Ward, D. (Bristol R), 1959 v E; (with Cardiff C), 1962 v E (2)

Warner, J. (Swansea T), 1937 v E; (with Manchester U), 1939 v F (2)

Warren, F. W. (Cardiff C), 1929 v Ni; (with Middlesbrough), 1931 v Ni; 1933 v F, E; (with Hearts), 1937 v Ni; 1938 v Ni (6)

Watkins, A. E. (Leicester Fosse), 1898 v E, S; (with Aston Villa), 1900 v E, S; (with Millwall), 1904 v Ni (5)

Watkins, W. M. (Stoke C), 1902 v E; 1903 v E, S; (with Aston Villa); 1904 v E, S, Ni; (with Sunderland), 1905 v E, S, Ni; (with Stoke C), 1908 v Ni (10)

Webster, C (Manchester U), 1957 v Cz; 1958 v H, M, Br (4)

Whatley, W. J. (Tottenham H), 1939 v E, S (2)

White, P. F. (London Welsh), 1896 v Ni (1)

Wilcock, A. R. (Oswestry), 1890 v Ni (1)

Wilding, J. (Wrexham Olympians), 1885 v E, S, Ni; 1886 v E, Ni; (with Bootle), 1887 v E; 1888 v S, Ni; (with Wrexham), 1892 v S (9)

Williams, A. (Reading), 1994 v Es; 1995 v Alb, Mol, G (sub), Ge; 1996 v Mol, I; (with Wolverhampton W), 1998 v Br (sub), Jam (9)

Williams, A. L. (Wrexham), 1931 v E (1)

Williams, A. P. (Southampton), 1998 v Br (sub), Ma (2)

Williams, B. (Bristol C), 1930 v Ni (1)

Williams, B. D. (Swansea T), 1928 v Ni, E; 1930 v E, S; (with Everton), 1931 v Ni; 1932 v E; 1933 v E, S, Ni; 1935 v Ni (10)

Williams, D. G. (Derby Co), 1988 v Cz, Y, Se, Ma, I; 1989 v Ho, Is, Se, WG; 1990 v Fi, Ho; (with Ipswich T), 1993 v Ei; 1996 v G (sub) (13)

Williams, D. M. (Norwich C), 1986 v S.Ar (sub), U, Ca (2); 1987 v Fi (5)

Williams, D. R. (Merthyr T), 1921 v E, S; (with Sheffield W), 1923 v S; 1926 v S; 1927 v E, Ni; (with Manchester U), 1929 v E, S (8)

Williams, E. (Crewe Alex), 1893 v E, S (2)

Williams, E. (Druids), 1901 v E, Ni, S; 1902 v E, Ni (5)

Williams, G. (Chirk), 1893 v S; 1894 v S; 1895 v E, S, Ni; 1898 v Ni (6)

Williams, G. E. (WBA), 1960 v Ni; 1961 v S, E, Ei; 1963 v Ni, H; 1964 v E, S, Ni; 1965 v S, E, Ni, D, Gr (2), USSR, I; 1966 v Ni, Br (2), Ch; 1967 v S, E, Ni; 1968 v Ni; 1969 v I (26)

Williams, G. G. (Swansea T), 1961 v Ni, H, Sp (2); 1962 v E (5)

Williams, G. J. J. (Cardiff C), 1951 v Sw (1)

Williams, G. O. (Wrexham), 1907 v Ni (1)

Williams, H. J. (Swansea), 1965 v Gr (2); 1972 v R (3)

Williams, H. T. (Newport Co), 1949 v Ni, Sw; (with Leeds U), 1950 v Ni; 1951 v S (4)

Williams, J. H. (Oswestry), 1884 v E (1)

Williams, J. J. (Wrexham), 1939 v F (1)

Williams, J. T. (Middlesbrough), 1925 v Ni (1)

Williams, J. W. (C Palace), 1912 v S, Ni (2)

Williams, R. (Newcastle U), 1935 v S, E (2)

Williams, R. P. (Caernarvon), 1886 v S (1)

Williams, S. G. (WBA), 1954 v A; 1955 v E, Ni; 1956 v E, S, A; 1958 v E, S, Ni, Is (2), H (2), M, Se, Br; 1959 v E, S, Ni; 1960 v E, S, Ni; 1961 v Ni, Ei, H, Sp (2); 1962 v E, S, Ni, Br (2), M; (with Southampton), 1963 v S, E, H (2); 1964 v E, S; 1965 v S, E, D; 1966 v D (43)

Williams, W. (Druids), 1876 v S; 1878 v S; (with Oswestry), 1879 v E, S; (with Druids), 1880 v E; 1881 v E, S; 1882 v E, S, Ni; 1883 v Ni (11)

Williams, W. (Northampton T), 1925 v S (1)

Witcomb, D. F. (WBA), 1947 v E, S; (with Sheffield W), v Ni (3)

Woosnam, A. P. (Leyton Orient), 1959 v S; (with West Ham U), E; 1960 v E, S, Ni; 1961 v S, E, Ni, Ei, Sp, H; 1962 v E, S, Ni, Br; (with Aston Villa), 1963 v Ni, H (17)

Woosnam, G. (Newton White Star), 1879 v S (1)

Worthington, T. (Newtown), 1894 v S (1)

Wynn, G. A. (Wrexham), 1909 v E, S, Ni; (with Manchester C), 1910 v E; 1911 v Ni; 1912 v E, S; 1913 v E, S; 1914 v E, S (11)

Wynn, W. (Chirk), 1903 v Ni (1)

Yorath, T. C. (Leeds U), 1970 v I; 1971 v E, S, Ni; 1972 v Cz, E, S, Ni; 1973 v E, Pol, S; 1974 v Pol, E, S, Ni; 1975 v A, H (2), L (2), S; 1976 v A, E, S, Y (2), E, Ni; (with Coventry C), 1977 v WG, S (2), Cz, E, Ni; 1978 v K (2), S, Cz, WG, Ir, E, S, Ni; 1979 v T, WG, S, E, Ni; (with Tottenham H) 1980 v Ei, T, E, S, Ni, Ic; 1981 v T, Cz; (with Vancouver W), Ei, T, USSR (59)

Young, E. (Wimbledon), 1990 v Cr; (with C Palace), 1991 v D, Bel (2), L, Ei; 1992 v G, L, Ei, A; 1993 v Fa, Cy, Bel, Ei, Bel, Fa; 1994 v RCS, Cy, R, N; (with Wolverhampton W) 1996 v Alb (21)

## REPUBLIC OF IRELAND

Aherne, T. (Belfast C), 1946 v P, Sp; (with Luton T), 1950 v Fi, E, Fi, Se, Bel; 1951 v N, Arg, N; 1952 v WG (2), A, Sp; 1953 v F; 1954 v F (16)

Aldridge, J. W. (Oxford U), 1986 v W, U, Ic, Cz; 1987 v Bel, S, Pol; (with Liverpool), S, Bul, Bel, Br, L; 1988 v Bul, Pol, N, E, USSR, Ho; 1989 v Ni, Tun, Sp, F (sub), H, Ma (sub), H; 1990 v WG; (with Real Sociedad), Ni, Ma, Fi (sub), T, E, Eg, Ho, R, I; 1991 v T, E (2), Pol; (with Tranmere R), 1992 v H (sub), T, W (sub), Sw (sub), US (sub), Alb, I, P (sub); 1993 v La, D, Sp, D, Alb, La, Li; 1994 v Li, Ni, CzR, I (sub), M (sub), N; 1995 v La, Ni, P, Lie; 1996 v La, P, Ho, Ru; 1997 v Mac (sub) (69)

Ambrose, P. (Shamrock R), 1955 v N, Ho; 1964 v Pol, N, E (5)

Anderson, J. (Preston NE), 1980 v Cz (sub), US (sub); 1982 v Ch, Br, Tr; (with Newcastle U), 1984 v Chn; 1986 v W, Ic, Cz; 1987 v Bul, Bel, Br, L; 1988 v Y (sub); 1989 v Tun (16)

Andrews, P. (Bohemians), 1936 v Ho (1)

Arrigan, T. (Waterford), 1938 v N (1)

Babb, P. A. (Coventry C), 1994 v Ru, Ho, Bol, G, CzR (sub), I, M, N, Ho; (with Liverpool), 1995 v La, Lie, Ni (2), P, Lie, A; 1996 v La, P, Ho, CzR; 1997 v Ic; 1998 v Li (sub), R, Arg (sub), M (25)

Bailham, E. (Shamrock R), 1964 v E (1)

Barber, E. (Shelbourne), 1966 v Sp; (with Birmingham C), 1966 v Bel (2)

Barry, P. (Fordsons), 1928 v Bel; 1929 v Bel (2)

Beglin, J. (Liverpool), 1984 v Chn; 1985 v M, D, I, Is, E, N, Sw; 1986 v Sw, USSR, D, W; 1987 v Bel (sub), S, Pol (15)

Bermingham, J. (Bohemians), 1929 v Bel (1)

Bermingham, P. (St James' Gate), 1935 v H (1)

Braddish, S. (Dundalk), 1978 v T (sub), Pol (2)

Bonner, P. (Celtic), 1981 v Pol; 1982 v Alg; 1984 v Ma, Is, Chn; 1985 v I, Is, E, N; 1986 v U, Ic; 1987 v Bel (2), S (2), Pol, Bul, Br, L; 1988 v Bul, R, Y, N, E, USSR, Ho; 1989 v Sp, F, H, Sp, Ma, H; 1990 v WG, Ni, Ma, W, Fi, T, E, Eg, Ho, R, I; 1991 v Mor, T, E (2), W, Pol, US; 1992 v H, Pol, T, W, Sw, Alb, I; 1993 v La, D, Sp, W, Ni, D, Alb, La, Li; 1994 v Li, Sp, Ni, Ru, Ho, Bol, CzR, I, M, N, Ho; 1995 v Lie; 1996 v M, Bol (sub) (80)

Bradshaw, P. (St James' Gate), 1939 v Sw, Pol, H (2), G (5)

Brady, F. (Fordsons), 1926 v I; 1927 v I (2)

Brady, T. R. (QPR), 1964 v A (2), Sp (2), Pol, N (6)

Brady, W. L. (Arsenal), 1975 v USSR, T, Sw, USSR, Sw, WG; 1976 v T, N, Pol; 1977 v E, T, F (2), Sp, Bul; 1978 v Bul, N; 1979 v Ni, E, D, Bul, WG; 1980 v W, Bul, E, Cy; (with Juventus), 1981 v Ho, Bel, F, Cy, Bel; 1982 v Ho, F, Ch, Br, Tr; (with Sampdoria), 1983 v Ho, Sp, Ic, Ma; 1984 v Ic, Ho, Ma, Pol, Is; (with Internazionale), 1985 v USSR, N, D, I, E, N, Sp, Sw; 1986 v Sw, USSR, D, W; (with Ascoli), 1987 v Bel, S (2), Pol; (with West Ham U), Bul, Bel, Br, L; 1988 v L, Bul; 1989 v F, H (sub), H (sub); 1990 v WG, Fi (72)

Branagan, K. G. (Bolton W), 1997 v W (1)

Breen, G. (Birmingham C), 1996 v P (sub), Cro, Ho, US, M, Bol (sub); 1997 v Lie, Mac, Ic; (with Coventry C), v Mac; 1998 v Li (sub), R, CzR, Arg, M (15)

Breen, T. (Manchester U), 1937 v Sw, F; (with Shamrock R), 1947 v E, Sp, P (5)

Brennan, F. (Drumcondra), 1965 v Bel (1)

Brennan, S. A. (Manchester U), 1965 v Sp; 1966 v Sp, A, Bel; 1967 v Sp, T, Sp; 1969 v Cz, D, H; 1970 v S, Cz, D, H, Pol (sub), WG; (with Waterford), 1971 v Pol, Se, I (19)

Brown, J. (Coventry C), 1937 v Sw, F (2)

Browne, W. (Bohemians), 1964 v A, Sp, E (3)

Buckley, L. (Shamrock R), 1984 v Pol (sub); (with Waregem), 1985 v M (2)

Burke, F. (Cork Ath), 1952 v WG (1)

Burke, J. (Cork), 1934 v Bel (1)

Burke, J. (Shamrock R), 1929 v Bel (1)

Byrne, A. B. (Southampton), 1970 v D, Pol, WG; 1971 v Pol, Se (2), I (2), A; 1973 v F, USSR (sub), F, N; 1974 v Pol (14)

Byrne, D. (Shelbourne), 1929 v Bel; (with Shamrock R), 1932 v Sp; (with Coleraine), 1934 v Bel (3)

Byrne, J. (Bray Unknowns), 1928 v Bel (1)

Byrne, J. (QPR), 1985 v I, Is (sub), E (sub), Sp (sub); 1987 v S (sub), Bel (sub), Br, L (sub); 1988 v L, Bul (sub), Is, R, Y (sub), Pol (sub); (with Le Havre), 1990 v WG (sub), W, Fi, T (sub), Ma; (with Brighton & HA), 1991 v W; (with Sunderland), 1992 v T, W; (with Millwall), 1993 v W (23)

Byrne, P. (Shamrock R), 1984 v Pol, Chn; 1985 v M; 1986 v D (sub), W (sub), U (sub), Ic (sub), Cz (8)

Byrne, P. (Dolphin), 1931 v Sp; 1932 v Ho; (with Drumcondra), 1934 v Ho (3)

Byrne, S. (Bohemians) 1931 v Sp (1)

Campbell, A. (Santander), 1985 v I (sub), Is, Sp (3)

Campbell, N. (St Patrick's Ath), 1971 v A (sub); (with Fortuna, Cologne), 1972 v Ir, Ec, Ch, P; 1973 v USSR, F (sub); 1975 v WG; 1976 v N; 1977 v Sp, Bul (sub) (11)

Cannon, H. (Bohemians), 1926 v I; 1928 v Bel (2)

Cantwell, N. (West Ham U), 1954 v L; 1956 v Sp, Ho; 1957 v D, WG, E (2); 1958 v D, Pol, A; 1959 v Pol, Cz (2); 1960 v Se, Ch, Se; 1961 v N; (with Manchester U), S (2); 1962 v Cz (2), A; 1963 v Ic (2), S; 1964 v A. Sp. E; 1965 v Pol, Sp; 1966 v Sp (2), A, Bel; 1967 v Sp, T (36)

Carey, B. P. (Manchester U), 1992 v US (sub); 1993 v W; (with Leicester C), 1994 v Ru (3)

Carey, J. J. (Manchester U), 1938 v N, Cz, Pol; 1939 v Sw, Pol, H (2), G; 1946 v P, Sp; 1947 v E, Sp, P; 1948 v P, Sp; 1949 v Sw, Bel, P, Se, Sp; 1950 v Fi, E, Fi, Se; 1951 v N, Arg, N; 1953 v F, A (29)

Carolan, J. (Manchester U), 1960 v Se, Ch (2)

Carroll, B. (Shelbourne), 1949 v Bel; 1950 v Fi (2)

Carroll, T. R. (Ipswich T), 1968 v Pol; 1969 v Pol, A, D; 1970 v Cz, Pol, WG; 1971 v Sp; (with Birmingham C), 1972 v Ir, Ec, Ch, P; 1973 v USSR (2), Pol, F, N (17)

Carsley, L. K. (Derby Co), 1998 v R, Bel (1 + sub), CzR, Arg, M (6)

Cascarino, A. G. (Gillingham), 1986 v Sw, USSR, D; (with Millwall), 1988 v Pol, N (sub), USSR (sub), Ho (sub); 1989 v Ni, Tun, Sp, F, H, Sp, Ma, H; 1990 v WG (sub), Ni, Ma; (with Aston Villa), W, Fi, T, E, Eg, Ho (sub), R (sub), I (sub); 1991 v Mor (sub),T(sub), E (2 sub), Pol (sub), Ch (sub), US; (with Celtic), 1992 v Pol, T; (with Chelsea), W, Sw, US (sub); 1993 v W, Ni (sub), D (sub), Alb (sub), La (sub); 1994 v Li (sub), Sp (sub), Ni (sub), Ru, Bol (sub), G, CzR, Ho (sub); (with Marseille), 1995 v La (sub), Ni (sub), P (sub), Lie (sub), A (sub); 1996 v A (sub), P (sub), Ho, Ru (sub), P, Cro (sub), Ho; 1997 v Lie (sub), Mac, Ic; (with Nancy), v W, Mac, R (sub), Lie (sub); 1998 v Li (sub), Ic (sub), Li, R, Bel (2) (76)

Chandler, J. (Leeds U), 1980 v Cz (sub), US (2)

Chatton, H. A. (Shelbourne), 1931 v Sp; (with Dumbarton), 1932 v Sp; (with Cork), 1934 v Ho (3)

Clarke, J. (Drogheda U), 1978 v Pol (sub) (1)

Clarke, K. (Drumcondra), 1948 v P, Sp (2)

Clarke, M. (Shamrock R), 1950 v Bel (1)

Clinton, T. J. (Everton), 1951 v N; 1954 v F, L (3)

Coad, P. (Shamrock R), 1947 v E, Sp, P; 1948 v P, Sp; 1949 v Sw, Bel, P, Se; 1951 v N (sub); 1952 v Sp (11)

Coffey, T. (Drumcondra), 1950 v Fi (1)

Colfer, M. D. (Shelbourne), 1950 v Bel; 1951 v N (2)

Collins, E. (Jacobs), 1927 v I (1)

Conmy, O. M. (Peterborough U), 1965 v Bel; 1967 v Cz; 1968 v Cz, Pol; 1970 v Cz (5)

Connolly, D. J. (Watford), 1996 v P, Ho, US, M; 1997 v R, Lie; (with Feyenoord), 1998 v Li, Ic, Li, Bel (1 + sub), CzR, M (13)

Connolly, H. (Cork), 1937 v G (1)

Connolly, J. (Fordsons), 1926 v I (1)

Conroy, G. A. (Stoke C), 1970 v Cz, D, H, Pol, WG; 1971 v Pol, Se (2), I; 1973 v USSR, F, USSR, N; 1974 v Pol, Br, U, Ch; 1975 v T, Sw, USSR, Sw, WG (sub); 1976 v T (sub), Pol; 1977 v E, T, Pol (27)

Conway, J. P. (Fulham), 1967 v Sp, T, Sp; 1968 v Cz; 1969 v A (sub), H; 1970 v S, Cz, D, H, Pol, WG; 1971 v I, A; 1974 v U, Ch; 1975 v WG (sub); 1976 v N, Pol; (with Manchester C), 1977 v Pol (20)

Corr, P. J. (Everton), 1949 v P, Sp; 1950 v E, Se (4)

Courtney, E. (Cork U), 1946 v P (1)

Coyle, O. C. (Bolton W), 1994 v Ho (sub) (1)

Coyne, T. (Celtic), 1992 v Sw, US, Alb (sub), US (sub), I (sub), P (sub); 1993 v W (sub), La (sub); (with Tranmere R), Ni; (with Motherwell), 1994 v Ru (sub), Ho, Bol, G (sub), CzR (sub), I, M, Ho; 1995 v Lie, Ni (sub), A; 1996 v Ru (sub); 1998 v Bel (sub) (22)

Cummins, G. P. (Luton T), 1954 v L (2); 1955 v N (2), WG; 1956 v Y, Sp; 1958 v D, Pol, A; 1959 v Pol, Cz (2); 1960 v Se, Ch, WG, Se; 1961 v S (2) (19)

Cuneen, T. (Limerick), 1951 v N (1)

Cunningham, K. (Wimbledon), 1996 v CzR, P, Cro, Ho (sub), US, Bol; 1997 v Ic (sub), W, R, Lie; 1998 v Li, Ic, Li, Bel (2); CzR (16)

Curtis, D. P. (Shelbourne), 1957 v D, WG; (with Bristol C), 1957 v E (2); 1958 v D, Pol, A; (with Ipswich T), 1959 v Pol; 1960 v Se, Ch, WG, Se; 1961 v N, S; 1962 v A; 1963 v Ic; (with Exeter C), 1964 v A (17)

Cusack, S. (Limerick), 1953 v F (1)

Daish, L. S. (Cambridge U), 1992 v W, Sw (sub); (with Coventry C), 1996 v CzR (sub), Cro, M (5)

Daly, G. A. (Manchester U), 1973 v Pol (sub), N; 1974 v Br (sub), U (sub); 1975 v Sw (sub), WG; 1977 v E, T, F; (with Derby Co), F, Bul; 1978 v Bul, T, D; 1979 v Ni, E, D, Bul; 1980 v Ni, E, Cy, Sw, Arg; (with Coventry C), 1981 v WG'B', Ho, Bel, Cy, W, Bel, Cz, Pol (sub); 1982 v Alg, Ch, Br, Tr; 1983 v Ho, Sp (sub); 1984 v Is (sub), Ma; (with Birmingham C), 1985 v M (sub), N, Sp, Sw; 1986 v Sw; (with Shrewsbury T), U, Ic (sub), Cz (sub); 1987 v S (sub) (48)

Daly, J. (Shamrock R), 1932 v Ho; 1935 v Sw (2)

Daly, M. (Wolverhampton W), 1978 v T, Pol (2)

Daly, P. (Shamrock R), 1950 v Fi (sub) (1)

Davis, T. L. (Oldham Ath), 1937 v G, H; (with Tranmere R), 1938 v Cz, Pol (4)

Deacy, E. (Aston Villa), 1982 v Alg (sub), Ch, Br, Tr (4)

Delap, R. J. (Derby Co), 1998 v CzR (sub), Arg (sub), M (sub) (3)

De Mange, K. J. P. P. (Liverpool), 1987 v Br (sub); (with Hull C), 1989 v Tun (sub) (2)

Dempsey, J. T. (Fulham), 1967 v Sp, Cz; 1968 v Cz, Pol; 1969 v Pol, A, D; (with Chelsea), 1969 v Cz, D; 1970 v H, WG; 1971 v Pol, Se (2), I; 1972 v Ir, Ec, Ch, P (19)

Dennehy, J. (Cork Hibernians), 1972 v Ec (sub); (with Nottingham F), 1973 v USSR (sub), Pol, F, N; 1974 v Pol (sub); 1975 v T (sub), WG (sub); (with Walsall), 1976 v Pol (sub); 1977 v Pol (sub) (11)

Desmond, P. (Middlesbrough), 1950 v Fi, E, Fi, Se (4)

Devine, J. (Arsenal), 1980 v Cz, Ni; 1981 v WG'B', Cz; 1982 v Ho, Alg; 1983 v Sp, Ma; (with Norwich C), 1984 v Ic, Ho, Is; 1985 v USSR, N (13)

Donnelly, J. (Dundalk), 1935 v H, Sw, G; 1936 v Ho, Sw, H, L; 1937 v G, H; 1938 v N (10)

Donnelly, T. (Drumcondra), 1938 v N; (Shamrock R), 1939 v Sw (2)

Donovan, D. C. (Everton), 1955 v N, Ho, N, WG; 1957 v E (5)

Donovan, T. (Aston Villa), 1980 v Cz; 1981 v WG'B'(sub) (2)

Dowdall, C. (Fordsons), 1928 v Bel; (with Barnsley), 1929 v Bel; (with Cork), 1931 v Sp (3)

Doyle, C. (Shelbourne), 1959 v Cz (1)

Doyle, D. (Shamrock R), 1926 v I (1)

Doyle, L. (Dolphin), 1932 v Sp (1)

Duff, D. A. (Blackburn R), 1998 v CzR, M (2)

Duffy, B. (Shamrock R), 1950 v Bel (1)

Duggan, H. A. (Leeds U), 1927 v I; 1930 v Bel; 1936 v H, L; (with Newport Co), 1938 v N (5)

Dunne, A. P. (Manchester U), 1962 v A; 1963 v Ic, S; 1964 v A, Sp, Pol, N, E; 1965 v Pol, Sp; 1966 v Sp (2), A, Bel; 1967 v Sp, T, Sp; 1969 v Pol, D, H; 1970 v H; 1971 v Se, I, A; (with Bolton W), 1974 v Br (sub), U, Ch; 1975 v T, Sw, USSR, Sw, WG; 1976 v T (33)

Dunne, J. (Sheffield U), 1930 v Bel; (with Arsenal), 1936 v Sw, H, L; (with Southampton), 1937 v Sw, F; (with Shamrock R), 1938 v N (2), Cz, Pol; 1939 v Sw, Pol, H (2), G (15)

Dunne, J. C. (Fulham), 1971 v A (1)

Dunne, L. (Manchester C), 1935 v Sw, G (2)

Dunne, P. A. J. (Manchester U), 1965 v Sp; 1966 v Sp (2), WG; 1967 v T (5)

Dunne, S. (Luton T), 1953 v F, A; 1954 v F, L; 1956 v Sp, Ho; 1957 v D, WG, E; 1958 v D, Pol, A; 1959 v Pol; 1960 v WG, Se (15)

Dunne, T. (St Patrick's Ath), 1956 v Ho; 1957 v D, WG (3)

Dunning, P. (Shelbourne), 1971 v Se, I (2)

Dunphy, E. M. (York C), 1966 v Sp; (with Millwall), 1966 v WG; 1967 v T, Sp, T, Cz; 1968 v Cz, Pol; 1969 v Pol, A, D (2), H; 1970 v D, H, Pol, WG (sub); 1971 v Pol, Se (2), I (2), A (23)

Dwyer, N. M. (West Ham U), 1960 v Se, Ch, WG, Se; (with Swansea T), 1961 v W, N, S (2); 1962 v Cz (2); 1964 v Pol (sub), N, E; 1965 v Pol (14)

Eccles, P. (Shamrock R), 1986 v U (sub) (1)

Egan, R. (Dundalk), 1929 v Bel (1)
Eglington, T. J. (Shamrock R), 1946 v P, Sp; (with Everton), 1947 v E, Sp, P; 1948 v P; 1949 v Sw, P, Se; 1951 v N, Arg; 1952 v WG (2), A, Sp; 1953 v F, A; 1954 v F, L, F; 1955 v N, Ho, WG; 1956 v Sp (24)
Ellis, P. (Bohemians), 1935 v Sw, G; 1936 v Ho, Sw, L; 1937 v G, H (7)
Evans, M. J. (Southampton), 1998 v R (sub) (1)
Fagan, E. (Shamrock R), 1973 v N (sub) (1)
Fagan, F. (Manchester C), 1955 v N; 1960 v Se; (with Derby Co), 1960 v Ch, WG, Se; 1961 v W, N, S (8)
Fagan, J. (Shamrock R), 1926 v I (1)
Fairclough, M. (Dundalk), 1982 v Ch (sub), Tr (sub) (2)
Fallon, S. (Celtic), 1951 v N; 1952 v WG (2), A, Sp; 1953 v F; 1955 v N, WG (8)
Fallon, W. J. (Notts Co), 1935 v H; 1936 v H; 1937 v H, Sw, F; 1939 v Sw, Pol; (with Sheffield W), 1939 v H, G (9)
Farquharson, T. G. (Cardiff C), 1929 v Bel; 1930 v Bel; 1931 v Sp; 1932 v Sp (4)
Farrell, P. (Hibernian), 1937 v Sw, F (2)
Farrell, P. D. (Shamrock R), 1946 v P, Sp; (with Everton), 1947 v Sp, P; 1948 v P; 1949 v Sw, P (sub), Sp; 1950 v E, Fi, Se; 1951 v Arg, N; 1952 v WG (2), A, Sp; 1953 v F, A; 1954 v F (2); 1955 v N, Ho, WG; 1956 v Y, Sp; 1957 v E (28)
Farrelly, G. (Aston Villa), 1996 v P, US, Bol; (with Everton), 1998 v CzR, M (5)
Feenan, J. J. (Sunderland), 1937 v Sw, F (2)
Finucane, A. (Limerick), 1967 v T, Cz; 1969 v Cz, D, H; 1970 v S, Cz; 1971 v Se, I (1+1 sub); 1972 v A (11)
Fitzgerald, F. J. (Waterford), 1955 v Ho; 1956 v Ho (2)
Fitzgerald, P. J. (Leeds U), 1961 v W, N, S; (with Chester), 1962 v Cz (2) (5)
Fitzpatrick, K. (Limerick), 1970 v Cz (1)
Fitzsimons, A. G. (Middlesbrough), 1950 v Fi, Bel; 1952 v WG (2), Sp; 1953 v F, A; 1954 v F, L, F; 1955 v Ho, N, WG; 1956 v Y, Sp, Ho; 1957 v D, WG, E (2); 1958 v D, Pol, A; 1959 v Pol; (with Lincoln C), 1959 v Cz (26)
Fleming, C. (Middlesbrough), 1996 v CzR (sub), P, Cro (sub), Ho (sub), US (sub), M, Bol; 1997 v Lie (sub); 1998 v R (sub), M (10)
Flood, J. J. (Shamrock R), 1926 v I; 1929 v Bel; 1930 v Bel; 1931 v Sp; 1932 v Sp (5)
Fogarty, A. (Sunderland), 1960 v WG, Se; 1961 v S; 1962 v Cz (2); 1963 v Ic (2), S (sub); 1964 v A (2); (with Hartlepools U), Sp (11)
Foley, J. (Cork), 1934 v Bel, Ho; (with Celtic), 1935 v H, Sw, G; 1937 v G, H (7)
Foley, M. (Shelbourne), 1926 v I (1)
Foley, T. C. (Northampton T), 1964 v Sp, Pol, N; 1965 v Pol, Bel; 1966 v Sp (2), WG; 1967 v Cz (9)
Foy, T. (Shamrock R), 1938 v N; 1939 v H (2)
Fullam, J. (Preston NE), 1961 v N; (with Shamrock R), 1964 v Sp, Pol, N; 1966 v A, Bel; 1968 v Pol; 1969 v Pol, A, D; 1970 v Cz (sub) (11)
Fullam, R. (Shamrock R), 1926 v I; 1927 v I (2)

Gallagher, C. (Celtic), 1967 v T, Cz (2)
Gallagher, M. (Hibernian), 1954 v L (1)
Gallagher, P. (Falkirk), 1932 v Sp (1)
Galvin, A. (Tottenham H), 1983 v Ho, Ma; 1984 v Ho (sub), Is (sub); 1985 v M, USSR, N, D, I, N, Sp; 1986 v U, Ic, Cz; 1987 v Bel (2), S, Bul, L; (with Sheffield W), 1988 v L, Bul, R, Pol, N, E, USSR, Ho; 1989 v Sp; (with Swindon T), 1990 v WG (29)
Gannon, E. (Notts Co), 1949 v Sw; (with Sheffield W), 1949 v Bel, P, Se, Sp; 1950 v Fi; 1951 v N; 1952 v WG, A; 1954 v L, F; 1955 v N; (with Shelbourne), 1955 v N, WG (14)
Gannon, M. (Shelbourne), 1972 v A (1)
Gaskins, P. (Shamrock R), 1934 v Bel, Ho; 1935 v H, Sw, G; (with St James' Gate), 1938 v Cz, Pol (7)
Gavin, J. T. (Norwich C), 1950 v Fi (2); 1953 v F; 1954 v L; (with Tottenham H), 1955 v Ho, WG; (with Norwich C), 1957 v D (7)
Geoghegan, M. (St James' Gate), 1937 v G; 1938 v N (2)
Gibbons, A. (St Patrick's Ath), 1952 v WG; 1954 v L; 1956 v Y, Sp (4)
Gilbert, R. (Shamrock R), 1966 v WG (1)
Giles, C. (Doncaster R), 1951 v N (1)
Giles, M. J. (Manchester U), 1960 v Se, Ch; 1961 v W, N, S (2); 1962 v Cz (2), A; 1963 v Ic, S; (with Leeds U), 1964 v A (2), Sp (2), Pol, N, E; 1965 v Sp; 1966 v Sp (2), A, Bel; 1967 v Sp, T (2); 1969 v A, D, Cz; 1970 v S, Pol, WG; 1971 v I; 1973 v F, USSR; 1974 v Br, U, Ch; 1975 v USSR, T, Sw, USSR, Sw; (with WBA), 1976 v T; 1977 v E, T, F (2), Pol, Bul; (with Shamrock R), 1978 v Bul, T, Pol, N, D; 1979 v Ni, D, Bul, WG (59)

Given, S. J. J. (Blackburn R), 1996 v Ru, CzR, P, Cro, Ho, US, Bol; 1997 v Lie (2); (with Newcastle U), 1998 v Li, Ic, Li, Bel (2), CzR, Arg, M (17)
Givens, D. J. (Manchester U), 1969 v D, H; 1970 v S, Cz, D, H; (with Luton T), 1970 v Pol, WG; 1971 v Se, I (2), A; 1972 v Ir, Ec, P; (with QPR), 1973 v F, USSR, Pol, F, N; 1974 v Pol, Br, U, Ch; 1975 v USSR, T, Sw, USSR, Sw, WG; 1976 v T, N, Pol; 1977 v E, T, F (2), Sp, Bul; 1978 v Bul, N, D; (with Birmingham C), 1979 v Ni (sub), E, D, Bul, WG; 1980 v US (sub), Ni (sub), Sw, Arg; 1981 v Ho, Bel, Cy (sub), W; (with Neuchatel X), 1982 v F (sub) (56)
Glen, W. (Shamrock R), 1927 v I; 1929 v Bel; 1930 v Bel; 1932 v Sp; 1936 v Ho, Sw, H, L (8)
Glynn, D. (Drumcondra), 1952 v WG; 1955 v N (2)
Godwin, T. F. (Shamrock R), 1949 v P, Se, Sp; 1950 v Fi, E; (with Leicester C), 1950 v Fi, Se, Bel; 1951 v N; (with Bournemouth), 1956 v Ho; 1957 v E; 1958 v D, Pol (13)
Golding, J. (Shamrock R), 1928 v Bel; 1930 v Bel (2)
Goodman, J. (Wimbledon), 1997 v W, Mac, R (sub), Lie (sub) (4)
Gorman, W. C. (Bury), 1936 v Sw, H, L; 1937 v G, H; 1938 v N, Cz, Pol; 1939 v Sw, Pol (with Brentford) H; 1947 v E, P (13)
Grace, J. (Drumcondra), 1926 v I (1)
Grealish, A. (Orient), 1976 v N, Pol; 1978 v N, D; 1979 v Ni, E, WG; (with Luton T), 1980 v W, Cz, Bul, US, Ni, E, Cy, Sw, Arg; 1981 v WG'B', Ho, Bel, F, Cy, W, Bel, Pol; (with Brighton & HA), 1982 v Ho, Alg, Ch, Br, Tr; 1983 v Ho, Sp, Ic, Sp; 1984 v Ic, Ho; (with WBA), Pol, Chn; 1985 v M, USSR, N, D, Sp (sub); Sw; 1986 v USSR, D (45)
Gregg, E. (Bohemians), 1978 v Pol, D (sub); 1979 v E (sub), D, Bul, WG; 1980 v W, Cz (8)
Griffith, R. (Walsall), 1935 v H (1)
Grimes, A. A. (Manchester U), 1978 v T, Pol, N (sub); 1980 v Bul, US, Ni, E, Cy; 1981 v WG'B' (sub), Cz, Pol; 1982 v Alg; 1983 v Sp (2); (with Coventry C), 1984 v Pol, Is; (with Luton T), 1988 v L, R (18)

Hale, A. (Aston Villa), 1962 v A; (with Doncaster R), 1963 v Ic; 1964 v Sp (2); (with Waterford), 1967 v Sp; 1968 v Pol (sub); 1969 v Pol, A, D; 1970 v S, Cz; 1971 v Pol (sub); 1972 v A (sub); 1974 v Pol (sub) (14)
Hamilton, T. (Shamrock R), 1959 v Cz (2) (2)
Hand, E. K. (Portsmouth), 1969 v Cz (sub); 1970 v Pol, WG; 1971 v Pol, A; 1973 v USSR, F, USSR, Pol, F; 1974 v Pol, Br, U, Ch; 1975 v T, Sw, USSR, Sw, WG; 1976 v T (20)
Harrington, W. (Cork), 1936 v Ho, Sw, H, L; 1938 v Pol (sub) (5)
Harte, I.P. (Leeds U), 1996 v Cro (sub), Ho, M, Bol; 1997 v Lie, Mac, Ic (sub), W, Mac (sub), R, Lie; 1998 v Li, Ic, Li, Bel (2), Arg, M (18)
Hartnett, J. B. (Middlesbrough), 1949 v Sp; 1954 v L (2)
Haverty, J. (Arsenal), 1956 v Ho; 1957 v D, WG, E (2); 1958 v D, Pol, A; 1959 v Pol; 1960 v Se, Ch; 1961 v W, N, S (2); (with Blackburn R), 1962 v Cz (2); (with Millwall), 1963 v S; 1964 v A, Sp, Pol, N, E; (with Celtic), 1965 v Pol; (with Bristol R), 1965 v Sp; (with Shelbourne), 1966 v Sp (2), WG, A, Bel; 1967 v T, Sp (32)
Hayes, A. W. P. (Southampton), 1979 v D (1)
Hayes, W. E. (Huddersfield T), 1947 v E, P (2)
Hayes, W. J. (Limerick), 1949 v Bel (1)
Healey, R. (Cardiff C), 1977 v Pol; 1980 v E (sub) (2)
Heighway, S. D. (Liverpool), 1971 v Pol, Se (2), I, A; 1973 v USSR; 1975 v USSR, T, USSR, WG; 1976 v T, N; 1977 v E, F (2), Sp, Bul; 1978 v Bul, N, D; 1979 v Ni, Bul; 1980 v Bul, US, Ni, E, Cy, Arg; 1981 v Bel, F, Cy, W, Bel; (with Minnesota K), 1982 v Ho (34)
Henderson, B. (Drumcondra), 1948 v P, Sp (2)
Hennessy, J. (Shelbourne), 1965 v Pol, Bel, Sp; 1966 v WG; (with St Patrick's Ath), 1969 v A (5)
Herrick, J. (Cork Hibernians), 1972 v A, Ch (sub); (with Shamrock R), 1973 v F (sub) (3)
Higgins, J. (Birmingham C), 1951 v Arg (1)
Holmes, J. (Coventry C), 1971 v A (sub); 1973 v F, USSR, Pol, F, N; 1974 v Pol, Br; 1975 v USSR, Sw; 1976 v T, N, Pol; 1977 v E, T, F, Sp; (with Tottenham H), F, Pol, Bul; 1978 v Bul, T, Pol, N, D; 1979 v Ni, E, D, Bul; (with Vancouver W), 1981 v W (30)
Horlacher, A. F. (Bohemians), 1930 v Bel; 1932 v Sp, Ho; 1934 v Ho (sub); 1935 v H;1936 v Ho, Sw (7)
Houghton, R. J. (Oxford U), 1986 v W, U, Ic, Cz; 1987 v Bel (2), S (2), Pol, L; 1988 v L, Bul; (with Liverpool), Is, Y, N, E, USSR, Ho; 1989 v Ni, Tun, Sp, F, H, Sp, Ma, H; 1990 v Ni, Ma, Fi, E, Eg, Ho, R, I; 1991 v Mor, T, E (2), Pol, Ch, US; 1992 v H, Alb, US, I, P; (with Aston Villa), 1993 v D, Sp, Ni, D, Alb, La, Li; 1994 v Li, Sp, Ni, Bol, G (sub), I, M, N, Ho; (with C Palace), 1995 v P, A; 1996 v A, CzR; 1997 v Lie, Lie; (with Reading), 1998 v Li, R, Bel (1 + sub) (73)

Howlett, G. (Brighton & HA), 1984 v Chn (sub) (1)

Hoy, M. (Dundalk), 1938 v N; 1939 v Sw, Pol, H (2), G (6)

Hughton, C. (Tottenham H), 1980 v US, E, Sw, Arg; 1981 v Ho, Bel, F, Cy, W, Bel, Pol; 1982 v F; 1983 v Ho, Sp, Ma, Sp; 1984 v Ic, Ho, Ma; 1985 v M (sub), USSR, N, I, Is, E, Sp; 1986 v Sw, USSR, U, Ic; 1987 v Bel, Bul; 1988 v Is, Y, Pol, N, E, USSR, Ho; 1989 v Ni, F, H, Sp, Ma, H; 1990 v W (sub), USSR (sub), Fi, T (sub), Ma; 1991 v T; (with West Ham U), Ch; 1992 v T (53)

Hurley, C. J. (Millwall), 1957 v E; (with Sunderland), 1958 v D, Pol, A; 1959 v Cz (2); 1960 v Se, Ch, WG, Se; 1961 v W, N, S (2); 1962 v Cz (2), A; 1963 v Ic (2), S; 1964 v A (2), Sp (2), Pol, N; 1965 v Sp; 1966 v WG, A, Bel; 1967 v T, Sp, T, Cz; 1968 v Cz, Pol; 1969 v Pol, D, Cz, (with Bolton W), H (40)

Hutchinson, F. (Drumcondra), 1935 v Sw, G (2)

Irwin, D. J. (Manchester U), 1991 v Mor, T, W, E, Pol, US; 1992 v H, Pol, W, US, Alb, US (sub), I; 1993 v La, D, Sp, Ni, D, Alb, La, Li; 1994 v Li, Sp, Ni, Bol, G, I, M; 1995 v La, Lie, Ni, E, Ni, P, Lie, A; 1996 v A, P, Ho; 1997 v Lie, Mac, Ic, Mac, R; 1998 v Li, Bel, Arg (sub) (48)

Jordan, D. (Wolverhampton W), 1937 v Sw, F (2)

Jordan, W. (Bohemians), 1934 v Ho; 1938 v N (2)

Kavanagh, G. A. (Stoke C), 1998 v CzR (sub) (1)

Kavanagh, P. J. (Celtic), 1931 v Sp; 1932 v Sp (2)

Keane, R. D. (Wolverhampton W), 1998 v CzR (sub), Arg, M (3)

Keane, R. M. (Nottingham F), 1991 v Ch; 1992 v H, Pol, W, Sw, Alb, US; 1993 v La, D, Sp, W, Ni, D, Alb, La, Li; (with Manchester U), 1994 v Li, Sp, Ni, Bol, G, CzR (sub), I, M, N, Ho; 1995 v Ni (2); 1996 v A, Ru; 1997 v Ic, W, Mac, R, Lie; 1998 v Li, Ic, Li (38)

Keane, T. R. (Swansea T), 1949 v Sw, P, Se, Sp (4)

Kearin, M. (Shamrock R), 1972 v A (1)

Kearns, F. T. (West Ham U), 1954 v L (1)

Kearns, M. (Oxford U), 1971 v Pol (sub); (with Walsall), 1974 v Pol (sub), U, Ch; 1976 v N, Pol; 1977 v E, T, F (2), Sp, Bul; 1978 v N, D; 1979 v Ni, E; (with Wolverhampton W), 1980 v US, Ni (18)

Kelly, A. T. (Sheffield U), 1993 v W (sub); 1994 v Ru (sub), G; 1995 v La, Ni, E, Ni, P, Lie, A; 1996 v A, La, P, Ho; 1997 v Mac, Ic, Mac, R; 1998 v R, Arg (sub) (20)

Kelly, D. T. (Walsall), 1988 v Is, R, Y; (with West Ham U), 1989 v Tun (sub); (with Leicester C), 1990 v USSR, Ma; 1991 v Mor, W (sub), Ch, US; 1992 v H; (with Newcastle U), I (sub), P; 1993 v Sp (sub), Ni; (with Wolverhampton W), 1994 v Ru, N (sub); 1995 v E, Ni; (with Sunderland), 1996 v La (sub); 1997 v Ic, W (sub), Mac (sub); (with Tranmere R), 1998 v Li (sub), R (sub), Bel (sub) (26)

Kelly, G. (Leeds U), 1994 v Ru, Ho, Bol (sub), G (sub), CzR, N, Ho; 1995 v La, Lie, Ni (2), P, Lie, A; 1996 v A, La, P, Ho; 1997 v W (sub), R, Lie; 1998 v Ic, Li, Bel (2), CzR, Arg, M (28)

Kelly, J. (Derry C), 1932 v Ho; 1934 v Bel; 1936 v Sw, L (4)

Kelly, J. A. (Drumcondra), 1957 v WG, E; (with Preston NE), 1962 v A; 1963 v Ic (2), S; 1964 v A (2), Sp (2), Pol; 1965 v Bel; 1966 v A, Bel; 1967 v Sp (2), T, Cz; 1968 v Pol, Cz; 1969 v Pol, A, D, Cz, D, H; 1970 v S, D, H, Pol, WG; 1971 v Pol, Se (2), I (2), A; 1972 v Ir, Ec, Ch, P; 1973 v USSR, F, USSR, Pol, F, N (47)

Kelly, J. P. V. (Wolverhampton W), 1961 v W, N, S; 1962 v Cz (2) (5)

Kelly, M. J. (Portsmouth), 1988 v Y, Pol (sub); 1989 v Tun; 1991 v Mor (4)

Kelly, N. (Nottingham F), 1954 v L (1)

Kendrick, J. (Everton), 1927 v I; (with Dolphin) 1934 v Bel, Ho; 1936 v Ho (4)

Kenna, J. J. (Blackburn R), 1995 v P (sub), Lie (sub), A (sub); 1996 v La, P, Ho, Ru (sub), CzR, P, Cro, Ho, US; 1997 v Lie, Mac, Ic, R (sub), Lie; 1998 v Li, Ic, R, Bel (1 + sub), CzR, Arg (24)

Kennedy, M. (Liverpool), 1996 v A, La (sub), P, Ru, CzR, Cro, Ho (sub), US (sub), M, Bol (sub); 1997 v R, Lie; 1998 v Li, Ic (sub), R, Bel (2), M (sub) (18)

Kennedy, M. F. (Portsmouth), 1986 v Ic, Cz (sub) (2)

Kennedy, W. (St James' Gate), 1932 v Ho; 1934 v Bel, Ho (3)

Keogh, J. (Shamrock R), 1966 v WG (sub) (1)

Keogh, S. (Shamrock R), 1959 v Pol (1)

Kernaghan, A. N. (Middlesbrough), 1993 v La, D (2), Alb, La, Li; 1994 v Li; (with Manchester C), Sp, Ni, Bol (sub), CzR; 1995 v Lie, E; 1996 v A, P (sub), Ho (sub), Ru, P, Cro (sub), Ho, US, Bol (22)

Kiernan, F. W. (Shamrock R), 1951 v Arg, N; (with Southampton), 1952 v WG (2), A (5)

Kilbane, K. D. (WBA), 1998 v Ic, CzR (sub), Arg (3)

Kinnear, J. P. (Tottenham H), 1967 v T; 1968 v Cz, Pol; 1969 v A; 1970 v Cz, D, H, Pol; 1971 v Se (sub), I; 1972 v Ir, Ec, Ch, P; 1973 v USSR, F; 1974 v Pol, Br, U, Ch; 1975 v USSR, T, Sw, USSR, WG; (with Brighton & HA), 1976 v T (sub) (26)

Kinsella, J. (Shelbourne), 1928 v Bel (1)

Kinsella, M. A. (Charlton Ath), 1998 v CzR, Arg (2)

Kinsella, O. (Shamrock R), 1932 v Ho; 1938 v N (2)

Kirkland, A. (Shamrock R), 1927 v I (1)

Lacey, W. (Shelbourne), 1927 v I; 1928 v Bel; 1930 v Bel (3)

Langan, D. (Derby Co), 1978 v T, N; 1980 v Sw, Arg; (with Birmingham C), 1981 v WG'B', Ho, Bel, F, Cy, W, Bel, Cz, Pol; 1982 v Ho, F; (with Oxford U), 1985 v N, Sp, Sw; 1986 v W, U; 1987 v Bel, S, Pol, Br (sub), L (sub); 1988 v L (26)

Lawler, J. F. (Fulham), 1953 v A; 1954 v L, F; 1955 v N, H, N, WG; 1956 v Y (8)

Lawlor, J. C. (Drumcondra), 1949 v Bel; (with Doncaster R), 1951 v N, Arg (3)

Lawlor, M. (Shamrock R), 1971 v Pol, Se (2), I (sub); 1973 v Pol (5)

Lawrenson, M. (Preston NE), 1977 v Pol; (with Brighton), 1978 v Bul, Pol, N (sub); 1979 v Ni, E; 1980 v E, Cy, Sw; 1981 v Ho, Bel, F, Cy, Pol; (with Liverpool), 1982 v Ho, F; 1983 v Ho, Sp, Ic, Ma, Sp; 1984 v Ic, Ho, Ma, Is; 1985 v USSR, N, D, I, E, N; 1986 v Sw, USSR, D; 1987 v Bel, S; 1988 v Bul, Is (38)

Leech, M. (Shamrock R), 1969 v Cz, D, H; 1972 v A, Ir, Ec, P; 1973 v USSR (sub) (8)

Lennon, C. (St James' Gate), 1935 v H, Sw, G (3)

Lennox, G. (Dolphin), 1931 v Sp; 1932 v Sp (2)

Lowry, D. (St Patrick's Ath), 1962 v A (sub) (1)

Lunn, R. (Dundalk), 1939 v Sw, Pol (2)

Lynch, J. (Cork Bohemians), 1934 v Bel (1)

McAlinden, J. (Portsmouth), 1946 v P, Sp (2)

McAteer, J. W. (Bolton W), 1994 v Ru, Ho (sub), Bol (sub), G, CzR (sub), I (sub), M (sub), N, Ho (sub); 1995 v La, Lie, Ni (2 sub), Lie; (with Liverpool), 1996 v La, P, Ho (sub), Ru; 1997 v Mac, Ic, W, Mac; 1998 v Ic (sub), Li, R (25)

McCann, J. (Shamrock R), 1957 v WG (1)

McCarthy, J. (Bohemians), 1926 v I; 1928 v Bel; 1930 v Bel (3)

McCarthy, M. (Manchester C), 1984 v Pol, Chn; 1985 v M, D, I, Is, E, Sp, Sw; 1986 v Sw, USSR, W (sub), U, Ic, Cz; 1987 v S (2), Pol, Bul, Bel (with Celtic), Br, L; 1988 v Bul, Is, R, Y, N, E, USSR, Ho; 1989 v Ni, Tun, Sp, F, H, Sp; (with Lyon), 1990 v WG, Ni (with Millwall), W, USSR, Fi, T, E, Eg, Ho, R, I; 1991 v Mor, T, E, US; 1992 v H, T, Alb (sub), US, I, P (57)

McCarthy, M. (Shamrock R), 1932 v Ho (1)

McConville, T. (Dundalk), 1972 v A; (with Waterford), 1973 v USSR, F, USSR, Pol, F (6)

McDonagh, Jacko (Shamrock R), 1984 v Pol (sub), Ma (sub); 1985 v M (sub) (3)

McDonagh, J. (Everton), 1981 v WG'B', W, Bel, Cz; (with Bolton W), 1982 v Ho, F, Ch, Br; 1983 v Ho, Sp, Ic, Ma, Sp; (with Notts Co), 1984 v Ic, Ho, Pol; 1985 v M, USSR, N, D, Sp, Sw; 1986 v Sw, USSR (with Wichita Wings) D (25)

McEvoy, M. A. (Blackburn R), 1961 v S (2); 1963 v S; 1964 v A, Sp (2), Pol, N, E; 1965 v Pol, Bel, Sp; 1966 v Sp (2); 1967 v Sp, T, Cz (17)

McGee, P. (QPR), 1978 v T, N (sub), D (sub); 1979 v Ni, E, D (sub), Bul (sub); 1980 v Cz, Bul; (with Preston NE), US, Ni, Cy, Sw, Arg; 1981 v Bel (sub) (15)

McGoldrick, E. J. (C Palace), 1992 v Sw, US, I, P (sub); 1993 v D, W, Ni (sub), D; (with Arsenal), 1994 v Ni, Ru, Ho, CzR; 1995 v La (sub), Lie, E (15)

McGowan, D. (West Ham U), 1949 v P, Se, Sp (3)

McGowan, J. (Cork U), 1947 v Sp (1)

McGrath, M. (Blackburn R), 1958 v A; 1959 v Pol, Cz (2); 1960 v Se, WG, Se; 1961 v W; 1962 v Cz (2); 1963 v S; 1964 v A (2); 1965 v Pol, Bel, Sp; 1966 v Sp; (with Bradford), 1966 v WG, A, Bel; 1967 v T (22)

McGrath, P. (Manchester U), 1985 v I (sub), Is, E, N (sub), Sw; 1986 v Sw (sub), D, W, Ic, Cz; 1987 v Bel (2), S (2), Pol, Bul, Br, L; 1988 v L, Bul, Y, Pol, N, E, Ho; 1989 v Ni, F, H, Sp, Ma, H; (with Aston Villa), 1990 v WG, Ma, USSR, Fi, T, E, Eg, Ho, R, I; 1991 v E (2), W, Pol, Ch (sub), US; 1992 v Pol, T, Sw, US, Alb, US, I, P; 1993 v La, Sp, Ni, D, La; 1994 v Sp, Ni, G, CzR, I, M, N, Ho; 1995 v La, Ni, E, Ni, P, Lie, A; 1996 v A, La, P, Ho, Ru, CzR; (with Derby Co), 1997 v W (83)

McGuire, M. (Bohemians), 1936 v Ho (1)

McKenzie, G. (Southend U), 1938 v N (2), Cz, Pol; 1939 v Sw, Pol, H (2), G (9)

Mackey, G. (Shamrock R), 1957 v D, WG, E (3)
McLoughlin, A. F. (Swindon T), 1990 v Ma, E (sub), Eg (sub); 1991 v Mor (sub), E (sub); (with Southampton), W, Ch (sub); 1992 v H (sub), W (sub); (with Portsmouth), US (1+sub), I (sub), P; 1993 v W; 1994 v Ni (sub), Ru, Ho (sub); 1995 v Lie (sub); 1996 v P, Cro, Ho, US, M, Bol (sub); 1997 v Lie, Mac, Ic, W, Mac; 1998 v Li (sub), Ic, Li, R, Bel, CzR (sub) (35)
McLoughlin, F. (Fordsons), 1930 v Bel; (with Cork), 1932 v Sp (2)
McMillan, W. (Belfast Celtic), 1946 v P, Sp (2)
McNally, J. B. (Luton T), 1959 v Cz; 1961 v S; 1963 v Ic (3)
Macken, A. (Derby Co), 1977 v Sp (1)
Madden, O. (Cork), 1936 v H (1)
Maguire, J. (Shamrock R), 1929 v Bel (1)
Malone, G. (Shelbourne), 1949 v Bel (1)
Mancini, T. J. (QPR), 1974 v Pol, Br, U, Ch; (with Arsenal), 1975 v USSR (5)
Martin, C. (Bo'ness), 1927 v I (1)
Martin, C. J. (Glentoran), 1946 v P (sub), Sp; 1947 v E; (with Leeds U), 1947 v Sp; 1948 v P, Sp; (with Aston Villa), 1949 v Sw, Bel, P, Se, Sp; 1950 v Fi, E, Fi, Se, Bel; 1951 v Arg; 1952 v WG, A, Sp; 1954 v F (2), L; 1955 v N, Ho, N, WG; 1956 v Y, Sp, Ho (30)
Martin, M. P. (Bohemians), 1972 v A, Ir, Ec, Ch, P; 1973 v USSR; (with Manchester U), 1973 v USSR, Pol, F, N; 1974 v Pol, Br, U, Ch; 1975 v USSR, T, Sw, USSR, Sw, WG; (with WBA), 1976 v T, N, Pol; 1977 v E, T, F (2), Sp, Pol, Bul; (with Newcastle U), 1979 v D, Bul, WG; 1980 v W, Cz, Bul, US, Ni; 1981 v WG'B', F, Bel, Cz; 1982 v Ho, F, Alg, Ch, Br, Tr; 1983 v Ho, Sp, Ma, Sp (52)
Maybury, A. (Leeds U), 1998 v CzR (1)
Meagan, M. K. (Everton), 1961 v S; 1962 v A; 1963 v Ic; 1964 v Sp; (with Huddersfield T), 1965 v Bel; 1966 v Sp (2), A, Bel; 1967 v Sp, T, Sp, T, Cz; 1968 v Cz, Pol; (with Drogheda), 1970 v S (17)
Meehan, P. (Drumcondra), 1934 v Ho (1)
Milligan, M. J. (Oldham Ath), 1992 v US (sub) (1)
Monahan, P. (Sligo R), 1935 v Sw, G (1)
Mooney, J. (Shamrock R), 1965 v Pol, Bel (2)
Moore, A. (Middlesbrough), 1996 v CzR, Cro (sub), Ho, M, Bol; 1997 v Lie (sub), Mac (sub), Ic (sub) (8)
Moore, P. (Shamrock R), 1931 v Sp; 1932 v Ho; (with Aberdeen), 1934 v Bel, Ho; 1935 v H, G; (with Shamrock R), 1936 v Ho; 1937 v G, H (9)
Moran, K. (Manchester U), 1980 v Sw, Arg; 1981 v WG'B', Bel, F, Cy, W (sub), Bel, Cz, Pol; 1982 v F, Alg; 1983 v Ic; 1984 v Ic, Ho, Ma, Is; 1985 v M; 1986 v D, Ic, Cz; 1987 v Bel (2), S (2), Pol, Bul, Br, L; 1988 v L, Bul, Is, R, Y, Pol, N, E, USSR, Ho; (with Sporting Gijon), 1989 v Ni, H, Sp, Ma, H; 1990 v Ni, Ma; (with Blackburn R), W, USSR (sub), Ma, E, Eg, Ho, R, I; 1991 v T (sub), W, E, Pol, Ch, US; 1992 v Pol, US; 1993 v D, Sp, Ni, Alb; 1994 v Li, Sp, Ho, Bol (71)
Moroney, T. (West Ham U), 1948 v Sp; 1949 v P, Se, Sp; 1950 v Fi, E, Fi, Bel; 1951 v N (2); 1952 v WG; (with Evergreen U), 1954 v F (12)
Morris, C. B. (Celtic), 1988 v Is, R, Y, Pol, N, E, USSR, Ho; 1989 v Ni, Tun, Sp, F, H (1+1 sub); 1990 v WG, Ni, Ma (sub), W, USSR, Fi (sub), T, E, Eg, Ho, R, I; 1991 v E; 1992 v H (sub), Pol, W, Sw, US (2), P; (with Middlesbrough), 1993 v W (35)
Moulson, C. (Lincoln C), 1936 v H, L; (with Notts Co), 1937 v H, Sw, F (5)
Moulson, G. B. (Lincoln C), 1948 v P, Sp; 1949 v Sw (3)
Mucklan, C. (Drogheda U), 1978 v Pol (1)
Muldoon, T. (Aston Villa), 1927 v I (1)
Mulligan, P. M. (Shamrock R), 1969 v Cz, D, H; 1970 v S, Cz, D; (with Chelsea), 1970 v H, Pol, WG; 1971 v Pol, Se, I; 1972 v A, Ir, Ec, Ch, P; (with C Palace), 1973 v F, USSR, Pol, F, N; 1974 v Pol, Br, U, Ch; 1975 v USSR, T, Sw, USSR, Sw; (with WBA), 1976 v T, Pol; 1977 v E, T, F (2), Pol, Bul; 1978 v Bul, N, D; 1979 v E, D, Bul (sub), WG; (with Shamrock R), 1980 v W, Cz, Bul, US (sub) (50)
Munroe, L. (Shamrock R), 1954 v L (1)
Murphy, A. (Clyde), 1956 v Y (1)
Murphy, B. (Bohemians), 1986 v U (1)
Murphy, J. (C Palace), 1980 v W, US, Cy (3)
Murray, T. (Dundalk), 1950 v Bel (1)

Newman, W. (Shelbourne), 1969 v D (1)
Nolan, R. (Shamrock R), 1957 v D, WG, E; 1958 v Pol; 1960 v Ch, Se; 1962 v Cz (2); 1963 v Ic (10)

O'Brien, F. (Philadelphia F), 1980 v Cz, E, Cy (sub) (3)
O'Brien, L. (Shamrock R), 1986 v U; (with Manchester U), 1987 v Br; 1988 v Is (sub), R (sub), Y (sub), Pol (sub); 1989 v Tun; (with Newcastle U), 1992 v Sw

(sub); 1993 v W; (with Tranmere R), 1994 v Ru; 1996 v Cro, Ho, US, Bol; 1997 v Mac (sub) (16)
O'Brien, M. T. (Derby Co), 1927 v I; (with Walsall), 1929 v Bel; (with Norwich C), 1930 v Bel; (with Watford), 1932 v Ho (4)
O'Brien, R. (Notts Co), 1976 v N, Pol; 1977 v Sp, Pol; 1980 v Arg (sub) (5)
O'Byrne, L. B. (Shamrock R), 1949 v Bel (1)
O'Callaghan, B. R. (Stoke C), 1979 v WG (sub); 1980 v W, US; 1981 v W; 1982 v Br, Tr (6)
O'Callaghan, K. (Ipswich T), 1981 v WG'B', Cz, Pol; 1982 v Alg, Ch, Br, Tr (sub); 1983 v Sp, Ic (sub), Ma (sub), Sp (sub); 1984 v Ic, Ho, Ma; 1985 v M (sub), N (sub), D (sub), (with Portsmouth) E (sub); 1986 v Sw (sub), USSR (sub); 1987 v Br (21)
O'Connell, A. (Dundalk), 1967 v Sp; (with Bohemians), 1971 v Pol (sub) (2)
O'Connor, T. (Shamrock R), 1950 v Fi, E, Fi, Se (4)
O'Connor, T. (Fulham), 1968 v Cz; (with Dundalk), 1972 v A, Ir (sub), Ec (sub), Ch; (with Bohemians), 1973 v F (sub), Pol (sub) (7)
O'Driscoll, J. F. (Swansea T), 1949 v Sw, Bel, Se (3)
O'Driscoll, S. (Fulham), 1982 v Ch, Br, Tr (sub) (3)
O'Farrell, F. (West Ham U), 1952 v A; 1953 v A; 1954 v F; 1955 v Ho, N; 1956 v Y, Ho; (with Preston NE), 1958 v D; 1959 v Cz (9)
O'Flanagan, K. P. (Bohemians), 1938 v N, Cz, Pol; 1939 v Pol, H (2), G; (with Arsenal), 1947 v E, Sp, P (10)
O'Flanagan, M. (Bohemians), 1947 v E (1)
O'Hanlon, K. G. (Rotherham U), 1988 v Is (1)
O'Kane, P. (Bohemians), 1935 v H, Sw, G (3)
O'Keefe, E. (Everton), 1981 v W; (with Port Vale), 1984 v Chn; 1985 v M, USSR (sub), E (5)
O'Keefe, T. (Cork), 1934 v Bel; (with Waterford), 1938 v Cz, Pol (3)
O'Leary, D. (Arsenal), 1977 v E, F (2), Sp, Bul; 1978 v Bul, N, D; 1979 v E, Bul, WG; 1980 v W, Bul, Ni, E, Cy; 1981 v WG'B',Ho, Cz, Pol; 1982 v Ho, F; 1983 v Ho, Ic, Sp; 1984 v Pol, Is, Chn; 1985 v USSR, N, D, Is, E (sub), N, Sp, Sw; 1986 v Sw, USSR, D, W; 1989 v Sp, Ma, H; 1990 v WG, Ni (sub), Ma, W (sub), USSR, Fi, T, Ma, R (sub); 1991 v Mor, T, E (2), Pol, Ch; 1992 v H, Pol, T, W, Sw, US, Alb, I, P; 1993 v W (68)
O'Leary, P. (Shamrock R), 1980 v Bul, US, Ni, E (sub), Cz, Arg; 1981 v Ho (7)
O'Mahoney, M. T. (Bristol R), 1938 v Cz, Pol; 1939 v Sw, Pol, H, G (6)
O'Neill, F. S. (Shamrock R), 1962 v Cz (2); 1965 v Pol, Bel, Sp; 1966 v Sp (2), WG, A; 1967 v Sp, T, Sp, T; 1969 v Pol, A, D, Cz, D (sub), H (sub); 1972 v A (20)
O'Neill, J. (Everton), 1952 v Sp; 1953 v F, A; 1954 v F, L, F; 1955 v N, Ho, N, WG; 1956 v Y, Sp; 1957 v D; 1958 v A; 1959 v Pol, Cz (2) (17)
O'Neill, J. (Preston NE), 1961 v W (1)
O'Neill, K. P. (Norwich C), 1996 v P (sub), Cro, Ho (sub), US (sub), M, Bol; 1997 v Lie, Mac (1 + sub) (9)
O'Neill, W. (Dundalk), 1936 v Ho, Sw, H, L; 1937 v G, H, Sw, F; 1938 v N; 1939 v H, G (11)
O'Regan, K. (Brighton & HA), 1984 v Ma, Pol; 1985 v M, Sp (sub) (4)
O'Reilly, J. (Brideville), 1932 v Ho; (with Bohemians), 1934 v Bel, Ho; (with Brideville), 1936 v Ho; Sw, H, L; (with St James' Gate), 1937 v G, H, Sw, F; 1938 v N (2), Cz, Pol; 1939 v Sw, Pol, H (2), G (20)
O'Reilly, J. (Cork U), 1946 v P, Sp (2)

Peyton, G. (Fulham), 1977 v Sp (sub); 1978 v Bul, T, Pol; 1979 v D, Bul, WG; 1980 v W, Cz, Bul, E, Cy, Sw, Arg; 1981 v Ho, Bel, F, Cy; 1982 v Tr; 1985 v M (sub); 1986 v W, Cz; (with Bournemouth), 1988 v L, Pol; 1989 v Ni, Tun; 1990 v USSR, Ma; 1991 v Ch; (with Everton) 1992 v US (2), I (sub), P (33)
Peyton, N. (Shamrock R), 1957 v WG; (with Leeds U), 1960 v WG, Se (sub); 1961 v W; 1963 v Ic, S (6)
Phelan, T. (Wimbledon), 1992 v H, Pol (sub), T, W, Sw, US, I (sub), P; (with Manchester C), 1993 v La (sub), D, Sp, Ni, Alb, La, Li; 1994 v Li, Sp, Ni, Ho, Bol, G, CzR, I, M, Ho; 1995 v E; 1996 v La; (with Chelsea), Ho, Ru, P, Cro, Ho, US, M (sub), Bol; (with Everton), 1997 v W, Mac; 1998 v R (38)

Quinn, N. J. (Arsenal), 1986 v Ic (sub), Cz; 1987 v Bul (sub), Br (sub); 1988 v L (sub), Bul (sub), Is, R (sub), Pol (sub), E (sub); 1989 v Tun (sub), Sp (sub), H (sub); (with Manchester C), 1990 v USSR, Ma, Eg (sub), Ho, R, I; 1991 v Mor, T, E(2) W, Pol; 1992 v H, W (sub), US, Alb, US, I, P; 1993 v La, D, Sp, Ni, D, Alb, La, Li; 1994 v Li, Sp, Ni; 1995 v La, Lie, Ni, E, Ni, P, Lie, A; 1996 v A, La,

P, Ru, CzR, P (sub), Cro, Ho (sub), US; (with Sunderland), 1997 v Lie; 1998 v Li, Arg (63)

Reid, C. (Brideville), 1931 v Sp (1)
Richardson, D. J. (Shamrock R), 1972 v A (sub); (with Gillingham), 1973 v N (sub); 1980 v Cz (3)
Rigby, A. (St James' Gate), 1935 v H, Sw, G (3)
Ringstead, A. (Sheffield U), 1951 v Arg, N; 1952 v WG (2), A, Sp; 1953 v A; 1954 v F; 1955 v N; 1956 v Y, Sp, Ho; 1957 v E (2); 1958 v D, Pol, A; 1959 v Pol, Cz (2) (20)
Robinson, J. (Bohemians), 1928 v Bel; (with Dolphin), 1931 v Sp (2)
Robinson, M. (Brighton & HA), 1981 v WG'B', F, Cy, Bel, Pol; 1982 v Ho, F, Alg, Ch; 1983 v Ho, Sp, Ic, Ma; (with Liverpool), 1984 v Ic, Ho, Is; 1985 v USSR, N; (with QPR), N, Sp, Sw; 1986 v D (sub), W, Cz (24)
Roche, P. J. (Shelbourne), 1972 v A; (with Manchester U), 1975 v USSR, T, Sw, USSR, Sw, WG; 1976 v T (8)
Rogers, E. (Blackburn R), 1968 v Cz, Pol; 1969 v Pol, A, D, Cz, D, H; 1970 v S, D, H; 1971 v I (2), A; (with Charlton Ath), 1972 v Ir, Ec, Ch, P; 1973 v USSR (19)
Ryan, G. (Derby Co), 1978 v T; (with Brighton & HA), 1979 v E, WG; 1980 v W, Cy (sub), Sw, Arg (sub); 1981 v WG'B' (sub), F (sub), Pol (sub); 1982 v Br (sub), Ho (sub), Alg (sub), Ch (sub), Tr; 1984 v Pol, Chn; 1985 v M (18)
Ryan, R. A. (WBA), 1950 v Se, Bel; 1951 v N, Arg, N; 1952 v WG (2), A, Sp; 1953 v F, A; 1954 v F, L, F; 1955 v N; (with Derby Co), 1956 v Sp (16)

Savage, D. P. T. (Millwall), 1996 v P (sub), Cro (sub), US (sub), M, Bol (5)
Saward, P. (Millwall), 1954 v L; (with Aston Villa), 1957 v E (2); 1958 v D, Pol, A; 1959 v Pol, Cz; 1960 v Se, Ch, WG, Se; 1961 v W, N; (with Huddersfield T), 1961 v S; 1962 v A; 1963 v Ic (2) (18)
Scannell, T. (Southend U), 1954 v L (1)
Scully, P. J. (Arsenal), 1989 v Tun (sub) (1)
Sheedy, K. (Everton), 1984 v Ho (sub), Ma; 1985 v D, I, Is, Sw; 1986 v Sw, D; 1987 v S, Pol; 1988 v Is, R, Pol, E (sub), USSR; 1989 v Ni, Tun, H, Sp, Ma, H; 1990 v Ni, Ma, W (sub), USSR, Fi (sub), T, E, Eg, Ho, R, I; 1991 v E, Pol, Ch, US; 1992 v H, Pol, T, W; (with Newcastle U), Sw (sub), Alb; 1993 v La, W (sub) (45)
Sheridan, J. J. (Leeds U), 1988 v R, Y, Pol, N (sub); 1989 v Sp; (with Sheffield W), 1990 v W, T (sub), Ma, I (sub); 1991 v Mor (sub), T, Ch, US (sub); 1992 v H; 1993 v La; 1994 v Sp (sub), Ho, Bol, G, CzR, I, M, N, Ho; 1995 v La, Lie, Ni, E, Ni, P, Lie, A; 1996 v A, Ho (34)
Slaven, B. (Middlesbrough), 1990 v W, Fi, T (sub), Ma; 1991 v W, Pol (sub); 1993 v W (7)
Sloan, J. W. (Arsenal), 1946 v P, Sp (2)
Smyth, M. (Shamrock R), 1969 v Pol (sub) (1)
Squires, J. (Shelbourne), 1934 v Ho (1)
Stapleton, F. (Arsenal), 1977 v T, F, Sp, Bul; 1978 v Bul, N, D; 1979 v Ni, E (sub), D, WG; 1980 v W, Bul, Ni, E, Cy; 1981 v WG'B', Ho, Bel, F, Cy, Bel, Cz, Pol; (with Manchester U), 1982 v Ho, F, Alg; 1983 v Ho, Sp, Ic, Ma, Sp; 1984 v Ic, Ho, Ma, Pol, Is, Chn; 1985 v N, D, I, Is, E, N, Sw; 1986 v Sw, USSR, D, U, Ic, Cz (sub); 1987 v Bel (2), S (2), Pol, Bul, L; (with Ajax), 1988 v L, Bul, R, Y, N, E, USSR, Ho; (with Le Havre), 1989 v F, Sp, Ma; (with Blackburn R), 1990 v WG, Ma (sub) (71)
Staunton, S. (Liverpool), 1989 v Tun, Sp (2), Ma, H; 1990 v WG, Ni, Ma, W, USSR, Fi, T, Ma, E, Eg, Ho, R, I; 1991 v Mor, T, E (2), W, Pol, Ch, US; (with Aston Villa), 1992 v Pol, T, Sw, US, Alb, US, I, P; 1993 v La, Sp, Ni, D, Alb, La, Li; 1994 v Li, Sp, Ho, Bol, G, CzR, I, M, N, Ho; 1995 v La, Lie, Ni, E, Ni, P, Lie, A; 1996 v La, P, Ru; 1997 v Lie, Mac (2), W, R, Lie; 1998 v Lit, Ic, Li, Bel (2), Arg (74)

Stevenson, A. E. (Dolphin), 1932 v Ho; (with Everton), 1947 v E, Sp, P; 1948 v P, Sp; 1949 v Sw (7)
Strahan, F. (Shelbourne), 1964 v Pol, N, E; 1965 v Pol; 1966 v WG (5)
Sullivan, J. (Fordsons), 1928 v Bel (1)
Swan, M. M. G. (Drumcondra), 1960 v Se (sub) (1)
Synnott, N. (Shamrock R), 1978 v T, Pol; 1979 v Ni (3)

Taylor, T. (Waterford), 1959 v Pol (sub) (1)
Thomas, P. (Waterford), 1974 v Pol, Br (2)
Townsend, A. D. (Norwich C), 1989 v F, Sp (sub), Ma (sub), H; 1990 v WG (sub), Ni, Ma, W, USSR, Fi (sub), T, Ma (sub), E, Eg, Ho, R, I; (with Chelsea), 1991 v Mor, T, E (2), W, Pol, Ch, US; 1992 v Pol, W, US, Alb, US, I; 1993 v La, D, Sp, Ni, D, Alb, La, Li; (with Aston Villa), 1994 v Li, Ni, Ho, Bol, G, CzR, I, M, N, Ho; 1995 v La, Ni, E, Ni, P; 1996 v A, La, Ho, Ru, CzR, P; 1997 v Lie, Mac (2), Ic, R, Lie; 1998 v Li; (with Middlesbrough), Ic, Bel (2) (70)
Traynor, T. J. (Southampton), 1954 v L; 1962 v A; 1963 v Ic (2), S; 1964 v A (2), Sp (8)
Treacy, R. C. P. (WBA), 1966 v WG; 1967 v Sp, Cz; 1968 v Cz; (with Charlton Ath), 1968 v Pol; 1969 v Pol, Cz, D; 1970 v S, D, H (sub), Pol (sub), WG (sub); 1971 v Pol, Se (sub+1), I, A; (with Swindon T), 1972 v Ir, Ec, Ch, P; 1973 v USSR, F, USSR, Pol, F, N; 1974 v Pol; (with Preston NE), Br; 1975 v USSR, Sw (2), WG; 1976 v T, N (sub), Pol (sub); (with WBA), 1977 v F, Pol; (with Shamrock R), 1978 v T, Pol; 1980 v Cz (sub) (42)
Tuohy, L. (Shamrock R), 1956 v Y; 1959 v Cz (2); (with Newcastle U), 1962 v A; 1963 v Ic (2); (with Shamrock R), 1964 v A; 1965 v Bel (8)
Turner, C. J. (Southend U), 1936 v Sw; 1937 v G, H, Sw, F; 1938 v N (2), (with West Ham U) Cz, Pol; 1939 v H (10)
Turner, P. (Celtic), 1963 v S; 1964 v Sp (2)

Vernon, J. (Belfast C), 1946 v P, Sp (2)

Waddock, G. (QPR), 1980 v Sw, Arg; 1981 v W, Pol (sub); 1982 v Alg; 1983 v Ic, Ma, Sp, Ho (sub); 1984 v Ma (sub), Ic, Ho, Is; 1985 v I, Is, E, N, Sp; 1986 v USSR; (with Millwall), 1990 v USSR, T (21)
Walsh, D. J. (Linfield), 1946 v P, Sp; (with WBA), 1947 v Sp, P; 1948 v P, Sp; 1949 v Sw, P, Se, Sp; 1950 v E, Fi, Se; 1951 v N; (with Aston Villa), Arg, N; 1952 v Sp; 1953 v A; 1954 v F (2) (20)
Walsh, J. (Limerick), 1982 v Tr (1)
Walsh, M. (Blackpool), 1976 v N, Pol; 1977 v F (sub), Pol; (with Everton), 1979 v Ni (sub); (with QPR), D (sub), Bul, WG (sub); (with Porto), 1981 v Bel (sub), Cz; 1982 v Alg (sub); 1983 v Sp, Ho (sub), Sp (sub); 1984 v Ic (sub), Ma, Pol, Chn; 1985 v USSR, N (sub), D (21)
Walsh, M. (Everton), 1982 v Ch, Br, Tr; 1983 v Ic (4)
Walsh, W. (Manchester C), 1947 v E, Sp, P; 1948 v P, Sp; 1949 v Bel; 1950 v E, Se, Bel (9)
Waters, J. (Grimsby T), 1977 v T; 1980 v Ni (sub) (2)
Watters, F. (Shelbourne), 1926 v I (1)
Weir, E. (Clyde), 1939 v H (2), G (3)
Whelan, R. (St Patrick's Ath), 1964 v A, E (sub) (2)
Whelan, R. (Liverpool), 1981 v Cz (sub); 1982 v Ho (sub), F; 1983 v Ic, Ma, Sp; 1984 v Is; 1985 v USSR, N, I (sub), Is, E, N (sub), Sw (sub); 1986 v USSR (sub), W; 1987 v Bel (sub), S, Bul, Bel, Br, L; 1988 v L, Bul, Pol, N, E, USSR, Ho; 1989 v Ni, F, H, Sp, Ma; 1990 v WG, Ni, Ma, W, Ho (sub); 1991 v Mor, E; 1992 v Sw; 1993 v La, W (sub), Li (sub); 1994 v Li (sub), Sp, Ru, Ho, G (sub), N (sub); (with Southend U), 1995 v Lie, A (53)
Whelan, W. (Manchester U), 1956 v Ho; 1957 v D, E (2) (4)
White, J. J. (Bohemians), 1928 v Bel (1)
Whittaker, R. (Chelsea), 1959 v Cz (1)
Williams, J. (Shamrock R), 1938 v N (1)

# BRITISH AND IRISH INTERNATIONAL GOALSCORERS SINCE 1872

Where two players with the same surname and initials have appeared for the same country, and one or both have scored, they have been distinguished by reference to the club which appears *first* against their name in the international appearances section.

## ENGLAND

|  | |  | |  | |  | |
|---|---|---|---|---|---|---|---|
| A'Court, A. | 1 | Carter, H. S. | 7 | Grainger, C. | 3 | Mabbutt, G. | 1 |
| Adams, T. A. | 4 | Carter, J. H. | 4 | Greaves, J. | 44 | Macdonald, M. | 6 |
| Adcock, H. | 1 | Chadwick, E. | 3 | Grosvenor, A. T. | 2 | Mannion, W. J. | 11 |
| Alcock, C. W. | 1 | Chamberlain, M. | 1 | Gunn, W. | 1 | Mariner, P. | 13 |
| Allen, A. | 3 | Chambers, H. | 5 | | | Marsh, R. W. | 1 |
| Allen, R. | 2 | Channon, M. R. | 21 | Haines, J. T. W. | 2 | Matthews, S. | 11 |
| Anderson, V. | 2 | Charlton, J. | 6 | Hall, G. W. | 9 | Matthews, V. | 1 |
| Anderton, D. R. | 6 | Charlton, R. | 49 | Halse, H. J. | 2 | McCall, J. | 1 |
| Astall, G. | 1 | Chenery, C. J. | 1 | Hampson, J. | 5 | McDermott, T. | 3 |
| Athersmith, W. C. | 3 | Chivers, M. | 13 | Hampton, H. | 2 | Medley, L. D. | 1 |
| Atyeo, P. J. W. | 5 | Clarke, A. J. | 10 | Hancocks, J. | 2 | Melia, J. | 1 |
| | | Cobbold, W. N. | 7 | Hardman, H. P. | 1 | Mercer, D. W. | 1 |
| Bache, J. W. | 4 | Cock, J. G. | 2 | Harris, S. S. | 2 | Merson, P. C. | 2 |
| Bailey, N. C. | 2 | Common, A. | 2 | Hassall, H. W. | 4 | Milburn, J. E. T. | 10 |
| Baily, E. F. | 5 | Connelly, J. M. | 7 | Hateley, M. | 9 | Miller, H. S. | 1 |
| Baker, J. H. | 3 | Coppell, S. J. | 7 | Haynes, J. N. | 18 | Mills, G. R. | 3 |
| Ball, A. J. | 8 | Cotterill, G. H. | 2 | Hegan, K. E. | 4 | Milward, A. | 3 |
| Bambridge, A. L. | 1 | Cowans, G. | 2 | Henfrey, A. G. | 2 | Mitchell, C. | 5 |
| Bambridge, E. C. | 12 | Crawford, R. | 1 | Hilsdon, G. R. | 14 | Moore, J. | 1 |
| Barclay, R. | 2 | Crawshaw, T. H. | 1 | Hine, E. W. | 4 | Moore, R. F. | 2 |
| Barmby, N. J. | 3 | Crayston, W. J. | 1 | Hirst, D. E. | 1 | Moore, W. G. B. | 2 |
| Barnes, J. | 11 | Creek, F. N. S. | 1 | Hitchens, G. A. | 5 | Morren, T. | 1 |
| Barnes, P. S. | 4 | Crooks, S. D. | 7 | Hobbis, H. H. F. | 1 | Morris, F. | 1 |
| Barton, J. | 1 | Currey, E. S. | 2 | Hoddle, G. | 8 | Morris, J. | 3 |
| Bassett, W. I. | 7 | Currie, A. W. | 3 | Hodgetts, D. | 1 | Mortensen, S. H. | 23 |
| Bastin, C. S. | 12 | Cursham, A. W. | 2 | Hodgson, G. | 1 | Morton, J. R. | 1 |
| Beardsley, P. A. | 9 | Cursham, H. A. | 5 | Holley, G. H. | 8 | Mosforth, W. | 3 |
| Beasley, A. | 1 | | | Houghton, W. E. | 5 | Mullen, J. | 6 |
| Beattie, T. K. | 1 | Daft, H. B. | 3 | Howell, R. | 1 | Mullery, A. P. | 1 |
| Beckham, D. R. J. | 1 | Davenport, J. K. | 2 | Hughes, E. W. | 1 | | |
| Becton, F. | 2 | Davis, G. | 1 | Hulme, J. H. A. | 4 | Neal, P. G. | 5 |
| Bedford, H. | 1 | Davis, H. | 1 | Hunt, G. S. | 1 | Needham, E. | 3 |
| Bell, C. | 9 | Day, S. H. | 2 | Hunt, R. | 18 | Nicholls, J. | 1 |
| Bentley, R. T. F. | 9 | Dean, W. R. | 18 | Hunter, N. | 2 | Nicholson, W. E. | 1 |
| Bishop, S. M. | 1 | Devey, J. H. G. | 1 | Hurst, G. C. | 24 | | |
| Blackburn, F. | 1 | Dewhurst, F. | 11 | | | O'Grady, M. | 3 |
| Blissett, L. | 3 | Dix, W. R. | 1 | Ince, P. E. C. | 2 | Osborne, F. R. | 3 |
| Bloomer, S. | 28 | Dixon, K. M. | 4 | | | Owen, M. J. | 3 |
| Bond, R. | 2 | Dixon, L. M. | 1 | Jack, D. N. B. | 3 | Own goals | 23 |
| Bonsor, A. G. | 1 | Douglas, B. | 11 | Johnson, D. E. | 6 | | |
| Bowden, E. R. | 1 | Drake, E. J. | 6 | Johnson, E. | 2 | Page, L. A. | 1 |
| Bowers, J. W. | 2 | Ducat, A. | 1 | Johnson, J. A. | 2 | Paine, T. L. | 7 |
| Bowles, S. | 1 | Dunn, A. T. B. | 2 | Johnson, T. C. F. | 5 | Palmer, C. L. | 1 |
| Bradford, G. R. W. | 1 | | | Johnson, W. H. | 1 | Parry, E. H. | 1 |
| Bradford, J. | 7 | Eastham, G. | 2 | | | Parry, R. A. | 1 |
| Bradley, W. | 2 | Edwards, D. | 5 | Kail, E. I. L. | 2 | Pawson, F. W. | 1 |
| Bradshaw, F. | 3 | Elliott, W. H. | 3 | Kay, A. H. | 1 | Payne, J. | 2 |
| Bridges, B. J. | 1 | Evans, R. E. | 1 | Keegan, J. K. | 21 | Peacock, A. | 3 |
| Bridgett, A. | 3 | | | Kelly, R. | 8 | Pearce, S. | 5 |
| Brindle, T. | 1 | Ferdinand, L. | 5 | Kennedy, R. | 3 | Pearson, J. S. | 5 |
| Britton, C. S. | 1 | Finney, T. | 30 | Kenyon-Slaney, W. S. | 2 | Pearson, S. C. | 5 |
| Broadbent, P. F. | 2 | Fleming, H. J. | 9 | Keown, M. R. | 1 | Perry, W. | 2 |
| Broadis, I. A. | 8 | Flowers, R. | 10 | Kevan, D. T. | 8 | Peters, M. | 20 |
| Brodie, J. B. | 1 | Forman, Frank | 1 | Kidd, B. | 1 | Pickering, F. | 5 |
| Bromley-Davenport, W. | 2 | Forman, Fred | 3 | Kingsford, R. K. | 1 | Platt, D. | 27 |
| Brook, E. F. | 10 | Foster, R. E. | 3 | Kirchen, A. J. | 2 | Pointer, R. | 2 |
| Brooking, T. D. | 5 | Fowler, R. B. | 2 | Kirton, W. J. | 1 | | |
| Brooks, J. | 2 | Francis, G. C. J. | 3 | | | Quantrill, A. | 1 |
| Broome, F. H. | 3 | Francis, T. | 12 | Langton, R. | 1 | | |
| Brown, A. | 4 | Freeman, B. C. | 3 | Latchford, R. D. | 5 | Ramsay, A. E. | 3 |
| Brown, A. S. | 1 | Froggatt, J. | 2 | Latherton, E. G. | 1 | Revie, D. G. | 4 |
| Brown, G. | 5 | Froggatt, R. | 2 | Lawler, C. | 1 | Reynolds, J. | 3 |
| Brown, J. | 3 | | | Lawton, T. | 22 | Richardson, J. R. | 2 |
| Brown, W. | 1 | Galley, T. | 1 | Lee, F. | 10 | Rigby, A. | 3 |
| Buchan, C. M. | 4 | Gascoigne, P. J. | 10 | Lee, J. | 1 | Rimmer, E. J. | 2 |
| Bull, S. G. | 4 | Geary, F. | 3 | Lee, R. M. | 2 | Roberts, H. | 1 |
| Bullock, N. | 2 | Gibbins, W. V. T. | 3 | Lee, S. | 2 | Roberts, W. T. | 2 |
| Burgess, H. | 4 | Gilliatt, W. E. | 3 | Le Saux, G. P. | 1 | Robinson, J. | 3 |
| Butcher, T. | 3 | Goddard, P. | 1 | Lindley, T. | 15 | Robson, B. | 26 |
| Byrne, J. J. | 8 | Goodall, J. | 12 | Lineker, G. | 48 | Robson, R. | 4 |
| | | Goodyer, A. C. | 1 | Lofthouse, J. M. | 3 | Rowley, J. F. | 6 |
| Camsell, G. H. | 18 | Gosling, R. C. | 2 | Lofthouse, N. | 30 | Royle, J. | 2 |
| | | Goulden, L. A. | 4 | Hon. A. Lyttelton | 1 | Rutherford, J. | 3 |

|  | |  | |  | |  | |
|---|---|---|---|---|---|---|---|
| Campbell, John | 4 | Harrower, W. | 5 | McClair, B. J. | 2 | Robertson, A. | 2 |
| *(Rangers)* | | Hartford, R. A. | 4 | McCoist, A. | 19 | Robertson, J. | 2 |
| Campbell, P. | 2 | Heggie, C. | 5 | McColl, R. S. | 13 | Robertson, J. N. | 9 |
| Campbell, R. | 1 | Henderson, J. G. | 1 | McCulloch, D. | 3 | Robertson, J. T. | 2 |
| Cassidy, J. | 1 | Henderson, W. | 5 | McDougall, J. | 4 | Robertson, T. | 1 |
| Chalmers, S. | 3 | Hendry, E. C. J. | 1 | McFarlane, A. | 1 | Robertson, W. | 1 |
| Chambers, T. | 1 | Herd, D. G. | 3 | McFadyen, W. | 2 | Russell, D. | 1 |
| Cheyne, A. G. | 4 | Herd, G. | 1 | McGhee, M. | 2 | | |
| Christie, A. J. | 1 | Hewie, J. D. | 2 | McGinlay, J. | 4 | Scott, A. S. | 5 |
| Clunas, W. L. | 1 | Higgins, A. | 1 | McGrory, J. | 6 | Sellar, W. | 4 |
| Collins, J. | 11 | *(Newcastle U)* | | McGuire, W. | 1 | Sharp, G. | 1 |
| Collins, R. Y. | 10 | Higgins, A. (*Kilmarnock*) | 4 | McInally, A. | 3 | Shaw, F. W. | 1 |
| Combe, J. R. | 1 | Highet, T. C. | 1 | McInnes, T. | 2 | Shearer, D. | 2 |
| Conn, A. | 1 | Holton, J. A. | 2 | McKie, J. | 2 | Simpson, J. | 1 |
| Cooper, D. | 6 | Hopkin, D. | 2 | McKimmie, S. | 1 | Smith, A. | 5 |
| Craig, J. | 1 | Houliston, W. | 2 | McKinlay, W. | 4 | Smith, G. | 4 |
| Craig, T. | 1 | Howie, H. | 1 | McKinnon, A. | 1 | Smith, J. | 1 |
| Crawford, S. | 1 | Howie, J. | 2 | McKinnon, R. | 1 | Smith, John | 13 |
| Cunningham, A. N. | 5 | Hutchison, T. | 1 | McKinnon, W. W. | 5 | Somerville, G. | 1 |
| Curran, H. P. | 1 | Hutton, J. | 1 | McLaren, A. | 4 | Souness, G. J. | 4 |
| | | Hyslop, T. | 1 | McLaren, J. | 1 | Speedie, F. | 2 |
| Dailly, C. | 1 | | | McLean, A. | 1 | St John, I. | 9 |
| Dalglish, K. | 30 | Imrie, W. N. | 1 | McLean, T. | 1 | Steel, W. | 12 |
| Davidson, D. | 1 | | | McLintock, F. | 1 | Stein, C. | 10 |
| Davidson, J. A. | 1 | Jackson, A. | 8 | McMahon, A. | 6 | Stevenson, G. | 4 |
| Delaney, J. | 3 | Jackson, C. | 1 | McMenemy, J. | 5 | Stewart, R. | 1 |
| Devine, A. | 1 | Jackson, D. | 4 | McMillan, I. L. | 2 | Stewart, W. E. | 1 |
| Dewar, G. | 1 | James, A. W. | 4 | McNeil, H. | 5 | Strachan, G. | 5 |
| Dewar, N. | 4 | Jardine, A. | 1 | McNeill, W. | 3 | Sturrock, P. | 3 |
| Dickson, W. | 4 | Jenkinson, T. | 1 | McPhail, J. | 3 | | |
| Divers, J. | 1 | Jess, E. | 1 | McPhail, R. | 7 | Taylor, J. D. | 1 |
| Docherty, T. H. | 1 | Johnston, L. H. | 1 | McPherson, J. | 8 | Templeton, R. | 1 |
| Dodds, D. | 1 | Johnston, M. | 14 | McPherson, R. | 1 | Thomson, A. | 1 |
| Donaldson, A. | 1 | Johnstone, D. | 2 | McQueen, G. | 5 | Thomson, C. | 4 |
| Donnachie, J. | 1 | Johnstone, J. | 4 | McStay, P. | 9 | Thomson, R. | 1 |
| Dougall, J. | 1 | Johnstone, Jas. | 1 | Meiklejohn, D. D. | 3 | Thomson, W. | 1 |
| Drummond, J. | 2 | Johnstone, R. | 9 | Millar, J. | 2 | Thornton, W. | 1 |
| Dunbar, M. | 1 | Johnstone, W. | 1 | Miller, T. | 2 | | |
| Duncan, D. | 7 | Jordan, J. | 11 | Miller, W. | 1 | | |
| Duncan, D. M. | 1 | | | Mitchell, R. C. | 1 | Waddell, T. S. | 1 |
| Duncan, J. | 1 | Kay, J. L. | 5 | Morgan, W. | 1 | Waddell, W. | 6 |
| Dunn, J. | 2 | Keillor, A. | 3 | Morris, D. | 1 | Walker, J. | 2 |
| Durie, G. S. | 7 | Kelly, J. | 1 | Morris, H. | 3 | Walker, R. | 7 |
| | | Kelso, J. | 1 | Morton, A. L. | 5 | Walker, T. | 9 |
| Easson, J. F. | 1 | Ker, G. | 10 | Mudie, J. K. | 9 | Wallace, I. A. | 1 |
| Ellis, J. | 1 | King, A. | 1 | Mulhall, G. | 1 | Wark, J. | 7 |
| | | King, J. | 1 | Munro, A. D. | 1 | Watson, J. A. K. | 1 |
| Ferguson, J. | 6 | Kinnear, D. | 1 | Munro, N. | 1 | Watt, F. | 2 |
| Fernie, W. | 1 | | | Murdoch, R. | 5 | Watt, W. W. | 1 |
| Fitchie, T. T. | 1 | Lambie, W. A. | 5 | Murphy, F. | 1 | Weir, A. | 1 |
| Flavell, R. | 2 | Lang, J. J. | 1 | Murray, J. | 1 | Weir, J. B. | 2 |
| Fleming, C. | 2 | Law, D. | 30 | | | White, J. A. | 3 |
| Fleming, J. W. | 3 | Leggat, G. | 8 | Napier, C. E. | 3 | Wilson, A. | 2 |
| Fraser, M. J. E. | 3 | Lennie, W. | 1 | Narey, D. | 1 | Wilson, A. N. | 13 |
| | | Lennox, R. | 3 | Neil, R. G. | 2 | Wilson, D. | 2 |
| Gallacher, H. K. | 23 | Liddell, W. | 6 | Nevin, P. K. F. | 5 | *(Queen's Park)* | |
| Gallacher, K. W. | 8 | Lindsay, J. | 6 | Nicholas, C. | 5 | Wilson, D. (*Rangers*) | 9 |
| Gallacher, P. | 1 | Linwood, A. B. | 1 | Nisbet, J. | 2 | Wilson, H. | 1 |
| Galt, J. H. | 1 | Logan, J. | 1 | | | Wylie, T. G. | 1 |
| Gemmell, T. (*St Mirren*) | 1 | Lorimer, P. | 4 | O'Donnell, F. | 2 | | |
| Gemmell, T. (*Celtic*) | 1 | Love, A. | 1 | O'Hare, J. | 5 | Young, A. | 5 |
| Gemmill, A. | 8 | Lowe, J. (*Cambuslang*) | 1 | Ormond, W. E. | 1 | | |
| Gibb, W. | 1 | Lowe, J. (*St Bernards*) | 1 | O'Rourke, F. | 1 | **WALES** | |
| Gibson, D. W. | 3 | | | Orr, R. | 1 | Allchurch, I. J. | 23 |
| Gibson, J. D. | 1 | Macari, L. | 5 | Orr, T. | 1 | Allen, M. | 3 |
| Gibson, N. | 1 | MacDougall, E. J. | 3 | Oswald, J. | 1 | Astley, D. J. | 12 |
| Gillespie, Jas. | 3 | MacLeod, M. | 1 | Own goals | 14 | Atherton, R. W. | 2 |
| Gillick, T. | 3 | Mackay, D. C. | 4 | | | | |
| Gilzean, A. J. | 12 | Mackay, G. | 1 | Parlane, D. | 1 | Bamford, T. | 1 |
| Gossland, J. | 2 | MacKenzie, J. A. | 1 | Paul, H. McD. | 2 | Barnes, W. | 1 |
| Goudie, J. | 1 | Madden, J. | 5 | Paul, W. | 6 | Bellamy, C. D. | 1 |
| Gough, C. R. | 6 | Marshall, H. | 1 | Pettigrew, W. | 2 | Blackmore, C. G. | 1 |
| Gourlay, J. | 1 | Marshall, J. | 1 | Provan, D. | 1 | Blake, N. A. | 2 |
| Graham, A. | 2 | Mason, J. | 4 | | | Bodin, P. J. | 3 |
| Graham, G. | 3 | Massie, A. | 1 | Quinn, J. | 7 | Boulter, L. M. | 1 |
| Gray, A. | 5 | Masson, D. S. | 5 | Quinn, P. | 1 | Bowdler, J. C. H. | 3 |
| Gray, E. | 3 | McAdam, J. | 1 | | | Bowen, D. L. | 1 |
| Gray, F. | 1 | McAllister, G. | 5 | Rankin, G. | 2 | Bowen, M. | 3 |
| Greig, J. | 3 | McAulay, J. | 1 | Rankin, R. | 2 | Boyle, T. | 1 |
| Groves, W. | 4 | McAvennie, F. | 1 | Reid, W. | 4 | Bryan, T. | 1 |
| | | McCall, J. | 1 | Reilly, L. | 22 | Burgess, W. A. R. | 1 |
| Hamilton, G. | 4 | McCall, S. M. | 1 | Renny-Tailyour, H. W. | 1 | Burke, T. | 1 |
| Hamilton, J. | 3 | McCalliog, J. | 1 | Richmond, J. T. | 1 | Butler, W. T. | 1 |
| *(Queen's Park)* | | McCallum, N. | 1 | Ring, T. | 2 | | |
| Hamilton, R. C. | 14 | | | Rioch, B. D. | 6 | Chapman, T. | 2 |
| Harper, J. M. | 2 | | | Ritchie, J. | 1 | Charles, J. | 1 |

| Name | Goals |
|---|---|
| Charles, M. | 6 |
| Charles, W. J. | 15 |
| Clarke, R. J. | 5 |
| Coleman, C. | 3 |
| Collier, D. J. | 1 |
| Crosse, K. | 1 |
| Cumner, R. H. | 1 |
| Curtis, A. | 6 |
| Curtis, E. R. | 3 |
| Davies, D. W. | 1 |
| Davies, E. Lloyd | 1 |
| Davies, G. | 2 |
| Davies, L. S. | 6 |
| Davies, R. T. | 9 |
| Davies, R. W. | 6 |
| Davies, S. | 5 |
| Davies, W. | 6 |
| Davies, W. H. | 1 |
| Davies, William | 5 |
| Davis, W. O. | 1 |
| Deacy, N. | 4 |
| Doughty, J. | 6 |
| Doughty, R. | 2 |
| Durban, A. | 2 |
| Dwyer, P. | 2 |
| Edwards, G. | 2 |
| Edwards, R. I. | 4 |
| England, H. M. | 4 |
| Evans, I. | 1 |
| Evans, J. | 1 |
| Evans, R. E. | 2 |
| Evans, W. | 1 |
| Eyton-Jones, J. A. | 1 |
| Flynn, B. | 7 |
| Ford, T. | 23 |
| Foulkes, W. I. | 1 |
| Fowler, J. | 3 |
| Giles, D. | 2 |
| Giggs, R. J. | 5 |
| Glover, E. M. | 7 |
| Godfrey, B. C. | 2 |
| Green, A. W. | 3 |
| Griffiths, A. T. | 6 |
| Griffiths, M. W. | 2 |
| Griffiths, T. P. | 3 |
| Harris, C. S. | 1 |
| Hartson, J. | 2 |
| Hersee, R. | 1 |
| Hewitt, R. | 1 |
| Hockey, T. | 1 |
| Hodges, G. | 2 |
| Hole, W. J. | 1 |
| Hopkins, I. J. | 2 |
| Horne, B. | 2 |
| Howell, E. G. | 3 |
| Hughes, L. M. | 16 |
| James, E. | 2 |
| James, L. | 10 |
| James, R. | 7 |
| Jarrett, R. H. | 3 |
| Jenkyns, C. A. | 1 |
| Jones, A. | 1 |
| Jones, Bryn | 6 |
| Jones, B. S. | 2 |
| Jones, Cliff | 16 |
| Jones, C. W. | 1 |
| Jones, D. E. | 1 |
| Jones, Evan | 1 |
| Jones, H. | 1 |
| Jones, I. | 1 |
| Jones, J. L. | 1 |
| Jones, J. O. | 1 |
| Jones, J. P. | 1 |
| Jones, Leslie J. | 1 |
| Jones, R. A. | 2 |
| Jones, W. L. | 6 |
| Keenor, F. C. | 2 |
| Krzywicki, R. L. | 1 |
| Leek, K. | 5 |
| Lewis, B. | 4 |
| Lewis, D. M. | 2 |
| Lewis, W. | 8 |
| Lewis, W. L. | 3 |
| Lovell, S. | 1 |
| Lowrie, G. | 2 |
| Mahoney, J. F. | 1 |
| Mays, A. W. | 1 |
| Medwin, T. C. | 6 |
| Melville, A. K | 3 |
| Meredith, W. H. | 11 |
| Mills, T. J. | 1 |
| Moore, G. | 1 |
| Morgan, J. R. | 2 |
| Morgan-Owen, H. | 1 |
| Morgan-Owen, M. M. | 2 |
| Morris, A. G. | 9 |
| Morris, H. | 2 |
| Morris, R. | 1 |
| Morris, S. | 2 |
| Nicholas, P. | 2 |
| O'Callaghan, E. | 3 |
| O'Sullivan, P. A. | 1 |
| Owen, G. | 2 |
| Owen, W. | 4 |
| Owen, W. P. | 6 |
| Own goals | 13 |
| Palmer, D. | 3 |
| Parry, T. D. | 3 |
| Paul, R. | 1 |
| Peake, E. | 1 |
| Pembridge, M. | 5 |
| Perry, E. | 1 |
| Phillips, C. | 5 |
| Phillips, D. | 2 |
| Powell, A. | 1 |
| Powell, D. | 1 |
| Price, J. | 4 |
| Price, P. | 1 |
| Pryce-Jones, W. E. | 3 |
| Pugh, D. H. | 2 |
| Reece, G. I. | 2 |
| Rees, R. R. | 3 |
| Richards, R. W. | 1 |
| Roach, J. | 2 |
| Robbins, W. W. | 4 |
| Roberts, J. (*Corwen*) | 1 |
| Roberts, Jas. | 1 |
| Roberts, P. S. | 1 |
| Roberts, R. (*Druids*) | 1 |
| Roberts, W. (*Llangollen*) | 2 |
| Roberts, W. (*Wrexham*) | 1 |
| Roberts, W. H. | 1 |
| Robinson, J. R. C. | 1 |
| Rush, I. | 28 |
| Russell, M. R. | 1 |
| Sabine, H. W. | 1 |
| Saunders, D. | 21 |
| Savage, R. W. | 1 |
| Shaw, E. G. | 2 |
| Sisson, H. | 4 |
| Slatter, N. | 2 |
| Smallman, D. P. | 1 |
| Speed, G. A. | 3 |
| Symons, C. J. | 1 |
| Tapscott, D. R. | 4 |
| Thomas, M. | 4 |
| Thomas, T. | 1 |
| Toshack, J. B. | 12 |
| Trainer, H. | 2 |
| Vaughan, John | 2 |
| Vernon, T. R. | 8 |
| Vizard, E. T. | 1 |
| Walsh, I. | 7 |
| Warren, F. W. | 3 |
| Watkins, W. M. | 4 |
| Wilding, J. | 4 |
| Williams, D. R. | 2 |
| Williams, G. E. | 1 |
| Williams, G. G. | 1 |
| Williams, W. | 1 |
| Woosnam, A. P. | 3 |
| Wynn, G. A. | 1 |
| Yorath, T. C. | 2 |
| Young, E. | 1 |

**EIRE**

| Name | Goals |
|---|---|
| Aldridge, J. | 19 |
| Ambrose, P. | 1 |
| Anderson, J. | 1 |
| Bermingham, P. | 1 |
| Bradshaw, P. | 4 |
| Brady, L. | 9 |
| Breen, G. | 2 |
| Brown, D. | 1 |
| Byrne, J. (*Bray*) | 1 |
| Byrne, J. (*QPR*) | 4 |
| Cantwell, J. | 14 |
| Carey, J. | 3 |
| Carroll, T. | 1 |
| Cascarino, A. | 19 |
| Coad, P. | 3 |
| Connolly, D. J. | 6 |
| Conroy, T. | 2 |
| Conway, J. | 3 |
| Coyne, T. | 6 |
| Cummings, G. | 5 |
| Curtis, D. | 8 |
| Daly, G. | 13 |
| Davis, T. | 4 |
| Dempsey, J. | 1 |
| Dennehy, M. | 2 |
| Donnelly, J. | 3 |
| Donnelly, T. | 1 |
| Duffy, B. | 1 |
| Duggan, H. | 1 |
| Dunne, J. | 12 |
| Dunne, L. | 1 |
| Eglington, T. | 2 |
| Ellis, P. | 2 |
| Fagan, F. | 5 |
| Fallon, S. | 2 |
| Fallon, W. | 2 |
| Farrell, P. | 3 |
| Fitzgerald, P. | 2 |
| Fitzgerald, J. | 1 |
| Fitzsimmons, A. | 7 |
| Flood, J. J. | 4 |
| Fogarty, A. | 3 |
| Fullam, J. | 1 |
| Fullam, R. | 1 |
| Galvin, A. | 1 |
| Gavin, J. | 2 |
| Geoghegan, M. | 2 |
| Giles, J. | 5 |
| Givens, D. | 19 |
| Glynn, D. | 1 |
| Grealish, T. | 8 |
| Grimes, A. A. | 1 |
| Hale, A. | 2 |
| Hand, E. | 2 |
| Harte, I. P. | 2 |
| Haverty, J. | 3 |
| Holmes, J. | 1 |
| Horlacher, A. | 2 |
| Houghton, R. | 6 |
| Hughton, C. | 1 |
| Hurley, C. | 2 |
| Irwin, D. | 2 |
| Jordan, D. | 1 |
| Keane, R. M. | 3 |
| Kelly, D. | 9 |
| Kelly, G. | 1 |
| Kelly, J. | 2 |
| Kernaghan, A. N. | 1 |
| Lacey, W. | 1 |
| Lawrenson, M. | 5 |
| Leech, M. | 2 |
| McAteer, J. W. | 1 |
| McCann, J. | 1 |
| McCarthy, M. | 2 |
| McEvoy, A. | 6 |
| McGee, P. | 4 |
| McGrath, P. | 8 |
| McLoughlin, A. F. | 2 |
| Mancini, T. | 1 |
| Martin, C. | 6 |
| Martin, M. | 4 |
| Mooney, J. | 1 |
| Moore, P. | 7 |
| Moran, K. | 6 |
| Moroney, T. | 1 |
| Mulligan, P. | 1 |
| O'Callaghan, K. | 1 |
| O'Connor, T. | 2 |
| O'Farrell, F. | 2 |
| O'Flanagan, K. | 3 |
| O'Keefe, E. | 1 |
| O'Leary, D. A. | 1 |
| O'Neill, F. | 1 |
| O'Neill, K. P. | 4 |
| O'Reilly, J. (*Brideville*) | 2 |
| O'Reilly, J. (*Cork*) | 1 |
| Own goals | 7 |
| Quinn, N. | 16 |
| Ringstead, A. | 7 |
| Robinson, M. | 4 |
| Rogers, E. | 5 |
| Ryan, G. | 1 |
| Ryan, R. | 3 |
| Sheedy, K. | 9 |
| Sheridan, J. | 5 |
| Slaven, B. | 1 |
| Sloan, W. | 1 |
| Squires, J. | 1 |
| Stapleton, F. | 20 |
| Staunton, S. | 5 |
| Strahan, J. | 1 |
| Sullivan, J. | 1 |
| Townsend, A. D. | 7 |
| Treacy, R. | 5 |
| Touhy, L. | 4 |
| Waddock, G. | 3 |
| Walsh, D. | 5 |
| Walsh, M. | 3 |
| Waters, J. | 1 |
| White, J. J. | 2 |
| Whelan, R. | 3 |

# EUROPEAN FOOTBALL CHAMPIONSHIP
## (formerly EUROPEAN NATIONS' CUP)

| Year | Winners | | Runners-up | | Venue | Attendance |
|------|---------|---|-----------|---|-------|-----------|
| 1960 | USSR | 2 | Yugoslavia | 1 | Paris | 17,966 |
| 1964 | Spain | 2 | USSR | 1 | Madrid | 120,000 |
| 1968 | Italy | 2 | Yugoslavia | 0 | Rome | 60,000 |
| | After 1-1 draw | | | | | 75,000 |
| 1972 | West Germany | 3 | USSR | 0 | Brussels | 43,437 |
| 1976 | Czechoslovakia | 2 | West Germany | 2 | Belgrade | 45,000 |
| | *(Czechoslovakia won on penalties)* | | | | | |
| 1980 | West Germany | 2 | Belgium | 1 | Rome | 47,864 |
| 1984 | France | 2 | Spain | 0 | Paris | 48,000 |
| 1988 | Holland | 2 | USSR | 0 | Munich | 72,308 |
| 1992 | Denmark | 2 | Germany | 0 | Gothenburg | 37,800 |
| 1996 | Germany | 2 | Czech Republic | 1 | Wembley | 73,611 |

*(Germany won on sudden death)*

# EURO 2000

**GROUP 1**
Italy, Denmark, Switzerland, Wales, Belarus
05.09.98 Wales v Italy
05.09.98 Belarus v Denmark
10.10.98 Denmark v Wales
10.10.98 Italy v Switzerland
14.10.98 Wales v Belarus
14.10.98 Switzerland v Denmark
27.03.99 Denmark v Italy
27.03.99 Belarus v Switzerland
31.03.99 Italy v Wales
31.03.99 Switzerland v Wales
05.06.99 Denmark v Belarus
05.06.99 Italy v Wales
09.06.99 Wales v Denmark
09.06.99 Switzerland v Italy
04.09.99 Denmark v Switzerland
04.09.99 Belarus v Wales
08.09.99 Italy v Denmark
08.09.99 Switzerland v Belarus
09.10.99 Wales v Switzerland
09.10.99 Belarus v Italy

**GROUP 2**
Norway, Greece, Georgia, Latvia, Slovenia, Albania
05.09.98 Georgia v Albania
06.09.98 Greece v Slovenia
06.09.98 Norway v Latvia
10.10.98 Albania v Greece
10.10.98 Slovenia v Norway
10.10.98 Latvia v Georgia
14.10.98 Norway v Albania
14.10.98 Greece v Georgia
14.10.98 Slovenia v Latvia
27.03.99 Greece v Norway
27.03.99 Georgia v Slovenia
31.03.99 Slovenia v Albania
31.03.99 Latvia v Greece
28.04.99 Albania v Latvia
28.04.99 Georgia v Norway
30.05.99 Norway v Georgia
05.06.99 Albania v Norway
05.06.99 Georgia v Greece
05.06.99 Latvia v Slovenia
09.06.99 Albania v Slovenia
09.06.99 Greece v Latvia
04.09.99 Norway v Greece
04.09.99 Latvia v Albania
04.09.99 Slovenia v Georgia
08.09.99 Greece v Albania
08.09.99 Norway v Slovenia
08.09.99 Georgia v Latvia
09.10.99 Albania v Georgia
09.10.99 Slovenia v Greece
09.10.99 Latvia v Norway

**GROUP 3**
Germany, Turkey, Finland, Northern Ireland, Moldova
05.09.98 Finland v Moldova
05.09.98 Turkey v Northern Ireland
10.10.98 Turkey v Germany
10.10.98 Northern Ireland v Finland

14.10.98 Moldova v Germany
14.10.98 Turkey v Finland
18.11.98 Northern Ireland v Moldova
27.03.99 Northern Ireland v Germany
27.03.99 Turkey v Moldova
31.03.99 Germany v Finland
31.03.99 Moldova v Northern Ireland
04.06.99 Germany v Moldova
05.06.99 Finland v Turkey
09.06.99 Moldova v Finland
04.09.99 Finland v Germany
04.09.99 Northern Ireland v Turkey
08.09.99 Germany v Northern Ireland
08.09.99 Moldova v Turkey
09.10.99 Germany v Turkey
09.10.99 Finland v Northern Ireland

**GROUP 4**
Russia, France, Ukraine, Iceland, Armenia, Andorra
05.09.98 Armenia v Andorra
05.09.98 Ukraine v Russia
05.09.98 Iceland v France
10.10.98 Andorra v Ukraine
10.10.98 Russia v France
10.10.98 Armenia v Iceland
14.10.98 Ukraine v Armenia
14.10.98 France v Andorra
14.10.98 Iceland v Russia
27.03.99 Andorra v Iceland
27.03.99 France v Ukraine
27.03.99 Armenia v Russia
31.03.99 Ukraine v Iceland
31.03.99 Russia v Andorra
31.03.99 France v Armenia
05.06.99 Ukraine v Andorra
05.06.99 France v Russia
05.06.99 Iceland v Armenia
09.06.99 Andorra v France
09.06.99 Russia v Iceland
09.06.99 Armenia v Ukraine
04.09.99 Ukraine v France
04.09.99 Iceland v Andorra
04.09.99 Russia v Armenia
08.09.99 Andorra v Russia
08.09.99 Iceland v Ukraine
08.09.99 Armenia v France
09.10.99 France v Iceland
09.10.99 Russia v Ukraine
09.10.99 Andorra v Armenia

**GROUP 5**
England, Bulgaria, Sweden, Poland, Luxembourg
05.09.98 Sweden v England
06.09.98 Bulgaria v Poland
10.10.98 Poland v Luxembourg
10.10.98 England v Bulgaria
14.10.98 Luxembourg v England
14.10.98 Bulgaria v Sweden
27.03.99 Sweden v Luxembourg
27.03.99 England v Poland
31.03.99 Poland v Sweden
31.03.99 Luxembourg v Bulgaria

05.06.99  Poland v Bulgaria
05.06.99  England v Sweden
09.06.99  Luxembourg v Poland
09.06.99  Bulgaria v England
04.09.99  England v Luxembourg
05.09.99  Sweden v Bulgaria
08.09.99  Poland v England
08.09.99  Luxembourg v Sweden
09.10.99  Sweden v Poland
10.10.99  Bulgaria v Luxembourg

**GROUP 6**
Spain, Austria, Israel, Cyprus, San Marino
05.09.98  Austria v Israel
05.09.98  Cyprus v Spain
10.10.98  Cyprus v Austria
10.10.98  San Marino v Israel
14.10.98  San Marino v Austria
14.10.98  Israel v Spain
18.11.98  San Marino v Cyprus
10.02.99  Cyprus v San Marino
27.03.99  Spain v Austria
28.03.99  Israel v Cyprus
31.03.99  San Marino v Spain
28.04.99  Austria v San Marino
05.06.99  Spain v San Marino
06.06.99  Israel v Austria
04.09.99  Austria v Spain
05.09.99  Cyprus v Israel
08.09.99  Israel v San Marino
08.09.99  Spain v Cyprus
09.10.99  Spain v Israel
10.10.99  Austria v Cyprus

**GROUP 7**
Romania, Portugal, Slovakia, Hungary, Liechtenstein,
Azerbaijan
02.09.98  Romania v Liechtenstein
05.09.98  Slovakia v Azerbaijan
06.09.98  Hungary v Portugal
10.10.98  Portugal v Romania
10.10.98  Liechtenstein v Slovakia
10.10.98  Azerbaijan v Hungary
14.10.98  Liechtenstein v Azerbaijan
14.10.98  Hungary v Romania
14.10.98  Slovakia v Portugal
26.03.99  Portugal v Azerbaijan
27.03.99  Hungary v Liechtenstein
27.03.99  Romania v Slovakia
31.03.99  Liechtenstein v Portugal
31.03.99  Azerbaijan v Romania
31.03.99  Slovakia v Hungary
05.06.99  Portugal v Slovakia
05.06.99  Azerbaijan v Liechtenstein
05.06.99  Romania v Hungary
09.06.99  Portugal v Liechtenstein
09.06.99  Hungary v Slovakia
09.06.99  Romania v Azerbaijan
03.09.99  Azerbaijan v Portugal
04.09.99  Liechtenstein v Hungary
04.09.99  Slovakia v Romania
08.09.99  Hungary v Azerbaijan
08.09.99  Romania v Portugal
08.09.99  Slovakia v Liechtenstein
09.10.99  Liechtenstein v Romania
09.10.99  Azerbaijan v Slovakia
10.10.99  Portugal v Hungary

**GROUP 8**
Yugoslavia, Croatia, Rep. of Ireland, Macedonia, Malta
05.09.98  Rep. of Ireland v Croatia
06.09.98  Macedonia v Malta
10.10.98  Malta v Croatia
10.10.98  Yugoslavia v Rep. of Ireland
14.10.98  Rep. of Ireland v Malta
14.10.98  Croatia v Macedonia
18.11.98  Malta v Macedonia
10.02.99  Malta v Yugoslavia
27.03.99  Macedonia v Rep. of Ireland
27.03.99  Yugoslavia v Croatia
31.03.99  Croatia v Malta
31.03.99  Yugoslavia v Macedonia
05.06.99  Macedonia v Croatia
05.06.99  Rep. of Ireland v Yugoslavia
09.06.99  Yugoslavia v Malta
04.09.99  Croatia v Rep. of Ireland
08.09.99  Malta v Rep. of Ireland
08.09.99  Macedonia v Yugoslavia
10.10.99  Croatia v Yugoslavia
10.10.99  Rep. of Ireland v Macedonia

**GROUP 9**
Scotland, Czech Republic, Lithuania, Bosnia, Faeroes,
Estonia

**Tallinn, 4 June 1998, 3500**

**Estonia (2) 5** *(Viikmae 13, Reim 43 (pen), Terehhov 76,
Oper 87, Kirs 90)*
**Faeroes (0) 0**

*Estonia:* Poom; Lemsalu, Kirs, Hohlov-Simson, Meet,
    Viikmae (O'Konnel-Bronin 80), Terehhov, Oper,
    Kristal, Reim, Zelinski.
*Faeroes:* Knudsen; Dam, Hansen J, Thorsteinsson,
    Hansen O (Jarnskor H 83), Morkore A, Joensen,
    Johnsson, Petersen, Muller (Mikkelsen 41), Jonsson
    (Arge 83).

19.08.98  Bosnia v Faeroes
05.09.98  Bosnia v Estonia
05.09.98  Lithuania v Scotland
06.09.98  Faeroes v Czech Republic
10.10.98  Bosnia v Czech Republic
10.10.98  Lithuania v Faeroes
10.10.98  Scotland v Estonia
14.10.98  Lithuania v Bosnia
14.10.98  Scotland v Faeroes
14.10.98  Czech Republic v Estonia
27.03.99  Czech Republic v Lithuania
27.03.99  Scotland v Bosnia
31.03.99  Lithuania v Estonia
31.03.99  Scotland v Czech Republic
05.06.99  Bosnia v Lithuania
05.06.99  Estonia v Czech Republic
05.06.99  Faeroes v Scotland
09.06.99  Estonia v Lithuania
09.06.99  Faeroes v Bosnia
09.06.99  Czech Republic v Scotland
04.09.99  Bosnia v Scotland
04.09.99  Faeroes v Estonia
04.09.99  Lithuania v Czech Republic
08.09.99  Czech Republic v Bosnia
08.09.99  Faeroes v Lithuania
08.09.99  Estonia v Scotland
09.10.99  Estonia v Bosnia
09.10.99  Czech Republic v Faeroes
09.10.99  Scotland v Lithuania

# SOUTH AMERICA

## COPA LIBERTADORES 1998

**FIRST ROUND**

**Group 1**

|  | P | W | D | L | F | A | Pts |
|---|---|---|---|---|---|---|---|
| America (Col) | 6 | 3 | 2 | 1 | 10 | 5 | 11 |
| Barcelona | 6 | 2 | 3 | 1 | 5 | 3 | 9 |
| Bucaramanga | 6 | 2 | 1 | 3 | 5 | 6 | 7 |
| Dep. Quito | 6 | 1 | 2 | 3 | 3 | 9 | 5 |

**Group 2**

|  | P | W | D | L | F | A | Pts |
|---|---|---|---|---|---|---|---|
| Gremio | 6 | 4 | 0 | 2 | 6 | 5 | 12 |
| Vasco da Gama | 6 | 2 | 2 | 2 | 7 | 4 | 8 |
| America (Mex) | 6 | 2 | 2 | 2 | 6 | 5 | 8 |
| Guadalajara | 6 | 2 | 0 | 4 | 2 | 7 | 6 |

**Group 3**

|  | P | W | D | L | F | A | Pts |
|---|---|---|---|---|---|---|---|
| Olimpia | 6 | 4 | 1 | 1 | 14 | 6 | 13 |
| Colo Colo | 6 | 2 | 1 | 3 | 8 | 10 | 7 |
| Cerro Porteno | 6 | 2 | 1 | 3 | 6 | 9 | 7 |
| Univ. Catolica | 6 | 2 | 1 | 3 | 5 | 8 | 7 |

**Group 4**

|  | P | W | D | L | F | A | Pts |
|---|---|---|---|---|---|---|---|
| Bolivar | 6 | 4 | 1 | 1 | 9 | 7 | 13 |
| Penarol | 6 | 3 | 1 | 2 | 12 | 5 | 10 |
| Nacional | 6 | 2 | 0 | 4 | 11 | 12 | 6 |
| Oriente Petrolero | 6 | 1 | 2 | 3 | 7 | 15 | 5 |

**Group 5**

|  | P | W | D | L | F | A | Pts |
|---|---|---|---|---|---|---|---|
| River Plate | 6 | 5 | 1 | 0 | 15 | 7 | 16 |
| Alianza | 6 | 2 | 1 | 3 | 5 | 7 | 7 |
| Colon | 6 | 2 | 1 | 3 | 5 | 8 | 7 |
| Sporting Cristal | 6 | 1 | 1 | 4 | 8 | 11 | 4 |

**SECOND ROUND, FIRST LEG**
Vasco de Gama 2, Cruzeiro 1
Cerro Porteno 1, America (Col) 0
Nacional 1, Gremio 1
Barcelona 2, Colo Colo 1
Bucaramanga 1, Bolivar 2
Alianza 1, Penarol 0
America (Mex) 1, River Plate 1
Colon 3, Olimpia 2

**SECOND ROUND, SECOND LEG**
Gremio 4, Nacional 0
Bolivar 1, Bucaramanga 0
Penarol 2, Alianza 1
*(Penarol won 3-1 on penalties)*
America (Col) 1, Cerro Porteno 2
Colo Colo 2, Barcelona 2
Olimpia 1, Colon 0
*(Colon won 2-1 on penalties).*
River Plate 1, America (Mex) 0

**QUARTER-FINALS, FIRST LEG**
Bolivar 1, Barcelona 1
Penarol 2, Cerro Porteno 0
River Plate 2, Colon 1

**QUARTER-FINALS, SECOND LEG**
Barcelona 4, Bolivar 0
Cerro Porteno 3, Penarol 0
Colon 1, River Plate 3

## CENTENARIO CUP

**GROUP A**
America (Br) 1, Corinthians 1
Atletico Mineiro 2, AC Milan 2
Corinthians 0, AC Milan 0
America (Br) 2, Atletico Mineiro 2
Atletico Mineiro 4, Corinthians 2
America (Br) 1, AC Milan 1

**GROUP B**
Flamengo 2, Olimpia 2
Cruzeiro 4, Benfica 1
Cruzeiro 1, Olimpia 0
Flamengo 5, Benfica 2
Benfica 0, Olimpia 0
Cruzeiro 2, Flamengo 1

**FINAL**
Atletico Mineiro 2, Cruzeiro 1

## SOUTH AMERICAN SUPER CUP

**GROUP 1**
Colo Colo 4, Cruzeiro 2
Boca Juniors 1, Independiente 1
Colo Colo 2, Independiente 0
Boca Juniors 1, Cruzeiro 0
Colo Colo 2, Boca Juniors 1
Cruzeiro 2, Independiente 1
Cruzeiro 2, Colo Colo 0
Independiente 2, Boca Juniors 1
Cruzeiro 2, Boca Juniors 1
Independiente 2, Colo Colo 2
Boca Juniors 2, Colo Colo 2
Independiente 3, Cruzeiro 1

**GROUP 2**
Flamengo 3, Sao Paulo 2
Olimpia 1, Velez Sarsfield 0
Olimpia 0, Flamengo 1
Sao Paulo 5, Velez Sarsfield 1
Olimpia 1, Sao Paulo 0
Flamengo 0, Velez Sarsfield 1
Velez Sarsfield 1, Olimpia 1
Sao Paulo 1, Flamengo 0
Flamengo 3, Olimpia 3

Velez Sarsfield 3, Sao Paulo 3
Velez Sarsfield 0, Flamengo 3
Sao Paulo 4, Olimpia 1

**GROUP 3**
River Plate 3, Racing 2
Vasco da Gama 2, Santos 1
Vasco da Gama 1, Racing 0
River Plate 3, Santos 2
River Plate 5, Vasco da Gama 1
Racing 2, Santos 0
Racing 2, River Plate 3
Santos 1, Vasco da Gama 2
Racing 2, Vasco da Gama 3
Santos 2, River Plate 1
Santos 3, Racing 2
Vasco da Gama 0, River Plate 2

**GROUP 4**
Gremio 1, Penarol 1
Estudiantes 1, Nacional (Col) 0
Penarol 3, Nacional (Col) 1
Estudiantes 0, Gremio 0
Gremio 2, Nacional (Col) 2

Penarol 2, Estudiantes 2
Nacional (Col) 2, Estudiantes 0
Penarol 3, Gremio 2
Nacional (Col) 1, Penarol 0
Gremio 3, Estudiantes 2
Nacional (Col) 3, Gremio 1
Estudiantes 3, Penarol 1

**SEMI-FINALS, FIRST LEG**
River Plate 2, Nacional (Col) 0
Sao Paulo 3, Colo Colo 1

**SEMI-FINALS, SECOND LEG**
Nacional (Col) 2, River Plate 1
Colo Colo 0, Sao Paulo 1

**FINAL, FIRST LEG**
Sao Paulo 0, River Plate 0

**FINAL, SECOND LEG**
River Plate 2, Sao Paulo 1

## CONMEBOL CUP

**PRELIMINARY ROUND, FIRST LEG**
Estudiantes 1, Union Tachira 0

**PRELIMINARY ROUND, SECOND LEG**
Union Tachira 3, Estudiantes 2
*(Union Tachira won 3-2 on penalties)*

**FIRST ROUND, FIRST LEG**
Tolima 2, Rio Branco 1
Universitario 3, Tecnico 0
Vitoria 2, Sportivo 0
Santa Cruz 1, Lanus 1
Univ de Chile 2, Colon 1
Defensor 3, Danubio 3
Union Tachira 1, America Cali 1
Atletico Mineiro 4, Portuguesa 1

**FIRST ROUND, SECOND LEG**
Rio Branco 1, Tolima 0
*(Tolima won 3-1 on penalties)*
Tecnico 0, Universitario 0
Sportivo 1, Vitoria 4
Lanus 5, Santa Cruz 0
Colon 2, Univ de Chile 1
*(Colon won 3-2 on penalties)*
Danubio 3, Defensor 2
America Cali 3, Union Tachira 1
Portuguesa 0, Atletico Mineiro 0

**SECOND ROUND, FIRST LEG**
America Cali 1, Atletico Mineiro 2
Vitoria 1, Lanus 0
Tolima 1, Universitario 0
Danubio 1, Colon 1

**SECOND ROUND, SECOND LEG**
Atletico Mineiro 1, America Cali 1
Universitario 2, Tolima 0
Lanus 3, Vitoria 1
Colon 1, Danubio 1
*(Colon won 3-2 on penalties)*

**SEMI-FINALS, FIRST LEG**
Colon 0, Lanus 2
Universitario 0, Atletico Mineiro 2

**SEMI-FINALS, SECOND LEG**
Lanus 0, Colon 0
Atletico Mineiro 4, Universitario 0

**FINAL FIRST LEG**
Lanus 1, Atletico Mineiro 4

**FINAL SECOND LEG**
Atletico Mineiro 1, Lanus 4

# AFRICA

## AFRICAN NATIONS' CUP 1998

**GROUP 1**
Ghana 2, Angola 1
Sudan 0, Zimbabwe 3
Zimbabwe 0, Ghana 0
Zimbabwe 1, Angola 0

**GROUP 2**
Algeria 4, Ivory Coast 1
Benin 1, Mali 2
Ivory Coast 1, Benin 0
Mali 1, Algeria 0
Benin 1, Algeria 1
Mali 1, Ivory Coast 2

**GROUP 3**
Egypt 1, Morocco 1
Ethiopia 1, Senegal 2
Senegal 2, Egypt 0
Senegal 0, Morocco 0
Ethiopia 1, Egypt 1

**GROUP 4**
Tunisia 2, Sierra Leone 0
Central Africa 2, Guinea 3
Guinea 1, Tunisia 0
Guinea 1, Sierra Leone 0

**GROUP 5**
Namibia 1, Kenya 0
Gabon 0, Cameroon 0
Kenya 1, Gabon 0
Cameroon 4, Namibia 0
Kenya 0, Cameroon 0
Namibia 1, Gabon 1

**GROUP 6**
Togo 2, Tanzania 1
Zaire 0, Liberia 0
Tanzania 1, Zaire 2
Liberia 1, Togo 2
Tanzania 1, Liberia 1
Togo 1, Zaire 1

**GROUP 7**
Mauritius 1, Malawi 2
Zambia 1, Mozambique 0
Malawi 0, Zambia 2
Mozambique 3, Mauritius 0
Malawi 2, Mozambique 0
Mauritius 0, Zambia 0

**Group A**

| | P | W | D | L | F | A | Pts |
|---|---|---|---|---|---|---|---|
| Cameroon | 3 | 2 | 1 | 0 | 5 | 3 | 7 |
| Burkina Faso | 3 | 2 | 0 | 1 | 3 | 2 | 6 |
| Guinea | 3 | 1 | 1 | 1 | 3 | 3 | 4 |
| Algeria | 3 | 0 | 0 | 3 | 2 | 5 | 0 |

**Group B**

| | P | W | D | L | F | A | Pts |
|---|---|---|---|---|---|---|---|
| Tunisia | 3 | 2 | 0 | 1 | 5 | 4 | 6 |
| Congo | 3 | 2 | 0 | 1 | 4 | 3 | 6 |
| Ghana | 3 | 1 | 0 | 2 | 3 | 3 | 3 |
| Togo | 3 | 1 | 0 | 2 | 4 | 6 | 3 |

**Group C**

| | P | W | D | L | F | A | Pts |
|---|---|---|---|---|---|---|---|
| Ivory Coast | 3 | 2 | 1 | 0 | 10 | 6 | 7 |
| South Africa | 3 | 1 | 2 | 0 | 5 | 2 | 5 |
| Angola | 3 | 0 | 2 | 1 | 5 | 8 | 2 |
| Namibia | 3 | 0 | 1 | 2 | 7 | 11 | 1 |

**Group D**

| | P | W | D | L | F | A | Pts |
|---|---|---|---|---|---|---|---|
| Morocco | 3 | 2 | 1 | 0 | 5 | 1 | 7 |
| Egypt | 3 | 2 | 0 | 1 | 6 | 1 | 6 |
| Zambia | 3 | 1 | 1 | 1 | 4 | 6 | 4 |
| Mozambique | 3 | 0 | 0 | 3 | 1 | 8 | 0 |

**QUARTER-FINALS**
Congo 1, Cameroon 0
Egypt 0, Ivory Coast 0
*(Egypt won 5-4 on penalties)*
Burkina Faso 1, Tunisia 1
*(Burkina Faso won 8-7 on penalties)*
South Africa 2, Morocco 1

**SEMI-FINALS**
South Africa 2, Congo 1
Egypt 2, Burkina Faso 0

**THIRD/FOURTH PLACE**
Burkina Faso 4, Congo 4
*(Congo won 4-1 on penalties)*

**FINAL**
Egypt 2, South Africa 0

# UEFA UNDER-21 CHAMPIONSHIP 1996–98

**GROUP 1**
Greece 0, Slovenia 2
Greece 3, Bosnia 0
Slovenia 0, Denmark 3
Denmark 1, Greece 3
Slovenia 2, Bosnia 0
Bosnia 3, Croatia 1
Croatia 0, Greece 1
Croatia 2, Denmark 0
Bosnia 0, Greece 0
Croatia 2, Slovenia 0
Denmark 2, Slovenia 1
Greece 2, Croatia 0
Denmark 5, Bosnia 0
Croatia 6, Bosnia 1
Slovenia 1, Greece 3
Denmark 1, Croatia 0
Greece 2, Denmark 3
Slovenia 1, Croatia 2
Bosnia 1, Denmark 1
Bosnia 1, Slovenia 2

**GROUP 2**
Moldova 0, England 2
Moldova 0, Italy 3
England 0, Poland 0
Georgia 0, England 1
Italy 6, Georgia 0
Poland 1, Moldova 3
England 1, Italy 0
Italy 6, Moldova 0
Poland 1, Italy 1
England 0, Georgia 0
Italy 1, Poland 1
Poland 1, England 1
Georgia 1, Moldova 0
Poland 2, Georgia 2
England 1, Moldova 0
Georgia 2, Italy 0
Moldova 2, Poland 3
Georgia 5, Poland 1
Italy 0, England 1
Moldova 0, Georgia 0

**GROUP 3**
France 1, Switzerland 0
Finland 1, Switzerland 1
France 2, Hungary 0
Switzerland 3, Norway 7
Norway 4, Hungary 1
Norway 1, France 1
Hungary 0, Finland 1
Norway 3, Finland 0
Switzerland 4, Hungary 1
France 2, Finland 1
Finland 1, France 1
Hungary 2, Norway 0
Finland 0, Norway 0
Hungary 2, Switzerland 2
Hungary 2, France 4
Norway 4, Switzerland 1
Switzerland 2, Finland 1
Finland 3, Hungary 1
Switzerland 0, France 1
Norway 3, France 2

**GROUP 4**
Austria 4, Scotland 0
Estonia 1, Belarus 1

Latvia 0, Scotland 0
Belarus 2, Latvia 0
Sweden 1, Belarus 3
Belarus 3, Estonia 1
Sweden 4, Austria 1
Estonia 0, Scotland 1
Latvia 0, Sweden 2
Austria 0, Latvia 0
Scotland 1, Sweden 4
Scotland 4, Estonia 0
Scotland 1, Austria 2
Austria 7, Estonia 1
Sweden 2, Scotland 1
Latvia 0, Belarus 3
Estonia 0, Sweden 2
Latvia 1, Austria 0
Belarus 1, Scotland 0
Estonia 0, Latvia 1
Estonia 0, Austria 1
Belarus 0, Sweden 1
Sweden 5, Latvia 0
Belarus 1, Austria 1
Austria 0, Sweden 4
Scotland 0, Belgium 3
Latvia 0, Estonia 1
Scotland 2, Latvia 4
Austria 2, Belarus 3
Sweden 5, Estonia 0

**GROUP 5**
Israel 2, Bulgaria 0
Russia 2, Cyprus 1
Cyprus 1, Israel 1
Luxembourg 0, Bulgaria 4
Israel 1, Russia 0
Luxembourg 1, Russia 7
Cyprus 3, Bulgaria 0
Israel 2, Luxembourg 1
Cyprus 0, Russia 4
Luxembourg 0, Israel 5
Bulgaria 3, Cyprus 1
Israel 4, Cyprus 3
Russia 1, Israel 1
Bulgaria 3, Israel 1
Bulgaria 1, Russia 2
Luxembourg 1, Cyprus 2
Russia 3, Bulgaria 2
Cyprus 5, Luxembourg 0

**GROUP 6**
Czech Repblic 4, Malta 0
Yugoslavia 1, Malta 0
Slovakia 3, Malta 0
Czech Republic 1, Spain 2
Yugoslavia 3, Czech Republic 0
Spain 1, Slovakia 1
Spain 1, Yugoslavia 0
Malta 0, Spain 3
Spain 1, Malta 0
Malta 0, Slovakia 6
Czech Republic 0, Yugoslavia 1
Yugoslavia 1, Spain 2
Spain 4, Czech Republic 0
Yugoslavia 1, Slovakia 0
Slovakia 0, Czech Republic 1
Slovakia 0, Yugoslavia 1
Czech Republic 2, Slovakia 3

Malta 0, Yugoslavia 6
Malta 0, Czech Republic 5
Slovakia 3, Spain 4

**GROUP 7**
Wales 4, San Marino 0
Wales 0, Holland 2
San Marino 0, Wales 3
Belgium 1, Turkey 2
San Marino 1, Belgium 5
Turkey 3, San Marino 0
Holland 0, Wales 1
Turkey 0, Holland 1
Holland 6, San Marino 0
Wales 0, Turkey 3
Belgium 2, Holland 2
Wales 1, Belgium 0
Turkey 1, Belgium 2
San Marino 0, Holland 7
Belgium 3, San Marino 0
Turkey 3, Wales 0
San Marino 1, Turkey 4
Holland 5, Belgium 2
Holland 3, Turkey 0
Belgium 1, Wales 0

**GROUP 8**
Republic of Ireland 0, Iceland 1
Lithuania 0, Iceland 3
Iceland 2, Macedonia 0
Romania 2, Lithuania 1
Republic of Ireland 4, Macedonia 0
Iceland 2, Romania 3
Macedonia 0, Romania 1
Lithuania 1, Romania 2
Macedonia 0, Republic of Ireland 4
Romania 1, Republic of Ireland 0
Macedonia 1, Iceland 1
Iceland 0, Lithuania 2
Republic of Ireland 2, Lithuania 0
Romania 3, Macedonia 0
Romania 4, Iceland 0
Lithuania 2, Republic of Ireland 1
Iceland 0, Republic of Ireland 0
Lithuania 1, Macedonia 0
Republic of Ireland 0, Romania 2
Lithuania 1, Macedonia 2

**GROUP 9**
Albania 3, Armenia 2
Ukraine 1, Portugal 0
Armenia 3, Portugal 4
Portugal 1, Ukraine 0
Albania 2, Portugal 4
Armenia 0, Germany 1
Portugal 1, Germany 2
Albania 0, Ukraine 3
Albania 0, Germany 4
Ukraine 7, Armenia 0
Germany 2, Ukraine 0
Portugal 1, Albania 1
Ukraine 1, Germany 1
Portugal 8, Armenia 1
Ukraine 1, Albania 0
Germany 7, Armenia 0
Germany 1, Portugal 1
Armenia 2, Albania 0
Armenia 0, Ukraine 1
Georgia 2, Albania 0

| GROUP 1 | P | W | D | L | F | A | Pts |
|---|---|---|---|---|---|---|---|
| Denmark | 8 | 5 | 1 | 2 | 16 | 9 | 16 |
| Greece | 8 | 5 | 1 | 2 | 12 | 7 | 16 |
| Croatia | 8 | 4 | 0 | 4 | 13 | 9 | 12 |
| Slovenia | 8 | 3 | 0 | 5 | 9 | 13 | 9 |
| Bosnia | 8 | 1 | 2 | 5 | 6 | 18 | 5 |

| GROUP 2 | P | W | D | L | F | A | Pts |
|---|---|---|---|---|---|---|---|
| England | 8 | 5 | 3 | 0 | 7 | 1 | 18 |
| Georgia | 8 | 3 | 3 | 2 | 10 | 10 | 12 |
| Italy | 8 | 3 | 2 | 3 | 17 | 6 | 11 |
| Poland | 8 | 1 | 5 | 2 | 10 | 15 | 8 |
| Moldova | 8 | 1 | 1 | 6 | 5 | 17 | 4 |

| GROUP 3 | P | W | D | L | F | A | Pts |
|---|---|---|---|---|---|---|---|
| Norway | 8 | 5 | 2 | 1 | 22 | 10 | 17 |
| France | 8 | 4 | 3 | 1 | 13 | 8 | 15 |
| Finland | 8 | 2 | 3 | 3 | 8 | 10 | 9 |
| Switzerland | 8 | 2 | 3 | 3 | 13 | 17 | 9 |
| Hungary | 8 | 1 | 1 | 6 | 9 | 20 | 4 |

| GROUP 4 | P | W | D | L | F | A | Pts |
|---|---|---|---|---|---|---|---|
| Sweden | 10 | 9 | 0 | 1 | 30 | 6 | 27 |
| Belarus | 10 | 6 | 2 | 2 | 17 | 7 | 20 |
| Austria | 10 | 6 | 2 | 2 | 21 | 12 | 20 |
| Latvia | 10 | 2 | 2 | 6 | 6 | 18 | 8 |
| Scotland | 10 | 2 | 1 | 7 | 10 | 20 | 7 |
| Estonia | 10 | 1 | 1 | 8 | 4 | 25 | 4 |

| GROUP 5 | P | W | D | L | F | A | Pts |
|---|---|---|---|---|---|---|---|
| Russia | 8 | 6 | 1 | 1 | 27 | 7 | 19 |
| Israel | 8 | 5 | 2 | 1 | 17 | 9 | 17 |
| Bulgaria | 8 | 4 | 0 | 4 | 16 | 12 | 12 |
| Cyprus | 8 | 3 | 1 | 4 | 16 | 15 | 10 |
| Luxembourg | 8 | 0 | 0 | 8 | 3 | 36 | 0 |

| GROUP 6 | P | W | D | L | F | A | Pts |
|---|---|---|---|---|---|---|---|
| Spain | 8 | 7 | 1 | 0 | 18 | 6 | 22 |
| Yugoslavia | 8 | 6 | 0 | 2 | 14 | 3 | 18 |
| Slovakia | 8 | 3 | 1 | 4 | 16 | 10 | 10 |
| Czech Republic | 8 | 3 | 0 | 5 | 13 | 13 | 9 |
| Malta | 8 | 0 | 0 | 8 | 0 | 29 | 0 |

| GROUP 7 | P | W | D | L | F | A | Pts |
|---|---|---|---|---|---|---|---|
| Holland | 8 | 6 | 1 | 1 | 26 | 5 | 19 |
| Turkey | 8 | 5 | 0 | 3 | 16 | 8 | 15 |
| Belgium | 8 | 4 | 1 | 3 | 16 | 12 | 13 |
| Wales | 8 | 4 | 0 | 4 | 9 | 9 | 12 |
| San Marino | 8 | 0 | 0 | 8 | 2 | 35 | 0 |

| GROUP 8 | P | W | D | L | F | A | Pts |
|---|---|---|---|---|---|---|---|
| Romania | 8 | 8 | 0 | 0 | 18 | 4 | 24 |
| Iceland | 8 | 4 | 1 | 3 | 10 | 10 | 13 |
| Republic of Ireland | 8 | 3 | 0 | 5 | 11 | 7 | 9 |
| Lithuania | 8 | 3 | 0 | 5 | 8 | 12 | 9 |
| Macedonia | 8 | 1 | 1 | 6 | 3 | 17 | 4 |

| GROUP 9 | P | W | D | L | F | A | Pts |
|---|---|---|---|---|---|---|---|
| Germany | 8 | 6 | 2 | 0 | 20 | 3 | 20 |
| Ukraine | 8 | 5 | 1 | 2 | 14 | 4 | 16 |
| Portugal | 8 | 4 | 2 | 2 | 20 | 11 | 14 |
| Albania | 8 | 1 | 1 | 6 | 6 | 19 | 4 |
| Armenia | 8 | 1 | 0 | 7 | 8 | 31 | 3 |

**QUALIFYING PLAY-OFF**
Greece 2, England 0
England 4, Greece 2

**QUARTER-FINALS**

**GROUP A**
Germany 0, Greece 1
Holland 2, Romania 1

**GROUP B**
Norway 1, Sweden 0
Spain 1, Russia 0

**SEMI-FINALS**
Greece 3, Holland 0
Spain 1, Norway 0

**3RD/4TH PLACE**
Norway 2, Holland 0

**5TH/6TH PLACE**
Germany 2, Sweden 1

**7TH/8TH PLACE**
Russia 2, Romania 1

**FINAL**
Spain 1, Greece 0

# 16th UEFA UNDER-16 CHAMPIONSHIP

## (Finals in Scotland)

**GROUP A**
Denmark 1, Sweden 1
Greece 2, Iceland 0
Sweden 1, Iceland 1
Denmark 0, Greece 0
Iceland 0, Denmark 1
Sweden 0, Greece 2

**GROUP B**
Liechtenstein 0, Norway 5
Portugal 1, Italy 1
Liechtenstein 0, Portugal 1
Norway 1, Italy 4
Italy 2, Liechtenstein 0
Norway 1, Portugal 2

**GROUP C**
Scotland 0, Republic of Ireland 0
Spain 1, Finland 0
Scotland 1, Spain 1
Republic of Ireland 2, Finland 0
Finland 2, Scotland 0
Republic of Ireland 1, Spain 0

**GROUP D**
Russia 1, Israel 1
Croatia 2, Ukraine 0
Israel 1, Ukraine 1
Russia 0, Croatia 0
Ukraine 2, Russia 1
Israel 2, Croatia 0

**QUARTER-FINALS**
Greece 1, Spain 2
Republic of Ireland 2, Denmark 0
Italy 2, Croatia 1
Israel 1, Portugal 4

**SEMI-FINALS**
Spain 1, Italy 2
Republic of Ireland 2, Portugal 0

**3RD/4TH PLACE**
Spain 2, Portugal 1

**FINAL**
Italy 1, Republic of Ireland 2

# 4th WORLD UNDER-17 CHAMPIONSHIP

## (In Egypt)

**GROUP A**
Egypt 3, Thailand 2
Chile 0, Germany 1
Egypt 1, Chile 1
Thailand 0, Germany 3
Egypt 1, Germany 1
Thailand 2, Chile 6

**GROUP B**
New Zealand 0, Mali 4
Mexico 2, Spain 3
Mali 0, Spain 1
New Zealand 0, Mexico 5
New Zealand 0, Spain 13
Mali 3, Mexico 1

**GROUP C**
Oman 4, USA 0
Austria 0, Brazil 7
USA 0, Brazil 3
Oman 3, Austria 1
Oman 1, Brazil 3
USA 4, Austria 0

**GROUP D**
Argentina 0, Ghana 0
Costa Rica 1, Bahrain 3
Ghana 5, Bahrain 1
Argentina 1, Costa Rica 0
Argentina 2, Bahrain 0
Ghana 2, Costa Rica 0

**QUARTER-FINALS**
Brazil 2, Argentina 0
Germany 0, Mali 0
aet; Germany won 4-3 on penalties.
Ghana 4, Oman 1
Spain 2, Egypt 1

**SEMI-FINALS**
Germany 0, Brazil 4
Spain 1, Ghana 2

**3RD/4TH PLACE**
Germany 1, Spain 2

**FINAL**
Brazil 2, Ghana 1

# 13th EUROPEAN UNDER-18 YOUTH CHAMPIONSHIP

## (Finals in Iceland)

**GROUP A**
Portugal 2, Hungary 0
Iceland 1, Spain 1
Spain 2, Hungary 1
Iceland 0, Portugal 1
Spain 0, Portugal 2
Hungary 2, Iceland 2

**GROUP B**
France 3, Republic of Ireland 2
Israel 0, Switzerland 3

Israel 0, France 2
Switzerland 0, Republic of Ireland 1
Republic of Ireland 1, Israel 1
Switzerland 0, France 1

**3RD/4TH PLACE**
Spain 2, Republic of Ireland 1

**FINAL**
France 1, Portugal 0

# OLYMPIC FOOTBALL

**Previous medallists**

| 1896 Athens* | 1 Denmark | 1932 Los Angeles | | 1968 Mexico City | 1 Hungary |
| | 2 Greece | no tournament | | | 2 Bulgaria |
| 1900 Paris* | 1 Great Britain | 1936 Berlin | 1 Italy | | 3 Japan |
| | 2 France | | 2 Austria | 1972 Munich | 1 Poland |
| 1904 St Louis** | 1 Canada | | 3 Norway | | 2 Hungary |
| | 2 USA | 1948 London | 1 Sweden | | 3 E Germany/USSR |
| 1908 London | 1 Great Britain | | 2 Yugoslavia | 1976 Montreal | 1 East Germany |
| | 2 Denmark | | 3 Denmark | | 2 Poland |
| | 3 Holland | 1952 Helsinki | 1 Hungary | | 3 USSR |
| 1912 Stockholm | 1 England | | 2 Yugoslavia | 1980 Moscow | 1 Czechoslovakia |
| | 2 Denmark | | 3 Sweden | | 2 East Germany |
| | 3 Holland | 1956 Melbourne | 1 USSR | | 3 USSR |
| 1920 Antwerp | 1 Belgium | | 2 Yugoslavia | 1984 Los Angeles | 1 France |
| | 2 Spain | | 3 Bulgaria | | 2 Brazil |
| | 3 Holland | 1960 Rome | 1 Yugoslavia | | 3 Yugoslavia |
| 1924 Paris | 1 Uruguay | | 2 Denmark | 1988 Seoul | 1 USSR |
| | 2 Switzerland | | 3 Hungary | | 2 Brazil |
| | 3 Sweden | 1964 Tokyo | 1 Hungary | | 3 West Germany |
| 1928 Amsterdam | 1 Uruguay | | 2 Czechoslovakia | 1992 Barcelona | 1 Spain |
| | 2 Argentina | | 3 East Germany | | 2 Poland |
| | 3 Italy | | | | 3 Ghana |
| | | | | 1996 Atlanta | 1 Nigeria |
| | | | | | 2 Argentina |
| | | | | | 3 Brazil |

* No official tournament
** No official tournament but gold medal later awarded by IOC

# ENGLAND UNDER-21 RESULTS 1976–98

EC UEFA Competition for Under-21 Teams

### v ALBANIA

| Year | Date | | Venue | Eng | Alb |
|---|---|---|---|---|---|
| EC1989 | Mar | 7 | Shkroda | 2 | 1 |
| EC1989 | April | 25 | Ipswich | 2 | 0 |

### v ANGOLA

| Year | Date | | Venue | Eng | Ang |
|---|---|---|---|---|---|
| 1995 | June | 10 | Toulon | 1 | 0 |
| 1996 | May | 28 | Toulon | 0 | 2 |

### v ARGENTINA

| Year | Date | | Venue | Eng | Arg |
|---|---|---|---|---|---|
| 1998 | May | 18 | Toulon | 0 | 2 |

### v AUSTRIA

| Year | Date | | Venue | Eng | Aus |
|---|---|---|---|---|---|
| 1994 | Oct | 11 | Kapfenberg | 3 | 1 |
| 1995 | Nov | 14 | Middlesbrough | 2 | 1 |

### v BELGIUM

| Year | Date | | Venue | Eng | Bel |
|---|---|---|---|---|---|
| 1994 | June | 5 | Marseille | 2 | 1 |
| 1996 | May | 24 | Toulon | 1 | 0 |

### v BRAZIL

| Year | Date | | Venue | Eng | B |
|---|---|---|---|---|---|
| 1993 | June | 11 | Toulon | 0 | 0 |
| 1995 | June | 6 | Toulon | 0 | 2 |
| 1996 | June | 1 | Toulon | 1 | 2 |

### v BULGARIA

| Year | Date | | Venue | Eng | Bul |
|---|---|---|---|---|---|
| EC1979 | June | 5 | Pernik | 3 | 1 |
| EC1979 | Nov | 20 | Leicester | 5 | 0 |
| 1989 | June | 5 | Toulon | 2 | 3 |

### v CROATIA

| Year | Date | | Venue | Eng | Cro |
|---|---|---|---|---|---|
| 1996 | Apr | 23 | Sunderland | 0 | 1 |

### v CZECHOSLOVAKIA

| Year | Date | | Venue | Eng | Cz |
|---|---|---|---|---|---|
| 1990 | May | 28 | Toulon | 2 | 1 |
| 1992 | May | 26 | Toulon | 1 | 2 |
| 1993 | June | 9 | Toulon | 1 | 1 |

### v DENMARK

| Year | Date | | Venue | Eng | Den |
|---|---|---|---|---|---|
| EC1978 | Sept | 19 | Hvidovre | 2 | 1 |
| EC1979 | Sept | 11 | Watford | 1 | 0 |
| EC1982 | Sept | 21 | Hvidovre | 4 | 1 |
| EC1983 | Sept | 20 | Norwich | 4 | 1 |
| EC1986 | Mar | 12 | Copenhagen | 1 | 0 |
| EC1986 | Mar | 26 | Manchester | 1 | 1 |
| 1988 | Sept | 13 | Watford | 0 | 0 |
| 1994 | Mar | 8 | Brentford | 1 | 0 |

### v EAST GERMANY

| Year | Date | | Venue | Eng | EG |
|---|---|---|---|---|---|
| EC1980 | April | 16 | Sheffield | 1 | 2 |
| EC1980 | April | 23 | Jena | 0 | 1 |

### v FINLAND

| Year | Date | | Venue | Eng | Fin |
|---|---|---|---|---|---|
| EC1977 | May | 26 | Helsinki | 1 | 0 |
| EC1977 | Oct | 12 | Hull | 8 | 1 |
| EC1984 | Oct | 16 | Southampton | 2 | 0 |
| EC1985 | May | 21 | Mikkeli | 1 | 3 |

### v FRANCE

| Year | Date | | Venue | Eng | Fra |
|---|---|---|---|---|---|
| EC1984 | Feb | 28 | Sheffield | 6 | 1 |
| EC1984 | Mar | 28 | Rouen | 1 | 0 |
| 1987 | June | 11 | Toulon | 0 | 2 |
| EC1988 | April | 13 | Besancon | 2 | 4 |
| EC1988 | April | 27 | Highbury | 2 | 2 |
| 1988 | June | 12 | Toulon | 2 | 4 |
| 1990 | May | 23 | Toulon | 7 | 3 |
| 1991 | June | 3 | Toulon | 1 | 0 |
| 1992 | May | 28 | Toulon | 0 | 0 |
| 1993 | June | 15 | Toulon | 1 | 0 |
| 1994 | May | 31 | Aubagne | 0 | 3 |
| 1994 | Sept | 6 | Leicester | 0 | 0 |
| 1995 | June | 10 | Toulon | 0 | 2 |
| 1998 | May | 14 | Toulon | 1 | 1 |

### v GEORGIA

| Year | Date | | Venue | Eng | Geo |
|---|---|---|---|---|---|
| EC1996 | Nov | 8 | Batumi | 1 | 0 |
| EC1997 | April | 29 | Charlton | 0 | 0 |

### v GERMANY

| Year | Date | | Venue | Eng | Ger |
|---|---|---|---|---|---|
| 1991 | Sept | 10 | Scunthorpe | 2 | 1 |

### v GREECE

| Year | Date | | Venue | Eng | Gre |
|---|---|---|---|---|---|
| EC1982 | Nov | 16 | Piraeus | 0 | 1 |
| EC1983 | Mar | 29 | Portsmouth | 2 | 1 |
| 1989 | Feb | 7 | Patras | 0 | 1 |
| EC1997 | Nov | 13 | Heraklion | 0 | 2 |
| EC1997 | Dec | 17 | Norwich | 4 | 2 |

### v HOLLAND

| Year | Date | | Venue | Eng | H |
|---|---|---|---|---|---|
| EC1993 | April | 27 | Portsmouth | 3 | 0 |
| EC1993 | Oct | 12 | Utrecht | 1 | 1 |

### v HUNGARY

| Year | Date | | Venue | Eng | Hun |
|---|---|---|---|---|---|
| EC1981 | June | 5 | Keszthely | 2 | 1 |
| EC1981 | Nov | 17 | Nottingham | 2 | 0 |
| EC1983 | April | 26 | Newcastle | 1 | 0 |
| EC1983 | Oct | 11 | Nyiregyhaza | 2 | 0 |
| 1990 | Sept | 11 | Southampton | 3 | 1 |
| 1992 | May | 12 | Budapest | 2 | 2 |

### v ITALY

| Year | Date | | Venue | Eng | Italy |
|---|---|---|---|---|---|
| EC1978 | Mar | 8 | Manchester | 2 | 1 |
| EC1978 | April | 5 | Rome | 0 | 0 |
| EC1984 | April | 18 | Manchester | 3 | 1 |
| EC1984 | May | 2 | Florence | 0 | 1 |
| EC1986 | April | 9 | Pisa | 0 | 2 |
| EC1986 | April | 23 | Swindon | 1 | 1 |
| EC1997 | Feb | 12 | Bristol | 1 | 0 |
| EC1997 | Oct | 10 | Rieti | 1 | 0 |

### v ISRAEL

| Year | Date | | Venue | Eng | Isr |
|---|---|---|---|---|---|
| 1985 | Feb | 27 | Tel Aviv | 2 | 1 |

### v LATVIA

| Year | Date | | Venue | Eng | Lat |
|---|---|---|---|---|---|
| 1995 | April | 25 | Riga | 1 | 0 |
| 1995 | June | 7 | Burnley | 4 | 0 |

### v MALAYSIA

| Year | Date | | Venue | Eng | Mal |
|---|---|---|---|---|---|
| 1995 | June | 8 | Toulon | 2 | 0 |

### v MEXICO

| Year | Date | | Venue | Eng | Mex |
|---|---|---|---|---|---|
| 1988 | June | 5 | Toulon | 2 | 1 |
| 1991 | May | 29 | Toulon | 6 | 0 |
| 1992 | May | 25 | Toulon | 1 | 1 |

### v MOLDOVA

| Year | Date | | Venue | Eng | Mol |
|---|---|---|---|---|---|
| EC1996 | Aug | 31 | Chisinau | 2 | 0 |
| EC1997 | Sept | 9 | Wycombe | 1 | 0 |

### v MOROCCO

| Year | Date | | Venue | Eng | Mor |
|---|---|---|---|---|---|
| 1987 | June | 7 | Toulon | 2 | 0 |
| 1988 | June | 9 | Toulon | 1 | 0 |

### v NORWAY

| Year | Date | | Venue | Eng | Nor |
|---|---|---|---|---|---|
| EC1977 | June | 1 | Bergen | 2 | 1 |
| EC1977 | Sept | 6 | Brighton | 6 | 0 |
| 1980 | Sept | 9 | Southampton | 3 | 0 |
| 1981 | Sept | 8 | Drammen | 0 | 0 |
| EC1992 | Oct | 13 | Peterborough | 0 | 2 |
| EC1993 | June | 1 | Stavanger | 1 | 1 |
| 1995 | Oct | 10 | Stavanger | 2 | 2 |

### v POLAND

| Year | Date | | Venue | Eng | Pol |
|---|---|---|---|---|---|
| EC1982 | Mar | 17 | Warsaw | 2 | 1 |
| EC1982 | April | 7 | West Ham | 2 | 2 |
| EC1989 | June | 2 | Plymouth | 2 | 1 |
| EC1989 | Oct | 10 | Jastrzebie | 3 | 1 |
| EC1990 | Oct | 16 | Tottenham | 0 | 1 |
| EC1993 | May | 28 | Zdroj | 4 | 1 |
| EC1993 | Sept | 7 | Millwall | 1 | 2 |
| EC1996 | Oct | 8 | Wolverhampton | 0 | 0 |
| EC1997 | May | 30 | Katowice | 1 | 1 |

### v PORTUGAL

| Year | Date | | Venue | Eng | Por |
|---|---|---|---|---|---|
| 1987 | June | 13 | Toulon | 0 | 0 |
| 1990 | May | 21 | Toulon | 0 | 1 |
| 1993 | June | 7 | Toulon | 2 | 0 |
| 1994 | June | 7 | Toulon | 2 | 0 |
| 1995 | Sept | 2 | Lisbon | 0 | 2 |
| 1996 | May | 30 | Toulon | 1 | 3 |

### v REPUBLIC OF IRELAND

| Year | Date | | Venue | Eng | RoI |
|---|---|---|---|---|---|
| 1981 | Feb | 25 | Liverpool | 1 | 0 |
| 1985 | Mar | 25 | Portsmouth | 3 | 2 |
| 1989 | June | 9 | Toulon | 0 | 0 |
| EC1990 | Nov | 13 | Cork | 3 | 0 |
| EC1991 | Mar | 26 | Brentford | 3 | 0 |
| 1994 | Nov | 15 | Newcastle | 1 | 0 |
| 1995 | Mar | 27 | Dublin | 2 | 0 |

### v ROMANIA

| Year | Date | | Venue | Eng | Rom |
|---|---|---|---|---|---|
| EC1980 | Oct | 14 | Ploesti | 0 | 4 |
| EC1981 | April | 28 | Swindon | 3 | 0 |
| EC1985 | April | 30 | Brasov | 0 | 0 |
| EC1985 | Sept | 10 | Ipswich | 3 | 0 |

### v RUSSIA

| Year | Date | | Venue | Eng | Rus |
|---|---|---|---|---|---|
| 1994 | May | 30 | Bandol | 2 | 0 |

| v SAN MARINO | | | Eng | SM |
|---|---|---|---|---|
| EC1993 | Feb | 16 | Luton 6 | 0 |
| EC1993 | Nov | 17 | San Marino 4 | 0 |

| v SENEGAL | | | Eng | Sen |
|---|---|---|---|---|
| 1989 | June | 7 | Toulon 6 | 1 |
| 1991 | May | 27 | Toulon 2 | 1 |

| v SCOTLAND | | | Eng | Sco |
|---|---|---|---|---|
| 1977 | April | 27 | Sheffield 1 | 0 |
| EC1980 | Feb | 12 | Coventry 2 | 1 |
| EC1980 | Mar | 4 | Aberdeen 0 | 0 |
| EC1982 | April | 19 | Glasgow 1 | 0 |
| EC1982 | April | 28 | Manchester 1 | 1 |
| EC1988 | Feb | 16 | Aberdeen 1 | 0 |
| EC1988 | Mar | 22 | Nottingham 1 | 0 |
| 1993 | June | 13 | Toulon 1 | 0 |

| v SOUTH AFRICA | | | Eng | SA |
|---|---|---|---|---|
| 1998 | May | 16 | Toulon 3 | 1 |

| v SPAIN | | | Eng | Spa |
|---|---|---|---|---|
| EC1984 | May | 17 | Seville 1 | 0 |
| EC1984 | May | 24 | Sheffield 2 | 0 |
| 1987 | Feb | 18 | Burgos 2 | 1 |
| 1992 | Sept | 8 | Burgos 1 | 0 |

| v SWEDEN | | | Eng | Swe |
|---|---|---|---|---|
| 1979 | June | 9 | Vasteras 2 | 1 |
| 1986 | Sept | 9 | Ostersund 1 | 1 |
| EC1988 | Oct | 18 | Coventry 1 | 1 |
| EC1989 | Sept | 5 | Uppsala 0 | 1 |

| v SWITZERLAND | | | Eng | Swit |
|---|---|---|---|---|
| EC1980 | Nov | 18 | Ipswich 5 | 0 |
| EC1981 | May | 31 | Neuenburg 0 | 0 |
| 1988 | May | 28 | Lausanne 1 | 1 |

| | | | Eng | Swit |
|---|---|---|---|---|
| 1996 | April | 1 | Swindon 0 | 0 |
| 1998 | Mar | 24 | Brugglifeld 0 | 2 |

| v USA | | | Eng | USA |
|---|---|---|---|---|
| 1989 | June | 11 | Toulon 0 | 2 |
| 1994 | June | 2 | Toulon 3 | 0 |

| v TURKEY | | | Eng | Tur |
|---|---|---|---|---|
| EC1984 | Nov | 13 | Bursa 0 | 0 |
| EC1985 | Oct | 15 | Bristol 3 | 0 |
| EC1987 | April | 28 | Izmir 0 | 0 |
| EC1987 | Oct | 13 | Sheffield 1 | 1 |
| EC1991 | April | 30 | Izmir 2 | 2 |
| 1991 | Oct | 15 | Reading 2 | 0 |
| EC1992 | Nov | 17 | Orient 0 | 1 |
| EC1993 | Mar | 30 | Izmir 0 | 0 |

| v USSR | | | Eng | USSR |
|---|---|---|---|---|
| 1987 | June | 9 | Toulon 0 | 0 |
| 1988 | June | 7 | Toulon 1 | 0 |
| 1990 | May | 25 | Toulon 2 | 1 |
| 1991 | May | 31 | Toulon 2 | 1 |

| v WALES | | | Eng | Wales |
|---|---|---|---|---|
| 1976 | Dec | 15 | Wolverhampton 0 | 0 |
| 1979 | Feb | 6 | Swansea 1 | 0 |
| 1990 | Dec | 5 | Tranmere 0 | 0 |

| v WEST GERMANY | | | Eng | WG |
|---|---|---|---|---|
| EC1982 | Sept | 21 | Sheffield 3 | 1 |
| EC1982 | Oct | 12 | Bremen 2 | 3 |
| 1987 | Sept | 8 | Ludenscheid 0 | 2 |

| v YUGOSLAVIA | | | Eng | Yugo |
|---|---|---|---|---|
| EC1978 | April | 19 | Novi Sad 1 | 2 |
| EC1978 | May | 2 | Manchester 1 | 1 |
| EC1986 | Nov | 11 | Peterborough 1 | 1 |
| EC1987 | Nov | 10 | Zemun 5 | 1 |

# ENGLAND B RESULTS 1949–98

| Year | Date | | Venue | | |
|---|---|---|---|---|---|

| v ALGERIA | | | Eng | Alg |
|---|---|---|---|---|
| 1990 | Dec | 11 | Algiers 0 | 0 |

| v AUSTRALIA | | | Eng | Aust |
|---|---|---|---|---|
| 1980 | Nov | 17 | Birmingham 1 | 0 |

| v AUSTRIA | | | Eng | Aus |
|---|---|---|---|---|
| 1979† | June | 12 | Klagenfurt 1 | 0 |

†Abandoned 60 mins; waterlogged pitch.

| v CHILE | | | Eng | Ch |
|---|---|---|---|---|
| 1998 | Feb | 10 | West Bromwich 1 | 2 |

| v CIS | | | Eng | CIS |
|---|---|---|---|---|
| 1992 | April | 28 | Moscow 1 | 1 |

| v CZECHOSLOVAKIA | | | Eng | Cz |
|---|---|---|---|---|
| 1978 | Nov | 28 | Prague 1 | 0 |
| 1990 | April | 24 | Sunderland 2 | 0 |
| 1992 | Mar | 24 | Budejovice 1 | 0 |

| v FINLAND | | | Eng | Fin |
|---|---|---|---|---|
| 1949 | May | 15 | Helsinki 4 | 0 |

| v FRANCE | | | Eng | Fra |
|---|---|---|---|---|
| 1952 | May | 22 | Le Havre 1 | 7 |
| 1992 | Feb | 18 | Loftus Road 3 | 0 |

| v WEST GERMANY | | | Eng | WG |
|---|---|---|---|---|
| 1954 | Mar | 24 | Gelsenkirchen 4 | 0 |
| 1955 | Mar | 23 | Sheffield 1 | 1 |
| 1978 | Feb | 21 | Augsburg 2 | 1 |

| v HOLLAND | | | Eng | Hol |
|---|---|---|---|---|
| 1949 | May | 18 | Amsterdam 4 | 0 |
| 1950 | Feb | 22 | Newcastle 1 | 0 |
| 1952 | Mar | 26 | Amsterdam 1 | 0 |

| v ICELAND | | | Eng | Ice |
|---|---|---|---|---|
| 1989 | May | 19 | Reykjavik 2 | 0 |
| 1991 | April | 27 | Watford 1 | 0 |

| v ITALY | | | Eng | Italy |
|---|---|---|---|---|
| 1950 | May | 11 | Milan 0 | 5 |
| 1989 | Nov | 14 | Brighton 1 | 1 |

| v LUXEMBOURG | | | Eng | Lux |
|---|---|---|---|---|
| 1950 | May | 21 | Luxembourg 2 | 1 |

| v MALAYSIA | | | Eng | Mal |
|---|---|---|---|---|
| 1978 | May | 30 | Kuala Lumpur 1 | 1 |

| v MALTA | | | Eng | Mal |
|---|---|---|---|---|
| 1987 | Oct | 14 | Ta'Qali 2 | 0 |

| v NEW ZEALAND | | | Eng | NZ |
|---|---|---|---|---|
| 1978 | June | 7 | Christchurch 4 | 0 |
| 1978 | June | 11 | Wellington 3 | 1 |
| 1978 | June | 14 | Auckland 4 | 0 |
| 1979 | Oct | 15 | Leyton 4 | 1 |
| 1984 | Nov | 13 | Nottingham 2 | 0 |

| v NORTHERN IRELAND | | | Eng | NI |
|---|---|---|---|---|
| 1994 | May | 10 | Sheffield 4 | 2 |

| v NORWAY | | | Eng | Nor |
|---|---|---|---|---|
| 1989 | May | 22 | Stavanger 1 | 0 |

| v REPUBLIC OF IRELAND | | | Eng | RoI |
|---|---|---|---|---|
| 1990 | Mar | 27 | Cork 1 | 4 |
| 1994 | Dec | 13 | Liverpool 2 | 0 |

| v RUSSIA | | | Eng | Rus |
|---|---|---|---|---|
| 1998 | Apr | 21 | Loftus Road 4 | 1 |

| v SCOTLAND | | | Eng | Sco |
|---|---|---|---|---|
| 1953 | Mar | 11 | Edinburgh 2 | 2 |
| 1954 | Mar | 3 | Sunderland 1 | 1 |
| 1956 | Feb | 29 | Dundee 2 | 2 |
| 1957 | Feb | 6 | Birmingham 4 | 1 |

| v SINGAPORE | | | Eng | Sin |
|---|---|---|---|---|
| 1978 | June | 18 | Singapore 8 | 0 |

| v SPAIN | | | Eng | Sp |
|---|---|---|---|---|
| 1980 | Mar | 26 | Sunderland 1 | 0 |
| 1981 | Mar | 25 | Granada 2 | 3 |
| 1991* | Dec | 18 | Castellon 1 | 0 |

*Spanish Olympic XI

| v SWITZERLAND | | | Eng | Swit |
|---|---|---|---|---|
| 1950 | Jan | 18 | Sheffield 5 | 0 |
| 1954 | May | 22 | Basle 0 | 2 |
| 1956 | Mar | 21 | Southampton 4 | 1 |
| 1989 | May | 16 | Winterthur 2 | 0 |
| 1991 | May | 20 | Walsall 2 | 1 |

| v USA | | | Eng | USA |
|---|---|---|---|---|
| 1980 | Oct | 14 | Manchester 1 | 0 |

| v WALES | | | Eng | Wales |
|---|---|---|---|---|
| 1991 | Feb | 5 | Swansea 1 | 0 |

| v YUGOSLAVIA | | | Eng | Yugo |
|---|---|---|---|---|
| 1954 | May | 16 | Ljubljana 1 | 2 |
| 1955 | Oct | 19 | Manchester 5 | 1 |
| 1989 | Dec | 12 | Millwall 2 | 1 |

# BRITISH AND IRISH UNDER-21 TEAMS 1997–98

## ENGLAND UNDER-21 INTERNATIONALS

**9 Sept**

**England (0) 1** *(Hall 72)*

**Moldova (0) 0**                                                5534

*England:* Wright; Dyer K, Granville (Quinn 58), Duberry, Scimeca, Hall, Murphy (Carragher 69), Quashie, Dyer B, Hughes, Bowyer (Bradbury 58).

**10 Oct**

**Italy (0) 0**

**England (0) 1** *(Dyer K 88)*                                 8800

*England:* Wright; Dyer K, Quinn, Scimeca, Ferdinand R, Thatcher, Murray, Carragher, Hughes (Curtis 51), Eadie, Heskey (Bradbury 46).

**13 Nov**

**Greece (0) 2** *(Dellas 78, Lymperopoulos 90 (pen))*

**England (0) 0**                                               4000

*England:* Wright; Curtis, Dyer K (Murphy 79), Lampard, Scimeca, Hall, Serrant, Quashie, Dyer B (Moses 60), Hughes, Heskey (Davies 79).

**17 Dec**

**England (2) 4** *(Heskey 21, 34, Owen 60, Hall 78)*

**Greece (2) 2** *(Konstantinidis 28, Hall 30 (og))*          14,114

*England:* Wright; Scimeca, Serrant (Scowcroft 50), Duberry (Bullock 57), Ferdinand R, Hall, Murray, Carragher, Owen, Lampard, Heskey.

**24 Mar**

**Switzerland (2) 2** *(Haas 5, De Napoli 30)*

**England (0) 0**                                               1300

*England:* Hislop; Curtis, Dyer K, Redknapp (Holloway 71), Matteo (Williams 71), Guppy, Sinclair, Quashie, Barmby, Lampard (Hendrie 79), Heskey (Hughes 71).

**14 May**

**England (1) 1** *(Heskey 11)*

**France (0) 1** *(Saha 69)*                                    2200

*England:* Simonsen; Curtis, Rogers, Purse, Marsh (Elliott 58), Kosluk (Clegg 62), Carragher, Lampard, Oakley, Euell (Allen 73), Heskey.

**16 May**

**England (2) 3** *(Lampard 37, Heskey 40, 55)*

**South Africa (0) 1** *(Salmon 58)*                           500

*England:* Wright; Dyer K, Rogers, Purse, Curtis, Elliott, Carragher (Clegg 57), Lampard, Oakley, Allen (Howe 73), Heskey (Bent 57).

**18 May**

**England (0) 0**

**Argentina (2) 2** *(Quintana 6, Guerrero 16)*                500

*England:* Wright; Dyer K, Rogers, Howe (Euell 64), Curtis, Elliott (Allen 46), Carragher, Lampard, Oakley, Bent (Kosluk 50), Heskey.

## SCOTLAND UNDER-21 INTERNATIONALS

**5 Sept**

**Scotland (0) 0**

**Belarus (0) 3** *(Makovski 51, Lissovski 78, Skripchenko 82)*                                                      2741

*Scotland:* Alexander; McEwan (Seaton), Horn, McCluskey, Buchan, Brebner, Easton, Ferguson, Anderson I, Craig (Graham), Thompson (McCulloch).

**10 Oct**

**Scotland (2) 2** *(Anderson I 32 (pen), Graham 41)*

**Latvia (2) 4** *(Polakovs 9, Slesaruks 21, Pelcis 54, Lidaks 57)*                                                     1780

*Scotland:* Mathieson; Horn, McCluskey, Buchan, McEwan (Anderson R), Brebner (Young), Ferguson, Naysmith, Anderson I, Thompson, Craig (Graham).

**24 Mar**

**Scotland (0) 1** *(Ferguson 86)*

**Denmark (2) 2** *(Gronkjaer 18, Madsen 23)*                  2227

*Scotland:* Scrimgour; McEwan, Naysmith, McCluskey (Horn), Carey, Brebner (Anderson I), Campbell (Ferguson), Strachan, McCulloch, Graham (Burchill), Easton.

**21 Apr**

**Scotland (0) 1** *(Anderson R 89)*

**Finland (1) 1** *(Hietanen 4)*                               1113

*Scotland:* Robertson; McEwan, Buchan (Campbell), Easton, Archibald, Anderson R, Anderson I, Burchill (McCulloch), Dargo (Graham), Ferguson, Brebner (McAnespie).

**18 May**

**Republic of Ireland (1) 3** *(Connolly 12, Hawkins 68, Grant 86)*

**Scotland (0) 0**                                             700

*Scotland:* Alexander; McEwan, Lauchlan, Anderson R (McCluskey), Archibald, Strachan, Easton (Burke), Dargo, McCulloch (Graham), Ferguson, Campbell (Anderson I).

**20 May**

**Northern Ireland (1) 1** *(Mulryne 29)*

**Scotland (1) 1** *(McCluskey 22)*                            500

*Scotland:* Robertson; McEwan, Lauchlan, McCluskey, Archibald, Easton, Anderson I (McBride), McCulloch (Campbell), Graham, Ferguson, Elliot (Dargo).

**23 May**

**Italy (0) 4** *(Longo 56, Ventola 64, Gattuso 71, Firmani 78)*

**Scotland (0) 0**                                             1000

*Scotland:* Alexander; McCluskey (McBride), McEwan, Anderson R, Archibald, Lauchlan, Easton, Dargo, Graham, Ferguson, Campbell.

## WALES UNDER-21 INTERNATIONALS

**19 Aug**
**Turkey (1) 3** *(Goghan S 25, Ozkan 60, 82)*
**Wales (0) 0** 4000
*Wales:* Tony Williams; Brace, Roberts, Hughes, Edwards, Jarman (Jenkins 79), Bellamy, Thomas D, Haworth (Llewellyn 82), Oster, Ramasut (Coates 69).

**10 Oct**
**Belgium (0) 1** *(Jbari 78)*
**Wales (0) 0** 500
*Wales:* Tony Williams; Andrew Williams, Thomas J, Jones, Hughes, Jarman, Bellamy, Thomas D (Llewellyn 68), Haworth, Oster, Wright.

**22 Apr**
**Italy (2) 2** *(Rossini 41, Zambrotta 43)*
**Wales (0) 1** *(Haworth 78)* 1000
*Wales:* Tony Williams; Andrew Williams (Price 74), Roberts, Green, Hughes, Williams D, Bellamy, Llewellyn (Tipton 65), Haworth, Oster, Ramasut (Wright 61).

## NORTHERN IRELAND UNDER-21 INTERNATIONALS

**21 Apr**
**Northern Ireland (1) 2** *(Mulryne (pen), Coote)*
**Switzerland (0) 1** *(Yakin (pen))* 300
*Northern Ireland:* Taylor; Lyttle (McCallion), McGlinchey, Burns, Waterman, Mulryne, Johnson (Boyle), Jeff Whitley, McKnight, Fitzgerald (Coote), Friars.

**20 May**
**Scotland (1) 1** *(McCluskey 22)*
**Northern Ireland (1) 1** *(Mulryne 29)* 500
*Northern Ireland:* Carroll; Lyttle (Griffin 46), McGlinchey, Burns, Waterman, Mulryne, Johnson, Jeff Whitley (Boyle 74), Coote, Fitzgerald (McVeigh 64), Friars.

**22 May**
**Republic of Ireland (0) 0**
**Northern Ireland (0) 1** *(Coote 54)* 3000
*Northern Ireland:* Carroll; Griffin, McGlinchey, Burns, Waterman, Mulryne, Johnson, Jeff Whitley, Coote, McVeigh (Feeney 46), Friars.

## REPUBLIC OF IRELAND UNDER-21 INTERNATIONALS

**19 Aug**
**Republic of Ireland (0) 2** *(Fenn 55, 90)*
**Lithuania (0) 0** 2000
*Republic of Ireland:* Murphy; Maher, Worrell, Quinn, Ryan, Finnan, Boland, Farrelly, Kilbane, Fenn, Delap (Kelly 53).

**5 Sept**
**Iceland (1) 1** *(Thordarson 27)*
**Republic of Ireland (0) 0** 1200
*Republic of Ireland:* Murphy; Carr, Ryan (Scully 68), Boland, Quinn, Worrell, Finnan, Kelly (Foley 46), Fenn, Farrelly, Mahon.

**9 Sept**
**Lithuania (0) 2** *(Fomenko 69, Buitkus 72)*
**Republic of Ireland (0) 1** *(Gain 65)* 600
*Republic of Ireland:* Murphy; Morgan (Boland 11), Quinn, Worrell, Darcy, Maher, Finnan, Mahon, Kelly (Scully 70), Foley, Gain.

**10 Oct**
**Romania (2) 2** *(Petre 3, Rosu 28)*
**Republic of Ireland (0) 0** 3100
*Republic of Ireland:* O'Connor; Maybury, Ryan, Hawkins, Worrell, Burns (Folan 46), Morgan, Inman, Mahon (Molloy 75), Conlon (Baker 46), Kilbane.

**24 Mar**
**Czech Republic (1) 3** *(Sionko 14, Vozabal 83, Zakopal 89)*
**Republic of Ireland (0) 0** 1800
*Republic of Ireland:* O'Connor (O'Reilly 70); Folan, McKeever (Dillon 46), Whittle (McClare 63), Boxall, Darcy, Inman (Kirby 46), Armstrong, Boylan (Baker 22), Crowe, Mahon.

## ENGLAND B INTERNATIONALS

**10 Feb**
**England (0) 1** *(Heskey 90)*
**Chile (0) 2** *(Neira 70, 82)* 13,970
*England:* Pressman; Dyer K (Guppy 55), Wilcox (Carragher 81), Scimeca, Matteo, Hall, Parlour (Murray 62), Quashie (Lampard 33), Huckerby, Merson, Heskey.

**21 Apr**
**England (2) 4** *(Ferdinand L 2, Le Tissier 13, 84, 90)*
**Russia (0) 1** *(Bouznikine 83)* 7845
*England:* Walker; Watson (Curtis 81), Serrant, Williams, Quinn, Sinclair (Dyer K 46), Anderton (Hendrie 84), Barmby (Johnson 81), Ferdinand L (Phillips 81), Carragher, Le Tissier.

## SCOTLAND B INTERNATIONALS

**24 Mar**
**Scotland (1) 4** *(McIntosh 41, Cleland 47, Wright 54, Cameron 55)*
**Wales (0) 0** 5989
*Scotland:* Gould (Douglas); Cleland, McKinlay T, Rae (Johnston), McIntosh, Ritchie, Cameron, Crawford (Dodds), Wright (Freedman), Fulton (Glass), McCann.

**21 Apr**
**Scotland (0) 1** *(Crawford 69)*
**Norway (1) 2** *(Aarsheim 33, Helstad 65)* 7845
*Scotland:* Gould (Main); Cleland, McKinlay T, Rae (Reilly), McIntosh, Ritchie, Crawford, Hopkin, Smith (McIntyre), Wright (Johnston), McCann.

# BRITISH UNDER-21 APPEARANCES 1976–1998

**ENGLAND**

Ablett, G. (Liverpool), 1988 v F (1)

Adams, A. (Arsenal). 1985 v Ei, Fi; 1986 v D; 1987 v Se, Y (5)

Adams, N. (Everton), 1987 v Se (1)

Allen, B. (QPR), 1992 v H, M, Cz, F; 1993 v N (sub), T, P, Cz (sub) (8)

Allen, C. A. (Oxford U), 1995 v Br (sub), F (sub) (2)

Allen, C. (QPR), 1980 v EG (sub); (with C Palace), 1981 v N, R (3)

Allen, M. (QPR), 1987 v Se (sub); 1988 v Y (sub) (2)

Allen, P. (West Ham U), 1985 v Ei, R; (with Tottenham H, 1986 v R (3)

Allen, R. W. (Tottenham H), 1998 v F (sub), S.Af, Arg (sub) (3)

Anderson, V. A. (Nottingham F), 1978 v I (1)

Anderton, D. R. (Tottenham H), 1993 v Sp, Sm, Ho, Pol, N, P, Cz, Br, S, F; 1994 v Pol, Sm (12)

Andrews, I. (Leicester C), 1987 v Se (1)

Ardley, N. C. (Wimbledon), 1993 v Pol, N, P, Cz, Br, S, F, 1994 v Pol (sub), Ho, Sm (10)

Ashcroft, L. (Preston NE), 1992 v H (sub) (1)

Atherton, P. (Coventry C), 1992 v T (1)

Atkinson, B. (Sunderland), 1991 v W (sub), Sen, M, USSR (sub); F; 1992 v Pol (sub) (6)

Awford, A. T. (Portsmouth), 1993 v Sp, N, T, P, Cz, Br, S, F; 1994 v Ho (9)

Bailey, G. R. (Manchester U), 1979 v W, Bul; 1980 v D, S (2), EG; 1982 v N; 1983 v D, Gr; 1984 v H, F (2), I, Sp (14)

Baker, G. E. (Southampton), 1981 v N, R (2)

Barker, S. (Blackburn R), 1985 v Is (sub), Ei, R; 1986 v I (4)

Barmby, N. J. (Tottenham H), 1994 v D; 1995 v P, A (sub); (with Everton), 1998 v Sw (4)

Bannister, G. (Sheffield W), 1982 v Pol (1)

Barnes, J. (Watford), 1983 v D, Gr (2)

Barnes, P. S. (Manchester C), 1977 v W (sub), S, Fi, N; 1978 v N, Fi, I (2), Y (9)

Barrett, E. D. (Oldham Ath), 1990 v P, F, USSR, Cz (4)

Bart-Williams, C. G. (Sheffield W), 1993 v Sp, N, T; 1994 v D, Ru, F, Bel, P; 1995 v P, A, Ei (2), La (2); ( with Nottingham F) 1996 v P (sub), A (16)

Batty, D. (Leeds U), 1988 v Sw (sub); 1989 v Gr (sub), Bul, Sen, Ei, US; 1990 v Pol (7)

Bazeley, D. S. (Watford), 1992 v H (sub) (1)

Beagrie, P. (Sheffield U), 1988 v WG, T (2)

Beardsmore, R. (Manchester U), 1989 v Gr, Alb (sub), Pol, Bul, USA (5)

Beckham, D. R. J. (Manchester U), 1995 v Br, Mal, An, F; 1996 v P, A (sub), Bel, An, P (9)

Bent, M. N. (Crystal Palace), 1998 v S.Af (sub), Arg (2)

Beeston, C (Stoke C), 1988 v USSR (1)

Bertschin, K. E. (Birmingham C), 1977 v S; 1978 v Y (2) (3)

Birtles, G. (Nottingham F), 1980 v Bul, EG (sub) (2)

Blackwell, D. R. (Wimbledon), 1991 v W, T, Sen (sub), M, USSR, F (6)

Blake, M. A. (Aston Villa), 1990 v F (sub), Cz (sub); 1991 v H, Pol, Ei (2), W; 1992 v Pol (8)

Blissett, L. L. (Watford), 1979 v W, Bul (sub), Se; 1980 v D (4)

Booth, A. D. (Huddersfield T), 1995 v La (2 subs); 1996 v N (3)

Bowyer, L. D. (Charlton Ath), 1996 v N (sub), Bel, P, Br; (with Leeds U), 1997 v Mol, I, Sw, Ge; 1998 v Mol (9)

Bracewell, P. (Stoke C), 1983 v D, Gr (1 + 1 sub), H; 1984 v D, H, F (2), I (2), Sp (2); 1985 v T (13)

Bradbury, L. M. (Portsmouth), 1997 v Pol; (with Manchester C), 1998 v Mol (sub), I (sub) (3)

Branch, M. (Everton), 1997 v Pol (sub) (1)

Bradshaw, P. W. (Wolverhampton W), 1977 v W, S; 1978 v Fi, Y (4)

Breacker, D. (Luton T), 1986 v I (2) (2)

Brennan, M. (Ipswich T), 1987 v Y, Sp, T, Mor, F (5)

Bridges, M. (Sunderland), 1997 v Sw (sub) (1)

Brightwell, I. (Manchester C), 1989 v D, Alb; 1990 v Se (sub), Pol (4)

Briscoe, L. S. (Sheffield W), 1996 v Cro, Bel (sub), An, Br; 1997 v Sw (sub) (5)

Brock, K. (Oxford U), 1984 v I, Sp (2); 1986 v I (4)

Broomes, M. C. (Blackburn R), 1997 v Sw, Ge (2)

Brown, M. R. (Manchester C), 1996 v Cro, Bel, An, P (4)

Bull, S. G. (Wolverhampton W), 1989 v Alb (2) Pol; 1990 v Se, Pol (5)

Bullock, M. J. (Barnsley), 1998 v Gr (sub) (1)

Burrows, D. (WBA), 1989 v Se (sub); (with Liverpool), Gr, Alb (2), Pol; 1990 v Se, Pol (7)

Butcher, T. I. (Ipswich T), 1979 v Se; 1980 v D, Bul, S (2), EG (2) (7)

Butt, N. (Manchester U), 1995 v Ei (2), La; 1996 v P, A; 1997 v Ge, Pol (7)

Butters, G. (Tottenham H), 1989 v Bul, Sen (sub), Ei (sub) (3)

Butterworth, I. (Coventry C), 1985 v T, R; (with Nottingham F) 1986 v R, T, D (2), I (2) (8)

Caesar, G. (Arsenal), 1987 v Mor, USSR (sub), F (3)

Callaghan, N. (Watford), 1983 v D, Gr (sub), H (sub); 1984 v D, H, F (2), I, Sp (9)

Campbell, K. J. (Arsenal), 1991 v H, T (sub); 1992 v G, T (4)

Campbell, S. (Tottenham), 1994 v D, Ru, F, US, Bel, P; 1995 v P, A, Ei; 1996 v N, A (11)

Carbon, M. P. (Derby Co), 1996 v Cro (sub); 1997 v Ge, I, Sw (4)

Carr, C. (Fulham), 1985 v Ei (sub) (1)

Carr, F. (Nottingham F), 1987 v Se, Y, Sp (sub), Mor, USSR; 1988 v WG (sub), T, Y, F (9)

Carragher, J. L. (Liverpool), 1997 v I (sub), Sw, Ge, Pol; 1998 v Mol (sub), I, Gr, Sw (sub), F, S.Af, Arg (11)

Casper, C. M. (Manchester U), 1995 v Mal (1)

Caton, T. (Manchester C), 1982 v N, H (sub), Pol (2), S; 1983 v WG (2), Gr; 1984 v D, H, F (2), I (2) (14)

Challis, T. M. (QPR), 1996 v An, P (2)

Chamberlain, M. (Stoke C), 1983 v Gr; 1984 v F (sub), I, Sp (4)

Chapman, L. (Stoke C), 1981 v Ei (1)

Charles, G. A. (Nottingham F), 1991 v H, W (sub), Ei; 1992 v T (4)

Chettle, S. (Nottingham F), 1988 v M, USSR, Mor, F; 1989 v D, Se, Gr, Alb (2), Bul; 1990 v Se, Pol (12)

Clark, L. R. (Newcastle U), 1992 v Cz, F; 1993 v Sp, N, T, Ho (sub), Pol (sub), Cz, Br, S; 1994 v Ho (11)

Clegg, M. J. (Manchester U), 1998 v Fr (sub), S.Af (sub) (2)

Clough, N. (Nottingham F), 1986 v D (sub); 1987 v Se, Y, T, USSR, F (sub), P; 1988 v WG, T, Y, S (2), M, Mor, F (15)

Cole, A. A. (Arsenal), 1992 v H, Cz (sub), F (sub); (with Bristol C), 1993 v Sm; (with Newcastle U), Pol, N; 1994 v Pol, Ho (8)

Coney, D. (Fulham), 1985 v T (sub); 1986 v R; 1988 v T, WG (4)

Connor, T. (Brighton & HA), 1987 v Y (1)

Cooke, R. (Tottenham H), 1986 v D (sub) (1)

Cooke, T. J. (Manchester U), 1996 v Cro, Bel, An (sub), P (4)

Cooper, C. (Middlesbrough), 1988 v F (2), M, USSR, Mor; 1989 v D, Se, Gr (8)

Corrigan, J. T. (Manchester C), 1978 v I (2), Y (3)

Cottee, A. (West Ham U), 1985 v Fi (sub), Is (sub), Ei, R, Fi; 1987 v Sp, P; 1988 v WG (8)

Couzens, A. J. (Leeds U), 1995 v Mal (sub), An, F (sub) (3)

Cowans, G. S. (Aston Villa), 1979 v W, Se; 1980 v Bul, EG; 1981 v R (5)

Cox, N. J. (Aston Villa), 1993 v T, Ho, Pol, N; 1994 v Pol, Sm (6)

Cranson, I. (Ipswich T), 1985 v Fi, Is, R; 1986 v R, I (5)

Croft, G. (Grimsby T), 1995 v Br, Mal, An, F (4)

Crooks, G. (Stoke C), 1980 v Bul, S (2), EG (sub) (4)

Crossley, M. G. (Nottingham F), 1990 v P, USSR, Cz (3)

Cundy, J. V. (Chelsea), 1991 v Ei (2); 1992 v Pol (3)

Cunningham, L. (WBA), 1977 v S, Fi, N (sub); 1978 v N, Fi, I (6)

Curbishley, L. C. (Birmingham C), 1981 v Sw (1)

Curtis, J. C. K. (Manchester U), 1998 v I (sub), Gr, Sw, F, S.Af, Arg (6)

Daniel, P. W. (Hull C), 1977 v S, Fi, N; 1978 v Fi, I, Y (2) (7)

Davies, K. C. (Southampton), 1998 v Gr (sub) (1)

Davis, K. G. (Luton T), 1995 v An; 1996 v Cro (sub), P (3)

Davis, P. (Arsenal), 1982 v Pol, S; 1983 v D, Gr (1 + 1 sub), H (sub); 1987 v T; 1988 v WG, T, Y, Fr (11)

Day, C. N. (Tottenham H), 1996 v Cro, Bel, Br; (with Crystal Palace), 1997 v Mol, Ge, Sw (6)

D'Avray, M. (Ipswich T), 1984 v I, Sp (sub) (2)

Deehan, J. M. (Aston Villa), 1977 v N; 1978 v N, Fi, I; 1979 v Bul, Se (sub); 1980 v D (7)

Dennis, M. E. (Birmingham C), 1980 v Bul; 1981 v N, R (3)

Dichio, D. S. E. (QPR), 1996 v N (sub) (1)

Dickens, A. (West Ham U), 1985 v Fi (sub) (1)

Dicks, J. (West Ham U), 1988 v Sw (sub), M, Mor, F (4)

Digby, F. (Swindon T), 1987 v Sp (sub), USSR, P; 1988 v T; 1990 v Pol (5)

Dillon, K. P. (Birmingham C), 1981 v R (1)

Dixon, K. (Chelsea), 1985 v Fi (1)

Dobson, A. (Coventry C), 1989 v Bul, Sen, Ei, US (4)

Dodd, J. R. (Southampton), 1991 v Pol, Ei, T, Sen, M, F; 1992 v G, Pol (8)

Donowa, L. (Norwich C), 1983 v Is, R (sub), Fi (sub) (3)

Dorigo, A. (Aston Villa), 1987 v Se, Sp, T, Mor, USSR, F, P; 1988 v WG, Y, S (2) (11)

Dozzell, J. (Ipswich T), 1987 v Se, Y (sub), Sp, USSR, F, P; 1989 v Se, Gr (sub); 1990 v Se (sub) (9)

Draper, M. A. (Notts Co), 1991 v Ei (sub); 1992 v G, Pol (3)

Duberry, M. W. (Chelsea), 1997 v Mol, Pol, Ge; 1998 v Mol, Gr (5)

Duxbury, M. (Manchester U), 1981 v Sw (sub), Ei (sub), R (sub), Sw; 1982 v N; 1983 v WG (2) (7)

Dyer, B. A. (Crystal Palace), 1994 v Ru, F, US, Bel, P; 1995 v P (sub); 1996 v Cro; 1997 v Mol, Ge; 1998 v Mol, Gr (10)

Dyer, K. C. (Ipswich T), 1998 v Mol, I, Gr, Sw, S.Af, Arg (6)

Dyson, P. I. (Coventry C), 1981 v N, R, Sw, Ei (4)

Eadie, D. M. (Norwich C), 1994 v F (sub), US; 1997 v Mol, Ge (2), I; 1998 v I (7)

Ebbrell, J. (Everton), 1989 v Sen, Ei, US (sub); 1990 v P, F, USSR, Cz; 1991 v H, Pol, Ei, W, T; 1992 v G, T (14)

Edghill, R. A. (Manchester C), 1994 v D, Ru; 1995 v A (3)

Ehiogu, U. (Aston Villa), 1992 v H, M, Cz, F; 1993 v Sp, N, T, Sm, T, Ho, Pol, N; 1994 v Pol, Ho, Sm (15)

Elliott, P. (Luton T), 1985 v Fi; 1986 v T, D (3)

Elliott, R. J. (Newcastle U), 1996 v P, A (2)

Elliott, S. W. (Derby Co), 1998 v F, Arg (sub) (2)

Euell, J. J. (Wimbledon), 1998 v F, Arg (sub) (2)

Fairclough, C. (Nottingham F), 1985 v T, Is, Ei; 1987 v Sp, T; (with Tottenham H), 1988 v Y, F (7)

Fairclough, D. (Liverpool), 1977 v W (1)

Fashanu, J. (Norwich C), 1980 v EG; 1981 v N (sub), R, Sw, Ei (sub), H; (with Nottingham F), 1982 v N, H, Pol, S; 1983 v WG (sub) (11)

Fear, P. (Wimbledon), 1994 v Ru, F, US (sub) (3)

Fenton, G. A. (Aston Villa), 1995 v Ei (1)

Fenwick, T. W. (C Palace), 1981 v N, R, Sw, Ei; (with QPR), R; 1982 v N, H, S (2); 1983 v WG (2) (11)

Ferdinand, R. G. (West Ham U), 1997 v Sw, Ge; 1998 v I, Gr (4)

Fereday, W. (QPR), 1985 v T, Ei (sub). Fi; 1986 v T (sub), I (5)

Flitcroft, G. W. (Manchester C), 1993 v Sm, Hol, N, P, Cz, Br, S, F; 1994 v Pol, Ho (10)

Flowers, T. (Southampton), 1987 v Mor, F; 1988 v WG (sub) (3)

Ford, M. (Leeds U), 1996 v Cro; 1997 v Mol (2)

Forster, N. M. (Brentford), 1995 v Br, Mal, An, F (4)

Forsyth, M. (Derby Co), 1988 v Sw (1)

Foster, S. (Brighton & HA), 1980 v EG (sub) (1)

Fowler, R. B. (Liverpool), 1994 v Sm, Ru (subs), F, US; 1995 v P, A; 1996 v P, A (8)

Froggatt, S. J. (Aston Villa), 1993 v Sp, Sm (sub) (2)

Futcher, P. (Luton T), 1977 v W, S, Fi, N; (with Manchester C), 1978 v N, Fi, I (2), Y (2); 1979 v D (11)

Gabbiadini, M. (Sunderland), 1989 v Bul, USA (2)

Gale, A. (Fulham), 1982 v Pol (1)

Gallen, K. A. (QPR), 1995 v Ei, La (2); 1996 v Cro (4)

Gascoigne, P. (Newcastle U), 1987 v Mo, USSR, P; 1988 v WG, Y, S (2), F (2), Sw, M, USSR (sub), Mor (13)

Gayle, H. (Birmingham C), 1984 v I, Sp (2) (3)

Gernon, T. (Ipswich T), 1983 v Gr (1)

Gerrard, P. W. (Oldham Ath), 1993 v T, Ho, Pol, N, P, Cz, Br, S, F; 1994 v D, Ru; 1995 v P, A, Ei (2), La (2); 1996 v P (18)

Gibbs, N. (Watford), 1987 v Mor, USSR, F, P; 1988 v T (5)

Gibson, C. (Aston Villa), 1982 v N (1)

Gilbert, W. A. (C Palace), 1979 v W, Bul; 1980 v Bul; 1981 v N, R, Sw, R, Sw, H; 1982 v N (sub), H (11)

Goddard, P. (West Ham U), 1981 v N, Sw, Ei (sub); 1982 v N (sub), Pol, S; 1983 v WG (2) (8)

Gordon, D. (Norwich C), 1987 v T (sub), Mor (sub), F, P (4)

Gordon, D. D. (Crystal Palace), 1994 v Ru, F, US, Bel, P; 1995 v P, A, Ei (2), La (2); 1996 v P, N (13)

Grant, A. J. (Everton), 1996 v An (sub) (1)

Granville, D. P. (Chelsea), 1997 v Ge (sub), Pol; 1998 v Mol (3)

Gray, A. (Aston Villa), 1988 v S, F (2)

Guppy, S. A. (Leicester C), 1998 v Sw (1)

Haigh, P. (Hull C), 1977 v N (sub) (1)

Hall, M. T. J. (Coventry C), 1997 v Pol (2), I, Sw, Ge; 1998 v Mol, Gr (2) (8)

Hall, R. A. (Southampton), 1992 v H (sub), F; 1993 v Sm, T, Ho, Pol, P, Cz, Br, S, F (11)

Hamilton, D. V. (Newcastle U), 1997 v Pol (1)

Hardyman, P. (Portsmouth), 1985 v Ei; 1986 v D (2)

Hateley, M. (Coventry C), 1982 v Pol, S; 1983 v Gr (2), H; (with Portsmouth), 1984 v F (2), I, Sp (2) (10)

Hayes, M. (Arsenal), 1987 v Sp, T; 1988 v F (sub) (3)

Hazell, R. J. (Wolverhampton W), 1979 v D (1)

Heaney, N. A. (Arsenal), 1992 v H, M, Cz, F; 1993 v N, T (6)

Heath, A. (Stoke C), 1981 v R, Sw, H; 1982 v N, H; (with Everton), Pol, S; 1983 v WG (8)

Hendon, I. M. (Tottenham H), 1992 v H, M, Cz, F; 1993 v Sp, N, T (7)

Hendrie, L. A. (Aston Villa), 1996 v Cro (sub); 1998 v Sw (sub) (2)

Hesford, I. (Blackpool), 1981 v Ei (sub), Pol (2), S (2); 1983 v WG (2) (7)

Heskey, E. W. I. (Leicester C), 1997 v I, Ge, Pol (2); 1998 v I, Gr (2), Sw, F, S.Af, Arg (11)

Hilaire, V. (C Palace), 1980 v Bul, S (1+1 sub), EG (2); 1981 v N, R, Sw (sub); 1982 v Pol (sub) (9)

Hill, D. R. L. (Tottenham H), 1995 v Br, Mal, An, F (4)

Hillier, D. (Arsenal), 1991 v T (1)

Hinchcliffe, A. (Manchester C), 1989 v D (1)

Hinshelwood, P. A. (C Palace), 1978 v N; 1980 v EG (2)

Hirst, D. (Sheffield W), 1988 v USSR, F; 1989 v D, Bul (sub), Sen, Ei, US (7)

Hislop, N. S. (Newcastle U), 1998 v Sw (1)

Hoddle, G. (Tottenham H), 1977 v W (sub); 1978 v Fi (sub), I (2), Y; 1979 v D, W, Bul; 1980 v S (2), EG (2) (12)

Hodge, S. (Nottingham F), 1983 v Gr (sub); 1984 v D, F, I, Sp (2); (with Aston Villa), 1986 v R, T (8)

Hodgson, D. J. (Middlesbrough), 1981 v N, R (sub), Sw, Ei; 1982 v Pol; 1983 v WG (6)

Holdsworth, D. (Watford), 1989 v Gr (sub) (1)

Holland, C. J. (Newcastle U), 1995 v La; 1996 v N (sub), A (sub), Cro, Bel, An, Br; 1997 v Mol, Pol, Sw (10)

Holland, P. (Mansfield T), 1995 v Br, Mal, An, F (4)

Holloway, D. (Sunderland), 1998 v Sw (sub) (1)

Horne, B. (Millwall), 1989 v Gr (sub), Pol, Bul, Ei, US (5)

Howe, E. J. F. (Bournemouth), 1998 v S.Af (sub), Arg (2)

Hucker, P. (QPR), 1984 v I, Sp (2)

Huckerby, D. (Coventry C), 1997 v I (sub), Sw, Ge (sub), Pol (sub) (4)

Hughes, S. J. (Arsenal), 1997 v I, Sw, Ge, Pol; 1998 v Mol, I, Gr, Sw (sub) (8)

Humphreys, R. J. (Sheffield W), 1997 v Pol, Ge (sub), Sw (3)

Impey, A. R. (QPR), 1993 v T (1)

Ince, P. (West Ham U), 1989 v Alb; 1990 v Se (2)

Redmond, S. (Manchester C), 1988 v F (2), M, USSR, Mor, F; 1989 v D, Se, Gr, Alb (2), Pol; 1990 v Se, Pol (14)

Reeves, K. P. (Norwich C), 1978 v I, Y (2); 1979 v N, W, Bul, Sw; 1980 v D, S; (with Manchester C), EG (10)

Regis, C. (WBA), 1979 v D, Bul, Se; 1980 v S, EG; 1983 v D (6)

Reid, N. S. (Manchester C), 1981 v H (sub); 1982 v H, Pol (2), S (2) (6)

Reid, P. (Bolton W), 1977 v S, Fi, N; 1978 v Fi, I, Y (6)

Richards, D. I. (Wolverhampton W), 1995 v Br, Mal, An, F (4)

Richards, J. P. (Wolverhampton W), 1977 v Fi, N (2)

Rideout, P. (Aston Villa), 1985 v Fi, Is, Ei (sub), R; (with Bari), 1986 v D (5)

Ripley, S. (Middlesbrough), 1988 v USSR, F (sub); 1989 v D (sub), Se, Gr, Alb (2); 1990 v Se (8)

Ritchie, A. (Brighton & HA), 1982 v Pol (1)

Rix, G. (Arsenal), 1978 v Fi (sub), Y; 1979 v D, Se; 1980 v D (sub), Bul, S (7)

Roberts, A. J. (Millwall), 1995 v Ei, La (2); (with C Palace), 1996 v N, A (5)

Roberts, B. J. (Middlesbrough), 1997 v Sw (sub) (1)

Robins, M. G. (Manchester U), 1990 v P, F, USSR, Cz; 1991 v H (sub), Pol (6)

Robson, B. (WBA), 1979 v W, Bul (sub), Se; 1980 v D, Bul, S (2) (7)

Robson, S. (Arsenal), 1984 v I; 1985 v Fi, Is, Fi; 1986 v R, I (with West Ham U); 1988 v S, Sw (8)

Rocastle, D. (Arsenal), 1987 v Se, Y, Sp, T; 1988 v WG, T, Y, S (2), F (2 subs), M, USSR, Mor (14)

Rodger, G. (Coventry C), 1987 v USSR, F, P; 1988 v WG (4)

Rogers, A. (Nottingham F), 1998 v F, S.Af, Arg (3)

Rosario, R. (Norwich C), 1987 v T (sub), Mor, F, P (sub) (4)

Rose, M. (Arsenal), 1997 v Ge (sub), I (2)

Rowell, G. (Sunderland), 1977 v Fi (1)

Ruddock, N. (Southampton), 1989 v Bul (sub), Sen, Ei, US (4)

Rufus, R. R. (Charlton Ath), 1996 v Cro, Bel, An, P, Br; 1997 v I (6)

Ryan, J. (Oldham Ath), 1983 v H (1)

Ryder, S.H. (Walsall), 1995 v Br, An, F (3)

Samways, V. (Tottenham H), 1988 v Sw (sub), USSR, F; 1989 v D, Se (5)

Sansom, K. G. (C Palace), 1979 v D, W, Bul, Se; 1980 v S (2), EG (2) (8)

Scimeca, R. (Aston Villa), 1996 v P; 1997 v Mol, Pol, Ge, I; 1998 v Mol, I, Gr (2) (9)

Scowcroft, J. B. (Ipswich T), 1997 v Pol, Ge (2), I (sub); 1998 v Gr (sub) (5)

Seaman, D. (Birmingham C), 1985 v Fi, T, Is, Ei, R, Fi; 1986 v R, F, D, I (10)

Sedgley, S. (Coventry C), 1987 v USSR, F (sub), P; 1988 v F; 1989 v D (sub), Se, Gr, Alb (2), Pol; (with Tottenham H), 1990 v Se (11)

Sellars, S. (Blackburn R), 1988 v S (sub), F, Sw (3)

Selley, I. (Arsenal), 1994 v Ru (sub), F (sub), US (3)

Serrant, C. (Oldham Ath), 1998 v Gr (2) (2)

Sharpe, L. (Manchester U), 1989 v Gr; 1990 v P (sub), F, USSR, Cz; 1991 v H, Pol (sub), Ei (8)

Shaw, G. R. (Aston Villa), 1981 v Ei, Sw, H; 1982 v H, S; 1983 v WG (2) (7)

Shearer, A. (Southampton), 1991 v Ei (2), W, T, Sen, M, USSR, F; 1992 v G, T, Pol (11)

Shelton, G. (Sheffield W), 1985 v Fi (1)

Sheringham, T. (Millwall), 1988 v Sw (1)

Sheron, M. N. (Manchester C), 1992 v H, F; 1993 v N (sub), T (sub), Sm, Ho, Pol, N, P, Cz, Br, S, F; 1994 v Pol (sub), Ho, Sm (16)

Sherwood, T. A. (Norwich C), 1990 v P, F, USSR, Cz (4)

Shipperley, N. J. (Chelsea), 1994 v Sm (sub); (with Southampton) 1995 v Ei, La (2); 1996 v P, N, A (7)

Simonsen, S. P. A. (Tranmere R), 1998 v F (1)

Simpson, P. (Manchester C), 1986 v D (sub); 1987 v Y, Mor, F, P (5)

Sims, S. (Leicester C), 1977 v W, S, Fi, N; 1978 v N, Fi, I (2), Y (2) (10)

Sinclair, T. (QPR), 1994 v Ho, Sm, D, Ru, F, US, Bel, P; 1995 v P, Ei (2), La; 1996 v P; (with West Ham U), 1998 v Sw (5)

Sinnott, L. (Watford), 1985 v Is (sub) (1)

Slade, S. A. (Tottenham H), 1996 v Bel, An, P, Br (4)

Slater, S. I. (West Ham U), 1990 v P, USSR (sub), Cz (sub) (3)

Small, B. (Aston Villa), 1993 v Sm, T, Ho, Pol, N, P, Cz, Br, S, F; 1994 v Pol, Sm (12)

Smith, D. (Coventry C), 1988 v M, USSR (sub), Mor; 1989 v D, Se, Alb (2), Pol; 1990 v Se, Pol (10)

Smith, M. (Sheffield W), 1981 v Ei, R, Sw, H; 1982 v Pol (sub) (5)

Smith, M. (Sunderland), 1995 v Ei (sub) (1)

Snodin, I. (Doncaster R), 1985 v T, Is, R, Fi (4)

Statham, B. (Tottenham H), 1988 v Sw; 1989 v D (sub), Se (3)

Statham, D. J. (WBA), 1978 v Fi, 1979 v W, Bul, Se; 1980 v D; 1983 v D (6)

Stein, B. (Luton T), 1984 v D, H, I (3)

Sterland, M. (Sheffield W), 1984 v D, H, F (2), I, Sp (2) (7)

Steven, T. (Everton), 1985 v Fi, T (2)

Stevens, G. (Brighton & HA), 1983 v H; (with Tottenham H), 1984 v H, F (1+1 subs), I (sub), Sp (1+1 sub); 1986 v I (8)

Stewart, P. (Manchester C), 1988 v F (1)

Stuart, G. C. (Chelsea), 1990 v P (sub), F, USSR, Cz; 1991 v T (sub) (5)

Stuart, J. C. (Charlton Ath), 1996 v Bel, An, P, Br (4)

Suckling, P. (Coventry C), 1986 v D; (with Manchester C), 1987 v Se (sub), Y, Sp, T; (with C Palace), 1988 v S (2), F (2), Sw (10)

Summerbee, N.J. (Swindon T), 1993 v P (sub), S (sub), F (3)

Sunderland, A. (Wolverhampton W), 1977 v W (1)

Sutton, C. R. (Norwich), 1993 v Sp (sub), T (sub + 1),Ho, P (sub), Cz, Br, S, F; 1994 v Pol, Ho, Sm, D (13)

Swindlehurst, D. (C Palace), 1977 v W (1)

Sutch, D. (Norwich C), 1992 v H, M, Cz; 1993 v T (4)

Talbot, B. (Ipswich T), 1977 v W (1)

Thatcher, B. D. (Millwall), 1996 v Cro; (with Wimbledon), 1997 v Mol, Pol; 1998 v I (4)

Thomas, D. (Coventry C), 1981 v Ei; 1983 v WG (2), Gr, H; (with Tottenham H), I, Sp (7)

Thomas, M. (Luton T), 1986 v T, D, I (3)

Thomas, M. (Arsenal), 1988 v Y, S, F (2), M, USSR, Mor; 1989 v Gr, Alb (2), Pol; 1990 v Se (12)

Thomas, R. E. (Watford), 1990 v P (1)

Thompson, A. (Bolton W), 1995 v La; 1996 v P (2)

Thompson, D. A. (Liverpool), 1997 v Pol (sub), Ge (2)

Thompson, G. L. (Coventry C), 1981 v R, Sw, H; 1982 v N, H, S (6)

Thorn, A. (Wimbledon), 1988 v WG (sub). Y, S, F, Sw (5)

Thornley, B. L. (Manchester U), 1996 v Bel, P, Br (3)

Tiler, C. (Barnsley), 1990 v P, USSR, Cz; 1991 v H, Pol, Ei (2), T, Sen, USSR, F; (with Nottingham F), 1992 v G, T (13)

Unsworth, D. G. (Everton), 1995 v A, Ei (2), La; 1996 v N, A (6)

Venison, B. (Sunderland), 1983 v D, Gr; 1985 v Fi, T, Is, Fi; 1986 v R, T, D (2) (10)

Vinnicombe, C. (Rangers), 1991 v H (sub), Pol, Ei (2), T, Sen, M, USSR (sub), F; 1992 v G, T, Pol (12)

Waddle, C. (Newcastle U), 1985 v Fi (1)

Wallace, D. (Southampton), 1983 v Gr, H; 1984 v D, H, F (2), I, Sp (sub); 1985 v Fi, T, Is; 1986 v R, D, I (14)

Wallace, Ray (Southampton), 1989 v Bul, Sen (sub), Ei; 1990 v Se (4)

Wallace, Rod (Southampton), 1989 v Bul, Ei (sub), US; 1991 v H, Pol, Ei, T, Sen, M, USSR, F (11)

Walker, D. (Nottingham F), 1985 v Fi; 1987 v Se, T; 1988 v WG, T, S (2) (7)

Walker, I. M. (Tottenham H), 1991 v W; 1992 v H, Cz, F; 1993 v Sp, N, T, Sm; 1994 v Pol (9)

Walsh, G. (Manchester U), 1988 v WG, Y (2)

Walsh, P. M. (Luton T), 1983 v D (sub), Gr (2), H (4)

Walters, K. (Aston Villa), 1984 v D (sub), H (sub); 1985 v Is, Ei, R; 1986 v R, T, D, I (sub) (9)

Ward, P. D. (Brighton & HA), 1979 v N; 1980 v EG (2)

Warhurst, P. (Oldham Ath), 1991 v H, Pol, W, Sen, M (sub), USSR, F (sub); (with Sheffield W), 1992 v G (8)

Watson, D. (Norwich C), 1984 v D, F (2), I (2), Sp (2) (7)

Watson, D. N. (Barnsley), 1994 v Ho, Sm; 1995 v Br, F; 1996 v N (5)

Watson, G. (Sheffield W), 1991 v Sen, USSR (2)

Watson, S. C. (Newcastle U), 1993 v Sp (sub), N; 1994 v Sm (sub), D; 1995 v P, A, Ei (2), La (2); 1996 v N, A (12)

Webb, N. (Portsmouth), 1985 v Ei; (with Nottingham F), 1986 v D (2) (3)

Whelan, P. J. (Ipswich T), 1993 v Sp, T (sub), P (3)

Whelan, N. (Leeds U), 1995 v A (sub), Ei (2)

White, D. (Manchester C), 1988 v S (2), F, USSR; 1989 v Se; 1990 v Pol (6)

Whyte, C. (Arsenal), 1982 v S (1+1 sub); 1983 v D, Gr (4)

Wicks, S. (QPR), 1982 v S (1)

Wilkins, R. C. (Chelsea), 1977 v W (1)

Wilkinson, P. (Grimsby T), 1985 v Ei, R (sub); (with Everton), 1986 v R (sub), I (4)

Williams, D. (Sunderland), 1998 v Sw (sub) (1)

Williams, P. (Charlton Ath), 1989 v Bul, Sen, Ei, US (sub) (4)

Williams, P. D. (Derby Co), 1991 v Sen, M, USSR; 1992 v G, T, Pol (6)

Williams, S. C. (Southampton), 1977 v S, Fi, N; 1978 v N, I (1 + 1 sub), Y (2); 1979 v D, Bul, Se (sub); 1980 v D, EG (2) (14)

Winterburn, N. (Wimbledon), 1986 v I (1)

Wise, D. (Wimbledon), 1988 v Sw (1)

Woodcook, A. S. (Nottingham F), 1978 v Fi, I (2)

Woods, C. C. E. (Nottingham F), 1979 v W (sub), Se; (with QPR), 1980 v Bul, EG; 1981 v Sw; (with Norwich C), 1984 v D (6)

Wright, A. G. (Blackburn), 1993 v Sp, N (2)

Wright, M. (Southampton), 1983 v Gr, H; 1984 v D, H (4)

Wright, R. I. (Ipswich T), 1997 v Ge, Pol; 1998 v Mol, I, Gr (2), S.Af, Arg (8)

Wright, W. (Everton), 1979 v D, W, Bul; 1980 v D, S (2) (6)

Yates, D. (Notts Co), 1989 v D (sub), Bul, Sen, Ei, US (5)

**SCOTLAND**

Aitken, R. (Celtic), 1977 v Cz, W, Sw; 1978 v Cz, W; 1979 v P, N (2); 1980 v Bel, E; 1984 v EG, Y (2); 1985 v WG, Ic, Sp (16)

Albiston, A. (Manchester U), 1977 v Cz, W, Sw; 1978 v Sw, Cz (5)

Alexander, N. (Stenhousemuir), 1997 v P (sub); 1998 v Bl, Ei, I (4)

Anderson, I. (Dundee), 1997 v Co (sub), US, CzR, P; 1998 v Bl, La, Fi, D (sub), Ei (sub), Ni (10)

Anderson, R. (Aberdeen), 1997 v Es, A, Se; 1998 v La (sub), Fi, Ei, I (7)

Anthony, M. (Celtic), 1997 v La (sub), Es (sub), Col (3)

Archdeacon, O. (Celtic), 1987 v WG (sub) (1)

Archibald, A. (Partick T), 1998 v Fi, Ei, Ni, I (4)

Archibald, S. (Aberdeen), 1980 v B, E (2), WG; (with Tottenham H), 1981 v D (5)

Bagen, D. (Kilmarnock), 1997 v Es, A (sub), Se (sub), Bl (4)

Bain, K. (Dundee), 1993 v P, I, Ma, P (4)

Baker, M. (St. Mirren), 1993 v F, M, E; 1994 v Ma, A; 1995 v Gr, M, F (sub), Sk (sub); 1996 v H (sub) (10)

Bannon, E. J. P. (Hearts), 1979 v US; (with Chelsea), P, N (2); (with Dundee U), 1980 v Bel, WG, E (7)

Beattie, J. (St Mirren), 1992 v D, US, P, Y (4)

Beaumont, D. (Dundee U), 1985 v Ic (1)

Bell, D. (Aberdeen), 1981 v D; 1984 v Y (2)

Bernard, P. R. J. (Oldham Ath), 1992 v R (sub), D, Se (sub), US; 1993 v Sw, P, I, Ma, P, F, Bul, M, E; 1994 v I, Ma (15)

Bett, J. (Rangers), 1981 v Se, D; 1982 v Se, D, I, E (2) (7)

Black, E. (Aberdeen), 1983 v EG, Sw (2), Bel; 1985 v Ic, Sp (2), Ic (8)

Blair, A. (Coventry C), 1980 v E; 1981 v Se; (with Aston Villa), 1982 v Se, D, I (5)

Bollan, G. (Dundee U), 1992 v D, G (sub), US, P, Y; 1993 v Sw, P, I, P, F, Bul, M, E; 1994 v Sw; 1995 v Gr; (with Rangers) v Ru, Sm (17)

Bonar, P. (Raith R), 1997 v A, La, Es (sub), Se (4)

Booth, S. (Aberdeen), 1991 v R (sub), Bul (sub + 1), Pol, F (sub); 1992 v Sw, R, D, Se, US, P, Y; 1993 v Ma, P (14)

Bowes, M. J. (Dunfermline Ath), 1992 v D (sub) (1)

Bowman, D. (Hearts), 1985 v WG (sub) (1)

Boyack, S. (Rangers), 1997 v Se (1)

Boyd, T. (Motherwell), 1987 v WG, Ei (2), Bel; 1988 v Bel (5)

Brazil, A. (Hibernian), 1978 v W (1)

Brazil, A. (Ipswich T), 1979 v N; 1980 v Bel (2), E (2), WG; 1981 v Se; 1982 v Se (8)

Brebner, G. I. (Manchester U), 1997 v Col, CzR (sub), US (sub), P; 1998 v Bl, La, Fi, D (8)

Brough, J. (Hearts), 1981 v D (1)

Browne, P. (Raith R), 1997 v A (1)

Buchan, J. (Aberdeen), 1997 v Se, Col, CzR, P; 1998 v Bl, La, Fi (7)

Burchill, M. (Celtic), 1998 v Fi, D (sub) (2)

Burke, A. (Kilmarnock), 1997 v Es, A, Bl (sub); 1998 v Ei (sub) (4)

Burley, G. E. (Ipswich T), 1977 v Cz, W, Sw; 1978 v Sw, Cz (5)

Burley, C. (Chelsea), 1992 v D; 1993 v Sw, P, I, P; 1994 v Sw, I (sub) (7)

Burns, H. (Rangers), 1985 v Sp, Ic (sub) (2)

Burns, T. (Celtic), 1977 v Cz, W, E; 1978 v Sw; 1982 v E (5)

Campbell, S. (Dundee), 1989 v N (sub), Y, F (3)

Campbell, S. P. (Leicester C), 1998 v Fi (sub), D, Ei, Ni (sub), I (5)

Carey, L. A. (Bristol C), 1998 v D (1)

Casey, J. (Celtic), 1978 v W (1)

Christie, M. (Dundee), 1992 v D, P (sub), Y (3)

Clark, R. (Aberdeen), 1977 v Cz, W, Sw (3)

Clarke, S. (St Mirren), 1984 v Bel, EG, Y; 1985 v WG, Ic, Sp (2), Ic (8)

Cleland, A. (Dundee U), 1990 v F, N (2); 1991 v R, Sw, Bul; 1992 v Sw, R, G, Se (2) (11)

Collins, J. (Hibernian), 1988 v Bel, E; 1989 v N, Y, F; 1990 v Y, F, N (8)

Connolly, P. (Dundee U), 1991 v R (sub), Sw, Bul (3)

Connor, R. (Ayr U), 1981 v Se; 1982 v Se (2)

Cooper, D. (Clydebank), 1977 v Cz, W, Sw, E; (with Rangers), 1978 v Sw, Cz (6)

Cooper, N. (Aberdeen), 1982 v D, E (2); 1983 v Bel, EG, Sw (2); 1984 v Bel, EG, Y; 1985 v Ic, Sp, Ic (13)

Crabbe, S. (Hearts), 1990 v Y (sub), F (2)

Craig, M. (Aberdeen), 1998 v Bl, La (2)

Craig, T. (Newcastle U), 1977 v E (1)

Crainie, D. (Celtic), 1983 v Sw (sub) (1)

Crawford, S. (Raith R), 1994 v A, Eg, P, Bel; 1995 v Fi, Ru,Gr, Ru, Sm, M, F (sub), Sk (sub), Br (sub); 1996 v Gr, Fi (sub), H (1 + sub), Sp (sub), F (sub) (19)

Creaney, G. (Celtic), 1991 v Sw, Bul (2), Pol, F; 1992 v Sw, R, G (2), Se (2) (11)

Dailly, C. (Dundee U), 1991 v R; 1992 v US, R; 1993 v Sw, P, I, Ic, P, F, Bul, M, E; 1994 v Sw, I, Ma, A, Eg, P, Bel; 1995 v Fi, Ru, Gr, Ru, Sm, M, F, Sk, Br; 1996 v Fi, Sm, H (2), Sp, F (34)

Dargo, C. (Raith R), 1998 v Fi, Ei, Ni (sub), I (4)

Davidson, C. (St Johnstone), 1997 v Se, Bl (2)

Dawson, A. (Rangers), 1979 v P, N (2); 1980 v B (2), E (2), WG (8)

Deas, P. A. (St Johnstone), 1992 v D (sub); 1993 v Ma (2)

Dennis, S. (Raith R), 1992 v Sw (1)

Dickov, P. (Arsenal), 1992 v Y; 1993 v F, M, E (4)

Dodds, D. (Dundee U), 1978 v W (1)

Dods, D. (Hibernian), 1997 v La, Es, Se (2), Bl (5)

Donald, G. S. (Hibernian), 1992 v US (sub), P, Y (sub) (3)

Donnelly, S. (Celtic), 1994 v Eg, P, Bel; 1995 v Fi, Gr (sub); 1996 v Gr (sub), Sm, H (2), Sp, F (11)

Dow, A. (Dundee), 1993 v Ma (sub), Ic; (with Chelsea) 1994 v I (3)

Duffy, J. (Dundee), 1987 v Ei (1)

Durie, G. S. (Chelsea), 1987 v WG, Ei, Bel; 1988 v Bel (4)

Durrant, I. (Rangers), 1987 v WG, Ei, Bel; 1988 v E (4)

Doyle, J. (Partick Th), 1981 v D, I (sub) (2)

Easton, C. (Dundee U), 1997 v Col, US, CzR, P; 1998 v Bl, Fi, D, Ei, Ni, I (10)

Elliot, B. (Celtic), 1998 v Ni (1)

Ferguson, B. (Rangers), 1997 v Col (sub), US, CzR, P; 1998 v Bl, La, Fi, D (sub), Ei, Ni, I (11)

Ferguson, D. (Rangers), 1987 v WG, Ei, Bel; 1988 v E; 1990 v Y (5)

Ferguson, D. (Dundee U), 1992 v D, G, Se (2); 1993 v Sw, I, Ma (7)

Ferguson, D. (Manchester U), 1992 v US, P (sub), Y; 1993 v Sw, Ma (5)

Ferguson, I. (Dundee), 1983 v EG (sub), Sw (sub); 1984 v Bel (sub), EG (4)

Ferguson, I. (Clyde), 1987 v WG (sub), Ei; (with St Mirren), Ei, Bel; 1988 v Bel; (with Rangers), E (sub) (6)

Ferguson, R. (Hamilton A), 1977 v E (1)

Findlay, W. (Hibernian), 1991 v R, Pol, Bul (2), Pol (5)

Fitzpatrick, A. (St Mirren), 1977 v W (sub), Sw (sub), E; 1978 v Sw, Cz (5)

Flannigan, C. (Clydebank), 1993 v Ic (sub) (1)

Fleck, R. (Rangers), 1987 v WG (sub), Ei, Bel; (with Norwich C), 1988 v E (2); 1989 v Y (6)

Freedman, D. A. (Barnet), 1995 v Ru (sub + 1), Sm, M, F, Sk, Br; (with C Palace) 1996 v Sm (sub) (8)

Fridge, L. (St Mirren), 1989 v F; 1990 v Y (2)

Fullarton, J. (St. Mirren), 1993 v F, Bul; 1994 v Ma, A, Eg, P, Bel; 1995 v M, F, Sk, Br; 1996 v Gr, Fi, H (sub + 1), Sp (sub), F (17)

Fulton, M. (St Mirren), 1980 v Bel, WG, E; 1981 v Se, D (sub) (5)

Fulton, S. (Celtic), 1991 v R, Sw, Bul, Pol, F; 1992 v G (2) (7)

Gallacher, K. (Dundee U), 1987 v WG, Ei (2), Bel (sub); 1988 v E (2); 1990 v Y (7)

Galloway, M. (Hearts), 1989 v F; (with Celtic), 1990 v N (2)

Gardiner, J. (Hibernian), 1993 v F (1)

Geddes, R. (Dundee), 1982 v Se, D, E (2); 1988 v E (5)

Gemmill, S. (Nottingham F), 1992 v Sw, R (sub), G (sub), Se (sub) (4)

Germaine, G. (WBA), 1997 v Se (1)

Gilles, R. (St Mirren), 1997 v A (1 + sub), La, Es (2), Se, Bl (7)

Gillespie, G. (Coventry C), 1979 v US; 1980 v E; 1981 v D; 1982 v Se, D, I (2), E (8)

Glass, S. (Aberdeen), 1995 v M, F, Sk, Br; 1996 v Gr, Fi, H, Sp; 1997 v A (2), Es (11)

Glover, L. (Nottingham F), 1988 v Bel (sub); 1989 v N; 1990 v Y (3)

Goram, A. (Oldham Ath), 1987 v Ei (1)

Gough, C. R. (Dundee U), 1983 v EG, Sw, Bel; 1984 v Y (2) (5)

Graham, D. (Rangers), 1998 v Bl (sub), La (sub), Fi (sub), D, Ei (sub), Ni, I (7)

Grant, P. (Celtic), 1985 v WG, Ic, Sp; 1987 v WG, Ei (2), Bel; 1988 v Bel, E (2) (10)

Gray S. (Celtic), 1995 v F, Sk, Br; 1996 v Gr, H, Sp, F (7)

Gray, S. (Aberdeen), 1987 v WG (1)

Gunn, B. (Aberdeen), 1984 v EG, Y (2); 1985 v WG, Ic, Sp (2), Ic; 1990 v F (9)

Hagen, D. (Rangers), 1992 v D (sub), US (sub), P, Y; 1993 v Sw (sub), P, Ic, P (8)

Hamilton, B. (St Mirren), 1989 v Y, F (sub); 1990 v F, N (4)

Hamilton, J. (Dundee) 1995 v Sm (sub), Br; 1996 v Fi (sub), Sm, H (sub), Sp (sub), F; 1997 v A, La, Es, Se; (with Hearts), Es, A, Se (14)

Handyside, P. (Grimsby T), 1993 v Ic (sub), Bul, M, E; 1995 v Ru; 1996 v Fi, Sm (7)

Hannah, D. (Dundee U), 1993 v F (sub), Bul, M; 1994 v A, Eg, P, Bel; 1995 v Fi, Ru (sub), Gr, Ru, M, F, Sk, Br; 1996 v Gr (16)

Harper, K. (Hibernian), 1995 v Ru (sub); 1996 v Fi; 1997 v A (2), La, Es, Se (7)

Hartford, R. A. (Manchester C), 1977 v Sw (1)

Hartley, P. (Millwall), 1997 v A (sub) (1)

Hegarty, P. (Dundee U), 1987 v WG, Bel; 1988 v E (2); 1990 v F, N (6)

Hendry, J. (Tottenham H), 1992 v D (sub) (1)

Hetherston, B. (St Mirren), 1997 v Es (sub) (1)

Hewitt, J. (Aberdeen), 1982 v I; 1983 v EG, Sw (2); 1984 v Bel, Y (sub) (6)

Hogg, G. (Manchester U), 1984 v Y; 1985 v WG, Ic, Sp (4)

Hood, G. (Ayr U), 1993 v F, E (sub); 1994 v A (3)

Horn, R. (Hearts), 1997 v US, CzR, P; 1998 v Bl, La, D (sub) (6)

Howie, S. (Cowdenbeath), 1993 v Ma, Ic, P; 1994 v Sw, I (5)

Hunter, G. (Hibernian), 1987 v Ei (sub); 1988 v Bel, E (3)

Hunter, P. (East Fife), 1989 v N (sub), F (sub); 1990 v F (sub) (3)

James, K. F. (Falkirk), 1997 v Bl (1)

Jardine, I. (Kilmarnock), 1979 v US (1)

Jess, E. (Aberdeen), 1990 v F (sub), N (sub); 1991 v R, Sw, Bul (2), Pol, F; 1992 v Sw, R, G (2), Se (1 + 1 sub) (14)

Johnson, G. I. (Dundee U), 1992 v US, P, Y; 1993 v Sw, P, Ma (6)

Johnston, A. (Hearts), 1994 v Bel; 1995 v Ru, 1996 v Sp (3)

Johnston, F. (Falkirk), 1993 v Ic (1)

Johnston, M. (Partick Th), 1984 v EG (sub); (with Watford), Y (2) (3)

Jupp, D. A. (Fulham), 1995 v Fi, Ru (2), Sm, M, F, Sk, Br; 1997 v Se (9)

Kirkwood, D. (Hearts), 1990 v Y (1)

Kerr, S. (Celtic), 1993 v Bul, M, E; 1994 v Ma, A, Eg, P, Bel; 1995 v Fi, Gr (10)

Lambert, P. (St Mirren), 1991 v R, Sw, Bul (2), Pol, F; 1992 v Sw, R, G (2), Se (11)

Lauchlan, J. (Kilmarnock), 1998 v Ei, Ni, I (3)

Lavety, B. (St. Mirren), 1993 v Ic, Bul (sub), M (sub), E; 1994 v Ma, A (sub), Eg (sub), Bel (sub); 1995 v Fi (sub) (9)

Lavin, G. (Watford), 1993 v F, Bul, M; 1994 v Ma, Eg, P, Bel (7)

Leighton, J. (Aberdeen), 1982 v I (1)

Levein, C. (Hearts), 1985 v Sp, Ic (2)

Liddell, A. M. (Barnsley), 1994 v Ma (sub); 1995 v Sm (sub), M (sub), F, Sk; 1996 v Gr, Fi, Sm, H (2), Sp, F (sub) (12)

Lindsey, J. (Motherwell), 1979 v US (1)

Locke, G. (Hearts), 1994 v Ma, A, Eg, P; 1995 v Fi; 1996 v Fi, H; 1997 v Es, A, Bl (10)

Love, G. (Hibernian), 1995 v Ru (1)

McAllister, G. (Leicester C), 1990 v N (1)

McAlpine, H. (Dundee U), 1983 v EG, Sw (2), Bel; 1984 v Bel (5)

McAnespie, K. (St Johnstone), 1998 v Fi (sub) (1)

McAuley, S. (St. Johnstone), 1993 v P (sub) (1)

McAvennie, F. (St Mirren), 1982 v I, E; 1985 v Is, Ei, R (5)

McBride, J. (Everton), 1981 v D (1)

McBride, J. P. (Celtic), 1998 v Ni (sub), I (sub) (2)

McCall, S. (Bradford C), 1988 v E; (with Everton), 1990 v F (2)

McCann, N. (Dundee), 1994 v A, Eg, P, Bel; 1995 v Fi, Gr (sub); Sm; 1996 v Fi, Sm (9)

McClair, B. (Celtic), 1984 v Bel (sub), EG, Y (1 + 1 sub); 1985 v WG, Ic, Sp, Ic (8)

McCluskey, G. (Celtic), 1979 v US, P; 1980 v Bel (2); 1982 v D, I (6)

McCluskey, S. (St Johnstone), 1997 v Es (2), A, Se, Col, US, CzR; 1998 v Bl, La, D, Ei (sub), Ni, I (13)

McCoist, A. (Rangers), 1984 v Bel (1)

McConnell, I. (Clyde), 1997 v A (sub) (1)

McCulloch, A. (Kilmarnock), 1981 v Se (1)

McCulloch, I. (Notts Co), 1982 v E (2)

McCulloch, L. (Motherwell), 1997 v La (sub), Es (1 + sub), Se (sub + 1), A (sub), Col (sub); 1998 v Bl (sub), Fi (sub), D, Ei, Ni (12)

MacDonald, J. (Rangers), 1980 v WG (sub); 1981 v Se; 1982 v Se (sub), L, I (2), E (2 sub) (8)

McDonald, C. (Falkirk), 1995 v Fi (sub), Ru, M (sub), F (sub), Br (sub) (5)

McEwan, C. (Clyde), 1997 v Col, US (sub), CzR (sub), P; (with Raith R), 1998 v Bl, La, Fi, D, Ei, Ni, I (11)

McFarlane, D. (Hamilton A), 1997 v Col, US (sub), P (sub) (3)

McGarry, S. (St Mirren), 1997 v US, CzR, P (sub) (3)

McGarvey, F. (St Mirren), 1977 v E; 1978 v Cz; (with Celtic), 1982 v D (3)

McGarvey, S. (Manchester U), 1982 v E (sub); 1983 v Bel, Sw; 1984 v Bel (4)

McGhee, M. (Aberdeen), 1981 v D (1)

McGinnis, G. (Dundee U), 1985 v Sp (1)

McGrillen, P. (Motherwell), 1994 v Sw (sub), I (2)

McInally, J. (Dundee U), 1989 v F (1)

McKenzie, R. (Hearts), 1997 v Es, Bl (2)

McKimmie, S. (Aberdeen), 1985 v WG, Ic (2) (3)

McKinlay, T. (Dundee), 1984 v EG (sub); 1985 v WG, Ic, Sp (2), Ic (6)

McKinlay, W. (Dundee U), 1989 v N, Y (sub), F; 1990 v Y, F, N (6)

McKinnon, R. (Dundee U), 1991 v R, Pol (sub); 1992 v G (2), Se (2) (6)

McLaren, A, (Hearts), 1989 v F; 1990 v Y, N; 1991 v Sw, Bul, Pol, F; 1992 v R, G, Se (2) (11)

McLaren, A. (Dundee U), 1993 v I, Ma (sub); 1994 v Sw, I (sub) (4)

McLaughlin, B. (Celtic), 1995 v Ru, Sm, M, Sk (sub); Br (sub); 1996 v Gr (sub), Sm (sub), H (8)

McLaughlin, J. (Morton), 1981 v D; 1982 v Se, D, I, E (2); 1983 v EG, Sw (2), Bel (10)

McLeish, A. (Aberdeen), 1978 v W; 1979 v US; 1980 v Bel, E (2); 1987 v Ei (6)

MacLeod, A. (Hibernian), 1979 v P, N (2) (3)

McLeod, J. (Dundee U), 1989 v N; 1990 v F (2)

MacLeod, M. (Dumbarton), 1979 v US; (with Celtic), P (sub), N (2); 1980 v Bel (5)

McMillan, S. (Motherwell), 1997 v A (sub + sub), Se, Bl (4)

McNab, N. (Tottenham H), 1978 v W (1)

McNally, M. (Celtic), 1991 v Bul; 1993 v Ic (2)

McNamara, J. (Dunfermline Ath), 1994 v A, Bel; 1995 v Gr, Ru, Sm; 1996 v Gr, Fi; (with Celtic), Sm, H (2), Sp, F (12)

McNichol, J. (Brentford), 1979 v P, N (2); 1980 v Bel (2), WG, E (7)

McNiven, D. (Leeds U), 1977 v Cz, W (sub), Sw (sub) (3)

McNiven, S. A. (Oldham Ath), 1996 v Sm (sub) (1)

McPherson, D. (Rangers), 1984 v Bel; 1985 v Sp; (with Hearts), 1989 v N, Y (4)

McQuilken, J. (Celtic), 1993 v Bul, E (2)

McStay, P. (Celtic), 1983 v EG, Sw (2); 1984 v Y (2) (5)

McWhirter, N. (St Mirren), 1991 v Bul (sub) (1)

Main, A. (Dundee U), 1988 v E; 1989 v Y; 1990 v N (3)

Malpas, M. (Dundee U), 1983 v Bel, Sw (1+1 sub); 1984 v Bel, EG, Y (2); 1985 v Sp (8)

Marshall, S. R. (Arsenal), 1995 v Ru, Gr; 1996 v H, Sp, F (5)

Mathieson, D. (Queen of the South), 1997 v Col; 1998 v La (2)

May, E. (Hibernian), 1989 v Y (sub), F (2)

Meldrum, C. (Kilmarnock), 1996 v F (sub); 1997 v A (2), La, Es, Se (6)

Melrose, J. (Partick Th), 1977 v Sw; 1979 v US, P, N (2); 1980 v Bel (sub), WG, E (8)

Miller, C. (Rangers), 1995 v Gr, Ru; 1996 v Gr, Sp, F; 1997 v A, La, Es (8)

Miller, J. (Aberdeen), 1987 v Ei (sub); 1988 v Bel; (with Celtic), E; 1989 v N, Y; 1990 v F, N (7)

Miller, W. (Aberdeen), 1978 v Sw, Cz (2)

Miller, W. (Hibernian), 1991 v R, Sw, Bul, Pol, F; 1992 v R, G (sub) (7)

Milne, R. (Dundee U), 1982 v Se (sub); 1984 v Bel, EG (3)

Money, I. C. (St Mirren), 1987 v Ei; 1988 v Bel; 1989 v N (3)

Muir, L. (Hibernian), 1977 v Cz (sub) (1)

Murray, N. (Rangers), 1993 v P (sub), Ma, Ic, P; 1994 v Sw, I; 1995 v Fi, Ru, Gr, Sm; 1996 v Gr (sub), Fi, Sm, H (2), F (16)

Murray, R. (Bournemouth), 1993 v Ic (sub) (1)

Narey, D. (Dundee U), 1977 v Cz, Sw; 1978 v Sw, Cz (4)

Naysmith, G. (Hearts), 1997 v La, Es (1 + sub), Se, A, Col, US, CzR, P; 1998 v La, D (11)

Nevin, P. (Chelsea), 1985 v WG, Ic, Sp (2), Ic (5)

Nicholas, C. (Celtic), 1981 v Se; 1982 v Se; 1983 v EG, Sw, Bel; (with Arsenal), 1984 v Y (6)

Nicol, S. (Ayr U), 1981 v Se; 1982 v Se, D; (with Liverpool), I (2), E (2); 1983 v EG, Sw (2), Bel; 1984 v Bel, EG, Y (14)

Nisbet, S. (Rangers), 1989 v N, Y, F; 1990 v Y, F (5)

O'Donnell, P. (Motherwell), 1992 v Sw (sub), R, D, G (2), Se (1 + 1 sub); 1993 v P (8)

O'Neil, B. (Celtic), 1992 v D, G, Se (2); 1993 v Sw, P, I (7)

O'Neil, J. (Dundee U), 1991 v Bul (sub) (1)

O'Neill, M. (Clyde), 1995 v Ru (sub), F, Sk, Br; 1997 v Se (sub), Bl (sub) (6)

Orr, N. (Morton), 1978 v W (sub); 1979 v US, P, N (2); 1980 v Bel, E (7)

Parlane, D. (Rangers), 1977 v W (1)

Paterson, C. (Hibernian), 1981 v Se; 1982 v I (2)

Paterson, J. (Dundee U), 1997 v Col, US, CzR (3)

Payne, G. (Dundee U), 1978 v Sw, Cz, W (3)

Peacock, L. A. (Carlisle U), 1997 v Bl (1)

Pressley, S. (Rangers), 1993 v Ic, F, Bul, M, E; 1994 v Sw, I, M, A, Eg, P, Bel; 1995 v Fi; (with Coventry C), Ru

(2), Sm, M, F, Sk, Br; (with Dundee U), 1996 v Gr, Sm, H (2), Sp, F (26)

Provan, D. (Kilmarnock), 1977 v Cz (sub) (1)

Rae, A. (Millwall), 1991 v Bul (sub + 1), F (sub); 1992 v Sw, R, G (sub), Se (2) (8)

Redford, I. (Rangers), 1981 v Se (sub); 1982 v Se, D, I (2), E (6)

Reid, B. (Rangers), 1991 v F; 1992 v D, US, P (4)

Reid, C. (Hibernian), 1993 v Sw, P, I (3)

Reid, M. (Celtic), 1982 v E; 1984 v Y (2)

Reid, R. (St Mirren), 1977 v W, Sw, E (3)

Renicks, S. (Hamilton A), 1997 v Bl (1)

Rice, B. (Hibernian), 1985 v WG (1)

Richardson, L. (St Mirren), 1980 v WG, E (sub) (2)

Ritchie, A. (Morton), 1980 v Bel (1)

Ritchie, P. R. (Hearts), 1996 v H; 1997 v A (2), La, Es (2), Se (7)

Robertson, A. (Rangers) 1991 v F (1)

Robertson, C. (Rangers), 1977 v E (sub) (1)

Robertson, D. (Aberdeen), 1987 v Ei (sub); 1988 v E (2); 1989 v N, Y; 1990 v Y, N (7)

Robertson, H. (Aberdeen), 1994 v Eg; 1995 v Fi (2)

Robertson, J. (Hearts), 1985 v WG, Ic (sub) (2)

Robertson, L. (Rangers), 1993 v F, M (sub), E (sub) (3)

Robertson, S. (St Johnstone), 1998 v Fi, Ni (2)

Roddie, A. (Aberdeen), 1992 v US, P; 1993 v Sw (sub), P, Ic (5)

Ross, T. W. (Arsenal), 1977 v W (1)

Rowson, D. (Aberdeen), 1997 v La, Es, Se (2), Bl (5)

Russell, R. (Rangers), 1978 v W; 1980 v Bel; 1984 v Y (3)

Salton, D. B. (Luton T), 1992 v D, US, P, Y; 1993 v Sw, I (6)

Scott, P. (St Johnstone), 1994 v A (sub), Eg (sub), P, Bel (4)

Scrimgour, D. (St Mirren), 1997 v US, CzR; 1998 v D (3)

Seaton, A. (Falkirk), 1998 v Bl (sub) (1)

Shannon, R. (Dundee), 1987 v WG, Ei (2), Bel; 1988 v Bel, E (2) (7)

Sharp, G. (Everton), 1982 v E (1)

Sharp, R. (Dunfermline Ath), 1990 v N (sub); 1991 v R, Sw, Bul (4)

Sheerin, P. (Southampton), 1996 v Sm (1)

Shields, G. (Rangers), 1997 v A, La (2)

Simpson, N. (Aberdeen), 1982 v I (2), E; 1983 v EG, Sw (2), Bel; 1984 v Bel, EG, Y; 1985 v Sp (11)

Sinclair, G. (Dumbarton), 1977 v E (1)

Skilling, M. (Kilmarnock), 1993 v Ic (sub); 1994 v I (2)

Smith, B. M. (Celtic), 1992 v G (2), US, P, Y (5)

Smith, G. (Rangers), 1978 v W (1)

Smith, H. G. (Hearts), 1987 v WG, Bel (2)

Sneddon, A. (Celtic), 1979 v US (1)

Speedie, D. (Chelsea), 1985 v Sp (1)

Spencer, J. (Rangers), 1991 v Sw (sub), F; 1992 v Sw (3)

Stanton, P. (Hibernian), 1977 v Cz (1)

Stark, W. (Aberdeen), 1985 v Ic (1)

Stephen, R. (Dundee), 1983 v Bel (sub) (1)

Stevens, G. (Motherwell), 1977 v E (1)

Stewart, J. (Kilmarnock), 1978 v Sw, Cz; (with Middlesbrough), 1979 v P (3)

Stewart, R. (Dundee U), 1979 v P, N (2); (with West Ham U), 1980 v Bel (2), E (2), WG; 1981 v D; 1982 v I (2), E (12)

Stillie, D. (Aberdeen), 1995 v Ru (2), Sm, M, F, Sk, Br; 1996 v Gr, Fi, Sm, H (2), Sp, F (14)

Strachan, G. D. (Aberdeen), 1980 v Bel (1)

Strachan, G. D. (Coventry C), 1998 v D, Ei (2)

Sturrock, P. (Dundee U), 1977 v Cz, W, Sw, E; 1978 v Sw, Cz; 1982 v Se, I, E (9)

Sweeney, S. (Clydebank), 1991 v R, Sw (sub), Bul (2), Pol; 1992 v Sw, R (7)

Teale, G. (Clydebank), 1997 v La (sub), Es, Bl (3)

Telfer, P. (Luton T), 1993 v Ma, P; 1994 v Sw (3)

Thomas, K. (Hearts), 1993 v F (sub), Bul, M, E; 1994 v Sw, Ma; 1995 v Gr; 1997 v A (8)

Thompson, S. (Dundee U), 1997 v US, CzR, P; 1998 v Bl, La (5)

Thomson, W. (Partick Th), 1977 v E (sub); 1978 v W; (with St Mirren), 1979 v US, N (2); 1980 v Bel (2), E (2), WG (10)

Tolmie, J. (Morton), 1980 v Bel (sub) (1)

Tortolano, J. (Hibernian), 1987 v WG, Ei (2)

Tweed, S. (Hibernian), 1993 v Ic; 1994 v Sw, I (3)

Walker, A. (Celtic), 1988 v Bel (1)

Wallace, I. (Coventry C), 1978 v Sw (1)

Walsh, C. (Nottingham F), 1984 v EG, Sw (2), Bel; 1984 v EG (5)
Wark, J. (Ipswich T), 1977 v Cz, W, Sw; 1978 v W; 1979 v P; 1980 v E (2), WG (8)
Watson, A. (Aberdeen), 1981 v Se, D; 1982 v D, I (sub) (4)
Watson, K. (Rangers), 1977 v E; 1978 v Sw (sub) (2)
Watt, M. (Aberdeen), 1991 v R, Sw, Bul (2), Pol, F; 1992 v Sw, R, G (2), Se (2) (12)
Whiteford, A. (St Johnstone), 1997 v US (1)
Whyte, D. (Celtic), 1987 v Ei (2), Bel; 1988 v E (2); 1989 v N, Y; 1990 v Y, N (9)
Will, J. A. (Arsenal), 1992 v D (sub), Y; 1993 v Ic (sub) (3)
Wilson, T. (St Mirren), 1983 v Sw (sub) (1)
Wilson, T. (Nottingham F), 1988 v E; 1989 v N, Y; 1990 v F (4)
Winnie, D. (St Mirren), 1988 v Bel (1)
Wright, P. (Aberdeen), 1989 v Y, F; (with QPR), 1990 v Y (sub) (3)
Wright, S. (Aberdeen), 1991 v Bul, Pol, F; 1992 v Sw, G (2), Se (2); 1993 v Sw, P, I, Ma; 1994 v I, Ma (14)
Wright, T. (Oldham Ath), 1987 v Bel (sub) (1)

Young, D. (Aberdeen), 1997 v Es (sub), Se, Col, CzR (sub), P; 1998 v La (sub) (6)

# WALES

Aizlewood, M. (Luton T), 1979 v E; 1981 v Ho (2)

Baddeley, L. M. (Cardiff C), 1996 v Mol (sub), G (sub) (2)
Balcombe, S. (Leeds U), 1982 v F (sub) (1)
Barnhouse, D. J. (Swansea), 1995 v Mol; 1996 v Mol, Sm (3)
Bater, P. T. (Bristol R), 1977 v E, S (2)
Bellamy, C. D. (Norwich C), 1996 v Sm (sub); 1997 v Sm, T, Bel; 1998 v T, Bel, I (7)
Bird, A. (Cardiff C), 1993 v Cy (sub); 1994 v Cy (sub); 1995 v Mol, Ge (sub), Bul; 1996 v G (sub) (6)
Blackmore, C. (Manchester U), 1984 v N, Bul, Y (3)
Blake, N. (Cardiff C), 1991 v Pol (sub); 1993 v Cy, Bel, RCS; 1994 v RCS (5)
Blaney, S. D. (West Ham U), 1997 v Sm, Ho, T (3)
Bodin, P. (Cardiff C), 1983 v Y (1)
Bowen, J. P. (Swansea C), 1993 v Cy, Bel (2); 1994 v RCS, R (sub) (5)
Bowen, M. (Tottenham H), 1983 v N; 1984 v Bul, Y (3)
Boyle, T. (C Palace), 1982 v F (1)
Brace, D. P. (Wrexham), 1995 v Ge, Bul (2); 1997 v Sm Ho; 1998 v T (6)

Cegielski, W. (Wrexham), 1977 v E (sub), S (2)
Chapple, S. R. (Swansea C), 1992 v R; 1993 v Cy, Bel (2), RCS; 1994 v RCS; Bul (2) (8)
Charles, J. M. (Swansea C), 1979 v E; 1981 v Ho (2)
Clark, J. (Manchester U), 1978 v S; (with Derby Co), 1979 v E (2)
Coates, J. S. (Swansea C), 1996 v Mol, G; 1997 v Ho, T (sub); 1998 v T (sub) (5)
Coleman, C. (Swansea C), 1990 v Pol; 1991 v E, Pol (3)
Coyne, D. (Tranmere R), 1992 v R; 1994 v Cy (sub), R; 1995 v Mol, Ge, Bul (2) (7)
Curtis, A. T. (Swansea C), 1977 v E (1)

Davies, A. (Manchester U), 1982 v F (2), Ho; 1983 v N, Y, Bul (6)
Davies, G. M. (Hereford U), 1993 v Bel, RCS; 1995 v Mol (sub), Ge, Bul (2); (with C Palace) 1996 v Mol (7)
Davies, I. C. (Norwich C), 1978 v S (sub) (1)
Deacy, N. (PSV Eindhoven), 1977 v S (1)
Dibble, A. (Cardiff C), 1983 v Bul; 1984 v N, Bul (3)
Doyle, S. C. (Preston NE), 1979 v E (sub); (with Huddersfield T), 1984 v N (2)
Dwyer, P. J. (Cardiff C), 1979 v E (1)

Ebdon, M. (Everton), 1990 v Pol; 1991 v E (2)
Edwards, C. N. H. (Swansea C), 1996 v G; 1997 v Sm, Ho (2), T, Bel; 1998 v T (7)
Edwards, R. I. (Chester), 1977 v S; 1978 v W (2)
Edwards, R. W. (Bristol C), 1991 v Pol; 1992 v R; 1993 v Cy, Bel (2), RCS; 1994 v RCS, Cy, R; 1995 v Ge, Bul; 1996 v Mol, G (13)
Evans, A. (Bristol R), 1977 v E (1)
Evans, P. S. (Shrewsbury T), 1996 v G (1)

Evans, T. (Cardiff C), 1995 v Bul (sub); 1996 v Mol, G (3)

Foster, M. G. (Tranmere R), 1993 v RCS (1)
Freestone, R. (Chelsea), 1990 v Pol (1)

Gale, D. (Swansea C), 1983 v Bul; 1984 v N (sub) (2)
Giggs, R. (Manchester U), 1991 v Pol (1)
Giles, D. C. (Cardiff C), 1977 v S; 1978 v S; (with Swansea C), 1981 v Ho; (with C Palace), 1983 v Y (4)
Giles, P. (Cardiff C), 1982 v F (2), Ho (3)
Graham, D. (Manchester U), 1991 v E (1)
Green, R. M. (Wolverhampton W), 1998 v I (1)
Griffith, C. (Cardiff C), 1990 v Pol (1)
Griffiths, C. (Shrewsbury T), 1991 v Pol (sub) (1)

Hall, G. D. (Chelsea), 1990 v Pol (1)
Hartson, J. (Luton T), 1994 v Cy, R; 1995 v Mol, Ge, Bul; (with Arsenal), 1996 v G, Sm; 1997 v Sm, Ho (9)
Haworth, S. O. (Cardiff C), 1997 v Ho, T, Bel; (with Coventry C), 1998 v T, Bel; I (6)
Hodges, G. (Wimbledon), 1983 v Y (sub), Bul (sub); 1984 v N, Bul, Y (5)
Holden, A. (Chester C), 1984 v Y (sub) (1)
Hopkins, J. (Fulham), 1982 v F (sub), Ho; 1983 v N, Y, Bul (5)
Huggins, D. S. (Bristol C), 1996 v Sm (1)
Hughes, D. R. (Southampton), 1994 v R (1)
Hughes, R. D. (Aston Villa), 1996 v Sm; 1997 v Sm (sub), Ho (2), T, Bel; 1998 v T, Bel, I (9)
Hughes, I. (Bury), 1992 v R; 1993 v Cy, Bel (sub), RCS; 1994 v Cy, R; 1995 v Mol, Ge, Bul; 1996 v Mol (sub), G (11)
Hughes, L. M. (Manchester U), 1983 v N, Y; 1984 v N, Bul, Y (5)
Hughes, W. (WBA), 1977 v E, S; 1978 v S (3)

Jackett, K. (Watford), 1981 v Ho; 1982 v F (2)
James, R. M. (Swansea C), 1977 v E, S; 1978 v S (3)
Jarman, L. (Cardiff C), 1996 v Sm; 1997 v Sm, Ho (2), Bel; 1998 v T, Bel (7)
Jenkins, L. D. (Swansea C), 1998 v T (sub) (1)
Jenkins, S. R. (Swansea C), 1993 v Cy (sub), Bel (2)
Jones, F. (Wrexham), 1981 v Ho (1)
Jones, L. (Cardiff C), 1982 v F (2), Ho (3)
Jones, M. G. (Leeds U), 1998 v Bel (1)
Jones, P. L. (Liverpool), 1992 v R; 1993 v Cy, Bel (2), RCS; 1994 v RCS (sub), Cy, R; 1995 v Mol, Ge; 1996 v Mol, G (12)
Jones, R. (Sheffield W), 1994 v R; 1995 v Bul (2) (3)
Jones, V. (Bristol R), 1979 v E; 1981 v Ho (2)

Kendall, M. (Tottenham H), 1978 v S (1)
Kenworthy, J. R. (Tranmere R), 1994 v Cy; 1995 v Mol, Bul (3)
Knott, G. R. (Tottenham H), 1996 v Sm (1)

Law, B. J. (QPR), 1990 v Pol; 1991 v E (2)
Letheran, G. (Leeds U), 1977 v E, S (2)
Lewis, D. (Swansea C), 1982 v F (2), Ho; 1983 v N, Y, Bul; 1984 v N, Bul, Y (9)
Lewis, J. (Cardiff C), 1983 v N (1)
Llewellyn, C. M. (Norwich C), 1998 v T (sub), Bel (sub), I (3)
Loveridge, J. (Swansea C), 1982 v Ho; 1983 v N, Bul (3)
Lowndes, S. R. (Newport Co), 1979 v E; 1981 v Ho; (with Millwall), 1984 v Bul, Y (4)

McCarthy, A. J. (QPR), 1994 v RCS, Cy, R (3)
Maddy, P. (Cardiff C), 1982 v Ho; 1983 v N (sub) (2)
Margetson, M. W. (Manchester C), 1992 v R; 1993 v Cy, Bel (2), RCS; 1994 v RCS, Cy (7)
Marustik, C. (Swansea C), 1982 v F (2); 1983 v Y, Bul; 1984 v N, Bul, Y (7)
Meaker, M. J. (QPR), 1994 v RCS (sub), R (sub) (2)
Melville, A. K. (Swansea C), 1990 v Pol; (with Oxford U), 1991 v E (2)
Micallef, C. (Cardiff C), 1982 v F, Ho; 1983 v N (3)
Morgan, A. M. (Tranmere R), 1995 v Mol, Bul; 1996 v Mol, G (4)
Mountain, P. D. (Cardiff C), 1997 v Ho, T (2)

Nardiello, D. (Coventry C), 1978 v S (1)
Neilson, A. B. (Newcastle U), 1993 v Cy, Bel (2), RCS; 1994 v RCS, Cy, R (7)
Nicholas, P. (C Palace), 1978 v S; 1979 v E; (with Arsenal), 1982 v F (3)
Nogan, K. (Luton T), 1990 v Pol; 1991 v E (2)
Nogan, L. (Oxford U) 1991 v E (1)

Oster, J. M. (Grimsby T), 1997 v Sm (sub), Ho (sub), T, Bel; (with Everton), 1998 v T, Bel, I (7)
Owen, G. (Wrexham), 1991 v E (sub), Pol; 1992 v R; 1993 v Cy, Bel (2); 1994 v Cy, R (8)

Page, R. J. (Watford), 1995 v Mol, Ge, Bul; 1996 v Mol (4)
Partridge, D. W. (West Ham U), 1997 v T (1)
Pascoe, C. (Swansea C), 1983 v Bul (sub); 1984 v N (sub), Bul, Y (4)
Pembridge, M. (Luton T), 1991 v Pol (1)
Perry, J. (Cardiff C), 1990 v Pol; 1991 v E, Pol (3)
Peters, M. (Manchester C), 1992 v R; (with Norwich C), 1993 v Cy, RCS (3)
Phillips, D. (Plymouth Arg), 1984 v N, Bul, Y (3)
Phillips, L. (Swansea C), 1979 v E; (with Charlton Ath), 1983 v N (2)
Pontin, K. (Cardiff C), 1978 v S (1)
Powell, L. (Southampton), 1991 v Pol (sub); 1992 v R (sub); 1993 v Bel (sub); 1994 v RCS (4)
Price, J. J. (Swansea C), 1998 v I (sub) (1)
Price, P. (Luton T), 1981 v Ho (1)
Pugh, D. (Doncaster R), 1982 v F (2) (2)
Pugh, S. (Wrexham), 1993 v Bel (2 subs) (2)

Ramasut, M. W. T. (Bristol R), 1997 v Ho, Bel; 1998 v T, I (4)
Ratcliffe, K. (Everton), 1981 v Ho; 1982 v F (2)
Ready, K. (QPR), 1992 v R; 1993 v Bel (2); 1994 v RCS, Cy (5)
Rees, A. (Birmingham C), 1984 v N (1)
Rees, J. (Luton T), 1990 v Pol; 1991 v E, Pol (3)
Roberts, A. (QPR), 1991 v E, Pol (2)
Roberts, G. (Hull C), 1983 v Bul (1)
Roberts, G. W. (Liverpool), 1997 v Ho, T, Bel; 1998 v T, I (5)
Roberts, J. G. (Wrexham), 1977 v E (1)
Roberts, P. (Porthmadog), 1990 v Ho (sub) (1)
Robinson, C. P. (Wolverhampton W), 1996 v Sm; 1997 v Sm, Ho (2), T, Bel (6)
Robinson, J. (Brighton & HA), 1992 v R; (with Charlton Ath), 1993 v Bel; 1994 v RCS, Cy, R (5)
Rowlands, A. J. R. (Manchester C), 1996 v Sm; 1997 v Sm, Ho (1 + sub), T (sub) (5)
Rush, I. (Liverpool), 1981 v Ho; 1982 v F (2)

Savage, R. W. (Crewe Alex), 1995 v Bul; 1996 v Mol, G (3)
Sayer, P. A. (Cardiff C), 1977 v E, S (2)
Searle, D. (Cardiff C), 1991 v Pol (sub); 1992 v R; 1993 v Cy, Bel (2), RCS; 1994 v RCS (6)
Slatter, N. (Bristol R), 1983 v N, Y, Bul; 1984 v N, Bul, Y (6)
Speed, G. A. (Leeds U), 1990 v Pol; 1991 v E, Pol (3)
Stevenson, N. (Swansea C), 1982 v F, Ho (2)
Stevenson, W. B. (Leeds U), 1977 v E, S; 1978 v S (3)
Symons, K. (Portsmouth), 1991 v E, Pol (2)

Taylor, G. K. (Bristol R), 1995 v Ge, Bul (2); 1996 v Mol (4)
Thomas, D. J. (Watford), 1998 v T, Bel (2)
Thomas, J. A. (Blackburn R), 1996 v Sm; 1997 v Sm, Ho (2), T, Bel; 1998 v Bel (7)
Thomas, Martin R. (Bristol R), 1979 v E; 1981 v Ho (2)
Thomas, Mickey R. (Wrexham), 1977 v E; 1978 v S (2)
Thomas, D. G. (Leeds U), 1977 v E; 1979 v E; 1984 v N (3)
Tibbott, L. (Ipswich T), 1977 v E, S (2)
Tipton, M. J. (Oldham Ath), 1998 v I (sub) (1)
Twiddy, C. (Plymouth Arg), 1995 v Mol, Ge; 1996 v G (sub) (3)

Vaughan, N. (Newport Co), 1982 v F, Ho (2)

Walsh, I. P. (C Palace), 1979 v E; (with Swansea C), 1983 v Bul (2)
Walton, M. (Norwich C.), 1991 v Pol (sub) (1)
Ward, D. (Notts Co), 1996 v Mol, G (2)
Williams, A. P. (Southampton), 1998 v Bel, I )2)
Williams, A. S. (Blackburn R), 1996 v Sm; 1997 v Sm, Ho, Bel; 1998 v T, Bel, I (7)
Williams, D. (Bristol R), 1983 v Y (1)
Williams, D. I. L. (Liverpool), 1998 v I (1)
Williams, E. (Caernarfon T), 1997 v Ho (sub), T (sub) (2)
Williams, G. (Bristol R), 1983 v Y, Bul (2)
Williams, S. J. (Wrexham), 1995 v Mol, Ge, Bul (2) (4)

Wilmot, R. (Arsenal), 1982 v F (2), Ho; 1983 v N, Y; 1984 v Y (6)
Wright, A. A. (Oxford U), 1998 v Bel, I (sub) (2)

Young, S. (Cardiff C), 1996 v Sm; 1997 v Sm, Ho (2), Bel (sub) (5)

**NORTHERN IRELAND**
Bailie, N. (Linfield), l990 v Is; 1994 v R (sub) (2)
Beatty, S. (Chelsea), 1990 v Is; (with Linfield), 1994 v R (2)
Black, K. T. (Luton T), 1990 v Is (1)
Blackledge, G. (Portadown), 1978 v Ei (1)
Boyle, W. S. (Leeds U), 1998 v Sw (sub), S (sub) (2)
Brotherston, N. (Blackburn R), 1978 v Ei (sub) (1)
Burns, L. (Port Vale), 1998 v Sw, S, Ei (3)

Carroll, R. E. (Wigan Ath), 1998 v S, Ei (2)
Connell, T. E. (Coleraine), 1978 v Ei (sub) (1)
Coote, A. (Norwich C), 1998 v Sw (sub), S, Ei (3)

Devine, D. (Omagh T), 1994 v R (1)
Devine, J. (Glentoran), 1990 v Is (1)
Donaghy, M. M. (Larne), 1978 v Ei (1)
Dowie, I. (Luton T), 1990 v Is (1)

Feeney, L. (Linfield), 1998 v Ei (sub) (1)
Fitzgerald, D. (Rangers), 1998 v Sw, S (2)
Friars, S. M. (Liverpool), 1998 v Sw, S, Ei (3)

Gillespie, K. R. (Manchester U), 1994 v R (1)
Glendinning, M. (Bangor), 1994 v R (1)
Gray, P. (Luton T), 1990 v Is (sub) (1)
Griffin, D. J. (St Johnstone), 1998 v S (sub), Ei (2)

Hamilton, W. R. (Linfield), 1978 v Ei (1)
Harvey, J. (Arsenal), 1978 v Ei (1)
Hayes, T. (Luton T), 1978 v Ei (1)
Hughes, M. E. (Manchester C), 1990 v Is (sub)

Johnson, D. (Blackburn R), 1998 v Sw, S, Ei (3)
Johnston, B. (Cliftonville), 1978 v Ei (1)

Kee, P. V. (Oxford U), 1990 v Is (1)
Kelly, N. (Oldham Ath), 1990 v Is (sub) (1)

Lennon, N. F. (Manchester C), 1990 v Is; (with Crewe Alex), 1994 v R (2)
Lyttle, G. (Celtic), 1998 v Sw, S (2)

Magee, J. (Bangor), 1994 v R (sub) (1)
Magilton, J. (Liverpool), 1990 v Is (1)
Matthews, N. P. (Blackpool), 1990 v Is (1)
McBride, J. (Glentoran), 1994 v R (sub) (1)
McCallion, E. (Coleraine), 1998 v Sw (sub) (1)
McCoy, R. K. (Coleraine), 1990 v Is (1)
McCreery, D. (Manchester U), 1978 v Ei (1)
McGibbon, P. C. G. (Manchester U), 1994 v R (1)
McGlinchey, B. (Manchester C), 1998 v Sw, S, Ei (3)
McIlroy, T. (Linfield), 1994 v R (sub) (1)
McKnight, P. (Rangers), 1998 v Sw (1)
McMahon, G. J. (Tottenham H),1994 v R (sub) (1)
McVeigh, P. (Tottenham H), 1998 v S (sub), Ei (2)
Millar, W. P. (Port Vale), 1990 v Is (1)
Moreland, V. (Glentoran), 1978 v Ei (sub) (1)
Mulryne, P. P. (Manchester U), Sw, S, Ei (3)
Murray, W. (Linfield), 1978 v Ei (sub) (1)

Nicholl, J. M. (Manchester U), 1978 v Ei (1)

O'Hara, G. (Leeds U), 1994 v R (1)
O'Neill, M. A. M. (Hibernian), 1994 v R (1)
O'Neill, J. P. (Leicester C), 1978 v Ei (1)

Patterson, D. J. (Crystal Palace), 1994 v R (1)

Quinn, S. J. (Blackpool), 1994 v R (1)

Robinson, S. (Tottenham H), 1994 v R (1)

Sloan, T. (Ballymena U), 1978 v Ei (1)

Taylor, M. S. (Fulham), 1998 v Sw (1)

Waterman, D. G. (Portsmouth), 1998 v Sw, S, Ei (3)
Whitley, Jeff (Manchester C), 1998 v Sw, S, Ei (3)

# INTERNATIONAL RECORDS

## MOST GOALS IN AN INTERNATIONAL

| | | |
|---|---|---|
| Record | Sophus Nielsen (Denmark) 10 goals v France, at White City (Olympics) | 22.10.1908 |
| | Gottfried Fuchs (Germany) 10 goals v Russia, in Stockholm (Olympics) | 1.7.1912 |
| World Cup | Gary Cole (Australia) 7 goals v Fiji, in Melbourne | 14.8.1981 |
| | Karim Bagheri (Iran) 7 goals v Maldives, in Damascus | 2.6.1997 |
| England | Malcolm Macdonald (Newcastle U) 5 goals v Cyprus, at Wembley | 16.4.1975 |
| | Willie Hall (Tottenham H) 5 goals v Ireland, at Old Trafford | 16.11.1938 |
| | Steve Bloomer (Derby Co) 5 goals v Wales, at Cardiff | 16.3.1896 |
| | Howard Vaughton (Aston Villa) 5 goals v Ireland, at Belfast | 18.2.1882 |
| Ireland | Joe Bambrick (Linfield) 6 goals v Wales, at Belfast | 1.2.1930 |
| Wales | John Price (Wrexham) 4 goals v Ireland, at Wrexham | 25.2.1882 |
| | Mel Charles (Cardiff C) 4 goals v Ireland, at Cardiff | 11.4.1962 |
| | Ian Edwards (Chester) 4 goals v Malta, at Wrexham | 25.10.1978 |

## MOST GOALS IN AN INTERNATIONAL CAREER

| | | Goals | Games |
|---|---|---|---|
| England | Bobby Charlton (Manchester U) | 49 | 106 |
| Scotland | Denis Law (Huddersfield T, Manchester C, Torino, Manchester U) | 30 | 55 |
| | Kenny Dalglish (Celtic, Liverpool) | 30 | 102 |
| Ireland | Colin Clarke (Bournemouth, Southampton, QPR, Portsmouth) | 13 | 38 |
| Wales | Ian Rush (Liverpool, Juventus) | 28 | 73 |
| Republic of Ireland | Frank Stapleton (Arsenal, Manchester U, Ajax, Derby Co, Le Havre, Blackburn R) | 20 | 70 |

## HIGHEST SCORES

| | | | | | |
|---|---|---|---|---|---|
| World Cup Match | Iran | 17 | Maldives | 0 | 1997 |
| European Championship | Spain | 12 | Malta | 1 | 1983 |
| Olympic Games | Denmark | 17 | France | 1 | 1908 |
| | Germany | 16 | USSR | 0 | 1912 |
| Other International Match | Germany | 13 | Finland | 0 | 1940 |
| | Spain | 13 | Bulgaria | 0 | 1933 |
| European Cup | Feyenoord | 12 | K R Reykjavik | 2 | 1969 |
| European Cup-Winners' Cup | Sporting Lisbon | 16 | Apoel Nicosia | 1 | 1963 |
| Fairs & UEFA Cups | Ajax | 14 | Red Boys | 0 | 1984 |

## GOALSCORING RECORDS

| | | |
|---|---|---|
| World Cup Final | Geoff Hurst (England) 3 goals v West Germany | 1966 |
| World Cup Final tournament | Just Fontaine (France) 13 goals | 1958 |
| Career | Artur Friedenreich (Brazil) 1329 goals | 1910–30 |
| | Pelè (Brazil) 1281 goals | *1956–78 |
| | Franz 'Bimbo' Binder (Austria, Germany) 1006 goals | 1930–50 |

*Pelé subsequently scored two goals in Testimonial matches making his total 1283.*

## MOST CAPPED INTERNATIONALS IN BRITISH ISLES

| | | | |
|---|---|---|---|
| England | Peter Shilton | 125 appearances | 1970–90 |
| Northern Ireland | Pat Jennings | 119 appearances | 1964–86 |
| Scotland | Kenny Dalglish | 102 appearances | 1971–86 |
| Wales | Neville Southall | 92 appearances | 1982–97 |
| Republic of Ireland | Paul McGrath | 83 appearances | 1984–97 |

# BRITISH & IRISH INTERNATIONAL MANAGERS

**England**

Walter Winterbottom 1946–1962 (after period as coach); Alf Ramsey 1963–1974; Joe Mercer (caretaker) 1974; Don Revie 1974–1977; Ron Greenwood 1977–1982; Bobby Robson 1982–1990; Graham Taylor 1990–1993; Terry Venables (coach) 1994–1996; Glenn Hoddle from May 1996.

**Northern Ireland**

Billy Bingham 1967–1971; Terry Neill 1971–1975; Dave Clements (player-manager) 1975–1976; Danny Blanchflower 1976–1979; Billy Bingham 1980–1993; Bryan Hamilton 1994–1998; Lawrie McMenemy from February 1998

**Scotland**

Bobby Brown 1967–1971; Tommy Docherty 1971–1972; Willie Ormond 1973–1977; Ally MacLeod 1977–1978;

Jock Stein 1978–1985; Alex Ferguson (caretaker) 1985–1986 Andy Roxburgh (coach) 1986–1993; Craig Brown from September 1993.

**Wales**

Mike Smith 1974–1979; Mike England 1980–1988; David Williams (caretaker) 1988; Terry Yorath 1988–1993; John Toshack 1994 for one match; Mike Smith 1994–1995; Bobby Gould from August 1995.

**Republic of Ireland**

Liam Tuohy 1971–1972; Johnny Giles 1973–1980 (after period as player-manager); Eoin Hand 1980–1985; Jack Charlton 1986–1996; Mick McCarthy from February 1996.

# FA YOUTH GAMES 1997–98

## ENGLAND UNDER-18

### 9 Sept
### England 0
### Yugoslavia 0

*England:* Simonsen (Tranmere R); Cooper (Nottingham F), Ball (Everton), Brown (Manchester U), Woodgate (Leeds U), Upson (Arsenal), Noel-Williams (Watford), Dixon (Leeds U) [Dudley (Notts Co) 46] [Smith (Watford) 84], Owen (Liverpool), Nicholls (Charlton Ath), Stanton (Blackburn R) Wellens (Manchester U) 67].

### 11 Oct
### England 4 *(Ormerod 2, Matthews, Brown)*
### Yugoslavia 0

*England:* Simonsen (Tranmere R); Cooper (Nottingham F), Ball (Everton), Brown (Manchester U), Woodgate (Leeds U), Upson (Arsenal), Ormerod (Middlesbrough), Johnson (Crewe Alex), Cadamarteri (Everton) [Campbell (Middlesbrough) 77], Nicholls (Charlton Ath), Matthews (Leeds U).

### 27 Oct
### England 1 *(Matthews 32)*
### Russia 2

*England:* Simonsen (Tranmere R); Cooper (Nottingham F), Ball (Everton), Haslam (Sheffield W), Woodgate (Leeds U), Upson (Arsenal), Ormerod (Middlesbrough) [Griffin (Stoke C) 50], Johnson (Crewe Alex) [Morris (Sheffield U) 80], Matthews (Leeds U), Nicholls (Charlton Ath), Hackworth (Leeds U) [Dudley (Notts Co) 52].

### 14 Nov
### England 3 *(Cooper, Cadamarteri, Johnson*
### Russia 2

*England:* Simonsen (Tranmere R); Haslam (Sheffield W), Ball (Everton), Cooper (Nottingham F), Woodgate (Leeds U), Upson (Arsenal), Griffin (Stoke C) [Hulbert (Swindon T) 85], Cadamarteri (Everton), Matthews (Leeds U), Nicholls (Charlton Ath) [Dunn (Blackburn R) 70], Johnson (Crewe Alex).

### 12 Feb
### England 1 *(Dudley 80)*
### Israel 0

*England:* Knight (Derby Co); Young (Tottenham H), Konchesky (Charlton Ath) [Dunn (Blackburn R) 75], Fenton (Manchester C), Taylor (Blackburn R), Holden (Bolton W) [Haslam (Sheffield W) 50], Piercy (Tottenham H), Dunn (Blackburn R) [Cooper (Nottingham F) 45], Smith (Leeds U), Dudley (Notts Co), Vernazza (Arsenal) [Butterfield (Grimsby T) 50].

### 26 Mar
### England 3 *(Cooper 13, Woodgate 30, own goal)*
### France 0

*England:* Simonsen (Tranmere R); Brown (Manchester U), Ball (Everton), Cooper (Nottingham F), Woodgate (Leeds U), Upson (Arsenal), Griffin (Stoke C), Cadamarteri (Everton) [Piercy (Tottenham H) 91], Matthews (Leeds U) [Smith (Leeds U) 89], Vernazza (Arsenal), Johnson (Crewe Alex).

### 23 April
### England 0
### France 1

*England:* Simonsen (Tranmere R); Brown (Manchester U), Ball (Everton), Cooper (Nottingham F), Woodgate (Leeds U), Upson (Arsenal), Griffin (Stoke C), Cadamarteri (Everton ) [Greening (Manchester U) 68], Matthews (Leeds U), Vernazza (Arsenal), Johnson (Crewe Alex).

### 30 May
### England 1 *(Piercy 78)*
### Cyprus 0

*England:* Green (Norwich C); Young (Tottenham H), Evans (Leeds U), Haslam (Sheffield W), Taylor (Blackburn R), Fenton (Manchester C), Hulbert (Swindon T) [Lunt (Crewe Alex) 65], Piercy (Tottenham H), Crouch (Tottenham H) [Hackworth (Leeds U) 70], Morris (Sheffield U), Milligan (Everton).

### 1 June
### England 0
### France 3

*England:* Green (Norwich C) [Taylor (Arsenal) 10]; Young (Tottenham H), Holden (Bolton W), Haslam (Sheffield W), Taylor (Blackburn R), Fenton (Manchester C), Lunt (Crewe Alex), Piercy (Tottenham H), Hackworth (Leeds U), Morris (Sheffield U) [Crouch (Tottenham H) 75], Milligan (Everton).

# WOMEN'S FOOTBALL 1997–98

Massive strides have been taken in the past twelve months to promote women's and girls' football in this country. The Women's Football Alliance is now one of the forty-seven County Football Associations, whilst a structure plan entitled the FA's Talent Development Plan for Women's Football has been launched. As its name suggests its intention is to identify and subsequently develop talented female players from as young as ten years of age through to the England Senior team. With the men's Premier League developing academies throughout its membership, this plan will attempt to establish a network of Centres of Excellence within those Premiership clubs and also those of the Nationwide League. The plan also includes the intended appointment of a National Coach, further Regional Officers of whom there are five at present plus the introduction of player and coaching schemes. At the first conference of the newly formed FA Coaches Association an afternoon was devoted to women's football and the same situation will occur at the second annual conference this year.

Hope Powell becomes the first ever Women's National Coach. An England international, Ms Powell has responsibility for the England Senior team plus the Under-18 and Under-16 sides.

The current structure of women's football consists of Mr Ray Kiddell, the Chairman of the FA Women's Football Committee; Kelly Simmons, the women's Football Co-ordinator plus five Regional Directors. These are Julie Lewis (the North); Ros Potts (South East); Lucy Wellings (South West); Donna McIvor (East Midlands) and Rachel Pavlou (West Midlands).

The Secretary of the FA Women's Premier League is Ms Sue Barwick. Although there is a Women's Football department at the FA's Headquarters at Lancaster Gate, most of the administrative functions are carried out from the FA's other address at 9 Wylotts Place, Potters Bar, Hertfordshire EN6 2JD – Phone Number 01707-671805. Fax 01707-644190.

## The 1997–98 Season – The Records

Arsenal Ladies continue to dominate the women's competitive football scene and completed yet another 'double' last season, virtually emulating their male counterparts. The Gunners annexed both Cups winning the Premier League Cup on the 22nd March 1998 by beating Croydon Ladies in a penalty shoot-out after the initial 0-0 draw. Croydon were again Arsenal's victims on the 4th May when in normal time the Gunners won by 3-2.

The FA Women's Premier League National Division was won by Everton, with Arsenal as runners up. The Southern Division was won by Southampton Saints with Brighton & Hove Albion second. The Northern Division was won by Ilkeston Town by the wide margin of 12 points from Garswood Saints.

This all means that the Premier sides, Berkhamsted Town and Wembley are relegated to the Northern and Southern Divisions respectively, with Southampton Saints and Ilkeston Town promoted to the top Division. Finally being bottom of their respective Divisions means dropping out of the Leagues altogether for Rushden & Diamonds in the South and Bloxwich Town in the North. They are, respectively, replaced by Reading Royals and Leeds.

KEN GOLDMAN

## The Full Historical List of Achievers is as follows:

| National Division League Winners | | | Women's FA Cup Winners | | League Cup | |
|---|---|---|---|---|---|---|
| 1992/93 | Arsenal | 1992/93 | Arsenal (WFA Competition) | 1992/93 | Arsenal (WFA Competition) | |
| 1993/94 | Doncaster Belles | 1993/94 | Doncaster Belles | 1993/94 | Arsenal (WFA Competition) | |
| 1994/95 | Arsenal | 1994/95 | Arsenal | 1994/95 | Wimbledon | |
| 1995/96 | Croydon | 1995/96 | Croydon | 1995/96 | Wembley | |
| 1996/97 | Arsenal | 1996/97 | Millwall Lionesses | 1996/97 | Millwall Lionesses | |
| 1997/98 | Everton | 1997/98 | Arsenal | 1997/98 | Arsenal | |

## FA WOMEN'S PREMIER LEAGUE

### NATIONAL DIVISION

| | P | W | D | L | F | A | GD | Pts |
|---|---|---|---|---|---|---|---|---|
| Everton | 18 | 13 | 4 | 1 | 54 | 14 | +40 | 43 |
| Arsenal | 18 | 12 | 4 | 2 | 55 | 22 | +33 | 40 |
| Doncaster Belles | 18 | 12 | 2 | 4 | 54 | 18 | +36 | 38 |
| Croydon | 18 | 10 | 5 | 3 | 46 | 14 | +32 | 35 |
| Millwall Lionesses | 18 | 8 | 5 | 5 | 37 | 15 | +22 | 29 |
| Liverpool Ladies | 18 | 8 | 3 | 7 | 33 | 25 | +8 | 27 |
| Tranmere Rovers | 18 | 5 | 4 | 9 | 33 | 43 | −10 | 19 |
| Bradford City | 18 | 3 | 3 | 12 | 39 | 52 | −13 | 12 |
| Berkhamsted Town | 18 | 3 | 2 | 13 | 22 | 64 | −42 | 11 |
| Wembley | 18 | 0 | 0 | 18 | 3 | 109 | −106 | 0 |

### SOUTHERN DIVISION

| | P | W | D | L | F | A | GD | Pts |
|---|---|---|---|---|---|---|---|---|
| Southampton Saints | 18 | 12 | 6 | 0 | 50 | 14 | +36 | 42 |
| Brighton & Hove Albion | 18 | 12 | 2 | 4 | 64 | 21 | +43 | 38 |
| Wimbledon | 18 | 11 | 3 | 4 | 64 | 30 | +34 | 36 |
| Langford | 18 | 10 | 4 | 4 | 52 | 33 | +19 | 34 |
| Whitehawk | 18 | 9 | 4 | 5 | 69 | 30 | +39 | 31 |
| Barry Town | 18 | 3 | 5 | 7 | 23 | 29 | −6 | 23 |
| Three Bridges | 18 | 7 | 1 | 10 | 47 | 37 | +10 | 22 |
| Ipswich Town | 18 | 5 | 3 | 9 | 33 | 31 | +2 | 18 |
| Leyton Orient | 18 | 3 | 2 | 13 | 23 | 62 | −39 | 11 |
| Rushden & Diamonds | 18 | 0 | 0 | 18 | 10 | 148 | −138 | 0 |

### NORTHERN DIVISION

| | P | W | D | L | F | A | GD | Pts |
|---|---|---|---|---|---|---|---|---|
| Ilkeston Town | 18 | 17 | 0 | 1 | 68 | 6 | +62 | 51 |
| Garswood Saints | 18 | 12 | 3 | 3 | 43 | 23 | +20 | 39 |
| Aston Villa Ladies | 18 | 10 | 2 | 6 | 38 | 23 | +15 | 32 |
| Wolverhampton Wanderers | 18 | 8 | 5 | 5 | 33 | 20 | +13 | 29 |
| Blyth Spartans Kestrels | 18 | 8 | 4 | 6 | 40 | 23 | +17 | 28 |
| Sheffield Wednesday | 18 | 8 | 3 | 7 | 39 | 40 | −1 | 27 |
| Huddersfield Town | 18 | 7 | 3 | 8 | 32 | 31 | +1 | 24 |
| Coventry City | 18 | 2 | 6 | 10 | 22 | 62 | −40 | 12 |
| Arnold Town | 18 | 2 | 4 | 12 | 11 | 36 | −25 | 10 |
| Bloxwich Town | 18 | 0 | 2 | 16 | 12 | 74 | −62 | 2 |

## CSI FA WOMEN'S CUP 1997–98

**FIRST ROUND**

| | |
|---|---|
| Thorpe Tigers v Newsham PH | 0-6 |
| Doncaster Rovers v Wigan | 3-1 |
| Preston North End v Manchester United | 3-2 |
| Chester-Le-Street v Leeds United | 3-8 |
| Leeds City Vixens v Barnsley | 4-1 |
| Blackburn Rovers v Chesterfield | 3-2 |
| Chester City v Trafford | 3-2 |
| Stockport Celtic v Haslingden | 0-2 |
| Droylsden v York City | 11-3 |
| Hull City v Bangor City | 0-4 |
| Darlington v Wrexham | 6-0 |
| Sheffield Hallam United v Stockport | 0-10 |
| Norton v Scunthorpe Ironesses | 2-2, 1-3 |
| Selby Town v Newcastle | 1-6 |
| Oldham Athletic v Middlesbrough | 2-1 |
| Rochdale v Liverpool Feds | 0-9 |
| Warrington Grange v Kirklees | 6-0 |
| Newcastle Town v Stockport County | 4-1 |
| Hemsworth Town v Mond Rangers | 3-2 |
| Sunderland v Bury | 2-3 |
| Shrewsbury Town v Nettleham | 3-1 |
| Belper Town v Gorleston | 3-5 |
| Bedford Bells v Derby County | 0-1 |
| Ilkeston v Canary Rangers | 3-6 |
| Milton Keynes Athletic w.o. v Cambridge withdrew | |
| Birmingham City v Leicester City | 5-3 |
| Loughborough Students v Haverhill Rovers | 3-1 |
| Southwold Town v Derby City | 3-4 |
| Clacton withdrew v Mansfield Town w.o. | |
| Highfield Rangers v Cambridge United | 6-0 |
| Calverton MW v Mowbray Villa | 6-1 |
| Rea Valley Rovers v Pye | 7-0 |
| Harlow Town v Wembley Mill Hill | 3-7 |
| Charlton v Hassocks | 3-0 |
| Collier Row v Chelsea | 1-2 |
| London Ladies v Abbey Rangers | 1-2 |
| Maidstone United v Fulham | 0-2 |
| St Georges (Eltham) v Egham Town | 24-0 |
| Watford & Evergreen v Newham | 9-0 |
| Teynham Gunners v Hastings Town | 4-2 |
| Luton v Sawbridgeworth Town | 4-0 |
| *Abandoned 59 minutes; Sawbridgeworth Town withdrew due to injury sustained by a player, result stands.* | |
| London Womens v Leatherhead | 4-0 |
| Dulwich Hamlet v Tesco Country Club | 6-1 |
| Camberley Town v Welwyn Garden City | 0-6 |
| Walkern v Malling | 1-5 |
| Gillingham Girls v Stevenage Borough | 12-0 |
| West Ham United v Redbridge Wanderers | 5-0 |
| Queens Park Rangers v Enfield | 2-1 |
| Clapton v Barnet | 2-0 |
| Redhill v Tottenham Hotspur | 2-8 |
| Hampton v Great Wakering Rovers | 11-0 |
| Stanway v Surbiton | 1-2 |
| Hackney v Queens Park Rangers LSA | 9-1 |
| Chesham United v Hendon | 4-5 |
| Chelmsford v Aylesbury Stocklake | 3-0 |
| Oxford United v Protel Super Strikers | 14-0 |
| Okeford United w.o. v Slough Town withdrew | |
| Reading Royals w.o. v Thame United failed to fulfil fixture | |
| Freeway v Swindon Town | 0-6 |
| Basingstoke Town v Bristol City | 4-2 |
| Elmore Eagles v Worcester City | 7-3 |
| Risborough Rangers v Clevedon United | 3-1 |
| Truro City v Exeter Rangers | 2-1 |
| Portsmouth v Wokingham Town | 5-1 |
| Sherborne v Saltash Pilgrims | 3-4 |
| Cabeltel (Newport) v Binfield | 1-3 |
| Cardiff County v Barnstaple Town | 15-1 |
| Newton Abbot v Swindon Spitfires | 0-4 |

**SECOND ROUND**

| | |
|---|---|
| Bangor City v Oldham Athletic | 1-2 |
| Garswood Saints v Droylsden | 7-1 |
| Preston North End v Darlington | 14-1 |
| Scunthorpe Ironesses v Stockport | 1-4 |
| Bury v Liverpool Feds | 2-4 |
| Chester City v Huddersfield Town | 2-4 |
| Blyth Spartans Kestrels v Leeds United | 6-3 |
| Sheffield Wednesday v Doncaster Rovers | 3-2 |

| | |
|---|---|
| Newcastle Town v Newcastle | 2-1 |
| Hemsworth Town v Leeds City Vixens | 1-5 |
| Blackburn Rovers v Haslingden | 6-1 |
| Warrington Grange v Newsham PH | 1-0 |
| Milton Keynes Athletic v Derby County | 1-6 |
| Ipswich Town v Ilkeston Town | 0-5 |
| Coventry City v Mansfield Town | 2-1 |
| Loughborough Students v Highfield Rangers | 4-4, 1-2 |
| Gorleston v Birmingham City | 0-2 |
| Calverton MW v Arnold Town | 0-1 |
| Bloxwich Town v Shrewsbury Town | 3-1 |
| Wolverhampton Wanderers v Rushden & Diamonds | 14-0 |
| Rea Valley Rovers v Aston Villa | 0-8 |
| Derby City v Canary Racers | 1-5 |
| Fulham v Teynham Gunners | 7-1 |
| Brighton & Hove Albion v Hampton | 0-0, 2-1 |
| Clapton v Tottenham Hotspur | 0-4 |
| London Womens v Leyton Orient | 1-2 |
| St Georges (Eltham) v Surbiton | 1-1, 3-0 |
| Langford v Chelmsford | 1-1, 4-0 |
| West Ham United v Risborough Rangers | 3-1 |
| Luton v Queens Park Rangers | 0-1 |
| Hendon v Hackney | 5-5, 3-0 |
| Three Bridges v Chelsea | 4-2 |
| Welwyn Garden City v Whitehawk | 1-10 |
| Dulwich Hamlet v Wimbledon | 0-16 |
| Charlton v Abbey Rangers | 1-1, 2-0 |
| Wembley Mill Hill v Gillingham Girls | 7-1 |
| Watford & Evergreen v Malling | 3-0 |
| Basingstoke Town v Reading Royals | 0-8 |
| Swindon Town v Cardiff County | 0-2 |
| Truro City v Swindon Spitfires | 2-2, 2-1 |
| Southampton Saints v Oxford United | 3-1 |
| Saltash Pilgrims v Portsmouth | 2-5 |
| Elmore Eagles v Barry Town | 0-7 |
| Binfield v Okeford United | 1-0 |

**THIRD ROUND**

| | |
|---|---|
| Huddersfield Town v Leeds City Vixens | 4-2 |
| Liverpool Feds v Sheffield Wednesday | 1-5 |
| Blyth Spartans Kestrels v Garswood Saints | 1-3 |
| Oldham Athletic v Preston North End | 0-2 |
| Warrington Grange v Newcastle Town | 3-5 |
| Stockport v Blackburn Rovers | 4-2 |
| Bloxwich Town v Highfield Rangers | 6-1 |
| Canary Racers v Arnold Town | 6-0 |
| Coventry City v Birmingham City | 4-4, 5-0 |
| Aston Villa v Wolverhampton Wanderers | 1-0 |
| Ilkeston Town v Derby County | 6-0 |
| Wembley Mill Hill v Whitehawk | 1-4 |
| Brighton & Hove Albion v Langford | 3-3, 3-2 |
| Three Bridges v Watford & Evergreen | 0-6 |
| Queens Park Rangers v Wimbledon | 3-4 |
| Leyton Orient v Reading Royals | 2-2, 0-1 |
| Fulham v Tottenham Hotspur | 4-7 |
| West Ham United v Charlton | 0-7 |
| Hendon v St Georges (Eltham) | 0-6 |
| Truro City v Barry Town | 0-4 |
| Binfield v Southampton Saints | 0-6 |
| Cardiff County v Portsmouth | 3-0 |

**FOURTH ROUND**

| | |
|---|---|
| Huddersfield Town v Wimbledon | 3-2 |
| Bradford City v Aston Villa | 5-1 |
| Tranmere Rovers v Berkhamsted Town | 4-2 |
| Bloxwich Town v Ilkeston Town | 0-2 |
| Whitehawk v Coventry City | 5-0 |
| Cardiff County v Millwall Lionesses | 0-6 |
| Tottenham Hotspur v Brighton & Hove Albion | 2-1 |
| Wembley v Croydon | 0-10 |
| Doncaster Belles v St Georges (Eltham) | 10-0 |
| Southampton Saints v Newcastle Town | 2-1 |
| Garswood Saints v Preston North End | 4-1 |
| Sheffield Wednesday v Watford & Evergreen | 3-2 |
| Everton v Liverpool | 0-1 |
| Canary Racers v Arsenal | 0-12 |
| Charlton v Stockport | 1-2 |
| Reading Royals v Barry Town | 0-2 |

**FIFTH ROUND**

| | |
|---|---|
| Tranmere Rovers v Garswood Saints | 1-2 |
| Doncaster Belles v Huddersfield Town | 6-0 |
| Liverpool v Ilkeston Town | 2-0 |
| Millwall Lionesses v Whitehawk | 2-0 |
| Bradford City v Sheffield Wednesday | 4-1 |
| Barry Town v Stockport | 2-1 |
| Southampton Saints v Arsenal | 0-1 |
| Croydon v Tottenham Hotspur | 4-1 |

**SIXTH ROUND**

| | |
|---|---|
| Croydon v Bradford City | 3-2 |
| Garswood Saints v Barry Town | 1-2 |
| Doncaster Belles v Arsenal | 1-2 |
| Millwall Lionesses v Liverpool | 2-2, 1-3 |

**SEMI-FINALS**

| | |
|---|---|
| Arsenal v Millwall Lionesses | 1-0 |
| Barry Town v Croydon | 0-1 |

**FINAL (at New Den)**

**3 MAY**

**Arsenal (1) 3** *(Spacey, Yankey, Few)*

**Croydon (1) 2** *(Broadhurst (pen), Powell)* 2205

*Arsenal:* Reed; White, Harwood, Few, Pealling, Slee, Mapes (Daly), Williams, Jerray-Silver, Spacey, Yankey. *Croydon:* Cooper; Wylie, Darby, Cottier, Davis, Proctor, Bampton, Powell, Fletcher, Britton, Broadhurst. *Referee:* A. Wiley (Burntwood).

## FA WOMEN'S LEAGUE CUP 1997–98

**FIRST ROUND**

Arsenal 6, Huddersfield 2
Barry Town Ladies 3, Wolverhampton 6
Blyth Spartans 5, Ipswich Town 3
Bradford City 6, Arnold Town 0
Doncaster Belles 1, Liverpool 1
*Liverpool won on penalties*
Leyton Orient 1, Southampton 4
Sheffield Wednesday 6, Coventry City 0
Three Bridges 2, Croydon 3
Tranmere Rovers 3, Brighton & Hove Albion 1
Wembley 3, Bloxwich Town 1
Berkhamsted 11, Rushden & Diamonds 1
Garswood Saints 1, Ilkeston Town 4
Langford 0, Wimbledon 9
Whitehawk 2, Aston Villa 1

**SECOND ROUND**

Arsenal 2, Millwall Lionesses 1
Ilkeston Town 2, Croydon 3
Liverpool 7, Whitehawk 0

Sheffield Wednesday 0, Berkhamsted 2
Tranmere Rovers 1, Blyth Spartans 1
*Tranmere Rovers won 5-4 on penalties.*
Wembley 0, Bradford City 5
Wimbledon 2, Southampton 3
Wolverhampton 0, Everton 8

**THIRD ROUND**

Bradford City 4, Southampton 2
Croydon 2, Liverpool 1
Everton 2, Tranmere Rovers 1
Arsenal 4, Berkhamsted 0

**SEMI-FINALS**

Bradford City 2, Arsenal 2
Croydon 2, Everton 0

**FINAL**

Arsenal 0, Croydon 0
*aet; Arsenal won 4-2 on penalties.*

## ENGLAND INTERNATIONALS

**WORLD CUP QUALIFYING**

Germany 3, England 0; England 1 (Smith), Holland 0; England 0, Germany 1; England 1 (White), Norway 2.

| | P | W | D | L | F | A | Pts |
|---|---|---|---|---|---|---|---|
| Germany | 5 | 4 | 0 | 1 | 7 | 2 | 12 |
| Norway | 4 | 2 | 1 | 1 | 8 | 3 | 7 |
| Holland | 5 | 1 | 1 | 3 | 3 | 9 | 4 |
| England | 4 | 1 | 0 | 3 | 2 | 6 | 3 |

Later result: Holland 2, England 1.

Friendly match: France 3, England 2 (Davis, Burke).

**EUROPEAN UNDER-18 CHAMPIONSHIP**

Mini-Tournament: Belgium 1, England 2; England 1, France 1, France 2, Belgium 0

# FOOTBALL CONFERENCE 1997–98

## FOOTBALL CONFERENCE TABLE 1997–98

| | | Home | | | Goals | | Away | | | Goals | | |
|---|---|---|---|---|---|---|---|---|---|---|---|---|
| | P | W | D | L | F | A | W | D | L | F | A | Pts |
| Halifax Town | 42 | 17 | 4 | 0 | 51 | 15 | 8 | 8 | 5 | 23 | 28 | 87 |
| Cheltenham Town | 42 | 15 | 4 | 2 | 39 | 15 | 8 | 5 | 8 | 24 | 28 | 78 |
| Woking | 42 | 14 | 3 | 4 | 47 | 22 | 8 | 5 | 8 | 25 | 24 | 74 |
| Rushden & Diamonds | 42 | 12 | 4 | 5 | 44 | 26 | 11 | 1 | 9 | 35 | 31 | 74 |
| Morecambe | 42 | 11 | 4 | 6 | 35 | 30 | 10 | 6 | 5 | 42 | 34 | 73 |
| Hereford United | 42 | 11 | 7 | 3 | 30 | 19 | 7 | 6 | 8 | 26 | 30 | 67 |
| Hednesford Town | 42 | 14 | 4 | 3 | 28 | 12 | 4 | 8 | 9 | 31 | 38 | 66 |
| Slough Town | 42 | 10 | 6 | 5 | 34 | 21 | 8 | 4 | 9 | 24 | 28 | 64 |
| Northwich Victoria | 42 | 8 | 9 | 4 | 34 | 24 | 7 | 6 | 8 | 29 | 35 | 60 |
| Welling United | 42 | 11 | 5 | 5 | 39 | 27 | 6 | 4 | 11 | 25 | 35 | 60 |
| Yeovil Town | 42 | 14 | 3 | 4 | 45 | 24 | 3 | 5 | 13 | 28 | 39 | 59 |
| Hayes | 42 | 10 | 4 | 7 | 36 | 25 | 6 | 6 | 9 | 26 | 27 | 58 |
| Dover Athletic | 42 | 10 | 4 | 7 | 34 | 29 | 5 | 6 | 10 | 26 | 41 | 55 |
| Kettering Town | 42 | 8 | 6 | 7 | 29 | 29 | 5 | 7 | 9 | 24 | 31 | 52 |
| Stevenage Borough | 42 | 8 | 8 | 5 | 35 | 27 | 5 | 4 | 12 | 24 | 36 | 51 |
| Southport | 42 | 9 | 5 | 7 | 32 | 26 | 4 | 6 | 11 | 24 | 32 | 50 |
| Kidderminster Harriers | 42 | 6 | 8 | 7 | 32 | 31 | 5 | 6 | 10 | 24 | 32 | 47 |
| Farnborough Town | 42 | 10 | 3 | 8 | 37 | 27 | 2 | 5 | 14 | 19 | 43 | 44 |
| Leek Town | 42 | 8 | 8 | 5 | 34 | 26 | 2 | 6 | 13 | 18 | 41 | 44 |
| Telford United | 42 | 6 | 7 | 8 | 25 | 31 | 4 | 5 | 12 | 28 | 45 | 42 |
| Gateshead | 42 | 7 | 6 | 8 | 32 | 35 | 1 | 5 | 15 | 19 | 52 | 35 |
| Stalybridge Celtic | 42 | 6 | 5 | 10 | 33 | 38 | 1 | 3 | 17 | 15 | 55 | 29 |

## ATTENDANCES BY CLUB 1997–98

| | Aggregate 1997–98 | Average 1997–98 | Average 1996–97 | % Change |
|---|---|---|---|---|
| Cheltenham Town | 38,586 | 1,837 | 995 | +85 |
| Dover Athletic | 22,455 | 1,069 | 1,070 | — |
| Farnborough Town | 17,137 | 816 | 806 | +1 |
| Gateshead | 12,843 | 612 | 588 | +4 |
| Halifax Town | 53,358 | 2,541 | 841 | +202 |
| Hayes | 13,887 | 661 | 663 | — |
| Hednesford Town | 29,776 | 1,418 | 1,313 | +8 |
| Hereford United | 52,009 | 2,477 | 2,931 | –15 |
| Kettering Town | 31,313 | 1,491 | 1,709 | –13 |
| Kidderminster Harriers | 42,484 | 2,023 | 2,660 | –24 |
| Leek Town | 16,419 | 782 | 509 | +54 |
| Morecambe | 32,163 | 1,532 | 1,010 | +52 |
| Northwich Victoria | 21,212 | 1,101 | 967 | +14 |
| Rushden & Damonds | 53,600 | 2,552 | 2,514 | +1 |
| Slough Town | 16,111 | 767 | 1,069 | –28 |
| Southport | 22,146 | 1,055 | 970 | +9 |
| Stalybridge Celtic | 16,927 | 806 | 648 | +24 |
| Stevenage Borough | 47,286 | 2,252 | 2,881 | –22 |
| Telford United | 16,785 | 799 | 885 | –10 |
| Welling United | 14,879 | 709 | 714 | — |
| Woking | 58,828 | 2,801 | 2,595 | +8 |
| Yeovil Town | 51,596 | 2,457 | 2,779 | –11 |

## HIGHEST ATTENDANCES 1997–98

| | | | | | | |
|---|---|---|---|---|---|---|
| 6,357 | Halifax Town v Cheltenham Town (1-1) | 25.4.98 | 3,930 | Woking v Rushden & Diamonds (0-2) | 14.3.98 |
| 4,701 | Halifax Town v Southport (4-3) | 13.4.98 | 3,866 | Rushden & Diamonds v Kettering | |
| 4,693 | Kidderminster Harriers v Hereford | | | Town (1-0) | 25.11.97 |
| | United (1-4) | 1.1.98 | 3,857 | Rushden & Diamonds v Cheltenham | |
| 4,671 | Hereford United v Kidderminster | | | Town (4-1) | 7.3.98 |
| | Harriers (1-0) | 26.12.98 | 3,704 | Hereford United v Cheltenham Town (3-2) | 25.8.97 |
| 4,124 | Woking v Farnborough Town (3-0) | 26.12.97 | 3,675 | Rushden & Diamonds v Halifax Town (4-0) | 7.2.98 |
| 4,016 | Kettering Town v Rushden & | | 3,657 | Yeovil Town v Cheltenham Town (1-1) | 1.1.98 |
| | Diamonds (0-4) | 21.2.98 | 3,602 | Yeovil Town v Stevenage Borough (2-1) | 16.8.97 |
| 3,951 | Halifax Town v Rushden & Diamonds (2-0) | 21.3.98 | 3,527 | Rushden & Diamonds v Stevenage | |
| 3,940 | Morecambe v Halifax Town (1-1) | 28.10.97 | | Borough (2-0) | 26.12.97 |

## FOOTBALL CONFERENCE LEADING GOALSCORERS 1997–98

| Conf. | | | FAC | SCC | FAT |
|---|---|---|---|---|---|
| 30 | Geoff Horsfield (Halifax Town) | + | 4 | — | — |
| 29 | Darren Collins (Rushden & Diamonds) | + | — | — | 3 |
| 20 | Darran Hay (Woking) | + | — | 1 | — |
| 18 | Mark Cooper (Welling United) | + | 1 | — | — |
| | John Norman (Morecambe) | + | — | 3 | — |
| 17 | Neil Grayson (Cheltenham Town) | + | 4 | 1 | — |
| | Owen Pickard (Yeovil Town) | + | 6 | 1 | — |
| | Dale Watkins (Cheltenham Town) | + | 4 | 1 | 7 |
| 16 | Mike Bignall (Kidderminster Harriers) | + | 1 | — | — |
| | Brendan Burke (Stalybridge Celtic) | + | 2 | 1 | 1 |
| | Jason Eaton (Cheltenham Town) | + | 2 | — | 4 |
| | David Mehew (Rushden & Diamonds) | + | 1 | — | — |
| | Warren Patmore (Yeovil Town) | + | — | 1 | — |
| 15 | Ritchie Hanlon (Welling United) | + | — | — | 2 |
| | Martin Randall (Hayes) | + | — | 2 | 2 |
| 14 | Jamie Paterson (Halifax Town) | + | 3 | — | 1 |
| | Grant Payne (Woking) | + | — | 1 | — |
| | Chris Pearson (Kettering Town) | + | — | — | — |
| 13 | Andy Milner (Morcambe) | + | — | 2 | — |
| 12 | Steve Bowey (Gateshead) | + | 1 | — | 1 |
| | Jimmy Strouts (Dover Athletic) | + | — | 1 | — |

FAC: FA Cup; SCC: Spalding Challenge Cup; FAT: FA Trophy.

## CLUB REVIEW

| | FC | FAT | SCC | FAC |
|---|---|---|---|---|
| Cheltenham Town | 2 | W | 1 | 3 |
| 1996-97 | 2DM | 1 | – | 1 |
| Dover Athletic | 13 | SF | 1 | 2q |
| | 17 | 1 | 1 | 3q |
| Farnborough Town | 18 | 1 | 3 | 1 |
| | 7 | 7 | S-F | 1 |
| Gateshead | 21 | 2 | 3 | 2q |
| | 10 | 1 | 2 | 4q |
| Halifax Town | 1 | 2 | 1 | 4q |
| | 19 | 2 | 1 | 2q |
| Hayes | 12 | QF | SF | 1 |
| | 15 | 2 | 1 | 1 |
| Hednesford Town | 7 | 3 | 3 | 2 |
| | 8 | 1 | 2 | 4 |
| Hereford United | 6 | 2 | 2 | 3 |
| | 24D3 | – | – | 1 |
| Kettering Town | 14 | 2 | 2 | 3q |
| | 14 | 1 | 2 | 3q |
| Kidderminster H. | 17 | 2 | 2 | 4q |
| | 2 | 3 | W | 1 |
| Leek Town | 19 | 2 | 2 | 1q |
| | 1UL | 1q | – | 4q |
| Morecambe | 5 | 2 | W | 1 |
| | 4 | 3 | SF | 1 |
| Northwich Victoria | 9 | 3 | SF | 1 |
| | 6 | 2 | 2 | 1 |
| Rushden & D'mnds | 4 | 2 | 1 | 4q |
| | 12 | 1 | QF | 1 |
| Slough Town | 8 | SF | 2 | 1 |
| | 16 | 1 | 1 | 4q |
| Southport | 16 | F | 1 | 1 |
| | 11 | 2 | 2 | 1 |
| Stalybridge Celtic | 22 | 1 | 2 | 4q |
| | 13 | 1 | QF | 1 |
| Stevenage Borough | 15 | QF | 2 | 4 |
| | 3 | SF | 2 | 3 |
| Telford United | 20 | 2 | 2 | 1q |
| | 9 | 1 | 1 | 4q |
| Welling United | 10 | 1 | 1 | 2q |
| | 18 | 2 | QF | 1 |
| Woking | 3 | 1 | F | 1 |
| | 5 | W | 2 | 3 |
| Yeovil Town | 11 | 1 | 3 | 4q |
| | 1IL | 1 | – | 4q |

FC: Football Conference; FAT FA Trophy; SCC: Spalding Challenge Cup; FAC: FA Cup; DM: Dr Martens League; UL: Unibond League; IL: ICIS League.

### HIGHEST AGGREGATE SCORE

| | |
|---|---|
| 6-4 | Hayes v Yeovil Town 14.2.98 |
| 5-5 | Rushden & Diamonds v Farnborough Town 13.9.97 |

### LARGEST HOME MARGIN

| | |
|---|---|
| 6-0 | Farnborough Town v Stalybridge Celtic 20.12.97 |
| 6-1 | Stalybridge Celtic v Leek Town 25.8.97 |
| 6-1 | Halifax Town v Telford United 16.9.97 |
| 6-1 | Stevenage Borough v Gateshead 4.10.97 |

### LARGEST AWAY MARGIN

| | |
|---|---|
| 1-5 | Stevenage Borough v Hayes 1.9.97 |
| 1-5 | Morecambe v Hereford United 1.11.97 |
| 0-4 | Dover Athletic v Kidderminster Harriers 20.9.97 |
| 0-4 | Kettering Town v Rushden & Diamonds 21.2.98 |
| 0-4 | Leek Town v Kettering Town 31.3.98 |

### CONSECUTIVE VICTORIES

| | |
|---|---|
| 8 | Halifax Town |
| 5 | Morecambe, Northwich Victoria, Welling United |

### CONSECUTIVE DEFEATS

| | |
|---|---|
| 7 | Farnborough Town, Stalybridge Celtic |
| 5 | Stevenage Borough, Yeovil Town |

### MATCHES WITHOUT DEFEAT

| | |
|---|---|
| 17 | Cheltenham Town |
| 13 | Hereford United |
| 12 | Halifax Town |

### MATCHES WITHOUT SUCCESS

| | |
|---|---|
| 18 | Gateshead |
| 14 | Stalybridge Celtic |
| 13 | Kettering Town |
| 10 | Kidderminster Harriers, Leek Town, Northwich Victoria |

# FOOTBALL CONFERENCE 1997–98

## APPEARANCES AND GOALSCORERS

### Cheltenham Town

**Conference Appearances:** Banks, C. 39(1); Benton, S. 5(6); Bloomer, B. 32; Book, S. 42; Casey, R. 1(2); Clark, B. 6; Crisp, M. 6(15); Duff, M. 41; Eaton, J. 28(6); Freeman, M. 28; Grayson, N. 13(2); Howells, L. 31; Jackson, M. 4(2); Knight, K. 26(8); Milton, R. 21(4); Smith, J. 20(7); Teague, S. 0(1); Thorp, M. 2; Victory, J. 42; Walker, C. 23(3); Watkins, D. 35(5); Wright, D. 17(8).

**Goals (63):** Bloomer 1, Eaton 15, Freeman 2, Grayson 6, Howells 3, Knight 2, Smith 5, Victory 6, Walker 4, Watkins 17, OG 2.

### Dover Athletic

**Conference Appearances:** Adams, D. 25(8); Alford, C. 15; Ayorinde, S. 18(1); Barber, P. 12(1); Budden, J. 37; Clarke, D. 12(2); Daniels, S. 15; Davies, M. 28; Dempsey, M. 5; Dobbs, G. 12(10); Fearon, R. 12; French, J. 0(1); Godden, R. 1(6); Hanson, D. 4; Henry, L. 29(6); Hogg, A. 1(1); Jones, S. 2(3); Leberl, J. 19(4); Le Bihan, N. 30(2); McCabe, R. 0(1); McRobert, L. 6(3); Mitten, C. 2; Munday, S. 28; Palmer, L. 38(1); Reina, R. 5; Shearer, L. 25; Stebbing, G. 35(2); Strouts, J. 34(1); Wilson, P. 12(4).

**Goals (60):** Adams 7, Alford 7, Ayorinde 5, Barber 2, Budden 4, Dobbs 1, Godden 1, Hanson 1, Henry 4, Le Bihan 3, McRobert 3, Munday 1, Reina 2, Shearer 1, Strouts 13, Wilson 2, OG 3.

### Farnborough Town

**Conference Appearances:** Baker, N. 27(8); Baker, S. 37; Boothe, C. 8(2); Coles, D. 3; Dobson, R. 0(2); Harford, P. 30(1); Harlow, D. 37(3); Harte, S. 2(5); Hooper, N. 2(2); Horne, B. 9; Kelly, M. 1; Kemp, S. 1(1); Laidlaw, J. 13(9); MacKenzie, S. 29; Mehew, D. 32; Miller, B. 25(7); Mintram, S. 20(1); Robson, D. 26(10); Rowe, A. 1; Rowlands, K. 12(14); Rowlands, M. 29(5); Stemp, W. 42; Underwood, J. 31(5); White, C. 9(1); Wingfield, D. 36(1).

**Goals (56):** Baker N. 1, Baker S. 1, Boothe 2, Harford 1, Harlow 2, Laidlaw 4, Mehew 15, Miller 1, Robson 4, Rowlands K. 8, Rowlands M. 7, Underoowd 1, Wingfield 9.

### Gateshead

**Conference Appearances:** Bochenski, S. 2; Bowey, S. 40(1); Byrne, W. 8(1); Carter, M. 9; Clyde, D. 4; Connor, P. 5; Currie, D. 2(1); Edgcumbe, W. 4(4); Hall, T. 12(2); Harkus, S. 10(12); Heron, C. 0(1); Hunter, D. 2; Hutchinson, S. 3(4); Innes, G. 10(15); Johnson, F. 2; Kitchen, S. 36; Lowe, K. 21; McGargle, S. 0(7); Marquis, P. 25(1); Moore, R. 10; Ord, D. 26(4); Patterson, M. 1(4); Pearson, G. 4; Peverell, N. 14(2); Platt, D. 6; Proudlock, P. 27(6); Robinson, G. 20(4); Robson, G. 31; Robson, J. 15(3); Rose, C. 4(1); Rowe, B. 15(4); Scott, M. 23(6); Skedd, S. 0(1); Sunderland, J. 2(3); Twynham, G. 2(8); Wells, M. 21(3); West, G. 4; Willgrass, A. 19(1); Williams, D. 24.

**Goals (51):** Bowey 12, Carter 1, Connor 3, Hall 1, Harkus 5, Hutchinson 1, Innes 4, Kitchen 1, Marquis 3, Pearson 1, Peverell 3, Proudlock 7, Robinson 2, Robson G. 1, OG 1.

### Halifax Town

**Conference Appearances:** Boardman, C. 4; Bradshaw, M. 42; Brook, G. 18(4); Borwn, J. 37; Griffiths, W. 0(2); Hanson, D. 6(5); Horner, N. 10(8); Horsfield, G. 40; Hulme, K. 30; Hurst, C. 2(1); Jackson, P. 8; Kilcline, B. 23(1); Kiwomya, A. 0(5); Lyons, D. 13(11); Martin, L. 32; Midwood, M. 5; Morgan, P. 1; Murphy, J. 27(1); O'Regan, K. 36(1); Paterson, J. 36; Philliskirk, T. 4; Place, D. 0(1); Rhodes, A. 8; Stoneman, P. 38; Thackeray, A. 41; Woods, A. 1.

**Goals (74):** Bradshaw 5, Brook 3, Hanson 2, Horsfield 30, Hulme 7, Kilcline 2, Lyons 3, O'Regan 1, Paterson 14, Philliskirk 2, Stoneman 2, Thackeray 2, OG 1.

### Hayes

**Conference Appearances:** Beccles, K. 1; Beer, J. 13; Boothe, C. 22; Brady, J. 40; Bunce, N. 34; Cox, A. 24; Craft, D. 3; Dell, S. 3; Djemai, H. 1; Domingos, A. 9; Duncan, I. 12; Flynn, L. 33; Francis, J. 21; Gallagher, K. 5;

Goodliffe, J. 18; Hall, M. 37; Hammett, B. 23; Haynes, J. 23; Meara, R. 41; Metcalfe, C. 12; Passmore, L. 1; Pye, M. 22; Randall, M. 37; Roberts, J. 7; Roddis, N. 24; Sparkes, C. 29; Taylor, A. 11; Watts, A. 18; Wilkinson, D. 36.

**Goals (62):** Boothe 4, Brady 1, Bunce 4, Cox 2, Domingos 1, Duncan 1, Flynn 5, Francis 1, Goodliffe 1, Hall 6, Hammett 1, Haynes 3, Metcalfe 2, Randall 16, Roberts 5, Roddis 3, Sparkes 1, Wilkinson 2, OG 3.

### Hednesford Town

**Conference Appearances:** Anderton, D. 4(3); Beeston, C. 25; Blades, P. 37(1); Brindley, C. 14; Broadhurst 2(3); Carty, P. 32(4); Colkin, L. 7; Collins, K. 29(1); Comyn, A. 32(1); Cooksey, S. 42; Dandy, R. 2; Dennison, R. 26(4); Eccleston, T. 9(5); Fitzpatrick, G. 34; Francis, D. 15(4); Hemmings, T. 11(2); Jeffers, J. 0(1); Knight, L. 0(1); Lake, S. 19(6); Landon, R. 3(1); Mckenzie, O. 0(3); Niblett, N. 6; Norbury, M. 20(4); Ntamark, C. 18(2); O'Connor, J. 25(2); Sedgemore, J. 13; Simpson, W. 8; Smith, N. 0(2); Ware, P. 32.

**Goals (59):** Anderson 3, Beeston 1, Carty 8, Comyn 3, Dennison 4, Eccleston 5, Fitzpatrick 7, Francis 3, Hemmings 1, Lake 1, Norbury 6, Ntamark 1, O'Connor 8, Sedgemore 1, Ware 7.

### Hereford United

**Conference Appearances:** Agana, T. 17(5); Brough, J. 31(2); Cook, G. 7(10); deBont, A. 2; Fishlock, M. 36(1); Foster, I. 13(4); Gayle, M. 5; Grayson, N. 23(2); Hargreaves, C. 38; Leadbeater, R. 12; Mackenzie, C. 7; Mahon, G. 42; Mansell, C. 0(4); Matthewson, T. 28; McCue, J. 5(2); McGorry, B. 30(2); Milner, A. 8; Norton, D. 5(1); Parry, P. 0(2); Pitman, J. 29(1); Quy, A. 28; Rodgerson, I. 35(2); Walker, R. 34; Warner, R. 21(6); Williams, G. 3(7).

**Goals (56):** Agana 7, Brough 4, Cook 2, Fishlock 2, Foster 3, Grayson 11; Hargreaves 4, Leadbeater 7, Matthewson 2, McGorry 1, Milner 5, Pitman 5, Williams 1, OG 2.

### Kettering Town

**Conference Appearances:** Adams, C. 31(4); Berry, S. 27(6); Brown, A. 0(1); Costello, P. 31(6); Cox, P. 17(7); De Vito, C. 9; Gaunt, C. 10; Hercock, D. 7(2); Holliday, D. 0(4); Leczynski, A. 1; Miles, P. 0(20); Moore, D. 14; Mutchell, R. 41; Norman, C. 27(10); Nuttell, M. 12(8); Pack, L. 0(1); Pearson, C. 31(3); Pick, G. 5; Quy, A. 2; Ridgway, I. 25(11); Rowe, Z. 2; Sandeman, B. 23; Sheppard, S. 12(1); Shoemake, K. 1(5); Sinden, S. 1(6); Taylor, C. 27; Tucker, M. 33(5); Van Dullemen, R. 10(1); Venables, D. 3(3); Vowden, C. 39(1); Wilkes, T. 22(20).

**Goals (53):** Adams 5, Berry 1, Costello 5, Mutchell 2, Norman 8, Nuttell 1, Pearson 14, Sandeman 3, Tucker 1, Van Dullemen 1, Vowden 5, Wilkes 7.

### Kidderminster Harriers

**Conference Appearances:** Arnold, I. 39; Barber, F. 3; Beard, M. 4(1); Bignall, M. 22(1); Bignot, M. 4; Brighton, S. 2(3); Brindley, C. 22; Brock, S. 4; Cartwright, N. 3; Casey, K. 3(8); Clarke, M. 10(1); Davies, P. 14(1); Deakin, J. 30(4); Doherty, N. 26(3); Fraser, J. 1(1); Lilwall, S. 4(3); McCue, J. 0(7); Moore, P. 0(2); Niblett, N. 7; Olney, I. 11; Pope, S. 12; Prindiville, S. 29; Robinson, A. 6(9); Shepherd, M. 4; Skelding, J. 15; Smith, A. 23; Steadman, D. 33; Thomas, W. 8; Webb, P. 23(4); Weir, M. 28(2); Westhead, M. 2; Willetts, K. 29(1); Yates, M. 41.

**Goals (56):** Arnold 9, Beard 1, Bignall 11, Brindley 1, Cartwright 1, Davies 5, Deakin 2, Doherty 9, Robinson 3, Smith 3, Thomas 1, Willetts 2, Yates 5, OG 3.

### Leek Town

**Conference Appearances:** Bauress, G. 2; Beeby, M. 25(4); Biggins, W. 33(6); Birch, J. 7; Brunskill, I. 35(2); Callan, A. 21(8); Cunningham, D. 16(15); Cutler, N. 11; Diskin, J. 32; Ellis, N. 34(2); Filson, M. 12(0); Germaine, G. 10; Hassall, J. 1(1); Hawkes, M. 0(1); Hawtin, D. 31(2); Jones, S. 0(2); Knowles, M. 1; Leicester, S. 23(4); McAuley, H. 30(5); Newland, R. 21; Parker, J. 13; Soley, S. 36; Tobin, S. 24(5); Trott, D. 24(10); Walker, R. 36(1).

**Goals (52):** Beeby 2, Biggins 8, Cunningham 1, Diskin 1, Ellis 2, Hawtin 1, Leicester 1, McAuley 11, Soley 12, Tobin 5, Trott 5, Walker 2, OG 1.

## Morecambe

**Conference Appearances:** Banks, A. 14; Bignall, M. 7(3); Burns, P. 25(7); Ceroalo, M. 8(10); Curtis, W. 4; Drummond, S. 18(8); Grimshaw, A. 24; Hayton, K. 0(1); Healy, B. 39; Hodgson, S. 6(5); Hughes, A. 8; Hughes, D. 8(2); Hunt, S. 1(3); Kennedy, J. 13; Knowles, M 10(9); Lowe, D. 4(2); McKearney, D. 33; McIlhargey, S. 28; Mayers, K. 26(15); Miller, D. 16; Milner, A. 21; Mitchell, N. 2(4); Monk, I. 31(3); Norman, J. 40(2); Parkinson, S. 4(15); Rushton, P. 26(2); Shirley, M. 38(1); Takano, K. 6(1); Williams, G. 2(7).
**Goals (77):** Bignall 5, Burns 2, Ceroalo 7, Curtis 2, Drummond 1, Grimshaw 2, Healy 7, Hughes 1, McKearney 4, Mayers 3, Milner 8, Monk 2, Norman 18, Parkinson 1, Rushton 1, Shirley 10, OG 3.

## Northwich Victoria

**Conference Appearances:** Billing, P. 14(1); Bishop, E. 16(7); Carroll, T. 4(12); Collins, J. 5(3); Cooke, I. 28(9); Crookes, D. 37(2); Dowell, W. 0(1); Duffy, C. 29(5); Fairclough, W. 32(1); Gardiner, M. 21; Greygoose, D. 42; Hussin, E. 4(4); Illman, N. 14; Lampkin, R. 0(1); Milligan, M. 10(2); Sandeman, B. 5; Simpson, W. 36; Stannard, J. 16(13); Tait, P. 36(4); Vicary, D. 23(10); Walters, S. 41; Ward, D. 27(7); Ward, M. 6(1); Williams, C. 16(8).
**Goals (63):** Bishop 4, Carroll 1, Collins 3, Cooke 8, Crookes 3, Duffy 1, Gardiner 1, Illman 9, Milligan 1, Stannard 3, Tait 12, Vicary 2, Walters 7, Ward 1, Williams 4, OG 3.

## Rushden & Diamonds

**Conference Appearances:** Alford, C. 4(2); Barnwell, J. 4(1); Butterworth, G. 28; Bradshaw, D. 29; Branston, G. 10(1); Cann, A. 0(1); Capone, J. 18(12); Chapman, A. 0(2); Cherry, S. 8; Collins, D. 39; Cooper, M. 9(5); Cramman, K. 36(1); Foster, A. 13(7); Fuff, G. 4; Hackett, B. 22(6); Hamsher, J. 21(8); Hodson, S. 4; Kelly, W. 11(4); Mehew, D. 5(6); Mison, M. 29; Ndah, J. 4(1); Ndekwe, M. 0(2); O'Shea, D. 1; Peaks, A. 5; Rawle, M. 0(8); Rodwell, J. 12(4); Smith, M. 30; Underwood, P. 24(4); West, C. 14(1); Watts, D. 4; Whyte, C. 34; Wooding, T. 28.
**Goals (79):** Alford 2, Barnwell 3, Butterworth 1, Capone 4, Collins 29, Cooper 3, Cramman 2, Foster 9, Hackett 2, Hamsher 1, Mehew 1, Mison 7, Ndal 1, Rawle 1, Underwood 6, West 6, OG 1.

## Slough Town

**Conference Appearances:** Abbott, G. 36; Angus, T. 33; Bailey, D. 40; Bolt, D. 40; Brazil, D. 38; Browne, C. 32; Duffy, G. 2; Fiore, M. 13; Hardyman, P. 29; Hercules, C. 37; McGinnis, G. 24; Miles, B. 11; Nolan, T. 6; Owusu, L. 27; Randall, L. 15; Simpson, D. 12; Smart, G. 42; Smith, R. 8; Stowell, M. 24; West, M. 24; Wilkerson, P. 31.
**Goals (57):** Abbott 9, Angus 1, Bolt 11, Brazil 4, Browne 4, Fiore 2, Hardyman 2, Hercules 7, Owusu 9, Randall 2, Smart 1, Stowell 1, West 4.

## Southport

**Conference Appearances:** Bagnall, J. 5; Blakeman, C. 0(1); Blythe, A. 1(1); Bolland, P. 22(4); Butler, B. 35; Clarke, P. 1(2); Deary, J. 13; Dove, L. 7; Farley, A. 36; Formby, K. 35; Futcher, P. 37(1); Gamble, D. 27(7); Horner, P. 23; Jones, P. 11(9); Kielty, G. 33(4); Mitten, P. 14(11); Moore, M. 2(4); Moran, S. 0(1); Morgan, J. 2(2); O'Reilly, J. 10(1); Pepper, J. 0(4); Powell, F. 0(1); Ross, B. 20(7); Ryan, T. 36(1); Stewart, W. 37; Taylor, P. 0(1); Thompson, D. 28(9); Whittaker, A. 22(2).
**Goals (56):** Ryan 1, Butler 4, Formby 4, Kielty 5, Thompson 3, Gamble 4, Horner 1, Bolland 1, Whittaker 8, Ross 6, Mitten 4, Deary 4, O'Reilly 6, Morris 1, OG 4.

## Stalybridge Celtic

**Conference Appearances:** Anderson, L. 0(1); Bates, J. 30(7); Burke, B. 39(1); Brien, A. 3; Brownrigg, A. 10(1); Butler, J. 6(1); Coathup, L. 30(1); Charles, S. 3(3); Cherry, S. 10; Crossley, R. 8(1); Curtis, L. 4; Cutler, N. 7; Daly, M. 6(5); Dolby, C. 11(4); Dove, L. 16(3); Edey, C. 2; Golbourne, R. 8(11); Hall, D. 21(6); Hammond, A. 2(1); Heath, S. 8; Highfield, M. 13(3); Hine, M. 24(4); Hoe, M. 0(5); Horner, R. 4(3); Howard, S. 0(1); Ingham, G. 8; Jones, S. 44; Levendis, A. 0(1); Lonergan, D. 2; Martin, D. 11(1); Marsh, N. 0(3); McCord, B. 2; Powell, M. 35(7); Pickess, J. 1; Ramsey, J. 2; Rawstron, M. 0(1); Shearer, L. 0(1); Statham, M. 17; Storey, B. 9(11); Sullivan, A. 19(11); Thomas, G. 9(1); Trees, R. 21(7); Trundle, L. 22(5); Utley, D. 1(1); Varadi, I. 0(1); Vine, D.

3(13); Walker, G. 3(4); Watson, J. 1; Williams, C. 10; Whittaker, S. 3(1); Wrightson, J. 2.
**Goals (48):** Bates 1, Burke 16, Charles 1, Dolby 1, Hall 1, Heath 1, Highfield 1, Hine 1, Jones 4, Martin 1, Powell 2, Ramsey 1, Storey 1, Sullivan 6, Thomas 1, Trees 1, Trundle 7, Williams 1.

## Stevenage Borough

**Conference Appearances:** Beevor, S. 26(3); Catlin, N. 8; Crawshaw, G. 35(2); Dean, P. 2(2); Dillnutt, J. 9(3); Fenton, D. 6(4); Gallagher, D. 31; Grazioli, G. 11(1); Harvey, L. 7(3); Holden, S. 8(4); Johansen, T. 3(1); Kirby, R. 31; Love, M. 26(1); March, J. 29(3); Marshall, R. 1; Meah, J. 3(2); Perkins, S. 25(1); Rogers, D. 1, Smith, M. 32; Soloman, J. 27(4); Stapleton, S. 4(3); Thompson, P. 5(3); Trebble, N. 31(4); Trott, R. 39; Wilmot, R. 11; Wordsworth, D. 15(5).
**Goals (59):** Beevor 4, Catlin 2, Crawshaw 11, Grazioli 7; Kirby 1, Love 1, Perkins 4, Smith 4, Soloman 3, Stevens 1, Thompson 1, Trebble 8, Trott 3, Wordsworth 8, OG 1.

## Telford United

**Conference Appearances:** Anderson, D. 1; Ashley, K. 15(1); Atkinson, C. 1; Bennett, D. 2; Bentley, J. 31; Bryan, S. 0(1); Bytheway, M. 12(1); Bywater, P. 17; Carlwright, N. 13(6); Challinor, P. 16(5); Charlton, A. 4(6); Colcombe, S. 15(2); Colley, N. 3(14); Collins, T. 0(5); Corns, S. 0(1); Daley, R. 4(14); Dudley, D. 6(2); Duerden, I. 4(3); Eastwood, P. 8; Eccleston, S. 17(4); Fowler, L. 30; Gray, B. 25(10); Hodson, S. 17; Jones, Mark 28(1); Jones, Marcus 13; Joseph, A. 1(2); Langford, T. 7(5); Moore, M. 7(1); Murphy, G. 9; Norbury, M. 6(3); Palmer, S. 17(8); Parkes, G. 0(1); Purdie, J. 6(3); Shakespeare, C. 8; Simpson, P. 7; Taylor, S. 12(2); Turner, M. 38(1); Ward, N. 2; Westhead, M. 8; Wilcox, B. 13(3); Wright, E. 7.
**Goals (53):** Ashley 1, Bentley 5, Colley 1, Daley 1, Eastwood 2, Fowler 3, Gray 10, Langford 5, Moore 2, Murphy 8, Norbury 1, Palmer 4, Shakespeare 1, Taylor 2, Turner 4, Wright 2, OG 1.

## Welling United

**Conference Appearances:** Abbott, S. 0(8); Appiah, S. 9; Braithwaite, L. 5; Brown, D. 13(4); Chapman, D. 33(1); Cooper, M. 35; Copley, P. 29; Dimmock, R. 0(6); Dolby, T. 32(2); Farley, J. 33(7); Hanlon, R. 31(4); Horton, D. 30; Hynes, M. 14(2); Ilic, S. 2; King, T. 4(3); Knight, G. 40; Lakin, B. 9; Lindsey, S. 1; Martin, D. 6; Omigie, J. 0(1); Perkins, S. 4(1); Rutherford, M. 38; Side, C. 0(1); Simpson, C. 0(1); Skiverton, T. 29; Vercesi, R. 11(15); Watson, M. 15(9); Watts, L. 39; Watts, S. 0(1).
**Goals (64):** Appiah 2, Braithwaite 1, Cooper 18, Copley 4, Dolby 7, Farley 1, Hanlon 15, Hynes 6, Rutherford 2, Skiverton 1, Watson 2, Watts 1, Vercesi 4.

## Woking

**Conference Appearances:** Abbey, N. 4; Barry, L. 39; Betsy, K. 39(2); Brown, K. 25; Danzey, M. 25(1); Ellis, A. 32(2); Girdler, S. 1(1); Goddard, R. 7; Hay, D. 29(4); Hayward, A. 6; Howard, T. 15(1); Hunter, J. 1; Jackson, J. 9; Jones, T. 9(3); Kamara, B. 4(2); Kilner, A. 0(3); McAree, R. 9(2); Payne, G. 34(4); Saunders, E. 24; Smith, S. 22(9); Steele, S. 30(6); Stewart, S. 7; Sutton, W. 17(1); Taylor, R. 31; Thompson, S. 26; Timothy, D. 7(2); West, S. 17(5); Wood, S. 1.
**Goals (72):** Betsy 6, Danzey 3, Hay 19, Hayward 4, Howard 1, Jackson 1, McAree 2, Payne 15, Saunders 1, Steele 4, Taylor 3, Thompson 2, West 8, OG 3.

## Yeovil Town

**Conference Appearances:** Archer, L. 20(10); Birkby, D. 7(8); Braybrook, H. 1(2); Brown, H. 11; Brown, S. 19(4); Calderhead, W. 2(3); Cousins, R. 41; Denys, R. 2(3); Engwell, M. 17(2); Fielder, C. 28(7); Freeman, A. 2; Hannigan, A. 36(1); Harvey, L. 8(3); Hayfield, M. 5; Howard, T. 6(1); Kemp, G. 11(10); Omogbehin, C. 1; Parmenter, S. 14(5); Patmore, W. 36(1); Pennock, T. 42; Pickard, O. 37(2); Piper, D. 14; Pounder, T. 3(11); Roberts, G. 5(1); Smith, B. 14; Spencer, S. 0(1); Stott, S. 35; Thompson, D. 5; Thompson, S. 12; White, C. 12; Wimble, S. 1(2); Winston, S. 5(9); Winter, S. 2(6).
**Goals (73):** Archer 8, Chandler 1, Denys 1, Engwell 1, Fielder 2, Hannigan 1, Hayfield 1, Parmenter 3, Patmore 16, Pickard 17, Pounder 1, Roberts 1, Smith 5, Stott 7, Thompson 2, Winston 6.

# FOOTBALL CONFERENCE: MEMBERS CLUBS SEASON 1998–99

Club: BARROW
Colours: White shirts blue trim, white shorts blue trim
Ground: Holker Street Stadium, Wilkie Road, Barrow in Furness, Cumbria LA14 5UW
Tel: 01229 820346
Year Formed: 1901
Record Gate: 6,002 (v Enfield 1988)
Nickname: Bluebirds
Manager: Owen Brown
Secretary: Patricia Brewer

Club: CHELTENHAM TOWN
Colours: Red and white striped shirts, white shorts
Ground: Whaddon Road, Cheltenham, Glos, GL52 5NA
Tel: 01242 573558
Year Formed: 1892
Record Gate: 8236 (1956 v Reading)
Nickname: The Robins
Manager: Steve Cotterill
Secretary: Reg Woodward

Club: DONCASTER ROVERS
Colours: Red shirts, red shorts
Ground: Belle Vue, Doncaster, DN4 5HT
Tel: 01302 539441
Year Formed: 1879
Record Gate: 37,149 (v Hull City 1948)
Nickname: Rovers
Manager: Mark Weaver
Secretary: Joan Oldale

Club: DOVER ATHLETIC
Colours: White shirts, black shorts
Ground: Crabble Athletic Ground, Lewisham Road, River, Dover, Kent CT17 0PB
Tel: 01304 822373
Year Formed: 1983
Record Gate: 4035 (1992 v Bromsgrove Rovers)
Nickname: The Lillywhites
Manager: Bill Williams
Secretary: John Durrant

Club: FARNBOROUGH TOWN
Colours: Yellow and blue shirts, blue shorts
Ground: Cherrywood Road, Farnborough, Hampshire GU14 8UD
Tel: 01252 541469
Year Formed: 1967
Record Gate: 3069 (1991 v Colchester U)
Nickname: Boro
Manager: Alan Taylor
Secretary: Terry Parr

Club: FOREST GREEN ROVERS
Colours: Black and white striped shirts, black shorts
Ground: The Lawn, Nympsfield Road, Forest Green, Nailsworth, Glos GL6 0ET
Tel: 01453 834860
Year Formed: 1890
Record Gate: 2,891 (1998 v Merthyr Tydfil)
Nickname: Rovers
Manager: Frank Gregan
Managing Director: Colin Peake

Club: HAYES
Colours: Red and white striped shirts, black shorts
Ground: Townfield House, Church Road, Hayes, Middlesex UB3
Tel: 0181 573 2075
Year formed: 1909
Record Gate: 15,370 (1951 v Bromley)
Nickname: Missioners
Manager: Terry Brown
Secretary: John Bond (Jnr)

Club: HEDNESFORD TOWN
Colours: Black and white striped shirts, black shorts, red and white trim
Ground: Keys Park, Hill Street, Hednesford, Staffordshire WS12 5DW
Tel: 01543 422870
Year Formed: 1880
Record Gate: 10,000 (1927 v Walsall)
Nickname: The Pitmen
Manager: John Baldwin
Secretary: Richard Murning

Club: HEREFORD UNITED
Colours: White shirts black trim, black shorts white trim
Ground: Edgar Street, Hereford, HR4 9JU
Tel: 01432 276666
Year Formed: 1924
Record Gate: 18,114 (1958 v Sheffield Wednesday)
Nickname: United
Manager: Graham Turner
Secretary: Joan Fennessy

Club: KETTERING TOWN
Colours: Red and black shirts, red shorts black trim
Ground: Rockingham Road, Kettering, Northants NN16 9AW
Tel: 01536 483028/410815
Year Formed: 1875
Record Gate: 11,536 (1947 v Peterborough)
Nickname: The Poppies
Manager: Peter Morris
Secretary: Gerry Knowles

Club: KIDDERMINSTER HARRIERS
Colours: Red and white halved shirts, red shorts
Ground: Aggborough, Hoo Road, Kidderminster DY10 1NB
Tel: 01562 823931
Year Formed: 1886
Record Gate: 9155 (1948 v Hereford)
Nickname: The Harriers
Manager: Graham Allner
Secretary: Roger Barlow

Club: KINGSTONIAN
Colours: Red and white hooped shirts, black shorts
Ground: Kingsmeadow Stadium
Tel: 0181 547 3335
Year Formed: 1885
Record Gate: 4,582 (v Chelsea 1995)
Nickname: The K's
Manager: Geoff Chapple
Secretary: WR McNally

Club: LEEK TOWN
Colours: Blue shirts yellow collar and cuffs, blue and yellow striped shorts
Ground: Harrison Park, Macclesfield Road, Leek, Staffs ST13 8LD
Tel: 01538 399278
Year Formed: 1947
Record Gate: 5312 (1973 v Macclesfield Town)
Nickname: The Blues
Manager: Ernie Moss
Secretary: Michael Rowley

Club: MORECAMBE
Colours: Red shirts, black shorts
Ground: Christie Park, Lancaster Road, Morecambe, Lancashire LA4 5TJ
Tel: 01524 411797
Year Formed: 1920
Record Gate: 9326 (1962 FA Cup Third Round Proper v Weymouth)
Nickname: The Shrimps
Manager: Jim Harvey
Secretary: Neil Marsdin

Club: NORTHWICH VICTORIA
Colours: Green shirts, white shorts green trim
Ground: The Drill Field, Northwich, Cheshire CW9 5HN
Tel: 01606 41450
Year Formed: 1874
Record Gate: 11,290 (1949 v Witton A) 12,000 (1977 v Watford FAC4)
Nickname: The Vics
Manager: Phil Wilson
Secretary: Derek Nuttall

Club: RUSHDEN & DIAMONDS
Colours: White shirts, blue shorts
Ground: Nene Park, Station Road, Irthlingborough, Northants NN9 5QF
Tel: 01933 652000
Year Formed: 1992
Record Gate: 5170 (1997 v Kettering Town)
Nickname: Diamonds
Head Coach: Brian Talbot
Secretary: David Joyce

Club: SOUTHPORT
Colours: Old gold and black shirts, black shorts
Ground: Haig Avenue, Southport PR8 6JZ
Tel: 01704 533422
Year Formed: 1881
Record Gate: 20,010 (1932 v Newcastle United)
Nickname: The Sandgrounders
Manager: Paul Futcher
Secretary: Ken Hilton

Club: STEVENAGE BOROUGH
Colours: Red shirts, black shorts
Ground: Broadhall Way, Stevenage, Herts SG2 8RH
Tel: 01438 743322
Year Formed: 1976
Record Gate: 15,365 (1997 v Birmingham City at St Andrews)
Nickname: The Boro
Manager: Paul Fairclough
Secretary: Frank Radcliffe

Club: TELFORD UNITED
Colours: White shirts black trim, white shorts black trim
Ground: Bucks Head, Watling Street, Telford TF1 2NJ
Tel: 01952 640064
Year Formed: 1877
Record Gate: 13,000 (1935 v Shrewsbury)
Nickname: The Lillywhites
Manager: Jimmy Mullen
Secretary: Mike Ferriday

Club: WELLING UNITED
Colours: Red shirts, red shorts
Ground: Park View Road Ground, Welling, Kent DA16 1SY
Tel: 0181-301 1196
Year Formed: 1963
Record Gate: 4020 (1989 v Gillingham)
Nickname: The Wings
Manager: Kevin Hales
Secretary: Barrie Hobbins

Club: WOKING
Colours: Red and white halved shirts, black shorts
Ground: Kingfield Sports Ground, Kingfield, Woking, Surrey GU22 9AA
Tel: 01483 772470
Year Formed: 1889
Record Gate: 6084 (1997 v Coventry City)
Nickname: The Cardinals
Manager: John McGovern
Secretary: Phil Ledger, JP

Club: YEOVIL TOWN
Colours: Green and white shirts, green shorts
Ground: Huish Park, Lufton Way, Yeovil, Somerset BA22 8YF
Tel: 01935 423662
Year Formed: 1896
Record Gate: 8612 (1993 v Arsenal)
Nickname: The Glovers
Coach: Colin Lippiatt
Secretary: Jean Cotton

FOOTBALL CONFERENCE RESULTS 1997-98

| | Cheltenham Town | Dover Athletic | Farnborough Town | Gateshead | Halifax Town | Hayes | Hednesford Town | Hereford United | Kettering Town | Kidderminster Harriers | Leek Town | Morecambe | Northwich Victoria | Rushden & Diamonds | Slough Town | Southport | Stalybridge Celtic | Stevenage Borough | Telford United | Welling United | Woking | Yeovil Town |
|---|---|---|---|---|---|---|---|---|---|---|---|---|---|---|---|---|---|---|---|---|---|---|
| Cheltenham Town | — | 3-1 | 1-0 | 2-0 | 4-0 | 2-1 | 1-0 | 1-2 | 2-0 | 0-1 | 1-1 | 2-1 | 3-2 | 2-0 | 1-1 | 2-0 | 2-0 | 1-1 | 3-1 | 1-1 | 3-2 | 2-0 |
| Dover Athletic | 3-0 | — | 2-2 | 0-1 | 0-1 | 1-0 | 1-3 | 1-1 | 0-0 | 0-4 | 2-1 | 2-3 | 4-0 | 0-3 | 2-1 | 3-1 | 3-1 | 1-1 | 6-3 | 2-1 | 0-2 | 1-0 |
| Farnborough Town | 1-2 | 1-0 | — | 4-0 | 1-2 | 0-2 | 1-3 | 0-2 | 3-2 | 3-3 | 2-0 | 0-2 | 2-3 | 2-0 | 1-0 | 3-2 | 6-0 | 1-2 | 1-0 | 0-0 | 3-0 | 2-2 |
| Gateshead | 0-0 | 1-2 | 3-0 | — | 2-2 | 1-1 | 2-5 | 1-1 | 2-0 | 2-0 | 2-1 | 1-4 | 2-2 | 2-1 | 5-1 | 0-2 | 3-3 | 2-1 | 0-2 | 2-1 | 1-2 | 0-3 |
| Halifax Town | 1-1 | 1-1 | 1-0 | 1-2 | — | 1-1 | 1-1 | 3-0 | 3-0 | 2-0 | 2-1 | 5-1 | 4-2 | 2-0 | 1-0 | 4-3 | 3-1 | 4-0 | 6-1 | 1-0 | 1-0 | 3-1 |
| Hayes | 1-1 | 0-0 | 3-1 | 1-0 | 1-1 | — | 4-0 | 2-0 | 0-1 | 1-1 | 1-0 | 0-3 | 1-1 | 1-2 | 0-1 | 2-0 | 1-2 | 1-3 | 2-1 | 3-1 | 3-0 | 1-0 |
| Hednesford Town | 0-1 | 1-0 | 1-0 | 3-0 | 0-0 | 2-1 | — | 1-1 | 1-1 | 3-0 | 1-0 | 0-1 | 2-0 | 0-1 | 2-1 | 2-1 | 1-0 | 2-1 | 1-0 | 3-2 | 1-1 | 1-0 |
| Hereford United | 3-2 | 0-1 | 2-1 | 1-0 | 0-0 | 3-0 | 2-1 | — | 3-2 | 1-0 | 1-0 | 1-0 | 2-2 | 1-1 | 1-1 | 2-1 | 3-0 | 0-2 | 1-1 | 1-2 | 2-1 | 1-1 |
| Kettering Town | 0-1 | 2-1 | 2-1 | 3-0 | 3-0 | 1-1 | 2-1 | 1-2 | — | 2-2 | 1-0 | 1-1 | 1-3 | 0-4 | 1-1 | 1-1 | 3-1 | 2-0 | 1-3 | 0-1 | 0-1 | 1-1 |
| Kidderminster Harriers | 1-2 | 3-3 | 2-0 | 1-1 | 0-2 | 1-0 | 1-1 | 1-4 | 4-1 | — | 1-1 | 1-4 | 1-1 | 1-2 | 3-3 | 1-1 | 5-0 | 1-3 | 1-1 | 2-1 | 1-1 | 3-1 |
| Leek Town | 0-0 | 5-1 | 3-1 | 2-2 | 2-0 | 1-0 | 3-3 | 2-2 | 0-4 | 0-0 | — | 1-1 | 1-1 | 2-0 | 0-1 | 0-1 | 2-2 | 2-1 | 3-1 | 1-2 | 2-0 | 2-0 |
| Morecambe | 1-0 | 3-3 | 3-3 | 1-1 | 1-1 | 0-2 | 1-3 | 1-5 | 1-3 | 3-1 | 1-1 | — | 3-1 | 3-1 | 0-2 | 0-0 | 3-1 | 0-2 | 1-0 | 4-2 | 1-2 | 1-0 |
| Northwich Victoria | 2-1 | 2-1 | 3-3 | 1-1 | 2-0 | 1-1 | 1-1 | 0-2 | 0-0 | 4-1 | 3-1 | 5-0 | — | 2-4 | 2-1 | 1-0 | 1-0 | 1-1 | 2-2 | 5-1 | 0-2 | 2-1 |
| Rushden & Diamonds | 4-1 | 4-1 | 5-5 | 3-2 | 4-0 | 1-3 | 1-1 | 1-0 | 1-0 | 2-0 | 2-2 | 3-3 | 2-4 | — | 0-1 | 3-2 | 3-0 | 2-0 | 3-2 | 1-2 | 2-1 | 2-2 |
| Slough Town | 1-2 | 2-4 | 1-0 | 1-0 | 1-1 | 0-0 | 2-0 | 1-0 | 1-0 | 1-2 | 2-2 | 3-3 | 0-1 | 1-2 | — | 1-0 | 4-0 | 3-1 | 1-0 | 3-1 | 1-3 | 1-1 |
| Southport | 1-2 | 0-1 | 3-1 | 3-1 | 0-0 | 0-2 | 4-1 | 3-0 | 1-0 | 1-3 | 6-1 | 1-1 | 1-0 | 3-2 | 0-1 | — | 4-2 | 1-0 | 1-2 | 2-1 | 0-0 | 2-1 |
| Stalybridge Celtic | 1-4 | 1-0 | 1-1 | 2-2 | 0-1 | 1-1 | 1-1 | 0-0 | 4-2 | 2-1 | 5-2 | 3-1 | 1-0 | 2-4 | 1-0 | 1-3 | — | 1-1 | 1-2 | 0-0 | 0-3 | 3-2 |
| Stevenage Borough | 1-2 | 2-2 | 5-0 | 6-1 | 1-2 | 1-5 | 1-1 | 2-3 | 0-0 | 3-1 | 3-0 | 0-3 | 2-0 | 2-1 | 1-2 | 1-0 | 1-1 | — | 1-1 | 0-3 | 0-0 | 2-1 |
| Telford United | 0-0 | 0-1 | 0-1 | 4-4 | 0-3 | 1-0 | 1-1 | 2-0 | 1-1 | 1-1 | 2-0 | 1-3 | 3-2 | 4-2 | 0-1 | 2-2 | 1-0 | 3-0 | — | 0-3 | 0-3 | 1-4 |
| Welling United | 2-1 | 2-2 | 1-0 | 2-0 | 6-2 | 2-0 | 3-2 | 3-0 | 2-2 | 0-3 | 5-2 | 2-2 | 0-1 | 0-1 | 4-2 | 3-5 | 3-1 | 1-0 | 4-1 | — | 1-1 | 1-3 |
| Woking | 2-0 | 4-0 | 3-0 | 3-1 | 2-2 | 3-0 | 4-2 | 3-0 | 0-1 | 1-1 | 3-1 | 0-2 | 2-1 | 0-2 | 0-1 | 1-1 | 2-0 | 5-3 | 1-1 | 3-1 | — | 2-0 |
| Yeovil Town | 3-1 | 4-1 | 0-1 | 6-3 | 0-1 | 4-3 | 1-0 | 2-0 | 2-0 | 1-0 | 3-1 | 2-3 | 1-2 | 1-2 | 1-1 | 0-0 | 2-1 | 2-1 | 5-3 | 1-1 | 2-0 | — |

## SPALDING CHALLENGE CUP 1997–98

**First Round**

Dover Athletic 1 *(McRobert)*
Kettering Town 3 *(Wilkes, Costello, Norman)* — 404

Hayes 2 *(Roddis, Hammatt)*
Rushden & Diamonds 0 — 438

Leek Town 3 *(Filson, McAuley 2)*
Southport 1 *(Beckford)* — 349

Slough Town 1 *(Abbott)*
Welling United 0 — 293

Stalybridge Celtic 3 *(Butler, Trees, Trundle)*
Halifax Town 1 *(Boardman)* — 489

Yeovil Town 3 *(Birkby 3)*
Cheltenham Town 1 *(Watkins)* — 1005

**Second Round**

Farnborough Town 2 *(Robson, Underwood)*
Hereford United 1 *(Grayson)* — 256

Hayes 2 *(Hammatt, Haynes)*
Slough Town 0 — 374

Kidderminster Harriers 0
Hednesford Town 2 *(Francis, Hemmings)* — 734

Morecambe 3 *(Norman, OG, McKearney)*
Leek Town 2 *(OG, Ellis)* — 356

Stalybridge Celtic 3 *(Burke, Sullivan 2)*
Gateshead 4 *(Carter, Twynham 2, OG)* — 224

Stevenage Borough 0
Yeovil Town 3 *(Pickard, Patmore, Calderhead)* — 816

Telford United 1 *(Cartwright)*
Northwich Victoria 2 *(Ward, Cooke)* — 307

Woking 4 *(Steele 2, Timothy, West)*
Kettering Town 0 — 559

**Third Round**

Hayes 3 *(Roddis, Randall, Hammatt)*
Yeovil Town 0 — 171

Gateshead 1 *(Harkus)*
Morecambe 1 *(Drummond)* — 204

Morecambe 3 *(Monk, Miller, Drummond)*
Gateshead 1 *(Marquis)* — 305

Northwich Victoria 3 *(Williams, Stannard, Steele)*
Hednesford Town 2 *(Fitzpatrick, Norbury)* — 447

Woking 3 *(Smith, Hay, Saunders)*
Farnborough Town 1 *(Harford)* — 998

**Semi-Final** (two legs)

Hayes 0
Woking 2 *(Payne, Smith)* — 647

Woking 3 *(West 2, Betsy)*
Hayes 1 *(Randall)* — 826

Morecambe 3 *(Milner, Mayers, Norman)*
Northwich Victoria 0 — 608

Northwich Victoria 3 *(Stannard 2, Illman)*
Morecambe 1 *(Norman)* — 457

**Final** (two legs)

Morecambe 1 *(Healy)*
Woking 1 *(Hayward)* — 782

Woking 1 *(Hay)*
Morecambe 1 *(Healy)* — 2045
*(Morecambe won 4-3 on penalties)*

## THE MAIL ON SUNDAY
### Monthly Awards

| **Goalscorer Of The Month** | | **Team Performance Of The Month** | **Manager Of The Month** |
|---|---|---|---|
| **AUGUST** | | | |
| Mike Bignall | | *Stalybridge Celtic* | Jim Harvey |
| *Kidderminster Harriers* | | (6-1 v Leek Town (H) 25/8) | *Morecambe* |
| Brendan Burke | Warren Patmore | | |
| *Stalybridge Celtic* | *Yeovil Town* | | |
| Neil Grayson | Owen Pickard | | |
| *Hereford United* | *Yeovil Town* | | |
| **SEPTEMBER** | | | |
| Geoff Horsfield | | *Hayes* | George Mulhall |
| *Halifax Town* | | (5-1 v Stevenage Borough (A) 1/9) | *Halifax Town* |
| **OCTOBER** | | | |
| Geoff Horsfield | | *Halifax Town* | Brian McDermott |
| *Halifax Town* | | (4-0 v Stevenage Borough (H) 18/10) | *Slough Town* |
| Brendan Burke | | | |
| *Stalybridge Celtic* | | | |
| **NOVEMBER** | | | |
| Neil Doherty | | *Cheltenham Town* | John Baldwin |
| *Kidderminster Harriers* | | (4-0 v Halifax Town (H) 1/11) | *Hednesford Town* |
| **DECEMBER** | | | |
| Darren Collins | | *Kettering Town* | Brian Talbot |
| *Rushden & Diamonds* | | (3-1 v Morecambe (A) 20/12) | *Rushden & Diamonds* |
| **JANUARY** | | | |
| Dale Watkins | | *Yeovil Town* | Phil Wilson |
| *Cheltenham Town* | | (3-1 v Cheltenham Town (H) 1/1) | *Northwich Victoria* |
| **FEBRUARY** | | | |
| Mike Bignall | | *Gateshead* | Steve Cotterill |
| *Kidderminster Harriers* | | (2-1 v Rushden & Diamonds (H) 14/2) | *Cheltenham Town* |
| | | | Paul Fairclough |
| | | | *Stevenage Borough* |
| **MARCH** | | | |
| Giuliano Grazioli | | *Northwich Victoria* | Steve Berry |
| *Stevenage Borough* | | (5-0 v Morecambe (H) 14/3) | *Kettering Town* |
| Brain Ross | | | |
| *Southport* | | | |
| Sam Winston | | | |
| *Yeovil Town* | | | |
| **APRIL** | | | |
| Darren Collins | | *Leek Town* | Jim Harvey |
| *Rushden & Diamonds* | | (1-0 v Rushden & Diamonds (A) 18/4) | *Morecambe* |
| Justin O'Reilly | | | |
| *Southport* | | | |
| Dale Watkins | | | |
| *Cheltenham Town* | | | |

# UNIBOND LEAGUE 1997-98

## UNIBOND LEAGUE

**Premier Division**

| | P | W | D | L | F | A | W | D | L | F | A | Pts |
|---|---|---|---|---|---|---|---|---|---|---|---|---|
| | | | Home | | Goals | | | Away | | Goals | | |
| Barrow | 42 | 13 | 3 | 5 | 29 | 13 | 12 | 5 | 4 | 32 | 16 | 83 |
| Boston United | 42 | 11 | 6 | 4 | 29 | 23 | 11 | 6 | 4 | 26 | 17 | 78 |
| Leigh | 42 | 12 | 6 | 3 | 32 | 15 | 9 | 7 | 5 | 31 | 26 | 76 |
| Runcorn | 42 | 13 | 5 | 3 | 43 | 19 | 9 | 4 | 8 | 37 | 31 | 75 |
| Gainsborough Trinity | 42 | 14 | 2 | 5 | 32 | 16 | 8 | 7 | 6 | 28 | 23 | 75 |
| Emley | 42 | 14 | 5 | 2 | 45 | 21 | 8 | 3 | 10 | 36 | 40 | 74 |
| Winsford United | 42 | 9 | 8 | 4 | 26 | 15 | 10 | 4 | 7 | 28 | 28 | 69 |
| Altrincham | 42 | 14 | 4 | 3 | 51 | 15 | 4 | 7 | 10 | 25 | 29 | 65 |
| Guiseley | 42 | 7 | 9 | 5 | 35 | 31 | 9 | 7 | 5 | 26 | 22 | 64 |
| Bishop Auckland | 42 | 9 | 6 | 6 | 46 | 34 | 8 | 6 | 7 | 32 | 26 | 63 |
| Marine | 42 | 8 | 5 | 8 | 27 | 28 | 7 | 6 | 8 | 29 | 31 | 56 |
| Hyde United | 42 | 8 | 6 | 7 | 32 | 29 | 5 | 10 | 6 | 28 | 26 | 55 |
| Colwyn Bay | 42 | 10 | 5 | 6 | 37 | 28 | 5 | 4 | 12 | 16 | 29 | 54 |
| Spenymoor United −1 | 42 | 6 | 8 | 7 | 26 | 31 | 8 | 3 | 10 | 32 | 41 | 52 |
| Chorley | 42 | 9 | 4 | 8 | 27 | 28 | 5 | 3 | 13 | 24 | 42 | 49 |
| Frickley Athletic | 42 | 11 | 4 | 6 | 28 | 22 | 1 | 8 | 12 | 17 | 40 | 48 |
| Lancaster City | 42 | 10 | 5 | 6 | 35 | 26 | 3 | 3 | 15 | 20 | 48 | 47 |
| Blyth Spartans −10 | 42 | 6 | 6 | 9 | 26 | 33 | 6 | 7 | 8 | 26 | 30 | 39 |
| Bamber Bridge | 42 | 6 | 5 | 10 | 32 | 36 | 3 | 7 | 11 | 19 | 38 | 39 |
| Accrington Stanley | 42 | 5 | 9 | 7 | 28 | 30 | 3 | 5 | 13 | 21 | 38 | 38 |
| Radcliffe Borough | 42 | 2 | 6 | 13 | 20 | 32 | 4 | 6 | 11 | 19 | 38 | 30 |
| Alfreton Town | 42 | 2 | 7 | 12 | 19 | 40 | 1 | 6 | 14 | 13 | 46 | 22 |

−1pt, −10pts for breach of rules

**First Division**

| | P | W | D | L | F | A | W | D | L | F | A | Pts |
|---|---|---|---|---|---|---|---|---|---|---|---|---|
| | | | Home | | Goals | | | Away | | Goals | | |
| Whitby Town | 42 | 15 | 3 | 3 | 50 | 27 | 15 | 5 | 1 | 49 | 21 | 98 |
| Worksop Town | 42 | 14 | 4 | 3 | 49 | 21 | 14 | 3 | 4 | 44 | 23 | 91 |
| Ashton United | 42 | 16 | 2 | 3 | 50 | 24 | 10 | 7 | 4 | 43 | 19 | 87 |
| Droylsden | 42 | 13 | 3 | 5 | 39 | 25 | 11 | 5 | 5 | 31 | 24 | 80 |
| Lincoln United | 42 | 11 | 5 | 5 | 37 | 25 | 9 | 6 | 6 | 39 | 37 | 71 |
| Farsley Celtic | 42 | 11 | 6 | 4 | 41 | 28 | 9 | 4 | 8 | 31 | 38 | 70 |
| Witton Albion | 42 | 11 | 5 | 5 | 44 | 20 | 8 | 4 | 9 | 33 | 35 | 66 |
| Eastwood Town | 42 | 8 | 10 | 3 | 36 | 25 | 10 | 2 | 9 | 32 | 26 | 66 |
| Bradford Park Avenue | 42 | 9 | 5 | 7 | 37 | 24 | 9 | 6 | 6 | 25 | 22 | 65 |
| Belper Town | 42 | 10 | 2 | 9 | 37 | 38 | 8 | 5 | 8 | 31 | 28 | 61 |
| Stocksbridge Park Steels | 42 | 10 | 5 | 6 | 38 | 29 | 7 | 4 | 10 | 30 | 34 | 60 |
| Trafford | 42 | 9 | 3 | 9 | 29 | 25 | 7 | 3 | 11 | 30 | 36 | 54 |
| Whitley Bay | 42 | 7 | 6 | 8 | 32 | 30 | 7 | 6 | 8 | 28 | 33 | 54 |
| Matlock Town | 42 | 10 | 4 | 7 | 44 | 28 | 4 | 7 | 10 | 24 | 36 | 53 |
| Gretna | 42 | 8 | 6 | 7 | 32 | 26 | 5 | 3 | 13 | 26 | 38 | 48 |
| Netherfield | 42 | 8 | 2 | 11 | 32 | 42 | 4 | 9 | 8 | 23 | 33 | 47 |
| Flixton | 42 | 6 | 6 | 9 | 22 | 27 | 4 | 6 | 11 | 23 | 46 | 42 |
| Congleton Town | 42 | 7 | 5 | 9 | 32 | 42 | 4 | 3 | 14 | 33 | 59 | 41 |
| Harrogate Town | 42 | 4 | 8 | 9 | 26 | 34 | 4 | 6 | 11 | 31 | 46 | 38 |
| Great Harwood Town | 42 | 2 | 8 | 11 | 21 | 43 | 6 | 4 | 11 | 20 | 45 | 36 |
| Workington | 42 | 4 | 3 | 14 | 18 | 40 | 4 | 4 | 13 | 20 | 44 | 31 |
| Buxton | 42 | 4 | 2 | 15 | 24 | 40 | 3 | 1 | 17 | 17 | 47 | 24 |

## LEADING GOALSCORERS

**(In order of League Goals)**

**Premier Division**

| Lge | Cup | Tot | |
|---|---|---|---|
| 31 | 10 | 41 | Liam Watson (Runcorn) |
| 19 | 7 | 26 | Neil Matthews (Guiseley) |
| 18 | 2 | 20 | Ian Banks (Emley) |
| 16 | 4 | 20 | Keith Russell (Altrincham) |
| 15 | 8 | 23 | Andy Shaw (Bishop Auckland) |
| 15 | 6 | 21 | Niell Hardy (Altrincham) |
| 15 | 5 | 20 | Matt Swailes (Chorley) |
| 15 | 3 | 18 | Phil Brown (Gainsborough Trinity) |
| 15 | 1 | 16 | Lutel James (Hyde United) |
| 14 | 6 | 20 | Bobby Davison (Guiseley) |
| 14 | 3 | 17 | Keith Evans (Leigh) |
| 14 | 2 | 16 | Paul David (Emley) |
| 13 | 10 | 23 | Lee Ellison (Bishop Auckland) |
| 13 | 7 | 20 | Paul McNally (Runcorn) |
| 13 | 6 | 19 | Keith Fletcher (Blyth Spartans) |
| 13 | 2 | 15 | Lee Cryer (Leigh) |
| 13 | 2 | 15 | Neil Morton (Barrow) |
| 13 | 2 | 15 | Tony Wright (Barrow − 7 + 1 for Droylsden) |
| 13 | 0 | 13 | Brian Welch (Accrington Stanley) |

**First Division**

| Lge | Cup | Tot | |
|---|---|---|---|
| 31 | 3 | 39 | Darren Washington (Witton Albion) |
| 23 | 7 | 30 | Paul Pitman (Whitby Town) |
| 21 | 8 | 29 | Kenny Clark (Matlock Town) |
| 20 | 4 | 24 | Andrew Fletcher (Netherfield − 8 + 4 for Whitby Town) |
| 20 | 2 | 22 | Martin Henderson (Whitley Bay; 2 for Workington) |
| 20 | 1 | 21 | Glenn Kirkwood (Eastwood Town) |
| 18 | 3 | 21 | Darren Emmett (Netherfield) |
| 18 | 2 | 20 | Graham Dodd (Congleton Town) |
| 18 | 0 | 18 | Scott Jackson (Farsley Celtic) |
| 17 | 7 | 24 | Gary Hurlstone (Stocksbridge Park Steels) |
| 17 | 2 | 19 | Jimmy Bell (Ashton United) |
| 16 | 3 | 19 | Carl Cunningham (Belper Town; 2 for Alfreton Town) |
| 15 | 2 | 17 | Gavin Bailey (Stocksbridge Park Steels) |
| 15 | 0 | 15 | John Coleman (Ashton United) |
| 14 | 5 | 19 | Eamonn Elliott (Ashton United) |
| 14 | 0 | 14 | Gavin Worboys (Eastwood Town) |

## UNIBOND CLUB OF THE MONTHS AWARD

| | |
|---|---|
| Aug/Sept | Winsford United |
| October | Gainsborough Trinity |
| November | Emley |
| December | Leigh |
| January | Barrow |
| February | Runcorn |
| March | Gainsborough Trinity |
| April/May | Gainsborough Trinity |

## UNIBOND CLUB OF THE MONTHS AWARD

| | |
|---|---|
| Aug/Sept | Gretna |
| October | Whitby Town |
| November | Worksop Town |
| December | Whitley Bay |
| January | Ashton United |
| February | Whitby Town |
| March | Lincoln United |
| April/May | Trafford |

## UNIBOND LEAGUE — PREMIER DIVISION RESULTS 1997–98

| | Accrington Stanley | Alfreton Town | Altrincham | Bamber Bridge | Barrow | Bishop Auckland | Blyth Spartans | Boston United | Chorley | Colwyn Bay | Emley | Frickley Athletic | Gainsborough Trinity | Guiseley | Hyde United | Lancaster City | Leigh | Marine | Radcliffe Borough | Runcorn | Spennymoor United | Winsford United |
|---|---|---|---|---|---|---|---|---|---|---|---|---|---|---|---|---|---|---|---|---|---|---|
| Accrington Stanley | — | 1-1 | 1-1 | 1-1 | 0-1 | 1-1 | 2-0 | 1-1 | 0-3 | 1-2 | 4-2 | 3-0 | 0-2 | 2-3 | 1-1 | 1-1 | 1-3 | 1-1 | 2-2 | 0-3 | 3-0 | 2-1 |
| Alfreton Town | 0-1 | — | 0-3 | 1-2 | 0-3 | 2-6 | 0-3 | 1-2 | 1-1 | 1-1 | 1-1 | 2-1 | 2-3 | 1-1 | 0-0 | 1-0 | 3-2 | 0-0 | 0-2 | 1-3 | 2-3 | 0-1 |
| Altrincham | 1-0 | 5-0 | — | 5-0 | 2-2 | 1-1 | 3-0 | 1-2 | 3-0 | 0-3 | 2-1 | 2-1 | 0-0 | 2-0 | 1-3 | 0-1 | 2-2 | 3-1 | 3-0 | 2-1 | 4-0 | 0-1 |
| Bamber Bridge | 2-1 | 4-1 | 0-3 | — | 2-2 | 3-1 | 1-4 | 2-2 | 4-0 | 0-2 | 2-3 | 3-0 | 2-2 | 1-2 | 1-1 | 1-0 | 0-1 | 1-2 | 1-0 | 1-0 | 2-2 | 2-3 |
| Barrow | 2-0 | 2-0 | 2-2 | 2-0 | — | 1-1 | 3-1 | 1-0 | 0-2 | 1-1 | 1-0 | 2-1 | 2-0 | 0-1 | 2-2 | 1-0 | 3-2 | 0-1 | 3-0 | 1-0 | 1-2 | 1-2 |
| Bishop Auckland | 2-2 | 1-1 | 5-2 | 1-1 | 0-2 | — | 1-1 | 0-2 | 5-2 | 0-2 | 4-3 | 4-1 | 1-3 | 1-1 | 2-1 | 3-1 | 0-1 | 2-4 | 3-0 | 1-2 | 1-1 | 6-0 |
| Blyth Spartans | 2-2 | 4-2 | 3-3 | 1-1 | 2-1 | 1-4 | — | 0-1 | 2-1 | 3-1 | 0-2 | 2-3 | 0-0 | 1-1 | 1-1 | 0-1 | 1-0 | 1-0 | 1-0 | 0-4 | 2-3 | 0-1 |
| Boston United | 1-3 | 2-0 | 1-0 | 1-1 | 0-2 | 1-0 | 2-2 | — | 1-1 | 1-0 | 3-2 | 3-0 | 1-0 | 2-1 | 1-1 | 2-0 | 0-1 | 1-1 | 2-2 | 0-3 | 1-3 | 2-1 |
| Chorley | 1-1 | 2-0 | 1-0 | 2-1 | 0-2 | 1-0 | 1-3 | 1-1 | — | 1-1 | 1-2 | 0-0 | 1-1 | 1-0 | 1-5 | 2-3 | 2-3 | 0-3 | 1-1 | 4-2 | 4-1 | 2-0 |
| Colwyn Bay | 2-1 | 3-0 | 0-0 | 3-1 | 1-1 | 0-1 | 2-0 | 0-2 | 3-3 | — | 1-3 | 1-1 | 1-1 | 0-1 | 3-1 | 5-2 | 2-2 | 4-1 | 2-1 | 2-1 | 2-0 | 0-3 |
| Emley | 5-3 | 2-0 | 2-1 | 0-0 | 3-0 | 1-2 | 1-1 | 0-3 | 3-1 | 1-0 | — | 1-0 | 1-0 | 3-3 | 2-1 | 5-3 | 0-0 | 2-0 | 2-0 | 6-2 | 3-0 | 0-2 |
| Frickley Athletic | 2-1 | 2-1 | 2-1 | 1-0 | 0-1 | 2-3 | 0-0 | 0-0 | 2-0 | 1-3 | 2-1 | — | 1-1 | 0-1 | 3-1 | 2-1 | 3-0 | 1-1 | 1-0 | 1-3 | 2-3 | 3-0 |
| Gainsborough Trinity | 0-0 | 4-0 | 2-1 | 3-2 | 0-3 | 1-0 | 0-0 | 1-0 | 2-1 | 1-0 | 2-1 | 3-1 | — | 1-3 | 4-1 | 2-1 | 2-1 | 2-0 | 3-0 | 1-0 | 0-1 | 0-2 |
| Guiseley | 1-0 | 1-2 | 2-2 | 1-1 | 1-1 | 3-3 | 1-3 | 0-1 | 0-2 | 3-1 | 0-2 | 4-0 | 1-3 | — | 1-1 | 2-1 | 2-1 | 2-2 | 4-1 | 2-2 | 1-1 | 0-2 |
| Hyde United | 1-1 | 4-1 | 0-1 | 1-1 | 0-3 | 1-2 | 1-0 | 1-1 | 0-2 | 2-0 | 1-0 | 1-1 | 4-1 | 1-1 | — | 4-1 | 3-3 | 1-1 | 0-1 | 0-2 | 3-2 | 4-3 |
| Lancaster City | 3-2 | 1-1 | 2-2 | 1-0 | 0-2 | 1-3 | 3-1 | 0-2 | 4-1 | 0-1 | 2-2 | 2-1 | 0-1 | 3-2 | 0-1 | — | 0-1 | 3-2 | 0-1 | 3-0 | 3-2 | 1-1 |
| Leigh | 1-0 | 2-2 | 2-2 | 4-0 | 0-1 | 1-3 | 1-1 | 3-1 | 1-2 | 3-0 | 2-1 | 3-0 | 2-1 | 2-1 | 3-3 | 2-0 | — | 1-0 | 0-0 | 3-2 | 4-2 | 2-0 |
| Marine | 3-1 | 2-0 | 1-0 | 3-1 | 1-0 | 0-0 | 1-2 | 0-1 | 1-2 | 1-0 | 3-5 | 1-1 | 1-3 | 0-1 | 0-2 | 2-0 | 1-1 | — | 1-2 | 0-0 | 0-4 | 0-0 |
| Radcliffe Borough | 1-2 | 1-1 | 0-1 | 3-0 | 1-2 | 1-2 | 1-2 | 1-2 | 1-2 | 1-1 | 1-2 | 2-1 | 2-0 | 0-2 | 0-0 | 6-2 | 0-1 | 0-3 | — | 3-2 | 0-2 | 0-2 |
| Runcorn | 3-0 | 3-1 | 1-0 | 4-2 | 0-1 | 2-1 | 1-1 | 1-1 | 2-3 | 0-0 | 1-0 | 2-1 | 1-4 | 1-1 | 0-1 | 3-0 | 2-2 | 3-0 | 6-3 | — | 2-0 | 0-0 |
| Spennymoor United | 2-0 | 1-1 | 2-1 | 0-3 | 3-2 | 1-1 | 2-1 | 3-0 | 2-0 | 2-1 | 2-2 | 0-0 | 1-1 | 1-2 | 2-2 | 1-1 | 0-3 | 1-2 | 1-1 | 0-1 | — | 1-1 |
| Winsford United | 3-0 | 0-0 | 2-1 | 0-1 | 0-0 | 0-0 | 3-0 | 1-2 | 1-0 | 2-0 | 0-1 | 2-1 | 1-1 | 2-1 | 1-1 | 3-0 | 0-1 | 2-4 | 2-2 | 1-1 | 1-0 | — |

## UNIBOND LEAGUE — FIRST DIVISION RESULTS 1997–98

| | Ashton United | Belper Town | Bradford Park Avenue | Buxton | Congleton Town | Droylsden | Eastwood Town | Farsley Celtic | Flixton | Great Harwood Town | Gretna | Harrogate Town | Lincoln United | Matlock Town | Netherfield | Stocksbridge Park Steels | Trafford | Whitby Town | Whitley Bay | Witton Albion | Workington | Worksop Town |
|---|---|---|---|---|---|---|---|---|---|---|---|---|---|---|---|---|---|---|---|---|---|---|
| Ashton United | — | 3-4 | 0-1 | 1-0 | 3-2 | 4-2 | 1-0 | 3-1 | 2-1 | 3-0 | 1-1 | 3-0 | 2-0 | 5-1 | 4-1 | 3-3 | 3-1 | 2-0 | 1-4 | 3-1 | 1-0 | 2-1 |
| Belper Town | 0-7 | — | 0-1 | 2-1 | 4-0 | 0-3 | 0-0 | 2-3 | 4-0 | 1-2 | 4-3 | 2-1 | 1-3 | 1-1 | 1-0 | 2-1 | 3-1 | 0-1 | 1-1 | 3-2 | 5-0 | 0-4 |
| Bradford Park Avenue | 0-0 | 0-0 | — | 4-1 | 1-0 | 1-0 | 0-0 | 5-2 | 4-0 | 1-2 | 4-0 | 3-1 | 1-1 | 1-2 | 3-1 | 2-3 | 0-1 | 1-1 | 3-0 | 1-3 | 3-3 | 2-3 |
| Buxton | 1-4 | 0-2 | 0-1 | — | 4-1 | 0-1 | 2-0 | 1-3 | 2-2 | 1-2 | 1-3 | 2-0 | 1-3 | 1-2 | 1-0 | 1-1 | 0-2 | 1-2 | 2-3 | 1-3 | 2-3 | 0-1 |
| Congleton Town | 0-3 | 0-4 | 2-1 | 3-1 | — | 2-2 | 1-0 | 1-3 | 1-3 | 1-1 | 1-0 | 2-4 | 3-3 | 3-1 | 2-0 | 2-2 | 1-4 | 1-2 | 2-1 | 3-3 | 1-3 | 0-1 |
| Droylsden | 2-1 | 2-0 | 2-2 | 1-0 | 3-1 | — | 0-2 | 3-0 | 1-2 | 3-3 | 1-0 | 2-0 | 2-3 | 2-1 | 0-0 | 2-1 | 3-1 | 2-3 | 1-0 | 0-4 | 3-0 | 1-0 |
| Eastwood Town | 1-0 | 0-1 | 1-1 | 2-0 | 5-0 | 2-2 | — | 3-3 | 1-1 | 1-1 | 3-1 | 1-0 | 0-3 | 0-0 | 4-4 | 3-1 | 2-1 | 0-0 | 2-3 | 1-1 | 2-0 | 2-2 |
| Farsley Celtic | 2-1 | 5-3 | 1-1 | 2-1 | 1-1 | 0-1 | 5-0 | — | 1-0 | 6-1 | 3-2 | 3-3 | 2-1 | 1-1 | 1-0 | 0-2 | 5-2 | 1-2 | 2-0 | 0-2 | 2-1 | 1-1 |
| Flixton | 2-2 | 1-1 | 1-3 | 1-2 | 0-2 | 0-1 | 2-2 | 3-3 | — | 1-0 | 2-0 | 0-3 | 0-0 | 1-0 | 1-0 | 0-4 | 0-1 | 1-4 | 0-1 | 3-1 | 6-0 | 1-1 |
| Great Harwood Town | 0-1 | 3-1 | 0-2 | 0-0 | 2-5 | 0-1 | 1-5 | 1-0 | 1-1 | — | 0-1 | 1-1 | 1-2 | 3-1 | 0-0 | 2-2 | 2-2 | 0-7 | 1-1 | 1-2 | 0-3 | 2-3 |
| Gretna | 1-1 | 4-3 | 1-0 | 4-0 | 4-0 | 3-2 | 2-3 | 1-1 | 1-1 | 1-2 | — | 2-2 | 2-1 | 3-1 | 0-0 | 2-1 | 0-1 | 1-1 | 0-1 | 1-1 | 1-0 | 2-3 |
| Harrogate Town | 1-1 | 2-0 | 2-4 | 2-0 | 0-3 | 1-0 | 1-0 | 2-0 | 1-3 | 1-2 | 1-1 | — | 2-3 | 2-2 | 2-4 | 2-1 | 4-1 | 1-1 | 2-2 | 0-0 | 1-1 | 0-2 |
| Lincoln United | 0-2 | 1-0 | 0-0 | 0-1 | 3-3 | 3-0 | 4-1 | 2-0 | 4-1 | 1-1 | 2-1 | 2-1 | — | 4-3 | 2-2 | 3-0 | 1-2 | 2-5 | 3-0 | 1-0 | 1-1 | 1-0 |
| Matlock Town | 1-4 | 0-3 | 2-0 | 3-0 | 3-0 | 2-3 | 1-0 | 1-1 | 6-1 | 1-1 | 1-1 | 6-0 | 4-3 | — | 2-3 | 1-0 | 2-1 | 3-3 | 1-1 | 4-1 | 3-0 | 1-2 |
| Netherfield | 1-3 | 0-2 | 1-1 | 2-1 | 3-2 | 2-0 | 2-0 | 0-3 | 2-0 | 0-1 | 0-3 | 1-4 | 0-3 | 1-1 | — | 0-3 | 2-1 | 1-4 | 4-3 | 3-1 | 0-0 | 2-6 |
| Stocksbridge Park Steels | 1-4 | 2-0 | 0-1 | 2-1 | 2-1 | 2-1 | 3-1 | 4-0 | 5-1 | 4-0 | 3-0 | 4-2 | 5-1 | 2-2 | 0-1 | — | 2-1 | 1-4 | 2-2 | 3-0 | 0-0 | 1-0 |
| Trafford | 2-1 | 1-1 | 1-1 | 4-0 | 1-3 | 1-0 | 2-0 | 2-2 | 3-1 | 1-0 | 3-0 | 2-4 | 1-1 | 0-1 | 4-1 | 1-2 | — | 1-3 | 0-1 | 3-0 | 2-1 | 1-2 |
| Whitby Town | 1-1 | 2-2 | 5-2 | 4-3 | 2-1 | 1-0 | 2-0 | 2-1 | 6-1 | 3-0 | 2-0 | 1-0 | 3-5 | 1-0 | 1-1 | 1-0 | 2-1 | — | 3-2 | 4-1 | 2-3 | 2-3 |
| Whitley Bay | 1-1 | 0-2 | 1-0 | 3-1 | 4-4 | 1-1 | 4-0 | 1-2 | 1-2 | 2-0 | 2-0 | 1-1 | 2-2 | 1-0 | 2-2 | 5-0 | 0-0 | 1-3 | — | 0-3 | 3-0 | 1-3 |
| Witton Albion | 1-1 | 2-0 | 1-2 | 4-0 | 5-3 | 2-2 | 5-1 | 1-1 | 4-1 | 1-0 | 0-2 | 4-0 | 3-0 | 0-1 | 0-2 | 1-0 | 2-0 | 1-1 | 0-0 | — | 2-1 | 1-2 |
| Workington | 0-3 | 0-2 | 0-1 | 0-2 | 4-0 | 0-1 | 2-2 | 0-1 | 2-0 | 1-4 | 0-4 | 1-1 | 1-1 | 4-2 | 0-0 | 0-1 | 1-5 | 1-1 | 1-2 | 1-4 | — | 0-4 |
| Worksop Town | 1-2 | 0-0 | 1-0 | 3-2 | 5-1 | 2-2 | 3-1 | 1-2 | 2-0 | 3-0 | 3-2 | 3-3 | 3-0 | 3-1 | 4-1 | 1-2 | 1-1 | 1-3 | 2-0 | 2-0 | 3-0 | — |

# UNIBOND CHALLENGE CUP

**FIRST ROUND**
Alfreton Town 1, Matlock Town 3 *(after 1-1 draw)*
Bamber Bridge 2, Gretna 1
Belper Town 3, Buxton 0
Bradford Park Avenue 1, Lincoln United 0
Droylsden 2, Witton Albion 1
Flixton 0, Ashton United 1 *(after 2-2 draw)*
Leigh 3, Workington 1 *(after 1-1 draw)*
Radcliffe Borough 3, Great Harwood Town 0
Stocksbridge Park Steels 3, Farsley Celtic 0
Trafford 1, Congleton Town 2
Whitby Town 6, Harrogate Town 1
Whitley Bay 8, Netherfield 3
Worksop Town 1, Eastwood Town 4

**SECOND ROUND**
Altrincham 3, Droylsden 0
Ashton United 1, Runcorn 2
Bamber Bridge 0, Chorley 1
Barrow 0, Lancaster City 3
Belper Town 1, Stocksbridge Park Steels 0
Blyth Spartans 1, Whitley Bay 0
Boston United 1, Emley 0
Bradford Park Avenue 0, Frickley Athletic 2
Colwyn Bay 1, Hyde United 0
Congleton Town 3, Winsford United 2 *(after 3-3 draw; Congleton expelled for fielding an ineligible player)*
Gainsborough Trinity 2, Matlock Town 0
Guiseley 0, Bishop Auckland 3
Leigh 2, Radcliffe Borough 0 *(after 0-0 draw)*
Marine 2, Accrington Stanley 0 *(after 4-4 draw)*
Whitby Town 0, Spennymoor United 1 *(after 1-1 draw)*

Eastwood Town - bye

**THIRD ROUND**
Altrincham 4, Colwyn Bay 2
Belper Town 3, Bishop Auckland 2 *(after 1-1 draw; Belper expelled for fielding an ineligible player)*
Blyth Spartans 4, Frickley Athletic 1
Chorley 5, Leigh 2
Gainsborough Trinity 4, Eastwood Town 2
Marine 1, Runcorn 0
Spennymoor United 1, Boston United 3
Winsford United 1, Lancaster City 0

**FOURTH ROUND**
Altrincham 2, Boston United 1 *(after 1-1 draw)*
Blyth Spartans 2, Marine 0
Gainsborough Trinity 2, Bishop Auckland 1 *(after 0-0 draw)*
Winsford United 0, Chorley 1 *(after 0-0 draw)*

**SEMI-FINALS (TWO LEGS)**
Altrincham 2, Chorley 0
Chorley 3, Altrincham 2
Blyth Spartans 1, Gainsborough Trinity 2
Gainsborough Trinity 2, Blyth Spartans 1

**FINAL**
Altrincham 2, Gainsborough Trinity 1 *(aet; at Chesterfield)*

# UNIBOND LEAGUE PRESIDENT'S CUP

**FIRST ROUND**
Altrincham 0, Leigh 1
Ashton United 2, Worksop Town 1
Barrow 2, Marine 5
Blyth Spartans 3, Bishop Auckland 2
Boston United 1, Bradford Park Avenue 0
Emley 2, Stocksbridge Park Steels 0
Farsley Celtic 0, Guiseley 1
Runcorn 3, Radcliffe Borough 1 *(after 0-0 draw)*

**SECOND ROUND**
Ashton United 2, Emley 1
Blyth Spartans 4, Boston United 2 *(after 3-3 draw)*
Guiseley 0, Leigh 0 *(after 0-0 draw)*

Runcorn 2, Marine 1

**SEMI-FINALS (TWO LEGS)**
Ashton United 1, Guiseley 2
Guiseley 1, Ashton United 1
Blyth Spartans 2, Runcorn 1
*(Blyth expelled for fielding an ineligible player)*

**FINAL (TWO LEGS)**
Guiseley 1, Runcorn 2
Runcorn 3, Guiseley 2
*(Runcorn won 5-3 on aggregate)*

# UNIFILLA FIRST DIVISION CUP

**FIRST ROUND**
Belper Town 5, Congleton Town 2
Gretna 2, Workington 0
Matlock Town 1, Eastwood Town 2
Netherfield 0, Great Harwood Town 2
Whitley Bay 1, Whitby Town 2 *(after 2-2 draw)*
Witton Albion 0, Trafford 2

**SECOND ROUND**
Belper Town 3, Buxton 2
Bradford Park Avenue 2, Whitby Town 0
Droylsden 4, Flixton 2
Eastwood Town 0, Farsley Celtic 1
Great Harwood Town 0, Ashton United 1 *(after 1-1 draw)*
Harrogate Town 2, Lincoln United 3
Stocksbridge Park Steels 1, Worksop Town 0
Trafford 2, Gretna 0

**THIRD ROUND**
Belper Town 1, Ashton United 2
Bradford Park Avenue 3, Droylsden 1 *(after 1-1 draw)*
Farsley Celtic 0, Lincoln United 3
Stocksbridge Park Steels 2, Trafford 3

**SEMI-FINALS (TWO LEGS)**
Ashton United 2, Lincoln United 4
Lincoln United 0, Ashton United 1
Trafford 1, Bradford Park Avenue 2
Bradford Park Avenue 0, Trafford 2

**FINAL**
Lincoln United 1, Trafford 3
*(aet; at Lincoln United)*

# DR MARTENS LEAGUE 1997–98

## Premier Division

| | P | W | D | L | F | A | Pts |
|---|---|---|---|---|---|---|---|
| Forest Green Rovers | 42 | 27 | 8 | 7 | 93 | 55 | 89 |
| Merthyr Tydfil | 42 | 24 | 12 | 6 | 80 | 42 | 84 |
| Burton Albion | 42 | 21 | 8 | 13 | 64 | 43 | 71 |
| Dorchester Town | 42 | 19 | 13 | 10 | 63 | 38 | 70 |
| Halesowen Town | 42 | 18 | 15 | 9 | 70 | 38 | 69 |
| Bath City | 42 | 19 | 12 | 11 | 72 | 51 | 69 |
| Worcester City | 42 | 19 | 12 | 11 | 54 | 44 | 69 |
| King's Lynn | 42 | 18 | 11 | 13 | 64 | 65 | 65 |
| Atherstone United | 42 | 17 | 12 | 13 | 55 | 49 | 63 |
| Crawley Town | 42 | 17 | 8 | 17 | 63 | 60 | 59 |
| Gloucester City | 42 | 16 | 11 | 15 | 57 | 57 | 59 |
| Nuneaton Borough | 42 | 17 | 6 | 19 | 68 | 61 | 57 |
| Cambridge City | 42 | 16 | 8 | 18 | 62 | 70 | 56 |
| Hastings Town | 42 | 14 | 12 | 16 | 67 | 70 | 54 |
| Tamworth | 42 | 14 | 11 | 17 | 68 | 65 | 53 |
| Rothwell Town | 42 | 11 | 16 | 15 | 55 | 73 | 49 |
| Gresley Rovers | 42 | 14 | 6 | 22 | 59 | 77 | 48 |
| Salisbury City | 42 | 12 | 12 | 18 | 53 | 72 | 48 |
| Bromsgrove Rovers | 42 | 13 | 6 | 23 | 67 | 85 | 45 |
| Sittingbourne | 42 | 12 | 8 | 22 | 47 | 66 | 44 |
| Ashford Town | 42 | 8 | 5 | 29 | 34 | 85 | 29 |
| St Leonards Stamcroft | 42 | 5 | 10 | 27 | 48 | 97 | 25 |

## Midland Division

| | P | W | D | L | F | A | Pts |
|---|---|---|---|---|---|---|---|
| Grantham Town | 40 | 30 | 4 | 6 | 87 | 39 | 94 |
| Ilkeston Town | 40 | 29 | 6 | 5 | 123 | 39 | 93 |
| Solihull Borough | 40 | 22 | 9 | 9 | 81 | 48 | 75 |
| Raunds Town | 40 | 20 | 8 | 12 | 73 | 44 | 68 |
| Wisbech Town | 40 | 20 | 7 | 13 | 79 | 57 | 67 |
| Moor Green | 40 | 20 | 7 | 13 | 72 | 55 | 67 |
| Bilston Town | 40 | 20 | 5 | 15 | 69 | 57 | 65 |
| Blakenall | 40 | 17 | 13 | 10 | 66 | 55 | 64 |
| Stafford Rangers | 40 | 18 | 6 | 16 | 57 | 56 | 60 |
| Redditch United | 40 | 16 | 11 | 13 | 59 | 41 | 59 |
| Stourbridge | 40 | 16 | 9 | 15 | 57 | 55 | 57 |
| Hinckley United | 40 | 15 | 11 | 14 | 59 | 56 | 56 |
| Brackley Town | 40 | 15 | 7 | 18 | 45 | 57 | 52 |
| Bedworth United | 40 | 15 | 5 | 20 | 50 | 73 | 50 |
| Racing Club Warwick | 40 | 11 | 9 | 20 | 49 | 56 | 42 |
| Shepshed Dynamo | 40 | 9 | 14 | 17 | 55 | 74 | 41 |
| Sutton Coldfield Town | 40 | 9 | 12 | 19 | 42 | 68 | 39 |
| Paget Rangers | 40 | 9 | 12 | 19 | 40 | 75 | 39 |
| VS Rugby | 40 | 8 | 12 | 20 | 53 | 93 | 36 |
| Evesham United | 40 | 7 | 9 | 24 | 47 | 94 | 30 |
| Corby Town | 40 | 2 | 8 | 30 | 41 | 112 | 14 |

## Southern Division

| | P | W | D | L | F | A | Pts |
|---|---|---|---|---|---|---|---|
| Weymouth | 42 | 32 | 2 | 8 | 107 | 48 | 98 |
| Chelmsford City | 42 | 29 | 8 | 5 | 86 | 39 | 95 |
| Bashley | 42 | 29 | 4 | 9 | 101 | 59 | 91 |
| Newport IOW | 42 | 25 | 9 | 8 | 72 | 34 | 84 |
| Fisher Athletic London | 42 | 25 | 5 | 12 | 87 | 50 | 80 |
| Margate | 42 | 23 | 8 | 11 | 71 | 42 | 77 |
| Newport AFC | 42 | 21 | 6 | 15 | 83 | 65 | 69 |
| Witney Town | 42 | 20 | 9 | 13 | 74 | 58 | 69 |
| Clevedon Town | 42 | 20 | 7 | 15 | 57 | 55 | 67 |
| Waterlooville | 42 | 17 | 7 | 18 | 69 | 64 | 58 |
| Dartford | 42 | 17 | 7 | 18 | 60 | 60 | 58 |
| Havant Town | 42 | 13 | 14 | 15 | 65 | 70 | 53 |
| Fleet Town | 42 | 16 | 5 | 21 | 63 | 83 | 53 |
| Tonbridge Angels | 42 | 14 | 10 | 18 | 49 | 55 | 52 |
| Trowbridge Town | 42 | 14 | 6 | 22 | 55 | 69 | 48 |
| Erith & Belvedere | 42 | 11 | 13 | 18 | 47 | 68 | 46 |
| Fareham Town | 42 | 12 | 9 | 21 | 75 | 87 | 45 |
| Cirencester Town | 42 | 12 | 7 | 23 | 63 | 88 | 43 |
| Weston-Super-Mare | 42 | 12 | 5 | 25 | 49 | 86 | 41 |
| Baldock Town | 42 | 10 | 5 | 27 | 53 | 81 | 35 |
| Cinderford Town | 42 | 6 | 5 | 31 | 40 | 112 | 23 |
| Yate Town | 42 | 5 | 7 | 30 | 44 | 97 | 22 |

## LEADING GOALSCORERS
### (League and Cup)

### Premier Division

| | |
|---|---|
| I. Mitchell (Merthyr Tydfil) | 25 |
| P. Hunt (Forest Green Rovers) | 24 |
| S. Browne (Hastings Town) | 23 |
| E. Wright (Halesowen Town) | 23 |
| P. Evans (Merthyr Tydfil) | 22 |
| A. Mainwaring (Gloucester City) | 22 |
| S. Piearce (Halesowen Town) | 22 |
| S. Bowan (Worcester City) | 21 |
| M. Shepherd (Dorchester Town) | 19 |
| G. Colbourne (Bath City) | 18 |
| A. Garner (Burton Albion) | 18 |

### Midland Division

| | |
|---|---|
| C. Moore (Ilkeston Town) | 29 |
| S. Keeble (Wisbech Town) | 28 |
| K. Slinn (Raunds Town) | 25 |
| M. Carmichael (Ilkeston Town) | 23 |
| N. Dowling (Solihull Borough) | 23 |
| M. Whitehouse (Moor Green) | 22 |
| D. King (Grantham Town) | 21 |
| D. Taylor (Grantham Town) | 21 |
| G. Russell (Moor Green) | 17 |

### Southern Division

| | |
|---|---|
| D. Laws (Weymouth) | 40 |
| A. Romasz (Fareham Town) | 33 |
| J. Taylor (Bashley) | 33 |
| P. Sales (Bashley) | 26 |
| S. Tate (Waterlooville) | 24 |
| J. Lovell (Fisher Athletic London) | 22 |
| A. Cook (Clevedon Town) | 21 |
| E. Fearon (Newport IOW) | 21 |
| S. Tapp (Trowbridge Town) | 21 |
| P. Hambley (Fisher Athletic London) | 20 |
| M. Rawlins (Clevedon Town) | 20 |
| P. Sykes (Margate) | 20 |
| S. Watts (Fisher Athletic London) | 20 |
| P. Andrews (Bashley) | 19 |
| A. Rice (Havant Town) | 19 |
| W. Goddard (Chelmsford City) | 17 |
| M. Munday (Margate) | 17 |

## DR MARTENS CUP

**PRELIMINARY ROUND, FIRST LEG**
Tamworth 4, Gresley Rovers 3
Weston-Super-Mare 0, Gloucester City 2

**PRELIMINARY ROUND, SECOND LEG**
Gloucester City 1, Weston-Super-Mare 0
Gresley Rovers 2, Tamworth 2

**FIRST ROUND, FIRST LEG**
Cinderford Town 0, Gloucester City 3
Atherstone United 1, Moor Green 4
Witney Town 1, Newport AFC 3
Worcester City 6, Stafford Rangers 3
Ashford Town 2, Chelmsford City 1
Bashley 4, Fleet Town 0
Bedworth United 1, Nuneaton Borough 1
Bilston Town 3, Halesowen Town 1
Clevedon Town 3, Cirencester Town 2
Crawley Town 3, Sittingbourne 3
Fisher Athletic 5, Dartford 3
Grantham Town 1, Wisbech Town 0
Ilkeston Town 2, Kings Lynn 1
Hinckley United 3, VS Rugby 1
Merthyr Tydfil 0, Forest Green Rovers 0
Newport (IOW) 2, Waterlooville 1
Redditch United 2, Bromsgrove Rovers 1
Shepshed Dynamo 3, Cambridge City 3
Stourbridge 4, Evesham United 0
Sutton Coldfield Town 2, Racing Club Warwick 1
Tamworth 0, Burton Albion 2
Tonbridge Angels 0, Margate 0
Yate Town 0, Bath City 1
Baldock Town 0, Hastings Town 1
Corby Town 1, Brackley Town 2
Fareham Town 1, Dorchester Town 4
Paget Rangers 2, Solihull Borough 1
Raunds Town 6, Rothwell Town 1
Salisbury City 2, Trowbridge Town 3
Havant Town 1, Weymouth 1
St Leonards Stamcroft 2, Erith & Belvedere 3

**FIRST ROUND, SECOND LEG**
Dartford 0, Fisher Athletic 2
Chelmsford City 4, Ashford Town 1
Bath City 2, Yate Town 1
Bromsgrove Rovers 0, Redditch United 2
Cambridge City 3, Shepshed Dynamo 0
Cirencester Town 1, Clevedon Town 3
Dorchester Town 3, Fareham Town 1
Evesham United 0, Stourbridge 2
Halesowen Town 0, Bilston Town 0
Hastings United 3, Baldock Town 0
Kings Lynn 2, Ilkeston Town 2
Margate 4, Tonbridge Angels 0
Moor Green 2, Atherstone United 3
Nuneaton Borough 0, Bedworth United 2
Rothwell Town 0, Raunds Town 3
Stafford Rangers 2, Worcester City 0
Waterlooville 2, Newport (IOW) 2
Erith & Belvedere 0, St Leonards Stamcroft 2
Forest Green Rovers 3, Merthyr Tydfil 1
Racing Club Warwick 2, Sutton Coldfield Town 2
Trowbridge Town 3, Salisbury City 4
VS Rugby 0, Hinckley United 1
Brackley Town 0, Corby Town 2

Burton Albion 1, Tamworth 1
Fleet Town 1, Bashley 1
Weymouth 0, Havant Town 2
Sittingbourne 3, Crawley Town 5
Wisbech Town 1, Grantham Town 4
Solihull Borough 3, Paget Rangers 1
Gloucester City 2, Cinderford Town 0
Newport AFC 2, Witney Town 1
Blakenall bye; Dudley Town withdrew

**SECOND ROUND**
Gloucester City 2, Newport AFC 2
*Replay* Newport AFC 1, Gloucester City 2
Bedworth United 1, Worcester City 0
Crawley Town 0, St Leonards Stamcroft 1
Fisher Athletic 2, Chelmsford City 0
Grantham Town 3, Raunds Town 3
*Replay* Raunds Town 3, Grantham Town 1
Sutton Coldfield Town 4, Blakenall 0
Havant Town 1, Dorchester Town 1
*Replay* Dorchester Town 3, Havant Town 0
Salisbury City 1, Bashley 6
Bath City 1, Newport (IOW) 2
Burton Albion 1, Moor Green 3
Cambridge City 1, Hinckley United 0
Hastings Town 1, Margate 2
Stourbridge 0, Solihull Borough 0
*Replay* Solihull Borough 0, Stourbridge 1
Bilston Town 0, Redditch United 1
Corby Town 1, Ilkeston Town 2
Clevedon Town 4, Forest Green Rovers 1

**THIRD ROUND**
Margate 4, St Leonards Stamcroft 0
Moor Green 1, Sutton Coldfield Town 0
Raunds Town 0, Ilkeston Town 3
Redditch United 1, Stourbridge 0
Bedworth United 0, Gloucester City 3
Dorchester Town 4, Clevedon Town 1
Fisher Athletic 3, Cambridge City 4
Newport (IOW) 0, Bashley 3

**FOURTH ROUND**
Moor Green 3, Ilkeston Town 3
*Replay* Ilkeston Town 4, Moor Green 0
Dorchester Town 1, Bashley 1
*Replay* Bashley 2, Dorchester Town 0
Margate 2, Cambridge City 1
Gloucester City 2, Redditch United 2
*Replay* Redditch United 4, Gloucester City 1

**SEMI-FINALS, FIRST LEG**
Bashley 0, Margate 3
Ilkeston Town 1, Redditch United 0

**SEMI-FINALS, SECOND LEG**
Margate 1, Bashley 2
Redditch United 3, Ilkeston Town 1

**FINAL, FIRST LEG**
Margate 2, Redditch United 0

**FINAL, SECOND LEG**
Redditch United 1, Margate 0

## DR MARTENS LEAGUE — PREMIER DIVISION RESULTS 1997-98

| | Ashford Town | Atherstone United | Bath City | Bromsgrove Rovers | Burton Albion | Cambridge City | Crawley Town | Dorchester Town | Forest Green Rovers | Gloucester City | Gresley Rovers | Halesowen Town | Hastings Town | King's Lynn | Merthyr Tydfil | Nuneaton Borough | Rothwell Town | Salisbury City | Sittingbourne | St Leonards Stamcroft | Tamworth | Worcester City |
|---|---|---|---|---|---|---|---|---|---|---|---|---|---|---|---|---|---|---|---|---|---|---|
| Ashford Town | — | 2-0 | 0-1 | 3-0 | 4-0 | 2-0 | 0-1 | 0-4 | 0-1 | 0-1 | 1-0 | 0-5 | 1-2 | 0-3 | 2-2 | 2-1 | 1-1 | 1-1 | 0-1 | 4-0 | 1-1 | 0-2 |
| Atherstone United | 2-1 | — | 0-0 | 2-1 | 0-1 | 1-2 | 3-0 | 0-0 | 1-1 | 2-2 | 2-3 | 0-0 | 3-1 | 1-1 | 0-2 | 2-2 | 3-1 | 0-3 | 2-1 | 4-0 | 0-0 | 0-2 |
| Bath City | 3-0 | 0-0 | — | 3-1 | 0-0 | 1-1 | 2-1 | 1-0 | 1-1 | 1-0 | 0-0 | 1-3 | 2-2 | 2-0 | 3-0 | 5-0 | 1-1 | 5-0 | 1-0 | 4-0 | 3-3 | 1-0 |
| Bromsgrove Rovers | 3-0 | 0-1 | 0-0 | — | 1-2 | 3-0 | 1-1 | 0-2 | 1-1 | 4-2 | 3-1 | 2-0 | 3-2 | 0-1 | 0-1 | 2-1 | 3-0 | 1-2 | 3-0 | 2-1 | 3-0 | 3-0 |
| Burton Albion | 4-0 | 0-1 | 3-1 | 5-1 | — | 1-3 | 5-2 | 1-2 | 4-1 | 2-1 | 0-1 | 0-0 | 0-1 | 0-0 | 3-0 | 1-0 | 3-0 | 2-2 | 3-2 | 4-0 | 1-0 | 2-0 |
| Cambridge City | 2-0 | 1-2 | 0-1 | 4-0 | 1-2 | — | 3-2 | 1-2 | 1-2 | 1-1 | 0-0 | 0-0 | 2-1 | 2-0 | 0-3 | 3-1 | 3-3 | 3-1 | 2-1 | 2-1 | 2-2 | 1-4 |
| Crawley Town | 1-2 | 3-0 | 2-1 | 4-2 | 3-2 | 0-1 | — | 0-1 | 1-1 | 3-1 | 0-1 | 2-0 | 3-0 | 3-4 | 1-2 | 1-2 | 2-3 | 1-0 | 0-0 | 2-1 | 3-2 | 2-3 |
| Dorchester Town | 5-1 | 0-0 | 2-0 | 4-0 | 1-2 | 0-1 | 3-2 | — | 1-1 | 3-0 | 1-0 | 2-0 | 3-0 | 4-2 | 3-1 | 4-2 | 2-0 | 3-2 | 3-0 | 1-1 | 2-0 | 0-0 |
| Forest Green Rovers | 3-0 | 3-1 | 2-0 | 2-1 | 1-3 | 2-2 | 3-2 | 1-0 | — | 1-1 | 1-0 | 2-0 | 5-2 | 4-2 | 3-1 | 1-0 | 0-1 | 1-1 | 2-1 | 2-2 | 5-0 | 0-0 |
| Gloucester City | 2-3 | 1-2 | 3-5 | 4-2 | 4-2 | 1-1 | 3-2 | 1-0 | 1-4 | — | 1-1 | 1-0 | 1-1 | 3-0 | 1-0 | 1-0 | 0-1 | 1-1 | 2-1 | 1-1 | 1-0 | 2-2 |
| Gresley Rovers | 2-0 | 2-0 | 0-1 | 4-2 | 2-0 | 3-1 | 0-1 | 2-1 | 1-5 | 2-3 | — | 1-1 | 2-1 | 2-4 | 2-0 | 0-1 | 5-2 | 1-1 | 2-1 | 5-1 | 0-3 | 2-0 |
| Halesowen Town | 1-0 | 3-1 | 1-1 | 2-0 | 2-0 | 1-2 | 0-1 | 3-0 | 3-0 | 0-1 | 5-0 | — | 2-1 | 4-1 | 2-2 | 3-0 | 1-3 | 4-1 | 3-1 | 3-0 | 1-1 | 3-1 |
| Hastings Town | 4-1 | 3-1 | 2-2 | 3-2 | 0-1 | 1-2 | 0-1 | 0-2 | 1-1 | 1-1 | 4-1 | 2-2 | — | 3-2 | 0-1 | 2-4 | 3-1 | 2-0 | 3-0 | 1-1 | 2-2 | 3-1 |
| King's Lynn | 2-1 | 1-4 | 2-3 | 3-1 | 2-1 | 2-1 | 1-2 | 2-0 | 0-2 | 1-2 | 1-0 | 0-0 | 1-1 | — | 1-1 | 1-0 | 1-1 | 3-0 | 0-1 | 1-1 | 2-1 | 2-2 |
| Merthyr Tydfil | 3-0 | 1-1 | 3-3 | 4-2 | 2-1 | 2-1 | 2-1 | 4-0 | 4-0 | 1-0 | 3-1 | 1-0 | 2-1 | 4-0 | — | 0-1 | 3-0 | 2-1 | 3-1 | 4-0 | 3-1 | 2-1 |
| Nuneaton Borough | 2-1 | 0-1 | 1-4 | 2-1 | 0-1 | 1-2 | 2-1 | 4-0 | 4-0 | 1-0 | 6-0 | 1-0 | 2-0 | 4-0 | 0-1 | — | 3-0 | 2-1 | 3-1 | 1-1 | 0-2 | 2-0 |
| Rothwell Town | 1-2 | 2-2 | 2-0 | 2-0 | 1-0 | 1-2 | 1-2 | 0-0 | 2-5 | 2-3 | 1-0 | 5-1 | 2-0 | 1-2 | 1-1 | 1-6 | — | 0-0 | 4-0 | 0-0 | 1-0 | 1-1 |
| Salisbury City | 0-0 | 2-1 | 1-1 | 2-0 | 0-3 | 1-1 | 2-6 | 0-3 | 0-2 | 2-3 | 1-0 | 1-1 | 2-0 | 2-2 | 2-5 | 2-2 | 0-0 | — | 4-0 | 0-3 | 3-2 | 1-1 |
| Sittingbourne | 3-2 | 0-2 | 4-2 | 0-2 | 2-2 | 3-1 | 2-1 | 1-0 | 4-5 | 2-0 | 2-3 | 0-0 | 1-0 | 1-0 | 1-2 | 1-0 | 3-2 | 0-0 | — | 1-3 | 0-1 | 0-0 |
| St Leonards Stamcroft | 4-1 | 1-2 | 0-2 | 2-4 | 1-1 | 5-1 | 0-2 | 1-0 | 1-2 | 0-0 | 1-3 | 2-5 | 1-4 | 2-4 | 0-0 | 1-5 | 1-1 | 6-2 | 0-4 | — | 1-2 | 1-1 |
| Tamworth | 4-0 | 0-2 | 1-2 | 2-4 | 1-0 | 2-2 | 2-1 | 3-2 | 1-2 | 1-3 | 6-3 | 0-2 | 1-0 | 3-0 | 2-4 | 2-1 | 1-1 | 1-1 | 4-1 | 1-1 | — | 3-0 |
| Worcester City | 2-1 | 2-1 | 1-1 | 2-0 | 2-1 | 1-1 | 1-3 | 1-0 | 2-3 | 2-1 | 1-0 | 1-1 | 3-1 | 3-1 | 1-1 | 1-0 | 3-0 | 2-0 | 1-0 | 2-0 | 3-1 | — |

## DR MARTENS LEAGUE — MIDLAND DIVISION RESULTS 1997–98

| | Bedworth United | Bilston Town | Blakenall | Brackley Town | Corby Town | Evesham United | Grantham Town | Hinckley United | Ilkeston Town | Moor Green | Paget Rangers | Racing Club Warwick | Raunds Town | Redditch United | Shepshed Dynamo | Solihull Borough | Stafford Rangers | Stourbridge | Sutton Coldfield Town | VS Rugby | Wisbech Town |
|---|---|---|---|---|---|---|---|---|---|---|---|---|---|---|---|---|---|---|---|---|---|
| Bedworth United | — | 4-0 | 0-0 | 1-0 | 0-0 | 0-0 | 1-3 | 1-3 | 0-3 | 0-1 | 1-1 | 1-0 | 0-2 | 3-2 | 2-1 | 1-4 | 0-1 | 3-1 | 3-0 | 3-3 | 2-5 |
| Bilston Town | 3-1 | — | 1-0 | 3-0 | 6-0 | 1-0 | 1-2 | 1-0 | 2-2 | 2-1 | 3-1 | 2-0 | 3-2 | 0-3 | 1-2 | 1-0 | 2-3 | 2-0 | 3-1 | 3-4 | 0-1 |
| Blakenall | 1-1 | 2-1 | — | 1-1 | 4-2 | 5-0 | 1-3 | 2-2 | 2-1 | 2-1 | 2-2 | 2-0 | 1-3 | 1-1 | 4-3 | 2-2 | 4-1 | 3-3 | 2-2 | 3-1 | 1-0 |
| Brackley Town | 0-2 | 2-0 | 4-1 | — | 3-1 | 1-1 | 0-2 | 0-1 | 0-2 | 2-5 | 0-1 | 0-1 | 2-1 | 1-0 | 2-1 | 0-2 | 1-2 | 2-1 | 2-0 | 3-1 | 4-6 |
| Corby Town | 2-4 | 2-2 | 1-2 | 0-2 | — | 4-4 | 1-4 | 0-1 | 1-5 | 1-2 | 2-2 | 2-1 | 1-1 | 0-2 | 1-3 | 1-7 | 1-2 | 1-2 | 2-3 | 1-3 | 0-1 |
| Evesham United | 1-2 | 1-5 | 3-4 | 2-0 | 0-1 | — | 0-2 | 3-1 | 0-5 | 0-2 | 1-1 | 2-1 | 1-0 | 0-2 | 0-0 | 2-4 | 1-0 | 2-3 | 2-4 | 1-3 | 0-1 |
| Grantham Town | 2-0 | 3-1 | 2-1 | 3-1 | 6-5 | 1-0 | — | 1-1 | 6-0 | 2-1 | 3-0 | 1-2 | 1-0 | 1-0 | 4-0 | 2-2 | 1-0 | 1-1 | 1-0 | 2-1 | 3-2 |
| Hinckley United | 2-0 | 4-1 | 1-2 | 0-1 | 0-0 | 4-1 | 1-2 | — | 3-4 | 2-1 | 1-0 | 2-1 | 1-1 | 0-4 | 3-2 | 2-2 | 0-0 | 3-0 | 1-3 | 2-1 | 3-1 |
| Ilkeston Town | 3-1 | 6-0 | 0-1 | 5-1 | 3-0 | 8-1 | 3-2 | 3-0 | — | 1-0 | 5-0 | 2-0 | 3-0 | 2-0 | 1-0 | 2-1 | 2-1 | 3-1 | 3-0 | 11-1 | 3-3 |
| Moor Green | 2-0 | 0-0 | 1-3 | 0-1 | 2-1 | 0-0 | 2-1 | 3-0 | 2-2 | — | 2-4 | 1-0 | 3-0 | 2-0 | 4-0 | 0-3 | 4-3 | 1-1 | 3-0 | 2-2 | 3-2 |
| Paget Rangers | 3-2 | 0-4 | 2-2 | 1-1 | 2-1 | 0-0 | 3-4 | 3-1 | 2-2 | 0-3 | — | 2-3 | 1-5 | 0-2 | 1-3 | 0-3 | 3-1 | 0-0 | 2-0 | 1-0 | 0-3 |
| Racing Club Warwick | 2-0 | 0-2 | 0-0 | 0-0 | 1-1 | 4-0 | 0-1 | 2-2 | 0-0 | 4-1 | 3-0 | — | 2-2 | 0-2 | 2-2 | 0-3 | 0-1 | 1-0 | 1-0 | 0-2 | 4-1 |
| Raunds Town | 7-1 | 3-2 | 2-0 | 3-0 | 3-3 | 4-0 | 3-0 | 2-1 | 1-0 | 2-1 | 1-1 | 1-2 | — | 1-2 | 6-0 | 2-1 | 1-2 | 0-0 | 5-1 | 3-0 | 0-0 |
| Redditch United | 0-2 | 0-1 | 0-1 | 1-1 | 2-0 | 3-1 | 0-2 | 3-1 | 1-1 | 1-1 | 0-0 | 2-0 | 0-1 | — | 3-2 | 1-2 | 0-0 | 3-1 | 5-1 | 3-0 | 0-0 |
| Shepshed Dynamo | 0-1 | 0-4 | 4-1 | 2-0 | 1-0 | 1-1 | 0-5 | 0-0 | 1-2 | 1-3 | 0-0 | 1-1 | 1-5 | 2-1 | — | 3-3 | 2-0 | 0-0 | 0-0 | 2-2 | 2-2 |
| Solihull Borough | 3-0 | 1-2 | 1-0 | 1-1 | 1-0 | 2-0 | 0-5 | 0-0 | 0-4 | 3-2 | 1-3 | 2-0 | 1-1 | 1-2 | 3-1 | — | 2-0 | 3-1 | 2-2 | 4-1 | 4-0 |
| Stafford Rangers | 1-2 | 3-1 | 1-0 | 0-1 | 1-0 | 2-5 | 0-2 | 0-0 | 2-2 | 1-3 | 2-0 | 3-1 | 2-1 | 0-1 | 3-1 | 2-1 | — | 5-1 | 0-3 | 3-2 | 0-2 |
| Stourbridge | 4-1 | 0-2 | 1-2 | 2-0 | 5-0 | 2-3 | 2-0 | 1-0 | 1-5 | 1-1 | 0-0 | 1-0 | 4-1 | 3-3 | 1-2 | 0-1 | 1-2 | — | 1-0 | 4-0 | 1-0 |
| Sutton Coldfield Town | 1-2 | 0-0 | 0-0 | 1-2 | 3-2 | 3-3 | 1-0 | 0-2 | 1-4 | 0-1 | 1-0 | 3-1 | 1-1 | 0-4 | 2-2 | 1-3 | 0-2 | 0-2 | — | 1-3 | 1-1 |
| VS Rugby | 0-1 | 1-1 | 0-0 | 1-1 | 3-0 | 2-2 | 1-3 | 1-1 | 0-7 | 3-3 | 4-1 | 0-5 | 0-1 | 1-1 | 0-5 | 1-3 | 1-1 | 0-1 | 1-1 | — | 0-3 |
| Wisbech Town | 4-0 | 2-0 | 2-1 | 1-0 | 5-0 | 4-3 | 1-1 | 4-2 | 2-5 | 3-0 | 3-0 | 3-1 | 0-1 | 2-1 | 2-2 | 4-0 | 0-2 | 0-1 | 0-1 | 4-1 | — |

## DR MARTENS LEAGUE — SOUTHERN DIVISION RESULTS 1997-98

| | Baldock Town | Bashley | Chelmsford City | Cinderford Town | Cirencester Town | Clevedon Town | Dartford | Erith & Belvedere | Fareham Town | Fisher Athletic London | Fleet Town | Havant Town | Margate | Newport AFC | Newport IOW | Tonbridge Angels | Trowbridge Town | Waterlooville | Weston-Super-Mare | Weymouth | Witney Town | Yate Town |
|---|---|---|---|---|---|---|---|---|---|---|---|---|---|---|---|---|---|---|---|---|---|---|
| Baldock Town | — | 1-2 | 0-2 | 3-2 | 1-4 | 1-3 | 3-1 | 1-2 | 3-1 | 1-2 | 5-0 | 5-3 | 2-0 | 3-1 | 2-1 | 1-0 | 2-0 | 2-1 | 1-2 | 3-1 | 2-3 | 2-0 |
| Bashley | 2-0 | — | 3-2 | 6-1 | 2-1 | 2-0 | 2-2 | 6-2 | 5-0 | 1-2 | 2-1 | 0-2 | 1-1 | 4-2 | 1-1 | 3-1 | 6-1 | 3-0 | 2-1 | 4-1 | 2-0 | 2-1 |
| Chelmsford City | 1-0 | 3-1 | — | 3-0 | 4-1 | 2-0 | 1-4 | 6-0 | 1-0 | 1-2 | 2-2 | 3-3 | 2-2 | 1-2 | 1-4 | 0-2 | 1-1 | 1-2 | 4-0 | 1-2 | 1-2 | 1-2 |
| Cinderford Town | 1-1 | 0-4 | 6-1 | — | 2-5 | 1-2 | 2-0 | 1-2 | 3-3 | 2-2 | 3-0 | 1-2 | 4-0 | 2-1 | 2-3 | 3-0 | 0-0 | 3-1 | 0-2 | 9-0 | 3-1 | 2-1 |
| Cirencester Town | 1-0 | 2-3 | 1-2 | 1-2 | — | 0-1 | 1-1 | 1-1 | 1-0 | 1-2 | 2-1 | 3-1 | 2-3 | 3-1 | 1-0 | 5-1 | 3-1 | 3-1 | 1-3 | 3-1 | 4-2 | 2-2 |
| Clevedon Town | 0-0 | 0-4 | 1-1 | 4-1 | 2-4 | — | 1-3 | 1-1 | 2-0 | 1-0 | 1-0 | 0-3 | 3-1 | 3-2 | 0-2 | 0-2 | 1-3 | 0-1 | 0-0 | 2-0 | 6-1 | 0-2 |
| Dartford | 2-1 | 2-0 | 0-1 | 0-3 | 0-3 | 0-1 | — | 2-1 | 1-1 | 2-1 | 1-3 | 3-2 | 0-1 | 1-1 | 3-1 | 2-1 | 2-1 | 1-2 | 2-1 | 0-0 | 3-1 | 0-1 |
| Erith & Belvedere | 1-2 | 0-3 | 2-2 | 0-1 | 4-0 | 2-1 | 2-1 | — | 1-1 | 3-2 | 2-1 | 3-1 | 1-2 | 2-1 | 2-1 | 1-1 | 1-1 | 5-0 | 1-0 | 1-0 | 1-1 | 2-2 |
| Fareham Town | 6-6 | 5-2 | 2-2 | 7-0 | 5-1 | 2-2 | 1-3 | 0-0 | — | 2-1 | 2-1 | 3-4 | 1-2 | 3-1 | 0-5 | 1-0 | 2-0 | 0-4 | 2-1 | 3-3 | 3-1 | 1-0 |
| Fisher Athletic London | 5-1 | 5-2 | 1-1 | 4-1 | 2-2 | 1-2 | 2-1 | 3-0 | 3-0 | — | 1-1 | 2-2 | 2-2 | 2-3 | 2-1 | 1-0 | 1-1 | 1-1 | 3-3 | 1-2 | 1-2 | 2-0 |
| Fleet Town | 2-1 | 1-2 | 2-2 | 2-3 | 4-1 | 2-0 | 1-3 | 2-2 | 2-2 | 1-1 | — | 2-2 | 0-2 | 1-0 | 4-0 | 1-0 | 1-1 | 1-1 | 5-2 | 0-2 | 3-3 | 1-0 |
| Havant Town | 5-3 | 0-2 | 1-1 | 2-0 | 3-1 | 0-3 | 3-2 | 3-1 | 0-2 | 2-2 | 0-0 | — | 1-0 | 3-2 | 1-4 | 2-3 | 1-0 | 2-1 | 4-0 | 3-1 | 4-3 | 2-2 |
| Margate | 2-0 | 1-1 | 2-2 | 4-0 | 2-3 | 3-1 | 0-1 | 1-2 | 0-2 | 2-2 | 3-0 | 1-0 | — | 2-3 | 0-2 | 3-0 | 5-1 | 2-0 | 1-2 | 2-3 | 3-3 | 0-3 |
| Newport AFC | 3-1 | 4-2 | 1-2 | 2-1 | 3-1 | 3-2 | 1-1 | 2-1 | 7-1 | 1-0 | 1-0 | 3-2 | 2-3 | — | 2-2 | 2-0 | 1-1 | 1-1 | 2-1 | 2-4 | 0-1 | 2-0 |
| Newport IOW | 2-1 | 1-1 | 1-4 | 2-3 | 1-0 | 0-2 | 3-1 | 2-1 | 2-1 | 2-1 | 4-0 | 0-0 | 2-2 | 2-0 | — | 1-0 | 0-0 | 1-0 | 1-1 | 1-3 | 1-1 | 2-1 |
| Tonbridge Angels | 1-0 | 3-1 | 0-2 | 3-0 | 5-1 | 0-2 | 3-0 | 1-1 | 1-1 | 1-0 | 1-3 | 3-0 | 3-0 | 1-0 | 1-0 | — | 2-0 | 2-0 | 1-0 | 2-0 | 3-3 | 1-0 |
| Trowbridge Town | 2-0 | 1-2 | 1-2 | 0-0 | 3-1 | 1-3 | 2-1 | 1-2 | 4-2 | 0-2 | 1-1 | 2-3 | 2-2 | 3-1 | 3-1 | 4-1 | — | 4-2 | 3-2 | 1-2 | 5-3 | 5-1 |
| Waterlooville | 2-1 | 2-1 | 1-2 | 3-1 | 3-1 | 0-1 | 1-2 | 5-0 | 0-4 | 1-1 | 1-1 | 0-3 | 1-1 | 2-0 | 1-0 | 2-0 | 4-0 | — | 1-0 | 4-2 | 0-4 | 2-0 |
| Weston-Super-Mare | 1-2 | 2-1 | 0-3 | 0-2 | 1-3 | 0-0 | 2-1 | 1-0 | 2-1 | 3-3 | 1-2 | 2-4 | 1-2 | 2-1 | 1-1 | 4-0 | 4-0 | 0-1 | — | 4-0 | 3-1 | 2-1 |
| Weymouth | 3-1 | 4-1 | 1-2 | 9-0 | 3-1 | 2-0 | 0-0 | 1-0 | 2-1 | 0-2 | 0-2 | 3-3 | 1-2 | 2-4 | 1-2 | 1-2 | 1-1 | 1-2 | 4-0 | — | 1-2 | 4-2 |
| Witney Town | 0-0 | 4-0 | 0-1 | 3-0 | 4-2 | 6-1 | 3-1 | 1-1 | 3-1 | 2-1 | 3-3 | 1-0 | 3-3 | 1-1 | 1-1 | 1-1 | 5-3 | 0-2 | 3-1 | 1-2 | — | 2-3 |
| Yate Town | 0-1 | 0-5 | 2-3 | 2-1 | 2-2 | 0-2 | 0-1 | 2-2 | 5-0 | 2-0 | 1-0 | 1-2 | 0-3 | 0-2 | 0-3 | 2-1 | 0-1 | 2-2 | 2-1 | 1-2 | 2-3 | — |

# RYMAN FOOTBALL LEAGUE 1997–98

## Premier Division

| | P | Home W | D | L | Away W | D | L | Total W | D | L | Goals F | A | Pts |
|---|---|---|---|---|---|---|---|---|---|---|---|---|---|
| Kingstonian | 42 | 14 | 4 | 3 | 11 | 8 | 2 | 25 | 12 | 5 | 84 | 35 | 87 |
| Boreham Wood | 42 | 11 | 6 | 4 | 12 | 5 | 4 | 23 | 11 | 8 | 81 | 42 | 80 |
| Sutton United | 42 | 14 | 3 | 4 | 8 | 9 | 4 | 22 | 12 | 8 | 83 | 56 | 78 |
| Dagenham & Redbridge | 42 | 11 | 6 | 4 | 10 | 4 | 7 | 21 | 10 | 11 | 73 | 50 | 73 |
| Hendon | 42 | 15 | 2 | 4 | 6 | 8 | 7 | 21 | 10 | 11 | 69 | 50 | 73 |
| Heybridge Swifts | 42 | 9 | 6 | 6 | 9 | 5 | 7 | 18 | 11 | 13 | 74 | 62 | 65 |
| Enfield | 42 | 9 | 4 | 8 | 9 | 4 | 8 | 18 | 8 | 16 | 66 | 58 | 62 |
| Basingstoke Town | 42 | 9 | 6 | 6 | 8 | 5 | 8 | 17 | 11 | 14 | 56 | 60 | 62 |
| Walton & Hersham | 42 | 9 | 6 | 6 | 9 | 0 | 12 | 18 | 6 | 18 | 50 | 70 | 60 |
| Purfleet | 42 | 10 | 4 | 7 | 5 | 9 | 7 | 15 | 13 | 14 | 57 | 58 | 58 |
| St Albans City | 42 | 9 | 3 | 9 | 8 | 4 | 9 | 17 | 7 | 18 | 54 | 59 | 58 |
| Harrow Borough | 42 | 10 | 3 | 8 | 5 | 7 | 9 | 15 | 10 | 17 | 60 | 67 | 55 |
| Gravesend & Northfleet | 42 | 10 | 5 | 6 | 5 | 3 | 13 | 15 | 8 | 19 | 65 | 67 | 53 |
| Chesham United | 42 | 8 | 7 | 6 | 6 | 3 | 12 | 14 | 10 | 18 | 71 | 70 | 52 |
| Bromley | 42 | 7 | 6 | 8 | 6 | 7 | 8 | 13 | 13 | 16 | 53 | 53 | 52 |
| Dulwich Hamlet | 42 | 10 | 3 | 8 | 3 | 8 | 10 | 13 | 11 | 18 | 56 | 67 | 50 |
| Carshalton Athletic | 42 | 7 | 4 | 10 | 6 | 5 | 10 | 13 | 9 | 20 | 54 | 77 | 48 |
| Aylesbury United | 42 | 8 | 6 | 7 | 5 | 2 | 14 | 13 | 8 | 21 | 55 | 70 | 47 |
| Bishop's Stortford | 42 | 9 | 4 | 8 | 5 | 1 | 15 | 14 | 5 | 23 | 53 | 69 | 47 |
| Yeading | 42 | 4 | 7 | 10 | 8 | 4 | 9 | 12 | 11 | 19 | 49 | 65 | 47 |
| Hitchin Town | 42 | 3 | 9 | 9 | 5 | 6 | 10 | 8 | 15 | 19 | 45 | 62 | 39 |
| Oxford City | 42 | 4 | 6 | 11 | 3 | 3 | 15 | 7 | 9 | 26 | 35 | 76 | 30 |

## Division One

| | P | Home W | D | L | Away W | D | L | Total W | D | L | Goals F | A | Pts |
|---|---|---|---|---|---|---|---|---|---|---|---|---|---|
| Aldershot Town | 42 | 16 | 3 | 2 | 12 | 5 | 4 | 28 | 8 | 6 | 89 | 36 | 92 |
| Billericay Town | 42 | 13 | 3 | 5 | 12 | 3 | 6 | 25 | 6 | 11 | 78 | 44 | 81 |
| Hampton | 42 | 13 | 6 | 2 | 9 | 9 | 3 | 22 | 15 | 5 | 75 | 47 | 81 |
| Maidenhead United | 42 | 14 | 3 | 4 | 11 | 2 | 8 | 25 | 5 | 12 | 76 | 37 | 80 |
| Uxbridge Town | 42 | 13 | 5 | 3 | 10 | 1 | 10 | 23 | 6 | 13 | 66 | 59 | 75 |
| Grays Athletic | 42 | 11 | 6 | 4 | 10 | 4 | 7 | 21 | 10 | 11 | 79 | 49 | 73 |
| Romford | 42 | 11 | 4 | 6 | 10 | 4 | 7 | 21 | 8 | 13 | 92 | 59 | 71 |
| Bognor Regis Town | 42 | 12 | 2 | 7 | 8 | 7 | 6 | 20 | 9 | 13 | 77 | 45 | 69 |
| Leatherhead | 42 | 11 | 6 | 4 | 7 | 5 | 9 | 18 | 11 | 13 | 70 | 51 | 65 |
| Leyton Pennant | 42 | 9 | 5 | 7 | 8 | 6 | 7 | 17 | 11 | 14 | 66 | 58 | 62 |
| Chertsey Town | 42 | 8 | 6 | 7 | 8 | 7 | 6 | 16 | 13 | 13 | 83 | 70 | 61 |
| Worthing | 42 | 10 | 4 | 7 | 7 | 2 | 12 | 17 | 6 | 19 | 64 | 71 | 57 |
| Berkhamsted Town | 42 | 9 | 5 | 7 | 6 | 3 | 12 | 15 | 8 | 19 | 59 | 69 | 53 |
| Staines Town | 42 | 8 | 4 | 9 | 5 | 6 | 10 | 13 | 10 | 19 | 54 | 71 | 49 |
| Croydon | 42 | 10 | 4 | 7 | 3 | 6 | 12 | 13 | 10 | 19 | 47 | 64 | 49 |
| Barton Rovers | 42 | 6 | 9 | 6 | 5 | 4 | 12 | 11 | 13 | 18 | 53 | 72 | 46 |
| Wembley | 42 | 5 | 7 | 9 | 5 | 8 | 8 | 10 | 15 | 17 | 38 | 61 | 45 |
| Molesey | 42 | 8 | 4 | 9 | 2 | 7 | 12 | 10 | 11 | 21 | 47 | 65 | 41 |
| Whyteleafe | 42 | 5 | 6 | 10 | 5 | 4 | 12 | 10 | 10 | 22 | 48 | 83 | 40 |
| Wokingham Town | 42 | 5 | 4 | 12 | 2 | 6 | 13 | 7 | 10 | 25 | 41 | 74 | 31 |
| Abingdon Town | 42 | 5 | 2 | 14 | 4 | 2 | 15 | 9 | 4 | 29 | 47 | 101 | 31 |
| Thame United | 42 | 4 | 6 | 11 | 3 | 3 | 15 | 7 | 9 | 26 | 33 | 96 | 30 |

## Division Two

| | P | Home W | D | L | Away W | D | L | Total W | D | L | Goals F | A | Pts |
|---|---|---|---|---|---|---|---|---|---|---|---|---|---|
| Canvey Island | 42 | 17 | 3 | 1 | 13 | 5 | 3 | 30 | 8 | 4 | 116 | 41 | 98 |
| Braintree Town | 42 | 16 | 3 | 2 | 13 | 8 | 0 | 29 | 11 | 2 | 117 | 45 | 98 |
| Wealdstone | 42 | 13 | 6 | 2 | 11 | 5 | 5 | 24 | 11 | 7 | 81 | 46 | 83 |
| Bedford Town | 42 | 13 | 5 | 3 | 9 | 7 | 5 | 22 | 12 | 8 | 55 | 25 | 78 |
| Metropolitan Police | 42 | 12 | 2 | 7 | 9 | 6 | 6 | 21 | 8 | 13 | 80 | 65 | 71 |
| Wivenhoe Town | 42 | 9 | 6 | 6 | 9 | 6 | 6 | 18 | 12 | 12 | 84 | 66 | 66 |
| Edgware Town | 42 | 11 | 4 | 6 | 7 | 6 | 8 | 18 | 10 | 14 | 81 | 65 | 64 |
| Chalfont St Peter | 42 | 9 | 7 | 5 | 8 | 6 | 7 | 17 | 13 | 12 | 63 | 60 | 64 |
| Northwood | 42 | 8 | 7 | 6 | 9 | 4 | 8 | 17 | 11 | 14 | 65 | 69 | 62 |
| Windsor & Eton | 42 | 10 | 4 | 7 | 7 | 3 | 11 | 17 | 7 | 18 | 74 | 72 | 58 |
| Tooting & Mitcham | 42 | 9 | 5 | 7 | 7 | 4 | 10 | 16 | 9 | 17 | 58 | 56 | 57 |
| Barking | 42 | 7 | 6 | 8 | 8 | 6 | 7 | 15 | 12 | 15 | 62 | 75 | 57 |
| Banstead Athletic | 42 | 7 | 6 | 8 | 8 | 3 | 10 | 15 | 9 | 18 | 60 | 63 | 54 |
| Marlow | 42 | 11 | 2 | 8 | 5 | 3 | 13 | 16 | 5 | 21 | 64 | 78 | 53 |
| Horsham | 42 | 8 | 3 | 10 | 5 | 6 | 10 | 13 | 9 | 20 | 67 | 75 | 48 |
| Bracknell Town | 42 | 8 | 4 | 9 | 5 | 4 | 12 | 13 | 8 | 21 | 68 | 93 | 47 |
| Leighton Town | 42 | 8 | 3 | 10 | 5 | 3 | 13 | 13 | 6 | 23 | 45 | 78 | 45 |
| Hungerford Town | 42 | 7 | 5 | 9 | 4 | 6 | 11 | 11 | 11 | 20 | 66 | 77 | 44 |
| Witham Town | 42 | 5 | 7 | 9 | 4 | 6 | 11 | 9 | 13 | 20 | 55 | 68 | 40 |
| Tilbury | 42 | 4 | 9 | 8 | 5 | 3 | 13 | 9 | 12 | 21 | 57 | 88 | 39 |
| Egham Town | 42 | 8 | 4 | 9 | 1 | 1 | 19 | 9 | 5 | 28 | 47 | 101 | 32 |
| Cheshunt | 42 | 1 | 5 | 15 | 3 | 5 | 13 | 4 | 10 | 28 | 31 | 90 | 22 |

## Division Three

| | P | W | D | L | W | D | L | W | D | L | F | A | Pts |
|---|---|---|---|---|---|---|---|---|---|---|---|---|---|
| | | Home | | | Away | | | Total | | | Goals | | |
| Hemel Hempstead | 38 | 15 | 3 | 1 | 12 | 3 | 4 | 27 | 6 | 5 | 86 | 28 | 87 |
| Hertford Town | 38 | 13 | 4 | 2 | 13 | 1 | 5 | 26 | 5 | 7 | 77 | 31 | 83 |
| Harlow Town | 38 | 10 | 6 | 3 | 14 | 5 | 0 | 24 | 11 | 3 | 81 | 43 | 83 |
| Camberley Town | 38 | 13 | 1 | 5 | 11 | 6 | 2 | 24 | 7 | 7 | 93 | 43 | 79 |
| Ford United | 38 | 11 | 5 | 3 | 12 | 4 | 3 | 23 | 9 | 6 | 90 | 34 | 78 |
| East Thurrock United | 38 | 11 | 3 | 5 | 12 | 4 | 3 | 23 | 7 | 8 | 70 | 40 | 76 |
| Epsom & Ewell | 38 | 10 | 2 | 7 | 7 | 4 | 8 | 17 | 6 | 15 | 69 | 57 | 57 |
| Ware | 38 | 9 | 2 | 8 | 8 | 4 | 7 | 17 | 6 | 15 | 69 | 57 | 57 |
| Aveley | 38 | 10 | 3 | 6 | 6 | 4 | 9 | 16 | 7 | 15 | 65 | 57 | 55 |
| Corinthian-Casuals | 38 | 7 | 3 | 9 | 9 | 3 | 7 | 16 | 6 | 16 | 59 | 57 | 54 |
| Hornchurch | 38 | 6 | 7 | 6 | 6 | 2 | 11 | 12 | 9 | 17 | 55 | 68 | 45 |
| Clapton | 38 | 8 | 4 | 7 | 5 | 2 | 12 | 13 | 6 | 19 | 46 | 61 | 45 |
| Flackwell Heath | 38 | 7 | 4 | 8 | 5 | 5 | 9 | 12 | 9 | 17 | 50 | 76 | 45 |
| Croydon Athletic | 38 | 8 | 3 | 8 | 4 | 4 | 11 | 12 | 7 | 19 | 58 | 63 | 43 |
| Tring Town | 38 | 5 | 5 | 9 | 7 | 2 | 10 | 12 | 7 | 19 | 51 | 69 | 43 |
| Southall | 38 | 7 | 3 | 9 | 3 | 3 | 13 | 10 | 6 | 22 | 41 | 85 | 36 |
| Dorking | 38 | 7 | 4 | 8 | 2 | 2 | 15 | 9 | 6 | 23 | 49 | 94 | 33 |
| Wingate & Finchley | 38 | 4 | 3 | 12 | 3 | 5 | 11 | 7 | 8 | 23 | 46 | 80 | 29 |
| Lewes | 38 | 7 | 1 | 11 | 0 | 4 | 15 | 7 | 5 | 26 | 34 | 88 | 26 |
| Kingsbury Town | 38 | 3 | 2 | 14 | 2 | 1 | 16 | 5 | 3 | 30 | 35 | 93 | 18 |

## LEADING GOALSCORERS

| **Premier Division** | | Lge | GIC | PC |
|---|---|---|---|---|
| 37 | Shaun Marshall (Boreham Wood) | 30 | 6 | 1 |
| 33 | Joff Vansittart (Sutton United) | 22 | 11 | 1 |
| 30 | Steve Portway (Gravesend & Northfleet) | 27 | 2 | 1 |
| | *(includes 2 league and 1 GIC goals for Purfleet)* | | | |
| 28 | Paul Cobb (Dagenham & Redbridge) | 24 | 2 | 2 |
| 25 | David Leworthy (Kingstonian) | 22 | 1 | 2 |
| 21 | Andy Sayer (Walton & Hersham) | 21 | | |
| | Steve Clark (St Albans City) | 19 | 2 | |

| **Division One** | | | | |
|---|---|---|---|---|
| 36 | Leon Gutzmore (Billericay Town) | 34 | 2 | |
| 30 | Adie Miles (Bognor Regis Town) | 24 | 4 | 2 |
| 29 | Wade Falana (Romford) | 25 | 4 | |
| | *(includes 6 league goals for Harlow Town)* | | | |
| 27 | Vinny John (Romford) | 27 | | |
| 24 | Steve Lunn (Leatherhead) | 22 | | 2 |
| 23 | Roy Young (Aldershot) | 20 | 3 | |

| **Division Two** | | | | VT |
|---|---|---|---|---|
| 39 | Gary Bennett (Braintree Town) | 36 | 3 | |
| 30 | Andy Jones (Canvey Island) | 27 | 1 | 2 |
| 25 | Simon Liddle (Canvey Island) | 19 | 3 | 3 |
| 24 | Jason Prins (Metropolitan Police) | 24 | | |

| **Division Three** | | | | |
|---|---|---|---|---|
| 33 | Jeff Wood (Ford United) | 30 | 1 | 2 |
| 26 | Josh Price (Hemel Hempstead) | 24 | 2 | |
| 23 | Ian Jopling (Camberley Town) | 22 | 1 | |
| | Tim Sills (Camberley Town) | 21 | 2 | |

Lge: Ryman League; GIC: Guardian Insurance Cup; PC: Puma Cup; VT: Vandanel Trophy

## ATTENDANCES

**Premier Divison**
Aggregate: 206,753
Highest Individual crowd: 2019 Kingstonian v Sutton United

**Division One**
Aggregate: 142,581
Highest Individual crowd: 4289 Aldershot Town v Berkhamsted Town

**Division Two**
Aggregate: 78,171
Highest Individual crowd: 1108 Canvey Island v Braintree Town

**Division Three**
Aggregate: 28,949
Highest Individual crowd: 480 Hertford Town v Ware

## PREVIOUS SEASONS

| SEASON | CLUBS | GAMES | AGG | AVE |
|---|---|---|---|---|
| 1988–1989 | 86 | 1764 | 323,197 | 183 |
| 1989–1990 | 87 | 1806 | 387,441 | 215 |
| 1990–1991 | 88 | 1848 | 404,703 | 219 |
| 1991–1992 | 86 | 1764 | 397,553 | 225 |
| 1992–1993 | 85 | 1724 | 430,518 | 247 |
| 1993–1994 | 87 | 1806 | 423,306 | 234 |
| 1994–1995 | 87 | 1806 | 433,703 | 240 |
| 1995–1996 | 86 | 1764 | 440,285 | 250 |
| 1996–1997 | 83 | 1658 | 461,944 | 278 |
| 1997–1998 | 86 | 1766 | 456,454 | 258 |

## RYMAN FOOTBALL LEAGUE—PREMIER DIVISION RESULTS 1997-98

| | AYL | BAS | BIS | BOR | BRO | CAR | CHE | DAG | DUL | ENF | GRA | HAR | HEN | HEY | HIT | KIN | OXF | PUR | STA | SUT | WAL | YEA |
|---|---|---|---|---|---|---|---|---|---|---|---|---|---|---|---|---|---|---|---|---|---|---|
| Aylesbury United | — | 1-2 | 2-0 | 2-2 | 1-2 | 4-1 | 0-0 | 1-2 | 0-0 | 1-1 | 0-2 | 1-0 | 3-0 | 1-3 | 1-0 | 2-0 | 4-1 | 0-2 | 1-2 | 1-1 | 4-0 | 1-1 |
| Basingstoke Town | 1-0 | — | 3-1 | 2-2 | 0-3 | 1-2 | 2-0 | 1-2 | 4-3 | 0-0 | 2-1 | 2-2 | 1-1 | 2-0 | 3-0 | 0-0 | 2-1 | 0-2 | 3-1 | 1-1 | 1-2 | 1-2 |
| Bishop's Stortford | 1-0 | 1-0 | — | 3-1 | 2-0 | 4-3 | 4-2 | 1-1 | 1-1 | 0-2 | 1-2 | 1-2 | 1-2 | 2-2 | 0-2 | 0-1 | 0-1 | 2-0 | 1-0 | 0-1 | 3-1 | 2-1 |
| Boreham Wood | 2-1 | 5-0 | 1-0 | — | 0-0 | 2-2 | 3-1 | 0-0 | 4-0 | 2-1 | 4-1 | 2-2 | 1-2 | 2-3 | 0-0 | 0-1 | 3-1 | 3-1 | 2-3 | 2-2 | 3-0 | 3-1 |
| Bromley | 3-0 | 0-2 | 3-2 | 0-0 | — | 3-0 | 1-2 | 2-0 | 1-1 | 3-1 | 2-0 | 2-1 | 0-0 | 2-2 | 0-0 | 0-2 | 1-2 | 2-3 | 1-1 | 1-1 | 0-1 | 0-2 |
| Carshalton Athletic | 2-3 | 0-1 | 1-2 | 0-2 | 3-0 | — | 0-1 | 0-2 | 3-3 | 2-0 | 2-0 | 1-5 | 3-1 | 1-1 | 1-2 | 1-1 | 2-0 | 1-0 | 0-2 | 1-5 | 1-2 | 1-0 |
| Chesham United | 4-2 | 0-1 | 1-1 | 1-1 | 2-3 | 3-0 | — | 0-0 | 5-1 | 2-0 | 4-2 | 1-5 | 3-1 | 1-1 | 3-3 | 1-1 | 6-0 | 1-1 | 1-2 | 3-3 | 2-0 | 3-1 |
| Dagenham & Redbridge | 2-3 | 0-1 | 2-1 | 1-1 | 2-0 | 3-0 | 2-0 | — | 2-1 | 0-2 | 2-0 | 1-2 | 1-1 | 6-2 | 1-0 | 2-2 | 7-0 | 2-2 | 1-1 | 0-2 | 4-2 | 1-1 |
| Dulwich Hamlet | 2-1 | 0-1 | 5-0 | 0-1 | 3-3 | 0-3 | 3-1 | 0-2 | — | 2-0 | 1-1 | 1-2 | 1-2 | 1-2 | 2-2 | 2-2 | 3-2 | 2-1 | 1-2 | 1-0 | 1-3 | 2-1 |
| Enfield | 2-1 | 2-1 | 4-1 | 1-1 | 1-1 | 3-0 | 0-1 | 1-2 | 2-0 | — | 1-2 | 3-3 | 3-3 | 4-2 | 2-1 | 0-1 | 2-0 | 0-0 | 0-2 | 0-2 | 3-0 | 2-0 |
| Gravesend & Northfleet | 6-0 | 3-0 | 1-2 | 1-1 | 1-0 | 3-3 | 3-2 | 2-2 | 2-0 | 1-3 | — | 3-0 | 4-0 | 1-0 | 2-0 | 1-2 | 3-2 | 0-0 | 2-1 | 2-2 | 1-2 | 1-2 |
| Harrow Borough | 1-1 | 2-0 | 3-0 | 1-0 | 2-3 | 1-3 | 1-0 | 0-5 | 2-0 | 2-1 | 2-1 | — | 0-0 | 0-2 | 1-1 | 0-2 | 0-3 | 3-0 | 1-0 | 0-2 | 2-0 | 2-1 |
| Hendon | 3-0 | 2-1 | 3-0 | 2-1 | 1-0 | 4-0 | 1-2 | 3-0 | 2-0 | 0-3 | 0-0 | 2-1 | — | 0-2 | 1-2 | 1-1 | 1-0 | 1-1 | 2-1 | 4-2 | 4-0 | 1-0 |
| Heybridge Swifts | 5-1 | 5-1 | 1-0 | 2-1 | 2-2 | 0-0 | 0-3 | 2-5 | 3-1 | 4-1 | 2-2 | 0-2 | 1-1 | — | 1-2 | 1-3 | 3-0 | 0-1 | 3-2 | 1-1 | 0-1 | 2-2 |
| Hitchin Town | 2-3 | 1-2 | 1-0 | 0-2 | 1-1 | 1-2 | 1-2 | 0-1 | 2-0 | 1-1 | 4-0 | 2-2 | 1-1 | 1-2 | — | 0-0 | 0-0 | 3-3 | 1-1 | 0-3 | 1-0 | 0-2 |
| Kingstonian | 3-0 | 2-0 | 1-0 | 2-5 | 4-1 | 5-1 | 3-1 | 0-2 | 2-1 | 0-0 | 3-1 | 5-2 | 2-1 | 3-0 | 2-0 | — | 0-0 | 2-2 | 5-0 | 0-0 | 7-0 | 0-1 |
| Oxford City | 2-2 | 0-1 | 1-0 | 0-1 | 1-1 | 1-1 | 2-1 | 2-0 | 0-1 | 1-2 | 2-1 | 2-4 | 0-2 | 0-2 | 2-2 | 0-1 | — | 0-0 | 0-0 | 1-2 | 0-1 | 0-3 |
| Purfleet | 0-2 | 1-2 | 3-1 | 0-2 | 3-0 | 1-2 | 3-2 | 2-0 | 1-0 | 4-0 | 2-0 | 2-2 | 1-0 | 0-3 | 1-0 | 0-1 | 2-1 | — | 0-1 | 0-6 | 1-0 | 1-3 |
| St Albans City | 1-3 | 2-2 | 3-1 | 0-2 | 2-4 | 3-0 | 3-0 | 2-1 | 3-0 | 0-4 | 0-1 | 0-0 | 1-2 | 0-3 | 4-1 | 0-3 | 4-1 | 3-2 | — | 4-2 | 1-0 | 0-1 |
| Sutton United | 3-0 | 1-1 | 2-4 | 1-2 | 1-0 | 3-4 | 2-4 | 2-1 | 1-1 | 0-5 | 3-1 | 2-1 | 2-1 | 4-1 | 2-0 | 3-3 | 2-1 | 3-0 | 3-1 | — | 2-0 | 1-1 |
| Walton & Hersham | 3-0 | 1-1 | 3-0 | 1-4 | 0-2 | 3-4 | 1-1 | 1-4 | 2-4 | 3-1 | 0-1 | 0-0 | 2-2 | 1-0 | 2-1 | 1-4 | 1-0 | 2-4 | 1-0 | 1-1 | — | 1-1 |
| Yeading | 1-0 | 2-2 | 0-2 | 0-1 | 1-1 | 0-0 | 2-0 | 2-2 | 2-2 | 0-2 | 4-3 | 2-2 | 0-2 | 0-3 | 1-2 | 1-3 | 1-1 | 0-0 | 0-2 | 3-1 | 2-4 | — |

## RYMAN FOOTBALL LEAGUE—DIVISION ONE RESULTS 1997–98

| | Abingdon Town | Aldershot Town | Barton Rovers | Berkhamsted Town | Billericay Town | Bognor Regis Town | Chertsey Town | Croydon | Grays Athletic | Hampton | Leatherhead | Leyton Pennant | Maidenhead United | Molesey | Romford | Staines Town | Thame United | Uxbridge | Wembley | Whyteleafe | Wokingham Town | Worthing |
|---|---|---|---|---|---|---|---|---|---|---|---|---|---|---|---|---|---|---|---|---|---|---|
| Abingdon Town | — | 0-2 | 3-3 | 0-2 | 0-1 | 1-3 | 0-2 | 1-2 | 0-2 | 0-2 | 1-2 | 0-4 | 1-4 | 0-3 | 1-6 | 2-0 | 1-0 | 1-2 | 2-0 | 1-0 | 2-2 | 3-0 |
| Aldershot Town | 3-1 | — | 1-0 | 3-0 | 2-0 | 1-1 | 0-1 | 1-1 | 2-1 | 2-0 | 1-0 | 8-1 | 0-2 | 3-1 | 2-0 | 2-0 | 1-1 | 4-0 | 3-1 | 3-0 | 4-0 | 3-1 |
| Barton Rovers | 1-2 | 1-1 | — | 2-2 | 2-0 | 1-1 | 0-0 | 1-0 | 1-2 | 1-1 | 4-4 | 0-0 | 1-0 | 3-0 | 2-4 | 0-0 | 3-0 | 0-1 | 0-0 | 3-0 | 0-3 | 1-4 |
| Berkhamsted Town | 0-1 | 4-2 | 1-0 | — | 1-5 | 3-2 | 3-1 | 1-0 | 1-0 | 1-2 | 2-1 | 3-3 | 5-0 | 2-2 | 2-4 | 4-2 | 3-3 | 0-2 | 1-2 | 1-3 | 1-1 | 0-0 |
| Billericay Town | 3-1 | 1-2 | 4-0 | 1-1 | — | 0-2 | 1-5 | 2-1 | 2-1 | 1-2 | 1-0 | 1-2 | 0-2 | 2-1 | 2-1 | 2-0 | 4-0 | 1-1 | 4-0 | 4-1 | 3-0 | 4-0 |
| Bognor Regis Town | 7-0 | 1-2 | 4-0 | 0-0 | 4-2 | — | 2-3 | 0-1 | 2-0 | 1-2 | 2-0 | 0-2 | 2-1 | 4-1 | 3-0 | 1-1 | 4-0 | 2-1 | 1-2 | 2-0 | 3-0 | 1-2 |
| Chertsey Town | 1-1 | 2-0 | 3-2 | 4-2 | 1-3 | 1-1 | — | 5-1 | 3-3 | 1-1 | 3-4 | 1-1 | 0-2 | 1-1 | 2-4 | 4-0 | 3-0 | 1-3 | 4-1 | 1-3 | 4-1 | 1-4 |
| Croydon | 3-1 | 2-1 | 3-5 | 1-0 | 1-3 | 0-0 | 5-1 | — | 1-2 | 2-1 | 3-2 | 2-1 | 2-1 | 0-0 | 1-2 | 1-2 | 1-1 | 0-1 | 0-1 | 1-0 | 2-0 | 1-0 |
| Grays Athletic | 7-1 | 2-1 | 2-2 | 2-0 | 2-1 | 2-2 | 3-0 | 1-1 | — | 1-2 | 3-1 | 1-2 | 1-0 | 2-0 | 2-2 | 0-1 | 2-0 | 2-3 | 2-0 | 1-1 | 1-1 | 1-0 |
| Hampton | 4-2 | 1-1 | 1-2 | 3-2 | 0-2 | 2-1 | 2-2 | 2-2 | 1-2 | — | 2-0 | 3-1 | 1-0 | 1-0 | 1-0 | 3-1 | 4-1 | 1-0 | 1-1 | 2-1 | 3-3 | 2-0 |
| Leatherhead | 3-4 | 0-0 | 2-0 | 3-0 | 1-1 | 0-0 | 3-0 | 1-1 | 2-2 | 0-0 | — | 1-2 | 2-1 | 1-0 | 3-1 | 1-0 | 1-2 | 5-2 | 0-0 | 2-0 | 2-1 | 5-1 |
| Leyton Pennant | 2-1 | 3-3 | 2-0 | 0-1 | 2-3 | 0-0 | 1-1 | 2-0 | 1-1 | 1-0 | 1-3 | — | 1-2 | 3-1 | 3-1 | 1-2 | 4-1 | 4-0 | 2-1 | 1-1 | 2-2 | 1-3 |
| Maidenhead United | 2-1 | 0-2 | 3-0 | 2-1 | 1-0 | 1-0 | 4-1 | 6-1 | 0-1 | 1-1 | 2-1 | 0-0 | — | 1-1 | 1-3 | 3-0 | 5-0 | 2-1 | 4-0 | 5-0 | 2-1 | 1-2 |
| Molesey | 1-0 | 0-1 | 2-1 | 0-1 | 1-0 | 2-3 | 2-4 | 3-2 | 3-3 | 1-1 | 1-0 | 0-1 | 0-3 | — | 1-1 | 3-2 | 2-3 | 2-3 | 0-0 | 0-0 | 1-0 | 1-0 |
| Romford | 3-2 | 1-2 | 6-1 | 2-1 | 2-3 | 5-0 | 2-2 | 3-2 | 1-4 | 0-1 | 1-0 | 0-1 | 0-1 | 0-0 | — | 2-1 | 3-1 | 3-1 | 1-2 | 1-0 | 1-0 | 4-0 |
| Staines Town | 2-1 | 2-5 | 2-3 | 3-2 | 1-2 | 1-2 | 2-2 | 3-1 | 2-0 | 2-2 | 1-1 | 1-0 | 0-4 | 2-3 | 1-4 | — | 4-1 | 0-1 | 1-1 | 3-1 | 3-0 | 1-1 |
| Thame United | 3-0 | 1-4 | 1-1 | 0-1 | 0-3 | 3-0 | 0-1 | 1-2 | 3-2 | 0-5 | 0-3 | 0-0 | 0-0 | 2-1 | 0-1 | 1-1 | — | 0-1 | 1-1 | 0-2 | 0-0 | 3-2 |
| Uxbridge | 5-2 | 1-2 | 2-1 | 3-1 | 0-0 | 2-1 | 1-1 | 2-1 | 3-2 | 1-2 | 1-1 | 1-0 | 1-1 | 1-0 | 3-2 | 0-0 | 3-1 | — | 3-0 | 1-3 | 1-0 | 2-1 |
| Wembley | 1-0 | 0-1 | 0-1 | 1-0 | 1-0 | 0-5 | 2-2 | 0-0 | 0-1 | 1-3 | 1-1 | 2-3 | 0-2 | 1-1 | 3-3 | 0-0 | 5-0 | 1-3 | — | 0-0 | 2-1 | 1-3 |
| Whyteleafe | 0-3 | 0-4 | 1-1 | 0-1 | 1-3 | 2-2 | 4-1 | 2-1 | 0-3 | 1-1 | 0-3 | 3-5 | 1-2 | 2-2 | 2-8 | 2-2 | 4-0 | 3-2 | 0-0 | — | 2-1 | 0-1 |
| Wokingham Town | 1-1 | 0-3 | 4-0 | 0-1 | 0-1 | 0-2 | 1-1 | 1-1 | 1-2 | 3-4 | 2-2 | 2-1 | 0-1 | 2-1 | 1-1 | 1-3 | 0-1 | 2-1 | 0-2 | 1-2 | — | 2-1 |
| Worthing | 7-2 | 2-2 | 0-2 | 3-1 | 1-1 | 0-2 | 2-1 | 2-0 | 1-7 | 2-2 | 0-3 | 1-0 | 2-1 | 4-1 | 0-4 | 0-1 | 3-1 | 3-0 | 1-1 | 4-0 | 0-1 | — |

## RYMAN FOOTBALL LEAGUE—DIVISION TWO RESULTS 1997-98

| | Banstead Athletic | Barking | Bedford Town | Bracknell Town | Braintree Town | Canvey Island | Chalfont St Peter | Cheshunt | Edgware Town | Egham Town | Horsham | Hungerford Town | Leighton Town | Marlow | Metropolitan Police | Northwood | Tilbury | Tooting & Mitcham United | Wealdstone | Windsor & Eton | Witham Town | Wivenhoe Town |
|---|---|---|---|---|---|---|---|---|---|---|---|---|---|---|---|---|---|---|---|---|---|---|
| Banstead Athletic | — | 1-2 | 0-2 | 3-1 | 0-0 | 2-2 | 1-2 | 3-2 | 2-2 | 1-0 | 1-2 | 0-4 | 1-3 | 1-2 | 3-1 | 1-1 | 5-2 | 1-1 | 4-1 | 2-1 | 0-0 | 1-3 |
| Barking | 3-1 | — | 1-2 | 3-3 | 1-3 | 0-4 | 1-1 | 0-0 | 0-0 | 2-1 | 0-1 | 4-2 | 0-1 | 1-0 | 0-2 | 1-1 | 0-3 | 1-2 | 2-1 | 3-0 | 2-2 | 4-3 |
| Bedford Town | 2-0 | 2-0 | — | 1-1 | 0-1 | 2-3 | 0-0 | 3-1 | 3-2 | 2-0 | 0-0 | 2-0 | 1-0 | 0-1 | 1-0 | 4-0 | 3-0 | 2-0 | 0-0 | 3-0 | 1-0 | 1-1 |
| Bracknell Town | 1-0 | 1-2 | 2-0 | — | 1-4 | 1-1 | 1-2 | 1-1 | 0-0 | 3-1 | 3-2 | 4-1 | 1-2 | 3-2 | 2-0 | 2-4 | 1-2 | 1-2 | 3-4 | 5-3 | 1-1 | 1-8 |
| Braintree Town | 4-0 | 1-1 | 3-0 | 4-2 | — | 2-1 | 4-1 | 0-1 | 1-1 | 4-1 | 5-1 | 3-1 | 4-0 | 5-3 | 7-0 | 4-0 | 4-1 | 3-0 | 0-1 | 3-0 | 1-0 | 4-4 |
| Canvey Island | 1-2 | 6-0 | 1-0 | 5-1 | 1-1 | — | 4-0 | 3-0 | 3-2 | 6-1 | 2-0 | 7-2 | 2-0 | 3-1 | 1-1 | 4-0 | 5-1 | 3-0 | 2-0 | 5-1 | 3-0 | 3-3 |
| Chalfont St Peter | 2-1 | 2-2 | 0-0 | 5-5 | 1-4 | 0-5 | — | 0-0 | 0-3 | 4-2 | 1-0 | 1-2 | 2-0 | 3-5 | 1-1 | 4-0 | 1-1 | 2-0 | 1-1 | 4-0 | 0-1 | 2-0 |
| Cheshunt | 0-1 | 1-2 | 0-1 | 1-0 | 1-2 | 1-2 | 0-2 | — | 2-2 | 0-3 | 0-0 | 2-3 | 1-1 | 3-5 | 0-3 | 0-0 | 0-2 | 0-3 | 0-2 | 0-3 | 0-0 | 0-2 |
| Edgware Town | 2-0 | 2-2 | 0-0 | 2-0 | 0-2 | 3-0 | 2-1 | 8-0 | — | 3-1 | 5-2 | 2-1 | 1-2 | 3-2 | 3-4 | 3-1 | 2-1 | 2-1 | 0-2 | 0-4 | 1-2 | 2-1 |
| Egham Town | 0-4 | 1-0 | 1-2 | 0-1 | 1-1 | 4-3 | 0-2 | 1-0 | 1-0 | — | 3-2 | 2-0 | 0-0 | 3-0 | 0-3 | 2-0 | 2-2 | 1-4 | 3-5 | 0-1 | 1-2 | 2-2 |
| Horsham | 0-4 | 1-2 | 1-0 | 0-1 | 1-1 | 0-3 | 2-2 | 2-3 | 1-3 | 2-0 | — | 1-1 | 4-0 | 3-0 | 0-2 | 0-1 | 5-2 | 2-1 | 0-2 | 3-0 | 3-1 | 0-1 |
| Hungerford Town | 4-1 | 0-2 | 1-1 | 1-2 | 2-3 | 1-1 | 1-1 | 1-0 | 1-0 | 7-1 | 2-4 | — | 4-0 | 1-2 | 1-3 | 1-3 | 2-0 | 1-3 | 1-1 | 1-2 | 3-1 | 2-2 |
| Leighton Town | 0-2 | 2-2 | 0-0 | 1-0 | 0-4 | 2-4 | 2-0 | 3-2 | 0-3 | 2-0 | 2-1 | 2-1 | — | 2-1 | 1-3 | 1-3 | 2-3 | 1-3 | 0-1 | 1-1 | 2-0 | 1-3 |
| Marlow | 0-3 | 5-2 | 2-0 | 2-1 | 1-3 | 1-3 | 1-3 | 3-1 | 1-3 | 2-1 | 2-2 | 1-1 | 2-0 | — | 2-1 | 1-2 | 1-0 | 2-1 | 0-2 | 4-1 | 4-2 | 0-1 |
| Metropolitan Police | 3-1 | 5-1 | 0-1 | 5-0 | 4-4 | 1-2 | 1-4 | 3-1 | 2-2 | 1-0 | 1-7 | 4-2 | 3-0 | 3-2 | — | 2-1 | 2-0 | 4-3 | 1-0 | 0-2 | 2-1 | 1-2 |
| Northwood | 3-1 | 1-1 | 0-3 | 2-1 | 1-2 | 1-2 | 3-1 | 6-0 | 1-0 | 2-1 | 2-2 | 1-1 | 2-1 | 1-1 | 3-3 | — | 4-2 | 0-1 | 0-0 | 1-4 | 1-2 | 0-3 |
| Tilbury | 0-0 | 2-1 | 1-1 | 3-4 | 1-4 | 1-2 | 1-2 | 2-1 | 3-4 | 1-1 | 1-1 | 1-0 | 3-2 | 1-1 | 2-2 | 1-2 | — | 1-1 | 1-2 | 0-0 | 2-2 | 1-3 |
| Tooting & Mitcham United | 2-0 | 1-1 | 0-0 | 2-3 | 1-1 | 0-1 | 0-3 | 1-2 | 3-0 | 4-0 | 1-2 | 1-1 | 3-0 | 2-0 | 1-0 | 0-1 | 1-2 | — | 2-2 | 2-1 | 1-0 | 1-0 |
| Wealdstone | 1-1 | 4-2 | 0-1 | 2-0 | 1-1 | 1-1 | 2-0 | 5-1 | 3-1 | 4-2 | 4-2 | 3-1 | 2-1 | 5-0 | 0-2 | 1-1 | 3-1 | 2-0 | — | 2-0 | 1-1 | 1-1 |
| Windsor & Eton | 0-2 | 2-3 | 0-4 | 4-2 | 3-3 | 0-3 | 3-0 | 3-0 | 2-3 | 7-1 | 1-0 | 0-0 | 2-2 | 2-1 | 1-1 | 2-4 | 5-0 | 1-0 | 1-2 | — | 3-1 | 5-1 |
| Witham Town | 1-1 | 1-2 | 1-1 | 3-0 | 2-3 | 1-2 | 1-1 | 1-1 | 2-4 | 3-1 | 3-3 | 1-2 | 0-2 | 0-1 | 1-2 | 1-2 | 2-1 | 5-2 | 3-4 | 0-0 | — | 2-1 |
| Wivenhoe Town | 0-2 | 1-3 | 1-3 | 2-2 | 2-3 | 1-1 | 1-1 | 1-0 | 3-1 | 2-2 | 6-2 | 2-2 | 3-1 | 0-0 | 0-2 | 3-1 | 2-2 | 2-1 | 2-1 | 0-3 | 2-1 | — |

## RYMAN FOOTBALL LEAGUE—DIVISION THREE RESULTS 1997-98

| | Aveley | Camberley Town | Clapton | Corinthian-Casuals | Croydon Athletic | Dorking | East Thurrock United | Epsom & Ewell | Flackwell Heath | Ford United | Harlow Town | Hemel Hempstead | Hertford Town | Hornchurch | Kingsbury Town | Lewes | Southall | Tring Town | Ware | Wingate & Finchley |
|---|---|---|---|---|---|---|---|---|---|---|---|---|---|---|---|---|---|---|---|---|
| Aveley | — | 1-3 | 3-0 | 2-1 | 2-0 | 2-0 | 0-1 | 1-2 | 1-3 | 2-2 | 3-4 | 2-0 | 3-0 | 2-0 | 2-1 | 1-1 | 1-0 | 1-1 | 0-1 | 2-0 |
| Camberley Town | 1-3 | — | 3-0 | 0-1 | 4-2 | 7-2 | 0-2 | 1-1 | 4-0 | 1-2 | 2-3 | 2-1 | 1-0 | 4-0 | 2-1 | 5-0 | 2-1 | 6-0 | 1-0 | 2-0 |
| Clapton | 0-3 | 3-0 | — | 3-3 | 1-3 | 1-0 | 0-1 | 0-1 | 2-2 | 1-3 | 4-5 | 2-0 | 1-0 | 1-0 | 2-1 | 3-0 | 1-0 | 1-0 | 0-2 | 3-0 |
| Corinthian-Casuals | 3-1 | 1-3 | 3-3 | — | 3-2 | 3-0 | 0-0 | 4-2 | 1-1 | 0-2 | 1-3 | 0-3 | 2-4 | 0-2 | 3-0 | 1-1 | 3-0 | 2-4 | 3-2 | 2-0 |
| Croydon Athletic | 3-2 | 1-4 | 2-0 | 3-2 | — | 7-1 | 1-2 | 5-2 | 2-1 | 0-1 | 1-1 | 0-0 | 0-3 | 2-1 | 2-1 | 3-1 | 1-2 | 1-4 | 2-2 | 5-1 |
| Dorking | 3-2 | 1-4 | 1-0 | 7-1 | 2-1 | — | 1-4 | 4-3 | 0-3 | 3-3 | 1-2 | 0-2 | 0-3 | 0-5 | 1-2 | 3-1 | 1-2 | 2-3 | 2-2 | 1-2 |
| East Thurrock United | 1-1 | 1-0 | 1-0 | 0-0 | 1-4 | 3-0 | — | 3-1 | 1-0 | 1-0 | 2-3 | 2-1 | 0-0 | 2-1 | 2-0 | 3-0 | 2-1 | 3-0 | 3-1 | 0-2 |
| Epsom & Ewell | 4-2 | 1-0 | 0-1 | 0-1 | 5-2 | 2-1 | 7-2 | — | 1-0 | 0-1 | 1-3 | 1-3 | 1-2 | 2-2 | 3-0 | 4-0 | 1-1 | 1-2 | 1-2 | 2-0 |
| Flackwell Heath | 1-1 | 1-3 | 1-1 | 3-1 | 0-3 | 4-1 | 1-1 | 6-1 | — | 2-3 | 1-1 | 0-6 | 3-2 | 2-3 | 8-0 | 2-1 | 6-0 | 2-1 | 0-2 | 1-1 |
| Ford United | 1-1 | 2-0 | 6-0 | 0-0 | 0-1 | 3-1 | 2-0 | 1-1 | 8-0 | — | 1-3 | 0-1 | 0-1 | 3-1 | 2-0 | 5-0 | 2-1 | 3-2 | 3-0 | 6-0 |
| Harlow Town | 1-0 | 1-1 | 2-0 | 3-0 | 1-1 | 3-0 | 6-0 | 1-0 | 7-0 | 1-3 | — | 0-1 | 2-4 | 1-0 | 3-2 | 2-1 | 2-1 | 1-0 | 2-0 | 2-2 |
| Hemel Hempstead | 3-1 | 1-1 | 2-0 | 3-0 | 0-0 | 2-1 | 2-2 | 2-1 | 2-0 | 0-0 | 2-2 | — | 1-2 | 6-1 | 4-2 | 2-0 | 2-1 | 1-0 | 1-1 | 3-0 |
| Hertford Town | 4-2 | 2-3 | 3-0 | 1-0 | 0-2 | 2-0 | 1-2 | 2-1 | 0-0 | 1-0 | 1-2 | 1-1 | — | 0-4 | 0-2 | 3-0 | 0-1 | 5-0 | 4-2 | 1-0 |
| Hornchurch | 1-2 | 3-3 | 1-1 | 3-1 | 0-3 | 0-0 | 0-3 | 0-1 | 0-1 | 0-2 | 0-3 | 2-4 | 0-4 | — | 0-2 | 2-0 | 2-0 | 4-2 | 1-1 | 4-4 |
| Kingsbury Town | 0-3 | 1-4 | 2-1 | 1-2 | 2-3 | 4-4 | 0-5 | 0-1 | 1-4 | 0-3 | 1-5 | 3-0 | 3-0 | 0-2 | — | 1-1 | 1-1 | 0-3 | 1-0 | 0-2 |
| Lewes | 3-2 | 1-4 | 2-0 | 1-4 | 3-0 | 3-1 | 1-2 | 1-2 | 2-2 | 0-2 | 0-1 | 0-7 | 0-1 | 2-0 | 4-1 | — | 2-2 | 2-3 | 1-6 | 1-0 |
| Southall | 0-2 | 3-2 | 1-3 | 1-1 | 1-4 | 2-0 | 0-2 | 1-0 | 3-1 | 1-3 | 2-2 | 0-1 | 0-3 | 2-0 | 0-0 | 2-0 | — | 2-3 | 1-7 | 2-1 |
| Tring Town | 2-0 | 1-7 | 0-1 | 0-1 | 1-0 | 0-4 | 3-3 | 1-1 | 5-0 | 0-2 | 1-2 | 0-2 | 0-5 | 4-2 | 4-1 | 3-1 | 1-2 | — | 1-3 | 1-1 |
| Ware | 2-0 | 4-2 | 2-1 | 3-2 | 2-2 | 2-3 | 0-3 | 2-3 | 0-2 | 0-2 | 3-6 | 0-2 | 0-1 | 1-1 | 3-1 | 1-1 | 4-1 | 1-0 | — | 1-0 |
| Wingate & Finchley | 4-5 | 2-2 | 0-4 | 1-3 | 2-2 | 2-3 | 0-3 | 1-2 | 1-0 | 0-0 | 1-3 | 1-3 | 0-1 | 4-4 | 4-1 | 2-0 | 5-0 | 0-1 | 1-0 | — |

## GUARDIAN INSURANCE CUP 1997–98

**PRELIMINARY ROUND**
Aveley 3, Epsom & Ewell 0
Bedford Town 1, Windsor & Eton 0
Camberley Town 1, Witham Town 0
Cheshunt 0, Marlow 5
Corinthian-Casuals 2, Wingate & Finchley 2
*Replay* Corinthian-Casuals 0, Wingate & Finchley 2
Croydon Athletic 3, Ware 3
*Replay* Croydon Athletic 1, Ware 0
East Thurrock United 2, Ford United 4
Egham Town 2, Braintree Town 4
Flackwell Heath 1, Lewes 2
Hemel Hempstead 4, Kingsbury Town 2
Hertford Town 1, Clapton 1
*Replay* Hertford Town 0, Clapton 2
Horsham 2, Harlow Town 4
Hungerford Town 2, Northwood 1
Leatherhead 0, Canvey Island 1
Metropolitan Police 2, Barking 1
Southall 1, Hornchurch 2
Tilbury 2, Chalfont St Peter 1
Tooting & Mitcham United 5, Dorking 2
Tring Town 0, Bracknell Town 2
Wealdstone 2, Edgware Town 1
Wembley 2, Leighton Town 1
Wivenhoe Town 3, Banstead Athletic 0

**FIRST ROUND**
Croydon 4, Metropolitan Police 0
Aveley 4, Abingdon Town 2
Basingstoke Town 3, Dulwich Hamlet 1
Bedford Town 1, Whyteleafe 0
Berkhamsted Town 1, Walton & Hersham 2
Bracknell Town 0, Sutton United 2
Bromley 3, Bishops Stortford 1
Camberley Town 2, Kingstonian 1
Carshalton Athletic 3, Hungerford Town 2
Chesham United 1, Boreham Wood 4
Enfield 1, St Albans City 2
Ford United 1, Dagenham & Redbridge 3
Gravesend & Northfleet 1, Aylesbury United 0
Harrow Borough 0, Canvey Island 3
Hitchin Town 2, Wembley 0
Lewes 0, Clapton 4
Leyton Pennant 2, Uxbridge 2
*Replay* Uxbridge 3, Leyton Pennant 0
Maidenhead United 1, Romford 2
Molesey 0, Hampton 4
Marlow 1, Harlow Town 4
Staines Town 1, Hendon 8
Thame United 1, Heybridge Swifts 2
Tilbury 0, Bognor Regis Town 2
Oxford City 4, Braintree Town 1
Wingate & Finchley 1, Chertsey Town 2
Billericay Town 5, Hornchurch 2
Aldershot Town 4, Croydon Athletic 0
Wealdstone 4, Barton Rovers 1
Wivenhoe Town 0, Purfleet 2
Wokingham Town 1, Grays Athletic 0
Worthing 0, Tooting & Mitcham United 1
Yeading 3, Hemel Hempstead 2

**SECOND ROUND**
Aldershot Town 0, Dagenham & Redbridge 1
Basingstoke Town 1, Aveley 1
*Replay* Aveley 1, Basingstoke Town 3
Billericay Town 0, Purfleet 0
*Replay* Purfleet 1, Billericay Town 2
Boreham Wood 4, Bognor Regis Town 3
Carshalton Athletic 1, Yeading 0
Clapton 1, St Albans City 2
Gravesend & Northfleet 3, Wokingham Town 2
*Gravesend & Northfleet were removed from the competition*
Hampton 2, Walton & Hersham 3
Hendon 2, Canvey Island 4
Heybridge Swifts 0, Oxford City 1
Romford 4, Chertsey Town 1
Sutton United 3, Uxbridge 0
Harlow Town 2, Bromley 3
Hitchin Town 4, Wealdstone 4
*Replay* Wealdstone 2, Hitchin Town 6
Tooting & Mitcham United 0, Camberley Town 2
Croydon 1, Bedford Town 2

**THIRD ROUND**
Canvey Island 2, Hitchin Town 0
Carshalton Athletic 1, Billericay Town 0
Romford 3, Bromley 1
St Albans City 1, Bedford Town 1
*Replay* Bedford Town 3, St Albans City 3
*St Albans City won 4-2 on penalties.*
Wokingham Town 1, Walton & Hersham 0
Boreham Wood 1, Dagenham & Redbridge 0
Camberley Town 0, Oxford City 3
Sutton United 2, Basingstoke Town 2
*Replay* Basingstoke Town 1, Sutton United 3

**FOURTH ROUND**
Wokingham Town 0, St Albans City 3
Boreham Wood 2, Canvey Island 0
Carshalton Athletic 0, Oxford City 1
Romford 2, Sutton United 2
*Replay* Sutton United 5, Romford 3

**SEMI-FINALS FIRST LEG**
Sutton United 0, St Albans City 0
Oxford City 2, Boreham Wood 1

**SEMI-FINALS SECOND LEG**
Boreham Wood 0, Oxford City 3
St Albans City 0, Sutton United 3

**FINAL**
Oxford City 1, Sutton United 6
(At Harrow Borough)

## PUMA CUP

**FIRST ROUND**
Abingdon Town 0, Basingstoke Town 1
Bishops Stortford 0, Leyton Pennant 2
Bromley 2, Maidenhead United 3
Chertsey Town 3, Wokingham Town 3
*Chertsey Town won 5-4 on penalties.*
Gravesend & Northfleet United 4, Berkhamsted Town 3
Hendon 3, Purfleet 0
Hitchin Town 1, Boreham Wood 2
Molesey 0, Worthing 1
St Albans City 5, Enfield 1
Walton & Hersham 3, Staines Town 4
Dulwich Hamlet 0, Kingstonian 3
Wembley 2, Billericay Town 0

**SECOND ROUND**
Barton Rovers 0, Harrow Borough 2

Chesham United 0, Gravesend & Northfleet 3
Staines Town 3, Sutton United 0
Uxbridge 1, Heybridge Swifts 1
*Uxbridge won 5-4 on penalties.*
Yeading 3, Wembley 2
Bognor Regis Town 3, Worthing 1
Leyton Pennant 3, Grays Athletic 0
Oxford City 3, Thame United 1
Leatherhead 2, Chertsey Town 1
Carshalton Athletic 1, Aldershot Town 0
Croydon 0, Whyteleafe 2
Dagenham & Redbridge 3, Romford 0
Basingstoke Town 3, Kingstonian 2
Boreham Wood 6, Aylesbury United 1
Hampton 0, Maidenhead United 4
Hendon 6, St Albans City 1

**THIRD ROUND**
Dagenham & Redbridge 3, Harrow Borough 1
Carshalton Athletic 3, Bognor Regis Town 2
Hendon 1, Gravesend & Northfleet 0
Oxford City 1, Basingstoke Town 2
Whyteleafe 1, Staines Town 3
Leatherhead 1, Maidenhead United 0
*Leatherhead removed from competition.*
Boreham Wood 2, Uxbridge 1
Leyton Penant 1, Yeading 2

**FOURTH ROUND**
Carshalton Athletic 1, Leatherhead 2
*Match void.*

Carshalton Athletic 1, Maidenhead United 2
Hendon 3, Dagenham & Redbridge 1
Staines Town 1, Basingstoke Town 4
Boreham Wood 2, Yeading 2
*Yeading won 3-0 on penalties.*

**SEMI-FINALS**
Hendon 2, Maidenhead United 1
Yeading 2, Basingstoke Town 4

**FINAL**
Basingstoke Town 1, Hendon 4

# VANDANEL TROPHY

**FIRST ROUND**
Banstead Athletic 2, Camberley Town 1
Clapton 1, Ford United 4
East Thurrock United 4, Witham Town 3
Egham Town 1, Chalfont St Peter 0
Flackwell Heath 3, Tring Town 1
Hertford Town 0, Canvey Island 3
Kingsbury Town 0, Braintree Town 4
Ware 2, Aveley 2
*Aveley won 10-9 on penalties.*
Wingate & Finchley 1, Marlow 8
Croydon Athletic 0, Corinthian-Casuals 2

**SECOND ROUND**
Banstead Athletic 2, Marlow 4
Barking 5, Braintree Town 4
Bracknell Town 1, Epsom & Euell 2
Canvey Island 4, Harlow Town 1
Egham Town 4, Hungerford Town 0
Ford United 1, Edgware Town 4
Flackwell Heath 2, Dorking 0
Hemel Hempstead 0, East Thurrock United 2
Leighton Town 1, Bedford Town 2
Lewes 0, Horsham 2
Metropolitan Police 1, Windsor & Eton 4
Northwood 4, Wivenhoe Town 0
Southall 1, Hornchurch 1
*Southall won 5-4 on penalties.*

Tilbury 1, Wealdstone 2
Tooting & Mitcham United 0, Corinthian-Casuals 1
Aveley 1, Cheshunt 0

**THIRD ROUND**
Aveley 2, East Thurrock United 3
Barking 0, Bedford Town 3
Corinthian-Casuals 4, Southall 1
Edgware Town 1, Wealdstone 2
Epsom & Euell 4, Windsor & Eton 1
Egham Town 6, Flackwell Heath 1
Marlow 3, Horsham 2
Northwood 3, Canvey Island 1

**FOURTH ROUND**
Bedford Town 2, Northwood 1
East Thurrock United 1, Wealdstone 2
Egham Town 3, Corinthian-Casuals 0
Epsom & Euell 2, Marlow 1

**SEMI-FINALS**
Egham Town 0, Bedford Town 1
Wealdstone 0, Epsom & Euell 1

**FINAL**
Bedford Town 2, Epsom & Euell 0
(At Hendon).

# CUP ATTENDANCES

| | |
|---|---|
| Guardian Insurance Cup | 16,301 |
| Puma Cup | 6,695 |
| Vandanel Trophy | 4,085 |

# AWARDS

**William Hill Managers of the Season Awards**

| Premier Division | Geoff Chapple | Kingstonian |
|---|---|---|
| Division One | George Borg | Aldershot Town |
| Division Two | Jeff King | Canvey Island |
| Division Three | Mike Vipond | Hemel Hempstead |

**Divisional Goalscoring—sponsored by Cryuff/Spall Sports**

| Premier Division | Shaun Marshall | Boreham Wood |
|---|---|---|
| Division One | Leon Gutzmore | Billericay Town |
| Division Two | Gary Bennett | Braintree United |
| Division Three | Jeff Wood | Ford United |

**Team Award**
Braintree Town (117)

# FA UMBRO TROPHY 1997–98

## FIRST QUALIFYING ROUND

| | |
|---|---|
| Stafford Rangers v Hinckley United | 1-1, 0-1 |
| Moor Green v Atherstone United | 1-0 |
| Buxton v Alfreton Town | 0-1 |
| Bedworth United v Stocksbridge Park Steels | 3-1 |
| Solihull Borough v Shepshed Dynamo | 3-0 |
| Lincoln United v Trafford | 5-2 |
| Tamworth v Congleton Town | 5-1 |
| Paget Rangers v Bilston Town | 0-0, 2-2 |

*Bilston Town won 5-3 on penalties.*

| | |
|---|---|
| Witton Albion v Farsley Celtic | 3-0 |
| Radcliffe Borough w.o. v Dudley Town withdrew | |
| Eastwood Town v Redditch United | 1-1, 0-3 |
| Blakenall v Spennymoor United | 2-3 |
| Belper Town v Droylsden | 2-2, 3-2 |
| Winsford United v Ilkeston Town | 2-0 |
| Flixton v Matlock Town | 0-3 |
| Netherfield v Whitby Town | 1-1, 3-3 |

*Whitby Town won 4-3 on penalties.*

| | |
|---|---|
| Frickley Athletic v Leigh RMI | 1-1, 1-2 |
| Knowsley United withdrew v Great Harwood Town w.o. | |
| Sutton Coldfield Town v Gretna | 2-1 |
| Whitley Bay v Worksop Town | 0-1 |
| Wembley v Gravesend & Northfleet | 2-6 |
| Whyteleafe v Margate | 1-5 |
| Corby Town v Newport AFC | 4-3 |
| Yate Town v Molesey | 1-3 |
| Tonbridge v Newport (IOW) | 1-0 |
| Oxford City v Cinderford Town | 6-0 |
| Havant Town v Hendon | 2-2, 1-2 |
| Trowbridge Town v Raunds Town | 1-2 |
| Bognor Regis Town v Thame United | 4-0 |
| Walton & Hersham v Staines Town | 3-0 |
| Aldershot Town v Croydon | 5-1 |
| Waterlooville v Fisher Athletic | 2-1 |
| Crawley Town v Kingstonian | 2-1 |
| Brackley Town v Worcester City | 2-2, 0-5 |
| Ashford Town v VS Rugby | 2-1 |
| Hampton v Wokingham Town | 0-1 |
| Evesham United v Rothwell Town | 1-2 |
| Billericay Town v Grays Athletic | 3-2 |
| Romford v Chertsey Town | 2-0 |
| Harrow Borough v Weston-Super-Mare | 1-1, 2-1 |
| Hitchin Town v Erith & Belvedere | 7-1 |
| Basingstoke Town v Leatherhead | 2-0 |
| Leyton Pennant v Baldock Town | 0-1 |
| Cambridge City v Maidenhead United | 2-1 |
| Wisbech Town v Clevedon Town | 4-3 |
| Carshalton Athletic v Racing Club Warwick | 2-0 |
| Fleet Town v Abingdon Town | 2-2, 0-2 |
| Uxbridge v Weymouth | 2-2, 1-1 |
| Fareham Town v Witney Town | 0-3 |

## SECOND QUALIFYING ROUND

| | |
|---|---|
| Redditch United v Worksop Town | 1-3 |
| Winsford United v Spennymoor United | 1-0 |
| Hinckley United v Whitby Town | 3-1 |
| Radcliffe Borough v Leigh RMI | 1-1, 0-1 |
| Stourbridge v Great Harwood Town | 1-1, 1-3 |
| Witton Albion v Bilston Town | 0-0, 2-2 |

*Witton Albion won 6-5 on penalties.*

| | |
|---|---|
| Solihull Borough v Alfreton Town | 9-1 |
| Gainsborough Trinity v Bedworth United | 3-0 |
| Workington v Harrogate Town | 1-1, 0-0 |

*Harrogate Town won 5-4 on penalties.*

| | |
|---|---|
| Matlock Town v Sutton Coldfield Town | 4-1 |
| Lincoln United v Belper Town | 1-2 |
| Tamworth v Moor Green | 4-3 |
| Abingdon Town v Wokingham Town | 2-0 |
| Margate v Waterlooville | 3-2 |
| Billericay Town v Forest Green Rovers | 4-0 |
| Carshalton Athletic v Aldershot Town | 0-0, 0-3 |
| Cambridge City v Dartford | 1-1, 1-0 |
| Crawley Town v Bishop's Stortford | 1-2 |
| Berkhamsted Town v Worcester City | 3-2 |
| Baldock Town v Corby Town | 1-2 |
| Basingstoke Town v Witney Town | 2-0 |
| Tonbridge v Hastings Town | 0-3 |
| Uxbridge v Worthing | 0-1 |
| Bognor Regis Town v Chesham United | 2-3 |

| | |
|---|---|
| Oxford City v Wisbech Town | 0-2 |
| Ashford Town v Raunds Town | 1-2 |
| Cirencester Town v Gravesend & Northfleet | 1-0 |
| Bromley v Hendon | 2-1 |
| Hitchin Town v Barton Rovers | 3-0 |
| Romford v Rothwell Town | 5-1 |
| Harrow Borough v Molesey | 5-0 |
| Walton & Hersham v Bashley | 0-0, 0-2 |

## THIRD QUALIFYING ROUND

| | |
|---|---|
| Marine v Grantham Town | 1-1, 0-1 |
| Bradford Park Avenue v Leigh RMI | 1-1, 0-1 |
| Tamworth v Lancaster City | 0-1 |
| Belper Town v Boston United | 1-5 |
| Bromsgrove Rovers v Worksop Town | 1-2 |
| Accrington Stanley v Runcorn | 0-5 |
| Solihull Borough v Emley | 2-1 |
| Barrow v Hinckley United | 4-1 |
| Great Harwood Town v Witton Albion | 0-1 |
| Matlock Town v Winsford United | 1-1, 0-0 |

*Winsford United won 5-3 on penalties.*

| | |
|---|---|
| Gainsborough Trinity v Bamber Bridge | 1-0 |
| Halesowen Town v Burton Albion | 1-2 |
| Harrogate Town v Blyth Spartans | 0-3 |
| Nuneaton Borough v Altrincham | 0-2 |
| Bromley v Purfleet | 1-4 |
| St Albans City v Bishop's Stortford | 5-2 |
| Harrow Borough v Bath City | 1-3 |
| Hitchin Town v Boreham Wood | 0-2 |
| Berkhamsted Town v Salisbury City | 2-1 |
| Wisbech Town v Raunds Town | 2-2, 2-3 |
| Dorchester Town v Worthing | 3-0 |
| Aylesbury United v Dulwich Hamlet | 0-3 |
| Bashley v Cirencester Town | 4-1 |
| Corby Town v Margate | 2-2, 1-5 |
| Kings Lynn v Chelmsford City | 1-4 |
| Basingstoke Town v Romford | 4-0 |
| Merthyr Tydfil v Cambridge City | 2-2, 3-6 |
| Hastings Town v Heybridge Swifts | 3-2 |
| Chesham United v Sutton United | 2-1 |
| Yeading v St Leonards Stamcroft | 2-0 |
| Billericay Town v Aldershot Town | 2-1 |
| Sittingbourne v Abingdon Town | 1-1, 2-1 |

## FIRST ROUND

| | |
|---|---|
| Barrow v Worksop Town | 1-1, 4-2 |
| Grantham Town v Leigh RMI | 1-1, 0-0 |

*Grantham Town won 4-3 on penalties.*

| | |
|---|---|
| Halifax Town v Blyth Spartans | 2-1 |
| Lancaster City v Northwich Victoria | 0-3 |
| Hednesford Town v Gainsborough Trinity | 2-1 |
| Burton Albion v Witton Albion | 2-1 |
| Guiseley v Telford United | 0-0, 2-3 |
| Morecambe v Solihull Borough | 3-2 |
| Hyde United v Boston United | 2-1 |
| Altrincham v Runcorn | 3-1 |
| Stalybridge Celtic v Gateshead | 2-4 |
| Bishop Auckland v Colwyn Bay | 3-1 |
| Southport v Winsford United | 3-0 |
| Gresley Rovers v Leek Town | 4-4, 1-3 |
| Ashton United v Chorley | 0-0, 2-1 |
| Kettering Town v Dorchester Town | 1-0 |
| Welling United v Slough Town | 1-1, 1-2 |
| Dagenham & Redbridge v Billericay Town | 1-0 |
| Bashley v Raunds Town | 3-0 |
| Hayes v Cambridge City | 3-2 |
| Kidderminster Harriers v Berkhamsted Town | 4-1 |
| Bath City v Hastings Town | 0-0, 1-0 |
| Stevenage Borough v Chesham United | 2-2, 3-0 |
| Woking v Margate | 0-1 |
| Rushden & Diamonds v Farnborough Town | 3-2 |
| Enfield v Cheltenham Town | 1-1, 1-5 |
| Hereford United v Dulwich Hamlet | 3-0 |
| Boreham Wood v Chelmsford City | 2-1 |
| Purfleet v Dover Athletic | 0-1 |
| Yeovil Town v Yeading | 0-0, 0-1 |
| St Albans City v Sittingbourne | 0-0, 1-0 |
| Basingstoke Town v Gloucester City | 0-1 |

**SECOND ROUND**

| | |
|---|---|
| Altrincham v Morecambe | 2-0 |
| Bath City v Grantham Town | 2-3 |
| Barrow v St Albans City | 2-1 |
| Hednesford Town v Leek Town | 5-0 |
| Yeading v Southport | 0-6 |
| Hayes v Kidderminster Harriers | 5-0 |
| Halifax Town v Slough Town | 1-1, 0-2 |
| Gloucester City v Burton Albion | 1-1, 2-2 |
| *Gloucester City won 6-5 on penalties.* | |
| Bishop Auckland v Boreham Wood | 1-4 |
| Hereford United v Dover Athletic | 0-2 |
| Margate v Bashley | 1-2 |
| Dagenham & Redbridge v Hyde United | 0-5 |
| Cheltenham Town v Rushden & Diamonds | 3-1 |
| Telford United v Ashton United | 0-1 |
| Northwich Victoria v Kettering Town | 4-0 |
| Gateshead v Stevenage Borough | 1-2 |

**THIRD ROUND**

| | |
|---|---|
| Grantham Town v Hednesford Town | 2-1 |
| Hyde United v Dover Athletic | 0-2 |
| Stevenage Borough v Gloucester City | 1-1, 2-1 |
| Slough Town v Boreham Wood | 1-1, 2-1 |
| Barrow v Northwich Victoria | 1-0 |
| Altrincham v Southport | 0-2 |
| Hayes v Bashley | 2-0 |
| Ashton United v Cheltenham Town | 0-1 |

**FOURTH ROUND**

| | |
|---|---|
| Dover Athletic v Barrow | 1-1, 0-0 |
| *Dover Athletic won 5-4 on penalties.* | |
| Stevenage Borough v Slough Town | 0-1 |
| Cheltenham Town v Hayes | 1-0 |
| Grantham Town v Southport | 1-1, 1-3 |

**SEMI-FINAL (FIRST LEG)**

| | |
|---|---|
| Cheltenham Town v Dover Athletic | 2-1 |
| Slough Town v Southport | 0-1 |

**SEMI-FINAL (SECOND LEG)**

| | |
|---|---|
| Dover Athletic v Cheltenham Town | 2-2 |
| Southport v Slough Town | 1-1 |

**FINAL (at Wembley)**

**17 MAY**

**Cheltenham Town (0) 1** *(Eaton)*

**Southport (0) 0**                                    26,837

*Cheltenham Town:* Book; Duff, Victory, Freeman, Banks, Knight (Milton), Howells, Bloomer, Eaton, Walker (Smith J), Watkins.

*Southport:* Stewart; Farley, Formby (Whittaker), Horner, Futcher, Ryan, Kielty, Butler, Thompson (Bolland), Ross, Gamble.

*Referee:* G. Willard (Worthing).

Cheltenham Town players celebrate their FA Trophy win at Wembley. (Action Images)

# FA CARLSBERG VASE 1997–98

**First Qualifying Round**

| | |
|---|---|
| Easington Colliery v Norton & Stockton Ancients | 1-0 |
| Brandon United v Penrith | 0-2 |
| Glapwell v Hall Road Rangers | 1-3 |
| Oldham Town v Thackley | 3-4 |
| Burscough v Blackpool (Wren) Rovers | 2-2, 2-0 |
| Long Eaton United removed v Harworth CI w.o. | |
| Glossop North End v Vauxhall GM | 2-4 |
| Maltby Main v Arnold Town | 1-2 |
| Ramsbottom United v Chadderton | 4-5 |
| St Helens Town v Ossett Town | 3-1 |
| Pershore Town v Wellingborough Town | 3-4 |
| Shifnal Town v Wednesfield | 0-7 |
| Barrow Town v Meir KA | 1-5 |
| Stapenhill v Gornal Athletic | 3-2 |
| Fakenham Town v Holbeach United | 2-0 |
| Braintree Town v Brightlingsea United | 6-1 |
| Somersham Town v Worboys Town | 1-6 |
| Ipswich Wanderers v Lowestoft Town | 3-0 |
| Stansted v East Thurrock United | 1-2 |
| Biggleswade Town v Beaconsfield SYCOB | 0-1 |
| Chalfont St Peter v Ilford | 4-2 |
| Hertford Town v Flackwell Heath | 0-3 |
| Hornchurch v Wealdstone | 4-5 |
| Hanwell Town v Harlow Town | 2-2, 2-1 |
| Saltdean United v Three Bridges | 2-5 |
| Folkestone Invicta v East Preston | 3-1 |
| Pagham v Redhill | 2-4 |
| Erith Town v Farnham Town | 3-5 |
| Mile Oak v Lancing | 1-2 |
| Slade Green v Dorking | 3-0 |
| Christchurch v Sandhurst Town | 0-2 |
| Brockenhurst v Cowes Sports | 1-2 |
| Bodmin Town w.o. v Bishop Sutton withdrew | |
| Odd Down v Torrington | 1-0 |
| Melksham Town v St Blazey | 1-0 |

**Second Qualifying Round**

| | |
|---|---|
| Easington Colliery v Penrith | 2-1 |
| Washington v RTM Newcastle | 2-3 |
| Shildon v West Allotment Celtic | 1-4 |
| Whickham v Stockton | 0-2 |
| Northallerton v Morpeth Town | 3-2 |
| Ryhope CA v Willington | 1-3 |
| Horden CW v Jarrow Roofing Boldon CA | 1-2 |
| Billingham Town v Evenwood Town | 3-1 |
| Tadcaster Albion v Pickering Town | 1-0 |
| Marske United v Consett | 1-1, 3-0 |
| Shotton Comrades v Peterlee Newtown | 0-3 |
| Harrogate Railway v Ashington | 0-5 |
| South Shields v Crook Town | 3-0 |
| Eccleshill United v Leek CSOB | 3-0 |
| Douglas High School OB v Glasshoughton Welfare | 2-3 |
| Hatfield Main v Garforth Town | 3-2 |
| Yorkshire Amateur v Borrowash Victoria | 0-3 |
| Kidsgrove Athletic v Vauxhall GM | 4-2 |
| Paulton Victoria v Selby Town | 4-1 |
| Heanor Town v Atherton Collieries | 3-0 |
| East Manchester v Cheadle Town | 2-2, 5-5 |
| *East Manchester won 3-2 on penalties.* | |
| Armthorpe Welfare v Pontefract Collieries | 2-1 |
| Hall Road Rangers v Bacup Borough | 3-0 |
| Liversedge v Bootle | 0-2 |
| Arnold Town v Main Road | 1-0 |
| Burscough v Salford City | 2-0 |
| Louth United v Sheffield | 0-1 |
| Parkgate v Castletown Gabriels | 0-2 |
| Nettleham v St Helens Town | 0-1 |
| Skelmersdale United v Hallam | 4-2 |
| Brodsworth v Darwen | 4-1 |
| Holker Old Boys v Prescot Cables | 0-2 |
| Haslingden v Rossington Main | 0-0, 0-6 |
| Chadderton v Rainworth MW | 2-0 |
| Grimthorpe MW v Thackley | 1-1, 2-3 |
| Worsbro Bridge MW v Rossendale United | 0-2 |
| Ossett Albion v Staveley MW | 2-3 |
| Ford Sports Daventry v Oldbury United | 2-1 |
| Wellingborough Town v Birstall United | 2-3 |
| Oadby Town v Halesowen Harriers | 3-2 |

| | |
|---|---|
| Worcester Athletico v Dunkirk | 2-1 |
| St Andrews v Knypersley Victoria | 0-2 |
| Desborough Town v Banbury United | 0-2 |
| Stourport Swifts v Cradley Town | 5-0 |
| Sandwell Borough v Meir KA | 3-3, 5-2 |
| Chasetown v Shirebrook Town | 2-1 |
| Kings Heath v Gedling Town | 1-0 |
| Friar Lane OB v Willenhall Town | 2-1 |
| Stewarts & Lloyds v Bolehall Swifts | 2-0 |
| Pelsall Villa v Northampton Spencer | 4-3 |
| Tivedale v Wednesfield | 0-0, 0-1 |
| Coleshill Town v Newport Pagnell Town | 1-3 |
| Kimberley Town v Rocester | 1-2 |
| West Midlands Police v Sandiacre Town | 1-2 |
| Walsall Wood v Highgate United | 2-1 |
| Lye Town v Long Buckby | 3-2 |
| Stratford Town v Ibstock Welfare | 1-0 |
| Holewell Sports v Rushall Olympic | 2-4 |
| Bloxwich Town v Anstey Nomads | 7-2 |
| Westfields v Stapenhill | 1-4 |
| Whitton United w.o. v Saffron Walden Town removed. | |
| Boston Town v Eynesbury Rovers | 3-1 |
| Mirrlees Blackstone v Clapton Town | 5-1 |
| Sawbridgeworth Town v Hadleigh United | 2-2, 2-1 |
| Fakenham Town v March Town United | 3-0 |
| Stowmarket Town v Great Yarmouth Town | 3-3, 3-4 |
| Soham Town Rangers v Worboys Town | 0-1 |
| Burnham Ramblers v Harwich & Parkstone | 2-4 |
| Maldon Town v Felixstowe Port & Town | 2-1 |
| Ely City v Thetford Town | 2-1 |
| Basildon United v Newmarket Town | 0-0, 1-0 |
| Downham Town v St Neots Town | 1-3 |
| Stanway Rovers v Sudbury Town | 0-3 |
| Gorleston v Sudbury Wanderers | 1-2 |
| Wotton United v Norwich United | 0-3 |
| Braintree Town v Swaffham Town | 1-0 |
| Bourne Town v Haverhill Rovers | 2-1 |
| Ipswich Wanderers v Tiptree United | 1-2 |
| Mildenhall Town v Cornard United | 3-2 |
| Needham Market v Witham Town | 1-3 |
| Yaxley v Great Wakering Rovers | 0-3 |
| Brimsdown Rovers v Milton Keynes | 2-2, 1-5 |
| East Thurrock United v Bowers United | 1-4 |
| Hanwell Town v Tring Town | 1-2 |
| Potters Bar Town v Potton United | 3-0 |
| Ware v Harpenden Town | 3-2 |
| Ford United v Bedford Town | 2-1 |
| Wootton Blue Cross v Tilbury | 4-1 |
| Brache Sparta v Chalfont St Peter | 3-0 |
| Edgware Town v Kingsbury Town | 6-0 |
| Harefield United v Wealdstone | 1-4 |
| London Colney v Langford | 9-0 |
| Aveley v Clapton | 3-1 |
| Viking Sports v Welwyn Garden City | 3-4 |
| Hillingdon Borough v Beaconsfield SYCOB | 3-0 |
| Shillington v Waltham Abbey | 0-2 |
| Wingate & Finchley v Amersham Town | 2-3 |
| Leighton Town v Southall | 3-1 |
| Hoddesdon Town v Cheshunt | 4-3 |
| Royston Town v Barkingside | 2-2, 0-3 |
| Brook House v Harringey Borough | 3-2 |
| Ruislip Manor v Hemel Hempstead | 2-3 |
| Stotfold v Bedford United | 2-0 |
| Letchworth v Flackwell Heath | 0-1 |
| Godalming & Guildford v Ringmer | 3-2 |
| Ramsgate v Redhill | 3-1 |
| Bracknell Town v East Grinstead | 1-2 |
| Whitehawk v Slade Green | 2-2, 1-4 |
| *Replay ordered; incorrect pitch dimensions, 0-1.* | |
| Portfield v Camberley Town | 2-3 |
| Arundel v Windsor & Eton | 0-6 |
| Bedfont v Oakwood | 2-1 |
| Hassocks v Littlehampton Town | 1-2 |
| Southwick v Eastbourne Town | 1-2 |
| Ashford Town (Middlesex) v Corinthian-Casuals | 2-2, 3-1 |
| Horsham w.o. v Beckenham Town removed. | |
| Langney Sports v Raynes Park Vale | 1-0 |
| Lancing v Faversham Town | 0-2 |
| Sheppey United v Ash United | 4-3 |
| Chatham Town v Selsey | 2-1 |

| | |
|---|---|
| Corinthian v Merstham | 2-1 |
| Deal Town v Thamesmead Town | 2-1 |
| Crowborough Athletic v Egham Town | 0-4 |
| Hailsham Town v Croydon Athletic | 1-1, 2-1 |
| Lewes v Chipstead | 0-5 |
| Three Bridges v Epsom & Ewell | 0-3 |
| Farnham Town v Chichester City | 5-0 |
| Canterbury City v Shoreham | 3-5 |
| Folkestone Invicta v Cobham | 3-2 |
| Tonbridge Wells v Hythe United | 3-2 |
| Horsham YMCA v Sidley United | 2-2, 1-1 |

*Sidley United won 4-3 on penalties.*

| | |
|---|---|
| Sandhurst Town v Cowes Sports | 1-4 |
| Didcot Town v North Leigh | 1-3 |
| Bicester Town v Stoney Stratford Town | 2-1 |
| Calne Town v Andover | 2-3 |
| Downtown v Gosport Borough | 0-1 |
| Totton v Cove | 3-0 |
| Romsey Town v Hungerford Town | 0-1 |
| Portsmouth Royal Navy v Newbury | 2-4 |
| Whitchurch United v Swindon Supermarine | 0-5 |
| Kintbury Rangers v BAT Sports | 0-2 |
| Bournemouth v Wantage Town | 4-1 |
| Eastleigh v Petersfield Town | 4-0 |
| First Tower United v Carterton Town | 3-1 |

*Replay ordered due to First Tower United fielding ineligible player, 3-1.*

| | |
|---|---|
| Backwell United v Bridgwater Town | 0-1 |
| Devizes Town v Shortwood United | 2-1 |
| Hallen v Barnstaple Town | 2-1 |
| Paulton Rovers v Odd Down | 2-1 |
| Elmore v Warminster Town | 4-1 |
| Newquay v Chard Town | 1-2 |
| Bideford v Bridport | 0-1 |
| Westbury United v Dawlish Town | 3-1 |
| Tuffley Rovers v Fairford Town | 1-2 |
| Almondsbury Town v Endsleigh | 0-2 |
| Melksham Town v Ilfracombe Town | 4-0 |
| Keynsham Town v Wellington Town | 2-0 |
| Welton Rovers v Bodmin Town | 1-3 |
| Crediton United v Porthleven | 2-6 |
| Minehead v Frome Town | 5-1 |
| Brislington v Glastonbury | 3-0 |

**First Round**

| | |
|---|---|
| Willington v Stockton | 1-4 |
| Skelmersdale United v West Auckland Town | 0-3 |
| South Shields v Chadderton | 2-3 |
| East Manchester v Rossendale United | 2-3 |
| Tow Law Town v St Helens Town | 2-1 |
| Tadcaster Albion v Thackley | 1-4 |
| Prudhoe Town v Brodsworth | 1-2 |
| Paulton Victoria v Ashington | 4-2 |
| Prescot Cables v Sheffield | 0-2 |
| Murton v Rossington Main | 3-1 |
| Seaham Red Star v Hall Road Rangers | 1-0 |
| Jarrow Roofing Boldon CA v Bootle | 2-0 |
| Borrowash Victoria v Northallerton | 1-0 |
| Easington Colliery v Burscough | 2-4 |
| Glasshoughton Welfare v Billingham Town | 1-2 |
| Kidsgrove Athletic v RTM Newcastle | 2-2, 1-0 |
| Hebburn v Chester-Le-Street Town | 2-2, 0-2 |
| Armthorpe Welfare v West Allotment Celtic | 1-1 |

*(abandoned 89 minutes due to player injury), 3-2*

| | |
|---|---|
| Billingham Synthonia v Eccleshill United | 5-1 |
| Castleton Gabriels v Marske United | 1-2 |
| Hatfield Main v Nantwich Town | 1-2 |
| Peterlee Newtown v Heanor Town | 4-2 |
| Blidworth MW v Boston Town | 0-8 |
| Kings Heath v Wednesfield | 2-2, 0-4 |
| Bridnorth Town v Boldmere St Michaels | 0-5 |
| Stewarts & Lloyds v Rocester | 0-3 |
| Bloxwich Town v Rushall Olympic | 2-0 |
| Sandwell Borough v Staveley MW | 0-4 |
| Walsall Wood v Worcester Athletico | 1-2 |
| Stratford Town v Birstall United | 0-2 |
| Mirrlees Blackstone v Coggenhoe United | 4-2 |
| Banbury United v Oadby Town | 1-2 |
| Arnold Town v Stapenhill | 4-2 |
| Newcastle Town v Pelsall Villa | 1-0 |
| Knypersley Victoria v Sandiacre Town | 3-0 |
| Barwell v Ford Sports Daventry | 2-0 |
| Hucknall Town v Chase Town | 2-0 |
| Lye Town v Stourport Swifts | 2-4 |
| Newport Pagnell Town v Friar Lane OB | 0-4 |

| | |
|---|---|
| Flackwell Heath v Leighton Town | 2-1 |
| Harwich & Parkstone v Tring Town | 3-1 |
| London Colney v Brache Sparta | 1-2 |
| Braintree Town v Bury Town | 3-0 |
| Ely City v Wivenhoe Town | 2-1 |
| Concord Rangers v Great Yarmouth Town | 1-0 |
| Woodbridge Town v Southend Manor | 5-1 |
| Whitton United v Wealdstone | 1-3 |
| Wootton Blue Cross v Edgware Town | 0-1 |
| Ford United v Sudbury Wanderers | 2-3 |
| Norwich United v Welwyn Garden City | 3-1 |
| Aveley v St Neots Town | 4-2 |
| Stotfold v Maldon Town | 2-0 |
| Histon v Witham Town | 2-0 |
| Amersham Town v Halstead Town | 0-7 |
| Hoddesdon Town v Bowers United | 3-5 |
| Fakenham Town v Potters Bar Town | 1-2 |
| Sudbury Town v Bourne Town | 5-1 |
| Milton Keynes v Great Wakering Rovers | 0-3 |
| Worboys Town v Basildon United | 0-1 |
| Hemel Hempstead v Barkingside | 3-1 |
| Hillingdon Borough v Ware | 1-1, 4-2 |
| Tiptree United v Sawbridgeworth Town | 0-1 |
| Waltham Abbey v Mildenhall Town | 2-1 |
| East Grinstead Town v Folkestone Invicta | 0-2 |
| Thatcham Town v Reading Town | 3-0 |
| Bedfont v Faversham Town | 1-2 |
| Burnham v Egham Town | 1-0 |
| Langney Sports v Farnham Town | 2-1 |
| Sidley United v Brook House | 0-2 |
| Chatham Town v Hailsham Town | 3-1 |
| Ashford Town v Sheppey United | 2-1 |
| Metropolitan Police v North Leigh | 3-1 |
| Horsham v Ramsgate | 0-1 |
| Cowes Sports v Epsom & Ewell | 5-2 |
| Tunbridge Wells v Wick | 2-4 |
| Windsor & Eton v Shoreham | 0-1 |
| Corinthian v Slade Green | 1-0 |
| Deal Town v Godalming & Guildford | 3-1 |
| Bicester Town v Littlehampton Town | 2-5 |
| Abingdon United v Camberley Town | 1-3 |
| Eastbourne Town v Chipstead | 1-4 |
| Bodmin Town v Bournemouth | 2-0 |
| Chard Town v First Tower United | 1-0 |
| Chippenham Town v Devizes Town | 1-1, 4-0 |
| Melksham Town v Wimborne Town | 4-6 |
| Swindon Supermarine v Porthleven | 1-1, 1-2 |
| Paulton Rovers v Minehead | 4-0 |
| BAT Sports v Hallen | 3-2 |
| Hungerford Town v Westbury United | 2-1 |
| Eastleigh v Bridport | 1-2 |
| Falmouth Town v Bridgwater Town | 0-1 |
| Brislington v Elmore | 2-3 |
| Bemerton Heath Harlequins v Totton AFC | 2-0 |
| Endsleigh v Newbury AFC | 2-2, 1-0 |
| Fairford Town v Gosport Borough | 2-3 |
| Andover v Keynsham Town | 5-0 |

**Second Round**

| | |
|---|---|
| Dunston FB v Atherton LR | 1-0 |
| Seaham Red Star v Chadderton | 2-1 |
| Rossendale United v Tow Law Town | 1-2 |
| West Auckland Town v Curzon Ashton | 1-0 |
| Armthorpe Welfare v Denaby United | 1-1 |

*(Abandoned 70 minutes; fog), 0-0, 0-1.*

| | |
|---|---|
| North Ferriby United v Murton | 7-0 |
| Peterlee Newtown v Brigg Town | 1-3 |
| Warrington Town v Paulton Victoria | 0-1 |
| Kidsgrove Athletic v Brodsworth | 2-2, 2-0 |
| Nantwich Town v Burscough | 1-3 |
| Stockton v Sheffield | 3-1 |
| Mossley v Jarrow Roofing Boldon CA | 1-1, 5-1 |
| Thackley v Borrowash Victoria | 6-1 |
| Chester-Le-Street Town v Billingham Town | 4-4, 4-6 |
| Clitheroe v Guisborough Town | 5-0 |
| Bedlington Terriers v Billingham Synthonia | 5-0 |
| Durham City v Marske United | 0-1 |
| Newcastle Town v Birstall United | 0-1 |
| Friar Lane OB v Wednesfield | 1-0 |
| Boldmere St Michaels v Arnold Town | 0-0, 1-2 |
| Spalding United v Mirrlees Blackstone | 2-0 |
| Barwell v Boston Town | 1-4 |
| Knypersley Victoria v Stamford AFC | 0-1 |
| Ely City v Worcester Athletico | 1-0 |
| Oadby Town v Norwich United | 5-1 |

| | |
|---|---|
| Staveley MW v Wroxham | 1-3 |
| Bloxwich Town v Diss Town | 2-1 |
| Rocester v Histon | 2-2, 0-1 |
| Hucknall Town v Stourport Swifts | 2-1 |
| Ashford Town (Middlesex) v Littlehampton Town | 5-3 |
| Deal Town v Great Wakering Rovers | 2-2, 1-2 |
| Shoreham v Sudbury Town | 2-4 |
| Basildon United v Edgware Town | 3-2 |
| Potters Bar Town v Whitstable Town | 4-2 |
| Faversham Town v Banstead Athletic | 1-2 |
| Braintree Town v Concord Rangers | 8-1 |
| Peacehaven & Telscombe v Chatham Town | 1-0 |
| Harwich & Parkstone v Folkestone Invicta | 1-1, 1-5 |
| Chipstead v Barking | 2-1 |
| Metropolitan Police v Tooting & Mitcham United | 0-1 |
| Hillingdon Borough v Brook House | 1-6 |
| Hemel Hempstead v Wick | 3-2 |
| Camberley Town v Corinthian | 3-0 |
| Brache Sparta v Halstead Town | 2-1 |

*(abandoned 80 minutes; waterlogged pitch)*, 5-1.

| | |
|---|---|
| Sawbridgeworth Town v Stotfold | 1-5 |
| Burgess Hill Town v Canvey Island | 2-1 |
| Sudbury Wanderers v Flackwell Heath | 4-0 |
| Bowers United v Buckingham Town | 3-0 |
| Northwood v Woodbridge Town | 0-2 |
| Arlesey Town v Waltham Abbey | 3-2 |
| Herne Bay v Langney Sports | 1-1 |

*(abandoned 46 minutes; floodlight failure)*, 2-0.

| | |
|---|---|
| Aveley v Burnham | 2-2, 2-0 |
| Ramsgate v Wealdstone | 0-1 |
| Wimbourne Town v Gosport Borough | 3-1 |
| Elmore v Chard Town | 2-4 |
| Paulton Rovers v Porthleven | 2-4 |
| Chippenham Town v Andover | 3-2 |
| Tiverton Town v Mangotsfield United | 5-1 |
| Bridport v Bridgwater Town | 3-0 |
| Taunton Town v Hungerford Town | 5-1 |
| Thatcham Town v Marlow | 2-0 |
| BAT Sports v Bodmin Town | 1-3 |
| Lymington AFC v Bemerton Heath Harlequins | 0-0, 2-1 |
| Endsleigh v Cowes Sports | 0-2 |

**Third Round**

| | |
|---|---|
| Marske United v Bedlington Terriers | 1-2 |
| Stockton v Burscough | 1-2 |
| Mossley v West Auckland Town | 0-2 |
| Paulton Victoria v Kidsgrove Athletic | 1-4 |
| Tow Law Town v Dunston FB | 2-1 |
| Billingham Town v Friar Lane OB | 1-0 |
| Arnold Town v North Ferriby United | 1-3 |
| Clitheroe v Boston Town | 3-0 |
| Oadby Town v Seaham Red Star | 4-1 |
| Brigg Town v Hucknall Town | 1-2 |
| Denaby United v Birstall United | 0-1 |
| Thackley v Stamford | 2-3 |
| Bloxwich Town v Spalding United | 1-3 |
| Braintree Town v Banstead Athletic | 4-2 |
| Hemel Hempstead v Taunton Town | 2-3 |
| Lymington AFC v Woodbridge Town | 2-0 |
| Bodmin Town v Bowers United | 5-3 |
| Wimbourne Town v Tiverton Town | 0-4 |
| Basildon United v Herne Bay | 1-3 |
| Cowes Sports v Chard Town | 1-1, 0-0 |

*Cowes Sports won 4-1 on penalties.*

| | |
|---|---|
| Porthleven v Arlesey Town | 3-2 |
| Bridport v Potters Bar Town | 0-4 |
| Folkestone Invicta v Chipstead | 2-1 |

| | |
|---|---|
| Brook House v Histon | 0-0, 0-3 |
| Peacehaven & Telscombe v Sudbury Town | 1-2 |
| Aveley v Wroxham | 1-2 |
| Stotfold v Ashford Town (Middlesex) | 2-1 |
| Thatcham Town v Burgess Hill Town | 0-3 |
| Great Wakering Rovers v Wealdstone | 2-1 |
| Brache Sparta v Ely City | 8-1 |
| Chippenham Town v Tooting & Mitcham United | 2-3 |
| Camberley Town v Sudbury Wanderers | 3-3, 1-3 |

**Fourth Round**

| | |
|---|---|
| Taunton Town v Herne Bay | 5-2 |
| Sudbury Wanderers v Bedlington Terriers | 3-0 |
| Oadby Town v Tooting & Mitcham United | 2-2, 4-1 |
| Hucknall Town v Wroxham | 2-1 |
| Billingham Town v Bodmin Town | 3-1 |
| Tow Law Town v Histon | 3-0 |
| Kidsgrove Athletic v Brache Sparta | 2-2, 3-0 |
| Braintree Town v Lymington | 0-0, 1-2 |
| Stamford v Potters Bar Town | 0-1 |
| Cowes Sports v North Ferriby United | 1-1, 1-3 |
| Sudbury Town v Burscough | 1-0 |
| Tiverton Town v West Auckland Town | 9-0 |
| Spalding United v Birstall United | 2-1 |
| Stotfold v Porthleven | 1-2 |
| Clitheroe v Burgess Hill Town | 0-0, 0-3 |
| Great Wakering Rovers v Folkestone Invicta | 2-1 |

**Fifth Round**

| | |
|---|---|
| Tiverton Town v Oadby Town | 2-1 |
| Sudbury Wanderers v Burgess Hill Town | 1-0 |
| Porthleven v Hucknall Town | 1-0 |
| Sudbury Town v Tow Law Town | 1-2 |
| Kidsgrove Athletic v Lymington | 3-2 |
| Spalding United v Billingham Town | 2-0 |
| North Ferriby United v Taunton Town | 0-2 |
| Great Wakering Rovers v Potters Bar Town | 0-1 |

**Sixth Round**

| | |
|---|---|
| Taunton Town v Porthleven | 2-0 |
| Spalding United v Tiverton Town | 1-2 |
| Sudbury Wanderers v Tow Law Town | 1-1, 0-2 |
| Kidsgrove Athletic v Potters Bar Town | 2-0 |

**Semi-finals (two legs)**

| | |
|---|---|
| Taunton Town v Tow Law Town | 4-4, 0-1 |
| Tiverton Town v Kidsgrove Athletic | 2-0, 1-2 |

**FINAL (at Wembley)**

**9 MAY**

**Tiverton Town (0) 1** (*Varley*)
**Tow Law Town (0) 0** 13,193

*Tiverton Town:* Edwards; Fallon, Saunders, Tatterton, Smith J, Conning, Mancekivell (Rogers), Smith K (Varley), Everett, Daly, Leonard (Waters).
*Tow Law Town:* Dawson; Pickering, Darwent, Bailey, Hague, Moan, Johnson, Nelson, Suddick, Laidler (Bennett), Robinson.
*Referee:* M. Riley (Leeds).

# THE TIMES FA YOUTH CUP 1997–98

**PRELIMINARY ROUND**

| | |
|---|---|
| Lancaster City v Yorkshire Amateur | 0-3 |
| Wigan Athletic v Billingham Town | 3-2 |
| Guisborough Town v Hartlepool United | 0-0, 2-3 |
| Farsley Celtic w.o. v Barrow withdrew | |
| Shotton Comrades withdrew v Carlisle United w.o. | |
| Stocksbridge Park Steels v Preston North End | 1-3 |
| Chester City v Runcorn | 10-1 |
| Scunthorpe United v Lincoln City | 0-0, 2-1 |
| Louth United v Notts County | 0-9 |
| Hull City v Frickley Athletic | 3-1 |
| Nantwich Town v Stockport County | 0-10 |
| Southport v Mansfield Town | 1-2 |
| Warrington Town v Chadderton | 2-2, 2-2, 5-3 |
| Ilkeston Town v Morecambe | 2-2, 3-1 |
| Halifax Town v Denaby United | 4-4, 0-3 |
| Atherton LR v Leigh RMI | 5-0 |
| Doncaster Rovers v Ashton United | 4-0 |
| Curzon Ashton v Rochdale | 0-9 |
| Kidderminster Harriers v Chase Town | 4-0 |
| Birstall United v Lye Town | 3-2 |
| Redditch United v Bromsgrove Rovers | 1-3 |
| Pershore Town v Racing Club Warwick | 2-2, 2-1 |
| Ibstock Welfare v Halesowen Town | 0-2 |
| Bedworth United v Rothwell Town | 4-2 |
| Hinckley United v Banbury United | 4-1 |
| Gresley Rovers v Willenhall Town | 7-0 |
| Somersham Town v VS Rugby | 3-0 |
| Westfields v Histon | 2-5 |
| Eynesbury Rovers v Wednesfield | 0-10 |
| Cambridge United v Solihull Borough | 8-1 |
| Harlow Town v Sudbury Town | 2-1 |
| Gorleston v Wivenhoe Town | 4-7 |
| Basildon United v Fakenham Town | 3-2 |
| Felixstowe Port & Town v Ipswich Wanderers | 0-2 |
| Walton & Hersham v Royston Town | 10-0 |
| Chesham United v Bedfont | 4-2 |
| Ruislip Manor v Wembley | 0-7 |
| Barnet v Hillingdon Borough | 4-1 |
| Chelmsford City v Boreham Wood | 5-2 |
| Kingsbury Town v Wingate & Finchley | 0-4 |
| Hayes v Bedford Town | 2-3 |
| Marlow v Hampton | 4-2 |
| Waltham Abbey v Cheshunt | 2-3 |
| Stevenage Borough v Arlesey Town | 10-0 |
| East Thurrock United v Purfleet | 4-2 |
| Leyton Sports v Concord Rangers | 3-5 |
| Hendon v Northwood | 4-3 |
| Tilbury v Stanway Rovers | 1-1, 1-2 |
| Harefield United withdrew v Dartford w.o. | |
| Thamesmead Town w.o. v Baldock Town withdrew | |
| Welwyn Garden City v Yeading | 3-3, 0-5 |
| Corinthian v Tonbridge | 1-3 |
| Herne Bay v Ashford Town (Middlesex) | 5-1 |
| Carshalton Athletic v Camberley Town | 0-3 |
| Farnborough Town v Sittingbourne | 0-6 |
| Croydon v Faversham Town | 5-1 |
| Whitstable Town v Chipstead | 1-5 |
| Chatham Town v Kingstonian | 0-1 |
| Bromley v Hastings Town | 3-2 |
| Chichester City v Hythe United | 6-2 |
| Redhill v Dover Athletic | 0-3 |
| Ringmer v Folkestone Invicta | 0-9 |
| Eastbourne Town v Raynes Park Vale | 7-0 |
| Crawley Town v Portfield | 1-0 |
| Aldershot Town v Reading Town | 1-0 |
| Merstham v Basingstoke Town | 2-1 |
| Fisher Athletic v Leatherhead | 3-0 |
| Wokingham Town v Dorking | 7-3 |
| Egham Town v Tooting & Mitcham United | 0-4 |
| Carterton Town v Newbury AFC | 2-3 |
| Bashley v Romsey Town | 2-3 |
| Havant Town withdrew v Abingdon Town w.o. | |
| Thame United v Weymouth | 3-1 |
| Oxford City v Eastleigh | 3-1 |
| Warminster Town v Salisbury City | 1-1, 3-2 |
| Cinderford Town v Cheltenham Town | 2-3 |
| Mangotsfield United v Yeovil Town | 1-2 |
| Forest Green Rovers v Gloucester City | 0-0, 1-2 |
| Yate Town v Cirencester Town | 1-3 |

**FIRST QUALIFYING ROUND**

| | |
|---|---|
| Wigan Athletic v Darlington | 2-1 |
| Scarborough v Farsley Celtic | 7-1 |
| Hartlepool United v Harrogate Town | 4-1 |

| | |
|---|---|
| Yorkshire Amateur v Carlisle United | 0-4 |
| Chester City v Barnsley | 2-1 |
| Northwich Victoria v Notts County | 0-5 |
| Scunthorpe United v Marine | 5-1 |
| Preston North End v Sheffield Wednesday | 1-0 |
| Stockport County v Chesterfield | 0-3 |
| Stalybridge Celtic v Warrington Town | 0-7 |
| Mansfield Town v Worksop Town | 7-2 |
| Hull City v Cheadle Town | 11-1 |
| Denaby United withdrew v Brigg Town w.o. | |
| Emley v Doncaster Rovers | 1-3 |
| Atherton LR v Bamber Bridge | 0-2 |
| Ilkeston Town v Rochdale | 2-1 |
| Kidderminster Harriers v Gornal Athletic | 3-1 |
| Northampton Spencer v Bromsgrove Rovers | 0-2 |
| Birstall United v Bilston Town | 0-3 |
| Walsall Wood v Burton Albion | 0-5 |
| Halesowen Town v Atherstone United | 0-0, 2-0 |
| Holwell Sports v Hinckley United | 0-4 |
| Bedworth United v Stourbridge | 4-0 |
| Pershore Town v Gresley Rovers | 0-4 |
| Histon v Tividale | 7-2 |
| Cradley Town v Cambridge United | 0-5 |
| Wednesfield v Cambridge City | 0-2 |
| Somersham Town v Tamworth | 1-0 |
| Wivenhoe Town v Maldon Town | 3-3, 4-0 |
| Great Wakering Rovers v Ipswich Wanderers | 4-0 |
| Basildon United v Kings Lynn | 2-4 |
| Harlow Town v Braintree Town | 3-1 |
| Chesham United v Hornchurch | 0-2 |
| Staines Town v Barnet | 5-3 |
| Wembley v Beaconsfield SYCOB | 4-0 |
| Walton & Hersham v Leighton Town | 8-0 |
| Wingate & Finchley v Romford | 2-3 |
| Hitchin Town v Marlow | 5-1 |
| Bedford Town v Hemel Hempstead | 2-0 |
| Chelmsford City v Cheshunt | 5-1 |
| East Thurrock United v Uxbridge | 2-0 |
| *Ordered to be replayed; referee allowed only 80 minutes,* 2-1 | |
| Grays Athletic v Hendon | 1-0 |
| Concord Rangers v Hoddesdon Town | 3-5 |
| Stevenage Borough v Potters Bar Town | 6-1 |
| Dartford v Bishop's Stortford | 1-0 |
| St Albans City v Yeading | 1-1, 4-1 |
| Thamesmead Town v Erith & Belvedere | 1-3 |
| Stanway Rovers v Southend Manor | 1-0 |
| Herne Bay v Sutton United | 1-2 |
| Southwick v Sittingbourne | 0-3 |
| Camberley Town v Bracknell Town | 3-1 |
| Tonbridge v Welling United | 0-5 |
| Chipstead v Margate | 5-1 |
| Banstead Athletic v Bromley | 2-1 |
| Kingstonian v Burgess Hill Town | 0-0, 1-2 |
| Croydon v Horsham | 2-1 |
| Dover Athletic v Whitehawk | 5-0 |
| Horsham YMCA v Eastbourne Town | 0-7 |
| Folkestone Invicta v Three Bridges | 0-2 |
| Chichester City v Crawley Town | 1-3 |
| Merstham v Whyteleafe | 4-2 |
| Maidenhead United v Wokingham Town | 3-0 |
| Fisher Athletic v Saltdean United | 4-2 |
| Aldershot Town v Tooting & Mitcham United | 1-3 |
| Romsey Town v Fareham Town | 0-3 |
| Thatcham Town v Thame United | 4-2 |
| Abingdon Town v Witney Town | 7-2 |
| Newbury AFC v Oxford City | 1-3 |
| Cheltenham Town v Odd Down | 4-0 |
| Paulton Rovers v Gloucester City | 0-5 |
| Yeovil Town v Chippenham Town | 1-2 |
| Warminster Town v Cirencester Town | 0-14 |

**SECOND QUALIFYING ROUND**

| | |
|---|---|
| Hartlepool United v Wigan Athletic | 4-1 |
| Scarborough v Carlisle United | 3-2 |
| Scunthorpe United v Chester City | 1-2 |
| Notts County v Preston North End | 2-1, 2-1 |
| Mansfield Town v Chesterfield | 2-1 |
| Warrington Town v Hull City | 0-8 |
| Bamber Bridge v Brigg Town | 4-0 |
| Doncaster Rovers v Ilkeston Town | 2-1 |
| Bilston Town v Kidderminster Harriers | 1-2 |
| Bromsgrove Rovers v Burton Albion | 1-1, 2-3 |
| Bedworth United v Halesowen Town | 2-1 |
| Hinckley United v Gresley Rovers | 5-0 |
| Cambridge City v Histon | 2-3 |
| Cambridge United v Somersham Town | 2-3 |

| | |
|---|---|
| Kings Lynn v Wivenhoe Town | 5-1 |
| Great Wakering Rovers v Harlow Town | 2-2, 2-0 |
| Wembley v Hornchurch | 2-2, 2-1 |
| Staines Town v Walton & Hersham | 0-0, 1-2 |
| Bedford Town v Romford | 3-1 |
| Hitchin Town v Chelmsford City | 2-4 |
| Hoddesdon Town v East Thurrock United | 5-1 |
| Grays Athletic v Stevenage Borough | 1-3 |
| Erith & Belvedere v Dartford | 3-1 |
| St Albans City v Stanway Rovers | 2-1 |
| Camberley Town v Sutton United | 1-1, 1-2 |
| Sittingbourne v Welling United | 1-1, 1-2 |
| Burgess Hill Town v Chipstead | 0-1 |
| Bromley v Croydon | 1-2 |
| Three Bridges v Dover Athletic | 1-0 |
| Eastbourne Town v Crawley Town | 0-2 |
| Fisher Athletic v Merstham | 2-2, 2-2 |
| *Merstham won 5-4 on penalties.* | |
| Maidenhead United v Tooting & Mitcham United | 1-3 |
| Abingdon Town v Fareham Town | 6-1 |
| Thatcham Town v Oxford City | 1-3 |
| Yeovil Town v Cheltenham Town | 1-1, 1-3 |
| Gloucester Town v Cirencester Town | 2-0 |

**THIRD QUALIFYING ROUND**

| | |
|---|---|
| Scarborough v Hartlepool United | 5-2 |
| Notts County v Chester City | 5-1 |
| Hull City v Mansfield Town | 2-0 |
| Doncaster Rovers v Bamber Bridge | 3-1 |
| Burton Albion v Kidderminster Harriers | 3-2 |
| Hinckley United v Bedworth United | 2-3 |
| Somersham Town v Histon | 2-2, 2-6 |
| Great Wakering Rovers v Kings Lynn | 3-2 |
| Walton & Hersham v Wembley | 3-3, 3-2 |
| Chelmsford City v Bedford Town | 2-3 |
| Stevenage Borough v Hoddesdon Town | 5-0 |
| St Albans City v Erith & Belvedere | 0-2 |
| Welling United v Sutton United | 4-1 |
| Croydon v Chipstead | 0-1 |
| Crawley Town v Three Bridges | 1-0 |
| Tooting & Mitcham United v Merstham | 3-1 |
| Oxford City v Abingdon Town | 1-1, 1-1 |
| *Abingdon Town won 4-3 on penalties.* | |
| Gloucester City v Cheltenham Town | 1-0 |

**FIRST ROUND**

| | |
|---|---|
| Shrewsbury Town v Boldmere St Michaels | 5-1 |
| Rotherham United v Bury | 0-1 |
| Bradford City v Nuneaton Borough | 9-0 |
| Bolton Wanderers v Scarborough | 1-2 |
| Stoke City v Wolverhampton Wanderers | 3-0 |
| Burton Albion v Bedworth United | 3-1 |
| Burnley v Wrexham | 2-0 |
| Peterborough United v Doncaster Rovers | 2-1 |
| Grimsby Town v Leicester City | 0-1 |
| Walsall v Port Vale | 4-4, 2-1 |
| Derby County v Blackpool | 0-2 |
| Newcastle United v Hull City | 0-1 |
| Birmingham City v Crewe Alexandra | 1-2 |
| Huddersfield Town v York City | 1-2 |
| Aston Villa v Notts County | 2-4 |
| Enfield v Stevenage Borough | 5-1 |
| Torquay United v Leyton Orient | 3-3, 4-0 |
| Reading v Oxford United | 3-2 |
| Erith & Belvedere v Tooting & Mitcham United | 2-0 |
| Crawley Town v Great Wakering Rovers | 2-5 |
| Welling United v Dulwich Hamlet | 2-2, 1-0 |
| Bournemouth AFC v Gillingham | 0-3 |
| Exeter City v Colchester United | 4-2 |
| Gloucester City v Southampton | 0-6 |
| Histon v Gravesend & Northfleet | 3-2 |
| Chipstead v Chelsea | 0-9 |
| Plymouth Argyle v Hereford United | 4-2 |
| Croydon Athletic v Northampton Town | 2-5 |
| Woking v Brighton & Hove Albion | 3-3, 3-1 |
| Wycombe Wanderers v Cardiff City | 2-1 |
| Fulham v Abingdon Town | 3-1 |
| Swindon Town v Bristol Rovers | 1-1, 0-0 |
| *Bristol Rovers won 10-9 on penalties.* | |
| Swansea City v Bedford Town | 3-2 |
| Walton & Hersham v Rushden & Diamonds | 0-3 |

**SECOND ROUND**

| | |
|---|---|
| Burton Albion v Nottingham Forest | 0-5 |
| Blackpool v Everton | 0-1 |
| Leicester City v Liverpool | 2-3 |
| Bury v Peterborough United | 0-2 |
| Notts County v Walsall | 2-1 |
| Bradford City v Scarborough | 2-1 |
| Shrewsbury Town v Stoke City | 1-2 |
| Sheffield United v Tranmere Rovers | 3-3, 3-5 |

| | |
|---|---|
| Sunderland v Crewe Alexandra | 1-2 |
| Leeds United v Oldham Athletic | 3-2 |
| York City v Middlesbrough | 0-1 |
| Hull City v Burnley | 1-0 |
| West Bromwich Albion v Manchester City | 1-1, 2-3 |
| Hull City v Burnley | 1-0 |
| Blackburn Rovers v Manchester United | 1-1, 3-2 |
| Rushden & Diamonds v Charlton Athletic | 1-6 |
| Southampton v Histon | 6-0 |
| West Ham United v Millwall | 2-0 |
| Torquay United v Bristol City | 0-3 |
| Watford v Northampton Town | 6-3 |
| Norwich City v Crystal Palace | 0-0, 1-2 |
| Enfield v Bristol Rovers | 0-1 |
| Chelsea v Wimbledon | 2-2, 3-1 |
| Portsmouth v Erith & Belvedere | 5-0 |
| Ipswich Town v Great Wakering Rovers | 4-1 |
| Swansea City v Brentford | 2-2, 1-0 |
| Exeter City v Arsenal | 1-1, 0-1 |
| Queens Park Rangers v Southend United | 3-2 |
| Tottenham Hotspur v Reading | 1-0 |
| Coventry City v Luton Town | 0-4 |
| Plymouth Argyle v Fulham | 0-3 |
| Wycombe Wanderers v Welling United | 2-0 |
| Woking v Gillingham | 1-2 |

**THIRD ROUND**

| | |
|---|---|
| Watford v Fulham | 2-0 |
| Middlesbrough v Charlton Athletic | 3-2 |
| Liverpool v Queens Park Rangers | 1-2 |
| West Ham United v Blackburn Rovers | 1-4 |
| Leeds United v Crystal Palace | 3-1 |
| Everton v Stoke City | 1-0 |
| Tranmere Rovers v Chelsea | 2-5 |
| Portsmouth v Gillingham | 2-0 |
| Southampton v Nottingham Forest | 3-0 |
| Ipswich Town v Bradford City | 2-1 |
| Peterborough United v Wycombe Wanderers | 2-0 |
| Hull City v Bristol Rovers | 3-1 |
| Bristol City v Swansea City | 2-0 |
| Luton Town v Tottenham Hotspur | 2-2, 2-4 |
| Notts County v Arsenal | 1-6 |
| Crewe Alexandra v Manchester City | 2-0 |

**FOURTH ROUND**

| | |
|---|---|
| Portsmouth v Chelsea | 1-3 |
| Middlesbrough v Leeds United | 0-0, 0-2 |
| Hull City v Ipswich Town | 1-1, 0-1 |
| Queens Park Rangers v Blackburn Rovers | 1-5 |
| Arsenal v Bristol City | 3-1 |
| Southampton v Peterborough United | 1-2 |
| Watford v Everton | 2-3 |
| Crewe Alexandra v Tottenham Hotspur | 1-0 |

**FIFTH ROUND**

| | |
|---|---|
| Everton v Ipswich Town | 3-2 |
| Chelsea v Blackburn Rovers | 1-1, 0-2 |
| Peterborough United v Crewe Alexandra | 1-1, 3-1 |
| Arsenal v Leeds United | 0-1 |

**SEMI-FINALS (TWO LEGS)**

| | |
|---|---|
| Leeds United v Everton | 0-1, 1-2 |
| Blackburn Rovers v Peterborough United | 1-0, 1-0 |

**FINAL FIRST LEG**

**2 MAY**

**Blackburn Rovers (1) 1** *(Taylor)*

**Everton (2) 3** *(Jevons, Cadamarteri, Osman)*     9280

*Blackburn Rovers:* Stewart; Richardson, Murphy, McAvoy, Taylor, Brown, Scates, Dunn, Topley (Woodfield), Hamilton, Ryan (Baldacchino).
*Everton:* Delany; Regan, Eaton, O'Brien (Hibbert), Farley, Dunne, Poppleton, Osman, Cadamarteri, Jevons (Jeffers), Milligan.
*Referee:* N. Barry (Scunthorpe).

**FINAL SECOND LEG**

**7 MAY**

**Everton (1) 2** *(Jeffers, Milligan)*

**Blackburn Rovers (0) 2** *(Hamilton, Hawe)*     15,258

*Everton:* Delany; Regan, Eaton, O'Brien, Farley, Dunne, Poppleton, Jevons, Cadamarteri, Jeffers (Hibbert), Milligan.
*Blackburn Rovers:* Stewart; Richardson, Murphy, McAvoy, Taylor, Brown (Hawe), Scates, Dunn, Topley, Hamilton, Baldacchino (Ryan).
*Referee:* N. Barry (Scunthorpe).

# FA SUNDAY CUP 1997–98

## FIRST ROUND

| | |
|---|---|
| Lion & Unicorn v Rob Roy | 1-4 |
| Albion Sports v Boulevard Mode Force | 0-4 |
| Hartlepool Rovers v Seymour | 6-1 |
| BRNESC v Caldway | 2-1 |
| Bulford v Hartlepool Staincliffe Hotel | 1-3 |
| Allerton v Baildon Junction Athletic | 3-0 |
| Britannia v Tanhouse Upholland Labour | 0-2 |
| Clubmoor Nalgo v Packaging DKS | 1-0 |
| Hudsons v Shankhouse United | 5-3 |
| Littlewoods Athletic v Nicosia | 2-1 |
| Humbledon Plains Farm v Salerno | 0-2 |
| Lobster v Mainstay | 3-2 |
| Newfield v Queens Park | 2-2, 0-3 |
| Bolton Woods v Manfast | 1-1, 4-1 |
| Grosvenor Park v Sandon | 0-2 |
| Birmingham Celtic v Cheadle United | 2-1 |
| Rovers Sports w.o. v Tuddenham Rovers withdrew | |
| Sawston Keys v Slade Celtic | 3-4 |
| Melton Youth Old Boys v Olympic Star | 0-2 |
| Hundred Acre v Mackadown Lane S&S | 0-1 |
| Lodge Cottrell v Sandwell | 4-2 |
| Heathfield v Leicester City Bus | 4-1 |
| Ford Basildon v Holderness United | 1-3 |
| Broad Plain House v Cobham | 2-3 |
| Fryerns v Winter Royals | 3-2 |
| BRSC Aidan v Duke of York | 2-0 |
| Mailcoach v Pitsea | 1-1, 1-6 |
| Continental v Golden Bottle | 2-1 |
| Northampton St Margarets v Ouzavich | 1-3 |
| Caversham Park Village v Hanham Sunday | 3-5 |
| Luton Old Boys v Theale | 0-0, 2-3 |
| Lebeq Tavern w.o. v Lomax Chestnuts withdrew | |
| New Inn Keynsham v St Josephs (Luton) | 2-5 |
| Belstone v Courage | 3-1 |
| St Joseph's (Bristol) v St Joseph's (Sth Oxhey) | 0-2 |
| Northfield Rangers v Oxford Road Social | 2-0 |
| Kendall Albion v The Cutters Friday | 3-2 |
| Old Oak v Reading Borough | 2-1 |
| Active Signs w.o. v Shenley Hotel withdrew | |
| Chequers v Gossoms End | 3-0 |
| Greenacres v Watford Labour | 4-1 |
| Italia Wasteels v Morden Nomads | 0-2 |

## SECOND ROUND

| | |
|---|---|
| Hartlepool Rovers v Boulevard Mode Force | 1-3 |
| Rob Roy v Hudsons | 3-0 |
| Eden Vale v Blyth Comrades Social | 5-1 |
| Tanhouse Upholland Labour v Allerton | 4-1 |
| Northwood v Queens Park | 0-2 |
| Bolton Woods v BRNESC | 8-0 |
| East Bowling Unity v Clubmoor Nalgo | 4-2 |
| Crown v Hartlepool Staincliffe Hotel | 3-1 |
| Lobster v Hartlepool Lion Hotel | 0-3 |
| A3 v Stanley Road | 3-2 |
| Rovers Sports v Littlewoods Athletic | 3-0 |
| Birmingham Celtic v Sandon | 2-3 |
| Mackadown Lane S&S v Salerno | 0-2 |
| Park Inn v Slade Celtic | 2-0 |
| Chequers v Olympic Star | 0-1 |
| Hanham Sunday v Marston Sports | 1-2 |
| Theale v Brookvale Athletic | 0-4 |
| Ouzavich v BRSC Aidan | 1-1, 1-2 |

| | |
|---|---|
| Cobham v Lodge Cottrell | 3-5 |
| Holderness United v Heathfield | 1-4 |
| Lebeq Tavern v Fryerns | 1-0 |
| Continental v Pitsea | 2-4 |
| Old Oak v St Josephs (Luton) | 0-5 |
| St Joseph's (Sth Oxhey) v Belstone | 3-0 |
| Greenacres v Northfield Rangers | 1-2 |
| Active Signs v Kendall Albion | 6-0 |
| Capel Plough v Arras | 2-4 |
| Coach & Horses v Bournemouth | 4-2 |
| Forest Athletic v Bournemouth Electric | 3-2 |
| Clifton Albion v Celtic SC (Luton) | 0-1 |
| *(Celtic SC (Luton) removed from the competition for fielding an ineligible player; Clifton Albion re-instated).* | |
| Morden Nomads v Hammer | 3-0 |
| Warriors v Oakwood Sports | 5-0 |

## THIRD ROUND

| | |
|---|---|
| Salerno v Queens Park | 1-0 |
| Bolton Woods v Rob Roy | 2-0 |
| Crown v Tanhouse Upholland Labour | 2-1 |
| Park Inn v Hartlepool Lion Hotel | 0-3 |
| A3 v Sandon | 1-3 |
| Rovers Sports v East Bowling Unity | 3-1 |
| Eden Vale v Boulevard Mode Force | 1-0 |
| Lebeq Tavern v Marston Sports | 1-3 |
| St Josephs (Luton) v Lodge Cottrell | 4-0 |
| Forest Athletic v Clifton Albion | 4-1 |
| BRSC Aidan v Olympic Star | 1-3 |
| St Josephs (South Oxhey) v Pitsea | 2-6 |
| Warriors v Active Signs | 5-6 |
| Brookvale Athletic v Arras | 4-0 |
| Northfield Rangers v Morden Nomads | 0-1 |
| Heathfield v Coach & Horses | 4-0 |

## FOURTH ROUND

| | |
|---|---|
| Hartlepool Lion Hotel v Olympic Star | 0-1 |
| Sandon v Bolton Woods | 0-2 |
| Crown v Eden Vale | 2-5 |
| Rovers Sports v Salerno | 0-1 |
| Pitsea v Heathfield | 2-0 |
| Active Signs v Forest Athletic | 2-4 |
| Marston Sports v Morden Nomads | 0-0, 4-1 |
| Brookvale Athletic v St Josephs (Luton) | 1-3 |

## FIFTH ROUND

| | |
|---|---|
| Eden Vale v Salerno | 2-1 |
| Bolton Woods v Olympic Star | 1-2 |
| Marston Sports v St Josephs (Luton) | 1-2 |
| Forest Athletic v Pitsea | 1-6 |

## SEMI-FINALS

| | |
|---|---|
| Eden Vale v St Josephs (Luton) | 1-2 |
| Olympic Star v Pitsea | 3-1 |

## FINAL

| | |
|---|---|
| Olympic Star v St Josephs (Luton) | 1-1 |
| *Olympic Star won 5-4 on penalties.* | |

# FA COUNTY YOUTH CHALLENGE CUP 1997–98

**FIRST ROUND**

| | |
|---|---|
| Sheffield & Hallamshire v Cumberland | 3-2 |
| Cheshire v Westmoreland | 6-0 |
| Nottinghamshire v Liverpool | 2-4 |
| Derbyshire v Shropshire | 3-4 |
| Lincolnshire v Manchester | 2-1 |
| Middlesex v Worcestershire | 1-4 |
| Hertfordshire v Gloucestershire | 1-2 |
| Bedfordshire v Kent | 1-3 |
| Oxfordshire v Leicestershire & Rutland | 1-3 |
| Berks & Bucks v Sussex | 1-3 |
| Northamptonshire v Hampshire | 2-1 |
| Royal Navy v Somerset | 2-8 |
| Army v Wiltshire | 1-3 |

**SECOND ROUND**

| | |
|---|---|
| Durham v Sheffield & Hallamshire | 2-0 |
| Northumberland v Cheshire | 3-0 |
| North Riding v Liverpool | 2-0 |
| Lancashire v Staffordshire | 4-1 |
| East Riding v Shropshire | 4-3 |
| West Riding v Lincolnshire | 4-2 |
| Cambridgeshire v Herefordshire | 7-1 |
| Huntingdonshire v Worcestershire | 2-3 |
| Birmingham v Gloucestershire | 1-3 |
| Norfolk v Kent | 2-1 |
| Suffolk v Leicestershire & Rutland | 2-2, 2-6 |
| Essex v Sussex | 0-4 |

| | |
|---|---|
| Surrey v Dorset | 6-1 |
| London v Northamptonshire | 2-1 |
| Cornwall v Somerset | 2-2, 1-1 |
| *Cornwall won 5-4 on penalties.* | |
| Devon v Wiltshire | 4-4, 1-4 |

**THIRD ROUND**

| | |
|---|---|
| Northumberland v Durham | 2-0 |
| North Riding v West Riding | 1-5 |
| Lancashire v East Riding | 1-4 |
| Sussex v Norfolk | 2-0 |
| Leicestershire & Rutland v Wiltshire | 0-8 |
| Worcestershire v Surrey | 1-0 |
| Cambridgeshire v Gloucestershire | 0-2 |
| Cornwall v London | 1-0 |

**FOURTH ROUND**

| | |
|---|---|
| Sussex v Worcestershire | 2-0 |
| Northumberland v Gloucestershire | 4-2 |
| West Riding v East Riding | 2-1 |
| Wiltshire v Cornwall | 1-1, 2-0 |

**SEMI-FINALS**

| | |
|---|---|
| Northumberland v Wiltshire | 3-2 |
| West Riding v Sussex | 2-1 |

**FINAL**

| | |
|---|---|
| West Riding v Northumberland | 1-2 |

# FA PREMIER YOUTH LEAGUE

## CONFERENCE 1

| | | Home | | | Goals | | Away | | | Goals | | | |
|---|---|---|---|---|---|---|---|---|---|---|---|---|---|
| | P | W | D | L | F | A | W | D | L | F | A | GD | Pts |
| Sheffield W | 22 | 5 | 3 | 3 | 19 | 15 | 7 | 2 | 2 | 21 | 13 | +12 | 41 |
| Sunderland | 22 | 7 | 1 | 3 | 23 | 15 | 5 | 1 | 5 | 18 | 15 | +11 | 38 |
| Nottingham F | 22 | 5 | 1 | 5 | 21 | 23 | 6 | 3 | 2 | 22 | 10 | +10 | 37 |
| Middlesbrough | 22 | 4 | 3 | 4 | 15 | 18 | 5 | 3 | 3 | 22 | 17 | +2 | 33 |
| Leeds U | 22 | 3 | 5 | 3 | 26 | 24 | 2 | 6 | 3 | 18 | 20 | 0 | 26 |
| Derby Co | 22 | 4 | 2 | 5 | 16 | 21 | 2 | 5 | 4 | 16 | 19 | −8 | 25 |
| Coventry C | 22 | 4 | 4 | 3 | 10 | 10 | 1 | 1 | 9 | 11 | 37 | −26 | 20 |
| Barnsley | 22 | 1 | 2 | 8 | 9 | 24 | 2 | 3 | 6 | 9 | 20 | −26 | 14 |

## CONFERENCE 2

| | | Home | | | Goals | | Away | | | Goals | | | |
|---|---|---|---|---|---|---|---|---|---|---|---|---|---|
| | P | W | D | L | F | A | W | D | L | F | A | GD | Pts |
| Arsenal | 22 | 5 | 3 | 3 | 26 | 13 | 9 | 1 | 1 | 34 | 10 | +37 | 46 |
| Tottenham H | 22 | 5 | 3 | 3 | 15 | 16 | 5 | 3 | 3 | 20 | 18 | +1 | 36 |
| Crystal Palace | 22 | 5 | 3 | 3 | 16 | 8 | 5 | 2 | 4 | 22 | 17 | +13 | 35 |
| Southampton | 22 | 6 | 2 | 3 | 22 | 20 | 4 | 3 | 4 | 18 | 19 | +1 | 35 |
| West Ham U | 22 | 5 | 3 | 3 | 19 | 16 | 3 | 2 | 6 | 16 | 21 | −2 | 29 |
| QPR | 22 | 4 | 2 | 5 | 23 | 21 | 2 | 5 | 4 | 11 | 14 | −1 | 25 |
| Chelsea | 22 | 3 | 4 | 4 | 18 | 18 | 2 | 3 | 6 | 13 | 20 | −7 | 22 |
| Wimbledon | 22 | 3 | 4 | 4 | 10 | 17 | 2 | 2 | 7 | 8 | 18 | −17 | 21 |

## PLAY-OFFS

**First Round**
Arsenal 5, Barnsley 2
Middlesbrough 0, West Ham U 2
Sunderland 1, Chelsea 0
Crystal Palace 2, Derby Co 0
Sheffield W 3, Wimbledon 2
Southampton 7, Leeds U 1
Tottenham H 2, Coventry C 0
Nottingham F 2, QPR 0

**Second Round**
Arsenal 3, West Ham U 0

Sunderland 2, Crystal Palace 1
Sheffield W 4, Southampton 0
Tottenham H 2, Nottingham F 0

**Semi-Finals**
Arsenal 3, Sunderland 2
Tottenham H 2, Sheffield W 0

**Final (two legs)**
Arsenal 2, Tottenham H 0
Tottenham H 1, Arsenal 0

# UNIVERSITY FOOTBALL 1997–98

## 114th UNIVERSITY MATCH

(at Craven Cottage, Fulham)

**Oxford 4, Cambridge 0** (h-t 1-0)

*Oxford:* Park; Loebinger (Wardle), Buckley, Lea, O'Brien, Spencer, Parker, Probert, Cairnes, Goff (Richards), Kintish (Calver).
*Scorers:* Parker, Probert, Cairnes, Richards.
*Cambridge:* Gort; Ball, House (Ghaemmaghami), Dobson (Miller), Pett, Mowart, Fearnley A, Eales, Walsh, Fearnley T, Arhmed (Elliot).
*Referee:* D. Elleray (Harrow).
Cambridge have not won the fixture for ten years, but still lead Oxford by 45 wins to 43 with 26 drawn.

## LONDON UNIVERSITY XI REPRESENTATIVE MATCH RESULTS

Old Boys' League Lost 2-3
Ulysses Won 1-0
Southern Amateur League Won 0-4
BUSA South-East Lost 1-3
Arthurian League Won 0-6
Southern Olympian League Lost 1-2
Cambridge University Lost 1-2
Amateur Football Alliance Lost 0-5
London Legal League Lost 0-1
Metropolitan Police Lost 1-2
*Oxford University, Fulham, & Army Crusaders cancelled the arranged games*

## UNIVERSITY OF LONDON INTER-COLLEGIATE MENS' LEAGUE

| PREMIER DIVISION | P | W | D | L | F | A | Pts |
|---|---|---|---|---|---|---|---|
| Q. Mary Westfield College | 14 | 11 | 1 | 2 | 44 | 17 | 34 |
| London School of Economics | 14 | 8 | 2 | 4 | 33 | 25 | 26 |
| University College | 14 | 8 | 1 | 5 | 38 | 28 | 25 |
| Imperial College | 14 | 6 | 3 | 5 | 41 | 33 | 21 |
| King's College | 14 | 5 | 3 | 6 | 27 | 35 | 18 |
| Goldsmiths' College | 14 | 4 | 2 | 8 | 24 | 30 | 14 |
| Royal Holloway College | 13 | 2 | 5 | 6 | 28 | 32 | 11 |
| U.M.D.S. | 13 | 2 | 1 | 10 | 11 | 46 | 7 |

| DIVISION ONE | P | W | D | L | F | A | Pts |
|---|---|---|---|---|---|---|---|
| University College Res. | 18 | 13 | 3 | 2 | 51 | 15 | 42 |
| R. Holloway College Res. | 17 | 13 | 2 | 2 | 48 | 16 | 41 |
| Goldsmiths' College Res. | 18 | 13 | 0 | 5 | 46 | 27 | 39 |
| Q. Mary Westfield College Res. | 18 | 10 | 1 | 7 | 38 | 42 | 31 |
| London School Economics Res. | 18 | 6 | 4 | 8 | 41 | 41 | 22 |
| Royal School of Mines (IC) | 17 | 6 | 2 | 9 | 28 | 36 | 20 |
| Ch. Cross & W'min. Hosp. MS | 18 | 6 | 2 | 10 | 35 | 49 | 20 |
| UCL & Middx Hosp Med. Sch. | 18 | 6 | 1 | 11 | 42 | 55 | 19 |
| Royal Holloway College 3rd | 18 | 4 | 2 | 12 | 29 | 41 | 14 |
| King's College Hosp. Med. Sch. | 18 | 3 | 1 | 14 | 30 | 66 | 10 |

**Division Two**–10 Teams–Won by R. London & St. Bart's Med. Sch.
**Division Three**–10 Teams–Won by Imperial College 3rd.
**Division Four**–10 Teams–Won by King's College 4th.
**Division Five**–10 Teams–Won by King's College 5th.
**Division Six**–11 Teams–Won by by St. Mary's Hospital Med. Sch. Res.
**Challenge Cup**–Imperial College 0, London School of Economics 4
**Upper Reserves Cup**–St. Mary's Hosp Med. Sch. 3, University College Hosp Med. Sch. 2
**Lower Reserves Cup**–R. Academy of Music 7, London School of Economics 6th 3

## BRITISH UNIVERSITIES SPORTS ASSOCIATION CHAMPIONSHIP

**Finals (Men)**
**First XI**
Brunel (West London) 1, Luton 0 aet
**Second XI**
Loughborough 3, Crewe & Alsager 0
**Third XI**
Loughborough 0, Exeter 1
**Fourth XI**
Loughborough 1, Crewe & Alsager 0

**Women's**
Loughborough 1, Leeds Metropolitan 0

**BUSA Games (Men's)**
England 2, N. Ireland 2; England 0, Scotland 0; England 2, Wales 0; N. Ireland 8, Scotland 0; N. Ireland 2, Wales 0; Scotland 2, Wales 7.
**BUSA Games (Women's)**
England 2, N. Ireland 1; England 5, Scotland 0; England 5, Wales 0; N. Ireland 3, Scotland 0; N. Ireland 2, Wales 0; Scotland 1, Wales 0.

**Men's International**
English Universities v RAF 3-2; v Stoke City Reserves 0-4; v Prison Service 7-1.
British Universities v N. Ireland Under-18 1-0; v FA XI 2-1.

**Women's International**
English Universities v Aston Villa Ladies 1-0; v Civil Service 2-3; v Tranmere Rovers Ladies 3-7.

## UNIVERSITY OF LONDON INTER-COLLEGIATE WOMENS' LEAGUE

| PREMIER DIVISION | P | W | D | L | F | A | Pts |
|---|---|---|---|---|---|---|---|
| R.Lon'n Hosp & Q. Mary Westf'd | 14 | 13 | 1 | 0 | 75 | 6 | 40 |
| University College | 14 | 11 | 1 | 2 | 56 | 22 | 34 |
| Royal Holloway College | 14 | 10 | 1 | 3 | 79 | 15 | 31 |
| London School of Economics | 12 | 4 | 2 | 6 | 31 | 22 | 14 |
| Imperial College | 14 | 4 | 1 | 9 | 21 | 61 | 13 |
| King's College | 13 | 4 | 0 | 9 | 19 | 57 | 12 |
| St. George's Hospital MS | 13 | 2 | 1 | 10 | 19 | 69 | 7 |
| R.Free Hos. Sch. Med. Res | 12 | 1 | 1 | 10 | 2 | 50 | 4 |

| FIRST DIVISION | P | W | D | L | F | A | Pts |
|---|---|---|---|---|---|---|---|
| Wye College | 12 | 10 | 0 | 2 | 60 | 13 | 30 |
| U.M.D.S. | 12 | 9 | 1 | 2 | 42 | 6 | 28 |
| Royal Free Hospital Res | 12 | 7 | 1 | 4 | 26 | 26 | 22 |
| University College Hospital | 12 | 6 | 1 | 5 | 27 | 22 | 19 |
| University College Res | 12 | 4 | 0 | 8 | 25 | 42 | 12 |
| Royal Holloway College Res | 12 | 2 | 1 | 9 | 13 | 44 | 7 |
| Goldsmiths' College | 12 | 2 | 0 | 10 | 11 | 51 | 6 |

**Women's Challenge Cup**–University College 3, King's College 1

# SCHOOLS FOOTBALL 1997–98

## ESFA FUJI FILM TROPHY

**FINAL: 1ST LEG**
Bristol 0, Barnsley 1
*Played at Bristol City 30 April*

**FINAL: 2ND LEG**
Barnsley 0, Bristol 1
*Played at Barnsley 11 May*
*Bristol and Barnsley shared Trophy*

## ESFA SNICKERS U.19 SCHOOLS AND COLLEGES COMPETITION

**FINAL:**
Cirencester College 3, Knowsley College 0
*Played at Villa Park 11 May*

## ESFA SNICKERS U.19 INDIVIDUAL SCHOOLS COMPETITION

**FINAL:**
Turnford School (Hertfordshire) 0, Aston School (South Yorkshire) 0
*Played at Villa Park 11 May*
*Turnford and Aston shared Trophy*

## ESFA GOODYEAR U.16 COMPETITION
(with Channel 4)

**FINAL:**
Blue Coat School (Merseyside) 6, Douay Martyrs School (Middlesex) 2
*Played at Wolverhampton Wanderers 26 April*

## ESFA PREMIER LEAGUE U.16 INTER COUNTY COMPETITION

**FINAL:**
Lancashire 2, Berkshire 1
*Played at Blackburn Rovers 14 May*

## ESFA PREMIER LEAGUE U.19 INTER COUNTY COMPETITION

**FINAL:**
Essex 2, Northumberland 1
*Played at Southend United 12 May*

## ESFA VIMTO GIRLS U.16 COMPETITION

**FINAL:**
Darrick Wood School (Kent) 3, Valley School (Nottinghamshire) 4
*Played at Millwall 15 May*

## ESFA WAGON WHEELS 5-A-SIDE COMPETITION

**GIRLS FINAL:**
Mountain Ash School (Cynon Valley) 1, Cockshut Hill School (Birmingham) 0

**BOYS FINAL:**
Nicholas Chamberlaine (Nuneaton) 2, Kings School (Chester) 1
*Staged at Aston Villa Sports Centre 28 March*

## ESFA PREDATOR PREMIER 7-A-SIDE TROPHY

**SEMI-FINALS:**
Newham* 0, Stoke-on-Trent 0
Peterlee 1, Bristol* 1
* won on corners

**THIRD PLACE:**
Peterlee 1, Stoke-on-Trent 0

**FINAL:**
Newham 0, Bristol 0
*Played at Wembley, 14 March*
*Newham and Bristol shared Trophy*

## ESFA PREDATOR 6-A-SIDE TROPHY

**SEMI-FINALS:**
St Vincent's RC, Newcastle 0, St Philip Neri's RC, Mansfield 1
Botwell House RC, Hayes* 1, Courthouse Junior, Maidenhead 1
* won on corners

**THIRD PLACE:**
St Vincent's RC 4, Courthouse 0

**FINAL:**
St Philip Neri's RC 0, Botwell House RC 3
*Played at Old Trafford, Manchester 9 May*

## ESFA SMALL PRIMARY SCHOOLS 6-A-SIDE COMPETITION

**FINAL:**
Newstead School (Notts) 0, Crick School (Northants) 1
*Played at Leicester City 20 April*

## PANINI U.11 6-A-SIDE COMPETITION
*(ESFA/PFA Community Scheme Activity)*

**FINAL:**
Fernwood School 1, Headlington Middle School 0
*Played at Wembley 19 April*

## NATIONWIDE SCHOOLS CHALLENGE

**FINAL: DIVISION 3 PLAY-OFF: 22 MAY**
The Gilberd School (*Colchester United FC*) 1, Westlands School (*Torquay United FC*) 1

**FINAL: DIVISION 2 PLAY-OFF: 24 MAY**
Waltham Toll Bar School (*Grimsby Town FC*) 4, The Ferrers School (*Northampton Town FC*) 0

**FINAL: DIVISION 1 PLAY-OFF: 25 MAY**
Hylton Red House School (*Sunderland FC*) 1, Bexley & Erith Technical High (*Charlton Athletic FC*) 2

## BOODLE & DUNTHORNE INDEPENDENT SCHOOLS FA CUP 1997–98

**PRELIMINARY ROUND**
Wolverhampton GS 3, City of London 1
Eton 2, Alleyn's 0 *(aet)*
QEGS, Blackburn 3, Highgate 0

**FIRST ROUND**
Oswestry 2, Batley GS 2 *(aet)*
*(Oswestry won 4-2 on penalties)*
St Bede's 3, Charterhouse 3 *(aet)*
*(St Bede's won 4-2 on penalties)*
Ardingly 6, Victoria College 0
Malvern 0, St Edmund's, Canterbury 0 *(aet)*
*(St Edmund's won 3-2 on penalties)*
Wellingborough 0, Lancing 0 *(aet)*
*(Wellingborough won 4-3 on penalties)*
Hulme GS 6, John Lyon 3
QEGS, Blackburn 3, Chigwell 1 *(aet)*
Repton 3, Hampton 2
Eton 3, Latymer Upper 1
Kimbolton 0, Brentwood 3
Manchester GS 2, Bolton 6
Aldenham 3, Forest 2
Westminster 4, Bradfield 3 *(aet)*
K.E.S. Witley 1, Shrewsbury 4
Wolverhampton GS 1, King's, Chester 3
Bury GS 1, Haileybury 3

**SECOND ROUND**
Bolton 10, Wellingborough 0
Oswestry 2, King's School, Chester 3
Haileybury 1, Eton 3
St Edmund's, Canterbury 1, Brentwood 2
Hulme GS 0, QEGS, Blackburn 6
Ardingly 10, Westminster 1
Shrewsbury 4, St Bede's 2
Aldenham 1, Repton 6 *(aet)*

**THIRD ROUND**
Brentwood 0, Bolton 5
Repton 2, Eton 1
QEGS, Blackburn 5, King's School, Chester 0
Ardingly 3, Shrewsbury 1

**SEMI-FINALS**
Ardingly 4, QEGS, Blackburn 2
Repton 3, Bolton 4 *(aet)*

**FINAL (AT SIXFIELDS STADIUM, NORTHAMPTON TOWN FC)**
**Ardingly 3** *(Beech 2, Montomery)*
**Bolton 1** *(Whittaker)*
*Ardingly:* K Monem; J Lindsten, Y Mihata, F Cornwall, J Fairbrother, D Menzies, D Marney, T Beech, N Holloway (G Rowley), P Montomery, T Swann.
*Bolton:* R Sellers; R Thompson, D Williams, C Jolley, R Farnie, M Brookes, R Meadows, A Myers, D Barrett, T Whittaker (J Chadwick), M Dewhurst (J Ducker).
*Referee:* S. Lodge (Barnsley).

### INTERNATIONAL PROGRAMME 1997–98

**UNDER 15**
England 4, Belgium 2 - Brussels, 26 November
England 1, Wales 0 - Bury, 23 January
England 3, N Ireland 0 - Barnsley, 20 February
England 0, Brazil 0 - Wembley, 14 March
England 1, Brazil 2 - Middlesbrough, 17 March
England 1, Scotland 3 - Kirkcaldy, 27 March
England 1, Hungary 0 - Old Trafford, 9 May
England 1, Germany 0 - Berlin, 26 May
**Overall Record**...Played 8, Won 5, Drew 1, Lost 2, Goals For 12, Goals Against 7
*Scorers:* Bothroyd (4), Davis (2), Dodd (2), Parnaby (2), Clarke, Nardiello.

### MONTAIGU TOURNAMENT – FRANCE

England 0, Tunisia 0; England 5, Romania 0; England 1, Republic of Ireland 0; England 3, Colombia 2; England 5, Ukraine 0.

**SEMI-FINAL**
France 1, England 0

**THIRD/FOURTH PLACE**
England 0, Italy 0
*(England won on penalties)*

**TOURNAMENT FINAL**
France 0, Cameroon 0
*(France won on penalties)*

**UNDER 18**
England 1, Belgium 1 - Yeovil, 25 February
England 1, N Ireland 2 - Belfast, 4 March
England 0, Austria 4 - Vienna, 31 March
England 2, Wales 1 - Scunthorpe, 28 April

**OVERALL RECORD**...Played 4, Won 1, Drew 1, Lost 2, Goals For 4, Goals Against 8
*Scorers:* Parkin 2, Baker, Preston.

### ADIDAS VICTORY SHIELD SEASON 1997–98

England 1, Wales 0 - Bury, 23 January
England 3, N. Ireland 0 - Barnsley, 20 February
Wales 2, N. Ireland 0 - Cardiff, 27 February
Wales 0, Scotland 1 - Wrexham, 13 March
N. Ireland 0, Scotland 3 - Linfield, 20 March
Scotland 3, England 1 - Kirkcaldy, 27 March

|            | P | W | D | L | F | A | Pts |
|------------|---|---|---|---|---|---|-----|
| Scotland   | 3 | 3 | 0 | 0 | 7 | 1 | 6   |
| England    | 3 | 2 | 0 | 1 | 5 | 3 | 4   |
| Wales      | 3 | 1 | 0 | 2 | 2 | 2 | 2   |
| N. Ireland | 3 | 0 | 0 | 3 | 0 | 8 | 0   |

### THE GOODYEAR CENTENARY SHIELD SEASON 1997–98

**SEMI-FINAL**
N. Ireland 2, England 1 - Belfast, 4 March
Scotland 2, Wales 0 - Banff, 6 March

**THIRD/FOURTH PLACE**
England 2, Wales 1 - Scunthorpe, 28 April

**FINAL**
N. Ireland 4, Scotland 3 - Larne, 3 April

**ENGLAND BOYS:** *Back Row:* Jay Bothroyd, Ben Clark, Rhys Evans, Matthew Hamshaw, Philip Senior, Richard Logan, Daniel Nardiello
*Middle Row:* Dr. Arthur Tabor, Stuart Parnaby, Ashley Dodd, Mrek Szmid, Peter Clarke, Alexander Tapp, Jonathan Bewers, James Davis
*Front Row:* Ian Shead (Goalkeeping Coach), Mark Eales (Physiotherapist), Jermain Defoe, Alan Heads (Chariman), Chris O'Brien, Dave Parnaby (Manager), Vic Bragg (Assistant Manager)

# AVON INSURANCE COMBINATION 1997–98

Charlton Athletic won the Avon Insurance Combination Championship for the first time since 1950 and for only the second time in their history, winning the title by a massive seven point margin over their nearest challengers, Tottenham Hotspur.

Charlton's success was sweet revenge for 1995, when Tottenham Hotspur's last game of the season win over Charlton denied them the title.

Ably managed by Keith Peacock, Charlton won the title in style with an unbeaten run of twenty-five matches and just three defeats, twenty-two clean sheets and only nineteen goals conceded all season.

Their squad contained a successful blend of experienced professionals such as Bradley Allen, top scorer in the Avon Insurance Combination with twenty-three goals and Andy Petterson and exciting young talent like Scott Parker, Paul Konchesky, Kevin Nicholls and Kevin Lisbie.

Arsenal and Tottenham also challenged for the title and credit should also go to Millwall who finished in fifth place.

The main purpose of the Avon Insurance Combination is to encourage the development of young talent and names to watch out for in the near future include the aforementioned Charlton youngsters, Arsenal's Isiah Rankin, Liam George of Luton Town, Chelsea's Jon Harley and Steven Hampshire and West Ham goalkeeper Stephen Bywater.

Stars who graced the Avon Insurance Combination throughout the season included Matthew Le Tissier, Ian Wright, Tony Adams, Dennis Bergkamp, and David Ginola.

Norwich City and Charlton Athletic shared the Avon Insurance Enterprise Award for their Family Night Football schemes which saw gates rise dramatically for Reserve matches at Carrow Road and the crucial Charlton versus Arsenal game attracted a crowd of over 7,500.

Avon Insurance are about to enter the fifth year of their sponsorship which has been extended until 2003 and the Avon Insurance Combination will welcom eleven new teams for the 1998–99 season giving a total of twenty-nine member clubs.

| | P | W | D | L | F | A | GD | Pts |
|---|---|---|---|---|---|---|---|---|
| Charlton Athletic* | 33 | 25 | 5 | 3 | 81 | 19 | +62 | 80 |
| Tottenham Hotspur | 34 | 22 | 7 | 5 | 75 | 29 | +46 | 73 |
| Arsenal | 34 | 20 | 9 | 5 | 71 | 26 | +45 | 69 |
| Southampton | 34 | 13 | 13 | 8 | 54 | 42 | +12 | 52 |
| Millwall | 34 | 15 | 6 | 13 | 39 | 41 | –2 | 51 |
| Crystal Palace* | 33 | 16 | 2 | 15 | 45 | 39 | +6 | 50 |
| Norwich City | 34 | 12 | 13 | 9 | 42 | 44 | –2 | 49 |
| Watford | 34 | 11 | 11 | 12 | 37 | 50 | –13 | 44 |
| Portsmouth | 34 | 12 | 7 | 15 | 45 | 51 | –6 | 43 |
| Ipswich Town | 34 | 11 | 10 | 13 | 48 | 60 | –12 | 43 |
| Luton Town* | 32 | 11 | 9 | 12 | 48 | 47 | +1 | 42 |
| Wimbledon | 34 | 11 | 9 | 14 | 42 | 42 | 0 | 42 |
| Oxford United | 34 | 11 | 8 | 15 | 41 | 63 | –22 | 41 |
| QPR* | 32 | 9 | 10 | 13 | 45 | 44 | +1 | 37 |
| Chelsea | 34 | 8 | 12 | 14 | 45 | 61 | –16 | 36 |
| Swindon Town | 34 | 9 | 3 | 22 | 48 | 74 | –26 | 30 |
| West Ham United* | 30 | 6 | 9 | 15 | 33 | 54 | –21 | 27 |
| Brighton & HA | 34 | 3 | 9 | 22 | 28 | 81 | –53 | 18 |

*Failed to complete all fixtures.*

## 1997–98 SEASON SUMMARY
**Champions** – Charlton Athletic
**Top Scorer** – Bradley Allen (Charlton Athletic)
**Fair Play Award** – Charlton Athletic
**Avon Insurance Enterprise Award** – Norwich City/Charlton Athletic
**Avon Insurance Programme Award** – Arsenal/Ipswich Town

## Charlton Athletic Avon Insurance Combination Champions
**League Appearances:** Allen 20; Allman 7+7; Balmer 15; Barness 10; Beale 1; Bowen 3; Bright 6; Brown 7; Chapple 6; Emblen 22; Fairhurst 1; Fortune 9+9; Goldup 5+1; Hales 4+5; Heaney 1; Hockley 0+2; Holmes 5+1; Ifejiagwa 10; Ilic 8; Izzet 0+1; James 2+2; Jones K 1; Jones S 11; Konchesky 25+2; Leaburn 7; Lee 24+2; Linger 4; Lisbie 26+1; Lyons 2; MacDonald 6+13; Mendonca 1; Minors 1+3; Mortimer 9; Newton 5; Nicholls 8; Parker 17; Petterson 10; Salmon 12; Sharman 0+1; Skeldon 3; Stuart 11; Tindall 28+3; Toms 8+7; Turner 3.
**Goals:** Allen 23, Lisbie 10, Jones S 6, Bright 4, Emblen 4, Leaburn 4, Tindall 4, Hales 3, Konchesky 3, Mortimer 3, Parker 3, Balmer 2, Brown 2, Fortune 2, MacDonald 2, Newton 2, Chapple 1, James 1, Stuart 1, Toms 1.

# PONTIN'S LEAGUE 1997-98

Leeds United entered the old Central League in 1921-22 and won the championship for the first time in 1936-37. They entered their last game against Oldham Athletic requiring one point to overtake Preston North End.

They won with goals from George Ainsley, Jack Hargreaves and John Thomson for a 3-0 win. The same season the club's third team won the Yorkshire League Cup in the evening of the same day the reserves had been successful.

In 1997-98 the Leeds United youth team reached the semi-final of the Times FA Youth Cup to underline the progress made by the club at various levels.

Sheffield United completed an all-Yorkshire success in the competition by winning the Pontin's League Cup, defeating Rotherham United 1-0 in the final.

## PONTIN'S LEAGUE CUP
### Group 1
Bradford C 5, Oldham Ath 1
Wrexham 3, Bradford C 0
Oldham Ath 2, Burnley 1
Bradford C 1, Burnley 4
Wrexham 0, Oldham Ath 0
Burnley 1, Wrexham 1

### Group 2
Scunthorpe U 1, Huddersfield T 0
Leeds U 2, Sheffield U 2
Sheffield U 4, Scunthorpe U 1
Huddersfield T 1, Sheffield U 2
Scunthorpe U 2, Leeds U 2
Huddersfield T 0, Leeds U 2

### Group 3
Walsall 1, Notts Co 0
Derby Co 2, Walsall 1
Walsall 4, Leicester C 2
Leicester C 0, Derby Co 1
Notts Co 0, Derby Co 2
Notts Co 0, Leicester C 1

### Group 4
Bury 4, Wigan Ath 1
Stoke C 2, Stockport Co 1
Bury 2, Chesterfield 0
Wigan Ath 1, Stoke C 5
Stockport Co 1, Chesterfield 1
Chesterfield 1, Stoke C 0
Wigan Ath 1, Stockport Co 3
Stockport Co 4, Bury 0
Stoke C 3, Bury 0

### Group 5
York C 2, Newcastle U 0
Barnsley 1, York C 1
York C 1, Barnsley 2
Newcastle U 0, York C 1
Newcastle U 0, Barnsley 3
Barnsley 2, Newcastle U 2

### Group 6
Tranmere R 1, Rotherham U 1
Rotherham U 1, Scarborough 0
Rotherham U 1, Blackpool 1
Tranmere R 6, Scarborough 3
Scarborough 1, Tranmere R 5
Blackpool 2, Rotherham U 0
Rotherham U 3, Tranmere R 3
Blackpool 3, Tranmere R 1
Scarborough 0, Rotherham U 1
Tranmere R 3, Blackpool 4

### QUARTER-FINALS
Blackpool 1, Stockport Co 0
Rotherham U 1, Barnsley 0
Stoke C 1, Sheffield U 1
*aet; Sheffield U won 3-2 on penalties.*
Wrexham 1, Derby Co 0

### SEMI-FINALS
Blackpool 2, Rotherham U 3
Sheffield U 7, Wrexham 1

### FINAL
Sheffield U 1, Rotherham U 0

**Leeds United Pontin's League Appearances:**
Beeney 22; Blunt 4+6; Bowyer 4; Boyle 13+4; Brolin 2+1; Dixon 0+1; Doyle 0+1; Foster 10+2; Gray 19+1; Hackworth 0+1; Halle 1; Harte 9; Hasselbaink 2; Hessey 2; Hopkin 8; Jackson 23; Jobson 0+5; Jones 0+1; Kewell 4; Knarvik 3+2; Laurent 11; Lilley 21+1; Lynch 8; McPhail 18+1; Matthews 8+4; Maybury 11+1; Molenaar 10; Palmer 5; Robertson 7; Robinson 2; Rush 1; Sharpe 2+2; Shepherd 16+1; Smith 1; Wallace 3; Woodgate 10+1; Wright 4+4.
**Goals:** Lilley 13, Brolin 5, Gray 5, Boyle 3, Hopkin 3, Laurent 3, Matthews 3, Woodgate 3, Hasselbaink 2, McPhail 2, Wallace 2, Foster 1, Harte 1, Jackson 1, Knarvik 1, Shepherd 1, Wright 1.

### Premier Division
|                    | P  | W  | D | L  | F  | A  | Pts |
|--------------------|----|----|---|----|----|----|-----|
| Leeds United       | 24 | 15 | 3 | 6  | 50 | 27 | 48  |
| Manchester United  | 24 | 14 | 4 | 6  | 55 | 29 | 46  |
| Blackburn Rovers   | 24 | 11 | 7 | 6  | 41 | 33 | 40  |
| Aston Villa        | 24 | 10 | 7 | 7  | 34 | 24 | 37  |
| Birmingham City    | 24 | 9  | 7 | 8  | 33 | 29 | 34  |
| Stoke City         | 24 | 10 | 4 | 10 | 35 | 41 | 34  |
| Everton            | 24 | 9  | 6 | 9  | 33 | 32 | 33  |
| Derby County       | 24 | 10 | 3 | 11 | 34 | 36 | 33  |
| Preston North End  | 24 | 10 | 3 | 11 | 32 | 48 | 33  |
| Liverpool          | 24 | 8  | 5 | 11 | 32 | 43 | 29  |
| Nottingham Forest  | 24 | 7  | 5 | 12 | 37 | 51 | 26  |
| Tranmere Rovers    | 24 | 4  | 9 | 11 | 38 | 48 | 21  |
| Sheffield Wednesday| 24 | 4  | 7 | 13 | 27 | 40 | 19  |

### Division One
|                    | P  | W  | D | L  | F  | A  | Pts |
|--------------------|----|----|---|----|----|----|-----|
| Sunderland         | 24 | 14 | 5 | 5  | 43 | 29 | 47  |
| Leicester City     | 24 | 13 | 5 | 6  | 48 | 30 | 44  |
| Port Vale          | 24 | 11 | 7 | 6  | 38 | 33 | 40  |
| Coventry City      | 24 | 11 | 4 | 9  | 34 | 28 | 37  |
| Grimsby Town       | 24 | 11 | 4 | 9  | 31 | 26 | 37  |
| Middlesbrough      | 24 | 9  | 8 | 7  | 33 | 27 | 35  |
| Oldham Athletic    | 24 | 9  | 5 | 10 | 37 | 30 | 32  |
| Bolton Wanderers   | 24 | 8  | 7 | 9  | 36 | 34 | 31  |
| Wolverhampton Wdrs | 24 | 7  | 8 | 9  | 28 | 33 | 29  |
| Manchester City    | 24 | 6  | 9 | 9  | 37 | 44 | 27  |
| West Bromwich Albion | 24 | 7 | 6 | 11 | 28 | 39 | 27  |
| Huddersfield Town  | 24 | 7  | 5 | 12 | 38 | 45 | 26  |
| Notts County       | 24 | 3  | 7 | 14 | 23 | 56 | 16  |

### Division Two
|                    | P  | W  | D | L  | F  | A  | Pts |
|--------------------|----|----|---|----|----|----|-----|
| Burnley            | 24 | 14 | 5 | 5  | 56 | 29 | 47  |
| Barnsley           | 24 | 13 | 7 | 4  | 42 | 20 | 46  |
| Shrewsbury Town    | 24 | 14 | 4 | 6  | 42 | 32 | 46  |
| Rotherham United   | 24 | 11 | 6 | 7  | 50 | 28 | 39  |
| Blackpool          | 24 | 10 | 8 | 6  | 40 | 35 | 38  |
| Sheffield United   | 24 | 11 | 1 | 12 | 46 | 43 | 34  |
| York City          | 24 | 8  | 7 | 9  | 36 | 34 | 31  |
| Stockport County   | 24 | 8  | 6 | 10 | 40 | 46 | 30  |
| Wrexham            | 24 | 8  | 4 | 12 | 41 | 43 | 28  |
| Bradford City      | 24 | 8  | 4 | 12 | 46 | 51 | 28  |
| Lincoln City       | 24 | 8  | 3 | 13 | 40 | 57 | 27  |
| Carlisle United    | 24 | 5  | 6 | 13 | 26 | 55 | 21  |
| Rochdale           | 24 | 6  | 3 | 15 | 26 | 58 | 21  |

### Division Three
|                    | P  | W  | D | L  | F  | A  | Pts |
|--------------------|----|----|---|----|----|----|-----|
| Scarborough        | 18 | 13 | 3 | 2  | 42 | 22 | 42  |
| Newcastle United   | 18 | 10 | 5 | 3  | 24 | 10 | 35  |
| Scunthorpe United  | 18 | 10 | 2 | 6  | 31 | 24 | 32  |
| Chester City       | 18 | 8  | 5 | 5  | 31 | 29 | 29  |
| Wigan Athletic     | 18 | 7  | 4 | 7  | 33 | 30 | 25  |
| Chesterfield       | 18 | 7  | 1 | 10 | 28 | 29 | 22  |
| Walsall            | 18 | 5  | 4 | 9  | 24 | 26 | 19  |
| Hull City          | 18 | 5  | 3 | 10 | 18 | 26 | 18  |
| Bury               | 18 | 4  | 5 | 9  | 19 | 29 | 17  |
| Doncaster Rovers   | 18 | 3  | 4 | 11 | 24 | 49 | 13  |

# NON-LEAGUE TABLES 1997–98

## ENDSLEIGH INSURANCE MIDLAND FOOTBALL COMBINATION

| Premier Division | P | W | D | L | F | A | Pts |
|---|---|---|---|---|---|---|---|
| Worcester Athletico | 40 | 26 | 12 | 2 | 111 | 41 | 90 |
| Southam United | 40 | 24 | 11 | 5 | 84 | 38 | 83 |
| Bolehall Swifts | 40 | 25 | 8 | 7 | 76 | 43 | 83 |
| Studley BKL | 40 | 24 | 4 | 12 | 79 | 36 | 76 |
| Coleshill Town | 40 | 21 | 9 | 10 | 78 | 38 | 72 |
| GPT (Coventry) | 40 | 20 | 8 | 12 | 71 | 46 | 68 |
| Meir KA | 40 | 20 | 7 | 13 | 81 | 58 | 67 |
| David Lloyd AFC | 40 | 19 | 7 | 14 | 80 | 66 | 64 |
| Kings Heath | 40 | 17 | 12 | 11 | 62 | 45 | 63 |
| Continental Star | 40 | 18 | 7 | 15 | 78 | 69 | 61 |
| Knowle | 40 | 14 | 12 | 14 | 81 | 72 | 54 |
| Bilston Community Col | 40 | 15 | 9 | 16 | 69 | 76 | 54 |
| Coventry Sphinx* | 40 | 15 | 9 | 16 | 72 | 78 | 51 |
| Cheslyn Hay | 40 | 14 | 9 | 17 | 66 | 86 | 51 |
| Highgate United | 40 | 12 | 14 | 14 | 59 | 54 | 50 |
| Handrahan Timbers | 40 | 11 | 10 | 19 | 52 | 53 | 43 |
| Alvechurch | 40 | 12 | 6 | 22 | 67 | 88 | 42 |
| Massey Ferguson | 40 | 12 | 5 | 23 | 49 | 73 | 41 |
| Kenilworth Town | 40 | 6 | 8 | 26 | 43 | 98 | 26 |
| Dudley Sports | 40 | 4 | 7 | 29 | 54 | 137 | 19 |
| Wellesbourne | 40 | 1 | 6 | 33 | 38 | 155 | 9 |

*= 3 points deducted

## COMBINED COUNTIES LEAGUE

| Premier Division | P | W | D | L | F | A | Pts |
|---|---|---|---|---|---|---|---|
| Ashford Town (Middx) | 38 | 30 | 3 | 5 | 123 | 31 | 93 |
| Reading Town | 38 | 28 | 5 | 5 | 102 | 26 | 89 |
| Ash United | 38 | 28 | 3 | 7 | 107 | 52 | 87 |
| Raynes Park Vale | 38 | 24 | 5 | 9 | 86 | 61 | 77 |
| Chipstead | 38 | 23 | 5 | 10 | 79 | 43 | 74 |
| Farnham Town | 38 | 22 | 4 | 12 | 94 | 60 | 70 |
| Bedfont | 38 | 18 | 5 | 15 | 75 | 70 | 59 |
| Godalming & Guildford | 38 | 15 | 10 | 13 | 77 | 69 | 55 |
| Sandhurst Town | 38 | 16 | 7 | 15 | 67 | 64 | 55 |
| Chessington & Hook | 38 | 16 | 6 | 16 | 63 | 65 | 54 |
| Feltham | 38 | 15 | 7 | 16 | 70 | 71 | 52 |
| Netherne | 38 | 13 | 8 | 17 | 61 | 88 | 47 |
| Westfield | 38 | 12 | 7 | 19 | 54 | 63 | 43 |
| Viking Sports | 38 | 11 | 7 | 20 | 52 | 82 | 40 |
| Merstham | 38 | 12 | 4 | 22 | 58 | 91 | 40 |
| Hartley Wintney | 38 | 10 | 6 | 22 | 47 | 91 | 36 |
| Cobham | 39 | 9 | 7 | 22 | 55 | 73 | 34 |
| Walton Casuals | 38 | 8 | 10 | 20 | 45 | 84 | 34 |
| Cranleigh | 38 | 8 | 3 | 27 | 53 | 110 | 27 |
| Cove | 38 | 5 | 2 | 31 | 33 | 107 | 17 |

## UNIJET SUSSEX COUNTY LEAGUE

| Division One | P | W | D | L | F | A | Pts |
|---|---|---|---|---|---|---|---|
| Burgess Hill Town | 38 | 29 | 5 | 4 | 105 | 34 | 92 |
| Littlehampton Town | 38 | 27 | 6 | 5 | 102 | 45 | 87 |
| Wick | 38 | 23 | 7 | 8 | 81 | 39 | 76 |
| Langney Sports | 38 | 23 | 5 | 10 | 77 | 46 | 74 |
| Redhill | 38 | 21 | 5 | 12 | 85 | 38 | 68 |
| Saltdean United | 38 | 20 | 6 | 12 | 76 | 67 | 66 |
| Ringmer | 38 | 16 | 10 | 12 | 67 | 59 | 58 |
| Selsey | 38 | 14 | 12 | 12 | 60 | 51 | 54 |
| Pagham | 38 | 14 | 12 | 12 | 41 | 42 | 54 |
| Shoreham | 38 | 16 | 6 | 16 | 55 | 58 | 54 |
| Whitehawk | 38 | 12 | 12 | 14 | 50 | 54 | 48 |
| Hassocks | 38 | 11 | 11 | 16 | 53 | 62 | 44 |
| Horsham YMCA | 38 | 13 | 5 | 20 | 72 | 83 | 44 |
| Eastbourne Town | 38 | 12 | 7 | 19 | 54 | 73 | 43 |
| Portfield | 38 | 11 | 8 | 19 | 58 | 87 | 41 |
| Chichester City | 38 | 10 | 9 | 19 | 62 | 76 | 39 |
| Hailsham Town | 38 | 12 | 1 | 25 | 60 | 96 | 37 |
| Mile Oak | 38 | 8 | 10 | 20 | 45 | 71 | 34 |
| Peacehaven & Telscombe | 38 | 7 | 8 | 23 | 40 | 88 | 29 |
| Arundel | 38 | 6 | 5 | 27 | 44 | 120 | 23 |

## Division Two

| Division Two | P | W | D | L | F | A | Pts |
|---|---|---|---|---|---|---|---|
| East Preston | 34 | 25 | 5 | 4 | 113 | 42 | 80 |
| Eastbourne United | 34 | 21 | 6 | 7 | 82 | 36 | 69 |
| Broadbridge Heath | 34 | 20 | 3 | 11 | 72 | 46 | 63 |
| Sidley United | 34 | 18 | 9 | 7 | 68 | 42 | 63 |
| Sidlesham | 34 | 17 | 9 | 8 | 72 | 49 | 60 |
| Shinewater Association | 34 | 17 | 5 | 12 | 62 | 50 | 56 |
| Three Bridges | 34 | 16 | 6 | 12 | 63 | 52 | 54 |
| Southwick | 34 | 16 | 6 | 12 | 70 | 64 | 54 |
| Worthing United | 34 | 13 | 7 | 14 | 68 | 68 | 46 |
| East Grinstead Town | 34 | 13 | 6 | 15 | 51 | 51 | 45 |
| Crawley Down Village | 34 | 12 | 8 | 14 | 56 | 68 | 44 |
| Crowborough Athletic | 34 | 12 | 6 | 16 | 53 | 65 | 42 |
| Lancing | 34 | 12 | 4 | 18 | 57 | 84 | 40 |
| Oakwood | 34 | 10 | 9 | 15 | 70 | 60 | 39 |
| Withdean | 34 | 9 | 8 | 17 | 52 | 75 | 35 |
| Newhaven | 34 | 7 | 9 | 18 | 40 | 80 | 30 |
| Midhurst & Easebourne | 34 | 8 | 4 | 22 | 47 | 115 | 28 |
| Bexhill Town | 34 | 4 | 2 | 28 | 42 | 91 | 14 |

## HIGHLAND LEAGUE

| | P | W | D | L | F | A | Pts |
|---|---|---|---|---|---|---|---|
| Huntly | 30 | 22 | 5 | 3 | 92 | 32 | 71 |
| Fraserburgh | 30 | 21 | 4 | 5 | 69 | 31 | 67 |
| Peterhead | 30 | 20 | 5 | 5 | 88 | 34 | 65 |
| Cove Rangers | 30 | 19 | 4 | 7 | 100 | 39 | 61 |
| Elgin City | 30 | 16 | 7 | 7 | 59 | 33 | 55 |
| Keith | 30 | 15 | 6 | 9 | 65 | 54 | 51 |
| Forres Mechanics | 30 | 13 | 6 | 11 | 64 | 58 | 45 |
| Clachnacuddin | 30 | 14 | 3 | 13 | 59 | 57 | 45 |
| Deveronvale | 30 | 11 | 6 | 13 | 59 | 61 | 39 |
| Buckie Thistle | 30 | 11 | 6 | 13 | 42 | 47 | 39 |
| Brora Rangers | 30 | 10 | 4 | 16 | 54 | 66 | 34 |
| Lossiemouth | 30 | 9 | 6 | 15 | 39 | 66 | 33 |
| Rothes | 30 | 7 | 8 | 15 | 41 | 56 | 29 |
| Wick Academy | 30 | 5 | 5 | 20 | 40 | 74 | 20 |
| Fort William | 30 | 3 | 4 | 23 | 31 | 130 | 13 |
| Nairn County | 30 | 3 | 3 | 24 | 30 | 94 | 12 |

## LANCASHIRE FOOTBALL LEAGUE

| Division One | P | W | D | L | F | A | Pts |
|---|---|---|---|---|---|---|---|
| Manchester United A | 30 | 22 | 6 | 2 | 80 | 29 | 72 |
| Crewe Alexandra Res | 30 | 19 | 4 | 7 | 71 | 39 | 61 |
| Everton A | 30 | 16 | 7 | 7 | 68 | 37 | 55 |
| Blackburn Rovers A | 30 | 13 | 9 | 8 | 61 | 36 | 48 |
| Oldham Athletic A | 30 | 14 | 6 | 10 | 49 | 40 | 48 |
| Bury A | 30 | 13 | 9 | 8 | 45 | 43 | 48 |
| Burnley A | 30 | 13 | 6 | 11 | 55 | 55 | 45 |
| Liverpool A | 30 | 13 | 5 | 12 | 43 | 43 | 44 |
| Bolton Wanderers A | 30 | 12 | 6 | 12 | 37 | 39 | 42 |
| Manchester City A | 30 | 11 | 8 | 11 | 47 | 39 | 41 |
| Tranmere Rovers A | 30 | 10 | 7 | 13 | 57 | 67 | 37 |
| Wrexham A | 30 | 10 | 4 | 16 | 59 | 78 | 34 |
| Morecambe Reserves | 30 | 7 | 11 | 12 | 41 | 56 | 32 |
| Stoke City A | 30 | 8 | 6 | 16 | 37 | 49 | 30 |
| Preston North End A | 30 | 3 | 7 | 20 | 23 | 65 | 16 |
| Marine Reserve | 30 | 4 | 3 | 23 | 24 | 82 | 15 |

| Division Two | P | W | D | L | F | A | Pts |
|---|---|---|---|---|---|---|---|
| Blackburn Rovers B | 36 | 28 | 5 | 3 | 113 | 28 | 89 |
| Everton B | 36 | 25 | 7 | 4 | 88 | 33 | 82 |
| Tranmere Rovers B | 36 | 21 | 8 | 7 | 78 | 51 | 71 |
| Blackpool A | 36 | 22 | 4 | 10 | 67 | 49 | 70 |
| Manchester United B | 36 | 21 | 3 | 12 | 110 | 57 | 66 |
| Wigan Athletic A | 36 | 18 | 5 | 13 | 60 | 56 | 59 |
| Stockport County A | 36 | 17 | 6 | 13 | 101 | 81 | 57 |
| Oldham Athletic B | 36 | 17 | 6 | 13 | 53 | 43 | 57 |
| Crewe Alexandra A | 36 | 15 | 6 | 15 | 67 | 65 | 51 |
| Wrexham B | 36 | 15 | 5 | 16 | 52 | 55 | 50 |
| Liverpool B | 36 | 14 | 7 | 15 | 68 | 59 | 49 |
| Manchester City B | 36 | 15 | 4 | 17 | 70 | 62 | 49 |
| Carlisle Utd A | 36 | 11 | 8 | 17 | 54 | 74 | 41 |
| Chester City A | 36 | 11 | 6 | 19 | 69 | 86 | 39 |
| Burnley B | 36 | 11 | 6 | 19 | 53 | 75 | 39 |
| Rochdale A | 36 | 10 | 8 | 18 | 52 | 76 | 38 |
| Bury B | 36 | 9 | 4 | 23 | 33 | 87 | 31 |
| Marine Youth | 36 | 5 | 4 | 27 | 42 | 88 | 19 |
| Morecambe A | 36 | 3 | 6 | 27 | 36 | 141 | 15 |

## NORTH WEST COUNTIES LEAGUE

| Division One | P | W | D | L | F | A | Pts |
|---|---|---|---|---|---|---|---|
| Kidsgrove Athletic | 42 | 32 | 3 | 7 | 127 | 50 | 99 |
| Burscough | 42 | 29 | 7 | 6 | 101 | 30 | 94 |
| Newcastle Town | 42 | 23 | 16 | 3 | 82 | 32 | 85 |
| Vauxhall GM | 42 | 24 | 9 | 9 | 91 | 52 | 81 |
| St Helens Town | 42 | 22 | 12 | 8 | 91 | 59 | 78 |
| Clitheroe | 42 | 21 | 10 | 11 | 72 | 51 | 73 |
| Prescot Cables | 42 | 19 | 11 | 12 | 72 | 57 | 68 |
| Glossop North End | 42 | 19 | 7 | 16 | 78 | 69 | 64 |
| Mossley | 42 | 16 | 14 | 12 | 67 | 52 | 62 |
| Nantwich Town | 42 | 17 | 6 | 19 | 71 | 79 | 57 |
| Maine Road | 42 | 15 | 10 | 17 | 56 | 70 | 55 |
| Chadderton | 42 | 15 | 8 | 19 | 63 | 59 | 53 |
| Rossendale United | 42 | 15 | 6 | 21 | 61 | 80 | 51 |
| Blackpool Rovers | 42 | 13 | 9 | 20 | 68 | 84 | 48 |
| Atherton LR | 42 | 12 | 11 | 19 | 54 | 73 | 47 |
| Haslingden | 42 | 12 | 10 | 20 | 68 | 95 | 46 |
| Ramsbottom United | 42 | 12 | 9 | 21 | 58 | 85 | 45 |
| Salford City | 42 | 13 | 4 | 25 | 64 | 92 | 43 |
| Warrington Town | 42 | 10 | 10 | 22 | 56 | 72 | 40 |
| Holker Old Boys | 42 | 7 | 12 | 23 | 46 | 96 | 33 |
| Darwen | 42 | 6 | 13 | 23 | 42 | 93 | 31 |
| Atherton Collieries | 42 | 7 | 9 | 26 | 42 | 100 | 30 |

| Division Two | P | W | D | L | F | A | Pts |
|---|---|---|---|---|---|---|---|
| Oldham Town | 40 | 27 | 8 | 5 | 118 | 49 | 89 |
| Skelmersdale United | 40 | 26 | 7 | 7 | 111 | 50 | 85 |
| Leek CSOB | 40 | 26 | 7 | 7 | 76 | 38 | 85 |
| Cheadle Town | 40 | 24 | 9 | 7 | 108 | 58 | 81 |
| Woodley Sports | 40 | 22 | 7 | 11 | 116 | 73 | 73 |
| Formby | 40 | 22 | 7 | 11 | 90 | 63 | 73 |
| Bootle | 40 | 19 | 15 | 6 | 82 | 60 | 72 |
| Garswood United | 40 | 19 | 10 | 11 | 98 | 62 | 67 |
| Tetley Walker | 40 | 19 | 9 | 12 | 98 | 62 | 66 |
| Castleton Gabriels | 40 | 18 | 7 | 15 | 86 | 59 | 61 |
| Maghull | 40 | 16 | 10 | 14 | 67 | 62 | 58 |
| Fleetwood Freeport | 40 | 15 | 11 | 14 | 73 | 55 | 56 |
| Nelson | 40 | 17 | 5 | 18 | 69 | 76 | 56 |
| Bacup Borough | 40 | 13 | 8 | 19 | 58 | 83 | 47 |
| Squires Gate | 40 | 11 | 9 | 20 | 72 | 88 | 42 |
| Daisy Hill | 40 | 11 | 9 | 20 | 60 | 86 | 42 |
| Middlewich Athletic | 40 | 11 | 8 | 21 | 48 | 90 | 41 |
| Colne | 40 | 8 | 7 | 25 | 48 | 91 | 31 |
| Ashton Town | 40 | 6 | 6 | 28 | 73 | 137 | 24 |
| Stantondale | 40 | 4 | 4 | 32 | 50 | 146 | 16 |
| Blackpool Mechanics | 40 | 2 | 5 | 33 | 33 | 165 | 11 |

## VAUX WEARSIDE LEAGUE

| | P | W | D | L | F | A | Pts |
|---|---|---|---|---|---|---|---|
| Annfield Plain | 36 | 26 | 3 | 7 | 121 | 43 | 81 |
| Kennek Roker | 36 | 23 | 8 | 5 | 103 | 44 | 77 |
| Birtley Town (–3) | 36 | 25 | 3 | 8 | 103 | 49 | 75 |
| Gateshead Reserves | 36 | 22 | 5 | 9 | 106 | 53 | 71 |
| Ryhope CW | 36 | 19 | 6 | 11 | 80 | 47 | 63 |
| Washington Nissan | 36 | 17 | 11 | 8 | 80 | 54 | 62 |
| Boldon CA | 36 | 19 | 5 | 12 | 90 | 79 | 62 |
| Cleadon SC | 36 | 18 | 7 | 11 | 71 | 49 | 61 |
| Windscale | 36 | 17 | 5 | 14 | 98 | 56 | 56 |
| South Tyneside U | 36 | 14 | 9 | 13 | 90 | 76 | 51 |
| North Shields Ath | 36 | 14 | 7 | 15 | 67 | 71 | 49 |
| Stanley United | 36 | 14 | 6 | 16 | 98 | 91 | 48 |
| Hartlepool BWOB | 36 | 13 | 9 | 14 | 67 | 70 | 48 |
| Wolviston | 36 | 14 | 4 | 18 | 71 | 77 | 46 |
| Harton & Westoe | 36 | 11 | 8 | 17 | 67 | 95 | 41 |
| Jarrow | 36 | 6 | 7 | 23 | 56 | 95 | 25 |
| Whitehaven Amtrs | 36 | 7 | 4 | 25 | 55 | 133 | 25 |
| South Bank | 36 | 7 | 2 | 27 | 42 | 118 | 23 |
| Horden Athletic | 36 | 1 | 1 | 34 | 26 | 191 | 4 |

## THE JEWSON SOUTH-WESTERN FOOTBALL LEAGUE

| | P | W | D | L | F | A | Pts |
|---|---|---|---|---|---|---|---|
| Truro City | 30 | 23 | 3 | 4 | 76 | 15 | 72 |
| Falmouth Town | 30 | 22 | 5 | 3 | 76 | 33 | 71 |
| Porthleven | 30 | 20 | 6 | 4 | 88 | 24 | 66 |
| St Blazey | 30 | 16 | 3 | 11 | 60 | 39 | 51 |
| Torpoint Athletic | 30 | 15 | 4 | 11 | 71 | 56 | 49 |
| Millbrook | 30 | 14 | 7 | 9 | 52 | 42 | 49 |
| Bodmin Town | 30 | 15 | 4 | 11 | 51 | 48 | 49 |
| Penzance | 30 | 13 | 8 | 9 | 54 | 46 | 47 |
| Saltash United | 30 | 14 | 3 | 13 | 63 | 60 | 45 |
| Holsworthy | 30 | 13 | 5 | 12 | 61 | 67 | 44 |
| Wadebridge Town | 30 | 11 | 2 | 17 | 40 | 53 | 35 |
| Liskeard Athletic | 30 | 7 | 6 | 17 | 45 | 64 | 27 |
| Newquay | 30 | 8 | 3 | 19 | 37 | 73 | 27 |
| St Austell | 30 | 5 | 8 | 17 | 33 | 82 | 23 |
| Tavistock | 30 | 3 | 6 | 21 | 38 | 87 | 15 |
| Launceston | 30 | 3 | 3 | 24 | 27 | 83 | 12 |

## NORTHERN ALLIANCE LEAGUE

| Premier Division | P | W | D | L | F | A | Pts |
|---|---|---|---|---|---|---|---|
| West Allotment C | 28 | 24 | 3 | 1 | 80 | 30 | 75 |
| Lemington Social | 28 | 21 | 3 | 4 | 79 | 31 | 66 |
| Ponteland United | 28 | 19 | 2 | 7 | 87 | 41 | 59 |
| Hartlepool United A | 28 | 15 | 6 | 7 | 72 | 45 | 51 |
| Carlisle City | 28 | 13 | 8 | 7 | 51 | 29 | 47 |
| Ryton | 28 | 11 | 3 | 14 | 56 | 69 | 36 |
| Benfield Park | 28 | 10 | 4 | 14 | 39 | 61 | 34 |
| Winlaton Hallgarth | 28 | 8 | 7 | 13 | 37 | 57 | 31 |
| Walker Ledwood | 28 | 7 | 9 | 12 | 35 | 43 | 30 |
| St Columbas | 28 | 8 | 6 | 14 | 42 | 76 | 30 |
| Hebburn Reyrolle (–3) | 28 | 8 | 7 | 13 | 54 | 53 | 28 |
| Seaton Delaval A | 28 | 7 | 6 | 15 | 43 | 60 | 27 |
| Gillford Park | 28 | 7 | 6 | 15 | 34 | 52 | 27 |
| Walker Central (–6) | 28 | 5 | 10 | 13 | 33 | 51 | 19 |
| Spittal Rovers | 28 | 5 | 4 | 19 | 31 | 75 | 19 |

| Division One | P | W | D | L | F | A | Pts |
|---|---|---|---|---|---|---|---|
| Shankhouse | 26 | 22 | 1 | 3 | 100 | 28 | 67 |
| Northbank Carlisle | 26 | 21 | 2 | 3 | 113 | 28 | 65 |
| Heaton Stannington | 26 | 20 | 1 | 5 | 99 | 31 | 61 |
| Heddon Institute (–3) | 26 | 16 | 3 | 7 | 82 | 47 | 48 |
| Amble Town | 26 | 15 | 3 | 8 | 78 | 51 | 48 |
| Newcastle University | 26 | 13 | 3 | 10 | 61 | 47 | 42 |
| Newbiggin CW (–3) | 26 | 14 | 1 | 11 | 72 | 65 | 40 |
| Percy Main Amateurs | 26 | 10 | 5 | 11 | 59 | 49 | 35 |
| Gosforth Bohemians | 26 | 8 | 5 | 13 | 56 | 83 | 29 |
| Hexham Swinton | 26 | 8 | 2 | 16 | 54 | 81 | 26 |
| Procter & Gamble | 26 | 6 | 3 | 17 | 37 | 74 | 21 |
| Longbenton | 26 | 4 | 3 | 19 | 45 | 95 | 15 |
| Ashington HP | 26 | 3 | 3 | 20 | 40 | 90 | 12 |
| Swalwell (–3) | 26 | 3 | 3 | 20 | 31 | 158 | 9 |

## WEST CHESHIRE LEAGUE

| Division One | P | W | D | L | F | A | Pts |
|---|---|---|---|---|---|---|---|
| Poulton Victoria | 30 | 24 | 3 | 3 | 100 | 27 | 75 |
| Ashville | 30 | 19 | 7 | 4 | 56 | 27 | 64 |
| Stork | 30 | 18 | 7 | 5 | 67 | 39 | 61 |
| Shell | 30 | 15 | 10 | 5 | 71 | 37 | 55 |
| Cammell Laird | 30 | 14 | 8 | 8 | 49 | 38 | 50 |
| Heswall | 30 | 16 | 4 | 11 | 67 | 48 | 49 |
| Christleton | 30 | 13 | 5 | 12 | 66 | 40 | 44 |
| Blacon YC | 30 | 11 | 9 | 10 | 70 | 56 | 42 |
| Newton | 30 | 11 | 9 | 10 | 67 | 50 | 42 |
| Mersey Royal | 30 | 11 | 8 | 11 | 58 | 44 | 41 |
| Vauxhall Motors | 30 | 11 | 6 | 13 | 62 | 66 | 39 |
| Mond Rangers | 30 | 10 | 4 | 16 | 57 | 60 | 34 |
| Mersey Police | 30 | 9 | 5 | 16 | 53 | 65 | 32 |
| Capenhurst | 30 | 7 | 4 | 19 | 37 | 70 | 25 |
| Bromboro Pool | 30 | 5 | 2 | 23 | 40 | 104 | 17 |
| Moreton | 30 | 2 | 2 | 28 | 29 | 128 | 2 |

## NOTTS FOOTBALL ALLIANCE

| Senior Division | P | W | D | L | F | A | Pts |
|---|---|---|---|---|---|---|---|
| Boots Athletic | 30 | 27 | 1 | 2 | 116 | 29 | 82 |
| Wellbeck CW | 30 | 22 | 3 | 5 | 91 | 37 | 69 |
| Pelican | 30 | 18 | 7 | 5 | 73 | 40 | 61 |
| Notts Police | 30 | 18 | 4 | 8 | 57 | 32 | 58 |
| Rainworth MW | 30 | 14 | 7 | 9 | 53 | 45 | 49 |
| Linby CW | 30 | 14 | 7 | 9 | 52 | 50 | 49 |
| Southwell City | 30 | 13 | 4 | 13 | 54 | 42 | 43 |
| Attenborough | 30 | 13 | 4 | 13 | 61 | 58 | 43 |
| Ruddington United | 30 | 11 | 6 | 13 | 52 | 60 | 39 |
| Ollerton Town | 30 | 10 | 4 | 16 | 63 | 72 | 34 |
| Keyworth United | 30 | 8 | 6 | 16 | 50 | 86 | 30 |
| Thoresby CW | 30 | 8 | 6 | 16 | 39 | 76 | 30 |
| Wollaton | 30 | 7 | 6 | 17 | 37 | 58 | 27 |
| Cotgrave CW | 30 | 7 | 4 | 19 | 51 | 88 | 25 |
| Retford United | 30 | 6 | 4 | 20 | 33 | 62 | 22 |
| Awsworth Villa | 30 | 5 | 4 | 21 | 40 | 86 | 19 |

## MIDLAND FOOTBALL ALLIANCE

| | P | W | D | L | F | A | Pts |
|---|---|---|---|---|---|---|---|
| Bloxwich Town | 38 | 28 | 4 | 6 | 77 | 31 | 88 |
| Rocester | 38 | 23 | 7 | 8 | 74 | 36 | 76 |
| Oldbury United | 38 | 20 | 11 | 7 | 73 | 43 | 71 |
| Boldmere St Michaels | 38 | 19 | 11 | 8 | 54 | 38 | 68 |
| Kings Norton Town | 38 | 18 | 13 | 7 | 57 | 37 | 67 |
| Barwell | 38 | 16 | 12 | 10 | 68 | 56 | 60 |
| Bridgnorth Town | 38 | 15 | 13 | 10 | 64 | 47 | 58 |
| West Midlands Police | 38 | 15 | 12 | 11 | 58 | 42 | 57 |
| Halesowen Harriers | 38 | 17 | 5 | 16 | 53 | 63 | 56 |
| Chasetown | 38 | 14 | 11 | 13 | 57 | 43 | 53 |
| Wednesfield | 38 | 14 | 11 | 13 | 56 | 49 | 53 |
| Knypersley Vics | 38 | 11 | 17 | 10 | 52 | 53 | 50 |
| Willenhall Town | 38 | 12 | 13 | 13 | 45 | 44 | 49 |
| Pelsall Villa | 38 | 10 | 15 | 13 | 66 | 66 | 45 |
| Sandwell Borough | 38 | 10 | 15 | 13 | 57 | 62 | 45 |
| Rushall Olympic | 38 | 12 | 8 | 18 | 51 | 57 | 44 |
| Stapenhill | 38 | 7 | 12 | 19 | 39 | 74 | 33 |
| Stratford Town | 38 | 8 | 7 | 23 | 39 | 69 | 31 |
| Pershore Town | 38 | 4 | 6 | 28 | 36 | 97 | 18 |
| Shifnal Town | 38 | 3 | 5 | 30 | 35 | 103 | 14 |

## MANCHESTER LEAGUE

| Premier Division | P | W | D | L | F | A | Pts |
|---|---|---|---|---|---|---|---|
| Springhead | 30 | 21 | 3 | 6 | 80 | 32 | 66 |
| Abbey Hey | 30 | 19 | 4 | 7 | 81 | 44 | 61 |
| Tottington United | 30 | 15 | 7 | 8 | 58 | 43 | 52 |
| Stand Athletic (–3) | 30 | 14 | 9 | 7 | 60 | 36 | 48 |
| Atherton Town | 30 | 14 | 6 | 10 | 50 | 43 | 48 |
| Dukinfield Town | 30 | 13 | 7 | 10 | 52 | 46 | 46 |
| BICC | 30 | 13 | 5 | 12 | 71 | 59 | 44 |
| Wythenshawe Amateurs | 30 | 12 | 8 | 10 | 46 | 41 | 44 |
| Monton Amateurs | 30 | 12 | 6 | 12 | 44 | 49 | 42 |
| East Manchester | 30 | 11 | 7 | 12 | 52 | 51 | 40 |
| Little Hulton (–1) | 30 | 10 | 8 | 12 | 51 | 50 | 37 |
| Prestwich Heys | 30 | 11 | 4 | 15 | 42 | 47 | 37 |
| Elton Fold | 30 | 8 | 7 | 15 | 47 | 65 | 31 |
| Mitchell Shackleton | 30 | 8 | 5 | 17 | 42 | 66 | 29 |
| Stockport Georgians | 30 | 5 | 8 | 17 | 38 | 75 | 23 |
| Wythenshawe Town | 30 | 6 | 2 | 22 | 36 | 103 | 20 |

## WINSTONLEAD KENT LEAGUE

| Division One | P | W | D | L | F | A | Pts |
|---|---|---|---|---|---|---|---|
| Herne Bay | 42 | 34 | 5 | 3 | 105 | 29 | 107 |
| Folkestone Invicta | 42 | 31 | 4 | 7 | 127 | 41 | 97 |
| Sheppey United | 42 | 27 | 10 | 5 | 110 | 63 | 91 |
| Swanley Furness | 42 | 22 | 9 | 11 | 86 | 50 | 75 |
| Greenwich Borough | 42 | 21 | 11 | 10 | 83 | 42 | 74 |
| Cray Wanderers | 42 | 20 | 11 | 11 | 70 | 50 | 71 |
| Beckenham Town | 42 | 21 | 7 | 14 | 67 | 54 | 70 |
| Whitstable Town | 42 | 19 | 11 | 12 | 72 | 54 | 68 |
| VCD Athletic | 42 | 17 | 14 | 11 | 88 | 62 | 65 |
| Lordswood | 42 | 18 | 9 | 15 | 70 | 64 | 63 |
| Tunbridge Wells | 42 | 17 | 6 | 19 | 73 | 76 | 57 |
| Thamesmead Town | 42 | 15 | 9 | 18 | 69 | 70 | 54 |
| Ramsgate | 42 | 14 | 9 | 19 | 80 | 85 | 51 |
| Hythe United | 42 | 15 | 5 | 22 | 75 | 103 | 50 |
| Faversham Town (–5) | 42 | 14 | 12 | 16 | 62 | 68 | 49 |
| Slade Green | 42 | 12 | 13 | 17 | 58 | 67 | 49 |
| Deal Town | 42 | 15 | 4 | 23 | 75 | 97 | 49 |
| Chatham Town | 42 | 12 | 12 | 18 | 56 | 66 | 48 |
| Erith Town | 42 | 12 | 6 | 24 | 48 | 86 | 42 |
| Canterbury City | 42 | 8 | 6 | 28 | 45 | 96 | 30 |
| Crockenhill | 42 | 6 | 2 | 34 | 31 | 133 | 20 |
| Corinthian | 42 | 2 | 5 | 35 | 36 | 130 | 11 |

## SCREWFIX DIRECT LEAGUE

| Premier Division | P | W | D | L | F | A | Pts |
|---|---|---|---|---|---|---|---|
| Tiverton Town | 38 | 36 | 2 | 0 | 154 | 20 | 110 |
| Taunton Town | 38 | 31 | 3 | 4 | 107 | 28 | 96 |
| Melksham Town | 38 | 22 | 7 | 9 | 75 | 37 | 73 |
| Bridgwater Town | 38 | 22 | 6 | 10 | 73 | 43 | 72 |
| Paulton Rovers | 38 | 19 | 6 | 13 | 76 | 69 | 63 |
| Mangotsfield United | 38 | 18 | 8 | 12 | 76 | 50 | 62 |
| Barnstaple Town | 38 | 18 | 5 | 15 | 79 | 64 | 59 |
| Brislington | 38 | 17 | 8 | 13 | 62 | 55 | 59 |
| Calne Town | 38 | 16 | 9 | 13 | 68 | 67 | 57 |
| Backwell United | 38 | 15 | 7 | 16 | 70 | 68 | 52 |
| Bridport | 38 | 16 | 4 | 18 | 62 | 72 | 52 |
| Chippenham Town | 38 | 13 | 11 | 14 | 53 | 57 | 50 |
| Bideford | 38 | 14 | 6 | 18 | 68 | 90 | 48 |
| Elmore | 38 | 10 | 8 | 20 | 54 | 100 | 38 |
| Westbury United | 38 | 9 | 8 | 21 | 39 | 65 | 35 |
| Bristol Manor Farm | 38 | 8 | 10 | 20 | 37 | 73 | 34 |
| Keynsham Town | 38 | 10 | 4 | 24 | 46 | 94 | 34 |
| Odd Down | 38 | 9 | 6 | 23 | 33 | 80 | 33 |
| Chard Town | 38 | 8 | 8 | 22 | 44 | 77 | 32 |
| Torrington | 38 | 2 | 8 | 28 | 21 | 88 | 14 |

| Division One | P | W | D | L | F | A | Pts |
|---|---|---|---|---|---|---|---|
| Bishop Sutton | 36 | 26 | 8 | 2 | 86 | 25 | 86 |
| Yeovil Town | 36 | 24 | 6 | 6 | 95 | 47 | 78 |
| Devizes Town | 36 | 22 | 7 | 7 | 83 | 38 | 73 |
| Street | 36 | 21 | 7 | 8 | 61 | 32 | 70 |
| Clyst Rovers** | 36 | 20 | 10 | 6 | 89 | 39 | 67 |
| Minehead | 36 | 16 | 14 | 6 | 60 | 39 | 62 |
| Dawlish Town** | 36 | 17 | 10 | 9 | 78 | 48 | 58 |
| Crediton United | 36 | 15 | 8 | 13 | 65 | 67 | 53 |
| Exmouth Town | 36 | 15 | 6 | 15 | 68 | 60 | 51 |
| Bitton | 36 | 14 | 8 | 14 | 55 | 53 | 50 |
| Wellington | 36 | 13 | 10 | 13 | 72 | 54 | 49 |
| Ilfracombe Town | 36 | 14 | 7 | 15 | 75 | 67 | 49 |
| Larkhall Athletic | 36 | 12 | 7 | 17 | 45 | 58 | 43 |
| Welton Rovers | 36 | 9 | 6 | 21 | 51 | 78 | 33 |
| Warminster Town | 36 | 9 | 5 | 22 | 40 | 83 | 32 |
| Glastonbury | 36 | 9 | 4 | 23 | 41 | 86 | 31 |
| Frome Town | 36 | 8 | 6 | 22 | 47 | 74 | 30 |
| Heavitree United | 36 | 3 | 7 | 26 | 34 | 135 | 16 |
| Pewsey Vale** | 36 | 3 | 8 | 25 | 40 | 102 | 14 |

**3 points deducted

## ESSEX SENIOR LEAGUE

| Premier Division | P | W | D | L | F | A | Pts |
|---|---|---|---|---|---|---|---|
| Concorde Rangers | 26 | 23 | 2 | 1 | 74 | 20 | 71 |
| Basildon United | 26 | 22 | 3 | 1 | 75 | 15 | 69 |
| Bowers United | 26 | 19 | 2 | 5 | 65 | 25 | 59 |
| Stansted | 26 | 15 | 3 | 8 | 71 | 43 | 48 |
| Burnham Ramblers | 26 | 13 | 5 | 8 | 52 | 33 | 44 |
| Hullbridge Sports | 26 | 11 | 5 | 10 | 44 | 37 | 38 |
| Great Wakering Rovers | 26 | 10 | 5 | 11 | 39 | 42 | 35 |
| Brentwood | 26 | 9 | 4 | 13 | 34 | 44 | 31 |
| East Ham United | 26 | 9 | 3 | 14 | 41 | 61 | 30 |
| Sawbridgeworth Town | 26 | 8 | 3 | 15 | 32 | 57 | 27 |
| Ilford | 26 | 7 | 5 | 14 | 38 | 48 | 26 |
| Southend Manor | 26 | 4 | 6 | 16 | 27 | 66 | 18 |
| Eton Manor | 26 | 3 | 4 | 19 | 34 | 59 | 13 |
| Saffron Walden Town | 26 | 3 | 2 | 21 | 24 | 100 | 11 |

## JEWSON (EAST COUNTIES) LEAGUE

| Premier Division | P | W | D | L | F | A | Pts |
|---|---|---|---|---|---|---|---|
| Wroxham | 42 | 30 | 7 | 5 | 80 | 26 | 97 |
| Ely City | 42 | 29 | 8 | 5 | 91 | 43 | 95 |
| Histon | 42 | 27 | 7 | 8 | 102 | 46 | 88 |
| Sudbury Wanderers | 42 | 25 | 4 | 13 | 100 | 56 | 79 |
| Great Yarmouth Town | 42 | 21 | 8 | 13 | 80 | 60 | 71 |
| Sudbury Town | 42 | 19 | 13 | 10 | 81 | 43 | 70 |
| Halstead Town | 42 | 19 | 8 | 15 | 80 | 64 | 65 |
| Felixstowe Port & Town | 42 | 20 | 4 | 18 | 58 | 43 | 64 |
| Lowestoft Town | 42 | 18 | 10 | 14 | 82 | 70 | 64 |
| Fakenham Town | 42 | 18 | 9 | 15 | 68 | 61 | 63 |
| Newmarket Town | 42 | 18 | 7 | 17 | 68 | 52 | 61 |
| Woodbridge Town | 42 | 15 | 14 | 13 | 74 | 71 | 59 |
| Stowmarket Town | 42 | 17 | 4 | 21 | 63 | 81 | 55 |
| Gorleston | 42 | 14 | 12 | 16 | 62 | 63 | 54 |
| Soham Town Rangers* | 42 | 16 | 5 | 21 | 86 | 88 | 52 |
| Warboys Town | 42 | 16 | 4 | 22 | 72 | 78 | 52 |
| Diss Town | 42 | 13 | 10 | 19 | 64 | 76 | 49 |
| Bury Town | 42 | 13 | 8 | 21 | 58 | 71 | 47 |
| Harwich & Parkeston | 42 | 12 | 7 | 23 | 61 | 85 | 43 |
| Watton United | 42 | 7 | 7 | 28 | 44 | 126 | 28 |
| Clacton Town | 42 | 6 | 8 | 28 | 46 | 140 | 26 |
| Tiptree United | 42 | 3 | 8 | 31 | 46 | 123 | 17 |

*One point deducted – ineligible player

| Division One | P | W | D | L | F | A | Pts |
|---|---|---|---|---|---|---|---|
| Ipswich Wanderers | 34 | 29 | 2 | 3 | 100 | 35 | 89 |
| Maldon Town | 34 | 26 | 2 | 6 | 84 | 29 | 80 |
| Swaffham Town | 34 | 21 | 7 | 6 | 67 | 26 | 70 |
| Needham Market | 34 | 17 | 7 | 10 | 53 | 39 | 58 |
| Stanway Rovers | 34 | 16 | 9 | 9 | 64 | 37 | 57 |
| Cambridge City Res | 34 | 16 | 8 | 10 | 63 | 44 | 56 |
| Chatteris Town | 34 | 16 | 8 | 10 | 56 | 53 | 56 |
| Norwich United | 34 | 16 | 3 | 15 | 51 | 46 | 51 |
| Whitton United | 34 | 14 | 8 | 12 | 66 | 55 | 50 |
| Haverhill Rovers | 34 | 14 | 7 | 13 | 54 | 56 | 49 |
| Mildenhall Town | 34 | 10 | 12 | 12 | 46 | 57 | 42 |
| Downham Town | 34 | 10 | 7 | 17 | 50 | 72 | 37 |
| Thetford Town | 34 | 9 | 5 | 20 | 47 | 74 | 32 |
| Cornard United | 34 | 8 | 8 | 18 | 41 | 71 | 32 |
| March Town United | 34 | 7 | 7 | 20 | 34 | 75 | 28 |
| Hadleigh United | 34 | 6 | 8 | 20 | 32 | 60 | 26 |
| Brightlingsea United | 34 | 5 | 7 | 22 | 30 | 67 | 22 |
| Somersham Town | 34 | 4 | 9 | 21 | 46 | 88 | 21 |

## REDFERNS INTERNATIONAL REMOVERS CENTRAL MIDLANDS LEAGUE

| Supreme Division | P | W | D | L | F | A | Pts |
|---|---|---|---|---|---|---|---|
| Gedling Town | 30 | 26 | 1 | 3 | 100 | 35 | 79 |
| Kimberley Town | 30 | 20 | 3 | 7 | 78 | 46 | 63 |
| Mickleover Sports | 30 | 17 | 6 | 7 | 71 | 43 | 57 |
| Dunkirk | 30 | 17 | 4 | 9 | 64 | 38 | 55 |
| Heanor Town | 30 | 14 | 7 | 9 | 62 | 45 | 49 |
| Nettleham | 30 | 15 | 1 | 14 | 59 | 50 | 46 |
| Clipstone Welfare | 30 | 13 | 6 | 11 | 62 | 63 | 45 |
| Collingham | 30 | 11 | 7 | 12 | 49 | 52 | 40 |
| Rossington | 30 | 11 | 5 | 14 | 60 | 60 | 38 |
| Graham Street Prims | 30 | 11 | 5 | 14 | 49 | 63 | 38 |
| Long Eaton United | 30 | 11 | 2 | 17 | 48 | 57 | 35 |
| Grimethorpe MW | 30 | 10 | 4 | 16 | 36 | 53 | 34 |
| Harworth Colliery Inst | 30 | 8 | 7 | 15 | 38 | 58 | 31 |
| Shirebrook Town | 30 | 7 | 9 | 14 | 43 | 68 | 30 |
| Sandiacre Town | 30 | 9 | 3 | 18 | 38 | 65 | 30 |
| Thorne Colliery | 30 | 4 | 2 | 24 | 23 | 82 | 14 |

## Premier Division

| | P | W | D | L | F | A | Pts |
|---|---|---|---|---|---|---|---|
| Goole | 32 | 27 | 4 | 1 | 101 | 18 | 85 |
| Hucknall Rolls Royce | 32 | 23 | 4 | 5 | 89 | 35 | 73 |
| Sneinton | 32 | 21 | 4 | 7 | 96 | 44 | 67 |
| Askern Welfare (–3) | 32 | 21 | 3 | 8 | 100 | 39 | 63 |
| S. Normanton Athletic | 32 | 17 | 3 | 12 | 61 | 49 | 54 |
| Greenwood Meadows | 32 | 16 | 4 | 12 | 70 | 59 | 52 |
| Hemsworth Town | 32 | 14 | 8 | 10 | 54 | 52 | 50 |
| Selston | 32 | 14 | 7 | 11 | 62 | 52 | 49 |
| Radford | 32 | 13 | 6 | 13 | 50 | 67 | 45 |
| Holbrook | 32 | 14 | 3 | 15 | 47 | 66 | 45 |
| Shardlow St James (–1) | 32 | 13 | 4 | 15 | 54 | 61 | 42 |
| Stanton Ilkeston | 32 | 9 | 6 | 17 | 52 | 66 | 33 |
| Sheepbridge | 32 | 8 | 6 | 18 | 46 | 86 | 30 |
| Mickleover RBL | 32 | 6 | 10 | 16 | 46 | 76 | 28 |
| Sheffield Hallam Univ | 32 | 8 | 2 | 22 | 47 | 75 | 26 |
| Mexborough Athletic | 32 | 5 | 4 | 23 | 37 | 84 | 19 |
| Blackwell MW | 32 | 2 | 4 | 26 | 22 | 105 | 10 |

## NORTHERN COUNTIES (EAST) LEAGUE

### Premier Division

| | P | W | D | L | F | A | Pts |
|---|---|---|---|---|---|---|---|
| Hucknall Town | 38 | 26 | 8 | 4 | 90 | 34 | 86 |
| North Ferriby United | 38 | 25 | 6 | 7 | 89 | 37 | 81 |
| Ossett Albion | 38 | 21 | 11 | 6 | 59 | 25 | 74 |
| Brigg Town | 38 | 20 | 10 | 8 | 76 | 40 | 70 |
| Glasshoughton Welfare | 38 | 17 | 9 | 12 | 66 | 64 | 60 |
| Maltby Main | 38 | 17 | 8 | 13 | 51 | 40 | 59 |
| Ossett Town | 38 | 17 | 7 | 14 | 67 | 53 | 58 |
| Eccleshill United | 38 | 16 | 9 | 13 | 64 | 58 | 57 |
| Armthorpe Welfare | 38 | 16 | 8 | 14 | 60 | 44 | 56 |
| Selby Town | 38 | 15 | 6 | 17 | 60 | 75 | 51 |
| Thackley | 38 | 12 | 12 | 14 | 48 | 55 | 48 |
| Denaby United | 38 | 14 | 6 | 18 | 55 | 68 | 48 |
| Pontefract Collieries | 38 | 13 | 9 | 16 | 60 | 76 | 48 |
| Arnold Town | 38 | 10 | 16 | 12 | 55 | 52 | 46 |
| Sheffield | 38 | 13 | 7 | 18 | 62 | 72 | 46 |
| Pickering Town | 38 | 12 | 8 | 18 | 56 | 68 | 44 |
| Hallam | 38 | 10 | 10 | 18 | 52 | 77 | 40 |
| Liversedge | 38 | 7 | 9 | 22 | 41 | 88 | 30 |
| Curzon Ashton | 38 | 7 | 8 | 23 | 42 | 75 | 29 |
| Hatfield Main | 38 | 6 | 5 | 27 | 46 | 98 | 23 |

### Division One

| | P | W | D | L | F | A | Pts |
|---|---|---|---|---|---|---|---|
| Garforth Town | 28 | 23 | 3 | 2 | 77 | 17 | 72 |
| Staveley MW | 28 | 15 | 9 | 4 | 51 | 30 | 54 |
| Hall Road Rangers | 28 | 16 | 4 | 8 | 68 | 34 | 52 |
| Glapwell | 28 | 14 | 4 | 10 | 59 | 50 | 46 |
| Parkgate | 28 | 14 | 3 | 11 | 61 | 47 | 45 |
| Louth United | 28 | 14 | 2 | 12 | 73 | 50 | 44 |
| Worsbrough Bridge | 28 | 13 | 4 | 11 | 58 | 57 | 43 |
| Borrowash Victoria | 28 | 11 | 8 | 9 | 67 | 50 | 41 |
| Rossington Main | 28 | 11 | 4 | 13 | 41 | 46 | 37 |
| Winterton Rangers | 28 | 11 | 3 | 14 | 41 | 55 | 36 |
| Harrogate Railway | 28 | 10 | 4 | 14 | 58 | 52 | 34 |
| Brodsworth MW | 28 | 8 | 9 | 11 | 53 | 43 | 33 |
| Tadcaster Albion | 28 | 8 | 6 | 14 | 56 | 46 | 30 |
| Yorkshire Amateur | 28 | 8 | 5 | 15 | 49 | 57 | 29 |
| Blidworth Welfare | 28 | 0 | 0 | 28 | 8 | 186 | 0 |

## BANKS'S BREWERY WEST MIDLANDS LEAGUE

### Premier Division

| | P | W | D | L | F | A | Pts |
|---|---|---|---|---|---|---|---|
| Lye Town | 34 | 26 | 6 | 2 | 91 | 35 | 84 |
| Stourport Swifts | 34 | 23 | 6 | 5 | 101 | 34 | 75 |
| Brierley Hill Town | 34 | 21 | 5 | 8 | 64 | 34 | 68 |
| Kington Town | 34 | 21 | 3 | 10 | 97 | 67 | 66 |
| Bloxwich Strollers | 34 | 18 | 4 | 12 | 81 | 49 | 58 |
| Malvern Town | 34 | 17 | 4 | 13 | 73 | 59 | 55 |
| W'pton Casuals | 34 | 15 | 6 | 13 | 64 | 52 | 51 |
| Gornal Athletic | 34 | 15 | 5 | 14 | 56 | 50 | 50 |
| Darlaston Town | 34 | 15 | 3 | 16 | 78 | 70 | 48 |
| Tividale | 34 | 15 | 3 | 16 | 64 | 57 | 48 |
| Ludlow Town | 34 | 14 | 3 | 17 | 58 | 71 | 45 |
| Stafford Town | 34 | 12 | 7 | 15 | 49 | 57 | 43 |
| Walsall Wood | 34 | 11 | 7 | 16 | 49 | 64 | 40 |
| Westfields | 34 | 11 | 5 | 18 | 57 | 69 | 38 |
| Bustleholme | 34 | 11 | 3 | 20 | 48 | 76 | 36 |
| Cradley Town | 34 | 9 | 5 | 20 | 54 | 80 | 32 |
| Ettinghall HT | 34 | 5 | 7 | 22 | 37 | 100 | 22 |
| W'pton United | 34 | 2 | 5 | 27 | 19 | 116 | 11 |

## SOUTH EAST COUNTIES LEAGUE

### Division One

| | P | W | D | L | F | A | Pts |
|---|---|---|---|---|---|---|---|
| West Ham United | 30 | 23 | 4 | 3 | 88 | 23 | 73 |
| Portsmouth | 30 | 20 | 5 | 5 | 67 | 33 | 65 |
| Fulham | 30 | 16 | 5 | 9 | 47 | 48 | 53 |
| Charlton Athletic | 30 | 14 | 8 | 8 | 76 | 50 | 50 |
| Leyton Orient | 30 | 15 | 3 | 12 | 56 | 58 | 48 |
| Millwall | 30 | 14 | 5 | 11 | 48 | 36 | 47 |
| Ipswich Town | 30 | 13 | 4 | 13 | 43 | 49 | 43 |
| Arsenal | 30 | 12 | 5 | 13 | 51 | 55 | 41 |
| Watford | 30 | 11 | 7 | 12 | 50 | 52 | 40 |
| Norwich City | 30 | 9 | 11 | 10 | 38 | 41 | 38 |
| Cambridge United | 30 | 9 | 10 | 11 | 52 | 53 | 37 |
| Tottenham Hotspur | 30 | 10 | 5 | 15 | 46 | 60 | 35 |
| Crystal Palace | 30 | 8 | 6 | 16 | 46 | 61 | 30 |
| Gillingham | 30 | 7 | 8 | 15 | 41 | 58 | 29 |
| Queens Park Rangers | 30 | 6 | 3 | 21 | 30 | 72 | 21 |
| Southend United | 30 | 3 | 11 | 16 | 34 | 64 | 20 |

### Division Two

| | P | W | D | L | F | A | Pts |
|---|---|---|---|---|---|---|---|
| Luton Town | 28 | 18 | 7 | 3 | 71 | 24 | 61 |
| Bristol City | 28 | 17 | 6 | 5 | 54 | 35 | 57 |
| Brentford | 28 | 15 | 9 | 4 | 49 | 31 | 54 |
| Wycombe Wanderers | 28 | 11 | 10 | 7 | 42 | 30 | 43 |
| Colchester United | 28 | 11 | 8 | 9 | 49 | 42 | 41 |
| Swindon Town | 28 | 13 | 2 | 13 | 46 | 46 | 41 |
| Wimbledon | 28 | 11 | 5 | 12 | 46 | 50 | 38 |
| Oxford United | 28 | 11 | 5 | 12 | 50 | 59 | 38 |
| Southampton | 28 | 10 | 5 | 13 | 53 | 56 | 35 |
| Bristol Rovers | 28 | 9 | 7 | 12 | 53 | 49 | 34 |
| AFC Bournemouth | 28 | 8 | 8 | 12 | 43 | 58 | 32 |
| Reading | 28 | 8 | 6 | 14 | 37 | 49 | 30 |
| Tottenham Hotspur | 28 | 8 | 6 | 14 | 36 | 49 | 30 |
| Barnet | 28 | 7 | 7 | 14 | 47 | 61 | 28 |
| Brighton & Hove Albion | 28 | 4 | 7 | 17 | 32 | 69 | 19 |

## HELLENIC LEAGUE

### Premier Division

| | P | W | D | L | F | A | Pts |
|---|---|---|---|---|---|---|---|
| Swindon Supermarine | 34 | 27 | 3 | 4 | 83 | 20 | 84 |
| Endsleigh | 34 | 26 | 4 | 4 | 75 | 24 | 82 |
| Burnham | 34 | 18 | 10 | 6 | 65 | 35 | 64 |
| Banbury United | 34 | 17 | 7 | 10 | 69 | 42 | 58 |
| Almondsbury Town | 34 | 17 | 4 | 13 | 51 | 37 | 55 |
| Tuffley Rovers | 34 | 16 | 7 | 11 | 57 | 49 | 55 |
| Highworth Town | 34 | 14 | 7 | 13 | 52 | 56 | 49 |
| North Leigh | 34 | 13 | 8 | 13 | 51 | 46 | 47 |
| Fairford Town | 34 | 13 | 8 | 13 | 54 | 53 | 47 |
| Abingdon United | 34 | 12 | 10 | 12 | 60 | 57 | 46 |
| Wantage Town | 34 | 12 | 4 | 18 | 45 | 72 | 40 |
| Didcot Town | 34 | 9 | 12 | 13 | 48 | 49 | 39 |
| Carterton Town | 34 | 9 | 10 | 15 | 50 | 57 | 37 |
| Shortwood United | 34 | 10 | 6 | 18 | 57 | 78 | 36 |
| Hallen | 34 | 9 | 6 | 19 | 39 | 57 | 33 |
| Harrow Hill | 34 | 8 | 7 | 19 | 38 | 70 | 31 |
| Bicester Town | 34 | 7 | 8 | 19 | 43 | 73 | 29 |
| Kintbury Rangers* | 34 | 6 | 5 | 23 | 32 | 94 | 20 |

*3 points deducted

### Division One

| | P | W | D | L | F | A | Pts |
|---|---|---|---|---|---|---|---|
| Ardley United | 32 | 23 | 5 | 4 | 104 | 36 | 74 |
| Cirencester Academy* | 32 | 21 | 9 | 2 | 66 | 22 | 69 |
| Cheltenham Saracens | 32 | 21 | 6 | 5 | 71 | 41 | 69 |
| Purton | 32 | 18 | 6 | 8 | 71 | 44 | 60 |
| Kidlington | 32 | 16 | 8 | 8 | 71 | 49 | 56 |
| Easington Sports | 32 | 15 | 5 | 12 | 60 | 56 | 50 |
| Pegasus Juniors | 32 | 14 | 6 | 12 | 62 | 50 | 48 |
| Clanfield | 32 | 14 | 5 | 13 | 64 | 56 | 47 |
| Ross Town | 32 | 13 | 6 | 13 | 56 | 57 | 45 |
| Wootton Bassett | 32 | 12 | 6 | 4 | 67 | 58 | 42 |
| Cirencester United | 32 | 11 | 7 | 14 | 51 | 57 | 40 |
| Bishops Cleeve | 32 | 12 | 3 | 17 | 42 | 63 | 39 |
| Watlington | 32 | 11 | 3 | 18 | 42 | 59 | 36 |
| Headington Amateurs | 32 | 9 | 7 | 16 | 47 | 56 | 34 |
| Letcombe | 32 | 8 | 3 | 21 | 40 | 82 | 27 |
| Milton United | 32 | 6 | 4 | 22 | 37 | 82 | 22 |
| Yarnton | 32 | 2 | 3 | 27 | 29 | 112 | 9 |

*3 points deducted

## MINERVA FOOTBALLS SOUTH MIDLANDS LEAGUE

### Premier Division North

| | P | W | D | L | F | A | Pts |
|---|---|---|---|---|---|---|---|
| Brache Sparta | 28 | 23 | 2 | 3 | 75 | 17 | 71 |
| Potters Bar Town | 28 | 20 | 7 | 1 | 62 | 21 | 67 |
| London Colney | 28 | 16 | 4 | 8 | 67 | 46 | 52 |
| Royston Town | 28 | 14 | 5 | 9 | 52 | 34 | 47 |
| Hoddesdon Town | 28 | 15 | 2 | 11 | 50 | 36 | 47 |
| Welwyn Garden City | 28 | 12 | 10 | 6 | 47 | 42 | 46 |
| Arlesey Town | 28 | 13 | 5 | 10 | 51 | 41 | 44 |
| Harpenden Town | 28 | 12 | 5 | 11 | 46 | 45 | 41 |
| Toddington Rovers | 28 | 10 | 5 | 13 | 39 | 52 | 35 |
| Buckingham Athletic | 28 | 9 | 6 | 13 | 46 | 55 | 33 |
| Letchworth | 28 | 8 | 5 | 15 | 50 | 63 | 29 |
| Biggleswade Town | 28 | 7 | 7 | 14 | 41 | 53 | 28 |
| Milton Keynes* | 28 | 8 | 5 | 15 | 40 | 52 | 28 |
| Bedford United** | 28 | 3 | 8 | 17 | 25 | 67 | 14 |
| Langford | 28 | 1 | 2 | 25 | 23 | 90 | 5 |

*1 point deducted
**3 points deducted

### Premier Division South

| | P | W | D | L | F | A | Pts |
|---|---|---|---|---|---|---|---|
| Brook House | 28 | 18 | 6 | 4 | 66 | 27 | 60 |
| Beaconsfield SYCOB | 28 | 16 | 8 | 4 | 59 | 27 | 56 |
| Ruislip Manor | 28 | 17 | 4 | 7 | 61 | 29 | 55 |
| Hillingdon Borough | 28 | 15 | 7 | 6 | 73 | 35 | 52 |
| Barkingside | 28 | 12 | 7 | 9 | 44 | 34 | 43 |
| Waltham Abbey | 28 | 12 | 6 | 10 | 54 | 42 | 42 |
| Haringey Borough | 28 | 12 | 4 | 12 | 42 | 44 | 40 |
| Brimsdown Rovers | 28 | 11 | 4 | 13 | 46 | 58 | 37 |
| St Margaretsbury* | 28 | 11 | 4 | 13 | 46 | 58 | 36 |
| Islington St Marys* | 28 | 10 | 4 | 14 | 42 | 52 | 33 |
| Woodford Town | 28 | 7 | 9 | 12 | 48 | 59 | 30 |
| Hanwell Town | 28 | 8 | 4 | 16 | 45 | 76 | 28 |
| Harefield United | 28 | 7 | 6 | 15 | 27 | 67 | 27 |
| Amersham Town | 28 | 8 | 2 | 18 | 26 | 45 | 26 |
| Cockfosters | 28 | 5 | 7 | 16 | 35 | 61 | 22 |

*1 point deducted

### Senior Division

| | P | W | D | L | F | A | Pts |
|---|---|---|---|---|---|---|---|
| New Bradwell St Peter | 30 | 21 | 5 | 4 | 86 | 30 | 68 |
| Tring Athletic | 30 | 21 | 5 | 4 | 84 | 30 | 68 |
| Mercedes Benz | 30 | 21 | 2 | 7 | 84 | 51 | 65 |
| Holmer Green | 30 | 20 | 3 | 7 | 94 | 41 | 63 |
| Biggleswade United | 30 | 16 | 8 | 6 | 74 | 40 | 56 |
| Houghton Town | 30 | 16 | 6 | 8 | 69 | 51 | 54 |
| Leverstock Green | 30 | 15 | 7 | 8 | 66 | 43 | 52 |
| Caddington | 30 | 15 | 4 | 11 | 57 | 61 | 49 |
| Shillington | 30 | 12 | 5 | 13 | 56 | 61 | 41 |
| Risborough Rangers | 30 | 8 | 9 | 13 | 50 | 65 | 33 |
| Winslow United | 30 | 10 | 2 | 18 | 55 | 78 | 32 |
| Totternhoe | 30 | 8 | 3 | 19 | 53 | 78 | 27 |
| Stony Stratford Town | 30 | 7 | 2 | 21 | 46 | 78 | 23 |
| The 61 FC (Luton) | 30 | 5 | 3 | 22 | 35 | 99 | 18 |
| Kent Athletic* | 30 | 5 | 4 | 21 | 44 | 88 | 16 |
| Ampthill Town | 30 | 4 | 4 | 22 | 33 | 92 | 16 |

*3 points deducted

## EVERARDS BREWERY LEICESTERSHIRE SENIOR LEAGUE

### Premier Division

| | P | W | D | L | F | A | Pts |
|---|---|---|---|---|---|---|---|
| Oadby Town | 34 | 27 | 2 | 5 | 101 | 34 | 83 |
| Kirby Muxloe SC | 34 | 24 | 5 | 5 | 83 | 38 | 77 |
| Friar Lane OB | 34 | 24 | 2 | 8 | 88 | 33 | 74 |
| Holwell Sports | 34 | 22 | 7 | 5 | 86 | 41 | 73 |
| St Andrews SC | 34 | 19 | 6 | 9 | 81 | 39 | 63 |
| Ibstock Welfare | 34 | 19 | 3 | 12 | 76 | 52 | 60 |
| Downes Sports | 34 | 18 | 4 | 12 | 67 | 57 | 58 |
| Birstall United | 34 | 16 | 6 | 12 | 52 | 41 | 54 |
| Cottesmore Amateurs | 34 | 15 | 4 | 15 | 63 | 61 | 49 |
| Highfield Rangers | 34 | 15 | 3 | 16 | 46 | 62 | 48 |
| Quorn | 34 | 10 | 7 | 17 | 61 | 73 | 37 |
| Thringstone United | 34 | 9 | 10 | 15 | 34 | 47 | 37 |
| Ansley Nomads | 34 | 10 | 5 | 19 | 49 | 69 | 35 |
| Coalville | 34 | 9 | 5 | 20 | 42 | 72 | 32 |
| Aylestone Park OB | 34 | 8 | 6 | 20 | 49 | 81 | 30 |
| Lutterworth Town | 34 | 8 | 6 | 20 | 51 | 89 | 30 |
| Barrow Town | 34 | 5 | 7 | 22 | 41 | 87 | 22 |
| United Collieries (−3) | 34 | 4 | 0 | 30 | 30 | 124 | 9 |

### Division One

| | P | W | D | L | F | A | Pts |
|---|---|---|---|---|---|---|---|
| Thurnby Rangers | 30 | 24 | 2 | 4 | 89 | 33 | 74 |
| Stoney Stanton | 30 | 18 | 7 | 5 | 67 | 40 | 61 |
| Saffron Dynamo | 30 | 18 | 4 | 8 | 65 | 36 | 58 |
| Blaby & Whet. A | 30 | 17 | 6 | 7 | 52 | 38 | 57 |
| Fosse Imps | 30 | 17 | 5 | 8 | 71 | 36 | 56 |
| Leics Constabulary | 30 | 15 | 10 | 5 | 80 | 35 | 55 |
| Huncote S & S | 30 | 13 | 7 | 10 | 75 | 55 | 46 |
| Anstey Town | 30 | 12 | 6 | 12 | 60 | 53 | 42 |
| Bardon Hill | 30 | 11 | 7 | 12 | 56 | 52 | 40 |
| Loughborough D | 30 | 11 | 7 | 12 | 52 | 63 | 40 |
| Sileby Town | 30 | 10 | 7 | 13 | 44 | 53 | 37 |
| Earl Shilton Albion | 30 | 9 | 5 | 16 | 38 | 39 | 32 |
| Narb. & L'thorpe | 30 | 8 | 4 | 18 | 39 | 60 | 28 |
| Asfordby Amateurs | 30 | 6 | 5 | 19 | 29 | 74 | 23 |
| Harborough Town | 30 | 3 | 4 | 23 | 26 | 112 | 13 |
| North Kilworth | 30 | 2 | 6 | 22 | 32 | 96 | 12 |

## UNITED COUNTIES FOOTBALL LEAGUE

### Premier Division

| | P | W | D | L | F | A | Pts |
|---|---|---|---|---|---|---|---|
| Stamford | 40 | 29 | 6 | 5 | 113 | 45 | 93 |
| Northampton Spen | 40 | 27 | 2 | 11 | 105 | 59 | 83 |
| Spalding United | 40 | 24 | 10 | 6 | 77 | 47 | 82 |
| Desborough Town | 40 | 23 | 9 | 8 | 89 | 49 | 78 |
| S & L Corby | 40 | 24 | 6 | 10 | 68 | 39 | 78 |
| Ford Sports Daventry | 40 | 22 | 10 | 8 | 74 | 38 | 76 |
| Boston Town | 40 | 23 | 6 | 11 | 82 | 48 | 75 |
| Stotfold | 40 | 21 | 9 | 10 | 89 | 60 | 72 |
| Mirrlees Blackstone | 40 | 20 | 7 | 13 | 69 | 50 | 67 |
| St Neots Town | 40 | 20 | 3 | 17 | 67 | 60 | 63 |
| Buckingham Town | 40 | 18 | 7 | 15 | 58 | 49 | 61 |
| Cogenhoe United | 40 | 17 | 9 | 14 | 68 | 53 | 60 |
| Long Buckby | 40 | 14 | 8 | 18 | 64 | 68 | 50 |
| Potton United | 40 | 11 | 10 | 19 | 46 | 62 | 43 |
| Wellingborough Town | 40 | 11 | 5 | 24 | 46 | 77 | 38 |
| Holbeach United | 40 | 10 | 8 | 22 | 39 | 76 | 38 |
| Wootton Blue Cross | 40 | 9 | 6 | 25 | 53 | 99 | 33 |
| Yaxley | 40 | 9 | 3 | 28 | 57 | 102 | 30 |
| Bourne Town | 40 | 8 | 5 | 27 | 48 | 96 | 29 |
| Eynesbury Rovers | 40 | 6 | 10 | 24 | 29 | 72 | 28 |
| Kempston Rovers | 40 | 2 | 5 | 33 | 18 | 110 | 11 |

### Division One

| | P | W | D | L | F | A | Pts |
|---|---|---|---|---|---|---|---|
| Higham Town | 34 | 26 | 4 | 4 | 91 | 23 | 82 |
| Cottingham | 34 | 23 | 4 | 7 | 84 | 40 | 73 |
| Harrowby United | 34 | 20 | 4 | 10 | 94 | 61 | 64 |
| Bugbrooke St M. | 34 | 18 | 7 | 9 | 90 | 47 | 61 |
| Blisworth | 34 | 19 | 4 | 11 | 73 | 54 | 61 |
| Well. Whitworths | 34 | 17 | 5 | 12 | 78 | 55 | 56 |
| Daventry Town | 34 | 16 | 5 | 13 | 87 | 66 | 53 |
| St Ives Town | 34 | 15 | 7 | 12 | 66 | 57 | 52 |
| Newport Pagnell Town | 34 | 16 | 4 | 14 | 61 | 56 | 52 |
| Rothwell Corinthians | 34 | 14 | 8 | 12 | 77 | 58 | 50 |
| Olney Town | 34 | 15 | 5 | 14 | 65 | 55 | 50 |
| Northampton Vanaid | 34 | 14 | 5 | 15 | 90 | 54 | 47 |
| Thrapston Town | 34 | 12 | 7 | 15 | 74 | 59 | 43 |
| Burton Park Wanderers | 34 | 13 | 3 | 18 | 58 | 71 | 42 |
| ON Chenecks | 34 | 10 | 8 | 16 | 54 | 61 | 38 |
| Irchester United | 34 | 7 | 5 | 22 | 43 | 85 | 26 |
| Sharnbrook | 34 | 6 | 4 | 24 | 50 | 82 | 22 |
| Huntingdon United | 34 | 0 | 1 | 33 | 22 | 273 | 1 |

## JEWSON WESSEX FOOTBALL LEAGUE

**Division One**

| | P | W | D | L | F | A | Pts |
|---|---|---|---|---|---|---|---|
| AFC Lymington | 38 | 29 | 5 | 4 | 94 | 27 | 92 |
| Andover | 38 | 24 | 9 | 5 | 99 | 46 | 81 |
| AFC Newbury | 38 | 22 | 7 | 9 | 72 | 35 | 73 |
| Eastleigh | 38 | 20 | 11 | 7 | 74 | 31 | 71 |
| Bemerton Heath Har. | 38 | 19 | 11 | 8 | 69 | 38 | 68 |
| Cowes Sports | 38 | 20 | 6 | 12 | 67 | 51 | 66 |
| Wimborne Town | 38 | 18 | 9 | 11 | 89 | 63 | 63 |
| AFC Totton | 38 | 15 | 10 | 13 | 58 | 41 | 55 |
| Bournemouth | 38 | 16 | 7 | 15 | 64 | 68 | 55 |
| Thatcham Town | 38 | 16 | 6 | 16 | 64 | 54 | 54 |
| Christchurch | 38 | 15 | 6 | 17 | 55 | 69 | 51 |
| East Cowes Vics | 38 | 13 | 11 | 14 | 46 | 42 | 50 |
| Portsmouth Royal Navy | 38 | 13 | 7 | 18 | 64 | 79 | 46 |
| BAT | 38 | 12 | 7 | 19 | 60 | 82 | 43 |
| Gosport Borough | 38 | 9 | 10 | 19 | 48 | 65 | 37 |
| Aerostructures | 38 | 9 | 10 | 19 | 50 | 77 | 37 |
| Brockenhurst | 38 | 9 | 9 | 20 | 43 | 83 | 36 |
| Downton | 38 | 7 | 10 | 21 | 36 | 66 | 31 |
| Whitchurch United | 38 | 7 | 8 | 23 | 37 | 78 | 29 |
| Romsey Town | 38 | 5 | 5 | 28 | 40 | 134 | 20 |

## ARNOTT INSURANCE NORTHERN LEAGUE

**Division One**

| | P | W | D | L | F | A | Pts |
|---|---|---|---|---|---|---|---|
| Bedlington Terriers | 38 | 29 | 3 | 6 | 120 | 32 | 90 |
| Billingham Synthonia | 38 | 23 | 9 | 6 | 81 | 36 | 78 |
| Guisborough Town | 38 | 23 | 6 | 9 | 84 | 53 | 75 |
| Dunston Feds | 38 | 21 | 10 | 7 | 69 | 35 | 73 |
| RTM Newcastle | 38 | 20 | 5 | 13 | 92 | 70 | 65 |
| Penrith | 38 | 19 | 8 | 11 | 81 | 62 | 65 |
| Morpeth Town | 38 | 16 | 14 | 8 | 75 | 48 | 62 |
| South Shields (–3) | 38 | 15 | 19 | 4 | 65 | 38 | 61 |
| Shildon | 38 | 16 | 7 | 15 | 77 | 87 | 55 |
| Billingham Town | 38 | 17 | 2 | 19 | 72 | 79 | 53 |
| Tow Law Town (–3) | 38 | 16 | 7 | 15 | 78 | 61 | 52 |
| Consett | 38 | 13 | 11 | 14 | 60 | 62 | 50 |
| Jarrow Roofing | 38 | 11 | 12 | 15 | 64 | 70 | 45 |
| Crook Town | 38 | 12 | 7 | 19 | 58 | 67 | 43 |
| Seaham Red Star | 38 | 12 | 7 | 19 | 60 | 83 | 43 |
| Easington Colliery (–3) | 38 | 13 | 6 | 19 | 77 | 97 | 42 |
| Stockton (–3) | 38 | 10 | 10 | 18 | 54 | 65 | 37 |
| Durham City | 38 | 10 | 7 | 21 | 55 | 67 | 37 |
| Northallerton | 38 | 4 | 6 | 28 | 39 | 102 | 18 |
| Murton (–3) | 38 | 2 | 0 | 36 | 23 | 170 | 3 |

**Division Two**

| | P | W | D | L | F | A | Pts |
|---|---|---|---|---|---|---|---|
| Chester-le-Street Town | 36 | 29 | 3 | 4 | 105 | 27 | 90 |
| West Auckland Town | 36 | 24 | 8 | 4 | 84 | 36 | 80 |
| Marske United | 36 | 24 | 5 | 7 | 78 | 30 | 77 |
| Prudhoe Town (–3) | 36 | 20 | 5 | 11 | 87 | 58 | 62 |
| Ashington | 36 | 18 | 7 | 11 | 75 | 52 | 61 |
| Willington | 36 | 16 | 6 | 14 | 87 | 65 | 54 |
| Peterlee Newtown (–3) | 36 | 16 | 7 | 13 | 60 | 55 | 52 |
| Evenwood Town | 36 | 14 | 9 | 13 | 62 | 62 | 51 |
| Alnwick Town | 36 | 15 | 5 | 16 | 68 | 63 | 50 |
| Norton & Stock A. | 36 | 14 | 7 | 15 | 58 | 56 | 49 |
| Shotton Comrades | 36 | 13 | 8 | 15 | 66 | 61 | 47 |
| Hebburn | 36 | 12 | 10 | 14 | 57 | 43 | 46 |
| Ryhope CA | 36 | 12 | 10 | 14 | 60 | 63 | 46 |
| Whickham (–6) | 36 | 14 | 7 | 15 | 51 | 66 | 43 |
| Esh Winning | 36 | 11 | 9 | 16 | 58 | 79 | 42 |
| Horden CW | 35 | 11 | 8 | 16 | 53 | 67 | 41 |
| Brandon United | 36 | 11 | 6 | 19 | 59 | 87 | 39 |
| Eppleton CW | 36 | 4 | 4 | 28 | 29 | 103 | 16 |
| Washington | 35 | 1 | 0 | 34 | 24 | 148 | 3 |

## SEMI-PROFESSIONAL INTERNATIONAL

**3 Mar**

**England 2** *(Grayson, Bradshaw)*
**Holland 1**     1561

*England:* Stewart (Southport) [Cooksey (Hednesford Town)]; Hooper (Kingstonian) [Comyn (Hednesford Town)], Bradshaw (Halifax Town) [Victory (Cheltenham Town)], Banks (Cheltenham Town), Smith (Stevenage Borough), Ryan (Southport), Howells (Cheltenham Town), Butterworth (Rushden & Diamonds), Grayson (Cheltenham Town) [Pickard (Yeovil Town)], Watkins (Cheltenham Town), Healy (Morecambe) [Betsy (Woking)].

## FA XI REPRESENTATIVE MATCHES

**4 Nov**

**FA XI 5** *(Tait, Horsfield, Farley, Monk, Ceraolo)*
**Northern Premier League 0**     175

*FA XI:* Stewart (Southport) [Greygoose (Northwich Victoria)]; Farley (Southport) [Vicary (Northwich Victoria)], Bradshaw (Halifax Town) [Monk (Morecambe)], Simpson (Northwich Victoria), Higgins (Barrow), Ryan (Southport), Proudlock (Gateshead), Healy (Morecambe), Tait (Northwich Victoria) [Ceraolo (Morecambe)], Horsfield (Halifax Town), Walters (Northwich Victoria).

**9 Dec**

**FA XI 2** *(Stott, own goal)*
**Southern League 1**     415

*FA XI:* Pennock (Yeovil Town) [Grayson (Hereford United)]; Banks (Cheltenham Town), Victory (Cheltenham Town), Cousins (Yeovil Town), Webb (Kidderminster Harriers), Yates (Kidderminster Harriers), Pitman (Hereford United), Howells (Cheltenham Town), Eaton (Cheltenham Town) [Brook (Cheltenham Town)], Watkins (Cheltenham Town), Stott (Yeovil Town).

**10 Dec**

**FA XI 2** *(Perkins 2)*
**Isthmian League 0**     350

*FA XI:* Mackenzie (Farnborough Town) [Meara (Hayes)]; Watts (Welling United) [Munday (Dover Athletic)], Sparks (Hayes) [Danzey (Woking)], Hercules (Slough Town) [Stemp (Farnborough Town)], Smith (Stevenage Borough), Perkins (Stevenage Borough), Betsey (Woking), Harlow (Farnborough Town), West (Woking), Randall (Farnborough Town) [Crawshaw (Stevenage Borough)], Wingfield (Farnborough Town).

# AMATEUR FOOTBALL ALLIANCE 1997–98

## AFA SENIOR CUP

**1st Round Proper**
Old Minchendenians 2, 1 Old Parkonians
Alleyn Old Boys 2, 4 National Westminster Bank
Polytechnic 4*, 2* Old Meadonians
Old Grammarians 1, 3 Barclays Bank
Carshalton 6, 0 Old Wokingians
Cardinal Manning Old Boys 4*:0, 4*:4 Civil Service
Old Kingsburians 3, 5 Old Finchleians
Old Woodhouseians 2, 3 Nottsborough
Latymer Old Boys 4, 3 Old Southallians
Old Danes 0, 3 Old Salesians
Old Bealonians 1*:0, 1*:5 Wake Green
Shene Old Grammarians 2*:2, 2*:6 Old Tenisonians
Old Latymerians 4*, 3* Old Salvatorians
Witan 0, 1 Alexandra Park
Old Bromleians 6, 4 Old Esthameians
Old Vaughanianss 6, 0 Mill Hill Village
City of London w/o, w/d Old Haberdashers
Cuaco 2, 6 Crouch End Vampires
West Wickham 3, 1 Ulysses
Lensbury 1, 0 Glyn Old Boys
Merton 0, 5 Norsemen
Brent 1*:0, 1*:7 Southgate County
Old Parmiterians w/d a w/o Old Tiffinian
Old Reptonian 2, 3 East Barnet Old Grammarians
Old Foresters 0, 2 Old Ignatians
Old Isleworthians 2*:2, 2*:4 Old Cholmeleians
Brentham 0, 5 Old Owens
Old Chigwellians 0, 4 Midland Bank
Old Stationers 11, 2 Old Camdenians
Old Buckwellians 4, 5 Enfield Old Grammarians
Old Aloysians 1, 0 Lloyds Bank
Old Wilsonians 3, 0 Old Salopians
(a *awarded after abandonment*) (* *after extra time*)

**2nd Round Proper**
Old Minchendenians 2, 5 National Westminster Bank
Polytechnic 3, 2 Barclays Bank

Carshalton 2, 1 Civil Service
Old Finchleians 5, 3 Nottsborough
Latymer Old Boys 2, 4 Old Salesians
Wake Green 0, 1 Old Tenisonians
Old Latymerians 3*:4*, 3*:6* Alexandra Park
Old Bromleians 3, 2 Old Vaughanians
City of London 1, 2 Crouch End Vampires
West Wickham 1, 0 Lensbury
Norsemen 3, 1 Southgate County
Old Tiffinian 2, 0 East Barnet Old Grammarians
Old Ignatians 4, 0 Old Cholmeleians
Old Owens 3, 1 Midland Bank
Old Stationers 3, 2 Enfield Old Grammarians
Old Aloysians 3, 2 Old Wilsonians

**3rd Round Proper**
National Westminster Bank 5, 2 Polytechnic
Carshalton 1*:0, 1*:4 Old Finchleians
Old Salesians 2, 1 Old Tenisonians
Alexandra Park 1, 3 Old Bromleians
Crouch End Vampires 2, 5 West Wickham
Norsemen 3, 1 Old Tiffinian
Old Ignatians 6*, 1* Old Owens
Old Stationers 3, 4 Old Aloysians

**4th Round Proper**
National Westminster Bank 0, 4 Old Finchleians
Old Salesians 4, 2 Old Bromleians
West Wickham 3*, 2* Norsemen
Old Ignatians 2, 5 Old Aloysians

**Semi-Finals**
Old Finchleians 4, 0 Old Salesians
West Wickham 1*, 2* Old Aloysians

**Final**
Old Finchleians 0*, 2* Old Aloysians

## OTHER A.F.A. CUP RESULTS

**Intermediate**
O. Actonians Ass'n Res. 3, Lloyds Bank Res 2
**Junior**
Polytechnic 3rd 2, Old Tenisonians 3rd 0
**Minor**
Midland Bank 4th 1*:1*, Silhill 4th 1*:0*
**Senior Novets**
Old Meadonians 5th 1, Old Finchleians 5th 5
**Intermediate Novets**
Midland Bank 6th 2, City of London 6th 1
**Junior Novets**
Norsemen 8th 3, Old Parmiterians 10th 0
**Veterans**
City of London 1, Old Grammarians 0
**Open Veterans**
Port of London Auth'ty 3, Snaresbrook 0
**Youth**
Old Salesians 3, Norsemen 1
**Essex Senior**
Old Bealonians 6*, Old Buckwellians 8*
**Middlesex Senior**
Old Aloysians 4, Old Ignatians 0
**Surrey Senior**
Old Salesians 0*:0, Nat'l Westminster Bank 0*:1
**Essex Intermediate**
Old Bealonians Res. 0, Hale End Athletic Res. 1
**Kent Intermediate**
Midland Bank Res 2, Chase Manhattan Bank 0
**Middlesex Intermediate**
Winchmore Hill Res 2, O. Actonians Ass'n Res 1
**Surrey Intermediate**
Carshalton Res 1, Kew Association Res 0
**Greenland Memorial**
Old Parmiterians 4, Old Foresters 1

### ARTHUR DUNN CUP FINAL

Old Foresters 3, Old Brentwoods 1

### ARTHURIAN LEAGUE

| PREMIER DIVISION | P | W | D | L | F | A | Pts |
|---|---|---|---|---|---|---|---|
| Old Foresters | 16 | 13 | 2 | 1 | 63 | 22 | 25* |
| Old Brentwoods | 16 | 11 | 3 | 2 | 39 | 17 | 25 |
| Lancing Old Boys | 16 | 9 | 3 | 4 | 50 | 30 | 21 |
| Old Etonians | 16 | 7 | 2 | 7 | 29 | 30 | 16 |
| Old Chigwellians | 16 | 6 | 2 | 8 | 36 | 31 | 14 |
| Old Carthusians | 16 | 6 | 2 | 8 | 34 | 39 | 14 |
| Old Salopians | 16 | 5 | 2 | 9 | 25 | 44 | 12 |
| Old Cholmeleians | 16 | 3 | 3 | 10 | 25 | 38 | 9 |
| Old Haberdashers | 16 | 2 | 1 | 13 | 18 | 68 | 5 |

| DIVISION 1 | P | W | D | L | F | A | Pts |
|---|---|---|---|---|---|---|---|
| Old Reptonians | 16 | 11 | 3 | 2 | 56 | 16 | 25 |
| Old Bradfieldians | 16 | 10 | 1 | 5 | 31 | 22 | 21 |
| Old Wellingburians | 16 | 8 | 2 | 6 | 45 | 25 | 18 |
| Old Harrovians | 16 | 8 | 2 | 6 | 51 | 46 | 18 |
| Old Aldenhamians | 16 | 7 | 4 | 5 | 27 | 30 | 18 |
| Old Witleians | 16 | 5 | 4 | 7 | 28 | 36 | 14 |
| Old Malvernians | 16 | 2 | 7 | 7 | 22 | 41 | 11 |
| Old Haileyburians | 16 | 3 | 4 | 9 | 29 | 40 | 10 |
| Old Wykehamists | 16 | 3 | 3 | 10 | 30 | 63 | 9 |

| DIVISION 2 | P | W | D | L | F | A | Pts |
|---|---|---|---|---|---|---|---|
| Old Etonians Res. | 14 | 12 | 0 | 2 | 33 | 10 | 24 |
| Old Brentwoods Res. | 14 | 9 | 1 | 4 | 34 | 20 | 19 |
| Old Etonians 3rd. | 14 | 6 | 4 | 4 | 28 | 25 | 16 |
| Old Chigwellians Res. | 14 | 6 | 3 | 5 | 31 | 32 | 15 |
| Old Cholmeleians 3rd. | 14 | 6 | 1 | 7 | 23 | 33 | 13 |
| Old Cholmeleians Res. | 14 | 4 | 3 | 7 | 22 | 23 | 11 |
| Old Foresters Res. | 14 | 4 | 1 | 9 | 29 | 39 | 6* |
| Old Carthusians Res. | 14 | 2 | 1 | 11 | 20 | 38 | 5 |

**DIVISION 3**

| | P | W | D | L | F | A | Pts |
|---|---|---|---|---|---|---|---|
| Old Millhillians | 16 | 12 | 2 | 2 | 46 | 17 | 26 |
| Lancing Old Boys Res. | 16 | 9 | 4 | 3 | 40 | 25 | 21* |
| Old Brentwoods 3rd. | 16 | 7 | 2 | 7 | 37 | 32 | 15* |
| Old Westminsters | 16 | 6 | 3 | 7 | 28 | 40 | 15 |
| Old Harrovians Res. | 16 | 7 | 0 | 9 | 31 | 40 | 14 |
| Old Cholmeleians 4th. | 16 | 5 | 4 | 7 | 22 | 31 | 14 |
| Old Salopians Res. | 16 | 7 | 3 | 6 | 30 | 28 | 13* |
| Old Eastbournians | 16 | 3 | 3 | 10 | 25 | 33 | 9 |
| Old Aldenhamians Res. | 16 | 4 | 3 | 9 | 37 | 50 | 9* |

(*\* Points deducted – breach of Rule*)

**Division 4**–Won By Old Reptonians Res.
**Division 5**–Won By Old Bradfieldians Res.
**Junior League Cup**–Lancing Old Boys Res 3, Old Brentwood Res 2
**Derrik Moore Veterans Cup**–Old Chigwellians 4, Old Cholmeleians 1
**Jim Dixson VI-a-Side**–Won by Old Bradfieldians

### LONDON FINANCIAL F.A.

**DIVISION ONE**

| | P | W | D | L | F | A | Pts |
|---|---|---|---|---|---|---|---|
| Kleinwort Benson | 16 | 11 | 3 | 2 | 38 | 25 | 36 |
| Churchill Insurance | 16 | 11 | 2 | 3 | 34 | 18 | 35 |
| Royal Sun Alliance | 16 | 9 | 1 | 6 | 40 | 30 | 28 |
| Bank America | 16 | 7 | 2 | 7 | 30 | 21 | 23 |
| Coutts & Co. | 16 | 7 | 1 | 8 | 35 | 34 | 22 |
| Morgan Guaranty | 16 | 4 | 6 | 6 | 33 | 39 | 18 |
| Allied Irish Bank | 16 | 5 | 2 | 9 | 18 | 33 | 17 |
| Royal Bank of Scotland | 16 | 4 | 2 | 10 | 42 | 48 | 14 |
| J & H Marsh & McLennan | 16 | 4 | 1 | 11 | 22 | 44 | 12* |

**DIVISION TWO**

| | P | W | D | L | F | A | Pts |
|---|---|---|---|---|---|---|---|
| C.F.I. Vantage | 18 | 15 | 2 | 1 | 64 | 23 | 47 |
| Union Bank of Switzl'd | 18 | 13 | 3 | 2 | 55 | 25 | 42 |
| Granby | 18 | 12 | 2 | 4 | 59 | 34 | 38 |
| Citibank | 18 | 9 | 3 | 6 | 63 | 36 | 30 |
| Chase Manhattan Bank | 18 | 8 | 6 | 4 | 40 | 26 | 30 |
| Eagle Star | 18 | 5 | 4 | 9 | 39 | 38 | 19 |
| Temple Bar | 18 | 6 | 1 | 11 | 52 | 56 | 19 |
| Salomon Brothers | 18 | 5 | 0 | 13 | 25 | 62 | 15 |
| Century Life | 18 | 4 | 2 | 12 | 26 | 51 | 14 |
| R Bank of Scotland Res. | 18 | 1 | 1 | 16 | 27 | 99 | 4 |

**DIVISION THREE**

| | P | W | D | L | F | A | Pts |
|---|---|---|---|---|---|---|---|
| Standard Chartered | 18 | 14 | 2 | 2 | 66 | 20 | 44 |
| J&H Marsh & McLennan Res. | 18 | 13 | 3 | 2 | 63 | 34 | 42 |
| Foreign & Commonwealth | 18 | 11 | 3 | 4 | 72 | 35 | 36 |
| Credit Suisse Finan'l Products | 18 | 9 | 3 | 6 | 48 | 37 | 29* |
| Lincoln | 18 | 8 | 3 | 7 | 41 | 34 | 27 |
| Bank America Res. | 18 | 8 | 2 | 8 | 37 | 41 | 26 |
| ANZ Banking Group | 18 | 5 | 5 | 8 | 35 | 42 | 20 |
| Noble Lowndes | 18 | 6 | 0 | 12 | 27 | 58 | 18 |
| Royal Sun Alliance Res. | 18 | 2 | 2 | 14 | 24 | 56 | 8 |
| Coutts & Co. Res. | 18 | 2 | 1 | 15 | 13 | 69 | 7 |

**DIVISION FOUR**

| | P | W | D | L | F | A | Pts |
|---|---|---|---|---|---|---|---|
| C Hoare & Co. | 20 | 17 | 1 | 2 | 73 | 25 | 52 |
| Abbey National | 20 | 14 | 4 | 2 | 88 | 36 | 46 |
| Royal Sun Alliance 3rd. | 20 | 14 | 2 | 4 | 48 | 27 | 44 |
| Eagle Star Res. | 20 | 12 | 3 | 5 | 60 | 31 | 39 |
| Citibank Res. | 20 | 9 | 3 | 8 | 43 | 40 | 30 |
| British Gas | 20 | 6 | 5 | 9 | 42 | 46 | 23 |
| Churchill Insurance Res. | 20 | 6 | 4 | 10 | 40 | 56 | 22 |
| Granby Res. | 20 | 5 | 3 | 12 | 38 | 56 | 18 |
| Bank of Ireland | 20 | 4 | 3 | 13 | 27 | 76 | 15 |
| Noble Lowndes Res. | 20 | 4 | 1 | 15 | 28 | 72 | 13 |
| Royal Bank of Scotland 3rd. | 20 | 2 | 5 | 13 | 40 | 62 | 11 |

**DIVISION FIVE**

| | P | W | D | L | F | A | Pts |
|---|---|---|---|---|---|---|---|
| J & H Marsh & McLennan 3rd. | 18 | 16 | 1 | 1 | 68 | 20 | 49 |
| Temple Bar Res. | 18 | 10 | 4 | 4 | 63 | 29 | 34 |
| Standard Chartered Res. | 18 | 9 | 1 | 8 | 60 | 54 | 28 |
| Royal Bank of Scotland 4th. | 18 | 7 | 5 | 6 | 28 | 28 | 26 |
| Gaflac | 18 | 8 | 1 | 9 | 45 | 48 | 25 |
| Lensbury 6th. | 18 | 2 | 3 | 13 | 24 | 56 | 9 |
| Eagle Star 3rd. | 18 | 2 | 3 | 13 | 30 | 85 | 9 |

(*\* Points deducted – breach of Rule*)

**Representative Matches**
v Southern Olympian League Drawn 1-1
v Royal Marines Lost 2-6
v Southern Amateur League "B" Lost 0-3
v Old Boys' League Drawn 2-2
v Bristol Insurance Institute Lost 1-6

v Stock Exchange FA Cancelled

### LONDON LEGAL LEAGUE

**DIVISION ONE**

| | P | W | D | L | F | A | Pts |
|---|---|---|---|---|---|---|---|
| Gray's Inn | 18 | 14 | 2 | 2 | 53 | 22 | 30 |
| Slaughter & May | 18 | 13 | 3 | 2 | 57 | 23 | 29 |
| Cameron McKenna | 18 | 8 | 1 | 9 | 46 | 35 | 17 |
| Lovell White Durrant | 18 | 6 | 5 | 7 | 25 | 31 | 17 |
| Pegasus (Inner Temple) | 18 | 8 | 1 | 9 | 39 | 45 | 17 |
| Herbert Smith | 18 | 6 | 4 | 8 | 39 | 49 | 16 |
| Wilde Sapte | 18 | 6 | 3 | 9 | 32 | 49 | 15 |
| Linklaters & Paines | 18 | 4 | 6 | 8 | 24 | 26 | 14 |
| Nabarro Nathanson | 18 | 6 | 2 | 10 | 25 | 38 | 14 |
| Taylor Joynson Garrett | 18 | 3 | 5 | 10 | 26 | 48 | 11 |

**DIVISION TWO**

| | P | W | D | L | F | A | Pts |
|---|---|---|---|---|---|---|---|
| Rosling King | 18 | 15 | 1 | 2 | 53 | 22 | 31 |
| Clifford Chance | 18 | 15 | 0 | 3 | 81 | 26 | 30 |
| Stephenson Harwood | 18 | 10 | 3 | 5 | 39 | 25 | 23 |
| Allen & Overy | 18 | 10 | 1 | 7 | 43 | 32 | 21 |
| Kennedy's | 18 | 7 | 3 | 8 | 40 | 35 | 17 |
| Norton Rose | 18 | 7 | 3 | 8 | 30 | 39 | 17 |
| Freshfields | 18 | 7 | 0 | 11 | 33 | 55 | 14 |
| D.J. Freeman | 18 | 4 | 2 | 12 | 19 | 55 | 10 |
| Macfarlanes | 18 | 4 | 1 | 13 | 22 | 47 | 9 |
| S.J. Berwin | 18 | 3 | 2 | 13 | 29 | 53 | 8 |

**DIVISION THREE**

| | P | W | D | L | F | A | Pts |
|---|---|---|---|---|---|---|---|
| K.P.M.G. | 18 | 14 | 3 | 1 | 61 | 11 | 31 |
| Denton Hall | 18 | 11 | 4 | 3 | 46 | 24 | 26 |
| Simmons & Simmons | 18 | 11 | 3 | 4 | 42 | 31 | 25 |
| Nicholson Graham & Jones | 18 | 9 | 1 | 8 | 31 | 29 | 19 |
| Titmus Sainer Dechert | 18 | 7 | 4 | 7 | 24 | 32 | 18 |
| Barlow Lyde & Gilbert | 18 | 6 | 3 | 9 | 32 | 29 | 15 |
| Watson Farley & Wlliams | 18 | 5 | 3 | 10 | 23 | 43 | 13 |
| Hammond Suddards | 18 | 6 | 1 | 11 | 32 | 58 | 13 |
| Richards Butler | 18 | 5 | 1 | 12 | 39 | 44 | 11 |
| Baker Mackenzie | 18 | 3 | 3 | 12 | 19 | 48 | 9 |

**League Challenge Cup**–Gray's Inn 0*, Lovell White Durrant 1*
**Weavers Arms Cup**–Wilde Sapte 3*, K.P.M.G. 2*
**Invitation Cup**–Rosling King 4, D.J. Freeman 0
(*\*after extra time*)

### LONDON OLD BOYS' CUP

**Senior**
Old Meadonians 4, 2 Enfield Old Grammarians
**Intermediate**
Old Salvatorians Res. 2, 0 Latymer Old Boys Res.
**Junior**
Old Meadonians 3rd.1*, 0 Alpertonians Res.
**Minor**
Old Alpertonians 3rd. 3, 0 City of London 4th.
**Novets**
Old Actonians Ass'n 5th. 3, 1Old Suttonians 5th.
**Drummond**
Albanian 6th. 4, 2 Old Addeyans 6th.
**Nemean**
Old Manorians 7th. 2, 1 Old Parmiterians 10th.
**Veterans**
Old Salvatorians Vets. 3, 2 Old Meadonians Vets.
(*\*after exta time*)

### OLD BOYS' INVITATION CUPS

**Senior**
Old Wilsonians 2, 0 Old Stationers
**Junior**
Old Tenisonians Res. 0, 1 Old Woodhouseians Res.
**Minor**
Old Finchleians 3rd. 2, 1 Old Colfeians 3rd.
**4th XI**
Glyn Old Boys 4th. 3, 4 Old Finchleians 4th.
**5th XI**
Old Stationers 5th. 6, 3 Old Suttonians 5th.
**6th XI**
Glyn Old Boys 6th. 5, 0 Old Stationers 6th.
**7th XI**
Old Stationers 7th. 1, 0 East Barnet Old Grammarians 7th.
**Veterans**
Old Bromleians Vets. 5, 1 Old Stationers Vets.

## OLD BOYS' LEAGUE

| Premier Division | P | W | D | L | F | A | Pts |
|---|---|---|---|---|---|---|---|
| Old Tenisonians | 20 | 13 | 5 | 2 | 48 | 18 | 31 |
| Old Aloysians | 20 | 14 | 2 | 4 | 55 | 24 | 30 |
| Old Hamptonians | 20 | 12 | 2 | 6 | 41 | 25 | 26 |
| Old Ignatians | 20 | 11 | 1 | 8 | 34 | 36 | 23 |
| Old Vaughanians | 20 | 7 | 5 | 8 | 27 | 33 | 19 |
| Old Meadonians | 20 | 7 | 4 | 9 | 29 | 38 | 18 |
| Enfield Old Grammarians | 20 | 7 | 3 | 10 | 26 | 39 | 17 |
| Glyn Old Boys | 20 | 5 | 6 | 9 | 34 | 40 | 16 |
| Cardinal Manning O.B. | 20 | 6 | 3 | 11 | 21 | 31 | 15 |
| Latymer Old Boys | 20 | 4 | 6 | 10 | 19 | 32 | 14 |
| Old Suttonians | 20 | 2 | 7 | 11 | 23 | 41 | 11 |

| Senior Division One | P | W | D | L | F | A | Pts |
|---|---|---|---|---|---|---|---|
| Old Buckwellians | 20 | 13 | 2 | 5 | 66 | 33 | 28 |
| Old Salvatorians | 20 | 11 | 4 | 5 | 37 | 27 | 26 |
| Phoenix Old Boys | 20 | 9 | 6 | 5 | 52 | 29 | 24 |
| Old Wilsonians | 20 | 9 | 4 | 7 | 48 | 37 | 22 |
| Old Kingsburians | 20 | 6 | 8 | 6 | 37 | 40 | 20 |
| Old Tiffinians | 20 | 9 | 3 | 8 | 33 | 33 | 19* |
| Old Reigatians | 20 | 7 | 5 | 8 | 30 | 30 | 19 |
| Old Isleworthians | 20 | 6 | 5 | 9 | 35 | 34 | 17 |
| Old Manorians | 20 | 7 | 3 | 10 | 32 | 45 | 17 |
| Clapham Old Xaverians | 20 | 6 | 2 | 12 | 29 | 56 | 14 |
| Chertsey Old Salesians | 20 | 5 | 2 | 13 | 23 | 58 | 12 |

| Senior Division Two | P | W | D | L | F | A | Pts |
|---|---|---|---|---|---|---|---|
| Old Dorkinians | 20 | 14 | 1 | 5 | 38 | 20 | 29 |
| Shene Old Grammarians | 20 | 11 | 5 | 4 | 55 | 32 | 27 |
| Old Tollingtonians | 20 | 9 | 6 | 5 | 48 | 33 | 24 |
| Old Camdenians | 20 | 9 | 3 | 8 | 46 | 46 | 21 |
| Old Tenisonians Res. | 20 | 9 | 3 | 8 | 40 | 44 | 21 |
| Old Danes | 20 | 7 | 6 | 7 | 41 | 36 | 20 |
| Old Sinjuns | 20 | 7 | 6 | 7 | 59 | 44 | 18* |
| Old Meadonians Res. | 20 | 7 | 2 | 11 | 44 | 47 | 16 |
| Old Minchendenians | 20 | 6 | 4 | 10 | 33 | 49 | 16 |
| Latymer Old Boys Res. | 20 | 5 | 3 | 12 | 31 | 53 | 13 |
| Mill Hill County O.B | 20 | 5 | 3 | 12 | 25 | 56 | 13 |

| Senior Division Three | P | W | D | L | F | A | Pts |
|---|---|---|---|---|---|---|---|
| John Fisher Old Boys | 20 | 14 | 1 | 5 | 50 | 26 | 29 |
| Old Vaughanians Res. | 20 | 12 | 4 | 4 | 37 | 24 | 28 |
| Old Wokingians | 20 | 10 | 4 | 6 | 46 | 26 | 24 |
| Old Uffingtonians | 20 | 11 | 2 | 7 | 45 | 33 | 24 |
| Old Addeyans | 20 | 9 | 3 | 8 | 39 | 31 | 21 |
| Old Aloysians Res. | 20 | 7 | 7 | 6 | 36 | 35 | 21 |
| Phoenix Old Boys Res. | 20 | 8 | 4 | 8 | 40 | 34 | 20 |
| Old Hamptonians Res. | 20 | 7 | 2 | 11 | 41 | 59 | 16 |
| Old St. Marys | 20 | 7 | 1 | 12 | 36 | 55 | 15 |
| Old Southallians | 20 | 5 | 1 | 14 | 35 | 51 | 11 |
| Enfield O. Grammarians Res. | 20 | 4 | 3 | 13 | 26 | 57 | 11 |

*(\* points deducted for breach of rule)*

**Intermediate Division North**–12 Teams–Won by Queen Mary College Old Boys
**Intermediate Division South**–12 Teams–Won by Old Dorkinians Res.
**Division One North**–9 Teams–Won by Old Edmontonians
**Division One South**–11 Teams–Won by Old Wilsonians Res.
**Division One West**–9 Teams–Won by Old Isleworthians Res.
**Division Two North**–10 Teams–Won by Wood Green Old Boys Res.
**Division Two South**–11 Teams–Won by Old Paulines
**Division Two West**–9 Teams–Won by Old Salvatorians 4th.
**Division Three North**–10 Teams–Won by Wood Green Old Boys 3rd.
**Division Three South**–12 Teams–Won by Fitzwilliam Old Boys
**Division Three West**–10 Teams–Won by Old Danes 3rd.
**Division Four North**–9 Teams–Won by Old Salvatorians 5th.
**Division Four South**–12 Teams–Won by John Fisher Old Boys 3rd.
**Division Four West**–10 Teams–Won by Old Salvatorians 6th.
**Division Five North**–10 Teams–Won by Enfield O.Grammarians 6th.
**Division Five South**–11 Teams–Won by Old Meadonians 7th.

**Division Five West**–9 Teams–Won by Old Challoners 3rd.
**Division Six North**–8 Teams–Won by Leyton County Old BOys 5th.
**Division Six South**–12 Teams–Won by Fitzwilliam Old Boys Res.
**Division Six West**–8 Teams–Won by Old Manorians 6th.
**Division Seven North**–8 Teams–Won by Davenant Wanderers 3rd.
**Division Seven South**–10 Teams–Won by Old Sinjuns 4th.
**Division Seven West**–7 Teams–Won by Holland Park Old Boys 5th.
**Division Eight South**–9 Teams–Won by Old Paulines Res.
**Division Eight West**–8 Teams–Won by Old Manorians 7th.
**Division Nine South**–10 Teams–Won by Old Thorntonians 5th.

## MIDLAND AMATEUR ALLIANCE

| PREMIER DIVISION | P | W | D | L | F | A | Pts |
|---|---|---|---|---|---|---|---|
| Beeston Old Boys Assn. | 22 | 19 | 0 | 3 | 75 | 31 | 57 |
| Old Elizabethans | 22 | 16 | 1 | 5 | 71 | 23 | 49 |
| Kirton B.W. | 22 | 15 | 2 | 5 | 71 | 31 | 47 |
| Derbyshire Amateurs | 22 | 15 | 1 | 6 | 70 | 31 | 46 |
| Beeston Town "A" | 22 | 12 | 6 | 4 | 75 | 46 | 42 |
| Lady Bay | 22 | 11 | 1 | 10 | 73 | 61 | 34 |
| P K F Steelers | 22 | 9 | 2 | 11 | 62 | 52 | 29 |
| Bassingfield | 22 | 9 | 2 | 11 | 53 | 54 | 29 |
| Caribbean Cavaliers | 22 | 7 | 3 | 12 | 50 | 66 | 24 |
| Racing Toton | 22 | 4 | 2 | 16 | 34 | 77 | 14 |
| Magdala Amateurs "A" | 22 | 3 | 4 | 15 | 34 | 72 | 13 |
| County Nalgo | 22 | 0 | 0 | 22 | 16 | 140 | 0 |

| DIVISION ONE | P | W | D | L | F | A | Pts |
|---|---|---|---|---|---|---|---|
| Tibshelf Old Boys | 22 | 18 | 0 | 4 | 73 | 32 | 54 |
| Parkhead Academicals | 22 | 16 | 4 | 2 | 58 | 22 | 52 |
| Dynamo Baptist | 22 | 12 | 4 | 6 | 59 | 35 | 40 |
| Nottinghamshire | 22 | 10 | 4 | 8 | 57 | 38 | 34 |
| Woodborough United | 22 | 9 | 6 | 7 | 50 | 53 | 33 |
| Edwinstowe J G | 22 | 9 | 4 | 9 | 51 | 50 | 31 |
| Bassingfield Res. | 22 | 8 | 5 | 9 | 39 | 52 | 29 |
| Old Elizabethans Res. | 22 | 8 | 4 | 10 | 45 | 53 | 28 |
| Radcliffe Olympic Res. | 22 | 7 | 4 | 11 | 43 | 54 | 25 |
| Ilkeston Rangers | 22 | 6 | 3 | 13 | 49 | 62 | 21 |
| Cadland Chilwell | 22 | 3 | 5 | 14 | 24 | 54 | 14 |
| Lady Bay Res. | 22 | 3 | 3 | 16 | 21 | 64 | 12 |

| DIVISION TWO | P | W | D | L | F | A | Pts |
|---|---|---|---|---|---|---|---|
| A S C Dayncourt | 24 | 24 | 0 | 0 | 136 | 15 | 72 |
| Hucknall Sports Y C | 24 | 18 | 1 | 5 | 93 | 61 | 55 |
| Derbyshire Amateurs Res. | 24 | 14 | 3 | 7 | 54 | 41 | 45 |
| Arnold & Carlton College | 24 | 11 | 6 | 7 | 70 | 55 | 39 |
| Old Elizabethans 3rd. | 24 | 10 | 4 | 10 | 53 | 57 | 34 |
| Southwell Amateurs | 24 | 10 | 3 | 11 | 52 | 52 | 33 |
| Gresham United | 24 | 10 | 2 | 12 | 59 | 70 | 32 |
| Magdala Amateurs Res. | 24 | 9 | 4 | 11 | 58 | 85 | 31 |
| Beeston Old Boys Res. | 24 | 7 | 3 | 14 | 48 | 70 | 24 |
| Brunts Old Boys | 24 | 7 | 2 | 15 | 45 | 65 | 23 |
| Nottinghamshire Res. | 24 | 5 | 8 | 11 | 52 | 74 | 23 |
| Ilkeston Rangers Res. | 24 | 4 | 5 | 15 | 42 | 85 | 17 |
| Racing Toton Res. | 24 | 4 | 4 | 16 | 38 | 70 | 16 |

| DIVISION THREE | P | W | D | L | F | A | Pts |
|---|---|---|---|---|---|---|---|
| Nottingham I.C. | 22 | 20 | 1 | 1 | 132 | 11 | 61 |
| A S C Dayncourt Res | 22 | 17 | 1 | 4 | 82 | 34 | 52 |
| Hucknall Sports Y C Res | 22 | 14 | 2 | 6 | 69 | 46 | 44 |
| Derbyshire Amateurs 3rd | 22 | 13 | 3 | 6 | 86 | 56 | 42 |
| Sherwood | 22 | 13 | 1 | 8 | 81 | 68 | 40 |
| E M T E C | 22 | 7 | 6 | 9 | 57 | 70 | 27 |
| Old Elizabethans 4th. | 22 | 8 | 3 | 11 | 49 | 80 | 27 |
| Dynamo Baptist Res. | 22 | 8 | 2 | 12 | 58 | 63 | 26 |
| Nottinghamshire 3rd. | 22 | 7 | 3 | 12 | 45 | 61 | 24 |
| Old Bemrosians | 22 | 5 | 3 | 14 | 39 | 61 | 18 |
| Tibshelf Old Boys Res. | 22 | 2 | 4 | 16 | 33 | 96 | 10 |
| West-Clif | 22 | 2 | 3 | 17 | 32 | 117 | 9 |

**League Cup Winners:**
**Senior:** Derbyshire Amateurs
**Intermediate:** Old Elizabethans Res.
**Minor:** A S C Dayncourt
**H.B. Poole Trophy:** Lady Bay

# SOUTHERN AMATEUR LEAGUE

**SENIOR SECTION:**

| FIRST DIVISION | P | W | D | L | F | A | Pts |
|---|---|---|---|---|---|---|---|
| Norsemen | 22 | 12 | 6 | 4 | 55 | 39 | 30 |
| Lensbury | 22 | 11 | 6 | 5 | 52 | 39 | 28 |
| E.Barnet O. Grammarians | 22 | 10 | 7 | 5 | 44 | 30 | 27 |
| Crouch End Vampires | 22 | 10 | 5 | 7 | 56 | 33 | 25 |
| O.Actonians Association | 22 | 10 | 3 | 9 | 35 | 34 | 23 |
| Lloyds Bank | 22 | 9 | 4 | 9 | 37 | 36 | 22 |
| Old Parmiterians | 22 | 9 | 4 | 9 | 42 | 43 | 22 |
| Polytechnic | 22 | 6 | 9 | 7 | 31 | 33 | 21 |
| Carshalton | 22 | 7 | 7 | 8 | 37 | 46 | 21 |
| West Wickham | 22 | 9 | 2 | 11 | 32 | 38 | 20 |
| Civil Service | 22 | 7 | 5 | 10 | 39 | 42 | 19 |
| South Bank Polytechnic | 22 | 3 | 0 | 19 | 26 | 79 | 6 |

| SECOND DIVISION | P | W | D | L | F | A | Pts |
|---|---|---|---|---|---|---|---|
| National Westmin'r Bank | 22 | 11 | 8 | 3 | 60 | 34 | 30 |
| Barclays Bank | 22 | 13 | 4 | 5 | 52 | 32 | 30 |
| Midland Bank | 22 | 11 | 7 | 4 | 49 | 21 | 29 |
| Old Esthameians | 22 | 9 | 7 | 6 | 43 | 26 | 25 |
| Old Owens | 22 | 11 | 3 | 8 | 45 | 41 | 25 |
| Old Parkonians | 22 | 8 | 8 | 6 | 33 | 28 | 24 |
| Old Salesians | 22 | 9 | 4 | 9 | 41 | 39 | 22 |
| Winchmore Hill | 22 | 8 | 6 | 8 | 28 | 41 | 22 |
| Alexandra Park | 22 | 6 | 9 | 7 | 31 | 38 | 21 |
| Old Lyonians | 22 | 3 | 10 | 9 | 17 | 40 | 16 |
| Cuaco | 22 | 1 | 9 | 12 | 20 | 48 | 11 |
| Old Latymerians | 22 | 2 | 5 | 15 | 25 | 56 | 9 |

| THIRD DIVISION | P | W | D | L | F | A | Pts |
|---|---|---|---|---|---|---|---|
| Old Stationers | 20 | 13 | 3 | 4 | 65 | 38 | 29 |
| Old Bromleians | 20 | 13 | 2 | 5 | 66 | 39 | 28 |
| Brentham | 20 | 11 | 6 | 3 | 38 | 21 | 28 |
| Bank of England | 20 | 11 | 4 | 5 | 43 | 22 | 26 |
| Broomfield | 20 | 11 | 4 | 5 | 47 | 33 | 26 |
| Kew Association | 20 | 11 | 2 | 7 | 42 | 30 | 24 |
| Alleyn Old Boys | 20 | 8 | 3 | 9 | 48 | 48 | 19 |
| Ibis | 20 | 6 | 4 | 10 | 34 | 45 | 16 |
| Southgate Olympic | 20 | 3 | 3 | 14 | 25 | 54 | 9 |
| Merton | 20 | 2 | 4 | 14 | 27 | 60 | 8 |
| O. Westminster Citizens | 20 | 1 | 5 | 14 | 23 | 69 | 7 |

**RESERVE TEAMS SECTION:**
**First Division**–12 Teams–Won by Old Actonians Association Res.
**Second Division**–12 Teams–Won by Carshalton Res.
**Third Division**–11 Teams–Won by Midland Bank Res.

**3rd. Teams Section:**
**First Division**–12 Teams–Won by Barclays Bank 3rd.
**Second Division**–12 Teams–Won by Southgate Olympic 3rd.
**Third Division**–11 Teams–Won by Old Owens 3rd.

**4th. Teams Section:**
**First Division**–12 Teams–Won by Old Actonians Association 4th.
**Second Division**–12 Teams–Won by Southgate Olympic 4th.
**Third Division**–11 Teams–Won by Broomfield 4th.

**5th. Teams Section:**
**First Division**–10 Teams–Won by Midland Bank 5th.
**Second Division**–11 Teams–Won by Old Esthameians 5th.
**Third Division**–11 Teams–Won by West Wickham 5th.

**6th. Teams Section:**
**First Division**–10 Teams–Won by Old Actonians Association 6th.
**Second Division**–9 Teams–Won by Midland Bank 6th.
**Third Division**–5 Teams–Won by Lloyds Bank 6th.

**Minor Section**
**First Division**–10 Teams–Won by Polytechnic 7th.
**Second Division**–10 Teams–Won by Old Actonians Association 9th.
**Third Division**–10 Teams–Won by Norsemen 8th.
**Fourth Division**–10 Teams–Won by National Westminster Bank 10th.

# SOUTHERN OLYMPIAN LEAGUE

**SENIOR SECTION:**

| Division One | P | W | D | L | F | A | Pts |
|---|---|---|---|---|---|---|---|
| Old Finchleians | 18 | 11 | 4 | 3 | 54 | 31 | 26 |
| Hon. Artillery Company | 18 | 9 | 4 | 5 | 35 | 20 | 22 |
| Nottsborough | 18 | 8 | 4 | 6 | 38 | 36 | 20 |
| Witan | 18 | 7 | 5 | 6 | 34 | 34 | 19 |
| Hale End Athletic | 18 | 7 | 5 | 6 | 28 | 32 | 19 |
| Parkfield | 18 | 6 | 6 | 6 | 32 | 33 | 18 |
| City of London | 18 | 6 | 4 | 8 | 36 | 37 | 16 |
| Southgate County | 18 | 6 | 4 | 8 | 34 | 39 | 16 |
| Ulysses | 18 | 6 | 3 | 9 | 25 | 38 | 15 |
| St Mary's College | 18 | 4 | 1 | 13 | 22 | 38 | 9 |

| Division Two | P | W | D | L | F | A | Pts |
|---|---|---|---|---|---|---|---|
| Old Grammarians | 18 | 10 | 7 | 1 | 38 | 16 | 27 |
| Old Woodhouseians | 18 | 11 | 3 | 4 | 39 | 28 | 25 |
| Albanian | 18 | 10 | 3 | 5 | 41 | 31 | 23 |
| Fulham Compton Old Boys | 18 | 9 | 1 | 8 | 53 | 44 | 19 |
| Hampstead Heathens | 18 | 6 | 6 | 6 | 38 | 35 | 18 |
| UCL Academicals | 18 | 8 | 2 | 8 | 30 | 33 | 18 |
| Mill Hill Village | 18 | 7 | 1 | 10 | 44 | 49 | 15 |
| Wandsworth Borough | 18 | 5 | 3 | 10 | 42 | 47 | 13 |
| Ealing Association | 18 | 5 | 2 | 11 | 39 | 53 | 12 |
| Westerns | 18 | 5 | 0 | 13 | 36 | 64 | 10 |

| Division Three | P | W | D | L | F | A | Pts |
|---|---|---|---|---|---|---|---|
| Old Bealonians | 18 | 15 | 2 | 1 | 80 | 27 | 32 |
| Pegasus (Inner Temple) | 18 | 11 | 4 | 3 | 50 | 30 | 26 |
| BBC | 18 | 6 | 8 | 4 | 46 | 38 | 20 |
| Hadley | 18 | 8 | 4 | 6 | 38 | 32 | 20 |
| Duncombe Sports | 18 | 9 | 2 | 7 | 51 | 46 | 20 |
| Inland Revenue | 18 | 8 | 1 | 9 | 36 | 47 | 17 |
| New Scotland Yard Comets | 18 | 6 | 3 | 9 | 26 | 45 | 15 |
| Old Colfeians | 18 | 5 | 4 | 9 | 32 | 38 | 14 |
| London Welsh | 18 | 4 | 1 | 13 | 32 | 63 | 9 |
| Mayfield Athletic | 18 | 2 | 3 | 13 | 28 | 53 | 7 |

| Division Four | P | W | D | L | F | A | Pts |
|---|---|---|---|---|---|---|---|
| Brent | 16 | 11 | 5 | 0 | 38 | 6 | 27 |
| Cardinal Pole Old Boys | 16 | 13 | 0 | 3 | 47 | 19 | 26 |
| Tesco Country Club | 16 | 8 | 2 | 6 | 32 | 26 | 18 |
| London Airways | 16 | 8 | 2 | 6 | 36 | 33 | 18 |
| Centymca | 16 | 6 | 3 | 7 | 30 | 29 | 15 |
| Birkbeck College | 16 | 5 | 2 | 9 | 23 | 32 | 12 |
| Old Fairlopians | 16 | 5 | 2 | 9 | 23 | 32 | 12 |
| Economicals | 16 | 5 | 1 | 10 | 32 | 45 | 11 |
| Tansley | 16 | 2 | 1 | 13 | 24 | 63 | 5 |

**Intermediate Section:**
**Division One**–10 Teams–Won by Old Finchleians Res.
**Division Two**–10 Teams–Won by Old Bealonians Res.
**Division Three**–10 Teams–Won by Old Finchleians 3rd.

**Junior Section:**
**Division One**–11 Teams–Won by The Cheshunt Club
**Division Two N**–10 Teams–Won by Parkfield 4th.
**Division Two S&W**–11 Teams–Won by BBC 3rd
**Division Three N**–10 Teams–Won by Hampstead Heathens 4th.
**Division Three S&W**–12 Teams–Won by Fulham Compton O.B. 4th.
**Division Four N**–10 Teams–Won by Parkfield 6th.
**Division Four S&W**–11 Teams–Won by City of London 6th.
**Division Five N**–9 Teams–Won by Parkfield 7th.

**Senior Challenge Bowl**–Won by City of London
**Senior Challenge Shield**–Won by Old Finchleians
**Intermediate Challenge Cup**–Won by Hale End Athletic Reserves
**Intermediate Challenge Shield**–Won by Parkfield Reserves
**Junior Challenge Cup**–Won by Old Finchleians 3rd
**Junior Challenge Shield**–Won by Old Bealonians 3rd
**Mander Cup**–Won by Albanian 4th
**Mander Shield**–Won by UCL Academicals 4th
**Burntwood Trophy**–Won by Southgate County 5th
**Burntwood Shield**–Won by BBC 5th
**Thomas Parmiter Cup**–Won by City of London 6th
**Thomas Parmiter Shield**–Won by Parkfield 6th
**Veterans' Challenge Cup**–Won by Old Fairlopians Vets
**Veterans' Challenge Shield**–Won by Old Finchleians Vets

# RECORDS

## Major British Records

### HIGHEST WINS

| | | | | | |
|---|---|---|---|---|---|
| **First-Class Match** | Arbroath | 36 | Bon Accord | 0 | 12 Sept 1885 |
| | *(Scottish Cup 1st Round)* | | | | |
| **International Match** | England | 13 | Ireland | 0 | 18 Feb 1882 |
| **FA Cup** | Preston NE | 26 | Hyde U | 0 | 15 Oct 1887 |
| | *(1st Round)* | | | | |
| **League Cup** | West Ham U | 10 | Bury | 0 | 25 Oct 1983 |
| | *(2nd Round, 2nd Leg)* | | | | |
| | Liverpool | 10 | Fulham | 0 | 23 Sept 1986 |
| | *(2nd Round, 1st Leg)* | | | | |

| | | | | | |
|---|---|---|---|---|---|
| **FA PREMIER LEAGUE** | | | | | |
| | *(Home)* | Manchester U | 9 | Ipswich T | 0 | 4 March 1995 |
| | *(Away)* | Sheffield W | 1 | Nottingham F | 7 | 1 April 1995 |

| | | | | | | |
|---|---|---|---|---|---|---|
| **FOOTBALL LEAGUE** | | | | | | |
| **Division 1** | *(Home)* | WBA | 12 | Darwen | 0 | 4 April 1892 |
| | | Nottingham F | 12 | Leicester Fosse | 0 | 21 April 1909 |
| | *(Away)* | Newcastle U | 1 | Sunderland | 9 | 5 Dec 1908 |
| | | Cardiff C | 1 | Wolverhampton W | 9 | 3 Sept 1955 |
| **Division 2** | *(Home)* | Newcastle U | 13 | Newport Co | 0 | 5 Oct 1946 |
| | *(Away)* | Burslem PV | 0 | Sheffield U | 10 | 10 Dec 1892 |
| **Division 3** | *(Home)* | Gillingham | 10 | Chesterfield | 0 | 5 Sept 1987 |
| | *(Away)* | Halifax T | 0 | Fulham | 8 | 16 Sept 1969 |
| **Division 3(S)** | *(Home)* | Luton T | 12 | Bristol R | 0 | 13 April 1936 |
| | *(Away)* | Northampton T | 0 | Walsall | 8 | 2 Feb 1947 |
| **Division 3(N)** | *(Home)* | Stockport Co | 13 | Halifax T | 0 | 6 Jan 1934 |
| | *(Away)* | Accrington S | 0 | Barnsley | 9 | 3 Feb 1934 |
| **Division 4** | *(Home)* | Oldham Ath | 11 | Southport | 0 | 26 Dec 1962 |
| | *(Away)* | Crewe Alex | 1 | Rotherham U | 8 | 8 Sept 1973 |
| **Aggregate Division 3(N)** | | Tranmere R | 13 | Oldham Ath | 4 | 26 Dec 1935 |

| | | | | | | |
|---|---|---|---|---|---|---|
| **SCOTTISH LEAGUE** | | | | | | |
| **Premier** | *(Home)* | Aberdeen | 8 | Motherwell | 0 | 26 March 1979 |
| **Division** | *(Away)* | Hamilton A | 0 | Celtic | 8 | 5 Nov 1988 |
| **Division 1** | *(Home)* | Celtic | 11 | Dundee | 0 | 26 Oct 1895 |
| | *(Away)* | Airdrieonians | 1 | Hibernian | 11 | 24 Oct 1950 |
| **Division 2** | *(Home)* | Airdrieonians | 15 | Dundee Wanderers | 1 | 1 Dec 1894 |
| | *(Away)* | Alloa Ath | 0 | Dundee | 10 | 8 March 1947 |

### LEAGUE CHAMPIONSHIP HAT-TRICKS

| | |
|---|---|
| **Huddersfield T** | 1923–24 to 1925–26 |
| **Arsenal** | 1932–33 to 1934–35 |
| **Liverpool** | 1981–82 to 1983–84 |

### MOST GOALS FOR IN A SEASON

| | | *Goals* | *Games* | *Season* |
|---|---|---|---|---|
| **FA PREMIER LEAGUE** | | | | |
| | Newcastle U | 82 | 42 | 1993–94 |
| **FOOTBALL LEAGUE** | | | | |
| **Division 1** | Aston V | 128 | 42 | 1930–31 |
| **Division 2** | Middlesbrough | 122 | 42 | 1926–27 |
| **Division 3(S)** | Millwall | 127 | 42 | 1927–28 |
| **Division 3(N)** | Bradford C | 128 | 42 | 1928–29 |
| **Division 3** | QPR | 111 | 46 | 1961–62 |
| **Division 4** | Peterborough U | 134 | 46 | 1960–61 |
| **SCOTTISH LEAGUE** | | | | |
| **Premier Division** | Rangers | 101 | 44 | 1991–92 |
| | Dundee U | 90 | 36 | 1982–83 |
| | Celtic | 90 | 36 | 1982–83 |
| | Celtic | 90 | 44 | 1986–87 |
| **Division 1** | Hearts | 132 | 34 | 1957–58 |
| **Division 2** | Raith R | 142 | 34 | 1937–38 |
| **New Division 1** | Dunfermline Ath | 93 | 44 | 1993–94 |
| | Motherwell | 92 | 39 | 1981–82 |
| **New Division 2** | Ayr U | 95 | 39 | 1987–88 |
| **New Division 3** | Alloa | 78 | 36 | 1997–98 |

## FEWEST GOALS FOR IN A SEASON

| FA PREMIER LEAGUE | | Goals | Games | Season |
|---|---|---|---|---|
| | Leeds U | 28 | 38 | 1996–97 |
| **FOOTBALL LEAGUE** | (minimum 42 games) | | | |
| **Division 1** | Stoke C | 24 | 42 | 1984–85 |
| **Division 2** | Watford | 24 | 42 | 1971–72 |
| | Leyton Orient | 30 | 46 | 1994–95 |
| **Division 3(S)** | Crystal Palace | 33 | 42 | 1950–51 |
| **Division 3(N)** | Crewe Alex | 32 | 42 | 1923–24 |
| **Division 3** | Stockport Co | 27 | 46 | 1969–70 |
| **Division 4** | Crewe Alex | 29 | 46 | 1981–82 |
| **SCOTTISH LEAGUE** | (minimum 30 games) | | | |
| **Premier Division** | Hamilton A | 19 | 36 | 1988–89 |
| | Dunfermline Ath | 22 | 44 | 1991–92 |
| **Division 1** | Brechin C | 30 | 44 | 1993–94 |
| | Ayr U | 20 | 34 | 1966–67 |
| **Division 2** | Lochgelly U | 20 | 38 | 1923–24 |
| **New Division 1** | Stirling Alb | 18 | 39 | 1980–81 |
| | Dumbarton | 23 | 36 | 1995–96 |
| **New Division 2** | Brechin C | 22 | 36 | 1994–95 |
| **New Division 3** | Alloa | 26 | 36 | 1995–96 |

## MOST GOALS AGAINST IN A SEASON

| FA PREMIER LEAGUE | | Goals | Games | Season |
|---|---|---|---|---|
| | Swindon T | 100 | 42 | 1993–94 |
| **FOOTBALL LEAGUE** | | | | |
| **Division 1** | Blackpool | 125 | 42 | 1930–31 |
| **Division 2** | Darwen | 141 | 34 | 1898–99 |
| **Division 3(S)** | Merthyr T | 135 | 42 | 1929–30 |
| **Division 3(N)** | Nelson | 136 | 42 | 1927–28 |
| **Division 3** | Accrington S | 123 | 46 | 1959–60 |
| **Division 4** | Hartlepools U | 109 | 46 | 1959–60 |
| **SCOTTISH LEAGUE** | | | | |
| **Premier Division** | Morton | 100 | 36 | 1984–85 |
| | Morton | 100 | 44 | 1987–88 |
| **Division 1** | Leith Ath | 137 | 38 | 1931–32 |
| **Division 2** | Edinburgh C | 146 | 38 | 1931–32 |
| **New Division 1** | Queen of the S | 99 | 39 | 1988–89 |
| | Cowdenbeath | 109 | 44 | 1992–93 |
| **New Division 2** | Meadowbank T | 89 | 39 | 1977–78 |
| **New Division 3** | Albion R | 82 | 36 | 1994–95 |

## FEWEST GOALS AGAINST IN A SEASON

| FA PREMIER LEAGUE | | Goals | Games | Season |
|---|---|---|---|---|
| | Manchester U | 26 | 38 | 1997–98 |
| **FOOTBALL LEAGUE** | (minimum 42 games) | | | |
| **Division 1** | Liverpool | 16 | 42 | 1978–79 |
| **Division 2** | Manchester U | 23 | 42 | 1924–25 |
| | West Ham U | 34 | 46 | 1990–91 |
| **Division 3(S)** | Southampton | 21 | 42 | 1921–22 |
| **Division 3(N)** | Port Vale | 21 | 46 | 1953–54 |
| **Division 3** | Gillingham | 20 | 46 | 1995–96 |
| **Division 4** | Lincoln C | 25 | 46 | 1980–81 |
| **SCOTTISH LEAGUE** | (minimum 30 games) | | | |
| **Premier Division** | Rangers | 19 | 36 | 1989–90 |
| | Rangers | 23 | 44 | 1986–87 |
| | Celtic | 23 | 44 | 1987–88 |
| **Division 1** | Celtic | 14 | 38 | 1913–14 |
| **Division 2** | Morton | 20 | 38 | 1966–67 |
| **New Division 1** | St Johnstone | 23 | 36 | 1996–97 |
| | Hibernian | 24 | 39 | 1980–81 |
| | Falkirk | 32 | 44 | 1993–94 |
| **New Division 2** | St Johnstone | 24 | 39 | 1987–88 |
| | Stirling Alb | 24 | 39 | 1990–91 |
| **New Division 3** | Brechin C | 21 | 36 | 1995–96 |

## MOST POINTS IN A SEASON

| FOOTBALL LEAGUE | (under old system of two points for a win) | *Points* | *Games* | *Season* |
|---|---|---|---|---|
| Division 1 | Liverpool | 68 | 42 | 1978–79 |
| Division 2 | Tottenham H | 70 | 42 | 1919–20 |
| Division 3 | Aston V | 70 | 46 | 1971–72 |
| Division 3(S) | Nottingham F | 70 | 46 | 1950–51 |
| | Bristol C | 70 | 46 | 1954–55 |
| Division 3(N) | Doncaster R | 72 | 42 | 1946–47 |
| Division 4 | Lincoln C | 74 | 46 | 1975–76 |
| **SCOTTISH LEAGUE** | | | | |
| Premier Division | Aberdeen | 59 | 36 | 1984–85 |
| | Rangers | 73 | 44 | 1992–93 |
| Division 1 | Rangers | 76 | 42 | 1920–21 |
| Division 2 | Morton | 69 | 38 | 1966–67 |
| New Division 1 | St Mirren | 62 | 39 | 1976–77 |
| | Falkirk | 66 | 44 | 1993–94 |
| New Division 2 | Forfar Ath | 63 | 39 | 1983–84 |
| **FA PREMIER LEAGUE** | (three points for a win) | | | |
| | Manchester U | 92 | 42 | 1993–94 |
| **FOOTBALL LEAGUE** | | | | |
| Division 1 | Bolton W | 98 | 46 | 1996–97 |
| | Everton | 90 | 42 | 1984–85 |
| | Liverpool | 90 | 40 | 1987–88 |
| Division 2 | Chelsea | 99 | 46 | 1988–89 |
| Division 3 | Notts Co | 99 | 46 | 1997–98 |
| Division 4 | Swindon T | 102 | 46 | 1985–86 |
| **SCOTTISH LEAGUE** | | | | |
| Premier Division | Rangers | 87 | 36 | 1995–96 |
| New Division 1 | St Johnstone | 80 | 36 | 1996–97 |
| New Division 2 | Stirling Alb | 81 | 36 | 1995–96 |
| New Division 3 | Forfar Ath | 80 | 36 | 1994–95 |

## FEWEST POINTS IN A SEASON

| FA PREMIER LEAGUE | | *Points* | *Games* | *Season* |
|---|---|---|---|---|
| | Ipswich T | 27 | 42 | 1994–95 |
| **FOOTBALL LEAGUE** | (minimum 34 games) | | | |
| Division 1 | Stoke C | 17 | 42 | 1984–85 |
| Division 2 | Doncaster R | 8 | 34 | 1904–05 |
| | Loughborough T | 8 | 34 | 1899–1900 |
| | Walsall | 31 | 46 | 1988–89 |
| Division 3 | Doncaster R | 20 | 46 | 1997–98 |
| Division 3(S) | Merthyr T | 21 | 42 | 1924–25 & 1929–30 |
| | QPR | 21 | 42 | 1925–26 |
| Division 3(N) | Rochdale | 11 | 40 | 1931–32 |
| Division 4 | Workington | 19 | 46 | 1976–77 |
| **SCOTTISH LEAGUE** | (minimum 30 games) | | | |
| Premier Division | St Johnstone | 11 | 36 | 1975–76 |
| | Morton | 16 | 44 | 1987–88 |
| Division 1 | Stirling Alb | 6 | 30 | 1954–55 |
| Division 2 | Edinburgh C | 7 | 34 | 1936–37 |
| New Division 1 | Queen of the S | 10 | 39 | 1988–89 |
| | Cowdenbeath | 13 | 44 | 1992–93 |
| New Division 2 | Berwick R | 16 | 39 | 1987–88 |
| | Stranraer | 16 | 39 | 1987–88 |
| New Division 3 | Albion R | 18 | 36 | 1994–95 |

## MOST WINS IN A SEASON

| FA PREMIER LEAGUE | | *Wins* | *Games* | *Season* |
|---|---|---|---|---|
| | Manchester U | 27 | 42 | 1993–94 |
| | Blackburn R | 27 | 42 | 1994–95 |
| **FOOTBALL LEAGUE** | | | | |
| Division 1 | Tottenham H | 31 | 42 | 1960–61 |
| Division 2 | Tottenham H | 32 | 42 | 1919–20 |
| Division 3(S) | Millwall | 30 | 42 | 1927–28 |
| | Plymouth Arg | 30 | 42 | 1929–30 |
| | Cardiff C | 30 | 42 | 1946–47 |
| | Nottingham F | 30 | 46 | 1950–51 |
| | Bristol C | 30 | 46 | 1954–55 |

| Division 3(N) | Doncaster R | 33 | 42 | 1946–47 |
|---|---|---|---|---|
| Division 3 | Aston V | 32 | 46 | 1971–72 |
| Division 4 | Lincoln C | 32 | 46 | 1975–76 |
| | Swindon T | 32 | 46 | 1985–86 |

**SCOTTISH LEAGUE**

| Premier Division | Rangers | 27 | 36 | 1995–96 |
|---|---|---|---|---|
| | Aberdeen | 27 | 36 | 1984–85 |
| | Rangers | 33 | 44 | 1991–92 |
| | Rangers | 33 | 44 | 1992–93 |
| Division 1 | Rangers | 35 | 42 | 1920–21 |
| Division 2 | Morton | 33 | 38 | 1966–67 |
| New Division 1 | Motherwell | 26 | 39 | 1981–82 |
| New Division 2 | Forfar Ath | 27 | 39 | 1983–84 |
| | Ayr U | 27 | 39 | 1987–88 |
| New Division 3 | Forfar Ath | 25 | 36 | 1994–95 |

## RECORD HOME WINS IN A SEASON

Brentford won all 21 games in Division 3(S), 1929–30

## UNDEFEATED AT HOME

Liverpool 85 games (63 League, 9 League Cup, 7 European, 6 FA Cup), Jan 1978–Jan 1981

## RECORD AWAY WINS IN A SEASON

Doncaster R won 18 of 21 games in Division 3(N), 1946–47

## FEWEST WINS IN A SEASON

| **FA PREMIER LEAGUE** | | *Wins* | *Games* | *Season* |
|---|---|---|---|---|
| | Swindon T | 5 | 42 | 1993–94 |
| **FOOTBALL LEAGUE** | | | | |
| Division 1 | Stoke C | 3 | 22 | 1889–90 |
| | Woolwich Arsenal | 3 | 38 | 1912–13 |
| | Stoke C | 3 | 42 | 1984–85 |
| Division 2 | Loughborough T | 1 | 34 | 1899–1900 |
| | Walsall | 5 | 46 | 1988–89 |
| Division 3(S) | Merthyr T | 6 | 42 | 1929–30 |
| | QPR | 6 | 42 | 1925–26 |
| Division 3(N) | Rochdale | 4 | 40 | 1931–32 |
| Division 3 | Rochdale | 2 | 46 | 1973–74 |
| Division 4 | Southport | 3 | 46 | 1976–77 |
| **SCOTTISH LEAGUE** | | | | |
| Premier Division | St Johnstone | 3 | 36 | 1975–76 |
| | Kilmarnock | 3 | 36 | 1982–83 |
| | Morton | 3 | 44 | 1987–88 |
| Division 1 | Vale of Leven | 0 | 22 | 1891–92 |
| Division 2 | East Stirlingshire | 1 | 22 | 1905–06 |
| | Forfar Ath | 1 | 38 | 1974–75 |
| New Division 1 | Queen of the S | 2 | 39 | 1988–89 |
| | Cowdenbeath | 3 | 44 | 1992–93 |
| New Division 2 | Forfar Ath | 4 | 26 | 1975–76 |
| | Stranraer | 4 | 39 | 1987–88 |
| New Division 3 | Albion R | 5 | 36 | 1994–95 |

## MOST DEFEATS IN A SEASON

| **FA PREMIER LEAGUE** | | *Defeats* | *Games* | *Season* |
|---|---|---|---|---|
| | Ipswich T | 29 | 42 | 1994–95 |
| **FOOTBALL LEAGUE** | | | | |
| Division 1 | Stoke C | 31 | 42 | 1984–85 |
| Division 2 | Tranmere R | 31 | 42 | 1938–39 |
| | Chester C | 33 | 46 | 1992–93 |
| Division 3 | Doncaster R | 34 | 46 | 1997–98 |
| Division 3(S) | Merthyr T | 29 | 42 | 1924–25 |
| | Walsall | 29 | 46 | 1952–53 |
| | Walsall | 29 | 46 | 1953–54 |
| Division 3(N) | Rochdale | 33 | 40 | 1931–32 |
| Division 4 | Newport Co | 33 | 46 | 1987–88 |

**SCOTTISH LEAGUE**

| | | | | |
|---|---|---|---|---|
| **Premier Division** | Morton | 29 | 36 | 1984–85 |
| **Division 1** | St Mirren | 31 | 42 | 1920–21 |
| **Division 2** | Brechin C | 30 | 36 | 1962–63 |
| | Lochgelly | 30 | 38 | 1923–24 |
| **New Division 1** | Queen of the S | 29 | 39 | 1988–89 |
| | Dumbarton | 31 | 36 | 1995–96 |
| | Cowdenbeath | 34 | 44 | 1992–93 |
| **New Division 2** | Berwick R | 29 | 39 | 1987–88 |
| **New Division 3** | Albion R | 28 | 36 | 1994–95 |

## HAT-TRICKS

**Career** 34 Dixie Dean (Tranmere R, Everton, Notts Co, England)
**Division 1 (one season post-war)** 6 Jimmy Greaves (Chelsea), 1960–61
**Three for one team one match**
West, Spouncer, Hooper, Nottingham F v Leicester Fosse, Division 1, 21 April 1909
Barnes, Ambler, Davies, Wrexham v Hartlepools U, Division 4, 3 March 1962
Adcock, Stewart, White, Manchester C v Huddersfield T, Division 2, 7 Nov 1987
Loasby, Smith, Wells, Northampton T v Walsall, Division 3S, 5 Nov 1927
Bowater, Hoyland, Readman, Mansfield T v Rotherham U, Division 3N, 27 Dec 1932

## FEWEST DEFEATS IN A SEASON
*(Minimum 20 games)*

| **FA PREMIER LEAGUE** | | *Defeats* | *Games* | *Season* |
|---|---|---|---|---|
| | Manchester U | 4 | 42 | 1993–94 |
| **FOOTBALL LEAGUE** | | | | |
| **Division 1** | Preston NE | 0 | 22 | 1888–89 |
| | Arsenal | 1 | 38 | 1990–91 |
| | Liverpool | 2 | 40 | 1987–88 |
| | Leeds U | 2 | 42 | 1968–69 |
| **Division 2** | Liverpool | 0 | 28 | 1893–94 |
| | Burnley | 2 | 30 | 1897–98 |
| | Bristol C | 2 | 38 | 1905–06 |
| | Leeds U | 3 | 42 | 1963–64 |
| | Chelsea | 5 | 46 | 1988–89 |
| **Division 3** | QPR | 5 | 46 | 1966–67 |
| | Bristol R | 5 | 46 | 1989–90 |
| | Notts Co | 5 | 46 | 1997–98 |
| **Division 3(S)** | Southampton | 4 | 42 | 1921–22 |
| | Plymouth Arg | 4 | 42 | 1929–30 |
| **Division 3(N)** | Port Vale | 3 | 46 | 1953–54 |
| | Doncaster R | 3 | 42 | 1946–47 |
| | Wolverhampton W | 3 | 42 | 1923–24 |
| **Division 4** | Lincoln C | 4 | 46 | 1975–76 |
| | Sheffield U | 4 | 46 | 1981–82 |
| | Bournemouth | 4 | 46 | 1981–82 |
| **SCOTTISH LEAGUE** | | | | |
| **Premier Division** | Rangers | 3 | 36 | 1995–96 |
| | Celtic | 3 | 44 | 1987–88 |
| **Division 1** | Rangers | 0 | 18 | 1898–99 |
| | Rangers | 1 | 42 | 1920–21 |
| **Division 2** | Clyde | 1 | 36 | 1956–57 |
| | Morton | 1 | 36 | 1962–63 |
| | St Mirren | 1 | 36 | 1967–68 |
| **New Division 1** | Partick T | 2 | 26 | 1975–76 |
| | St Mirren | 2 | 39 | 1976–77 |
| | Raith R | 4 | 44 | 1992–93 |
| | Falkirk | 4 | 44 | 1993–94 |
| **New Division 2** | Raith R | 1 | 26 | 1975–76 |
| | Clydebank | 3 | 26 | 1975–76 |
| | Forfar Ath | 3 | 39 | 1983–84 |
| | Raith R | 3 | 39 | 1986–87 |
| | Livingston | 6 | 36 | 1995–96 |
| **New Division 3** | Forfar Ath | 6 | 36 | 1994–95 |
| | Inverness T | 6 | 36 | 1996–97 |

## MOST DRAWN GAMES IN A SEASON

| **FA PREMIER LEAGUE** | | *Draws* | *Games* | *Season* |
|---|---|---|---|---|
| | Manchester C | 18 | 42 | 1993–94 |
| | Sheffield U | 18 | 42 | 1993–94 |
| | Southampton | 18 | 42 | 1994–95 |
| **FOOTBALL LEAGUE** | | | | |
| **Division 1** | Norwich C | 23 | 42 | 1978–79 |
| **Division 3** | Cardiff C | 23 | 46 | 1997–98 |
| | Hartlepool U | 23 | 46 | 1997–98 |
| **Division 4** | Exeter C | 23 | 46 | 1986–87 |
| **SCOTTISH LEAGUE** | | | | |
| **Premier Division** | Aberdeen | 21 | 44 | 1993–94 |
| **New Division 1** | East Fife | 21 | 44 | 1986–87 |

# MOST GOALS IN A GAME

| | | |
|---|---|---|
| **FA PREMIER LEAGUE** | Andy Cole (Manchester U) 5 goals v Ipswich T | 4 Mar 1995 |
| **FOOTBALL LEAGUE** | | |
| **Division 1** | Ted Drake (Arsenal) 7 goals v Aston V | 14 Dec 1935 |
| | James Ross (Preston NE) 7 goals v Stoke | 6 Oct 1888 |
| **Division 2** | Tommy Briggs (Blackburn R) 7 goals v Bristol R | 5 Feb 1955 |
| | Neville Coleman (Stoke C) 7 goals v Lincoln C | 23 Feb 1957 |
| **Division 3(S)** | Joe Payne (Luton T) 10 goals v Bristol R | 13 April 1936 |
| **Division 3(N)** | Bunny Bell (Tranmere R) 9 goals v Oldham Ath | 26 Dec 1935 |
| **Division 3** | Steve Earle (Fulham) 5 goals v Halifax T | 16 Sept 1969 |
| | Barrie Thomas (Scunthorpe U) 5 goals v Luton T | 24 April 1965 |
| | Keith East (Swindon T) 5 goals v Mansfield T | 20 Nov 1965 |
| | Alf Wood (Shrewsbury T) 5 goals v Blackburn R | 2 Oct 1971 |
| | Tony Caldwell (Bolton W) 5 goals v Walsall | 10 Sept 1983 |
| | Andy Jones (Port Vale) 5 goals v Newport Co | 4 May 1987 |
| | Steve Wilkinson (Mansfield T) 5 goals v Birmingham C | 3 April 1990 |
| **Division 4** | Bert Lister (Oldham Ath) 6 goals v Southport | 26 Dec 1962 |
| **FA CUP** | Ted MacDougall (Bournemouth) 9 goals v Margate (*1st Round*) | 20 Nov 1971 |
| **LEAGUE CUP** | Frankie Bunn (Oldham Ath) 6 goals v Scarborough | 25 Oct 1989 |
| **SCOTTISH LEAGUE** | | |
| **Premier Division** | Paul Sturrock (Dundee U) 5 goals v Morton | 17 Nov 1984 |
| **Division 1** | Jimmy McGrory (Celtic) 8 goals v Dunfermline Ath | 14 Sept 1928 |
| **Division 2** | Owen McNally (Arthurlie) 8 goals v Armadale | 1 Oct 1927 |
| | Jim Dyet (King's Park) 8 goals v Forfar Ath | 2 Jan 1930 |
| | John Calder (Morton) 8 goals v Raith R | 18 April 1936 |
| | Norman Hayward (Raith R) 8 goals v Brechin C | 20 Aug 1937 |
| **SCOTTISH CUP** | John Petrie (Arbroath) 13 goals v Bon Accord (*1st Round*) | 12 Sept 1885 |

# MOST LEAGUE GOALS IN A SEASON

| | | Goals | Games | Season |
|---|---|---|---|---|
| **FA PREMIER LEAGUE** | Andy Cole (Newcastle U) | 34 | 40 | 1993–94 |
| | Alan Shearer (Blackburn R) | 34 | 42 | 1994–95 |
| **Division 1** | Dixie Dean (Everton) | 60 | 39 | 1927–28 |
| **Division 2** | George Camsell (Middlesbrough) | 59 | 37 | 1926–27 |
| **Division 3(S)** | Joe Payne (Luton T) | 55 | 39 | 1936–37 |
| **Division 3(N)** | Ted Harston (Mansfield T) | 55 | 41 | 1936–37 |
| **Division 3** | Derek Reeves (Southampton) | 39 | 46 | 1959–60 |
| **Division 4** | Terry Bly (Peterborough U) | 52 | 46 | 1960–61 |
| **FA CUP** | Sandy Brown (Tottenham H) | 15 | 8 | 1900–01 |
| **LEAGUE CUP** | Clive Allen (Tottenham H) | 12 | 9 | 1986–87 |
| **SCOTTISH LEAGUE** | | | | |
| **Division 1** | William McFadyen (Motherwell) | 52 | 34 | 1931–32 |
| **Division 2** | Jim Smith (Ayr U) | 66 | 38 | 1927–28 |

# MOST LEAGUE GOALS IN A CAREER

| | | Goals | Games | Season |
|---|---|---|---|---|
| **FOOTBALL LEAGUE** | | | | |
| **Arthur Rowley** | WBA | 4 | 24 | 1946–48 |
| | Fulham | 27 | 56 | 1948–50 |
| | Leicester C | 251 | 303 | 1950–58 |
| | Shrewsbury T | 152 | 236 | 1958–65 |
| | | 434 | 619 | |
| **SCOTTISH LEAGUE** | | | | |
| **Jimmy McGrory** | Celtic | 1 | 3 | 1922–23 |
| | Clydebank | 13 | 30 | 1923–24 |
| | Celtic | 396 | 375 | 1924–38 |
| | | 410 | 408 | |

# MOST CUP GOALS IN A CAREER

**FA CUP (post-war)**

Ian Rush   42   (Chester, Liverpool)
**Pre-war:**  Henry Cursham  48  (Notts Co)

**LEAGUE CUP**

Geoff Hurst   49   (West Ham U, Stoke C)
Ian Rush   49   (Chester, Liverpool, Newcastle U)

## A CENTURY OF LEAGUE AND CUP GOALS IN CONSECUTIVE SEASONS

| | | | | |
|---|---|---|---|---|
| **George Camsell** | Middlesbrough | 59 Lge | 5 Cup | 1926–27 |
| (101 goals) | | 33 | 4 | 1927–28 |
| **Steve Bull** | Wolverhampton W | 34 Lge | 18 Cup | 1987–88 |
| (102 goals) | | 37 | 13 | 1988–89 |

(Camsell's cup goals were all scored in the FA Cup; Bull had 12 in the Sherpa Van Trophy, 3 Littlewoods Cup, 3 FA Cup in 1987–88; 11 Sherpa Van Trophy, 2 Littlewoods Cup in 1988–89.)

## LONGEST SEQUENCE OF CONSECUTIVE SCORING (Individual)

**FA PREMIER LEAGUE**
Mark Stein (Chelsea)         9 in 7 games      1993–94
**FOOTBALL LEAGUE
RECORD**
Dixie Dean (Everton)         23 in 12 games     1930–31

## LONGEST WINNING SEQUENCE

| **FOOTBALL LEAGUE** | | *Games* | *Season* |
|---|---|---|---|
| **Division 1** | Tottenham H | 13 | 1959–60 (2) |
| | | | and 1960–61 (11) |
| | Preston NE | 13 | 1891–92 |
| | Sunderland | 13 | 1891–92 |
| **Division 2** | Manchester U | 14 | 1904–05 |
| | Bristol C | 14 | 1905–06 |
| | Preston NE | 14 | 1950–51 |
| **Division 3** | Reading | 13 | 1985–86 |
| *From Season's start* | | | |
| **Division 1** | Tottenham H | 11 | 1960–61 |
| **Division 3** | Reading | 13 | 1985–86 |

## LONGEST WINNING SEQUENCE IN A SEASON

| **FOOTBALL LEAGUE** | | *Games* | *Season* |
|---|---|---|---|
| **Division 1** | Tottenham H | 11 | 1960–61 |
| **Division 2** | Manchester U | 14 | 1904–05 |
| **Division 2** | Bristol C | 14 | 1905–06 |
| **Division 2** | Preston NE | 14 | 1950–51 |
| **SCOTTISH LEAGUE** | | | |
| **Division 2** | Morton | 23 | 1963–64 |

## LONGEST UNBEATEN SEQUENCE

| **FOOTBALL LEAGUE** | | *Games* | *Seasons* |
|---|---|---|---|
| **Division 1** | Nottingham F | 42 | Nov 1977–Dec 1978 |

## LONGEST UNBEATEN CUP SEQUENCE

Liverpool 25 rounds League/Milk Cup 1980–84

## LONGEST UNBEATEN SEQUENCE IN A SEASON

| **FOOTBALL LEAGUE** | | *Games* | *Season* |
|---|---|---|---|
| **Division 1** | Burnley | 30 | 1920–21 |

## LONGEST UNBEATEN START TO A SEASON

| **FOOTBALL LEAGUE** | | *Games* | *Season* |
|---|---|---|---|
| **Division 1** | Leeds U | 29 | 1973–74 |
| **Division 1** | Liverpool | 29 | 1987–88 |

## LONGEST SEQUENCE WITHOUT A WIN IN A SEASON

| **FOOTBALL LEAGUE** | | *Games* | *Season* |
|---|---|---|---|
| **Division 2** | Cambridge U | 31 | 1983–84 |

## LONGEST SEQUENCE WITHOUT A WIN FROM SEASON'S START

| **Division 1** | Sheffield U | 16 | 1990–91 |
|---|---|---|---|

## LONGEST SEQUENCE OF CONSECUTIVE DEFEATS

| **FOOTBALL LEAGUE** | | *Games* | *Season* |
|---|---|---|---|
| **Division 2** | Darwen | 18 | 1898–99 |

## GOALKEEPING RECORDS (WITHOUT CONCEDING A GOAL)

**British record** (all competitive games)
Chris Woods, Rangers, in 1196 minutes from 26 November 1986 to 31 January 1987.

**Football League**
Steve Death, Reading, 1103 minutes from 24 March to 18 August 1979.

## PENALTIES

| | | Goals | Season |
|---|---|---|---|
| **Most in a Season (individual)** | | | |
| Division 1 | Francis Lee (Manchester C) | 13 | 1971–72 |
| **Most awarded in one game** | | | |
| Five | Crystal Palace (4 – 1 scored, 3 missed) v Brighton & HA (1 scored), Div 2 | | 1988–89 |
| **Most saved in a Season** | | | |
| Division 1 | Paul Cooper (Ipswich T) | 8 (of 10) | 1979–80 |

## MOST LEAGUE APPEARANCES (750+ matches)

1005 Peter Shilton (286 Leicester City, 110 Stoke City, 202 Nottingham Forest, 188 Southampton, 175 Derby County, 34 Plymouth Argyle, 1 Bolton Wanderers, 9 Leyton Orient)1966–97
863 Tommy Hutchison (165 Blackpool, 314 Coventry City, 46 Manchester City, 92 Burnley 178 Swansea City, 68 Alloa) 1965–91
824 Terry Paine (713 Southampton, 111 Hereford United) 1957–77
800 Tony Ford (355 Grimsby T, 9 Sunderland (loan), 112 Stoke C, 114 WBA, 68 Grimsby T, 5 Bradford C (loan), 76 Scunthorpe U, 61 Mansfield T) 1975–98
782 Robbie James (484 Swansea C, 48 Stoke C, 87 QPR, 23 Leicester C, 89 Bradford C, 51 Cardiff C) 1973–94
777 Alan Oakes (565 Manchester C, 211 Chester C, 1 Port Vale) 1959–84
771 John Burridge (27 Workington, 134 Blackpool, 65 Aston Villa, 6 Southend U (loan), 88 Crystal Palace, 39 QPR, 74 Wolverhampton W, 6 Derby Co (loan), 109 Sheffield U, 62 Southampton, 67 Newcastle U, 65 Hibernian, 3 Scarborough, 4 Lincoln C, 3 Aberdeen, 3 Dumbarton, 3 Falkirk, 4 Manchester C, 3 Darlington, 6 Queen of the South) 1968–96
770 John Trollope (all for Swindon Town) 1960–80†
764 Jimmy Dickinson (all for Portsmouth) 1946–65
761 Roy Sproson (all for Port Vale) 1950–72
758 Ray Clemence (48 Scunthorpe United, 470 Liverpool, 240 Tottenham Hotspur) 1966–87
758 Billy Bonds (95 Charlton Ath, 663 West Ham U) 1964–88
757 Pat Jennings (48 Watford, 472 Tottenham Hotspur, 237 Arsenal) 1963–86
757 Frank Worthington (171 Huddersfield T, 210 Leicester C, 84 Bolton W, 75 Birmingham C, 32 Leeds U, 195 Sunderland, 34 Southampton, 31 Brighton & HA, 59 Tranmere R, 23 Preston NE, 19 Stockport Co) 1966–88
† record for one club

Consecutive
401 Harold Bell (401 Tranmere R; 459 in all games) 1946–55

**FA CUP**
88 Ian Callaghan (79 Liverpool, 7 Swansea C, 2 Crewe Alex)

Most Senior Matches
1390 Peter Shilton (1005 League, 86 FA Cup, 102 League Cup, 125 Internationals, 13 Under-23, 4 Football League XI, 20 European Cup, 7 Texaco Cup, 5 Simod Cup, 4 European Super Cup, 4 UEFA Cup, 3 Screen Sport Super Cup, 3 Zenith Data Systems Cup, 2 Autoglass Trophy, 2 Charity Shield, 2 Full Members Cup, 1 Anglo-Italian Cup, 1 Football League play-offs, 1 World Club Championship)

## MOST FA CUP FINAL GOALS

Ian Rush (Liverpool) 5: 1986(2), 1989(2), 1992(1)

## MOST LEAGUE MEDALS

Phil Neal (Liverpool) 8: 1976, 1977, 1979, 1980, 1982, 1983, 1984, 1986
Alan Hansen (Liverpool) 8: 1979, 1980, 1982, 1983, 1984, 1986, 1988, 1990

## OTHER RECORDS

**YOUNGEST PLAYERS**
**FA Premier League** Andy Campbell, 16 years, 352 days, Middlesbrough v Sheffield W, 5.4.96.
**FA Premier League scorer** Andy Turner, 17 years 166 days, Tottenham H v Everton, 5.9.92.
**Football League** Albert Geldard, 15 years 158 days, Bradford Park Avenue v Millwall, Division 2, 16.9.29; and Ken Roberts, 15 years 158 days, Wrexham v Bradford Park Avenue, Division 3N, 1.9.51
**Football League scorer**
Ronnie Dix, 15 years 180 days, Bristol Rovers v Norwich City, Division 3S, 3.3.28.
**Division 1**
Derek Forster, 15 years 185 days, Sunderland v Leicester City, 22.8.84.
**Division 1 scorer**
Jason Dozzell, 16 years 57 days as substitute Ipswich Town v Coventry City, 4.2.84
**Division 1 hat-tricks**
Alan Shearer, 17 years 240 days, Southampton v Arsenal, 9.4.88
Jimmy Greaves, 17 years 10 months, Chelsea v Portsmouth, 25.12.57
**FA Cup (any round)**
Andy Awford, 15 years 88 days as substitute Worcester City v Boreham Wood, 3rd Qual. rd, 10.10.87
**FA Cup proper**
Scott Endersby, 15 years 288 days, Kettering v Tilbury, 1st rd, 26.11.77

**FA Cup Final**
  James Prinsep, 17 years 245 days, Clapham Rovers v Old Etonians, 1879
**FA Cup Final scorer**
  Norman Whiteside, 18 years 18 days, Manchester United v Brighton & Hove Albion, 1983
**FA Cup Final captain**
  David Nish, 21 years 212 days, Leicester City v Manchester City, 1969
**League Cup Final scorer**
  Norman Whiteside, 17 years 324 days, Manchester United v Liverpool, 1983
**League Cup Final captain**
  Barry Venison, 20 years 7 months 8 days, Sunderland v Norwich City, 1985

**OLDEST PLAYERS**
**Football League**
  Neil McBain, 52 years 4 months, New Brighton v Hartlepools United, Div 3N, 15.3.47 (McBain was New Brighton's manager and had to play in an emergency)
**Division 1**
  Stanley Matthews, 50 years 5 days, Stoke City v Fulham, 6.2.65

## SENDINGS-OFF

| | | |
|---|---|---|
| **Season** | 314 (League alone) | 1994–95 |
| **Day** | 15 (3 League, 12 FA Cup*) | 20 Nov 1982 |
| | *worst overall FA Cup total* | |
| **League** | 13 | 14 Dec 1985; 19 Aug 1995; 9 Sept 1995 |
| **Weekend** | 15 | 22/23 Dec 1990 |
| **FA Cup Final** | Kevin Moran, Manchester U v Everton | 1985 |
| **Quickest** | Mark Smith, Crewe Alex v Darlington (away) Div 3: 19 secs | 12 March 1994 |
| **Most one game** | Four: Northampton T (0) v Hereford U (4) Div 3 | 11 Nov 1992 |
| | Four: Crewe Alex (2) v Bradford PA (2) Div 3N | 8 Jan 1955 |
| | Four: Sheffield U (1) v Portsmouth (3) Div 2 | 13 Dec 1986 |
| | Four: Port Vale (2) v Northampton T (2) Littlewoods Cup | 18 Aug 1987 |
| | Four: Brentford (2) v Mansfield T (2) Div 3 | 12 Dec 1987 |

## RECORD ATTENDANCES

| | | | |
|---|---|---|---|
| **FA Premier League** | 55,306 | Manchester U v Wimbledon | 28.3.98 |
| **Football League** | 83,260 | Manchester U v Arsenal, Maine Road | 17.1.1948 |
| **Scottish League** | 118,567 | Rangers v Celtic, Ibrox Stadium | 2.1.1939 |
| **FA Cup Final** | 126,047* | Bolton W v West Ham U, Wembley | 28.4.1923 |
| **European Cup** | 135,826 | Celtic v Leeds U, semi-final at Hampden Park | 15.4.1970 |
| **Scottish Cup** | 146,433 | Celtic v Aberdeen, Hampden Park | 24.4.37 |
| **World Cup** | 199,854† | Brazil v Uruguay, Maracana, Rio | 16.7.50 |

* It has been estimated that as many as 70,000 more broke in without paying.
† 173,830 paid.

# IMPORTANT ADDRESSES

**The Football Association:** R. H. G. Kelly, F.C.I.S., 16 Lancaster Gate, London W2 3LW. *0171 262 4542*

**Scotland:** J. Farry, 6 Park Gardens, Glasgow G3 7YE. *0141-332 6372*

**Northern Ireland** (Irish FA): D. I. Bowen, 20 Windsor Avenue, Belfast BT9 6EG. *01232 669458*

**Wales:** A. Evans, 3 Westgate Street, Cardiff, South Glamorgan CF1 1JF. *01222 372325*

**Republic of Ireland** (FA of Ireland): B. O'Byrne, 80 Merrion Square South, Dublin 2. *00353 16766864*

**International Federation** (FIFA): The Secretary, P. O. Box 85 8030 Zurich, Switzerland. *00 411 384 9595. Fax: 00 411 384 9696*

**Union of European Football Associations:** G. Aigner, Chemin de la Redoute 54, Case Postale 303 CH-1260 Nyon, Switzerland. *01041 22 994 44 44. Fax: 0041 22 994 44 88*

## THE LEAGUES

**The Premier League:** P. Leaver, 11 Connaught Place, London W2 2ET *0171-298-1600*

**The Football League:** J. D. Dent, F.C.I.S., The Football League, Lytham St Annes, Lancs FY8 1JG. *01253-729421. Telex 67675*

**The Scottish League:** P. Donald, 188 West Regent Street, Glasgow G2 4RY. *0141-248 3844*

**The Irish League:** J. H. Wallace, 87 University Street, Belfast BT7 1HP. *01232 242888*

**Football League of Ireland:** E. Morris, 80 Merrion Square South, Dublin 2. *003531 765120*

**Football Conference:** J. A. Moules, Collingwood House, Schooner Court, Crossways, Dartford DA2 6QQ. *01322 303120*

**Central League:** A. Williamson, The Football League, Lytham St Annes, Lancs FY8 1JG. *01253 729421*

**North West Counties League:** M. Darby, 87 Hillary Road, Hyde, Cheshire SK14 4EB.

**Eastern Counties League:** C. Lamb, 26 Dunthorpe Road, Clacton, Essex CO12 8UJ. *01255 436398*

**Football Combination:** N. Chamberlain, 2 Vicarage Close, Old Costessey, Norwich NR8 5DL. *10603 743998*

**Hellenic League:** B. King, 83 Queens Road, Carterton, Oxon OX18 3YF. *01793 493502*

**Kent League:** R. Vinter, The Thatched Barn, Lower Hardres, Canterbury, Kent CT4 5PG

**Lancashire Amateur League:** R. G. Bowker, 13 Shores Green Drive, Wincham, Northwich, Cheshire CW9 6EE. *0161-480 7723*

**Lancashire Football League:** J. W. Howarth, 465 Whalley Road, Clapton-le-Moors, Accrington, Lancs BB5 5RP. *01254 398957*

**Leicestershire Senior League:** R. J. Holmes, 8 Huntsman Close, Markfield, Leics LE67 9XE. *01530 243093*

**London Spartan:** K. J. Cordell, 44 Greenleas, Waltham Abbey, Essex EN9 1SZ. *01992 712428*

**Manchester League:** J. A. Warrington, 17 Broadacre, Mottram Rise, Stalybridge, Cheshire SK15 2TX. *01457 764427*

**Midland Combination:** N. Harvey, 115 Millfield Road, Handsworth Wood, Birmingham B20 1ED. *0121 357 4172*

**Mid-Week Football League:** N. A. S. Matthews, Cedar Court, Steeple Aston, Oxford. *01869 40347*

**Northern Premier:** R. D. Bayley, 22 Woburn Drive, Hale, Altrincham, Cheshire WA15 8LZ. *0161-980 7007*

**Northern Intermediate League:** G. Thompson, Clegg House, 253 Pitsmoor Road, Sheffield S3 9AQ. *01742 27817*

**Northern League:** J. H. McLackland, 92 Appletree Gardens, Walkerville NE6 4SX

**North Midlands League:** G. Thompson, 7 Wren Park Close, Ridgway, Sheffield.

**Peterborough and District League:** M. J. Croson, 44 Storrington Way, Werrington, Peterborough, Cambs PE4 6QP.

**Isthmian League:** N. Robinson, 226 Rye Lane, Peckham SE15 4NL. *0181 409 1978. Fax: 0181 409 1979*

**Southern Amateur League:** S. J. Lucas, 23 Beaufort Close, North Weald Bassett, Epping, Essex CM16 6JZ. *0137882 3932*

**South-East Counties League:** A. Leather, 66 Green Acres, Chichester Road, Croydon, Surrey CR0 5UX. *0181-681 7100*

**Southern League:** D. J. Strudwick, P. O. Box 90, Worcester, WR3 8RX. *01905 757509*

**South Midlands League:** M. Mitchell, 26 Leighton Court, Dunstable, Beds LU6 1EW. *01582 667291*

**South Western League:** M. Goodenough, Rose Cottage, Horrelsford, Milton Damerel, Holsworthy, Devon EX22 7NJ. *01409 261402*

**United Counties League:** R. Gamble, 8 Bostock Avenue, Northampton. *01604 37766*

**Wearside League:** B. Robson, 12 Deneside, Howden-le-Wear, Crook, Co. Durham DL15 8JR. *01388 762034*

**Western League:** M. E. Washer, 16 Heathfield Road, Nailsea, Bristol BS19 1EB.

**The Welsh League:** K. J. Tucker, 16 The Parade, Merthyr Tydfil, Mid Glamorgan CF47 0ET. *01685 723884*

**West Midlands Regional League:** N. R. Juggins, 14 Badger Way, Blackwell, Bromsgrove, Worcs B60 1EX.

**West Yorkshire League:** W. Keyworth, 2 Hill Court Grove, Bramley, Yorks L13 2AP. *0113 74465*

**Northern Counties (East):** B. Wood, 6 Restmore Avenue, Guiseley, Nr Leeds LS20 9DG. *01943 874558*

## COUNTY FOOTBALL ASSOCIATIONS

**Bedfordshire:** P. D. Brown, Century House, Skimpot Road, Dunstable, Beds LU5 4JU. *01582 565111*

**Berks and Bucks:** B. G. Moore, 15a London Street, Faringdon, Oxon SN7 7HD. *01367 242099*

**Birmingham County:** M. Pennick, County FA Offices, Rayhall Lane, Great Barr, Birmingham B43 6JF. *0121 357 4278*

**Cambridgeshire:** A. K. Pawley, 3 Signet Court, Swanns Road, Cambridge CB5 8LA. *01223 576770*

**Cheshire:** A. Collins, The Cottage, Hartford Moss Rec Centre, Winnington, Northwich CW8 4BG.

**Cornwall:** B. Cudmore, 14 High Cross Street, St. Austell, Cornwall PL25 4AB. *01726 74080*

**Cumberland:** J. A. Murphy, 17 Oxford Street, Workington, Cumbria CA14 2AL. *01900 872310*

**Derbyshire:** K. Compton, The Grandstand, Moorways Stadium, Moor Lane, Derby DE2 8FB. *01332 361422*

**Devon County:** C. Davidson, County HQ, Coach Road, Newton Abbot, Devon TQ12 1EJ. *01626 332077*

**Dorset County:** P. Hough, County Ground, Blandford Close, Hamsworthy, Poole, Dorset BH15 4BF. *01202 682375*

**Durham:** J. Topping, 'Codeslaw', Ferens Park, Durham DH1 1JZ. *0191 3848653*

**East Riding County:** D. R. Johnson, 52 Bethune Ave, Hull HU4 7EJ. *01482 641458*

**Essex County:** P. Sammons, 31 Mildmay Road, Chelmsford, Essex CM2 0DN. *01245 357727*

**Gloucestershire:** P. Britton, Oaklands Park, Almondsbury, Bristol BS12 4AG. *01454 615888*

**Guernsey:** D. Dorey, Haut Regard, St. Clair Hill, St. Sampson's, Guernsey, GY2 4DT, CI. *01481 46231*

**Hampshire:** R. G. Barnes, 8 Ashwood Gardens, off Winchester Road, Southampton SO16 7PW. *01703 791110*

**Herefordshire:** J. S. Lambert, Muirfield Close, Holmer, Hereford HR1 1QB. *01432 270308*

**Hertfordshire:** R. G. Kibble, Marquis House, 68 Great North Road, Hatfield, Herts AL9 5ER. *01707 256891*

**Huntingdonshire:** M. M. Armstrong, 1 Chapel End, Great Giddings, Huntingdon, Cambs PE17 5NP. *01832 293262*

**Isle of Man:** Mrs A. Garrett, P.O. Box 53, The Bowl, Douglas IOM IM99 1GY. *01624 615576*

**Jersey:** S. Monks, Rocqueberg View, La Rue De Samares, St. Clement, Jersey JE2 6LS

**Kent County:** K. T. Masters, 69 Maidstone Road, Chatham, Kent ME4 6DT. *01634 843824*

**Lancashire:** J. Kenyon, 31a Wellington St, St John's, Blackburn, Lancs BB1 8AU. *01254 264333*

**Leicestershire and Rutland:** R. E. Barston, Holmes Park, Dog and Gun Lane, Whetstone, Leicester LE8 3LJ. *0116 2867828*

**Lincolnshire:** J. Griffin, PO Box 26, 12 Dean Road, Lincoln LN2 4DP. *01522 524917*

**Liverpool County:** F. L. J. Hunter, 23 Greenfield Road, Old Swann, Liverpool L13 3BN. *0151-220 6089*

**London:** D. Fowkes, Aldworth Grove, London SE13 6HY. *0181 690 9626*

**Manchester County:** P. Smith, Brantingham Road, Chorlton, Manchester M21 0TT. *0161-881 0299*

**Middlesex County:** P. J. Clayton, 39 Roxborough Road, Harrow, Middx HA1 1NS. *0181 424 8524*

**Norfolk County:** R. J. Howlett, Plantation Park, Blofield, Norwich, Norfolk, NR13 4PL. *01603 717177*

**Northamptonshire:** B. Walden, 2 Duncan Close, Moulton Park, Northampton NN3 6WL. *01604 670741*

**North Riding County:** M. Jarvis, 284 Linthorpe Road, Middlesbrough TS1 3QU. *01642 224585*

**Northumberland:** R. E. Maughan, Seymour House, 10 Brenkley Way, Blezard Bus Park, Seaton Burn, Newcastle upon Tyne NE13 6DT. *0191 236 8020*

**Nottinghamshire:** W. T. Annable, 7 Clarendon Street, Nottingham NG1 5HS. *0115 9418954*

**Oxfordshire:** P. J. Ladbrook, 3 Wilkins Road, Cowley, Oxford OX4 2HY. *01865 775432*

**Sheffield and Hallamshire:** G. Thompson, Clegg House, 5 Onslow Road, Sheffield S11 7AF. *011422 670068*

**Shropshire:** A. W. Brett, 5 Ebnal Road, Shrewsbury SY2 6PW. *01743 236145*

**Somerset & Avon (South):** Mrs H. Marchment, 30 North Road, Midsomer Norton, Bath BA3 2QD. *01761 410280*

**Staffordshire:** B. J. Adshead, County Showground, Weston Road, Stafford ST18 0DB. *01785 256994*

**Suffolk County:** W. M. Steward, 2 Millfields, Haughley, Stowmarket, Suffolk IP14 3PU. *01449 673481*

**Surrey County:** A. P. Adams, 321 Kingston Road, Leatherhead, Surrey KT22 7TU. *01372 373543*

**Sussex County:** D. M. Worsfold, County Office, Culver Road, Lancing, Sussex BN15 9AX. *01903 753547*

**Westmorland:** P. G. Ducksbury, 1 Dalton Road, Kendal LA9 6AG. *01539 730946*

**West Riding County:** R. Carter, Fleet Lane, Woodlesford, Leeds LS26 8NX. *0113 2821222*

**Wiltshire:** E. M. Parry, 44 Kennet Avenue, Swindon SN2 3LG. *01793 529036*

**Worcestershire:** M. R. Leggett Fermain, 12 Worcester Road, Evesham, Worcs WR11 4JU. *01905 612336*

## OTHER USEFUL ADDRESSES

**Amateur Football Alliance:** W. P. Goss, 55 Islington Park Street, London N1 1QB. *0171-359 3493*

**English Schools FA:** M. R. Berry, 1/2 Eastgate Street, Stafford ST16 2NN. *01785 51142*

**Oxford University:** M. H. Matthews, University College, Oxford OX1 4BH.

**Cambridge University:** Dr J. A. Little, St Catherine's College, Cambridge CB2 1RL.

**Army:** Major T. C. Knight ASCB (MOD), Clayton Barracks, Aldershot, Hants GU11 2BG. *01252 348571/4*

**Royal Air Force:** WG CDR W. E. Mahon, BA, RAF, SM 88 (RAF) Palmer Pavilion, Room V028, P. O. Box 69, RAF Wyton, Huntingdon, Cambs PE17 2DL. *01480 52451 Ex 4628*

**Royal Navy:** Lt-Cdr J. Danks, RN. Sports Office, H.M.S. Temeraire, Portsmouth, Hants PO1 2HB. *01705 722671*

**British Universities Sports Association:** G. Gregory-Jones, Chief Executive: BUSA, 8 Union Street, London SE1 1SZ. *0171-357 8555*

**Central Council of Physical Recreation:** General Secretary, 70 Brompton Road, London SW3 1HE. *0171-584 6651*

**British Olympic Association:** 6 John Prince's Street, London W1M 0DH. *0171-408 2029*

**National Federation of Football Supporters' Clubs:** Chairman: Ian D. Todd MBE, 8 Wyke Close, Wyke Gardens, Isleworth, Middlesex TW7 5PE. *0181-847-2905 (and fax). Mobile: 0961-558908.* National Secretary: Mark Agate, "The Stadium", 14 Coombe Close, Lordswood, Chatham, Kent ME5 8NU. *01634 319461 (and fax)*

**National Playing Fields Association:** Col R. Satterthwaite, O.B.E., 578b Catherine Place, London, SW1.

**The Scottish Football Commercial Managers Association:** J. E. Hillier (Chairman), c/o Keith FC Promotions Office, 60 Union Street, Keith, Banffshire, Scotland.

**Professional Footballers' Association:** G. Taylor, 2 Oxford Court, Bishopsgate, Off Lower Mosley Street, Manchester M2 3WQ. *0161-236 0575*

**Referees' Association:** A. Smith, 1 Westhill Road, Coundon, Coventry CV6 2AD *01203 601701*

**Women's Football Alliance:** Miss K. Simmons, 9 Wyllyotts Place, Potters Bar, Herts EN6 2JD. *01707 651840*

**Institute of Football Management and Administration:** 44 Holy Walk, Leamington Spa, Warwickshire, CV32 4YS. *01926 882313. Fax: 01926 886829*

**Football Administrators Association:** as above.

**Commercial and Marketing Managers Association:** as above.

**Management Statts Association:** as above.

**League Managers Association:** as above.

**The Association of Football Statisticians:** R. J. Spiller, PO Box 5828, Basildon, Essex SS15 5GQ. *01268 416020 (and fax 01268-543559)*

**The Football Programme Directory:** David Stacey, 'The Beeches', 66 Southend Road, Wickford, Essex SS11 8EN. *01268 732041 (and fax)*

**England Football Supporters Association:** Publicity Officer, David Stacey, 'The Beeches', 66 Southend Road, Wickford, Essex SS11 8EN. *01268 732041 (and fax)*

**World Cup (1966) Association:** as above.

**The Ninety-Two Club:** 104 Gilda Crescent, Whitchurch, Bristol BS14 9LD.

**Scottish 38 Club:** Mark Byatt, 6 Greenfields Close, Loughton, Essex IG10 3HG. *0181-508 6088*

**The Football Trust:** Second Floor, Walkden House, 10 Melton Street, London NW1 2EJ. *0171-388 4504*

**Association of Provincial Football Supporters Clubs in London:** Stephen Moon, 32 Westminster Gardens, Barking, Essex IG11 0BJ. *0181-594-2367.*

**World Association of Friends of English Football:** Carlisle Hill, Gluck, Habichthof 2, D24939 Flensburg, Germany. *0049 461 4700222.*

**Football Postcard Collectors Club:** PRO: Bryan Horsnell, 275 Overdown Road, Tilehurst, Reading RG3 6NX. *01734 424448*

**UK Programme Collectors Club:** Secretary, John Litster, 46 Milton Road, Kirkcaldy, Fife KY1 1TL. *01592 268718. Fax: 01592 595069*

**Programme Monthly:** as above.

**Scottish Football Historians Association:** as above.

**Phil Gould** (Licensed Football Agent), c/o Whoppit Management Ltd, P. O. Box 27204, London N11 2WS. *07071 732 468. Fax: 07070 732 469*

**The Scandinavian Union of Supporters of British Football:** Postboks, 15 Stovner, N-0913 Oslo, Norway.

# FOOTBALL AWARDS 1998

### FOOTBALLER OF THE YEAR
The Football Writers Association Award for the Footballer of the Year went to Dennis Bergkamp of Arsenal and Holland.

### THE PFA AWARDS 1998
**Player of the Year:** Dennis Bergkamp, Arsenal.
**Young Player of the Year:** Michael Owen, Liverpool.
**Merit Award:** Steve Ogrizovic, Coventry C.

### THE SCOTTISH PFA AWARDS 1998
**Player of the Year:** Jackie McNamara, Celtic.
**Young Player of the Year:** Gary Maysmith, Hearts.

### SCOTTISH FOOTBALL WRITERS ASSOCIATION
**Player of the Year:** Craig Burley, Celtic.

### EUROPEAN FOOTBALLER OF THE YEAR 1997
Ronaldo (Internazionale).

### WORLD PLAYER OF THE YEAR
Ronaldo (Internazionale).

### CARLING AWARD WINNERS 1997-98
**Carling Manager of the Month**

| | | |
|---|---|---|
| **August** | Roy Hodgson | Blackburn Rovers |
| **September** | Martin O'Neill | Leicester City |
| **October** | Alex Ferguson | Manchester United |
| **November** | George Graham | Leeds United |
| **December** | Roy Hodgson | Blackburn Rovers |
| **January** | Howard Kendall | Everton |
| **February** | Gordon Strachan | Coventry City |
| **March** | Arsène Wenger | Arsenal |
| **April** | Arsène Wenger | Arsenal |
| | | |
| **Carling Manager of the Year** | **Arsène Wenger** | **Arsenal** |

**Carling Player of the Month**

| | | |
|---|---|---|
| **August** | Dennis Bergkamp | Arsenal |
| **September** | Dennis Bergkamp | Arsenal |
| **October** | Paulo Wanchope | Derby County |
| **November** | Andy Cole | Manchester U |
| | Kevin Davies | Southampton |
| **December** | Steve McManaman | Liverpool |
| **January** | Dion Dublin | Coventry City |
| **February** | Chris Sutton | Blackburn Rovers |
| **March** | Alex Manninger | Arsenal |
| **April** | Emmanuel Petit | Arsenal |
| | | |
| **Carling Player of the Year** | **Michael Owen** | **Liverpool** |

*(Carling Sponsors of the Football Writers Association)*

**Carling No. 1 Awards**
Awarded for outstanding contributions to the national game.

**Jim Smith**, service to football.
**Ian Wright**, Arsenal record goalscorer.

# REFEREEING AND THE REFEREES

The major change to the Laws for the forthcoming season concern the unfair tackle from behind. Exceptionally the Law that came into force from July 1 was allowed to be introduced at the start of this year's World Cup in France. There, the referees were initially criticised by Sepp Blatter, the new President of FIFA and one of the main proponents of the change, for not enforcing it in the manner laid down in the new interpretation of Law 12. This now reads: "A tackle from behind which endangers the safety of an opponent must be sanctioned as serious foul play." The sub-text adds: "The above mentioned decision means that the player guilty of such an offence has to be sent off." Ultimately there was a change of climate towards the issuing of more red cards and there can be no doubt that this is a Law change which will cause considerable controversy in the new season, so far as interpretation is concerned and as to both its honouring and its breach.

At the start of last season there was a complete rewording of the Laws of the Game themselves, and although the seventeen Laws remain the same in essence, some simplification of the language and some shortening of the terms related to the offences has been implemented. However, brevity is not always advantageous in Law making and defining. The good intention of simplifying, by the dropping of substantial references to many of the offences previously encompassed by the "Indirect Free Kick" in Law 12, unfortunately led to discrepancies. This has now been remedied by the insertion of a new phrase to cover any omissions and reads: "An indirect free kick is also awarded to the opposing team if a player, in the opinion of the referee, commits any other offence not previously mentioned in Law 12 for which play is stopped, to caution or dismiss a player."

The sending-off offence for denying a goal-scoring opportunity has now been reworded so it becomes denying "an opposing team" rather than "an opponent"; thus widening the scope of the provision.

The 5/6 seconds Rule of holding the ball by the goalkeeper is now moved to the "International Board Decisions" from last season's recommendations and no doubt will be upgraded again, into the Laws next season. A player returning to the field after injury may now re-enter it from any boundary line if the ball is dead, but if in play only from the touchlines. The referee must still signal for his/her return, thus missing a golden opportunity to move this responsibility to the assistant referee or if available the fourth official.

There are still a number of provisions that apply in most professional games which are not written either into the Laws or the International Board Decisions. FIFA therefore intend to republish a booklet entitled "Additional Instructions for Referees" which should cover the crucial points many of which are otherwise hard to find.

Let us also hope the Premiership will this term follow last season's Nationwide League experiment of getting the fourth official (on the referee's sole instruction) to notify how much stoppage time will be played at the end of each half.

Finally FIFA have authorised an experiment to take place in Jersey during the 1998–99 season, whereby any defending player, or players, who do not retreat the appropriate distance at the taking of a free kick, will not only receive a caution, but will cause the ball to be moved ten yards (9.15 metres) closer towards their own goal.

The full National Review Board list of referees and assistant referees is set out below and those on the Premiership are marked with an asterisk and those new to that List are also duly signified.

This season there are eighteen Premier League referees of whom only one, Robert Harris from Oxford, is new to the List. There have been some notable retirements over the close season, namely ex-FIFA referees Gerald Ashby and Martin Bodenham, whilst the number is reduced by one from last season. One man who deserves a special mention is Paul Durkin from Portland in Dorset. Not only was he England's sole Referee for the France 98 World Cup but he also refereed last season's FA Cup Final and was appointed by UEFA to referee the Semi-Finals of two separate European club tournaments. The only English Assistant Referee at France 98 was Mark Warren of Walsall who has also been elevated to the National Referees' List for this season.

KEN GOLDMAN

# NATIONAL LIST OF REFEREES FOR SEASON 1998–99

*Alcock, P.E. (Halstead, Kent)
Baines, S.J. (Chesterfield)
*Barber, G.P. (Pyrford, Surrey)
*Barry, N.S. (Scunthorpe)
Bates, A. (Stoke-on-Trent)
Bennett, S.G. (Orpington, Kent)
Brandwood, M.J. (Lichfield, Staffs)
*Burge, K.W. (Tonypandy)
Burns, W.C. (Scarborough)
Butler, A.N. (Sutton-in-Ashfield)
Cable, L. (Woking)
Cain, G. (Bootle)
Coddington, B. (Sheffield)
Cowburn, M. (Blackpool)
Crick, D.R. (Worcester Park, Surrey)
Danson, P.S. (Leicester)
Dean, M.L. (Eastham, Wirral)
Dowd, P. (Stoke-on-Trent)
*Dunn, S.W. (Bristol)
*Durkin, P.A. (Portland, Dorset)
D'Urso, A.P. (Billericay, Essex)
*Elleray, D.R. (Harrow-on-the-Hill)
Finch, C.T. (Bury St Edmunds)
Fletcher, M. (Warley, West Midlands)
Foy, C.J. (St Helens)
Frankland, G.B. (Middlesbrough)
Furnandiz, R.D. (Doncaster)

*Gallagher, D.J. (Banbury, Oxon)
Hall, A.R. (Birmingham)
Halsey, M.R. (Welwyn Garden City, Herts)
*#Harris, R.J. (Oxford)
Heilbron, T. (Newton Aycliffe)
Hill, K. (Royston, Herts)
Jones, M.J. (Chester)
*Jones, P. (Loughborough)
Jones, T. (Barrow-in-Furness)
Jordan, B. (Tring, Herts)
Kirkby, J.A. (Sheffield)
Knight, B. (Orpington)
Laws, D. (Whitley Bay)
Laws, G. (Whitley Bay)
Leach, K.A. (Codsall, Staffs)
Leake, A.R. (Darwen, Lancashire)
*Lodge, S.J. (Barnsley)
Lomas, E. (Manchester)
Lynch, K.M. (Kirk Hammerton, Nr York)
Mathieson, S.W. (Stockport)
Messias, M.D. (York)
Olivier, R. (Sutton Coldfield)
Pearson, R. (Peterlee, Durham)
Pierce, M.E. (Portsmouth)
Pike, M.S. (Barrow-in-Furness)

*Poll, G. (Tring, Hertfordshire)
Pugh, D. (Wirral)
*Reed, M.D. (Birmingham)
Rejer, P. (Leamington Spa)
*Rennie, U.D. (Sheffield)
Richards, P.R. (Preston)
*Riley, M.A. (Leeds)
Robinson, J.P. (Hull)
Singh, G. (Wolverhampton)
Stretton, F.G. (Nottingham)
Styles, R. (Waterlooville, Hants)
Taylor, P. (Cheshunt, Hertfordshire)
Walton, P. (Winwick, Northants)
Warren, M. (Walsall)
Wiley, A.G. (Burntwood, Staffs)
Wilkes, C.R. (Gloucester)
*Wilkie, A.B. (Chester-le-Street)
*Willard, G.S. (Worthing, W. Sussex)
*Winter, J.T. (Stockton-on-Tees)
Wolstenholme, E.K. (Blackburn)

*Denotes Premiership Referee.
#Denotes promotion to list for first time.

## ASSISTANT REFEREES

Adcock, D.J. (Long Eaton, Notts)
Armstrong, P. (Thatcham, Berks)
Artis, S.G. (Norwich)
Aston, G.A. (Kingswinford)
*Atkins, G. (Bradford)
Atkinson, M. (Leeds)
*Babski, D.S. (Scunthorpe)
Baker, B.L. (Warminster, Wilts)
Baker, L. (Watchet, Somerset)
Bannister, N. (Goole, E Yorks)
Barker, C.A. (York)
Barnes, K. (Swindon)
*#Barnes, P.W. (Peterborough)
Barston, P.S. (Loughborough)
*Bassindale, C. (Doncaster)
*#Beale, G.A. (Taunton)
Beeby, R.J. (Northampton)
Bello, B. (Manchester)
Bentley, I.F. (Mitcham, Surrey)
Bishop, M. (Southfleet, Kent)
Blanchard, I. (Hull)
*#Bone, R. (Orpington, Kent)
*Booth, D.A. (Barnsley)
Booth, R.J. (Sutton-in-Ashfleet, Notts)
Boyeson, D. (Hull)
Brammer, D.S. (Weston-super-Mare)
*Brand, S.R. (Wirral)
Brayne, R.E. (Harlow, Essex)
Brittain, G.M. (Doncaster)
Brown, A.R. (Preston)
*Bryan, D.S. (Stamford)
Buller, K.R. (Bridgwater)
*Burton, R. (Burton-on-Trent)
*Butler, A.N. (Wigan)
*#Cairns, M.J. (Coventry)
*#Canadine, P. (Rotherham)
Carter, J.E. (Sunderland)
Castle, S. (Wolverhampton)
Chittenden, S. (St Albans)
Clingo, S.G. (Downham Market, Norfolk)
Clyde, A.L. (Doncaster)
Cockwill, N.R. (Barnstaple, N. Devon)
Coffey, S. (Liverpool)
Conn, T. (Royston, Herts)
*#Cooper, M.A. (Walsall)
Cooper, R.J. (Tynemouth)
Coxhead, R. (Huntingdon, Cambs)
Curson, B. (Hinckley, Leics)
*Dearing, M.D. (Northolt, Middlesex)
Desmond, R.P. (Swindon)
*Devine, J.P. (Middlesbrough)
Dexter, M.C. (Thurmaston, Leics)
Downs, D.G. (Shefford, Beds)
*#Drysdale, D. (Lincoln)
Eastwood, P. (Manchester)
Ebbage, M. (Burnham, Bucks)
Edwards, C.D. (Oldham)
Ellicott, B.P. (Redditch)
Evans, E.M. (Manchester)
Evans, R.J. (Beckenham, Kent)
Foulkes, G.W. (Liverpool)
Francis, C.J. (Ely, Cambs)
*French, S.J. (Wolverhampton)
*Gagen, S.L. (New Malden, Surrey)
Garratt, A.M. (Walsall)
Garratt, L.P. (Southend)
Gosling, I.J. (Broomfield, Kent)
*Gould, R. (Swadlincote, Derbyshire)
*Green, A.J. (Hinckley, Leics)
*Green, N.E. (Stourport-on-Severn, Worcs)
Griffin, D.P. (Hornchurch, Essex)
Griffiths, S.J. (Macclesfield)
Habgood, S. (Chippenham, Wilts)
Hall, G.A. (Hixon, Nr Stafford

*Hall, M. (Whitley Bay)
*Hancox, N. (Walsall Wood, W. Midlands)
Harris, I.R. (Torpoint, Cornwall)
Harris, P.I. (Warrington)
Harteveld, A.C. (York)
Harvey, A.C. (Croxley Green, Herts)
Hawken, M. (St Austell)
*Hawkes, K.J. (Quedgeley, Glos)
Haxby, M.D. (New Brighton, Wirral)
Head, S. (Stokenchurch, Bucks)
Hegley, G.K. (Bishops Stortford)
Hills, C.J. (Ely, Cambs)
Hine, D.J. (Worcester)
*Hogg, A.S. (Sheffield)
*Holbrook, J.H. (Telford)
*Horlick, D.M. (Liverpool)
Horton, A.J. (Wolverhampton)
Howells, A.C. (Port Talbot)
Howes, T.P. (Norwich)
Hubbard, J.R. (Leicester)
Ingram, K.R. (Kingswinford)
Ives, G.L. (Hornchurch)
Ives, M. (Biggleswade, Beds)
James, R.G. (Milton Keynes)
Jones, C. (Pontypridd)
Jones, L.C. (Bournemouth)
Jones, N.L. (Plymouth)
*Joslin, P.J. (Newark)
Kasey, J.R. (Epsom)
*Kaye, A. (Wakefield)
Kellett, D.G. (Bradford)
Kettle, T.M. (Shrewsbury)
King, E.A. (Newmarket)
Lee, R. (Brentwood, Essex)
Leech, J. (Wigan)
Lewis, R.L. (Shrewsbury)
Lilley, S.J. (Bury St Edmunds)
Lockhart, R. (Newcastle-upon-Tyne)
McGee, A. (Knowsley)
McGirl, P.J. (Bedford)
*Martin, A.J. (Stafford)
Martin, E.A.C. (Williton, Somerset)
Martin, R.W. (Sheffield)
Mason, L.S. (Bolton)
Massey, T. (Stockport)
Maynard, M. (Hertford)
Maynard, R. (Bristol)
Mazonowicz, M. (Swindon)
Meads, C.J. (Wetherby)
Melin, P.W. (Frimley, Surrey)
Melinn, R.J. (Bridgwater, Somerset)
Mellor, G.S. (Kimberworth Park, S. Yorks)
Merchant, K. (West Ewell, Surrey)
Millership, B.T. (Atherstone, Warks)
*Morrall, D.A. (Sheffield)
Morrison, D.P. (Littleover, Derbys)
Mullarkey M. (Exeter)
Nicholson, A.R. (Halifax)
Nicholson, P.W. (Durham)
Nind, K.J. (Bromsgrove)
*#Norman, P.V. (Sherborne, Dorset)
*#North, M.J. (Bournemouth)
Oldham, A.B. (Poulton-le-Fylde, Lancs)
Oliver, C.W. (Ashington, Northumberland)
Parish, G.B. (Harlow)
Parker, K.E. (Hartlepool)
*#Parkes, T.A. (Birmingham)
Pashley, R.A. (Chesterfield)
Pawson, P.M. (Sheffield)
Payne, R.G. (Flitwick, Beds)
Peacock, D. (Redcar, Cleveland)
Pearce, J.E. (Dagenham)
Pearson, G.D. (Kidderminster)
Peeke, S. (Northfleet, Kent)
Penn, A.M. (Kingswinford)

Penton, C. (Woodingdean, E. Sussex)
Perkin, N.F. (Gravesend)
Perlejewski, A.J. (Ryme Instrinseca, Dorset)
*Pettitt, J.W. (Welling, Kent)
*Pike, K. (Gillingham, Dorset)
Pollard, T.J. (Bury St Edmunds)
Pollock, R.M. (Liverpool)
Postles, M.D. (Coneyhurst Common, W. Sussex)
Powell, K. (Hartlepool)
Probert, L.W. (Bridgwater)
*#Prosser, P.J. (Innsworth, Glos)
Rawcliffe, A. (Manchester)
Reynolds, K.S. (East Barnet)
*Richards, D.C. (Llanelli, Carmarthen)
Robinson, M.G. (Darlington)
*Ross, J.J. (London)
Rushton, G.N. (Nelson, Lancashire)
*Ryan, M. (Preston)
Salisbury, G. (Preston)
*Sharp, P.R. (St Albans)
Shaw, G. (Bramhall, Cheshire)
Shaw, I.D. (Crewe)
Shaw, M.A. (Macclesfield)
Shaw, W. (Blackburn)
*Sheffield, J.A. (Burntwood, Staffs)
*Short, M.L. (Grantham, Lincs)
Smith, A.N. (Castleford, W. Yorks)
Smith, J.P. (Stockport)
Smith, R.A. (Loughborough)
Smith, R.G. (Chelmsford)
Spicer, D.R. (Totten, Hampshire)
Stott, G.T. (Manchester)
Sygmuta, B.C. (Northallerton)
Tanner, S.J. (Bristol)
Tarry, E.J. (Manchester)
Taylor, J.T. (Blackburn)
Thiarra, S.S. (Bedford)
Thorpe, M. (Ipswich)
Tiffin, R. (Houghton-le-Spring)
Tincknell, S.W. (Watford)
Tingey, M. (High Wycombe, Bucks)
*Tomlin, S.G. (Lewes, E. Sussex)
*Toms, Mrs W. (Poole)
Torrance, K.R. (Camberley, Surrey)
Townsend, K.N. (Brierley Hills, W. Mids)
*#Turner, G.B. (Chesterfield)
Unsworth, D. (Bolton)
*Vosper, P.A. (London)
Wade, B. (Isle of Wight)
Wallace, G. (New Herrington, Tyne & Wear)
*Walsh, E.J. (Bromsgrove)
Ward, J. (Ferryhill, Co Durham)
Ward, R.B. (Milton Keynes)
Wardle, K. (Houghton-le-Spring)
Webb, A.J. (Winnersh, Berks)
*#Webb, H.M. (Rotherham)
Webster, C.H. (Chester-le-Street)
Whitby, D. (Liverpool)
Whitehouse, I. (Calne, Wiltshire)
Wilkins, A.M. (Longfield, Kent)
*Williams, M.A. (Hereford)
*Wing, P.B. (Burbage, Leics)
Wood, A.R. (Birkenhead)
Wood, D. (Harrogate)
Wood, D.R. (Liverpool)
Wood, P.M. (Fleetwood, Lancs)
Woodroffe, J.D. (Wicken, Cambs)
Woolmer, K.A. (Northampton)
Yates, N.A. (Blackburn)
Yerbey, M.S. (Ashford, Kent)
Zipfel, R.J. (Thetford, Norfolk)

*Premiership*
*#New to Premiership list*

# FOOTBALL AND THE LAW

Arsenal's most celebrated or best connected supporter, Dr George Carey, is otherwise known as the Lord Archbishop of Canterbury. On the eve of Euro '96 he explained in a House of Lords debate on *'Society's Moral and Spiritual well being'*,

'We take it for granted that you cannot play a game of football without rules. Rules do not get in the way of the game: they make it possible'.

For rules read Laws; and Laws include not only the Laws of Play but also the penal laws of punishment on and off the field of play. Duncan Ferguson broke the penal Laws of Play as well as the criminal Law of the land when he head butted an opponent during the course of play and was prosecuted to conviction.

Not surprisingly, but perhaps not well known within and also outside the game, is that Clause 4 of the English FA's professional footballer's contract provides

'The Player undertakes to adhere to the Laws of the Game of Association Football in matches in which he participates'.

Breaches of those Laws do not necessarily end in criminal or civil courts. Yet in the growing jungle law of commerce which clouds so much of all national and international sport, including football, it does not follow that even lawyers recognise the border lines between the two levels of playing and national regulations and their enforcement.

On the eve of the 1994 World Cup, one of the FA's leading legal advisers allowed himself in the solicitors' in house weekly journal, the *Law Society's Gazette*, to be described as a 'commercial litigator who spends nearly a third of his time handling contentious work for the FA'. He explained:

'A rule change to prevent the types of soccer injury suffered by Spurs centre back Gary Mabbutt and Torquay defender John Uzzell would be extraordinarily difficult to draft'.

Yet during the opening days of the following season 1994–95, Philip Don, England's World Cup referee, explained to Michael Parkinson in the *Daily Telegraph*

'The laws weren't changed. All that FIFA did was to remind referees of what their responsibilities are'.

Four years on FIFA left no doubt about what those responsibilities would be. Yet no competition within living memory has inspired so much controversy for law enforcement as did France '98. Sepp Blatter, FIFA's newly elected President was reported to be unhappy at the illegal tactics increasingly used by players during the finals.

'It is incredible how many players are using their hands to grab an opponent's shirt', he said.

'It is as if they have been signed up by companies as textile testers'.

He is also fed up with players diving, too.

'The laws of the game need to be applied, Referees please intervene'.

Yet putting aside the insoluble problem of harmonising the Laws of the Game's interpretations in more countries than comprise United Nations' membership, one key factor emerged crystallised by Paul Hayward in the *Daily Telegraph*:

'For all the froth over refereeing, the lives of the most skilful athletes have been improved by the determination of FIFA to eliminate professional thuggery. The wonder is that it has taken this long to acknowledge the simple truth that people pay to seen the good players run with the ball than the bad ones kick them as they do it.'

For those who were born after England won the World Cup in 1966, or have forgotten about it or never see Brian Glanville's Word Cup film *GOAL*, they may not know how England's victory was contributed to by the elimination from the tournament of Pele in the graphic account he has explained in *My Life and the Beautiful Game* (1977, Pele with Robert L. Fish (pages 144–145))

'. . . against Bulgaria . . . I had been the target of merciless attacks from Zechev of Bulgaria throughout the entire game. Zechev did everything he could physically to cripple me, and the referee, Jim Finney* gave neither me nor any of the others on our team the protection we had a right to expect from an official in a game'.

. . .

'Morais, of Portugal, had a field day fouling me, eventually putting me out of the game. He tripped me, and when I was stumbling to the ground he leaped at me, feet first, and cut me down completely. It wasn't until I actually saw the films of the game that I realised what a terribly vicious double-foul it was. The stands came to their feet screaming at the foul, but the English referee, George McCabe allowed Morais to remain on the field, although again, even in the most inexperienced league in the world, he would have been thrown out for either of the two fouls, let alone both. Dr Gosling and Mario Americo came to help me from the field, and Brazil went on to play with ten men and ended up eliminated from the tournament.'

* NB Jack Rollin, football's leading statistician and author of the *Guiness Book of Soccer Records*, in his *World Cup Triumph 1966* records the referee as Herr Tschenscher of West Germany. Pele's text is as cited above.

While the arguments will rage well into the next World Cup and beyond, and perhaps in perpetuity, it is worth looking back to 1966 and realising what would have happened in France '98 if FIFA had NOT implemented the mandatory red card to enforce the Law of the Game *ON* the field. For their breaches Pele's assassins in 1966 could have been prosecuted and sued in the criminal and civil courts on the evidence clearly seen in Glanville's film and corroborated by the testimony of the victim, cited above. For the Law of the Land does not stop at the touchline; and without the Rule of Law there is anarchy in society and chaos in sport.

EDWARD GRAYSON

# The FOOTBALL TRUST
## *Helping the game*

A major new funding package made up of annual contributions from the Football Association, the FA Premier League, the English Sports Council, the Football League and the Professional Footballers' Association and in Scotland from the Scottish Football Association and the Scottish Sports Council, has been added to the Trust's pools derived income. It will secure the future of the Trust and enable it to continue to grant aid football at every level.

Under the incoming Chairmanship of Tom Pendry MP, and backed by its new funding partners, the Trust will continue the vital grant support for professional clubs and ensure the Taylor programme is completed successfully at lower division clubs.

Newly appointed Pendry said: 'The Trust has a vital role in the game and no one should underestimate the important contribution it has made to British football. Thanks to our investment in stadium redevelopment, England successfully hosted a major international football championship for the first time in 30 years. The venues chosen for Euro '96 were excellent examples of the tremendous progress which has been made as a result of Taylor progress. This has seen new grounds at Chester, Millwall, Northampton, Middlesbrough, Huddersfield, Sunderland, Bolton, Derby and Stoke. Reading's new stadium at Smallmead is another while ten more clubs have ambitions to relocate.

'Over 150 new and refurbished stands in the Premier League, the Football League and the Scottish Football League were all made possible by Trust grants along with countless other vital stadium improvements.'

Pendry also stated that the Trust's role in ventures such as the 'Kick it Out' campaign against racism is important and will continue. 'Our unique position at the heart of the game will ensure that the Trust continues to give priority to these issues and help mould opinion within the game.'

The new chairman together with Chief Executive Peter Lee will aim to deliver fresh ideas to aid the national game. The Trust, stressed Pendry, is unique in that it brings closer all the football authorities in one body, reinforced now by the involvement of the Sports Councils of England and Scotland. 'We attach great importance to helping clubs develop modern training facilities for players of all ages and abilities in the local community. We are about a great deal more than bricks and mortar, we can handle grant aid programmes of every sort, including revenue grants in community involvement and player development.'

The Trust will endeavour to play an essential part in the game at all levels throughout the UK in conjunction with football authorities and Sports Councils. 'Making full use of our huge grant aid experience and expertise,' stressed Pendry.

**What Does It Do?**

- For 22 years now the Football Trust has been providing support for the game at EVERY level throughout the UK.
- The Trust's present priority task is to provide grant aid for new grounds and redevelopment work at FA Premier League and Football League grounds which helps clubs to implement the recommendations of the Taylor Report.
- Grants are also available for safety and improvement work throughout the Pyramid to the first division of the Football League, for closed circuit television, transport projects and community initiatives.
- The youngsters are not overlooked as the Trust also runs a joint grass roots scheme with the Football Association.

| Club | Trust grant (£) | Project cost (£) | Project |
|---|---|---|---|
| Airdrieonians | 1,250,000 | 4,750,000 | New stadium |
| Bolton Wanderers | 2,500,000 | 16,000,000 | New stadium |
| Bradford City | 652,800 | 1,360,000 | New Midland Road Stand |
| Brentford | 71,250 | 306,097 | Seating to the South Stand Paddock |
| Brentford | 160,000 | 222,000 | Redevelopment of North Stand |
| Darlington | 750,000 | 2,500,000 | New East Stand |
| Derby County | 2,500,000 | 19,500,000 | New Stadium |
| East Fife | 750,000 | 2,150,000 | New Stadium |
| Gillingham | 1,000,000 | 1,432,000 | New Gordon Road Stand |
| Hartlepool | 6,000 (additional grant offer) | 370,000 | Additional works, New Town End Stand |
| Leyton Orient | 750,000 | 3,800,000 | New South Stand |
| Livingston | 250,000 | 783,949 | Third Stand at Almondvale Stadium |
| Oxford United | 2,000,000 | 16,000,000 | New Stadium |
| Raith Rovers | 1,500,000 | 3,399,307 | Three new stands |
| Stockport County | 40,000 | 79,605 | Replacement seating, Main Stand |
| Stoke City | 2,500,000 | 13,624,524 | New Stadium |

BOB HENNESSY

# FOOTBALL CLUB CHAPLAINCY

In the early 1970s, a small number of clubs had friendly contact with local clergy who were available to perform 'religious duties' or to help in times of crisis. Thus the work of Revs. Mike Pusey (Aldershot), Jack Bingham (Stockport County), Michael Chantry (Oxford United) and the late John Jackson (Leeds United) laid the foundations for chaplaincy developments in British football.

Their involvement with secular sporting institutions paralleled chaplaincy links in other areas of society. In education, hospitals, prisons and the armed forces, the work of the chaplain or padre had become both recognised and valued. By the 1980s football was clearly opening up to similar involvements. Indeed, the work of the chaplain grew beyond that of a minister contactable in a crisis, or when a religious activity was called for.

Chaplaincy developed so that the chaplain became closely involved with the club, being known to players and non-playing staff alike. He became regarded as a friend of the club, a listening ear, one to go to when advice or counsel might be sought; one who seeks to care for the needy, hospitalised, bereaved, and troubled; one who is trustworthy, confidential, a non-threatening source of pastoral care and spiritual input.

As those clubs with chaplains spoke of the benefits of such appointments, the number of 'official chaplains' grew, so that now there are about seventy clubs with chaplains in the various leagues in the United Kingdom. Clearly the chaplain does not claim to help all the people all the time, but for some of the staff, for some of the time, his involvement is vitally important.

The chaplain tries to be concerned for all at the club: office staff, administrators, players, cleaners, YTS trainees, coaches, groundsmen, commercial staff, management, maintenance personnel, directors, and others connected with the club, not least the fans. The community of the club is the chaplain's parish, so to speak, and in that community needs emerge.

Thus he is available to those facing bereavement, hospitalisation, major surgery, personal crises or problems, family illness, the ending of a career, redundancy, problems with police, drugs, relationships or whatever. He listens in absolute confidence and supports appropriately. As well as being a trusted friend and an experienced counsellor, he also offers input in the vital spiritual areas of life.

## GREATER UNDERSTANDING

Fortunately, there is now a greater understanding of the chaplain's role. Clubs know he does not claim to be a potential miracle worker, offering up incantations for success at his particular club. Neither is he a hot-headed evangelist, imposing his beliefs on unwilling listeners. His job is to be a pastoral and spiritual safety net to the whole club, and to serve with absolute integrity.

Usually the chaplain has a regular time to visit the club—although the amount of time varies. Some give three or four hours, some give a whole day each week to the task. Each chaplain demonstrates his commitment differently, yet all have a deep concern for people. Each desires to be available to offer help and support—and more—to the club in helpful and appropriate ways.

In recent years the Football Club Chaplains have met for an Annual Conference at Lilleshall which has been generously sponsored by the Premier League. The chaplains have taken steps to establish a 'Football Chaplains' Association' which broadly is seeking to be a defined reference point for football chaplaincy and to promote high standards for chaplaincy work.

Chaplaincy is not about obtaining a ticket for a game, a title, or status. It is about real involvement, a job, a task, a responsibility. We believe it adds something of significance to the life of a football club, and believe the right clergyman, working wisely and appropriately, can bring great benefits to a club and its staff.

THE REV

## OFFICIAL CHAPLAINS TO FA PREMIERSHIP AND FOOTBALL LEAGUE CLUBS

Rev John Bingham—Chesterfield
Rev Richard Chewter—Exeter C
Rev Michael Lowe—AFC Bournemouth
Rev Andrew Taggart—Torquay U
Rev David Jeans—Sheffield W
Rev Nigel Sands—Crystal Palace
Rev Graham Spencer—Leicester C
Rev Philip Miller—Ipswich T
Rev Allen Bagshawe—Hull C
Rev David Tully—Newcastle U
Rev Derek Cleave—Bristol City
Rev Brian Rice—Hartlepool U
Revs Andy Cowley and John Graham—Watford
Rev Michael Chantry—Oxford U
Rev Michael Futens—Derby C
Rev Ken Hawkins—Birmingham C
Rev Simon Stevenette—Bristol R
Rev Cannon Michael Hunter—Grimsby T
Rev Chris Cullwick—York C
Rev Stephen Cooper—Middlesbrough
Rev Tony Porter—Manchester C
Fr Joe Jordan—Cardiff City
Fr Andrew McMahon—Southampton
Rev Henry Corbett and Rev Harry Ross—Everton
Rev Jeff Howden—Plymouth Argyle

Rev Mervyn Terrett—Luton T
Rev Peter Bye—Carlisle U
Rev David Langdon—QPR
Rev Gary Piper—Fulham
Rev Peter Amos—Barnsley
Rev Barry Kirk—Reading
Rev Martin Short—Bradford C
Rev John Boyers—Manchester U
Rev Martin Butt—Walsall
Rev Steve Riley and Capt Andrew Vertigan—Leeds U
Rev Fr Alan Poulter and Fr Gerald Courell—Tranmere R
Rev Mark Kichenside and Rev Jeffrey Heskins—Charlton Ath
Rev Owen Beament—Millwall
Rev Elwin Cockett—West Ham U
Rev Mick Woodhead—Sheffield U
Rev Alan Comfort—Leyton Orient
Rev John Hall-Matthews—Wolverhampton W
Rev Mark Cockayne—Doncaster R
Rev Ken Baker—Northampton T
Rev Steve Halliwell—Barnet
Rev Richard Havton—Gillingham
Rev Clive Andrews—Notts Co
Rev Chris Nelson—Preston North End
Rev Paul Brown—Wrexham
Major Graham Carey—Portsmouth

*The chaplains hope that those who read this page will see the value and benefit of chaplaincy work in football and will take appropriate steps to spread the word where this is possible. They would also like to thank the editors of the* Rothmans Yearbook *for their continued support for this specialist and growing area of work.*

*The following addresses may be helpful; SCORE (Sports Chaplaincy Offering Resources and Encouragement), PO Box 123, Sale, Manchester M33 4ZA and Christians in Sport, PO Box 93, Oxford OX2 7YP.*

# OBITUARIES

**Harry Adamson** (b Kelty 27.8.24; d Dunfermline 23.5.97). A half-back who signed for Notts County in August, 1946 and played 233 League matches, scoring five times, before leaving for non-League football in the mid-fifties.

**Brian Alderson** (b Dundee 5.5.50; d Atlanta, United States 23.4.97). Brian starred initially for Coventry City in the early seventies and will be fondly remembered as a pacy winger who made 127 League appearances for the Sky Blues, scoring 29 times. In July, 1975, he moved to Leicester City and scored nine goals in 90 League outings. He was also capped by Scotland at Under-23 level.

**Ivor Allchurch** (b Swansea 16.12.29; d Monmouth 10.5.97). A thorough gentleman on and off the pitch, Ivor was a superbly gifted player. An old fashioned inside forward, he won his first cap for Wales at 20 years of age and made a total of 68 international appearances between 1950 and 1966. Ivor's career began with his home town League club Swansea in 1947 and he gave wonderful service, playing 330 League games and scoring 124 goals. In October, 1958 he moved to Newcastle for £27,000, in those days a massive fee. At St James' Park he was a real crowd pleaser and hit 46 goals in 143 League appearances. In July, 1962 he returned to his native Wales and Cardiff City. In three seasons he had a further 103 League outings and scored 39 times before completing a magnificent career with Swansea City, whom he rejoined in July, 1965. At the Vetch he again passed the 100 League appearances mark (118 in total) and found the net on 42 occasions.

**William Allsop** (b Ripley 29.1.12; d Halifax 24.4.97). Bill began with Bolton Wanderers in the early thirties, but moved to Port Vale without making a League appearance. A full-back, he had just six outings with the Burslem club before joining Halifax Town in 1934, where he remained until 1947. He became skipper and went on to make 239 League appearances for Town either side of the Second World War, during which he gave great additional service, playing 232 times.

**Stan Anderson** (b 22.6.39; d 12.97). A half back who served Hamilton Academicals, Rangers, Queen of the South and Clyde between the late fifties and 1970. In his final season at Shawfield Park (1969–70), he helped the club avoid relegation from the old First Division by just four points.

**George Antonio** (b Whitchurch 20.10.14; d 2.7.97). George signed for Stoke City in 1936 and played for the Potters during and after the Second World War. During hostilities he guested for nine other clubs but continued playing for Stoke until 1947 when he joined Derby County. A forward, he also had spells in the late forties with Doncaster Rovers and Mansfield Town.

**David Bairstow** (b Bradford 1.9.51; d 5.1.98). A fine all round sportsman who played cricket for Yorkshire and England for whom he kept wicket. He was no mean footballer, either, and signed for his local club Bradford City in December, 1971. He played 17 League matches for City in the early seventies and scored once.

**Anatoly Banishevsky** (b Azerbaijan 1948; d 1998). A very talented forward who played for the USSR in the sixties and will be remembered by many for his contribution during the 1966 World Cup finals when he helped his country to finish fourth in the competition.

**Bobby Blackwood** (b Edinburgh 20.8.34; d 25.6.97). Bobby started out with Hearts in the early fifties and played in the Tynecastle club's title winning team of 1958. A year later he helped the club win the League Cup and in 1960 he played a starring role up front, hitting 12 goals as Hearts won the League once again. In June, 1962 he came south to join Alf Ramsey's Ipswich Town where he scored 11 goals in 62 League outings. In May, 1965 he signed for Colchester United and amassed 105 League appearances, scoring six times.

**Don Bradley** (b Clipstone 11.9.24; d 26.6.97). Defender Don began his career with West Bromwich Albion, but made no League appearances and departed to Mansfield Town in August, 1949. He served the Stags with unflagging loyalty until 1961 and amassed 385 League appearances and five goals.

**Billy Bremner** (b Stirling 9.12.42; d Doncaster 7.12.97). The combative midfield dynamo was the driving force behind the success story of Leeds United in the sixties and seventies. A truly inspirational figure, Billy gave wonderful service to the club he joined as a 17-year-old in 1959. Always determined in the tackle and no mean passer, he made his Leeds debut alongside Don Revie against Chelsea in 1960. In 1964, Billy won a Second Division Championship medal which was a prelude to two League Championship titles (1969 and 1974), an FA Cup winners' medal (1972) and two European Fairs Cup successes in 1968 and 1971. In 1970, Billy was awarded the Football Writers' Player of the Year. He won 54 caps for Scotland between 1965 and 1975. In 1976, after 586 League games and 92 goals, he joined Hull City for £35,000 and scored on his debut. In 1978, he left Boothferry Park to become manager of Doncaster Rovers and was at the helm for two successful promotion campaigns of 1981 and 1984. A year later he was offered the ultimate post, manager of his beloved Leeds United, then in the Second Division. He wasn't able to repeat his success at Doncaster, however, and was dismissed in 1988. He rejoined Doncaster in 1989, but parted company in 1992.

**Cliff Bryant** (b Bristol 6.8.13; d 2.12.97). A central defender, Cliff joined his local club Bristol Rovers in 1931, but only made one League appearance. The following year he was transferred to Blackburn Rovers, but four League appearances later he was on his way to Wrexham. Unfortunately the Second World War interrupted his career and he had only eight League outings.

**John Carruthers** (b Dumfries 2.8.26; d 14.9.97). John signed for Carlisle United in July, 1949, but only managed two League appearances on the right wing before he departed to Workington Town two years later. Three League games followed before he eventually became a highly successful scout for Ipswich Town and latterly Sunderland.

**Gordon Clark** (b Gainsborough 16.4.14; d 10.97). A full-back who played for Southend United and Manchester City before the outbreak of the Second World War. He moved to Ireland after hostilities and became player-manager of Waterford. His first outright managerial role was at Distillery, but in 1950 he took over the helm at Aldershot. Following a five year spell at the Recreation Ground, he accepted the post of assistant manager and chief scout at West Bromwich Albion. In 1959, he became boss at The Hawthorns. Two years later he became assistant manager of Sheffield Wednesday. 1964 saw him take the reins of Peterborough United, where he spent three years. In 1967 he was appointed chief scout at Arsenal and spent ten valuable years with the Gunners. He then had two spells as assistant manager of Fulham and Queens Park Rangers in 1977 and 1979 respectively.

**Fred Cutting** (b North Walsham 4.12.21; d 1997). A forward, Fred had spells with Leicester and Norwich before enjoying two seasons with Colchester United, their first as a League club (1950–51, 1951–52) in the old Third Division (South). In 29 League outings, he scored 12 goals.

**Zoltan Czibor** (b Komaron, Hungary 1929; d 1.9.97). A wonderful left or right winger with dazzling dribbling ability in the peerless Hungary team of the fifties. He won domestic honours with Ferencvaros, Honved and Barcelona as well as a Fairs Cup medal in 1960 with the Spanish giants. He made 42 appearances for the Hungarian national side and scored 19 times.

**Gordon Dale** (b Worksop 20.5.25; d 14.3.97). Gordon, a clever left-winger, began his League career with Chesterfield in February, 1948. After 91 League games and three goals, he signed for Portsmouth in 1951, a year after they had won back-to-back First Division Championships. He made 115 League appearances for Pompey and scored 18 goals before completing his career with Exeter City, whom he joined in October, 1957. He had a further 122 League outings with the Grecians and found the net eight times.

**Ray Daniel** (b Swansea 2.11.28; d 7.11.97). A cultured centre-half, Ray played for his home town side, Swansea during the war but after hostilities he joined Arsenal. He made 87 League appearances for the Gunners which incorporated the First Division Championship winning season of 1952–53. At the end of that season he made a shock move to Sunderland and had 137 League outings for the Wearsiders, scoring six times. In October, 1957 he returned to his native Wales, where he spent a brief spell with Cardiff before completing his League career with Swansea. In July, 1960 he accepted the player-manager's job at Hereford United where he remained until 1967. On the international front, Ray won 21 caps for Wales between 1951 and 1957.

**Mel Daniel** (b Llanelli 26.1.16; d 15.9.97). Like his son Alan, inside forward Mel began his League career with Luton Town. Between 1946 and 1949, he scored 20 goals in 53 appearances before completing his League career with Aldershot, where he had 28 outings and scored once.

**Cyril Dean** (b Bournemouth 1915; d 9.97). A forward who made 15 appearances and scored three goals for Reading in the late thirties. The Second World War interrupted his League career but he played wartime games for Fulham, Lincoln City and Millwall.

**Justin Fashanu** (b Hackney 19.2.61; d 2.5.98). A former Barnardo's boy, Justin began with Norwich City, signing in December, 1978 and was an immediate hit … finishing the 1979–80 season as the club's top scorer with 11 League goals. Norwich finished that campaign in 12th position, but in 1980–81 they were relegated to Division Two. Nevertheless, there was no stopping Justin, who was once again top of City's scorers, this time with 19 in the League, including a 20 minute hat-trick against Stoke City. Then there was a stunning long range goal against Liverpool that has been replayed on television countless times since. The goals prompted a £1 million move to Nottingham Forest in August, 1981, but only 3 goals in 32 League games saw him sold to Southampton a year later. Four months on and he was on the move again, this time to Notts County. In his first season 1982–83, he hit 11 goals in 32 League games, which became 20 in 64 matches until injury put paid to his career at County. He made a brave attempt at a comeback with Brighton in 1985–86, but after 16 games and 2 goals he crossed the Atlantic where he coached in Canada and California. Justin came back to the UK in 1989 and had short spells with Manchester City (2 games), West Ham (2 games) and Leyton Orient (5 games). He returned to Canada, but was back in 1991 to have an unsuccessful trial with Newcastle. He became assistant manager at Torquay United in 1991 and also had a successful season on the playing field, finishing top scorer with ten goals. He made a total of 41 League appearances for Torquay scoring 15 goals before leaving for Airdrie in February, 1993. At Broomfield Park, he had 16 outings and scored five times. The 1993–94 season saw him at Hearts, where he made 11 League appearances (1 goal), but he didn't complete the campaign, leaving for America to work as a coach. On the international front, Justin made 11 Under-21 appearances and won one England 'B' cap.

**Charlie Fleming** (b Blairhall 12.7.27; d 14.8.97). Charlie earned initial fame with East Fife for whom he scored 164 goals between 1947 and 1955. He won two League Cup winners' medals (1949–50, 1953–54) and a Scottish Cup runners-up medal in 1950. Charlie moved to Sunderland in January, 1955, but in 1953, before he journeyed south he won an international cap for Scotland against Ireland and scored twice in the 3-1 success. The goals continued to flow with the Rokerites … 62 in only 107 League appearances, a phenomenal return. Following his departure from Sunderland in 1958, he held player-manager positions with Bath City and Trowbridge Town.

**Henry Freeman** (b Woodstock 4.11.18; d 19.3.97). A full-back, Henry made 178 League appearances for Fulham, scoring six times, but his career with the Cottagers spanned the Second World War, following his debut in March, 1939. As well as serving in the Royal Fusiliers, he played for Fulham and guested for Northampton Town. When

Jimmy Hagan

Ivor Allchurch

normal football resumed after hostilities, Henry picked up where he left off and served Fulham until 1952. In October of that year he moved to Walsall before leaving the League circuit in 1953. Player-manager and coaching posts followed with Dover, Ashford United, Windsor and Eton, and Woodstock.

**Joseph Gardiner** (b Dearpark 23.8.16; d 1997). A defender for Wolves prior to the Second World War, Joe won a runners-up medal in the Wanderers side that Major Frank Buckley took to the FA Cup final in 1939. He made 121 League appearances and scored twice before becoming trainer at Molineux during the fifties. Joe later served Birmingham City in the same capacity.

**Jimmy Hagan** (b Washington, Co Durham 21.1.18; d 27.2.98). Jimmy signed for Derby on his 17th birthday in January, 1935, but didn't settle and joined Sheffield United in November, 1938 for £2,500. Hagan became a hero at Bramall Lane, being instrumental in the club's promotion to the First Division in 1939. It was such a pity that the war years interrupted his career. He still managed more than 400 appearances for United either side of hostilities. Although he won 16 wartime caps for England (he once scored after only 50 seconds against Scotland), he only won one official cap, versus Denmark in 1948. On the domestic front, United were relegated in 1949, but Jimmy's inspirational performances helped them win their place back in 1953. He retired in 1958 and became manager of Peterborough United, taking them into the Football League in 1960. He was dismissed in 1962, but was appointed manager of West Brom in 1963. At Albion, he won a League Cup final in 1965 and lost at the same stage of the competiton two years later. In March, 1970 he took the manager's job at Benfica and won the Portuguese title three seasons running. The League and Cup double was achieved in 1972. He left Benfica in September, 1973 and subsequently held coaching positions in Kuwait, Sporting Lisbon and Oporto.

**John Hampshire** (b Goldthorpe 5.10.13; d 23.5.97). Father of John and Alan Hampshire, who both became cricketers; John later a test match umpire. John (senior) played cricket for his native Yorkshire, but on the football front he started out with Manchester City before joining Bristol City in 1936. He had 21 League outings in two years with the Ashton Gate club prior to joining Bath City.

**Dennis Hatsell** (b Preston 9.6.30; d 1.1.98). A one club man who signed for his local side, North End, in June, 1948 and went on to make 115 League appearances as a centre forward, scoring 54 times. Dennis left Deepdale in 1960 to join Southern League Chelmsford City.

**Jimmy Heale** (b Bristol 1914; d 22.5.97). Jimmy was an inside left who began with Bristol City, signing on a professional basis in 1931. After 26 League games and eight goals, he moved to Manchester City in January, 1934. He didn't play in City's FA Cup final victory the same year, but still managed an impressive 39 goals in 86 League matches.

**Tommy Holmes** (b County Durham 1902; d 3.6.97). A wing-half who played 138 League matches for Southport between 1929 and the mid-thirties.

**Percy Hooper** (b 17.12.14; d 3.7.97). Percy kept goal for Tottenham Hotspur before the Second World War, signing in 1935. He had 97 League outings for Spurs, but in 1938 he played in a sixth round FA Cup-tie against Sunderland in which Spurs established their record attendance of 75,038 at White Hart Lane. In March, 1947, he signed for Swansea Town and played 12 League games before completing his career with a short spell at Chingford, then five years with King's Lynn.

**Robbie James** (b Swansea 23.3.57 d 18.2.98). The winner of 47 Welsh caps, Robbie collapsed and died while playing for Llanelli, the club he also managed. He found fame with his home town club, Swansea City, for whom he signed in April, 1974. and went on to make 394 League appearances, scoring 99 goals. Robbie was in the entertaining Swansea team that won promotion from the Second Division in 1980–81 and was then an integral part of the side that took the old First Division by storm the following season when their charismatic displays not only captured the imagination of the locals but the whole country as they took on the so-called 'big boys'. Arsenal, Liverpool and Manchester United all came a cropper at the Vetch Field during the 1981–82 season when Robbie finished as the club's leading goalscorer with 14 in the League and the Swans finished sixth in the table. In July, 1983, he moved to Stoke City, where he made 48 League appearances, scoring six times. He subsequently had almost three seasons (1984–87) with Queens Park Rangers (87 League outings, 4 goals), before spending part of the 1987–88 campaign with Leicester City (23 League games), then returned 'home' to Swansea for whom he had another 90 League outings (16 goals), before completing his first class career with Bradford and Cardiff City in the early nineties.

**Jack Jennings** (b Wigan 27.8.02; d 14.4.97). A defender, Jack started out with his local club Wigan Borough (they changed their name to Wigan Athletic in 1932), but moved to Cardiff City after three years. He had 93 outings with Cardiff before moving to Middlesbrough in 1930, where he made 195 League appearances and scored 10 goals. In 1937 he was off to Preston North End, but his stay was brief and a year later he was transferred to Bradford City, where injury terminated his League career.

**Arthur Jepson** (b Basford 12.7.15; d 17.7.97). Arthur was a cricketer for Nottinghamshire and later became a test umpire, but he also played two games for Mansfield Town in the thirties, had a short spell with non-League Grantham Town, then signed for Port Vale in 1938. After turning out for Port Vale, Nottingham Forest, Notts County, Swansea, Watford and York City during the war years, he signed for Stoke City in September, 1946. He had 28 League outings for the Potters before joining Lincoln City in December, 1948. He completed his career in 1950 having kept goal on 58 occasions for the Red Imps.

**Frank Joyner** (b St Andrews, Fife 20.8.18; d 25.4.97). A winger, Frank had a remarkable career which began with Raith Rovers in the late thirties and continued with Sheffield United shortly before the Second World War. With both Raith and United he was an integral part of two promotion winning sides and it was a great shame that the war interrupted his League career. During hostilities he guested for Third Lanark, Norwich and Chelsea, apart from serving in India and Burma. After the war he played for Dundee, Raith Rovers, Hamilton Academicals, Falkirk, Forfar and Stirling Albion.

**George Marks** (b Figheldean 9.4.15; d 1.2.98) So many players lost much of their first class careers to the Second World War, but George must have been one of the most unfortunate. He had just made the Arsenal first team, keeping goal at the tail end of the 1938–39 season, before being selected for the first four League matches at the outset of the 1939–40 campaign, when the war intervened. He was England's first choice goalkeeper during the war years, but a head injury against Wales terminated his unofficial international career. In August, 1946 he joined Blackburn Rovers and made 67 League appearances before moving to Bristol City two years later. His stay at Ashton Gate lasted only two months, because after only nine League outings he joined Reading, where he completed his first class career, making 128 League appearances.

**John Marsh** (b Mansfield 8.10.22; d 5.12.97). John was an inside forward who began with Notts County and played 42 League games, scoring 18 times between 1946 and 1948, the year in which he was transferred to Coventry City. At Highfield Road he had 20 League outings and hit six goals before a move to Leicester came in March, 1950. Four goals in 14 games followed, then he was off to Chesterfield, where he completed his League career with four strikes in 27 games.

**John (Jack) Marshall** (b Bolton 29.5.17; d 6.1.98). 'Jolly Jack', as he was known, was a full-back who joined Burnley in 1936, but had to retire through injury ten years later. He then had coaching spells with Bury and Stoke City before becoming trainer coach of Sheffield Wednesday in 1954. He was also England trainer in the late fifties and served Rochdale as manager between October, 1958 and June, 1960. Three months later he became boss at Blackburn Rovers, where he remained until 1967. He took over the helm at Sheffield Wednesday from February, 1968 until May, 1969, then moved on to Bury, but Jack lasted only seven matches before becoming physiotherapist at Blackburn Rovers, a post he was to remain in for ten years.

**Slava Metreveli** (b Russia 1937; d 1998). A member of the USSR side who finished fourth in the 1966 World Cup. Slava played his club football for Moscow Torpedo and Dynamo Tbilisi.

**Arthur Milne** (b Brechin 1915; d Edinburgh 5.97). Arthur started out with his local side Brechin Vics, and went on to play for Dundee United and Hibernian before war was declared. During hostilities he continued to play for Hibs and scored the winner against Rangers in the Scottish Summer Cup final. He also appeared in a Scotland side that played England at Wembley in 1944. After the war, he spent three years with St Mirren.

**Jimmy Milne** (b Dundee 24.1.11; d Hinckley 13.12.97). A half-back, Jimmy was initially with Dundee United, signing in 1931, but a year later he had moved to Preston North End for whom he gave loyal service, making 230 League appearances. In the 1933–34 season, he celebrated as North End won promotion from the Second Division as runners-up. Three years later he was playing at Wembley in the Cup final. During the war he played for Preston and Bury, then joined Wigan as player-manager in the 1946–47 season. He subsequently held a similar post at Morecambe, became a trainer with Doncaster Rovers, then returned to Preston in 1949, first as a trainer, then as manager in the early sixties, a position he occupied until 1968.

**Ian Moores** (b Chesterton 5.10.54; d 12.1.98). Ian signed for Stoke City in June, 1972, having served his apprenticeship at the Victoria Ground. A year after his debut in 1974, he won two England Under-23 caps, playing in a 2-0 victory over Wales, then a one-all draw with Czechoslovakia. In August, 1976 he moved to Tottenham for £75,000. Just over two years later, having played 29 League matches, he joined Orient for £55,000. At Brisbane Road he had 117 League outings and found the net 26 times. In July, 1982, Ian left East London for Bolton. His stay at Burnden Park was brief, 26 League games and three goals, which included a three match loan period with Barnsley. He departed from Bolton in 1983 to play in Cyprus, where he had five successful years. On returning to England in the late eighties, Ian signed for Southern League Tamworth and helped them win the FA Vase in 1989 by scoring in the replay of the final.

**Frank Moss** (b Birmingham 16.9.17; d 5.97). A centre-half, Frank signed for Sheffield Wednesday in 1935. After 22 League games, he joined Aston Villa in 1938, but only made two appearances for the club before the outbreak of war. Following hostilities, Frank resumed his career at Villa Park and made a further 288 League appearances until the mid-fifties.

**Jimmy Munro** (b Garmouth 25.3.26; d 22.6.97). Signed by Manchester City from Waterford in 1947, Jimmy scored 4 goals from his right-wing position in 25 games before he was snapped up by Oldham in June, 1950. He played in 119 League games for the Latics, scoring 21 times, then made a further 161 League appearances (24 goals) for Lincoln City between February, 1953 and January, 1958. He then moved to Bury where he scored 8 goals in 41 outings before leaving the League in 1959. Spells with Weymouth, Poole Town and Ely followed.

**Keith Newton** (b Manchester 23.6.41; d 6.98). This stylish full-back started out with Blackburn Rovers, starring in their FA Youth Cup winning side of 1959, having signed for the club in October, 1958. In an eleven year period at Ewood Park he played 306 League games and made 19 appearances for England before being transferred to Everton in December, 1969 for £80,000. A further eight caps followed while he was on Merseyside and, in his first season at Goodison, he won a Championship medal. Keith left Everton for Burnley in June, 1972 and secured a Second Division Championship medal the following year. He had 209 League outings in a Turf Moor career that he completed in the late seventies.

**Eddie Quigley** (b Bury 13.7.21; d 4.97). Eddie was once the most costly player in Britain, having been signed by Preston North End from Sheffield Wednesday for £26,500 in December, 1949. He was originally with Bury and scored five times against Millwall on the day of a positional switch from defender to centre-forward. He left the Shakers for Sheffield Wednesday in October, 1947, having scored 18 goals in 42 League appearances. At Hillsborough, he amassed 50 goals in 74 games in only two years and he was unfortunate to win only England 'B' honours following such a rich vein of form. It was therefore a major surprise when he was allowed to leave for Preston but, although he won a Second Division Championship medal with North End, the goals per game ratio was 17 in 52 matches and by November, 1951, Eddie had been snapped up by Blackburn Rovers. There was an immediate transformation – 92 goals in just 159 League games followed before he returned to Bury in August, 1956. He went on to manage Stockport County and Blackburn Rovers.

**Derek Rees** (b Swansea 18.2.34; d 4.98). An inside forward, Derek signed for Portsmouth in May, 1954, but found it difficult to secure a regular spot in a Pompey side that was going through a transitional period after so much success in the late forties and early fifties. During his three year stay at Fratton Park, he had 47 League outings and scored 15 times before a move to Ipswich came in May, 1957. He remained at Portman Road until the early sixties and in 90 League appearances scored 29 times.

**Jack Rigby** (b Leigh 29.7.24; d 1997). A defender with Manchester City between 1946 and 1953, Jack made 100 League appearances before leaving Maine Road for Peterborough United.

**Tommy Ring** (b Glasgow 8.3.30; d 10.97). Tommy starred on the wing for Clyde in the mid-fifties and played a major role in helping them to win the Scottish Cup in 1955, when they beat Celtic 1-0 after a replay. Tommy scored the goal and was a Cup winner again in 1958 with a victory over Hibernian. He won 12 caps for Scotland, the first against Sweden in 1953 and scored two goals at international level, versus Hungary in 1954, and against England at Wembley in 1957. When Clyde won the Second Division Championship in 1952 and again in 1957, Tommy passed the 20 goal mark on both occasions. He came south to Everton in 1960 and made 27 League appearances, scoring six times. He completed his Football League career at Barnsley, scoring once in 21 games, before finishing his playing career with Aberdeen.

**Jack Rowley** (b Wolverhampton 7.10.20; d 28.6.98). Brother of Arthur, Jack began with Bournemouth, but made his name with Manchester United in a ten year period following the second world war. In 317 League games, he hit 163 goals. Thirty of those helped United to secure the First Division Championship in 1951–52. Jack also bagged a brace in the 1948 Cup final victory over Blackpool. That same year he made his full England debut against Switzerland at Highbury and celebrated with a goal in the 6-0 rout. In November, 1949, he scored four times in England's 9-2 demolition of Northern Ireland at Maine Road and later the same month hit one of the two goals that helped defeat Italy 2-0 at White Hart Lane, to bring his international total to six goals in six appearances. In February, 1955, he went to Plymouth Argyle as Player-Manager and hit a further 14 goals for Argyle in 56 League outings.

**Bob Royston** (b Newcastle 1.12.15; d 2.97). Bob began with Sunderland in 1935 but left to join Southport the following year where he played 70 League matches in defence. He was transferred to Plymouth Argyle shortly before the outbreak of World War Two and resumed his Home Park career after hostilities, to take his total number of League appearances for Argyle to 39.

George Male

Billy Bremner

**Charlie Rundle** (b Fowey 17.1.23; d 28.6.97). Scored on his Spurs debut in 1946 and went on to hit 12 goals in 28 League games for Tottenham before a move to Crystal Palace in June, 1950. where he played 38 League games and scored twice.

**John Saunders** (b Worksop 1.12.50; d 4.1.98). John served five League clubs, beginning with Mansfield Town for whom he made his debut in 1969. 90 League games and two goals followed for the centre-half, before he moved to Huddersfield Town in October, 1972. At Leeds Road he made a further 121 League appearances, scoring once. He made his next move in December, 1975, but stayed in Yorkshire with Barnsley for whom he had 149 outings, found the net seven times, and skippered the Tykes to promotion to the Third Division in May, 1979. The following month he joined Lincoln City, but after 26 League games and one goal he made his fifth move to Doncaster Rovers, for whom he scored twice in 28 League games and helped the club to promotion to the Third Division in 1981.

**Jimmy Scoular** (b Livingston 11.1.25; d 19.3.98). The son of a miner, Jimmy became a steel-foundry worker on leaving school, but when he joined the Royal Navy in 1943 he was posted hundreds of miles from his Scottish home to a base outside Portsmouth. He signed for Pompey in December, 1945 and was part of the famous half-back line that included Reg Flewin and Jimmy Dickinson, a partnership that helped win back-to-back Championship titles in 1949 and 1950. While at Fratton Park, Jimmy won nine caps for Scotland and demonstrated the same gritty, fear-some tackling that was the hallmark of his game. He never gave up a seemingly lost cause and it was these qualities that persuaded Newcastle to pay £22,250 in June, 1953. He played 247 League games for Pompey, scoring eight times. At Newcastle Jimmy became skipper and led the side to victory in the 1955 FA Cup final. At St James' Park he amassed an identical number of League games – 247 – and scored six goals. In January, 1961, he accepted the position of player-manager at Bradford Park Avenue and had a further 108 League outings, scoring five times. He retired from playing in 1964 and took over as manager of Cardiff City the same year, a position he held until 1973. During that period the Ninian Park club won the Welsh Cup seven times and reached the semi-finals of the European Cup-winners' Cup in 1967–68. Under his guidance, the Bluebirds were a formidable Second Division side and he was a popular figurehead amongst the Cardiff faithful. With admirable wit they adopted the chorus of Handel's Messiah to sing his praises – Hallelujah, Jimmy Scoular!

**John Sheen** (b Airdrie 30.8.20; d 5.7.97). A half-back, John signed for Sheffield United before the Second World War, but only played for them during hostilities. He moved to Hull City in July, 1946 and scored once in five appearances for the Tigers.

**Peter Sillett** (b Southampton 1.2.33; d 14.3.98). Peter started out with his local club, Southampton, signing in June, 1950. An accomplished full-back, he played 60 League games (four goals) for the Saints and won England youth plus three Under-23 caps before a move to Chelsea in June, 1953. Two years later, he helped the Blues win the First Division Championship, to this date their one and only title success. In all he made 260 League appearances for Chelsea and scored 29 times. Days after celebrating the Championship, Peter made his full England debut against France, then had two further outings against Spain and Portugal. He also won an England 'B' cap and represented the Football League.

**David Smith** (b Durham 12.10.15; d 1.98). Dave, a right-winger, joined Newcastle United in the mid-thirties but only made one League appearance before the outbreak of war. He left St. James' Park for Northampton Town during hostilities and when the war ended he was a fixture in the Cobblers line-up until the early fifties, making 128 League appearances and scoring 30 goals. He went on to become secretary of the club in 1951 and manager three years later.

**Peter Springett** (b Fulham 8.5.46 d 30.9.97). The younger brother of former England goalkeper, Ron, Peter died following a brave four year battle with a crippling illness. He signed for Queens Park Rangers in May, 1963 and played 139 League matches in a four year period. During that time, he helped Rangers win a 'double' of the Third Division Championship and the League Cup final. No team from Division Three had previously won a Cup final at Wembley. In a matter of weeks after that success he was on his way to Sheffield Wednesday in a swap deal with his brother. Peter amassed 180 League outings with Wednesday and won six England Under-23 caps. In July, 1975 he joined Barnsley and helped the Tykes win promotion to Division Three in 1979.

**Hugh Turner** (b Wigan 6.8.04; d 1997). Hugh played in goal for Huddersfield in the late twenties and played in the 1930 FA Cup final against Arsenal, winning a runners-up medal. The following year he won an England cap and also played in a Football League representative side against the Irish League. After 364 League games, he left Huddersfield to join Fulham in 1937 and had 68 League outings for the Cottagers prior to the war.

**Reg Weston** (b 16.1.18; d 17.2.98). After leaving the navy, Reg joined Swansea in May, 1946 and went on to make 227 League appearances, scoring once. A dominating centre-half, he was skipper of the Swansea Town side that won the Third Division South title in 1948–49. During that campaign, that impressive Swans team won 17 successive home matches, a record for the club which is still intact. In October, 1953, Reg left Vetch Field to become player-manager of Derby County, but a year later, having not played a League game, he took a similar post with Burton Albion, where he saw out his playing career.

**John (Jack) Wharton** (b Bolton 18.6.20; d 5.97). Father of Terry Wharton (Wolves, Bolton, Crystal Palace and Walsall), Jack was an outside right who signed for Plymouth Argyle in the late thirties and scored twice on his debut. After ten League appearances he was snapped up by Preston North End, but had to resume his career after the war. Following 25 League outings and seven goals, he moved to Manchester City, but Jack was at Maine Road for little more than a year (23 League games and two goals) before he was signed by Blackburn Rovers in June, 1948. He enjoyed almost five years at Ewood Park, playing 129 League matches and finding the net on 15 occasions. In February, 1953, he joined Newport County where he scored a further ten times in 74 League outings.

**Brian Whittaker** (b Glasgow 23.9.56; d 8.9.97). A defender, Brian started out with Partick Thistle in the mid-seventies and had a total of 300 outings before joining Celtic in 1983. He played ten League matches for the Celts, scoring twice before moving to Hearts, where he had 162 League outings and won a runners-up medal in the 1986 Scottish Cup final. Brian completed his career in the early nineties with Falkirk for whom he had 31 League outings, which included a First Division Championship medal in 1991. He was tragically killed in a motor accident.

**Ron Wigg** (b Dunmow 18.5.49; d 7.97). A forward, Ron was an apprentice at Leyton Orient in the mid sixties, but was snapped up by Ipswich Town in April, 1967. In two seasons at Portman Road, he scored 14 times in 37 games before a move to Watford came in June, 1970. With the Vicarage Road club he hit 20 goals in 97 matches. In early 1973 Ron was off to Rotherham where 22 goals in 65 League outings followed. Less than two years later, in January, 1975, Grimsby secured his services and he produced 11 goals in 63 League games. Barnsley became Ron's fifth port of call in March, 1977 and he scored five times for the Tykes in 18 League matches. In October of that year, he completed his League career by signing for Scunthorpe, where he made 50 League appearances and found the net six times.

# THE FA CARLING PREMIERSHIP and NATIONWIDE FOOTBALL LEAGUE FIXTURES 1998–99

**Saturday August 8 1998**

**Nationwide Football League Division 1**
Barnsley v WBA
Bradford C v Stockport Co
Bristol C v Oxford U
Bury v Huddersfield T
Crystal Palace v Bolton W
Norwich C v Crewe Alex
Port Vale v Birmingham C
Portsmouth v Watford
Sheffield U v Swindon T
Sunderland v QPR
Wolverhampton W v Tranmere R

**Nationwide Football League Division 2**
AFC Bournemouth v Lincoln C
Burnley v Bristol R
Colchester U v Chesterfield
Gillingham v Walsall
Macclesfield T v Fulham
Manchester C v Blackpool
Northampton T v Stoke C
Oldham Ath v Notts Co
Preston NE v York C
Reading v Wrexham – POSTPONED
Wigan Ath v Millwall
Wrexham v Reading
Wycombe W v Luton T

**Nationwide Football League Division 3**
Brentford v Mansfield T
Carlisle U v Brighton & HA
Chester C v Leyton Orient
Darlington v Barnet
Hartlepool U v Cardiff C
Peterborough U v Halifax T
Plymouth Arg v Rochdale
Rotherham U v Hull C
Scarborough v Southend U
Shrewsbury T v Scunthorpe U
Swansea C v Exeter C
Torquay U v Cambridge U

**Sunday August 9 1998**
**Nationwide Football League Division 1**
Grimsby T v Ipswich T (4:00)

**Friday August 14 1998**
**Nationwide Football League Division 2**
Fulham v Manchester C

**Saturday August 15 1998**
**FA Carling Premiership**
Blackburn R v Derby Co
Coventry C v Chelsea
Everton v Aston Villa
Manchester U v Leicester C
Middlesbrough v Leeds U
Newcastle U v Charlton Ath
Sheffield W v West Ham U
Wimbledon v Tottenham H

**Nationwide Football League Division 1**
Bolton W v Grimsby T
Crewe Alex v Barnsley
Huddersfield T v Port Vale
Ipswich T v Bury
Oxford U v Wolverhampton W
QPR v Bristol C
Stockport Co v Norwich C
Swindon T v Sunderland

Tranmere R v Portsmouth
Watford v Bradford C
WBA v Sheffield U

**Nationwide Football League Division 2**
Blackpool v Oldham Ath
Bristol R v Reading
Chesterfield v Burnley
Lincoln C v Wigan Ath
Luton T v Preston NE
Millwall v Wycombe W
Notts Co v AFC Bournemouth
Stoke C v Macclesfield T
Walsall v Northampton T
Wrexham v Colchester U
York C v Gillingham

**Nationwide Football League Division 3**
Barnet v Hartlepool U
Brighton & HA v Chester C
Cambridge U v Swansea C
Cardiff C v Peterborough U
Exeter C v Scarborough
Halifax T v Brentford
Hull C v Darlington
Leyton Orient v Rotherham U
Mansfield T v Plymouth Arg
Rochdale v Torquay U
Scunthorpe U v Carlisle U
Southend U v Shrewsbury T

**Sunday August 16 1998**
**FA Carling Premiership**
Southampton v Liverpool (4:00)

**Nationwide Football League Division 1**
Birmingham C v Crystal Palace (1:00)

**Monday August 17 1998**
**FA Carling Premiership**
Arsenal v Nottingham F (8:00)

**Friday August 21 1998**
**Nationwide Football League Division 1**
Barnsley v Stockport Co

**Nationwide Football League Division 3**
Shrewsbury T v Cardiff C

**Saturday August 22 1998**
**FA Carling Premiership**
Charlton Ath v Southampton
Chelsea v Newcastle U
Derby Co v Wimbledon
Leicester C v Everton
Liverpool v Arsenal
Nottingham F v Coventry C
Tottenham H v Sheffield W
West Ham U v Manchester U

**Nationwide Football League Division 1**
Bristol C v Watford
Bury v Crewe Alex
Crystal Palace v Oxford U
Grimsby T v Huddersfield T
Norwich C v QPR
Port Vale v WBA
Portsmouth v Ipswich T
Sheffield U v Birmingham C
Sunderland v Tranmere R
Wolverhampton W v Swindon T

**Nationwide Football League Division 2**
AFC Bournemouth v Millwall
Burnley v York C
Colchester U v Fulham
Gillingham v Bristol R
Macclesfield T v Lincoln C
Manchester C v Wrexham
Northampton T v Notts Co
Oldham Ath v Chesterfield
Preston NE v Stoke C
Reading v Luton T
Wigan Ath v Blackpool
Wycombe W v Walsall

**Nationwide Football League Division 3**
Brentford v Brighton & HA
Carlisle U v Rochdale
Darlington v Halifax T
Hartlepool U v Scunthorpe U
Peterborough U v Southend U
Plymouth Arg v Barnet
Rotherham U v Cambridge U
Scarborough v Mansfield T
Swansea C v Leyton Orient
Torquay U v Exeter C (12:00)

**Sunday August 23 1998**
**FA Carling Premiership**
Aston Villa v Middlesbrough (4:00)

**Nationwide Football League Division 1**
Bradford C v Bolton W (1:00)

**Nationwide Football League Division 3**
Chester C v Hull C

**Monday August 24 1998**
**FA Carling Premiership**
Leeds U v Blackburn R (8:00)

**Friday August 28 1998**
**Nationwide Football League Division 1**
Crewe Alex v Bradford C
Watford v Wolverhampton W

**Nationwide Football League Division 3**
Halifax T v Shrewsbury T

**Saturday August 29 1998**
**FA Carling Premiership**
Arsenal v Charlton Ath
Blackburn R v Leicester C
Coventry C v West Ham U
Everton v Tottenham H
Middlesbrough v Derby Co
Sheffield W v Aston Villa
Southampton v Nottingham F
Wimbledon v Leeds U

**Nationwide Football League Division 1**
Birmingham C v Barnsley
Bolton W v Sheffield U
Huddersfield T v Portsmouth
Ipswich T v Sunderland (6:00)
Oxford U v Grimsby T
QPR v Bury
Stockport Co v Crystal Palace
Swindon T v Port Vale
Tranmere R v Bristol C
WBA v Norwich C

**Nationwide Football League Division 2**
Blackpool v Gillingham
Bristol R v Wigan Ath
Chesterfield v Reading
Fulham v AFC Bournemouth
Lincoln C v Preston NE
Luton T v Colchester U
Millwall v Macclesfield T
Notts Co v Manchester C
Stoke C v Oldham Ath
Walsall v Burnley
Wrexham v Northampton T
York C v Wycombe W

**Nationwide Football League Division 3**
Barnet v Brentford
Brighton & HA v Torquay U
Cambridge U v Hartlepool U
Cardiff C v Rotherham U
Exeter C v Carlisle U
Hull C v Peterborough U
Leyton Orient v Scarborough
Mansfield T v Swansea C
Rochdale v Darlington
Scunthorpe U v Plymouth Arg
Southend U v Chester C

**Sunday August 30 1998**
**FA Carling Premiership**
Newcastle U v Liverpool (4:00)

**Monday August 31 1998**
**Nationwide Football League Division 1**
Barnsley v Oxford U
Bradford C v Birmingham C
Bristol C v Huddersfield T
Bury v Swindon T
Crystal Palace v Tranmere R
Grimsby T v WBA
Port Vale v Ipswich T
Portsmouth v QPR
Sheffield U v Crewe Alex (8:00)
Sunderland v Watford
Wolverhampton W v Stockport Co

**Nationwide Football League Division 2**
Colchester U v Stoke C
Macclesfield T v Notts Co
Northampton T v Lincoln C (7:45)
Preston NE v Chesterfield
Wigan Ath v Luton T
Wycombe W v Bristol R

**Nationwide Football League Division 3**
Brentford v Rochdale
Darlington v Cardiff C
Hartlepool U v Hull C (12:00)
Peterborough U v Exeter C
Plymouth Arg v Halifax T
Rotherham U v Mansfield T (7:45)
Scarborough v Brighton & HA
Shrewsbury T v Barnet
Swansea C v Scunthorpe U

**Tuesday September 1 1998**
**Nationwide Football League Division 1**
Norwich C v Bolton W

**Nationwide Football League Division 2**
AFC Bournemouth v Blackpool
Burnley v Millwall
Gillingham v Wrexham
Oldham Ath v Fulham

**Nationwide Football League Division 3**
Carlisle U v Southend U
Chester C v Cambridge U (7:30)
Torquay U v Leyton Orient

**Wednesday September 2 1998**
**Nationwide Football League Division 2**
Manchester C v Walsall
Reading v York C

**Friday September 4 1998**
**Nationwide Football League Division 1**
Tranmere R v Bradford C

**Nationwide Football League Division 3**
Halifax T v Hartlepool U

**Saturday September 5 1998**
**Nationwide Football League Division 1**
Birmingham C v Bury
Bolton W v Port Vale
Crewe Alex v Sunderland
Huddersfield T v Sheffield U
Ipswich T v Wolverhampton W
QPR v Barnsley
Stockport Co v Grimsby T
Swindon T v Bristol C
Watford v Norwich C
WBA v Crystal Palace

**Nationwide Football League Division 2**
Blackpool v Northampton T
Bristol R v Preston NE
Chesterfield v Gillingham
Fulham v Wycombe W
Lincoln C v Oldham Ath
Luton T v Burnley
Millwall v Manchester C
Notts Co v Wigan Ath
Stoke C v AFC Bournemouth
Walsall v Reading
Wrexham v Macclesfield T
York C v Colchester U

**Nationwide Football League Division 3**
Barnet v Peterborough U
Brighton & HA v Swansea C
Cambridge U v Scarborough
Cardiff C v Plymouth Arg (12:15)
Exeter C v Chester C
Hull C v Brentford
Leyton Orient v Carlisle U
Mansfield T v Darlington
Rochdale v Shrewsbury T
Scunthorpe U v Torquay U
Southend U v Rotherham U

**Sunday September 6 1998**
**Nationwide Football League Division 1**
Oxford U v Portsmouth (1:00)

**Tuesday September 8 1998**
**FA Carling Premiership**
Charlton Ath v Manchester U –
POSTPONED
Leeds U v Southampton
Nottingham F v Everton

**Nationwide Football League Division 1**
Barnsley v Norwich C
Birmingham C v Stockport Co
Bury v Portsmouth
Crewe Alex v Crystal Palace
Huddersfield T v Watford
Ipswich T v Bradford C
Port Vale v Wolverhampton W
QPR v Tranmere R
Sheffield U v Grimsby T
Sunderland v Bristol C
WBA v Bolton W

**Nationwide Football League Division 2**
Blackpool v Notts Co (7:30)
Bristol R v Chesterfield
Fulham v Stoke C
Gillingham v Northampton T
Manchester C v AFC Bournemouth
Oldham Ath v Macclesfield T
Walsall v York C
Wigan Ath v Colchester U
Wrexham v Luton T (7:30)
Wycombe W v Preston NE

**Nationwide Football League Division 3**
Cardiff C v Barnet (7:30)

Carlisle U v Swansea C
Darlington v Hartlepool U (7:30)
Exeter C v Brighton & HA
Hull C v Rochdale (7:30)
Leyton Orient v Mansfield T
Peterborough U v Chester C
Rotherham U v Plymouth Arg
Scunthorpe U v Cambridge U (7:30)
Southend U v Halifax T
Torquay U v Brentford

**Wednesday September 9 1998**
**FA Carling Premiership**
Aston Villa v Newcastle U
Chelsea v Arsenal (8:00)
Derby Co v Sheffield W
Leicester C v Middlesbrough
Liverpool v Coventry C
Manchester U v Charlton Ath (8:00)
Tottenham H v Blackburn R
West Ham U v Wimbledon

**Nationwide Football League Division 1**
Swindon T v Oxford U

**Nationwide Football League Division 2**
Millwall v Lincoln C
Reading v Burnley

**Nationwide Football League Division 3**
Scarborough v Shrewsbury T (7:30)

**Friday September 11 1998**
**Nationwide Football League Division 1**
Tranmere R v Huddersfield T

**Nationwide Football League Division 3**
Halifax T v Cardiff C

**Saturday September 12 1998**
**FA Carling Premiership**
Aston Villa v Wimbledon
Charlton Ath v Derby Co
Chelsea v Nottingham F
Everton v Leeds U
Leicester C v Arsenal
Manchester U v Coventry C
Newcastle U v Southampton
Sheffield W v Blackburn R
West Ham U v Liverpool

**Nationwide Football League Division 1**
Bolton W v Birmingham C
Bradford C v Sheffield U
Bristol C v WBA
Crystal Palace v Port Vale
Grimsby T v Barnsley
Oxford U v Ipswich T
Portsmouth v Swindon T
Stockport Co v Crewe Alex
Watford v QPR
Wolverhampton W v Sunderland

**Nationwide Football League Division 2**
AFC Bournemouth v Wigan Ath
Burnley v Wycombe W
Chesterfield v Walsall
Colchester U v Gillingham
Lincoln C v Blackpool
Luton T v Bristol R
Macclesfield T v Manchester C
Northampton T v Oldham Ath
Notts Co v Fulham
Preston NE v Reading
Stoke C v Millwall
York C v Wrexham

**Nationwide Football League Division 3**
Barnet v Hull C
Brentford v Rotherham U
Brighton & HA v Southend U
Cambridge U v Leyton Orient
Chester C v Torquay U
Hartlepool U v Exeter C
Mansfield T v Carlisle U
Plymouth Arg v Darlington

Rochdale v Scunthorpe U
Shrewsbury T v Peterborough U
Swansea C v Scarborough

**Sunday September 13 1998**
**FA Carling Premiership**
Tottenham H v Middlesbrough (4:00)

**Nationwide Football League Division 1**
Norwich C v Bury (1:00)

**Friday September 18 1998**
**Nationwide Football League Division 2**
Walsall v Notts Co

**Saturday September 19 1998**
**FA Carling Premiership**
Coventry C v Newcastle U
Derby Co v Leicester C
Leeds U v Aston Villa
Liverpool v Charlton Ath
Middlesbrough v Everton
Nottingham F v West Ham U
Southampton v Tottenham H
Wimbledon v Sheffield W

**Nationwide Football League Division 1**
Barnsley v Crystal Palace
Birmingham C v Grimsby T
Bury v Tranmere R
Crewe Alex v Bolton W
Huddersfield T v Wolverhampton W
Ipswich T v Bristol C
Port Vale v Portsmouth
QPR v Stockport Co
Sheffield U v Norwich C
Sunderland v Oxford U
Swindon T v Watford

**Nationwide Football League Division 2**
Blackpool v Luton T
Bristol R v Lincoln C
Fulham v York C
Gillingham v Burnley
Manchester C v Chesterfield
Millwall v Northampton T
Oldham Ath v Preston NE
Reading v Colchester U
Wigan Ath v Macclesfield T
Wrexham v Stoke C
Wycombe W v AFC Bournemouth

**Nationwide Football League Division 3**
Cardiff C v Rochdale
Carlisle U v Chester C
Darlington v Shrewsbury T
Exeter C v Barnet
Hull C v Halifax T
Leyton Orient v Brighton & HA
Peterborough U v Plymouth Arg
Rotherham U v Hartlepool U
Scarborough v Brentford
Scunthorpe U v Mansfield T
Southend U v Cambridge U
Torquay U v Swansea C

**Sunday September 20 1998**
**FA Carling Premiership**
Arsenal v Manchester U (4:00)

**Nationwide Football League Division 1**
WBA v Bradford C (1:00)

**Monday September 21 1998**
**FA Carling Premiership**
Blackburn R v Chelsea (8:00)

**Friday September 25 1998**
**Nationwide Football League Division 1**
Tranmere R v Swindon T

**Saturday September 26 1998**
**FA Carling Premiership**
Aston Villa v Derby Co

Charlton Ath v Coventry C
Chelsea v Middlesbrough
Everton v Blackburn R
Manchester U v Liverpool (11:15)
Newcastle U v Nottingham F
Sheffield W v Arsenal
Tottenham H v Leeds U

**Nationwide Football League Division 1**
Bolton W v Huddersfield T
Bradford C v Barnsley
Bristol C v Crewe Alex
Grimsby T v Port Vale
Norwich C v Birmingham C
Oxford U v QPR
Portsmouth v Sunderland
Stockport Co v WBA
Watford v Ipswich T
Wolverhampton W v Bury

**Nationwide Football League Division 2**
AFC Bournemouth v Oldham Ath
Burnley v Wigan Ath
Chesterfield v Wrexham
Colchester U v Wycombe W
Lincoln C v Fulham
Luton T v Walsall
Macclesfield T v Reading
Northampton T v Manchester C
Notts Co v Millwall
Preston NE v Gillingham
Stoke C v Blackpool
York C v Bristol R

**Nationwide Football League Division 3**
Barnet v Rotherham U
Brentford v Darlington
Brighton & HA v Scunthorpe U
Cambridge U v Exeter C
Chester C v Cardiff C
Halifax T v Torquay U
Hartlepool U v Peterborough U
Mansfield T v Hull C
Plymouth Arg v Scarborough
Rochdale v Leyton Orient
Shrewsbury T v Carlisle U
Swansea C v Southend U

**Sunday September 27 1998**
**FA Carling Premiership**
Leicester C v Wimbledon (4:00)

**Nationwide Football League Division 1**
Crystal Palace v Sheffield U (1:00)

**Monday September 28 1998**
**FA Carling Premiership**
West Ham U v Southampton (8:00)

**Tuesday September 29 1998**
**Nationwide Football League Division 1**
Bolton W v Swindon T (8:00)
Bradford C v Port Vale
Bristol C v Barnsley
Grimsby T v Crewe Alex
Norwich C v Sunderland
Oxford U v WBA
Portsmouth v Birmingham C
Stockport Co v Huddersfield T
Tranmere R v Ipswich T
Watford v Sheffield U
Wolverhampton W v QPR

**Wednesday September 30 1998**
**Nationwide Football League Division 1**
Crystal Palace v Bury

**Saturday October 3 1998**
**FA Carling Premiership**
Blackburn R v West Ham U
Coventry C v Aston Villa
Derby Co v Tottenham H
Leeds U v Leicester C
Middlesbrough v Sheffield W
Nottingham F v Charlton Ath

Southampton v Manchester U
Wimbledon v Everton

**Nationwide Football League Division 1**
Barnsley v Bolton W
Birmingham C v Tranmere R
Bury v Bristol C
Crewe Alex v Wolverhampton W
Huddersfield T v Oxford U
Ipswich T v Crystal Palace
Port Vale v Norwich C
QPR v Grimsby T
Sheffield U v Portsmouth
Sunderland v Bradford C
Swindon T v Stockport Co

**Nationwide Football League Division 2**
Blackpool v York C
Bristol R v AFC Bournemouth
Fulham v Luton T
Gillingham v Macclesfield T
Manchester C v Burnley
Millwall v Chesterfield
Oldham Ath v Colchester U
Reading v Stoke C
Walsall v Preston NE
Wigan Ath v Northampton T
Wrexham v Lincoln C
Wycombe W v Notts Co

**Nationwide Football League Division 3**
Cardiff C v Brighton & HA
Carlisle U v Barnet
Darlington v Swansea C
Exeter C v Mansfield T
Hull C v Cambridge U
Leyton Orient v Hartlepool U
Peterborough U v Brentford
Rotherham U v Shrewsbury T
Scarborough v Chester C
Scunthorpe U v Halifax T
Southend U v Rochdale
Torquay U v Plymouth Arg (12:00)

**Sunday October 4 1998**
**FA Carling Premiership**
Arsenal v Newcastle U
Liverpool v Chelsea (4:00)

**Nationwide Football League Division 1**
WBA v Watford (1:00)

**Friday October 9 1998**
**Nationwide Football League Division 2**
Colchester U v Burnley

**Nationwide Football League Division 3**
Mansfield T v Torquay U

**Saturday October 10 1998**
**Nationwide Football League Division 1**
Bradford C v Bury
Bristol C v Portsmouth
Crewe Alex v WBA
Norwich C v Grimsby T
Oxford U v Tranmere R
QPR v Ipswich T
Stockport Co v Bolton W
Sunderland v Crystal Palace
Swindon T v Huddersfield T
Watford v Birmingham C
Wolverhampton W v Sheffield U

**Nationwide Football League Division 2**
Blackpool v Millwall
Fulham v Reading
Gillingham v Wycombe W
Macclesfield T v AFC Bournemouth
Manchester C v Preston NE
Northampton T v Bristol R
Notts Co v Lincoln C
Oldham Ath v Wigan Ath
Wrexham v Walsall
York C v Luton T

**Nationwide Football League Division 3**
Barnet v Chester C
Cambridge U v Brighton & HA
Carlisle U v Scarborough
Darlington v Peterborough U
Hartlepool U v Shrewsbury T
Hull C v Cardiff C
Leyton Orient v Exeter C
Plymouth Arg v Brentford
Rochdale v Halifax T
Scunthorpe U v Southend U
Swansea C v Rotherham U

**Sunday October 11 1998**

**Nationwide Football League Division 1**
Barnsley v Port Vale (1:00)

**Monday October 12 1998**

**Nationwide Football League Division 2**
Stoke C v Chesterfield (8:00)

**Friday October 16 1998**

**Nationwide Football League Division 3**
Halifax T v Barnet

**Saturday October 17 1998**

**FA Carling Premiership**
Arsenal v Southampton
Chelsea v Charlton Ath
Everton v Liverpool
Manchester U v Wimbledon
Middlesbrough v Blackburn R
Newcastle U v Derby Co
Nottingham F v Leeds U
West Ham U v Aston Villa

**Nationwide Football League Division 1**
Birmingham C v Crewe Alex
Bolton W v Oxford U
Bury v Stockport Co
Crystal Palace v Norwich C
Grimsby T v Bradford C
Huddersfield T v QPR
Ipswich T v Swindon T
Port Vale v Bristol C
Portsmouth v Wolverhampton W
Sheffield U v Barnsley
Tranmere R v Watford

**Nationwide Football League Division 2**
AFC Bournemouth v Northampton T
Bristol R v Wrexham
Burnley v Notts Co
Chesterfield v York C
Lincoln C v Stoke C
Luton T v Oldham Ath
Millwall v Fulham
Preston NE v Colchester U
Reading v Gillingham
Walsall v Blackpool
Wigan Ath v Manchester C
Wycombe W v Macclesfield T

**Nationwide Football League Division 3**
Brentford v Hartlepool U
Brighton & HA v Mansfield T
Cardiff C v Cambridge U
Chester C v Swansea C
Exeter C v Scunthorpe U
Peterborough U v Rochdale
Rotherham U v Darlington
Scarborough v Hull C
Shrewsbury T v Plymouth Arg
Southend U v Leyton Orient
Torquay U v Carlisle U

**Sunday October 18 1998**

**FA Carling Premiership**
Coventry C v Sheffield W (4:00)

**Nationwide Football League Division 1**
WBA v Sunderland (1:00)

**Monday October 19 1998**

**FA Carling Premiership**
Leicester C v Tottenham H (8:00)

**Tuesday October 20 1998**

**Nationwide Football League Division 1**
Birmingham C v Swindon T
Bolton W v Watford (8:00)
Bury v Oxford U
Crystal Palace v Wolverhampton W
Grimsby T v Bristol C
Ipswich T v Norwich C
Port Vale v Crewe Alex
Portsmouth v Bradford C
Sheffield U v Stockport Co
Tranmere R v Barnsley

**Nationwide Football League Division 2**
AFC Bournemouth v Gillingham
Bristol R v Stoke C
Burnley v Oldham Ath
Chesterfield v Notts Co
Lincoln C v Manchester C
Luton T v Northampton T
Preston NE v Macclesfield T
Walsall v Colchester U
Wigan Ath v Fulham
Wycombe W v Wrexham

**Nationwide Football League Division 3**
Brentford v Scunthorpe U
Brighton & HA v Plymouth Arg
Cardiff C v Leyton Orient (7:30)
Chester C v Hartlepool U (7:30)
Exeter C v Hull C
Halifax T v Cambridge U
Peterborough U v Carlisle U
Rotherham U v Rochdale
Shrewsbury T v Swansea C
Southend U v Mansfield T
Torquay U v Darlington

**Wednesday October 21 1998**

**Nationwide Football League Division 1**
Huddersfield T v Sunderland
WBA v QPR

**Nationwide Football League Division 2**
Millwall v York C
Reading v Blackpool

**Nationwide Football League Division 3**
Scarborough v Barnet (7:30)

**Friday October 23 1998**

**Nationwide Football League Division 1**
Bristol C v Bolton W

**Saturday October 24 1998**

**FA Carling Premiership**
Aston Villa v Leicester C
Charlton Ath v West Ham U
Derby Co v Manchester U
Liverpool v Nottingham F
Sheffield W v Everton
Southampton v Coventry C
Tottenham H v Newcastle U
Wimbledon v Middlesbrough

**Nationwide Football League Division 1**
Barnsley v Portsmouth
Bradford C v Crystal Palace
Crewe Alex v Tranmere R
Norwich C v Huddersfield T
Oxford U v Sheffield U
Stockport Co v Ipswich T
Sunderland v Bury
Swindon T v WBA
Watford v Port Vale
Wolverhampton W v Grimsby T

**Nationwide Football League Division 2**
Blackpool v Chesterfield
Colchester U v AFC Bournemouth
Fulham v Walsall

Gillingham v Luton T
Macclesfield T v Burnley
Manchester C v Reading
Northampton T v Preston NE
Notts Co v Bristol R
Oldham Ath v Wycombe W
Stoke C v Wigan Ath
Wrexham v Millwall
York C v Lincoln C

**Nationwide Football League Division 3**
Barnet v Brighton & HA
Cambridge U v Shrewsbury T
Carlisle U v Cardiff C
Darlington v Exeter C
Hartlepool U v Torquay U
Hull C v Southend U
Leyton Orient v Halifax T
Mansfield T v Peterborough U
Plymouth Arg v Chester C
Rochdale v Scarborough
Scunthorpe U v Rotherham U
Swansea C v Brentford

**Sunday October 25 1998**

**FA Carling Premiership**
Blackburn R v Arsenal (4:00)
Leeds U v Chelsea

**Nationwide Football League Division 1**
QPR v Birmingham C (1:00)

**Saturday October 31 1998**

**FA Carling Premiership**
Chelsea v Aston Villa
Coventry C v Arsenal
Derby Co v Leeds U
Everton v Manchester U
Leicester C v Liverpool
Newcastle U v West Ham U
Sheffield W v Southampton
Wimbledon v Blackburn R

**Nationwide Football League Division 1**
Birmingham C v Huddersfield T
Bradford C v Bristol C
Bury v Watford
Grimsby T v Crystal Palace
Ipswich T v WBA
Oxford U v Crewe Alex
Port Vale v Sheffield U
Portsmouth v Norwich C
Swindon T v QPR
Tranmere R v Stockport Co
Wolverhampton W v Barnsley

**Nationwide Football League Division 2**
AFC Bournemouth v Preston NE
Blackpool v Fulham
Bristol R v Walsall
Burnley v Wrexham
Lincoln C v Gillingham
Luton T v Chesterfield
Macclesfield T v Northampton T
Manchester C v Colchester U
Millwall v Oldham Ath
Notts Co v Stoke C
Wigan Ath v York C
Wycombe W v Reading

**Nationwide Football League Division 3**
Barnet v Rochdale
Brentford v Carlisle U
Brighton & HA v Hartlepool U
Cardiff C v Exeter C
Chester C v Shrewsbury T
Halifax T v Swansea C
Leyton Orient v Scunthorpe U
Mansfield T v Cambridge U
Peterborough U v Rotherham U
Plymouth Arg v Hull C
Scarborough v Torquay U
Southend U v Darlington

**Sunday November 1 1998**
**FA Carling Premiership**
Middlesbrough v Nottingham F (4:00)

**Nationwide Football League Division 1**
Bolton W v Sunderland (1:00)

**Monday November 2 1998**
**FA Carling Premiership**
Tottenham H v Charlton Ath 8:00)

**Friday November 6 1998**
**Nationwide Football League Division 2**
Colchester U v Macclesfield T

**Saturday November 7 1998**
**FA Carling Premiership**
Arsenal v Everton
Aston Villa v Tottenham H
Blackburn R v Coventry C
Charlton Ath v Leicester C
Liverpool v Derby Co
Nottingham F v Wimbledon
Southampton v Middlesbrough

**Nationwide Football League Division 1**
Barnsley v Bury
Bristol C v Wolverhampton W
Crewe Alex v Swindon T
Crystal Palace v Portsmouth
Huddersfield T v Ipswich T
Norwich C v Bradford C
QPR v Bolton W
Sheffield U v Tranmere R
Sunderland v Grimsby T
Watford v Oxford U
WBA v Birmingham C (12:00)

**Nationwide Football League Division 2**
Chesterfield v Lincoln C
Fulham v Bristol R
Gillingham v Wigan Ath
Northampton T v Wycombe W
Oldham Ath v Manchester C
Preston NE v Burnley
Reading v AFC Bournemouth
Stoke C v Luton T
Walsall v Millwall
Wrexham v Blackpool
York C v Notts Co

**Nationwide Football League Division 3**
Cambridge U v Barnet
Carlisle U v Halifax T
Darlington v Brighton & HA
Exeter C v Southend U
Hartlepool U v Plymouth Arg
Hull C v Leyton Orient
Rochdale v Mansfield T
Rotherham U v Scarborough
Scunthorpe U v Chester C
Shrewsbury T v Brentford
Swansea C v Peterborough U
Torquay U v Cardiff C

**Sunday November 8 1998**
**FA Carling Premiership**
Leeds U v Sheffield W (4:00)
Manchester U v Newcastle U
West Ham U v Chelsea

**Nationwide Football League Division 1**
Stockport Co v Port Vale (1:00)

**Tuesday November 10 1998**
**Nationwide Football League Division 2**
Bristol R v Blackpool
Burnley v Stoke C
Chesterfield v AFC Bournemouth
Colchester U v Northampton T
Gillingham v Oldham Ath
Luton T v Notts Co
Preston NE v Millwall
Walsall v Lincoln C
Wrexham v Fulham (7:30)

Wycombe W v Manchester C
York C v Macclesfield T

**Nationwide Football League Division 3**
Barnet v Scunthorpe U
Brentford v Southend U
Cardiff C v Scarborough (7:30)
Darlington v Carlisle U (7:30)
Halifax T v Chester C
Hartlepool U v Mansfield T (7:30)
Hull C v Brighton & HA (7:30)
Peterborough U v Cambridge U
Plymouth Arg v Swansea C
Rochdale v Exeter C
Rotherham U v Torquay U
Shrewsbury T v Leyton Orient

**Wednesday November 11 1998**
**Nationwide Football League Division 2**
Reading v Wigan Ath

**Saturday November 14 1998**
**FA Carling Premiership**
Arsenal v Tottenham H
Charlton Ath v Middlesbrough
Chelsea v Wimbledon
Liverpool v Leeds U
Manchester U v Blackburn R
Newcastle U v Sheffield W
Southampton v Aston Villa
West Ham U v Leicester C

**Nationwide Football League Division 1**
Barnsley v Ipswich T
Birmingham C v Oxford U
Bolton W v Tranmere R
Bradford C v Swindon T
Crewe Alex v QPR
Crystal Palace v Bristol C
Grimsby T v Portsmouth
Norwich C v Wolverhampton W
Port Vale v Sunderland
Sheffield U v Bury
Stockport Co v Watford
WBA v Huddersfield T

**Sunday November 15 1998**
**FA Carling Premiership**
Coventry C v Everton (4:00)

**Monday November 16 1998**
**FA Carling Premiership**
Nottingham F v Derby Co (8:00)

**Friday November 20 1998**
**Nationwide Football League Division 3**
Mansfield T v Barnet

**Saturday November 21 1998**
**FA Carling Premiership**
Aston Villa v Liverpool
Blackburn R v Southampton
Leeds U v Charlton Ath
Leicester C v Chelsea
Middlesbrough v Coventry C
Sheffield W v Manchester U
Tottenham H v Nottingham F
Wimbledon v Arsenal

**Nationwide Football League Division 1**
Bristol C v Stockport Co
Bury v Grimsby T
Huddersfield T v Bradford C
Ipswich T v Bolton W
Oxford U v Port Vale
Portsmouth v WBA
QPR v Sheffield U
Sunderland v Barnsley
Swindon T v Crystal Palace
Tranmere R v Norwich C
Watford v Crewe Alex

**Nationwide Football League Division 2**
AFC Bournemouth v Burnley
Blackpool v Preston NE

Fulham v Chesterfield
Lincoln C v Luton T
Macclesfield T v Walsall
Manchester C v Gillingham
Millwall v Bristol R
Northampton T v Reading
Notts Co v Colchester U
Oldham Ath v Wrexham
Stoke C v York C
Wigan Ath v Wycombe W

**Nationwide Football League Division 3**
Brighton & HA v Halifax T
Cambridge U v Darlington
Carlisle U v Rotherham U
Chester C v Rochdale
Exeter C v Shrewsbury T
Leyton Orient v Brentford
Scarborough v Hartlepool U
Scunthorpe U v Hull C
Southend U v Plymouth Arg
Torquay U v Peterborough U

**Sunday November 22 1998**
**FA Carling Premiership**
Derby Co v West Ham U (4:00)

**Nationwide Football League Division 1**
Wolverhampton W v Birmingham C (1:00)

**Nationwide Football League Division 3**
Swansea C v Cardiff C (12:00)

**Monday November 23 1998**
**FA Carling Premiership**
Everton v Newcastle U (8:00)

**Friday November 27 1998**
**Nationwide Football League Division 1**
Barnsley v Huddersfield T

**Nationwide Football League Division 3**
Halifax T v Mansfield T

**Saturday November 28 1998**
**FA Carling Premiership**
Charlton Ath v Everton
Chelsea v Sheffield W
Coventry C v Leicester C
Manchester U v Leeds U
Newcastle U v Wimbledon
Nottingham F v Aston Villa
Southampton v Derby Co
West Ham U v Tottenham H

**Nationwide Football League Division 1**
Birmingham C v Bristol C
Bolton W v Bury
Bradford C v QPR
Crewe Alex v Ipswich T
Crystal Palace v Watford
Grimsby T v Swindon T
Port Vale v Tranmere R
Sheffield U v Sunderland
Stockport Co v Portsmouth

**Nationwide Football League Division 2**
Bristol R v Oldham Ath
Burnley v Blackpool
Chesterfield v Macclesfield T
Colchester U v Millwall
Gillingham v Fulham
Luton T v Manchester C
Preston NE v Wigan Ath
Reading v Lincoln C
Walsall v AFC Bournemouth
Wrexham v Notts Co
Wycombe W v Stoke C
York C v Northampton T

**Nationwide Football League Division 3**
Barnet v Torquay U
Brentford v Chester C
Cardiff C v Southend U

Darlington v Scarborough
Hartlepool U v Swansea C
Hull C v Carlisle U
Peterborough U v Scunthorpe U
Plymouth Arg v Leyton Orient
Rochdale v Cambridge U
Rotherham U v Exeter C
Shrewsbury T v Brighton & HA

**Sunday November 29 1998**
**FA Carling Premiership**
Arsenal v Middlesbrough
Liverpool v Blackburn R (4:00)

**Nationwide Football League Division 1**
Norwich C v Oxford U (1:00)
WBA v Wolverhampton W (1:00)

**Saturday December 5 1998**
**FA Carling Premiership**
Aston Villa v Manchester U
Blackburn R v Charlton Ath
Derby Co v Arsenal
Everton v Chelsea
Leeds U v West Ham U
Leicester C v Southampton
Tottenham H v Liverpool
Wimbledon v Coventry C

**Nationwide Football League Division 1**
Bristol C v Sheffield U
Bury v WBA
Huddersfield T v Crystal Palace
Ipswich T v Birmingham C
Oxford U v Bradford C
Portsmouth v Crewe Alex
QPR v Port Vale
Sunderland v Stockport Co
Swindon T v Norwich C
Tranmere R v Grimsby T
Watford v Barnsley
Wolverhampton W v Bolton W

**Sunday December 6 1998**
**FA Carling Premiership**
Middlesbrough v Newcastle U (4:00)

**Monday December 7 1998**
**FA Carling Premiership**
Sheffield W v Nottingham F (8:00)

**Friday December 11 1998**
**Nationwide Football League Division 1**
Bury v Sheffield U

**Nationwide Football League Division 3**
Brighton & HA v Rotherham U
(8:00)
Mansfield T v Shrewsbury T

**Saturday December 12 1998**
**FA Carling Premiership**
Aston Villa v Arsenal
Blackburn R v Newcastle U
Derby Co v Chelsea
Everton v Southampton
Leicester C v Nottingham F
Middlesbrough v West Ham U
Sheffield W v Charlton Ath
Tottenham H v Manchester U

**Nationwide Football League Division 1**
Bristol C v Crystal Palace
Huddersfield T v WBA
Ipswich T v Barnsley
Oxford U v Birmingham C
QPR v Crewe Alex
Sunderland v Port Vale
Swindon T v Bradford C
Tranmere R v Bolton W
Watford v Stockport Co
Wolverhampton W v Norwich C

**Nationwide Football League Division 2**
AFC Bournemouth v York C

Blackpool v Wycombe W
Fulham v Burnley
Lincoln C v Colchester U
Macclesfield T v Luton T
Manchester C v Bristol R
Millwall v Reading
Northampton T v Chesterfield
Notts Co v Preston NE
Oldham Ath v Walsall
Stoke C v Gillingham
Wigan Ath v Wrexham

**Nationwide Football League Division 3**
Cambridge U v Plymouth Arg
Carlisle U v Hartlepool U
Chester C v Darlington
Exeter C v Brentford
Leyton Orient v Peterborough U
Scarborough v Halifax T
Scunthorpe U v Cardiff C
Southend U v Barnet
Swansea C v Rochdale
Torquay U v Hull C

**Sunday December 13 1998**
**FA Carling Premiership**
Wimbledon v Liverpool (4:00)

**Nationwide Football League Division 1**
Portsmouth v Grimsby T (1:00)

**Monday December 14 1998**
**FA Carling Premiership**
Leeds U v Coventry C (8:00)

**Wednesday December 16 1998**
**FA Carling Premiership**
Manchester U v Chelsea (8:00)

**Friday December 18 1998**
**Nationwide Football League Division 2**
Bristol R v Macclesfield T
Colchester U v Blackpool

**Nationwide Football League Division 3**
Rotherham U v Chester C
Shrewsbury T v Torquay U

**Saturday December 19 1998**
**FA Carling Premiership**
Chelsea v Tottenham H
Coventry C v Derby Co
Liverpool v Sheffield W
Manchester U v Middlesbrough
Newcastle U v Leicester C
Nottingham F v Blackburn R
Southampton v Wimbledon
West Ham U v Everton

**Nationwide Football League Division 1**
Barnsley v Swindon T
Birmingham C v Sunderland
Bolton W v Portsmouth
Bradford C v Wolverhampton W
Crewe Alex v Huddersfield T
Crystal Palace v QPR
Grimsby T v Watford
Norwich C v Bristol C
Port Vale v Bury
Stockport Co v Oxford U
WBA v Tranmere R

**Nationwide Football League Division 2**
Burnley v Northampton T
Chesterfield v Wigan Ath
Gillingham v Notts Co
Luton T v Millwall
Preston NE v Fulham
Reading v Oldham Ath
Walsall v Stoke C
Wrexham v AFC Bournemouth
Wycombe W v Lincoln C
York C v Manchester C

**Nationwide Football League Division 3**
Barnet v Leyton Orient
Brentford v Cambridge U
Cardiff C v Mansfield T
Darlington v Scunthorpe U
Halifax T v Exeter C
Hartlepool U v Southend U
Hull C v Swansea C
Peterborough U v Scarborough
Plymouth Arg v Carlisle U
Rochdale v Brighton & HA

**Sunday December 20 1998**
**FA Carling Premiership**
Arsenal v Leeds U (4:00)

**Nationwide Football League Division 1**
Sheffield U v Ipswich T (1:00)

**Monday December 21 1998**
**FA Carling Premiership**
Charlton Ath v Aston Villa (8:00)

**Saturday December 26 1998**
**FA Carling Premiership**
Arsenal v West Ham U (12:00)
Blackburn R v Aston Villa (6:00)
Coventry C v Tottenham H
Everton v Derby Co
Manchester U v Nottingham F
Middlesbrough v Liverpool
Newcastle U v Leeds U
Sheffield W v Leicester C
Southampton v Chelsea
Wimbledon v Charlton Ath (12:00)

**Nationwide Football League Division 1**
Birmingham C v Sheffield U
Bolton W v Bradford C
Crewe Alex v Bury
Huddersfield T v Grimsby T
Ipswich T v Portsmouth
Oxford U v Crystal Palace
QPR v Norwich C (12:00)
Stockport Co v Barnsley
Swindon T v Wolverhampton W
Tranmere R v Sunderland
Watford v Bristol C (12:00)
WBA v Port Vale (1:00)

**Nationwide Football League Division 2**
Blackpool v Wigan Ath
Bristol R v Gillingham
Chesterfield v Oldham Ath
Fulham v Colchester U (12:00)
Lincoln C v Macclesfield T
Luton T v Reading (12:00)
Millwall v AFC Bournemouth (12:00)
Notts Co v Northampton T
Stoke C v Preston NE
Walsall v Wycombe W
Wrexham v Manchester C
York C v Burnley

**Nationwide Football League Division 3**
Barnet v Plymouth Arg (1:30)
Brighton & HA v Brentford (12:00)
Cambridge U v Rotherham U
Cardiff C v Shrewsbury T
Exeter C v Torquay U (11:00)
Halifax T v Darlington
Hull C v Chester C
Leyton Orient v Swansea C (1:30)
Mansfield T v Scarborough
Rochdale v Carlisle U
Scunthorpe U v Hartlepool U
Southend U v Peterborough U

**Monday December 28 1998**
**FA Carling Premiership**
Aston Villa v Sheffield W
Charlton Ath v Arsenal
Derby Co v Middlesbrough
Leicester C v Blackburn R
Liverpool v Newcastle U

Nottingham F v Southampton
Tottenham H v Everton
West Ham U v Coventry C

**Nationwide Football League Division 1**
Barnsley v QPR
Bradford C v Tranmere R
Bristol C v Swindon T
Bury v Birmingham C
Crystal Palace v WBA
Grimsby T v Stockport Co
Port Vale v Bolton W
Portsmouth v Oxford U
Sheffield U v Huddersfield T
Sunderland v Crewe Alex
Wolverhampton W v Ipswich T (1:00)

**Nationwide Football League Division 2**
AFC Bournemouth v Luton T
Burnley v Lincoln C
Colchester U v Bristol R
Macclesfield T v Blackpool
Manchester C v Stoke C
Northampton T v Fulham
Oldham Ath v York C
Preston NE v Wrexham
Reading v Notts Co
Wigan Ath v Walsall
Wycombe W v Chesterfield

**Nationwide Football League Division 3**
Brentford v Cardiff C
Carlisle U v Cambridge U
Chester C v Mansfield T
Darlington v Leyton Orient
Hartlepool U v Rochdale
Peterborough U v Brighton & HA
Plymouth Arg v Exeter C
Rotherham U v Halifax T (12:00)
Scarborough v Scunthorpe U
Shrewsbury T v Hull C
Swansea C v Barnet
Torquay U v Southend U

**Tuesday December 29 1998**
**FA Carling Premiership**
Chelsea v Manchester U (8:00)
Leeds U v Wimbledon

**Nationwide Football League Division 1**
Norwich C v Watford

**Nationwide Football League Division 2**
Gillingham v Millwall

**Saturday January 2 1999**
**Nationwide Football League Division 2**
AFC Bournemouth v Fulham
Burnley v Walsall
Colchester U v Luton T
Gillingham v Blackpool
Macclesfield T v Millwall
Manchester C v Notts Co
Northampton T v Wrexham
Oldham Ath v Stoke C
Preston NE v Lincoln C
Reading v Chesterfield
Wigan Ath v Bristol R
Wycombe W v York C

**Nationwide Football League Division 3**
Brentford v Barnet
Carlisle U v Exeter C
Chester C v Southend U
Darlington v Rochdale
Hartlepool U v Cambridge U
Peterborough U v Hull C
Plymouth Arg v Scunthorpe U
Rotherham U v Cardiff C
Scarborough v Leyton Orient
Shrewsbury T v Halifax T
Swansea C v Mansfield T
Torquay U v Brighton & HA

**Saturday January 9 1999**
**FA Carling Premiership**
Arsenal v Liverpool
Blackburn R v Leeds U
Coventry C v Nottingham F
Everton v Leicester C
Manchester U v West Ham U
Middlesbrough v Aston Villa
Newcastle U v Chelsea
Sheffield W v Tottenham H
Southampton v Charlton Ath
Wimbledon v Derby Co

**Nationwide Football League Division 1**
Birmingham C v Port Vale
Bolton W v Crystal Palace
Crewe Alex v Norwich C
Huddersfield T v Bury
Ipswich T v Grimsby T
Oxford U v Bristol C
QPR v Sunderland
Stockport Co v Bradford C
Swindon T v Sheffield U
Tranmere R v Wolverhampton W
Watford v Portsmouth
WBA v Barnsley

**Nationwide Football League Division 2**
Blackpool v Manchester C
Bristol R v Burnley
Chesterfield v Colchester U
Fulham v Macclesfield T
Lincoln C v AFC Bournemouth
Luton T v Wycombe W
Millwall v Wigan Ath
Notts Co v Oldham Ath
Reading v Wrexham
Stoke C v Northampton T
Walsall v Gillingham
Wrexham v Reading – POSTPONED
York C v Preston NE

**Nationwide Football League Division 3**
Barnet v Darlington
Brighton & HA v Carlisle U
Cambridge U v Torquay U
Cardiff C v Hartlepool U
Exeter C v Swansea C
Halifax T v Peterborough U
Hull C v Rotherham U
Leyton Orient v Chester C
Mansfield T v Brentford
Rochdale v Plymouth Arg
Scunthorpe U v Shrewsbury T
Southend U v Scarborough

**Friday January 15 1999**
**Nationwide Football League Division 2**
Colchester U v Wrexham

**Saturday January 16 1999**
**FA Carling Premiership**
Aston Villa v Everton
Charlton Ath v Newcastle U
Chelsea v Coventry C
Derby Co v Blackburn R
Leeds U v Middlesbrough
Leicester C v Manchester U
Liverpool v Southampton
Nottingham F v Arsenal
Tottenham H v Wimbledon
West Ham U v Sheffield W

**Nationwide Football League Division 1**
Barnsley v Birmingham C
Bradford C v Crewe Alex
Bristol C v Tranmere R
Bury v QPR
Crystal Palace v Stockport Co
Grimsby T v Oxford U
Norwich C v WBA
Port Vale v Swindon T
Portsmouth v Huddersfield T
Sheffield U v Bolton W
Sunderland v Ipswich T
Wolverhampton W v Watford

**Nationwide Football League Division 2**
AFC Bournemouth v Notts Co
Burnley v Chesterfield
Gillingham v York C
Macclesfield T v Stoke C
Manchester C v Fulham
Northampton T v Walsall
Oldham Ath v Blackpool
Preston NE v Luton T
Reading v Bristol R
Wigan Ath v Lincoln C
Wycombe W v Millwall

**Nationwide Football League Division 3**
Brentford v Halifax T
Carlisle U v Scunthorpe U
Chester C v Brighton & HA
Darlington v Hull C
Hartlepool U v Barnet
Peterborough U v Cardiff C
Plymouth Arg v Mansfield T
Rotherham U v Leyton Orient
Scarborough v Exeter C
Shrewsbury T v Southend U
Swansea C v Cambridge U
Torquay U v Rochdale

**Saturday January 23 1999**
**Nationwide Football League Division 2**
Blackpool v AFC Bournemouth
Bristol R v Wycombe W
Chesterfield v Preston NE
Fulham v Oldham Ath
Lincoln C v Northampton T
Luton T v Wigan Ath
Millwall v Burnley
Notts Co v Macclesfield T
Stoke C v Colchester U
Walsall v Manchester C
Wrexham v Gillingham
York C v Reading

**Nationwide Football League Division 3**
Barnet v Shrewsbury T
Brighton & HA v Scarborough
Cambridge U v Chester C
Cardiff C v Darlington
Exeter C v Peterborough U
Halifax T v Plymouth Arg
Hull C v Hartlepool U
Leyton Orient v Torquay U
Mansfield T v Rotherham U
Rochdale v Brentford
Scunthorpe U v Swansea C
Southend U v Carlisle U

**Saturday January 30 1999**
**FA Carling Premiership**
Arsenal v Chelsea
Blackburn R v Tottenham H
Charlton Ath v Manchester U
Coventry C v Liverpool
Everton v Nottingham F
Manchester U v Charlton Ath –
POSTPONED
Middlesbrough v Leicester C
Newcastle U v Aston Villa
Sheffield W v Derby Co
Southampton v Leeds U
Wimbledon v West Ham U

**Nationwide Football League Division 1**
Birmingham C v Bradford C
Bolton W v Norwich C
Crewe Alex v Sheffield U
Huddersfield T v Bristol C
Ipswich T v Port Vale
Oxford U v Barnsley
QPR v Portsmouth
Stockport Co v Wolverhampton W
Swindon T v Bury
Tranmere R v Crystal Palace
Watford v Sunderland
WBA v Grimsby T

**Nationwide Football League Division 2**
Blackpool v Macclesfield T
Bristol R v Colchester U
Chesterfield v Wycombe W
Fulham v Northampton T
Lincoln C v Burnley
Luton T v AFC Bournemouth
Millwall v Gillingham
Notts Co v Reading
Stoke C v Manchester C
Walsall v Wigan Ath
Wrexham v Preston NE
York C v Oldham Ath

**Nationwide Football League Division 3**
Barnet v Swansea C
Brighton & HA v Peterborough U
Cambridge U v Carlisle U
Cardiff C v Brentford
Exeter C v Plymouth Arg
Halifax T v Rotherham U
Hull C v Shrewsbury T
Leyton Orient v Darlington
Mansfield T v Chester C
Rochdale v Hartlepool U
Scunthorpe U v Scarborough
Southend U v Torquay U

**Friday February 5 1999**
**Nationwide Football League Division 2**
Colchester U v York C

**Nationwide Football League Division 3**
Swansea C v Brighton & HA

**Saturday February 6 1999**
**FA Carling Premiership**
Aston Villa v Blackburn R
Charlton Ath v Wimbledon
Chelsea v Southampton
Derby Co v Everton
Leeds U v Newcastle U
Leicester C v Sheffield W
Liverpool v Middlesbrough
Nottingham F v Manchester U
Tottenham H v Coventry C
West Ham U v Arsenal

**Nationwide Football League Division 1**
Barnsley v Crewe Alex
Bradford C v Watford
Bristol C v QPR
Bury v Ipswich T
Crystal Palace v Birmingham C
Grimsby T v Bolton W
Norwich C v Stockport Co
Port Vale v Huddersfield T
Portsmouth v Tranmere R
Sheffield U v WBA
Sunderland v Swindon T
Wolverhampton W v Oxford U

**Nationwide Football League Division 2**
AFC Bournemouth v Stoke C
Burnley v Luton T
Gillingham v Chesterfield
Macclesfield T v Wrexham
Manchester C v Millwall
Northampton T v Blackpool
Oldham Ath v Lincoln C
Preston NE v Bristol R
Reading v Walsall
Wigan Ath v Notts Co
Wycombe W v Fulham

**Nationwide Football League Division 3**
Brentford v Hull C
Carlisle U v Leyton Orient
Chester C v Exeter C
Darlington v Mansfield T
Hartlepool U v Halifax T
Peterborough U v Barnet
Plymouth Arg v Cardiff C
Rotherham U v Southend U
Scarborough v Cambridge U
Shrewsbury T v Rochdale
Torquay U v Scunthorpe U

**Friday February 12 1999**
**Nationwide Football League Division 2**
Colchester U v Wigan Ath

**Saturday February 13 1999**
**FA Carling Premiership**
Aston Villa v Leeds U
Charlton Ath v Liverpool
Chelsea v Blackburn R
Everton v Middlesbrough
Leicester C v Derby Co
Manchester U v Arsenal
Newcastle U v Coventry C
Sheffield W v Wimbledon
Tottenham H v Southampton
West Ham U v Nottingham F

**Nationwide Football League Division 1**
Bolton W v WBA
Bradford C v Ipswich T
Bristol C v Sunderland
Crystal Palace v Crewe Alex
Grimsby T v Sheffield U
Norwich C v Barnsley
Oxford U v Swindon T
Portsmouth v Bury
Stockport Co v Birmingham C
Tranmere R v QPR
Watford v Huddersfield T
Wolverhampton W v Port Vale

**Nationwide Football League Division 2**
AFC Bournemouth v Manchester C
Burnley v Reading
Chesterfield v Bristol R
Lincoln C v Millwall
Luton T v Wrexham
Macclesfield T v Oldham Ath
Northampton T v Gillingham
Notts Co v Blackpool
Preston NE v Wycombe W
Stoke C v Fulham
York C v Walsall

**Nationwide Football League Division 3**
Barnet v Cardiff C
Brentford v Torquay U
Brighton & HA v Exeter C
Cambridge U v Scunthorpe U
Chester C v Peterborough U
Halifax T v Southend U
Hartlepool U v Darlington
Mansfield T v Leyton Orient
Plymouth Arg v Rotherham U
Rochdale v Hull C
Shrewsbury T v Scarborough
Swansea C v Carlisle U

**Saturday February 20 1999**
**FA Carling Premiership**
Arsenal v Leicester C
Blackburn R v Sheffield W
Coventry C v Manchester U
Derby Co v Charlton Ath
Leeds U v Everton
Liverpool v West Ham U
Middlesbrough v Tottenham H
Nottingham F v Chelsea
Southampton v Newcastle U
Wimbledon v Aston Villa

**Nationwide Football League Division 1**
Barnsley v Grimsby T
Birmingham C v Bolton W
Bury v Norwich C
Crewe Alex v Stockport Co
Huddersfield T v Tranmere R
Ipswich T v Oxford U
Port Vale v Crystal Palace
QPR v Watford
Sheffield U v Bradford C
Sunderland v Wolverhampton W
Swindon T v Portsmouth
WBA v Bristol C

**Nationwide Football League Division 2**
Blackpool v Lincoln C
Bristol R v Luton T
Fulham v Notts Co
Gillingham v Colchester U
Manchester C v Macclesfield T
Millwall v Stoke C
Oldham Ath v Northampton T
Reading v Preston NE
Walsall v Chesterfield
Wigan Ath v AFC Bournemouth
Wrexham v York C
Wycombe W v Burnley

**Nationwide Football League Division 3**
Cardiff C v Halifax T
Carlisle U v Mansfield T
Darlington v Plymouth Arg
Exeter C v Hartlepool U
Hull C v Barnet
Leyton Orient v Cambridge U
Peterborough U v Shrewsbury T
Rotherham U v Brentford
Scarborough v Swansea C
Scunthorpe U v Rochdale
Southend U v Brighton & HA
Torquay U v Chester C

**Saturday February 27 1999**
**FA Carling Premiership**
Aston Villa v Coventry C
Charlton Ath v Nottingham F
Chelsea v Liverpool
Everton v Wimbledon
Leicester C v Leeds U
Manchester U v Southampton
Newcastle U v Arsenal
Sheffield W v Middlesbrough
Tottenham H v Derby Co
West Ham U v Blackburn R

**Nationwide Football League Division 1**
Bolton W v Crewe Alex
Bradford C v WBA
Bristol C v Ipswich T
Crystal Palace v Barnsley
Grimsby T v Birmingham C
Norwich C v Sheffield U
Oxford U v Sunderland
Portsmouth v Port Vale
Stockport Co v QPR
Tranmere R v Bury
Watford v Swindon T
Wolverhampton W v Huddersfield T

**Nationwide Football League Division 2**
AFC Bournemouth v Wycombe W
Burnley v Gillingham
Chesterfield v Manchester C
Colchester U v Reading
Lincoln C v Bristol R
Luton T v Blackpool
Macclesfield T v Wigan Ath
Northampton T v Millwall
Notts Co v Walsall
Preston NE v Oldham Ath
Stoke C v Wrexham
York C v Fulham

**Nationwide Football League Division 3**
Barnet v Exeter C
Brentford v Scarborough
Brighton & HA v Leyton Orient
Cambridge U v Southend U
Chester C v Carlisle U
Halifax T v Hull C
Hartlepool U v Rotherham U
Mansfield T v Scunthorpe U
Plymouth Arg v Peterborough U
Rochdale v Cardiff C
Shrewsbury T v Darlington
Swansea C v Torquay U

**Tuesday March 2 1999**
**Nationwide Football League Division 1**
Barnsley v Bradford C

Birmingham C v Norwich C
Bury v Wolverhampton W
Crewe Alex v Bristol C
Huddersfield T v Bolton W
Ipswich T v Watford
Port Vale v Grimsby T
Sheffield U v Crystal Palace
Sunderland v Portsmouth
WBA v Stockport Co

**Wednesday March 3 1999**
**Nationwide Football League Division 1**
QPR v Oxford U
Swindon T v Tranmere R

**Saturday March 6 1999**
**FA Carling Premiership**
Arsenal v Sheffield W
Blackburn R v Everton
Coventry C v Charlton Ath
Derby Co v Aston Villa
Leeds U v Tottenham H
Liverpool v Manchester U
Middlesbrough v Chelsea
Nottingham F v Newcastle U
Southampton v West Ham U
Wimbledon v Leicester C

**Nationwide Football League Division 1**
Barnsley v Bristol C
Birmingham C v Portsmouth
Bury v Crystal Palace
Crewe Alex v Grimsby T
Huddersfield T v Stockport Co
Ipswich T v Tranmere R
Port Vale v Bradford C
QPR v Wolverhampton W
Sheffield U v Watford
Sunderland v Norwich C
Swindon T v Bolton W
WBA v Oxford U

**Nationwide Football League Division 2**
Blackpool v Stoke C
Bristol R v York C
Fulham v Lincoln C
Gillingham v Preston NE
Manchester C v Northampton T
Millwall v Notts Co
Oldham Ath v AFC Bournemouth
Reading v Macclesfield T
Walsall v Luton T
Wigan Ath v Burnley
Wrexham v Chesterfield
Wycombe W v Colchester U

**Nationwide Football League Division 3**
Cardiff C v Chester C
Carlisle U v Shrewsbury T
Darlington v Brentford
Exeter C v Cambridge U
Hull C v Mansfield T
Leyton Orient v Rochdale
Peterborough U v Hartlepool U
Rotherham U v Barnet
Scarborough v Plymouth Arg
Scunthorpe U v Brighton & HA
Southend U v Swansea C
Torquay U v Halifax T

**Tuesday March 9 1999**
**Nationwide Football League Division 1**
Bolton W v Barnsley (8:00)
Bradford C v Sunderland
Bristol C v Bury
Crystal Palace v Ipswich T
Grimsby T v QPR
Norwich C v Port Vale
Oxford U v Huddersfield T
Portsmouth v Sheffield U
Stockport Co v Swindon T
Tranmere R v Birmingham C
Watford v WBA
Wolverhampton W v Crewe Alex

**Nationwide Football League Division 2**
AFC Bournemouth v Bristol R
Burnley v Manchester C
Chesterfield v Millwall
Colchester U v Oldham Ath
Lincoln C v Wrexham
Luton T v Fulham
Macclesfield T v Gillingham
Northampton T v Wigan Ath
Notts Co v Wycombe W
Preston NE v Walsall
York C v Blackpool

**Nationwide Football League Division 3**
Barnet v Carlisle U
Brentford v Peterborough U
Cambridge U v Hull C
Chester C v Scarborough (7:30)
Halifax T v Scunthorpe U
Hartlepool U v Leyton Orient (7:30)
Mansfield T v Exeter C
Plymouth Arg v Torquay U
Rochdale v Southend U
Shrewsbury T v Rotherham U
Swansea C v Darlington

**Wednesday March 10 1999**
**Nationwide Football League Division 2**
Stoke C v Reading

**Nationwide Football League Division 3**
Brighton & HA v Cardiff C (8:00)

**Friday March 12 1999**
**Nationwide Football League Division 2**
Bristol R v Fulham

**Saturday March 13 1999**
**FA Carling Premiership**
Chelsea v West Ham U
Coventry C v Blackburn R
Derby Co v Liverpool
Everton v Arsenal
Leicester C v Charlton Ath
Middlesbrough v Southampton
Newcastle U v Manchester U
Sheffield W v Leeds U
Tottenham H v Aston Villa
Wimbledon v Nottingham F

**Nationwide Football League Division 1**
Birmingham C v WBA
Bolton W v QPR
Bradford C v Norwich C
Bury v Barnsley
Grimsby T v Sunderland
Ipswich T v Huddersfield T
Oxford U v Watford
Port Vale v Stockport Co
Portsmouth v Crystal Palace
Swindon T v Crewe Alex
Tranmere R v Sheffield U
Wolverhampton W v Bristol C

**Nationwide Football League Division 2**
AFC Bournemouth v Reading
Blackpool v Wrexham
Burnley v Preston NE
Lincoln C v Chesterfield
Luton T v Stoke C
Macclesfield T v Colchester U
Manchester C v Oldham Ath
Millwall v Walsall
Notts Co v York C
Wigan Ath v Gillingham
Wycombe W v Northampton T

**Nationwide Football League Division 3**
Barnet v Cambridge U
Brentford v Shrewsbury T
Brighton & HA v Darlington
Cardiff C v Torquay U
Chester C v Scunthorpe U
Halifax T v Carlisle U
Leyton Orient v Hull C
Mansfield T v Rochdale

Peterborough U v Swansea C
Plymouth Arg v Hartlepool U
Scarborough v Rotherham U
Southend U v Exeter C

**Saturday March 20 1999**
**FA Carling Premiership**
Arsenal v Coventry C
Aston Villa v Chelsea
Blackburn R v Wimbledon
Charlton Ath v Tottenham H
Leeds U v Derby Co
Liverpool v Leicester C
Manchester U v Everton
Nottingham F v Middlesbrough
Southampton v Sheffield W
West Ham U v Newcastle U

**Nationwide Football League Division 1**
Barnsley v Wolverhampton W
Bristol C v Bradford C
Crewe Alex v Oxford U
Crystal Palace v Grimsby T
Huddersfield T v Birmingham C
Norwich C v Portsmouth
QPR v Swindon T
Sheffield U v Port Vale
Stockport Co v Tranmere R
Sunderland v Bolton W
Watford v Bury
WBA v Ipswich T

**Nationwide Football League Division 2**
Chesterfield v Luton T
Colchester U v Manchester C
Fulham v Blackpool
Gillingham v Lincoln C
Northampton T v Macclesfield T
Oldham Ath v Millwall
Preston NE v AFC Bournemouth
Reading v Wycombe W
Stoke C v Notts Co
Walsall v Bristol R
Wrexham v Burnley
York C v Wigan Ath

**Nationwide Football League Division 3**
Cambridge U v Mansfield T
Carlisle U v Brentford
Darlington v Southend U
Exeter C v Cardiff C
Hartlepool U v Brighton & HA
Hull C v Plymouth Arg
Rochdale v Barnet
Rotherham U v Peterborough U
Scunthorpe U v Leyton Orient
Shrewsbury T v Chester C
Swansea C v Halifax T
Torquay U v Scarborough

**Friday March 26 1999**
**Nationwide Football League Division 3**
Halifax T v Leyton Orient

**Saturday March 27 1999**
**Nationwide Football League Division 1**
Birmingham C v QPR
Bolton W v Bristol C
Bury v Sunderland
Crystal Palace v Bradford C
Grimsby T v Wolverhampton W
Huddersfield T v Norwich C
Ipswich T v Stockport Co
Port Vale v Watford
Portsmouth v Barnsley
Sheffield U v Oxford U
Tranmere R v Crewe Alex
WBA v Swindon T

**Nationwide Football League Division 2**
AFC Bournemouth v Colchester U
Bristol R v Notts Co
Burnley v Macclesfield T
Chesterfield v Blackpool
Lincoln C v York C
Luton T v Gillingham

Millwall v Wrexham
Preston NE v Northampton T
Reading v Manchester C
Walsall v Fulham
Wigan Ath v Stoke C
Wycombe W v Oldham Ath

**Nationwide Football League Division 3**
Brentford v Swansea C
Brighton & HA v Barnet
Cardiff C v Carlisle U
Chester C v Plymouth Arg
Exeter C v Darlington
Peterborough U v Mansfield T
Rotherham U v Scunthorpe U
Scarborough v Rochdale
Shrewsbury T v Cambridge U
Southend U v Hull C
Torquay U v Hartlepool U

**Friday April 2 1999**
**Nationwide Football League Division 2**
Colchester U v Preston NE (3:00)
Northampton T v AFC Bournemouth
(7:45)
Oldham Ath v Luton T (3:30)

**Saturday April 3 1999**
**FA Carling Premiership**
Aston Villa v West Ham U
Blackburn R v Middlesbrough
Charlton Ath v Chelsea
Derby Co v Newcastle U
Leeds U v Nottingham F
Liverpool v Everton
Sheffield W v Coventry C
Southampton v Arsenal
Tottenham H v Leicester C
Wimbledon v Manchester U

**Nationwide Football League Division 1**
Barnsley v Sheffield U
Bradford C v Grimsby T
Bristol C v Port Vale
Crewe Alex v Birmingham C
Norwich C v Crystal Palace
Oxford U v Bolton W
QPR v Huddersfield T
Stockport Co v Bury
Sunderland v WBA
Swindon T v Ipswich T
Watford v Tranmere R
Wolverhampton W v Portsmouth

**Nationwide Football League Division 2**
Blackpool v Walsall
Fulham v Millwall
Gillingham v Reading
Macclesfield T v Wycombe W
Manchester C v Wigan Ath
Notts Co v Burnley
Stoke C v Lincoln C
Wrexham v Bristol R
York C v Chesterfield

**Nationwide Football League Division 3**
Barnet v Halifax T
Cambridge U v Cardiff C
Carlisle U v Torquay U
Darlington v Rotherham U
Hartlepool U v Brentford
Hull C v Scarborough
Leyton Orient v Southend U
Mansfield T v Brighton & HA
Plymouth Arg v Shrewsbury T
Rochdale v Peterborough U
Scunthorpe U v Exeter C
Swansea C v Chester C

**Monday April 5 1999**
**FA Carling Premiership**
Chelsea v Leeds U
Coventry C v Southampton
Everton v Sheffield W
Manchester U v Derby Co
Middlesbrough v Wimbledon

Newcastle U v Tottenham H
Nottingham F v Liverpool
West Ham U v Charlton Ath

**Nationwide Football League Division 1**
Birmingham C v Watford
Bolton W v Stockport Co
Bury v Bradford C
Crystal Palace v Sunderland
Grimsby T v Norwich C
Huddersfield T v Swindon T
Ipswich T v QPR
Port Vale v Barnsley
Portsmouth v Bristol C
Sheffield U v Wolverhampton W
Tranmere R v Oxford U
WBA v Crewe Alex

**Nationwide Football League Division 2**
Bristol R v Northampton T
Burnley v Colchester U
Chesterfield v Stoke C
Lincoln C v Notts Co
Millwall v Blackpool
Preston NE v Manchester C
Reading v Fulham
Wigan Ath v Oldham Ath
Wycombe W v Gillingham

**Nationwide Football League Division 3**
Brentford v Plymouth Arg
Cardiff C v Hull C
Chester C v Barnet
Exeter C v Leyton Orient
Halifax T v Rochdale
Peterborough U v Darlington
Rotherham U v Swansea C
Scarborough v Carlisle U
Shrewsbury T v Hartlepool U
Southend U v Scunthorpe U (7:45)
Torquay U v Mansfield T

**Tuesday April 6 1999**
**FA Carling Premiership**
Arsenal v Blackburn R
Leicester C v Aston Villa

**Nationwide Football League Division 2**
AFC Bournemouth v Macclesfield T
Luton T v York C
Walsall v Wrexham

**Nationwide Football League Division 3**
Brighton & HA v Cambridge U (8:00)

**Friday April 9 1999**
**Nationwide Football League Division 3**
Swansea C v Shrewsbury T

**Saturday April 10 1999**
**FA Carling Premiership**
Aston Villa v Southampton
Blackburn R v Manchester U
Derby Co v Nottingham F
Leeds U v Liverpool
Leicester C v West Ham U
Middlesbrough v Charlton Ath
Sheffield W v Newcastle U
Tottenham H v Arsenal
Wimbledon v Chelsea

**Nationwide Football League Division 1**
Barnsley v Tranmere R
Bradford C v Portsmouth
Bristol C v Grimsby T
Crewe Alex v Port Vale
Norwich C v Ipswich T
Oxford U v Bury
QPR v WBA
Stockport Co v Sheffield U
Sunderland v Huddersfield T
Swindon T v Birmingham C
Watford v Bolton W
Wolverhampton W v Crystal Palace

**Nationwide Football League Division 2**
Blackpool v Reading
Colchester U v Walsall
Fulham v Wigan Ath
Gillingham v AFC Bournemouth
Macclesfield T v Preston NE
Manchester C v Lincoln C
Northampton T v Luton T
Notts Co v Chesterfield
Oldham Ath v Burnley
Stoke C v Bristol R
Wrexham v Wycombe W
York C v Millwall

**Nationwide Football League Division 3**
Barnet v Scarborough
Cambridge U v Halifax T
Carlisle U v Peterborough U
Darlington v Torquay U
Hartlepool U v Chester C
Hull C v Exeter C
Leyton Orient v Cardiff C
Mansfield T v Southend U
Plymouth Arg v Brighton & HA
Rochdale v Rotherham U
Scunthorpe U v Brentford

**Sunday April 11 1999**
**FA Carling Premiership**
Everton v Coventry C

**Tuesday April 13 1999**
**Nationwide Football League Division 2**
AFC Bournemouth v Walsall
Blackpool v Burnley (7:30)
Fulham v Gillingham
Lincoln C v Reading
Macclesfield T v Chesterfield
Northampton T v York C
Notts Co v Wrexham
Oldham Ath v Bristol R
Wigan Ath v Preston NE

**Nationwide Football League Division 3**
Brighton & HA v Shrewsbury T
(8:00)
Cambridge U v Rochdale
Carlisle U v Hull C
Chester C v Brentford (7:30)
Exeter C v Rotherham U
Leyton Orient v Plymouth Arg
Mansfield T v Halifax T
Scunthorpe U v Peterborough U
(7:30)
Southend U v Cardiff C
Swansea C v Hartlepool U
Torquay U v Barnet

**Wednesday April 14 1999**
**Nationwide Football League Division 2**
Manchester C v Luton T
Millwall v Colchester U
Stoke C v Wycombe W

**Nationwide Football League Division 3**
Scarborough v Darlington (7:30)

**Friday April 16 1999**
**Nationwide Football League Division 2**
Colchester U v Notts Co

**Saturday April 17 1999**
**FA Carling Premiership**
Arsenal v Wimbledon
Charlton Ath v Leeds U
Chelsea v Leicester C
Coventry C v Middlesbrough
Liverpool v Aston Villa
Manchester U v Sheffield W
Newcastle U v Everton
Nottingham F v Tottenham H
Southampton v Blackburn R
West Ham U v Derby Co

**Nationwide Football League Division 1**
Barnsley v Sunderland
Birmingham C v Wolverhampton W
Bolton W v Ipswich T
Bradford C v Huddersfield T
Crewe Alex v Watford
Crystal Palace v Swindon T
Grimsby T v Bury
Norwich C v Tranmere R
Port Vale v Oxford U
Sheffield U v QPR
Stockport Co v Bristol C
WBA v Portsmouth

**Nationwide Football League Division 2**
Bristol R v Millwall
Burnley v AFC Bournemouth
Chesterfield v Fulham
Gillingham v Manchester C
Luton T v Lincoln C
Preston NE v Blackpool
Reading v Northampton T
Walsall v Macclesfield T
Wrexham v Oldham Ath
Wycombe W v Wigan Ath
York C v Stoke C

**Nationwide Football League Division 3**
Barnet v Mansfield T
Brentford v Leyton Orient
Darlington v Cambridge U
Halifax T v Brighton & HA
Hartlepool U v Scarborough
Hull C v Scunthorpe U
Peterborough U v Torquay U
Plymouth Arg v Southend U
Rochdale v Chester C
Rotherham U v Carlisle U
Shrewsbury T v Exeter C

**Sunday April 18 1999**
**Nationwide Football League Division 3**
Cardiff C v Swansea C (12:00)

**Saturday April 24 1999**
**FA Carling Premiership**
Aston Villa v Nottingham F
Blackburn R v Liverpool
Derby Co v Southampton
Everton v Charlton Ath
Leeds U v Manchester U
Leicester C v Coventry C
Middlesbrough v Arsenal
Sheffield W v Chelsea
Tottenham H v West Ham U
Wimbledon v Newcastle U

**Nationwide Football League Division 1**
Bristol C v Birmingham C
Bury v Bolton W
Huddersfield T v Barnsley
Ipswich T v Crewe Alex
Oxford U v Norwich C
Portsmouth v Stockport Co
QPR v Bradford C
Sunderland v Sheffield U
Swindon T v Grimsby T
Tranmere R v Port Vale
Watford v Crystal Palace

**Nationwide Football League Division 2**
AFC Bournemouth v Chesterfield
Blackpool v Bristol R
Fulham v Wrexham
Lincoln C v Walsall
Macclesfield T v York C

Manchester C v Wycombe W
Millwall v Preston NE
Northampton T v Colchester U
Notts Co v Luton T
Oldham Ath v Gillingham
Stoke C v Burnley
Wigan Ath v Reading

**Nationwide Football League Division 3**
Brighton & HA v Hull C
Cambridge U v Peterborough U
Carlisle U v Darlington
Chester C v Halifax T
Exeter C v Rochdale
Leyton Orient v Shrewsbury T
Mansfield T v Hartlepool U
Scarborough v Cardiff C
Scunthorpe U v Barnet
Southend U v Brentford
Swansea C v Plymouth Arg
Torquay U v Rotherham U

**Sunday April 25 1999**
**Nationwide Football League Division 1**
Wolverhampton W v WBA (1:00)

**Saturday May 1 1999**
**FA Carling Premiership**
Arsenal v Derby Co
Charlton Ath v Blackburn R
Chelsea v Everton
Coventry C v Wimbledon
Liverpool v Tottenham H
Manchester U v Aston Villa
Newcastle U v Middlesbrough
Nottingham F v Sheffield W
Southampton v Leicester C
West Ham U v Leeds U

**Nationwide Football League Division 1**
Barnsley v Watford
Birmingham C v Ipswich T
Bolton W v Wolverhampton W
Bradford C v Oxford U
Crewe Alex v Portsmouth
Crystal Palace v Huddersfield T
Grimsby T v Tranmere R
Norwich C v Swindon T
Port Vale v QPR
Sheffield U v Bristol C
Stockport Co v Sunderland
WBA v Bury

**Nationwide Football League Division 2**
Bristol R v Manchester C
Burnley v Fulham
Chesterfield v Northampton T
Colchester U v Lincoln C
Gillingham v Stoke C
Luton T v Macclesfield T
Preston NE v Notts Co
Reading v Millwall
Walsall v Oldham Ath
Wrexham v Wigan Ath
Wycombe W v Blackpool
York C v AFC Bournemouth

**Nationwide Football League Division 3**
Barnet v Southend U
Brentford v Exeter C
Cardiff C v Scunthorpe U
Darlington v Chester C
Halifax T v Scarborough
Hartlepool U v Carlisle U
Hull C v Torquay U
Peterborough U v Leyton Orient

Plymouth Arg v Cambridge U
Rochdale v Swansea C
Rotherham U v Brighton & HA
Shrewsbury T v Mansfield T

**Saturday May 8 1999**
**FA Carling Premiership**
Aston Villa v Charlton Ath
Blackburn R v Nottingham F
Derby Co v Coventry C
Everton v West Ham U
Leeds U v Arsenal
Leicester C v Newcastle U
Middlesbrough v Manchester U
Sheffield W v Liverpool
Tottenham H v Chelsea
Wimbledon v Southampton

**Nationwide Football League Division 2**
AFC Bournemouth v Wrexham
Blackpool v Colchester U
Fulham v Preston NE
Lincoln C v Wycombe W
Macclesfield T v Bristol R
Manchester C v York C
Millwall v Luton T
Northampton T v Burnley
Notts Co v Gillingham
Oldham Ath v Reading
Stoke C v Walsall
Wigan Ath v Chesterfield

**Nationwide Football League Division 3**
Brighton & HA v Rochdale
Cambridge U v Brentford
Carlisle U v Plymouth Arg
Chester C v Rotherham U
Exeter C v Halifax T
Leyton Orient v Barnet
Mansfield T v Cardiff C
Scarborough v Peterborough U
Scunthorpe U v Darlington
Southend U v Hartlepool U
Swansea C v Hull C
Torquay U v Shrewsbury T

**Sunday May 9 1999**
**Nationwide Football League Division 1**
Bristol C v Norwich C (1:30)
Bury v Port Vale (1:30)
Huddersfield T v Crewe Alex (1:30)
Ipswich T v Sheffield U (1:30)
Oxford U v Stockport Co (1:30)
Portsmouth v Bolton W (1:30)
QPR v Crystal Palace (1:30)
Sunderland v Birmingham C (1:30)
Swindon T v Barnsley (1:30)
Tranmere R v WBA (1:30)
Watford v Grimsby T (1:30)
Wolverhampton W v Bradford C (1:30)

**Sunday May 16 1999**
**FA Carling Premiership**
Arsenal v Aston Villa (4:00)
Charlton Ath v Sheffield W (4:00)
Chelsea v Derby Co (4:00)
Coventry C v Leeds U (4:00)
Liverpool v Wimbledon (4:00)
Manchester U v Tottenham H (4:00)
Newcastle U v Blackburn R (4:00)
Nottingham F v Leicester C (4:00)
Southampton v Everton (4:00)
West Ham U v Middlesbrough (4:00)

# FA CARLING PREMIERSHIP FIXTURES 1998–99

*Copyright © The FA Premier League Ltd 1997. Copyright Licence No. NCH 98:001. Compiled in association with SEMA Group.*

| | Arsenal | Aston Villa | Blackburn R | Charlton Ath | Chelsea | Coventry C | Derby Co | Everton | Leeds U | Leicester C | Liverpool | Manchester U | Middlesbrough | Newcastle U | Nottingham F | Sheffield W | Southampton | Tottenham H | West Ham U | Wimbledon |
|---|---|---|---|---|---|---|---|---|---|---|---|---|---|---|---|---|---|---|---|---|
| Arsenal | — | 16.5 | 6.4 | 29.8 | 30.1 | 20.3 | 1.5 | 7.11 | 20.12 | 20.2 | 9.1 | 20.9 | 29.11 | 4.10 | 17.8 | 6.3 | 17.10 | 14.11 | 26.12 | 17.4 |
| Aston Villa | 12.12 | — | 6.2 | 8.5 | 20.3 | 27.2 | 26.9 | 16.1 | 13.2 | 24.10 | 21.11 | 5.12 | 23.8 | 9.9 | 24.4 | 28.12 | 10.4 | 7.11 | 3.4 | 12.9 |
| Blackburn R | 25.10 | 26.12 | — | 5.12 | 21.9 | 7.11 | 15.8 | 6.3 | 9.1 | 29.8 | 24.4 | 10.4 | 3.4 | 12.12 | 8.5 | 20.2 | 21.11 | 30.1 | 3.10 | 20.3 |
| Charlton Ath | 28.12 | 21.12 | 1.5 | — | 3.4 | 26.9 | 12.9 | 28.11 | 17.4 | 7.11 | 13.2 | 30.1 | 14.11 | 16.1 | 27.2 | 16.5 | 22.8 | 20.3 | 24.10 | 6.2 |
| Chelsea | 9.9 | 31.10 | 13.2 | 17.10 | — | 16.1 | 16.5 | 1.5 | 5.4 | 17.4 | 27.2 | 29.12 | 26.9 | 22.8 | 12.9 | 28.11 | 6.2 | 19.12 | 13.3 | 14.11 |
| Coventry C | 31.10 | 3.10 | 13.3 | 6.3 | 15.8 | — | 19.12 | 15.11 | 16.5 | 28.11 | 30.1 | 20.2 | 17.4 | 19.9 | 9.1 | 18.10 | 5.4 | 26.12 | 29.8 | 1.5 |
| Derby Co | 5.12 | 6.3 | 16.1 | 20.2 | 12.12 | 8.5 | — | 6.2 | 31.10 | 19.9 | 13.3 | 24.10 | 28.12 | 3.4 | 10.4 | 9.9 | 24.4 | 3.10 | 22.11 | 22.8 |
| Everton | 13.3 | 15.8 | 26.9 | 24.4 | 5.12 | 11.4 | 26.12 | — | 12.9 | 9.1 | 17.10 | 31.10 | 13.2 | 23.11 | 30.1 | 5.4 | 12.12 | 29.8 | 8.5 | 27.2 |
| Leeds U | 8.5 | 19.9 | 24.8 | 21.11 | 25.10 | 14.12 | 20.3 | 20.2 | — | 3.10 | 10.4 | 24.4 | 16.1 | 6.2 | 3.4 | 8.11 | 8.9 | 6.3 | 5.12 | 29.12 |
| Leicester C | 12.9 | 6.4 | 28.12 | 13.3 | 21.11 | 24.4 | 13.2 | 22.8 | 14.11 | — | 31.10 | 16.1 | 9.9 | 8.5 | 12.12 | 6.2 | 5.12 | 19.10 | 10.4 | 27.9 |
| Liverpool | 22.8 | 17.4 | 29.11 | 19.9 | 21.11 | 9.9 | 7.11 | 3.4 | 14.11 | 20.3 | — | 6.3 | 6.2 | 28.12 | 24.10 | 19.12 | 16.1 | 1.5 | 20.2 | 16.5 |
| Manchester U | 13.2 | 1.5 | 14.11 | 9.9 | 16.12 | 12.9 | 5.4 | 20.3 | 28.11 | 15.8 | 26.9 | — | 19.12 | 8.11 | 26.12 | 17.4 | 27.2 | 16.5 | 9.1 | 17.10 |
| Middlesbrough | 24.4 | 9.1 | 17.10 | 10.4 | 6.3 | 21.11 | 29.8 | 19.9 | 15.8 | 30.1 | 26.12 | 8.5 | — | 6.12 | 1.11 | 3.10 | 13.3 | 20.2 | 12.12 | 5.4 |
| Newcastle U | 27.2 | 30.1 | 16.5 | 15.8 | 9.1 | 13.2 | 17.10 | 17.4 | 26.12 | 19.12 | 30.8 | 13.3 | 1.5 | — | 26.9 | 14.11 | 12.9 | 5.4 | 31.10 | 28.11 |
| Nottingham F | 16.1 | 28.11 | 19.12 | 3.10 | 20.2 | 22.8 | 16.11 | 8.9 | 17.10 | 16.5 | 5.4 | 6.2 | 27.2 | 6.3 | — | 1.5 | 28.12 | 17.4 | 19.9 | 7.11 |
| Sheffield W | 26.9 | 29.8 | 12.9 | 12.12 | 24.4 | 18.10 | 30.1 | 24.10 | 8.11 | 6.2 | 19.12 | 17.4 | 3.10 | 14.11 | 1.5 | — | 31.10 | 9.1 | 15.8 | 13.2 |
| Southampton | 3.4 | 14.11 | 17.4 | 9.1 | 26.12 | 6.2 | 28.11 | 16.5 | 8.9 | 5.12 | 16.1 | 27.2 | 13.3 | 12.9 | 28.12 | 20.3 | — | 19.9 | 31.10 | 8.5 |
| Tottenham H | 10.4 | 13.3 | 9.9 | 2.11 | 8.5 | 27.2 | 27.2 | 28.12 | 6.3 | 19.10 | 1.5 | 16.5 | 20.2 | 5.4 | 17.4 | 22.8 | 13.2 | — | 24.4 | 15.8 |
| West Ham U | 6.2 | 17.10 | 27.2 | 5.4 | 8.11 | 17.4 | 26.9 | 8.5 | 5.12 | 10.4 | 20.2 | 9.1 | 12.12 | 31.10 | 19.9 | 24.4 | 31.10 | 28.11 | — | 9.9 |
| Wimbledon | 21.11 | 20.2 | 31.10 | 26.12 | 10.4 | 9.1 | 3.10 | 3.10 | 29.12 | 27.9 | 16.5 | 17.10 | 5.4 | 28.11 | 7.11 | 19.9 | 8.5 | 15.8 | 9.9 | — |

# NATIONWIDE FOOTBALL LEAGUE FIXTURES 1998-99

*Copyright © The Football League Ltd 1997. Copyright Licence No. NCH 98.001. Compiled in association with SEMA Group.*

## DIVISION ONE

| | Barnsley | Birmingham C | Bolton W | Bradford C | Bristol C | Bury | Crewe Alex | Crystal Palace | Grimsby T | Huddersfield T | Ipswich T | Norwich C | Oxford U | Port Vale | Portsmouth | QPR | Sheffield U | Stockport Co | Sunderland | Swindon T | Tranmere R | Watford | WBA | Wolverhampton W |
|---|---|---|---|---|---|---|---|---|---|---|---|---|---|---|---|---|---|---|---|---|---|---|---|---|
| Barnsley | — | 16.1 | 3.10 | 2.3 | 6.3 | 7.11 | 6.2 | 19.9 | 20.2 | 27.11 | 14.11 | 8.9 | 31.8 | 11.10 | 24.10 | 28.12 | 3.4 | 21.8 | 17.4 | 19.12 | 10.4 | 1.5 | 8.8 | 20.3 |
| Birmingham C | 29.8 | — | 20.2 | 30.1 | 28.11 | 5.9 | 17.10 | 16.8 | 9.1 | 31.10 | 1.5 | 12.9 | 14.11 | 9.1 | 6.3 | 27.3 | 26.12 | 8.9 | 19.12 | 20.10 | 3.10 | 5.4 | 13.3 | 17.4 |
| Bolton W | 9.3 | 12.9 | — | 26.12 | 27.3 | 28.11 | 27.2 | 9.1 | 15.8 | 26.9 | 17.4 | 5.9 | 17.10 | 5.9 | 19.12 | 13.3 | 29.8 | 5.4 | 9.3 | 29.9 | 14.11 | 20.10 | 13.2 | 1.5 |
| Bradford C | 26.9 | 31.8 | 23.8 | — | 31.10 | 10.10 | 16.1 | 24.10 | 3.4 | 17.4 | 13.2 | 13.3 | 1.5 | 29.9 | 10.4 | 28.11 | 12.9 | 8.8 | 9.3 | 14.11 | 28.12 | 6.2 | 27.2 | 19.12 |
| Bristol C | 29.9 | 24.4 | 23.10 | 20.3 | — | 9.3 | 26.9 | 12.12 | 10.4 | 31.8 | 27.2 | 9.5 | 8.8 | 3.4 | 10.10 | 6.2 | 5.12 | 21.11 | 13.2 | 28.12 | 16.1 | 22.8 | 12.9 | 7.11 |
| Bury | 13.3 | 28.12 | 24.4 | 5.4 | 3.10 | — | 22.8 | 6.3 | 21.11 | 8.8 | 6.2 | 20.2 | 20.10 | 9.5 | 8.9 | 16.1 | 11.12 | 17.10 | 27.3 | 7.11 | 19.9 | 31.10 | 5.12 | 2.3 |
| Crewe Alex | 15.8 | 3.4 | 19.9 | 28.8 | 2.3 | 26.12 | — | 8.9 | 6.3 | 19.12 | 28.11 | 9.1 | 20.3 | 10.4 | 1.5 | 14.11 | 30.1 | 20.2 | 5.9 | 7.11 | 24.10 | 17.4 | 10.10 | 3.10 |
| Crystal Palace | 27.2 | 6.2 | 8.8 | 28.8 | 14.11 | 26.12 | 13.2 | — | 20.3 | 1.5 | 9.3 | 17.10 | 22.8 | 12.9 | 7.11 | 19.12 | 27.9 | 16.1 | 5.4 | 17.4 | 31.8 | 28.11 | 28.12 | 20.10 |
| Grimsby T | 12.9 | 27.2 | 6.2 | 27.3 | 17.10 | 30.9 | 29.9 | 31.10 | — | 22.8 | 9.8 | 5.4 | 16.1 | 26.9 | 7.11 | 9.3 | 13.2 | 28.12 | 13.3 | 28.11 | 1.5 | 19.12 | 31.8 | 27.3 |
| Huddersfield T | 24.4 | 20.3 | 2.3 | 17.10 | 20.10 | 17.4 | 9.5 | 22.8 | 26.12 | — | 7.11 | 3.10 | 16.1 | 26.9 | 14.11 | 9.3 | 13.2 | 6.3 | 21.10 | 5.4 | 20.2 | 8.9 | 12.12 | 19.9 |
| Ipswich T | 12.12 | 5.12 | 21.11 | 8.9 | 19.9 | 15.8 | 13.9 | 22.8 | 9.1 | 13.3 | — | 20.10 | 20.2 | 30.1 | 29.8 | 17.10 | 1.5 | 6.2 | 29.9 | 13.2 | 6.3 | 29.12 | 3.10 | 5.9 |
| Norwich C | 13.2 | 26.9 | 1.9 | 7.11 | 19.12 | 13.9 | 8.8 | 3.4 | 10.10 | 24.10 | 10.4 | — | 29.11 | 9.3 | 20.3 | 22.8 | 27.2 | 6.2 | 29.9 | 1.5 | 17.4 | 13.3 | 16.1 | 14.11 |
| Oxford U | 30.1 | 12.12 | 3.4 | 6.3 | 17.10 | 10.4 | 31.10 | 26.12 | 20.2 | 9.3 | 12.9 | 21.11 | — | 29.11 | 6.9 | 26.9 | 24.10 | 8.11 | 20.3 | 8.11 | 10.10 | 13.3 | 29.9 | 15.8 |
| Port Vale | 5.4 | 8.8 | 28.12 | 6.3 | 8.9 | 9.5 | 10.4 | 9.5 | 26.9 | 15.8 | 27.2 | 9.3 | 21.11 | — | 19.9 | 1.5 | 31.10 | 13.3 | 14.11 | 16.1 | 28.11 | 27.3 | 22.8 | 8.9 |
| Portsmouth | 27.3 | 29.9 | 9.5 | 20.10 | 5.9 | 15.8 | 5.12 | 22.8 | 13.12 | 16.1 | 22.8 | 31.10 | 28.12 | 27.2 | — | 31.8 | 9.3 | 24.4 | 26.9 | 12.9 | 6.2 | 8.8 | 10.4 | 6.3 |
| QPR | 5.9 | 25.10 | 7.11 | 20.10 | 15.8 | 29.8 | 12.12 | 9.5 | 3.10 | 3.4 | 10.10 | 26.12 | 3.3 | 5.12 | 30.1 | — | 17.4 | 19.9 | 9.1 | 20.3 | 8.9 | 20.2 | 10.4 | 6.3 |
| Sheffield U | 17.10 | 22.8 | 16.1 | 20.2 | 1.5 | 14.11 | 31.8 | 2.3 | 8.9 | 28.12 | 20.12 | 19.9 | 27.3 | 20.3 | 3.10 | 17.4 | — | 20.10 | 28.11 | 8.8 | 7.11 | 6.3 | 6.2 | 5.4 |
| Stockport Co | 26.12 | 13.2 | 10.10 | 9.1 | 5.12 | 3.4 | 12.9 | 29.8 | 20.3 | 9.9 | 24.10 | 15.8 | 19.12 | 8.11 | 27.2 | 27.2 | 28.11 | — | 1.5 | 9.3 | 20.3 | 14.11 | 26.9 | 30.1 |
| Sunderland | 21.11 | 9.5 | 20.3 | 3.10 | 19.9 | 24.10 | 28.12 | 9.8 | 7.11 | 10.4 | 16.1 | 6.3 | 19.9 | 12.12 | 2.3 | 8.8 | 24.4 | 1.5 | — | 6.2 | 22.8 | 31.8 | 3.4 | 20.2 |
| Swindon T | 9.5 | 10.4 | 6.3 | 12.12 | 5.9 | 30.1 | 13.3 | 21.11 | 24.4 | 10.10 | 3.4 | 5.12 | 9.9 | 29.8 | 20.2 | 31.10 | 9.1 | 3.10 | 15.8 | — | 3.3 | 19.9 | 24.10 | 26.12 |
| Tranmere R | 20.10 | 9.3 | 12.12 | 4.9 | 29.8 | 27.2 | 27.3 | 30.1 | 5.12 | 11.9 | 29.9 | 21.11 | 5.4 | 24.4 | 15.8 | 13.2 | 13.3 | 31.10 | 26.12 | 25.9 | — | 17.10 | 24.10 | 26.12 |
| Watford | 5.12 | 10.10 | 10.4 | 15.8 | 12.12 | 20.3 | 21.11 | 13.2 | 9.5 | 11.9 | 29.9 | 5.9 | 7.11 | 24.10 | 15.8 | 12.9 | 29.9 | 12.12 | 30.1 | 27.2 | 3.4 | — | 9.3 | 28.8 |
| WBA | 9.1 | 7.11 | 8.9 | 20.9 | 5.9 | 1.5 | 5.4 | 28.12 | 30.1 | 14.11 | 20.3 | 29.8 | 6.3 | 26.12 | 17.4 | 21.10 | 15.8 | 2.3 | 18.10 | 27.3 | 19.12 | 4.10 | — | 29.11 |
| Wolverhampton W | 31.10 | 22.11 | 8.9 | 9.5 | 13.3 | 26.9 | 9.3 | 10.4 | 27.3 | 19.9 | 5.12 | 13.2 | 6.2 | 13.2 | 3.4 | 29.9 | 10.10 | 31.8 | 12.9 | 22.8 | 8.8 | 16.1 | 25.4 | — |

# NATIONWIDE FOOTBALL LEAGUE FIXTURES 1998–99

*Copyright © The Football League Ltd 1997. Copyright Licence No. NCH 98.001. Compiled in association with SEMA Group.*

## DIVISION TWO

| | Blackpool | AFC Bournemouth | Bristol R | Burnley | Chesterfield | Colchester U | Fulham | Gillingham | Lincoln C | Luton T | Macclesfield T | Manchester C | Millwall | Northampton T | Notts Co | Oldham Ath | Preston N E | Reading | Stoke C | Walsall | Wigan Ath | Wrexham | Wycombe W | York C |
|---|---|---|---|---|---|---|---|---|---|---|---|---|---|---|---|---|---|---|---|---|---|---|---|---|
| Blackpool | — | 23.1 | 24.4 | 13.4 | 24.10 | 8.5 | 31.10 | 29.8 | 20.2 | 19.9 | 30.1 | 9.1 | 10.10 | 5.9 | 8.9 | 15.8 | 21.11 | 10.4 | 6.3 | 3.4 | 26.12 | 13.3 | 12.12 | 3.10 |
| AFC Bournemouth | 1.9 | — | 9.3 | 21.11 | 8.9 | 30.1 | 2.1 | 20.10 | 9.1 | 28.12 | 6.4 | 13.2 | 22.8 | 17.10 | 16.1 | 26.9 | 31.10 | 13.3 | 6.2 | 13.4 | 12.9 | 8.5 | 27.2 | 12.12 |
| Bristol R | 10.11 | 3.10 | — | 9.1 | 8.9 | 30.1 | 12.3 | 26.12 | 19.9 | 20.2 | 18.12 | 1.5 | 17.4 | 5.4 | 27.3 | 28.11 | 5.9 | 15.8 | 10.11 | 31.10 | 29.8 | 17.10 | 23.1 | 6.3 |
| Burnley | 28.11 | 17.4 | 8.8 | — | 16.1 | 5.4 | 1.5 | 5.9 | 27.2 | 6.2 | 27.3 | 9.3 | 1.9 | 30.1 | 27.3 | 28.11 | 13.3 | 13.2 | 10.11 | 2.1 | 26.9 | 17.10 | 12.9 | 22.8 |
| Chesterfield | 27.3 | 10.11 | 13.2 | 15.8 | — | 9.1 | 17.4 | 5.9 | 7.11 | 20.3 | 27.3 | 27.2 | 9.3 | 19.12 | 16.4 | 20.10 | 23.1 | 29.8 | 5.4 | 12.9 | 19.12 | 26.9 | 30.1 | 17.10 |
| Colchester U | 18.12 | 24.10 | 28.12 | 9.10 | 8.8 | — | 22.8 | 12.9 | 3.10 | 2.1 | 6.11 | 20.3 | 28.11 | 10.11 | 16.4 | 9.3 | 2.4 | 27.2 | 31.8 | 10.4 | 12.2 | 15.1 | 26.9 | 5.2 |
| Fulham | 20.3 | 29.8 | 7.11 | 12.12 | 8.8 | 22.8 | — | 13.4 | 6.3 | 3.10 | 9.1 | 14.8 | 3.4 | 30.1 | 20.2 | 23.1 | 8.5 | 10.10 | 8.9 | 24.10 | 10.4 | 24.4 | 5.9 | 19.9 |
| Gillingham | 2.1 | 10.4 | 22.8 | 19.9 | 6.2 | 20.2 | 13.4 | — | 3.10 | 24.10 | 3.10 | 14.8 | 29.12 | 8.9 | 19.12 | 10.11 | 6.3 | 3.4 | 1.5 | 8.8 | 7.11 | 1.9 | 5.9 | 16.1 |
| Lincoln C | 12.9 | 9.1 | 27.2 | 30.1 | 13.3 | 20.3 | 6.3 | 21.11 | — | 21.11 | 26.12 | 20.10 | 13.2 | 23.1 | 5.4 | 5.9 | 29.8 | 13.4 | 17.10 | 24.4 | 15.8 | 9.3 | 8.5 | 27.3 |
| Luton T | 27.2 | 30.1 | 12.9 | 5.9 | 31.10 | 13.4 | 9.3 | 27.3 | 17.4 | — | 1.5 | 28.11 | 19.12 | 20.10 | 10.11 | 17.10 | 15.8 | 26.12 | 13.3 | 26.9 | 23.1 | 13.2 | 9.1 | 6.4 |
| Macclesfield T | 28.12 | 8.9 | 8.5 | 24.10 | 13.4 | 13.3 | 8.8 | 9.3 | 20.2 | 1.5 | — | 12.9 | 6.2 | 31.10 | 20.10 | 13.2 | 10.4 | 26.9 | 16.1 | 21.11 | 3.4 | 6.2 | 3.4 | 24.4 |
| Manchester C | 8.8 | 8.9 | 12.12 | 3.10 | 19.9 | 31.10 | 16.1 | 21.11 | 19.9 | 22.8 | 6.2 | — | 6.2 | 6.3 | 31.8 | 13.2 | 13.3 | 24.10 | 12.3 | 2.9 | 3.4 | 6.2 | 24.4 | 8.5 |
| Millwall | 5.4 | 26.12 | 21.11 | 23.1 | 3.10 | 28.11 | 17.10 | 30.1 | 13.2 | 19.12 | 2.1 | 5.9 | — | 19.9 | 6.3 | 31.10 | 24.4 | 12.12 | 20.2 | 13.3 | 9.1 | 27.3 | 15.8 | 21.10 |
| Northampton T | 6.2 | 2.4 | 10.10 | 8.5 | 12.12 | 24.4 | 21.11 | 13.2 | 23.1 | 20.10 | 14.8 | 5.9 | 27.2 | — | 26.12 | 9.1 | 24.10 | 21.11 | 8.8 | 16.1 | 9.3 | 2.1 | 7.11 | 13.4 |
| Notts Co | 8.9 | 16.1 | 27.3 | 27.3 | 16.4 | 16.4 | 20.2 | 19.12 | 5.4 | 10.11 | 20.10 | 31.8 | 6.3 | 26.12 | — | 8.8 | 12.12 | 30.1 | 31.10 | 24.10 | 11.11 | 28.11 | 1.5 | 28.12 |
| Oldham Ath | 16.1 | 6.3 | 13.4 | 10.4 | 22.8 | 6.2 | 1.9 | 24.4 | 2.4 | 8.9 | 7.11 | 5.4 | 24.4 | 20.2 | 8.8 | — | 19.9 | 8.5 | 2.1 | 12.12 | 10.10 | 21.11 | 24.10 | 13.3 |
| Preston N E | 17.4 | 20.3 | 6.2 | 7.11 | 31.8 | 2.1 | 19.12 | 26.9 | 29.8 | 15.8 | 10.4 | 7.11 | 24.4 | 24.10 | 12.12 | 19.9 | — | 30.1 | 22.8 | 9.3 | 10.10 | 28.12 | 13.2 | 2.9 |
| Reading | 21.10 | 7.11 | 16.1 | 9.9 | 23.1 | 19.9 | 5.4 | 17.10 | 13.4 | 26.12 | 28.12 | 19.12 | 20.3 | 9.1 | 28.12 | 29.8 | 26.12 | — | 3.10 | 6.2 | 11.11 | 9.1 | 20.3 | 8.8 |
| Stoke C | 26.9 | 5.9 | 10.4 | 24.4 | 5.4 | 3.4 | 8.9 | 8.5 | 10.10 | 7.11 | 15.8 | 30.1 | 12.9 | 24.10 | 19.12 | 28.12 | 26.12 | 10.3 | — | 8.5 | 24.10 | 27.2 | 14.4 | 2.1 |
| Walsall | 17.10 | 28.11 | 20.3 | 24.4 | 12.10 | 20.10 | 27.3 | 7.11 | 24.4 | 12.9 | 18.9 | 30.1 | 15.8 | 3.10 | 24.10 | 9.3 | 19.12 | 5.9 | 1.5 | — | 6.4 | 27.3 | 26.12 | 8.9 |
| Wigan Ath | 22.8 | 20.2 | 2.1 | 6.3 | 8.5 | 16.1 | 31.8 | 8.9 | 17.10 | 19.9 | 26.12 | 17.10 | 24.10 | 29.8 | 13.3 | 6.2 | 28.11 | 24.4 | 27.3 | 19.9 | — | 12.12 | 21.11 | 31.10 |
| Wrexham | 7.11 | 19.12 | 3.4 | 20.3 | 6.3 | 15.8 | 8.8 | 28.12 | 9.1 | 8.9 | 17.4 | 10.11 | 27.3 | 13.3 | 28.11 | 28.12 | 9.1 | 31.10 | 28.11 | 10.10 | 12.12 | — | 10.4 | 12.9 |
| Wycombe W | 1.5 | 19.9 | 31.8 | 20.2 | 28.12 | 6.3 | 6.2 | 5.4 | 27.3 | 9.1 | 6.2 | 24.4 | 15.8 | 7.11 | 17.4 | 24.10 | 13.2 | 8.8 | 19.9 | 22.8 | 17.4 | 10.4 | — | 2.1 |
| York C | 9.3 | 1.5 | 26.9 | 26.12 | 3.4 | 5.9 | 27.2 | 15.8 | 31.8 | 10.10 | 10.11 | 19.12 | 7.11 | 28.11 | 13.3 | 30.1 | 9.1 | 23.1 | 17.4 | 13.2 | 20.3 | 12.9 | 29.8 | — |

# NATIONWIDE FOOTBALL LEAGUE FIXTURES 1998–99

## DIVISION THREE

| | Barnet | Brentford | Brighton & H A | Cambridge U | Cardiff C | Carlisle U | Chester C | Darlington | Exeter C | Halifax T | Hartlepool U | Hull C | Leyton O | Mansfield T | Peterborough U | Plymouth Arg | Rochdale | Rotherham U | Scarborough | Scunthorpe U | Shrewsbury T | Southend U | Swansea C | Torquay U |
|---|---|---|---|---|---|---|---|---|---|---|---|---|---|---|---|---|---|---|---|---|---|---|---|---|
| Barnet | — | 29.8 | 24.10 | 13.3 | 13.2 | 9.3 | 10.10 | 9.1 | 27.2 | 3.4 | 15.8 | 12.9 | 19.12 | 17.4 | 5.9 | 26.12 | 31.10 | 26.9 | 10.4 | 10.11 | 23.1 | 1.5 | 30.1 | 28.11 |
| Brentford | 2.1 | — | 22.8 | 19.12 | 28.12 | 9.1 | 28.11 | 26.9 | 1.5 | 16.1 | 17.10 | 6.2 | 17.4 | 8.8 | 9.3 | 5.4 | 31.8 | 12.9 | 27.2 | 20.10 | 13.3 | 10.11 | 27.3 | 13.2 |
| Brighton & H A | 27.3 | 26.12 | — | 6.4 | 10.3 | 3.4 | 15.8 | 13.3 | 13.2 | 21.11 | 31.10 | 24.4 | 27.2 | 17.10 | 30.1 | 8.5 | 8.5 | 11.12 | 23.1 | 26.9 | 13.4 | 12.9 | 5.9 | 29.8 |
| Cambridge U | 7.11 | 8.5 | 10.10 | — | 3.4 | 30.1 | 6.3 | 24.4 | 26.9 | 20.10 | 3.10 | 9.3 | 20.2 | 15.8 | 24.10 | 12.12 | 13.4 | 8.9 | 5.9 | 13.2 | 27.3 | 27.2 | 15.8 | 9.1 |
| Cardiff C | 8.9 | 30.1 | 3.10 | 17.10 | — | 24.10 | 19.9 | 6.2 | 31.10 | 2.1 | 9.1 | 5.4 | 20.10 | 19.12 | 10.4 | 5.9 | 22.8 | 29.8 | 13.2 | 1.5 | 26.12 | 28.11 | 18.4 | 13.3 |
| Carlisle U | 3.10 | 8.8 | 8.8 | 30.1 | 24.10 | — | 19.9 | 23.1 | 26.9 | 20.10 | 6.3 | 31.8 | 7.11 | 16.1 | 24.4 | 8.5 | 2.1 | 13.4 | 10.10 | 16.1 | 6.3 | 1.9 | 8.9 | 3.4 |
| Chester C | 5.4 | 16.1 | 15.8 | 6.3 | 19.9 | 16.1 | — | 9.1 | 20.10 | 7.11 | 13.2 | 10.4 | 2.1 | 3.4 | 26.9 | 8.9 | 24.4 | 30.1 | 9.3 | 13.3 | 31.10 | 2.1 | 17.10 | 12.9 |
| Darlington | 8.8 | 26.9 | 13.3 | 24.4 | 6.2 | 23.1 | 9.1 | — | 12.9 | 1.9 | 3.10 | 5.4 | 17.4 | 2.1 | 8.5 | 12.9 | 28.11 | 27.2 | 15.8 | 19.12 | 19.9 | 20.3 | 3.10 | 10.4 |
| Exeter C | 19.9 | 1.5 | 13.2 | 26.9 | 31.10 | 26.9 | 20.10 | 12.9 | — | 24.10 | 23.8 | 27.2 | 6.2 | 21.11 | 28.12 | 31.8 | 2.1 | 9.1 | 7.11 | 17.10 | 21.11 | 7.11 | 10.4 | 26.12 |
| Halifax T | 16.10 | 16.1 | 21.11 | 20.10 | 2.1 | 20.10 | 7.11 | 1.9 | 24.10 | — | 30.1 | 27.2 | 22.8 | 5.4 | 6.2 | 13.4 | 2.4 | 15.8 | 1.5 | 9.3 | 28.8 | 13.2 | 31.10 | 26.9 |
| Hartlepool U | 16.1 | 17.10 | 31.10 | 3.10 | 9.1 | 6.3 | 13.2 | 3.10 | 23.8 | 30.1 | — | 9.3 | 28.12 | 10.11 | 10.10 | 20.3 | 8.9 | 23.1 | 17.4 | 22.8 | 10.10 | 19.12 | 26.9 | 24.10 |
| Hull C | 20.2 | 6.2 | 24.4 | 9.3 | 5.4 | 31.8 | 10.4 | 5.4 | 27.2 | 27.2 | 9.3 | — | 13.2 | 13.3 | 26.9 | 6.3 | 31.10 | 31.10 | 3.4 | 17.4 | 30.1 | 24.10 | 19.12 | 1.5 |
| Leyton O | 8.5 | 17.4 | 27.2 | 20.2 | 20.10 | 7.11 | 2.1 | 17.4 | 6.2 | 22.8 | 28.12 | 13.2 | — | 24.4 | 12.12 | 15.8 | 2.4 | 13.2 | 29.8 | 31.10 | 24.4 | 3.4 | 26.12 | 23.1 |
| Mansfield T | 20.11 | 8.8 | 17.10 | 15.8 | 19.12 | 16.1 | 3.4 | 2.1 | 21.11 | 5.4 | 10.11 | 13.3 | 24.4 | — | 24.10 | 2.1 | 8.8 | 16.1 | 26.12 | 27.2 | 11.12 | 10.4 | 29.8 | 9.10 |
| Peterborough U | 6.2 | 9.3 | 30.1 | 24.10 | 10.4 | 24.4 | 26.9 | 8.5 | 28.12 | 6.2 | 10.10 | 26.9 | 12.12 | 24.10 | — | 19.9 | 8.8 | 20.3 | 7.11 | 28.11 | 20.2 | 22.8 | 13.3 | 17.4 |
| Plymouth Arg | 22.8 | 5.4 | 8.5 | 12.12 | 5.9 | 8.5 | 8.9 | 12.9 | 31.8 | 13.4 | 20.3 | 6.3 | 15.8 | 2.1 | 19.9 | — | 19.9 | 8.9 | 24.10 | 9.1 | 3.4 | 17.4 | 10.11 | 9.3 |
| Rochdale | 20.3 | 31.8 | 8.5 | 13.4 | 22.8 | 2.1 | 24.4 | 28.11 | 2.1 | 2.4 | 8.9 | 31.10 | 2.4 | 8.8 | 8.8 | 19.9 | — | 10.4 | 20.10 | 27.3 | 5.9 | 9.3 | 1.5 | 15.8 |
| Rotherham U | 6.3 | 12.9 | 11.12 | 8.9 | 29.8 | 5.4 | 30.1 | 27.2 | 9.1 | 15.8 | 23.1 | 31.10 | 13.2 | 16.1 | 20.3 | 8.9 | 10.4 | — | 13.3 | 12.9 | 3.10 | 6.2 | 5.4 | 10.11 |
| Scarborough | 21.10 | 27.2 | 23.1 | 5.9 | 13.2 | 10.10 | 9.3 | 15.8 | 7.11 | 1.5 | 17.4 | 3.4 | 29.8 | 26.12 | 7.11 | 24.10 | 20.10 | 13.3 | — | 28.12 | 9.9 | 8.8 | 20.2 | 31.10 |
| Scunthorpe U | 24.4 | 20.10 | 26.9 | 13.2 | 1.5 | 16.1 | 13.3 | 19.12 | 17.10 | 9.3 | 22.8 | 17.4 | 31.10 | 27.2 | 28.11 | 9.1 | 27.3 | 12.9 | 30.1 | — | 9.1 | 10.10 | 23.1 | 5.9 |
| Shrewsbury T | 31.8 | 13.3 | 13.4 | 27.3 | 26.12 | 6.3 | 31.10 | 19.9 | 21.11 | 28.8 | 10.10 | 30.1 | 24.4 | 11.12 | 20.2 | 3.4 | 5.9 | 3.10 | 9.9 | 8.8 | — | 16.1 | 20.10 | 18.12 |
| Southend U | 12.12 | 10.11 | 12.9 | 27.2 | 28.11 | 1.9 | 2.1 | 20.3 | 7.11 | 13.2 | 19.12 | 24.10 | 3.4 | 10.4 | 22.8 | 17.4 | 9.3 | 6.2 | 8.8 | 5.4 | 15.8 | — | 6.3 | 30.1 |
| Swansea C | 28.12 | 27.3 | 5.9 | 15.8 | 18.4 | 8.9 | 17.10 | 3.10 | 10.4 | 31.10 | 26.9 | 19.12 | 26.12 | 29.8 | 13.3 | 10.11 | 1.5 | 5.4 | 20.2 | 31.8 | 9.4 | 26.9 | — | 19.9 |
| Torquay U | 13.4 | 13.2 | 29.8 | 9.1 | 13.3 | 3.4 | 12.9 | 10.4 | 26.12 | 26.9 | 24.10 | 1.5 | 23.1 | 9.10 | 17.4 | 9.3 | 15.8 | 10.11 | 20.3 | 6.2 | 8.5 | 28.12 | 27.2 | — |

# OTHER FIXTURES 1998–99

**July 1998**
| | |
|---|---|
| 18 Sat | UEFA Intertoto Cup 3 (1) |
| 22 Wed | Champions League 1Q (1) |
| | UEFA Cup 1Q (1) |
| 25 Sat | UEFA Intertoto Cup 3 (2) |
| 29 Wed | Champions League 1Q (2) |
| | UEFA Cup 1Q (2) |
| | UEFA Intertoto Cup 4 (1) |

**August**
| | |
|---|---|
| 5 Wed | UEFA Intertoto Cup 4 (2) |
| 8 Sat | Start of FL season |
| 9 Sun | FA Charity Shield |
| 11 Tue | UEFA Cup 2Q (1) |
| 12 Wed | Champions League 2Q (1) |
| 13 Thu | ECWC P (1) |
| 15 Sat | Start of FA Premier League season |
| 19 Wed | International (F) |
| 25 Tue | UEFA Cup 2Q (2) |
| 26 Wed | Champions League 2Q (2) |
| 27 Thu | ECWC P (2) |
| 28 Fri | UEFA Super Cup – Chelsea v Real Madrid – Monaco |
| 31 Mon | Bank Holiday |

**September**
| | |
|---|---|
| 5 Sat* | Sweden v England (EC) |
| | FA Cup P |
| | FA Youth Cup 1Q+ |
| 12 Sat | FA Vase 1Q |
| 15 Tue | UEFA Cup 1 (1) |
| 16 Wed | Champions League (1) |
| 17 Thu | ECWC 1 (1) |
| 19 Sat | FA Cup 1Q |
| 26 Sat | FA Youth Cup 2Q+ |
| 27 Sun | FA Women's Cup 1 |
| 29 Tue | UEFA Cup 1 (2) |
| 30 Wed | Champions League 1 (2) |

**October**
| | |
|---|---|
| 1 Thu | ECWC 1 (2) |
| 3 Sat | FA Cup 2Q |
| 10 Sat* | England v Bulgaria (EC) |
| | FA Vase 2Q |
| | FA County Youth Cup 1+ |
| 14 Wed | Luxemburg v England (EC) |
| 17 Sat | FA Cup 3Q |
| | FA Youth Cup 3Q+ |
| 20 Tue | UEFA Cup 2 (1) |
| 21 Wed | Champions League 2 (1) |
| 22 Thu | ECWC 2 (1) |
| 24 Sat | FA Trophy 1 |
| 25 Sun | FA Sunday Cup 1 |
| 31 Sat | FA Cup 4Q |

**November**
| | |
|---|---|
| 1 Sun | FA Women's Cup 2 |
| 3 Tue | UEFA Cup 2 (2) |
| 4 Wed | Champions League 2 (2) |
| 5 Thu | ECWC 2 (2) |

| | |
|---|---|
| 7 Sat | FA Vase 1P |
| | FA Youth Cup 1P+ |
| 10 Tue | FA XI v Northern Premier League |
| 14 Sat | International (F) |
| | FA Cup 1P |
| | FA County Youth Cup 2+ |
| 18 Wed | International (F) |
| 21 Sat | FA Trophy 2 |
| 22 Sun | FA Sunday Cup 2 |
| 24 Tue | UEFA Cup 3 (1) |
| 25 Wed | Champions League 3 (1) |
| 28 Sat | FA Vase 2P |
| | FA Youth Cup 2P+ |

**December**
| | |
|---|---|
| 5 Sat | FA Cup 2P |
| 6 Sun | FA Women's Cup 3 |
| 8 Tue | FA XI v Southern League |
| | UEFA Cup 3 (2) |
| 9 Wed | Champions League 3 (2) |
| | FA XI v Isthmian League |
| 12 Sat | FA Vase 3P |
| 13 Sun | FA Sunday Cup 3 |
| 19 Sat | FA County Youth Cup 3+ |
| 26 Sat | Boxing Day |

**January 1999**
| | |
|---|---|
| 1 Fri | New Year's Day |
| 2 Sat | FA Cup 3P |
| 5 Tue | FA XI v Combined Services |
| 9 Sat | International (not UEFA date) |
| | FA Vase 4P |
| | FA Youth Cup 3P+ |
| 10 Sun | FA Women's Cup 4 |
| 13 Wed | International (not UEFA date) |
| | FA Cup 3P replay |
| 16 Sat | FA Trophy 3 |
| 17 Sun | FA Sunday Cup 4 |
| 23 Sat | FA Cup 4P |
| 30 Sat | FA Vase 5P |
| | FA Youth Cup 4P+ |
| | FA County Youth Cup 4+ |

**February**
| | |
|---|---|
| 2 Tue | FA XI v British Students |
| 3 Wed | FA Cup 4P replay |
| 6 Sat | International (not UEFA date) |
| | FA Trophy 4 |
| 7 Sun | FA Women's Cup 5 |
| 10 Wed | International (F) |
| 13 Sat | FA Cup 5P |
| 14 Sun | FA Sunday Cup 5 |
| 20 Sat | FA Vase 6P |
| | FA Youth Cup 5P+ |
| 24 Wed | FA Cup 5P replay |
| 27 Sat | FA Trophy 5 |

**March**
| | |
|---|---|
| 2 Tue | Semi-Pro International |
| | UEFA Cup QF (1) |

| | |
|---|---|
| 3 Wed | Champions League QF (1) |
| 4 Thu | ECWC QF (1) |
| 6 Sat | FA Cup 6P |
| 7 Sun | FA Women's Cup 6 |
| 10 Wed | FA Cup 6P replay (prov) |
| 13 Sat | FA Vase SF (1) |
| | FA Youth Cup 6P+ |
| | FA County Youth Cup SF+ |
| 16 Tue | UEFA Cup QF (2) |
| 17 Wed | Champions League QF (2) |
| | FA Cup 6P replay (prov) |
| 18 Thu | ECWC QF (2) |
| 20 Sat | FA Vase SF (2) |
| 27 Sat | England v Poland (EC) |
| | FA Trophy 6 |
| 28 Sun | FA Sunday Cup SF |
| 30 Tue | Semi-Pro International |
| 31 Wed | International (EC) |

**April**

| | |
|---|---|
| 2 Fri | Good Friday |
| 4 Sun | FA Women's Cup SF |
| 5 Mon | Bank Holiday |
| 6 Tue | UEFA Cup SF (1) |
| 7 Wed | Champions League SF (1) |
| 8 Thu | ECWC SF (1) |
| 10 Sat | FA Trophy SF (1) |
| | FA Youth Cup SF+ |
| 11 Sun | FA Cup SF |
| 14 Wed | FA Cup SF Replay |
| 17 Sat | |
| | FA Trophy SF (2) |
| 20 Tue | UEFA Cup SF (2) |
| 21 Wed | Champions League SF (2) |
| 22 Thu | ECWC SF (2) |

| | |
|---|---|
| 24 Sat | FA County Youth Cup Final (fixed date) |
| 25 Sun | FA Sunday Cup Final |
| 28 Wed | International (F) |

**May**

| | |
|---|---|
| 3 Mon | FA Women's Cup Final |
| 8 Sat | End of Football League Season |
| 12 Wed | UEFA Cup Final |
| 15 Sat | FA Trophy Final – Wembley Stadium 3.00 |
| | FA Youth Cup Final+ |
| 16 Sun | FA Vase Final – Wembley Stadium 3.00 |
| | End of FA Premier League Season |
| | FL Play-Offs SF (1) |
| 19 Wed | European Cup Winners Cup Final |
| | FL Play-Offs SF (2) |
| 22 Sat | FA Cup Final – Wembley Stadium 3.00 |
| 26 Wed | European Champions League Final |
| 27 Thu | FA Cup Final Replay |
| 29 Sat | FL Play-Offs Final Div 3 |
| 30 Sun | FL Play-Offs Final Div 2 |
| 31 Mon | FL Play-Offs Final Div 1 |

to be dated – FA XI v Highland League

**June**

| | |
|---|---|
| 5 Sat | England v Sweden (EC) |
| 9 Wed | Bulgaria v England (EC) |

+ closing date of round
* no FA Premier League games
EC = UEFA European Championship

# STOP PRESS

New sponsors: Worthington (League) Cup £23m over five years; The AXA sponsored FA Cup £25m over four years; Scottish Premier Sky deal for £45m ... Peter Middleton, a former monk, becomes independent chairman of Football League ... Pay-per-view TV predicted for New Year ... Maldini out, Zoff in for Italian Job ... France's successful manager Aimé Jacquet moves upstairs with Roger Lemerre taking over ... After Walter Smith takes over at Everton, Gérard Houllier, France's No. 2 goes to Liverpool as joint manager as Ronnie Moran retires ... Brazil sack Mario Zagallo and his staff ... Shepherd and Hall back at Newcastle ... Arsenal to play European games at Wembley ... Crystal Palace sunk twice 2-0 by Samsunspor in the Inter-Toto ... Rangers spend £25m on seven signings ... South Korea want 2002 World Cup in September ... European Cup results: Celtic 0, St Patrick's Ath 0; Dynamo Kiev 8, Barry T 0; Cliftonville 1, Kosice 5; UEFA Cup: Omonia 5, Linfield 1; Newtown 0, Wisla 0; Shelbourne 3, Rangers 5; Zeljeznicar 1, Kilmarnock 1 ... Poland's Euro 2000 participation threatened ... Croatia beat our Under-18's, but Republic of Ireland win the title ... Posh's Matthew Etherington, 16, could go for a trainee record over the £2.3m paid by West Ham for Rochdale's Stephen Bywater.

Top Transfers:- Jaap Stam, Ajax to **Manchester U** £10.5m; Kevin Davies, Southampton to **Blackburn R** £7.5m; Andrei Kanchelskis, Fiorentina to **Rangers** £5.5m; Pierluigi Casiraghi, Lazio to **Chelsea** £5.4m; Georgi Kinkladze, Manchester C to **Ajax** £5.25m; Giovanni van Bronckhorst, Feyenoord to Rangers £5m; Dietmar Hamann, Bayern Munich to **Newcastle U** £5m; Arthur Numan, PSV Eindhoven to Rangers £5m; Marcel Desailly, AC Milan to **Chelsea** £4.6m; Alan Thompson, Bolton W to **Aston Villa** £4.5m; Jesper Blomqvist, Parma to **Manchester U** £4.4m; Gabriel Amato, Mallorca to Rangers £4.2m; Viorel Moldovan, Coventry C to **Fenerbahce** £4m; Olivier Dacourt, Strasbourg to **Everton** £4m; Vegard Heggem, Rosenborg to **Liverpool**, £3.5m; Stephane Guivarc'h, Auxerre to **Newcastle U** £3.5m.

*Other moves completed and pending:-* **Arsenal:** David Grodin (St Etienne); **Aston Villa:** Fabio Ferraresi (Cesena), David Unsworth (West Ham U); **Blackburn R:** Jim Corbett (Gillingham), Darren Peacock (Newcastle U), Sebastien Perez (Bastia); **Charlton Ath:** Chris Powell (Derby Co), Andy Hunt (WBA), Neil Redfearn (Barnsley), Simon Royce (Southend U); **Chelsea:** Brian Laudrup (Rangers), Albert Ferrer (Barcelona); **Coventry C:** Jean-Guy Wallemme (Lens), Philippe Clement (Genk), Ian Brightwell (Manchester C); **Derby Co:** Horatio Angel Carbonari (Rosario Central), Stefan Schnoor (Hamburg); **Everton:** John Collins (Monaco), Marco Materazzi (Perugia); **Leeds U:** Clyde Wijnhard (Willem II), Danny Granville (Chelsea); **Leicester C:** Gerry Taggart (Bolton W); **Liverpool:** Sean Dundee (Karlsruhe), Steve Staunton (Aston Villa); **Middlesbrough:** Gary Pallister (Manchester U), Dean Gordon (Crystal Palace); **Newcastle U:** Yorgos Yoryadis (Panathinaikos), Lionel Perez (Sunderland), Stephen Glass (Aberdeen), Carl Serrant (Oldham Ath), Laurent Charvet (Cannes), Gary Brady (Tottenham H); **Nottingham F:** Jean-Claude Darcheville (Rennes); **Southampton:** David Howells (Tottenham H), Stuart Ripley (Blackburn R), Martin Paul (Kings Lynn), James Beattie (Blackburn R), Mark Hughes (Chelsea), Scott Marshall (Arsenal); **Tottenham H:** Paolo Tramezzani (Piacenza); **West Ham U:** Shaka Hislop (Newcastle U), Marc Keller (Karlsruhe), Ian Wright (Arsenal); Ade Akinbiyi, Gillingham to Bristol C; David Amsalem, Beitar Jerusalem to Crystal Palace; Dean Austin, Tottenham H to Crystal Palace; Steve Agnew, Sunderland to York C; Luke Beckett, Barnsley to Chester C; Mohamed Berthe, West Ham to Bournemouth; Ademola Bankole, Crewe Alex to QPR; Grant Brebner, Manchester U to Reading; Chris Billy, Plymouth Arg to Notts Co; Mark Blake, Fulham to Cannes; David Bardsley, QPR to Blackpool; Roger Boli, Walsall to Dundee U; Paul Butler, Bury to Sunderland; Jimmy Carter, Portsmouth to Millwall; Trevor Challis, QPR to Bristol R; Lionel Charbonnier, Auxerre to Rangers; Carlo Corazzin, Plymouth Arg to Northampton T; Duane Darby, Hull C to Notts Co; Tony Daley, Wolverhampton W to Watford; John Finnigan, Nottingham F to Lincoln C; Darren Freeman, Fulham to Brentford; Jimmy Glass, Bournemouth to Swindon T; Marco Gabbiadini, York C to Darlington; Frode Grodas, Tottenham H to Schalke; Ricardo Gardener, Harbour View to Bolton W; Danny Hill, Tottenham H to Oxford U; Craig Hignett, Middlesbrough to Aberdeen; Richard Hughes, Arsenal to Bournemouth; Carl Hutchings, Brentford to Bristol C; Rodney Jack, Torquay U to Crewe Alex; Claus Jensen, Lyngby to Bolton W; Nikos Kyzeridis, Paniliakos to Portsmouth; Stuart McCall, Rangers to Bradford C; Graeme Murty, York C to Reading; Gavin McGowan, Arsenal to Luton T; Brian McClair, Manchester U to Motherwell; Fernando Nelson, Aston Villa to Porto; David Oldfield, Luton T to Stoke C; John Polston, Norwich C to Reading; Darren Patterson, Luton T to Dundee U; Daniel Prodan, Atletico Madrid to Rangers; Mark Pembridge, Sheffield W to Benfica; Kevin Richardson, Southampton to Barnsley; Alan Reeves, Wimbledon to Swindon T; Mark Reilly, Kilmarnock to Reading; John Salako, Bolton W to Fulham; Kit Symons, Manchester C to Fulham; Duncan Spedding, Southampton to Northampton T; Chris Short, Sheffield U to Stoke C; Bryan Small, Bury to Stoke C; Thomas Sorensen, Odense to Sunderland; Masa Sarr, Hajduk Split to Reading; Liazid Sandjak, Neuchatel Xamax to Portsmouth; Mathias Svensson, Portsmouth to Innsbruck; Ian Snodin, Scarborough to Doncaster R (as player/manager); Jamie Stuart, Charlton Ath to Millwall; Mark Stein, Chelsea to Bournemouth; Bob Taylor, WBA to Bolton W; Tony Thorpe, Fulham to Bristol C; Graeme Tomlinson, Manchester U to Macclesfield T; Jon Dahl Tomasson, Newcastle U to Feyenoord; Jason Tindall, Chelsea to Bournemouth; Michael Thomas, Liverpool to Benfica; Ben Thornley, Manchester U to Huddersfield T; Nico Vasen, Aalst to Huddersfield T; Robin Van der Laan, Derby Co to Barnsley; Rod Wallace, Leeds U to Rangers; Dean Windass, Aberdeen to Oxford U; Matthew Wicks, Arsenal to Crewe Alex; Neil Wainwright, Wrexham to Sunderland; Geraint Williams, Ipswich T to Colchester U; Shaun Wright-Phillips, Nottingham F to Manchester C.

**Coaching moves:-** Arrigo Sacchi to Atletico Madrid; Guus Hiddink to Real Madrid; Dr Jozef Venglos to Celtic; Dick Advocaat to Rangers; John Deehan as Sheffield U No. 2; Paddy Bonner as Reading No. 2.